Pronunciation table

Consonants

symbol	key word
b	back
d	day
ð	then
dʒ	jump
f	fat
g	get
h	hot
j	yet
k	key
l	led
m	sum
n	sun
ŋ	sung
p	pen
r	red
s	soon
ʃ	fishing
t	tea
tʃ	cheer
θ	thing
v	view
w	wet
x	loch
z	zero
ʒ	pleasure

Vowels

symbol	key word
iː	sheep
ɪ	ship
i	happy
e	bed
æ	bad
ɑː	calm
ɒ	pot
ɔː	caught
ʊ	put
u	actuality
uː	boot
ʌ	cut
ɜː	bird
ə	cupboard
eɪ	make
əʊ	note
aɪ	bite
aʊ	now
ɔɪ	boy
ɪə	here
ɪə	peculiar
eə	there
ʊə	poor
uə	ritual
eɪə	player
əʊə	lower
aɪə	tire
aʊə	tower
ɔɪə	employer

Special signs

‖	separates British and American pronunciations: British on the left, American on the right
/ˈ/	shows main stress
/ˌ/	shows secondary stress
/◄/	shows stress shift
/ʳ/	at the end of a word means that /r/ is usually pronounced in American English and is pronounced in British English when the next word begins with a vowel sound
/ɪ/	means that some speakers use /ɪ/ and others use /ə/
/ʊ/	means that some speakers use /ʊ/ and others use /ə/
/ə/	means that /ə/ may or may not be used

Editorial Director
Della Summers

Managing Editor
Sheila Dignen

Editorial Manager
Penny Stock

Publishing
Adam Gadsby
Andrew Delahunty

Senior lexicographer
Andrew Delahunty

Co-ordinating editors
Alison Steadman
Heather Gay

Lexicographers
Susan Axbey
Caroline Curry
Belinda Dean
Jessica Feinstein
Jock Graham
Sarah Hall
Colin Hope
Fred McDonald
Fiona McIntosh
Carole Owen
Valerie Smith
Jane Walsh
Joc Potter
Gillian Lazar

Illustrations editors
Lizzie Warren
Jane Walsh
Sarah Gumbrell

Design
Paul Price-Smith
Ken Brooks
Hilary Fletcher
Cathy May

Production
Clive McKeough

American lexicographers
Karen Cleveland Marwick
Dana Darby Johnson
Orin Hargraves
Brock N Brock

Illustrators
Martin Aitchison (John Martin and Artists)
Victor Ambrose (Virgil Pomfret Illustration Agency)
Rowan Barnes-Murphy
Neil Gower
Kim Harley (Young Artists)
Chris Molan
Steve Noon (Beehive Illustration Agency)
David Parkins
Francesca Pelizzoli (Virgil Pomfret Illustration Agency)
Technical Art Services
Cliff Wright

Pronunciation editor
Dinah Jackson

Geographical consultant
Harold Fullard OBE

Administrative Assistants
Denise Denney
Barbara Egerton
Jenny Thomson

The publishers and editorial team wish to express their gratitude to the many people who contributed advice on the making of the dictionary, particularly those on the Longman Dictionaries Advisory Committee, Linglex, Professor Sir Randolph Quirk, Professor Geoffrey Leech, Paul Meara, Professor John Wells, Professor Gill Brown, Philip Scholfield, Jean Aitchison, Karen Sparck-Jones, and Antonia Byatt. Special thanks are due to Susan Maingay, Maggy Hendry, Louise McConnell, Helen Pimblett, and to Shinsuke Suzuki for advice on Japanese entries. We would also like to thank those involved in the creation of the Longman Dictionary of Contemporary English, especially Michael Rundell, Susan Maingay, and Fiona McIntosh.

Longman

Dictionary of

English

Language and

Culture

Longman

Longman Group UK Limited
Longman House, Burnt Mill, Harlow,
Essex CM20 2JE, England
and Associated Companies throughout the world

The information contained in this book was correct insofar
as could be ascertained by the publishers at the time of
printing. The information of the definitions with regard to
people, institutions, products and companies represents
the meaning, connotations, and associations that English-
speaking people have, as ascertained by the editorial
team on the basis of their professional knowledge and/or
citational evidence from newspapers, books and
magazines.

First published 1992
Third impression (updated) 1993

British Library Cataloguing-in-Publication Data

A catalogue record for this book is available from the
British Library.

Cased Edition:
ISBN 0 582 23794 7

Paperback Edition:
ISBN 0 582 23720 3

Set in 6½/7¼ pt. Nimrod

Typesetting in England by OTS (Typesetting) Ltd
Printed in England by Clays Ltd, St Ives plc

Contents

The Dictionary A–Z

We are grateful to the following for their permission to reproduce copyright material:

Action Plus/R.Francis for page 884 (background), Tony Henshaw for page 758; Allsport (UK) Ltd for page 780, /Russell Cheyne for pages 492 and 1501, /J Daniel for page 884 (middle right), /Ken Levine for page 707, /Adrian Murell for page 884 (middle left), /Mike Powell for pages 722 and 884 (top left, top middle), /Rick Stewart for page 884 (bottom right), /Billy Stickland for page 884 (top right, bottom left); American Express Europe Limited for page 33; Amnesty International for page 34 (bottom); Ancient Art & Architecture for page 1426; Aquarius Picture Library for page 685 (top right); BBC Photolibrary for pages 686 (upper middle left, bottom left) and 1367; Photograph courtesy of J.Barbour & Sons Limited 82 (left); Barclays Bank PLC for pages 82 (top right) and 437; Bettman/UPI for pages 34 (top), 183 (top left), 355 and 1252; Anthony Blake for page 215; Bridgeman Art Library for pages 210, 1016 (top middle, top right, middle left, middle right, bottom middle, bottom right), / Bonhams, London for page 56, /Giraudon for page 1016 (top left), /National Coal Board for page 611, /Stedelijk Museum, Eindhoven for page 310, /Tate Gallery, London for page 931, /By courtesy of the board of Trustees of the V&A or pages 88 and 1401 (top); British Standards Institute for page 725; British Telecommunications PLC for page 146; Camera Press Ltd for pages 751 (middle left), 950 (top left) and 1017 (middle left); The J Allan Cash Photolibrary for pages 162 (middle left), 509, 556, 571, 601, 639, 711, 734, 755, 779, 1022 (bottom), 1026 (bottom), 1088, 1139, 1169, 1457, 1463, 1465; Channel 4 TV for pages 287, 686 (upper middle right, lower middle left and bottom right); "Coca-Cola" and "Coke" are registered trademarks which identify the same product of The Coca-Cola Company for page 237; Colorsport for page 26; Edifice for pages 161 (middle right) and 227 (middle right); English Tourist Board for page 426; Eurocard International for page 820; Euromap for pages 66 and 897; Greg Evans Photolibrary for pages 151, 158 (top), 875, 895, 989 (top, bottom), 1356 (top), 1493; Eye Ubiquitous/R.Friend for page 1406 (middle right); The Financial Times for page 896 (lower middle); Hilary Fletcher for page 98; Granada TV for pages 686 (top), /Julie Goodyear for page 793, /Jean Alexander for page 922; The Ronald Grant Archive for pages 228 (top left, top right), 496, 553 (top right), 649 and 848; Sally & Richard Greenhill Photography for pages 161 (top left), 483 and 950 (middle middle), 1061 (top left); Permission is granted by R.Grigg & Co., manufacturers of the Dr Marten 1460 boot for page 390; The Rt. Hon. The Lord Mayor of London, Sir Brian Jenkins GBE MP DSc - © Guild Hall for page 784; Sarah Gumbrell for page 570 (top); © Hanna Barbera for page 491; Robert Harding Picture Library for pages 162 (top right, middle right, bottom left), 227 (top left, top right, upper middle left, middle); © Herge/Sundancer for page 1390; HMV/Thorn EMI Patents Limited for page 629; Philip Hoult for page 1406 (top, bottom); House of Commons for page 949 (middle right); Hulton Deutsch Collection for pages 82 (bottom right), 150, 176 196, 217, 281, 295, 326, 392, 407, 415, 505, 534, 553 (upper middle left), 566 (top left), 632 (bottom), 717, 720, 751 (bottom), 752 (upper middle, middle right, bottom left, bottom right), 767, 854, 866, 880, 900, 911, 1022 (top), 1143, 1159, 1427, 1461; ITC Entertainment Group for page 686 (lower middle right); Image Bank/P.Beney for page 419, / Bowater for page 162 (bottom right), /Romilly Cockyer for page 227 (lower middle left), /John P.Kelly for page 868, / Bob Noble for page 632 (top), and /Marc Romanelli for page 161 (middle left); Imperial War Museum, London for page 724, 1434, 1526; The Kobal Collection for pages 61 (bottom), 87, 128, 160, 228 (top middle, lower middle middle, bottom middle left, bottom right), 234, 553 (top left, bottom middle), 560, 575, 621, 685 (top left, top middle, upper middle far left, upper middle left, upper middle right, upper middle far right, lower middle left, lower middle middle, lower middle right, bottom left, bottom middle, bottom right), 708, 816, 846, 925, 936, 998, 1085, 1144, 1277, 1281, 1318, 1332, 1354, 1484, 1528; Lego UK Ltd for page 753; London Transport Advertising & Publicity for page 1436; Metropolitan Police for page 1017 (right); Midland Bank PLC for page 6; William Morris Gallery for page 864; Network Photographers/Jordan for page 950 (top right), /Lewis for page 1406 (middle left), /Paul Lowe for page 752 (lower middle), /Quesada/Matrix for page 950 (middle left); The New York Times for page 896 (top right); News of the World, News Group Newspapers for page 896 (top left); P & Co., 1988 for page 948; Photo Edit/Paul Conklin for page 751 (top left), /1990 Tony Freeman for page 950 (bottom right), /JS for page 1017 (left), /Rhoda Sidnay for page 1017 (middle right); Photo Researchers for page 161 (bottom right); Pictor International for pages 584 and 751 (top right); Pitkin Pictorials for page 949 (top); The Picture Cube /Jeff Dunn for page 161 (top right), /Henryk Tomasz © Kaiser for page 161 (bottom left); Popperfoto Ltd for pages 81, 718 (left), 950 (middle right, bottom right), 1137, 1150 (right), 1359, 1362 and 1369; Quadrant Picture Library for page 166, 600, /Alan Felix for page 1299; Permission to reproduce the Red Cross and Red Crescent designations and emblems has been granted by the Ministry of Defence and the British Red Cross Society, London for page 1100; Redferns for pages 554 (top left, bottom right), 1067 and 1138; Retna Pictures/Phil Loftus for page 553 (bottom left), /Paul Rider for page 553 (lower middle left); Rex Features for pages 61 (top), 157, 169, 183 (bottom left), 197, 226, 228 (upper middle left, upper middle middle, upper middle right, lower middle left, bottom left, bottom middle right), 319, 352, 374, 398, 410, 553 (middle, middle right, bottom middle), 554 (top right, upper middle left, upper middle middle, upper middle right), 554 (upper middle left), 554 (lower middle middle left, lower middle left, lower middle middle left, lower middle middle right, lower middle right, bottom left), 561, 566 (bottom left), 615, 616, 617 (bottom left), 628, 718 (right), 730, 752 (top right), 759, 796, 813, 858, 947, 963, 1092, 1128, 1135, 1476, 1504; Photo courtesy of The Norman Rockwell Museum at Stockbridge for page 1368; The Scotsman for page 896 (bottom); Frank Spooner Pictures/ Edmonson/Gamma Liaison for page 752 (top left); Tony Stone Worldwide for pages 107 (left), 486 and 1517; Syndication International for pages 50, 107 (right), 228 (lower middle right), 627 and 1279; Telegraph Colour Library for pages 178, 185, 220, 261, 284, 294, 537, 570 (bottom), 1072, 1150 (left), 1158, 1187, 1356 (middle), 1389, 1479, 1491, 1496; Topham Picture Source/Associated Press for page 949 (bottom); PEANUTS Characters reproduced by permission of United Features syndicate, Inc. for pages 148 and 1255; Viewfinder Colour Library for pages 751 (middle right) and 1356 (bottom); Reproduced by permission of the Trustees of the Wallace Collection for page 1016 (bottom left); Andrew Ward for pages 19 and 1401 (bottom); Lizzie Warren for page 55; The Washington Post for page 896 (upper middle); Youth Hostel Association for page 1523; Zefa Picture Library (UK) Ltd for pages; 158 (bottom), 162 (top left, background), 227 (bottom), 404, 471, 562, 634, 838, 902, 969, 977, 989 (middle), 991, 1026 (top), 1061 (top right), 1066, 1099 (right), 1297, 1316, 1524.

The photographs on pages 114, 476, 489, 789, 1061 (bottom), 1099 (left), 1125, 1342, 1428 were taken by Longman Photographic Unit.

Back Cover photographs by Action Plus/Tony Henshaw (lower middle right); Bridgeman Art Library (top); Popperfoto (upper middle); Telegraph Colour Library (bottom).

This Dictionary has been produced to help students of English understand the words and phrases that make up the complex fabric of English-speaking life and culture.

The full text of the *Longman Dictionary of Contemporary English* is the basis for the book, but we have included a further 15,000 people, places, events, and institutions in order to provide advanced learners of English with a full reference resource in one book.

This is because we believe that when students come across references to *Rodeo Drive, triffids, Reuters, PSBR,* the *Teamsters' Union* or *Clarence Darrow* in their reading, they should be able to look them up in their dictionary just as they would other, more general language words.

The range of words and phrases included here should help students extend the breadth of their understanding of English, but information is also provided to increase the depth of their understanding.

The *connotations* of some of the items entered here, many of them for the first time in a reference book, are often essential to the full understanding of a passage. For example, what associations do native-speakers of English naturally have with items such as *Rolls Royce* or the *National Enquirer*? It is surely necessary to understand the reputation for high quality associated with the name *Rolls Royce* in order to understand a sentence like *Our company provides a Rolls Royce service,* and so this information is clearly stated in the definition.

The lexicographic work that has gone into the creation of this book is based on the analysis of authentic language as found in the many books and newspapers from Britain and America included in the Longman Corpus Network, an extensive resource of computerized language data collected over many years at Longman. The use of this data in our dictionaries ensures that the content is both up-to-date and accurate.

We very much hope that the understanding of language by advanced learners of English will be greatly enhanced by the use of the new Longman Dictionary of English Language and Culture.

Della Summers
Editorial Director

a·board /ə'bɔːd‖-ɔːrd/ adv, prep on or into (a ship, train, air-craft, bus, etc.): *The boat is ready to leave. All aboard!* | *The plane crashed, killing all 200 people aboard.* – compare **on board** (BOARD¹)

British and American pronunciations: page F30

an·ti·bi·ot·ic /ˌæntɪbaɪ'ɒtɪk◂‖-'ɑː-/ n a medical substance, such as PENICILLIN, that is produced by living things and is able to destroy or stop the growth of harmful bacteria that have entered the body: *a course of antibiotics to clear an infection* –**antibiotic** adj

word class (or "part of speech") labels: page F16

bad·ger¹ /'bædʒəʳ/ n **1** [C] an animal which has black and white fur, lives in holes in the ground, and is active at night **2** [U] the skin or hair of this animal
badger² v [T (**into**)] to (try to) persuade by asking again and again; PESTER: *The children badgered me into taking them to the cinema.* [+obj+to-v] *They kept badgering him to get a home computer.*

words with the same spelling but different use or meaning: page F10

Ad·ams /'ædəmz/ , **An·sel** /'ænsəl/ (1902–84) an American photographer known esp. for his photographs of the scenery of the West of the US
Adams , John (1735–1826) the second president of the US and an influential political leader of the movement towards independence from the British

people with the same name: page F11

blot·ter /'blɒtəʳ‖'blɑː-/ n **1** a large piece of blotting paper against which writing paper can be pressed to dry the ink **2** *AmE* a book where records are written every day, before the information is stored elsewhere (often in the phrase **police blotter**)

words having more than one meaning: page F13

clam·our¹ *BrE* ‖ **clamor** *AmE* /'klæməʳ/ n **1** [S] a loud continuous, usu. confused noise or shouting: *a clamour of voices*/of bells

spelling variation: page F11

cri·te·ri·on /kraɪ'tɪəriən/ n **-ria** /riə/ or **-rions** an established standard or principle, on which a judgment or decision is based

meanings explained in clear language: page F14

damage² v [T] to cause damage to: *to damage someone's reputation* | *The building was severely damaged by the explosion.* | *Smoking can damage your health.* | *The incident had a damaging effect on East-West relations.*

useful natural example sentences: page F15

birth·day /'bɜːθdeɪ‖'bɜːr-/ n **1** a day which is an exact year or number of years after one was born: *my 21st birthday* | *a birthday party* | *Happy birthday to you!* –compare ANNIVERSARY
▶CULTURAL NOTE People, esp. children, often celebrate their birthdays with a **birthday party** where people play games, sometimes wear special paper hats, eat **birthday cake**, and sing a special song called *Happy Birthday to you*. People are usu. given presents and **birthday cards** on their birthday.◀

Cultural Notes: page F27

drawing pin /'·· ·/ *BrE* ‖ **thumbtack** *AmE*– n a short pin with a broad flat head, used esp. for putting notices on boards or walls –see picture at PIN

British and American word differences: page F26

dry-clean /ˌ· '·/ v [T] to clean (clothes, material, etc.) with chemicals instead of water
dry clean·er's /ˌ· '··/ n a shop where clothes, curtains, etc., can be taken to be dry-cleaned
dry dock /'·· ·/ n a place in which a ship is held in position while the water is pumped out, leaving the ship dry for repairs: *The ship is in dry dock being painted.*

compound words shown as separate entries: page F10
stress patterns shown for compound words: page F29

flag² *v* **-gg-** [T] to put a special mark on (something) so it can be picked out from among others
  flag sthg./sbdy. ↔ **down** *phr v* [T] to cause (a vehicle or its driver) to stop by waving at the driver: *I tried to flag down a taxi.*

phrasal verbs: page F11

frying pan /'·· ˌ·/ also **skillet** *AmE*— *n* **1** a flat pan with a long handle, used for frying food: *a non-stick frying pan* **2 out of the frying pan into the fire** out of a bad position into an even worse one —see picture at PAN

idioms: page F12

fish·er /'fɪʃəʳ/ *n* **I will make you fishers of men** a phrase used in the Bible by Christ, telling his followers, who were fishermen, that they should stop trying to catch fish and instead should try to attract more people to follow him

well known sayings and quotations: page F12

fur·tive /'fɜːtɪv‖'fɜːr-/ *adj* quiet and secret; trying to escape notice or hide one's intentions: *She cast a furtive glance down the hotel corridor before leaving her room.* – ~**ly** *adv* – ~**ness** *n* [U]

derived words shown without definitions: page F13

gap /gæp/ *n* [(**in, between**)] **1** an empty space between two objects or two parts of an object: *The gate was locked but we went through a gap in the fence.*

guarantee² *v* [T] **1** to give a guarantee: *The manufacturers guarantee the watch for three years.* [+(*that*)] *They have guaranteed that any faulty parts will be replaced free of charge.* [+*to-v*] *Our products are guaranteed to last for years.* [+*obj*+*adj*] *All our food is guaranteed free of artificial preservatives*

grammar codes: page F18

hit man /'· ·/ *n infml, esp. AmE* a criminal who is employed to kill someone

labels showing style, region, etc.: page F23

hope·ful·ly /'həʊpfəli/ *adv* **1** in a hopeful way: *The little boy looked at her hopefully as she handed out the sweets.* **2** if our hopes succeed: *Hopefully we'll be there by dinnertime.*
  ▷ USAGE This second meaning of **hopefully** is now very common, especially in speech; but it is thought by some people to be incorrect.◁

Usage Notes: page F27

frog /frɒg‖fraːg, frɔːg/ *n* **1** a small hairless tailless animal, usu. brownish-green, that lives in water and on land, has long back legs for swimming and jumping, and CROAKS (=makes a deep rough sound). People sometimes make jokes about kissing frogs to make them turn into an attractive prince, because this happens in some children's fairy stories. —see also FROG PRINCE

"cross-references" directing you to other words: page F26

in·ci·dent /'ɪnsɪdənt/ *n* **1** an event; a happening, esp. one that is unusual: *one of the strangest incidents in my life* | *We completed the journey* **without further incident**. (=with nothing unusual happening)

words often used together, shown in dark type, page F15
explanation of example: page F15

lb *written abbrev. for:* pound (weight)
lbw /ˌel biː 'dʌbəljuː/ *abbrev. for:* leg before wicket (LEG¹)
LCD /ˌel siː 'diː/ *n* liquid crystal display; part of an APPARATUS on which numbers, letters, etc. are shown by passing an electric current through a special liquid, so that they light up

abbreviations and words using capital letters: page F10

mal- see WORD FORMATION

prefixes and suffixes: page F11

out·do /aʊt'duː/ *v* **-did** /'dɪd/, **-done** /'dʌn/, *3rd person sing. present tense* **-does** /'dʌz/ [T] to do or be better than (someone else):

irregular verb forms: page F17

o·vum /'əʊvəm/ *n* **ova** /'əʊvə/ *tech* an egg, esp. one that develops inside the mother's body

nouns with irregular plurals: page F17

1 Finding words and phrases

All dictionaries follow alphabetical order, but they do not all list words in exactly the same way. For example, in some dictionaries the expression **part of speech** may be listed in the entry for **part**, and in others it may come at **speech**. In this dictionary it has its own separate entry in the main alphabetical list, between **partnership** and **partook**. These main entries are called "headwords", but not all words and phrases appear as full headwords – you may have to look for them under another headword. In order to use this dictionary effectively, you need to know how the words are listed, and the purpose of this section is to explain exactly where to find the word or phrase you are looking for:

    1.1 Homographs
    1.2 Compound words
    1.3 Plural nouns
    1.4 Words that start with capital letters
    1.5 Abbreviations
    1.6 Prefixes and suffixes
    1.7 Different spellings
    1.8 Irregular inflections
    1.9 Phrasal verbs
    1.10 Idioms, Sayings and Quotations
    1.11 Derived words without definitions

1.1 Homographs

"Homographs" are words that have the same spelling but are different in some other way. They may have a different pronunciation, they may belong to a different word class (noun, verb, adjective, etc.), or they may be completely different in meaning. Homographs are shown as separate headwords and each one is given a raised number, like this:

flock¹ /flɒk‖flɑːk/ n [C+sing./pl. v] **1** a group of sheep, goats, or birds −compare HERD¹ (1) **2** [+of] infml a crowd; large number of people: a flock of tourists **3** the group of people who regularly attend a church: The priest warned his flock against breaking God's law.
flock² v [I+adv/prep] to gather or move in large numbers: People are flocking to the cinema to see the new film.
flock³ n [U] **1** small pieces of wool, cotton, etc., used for filling CUSHIONs, etc. **2** soft material that forms decorative patterns on the surface of wallpaper, curtains, etc.

In this example, **flock¹** and **flock²** are closely related in meaning, but they are shown as separate headwords because they belong to different word classes. And **flock³** is completely unrelated in meaning to the other two, so it also has a separate entry. The order in which homographs are listed depends on how common they are: the most frequently used words come first.

1.2 Compound words

A "compound word" is a combination of two or more separate words that functions as a single word and has its own special meaning.

hot air /ˌ· '·/ n [U] infml derog meaningless talk or ideas
hot·bed /'hɒtbed‖'hɑːt-/ n [+of] a place or condition where the stated undesirable thing can exist and develop: The city is a hotbed of crime. | a hotbed of intrigue
hot-blood·ed /ˌ· '···◄/ adj having strong excitable feelings; PASSIONATE
hotch·potch /'hɒtʃpɒtʃ‖'hɑːtʃpɑːtʃ/ esp. BrE ‖ usu. **hodgepodge** AmE− n [S] a number of things mixed up without any sensible order or arrangement
hot-cross bun /ˌ· · '·/ n a small sweet cake made of bread with a cross-shaped mark on top, which is eaten on Good Friday, just before Easter
hot dog /ˌ· '·‖'· ·/ n a cooked FRANKFURTER or other SAUSAGE in a long bread ROLL. In the US hot dogs and HAMBURGERS are considered to be very American foods and are very popular.
hot flush /ˌ· '·/ esp. BrE ‖ usu. **hot flash** AmE− n a sudden feeling of heat in the skin, esp. as experienced by women at the MENOPAUSE (=the time when they stop being able to bear children)

In this dictionary, compound words are always treated as separate headwords (not as part of another main headword like **hot**), whether they are written as a single word (like **hotbed**), or as two or three separate words (like **hot air**), or joined by hyphens (like **hot-blooded**).

It is important to distinguish between compound words, which have a fixed form and a special meaning, and groups of words that simply appear together in a particular sentence. Expressions like "a hot day", "a hot room", and "hot weather" are not shown as headwords because they are "free" combinations of an adjective and noun. Their form is not fixed, so one could equally say "the day was hot", "the weather was hot", and so on. This would not be possible with true compounds like **hot air** and **hot dog**.

1.3 Plural nouns

If a noun is always used in the plural form in one of its meanings, this meaning is shown as a separate headword:

bend² n **1** a curved part, esp. in a road or stream: a bend in the road/river **2** an act of bending: forward bends to stretch the spine **3** around/round the bend infml, often humor mad: This pink wallpaper would drive/send me around/round the bend. | That old man next door must be/have gone round the bend − he's been cutting the grass with a pair of scissors!
bends /bendz/ n [the+sing./pl. v] a painful and occasionally fatal condition caused by gas in the tubes through which blood flows, suffered esp. by deep-sea DIVERs who come to the surface too quickly

1.4 Words that start with capital letters

Some words are always written with capital letters, for example if they are the name of a particular place, organization, or event. These words are shown as separate headwords, even if they have the same spelling as another headword:

ref·or·ma·tion /ˌrefəˈmeɪʃən‖-fər-/ n [C;U] (an) improvement; the act of reforming or state of being reformed: *a complete reformation in his character*

Reformation [the] the religious movement in Europe in the 16th century leading to the establishment of the Protestant churches

Words that begin with capital letters may sometimes have more than one meaning. Each meaning has its own definition number and definition.

Entries for people are always shown as separate headwords, not as different meanings under one headword. They are listed in alphabetical order of the person's first name:

Arm·strong /ˈɑːmstrɒŋ‖ˈɑːrmstrɔːŋ/, **Lou·is** /ˈluːi/ (1900–71) an American JAZZ musician, singer, and bandleader, known esp. for the rough sound of his voice

Armstrong, Neil /niːl/ (1930–) an American ASTRONAUT who was the first man to step on the moon in 1969. He is remembered for saying "one small step for a man, one giant leap for mankind" as he first stepped onto the moon.

1.5 Abbreviations

"Abbreviations" are either shortened forms of words (like **Dr** for **Doctor**) or groups of letters made up from the first letters of the name of something (like **AIDS** for **Acquired Immune Deficiency Syndrome**). In both cases, they appear as headwords in their own alphabetical place, even if they have the same spelling as another headword:

haz·y /ˈheɪzi/ adj **1** misty; rather cloudy: *The mountains were hazy in the distance.* **2** unclear; uncertain: *I'm rather hazy about the details of the arrangement.* —**ily** adv —**iness** n [U]

H-bomb /ˈeɪtʃ bɒm‖-bɑːm/ n a HYDROGEN BOMB

HCF /ˌeɪtʃ siː ˈef/ abbrev. for: highest common factor —see FACTOR (2)

he¹ /i, hi; strong hiː/ pron (used as the subject of a sentence)

vat /væt/ n a very large barrel or other container for holding liquids, such as WHISKY, DYE, etc., esp. when they are being made

VAT /ˌviː eɪ ˈtiː, væt/ n [U] value-added tax; (in Britain and many other European countries) a tax added to the price of an article, and paid by the buyer to the seller, who then pays it to the government —compare SALES TAX

Vat·i·can /ˈvætɪkən/ [the] **1** the large palace in which the Pope (=head of the Roman Catholic Church) lives, in Rome: *At last, white smoke could be seen coming from the Vatican chimney.* **2** the government or office of the Pope: *The Vatican is taking a hard line on birth control.*

1.6 Prefixes and suffixes

There is a full list of prefixes and suffixes in the Word Formation section at the back of the dictionary (on page B4). But the most common ones are also shown in the main part of the dictionary with a note directing you to the full list, like this:

vice² esp. BrE ‖ **vise** AmE— n a tool with metal jaws that can be tightened, used for holding something firmly so that it can be worked on with both hands

vice- see WORD FORMATION

vice-chan·cel·lor /ˌ· ˈ···◄/ n **1** (often cap. V and C)

1.7 Different spellings

If a word has more than one spelling, the full definition is given at the most common spelling. But there will also be a short headword at the other spelling, directing you to the main entry:

caf·tan , kaftan /ˈkæftæn‖kæfˈtæn/ n a long loose garment, usu. of cotton or silk, worn in the Near and Middle East.

kaf·tan /ˈkæftæn‖kæfˈtæn/ n a CAFTAN

1.8 Irregular inflections

"Inflections" are the changes that are made in the form of a word according to the way the word is being used in a sentence. For example, **dog** becomes **dogs** when it is used in the plural, and **carry** becomes **carried** when it is used in the past tense. These are REGULAR inflections because they are formed according to regular rules. Regular inflections are not listed separately in the dictionary. But many words have IRREGULAR inflections, and to help you find the main entry these inflections are shown as separate headwords like this:

bounc·y /ˈbaʊnsi/ adj **1** full of life and confidence, and eager for action: *a bouncy person/manner* **2** that bounces well: *a bouncy ball* —**ily** adv —**iness** n [U]

bound¹ /baʊnd/ past tense & participle of BIND¹: *The prisoner was bound to a stake and shot.*

bound² adj **1** [F+to-v] very likely; certain

This means that the full definition of **bound**, when it is used as a verb, can be found at the headword for **bind**.

1.9 Phrasal verbs

A "phrasal verb" (sometimes called a two-part verb) is a fixed expression that consists of a verb followed by an adverb (like **give out**), or a preposition (like **look after**), or sometimes both (like **put up with**). Phrasal verbs have their own special meanings, and these are often quite different from the meaning of the main verb from which they are formed. Phrasal verbs are very common in English.

In this dictionary, phrasal verbs are shown as separate entries in a list following the main verb, like this:

back⁴ v **1** [I;T] to (cause to) go backwards: *She backed the car through the gate/into the parking space.* . . . .
. . . . **5** [I] tech (of the wind) to change direction, moving round the COMPASS in the order North–West–South–East —compare VEER (2) **6 back the wrong horse** to support the loser
back away also **back off** AmE— phr v [I (**from**)] to move away or back because of fear or dislike: *The dog backed away as the man raised his stick.* | (fig.) *The government has backed away from radical reshaping of the tax system.*
back down phr v [I (**over, on**)] to accept defeat in an argument, opinion, or claim; admit that one was wrong: *I saw that she was right, so I had to back down.*
back off phr v [I] AmE to stop trying to make (someone) to do or think (something): *I saw I was upsetting her so I backed off.* | *Just back off and leave me alone!*

In some cases, there is no simple verb form: that is, the verb is only ever found as part of a phrasal verb. In cases like this, the simple verb form is given, and the phrasal verbs are listed under it, like this:

knuckle² *v*
    knuckle down *phr v* [I (**to**)] to start working hard: *You'll really have to knuckle down if you want to pass the exam.* | *We knuckled down to the job/to finding the answer.*
    knuckle under *phr v* [I (**to**)] to be forced to accept the orders of someone more powerful: *He refused to knuckle under (to any dictatorship).*

It is important to distinguish between true phrasal verbs, which are fixed combinations of verb + adverb/preposition, and other expressions in which verbs freely combine with adverbs or prepositions in a particular sentence. In sentences like:
I **ran** *across the field*
She **ran** *into the room*
We **ran** *up the hill*
the verb **run** is being used with its usual meaning, and is followed by a phrase that begins with a preposition (*across the field*, *into the room*, *up the hill*). But the same expressions can also be used as phrasal verbs, and in this case their meaning is very different:
I **ran across** (= happened to meet) *an old friend today*
She **ran into** (= began to experience) *a few problems*
We **ran up** *a big bill* (= got it as a result of buying things) *at the restaurant*
It is only these SPECIAL meanings that are explained at the definitions for phrasal verbs:

    run across sbdy./sthg. *phr v* [T] to find or meet (esp. someone or something pleasant) by chance: *I ran across an old friend in the street.* —compare COME **across** (1)

For more information about phrasal verbs, see section 3.4 (Grammar and phrasal verbs).

1.10 Idioms, Sayings, and Quotations

An idiom is a fixed phrase that has its own special meaning. It is often impossible to guess the meaning of the whole phrase from the meanings of the separate words that it is formed from. For example, to **kick the bucket** is an idiom meaning "to die" – it has no connection with either kicking or buckets.

How to find idioms
In this dictionary idioms are printed in **dark type** and they are listed in alphabetical order after all the other meanings of a headword, like this:

jump¹ /dʒʌmp/ *v* **1** [I] to push oneself into the air or away from a surface by the force of one's legs; spring: *The children jumped up and down.* ....
...............**10 jump a claim** *esp. AmE* to try to claim valuable land which someone else already owns **11 jump down someone's throat** *infml* to attack someone in words, strongly and unexpectedly, esp. before they have finished talking **12 jump rope** *AmE for* SKIP¹(5) **13 jump the gun** *infml* to take action too soon or before the proper time: *I know he's a suspect, but isn't it jumping the gun a bit to arrest him immediately?* **14 jump the queue** *BrE* ‖ **cut in line** *AmE* to obtain an unfair advantage over others who have been waiting longer **15 jump to it** *infml* to hurry: *You'll have to jump to it if you want to catch the train.*

The dictionary lists idioms at the first MAIN word in the phrase (that is, not at words like **the**, **something**, or **with**), so **kick the bucket** has its definition at **kick**. But if you look for it at **bucket** you will find a note directing you to the right place:

buck·et¹ /ˈbʌkɪt/ *n* **1** an open metal, plastic, or wooden container with a handle for carrying liquids. .... **2** [(of)] also **buck·et·ful** /-fʊl/— the quantity held by a bucket: *She poured a bucket/two bucketfuls of water over me.* | (fig.) *The rain came down in buckets.* (=it rained very hard) —see also **kick the bucket** (KICK¹ (11)) **3 a drop in the bucket** a small amount which is not enough: *The money budgeted is a drop in the bucket compared to what is needed.*

There are two exceptions to this rule:
1 if the idiom starts with a VERY common verb (such as **have**, **get**, **make**, or **take**) it is shown at the next main word. So
    have one's head screwed on (= to be sensible and practical)
    is shown at **head**, not at **have**.
2 if one of the words in the idiom is variable, the idiom is shown at the main INVARIABLE word. So **take something with a pinch/grain of salt** (= not to believe something)
    is shown at **salt**, not at **pinch** or **grain**

When a noun is often used to form a suffix, in expressions like left-**handed**, clear-**headed**, or well-**mannered**, this suffix is treated like an idiom, and is shown under the noun as the last idiom in the list:

heart /hɑːt‖hɑːrt/ *n* **1** [C] the organ inside the chest which controls the flow of blood by pushing it round the body: .... **19 to one's heart's content** as much as one wants: *It's the weekend, so you can sleep to your heart's content.* **20 -hearted** /hɑːtɪd‖hɑːr-/ having a heart or character of the stated kind: *kind-hearted* | *cold-hearted* (=without kind feelings) | *stout-hearted* (=full of determination)

A saying is a fixed phrase that is usually used in a particular situation to give advice or to state a general truth. Sayings are shown in this dictionary in the same way as idioms, but they are labelled *saying*. The definition tells you what the saying means and in which situations it is used:

life /laɪf/ *n* **lives** /laɪvz/ **1** [U] the active force in animals and plants that makes them different from all other forms of matter, such as stones or machines or dead bodies: ....
(CREMATE) **22 life begins at forty** *saying* you can start to enjoy life once you are 40 years old

A quotation is a fixed phrase taken from a well known book, play, poem, speech, etc. Quotations are shown in this dictionary in the same way as idioms and sayings, but are labelled *quote*:

death /deθ/ *n* **1** [C;U] the end of life; time or manner of dying: .... **11 till death us do part** *BrE* ‖ **till us do us part** *AmE quote* a phrase from the Christian marriage service. Two people getting married promise that they will stay together and love each other "till death us do part" (=until one of them dies).

1.11 Derived words without definitions

The dictionary shows all the members of a word family, but they are not always treated as separate headwords. In many cases, related forms are shown under the main entry, like this:

> **grace·ful** /ˈgreɪsfəl/ *adj* **1** attractively and usu. effortlessly fine and smooth; full of grace: *a graceful dancer* | *her graceful movements* **2** showing a willingness to behave fairly and honourably: *a graceful apology* —see GRACIOUS (USAGE) — ~ly *adv* — ~ness *n* [U]

In this case, **gracefully** and **gracefulness** are not given their own separate entries because their meaning can easily be guessed from the base form (**graceful**) and the added endings:

    graceful + **-ly** means "in a graceful way"
    graceful + **-ness** means "the fact or quality of being graceful".

Derived forms come at the end of a headword entry, after all the definitions of the main word.
They NEVER have a definition.
They ALWAYS have a word class label (*adv*, *n*, etc.).
They SOMETIMES have a pronunciation and/or a grammar code and/or an example sentence.

> **af·firm** /əˈfɜːm‖-ɜːrm/ *v fml* **1** [T] to declare (usually again, or in answer to a question or doubt): *The minister affirmed the government's intention to reduce taxes.* [+*that*] *She affirmed that she was telling the truth.* —compare DENY (1) **2** [I] to promise to tell the truth in a court of law, but without mentioning God or religion in the promise — ~ation /ˌæfəˈmeɪʃən‖ˌæfər-/ *n* [C;U]

In this case, the pronunciation is given because the pronunciation of the base form (**affirm**) changes when the suffix (**-ation**) is added. The grammar code shows that the derived noun can be either countable or uncountable.

> **in·ves·ti·gate** /ɪnˈvestɪgeɪt/ *v* [I;T] to try to find out more information about, examine the reasons for (something), the character of (someone), etc.: *The police are investigating the crime.* | *He has been investigated and found blameless.* | *to investigate the causes of cancer* —**gator** *n* —**gation** /ɪnˌvestɪˈgeɪʃən/ *n* [C;U (**into**)] —**gative** /ɪnˈvestɪgətɪv‖-geɪtɪv/ *adj* : *investigative journalism* (=where newspapers try to find out things of public importance, uncover secrets, etc.)

In this case, an example is given to illustrate a common use of the derived form **investigative**, and there is also an added explanation to make the meaning as clear as possible.

Derived forms can be shown in three different ways:
1 with a wavy line, like this:

    grace·ful   — ~ness *n* [U]

In this case, the ending **-ness** is added directly to the base form **graceful**.

2 with a hyphen, like this:

    greas·y —**iness** *n* [U]

In this case, the base form changes slightly before the ending **-ness** can be added (the **y** becomes an **i**). The hyphen means that the derived word is formed by adding the ending shown (**-iness**) to the base word WITHOUT its last syllable. So in this example, the last syllable **-y** is removed from **greasy** and the ending **-iness** is added to it.

3 as a complete word, like this:

> **ar·chives** /ˈɑːkaɪvz‖ˈɑːr-/ *n* [P] (a place for storing) historical materials, such as old papers, letters, and reports concerning a government, family, organization, etc., kept esp. for historical interest: *an interesting old newsreel from the BBC archives* —**archive** *adj* [A] : *archive material*

In this example, the derived form is shown in full because it is shorter than the base word. In some cases, the derived form is actually the SAME as the base form, but it is shown (in full) because it belongs to a different word class:

> **am·e·thyst** /ˈæmɪθɪst/ *n* [C;U] (the colour of) a purple stone, used in jewellery —**amethyst** *adj*

The adjective form simply means "made of, or having the colour of amethyst", so it is shown as a derived form without a separate definition.

2 Understanding meaning

There are two ways in which the dictionary can help you to understand the meaning of a word or phrase. The definitions explain the meaning in clear and simple language. And the examples show how the word is normally used. The purpose of this section is to explain all the different kinds of information that the dictionary provides in its definitions and examples. This will help you to use the dictionary effectively as a guide to understanding meaning:

    2.1 Words with more than one meaning
    2.2 Definitions
    2.3 Synonyms
    2.4 Brackets in definitions
    2.5 Examples
    2.6 Figurative examples
    2.7 Brackets in examples

2.1 Words with more than one meaning

Most words have more than one meaning, and each meaning is given a number, like this:

> **horse¹** /hɔːs‖hɔːrs/ *n* **1** [C] a large strong four-legged animal with hard feet (HOOVES), which people ride on and use for pulling heavy things: *learning to ride a horse* | *A male horse is called a stallion, and a female horse is a mare.* | *We went to see the horse races.* —see BICYCLE (USAGE) —see also FOAL, NEIGH **2** [C] an exercise apparatus for jumping over; VAULTING HORSE **3** [P] *old use, esp. BrE* soldiers riding on horses; CAVALRY: *a regiment of horse* **4** [U] *sl for* HEROIN **5 a horse! a horse! my kingdom for a horse!** *quote* a phrase from Shakespeare's play *Richard III*, said by the King when he needs a horse very badly and now often used humorously when someone needs something badly **6 a horse of another/a different colour** a completely different thing or situation

The most common or most basic meanings are always shown first. These are followed by other meanings that are less common or more limited in their use: for example, they may be old-fashioned or literary or technical, or they may be used in only one variety of English (such as American English). Finally, if there are any idioms, these are listed in alphabetical order AFTER all the other definitions.

2.2 Definitions

Definitions in simple language

Definitions are the explanations of what words mean. All the definitions in this dictionary are written in clear and simple language, using a small "defining vocabulary" of about 2000 common words. This means that you will have no trouble in understanding even difficult or unfamiliar words, such as:

ped·i·ment /ˈpedᵻmənt/ n a three-sided piece of stone or other material placed above the entrance to a building, found esp. in the buildings of ancient Greece

The list of words that are used in the definitions is shown at the back of the dictionary on page B15. Every definition has been computer-checked to make sure that it is written ONLY using words from the list.

The use of words from outside the defining vocabulary

It is sometimes necessary in a definition to refer to a less common word that is not in the 2000-word defining vocabulary. When this happens, the word is written in SMALL CAPITAL LETTERS to show that it does not belong to the special list, like this:

white wed·ding /ˌ· ˈ··/ n esp. BrE a wedding at which the BRIDE (=woman being married) wears a long white dress

This means that **bride** is not one of the 2000 defining words. You may need to check its meaning at its own entry in the dictionary, but you already have some help from the words in brackets (= woman being married) which give a short explanation of what **bride** means.

Sometimes a definition includes a word that has its own definition very close by. If the other definition is no more than three entries away, the word is written in ordinary type, even if it is not in the 2000-word defining vocabulary. For example:

auc·tio·neer /ˌɔːkʃəˈnɪəʳ/ n a person who is in charge of an auction and who calls out the prices as they are reached

The word "auction" is not on the special list of defining words, but its own definition is only two entries away, so it can be found very easily.

2.3 Synonyms

A synonym is a word that has the same meaning, or almost the same meaning, as another word. In this dictionary, synonyms are usually shown directly after the full definition, like this:

plod /plɒd‖plɑːd/ v -dd- 1 [I+adv/prep] to walk slowly along, esp. with difficulty and great effort; TRUDGE: *The carthorse plodded along/plodded up the hill pulling the load behind it.* 2 [I+adv/prep, esp. AWAY, ON] to work steadily, esp. at something uninteresting: *She plods away quietly in her corner.* | *I'll plod on* (=continue to work) *for another hour and then take a break.*

This means that "trudge" is another way of saying "plod". Sometimes the added synonym at the end of a definition will be a more familiar word than the word you are looking up. If so, it will help you understand the definition better. For example:

rally³ v [T (**about, on**)] *old use* to make fun of (a person) in a friendly way; TEASE: *They rallied him about/on his strange appearance.*

On the other hand, the synonym may be a LESS common word than the one you are looking up, and in this case it will help to increase your vocabulary. For example:

hide¹ /haɪd/ v hid /hɪd/, hidden /ˈhɪdn/ [(**from**)] 1 [T] to put or keep out of sight; prevent from being seen or found; CONCEAL: *I hid the broken plate in the drawer.* | *The house was hidden from view by a row of tall trees.* |

2.4 Brackets in definitions

Sometimes part of a definition is shown in round brackets, like this:

pal·pi·tate /ˈpælpᵻteɪt/ v [I] 1 *med* (of the heart) to beat fast and irregularly 2 [(**with**)] *fml* (of a person or the body) to tremble: *He was positively palpitating with excitement.*

The definition explains what **palpitate** means, but the part in brackets shows that this word is only used when talking about the heart.

Brackets are used in definitions:
1 to give information about how and when a word is normally used
2 to show that part of a definition can be either included or left out

Here are some examples:

Information on word use

glau·cous /ˈglɔːkəs/ adj tech (of a leaf, fruit, etc.) covered with a fine whitish powdery surface

This means that **glaucous** is normally used to describe things like plants and fruit.

glean /gliːn/ v 1 [T] to gather (facts or information) in small amounts and often with difficulty: *From what I was able to glean, it appears they don't intend to take any action yet.* 2 [I;T] to collect (grain that has been left behind) after crops have been cut

This means that the usual object of this verb is "facts" or "information".

huh /hʌh/ *interj infml* (used for asking a question or for expressing surprise or disapproval): *It's pretty big, huh?*

Words like **huh**, **ouch**, and **shh** are not given proper definitions because they have no real meaning. Instead, they are given a note in brackets that explains the kind of situation in which they are normally used.

Inclusion or exclusion

pars·nip /ˈpɑːsnɪp‖ˈpɑːr-/ *n* [C;U] (a plant with) a thick white or yellowish root that is used as a vegetable

The brackets here are used to show that the first half of the definition can be left out. So **parsnip** can mean EITHER "a type of root that is used as a vegetable" OR "the plant that produces this root".

hur·ry¹ /ˈhʌri‖ˈhɜːri/ *v* **1** [I;T] to (cause to) be quick in action or movement, sometimes too quick: *There's no need to hurry; we're not late.* | *She hurried across the road to catch the bus.* | *Don't hurry me; I'm working as fast as I can!*

The brackets show that **hurry** can mean EITHER "to move quickly" (*She hurried across the road*) OR "to make someone move quickly" (*Don't hurry me*).

2.5 Examples

The dictionary includes a great many examples of words in use. The examples may be short phrases or whole sentences, and they are written in *italic letters* after the definition, like this:

ran·sack /ˈrænsæk/ *v* [T] **1** to search (a place) thoroughly and roughly, causing disorder: *The police ransacked the house, looking for drugs.* **2** to go through (a place) stealing and causing widespread damage: *Enemy soldiers ransacked the town.*

Examples are normally written in simple language, but if a difficult word or phrase is included it is usually explained by a note in brackets, like this:

groom² *v* **1** [T] to take care of (horses), esp. by rubbing, brushing, and cleaning them .... **4** [T (for)] to prepare (someone) for a special position or occasion: *They were grooming her for stardom.* (=to play big parts in plays or films)

The examples are used to help you understand the meaning of a new word and to show how it is actually used.
They have special functions:
1 to show context – the kinds of situation in which the headword is typically used
2 to show grammar – the way the headword can combine with other words in clauses or sentences
3 to show collocation – the particular words that are often used with the headword

Here are some examples:

Context

pelt¹ /pelt/ *v* **1** [T (**with**)] to attack (someone) by throwing a lot of things at them, quickly and repeatedly: *They pelted the speaker with rotten tomatoes.*

This example gives a typical situation in which **pelt** might be used, and it also shows the kind of things that people throw when they **pelt** someone.

Grammar

guess¹ /ges/ *v* **1** [I (**at**); T] to form a judgment (about) or risk giving an opinion (on) without knowing or considering all the facts: *"I don't know the answer." "Well just guess!"* | *Can you guess (at) the price?* [+(*that*)] *I guessed I'd find you in here!* [+*wh-*] *You'll never guess how much*|*what it cost.* [+*obj+to-v*] *I'd guess it to be about £300.*

These examples show how **guess** can be used as a transitive or intransitive verb (with or without an object) or with various kinds of clause. The sloping line (/) is used to show different uses of a word that are equally common or equally correct. So you can say:
You'll never guess what it cost.
OR *You'll never guess how much it cost.*

Collocation

herd¹ /hɜːd‖hɜːrd/ *n* **1** [C+*sing.*|*pl. v*] a group of animals of one kind which live and feed together: *a herd of cattle*|*elephants* —compare FLOCK¹ (1)

The definition explains what **herd** means, but it is the example that shows the kinds of animal that **herd** is used in connection with. This is an example of "collocation", or the way that some words are regularly used in combination with others. If a particular combination is very common or very fixed, it is shown in **dark type**, like this:

harm¹ /hɑːm‖hɑːrm/ *n* [U (**to**)] **1** damage or wrong: *His film was a complete failure, and this did his reputation a lot of harm.* .... | *I don't think you should punish them for this – it would probably* **do more harm than good.** (=have a damaging rather than helpful effect) —see also GRIEVOUS BODILY HARM **2 come to harm** [*usu. in negatives*] to be hurt: *My brother's ship was caught in a storm but he came to no harm.* **3 out of harm's way** in a position in which one is **a** safe from harm or **b** unable to cause harm

This means that the expression **do more harm than good** is a particularly common use of the noun **harm**. The note in brackets at the end of the example helps to make the meaning completely clear.

2.6 Figurative examples

Some words are used in an imaginative or "figurative" way, to suggest a meaning that is not the literal meaning but has some similarities with it. If a word is often used like this, the examples will include a figurative use, and this is shown by the note (fig.):

grab[1] /græb/ *v* **-bb-** [T]   **1** to take hold of (a person or thing) with a sudden rough movement, esp. for a bad or selfish purpose: *He grabbed the money and ran off.* | *They grabbed her by the arm and forced her into their car.* | (fig.) *Don't miss this chance to travel — grab it before the boss changes her mind.*

As the definition shows, **grab** describes a physical action or movement. But **grab** can also be used to express the idea of eagerly accepting a chance or opportunity. This is NOT a physical process, so the example is figurative.

2.7 Brackets in examples

Brackets are used in examples:
1 to make the meaning of the example sentence completely clear
2 to show the situation in which a particular expression would be used
3 to show that part of an example can be either included or left out

Here are some examples:

Explanation

ram[2] *v* **-mm-** [T]   **1** to run or drive into (something) very hard: *His car rammed mine.* **2** [+obj+adv|prep] to force into place with heavy pressure: *I rammed down the earth round the newly planted bush.* | (fig.) *The terrorist attack rammed home the need for tighter security.* (=forced people to recognize this need)

Explanations like this are often given as an additional way of making the meaning clear, and they are especially common if the example is figurative or includes a strong collocation in dark type.

Situation

sup·pose[1] /sə'pəʊz/ *v* [T *not usu. in progressive forms*]   **1** [+(that);obj] to consider to be probable; ASSUME: *As she's not here, I suppose she must have gone home.* | *There's no reason to suppose that his new book will be any better than his last one.* | *"He must have missed the train, then." "Yes, I suppose so."* | *I don't suppose she'll agree.* | (in polite requests) *I don't suppose you could give me a lift to the station, could you?*

In this case, the note in brackets explains that **suppose** is often used in expressions like this as a polite way of making a request.

Inclusion or exclusion

pass[1] /pɑːs‖pæs/ *v*   **1** [I (BY);T] to reach and move beyond (a person or place) . . . .
6 [I;T **(to)**] (in various sports) to kick, throw, hit, etc. (esp. a ball), esp. to a member of one's own side: *He passed (the ball) back to the goalkeeper.*

Pass can be used here either with or without an object. So "the ball" can be left out of this sentence, and is therefore shown in brackets.

3 Grammar

As well as explaining the meaning of words, the dictionary provides a great deal of information about grammar. It tells you the word class that a headword belongs to — whether it is a noun, an adjective, a verb, or some other type of word. It gives information about the inflections of words — how their form changes when they are used in the plural, or in the past tense, or in some other way. And it gives a full description of the word's syntax — the various patterns in which it can combine with other words to form sentences. The purpose of this section is to explain how to use the grammatical information in the dictionary.

3.1 Word classes

Most words in the dictionary are given a special sign to show their word class (or "part of speech"), like this:

harm·less /'hɑːmləs‖'hɑːrm-/ *adj* unable or unlikely to cause harm: *The dog seems fierce, but he's harmless.* — ~**ly** *adv* — ~**ness** *n* [U]

This means that **harmless** is an adjective. Derived forms are also given word class labels: **harmlessly** is an adverb and **harmlessness** is a noun. Some words belong to more than one word class, and these are usually shown as separate headwords, like this:

for·mat[1] /'fɔːmæt‖'fɔːr-/ *n*   **1** the size, shape, etc., in which something, esp. a book, is produced   **2** the general plan or arrangement of something: *a new format for the six o'clock TV news* | *Official reports are usually written to a set format.*
format[2] *v* **-tt-** [T] to arrange (a book, computer information, etc.) in a particular format

But occasionally a word belonging to two different word classes is dealt with in a single combined entry, like this:

fric·a·tive /'frɪkətɪv/ *adj, n tech* (a consonant sound such as /f/ or /z/) made by forcing air out through a narrow opening between the tongue or lip and another part of the mouth

Fricative can be a noun OR an adjective. The full definition describes its use as a noun. If the words in brackets are left out, the part that remains describes its use as an adjective.

Words referring to people, places, organizations, institutions, etc. are given no sign to show word class and no grammar code, e.g.:

High·grove House /ˌhaɪɡrəʊv 'haʊs/ a house in Gloucestershire, England, which is owned by the Prince and Princess of Wales

If the name of a place, institution, etc. is usually used with "the", it is given the grammar code [*the*]:

Grand Na·tion·al /ˌ· '···/ [*the*] a famous horse race held each year at the AINTREE course near Liverpool. Many people who never usu. show interest in racing risk their money on the horse they think will win the Grand National.

Table 3.1 shows the word classes used in the dictionary. You can find the exact meanings of these terms by looking up their definitions in the dictionary.

Table 3.1 Word classes

sign	word class	examples
abbrev.	abbreviation that can be written or spoken	domestic animals, e.g. cows and sheep Washington DC
adj	adjective	a **fast** car a **run-of-the-mill** book
adv	adverb	smiling **happily** Put it **away**.
conj	conjunction	You won't pass **unless** you work.
determiner	determiner	**this** week **my** younger brother
interj	interjection	**Hello** Jane! **Ouch!**
n	noun	a black **dog** a few **odds and ends**
phr v	phrasal verb	I've **given up** smoking. **Hand** the books **out**. I won't **put up with** this.
predeterminer	predeterminer	**all** the students **half** an hour
prep	preposition	Put it **in** the drawer. Don't drive **after** drinking.
pron	pronoun	**She** bought **it** for **herself**. **Who** said **that**?
short for	shortened form of a pronoun + verb combination	**I'll** do it. **They'd** already left.
v	verb	She **teaches** English. You **need** a rest.
written abbrev.	abbreviation that can be written but not spoken	**Fri.** 20th October 13,000 **Hz**

3.2 Inflections

General notes

Inflections are the changes that are made in the form of a word according to how it is being used in a sentence. Most words form their inflections according to regular rules. For example, nouns usually add **-s** OR **-es** to make the plural, and verbs usually end in **-ed** when they are used in the past tense. These "regular inflections" are not shown in the dictionary, except where there is a possibility of confusion or if the regular inflection has a difficult pronunciation.

"Irregular inflections" are always shown. They come directly after the word class sign and they are written in **dark type**, like this:

sheep /ʃiːp/ n **sheep** **1** a grass-eating animal that is farmed for its wool and its meat

This means the plural of **sheep** is **sheep** (NOT **sheeps**, which would be a regular plural).

For words of two or more syllables, only the part that changes is usually shown, like this:

hy·poth·e·sis /haɪˈpɒθ{ə}s{ɪ}s‖-ˈpɑː-/ n **-ses** /siːz/

So the plural of **hypothesis** is **hypotheses**.

Inflections that are formed by doubling the consonant at the end of a word are shown like this:

grab[1] /græb/ v **-bb-**
grim /grɪm/ adj **-mm-**

This means that **grab** becomes **grabbed** in the past, **grabbing** in the present participle, and so on. And **grim** becomes **grimmer** and **grimmest** when used in the comparative and superlative.

If an irregular inflection is very different from the base form, it also has its own separate entry directing you to the base form, like this:

fought /fɔːt/ past tense & participle of FIGHT[1]

Special rules for nouns, verbs, and adjectives

Noun inflections
If two or more plural forms are possible, they are shown like this:

hoof /huːf‖hʊf/ n **hoofs** or **hooves** /huːvz‖hʊfs/

Inflections are always shown for nouns ending in **-o** because it is impossible to know whether the plural of a particular noun will be **-os** OR **-oes**:

ga·ze·bo /ɡəˈziːbəʊ‖-ˈzeɪ-, -ˈziː-/ n **-bos** a shelter or hut, usu. in a garden, where one can sit and look at the view

Verb inflections
If only one inflection is shown at a verb, it is both the past tense and the past participle:

catch[1] /kætʃ/ v **caught** /kɔːt/

This means that **caught** is used for the past tense (*She caught the ball*) AND for the past participle (*The ball has been caught*).

If two inflections are shown, the first one is the past tense and the second one is the past participle:

for·give /fəˈɡɪv‖fər-/ v **-gave** /ˈɡeɪv/, **-given** /ˈɡɪvən/

If any variation is possible, it is shown like this:

sow[1] /səʊ/ v **sowed**, **sown** /səʊn/ or **sowed**

This means that the past tense is **sowed**, but the past participle can be either **sown** OR **sowed**.

If other irregular inflections are shown in addition to the past tense and past participle, they come after these two and are fully explained.

go[1] /gəʊ/ *v* **went** /went/, **gone** /gɒn‖gɔːn/*3rd person sing. present* **goes**

There is a full list of verbs with irregular inflections at the back of the book on page B23.

Adjective inflections

A small number of adjectives have irregular forms when used in the comparative and superlative. These irregular inflections are shown like this:

bad[1] /bæd/ *adj* **worse** /wɜːs‖wɜːrs/, **worst** /wɜːst‖wɜːrst/

The comparative is shown first, the superlative second.

In all other cases, the comparative and superlative forms of adjectives are produced EITHER by adding **-er** and **-est** (or **-r**, **-st**, **-ier**, **-iest**) OR by using **more** and **most** before the adjective. The choice of inflection types is governed by these general rules:

for words of one syllable
-er, **-est** are usual; **more**, **most** are possible but uncommon:
    rich   richer   richest

for words of two syllables
-er, **-est** and **more**, **most** are equally common:
  wealthy wealthier   wealthiest
OR   **more wealthy most wealthy**

for words of three or more syllables
more, **most** are always used:
    affluent more affluent most affluent

There are occasional exceptions to these general rules. The two main exceptions are:
1 adjectives formed from participles never use **-er**, **-est**:
    bored more bored most bored
    tiring more tiring most tiring
2 adjectives which have three syllables but start with **un-** can use **-er**, **-est**:
    unhappy unhappier unhappiest

3.3 Grammar codes

The dictionary uses a special system of easy-to-understand grammar codes. These codes give a complete description of the various ways in which a word can combine with other words to form sentences. The grammar codes are shown in square brackets, like this:

a·wake[1] /əˈweɪk/ *adj* [F] not asleep: *She lay awake for hours thinking about him.* | *The children are still* **wide awake.** (=not at all sleepy) | (fig.) *The company is awake to* (=conscious of) *these new developments.*

This code means that **awake** can only be used AFTER the noun it describes, not before it. So you can say:

The children are awake and making a lot of noise but NOT
The awake children are making a lot of noise.

There is a full list of all the grammar codes at the front of the dictionary.

This section will explain:

- The main types of code
- Where to find the codes in a dictionary entry
- What the special signs in codes mean
- The relationship between the codes and the examples
- How the codes are used with adjectives, nouns and verbs

The main types of code

The code system consists of four main types of information. These are:
1 the letter codes, like [I] [T] [C] [U]
   These give basic grammatical information, such as whether a verb is transitive or intransitive, and whether a noun is countable or uncountable.
2 Prepositions or adverbs, like [(to)] [(with)], that can or must be used after a particular word
3 sentence pattern codes like [+to-v] [+v-ing]
   These show the types of clause that can follow a word.
4 other limitations on a word's use, e.g. [*usu. sing.*] [*usu. in negatives*] [*not in progressive forms*]

Where to find the codes

Codes can be shown at three different placs in an entry. These are:
1 before ALL the definitions, like this:

fox[2] *v* [T] *infml* **1** *BrE* to confuse; to be too difficult for (someone) to understand: *The second question on the exam paper completely foxed me.* **2** to deceive cleverly; trick: *He managed to fox them by wearing a disguise.*

This means that, although **fox** has two separate meanings, they both have the same code.

2 at the beginning of a particular definition, like this:

rar·i·ty /ˈreərɪti/ *n* **1** [U] the state or quality of being RARE[1] (1): *These stamps have great rarity value.* **2** [C] something uncommon: *People who bake their own bread have become a rarity|something of a rarity.*

3 directly before a particular example, like this:

hunch[1] /hʌntʃ/ *n* an idea based on feeling rather than on reason or facts: *"How did you know that horse was going to win?" "It was just a hunch."* [+(that)] *I have a hunch that she didn't really want to go.*

This means that **hunch** can be followed by a clause with *that*, and an example of this pattern is shown straight after the code.

What the special signs in codes mean

Brackets

Round brackets ( ) are used to show parts of a code that can either be included or left out. Their main use is to show the prepositions or adverbs that are frequently used after a particular word, like this:

gap /gæp/ n [(in, between)] **1** an empty space between two objects or two parts of an object: *The gate was locked but we went through a gap in the fence.*

This means you can say:
> We went through a gap **in** the fence
OR We went through a gap **between** the houses.

But the brackets show that these prepositions are only "optional" – they do not have to be used – so you can also say, simply:
> We went through a gap.

Note that **in** and **between** are written in **dark type** because they are prepositions. When adverbs are shown in codes, they are written in SMALL CAPITAL LETTERS, like this:

heal /hiːl/ v **1** [I (OVER, UP)] (of a wounded part of the body) to become healthy again, esp. to grow new skin

The code here means you can say:
> The wound healed up
> The wound healed over
OR simply
> The wound healed.

The plus sign

The plus sign + is used to show part of a code that MUST be included. For example:

fraught /frɔːt/ adj **1** [F+with] full of something unpleasant: *The expedition through the jungle was fraught with difficulties and danger.* **2** infml troubled by anxieties; very TENSE

The code shows that **with** is 'obligatory' here. It MUST be used after **fraught** in this meaning, so you cannot say:
> The expedition **was fraught**.

Here is another example:

hare² v [I | adv/prep] BrE infml to run very fast: *He hared off down the road.*

The code [I] shows that **hare** is an intransitive verb, but in this case it MUST also be followed by an adverb or preposition. So you can say:
> We hared off down the road/She hared along the street/I hared after the bus, and so on.
But you cannot simply say:
> We hared.

Note that the + sign has a different function when it is used in codes that come directly before examples.

In these cases, the pattern shown is NOT obligatory: the + here simply means that this pattern can be used as well as any others that have already been mentioned.

The relationship between the codes and the examples

The codes give a complete description of the grammar of each word and each meaning. The examples illustrate most of the information shown in the codes, but simple grammatical points are not always illustrated with an example. For instance, if a noun can be both countable and uncountable, examples of each use will not necessarily be given, or if a code shows that a particular word can be used with several different prepositions, there will not always be an example of every one. But if the codes include a sentence pattern, such as [+v-ing] or [+to-v], this will always be shown in an example.

When there is a wide range of grammatical information for a particular word or meaning, the examples usually start by illustrating the simple uses and then move on to those which are more difficult or less common, like this:

re·mem·ber /rɪˈmembəʳ/ v [not usu. in progressive forms] **1** [I;T (as)] to (be able to) bring back to one's mind (information, past events, etc.); keep in the memory: *"What's her name?" "I can't remember."* | *I'll always remember that wonderful day.* | *I remember her as* (=I think she was, if my memory is correct) *rather a tall woman.* [+(that)] *She suddenly remembered that she had not locked the door.* [+wh-] *Can you remember where he lives/how to get there?* [+v-ing] *I don't remember agreeing to that.* | *Certainly I posted your letter – I remember posting it.* [+obj+v-ing] *Do you remember me asking you that same question?*

These examples show FIRST simple intransitive and transitive uses, THEN a sentence that shows how the verb can be used with the preposition **as**, and LASTLY some sentences that show the four different sentence patterns which can be used with **remember**.

Table 3.3 How the codes are used with adjectives, nouns, and verbs

code	meaning	examples	correct or incorrect
adjectives			
no code	Can be used before the noun it describes, after a verb, or after a verb and its object. Most adjectives can behave like this, and so they are not coded.	a **happy** smile She looks **happy**. It made her **happy**.	
[A]	Used only before the noun it describes.	an **indoor** swimming pool The pool is indoor.	✕
[F]	Used only after a verb.	The children are **asleep**. the asleep children	✕
[after *n*]	Used directly after the noun it describes	the director **designate** the director is designate. the designate director	✕ ✕
[also *n*, *the*+P]	Can be used with **the** to form a plural noun.	The **rich** (= rich people) have received tax cuts.	
[*no comp.*]	Not used in the comparative or superlative forms.	the **main** difficulty This is the mainest difficulty.	✕
optional or obligatory prepositions, such as [(**in**)] [(**about**)] [+**with**]	Many adjectives are followed by particular prepositions. The round brackets show that a preposition may or may not be used, but the plus sign means that the preposition MUST be used.	**interested** in football **glad** about your new job **fraught** with problems	
sentence patterns, such as [+*to-v*] [+*that*]	Some adjectives can be followed by sentence patterns, such as a *to*-infinitive or a *that*-clause.	**afraid** to tell her **hopeful** that she'll win	
nouns			
no code	Simple countable noun: a large number of nouns are of this type so they are not given a code.	Have you got a **dog**? The **dogs** were barking.	
	Most nouns can also be used before another noun as "modifiers". This use is not coded but is shown in examples when it is common.	**dog** food **office** equipment	
[C]	Countable noun: these are ONLY coded if they also have another code, e.g.: **illness** *n* [C;U].	serious **illnesses** absent due to **illness**	
[U]	Uncountable noun: not used in the plural and not usually used with **a**, **an**, or **one**.	a roomful of **furniture** some furnitures Here is the **information** you asked for. Here are the informations you asked for.	✕ ✕
[P]	Plural noun: used only with a plural verb or pronoun.	The police need public **support**. These **trousers** are new. This scissors is sharp.	✕
[S]	Singular noun: cannot be counted or used in the plural; usually used with **a** or **an**.	I'll have a **think** about it. I'll have one think about it. I'll have a few thinks about it.	✕ ✕
[*the*]	Special noun that is the name of an actual place, organization, event, etc., ALWAYS used with **the**.	the **Kremlin** the **Renaissance**	
[*the*+P]	Shows use with **the**: [*the*+code] means **the** is obligatory.	This place gives me the **creeps**! This place gives me creeps!	✕
[(*the*) U]	[(*the*) code] means **the** is common but not obligatory.	She's got the **measles**. She's got **measles**.	
[+*sing./pl. v*]	Noun representing a group or organization, which can be used with a	The **committee** has reached a decision.	

code	meaning	examples	correct or incorrect
	singular or plural verb when the noun is singular. (This use is common in British English but rare in American English.)	**The committee have reached a decision.**	
optional or obligatory prepositions, such as [(between, with)] [+of]	Many nouns are followed by particular prepositions. The round brackets show that a preposition may or may not be used, but the plus sign means that the preposition MUST be used.	**the frontier between Norway and Sweden** **Norway's frontier with Sweden** **a hotbed of crime**	
sentence patterns, such as [+to-v] [+wh-]	Many nouns can be followed by sentence patterns, such as a to-infinitive or a clause beginning with a wh- word.	**a decision to leave** **the reason why she went**	

verbs

code	meaning	examples	correct or incorrect
[I]	intransitive verb; a verb that does not take a direct object.	**He's sleeping.** **We got up early.**	
[T]	Transitive verb; a verb that must have a direct object, which may be a noun or pronoun, OR a clause. A verb with this code takes a noun or pronoun object. If a [T] verb can also take a clause as its object, a sentence pattern is added to the code.	**I enjoyed the book.** **I enjoyed it.** I enjoyed.	✗
[L]	"Linking" verb: a verb followed by a noun or adjective complement that refers to the subject of the verb. Most [L] verbs can have both nouns and adjectives as complements.	**I felt stupid.** **I felt a fool.**	
	If an [L] verb can ONLY take an adjective, or ONLY a noun as its complement, it is coded [L+adj] or [L+n]	**That sounds interesting.** **This represents a big improvement.**	
optional adverbs and prepositions, such as [I(together)] [I(against)] [T(of)]	Many verbs can be followed by a particular adverb or preposition, but the round brackets show that the verb can also be used without an adverb or preposition.	**The children huddled together.** **plotting against the government** **She was accused of murder.**	
obligatory adverbs and prepositions	Some verbs MUST be followed by a particular adverb or preposition. These verbs are treated as phrasal verbs. For example, **refer** is always used with **to**, so it is shown as **refer to** phr v.	**The writer refers to another book on this subject.**	
[I+adv/prep] [T+obj+adv/prep]	These verbs MUST be followed by an adverb or preposition, but many different adverbs or prepositions can be used. Verbs like this cannot be used on their own.	**My daughter lives along the road/ abroad/in Italy.** My daughter lives. **Put the box away/on the table/over there.** Put the box.	✗ ✗
sentence patterns, such as [+to-v] [+v-ing] [+(that)]	Many verbs can be followed by sentence patterns, such as a to-infinitive, a verb in the -ing form, or a that-clause.	**We decided to go.** **She's given up smoking.** **I think (that) he's gone home.**	

special sentence patterns only used with verbs

code	meaning	examples	correct or incorrect
[+obj(i) +obj(d)]	A verb that takes two objects, an indirect and a direct object. Verbs with this pattern can usually also be used in the pattern: verb + direct object + to + indirect object.	**I handed her the plate.** I handed her. **I handed the plate to her.**	✗

code	meaning	examples	correct or incorrect
	A transitive verb that is followed by an object AND a clause or complement is shown with a code that begins with [+ *obj* +].		
[+*obj*+*to-v*]	Verb + object + infinitive.	**I advised her to go.**	
		She was advised to go.	
		I advised to go.	×
[+*obj*+*to-v*]	Verb + object + infinitive without **to**. The **to** is used when the verb is passive.	**We saw him leave.**	
		He was seen to leave.	
		We saw leave.	×
[+*obj*+*v-ing*)	Verb + object + verb in **-ing** form.	**They heard someone laughing.**	
		Someone was heard laughing.	
		They heard laughing.	×
[+*obj*+*that*]	Verb + object + clause with **that**.	**I told the boss that I would be late.**	
		The boss was told that I would be late.	
		I told that I would be late.	×
[+*obj*+*wh-*]	Verb + object + clause with **wh-**.	**Tell us why you did it.**	
		We were told why she did it.	
		Tell why you did it.	×
[+*obj*+*v-ed*]	Verb + object + past participle.	**I want this work finished by tomorrow.**	×
		I want finished by tomorrow.	
[+*obj*+*adj*]	Verb + object + adjective.	**They believed her guilty.**	
		She was believed (to be) guilty.	
		They believed guilty.	×
[+*obj*+*n*]	Verb + object + noun.	**They consider this offer a big improvement.**	
		This offer is considered (to be) a big improvement.	
		They consider a big improvement.	×
[*obj*] e.g. (T+*that; obj*]	A transitive verb whose object is always a clause, NEVER a noun or pronoun.	**They reasoned that the murderer must have been a woman.**	
		They reasoned it.	×
[*not in progressive forms*]	A verb that is not used in the progressive aspect (i.e. not following the verb **be** in an **-ing** form).	**I like football.**	
		I am liking football.	×

3.4 Grammar and phrasal verbs

Phrasal verbs can be transitive or intransitive, exactly like ordinary verbs. Intransitive phrasal verbs are used in the same way as other intransitive verbs. But in order to use a transitive phrasal verb correctly, you need to know exactly where its object or objects can go. For example, you can say:

Take off your coat

OR **Take** your coat **off**.

But you can only say:

She **takes after** her mother

and NOT

She **takes** her mother **after**.

Every phrasal verb entry provides information about where the object can go. This information is shown by means of an easy-to-use system of signs, which is explained in the examples that follow. There are six main types of transitive phrasal verb.

Table 3.4 Main types of transitive phrasal verb

verb type	meaning	examples	correct or incorrect
send sbdy./sthg. ↔ **out**	sbdy. means "somebody" (= a person) and sthg. means "something" (= a non-human object). The sign ↔ means that the object can come either before **out** or after it. But if the object is a pronoun (**him, her,** etc.) it MUST come directly after the verb. This is the most common type of phrasal verb.	**We sent out the invitations.** **We sent the invitations out.** **We sent them out.** We sent out them.	×
push sbdy. **around.**	The object must come BETWEEN **push** and **around**.	**He always pushes his sister around.** He always pushes around his sister.	×
break into sthg.	The object must come AFTER **into**.	**They broke into the empty house.** They broke the empty house into.	×
put up with sbdy./sthg.	The object must come AFTER both **up** and **with**.	**I won't put up with this.** I won't put this up with. I won't put up this with.	× ×
acquaint sbdy. **wih** sthg.	There are two objects, one before **with** and one after it.	**She acquainted us with the facts.** She acquainted with us the facts.	×
see sbdy. **through** (sthg.)	The verb can have either one object, which comes before **through**, or two objects, one before **through** and one after it.	**Here's $10 to see you through.** **Here's $10 to see you through the weekend.** Here's $10 to see through you.	×

4 Style and usage – how the dictionary can help you to choose the right word

As well as explaining meaning and grammar, the dictionary provides a great deal of information about style and usage. A system of "labels" is used to show words and phrases that can only be used in certain styles of speaking or writing. There is also detailed information about word variation – how a particular meaning can be expressed by a variety of different words. And a system of cross-references notes that direct you from one entry to another – is used to draw your attention to points of difference or similarity in words of the same general type. Finally, the Usage Notes give detailed information about difficult points of grammar, about fine differences between words of roughly the same meaning, and about choosing the most suitable word or phrase to express a particular idea. All this information will help you to use words correctly and to increase your vocabulary by building on what you already know.

4.1 Labels

This section will explain:

* The purpose of labels
* The types of label used in the dictionary
* Where labels can be shown in dictionary entries

The purpose of labels

Most of the words in the dictionary could be used, either in speaking or writing, in any kind of situation, or in any variety of English. But if the use of a word is limited in some way, it will be given a label, like this:

vend /vend/ v [T]   **1** *law* to sell (esp. land or other property)

The label *law* shows that **vend** is only used as a technical legal term – for example, in contracts or other official papers. You would not say to a friend:

"I hear Susan's planning to **vend** her house". The meaning is correct, but the style is wrong.

There is another word with the same meaning:

flog /flɒg‖flɑːg/ v -**gg**- [T]   **1** to beat severely with a whip or stick, esp. as a punishment   **2** *BrE infml* to sell: *He makes a living flogging encyclopedias.*

In this case, the label shows that **flog** is an informal word: its use is limited to informal situations, and it is not usually used in writing (certainly not in offical writing). The label also shows that **flog** is "British English", that is, it would not be used by speakers of other varieties of English, such as Americans or Canadians.

The dictionary uses labels to show how the use of a particular word or meaning is limited to certain types of speech or writing, or to certain regions of the English-speaking world. Understanding these labels will help you to use the dictionary effectively in order to choose the right word for any situation.

Types of label used in the dictionary

This section explains the labels according to the type of information they show.

> There is a full list of all the labels at the back of the dictionary.

Labels showing region

Most words can be used in any variety of English, but some are limited to particular parts of the world. These are shown by the following labels:

AmE American English
BrE British English

These are the two main varieties of English. American English usually includes the English of both the US and Canada. British English is the variety of English spoken in Britain, and usually also includes the English of Ireland, Australia and New Zealand, India and Pakistan, Africa and the Caribbean. But if a word is strictly limited to one region, this is shown by one of the following labels:

AustrE	Australian English
CanE	Canadian English
CarE	Caribbean English
IndE & PakE	Indian & Pakistani English
IrE	Irish English
NZE	New Zealand English
SAfrE	South African English
ScotE	Scottish English

Words that are used in English but borrowed from other languages (such as **zeitgeist** or **je ne sais quoi**) are given labels that show their language or origin:

Fr	French
Ger	German
It	Italian
Lat	Latin
Sp	Spanish

Labels showing special fields or subjects

Some words are only used in certain fields of activity or certain types of writing. These are shown by the following labels:

bibl	used mainly in the Bible
law	legal term – used in contracts, courts of law, etc.
lit	used mainly in literature
med	medical term – used by doctors, nurses, etc.
naut	nautical term – used by sailors
poet	used mainly in poetry
tech	technical term – used by specialists in various fields

Labels showing situations in which words are used

Some words would only be suitable in certain types of situation. These are shown by the following labels:

infml	informal – used especially in conversation, in letters between friends, etc.
fml	formal – used especially in official papers, business letters, public speeches, etc.
sl	slang – very informal, rarely used in writing, used especially in the private language of particular social groups

Labels showing time

Some words are no longer used in modern English (though they will often be found in old books), and some are beginning to be used less often. These are shown by the following labels:

old-fash	old-fashioned – no longer common, used mainly by older people
old use	no longer used
rare or becoming rare	rarely used, or beginning to be used less often

Labels showing attitude

Some words are used to suggest a particular attitude. For example, the word **new-fangled** is similar in meaning to **modern**, but it also suggests an attitude of disapproval: if you call something **new-fangled**, it means that it is new but that you do not like it or regard it as necessary. Words that show the speaker's attitude are given one of the following labels:

apprec	appreciative – shows that the speaker likes or approves of something
derog	derogatory – shows that the speaker dislikes or disapproves of something
euph	euphemistic – a polite or indirect word for something unpleasant or embarrassing
humor	humorous – shows a joking or ironic attitude
pomp	pompous – shows a foolishly self-important attitude

Labels showing other limitations on use

dial	dialect – a word belonging to the local speech of a particular area
nonstandard	a word regarded as incorrect by most educated speakers
taboo	a very offensive word which should always be avoided
tdmk	a trademark, whose use is officially controlled

Where labels can be shown in dictionary entries

Labels can appear in any of the following parts of an entry:

1 before ALL the definitions, like this:

ob·lo·quy /ˈɒbləkwi‖ˈɑːb-/ n [U] *fml* **1** strong words spoken against someone; ABUSE **2** loss of respect and honour; DISGRACE

This means that **obloquy** is formal in both its meanings.

2 before a particular definition, like this:

liq·uid¹ /ˈlɪkwĭd/ n **1** [C;U] a substance which is not a solid or a gas, which flows, is wet, and has no fixed shape: *Water is a liquid.* **2** [C] *tech* either of the consonant sounds /l/ and /r/

This means that the second meaning is technical, but there are no limitations on the use of the first meaning.

3   in idioms, either before the definition:

9 dead as a doornail *infml* completely dead

or in the actual form of the idiom:

2 a new lease of life (*BrE*)|**on life** (*AmE*) the ability to be happy, active, and successful again, esp. after being weak or tired

This means that British speakers say "a new lease of life", and American speakers say "a new lease on life".

4   in or before a particular example, like this:

man·y /ˈmeni/ *determiner, pron*   **1** a large number (of): more than several but less than most: *Many people find this kind of film unpleasant. . . . . (fml) Many a good climber* (=many good climbers) *has met his death on this mountain.*

The label here shows that **many** is informal when it is used in this particular pattern (**many a . . .**) but its other uses are not limited.

5   with a particular pronunciation, like this:

lee·ward[1] /ˈliːwəd, *tech* ˈluːəd‖-ərd/ *adj, adv naut*

This means that the usual pronunciation is /ˈliːwəd/ but there is also a special technical pronunciation /ˈluːəd/. See also Section 5 on British and American pronunciations.

6   with a particular inflection, like this:

panel[2] *v* -ll- *BrE* ‖ -l- *AmE*

This means that the past tense of **panel** is **panelled** in British English and **paneled** in American English.

7   with a particular spelling, like this:

leu·ke·mia also -**kae**- *BrE* /luːˈkiːmiə/

This means that the usual spelling is **leukemia**, but in British English **leukaemia** can also be used.

8   with a variant, like this:

shoulder blade /ˈ·· ·/ also **scapula** *med*– *n*

This means that the usual word is **shoulder blade**, but there is also a special medical term **scapula**.

4.2 Word variation

Some words have several spellings, and some meanings can be expressed by several different words. For example, **judgment** can also be spelled **judgement**, and the substance **mother-of-pearl** can also be called **nacre**. These are examples of "word variation".

This section will explain:
- How spelling differences are shown
- How word differences are shown
- How British and American differences are shown

How spelling differences are shown

If a word has more than one spelling, the main definition is given at the most common spelling and any other spellings are shown directly after the headword, like this:

caf·tan , kaftan /ˈkæftæn‖kæfˈtæn/ *n* a long loose garment, usu. of cotton or silk, worn in the Near and Middle East.

This means that **caftan** is the most common spelling, but **kaftan** can also be used. If you look up **kaftan** you will find a short entry directing you to the main headword, like this:

kaf·tan /ˈkæftæn‖kæfˈtæn/ *n* a CAFTAN

But if the two spellings are very close in alphabetical order, there will only be one entry:

judg·ment, judgement /ˈdʒʌdʒmənt/ *n*

How word differences are shown

If two or more words share the same meaning, the main definition is given at the most common word and the other words are shown before the word class, like this:

mother-of-pearl /ˌ·· ·ˈ·◄/ also **nacre**– *n* [U] a hard smooth shiny pale variously coloured substance

This means that the usual name for this substance is **mother-of-pearl**, but it can also be called **nacre**.

Sometimes the alternative word is limited in its use (e.g. by being formal or technical). In cases like this, a label is added:

shoulder blade /ˈ·· ·/ also **scapula** *med*– *n*

Shoulder blade is the usual word, but the technical medical term is **scapula**.

Sometimes the alternative word applies to only ONE of the meanings of a headword. In this case, it is shown directly before that particular definition:

shroud[1] /ʃraʊd/ *n*   **1** also **winding sheet**– a cloth for covering a dead body for burial –see also TURIN SHROUD   **2** something that covers and hides: *A shroud of secrecy hangs over|surrounds the plan.*

This means that **winding sheet** is another word for **shroud**, but only in its first meaning.

In all these cases, the alternative word has its own short entry directing you to the main headword:

na·cre /ˈneɪkər/ *n* [U] *esp. BrE* MOTHER-OF-PEARL

scap·u·la /ˈskæpjələ/ *n med for* SHOULDER BLADE

winding sheet /ˈwaɪndɪŋ ʃiːt/ *n* a SHROUD[1] (1)

The only time a separate entry is NOT given is if the other word is very close in spelling to the main word, like this:

life-size /ˈ· ·/ also **life-sized** –

There are two other special cases where alternative forms are shown:
1 masculine and feminine forms
   For some nouns (especially names of professions or of animals) there are special masculine and feminine forms, and these are shown like this:

fox¹ /fɒks‖fɑːks/ n 1 [C] **vixen** *fem.*– a small doglike flesh-eating wild animal with a reddish coat and a wide furry tail. It is often hunted for sport in Britain and is said to have a clever and deceiving nature

This means that a female fox is called a **vixen**.

2 words that mean the same whether they are in the singular or plural form. Some words can be used in the plural to express a singular meaning. They are shown like this:

mak·er /ˈmeɪkəʳ/ n 1 a (*often in comb.*) a person who makes something: *a mapmaker* | *a filmmaker* | *a trouble-maker* b also **makers** *pl.*– a firm that makes something: *My watch has gone wrong; I'm sending it back to the makers.*

This means that the firm that makes something can be called "the maker" or "the makers". So you can express the same meaning by saying:
   I'm sending my watch back to the **maker**
OR I'm sending my watch back to the **makers**.

How British and American differences are shown

British and American spelling differences
Some words have different spellings according to whether they are used in British English or American English. For example:

col·our¹ *BrE* ‖ **color** *AmE* /ˈkʌləʳ/ n 1 [U] the quality in

The British spelling is **colour**; the American spelling is **color**. In cases like this, the main definition is shown at the British spelling, but there is also a short entry at **color**:

col·or /ˈkʌləʳ/ *AmE for* COLOUR

Notice the double bar ‖ which is used to indicate a British/American difference.

Some words have a main spelling that is used in both British and American English, AND a second spelling that can also be used in one of these varieties. For example:

or·gan·ize also **-ise** *BrE* /ˈɔːgənaɪz‖ˈɔːr-/ v 1 [T] to arrange

This means that both British and American speakers use the spelling **organize**, but British speakers also use the spelling **organise**.

British and American word differences
There are very many differences between British and American vocabulary. For example, a small farm that grows fruit and vegetables for sale is called a **truck farm** by American speakers and a **market garden** by British speakers. In cases like this, the main definition is given at the British word, and the American word is given as an alternative, like this:

market gar·den /ˌ·· ˈ··/ *BrE* ‖ **truck farm** *AmE*– n an area for growing vegetables and fruit for sale

The American form also has its own short entry:

truck farm /ˈ· ·/ n *AmE for* MARKET GARDEN

Sometimes the differences are less clear than this. For example, the word **truck** (meaning a heavy road vehicle) is used in both British and American English. But many British speakers call this vehicle a **lorry**, whereas Americans never use this word. In cases like this, the main definition goes at the "World English" form, like this:

truck¹ /trʌk/ n 1 also **lorry** *BrE*– a large motor vehicle for carrying goods in large quantities

Truck has no label, so it can be used in any variety of English, but **lorry** – as the label shows – would only be used by British speakers.

4.3 Cross-references

Cross-references are notes that direct your from one headword to another. They are used to draw your attention to other words that have some connection with the word you are looking up. The information these notes provide can help you to find the words you need, avoid mistakes, and increase your vocabulary.

There are four main kinds of cross-reference:
1 opposites
   When a word has an exact opposite, it is shown in **dark type** like this:

prov·i·dent /ˈprɒvɪdənt‖ˈprɑː-/ adj *apprec* careful and sensible in providing for future needs, esp. by saving or storing –opposite **improvident** – ~**ly** *adv*

The "opposite" note is especially useful when there is more than one opposite, according to the meaning:

of·fen·sive¹ /əˈfensɪv/ adj 1 causing offence; unpleasant: *offensive remarks/smells* | *I found him extremely offensive.* | *crude jokes that are offensive to women* –opposite **inoffensive** 2 of or for attacking: *offensive weapons* | *The troops took up offensive positions.* –opposite **defensive**

2 "compare" cross-references
   These are used to inform you of other words that are similar to (but not quite the same as) the word you are looking up. For example:

spa·ghet·ti /spəˈgeti/ n [U] Italian PASTA (=food made from flour mixed with water) in the shape of long strings, cooked in boiling water –compare MACARONI, TAGLIATELLE, VERMICELLI

All these words – **spaghetti**, **macaroni**, **tagliatelle**, **vermicelli** – are types of pasta, but if you look at each definition you will see how they differ from each other.

"Compare" notes are often used to draw your attention to words that are sometimes confused because they look or sound very similar. For example:

ef·fi·ca·cious /ˌefə'keɪʃəs◄/ *adj fml* (of a medicine, a course of action, etc.) producing the desired effect, esp. in curing an illness or dealing with a problem: *an efficacious remedy* —compare EFFECTIVE, EFFICIENT

3 "see also" cross-references are used to to direct you to words that give more information about the word you are looking up or about the typical context in which it is used. They also sometimes direct you to a word where a story or historical event is explained in detail. For example:

ball² *n* **1** [C] a large formal occasion for social dancing **2** [S] *infml* a very good time: *They all had a ball at the party.* **3 You 'shall go to the ball!** a phrase used by the FAIRY GODMOTHER to Cinderella in the story of Cinderella —see also CINDERELLA

The "see also" note is also used to draw your attention to other headwords that are formed using the word you are looking up. For example:

race¹ /reɪs/ *n* **1** [(against, between, with)] a competition in speed: *to have/run/lose/win a race* | *a ten-mile race* | *a boat race* | *a horse race* | (fig.) *a race against time* (=an attempt to complete something before it is too late) **2** *tech or lit* a strong flow of water: *A mill-race is the stream of water driving a water-mill.* —see also ARMS RACE, RAT RACE

The "see also" note is also used to direct you to the entry where an idiom has its definition. So if you look for the idiom **kick the bucket** at **bucket**, you will find a note directing you to **kick**, where the idiom has its definition:

buck·et¹ /'bʌkɪt/ *n* **1** an open metal, plastic, or wooden container with a handle for carrying liquids. .... —see also **kick the bucket** (KICK¹ (11)) **3 a drop in the bucket** a small amount which is not enough: *The money budgeted is a drop in the bucket compared to what is needed.*

4 "see" cross-references
These are used to direct you to Usage Notes, features, and illustrations, which are described in the next section.

4.4 Usage Notes, Cultural Notes, features and illustrations

In addition to the main dictionary entries, a great deal of information about language is provided in Usage Notes, Cultural Notes, features, and illustrations.

Usage Notes
The purpose of Usage Notes

The Usage Notes cover four main areas:
1 word sets
These notes explain the difference between words of roughly similar meaning: for example, a Usage Note at **fat** explains words like **chubby**, **stout**, and **overweight**.

2 difficult points of grammar and style
These notes explain, for example, whether a plural pronoun can be used after words like **anyone** and **someone** (can you say: *Someone has left their coat on my desk?*)
3 important British and American differences
These notes explain, for example, the different uses of the word **hire** in British and American English.
4 information about "pragmatics"
These notes explain the way some words and phrases can be used in conversation to suggest a meaning or attitude that could not be known simply through understanding the literal meaning of the words themselves. See, for example, the note at **mean** on the "pragmatic" use of the expressions "I mean" and "I mean to say".

Where Usage Notes are shown
Usage Notes come at the very end of a dictionary entry, in a separate paragraph:

hope·ful·ly /'hɔʊpfəli/ *adv* **1** in a hopeful way: *The little boy looked at her hopefully as she handed out the sweets.* **2** if our hopes succeed: *Hopefully we'll be there by dinnertime.*
■ USAGE This second meaning of **hopefully** is now very common, especially in speech, but it is thought by some people to be incorrect.

If a Usage Note deals with several different words, the Note itself is usually shown at the most common word, and there are cross-references to it at the other words:

o·bese /əʊ'biːs/ *adj fml* very fat; unhealthily fat – see FAT (USAGE) – **obesity** *n* [U]

Cultural Notes

The Cultural Notes give detailed information about the associations that words have for native speakers of English. Sometimes these associations are connected with old beliefs or traditions, sometimes with well known stories, and sometimes with historical or political events. They are also sometimes connected with particular aspects of British or American life.
Cultural notes come after the definition and examples of a particular meaning of a word:

flag¹ /flæg/ *n* **1** a square or OBLONG piece of material, usu. with a pattern or picture on it, that is put up as a sign of a country, organization, etc., or to make signals. Flags are often flown at HALF-MAST when an important person has died: *The French flags were flapping/fluttering in the breeze.* | *The danger flag was flying.* (=being shown) | *The children waved their flags as the queen passed by.* | (fig.) *Most of the countries that once lived under the British flag* (=were ruled by Britain) *are now independent.*
▶CULTURAL NOTE In the US the American flag is a very important SYMBOL of the country and is supposed to be treated with respect. Children repeat the Pledge of Allegiance to the flag (= promise to be loyal to the country and its flag) at school and are usually taught how to fold it correctly. In the 1960s some American people burned the flag to protest against the Vietnam War, and many Americans felt very strongly that this was wrong.◀

Features

The 16 features have been specially compiled to provide useful extra information on areas of particular cultural interest in Britain and the US. Cross references from relevant entries direct you to the features.

Illustrations

The dictionary includes over 650 carefully chosen illustrations. The illustrations and the definitions work together to ensure that important language points and aspects of Western culture are explained in the clearest possible way. There are four main types of illustration:

1 picture of common animals, plants, objects, etc. See for example **car**, **cottage**, **dog**.
2 pictures showing things that are not easily explained in words, such as shapes, complex actions, or small differences between words which are similar but not the same. See for example **cartwheel**, **jagged**, **pile**.
3 pictures showing groups of related objects. These explain the differences between similar objects, show the range of shapes and forms covered by a particular word, and serve as an important aid to vocabulary expansion. See for example **chair**, **pin**, **rack**.
4 pictures showing the basic physical meaning of words that are commonly used in an abstract or figurative way with the aim of making these abstract uses easier to understand. See for example **muzzle**, **pigeonhole**, **pioneer**.

5 Pronunciation

The dictionary provides detailed information about pronunciation and stress. The purpose of this section is to explain what the pronunciation symbols mean and where to find them in dictionary entries, how differences in British and American pronunciation are shown, and how the dictionary gives information about stress patterns in words and phrases.

5.1 Pronunciation symbols
5.2 Where pronunciations are shown
5.3 British and American differences
5.4 Stress
5.5 Special symbols

5.1 Pronunciation symbols

Pronunciations are shown using the standard system known as the International Phonetic Alphabet (IPA) and Table 5.1 shows the symbols that are used. The Table gives a common "key word" for each sound, and it also shows other ways in which the sound is often spelled. In addition to the symbols here, the dictionary uses a small number of special symbols: these are explained in section 5.5.

Table 5.1

CONSONANTS			VOWELS		
symbol	key word	other common spellings	symbol	key word	other common spellings
p	pen	happy	iː	sheep	field team key scene amoeba
b	back	rubber	ɪ	ship	savage guilt system women
t	tea	butter walked doubt	e	bed	any said bread bury friend
d	day	ladder called could	æ	bad	plaid laugh (AmE) calf (AmE)
k	key	cool soccer lock school cheque	ɑː	calm	father heart laugh (BrE) bother (AmE)
g	get	bigger ghost	ɒ	pot	watch (BrE) cough (BrE) laurel (BrE)
tʃ	cheer	match nature question cello	ɔː	caught	ball board draw four floor cough (AmE)
dʒ	jump	age edge soldier gradual	ʊ	put	wood wolf could
f	fat	coffee cough physics half	uː	boot	move shoe group flew blue rude
v	view	of navvy	ʌ	cut	some blood does
θ	thing		ɜː	bird	burn fern worm earn journal
ð	then		ə	cupboard	the colour actor nation danger
s	soon	city psychology mes scene listen	eɪ	make	pray prey steak vein gauge
z	zero	was dazzle example (/gz/)	əʊ	note	soap soul grow sew toe
ʃ	fishing	sure station tension vicious chevron	aɪ	bite	pie buy try guide sigh
ʒ	pleasure	vision rouge	aʊ	now	spout plough
h	hot	whole	ɔɪ	boy	poison lawyer
m	sum	hammer calm bomb	ɪə	here	beer weir appear fierce
n	sun	funny know gnaw	eə	there	hair bear bare their prayer
ŋ	sung	sink	ʊə	poor	tour sure
l	led	balloon battle	eɪə	player	
r	red	marry wriggle rhubarb	əʊə	lower	
j	yet	onion use few (/juː/) Europe	aɪə	tire	
w	wet	one when queen (/kw/)	aʊə	tower	
x	loch		ɔɪə	employer	

5.2 Where pronunciations are shown

Pronunciations are shown directly after the headword, like this:

ra·pa·cious /rəˈpeɪʃəs/ *adj fml* taking everything one can, esp. by force

As an additional help to pronouncing the word correctly, the headword is divided into its separate syllables (**ra-**, **-pa**, and **-cious**) by means of dots. These dots also show where you can break a word (or "hyphenate" it) at the end of a line of writing.

If a word has more than one correct pronunciation, all of them are shown:

leg·room /ˈlegrʊm, -ruːm/

This means that the second syllable can be pronounced /-rʊm/ or /-ruːm/.

If two words have the same spelling and the same pronunciation, the second entry is not given a pronunciation:

pend·ing¹ /ˈpendɪŋ/ *prep fml* while waiting for; until: *We delayed our decision pending his return from Europe.*

pending² *adj* 1 [F] *fml* not yet decided or settled

But for words with the same spelling that have different pronunciations, a full pronunciation is shown at each word:

wind¹ /wɪnd/ *n* 1 [C;U] moving air; a current of air, esp. one moving strongly or quickly

wind³ /waɪnd/ *v* **wound** /waʊnd/ 1 [T] to turn round and round with a number of circular movements

If a word has another form that does not have a separate entry in the dictionary, it is given its own pronunciation:

lat·tice /ˈlætɟs/ also **lat·tice·work** /ˈlætɟswɜːk‖-wɜːrk/

Compound words that are written with a space or a hyphen (like **bus stop** and **happy-go-lucky**) are not given pronunciations, provided that all the words from which they are formed have their own entries in the dictionary. Instead they are given stress patterns, like this:

happy-go-luck·y /ˌ··· ˈ···◂/

But if any of the words that make up a compound word does not have its own dictionary entry, a full pronunciation is given:

lap·is laz·u·li /ˌlæpɟs ˈlæzjʊli‖-ˈlæzəli/

The derived words which are formed using common suffixes and shown at the end of an entry do not usually have a pronunciation. For example:

lim·it·less /ˈlɪmɟtləs/ *adj* without limit or end: *limitless possibilities* — ~ **ly** *adv* — ~ **ness** *n* [U]

The pronunciation of **limitlessly** is the same as the pronunciation of **limitless** plus the pronunciation of **-ly**, and all the common suffixes are shown – with pronunciations – in the Word Formation section at the back of the dictionary.

But if the main word form changes when the suffix is added, a pronunciation will be shown. Here are some examples:

re·e·lect /ˌriːɟˈlekt/ *v* [T] to elect again: *He has been reelected to Parliament.* — ~**ion** /ˈlekʃən/ *n* [C;U] : *She is seeking reelection for a third term of office.*

The last syllable of the base form changes slightly in the derived form.

lyr·i·cal /ˈlɪrɪkəl/ *adj* — ~ **ly** /kli/ *adv*

The spelling suggests a pronunciation /ˈlɪrɪkɔli/, which would be incorrect.

le·gal·ize also **-ise** *BrE* /ˈliːgəlaɪz/ *v*
— **ization** /ˌliːgəlaɪˈzeɪʃən‖-gələ-/ *n* [U]

In this case, the sounds are the same as in the base form, but the stress is different.

Abbreviations which are only used in writing (such as **mm** or **lb**) are not given pronunciations. But pronunciations are shown for abbreviations that are commonly used in speech:

PC /ˌpiː ˈsiː/ *abbrev. for:* PERSONAL COMPUTER

Words that are "borrowed" from other languages are pronounced with English sounds and stress. We show the most common English pronunciation, although some speakers use a pronunciation closer to that of the original:

5.3 Names of people

Names which are pronounced the same as an ordinary word with the same spelling are listed after it and are not given a pronunciation:

cart·er /ˈkɑːtəʳ‖ˈkɑːr-/ *BrE old use n* a person whose job is driving carts
Carter, Jimmy (1924–) the president of the US from 1977 to 1981.

First names and titles are not given a pronunciation if they are the same as a name or title which has its own entry, or are pronounced and spelt the same as an ordinary word. In the above example, **Jimmy** is not given a pronunciation because **jimmy** is a word in the dictionary.
First names are given a pronunciation if they are pronounced differently from another entry with the same spelling, or have no entry of their own:

Co·le·ridge /ˈkəʊlərɪdʒ/, **Sam·u·el Tay·lor** /ˈsæmjuəl ˈteɪləʳ/

Initial are not included in the pronunciation unless they are always used when talking about the person:

Lee, General Rob·ert E /ˈrɒbət iː‖ˈrɑːbərt-/

5.4 Foreign names and words

Foreign names, and words "borrowed" from other languages are pronounced with English sounds and stress. We show the most common English pronunciations, although some speakers may use a pronunciation closer to that of the original:

je ne sais quoi /ˌʒə nə seɪ ˈkwɑː/

Gar·cí·a Lor·ca /gɑːˌsiːə ˈlɔːkə‖gɑːrˌsiːə ˈlɔːr-/,

5.5 British and American differences

The dictionary shows both British and American pronunciations. The British pronunciations are based on those in the *English Pronouncing Dictionary* (14th edition, edited by Professor A.C. Gimson, Dent 1977) and the *Longman Pronunciation Dictionary* by Professor J.C. Wells (1990). They represent the accent called "Received Pronunciation" (or "RP"), which is common among educated British speakers, especially in southern England. The American pronunciations represent one (sometimes two) of the more common accents used by American speakers, and are based on the pronunciations in Webster's *Ninth New Collegiate Dictionary* (1983). But in both varieties of English, many other accents are also used: for example, the British "RP" accent is not widely used outside southern England. So the pronunciations we show are not necessarily the only acceptable ones.

When only one pronunciation is shown, it can be used in both British and American English. When there is a difference, the British and American pronunciations are separated by a "double bar" (‖), with British pronunciation on the left and the American one on the right:

as·sume /əˈsjuːm‖əˈsuːm/

This means that the British pronunciation is /əˈsjuːm/ and the American pronunciation is /əˈsuːm/. For longer words, the pronunciation on the right of the double bar gives only the part that is different from the pronunciation on the left:

con·tra·dic·tion /ˌkɒntrəˈdɪkʃən‖ˌkɑːn-/

5.6 Stress

How stress is shown

When English words have two or more syllables, one syllable is pronounced more strongly than the rest: it has greater "stress". In order to show which is the strongest syllable in a word, we put the mark /ˈ/ directly before it. For example:

de·vel·op /dɪˈveləp/

let·ter /ˈletər/

This means that the main stress in **letter** is on the first syllable, and the main stress in **develop** is on the second syllable.

Some longer words also have a weaker stress on another syllable, called the "secondary stress". In these cases, the mark /ˌ/ is put before the syllable that has secondary stress. For example:

min·i·com·put·er /ˈmɪnikəmˌpjuːtər/

In this word the main stress is on the syllable -**put**- and the secondary stress in on **min**-. Some VERY long words have two secondary stresses. But the second of these is weaker than the first, and it is only shown with the mark /ˌ/ when it has /ɪ/ as its vowel, as in:

con·tra·in·di·ca·tion /ˌkɒntrəˌɪndʒˈkeɪʃən‖ˌkɑːn-/

This is because /ɪ/ is the only vowel that can be either strong or weak (/ə/ is always weak and the other vowels are always strong).

Stress patterns in compound words

Compound words written with a space or a hyphen are given "stress patterns" instead of pronunciations. Each syllable in the stress pattern is shown by a dot, and the stress marks /ˈ/ and /ˌ/ are shown before the dots which represent stressed syllables. For example:

word pro·cess·or /ˈ· ˌ···/

This means that **word** has the main stress and **pro**- has the secondary stress.

Stress shift

Some compound words have different stress patterns according to whether they are being used directly before a noun. For example, the usual stress pattern for **plate glass** is /ˌ· ˈ·/, in sentences like:
    The window is made of plate glass
and *We bought some plate glass for the window.*
But if **plate glass** comes directly before a noun which has a stronger stress, the word **glass** loses its stress altogether, as in:
    plate glass window /ˌ· · ˈ··/

In this case, **plate** has more stress than **glass**. This is called "stress shift" because the stress has "moved back" to another syllable. Stress shift is shown by the mark /◄/ after the stress pattern:

plate glass /ˌ· ˈ·◄/ˈ

Stress shift can happen with single words, such as:

in·de·pen·dent[1] /ˌɪndʒˈpendənt◄/

Stress marks in idioms

In idioms, the stress usually comes on the last "main" word (noun, adjective, verb, or adverb). So in the expression "mind your own business", the word "business" has the main stress. In these REGULAR cases, stress marks are not shown for idioms. But if the stress in an idiom is not where you might expect it to be, a stress mark is shown before the word with the main stress. For example:

as the ˈcrow flies

Search ˈme!

5.7 Special symbols

In addition to the standard IPA symbols, we use a number of special symbols. These are:

/ʳ/

For example:

fire¹ /faɪəʳ/

This symbol is used at the end of a word to show that in the British RP accent, the /r/ is only pronounced when a vowel follows. So British speakers say:

fire engine /'faɪər ˌendʒɪn/

BUT **fire brigade** /'faɪə brɪˌgeɪd/

In American speech however, the /r/ is ALWAYS pronounced, even if a consonant follows.

/ɪ̯/

For example:

def·i·ni·tion /ˌdefɪ̯'nɪʃən/

This symbol is used to show that in both British and American speech, some speakers use /ɪ/ and others use /ə/. So **definition** can be pronounced either as /ˌdefɪ'nɪʃən/ or as /ˌdefə'nɪʃən/.

/ʊ̯/

For example:

reg·u·lar¹ /'regjʊ̯ləʳ/

This symbol is used to show that in both British and American speech, some speakers use /ʊ/ and others /ə/. So **regular** can be pronounced either as /'regjələʳ/ or as /'regjʊləʳ/.

/i/

For example:

hap·py /'hæpi/

ob·vi·ate /'ɒbvieɪt‖'ɑːb-/

This symbol is used to show that many RP speakers say /ɪ/ and many American speakers say /iː/. It can also, for many speakers of both varieties, represent a sound that is somewhere between /ɪ/ and /iː/. This symbol usually appears EITHER at the end of a word (as in **happy**), and in this case it is also used when common suffixes are added (as in **happiness**), OR in an unstressed syllable in the middle of a word when the syllable that follows starts with a vowel (as in **obviate**).

/u/

For example:

punc·tu·al /'pʌŋktʃuəl/

This symbol is used to represent a sound that is similar to /uː/ but shorter. It usually appears in an unstressed syllable in the middle of a word when the syllable that follows starts with a vowel.

/ə/

For example:

trav·el¹ /'trævəl/

var·y /'veəri/

This symbol is used to show that the /ə/ sound can be left out when a word is pronounced. It is used in three ways:

1 to show a "syllabic consonant"

The sounds /l/, /m/, and /n/ can be "syllabic consonants": that is, they can form syllables on their own without a vowel. For example, **travel** is usually pronounced /'trævl/, without a vowel in the second syllable. But it can also be pronounced /'trævəl/, so in cases like this, the /ə/ symbol is used to show that either of these two pronunciations is possible. When a syllabic consonant is followed by a vowel sound, there are three possible pronunciations:

listener /'lɪsənəʳ/ can represent

/'lɪsənəʳ/ (= three syllables; three vowels)

/'lɪsnəʳ/ (= three syllables; two vowels and one syllabic consonant shown here as /n̩/)

/'lɪsnəʳ/ (= two syllables; two vowels)

2 after a vowel and usually before a /r/, to show that the /ə/ sound can be left out

For example, some speakers (especially in America) pronounce **vary** as /'veri/, and others pronounce it as /'veəri/. The pronunciation given in the dictionary, /'veəri/, shows that either of these is possible.

3 after a consonant and usually before /r/, to show that the /ə/ sound can be left out.

For example, there are two possible pronunciations for **liberal** /'lɪbərəl/:

/'lɪbərəl/ (= three syllables)

/'lɪbrəl/ (= two syllables)

/i/ and /j/

When /i/ appears in the middle of a word, followed by a syllable that starts with a vowel, it is often possible to use /j/ instead. For example:

fa·mil·i·ar·ize also **-ise** *BrE* /fə'mɪliəraɪz/

This can ALSO be pronounced /fə'mɪljəraɪz/. But the /j/ is not shown unless it is very common.

/n/ and /ŋ/

When /n/ is followed by /k/ or /g/ it is often possible to use /ŋ/ instead, but the /ŋ/ is not shown. For example:

en·gross /ɪn'grəʊs/

This can ALSO be pronounced /ɪŋ'grəʊs/.

Hyphens in pronunciations

Hyphens are used for two reasons:

1 to represent parts of a pronunciation that are not repeated

For example:

ac·cord·ance /ə'kɔːdəns‖-ɔːr-/

The second pronunciation is /ə'kɔːrdəns/ but the first and last parts of the first pronunciation are not repeated.

2 to prevent possible confusion

For example:

ar·cha·ic /ɑː'keɪ-ɪk‖ɑːr-/

A

A, a /eɪ/ A's, a's *or* As, as **1** the first letter of the English alphabet **2 from A to B** from one place to another: *What's the quickest way to get from A to B in London?* **3 from A to Z** from the beginning to the end; including everything

A¹ /eɪ/ n **1** a note in Western music; the musical KEY¹ (4) based on this note **2** a mark given to a student's work, showing the highest level of quality: *I got an A in algebra.| She's an A student.* —see also GRADE¹ (3) **3** one of the common blood groups: *His blood group is A positive.*

A² *abbrev. for:* AMP

a /ə; *strong* eɪ/ *also* **an** *(before a vowel sound)— indefinite article, determiner* **1** (before a noun that names someone or something not already mentioned or known about): *Have you got a car?| I had a pain in my leg. | This is a very good book. | That sounds like an excuse to me. | She's a doctor/a famous writer. | It's a pity you can't come. | He's a friend of mine.* (=one of my friends) | *She was a Jones* (=one of the Jones family) *before she married Bill* **2 a** one: *a thousand pounds | a dozen eggs* **b** (before certain words of quantity): *a few weeks | a lot of people | a little water | a great many times* **3** each; every; per: *six times a day | £2 a dozen* **4** the thing called; any; every: *A square has four sides. | I would say a parcel was bigger than a packet.* **5** (before the first one of a pair that seems to be a single whole): *a cup and saucer | a bucket and spade* **6** (before [U] nouns) a container or unit of: *I'd like a coffee, please.* **7** a certain amount of; some **a** (before [S] nouns, esp. words for actions): *Have a look at this. | You need a wash. | She has a good knowledge of chemistry.* **b** (before the -ing form of verbs when used as nouns): *He drove off with a crashing of gears and a screeching of tyres.* **8** a kind of: *Médoc is a (very good) wine. | This is a good Médoc.* **9** (before the name of a painter or other ARTIST) a work by: *This painting is a Rembrandt.* **10** one like or having the qualities of: *They say the young actress is a (new) Marilyn Monroe!* **11 a** (before names of people, showing that someone is unknown to the speaker) a certain: *A Mrs Smith wishes to speak to you.* **b** (before names of times and places) a particular one: *I can't remember a Christmas when it snowed so much.* (compare *It always snows at Christmas.*) **12 a** (after half/rather/such/what/ *(fml or lit)* many): *I've got rather a headache. | What a nice girl (she is)! | I've never met such a nice girl. | (fml or lit) Many a small business has failed* (=many small businesses have failed) **b** (after as/how/so/too +adj): *He's got as big a car as you have. | I've never met so nice a girl.* —see AN (USAGE)

A-1 /ˌeɪ ˈwʌn/ *adj old-fash* of the best quality; very good: *Our holiday was really A-1.*

A1 /ˌeɪ ˈwʌn/ *[the]* a main road which goes from London to Edinburgh

A3 /ˌeɪ ˈθriː/ n [U] a standard size of paper in the EC 29.7 x 42 centimetres: *a sheet of A3*

A4 /ˌeɪ ˈfɔːr/ n [U] a standard size of paper in the EC 21 x 29.7 centimetres: *a sheet of A4*

AA /ˌeɪ ˈeɪ/ **1** *abbrev. for:* ALCOHOLICS ANONYMOUS **2** *[the]* Automobile Association; a British organization which helps its members when their cars break down on the road: *I've joined the AA. | the AA handbook* **3** Associate of Arts; a US college degree

AAA¹ /ˌθriː ˈeɪz◀/ *[the]* Amateur Athletic Association; a British organization for ATHLETEs

AAA² /ˌtrɪpəl ˈeɪ◀/ American Automobile Association; an American organization which helps its members when their cars break down on the road

aard·vark /ˈɑːdvɑːk‖ˈɑːrdvɑːrk/ n a large animal of southern Africa, similar to an ANTEATER, which feeds on TERMITEs at night. People sometimes use this word as an example of the first word that is likely to appear in a dictionary or ENCYCLOPEDIA.

Aa·ron /ˈeərən/ in the Bible, a priest, the brother of Moses

Aaron , Hank (1934–) a BASEBALL player famous for hitting more HOME RUNs than Babe Ruth, who had held the record for almost 40 years

AARP /ˌeɪ eɪ ɑː ˈpiː‖-ɑːr-/ *abbrev. for:* AMERICAN ASSOCIATION OF RETIRED PERSONS

AB¹ /ˌeɪ· ˈ·/ *AmE abbrev. for:* BA (1)

AB² one the common blood types

ABA /ˌeɪ biː ˈeɪ/ n *abbrev. for:* AMERICAN BAR ASSOCIATION

a·back /əˈbæk/ adv **be taken aback** to be shocked, esp. by something unpleasant or unexpected: *I was rather taken aback by his rudeness.*

ab·a·cus /ˈæbəkəs/ n a frame holding wires on which small balls can be moved, used for counting and calculating, esp. in eastern countries

ab·a·lo·ne /ˌæbəˈləʊni/ n [C;U] (the shell of) a kind of SHELLFISH, used as food and known for its shell, which is lined with MOTHER-OF-PEARL

a·ban·don¹ /əˈbændən/ v [T] **1** to leave completely and for ever; DESERT: *He abandoned his wife and children. | When the fire got out of control, the captain told the sailors to* **abandon ship.** **2** to give up or bring an end to (something), esp. without finishing it or gaining the intended result: *The bad weather forced them to abandon their search. | They abandoned all hope of finding the child. | The party has now abandoned its earlier commitment to restoring full employment. | The game had to be abandoned because of crowd trouble.* —see also ABANDONED – ~ment n [U]

    abandon sbdy. to sthg. *phr v* [T] *lit* to allow (oneself) to be completely controlled by (a feeling, desire, etc.): *He abandoned himself to grief.*

abandon² n [U] the state when one's feelings and actions are uncontrolled: *People were shouting and cheering in* **gay abandon.**

a·ban·doned /əˈbændənd/ adj completely uncontrolled, esp. in a way that is thought to be immoral: *abandoned behaviour*

a·base /əˈbeɪs/ v [T (**to, before**)] *fml* to make (oneself) lose self-respect; make HUMBLE – ~ment n [U]

a·bashed /əˈbæʃt/ adj [F] uncomfortable and ashamed in the presence of others, esp. when one has done something wrong or stupid —opposite **unabashed**

a·bate /əˈbeɪt/ v *fml* **1** [I] (of winds, storms, sounds, pain, etc.) to become less strong; decrease: *The recent public anxiety about this issue may now be abating.* —see also UNABATED **2** [T] *law* to bring to an end (esp. in the phrase **abate a nuisance**) – ~ment n [U]

ab·at·toir /ˈæbətwɑːr/ n *BrE for* SLAUGHTERHOUSE

Ab·ba /ˈæbə/ a Swedish popular music group who became internationally successful when they won the Eurovision Song Contest in 1974, and whose music was popular with people of all ages

ab·bess /ˈæbɪs, ˈæbes/ n a woman who is the head of a CONVENT (=a religious establishment for women called NUNS) —compare ABBOT

ab·bey /ˈæbi/ n **1** (esp. formerly) a building in which MONKS or NUNS live and work; MONASTERY or CONVENT —compare PRIORY **2** (*often cap. as part of a name*) a large church where MONKS or NUNS once lived: *Westminster Abbey*

Abbey Na·tion·al /ˌ·· ˈ···◀/ *[the]* a British financial organization, formerly a BUILDING SOCIETY, now a bank and a PLC, branches of which are found in many towns and cities in Britain

ab·bot /ˈæbət/ n a man who is the head of a MONASTERY (=a religious establishment for men called MONKs) —compare ABBESS

Ab·bott and Cos·tel·lo /ˌæbət ənd kɒˈsteləʊ‖-ˌkɑː-/ , **Bud** (1896–1974) and **Lou** /luː/ (1908–1959) two popular American COMEDIANs who appeared in many films together

ab·bre·vi·ate /əˈbriːvieɪt/ v [T] to make (a word, story, etc.) shorter

ab·bre·vi·a·tion /əˌbriːviˈeɪʃən/ n **1** [C] a shortened form of a word, such as "*Dr*" for "Doctor" or "*PTO*" for "please turn over". In this dictionary some abbreviations (such as *Dr*) are marked *written abbrev.*, showing that they are only used in writing and not in speech. **2** [U] the act of abbreviating

ABC¹ /ˌeɪ biː ˈsiː/ n *BrE* || **ABC's** *AmE*— **1** [U] the alphabet, as taught to children: *children learning their ABC* **2** [*the*+S (**of**)] the simplest facts about something which have to be learnt first: *classes in the ABC of cooking*

ABC² American Broadcasting Company; one of the four national television networks in the US, supported by advertising

ab·di·cate /ˈæbdɪkeɪt/ v **1** [I (**from**);T] to give up officially (an official position, esp. that of king or queen): *The king abdicated (the throne).* **2** [T] *fml* to give up (a right, claim, or responsibility); RENOUNCE: *He accused the government of abdicating its responsibility for the economy.* —**cation** /ˌæbdɪˈkeɪʃən/ n [C;U (**of, from**)]

Abdication also **Abdication Crisis** /ˌ··ˈ·· ˌ··/ [*the*] the period in Britain in 1936, in which King Edward VIII was forced to abdicate so that he could marry Wallis Simpson, an American who had been divorced (DIVORCE). According to the law, he was not allowed to marry a divorced woman and still remain king.

ab·do·men /ˈæbdəmən, æbˈdəʊ-/ n *med* **1** a main part of the front of the body in animals, between the chest and legs, containing the stomach, bowels, etc.; the BELLY **2** the end part of an insect's body, joined to the THORAX – see picture at INSECT —**dominal** /æbˈdɒmɪnəl‖-ˈdɑː-/ adj: *abdominal pains*

ab·duct /əbˈdʌkt, æb-/ v [T] to take (a person) away illegally, often by force; KIDNAP: *The police think the boy has been abducted.* —**duction** /ˈdʌkʃən/ n [U]

Ab·dul-Jab·bar /ˌæbdʊl ˈdʒæbəʳ/ , **Ka·reem** /kəˈriːm/ (formerly **Lew Alcindor**) (1947–) an American BASKETBALL player considered to be one of the best players ever

a·bed /əˈbed/ adj [F] *lit* or *old use* in bed

A·bel /ˈeɪbəl/ (in the Bible) the second son of Adam and Eve, who was killed violently by his brother Cain

Ab·e·lard /ˈæbəlɑːd‖-lɑːrd/ , **Peter** (1079–1142) a French PHILOSOPHER and THEOLOGIAN best remembered for his love for Héloïse, shown in their famous letters to each other

Ab·er·deen /ˌæbəˈdiːn◂‖-bər-/ a port in north-east Scotland, which is the centre of the North Sea oil industry – see colour map on page 818

Aberdeen An·gus /ˌ··· ˈ··/ a type of cattle originally from NE Scotland and bred for meat

Ab·er·deen·shire /ˌæbəˈdiːnʃəʳ‖-bər-/ a former COUNTY in E Scotland, now part of Grampian REGION

Ab·er·fan /ˌæbəˈvæn‖-bər-/ a small mining (MINE) town in South Wales, where in 1966 a pile of coal waste slipped onto a school and killed more than 100 children

a·ber·rant /ˈæbərənt, əˈberənt/ adj **1** changed from what is usual, expected, or right: *aberrant behaviour under the influence of drugs* **2** *tech* not like the rest of its kind: *an aberrant example of a common insect*

ab·er·ra·tion /ˌæbəˈreɪʃən/ n [C;U] a change away from one's usual way of thinking or of behaving: *She hit him in a moment of aberration.* | *a statistical aberration*

Ab·er·ys·twyth /ˌæbəˈrɪstwɪθ/ a port and university town in a Welsh-speaking area of Wales

a·bet /əˈbet/ v -tt- [T (**in**)] *law* to encourage or give help to (a crime or criminal): *The police say he* **aided and abetted** *the thief in robbing the bank.* – – **tor** n

a·bey·ance /əˈbeɪəns/ n [U] *fml* the condition of not being in use for a certain time: *an old custom that has* **fallen into abeyance**

ab·hor /əbˈhɔːʳ, æb-/ v -rr- [T *not in progressive forms*] to hate very much; DETEST: *I abhor cruelty to animals.*

ab·hor·rent /əbˈhɒrənt‖-ˈhɔːr-/ adj [(**to**)] deeply disliked; REPUGNANT: *The killing of animals for food is (utterly) abhorrent to some people.* —**rence** n [U] : *The president expressed his abhorrence at the murder.*

a·bide /əˈbaɪd/ v **1** [T *usu. in questions and negatives*] to bear; TOLERATE: *I can't abide rude people.* [+*v-ing*] *I cannot abide seeing such cruelty.* –see BEAR (USAGE) **2** [I+*adv*/*prep*] (*past tense* also **abode**) *lit* or *old use* to stay, wait, or live (in a place or condition)
  abide by sthg. *phr v* [T] **1** to obey exactly or remain faithful to (laws, promises, etc.): *If you join the club you must abide by its rules.* **2** to accept without complaint: *You must abide by the consequences of your decision.*

Abide With Me /·ˌ· · ˌ·/ the title and first line of a religious song (HYMN)

a·bid·ing /əˈbaɪdɪŋ/ adj [A] lasting for a long time and unlikely to change: *The experience left me with an abiding hatred of dogs.*

a·bil·i·ty /əˈbɪlɪti/ n [C;U] **1** the fact of having the skill, power, or other qualities that are needed in order to do something: *a man of great musical ability* | *a job more suited to your abilities* [+*to-v*] *She has demonstrated*|*has got a remarkable ability to get things done.* | *I did the work* **to the best of my ability.** (=as well as I could) –see also MIXED ABILITY; see GENIUS (USAGE) **2 from each according to his abilities, to each according to his needs** *quote* a phrase from a work by Karl Marx, saying that in a society each person should give what they can, and each person should receive what they need

ab·ject /ˈæbdʒekt/ adj *fml* **1** (of a condition) as low as possible; pitiful; WRETCHED: *abject poverty* **2** (esp. of people or behaviour) showing lack of self-respect; very HUMBLE: *an abject apology* – ~ **ly** adv —**jection** /æbˈdʒekʃən, əb-/ n [U]

ab·jure /əbˈdʒʊəʳ, æb-/ v [T] *fml* to make a solemn promise, esp. publicly, to give up (an opinion, claim, etc.); RENOUNCE: *They abjured their religion.* —**juration** /ˌæbdʒʊˈreɪʃən/ n [U]

a·blaze /əˈbleɪz/ adj [F (**with**)] **1** burning strongly and uncontrollably: *The wooden house was quickly ablaze.* | (fig.) *ablaze with anger*|*excitement* **2** shining brightly: *The room was ablaze with light.*

a·ble /ˈeɪbəl/ adj **1** [F+*to-v*] having the skill, power, knowledge, time, or other qualities that are needed in order to do something: *Will you be able to come to our party?* | *I think David is more able*|*better able to deal with this problem than I am.* | *We are not yet able to predict the result.* | *They are willing and able to help.* **2** clever or skilful; COMPETENT: *She's an abler teacher*|*a more able teacher than he is.* [*also n, the*+P] *to assist the less able among us* –see also ABLY; see COULD (USAGE)

-able see WORD FORMATION

able-bod·ied /ˌ·· ˈ···◂/ adj physically strong and active, esp. as opposed to being DISABLED —**able-bodied** n [*the*+P]

able sea·man /ˌ·· ˈ··/ ‖ also **able-bod·ied sea·man** /ˌ·· ·· ˈ··/ *AmE* n a naval rank – see TABLE 3

a·blu·tion /əˈbluːʃən/ n [C;U] *fml* the washing of the hands or body as part of a religious ceremony

a·blu·tions /əˈbluːʃənz/ n [P] *pomp* or *humor* the act of washing oneself: *to perform one's ablutions*

a·bly /ˈeɪbli/ adv in an able manner; skilfully: *She controlled the meeting very ably.*

ABM /ˌeɪ biː ˈem/ n antiballistic missile; a weapon used for defence against MISSILES: *The ABM treaty was signed by Nixon and Brezhnev.*

ab·ne·ga·tion /ˌæbnɪˈgeɪʃən/ also **self-abnegation**– n [U] *fml* lack of concern for one's own wishes; SELF-DENIAL

ab·norm·al /æbˈnɔːməl‖-ˈnɔːr-/ adj different from what is expected, usual, or average, esp. in a bad or undesirable way; not NORMAL: *Is the child abnormal in any way?* | *abnormal behaviour* | *abnormal levels of radiation in the area of the power station* – ~ **ly** adv : *It was abnormally hot.* – ~ **ity** /ˌæbnɔːˈmælɪti‖-nər-/ n [C;U]

ab·o /ˈæbəʊ/ n **abos** *AustrE taboo derog* an Australian ABORIGINE

a·board /əˈbɔːd‖-ɔːrd/ adv, prep on or into (a ship, train, aircraft, bus, etc.): *The boat is ready to leave. All aboard!* | *The plane crashed, killing all 200 people aboard.* – compare on board (BOARD¹)

a·bode¹ /əˈbəʊd/ *past tense of* ABIDE (2)

abode² n [*usu. sing.*] *lit, humor,* or *law* the place where one lives; one's home: *Welcome to my humble abode!* | *a person of*|*with no fixed abode*

a·bol·ish /əˈbɒlɪʃ‖əˈbɑː-/ v [T] to bring to an end by law; stop: *Slavery was abolished in the US in the 19th century.* | *a government plan to abolish state pensions* —**ition** /ˌæbəˈlɪʃən/ n [U] : *They campaigned for the abolition of capital punishment.*

a·bo·li·tion·ist /ˌæbəˈlɪʃənɪst/ n someone who wants or tries to abolish something. The word is used esp. to describe the people who wanted to abolish SLAVERY in Britain in the 18th century and in the US in the 19th century, before and during the Civil War.

A-bomb /ˈeɪ bɒm‖-bɑːm/ n an ATOM BOMB

a·bom·i·na·ble /ə'bɒmɪnəbəl, -mənə-‖ə'baː-/ adj causing great dislike; hateful: *abominable treatment of prisoners* | *(infml) The food in this hotel is abominable.* —**bly** adv

abominable snow·man /·,·⸱·· '··/ n **1** a YETI **2** an evil character made of snow in an American television story for children

a·bom·i·nate /ə'bɒmɪneɪt‖ə'baː-/ v [T *not in progressive forms*] fml to hate very much; ABHOR

a·bom·i·na·tion /ə,bɒmɪ'neɪʃən‖ə,baː-/ n **1** [U] great hatred; DISGUST **2** [C] something deeply offensive or hateful

ab·o·rig·i·nal[1] /,æbə'rɪdʒɪnəl◂/ adj [A] of or concerning people or living things that have existed in a place from the earliest times; INDIGENOUS: *an aboriginal civilization*

aboriginal[2] n an aborigine

ab·o·rig·i·ne /,æbə'rɪdʒɪni/ n a member of the group of people that has lived in Australia from the earliest times

a·bort /ə'bɔːt‖-ɔːrt/ v **1** [T] to cause (a child) to be born too soon, or to end (a PREGNANCY) too soon, so that the child cannot live: *The doctor had to abort the baby/the pregnancy.* **2** [I;T] usu. **miscarry** AmE— to give birth too early to (a dead child) —compare MISCARRY (1) **3** [I;T] tech to end before the expected time because of some trouble: *The space flight had to be aborted because of difficulties with the computer.*

a·bor·tion /ə'bɔːʃən‖ə'bɔːr-/ n **1** [C;U] the act of stopping the development of a child inside a woman, esp. by a medical operation and usually before the 21st week: *She had an abortion.* | *Is abortion legal in your country?* | *drugs used to induce abortion* | *anti-abortion groups* compare MISCARRIAGE, STILLBIRTH —see also BACK-STREET ABORTION

▶ CULTURAL NOTE Abortion under certain specific conditions was made legal in Britain in 1967, but it remains a subject about which people have strong feelings and different opinions. It is legal in the US but some states have tried to limit the cases in which it can be used. Abortion is a very important political issue in the US and many people have strong feelings about it. Both in Britain and the US there are organizations which want to change the law either to limit or to widen the conditions under which abortion is legal. Very few people want to make abortion completely illegal again, though there are some groups, esp. in the US, which want this. —see also PRO-CHOICE, RIGHT TO LIFE, ROE VS. WADE◄

2 [C] rare a badly-formed creature produced by an abortion **3** [C] a plan or arrangement which goes wrong before it can develop properly

a·bor·tion·ist /ə'bɔːʃənɪst‖ə'bɔːr-/ n a person, esp. not a doctor, who gets money for doing abortions

a·bor·tive /ə'bɔːtɪv‖ə'bɔːr-/ adj failing to reach the result that was intended; unsuccessful: *an abortive attempt to build a railway* | *an abortive takeover bid* — ~**ly** adv

a·bound /ə'baʊnd/ v [I] fml to exist in large numbers or great quantity: *Theories/Questions abound as to the reasons for the president's decision.*
abound in/with sthg. phr v [T] to have in large numbers or great quantity: *The country abounds in valuable minerals.*

a·bout[1] /ə'baʊt/ prep **1** on the subject of: *a book about lions* | *talking about their holidays* | *Something should be done about unemployment.* | *She feels very strongly about this.* —see ON[1] (USAGE) **2** also **around** esp. AmE— here and there in; in all parts of: *They walked about the streets.* | *books lying about the room* —see ROUND[3] (USAGE) **3** in the character of: *There's something about her that I really don't like.* **4** lit, esp. BrE surrounding: *the high walls about the prison* **5** fml on the body of: *He had a gun hidden about his person.* (=in his clothes) **6** busy or concerned with (an activity): *going about one's day-to-day business* | *Do the shopping now, and while you're about it get me that book from the library.* | *Bring me a drink — and be quick about it!* **7** what/how about: a what news or plans have you concerning: *What about Jack? We can't just leave him here.* **b** (making a suggestion): *How/What about a drink?*

▷ USAGE In spoken English (**it's**) about is used to introduce a topic you want to discuss: *Now,* about *your exam results, David. They're not very good, are they?* | It's about *my little boy, doctor, he's not very well.*◁

about[2] adv **1** also **around** esp. AmE— here and there; in all directions or places: *They always go about together.* | *papers lying about on the floor* | *There are a lot of colds about at the moment.* (=Many people have colds just now.) **2** also **around** esp. AmE— somewhere near: *Is there anybody about?* **3** also **around** esp. AmE— a little more or less than: *about five miles/ten years* | *This year's profits are about the same as last year's.* **4** infml almost: *I'm about ready.* | *That looks about right.* **5** fml so as to face the opposite way: *The ship turned about and left the battle.* —see also **just about** (JUST[1]); see ROUND[3] (USAGE)

about[3] adj **1** [F] out of bed; active: *The doctor told me I'd be up and about again very soon.* —see also **out and about** (OUT[1]) **2** be about to to be just ready to; be going to: *We were about to start, when it rained.* **3** not about to infml, esp. AmE very unwilling to: *I'm not about to lend you any more money.*

about-turn /·,· '·•/ esp. BrE | **about-face** /·'·•/ esp. AmE— n [usu. sing.] **1** a change to the opposite position, opinion, or course of action: *The government has done a complete about-turn in its policy on military spending.* **2** (also interj) (a military order to) turn round and face in the opposite direction

a·bove[1] /ə'bʌv/ prep **1** higher than; over: *We flew above the clouds.* | *There's nothing in this shop (at/for) above £5.* | *Raise your arms above your head.* | *500 feet above sea level* | *The town's birthrate was well above the national average.* —opposite **below**; see USAGE **2** to a greater degree than: *The company values hard work above good ideas.* | *respected above all others* | *to be praised for a dedication* above and beyond *the call of duty* (=much greater than usual or expected) **3** higher in rank or power than: *A general is above a major.* —opposite **below 4** too good, proud, or honest for: *Her behaviour was above suspicion.* | *They're not above a bit of bribery if it will get them what they want.* **5 above all (else)** most important of all: *And above all, remember to send us your comments.* **6 get above oneself** to have too much trust in one's own cleverness —see also **over and above** (OVER[1] (13))

▷ USAGE The prepositions **above** and **over** can often be used in the same way: *Let's hang the painting* over/above *the fireplace.* If there is an idea of movement **over** is used: *The bird flew* over *the lake.* | *The sheep jumped* over *the wall.* **Over** is also used if there is an idea of covering: *He pulled the blanket* over *his head and fell asleep.* | *They built a roof* over *the courtyard.*◁

above[2] adv **1** in or to a higher place; higher: *I heard some noises coming from the room above.* | *A shout from above warned me of the danger.* **2** more; higher: *the numbers 20 and above* | *children of six or above* (=six or older) | *a military meeting for captains and above* (=of higher rank) **3** on an earlier page or higher on the same page: *the facts mentioned above* —opposite **below**

above[3] adj [A; after n] fml mentioned on an earlier page or higher on the same page: *For an explanation, see the above section/the section above.* [also n, the+C, pl. **above**] *The above is the profit before tax.* | *All the above are asked to attend tomorrow's meeting.*

a·bove·board /ə,bʌv'bɔːd◂, ə'bʌvbɔːd‖ə'bʌvbɔːrd/ adj [F] without any attempt to deceive: *Don't worry; it's all open and aboveboard.*

above-men·tioned /·,· '··◂/ adj [A] fml ABOVE[3]: *the above-mentioned facts* [also n, the+P] ... *Williams, Brown, and Jones. The above-mentioned will attend the course.* —compare UNDERMENTIONED

ab·ra·ca·dab·ra /,æbrəkə'dæbrə/ n, interj (a word spoken to help magic to be successful, when performing magic tricks for entertainment)

a·brade /ə'breɪd/ v [I;T] tech to wear away by hard rubbing

A·bra·ham /'eɪbrəhæm, -həm/ (in the Bible) a religious figure, considered to have established the Hebrews. Abraham was willing to kill his son Isaac because God asked him to. Then when God said it was not necessary, Abraham offered to kill a sheep instead.

a·bra·sion /ə'breɪʒən/ n tech **1** [U] loss of surface by rubbing; wearing away **2** [C] a place where the surface, esp. of the skin, has been rubbed or worn away: *suffering from multiple abrasions*

a·bra·sive[1] /ə'breɪsɪv/ adj **1** causing the wearing away of a surface **2** causing annoyance or dislike; rough: *an abrasive voice/personality* — ~**ly** adv

abrasive² *n* [C;U] a substance, such as sand, used for cleaning, polishing, or removing a surface

a·breast /ə'brest/ *adv* **1** next to one another and facing the same way: *They were cycling two abreast.* **2 keep/be abreast of** to know the most recent facts about: *Read the papers if you want to keep abreast of the times/of the latest developments in the news.*

a·bridge /ə'brɪdʒ/ *v* [T] to make (something written or spoken) shorter: *the abridged version of "War and Peace"* —see also UNABRIDGED

a·bridg·ment , abridgement /ə'brɪdʒmənt/ *n* **1** [C] something, such as a book or play, that has been made shorter: *an abridgment for radio in five parts* **2** [U] the act of making shorter

a·broad /ə'brɔːd/ *adv* **1** to or in another country or countries: *He lived abroad for many years.* | *Are you going abroad for your holidays?* | *products sold both at home and abroad* **2** *fml* over a wide area; everywhere: *The news soon spread abroad.* **3** *old use* out of doors: *There was no one abroad so early.*

ab·ro·gate /'æbrəgeɪt/ *v* [T] *fml* to put an end to the force of: *to abrogate a law/a treaty* —**gation** /ˌæbrə'geɪʃən/ *n* [C;U]

a·brupt /ə'brʌpt/ *adj* **1** sudden and unexpected: *The meeting came to an abrupt end.* | *an abrupt change of policy/drop in oil prices* **2** (of behaviour, character, etc.) not wanting to waste time being nice; BRUSQUE: *an abrupt manner* — **~ly** *adv* : *Our discussion was abruptly curtailed.* — **~ness** *n* [U]

ab·scess /'æbses/ *n* a swelling on or in the body where PUS (=a thick yellowish poisonous liquid) has gathered

ab·scond /əb'skɒnd, æb-‖æb'skænd/ *v* [I (**from, with**)] *fml* to go away suddenly and secretly because one has done something wrong

ab·seil /'æbseɪl/ *esp. BrE* ‖ *usu.* **rappel** *AmE v* [I (**down**)] to descend a steep slope using a rope —**abseil** *n*

ab·sence /'æbsəns/ *n* **1** [C;U (**from**)] the state or a period of being away: *Caroline will be in charge of the office during my absence.* | *She took a year's* **leave of absence** (=official pause) *from her job.* | *Jane was* **conspicuous by her absence.** (=people noticed she was not there) | *After a long absence, he has returned to doing TV work.* —opposite **presence** **2** [U (**of**)] non-existence; lack: *We were worried by the absence of definite figures in the report.* | **In the absence of** *any further evidence* (=because there was none) *the police were unable to solve the murder.* **3 absence makes the heart grow fonder** *saying* one likes a person better when one has been away from him/her for a little time; one forgets the less attractive things about a person

ab·sent¹ /'æbsənt/ *adj* **1** [(**from**)] not present: *How many students are absent (from class) today?* **2** [A] showing lack of attention: *an absent expression on his face* **3** *fml* not existing; lacking: *In the Manx type of cat, the tail is absent.* —see also ABSENTLY **4 absent friends** (a phrase used when drinking, to show that one is thinking about people who are not able to be present): *I propose a toast - absent friends.*

ab·sent² /əb'sent, æb-‖æb-/ *v* [T (**from**)] *fml* to keep (oneself) away: *He absented himself from the meeting.*

ab·sen·tee /ˌæbsən'tiː◂/ *n* a person who ought to be present but stays away: *There were many absentees from the meeting.* | *an absentee landlord* (=who does not live near the property he owns)

absentee bal·lot /ˌ··· '··/ *n AmE* an official paper used to vote by post when one cannot go to the place where voting is being done

ab·sen·tee·is·m /ˌæbsən'tiːɪzəm/ *n* [U] regular absence from work or duty without good cause: *an industry with a high rate of absenteeism*

absentee vote /ˌ··· '·/ *n AmE* a vote which is sent by post because one cannot go to the place where voting is being done

ab·sen·ti·a /æb'sentiə/ *n* **in absentia** *fml* for in his/her/their absence

ab·sent·ly /'æbsəntli/ *adv* in an absent-minded manner

absent-mind·ed /ˌ·· '··◂/ *adj* too concerned with one's thoughts to notice what is happening, what one is doing, etc.; PREOCCUPIED — **~ly** *adv* — **~ness** *n* [U]

absent-minded professor

absent-minded pro·fess·or /ˌ··· ·· ·'··/ *n* a STEREOTYPE of a university teacher who is usu. a fairly old man and is very clever, but too concerned with his work and ideas to notice or remember things that are happening around him

ab·sinth , absinthe /'æbsɪnθ/ *n* [U] a bitter green very strong alcoholic drink

ab·so·lute /'æbsəluːt/ *adj* **1** [A] complete; perfect: *a woman of absolute honesty* | *That's absolute nonsense!* **2** [A] not allowing any doubt: *We now have absolute proof of his guilt.* **3** having complete power; without limit: *an absolute ruler/monarchy* | *The general's power was absolute.* —see also ABSOLUTISM **4** not measured by comparison with other things: *In absolute terms, wages have risen, but not in comparison with the cost of living.* —opposite **relative** —see also DECREE ABSOLUTE — **~ness** *n* [U]

ab·so·lute·ly /'æbsəlutli, ˌæbsə'luːtli/ *adv* **1** completely: *I trust her discretion absolutely.* | *It's difficult to cross the desert by car, but not absolutely impossible.* | *I'm absolutely starving.* (=very hungry) **2** *infml* certainly: *"Do you think so?" "Absolutely!"*

▷ USAGE **1 Absolutely** is often used to give more strength to following adjectives or verbs which are already very strong. Compare: *I'm* **very** *hungry* and *I'm* **absolutely** *starving.* | *I* **quite** *like jazz* and *I* **absolutely** *adore pop music.* 2 The adverbs **absolutely** and **altogether** are pronounced /ˈ· · · ·/ when they come before the word they describe: *I* 'absolutely *refuse.* | 'altogether *different.* They are pronounced /ˌ· · ˈ· ·/ when they come after the word or when they stand alone: *different* ˌalto'gether | ˌAbso'lutely!◁

absolute mon·ar·chy /ˌ··· '···/ *n* a state ruled by a king or queen whose power is not limited by any system of laws —compare CONSTITUTIONAL MONARCHY

absolute ze·ro /ˌ··· '··/ *n* [U] the lowest temperature that is thought to be possible

ab·so·lu·tion /ˌæbsə'luːʃən/ *n* [U] (esp. in the Christian religion) forgiveness for a SIN. A priest declares that a person is forgiven, and the person is then freed from guilt for the sin: *to grant someone absolution* —see also ABSOLVE

ab·so·lut·is·m /'æbsəlutɪzəm/ *n* [U] a political system or principle in which unlimited power is held by one ruler

ab·solve /əb'zɒlv‖-aːlv/ *v* [T] **1** [(**of, from**)] to free (someone) from fulfilling a promise or from having to suffer for wrongdoing **2** (esp. of a priest) to forgive (a person) for doing wrong

ab·sorb /əb'sɔːb, əb'zɔːb‖-ɔːrb/ *v* [T] **1** to take or suck (esp. liquids) in, esp. gradually: *Salt absorbs moisture from the air.* | *The walls of the house absorb heat during the day.* | (fig.) *So many new ideas! It's all rather too much for me to absorb all at once.* | (fig.) *Defence spending absorbs almost 20% of the country's money.* —see also SHOCK ABSORBER **2** [(**in**) *usu. pass.*] to completely fill the attention of; ENGROSS: *I was absorbed in a book and didn't hear you call.* —see also ABSORBING **3** [(**into**)] (of a country or organization) to make (a smaller country or organization) into a part of itself; gain control over: *The company has gradually absorbed its smaller rivals.* —**sorption** /-ɔːpʃən‖-ɔːrp-/ *n* [U (**in, into, by**)] : *his complete absorption in his work* | *the absorption of a small company into a larger one*

ab·sor·bent /əb'sɔːbənt, -'zɔː-‖-ɔːr-/ *n, adj* (something) that is able to absorb: *to put an absorbent dressing on a cut*

ab·sorb·ing /əb'sɔːbɪŋ, -'zɔː-‖-ɔːr-/ adj taking all one's attention; very interesting: an absorbing task

ab·stain /əb'steɪn/ v [I (**from**)] **1** to intentionally not use one's vote: Five members voted for the proposal, twelve voted against, and three abstained. **2** to keep oneself from doing something that one enjoys: to abstain from smoking —see also ABSTENTION – ~ **er** n

ab·ste·mi·ous /əb'stiːmiəs/ adj allowing (oneself) only a little food, drink, or pleasure: an abstemious meal | You're being very abstemious today! – ~ **ly** adv – ~ **ness** n [U]

ab·sten·tion /əb'stenʃən/ n [C;U (**from**)] the act or an example of abstaining, esp. from voting: 50 votes for, 35 against, and 7 abstentions

ab·sti·nence /'æbstɪnəns/ n [U (**from**)] the act of keeping away from pleasant things, esp. from alcoholic drink: enforced abstinence —**nent** adj

abstract

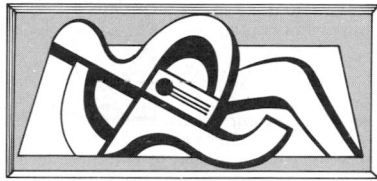

an abstract painting

ab·stract¹ /'æbstrækt/ adj **1** existing as a quality or CONCEPT rather than as something real or solid: Beauty is abstract but a house is not. —compare CONCRETE¹ (1) **2** general as opposed to particular: an abstract discussion of the crime problem, without reference to actual cases **3** (in art, said of paintings, drawings, etc.) not trying to show things as they would be seen by a camera – compare REPRESENTATIONAL

abstract² n **1** an abstract painting, drawing, or other work of art **2** [(**of**)] a shortened form of a statement, speech, etc. **3 in the abstract** in general; not related to particular examples or practical experience

ab·stract³ /əb'strækt, æb-/ v [T (**from**)] **1** to make a shortened form of (a statement, speech, etc.) by separating out what is important **2** euph to steal

ab·stract·ed /əb'stræktɪd, æb-/ adj not noticing what is happening; deep in thought – ~ **ly** adv

ab·strac·tion /əb'strækʃən, æb-/ n **1** [U] the state of not noticing what is happening; being ABSENT-MINDED: a look of abstraction **2** [C] an idea of a quality considered separately from any particular object or case: A good judge must consider the actual facts of a case as well as the abstraction "justice".

abstract noun /ˌ·· '·/ n a word that names a quality, state, or action: "Hunger" and "beauty" are examples of abstract nouns.

ab·struse /əb'struːs, æb-/ adj fml difficult to understand: an abstruse theory – ~ **ness** n [U]

ab·surd /əb'sɜːd, -'zɜːd‖-ɜːrd/ adj against reason or common sense; clearly false or foolish; RIDICULOUS: It's (patently) absurd not to wear a coat in such cold weather. | He looks absurd in that hat! – ~ **ly** adv : an absurdly overpriced hotel – ~ **ity** /əb'sɜːdɪti, -'zɜː-‖-ɜːr-/ n [C;U] : We had to laugh at the absurdity of the situation.

ABTA /'æbtə/ the Association of British Travel Agents; an organization whose job is to protect customers and make sure that they do not lose money and are not cheated when paying for their holiday. Many travel agencies (TRAVEL AGENCY) and TOUR OPERATORs are members of ABTA.

Ab·u Dha·bi /ˌæbuː 'dɑːbi‖ˌɑː-/ **1** island and largest EMIRATE of the United Arab Emirates **2** the capital city of the United Arab Emirates

a·bun·dance /ə'bʌndəns/ n [S (**of**);U] a great quantity; plenty: At the party there was food and drink in abundance. | The country has an abundance of skilled workers, but not enough jobs.

a·bun·dant /ə'bʌndənt/ adj more than enough; PLENTIFUL: The country has abundant supplies of oil and gas. – ~ **ly** adv : She made it **abundantly clear** (=very clear) that she wanted me to leave.

Ab·u Ni·dal /ˌæbuː niː'dæl‖ˌɑːbuː niː'dɑːl/ a Palestinian terrorist organization, named after a wealthy man of the same name, which was responsible for many events including the killing of Jewish CIVILIANs at Rome airport in 1985

a·buse¹ /ə'bjuːz/ v [T] **1** to say unkind, cruel, or rude things to or about: She abused him roundly for his neglect. **2** to put to wrong use; use badly, esp. for one's own advantage: to abuse one's power —see MISUSE (USAGE) **3** to treat (someone, esp. a child) in a cruel or immoral way: The child had been sexually abused. **4** to physically hurt: He abuses his wife.

abuse² /ə'bjuːs/ n **1** [U] unkind, cruel, or rude words: He greeted me with a **stream of abuse**. | a term of abuse | foul-mouthed abuse **2** [C;U] wrong use: I'm afraid the system is open to abuse. | the abuse of power/of drugs **3** [C] an unjust or harmful custom **4** [U] bad or cruel treatment, esp. of children: hundreds of children at risk from abuse —see also CHILD ABUSE

Abu Sim·bel /ˌæbuː 'sɪmbəl‖ˌɑː-/ a place on the river Nile in S Egypt where there are two ancient rock temples which were built in about 1250 BC

a·bu·sive /ə'bjuːsɪv/ adj using or containing unkind, cruel, or rude language: an abusive letter/person – ~ **ly** adv – ~ **ness** n [U]

a·but /ə'bʌt/ v
    abut on sthg. phr v -tt- [T no pass.] fml (of land or buildings) to lie next to or touch on one side: Their garden abuts on ours.

a·but·ment /ə'bʌtmənt/ n a support, esp. one on which a bridge or arch rests

a·bys·mal /ə'bɪzməl/ adj very bad: The food was abysmal. | abysmal weather

a·byss /ə'bɪs/ n a deep bottomless hole: (fig.) an abyss of despair

Ab·ys·sin·i·a /ˌæbɪ'sɪniə/ the former name for Ethiopia —Abyssinian n, adj

a/c also **A/C**— written abbrev. for: ACCOUNT¹ (2–5)

AC /ˌeɪ 'siː◁/ **1** abbrev. for ALTERNATING CURRENT —compare DC; see also AC/DC **2** AmE infml AIR-CONDITIONING: I'm going to turn on the AC.

a·ca·cia /ə'keɪʃə/ n -cias or -cia a mainly tropical tree from which GUM² (1) is obtained

Ac·a·deme /'ækədiːm, ˌækə'diːm/ **the groves of Academe** quote a phrase from a work by Horace, now often used humorously to describe the world of education, esp. universities: It was time to leave the groves of Academe and to look for a job.

ac·a·de·mi·a /ˌækə'diːmiə/ n [U] the world of education, esp. universities: Professor James had been living in academia for too long to ever be successful in the business world.

ac·a·dem·ic¹ /ˌækə'demɪk◁/ adj **1** concerning education, esp. college or university level: They publish academic books. **2** being or based on subjects that are taught to develop the mind rather than to provide practical skills: academic studies —compare TECHNICAL (1,2) **3** not related to practical situations; THEORETICAL: Where we ought to go for our holidays is a purely academic question because we can't afford a holiday at all! – ~ **ally** /kli/ adv: children who do well academically (=in academic subjects)

academic² n **1** a college or university teacher. In Britain and the US, academics are sometimes criticized as being people who think only about ideas and theories (THEORY), but do not know very much about the real world or real problems. **2** someone who looks at things in an ACADEMIC¹ (2) way

academic free·dom /ˌ···· '··/ n [U] the freedom of students, teachers, and educational institutions to express and study any ideas that they want to

academic year /ˌ···· '·/ BrE ‖ **school year** AmE n the period of a year in which school, college or university courses run. In Britain and the US the academic year usually begins in September or October and ends in June or July, with holidays at Christmas and Easter. Some schools in the US run **year round** (=all year) with several shorter holidays instead of the long break during the summer.

a·cad·e·mi·cian /əˌkædə'mɪʃən‖ˌækədə-/ n a member of an academy

a·cad·e·my /ə'kædəmi/ n (often cap. as part of a name) **1** a society of people interested in the advancement of art, science, or literature, to which members are usu. elected as an honour: the Hungarian Academy of Science **2** a school for training in a special art or skill: a military academy | an academy of music

Academy A·ward /·ˌ··· ·ˈ·/ n an OSCAR

A·ca·di·a /ə'keidiə/ the name of an area formerly consisting of Nova Scotia and several other parts of Canada and Maine, once settled by the French

a cap·pel·la also **a capella** /ˌæ kæ'pelə‖ˌɑː kə-/ adv, adj It (of singing) without musical instruments: She stood up and sang a cappella.

Ac·a·pul·co /ˌækə'pulkəu‖ˌɑːkə'puːl-/ a city on the west coast of Mexico, known as a holiday place for rich and famous people from all over the world

ACAS /'eikæs/ Advisory Conciliation and Arbitration Service; ACAS is an independent British organization working in the field of industrial relations and helping to find a way of dealing with disagreements between management and unions, esp. over pay and conditions at work: ACAS has been called in to try to end the dispute.

ac·cede /ək'siːd, æk-/ v [I (to)] fml **1** to agree to a suggestion, plan, demand, etc., often after first disagreeing: In the end she acceded to our request. **2** to take a high post or position after someone has left it **3** to join a group of people, countries, etc., in an agreement —see also ACCESSION

ac·cel·e·rate /ək'seləreit/ v **1** [I;T] to (cause to) move faster —opposite **decelerate 2** [T] fml to cause to happen faster or earlier than expected: accelerated promotion | economic policies that have accelerated the decline of manufacturing industry

ac·cel·e·ra·tion /ək,selə'reiʃən/ n [U] (the rate of) increasing speed: a car with good acceleration

ac·cel·e·ra·tor /ək'seləreitə*/ n **1** also **gas pedal** AmE— the instrument in a machine or vehicle (esp. a car) which is used to increase its speed: He put his foot down hard on the accelerator. —see picture at CAR **2** tech ‖ also **atom smasher** AmE infml a machine for making PARTICLES (=very small pieces of matter) move very quickly

ac·cent¹ /'æksənt‖'æksent/ n **1** a particular way of speaking, usu. connected with a country, area, or social class: He speaks English with a strong German accent. | Where are you from? I can't place (=recognize) your accent. —compare DIALECT

▶ CULTURAL NOTE Many different English accents can be heard in both Britain and the US, and an accent often shows where a person is from. In Britain, an accent often also suggests a person's educational background or social class, with the accent of educated people from southeast England considered the most standard.◀

2 [(on)] importance given to a word or part of a word by saying it with more force or on a different musical note: The accent in the word "important" is on the second syllable. **3** a mark used in writing or printing, esp. above a word or part of a word, to show what kind of sound is needed when it is spoken: In French there are three possible accents on the vowel "e". | an acute accent **4** [(on) usu. sing.] particular importance or interest, an EMPHASIS: The accent (of the report) is on safety.

ac·cent² /ək'sent‖'æksent/ v [T] **1** to pronounce (a word or a part of a word) with an ACCENT¹ (2) **2** to mark (a written word) with an ACCENT¹ (3) **3** to direct attention to; accentuate: A red belt accents the colour in her dress. | French herbs accent the flavour of the meat.

ac·cen·tu·ate /ək'sentʃueit/ v [T] **1** to direct attention to; EMPHASIZE: The dark frame accentuates the brightness of the picture. **2** to pronounce with great force —**-ation** /ək,sentʃu'eiʃən/ n [C;U]

ac·cept /ək'sept/ v **1** [I;T] to take or receive (something offered or given), esp. willingly: The police aren't allowed to accept rewards. | He asked her to marry him and she accepted (his offer). **2** [T] to take or receive as satisfactory or reasonable, often unwillingly: The company did not accept the report's criticisms. | Did she accept your reasons for being late? | He accepted her apology very graciously. | They accepted responsibility for the accident. | The work force has reluctantly agreed to accept a cut in pay. **3** [T] to recognize as being true or right: For a long time she could not accept the fact of her husband's death. |

I'm sorry, but I can't accept that. [+that] It is generally accepted that smoking causes bad health. | accepted principles of behaviour —see REFUSE (USAGE)

ac·cep·ta·ble /ək'septəbəl/ adj **1** good enough; satisfactory: This standard of work is not acceptable; do it again. **2** that can be allowed; TOLERABLE: an acceptable level of inflation | an acceptable risk | behaviour that is not socially acceptable —opposite **unacceptable 3** worth receiving; welcome: an acceptable gift —**·bly** adv —**·bility** /ək,septə'biləti/ n [U]

ac·cept·ance /ək'septəns/ n [C;U] **1** the act of accepting or being accepted **2** favour; approval: to gain acceptance for one's ideas **3** (in business) an agreement to pay

ac·cess¹ /'ækses/ n **1** [U (to)] means of entering; way in; entrance: The only means of access to the building is along a muddy track. **2** [U (to)] means or right of using, reaching, or obtaining: Students need easy access to books. | My ex-husband has access to the children at weekends. (=is allowed to see them then) **3** [C+of] lit or old use a sudden attack, as of anger or a disease **4** **easy/difficult of access** easy/ difficult to reach

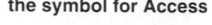

the symbol for Access

access² v [T] to obtain (stored information) from a computer's memory

Access card /'·· ˌ·/ n tdmk a CREDIT CARD given by British banks to their customers, who use it to obtain money, goods, and services which they pay for later: Do you take (=accept payment by) Access? | I've lost my Access card. —see CREDIT CARD

ac·ces·si·ble /ək'sesəbəl/ adj [(to, by)] **1** easy to reach, enter, or obtain: The island is accessible only by boat. —opposite **inaccessible 2** easy and friendly to speak to: A manager should be accessible to his/her staff. **3** in a form that is easy to understand: The information ought to be made more accessible. —**·bility** /ək,sesə'biləti/ n [U]

ac·ces·sion /ək'seʃən/ n fml **1** [U (to)] the act of acceding (ACCEDE) or coming to a high position: the Queen's accession to the throne —compare SUCCESSION (3) **2** [C;U (to)] (an) addition to a group or collection: an important new accession of scientific books to the library **3** [C;U (to)] agreement, esp. to a demand

ac·ces·so·ry /ək'sesəri/ n **1** [usu. pl.] something which is not a necessary part of something larger but which makes it more useful, effective, etc.: car accessories including the roof rack and radio **2** [usu. pl.] the bag, shoes, etc., that complete a woman's clothes; a formal word usually used to describe fashion clothes: a black dress with matching accessories **3** [C] also **accessary**— law a person who is not present at a crime but who helps someone else in doing it, either before the crime **(accessory before the fact)** or afterwards **(accessory after the fact):** an accessory to murder

access time /'·· ˌ·/ n [U] tech the time taken by a computer to find and use a piece of information in its memory; the length of time between asking the computer for information and getting it

ac·ci·dence /'æksɪdəns/ n [U] tech the rules of grammar which are concerned with changes in the form of words (their INFLECTION) according to their use in a sentence, as in sing, sang, sung, or in body, bodies

ac·ci·dent /'æksɪdənt/ n **1** something, esp. something unpleasant or damaging, that happens unexpectedly or by chance: I'm afraid I had an accident in the kitchen and broke all the glasses. | a bad/serious/fatal accident on the motorway —see also CHAPTER OF ACCIDENTS **2** something that happened that was not intentional and so cannot be blamed on anyone: I didn't break it on purpose, Mum, it was an accident! | He swears it was an accident. **3 by accident** by chance: I met her purely by accident. | The trip was a success, but **more by accident than design**. (=not because of good planning **4 by accident of** by the chance or fortune of: wealthy by accident of birth **5 accidents will happen** saying a phrase used when there has been an accident, meaning that it is impossible to avoid them and so not worth worrying about them

ac·ci·den·tal /ˌæksɪ'dentl◄/ adj happening by chance, not by plan or intention — ~**ly** *adv* : *She walked past and spilled my drink,* **accidentally on purpose.** (=She pretended that it was an accident, but really she did it on purpose)

accidental death /ˌ···· ˈ·/ *n law* one of the VERDICTS possible at a British INQUEST trying to discover the cause of someone's death

accident-prone /ˈ··· ·/ *adj* (of a person) more likely to have accidents than most people are

ac·claim[1] /əˈkleɪm/ *v* [T (**as**)] to greet with approval; publicly recognize: *The new drug has been acclaimed as the most important discovery for years.* [+obj+n] *They acclaimed him their leader.*

acclaim[2] *n* [U] strong expressions of approval and praise: *The book received considerable critical acclaim.*

ac·cla·ma·tion /ˌækləˈmeɪʃən/ *n* [C;U] *fml* loud expressions of approval or welcome

ac·cli·ma·tize also **-tise** *BrE* /əˈklaɪmətaɪz/ also **ac·cli·mate** /əˈklaɪmət‖ˈækləmeɪt, əˈklaɪmət/ *AmE*— *v* [I;T (**to**)] to (cause to) become used to the conditions of weather in a new part of the world: *We lived in Africa for five years, but we never really got acclimatized (to the hot weather).* | (fig.) *He can't acclimatize (himself) to working at night.* —-**tization** /əˌklaɪmətaɪˈzeɪʃən‖-tə-/ *n* [U]

ac·cliv·i·ty /əˈklɪvɪti/ *n fml or tech* an upward slope — compare DECLIVITY

ac·co·lade /ˈækəleɪd/ *n* strong praise and approval: *The film received/won accolades from all the critics.*

ac·com·mo·date /əˈkɒmədeɪt‖əˈkɑː-/ *v* [T] *fml* **1** to provide with a place in which to live or stay **2** to have enough space for: *Are there enough shelves to accommodate all our books?* **3** to make changes that take account of the wishes or demands of: *The union has made every possible effort to accommodate the management.* **4** [(**to**)] to change (esp. oneself) to fit new conditions **5** [(**with**)] to supply with something that is needed, esp. money: *He asked his uncle to accommodate him till his pay cheque arrived.*

ac·com·mo·dat·ing /əˈkɒmədeɪtɪŋ‖əˈkɑː-/ *adj fml apprec* willing to help or make changes to suit new conditions; OBLIGING — ~**ly** *adv*

ac·com·mo·da·tion /əˌkɒməˈdeɪʃən‖əˌkɑː-/ *n* **1** [U] a place to live or work in; house, flat, hotel room, etc.: *The travel agent fixed up/arranged our accommodation.* | *office accommodation* | *the high cost of rented accommodation in London* **2** [C;U] *fml* the settling of a disagreement: *efforts to come to/reach an accommodation with the US over imports*

accommodation a·gen·cy /·ˌ··ˈ·· ˌ····/ *n* (in Britain) an organization which finds houses and flats for people to rent, in return for payment

ac·com·mo·da·tions /əˌkɒməˈdeɪʃənz‖əˌkɑː-/ *n* [P] *AmE* **1** lodging, food, and services **2** a seat or place to sleep, esp. on a boat or train: *tourist accommodations on a boat*

ac·com·pa·ni·ment /əˈkʌmpənimənt/ *n* [(**to**)] **1** something which is used or provided with something else, esp. in order to improve it: *A green salad makes a good accompaniment to this dish.* **2** music played at the same time as singing or another instrument: *to play a piano accompaniment* | (fig.) *The election results were announced to* **the accompaniment** of *loud cheering.*

ac·com·pa·nist /əˈkʌmpənɪst/ *n* a person who plays a musical accompaniment

ac·com·pa·ny /əˈkʌmpəni/ *v* [T] **1** *rather fml* to go with, esp. on a journey: *Let me accompany you to your hotel.* **2** to exist or appear at the same time or same place as: *A series of colour photographs accompanies the text.* **3** to play a musical accompaniment for —see also UNACCOMPANIED

ac·com·plice /əˈkʌmplɪs‖əˈkɑːm-, əˈkʌm-/ *n* a person who helps another person to do wrong; usu. a criminal: *The kidnapper must have had an accomplice.*

ac·com·plish /əˈkʌmplɪʃ‖əˈkɑːm-, əˈkʌm-/ *v* [T] to succeed in doing; finish successfully; ACHIEVE: *She's accomplished a great deal in the last few weeks.* | *I don't feel our visit really accomplished anything.*

ac·com·plished /əˈkʌmplɪʃt‖əˈkɑːm-, əˈkʌm-/ *adj* skilled; good at something, esp. something artistic: *an accomplished singer*

ac·com·plish·ment /əˈkʌmplɪʃmənt‖əˈkɑːm-, əˈkʌm-/ *n* **1**

[C] a skill; something in which one is accomplished: *Being able to play the piano well is one of his many accomplishments.* **2** [U] the act of accomplishing or finishing work completely and successfully **3** [C] something accomplished; achievement: *This is the first house I've ever built – what an accomplishment (it is)!*

ac·cord[1] /əˈkɔːd‖-ɔːrd/ *n* **1** [C;U (**with**)] *fml* (an) agreement: *The two sides are completely in accord (with each other) on this matter.* **2** of one's own accord without being asked or ordered: *The children went to bed of their own accord, because they were so tired.* **3** with one accord with everyone expressing their agreement at the same time, either in words or in actions

accord[2] *v fml* **1** [I (**with**)] to be the same (as); agree: *What you have just said does not accord with what you told us yesterday.* **2** [T+obj(i)+obj(d)] to give or allow: *She was accorded a tremendous welcome at the party conference.*

ac·cord·ance /əˈkɔːdəns‖-ɔːr-/ *n* **in accordance with** in a way that fulfils or agrees with: *In accordance with your orders/your wishes, I cancelled the meeting.*

ac·cord·ing as /əˈkɔːdɪŋ əz, -æz‖əˈkɔːr-/ *conj BrE fml* depending on whether

ac·cord·ing·ly /əˈkɔːdɪŋli‖-ɔːr-/ *adv fml* **1** in a way suitable to what has been said or what has happened: *Please inform us of your decision and we will act accordingly.* **2** therefore; so: *They asked him to leave the meeting, and accordingly he went.*

according to /·ˈ··· ·/ *prep* **1** as stated or shown by: *According to our records, the books you have borrowed should now be returned to the library.* | *According to George, she's a really good teacher.* **2** in a way that agrees with: *We will be paid according to the amount of work we do.*

▷ USAGE 1 We use **according to** to show that the information comes from another person or place and not from our own knowledge: **According to** *these figures, the company is doing well.* It can also be used to suggest that you do not share someone's opinion: **According to** *George, I owe him £10.* (=but I don't agree) 2 We do not use **according to** with words like **opinion** or **view**. Compare: **According to** *the management ...* | *In the management's* **opinion/view** ...◁

ac·cor·di·on[1] /əˈkɔːdiən‖-ɔːr-/ *n* a musical instrument that is pressed in from each side so that the air in the middle part is forced through holes that can be opened and closed to produce different sounds. Accordion music is often played in films when the scene is in France, esp. Paris, and British people think of the accordion as a typically French musical instrument. In the US people think of the accordion in connection with old-fashioned dance music.

accordion[2] *adj AmE* having many folds like those of an accordion: *an accordion file* (=one that has sides which fold in or out to make it larger or smaller)

ac·cost /əˈkɒst‖əˈkɔːst, əˈkɑːst/ *v* [T] to go up to and speak to (someone, esp. a stranger), often threateningly or with the offer of sex: *A man accosted me in the street and asked for money.*

ac·count[1] /əˈkaʊnt/ *n* **1** [C (**of**)] a written or spoken report; description: *Give us your/an account of what happened.* | *a detailed account of the proceedings* | *He is a very good pianist,* **by all accounts.** (=according to what everyone says) | (fig.) *I thought Kevin* **gave a good account of himself** (=performed well) *in today's game.* **2** a sum of money kept in a bank, BUILDING SOCIETY, etc., which may be added to and taken from: *My salary is paid directly into my bank account.* | *Have you got an account with us?* — see also CHECKING ACCOUNT, CURRENT ACCOUNT, DEPOSIT ACCOUNT **3** *usu. pl.* a record or statement of money received and paid out, usually by a bank or business: *The accounts show that business is improving.* | *to audit the accounts* —see also ACCOUNTANT, EXPENSE ACCOUNT **4** a CREDIT ACCOUNT: *Please put the shoes on my account/charge the shoes to my account.* **5** a statement of money owed: *Please settle your account immediately.* (=pay what you owe) **6** a customer, esp. one who has regular dealings with a company: *Our sales manager has secured several big accounts recently.* **7 bring/call someone to account (for): a** to cause or force someone to give an explanation (of) **b** to punish someone (for) **8 of great/no/some account** of great/no/some importance **9 on account of** *fml* because of: *Why did you do it? Was it on account of what I said yesterday?* **10 on no**

account/not on any account not for any reason: *On no account must you tell him.* **11 on one's own account: a** for one's own advantage **b** at one's own risk **c** by oneself **12 on someone's account** out of consideration for someone's wishes **13 take account of something/take something into account** to give proper consideration to a fact, situation, etc., when making a judgment or decision: *His exam results were not very good, but we must take into account his long illness.* | *The teachers promised to take account of the wishes of the parents before making any changes.* | *Their estimate of the cost takes no account of inflation.* | *Your objections will be taken into account.* **14 to (good) account** so as to bring advantage or profit: *She put/turned her computing skills to good account.*

account² *v* [T+*obj*+*n*/*adj*] *fml* to consider: *He was accounted a wise man.*

account for sthg. *phr v* [T] **1** to give or be a satisfactory explanation for: *The defendant couldn't account for the fact that the money was found in his house.* [+*v-ing*] *How do you account for losing five games in a row?* – compare ANSWER² **for** (1); see also UNACCOUNTABLE **2** [(**to**)] to provide a satisfactory record, esp. of money received and paid out: *He has to account to the chairman for how he spends the company's money.* –compare ANSWER² **for** (1) **3** to be the cause or origin of: *North Sea oil accounts for a high proportion of our export earnings.* **4** *infml, becoming rare* to kill, shoot, or catch **5 There's no accounting for tastes** *infml* (said usu. when one disagrees with another person's judgment) it is impossible to explain why different people like different things

ac·coun·ta·bil·i·ty /ə,kauntə'bɪlˌti/ *n* [U] the condition or quality of being accountable: *demands for an increase in police accountability*

ac·coun·ta·ble /ə'kauntəbəl/ *adj* [F (**to, for**)] responsible; having to give an explanation for one's actions; ANSWERABLE: *If anything happens to the car, I will hold you accountable.* | *Should the police be more accountable to the public?* –compare UNACCOUNTABLE

ac·coun·tan·cy /ə'kauntənsi/ also **ac·coun·ting** /ə'kauntɪŋ/ *AmE*– *n* [U] the work or job of an accountant: *a degree in accountancy*

ac·coun·tant /ə'kauntənt/ *n* a person whose job is to control and examine the FINANCIAL accounts of businesses or people. In Britain, people often make jokes about accountants because they are considered to be very boring and dull.

ac·cou·tre·ments /ə'ku:trˌmənts/ also **-terments** /ə'ku:tə-mənts‖-tər-/ *AmE*– *n* [P] equipment, esp. everything a soldier carries, except his clothes and weapons

Ac·cra /ə'krɑː/ the capital city of Ghana

ac·cred·it·ed /ə'kredˌtˌd/ *adj* **1** [(**to**)] officially representing one's government in a foreign country, esp. as an AMBASSADOR **2** having the power to act for an organization: *an accredited representative of the firm* **3** officially recognized as reaching a certain standard or quality: *accredited milk from a herd of healthy cows* | *an accredited university*

ac·cre·tion /ə'kri:ʃən/ *n* [C;U (**to**)] *fml* (an) increase by natural growth or by the gradual addition of matter on the outside: *towers and other accretions to the castle*

ac·crue /ə'kru:/ *v fml* **1** [I;T] to become bigger or more by addition: *Interest accrues on a bank account.* | *You should accrue more interest this way.* **2** [I(**to**)] to come as a gain or additional advantage: *Great wealth will accrue to her when she marries the duke.* --**crual** *n* [U]

acct *written abbrev. for:* ACCOUNT¹ (2–5)

ac·cu·mu·late /ə'kju:mjˌleɪt/ *v* [I;T] to make or become greater in quantity or size, esp. over a long period; collect or grow into a mass: *He gradually accumulated an impressive collection of paintings.* –see GATHER (USAGE) --**lation** /ə,kju:mjˌ'leɪʃən/ *n* [C;U]: *an accumulation of work while I was ill*

ac·cu·mu·la·tive /ə'kju:mjˌlətɪv‖-leɪ-, -lə-/ *adj fml* CUMULATIVE – ~**ly** *adv*

ac·cu·mu·la·tor /ə'kju:mjˌleɪtə^r/ *n* **1** a part of a computer where numbers are stored **2** *esp. BrE* ‖ usu. **storage battery** *AmE* a type of BATTERY which can take in new supplies of electricity so that it has enough power to keep working **3** *BrE* a set of BETs on four or more horse races. The money won on each race is added to the money put on the next race until all the bets have been won or one is lost.

ac·cu·ra·cy /'ækjˌrəsi/ *n* [U] the quality of being accurate; exactness or correctness: *the accuracy of his account* | *to throw darts with pinpoint accuracy*

ac·cu·rate /'ækjˌrət/ *adj* exactly correct: *Her report of what happened was accurate in every detail/was an accurate reflection of the facts.* | *Is the station clock accurate?* – opposite **inaccurate** – ~**ly** *adv*

ac·curs·ed /ə'kɜːsˌd, ə'kɜːst‖-ɜːr-/ also **ac·curst** /ə'kɜːst ‖ -ɜːr-/ *lit*– *adj* **1** *lit* under a curse **2** hateful because causing bad fortune or great trouble

ac·cu·sa·tion /,ækjˌ'zeɪʃən/ *n* [C;U] (a statement) accusing someone of doing wrong or of breaking the law: [+*that*] *How do you answer the accusation that your policies have caused high unemployment?* | *You shouldn't make wild accusations without any evidence.*

ac·cu·sa·tive /ə'kju:zətɪv/ *n tech* a particular form of a noun in certain languages, such as Latin, Greek, and German, which shows that the noun is the DIRECT OBJECT of a verb –**accusative** *adj*

ac·cu·sa·to·ry /ə'kju:zətəri‖-tɔːri/ *adj esp. AmE* expressing accusation: *an accusatory remark* | *an accusatory attitude*

ac·cuse /ə'kju:z/ *v* [T (**of**)] to charge (someone) with doing wrong or breaking the law: *He was accused of murder.* | *Are you accusing me of cheating?* | *The report accused the government of shirking its responsibilities.* --**cuser** *n* --**cusingly** *adv* : *He looked at her accusingly.*

ac·cused /ə'kju:zd/ *adj* charged with doing something wrong, a crime, etc.: *The company* **stands accused of** *failing to safeguard the public.* [also *n, the*+C, *pl.* **accused**] *The accused (man) was asked to give his name.* | *Several of the accused were found guilty.*

ac·cus·tom /ə'kʌstəm/ *v* [T (**to**)] to make used to: *to accustom oneself to a new job*

ac·cus·tomed /ə'kʌstəmd/ *adj* **1** [F+**to**] in the habit of; used to: *I'm not accustomed to getting up so early.* **2** [A *no comp.*] regular; usual: *sitting in her accustomed place at the head of the table*

AC/DC /,eɪ si: 'di: si:/ *adj* [F] *sl* BISEXUAL² : *I think he's a bit AC/DC.*

ace¹ /eɪs/ *n* **1** [(**of**)] a CARD¹ (1) that has a single mark or spot and usu. has the highest or the lowest value –see CARDS (USAGE) **2** *infml* a person of the highest skill in the stated activity: *an ace at chess* **3** (in tennis and VOLLEYBALL) a very fast and strong SERVE (=beginning shot) that the opponent cannot hit back **4 an ace in the hole** *AmE infml* something that will give a person an advantage or help when it is needed **5 within an ace of** *infml* very close to (a condition): *within an ace of victory/ death*

ace² *adj infml* very good or very skilled; excellent: *an ace skier* | *Their new record is really ace.*

ace³ *v* [T] *AmE infml* to do (something) very well: *I think I aced the exam, but the interview was murder.*

a·cer·bic /ə'sɜːbɪk‖-ɜːr-/ *adj* (of a person or manner) clever in a rather cruel way: *her acerbic wit*

a·cer·bi·ty /ə'sɜːbˌti‖-ɜːr-/ *n* [U] *fml* bitterness; sourness

ac·e·tate /'æsˌteɪt/ *n* [U] a chemical made from acetic acid –see also CELLULOSE (2)

a·ce·tic /ə'si:tɪk/ *adj* of, concerning, or producing VINEGAR or acetic acid

acetic ac·id /·,·· '··/ *n* [U] the acid in VINEGAR (=a bitter liquid made from wine or beer)

a·cet·y·lene /ə'setˌli:n‖-lən, -li:n/ *n* [U] a gas which burns with a very bright flame and is used in certain types of lamp and in cutting and joining pieces of metal

ache¹ /eɪk/ *v* [I] **1** to have or suffer a continuous, but not violent, pain: *I ache all over.* | *My head aches.* **2** [+**for**/ **to**-*v*] to have an extremely strong desire: *aching for freedom* | (*infml*) *I'm aching to tell them the news.*

ache² *n* (*often in comb.*) a continuous, but not violent, pain: *I've got a bit of an ache in my back.* | *Take no notice of him complaining – he's always full of little aches and pains.* | *a headache* | (fig.) *heartache* –compare PAIN¹

▷ USAGE **1** Note the fixed phrase **aches and pains**. **2** Nouns formed from **ache** are treated as uncountable in British English when they mean a condition or a state: *Chocolate gives me* **toothache**. | *She suffers from* **backache**. When they mean a single attack of pain, they can be either countable or uncountable: *She often* *gets* **stomachaches/stomachache.** But **headache** is always a countable noun: *a nasty* **headache.** Words ending in **-ache** are more often treated as countable in American English: *a* **toothache** | *a* **stomachache.**◁

a·chieve /ə'tʃiːv/ *v* [T] **1** to finish successfully; succeed in doing or reaching: *He will never achieve anything/his objectives if he doesn't work harder.* **2** to get as the result of action or effort; gain: *The company has achieved a 100% increase in profitability.* —**achievable** *adj*

a·chieve·ment /ə'tʃiːvmənt/ *n* **1** [U] the successful finishing or gaining of something: *We felt a great* **sense of achievement** *when we reached the top of the mountain.* **2** [C] something successfully finished or gained, esp. through skill and hard work: *a remarkable achievement* | *Without wishing to detract from your achievement in any way, can I remind you that other people also worked very hard on this book.* | *He has broken two world records in one day, which is* **quite an achievement!**

a·chiev·er /ə'tʃiːvəʳ/ *n* someone who is successful, esp. through skill and hard work: *He is a real achiever – he's won three medals.* —see also HIGH ACHIEVER

A·chil·les /ə'kɪliːz/ *in* CLASSICAL MYTHOLOGY, a HERO of ancient Greece who quarrelled with his commander during the Trojan War and in anger refused to fight. Later he returned to kill Hector and was killed in turn by Paris, who wounded him in the heel.

Achilles' heel /·,·· '·/ *n* a small but important weakness, esp. in a person's character (from the story of Achilles, whose mother held him by his heel when she dipped him in the water of the river Styx as a baby, so that his heel was the only part of his body unprotected against harm): *His loyalty to his country may be his Achilles' heel.*

Achilles ten·don /·,·· '··/ *n* the strong TENDON in the heel

ac·id¹ /'æsɟd/ *n* **1** [C;U] a substance that forms a chemical salt when combined with an ALKALI. It may destroy things it touches: *The acid burnt a hole in the carpet.* — compare ALKALI **2** [U] *sl* the HALLUCINOGENIC drug LSD **3** **drop acid** *sl* to take the drug LSD

acid² *adj* **1** having an unpleasantly sour or bitter taste like that of VINEGAR or unripe fruit **2** saying bitter or unkind things; bad-tempered: *his acid remarks*

acid house par·ty /'··· ,··/ *n esp BrE* a party held at a secret place for a large number of paying guests, usu. young people. Acid house parties became popular in the late 1980s and are known for their loud music, and for the drugs that can often be obtained there.

a·cid·i·fy /ə'sɪdɟfaɪ/ *v* [I;T] to make into or become an acid

a·cid·i·ty /ə'sɪdɟti/ *n* [U] the quality of being acid; sourness

ac·i·doph·i·lus /,æsɟ'dɒfɟləs||-'dɑː-/ *n* [U] *tech* a kind of BACTERIA added to milk or YOGHURT to insure a healthy stomach and INTESTINE

acid rain /,· '·/ *n* [U] rain containing harmful quantities of acid (esp. SULPHURIC ACID and NITRIC ACID) as a result of industrial POLLUTION. Many people consider acid rain to be a serious threat to the environment.

acid rock /,·· '·/ *n* [U] a kind of popular music sung and played in the 1960s and 1970s involving very loud, electronic sounds and strange lighting suggesting the effects of taking certain drugs

acid test /,·· '·/ *n* [usu. sing.] a test which will prove whether something is as valuable as it is supposed to be

ac·knowl·edge /ək'nɒlɪdʒ||-'nɑː-/ *v* [T] **1** [(as)] to accept or admit (as); recognize the fact or existence (of): *When the results of the vote were announced the Prime Minister acknowledged defeat.* | *The terrorists refused to acknowledge the court.* | *She is acknowledged as an expert on the subject.* | *an acknowledged expert* [+v-ing/that] *He grudgingly acknowledged having made a mistake/that he had made a mistake.* [+obj+to-v] *He is generally acknowledged to have the finest collection of Dutch paintings in private hands.* [+obj+adj] *She acknowledged herself puzzled.* **2** to show that one is grateful for: *The producer wishes to acknowledge the assistance of the Los Angeles Police Department in the making of this film.* **3** to state that one has received (something): *We must acknowledge his interest/acknowledge receipt of his letter.* **4** to show that one recognizes (someone) by smiling, waving, etc.: *She walked right past me without even acknowledging me.*

ac·knowl·edg·ment , **-edgement** /ək'nɒlɪdʒmənt||-'nɑː-/ *n* **1** [U] the act of acknowledging: *He was given a gold watch*

in acknowledgment of *his work for the company.* **2** [C] something given, done, or said as a way of thanking, showing that something official has been received, etc.: *I wrote to the company three weeks ago, and I haven't received an acknowledgment yet.*

ACLU /,eɪ siː el 'juː/ [the] American Civil Liberties Union; an organization which examines legal cases involving the BILL OF RIGHTS and often provides arguments for defending those rights

ac·me /'ækmi/ *n* [(the) S (of)] *fml* the highest point of development, success, etc.: *the acme of perfection*

ac·ne /'ækni/ *n* [U] a skin disorder common among young people, esp. ADOLESCENTS, in which many small raised spots appear on the face and neck

ac·o·lyte /'ækəlaɪt/ *n* **1** a person who helps a priest to perform religious ceremonies **2** *esp. lit* an attendant or follower

a·corn /'eɪkɔːn||-ɔːrn, -ərn/ *n* **1** the nut of the OAK tree, which grows in a cuplike holder —see picture at TREE **2 Great oaks from little** '**acorns grow** *saying* small things grow into great things over time

a·cous·tic /ə'kuːstɪk/ *adj* **1** of sound or the sense of hearing: *the acoustic nerve* **2** (esp. of a musical instrument) making its natural sound, not helped by electrical apparatus: *an acoustic guitar* —~**ally** /kli/ *adv*

acoustic coup·ler /·,·· '··/ *n tech* an instrument which allows computers to send and receive information through a telephone; simple type of MODEM

a·cous·tics /ə'kuːstɪks/ *n* **1** [U] the scientific study of sound **2** [P] the qualities of a place, esp. a hall, which influence the way sounds can be heard in it: *The acoustics of the theatre are very good.*

ac·quaint /ə'kweɪnt/ *v*
acquaint *sbdy.* **with** *sthg.* *phr v* [T] *fml* **1** to provide with (information); make known to: *She acquainted them with the facts.* **2 be acquainted (with)** to have met socially: *We're already acquainted (with each other).*

ac·quaint·ance /ə'kweɪntəns/ *n* **1** [C] a person whom one knows, esp. through work or business, but who is not a close friend —see also NODDING ACQUAINTANCE **2** [S;U (with)] knowledge obtained through personal experience rather than careful study: *I have a passing/some acquaintance with the language.* **3 make someone's acquaintance** to meet someone for the first time

ac·quaint·ance·ship /ə'kweɪntənsʃɪp/ *n* [S (with)] the state of being socially acquainted

ac·qui·esce /,ækwi'es/ *v* [(in)] *fml* to agree, often unwillingly, but without complaining or arguing; accept quietly: *He acquiesced in the plans his parents had made for him.*

ac·qui·es·cent /,ækwi'esənt/ *adj* tending to acquiesce; ready to agree without argument — ~ **ly** *adv* —**cence** *n* [U]

ac·quire /ə'kwaɪəʳ/ *v* [T] to gain or come to possess, esp. by one's own work, skill, or action, often over a long period of time: *I managed to acquire two tickets for the concert.* | *The company has recently acquired new offices in central London.* | *to acquire mannerisms*

acquired taste /·,·· '·/ *n* [usu. sing.] something that one may learn to like after a while: *Most people don't like whisky at first — it's (something of) an acquired taste.*

ac·qui·si·tion /,ækwɟ'zɪʃən/ *n* **1** [U (of)] the act of acquiring **2** [C] something or someone acquired: *This painting is my latest acquisition.* | *She is a valuable acquisition to the firm.*

ac·quis·i·tive /ə'kwɪzɟtɪv/ *adj often derog* keen on getting and possessing things: *Squirrels are very acquisitive creatures.* — ~ **ly** *adv* — ~ **ness** *n* [U]

ac·quit /ə'kwɪt/ *v* **-tt-** [T] **1** [(of)] to give a decision that (someone) is not guilty of a crime: *The jury acquitted him (of murder).* | *He was acquitted on the charge of murder but convicted of manslaughter.* —opposite convict **2 acquit oneself** *fml* to carry out an activity with the stated degree of success: *She was interviewed on the radio but acquitted herself rather badly.*

ac·quit·tal /ə'kwɪtl/ *n* [C;U] the act of acquitting someone in a court of law, or the fact of being acquitted —opposite conviction

a·cre /'eɪkəʳ/ *n* a unit for measuring area: *They own 200 acres of farmland.* | *a 200-acre farm* —see TABLE 2

a·cre·age /ˈeɪkərɪdʒ/ n [S;U] the area of a piece of land measured in acres

ac·rid /ˈækrɪd/ adj (of taste or smell) very bitter; causing a stinging sensation: *the acrid smell of burning wood* | (fig.) *an acrid remark*

ac·ri·mo·ny /ˈækrɪˌmənɪ‖-məʊni/ n [U] bitterness, as of manner or language: *They parted without acrimony.* **—nious** /ˌækrɪˈməʊniəs◂/ adj : *an acrimonious dispute* **—niously** adv

ac·ro·bat /ˈækrəbæt/ n a person skilled in walking on ropes or wires, balancing, walking on their hands, etc., esp. at a CIRCUS

ac·ro·bat·ic /ˌækrəˈbætɪk◂/ adj of or like an acrobat; moving or changing position quickly and easily, esp. in the air **—~ally** /kli/ adv

ac·ro·bat·ics /ˌækrəˈbætɪks/ n **1** [U] the art and tricks of an acrobat **2** [P] a group of acrobatic tricks considered as a performance

ac·ro·nym /ˈækrənɪm/ n a word made up from the first letters of the name of something, such as *NATO* from *North Atlantic Treaty Organization*

ac·ro·pho·bi·a /ˌækrəˈfəʊbiə/ n [U] a fear of high places

A·crop·o·lis /əˈkrɒpəlɪs‖əˈkrɑː-/ , **The** the central area and highest point in the ancient Greek city of Athens, containing important religious and military buildings. The Acropolis is still standing and is visited by many tourists.

a·cross /əˈkrɒs‖əˈkrɔːs/ adv, prep **1** from one side to the other (of): *The stream is two metres across.* | *They built a bridge across the river.* | *He lay across the bed.* **2** to or on the opposite side (of): *Can you jump across?* | *They live just across the road (from us).* | *Their house is just* **across from** (=opposite) *ours.* | *I helped the old lady* **across** *the road.* (=helped her to cross it) **3** so as to cross: *The two lines cut across each other.*

▷ USAGE The prepositions **across** and **over** are both used to show movement from one side to another: *She drove* **across/over** *the bridge.* If there is an idea of crossing something high, **over** is used: *She climbed* **over** *the fence.* If there is an idea of crossing a level surface, **across** is usually better: *He walked* **across** *the stage and bowed to the audience.*◁

a·cross-the-board /ˌ·ˌ· · ˈ·◂/ adj [A] influencing or having effects on people or things of all kinds or at every level, esp. within a business or industry: *an across-the-board pay rise* | *a 25% across-the-board cut in military spending* **—across-the-board** adv : *Share prices this week have fallen by an average of 5% across-the-board.*

a·cros·tic /əˈkrɒstɪk‖əˈkrɔː-/ n a set of words or lines (often of a poem), written one below the other, in which particular sets of letters (such as the first letter of each line) form a word or phrase

a·cryl·ic /əˈkrɪlɪk/ n [C;U] a chemical substance used in paints and for making a threadlike material **(acrylic fibre)** used for clothes. Clothes made of acrylic are usu. cheaper than clothes made of wool or cotton.

act¹ /ækt/ v **1** [I **(as, on, for)**] to do something; take action: *The council must act quickly, before more people are killed on that road.* | *She acted on our suggestion.* (=did what we suggested) | *a lawyer acting for* (=in the interests of) *Mr Miller* | *A trained dog can act as* (=fulfil the purpose of) *a guide to a blind person.* —see also ACTING¹ **2** [I **(on, upon)**] to produce an effect; work: *Does the drug take long to act (on the nerve centres)?* **3 a** [I+adv/prep] to behave as stated: *He acted as if he'd never seen me before.* | *The report said that the doctor had acted correctly/very responsibly.* **b** [L+adj] infml to behave so as to seem: *Don't act so stupid!* **4** [I;T] to represent (a part in a play or film); perform, esp. on the stage: *Olivier is acting (the part of Othello) tonight.* | *I can't take her seriously because she always seems to be acting.* (=behaving as if she is in a play) | (fig.) *He's always acting the experienced man who has seen everything.* see also ACT ING², ACTOR, ACTRESS, PLAY-ACT **5 act your age** to behave in an adult way rather than a childish way

act sthg. ↔ **out** phr v [T] to express (thoughts, unconscious fears, etc.) in actions and behaviour, rather than in words: *a chance to act out one's fantasies*

act up also **play up** BrE— phr v [I] infml to behave or perform badly: *My old car is always acting up.*

act² n **1** fml something that someone has done; an action of a particular kind: *an act of great generosity/courage* |

This despicable act will not go unpunished. | *a right wing group responsible for several acts of terrorism* —see USAGE **2** (often cap.) a law made by a parliament or similar body: *The drug was banned by an act of parliament.* | *a right granted under the Shops and Factories Act, 1978* | *lobbying to amend the Gun Control Act* **3** (often cap.) one of the main divisions of a stage play: *Hamlet kills the king in Act 5, Scene 2.* | *at the end of the first act* **4** one of a number of short events in a theatre or CIRCUS performance: *The next act will be a snake charmer.* **5** [usu. sing.] infml an example of insincere behaviour used to influence people's feelings: *Don't be taken in by his flattery — it's just an act/he's just putting on an act.* **6 get in on the act** infml to begin to take part in an activity that someone else has started, esp. in order to share in any advantages that may come as a result **7 get one's act together** infml to begin to work together in an effective way: *little chance of the divided opposition parties getting their act together* **8 in the act (of doing)** while actually doing; at the moment of doing (esp. something bad): *I caught him in the act of reading my private letters.*

▷ USAGE Compare **act** and **action**. 1 **Action** used as a singular countable noun has almost the same meaning as **act**: *a kind act/action*. 2 Certain fixed phrases use **act** and not **action**: *an act of cruelty/mercy/kindness* | *caught in the act of stealing*.◁

ACT /ˌeɪ siː ˈtiː/ see AMERICAN CONSERVATORY THEATRE

act·ing¹ /ˈæktɪŋ/ adj [A] appointed to carry out the duties of an office or position for a short time: *Our director is in hospital, but the acting director can see you.*

acting² n [U] the art or profession of representing a character, esp. in a play or for a film or on television

ac·tion /ˈækʃən/ n **1** [U] the fact or process of doing things, with the intention of gaining a desired result: *The police had to take firm action to deal with the riots.* | *to formulate a plan of action* | *to urge strike action* | *We're tired of talking about the problem — now is the time for action!* | *an* **action-packed** *drama* (=full of exciting action) **2** [C] something done; a DEED: *His prompt action probably saved her life.* | *His suicide attempt was* **the action of** (=an action typical of) *a desperate man.* —see ACT² (USAGE) **3** [U] effect: *Photographs are produced by the action of light on film.* **4** [the] the main events in a play or book: *The action takes place in a mountain village.* **5** [C;U] fighting or a fight between armies or navies: *The action lasted five hours.* | *Many men were* **killed in action.** **6** [C] a charge or a matter for consideration by a court of law: *If he doesn't pay us soon we'll have to* **bring an action** *against him.* | *a libel action* **7** [S] the way in which something moves or works: *The horse had a fine jumping action.* | *Today we'll study the action of the heart.* **8** [C usu. sing.] the moving parts of a machine or instrument: *The action of this piano is becoming stiff.* **9 action!** (said by film DIRECTORS when they are just about to begin filming a scene) **10 actions speak louder than words** saying it is easier to see what someone is like or what they feel about something by what they do, rather than by what they say **11 in/into action** in/into operation or a typical activity: *He is a very good tennis player; you ought to see him in action.* **12 out of action** unable to move, operate, etc.: *The storm put the telephones out of action.* —see also INDUSTRIAL ACTION **13 piece of the action** AmE, infml — a share of the profits or benefits of an action; in films, often said by criminals planning a crime: *Do you want a piece of the action?* **14 where the action is** AmE, infml — where the decisions are made, or where exciting things are happening: *I want to be where the action is!*

ac·tio·na·ble /ˈækʃənəbəl/ adj giving enough cause for a charge in a court of law: *I regard these allegations as actionable.*

action fig·ure /ˈ·· ·ˌ··/ n a doll with legs and arms that move. The advertisers say "action figure" instead of "doll" because the figures are usu. played with by boys, in games about war or adventure. —see CULTURAL NOTE at DOLL

Action Man /ˈ·· ·ˌ/ n **1** tdmk a doll dressed as a soldier and played with usu. by boys **2** (used esp. by British newspapers) a man who has an exciting and dangerous style of life: *His Action Man image has always concealed a more complex man.*

action re·play /ˌ··· ˈ···/ BrE ‖ **instant replay** AmE— n a recording of a piece of action on television, esp. in a game of sport, that is shown again immediately after it happens

action sta·tions /'·· ‚··/ also **battle stations** *AmE— interj* (an order to soldiers, sailors, etc., to take up positions ready for battle or other urgent action)

ac·tiv·ate /'ækt‚veɪt/ *v* [T] **1** to make (esp. an electrical system) active; bring into use: *Treading on any part of this floor activates the alarm system.* **2** *tech* to cause (a chemical action) to happen more quickly, as by heating **3** *tech* to make (something) RADIOACTIVE **4** *tech* to make (SEWAGE) pure by passing air through it **—ation** /‚ækt‚'veɪʃən/ *n* [U]

ac·tive¹ /'æktɪv/ *adj* **1** doing things or always ready to do things; able or ready to take action: *Although he's over 80 he's still very active.* | *an active member of the club who goes to every meeting* | *soldiers who are abroad* **on active service** (=actually fighting) **2** able to produce the typical effects or act in the typical way: *an active volcano* | *Don't touch it! The bomb mechanism is still active!* — opposite **inactive** **3** [*no comp.*] *tech* (of a verb or sentence) having the person or thing doing the action as the subject. In *The boy kicked the ball*, "kicked" is an active verb. —compare PASSIVE¹ (2) **4 active duty** *AmE* (in the military) full-time employment by the armed forces, as compared with RETIREMENT: *He's still on active duty.* —~**ly** *adv*

active² also **active voice** /‚·· '·/— *n tech* [*the*+S] the active form of a verb: *"The boy kicked the ball" is in the active.* —compare PASSIVE²

ac·tiv·ist /'ækt‚vₐst/ *n sometimes derog* a person taking a very active part, esp. in a political movement: *party activists*

ac·tiv·i·ty /æk'tɪv‚ti/ *n* **1** [U] movement or action: *There's been a lot of activity in the town centre today.* | *a sudden rush/flurry of activity on the stock market* | *political/industrial activity* —opposite **inactivity** **2** [C *often pl.*] something that is done or is being done, esp. for interest or pleasure: *The centre provides facilities for a whole range of leisure activities.* | *classroom activities* | *a government that supports terrorist activities*

act of God /‚·· · '·/ *n* **acts of God** a natural event such as a violent storm or flood, which can be neither prevented nor controlled. Acts of God sometimes change the conditions of certain business contracts or insurance policies (POLICY).

Act of Par·lia·ment /‚·· '···/ *n* a law passed by the British government

Act of U·nion /‚·· '··/ [*the*] **1** the union of the parliaments of England and Scotland in 1707 **2** the similar union of Ireland with Great Britain in 1800

act of wor·ship /‚·· '··/ *n* **acts of worship** an example of the way in which followers of any given religion pay their respects to their god or gods

ac·tor /'æktəʳ/ *n* a person who acts in a play or film or on television: *a good actor*

Actors' Eq·ui·ty As·so·ci·a·tion /‚·· '··· ···‚··/ EQUITY (2)

Actors' Stu·di·o /'·· ‚··/ , **The** an institution for training actors established in New York in 1947 which became famous for the METHOD school of acting and influenced many actors including Marlon Brando and James Dean

ac·tress /'æktr‚s/ *n* **1** a woman who acts in a play or film or on television **2 as the actress said to the bishop** *BrE* (a phrase said when someone has said something that could be understood as completely harmless, but which could be understood as talking about sex)

ac·tu·al /'æktʃuəl/ *adj* [A *no comp.*] existing as a real fact: *He forecast that the repairs would cost £2000, but the actual cost was a lot less.* **In actual fact** (=really) *it was quite cheap.* | *He told the newspapermen about the conversation, but would not play them the actual tape of it.* | *No, I'm not joking; those were her actual words.* | *a survey of the problems, both actual and potential* | *a big difference between the opinion polls and the actual election results*

ac·tu·al·i·ty /‚æktʃu'æl‚ti/ *n fml* **1** [U] the state of being real; existence **2** [C *usu. pl.*] something that is real; a fact

ac·tu·al·ly /'æktʃuəli, -tʃəli/ *adv* **1** in actual fact; really: *She says it's a good film, though she hasn't actually seen it.* | *Yes, I know he looks very young, but he's actually 45.* | (showing surprise) *He not only invited me in but he actually offered me a drink!* | *For the first time in years, the*

rate of inflation has actually [...] sation, sometimes when one [...] ing, but often without any r[...] *owe me a little more than t*[...] *"Well, actually, I don't like* [...] *will stay up and watch the fi*[...] *go to bed.*

▷ USAGE 1 **Actually** (and a [...] present time" in English. [...] *Simon?" "Actually I me*[...] *the company doing well?* [...] *very well.*|*It's doing very* [...] sation, **actually** can be used to soften what you a[...] ing, esp. if you are correcting someone, disagreeing, or complaining: *"Happy Birthday, Tom." "Well, actually my birthday was yesterday."* But it can be used with the opposite effect, if you speak with sarcasm: *I didn't ask your opinion, actually.*◁

ac·tu·a·ry /'æktʃuəri‖-tʃueri/ *n* a person who advises insurance companies on how much to charge for insurance, after considering the risks of fire, death, etc. —**arial** /‚æktʃu'eəriəl◂/ *adj*

ac·tu·ate /'æktʃueɪt/ *v* [*often pass.*] *fml* to cause to act; ACTIVATE or MOTIVATE: *He is actuated not by kindness but by ambition.*

Act-Up /'· ·/ an organization formed in the US in the 1980s and now operating also in Britain which protests against unfair treatment of people with AIDS, usu. in ways that attract attention from the MEDIA and ordinary people: *an Act-Up demonstration*

a·cu·i·ty /ə'kjuː‚ti/ *n* [U] *fml* fineness or sharpness, esp. of the mind or the senses of sight or hearing

ac·u·men /'ækjʊmən, ə'kjuːmən/ *n* [U] *fml* ability to think and judge quickly and well: *business/political acumen*

ac·u·pres·sure /'ækjʊpreʃəʳ/ *n* [U] the method of stopping pain and other illnesses, which is similar to acupuncture but which uses pressure instead of needles —compare SHIATSU

ac·u·punc·ture /'ækjʊ‚pʌŋktʃəʳ/ *n* [U] the method of stopping pain and curing diseases by putting special needles into certain parts of the body, used first in China. Acupuncture is not generally accepted as an effective medical treatment in Britain or the US, but is used esp. by people interested in ALTERNATIVE MEDICINE. —compare SHIATSU

a·cute /ə'kjuːt/ *adj* **1** (of the senses) able to notice small differences; working very well; sharp: *Dogs have an acute sense of smell.* | *She has very acute hearing.* **2** showing an ability to understand things clearly and deeply; PENETRATING: *an acute analysis of the political situation* **3** severe; very great: *acute pain* | *an acute shortage of water* **4** *tech* (of a disease) coming quickly to a dangerous condition —compare CHRONIC(1) **5** *tech* (of an angle) less than 90 degrees —compare OBTUSE (2), and see picture at ANGLE **6** [A] (of an ACCENT put above a letter to show pronunciation) being the mark over é —compare CIRCUMFLEX, GRAVE³ — ~**ly** *adv* : *The president is acutely conscious of the need for more doctors and nurses.* | *acutely embarrassing* — ~**ness** *n* [U]

ad /æd/ *n infml* an advertisement —see also CLASSIFIED AD

AD /‚eɪ 'diː◂/ *abbrev. for:* Anno Domini; (in the year) since the birth of Christ: *in 1066 AD* —see BC (USAGE)

ad·age /'ædɪdʒ/ *n* an old wise phrase; PROVERB

a·da·gio /ə'dɑːdʒəʊ/ *adj, adv, n* (a piece of music) played slowly

A·dair /ə'deəʳ/ , **Red** an American fire-fighter known esp. for his experience and skill at putting out oil fires

Ad·am¹ /'ædəm/ **1** in the Jewish and Christian religions and in Islam, the first man. According to the Bible, Adam lived in the Garden of Eden with Eve, the first woman. —see also FALL —see colour picture on page 424 **2 not know someone from Adam** *infml* to have no idea who someone is

Adam² , **Rob·ert** /'rɒbət‖'rɑːbərt/ (1728–1792) a Scottish ARCHITECT who drew up plans for many famous houses in England and after whom a style of furniture is named

ad·a·mant /'ædəmənt/ *adj fml* (of a person or behaviour) firm and immovable in purpose: *I tried to talk her out of it, but she was adamant.* [+*that*] *He was (completely) adamant that they should go.* — ~**ly** *adv*

...dəmz/, **An·sel** /'ænsəl/ (1902–84) an American ...apher known esp. for his photographs of the ...ry of the West of the US

...**ns**, **John** (1735–1826) the second president of the US ...nd an influential political leader of the movement towards independence from the British

Adams, **John Quin·cy** /dʒɒn 'kwɪnsi‖dʒɑːn-/ (1767–1848) the 6th president of the US, son of John Adams, who helped to prepare the MONROE DOCTRINE

Adams, **Sam·u·el** /'sæmjuəl/ (1722–1803) an American politician and writer who was active and influential in the movement towards independence from the British

Adam's ale /ˌ·· '·/ n [U] humor water as a drink (from the idea that Adam, the first man, would only have had water to drink)

Adam's ap·ple /ˌ·· '··‖'·· ˌ·-/ n that part at the front of the throat that is seen to move when a person, esp. a man, talks or swallows

Adam Smith In·sti·tute /ˌ·· '· ˌ···/ [the] a right wing British Conservative Party organization which encourages ideas of the FREE MARKET. It is named after the ECONOMIST Adam Smith.

a·dapt /ə'dæpt/ v [I;T (**to**, **for**)] to make or become suitable for new needs or different conditions: He adapted an old car engine to fit his boat. | When we moved to France, the children adapted (to the change) very well. | I'm afraid he can't adapt to the idea of having a woman as his boss. — compare ADJUST

a·dap·ta·ble /ə'dæptəbəl/ adj often apprec able to change so as to be suitable for new needs or different conditions: I'm sure she'll cope with the changes very well; she's very adaptable. —**·bility** /əˌdæptə'bɪlɪti/ n [U]

ad·ap·ta·tion /ˌædæp'teɪʃən/ n [C;U] the act or an example of adapting: an adaptation of her play for radio

a·dapt·er, **-or** /ə'dæptər/ n **1** a person or thing that adapts **2** a PLUG that makes it possible to use more than one piece of electrical equipment from a single SOCKET (=electricity supply point)

ADC /ˌ· · '·/ abbrev. for: AIDE-DE-CAMP

add /æd/ v **1** [T (**to**)] to put together with something else so as to increase the number, size, or importance: Add a few more names to the list. | Mix the flour and butter together, then add the sugar. | Would you like to add anything to what I've said, John? | The decision to buy this weapon will add at least £5 billion to the defence budget. —see also ADDED **2** [I;T (**to**, TOGETHER, UP)] to join (numbers, or amounts) so as to find the total: If you add 5 and/to 3 you get 8. | Add up these figures for me, please. —compare SUBTRACT **3** [T+that; obj] to say also: Almost as an afterthought, he added that they were very pleased with the result. **4** **add fuel to the fire** infml to make a difficult situation even worse, esp. by making someone feel more strongly about something: Her tactless remarks just added fuel to the fire. **5** **add insult to injury** to make matters even worse, esp. by causing annoyance as well as harm

add to sthg. phr v [T] to increase: The rise in electricity costs has added to our difficulties. —compare DETRACT **from**

add up phr v [I not in progressive forms] infml to make sense; form a likely or believable explanation: The facts just don't add up.

add up to phr v [T not in progressive forms] to amount to: With a meal included in the cost of the ticket, it all adds up to a really good evening's entertainment.

Ad·dams Fam·i·ly /'ædəmz ˌfæməli/ [the] a group of characters made originally by Charles Addams in CARTOONs who later appeared in a television programme and a film. They are a strange family who wear unusual clothes, are very interested in death, and have abilities to do things that ordinary people cannot do.

ad·ded /'ædɪd/ adj [A] existing in addition to what is usual or expected; further: The new system is not only cheaper, but has the added advantage of being much faster than the old one.

added val·ue /ˌ·· '··/ n [U] **1** the amount by which the value of the product is increased at each stage of its making **2** things added to a basic article during the making which increase its value

ad·den·dum /ə'dendəm/ n **-da** /də/ tech something that is added or is to be added, as at the end of a speech or book

ad·der /'ædər/ n **1** a small poisonous snake of northern Europe and northern Asia **2** any of several non-poisonous North American snakes

ad·dict /'ædɪkt/ n a person who is unable to free themselves from a harmful habit, esp. of taking drugs: a heroin addict | (fig.) At the age of 10, he's already a confirmed television addict.

ad·dic·ted /ə'dɪktɪd/ adj [F (**to**)] dependent on something, esp. a drug; unable to stop having or taking: It doesn't take long to become addicted to these drugs. | (fig.) My children are hopelessly/absolutely addicted to television.

ad·dic·tion /ə'dɪkʃən/ n [C;U] the state of being addicted or a habit to which one is addicted: the growing problem of heroin addiction among young people

ad·dic·tive /ə'dɪktɪv/ adj (esp. of drugs) causing addiction; habit-forming —opposite **non-addictive**

Ad·dis Ab·a·ba /ˌædɪs 'æbəbə/ the capital city of Ethiopia

Ad·di·son /'ædɪsən/, **Joseph** (1672–1719) an English writer, best known for the ESSAYs he wrote in The Tatler and The Spectator

ad·di·tion /ə'dɪʃən/ n **1** [U] the act of adding, esp. of adding numbers together —compare SUBTRACTION **2** [C (**to**)] something added: Additions are made to the list from time to time. | Congratulations! I hear there's to be an addition to the family! (=a new baby) | a last-minute addition to the programme for the President's visit **3** AmE a room or part of a building which is added to the main building: We must get a new carpet for the addition. **4** **in addition** (**to**) as well (as); besides: In addition to giving a general introduction to computers, the course also provides practical experience.

ad·di·tion·al /ə'dɪʃənəl/ adj beyond what is usual; added: An additional charge is made for heavy bags. | one of the additional requirements | additional evidence — ~**ly** adv

ad·di·tive /'ædɪtɪv/ n a substance, esp. a chemical one, added in small quantities to something else to add colour or taste or to make it last longer: additive-free foods —see also FOOD ADDITIVE

ad·dled /'ædld/ adj **1** (of an egg) having gone bad **2** infml (of someone's brain) having become confused

add-on /'· ·/ n a piece of equipment that can be connected to a computer, such as a DISK DRIVE or a MODEM, that increases its usefulness —compare PERIPHERAL[2]

ad·dress¹ /ə'dres‖ə'dres, 'ædres/ n **1** the number of the building, name of the street and town, etc., where a person lives or works, esp. when written on a letter or parcel: I can't read the address on this envelope. | Please notify us of any change of address. **2** (the number showing) a place in the memory of a computer where particular information is stored

ad·dress² /ə'dres/ v [T] **1** [(**to**)] to write a name and address on (an envelope, parcel, etc.): There's a letter addressed to you. **2 a** to direct speech or writing to (a person or group): The Education Secretary had to address a hostile crowd of teachers. **b** [(**to**)] to direct (speech or writing) to a person or group: She addressed her remarks particularly to the young people in the crowd. **3** [(**as**)] to speak or write to, using a particular title of rank: The president should be addressed as "Mr President". **4** (in GOLF) to slightly change the position of the GOLF CLUB before hitting (a golf ball) **5** **address oneself to** fml to direct one's attention or efforts to: He ignored the side issues and addressed himself to the main problem.

address³ n **1** [C] a formal speech made to a group of people (AUDIENCE) who are gathered esp. to listen: a commencement address **2** [U] rare skill in conversation or in dealing with a situation

ad·dress·ee /ˌædre'siː, ə-/ n the person to whom a letter, parcel, etc., is addressed

ad·duce /ə'djuːs‖ə'duːs/ v [T] fml to give (an example, proof, or explanation): Can you adduce any reason for his strange behaviour?

Ad·e·laide /'ædɪleɪd, -dəl-/ a port and the capital city of S Australia

Ad·e·nau·er /'ædənauər, 'ɑː-/, **Kon·rad** /'kɒnræd‖'kɑːn-/ (1876–1967) a German politician. He was the first Chancellor of West Germany from 1949 to 1963 and he led the country's return to economic STABILITY and entry into the EEC.

ad·e·noids /'ædɪnɔɪdz, 'ædən-/ n **1** [P] the soft growth between the back of the nose and the throat **2** [U] *BrE infml* the condition in which these are swollen and sore —**noidal** /ˌædˈnɔɪdl/ *adj*

ad·ept¹ /ˈædept, əˈdept‖əˈdept/ *adj* [(at, in)] highly skilled: *He was very adept at making up excuses for his lateness.* — ~**ly** *adv*

ad·ept² /ˈædept/ *n* [(at, in)] a person who is adept at something

ad·e·quate /ˈædɪkwᵻt/ *adj* **1** [(for)] enough for the purpose: *The city's water supply is no longer adequate (for its needs).* | *adequate parking facilities* —compare AMPLE (1) **2** [F (to)] having the necessary qualities: *I hope he will prove adequate to the job.* **3** only just good enough: *Her performance was adequate, though hardly exciting.* — ~**ly** *adv*: *She wasn't adequately insured.* —**quacy** *n* [U (for)] : *He doubted your adequacy for the job.*

▷ USAGE 1 **Adequate, enough,** and **sufficient** can all be used before nouns to talk about quantity: *We had* **adequate/enough/sufficient** *money for the journey.* But in this meaning only **enough** and **sufficient** are used before plural nouns: *Are there* **enough/sufficient** *apples for everyone?* 2 If you want to talk only about quantity, do not use **adequate** in sentences where it might mean "good enough". Compare *The prisoners received* **adequate** *food* (="good enough" or "enough in quantity") and *The prisoners received* **sufficient/enough** *food* (="enough in quantity"). 3 **Adequate** and **sufficient** are both slightly more formal than **enough.**◁

Ad·es·te Fi·de·les /æˌdesteɪ fɪˈdeɪleɪz‖-ti fɪˈdeɪleɪs/ the Latin title and first line of a religious song (CAROL) sung at Christmas. The English title is *Oh Come All Ye Faithful.*

ad·here /ədˈhɪəʳ/ *v* [I (to)] to stick firmly (to another or each other), for example by means of GLUE
adhere to sthg. *phr v* [T] *often fml* to continue to follow or remain loyal to (an idea, belief, or plan): *They failed to adhere to our original agreement.*

ad·her·ence /ədˈhɪərəns/ *n* [U+to] the action of continuing to support or be loyal to something, esp. in spite of difficulties: *adherence to one's religious beliefs*

ad·her·ent /ədˈhɪərənt/ *n* a person who supports a particular idea, person, political party, etc.

ad·he·sion /ədˈhiːʒən/ *n* **1** [U (to)] the state or action of sticking together or to something: *adhesion to strict production timetables* **2** [U] *tech* the joining together of parts inside the body which should be separate **3** [C] *tech* an area of TISSUE (=fleshlike body substance) that has grown round a diseased or damaged part

ad·he·sive /ədˈhiːsɪv/ *n, adj* (a substance such as glue) that can stick or cause stickiness: *adhesive tape*

ad hoc /ˌæd ˈhɒk‖ˈhɑːk, ˈhoʊk/ *adj* [A] *Lat* made, arranged, etc., for a particular purpose: *an ad hoc committee set up to deal with the water shortage*

Ad·i·das /ˈædᵻdæs‖əˈdiːdɑːz/ *tdmk* a company that sells sports clothing and equipment

A·die /ˈeɪdi/ , **Kate** /keɪt/ (1945–) a television news reporter for the BBC, who is known esp. for being seen in foreign places where dangerous events are happening

a·dieu /əˈdjuː‖əˈduː/ *interj, n* **adieus** or **adieux** /əˈdjuːz‖əˈduːz/ *lit* (a) goodbye: *to bid someone adieu*

ad in·fi·ni·tum /ˌæd ɪnfᵻˈnaɪtəm/ *adv Lat* without end; for ever

ad·i·os /ˌædiˈɒs‖-ˈoʊs/ *interj, n Sp, AmE infml—* goodbye

ad·i·pose /ˈædᵻpəʊs/ *adj* [A] *tech* of or containing animal fat; fatty: *adipose tissue*

Ad·i·ron·dacks /ˌædᵻˈrɒndæks‖-ˈrɑːn-/ [the] an area of mountains and forests in NE New York, known for its great natural beauty

adj *written abbrev. for:* ADJECTIVE

ad·ja·cent /əˈdʒeɪsənt/ *adj* [(to)] *fml* very close; touching or almost touching: *The council offices are adjacent to the library.*

ad·jec·tive /ˈædʒᵻktɪv/ *n* a word that describes a noun or PRONOUN, such as *black* in *She wore a black hat* or *happy* in *The news made her happy.* —compare ADVERB —**tival** /ˌædʒᵻkˈtaɪvəl/ *adj: an adjectival phrase such as "with blonde hair" in "the woman with blonde hair"* —**tivally** *adv*

ad·join /əˈdʒɔɪn/ *v* [I;T] to be next to, very close to, or touching (another or each other): *Our house adjoins theirs.* | *adjoining rooms*

ad·journ /əˈdʒɜːn‖-ɜːrn/ *v* **1** [I;T (for, till, until)] **a** to bring (a meeting, trial, etc.) to a stop, esp. for a short period or until a slightly later time: *Shall we adjourn this discussion until tomorrow?* **b** to come to such a stop: *The committee adjourned for an hour for lunch.* —compare POSTPONE **2** [I+adv/prep, esp. to] *often humor* (of a group of people) to go to another place, esp. for a rest: *After the meeting we all adjourned to the pub.* — ~**ment** *n* [C;U] : *The court met again after an adjournment of two weeks.*

ad·judge /əˈdʒʌdʒ/ *v* [T] *fml or tech* **1** to decide or state officially: [+*that*] *The court adjudged that he was guilty.* [+*obj+adj*] *It adjudged him (to be) guilty.* **2** [+*obj+n/adj*] to declare to be; PRONOUNCE: *The show was adjudged a great success.*

ad·ju·di·cate /əˈdʒuːdᵻkeɪt/ *v* [I (on, upon);T] *fml or tech* to act as a judge, for example in a competition or in an argument between two groups or organizations; decide about: *Who will adjudicate (on this dispute)?* | *to adjudicate a claim* —**cator** *n* —**cation** /əˌdʒuːdᵻˈkeɪʃən/ *n* [U] : *The matter was brought up for adjudication.*

ad·junct /ˈædʒʌŋkt/ *n* **1** [(to)] something that is added or joined to something else but is not a necessary part of it **2** *tech* an ADVERBIAL word or phrase that adds meaning to another part of a sentence, such as *on Sunday* in *They arrived on Sunday.*

ad·jure /əˈdʒʊəʳ/ *v* [T+obj+to-v] *fml* to urge solemnly: *She adjured him to tell the truth.*

ad·just /əˈdʒʌst/ *v* [I;T (to)] to change slightly, esp. in order to make right or make suitable for a particular purpose or situation: *You can adjust the colour on the TV by turning this knob.* | *He adjusted (himself) very quickly to the heat of the country.* | *Your tie needs adjusting.* —compare ADAPT; see also WELL-ADJUSTED — ~**able** *adj: an adjustable chair* — ~**ment** *n* [C;U] : *We made a few minor adjustments to the plan.*

ad·ju·tant /ˈædʒᵻtənt/ *n* an army officer responsible for office work

ad·lib¹ /ˌæd ˈlɪb/ *v* -**bb-** [I;T] *infml* to invent and deliver (music, words, etc.) without preparation; IMPROVISE: *The actress forgot her lines but ad-libbed very amusingly.*

ad lib² *adv infml* **1** (speaking, playing, performing, etc.) without preparation: *a radio show in which people have to speak ad lib for ten minutes on a given subject* **2** without limit; freely: *a restaurant where you pay a fixed price and can eat ad lib* —**ad-lib** /ˌ⋅ˈ⋅◂/ *adj: ad-lib jokes*

ad·man /ˈædmæn/ *n* -**men** /men/ *infml* a member of the advertising profession

ad·min /ˈædmɪn/ *n* [U] *infml abbrev. for:* ADMINISTRATION; the management of business affairs, often personal matters such as paying bills: *I must do some admin this weekend.*

ad·min·is·ter /ədˈmɪnᵻstəʳ/ *v* [T] **1** to manage or direct (esp. the affairs of a business, government, etc.): *The company's finances have been badly administered.* | *The courts administer the law.* **2** [(to)] *fml* to give; DISPENSE: *to administer punishment* | *The priest administered the last rites.* (=Christian ceremony for someone who is dying) **3** [(to)] *fml* to cause to make (an official promise): *to administer the oath to a witness in court*

ad·min·is·tra·tion /ədˌmɪnᵻˈstreɪʃən/ *n* **1** [U] the management or direction of the affairs of a business, government, etc.: *the administration of the law* | *You will need some experience in administration before you can run the department.* **2** [S + *sing./pl. v*] the people who direct the affairs of a business: *I think the accountants will want to talk to the college administration.* **3** [U (of)] *fml* the act of giving; administering (ADMINISTER 2, 3) **4** [*the*] *AmE (often cap.)* the (period of) government, esp. of a particular president or ruling party: *during the Reagan Administration*

ad·min·is·tra·tive /ədˈmɪnᵻstrətɪv‖-streɪtɪv/ *adj* of or concerning administration: *The job is mainly administrative.* | *administrative responsibilities* — ~**ly** *adv*

ad·min·is·tra·tor /ədˈmɪnᵻstreɪtəʳ/ *n* **1** a person whose job is administration **2** *BrE* a person appointed by a court to manage or direct the affairs of a company near to INSOLVENCY, in order to try to save it

ad·mi·ra·ble /ˈædmərəbəl/ *adj* worthy of admiration; very good: *She showed admirable self-control.* | *The commission of inquiry has done an admirable job.* —**bly** *adv*

ad·mi·ral /ˈædmərəl/ *n* a naval rank —see TABLE 3 —see also RED ADMIRAL; see FATHER (USAGE)

Admiral's Cup /ˌ··· ˈ·/ [*the*] an international sailing competition held off the British coast every two years and consisting of four races, including the Fastnet Cup Race

Ad·mi·ral·ty /ˈædmərəlti/ *n* [*the*] the government department that controls the British navy

Admiralty Arch /ˌ···· ˈ·/ the large arch which stands between the Mall and Trafalgar Square in central London

ad·mi·ra·tion /ˌædməˈreɪʃən/ *n* **1** [U (for)] a feeling of pleasure and respect: *I was filled with admiration for her courage.* **2** [*the*+S+of] a person or thing that causes such feelings: *His new bike made him the admiration of his friends.*

ad·mire /ədˈmaɪəʳ/ *v* [T (for)] to think of or look at with pleasure and respect: *I admire (her for) the way she handles her staff.* | *You may not like him, but you've got to admire his persistence.* | *He gave her an admiring look.* | *He's always looking in the mirror, admiring himself!* —see WONDER (USAGE)

ad·mir·er /ədˈmaɪərəʳ/ *n* a person who admires, esp. a man who is attracted to a particular woman: *one of her many admirers*

ad·mis·si·ble /ədˈmɪsɪbəl/ *adj* that can be accepted or considered: *admissible evidence in a court of law* —opposite **inadmissible** —**bility** /ədˌmɪsɪˈbɪlɪti/ *n* [U]

ad·mis·sion /ədˈmɪʃən/ *n* **1** [U (to)] allowing or being allowed to enter or join a school, club, building, etc.: *They campaigned for the admission of women to the club.* **2** [U] the cost of entrance: *Admission £1* **3** [C (of)] a statement admitting that something is true; CONFESSION: *an admission of guilt/failure* [+that] *His admission that he was the thief surprised everyone.* | *He's a bad driver,* **by/on his own admission.** (=as he himself says)

▷ USAGE Compare **admission** and **admittance.** In the meaning "permission to go in", **admission** is the ordinary word. **Admittance** is more formal and is usually used literally, with the meaning "permission to enter a building": *No* **admittance** *(fml)/***admission** *after 10 p.m.* The entrance price is the **admission:** *Admission £2.*◁

ad·mit /ədˈmɪt/ *v* **-tt-** **1** [I (to);T] to state or agree to the truth of (usu. something bad); CONFESS: *He admitted his guilt/admitted to the murder.* [+v-ing] *She admitted stealing the bicycle/admitted having stolen the bicycle.* [+(that)] *She admitted that she had stolen the bicycle.* | *I must admit, it's more difficult than I thought it would be.* [+obj+to-v] *A fuel leak is now admitted to have been the cause of the trouble.* —compare DENY (1) **2** [T (into, to)] to permit to enter; let in: *He was admitted to hospital suffering from burns.* **3** [I+of; T] *fml* to leave a chance for being possible; allow: *The facts admit (of) no other explanation.*

ad·mit·tance /ədˈmɪtəns/ *n* [U] *fml* right of entrance: *Journalists were unable to gain admittance to the courtroom.* —see ADMISSION (USAGE)

ad·mit·ted /ədˈmɪtɪd/ *adj* [A] having admitted oneself to be; SELF-CONFESSED: *He is an admitted alcoholic.*

ad·mit·ted·ly /ədˈmɪtɪdli/ *adv* it must be admitted (that): *Admittedly, he works slowly, but his essays are always excellent.* | *The results of our poll, though admittedly taken from a smaller sample, are quite different from theirs.*

ad·mix·ture /ədˈmɪkstʃəʳ/ *n* [+of; usu. sing.] *fml or tech* a substance that is added to another in a mixture

ad·mon·ish /ədˈmɒnɪʃ‖-ˈmɑː-/ *v* [T (for, against)] *fml* to warn or speak to with gentle disapproval: *The witness was admonished by the judge for failing to answer the question.* —~**ingly** *adv*

ad·mo·ni·tion /ˌædməˈnɪʃən/ *n* [C;U] *fml* an act of admonishing

ad·mon·i·to·ry /ədˈmɒnɪtəri‖ədˈmɑːnɪˌtɔːri/ *adj fml* of or being warning advice or gentle disapproval: *admonitory remarks*

ad nau·se·am /ˌæd ˈnɔːziəm, -iæm/ *adv Lat* repeatedly and to an annoying degree: *We have heard your complaints ad nauseam.*

a·do /əˈduː/ *n* [U] delay or unnecessary activity (esp. in the phrase **without more/further ado**): *Without more ado,*

I'd like to introduce tonight's special guest.

a·do·be /əˈdəʊbi/ *n* [U] a building substance made of earth and STRAW dried in the sun, used in hot countries; esp. in the South West of the US and Mexico

ad·o·les·cent /ˌædəˈlesənt/ *adj, n* **1** (of) a boy or girl in the period between being a child and being an adult; young TEENAGER of about 13–16 —see CHILD (USAGE) **2** *derog* (of) an adult who behaves like an adolescent: *his adolescent humour* —**cence** *n* [S;U] : *the period of adolescence*

▶CULTURAL NOTE People think of adolescents as being difficult because their behaviour and emotions are not always reasonable or controlled. They often do things against the advice or wishes of their parents. Adolescents also suffer from physical problems, e.g. spots (ACNE).◀

A·do·nis /əˈdəʊnɪs/ in CLASSICAL MYTHOLOGY, an extremely beautiful boy: *He walked into the room looking like (an) Adonis.* —see also GREEK GOD

a·dopt /əˈdɒpt‖əˈdɑːpt/ *v* **1** [I;T] to take (someone else's child) into one's family for ever and to take on the full responsibilities in law of a parent: *He's not my real father; I'm adopted.* —compare FOSTER

▶CULTURAL NOTE When people adopt a child, they become the legal parents of the child. The child's BIRTH CERTIFICATE is changed so that the child has the same name as the new parents, and the child's natural parents do not usually have the right to see the child or know where the child is. In Britain when the child is 18 years old, he or she has the right to learn who his or her real parents are, and to find them if he or she wants to. In the US, state laws vary, but generally a person does not have the right to know who his or her natural parents are, although they may be able to find out if the natural parents are willing. It is not easy for people to adopt children in Britain, as there are many checks made on their age, financial position, relationships, etc. before they are considered suitable. In the US there are usually fewer rules about who may adopt a child.◀

2 [T] to take and use as one's own: *We adopted their production methods.* **3** [T] to begin to have (a quality or appearance): *to adopt a conciliatory attitude/a tough approach to the terrorists* **4** [T] to approve formally; accept: *The committee adopted my suggestions.* **5** [T (as)] to choose as a representative (CANDIDATE) for election

a·dop·tion /əˈdɒpʃən‖əˈdɑːp-/ *n* [C;U] (an example of) the act of adopting: *If you can't have children of your own, why not consider adoption?* | (fig.) *He was not born here, but this is his* **country of adoption.**

adoption a·gen·cy /·ˈ··· ˌ···/ *n* an organization whose purpose is to connect people wishing to adopt suitable children, not always officially and sometimes for financial profit

a·dop·tive /əˈdɒptɪv‖əˈdɑːp-/ *adj* [A] *fml* having adopted a child: *her adoptive parents*

a·dor·a·ble /əˈdɔːrəbəl/ *adj* **1** worthy of being loved deeply **2** *infml* charming or attractive: *What adorable curtains!*

ad·o·ra·tion /ˌædəˈreɪʃən/ *n* [U] **1** religious worship **2** deep love and respect

a·dore /əˈdɔːʳ/ *v* [T *not in progressive forms*] **1** to love deeply and respect highly: *He gave her an adoring look.* | *He adores his elder brother.* **2** [+obj/v-ing] *infml* to like very much: *She adores the cinema/going to the cinema.* **3** to worship in a religious way

a·dorn /əˈdɔːn‖-ɔːrn/ *v* [T (with)] *fml* to make more beautiful, attractive, or interesting: *He adorned his story with all sorts of adventures that never happened.* —see DECORATE (USAGE)

a·dorn·ment /əˈdɔːnmənt‖-ɔːr-/ *n* **1** [U] the act of adorning **2** [C] something that adorns

a·dren·a·lin /əˈdrenəl-ɪn/ *n* [U] a chemical substance (HORMONE) made by the body during a period of fear, anger, excitement, etc., causing quick or violent action: *It was one of those scary situations that really* **gets the adrenalin going.**

A·dri·at·ic /ˌeɪdriˈætɪk◀/ also **Adriatic Sea** /ˌ···· ˈ·/ [*the*] the long, narrow sea between Italy and Yugoslavia and Albania. Its chief port is Venice.

a·drift /əˈdrɪft/ *adj, adv* [F] **1** (esp. of boats) not fastened, and driven about by the sea or wind; loose **2** without purpose or direction: *Our plans seem to have gone adrift somewhere.*

a·droit /ə'drɔɪt/ *adj* [(at, in)] quick and skilful in using mind or hand — ~ *ly* *adv*: *The politician sidestepped the question very adroitly.* — ~ *ness* *n* [U]

a·du·ki bean /ə'duːki biːn/ *also* **ad·zu·ki bean** /æd'zuː-/ *n* a brown and red bean much used in Chinese and Japanese cooking, either dried or ground into flour

ad·u·la·tion /ˌædʒ͡ʊ'leɪʃən/ *n* [U] praise or admiration that is more than is necessary or deserved: *basking in the adulation of the crowd* —**·latory** /ˌædʒ͡ʊ'leɪtəri, 'ædʒ͡ʊleɪtəri‖'ædʒələtɔːri/ *adj*

ad·ult[1] /'ædʌlt, ə'dʌlt/ *n* a fully grown person or animal, esp. a person over an age stated by law, usually 18 or 21: *This film is for adults only* —see also CONSENTING ADULT — ~ *hood* /'ædʌlthʊd‖ə'dʌlthʊd/ *n* [U]

▶ CULTURAL NOTE In Britain a person who is 16 years old is allowed to get married if his or her parents agree to it, and is also allowed to have sex (AGE OF CONSENT). At 17 years old people can learn to drive a car. At 18 people **come of age**, and are considered to be adults by law. They are allowed to vote in elections, to buy and drink alcohol, and to watch films containing sex and violence. They can get married without the agreement of their parents. In the US, 18 is also the age when a person is considered to be an adult by law. At 18 a person can vote in elections and no longer needs permission from their parents to do things, e.g. get married. Driving licences are usually obtained at age 16, in some states 15. However, in most states there are restrictions on alcoholic drinking until age 21, with only beer and wine allowable from the age of 18 at the earliest. Many people celebrate their 18th birthday with a party. Some people also celebrate their 21st birthday, which used to be the age at which a person became an adult. In both Britain and the US, it is thought that adults should be able to control their feelings and behaviour, for example by not losing their temper, not showing feelings such as jealousy, and behaving in a reasonable and responsible way: *I would find it easier to get on with him if he'd behave like an adult!* —compare MATURE[1] (1)◀

adult[2] *adj* **1** fully grown: *an adult lion* **2** suitable for or typical of a fully grown person; MATURE: *They've dealt with the situation in a very adult way.* | *adult entertainment*

adult book·store /ˌ·· '··, ·ˌ· '··/ *n* AmE *euph* a shop which sells books, magazines, and pictures of people, esp. women, wearing little or no clothing and sometimes performing sex acts

adult ed·u·ca·tion /ˌ··· ··'··, ·ˌ· ··'··/ ‖ *also* **continuing education** *AmE n* [U] education provided for adults outside the formal educational system, usu. by means of classes that are held in the evening —compare FURTHER EDUCATION, HIGHER EDUCATION

a·dul·ter·ate /ə'dʌltəreɪt/ *v* [T (with)] to make (a substance) impure or of poorer quality by the addition of something of lower quality: *This milk has been adulterated with water.* —see also UNADULTERATED —**·ation** /əˌdʌltə'reɪʃən/ *n* [U]

a·dul·ter·er /ə'dʌltərər/ **a·dul·ter·ess** /-tər̬s/ *fem.*— *n old use* a married person who has had sexual relations with someone who is not their husband/wife

a·dul·ter·y /ə'dʌltəri/ *n* [U] sexual relations between a married person and someone who is not their husband/wife: *to commit adultery* —**·terous** *adj*

▶ CULTURAL NOTE Although many people do not approve of people who COMMIT adultery, it is not a crime in Britain or the US. If someone who is married has a relationship with another person, people would say that they are **having an affair**, rather than that they are committing adultery. In law, adultery is a reason someone can use in order to end a marriage. In the US, adultery is considered to be a more serious offence, and most people feel strongly that it is wrong.◀

ad·um·brate /'ædʌmbreɪt/ *v* [T] *pomp* to give an incomplete or faint idea of (esp. future events) —**·bration** /ˌædʌm'breɪʃən/ *n* [C;U *obfr*]

adv *written abbrev. for:* ADVERB

ad·vance[1] /əd'vɑːns‖əd'væns/ *v rather fml* **1** [I (on, upon, against)] to move forward in position, development, etc.: *Napoleon's army advanced on Moscow.* —compare RETREAT[2] **2** [T] to help, improve, or bring advantage to (esp. a process or development): *His provocative comments will do nothing to advance the cause of world peace.* |

She's not really concerned about this issue — she's just trying to advance her own interests. **3** [T] to bring forward to an earlier date or time: *to advance the date of the meeting from Wednesday to Monday* —opposite **postpone** **4** [T+obj(i)+obj(d)] to provide (money) earlier than the proper or usual time: *The company will advance you £200 until your salary is paid.* **5** [T] to introduce; suggest: *The report advances the suggestion that safety standards should be improved.*

advance[2] *n* **1** [C;U] forward movement: *The army's advance was halted by shortages of food.* | *her rapid advance in the company* | *the advance of old age* | (fig.) *There have been great advances* (=developments) *in medicine in the last 50 years.* —compare RETREAT[1] (1) **2** [C (of)] money provided before the proper time: *They gave me an advance of a month's pay.* **3 in advance** ahead in time; BEFOREHAND: *We had to pay the rent two weeks in advance.* **4 in advance (of)** ahead (of): *A small force was sent on in advance.* —see also ADVANCES

advance[3] *adj* [A] happening, coming, or done before the proper or usual time: *We sent advance copies of the new book to all the papers.* | *It's a popular show, so advance booking is essential.* | *We can get you a plane ticket if you give us plenty of advance warning.*

ad·vanced /əd'vɑːnst‖əd'vænst/ *adj* **1** far on in development: *advanced studies* | *the advanced industrial nations of the world* | *an advanced child* **2** modern: *advanced ideas* **3 advanced in years** *fml euph* old

advanced lev·el /·ˈ· ˌ··/ *n* [C;U] (in British education) A LEVEL

ad·vance·ment /əd'vɑːnsmənt‖əd'væn-/ *n* [U] *fml* improvement, development, or movement to a higher rank

ad·vanc·es /əd'vɑːnsᵻz‖əd'væn-/ *n* [P] attempts to gain someone's friendship, love, or favourable attention: *She didn't respond to his advances.*

ad·van·tage /əd'vɑːntɪdʒ‖əd'væn-/ *n* **1** [C (over)] something that may help one to be successful or to gain a favourable result: *Her teaching experience gave her a big advantage (over the other applicants for the job).* —opposite **disadvantage** **2** [C;U] a favourable condition resulting from a particular course of action; gain; BENEFIT: *Is there any advantage to be gained from getting there early?* | *One of the advantages of this method is that it saves a lot of fuel.* | *This method* **has the advantage** *of saving a lot of fuel.* | *The lawyer's letter said she would hear something* **to** *her* **advantage** *if she contacted him.* —opposite **disadvantage** **3 Advantage X** (said in tennis when X has won the point after DEUCE; X must then win the next point to win the game, or the number of points returns to deuce): *Advantage Miss Graf.* **4 take advantage of: a** to make use of; profit from: *You should take advantage of the fine weather to paint the fence.* **b** to make unfair use of (someone or someone's qualities); EXPLOIT: *She took advantage of his good nature.* **5 You have the advantage of me** *BrE* You know something that I don't

ad·van·ta·geous /ˌædvən'teɪdʒəs, ˌædvæn-/ *adj* [(to)] helpful to a particular aim; bringing advantage: *The new process should be particularly advantageous to small companies.* —opposite **disadvantageous** — ~ *ly* *adv*

ad·vent /'ædvent/ *n* [*the*+S+of] the arrival or coming of (an important event, period, invention, etc.): *People are much better informed since the advent of television.*

Advent (in Christian religions) the period of the four weeks before Christmas

Advent cal·en·dar /'·· ˌ···/ *n* a special CALENDAR given to children in December. The child opens a little window on the calendar on each day of the month until the 24th December, which is the day before Christmas. Behind each window is a picture connected with Christmas.

ad·ven·ti·tious /ˌædvən'tɪʃəs, ˌædven-/ *adj fml* not expected or planned; coming by chance; accidental — ~ *ly* *adv*

ad·ven·ture /əd'ventʃər/ *n* **1** [C] a journey, experience, etc., that is strange and exciting and often dangerous: *her exciting adventures in the Himalayas* **2** [U] excitement, for example in a journey or activity; risk: *a life of adventure* | *Come on! Where's your sense of adventure?* (=Why are you afraid to take a risk?) —see VENTURE (USAGE)

adventure play·ground /·ˌ·· '··/ *n* BrE a piece of ground where young children can play, provided by some local councils in Britain, which has more exciting and adventurous equipment than usual

ad·ven·tur·er /əd'ventʃərər/ n **1** a person who enjoys adventures **2** a person who hopes to gain wealth or high social position by dishonest, dangerous, or sexually immoral means

ad·ven·tur·ess /əd'ventʃərɪs/ n a female ADVENTURER (esp. 2)

ad·ven·tur·ous /əd'ventʃərəs/ adj **1** also **ad·ven·ture·some** /əd'ventʃəsəm‖-tʃər-/ AmE— eager for adventure; ready to take risks; daring **2** exciting and full of danger: an adventurous life/journey — ~ly adv

ad·verb /'ædvɜːb‖-ɜːrb/ n a word or group of words that describes or adds to the meaning of a verb, an adjective, another adverb, or a whole sentence, such as slowly in He ran slowly; very in It's very hot; tomorrow in Come tomorrow; away in Put it away; and naturally in Naturally (=of course), we want you to come. —compare ADJECTIVE

ad·ver·bi·al /əd'vɜːbiəl‖-ɜːr-/ n, adj (a word or phrase) used as an adverb: an adverbial phrase — ~ly adv

ad·ver·sa·ry /'ædvəsəri‖'ædvərseri/ n fml an opponent; enemy —**sarial** /ˌædvɜː'seəriəl◂‖-vɜːr-/ adj

ad·verse /'ædvɜːs‖-ɜːrs/ adj fml unfavourable; going against; opposing: The proposal has attracted a lot of adverse comment. | in adverse conditions — ~ly adv

ad·ver·si·ty /əd'vɜːsɪ̇ti‖-ɜːr-/ n [C;U] fml bad fortune; trouble: A good friend will not desert you in time of adversity. | to meet with adversities

ad·vert[1] /əd'vɜːt‖-ɜːrt/ v
advert to sthg. phr v [T] fml to mention

ad·vert[2] 'ædvɜːt‖-ɜːrt/ n BrE infml an advertisement

ad·ver·tise /'ædvətaɪz‖-ər-/ v **1** [I;T] to make (something for sale, services offered, a room to rent, etc.) known to the public, for example in a newspaper or on television: I advertised (my house) in the "Daily News". | a big poster advertising a new shampoo | Are lawyers allowed to advertise (their services)? **2** [I (for)] to ask (for someone or something) by placing an advertisement in a newspaper, shop window, etc.: We've advertised for someone to look after the garden. **3** [T] to make generally known (esp. something that should perhaps be kept secret): It was unwise of them to advertise their willingness to make concessions at the negotiations. —**tiser** n

ad·ver·tise·ment /əd'vɜːtɪ̇smənt‖ˌædvər'taɪz-/ n also **ad**, **ad·vert** BrE infml something used for advertising things, such as a notice on a wall or in a newspaper, a short film shown on television: to put an advertisement in the paper | TV adverts in between programmes | (fig.) He's not a very good advertisement for the driving school — he's failed his test six times!

ad·ver·tis·ing /'ædvətaɪzɪŋ‖-ər-/ n [U] the business of encouraging people to buy goods by means of advertisements: a job in advertising | an advertising campaign

advertising a·gen·cy /'····· ·ˌ···/ n an organisation which helps a company sell its goods or services by doing MARKET RESEARCH, producing advertising materials, and buying space for advertising in newspapers or on television

Advertising Stan·dards Au·thor·i·ty /ˌ···· '·· ·ˌ···/ (abbrev. **ASA**) [the] a British organization which controls the activities of the advertising industry. If people think an advertisement is wrong or offensive, they can complain to this organization, which may decide that the advertisement should not be used again.

ad·vice /əd'vaɪs/ n [U] opinion given to someone about what they should do in a particular situation: I asked the doctor for her advice. | Acting on her advice, I decided to give up smoking. | He gave them some good/sound advice. | Let me give you a piece of advice. | If you **take my advice**, you won't let anyone about this. (=this is what I advise)

advice col·umn /·'· ·ˌ·/ n a part of a newspaper or magazine containing letters from readers asking for advice, often about money, work, health, personal problems, etc., together with advice from the newspaper or magazine

advice col·umn·ist /·'· ·ˌ··/ n a person, often an EXPERT in a certain field, who gives advice in an advice column

advice note /·'· ·/ n a letter sent by a supplier to a customer stating that goods ordered have arrived at the place they were being sent to

ad·vi·sab·le /əd'vaɪzəbəl/ adj sensible; wise: It is advisable

always to wear a safety belt when you're driving. — opposite **inadvisable** —**sability** /əd,vaɪzə'bɪlɪ̇ti/ n [U]: I would question the advisability of such a course of action.

ad·vise /əd'vaɪz/ v **1** [I;T] to give advice to; say or write (something) as advice: We will do as you advise. | The doctor advised complete rest. | The lawyers have advised against signing the contract. [+obj+to-v] I advised her to wait. [+obj+that] I advised her that she should wait. [+obj+wh-] She advised us where to eat. [+v-ing/that] I advise leaving early/that you leave early. **2** [I;T (on)] not in progressive forms] to act as a professional adviser (to): It's a lawyer's job to advise on the law. | She advises the President on foreign affairs. **3** [T (of)] fml to inform: Please advise me of the cost. [+obj+that/wh-] I have advised her that we are coming/advised her when the bags will arrive. **4** **ill-advised/well-advised** unwise/wise: You would be well-advised to stay at home tonight.

ad·vis·ed·ly /əd'vaɪzɪ̇dli/ adv after careful thought; purposely: She is behaving like a dictator — and I use the term advisedly.

ad·vis·er ‖ also **-or** AmE /əd'vaɪzər/ n a person whose job is to give advice, esp. to a government or business or (in the US) to students: the government's special adviser on the Middle East

ad·vi·so·ry /əd'vaɪzəri/ adj giving advice; having the power or duty to advise: employed in an advisory capacity

advisory bod·y /·'··· ·ˌ·/ n an organization which has the authority to make suggestions about how other organizations, esp. in a certain field, should behave and run their affairs

ad·vo·ca·cy /'ædvəkəsi/ n [U] **1** [(of)] the act or action of supporting an idea, way of life, person, etc. **2** the profession or work of an advocate

ad·vo·cate[1] /'ædvəkɪ̇t, -keɪt/ n **1** law ScotE a lawyer who speaks in defence of or in favour of another person in court —compare BARRISTER, SOLICITOR; —see also LAWYER (CULTURAL NOTE) **2** [(of)] a person who speaks for or supports an idea, way of life, etc.: a strong advocate of prison reform —see also DEVIL'S ADVOCATE

ad·vo·cate[2] /'ædvəkeɪt/ v [T+obj/v-ing] to speak in favour of; support (an idea or plan), esp. publicly: He advocates a reduction in military spending/advocates reducing military spending.

adze also **adz** AmE /ædz/ n a sharp tool with the blade at a right angle to the handle, used for shaping large pieces of wood

Ae·ge·an Sea /ɪˌdʒiːən 'siː/ [the] the sea of SE Europe, between Greece and Turkey

ae·gis /'iːdʒɪ̇s/ n **under the aegis of** fml with the protection or support of: a refugee programme under the aegis of the United Nations

Ae·ne·as /ɪ'niːəs/ in CLASSICAL MYTHOLOGY, a Trojan leader who, after the fall of Troy, escaped to Carthage, where he met Dido, and then to Italy where he established Latium and the Roman state

Ae·ne·id /ɪ'niː-ɪd/ , **The** Virgil's poem about the adventures of Aeneas a HERO from Greek and Roman MYTHOLOGY

ae·on , eon /'iːən/ n a period of time too long to be measured

aer·ate /'eəreɪt/ v [T] tech **1** to put air or gas into (a liquid) as by pressure **2** to allow air to act upon: Blood is aerated in the lungs. —**ation** /eə'reɪʃən/ n [U]

aer·i·al[1] /'eəriəl/ also **antenna** AmE— n a wire, rod, etc., often on top of a house or on a car, for receiving radio or television signals —see pictures at CAR and HOUSE

aerial[2] adj of, from, or happening in the air: an aerial battle | an aerial photograph (=taken from the air) — ~ly adv

ae·rie /'ɪəri‖'eəri/ n AmE for EYRIE

Ae·ro /'eərəʊ/ n tdmk a type of chocolate bar made by Rowntree Mackintosh Limited; there are different FLAVOURS of Aero and Aero DESSERTS

aero- see WORD FORMATION

aer·o·bat·ics /ˌeərə'bætɪks, ˌeərəʊ-/ n [U] the art of doing tricks in an aircraft, such as rolling over sideways or flying upside down —**batic** adj

aer·o·bic /eə'rəʊbɪk/ adj tech needing oxygen in order to live, happen, or exist: aerobic bacteria

aer·o·bics /eə'rəʊbɪks/ n [U] a form of very active physical exercise which is usu. done in a class with music and is intended to strengthen the heart and lungs. It is esp.

popular with women and is considered by many people to be a fashionable form of exercise: *She goes to/does aerobics twice a week.* | *an aerobics class*

aer·o·drome /'eərədrəʊm/ *n old-fash, esp. BrE* an AIRFIELD

aer·o·dy·nam·ic /ˌeərəʊdaɪ'næmɪk◂/ *adj* **1** concerning aerodynamics **2** using the principles of aerodynamics, esp. to improve the effectiveness or performance of something: *one of the most aerodynamic cars on the market* — ~**ally** /kli/ *adv* : *aerodynamically designed*

aer·o·dy·nam·ics /ˌeərəʊdaɪ'næmɪks/ *n* **1** [U] the science that studies the forces that act on bodies moving through the air **2** [P] the qualities necessary for movement through the air

aer·o·gramme /'eərəgræm/ *n* an AIRLETTER

aer·o·nau·tics /ˌeərə'nɔːtɪks/ *n* [U] the science of the operation and flight of aircraft —**nautical, -nautic** *adj*

aer·o·plane /'eərəpleɪn/ *BrE* ‖ **airplane** *AmE*— *n* a flying vehicle that has wings and at least one engine; PLANE: *a passenger aeroplane*

aer·o·sol /'eərəsɒl‖-sɑːl/ *n* a small container from which liquid can be forced out in the form of a fine mist. Many people now avoid using aerosols because they believe that the chemicals used in aerosols, called CFCs, can cause damage to the OZONE LAYER. Some aerosols do not contain these chemicals, and are usu. marked "ozone-friendly".

aer·o·space /'eərəspeɪs, 'eərəʊ-/ *n* [U] the air around the Earth, the space beyond it, and the vehicles used there: *the aerospace industry*

Aes·chy·lus /'iːskɪləs‖'es / (525–456 BC) a Greek poet and writer of many plays, often said to have invented TRAGEDY

Ae·sop /'iːsɒp‖-sɑːp/ *n* (?620–?560 BC) a Greek writer who wrote moral short stories (FABLES) using animal characters. The stories are called *Aesop's Fables*.

aes·thete also **es-** *AmE* /'iːsθiːt‖'es-/ *n* a person who has a highly developed sense of beauty, esp. beauty in art

aes·thet·ic also **es-** *AmE* /iːs'θetɪk, es-‖es-/ *adj* **1** of or showing a highly developed sense of beauty, esp. in art: *The building is aesthetic but not very practical.* **2** of or concerning aesthetics: *From an aesthetic point of view it's a nice design.* — ~**ally** /kli/ *adj*

aes·thet·ics also **es-** *AmE* /iːs'θetɪks, es-‖es-/ *n* [U] the study or science of beauty, esp. in art

ae·ther /'iːθəʳ/ *n* [U] *lit or old use for* ETHER (2)

a·far /ə'fɑːʳ/ *adv lit* at a distance; far off: *I saw him from afar.*

AFDC /ˌeɪ ef diː 'siː/ *n* [U] Aid to Families with Dependent Children; a US government programme that gives money to poor families, esp. single parents —compare CHILD BENEFIT

af·fa·ble /'æfəbəl/ *adj* easy to talk to; ready to be friendly; pleasant —**bly** *adv* —**bility** /ˌæfə'bɪlɪti/ *n* [U]

af·fair /ə'feəʳ/ *n* **1** an event or set of connected events: *The meeting was a noisy affair./a stormy affair* | *the Watergate affair* **2** [*often pl.*] something needing action or attention; matter: *The minister is busy with important affairs of state.* | *the Ministry of Foreign Affairs* | *This is a very embarrassing state of affairs!* (=situation) | *I am not prepared to discuss my financial affairs.* **3** a sexual relationship between two people not married to each other, although at least one of them is married, esp. one that lasts for some time: *She's having an affair with her husband's best friend.* —see also LOVE AFFAIR

af·fect¹ /ə'fekt/ *v* [T] **1** to cause some result or change in; influence: *Smoking affects health.* | *Will the strike affect the price of coal?* | *an important decision that will affect the company's future* | *a disease that does not affect* (=attack) *humans* | *emergency relief for the areas affected by drought/for the drought-affected areas* **2** to cause feelings of sorrow, anger, love, etc, in: *She was deeply affected by the news of his death.* | *an affecting experience*

▷ USAGE Compare **affect** and **effect**. **1 Affect** is the usual verb and **effect** is the usual noun: *Government policy will not* **affect** (*v*) *us/will not have any* **effect** (*n*) *on us.* **2 Effect** used as a verb is very formal and means "to bring about, usually according to one's wishes": *He was able to* **effect** *certain changes in government policy.*◁

affect² *v* [T] *fml, often derog* **1** to pretend to feel, have, or do: *He affected illness so that he could stay off work.* [+*to-v*] *She affected not to care about her failure.* **2** to show a liking for; use: *He affects long words that people can't understand.*

af·fec·ta·tion /ˌæfek'teɪʃən/ *n* [C;U] *derog* (a piece of) behaviour which is not one's natural manner: *She is sincere and quite without affectation.* | *She's not really American — her accent is just an affectation.*

af·fect·ed /ə'fektɪd/ *adj derog* not real, natural, or sincere; showing affectation: *an affected smile* —opposite **unaffected** — ~**ly** *adv*

af·fec·tion /ə'fekʃən/ *n* [U] gentle lasting love, like that of a parent for a child; fondness: *He feels/has a deep affection for his old friend.* | *a display/show of affection*

af·fec·tion·ate /ə'fekʃənɪt/ *adj* showing gentle love: *an affectionate hug* | *an affectionate child* — ~**ly** *adv* : *He signed the letter "Affectionately, your brother Bill".*

af·fi·anced /ə'faɪənst/ *adj old use for* ENGAGED¹ (1)

af·fi·da·vit /ˌæfɪ'deɪvɪt/ *n law* a written statement made after an official promise (OATH) to tell the truth, for use as proof in a court of law

af·fil·i·ate¹ /ə'fɪlieɪt/ *v* [I;T (**with, to**)] (esp. of a group or organization) to join or connect (esp. to a larger group): *Our club is affiliated with/to a national organization of similar clubs.* —compare DISAFFILIATE —**ation** /ə,fɪli'eɪʃən/ *n* [C;U (**with**)] : *We have affiliations with several other societies in the town.* | *What are her political affiliations?*

af·fil·i·ate² /ə'fɪliɪt/ *n* a group or organization that is affiliated to another, esp. a SUBSIDIARY (or part-owned) company controlled by a parent company

affiliation or·der /·····' ···, ···/ *n* a decision made in a British court of law ordering a man to pay for the support of his child born to a woman to whom he is not married

af·fin·i·ty /ə'fɪnɪti/ *n* **1** [C;U (**between, with**)] relationship, close similarity, or connection: *The French and Italian languages have many affinities (with each other).* **2** [S (**for, to, between**)] a strong feeling of shared interests (with someone): *He feels a strong affinity for/to her.* | *There is a great affinity between them.*

affinity card /·'··· , ·/ also **affinity credit card, charity card** *n* a type of CREDIT CARD which lets the user send a small sum of money to a particular CHARITY every time the card is used

af·firm /ə'fɜːm‖-ɜːrm/ *v fml* **1** [T] to declare (usually again, or in answer to a question or doubt): *The minister affirmed the government's intention to reduce taxes.* [+*that*] *She affirmed that she was telling the truth.* —compare DENY (1) **2** [I] to promise to tell the truth in a court of law, but without mentioning God or religion in the promise — ~**ation** /ˌæfə'meɪʃən‖ˌæfər-/ *n* [C;U]

af·firm·a·tive /ə'fɜːmətɪv‖-ɜːr-/ *n, adj often fml* (a statement) saying or meaning "yes": *The answer to my request was a strong affirmative* | *an affirmative answer* | *She answered* **in the affirmative**. —opposite **negative** — ~**ly** *adv*

affirmative ac·tion /·,··· ' ··/ *n* [U] the practice or principle, when choosing people for a job or an education course, of favouring people who are often treated unfairly esp. because of their sex or race; POSITIVE DISCRIMINATION. Affirmative action is a political subject in the US about which many people feel very strongly: *The company is an affirmative action employer.* | *UCLA's affirmative action program* —compare REVERSE DISCRIMINATION

af·fix¹ /ə'fɪks/ *v* [T (**to**)] *fml* to fix, fasten, or stick: *A stamp should be affixed to the envelope.*

af·fix² /'æfɪks/ *n* a group of letters or sounds added to the beginning of a word (PREFIX) or to the end of a word (SUFFIX) to change its meaning or its use (as in "untie", "misunderstood", "kindness", "quickly")

af·flict /ə'flɪkt/ *v* [T (**with**)] *often pass.* to cause to suffer in the body or mind; trouble: *afflicted with bad eyesight* | *one of the major problems currently afflicting third world countries*

af·flic·tion /ə'flɪkʃən/ *n* [C;U] *fml* (something that causes) suffering or unhappiness: *the afflictions of old age*

af·flu·ent /'æfluənt/ *adj* having plenty of money or other possessions; wealthy: *an affluent society/family* —**ence** *n* [U]

af·ford /ə'fɔːd‖-ɔːrd/ *v* [T] **1** (usu. with **can, could, able**

to) to be able to buy or pay for: *Thanks to the success of the business, we can afford a holiday|a new car this year.* **2** (usu. with **can, could, able to**) to be able to spend, give, do, etc., without serious loss or damage: *I can't afford three weeks away from work.* | *I just can't afford the time.* [+to-v] *We can't afford to lose such an important member of the staff|to upset such an important customer.* **3** *fml or lit* to provide; give: *The top-floor windows afforded a magnificent view of the whole city.* [+obj(i)+obj(d)] *The tree afforded us shelter from the rain.* — ~**able** *adj* : *rents affordable to students living on grants*

af·for·est /ə'fɒrɪst‖ə'fɔːr-, ə'fɑː-/ *v* [T] to plant (hills, etc.) with trees in order to make a forest —opposite **dis-afforest, deforest** — ~**ation** /ə,fɒrɪ'steɪʃən‖ə,fɔːr-, ə,fɑːr-/ *n* [U]

af·fray /ə'freɪ/ *n esp. law* a fight or noisy quarrel in a public place, between small groups

af·fri·cate /'æfrɪkɪt/ *n tech* a consonant sound consisting of a PLOSIVE (such as /t/ or /d/) that is immediately followed by a FRICATIVE pronounced in the same part of the mouth (such as /ʃ/ or /ʒ/): *The word "church" contains the affricate /tʃ/.*

af·front¹ /ə'frʌnt/ *v* [T *often pass.*] to be rude to or hurt the feelings of, esp. intentionally or in public; offend

affront² *n* [(**to**)] an act, remark, etc., that is rude to someone or hurts their feelings, esp. when intentional or in public; INSULT: *an affront to one's dignity|pride*

Af·ghan /'æfgæn/ *n* **1** also **Af·gha·ni** /æf'gɑːni/ someone who comes from Afghanistan or whose parents come from Afghanistan **2** also **Afghan hound** /,··· '·/ a tall thin dog originally used for hunting, with a pointed nose and a coat of very long silky hair —see picture at DOG **3** a colourful BLANKET made of knitted (KNIT) or crocheted (CROCHET) squares —**Afghan** *adj*

Af·ghan·is·tan /æf'gænɪstɑːn, -stæn‖-stæn/ a country in Asia, south of Turkmenistan and Tajikistan and northwest of Pakistan; capital Kabul; population 15,814,000 (1989)

a·fi·cio·na·do /ə,fɪʃə'nɑːdəʊ/ *n* **-dos** *Sp* someone who is keenly interested in a particular activity or subject; FAN; DEVOTEE: *aficionados of football* | *a cinema aficionado*

a·field /ə'fiːld/ *adv* far away, esp. from home; to or at a great distance: *Don't go too* **far afield** *or you'll get lost.* | *We get a lot of tourists from Europe, and some from even further afield.*

a·fire /ə'faɪər/ *adj, adv* [F (**with**)] on fire: *He set the house afire.* | (fig.) *afire with enthusiasm*

a·flame /ə'fleɪm/ *adj, adv* [F (**with**)] on fire; ABLAZE: *The house was aflame.* | (fig.) *The gardens were aflame with red and orange leaves.*

AFL-CIO /,eɪ ef ,el ,siː aɪ 'əʊ/ [the] American Federation of Labor and Congress of Industrial Organizations; an association of American TRADE UNIONS, which is very influential in the US

a·float /ə'fləʊt/ *adj, adv* [F] **1** floating on water; at sea: *Help me get the boat afloat.* | *How long did you spend afloat?* (=on a ship) **2** covered with water; flooded **3** out of debt: *The company somehow managed to keep|stay afloat.*

a·foot /ə'fʊt/ *adj, adv* [F] **1** (esp. of something bad) being prepared or in operation: *There is a plan afoot to pull down the old building.* | *There is some strange business afoot.* **2** *old use* moving, esp. on foot

a·fore·said /ə'fɔːsed‖ə'fɔːr-/ also **a·fore·men·tioned** /ə'fɔːmenʃənd‖ə'fɔːr-/ — *adj* [A] *law* mentioned or named before or already: *The car belongs to the aforesaid Ms Jones.* [also *n, the*+C, *pl.* **aforesaid**] *The aforementioned was|were present at the trial.*

a·fore·thought /ə'fɔːθɔːt‖ə'fɔːr-/ *adj law* see **with malice aforethought** (MALICE)

a for·ti·o·ri /,eɪ fɔːti'ɔːraɪ, -ri‖-fɔːr-/ *adv Lat* for a still stronger reason; even more certainly: *If you can afford a car then, a fortiori, you can afford a bicycle.*

a·foul /ə'faʊl/ *adv* **run afoul of** to bring one into opposition or disagreement with: *His proposal runs afoul of government plans to curb expenditure on education.*

a·fraid /ə'freɪd/ *adj* [F] **1** [(**of, for**)] full of fear; frightened: *There's no need to be afraid.* | *Don't be afraid of the dog.* | *He was afraid for his job.* (=afraid that he might lose it) [+to-v] *I was afraid to go out of the house at night.* [+(that)] *They were afraid that the police would catch them.* —see

FRIGHTENED (USAGE) **2** [(**of**)] unwilling to do something, esp. because of worry about possible results: *I didn't tell her because I was afraid of upsetting her.* [+to-v] *Don't be afraid to ask for help.* | (*apprec*) *They're not afraid of hard work.* (=They work very hard.) **3** [+(that)] *polite* sorry for something that has happened or is likely to happen: *I am afraid (that) I've broken your pen.* | *"Are we late?" "I'm afraid so."* | *"Are we on time?" "I'm afraid not."* | *I'm afraid I'm going to have to ask you to leave.* **4** **afraid of one's own shadow** habitually frightened or nervous

▷ USAGE **I'm afraid** is often used as a polite phrase when you are giving someone unpleasant information: **I'm afraid** *I have some rather bad news for you.* | *"Did you pass your exam?"* **"I'm afraid not."** | *"Do I have to pay the full price?"* **"I'm afraid so."** | **We're afraid** *we're unable to offer you the job.* It can also be used when you want to disagree with someone: **I'm afraid** *I really can't agree with you there.* | *Yes, Sue, but* **I'm afraid** *you haven't quite understood my point.*◁

a·fresh /ə'freʃ/ *adv fml* once more from the beginning; again: *After his business collapsed he had to start afresh.*

Af·ri·ca /'æfrɪkə/ one of the seven main land masses (CONTINENTS) on the Earth, south of the Mediterranean Sea and connected to Asia

Af·ri·can /'æfrɪkən/ *n, adj* (someone who comes or whose parents come) from Africa

African A·mer·i·can /,··· ·'···/ *n AmE* an American who is descended from black Africans, esp. those who were brought to America as slaves before the middle of the 19th century

African Na·tion·al Con·gress /,··· ,··· '··/ *n* [the] see ANC

African vi·o·let /,··· '···/ *n* a house plant with small pink or purple flowers popular in Britain and the US

Af·ri·kaans /,æfrɪ'kɑːns/ *n* [U] a language of South Africa similar to Dutch

Af·ri·ka·ner /,æfrɪ'kɑːnər/ *n* a South African whose first language is Afrikaans, esp. a descendant of the Dutch settlers of the 17th century

Af·ro /'æfrəʊ/ *n* **Afros** a hairstyle for men and women in which the hair is shaped into a large round bushy mass

Afro- see WORD FORMATION

Afro-Car·ib·be·an /,··· ··'··◁/ *n, adj* (a person) of the Caribbean, whose family came from Africa: *How many British MPs are of Afro-Caribbean origin?*

aft /ɑːft‖æft/ *adj, adv* in or towards the STERN (=the back part) of a boat or aircraft —opposite **fore** —compare FORWARD⁴

af·ter¹ /'ɑːftər‖'æf-/ *prep* **1** following in time; later than: *We'll leave after breakfast.* | *They will be back the day after tomorrow.* | *I don't like going out after dark.* | *After the performance there was enthusiastic applause.* | *a film about life after a nuclear attack* | (*AmE*) *It's twenty after seven.* **2** following continuously: **Day after day** *the rain continued.* | *It seems to be just one problem after another.* **3** following in place or order: *He entered the room after his father.* | *Your name comes after mine in the list.* | *Shut the door after you.* (=when you have gone through) | *After you with the sugar, please.* (=can I have it next?) **4** as a result of; because of: *After the way he treated me I never want to see him again.* **5** in spite of: *After all my care in packing it, the clock arrived broken.* **6** in search of (esp. in order to punish); looking for: *The police are after me.* | *"What are you after?" "I'm looking for my coat."* **7** with the name of: *The boy was named after his uncle.* **8** *fml* in the manner or style of: *This is a painting after Rembrandt.* **9** **after all: a** in spite of everything: *So you see I was right after all!* **b** it must be remembered (that): *I know he hasn't finished the work but, after all, he's very busy.* —see also ASK **after, after one's own heart** (HEART), TAKE **after**

after² *conj* at a later time than (when): *I found your coat after you had left the house.* | *She started the job soon after|shortly after she left the university.*

after³ *adv* [after *n*] later; afterwards: *John came on Tuesday, and I arrived the day after.*

▷ USAGE **After** with the meaning "afterwards" usu. follows another time adverb: *We arrived just|soon|shortly* **after.** But in informal English it can follow other words: *We had dinner and went home* **after-wards**/*(infml)* **after.**◁

after⁴ *adj* [A] **1** *lit* later in time: *He grew weak in after years.* **2** *tech* in the back part of a boat or aircraft: *the after deck*

after- see WORD FORMATION

af·ter·birth /ˈɑːftəbɜːθ‖ˈæftərbɜːrθ/ *n* the material that comes out of a woman just after she has given birth to a child —compare PLACENTA

af·ter·care /ˈɑːftəkeəʳ‖ˈæftər-/ *n* [U] the care or treatment given to someone after a period in hospital, prison, etc.

af·ter·ef·fect /ˈɑːftərɪˌfekt‖ˈæf-/ *n* [*often pl.*] an effect (usu. unpleasant) that follows some time after the cause or after the main effect

After Eight /ˌ¹·· ¹·/ *n tdmk* a flat, square, chocolate-covered soft PEPPERMINT sweet which is popular esp. after formal meals

af·ter·glow /ˈɑːftəgləʊ‖ˈæftər-/ *n* [*usu. sing.*] **1** the light that remains in the western sky after the sun has set **2** a pleasant feeling that remains after a happy experience or event

af·ter·life /ˈɑːftəlaɪf‖ˈæftər-/ *n* **-lives** /laɪvz/ [*usu. sing.*] **1** life after death **2** the later part of a person's life, esp. after a particular event —compare HEREAFTER²

af·ter·math /ˈɑːftəmæθ‖ˈæftər-/ *n* [(of) *usu. sing.*] the result or period following a bad event such as an accident, storm, war, etc.: *the danger of disease in the aftermath of the earthquake*

af·ter·noon /ˌɑːftəˈnuːn◂‖ˌæftər-/ *n* [C;U] the period between midday and either sunset or the end of the day's work: *a hot afternoon* | *on Tuesday afternoons* | *I'll have a sleep in the afternoon.* | *tomorrow afternoon* | *an afternoon swim* | *in the early/late afternoon* —compare EVENING

af·ter·noons /ˌɑːftəˈnuːnz‖ˌæftər-/ *adv esp. AmE* in the afternoon repeatedly; during any afternoon: *I'm always out in the afternoons.*

afternoon tea /ˌ··· ¹·/ *n* [C;U] *BrE, AustrE* a drink of tea and sometimes a light meal taken at about four o'clock in the afternoon

▶CULTURAL NOTE In Britain, afternoon tea is thought of as a formal meal, served to visitors. People typically think of small sandwiches, esp. CUCUMBER sandwiches, and small cakes, and of people behaving in a very polite, formal way towards each other.◀

af·ters /ˈɑːftəz‖ˈæftərz/ *n* [P] *BrE infml* the part of a meal that comes after the main dish; DESSERT: *What are we having for afters?* —see DESSERT (USAGE)

after-sales ser·vice /ˌ·· ¹· ¹·¸/ *n* [U] the services such as providing SPARE PARTS, repairs, and advice offered to customers after they have bought something. *The company provides a very good after-sales service.*

af·ter·shave /ˈɑːftəʃeɪv‖ˈæftər-/ also **after shave lo·tion** /ˈ··· ¸·¹·/— *n* [C;U] a liquid with a pleasant smell for use on the face after shaving (SHAVE)

af·ter·taste /ˈɑːftəteɪst‖ˈæftər-/ *n* a taste, esp. an unpleasant taste, that stays in the mouth after the food that caused it is no longer there: (fig.) *The angry exchange of words left an unpleasant aftertaste.*

af·ter·thought /ˈɑːftəθɔːt‖ˈæftər-/ *n* **1** an idea that comes later **2** something added later, esp. something that was not part of the original plan: *The conservatory was an afterthought, added on to the building several years later.*

af·ter·wards /ˈɑːftəwədz‖ˈæftərwərdz/ also **af·ter·ward** /-wəd‖-wərd/*AmE—* *adv* later; after that —see AFTER³ (USAGE)

AFTRA /ˈæftrə/ American Federation of Television and Radio Artists; an American trade union for actors and actresses whose performances are TAPED (recorded) for television or radio —compare EQUITY, SAG

A·ga /ˈɑːgə/ *n tdmk* a cooker made of solid iron, like the kinds of cooker that people used to have in the past. Agas now usu. work by electricity, oil, or gas.

a·gain /əˈgen, əˈgeɪn‖əˈgen/ *adv* **1** once more; one more time: *Please say that again.* | *Let's start again from the beginning.* | *Never do that again!* | *He told the story once again/yet again.* | *The committee will meet again next Thursday.* **2** back to the place, condition, etc., as before: *She was ill but now she is well again.* | *He's home again*

now. **3** besides; further: *I could eat as much* (=the same amount) *again*. **4** however; on the other hand: *She might agree, and then again she might not.* **5 again and again** also **time and (time) again, over and over again**— very often; repeatedly: *I've told them again and again not to play there.* —see also **now and again** (NOW)

a·gainst /əˈgenst, əˈgeɪnst‖əˈgenst/ *prep* **1** in opposition to: *We will fight against the enemy.* | *There were 20 votes for her and 12 against her.* | *They are strongly against the idea.* | *Against all probability, she won a place in the finals.* | *Stealing is* **against the law.** (=illegal) | *They went ahead with the plan,* **against my wishes.** (=although I did not want them to) **2** in the direction of and touching or meeting: *The rain beat against the windows.* **3** touching, esp. for support: *She was leaning against the wall.* **4** in an opposite direction to: *We sailed against the wind.* **5** as a defence or protection from: *They were vaccinated against cholera.* **6** having as a background: *The picture looks good against that light wall.* **7** causing disadvantage to; having an unfavourable effect on: *The present economic climate works against the smaller companies.* | *His prison record will count against him.* **8** *fml* in preparation for: *They have saved some money against their old age.* —see also **over against** (OVER²) **9 He that is not with me is against me** *quote from the Bible* any person who does not openly support me is opposed to me

A·ga Khan /ˌɑːgə ˈkɑːn/ [*the*] (1936–) a very rich Arab leader who is known for owning many race-horses

Ag·a·mem·non /ˌægəˈmemnən, -nɒn‖-nɑːn/ in CLASSICAL MYTHOLOGY, a king of Argos, leader of the Greeks in the Trojan War

a·gape /əˈgeɪp/ *adj, adv* [F] **1** wide open: *They watched with their mouths agape.* —see also GAPE **2** [(with)] in a state of wonder: *The children were agape (with excitement) as they watched the programme.*

ag·ate /ˈægət/ *n* [C;U] a hard stone with bands of colour, used in jewellery

age¹ /eɪdʒ/ *n* **1** [C] the period of time a person has lived or a thing has existed: *She entered Parliament at the age of 26.* | *He doesn't look his age.* (=He looks younger than he actually is.) | *At your age you should know better.* | *What ages are* (not *have*) *your children?* | *She married a man who was twice her age.* (=twice as old as she was) **2** [U] one of the periods of a person's life: *Who is going to look after them in their* **old age?** (=when they are old) | *A person of 40 has reached* **middle age.** | *retirement age* | *men of military age* (=within the age range considered acceptable for soldiers) —see also TEENAGE **3** [U] the state of being old: *His back was bent with age.* **4** [U] the particular time of life at which a person becomes able or not able to do something: *You can't drive a car yet — you're still* **under age.** (=you're too young) | *He won't be called up for military service — he's* **over age.** —see also AGE OF CONSENT **5** [C *usu. sing.*] (*often cap.*) a particular period of history: *The period in which people learnt to make tools of iron is called the* **Iron Age.** | *We are living in the nuclear age/the space age.* —see also GOLDEN AGE **6** [C] also **ages** *pl.*— *infml* a long time: *It's been ages/an age since we met.* **7 come of age: a** to reach the particular age, usu. 18 or 21, at which one becomes responsible in law for one's own actions, and is allowed to vote, own property, etc. **b** to reach a stage of full development: *The company has now been successfully established for ten years, and has really come of age.* —see also COMING OF AGE **8 age before beauty** a phrase used humorously by someone letting another person go through a door first

age² *v* **aged, ageing** *or* **aging** [I;T] **1** to (cause to) become old or seem old: *After his illness he aged quickly.* | *His illness seems to have aged him quite noticeably.* —see also

AGEING¹ **2** to improve, esp. in taste, as time passes: *This cheese has aged for nearly two years.*

Age Con·cern /'· ·,·/ a British CHARITY which represents the interests of old people

aged¹ /eɪdʒd/ *adj* **1** [F] being of the stated number of years: *They've got two children, aged 3 and 7.* **2** (of cheese or wine) fully developed, esp. in taste

ag·ed² /'eɪdʒɪd/ *adj* very old: *an aged man* [also *n*, *the*+P] *special arrangements for the* **aged and infirm**

age di·scrim·i·na·tion /'· ···,··/ *n* [U] *AmE for* AGEISM

age group /'· ·/ also **age brack·et** /'· ,··/— *n* [C+*sing.*|*pl. v*] the people between two particular ages considered as a group: *a book written for children in the 12–14 age group*

age·ing¹ *BrE* ‖ usu. **aging** *AmE* /'eɪdʒɪŋ/ *adj* [A] becoming old; rather old, esp. older than is considered desirable or suitable: *We need to replace some of this ageing office equipment.* | *an ageing playboy|hippie*

ageing² *BrE* ‖ usu. **aging** *AmE n* [U] **1** the process of getting old: *a healthy diet which retards ageing* | *the ageing process* **2** the changes that happen (e.g. to wine or cheese) as time passes

age·is·m, **agism** /'eɪdʒɪzəm/ *BrE* ‖ **age discrimination** *AmE* – *n* [U] the making of unfair differences between people because of their age, esp. treating young people more favourably than old people: *He didn't get the job because he's over 40 – that's pure ageism.* –**ageist** *adj, n*

age·less /'eɪdʒləs/ *adj* never growing old or never showing signs of growing old: *an ageless song* | *ageless beauty* – ~ **ness** *n* [U]

age lim·it /'· ,··/ *n* an upper or lower age beyond which one is not allowed to do something

a·gen·cy /'eɪdʒənsi/ *n* **1** [C] a business that makes its money by bringing people into touch with others or the products of others: *I got this job through an employment agency.* | *an advertising agency* | *The company has agencies* (=offices representing it) *all over the world.* –see also DATING AGENCY, NEWS AGENCY **2** [C] *esp. AmE* a department of a government or of an international body: *a United Nations agency responsible for helping refugees* **3** [S (**of**)] the power or force which causes a result: *Iron is melted by the agency of heat.*

Agency for In·ter·na·tion·al De·vel·op·ment /,··· · ,····· ·'··/ (*abbrev.* **AID**) [*the*] an American government department which provides money to help less developed countries to improve their economic situation and the quality of life of their people

a·gen·da /ə'dʒendə/ *n* **-das** a list of the subjects to be dealt with or talked about at a meeting: *What's on the agenda for this afternoon's meeting?* | *the first item on the agenda* | *The question of salary increases is high on the agenda.* | (fig.) *Education has risen to the top of the political agenda.* –see also HIDDEN AGENDA

a·gent /'eɪdʒənt/ *n* **1** a person whose job is to represent another person, a company, etc., esp. one who brings people into touch with others or deals with the business affairs of a person or company: *Our agent in Rome deals with all our Italian business.* | *An estate agent* (*BrE*)|*real estate agent* (*AmE*) *arranges the buying and selling of houses.* | *A literary agent manages the business affairs of an author.* –see also DOUBLE AGENT, FREE AGENT, LAND AGENT, SECRET AGENT **2** *fml or tech* a person or thing that works to produce a result: *Rain and sun are the agents which help plants to grow.* | *Soap is a cleansing agent.*

Agent Or·ange /,·· '··/ *n* [U] a chemical weapon used by American soldiers in Vietnam to destroy crops, and now thought to have caused ABORTIONS, CANCERS, and deformities (DEFORMITY) in many Vietnamese people

a·gent pro·voc·a·teur /,æʒɒn prɒvɒkə'tɜːᵣ ‖ ,ɑːʒɑːn prəʊvɑː-/ *n* **agents provocateurs** (*same pronunciation*) *Fr* a person who is employed by the government or police, to encourage criminals or those working against the state to do something illegal so that they can be caught

age of con·sent /,· · ·'·/ *n* [*the*] the age at which a person is considered to be old enough to marry or have sexual relations without breaking the law. In Britain the age of consent is 16 for HETEROSEXUAL sex and 21 for HOMOSEXUAL sex between men. In the US, the age of consent varies from state to state, but usu. it is between 16 and 18. –see also ADULT (CULTURAL NOTE)

Age of En·light·en·ment /,· · ·'···/ also **Age of Rea·son**

/,·· '··/— [*the*] a period in European history, in the 18th century, when educated people thought that belief should depend on reason and scientific proof

ag·glom·er·ate¹ /ə'glɒməreɪt‖ə'glɑː-/ *v* [I;T] *fml* to collect or gather into a confused mass or pile –**agglomerate** /ə'glɒmərʌt‖ə'glɑː-/ *adj* –**ation** /ə,glɒmə'reɪʃən‖ə,glɑː-/ *n* [C;U] : *The town is surrounded by agglomerations of ugly new houses.*

ag·glom·er·ate² /ə'glɒmərʌt‖ə'glɑː-/ *n* [S;U] *fml or tech* a type of rock formed from pieces of hard material from a VOLCANO that have been melted and united by heat

ag·glu·ti·na·tion /ə,gluːtɪ'neɪʃən/ *n* [U] *tech* **1** sticking or becoming stuck together, esp. in a jelly-like form: *agglutination of bacteria|red blood cells* **2** the formation of new words by combining separate parts which each have their own meaning (such as *shipyard* from *ship* and *yard*) –**native** /ə'gluːtɪnətɪv ‖ -neɪtɪv/ *adj* : *an agglutinative language* (=in which words are formed by agglutination)

ag·gran·dize·ment also **-disement** *BrE* /ə'grændʌzmənt/ *n* [U] *usu. derog* increase in size, power, or rank, esp. when intentionally planned: *He is willing to tell lies and break promises for his own personal aggrandizement.*

ag·gra·vate /'ægrəveɪt/ *v* [T] **1** to make (a difficult situation) more serious or dangerous; make worse: *The lack of rain aggravated the already serious shortage of food.* | *Their debt problem was further aggravated by the rise in interest rates.* **2** *infml* to make angry, esp. by continual annoyance: *aggravating delays caused by heavy traffic* –**vatingly** *adv* –**vation** /,ægrə'veɪʃən/ *n* [C;U]

▷ USAGE Although **aggravate** is commonly used to mean "annoy", this is often thought by teachers to be incorrect: a *difficulty* is **aggravated** (=made worse); a *person* is **irritated** or **annoyed**. –see also ANGRY (USAGE), ANNOY (USAGE)◁

ag·gre·gate¹ /'ægrɪgʌt/ *n* **1** [C;U] *fml* a total: *The football team had a low goal aggregate last season.* | *What were the company's aggregate earnings for the year?* **2** [S;U] *tech* the materials, such as sand and small stones, that are mixed with CEMENT to form CONCRETE

ag·gre·gate² /'ægrɪgeɪt/ *v fml or tech* **1** [I;T] to bring or come together into a group or mass **2** [L+*n*] to reach a total of; add up to: *Her earnings from all sources aggregated £100,000.* –**gation** /,ægrɪ'geɪʃən/ *n* [C;U]

ag·gres·sion /ə'greʃən/ *n* [U] the act or tendency of starting a quarrel, fight, or war, esp. without just cause: *The military exercise was condemned as* **an act of aggression.** –see also NONAGGRESSION

ag·gres·sive /ə'gresɪv/ *adj* **1** *derog* always ready to quarrel or attack; BELLIGERENT: *an aggressive manner* **2** *approc* not afraid of opposition; determined and forceful; ASSERTIVE: *A successful businessman must be aggressive.* | *an aggressive marketing campaign* **3** (of weapons) made for use in attack – ~ **ly** *adv* – ~ **ness** *n* [U]

ag·gres·sor /ə'gresəᵣ/ *n* a person or country that begins a quarrel, fight, war, etc., with another, esp. without just cause

ag·grieved /ə'griːvd/ *adj* **1** showing hurt, angry, and bitter feelings, esp. because one has been unfairly treated **2** *esp. law* having suffered as a result of the illegal actions of someone else: *The allegations of fraud were proved and the court awarded the aggrieved parties substantial damages.*

ag·gro /'ægrəʊ/ *n* [U] *BrE sl* trouble, esp. fighting, e.g. between groups of young people; used esp. of the behaviour of young, aggressive men, who enjoy fighting

a·ghast /ə'gɑːst‖ə'gæst/ *adj* [F (**at**)] suddenly filled with great surprise, fear, and shock: *She was aghast when she was told of her husband's huge gambling debts.*

ag·ile /'ædʒaɪl‖'ædʒəl/ *adj* able to move quickly and easily; NIMBLE: *an agile animal* | (fig.) *an agile mind* – ~ **ly** *adv* –**ility** /ə'dʒɪlʌti/ *n* [U]

A·gin·court /'ædʒʌnkɔː, -kɔːt‖-kɔːrt/ a famous battle in France in 1415, which the English, led by King Henry V, won. There are scenes of this battle in the play *Henry V* by Shakespeare.

ag·ing /'eɪdʒɪŋ/ *n* [U] AGEING

ag·is·m /'eɪdʒɪzəm/ *n* [U] AGEISM

ag·i·tate /'ædʒʌteɪt/ *v* **1** [T] to make (someone) feel anxious and nervous: *He became quite agitated when he was asked about his criminal past.* **2** [I (**for**, **against**)] to argue strongly in public for or against some political or social change: *to agitate for cheaper school meals* **3** [T] to shake (a liquid) about

ag·i·ta·tion /ˌædʒɪˈteɪʃən/ *n* **1** [U] painful excitement of the mind or feelings; anxiety: *He was in a state of great agitation.* **2** [C;U (**for, against**)] public argument, action, unrest, etc., for or against political or social change

ag·i·ta·tor /ˈædʒɪteɪtəʳ/ *n* **1** *usu. derog* a person who excites and influences public feeling, esp. towards political change **2** a machine for shaking or mixing

a·glow /əˈgləʊ/ *adj* [F (**with**)] bright with colour or excitement: *The sky was aglow with the setting sun.* | *a face aglow with excitement*

AGM /ˌeɪ dʒiː ˈem/ *n BrE* ‖ usu. **annual meeting** *AmE* — annual general meeting; a meeting held once a year by the members of a company, club, or other organization, for the purpose of electing officials, reporting on the year's business, etc

ag·nos·tic /æɡˈnɒstɪk, əɡ-‖-ˈnɑː-/ *n, adj* (a person) who believes that nothing can be known about God or life after death —compare ATHEIST — ~ **ism** /æɡˈnɒstɪ̱sɪzəm, əɡ-‖ -ˈnɑː-/ *n* [U]

a·go /əˈgəʊ/ *adj* [after *n* or *adv*] back in time from now; in the past: *He left ten minutes ago|five years ago.* | *How long ago did he leave?* | *He died long ago|a long time ago.* — compare FOR¹ (7)

▷ USAGE 1 **Ago** is nearly always used with verbs in past forms and not with verbs formed with *have*. Compare *I came here a year* **ago** and *I have been here for a year|*since *1985.* 2 When we are contrasting a more distant time in the past with a nearer time we use **before** (**that**) or **previously** instead of *ago*: *My grandfather died five years* **ago**; *my grandmother had already died three years* **before** (**that**)/**previously** (=eight years ago).◁

a·gog /əˈgɒg‖əˈgɑːg/ *adj* [F (**with**)] *infml* full of eager excitement and expectation: *The children were all agog (with excitement) as the actor pulled a gun from his pocket.*

ag·o·nize also **-nise** *BrE* /ˈægənaɪz/ *v* [I (**over**)] *infml* to make a long and anxious effort when considering something or trying to make a decision: *After agonizing (over it) for days we finally made up our minds.*

ag·o·nized also **-nised** *BrE* /ˈægənaɪzd/ *adj* expressing great pain: *She let out an agonized cry.*

ag·o·niz·ing also **-nising** *BrE* /ˈægənaɪzɪŋ/ *adj* causing great pain or anxiety: *an agonizing decision|delay* — **~ly** *adv*

ag·o·ny /ˈægəni/ *n* [C;U] very great pain or suffering of mind or body: *He lay in agony until the doctor arrived.* | *I was in an agony of doubt|in agonies of doubt.*

agony aunt /ˈ··· ˌ·/ *BrE* ‖ **advice columnist** *AmE* — *n* a woman who gives advice to readers in an agony column. Famous agony aunts in Britain are Marjorie Proops and Claire Rayner, and in the US Dear Abby and Ann Landers.

agony col·umn /ˈ··· ˌ··/ *BrE* ‖ **advice column** *AmE* — *n* a part of a newspaper, esp. a TABLOID, or magazine containing letters from readers about their personal problems, together with advice from the newspaper or magazine

ag·o·ra·pho·bi·a /ˌægərəˈfəʊbiə/ *n* [U] fear of open spaces —compare CLAUSTROPHOBIA

ag·o·ra·pho·bic /ˌægərəˈfəʊbɪk◂/ *n, adj* (a person) suffering from agoraphobia

a·grar·i·an /əˈgreəriən/ *adj* concerning land, esp. farmland or who owns it: *a campaigner for agrarian reform*

a·gree /əˈgriː/ *v* **1** [I (**with, about, on**);T *obj; not in progressive forms*] to have or share the same opinion, feeling, or purpose; CONCUR: *I thought it was a good idea, but she didn't agree.* | *I agree with you about his latest book — it's awful.* | *We agreed on a price for the car.* [+to-v] *We agreed to leave at once.* [+(that)] *It is generally agreed* (=most people agree) *that she is the best tennis player in the country.* | *"I think it's a bad idea."* "**I couldn't agree more.**" (=I completely agree.) —opposite **disagree**; see REFUSE (USAGE) **2** [I (**to**)] to say yes to an idea, opinion, suggestion, etc., esp. after an unwillingness or argument; CONSENT: *I suggested that we should go on holiday and she agreed at once.* | *We'll never get him to agree to it.* **3** [I (**with**)] (of facts, statements, etc.) to be in accor-

dance with each other or with something else; CORRESPOND: *The witnesses' statements just don't agree (with each other).* **4** [T] *esp. BrE* to accept (an idea, opinion, etc.); reach an agreement about: *The workers have agreed the company's pay offer.* | *an agreed price|statement* **5 agree to differ** to stop trying to persuade each other; remain friends in spite of having different opinions

▷ USAGE **Agree to** is used with the same meaning as **accept** before words like "suggestion", "proposal", or "plan": *Do you think he will* **agree to/accept** *my suggestions?* Both **agree** and **accept** can be used before *that* when the meaning is "admit", but **accept** is more formal: *I* **agree/accept** *that the company has not done well this year.*◁

agree with sbdy./sthg. *phr v* [T *no pass.*] **1** [*usu. in negatives*] *infml* to suit the health of: *I love prawns, but unfortunately they don't agree with me.* —opposite **disagree with 2** *tech* (of an adjective, verb, etc.) to have the proper relationship to (the word it belongs to in grammar), e.g. by being plural if it is plural, female if it is female, etc. —see also AGREE (1, 3)

a·gree·a·ble /əˈgriːəbəl/ *adj* **1** pleasant: *agreeable weather* —opposite **disagreeable 2** [F (**to**)] ready to agree; willing: *Are you agreeable (to the suggestion)?*

a·gree·a·bly /əˈgriːəbli/ *adv* pleasantly: *We were agreeably surprised by their willingness to negotiate.*

a·gree·ment /əˈgriːmənt/ *n* **1** [U] the state of having the same opinion, feeling, or purpose; thinking in the same way: *We are* **in agreement with** *their decision.* | *The two sides were unable to reach agreement.* —opposite **disagreement 2** [C] an arrangement or promise of action, such as one made between people, groups, businesses, or countries: *You have broken (the terms of) our agreement by not finishing the job in time.* | *The two companies* **entered into an agreement** *with each other.* | *to sign an agreement* | *trade agreements* | *an arms-control agreement* **3** [U (**with**)] *tech* the fact of agreeing with another word in grammar: *the agreement of the pronoun "she" with the noun "Jane" to which it refers*

ag·ri·busi·ness /ˈægrɪˌbɪznɪ̱s/ *n* [U;C] (a company involved in) the producing and selling of farm products, esp. as a big business: *Agribusiness is pushing out the small farmer.* | *the agribusiness sector of the economy*

ag·ri·cul·ture /ˈægrɪˌkʌltʃəʳ/ *n* [U] the practice or science of farming, esp. of growing crops —compare HORTICULTURE — **~tural** /ˌægrɪˈkʌltʃərəl◂/ *adj* : *agricultural products| machinery* — **~tur(al)ist** /ˌægrɪˈkʌltʃərəlɪ̱st/ *n*

ag·ro·chem·i·cal /ˌægrəʊˈkemɪkəl/ *n* a chemical used in farming e.g. to help plants grow

a·ground /əˈgraʊnd/ *adj, adv* [F] (of a ship) on or onto the shore or bottom of a sea, lake, etc. (esp. in the phrase **run aground**)

a·gue /ˈeɪgjuː/ *n* [C;U] fever with regular attacks of coldness and shaking esp. when caused by the disease MALARIA

ah /ɑː/ *interj* (a cry of surprise, pity, pain, joy, dislike, etc.): *Ah, there you are!*

a·ha /ɑːˈhɑː/ *interj* (a cry of surprise, satisfaction, amused discovery, etc.): *Aha, so it's you hiding there!*

A·hab /ˈeɪhæb/ , **Captain** a character in Herman Melville's NOVEL *Moby-Dick*. Captain Ahab hunts a white WHALE called Moby-Dick to the risk of his own life and the lives of the other people on his ship.

a·head /əˈhed/ *adj, adv,* [F;after *n*] **1** in front; forward: *One man went ahead (of the others) to see if the road was clear.* | *The road ahead was full of sheep.* **2** in or into the future: *to plan ahead|plan for the months ahead* **3 ahead of: a** in advance of: *The time in London is five hours ahead of the time in New York.* **b** in or into a more successful position than: *Our company is well ahead of its main rivals.* | *The Democrats have moved ahead of the Republicans in the latest poll.* **c** higher in price, value, etc. than: *Their pay offer was well ahead of inflation.* **4 get ahead** to do well; succeed —see also GO-AHEAD

a·hem /mˈhm; *spelling pronunciation* əˈhem/ *interj* (a cough used to attract attention, give a slight warning, express doubts, etc.)

a·hoy /əˈhɔɪ/ *interj* **1** (a cry of greeting made by sailors, esp. from one ship to another) **2 ship ahoy!** (a cry used by sailors to say that they can see a ship approaching)

AI /ˌeɪ ˈaɪ/ *n* [U] ARTIFICIAL INTELLIGENCE

aid¹ /eɪd/ v [T (**with, in**)] fml to give support to; help: We were greatly aided in our investigation by the cooperation of the police. | He was accused of **aiding and abetting** the terrorists. (=helping them in criminal activities) | computer-aided design —see HELP (USAGE)

aid² n fml **1** [U] support or help: We went to the aid of the injured man. | a concert **in aid of** (=to make money for) the church repairs fund —see also FIRST AID, LEGAL AID **2** [C] something that provides help and makes a process easier or more effective: A dictionary is an invaluable aid in learning a new language. —see also HEARING AID, VISUAL AID **3** [U] help that is given by one country to another in the form of food, machines, or special skills: aid to the developing countries | the government's aid budget/emergency aid —see also FOREIGN AID **4** [C] AmE aide **5 what is something in aid of?** BrE infml what is something for?: "What's this little handle in aid of?" "It's for starting the machine."

AID /ˌeɪ aɪ ˈdiː/ **1** abbrev. for AGENCY FOR INTERNATIONAL DEVELOPMENT **2** Artificial Insemination by Donor; an artificial method of making a woman PREGNANT, by using SEMEN that has been collected from men and frozen

aide /eɪd/ also **aid** AmE— n a person who helps, esp. a person employed to help a government minister: a presidential aide

aide-de-camp /ˌeɪd də ˈkɑːmp/ n **aides-de-camp** (same pronunciation) Fr a military or naval officer who helps an officer of higher rank in his duties

aided school /ˈ·· ˌ·/ n (in Britain) a type of school (=VOLUNTARY SCHOOL) whose managers have control over religious education and the choice of teachers and are responsible for part of the cost of building work needed for the school —compare CONTROLLED SCHOOL

AIDS , Aids /eɪdz/ n [U] Acquired Immune Deficiency Syndrome; a very serious disease caused by a VIRUS which breaks down the body's natural defences against infection: the AIDS epidemic | He died of Aids.

▶ CULTURAL NOTE In many countries AIDS is believed to be a disease that mostly affects HOMOSEXUAL men and people who INJECT drugs. Because some people think that homosexual behaviour and drug-taking are wrong, they sometimes see AIDS as a punishment for wrong behaviour. Some people are also afraid of people who have AIDS because they think, wrongly, that they might catch the disease just from being with that person. AIDS is now the subject of important health education CAMPAIGNs in many countries. In the US, AIDS is a political issue because many people want the government to give more money to AIDS research. —see also SAFE SEX◀

ai·ki·do /aɪˈkiːdəʊ/ n [U] a Japanese fighting art based on using the opponent's strength against them in order to defend oneself.

ail /eɪl/ v **1** [I] to be ill and grow weak: My grandmother is ailing. | (fig.) the country's ailing economy **2** [T] old use to cause pain to; trouble (esp. in the phrase **What ails you?**)

ai·le·ron /ˈeɪlərɒn‖-rɑːn/ n the movable back edge of the wing of an aircraft, used to keep it level or help it turn —compare ELEVATOR (4), and see picture at AIRCRAFT

ail·ment /ˈeɪlmənt/ n an illness that is not serious: He's always complaining of some ailment or other. | a minor ailment

Ail·sa Craig /ˌeɪlsə ˈkreɪg/ a small island in Scotland

aim¹ /eɪm/ v **1** [I;T (**at**)] to point or direct (a weapon, shot, etc.) towards some object, with the intention of hitting it: I aimed at the door but hit the window. | He aimed the gun carefully. | He aimed it at the bottles. | (fig.) She hit back with well-aimed criticism. | (fig.) The programme is aimed at (=intended for) young teenagers. **2** [I (**at, for**)] to direct one's efforts (towards doing or obtaining something); intend (to): The factory must aim at increased production/aim for an increase in production. [+to-v] He aims to be a successful writer.

aim² n **1** [U] the act of directing a weapon, shot, etc.: The hunter **took aim** at the lion. | His aim was very good. **2** [C (**of**)] the desired result of one's efforts; intention or purpose; OBJECTIVE: What is your aim in life? | The project was set up with the aim of helping young unemployed people. | The aim of the meeting was to reach agreement about next year's prices. | long-term/short-term aims | literary aims

aim·less /ˈeɪmləs/ adj often derog without any clear purpose or direction: his aimless life | aimless discussions — ~ly adv — ~ness n [U]

ain't /eɪnt/ nonstandard short for: am not, is not, are not, has not, have not: We ain't coming. | They ain't got it. — see AREN'T (USAGE)

Ain·tree /ˈeɪntriː/ a race course in NW England where an important horse race, the Grand National, takes place each year

air¹ /eər/ n **1** [the+S;U] the mixture of gases which surrounds the Earth and which we breathe: breathing in the fresh morning air | There was a smell of burning leaves in the air. **2** [the+S;U] the sky or the space above the ground: He jumped into the air. | air travel/tickets/travellers | It's quicker by air than by sea. | an air crash/disaster **3** [C (**of**)] the general character or appearance of, or feeling caused by, a person or place: There was an air of excitement at the meeting. | He explained the procedure with the weary air of a man who had explained it many times before. **4** [C] that part of a piece of music that is easily recognized and remembered; tune **5 in the air** infml **a** (of stories, talk, etc.) being passed on from one person to another **b** not fully planned or settled; uncertain: We may be going skiing at Christmas, but it's still all up in the air. **6 on/off the air** broadcasting/not broadcasting: We shall be on the air in five minutes. —see also AIRS, HOT AIR, THIN AIR, **clear the air** (CLEAR³), **walk on air** (WALK¹)

air² v **1** [I;T] to (cause to) become dry in a place that is warm or has plenty of dry air: Leave the clothes out on the washing-line to air. **2** [I;T] to (cause to) become fresh by letting in air; VENTILATE: We aired the room by opening the windows. **3** [T] to make known to others (one's opinions, ideas, complaints, etc.), often in an unwelcome way: He's always airing his views about politics. | an opportunity to **air one's grievances 4** [T] esp. AmE to broadcast on the radio or television: a television interview to be aired this evening —see also AIRING

air·bag /ˈeəbæg‖ˈeər-/ n a large bag in a car which quickly unfolds and fills with air to protect the driver or passenger from hitting the DASHBOARD (=instrument board) in an accident

air·base /ˈeəbeɪs‖ˈeər-/ n a place where military aircraft land and take off

air·bed /ˈeəbed‖ˈeər-/ n a long rubber or plastic bag filled with air and used as a bed or for lying on in water

air·borne /ˈeəbɔːn‖ˈeərbɔːrn/ adj **1** [F] (esp. of aircraft) in the air; in flight: We will be airborne in five minutes. **2** (esp. of seeds) carried about by the air **3** (of soldiers) trained to fight in an area after being moved by aircraft or dropped from aircraft by means of PARACHUTES: airborne troops

air·brake /ˈeəbreɪk‖ˈeər-/ n a BRAKE for stopping a large vehicle, such as a bus or train, that is worked by air under pressure

air·brick /ˈeəbrɪk‖ˈeər-/ n a special brick with holes through it, used to let air pass through a wall

air·bus /ˈeəbʌs‖ˈeər-/ n an aircraft for carrying large numbers of passengers on short flights

air chief mar·shal /ˌ· · ˈ··◀/ n a British airforce rank —see TABLE 3

air com·mo·dore /ˌ· ˈ···◀/ n a British airforce rank —see TABLE 3

air-con·di·tion·ing /ˈ· ·ˌ···/ n [U] the system that uses machines (**air-conditioners**) to control the temperature of the air in a room or building to keep it cool and dry —**-tioned** adj : Our offices are fully air-conditioned.

air·craft /ˈeəkrɑːft‖ˈeərkræft/ n esp. BrE -**craft** a flying machine of any type, with or without an engine: a jet aircraft | The airline has ordered 25 new aircraft. | the aircraft industry —see also ANTIAIRCRAFT, LIGHT AIRCRAFT

aircraft car·ri·er /ˈ·· ˌ···/ n a WARSHIP that carries aircraft and has a large flat surface where they can take off and land

air·craft·man /ˈeəkrɑːftmən‖ˈeərkræft-/ also **air·crafts·man** /-krɑːfts-‖-kræfts-/ n -**men** /mən/ a British airforce rank —see TABLE 3

air·crew /ˈeəkruː‖ˈeər-/ n [C+sing./pl. v] the pilot and others responsible for flying an aircraft, together with those who look after the comfort of the passengers

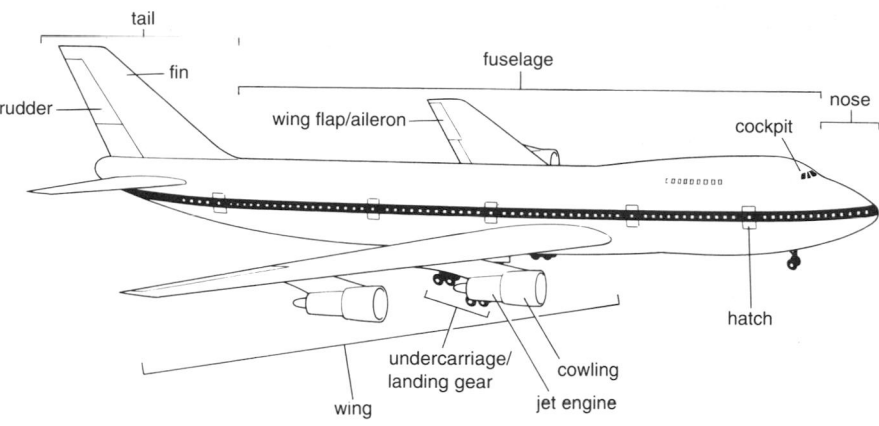

tail

fin

rudder

fuselage

wing flap/aileron

nose

cockpit

hatch

undercarriage/
landing gear

cowling

wing

jet engine

---

air·drop /ˈeədrɒp‖ˈeədrɑːp/ v **-pp-** [T] to deliver (supplies or soldiers) by dropping from an aircraft —**airdrop** n

Aire /eəʳ/ a river flowing through Yorkshire and Humberside to the North Sea

air·fare /ˈeəˌfeəʳ‖ˈeər-/ n the price of a journey by plane

air·field /ˈeəfiːld‖ˈeər-/ ‖ also **aerodrome** BrE — old-fash — n a place where aircraft can land and take off but which may not have any large buildings —compare AIRPORT

air·force /ˈeəfɔːs‖ˈeərfɔːrs/ n [C+sing./pl. v] the branch of a country's military forces that is concerned with attack and defence from the air

Air Force One /ˌ· · ˈ·/ the aircraft used by the American president

Air France /ˌ· ˈ·/ the main French AIRLINE. Like British Airways, Air France flies the Concorde aircraft.

air fresh·en·er /ˈ· ˌ··/ n [C;U] a substance used to make the air in a room smell fresh, sold either in a solid form, or as a liquid in an AEROSOL can

air·gun /ˈeəgʌn‖ˈeər-/ n a gun which uses strong air pressure to fire a bullet

air·head /ˈeəhed‖ˈeər-/ n esp. AmE sl derog a foolish or stupid person: That checkout girl was a real airhead, she couldn't even make change from five dollars.

air·host·ess /ˈeəˌhəʊstɪs‖ˈeər-/ esp. BrE ‖ usu. **stewardess** AmE— n a woman who looks after the comfort of the passengers in an aircraft during flight. Air hostesses are usu. young, and are typically thought of as being tall, attractive, and with a good figure.

air·i·ly /ˈeərɪli/ adv in a light AIRY (2, 3) manner; not seriously

air·ing /ˈeərɪŋ/ n **1** [U] the leaving of clothes, sheets, etc., in the open air or in a warm place to get thoroughly dry: Give the sheets a good airing. **2** [C usu. sing.] the making public of one's opinions, knowledge, ideas, etc., so that they can be freely talked about: We had a meeting and gave the subject a good airing.

airing cup·board /ˈ·· ˌ··/ n BrE a warm cupboard in which clothes, sheets, etc. are kept —see also LINEN CUPBOARD

air·lane /ˈeəleɪn‖ˈeər-/ n a path through the air regularly used by aircraft in flight

air·let·ter /ˈeəˌletəʳ‖ˈeər-/ also **aerogramme**— n a sheet of very thin paper already stamped for posting, on which a letter can be written and which is then folded and stuck at the edges and sent by air without an envelope

air·lift /ˈeəˌlɪft‖ˈeər-/ n an operation by which large numbers of people or large amounts of supplies are carried by aircraft, esp. to or from a place that is difficult to get to —**airlift** v [T (to)] : We airlifted food to the famine areas.

air·line /ˈeəlaɪn‖ˈeər-/ n a business that runs a regular service for carrying passengers and goods by air

air·lin·er /ˈeəˌlaɪnəʳ‖ˈeər-/ n old-fash a large passenger aircraft

air·lock /ˈeəlɒk‖ˈeərlɑːk/ n **1** a BUBBLE in a tube or pipe that prevents the flow of a liquid **2** an enclosed space or room into which or from which air cannot accidentally pass, e.g. in a spacecraft or apparatus for working under water

air·mail /ˈeəmeɪl‖ˈeər-/ n [U] **1** letters, parcels, etc., sent by air —compare SURFACE³ (2) **2** the system of sending things by air: Send it by airmail. —**airmail** adv : How much would it cost to send it airmail?

air·man /ˈeəmən‖ˈeər-/ **airwoman** fem.— n **-men** /mən/ **1** a person of or below NCO rank in an airforce **2** a US airforce rank —see TABLE 3 on page 0000

Air Miles /ˈ· ˌ·/ n [P] **1** tdmk a system of VOUCHERS (1) which are given away in Britain with certain items when one buys them, and which can be exchanged for flights with British Airways at a rate of roughly one voucher for each mile to be travelled **2** the organization which gives out the vouchers and controls their exchange

air·miss /ˈeəˌmɪs‖ˈeər-/ n a situation in which one plane nearly crashes into another one while both are in the air

air·plane /ˈeəpleɪn‖ˈeər-/ AmE ‖ **aeroplane** BrE— n a flying vehicle that has at least one engine; PLANE

air·pock·et /ˈeəˌpɒkɪt‖ˈeərˌpɑː-/ n a downward flow of air in the sky which can cause an aircraft to lose height suddenly

air·port /ˈeəpɔːt‖ˈeərpɔːrt/ n a place where aircraft can land and take off, which is regularly used by paying passengers and has several buildings (for waiting passengers, CUSTOMS, etc.): Heathrow Airport, London | airport security —compare AIRFIELD

air raid /ˈ· ·/ n an attack by military aircraft

alrs /eəz‖eərz/ also **airs and grac·es** /ˌ· · ˈ··/— n [P] derog unnatural manners or actions that are intended to make people think one is more important than one really is (esp. in the phrase **give oneself airs, put on airs**)

air-sea res·cue /ˌ· · ˈ··/ n [C;U] the saving of people in trouble at sea by both aircraft and ships or boats built for the purpose: The air-sea rescue services sent helicopters and lifeboats.

air·ship /ˈeəˌʃɪp‖ˈeər-/ n (esp. formerly) a large aircraft without wings, containing gas to make it lighter than air and an engine to make it move

air·sick /ˈeəˌsɪk‖ˈeər-/ adj sick because of the movement of an aircraft — **~ness** n [U]

air·space /ˈeəspeɪs‖ˈeər-/ n [U] the air or sky above a particular country, regarded as the property of that country: They claimed that foreign planes had entered Soviet airspace without permission.

air·speed /ˈeəspiːd‖ˈeər-/ n [S;U] the speed at which an aircraft travels through the air

air·strip /ˈeəˌstrɪp‖ˈeər-/ n a stretch of land that can be used by aircraft to take off and land, esp. in war or time of trouble —compare RUNWAY

air ter·mi·nal /ˈ· ˌ···/ *n* the building in which passengers come together before getting on board an aircraft or from which they leave at the end of their flight. It may be at the airport, or some distance away.

air·tight /ˈeətaɪt‖ˈeər-/ *adj* not allowing air to pass in or out: *airtight containers*

air·time /ˈeətaɪm‖ˈeər-/ *n* [U] the amount of time given to a record, subject, political party, etc. on the radio or television: *Her new single hasn't had much airtime.* | *Some of the smaller parties are trying to buy airtime.*

air-to-air /ˌ· · ˈ·◂/ *adj* [A] (of a weapon) intended to be fired from one aircraft in flight at another: *air-to-air missiles*

air traf·fic con·trol·ler /ˌ· ˈ·· ·ˌ··/ *n* also **air controller** /ˈ·· ·ˌ··/— a person at an airport who gives radio instructions to pilots about aircraft movement: *A strike by French air traffic controllers has led to the cancellation of nearly all flights.*

air vice-mar·shal /ˌ· · ˈ···◂/ *n* a British airforce rank —see TABLE 3

air·waves /ˈeəweɪvz‖ˈeər-/ *n* [*the* +P] the frequencies (FREQUENCY (3)) at which radio signals are broadcast, taken together: *That's not the sort of material you expect to hear coming over the airwaves.*

air·way /ˈeəweɪ‖ˈeər-/ *n* (*usu. cap. as part of a name*) an AIRLINE: *British Airways*

air·wom·an /ˈeəˌwʊmən‖ˈeər-/ *n* **-women** /ˌwɪmɪn/ a female AIRMAN

air·wor·thy /ˈeəˌwɜːði‖ˈeərˌwɜːrði/ *adj* (of an aircraft) in proper and safe working condition —**-thiness** *n* [U] : *a certificate of airworthiness*

air·y /ˈeəri/ *adj* **1** open to the fresh air: *The large window makes the room seem airy.* **2** also **airy-fair·y** /ˌ·· ˈ··◂/— *derog BrE* seeming not to be related to real facts or conditions; impractical: *She has these airy-fairy notions about going back to nature and growing all her own food.* **3** cheerful; not serious; NONCHALANT: *an airy smile*

aisle /aɪl/ *n* **1** a passage, usually one of two, leading through the length of a church and divided from the NAVE (=the central part) by a row of PILLARS —see picture at CHURCH **2** a narrow passage between rows of seats, shelves, etc., e.g. in a theatre, plane, or large shop —see picture at THEATRE —see also **roll in the aisles** (ROLL¹) **3** go/walk up the aisle *infml* to get married: *She was looking forward to the day when she would walk up the aisle.*

aitch /eɪtʃ/ *n* **1** a way of spelling the name of the letter *H, h* **2** drop one's aitches not to sound the letter *h* in one's speech, for example by saying *'ome* for *home*. In Britain, some people think that people who drop their aitches are from a low social class and uneducated.

a·jar /əˈdʒɑːʳ/ *adj, adv* [F] (of a door) not quite closed; slightly open

A·jax /ˈeɪdʒæks/ *n* [U] *tdmk* a cleaning substance made by Colgate-Palmolive Limited, used to remove dirt from esp. floors

AK *written abbrev. for:* ALASKA

ak·a /ˈækə, ˌeɪ keɪ ˈeɪ/ also known as; used to introduce another name that someone has: *John Wayne, aka "The Duke"*

Ak·a·bu·si /ˌækəˈbuːsi/, **Kriss** /krɪs/ (1958–) a British runner and captain of the British ATHLETICS team known for his lively personality and his CHRISTIAN faith

A·ke·la /ɑːˈkeɪlə/ *n* the title of one of the adult leaders of the Cub Scouts or Wolf Cubs in the Scout organization

Ak·i·hi·to /ˌækɪˈhiːtəʊ‖ˌɑː-/ (1933–) the EMPEROR of Japan, the son of the Emperor Hirohito

a·kim·bo /əˈkɪmbəʊ/ *adj, adv* [F] (of the arms) bent at the elbows and with hands on the HIPs; people stand with their arms akimbo when they are facing other people bravely or threateningly

a·kin /əˈkɪn/ *adj* [F (**to**)] having the same appearance, character, or nature; similar: *His position in the Soviet system is roughly akin to that of the US President's public relations adviser.*

AL *written abbrev. for:* ALABAMA

à la /ˈæ lə, ˈɑː lɑː/ *prep infml* in the manner of; like: *spy stories à la James Bond* | *She went about it à la Thatcher, putting her views very forcefully.*

Al·a·ba·ma /ˌæləˈbæmə◂/ *written abbrev.* **AL** a state in the south of the US, where the movement to win rights for black people began. —see also DEEP SOUTH and see colour map on pages 1374-5

al·a·bas·ter /ˈæləbɑːstəʳ‖-bæ-/ *n* [U] a transparent soft mainly white stone: *an alabaster vase* | (fig.) *her alabaster skin*

à la carte /ˌæ lə ˈkɑːt, ˌɑː lɑː-‖-ˌɑːrt/ *adj, adv* (of food in a restaurant) according to a list (MENU) where each dish has its own separate price —compare TABLE D'HOTE

a·lack /əˈlæk/ *interj old use* (a cry expressing sorrow)

a·lac·ri·ty /əˈlækrɪti/ *n* [U] *fml* quick and willing readiness: *She accepted our offer with alacrity.*

Aladdin

A·lad·din /əˈlædɪn/ a character in a story from the *Arabian Nights* who is employed by a MAGICIAN to obtain a lamp from an underground cave full of jewels and wonderful things. When Aladdin finds the lamp and rubs it, a GENIE appears and says that it will give Aladdin anything he wants. Aladdin keeps the lamp and makes himself rich until the magician takes possession of it from Aladdin's wife by pretending to be a MERCHANT (=a buyer and seller of goods) and offering "new lamps for old". Aladdin finally finds him, kills him, and regains the lamp. The story of Aladdin is often told in PANTOMIMEs in Britain. —see also ARABIAN NIGHTS

Aladdin's Cave

Aladdin's Cave /·ˌ·· ˈ·/ *n* a place filled with strange, lovely things: *an Aladdin's Cave of unusual ideas and gifts for the home*

Aladdin's lamp /·ˌ·· ˈ·/ *n* a magic lamp with a GENIE in it used by Aladdin

à la king /·· ˈ·/ *adj AmE* cooked in cream with green pepper and PIMENTOs: *chicken à la king*

Al·a·mein /ˈæləmeɪn/ also **El Alamein**— a place in N Africa where the British won an important battle against the Germans in the Second World War. The British side was led by Field-Marshal Montgomery, known as Monty.

Al·a·mo /ˈæləməʊ/ [*the*] an army building in San Antonio in Texas famous in American history because it was defended in 1836 against several THOUSAND Mexicans by only about 180 men led by Davy Crockett. The men all died, but their courage caused others to defeat the Mexicans. The phrase "Remember the Alamo!" is sometimes used to encourage people to continue doing something very difficult. —see also MEXICAN WAR

à la mode /ˌæ lə ˈməʊd, ˌɑː lɑː-/ *adj, adv* **1** [F] according to the latest fashion **2** [after *n*] *AmE* served with ice cream: *apple pie à la mode*

Al·a·mo·gor·do /ˌæləmə'gɔːdəʊ‖-'gɔːr-/ a town in the US state of New Mexico, near where the first test of an ATOMIC bomb was made

Al-A·non /ˌæl ə'nɒn‖-'nɑːn/ a society for people who believe they have been badly influenced by a relationship with an alcoholic, usually a member of their family. They meet often to try to change their behaviour —compare ALCOHOLICS ANONYMOUS

a·larm¹ /ə'lɑːm‖-ɑːrm/ n 1 [U] sudden fear and anxiety, esp. when caused by the possibility of danger: *There is no cause for alarm.* | *The news of the radiation leak caused widespread public alarm.*　2 [C] a warning of danger, given e.g. by ringing a bell or shouting: *I gave/raised the alarm as soon as I saw the smoke.*　3 [C] any apparatus, such as a bell, noise, or flag, by which a warning is given: *a burglar alarm* | *a fire alarm*　4 [C] an alarm clock —see also FALSE ALARM

alarm² v [T] to fill with fear, anxiety, and worry about the future: *The government is alarmed by the dramatic increase in violent crime.* | *an alarming increase in the number of heroin addicts* | *The problem is growing at an alarming rate.* — ~ingly adv: *Unemployment has risen alarmingly.*

alarm clock /·'· ·/ also **alarm**— n a clock that can be set to make a noise at any particular time to wake up someone who is asleep: *What time shall I set the alarm (clock) for?* —compare RADIO ALARM, and see picture at CLOCK

a·larm·ist /ə'lɑːmɪst‖ə'lɑːr-/ n derog a person who always expects danger, often without good reason, and alarms other people with fears and warnings —**alarmist** adj: *Don't be so alarmist — it's all under control.* —**ism** n [U]

a·las /ə'læs/ interj lit (a cry expressing sorrow or fear) —see also **alas, poor Yorick** (YORICK)

A·las·ka /ə'læskə/ written abbrev. **AK** the largest state in the US, separated from the rest of the country by Canada —see also BAKED ALASKA - **-kan** adj

Al·ba·ni·a /æl'beɪniə/ a country in Europe on the Adriatic Sea; capital Tirana; population 3,202,000 (1989) — **Albanian** adj

Al·ba·ni·an /æl'beɪniən/ n 1 [C] a person who comes from or whose parents come from Albania　2 [U] the language spoken in Albania

Al·ba·ny /'ɔːlbəni/ the capital city of the state of New York in the US

al·ba·tross /'ælbətrɒs‖-trɔːs, -trɑːs/ n **-trosses** or **-tross**　1 a large strong mostly white seabird that can fly long distances　2 **an albatross around/about one's neck** a continuous reminder that one has done something wrong (from Samuel Taylor Coleridge's poem *The Rime of the Ancient Mariner*, in which a sailor kills an albatross that is then hung around his neck to show that he has brought bad luck to the ship): *His remark has become a political albatross around his neck.* | *The new tax was proving to be an electoral albatross.*

Al·bee /'ælbiː/ , **Edward** (1928–) an American writer of plays, known esp. for the plays *Zoo Story* and *Who's Afraid of Virginia Woolf?*

al·be·it /ɔːl'biːɪt/ conj fml even though; although: *It was a very important, albeit small, mistake.* | *Attitudes to this question are changing, albeit slowly.*

Al·bert /'ælbət‖-bərt/ , **Prince** (1819–1861) the husband of Queen Victoria of Britain, known for his interest in the arts, and in social and industrial advancement

Al·ber·ta /æl'bɜːtə‖-ɜːr-/ a PROVINCE in W Canada

Albert Dock /ˌ·· '·/ a DOCK (1) in Liverpool, known for the Victorian WAREHOUSES built on it, now popular for its shops and restaurants

Albert Hall /ˌ·· '·/ also **Royal Albert Hall** fml— [the] a very large concert hall in London known esp. for its PROMENADE CONCERTS —see colour map on page 817

al·bi·no /æl'biːnəʊ‖æl'baɪ-/ n **-nos** a person or animal with a pale milky skin, very light hair, and eyes that are pink because of a lack of colouring matter

Al·bi·on /'ælbiən/ old use, poet England or Great Britain

al·bum /'ælbəm/ n 1 a book used for collecting photographs, stamps, etc.　2 an LP (=a long-playing RECORD)

al·bu·men /'ælbjʊmɪn‖æl'bjuː-/ n [U] the white or colourless part of an egg

Al·bu·quer·que /'ælbəkɜːki‖-ɜːr-/ the largest city in the state of New Mexico, US

Al·ca·traz /'ælkətræz/ a rocky island off San Francisco in California, US, which was used as a prison until 1963. The prison was known for its hard way of life and for being almost impossible to escape from.

al·che·my /'ælkəmi/ n [U] (esp. in the Middle Ages) the science concerned with finding a way to turn all metals into gold and finding a medicine to cure all diseases —**mist** n

Al·cock and Brown /ˌɔːlkɒk ənd 'braʊn‖-kɑːk-/ , **Sir John William** and **Sir Ar·thur Whit·ten** /'ɑːθə 'wɪtn‖ 'ɑːrθər-/ (1892–1919 and 1886–1948) the British pilot and NAVIGATOR respectively of the first aircraft to fly across the Atlantic without stopping, in 1919

al·co·hol /'ælkəhɒl‖-hɔːl/ n 1 [U] the pure colourless liquid present in drinks that can make one drunk, such as wine, beer, and SPIRITS　2 [U] drinks containing this: *The doctor told me to keep off alcohol.*　3 [C;U] any of a class of chemical substances of which the alcohol in wine is one

alcohol a·buse /'··· ·ˌ·/ n [U] tech the regular drinking of too much alcohol, so that it is harmful to a person's health

alcohol-free /ˌ··· '·◂/ adj (of a drink such as beer or wine) with all the alcohol removed. Alcohol-free drinks have become popular since the laws against DRINK-DRIVING were made firmer.

al·co·hol·ic¹ /ˌælkə'hɒlɪk◂‖-'hɔː-/ adj 1 containing alcohol: *alcoholic beverages/drinks* —opposite **non-alcoholic**　2 of or caused by the drinking of alcohol: *alcoholic self-pity* — ~**ally** /kli/ adv

alcoholic² n a person who is unable to stop the habit of drinking too much alcohol, esp. one whose health is damaged because of this —compare DRUNKARD

Alcoholics A·non·y·mous /ˌ····· ·'····/ also **AA** abbrev. an organization for alcoholics who want to cure themselves, and meet regularly to help each other —compare AL-ANON

al·co·hol·is·m /'ælkəhɒlɪzəm‖-hɔː-/ n [U] the diseased condition caused by the continued and habitual drinking of too much alcohol

Al·cott /'ɔːlkət‖-kɑːt/ , **Lou·i·sa May** /luˈiːzə 'meɪ/ (1832–88) an American writer whose books for children include *Little Women* and *Good Wives*

al·cove /'ælkəʊv/ n a small partly enclosed space in a room, in a garden wall, etc.; RECESS: *seats in the alcove*

Alde·burgh /'ɔːldbərə‖-bɜːrəʊ/ a town on the Suffolk coast of England where a music FESTIVAL is held every summer

al den·te /æl 'denti, -teɪ/ adj (of PASTA and vegetables) cooked just enough to be still firm when bitten

al·der·man /'ɔːldəmən‖-dər-/ n **-men** /mən/　1 (in Britain before 1974) a member of a town, city, or COUNTY council who was chosen by the elected members　2 (esp. in the US) a local government officer having various duties — ~**ic** /ˌɔːldə'mænɪk◂‖-ər-/ adj

Al·der·grove Air·port /ˌɔːldəgrəʊv 'eəpɔːt‖-dərgrəʊv 'eərpɔːrt/ the international airport in Belfast in Northern Ireland

Al·der·mas·ton /'ɔːldəˌmɑːstən‖-dərˌmæs-/ a village in Berkshire, England, which is known as a place near where RESEARCH is carried out into atomic weapons. People think of Aldermaston esp. in connection with the protest marches by CND in the 1950s and 60s, when many people walked from London to Aldermaston to show their strong feelings against the research.

Al·der·ney¹ /'ɔːldəni‖-dər-/ n a breed of cow kept for milk: *Alderney cattle*

Alderney² one of the islands in the English Channel, between England and France

Al·der·shot /'ɔːldəʃɒt‖-dərʃɑːt/ a town in Hampshire, S England known for its long association with the army

Al·diss /'ɔːldɪs/ , **Bri·an** /'braɪən/ (1925–) a British writer of SCIENCE FICTION

ale /eɪl/ n [U] any of several types of beer, esp. a kind that is particularly bitter, strong, and heavy —see also LIGHT ALE, REAL ALE

al·eck /'ælɪk/ n see SMART ALECK

ale·house /ˈeɪlhaʊs/ n -houses /ˌhaʊzᵻz/ old use a public drinking place

a·lert¹ /əˈlɜːt‖-ɜːrt/ adj 1 [(to)] watchful and ready to deal with danger; VIGILANT: alert to every possible danger 2 apprec quick to see and act; PERCEPTIVE: an alert mind — ~ly adv — ~ness n [U]

alert² n 1 a warning to be ready for danger: to sound the alert | a nuclear alert —opposite all clear; see also RED ALERT 2 on (the) alert (for) in a state of being ready to deal with danger, esp. after a warning

alert³ v [T (to)] to make (someone) watchful and ready for possible danger: a campaign to alert the public to the dangers of smoking

A·leu·tian Is·lands /əˈluːʃən ˌaɪləndz/ a group of islands off the coast of Alaska

A lev·el /ˈeɪ ˌlevəl/ also **advanced level**— n 1 [U] the higher standard of examination in the British education system, necessary for entrance to a university 2 [C] an examination of this standard in a particular subject, usually taken at the age of 18. Students usually take 3 or 4 A levels: She took A levels in physics, chemistry, and mathematics. –compare O LEVEL, GCSE see also extra information on page 408

ale·wife /ˈeɪlwaɪf/ -**wives** /waɪvz/ n a sea fish, related to the HERRING, which is found along the Atlantic coast of N America and used for food, BAIT, and FERTILIZER

Al·ex·an·der tech·nique /ˌælɪgˈzɑːndə tekˌniːk‖-ˈzændər-/ [the] a system of sitting, standing, and moving in a natural way, which is believed to help to improve general health or cure particular problems caused by using one's body carelessly: She teaches the Alexander technique.

Alexander the Great /ˌ··ˌ·· ˈ·/ (356–323 BC) the King of Macedonia who ruled over much of Asia and founded (FOUND (2)) Alexandria

Al·ex·an·dra Pal·ace /ˌælɪgzɑːndrə ˈpælᵻs‖-zæn-/ a large building in N London used for concerts since 1873, and famous because it was used as STUDIOs by the BBC

Al·ex·an·dri·a /ˌælɪgˈzɑːndriə‖-ˈzæn-/ a city and port in Egypt, on the Mediterranean coast, famous in the past as a place of great learning and for its library

ALF /ˌeɪ el ˈef/ abbrev. for: ANIMAL LIBERATION FRONT

al·fal·fa /ælˈfælfə/ n [U] esp. AmE a plant of the PEA family grown for animal food. The young undeveloped plants (**alfalfa sprouts**) are also eaten by people, esp. in SALADS

Al·fa Ro·me·o /ˌælfə rəʊˈmeɪəʊ/ n tdmk a type of Italian car which is fashionable and can go very fast

Al·fred the Great /ˌælfrᵻd θə ˈgreɪt/ (849–899) a king of Wessex, an area of southern England at that time, who fought several wars against the Danes. When British people think about King Alfred, they usually think about the well-known story in which he burnt some cakes in a woman's house where he was hiding.

al·fres·co /ælˈfreskəʊ/ adj, adv in the open air: We eat alfresco in summer. | an alfresco theatrical performance

al·gae /ˈældʒiː/ n [P] very simple, usu. very small plants that live in or near water

Al·garve /ælˈgɑːv‖ɑːlˈgɑːrvə/ [the] an area of southern Portugal which is popular for holidays

al·ge·bra /ˈældʒᵻbrə/ n [U] a branch of MATHEMATICS in which signs and letters are used to represent numbers and values — ~ic(al) /ˌældʒᵻˈbreɪ-ɪk(əl)/ adj — ~ically /kli/ adv

Al·ger /ˈældzəʳ/—, **Ho·ra·ti·o** /həˈreɪʃiəʊ/ (1832–99) an American writer, many of whose stories are about poor boys who became rich and successful men through hard work and taking advantage of lucky situations

Al·ge·ri·a /ælˈdʒɪəriə/ an oil producing country in NW Africa; capital Algiers; population 24,597,000 (1989) – **Algerian** adj, n

Al·giers /ælˈdʒɪəz‖-ɪərz/ the capital city of Algeria, an ancient Mediterranean port

ALGOL /ˈælgɒl‖-gɑːl/ n tech [U] a computer language: a program written in ALGOL | an ALGOL program

Al·gon·quin Round Ta·ble /ælˌgɒŋkwɪn raʊnd ˈteɪbəl‖-ˌgɑːŋ-/ [the] the place in New York's Algonquin Hotel where many writers met and exchanged ideas from the 1920s to the 1940s

al·go·rith·m /ˈælgərɪðəm/ n tech a list of instructions, esp. to a computer, which are carried out in a fixed order to find the answer to a question, calculate, etc. — ~ic /ˌælgəˈrɪðmɪk◂/ adj

Al·ham·bra /ælˈhæmbrə/ a palace near Granada in Spain, built between 1238 and 1358 for MUSLIM kings and considered to be a fine example of the Moorish (MOOR) style of building

A·li /ɑːˈli/, **Muhammad** (1942–) an American BOXER, born **Cassius Clay**, who won the world HEAVYWEIGHT title in 1964, 1974, and 1978. He was known esp. for his self-confidence, shown by the phrase "I am the greatest", which he often used.

Muhammad Ali

a·li·as¹ /ˈeɪliəs/ adv (esp. of a criminal) also known as; also called: Edward Ball alias John Smith

alias² n aliases a name other than one's usual or officially recognized name, used esp. by a criminal; a false name: He carried out a series of frauds using/under several different aliases.

A·li Ba·ba /ˌæli ˈbɑːbɑː‖ˌɑː-/ a character in a story from the Arabian Nights with the title of "Ali Baba and the Forty Thieves". Ali Baba sees 40 robbers enter a hidden cave by saying the words "Open Sesame!" He goes into the cave and takes some of the gold the robbers kept there. When the robbers discover that Ali Baba knows their secret, they decide to kill him and hide in 40 large, oil JARS which are delivered to Ali Baba's house, but his servant discovers the trick and pours boiling oil on them, killing them all. —see also ARABIAN NIGHTS, ALADDIN, SINDBAD

al·i·bi /ˈælᵻbaɪ/ n an argument or proof that a person who has been charged with a crime was in another place when the crime was done and that he/she therefore could not have done it: Jim's girlfriend gave him a **cast-iron** (=very strong) **alibi** by saying that he was with her on the night of the robbery. | (fig.) What's your alibi (=excuse) for being late this time?

Al·ice in Won·der·land /ˌælᵻs ɪn ˈwʌndələænd‖-dər-/ also **Alice's Ad·ven·tures in Won·der·land**— /ˌ···ˌ·· ˈ···/ a story by Lewis Carroll, in which a little girl called Alice falls down a rabbit hole and comes to a magical land where many strange animals and people appear and funny things happen. The expression **Alice-in-Wonderland** is sometimes used to describe something strange or unreal, as if in a dream: Medical practice has taken on an Alice-in-Wonderland quality: first the treatment, then the diagnosis. —see colour picture on page 619

Alice Springs /ˌælᵻs ˈsprɪŋz/ a town in Australia's Northern Territory, popular with tourists

a·li·en¹ /ˈeɪliən/ adj 1 belonging to another country or race; foreign: alien religious customs | an alien culture 2 [(to)] very different in nature or character, esp. so different as to cause dislike or opposition: Their ideas are quite alien to our way of thinking. | an alien concept

alien² n 1 (in films and stories) a creature from another world 2 a foreigner who has not become a citizen of the country where he/she is living —compare CITIZEN¹ (2), NATIONAL², SUBJECT¹ (5)

a·li·en·ate /ˈeɪliəneɪt/ v [T (from)] 1 to make (someone) become unfriendly, unsympathetic, or unwilling to give support: By adopting this policy, they risk alienating many of their supporters. 2 law to change who owns (land, property, etc.) —see also INALIENABLE

a·li·en·a·tion /ˌeɪliəˈneɪʃən/ n [U (from)] 1 separation from a person with whom one was formerly friendly 2 a feeling of not belonging to or being part of one's surroundings: The boring and repetitive nature of manufacturing jobs has led to the alienation of many workers.

a·light¹ /əˈlaɪt/ v alighted or alit /əˈlɪt/— [I (from, on)] fml to get off or down from something, esp. at the end of a journey; come down from above: The bird alighted on a branch. | Passengers should not alight from the train until it has stopped.

alight on/upon sthg. *phr v* [T] *fml becoming rare* to find or see unexpectedly; HAPPEN **on**

alight² *adj* [F] **1** on fire; in flames: *The dry leaves* **caught alight.** (=begin to burn) | *She poured kerosene over the rubbish and then* **set it alight.** (=lit it) **2** [(with)] having the lights on; lit up: *Every window was alight.* | (fig.) *eyes alight with happiness*

a·lign /ə'laɪn/ *v* [T] to bring, form, or arrange into a line or set of lines: *to align the wheels of a car*
align sbdy./sthg. **with** sbdy./sthg. *phr v* [T] **1** to cause to come into the same line as: *to align a picture with one directly opposite it* **2** to bring (oneself) into agreement or partnership with: *They aligned themselves with the opponents of the government.* | *They are closely aligned with the opponents of the government.* —see also NON-ALIGNED

a·lign·ment /ə'laɪnmənt/ *n* **1** [U] the state of being brought or arranged into a line or set of lines: *The wheels are* **out of alignment** *(with each other) — they need to be brought back into alignment.* **2** [U] (of people or countries with the same aims, ideas, etc.) the act of forming into groups, e.g. in order to fight a war —opposite **nonalignment** **3** [C] a group formed in this way: *a new alignment of left-wing parties*

a·like /ə'laɪk/ *adj, adv* [F] the same or similar; like one another: *The two brothers are very much alike.* | *She treats all her children alike.* | *a training course for employed and unemployed alike* (=for both equally)

al·i·men·ta·ry ca·nal /ˌælɪˈmentəri kəˈnæl/ *n* the tubelike passage leading from the mouth to the stomach and onward, in which food passes from the mouth and is digested (DIGEST¹)

al·i·mo·ny /ˈælɪməni‖-məʊni/ *n* [U] money that a man or woman has been ordered to pay regularly to his/her former partner after they have been legally separated or divorced (DIVORCE). It is usu. the man who is ordered to pay alimony to the woman to help her support their children until they are old enough to leave home. —compare PALIMONY

a·lit /ə'lɪt/ *past tense & participle of* ALIGHT¹

a·live /ə'laɪv/ *adj* [F] **1** [*no comp.*] having life; not dead; living: *Are your grandparents still alive?* | *He's the only man alive who could do it.* | (fig.) *local traditions that are still alive and well in rural regions* | (fig.) *The argument was kept alive by the politicians.* **2** full of life; active: *Although he's old, he's still very much alive.* | *The meeting really* **came alive** (=became lively) *when she stood up to make her speech.* **3** [(with)] covered with or full of living things: *The dead tree is alive with insects.* **4** [+to] having full knowledge of; AWARE: *He was alive to the dangers of the work.* **5** alive and kicking alive and very active **6** alive and well and living in… a phrase used, esp. in newspapers, when saying that someone who was believed dead is in fact still alive: *She is reported to be alive and well and living in South America.*

al·ka·li /ˈælkəlaɪ/ *n -lis or -lies* [C;U] *tech* a substance that forms a chemical salt when combined with an acid —compare ACID¹ (1) —**line** *adj*

Al·ka-Sel·tzer /ˌælkə ˈseltsəᵊ‖ˈælkə seltsəᵊ/ *tdmk* a medicine which is added to water to make a FIZZY drink and is used to treat stomach problems such as those caused by eating or drinking too much

all /ɔːl/ *determiner, predeterminer* **1** the complete amount or quantity of; the whole of: *He ate all his food.* | *He ate it all.* | *We walked all the way.* | *We worked hard all last year.* | *Not all water is suitable for drinking.* | *They danced all night.* (compare *They danced every night.*) | *She's on the telephone all the time.* (=very often) | *Every one of: All these questions must be answered.* | *Answer them all.* | *They must all be answered.* | *All children like toys.* | *We bought all kinds of things.* | *Ten students took the exam and they all passed.* | *She was,* **by all accounts** (=everyone says so) *an extraordinary woman.* **3** the greatest possible amount of: *The doctor came with all speed.* | *I must tell you, in all honesty, that I don't agree.* **4** influenced or controlled as if by (the stated body organ): *He was* **all ears** (=he listened very carefully) *as she recounted the strange story.* | *I can't play the piano today; I seem to be* **all thumbs.** **5 all in: a** *infml* very tired: *I felt all in by the end of the day.* **b** with everything included: *I sold the car, together with the radio and some spare parts, for £2000 all in.* | *an* **all-in** *price of £2000* — see also ALL-IN WRESTLING **6 all out** *infml* using all

possible strength and effort: *We* **went all out/made an all-out effort** *to finish the job by Christmas.* —see also ALL-PURPOSE, ALL-STAR, ALL-TIME, **all fours** (FOUR), **of all people** (PEOPLE¹), **(all) well and good** (WELL¹)

all² *adv* **1** [+adj|adv|prep] altogether; completely; wholly: *She sat all alone.* | *The old lady gets all confused when she has a lot of visitors.* | *I am* **all in favour of/all for** *your suggestion.* | *They were dressed all in black.* | *The programme was all about the dangers of smoking.* **2** (after numbers) for each side: *The match ended in a draw, with the score three all.* **3 all along** *infml* all the time from the beginning: *I suspected all along that he was lying.* **4 all at once** suddenly and unexpectedly **5 all but** almost; nearly: *It's all but impossible.* | *an all but impossible task* **6 all over: a** everywhere on an object or surface: *There was mud all over the floor.* | *Paint it green all over!* **b** everywhere in a place: *He looked all over for the lost book.* | *We travelled all over India.* **c** finished: *The referee has blown his whistle, and it's all over!* (=the game has finished) **d** *infml* very like; thoroughly typical: *He's always late; that's Billy all over.* **7 all the** (with COMPARATIVE adjectives and adverbs) by so much: *If we get help the work will be finished all the sooner.* | *The rise in prices is all the more serious because we are not selling enough goods abroad.* **8 all the same** *infml* even so; in any case: *She told me she hadn't enjoyed the film, but I decided to go and see it all the same.* **9 all the same to** *infml* not making any difference or causing any worry to: *It's all the same to me whether you stay or go.* | *If it's all the same to you, I'll turn the radio off.* (=Do you mind if I turn it off?) **10 all told** counting everyone; all together: *There are 48 members all told.* **11 all too** very; much more than is desirable: *These scenes of violence are all too familiar.* **12 all up (with)** *infml* at an end; ruined **13 not all that** *infml* not very: *I'm not all that hungry.* | *It's not as cold as all that.* **14 (not) all there** *infml* (not) clever or healthy in the mind: *I don't think he's quite all there.* —see also ALL CLEAR, ALL-POWERFUL, ALL RIGHT, ALL ROUND, ALL-ROUND

all³ *pron* **1** everyone or everything; the whole number, quantity, or amount: *I brought all of them.* | *He gave all he had.* | *We invited 100 people but not all of them came.* | *It'll cost all of* (=at least) *£5000.* | *They ate the whole fish; bones, tail,* **and all.** | *It's easy to put the fence up — all you need is a hammer and some nails.* **2 all and sundry** all types of people: *They've invited all and sundry to the wedding.* **3 all for one and one for all** *saying* we must all support each other and act together **4 all in all** considering everything; on the whole; generally: *All in all we had a good time.* **5 all one can do (not) to** *infml* very difficult (not) to: *It was all he could do not to cry.* **6 (not) at all** (*in questions and negatives*) (not) in any way: *I don't agree with you at all.* | *It was late, but they were not at all tired.* | *He's not looking at all well.* (=he looks ill) | *The government has done nothing at all to deal with the problem.* | *Is it at all possible that you have made a mistake?* —see also for all (FOR), in all (IN), not at all (NOT), once (and) for all (ONCE)

▷ USAGE 1 You can use **all** or **all of** before nouns with a determiner (such as *the, those, his*): **All (of)** *the students are coming to the party* (=the students we are talking about). **All**, not **all of** is used before nouns without a determiner: **All** *students hate exams.* (=students in general) 2 **All of** is used before personal pronouns: *I'd like* **all of** *you to come.* But you can put **all** after the pronoun: *They* **all** *like parties.* | *I'd like you* **all** *to come.* 3 **All** is singular with uncountable nouns: **All (of)** *the money is spent.* It is plural with plural nouns: **All (of)** *the people have gone.*◁

all⁴ *n* **one's all** *esp. lit* everything one possesses or considers valuable: *They gave their all in the struggle for freedom.*

all- see WORD FORMATION

Al·lah /ˈælə/ (the Muslim name for) God

all-A·mer·i·can¹ /ˌˌ ·¹····◄/ *adj* **1** having those qualities thought to be admired by Americans. Most British people have an idea of the all-American man or woman as being young, attractive, healthy, and rich, and very keen to be successful, but also insincere, and not very clever. Many Americans, though, see the all-American man or woman as usu. middle-class, white, and as representing American values that have been passed down from the past to the present: *a clean-cut all-American boy* | *an all-*

American family, cheerful and friendly **2** representing the best in American sports, esp. in university: *an All-American player out of UCLA*

All-American² *n* a player who has been chosen as one of the best in his or her sport in university: *He made All-American last year in football.*

Al·lan-a-Dale /ˌælən ə ˈdeɪl/ one of Robin Hood's companions and a musician —see ROBIN HOOD

all-a·round /ˌ· ·ˈ·◂/ *adj AmE for* ALL-ROUND

al·lay /əˈleɪ/ *v* [T] *fml* to make (fear, anger, doubt, etc.) less strong; calm; reduce in strength or severity: *I hope this statement will allay the public's fears.*

All Blacks /ˌ· ˈ·◂/ *n* [*the* + P] a New Zealand RUGBY UNION team

All-Bran /ˈ· ·/ *n tdmk* [U] a breakfast food which contains a lot of BRAN and is eaten with milk

all clear /ˌ· ˈ·/ *n* [*the*] **1** a signal (such as a whistle or loud cry) that danger is past: *to sound the all clear* —opposite alert **2** official permission for an intended action; GO-AHEAD: *We're ready to start the building work, and we're just waiting for the all clear from the council.*

all-com·ers /ˌɔːl ˈkʌməz‖-ˈərz/ *n* [P] anyone who arrives and wishes to compete: *He fiercely defended his right to speak out against all-comers.*

al·le·ga·tion /ˌælɪˈɡeɪʃən/ *n fml* a statement, which is not supported by proof, that someone has done something bad or criminal: *allegations of serious misconduct by government officials* | *If the allegations against him prove correct/prove to be well-founded, he will lose his job.*

al·lege /əˈledʒ/ *v* [T] *fml* to state or declare without proof or before finding proof: [+(*that*)] *The newspapers allege that the police shot the suspect without warning.* | *This is what they allege, but they are unlikely to be able to prove it.* [+*obj+to-v*] *He is alleged to have passed on secret information to a newspaper.* | *an alleged thief* | *under investigation for alleged fraud* —**allegedly** /əˈledʒɪdli/ *adv* : *He was allegedly involved in the great jewel robbery.* (=according to what is alleged)

Al·le·ghen·y Moun·tains /ˌælɪˌɡeɪni ˈmaʊntᵻnz/ also **Alleghenies** /ˌælɪˈɡeɪniz/ a range of mountains, part of the Appalachian range, which runs from Virginia to Pennsylvania in the US

al·le·giance /əˈliːdʒəns/ *n* [C;U (to)] loyalty, faith, and dutiful support to a leader, country, idea, etc.: *to swear allegiance to the Queen* | *His allegiances are divided.* | *Their marketing manager switched allegiance from the company to their main competitor.* —see also PLEDGE OF ALLEGIANCE

al·le·go·ry /ˈælɡəri‖-ɡɔːri/ *n* [C;U] (the style of) a story, poem, painting, etc., in which the characters and actions represent general truths, good and bad qualities, etc. —**gorical** /ˌælɪˈɡɒrɪkəl‖-ˈɡɔː-, -ˈɡɑː-/ *adj* —**gorically** /kli/ *adv*

al·le·gro /əˈleɡrəʊ, əˈleɪ-/ *n, adv, adj* -**gros** (a piece of music) played fast and with plenty of life

al·le·lu·ia /ˌælɪˈluːjə/ *n, interj* HALLELUJA

all-em·brac·ing /ˌ· ·ˈ···◂/ *adj* including everything or everyone: *Her speech was all-embracing—it covered every section of the community and every one of their concerns.*

Al·len /ˈælən/, **Woody** (1935–) an American COMIC actor and maker of humorous films, whose films include *Annie Hall*, *Manhattan*, and *Hannah and her Sisters* —see colour picture on page 553

Allende /aɪˈendi, -deɪ‖ɑːˈjen-/ , **Sal·va·dor** /ˈsælvədɔːʳ/ (1908–73) a Chilean COMMUNIST politician who was elected president of his country in 1970. He was killed when the army; supported by trees or bushes **4** a long brought down his government.

All-En·gland Club /ˌ· ˈ··· ˌ·/ [*the*] the All-England Lawn Tennis and Croquet Club in Wimbledon, London, where the famous Wimbledon grass court tennis competition is played every year

Al·len screw /ˈælən skruː/ *n* a screw with a six-sided hole in the top. An Allen screw is turned with an **Allen wrench**, which is an L-shaped bar of metal with six sides.

al·ler·gic /əˈlɜːdʒɪk‖-ɜːr-/ *adj* [(to)] suffering from an allergy: *She is allergic to the fur of cats.* | *an allergic reaction to cats* | (fig.) *He seems to be allergic to hard work.* (=he strongly dislikes it)

al·ler·gy /ˈælədʒi‖-ər-/ *n* [(to)] a condition of being unusually sensitive to something eaten, breathed in, or touched, in a way that causes pain or suffering: *an allergy to household dust/to penicillin*

al·le·vi·ate /əˈliːvieɪt/ *v* [T] to reduce (pain, suffering, difficulties, etc.), esp. for a short time; RELIEVE —**ation** /əˌliːviˈeɪʃən/ *n* [U]

al·ley /ˈæli/ *n* **1** a narrow street or path between buildings in a town —see also BLIND ALLEY **2** a narrow street allowing entry to garages or BACKYARDS **3** a path in a garden or park, esp. one bordered by trees or bushes **4** a long track along which balls are rolled in order to knock over bottle-shaped objects in BOWLING or SKITTLES **5 right up one's alley** *AmE* a person's area of interest or activity: *That job sounds like it's right up your alley.*

al·ley·way /ˈæliweɪ/ *n* an ALLEY (1)

All Fools' Day /ˌ· ˈ· ˌ·/ *n* [S] another name for APRIL FOOLS' DAY, April 1st

all fours /ˌ· ˈ·/ *n* on all fours with the hands and knees on the floor: *He was crawling around on all fours looking for his contact lens.*

All Hal·lows' Day /ˌ· ˈ·· ·/ also **All·hal·lows** /ɔːlˈhæləʊz/ —**All·hal·low·mas** /ɔːlˈhæləʊməs/ *n* [S] *old use* another name for ALL SAINTS' DAY, November 1st

al·li·ance /əˈlaɪəns/ *n* **1** [C (**with, between**)] a close agreement or connection made between countries, groups, families, etc. for a shared purpose or for the protection of their interests: *The two countries entered into a defensive alliance (with each other).* | *an alliance of moderate political groupings to oppose the government* —see also UNHOLY ALLIANCE **2** [C+*sing./pl. v*] a group or association formed in this way; combination of allies (ALLY): *The SDP-Liberal Alliance is holding a conference.* **3** [U (**with**)] the act of forming an alliance or the state of being in an alliance: *The steel union, in alliance with the railway workers, is planning a major strike.* **4** [C] *becoming rare* a union of families by marriage

Alliance [*the*] an association of the Liberal Party and the Social Democratic Party to fight the British elections together in 1983 and 1987.

Alliance & Leices·ter /·ˌ·· · ˈ··/ [*the*] a British BUILDING SOCIETY, branches of which are found in many towns and cities in Britain

al·lied /ˈælaɪd, əˈlaɪd/ *adj* [(to)] **1** joined by political agreement: *the allied forces* —see also ALLIES **2** related, esp. by shared qualities; similar: *a discussion of health and fitness and allied topics* **3** [F+**with/to**] connected; in addition: *The beautiful photography, allied with a very good script, makes it an excellent film.* —see also ALLY²

Al·lies /ˈælaɪz/ *n* [*the*+P] **1** the countries, including Britain, France, Russia, and the US, who fought together during the First World War **2** the countries, including Britain, the USSR, and the US, who fought together during the Second World War **3** the United Nations countries who fought together against Iraq during the Gulf War

al·li·ga·tor /ˈælɪɡeɪtəʳ/ *n* -**tors** *or* -**tor** **1** [C] a large cold-blooded REPTILE that lives on land and in lakes and rivers in the hot wet parts of America and China —compare CROCODILE **2** [U] its skin turned into leather **3 see you later, alligator** a phrase used, esp. by and to children, to say goodbye. The reply to this is "in a while, CROCODILE".

all-in·clu·sive /ˌ· ·ˈ···◂/ *adj* INCLUSIVE (1)

all-in wrest·ling /ˌ· · ˈ··/ *n* [U] a type of professional wrestling (WRESTLE) without limits on moves, holds, or methods

al·lit·er·a·tion /əˌlɪtəˈreɪʃən/ *n* [U] the appearance of the same sound or sounds at the beginning of two or more words that are next to or close to each other (as in "Round the rocks runs the river") —**tive** /əˈlɪtərətɪv‖-təreɪtɪv/ *adj* —**tively** *adv*

all-night·er /ˌɔːl ˈnaɪtəʳ/ *n AmE* a whole night spent studying or working: *Chip pulled an all-nighter* (=stayed up all night studying) *before his chemistry test.*

al·lo·cate /ˈæləkeɪt/ *v* [T (to)] **1** to set apart for a particular purpose; EARMARK: *The government has allocated over £100 million to the job creation programme.* | *That space has already been allocated for building a new hospital.* **2** to give as a share: *We've allocated accommodation to* *each of the refugees.* [+obj(i)+obj(d)] *Each of the refugees has been allocated accommodation.*

al·lo·ca·tion /ˌæləˈkeɪʃən/ n **1** [U] the act of allocating **2** [C] a share or amount that has been allocated

al·lo·path·ic medi·cine /ˌæləʊpæθɪk ˈmedsən‖-ˈmedˌsən/ n [U] the science and practice of medicine that is standard in the west; WESTERN MEDICINE

al·lot /əˈlɒt‖əˈlɑːt/ v **-tt-** [T (**to**)] to give as a share or set apart for a purpose; allocate: *Most of the money has already been allotted.* [+obj(i)+obj(d)] *They allotted us three weeks to finish the job.* | *We were unable to finish it* **in the allotted time.**

al·lot·ment /əˈlɒtmənt‖əˈlɑːt-/ n **1** [C] a share, e.g. of money or space **2** [U] the giving of shares; allocation **3** [C] (in Britain) a small piece of land rented out, esp. by a town council, to people who will grow vegetables on it

all-out /ˌ· ˈ·◄/ adj [A] total, complete, holding nothing back: *all-out war* | *an all-out assault on their opponents' goal*

al·low /əˈlaʊ/ v **1** [T] to let (someone) do something without opposing them or trying to prevent them; let (something) be done; permit: *They don't allow music after 10.30 at night.* [+v-ing] *Walking on the grass is not allowed.* [+obj+to-v] *His parents won't allow him to come.* | *He would like to come, but he's not allowed to.* | **Allow me to explain** (=I would like to explain) *that the government has no intention of raising taxes.* **2** [T+obj+adv/prep] to let come or go: *I don't allow dogs in the house.* | *They're not allowed out on Sundays.* **3** [T] to provide or give (esp. money or time), for a special purpose: *You'll have to allow three days for that job.* [+obj(i)+obj(d)] *My father allows me money for books.* | *We are only allowed a three-minute break.* **4** [I+of;T] to make possible (for): *The facts allow (of) no other explanation.* [+obj+to-v] *The extra money will allow us to buy a car.* | *A loophole in the law allowed them to escape prosecution.* **5** [T] to officially accept as correct, proper, etc.: *The referee refused to allow the goal.* | *Will the court allow her claim?* —opposite **disallow 6** [T+*that;obj*] *fml* to admit: *We must allow that.|It must be allowed that he is a very clever politician.*

allow for sbdy./sthg. *phr v* [T] to take into consideration: *The cost of the project will be £2 million, which allows for inflation at 5%.* [+v-ing] *We must start early, to allow for finding their house.* [+obj+v-ing] *Allowing for the train being late, we should be back by 10.30.*

al·low·a·ble /əˈlaʊəbəl/ adj that may be allowed or permitted —**bly** adv

al·low·ance /əˈlaʊəns/ n **1** [C] a something, esp. money, provided regularly or for a special purpose: *The scholarship includes an allowance (of £100) for books.* | *a travelling allowance* | AmE for POCKET MONEY (1) **2** [C] **a** money taken off the cost of something, usu. for a special reason; reduction **b** an amount of money one is allowed to earn free of tax: *a married man's tax allowance* **3** [C;U] the taking into consideration of facts that may change something, esp. an opinion or judgment: *She failed one of the exam papers, but we ought to* **make allowance(s) for** *the fact that she was ill.*

al·loy¹ /ˈælɔɪ‖ˈælɔɪ, əˈlɔɪ/ n [C;U] a metal that consists of two or more different metals mixed together: *Brass ts an alloy of copper and zinc.*

al·loy² /əˈlɔɪ‖əˈlɔɪ, ˈælɔɪ/ v [T] **1** *lit* to lower in value or quality; spoil —see also UNALLOYED **2** [(**with**)] *tech* to mix (one metal) with another

all-par·ty /ˌ· ˈ··◄/ adj involving Members of Parliament from different political parties: *An all-party committee of MPs has been set up to report on recent changes in the NHS.*

all-points bul·le·tin /ˌ· · ˈ···/ n AmE a police message, e.g. about a person wanted for questioning, broadcast to all police stations in an area

all-pow·er·ful /ˌ· ˈ···◄/ adj having the power to do anything; OMNIPOTENT

all-pur·pose /ˈ· ˌ··/ adj [A] able to be used in all conditions or for all purposes: *an all-purpose cleaning liquid*

all right /ˌ· ˈ·/ adj, adv [F no comp.] **1** safe, unharmed, or healthy: *The driver was rather shaken after the accident, but otherwise all right.* **2** *infml* satisfactory but not very good; acceptable; in a satisfactory or acceptable manner or state: *His work is all right (but he could be faster).* | *We're doing all right.* **3** allowable; acceptable: *Is it all right if I go now?* **4** also **right**— (in answer to a sug-

gestion, plan, etc.) I/we agree; yes: *"Come tomorrow." "All right! What time?"* **5** *infml* beyond doubt; certainly: *He's ill all right: he's got pneumonia.* —see ALRIGHT (USAGE) **6 That's/It's all right** (used as a reply when someone thanks you or says they are sorry for something they have done):*"Sorry I'm late." "That's all right."*

▷ USAGE 1 In a talk or lecture, **all right** can be used to show that the speaker is introducing a new topic or activity: **All right,** *now let's move on to the next point.* | **All right,** *now if you'll come over here, I'll show you how this machine works.* 2 In informal spoken English **all right** is often used to check that the listener has understood: *We switch it on and then press this button.* **(All) right?**◁

all round /ˌ· ˈ·/ adv *infml* in regard to everything; in every way: *Taken all round* (=when everything is considered) *it's not a bad car.*

all-round /ˈ· ·/ also **all-around** AmE— adj [A] having ability in many things, esp. in various sports: *an all-round athlete*

all-round·er /ˌ· ˈ··/ n **1** a person who has ability in many things: *He's a good all-rounder who likes sports, books, and music.* **2** (in cricket) a player who can both BAT and BOWL to a relatively high standard

All Saints' Day /ˌ· ˈ· ˌ·/ n [S] November 1st, when Christian churches remember all the SAINTS

all-seat·er /ˈ· ··/ adj [A] BrE (of a place where sports are played) having only seats and no places where people are allowed to stand, considered to be safer than places where people are allowed to stand: *an all-seater football stadium*

all-sing·ing all-danc·ing /ˌ·ˈ·· ˌ·ˈ··/ adj [A] *infml, BrE* using every possible means to attract attention

all·sorts /ˈɔːlsɔːts‖-sɔːrts/ n [P] sweets made from LIQUORICE in several different shapes: *liquorice allsorts*

All Souls' Day /ˌ· ˈ· ˌ·/ n [S] November 2nd, when people in Christian churches pray for the souls of those who have died

all·spice /ˈɔːlspaɪs/ n [U] a powder made from the berries of a tropical American tree, used for giving a special taste to food

all-star /ˈ· ·/ adj [A] including many famous actors: *a film with an all-star cast*

All-Star Game /ˌ· · ˈ·/ n (in the US) a BASEBALL game played mid-season in which the teams are made up of the best players in professional baseball

All's Well that Ends Well /ˌ· ˌ· ˌ· ˈ·/ the title of a humorous play by William Shakespeare about the love and marriage of two characters, Helena and Bertram

all-ter·rain bi·cy·cle /ˌ· ·· ˈ···/ n [C] a MOUNTAIN BIKE

all-ter·rain ve·hi·cle /ˌ· ·· ˈ···/ n [C] *esp. AmE* a motor vehicle with three or four wheels for use on rough ground, popular with young people —see OFF-ROAD VEHICLE

All Things Bright and Beau·ti·ful /ˌ· · ˌ· · ˈ···/ the title and first line of a religious song (HYMN), often sung by children:

All things bright and beautiful,
All creatures great and small,
All things wise and wonderful,
The Lord God made them all.

all-time /ˈ· ·/ adj [A] being the greatest, biggest, most, etc., ever known: *an all-time record* | *The shop's sales have reached an* **all-time high** *this year.*

al·lude /əˈluːd/ v

allude to sbdy./sthg. *phr v* [T] *fml* to speak about (someone or something), but in an indirect way: *She didn't mention Mr Smith by name, but it was clear she was alluding to him.*

al·lure¹ /əˈljʊər‖əˈlʊər/ v [T] to attract or charm by the offer of something pleasant; TEMPT: *The job offers alluring opportunities.*

allure² n [S;U] (an) attraction; charm: *the allure of fame/ foreign travel*

al·lure·ment /əˈljʊəmənt‖əˈlʊər-/ n something that attracts, charms, or TEMPTs

al·lu·sion /əˈluːʒən/ n [C;U (**to**)] *fml* (an example of) the act of alluding or speaking about something indirectly, esp. while speaking about something else: *She made several allusions to the previous government's failures.* —**sive**

/ə'lu:sɪv/ *adj* : *an allusive style of poetry which is hard to understand* —**sively** *adv*

al·lu·vi·al /ə'lu:viəl/ *adj* being, concerning, or made of soil put down by rivers, lakes, floods, etc.: *an alluvial plain*

al·lu·vi·um /ə'lu:viəm/ *n* -**viums** *or* -**via** /viə/ [C;U] *tech* soil put down by rivers, lakes, floods, etc.

al·ly¹ /'ælaɪ‖'ælaɪ, ə'laɪ/ *n* **1** a country that is joined to another by political agreement, esp. one that will provide support in war; member of an ALLIANCE: *a meeting of the European allies* —see also ALLIES **2** a person who regularly provides help or support; ASSOCIATE: *one of the Prime Minister's closest allies*

al·ly² /ə'laɪ‖ə'laɪ, 'ælaɪ/ *v* [I;T (**with, to**)] to join or unite, e.g. by political agreement or marriage: *The small country allied itself with/to the stronger power.* —see also ALLIED

Al·ly Pal·ly /,æli 'pæli/ *an informal name for* ALEXANDRA PALACE

al·ma ma·ter /,ælmə 'meɪtər, -'mɑ:-‖-'mɑ:-/ *n* [*usu. sing.*] *fml* **1** the school, college, or university which one attended **2** *AmE* (*usu. caps*) the song of a school, college, or university

al·ma·nac /'ɔːlmənæk‖'ɔːl-, 'æl-/ *n* a book giving a list of the days of a year, together with information, often in the form of tables, about the times of sunrise and sunset, changes in the moon, rise and fall of the sea, etc.

al·might·y /ɔːl'maɪti/ *adj* **1** (*often cap.*) able to do everything; OMNIPOTENT: *Almighty God | God Almighty* **2** [A] *infml* very big, strong, great, etc.: *I heard an almighty crash.*

al·mond /'ɑːmənd‖'ɑː-, 'æ-, 'æl-/ *n* **1** a fruit tree whose seeds are eaten as nuts **2** the nut of this tree —see picture at NUT

al·mo·ner /'ɑːmənər, 'æl-‖'æl-, 'ɑː-/ *n becoming rare* an official in a British hospital who looks after the material and social needs of the sick (now officially called a **medical social worker**)

al·most /'ɔːlməʊst‖'ɔːlməʊst, ɔːl'məʊst/ *adv* very nearly but not quite: *I almost dropped the plate.* | *She said almost nothing.* | *It's almost certain to succeed./It will almost certainly succeed.* | *almost everyone* | *an almost perfect performance* | *"Have you finished?" "Almost."*

▷ USAGE Compare **almost** and **nearly**, which have similar meanings. 1 You can use either **almost** or **nearly** before *all, every,* and *always,* and before negative verbs: *They almost/nearly always have coffee for breakfast.* | *Almost/nearly all the guests are here.* | *I almost/nearly didn't wake up on time.* 2 You can say *very/pretty/not* before **nearly**: *We pretty nearly missed the train.* | *I've not nearly finished,* but you cannot use these words before **almost**. 3 You can use **almost** before *any* and before negative words such as *no, none, never, nobody, nothing*: *Almost any bus will do.* | *I almost never see her,* but you cannot use **nearly** in this way. —see also PRACTICALLY (USAGE)◁

alms /ɑːmz‖ɑːmz, ɑːlmz/ *n* [P] *old use* money, food, clothes, etc., given to poor people

alms-house /'· ·/ *n* a house, usu. one of a group, provided in former times by a rich person, in which old or poor people could live without paying rent

a·loft /ə'lɒft‖ə'lɔːft/ *adv fml* high up, esp. in the air or among the sails of a ship: *The flag was flying aloft.*

a·lo·ha /ə'ləʊhə‖-hɑː/ *interj., n AmE* used as a greeting or to say goodbye, esp. in Hawaii

a·lone /ə'ləʊn/ *adj, adv* **1** [F] without or separated from others: *She lives alone.* | *The house stands alone on the hill.* | *I was (all) alone in the house.* | *I'm sure I'm* **not alone in thinking** (=not the only one who thinks) *that this is a mistake.* **2** [after *n*] only: *You alone can do it.* (=You are the only one who can do it.) | *The grant was awarded on merit alone.* | *Time alone will show who was right.* | *The price alone should have made you realize it was a trick.* (=without even considering other facts) | *She, alone of all the applicants* (=she was the only one), *had the qualifications we were looking for.* **3 leave/ let someone or something alone: a** to allow one to be by oneself **b** to allow someone or something to remain untouched or unchanged: *Leave that alone: it's mine.* —see also **go it alone** (GO¹), **let alone** (LET¹) **4 I want to be alone** a phrase which is believed to have been used by Greta Garbo, now often used humorously

▷ USAGE Being **alone** is neither good nor bad: *She lives on tea and cake when she's alone.* **Solitary** and **lone,** when used of things, mean that there is only one: *a* **solitary/lone** *tree in the garden,* but used of people they may show sadness, like **lonely** or **lonesome** (esp. *AmE*): *Come over and see me; I'm feeling a bit* **solitary/lonely/lonesome.** **Forlorn** suggests great sadness because of being left alone, and **desolate** is even stronger: *The death of his wife left him completely* **forlorn/desolate.**◁

a·long¹ /ə'lɒŋ‖ə'lɔːŋ/ *prep* **1** from one end of to the other; in a line in the direction of the length of: *We walked along the road.* **2** in a line next to the length of: *Trees grew along the river bank.* **3** at a point on the length of: *His room is along this passage.*

along² *adv* **1** forward; on: *She cycled along, singing happily.* **2** with others or oneself: *When we went to Paris we took my sister along (with us).* **3** to that place or this place: *I'll be along soon.* | *There's a meeting at the Town Hall and I'm thinking of going along.* | *She was just about to go home when along he came.* | *Along came her boyfriend, full of apologies.* (note word order) **4 along with** together with: *There was a bill along with the parcel.* —see also **all along** (ALL²)

a·long·side /ə,lɒŋ'saɪd‖ə,lɔːŋ-/ *adv, prep* close to and in line with the edge of (something); along the side (of): *We brought our boat alongside (their boat).* | (fig.) *videos, recordings, and other learning aids to be used alongside* (=together with or at the same time as) *the books*

a·loof¹ /ə'lu:f/ *adv* [(**from**)] apart; distant, esp. in feeling or interest: *He remained aloof from the other students.*

aloof² *adj* not very open or friendly in one's relations with other people; RESERVED: *I find her rather aloof/rather an aloof character.* — ~**ly** *adv* — ~**ness** *n* [U (**from**)]

a·loud /ə'laʊd/ *adv* **1** in a usual speaking voice; not silently: *The teacher asked me to read the poem aloud.* | *Party members are* **wondering aloud** (=openly asking) *whether he will resign.* **2** in a loud voice; so as to be heard at a distance: *The pain made him cry aloud.*

al·pac·a /æl'pækə/ *n* **1** [C] a sheeplike animal of Peru, related to the LLAMA **2** [U] cloth made from the wool of the alpaca

Al·pen /'ælpən/ *n* [U] *tdmk* a breakfast food made with grains, fruit, and nuts, and eaten with milk, and considered to be a healthy food

al·pha /'ælfə/ *n* the first letter (A, α) of the Greek alphabet, sometimes used as a mark for excellent work by a student

alpha and o·me·ga /,·· · '···‖,·· · '··/ *n* [*the*+S (**of**)] *lit* **1** the beginning and the end **2** the most necessary or important part

al·pha·bet /'ælfəbet/ *n* the set of letters used in writing any language, esp. when arranged in order: *the Greek/ Russian alphabet*

al·pha·bet·i·cal /,ælfə'betɪkəl◄/ *also* **al·pha·bet·ic** /,ælfə 'betɪk◄/ *rare*— *adj* of, belonging to, or in the order of the alphabet: *In a dictionary the words are arranged in alphabetical order.* — ~**ly** /kli/ *adv*

alphabet soup /'··· ,·/ *n* [U] *infml* speech or writing that is full of ABBREVIATIONS and ACRONYMS: *Education is all alphabet soup these days.*

al·pha·nu·mer·ic /,ælfənju:'merɪk◄-nu:-/ *adj tech* using or consisting of both letters and numbers as) *an alphanumeric character set/code*

al·pine /'ælpaɪn/ *adj* **1** of the Alps or other high mountains **2** (of plants) growing on parts of mountains that are too high for trees to grow on

Alps /ælps/ *n* [*the*+P] a mountain range in Europe, popular with tourists, esp. for skiing (SKI)

al·read·y /ɔːl'redi/ *adv* **1** by or before now or a particular time: *It's too late to give him any advice — he's already made up his mind.* | *By the time we got there, it was already getting dark.* | *He had already gone (when I arrived).* | *The new restaurant is unlikely to do well; there are too many restaurants here already.* **2** even before the time expected: *Are you leaving already?* | *She's here already; she must have come on the early train.* **3** on another occasion in the past; before: *I'm not going to watch that programme; I've seen it already.*

▷ USAGE 1 Compare **already** and **yet. Yet** is used in

negative forms: *I haven't finished* **yet** and also in most question forms: *Have you finished* **yet**? But compare *Have you had lunch* **yet**? (asking for information) and *Have you had your lunch* **already**? (expressing surprise) 2 Compare **already** and **all ready**. *We're* **all ready** means that all of us are ready. —see also JUST (USAGE), STILL (USAGE)◁

al·right /ˌɔːlˈraɪt/ *adj, adv* [F *no comp.*] ALL RIGHT
▷ USAGE **Alright** is very common now, but some people think **all right** is better English. —see also ALL RIGHT (USAGE)◁

Al·sa·tian /ælˈseɪʃən/ *esp.BrE* ‖ **German shepherd** *esp. AmE*— *n* a large dog, rather like a WOLF, often used by police or to guard property —see picture at DOG

al·so /ˈɔːlsəʊ/ *adv* as well; besides; too: *You'll have to get a passport, and you'll* **also** *need a visa.* | *The weather was* **not only** *cold,* **but also** *wet.* (=both cold and wet)
▷ USAGE 1 **Also**, **as well**, and **too** have similar meanings, but **as well** and **too** are more common than **also** at the end of a clause: *You'll need a new suitcase* **as well**. | *I must buy one* **too**. **Also** is slightly more formal: *She can sing and* **also** *dance.* | *She can sing, and dance* **too/as well** (less formal). 2 In negative expressions **neither** or **not** … **either** is used: *"Does she eat meat?" "No, and she* **doesn't** *eat fish* **either**/*No, and* **neither** *does he/he* **doesn't either**."◁

also-ran /ˈ··· ·/ *n* 1 a horse that ran in a race but was not one of the first three at the end 2 a person who has failed to win or do well, e.g. in a competition or election

al·tar /ˈɔːltəʳ/ *n* a table or raised level surface used in a religious ceremony, for example in the Christian service of Communion. The word is often used in connection with weddings. For example, if a woman talks about getting a man to the altar, she means marrying him in a church. —see picture at CHURCH

altar boy /ˈ·· ·/ *n* a boy who helps a Catholic priest during the church service

al·tar·piece /ˈɔːltəpiːs‖-ər-/ *n* a painting or other work of art placed above and behind an altar

al·ter /ˈɔːltəʳ/ *v* 1 [I;T] to make or become different, but without changing into something else: *This shirt will have to be altered; it's too large.* | *The village hasn't really altered much since the last time I was there.* 2 [T] *esp. AmE euph for* CASTRATE (an animal)

al·ter·a·tion /ˌɔːltəˈreɪʃən/ *n* 1 [U (of)] the act of making or becoming different: *My coat needs alteration.* 2 [C (to)] a change, esp. a slight one; something changed: *There have been a few alterations to the timetable.*

al·ter·ca·tion /ˌɔːltəˈkeɪʃən‖-tər-/ *n* [C;U] *fml* (a) noisy argument or quarrel

al·ter e·go /ˌæltər ˈiːɡəʊ, ˌɔːl-/ *n* **alter egos** *Lat* 1 a very close and trusted friend 2 a side of one's character which is different from one's usual character

al·ter·nate¹ /ɔːlˈtɜːnɪt‖ˈɔːltɜːr-, ˈæl-/ *adj* 1 (of two things) happening by turns; first one and then the other: *a week of alternate rain and sunshine* 2 one of every two; every second: *He works on alternate days.* 3 [A] *esp. AmE* instead of another; alternative: *an alternate plan/suggestion* — — **ly** *adv* : *The play is alternately sombre and comical.*

al·ter·nate² /ˈɔːltəneɪt‖-ər-/ *v* [I (with, between);T] to (cause to) follow by turns: *We alternated periods of work and sleep.* | *Work alternated with sleep.* | *His moods alternated between happiness and gloom.* | *She treated him with alternating affection and contempt.* — — **nation** /ˌɔːltəˈneɪʃən‖-tər-/ *n* [C;U]

al·ter·nat·ing cur·rent /ˌ····· ˈ···/ *n* [U] a flow of electricity that regularly changes direction at a very fast rate — compare DIRECT CURRENT

al·ter·na·tive¹ /ɔːlˈtɜːnətɪv‖ɔːlˈtɜːr-, æl-/ *adj* [A *no comp.*] 1 (of two or more things) that may be used, had, done, etc., instead of another; other: *We returned by the alternative road.* | *several alternative possibilities* 2 different from what is usual or TRADITIONAL: *alternative sources of energy, such as wave power and wind power* 3 (esp. of modern young people and what they do) not based on or not accepting the established standards of ordinary society: *the alternative press* | *alternative theatre* — — **ly** *adv* : *You're welcome to come with us now in our car. Alternatively you could go later with Mary.*

alternative² *n* [(to)] 1 a chance to choose or decide between two or more possible things, courses of action, etc.: *I'm afraid* **I have no alternative but to** *report you to the police.* 2 something, esp. a course of action, that may be taken or chosen instead of one or more others: *The only alternative to being taken prisoner was to die fighting.* | *We had to fight: there was no (other) alternative.* | *There are several alternatives to your plan.* 3 **there is no alternative** a phrase used by Margaret Thatcher to defend her economic policies (POLICY), now often used humorously
▷ USAGE Sentences such as *We have several* **alternatives** *to choose from* are very common, but are often thought to be incorrect because there should be only two **alternatives**.◁

alternative com·e·dy /·ˌ··· ˈ···/ *n* [U] a funny play, film, or other work which is different and modern in its attitudes, subject matter, etc., esp. by being non-RACIST, non-SEXIST, etc.

alternative med·i·cine /·ˌ··· ˈ··/ *n* [U] any method of preventing or treating illness other than that usu. used in Western countries. Alternative medicine includes ACUPUNCTURE, CHINESE MEDICINE, HERBAL MEDICINE, HOMEOPATHY, and osteopathy (OSTEOPATH). In Britain and the US these are not usu. covered by the NHS or health INSURANCE, so people who want to use them usu. have to pay for them. —see also COMPLEMENTARY MEDICINE

al·ter·na·tor /ˈɔːltəneɪtəʳ‖ˈɔːltər- ˈæl-/ *n* an electric GENERATOR for producing ALTERNATING CURRENT —see picture at ENGINE

al·though /ɔːlˈðəʊ/ *conj* 1 in spite of the fact that; THOUGH: *They are generous although they are poor.* | *Although my car is very old, it still runs very well.* 2 but; HOWEVER: *The price increase will obviously be unpopular, although it's unlikely to reduce demand.*

al·ti·me·ter /ˈæltɪˌmiːtəʳ‖ælˈtɪmɪtər/ *n* an instrument used, esp. in an aircraft, for recording height

al·ti·tude /ˈæltɪtjuːd‖-tuːd/ *n* 1 [*usu. sing.*] the height of an object or place above sea level: *The plane flew at an altitude of 30,000 feet.* | *What is the altitude of the top of the mountain?* —compare ELEVATION (2) 2 also **altitudes** *pl.*— a high area: *At high altitudes it is difficult to breathe.*

Alt·man /ˈɔːltmən/ , **Rob·ert** /ˈrɒbət‖ˈruːbərt/ (1925–) an American film director whose works include *Nashville*, *A Wedding*, and *Three Women*

al·to /ˈæltəʊ/ *n* **-tos** 1 also **counter tenor**— (a man with) a very high male singing voice, higher than TENOR 2 also **contralto**— (a woman with) a low female singing voice, lower than SOPRANO 3 a musical instrument with the same range of notes as these —*alto adj, adv* : *an alto saxophone/to sing alto*

al·to·geth·er¹ /ˌɔːltəˈɡeðəʳ/ *adv* 1 completely; thoroughly: *That's an altogether different matter/That's a different matter altogether.* | *We weren't altogether surprised when he arrived late.* 2 considering all things; on the whole: *It rained a lot, but altogether it was a good trip.* —see also ABSOLUTELY (USAGE)

al·to·geth·er² /ˌɔːltəˈɡeðəʳ/ *n* **in the altogether** *humor* without clothes; NUDE

Al·ton Tow·ers /ˌɔːltən ˈtaʊəz‖-ərz/ a large pleasure park in Staffordshire in England, where families go to enjoy the many rides and amusements

al·tru·is·m /ˈæltru-ɪzəm/ *n* [U] consideration of the happiness and good of others before one's own; unselfishness —compare EGOISM

al·tru·ist /ˈæltru-ɪst/ *n* a person who is habitually kind and helpful to others — — **ic** /ˌæltruˈɪstɪk◂/ *adj* — — **ically** /kli/ *adv*

al·u·min·i·um /ˌæljʊˈmɪniəm◂, ˌælə-/ *BrE* ‖ **a·lu·mi·num** /əˈluːmɪnəm/ *AmE*— *n* [U] a silver-white metal that is a simple substance (ELEMENT) light in weight, and easily shaped: *aluminium saucepans* | *aluminium foil*

aluminum foil /ˌ····· ˈ·/ *n* [U] *AmE for* TINFOIL

a·lum·nus /əˈlʌmnəs/ **a·lum·na** /-nə/ *fem.*— *n* **-ni** /naɪ/, **-nae** /niː/ *fem.*— *esp. AmE* a former student of a school, college, or university

al·ve·o·lar /ˈælviələʳ, ˌælviˈəʊləʳ◂‖ælˈviːələr/ *n, adj tech* (a consonant sound such as /t/ or /d/) made by putting the end of the tongue on the hard bony area at the top of the mouth just behind the upper front teeth

al·ways /ˈɔːlwз̆z, -weɪz/ *adv* **1** at all times; at each time: *The sun always rises in the east.* | *We've always lived here.* | *I'm always pleased to see her.* | *They always go to Italy for their holidays.* | *The job is interesting, but not always easy.* **2** for ever: *I will love you always.* **3** (used with the progressive form of a verb) all the time and often in an annoying way; repeatedly: *He's always asking silly questions.* **4** (used esp. with **can** or **could**) as a possible course of action: *If you can't start the car you can always go by bus instead.* —compare FOREVER (2); see NEVER (USAGE)

Alz·heim·er's dis·ease /ˈæltshaɪməz dɪˌziːz‖ˈɑːltshaɪmərz-/ also **presenile dementia**— *n* [U] an illness caused by the decay of the brain, which affects some older people, making them forget things and lose the ability to care for themselves

am /m, əm; *strong* æm/ *v 1st person sing. present tense of* BE: *I am (living) here now.* | *Here I am!* | *Am I the only person who's going?* —see AREN'T (USAGE)

AM /ˌeɪ ˈem◂/ *n* [U] amplitude modulation; a system of broadcasting in which the strength of the sound waves varies. Sometimes with this system, the sounds provided for the listener are not always very clear: *an AM radio* —compare FM and see MEDIUM WAVE (USAGE)

am, AM /ˌeɪ ˈem/ *abbrev. for:* ante meridiem (=*Lat*) before midday (used after numbers expressing time): *the 8 am (train) from London* —see also PM

A.M.A. AMA /ˌeɪ em ˈeɪ/ American Medical Association; the organization for doctors and RESEARCHERs in medicine

a·mal·gam /əˈmælgəm/ *n* **1** [C (**of**)] *fml* a mixture or combination of different things: *Her work is a strange amalgam of musical styles.* **2** [C;U] *tech* a mixture of metals, one of which is MERCURY, often used for filling holes in teeth

a·mal·gam·ate /əˈmælgəmeɪt/ *v* [I;T (**with**)] (of businesses, societies, groups, etc.) to join so as to form something larger; unite; combine —**-ation** /əˌmælgəˈmeɪʃən/ *n* [C;U (**with**)]: *The new company was formed by the amalgamation of three smaller businesses.*

a·man·u·en·sis /əˌmænjuˈensɹ̩s/ *n* **-ses** /siːz/ *pomp* a person employed to write down what someone else is saying or to copy what someone else has written

a·mass /əˈmæs/ *v* [T] to collect (money, goods, power, etc.) in great amounts, usu. over a long period; ACCUMULATE: *She amassed a fortune by speculating on the stock exchange.* | *to amass evidence/information* —see GATHER (USAGE)

am·a·teur /ˈæmətər, -tʃʊər, -tʃər, ˌæməˈtɜːr/ *adj, n* **1** [*no comp.*] (of, by, or being) a person who paints pictures, performs plays, takes part in sports, etc., for enjoyment and without being paid for it: *Only amateurs can compete in the Olympic Games.* | *an amateur photographer/actor/detective* | *amateur football/psychology* —compare DILETTANTE, PROFESSIONAL[1]; see also PRO-AM **2** *derog* (typical of) a person without experience or skill in a particular art, sport, etc.: *We made a rather amateur job of painting the house.*

amateur dra·mat·ics /ˌ··· ·ˈ··/ *n* [U] the performing of plays by people who are not paid for this and do it just for enjoyment. In Britain, most towns have an amateur dramatics group and because the standard is not always very high it is sometimes connected with bad, overemotional acting and so often considered humorous: *When they screamed at each other angrily and he walked out of the meeting, it was like amateur dramatics.*

am·a·teur·ish /ˈæmətərɪʃ, ˌæməˈtjʊərɪʃ, -ˈtɜːrɪʃ‖ ˌæməˈtʊər-, -ˈtɜːr-/ *adj derog* lacking skill; typical of an AMATEUR (2) — **~ly** *adv* — **~ness** *n* [U]

am·a·to·ry /ˈæmətəri‖ -tɔːri/ *adj lit or poet* concerning or expressing sexual love: *amatory verses*

a·maze /əˈmeɪz/ *v* [T] to fill with a feeling of great surprise or disbelief; cause wonder in; ASTONISH: *Your knowledge amazes me.* | *It amazed us to hear that you were leaving.* — **~ment** *n* [U]: *To my amazement I came first.* | *We watched in amazement as she tore up the contract and threw it in the bin.*

a·mazed /əˈmeɪzd/ *adj* [(**at, by**)] filled with great surprise or wonder: *I was amazed at/by his calmness.* | *We were amazed to hear the news/amazed (that) he could do it.* | *You would be amazed how difficult it was.* | *an amazed expression on her face*

a·maz·ing /əˈmeɪzɪŋ/ *adj usu. apprec* causing great surprise or wonder, esp. because of quantity or quality; EXTRAORDINARY: *The new car goes at an amazing speed.* | *What an amazing film!* | *It's quite amazing that he should be so unaware of what's going on!* — **~ly** *adv* : *an amazingly hot day* | *amazingly good/bad*

Amazing Grace /ˌ·ˌ·· ˈ·/ the title and first words of a religious song (HYMN)

Am·a·zon /ˈæməzən‖ -zɑːn, -zən/ *n* [*the*] a river in South America; the second longest river in the world

amazon *n* (*often cap.*) a tall strong woman, esp. one who likes sports. In CLASSICAL MYTHOLOGY, the Amazons were a nation of fierce, fighting women. — **~ian** /ˌæmə-ˈzəʊniən◂/ *adj*

am·bas·sa·dor /æmˈbæsədər/ *n* a DIPLOMAT of the highest rank who is the official representative of his/her country in another country: *Britain's ambassador to the Soviet Union* | (fig.) *Sportsmen who play abroad should remember that they are ambassadors of their country.* —compare CONSUL (1), HIGH COMMISSIONER — **~ship** *n* [C;U] — **~ial** /æmˌbæsəˈdɔːriəl/ *adj*

am·bas·sa·dress /æmˈbæsədrɹ̩s/ *n* **1** the wife of an ambassador **2** *pomp* a female representative or official messenger

am·ber /ˈæmbər/ *n* [U] (the colour of) a yellowish brown hard clear substance used for jewels, decorative objects, etc.: *an amber necklace* | *The traffic lights changed from green to amber to red.* —**amber** *adj*

am·bi·dex·trous /ˌæmbɪˈdekstrəs◂/ *adj* able to use either hand with equal skill — **~ly** *adv*

am·bi·ence, ambiance /ˈæmbiəns/ *n* the character, quality, feeling, etc., of a place; ATMOSPHERE: *This little restaurant has a pleasant ambience.*

am·bi·ent /ˈæmbiənt/ *adj* [A] *often tech* on all sides; completely surrounding: *The equipment will function in ambient temperatures of up to 40°C.*

am·big·u·ous /æmˈbɪgjuəs/ *adj* having more than one possible meaning or INTERPRETATION; unclear: *an ambiguous reply/attitude* –opposite **unambiguous**; compare AMBIVALENT — **~ly** *adv* **–guity** /ˌæmbɹ̩ˈgjuːɹ̩ti/ *n* [C;U]: *You should avoid ambiguity in your writing.* | *His reply was full of ambiguities.*

am·bit /ˈæmbɹ̩t/ *n* [*usu. sing.*] *fml* range or limit of power or influence

am·bi·tion /æmˈbɪʃən/ *n* **1** [U] strong desire, esp. over a long period, for success, power, wealth, etc.: *She's clever but she lacks ambition.* | *political ambition* | *his single-minded ambition* **2** [C] something that is desired in this way: *A big house in the country is my ambition.* | *One of her ambitions is to become a doctor.* | *He has at last achieved his lifetime ambition of launching a newspaper.*

am·bi·tious /æmˈbɪʃəs/ *adj* **1** having a strong desire for success, power, wealth, etc.: *an ambitious woman/politician* **2** showing or resulting from a desire to do something difficult or something that demands great effort, great skill, etc.: *His next production was a very ambitious musical.* | *We cooked nothing more ambitious than boiled eggs.* — **~ly** *adv* — **~ness** *n* [U]

am·biv·a·lent /æmˈbɪvələnt/ *adj* [(**towards, about**)] having opposing feelings towards, or opinions about, a person or thing: *an ambivalent attitude towards private enterprise* —compare AMBIGUOUS — **~ly** *adv* **–lence** *n* [U]

am·ble /ˈæmbəl/ *v* [I (**about, around**)] **1** to walk at an easy unhurried rate **2** (of a horse) to move at an easy unhurried rate by lifting the two legs on one side and then the two on the other —compare CANTER, GALLOP, TROT —**amble** *n* [S]

Am·bridge /ˈæmbrɪdʒ/ an imaginary village in the English countryside which is the setting for the popular British radio programme *The Archers*

am·bro·si·a /æmˈbrəʊziə‖ -ʒə/ *n* [U] *lit* something with a delightful taste or smell (from CLASSICAL MYTHOLOGY, where ambrosia was the food of the gods)

am·bu·lance /ˈæmbjɹ̩ləns/ *n* a motor vehicle for carrying sick or wounded people, esp. to a hospital: *They were taken by ambulance to the nearest hospital.*

ambulance chas·er /ˈ··· ˌ··/ *n AmE infml* a lawyer who tells people who have been in accidents that he or she will represent them if they want to SUE (=try to obtain money in court) the person who caused the accident

am·bu·lance·man /ˈæmbjʉlənsmæn/ *n* **-men** /men/ *BrE* a man whose job is to drive an ambulance or to look after sick or wounded people during their journey to hospital in an ambulance

am·bu·lance·wom·an /ˈæmbjʉlənsˌwʊmən/ *n* **-women** /ˌwɪmɪn/ *BrE* a woman whose job is to drive an ambulance or to look after sick or wounded people during their journey to hospital in an ambulance

am·bush¹ /ˈæmbʊʃ/ *v* [T] to attack from a place where one has hidden and waited

ambush² *n* **1** [C] a surprise attack from a place of hiding **2** [C;U] the place where the attackers hide: *waiting in ambush*

a·me·ba /əˈmiːbə/ *n AmE for* AMOEBA —**bic** *adj*

a·me·li·o·rate /əˈmiːliəreɪt/ *v* [I;T] *fml or pomp* to make or become better or less bad; improve: *Hiring an extra teacher will ameliorate the situation, but we still need more books and desks.* —**-ration** /əˌmiːliəˈreɪʃən/ *n* [U]

a·men /ɑːˈmen, eɪ-/ *interj* (used at the end of a prayer or HYMN) may this be true

a·me·na·ble /əˈmiːnəbəl/ *adj* **1** [(to)] ready to be guided or influenced (by): *I'm sure she'll be amenable to any sensible suggestions.* | *He's very amenable.* **2** [F+to] *fml* able to be tested by: *My scientific discoveries are amenable to the usual tests.*

a·mend /əˈmend/ *v* **1** [T] to make changes in the words of (a rule or law): *to amend the constitution* —compare EMEND **2** [I;T] *fml* to make or become better by getting rid of faults; improve; RECTIFY

a·mend·ment /əˈmendmənt/ *n* [C (to);U] **1** (the act of making) a change to improve a rule, law, statement, etc.: *Your plan needs some amendment.* | *So many amendments were made to the law that its original meaning was completely changed.* | *The opposition parties* **moved** (=suggested) **an amendment** *to the bill.* | *to debate/pass an amendment* **2** (*often cap.*) one of the list of rights included in the US Constitution —see also FIRST AMENDMENT

a·mends /əˈmendz/ *n* **make amends (for)** to pay for or show one is sorry for some harm, unkindness, damage, etc.; make REPARATION: *I'm sorry I forgot about your birthday. How can I make amends?*

a·me·ni·ty /əˈmiːnʉti‖əˈme-/ *n* [*often pl.*] something in a town, hotel, or other place, that helps to make life pleasant and provide enjoyment: *Parks and swimming pools are just some of the town's local amenities.*

Am·er·a·sian /ˌæməˈreɪʒən◂, -ʃən◂/ *n* a person whose father is American and whose mother is Asian; many Amerasians were born in Vietnam and Korea when Americans were fighting in wars there

A·mer·i·ca /əˈmerʉkə/ *infml* the UNITED STATES OF AMERICA

▷ USAGE People from different countries of North and South America sometimes protest when **America** is used to mean only the **United States**, but this meaning is commonly used and understood by English speakers all over the world.◁

A·mer·i·can /əˈmerʉkən/ *n, adj* (a person) from N, Central, or S America, esp. the United States of America

A·mer·i·ca·na /əˌmerʉˈkɑːnə/ *n* [U] (something) of a style which is esp. American, often associated with country or old-fashioned taste. Some Americana would be described as TACKY: *The movie is filled with Americana: shots of motels, gas stations, waffle houses, and old Ford pick-ups.* | *a collection of Americana including stetson hats and civil war memorabilia.*

American A·cad·e·my of Dra·mat·ic Arts /·,··· ·,··· ·,··· ·,··/ an American school for actors where many famous actors have studied

American As·so·ci·a·tion of Re·tired Per·sons /·,··· ···,·· · ·,· ˈ··/ also **AARP**— a group which represents the interests of older people, esp. those who have stopped working, when dealing with Congress

American Band·stand /·,··· ˈ··/ an American television programme popular esp. during the 1950s and 1960s which showed popular music bands and singers and had people dancing to them in the place where it was filmed

American Bar As·so·ci·a·tion /·,··· ˈ· ···,··/ also **ABA**— [*the*] a professional organization for lawyers in the US

American Can·cer So·ci·e·ty /·,··· ˈ·· ·,··/ also **ACS** (*abbrev.*) an American organization that works to find the causes, treatment, and cures of cancer

American cheese /·,··· ˈ·/ *n* [U] *AmE* a yellowish-orange, mild processed (PROCESS² (1)) cheese, not strong in taste, often bought in thin pieces wrapped in plastic

American Civ·il Lib·er·ties U·nion /·,··· ,·· ˈ··· ,··/ [*the*] see ACLU

American Civ·il War /·,··· ,·· ˈ·/ [*the*] see CIVIL WAR

American Con·ser·va·to·ry Thea·tre /·,··· ˈ···· ,··/ also **ACT** a REPERTORY theatre (=one that puts on different plays every few nights) and school for actors in San Francisco

American Dream /·,··· ˈ·/ [*the*] the idea that the US is a place where everyone has the chance of becoming rich and successful. Many IMMIGRANTS to the US in the early 20th century believed in the American Dream.

the symbol for American Express

American Ex·press /·,··· ·ˈ·/ *tdmk* a CHARGE CARD company with offices in many cities around the world. Well-known SLOGANs for American Express are "Don't leave home without it" and "That'll do nicely".

American football

American foot·ball /·,··· ˈ··/ *n* [U] *BrE for* FOOTBALL (2)

American Goth·ic /·,··· ˈ··/ a painting by Grant Wood, showing a very serious looking farmer holding a PITCHFORK, standing beside a young woman. It is often copied in a humorous way for advertising. —see colour picture on page 1016

American In·di·an /·,··· ˈ···/ also **Amerindian** *n* NATIVE AMERICAN

A·mer·i·can·is·m /əˈmerʉkənɪzəm/ *n* a word, phrase, speech sound, etc., of English as spoken in America, esp. in the US

a·mer·i·can·ize also **-ise** *BrE* /əˈmerʉkənaɪz/ *v* [T] to make something, such as a spelling, a place, a way of working, etc., American in character —**-ization** /əˌmerʉkənaɪˈzeɪʃən‖-kənə-/ *n* [U]

American League /·,··· ·ˈ·/ *n* [U] a group of PROFESSIONAL US BASEBALL teams which play against each other —see also BASEBALL, NATIONAL LEAGUE, WORLD SERIES

American Le·gion /·,··· ˈ··/ *n* [*the*] an association of people who served in the American armed forces during the war

American Re·vo·lu·tion·a·ry War /·,··· ···,···· '·/ *also* **American Revolution** *AmE* ‖ **American War of Independence** *esp. BrE* [*the*] (1775–83) the war in which the American colonies (COLONY) won their independence from Britain. Arguments which led to the war included Britain's **taxation** (of the colonies) **without representation** in Parliament, the presence and cost of a British army in the colonies, and Britain forbidding westward settlement beyond the Appalachian mountains. Anger on both sides resulted in the BOSTON MASSACRE and the BOSTON TEA PARTY. When fighting began in several areas near Boston in 1775, General George Washington led the American soldiers, and was later joined by help from France in 1777. In 1776, the colonies' **Continental Congress** rang the LIBERTY BELL to tell the people about the DECLARATION OF INDEPENDENCE. The war ended when the British surrendered in 1781; a peace agreement (TREATY) was signed in 1783. —see also CONSTITUTION, VALLEY FORGE, US

American Way /·,··· '·/ [*the*] a set of beliefs or values that many Americans hold but which are not laws or written down in any form. Examples of types of beliefs which would be considered part of the American Way are: working hard, believing in yourself and your ability to change your situation for the better, and treating people fairly. Sometimes people use the phrase "the American Way" in a negative way to mean that they think Americans believe that they deserve to have material wealth such as bigger cars and houses and expensive things: *It isn't part of the American Way to trample over the rights of the individual.* | *It's the American Way, isn't it? Better things and more of them.*

America's Cup /·,··· '·/ [*the*] a sailing competition in which teams from the US, Australia and other nations compete

America the Beau·ti·ful /·,··· · '···/ a PATRIOTIC song known to almost all Americans and taught to them as children. It begins:
O Beautiful for spacious skies,
for amber waves of grain;
for purple mountain majesties
above the fruited plain...

Am·er·in·di·an /ˌæməˈrɪndiən◂/ *n* NATIVE AMERICAN

am·e·thyst /ˈæmɪθɪst/ *n* [C;U] (the colour of) a purple stone, used in jewellery —**amethyst** *adj*

Am·ex /ˈæmeks/ *n tdmk abbrev. for* AMERICAN EXPRESS

a·mi·a·ble /ˈeɪmiəbəl/ *adj* pleasant and well-intentioned; likable; friendly: *an amiable young man* —**bly** *adv* —**bility** /ˌeɪmiəˈbɪlॢti/ *n* [U]

am·i·ca·ble /ˈæmɪkəbəl/ *adj* typical of friends; made or done in a friendly way: *We reached an amicable agreement.* —**bly** *adv* —**bility** /ˌæmॢkəˈbɪlॢti/ *n* [U]

a·mi·cus cu·ri·ae /əˈmaɪkəs ˈkjʊəri-iː, -aɪ/ *n* FRIEND OF THE COURT

a·mid /əˈmɪd/ *also* **a·midst** /əˈmɪdst/— *prep fml or lit* in the middle of; among: *He felt strange amid so many people.* | *Two shots were fired, and amid the confusion the killers got away.* | *The dollar fell in value today, amid rumours of weakness in the US economy.*

a·mid·ships /əˈmɪdˌʃɪps/ *adv tech* in the middle part of the ship

a·mi·go /əˈmiːgəʊ/ *amiga* /-gə/ *fem.*— *n* a friend

A·min Da·da /ɑːˌmiːn ˈdɑːdɑː/ , **Id·i** /ˈiːdi/ (1925–) the president of Uganda from 1971 to 1979. Many people suffered great cruelty and terror under his rule. In 1972, he forced 80,000 Asians to leave Uganda and many of these people came to live in Britain.

a·mi·no ac·id /əˌmiːnəʊ ˈæsॢd, əˌmaɪ-/ *n* any of several substances coming from and necessary to living matter. PROTEINs are chiefly built up from these substances.

a·mir /əˈmɪər/ *n* an EMIR

A·mis /ˈeɪmɪs/ , **Kingsley** (1922–) a British writer well known for his humorous NOVELs, such as *Lucky Jim* which is about a young university teacher

A·mish /ˈɑːmɪʃ/ *n* [*the*] a group of people who follow a branch of the Christian religion which has many rules about behaviour, e.g. they must wear a certain kind of clothing and must not use machinery. They live mainly in the American states of Pennsylvania and Ohio. The Amish have often gone to court to protect their religious

way of life. **Amish** *adj: an Amish town*

Amish dress

a·miss /əˈmɪs/ *adj, adv* [F *no comp.*] *fml* **1** wrong(ly) or imperfect(ly): *Is there something amiss?* | *A few words of introduction may not come amiss.* (=would be very suitable) **2 take something amiss** to be angry about something, esp. because of a misunderstanding

am·i·ty /ˈæmॢti/ *n* [U] *fml* friendship: *They lived in amity with their neighbours.*

Am·man /əˈmɑːn/ the capital city of Jordan

am·me·ter /ˈæmɪtər, ˈæmˌmiːtər/ *n* an instrument for measuring the strength of an electric current, in AMPS —see picture at METER

am·mo·ni·a /əˈməʊniə/ *n* [U] a strong gas with a sharp smell, used in explosives, in chemicals (FERTILIZERs) to help plants grow, etc.

am·mu·ni·tion /ˌæmjॢˈnɪʃən/ *also* **am·mo** /ˈæməʊ/ *infml*— *n* [U] bullets, bombs, explosives, etc., esp. things fired from a weapon: *They were desperately short of ammunition.* | (fig.) *The recent tax increases have provided the government's opponents with plenty of ammunition.*

am·ne·si·a /æmˈniːziə‖-ʒə/ *n* [U] loss of memory, either in part or completely: *She suffered amnesia after the car crash.* | *alcoholic amnesia* —**ac** /ziæk/ *adj, n*

am·nes·ty /ˈæmnॢsti/ *n* [C;U] (a) general act of forgiveness, esp. as allowed by a government to political criminals: *to declare an amnesty*

Amnesty In·ter·na·tion·al /ˌ··· ··'···/ an independent organization established in 1961 to defend human rights and freedom of expression in all parts of the world. It is known esp. for fighting against TORTURE and for trying to persuade governments to set free people who are held prisoner because of their political beliefs.

Amnesty International

am·ni·o·cen·te·sis /ˌæmniəʊsenˈtiːsॢs/ *n* [U] *med* a method of testing an unborn baby to find out if it has a condition such as DOWN'S SYNDROME by removing liquid from the mother's WOMB. The test is often given to PREGNANT women aged 35 or over.

Am·o·co /ˈæməkəʊ/ *tdmk* an American oil company

Am·o·co Ca·diz /ˌæməkəʊ kəˈdɪz/ [*the*] an OIL TANKER (=a very large ship carrying oil) which ran onto the sea bed off the coast of France in 1978, losing a great deal of oil in the **Amoco Cadiz disaster** —see also EXXON VALDEZ

a·moe·ba ‖ *also* **ameba** *AmE* /əˈmiːbə/ *n* **-bas** *or* **-bae** /biː/ a very small living creature consisting of only one cell

a·moe·bic ‖ *also* **amebic** *AmE* /əˈmiːbɪk/ *adj* of or caused by amoebas: *amoebic dysentery*

a·mok /əˈmɒk‖əˈmɑːk/ *also* **amuck**— *adv* **run amok** to go or run out of control, esp. with a desire to kill people: *a mad axeman running amok* | (fig.) *If public spending runs amok our money will lose its value.*

a·mong /əˈmʌŋ/ *also* **a·mongst** /əˈmʌŋst/— *prep* **1** in the middle of; surrounded by: *Their house is hidden among trees.* | *She was soon lost among the crowd.* **2** between or through the group of: *discontent among the unemployed* | *They talked about it among themselves.* (=together) **3** in the group of; being one of: *This mountain is among the highest in the world.* | *Among those who escaped was a man convicted for murder.* | *She's very keen on sport:* **among other things,** *she plays tennis twice a week.* **4** (when things are shared by more than two people) to each of: *Divide the money among the five of them.* (Compare *Divide the money between the two of them.*) — see BETWEEN (USAGE)

a·mor·al /eɪˈmɒrəl, æ-‖eɪˈmɔː-, -ˈmɑː-/ *adj* **1** having no understanding of right and wrong: *Young children and animals are amoral.* —compare IMMORAL, MORAL **2** not caring whether behaviour is right or wrong: *The killer was an amoral man who felt no remorse.* — ~**ity** /ˌɪcɪmɒ'rælɬti, ˌæ-‖ˌeɪmə-/ *n* [U]

am·o·rous /'æmərəs/ *adj* feeling or expressing love, esp. sexual love: *amorous glances* | *She refused his* **amorous advances.** (=attempts to start a sexual relationship) — ~**ly** *adv* — ~**ness** *n* [U]

a·mor·phous /ə'mɔːfəs‖-ɔːr-/ *adj* having no fixed form or shape: *an amorphous mass of metal* | *I can't understand his amorphous plans.* — ~**ly** *adv* — ~**ness** *n* [U]

a·mor·ti·za·tion ‖also -**tis**- *BrE* /ə,mɔːtaɪ'zeɪʃən‖,æmərtə-/ *n* [C;U] **1** the amortizing of a debt **2** the reduction in value from year to year of the equipment and property (ASSETS) of a business, which is calculated for the purpose of deciding the business's worth

a·mor·tize *also* -**tise** *BrE* /ə'mɔːtaɪz‖'æmər-/ *v* [T] *tech* to pay off (a debt), esp. by regular small amounts —**tizable** *adj*

A·mos and An·dy /ˌeɪmɒs ənd 'ændi‖-məs-/ two black characters in an old American radio programme, who were played by white actors. Because Amos and Andy were played as rather stupid and other characters were lazy or tried to make money without working, many people see this programme as an example of a white RACIST view of black people.

a·mount¹ /ə'maʊnt/ *n* **1** [(of)] a collection or mass considered as a unit in terms of its size, number, etc.: *Large amounts of money were spent on the bridge.* | *Her case has attracted an enormous amount of public sympathy.* | *He could only pay half the amount he owed.* | *These figures should be treated with* **a certain amount of** (=some) *caution/scepticism.* **2** **any amount of** a large quantity of; plenty of: *You'll have any amount of time after your examination.*

▷ USAGE **Amount** is usually used with uncountable nouns: *a large* **amount** *of money.* With most plurals it is better to use **number**: *a large* **number** *of mistakes.* However, **amount** is used when talking about goods which are handled in large quantities: *The shopkeeper had a large* **amount** *of oranges in his storeroom.*◁

amount² *v*
amount to sthg. *phr v* [T *not in progressive forms*] to be equal to, e.g. in quantity or in meaning: *Her reply amounts to a refusal* | *She hasn't actually refused, but it amounts to the same thing.* | *Our debts amount to over $1000.* [+*v-ing*] *Not punishing these hooligans amounts to condoning their behaviour.*

a·mour /ə'mʊər/ *n* becoming rare a sexual relationship, esp. one that is secret

amp /æmp/ *n* **1** *also* **ampere** /'æmpeər‖'æmpɪər/ *fml— tech* the standard measure of the flow of electrical current past a point; the current that flows when one VOLT meets a RESISTANCE of one OHM **2** *infml for* AMPLIFIER

am·per·age /'æmpərɪdʒ/ *n* [S;U] the strength of an electrical current measured in amps

am·per·sand /'æmpəsænd‖-ər-/ *n* the sign & for the word "and"

am·phet·a·mine /æm'fetəmiːn, -mɬn/ *n* [C;U] a drug used esp. formerly in medicine and, esp. illegally, by people wanting excitement

am·phib·i·an /æm'fɪbiən/ *n* an animal, such as a FROG, that is able to live both on land and in water

am·phib·i·ous /æm'fɪbiəs/ *adj* able to live or move both on land and in water: *Frogs are amphibious.* | *an amphibious vehicle* | *an amphibious aircraft* (=one that can land and take off on water)

am·phi·thea·tre *BrE* ‖ -**ter** *AmE* /'æmfɬθɪətər/ *n* a large roofless building with rows of seats on a slope all round a central area, used for competitions and plays, esp. in ancient Rome and Greece

am·pho·ra /'æmfərə/ *n* -**ras** *or* -**rae** /riː/ a narrow clay pot with two handles used, esp. in ancient Rome and Greece, for storing wine, oil, etc.

am·ple /'æmpəl/ *adj* **1** enough or more than enough: *We have ample money for the journey.* | *He was given ample opportunity to express his views.* —compare ADEQUATE (1) **2** with plenty of space; large; SPACIOUS: *a house with an ample garden* —**ply** *adv*: *Whoever finds the necklace will be amply rewarded.* (=given a lot of money)

am·pli·fi·er /'æmplɬfaɪər/ *also* **amp** *infml— n* an instrument, as used in radios and record players, that makes electrical current or power stronger, esp. so as to make sound louder

am·pli·fy /'æmplɬfaɪ/ *v* **1** [I **(on, upon)**;T] *fml* to increase in size, effect, etc., esp. by explaining in greater detail; EXPAND: *He amplified (on) his remarks with a graph showing the latest sales figures.* **2** [T] to increase the strength of (something, esp. sound coming through electrical instruments): *an amplified guitar* —**fication** /ˌæmplɬfɬ'keɪʃən/ *n* [S;U]

am·pli·tude /'æmplɬtjuːd‖-tuːd/ *n* [U] **1** *fml* the quality of being ample, esp. **a** great quantity; ABUNDANCE **b** largeness of space **2** *tech* the distance between the middle and the top (or bottom) of a wave such as a sound wave —see AM

am·poule /'æmpuːl/ *also* **am·pule** /'æmpjuːl/— *n* a small usu. glass container for medicine that is to be taken by INJECTION (=by being put under a person's skin through a needle)

am·pu·tate /'æmpjɬteɪt/ *v* [I;T] to cut off (all or part of a limb), esp. for medical reasons: *to amputate a finger* | *Her leg was so badly damaged that the doctors had to amputate (it).* —compare EXCISE² —**tation** /ˌæmpjɬ'teɪʃən/ *n* [C;U]

am·pu·tee /ˌæmpjɬ'tiː/ *n* a person who has had an arm or leg amputated

Am·rit·sar /æm'rɪtsər/ a city in the Punjab in north-west India. The Golden Temple in Amritsar is a holy place for Sikhs and the centre of the Sikh religion. In 1919 a peaceful gathering of Indian men, women, and children were trapped in Amritsar by British troops and fired at. Over 300 were killed and 1,000 injured. In 1984, about 1,000 Sikhs were killed in the Golden Temple by the Indian Army.

Am·ster·dam /'æmstədæm‖-tər-/ the capital city of the Netherlands in North Holland

Am·strad /'æmstræd/ *tdmk* a British company started by Alan Sugar best known for its low-cost personal computers used mainly for word processing

Am·trak /'æmtræk/ *tdmk* the company which runs passenger trains in the US: *Will you fly or take Amtrak?* —compare CONRAIL

a·muck /ə'mʌk/ *adv* AMOK

am·u·let /'æmjɬl̇t, -lɬt‖'æmjɬlət/ *n* an object worn in the belief that it will protect one against evil, disease, bad luck, etc.

Am·und·sen /'æməndsən‖'ɑː-/ , **Ro·ald** /'rəʊəld/ (1872–1928) a Norwegian EXPLORER who was the first person to reach the South Pole in 1911

a·muse /ə'mjuːz/ *v* [T] **1** to excite the sense of humour of; cause to laugh or smile: *His silly jokes amused the children.* | *We were greatly amused to hear about him sitting on the wet paint.* | *She was* **not at all amused** (=very annoyed) *when she heard what they had done.* | *an amused expression on her face* **2** to cause to spend time in a pleasant manner; entertain; DIVERT: *The new toys amused her/kept her amused for hours.* | *The children amused themselves by playing games.* **3** **we are not amused** a phrase which is believed to have been used by Queen Victoria, now often used humorously

a·muse·ment /ə'mjuːzmənt/ *n* **1** [U] the state of being amused; enjoyment: *I listened in amusement.* | **To everyone's amusement** *the actor fell off the stage.* **2** [C] something that makes one's time pass pleasantly; DIVERSION: *Big cities have theatres, films, football matches, and many other amusements.*

amusement ar·cade /·'··· ·ˌ·/ ‖ *usu.* **video arcade** *AmE— n* a place full of machines which spin numbers or with which one can play games after putting coins into them

amusement park /·'··· ·/ *n AmE* a park in which a person can ride on machines such as ROLLER COASTERS and perhaps play games of skill or chance. The most well known amusement parks in the US are Disneyland and Disneyworld.

a·mus·ing /ə'mjuːzɪŋ/ *adj* causing amusement; funny: *an amusing book/incident/person* | *I don't find his jokes very amusing.* — ~**ly** *adv*

Am·way /'æmweɪ/ *tdmk* **1** an American company which sells cleaning products. Amway does not sell its goods in stores but instead has an organization which allows people to sell the products in their spare time and then receive a payment from the company based on how much they sell. People who sell Amway are usually middle-class and often hold parties at which they sell Amway products: *an Amway party* **2** a cleaning product made by this company: *Jill and Bob sell Amway to earn extra cash.*

an /ən; *strong* æn/ *indefinite article, determiner* (used when the following word begins with a vowel sound) a: *an awful noise | an elephant | an hour | an RAF pilot | an LP*
▷ USAGE When putting **a** or **an** before a set of letters such as RAF, you must consider how the letters are said, not whether the letters themselves are vowels or consonants. RAF begins with the consonant *r*, but the letter is said with the vowel sound /ɑː/. Thus you say an *RAF officer* and a *UN official*◁

An·a·bap·tist /ˌænəˈbæptɪ̩st◂/ *n* a member of a group within the Christian religion that thinks that only people who believe (and therefore not very young children) should be baptized (BAPTIZE (1))

an·a·bol·ic ster·oid /ˌænəbɒlɪk ˈstɪərɔɪd, -ˈste-‖-baː-/ *n* any of various artificial substances that make muscles grow quickly and are taken, esp. by ATHLETEs, to increase strength. Many competitions, such as the Olympic Games, do not allow athletes who use anabolic steroids to compete.

a·nach·ro·nis·m /əˈnækrənɪzəm/ *n* a person, thing, or idea that is or appears to be in the wrong period of time: *Some people believe that the British House of Lords is an anachronism.* —**nistic** /əˌnækrəˈnɪstɪk◂/ *adj* —**nistically** /kli/ *adv*

an·a·con·da /ˌænəˈkɒndə‖-ˈkɑːn-/ *n* a large S American snake that crushes its food to death

a·nae·mi·a also **anemia** *AmE* /əˈniːmiə/ *n* [U] an unhealthy condition in which there are too few red cells in the blood

a·nae·mic also **anemic** *AmE* /əˈniːmɪk/ *adj* **1** suffering from anaemia **2** lacking forcefulness or spirit: *an anaemic performance* – ~ **ally** /kli/ *adv*

an·ae·ro·bic /ˌænəˈrəʊbɪk◂/ *adj tech* not needing oxygen in order to live or happen

an·aes·the·si·a also **anes-** *AmE* /ˌænɪ̩sˈθiːziə‖-ʒə/ *n* [U] the state of being unable to feel pain, esp. as a result of a physical wound, illness of the mind, drugs, etc.

an·aes·thet·ic also **anes-** *AmE* /ˌænɪ̩sˈθetɪk◂/ *n* [C;U] a substance that produces an inability to feel pain, either in a limited area (**local anaesthetic**) or in the whole body, together with unconsciousness (**general anaesthetic**): *The patient was under an anaesthetic when the operation was performed.*

an·aes·the·tist also **anes-** *AmE* /əˈniːsθɪ̩tɪst‖əˈnes-/ *n* a doctor who gives an anaesthetic to a patient

an·aes·the·tize also **anes-** *AmE*, **-tise** *BrE* /əˈniːsθɪ̩taɪz‖ əˈnes-/ *v* [T] to make unable to feel pain by giving an anaesthetic, esp. in order to perform an operation

an·a·gram /ˈænəɡræm/ *n* a word or phrase made by changing the order of the letters in another word or phrase: *"Silent" is an anagram of "listen".*

An·a·heim /ˈænəhaɪm/ a city in S California in the US, which contains the amusement centre, Disneyland, and has a large electronics industry

a·nal /ˈeɪnəl/ *adj* of, concerning, or near the ANUS

an·al·ge·si·a /ˌænəlˈdʒiːziə‖-ʒə/ *n* [U] *tech* the condition of being unable to feel pain even though conscious

an·al·ge·sic /ˌænəlˈdʒiːzɪk◂/ *n* [C;U] a substance that causes analgesia, such as a drug or a cream that is rubbed into the skin: *Aspirin is a mild analgesic.* —**analgesic** *adj*

a·nal·o·gous /əˈnæləɡəs/ *adj* [(to, with)] *fml* similar or alike in some ways; able to be compared (with): *The movement of particles in an atom is analogous to‖with the way the planets move round the sun.*

an·a·logue , **-log** /ˈænəlɒɡ‖-lɔːɡ, -lɑːɡ/ *n* [(of)] *fml* something that is in some way similar to something else

analogue com·put·er /ˌ··· ·ˈ··/ *n* a type of computer, now used only for certain special purposes, that performs operations by measuring continuously varying quantities rather than by a BINARY system of counting – compare DIGITAL COMPUTER

a·nal·o·gy /əˈnælədʒi/ *n* **1** [C (**to, with, between**)] a degree

of similarity between one thing or process and another, which makes it possible to explain something by comparing it to something else: *The author draws an analogy between the way water moves in waves and the way light travels.* **2** [U] the act of comparing one thing with another thing that is in some way similar, esp. in order to explain: *to explain the movement of light by analogy with that of water*

an·a·lyse also **-lyze** *AmE* /ˈænəlaɪz/ *v* [T] **1** to examine (something) by dividing it into its separate parts, in order to learn about its qualities, meaning, etc.: *He analysed the food and found it contained poison. | to analyse a sentence when studying grammar | Let's analyse the problem and see what went wrong.* —compare SYNTHESIZE **2** to PSYCHOANALYSE

a·nal·y·sis /əˈnælɪ̩sɪ̩s/ *n* **-ses** /siːz/ **1** [C;U] examination of something by dividing it into its separate parts: *The analysis of the food showed the presence of poison.* —compare SYNTHESIS **2** [C] an examination of something together with thoughts and judgments about it: *Our analysis shows that the company's failure was caused by lack of investment. | a detailed analysis of the week's news* **3** [U] PSYCHOANALYSIS **4 in the final‖last analysis** when everything has been considered; ULTIMATELY: *In the last analysis, the responsibility for this failure must lie with the minister.*

an·a·lyst /ˈænəlɪ̩st/ *n* **1** a person who makes an analysis, e.g. of chemical materials: *a food analyst | a political analyst* **2** a PSYCHOANALYST —see also SYSTEMS ANALYST

an·a·lyt·ic /ˌænəˈlɪtɪk◂/ also **an·a·lyt·i·cal** /-kəl/— *adj* using, or skilled in using, methods of careful examination, esp. in order to separate things into their parts: *She has a very analytic mind. | computer-based analytical techniques* – ~ **ally** /kli/ *adv*

an·a·paest /ˈænəpest, -piːst/ also **-pest** /pest/ *AmE*— *n tech* a measure of poetry consisting of two weak (or short) beats followed by one strong (or long) beat – ~ **ic** /ˌænəˈpestɪk◂, -ˈpiː-‖-ˈpe-/ *adj, n*

an·ar·chic /æˈnɑːkɪk‖-ɑːr-/ *adj* of, like, or likely to cause anarchy, esp. in lacking order or control: *The situation in the country is becoming increasingly anarchic. | an anarchic style of painting* – ~ **ally** /kli/ *adv*

an·ar·chis·m /ˈænəkɪzəm‖-nər-/ *n* [U] the political belief that society should have no government, laws, police, etc., but should be a free association of all its members

an·ar·chist /ˈænəkɪ̩st‖-ər-/ *n esp. derog* a person who believes that all forms of government or control are unnecessary or undesirable, and sometimes supports the use of violence to destroy governments – ~ **ic** /ˌænə ˈkɪstɪk◂‖-ər-/ *adj* – ~ **ically** /kli/ *adv*

an·ar·chy /ˈænəki‖-ər-/ *n* [U] **1** lawlessness and social and political disorder caused by absence of government or control **2** complete absence of government **3** any state of disorder and confusion: *a newspaper report on anarchy in our schools*

a·nath·e·ma /əˈnæθɪ̩mə/ *n* **1** [S;U (**to**)] something that one regards with strong dislike and disapproval: *His political views are (an) anathema to me.* **2** [C] *tech* someone or something that has been cursed by the Christian church

a·nath·e·ma·tize also **-tise** *BrE* /əˈnæθɪ̩mətaɪz/ *v* [T] *tech* (in the Christian church) to put a curse on

An·a·to·li·a /ˌænəˈtəʊliə/ the Asian part of Turkey —see ASIA MINOR

an·a·tom·i·cal /ˌænəˈtɒmɪkəl‖-ˈtɑː-/ *adj* of or concerned with anatomy: *an anatomical description of the leg* – ~ **ly** /kli/ *adv*

a·nat·o·mist /əˈnætəmɪ̩st/ *n* a person skilled in ANATOMY (1)

a·nat·o·my /əˈnætəmi/ *n* **1** [U] the scientific study of the bodies and body parts of people and animals —compare PHYSIOLOGY **2** [C] *often humor* the body of a person or animal: *The ball hit him on a rather delicate part of his anatomy.* **3** [C;U] the DISSECTION (=cutting into pieces) of a body or part of a person or animal to study the way it works or is built **4** [C] *usu. sing.* the way a living thing works or is built: *a lesson on the anatomy of the frog* | (fig.) *The book studies the anatomy of modern society.*

ANC /ˌeɪ en ˈsiː/ [*the*] the African National Congress; a political movement in South Africa, established in 1912, known for its fight against APARTHEID. Its most famous leader is Nelson Mandela.

an·ces·tor /'ænsəstə^r, -ses-‖-ses-/ **an·ces·tress** /-trɪs/ *fem.*— *n* [(of)] a person from whom one is descended, esp. one who lived a long time ago: *My ancestors came from Spain.*| (fig.) *This machine is the ancestor of the modern computer.* —compare DESCENDANT

▶ CULTURAL NOTE Most people do not know the names of their ancestors but some people, esp. in the US and Canada do try to find out about them.◀

an·ces·tral /æn'sestrəl/ *adj* [A] belonging to or coming from one's ancestors: *my ancestral home*

an·ces·try /'ænsestri, -ses-‖-ses-/ *n* [C *usu. sing.*;U] a person's ancestors considered as a group or as a continuous line: *a woman of noble ancestry*|*Scottish ancestry* | *to trace one's ancestry* (=find out who one's ancestors were)

an·chor[1] /'æŋkə^r/ *n* **1** a piece of heavy metal, usu. a hook with two arms, at the end of a chain or rope, for lowering into the water to keep a ship from moving: *We sailed round the coast and* **came to anchor** (=stopped sailing and lowered the anchor) *in a pleasant little bay. In the morning we* **weighed anchor** (=pulled it up) *and sailed on.* | *fishing boats* **riding/lying at anchor** (=floating and held by their anchors) | *The ship* **dropped anchor** (=lowered the anchor) *at Plymouth.* **2** a person or thing that provides support and a feeling of safety **3** *AmE* an ANCHORPERSON —see also SHEET ANCHOR

anchor[2] *v* **1** [I] to stop sailing and lower the anchor **2** [T] to fix firmly in position: *to anchor the roof of a house* **3** [T] *esp. AmE* to serve as an anchorperson of: *She anchors the top-rated news show.*

an·chor·age /'æŋkərɪdʒ/ *n* **1** [C] a place where ships may anchor **2** [C;U] a means of making firm: *Rub the door with sandpaper to provide anchorage for the next coat of paint.*

Anchorage the largest city in Alaska, US, with a large port and a busy industrial airport

an·cho·rite /'æŋkəraɪt/ *n* a person who lives alone for religious reasons; HERMIT

an·chor·per·son /'æŋkə,pɜːsən‖'æŋkər,pɜːrsən/ also **-man** /,mæn/ *masc.*, **-wom·an** /,wumən/ *fem.*— *n esp. AmE* a broadcaster, usu. on television, who is in charge of a news broadcast and appears on it to connect one part of the broadcast with the next

an·cho·vy /'æntʃəvi‖'æntʃəuvi/ *n* **-vies** *or* **-vy** [C;U] a small strong-tasting fish: *The pizza was decorated with slices of anchovy.* | *anchovy paste*

an·cient[1] /'eɪnʃənt/ *adj* **1** [A] in or of times long ago: *ancient Rome and Greece* | *a course in ancient history* **2** having existed for a very long time: *ancient customs/ruins* **3** *usu. humor* (of people or objects) very old: *my ancient car* | *My grandparents are rather ancient.*

▷ USAGE **Ancient** can be used to talk about the people of civilizations long ago: *the ancient Romans.* But it is usu. derogatory or humorous when used of a living person with the meaning "very old": *the ancient caretaker of the building.* —see OLD (USAGE)◁

ancient[2] *n* old use an old man

Ancient Mar·i·ner /,··· '···/ [the] the main character in the poem *The Rime of the Ancient Mariner* by Samuel Taylor Coleridge. He is an old sailor (MARINER) who shot down an ALBATROSS and, because the other sailors thought he had brought bad luck to the ship, wore the albatross on a rope round his neck. Many unlucky and terrible things happen and the sailor later tells his story to anyone who will listen: *He was like the Ancient Mariner, condemned for ever to tell and re-tell the story of his past.* —see also ALBATROSS

an·cients /'eɪnʃənts/ *n* [the+P] (*often cap.*) the European nations of ancient times, esp. as represented by the writers of ancient Greece and Rome: *to study the scientific beliefs of the ancients*

an·cil·la·ry /æn'sɪləri‖'ænsɪleri/ *adj* providing help, support, or additional services: *the ancillary staff of a hospital* (=the people who do cleaning work, cooking, etc.) — **ancillary** *n* : *hospital ancillaries*

and /ənd, ən, *strong* ænd/ *conj* **1** (used to join two things, esp. words of the same type or parts of sentences of the same importance) as well as; also: *a knife and fork* | *John and I* | *He started to shout and sing.* | *a mixture of sugar, flour, and water* | *We were cold and hungry.* | *We solved the problem by reducing our costs and borrowing more*

money. **2** then; afterwards: *She knocked on the door and went in.* | *I woke up and got out of bed.* | *We don't know yet if the operation was a success — we'll just have to* **wait and see.** **3** (expresses a result or explanation): *Water the seeds and they will grow.* | *She was sick and took some medicine.* (=because she was sick) Compare *She took some medicine and was sick.* (=because she took the medicine) **4** (joins repeated words) **a** to show that something continues to happen: *We ran and ran.* | *We waited for hours and hours.* | *It came nearer and nearer.* **b** *infml* to show a difference in quality or kind: *There are dictionaries and dictionaries.* (=some are much better than others) **5 a** (used instead of **to** after **come, go, try,** etc.): *Come and have tea with me.* | *Try and get here before 4 o'clock.* **b** (used after **nice** or **good** to add force): *It's nice and sunny today.* | *The soup was good and hot.* **6** (in saying numbers, used before the numbers 1 to 99 and after the word **hundred**, but sometimes left out in *AmE*): *one million, two hundred and fifty-three thousand, four hundred and twenty-six* (=1,253,426) **7** (in descriptions of food or drinks) served with: *bacon and eggs* | *a gin and tonic* | *bread and butter* (=bread spread with butter) **8 and how!** *sl* (used to give force to the idea just expressed) very much so: *"Did you enjoy yourselves?" "And how!"* **9 and so on/forth** and other things of that kind: *pots, pans, dishes, and so on*

an·dan·te /æn'dænti, -teɪ‖ɑːn'dɑːn-/ *n, adj, adv* (a piece of music) played rather slowly

An·der·sen /'ændəsən‖-dər-/, **Hans Chris·tian** /hæns 'krɪstʃən/ (1805–75) a Danish writer famous for his many FAIRY TALES which include *The Snow Queen, The Little Match Girl,* and *The Ugly Duckling*

Anderson, Sher·wood /'ʃɜːwʊd‖'ʃɜːr-/ (1876–1941) an American writer best known for his NOVEL *Winesburg, Ohio* about the loneliness and dissatisfaction of life in a small town

Anderson shel·ter /'··· ,··/ *n* a small metal AIR-RAID shelter used in Britain during the Second World War

An·des /'ændiːz/ [the] the mountains in the west of South America which separate the narrow coastal area from the rest of the CONTINENT

an·di·ron /'ændaɪən‖-ərn/ also **firedog**— *n* either of a pair of supports for burning logs in a fireplace

An·dor·ra /æn'dɔːrə/ a small, mountainous, partly independent state on the border between France and Spain, popular as a place for holidays and skiing (SKI[2]); population 50,000 (1989) —**Andorran** *n, adj*

-andr- see WORD FORMATION

An·dret·ti /æn'dreti/, **Mar·i·o** /'mæriəʊ‖'mɑː-/ (1940–) an Italian-born American race car driver: *Stop driving so fast! Who do you think you are, Mario Andretti?*

An·drew /'ændruː/, **Prince** the third child of Queen Elizabeth II of Great Britain, a pilot in the Royal Navy, who married Sarah Ferguson in 1986. His title is the Duke of York. In 1992 he and his wife separated.

Andrew, St. see SAINT ANDREW

An·drews /'ændruːz/, **Ju·lie** /'dʒuːli/ (1935–) an English singer and actress whose appearance in the films *Mary Poppins* and *The Sound of Music* helped to give her a pure and healthy image —see colour picture on page 685

Andrews, Éa·monn /'eɪmən/ (1922–87) a television and radio personality from Ireland known esp. as the presenter of the British television programme *This is Your Life*

An·drex /'ændreks/ *n* [U] *tdmk* a type of TOILET PAPER

An·dro·cles and the Li·on /,ændrəkliːz ənd ðə 'laɪən/ an old story of a slave (Androcles) who escapes from a cruel master and meets a lion with a THORN in its foot. Androcles removes the thorn and is later caught and made to fight with a lion in the ARENA as a punishment for running away from his master. However, the lion he is supposed to fight is the one he helped, and instead of attacking, it greets Androcles as a friend. George Bernard Shaw wrote an amusing play based on this story.

an·drog·y·nous /æn'drɒdʒɪnəs‖-'drɑː-/ *adj* (esp. of plants) having both male and female characteristics

an·droid /'ændrɔɪd/ *n* (in stories) a ROBOT in human form

An·drop·ov /æn'drɒpɒf‖ɑːn'drɔːpəf/, **Yu·ri** /'juəri/ (1914–84) a Soviet politician who was general secretary of the Communist Party (1982–4)

An·dy Capp /ˌændi ˈkæp/ a character in a CARTOON, originally in a British newspaper, who wears a flat cap. He is considered to be a STEREOTYPE of a rather old-fashioned British working-class man who is lazy, ignores his wife, and enjoys drinking beer in the pub: *an Andy Capp-like shirker*

Andy Pan·dy /ˌændi ˈpændi/ a PUPPET character in a British children's television programme in the 1950s and 1960s, who wore a blue and white STRIPED suit

an·ec·dot·al /ˌænɪkˈdəʊtl◂/ *adj* of, containing, telling, or full of anecdotes: *an anecdotal lecture about his travels* | *The theory relies more on anecdotal evidence than genuine statistics.*

an·ec·dote /ˈænɪkdəʊt/ *n* a short interesting or amusing story about a person or event

a·ne·mi·a /əˈniːmiə/ *n* [U] *esp. AmE for* ANAEMIA **–anemic** *adj* **–anemically** /kli/ *adv*

an·e·mom·e·ter /ˌænɪˈmɒmɪtəʳ‖-ˈmɑː-/ *n* a machine for measuring the strength of wind –see picture at METER

a·nem·o·ne /əˈneməni/ *n* **1** a plant with red, white, or blue flowers **2** a SEA ANEMONE –see picture at SEA

an·e·roid ba·rom·e·ter /ˌænərɔɪd bəˈrɒmɪtəʳ‖-ˈrɑː-/ *n* an instrument (BAROMETER) that measures changes in air pressure in order to tell what the weather is going to be or how high one is above sea level. It works by measuring the action of air pressure on a metal container emptied of air.

an·es·the·si·a /ˌænɪsˈθiːziə‖-ʒə/ *n* [U] *esp. AmE for* ANAESTHESIA **–anesthetic** /-ˈθetɪk/ *n* **–anesthetist** /əˈniːsθɪtɪst‖əˈnes-/ *n* **–anesthetize** /-θɪtaɪz/ *v* [T]

a·new /əˈnjuː‖əˈnuː/ *adv esp. lit* in a new or different way; again

An·field /ˈænfiːld/ the ground where Liverpool Football Club plays

an·gel /ˈeɪndʒəl/ *n* **1** a servant of God, who is believed by religious people to appear sometimes to people and bring them messages from God. Angels are usu. represented as a person with wings and dressed in white. –see also GUARDIAN ANGEL **2** a person who is very kind, beautiful, etc. **3** *infml* someone who is ready to support something, esp. a play or a film, by lending money **4 on the side of the angels** supporting the side that is morally right **– ~ic** /ænˈdʒelɪk/ *adj* : *Don't be deceived by his angelic smile!* **– ~ically** /kli/ *adv*

angel

angel dust /ˈ·· ·ˌ·/ *n* [U] *AmE sl for* PCP

Angel Falls /ˌ·· ˈ·/ a waterfall in SE Venezuela which has the world's highest uninterrupted fall

angel-food cake /ˈ··· · ˌ·/ *n* [C;U] *AmE* a very light white cake made with beaten egg whites

An·gel·i·co /ænˈdʒelɪkəʊ, Fra /frɑː/ (1400?–1455) an Italian MONK (Christian holy man) and painter, known esp. for his pictures on church walls

An·ge·lou /ˈændʒluː/, **May·a** /ˈmaɪə/ (1928–) a black American writer whose best known book is *I know why the Caged Bird Sings*

an·ge·lus /ˈændʒɪləs/ *n* [*the*+S] (*often cap.*) a bell that is rung three times a day in Roman Catholic churches to tell the people when to say a particular prayer

an·ger[1] /ˈæŋgəʳ/ *n* [U] a strong and sometimes violent feeling of displeasure, usu. leading to a desire to hurt or stop the person or thing causing it; extreme annoyance. Anger is one of the Seven Deadly Sins: *She could hardly contain* (=control) *her anger.* | *The workers reacted with anger and frustration to the closure of the factory.* | *suppressed anger* –see also SEVEN DEADLY SINS

anger[2] *v* [T] to make angry; INFURIATE

an·gi·na pec·to·ris /ænˌdʒaɪnə ˈpektərɪs/ also **angina** *n* [U] a heart disease causing sudden sharp pains in the chest

an·gle[1] /ˈæŋgəl/ *n* **1** the space between two lines or surfaces that meet or cross each other, measured in degrees that represent the amount of a circle that can fit into that space: *An angle of 90° is called a* **right angle**. | *a sharp angle* | *The plant was growing* **at an angle**. (=not straight or upright) | *He took photographs of the statue from several different angles.* **2** a corner, e.g. of a building or piece of furniture **3** *infml* a point of view; STANDPOINT: *If you look at the accident from another angle you will see how funny it all was.*

obtuse angle

angle

acute angle　　　　　　　　right angle

angle[2] *v* [T] **1** to turn or move at an angle: *a mirror angled so as to reflect light from a window* **2** *often derog* to represent (something) from a particular point of view; SLANT[1] (2): *She angles her reports to suit the people she is speaking to.*

angle[3] *v esp. BrE* [I] to try to catch fish with a hook and line: *He loves (to go) angling on a fine summer day.* –compare FISH[2] (1)

angle for sthg. *phr v* [T] *often derog* to try to get, esp. by means of indirect remarks or requests: *She's angling for an invitation/for compliments.*

An·gle·poise /ˈæŋgəlpɔɪz/ *n* , **Anglepoise lamp** /ˈ··· ·ˈ·/ **–** *BrE tdmk* a type of lamp which can be moved on its support into different positions, often used on desks –see picture at LIGHT

an·gler /ˈæŋgləʳ/ *n* a person who tries to catch fish with a hook and line

An·gle·sey /ˈæŋgəlsi/ an island off the NW coast of Wales connected to the mainland by road and railway bridges – see colour map on page 818

An·gli·a /ˈæŋgliə/ one of the British television companies controlled by the ITC, TRANSMITTING programmes to East Anglia

Anglian Wa·ter /ˌ··· ˈ··/ a water company in E England that deals with the supply of water to people and businesses, and the removal and treatment of SEWAGE

An·gli·can /ˈæŋglɪkən/ *n, adj* (a member) of the Church of England, a branch of the Christian religion – **~ ism** *n* [U]

Anglican Com·mu·nion /ˌ··· ·ˈ··/ [*the*] the group of churches around the world, mostly in English-speaking countries, that are descended from the Church of England and are closely related to it in practice and belief

an·gli·cis·m /ˈæŋglɪsɪzəm/ *n* an English word or phrase that is in common use in another language

an·gli·cize also **-cise** *BrE* /ˈæŋglɪsaɪz/ *v* [T] to make English or British in appearance, sound, character, etc.

Anglo- see WORD FORMATION,

Anglo-A·mer·i·can[1] /ˌ··· ·ˈ···◂/ *adj* of or between both Britain and America, esp. the US: *Anglo-American trade*

Anglo-American[2] *n* an American, esp. of the US, who is descended from a British family

Anglo-Cath·o·lic /ˌ··· ˈ···◂/ *n, adj* (a member) of the part of the Church of England whose beliefs and ceremonies are similar to those of the Roman Catholic Church – **~ ism** /ˌ··· ·ˈ····/ *n* [U]

Anglo-In·di·an /ˌ··· ˈ···◂/ *n* **1** a person who is descended from both British and Indian families **2** *old use* a British person born or living in India **–Anglo-Indian** *adj*

Anglo-I·rish A·gree·ment /ˌ··· ·ˈ·· ·ˈ··/ [*the*] an agreement, signed in 1985, between the governments of Britain and the Republic of Ireland. It gave the Republic of Ireland the right to take part in discussions on the affairs of Northern Ireland.

an·glo·phile /ˈæŋgləʊfaɪl, -glə-/ *n* a non-British person who is interested in and likes British people and things

an·glo·phil·i·a /ˌæŋgləʊˈfɪliə, -glə-/ *n* [U] interest in and liking for Britain

an·glo·phobe /ˈæŋgləʊfəʊb, -glə-/ *n* a non-British person who hates British people and things

an·glo·pho·bi·a /ˌæŋgləʊˈfəʊbiə, -glə-/ *n* [U] hatred of Britain

Anglo-Sax·on /ˌ··· ˈ··/ *n* **1** [C] also **Saxon–** a member of the people who lived in England in early times, from about 600 AD **2** [U] the language of the Anglo-Saxons —**Anglo-Saxon** /ˌ··· ˈ···/ *adj*

An·go·la /æŋˈgəʊlə/ a country in SW Africa which was called Portuguese West Africa until it became independent in 1975; capital Luanda; population 9,747,000 (1989) —**Angolan** *n, adj*

an·go·ra /æŋˈgɔːrə/ *n* **1** [C] (*often cap.*) a type of goat (**angora goat**) or rabbit (**angora rabbit**) with long silky hair **2** [U] woollen material or thread made from the hair of an angora rabbit. Things made from angora are expensive and are considered to be LUXURY goods. —compare MOHAIR

an·gos·tur·a /ˌæŋgəˈstjʊərə‖-ˈstʊərə/ *n* [U] a bitter liquid used for adding taste to alcoholic drinks

an·gry /ˈæŋgri/ *adj* [(**with, at**)] **1** feeling or showing anger: *Angry demonstrators jeered at the President.* | *an angry look on her face* | *angry criticism/words* | *I was angry with him for keeping me waiting.* | *I was angry at the delay.* | *Her rudeness made me really angry.* | *an angry exchange of views* **2** (of the sky or clouds) stormy — **angrily** *adv*

▷ USAGE When talking about a person's general character, we do not describe the person as **angry**. Instead, we use words like **quick-tempered** (not too derogatory), **irritable** (fairly weak), **bad-tempered, ill-tempered, ill-natured** (stronger and more derogatory). —see also ANNOY (USAGE)◁

Angry Young Man /ˌ··· · ˈ·/ *n BrE* a person who strongly criticizes established social and political institutions, first used to describe John Osborne and other British working-class or lower-middle-class writers in the 1950s. John Osborne's most famous play was *Look Back in Anger* and the main character, Jimmy Porter, was a typical Angry Young Man.

angst /æŋst/ *n* [U] anxiety and anguish caused esp. by considering the sad state of the world and/or the human condition

an·guish /ˈæŋgwɪʃ/ *n* [U] very great pain and suffering, esp. of the mind: *She was in anguish over her missing child.* —**anguished** *adj*: *anguished cries*

an·gu·lar /ˈæŋgjʊləʳ/ *adj* **1** having sharp corners **2** (of a person's body) with the bones able to be clearly seen; not rounded: *her sharp angular face* **3** [A] having or forming an angle or angles — ~ **ity** /ˌæŋgjʊˈlærˌti/ *n* [C;U]

An·gus /ˈæŋgəs/ a former COUNTY in E Scotland, now part of Tayside REGION

An·heu·ser-Busch /ˌænhaɪzə ˈbʊʃ‖-zər-/ *n* an American company which makes beer

an·i·mad·vert /ˌænɪmædˈvɜːt‖-ɜːrt/ *v* [I (**on, upon, about**)] *pomp* to speak about, esp. in a way that finds fault — **version** /ˈvɜːʃən‖ˈvɜːrʒən/ *n*

Animal, Vege·ta·ble or Min·e·ral /ˌ··· ˌ··· · ˈ···/ *AmE* for TWENTY QUESTIONS

an·i·mal¹ /ˈænˌməl/ *n* **1** a living creature, not a plant, that has senses and is able to move itself when it wants to: *Snakes, fish, and birds are all animals.* | *Humans are the most intelligent of all the animals.* | *Man is a political animal.* **2** all this group except human beings: *farm animals* | *Should animals be kept in cages?* **3** a MAMMAL **4** a person considered as behaving like a wild non-human creature **5** all animals are equal, but some animals are more equal than others *quote* a phrase from the book *Animal Farm* by George Orwell —see ANIMAL FARM **6** animal, vegetable or mineral a phrase used in popular British and American game shows on television and radio. In the games, people had to discover what an unknown object was by asking a number of questions.

animal² *adj* **1** [A] of, concerning, or made from animals: *cooking with animal fats* | *animal feed* **2** of the body, not the mind or the spirit, esp. concerning one's APPETITEs for food and sex: *animal desires*

animal crack·er /ˌ··· ˈ··/ *n* a small BISCUIT baked in the shape of an animal, usu. eaten by small children: *He ate a lion from his box of animal crackers.*

Animal Farm /ˌ··· ˈ·/ a book by George Orwell. In the story, a group of animals decide to live in a society in which they are all equal, but the pigs soon become the leaders and state that they are in fact better than the others. They say that "All animals are equal, but some animals are

more equal than others." This phrase is often used when saying that it is impossible to organize a society as a COMMUNIST society, with everyone equal, because some people will always become the leaders sooner or later.

animal hus·band·ry /ˌ··· ˈ···/ *n* [U] the branch of farming concerned with the keeping of animals and the production of animal materials, such as milk and meat

Animal Lib·e·ra·tion Front /ˌ··· ··ˈ·· ˌˈ·/ (*abbrev.* **ALF**) [*the*] a British organization which protests against the use of animals for scientific EXPERIMENTs, such as testing drugs and beauty products. Some of its members have been involved in freeing the animals.

animal rights group /ˌ··· ˈ· ˌˈ·/ *n* a group of people who protest against cruel treatment of animals

an·i·mate¹ /ˈænˌmɨt/ *adj* (of plants and animals) having life; alive —opposite **inanimate**

an·i·mate² /ˈænˌmeɪt/ *v* [T] *rather fml* to give life or excitement to; ENLIVEN: *Laughter animated his face.*

an·i·ma·ted /ˈænˌmeɪtˌd/ *adj* full of spirit and excitement; lively: *an animated argument/debate* — ~ **ly** *adv*

animated car·toon /ˌ··· · ˈ·/ *n fml for* CARTOON (2)

an·i·ma·tion /ˌænˌˈmeɪʃən/ *n* [U] **1** excitement; spirit; liveliness: *They were full of animation as they talked about their holiday.* **2** the making of CARTOONs

an·i·mis·m /ˈænˌmɪzəm/ *n* [U] a religion according to which natural objects, animals, and plants are believed to have souls —**mist** *n, adj*

an·i·mos·i·ty /ˌænˌˈmɒsˌti‖-ˈmɑː-/ *n* [C;U (**towards, between**)] (an example of) powerful, often active, hatred; HOSTILITY

an·i·seed /ˈænˌsiːd/ *n* [U] the strong-tasting seeds of a plant (**anise** /ˈænˌs/), used esp. in alcoholic drinks

An·ka·ra /ˈæŋkərə/ the capital city of Turkey

an·kle /ˈæŋkəl/ *n* **1** the joint between the foot and the leg **2** the part of the leg just above the heel: *ankle socks* (=that do not reach beyond the ankles) —see picture at FOOT

an·klet /ˈæŋklˌt/ *n* a ring or BRACELET worn round the ankle as a decoration

An·na Ka·ren·in·a /ˌænə kəˈrenɪnə/ a NOVEL by the Russian writer Count Leo Tolstoy which is considered to be one of the greatest works of Russian literature. It tells the sad story of a married woman who loves a young army officer.

an·nals /ˈænlz/ *n* [P (**of**)] *fml* a record of events or activities that is arranged in yearly parts, such as a record of the activities of a scientific society produced every year: *the Annals of the Zoological Society* | (fig.) *one of the most disgraceful episodes in the annals* (=history) *of British politics* —**annalist** *n*

An·nap·o·lis /əˈnæpəlɪs/ the capital of the US state of Maryland, where the United States Naval Academy, the place where the navy trains its officers, is based. Annapolis is often used to mean the academy itself: *He'll be attending Annapolis in the fall.*

Anne /æn/, **Princess** (1950–) the second child and only daughter of Queen Elizabeth II of Great Britain. Her title is the Princess Royal. She won a gold MEDAL for horse-riding in the 1972 Olympic Games and is known for her CHARITY work as President of the Save the Children Fund. She was divorced (DIVORCE) from her first husband, Captain Mark Phillips, and remarried Commander Tim Laurence in 1992.

Anne, Queen (1665–1714) a queen of Great Britain and Ireland (1702–14) and daughter of James II —see also QUEEN ANNE

an·neal /əˈniːl/ *v* [T] to make (metal, glass, etc.) hard by allowing slowly to become cool after heating until soft

an·nex /əˈneks‖əˈneks, ˈæneks/ *v* [T (**to**)] to take control and possession of (land, a small country, etc.), esp. by force — ~ **ation** /ˌænekˈseɪʃən/ *n* [C;U] : *Rome's annexation of Britain in 43 AD*

an·nexe *esp. BrE* ‖ **annex** *esp. AmE* /ˈæneks/ *n* a building joined or added to a larger one: *a hospital annexe*

An·ni·go·ni /ˌænɪˈgəʊni/, **Piet·ro** /ˈpjetrəʊ/ (1910–88) an Italian PORTRAIT painter who has painted pictures of John F. Kennedy and Queen Elizabeth

an·ni·hi·late /əˈnaɪəleɪt/ *v* [T] to destroy completely: *We annihilated the enemy.* | (fig.) *His arguments were annihilated.* —**lation** /əˌnaɪəˈleɪʃən/ *n* [U]: *the threat of* *annihilation by nuclear weapons/nuclear annihilation*

an·ni·ver·sa·ry /ˌænɪˈvɜːsəri‖-ɜːr-/ n [(of)] a day which is an exact year or number of years after a particular event: *a wedding anniversary | It's the twentieth anniversary of our country's independence.* (=exactly 20 years since it became independent) | *anniversary celebrations* —compare BIRTHDAY

An·no Dom·i·ni /ˌænəʊ ˈdɒmɪnaɪ‖-ˈdɑː-/ fml for AD

an·no·tate /ˈænəteɪt/ v [T] fml to add short notes to (a book) to explain certain parts: *an annotated edition of Shakespeare's plays* —**-tation** /ˌænəˈteɪʃən/ n [C;U]

an·nounce /əˈnaʊns/ v [T] 1 to make known publicly: *They announced the date of their wedding in the paper.* [+that] *The government has announced that electricity charges will go up in the spring.* | (fig.) *The bright flowers announced that spring was here.* 2 to state in a loud voice: *Everyone was silent as he announced the winner of the competition.* 3 to read (news) or introduce (a person or act) on the radio, television, etc. —see also UNANNOUNCED

an·nounce·ment /əˈnaʊnsmənt/ n 1 [C] a statement making publicly known something that has happened or will happen: *flight arrival announcements at the airport | a news/wedding announcement | I've got an important announcement to make.* 2 [U] the act of announcing something: *The announcement of the trade figures was delayed until after the election.*

an·nounc·er /əˈnaʊnsəʳ/ n a person who reads news or introduces people, acts, etc., esp. on radio or television

an·noy /əˈnɔɪ/ v [T] to make (someone) a little angry or impatient, esp. by repeated troublesome actions or attacks; IRRITATE: *These flies are annoying me.* | *I was annoyed with him because he kept interrupting.* | *an annoying delay* | *It annoyed me to think how much time we had wasted.*

▷ USAGE Things that make you fairly angry **annoy** you, **irritate** you or, less commonly, **provoke** you, **incense** you, or **rile** you. In informal speech they can also be said to **aggravate** you, but some people do not like this use of the word —see also AGGRAVATE (USAGE). You find these things **annoying, irritating, provoking,** or **aggravating.** Things which make you very angry **infuriate** you, and you find them **infuriating.**◁

an·noy·ance /əˈnɔɪəns/ n 1 [U] the feeling of being annoyed: *"Go away!" she replied with annoyance.* 2 [C] something which causes this: *The noisy traffic is a continual annoyance.*

an·nu·al¹ /ˈænjuəl/ adj 1 (happening, appearing, etc.) every year or once a year: *an annual event/festival/convention* 2 of or for one year: *What's your annual salary?* —see also AGM — ~ **ly** adv

annual² n 1 a plant that lives for only one year or season —compare BIENNIAL 2 a book produced once each year having the same title but containing different stories, pictures, information, etc.: *the Football Annual for 1993*

annual ac·counts /ˌ··· ·ˈ·/ n [P] a company's financial statement including the PROFIT AND LOSS ACCOUNT and the BALANCE SHEET. In Britain public limited companies (PUBLIC LIMITED COMPANY) and in the US CORPORATIONS must, by law, produce annual accounts for people to see.

annual meet·ing /ˌ··· ˈ·-/ n AmE for AGM

annual re·port /ˌ··· ·ˈ·/ n the report which a company sends to its SHAREHOLDERS each year, which may include annual accounts

annual re·turn /ˌ··· ·ˈ·/ n a tax form that self-employed people in Britain complete each year, giving details of their income, etc., so that the amount of tax they must pay can be calculated

an·nu·i·ty /əˈnjuːɪti‖əˈnuː-/ n a fixed sum of money paid each year to a person for a stated number of years or until death: *pension annuities*

an·nul /əˈnʌl/ v -ll- [T] tech to cause (a marriage, agreement, law, etc.) to no longer exist and to have no legal force. Catholics are not allowed to DIVORCE, but there are sometimes reasons for annulling a marriage —see also RESCIND — ~ **ment** n [C;U]

An·nun·ci·a·tion /əˌnʌnsiˈeɪʃən/ n [the] the occasion (celebrated by Christians on 25 March) on which the ANGEL (1) Gabriel appeared and told the Virgin Mary that she would bear the baby Jesus Christ

an·ode /ˈænəʊd/ also **positive pole—** n tech the part of an

electrical instrument (such as a BATTERY) which collects ELECTRONS, often a rod or wire represented by the sign (+) —compare CATHODE

an·o·dyne¹ /ˈænədaɪn/ adj often derog unlikely to offend or annoy anyone; BLAND: *After their meeting, the two leaders produced an anodyne statement that didn't really say anything at all.*

anodyne² n fml something which comforts a troubled mind or turns the attention away from more important matters

a·noint /əˈnɔɪnt/ v [T (with)] to put oil on (a person, head, or body), esp. in a religious ceremony: *The priest anointed her with oil.* [+obj+n] *They anointed him king.* (=put oil on him as a formal sign that he had become king) — ~ **ment** n [C;U]

a·nom·a·ly /əˈnɒməli‖əˈnɑː-/ n fml 1 [C] a person, thing, or situation that is different from the usual or accepted type: *A cat with no tail is an anomaly.* | *a statistical anomaly* 2 [U] unusual irregularity: *The anomaly of his position is that he is the chairman of the committee but isn't allowed to vote.* —**lous** adj : *in an anomalous position* —**lously** adv

a·non¹ /əˈnɒn‖əˈnɑːn/ adv old use or poet in a short time; soon —see also **ever and anon** (EVER)

anon² abbrev. for: (esp. at the end of a poem, letter, etc.) anonymous

an·o·nym·i·ty /ˌænəˈnɪmɪti/ n [U] the condition of being anonymous: *The defendants' anonymity was maintained until they were brought to court.*

a·non·y·mous /əˈnɒnɪməs‖əˈnɑː-/ adj 1 (of a person) with name unknown: *The flowers were sent by an anonymous admirer.* | *The writer of this article wishes to remain anonymous.* 2 done or made by someone whose name is not known or stated: *an anonymous letter/phone call/bomb threat | The Disaster Fund received an anonymous donation of £5000.* — ~ **ly** adv

a·noph·e·les /əˈnɒfɪliːz‖əˈnɑː-/ n tech a type of MOSQUITO, esp. the sort that spreads MALARIA

an·o·rak /ˈænəræk/ n esp. BrE a short coat that has a HOOD (=a cover for the head) and keeps out wind and rain

an·o·rex·i·a /ˌænəˈreksiə◂/ also **anorexia ner·vo·sa** /nɜːˈvəʊsə‖nɜːr-/— n [U] tech a serious illness in which there is loss of the desire for food and refusal to eat. The disease is suffered esp. by young women, who feel that they are unattractive because they are too fat, even when they are not. Some people believe that anorexia is partly caused by Western Society's belief that thin people are more attractive. —see also EATING DISORDER

an·o·rex·ic /ˌænəˈreksɪk◂/ n, adj (a person) suffering from anorexia

an·oth·er /əˈnʌðəʳ/ determiner, pron 1 (being) one more of the same kind: *Have another drink and another of these cakes.* | *He finished his sausage and asked for another (one).* | *He poured out yet another drink.* (=he had already had several) 2 more; in addition; FURTHER² (2): *If you want a double room that will cost another £15.* | *In another two weeks we'll be on holiday.* 3 a different one; some other: *There must be another way of doing it.* | *She lost her book and borrowed one from another girl/from another of the girls.* | *I'm in a hurry now; I'll do it another time.* | *They asked the advice of an outsider so as to get another perspective on the problem.* | *one law for the rich and another for the poor* | *It tastes delicious, but whether it's good for you is another matter altogether!* (=it probably is not good for you) —see also ONE ANOTHER; see OTHER (USAGE)

A N Oth·er /ˌeɪ en ˈʌðəʳ/ BrE another person whose name is not known: *The classes will be taught by Joanne Brown, Robert Smith and A N Other.*

An·ou·ilh /ˈænuːiː‖ɑːˈnuːjə, **Jean** /ʒɒn‖ʒɑːn/ (1910–87) a French writer of plays, including *Antigone* and *Becket*

An·sa·phone /ˈɑːnsəfəʊn‖ˈæn-/ n tdmk a telephone answering machine: *Leave a message on the Ansaphone.*

An·schluss /ˈænʃlʊs‖ˈɑːn-/ n the taking over of Austria by Hitler's Germany in 1938

ANSI /ˈænsi/ American National Standards Institute; an organization which sets standards for the DESIGN and performance of esp. electronic and scientific equipment: *The network conforms to ANSI X3T9.5.*

an·swer¹ /ˈɑːnsəʳ‖ˈæn-/ n 1 [C (to)] what is said, written, or done as a result of someone asking a question, sending a letter, etc.; reply: *a written/spoken answer | an official/unofficial answer | Although I wrote a month ago, I've had no answer (to my letter) yet. | We've made her an offer and we're now waiting for an answer. | I rang the doorbell but there was no answer.* | **In answer to** *my shouts people ran to help. | His only answer to their threat was to laugh. | a question-and-answer session with the leader of the Democrats | She gave/made no answer to his questions.* **2** [C] something which is discovered as a result esp. of thinking, calculating, etc.; SOLUTION: *The answer was 279. | The correct/wrong answer | There are no easy answers to the problem of unemployment.* | (fig.) *I'm getting too fat – the only answer is to eat less.* **3** [C] a piece of usu. written work to show knowledge or ability, e.g. in an examination: *Please write your answers on both sides of the paper.* **4** [S+to] a person or thing that is regarded as equal or similar to someone or something from another place; EQUIVALENT: *He's been described as Scotland's answer to Frank Sinatra.*

answer² *v* **1** [I;T] to give an answer (to); reply (to): *Why didn't you answer (me)? | The President answered the reporters' questions.* **2** [T+that;obj] to say as an answer: *I asked her the time, but she answered that she didn't know. | "I don't know," she answered.* **3** [I;T (with)] to do something as a reply (to): *She answered me with an angry look.* **4** [I;T] to act in reply to (a sign such as a telephone ringing or a knock on a door): *I knocked at the door but no one answered. | The phone's ringing – shall I answer it?* (=pick it up) | *a telephone answering machine* **5** [T] to give an explanation in reply to (a charge or argument): *How would you answer the criticism that your government has increased the level of taxation?* **6** [I+to;T] to be as described in; fit; CORRESPOND to: *He answers (to) the description given by the police, so he must be the criminal.* **7** [T] *fml* to be satisfactory for; fulfil: *This machinery will answer the company's needs very well. | The new government just didn't answer our hopes.*

▷ USAGE Compare **answer, reply, respond, retort, and rejoin. Answer** and **reply** are the usual verbs for answering questions; **respond** (*fml*) means the same thing but is less common: *"Are you coming?" "Yes," he answered/replied/responded.* With an object we use **answer, reply, respond to:** *We must answer/reply to/respond to these questions as soon as possible.* **Retort** or **rejoin** (rare) mean "to answer showing disagreement" and are usually used when reporting the actual words spoken: *"Are you ready?" "Why should I be ready when you're not?" she retorted.*◁

answer (sbdy.) **back** *phr v* [I;T *no pass.*] *infml* (esp. of children talking to adults) to reply rudely (to): *Don't answer (your grandmother) back: it's not polite.*

answer for sbdy./sthg. *phr v* [T (**to**)] **1** to accept responsibility for: *I will answer (to you) for his safety.* – compare ACCOUNT **for** (1,2) **2** to pay, suffer, or be punished as a result of: *You will have to answer for your violent behaviour in court. | It was his policies that got the country into this mess –* **he's got a lot to answer for!** (=he deserves the blame for a lot of things)

answer to sthg. *phr v* [T] **1** to act in reply to; obey: *The dog answers to his name.* **2 answer to the name of** pomp or humor to be called: *They had an old servant, who answered to the name of Brown.*

an·swer·a·ble /ˈɑːnsərəbəl‖ˈæn-/ *adj* **1** [F (**to, for**)] having to explain or defend one's actions; responsible; AC-COUNTABLE: *I am answerable to the government for any decision I make.* **2** able to be answered –**-bly** *adv* –**-bility** /ˌɑːnsərəˈbɪləti‖ˌæn-/ *n* [U]

answering ma·chine /ˈ··· ·ˌ·/ also **answerphone** *n* a machine attached to a telephone which records messages when one is unable to answer the telephone

an·swer·phone /ˈɑːnsəfəʊn‖ˈænsər-/ *n* an answering machine

ant /ænt/ *n* a small insect living on the ground in large social groups and known for hard work –see picture at INSECT

an·tag·o·nis·m /ænˈtægənɪzəm/ *n* [C;U (**to, towards**)] (an example of) active opposition or hatred, esp. between people or groups: *religious/ethnic antagonism | their obvious antagonism towards this proposal*

an·tag·o·nist /ænˈtægənɪst/ *n* a person who is opposed to another, esp. actively; opponent; ADVERSARY –compare

PROTAGONIST – – ~**ic** /ænˌtægəˈnɪstɪk◂/ *adj* [(**to, towards**)] – ~**ically** /kli/ *adv*

an·tag·o·nize also **-nise** *BrE* /ænˈtægənaɪz/ *v* [T] to cause to become an enemy or opponent: *His rudeness only antagonizes people.* (=makes them dislike him)

Ant·arc·tic /ænˈtɑːktɪk‖-ɑːr-/ *n* [the] the very cold most southern part of the world –compare ARCTIC **–Antarctic** *adj*

Ant·arc·tic·a /ænˈtɑːktɪkə‖-ɑːr-/ the large land mass (CONTINENT) surrounding the South Pole

Antarctic Cir·cle /·ˌ·· ˈ··/ *n* [the] an imaginary line drawn round the world at a certain distance from the most southern point (the South Pole), south of which there is no darkness for six months of each year and almost no light for the other six months –compare ARCTIC CIRCLE, and see picture at GLOBE

an·te¹ /ˈænti/ *n* **1** [C *usu. sing.*] an amount that is risked in the card game of POKER; a STAKE¹ (4): *a £2 ante* **2** [*the*+S] *infml, esp. AmE* an amount paid; price: *an attempt to up the ante*

ante² *v*

ante up (sthg.) *phr v* **-ted** *or* **-teed, -teing** [I;T] *AmE infml* to pay (an amount of money), esp. in a game of chance; to provide (one's share of the money)

ante- see WORD FORMATION

ant·eat·er /ˈæntˌiːtəʳ/ *n* an animal that eats ants, esp. one with a long sticky tongue

an·te·ced·ent¹ /ˌæntɪˈsiːdənt/ *n* **1** *fml* an event that comes before or causes another event **2** *tech* (in grammar) the word, phrase, or sentence that is represented by another word such as a PRONOUN. In the sentence "I saw John and spoke to him", *John* is the antecedent of *him.*

antecedent² *adj* [(**to**)] *fml* coming or being before

an·te·ced·ents /ˌæntɪˈsiːdənts/ *n* [P] *fml* past family or past history: *a person of unknown antecedents*

an·te·cham·ber /ˈæntɪˌtʃeɪmbəʳ/ also **anteroom**– *n* a small room leading to a larger one

an·te·date /ˈæntɪdeɪt, ˌæntɪˈdeɪt/ *v* [T] **1** to be earlier in history than: *This old carriage antedates the invention of the car.* **2** to write a date earlier than the date of writing on (a letter, cheque, etc.) –compare POSTDATE, BACKDATE

an·te·di·lu·vi·an /ˌæntɪdɪˈluːviən◂/ *adj humor* very old-fashioned; OUTDATED: *antediluvian ideas about marriage*

an·te·lope /ˈæntɪləʊp‖ˈæntəl-/ *n* **-lopes** *or* **-lope** a graceful grass-eating animal that has horns and is able to run very fast –see picture at DEER

ante me·rid·i·em /ˌænti məˈrɪdiəm, -diem/ *adv fml rare for* AM

an·te·na·tal /ˌæntiˈneɪtl◂/ *BrE* ‖ **prenatal** *AmE*– *adj tech* of or for the time before a birth: *antenatal care | An* **antenatal clinic** *is a place where women who are expecting babies go for medical examinations and exercises.* –compare POSTNATAL

an·ten·na /ænˈtenə/ *n* **1** (*pl.* **-nae** /niː/) a long thin sensitive hairlike organ, usu. growing in pairs, on the heads of some insects and CRUSTACEANS (=animals that live in shells), and used to feel with; FEELER –see picture at INSECT **2** (*pl.* **-nas**) *esp. AmE for* AERIAL: *a television antenna* –see picture at HOUSE

an·te·ri·or /ænˈtɪəriəʳ/ *adj* [no comp.] **1** [F+to] *fml* earlier (than); before; PRIOR **2** [A] (in BIOLOGY) nearer the front –opposite posterior

an·te·room /ˈæntɪrʊm, -ruːm/ *n* **1** an ANTECHAMBER **2** a WAITING ROOM

an·them /ˈænθəm/ *n* **1** a religious song to be sung in a church, esp. by a CHOIR, often with words taken from the Bible **2** any ceremonial song of praise –see also NATIONAL ANTHEM

an·ther /ˈænθəʳ/ *n* the part of a male flower which contains POLLEN (=the substance that makes the female flower bear fruit or seeds) –see picture at FLOWER

ant·hill /ˈæntˌhɪl/ *n* a raised mass of earth, little pieces of wood, etc., in which ants live

an·thol·o·gy /ænˈθɒlədʒi‖ænˈθɑː-/ *n* a collection of poems or other writings, often on the same subject, that have been chosen from different books or writers –compare OMNIBUS (1) **–-gist** *n*

An·tho·ny /ˈæntəni/, **Su·san** /ˈsuːzən/ **B.** (1820–1906) an American woman who fought to get the vote for women. Her picture is on the dollar coin.

an·thra·cite /ˈænθrəsaɪt/ n [U] a very hard kind of coal that burns slowly and without smoke

an·thrax /ˈænθræks/ n [U] a serious disease which attacks cattle, sheep, and sometimes humans

an·thro·po·cen·tric /ˌænθrəpəʊˈsentrɪk◂‖-pəˈsen-/ adj fml regarding human existence as the most important and central fact in the world — ~ **ally** /kli/ adv

an·thro·poid /ˈænθrəpɔɪd/ adj **1** [A] (of an animal) like a person: anthropoid apes such as the chimpanzee and the gorilla **2** infml derog (of a person) like a monkey

an·thro·pol·o·gy /ˌænθrəˈpɒlədʒi‖-ˈpɑː-/ n [U] the scientific study of the human race, including its different types and its beliefs, social habits and organization, etc. —compare ETHNOLOGY, SOCIOLOGY —**gist** n —**gical** /ˌænθrəpəˈlɒdʒɪkəl◂‖-ˈlɑː-/ adj —**gically** /kli/ adv

an·thro·po·mor·phic /ˌænθrəpəˈmɔːfɪk◂‖-ɔːr-/ adj fml (of a god or animal) having the form or qualities of a person

an·thro·po·mor·phis·m /ˌænθrəpəˈmɔːfɪzəm‖-ɔːr-/ n [U] fml or tech the idea that gods or animals have human forms or qualities

anti- see WORD FORMATION

an·ti·air·craft /ˌæntiˈeəkrɑːft‖-ˈeərkræft/ adj [A] (esp. of gunfire) directed against enemy aircraft: antiaircraft missiles

An·tibes /ɒnˈtiːb‖ɑːn-/ a fashionable holiday RESORT on the French Riviera

an·ti·bi·ot·ic /ˌæntɪbaɪˈɒtɪk◂‖-ˈɑː-/ n a medical substance, such as PENICILLIN, that is produced by living things and is able to destroy or stop the growth of harmful bacteria that have entered the body: a course of antibiotics to clear an infection —**antibiotic** adj

an·ti·bod·y /ˈæntɪˌbɒdi‖-ˌbɑː-/ n a substance produced in the body which fights against disease

An·ti·christ /ˈæntɪˌkraɪst/ [the] in the Christian religion, a great enemy of Christ who represents the power of evil and is expected to appear just before the end of the world

an·tic·i·pate /ænˈtɪsɪpeɪt/ v [T] **1** to think likely to happen; expect: Are you anticipating any trouble when the factory opens again? [+v-ing/that] We anticipate meeting/that we will meet a certain amount of resistance to our plan. | an anticipated growth rate of 4.2% **2** to guess or imagine in advance (what will happen) and take the necessary action in order to be ready: I tried to anticipate the kind of questions they were likely to ask me at the interview. [+wh-] In business, you've got to anticipate how your competitors will act. [+that] We anticipated that the enemy would try to cross the river so we destroyed the bridge. **3** to do something before (someone else): We anticipated our competitors by getting our book into the shops first. **4** fml to consider, mention, or make use of before the proper time: It is unwise to anticipate your earnings by spending a lot of money. —**patory** /ænˌtɪsɪˈpeɪtəri‖ænˈtɪsəpətɔːri/ adj

▷ USAGE Although **anticipate** is commonly used to mean "expect", this is thought by some teachers to be incorrect.◁

an·tic·i·pa·tion /ænˌtɪsɪˈpeɪʃən/ n [U (of)] the act of anticipating: I had taken my coat and umbrella in **anticipation of** rain. | The crowd waited outside the theatre in eager anticipation.

an·ti·cler·i·cal /ˌæntiˈklerɪkəl◂/ adj opposed to the influence of priests in public and political life — ~ **ism** n [U]

an·ti·cli·max /ˌæntiˈklaɪmæks/ n **1** something unexciting, ordinary, or disappointing coming after something important or exciting: To be back in the office after climbing mountains for a week was a bit of an anticlimax. **2** a sudden often funny change from something noble, serious, exciting, etc., to something foolish, unimportant, or uninteresting, esp. in a speech or piece of formal writing —see also CLIMAX

an·ti·clock·wise /ˌæntiˈklɒkwaɪz‖-ˈklɑːk-/ BrE ‖ **counterclockwise** AmE— adj, adv in the opposite direction to the movement of the hands of a clock: To remove the lid, turn it anticlockwise. —opposite **clockwise**

Anti-Corn Law League /ˌ·· ·· ·ˌ·/ [the] a group of people, led by Richard Cobden and John Bright, who protested against the corn laws in Britain in the 1840s

an·tics /ˈæntɪks/ n [P] strange or foolish behaviour that is usu. regarded with disapproval: The public eventually grew tired of his antics on the tennis court.

an·ti·cy·clone /ˌæntɪˈsaɪkləʊn/ n tech a mass of air that is heavy, causing calm weather, either hot or cold, in the area over which it moves —see also CYCLONE

an·ti·de·pres·sant /ˌæntidɪˈpresənt/ n a type of drug used in the treatment of DEPRESSION

an·ti·dote /ˈæntɪdəʊt/ n (**to**) a substance that stops a poison working inside a person or prevents the bad effects of a disease: a dangerous poison for which there is no known antidote | (fig.) Do you think there is any antidote to the nation's economic troubles?

an·ti·freeze /ˈæntɪfriːz/ n [U] a chemical substance put in water to stop it from freezing in very cold weather, used esp. in car engines

an·ti·gen /ˈæntɪdʒən/ n a harmful substance such as a bacterium or VIRUS which causes the body to produce antibodies (ANTIBODY) to fight it

An·tig·o·ne /ænˈtɪgəni/ in CLASSICAL MYTHOLOGY, a daughter of Oedipus, who, torn between her religious and legal duties, disobeyed the king and then killed herself. Her story is told by Sophocles in his play Antigone.

An·ti·gua /ænˈtiːgə/ an island in the Caribbean which is a centre of business and COMMUNICATIONS for the area — **Antiguan** adj,n

an·ti·her·o /ˈæntiˌhɪərəʊ/ n **-oes** the main character in a work of literature, who is represented as being no braver, stronger, or cleverer than ordinary people —compare HERO

an·ti·his·ta·mine /ˌæntiˈhɪstəmiːn, -mɪn/ n [C;U] a chemical substance that is used in the treatment of colds and allergies (ALLERGY)

an·ti·knock /ˌæntiˈnɒk‖-ˈnɑːk/ n [U] a chemical substance that is added to petrol to make car engines run smoothly, without knocking (KNOCK[1] (4))

an·ti·log·a·rith·m /ˌæntiˈlɒgərɪðəm‖-ˈlɑː-, -ˈlɔː-/ also **an·ti·log** /ˈæntɪlɒg‖-lɑːg, -lɔːg/— n infml the number whose LOGARITHM is a stated number: The antilogarithm of 2 is 100 because $10^2 = 100$.

an·ti·ma·cas·sar /ˌæntɪməˈkæsər/ n a piece of cloth put on the back of a chair, as a decoration and to protect it from marks left by hair oil. Antimacassars were widely used in the past, but are now considered old-fashioned.

an·ti·mat·ter /ˈæntɪmætər/ n [U] matter which is made up of antiparticles

an·ti·nu·cle·ar /ˌæntiˈnjuːkliər◂‖-ˈnuː-/ adj opposing the use of atomic power (for producing electricity) and the production and use of atomic weapons: an antinuclear demonstration | the antinuclear movement

an·ti·par·ti·cle /ˈæntiˌpɑːtɪkəl‖-ˌpɑːr-/ n an ELEMENTARY PARTICLE (=very small unit of matter in an atom) that carries the opposite electrical charge of the matter usu. found in atoms. Antiparticles are very rare in the known parts of the universe but they can be made in special scientific tests.

an·ti·pas·to /ˈæntipæstəʊ‖ˌæntiˈpɑː-/ n **-tos** or **-ti** /-tiː/ It a dish of food, usu. cold food, eaten before the main dish of a meal

an·ti·pa·thet·ic /ˌæntɪpəˈθetɪk◂/ adj [(to)] feeling, causing, or showing antipathy: He has always been strongly antipathetic to the views of the women's movement. — ~ **ally** /kli/ adv

an·tip·a·thy /ænˈtɪpəθi/ n [C;U (to, towards)] (an example of) a fixed and strong dislike or opposition; AVERSION: the President's well-known antipathy towards trade unions

an·ti·per·son·nel /ˌæntɪpɜːsəˈnel‖-ɜːr-/ adj euph (of bombs) intended to hurt people, not destroy property, by exploding into small pieces

an·ti·per·spi·rant /ˌæntɪˈpɜːspərənt‖-ˈpɜːr-/ n a chemical substance that helps to stop the skin from sweating (SWEAT) —compare DEODORANT

An·tip·o·des /ænˈtɪpədiːz/ n [the+P] lit or humor Australia and New Zealand —**Antipodean** /ænˌtɪpəˈdiːən/ adj

an·ti·quar·i·an¹ /ˌæntɪˈkweəriən◂/ also **an·ti·qua·ry** /ˈæntɪkwəri‖-kweri/— n a person who studies, collects, or sells antiquities or antiques

antiquarian² adj of or concerning antiquities or antiques or people who study, collect, or sell such things: an antiquarian bookseller

an·ti·quat·ed /ˈæntɪˌkweɪtɪd/ *adj* old and not suited to modern needs or conditions; old-fashioned; OUTDATED: *antiquated laws|machinery*

an·tique¹ /ænˈtiːk/ *adj* **1** made in an earlier period and usu. valuable: *an antique vase* **2** [A] *fml* of or connected with ancient times, esp. ancient Rome or Greece

antique² *n* a piece of furniture, decorative object, jewellery, etc., that was made in an earlier period and that is rare or valuable: *The palace is full of priceless antiques.* | *an antique dealer*

an·tiq·ui·ty /ænˈtɪkwɪti/ *n* **1** [U] the state of being very old; great age: *a building of great antiquity* **2** [C;U] (a building, work of art, etc., remaining from) ancient times, esp. before the Middle Ages: *to photograph the antiquities in the museum* | *one of the great writers of antiquity*

an·tir·rhi·num /ˌæntɪˈraɪnəm/ *n* a SNAPDRAGON

an·ti-Sem·i·tis·m /ˌænti ˈsemɪtɪzəm/ *n* [U] hatred of Jews —see also SEMITIC —-**Semitic** /sɪˈmɪtɪk◂/ *adj* —-**Semite** /ˈsiːmaɪt‖ˈsemaɪt/ *n*

an·ti·sep·tic /ˌæntɪˈseptɪk◂/ *n* a chemical substance that prevents disease in a wound, esp. by killing bacteria — **antiseptic** *adj*

an·ti·so·cial /ˌæntɪˈsəʊʃəl◂/ *adj* **1** causing harm to the way in which people live together peacefully, esp. by showing no concern for other people: *Playing music so loud that it annoys everyone else in the street is antisocial.* | *antisocial behaviour* **2** not liking to mix with other people; UNSOCIABLE: *Jane's very friendly, but her husband's rather antisocial.* **3** damaging to social life; UNSOCIAL: *antisocial work hours*

an·tith·e·sis /ænˈtɪθəsɪs/ *n* [(the) S (of, to)] *fml* the direct opposite: *The antithesis of death is life.* | *Their political views are the complete antithesis of mine.*

an·ti·thet·i·cal /ˌæntɪˈθetɪkəl/ also **an·ti·thet·ic** /-ˈθetɪk◂/— *adj* [(to)] being an antithesis; directly and completely opposed: *Those two ideas are absolutely antithetical (to each other).* —-**ically** /kli/ *adv*

an·ti·trust law /ˌæntiˈtrʌst ˌlɔː/ *n* [C;U] *tech* any law in the US directed against TRUSTs or business monopolies (MONOPOLY) because of their bad effect on trade —compare MONOPOLIES AND MERGERS COMMISSION

ant·ler /ˈæntləʳ/ *n* either of the pair of branched horns of a STAG (=a male deer) —see picture at DEER

Antoinette, Marie see MARIE ANTOINETTE

An·to·ny /ˈæntəni/, **Mark** (about 83–30 BC) a Roman politician and soldier who supported Julius Caesar and after his death became one of the rulers of the Roman Empire. He was in love with Cleopatra, and after they were defeated in battle they both killed themselves. Mark Antony appears in Shakespeare's play *Antony and Cleopatra*, and also *Julius Caesar*, in which he makes a famous speech beginning with the words "Friends, Romans, Countrymen, lend me your ears..." —see also CLEOPATRA and see colour picture on page 1146

Antony and Cle·o·pat·ra /ˌ··· · ··ˈ··/ the title of a play by William Shakespeare, about the love between Mark Antony, and the queen of Egypt

an·to·nym /ˈæntənɪm/ *n* a word that is opposite in meaning to another word in the same language: *"Pain" is the antonym of "pleasure".* —compare SYNONYM

An·trim /ˈæntrɪm/ a former COUNTY in Northern Ireland, now a local government DISTRICT, whose main town was Belfast

An·twerp /ˈæntwɜːp‖-ɜːrp/ a city and port in N Belgium

a·nus /ˈeɪnəs/ *n med* the hole through which solid food waste leaves the bowels —compare COLON¹, RECTUM

an·vil /ˈænvɪl/ *n* a heavy iron block on which metals are shaped by hammering

anx·i·e·ty /æŋˈzaɪəti/ *n* **1** [C;U (for, about)] an uncomfortable feeling in the mind usu. caused by the fear or expectation that something bad will happen: *There's a lot of anxiety among the staff about possible job losses.* | *We waited with great anxiety for more news about the accident.* | *Her statement was an attempt to allay* (=lessen) *public anxieties about the economic situation.* **2** [C (to)] a cause of anxiety: *Her sick child is a great anxiety to her.* **3** [U] a feeling of worried eagerness: *[+to-v] his obvious anxiety to please the boss*

anx·ious /ˈæŋkʃəs/ *adj* **1** [(for, about)] feeling anxiety; worried and frightened: *I was terribly anxious about the children when they didn't come home from school.* | *anxious for their safety* | *anxious inquiries from relatives of those on board the crashed plane* **2** causing anxiety; worrying: *an anxious wait for the results of our exams* | *It was an anxious time for us.* **3** [F+to-v|that] having a strong wish mixed with a feeling of anxiety; eager: *The government is anxious to reassure everyone that the situation is under control.* | *We were anxious that she should know the truth.* | *He was anxious for them to go.* —see NERVOUS (USAGE) — **~ly** *adv* : *She waited anxiously by the phone.*

an·y¹ /ˈeni/ *determiner, pron* **1** every; (of more than two), no matter which: *They're all free — take any (of them) you like.* | *Any child would know that.* | *You can use this printer with any computer|with any of our computers.* | *They haven't arrived yet but we're expecting them* **at any moment.** (=soon) | *The manufacturers will pay the cost of any repairs in the first 12 months.* **2** [*usu. in questions or negatives*] a some; even the smallest number or amount: *Have you got any money?* | *I need some nails — have you got any?* | *He hasn't got any imagination.* | *The soldiers fired at the crowd without any reason.* | *I admire her for her determination, but not for any other reason.* | *Are there any letters for me?* | *I never seem to get any.* (Compare *There are* **some** (*letters*) *for you.*) | *Come and see me if you have any time.* | *It isn't* **any** *use looking for her; she's already gone home.* | *Very few people,* **if any,** *still support this idea.* (=there may be no one who supports it) **b** (esp. with **just**) of an ordinary kind: *You can't just wear any (old) clothes if you're going there — you have to dress very smartly.* **3** as much as possible; all: *They will need any help they can get.* **4** in **'any case: a** also at **'any rate**— no matter what may happen: *We may miss the next bus, but in any case we'll be there before midday.* **b** besides; also: *I don't want to go out tonight, and in any case we can't afford it.* —see also **any amount of** (AMOUNT¹); see MORE (USAGE), SOME (USAGE)

any² *adv* [*usu. in questions or negatives*] in the least; at all: *I can't stay any longer.* | *I asked her to polish the floor but it doesn't look any different to me.* | (*AmE infml*) *We tried turning off the tap, but that didn't help any.*

an·y·bod·y /ˈeniˌbɒdi, ˈenibədi‖-ˌbɑːdi/ *pron* any person or all people; anyone —see EVERYONE (USAGE), SOMETHING (USAGE)

an·y·how /ˈenihaʊ/ *adv infml* **1** carelessly; without regular order: *Her clothes were thrown down just anyhow.* **2** in spite of that; anyway: *He told me not to buy it, but I bought it anyhow.* **3** (used when going on with a story, changing a subject in conversation, etc.) anyway: *"Well, anyhow, I rang the bell ... "* —see ANYWAY (USAGE)

an·y·one /ˈeniwʌn/ also **anybody**— *pron* **1** any person, no matter who; all people: *Anyone can cook — it's easy.* | *He's cleverer than anyone I know.* | *Anyone else would have been too embarrassed, but he just walked up and asked her for her autograph.* **2** [*usu. in questions or negatives*] any person; some person: *Is anyone listening?* | *There wasn't anyone on the information desk.* | *I can't find my pen — has anyone seen it?* | *If anyone finds my pen I hope they|he will tell me.* | *John can do it, if anyone can.* —see EVERYONE (USAGE), SOME (USAGE)

an·y·place /ˈenipleɪs/ *adv AmE for* ANYWHERE

Any Ques·tions /ˌ·· ˈ··/ a British radio programme in which members of the public put questions about current affairs to a group of politicians or public figures

an·y·thing /ˈeniθɪŋ/ *pron* **1** any object, act, event, etc., no matter what: *He will do anything for a quiet life.* | *It's a great pity, but I can't do anything about it.* (=I can't change the situation) | *Anything will do to keep the door open.* | *If you believe that, you'll believe anything!* **2** [*usu. in questions or negatives*] any one thing; something: *Is there anything in that box?* | *You can't believe anything she says.* | *Has anything interesting happened?* | *Don't do anything stupid* | *Did you notice anything unusual?* | *She doesn't know anything about current affairs.* | *Do you want* **anything else?** (=any other thing) | *Is there anything to eat?* | *We're not doing anything much at the weekend.* (=we have no particular plans) **3 anything but** not at all; far from: *That old bridge is anything but safe.* **4 anything like** at all like; at all: *It isn't anything like as cold as it was yesterday.* **5 as easy/fast/strong, etc., as anything** *infml* very easy/fast/strong, etc.: *It's as dark as anything outside.* **6 or anything** (used when there are other possibilities): *If you want to call me or any-thing, I'll be here all day.* **7 anything you say may be taken down and used in evidence against you** a phrase which is similar to the one used by the British police when charging someone with a crime. Although these are not the exact words used by the police, they are the words that most people believe are used by the police, and they are often used humorously. —see also LIKE² (5), see SOME (USAGE), SOMETHING (USAGE)

an·y·way /ˈeniweɪ/ *adv infml* **1** in spite of everything; in any case; anyhow: *It doesn't make much difference because we're going to be late anyway.* **2** (used when going on with a story, changing a subject in conversation, etc.): *"Well anyway, I rang the bell … "*
▷ USAGE In informal spoken English **anyway** (or **any-how**) is used 1 to show that the speaker wants to return to the main topic: *That's an interesting comment. But* **anyway**, *as I was saying … ,* or 2 to finish one topic and continue with another: **Anyway,** *shall we go on to the next point now?*◁

an·y·where /ˈeniweəʳ/ ‖ also **anyplace** *AmE adv* **1** in, at, or to any place at all: *Sit anywhere you like.* | *I looked all over for that book but I couldn't find it anywhere.* | *the best curry anywhere in London* **2** [*usu. in questions or negatives*] (in, at, or to) any place; some place: *Did you go anywhere yesterday?* | *It must be in the bathroom — it can't be* **anywhere else.** (=in any other place) | *Do they need anywhere to stay?* | *Are you going anywhere nice for your holidays?* | (*fig.*) *This argument isn't getting us any-where.* (=isn't doing any good) **3** any number or amount: *anywhere from 40 to 60 students* | *anywhere between 40 and 60 students* **4 anywhere near** *infml* at all near or nearly: *She isn't anywhere near as clever as her sister.* | *Are we anywhere near finishing?* **5 or anywhere** or in/at/to any other place: *Would you like to go to the beach or anywhere?* —see SOME (USAGE), SOMETHING (USAGE)

An·zac /ˈænzæk/ *n* a soldier from Australia or New Zealand, esp. in the First World War

Anzac Day /ˈ·· ˌ·/ (in Australia and New Zealand) April 25th each year, remembered as the date of the landing at Gallipoli in 1915

AOB /ˌeɪ əʊ ˈbiː/ *BrE* any other business; anything else that needs to be discussed at a meeting, that is not mentioned on the list of things to be discussed

A-OK A-Okay /ˌeɪ əʊˈkeɪ/ *adj AmE infml* very good: *You did an A-O.K. job on this project.*

AONB /ˌeɪ əʊ en ˈbiː/ *n BrE* Area of Outstanding Natural Beauty; an area which should be kept as it is, and not used for building on

a·or·ta /eɪˈɔːtə‖-ˈɔːr-/ *n* the largest ARTERY (=tube for car-rying blood) in the body, taking blood from the heart

AP /ˌeɪ ˈpiː/ *n* Associated Press; a company that gathers news stories, mostly in the US, and sells them to newspapers, television stations, etc.

a·pace /əˈpeɪs/ *adv lit or old use* quickly

A·pa·che /əˈpætʃi/ *n* [C; *the*+P] (a member of) a Native American people of the Western US —see also NATIVE AMERICAN (CULTURAL NOTE)

a·part /əˈpɑːt‖-ɑːrt/ *adv* **1** separated by a distance: *The boxers stood apart, waiting for the signal to start fight-ing.* | *We planted the trees wide apart.* | *He and his wife are living apart.* [after *n*] *The two villages are three miles apart.* | (*fig.*) *The two sides in the dispute are still a long way apart and it is unlikely that any agreement will be reached.* **2** in or into two or more separate parts: *He took the clock apart to repair it.* | *It just came apart in my hands.* **3** [after *n*] without considering; ASIDE: **Joking apart** (=speaking seriously), *we really must do something about that hole.* **4 apart from: a** without considering; except for: *a good piece of work, apart from a few slight faults* **b** as well as: *Apart from being too large, it just doesn't suit me.* **5 tell/know apart** to be able to see the difference between: *I can't tell the twins apart.* —see also **poles apart** (POLE¹), **worlds apart** (WORLD)

a·part·heid /əˈpɑːtheɪt, -teɪt, -taɪt, -taɪd‖-ɑːr-/ *n* [U] **1** (in South Africa) the system established by the government of keeping different races separate, esp. so as to give ad-vantage to white people. Many people all over the world believe very strongly that apartheid is wrong. The South African government is now removing the apartheid laws and ending this system. —compare SEGREGATION **2** any

system of separating groups of people, esp. to give advan-tage to one group: *cultural apartheid*

a·part·ment /əˈpɑːtmənt‖-ɑːr-/ *n* **1** *AmE* ‖ also **flat** *BrE* — a set of rooms in a building, esp. on one floor, including a kitchen and a bathroom —see HOUSE (USAGE) **2** [*often pl.*] a room, esp. a large or splendid one: *the Royal Apartments*

apartment building /·ˈ·· ˌ·/ also **apartment house** /·ˈ·· ·/ — *n AmE* a large building containing many apartments —see colour picture on page 161

ap·a·thet·ic /ˌæpəˈθetɪk◄/ *adj* lacking interest, strong feel-ings, or a desire to take action: *A few of the students got involved in the campaign but most of them were fairly apathetic.* — ~ **ally** /kli/ *adv*

ap·a·thy /ˈæpəθi/ *n* [U] lack of interest or strong feelings about something or everything; unwillingness or inabil-ity to act or take an active interest: *He was* **sunk in apa-thy** *after his failure.* | *We lost the election because of the apathy of our supporters.*

APB /ˌeɪ piː ˈbiː/ *n AmE* all points bulletin; a statement broadcast to police and others to call their attention to a particular person: *Police have issued an APB about the suspect who is believed to be hiding in the area.*

apes

orangutang

chimpanzee

gorilla

ape¹ /eɪp/ *n* a large monkey without a tail or with a very short tail, such as a GORILLA or CHIMPANZEE

ape² *v* [T] *derog* to copy (a person or a person's behaviour, manners, speech, etc.), in a stupid or unsuccessful way; IMITATE

ape³ *adj* [F] *AmE sl* uncontrollably angry: *The boss went ape when he saw the sales report.*

Ap·en·nines /ˈæpɪnaɪnz/ the range of mountains which runs the whole length of Italy

a·per·i·tif /əˌperɪˈtiːf/ *n* a small alcoholic drink drunk be-fore a meal. People usu. only drink aperitifs before spe-cial meals, on social occasions.

ap·er·ture /ˈæpətʃəʳ‖ˈæpərtʃuər/ *n* a hole, crack, or other narrow opening, esp. one that admits light into a camera

ape·shit /ˈeɪpʃɪt/ *adj AmE taboo sl* uncontrollably angry: *He went apeshit when we told him about the mistake.*

a·pex /ˈeɪpeks/ *n* **apexes** or **apices** /ˈeɪpɪsiːz/ *fml or tech* the top or highest point of anything: *the apex of a triangle* | (*fig.*) *the apex of his career*

APEX , Apex /ˈeɪpeks/ advance purchase excursion; a sys-tem of air travel ticket prices that are cheaper than the usual prices, but only available under certain conditions: *a New York–Paris APEX fare of $650*

a·phid /ˈeɪfɪd, ˈæfɪd/ also **a·phis** /ˈeɪfɪs, ˈæfɪs/— *n* any of various small insects (such as the GREENFLY) that live on the juices of plants; aphids are a PEST to farmers and gardeners, as they can damage plants

aph·o·ris·m /ˈæfərɪzəm/ *n* a true or wise saying or principle expressed in a few words; MAXIM —**aphoristic** /ˌæfəˈrɪstɪk◄/ *adj*

aph·ro·dis·i·ac /ˌæfrəˈdɪziæk/ *n, adj* (a medicine, drug, etc.) causing sexual excitement

Aph·ro·di·te /ˌæfrəˈdaɪti/ (in CLASSICAL MYTHOLOGY) the Greek goddess of love and beauty (Roman name Venus)

a·pi·a·ry /ˈeɪpiəri‖ˈeɪpieri/ *n* a place where bees are kept

a·piece /əˈpiːs/ *adv* to, for, or from each person or thing; each: *The apples cost ten pence apiece.* | *We gave them three tickets apiece.*

a·plen·ty /əˈplenti/ *adj* [after *n*] *old use or lit* in great quantity; in plentiful supply: *They had money aplenty.*

a·plomb /əˈplɒm‖əˈplɑːm/ *n* [U] the power to remain calm and steady in manner and behaviour in difficult situations; SELF-POSSESSION; COMPOSURE: *She handled their hostile questioning with great aplomb.*

APO /ˌeɪ piː ˈəʊ/ *n AmE* Army Post Office; used in addresses of soldiers serving on land outside the US — compare FPO

a·poc·a·lypse /əˈpɒkəlɪps‖əˈpɑː-/ *n* a description about the future, esp. about terrible things that will happen when the world ends: *To its opponents, genetic engineering is a test-tube apocalypse.*

a·poc·a·lyp·tic /əˌpɒkəˈlɪptɪk◂‖əˌpɑː-/ *adj* **1** telling of great misfortunes in the future: *apocalyptic warnings about the coming of wars and hunger* **2** of or like the end of the world: *apocalyptic scenes of death and destruction*

a·poc·ry·phal /əˈpɒkrɪfəl‖əˈpɑː-/ *adj* (esp. of a story concerning someone well-known or important) widely believed, but probably untrue: *an apocryphal story about the Prime Minister*

ap·o·gee /ˈæpədʒiː/ *n* **1** *tech* the point where the path of an object through space is farthest from the Earth — compare PERIGEE **2** *fml* the highest point of power or success: *the apogee of his political career*

a·po·lit·i·cal /ˌeɪpəˈlɪtɪkəl◂/ *adj* having no connection with politics or no interest in politics

A·pol·lo /əˈpɒləʊ‖əˈpɑː-/ **1** (in CLASSICAL MYTHOLOGY) the Greek and Roman god of the sun, medicine, poetry, music and PROPHECY **2** a young man of great physical beauty

Apollo Pro·gram /ˈ·ˌ··/ [*the*] the US space programme to put a man on the moon. It ended in 1974 after six successful moon landings —see also Neil ARMSTRONG

a·pol·o·get·ic /əˌpɒləˈdʒetɪk◂‖əˌpɑː-/ *adj* showing or saying that one is sorry for some fault or wrong: *She was most apologetic when she heard I had been kept waiting.* | *an apologetic letter* — ~**ally** /kli/ *adv*

a·pol·o·get·ics /əˌpɒləˈdʒetɪks‖əˌpɑː-/ *n* [P;U] *fml* the art or skill of giving arguments in defence of something, esp. of a religious belief —**apologetic** *adj* [A]

ap·o·lo·gi·a /ˌæpəˈləʊdʒiə, -dʒə/ *n* [(for, of)] *fml* a formal defence or explanation, esp. of a belief

a·pol·o·gist /əˈpɒlədʒɪst‖əˈpɑː-/ *n* [(for)] *fml* a person who strongly supports a particular belief and can give arguments in defence of it: *one of the leading apologists for the government's economic strategy*

a·pol·o·gize also **-gise** *BrE* /əˈpɒlədʒaɪz‖əˈpɑː-/ *v* [I (**to, for**)] to say one is sorry, e.g. for having done something wrong, or for causing pain or trouble: *I apologized (to her) for stepping on her foot.* | *I must apologize for not replying sooner to your letter.* | *She kept us waiting for a whole hour and she didn't even apologize!*

a·pol·o·gy /əˈpɒlədʒi‖əˈpɑː-/ *n* **1** [(for)] a statement expressing that one is sorry for having done something wrong, for causing pain or trouble, etc.: *I make no apology for what I said — it was a fair comment.* | *Please accept our apologies for any inconvenience we have caused.* | *Your allegations are completely untrue, and I demand an immediate apology.* | *I'm afraid I was rather bad-tempered yesterday — I think* **I owe you an apology.** | *The Finance Director* **sends her apologies** *and is unable to attend the meeting* **2** [(for)] *lit* a defence or explanation of a belief, idea, etc.: *Shelley's "Apology for Poetry"* **3** *infml, often humor* a very bad example of something

ap·o·plec·tic /ˌæpəˈplektɪk◂/ *adj* **1** violently excited and angry, and often having a red face: *The old general was apoplectic with rage.* **2** having or concerning apoplexy — ~**ally** /kli/ *adv*

ap·o·plex·y /ˈæpəpleksi/ *n* [U] the sudden loss of the ability to move, feel, think, etc., usu. caused by too much blood in the brain or by the bursting of one of the BLOOD VESSELs there; STROKE² (2)

a·pos·ta·sy /əˈpɒstəsi‖əˈpɑː-/ *n* [U] *fml* leaving or giving up of one's religious faith, political party, beliefs, etc.

a·pos·tate /əˈpɒsteɪt, -stət‖əˈpɑː-/ *n* a person guilty of apostasy

a pos·ter·i·o·ri /ˌeɪ pɒsteriˈɔːraɪ, ˌɑː pɒsteriˈɔːriː‖ˌɑː pəʊstɪəriˈɔːri, ˌeɪ pɑː-/ *adj, adv Lat* (of an argument) using actual facts or results to form a judgment about cause (as in the statement *The streets are wet so it must have rained.*) —compare A PRIORI

a·pos·tle /əˈpɒsəl‖əˈpɑː-/ *n* **1** any of the 12 followers of Christ chosen by him to spread his message to the world **2** [(of)] a leader of a new political or other belief or idea: *one of the apostles of non-violent protest*

Apostles' Creed /·ˌ·· ˈ·/ [*the*] a statement of religious belief in the Christian religion, beginning "I believe in God the Father Almighty..."

ap·o·stol·ic /ˌæpəˈstɒlɪk◂‖-ˈstɑː-/ *adj* **1** of or concerning one of Christ's 12 apostles **2** of or concerning the POPE (the leader of the Roman Catholic Church); PAPAL

a·pos·tro·phe /əˈpɒstrəfi‖əˈpɑː-/ *n* the sign (') used in writing **a** to show that one or more letters or numbers have been left out of a word or number (as in *don't* and *'86* for *do not* and *1986*) **b** before or after *s* to show possession (as in *John's book, James' book, children's books, company's product, companies' products*) **c** before *s* to show the plural of letters and numbers (as in *There are two f's in off* and *Your 8's look like S's*)

a·pos·tro·phize also **-phise** *BrE* /əˈpɒstrəfaɪz‖əˈpɑː-/ *v* [T] *fml* to address a speech to (an absent person, or an idea or quality as if it were a person)

a·poth·e·ca·ry /əˈpɒθɪkəri‖əˈpɑːθɪkeri/ *n old use* a person with a knowledge of chemistry who mixed and sold medicines; PHARMACIST

a·poth·e·o·sis /əˌpɒθiˈəʊsɪs‖əˌpɑː-, ˌæpəˈθiəsɪs/ *n* **-ses** /siːz/ [(**of**)] **1** the raising of a person or thing to the highest possible honour and glory, or the state reached in this way **2** *lit* the perfect example; QUINTESSENCE: *Christ's mother is the apotheosis of womanhood.*

ap·pal *BrE* ‖ **appall** *AmE* /əˈpɔːl/ *v* **-ll-** [T] to shock deeply; fill with fear, hatred, terror, etc.: *We were appalled when we heard that she had been murdered.* | *The prospect of another war appalled us.* | *They were appalled at/by the reports of the famine.*

Ap·pa·la·chi·a /ˌæpəˈleɪtʃiə/ an area in the Appalachian mountains in the American SOUTH, known esp. for its POVERTY. Many old ways have been preserved by the people in Appalachia, including CRAFTs, country skills, and music.

Ap·pa·la·chi·ans /ˌæpəˈleɪtʃiənz/ [*the*] the mountains in N America which run SW from the Quebec area in Canada to Alabama, US, with the highest point in North Carolina — see colour map on pages 1374-5

ap·pal·ling /əˈpɔːlɪŋ/ *adj* **1** causing fear and hatred; shocking; terrible: *appalling cruelty* **2** *infml* very bad: *an appalling waste* | *appalling food* — ~**ly** *adv*: *an appallingly bad driver*

ap·pa·loo·sa /ˌæpəˈluːsə/ *n AmE* a horse having many dark spots on a light-coloured coat

ap·par·at·chik /ˌɑːpəˈrɑːtʃɪk/ *n* an official working for a government or another organization, esp. when considered too ready to obey orders

ap·pa·ra·tus /ˌæpəˈreɪtəs‖-ˈræ-/ *n* **-tuses** or **-tus** [C;U] **1** a set of equipment, machines, tools, materials, etc., that work together for a particular purpose: *a piece of apparatus in a gymnasium* | *sports apparatus* | *The television men set up their apparatus.* | *The astronauts have special breathing apparatus.* **2** an organization or system made up of many parts: *the government's apparatus for settling industrial disputes*

ap·par·el¹ /əˈpærəl/ *n* [U] **1** *lit or old use* clothes, esp. of a fine or special sort; GARB: *the Queen's ceremonial apparel* **2** *esp. AmE* (in comb.) clothes; clothing: *ladies' ready-to-wear apparel*

apparel² *v* **-ll-** *BrE* ‖ **-l-** *AmE* [T (**in**)] *usu. pass.] lit or old use* to dress, esp. in fine or special clothes

ap·par·ent /əˈpærənt/ *adj* **1** [(**to**)] easily seen or understood; EVIDENT: *Her anxiety was apparent to everyone.* | *The reasons for his sudden departure soon became apparent.* (=were soon understood) | *It's quite apparent that she has no intention of changing her mind.* **2** seeming to be real but not necessarily so: *The teacher was shocked by the parents' apparent lack of concern about their child's* *behaviour.* | *The apparent improvement in this year's profits is due to the selling off of some of the company's property.* —see also HEIR APPARENT

ap·par·ent·ly /əˈpærəntli/ *adv* **1** it seems (that); according to what I have heard: *I wasn't there, but apparently it was a good party.* | *Apparently they're intending to put up the price of electricity.* | *"Did she pass her test?" "Apparently not."* **2** it is clear (that): *Apparently she never got my letter after all.* —compare EVIDENTLY, OBVIOUSLY

ap·pa·ri·tion /ˌæpəˈrɪʃən/ *n* the spirit of a dead person moving in bodily form; GHOST: *He saw the apparition of his dead wife.*

ap·peal /əˈpiːl/ *n* **1** [C;U (to, for)] (a) strong request for help, support, kindness, etc.: *His appeal for forgiveness went unanswered.* | *a personal appeal from the President on behalf of the victims* | *an appeal for money to build a new hall* **2** [U] power to move the feelings; attraction; interest: *Films of that sort have lost their appeal for me.* | *Her novels have wide appeal.* | *He hasn't got much* **sex appeal.** **3** [C;U] a formal request to a higher law court to change the decision of a lower court: *the* **right of appeal** | *a court of appeal* | *She has been convicted but her lawyer says she will* **lodge** (=make) **an appeal.** | *The court rejected his appeal.* **4** [C] (in sports) a call from a player for a decision from the UMPIRE or REFEREE (=the person who judges the rules of the game): *There was a loud appeal from the bowler and wicket keeper.*

appeal² *v* [I] **1** [(to, for)] to make a strong request for help, support, mercy, etc.: *The police are appealing to the public for any information about the murder victim.* | *They are appealing for funds to build a new church.* | *The government is appealing to everyone to save water.* **2** [(to) *not in progressive forms*] to please, attract, or interest: *Does the idea of working abroad appeal (to you)?* | *inexpensive jewellery which appeals to the 13 to 30 age group* **3** [(to, against)] to formally ask a higher law court to change the decision of a lower court: *I intend to appeal against this sentence/verdict.* | *The defendant has been* **given leave to appeal** *(to the High Court).* **4** (in sports) to make an appeal to the UMPIRE or REFEREE
appeal to sbdy./sthg. *phr v* [T] to look for support in: *By* **appealing to his better nature** (=the good side of his character), *we persuaded him to change his mind.*

Appeal Court /·ˈ· ·/ *n* COURT OF APPEAL

ap·peal·ing /əˈpiːlɪŋ/ *adj* **1** able to move the feelings: *the appealing eyes of a hungry dog* **2** attractive, pleasing, or interesting: *What an appealing little baby!* | *The idea of a free holiday is rather appealing.* —opposite **unappealing** (for 2) — ~ **ly** *adv*

ap·pear /əˈpɪər/ *v* **1** [I] to become able to be seen; come into sight or become noticeable: *A car appeared over the hill.* | *In this disease spots appear on the skin.* | *If I don't appear* (=arrive) *by 7 o'clock, I won't be coming at all.* | *Her new book will be appearing in the shops very soon.* **2** [L *not in progressive forms*] to seem; to give to other people a particular idea or feeling (e.g. about one's character, feelings, or intentions): *She appeared rather upset about something.| He may appear a fool but actually he's quite clever.* | *It now appears certain that the fire was caused deliberately.* [+*to-v*] *He appears to be sincere but I don't completely trust him.* | *The discussion appears to have been friendly and fruitful.* | *There appears to have been a mistake over the numbers.* [+*(that)*] *It appears she won't be coming after all.* | *It appears that I was wrong.|* *"Will she have to have an operation?" "It appears so/not."* | *It appears as if they've lost interest.* | *(fml or pomp)* **It would appear that** *the driver of the car was drunk.* **3** [I+*adv/prep*] to be present officially, e.g. in a court of law: *He had to appear before the committee to explain his behaviour.* | *Mr Jones will appear for you* (=be your lawyer) *in court tomorrow.* **4** [I+*adv/prep*] to perform publicly, e.g. in a play or film: *She has appeared in dozens of films.* | *He is currently appearing in Othello at the National Theatre.* **5** [I+*adv/prep; not in progressive forms*] to be found; exist: *This theme appears in several of her books.* | *I wasn't expecting that item to appear on the agenda.*

ap·pear·ance /əˈpɪərəns/ *n* **1** [C;U] (an example of) the act of appearing: *The last stage of the disease is marked by the appearance of blisters on the skin.* | *She's made a number of appearances on television/a number of television appearances.* | *He* **put in an appearance** *at the party* (=went there for a time), *but didn't stay long.* **2** [C;U]

the outside qualities of a person or thing, which can be seen by other people; the way a person or thing looks to other people: *His skin had an unhealthy appearance.* | *They changed the whole appearance of the house just by painting it.* | *I tried to give the appearance of being interested in his boring story.* | *Don't* **judge by appearances.** | **To/By all appearances** (=judging by what can be seen) *they're good friends.* **3 keep up appearances** to continue to live or behave in one's usual way, esp. in order to hide from other people a loss of money, social position, etc.

ap·pease /əˈpiːz/ *v* [T] to satisfy or make calm, esp. by giving in to demands or by doing something to fulfil a need: *I tried to appease them by offering to replace the car with a brand new one.* | *to appease one's curiosity by asking a few questions*

ap·pease·ment /əˈpiːzmənt/ *n* **1** [C;U] the act of appeasing **2** [U] *usu. derog* the political idea that peace can be continued by allowing one's enemies to have what they demand. In Britain the word is esp. used in association with Britain's POLICY of appeasement towards Hitler before the Second World War. —see also MUNICH AGREEMENT

ap·pel·late court /əˌpelət ˈkɔːt‖-ˈkɔːrt/ *n* a court which hears cases in which people are appealing (APPEAL (2)) against decisions made in other courts —see also extra information on page 742

ap·pel·la·tion /ˌæpəˈleɪʃən/ *n fml or pomp* a name or title, esp. one that is formal or descriptive

ap·pend /əˈpend/ *v* [T (to)] *fml* to add or join (esp. something written or printed onto the end of a larger piece of written material): *They appended their signatures to the statement.*

ap·pend·age /əˈpendɪdʒ/ *n* **1** something that is added to, connected to, or hanging from something else, esp. if it is larger or more important **2** *med or fml* an arm or leg

ap·pen·dec·to·my /ˌæpənˈdektəmi/ *n* [C;U] the medical operation of removing the appendix

ap·pen·di·ci·tis /əˌpendɪˈsaɪtɪs/ *n* [U] the diseased state of the appendix, usu. causing it to be removed by means of a medical operation

ap·pen·dix /əˈpendɪks/ *n* **-dixes** or **-dices** /dɪsiːz/ **1** also **vermiform appendix**— a short worm-shaped organ leading off the bowel, and having little or no use: *to have one's appendix out* (=have it removed by means of a medical operation) **2** a part at the end of a book containing additional information

ap·per·tain /ˌæpəˈteɪn‖-ər-/ *v*
appertain to sthg. *phr v* [T *no pass.*] *fml* to concern or belong to (something) by right: *the responsibilities appertaining to the chairmanship*

ap·pe·tite /ˈæpɪtaɪt/ *n* [C;U] a desire or wish to have something, esp. food: *Don't eat chocolate; it will spoil your appetite for dinner.* | *The baby has a good/healthy appetite.* (=eats well and enjoys its food) | (fig.) *He had no appetite for hard work.* | *sexual appetites* —see also **whet someone's appetite** (WHET); see DESIRE (USAGE)

ap·pe·tiz·er also **-tiser** *BrE* /ˈæpɪtaɪzər/ *n* something eaten or drunk before or at the beginning of a meal to increase the desire for food

ap·pe·tiz·ing also **-tising** *BrE* /ˈæpɪtaɪzɪŋ/ *adj* increasing one's appetite: *an appetizing smell* —opposite **unappetizing** — ~ **ly** *adv* : *food appetizingly cooked*

ap·plaud /əˈplɔːd/ *v* [I;T] **1** to show approval or enjoyment of (a play, actor, performer, etc.) esp. by striking one's hands together; CLAP **2** to express strong approval of (a person, idea, etc.): *We all applauded the authority's decision not to close the hospital.*

ap·plause /əˈplɔːz/ *n* [U] loud praise for a performance or performer, esp. by striking the hands together; clapping (CLAP): *The band got a big* **round of applause** *at the end of the concert.* | *polite/enthusiastic applause*

ap·ple /ˈæpəl/ *n* **1** a hard round fruit with white juicy flesh and a red, green, or yellow skin: *She ate the entire apple, core and all.* | *an apple tree* —see picture at FRUIT

▶ CULTURAL NOTE The apple is sometimes mentioned in connection with the story in the Bible of Adam and Eve, the first man and woman, who ate an apple that God had told them not to eat. As a result, they were sent away from the Garden of Eden —see also TREE OF KNOWLEDGE The apple is also sometimes mentioned in connection with Isaac

Newton and William Tell. —see Isaac NEWTON, William TELL◀

2 an apple a day keeps the doctor away an old saying meaning that apples are good for your health **3 the apple of one's eye** *infml* one's favourite person or thing

apple but·ter /ˈ·· ˈ··‖ˈ·· ·/ *n* [U] *AmE* a kind of JAM made from apples

apple cart /ˈ·· ·/ *n* upset the/someone's apple cart *infml* to spoil someone's plans

ap·ple·jack /ˈæpəldʒæk/ *n* [U] *AmE* a SPIRIT (=very strong alcoholic drink) made from apples

Ap·ple·mac /ˌæpəlˈmæk/ *n tdmk* also **Apple Macintosh** a type of personal computer which is simple, quick, and easy to use

apple of dis·cord /ˌ·· ˈ··/ *n* a cause of argument (from the story in CLASSICAL MYTHOLOGY in which a golden apple with "For the Fairest" written on it causes an argument between the goddesses Hera, Athena, and Aphrodite)

apple pie /ˌ·· ˈ·◀/ *n* **1** [C;U] apples cooked in pastry. Apple pie is considered by Americans to be something that is typically American: *as American as apple pie* **2 in apple-pie order** *BrE infml* in perfect arrangement or order: *He kept all his tools in apple-pie order.*

apple-pie bed /ˌ·· · ˈ·/ *n BrE* a bed where the sheets have been folded in a special way so that no one can get into it. People make apple-pie beds for other people as a joke —compare SHORT-SHEET

apple pol·ish·er /ˈ·· ˌ··/ *n AmE derog* a person who tries to win favour by being very helpful and praising someone in an insincere way

apple sauce /ˌ·· ˈ·‖ˈ·· ·/ *n BrE* [U] cooked, crushed apples served as a thick liquid, usu. with ROAST PORK

ap·ple·sauce /ˈæpəlsɔːs/ *n* [U] *AmE* **1** cooked, crushed apples used as a DESSERT (=sweet food eaten after a meal) or as baby food **2** *infml* nonsense

Ap·ples·eed /ˈæpəlsiːd/, **John·ny** /ˈdʒɒni‖ˈdʒɑː-/ the popular name of **John Chapman** (1774–1845), who walked around the eastern US planting apple trees and encouraging other people to plant them

ap·pli·ance /əˈplaɪəns/ *n* an apparatus, instrument, or tool for a particular purpose, esp. an electrical machine that is used in the house: **domestic appliances** *such as dishwashers and washing machines* —see MACHINE (USAGE)

ap·plic·a·ble /əˈplɪkəbəl, ˈæplɪkəbəl/ *adj* **1** [(to)] directed towards or concerning a particular person or group. *This section of the form is not applicable in your case.* | *The rule is only applicable to UK citizens.* **2** able to have an effect: *The new law becomes applicable from Monday.*

ap·pli·cant /ˈæplɪkənt/ *n* [(for)] a person who makes a request, esp. officially and in writing, for a job, for entrance to a school or university, for theatre tickets, etc.· *We had 250 applicants for the job.*

ap·pli·ca·tion /ˌæplɪˈkeɪʃən/ *n* **1** [C;U (for, to)] (the act of making) a request, esp. officially and in writing: *Tickets may be bought on application to the theatre.* | *I wrote five applications for jobs but didn't get a single reply.* | *Have you filled in the application form for a new passport?* | *His lawyer made an application for bail.* | *a membership application* **2** [U (of, to)] the act of putting something to use: *The application of new scientific discoveries to industrial processes usually makes jobs easier to do.* **3** [C] a particular practical use: *a new discovery that had a number of industrial applications* | *application software* **4** [C;U (to)] the putting of one thing onto another, e.g. of medicine onto the skin or paint onto a surface: *Your foot will feel better after the application of this ointment.* | *The door may need another application of paint.* **5** [U] careful and continuous attention or effort; DILIGENCE: *She worked with great application.* **6** [U (to)] the quality of being related or applicable: *That rule has no application to this particular case.*

ap·plied /əˈplaɪd/ *adj* (esp. of a science) able to be put to practical use: *applied physics* —compare PURE (6)

applied math·e·mat·ics /·,· ··ˈ··/ also **applied maths** /·,· ˈ·/ *BrE infml* — *n* [U] the science of numbers developed for practical purposes —compare PURE MATHEMATICS

ap·pli·qué /əˈpliːkeɪ‖ˌæplɪˈkeɪ/ *n* [U] (esp. in dressmaking) decorative work of one material sewn or stuck onto a larger surface of another material

ap·ply /əˈplaɪ/ *v* **1** [I (to, for)] to request something, esp.

officially and in writing: *I'll apply (for the job) today.* | *We've applied to the council for a home improvement grant.* | *Anyone under 30 need not apply.* (=is not considered suitable) **2** [T (to)] to bring or put into use or operation: *Apply as much force as is necessary.* | *Scientific discoveries are often applied to industrial processes.* | *to apply the brakes* | *to apply one's mind to a problem* **3** [T (to)] to put or spread on a surface: *Apply the paint evenly to both sides of the door.* **4** [I;T (to) *not in progressive forms*] to (cause to) have an effect; be directly related: *This rule does not apply in your particular case/cannot be applied to every case.* | *The questions in the second half of the form apply only to married men.* **5 apply oneself (to)** to work hard or with careful attention (at): *He has a lot of talent, but he won't apply himself.*

ap·point /əˈpɔɪnt/ *v* [T] **1** [(as, to)] to choose for a position or job: *We have decided to appoint a new teacher.* | *She's been appointed as sales director/to the post of sales director.* [+obj+n] *They appointed him chairman.* | *He was appointed chairman.* [+obj+to-v] *I've been appointed to run the overseas section.* | *A committee was appointed to investigate these complaints.* —see HIRE (USAGE) **2** *fml* to arrange or decide (esp. a time or place when something will happen): *The committee has appointed a day in July for your case to be heard.* | *She wasn't there at the appointed time.* —see also SELF-APPOINTED, WELL-APPOINTED —**pointee** *n* : *a presidential appointee* (=appointed by the president)

ap·point·ment /əˈpɔɪntmənt/ *n* **1** [C (with)] an arrangement for a meeting at an agreed time and place, esp. a formal meeting with an important or official person: *The director won't see you unless you have an appointment.* | *I have an appointment at 10.30 with the doctor.* [+to-v] *Can I make an appointment to see the manager?* | *a hairdressing appointment* | *a 12 o'clock appointment* **2** [U] the agreement of a time and place for meeting: *He will only see you by appointment.* **3** [C;U (as, of, to)] (the choosing of someone for) a position or job: *We were all pleased about the appointment of John as chairman/to be chairman.* | *I hope to get a teaching appointment at the new school.* | *(fml) Smiths Ltd., wine merchants by appointment to the Queen*

▷ USAGE When you arrange to see someone at a fixed time you **make an appointment**. If you then actually see the person as arranged, you **keep the appointment**. If you cannot come, you write or telephone to **cancel the appointment**. Because appointment is somewhat formal, we usually don't use it to talk about an arranged meeting with our friends. —compare MEETING³ and DATE³◁

Ap·po·mat·tox /ˌæpəˈmætəks/ a town in Virginia, US, where the Confederate general Robert E Lee gave up control to the Union army in 1865 bringing the Civil War to an end at a place which has now become a national historical park

ap·por·tion /əˈpɔːʃən‖-ɔːr-/ *v* [T (between, among)] to divide and share out: *We must apportion the money fairly.* | *It was difficult to apportion the blame for the accident between the two drivers.* — ~ **ment** *n* [C;U]

ap·po·site /ˈæpəzət/ *adj* [(to, for)] *fml* exactly suitable to or directly connected with the present moment or situation: *an apposite remark*

ap·po·si·tion /ˌæpəˈzɪʃən/ *n* [(in) U (to)] *tech* (in grammar) an arrangement in which one simple sentence contains two or more noun phrases that describe the same person or thing and are used in the same way. In the sentence *"The defendant, a woman of 35, denies kicking the policeman"* the two phrases *"the defendant"* and *"a woman of 35"* are in apposition (to each other).

ap·prais·al /əˈpreɪzəl/ *n* [(of)] (a statement or opinion based on) an act of appraising: *What's your appraisal of the situation?* | *a system for the annual appraisal of employees' work*

ap·praise /əˈpreɪz/ *v* [T] *fml* to judge the worth, quality, or condition of; find out the value of; EVALUATE: *They employed a consultant to appraise the relative merits of the two computer systems.* | *It's difficult to appraise the damage this might do to his political reputation.*

ap·pre·cia·ble /əˈpriːʃəbəl/ *adj* enough to be felt, noticed, or considered important: *an appreciable difference* —**bly** *adv* : *The temperature dropped appreciably last night.*

ap·pre·ci·ate /ə'priːʃieɪt/ v 1 [T] to recognize and enjoy the good qualities or worth of: *She doesn't appreciate good wine.* | *His abilities were not appreciated in his job.* 2 [T *not in progressive forms*] to understand fully; recognize: *I don't think you appreciate the difficulties this will cause.* [+that] *I appreciate that this is not an easy decision for you to make.* 3 [T] to be thankful or grateful for: *I appreciate your help.* | *I'd appreciate it if you would turn the radio down.* (=please turn it down) 4 [I (in)] (of property, possessions, etc.) to increase in value over a period of time: *Houses in this area have all appreciated (in value) since the new road was built.* —opposite **depreciate** (for 4)

ap·pre·ci·a·tion /ə,priːʃi'eɪʃən/ n 1 [U] understanding of the good qualities or worth of something: *The audience showed their appreciation with loud cheers.* 2 [C;U (of)] a judgment of the worth or facts of something: *The pupils wrote an appreciation of the play they had just seen.* | a realistic appreciation of the situation 3 [S;U (in)] (a) rise in value, esp. of land or possessions: *an appreciation of 50% in property values*

ap·pre·cia·tive /ə'priːʃətɪv/ adj [(of)] feeling or showing admiration or thanks; showing appreciation: *an appreciative audience* | *He was very appreciative of his colleagues' support during his illness.* —opposite **unappreciative** –~ly adv

ap·pre·hend /,æprɪ'hend/ v [T] 1 fml to take (a person who breaks the law) into police control; ARREST 2 old use to understand

ap·pre·hen·sion /,æprɪ'henʃən/ n 1 [C;U] anxiety about the future; expectation of something unpleasant: *We waited for their decision with a great deal of apprehension.* 2 [U] fml the act of apprehending someone; ARREST 3 [U] old use ability to understand; understanding

ap·pre·hen·sive /,æprɪ'hensɪv/ adj [(about, for)] full of fear or anxiety about the future; worried: *He looked apprehensive as he waited for the result to be broadcast.* | *She was apprehensive about her son's safety.* – –ly adv

ap·pren·tice¹ /ə'prentɪs/ n [(to)] a person who is under an agreement to work, for a number of years and usu. for low wages, for a person who is skilled in a trade, in order to learn that person's skill: *an apprentice electrician* | *The company is taking on four new apprentices.*

apprentice² v [T (to) usu. pass.] to make someone an apprentice: *She's apprenticed to a plumber.*

ap·pren·tice·ship /ə'prentɪsʃɪp/ n [C;U] (the condition or period of having) a job as an apprentice. In Britain and the US the state does not have an official system of apprenticeships. Apprenticeships are usu. offered by companies or by skilled workers who need someone to help them and are willing to teach their skill in return for this help: *The number of apprenticeships has declined sharply in recent years.* | *At the end of your apprenticeship your pay will be doubled.*

ap·prise /ə'praɪz/ v [T (of)] fml, becoming rare to inform; tell: *We apprised him of our arrival.*

ap·proach¹ /ə'prəutʃ/ v 1 [I;T] to come near or nearer (to) in space, time, quality, or quantity: *Silently we approached the enemy's camp.* | *The time is approaching when we will have to leave.* | *He's approaching 80.* (=is nearly 80 years old) | *They had to work in temperatures approaching 35°.* | *He's a good player, but doesn't approach international standard.* 2 [T (about)] to speak to (someone), esp. in order to make a request or suggestion for the first time: *Did he approach you about lending him some money?* —see also APPROACHABLE 3 [T] to begin to consider or deal with: *There are several ways of approaching this problem.*

approach² n 1 [U (of)] the act of approaching: *Our approach drove away the wild animals.* | *The approach of winter brings cold weather.* 2 [C (to)] a way of getting in: *All approaches to the town were blocked.* 3 [C (to)] a method of doing something or dealing with a problem: *a new approach to cancer treatment* | *a diplomatic approach* 4 [C (to)] an act of speaking to someone (about something) for the first time: *We have made approaches to them with a view to forming a business partnership.*

ap·proa·cha·ble /ə'prəutʃəbəl/ adj 1 easy to speak to or deal with; friendly: *You'll find the director a very approachable person.* —opposite **unapproachable** 2 able to be reached

approach shot /·'· ,·/ n (in GOLF) a shot from the FAIRWAY to the GREEN

ap·pro·ba·tion /,æprə'beɪʃən/ n [U] fml praise or approval, esp. when official

ap·pro·pri·ate¹ /ə'prəupriɪt/ adj [(for, to)] correct or suitable for a particular situation or occasion: *His bright clothes were hardly appropriate for such a solemn occasion.* | *I think this is an appropriate moment to raise the question of my promotion.* | *Complaints must be addressed to the appropriate authority.* —opposite **inappropriate** – ~ly adv – –ness n [U]

ap·pro·pri·ate² /ə'prəuprieɪt/ v [T] 1 [(for)] to set aside for a particular purpose; ALLOCATE: *The government has appropriated a large sum of money for building hospitals.* 2 fml to take for oneself or for one's own use, esp. without permission: *The minister was found to have appropriated government money.* —see also MISAPPROPRIATE —**-ation** /ə,prəupri'eɪʃən/ n [C;U (of)] : *appropriation of public money for a new hospital* | *an appropriation of £5,000,000 for a new hospital*

ap·prov·al /ə'pruːvəl/ n [U] 1 favourable opinion or judgment: *The audience showed its approval by cheering loudly.* | *(fml) I hope that the arrangements* **meet with your approval.** | *The new proposals have won the approval of the board.* | *By inviting her to the palace, the Queen has given her the royal* **seal of approval.** – opposite **disapproval** 2 official permission: *We can't start building without the council's approval.* 3 **on approval** (of goods taken or sent from a shop) to be returned without payment if the customer is not satisfied

ap·prove /ə'pruːv/ v 1 [I (of) *not in progressive forms*] to have a favourable opinion, esp. of a course of action or type of behaviour; regard as good, right, sensible, etc.: *I don't approve of smoking in bed/of people who smoke in bed.* | *You made a good decision, and I thoroughly/heartily approve of it.* | *You can join the class if your mother approves.* 2 [T] to agree officially to; RATIFY: *The city council approved the building plans.* | *The equipment must be bought from a supplier approved by the company.* | *an approved course in computer programming* —**provingly** adv

approved school /·'· ·/ n [C;U] a special school where children in Britain who have broken the law are sent if they are under 18 years old and so cannot be sent to prison. These schools are now officially called COMMUNITY HOMES.

approx written abbrev. for: approximately

ap·prox·i·mate¹ /ə'prɒksɪmɪt/ adj nearly correct but not exact: *The approximate number of children in the school is 300.* | *This is just an approximate figure.* – ~ly adv : *The plane will be landing in approximately 15 minutes.*

ap·prox·i·mate² /ə'prɒksɪmeɪt‖ə'prɑːk-/ v [I+to;L] fml to come near (to) in amount, nature, etc.: *Your story only approximates to the real facts.* | *The cost will approximate £5,000,000.*

ap·prox·i·ma·tion /ə,prɒksɪ'meɪʃən‖ə,prɑːk-/ n [C;U (to, of)] a result, calculation, etc., that is not exact but is good enough: *Could you give us a* **rough approximation** of the likely cost?

ap·pur·te·nance /ə'pɜːtɪnəns, -tən-‖ə'pɜːrtənəns/ n [usu. pl.] law something connected with something else, esp. the rights or responsibilities that go with owning property

APR /,eɪ piː 'ɑːr/ n Annual Percentage Rate; the annual rate of interest payable by anyone buying something over a period of time by borrowing money: *credit price £199.95, APR 25.3%, 20 weeks at £10 per week*

ap·rès-ski /,æpreɪ 'skiː◄‖,ɑː-/ n,adj (of or suitable for) activities taken part in after skiing (SKI), esp. eating, drinking, etc.

a·pri·cot /'eɪprɪkɒt‖'æprɪkɑːt/ n 1 [C] a round soft orange or yellow fruit with a furry outside like a PEACH but smaller and with a single large stone 2 [U] the colour of this fruit

A·pril /'eɪprəl/ (written abbrev. **Apr.**) n [C;U] the fourth month of the year, between March and May. When people think of April, they typically think of Easter, spring flowers, lambs, and **April showers** (=a light rain which often falls in April). They also think of **April Fools' Day**, which is April 1st. *It happened on April the seventeenth/on the seventeenth of April/(AmE) on April seventeenth.* | *This office opened in April 1991.* | *She started work here last April/the April before last.*

April fool /ˌ·· '·/ n (a person who has been deceived or made fun of by) a trick played on April 1st

April Fools' Day /ˌ·· '· ·/ April 1st, a day when people play tricks on others, esp. by telling them something that is not true, also called **All Fools' Day**

a pri·o·ri /ˌeɪ praɪˈɔːraɪ, ˌɑː priˈɔːriː/ adj, adv Lat (of an argument) using a cause to form a judgment about probable results (as in the statement It is raining so the streets must be wet) —compare A POSTERIORI

a·pron /ˈeɪprən/ n **1** a simple piece of clothing worn over the front part of one's clothes to keep them clean while one is cooking, doing something dirty, etc. Aprons are usu. worn by women in the home, and by people such as CHEFS at work. **2** also **apron stage** /ˌ·· '·/— that part of a stage in a theatre that comes forward towards where the public sit **3** (in an airport) the hard surface on which planes are turned round, loaded, unloaded, etc.

apron strings /ˈ·· ·/ n [P] infml the strings of an apron regarded as a sign of the control of a boy or man by his mother or wife: Though he's nearly 40, he's still **tied to his mother's apron strings**, and has never married.

ap·ro·pos[1] /ˌæprəˈpəʊ, ˈæprəpəʊ/ adv, prep [(of)] (used to introduce a new subject connected with what has just been mentioned): John was here yesterday; apropos, (=it's suitable to say this now) he's got a new job. | Apropos (of) John's new job (=while we're talking about it), what's he earning?

apropos[2] adj [F] very suitable for the time or situation; PERTINENT: I thought her remarks were very apropos.

apse /æps/ n the curved or many-sided end of a building, esp. the east end of a church

apt /æpt/ adj **1** [F+to-v] having a natural or habitual tendency to do something; likely: This kind of shoe is apt to slip on wet ground. **2** exactly suitable; PERTINENT: an apt remark **3** [(at)] fml quick to learn and understand: an apt student — ~**ly** adv — ~**ness** n [U]

▷ USAGE Compare He is apt to/He is inclined to/He tends to lose his temper in difficult situations (=this is one of his general characteristics) and When he finds out what you said, he is likely to lose his temper (=I think that this will happen in this particular situation)◁

ap·ti·tude /ˈæpt‿tjuːd‖-tuːd/ n [C;U (for)] natural ability or skill, esp. in learning: She showed great aptitude/an aptitude for learning languages. | an aptitude test

aq·ua·lung /ˈækwəlʌŋ/ n an apparatus that provides air for a swimmer under water, esp. a container of special air that is carried on the back and has a tube that takes the air to the mouth or nose

aq·ua·ma·rine /ˌækwəməˈriːn/ n **1** [C] a glass-like blue-green stone used for jewellery **2** [U] the colour of this stone —**aquamarine** adj

aq·ua·plane[1] /ˈækwəpleɪn/ n a thin board, used in a sporting activity, on which a person stands to be pulled quickly along the surface of the sea, a lake, etc., by a rope from a fast motorboat

aquaplane[2] v [I] **1** to ride on an aquaplane **2** BrE ‖ **hydroplane** AmE— (of a car) to slide forwards without control on a wet road, not touching the actual road surface at all

a·quar·i·um /əˈkweəriəm/ n -**iums** or -**ia** /iə/ **1** a transparent container for fish and other water animals **2** a building (esp. in a ZOO) containing many of these

A·quar·i·us /əˈkweəriəs/ n **1** [U] the eleventh (ELEVEN) sign of the ZODIAC, represented by a person pouring water **2** [C] a person born between January 21 and February 19 —see ZODIAC (USAGE) and see picture at ZODIAC

Aq·ua·scu·tum /ˌækwəˈskjuːtəm/ tdmk an expensive clothing shop in London

a·quat·ic /əˈkwætɪk, əˈkwɒ-‖əˈkwæ-, əˈkwɑː-/ adj living or happening in or on water: aquatic plants/animals | Aquatic sports include swimming and rowing. — ~**ally** /kli/ adv

aq·ua·tint /ˈækwətɪnt/ n **1** [U] the method of producing a picture on a flat piece of copper by letting a strong acid eat away the parts that have not been protected by WAX or some other material **2** [C] a picture printed from such a piece of copper

aq·ue·duct /ˈækw‿dʌkt/ n a bridge, pipe, or CANAL that carries a water supply, esp. one that is built higher than the land around it or that goes across a valley

a·que·ous /ˈeɪkwiəs, ˈækwiəs/ adj tech of, like, containing, or in water

aq·ui·line /ˈækwɪlaɪn‖-laɪn, -lən/ adj of or like an EAGLE: An aquiline nose is one that curves like an eagle's beak. | her sharp aquiline profile

A·qui·nas /əˈkwaɪnəs/, **St Thomas** (about 1225–74) an Italian religious writer and thinker whose ideas have been influential and important in the Catholic Church

A·qui·no /əˈkiːnəʊ/, **Ma·ri·a Co·ra·zón** /məˈriːə kɔːrəˈzɒn‖ -ˈzɑːn/ (1933–) a former president of the Philippines who became president after helping to remove President Marcos from power

AR written abbrev. for ARKANSAS

Ar·ab /ˈærəb/ n **1** a person descended from the people of the Arabian PENINSULA, and whose first language is usually Arabic **2** BrE ‖ **arabian** AmE a type of fast graceful horse

ar·a·besque /ˌærəˈbesk/ n **1** a position in BALLET dancing **2** a flowing decorative line or pattern

A·ra·bi·a /əˈreɪbiə/ the PENINSULA which contains Saudi Arabia, Yemen, and several other countries

A·ra·bi·an /əˈreɪbiən/ adj of Arabia: the Arabian desert

Arabian Nights /ˌ·, ··· '·/ [the] the popular name for the Thousand and One Nights, a book of Arabic stories from the tenth century AD, in which Scheherazade prevents her husband from killing her by amusing him with a different story for a THOUSAND and one nights —see ALADDIN, ALI BABA, SINDBAD

Ar·a·bic /ˈærəbɪk/ n [U] the SEMITIC language or writing of the Arabs, which is the main language of North Africa, the Middle East, and Arabia: She is studying Arabic. — **Arabic** adj

Arabic nu·me·ral /ˌ··· '···/ n **1** any of the signs (such as 1, 2, 3, 4) used for numbers in the English and many other alphabets —compare ROMAN NUMERAL **2** any of the signs used for numbers in the Arabic alphabet, on which the above number signs were based

Arab-Is·rae·li War /ˌ·· ·,·· '·/ n [the] any of the wars between Israel and the Arab countries, e.g. the 1967-1973 war.

ar·a·ble /ˈærəbəl/ adj (of land) suitable or used for growing crops —compare PASTURE

Arab League /ˌ·· '·/ [the] an association of Arab countries formed in 1945

Ar·a·fat /ˈærəfæt/, **Yas·ser** /ˈjæsəʳ/ (1929–) a Palestinian nationalist politician and president of the PLO

Ar·al·dite /ˈærəldaɪt/ n [U] tdmk a type of strong glue

Aral Sea /ˌærəl ˈsiː/ an inland sea between Kazakhstan and Uzbekistan which is now often much reduced in size or even dry

Ar·a·ma·ic /ˌærəˈmeɪ-ɪk◂/ n [U] a Semitic language spoken in SW Asia as a LINGUA FRANCA, and still spoken in parts of Syria and Lebanon —**Aramaic** adj

Ar·an Is·lands /ˈærən ˌaɪləndz/ [the+P] a group of three islands off the SW coast of the Irish Republic

Aran jum·per /ˌ·· '··/ also **Aran sweater** n a thick woollen JUMPER with a raised pattern of many different stitches, usu. made from natural-coloured wool

A·rap·a·ho /əˈræpəhəʊ/ n [C; the+P] (a member of) a Native American people from the GREAT PLAINS of the US —see NATIVE AMERICAN (CULTURAL NOTE)

Ar·a·rat /ˈærəræt/, **Mount** a mountain in E Turkey which according to old stories was the landing place of Noah's ARK

Aran jumper

ar·bi·ter /ˈɑːb‿təʳ‖ˈɑːr-/ n someone who is in a position to make influential judgments or to settle an argument: She became the supreme arbiter of fashion in beachwear. | the arbiter of a conflict/crisis

ar·bi·trage /ˈɑːbɪtrɑːʒ‖ˈɑːr-/ *n* [U] the process of buying something (esp. a COMMODITY or CURRENCY) in one place and selling it in another place at the same time in order to profit from differences in price between the two places —**trageur** /ˌɑːbɪtrɑːˈɜːrˑ‖ˌɑːr-/— *n*

ar·bi·tra·ry /ˈɑːbɪtrəri, -tri‖ˈɑːrbʒtreri/ *adj often derog* **1** typical of power that is uncontrolled and used without considering the wishes of others: *arbitrary arrests/ punishments | an arbitrary ruler* **2** decided by or based on chance or personal opinion rather than facts or reason; RANDOM: *I didn't know anything about any of the books so my choice was quite arbitrary.* —**rily** /ˈɑːbʒtrərʒli‖ˌɑːrbʒˈtreərʒli/ *adv* —**riness** *n* [U]

ar·bi·trate /ˈɑːbʒtreɪt‖ˈɑːr-/ *v* [I;T (**between**)] to act as a judge in (an argument), esp. at the request of both sides: *They've appointed a committee to arbitrate the dispute/to arbitrate between the management and unions.* —compare INTERMEDIARY; see also ACAS —**trator** *n*

ar·bi·tra·tion /ˌɑːbʒˈtreɪʃən‖ˌɑːr-/ *n* [U] the settling of an argument by the decision of a person or group that has been chosen by both sides: *The men agreed to* **go to arbitration** *to settle their pay claim.*

Ar·bor Day /ˈɑːbə deɪ‖ˈɑːrbər-/ an unofficial US holiday when people plant trees. Arbor Day is celebrated on different days in different states and school children often take part in it.

ar·bo·re·al /ɑːˈbɔːriəl‖ɑːr-/ *adj tech* of or living in trees: *arboreal animals*

ar·bo·re·tum /ˌɑːbəˈriːtəm‖ˌɑːr-/ **-ta** /tə/ *or* **-tums** *n* a place where trees are grown for study or for people to learn about them

ar·bour *BrE* ‖ **arbor** *AmE* /ˈɑːbəʳ‖ˈɑːr-/ *n* a sheltered place in a garden, usu. made by making trees or bushes grow so as to form an arch

arc /ɑːk‖ɑːrk/ *n* **1** part of a curved line or circle: *an arc of 110° | The sun appears to move in an arc across the sky.* **2** a very powerful flow of electricity through the air or of gas between two points, esp. as used to produce light in an **arc lamp** —see also ARC WELDING

ar·cade /ɑːˈkeɪd‖ɑːr-/ *n* a covered passage, esp. one with a roof supported by arches or with a row of shops on one or both sides: *a shopping arcade* —see also AMUSEMENT ARCADE

arcade game /·ˈ· ˌ·/ *n AmE* a coin-operated electronic machine with a VIDEO SCREEN and controls which is played for amusement

Ar·ca·di·a /ɑːˈkeɪdiə‖ɑːr-/ an area or scene of simple pleasant country life (from the REGION of ancient Greece called Arcadia, where people lived this kind of life)

ar·cane /ɑːˈkeɪn‖ɑːr-/ *adj lit* mysterious and secret; ESOTERIC: *arcane knowledge/rituals*

arch¹ /ɑːtʃ‖ɑːrtʃ/ *n* **1** a curved top on two supports, e.g. under a bridge or a church roof or above a door or window: *The bridge had seven arches.* **2** something with this shape, esp. the middle of the bottom of the foot —see picture at FOOT

arch² *v* [I;T] to form an arch or make into the shape of an arch: *The trees arched over the path. | The cat arched its back in anger.*

arch³ *adj* making fun of people in a clever or playful way: *an arch smile* – ~ **ly** *adv* : *"I know what you're thinking!" said the old lady archly.*

arch- see WORD FORMATION

ar·chae·ol·o·gy, **archeology** /ˌɑːkiˈɒlədʒi‖ˌɑːrkiˈɑː-/ *n* [U] the study of the buried remains of ancient times, such as houses, pots, tools, and weapons —see also INDUSTRIAL ARCHAEOLOGY —**gist** *n* —**gical** /ˌɑːkiəˈlɒdʒɪkəl◂‖ˌɑːrkiə ˈlɑː-/ *adj* : *archaeological excavations* —**gically** /kli/ *adv*

ar·cha·ic /ɑːˈkeɪ-ɪk‖ɑːr-/ *adj* belonging to the past; no longer used – ~ **ally** /kli/ *adv*

ar·cha·is·m /ɑːˈkeɪ-ɪzəm, ˈɑːkeɪ-‖ˈɑːrki-/ *n* a word or phrase that is no longer in general use

arch·an·gel /ˈɑːkeɪndʒəl‖ˈɑːrk-/ *n* a chief ANGEL in the Jewish, Christian, and Muslim religions: *the archangel Gabriel*

arch·bish·op /ˌɑːtʃˈbɪʃəp‖ˌɑːrtʃ-/ *n* (*often cap.*) (in some branches of the Christian church) a priest in charge of the churches and BISHOPs in a very large area: *Archbishop Jones | His Grace the Archbishop of York*

Archbishop of Can·ter·bu·ry /ˌ·ˌ·· · ˈ····/ [*the*] the head of the Anglican church in England —see CANTERBURY

Archbishop of West·min·ster /ˌ·ˌ·· · ˈ····/ [*the*] the head of the Roman Catholic church in Britain

arch·bish·op·ric /ˌɑːtʃˈbɪʃəprɪk ‖ˌɑːrtʃ-/ *n* the rank of, period in office of, or area governed by an archbishop

arch·dea·con /ˌɑːtʃˈdiːkən◂‖ ˌɑːrtʃ-/ *n* (in the Anglican branch of the Christian church) a priest of high rank who serves directly under a BISHOP

arch·di·o·cese /ˌɑːtʃˈdaɪəsʒs, -siːs‖ˌɑːrtʃ-/ *n* the church area under the government of an archbishop

arch·duke /ˌɑːtʃˈdjuːk◂‖ˌɑːrtʃ ˈduːk◂/ *n* (*often cap.*) a royal prince, esp. of the royal family of Austria in former times: *Archduke Charles*

arch·en·e·my /ˌɑːtʃˈenəmi‖ˌɑːrtʃ-/ *n* **1** [C] a main enemy **2** [*the*] (*often cap.*) the devil

ar·che·ol·o·gy /ɑːkiˈɒlədʒi‖ɑːrkiˈɑː-/ *n* ARCHAEOLOGY

ar·cher /ˈɑːtʃəʳ‖ˈɑːr-/ *n* a person who shoots ARROWs from a BOW³ (=piece of bent wood), either as a sport or (formerly) in war

Archer, Jef·frey /ˈdʒefri/ (1940–) an English Conservative politician and writer of best-selling NOVELs, including *First Among Equals*. He became Lord Archer in 1992.

Ar·chers /ˈɑːtʃəz‖ˈɑːrtʃərz/, **The** a British radio programme about a farming family, which has been running since 1951 and is very popular. It is set in a small imaginary country village called Ambridge.

ar·cher·y /ˈɑːtʃəri‖ˈɑːr-/ *n* [U] the art or sport of shooting arrows —see picture at TARGET

ar·che·type /ˈɑːkɪtaɪp‖ˈɑːr-/ *n* [(**of**)] **1** the original model of something, of which others are copies: *"the House of Commons, the archetype of all the representative assemblies"* (T.B. Macaulay) **2** a perfectly typical example of something —**typal** /ˈɑːkɪtaɪpəl, ˌɑːkɪˈtaɪ-‖ˌɑːrkɪˈtaɪ-/, —**typical** /ˌɑːkɪˈtɪpɪkəl‖ˌɑːr-/ *adj* : *the archetypal wealthy American tourist* —**typically** /kli/ *adv*

ar·chi·man·drite /ˌɑːkʒˈmændraɪt‖ˌɑːr-/ *n* the head of a group of MONKs of an Eastern branch of the Christian church

The Archbishop of Canterbury

Archimedes

EUREKA

Ar·chi·me·des /ˌɑːkɪˈmiːdiːz◂‖ˌɑːr-/ (287–212 B.C) a Greek MATHEMATICIAN and INVENTOR who established the rules for measuring DENSITY. He is believed to have discovered these rules while in his bath, and to have jumped out of his bath and run through the streets with no clothes on shouting "Eureka! Eureka!" ("I have found it! I have found it!").

Archimedes' prin·ci·ple /ˌ·ˈ···· ˈ···/ *n* [*the*] the principle which states that an object in a liquid is kept up by a force equal to the weight of the displaced (DISPLACE) liquid

ar·chi·pel·a·go /ˌɑːkʒˈpeləgəʊ‖ˌɑːr-/ *n* **-goes** *or* **-gos** a group of small islands and the area of sea round them

ar·chi·tect /ˈɑːkɟtekt‖ˈɑːr-/ n a person who plans new buildings and is responsible for making sure that they are built properly: *Who was the architect of St Paul's Cathedral?* | (fig.) *He was a fine politician, and many people regard him as the architect of the modern welfare state.*

ar·chi·tec·ture /ˈɑːkɟtektʃəʳ‖ˈɑːr-/ n [U] **1** the art and science of building, including its planning, making, and decoration **2** the style or manner of building in a particular country or period of history: *the architecture of ancient Greece* | *Gothic architecture* —see colour picture on page 227 **3** the INTERNAL arrangements of computer HARDWARE or SOFTWARE, esp. of the different parts in relation to each other —**-tural** /ˌɑːkɟˈtektʃərəl◂‖ˈɑːr-/ adj : *architectural plans* —**-turally** adv : *Architecturally, Venice is very beautiful.*

ar·chi·val /ɑːˈkaɪvəl‖ɑːr-/ adj of, contained in, or being archives

ar·chives /ˈɑːkaɪvz‖ˈɑːr-/ n [P] (a place for storing) historical materials, such as old papers, letters, and reports concerning a government, family, organization, etc., kept esp. for historical interest: *an interesting old newsreel from the BBC archives* —**archive** adj [A] : *archive material*

ar·chi·vist /ˈɑːkɟvɟst‖ˈɑːr-/ n a person who looks after archives

arch·way /ˈɑːtʃweɪ‖ˈɑːrtʃ-/ n **1** a passage under an arch or arches **2** an arch over an entrance: *an archway between the two rooms*

arc·tic /ˈɑːktɪk‖ˈɑːr-/ adj **1** (usu. cap.) of or concerning the most northern part of the world **2** extremely cold: *My bedroom was arctic.* | *arctic conditions*

Arctic n [the] the large land mass surrounding the North Pole —compare ANTARCTIC

Arctic Cir·cle /ˌ·· ˈ··/ [the] an imaginary line drawn round the world at a certain distance from the most northern point (the North Pole) —compare ANTARCTIC CIRCLE, and see picture at GLOBE

Arctic O·cean /ˌ·· ˈ··/ [the] the smallest ocean in the world, at the North Pole and covered with ice all year round

arc weld·ing /ˈ· ˌ··/ n [U] the joining together of pieces of metal by means of an ARC (2) of electricity

Ar·den /ˈɑːdn‖ˈɑːr-/ an area in Warwickshire, England, formerly part of a large forest which was the setting for Shakespeare's play *As You Like It*

Ar·dennes /ɑːˈden‖ɑːr-/ an area of hilly land with many trees in SE Belgium, N Luxembourg and N France where there was heavy fighting in the First and Second World Wars

ar·dent /ˈɑːdənt‖ˈɑːr-/ adj showing strong feeling or desire; eager; PASSIONATE: *an ardent supporter/admirer of the government* | *an ardent feminist* — **~ly** adv

ar·dour BrE ‖ **ardor** AmE /ˈɑːdəʳ‖ˈɑːr-/ n [U] fml or lit strong excitement or eagerness; ZEAL: *patriotic ardour* | *Her lack of enthusiasm dampened his ardour.*

ar·du·ous /ˈɑːdjuəs‖ˈɑːrdʒuəs/ adj fml needing hard and continuous effort; difficult: *a long and arduous climb* | *arduous work* — **~ly** adv — **ness** n [U]

are¹ /əʳ; strong ɑːʳ/ present tense pl. of BE: *They are (living) here now.* | *Here we are!* —see NOT (USAGE)

are² /ɑːʳ/ n a unit of area —see TABLE 2

ar·e·a /ˈeəriə/ n **1** [C;U] the size of a surface measured by multiplying the length by the width: *What's the area of your garden?* | *a room 16 square metres in area* —compare VOLUME (2) **2** [C] **a** a part or division of the world, of a country, etc.; REGION: *There aren't any big stores in this area (of the town).* | *He's the area sales manager for southern California.* | *The new factory will be built somewhere in the London area.* **b** such a part or division having a particular character or purpose: *an area of high unemployment* | *the commercial area of a big city* | (fig.) *her lack of organization is an area of concern.* | (fig.) *She's doing brilliantly in her career, but her personal life is a* **disaster area**. | (fig.) *The question of who is responsible for the safety of the machinery is rather a* **grey area**. (=not certain) **3** [C] a particular space or surface: *There's a parking area behind the cinema.* | *a large room with a dining area at one end* **4** [C] (the range or limits of) a subject, activity, etc.: *new developments in the area of language teaching*

▷ USAGE **Area**, **region**, and **district** can all be used when speaking about parts of the Earth's surface. **Area** is the most general word. An **area** can be small or large, and is not thought of as a fixed land division: *I find the people in this area very friendly.* A **region** is usually large, is usually part of a country, and may or may not be thought of as a fixed land division: *The south east is the richest region in England.* | *Edinburgh is in the Lothian region of Scotland.* A **district** is smaller than a **region**, and is usually a fixed land division of a country or city: *The letters SW1 stand for a postal district of London.*◁

area code /ˈ··· ˌ·/ n AmE a telephone CODE¹ (3). Area codes in the US and Canada contain three numbers and the middle number is always 1 or 0. Numbers beginning with the area code 800 are TOLL-FREE (=paid for by the receiver of the call).

a·re·na /əˈriːnə/ n **1** an enclosed area used for sports, public entertainments, etc.: *The circus elephants were led into the arena.* **2** a place of great activity, esp. of competition or fighting: *She entered the political arena at the age of 25.*

A·rendt /ˈeərənt/, **Han·nah** /ˈhænə/ (1906–75) an American political thinker, writer and teacher who was born in Germany but left in 1941 to escape the Nazis

aren't /ɑːnt‖ˈɑːrənt/ short for: **1** are not: *They aren't here.* **2** (in questions) am not: *I'm your friend, aren't I?*
▷ USAGE There is no natural short form of **am I not?** Compare: *I am your friend,* **am I not?** (fml) | *I'm your friend,* **aren't I?** (infml) | *I'm your friend,* **ain't I?** (nonstandard)◁

a·rête /əˈret, əˈreɪt/ n tech a part of a mountain in the form of a long sharp edge with steep sides; RIDGE

ar·gent /ˈɑːdʒənt‖ˈɑːr-/ n [U] poet (the colour of) silver: *He carried an argent shield.* —**argent** adj

Ar·gen·ti·na /ˌɑːdʒənˈtiːnə‖ˌɑːr-/ a country in South America, also called **the Argentine**. In 1982 Argentina and Britain fought the Falklands War. —**Argentinian** /-ˈtɪniən/ n,adj

Ar·gie, **Argy** /ˈɑːdʒi‖ˈɑːr-/ n BrE derog an Argentinian; used esp. in Britain during the Falklands War

ar·gon /ˈɑːgɒn‖ˈɑːrgɑːn/ n [U] a chemically inactive gas that is a simple substance (ELEMENT), is found in the air, and is used in some electric lights

Ar·go·nauts /ˈɑːgənɔːts‖ˈɑːr-/ in CLASSICAL MYTHOLOGY, a group of strong, brave men who sailed with Jason in the ship Argo —see JASON

Ar·gos /ˈɑːgɒs‖ˈɑːrgɑːs/ tdmk one of a group of shops in Britain, selling electrical goods and other things for the home. Argos produce a CATALOGUE which people order from, and are known for being cheaper than other shops: *the new Argos catalogue* | *I got it from Argos.*

ar·got /ˈɑːgəʊ‖ˈɑːrgət/ n [C;U] informal speech spoken and understood by only a small group of people, esp. criminals

ar·gu·a·ble /ˈɑːgjuəbəl‖ˈɑːr-/ adj **1** able to be supported with reasons: *an arguable theory* | *It is arguable that the government has no right to interfere in this matter.* **2** doubtful in some degree; QUESTIONABLE: *an arguable decision* —opposite **unarguable** (for 2) —**-bly** adv : *Arguably, the criminal is a necessary member of society.*

ar·gue /ˈɑːgjuː‖ˈɑːr-/ v **1** [I (with, over, about)] to express disagreement in words, often with strong feeling; quarrel: *Do what you are told and don't argue (with me).* | *They're always arguing about/over money.* **2** [I;T] to provide reasons for or against (something) clearly and in proper order: *We could argue this point for hours without reaching any conclusions.* | *They argued the case for a non-nuclear defence policy.* | *a well-argued speech in favour of the proposal* | *He argued for/against the proposed tax cuts.* [+that] *I would argue that/It could be argued that sending men to the moon is a waste of money.* **3** [T+obj+into/out of] to persuade (someone) by showing reasons for or against an idea or course of action, often with strong feeling: *She argued him into/out of leaving his job.* **4** [T] fml to show; give signs (of); INDICATE: *Her essay argued a very good grasp of the facts.* [+that] *The way he spends money argues that he is rich.* **5 argue the toss** BrE infml to argue about a decision that has already been made and cannot be changed —see QUARREL (USAGE)

ar·gu·ment /ˈɑːgjɟmənt‖ˈɑːr-/ n **1** [C] a disagreement, esp.

one that is noisy; quarrel: *They were having an argument about whose turn it was to do the cooking.* | *They got into an argument about politics.* **2** [C **(for, against)**] a reason given to support or disprove something: *The committee listened to all the arguments for and against the proposal.* | *The risk of heart disease is a powerful argument against smoking.* | *He made a strong|convincing argument against accepting the offer.* [+*that*] *the familiar argument that the cost would outweigh the benefits* **3** [U] the use of reason to decide something or persuade someone: *We should try to settle this affair by argument, not by fighting.* | *Let's say,* **for the sake of argument** (=in order to help in deciding or understanding something), *that the sale price will be £25: how much profit will that give us?* **4** [C] *lit* a short account of the story or subject of a book, poem, etc.; SUMMARY

ar·gu·men·ta·tive /ˌɑːgjⁱˈmentətɪv||ˌɑːr-/ *adj derog* (of a person) liking to ARGUE (1); QUARRELSOME — **~ly** *adv*

Ar·gus /ˈɑːgəs||ˈɑːr-/ in CLASSICAL MYTHOLOGY, a many-eyed creature that Hera used as a guard and who was killed by Hermes, after which Hera put its eyes into the tail of a PEACOCK. Newspapers are sometimes called the "Argus" to suggest that they are continually awake to bring the news.

Ar·gyll /ɑːˈgaɪl||ɑːr-/ a former COUNTY in W Scotland, now part of Strathclyde REGION

a·ri·a /ˈɑːriə/ *n* a song that is sung by only one person in an OPERA or ORATORIO

ar·id /ˈærⱼd/ *adj* (of land) having so little rain as to be very dry and unproductive: *the arid wastes of the Sahara* | (fig.) *arid studies that produce no new ideas* — **~ity** /əˈrɪdⱼti/ *n* [U]

A·ri·el /ˈeəriəl/ *n* [U] *tdmk* a type of washing powder or liquid sold in Britain

Ar·ies /ˈeəriːz, ˈæri-iːz/ *n* **1** [U] the first sign of the ZODIAC, represented by a RAM (=male sheep) **2** [C] a person born between March 21 and April 20 —see ZODIAC (USAGE) and see picture at ZODIAC

a·right /əˈraɪt/ *adv fml* correctly; properly: *Have I understood you aright?*

a·rise /əˈraɪz/ *v* **arose** /əˈrəʊz/, **arisen** /əˈrɪzən/ [I] **1** [(**from, out of**)] to come into being or begin to be noticed; happen; appear: *Some unexpected difficulties|opportunities have arisen.* | *A strong wind arose.* | *a meeting to discuss any matters arising from the recent changes in the law* | *The bank will extend your loan,* **should the need arise.** (=if it becomes necessary) **2** *old use or poet* to stand up from sitting, kneeling, or lying: *"I will arise and go now, and go to Innisfree."* (W.B. Yeats) The words "Arise, Sir..." are used in the ceremony that takes place when someone is made a KNIGHT —see also DUB

Ar·is·tide /ˌæriˈstiːd/, **Jean-Ber·trand** /ʒɒn ˈbeətrɒn||ʒɑːn beərˈtrɑːn/ (1953–) a Haitian Roman Catholic priest who was elected president of his country in 1990 but was forced by soldiers to leave office in late 1991

ar·is·toc·ra·cy /ˌærⱼˈstɒkrəsi||-ˈstɑː-/ *n* **1** [C+*sing.|pl. v*] the people of the highest social class, esp. people from noble families who have titles of rank —see also UPPER CLASS **2** [C **(of)**] the finest, best, or most powerful members of any group or class: *The drivers are the aristocracy of the railwaymen's union.* **3** [U] government by people of the highest social class, esp. a class depending on birth or wealth —compare DEMOCRACY

▶ CULTURAL NOTE Britain has an offical aristocracy of titled people, but in the US, where no aristocracy is recognized, the word is often used with humour or SARCASM. ◀

ar·is·to·crat /ˈærⱼstəkræt, əˈrɪ-||əˈrɪ-/ *n* a member of an aristocracy

ar·is·to·crat·ic /ˌærⱼstəˈkrætɪk◂, əⱼrɪ-||əⱼrɪ-/ *adj* of, like, or typical of an aristocrat: *an aristocratic family* | *her aristocratic manners*

Ar·i·stoph·a·nes /ærⱼˈstɒfəniːz||-ˈstɑː-/ (about 445 BC – after 388 BC) a Greek writer of plays and poems considered to be the greatest ancient writer of humorous plays

Ar·is·tot·le /ˈærⱼstɒtl||-tɑːtl/ (384–322 BC) a Greek PHILOSOPHER who has had great influence on Western thought

a·rith·me·tic¹ /əˈrɪθmətɪk/ *n* [U] the science of numbers; the adding, subtracting, multiplying, etc., of numbers; calculation by numbers —compare MATHEMATICS

ar·ith·met·ic² /ˌærɪθˈmetɪk◂/ also **-ical** /ɪkəl/— *adj* of or concerning arithmetic — **~ally** /kli/ *adv*

a·rith·me·ti·cian /əˌrɪθməˈtɪʃən/ *n* a person who studies and understands arithmetic

ar·ith·met·ic pro·gres·sion /ˌ···· ·ˈ··/ also **arithmetical progression** /·····ˈ··/ *n* a set of numbers in order, in which a fixed number is added to each to produce the next (as in *2, 4, 6, 8, 10,* ...) —compare GEOMETRIC PROGRESSION

Ar·i·zo·na /ˌærⱼˈzəʊnə◂/ *written abbrev.* **AZ** a state in the SW of the USA known for its desert CLIMATE —see colour map on pages 1374-5

ark /ɑːk||ɑːrk/ *n* a large ship

Ark [*the*] **1** the large boat built by Noah in the Bible in which he saved his family and two of every kind of animal from the flood that covered the world —see also FLOOD **2 out of the Ark** *infml* very old or old-fashioned: *his jacket looks as if it came out of the Ark.*

Ar·kan·sas /ˈɑːkənsɔː||ˈɑːr-/ *written abbrev.* **AR** a state in S central USA – see colour map on pages 1374-5

Ark of the Cov·e·nant /ˌ· · · ˈ··/ *n* [*the*] a box that represented to the Jews the presence of God and contained the laws of their religion (the TEN COMMANDMENTS)

Ark Roy·al /ˌ· ˈ··/ a British Royal Navy AIRCRAFT CARRIER built in 1936 and sunk in 1941 off Gibraltar

Ark·wright /ˈɑːkraɪt||ˈɑːrk-/, **Sir Richard** (1732–92) an English inventor whose machine for spinning cotton replaced hand labour, making him and the factory owners very wealthy and causing widespread unemployment and anger among the workers —see also INDUSTRIAL REVOLUTION

Ar·ling·ton Na·tion·al Cem·e·tery /ˌɑːlɪŋtən næʃənəln ˈsemⱼtri ||ˌɑːr-, -ˈsemⱼteri/ a CEMETERY (=place where dead people are buried) in Arlington, Virginia, near Washington, D.C., where people in the armed forces or the government may be buried. John F. Kennedy is buried there and the cemetery also contains the **Tomb of the Unknown Soldier**, a building to honour soldiers who have died in wars but whose names are not known.

Ar·lott /ˈɑːlɒt||ˈɑːr-/, **John** (1914–91) a well known and much loved English cricket COMMENTATOR and writer who broadcast on radio and television over many years, becoming thought of as the "voice of cricket"

arm¹ /ɑːm||ɑːrm/ *n* **1** either of the two upper limbs of a human being or other animal that stands on two legs: *She carried the box under her arm.* | *The soldier was wounded in the right arm.* | *He put his arm round his elderly mother and walked her to the car.* | *He* **took her in his arms** (=held her closely) *and kissed her.* | *They walked down the road* **arm in arm.** (=with arms joined) | *He's still only a* **babe in arms.** (=a small child needing to be carried) **2** something that is shaped like or moves like an arm: *the arm of my coat|of the chair|of a record player* | *a long narrow arm of the sea* —see picture at GLASSES **3** a part or division of a group, esp. of the military forces: *the Fleet Air Arm* (=the branch of the British Navy that uses aircraft) | *the UK arm of an international corporation* | *the company's research arm* **4** **keep someone at arm's length** to keep a safe distance away from; avoid being friendly with someone —see also ARMS, **cost an arm and a leg** (COST²), **a shot in the arm** (SHOT¹), **twist someone's arm** (TWIST¹) — **~less** *adj*

arm² *v* [I;T **(with)**] to supply (oneself or others) with weapons or armour: *The crowd armed themselves with broken bottles.* | *The country armed (itself) in preparation for war.* —opposite **disarm** —see also ARMED; UNARMED

Ar·ma·da /ɑːˈmɑːdə||ɑːr-/ [*the*] a collection of armed ships sent by Spain in 1588 against England but defeated by the English navy led by Sir Francis Drake. The word is sometimes used to describe any large group of ships.

ar·ma·dil·lo /ˌɑːməˈdɪləʊ||ˌɑːr-/ *n* **-los** a small animal which comes from the warm parts of the Americas, covered in hard bands of bonelike shell

Ar·ma·ged·don /ˌɑːməˈgedn||ˌɑːr-/ a great battle or war causing terrible destruction and bringing the end of the world (from the place, Armageddon, in the Bible, where it is said that a great battle will take place): *Millions of dollars were spent on bomb shelters and weapons ready for a nuclear Armageddon.*

Ar·magh /ˌɑːˈmɑː◂||ˌɑːr-/ **1** a town in Northern Ireland

2 a former COUNTY of Northern Ireland, now a local government DISTRICT

Ar·ma·gnac /ˈɑːməmjæk‖ˌɑːrmɔnˈjæk/ n [C;U] a strong alcoholic drink (BRANDY) made in SW France and usu. drunk from a small glass after a meal

ar·ma·ment /ˈɑːməmənt‖ˈɑːr-/ n **1** [C often pl.] the arms and other fighting equipment of an army, navy, etc., or on a warship or military aircraft: chemical armaments | the armaments industry **2** [C often pl.] an armed force or the total armed forces of a country **3** [U] the act of preparing for war —compare DISARMAMENT

Ar·ma·ni /ɑːˈmɑːni‖ɑːr-/, **Gior·gio** /ˈdʒɔːdʒəʊ‖ˈdʒɔːr-/ (1935–) an Italian fashion DESIGNER whose suits are expensive and very fashionable: smart young men in Armani suits

ar·ma·ture /ˈɑːmətʃəʳ‖ˈɑːr-/ n **1** the part of a GENERATOR (=a machine producing electricity) consisting of a piece of metal with wire wound around it, that goes round and round so as to produce electricity **2** a similar part in an electric motor that goes round and round so as to produce movement **3** a frame on which clay or other soft material can be put to make a figure or model

arm·band /ˈɑːmbænd‖ˈɑːrm-/ n **1** a band of material worn round the arm to show the wearer's official position, as a sign of MOURNING, etc. **2** a band of plastic filled with air, which children wear on their arms to help them float in water while they learn to swim

arm·chair¹ /ˈɑːmtʃeəʳ, ˌɑːmˈtʃeəʳ‖ˈɑːrm-, ˌɑːrm-/ n a comfortable chair with supports for the arms —see picture at CHAIR and at LIVING ROOM

armchair² /ˈɑːmtʃeəʳ‖ˈɑːrm-/ adj [A] usu. derog ready to give advice or pass judgment, but not taking an active part: an armchair critic/revolutionary

armed /ɑːmd‖ɑːrmd/ adj **1** [(with)] having or using weapons or armour: I warn you that I am armed. | The police were armed with truncheons and riot shields. | They were convicted of **armed robbery**. | Could the situation lead to **armed conflict**? (=war) | (fig.) She came to the meeting armed with all the facts and figures to prove her case. **2 armed to the teeth** very heavily armed

armed forc·es /ˌ· ˈ··/ n [(the) P] the military forces of a country, usu. the army, navy, and air force

Ar·me·ni·a /ɑːˈmiːniə‖ɑːr-/ a country in SE Europe bordering on Turkey, Iran, Georgia, and Azerbaijan; capital Yerevan; population 3,283,000 (1989) —**nian** n, adj

arm·ful /ˈɑːmfʊl‖ˈɑːrm-/ n [(of)] all that a person can hold in one or both arms: an armful of fresh flowers

arm·hole /ˈɑːmhəʊl‖ˈɑːrm-/ n a hole in a shirt, coat, etc., through which the arm is put

ar·mi·stice /ˈɑːmɪstɪs‖ˈɑːrm-/ n an agreement to stop fighting, usu. for a short time. The word is esp. used to mean the armistice that brought the end of the First World War, on November 11th 1918. —compare CEASE-FIRE, TRUCE

Armistice Day /ˈ··· ˌ·/ November 11th, celebrated as the ANNIVERSARY of the end of the First World War in 1918 — see also REMEMBRANCE DAY, VETERANS DAY

ar·mour BrE ‖ **armor** AmE /ˈɑːməʳ‖ˈɑːr-/ n [U] **1** strong protective metal or leather covering for the body as worn formerly in battle by fighting men and their horses: a suit of armour | (fig.) He seems immovable in his opposition to our plan, but I think I detect a **chink in his armour**. (=a weak point in his position) **2** strong protective metal covering on modern vehicles of war: armour-clad warships/tanks **3** the protective covering of some plants and animals

ar·moured BrE ‖ **armored** AmE /ˈɑːməd‖ˈɑːrmərd/ adj **1** protected by armour: armoured vehicles **2** [A] having fighting vehicles protected by armour: an armoured division

armoured car /ˌ·· ˈ·/ n **1** an armoured military vehicle, usu. with a powerful gun **2** a car protected by armour, used esp. by important people: The president rode in an armoured car.

ar·mour·er BrE ‖ **armorer** AmE /ˈɑːmərəʳ‖ˈɑːr-/ n a person who makes, repairs, and tests weapons and armour

armour plate /ˌ·· ˈ·‖ˈ··-/ also **armour pla·ting** /ˌ·· ˈ··‖ˈ··ˌ··/ n [U] a specially hardened metal cover used as protection for military vehicles —**armour-plated** /ˌ·· ˈ··◂‖ˈ·· ˌ··/ adj

ar·mour·y BrE ‖ **armory** AmE /ˈɑːməri‖ˈɑːr-/ n a place where weapons are stored

arm·pit /ˈɑːmˌpɪt‖ˈɑːrm-/ n the hollow place under the arm at the shoulder

arms /ɑːmz‖ɑːrmz/ n [P] **1** weapons of war: The government intends to cut expenditure on arms. | an arms control agreement | They have 50,000 men **under arms**. (=armed and ready to fight) | The general called on the defeated army to **lay down their arms**. (=stop fighting) | (lit) They **took up arms** (=became soldiers) in defence of their country. **2** a COAT OF ARMS. The word is sometimes used in the names of PUBS, such as The Farmer's Arms. —see also COLLEGE OF ARMS **3 up in arms** infml very angry and ready to argue or fight: The women are up in arms over/about their low rate of pay. —see also SMALL ARMS

arms con·trol /ˈ· ·ˌ·/ n [U] the attempt by powerful countries to limit the number and kind of weapons of war owned by themselves and other countries

arms race /ˈ· ·/ n [usu. sing.] a continuing struggle between two opposing countries in which each tries to produce more and better weapons of war than the other

Arm·strong /ˈɑːmstrɒŋ‖ˈɑːrmstrɔːŋ/, **Lou·is** /ˈluːi/ (1900–71) an American JAZZ musician, singer, and bandleader, known esp. for the rough sound of his voice

Armstrong, Neil /niːl/ (1930–) an American ASTRONAUT who was the first man to step on the moon in 1969. He is remembered for saying "one small step for a man, one giant leap for mankind" as he first stepped onto the moon. —see colour picture on page 752

ar·my /ˈɑːmi‖ˈɑːr-/ n [C+sing./pl. v] **1 a** the branch of a country's military forces that is concerned with attack and defence on land: to join the army | a modern well-equipped army | an army officer **b** any military force trained to fight on land: The radio station was seized by a rebel army. **2** any large group, esp. one that is brought together for some purpose: An army of workmen was brought in to build the stadium. **3 an army marches on its stomach** a phrase which is believed to have been said by Napoleon, meaning that soldiers need good food in order to walk and fight

army brat /ˈ·· ˌ·/ n AmE a person whose father was in one of the armed forces, and who therefore probably moved often from place to place as a child

Arn·hem /ˈɑːnəm‖ˈɑːr-/ a city in the Netherlands where British and ALLIED forces landed in the SECOND WORLD WAR and where there was a great loss of life

Ar·nold /ˈɑːnəld‖ˈɑːr-/, **Ben·e·dict** /ˈbenɪdɪkt/ (1741–1801) an American military leader, famous for betraying (BETRAY) his country to the British during the American Revolution

Arnold, Mat·thew /ˈmæθjuː/ (1822–88) an English poet, known for his poems such as Dover Beach and The Scholar Gypsy as well as works of criticism about literature and society

Arnold, Roseanne an American actress and COMEDIAN, formerly called Roseanne Barr, who is best known for the television programme Roseanne —see picture at ROSEANNE

A-road /ˈeɪ rəʊd/ n in Britain, a road (often shown in red on maps) with the letter A before its number, showing that it is an important main road but is not a full MOTORWAY

a·ro·ma /əˈrəʊmə/ n **1** a strong usu. pleasant smell: the aroma of hot coffee **2** a noticeable feeling or quality connected with a place or situation; AURA: An aroma of mystery hung about the place.

a·ro·ma·ther·a·py /əˌrəʊməˈθerəpi/ n [U] a kind of treatment using special oils to MASSAGE the body. This is usu. regarded as a form of ALTERNATIVE MEDICINE.

ar·o·mat·ic /ˌærəˈmætɪk◂/ adj having a strong pleasant smell: Aromatic herbs are often used in cooking. — ~**ally** /kli/ adv

a·rose /əˈrəʊz/ past tense of ARISE

a·round¹ /əˈraʊnd/ adv **1** esp. AmE from one place to another; to various places; about: I travelled around for a few years. | The company is looking around for a suitable site for the factory. | Do you know your way around? **2** esp. AmE in various places; here and there; about: Why are all these books lying around? | I haven't seen him *around lately.* | **See you around!** (=I'll see you some-where soon.) **3** *esp. AmE* on all sides; surrounding a centre: *a prison with high walls all around* | *The children gathered around to hear the story.* **4** in all directions from a centre: *not a single house for miles around* **5** somewhere near; in the area: *Is there anyone around?* | *I'll wait around for a while.* **6** *esp. AmE* so as to face the other way; round: *He turned around when he heard a noise behind him.* **7** *esp. AmE* moving in a circle; round: *turning around and around* **8** *esp. AmE* measured in a circle; round: *a tree ten feet around* **9** *infml* in existence or activity: *one of the best artists around* **10 have been around** *infml* to have had a lot of experience of life —see ROUND³ (USAGE)

around² *prep* **1** *esp. AmE* on all sides of; all round; sur-rounding: *We sat around the table.* | *a long wall around the grounds* | *He had a towel wrapped around his waist.* **2** from one place to another in; to or in various parts of; about: *They walked around the town.* | *books lying around the room* | *The store has about 20 branches dotted around the country.* **3** in some place near (to); in the area of: *He lives somewhere around London.* | *There must be a bank around here somewhere.* **4** a little more or less than; about: *There were around 200 people at the meeting.* | *The price has risen to around £5000.* | *I'll be home around seven.* **5** so as to avoid or get past; round: *Let's go around the town, not through it.* | *I don't think we can get around that problem.* **6** having a centre or base in: *Their soci-ety was built around a belief in God.* —see ROUND³ (USAGE)

Around the World in Eigh·ty Days /ˌ·ˌ·ˌ·ˌ·ˌ·· ˈ·/ a book by Jules Verne about an Englishman, Phileas Fogg, who travels around the world in 80 days with his ASSISTANT, Passepartout. It has been made into a successful film. — see colour picture on page 1145

a·rous·al /əˈrauzəl/ *n* [U] the act of arousing or state of being aroused, esp. sexually

a·rouse /əˈrauz/ *v* [T] **1** [(**from**)] *fml* to cause to wake; ROUSE: *We aroused him from his deep sleep.* **2** to cause to become active; excite: *Her behaviour aroused the sus-picions of the police.* | *sexually aroused*

ar·peg·gi·o /ɑːˈpedʒiəu‖ɑːr-/ *n* **-gios** the notes of a musical CHORD played separately in upward or downward order, rather than all at once

arr *written abbrev. for:* **1** arranged (by): *music by Mozart, arr Britten* **2 a** arrives **b** arrival —compare DEP

ar·raign /əˈreɪn/ *v* [T (**for, on**)] *tech* to call or bring before a court of law, esp. to face a serious charge: *arraigned on a charge of manslaughter* — ~ **ment** *n* [C;U]

Ar·ran /ˈærən/ an island at the mouth of the Firth of Clyde in Scotland

ar·range /əˈreɪndʒ/ *v* **1** [T] to put into a correct, pleasing, or desired order: *to arrange flowers in a vase* | *The books are arranged on the shelves in alphabetical order.* **2** [I+**about, for**; T] to make preparations (for); plan or set-tle in advance: *I've arranged for a taxi.* | *We must arrange about dinner.* | *Let's arrange a meeting for next Friday.* | *He called at 9.00, as arranged.* [+to-v] *We've arranged to meet them at the restaurant.* | *We've arranged with them to meet at the restaurant.* | *I've arranged for a doctor to see him/arranged for him to be seen by a doctor.* | *I've ar-ranged with the electrician to call tomorrow.* [+wh-] *We still have to arrange where to meet.* [+ that] *I've arranged that one of our representatives will meet you at the airport.* **3** [T (**for**)] to set out (a piece of music) in a certain way, e.g. for different instruments: *a symphony arranged for the piano*

arranged mar·riage /ˌ·ˌ· ˈ··/ *n* [C;U] a marriage where the parents choose a husband or wife for their child, usu. on grounds of religion, social class, etc. In Western society marriages are not usu. arranged by the parents of the two people involved.

ar·range·ment /əˈreɪndʒmənt/ *n* **1** [C *usually pl.*] a plan made in preparation for something: *We must make arrangements for the wedding.* | *He's in charge of the secu-rity arrangements for the president's visit.* **2** [C;U] some-thing that has been settled or agreed on; agreement: *By (a) special arrangement with the bank, we are being allowed to borrow a further £10,000.* | *It would normally cost £500 but I'm sure we can* **come to some arrange-ment.** [+to-v] *I have an arrangement with my ex-wife to see the children every weekend.* **3** [U (**of**)] the act of

arranging: *the art of flower arrangement* **4** [C] some-thing that has been put in order: *a beautiful flower arrangement* **5** [C;U] (an example of) the setting out of a piece of music in a certain way, e.g. for different instru-ments: *an arrangement of an old song for the piano*

ar·rant /ˈærənt/ *adj* [A] *esp. BrE* very bad; complete; extreme: *arrant nonsense*

ar·ray¹ /əˈreɪ/ *v* [T] *fml or lit* **1** to set in order: *The enemy forces were arrayed on the opposite hill.* **2** to dress, esp. splendidly: *arrayed in all her finery*

array² *n* **1** [C (**of**);U] *fml* a collection or ordered group: *troops lined up in battle array* | *a baffling array of facts and figures* **2** [C;U] *lit* fine clothes, esp. for a special oc-casion **3** *tech* a set of numbers or signs, or of computer memory units, arranged in rows and COLUMNs —see also DISARRAY

ar·rears /əˈrɪəz‖-ɪərz/ *n* [P] *esp. BrE* **1** money that is owed from the past and should have been paid: *He was in ar-rears with the rent.* | *The rent was two months in arrears.* **2** work that is still waiting to be done: *arrears of work that have piled up*

ar·rest¹ /əˈrest/ *v* [T] **1** to seize by the power of the law: *He has been arrested on suspicion of murder and taken into custody.* **2** *fml* to bring to an end; stop: *The treat-ment arrested the growth of the disease.* | *arrested develop-ment* **3** *fml* to catch and fix (esp. someone's attention); ENGAGE (3): *The bright lights arrested the baby's attention.*

arrest² *n* [C;U] the act or an example of arresting: *The police made several arrests.* | *He was soon put/placed* **under arrest.** —see also CITIZEN'S ARREST

ar·riv·al /əˈraɪvəl/ *n* **1** [U] the act of arriving: *We apolo-gize for the late arrival of the aircraft.* | *He was rushed to hospital but was* **dead on arrival.** | *The arrival of the computer has revolutionized the publishing industry* **2** [C] a person or thing that has arrived: *They went out to welcome the new arrivals.* | *The new arrival was a healthy baby boy.*

ar·rive /əˈraɪv/ *v* [I] **1** to reach a place at the end of a jour-ney: *We arrived home safely.* | *What time does the plane arrive in New York?* —compare DEPART (1) **2** to come to a place, esp. by arrangement: *Shall we start now, or shall we wait for the others to arrive?* **3** to be brought or deli-vered to a place: *Has the post arrived yet?* | *I'm still wait-ing for those books I ordered to arrive.* **4** to happen as expected or arranged; come: *At last the great day ar-rived.* | *Her baby arrived* (=was born) *yesterday.* **5** to win success: *They felt they had really arrived when they made their first record.*

arrive at sthg. *phr v* [T] to reach, esp. after much ef-fort or thought; come to: *After many hours' talk, the com-mittee arrived at a decision.*

ar·ro·gant /ˈærəgənt/ *adj* unpleasantly proud, with an un-reasonably strong belief in one's own importance, and a lack of respect for other people: *an arrogant official* | *arrogant behaviour* — ~ **ly** *adv* —**gance** *n* [U] : *his in-sufferable arrogance*

ar·ro·gate /ˈærəgeɪt/ *v* [T (**to**)] *fml* to take or claim (for one-self) without a proper or legal right: *Having seized power in the country, he arrogated to himself the right to change the law.*

ar·row /ˈærəu/ *n* **1** a thin straight stick with a point at one end and feathers at the other, which is shot from a BOW¹ in fighting or sport **2** a sign like an arrow (→) used to show direction or the position of something: *The casualty department is in the east wing – take the next left and follow the arrows.*

ar·row·head /ˈærəuhed/ *n* a pointed piece of stone or metal fixed to the front end of an arrow

ar·row·root /ˈærəuruːt, ˈærəruːt/ *n* [U] flour made from the root of a tropical American plant

arse¹ /ɑːs‖ɑːrs/ *n BrE taboo sl* **1** also **ass** *AmE*– the part of the body one sits on; BOTTOM **2** also **arse·hole** /ˈɑːshəul ‖ ˈɑːrs-/‖ **asshole** *AmE*– **a** the ANUS **b** a stupid annoying person

arse² *v*

arse about/around *phr v* [I] *BrE taboo sl* to waste time

ar·se·nal /ˈɑːsənəl‖ˈɑːr-/ *n* **1** a government building where weapons and explosives are made or stored **2** a store of weapons: *The police found an arsenal of knives and guns in the terrorists' hideout.*

Arsenal an English football team from North London

ar·se·nic /ˈɑːsənɪk‖ˈɑːr-/ *n* [U] a very poisonous substance, of which one chemical form is used in medicine and for killing rats

Arsenic and Old Lace /ˌ··· · · ˈ·/ the title of a humorous play by Joseph Kasselring which was later made into a film

ar·son /ˈɑːsən‖ˈɑːr-/ *n* [U] the crime of setting fire to property: *The police suspect arson.* — ~**ist** *n*

art¹ /ɑːt‖ɑːrt/ *n* **1** [U] the making or expression of what is beautiful, e.g. in music, literature, or esp. painting: *The museum contains some priceless* **works of art.** | *Dance is an exciting* **art form.** **2** [U] things produced by art, esp. paintings and SCULPTURE: *an exhibition of African art* **3** [C;U] skill in the making or doing of anything: *Driving a car in Central London is* **quite an art!** (=needs great skill) | *Television is ruining the art of conversation.* **4 art for art's sake** art is important simply because it is art, and not because it makes money or has any practical use —see also ARTS, BLACK ART, FINE ART, FINE ARTS, PLASTIC ART, POP ART

art² *v* **thou art** *old use or bibl* (when talking to one person) you are

art deco

art dec·o /ˌɑː ˈdekəʊ, ˌɑːt-‖ˌɑːr ˈdeɪkəʊ, ˌɑːrt-/ *n* [U] a style of art and decoration popular in the 1920s and 1930s in Europe and America, using esp. simple shapes and man-made materials

art di·rec·tor /ˈ· ·ˌ··/ *n* the person who arranges the clothes, lighting, and scenery for a film

ar·te·fact /ˈɑːtɪfækt‖ˈɑːr-/ *n* an ARTIFACT

Ar·te·mis /ˈɑːtɪmɪs‖ˈɑːr-/ in CLASSICAL MYTHOLOGY, the Greek goddess of the hunt and the moon (Roman name Diana)

ar·te·ri·al /ɑːˈtɪəriəl‖ɑːr-/ *adj* [A] **1** (of blood) sent from the heart in the arteries: *Arterial blood is bright red.* —compare VENOUS **2** (of a road, railway, etc.) main; forming one of the chief parts of a large system: *arterial roads leading into London*

ar·te·ri·o·scle·ro·sis /ɑːˌtɪəriəʊsklɪˈrəʊsɪs‖ɑːr-/ *n* [U] a diseased condition in which the walls of the arteries become thick and hard and so prevent the easy flow of blood through the body. The condition is often called **hardening of the arteries.** —see also ATHEROSCLEROSIS

ar·te·ry /ˈɑːtəri‖ˈɑːr-/ *n* **1** one of the tubes that carry blood from the heart to the rest of the body —compare VEIN **2** a main road, railway, river, etc.

ar·te·si·an well /ɑːˌtiːziən ˈwel‖ɑːrˌtiːʒən-/ *n* a well in which the water is forced to the surface by natural pressure

Ar·tex /ˈɑːteks‖ˈɑːr-/ *n* [U] *tdmk* a substance like thick lumpy paint used for covering the CEILING and walls inside a house

art·ful /ˈɑːtfəl‖ˈɑːr-/ *adj* cleverly deceitful; CUNNING: *He's very artful and usually succeeds in getting what he wants.* — ~**ly** *adv* — ~**ness** *n* [U]

Artful Dodg·er /ˌ··· ˈ··/ [*the*] a character from the book *Oliver Twist* by Charles Dickens. He is a young thief (PICKPOCKET) who is very successful at stealing from people and not getting caught

art gal·le·ry /ˈ· ˌ···/ *n* a building in which works of art are put on show to the public, either for sale or purely for them to be admired or studied

ar·thri·tis /ɑːˈθraɪtɪs‖ɑːr-/ *n* [U] a serious, often long-lasting disease causing pain and swelling in the joints of the body —**tic** /ɑːˈθrɪtɪk‖ɑːr-/ *adj, n*

Ar·thur /ˈɑːθəʳ‖ˈɑːr-/ a LEGENDARY king of Britain —see ARTHURIAN LEGEND —**Arthurian** /ɑːˈθjʊəriən‖ɑːrˈθʊə-/ *adj* : *Arthurian literature*

Arthur, Chester (1830–86) the president of the US from 1881 to 1885

Arthur An·der·son /ˌ··· ˈ···/ a large international ACCOUNTANCY firm

Arthur Daley /ˌɑːθə ˈdeɪli/ a character in the humorous British television SERIES *Minder*, who is dishonest but also likeable. He is a used-car salesman who also buys and sells other goods, including stolen goods, without much success.

Ar·thu·ri·an Le·gend /ɑːˌθjʊəriən ˈledʒənd‖ɑːrˌθʊə-/ stories about Arthur, who became king of England when he pulled out the sword in the stone (Excalibur) which noone except the king could do. His court at Camelot was famous for bravery, CHIVALRY, ROMANTIC love, and magic which was practised esp. by the MAGICIAN Merlin, and the SORCERESS Morgan le Fay. Here, at a round table, sat the bravest and most noble KNIGHTs in the land (the KNIGHTS OF THE ROUND TABLE), Sir Galahad, Sir Lancelot, Sir Bevidere, and others. England and Arthur's power began to fail when he discovered the love between his wife, Guinevere, and his best friend, Lancelot. Then began the long search for the Holy Grail (=the wine cup at Christ's last meal) which was finally found and brought back by Galahad. Arthur's strength returned and he went into battle to save England from Mordred whom he killed, but Arthur himself was very seriously wounded. He gave Excalibur to Bevidere and ordered him to throw it into a lake. The hand of the Lady of the Lake came out of the water, caught the sword, and took it under, then three women arrived on a boat and took Arthur to his final resting place at Avalon. It is said that Arthur will return if England is ever in danger again.

ar·tic /ɑːˈtɪk‖ɑːr-/ *n BrE infml* an articulated (ARTICULATE² (3)) lorry

ar·ti·choke /ˈɑːtɪtʃəʊk‖ɑːr-/ *n* [C;U] **1** also **globe artichoke**– a plant whose leafy flower is eaten as a vegetable. It is thought of as a DELICACY, and is quite difficult to eat because of its shape **2** also **Jerusalem artichoke**– a plant whose potato-like root is eaten as a vegetable see picture at VEGETABLE

ar·ti·cle¹ /ˈɑːtɪkəl‖ˈɑːr-/ *n* **1** a particular or separate thing or object, esp. one of a group: *an article of clothing* | *The burglars took no articles of value.* **2** a separate piece of writing on a particular subject in a newspaper, magazine, etc., that is not FICTION: *an article on the new football manager|on the Chinese way of life* **3** a complete separate part in a legal agreement, CONSTITUTION, etc. **4** *tech* a word used with a noun to show whether the noun refers to a particular example of something (the **definite article – the** in English) or to a general or not already mentioned example of something (the **indefinite article – a** or **an** in English)

article² *v* [T (**to, with**)] to place under ARTICLES: *I am articled to a firm of solicitors.*

articled clerk /ˌ··· ˈ·/ *n* a person training to be a lawyer in England and Wales who has taken some of his or her examinations and works for two years for a trained lawyer to learn how the law works in practice. Articled clerks are now usu. called **trainee solicitors**

ar·ti·cles /ˈɑːtɪkəlz‖ˈɑːr-/ *n* [P] a written agreement in law between an employer and someone learning a profession or job

Articles of Con·fed·e·ra·tion /ˌ··· · ···ˌ··/ [*the*+P] the agreement drawn up in 1781 by the 13 original colonies, (COLONY) of the US which served as the basic law for the government until the US Constitution was agreed upon in 1788

ar·tic·u·late¹ /ɑːˈtɪkj̵l̵ɪ̵t‖ɑːr-/ *adj* **1** expressing or able to express thoughts and feelings clearly and effectively: *a very articulate child* **2** (of speech) having clear separate sounds or words —opposite **inarticulate**; compare INTELLIGIBLE **3** *tech* having joints: *Insects are articulate animals.* — ~**ly** *adv* — ~**ness** *n* [U]

ar·tic·u·late² /ɑːˈtɪkj̵l̵eɪt‖ɑːr-/ *v* **1** [T] to express thoughts and feelings clearly: *He finds it very difficult to articulate his distress.* **2** [I;T] to speak or pronounce, esp. clearly and carefully **3** [T] to unite by joints that allow movement: *The bones of our fingers are articulated.* | *An* articulated vehicle/lorry/bus *can turn corners more easily.* —see picture at TRUCK

ar·tic·u·la·tion /ɑːˌtɪkjʊˈleɪʃən‖ɑːr-/ n 1 [U] the production of speech sounds: *clear articulation* 2 [U] the expression of thoughts and feelings in words 3 [C] *tech* a joint, esp. in a plant

ar·ti·fact , arte- /ˈɑːtɪfækt‖ˈɑːr-/ n an object made by human work, esp. a tool, weapon, or decorative object that has special historical interest: *an exhibition of ancient Egyptian artifacts*

ar·ti·fice /ˈɑːtɪfɪs‖ˈɑːr-/ n *fml* 1 [C] a clever trick: *The use of mirrors in a room is an artifice to make the room look larger.* 2 [U] clever skill; CUNNING

ar·tif·i·cer /ɑːˈtɪfɪsər‖ɑːr-/ n 1 *lit* a skilled workman 2 a naval or military MECHANIC

ar·ti·fi·cial /ˌɑːtɪˈfɪʃəl◂‖ˌɑːr-/ adj 1 made by humans, esp. as a copy of something natural: *This drink contains no artificial flavouring or colouring.* | *artificial flowers* | *artificial silk* 2 lacking true feelings; insincere: *She welcomed me with an artificial smile.* 3 happening as a result of human action, not through a natural process: *High import taxes give their homemade goods an artificial advantage in the market.* – ~ **ly** *adv* : *Government subsidies have kept the price of food artificially low.* – ~**ity** /ˌɑːtɪfɪʃiˈælɪti‖ˌɑːr-/ n [U]

artificial in·sem·i·na·tion /ˌ····· ··ˈ···/ n [U] the process of putting a male seed into a female animal or human, with an instrument rather than naturally. Women who find it difficult to become PREGNANT can be treated by using artificial insemination. —see also AID

artificial in·tel·li·gence /ˌ···· ·ˈ···/ also **AI** – n [U] a branch of computer science which aims to produce machines that can understand, make judgments, etc., in the way that humans do

artificial res·pi·ra·tion /ˌ···· ··ˈ··/ also **mouth-to-mouth resuscitation, kiss of life** n [U] the forcing of air into and out of the lungs of a person who has stopped breathing by blowing into the mouth —compare CPR

ar·til·le·ry /ɑːˈtɪləri‖ɑːr-/ n 1 [U] large guns, esp. on wheels or fixed in one place, e.g. on a ship or in a fort 2 [*the*+S+*sing./pl. v*] the part of the army that uses these weapons

ar·ti·san /ˌɑːtɪˈzæn‖ˈɑːrtɪzən/ n someone who does skilled work with their hands; CRAFTSMAN

art·ist /ˈɑːtɪst‖ˈɑːr-/ n 1 a person who produces works of art, esp. paintings or drawings 2 an inventive and skilled worker: *He's no ordinary baker – he's an artist.* 3 an ARTISTE 4 (*in comb.*) *infml* someone who is skilled in a particular activity, esp. a bad one: *a rip-off artist*

artist

ar·tiste /ɑːˈtiːst‖ɑːr-/ n a professional singer, actor, dancer, etc., who performs in a show

ar·tis·tic /ɑːˈtɪstɪk‖ɑːr-/ adj 1 [no comp.] of, concerning, or typical of art or artists: *the artistic temperament* 2 *approc* having or showing inventive skill and imagination in art: *He's very artistic.* | *an artistic flower arrangement* – ~ **ally** /kli/ adv : *My daughter is artistically inclined.*

art·ist·ry /ˈɑːtɪstri‖ˈɑːr-/ n [U] *apprec* inventive imagination and ability; artistic skill: *the artistry of the violinist*

art·less /ˈɑːtləs‖ˈɑːr-/ adj simple and natural, without any deceit or insincerity: *artless grace* | *an artless village girl* – ~**ly** adv – ~**ness** n [U]

art nou·veau /ˌɑː nuːˈvəʊ, ˌɑːt-‖ˌɑːr-/ n [U] a style of art and decoration common at the end of the 19th century in Europe and America, using flowing lines and plant forms. In Britain, art nouveau is connected esp. with the work of Aubrey Beardsley, Charles Rennie Mackintosh, and William Morris.

arts /ɑːts‖ɑːrts/ n [*the*+P] 1 also **humanities** ‖ **arts and letters** *AmE* – those subjects of study that are not considered to be part of science, such as history and languages, esp. as taught at a university: *an arts graduate* —see also BA, MA, LIBERAL ARTS 2 art, esp. the FINE ARTS: *Should the government provide money to support the arts?* | *Timothy Renton, the Arts Minister*

arts and crafts /ˌ· · ·ˈ·/ n [P] the arts that are concerned with making ordinary things by hand, such as POTTERY, weaving, furniture-making, etc.

Arts Coun·cil /ˈ· ˌ··/ [*the*] an organization in Britain which is supported by the government and provides financial help for many different organizations involved in the theatre, art, music, etc.

art thea·ter /ˈ· ˌ··/ n *AmE* a cinema which shows mainly foreign films or films which were made by independent producers rather than big companies

art nouveau

A Lalique vase

art·y /ˈɑːti‖ˈɑːr-/ ‖ usu. **art·sy** /ˈɑːtsi‖ˈɑːr-/ *AmE adj* often *derog* trying to appear artistic: *arty lighting/photography* —**iness** n [U]

art·y-craft·y /ˌɑːti ˈkrɑːfti‖ˌɑːrti ˈkræfti/ *BrE* ‖ **art·sy-craft·sy** /ˌɑːtsi ˈkrɑːftsi‖ˌɑːrtsi ˈkræftsi/ *AmE adj usu. derog* arty in a simple or country style: *They're a very arty-crafty couple – she makes clothes and he's a potter.*

arty-far·ty /ˌ·· ˈ···◂/ ‖ usu. **art·sy-fart·sy** /ˌɑːtsi ˈfɑːtsi‖ˌɑːrtsi ˈfɑːr-/ *AmE adj infml derog* arty

A·ry·an /ˈeəriən/ n, adj (of or concerning) a person from Northern Europe, esp. one with fair hair and blue eyes, considered by the Nazis in Germany as being a member of the best race of people

as¹ /əz; *strong* æz/ adv, prep 1 (used in comparisons and examples) equally; like: *He's not as old as me.* | *He's as strong as an ox.* | *She's clever, but her brother is just as clever.* | *I only like small animals,* **such as** *cats and dogs.* | *The disease attacks such animals as cats and dogs.* 2 in the condition of; when considered as being: *I like her as a person, but I don't think much of her as a writer.* | *He works as a farmer.* | *This is regarded as* (=thought to be) *his best film.* | *She was dressed as a man.* | *Speaking as a teacher, I am in favour of these reforms.* | *His talents as a film actor were soon recognized.* | *Several businesses went bankrupt as a result of the oil crisis.* —see LIKE² (USAGE)

as² conj 1 (used in comparisons): *She doesn't run as fast as she used to.* | *He works in the same office as my sister.* | *I was as surprised as anyone when they offered me the job.* (=no one was more surprised than me) | *Two is to four as four is to eight.* 2 in the way or manner that: *Do as I say!* | *He was late, as usual.* | *David, as you know* (=and you know this), *is a photographer.* | *As I said in my last letter, I am taking the exam in July.* 3 while; when: *He saw her as he was getting off the bus.* | *As the election approached, the violence got worse.* 4 because: *As she has no car, she can't get there easily.* 5 though: *Improbable as it seems, it's true.* | *Tired as I was, I tried to help them.* | (*esp. AmE*) *As popular as he is* (=even though he is popular) *the President has not been able to get his own way on every issue.* 6 (with **so** or **such**, showing a result): *so cold as to make swimming impossible* | *such an expression on his face as left no doubt of his decision* —see also SO¹, SUCH¹ 7 (showing a purpose): *He ran away* **so** *as not to be caught.* 8 **as against** in comparison with: *Our profits this year amount to £20,000 as against £15,000 last year.* 9 **as for** *sometimes derog* (used when starting to talk about a new subject, connected with what came before) when we speak of; concerning: *You can have a bed; as for him, he'll have to sleep on the floor.* 10 **as if/though: a** as it would be if (something were true): *I couldn't move my legs. It was as if they were stuck to the floor.* | *Why doesn't she buy us a drink? It isn't as if she had no money.* (=she has plenty of money) **b** in a way that suggests that (something is true): *He shook his head as if to say "don't trust her".* | *We've missed the bus. It looks as if* (=it seems) *we'll have to walk.* **c** (showing a strong negative): *"He's gone." "As if I cared!"* (=I don't care at all). 11 **as it is: a** in reality; in the situation that actually exists: *We had hoped to finish it today, but as it is we probably won't finish until tomorrow.* **b** already: *Don't say anything else; you're in enough trouble as it is.* 12 **as it were** as one might say; in a sort of way: *He is, as it were, a modern Sherlock Holmes.* **13 as of/from** starting from (the time stated): *As of today, you are in charge of the office.* **14 as to: a** (used esp. when speaking of arguments and decisions) on the subject of; concerning: *He's very uncertain as to whether it's the right job for him.* **b** according to; by: *correctly placed as to size and colour* **15 as yet** *fml* (*with negatives*) until now: *I have received no answer from them as yet.* —see also **as long as** (LONG²), **as often as not** (OFTEN), and **so far**

▷ USAGE In comparisons, you can use **as** or **so** after **not**: *He's not as/so old as I am.* Otherwise use **as**: *She's as pretty as her sister.* In AmE the first **as** in such comparisons is sometimes omitted: *He's old as the hills.* | *She turned red as a beet.*◁

ASA /ˌeɪ es ˈeɪ/ *abbrev. for* ADVERTISING STANDARDS AUTHORITY

asap /ˌeɪ es eɪ ˈpiː, ˈeɪsæp/ *abbrev. for:* as soon as possible

as·bes·tos /æsˈbestəs, æz-/ *n* [U] a soft grey mineral that is used as a building material (esp. when made into solid sheets against fire and heat) and for other industrial purposes, such as protecting things. In recent years asbestos used in building has been found to be harmful to humans.

as·cend /əˈsend/ *v* [I;T] *often fml* to climb; go, come, or move from a lower to a higher level: *The stairs ascended in a graceful curve.* | *He ascended the stairs.* | *Victoria ascended the throne* (=became queen) *in 1837.* | *an ascending scale of (musical) notes* —opposite **descend**

as·cen·dan·cy, **-dency** /əˈsendənsi/ *n* [U (**over, in**)] a position of power, influence, or control: *He slowly gained ascendancy over/in the group.*

as·cen·dant¹, **-dent** /əˈsendənt/ *n* **in the ascendant** having a controlling influence: *During this period, the radical wing of the party was in the ascendant.*

ascendant², **-dent** *adj fml* **1** rising **2** greater in influence: *ascendant power*

as·cen·sion /əˈsenʃən/ *n* [U] *fml* the process of ascending

Ascension Day /·ˈ··· ·/ *n* [C;U] a Christian holy day on the Thursday 40 days after Easter, when Christians remember Christ's ascent to heaven (**the Ascension**)

as·cent /əˈsent/ *n* **1** [C;U] the act or process of going up: *We made a successful ascent of the mountain.* | (fig.) *the ascent of man from his original state to modern civilization* **2** [C] a way up; upward slope, path, etc.: *a steep ascent* —opposite **descent**

as·cer·tain /ˌæsəˈteɪn, ˌæsər-/ *v* [T] *fml* to discover (the truth about something); to make certain: *to ascertain the facts* [+that] *I ascertained that he was dead.* [+wh-] *The police are trying to ascertain exactly who was at the party.* — **~able** *adj*

as·cet·ic /əˈsetɪk/ *n, adj* (a person) avoiding physical pleasures and comforts, generally for religious reasons: *the ascetic life of Buddhist monks* — **~ally** /kli/ *adv* — **~ism** /əˈset̬sɪzəm/ *n* [U]

ASCII /ˈæski/ *n* [U] American Standard Code for Information Interchange; a set of 128 letters, numbers, etc., used for easy exchange of information between a computer and other DATA PROCESSING machinery: *in ASCII format* —see also EBCDIC

as·cot /ˈæskɒt‖-kət/ *n AmE for* CRAVAT

Ascot see ROYAL ASCOT

as·cribe /əˈskraɪb/ *v*
ascribe sthg. to sthg./sbdy. *phr v* [T] to believe (something) to be the result or work of: *He ascribes his success to luck.* | *This song is often ascribed to Bach.* —**-cribable** *adj* [F+**to**]

As·da /ˈæzdə/ *tdmk* one of a group of large SUPERMARKETS in Britain which sell food and clothes, usu. at low prices

ASEAN /ˈæsiˌæn/ Association of South-East Asian Nations; an association consisting of Indonesia, Malaysia, the Philippines, Singapore, Thailand, and Brunei, which was formed in 1967 and works for social, political, and economic success in SE Asia: *the ASEAN countries* | *throughout the ASEAN region*

a·sep·tic /eɪˈseptɪk, ə-/ *adj tech* (of a wound or its covering) free from bacteria; clean

a·sex·u·al /eɪˈsekʃuəl/ *adj* **1** without sex or sexual organs **2** having no interest in sexual relations; without

sexuality — **~ly** *adv* : *to reproduce asexually* — **~ity** /ˌeɪsekʃuˈæləti/ *n* [U]

As·gard /ˈæsgɑːd‖-ɑːrd/ in Norse MYTHOLOGY, the home of the gods which consisted of beautiful, rich palaces and halls —see also VALHALLA

ash¹ /æʃ/ also **ashes** *pl.*— *n* [U] **1** the soft grey powder that remains after something has been burnt: *cigarette ash* | *The house burnt to ashes.* —see also ASHES **2 ashes to ashes, dust to dust** a phrase used as part of a Christian prayer at a funeral, usu. spoken as the dead person is about to be buried

ash² *n* [C;U] (the hard wood of) a forest tree common in Britain and throughout North America

ASH /æʃ/ *abbrev. for* Action on Smoking and Health; a British organization which is opposed to the practice of smoking: *A spokesperson from ASH called for higher taxes on tobacco.*

a·shamed /əˈʃeɪmd/ *adj* [F] **1** (**of**)] feeling shame or guilt because of something done: *You ought to be ashamed of yourself/of your behaviour.* | *He was ashamed of having lied to her.* [+that] *He was ashamed that he had lied.* [+to-v] *Their disgraceful behaviour made me ashamed to be British!* **2** (**of**)] feeling foolish or uncomfortable because of something: *He was ashamed of his dirty old clothes.* | *You shouldn't worry about failing the exam — it's nothing to be ashamed of.* **3** [+to-v] unwilling to do something because of fear that it might bring shame: *I was too ashamed to tell her I had failed.* — **~ly** /əˈʃeɪmᵻdli/ *adv*

ash·can /ˈæʃkæn/ *n AmE old fash* a DUSTBIN

Ash·croft /ˈæʃkrɒft‖-ɔːft/, **Dame Peg·gy** /ˈpegi/ (1907–91) a well-loved English actress who acted in many Shakespeare plays and in films such as *A Passage to India*

Ash·down /ˈæʃdaʊn/, **Paddy** (1941–) a British MP and the leader of the Liberal Democrats from 1988. It is often mentioned that he was once a COMMANDO in the Royal Marines.

Ashe /æʃ/, **Arthur** (1943–93) an American tennis player who became the first black person to win at Wimbledon, in 1975

ash·en /ˈæʃən/ *adj* of the colour of ash; pale grey: *His ashen face showed how shocked he was.*

ash·es /ˈæʃᵻz/ *n* [P] the remains of a dead body after it has been cremated (CREMATE): *Her ashes were scattered over the sea.*

Ashes *n* [*the*+P] the name given to the competition between the English and Australian cricket teams: *England have retained the Ashes for the third year running.*

Ash·ke·na·zy /ˌæʃkəˈnɑːzi/, **Vlad·i·mir** /ˈvlædᵻmɪər/ (1937–) a pianist and CONDUCTOR born in the Soviet Union, who came to live in England and then Iceland in the 1960s. He was musical director of the Royal Philharmonic in London from 1987.

Ash·ley /ˈæʃli/, **Lau·ra** /ˈlɔːrə/ (1926–85) a Welsh DESIGNER of dress materials, wall-coverings and clothes in a pretty Victorian style usu. with flowers. She started a chain of shops in Britain under her own name in the 1960s which later became successful in many other countries. —see also LAURA ASHLEY

Ash·mo·le·an Mu·se·um /æʃˌməʊliən mjuːˈziːəm/ [*the*] an important MUSEUM of ARCHAEOLOGY, paintings, and silver at the University of Oxford

a·shore /əˈʃɔːʳ/ *adv* on, onto, or to the shore: *Passengers may go ashore at Kingston.*

ash·ram /ˈæʃrəm/ *n* **1** a place where a Hindu holy man lives alone **2** a house where people live together practising Hinduism. They are often connected with the HIPPIE movement of the 1960s and 1970s.

Ash·ton /ˈæʃtən/, **Fred·e·rick** /ˈfredərɪk/ (1904–88) an English dancer and CHOREOGRAPHER who was director of the Royal Ballet from 1963 to 1970. He helped to make BALLET more popular.

ash·tray /ˈæʃtreɪ/ *n* a small dish for tobacco ash —see picture at TRAY

Ash Wednes·day /ˌ· ˈ··/ *n* [C;U] the first day of Lent, when some Christians put ashes on their foreheads as a sign of PENITENCE

ash·y /ˈæʃi/ *adj* **1** covered with ash **2** grey; ASHEN

A·sia /ˈeɪʃə, -ʒə‖-ʒə, -ʃə/ a large land mass (CONTINENT), which includes the **Middle East**, the **Far East**, and part of the former USSR

Asia Mi·nor /ₗ·· ¹··/ n the historic name for part of W Asia between the Black Sea on the N, the Mediterranean Sea on the S, and the Aegean Sea on the W, and which now forms most of Turkey

A·sian /ˈeɪʃən, ˈeɪʒən‖ˈeɪʒən, ˈeɪʃən/ also **A·si·at·ic** /ₗₑɪʃiˈætɪk◂, ₗeɪzi-, ₗeɪʒi-‖ₗeɪʒi-, ₗeɪzi-/ — n, adj (a person who comes from or whose parents come) from Asia. In Britain this usu. means from India, Pakistan, or Bangladesh. In the US, it usu. means a person from Japan, China, Korea, Vietnam, etc.

Asian flu /ₗ·· ¹·/ n [U] a variety of INFLUENZA (=flu) which spread from Asia to become a world wide EPIDEMIC in 1957

a·side¹ /əˈsaɪd/ adv 1 to the side: *She stepped aside to let them pass.* | (fig.) *Let's leave that problem aside for the moment.* 2 **aside from** esp. AmE a except for: *Everything was quiet, aside from the occasional sound of a car in the distance.* b as well as: *I didn't accept the job because it was badly paid and aside from that, it wasn't very interesting.*

aside² n 1 words spoken by an actor to those watching a play, and not intended to be heard by the other characters in the play 2 a remark in a low voice not intended to be heard by everyone present 3 a remark made or story told during a speech but which is not part of the main subject

As·i·mov /ˈæsɪmɒv‖ˈæzəmɑːf/, **Isaac** (1920–92) an American scientist and writer, born in the USSR, best known for his SCIENCE FICTION stories

as·i·nine /ˈæsₗnaɪn/ adj extremely foolish; stupid: *What an asinine remark!*

ask /ɑːsk‖æsk/ v 1 [I;T (**about**)] to request (information) from (someone); put a question to (someone), or call for an answer to (a question): *She asked about his new job.* | *"Have you seen my pen?" she asked.* | *Don't ask so many questions.* | *"Where's Tom?"* **"Don't ask me!"** (=I don't know) | *"What crazy scheme has he got in mind now?"* **"You may well ask!"** (=That is a good question because it certainly is something crazy) | *"I think he likes her."* **"If you ask me, he's in love."** | *"Do you know of a good dentist?" "No. You'll have to* **ask around.** *"* (=ask a lot of people) [+wh-] *The committee asked whether the minister knew about these facts.* [+obj+wh-] *Ask him where to go|who he is|if he'd like a drink.* | *Might I ask what you are doing in my bedroom?* [+obj(i)+obj(d)] *Ask him his name.* 2 [I;T (**for**)] to make a request for (something) or to (someone): *If you need any help, just ask.* | *She asked (me) for a drink.* | *He asked my advice.* | *They asked permission (to go).* [+to-v] *I asked to see the manager.* [+obj+to-v] *She asked him to wake her at 6 o'clock.* [+that] *(fml) He asked that they (should) be allowed to leave.* | *She asked him if he would lend her his car.* | *I think the job's yours* **for the asking.** (=if you show that you want it) [+obj (i) +obj (d)] *Can I* **ask you a favour?** (=ask you to do something for me) *I'm not* **asking the world,** (=asking for something unreasonable) *I only want five minutes of your time.* —see ORDER (USAGE), REQUEST (USAGE) 3 [T (**for, of**)] to expect or demand (something) from someone: *They're asking a lot of money for their house.* | *You're asking a lot|too much (of them) if you expect them to work at the weekend.* 4 [T (**to, for**)] to invite: *I've asked some friends to tea|for dinner.* | *I asked her in|up|down for a drink.* | *He wanted to ask her out* (=to go out with her socially), *but he didn't have the courage to do it.* [+obj+to-v] *Let's ask them to stay for the weekend.* | *"Are you going to the party?" "No, I haven't been asked."* 5 **Ask, and it shall be given you** quote a phrase from the Bible, now often used humorously

▷ USAGE Compare **ask, inquire, question,** and **interrogate. Ask** is the usual verb for questions: *"Where do you live?" he asked.* | *He asked a question.* **Inquire** (or **enquire**) has the same meaning, but is more formal, and is not followed by a noun or pronoun object: *"Where do you live?" he inquired.* | *He inquired where they lived.* To **question** a person is to ask them many questions, and to **interrogate** suggests that the person is being held by force and asked questions which they are unwilling to answer.◁

ask after sbdy. phr v [T] to ask about the health of; ask for news of: *"My mother asked after you." "How kind of her!"*

ask for sthg. phr v [T] infml to behave in a way that is likely to bring (a bad result): *Letting the children play*

with those matches was just **asking for trouble!** — compare HEAD² for

a·skance /əˈskæns, əˈskɑːns‖əˈskæns/ adv **look askance (at)** to look (at) or regard with disapproval or distrust

a·skew /əˈskjuː/ adv not properly straight: *The soldier's cap was slightly askew.*

asking price /ˈ·· ·/ n the price that a seller asks for his/her goods: *Did you get the asking price for your house?*

a·slant /əˈslɑːnt‖əˈslænt/ adj, adv [F] at an angle; not straight or level

a·sleep /əˈsliːp/ adj [F] 1 sleeping: *He was* **sound/fast asleep.** (=completely asleep) —opposite **awake** 2 (of an arm or leg that has been in one position too long) unable to feel; NUMB —see also **go to sleep** (SLEEP¹) 3 **fall asleep: a** to go into a state of sleep **b** euph to die

ASLEF /ˈæzlef/ the Associated Society of Locomotive Engineers and Firemen; the smaller of two British TRADE UNIONS which represent people who work on the railways —see also NUR

A/S lev·el /ₗ·ˈ· ₗ··/ n 1 [U] a middle standard of examination in British schools from 1989 onwards, for pupils who have taken GCSEs and wish to study a wider range of subjects than is possible at A LEVEL 2 [C] an examination of this standard in a particular subject

asp /æsp/ n a small poisonous snake of N Africa. Cleopatra is believed to have killed herself with an asp.

as·par·a·gus /əˈspærəgəs/ n [U] a plant whose young green stems are eaten as a vegetable and thought of as a DELICACY

ASPCA /ₗeɪ es ₗpi siː ˈeɪ/ [the] the American Society for the Prevention of Cruelty to Animals; a CHARITY which looks after animals, esp. unwanted pets, and tries to find homes for them

as·pect /ˈæspekt/ n 1 [C (**of**)] a particular side of a many-sided situation, idea, plan, etc.: *The training programme covers every aspect of the job.* | *The rise in violent crime is one of the more worrying aspects of the current situation.* 2 [C] the direction in which a window, room, front of a building, etc., faces: *The house has a south-facing aspect.* 3 [C;U] lit appearance: *a man melancholy in aspect* 4 [C;U] tech (in grammar) the particular form of a verb which shows whether the action that is described is a continuing action or an action that happens always, repeatedly, or for a moment: *"He sings" differs from "He is singing" in aspect.*

As·pel /ˈæspəl/, **Mi·chael** /ˈmaɪkəl/ (1933–) a British television host and personality who started as a news reader before getting his own talk show

as·pen /ˈæspən/ n a kind of tree which is common in the American Southwest

as·per·i·ty /æˈsperₗti, ə-/ n [C;U] fml (an example of) roughness or severity, esp. in speech, manner, or weather: *He answered our questions with some asperity.* | *the asperities of a Russian winter*

as·per·sion /əˈspɜːʃən, -ʒən‖-ɜːr-/ n fml or humor an unkind remark or unfavourable judgment: *Are you* **casting aspersions on** (=raising doubts about) *my ability to drive?*

as·phalt /ˈæsfælt‖ˈæsfɔːlt/ n [U] a black sticky material that is firm when it hardens, used for the surface of roads — **asphalt** v [T]

as·phyx·i·ate /æsˈfɪksieɪt, ə-/ v [I;T] fml to (cause to) be unable to breathe air; esp. to die or kill someone in this way; SUFFOCATE —**-ation** /æsₗfɪksiˈeɪʃən, ə-/ n [U]

as·pic /ˈæspɪk/ n [U] a clear brownish jelly made from meat bones: *chicken in aspic*

as·pi·dis·tra /ₗæspₗˈdɪstrə/ n a plant with broad green pointed leaves, often grown in houses

As·pin /ˈæspɪn/, **Les** /lez/ (1938–) a US Congressman who was named as Secretary of Defense by President Clinton in 1992

as·pi·rant /əˈspaɪərənt, ˈæspₗrənt/ n [(**to, for**)] fml a person who hopes for and tries to get a position of importance or honour: *one of the aspirants to the vice-presidency*

as·pi·rate¹ /ˈæspₗreɪt/ v [T] tech to pronounce (a word or letter) with the sound of the letter H (as in (a) human but not in (an) honour) or with ASPIRATION (2)

as·pi·rate² /ˈæspₗrₗt/ n tech the sound of the letter H, or the letter itself

as·pi·ra·tion /ˌæspɨˈreɪʃən/ n 1 [C;U] (a) strong desire to do something or have something, esp. something great or important: *The colonial government could no longer ignore the political aspirations of the local people.* [+to-v] *She has aspirations to become a great writer.* 2 [U] *tech* the blowing out of air that follows when some consonants are pronounced, such as the /p/in *pin*

as·pire /əˈspaɪəʳ/ v [I] to direct one's hopes and efforts to some important aim: *an aspiring young actress* [+to, after] *He aspired after a political career/to the leadership of the party.* [+to-v] *She aspires to become president.*

as·pirin /ˈæsprɨn/ n aspirin or aspirins [C;U] (a TABLET of) a medicine that reduces pain, INFLAMMATION, and fever: *Take a couple of aspirins for your headache.*

As·quith /ˈæskwɪθ/, Herbert Henry (1852–1928) a British Liberal politician and PRIME MINISTER from 1908 to 1916

ass¹ /æs/ n 1 an animal like a horse but smaller and with longer ears, e.g. the DONKEY 2 *infml* a stupid foolish person: *a pompous ass*

ass² n AmE for ARSE¹ (1)

As·sad /ˈæsæd/, Ha·fez al- /ˈhɑːfez æl/ (1928–) a former general and the president of Syria since 1971

as·sail /əˈseɪl/ v [T (with)] *fml* to attack violently: *The police were assailed with rocks and petrol bombs.* | *I was assailed by doubts/worries.*

as·sai·lant /əˈseɪlənt/ n *fml* an attacker

As·sam /əˈsæm/ n [U] a type of tea from the Assam state in NE India

as·sas·sin /əˈsæsɨn/ n a person who murders someone important, such as a ruler or politician: *Kennedy's assassin*

as·sas·sin·ate /əˈsæsɨneɪt/ v [T] to murder (a ruler, politician, or other important person): *a plot to assassinate the president* —see KILL (USAGE) —**ation** /əˌsæsɨˈneɪʃən/ n [C;U] : *a spate of assassinations* | *an assassination attempt*

as·sault¹ /əˈsɔːlt/ n [C;U(on)] (a) violent attack, esp. a sudden one: *The army launched a major assault against the rebel town.* | (fig.) *They made an assault on* (=an attempt to climb) *Mount Everest.* | *He was sent to prison for assault.* (=an attack on another person) —see also INDECENT ASSAULT

assault² v [T] to make an assault on, often an INDECENT ASSAULT: *She was too shaken after being assaulted to report the incident to the police.* | *The minister was assaulted by a barrage of abuse from the angry strikers.*

assault and bat·ter·y /·,·· ˈ···/ n [U] *law* an attack which includes not only threats but the actual use of violence

assault course /·ˈ· ˌ·/ BrE ‖ **obstacle course** AmE n an area of land on which soldiers and other people train by climbing or jumping over objects, through water, etc., in order to develop their fitness and courage

as·say /əˈseɪ/ v [T] 1 to test (metal-bearing soil, a gold ring, etc.) to discover what materials are present 2 *lit* to attempt (something difficult): *to assay the impossible* – **assay** n

as·se·gai /ˈæsɨgaɪ/ n a long thin wooden spear with an iron point, used in southern Africa

as·sem·blage /əˈsemblɪdʒ/ n *fml* 1 [C+*sing./pl.* v] a group of people or a collection of articles 2 [U] the act of coming or putting together

as·sem·ble /əˈsembəl/ v 1 [I;T] to gather or collect together into a group or into one place: *At the beginning of the day, we all assemble in the main hall to be addressed by the head teacher.* | *He called us all together, and told* **the assembled company** (=the group that had assembled) *that the exams had been cancelled.* | *to assemble a vast collection of old books* 2 [T] to put (something) together: *This bookcase is very easy to assemble.* | *to assemble cars/ radios/a model aeroplane*

as·sem·bly /əˈsembli/ n 1 [C+*sing./pl.* v] a group of people, esp. one gathered together for a special purpose, such as worship 2 [U] a meeting together of people: *to deny citizens the right of assembly* 3 [C;U] a meeting of all the teachers and pupils of a school. Many schools in Britain have assembly every morning before classes begin for the day. In American schools, assemblies are less frequent and used for a lesson, presentation, or ceremony. 4 [C+*sing./pl.* v] (*often cap.*) a law-making body, esp. the lower of two such bodies: *the New York State Assembly*

assembly lan·guage /·ˈ·· ˌ··/ n [C;U] a language used for writing computer PROGRAMS in a form which the computer can translate into MACHINE CODE

assembly line /·ˈ·· ·/ n an arrangement of workers and machines in which each person has a particular job and the work is passed, often on a moving band, directly from one worker to the next until the product is complete

as·sem·bly·man /əˈsemblimən/ **as·sem·bly·wom·an** /-ˌwʊmən/ *fem.*— n -**men** /mən/ AmE a member of an ASSEMBLY (4)

as·sent¹ /əˈsent/ v [I (to)] *fml* to agree to a suggestion, idea, etc. after careful consideration: *The chairman assented to the committee's proposals.* [+to-v] *The judge assented to allow the prisoner to speak.*

assent² n [U] agreement to a suggestion or idea: *We're waiting for the director to give his assent.* —opposite **dissent**

as·sert /əˈsɜːt‖-ɜːrt/ v [T] 1 to state or declare forcefully: *She asserted her opinions.* | *Although she was found guilty, she continued to assert her innocence.* [+that] *The government has repeatedly asserted that it will not change its policy.* 2 to make a claim to; defend (a right or claim) by forceful action: *to assert one's rights/independence* | *He asserted his authority by making them be quiet.* 3 **assert oneself** to show one's power, control, importance, etc.

as·ser·tion /əˈsɜːʃən‖-ɜːr-/ n a forceful statement or claim: *She could provide no evidence to back up her assertions.* [+that] *He repeated his assertion that he was not guilty.*

as·ser·tive /əˈsɜːtɪv‖-ɜːr-/ adj expressing or tending to express strong opinions or claims; showing a confident belief in one's own ability: *If you want to succeed in this business, you should be more assertive.* —see also SELF-ASSERTIVE — ~**ly** adv — ~**ness** n [U]

assertiveness train·ing /·ˈ··· ˌ··/ n [U] a course of lessons taken by someone to teach them how to become more assertive, so that they are able to express their opinions and make known their wishes

as·sess /əˈses/ v [T] 1 [(at)] to calculate or decide the value or amount of: *to assess the damage caused by a storm* | *They assessed the value of the house at £60,000.* 2 to judge the quality, importance, or worth of; EVALUATE: *He's so lazy that it's difficult to assess his ability.* | *It's too early to assess the effects of the new legislation.*

as·sess·ment /əˈsesmənt/ n 1 [C;U] (an example of) the act of assessing: *a very perceptive assessment of the situation* | *What's your assessment of her chances of winning?* —see also CONTINUOUS ASSESSMENT 2 [C] the value or amount at which something is calculated: *my tax assessment for 1990*

as·ses·sor /əˈsesəʳ/ n 1 a person whose job is to calculate the value of property or the amount of income or taxes 2 a person who advises a judge or official committee on matters that demand special knowledge

as·set /ˈæset/ n 1 the property of a person, company, etc. that has value and that may be sold to pay a debt: *The company's* **liquid assets** (=money, or property that can easily be sold for money) *are enormous.* 2 a valuable quality, skill, or person: *A sense of humour is a great asset in this job.* | *She's a tremendous asset to the company.* —compare LIABILITY (3,4) —see also CURRENT ASSETS, FIXED ASSETS, LIQUID ASSETS

asset-strip·ping /·ˈ·· ˌ··/ n [U] *tech* the practice of buying a company cheaply, selling all its assets to make a profit, and then closing it down

as·sev·e·rate /əˈsevəreɪt/ v [T+*obj/that*] *fml* to declare solemnly and forcefully —**ration** /əˌsevəˈreɪʃən/ n [C;U]

ass·hole /ˈæshəʊl/ n AmE for ARSE² (2)

as·sid·u·ous /əˈsɪdjuəs‖-dʒuəs/ adj showing careful and continuous attention; DILIGENT — ~**ly** adv — ~**ness**, —**ity** /ˌæsɨˈdjuːɨti‖-ˈduː-/ n [U]

as·sign /əˈsaɪn/ v [T] 1 [(to)] to give as a share or duty; ALLOT: [+obj(i)+obj(d)] *I've been assigned the job of looking after the new students.* | *They've assigned the job to me.* 2 to fix or set aside for a purpose; decide on; name: *We assigned a day for our meeting.* [+obj+to-v] *I've been assigned to take notes.* 3 [(to)] to give (property, rights, etc.) by a legal process: *She assigned her whole estate to a charitable organization.* — ~**able** adj

as·sig·na·tion /ˌæsɨgˈneɪʃən/ n *fml or humor* a meeting, esp. a secret meeting with a lover

as·sign·ment /ə'saɪnmənt/ *n* **1** [C] a duty or piece of work that is given to a particular person or people: *She's going to India on a special assignment for her newspaper.* | *His assignment was to follow the spy.* **2** [U (**of**)] the act of assigning: *the assignment of the chores*

as·sim·i·late /ə'sɪmɬleɪt/ *v* **1** [I;T] *tech* **a** to take (food) into the body and DIGEST it **b** (of food) to be taken into the body and digested **2** [T] to understand completely and be able to use properly: *You have to assimilate the facts, not just remember them.* **3** [I;T (**into**)] to make or become like the people of a country, race, or other group, esp. in ways of behaving or thinking: *America has assimilated many people from Europe.* | *They assimilated easily into the new community.*

as·sim·i·la·tion /ə,sɪmɬ'leɪʃən/ *n* [U] **1** the act of assimilating or of being assimilated **2** *tech* the changing of a speech sound because of the influence of another speech sound next to it (e.g. the *p* in *cupboard*)

Assisi see SAINT FRANCIS OF ASSISI

as·sist /ə'sɪst/ *v* [I;T (**in, with**)] *fml* to help or support: *A team of nurses assisted (the doctor) in performing the operation.* | *A man is* **assisting police (with their inquiries).** (=has been taken by the police for questioning) —see HELP (USAGE)

as·sist·ance /ə'sɪstəns/ *n* [U (**in**)] *rather fml* help or support: *Unless we receive more financial assistance from the government, the hospital will have to close.* | *Can I be of any assistance?* | *I was given some assistance in coming to my decision.* | *She* **came to my assistance.**

as·sis·tant /ə'sɪstənt/ *n* a person who helps another in a job or piece of work, and is under that person's direction: *When the shop is busy he employs an assistant.* | *a clerical assistant* | *an assistant cook/manager* | *the Assistant Director of Education in the London area* —see also SHOP ASSISTANT; see ATTEND (USAGE)

assistant pro·fes·sor /·,···· ·'··/ *n* a PROFESSOR (=teacher) at an American university who has a middle rank — compare ASSOCIATE PROFESSOR, FULL PROFESSOR

as·siz·es /ə'saɪzɬz/ *n* [(*the*)P] (in Britain until 1971) a meeting or meetings of a special court held by an important judge travelling from one county town to another — **assize** *adj* [A]

assoc *written abbrev. for:* **1** associated **2** also **assn**— association

as·so·ci·ate[1] /ə'səʊʃieɪt, ə'səʊsi-/ *v* **1** [I;T (**with**)] to join in a relationship based on friendship, business, or a shared purpose; combine as friends or partners: *The military régime dealt ruthlessly with anyone who was associated with the former government.* | *He associates with criminals.* **2** [T (**with**)] to connect in thought, memory, or imagination: *I associate summer with holidays.* | *The scientist decided he didn't want to be associated with the project, and left.*

as·so·ci·ate[2] /ə'səʊʃiɬt, -ɬt/ *n* **1** a person connected with another, esp. in work; partner: *He's not a friend; he's a business associate.* **2** (*often cap.*) the holder of an associate degree: *an associate of arts*

associated com·pa·ny /·,···· '···/ *n* a company of which 20 to 50 per cent of SHARES[1] (2) are owned by the parent company —compare SUBSIDIARY

as·so·ci·ate de·gree /·,···· ·'·/ *n* a degree given after two years of study in the US, usu. at a JUNIOR COLLEGE

associate pro·fes·sor /·,···· ·'··/ *n* a PROFESSOR (=teacher) at an American university who has the lowest rank — compare ASSISTANT PROFESSOR, FULL PROFESSOR

as·so·ci·a·tion /ə,səʊsi'eɪʃən, ə,səʊʃi-/ *n* **1** [C+*sing./pl. v*] an organization of people joined together for a shared purpose: *The Association of Scientific Workers is/are having its/their annual conference next week.* | *She set up/formed an association to help blind people.* —see also HOUSING ASSOCIATION **2** [U (**with**)] the act of associating or fact of being associated: *Our long association with your company has brought great benefits.* | *The council is working in association with the police on this.* **3** [C;U] (a) connection made in the mind between different things, ideas, etc.: *the association of ideas* | *Hospitals have rather unpleasant associations for me.* —see also FREE ASSOCIATION

Association foot·ball /·,···· '··/ *n* [U] *BrE fml for* FOOTBALL (1)

as·so·nance /'æsənəns/ *n* [U] *tech* similarity in the sounds of words, esp. the vowels of words (e.g. between *born* and *warm*)

as·sort /ə'sɔːt‖-ɔːrt/ *v* [T] to divide into different sorts **assort with** *phr v* **1** [T] *BrE fml* to match; agree with: *This does not assort with his earlier statement.* **2** to be friendly with (esp. bad company): *He is known to assort with criminal types.*

as·sort·ed /ə'sɔːtɬd‖-ɔːr-/ *adj* **1** of various types mixed together: *a bag of assorted sweets* **2** *fml* (*in comb.*) suited by nature or character; matched: *Anne and David are an ill-assorted pair.*

as·sort·ment /ə'sɔːtmənt‖-ɔːr-/ *n* [C+*sing./pl. v*] a group or quantity of mixed things or of various kinds of the same thing; mixture: *an assortment of sweets* | *She has an odd assortment of friends.*

asst *written abbrev. for:* ASSISTANT

as·suage /ə'sweɪdʒ/ *v* [T] *fml* to make (suffering, desire, etc.) less strong or severe; RELIEVE: *to assuage one's thirst*

as·sume /ə'sjuːm‖ə'suːm/ *v* [T] **1** to believe (something) to be true without actually having proof that it is; suppose: *We can't just assume her guilt.* [+(*that*)] *If he's not here in five minutes, we'll assume (that) he isn't coming.* | **Assuming (that)** *you're right about this, what shall we do?* [+*obj+to-v*] *He was with an elderly man and woman, who I assumed were his grandparents.* **2** to take or claim for oneself (sometimes without the right to do so); begin to have or use: *You will assume your new responsibilities tomorrow.* | *The army assumed control of the government.* **3** to begin to have (a quality or appearance): *The problem is beginning to assume massive proportions.* **4** to pretend to have; FEIGN: *He assumes a well-informed manner but in fact he knows very little.* | *to write under an assumed name*

as·sump·tion /ə'sʌmpʃən/ *n* **1** [C] something that is taken as a fact or believed to be true without proof: *Don't rely on the information she gave you — it's pure assumption (on her part).* | *The results of the experiment shook the basic assumptions of his theory.* [+*that*] *our mistaken assumption that the price would fall* | *Let's work* **on the assumption** (=taking it as likely) *that our proposal will be accepted.* **2** [U (**of**)] the act of assuming: *the army's assumption of power*

Assumption , The 1 (in the ROMAN CATHOLIC religion) the bodily taking up of the VIRGIN MARY (=Jesus' mother) into heaven **2** the day (August 15th) on which this event is celebrated

as·sur·ance /ə'ʃʊərəns/ *n* **1** [C (**of, about**)] a firm statement that something is certainly true or will certainly happen; promise: *In spite of all his assurances, he did not come back.* | *She gave repeated assurances of her loyalty.* [+*that*] *Let me give you my assurance that the work will be finished by the agreed date.* **2** [U] confident belief in one's own ability and powers: *The new teacher lacked assurance in front of his class.* —see also SELF-ASSURED **3** [U] *BrE* insurance against events that are certain rather than possible: *life assurance*

as·sure /ə'ʃʊər/ *v* [T] **1** [(**of**)] to tell firmly and with confidence with the aim of removing doubt; promise: *He assured us of his ability to solve the problem.* [+*obj+(that*)] *I can assure you (that) the medicine is perfectly safe.* | *You can* **rest assured** (=feel certain) *that your son will be happy here.* **2** to make (something) certain to happen or be gained; ENSURE: *The excellent reviews given to the film have assured its success.* **3** [(**of**)] to make (someone) feel certain of having or gaining something: *We booked early to assure ourselves of (getting) good seats.* | *Our clients are assured of an enjoyable and trouble-free holiday.* **4** *BrE* to INSURE, esp. against death —see INSURE (USAGE)

as·sured[1] /ə'ʃʊəd‖ə'ʃʊərd/ *adj* **1** also **self-assured**— confident in one's own abilities: *an assured manner* **2** having or showing certainty: *There is an assured demand for these products.* | *Her political future looks assured.* — **~ly** /ə'ʃʊərɬdli/ *adv*

as·sured[2] *n* assured [*the*+C] *BrE tech* a person whose life has been insured (INSURE): *On the death of the assured his family will receive a lump sum and an annual income.*

As·syr·i·a /ə'sɪriə/ an ancient civilization of W Asia around the city of Ashur, on the Tigris river. It was esp. important between the ninth and seventh centuries BC.

As·syr·i·an /ə'sɪrɪən/ *adj* of or about the people or language of Assyria —**Assyrians** *n* [*the* | P]

As·taire /ə'steə^r/, **Fred** /fred/ (1899–1987) an American dancer, singer, and actor who made many films, often with his dancing partner, **Ginger Rogers**, and who is known for his stylishness

Fred Astaire and Ginger Rogers

as·te·risk /'æstərɪsk/ also **star—** *n* a mark like a star (*) used **a** to draw attention to a note at the bottom of a page **b** to mark that certain letters are missing from a word **c** (*tech*) to show that a word, phrase, sound, etc., is incorrect (as in the example "In English we say *three boys*, not **three boy.*") —**asterisk** *v* [T] *BrE*

As·te·rix /'æstərɪks/ a CARTOON (1) character of French origin, who is a small, humorous GALLIC soldier. The CARTOON is very popular in book form and also in the films made from the stories

Asterix

a·stern /ə'stɜːn‖-ɜːrn/ *adv* in or at the back part (STERN) of a ship

as·te·roid /'æstərɔɪd/ also **minor planet—** *n* one of many small PLANETS between Mars and Jupiter

asth·ma /'æsmə‖'æzmə/ *n* [U] a long-lasting disease which causes difficulty in breathing — — **tic** /æs'mætɪk‖æz-/ *n, adj* : *He is (an) asthmatic.* — — **tically** /kli/ *adv*

as·tig·ma·tis·m /ə'stɪgmətɪzəm/ *n* [U] the inability of the eye to see properly or clearly because of its shape —**tic** /ˌæstɪg'mætɪk◂/ *adj*

a·stir /ə'stɜː^r/ *adj* [F] *esp. lit* **1** awake and out of bed: *No one was astir so early.* **2** [(with)] in a state of excitement: *The ship was astir with anxious passengers.*

As·ti spu·man·te /ˌæsti spuː'mænti‖-'maːn-/ *n* [U] a SPARKLING white wine from the town of Asti in Italy, which people sometimes drink instead of CHAMPAGNE when they want to celebrate, because it is cheaper

as·ton·ish /ə'stɒnɪʃ‖ə'staː-/ *v* [T] to fill with great surprise and perhaps disbelief: *She's been promoted again?* — *You astonish me!* | *an astonishing piece of news* | *We were all astonished by the news|astonished to hear that he had passed his driving test.* — — **ingly** *adv*

as·ton·ish·ment /ə'stɒnɪʃmənt‖ə'staː-/ *n* [U] great surprise or wonder: *To our astonishment he actually arrived on time.* | *She stared in astonishment at the document.*

As·ton /'æstən/ the name of a university in Birmingham, central England

Aston Mar·tin /ˌ·· '··/ *tdmk* a British car maker known esp. for their good quality, expensive sports cars

Aston Vil·la /ˌ·· '··◂/ the name of a British football club based in Birmingham

as·tound /ə'staʊnd/ *v* [T] to fill with shocked surprise, esp. because of something completely unexpected: *The news of their divorce astounded me.* | *an astounding defeat in the election* | *We were astounded by his success|astounded to hear that he had won.*

As·tra /'æstrə/ *n tdmk* a popular, small to middle sized car made by the British company Vauxhall

as·tra·khan /ˌæstrə'kæn◂‖'æstrəkən/ *n* [U] lamb's skin with the wool in tight little curls: *astrakhan coats*

as·tral /'æstrəl/ *adj* of or concerning stars

a·stray /ə'streɪ/ *adv* away from the right path or way: *One of the sheep went astray and got lost.* | (fig.) *I seem to have gone astray* (=made a mistake) *somewhere in my calculations.* | (fig.) *The attractions of the big city soon* **led him astray.** (=into bad ways)

a·stride /ə'straɪd/ *adv, prep* with a leg on each side (of): *sitting astride his horse*

as·trin·gent¹ /ə'strɪndʒənt/ *adj* **1** able to tighten up the skin or stop bleeding: *astringent lotions* **2** severe; bitter: *astringent criticism* — — **ly** *adv* —**gency** *n* [U]

astringent² *n* [C;U] *tech* a substance or medicine that tightens up the skin and stops bleeding

astro- see WORD FORMATION

as·trol·o·ger /ə'strɒlədʒə^r‖ə'straː-/ *n* a person who practises astrology

as·trol·o·gy /ə'strɒlədʒi‖ə'straː-/ *n* [U] the art of understanding the supposed influence of the sun, moon, stars, and PLANETS on events and on people's character. Astrology is not considered to be a proper science, and is not taken seriously by most people. —see ZODIAC (USAGE) —**gical** /ˌæstrə'lɒdʒɪkəl◂‖-'laː-/ *adj* —**gically** /kli/ *adv*

as·tro·naut /'æstrənɔːt‖-nɑːt/ *n* a person who travels in a spacecraft —see colour picture on page 752 and see also picture at HELMET

as·tro·nom·i·cal /ˌæstrə'nɒmɪkəl‖-'naː-/ also **as·tro·nom·ic** /ˌæstrə'nɒmɪk◂‖-'naː-/ *adj* **1** [A *no comp.*] of the stars or for the study of the stars: *an astronomical telescope* **2** *infml* (usu. of an amount or number) extremely large: *astronomical sums of money* | *a failure of astronomical proportions* — — **ly** /kli/ *adv*

as·tron·o·my /ə'strɒnəmi‖ə'straː-/ *n* [U] the scientific study of the sun, moon, stars, etc.

as·tro·phys·ics /ˌæstrəʊ'fɪzɪks, ˌæstrə-/ *n* [U] the scientific study of the chemical nature of the stars and the natural forces that influence them —**ical** *adj* —**icist** /-'fɪzɪsɪst/ *n*

As·tro·turf /'æstrəʊtɜːf‖-tɜːrf/ *n* [U] *tdmk* artificial grass used as a playing surface for sports

as·tute /ə'stjuːt‖ə'stuːt/ *adj* clever and able to see quickly something that is to one's advantage; SHREWD: *an astute businesswoman|investment* — — **ly** *adv* — **ness** *n* [U]

a·sun·der /ə'sʌndə^r/ *adv lit* **1** apart or into separate pieces: *The boat was torn asunder on the rocks.* **2** **Those whom God hath joined together let no man put asunder** let no one try to destroy this marriage (part of the Christian marriage service)

As·wan High Dam /ˌæswɑːn haɪ 'dæm/ one of the world's largest DAMs built across the River Nile in Egypt

a·sy·lum /ə'saɪləm/ *n* **1** [U] protection and shelter, esp. as given by one country to people who have left another for political reasons: *to seek|be granted political asylum* **2** [C] *becoming rare* a MENTAL HOSPITAL

a·sy·lum seek·er /·'··, ·'··/ *n* a person who has left one country usu. for political reasons and is asking for protection and shelter in another

a·sym·met·ric /ˌeɪsɪ'metrɪk◂, ˌæ-/ also **-rical** /kəl/— *adj* having sides that are not alike; lacking SYMMETRY — opposite **symmetrical** — — **ally** /kli/ *adv*

a·syn·chro·nous /eɪ'sɪŋkrənəs/ *adj tech* of or being a method of sending computer information over telephone lines in which specific BITS are used to show the beginning and end of each character sent —compare SYN-CHRONOUS

As You Like It /ˌ· · '· ·/ the title of a play by William Shakespeare, a ROMANTIC¹ (2) COMEDY (1)

at /ət; *strong* æt/ *prep* **1** (shows a point in space): *at my house* | *at the bottom of the page* | *He was standing at the door|at the bus stop.* | *We arrived at the airport.* **2 a** (shows an exact point in time): *at 10 o'clock* | *I'm busy* **at the moment.** (=now) **b** (shows a period of time) | *I often work at night.* | *It sometimes snows at Christmas.* **3** (shows an intended aim or object towards which a thing or action is directed): *Aim at the target.* | *He shot at the bird, but missed it.* (compare *He shot the bird.* (=he did not miss it)) | *Look at this!* | *She shouted at the boy.* | *to guess at the answer* **4** (shows the cause of an action or feeling): *I was surprised|amused|pleased at* (=by) *his behaviour.* | *I laughed at him|at his joke.* | *(AmE) Don't be mad at me.* (=angry with me) **5** (shows the subject or activity in which a judgment about someone's ability is made): *He's clever at arranging things.* | *He's bad at games.* | *She's a genius at chemistry.* | *She's getting on very well at her job.* **6** (shows a state or continued activity): *I never smoke at work|at school.* | *at liberty* | *at rest* | *The two countries are at war.* **7** (shows a price, rate, level, age, speed, etc.): *sold at (a price of) ten cents each|*

The temperature stood at 40°. | *to stop working at (the age of) 60* | *to drive at 100 kilometres an hour* | *The horse set off at a gallop.* | *I saw it at a distance.* (=a long way off) **8**(used before a SUPERLATIVE): *It will cost at least £1000.* | *The disease could affect, at worst, up to half the population.* **9 at a/an** as a result of only one; in only one: to reduce prices at a stroke (=by a single action or decision) | two at a time **10 at that:** a as well; besides: *It's a new idea, and a good one, at that.* **b** following or as a result of that; then: *She called him a liar, and at that he s̲.ˉrmed out of the room.* **11 where it's at** *infml* the most important thing: *Making lots of money and driving a big car – that's where it's at!* –see also **(not) at all** (ALL³)

AT&T /ˌeɪ tiː ənd ˈtiː/ American Telephone and Telegraph; an American maker of telephone, computer, and electronic equipment and services

At·a·türk /ˈætətɜːk‖-tɜːrk/, **Ke·mal** /keˈmɑːl/ (1881–1938) a Turkish politician whose real name was **Mustafa Kemal Pasha**. He was the first president of Turkey, and established it as a modern republic.

ate /et, eɪt‖eɪt/ *past tense of* EAT

▷ USAGE The usual British pronunciation is /et/, though some people say /eɪt/. Most Americans say /eɪt/, and /et/ is thought to be nonstandard by most Americans.◁

a·the·is·m /ˈeɪθi-ɪzəm/ *n* [U] disbelief in the existence of God

a·the·ist /ˈeɪθi-ɟ̩st/ *n* a person who does not believe in the existence of God: *a confirmed atheist* –compare AGNOSTIC, PAGAN¹ – **~ic(al)** /ˌeɪθiˈɪstɪk(əl)/ *adj* – **~ically** /kli/ *adv*

A·the·na /əˈθiːnə/ also **A·the·ne** /əˈθiːni/– in CLASSICAL MYTHOLOGY, the Greek goddess of wisdom and the arts (Roman name Minerva)

A·the·nae·um Club /əˈθiːniəm ˌklʌb/ [*the*] (in Britain) a gentleman's CLUB¹ (3) in Pall Mall in London

Ath·ens /ˈæθənz/ the capital city of Greece. Athens was the centre of ancient Greek civilization and many tourists now go there to see places of historical importance such as the Acropolis.

ath·e·ro·scle·ro·sis /ˌæθərəʊsklɟ̩ˈrəʊsɟ̩s/ *n* [U] *med* a form of ARTERIOSCLEROSIS in which the arteries (ARTERY) become blocked by fatty material (containing CHOLESTEROL), which gradually reduces the blood flow through the body –see also ARTERIOSCLEROSIS

ath·lete /ˈæθliːt/ *n* a person who practises athletics

athlete's foot /ˌ·· ˈ·/ *n* [U] a disease in which the skin cracks between the toes

ath·let·ic /æθˈletɪk, əθ-/ *adj* **1** [*no comp.*] of or concerning athletes or athletics **2** (of people) physically strong and active, with plenty of muscle and great ease: *of athletic build*

ath·let·ics /æθˈletɪks, əθ-‖ *BrE* ‖ **track and field** *AmE n* [U] the practice of physical exercises and of sports demanding strength and speed, such as running and jumping: *an athletics club/meeting*

athletic sup·por·ter /·ˈ·· ·ˌ··/ *n AmE fml for* JOCKSTRAP

a·thwart /əˈθwɔːt‖-ɔːrt/ *prep rare* across, esp. in a sloping direction

a·tish·oo /əˈtɪʃuː/ *interj* the word used to represent the sound of a SNEEZE

At·kin·son /ˈætkɪnsən/, **Rowan** (1955–) a British COMEDIAN and actor known esp. for his leading parts in television programmes such as *Blackadder* and *Mr Bean*

At·lan·ta /ətˈlæntə/ the capital city of the state of Georgia in the US – see colour map on pages 1374-5

At·lan·tic¹ /ətˈlæntɪk/ [*the*] the Atlantic Ocean. British people sometimes use the expressions "across the Atlantic" and "on the other side of the Atlantic", when they are talking about America.

Atlantic² *adj* in or near the Atlantic Ocean: *the Atlantic countries* | *the Atlantic community*

Atlantic Cit·y /·,·· ˈ··/ a city on the coast of New Jersey in the US, famous today for its many CASINOS

Atlantic O·cean /·,·· ˈ··/ [*the*] the second largest ocean in the world, which separates N and S America from Europe and Africa – see colour map on pages 1374-5

At·lan·tis /ətˈlæntɟ̩s/ an island which, according to an old story, sank beneath the sea in the Atlantic Ocean west of Gibraltar: *as far out of reach as Atlantis*

at·las /ˈætləs/ *n* a book of maps: *a world atlas*

Atlas in Greek MYTHOLOGY, a member of a race called the Titans, who, after their defeat by the Olympians, had to hold the sky on his shoulders forever. In pictures, Atlas is usually shown holding the world, rather than the sky, on his shoulders. –see colour picture on page 423. Because of this story an American BODYBUILDER called himself Charles Atlas and the word Atlas is now sometimes used to describe someone who is very strong: *Mr Atlas* | *He thinks he's Charles Atlas* | *Have you been working out? You look like Charles Atlas.*

ATM /ˌeɪ tiː ˈem/ *n* automatic teller machine; *AmE for* CASH DISPENSER

at·mo·sphere /ˈætməsfɪəʳ/ *n* **1** [C; *the*+S] the mixture of gases that surrounds the Earth, a star, etc. **2** [S] the air, esp. in a room: *a smoky atmosphere* **3** [C *usu. sing.*] the general character or feeling of a place: *Ever since their quarrel, there has been an unpleasant atmosphere in the office.*

at·mo·spher·ic /ˌætməsˈferɪk◀/ *adj* **1** [A] of or concerning the Earth's atmosphere: *atmospheric pressure* **2** mysteriously beautiful and strange: *That music's very atmospheric.*

at·mo·spher·ics /ˌætməsˈferɪks/ *n* [P] (a continuous light cracking noise in a radio caused by) electrical forces in the atmosphere

at·oll /ˈætɒl‖ˈætɑːl, ˈætɔːl, ˈætəʊl/ *n* a ring-shaped island made of CORAL, partly or completely enclosing an area of sea water (LAGOON)

at·om /ˈætəm/ *n* the smallest piece of a simple substance (ELEMENT) that can exist alone or combine with other substances (to form MOLECULES): (fig.) *There's not an atom* (=not even the smallest bit) *of truth in that statement.*

atom bomb /ˈ··· ·/ also **atomic bomb** /·ˌ·· ˈ·/, **A-bomb**– *n becoming old-fash* a bomb that uses the explosive power of NUCLEAR ENERGY

a·tom·ic /əˈtɒmɪk‖əˈtɑː-/ *adj* of or concerning atoms, NUCLEAR weapons, or NUCLEAR ENERGY: *an atomic submarine* | *atomic power/warfare* – **~ally** /kli/ *adv*

atomic en·er·gy /·ˌ·· ˈ···/ *n* [U] NUCLEAR ENERGY

atomic pile /·ˌ·· ˈ·/ *n* a NUCLEAR REACTOR

at·om·izer /ˈætəmaɪzəʳ/ *n* an instrument that changes a liquid, such as a PERFUME, into a mist of very small drops by forcing it out through a very small hole

atom smash·er /ˈ··· ˌ··/ *n infml* ACCELERATOR (2)

a·ton·al /eɪˈtəʊnl, æ-/ *adj* (of music) not based on any ordered SCALE (=set of notes) – **~ly** *adv* – **~ity** /ˌeɪtəʊˈnælɟ̩ti, æ-/ *n* [U]

a·tone /əˈtəʊn/ *v* [I (**for**)] to make repayment (for a crime, for failing to do something, etc.): *He tried to atone for his rudeness by sending her some flowers.* – **~ment** *n* [U] – see also DAY OF ATONEMENT

a·top /əˈtɒp‖əˈtɑːp/ *prep lit* on, to, or at the top of

A to Z /ˌeɪ tə ˈzed‖-ˈziː/ see A-Z

a·tri·um /ˈeɪtriəm/ *n* **-ria** /riə/ *or* **-ums** **1** either of the two spaces in the top of the heart that force blood into the VENTRICLES **2** a large open space on the ground floor of a tall building sometimes open to the sky and sometimes going up several levels of the building

a·tro·cious /əˈtrəʊʃəs/ *adj* **1** extremely cruel, evil, shameful, shocking, etc.: *an atrocious crime* | *atrocious working conditions* **2** *infml* very bad or unpleasant: *an atrocious meal* – **~ly** *adv*

a·troc·i·ty /əˈtrɒsɟ̩ti‖əˈtrɑː-/ *n* **1** [C;U] (an act of) great evil, esp. cruelty: *war criminals who committed appalling atrocities/acts of appalling atrocity* **2** [C] *infml* something that is very unpleasant or ugly: *The new library building is an atrocity.*

at·ro·phy /ˈætrəfi/ *v* [I;T] to (cause to) weaken and lose flesh and muscle through lack of blood or lack of use: *The disease atrophied her leg.* | *Her leg quickly atrophied.* | (fig.) *a boring repetitive job that atrophied my mind* –**atrophy** *n* [U]

at·tach /əˈtætʃ/ *v* [T] **1** [(**to**)] to fasten in position; fix or connect: *Be careful of the handle – it's not very well attached.* | *She attached a cheque to the order form.* | *"Their offer seems too good to be true." "Don't worry – there are* **no strings attached.**" (=no hidden conditions)–

compare DETACH **2** *law* to seize (goods or a person) because of an unpaid debt

attach to *phr v* [T] **1** (**attach** sbdy. **to** sthg.) to cause to belong to (a group or organization), esp. for a limited period: *During the war I was attached to the naval college as a gunnery instructor.* | *I got lost so I attached myself to another party of tourists.* **2** (**attach** sthg. **to** sthg.) to regard as having (special meaning or importance): *She attaches great importance to regular exercise.* | *It would be unwise to attach too much significance to these opinion polls.* **3** (**attach to** sthg.) *fml* to belong to or be connected with: *No blame attaches to him for the accident.* [+*v-ing*] *the responsibilities that attach to being president* **4 be attached to** to be fond of and feel a strong connection with: *I am deeply/very attached to this old car.*

at·tach·é /əˈtæʃeɪ‖ˌætəˈʃeɪ/ *n* a person with specialist knowledge who works in an EMBASSY: *a naval attaché*

attaché case /·ˈ·· ·‖ˌ··ˈ· ·/ *n* a thin hard case with a handle, for carrying papers —compare BRIEFCASE

at·tach·ment /əˈtætʃmənt/ *n* **1** [C] something that is fixed to something else: *a vacuum cleaner with a special attachment for dusting books* **2** [C (**to**)] fondness or friendship (for): *She has already formed a strong attachment to her baby brother.* **3** [U (**to**)] the act of attaching or state of being attached: *an officer on attachment to the drugs squad* **4** [C;U] *law* the seizure of a person or their goods in order to clear a debt

at·tack¹ /əˈtæk/ *v* **1** [I;T] to use violence (against), esp. with weapons: *The enemy attacked (us) at night.* **2** [T] to speak or write strongly against with the intention of showing something to be bad or worthless: *a powerful speech attacking government policy* **3** [T] to have a harmful or damaging effect on, esp. by a continuing action: *The disease attacks cereal crops/the central nervous system.* **4** [T] to begin to deal with (something) with eagerness and determination: *She attacked the problem at once.* | *He attacked the food as if he hadn't eaten for a week.* — ~**er** *n* : *armed attackers*

attack² *n* **1** [C (**on**);U] (an act of) violence intended to harm: *Security will be increased after yesterday's attack on the president's life.* | *The city came* **under attack** *during the night.* **2** [C (**on**)] writing, words, or action directed forcefully against a person, plan, etc., intended to hurt or damage: *The speaker made a scathing attack on the government's record.* | *The police are launching a major attack on drug dealers.* **3** [C (**of**)] a sudden and usu. severe period of illness, esp. one which tends to return: *an attack of malaria/asthma* | (fig.) *He was overcome by a sudden attack of shyness.* —see also HEART ATTACK

at·tain /əˈteɪn/ *v* [T] *fml* to gain or arrive at after long effort; reach: *She attained the rank of deputy director.* | *to attain one's objectives* — ~**able** *adj*

attain to sthg. *phr v* [T *no pass.*] *fml* to reach (a desired state or condition)

at·tain·ment /əˈteɪnmənt/ *n fml* **1** [U] the act of attaining: *the attainment of happiness* **2** [C] something that has been successfully gained or learned, often a skill: *The ability to speak Chinese is among his attainments.*

at·tempt¹ /əˈtempt/ *v* [T] to make an effort at; try (to do something), esp. without succeeding: *The second question was so difficult I didn't even attempt it.* [+*to-v*] *He attempted to leave but was stopped.* [+*v-ing*] *I attempted walking along the rope.* | *The old lady lived, so her attacker was charged with* **attempted murder**, *not murder.*

attempt² *n* [(**at, on**)] an effort made to do something: *He failed to set a new record, but it was a good attempt.* | *I passed my driving test at the third attempt.* | *After the* **attempt on her life** (=the attempt to kill her) *she retired from politics.* [+*to-v*] *The government announced big tax cuts in an attempt to regain its lost popularity.* | *Could you at least make an attempt to smile?*

At·ten·bo·rough /ˈætənbərə‖-bɜːrəʊ/, **Sir David** (1926–) an English NATURALIST who has made many films and television programmes about nature and animals all around the world, including a very popular SERIES called *Life on Earth*

Attenborough, Sir Richard (1923–) an English actor and film DIRECTOR, well known for making such films as *Gandhi* and *Cry Freedom*

at·tend /əˈtend/ *v* **1** [I;T] to be present at; go to: *Will you be attending the meeting?* | *The dance was* **well attended**.

(=there were many people there) | *Please let us know if you are unable to attend.* **2** [I (**on, upon**); T] to go with or be with, esp. to give protection, help, or care: *The queen had a good doctor attending (on) her.* | *He was constantly attended by his bodyguard.* **3** [I (**to**)] *fml* to give one's attention: *Are you attending (to what is being said)?* **4** [T] *fml* to happen in connection with; ACCOMPANY (2): *The rescue attempt was attended by difficulties.*

▷ USAGE People who **attend** a play or concert are the **audience;** people who **attend** a religious service are the **congregation;** people who **attend** a game, such as football, are **spectators.** But an **attendant** is someone who is employed to look after a public place or the people who use it: *a swimming-pool* **attendant.** Someone who works in a shop is an **assistant,** or **shop assistant** (*BrE*)/**salesclerk** (*AmE*).◁

attend to sbdy./sthg. *phr v* [T] to direct one's efforts and interest towards; deal with or look after: *Excuse me, but I have an urgent matter to attend to.* | *You'd better attend to the children first – they need their breakfast.*

at·tend·ance /əˈtendəns/ *n* **1** [C;U (**at**)] the act or fact of attending, usu. regularly: *Attendance at school is demanded by law.* | *a poor attendance record* **2** [S (**at**)] the number of people present: *an attendance of over 5000* **3** [U (**on**)] *fml* the act of going with or being with someone: *There is a doctor in attendance on the queen.* **4 be in attendance** to be a BRIDESMAID at a wedding: *In attendance were his sisters Joanna and Mary.* —see also **dance attendance on** *someone* (DANCE¹ (5))

at·tend·ant¹ /əˈtendənt/ *n* **1** a person employed to look after and help visitors or customers in a public place: *a car park/museum attendant* —see ATTEND (USAGE) **2** a person who goes with and serves or looks after another **3** a BRIDESMAID: *Attendants were Miss J. Brown and Miss L. Paton.*

attendant² *adj* [(**on, upon**)] *fml* **1** happening at the same time as, or as a result of, something else: *One of the difficulties attendant on shift work is lack of sleep.* | *bad weather and its attendant problems* **2** on duty to help and look after someone

at·ten·tion¹ /əˈtenʃən/ *n* **1** [U] the act of fixing the mind on something, esp. by watching or listening; full thought and consideration: *You must* **pay attention to** *the teacher. Don't let your attention wander.* | *He likes to be the* **centre of attention.** | *She waved her hand to* **attract/catch my attention.** | *If you distract his attention, I'll slip out of the room when he isn't looking.* | *She was convicted of driving* **without due care and attention.** | *He's got a very short* **attention span.** (=he can only keep his attention on something for a short time) **2** [U] particular care or consideration given to something, esp. with the aim of taking action: *Old cars need a lot of care and attention to keep them working.* | *This letter is* **for the attention of** *Mr Robinson.* | *The police should pay more attention to catching criminals.* | *The company is now turning its attention to the luxury car market.* **3** [C *usu. pl.*] *becoming rare* a kind or polite act showing respect or love, esp. of a man to a woman: *She felt embarrassed by his persistent attentions.* **4** [U] a military position in which a soldier stands straight and still: *to come to attention* | *to stand at attention* —compare EASE¹ (3) **5 attention all shipping** the phrase used on the British radio before the special report about the weather for people on the sea

attention² also **'shun–** *interj* a military order to come to ATTENTION¹ (4)

at·ten·tive /əˈtentɪv/ *adj* **1** taking careful notice; listening carefully: *an attentive audience/class* —opposite **inattentive 2** [(**to**)] politely helpful: *He was very attentive to the old lady and did everything for her.* — ~**ly** *adv* – ~**ness** *n* [U]

at·ten·u·ate /əˈtenjueɪt/ *v* [I;T] *fml or tech* to (cause to) become thin, weak, less valuable, etc.: *a powerful drug, used in an attenuated form as a medicine* —**-ation** /əˌtenjuˈeɪʃən/ *n* [U]

at·test /əˈtest/ *v fml* **1** [T] to declare to be true, esp. by signing something: *Witnesses attested his account of the attack.* **2** [I+**to**; T] to be proof of; DEMONSTRATE: *The luxurious furnishings attested (to) the family's wealth.*

at·tes·ta·tion /ˌæteˈsteɪʃən/ *n* [C;U] *fml* (the making of) a statement which the maker solemnly declares to be true

attested milk /ˌ·ˌ·· ·ˈ·/ *BrE* ‖ **certified milk** *AmE*– *n* [U] milk produced under official medical control

at·tic /ˈætɪk/ *n* the space in a building, esp. a house, just below the roof, which is often made into a room or used for storing furniture. In the past, attic rooms were often cheap to rent and people with little money often used to live in them. –compare GARRET

At·til·a /əˈtɪlə/ also **Attila the Hun** /ˌ·ˌ·· ·ˈ·/– (c. 406–53) king of the Huns (= an ancient people from Asia) who attacked and succeeded in controlling parts of the Roman Empire. He is usu. thought of as a cruel and violent man.

at·tire¹ /əˈtaɪəʳ/ *n* [U] *fml* clothes, esp. of a particular type: *in formal attire*

attire² *v* [T (in)] *fml* to put on clothes; dress: *attired in her academic robes*

at·ti·tude /ˈætɪtjuːd‖-tuːd/ *n* **1** [(to, towards)] a way of feeling or thinking about someone or something, esp. as this influences one's behaviour: *I don't like her (unhelpful) attitude.* | *What is the company's attitude to|towards this idea?* | *a pessimistic attitude of mind* **2** *fml* a position of the body; POSTURE: *He adopted a threatening attitude.* | *to* **strike an attitude** (=get into an unnatural position for effect) *in front of the mirror*

Att·lee /ˈætliː/, **Clement** (1883–1967) a British Labour politician and PRIME MINISTER (1945–51)

at·tor·ney /əˈtɜːniː‖-ɜːr-/ *n AmE* a lawyer. Lawyers in the US have to be licensed (LICENSE) by the state in which they practise, which allows them to practise in FEDERAL courts, but not necessarily in other states: *She refused to make a statement until she had spoken to her attorney.* –see also POWER OF ATTORNEY

attorney gen·e·ral /ˌ·ˌ·· ˈ···/ *n* **attorneys general** *or* **attorney generals** [(usu. caps.)] the chief law officer of a state or nation. In Britain the Attorney General is a Member of Parliament and BARRISTER. He is the chief law officer of the Crown and head of the English Bar. In the US the Attorney General is a member of the CABINET appointed by the President. He is the head of the Justice Department and the government's lawyer. –see also LORD ADVOCATE

at·tract /əˈtrækt/ *v* [T] **1** to excite the admiration, interest, or feelings of: *He was attracted by her smile.* | *She's always attracted to* (=she likes) *foreign men.* | *His new book has attracted a lot of attention.* **2** to draw or pull towards oneself; cause to come near: *A magnet attracts iron.* | *Flowers attract bees.* | *The company is trying to attract overseas investors.* | *a proposal that attracted widespread criticism* | *They say that opposites attract.*

at·trac·tion /əˈtrækʃən/ *n* **1** [U] the action or power of attracting: *The idea of travelling to the moon holds little attraction for me.* | *What's the attraction of going* (=why do you want to go) *on the stage?* **2** [C] something which attracts: *Our main attraction on tonight's show is an interview with Clint Eastwood.* –see also TOURIST ATTRACTION

at·trac·tive /əˈtræktɪv/ *adj* **1** able to attract; exciting interest or pleasure: *I find the idea of travel very attractive.*| *an attractive smile|offer|investment* **2** having good looks; pretty *or* HANDSOME: *an attractive girl|young man* – opposite **unattractive** –see BEAUTIFUL (USAGE) – ~ **ly** *adv* – ~ **ness** *n* [U]

at·tri·bute¹ /ˈætrɪbjuːt/ *n* a quality forming part of the nature of a person or thing: *Kindness is one of his best attributes.*

at·tri·bute² /əˈtrɪbjuːt‖-bjət/ *v*
attribute sthg. to sbdy./sthg. *phr v* [T] to believe (something) to be the result or work of: [+*obj/v-ing*] *He attributes his success to hard work|to working hard.* | *This song is usually attributed to Schubert.* –**attributable** *adj* [F+to] : *The fall in the price is attributable to a sharp reduction in demand.* –**attribution** /ˌætrɪˈbjuːʃən/ *n* [U (to)]

at·trib·u·tive /əˈtrɪbjŭtɪv/ *adj* (of an adjective, noun, or phrase) describing and coming before a noun: *In "a major success" "major" is an attributive adjective, and in "the school bus" "school" is a noun in attributive position.* –compare PREDICATIVE – ~ **ly** *adv*

at·tri·tion /əˈtrɪʃən/ *n* [U] the process of tiring, weakening, or destroying by continual worry, hardship, or repeated attacks: *to wage a* **war of attrition**

at·tune /əˈtjuːn‖əˈtuːn/ *v*
attune sbdy./sthg. to sthg. *phr v* [T *usu. pass.*] to make

used to or ready for: *I'm not really attuned to his way of thinking yet.*

At·wood /ˈætwʊd/, **Margaret** (1939–) a Canadian writer of short stories, poems, and NOVELs including *The Handmaid's Tale* and *Cat's Eye*

a·typ·i·cal /eɪˈtɪpɪkəl/ *adj* not typical; different from what is usual: *Her reaction to the drug was atypical.* – ~ **ly** /kli/ *adv*

au·ber·gine /ˈəʊbəʒiːn‖-bər-/ usu. **eggplant** *AmE*– *n* [C;U] (a type of plant with) a large purple fruit that is eaten as a vegetable, usu. cooked, e.g. in MOUSSAKA or RATATOUILLE –see picture at VEGETABLE

au·burn /ˈɔːbən‖-ərn/ *adj* (esp. of hair) reddish-brown – **auburn** *n* [U]

Auck·land /ˈɔːklənd/ **1** an area of North Island, New Zealand **2** the largest port and city of North Island, New Zealand

auc·tion¹ /ˈɔːkʃən/ *n* a public meeting at which land, buildings, or valuable goods are sold to the person who offers the most money. The auctioneer calls out a fairly low price, called the **starting price**, then people show in some way if they are willing to pay more than this, until finally one person offers more than anyone else is willing to pay, and the goods are sold to them: *to bid at a furniture auction* | *They've* **put** *the contents of their house* **up for auction.** | *It was sold* **at/by auction.** –see also DUTCH AUCTION

auction² *v* [T (OFF)] to sell by auction

auction bridge /ˈ·· ˌ·/ *n* [U] a card game for four people where the players BID² (3) to be allowed to choose the TRUMP suit –see also BRIDGE³, CONTRACT BRIDGE

auc·tio·neer /ˌɔːkʃəˈnɪəʳ/ *n* a person who is in charge of an auction and who calls out the prices as they are reached

auction house /ˈ·· ·/ *n* a company which arranges auctions. The most well-known auction houses in Britain and the US are Christie's and Sotheby's

au·da·cious /ɔːˈdeɪʃəs/ *adj* **1** daring, often to a degree that is considered foolish; ready to take dangerous risks **2** daringly impolite and disrespectful – ~ **ly** *adv*

au·dac·i·ty /ɔːˈdæsŭti/ *n* [U] **1** daring bravery **2** daring rudeness; lack of respect: *How you have the audacity to say such a thing, I don't know!*

Au·den /ˈɔːdn/, **W H** (1907–73) an English poet who wrote his most important poems in the 1930s. He became a US citizen in 1946.

au·di·ble /ˈɔːdŭbəl/ *adj* able to be heard: *His voice was barely audible above the noise of the machinery.* – opposite **inaudible** –**bly** *adv* –**bility** /ˌɔːdŭˈbɪlŭti/ *n* [U]

au·di·ence /ˈɔːdiəns‖ˈɔː-, ˈɑː-/ *n* **1** [C+*sing.|pl. v*] the people listening to or watching a performance, speech, television show, etc.: *The audience applauded loudly at the end of the concert.* | *Some members of the audience were shocked by the scenes of violence.* | *an appreciative audience* | *a TV programme with an audience of 12 million viewers* | *a show with a lot of* **audience participation** –see ATTEND (USAGE) **2** [C] a formal meeting between someone important and someone less important: *to have|seek|be granted an audience with the Pope* **3** [U] *law* freedom to be heard and to express one's views in a law court

au·di·o /ˈɔːdiəʊ/ *adj* [A] *tech* connected with or used in the broadcasting or receiving of sound radio signals – compare VIDEO

au·di·o·tape /ˈɔːdiəʊˌteɪp/ *n* [C,U] (a) TAPE¹ (2) used for recording sound on

audio-typ·ist /ˈ··· ˌ··/ *n* a typist who can type letters, etc. which have been recorded onto TAPE¹ (2) –**audiotyping** *n* [U]

audio-vis·u·al /ˌ··· ˈ···◄/ *adj* of, using, or being educational materials that provide information which can be seen and heard: *The school's audio-visual equipment includes videos and cassettes.* | *the use of audio-visual aids in teaching*

au·dit /ˈɔːdŭt/ *v* [T] to make an official examination of (the accounts of a business). Every British company must by law keep proper financial records and have them audited regularly by an independent auditor who is a fully trained accountant. –**audit** *n* : *The yearly audit takes place each December.*

au·di·tion¹ /ɔːˈdɪʃən/ n a performance given by a singer, actor, etc., as a test of their ability or suitability for a particular job: *They're holding auditions for the part next week.*

audition² v [I;T] to give or cause (someone) to give an audition: *He (was) auditioned for the role of Julius Caesar.*

au·di·tor /ˈɔːdɪtəʳ/ n **1** a person who audits the accounts of businesses **2** *rare* a person who listens; hearer

au·di·to·ri·um /ˌɔːdɪˈtɔːriəm/ n the space in a theatre, hall, etc., where people sit when listening to or watching a performance

au·di·to·ry /ˈɔːdɪtəriǁ-tɔːri/ adj tech of, by, or for hearing: *auditory difficulties for which an ear operation was necessary*

Au·du·bon /ˈɔːdəbɒnǁ-bɑːn/, **John James** (1785–1851) an American NATURALIST and painter of North American birds

Au·er·bach /ˈaʊəbɑːk ǁ ˈaʊər-/, **Arnold "Red"** (1917–　) a successful BASKETBALL COACH in the US

au fait /ˌəʊ ˈfeɪ/ adj [F (**with**)] fully informed; familiar: *I'm new to the job and not quite au fait with all the procedures yet.*

Auf Wie·der·seh·en /aʊf ˈviːdəzeɪənǁ-dər-/ the German for "goodbye"

Au·ge·an sta·bles /ɔːˌdʒiːən ˈsteɪbəlz/ n [P] **1** in Greek MYTHOLOGY, a place where King Augeas kept a large number of cattle, and which had not been cleaned for many years. Hercules cleaned the STABLES by changing the course of a river so that it flowed through them. **2** **clean out/cleanse the Augean stables** *fml* to do a very difficult job

au·ger /ˈɔːgəʳ/ n a tool for making large holes in wood or in the ground

aught /ɔːtǁɔːt, ɑːt/ pron **1** *old use* anything **2** **for aught I know/care** *lit* for all I know/care; but I do not know/care: *He may be dead for aught I know.*

aug·ment /ɔːgˈment/ v [I;T] *fml* to (cause to) become bigger, more valuable, better, etc.: *He augments his income by teaching in the evenings.* — ~ation /ˌɔːgmenˈteɪʃənǁ-mən-, -men-/ n [C;U]

au grat·in /əʊ ˈgrætæn ǁ -ˈgrɑːtn/ adj [after n] Fr cooked or baked with a covering of cheese or small pieces of bread mixed with butter: *potatoes au gratin*

au·gur /ˈɔːgəʳ/ v **1** [T] *lit* to be a sign of (something) in the future **2** [I] **augur well/ill (for)** to be a sign of good/bad things in the future: *This rain augurs well for this year's harvest.*

au·gu·ry /ˈɔːgjʊri/ n **1** [C] a sign of coming events **2** [U] the art of telling the future as practised by the ancient Romans

au·gust /ɔːˈgʌst/ adj *lit* noble and grand: *an august gathering* — ~ly adv

Au·gust /ˈɔːgəst/ (written abbrev. **Aug.**) n [C;U] the eighth month of the year, between July and September. When people think of August, they typically think of summer holidays, no school for children, hot weather, and long days: *It happened on August the fifteenth/the fifteenth of August/(AmE) on August fifteenth.* | *This office opened in August 1991.* | *She started work here last August/the August before last.*

August Bank Hol·i·day /ˌ··· ˈ···/ also **Late Summer Holiday** n (in Britain) an official public holiday on the last Monday in August. Many people travel by car to the coast, causing traffic problems in many places.

auk /ɔːk/ n a northern seabird with short wings

au lait /əʊ ˈleɪ/ adj Fr with milk: *café au lait*

Auld Lang Syne /ˌɔːld læŋ ˈzaɪn, ˌaʊld-, -ˈsaɪn/ a Scottish song sung by British people when they celebrate the beginning of the new year at 12 o'clock (MIDNIGHT) on December 31st. The first line of the song is: *Should auld* (=old) *acquaintance be forgot...*

aunt /ɑːntǁænt/ also **aunt·ie, aunt·y** /ˈɑːntiǁˈænti/ *infml* n (often cap.) **1** the sister of one's father or mother, or the wife of one's uncle: *Take me swimming, Auntie (Jane)!* | *My sister had a baby last week, so I'm now an aunt.* **2** BrE a woman who is a friend or neighbour of a small child or its parents —see FATHER (USAGE), UNCLE (USAGE)

►CULTURAL NOTE In Britain, many older people feel offended if children call them by their first name because it does not seem to show enough respect. So, for example, if a woman's name is Mary, she might prefer children to call her "auntie Mary", or if a man's name is John, he might prefer children to call him "uncle John". Most younger people feel happy for children to call them just by their first name.◄

Aunt·ie /ˈɑːntiǁˈæn-/ a name for the BBC used humorously to suggest that it is familiar, well-intentioned but rather unadventurous

Aunt Sal·ly /ˌ·ˈ··/ n BrE a person or thing at which people direct their laughter, anger, or general bad feeling (from the old game called Aunt Sally, in which people throw sticks or balls at a wooden model of a woman's head in order to win a prize: *those popular Aunt Sallys, central government and bureaucrats*

au pair /ˌəʊ ˈpeəʳ/ also **au pair girl** /· ˈ· ˌ·/— n a young foreign woman who lives with a family, usu. in order to learn their language, in return for doing light work in the house or looking after children. In Britain, au pairs are often thought of as sexy and attractive, esp. if they come from Scandinavia or France.

au·ra /ˈɔːrə/ n an effect or feeling that seems to surround and come from a person or place: *an aura of decay/mystery in the empty village*

au·ral /ˈɔːrəl/ adj tech of or related to the sense of hearing: *aural skills* — ~ly adv

▷ USAGE In language teaching, **aural** is sometimes pronounced /ˈaʊrəl/ to show the difference from **oral** /ˈɔːrəl/, esp. in the phrase **oral/aural**. —see also ORAL (USAGE)◁

Au·rang·zeb, **Aurungzeb** /ˈɔːrənzeb/ (1618–1707) a Mogul EMPEROR of N India

au·re·ole /ˈɔːriəʊl/ n a bright circle of light; HALO

au re·voir /ˌəʊ rəˈvwɑːʳ, ˌɒ-ǁˌəʊ-, ˌɒ-/ interj Fr till we meet again; goodbye. People sometimes use this expression to someone they love when goodbye seems too final, or as a joke when pretending to know French: *"Goodbye, darling." "No, not goodbye, au revoir."* | *Goodbye then, or au revoir as the French say.*

au·ri·cle /ˈɔːrɪkəl/ n tech **1** the outside part of the ear **2** either of the two spaces in the top of the heart; ATRIUM

au·ric·u·lar /ɔːˈrɪkjʊləʳ/ adj tech of or concerning the ear

au·ro·ra /əˈrɔːrə, ɔː-/ n -ras or -rae /riː/ bands or arches of coloured light in the night sky seen either in the most northern parts of the world (**aurora borealis** or **northern lights**) or in the most southern parts (**aurora australis** or **southern lights**)

Aurora in Roman MYTHOLOGY, the goddess of the DAWN (=first light of day) (Greek name Eos)

Ausch·witz /ˈaʊʃwɪts, -vɪts/ a town in Poland where the Germans built a CONCENTRATION CAMP during the Second World War. Millions of people, esp. Jews, died in Auschwitz, and its name has come to represent terrible suffering, cruelty, and inhumanity.

aus·cul·ta·tion /ˌɔːskəlˈteɪʃən/ n [U] tech the act of listening to the sounds coming from the organs inside the body as a method of discovering their health

aus·pic·es /ˈɔːspɪsɪz/ n [P] fml help, support, and favour: *This conference has been arranged under the auspices of the United Nations.*

aus·pi·cious /ɔːˈspɪʃəs/ adj fml giving, promising, or showing signs of future success: *an auspicious occasion* — opposite **inauspicious** — ~ly adv : *The year began auspiciously with good trade figures for January.*

Aus·sie /ˈɒziǁˈɔːsi, ˈɑːsi/ n sl an Australian

Aus·ten /ˈɒstənǁˈɔːs-/, **Jane** (1775–1817) an English writer who wrote, often humorously, about the way of life of middle class people of her time, in books such as *Pride and Prejudice* and *Emma*

aus·tere /ɔːˈstɪəʳ, ɒ-ǁɔː-/ adj **1** plain and severe; without comfort or enjoyment: *The monks led an austere life in the mountains.* | *an austere person/manner* **2** without decoration; plain: *the austere grandeur of the old cathedral* — ~ly adv

aus·ter·i·ty /ɔːˈsterəti, ɒ-ǁɔː-/ n **1** [U] the quality of being austere **2** [C usu. pl.] an austere act or manner: *The group practises religious austerities, such as fasting.* **3** [U] a situation, esp. one resulting from an intentional government plan, in which there is little money for spending on comfort and enjoyment: *a period of austerity* | *a package of austerity measures aimed at restoring the country's economic health*

Aus·tin¹ /ˈɒstɪn‖ˈɔːs-/ a once independent popular British car maker, started in 1905: *He still drives an old Austin 1100.*

Austin² *n* the capital of Texas in the US, on the Colorado River. It is the centre of a rich farming area and home to the University of Texas. – see colour map on pages 1374-5

Austin Reed /ˌ·· ˈ·/ one of a group of British men's clothing shops selling expensive, good quality clothes: *an Austin Reed suit*

Aus·tra·la·sia /ˌɒstrəˈleɪʒə,-ʃə‖ˌɔː-,ˌɑː-/ the name given to the group of islands in the Pacific Ocean, including Australia, New Zealand, and Papua New Guinea

Aus·tra·la·sian /ˌɒstrəˈleɪʒən, -ʃən‖ˌɔː-, ˌɑː-/ *n, adj* (a person who comes from or whose parents come) from Australia, New Zealand, or the surrounding islands

Australia

Darwin
Cairns
NORTHERN TERRITORY
WESTERN AUSTRALIA
Alice Springs
QUEENSLAND
Brisbane
SOUTH AUSTRALIA
NEW SOUTH WALES
Perth
Adelaide
Sydney
Canberra
VICTORIA
Melbourne
TASMANIA
Hobart

Aus·tra·li·a /ɒˈstreɪliə‖ɔː-,ɑː-/ a large country lying between the Indian and Pacific Oceans; capital Canberra; population 16,807,000 (1989). Many of the people who live there are of British DESCENT. ABORIGINALs account for about 1% of the population.

Australia Day /·ˈ··· ˌ·/ (in Australia) a national holiday on or near January 26th each year in memory of the landing of the British in 1788

Aus·tra·li·an /ɒˈstreɪliən‖ɔː-, ɑː-/ *n, adj* (a person who comes from or whose parents come) from Australia

Australian Rules foot·ball /·ˌ··· ˈ··/ *n* [U] a game played between two teams of 18 players on an OVAL field with an oval ball which is passed by kicking or striking with the hand, the object being to get points by putting the ball between a set of four posts which are placed at either end of the field

Australian Cap·i·tal Ter·ri·to·ry /·ˌ··· ˌ··· ˈ···/ [*the*] an area in SE Australia including the capital of Australia, Canberra, and Jervis Bay; population 258,900 (1986)

Aus·tri·a /ˈɒstriə‖ˈɔː-,ˈɑː/ a country in central Europe; capital Vienna —**Austrian** *adj*: *the Austrian mountains*

Aus·tri·an /ˈɒstriən‖ˈɔː-, ˈɑː-/ *n* 1 [C] a person who comes from or whose parents come from Austria: *He's an Austrian.* 2 [U] the (German) language spoken in Austria: *She's speaking Austrian.*

Austro- see WORD FORMATION

au·tar·chy /ˈɔːtɑːki‖-ɑːr-/ *n* [U] government of a country by one person with unlimited power

au·tar·ky , -chy /ˈɔːtɑːki‖-ɑːr-/ *n* 1 [U] the production by a country of everything that it needs 2 [C] a country that practises this system

au·then·tic /ɔːˈθentɪk/ *adj* 1 known to have been made, painted, written, etc., by the person who is claimed to have done it; GENUINE: *Is that an authentic Roman statue, or a modern copy?* 2 true and deserving to be believed or trusted; dependable: *an authentic testimony* – –**ally** /kli/ *adv*

au·then·ti·cate /ɔːˈθentɪkeɪt/ *v* [T] to prove (something) to be true or authentic: *This painting has been authenticated as a Rembrandt.* —**ation** /ɔːˌθentɪˈkeɪʃən/ *n* [U]

au·then·tic·i·ty /ˌɔːθenˈtɪsɪti/ *n* [U] the quality of being true or authentic: *The results of these chemical tests have cast doubt on the authenticity of this painting.* (=shown that it may not be authentic)

au·thor¹ /ˈɔːθər/ **au·thor·ess** /ˈɔːθərɪs‖*fem. rare*– *n* 1 the writer of a book, newspaper article, play, poem, etc.: *a prolific author* 2 the person who creates or begins something, esp. an idea or plan: *the chief author of the government's youth training programme*

author² *v* [T] *esp. AmE* to produce or begin (something); be the AUTHOR¹ (2) of: *The senator authored the bill to help the unemployed.*

au·thor·i·tar·i·an /ɔːˌθɒrɪˈteəriən◄‖ɔːˌθɑː-, əˌθɒː-/ *adj* believing or demanding that rules and laws must always be obeyed whether or not they are right: *an authoritarian style of government* —**authoritarian** *n* : *He's a strict authoritarian.* – ~ **ism** *n* [U]

au·thor·i·ta·tive /ɔːˈθɒrɪtətɪv, ə-‖əˈθɑːrəteɪtɪv, əˌθɒː-/ *adj* 1 having or showing authority; demanding or deserving respect and obedience: *an authoritative manner|tone* 2 generally regarded as providing knowledge or information that can be trusted: *an authoritative dictionary* – compare DEFINITIVE (2) – ~ **ly** *adv*

au·thor·i·ty /ɔːˈθɒrɪti, ə-‖əˈθɑː-, əˈθɒː-/ *n* 1 [U] (a position that gives someone) the ability, power, or right to control and command: *Who is in authority here?* | *He enjoys exercising his authority over his staff.* | *She thinks that young people have no respect for authority.* [+to-v] *He doesn't have the necessary authority to make this sort of decision.* 2 [C *often pl.*] a person or group with this power or right, esp. in public affairs: *The government is the highest authority in the country.* | *the local education|water authority* | *The authorities in Spain have refused to allow him to enter the country.* | *to approach the proper authorities for permission* —see also LOCAL AUTHORITY 3 [C *usu. sing.*] a paper giving this power or right: *May I see your authority?* 4 [U] power to influence: *Although she has no official position in the party, her opinions carry a lot of authority.* 5 [C(**on**)] a person, book, etc., whose knowledge or information is dependable, good, and respected: *He is a leading authority on plant diseases.*

au·thor·i·za·tion also **-isation** *BrE* /ˌɔːθəraɪˈzeɪʃən‖ˌɔːθərə-/ *n* [C;U] (a paper giving) right or official power to do something: *I can't spend this money without authorization from Head Office.* [+to-v] *Do you have the owner's authorization to drive this car?*

au·thor·ize, also **-ise** *BrE* /ˈɔːθəraɪz/ *v* [T] to give formal permission to or for: *Who authorized the payment of this bill?* [+obj+to-v] *I've been authorized (by the court) to repossess this property.*

authorized cap·i·tal /ˌ··· ˈ···/ *n* [U] *tech* the largest amount of money a company is allowed to raise by selling SHARES¹(2) to the general public

Authorized Ver·sion /ˌ··· ˈ··/ *esp. BrE* ‖ also **King James Version**– [*the*] the English translation of the Bible made in England in 1611, when James the First was king

au·thor·ship /ˈɔːθəʃɪp‖ˈɔːθər-/ *n* [U] 1 the name of the person who wrote a book, play, poem, etc.; IDENTITY of the AUTHOR: *a book of unknown authorship* 2 the profession of writing books

au·tis·m /ˈɔːtɪzəm/ *n* [U] an illness of the mind, esp. in children, in which the imagination becomes too important and good personal relationships cannot be formed

au·tis·tic /ɔːˈtɪstɪk/ *adj* suffering from autism: *autistic children* – ~ **ally** /kli/ *adv*

au·to /ˈɔːtəʊ/ *n* **-tos** *esp. AmE* a car: *second-hand autos* | *the auto industry*

auto- see WORD FORMATION

au·to·bi·og·ra·phy /ˌɔːtəbaɪˈɒɡrəfi‖-ˈɑːɡ-/ *n* 1 [C] an account of a person's life written by that person 2 [U] this branch of literature —compare BIOGRAPHY —**phical** /ˌɔːtəbaɪəˈɡræfɪkəl/, **-phic** *adj* —**phically** /kli/ *adv*

au·toc·ra·cy /ɔːˈtɒkrəsi‖ɔːˈtɑː-/ *n* 1 [U] government by one person with unlimited power 2 [C] a country, group, etc., ruled in this way

au·to·crat /ˈɔːtəkræt/ *n* 1 a ruler with unlimited power 2 a person who gives orders to others without considering their wishes – ~ **ic** /ˌɔːtəˈkrætɪk◄/ *adj* – ~ **ically** /kli/ *adv*

au·to·cross /'ɔ:təʊkrɒs‖-krɔ:s/ n [U] BrE the sport of racing motor cars around open fields or country rather than on roads

au·to·cue /'ɔ:təʊkju:/ n a machine similar to a TELEPROMPTER

au·to·graph¹ /'ɔ:təgrɑ:f‖-græf/ n a person's name in their own writing (SIGNATURE), esp. the signature of someone famous. Some people, esp. children, collect the autographs of famous people: *The little boys asked the footballer for his autograph.*

autograph² v [T] (esp. of a famous person) to sign (a letter, statement, book, etc.) with one's own name to show that one has written it: *an autographed copy of a book*

au·to·harp /'ɔ:təʊhɑ:p‖-hɑ:rp/ n a musical instrument played by pressing a button for a combination of notes (CHORD) and then passing one's fingers over the strings

au·to·im·mune dis·ease /ˌɔ:təʊɪmjuːn dɪˈziːz/ n an illness or unhealthy condition in which substances which usu. fight against illness are produced by the body and damage or destroy one or more of its own substances

au·to·mat /'ɔ:təmæt/ n tdmk a type of American restaurant where food can be obtained from machines into which coins are dropped. Automats were popular in the 1950s and 60s but are now rare.

au·to·mate /'ɔ:təmeɪt/ v [I;T] to make (a business or industrial process) work by machinery with little or no work by people: *a fully automated production line*

au·to·mat·ic¹ /ˌɔ:təˈmætɪk◂/ adj **1** (esp. of a machine) able to work or move by itself without operation by a person: *This heating system has an automatic temperature control.* | *an automatic pistol/rifle* (=able to fire continuously because the bullets are loaded automatically) **2** done without conscious thought, esp. as a habit: *The movements needed to ride a bicycle soon become automatic.* | *an automatic response* **3** certain to happen: *an automatic increase in pay every year* — ~ **ally** /kli/ adv

automatic² n a machine or apparatus, such as a car or a gun, that operates automatically —see picture at GUN

automatic pi·lot /ˌ·... '··/ also **autopilot** n an instrument that guides aircraft, spacecraft, ships, etc., without needing human operation: (fig.) *She's absolutely exhausted; she's just working on automatic pilot.*

Automatic Tel·ler Ma·chine /ˌ··· '·· ·ˌ·/ also **ATM** n AmE for CASH DISPENSER

automatic trans·mis·sion /ˌ···· ·'··/ n [U] a system which operates the GEARs of a car automatically, so that the driver does not need to move them by hand. Most cars in the US have automatic transmission but it is still rare in Britain: *My car has automatic transmission.*

au·to·ma·tion /ˌɔ:təˈmeɪʃən/ n [U] the use of machines that need little or no human control, esp. in place of workers: *redundancies owing to increased automation*

au·tom·a·ton /ɔ:ˈtɒmətən‖ɔ:ˈtɑ:-/ n -ta /tə/ or -tons **1** a machine that moves or works by itself, esp. a ROBOT **2** derog a person who acts without thought or feeling, like a machine

au·to·mo·bile /'ɔ:təməbi:l‖-məʊ-/ n fml, esp. AmE a car: *the automobile industry*

Automobile As·so·ci·a·tion /'···· ···ˌ··/ [the] see AA²

au·ton·o·mous /ɔ:ˈtɒnəməs‖ɔ:ˈtɑ:-/ adj having autonomy: *an autonomous region* — ~ **ly** adv

automatic ner·vous sys·tem /ˌ···· '·· ˌ··/ n med the part of the nervous system which controls those parts of the body which do not require conscious effort, such as the DIGESTION, the CIRCULATION, and the production of HORMONES

au·ton·o·my /ɔ:ˈtɒnəmi‖ɔ:ˈtɑ:-/ n [U] the right of self-government or management of one's own affairs, esp. of a state or group within a country: *a political system that allows a high degree of local autonomy*

au·to·pi·lot /'ɔ:təʊˌpaɪlət/ n see AUTOMATIC PILOT

au·top·sy /'ɔ:tɒpsi‖-tɑ:p-/ n a POSTMORTEM: *to carry out an autopsy on the victim*

au·to·sug·ges·tion /ˌɔ:təʊsəˈdʒestʃən‖-səgˈdʒe-, -səˈdʒe-/ n [U] the influencing of one's feelings about things, physical condition, etc., by suggestion coming from within oneself rather than from another person or from the outside world: *Many forms of relaxation use techniques of autosuggestion.* —**tive** adj

au·tumn /'ɔ:təm/ also **fall** AmE— n [C;U] the season between summer and winter, when leaves change colour and fruits become ripe: *I go on holiday in the autumn.* | *a cold autumn* | *last autumn* | *autumn colours* (=brown, orange, gold, etc.) —see colour picture on page 1211

au·tum·nal /ɔ:ˈtʌmnəl/ adj of, like, or in autumn — ~ **ly** adv

autumn state·ment /ˌ·· '··/ n an official printed statement produced for parliament by the British Government every year, usu. in November, about the future of the ECONOMY and the Government's spending plans for the next three years

aux·il·ia·ry¹ /ɔːɡˈzɪljəri, ɔ:k-‖ɔ:ɡˈzɪljəri, -ˈzɪləri/ adj providing (additional) help or support, esp. with lower rank or of less importance: *auxiliary nursing staff* | *an auxiliary petrol tank*

auxiliary² n **1** fml or tech a helper; ASSISTANT **2** [usu. pl.] a member of a group of foreign soldiers in the service of a country at war **3** an auxiliary verb

auxiliary verb /·ˌ··· '·/ n tech a verb that is used with another verb to show differences such as tense, person, and VOICE¹ (4). In English the auxiliary verbs are **be**, **do**, and **have** (as in *I am running, I didn't go, they have gone*) and all the MODALs

av written abbrev. for: average

a·vail¹ /əˈveɪl/ n [U] good result; advantage; use: *We tried and tried, but it was all to no avail.*

avail² v **1** [I usu. in questions and negatives] lit to be of use or advantage: *It avails nothing to cry.* **2** [I] **avail oneself of** to make good or profitable use of: *I availed myself of this opportunity to improve my English.*

a·vai·la·ble /əˈveɪləbəl/ adj [(to)] able to be had, obtained, used, seen, etc.: *I'm sorry, sir, those shoes are not available in your size.* | *Every available ambulance was rushed to the scene of the accident.* | *Details of the competition are available from our head office.* | *Is the new timetable available yet?* | *We want to make our products available to a wider market.* | *We tried to find out the Senator's opinion on this matter, but he was not available for comment.* — opposite **unavailable** —**bly** adv —**bility** /əˌveɪləˈbɪlˌti/ n [U] : *limited availability*

av·a·lanche /'ævəlɑ:nʃ‖-læntʃ/ n a large mass of snow and ice crashing down the side of a mountain: *He was swept away in an avalanche.* | (fig.) *We received an avalanche of inquiries.*

Av·a·lon, Avallon /'ævəlɒn‖-lɑ:n/ a LEGENDARY holy island, thought by some people to be near Glastonbury in SW England, where, according to the old stories, the wounded King Arthur was carried after his last battle —see also ARTHURIAN LEGEND

av·ant-garde /ˌævɒːŋ ˈɡɑːd◂‖ˌævɑːŋ ˈɡɑːrd◂/ n [(the) S+sing./pl. v] the writers, painters, musicians, etc., whose work is based on the newest ideas and methods. *a member of the avant-garde* —**avant-garde** adj : *an avant-garde novelist*

av·a·rice /'ævərəs/ n [U] fml extreme eagerness and desire to get or keep wealth; GREED —**ricious** /ˌævəˈrɪʃəs/ adj —**riciously** adv

av·a·tar /ˌævəˈtɑ:r/ n **1** the appearance of a Hindu god, esp. Vishnu, in human or animal form: *Krishna was an avatar of the god Vishnu.* **2** a person who represents (an idea, etc.) completely; EMBODIMENT

Ave written abbrev. for: AVENUE (1): *109 Lexington Ave*

Ave·bu·ry /'eɪvbəri‖-beri/ a prehistoric SITE in Wiltshire, S England, where there is a large ring of STANDING STONEs

a·venge /əˈvendʒ/ v [T] esp. lit **1** to get satisfaction for (something bad done to oneself, one's family, etc.) by punishing the person who did it: *They avenged his death by burning the village.* **2** [(on)] to punish someone for something bad done to (oneself, one's family, etc.): *He swore to avenge his brother.* | *They avenged themselves on their enemy.* —compare VENGEANCE —**avenger** n

A·ven·gers /əˈvendʒəz‖-ərz/ , **The** a popular British television programme of the 1960s, whose main characters were **Steed**, a very well dressed wealthy gentleman, and his young female companion, **Emma Peel**. They fought against crime and criminals, and are esp. remembered for their skill at fighting with their hands.

av·e·nue /'ævɪnju:‖-nu:/ n **1** (written abbrev. **Ave.**) a broad street in a town, sometimes having trees on each side: *Fifth Avenue* **2** a road or way between two rows of trees, esp. one that leads to a house **3** a means of reaching a desired result: *They* **explored every avenue** (=tried every method) *but could not find a solution.*

a·ver /ə'vɜːʳ/ *v* **-rr-** [T+*obj/that*] *fml* to state forcefully; declare

av·e·rage¹ /'ævərɪdʒ/ *n* **1** [C] the amount calculated by adding together several quantities and then dividing by the number of quantities: *The average of 3, 8, and 10 is 7.* | *Wages for industrial workers have increased by an average of 7½%.* **2** [C;U] a level or standard regarded as usual or ordinary: *His school work is well* **above/ below average.** | *We receive 20 letters a day* **on average.** | *a higher than average attendance*

average² *adj* **1** [A *no comp.*] calculated by making an average of a number of quantities: *What is the average rainfall for July?* | *Average earnings in the country are about $500 a month.* **2** of the usual or ordinary kind: *There was nothing special about the film — it was only average.* | *the average man in the street* | *of average height/intelligence*

average³ *v* **1** [L] to be as an average: *Our mail averages 20 letters a day.* **2** [T *no pass.*] to do, get, or have as an average or usual quantity: *I average eight hours' work a day.* **3** [T (OUT)] to calculate the average of (figures) **average out** *phr v* [I (at, to)] *infml* to come to an average or ordinary level or standard, esp. after being higher or lower: *Months of high and low sales average out over the year.* | *The weekly profits averaged out at 20%.*

a·verse /ə'vɜːs‖-ɜːrs/ *adj* [F+to] *fml or humor* not liking; opposed: *I don't smoke cigarettes, but I'm not averse to (having) the occasional cigar.*

a·ver·sion /ə'vɜːʃən‖ə'vɜːrʒən/ *n* **1** [S;U (to)] a feeling of strong dislike or unwillingness: *She has an aversion to cats/to doing the housework.* **2** [C] a person or thing that causes this feeling: *Housework is my* **pet aversion.**

aversion ther·a·py /·'··· ,···/ *n* [U] the treatment of a bad habit or behaviour pattern (e.g. ALCOHOLISM) by its association with unpleasant sensations

a·vert /ə'vɜːt‖-ɜːrt/ *v* [T] **1** to prevent (something unpleasant) from happening: *An accident was averted by his quick thinking.* **2** [(**from**)] *fml* to turn away (one's eyes, thoughts, etc.): *She averted her eyes/her gaze from the terrible sight.*

a·vi·a·ry /'eɪviəri‖'eɪvieri/ *n* a large cage or enclosed space for keeping birds in

a·vi·a·tion /ˌeɪvi'eɪʃən‖ˌeɪ-, ˌæ-/ *n* [U] **1** the science or practice of flying in aircraft **2** the aircraft industry

a·vi·a·tor /'eɪvieɪtəʳ‖'eɪ-, 'æ-/ *n old use* the pilot of an aircraft

av·id /'ævɪd/ *adj* [(**for**)] extremely eager or keen: *an avid* **reader** | *avid for success* — **ly** *adv* — **ity** /ə'vɪdᶾti/ *n* [U]

Av·ie·more /ˌævi'mɔːʳ/ a town in N central Scotland, a centre for winter sports, esp. skiing (SKI²)

A·vis /'eɪvᶾs/ *tdmk* a car rental company which has offices at many international airports

av·o·ca·do /ˌævə'kɑːdəʊ◄/ also **avocado pear** /ˌ···· '·/ — *n* **-dos** *or* **-does** a green or purple-black tropical fruit with a large stone and smooth oily flesh, usu. eaten as the first part of a meal: *avocado vinaigrette*

av·o·ca·tion /ˌævə'keɪʃən/ *n fml* something done for pleasure; a HOBBY

a·void /ə'vɔɪd/ *v* [T] **1** to keep away from or keep out of the way of, esp. on purpose: *I swerved to the side of the road to avoid the other car.* | *To avoid the city centre, turn right here.* | *These drugs are very dangerous; I'd* **avoid them like the plague** (=never go near them) *if I were you.* **2** to prevent (something) from happening, or stop oneself from doing (something): *I swerved to the side of the road to avoid a collision.* | *Nuclear war is to be* **avoided at all costs.** [+*v-ing*] *He tried to avoid answering my questions.* — ~**able** *adj*

a·void·ance /ə'vɔɪdəns/ *n* [U] the act of avoiding: *avoidance of danger* | *a scheme for* **tax avoidance** (=avoiding the payment of tax, but by legal means)

av·oir·du·pois /ˌævədə'pɔɪz, ˌævwɑːdju:'pwɑː‖ˌævərdə 'pɔɪz/ *n* [U] the system of weights in which the standard measures are the OUNCE, POUND, and TON: *16 ounces avoirdupois* —compare METRIC SYSTEM; see TABLE 2

A·von¹ /'eɪvən/ **1** a COUNTY in SW England **2** [*the*] one

of various English rivers, esp. the one that flows through Stratford-upon-Avon

Avon² /'eɪvɒn‖-vɑːn/ *n tdmk* an American company which sells products for the skin and hair

A·von la·dy /'eɪvɒn ˌleɪdi‖-vɑːn-/ *n* a woman who sells products made by Avon by calling at people's houses. Many people remember an old advertisement for Avon products, in which a woman rings at a front door and says "Avon calling!"

a·vow /ə'vaʊ/ *v* [T] *fml* to state openly; admit: *The prisoner avowed his guilt.* [+*that*] *He avowed that he was guilty.* | *Their avowed aim* (=which they have openly admitted) *is to overthrow the government.* — ~**al** *n* [C;U]

a·vun·cu·lar /ə'vʌŋkjᶷləʳ/ *adj* of or like an uncle, esp. by being kind and caring: *his friendly avuncular manner* — ~**ly** *adv*

AWACS /'eɪwæks/ *n* [U] Airborne Warning and Control System; an American military aircraft which looks at where enemy armies are and helps direct what American soldiers should do to attack or defend against them

a·wait /ə'weɪt/ *v* [T] **1** *fml* to wait for: *I am awaiting their reply.* | *She is in prison awaiting trial.* | *a* **long-awaited** *holiday* **2** to be ready for: *A warm welcome awaits you.* —see WAIT (USAGE)

a·wake¹ /ə'weɪk/ *adj* [F] not asleep: *She lay awake for hours thinking about him.* | *The children are still* **wide awake.** (=not at all sleepy) | (fig.) *The company is awake to* (=conscious of) *these new developments.*

a·wake² *v* **awoke** /ə'wəʊk/ *or* **awaked, awoken** /ə'wəʊkən/ [I;T] **1** to (cause to) stop sleeping; wake: *The noise awoke me.* | *I awoke to the sound of birds chirruping.* | *He awoke to find himself alone.* (=When he awoke, he found he was alone.) **2** [(**to**)] to (cause to) become conscious or active: *His letter awoke old memories.* | *They awoke to the danger of the situation too late to do anything about it.* —see WAKE (USAGE)

a·wak·en /ə'weɪkən/ *v* [I;T] to awake: *I was awakened by their shouts.* —see WAKE (USAGE) **awaken sbdy. to** sthg. *phr v* [T] to cause to understand or become conscious of: *We must awaken people to the need to protect our environment.*

a·wak·en·ing /ə'weɪkənɪŋ/ *n* **1** the act of waking from sleep: (fig.) *a spiritual awakening* **2** **rude awakening** a sudden consciousness of an unpleasant or threatening situation

a·ward¹ /ə'wɔːd‖-ɔːrd/ *v* [T (**to**)] to give, esp. as the result of an official decision: *The referee awarded a free kick.* | *The judge awarded substantial damages to the victims of the explosion.* [+*obj(i)*+*obj(d)*] *She's been awarded a scholarship to study at Oxford.*

award² *n* something, esp. a prize or money, given as the result of an official decision: *an award of £5000 to those injured in the explosion* | *The award for this year's best actress went to Meryl Streep.*

a·ware /ə'weəʳ/ *adj* **1** [F] having knowledge or understanding: [+*of*] *He said that the government was acutely* (=very) *aware of the problem.* [+*that/wh-*] *I'm well aware that this is a risky investment/well aware how risky this investment is.* —opposite **unaware** **2** [after *adv*] having knowledge or consciousness of the stated type: *politically/artistically aware* **3** showing understanding of oneself, one's surroundings, and other people; SENSITIVE: *She's a very aware person.* — ~**ness** *n* [U]

a·wash /ə'wɒʃ‖ə'wɔːʃ, ə'wɑːʃ/ *adj* [F (**with**)] level with and washed over by waves: *The river overflowed until the streets were awash.* | (fig.) *The country is awash with oil.* (=has a large amount of it)

a·way¹ /ə'weɪ/ *adv* **1** [(**from**)] from here or from there; to or at another place: *Go away!* | *They're away on holiday.* (compare *They're* **out** *for lunch.*) | *The ship moved slowly away from the shore.* | *The police tried to keep people away from the accident.* **2** [after *n*] at a stated distance in space or time: *He lives three miles away.* | *The exams are still six weeks away.* **3** into a safe or enclosed place: *I've put the milk away (in the fridge).* **4** so as to be gone or used up: *The sounds died away.* | *Their house was swept away in the flood.* | *He gave all his money away.* | *Don't throw this opportunity away.* | *They danced the night away.* (=danced all night) | *He cut away the dead branch.* **5** all the time; continuously: *They worked away all day.* | *I heard him hammering away.* **6 away with!**

lit take away; remove: *Away with him, guards!* –see also **far and away** (FAR[1]), **right away** (RIGHT[5]) **7 get away (with you)!** *infml, esp. BrE* You can't deceive me!; I don't believe you! (used in answer to something the speaker thinks is improbable or untrue): *"I'm getting married." "Get away (with you)!"* **8 get away from it all** *infml* to escape from the problems and worries of daily life, esp. by taking a holiday: *You need to go away for a while and get away from it all.*

away² *adj* [A] (of a sports match) played at the place, sports field, etc., of one's opponent: *an away match* –opposite **home**

A·way·day /əˈweɪdeɪ/ *n tdmk* a type of British Rail ticket sold at a reduced price, for use on a day out for pleasure, rather than by business travellers

awe¹ /ɔː/ *n* [U] a feeling of respect mixed with fear and wonder: *The sight filled us with awe.* | *He always* **stood in awe of** *his father.*

awe² *v present participle* **aweing** [T (**into**)] *fml* to fill with awe: *They were awed into silence by the enormous ancient buildings.*

awe-in·spir·ing /ˈ· ·ˌ··/ *adj* causing feelings of awe – **~ly** *adv*

awe·some /ˈɔːsəm/ *adj* **1** expressing or causing feelings of awe: *an awesome account of the terrors of war* | *an awesome achievement/task/responsibility* **2** *AmE infml* very good; MARVELLOUS

awe·struck /ˈɔːstrʌk/ also **awe·strick·en** /ˈɔːstrɪkən/– *adj* filled with, made silent by, or showing awe: *We sat in awestruck silence after hearing the truth at last.*

aw·ful /ˈɔːfəl/ *adj* **1** very bad or unpleasant; terrible; shocking: *The pain was awful.* | *What awful weather!* | *It must have been awful for you/an awful dilemma for you.* | *It was awful to see him in such pain.* | *an awful thing to say* | *It would be awful if they found out.* **2** [A] *infml* (used to add force) very great: *I've got an awful lot of work to do.* | *He made an awful fuss about me being late.* **3** *lit or old use* awe-inspiring – **~ness** *n* [U]

aw·ful·ly /ˈɔːfəli/ *adv infml* very: *awfully cold* | *awfully nice*

a·while /əˈwaɪl/ *adv esp. lit* for a short time: *We rested awhile at the side of the road.*

awk·ward /ˈɔːkwəd‖-wərd/ *adj* **1** lacking skill in moving (parts of) the body easily; CLUMSY: *an awkward movement* | *He's rather awkward with his hands.* **2** difficult to use or handle: *It's rather an awkward shape.* | *I had to bang in the nail at a rather awkward angle.* [+*to-v*] *It's an awkward machine to use.* **3** causing difficulty or uncomfortable feelings; inconvenient or embarrassing: *Our visitors came at an awkward time.* [+*to-v*] *It was an awkward time to call.* | *a long awkward silence* | *He made things* (–the situation) *very awkward for me taking me into his confidence.* | *They've been asking some very awkward questions.* | *Don't go too near the dog – he's an* **awkward customer**. (=is dangerous to deal with) **4** unwilling to help or agree; PERVERSE (2): *Don't be so awkward – we've got to get this finished by tonight.* **5 awkward age** the time when a child is changing into an adult and is known as an ADOLESCENT: *He'll soon be reaching that awkward age – too young to do all the things he wants to do and too old to act like a baby.* – **~ly** *adv* – **~ness** *n* [U]

awl /ɔːl/ *n* a small pointed tool, often with a broad handle, for making holes in leather

aw·ning /ˈɔːnɪŋ/ *n* a movable soft covering, esp. one made of CANVAS, used to protect shop windows, ships' DECKS, etc., from sun or rain

a·woke /əˈwəʊk/ *past tense of* AWAKE

a·wok·en /əˈwəʊkən/ *past participle of* AWAKE

A.W.O.L. /ˌeɪ ˌdʌbəljuː əʊ ˈel, ˈeɪwɒl‖-wɔːl/ *adj* [F] *infml* absent without leave; (of a member of the armed forces) absent from one's place of duty without permission – compare MIA

a·wry /əˈraɪ/ *adj, adv* [F] **1** not in the way that was planned or intended; wrong: *a police operation that went badly awry* **2** not in the correct position or shape; twisted; bent.

axe¹ also **ax** *AmE* /æks/ *n* **axes** /ˈæksɨz/ **1** a tool with a heavy metal blade on the end of a long handle, used to cut down trees or split logs –see also HATCHET **2 get the axe** *infml* **a** to be dismissed from one's job **b** (of a plan)

axes

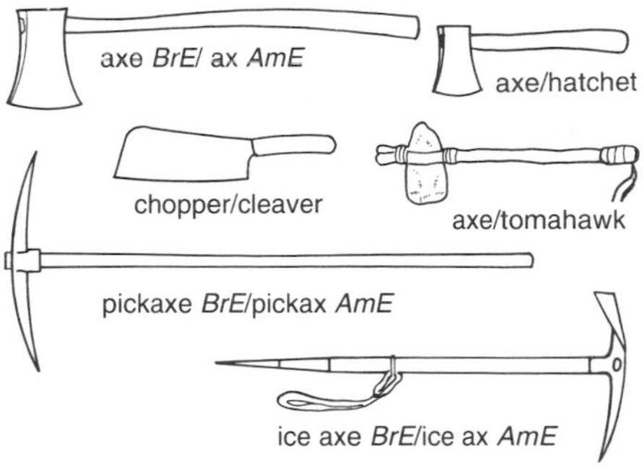
axe *BrE*/ ax *AmE*
axe/hatchet
chopper/cleaver
axe/tomahawk
pickaxe *BrE*/pickax *AmE*
ice axe *BrE*/ice ax *AmE*

to be ended because of lack of money or official support: *Several of our plans got the axe when the new government came in.* **3 have an ˈaxe to grind** *infml* to have personal and often selfish reasons for one's actions or statements: *The judge's criticisms of this policy must be taken seriously because he has no political axe to grind.* (=he does not have political reasons for finding fault)

axe² also **ax** *AmE v* [T] *infml* to put an end suddenly and usu. without warning to (a job, plans, etc.): *750 jobs were axed as a result of government spending cuts.*

ax·i·om /ˈæksiəm/ *n* a rule, principle, etc. that is generally accepted as true

ax·i·o·mat·ic /ˌæksiəˈmætɪk◂/ *adj fml* not needing to be proved; SELF-EVIDENT – **~ally** /kli/ *adv*

ax·is /ˈæksɨs/ *n* **axes** /ˈæksiːz/ *tech* **1** the usu. imaginary line around which a spinning body moves: *The Earth rotates about an axis between the North Pole and the South Pole.* –see picture at GLOBE **2** a line (e.g. across the middle of a circle) that divides a regular shape into two equal parts **3** a fixed line against which the positions of points are measured, esp. the HORIZONTAL (=flat) and VERTICAL (=upright) lines around a GRAPH –see picture at CHART

Axis also **Axis pow·ers, Axis coun·tries** /ˈ·· ˌ··/ *n* [*the*] the countries, including Germany, Italy, and Japan, who fought together during the Second World War against the ALLIES.

ax·le /ˈæksəl/ *n* a bar with a wheel on either end, around which the wheels turn or which turns with the wheels, as on a car –see picture at BICYCLE

Ax·min·ster /ˈæksmɪnstəʳ/ *n tdmk.* any of several kinds of carpet made in the town of Axminster, Devon, by a machine process which produces the effect of being hand-made

ay·ah /ˈaɪə/ *n IndE & PakE* an Indian nurse who looks after children

a·ya·tol·lah /ˌaɪəˈtɒlə‖-ˈtəʊ-/ *n* a religious leader among the Shiite Muslims: *Ayatollah Khomeini*

Ayatollah Khomeini see KHOMEINI

Ayck·bourn /ˈeɪkbɔːn‖-bɔːrn/, **Al·an** /ˈælən/ (1939–) an English writer of humorous plays such as *The Norman Conquests* and *A Chorus of Disapproval*

aye¹ /eɪ, aɪ/ *adv ScotE, esp. old use or poet* always; continually

aye² /aɪ/ *adv dial or lit* (often used when voting or by sailors) yes: *Aye, aye, sir; I'll do that at once.* | *All in favour say "Aye".*

aye³ /aɪ/ *n* a vote or voter in favour of an idea, plan, law, etc. –opposite **nay**

Ayer /eəʳ/, **A J** (1910–89) an English PHILOSOPHER who wrote *Language, Truth and Logic* in 1936

Ayers Rock /ˌeəz ˈrɒk‖ˌeərz ˈrɑːk/ an extremely large rock, part of a group, in SW Northern Territory, Australia. It is thought to be the world's largest MONOLITH and very popular as a tourist attraction because of its beautiful colours.

Ayles·bu·ry /ˈeɪlzbəri‖-beri/ a town in England, where the local government for Buckinghamshire is based

Ayr·shire /ˈeəʃəʳ‖ˈeər-/ **1** a former COUNTY in SW Scotland, now part of Strathclyde REGION **2** a brown and white cow of a breed that gives a large quantity of milk

AZ *written abbrev. for* ARIZONA

A – Z /ˌeɪ tə ˈzed‖-ˈziː/ *n* in Britain, a book of street plans of a town with a list of the street names at the end: *Look up Mortimer Road in the A–Z, will you?*

A·zer·bai·jan /ˌæzəbaɪˈdʒɑːn‖ˌɑːzər-/ a country in SE Europe next to the Caspian Sea, bordered by Russia, Armenia, and Iran; capital Baku; population 7,029,000 (1989) —**jani** *n, adj*

az·i·muth /ˈæzˌməθ/ *n* the angle on the Earth's surface between a north-south line and the position or direction of something, esp. a star, seen from a place on the Earth

A·zores /əˈzɔːz‖ˈeɪzɔːrz/ [*the*] a group of islands in the Atlantic, west of Portugal

AZT /ˌeɪ zed ˈtiː‖-ziː-/ *n* a medicine used by people with AIDS to slow down the progress of the illness

Az·tecs /ˈæzteks/ [*the*] an Indian people who lived in Mexico and were conquered (CONQUER) by the Spanish in 1519. They are remembered esp. for their great riches, esp. gold, and their fine buildings.

az·ure /ˈæʒəʳ, ˈæʒjuəʳ, ˈæzjuəʳ‖ˈæʒər/ *adj* having a bright blue colour, like the sky —**azure** *n* [U]

B

B, b /biː/ **B's, b's** or **Bs, bs** the second letter of the English alphabet

b written abbrev. for: born: b 1885

B **1** a note in Western music; the musical KEY¹ (4) based on this note **2** the second level of quality, e.g. as a mark given to student's work, usu. meaning good but not excellent: *I got a B for|in English.* —see also B-MOVIE, B-SIDE, GRADE¹ (3) **3** (of a pencil) having a soft centre and producing a dark black mark; 2B is softer than B **4** one of the common blood groups

B-2 bomb·er /ˌbiː ˈtuː ˈbɒməʳ‖-ˈbɑː-/ n a STEALTH BOMBER

B-52 /ˌbiː ˈfɪfti ˈtuː/ n a large military aircraft made in the US and used by the US to drop bombs in the Vietnam War and the Gulf War

BA /ˌbiː ˈeɪ/ abbrev. for: **1** Bachelor of Arts; (a title for someone who has) a first university degree: *Susan Potter, BA | He has a BA.* —compare BSc **2** BRITISH AIRWAYS **3** BUENOS AIRES

baa /bɑː/ v **baaed** [I] to make the sound that a sheep or lamb makes —**baa** n

Baa, Baa, Black Sheep /ˌ· · ˈ· ˌ·/ a NURSERY RHYME (=an old song or poem for children):
Baa, baa, black sheep,
Have you any wool?
Yes sir, yes sir,
Three bags full.

Baa·der-Mein·hof gang /ˌbɑːdə ˈmaɪnhɒf ˌgæŋ‖-dər ˈmaɪnhaʊf-/ l the| an extreme left-wing TERRORIST group in W Germany, also called the **Red Army Faction**, who carried out some terrorist acts in W Germany in the 1970s. The group is named after two of its early leaders, Andreas Baader (1943–77) and Ulrike Meinhoff (1934–76).

Ba·bar /ˈbɑːbɑːʳ/ an elephant in stories for children by Jean de Brunhoff

Bab·bage /ˈbæbɪdʒ/, **Charles** (1792–1871) an English MATHEMATICIAN who drew the plans for a machine on which the modern computer is based

bab·ble¹ /ˈbæbəl/ v **1** [I;T] to say or talk quickly and foolishly or in a way that is hard to understand: *She babbled her thanks in a great hurry. | I have no idea what he was babbling on about. | a babbling idiot* **2** [I] to make continuous sounds like water running gently over rounded stones: *a babbling brook* —**bler** n

babble² n [S] **1** a confused sound of many people talking at the same time: *a babble of voices* **2** a sound like that of a stream running gently over rounded stones: *the babble of running water*

babe /beɪb/ n **1** lit a baby: *a babe in arms* (=that needs to be carried) **2** AmE infml (used for addressing a usu. young woman): *Hi, babe.* **3 babe in the woods** AmE a person who can be easily deceived; a NAIVE person: *Many people are like babes in the woods when it comes to insurance scams.*

ba·bel /ˈbeɪbəl‖ˈbeɪ-, ˈbæ-/ n [S;U] a scene of confusion, disorder, and the noise of many voices (from story of the Tower of Babel in the Bible): *a Babel of French, German and Italian voices* —see also TOWER OF BABEL

Babes in the Wood /ˌ· · · ˈ·/ an old story about a young brother and sister (the babes) who are left in a wood by their wicked uncle who wants their property. The children die and are covered with leaves by a bird. Soon after the uncle loses his own sons and his goods, and finally dies.

ba·boon /bəˈbuːn‖bæ-/ n a large monkey of Africa or S Asia

ba·bu, baboo /ˈbɑːbuː/ n IndE **1** usu. derog an Indian clerk **2** (used esp. formerly as a Hindu title, like Mr)

ba·by¹ /ˈbeɪbi/ n **1** a very young child, esp. one who has not yet learnt to speak or walk: *a newborn baby | a baby girl | a three-month-old baby | My sister is expecting a baby.* (=is PREGNANT) —see CHILD (USAGE) **2** a very young animal or bird: *a baby monkey* **3** the youngest or smallest of a group: *My brother Peter is still at college; he's the baby of our family.* **4** usu. derog a person who

behaves like a baby: *Don't be such a baby! Take your medicine.* **5** infml something that is the special responsibility of a particular person: *Don't ask me about the building contract – that's Robert's baby.* **6** AmE infml a person, esp. a girl or woman **7 throw the baby out with the ˈbath water** to lose the most important part of something when getting rid of the bad or unwanted part

baby² v [T] infml to treat like a baby; give a great deal of care or attention to; MOLLYCODDLE: *babying his old car*

baby blues /ˈ·· ˌ·/ n [the+P] infml for POSTNATAL DEPRESSION: *an attack of the baby blues*

baby-boom /ˈ·· ·/ n a period when there is a large increase in the number of babies born, esp. the period after the SECOND WORLD WAR: *the baby-boom of the 1950s*

baby-boom·er /ˈ·· ˌ··/ n a person born during a baby-boom, esp. during the 1950s

baby bounc·er /ˈ·· ˌ··/ n a seat hanging from springs fixed to a frame in which a baby can stand with feet touching the floor and legs taking part of the body weight

baby car·riage /ˈ·· ˌ··/ also **baby buggy**– n AmE for PRAM

Ba·by·cham /ˈbeɪbiʃæm/ n [C;U] BrE, tdmk a sweet, SPARKLING, alcoholic drink which comes in a small bottle. It is usu. considered to be a woman's drink.

baby grand /ˌ·· ˈ·/ n infml a small GRAND PIANO (a piano with its strings set parallel to the ground, not up and down): *They have a baby grand in their living room.*

Ba·by·gro /ˈbeɪbigrəʊ/ also **babystretch ‖ stretch coveralls** AmE– n tdmk a piece of clothing for a baby made of stretchy material which covers the body, arms, legs, and feet

ba·by·hood /ˈbeɪbihʊd/ n [U] the period of time when one is a baby

ba·by·ish /ˈbeɪbi-ɪʃ/ adj derog (esp. of someone who is not a baby) like a baby: *It's babyish to cry about having a tooth out at your age!*

Bab·y·lon /ˈbæbɪlən, -lɒn‖-lɑːn/ an ancient city and capital of the **Babylonian Empire**, sometimes mentioned as an example of a city which valued pleasure and LUXURY above all else

baby milk /ˈ·· ·/ n [U] dried milk which is mixed with water and fed to babies instead of breast milk

baby-mind·er /ˈ·· ˌ··/ n BrE someone who looks after other people's babies, usu. when both parents are at work — compare BABY-SITTER

baby's breath /ˌ·· ˈ·/ also **babies' breath**– n [U] a plant with many small white or pink flowers, often dried and used in groups of cut flowers (BOUQUETS) and at weddings

baby-sit /ˈ·· ·/ also **sit** AmE– v **-sat**, present participle **-tt-** [I (for)] to act as a baby-sitter

baby-sit·ter /ˈ·· ˌ··/ also **sitter**– n **1** a person who takes care of babies or children while their parents are out, esp. in the evening. A baby-sitter is usu. paid. —compare BABY-MINDER **2** AmE for CHILDMINDER

ba·by·stretch /ˈbeɪbiˌstretʃ/ n a BABYGRO

baby talk /ˈ·· ·/ n [U] **1** the speechlike sounds made by babies when they are learning to talk **2** the way adults sometimes talk to babies, often repeating words or sounds or using words with no meaning

baby tooth /ˈ·· ·/ n AmE for MILK TOOTH

ba·by·walk·er /ˈbeɪbiwɔːkəʳ/ n a WALKER (2)

Ba·call /bəˈkɔːl/, **Lau·ren** /ˈlɔːrən/ (1924–) an American actress who made films with Humphrey Bogart, such as *The Big Sleep*, and married him in 1945

Ba·car·di /bəˈkɑːdi‖-ɑːr-/ n [C;U] tdmk a type of white RUM

bac·ca·lau·re·ate /ˌbækəˈlɔːriət/ n fml for BACHELOR'S DEGREE

bac·ca·rat, -ra /ˈbækərɑː‖ˌbækəˈrɑː/ n [U] a card game usu. played for money

bac·cha·nal /ˌbækəˈnæl, ˈbækənəl/ n esp. lit a noisy party with a lot of drinking and disorderly behaviour, perhaps including sex —see also BACCHUS – **~ian** /ˌbækəˈneɪliən◂/ adj

Bac·chus /ˈbækəs/ in CLASSICAL MYTHOLOGY, the god of wine, fertility (FERTILE), and REVELRY, also known by his Greek name Dionysus. He is usu. connected with drunkenness and wild drunken behaviour, esp. involving sex —see also BACCHANAL

bac·cy /ˈbæki/ n [U] sl tobacco

bach /bætʃ/ v [I] AmE infml (of a man) to cook, keep house, etc. without the help or presence of a woman; to live as a BACHELOR (1): He's baching while his wife is in the hospital.

Bach /bɑːk; bɑːx/, **Jo·hann Se·bas·ti·an** /ˈjəuhæn səˈbæstiən‖ˈhɑːn-/ (1685–1750) a German musician and COMPOSER, one of the best known and most admired of all time, well-known for his ORGAN music

Bach, P.D.Q. see Peter SCHICKELE

Bach·a·rach /ˈbækəræk/, **Burt** /bɜːt‖bɜːrt/ (1929–) an American songwriter whose music has been recorded by many different singers, and is esp. enjoyed by older people

bach·e·lor /ˈbætʃələʳ/ n **1** an unmarried man: He's a **confirmed bachelor**. (=He's unlikely to get married.) | an **eligible bachelor** (=who is regarded as very suitable to be chosen as a husband) | a bachelor flat —compare SPINSTER

▶ CULTURAL NOTE It is socially acceptable for a man to be unmarried in Western society, esp. if he is young and enjoying his life before getting married. If he is older, people may think he is HOMOSEXUAL. People do not feel sorry for unmarried men, but they do sometimes feel sorry for unmarried women.

◀**2** (often cap.) a person, male or female, who has a bachelor's degree: a Bachelor of Arts | a Bachelor of Science

bachelor's de·gree /ˈ··· ·ˌ·/ also **bachelor's** n a first university degree —see also BA, BSC

ba·cil·lus /bəˈsɪləs/ n -cilli /ˈsɪlaɪ/ tech any of several kinds of rod-shaped bacteria, some of which carry disease

back¹ /bæk/ n **1** the part of a person's or animal's body that is the side opposite the chest, and goes from the neck to the bottom of the SPINE or the tail: She was carrying the baby on her back. | You'll make your back ache if you carry those heavy buckets. | He was (**flat**) **on his back** (=ill in bed) for three months. **2** [(of) usu. sing.] the part furthest from the direction that something moves in or faces: Sit at the back of the aircraft. | The back of the house looks out onto the river. | He wrote "Just Married" on the back of their car. | Three people can sit in the back of this car. (=in the seats behind the driver) | There's a garden **at the back of**|(AmE) **in back of** the house. (=behind it) | (fig.) It was **at the back of** my mind that I had to phone you, but I completely forgot. **3** [(of) usu. sing.] the less important side or surface of something: She scribbled some notes on the back of an envelope. | The back of the knife won't cut. —compare BACKSIDE **4** [(of)] the part of a chair that one leans against when sitting **5** [(of) usu. sing.] the end of a book or newspaper: There is a lot of useful information at the back of the dictionary. **6** (in games like football) one of the defending players in a team —compare FORWARD⁵, CENTRE¹ (5) **7 at one's back** supporting one: Caesar marched into Rome with an army at his back. **8 back to back: a** with the backs facing each other: Stand back to back and we'll see which of you is taller. **b** esp. AmE happening one after the other: two football games played back to back **9 back to front:** BrE **a** in such a way that the back and front are opposite in position: You've got your sweater on back to front. **b** thoroughly: She knows the system back to front. **10 behind someone's back** unknown to the person concerned: This decision was taken behind my back. **11 get off someone's back** infml to stop putting unwanted pressure on someone to do something: I wish the boss would get off my back and let me do the job in my own way. **12 have/with one's back to the wall** infml (to be) in a position of great difficulty: With the continuing fall in demand, the steel producers really have their backs to the wall. **13 know somewhere like the back of one's hand** infml to know somewhere very well: She knows New York like the back of her hand. **14 put one's back into** to work very hard at: If we really put our backs into the job we can finish it today. **15 put someone's back up** infml to annoy someone **16 turn one's back on** to avoid or refuse to help, esp. unfairly or unkindly: He's always been kind to me – I can't just turn my back on him now that he needs my help. —see also BACK OF BEYOND, SHORT BACK AND SIDES, **break the back of** (BREAK¹ (22)), **see the back of** (SEE¹ (24)), **the straw that breaks the camel's back** (STRAW) and see picture at HORSE – ~ **less** adj : a backless swimming costume

back² adv **1** in or into the place or position where someone or something was before: Put the book back on the shelf when you've finished it. | Back in Nigeria (where I come from) we used to play a lot of tennis. | She came back to get the box that she'd left behind. | I bought a paper on the way back from school. | I came out of the mosque and put my shoes back on. | She was away for three weeks but she's back at work now. | (fig.) Hats are back in fashion/are coming back into fashion. **2** towards or at the back; away from the front: Sit well back or you won't be able to fasten your seat belt. | The police kept the crowd back as the President's car passed. **3** away from the speaker: Stand back! This dog bites. **4** towards or in an earlier time: We met him three years back/back in 1980.| to put the clock back (=so that it shows an earlier time) | She's been working there as far back as I can remember. | Looking back on it, it was a mistake. **5** in return; in reply: Phone me back when you know the answer. | I'll **pay her back** for her rudeness! **6** towards the beginning of a book: There's a picture six pages further back. **7** so as to be delayed or made slower: His bad health has **kept/held him back** at school.

back³ adj [A] **1** at the back: the back yard/garden | the back wheel of a bicycle —see also BACK DOOR, BACK BURNER **2** of or from the past: back pay/back rent (=money owed from an earlier time) | a **back number**/back copy/back **issue** of a magazine (=not the most recent one) **3** tech (of a vowel sound) made by raising the tongue at the back of the mouth —opposite **front**

back⁴ v **1** [I;T] to (cause to) go backwards: She backed the car through the gate/into the parking space. **2** [T] to support and encourage, often with money; provide BACKING for: The bank refused to back the scheme. | The union leaders decided to back the Government in its action. | The American-backed rebel forces (=who are supported by the Americans) **3** [T] to put money on the success of (a horse, dog, etc. in a race); BET on: Jane backed the winner and won £5. **4** [T (**with**)] to provide with a back or LINING: curtains backed with a plastic material **5** [I] tech (of the wind) to change direction, moving round the COMPASS in the order North–West–South–East —compare VEER (2) **6 back the wrong horse** to support the loser

back away also **back off** AmE– phr v [I (**from**)] to move away or back because of fear or dislike: The dog backed away as the man raised his stick. | (fig.) The government has backed away from radical reshaping of the tax system.

back down phr v [I (**over, on**)] to accept defeat in an argument, opinion, or claim; admit that one was wrong: I saw that she was right, so I had to back down.

back off phr v [I] AmE to stop trying to make (someone) do or think (something): I saw I was upsetting her so I backed off. | Just back off and leave me alone!

back onto sthg. phr v [T] (of a place or building) to be near to or have at the back: The house backs onto the river.

back out phr v [I (**from, of**)] to fail to fulfil a promise, contract, etc.: I hope I can depend on you not to back out at the last moment.

back sbdy./sthg. **up** phr v **1** [T] to support, esp. in an argument: The policeman wouldn't have believed me if you hadn't backed me up. **2** [I;T] to make a copy of (a DISK): Make sure you back up (the disk) before you turn the computer off. —see also BACKUP

back·ache /ˈbækeɪk/ n [C;U] (a) pain in the back: suffering from (a) backache —see ACHE² (USAGE)

back·bench /ˌbækˈbentʃ◂/ n any of the seats in the British parliament on which members who do not hold an official position in the government or opposition may sit: the Tory backbenches | backbench support/rebellion – compare FRONTBENCH

back·bench·er /ˌbækˈbentʃəʳ◂/ n a member of the British parliament who does not hold an official position in the government or opposition, and who sits on one of the back seats: angry backbenchers —compare FRONTBENCHER

back·bit·ing /ˈbækbaɪtɪŋ/ n [U] unkind and unpleasant talk about someone who is absent: I didn't enjoy working there – there was too much backbiting. —**-er** n

back·board /ˈbækbɔːd‖-bɔːrd/ n (in BASKETBALL) the board behind the basket

back·bone /ˈbækbəʊn/ n **1** [C] the row of bones in the centre of a person's or animal's back; SPINE **2** [the (**of**)] the part of a group, organization, etc. that provides the main support: The small farmers form the backbone of *the country's economy.*   **3** [U] firmness of mind; strength of character: *"No backbone," said the old general. "That's the trouble with young people today!"*

back·break·ing /ˈbækbreɪkɪŋ/ *adj* (of work) very hard and heavy: *a backbreaking job*

back burn·er /ˌ· ˈ··/ *n infml* **on the back burner** left to be dealt with later: *We put the Thompson project on the back burner while we rushed to meet the deadline on the Italo contract.*

back·chat /ˈbæktʃæt/ *BrE* ‖ **back talk** *AmE*— *n* [U] rude talk in reply to someone: *Just listen to me! I don't want any backchat!*

back·cloth /ˈbæk-klɒθ‖-klɔːθ/ *n BrE for* BACKDROP

back·comb /ˈbæk-kəʊm/ *v* [T] to comb (hair) against the direction of growth, in order to make it look thicker

back coun·try /ˈ· ˌ··/ *n [the]* **1** *esp. AustrE* a country area where few people live **2** *AmE* an area, esp. in the mountains, away from roads and towns: *hiking in the back country of Yosemite National Park*

back·date /ˌbækˈdeɪt‖ˈbækdeɪt/ *v* [T (**to**)] to make effective from an earlier date: *The pay increase agreed in June will be backdated to January.* —compare ANTEDATE, POSTDATE

back door /ˌ· ˈ·/ *n* **1** a door at the back or side of a building **2 get in through/by the back door** to get a job, a place in a university, etc. through having some unfair advantage

back·drop /ˈbækdrɒp‖-drɑːp/ also **backcloth** *BrE*— *n* **1** a painted cloth hung across the back of a stage **2** the conditions in which something happens; BACKGROUND: *The stormy political events of the 1930s provided the backdrop for the film.*

back·er /ˈbækəʳ/ *n* **1** someone who supports a plan, esp. with money: *We'll stage the play as soon as we've found a backer.* **2** someone who BACKs[4] (3) a horse

back·fire /ˌbækˈfaɪəʳ‖ˈbækfaɪəʳ/ *v* [I] **1** (of a motor vehicle) to make a loud noise because the explosion in the engine comes too soon **2** [(**on**)] to have an unexpected effect opposite to the effect intended: *His plan backfired (on him), and he lost all his money.*

back for·ma·tion /ˈ· ˌ··/ *n tech* a word formed from another word that seems to be formed from it, esp. by removing a SUFFIX: *The verb "televise" is a back formation from "television".*

back·gam·mon /ˈbækgæmən/ *n* [U] an indoor game for two players, using round wooden pieces and DICE on a special board

back·ground /ˈbækgraʊnd/ *n* **1** [C] the scenery or space behind the main objects or people in a view, a picture, or a photograph: *The mountains form a background to this photograph of the family.* | (fig.) *She has a lot of power, but likes to remain* **in the background.** (=as unnoticeable as possible) —compare FOREGROUND **2** [C;U] the conditions that exist when something happens, and that help to explain it. *The riots took place* **against a background of** *widespread unemployment.* | *You'll have to give me a bit more background (information) before I can help you.* **3** [C] a person's family, social class, experience, and education: *She has a background in child psychology.* | *children from disadvantaged backgrounds*

back·hand /ˈbækhænd/ *n* (in games such as tennis) (the ability to make) a stroke with the back of the hand turned in the direction of movement: *He's got an excellent backhand.* —compare FOREHAND —**backhand** *adj, adv: He returned it backhand.*

back·hand·ed /ˌbækˈhændɪd◄‖ˈbækhændɪd/ *adj* **1** using or made with a backhand **2** (of a remark) indirect, esp. SARCASTIC: *a backhanded compliment* —**backhanded** *adv*

back·hand·er /ˈbækhændəʳ/ *n* **1** a backhanded blow or stroke **2** *BrE infml* a BRIBE

back·ing /ˈbækɪŋ/ *n* **1** [U] help or support, esp. with money: *He's won the backing of the Congress for his scheme.* **2** [C;U] something that is used to make the back of an object: *(a) backing of cardboard* **3** [C] the musical ACCOMPANIMENT that supports a singer or musician

back·lash /ˈbæklæʃ/ *n* **1** [(**against**)] a strong but usu. delayed feeling of opposition among many people towards a belief or practice, esp. towards a political or social development: *The continual rise in violent crime eventually provoked a backlash against the liberal gun-control laws.* **2** a sudden backward movement

back·log /ˈbæklɒg‖-lɔːg, -lɑːg/ *n* [usu. sing.] a number of jobs that have to be done that were not done at the proper time: *a backlog of work after the holidays*

back num·ber /ˌ· ˈ··/ *n* a newspaper, magazine, etc. that is out of date, but may still be interesting or valuable — see also BACK[3] (2)

back of be·yond /ˌ· · · ·ˈ·/ *n [the] infml, esp. BrE* a very distant place which is difficult to get to: *They live on a farm somewhere at/in the back of beyond.*

back·pack[1] /ˈbækpæk/ *n esp. AmE* a RUCKSACK carried on one's back, often supported by a light metal frame, used by climbers and walkers or for carrying a baby or small child — ~ **er** *n*

backpack[2] *v* [I] *AmE* to walk and camp overnight carrying a backpack: *They went backpacking along the Appalachian Trail.*

back pas·sage /ˌ· ˈ··/ *n euph for* RECTUM

back·ped·al /ˌbækˈpedl‖ˈbækˌpedl/ *v* -ll- *BrE* ‖ -l- *AmE* [I] **1** to PEDAL backwards on a bicycle **2** *infml* to change an earlier principle or draw back from some promised action: *They promised to cut taxes, but they're beginning to backpedal now.*

back·room boy /ˈbækrʊm ˌbɔɪ, -ruːm-/ *n [often pl.] infml, esp. BrE* a person whose work is important but who does not receive recognition from the public, often because they are working to support someone else: *Engineers are often seen as the backroom boys of British industry.*

back seat /ˌ· ˈ·◄/ *n* **1** [C] a seat at the back of a car, behind where the driver sits **2** [S] a less important position: *After five years as a director, she's decided to* **take a back seat.**

back-seat dri·ver /ˌ· · ˈ··/ *n* a passenger in a motor vehicle who gives unwanted advice to the driver about how to drive: (fig.) *Mrs Thatcher promised that she wouldn't be a back-seat driver in the House of Commons.*

back·side /ˈbæksaɪd/ *n infml* the part of the body on which one sits —compare BACK[1] (3)

back·slap·ping /ˈbækslæpɪŋ/ *n* [U] (too much) noisy cheerfulness, showing admiration for one's own success: *The cast indulged in a great deal of backslapping when the show became an overnight success.* —**per** *n*

back·slide /ˌbækˈslaɪd‖ˈbækslaɪd/ *v* [I] to become less good, work less hard, etc., and esp. to go back to a worse condition after some improvement: *I managed to keep off cigarettes for two months, but recently I'm afraid I've begun to backslide.* —**slider** *n*

back·space /ˈbækspeɪs/ *n* [usu. sing.] the part that one presses to make the movable part of a TYPEWRITER move back one or more spaces towards the beginning of the line

back·spin /ˈbækspɪn/ *n* [U] turning movement given to a ball in such a way that it turns in the opposite direction to which it is being moved forward

back·stage /ˌbækˈsteɪdʒ/ *adv* **1** behind the stage in a theatre, esp. in(to) the dressing rooms of the actors: *After the performance we were invited backstage.* **2** in private; not seen publicly; secretly: *That's what they say, but who knows what really goes on backstage?* —**backstage** /ˈbæksteɪdʒ/ *adj* [A] : *backstage workers*

back·stairs /ˈbæksteəz‖-steərz/ *adj* [A] secret and perhaps unfair: *backstairs influence*

back street /ˈ· ·/ *n [usu. pl.]* a street away from the main streets, esp. in a poor area of a town —compare SIDE STREET

back-street a·bor·tion /ˌ· · · ·ˈ··/ also **back-al·ley abortion** *AmE* /ˌ· · ·ˈ··/— *n* an ABORTION performed illegally, usu. in poor, dirty conditions. People who are in favour of legal abortions often argue that if abortions are made illegal again, as they were in the past, there will be a return to back-street abortions.

back·stroke /ˈbækstrəʊk/ *n [(the)* S] a way of swimming on one's back by moving first one arm and then the other backwards while kicking the feet

back·swing /ˈbækswɪŋ/ *n* the movement of a CLUB, BAT, etc. backwards to a position from which the forward or downward swing is made

back talk /ˈ· ·/ *n* [U] *esp. AmE for* BACKCHAT

back-to-back /ˌ· · ·ˈ·◄/ *n BrE* a house in a row (=TERRACE) built with its back against the back of a house in a parallel row. This kind of house was once typical of industrial towns in the north of England.

back·track /ˈbæktræk/ v [I] **1** to go back over the same path **2** to draw back from a former position, promise, etc.; BACKPEDAL (2): *The government is already backtracking from its more expensive plans.*

back·up /ˈbækʌp/ n [C;U] a thing or person ready to be used in place of or to help another: *We won't be able to do it unless we have a lot of technical backup.* | *We have a backup computer in case the main one breaks down.* —see also BACK⁴ **up**

back·ward /ˈbækwəd‖-wərd/ adj **1** [A] directed towards the back, the beginning, or the past: *a backward glance* **2** late in development: *a backward child* | *Some backward parts of the country have no electricity.* —compare FORWARD² – ~ **ly** adv – ~ **ness** n [U]

back·ward·a·tion /ˌbækwəˈdeɪʃən‖-wər-/ n [U] BrE, tech the money paid by someone selling STOCK for the right to delay delivery until the following account —compare CONTANGO

back·wards /ˈbækwədz‖-wərdz/ also **backward** AmE— adv **1** towards the back, the beginning, or the past: *I walked backwards down the stairs, carrying the heavy box.* | *Can you say the alphabet backwards?* (=from Z to A) **2** with the back part in front: *to walk backwards* | *You've put your hat on backwards.* **3** towards a worse state: *The new measures are seen by some as a major step backwards.* **4 backwards and forwards** first in one direction and then in the opposite direction **5 bend/lean over backwards** to try as hard as possible to help or please someone: *We bent over backwards to help them.* **6 know something backwards** BrE ‖ **know something backwards and forwards** AmE to know something perfectly: *All the actors know the play backwards.* —compare FORWARD¹

back·wa·ter /ˈbækwɔːtəʳ‖-wɔː-, -wɑː-/ n **1** a part of a river out of the main stream, where the water does not move **2** *often derog* a place not influenced by outside events or new ideas: *There aren't any good shops in this village, it's a real backwater.* | *a cultural backwater*

back·woods /ˈbækwʊdz/ n [the+sing./pl. v] **1** (esp. in N America) uncleared land far away from towns **2** a distant or backward area

back·woods·man /ˈbækwʊdzmən/ n **-men** /mən/ **1** someone who lives in the backwoods **2** BrE infml a member of the House of Lords who lives in the country and hardly ever attends its meetings

back·yard /ˌbækˈjɑːd◄‖-ˈjɑːrd◄/ n **1** BrE a yard behind a house, covered with a hard surface **2** AmE an area of land behind a house, usu. covered with grass; a back garden: *The children are playing in the backyard.* —see GARDEN **3 not in my backyard** not in or near the place where I live. This phrase is used when discussing new industrial buildings, prisons, or processes which are thought to be harmful to the environment: *When it comes to setting up disposal sites for nuclear waste, the reaction of most people is "not in my backyard!"* —see also NIMBY

ba·con /ˈbeɪkən/ n [U] **1** salted or smoked meat from the back or sides of a pig, often served in narrow thin pieces. Bacon and eggs, cooked together in fat, is thought of as being the typical English breakfast. —compare GAMMON, HAM (1); see MEAT (USAGE) **2 bring home the bacon** infml to succeed, esp. in providing food for one's family —see also **save one's bacon** (SAVE¹)

Bacon, Francis (1909–92) an Irish artist known for his richly coloured paintings with twisted human and animal shapes

Bacon, Sir Francis (1561–1626) an English politician, PHILOSOPHER, and writer. He is known esp. because of the suggestion that he may have written some or all of Shakespeare's plays.

bac·te·ri·a /bækˈtɪəriə/ n sing. **-rium** /riəm/ [P] very small living things related to plants, some of which cause disease; MICROBEs —compare VIRUS —**·rial** adj : *a bacterial infection*

bac·te·ri·ol·o·gy /bækˌtɪəriˈɒlədʒi‖-ˈɑːl-/ n [U] the scientific study of bacteria —**·gist** n

Bac·tri·an /ˈbæktriən/ adj see CAMEL (1b)

bad¹ /bæd/ adj worse /wɜːs‖wɜːrs/, worst /wɜːst‖wɜːrst/ **1** not good; unpleasant, unwanted, or unacceptable: *a very bad performance* (=not of acceptable quality) | *The rain*

has had a very bad (=unfavourable) *effect on the crops.*| *You're a bad* (=disobedient) *boy!* | *bad* (=unpleasant) *news* | *The company's failure was due to bad* (=ineffective) *management.* | *Play in the cricket match was stopped because of bad light.* (=because it was too dark) | *bad* (=incorrect) *grammar* | *I'm rather bad at sums.* (=can't do them very well) | *He's in a bad temper.* (=angry) | *I felt bad* (=ashamed or sorry) *about not being able to come last night.* | *It was bad of him* (=dishonourable) *to change his mind once he had given his promise.* | *He made a very bad job of repairing it.* | *The situation is* **nothing like as bad/nowhere near as bad** (=much less bad) *as the newspapers say it is.* **2** unhealthy or unwell: *She's got a bad heart.* | *My leg's bad again.* (=is hurting) | (*infml*) *He was* **taken bad** (=became ill) *in the middle of the night.* **3** [(**for**)] having a harmful effect on one's health; damaging: *bad eating habits* | *Smoking is bad for you/bad for your health.* **4** serious; severe: *a bad cold* | *a bad defeat* | *a bad case of measles* **5** unfit to eat because of decay; ROTTEN: *bad apples* | *This fish has gone bad.* **6** not suitable; INOPPORTUNE: *The rise in interest rates happened at the worst possible time for the company.* [+to-v] *It was a bad moment to call because they were in the middle of an argument.* **7** AmE sl good **8** (**act**) **in bad faith** (to act) dishonestly; without intending to carry out a promise **9 bad lot/egg/hat/type** old-fash a person of dishonourable character **10 go from bad to worse** to get much worse even than before **11 have/get a bad name** to lose or have lost people's respect; have/get a bad REPUTATION: *Those cars have begun to get a bad name for rust.* **12 in a bad way** very ill or in serious trouble **13 (It's/That's) too bad** infml **a** It is unfortunate (that); I'm sorry: *Too bad you couldn't come last night.* **b** BrE It is very annoying or unreasonable: *They can't just double the price like that – it's too bad!* **14 not bad** infml (often used when a stronger expression of pleasure or approval is really meant) really rather good: *"How are you feeling?" "Not (so) bad."* | *This cake isn't bad.* | *That's not a bad idea!* —see also BADLY, **make the best of a bad job** (JOB) – ~ **ness** n [U]

bad² n **1 go to the bad** to begin living in a wrong or evil way: *He's gone to the bad since he won all that money.* **2 take the bad with the good** to accept not only the good things but also the bad things in life **3 to the bad** in debt by (an amount): *I've spent so much that I'm £100 to the bad this month.*

bad blood /ˌ· ˈ·/ also **bad feel·ing** /ˌ· ˈ··/ n [U (**between**)] angry or bitter feeling; HOSTILITY: *I don't think they'll ever work together again – there's too much bad blood between them.*

bad debt /ˌ· ˈ·/ n a debt that is unlikely to be paid

bad·die, **bad·dy** /ˈbædi/ BrE ‖ **bad guy** AmE— n someone who is bad or an opponent of good people, esp. in books, films, etc.: *He's a real baddie.* | *Look out, the baddies are coming!*

bade /bæd, beɪd/ past tense & participle of BID³

Ba·den-Po·well /ˌbeɪn ˈpəʊəl/, **Lord Rob·ert** /ˈrɒbət‖ ˈrɑːbərt/ (1857–1941) a British GENERAL who became famous in the Boer War and later started the SCOUTs association

Ba·der /ˈbɑːdəʳ/, **Douglas** (1910–82) a British airforce pilot who became famous flying fighter planes in the Battle of Britain, in spite of having lost both his legs in an accident in 1931

bad form /ˌ· ˈ·/ n [U] old-fash BrE socially unacceptable behaviour: *It's bad form to argue with the umpire.*

badge /bædʒ/ n **1** BrE ‖ **button, pin, patch** AmE anything, esp. a small piece of metal or plastic with a picture or words on it, worn to show rank, membership of a group, support for a political idea or belief, etc.: *They were wearing badges that said "Nuclear Power – No thanks!".* | *a school blazer with a badge sewn on it* | *Mayors wear chains round their necks as* **badges of office.** —compare BROOCH; see also BUTTON¹ (3) **2** AmE a small piece of metal with words or pictures on it which shows authority: *a sheriff's badge* | *He had to show me his badge before I would believe he was from the F.B.I.* **3** a small piece of cloth with a picture on it given to SCOUTs, GUIDEs, etc. when they have done certain things to earn it: *I got my photography and music badges today.*

bad·ger¹ /ˈbædʒəʳ/ n **1** [C] an animal which has black and white fur, lives in holes in the ground, and is active at night **2** [U] the skin or hair of this animal

badger² v [T (into)] to (try to) **badger** persuade by asking again and again; PESTER: *The children badgered me into taking them to the cinema.* [+obj+to-v] *They kept badgering him to get a home computer.*

bad guy /ˈ· ˌ·/ n AmE infml BADDIE

bad·i·nage /ˈbædɪnɑːʒ‖ˌbædənˈɑːʒ/ n [U] fml or humor playful joking talk; BANTER: *Enough of this badinage: let's talk seriously.*

bad·lands /ˈbædlændz/ n [P] (in N America) an area of unproductive land with strangely-shaped rocks and hills that have been worn away by the weather

Badlands also **Badlands Na·tion·al Park** /ˌ··· ˌ··· ˈ·/ [the] an area of badlands in S Dakota

bad lan·guage /ˌ· ˈ··/ n [U] language which includes swear words and is likely to offend people: *You won't like that film, it's got a lot of bad language in it.* | *Stop using bad language in front of the children.*

bad·ly /ˈbædli/ adv **worse** /wɜːs‖wɜːrs/, **worst** /wɜːst‖wɜːrst/ **1** in a bad manner: *badly made clothes* | *to play badly* | *badly wounded* | *The company had been badly managed.*| *He felt very badly* (=was very sorry) *about not being able to give more help.* —opposite **well** **2** to a great or serious degree: *My horse was badly beaten in the race.* | *badly wounded* | *It badly needs repainting.* | *He's* **badly in need of** *a haircut.* | *The north of the country is the most badly-affected area/the worst-affected area.*

badly-off /ˌ·· ˈ·/ also **bad-off** AmE– adj **worse-off, worst-off** [F] **1** not having much money; poor: *They're too badly off to have a holiday.* **2** [(for)] not having enough (of something needed); lacking: *The school is rather badly-off for equipment.* —opposite **well-off**

bad·min·ton /ˈbædmɪntən/ n [U] a game like tennis played by two or four people who hit a small feathered object (SHUTTLECOCK) over a high net with a RACKET

Badminton Horse Tri·als /ˌ···· ˈ· ˌ··/ [the] an important British horseriding competition held every year at Badminton House

bad-mouth /ˈ· ·/ v [T] sl, esp. AmE to speak badly of; criticize: *He was bad-mouthing the way the company was run and the boss overheard him.*

bad-off /ˌ· ˈ·/ adj AmE for BADLY-OFF

bad pen·ny /ˌ· ˈ··/ n infml **1** a person or thing that is not liked or wanted but is difficult to avoid **2 turn up like a bad penny** (of a person or thing not liked or wanted) to appear continually: *My ex-boyfriend turns up like a bad penny every time I go out.*

bad-tem·pered /ˌ· ˈ··◂/ adj having a bad or angry state of mind: *He's a bit bad-tempered now, he's just woken up.* see also ANGRY (USAGE)

BAe /ˌbiː eɪ ˈiː/ abbrev for BRITISH AEROSPACE

Bae·dek·er /ˈbeɪdɪkəʳ/ n a travel guide, in a SERIES begun by Karl Baedeker in Germany, used by travellers abroad: *Look it up in Baedeker.* | *Have you got the Baedeker for France?*

Ba·ez /ˈbaɪez/, **Joan** (1941–) an American FOLK singer popular esp. in the 1960s when she opposed the Vietnam War and supported the CIVIL RIGHTS movement in the US. She is known esp. for the song *We Shall Overcome* which is still sung on protest marches and at political meetings.

baf·fle¹ /ˈbæfəl/ v [T] to cause to have difficulty in understanding and confuse so much that effective action is impossible; BEWILDER: *The question baffled me completely.*| *The police admitted that they were completely baffled (by the lack of evidence).* – **–ment** n [U] **—fling** adj

baffle² n tech a board, sheet of metal, etc., that controls the flow of air, water, or sound into or out of an enclosed space

Baf·ta /ˈbæftə/ n a prize given for films and television programmes in Britain: *It won two Baftas.* | *the Bafta award ceremony*

bag¹ /bæg/ n **1 a** a container made of soft material which

usu. opens at the top: *a shopping bag* | *a golf bag* | *a paper/polythene bag* **b** a small bag used esp. by a woman for her personal things; HANDBAG: *Don't leave your bag in the office when you go to lunch.* **c** a bag used by someone travelling; piece of LUGGAGE: *to pack one's bags* **2** [(of)] also **bag·ful** /-fʊl/ (pl. **bagfuls, bagsful**)– the amount a bag will hold: *a bag of sweets* | *two bags of rice* **3** derog an unpleasant or unattractive woman; BAGGAGE (4): *You silly old bag!* **4** [usu. sing.] the number of birds or animals shot or caught on any one occasion: *We had a good bag that day.* **5 bag and baggage** with all one's belongings: *They threw her out of the house bag and baggage.* **6 bag of bones** a very thin person or animal **7 in the bag** infml certain to be won, gained, etc.: *We're sure to win. The match is in the bag.* **8 one's bag** infml something one particularly likes, is good at, or has special knowledge about: *I'm afraid I can't tell you anything about it – computers aren't really my bag.* **9 pull something out of the bag** to succeed by making an effort at a late stage: *He was exhausted but still managed to pull something out of the bag to win the race.* —see also BAGS, MIXED BAG, SLEEPING BAG, **let the cat out of the bag** (CAT), **be left holding the bag** (HOLD¹)

bag² v **-gg- 1** [T] to put (material or objects in large quantities) into a bag or bags **2** [T] to kill or catch (animals or birds): *We bagged a rabbit.* **3** [T] infml to take possession of: *Try to bag a couple of seats at the back for us.* **4** [I (OUT)] infml to hang loosely, like a bag: *His trousers bagged (out) at the knees.*

bag·a·telle /ˌbægəˈtel/ n **1** [U] a game played on a board with holes in which balls must be put **2** [S] something considered to be small and unimportant; TRIFLE: *It cost about £25,* **a mere bagatelle** *for someone as rich as her.*

ba·gel /ˈbeɪgəl/ n a ring-shaped bread ROLL, typical of Jewish cooking

bag·gage /ˈbægɪdʒ/ n **1** [U] esp. AmE the cases, bags, boxes, etc. of a traveller; LUGGAGE: *to see one's baggage through customs at the airport* | *a baggage check* **2** [U] the tents, beds, and other equipment of an army **3** [C] old-fash humor a good-for-nothing young woman; MINX **4** [C] infml an unpleasant or annoying old woman – see also **bag and baggage** (BAG¹ (5))

baggage car /ˈ·· ˌ·/ n AmE for LUGGAGE VAN

baggage room /ˈ·· ·/ n AmE for LEFT LUGGAGE OFFICE

Bag·gie /ˈbægi/ n AmE tdmk a small plastic bag used esp. to keep food in

Bag·gins /ˈbægɪnz/, **Bil·bo** /ˈbɪlbəʊ/ an imaginary creature (HOBBIT) who is the main character in the story *The Hobbit* by JRR Tolkien

bag·gy /ˈbægi/ adj infml hanging in loose folds; not tight: *His trousers were baggy at the knees.*

Bagh·dad /ˌbægˈdæd‖ˈbægdæd/ the capital city of Iraq

bag la·dy /ˈ· ˌ··/ n a homeless woman who walks around carrying all her possessions with her; female TRAMP

bag·pipes /ˈbægpaɪps/ also **pipes** infml– n [(the) P] a musical instrument played esp. in Scotland in which air stored in a bag is forced out through pipes to produce the sound: *to play the bagpipes* —see colour map on page 818 **—bagpipe** adj [A] : *bagpipe music*

bags¹ /bægz/ n [P+of] infml, esp. BrE lots; plenty: *She's got bags of money!* | *We've got bags of time.*

bags² n [P] BrE old-fash trousers, esp. loose-fitting trousers

bags³ interj BrE sl **Bags I!** (used by children) **a** Let me have it, not you: *Bags I the biggest one!* **b** I'll do it, not you: *Bags I sleep in the bathroom!*

ba·guette /bæˈget/ n a long, **baguette** thin French loaf

bah /bɑː/ interj (used to show disapproval or a low opinion of someone or something)

Ba·ha'i Faith /bəˌhaɪ ˈfeɪθ/ n [U] (members of) a religion which believes that all people should act peacefully as brothers and ignore differences of race and religion

Ba·ha·mas /bəˈhɑːməz/ [the+P] a country consisting of a group of islands in the Atlantic, SE of Florida. It is a popular centre for tourism – **Bahamian** /bəˈheɪmiən/ n, adj

Bah·rain , Bahrein /bɑːˈreɪn/ a country and group of islands in the Gulf off the coast of Arabia; capital Manama; population 489,000 (1989).Bahrain produces oil and is an important financial centre — **raini** *n*, *adj*

bail¹ /beɪl/ *n* [U] **1** money left with a court of law so that a prisoner can be set free until he/she is tried. If the prisoner returns to be tried, the money is returned: *She was* **released on bail** *of £5000.* | *The judge refused to* **grant him bail.** (=to allow him to be set free in this way) **2 stand/put up/go bail for someone** to pay money so that someone can be set free in this way **3 jump bail** to not come back for trial after bail has been paid

bail² *v*
bail out *phr v* **1** [T] (**bail** sbdy. ↔ **out**) to obtain freedom for (someone) by paying bail to make sure they appear in court at a future date: *Clark was charged with robbing the bank, so his family paid £500 to bail him out.* **2** [I;T] (=**bail** sthg. ↔ **out**) also **bale out** *BrE*— to remove water from (a boat): *When the storm rose on the lake, we had to bail out to reach the shore safely.* **3** [T] (**bail** sbdy./sthg. ↔ **out**) to help (esp. a business) out of difficulties by providing money: *The government can't expect the taxpayer to bail this company out indefinitely.* —see also BAIL-OUT **4** [I] **a** *AmE for* BALE **out** (1) **b** *AmE sl* to leave quickly, esp. because of danger or fear: *When we heard that weird moan, we bailed out of there as fast as we could.*

bail³ *n* (in cricket) either of two small pieces of wood laid on top of the STUMPS —see picture at CRICKET

bai·ley /ˈbeɪli/ *n* an open area (COURTYARD) inside the outer wall of a castle

Bai·ley's /ˈbeɪliz/ *n* [U] *tdmk* a strong, sweet alcoholic drink made of Irish WHISKEY mixed with cream, usu. drunk from a small glass after a meal

bail hos·tel /ˈ· ˌ··/ *n* a place in Britain with unpaid managers, which provides temporary housing and support for people on PROBATION or BAIL —compare PROBATION HOSTEL

bai·liff /ˈbeɪlɪf/ *n* **1** (in British law) an official who takes possession of a person's goods or property when they owe money, esp. for their rent **2** (in US law) an official who watches prisoners and keeps order in a court of law **3** *BrE* a person who looks after a farm or land for the owner

bail-out /ˈ· ·/ *n* help given, esp. financially, to a company which is in difficulty: *The director was hoping for a bailout to save the company.*

Bain·bridge /ˈbeɪnbrɪdʒ/, **Beryl** (1934–) an English writer, best known for her NOVELs *The Dressmaker* and *The Bottle Factory Outing*

Baird /beəd‖beərd/, **John Lo·gie** /dʒɒn ˈləʊgi‖dʒɑːn-/ (1888– 1946) a Scottish engineer who invented a television system

bairn /beən‖beərn/ *n ScotE & N EngE* a child

bait¹ /beɪt/ *n* [S;U] food or something like food used to attract fish, animals, or birds which are then caught: *fishing bait* | (fig.) *The shop used free gifts as a bait to attract new customers.* | (fig.) *She made some nasty remarks about his lack of experience, but he didn't* **rise to the bait.** (=he refused to get angry)

bait² *v* [T] **1** (**with**) to put bait on (a hook) to catch fish, or in (a trap) to catch animals: *to bait a mousetrap with cheese* **2** to try intentionally to make (someone) angry; TORMENT: *At school they baited him mercilessly because of his strange clothes.*

baize /beɪz/ *n* [U] thick woollen cloth, usu. green, used esp. to cover tables on which certain games (e.g. BILLIARDS) are played

Ba·ja Cal·i·for·ni·a /ˌbɑːhɑː kælɪˈfɔːniə‖-ˈfɔːrnjə/ also **Baja** a PENINSULA (=long finger of land) in Mexico that lies S of California and has several holiday towns

bake /beɪk/ *v* **1** [I;T] to (cause to) cook using dry heat in an OVEN: *to bake bread* | *The bread is baking.* | *baked potatoes in their jackets* (=with the skin on) —see COOK (USAGE) **2** [I;T] to (cause to) become hard by heating: *In former times, bricks were baked in the sun.* **3** [I] *infml* to be or become uncomfortably hot: *Open a window — I'm baking!It's baking in here!* —see also HALF-BAKED

baked A·las·ka /ˌ· ·ˈ··/ *n* [C;U] a sweet dish consisting of ice cream covered with MERINGUE, which is baked at a high temperature for a short time

baked beans /ˌ· ˈ·/ *n* [P] **1** in Britain, baked HARICOT BEANS (=a kind of white bean) in a TOMATO SAUCE, sold in tins. Baked beans are a favourite food of many children in Britain. **2** also **Boston baked beans** *AmE* in the US, beans cooked with PORK and brown sugar

Ba·ke·lite /ˈbeɪkəlaɪt/ *n* [U] *tdmk* any of a number of related RESINS (2), best known for being used to make the older type of telephones and radio sets

bak·er /ˈbeɪkəʳ/ *n* a person who bakes bread and cakes, esp. in order to sell them in a shop (**baker's**): *I bought these buns at the baker's (shop).*

Baker, James (1930–) an American Republican politician who was made Secretary of State under President Bush in 1989

Baker, Dame Jan·et /ˈdʒænɪt/ (1933–) an English OPERA singer

Baker, Ken·neth /ˈkenɪθ/ (1934–) a British Conservative politician

Baker, Richard (1925–) a British broadcaster and writer whose main interest is classical music, but who was formerly a television news reader

Baker day /ˈ·· ·/ *n infml* (in Britain) one of a number of days during the usual school year when teachers receive training and children do not attend school

baker's doz·en /ˌ·· ˈ··/ *n* [S] *old-fash* 13

Baker Street /ˈ·· ·/ a street in London where the DETECTIVE Sherlock Holmes lived in the stories about him by Arthur Conan Doyle —see colour map on page 817

bak·er·y /ˈbeɪkəri/ *n* a place where bread and sometimes cakes are baked and/or sold

Bake·well tart /ˌbeɪkwel ˈtɑːt‖-ˈtɑːrt/ *n* [C;U] a pastry TART filled with JAM and covered with a PASTE containing ALMONDS

bak·ing pow·der /ˈ·· ˌ··/ *n* [U] a powder used in baking cakes, etc. to make them light

baking sheet /ˈ·· ·/ *n AmE* a flat metal pan used for baking BISCUITS

baking so·da /ˈ·· ˌ··/ *n* [U] BICARBONATE

Bak·ke Case /ˈbɑːki keɪs/ [*the*] a legal case taken to the US Supreme Court which decided that a university could not refuse a student only because the university wanted to give a place to another student of a different RACE³. —see also AFFIRMATIVE ACTION, REVERSE DISCRIMINATION

Bak·ker /ˈbeɪkəʳ/, **James (Jim** /dʒɪm/) an American religious leader who ran a popular religious television show but admitted having sex with a PROSTITUTE and in 1989 was found guilty of misusing money given by the people who watched his programme

ba·kla·va /ˈbɑːkləvɑː/ *n* [U] a sweet food from the Middle East made from FILO PASTRY, nuts, and HONEY or SYRUP. Baklava is usu. TRIANGLE-shaped

Bal·a /ˈbælə/ a small town in NW Wales, at the NE end of **Bala Lake** (Llyn Tegid), the largest natural lake in Wales

bal·a·cla·va /ˌbæləˈklɑːvə◂/ *n* a warm woollen head covering that leaves the face free but covers the head, ears, and neck

bal·a·lai·ka /ˌbæləˈlaɪkə/ *n* a stringed musical instrument with a three-sided body, played esp. in Russia

bal·ance¹ /ˈbæləns/ *n* **1** [S;U] a state in which all weights and forces are evenly spread, so as to produce a condition of steadiness; EQUILIBRIUM: *I found it hard to* **keep my balance** *on the icy path.* | *He* **lost his balance** *and fell off his bicycle.* **2** [S;U] a state in which opposite or competing influences are evenly matched or are given equal importance: *We try to* **strike a balance** *between justice and mercy.* | *a new weapon that may upset the nuclear balance between the two superpowers* | *good reporting that covers the news with fairness and balance* —opposite **imbalance 3** [U] steadiness of the mind or feelings: *She temporarily lost her balance during the long months of solitude.* **4** [C (**to**)] a force or influence on one side which equals a force or influence on the other; COUNTERBALANCE: *They work well together — her steadiness acts as a balance to his clever but often impractical ideas.* **5** [*the*] the weight, force, or amount that is more on one side than another: *The balance of evidence lies against her.* **6** [C] an instrument for weighing things by seeing whether the amounts in two hanging pans are equal — see picture at LABORATORY **7** [C] an amount that remains or is left over: *My bank balance isn't very large.* (=I haven't got much money in the bank.) | *I'd like to take the balance of my holidays* (=the part I have not yet taken) *in September.* **8 in the balance** in a state of uncertainty: *The future of the nation is/hangs in the balance.* **9 on balance** when everything has been considered: *I think on balance I prefer the old system.*

balance² *v* **1** [I;T] to (cause to) be steady and keep in BALANCE¹ (1), esp. in a difficult position: *The dog balanced a ball on its nose.* | *When you learn to ride a bicycle you must learn to balance.* **2** [I;T (OUT)] to (cause to) have or be given equal weight, amount, importance, or influence to (something else/each other): *The weight here balances the weight there.* | *The company's accounts did not balance (out).* (=did not show money spent to be equal to money received) | *the problem of balancing the need for military secrecy with the public's right to be informed* **3** [T (**against**)] to consider in relation to something else; compare: *You have to balance the advantages of living in a big city against the disadvantages.*

balance beam /ˈ··· ·/ *n* a long narrow piece of wood in the air on which a GYMNAST performs

bal·anced /ˈbælənst/ *adj* **1** giving equal attention to all sides or all opinions; fair; showing BALANCE¹ (2): *balanced and impartial reporting of the election campaign* | *a balanced judgment* **2** in which money spent and money earned are equal: *a balanced budget* **3** having or showing a firm sensible mind: *She's very well balanced.* | *a balanced judgment* —compare UNBALANCE

balanced di·et /ˌ·· ˈ··/ *n* the right quantities and kinds of food needed for good health

balance of pay·ments /ˌ··· ˈ··/ *n* [S] the difference between the amount of money coming into a country and the amount going out, taking into account all international business such as trade in goods, services, insurance, and banking —compare BALANCE OF TRADE

balance of pow·er /ˌ··· ˈ··/ *n* [*the*] **1** a position in which political or military power is evenly balanced on all sides: *The growth of the new political party upset the balance of power.* | *the nuclear balance of power* **2 hold the balance of power** to be able to make either side more powerful than the other by favouring it: *The two big parties had an almost equal number of seats in Parliament, so a small party could hold the balance of power.*

balance of trade /ˌ··· ˈ·/ *n* [S] the difference in value between a country's IMPORTS (=the goods it brings into the country) and EXPORTS (=the goods it sends out of the country for sale) —compare BALANCE OF PAYMENTS

balance sheet /ˈ··· ·/ *n* a statement of how much money has come in and how much has gone out

Bal·an·chine /ˈbæləntʃiːn/ˌbælənˈtʃiːn, -ˈtʃiːn/, George (1904–83) a Russian-born American CHOREOGRAPHER who helped start the New York City Ballet

Bal·bo·a /bælˈbəʊə/, **Vas·co Nú·ñez de** /ˈvæskəʊ ˈnuːnjez də/ˈvɑːs-/ (1475–1519) a Spanish EXPLORER who was the first European to discover the Pacific Ocean

bal·co·ny /ˈbælkəni/ *n* **1** a raised flat surface which is built out from the upstairs wall of a building: *You can see the sea from our balcony.* —see picture at HOUSE **2** also **circle**— the seats upstairs in a theatre —see picture at THEATRE

bald /bɔːld/ *adj* **1** with little or no hair on the head: *He's going bald.* | (*humor*) *He's as bald as a coot.* (=completely bald) **2** with little or no decoration or detail; plain: *a bald statement of the facts* — ~**ness** *n* [U]

bald ea·gle /ˌ· ˈ··/ *n* a large bird (EAGLE) with a white head which is the national bird of the US

bald eagle

bal·der·dash /ˈbɔːldədæʃ/ǁ-dər-/ *n* [U] *old-fash infml* foolish talk or writing; nonsense

bald·ing /ˈbɔːldɪŋ/ *adj* going bald: *a balding man/ head*

bald·ly /ˈbɔːldli/ *adv* spoken plainly, without attempting to hide unpleasant facts: **To put it baldly,** *if you don't stop smoking you'll be dead in a year.*

Bald·win /ˈbɔːldwɪn/, **James** (1924–87) an American writer known for his NOVELS about black Americans, such as *Go Tell It on the Mountain* and *Another Country*

Baldwin, Stanley (1867–1947) a British Conservative politician who was PRIME MINISTER in the 1920s and 1930s

bale¹ /beɪl/ *n* a large tightly tied mass of esp. soft material ready to be taken away: *a bale of paper/hay/cotton*

bale² *v*

bale out *phr v* **1** [I (**of**)] *BrE* ǁ **bail out** *AmE*— to escape from an aircraft by PARACHUTE **2** [I;T (=**bale** sthg. ↔ **out**)] *BrE for* BAIL **out** (2)

Bal·e·a·ric Is·lands /ˌbæliærɪk ˈaɪləndz/ also **Bal·e·a·rics** /ˌbæliˈærɪks/ ǁ *the*+P/ a group of islands in the W Mediterranean, including Ibiza, Majorca, and Minorca

bale·ful /ˈbeɪlfəl/ *adj* full of hate and desire to do harm; evil; threatening: *a baleful look* —**fully** *adv*

Bal·four /ˈbælfər, -fɔːr/, **Arthur James** (1848–1930) a British Conservative politician who was PRIME MINISTER from 1902 to 1905, and FOREIGN SECRETARY from 1916 to 1919, when he was responsible for the **Balfour Declaration** (which expressed the belief that a national home for the Jews should be made in Palestine)

Ba·li /ˈbɑːli/ an island in Indonesia, to the east of Java

balk¹ also **baulk** /bɔːk, bɔːlk/ *v* **1** [I (**at**)] to be unwilling to do or agree to something difficult or unpleasant: *I wanted to buy the dress, but I balked at the high price.* **2** [T] to stop or intentionally get in the way of **3** (in BASE-BALL) to stop in the act of throwing the ball towards the player who is trying to hit it

balk² also **baulk** *BrE*— *n* a thick rough wooden beam

Bal·kans /ˈbɔːlkənz/ also **Balkan States** /ˌ·· ˈ·/ [*the*] a part of SE Europe which includes Greece, Romania, Bulgaria, Albania, Yugoslavia, Slovenia, Croatia, and Bosnia

ball¹ /bɔːl/ *n* **1 a** a usu. round object used in a game or sport: *The children were kicking a ball around the garden.* | *to bounce a ball* | *a tennis ball* **b** anything of a similar shape: *a ball of string* | *a snowball* | *a meatball* **2** a rounded part of the body: *the ball of the foot* (=at the base of the toes) | *an eyeball* —see picture at FOOT and HAND **3** an act or style of throwing a ball: *a fast ball* | *What a good ball!* —see also NO BALL **4** (in BASEBALL) a thrown ball which a player is not expected to swing at with his BAT because it is not within a certain area. After four such balls, the player may walk to first base **5** a round bullet or SHELL¹ (4) to be fired from a gun of a type now no longer used **6 ball and chain** a heavy ball of metal with a chain attached, that used to be fixed to prisoners' legs to stop them from escaping —see PRISONER **7 carry the ball** *AmE* to take responsibility, esp. in a difficult situation: *He's always left carrying the ball when things get rough.* **8 on the ball** *infml apprec* showing up-to-date knowledge and/or an ability to think and act quickly: *That new teacher is really on the ball.* **9 play ball** *AmE* to work well with someone; COOPERATE: *We tried to work out a fair deal but the other company's people just wouldn't play ball.* **10 set/start/keep the 'ball rolling** to begin/continue something, such as a conversation or a plan **11 The ball is in 'your/his/her court** Now it's your/his/her turn to take action or reply —see also BALLS

ball² *n* **1** [C] a large formal occasion for social dancing **2** [S] *infml* a very good time: *They all had a ball at the party.* **3 You 'shall go to the ball!** a phrase used by the FAIRY GODMOTHER to Cinderella in the story of Cinderella —see also CINDERELLA

Ball, Lu·cille /luːˈsiːl/ (1911–89) an American COMEDY actress known for her television shows *I Love Lucy*, *The Lucy Show*, and *Here's Lucy* which ran for many years and are still shown around the world

bal·lad /ˈbæləd/ *n* **1** a short story in the form of a poem **2** a simple song, esp. a popular love song

bal·lade /bæˈlɑːd/bə-/ *n* a poem with usu. three groups of lines and a shorter fourth group all having the same last line and using a very small number of RHYMES

Bal·lard /ˈbælɑːd/-ɑːrd/, **J G** (1930–) an English writer, best known for his SCIENCE FICTION books and for his NOVEL *Empire of the Sun*

bal·last¹ /ˈbæləst/ *n* [U] heavy material, such as broken stones, which is **a** carried by a ship to keep it steady **b** thrown from a BALLOON to make it rise **c** used as the bottom surface of a road or as the surface on which railway lines are placed

ballast² v [T (**with**)] to fill or supply with ballast

ball bear·ing /ˌ· ˈ··/ n **1** an arrangement of metal balls moving in a ring round a bar in a machine so that the bar can turn more easily **2** any one of these metal balls

ball boy /ˈ· ·/ **ball girl** fem.– n a young person who picks up balls for people playing in important tennis matches –see picture at TENNIS

ball·cock /ˈbɔːlkɒk‖-kɑːk/ n an apparatus for opening and closing a hole through which water passes, worked by a hollow floating ball which rises and falls with the level of the water

bal·le·ri·na /ˌbæləˈriːnə/ n a female ballet dancer

Bal·les·te·ros /ˌbælᵻˈstiərɒs‖ˌbaɪəˈsteərəʊs/, **Sev·e·ri·a·no** /ˌseveriˈɑːnəʊ/ (1957–) a Spanish GOLFER who has won many competitions around the world

bal·let /ˈbæleɪ‖bæˈleɪ, ˈbæleɪ/ n **1** [C] (the music for) a theatrical performance in which a story is told using artistic dancing and music, but without speech or singing: *Tchaikovsky wrote (the music for) several famous ballets.* **2** [(the)] U] such dancing as a form of art: *She has studied (the) ballet for six years.* | *a ballet dancer* **3** [C+sing./pl. v] also **corps de ballet**– a group of ballet dancers who work together: *the Bolshoi Ballet*

ball game /ˈ· ·/ n [usu. sing.] infml **1** AmE a BASEBALL game **2** a state of affairs; situation: *I used to be a teacher, so working in an office is a whole new ball game for me.*

bal·lis·tic mis·sile /bəˌlɪstɪk ˈmɪsaɪl‖-ˈmɪsəl/ n a MISSILE that is guided as it rises into the air but then falls freely such as bullets fired from a gun

bal·lis·tics /bəˈlɪstɪks/ n [U] the scientific study of the movement of objects that are thrown or forced through the air, such as bullets fired from a gun

bal·loon¹ /bəˈluːn/ n **1** also **hot-air balloon** AmE a large bag of strong light material filled with gas or heated air so that it can float in the air: *They crossed the English Channel in a hot-air balloon.* **2** a small usu. brightly coloured rubber bag that can be blown up, used as a toy or decoration for parties, etc.: *All the children were given balloons.* **3** the line round the words spoken by the figures in a CARTOON **4** AmE money borrowed, esp. for a MORTGAGE, which must be paid in one large sum after several smaller payments have been made: *a 10% mortgage with a five-year balloon* **5 go down like a lead balloon** infml (of a remark, joke, suggestion, etc.) to fail to have the intended effect and esp. to produce disapproval: *His jokes about women drivers went down like a lead balloon.* **6 when the balloon goes up** BrE when the action starts or the moment of great danger arrives –see also TRIAL BALLOON

balloon² v [I (OUT, UP)] to get bigger and bigger, or rounder and rounder, like a balloon being blown up: *His cheeks ballooned (out) as he played his trumpet.*

bal·loon·ing /bəˈluːnɪŋ/ n [U] the sport of flying in a balloon –**ist** n

bal·lot¹ /ˈbælət/ n **1** [C] a sheet of paper used to make a secret vote: *They're counting the ballots now.* **2** [(the) S] the process or system of secret voting: *The ballot is a vital part of the democratic process.* | *The leaders were accused of* **rigging the ballot.** (=arranging false results) | *When we* **put it to the ballot** (=had a vote) *the members decided to accept the management's offer.* **3** [C] an occasion of voting or a chance to vote: *The members have demanded a ballot.* | *a strike ballot* | *a postal ballot* **4** [C] the number of votes recorded; POLL

ballot² v **1** [I (**for**)] to vote or decide by secret voting: *They've balloted for the new chairman, but nobody knows the result yet.* **2** [T] to find out the views of (a group) by holding a vote: *They'll have to ballot the membership before they can declare a strike.*

ballot box /ˈ··· ·/ n **1** [C] a large (usu. tin) box into which the pieces of paper on which people record their votes are placed **2** [the] elections; the system or process of voting in an election: *Their popularity will be put to the test at/through the ballot box.*

ball park /ˈ· ·/ n [S] **1** infml a range of numbers, prices, etc. within which the correct figure is likely to be: *Their estimate was in the right ball park.* | *a ball-park figure* **2** AmE a playing field for BASEBALL, usu. with seats from which to watch the game

ball·play·er /ˈbɔːlpleɪəʳ/ n AmE a person who plays BASEBALL: *a scout looking at the high school ballplayers*

ball·point /ˈbɔːlpɔɪnt/ also **ballpoint pen** /ˌ·· ˈ·/ fml, **biro** BrE tdmk– n a pen with a ball at the end that rolls thick ink onto the paper

ball·room /ˈbɔːlrum, -ruːm/ n a large room for dancing – see BALL² (1)

ballroom danc·ing /ˌ·· ˈ··/ n [U] a formal kind of dancing done in pairs or groups to special music, such as the WALTZ or the FOXTROT. Ballroom dancing is usu. done by older people, and considered old-fashioned by many young people.

balls¹ /bɔːlz/ n taboo sl **1** [P] TESTICLES **2** [U] derog nonsense: *That's a load of balls.* **3** [U] daring self-confidence; CHEEK: *It must have taken a lot of balls to tell the director he was wrong.*

balls² v
   balls sthg. up BrE ‖ **ball sthg. up** AmE– phr v [T] taboo sl to do badly or unsuccessfully; spoil –**balls-up** /ˈ· ·/ n BrE sl: *He made a complete balls-up of the arrangements.*

ball·sy /ˈbɔːlzi/ adj sl having a lot of spirit or courage: *He's a ballsy kind of guy.*

bal·ly /ˈbæli/ adj, adv [A] BrE old-fash BLOODY²; used esp. by older, upper-class people

bal·ly·hoo /ˌbæliˈhuː‖ˈbælihuː/ n [U] infml ways of trying to gain public attention by making a lot of noise or through exciting kinds of advertising

balm /bɑːm‖bɑːm, bɑːlm/ n [C;U] **1** (an) oily liquid with a strong but pleasant smell, often from trees, used as medicine or to lessen pain **2** esp. lit something that gives comfort to the spirit

Bal·mor·al /bælˈmɒrəl‖-ˈmɔːr-/ also **Balmoral Cas·tle** /·ˌ·· ˈ··/– a castle in Scotland, NE of Braemar, which is one of the homes of the British royal family: *After their holiday in Spain, Charles and Diana will join the Queen at Balmoral.*

balm·y /ˈbɑːmi‖ˈbɑːmi, ˈbɑːlmi/ adj apprec (of air) soft and warm; MILD: *a balmy breeze* | *balmy days*

ba·lo·ney /bəˈləʊni/ n [U] sl BOLONEY

bal·sa /ˈbɔːlsə/ n [C;U] (the very light wood of) a tropical American tree

bal·sam /ˈbɔːlsəm/ n [C;U] (a tree that produces) BALM

Bal·tic /ˈbɔːltɪk/ [the] a sea which is part of the Atlantic, enclosed by Denmark, Sweden, the Baltic States, and Poland

Baltic States /ˌ·· ˈ·/ [(the)+P] the independent countries of Estonia, Latvia, and Lithuania

Bal·ti·more /ˈbɔːltᵻmɔːʳ/ a city on the E coast of the US, in the state of Maryland. Baltimore is one of the busiest sea ports in the US. – see colour maps on pages 1374–5

bal·us·trade /ˌbæləˈstreɪd‖ˈbæləstreɪd/ n a row of upright pieces of stone or wood with a bar along the top, guarding the outer edge of any place from which people might fall

Bal·zac /ˈbælzæk‖ˈbɔːl-/, **Hon·o·ré de** /ˈɒnəreɪ də‖ˌɑːnəˈreɪ-/ (1799–1850) a French writer who wrote about French society in NOVELs such as *La Comédie humaine*

Bam·bi /ˈbæmbi/ the title of a CARTOON film by Walt Disney about a young DEER called Bambi. Bambi is remembered as being an attractive, gentle animal, and the film is remembered for being sad.

bam·boo /ˌbæmˈbuː◂/ n -boos [C;U] a tall tropical plant of the grass family or its hard, hollow, jointed stems, which are used e.g. for making furniture

Bamboo Cur·tain /ˌ·· ˈ··/ [the] a political BARRIER between China and the other important powers e.g. the US and the former USSR, esp. during the time of Mao Ze-dong –compare IRON CURTAIN

bam·boo·zle /bæmˈbuːzəl/ v [T (**into, out of**)] sl to deceive; trick; HOODWINK

ban¹ /bæn/ v -**nn**- [T (**from**)] **1** to forbid, esp. by law: *The new military government has banned strikes and demonstrations.* | *After the accident, he was banned from driving.* | *banned books/films* **2 Ban the Bomb** a phrase used by people who marched in protests against the use of NUCLEAR WEAPONS, esp. in the 1960s

ban² n [(**on**)] an order banning something: *The union has imposed* (=established) *a ban on overtime/lifted*

(=removed) *the ban on overtime.* | *an alcohol ban* —see also TEST BAN

ba·nal /bəˈnɑːl, bəˈnæl/ *adj derog* uninteresting because very common; lacking new or original ideas: *a banal remark* —**banality** /bəˈnælˌti/ *n* [C;U]

ba·na·na /bəˈnɑːnə‖-ˈnæ-/ *n* **1** a long thick curved tropical fruit, having a yellow skin and a soft, sweet inside when ripe —see picture at FRUIT **2 top banana** *AmE infml* the most important person in an organization; the BOSS: *He's the top banana at a record company.*

banana re·pub·lic /·ˌ·· ˈ··ˌ/ *n infml derog* a small country, esp. in Central or S America, that is industrially underdeveloped, politically unsteady, and often dependent on financial support from abroad

ba·na·nas /bəˈnɑːnəz‖-ˈnæ-/ *adj AmE sl* **1** mad; crazy: *Everyone on the block thinks Mr. Allan is bananas because he walks his dog at midnight.* **2 go bananas** become wild or angry: *Dad will go bananas when he sees the mess you've made with his tools.*

banana skin /·ˈ·· ˌ·/ *n BrE infml* an event or situation likely to cause difficulty or make one look foolish (from a typical humorous situation in British COMEDY, in which a person slips on a banana skin and falls over): *This incident could turn into another banana skin for the government.*

banana split /·ˌ·· ˈ·/ *n* a sweet dish made of a banana split in two with ICE CREAM, chocolate liquid (SAUCE), whipped cream, and nuts

Ban·bu·ry /ˈbænbəri‖-beri/ a market town in Oxfordshire, England, known for the stone cross which features in a NURSERY RHYME: *Ride a cock horse to Banbury Cross*

band¹ /bænd/ *n* **1** a flat narrow often endless piece of material **a** for fastening things together or for putting round something to strengthen it: *She tied her hair back with a rubber band.* **b** forming part of an article of clothing: *the neckband of a shirt* | *the waistband of a pair of trousers* **2** a line of a colour or pattern different to that of the area on either side of it; STRIPE: *There was an orange band along the snake's back.* **3** a range of values, amounts, radio waves, etc.: *people within the $20,000 – $30,000 income band*

band² *n* [C+*sing.*/*pl. v*] **1** a group of people formed for some common purpose and often with a leader: *a band of robbers* **2** a group of musicians, esp. a group that play popular music: *a dance band* | *a brass band* | *a rock*/*jazz band* —compare ORCHESTRA; see also ONE-MAN BAND —see **to beat the band** (BEAT¹ (20))

band³ *v*
band together *phr v* [I (**against**)] to unite with some special purpose: *The two parties banded together to form an alliance.*

Ban·da /ˈbændə/, **Hastings** (1902–) a Malawi politician, president from 1964, who led the movement for independence in his country

ban·dage¹ /ˈbændɪdʒ/ *BrE* ‖ also **gauze** *AmE*– *n* **1** a long narrow piece of material, usu. cloth, for tying round a wound or round a part of the body that has been hurt **2** *AmE* also **Band-Aid** (*tdmk*) PLASTER¹ (2)

bandage² *v* [T (UP)] to tie up or bind round with a bandage: *The doctor bandaged (up) her broken ankle.* | *a band-aged arm*

Band Aid /·ˈ··/ *tdmk* a CHARITY set up by Bob Geldof in 1984 to raise money for people dying of hunger in Ethiopia, by getting many famous POP singers to make a record together, called *Do They Know It's Christmas?* They also organized the **Live Aid** concerts in London and Philadelphia in 1985.

Band-Aid *n tdmk, AmE for* PLASTER¹ (2)

ban·dan·na, -dana /bænˈdænə/ *n* a large brightly coloured handkerchief, worn round the neck or head

Ban·da·ra·na·i·ke /ˌbændərəˈnaɪkə/, **Sir·i·ma·vo** /sɪrɪˈmɑːvəʊ/ (1916–) a Sri Lankan politician who in 1960 became the first woman PRIME MINISTER in the world after the death of her husband Solomon Bandaranaike

b and b, B and B /ˌbiː ənd ˈbiː/ *abbrev. for:* BED AND BREAKFAST

ban·dit /ˈbændɪt/ *n* an armed robber, esp. one of an armed band who attack travellers in wild places —see also ONE-ARMED BANDIT

band·mas·ter /ˈbændˌmɑːstəʳ‖-ˌmæ-/ *n* a man who

CONDUCTS (=directs the playing of) a military band, brass band, etc.

ban·do·leer , bandolier /ˌbændəˈlɪəʳ/ *n* a belt that goes over a person's shoulder, and is used for carrying bullets

B & Q /ˌbiː ənd ˈkjuː/ one of a group of shops in Britain selling goods used for decorating or improving the home and garden, usu. at low prices

bands·man /ˈbændzmən/ *n* **-men** /mən/ a musician who plays in a military band, brass band, etc.

band·stand /ˈbændstænd/ *n* a raised place, open at the sides but with a roof, for a band playing music in the open air

band·wa·gon /ˈbændˌwægən/ *n* **1** a group, political party, movement, etc. that attracts support or followers because of its quick success or growth of popularity **2 jump**/**climb**/**get on the bandwagon** to begin to do something that a lot of other people are doing, esp. in the hope of personal advantage

ban·dy¹ /ˈbændi/ *adj* **1** (of legs) curving outwards at the knees **2** also **bandy-legged** /ˌ·· ˈ·◂‖ˈ·· ·/– having bandy legs
bandy sthg. **about**/**around** *phr v* [T] to spread (unfavourable or untrue ideas) by talking: *Several different figures have been bandied about, but these are the only correct ones.*

bandy² *v* **bandy words (with)** *old-fash* to quarrel (with)

bane /beɪn/ *n* **the bane of one's existence**/**life** a cause of continual trouble: *That car is the bane of my life!*

bane·ful /ˈbeɪnfəl/ *adj esp. lit* harmful; evil: *a baneful influence* – ~**ly** *adv*

Banff /bænf/ a holiday town in **Banff National Park** in the Rocky Mountains in Alberta, Canada

Banff·shire /ˈbænʃʃəʳ/ a former COUNTY in NE Scotland, now part of Grampian REGION

bang¹ /bæŋ/ *v* **1** [T] to hit sharply, esp. by accident; BUMP: *He fell and banged his knee.* | *I banged my head on the low ceiling.* **2** [I+*adv*/*prep*;T+*obj*+*adv*/*prep*] to (cause to) knock, beat, or move violently and with a loud noise: *She banged the chair against the wall.* | *They were banging on the door with their fists.* | *He banged the book down on the table.* **3** [I] to make a sharp loud noise or noises: *There is someone banging about upstairs.* | *I could hear the garage door banging (in the wind).* —see also **bang one's head against a brick wall** (HEAD¹)

bang² *n* **1** [C] a sharp knock or blow: *She fell and got a nasty bang on the knee.* **2** a sudden loud noise: *The door shut with a bang.* **3** [S] *infml* a strong or powerful effect; IMPACT: *The publication of the new magazine has made less of a bang than the publishers hoped for.* **4** *AmE infml* a strong feeling of pleasure: *She got a real bang out of the song the kids made up about her.* **5 go off with a bang** *BrE* ‖ **go over with a bang** *AmE* to be very successful: *The party really went off with a bang!* **6 not with a bang but a whimper** *quote* a phrase from a poem by T S Eliot, often used when saying that something does not end in an exciting way, but just stops in a very uninteresting and unexciting way: *That is the way the revolution ends, not with a bang but a whimper.* —see also BIG BANG THEORY

bang³ *adv* [+*adv*/*prep*] *infml* **1** directly or exactly: *The sales figures are bang on target.* | *Your answer's* **bang on.** (=exactly correct) | *The lights went out bang in the middle of the performance.* **2 bang goes (something)** that is the end of (something): *If we don't keep the price down, bang go our chances of getting the contract.*

bang⁴ also **bangs** *pl.*– *AmE n* hair cut straight across the forehead; FRINGE

bang·er /ˈbæŋəʳ/ *n BrE infml* **1** a SAUSAGE **2** an old car in poor condition; JALOPY **3** a cheap, noisy FIREWORK

bangers and mash /ˌ·· ˈ·/ *n* [U] *BrE infml* cooked SAUSAGES and mashed (MASH¹) potatoes, considered to be a typical British meal

Bang·kok /bæŋˈkɒk‖ˈbæŋkɑːk/ the capital city and main port of Thailand. It is famous for its TEMPLEs and other beautiful buildings.

Ban·gla·desh /ˌbæŋɡləˈdeʃ/ *n* a country in S Asia which is a member of the COMMONWEALTH (1), and often has bad floods in the rainy season; capital Dhaka; population 106,507,000 (1989) —**deshi** *n, adj*

ban·gle /ˈbæŋɡəl/ *n* a hard narrow band of gold, silver, etc.

worn round the arm or ankle as a decoration —compare BRACELET

bang-on /ˌ· ˈ-◂/ adj BrE infml exactly correct or highly AC-CURATE: *His estimate of how long the journey would take was bang-on.*

Ban·gor /ˈbæŋgəʳ/ a city and port on the NW coast of Wales, which has a university

bang-up /ˈ· ·/ adj AmE infml very good: *He did a bang-up job fixing the plumbing.*

ban·ish /ˈbænɪʃ/ v [T (from)] **1** to send away by official order, usu. from one's own country, esp. as a punishment: *She was banished by the government for political reasons.* —compare EXILE **2** to force to leave; drive away: *Those noisy children should be banished from the library.* | *You can banish that idea from your mind.* — ~ment n [U] : *to go/be sent into banishment*

ban·is·ter /ˈbænₐstəʳ/ also **banisters** pl.— n a row of upright pieces of wood or metal with a bar along the top guarding the outer edge of stairs: *The children were sliding down the banister/the banisters.* —compare HANDRAIL, RAILING

ban·jo /ˈbændʒəʊ/ n -jos or -joes a musical instrument with four or more strings, a long neck, and a body like a drum, used esp. to play popular music

bank¹ /bæŋk/ n **1** (a local office of) a business organization which performs services connected with money, esp. keeping money for customers and paying it out on demand, or lending money to customers: *The major banks have announced an increase in interest rates.* | *She works at the bank in the High Street.* | *I think she's a lot more interested in your* **bank balance** (=your money) *than your personality!* **2** a place where something is kept until it is ready for use, esp. products of human origin for medical use: *a kidney bank* | *Hospital blood banks have saved many lives.* **3** (a person who keeps) a supply of money or pieces for payment or use in a game of chance —see also **break the bank** (BREAK¹ (23)) and CLEARING BANK, MERCHANT BANK

bank² v **1** [T] to put or keep (money) in a bank **2** [I (with)] to keep one's money (in the stated bank): *Who do you bank with?*
　　bank on/upon sbdy./sthg. phr v [T] to depend on; trust in: *I'm banking on/you/on your help.* [+v-ing] *We mustn't bank on getting their agreement.* [+obj+to-v] *I'm banking on you to help me with the arrangements.* [+obj+v-ing] *We were banking on John knowing the way.*

bank³ n **1** land along the side of a river, lake, etc.: *the left bank of the Seine* | *the banks of the River Nile* —see SHORE (USAGE) **2** a pile or RIDGE of earth, mud, snow, etc.: *They sat on a grassy bank at the edge of the field watching the game of cricket.* **3** a mass of clouds, mist, etc.: *The banks of dark cloud promised rain.* **4** a slope made at bends in a road or racetrack, so that they are safer for cars to go round **5** a SANDBANK: *the Dogger Bank in the North Sea*

bank⁴ v [I] (of a car or aircraft) to move with one side higher than the other when making a turn
　　bank up phr v [I;T (=**bank** sthg. ↔ **up**)] to form into a mass or pile: *The wind had banked the snow up against the wall.* | *At night we bank up the fire so that it's still burning in the morning.*

bank⁵ n [(of)] a set of things arranged in a row, esp. a row of OARs in an ancient boat or of KEYs on a TYPEWRITER

bank ac·count /ˈ· ·ˌ·/ n an arrangement between a bank and a customer under which the customer can pay in and take out money: *I'd like to open* (=start) *a bank account.* —see also CURRENT ACCOUNT, DEPOSIT ACCOUNT, SAVINGS ACCOUNT

Bank·A·mer·i·ca /ˌbænkəˈmerₐkə/ the second largest bank in the US, with its main offices in San Francisco

bank bal·ance /ˈ· ˌ·◂/ n [S] the amount of money a person has in their bank account, or the amount of money they have generally: *The profits from his company have given him a very healthy bank balance.*

bank·book /ˈbæŋkbʊk/ n a book in which a record of the money one puts into and takes out of a bank is kept — compare PASSBOOK

bank draft /ˈ· ·/ also **bank·bill** /ˈbæŋkbɪl/, **banker's draft** /ˈ·· ·/— n an order by one bank to another (esp. a foreign bank) to pay a certain sum of money to a named person or organization

bank·er /ˈbæŋkəʳ/ n **1** a person who owns or manages a BANK¹ (1) **2** the player who keeps the BANK¹ (3) in various games of chance

banker's card /ˈ·· ·/ n BrE a CHEQUE CARD —compare DEBIT CARD

banker's or·der /ˌ·· ˈ·◂/ n a STANDING ORDER

bank hol·i·day /ˌ· ˈ··◂/ n **1** BrE ‖ **public holiday** AmE an official public holiday, not a Saturday or Sunday, when banks and most businesses are closed, esp. one in the Spring (**Spring bank holiday**) and one in August (**August bank holiday**, also called **Late Summer Holiday**). These two bank holidays are always on a Monday (**Bank Holiday Monday**), and the weekend when they take place is known as a **bank holiday weekend**: *There are bound to be traffic jams over the bank holiday weekend as people head for the coast.* —see also extra information on page 632 **2** AmE a period when banks are closed, usu. by government order, to prevent money difficulties

bank·ing /ˈbæŋkɪŋ/ n [U] the business of a bank or a banker: *a career in banking* | *the international banking system*

bank man·a·ger /ˈ· ˌ···/ n a person who manages a bank. The British STEREOTYPE of a bank manager is a boring, old-fashioned, MIDDLE-AGED man wearing a suit.

bank note /ˈ· ·/ n a piece of paper money printed for the national bank of a country for public use

Bank of Cred·it and Com·merce In·ter·na·tion·al /ˌ· · ˌ· ˌ·· ˌ· ··ˈ···/ see BCCI

Bank of Eng·land /ˌ· · ˈ··◂/ n [the] the central bank in Britain, which acts as banker to the government and to the HIGH STREET BANKS

Bank of Scot·land /ˌ· · ˈ··◂/ n [the] one of the main banks in Scotland. Like other Scottish banks, it prints its own banknotes.

bank rate /ˈ· ·/ n [the;U] the rate of interest fixed by a central bank, such as the Bank of England. The bank rate influences the rates of interest charged by all banks and building societies (BUILDING SOCIETY) for the LOAN of money, and the rate of interest paid to savers.

bank·roll¹ /ˈbæŋkrəʊl/ n AmE a supply of money

bankroll² v [T] AmE infml to supply money for or pay the cost of (a business, plan, etc.)

bank·rupt¹ /ˈbæŋkrʌpt/ adj **1** unable to pay one's debts. When people declare that they are bankrupt lawyers take charge of all their money and goods and sell them in order to pay their debts: *He started a small business, but went bankrupt when the recession started.* —compare IN-SOLVENT **2** lacking in a particular desirable quality: *morally bankrupt* (=completely without moral principles) | *bankrupt of new ideas*

bankrupt² n a person who is bankrupt

bankrupt³ v [T] to make bankrupt or very poor: *The cost of defending the libel action almost bankrupted the small magazine.*

bank·rupt·cy /ˈbæŋkrʌptsi/ n [C;U] (an example of) the state of being or becoming bankrupt: *The company is threatened with bankruptcy.* | *There has been a sharp increase in bankruptcies in the last two years.* | *the bankruptcy of the government's plans* (=their failure to produce good results, etc.)

Banks /bæŋks/, **Gordon** (1937–) an English football player, generally thought to be one of the best GOALKEEPERS to have played for England

bank state·ment /ˈ· ˌ··/ n a document sent regularly by a bank to a customer holding a CURRENT ACCOUNT. It lists all the amounts received by and paid out from the account.

ban·ner /ˈbænəʳ/ n **1** a long piece of cloth on which a sign is painted, often carried between two poles: *The marchers waved banners saying "We want work".* **2** lit a flag **3** **under the banner of** in the name of (a principle or aim); for the cause of: *The new government came to power under the banner of fighting poverty.*

banner head·line /ˌ·· ˈ··◂/ n a HEADLINE that goes across the whole width of a newspaper

Ban·nis·ter /ˈbænₐstəʳ/, **Sir Roger** (1929–) an English ATHLETE who, in 1954, was the first person to run a mile in under four minutes

ban·nock /ˈbænək/ n esp. ScotE a flat cake made of OATMEAL or MAIZE

Ban·nock·burn /ˈbænəkbɜːn‖ -bɜːrn/ a village in the central part of Scotland close to a famous battlefield where, in 1314, Robert the Bruce, King of the Scots, defeated the English

Roger Bannister

banns /bænz/ n [P] a public declaration, usu. made in church, of an intended marriage. In Britain, banns are read out on three separate Sundays before a marriage takes place. They include the words, "If any of you know cause or just impediment, why these two persons should not be joined together in holy Matrimony, ye are to declare it". In the US banns are not usu. declared now.

ban·quet¹ /ˈbæŋkwɪt/ n a formal dinner for many people in honour of a particular person or occasion

banquet² v [I] to take part in a banquet

Ban·quo /ˈbæŋkwəʊ/ a character in Shakespeare's play *Macbeth*, who is murdered by Macbeth but returns during a FEAST (=large meal) as a GHOST to HAUNT Macbeth and remind him of his crime

ban·shee /bænˈʃiː‖ˈbænʃiː/ n (esp. in Ireland) a spirit whose cry is believed to mean that there will be a death in the house

ban·tam /ˈbæntəm/ n a small kind of farm chicken

ban·tam·weight /ˈbæntəmweɪt/ n a BOXER heavier than a FLYWEIGHT but lighter than a FEATHERWEIGHT

ban·ter¹ /ˈbæntər/ n [U] light joking talk; REPARTEE: *The actress exchanged banter with reporters.*

banter² v [I] to speak or act playfully or jokingly — ~ing adj : *bantering remarks* − − ingly adv

Ban·tu /ˌbænˈtuː◂/ n **Bantu 1** [the+P] a race of black people who live in central, Eastern, and Southern Africa **2** [U] one of a group of African languages spoken in central and Southern Africa

Ban·tu·stan /ˌbæntuːˈstaːn/ n one of the partly self-governing areas in the Republic of South Africa set aside by the government for black citizens. The official name for these areas is HOMELANDS

ban·yan /ˈbænjən, ˈbænjæn/ also **banyan tree** /ˈ·· ˌ·/− n an Indian fruit tree whose branches grow down towards the ground and form new roots

bap /bæp/ n BrE a large soft bread ROLL, usu. with a fine covering of flour on top

bap·tis·m /ˈbæptɪzəm/ n **1** [C;U] a Christian religious ceremony in which a person is touched or covered with water to make them pure and free from guilt or SIN and show that they have been accepted as a member of the Church. Baptism is often also used as a ceremony for officially giving a name to a baby. −see also CHRISTEN, GOD-PARENT **2 baptism of fire** a difficult or unpleasant first experience of something −−mal /bæpˈtɪzməl/ adj

Bap·tist /ˈbæptɪst/ n a member of a Christian group which believes that baptism should be only for people old enough to understand its meaning and that they should be covered completely with water. The Baptists are the largest PROTESTANT group in the US, with many churches, esp. in the South −see also SOUTHERN BAPTIST

bap·tize also **-tise** BrE /bæpˈtaɪz/ v [T] **1** to perform the ceremony of baptism on (a person). In many Christian Churches babies are baptized when they are quite young, but some Churches believe that only adults can be baptized, when they are able to make their own choice to do it. **2** [+obj+n] to admit as a member of the stated church by baptism: *He was baptized a Roman Catholic.* **3** [+obj+n] to give (someone) a name at baptism: *She was baptized Sheila Jane.*

bar¹ /baːr/ n **1** a piece of solid material that is longer than it is wide: *a bar of soap/chocolate/gold/iron* −see picture at PIECE **2** a length of wood or metal across a door, gate, or window to keep it shut or prevent movement through

it: *There were bars across the windows of the prison.* | (fig.) *His bad English is a bar to* (=prevents) *his getting a job.* | (fig.) *The government has announced a total bar on imports of luxury cars.* **3** (a place with) a COUNTER¹ where **a** alcoholic drinks are served: *There are several bars in the hotel.* | *There were no free tables, so they stood at the bar.* | *What time does the bar close?* **b** a particular kind of food or drink is served: *a coffee bar* | *a snack bar* | *a sandwich bar* −see also WINE BAR **4** (in a court of law) a division between the part in which the business of the court is carried on and the part intended for the prisoner or the public: *the* **prisoner at the bar** (=the person being tried) | (fig.) *Your policies will be judged* **at the bar of public opinion.** (=by the public) −see also BAR **5** a group of notes and rests in music that add up to a particular time value: *She sang the first three bars of the song, and then stopped.* **6** a bank of sand or stones under the water parallel to a shore, at the entrance to a HARBOUR, etc. **7** esp. lit a narrow band of colour or light: *bars of sunlight* **8** a narrow band of metal or cloth worn on a military uniform to show rank, service, or good performance **9** a CROSSBAR **10 behind bars** in prison −see also BARRED (1), COLOUR BAR

bar² v **-rr-** [T] **1** [(UP)] to close firmly with a bar: *to bar the door* | *The empty house was barred up for the winter.* (=closed completely) −opposite **unbar 2** [+obj+adv/prep] to keep in or out by barring a door, gate, etc.: *They barred themselves in.* | *She barred them out of her room.* **3** [often pass.] to prevent movement through or into; block: *After the bombing, the whole area was barred to the public.* | *The road ahead was barred by a solid line of policemen.* **4** [(from)] **a** to prevent from entering; keep out: *The members voted to bar women from the club.* | *Traffic has been barred from the city centre.* **b** to forbid; PROHIBIT: *He has been barred from playing for two weeks because of bad behaviour.* −see also **no holds barred** (HOLD²)

bar³ prep except: *The whole group was at the party, bar John.* | *He's the best singer in the country,* **bar none.** (=without any exceptions) −see also BARRING

Bar n [the+sing./pl. v] **1** BrE (the members of) the profession of BARRISTER **2** AmE (the members of) the profession of lawyer **3 be called to the Bar: a** BrE to become a BARRISTER **b** AmE to become a lawyer

barb /baːb‖baːrb/ n **1** the sharp point of a fish hook, ARROW, etc., with a curved shape which prevents it from being easily pulled out **2** a remark that is clever or amusing but also cruel and sharp −see also BARBED

Bar·ba·dos /baːˈbeɪdɒs‖baːrˈbeɪdəs, -daːs/ an island in the British West Indies, part of the COMMONWEALTH since 1966; capital Bridgetown; population 256,000 (1989) −−dian n, adj

bar·bar·i·an /baːˈbeəriən‖baːr-/ n often derog an uncivilized person, esp. one who is rough and wild in behaviour: *The barbarians conquered Rome.* | (fig.) *barbarians who had never even heard of the great composer* −**barbarian** adj : *barbarian manners*

Bar·bar·i·ans /baːˈbeəriənz‖baːr-/ [the] a Rugby Union team based in Britain, with players from several countries. Teams from other countries which come to Britain often play against the Barbarians.

bar·bar·ic /baːˈbærɪk‖baːr-/ adj usu. derog **1** very cruel; BRUTAL: *a barbaric act of terrorism* | *barbaric tortures* **2** of or like a barbarian; BARBAROUS: *barbaric people/customs* − − ally /kli/ adv

bar·bar·is·m /ˈbaːbərɪzəm‖ˈbaːr-/ n usu. derog **1** [U] the rough uncivilized condition of being a barbarian: *At that time, most of the peoples of northern Europe were in a state of barbarism.* **2** [C] fml an offensive word or action, esp. a mistake in the use of language

bar·bar·i·ty /baːˈbærɪti‖baːr-/ n [C;U] (an example of) cruelty of the worst kind: *The barbarities of the last war must not be repeated.*

bar·bar·ize also **-ise** BrE /ˈbaːbəraɪz‖ˈbaːr-/ v [T] to make cruel and rough in manners

bar·bar·ous /ˈbaːbərəs‖ˈbaːr-/ adj usu. derog **1** rough and uncivilized: *barbarous people* **2** very cruel; BARBARIC **3** fml offensive in behaviour or manners, esp. by making mistakes in the use of language: *a barbarous writer/style* − − ly adv

bar·be·cue¹ /ˈbaːbɪkjuː‖ˈbaːr-/ also **barbie** AustrE and BrE *infml* −**bbq** *AmE infml*− *n* **1** a metal frame on which to cook food, esp. meat, over an open fire, usu. outdoors **2** a party at which food is prepared in this way and eaten: *We had a barbecue on the beach.*

barbecue² *v* [T] to cook (meat) **a** on a barbecue: *barbecued chicken* **b** in a very hot SAUCE

barbed /bɑːbd‖bɑːrbd/ *adj* **1** with one or more BARBS or short sharp points: *a barbed hook* **2** (of something spoken or written) sharp and unkind, esp. in judging a person, their ideas, etc.: *a barbed remark*

barbed wire /ˌ· ˈ·◂/ also **barbwire** *AmE*− *n* [U] wire with short sharp points on it: *a barbed-wire fence to keep the cattle in*

bar·bell /ˈbɑːˌbel‖ˈbɑːr-/ *n AmE* a metal stick with round weights at each end which is lifted to build strength

bar·ber /ˈbɑːbəʳ‖ˈbɑːr-/ *n* a person (usu. a man) who cuts men's hair, sometimes SHAVES them, and who usu. works in a shop (**barber's** *BrE* ‖ **barbershop** *AmE*): *I've got an appointment at the barber's.* −compare HAIRDRESSER

Barber, Sam·u·el /ˈsæmjuəl/ (1910−81) an American COMPOSER whose main works are *Adagio for Strings* and the OPERA *Antony and Cleopatra*

Barber of Se·ville /ˌ··· ˈ·-/, **The** an OPERA by Rossini, based on a French play by Beaumarchais

bar·ber·shop /ˈbɑːbəʃɒp‖-bərʃɑːp/ *adj* describing a style of singing popular songs in four parts in close HARMONY (=with the notes of each part close together in sound): *a barbershop quartet*

barber's pole /ˌ·· ˈ·/ *n* a pole painted in red and white STRIPES (1), used as a street sign outside an old-fashioned men's hairdresser's (HAIRDRESSER)

bar·bi·can /ˈbɑːbɪkən‖ˈbɑːr-/ *n* a tower for defence at a gate or bridge −see picture at CASTLE

Barbican [*the*] an area of modern buildings in the City of London, including the Barbican Arts Centre: *We went to see a film at the Barbican.* −see colour map on page 817

bar·bie /ˈbɑːbi‖ˈbɑːr-/ *n Austr and BrE infml* a BARBECUE

Barbie doll /ˈ··· ·/ *n tdmk* a DOLL in the shape of an attractive young woman, with a range of fashionable clothes, shoes, etc., used as a child's toy. In the US, a woman is sometimes said to be like a Barbie doll if she is attractive and likes clothes but is not very clever. −compare SINDY

bar bil·liards /ˌ· ˈ···/ *n* [U] a game usu. played in pubs, in which players use long sticks (CUEs) to push balls into holes in a table, without knocking over any of the small pieces of wood which stand near the holes

bar·bi·tu·rate /bɑːˈbɪtʃɣrɨt‖bɑːrˈbɪtʃɣrɨt, -reɪt/ *n* [C;U] *med* a powerful drug that makes people calm and puts them to sleep

Bar·bour /ˈbɑːbəʳ‖ˈbɑːr-/ *n tdmk* in Britain, a good quality, expensive coat which is quite short and made of a special material to protect one from rain and wind. Barbours are worn esp. by people who live or spend time in the country, but have also become fashionable with people who live in cities. − see also GREEN WELLIE BRIGADE

Barbour jackets

barb·wire /ˌbɑːbˈwaɪəʳ‖ˌbɑːrb-/ *n AmE* BARBED WIRE

Bar·ce·lo·na /ˌbɑːsɨˈləʊnə‖ˌbɑːr-/ a city and port in N Spain, on the Mediterranean

bar chart /ˈ· ·/ also **bar graph** *AmE*− *n* a way of showing changes in amounts, e.g. of population or profits, which is similar to a GRAPH but uses RECTANGULAR shapes positioned side by side instead of a line or curve −see picture at CHART, and see also FLOWCHART, PIE CHART

Bar·clay·card /ˈbɑːklɪkɑːd‖ˈbɑːrklɪkɑːrd/ *n tdmk* [C;U] a CREDIT CARD available from Barclays Bank: *Do you take* (=accept payment by) *Barclaycard? | I've lost my Barclaycard.*

Bar·clays Bank /ˌbɑːklɪz ˈbæŋk‖ˌbɑːr-/ also **Barclays** one

of the main British banks, branches of which can be found in many towns and cities in Britain

bar code /ˈ· ·/ *n* a system of representing information in a way that can be read by a computer, consisting of a special LABEL made up of thick and thin lines on products in shops, factories, etc.

bard /bɑːd‖bɑːrd/ *n lit* a poet

Bard of A·von /ˌbɑːd əv ˈeɪvən‖ˌbɑːrd-/ [*the*] a poetic name for William Shakespeare, after the river Avon at Stratford, where he was born

Bar·dot /bɑːˈdəʊ‖bɑːr-/, **Bri·gitte** /brɪˈʒiːt/ (1934−) a French film actress esp. famous in the 1950s and 60s, one of the main SEX SYMBOLs of that time

Brigitte Bardot

bare¹ /beəʳ/ *adj* **1** without clothes or covering: *bare skin | You'll cut yourself if you walk around here in* **bare feet.** *| The trees are bare.* (=without leaves) *| bare floorboards* (=not covered by any material) **2** not hidden; open to view or examination: *The investigation has* **laid bare** *their fraudulent scheme. | the bare truth* **3** [(of)] empty: *The cupboard was bare. | The thieves stripped the house bare.* (=took everything) *| a room bare of furniture* **4** [A] with nothing added: *I killed it* **with my bare hands.** (=without any weapon) *| Just give us the bare facts of the case. | the bare necessities of life | He did the bare minimum of revision* (=the smallest amount possible) *necessary to pass the exam.* −see also BARELY −− **ness** *n* [U]

bare² *v* [T] **1** to bring to view, esp. by taking off a covering; EXPOSE: *The dog* **bared its teeth.** *| He* **bared his head** (=took his hat off) *as a sign of respect when the funeral passed by.* **2 bare one's heart/soul** to make known one's deepest feelings

bare·back /ˈbeəbæk‖ˈbeər-/ *adj, adv* [A] on the bare back of a horse; without a SADDLE: *a bareback rider | to ride bareback*

bare bones /ˌ· ˈ·/ *n* [P (**of**)] the simplest but most important parts or facts: *the bare bones of the matter*

bare·faced /ˌbeəˈfeɪst◂‖ˈbeərfeɪst/ *adj* shameless and noticeable in an offensive way; BLATANT: *a barefaced lie* −− **ly** /ˌbeəˈfeɪstli, -sɨdli◂‖ˈbeərfeɪsɨdli, -stli/ *adv*

bare·foot /ˈbeəfʊt‖ˈbeər-/ also **bare·foot·ed** /ˌbeəˈfʊtɨd◂‖ˌbeər-/ *adj, adv* without shoes or other covering on the feet: *The children go* **barefoot** *in summer.*

bare·head·ed /ˌbeəˈhedɨd◂‖ˈbeərhedɨd/ *adj, adv* without a hat or other covering on the head

bare·leg·ged /ˌbeəˈlegɨd, -ˈlegd◂‖ˌbeər-/ *adj, adv* with no covering on the legs

bare·ly /ˈbeəli‖ˈbeərli/ *adv* **1** almost not; only just; hardly: *She had barely arrived when she had to leave again. | We* *have barely enough money to last the weekend.* | *The scar on her cheek is now barely noticeable.* —see HARDLY (USAGE)   **2** in a bare way: *The room was furnished barely.* (–with very little furniture)

Bar·en·boim /ˈbærənbɔɪm/, **Daniel** (1942–) an Israeli PIANIST and CONDUCTOR born in Argentina

barf /bɑːf‖bɑːrf/ v [I] *AmE infml* VOMIT[1]: *He'd been drinking too much and barfed all over the sidewalk.* —**barf** n [U] : *the smell of barf on the sidewalk*

barf bag /ˈ· ·/ n *AmE infml* a small paper bag used on passenger aircraft by people who need to be sick

bar food /ˈ· ˌ·/ n [U] food obtainable at the bar of a PUB, usu. plain but filling hot meals or cold sandwiches (SANDWICH[1] (1))

bar·gain[1] /ˈbɑːgɪn‖ˈbɑːr-/ n   **1** an agreement, made between two people or groups, to do something in return for something else: *We've made a bargain that he will do the shopping and I'll cook.* | *The management and the union leaders have* **struck a bargain.** (=reached an agreement) | *They haven't kept their* **side of the bargain.**| *Be careful if you're doing business with him; he* **drives a hard bargain.** (=tends to make agreements that are very much in his favour)   **2** something for sale or bought for less than its real value: *These shoes are a real bargain at such a low price.* | *a bargain price* | *to go* **bargain hunting** (=looking for cheap things to buy)   **3** any piece of business taking place on the STOCK EXCHANGE   **4 into the bargain** *BrE* **in the bargain** *AmE* in addition to everything else: *She had to look after four children, and her sick mother into the bargain.*   **5 make the best of a bad bargain** to do the best one can under difficult conditions

bargain[2] v [I (**with, about**)] to talk about the conditions of a sale, agreement, or contract; NEGOTIATE: *If you bargain with them they might reduce the price.* | *The increased demand for their skills has given these workers greater* **bargaining power.** – –**er** n : *wage bargainers*
   bargain sthg. ↔ **away** *phr v* [T] to give away or give up in return for something of less value: *The unions bargained away their rights in exchange for a small pay rise.*
   bargain for sbdy./sthg. , also **bargain on** sbdy./sthg. *AmE*– *phr v* [T *usu. in negatives*] to take into account; consider as likely or possible; expect: *I hadn't bargained for such heavy rain, and I got very wet.* [+v-ing] *We didn't bargain on spending so much money on hotels.* | *I just asked for a sandwich but I got more than I'd bargained for – they brought me an enormous plate of food!*

bargain base·ment /ˈ·· ˌ··/ n *esp. AmE* a part of a large shop, usu. the BASEMENT (=floor below ground level), where goods are sold at reduced prices

barge[1] /bɑːdʒ‖bɑːrdʒ/ n   **1** a large low flat-bottomed boat used mainly for carrying heavy goods on a CANAL or river   **2** a motorboat carried by naval ships for the use of officers   **3** a large rowing boat used chiefly on rivers for important people on ceremonial occasions

barge[2] v [I+*adv/prep*] (of a person) to move in a heavy ungraceful way, often hitting against things: *He barged onto the bus before everyone else.* | *She ran round the corner and barged into* one of the teachers.
   barge in *phr v* [I (**on**)] to enter or rush in rudely; interrupt: *The door burst open and the children barged in.*| *He's always barging in on other people's conversations.*

barg·ee /bɑːˈdʒiː‖bɑːr-/ *BrE* ‖ **barge·man** /ˈbɑːdʒmən‖ˈbɑːrdʒ-/*AmE*– n a person who drives or works on a barge on a CANAL

barge pole /ˈ· ·/ n   **1** a long pole used in pushing along and guiding a barge   **2 I wouldn't touch it/him/her, etc. with a barge pole** *(BrE)*/**with a ten-foot pole** *(AmE)* I want nothing to do with it/him/her

bar graph /ˈ· ·/ n *AmE for* BAR CHART

bar·i·tone /ˈbærɨtəʊn/ n (a man with) a male singing voice lower than TENOR and higher than BASS

ba·ri·um meal /ˌbeəriəm ˈmiːl/ n a chemical substance that people drink before they have X-RAYS, so that their inner organs will show up more clearly

bark[1] /bɑːk‖bɑːrk/ v   **1** [I (**at**)] to make the short sharp sound that dogs and some other animals make: *The dog always barks at the postman.*   **2** [T (OUT)] to say (something) in a sharp loud voice: *The officer barked (out) an order.*   **3 bark at the moon** *AmE* to make a great effort to do something useless   **4 bark up the wrong tree**

infml to direct one's efforts or actions at the wrong person or in the wrong direction; have a mistaken idea: *You're barking up the wrong tree if you think she'll be able to help you.*

bark[2] n   **1** the sharp loud sound made by a dog –see also WOOF[1]   **2** [*usu. sing.*] a sound or voice like this: *the bark of the guns*   **3 his bark is worse than his bite** *infml* he might shout a lot and seem frightening, but he is really quite nice

bark[3] n [U] the strong outer covering of a tree

bark[4] v [T] to rub the skin off (a knee, elbow, etc.) e.g. by falling: *She* **barked her shins** *against the wheelbarrow.*

bark[5] also **barque**– n   **1** a sailing ship with three MASTS, having square sails on the first two and a three-cornered sail on the third   **2** *lit* a small sailing ship of any type

bar keep·er /ˈ· ˌ··/ n *AmE* BARMAN

bark·er /ˈbɑːkəʳ‖ˈbɑːr-/ n a person who stands outside a place of public amusement, esp. a CIRCUS, shouting to people to come in

Bar·ker, Ron·nie /ˈrɒni‖ˈrɑː-/ (1929–) an English actor and COMEDIAN best-known for his parts in the British television programmes *Porridge*, *Open All Hours*, and esp. *The Two Ronnies*, in which he performed with Ronnie Corbett

bar·ley /ˈbɑːli‖ˈbɑːrli/ n [U] a grasslike grain plant grown as a food crop for people and cattle, and also used in the making of alcoholic drinks, such as beer –see picture at CEREAL

Bar·ley·corn, John see JOHN BARLEYCORN

barley sug·ar /ˈ·· ˌ··/ n [C;U] *BrE* a kind of sweet formerly made with barley, often eaten to prevent sickness during travelling

barley wa·ter /ˈ·· ˌ··/ n [U] *BrE* a drink made from barley and fruit juice

barley wine /ˌ·· ˈ·/ n [U] *esp. BrE* a type of very strong beer

Bar·low /ˈbɑːləʊ‖ˈbɑːr-/, **Ken** a character in the British television programme *Coronation Street*, sometimes mentioned as being a very boring character –see also CORONATION STREET

bar·maid /ˈbɑːmeɪd‖ˈbɑːr-/ n *esp. BrE* a woman who serves drinks in a BAR[1] (3a). The British STEREOTYPE of a barmaid is a friendly, attractive woman, usu. wearing a lot of MAKE-UP and often with large breasts.

bar·man /ˈbɑːmən‖ˈbɑːr-/ also **bartender, bar keeper** *esp. AmE*– n **-men** /mən/ a man who serves drinks in a BAR[1] (3a)

bar mitz·vah /ˌbɑː ˈmɪtsvə‖ˌbɑːr-/ n   **1** the religious ceremony held when a Jewish boy reaches the age of 13, the age of religious duty and responsibility   **2** a boy for whom this ceremony is held

barm·y /ˈbɑːmi‖ˈbɑːrmi/ adj *BrE infml* foolish or a little mad: *You must be barmy to go out playing football in weather like this.*

barn /bɑːn‖bɑːrn/ n   **1** a farm building for storing crops and food for animals, or for keeping animals in   **2** *infml* a big bare plain building: *a great barn of a house* –see also DUTCH BARN

bar·na·cle /ˈbɑːnəkəl‖ˈbɑːr-/ n a small SHELLFISH which collects in large numbers on rocks and on the bottoms of ships, and which is hard to remove

Bar·nard /ˈbɑːnɑːd‖ˈbɑːrnɑːrd/, **Chris·ti·aan** /ˈkrɪstiən/ (1922–) a South African SURGEON who was the first to successfully TRANSPLANT a human heart into a patient

Bar·nar·do Home /bəˈnɑːdəʊ ˌhəʊm‖bərˈnɑːr-/ n in Britain, one of a group of special homes for very poor children or those who have no parents. The first Barnardo home was opened in London in 1867 by T. J. Barnardo

barn dance /ˈ· ·/ n   **1** a social gathering at which COUNTRY DANCEs are performed, originally held in a barn   **2** *esp. BrE* a dance performed at such a gathering

Barnes /bɑːnz‖bɑːrnz/, **John** (1963–) an English international attacking footballer who played for Liverpool football club

bar·ney /ˈbɑːni‖ˈbɑːrni/ n [*usu. sing.*] *infml, esp. BrE* a noisy quarrel

Barns·ley /ˈbɑːnzli‖ˈbɑːr-/ a town in S Yorkshire in N England, known esp. for its coal mines

barn·storm /ˈbɑːnstɔːm‖ˈbɑːrnstɔːrm/ v [I] to travel from place to place making short stops to give theatre performances or make political speeches — ~**er** *n*

Bar·num /ˈbɑːnəm‖ˈbɑːr-/, **P T** (1810–91) an American most famous for the CIRCUS he began with James Bailey in 1881, which they called the "Greatest Show on Earth"

barn·yard /ˈbɑːnjɑːd‖ˈbɑːrnjɑːrd/ *n* a FARMYARD

ba·rom·e·ter /bəˈrɒmɪtəʳ‖-ˈrɑː-/ *n* **1** an instrument for measuring the air pressure in order to judge probable changes in the weather or to calculate height above sea level **2** something that shows or gives an idea of changes e.g. in public opinion: *Tomorrow's by-election will be a barometer of the mood in the whole country.* —**tric** /ˌbærəˈmetrɪk◂/ *adj* —**trically** /kli/ *adv*

bar·on /ˈbærən/ *n* **1** a British nobleman of the lowest rank **2** (*usu. in comb.*) a man, esp. a businessman, who has great power or influence: *an oil baron* | *a press baron who owns three national newspapers* | *union barons*

bar·on·ess /ˈbærənɪs/ *n* (in Britain) a woman who is **a** the wife of a baron **b** of that rank in her own right

bar·on·et /ˈbærənɪt, -net/ *n* a British KNIGHT¹ (2), lower in rank than a baron, whose title passes on to his son when he dies

bar·on·et·cy /ˈbærənɪtsi/ *n* the rank of a baronet

ba·ro·ni·al /bəˈrəʊniəl/ *adj* **1** of or related to a BARON **2** large, rich, and noble: *a baronial hall*

bar·on·y /ˈbærəni/ *n* the rank of a BARON

ba·roque /bəˈrɒk, bəˈrəʊk‖bəˈrəʊk, -ˈrɑːk/ *adj* in a highly decorated style which was fashionable in art, buildings, music, etc. in Europe during the 17th century —compare ROCOCO —**baroque** *n* [*the*]

barque /bɑːk‖bɑːrk/ *n* a BARK⁵

Barr /bɑːʳ/, **Ro·seanne** /rəʊˈzæn/ the former name of Roseanne Arnold —see Roseanne ARNOLD

Bar·ra /ˈbærə/ an island of the Outer Hebrides, in the Western Isles of Scotland

bar·rack /ˈbærək/ *v* [I;T] **1** *BrE* to interrupt by shouting or pretended cheering; JEER (at): *They barracked (the speaker) throughout the meeting.* **2** *AustrE* to cheer in support (of)

bar·racks /ˈbærəks/ *n* **barracks** [C+*sing./pl. v*] a building or group of buildings that soldiers live in

bar·ra·cu·da /ˌbærəˈkjuːdə‖-ˈkuːdə/ *n* **-da** *or* **-das** a large fierce flesh-eating tropical fish

bar·rage¹ /ˈbærɑːʒ‖ˈbɑːrɪdʒ/ *n* a bank of earth, stones, etc. built across a river to provide water for farming or to prevent flooding

bar·rage² /ˈbærɑːʒ‖bəˈrɑːʒ/ *n* **1** the continuous firing of a number of heavy guns, done esp. to give protection to soldiers as they advance upon the enemy **2** [(of)] a large number of questions, statements, etc., made at almost the same time or very quickly one after the other: *a nonstop barrage of questions* | *a barrage of criticism*

barred /bɑːd‖bɑːrd/ *adj* **1** having bars, esp. of the stated number: *a five-barred gate* **2** *fml* having bands of different colours: *barred feathers*

bar·rel¹ /ˈbærəl/ *n* **1** a round usu. wooden container with curved sides and a flat top and bottom: *a beer barrel* | *The wine is left to mature in oak barrels.* **2** [(of)] also **bar·rel·ful** /-fʊl/— the amount of liquid that a barrel contains, esp. used as a unit of oil production: *This country produces almost 2 million barrels of oil per day.* | *The price of crude oil has gone up by 50 cents a barrel.* **3** a long tube-shaped part of a gun: *a rifle barrel* —see picture at GUN **4 over a barrel** *infml* in a position of serious disadvantage: *They're charging an exorbitant price for fixing the car, but they've got us over a barrel because we can't do without it.* —see picture at CONTAINER, and see also **lock, stock, and barrel** (LOCK¹), **scrape the (bottom of the) barrel** (SCRAPE¹)

barrel² *v* **-l-** [I] *AmE infml* to move fast esp. unsafely: *He barreled along the road at 90 miles an hour.* | *She went barreling into the teacher as she ran around the corner.*

barrel or·gan /ˈ··· ˌ··/ *n* a big musical instrument which can be moved from place to place and is played by turning a handle, usu. by street musicians for money. In the past, when street musicians played barrel organs, they often had a pet monkey who sat on the barrel organ.

bar·ren /ˈbærən/ *adj* **1** (of women or female animals) not able to produce children or young; INFERTILE **2** (of trees

or plants) producing no fruit or seed **3** (of soil) too poor to produce a good crop: *barren wastelands* **4** useless; empty; producing no result: *a barren discussion* — ~**ness** *n* [U]

Bar·rett /ˈbærət/ a British building firm which builds houses in many parts of the country and is known esp. for its low-cost houses

bar·rette /bəˈret, bɑː-/ *n AmE for* HAIR SLIDE

bar·ri·cade¹ /ˈbærɪkeɪd, ˌbærɪˈkeɪd/ *n* a quickly-built structure of trees, earth, bricks, etc., put across a road or passage to stop anyone from passing or entering, and usu. intended for use over a limited time only

barricade² *v* [T] **1** to block off or close off with a barricade: *to barricade the street/the windows* **2** [+*obj+adv/ prep*] to defend or shut in with a barricade: *The terrorists barricaded themselves in (the embassy).*

Bar·rie /ˈbæri/, **J M** (1860–1937) a Scottish writer of plays and stories, best known for his children's story *Peter Pan* —see also PETER PAN

bar·ri·er /ˈbæriəʳ/ *n* **1** something that is used to keep people or things apart or to prevent or control their movement: *The police put up barriers to control the crowd.* | *Show your ticket at the barrier before you board the train.* | *The football fans broke through the barriers and rushed onto the pitch.* | *The cream acts as a barrier against infection.* **2** [(to)] something non-physical that keeps people apart or prevents activity, movement, etc.: *social/ethnic/language barriers* | *Lack of confidence is the biggest barrier to investment in the region.* | *trade barriers such as import taxes*

bar·ring /ˈbɑːrɪŋ/ *prep* except for: *Barring any last-minute problems* (=if there are none) *we should finish the job by tonight.* —see also BAR³

bar·ri·o /ˈbæriəʊ/ *n AmE* a poor part of an American town or city where many Spanish-speaking people live; GHETTO: *the barrios of Los Angeles*

bar·ris·ter /ˈbærɪstəʳ/ *n* esp. in England and Wales, a lawyer who has the right of speaking in the higher courts of law —compare ADVOCATE, SOLICITOR

bar·row¹ /ˈbærəʊ/ *n* **1** a small cart with two or four wheels, on which fruit, vegetables, etc. are put to be sold in street markets **2** a WHEELBARROW

barrow² *n* a TUMULUS

barrow boy /ˈ··· ˌ·/ *n esp. BrE* a man or boy who sells goods, e.g. fruit or vegetables, from a barrow; COSTERMONGER

Bar·row-in-Fur·ness /ˌbærəʊ ɪn ˈfɜːnɪs‖-ˈfɜːr-/ an industrial town in NW England

bar snack /ˈ· ·/ *n BrE* a light meal served in a PUB

Bart /bɑːt‖bɑːrt/ *written abbrev. for:* BARONET: *Sir John Brown, Bart.*

bar·tend·er /ˈbɑːˌtendəʳ‖ˈbɑːr-/ *n esp. AmE for* BARMAN

bar·ter /ˈbɑːtəʳ‖ˈbɑːr-/ *v* [I;T (**for, with**)] to exchange (goods) for other goods rather than for money; TRADE: *They bartered farm products for machinery.* | (fig.) *He bartered his freedom away for a little comfort.* —**barter** *n* [U]: *The system of barter was superseded by the use of money.*

Bar·ton /ˈbɑːtn‖ˈbɑːr-/, **Cla·ra** /ˈkleərə/ (1821–1912) an American nurse called the Angel of the Battlefield who worked in army camps during the American Civil War and the Franco-Prussian War and then set up and led the American Red Cross

Bart's /bɑːts‖bɑːrts/ also **St. Bartholomew's Hospital** a famous London teaching hospital whose history goes back to 1123

Ba·rysh·ni·kov /bəˈrɪʃnɪkɒf‖-kɔːf/, **Mik·hail** /mɪˈkaɪl/ (1948–) a Russian-born BALLET dancer and CHOREOGRAPHER who DEFECTed (left as a political protest) to the US

bas·alt /ˈbæsɔːlt, bəˈsɔːlt‖ˈbæ-, ˈbeɪ-/ *n* [U] a dark greenish-black rock

base¹ /beɪs/ *n* **1** [(the)] S (**of**)] the lowest part of something, esp. the part on which something stands: *the base of a mountain/statue/pillar* | *Draw a square with the line "xy" as its base.* | *The coccyx is a small bone at the base of the spine.* **2** [*usu. sing.*] the original part or substance from which something develops or from which a mixture is made: *Many languages have Latin as their base.* | *soup with a vegetable base* | *a paint with an oil base* **3** [C] a centre from which something is controlled and where

▶ Baseball

Baseball is a very popular sport in the US where it is often called the **national pastime**. Many people, esp. men, support a particular team and watch the games that their team plays.

Each team has a name, which usually includes the name of the town or city that the team is associated with. Some examples of names are: **Boston Red Sox, Minnesota Twins, Chicago Cubs,** and **Houston Astros.**

The two leagues together are known as the MAJOR LEAGUES. The playing season runs from late spring to October. The winning team in each league is called the PENNANT (2) champion. In October, the two pennant champions play against each other in seven games called the WORLD SERIES. The team that wins four games is the champion.

Professional baseball games are organised in the US in the following way:

National League   American League
(12 teams)   (14 teams)

↙   ↘   ↙   ↘

Eastern   Western   Eastern   Western
division   division   division   division

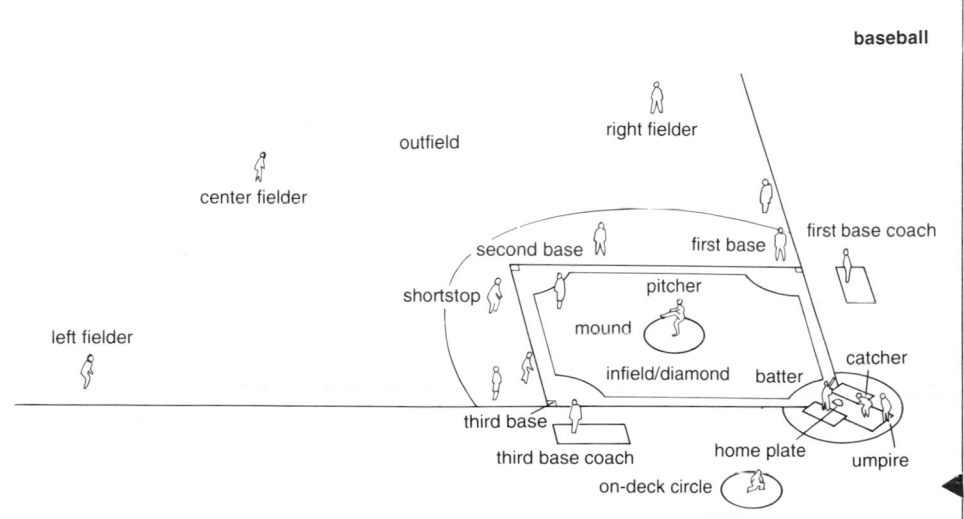

baseball

plans are made: *After we had reached the top of the mountain, we returned to our* **base camp.** | *Our company's base is in London, but we have branches all over the world.* | *a military/naval base* | *a cruise missile base* **4** [C] something that provides the conditions which are necessary for a particular activity or situation: *The party's main* **power base** (=the group that provides support for its political power) *is the middle class and the skilled manual workers.* | *the nation's* **manufacturing base** (=its factories, systems for producing important materials, etc.) | *The company is hoping to expand its* **customer base** *to include large business customers.* | *To finance these plans, the government will have to broaden the* **tax base.** (=to get tax from different kinds of people or activity) **5** [C] *tech* a chemical substance which combines with an acid to form a salt **6** [C] (in the game of BASEBALL) any of the four points which a player must touch in order to make a run —see picture at BASEBALL **7** [C *usu. sing.*] *tech* a line from which to calculate the distances and positions of distant points when making maps **8** [*usu. sing.*] *tech* the number in relation to which a number system or table is built up: *Ordinary numbers use base 10, but most computers work to base 2.* —see also DATA BASE **9 off base** *AmE infml* completely wrong: *You're way off base if you think I'm going to do that much overtime.*

base² *v* [T+*obj*+*adv*/*prep*; *usu. pass.*] to place or establish; provide with a base or centre: *Where is your company based?* | *It's based overseas/based in Paris.* | *a London-based firm* | *land-based missiles*
   base sthg. **on/upon** sthg. *phr v* [T] to form or make (something) using (something else) as the starting point: *Their marketing strategy is based on a study of consumer spending.* | *They based their estimate on the figures for the last three years.* | *The film is based on a novel by D.H. Lawrence.*

base³ *adj esp. lit* (of people, actions, etc.) showing a complete lack of moral principles; dishonourable: *base motives* | *base conduct* —see also BASE METAL — **~ ly** *adv* — **~ ness** *n* [U]

base-ball /ˈbeɪsbɔːl/ *n* [U] a game played with a BAT and ball (the **baseball**) between two teams of nine players each, on a large field which has four bases which a player must touch in order to make a RUN² (10b): *a baseball player/team* —see LITTLE LEAGUE, MAJOR LEAGUES, MINOR LEAGUE, NATIONAL LEAGUE REFEREE (USAGE) and see picture at GLOVE and colour picture on page 884

baseball cap /ˈ·· ·/ also **baseball hat** *n* a brightly coloured hat which fits close to the head and has a part that sticks out in front to shade the eyes —see picture at HAT

baseball card /ˈ·· ·/ *n* in the US, a small stiff piece of paper with a picture of a baseball player on the front and information about that player on the back: *a baseball card collector* | *children trading baseball cards*

baseball glove /ˈ·· ·/ also **baseball mitt, mitt**— *n* a thick, large leather hand covering worn to protect the hand when playing baseball

base-board /ˈbeɪsbɔːd‖-bɔːrd/ *n AmE for* SKIRTING BOARD

base hit /ˈ· ·/ *n* (in BASEBALL) an action of hitting the ball so that one reaches the first BASE (one of the four points a player must touch to win a point)

Ba-sel /ˈbɑːzəl/ also **Basle, Bâle** the second largest city in N Switzerland, on the river Rhine

base-less /ˈbeɪsləs/ *adj* without a good reason: *baseless fears/accusations*

base-line /ˈbeɪslaɪn/ *n* **1** [C *usu. sing.*] a line or level used as a base, e.g. when measuring or making comparisons

▶ Basketball

Basketball is a very popular sport in the US. Many people, esp. men, support a particular team and watch the games that their team plays.

Each team has a name, which usually includes the name of the town or city that the team is associated with. Some examples of names are: **Boston Celtics, Chicago Bulls, Denver Nuggets**, and **Los Angeles Lakers**.

The playing season runs from autumn to late spring. Teams within each division play against each other, and against teams from the other divisions within the conferences. The best teams from each conference then play a group of seven games against each other (the **NBA Championship**). The first team to win four of these games is the NBA champion.

Professional basketball games are organised in the US in the following way:

National Basketball Association (NBA)

↙ ↘

Eastern conference — Western conference

↙ ↘ ↙ ↘

Atlantic division (6 teams) — Central division (7 teams) — Midwest division (7 teams) — Pacific division (7 teams)

◀

2 [*the*] the back line at each end of a court in games like tennis —see picture at TENNIS

base·man /'beismən/ n -men /mən/ (in BASEBALL) the player who defends first, second, or third BASE¹ (6): *Cey is the third baseman tonight.*

base·ment /'beismənt/ n a room or rooms completely or partly below street level: *She lives in a basement/in a basement apartment.* —compare CELLAR

base met·al /ˌ· '··/ n *old use* a metal such as iron or lead which is not regarded as precious

base rate /'· ·/ n the standard rate of interest on which a bank bases its charges for lending and interest on borrowing —compare DISCOUNT RATE

bas·es /'beisi:z/ *pl. of* BASIS

bash¹ /bæʃ/ v [T] *infml* **1** [(IN, UP)] to hit hard so as to crush, break, or hurt: *She bashed her head (on the door).* | *They bashed the door in and rushed into the room.* **2** *infml, esp. BrE* to attack with words; find fault with: *The prime minister is always bashing the unions.*

bash² n usu. infml **1** a hard or painful blow: *He gave me a bash on the nose.* **2** *infml old-fash* an enjoyable party with a lot of noise, laughter, etc. **3 have a bash (at)** *BrE infml* to make an attempt (at): *I've never rowed a boat before, but I don't mind having a bash (at it).*

bash·ful /'bæʃfəl/ adj uncomfortable in social situations; SHY; SELF-CONSCIOUS: *a bashful smile* | *bashful teenagers* — ~ly adv — ~ness n [U]

Bash Street Kids /ˌ· · ˌ·/, **The** a group of children from a COMIC, who are difficult to control and who are always playing tricks on their teacher

ba·sic /'beisik/ adj **1** [(to)] more necessary than anything else; on which everything else rests, depends, or is built; FUNDAMENTAL: *the basic principles of mathematics* | *The industry's basic problem is the lack of demand.* | *A knowledge of her upbringing is basic to an understanding of her books.* **2** [A] being a starting point, to which more can be added: *my basic salary* (=before any additional payments) | *a course in basic computer skills* **3** [F] *infml* simple and without anything more than is necessary; RUDIMENTARY: *The hotel is a bit basic.* | *My knowledge of car engines is pretty basic.* —see also BASICS

Basic , basic n [U] a very commonly used computer language, which was developed to make computers easy for non-specialists to use

ba·sic·al·ly /'beisikli/ adv with regard to what is most important and basic; in reality; FUNDAMENTALLY: *Basically, he's a nice person, but he doesn't always show it.* | *He's basically nice.* | *Basically* (=the simple and most important fact is), *the company is in a mess.*

ba·sics /'beisiks/ n [(the)] P (of) the basic parts or principles of a subject, process, etc.: *The basics of education are reading, writing, and simple arithmetic.* | *We need to get back to (the) basics.* | *a back-to-basics approach*

basic train·ing /ˌ·· '··/ n [U] *AmE* the period in which a new soldier is taught military rules and how to fight and is given much physical exercise

Ba·sie /'beisi/, **Count** (1904–84) an American JAZZ musician who played the piano and led one of the best known big bands of the SWING period

bas·il /'bæzəl/ n [U] a type of sweet-smelling plant (HERB) used in cooking

ba·sil·i·ca /bə'silikə, -'zil-/ n **1** (in ancient Rome) a long room, round at one end, with a roof resting on two lines of stone supports, used as a law court **2** a church with a form like this: *St Peter's Basilica in Rome is the largest Roman Catholic church.*

bas·i·lisk /'bæsilisk, 'bæz-/ n an imaginary snakelike creature, whose breath and look were thought able to kill

ba·sin /'beisən/ n **1** *esp. BrE* a round container that is wide but not very deep, used for holding liquids or food; bowl: *a pudding basin* **2** a WASHBASIN **3** [(of)] also **ba·sin·ful** /-ful/— the amount a basin will hold: *a basin of hot water* **4** a hollow place containing water, or where water collects: *the basin of a fountain* **5** an area of land from which water runs down into a river; a large valley: *the Amazon Basin* **6** the deep part of a HARBOUR almost surrounded by land

Ba·sin·ger /'bæsindʒər/, **Kim** /kim/ (1954–) an American film actress, known esp. for playing attractive, sexy women

Ba·sin Street /'·· ˌ·/ a street in New Orleans, US, associated with JAZZ music and made famous by the song *Basin Street Blues* which many musicians have recorded

ba·sis /'beisis/ n bases /'beisi:z/ **1** [(of, for)] the facts, principles, statements, etc. from which something is formed, started, or developed: *What is the basis of/for your opinion?* | *There is no scientific basis for these claims.* | *This series of lectures formed the basis of a new book.* | *Is it safe to predict the result on the basis of one opinion poll?* **2** the stated way of carrying out an action, process, etc.: *She works for us on a part-time basis.* | *He gives advice on an individual basis.* | *The machine has been installed on a trial basis.* **3** the main or most important part of something: *The basis of the drink is orange juice.*

bask /ba:sk||bæsk/ v [I (in)] to sit or lie in pleasant warmth: *to lie on the sand, basking in the sunshine* | (fig.) *He basked in* (=enjoyed) *his employer's approval.*

Baskervilles see HOUND OF THE BASKERVILLES

bas·ket /'ba:skət||'bæ-/ n **1** a light container made of narrow pieces of wood, plastic, wire, etc., woven together, and used for carrying or holding things: *a shopping basket* | *a basket of eggs* | *a wastepaper basket* —see picture at CONTAINER **2** [(of)] also **basket·ful** /-ful/— the amount a basket will hold: *a basket of fruit* **3** an open net fixed to a metal ring high up off the ground, through which players try to throw the ball in the game of basketball **4** a point in this game: *He shot* (=made) *10 baskets.*

bas·ket·ball /'ba:skətbɔ:l||'bæs-/ n [U] an indoor game between two teams of usu. five players each, in which each team tries to throw a large ball (the **basketball**) through the other team's BASKET (3) —see REFEREE (USAGE) and see colour picture on page 884

basket case /'·· ˌ·/ n *infml* a person who is unable to do anything useful, usu. as the result of being very tired or frightened

bas·ket·ry /'ba:skətri||'bæs-/ also **bas·ket·work** /'ba:skətwɜ:k||'bæskətwɜːrk/— n [U] (the art of making) baskets or objects woven like baskets

basket weav·ing /ˈ·· ˌ··/ n [U] the activity of making baskets. In the US, people often make jokes about basket weaving, as an activity that takes little skill, knowledge, or work: *What did you study in college, basket weaving?*

Bas·kin-Rob·bins /ˌbæskɪn ˈrɒbɪnz‖-ˈrɑː-/ tdmk an American company which makes a well-known type of ICE CREAM

Basle /bɑːl/ see BASEL

Bas·mat·i rice /bəzˌmæti ˈraɪs/ n [U] a type of high quality rice from India and Pakistan, popular with British people esp. when cooking Indian food

basque /bæsk/ n a woman's close-fitting undergarment reaching from under the arms to the tops of the legs

Basque /bæsk, bɑːsk‖bæsk/ n **1** [C] a person from the mountainous REGION that is on the border between France and Spain and is partly in France and partly in Spain. In recent years some Basques in Spain (**Basque Separatists**) have tried to gain political independence for the region. **2** [U] the language of these people

bas-re·lief /ˌbɑː rɪˈliːf, ˌbæs-/ n [C;U] Fr (an example of) a form of art in which shapes stand out slightly from the surrounding surface, which has been cut away − compare HIGH RELIEF

bass¹ /beɪs/ n **1** [C] (a man with) the lowest male singing voice, below BARITONE **2** [U] the lower half of the whole range of musical notes −compare TREBLE³ (2) **3** [C] a BASS GUITAR: *He's formed a new band with his brother on bass/playing bass.* **4** [C] a DOUBLE BASS −**bass** adj, adv: *a bass saxophone/drum | to sing bass*

bass² /bæs/ n bass or basses a fresh-water or salt-water fish that can be eaten

Bass /bæs/ n tdmk a company which makes different types of beer and which owns many PUBS in the UK

bass clef /ˌbeɪs ˈklef/ n tech a sign (𝄢) on a musical STAVE showing that a note written on the top line of the stave is the A below MIDDLE C −compare TREBLE CLEF

bas·set /ˈbæsɪt/ also **basset hound** /ˈ·· ˌ·/ − n a sporting dog with a long body, short legs, and large ears

Bas·sey /ˈbæsi/, **Shir·ley** /ˈʃɜːli‖ˈʃɜːr-/ (1937−) a British popular music singer, born in Wales, known for her sexually attractive appearance and exciting stage performances whose well-known songs include *Hey, Big Spender*

bass gui·tar /ˌbeɪs ɡɪˈtɑːʳ/ also **bass**− n an electric GUITAR (musical instrument with six strings and a long neck) used for playing low musical notes

bas·si·net /ˌbæsɪˈnet/ n a baby's bed or carriage that looks like a basket, often with a covering at one end

bas·sist /ˈbeɪsɪst/ n a person who plays the BASS GUITAR or the DOUBLE BASS

bas·soon /bəˈsuːn/ n a large musical instrument of the WOODWIND family, with a double REED (2) −see picture at WOODWIND − ~ist n

bast /bæst/ n [U] the FIBRE from certain trees, used for making mats, baskets, etc.

bas·tard /ˈbæstəd, ˈbɑː-‖ˈbæstərd/ n **1** often derog a child of unmarried parents **2** sl an unpleasant, disagreeable, or cruel person: *You bastard! | She's a real bastard to work for.* **3** sl any person, esp. a man, of the stated kind: *That lucky bastard! | The poor bastard's been sacked.* **4** sl something difficult or troublesome: *This pan is a bastard to clean. | a bastard of a traffic jam*

bas·tard·ize also **-ise** BrE /ˈbæstədaɪz, ˈbɑː-‖ˈbæstər-/ v [T] fml to spoil by making false: *a bastardized account of the trial*

bas·tard·y /ˈbæstədi, ˈbɑː-‖ˈbæstər-/ n [U] fml or law the state of being a BASTARD

baste¹ /beɪst/ v [I;T] (in sewing) to TACK² (3)

baste² v [T] to cover (meat, etc.) with melted fat during cooking

Bas·tille /bæˈstiːl/ [the] an old prison in Paris, attacked and destroyed on 14 July 1789 during the French REVOLUTION. This date is now celebrated each year as a French national holiday (**Bastille Day**): *The storming of the Bastille really marked the beginning of the French Revolution.*

bas·ti·na·do /ˌbæstɪˈneɪdəʊ, -ˈnɑː-/ n **-does** old use a form of punishment consisting of beating someone with a stick across the bottoms of the feet −**bastinado** v [T]

bas·ti·on /ˈbæstiən‖-tʃən/ n **1** a part of the wall of a castle or fort that stands out from the main part **2** [(of)] someone or something that is regarded as strongly defending a particular principle or activity; STRONGHOLD: *a bastion of freedom during the war | The club is one of the last bastions of male chauvinism.*

bat¹ /bæt/ n **1** a specially shaped wooden stick for hitting the ball in games such as cricket, BASEBALL, and TABLE TENNIS −see picture at CRICKET **2** BrE a BATSMAN: *one of the best bats in the game* **3** at bat (in BASEBALL) having a turn to hit the ball: *Who's at bat now?* **4** off one's own bat BrE through one's own efforts; without being told to: *Have you done all this work off your own bat?* **5** off the bat infml, esp. AmE without delay: *I asked her to help us, and (right) off the bat she said she would.*

bat

bat² v **-tt-** **1** [T] to hit (as if) with a bat **2** [I] (in cricket and BASEBALL) to hit a ball with a bat or have a turn to bat: *He's better at batting than at catching. | They both bat left-handed. | Who's batting now?* **3** bat a thousand AmE infml to perform an activity or job very well, often without making mistakes: *She's been batting a thousand ever since she got her promotion.* **4** go to bat for AmE infml to give support to; defend

bat³ n **1** a flying mouselike animal that usu. eats insects or fruit and is active at night **2** be/have bats in the belfry infml to be mad −see also BATS, BATTY, as blind as a bat (BLIND¹ (9)) **3** like a bat out of hell infml extremely quickly: *I ran out of there like a bat out of hell.*

bat⁴ v [T] **1** to close and open (the eyes) quickly, sometimes as a sexual invitation; WINK **2** not bat an eye(lid) infml to show no sign of surprise or shock: *She paid the exorbitant bill without batting an eyelid.*

batch /bætʃ/ n [(of)] **1** a quantity of material produced in or prepared for one operation: *a batch of bread/loaves | to test a batch of medicine* **2** a group of people or things considered as a set: *The prisoners were released in batches of 10. | a new batch of students*

batch pro·ces·sing /ˈ· ˈ···/ n [U] a type of computer processing in which a group of PROGRAMS or jobs are run on a computer at one time without interruption − compare INTERACTIVE (2) −**batch process** v [T] : *Each branch of the bank has a computer which can batch process up to four million transactions a day.*

bat·ed /ˈbeɪtɪd/ adj with bated breath hardly breathing at all because of fear, anxious waiting, or other strong feeling: *We waited for the news with bated breath.*

Bates /beɪts/, **H E** (1905−74) an English writer of NOVELS and short stories, best known for his novel *The Darling Buds of May*

Bates, Norman the main character in the film *Psycho*. He runs the **Bates Motel** and is quite mad and dangerous, although he appears to be very kind and gentle. −see colour picture on page 685

Norman Bates

bath¹ /bɑːθ‖bæθ/ n **baths** /bɑːðz, bɑːθs‖bæðz, bæθs/ **1** also **bathtub** AmE− a large basin in which one sits to wash the whole body: *a white enamel bath with brass taps* **2** an act of washing one's whole body at one time: *I have (BrE)/take (AmE) a bath every morning. | I'm just* running/drawing a bath. (=pouring the water for a bath) *| a bath towel* −see also SAUNA, TURKISH BATH **3** (a container for holding) a liquid used for a special purpose: *an oil bath | The fabric is plunged into a bath of black dye.* **4** (in advertisements for houses, etc.) a bathroom: *two bedrooms, kitchen, and bath* −see BATH² (USAGE); see also BATHS

bath² *BrE* ‖ **bathe** *AmE v* **1** [T] to give a bath to (a person): *He's bathing the baby.* **2** [I] to have a bath

▷ USAGE 1 In *BrE* **bath** and **bathe** have slightly different meanings. You **bath** to get clean: *He* **baths** *every morning.* | *to* **bath** *a baby.* You **bathe** something to make it clean in a medical way: *to* **bathe** *a wound/**bathe** one's eyes.* This difference doesn't exist in *AmE*, which uses **bathe** for both meanings. In *BrE* **Bathe** is also the word for swimming: *to* **bathe** *in the sea.* 2 Note the spelling of **bathing, bathed.** These words can be formed from **bath** with the pronunciation /ˈbɑːθɪŋ, bɑːθt‖ˈbæ-/. But they can also be formed from **bathe**, with the pronunciation /ˈbeɪðɪŋ, beɪðd/. The large basin in which you **bath** is a **bath**, or **bathtub** (*AmE*). 3 It is more common to say **have/take a bath** than to use the verb **bath** alone: *I* **have/take** *a bath every day.*◁

Bath a town in SW England famous for many centuries for its health-giving waters, and visited by tourists for its old Roman baths and its Georgian buildings. Bath also has a university. —see also WIFE OF BATH and see colour map on page 818

bath chair /ˈ· ·/ *n* (*sometimes cap.* B) a wheeled chair for an old, sick person to be pushed in, with a covering for the top and sometimes for the sides —compare WHEELCHAIR

bathe¹ /beɪð/ *v* **1** [I] *esp. BrE* to swim in the sea, a river, etc. for pleasure **2** [I] *AmE* to have a bath **3** [T] to cover with or place in water or other liquid, usu. for medical reasons: *Bathe your ankle twice a day.* **4** [T] *lit* to flow along the edge of: *The Mediterranean Sea bathes the sunny shores of Italy.* **5** [T (in, with)] *often pass.*] to spread over with or as if with light, water, etc.; SUFFUSE: *The fields were bathed in sunlight.* | *The child's eyes were bathed with/in tears.* —see BATH² (USAGE) —**bather** *n*

bathe² *n* [S] *BrE* an act of bathing, esp. in the sea; a swim: *Let's go for a bathe.*

bath·ing /ˈbeɪðɪŋ/ *n* [U] *BrE* the act of going into water to bathe or swim: *The bathing is safe here.* | *a bathing accident* | *topless bathing*

bathing beau·ty /ˈ·· ¸··/ *n old-fash* an attractive young woman in a bathing suit, esp. one taking part in a BEAUTY CONTEST

bathing cap /ˈ·· ¸·/ *n* a cap worn in a swimming pool, mostly by women, to keep the hair dry

bathing ma·chine /ˈ··· ¸·/ *n* a wooden hut on wheels pulled down to the sea to allow bathers to dress and undress, used in Britain in the 18th and 19th centuries

bathing suit /ˈ·· ·/ also **bathing cos·tume** /ˈ·· ¸··/*BrE* — *n becoming rare* a SWIMSUIT

bath mat /ˈ· ·/ *n* a washable mat used in a bathroom to protect the floor from water

Bath Ol·i·ver /ˌbɑːθ ˈɒlɪvəʳ‖ˌbæθ ˈɑː-/ *n* a type of British dry, unsweetened BISCUIT, usu. eaten with cheese

ba·thos /ˈbeɪθɒs‖-θɑːs/ *n* [U] a sudden change from very beautiful or noble ideas, words, etc., to very ordinary or foolish ones

bath·robe /ˈbɑːθrəʊb‖ˈbæθ-/ *n* **1** a garment like a loose coat worn before and after having a bath, etc. **2** *AmE for* DRESSING GOWN

bath·room /ˈbɑːθrʊm, -ruːm‖ˈbæθ-/ *n* **1** a room containing a bath and usu. a TOILET **2** *AmE* a TOILET: *Is there a bathroom in this restaurant?* —see TOILET (USAGE)

bathroom tis·sue /ˈ·· ¸··/ *n* [U] *fml* TOILET PAPER

baths /bɑːðz, bɑːθs‖bæðz, bæθs/ *n* **baths** [C+*sing./pl. v*] *esp. BrE* a public building with an indoor swimming pool and/or bathrooms: *the public baths*

bath salts /ˈ· ·/ *n* [P] mineral salts that are added to bath water to soften it and make it smell nice

bath sheet /ˈ· ·/ *n* a very large TOWEL

bath·tub /ˈbɑːθtʌb‖ˈbæθ-/ *n also* **tub** *infml*— *n esp. AmE* a BATH¹ (1) —see BATH² (USAGE)

bath·y·scaph /ˈbæθɪskæf/ *n* a ship that can be driven deep under the sea, used in scientific tests

bath·y·sphere /ˈbæθɪsfɪəʳ/ *n* a strongly built container used for going deep into the sea for the purpose of watching plant life, animal life, etc.

ba·tik /bəˈtiːk, ˈbætɪk/ *n* [U] (cloth decorated by) an Indonesian method of printing coloured patterns on cloth by

putting WAX on the part that is not to be coloured

batik

BAT In·dus·tries /ˌbiː eɪ tiː ˈɪndəstriz/ a very large British company dealing in tobacco, paper, and other things

Ba·tis·ta /bəˈtiːstə/, **Ful·gen·ci·o** /fʊlˈhenθɪəʊ/ (1901–73) the leader of Cuba who ruled until he was forced to leave the country in 1959, after the successful military opposition led by Fidel Castro. Many Cuban REFUGEES in the US still support the principles and failed government of Batista.

bat·man /ˈbætmən/ *n* **-men** /mən/ an officer's personal servant in the British armed forces

Bat·man /ˈbætmæn/ a character found in COMICS, on television, and in films, who fights criminals and protects ordinary people, usu. helped by his partner, Robin, who is sometimes called the **Boy Wonder**. He wears a large black CLOAK and a black MASK, and has a special car called the **Batmobile** that can travel very fast and has many special pieces of equipment fitted to it. People sometimes use the phrase "Good thinking, Batman", which is often used by Robin when Batman has thought of a good idea.

bat·on /ˈbætɒn‖bæˈtɑːn, bə-/ *n* **1** a short thin stick used by a CONDUCTOR (=the leader of a group of musicians) to show the beat of the music **2** a short thick stick used as a weapon by a policeman; TRUNCHEON: *riot police with batons and tear gas* | *a baton charge* —see picture at CLUB **3** a short stick showing that the person who carries it has some special office or rank: *a General's baton* **4** a stick passed by one member of a team of runners to the next runner —see picture at STICK **5** a light metal tube with decorated ends which is spun, thrown into the air and caught by a MAJORETTE

baton charge /ˈ·· ¸·‖·ˈ· ¸·/ *n* a charge by police carrying batons, made in order to break up a crowd or a violent DEMONSTRATION (2)

Bat·on Rouge /ˌbætn ˈruːʒ/ the capital of the state of Louisiana in the US – see colour map on pages 1374-5

bats /bæts/ *adj* [F] *infml, esp. BrE* slightly mad; BATTY

bats·man /ˈbætsmən/ *n* **-men** /mən/ a person who BATS² (2) in cricket –see picture at CRICKET, and compare BATTER³

bat·tal·ion /bəˈtæljən/ *n* [C+*sing./pl. v*] a group of usu. 500–1000 soldiers made up of four or more companies (COMPANY (6a)): *The second battalion is/are going abroad.*

bat·ten¹ /ˈbætn/ *n* a long board used for fastening other pieces of wood

batten² *v*
batten sthg.↔**down** *phr v* [T] (on ships) to fasten with boards of wood: *There's a storm coming, so let's* **batten down the hatches.** (=fasten the entrances to the lower parts of the ship)
batten on/upon sbdy. *phr v* [T *pass. rare*] *esp. lit* to live well by using the work or generosity of (someone) for one's own advantage; EXPLOIT

Bat·ten·burg /ˈbætnbɜːg‖-bɜːrg/ *n* [U] a cake eaten in Britain, which is square in shape and divided into four parts, two pink and two yellow, and covered with MARZIPAN

bat·ter¹ /ˈbætəʳ/ *v* **1** [T] to damage, break, or cause to lose shape by continual hard use or beating: *The ship was battered against the rocks/battered to pieces by the storm.* | *an increase in the incidence of* **baby battering** (=violence by parents against small children) | *a battered old car/ hat* | (fig.) *to restore one's battered pride* **2** [I+*adv/prep*] to beat hard and repeatedly: *The police battered at/on the door.* | *waves battering against the shore*

batter² *n* [U] a mixture of flour, eggs, and milk, beaten together and used in cooking: *pancake batter*

batter³ *n* a person who BATS² (2), esp. in BASEBALL — compare BATSMAN and see picture at BASEBALL

bat·tered /ˈbætəd‖-tərd/ *adj* (of a person) having been physically harmed, usu. by a member of his or her family: *a battered baby* | *a shelter for battered women*

battered wife /ˌ·· ˈ·/ *n* a woman who has been physically harmed by her husband

bat·ter·ing ram /'··· ·ˌ·/ also **ram** — *n* a large heavy log with an iron end, used formerly in war for breaking through the doors and walls of castles and towns

Bat·ter·sea /'bætəsiǁ-tər-/ an area and former BOROUGH of SW London

Battersea Dogs' Home /ˌ··· '·· ·/ a place in Battersea in S London where dogs are kept when they have been thrown out by or taken away from their owners

Battersea Pow·er Sta·tion /ˌ··· '·· ˌ··/ a now disused power station in Battersea, SW London, which because of its four large chimneys looks like a table turned upside down

bat·ter·y /'bætəri/ *n* **1** [C] an apparatus for producing electricity, consisting of a group of connected electric CELLS: *The car won't start because the battery has gone flat.* (=has lost all its power) | *The radio takes four small batteries.* —see picture at ENGINE, and see also DRY BATTERY **2** [C] a number of big guns together with the men who make them work; set of guns fixed in a warship or fort **3** [C] *BrE* a line of small boxes in which hens are kept and specially treated so that they will lay eggs frequently: *battery hens* —compare FREE-RANGE **4** [C (**of**)] a group or set of things like tools, kitchen containers, knives, etc., that are kept together: *a battery of cooking utensils* **5** [C (**of**)] a set or number of things of the same kind coming together, esp. things that are difficult or unpleasant to deal with; ARRAY: *He faced a whole battery of newspaper cameras.* | *a battery of tests* | (fig.) *They've hired a battery of lawyers and experts to prove their case.* **6** [U] *law* the criminal offence of hitting another person —see also ASSAULT AND BATTERY

battery farm /'··· ·ˌ·/ *n* a farm on which hens are kept in batteries (BATTERY (3))

Battery Park /'··· '·/ a park at the extreme SW end of Manhattan, from where ferries (FERRY[1]) go to the Statue of Liberty

batting av·e·rage /'·· ·ˌ···/ *n* **1** (in BASEBALL) a set of numbers which tells how often a player has hit the ball in comparison to how many times he has had a chance to hit it: *His batting average is 347.* **2** (in CRICKET) a number which shows how many RUNS a player has scored during a given period as an AVERAGE **3** a record of performance: *His new car doesn't have much of a batting average, it's broken down twice in the last week.*

bat·tle[1] /'bætl/ *n* **1** a fight between enemy forces, esp. forming part of a larger struggle: *The Battle of Waterloo* | *It was one of the most crucial battles in the whole war.* | *a naval battle* | *He was killed* **in battle.** —see also PITCHED BATTLE; compare WAR **2** any struggle between opposing or competing groups, or against an undesirable situation: *a battle for power between the President's closest advisers* | *The two companies are engaged in a legal battle over the ownership of the land.* | *the battle against disease and poverty* | *The negotiations were a real* **battle of wits** *between the two sides.* (=a struggle to see who was the most clever) | *Today's football game will be a* **battle of the giants** *between the two strongest teams in the country.* —see also **half the battle** (HALF (2))

battle[2] *v* [I] **1** to take part in a struggle, esp. when trying to gain something or get somewhere: [+*adv/prep*] *The mountaineers battled on in spite of the bad weather conditions.* | *women battling for equal rights* | *After a sleepless night battling with her conscience, she decided to admit the truth.* [+*to-v*] *The firemen battled to control the flames.* | *battling to keep control of his company* **2** *esp. lit* to take part in a battle; fight: *The two armies battled (with each other) for half an hour.*

bat·tle·axe *BrE* ǁ **-ax** *AmE* /'bætl-æks/ *n* **1** a heavy AXE formerly used as a weapon **2** *infml* a fierce argumentative woman: *My boss is a real old battleaxe.*

battle cruis·er /'·· ·ˌ·/ *n* a large fast warship with heavy guns, but with lighter armour than a BATTLESHIP

battle cry /'··· ·/ *n* a WAR CRY

battle fa·tigue /'··· ·ˌ·/ *n* also **combat fatigue** [U] a type of mental illness in which a person suffers from severe anxiety and DEPRESSION, caused by the shock of being involved in a battle

bat·tle·field /'bætlfiːld/ also **bat·tle·ground** /-graʊnd/— *n* a place at which a battle is or has been fought: (fig.) *a political battlefield* (=area of disagreement)

bat·tle·ments /'bætlmənts/ *n* [P] a low wall round the flat

roof of a castle or fort, with spaces to shoot through — see picture at CASTLE

Battle of Brit·ain /ˌ··· '··/ [*the*] the British name given to the fighting between British and German aircraft during the summer and autumn of 1940, when German aircraft repeatedly bombed British cities, and British aircraft tried to fight them off. The bombing stopped late in 1940, and this was seen by British people as a great victory for them. Winston Churchill said about the British PILOTS who fought in the Battle of Britain, "Never in the field of human conflict was so much owed by so many to so few."

Battle of the Boyne see BOYNE

Battle of the Bulge /ˌ··· '·/ [*the*] **1** the last strong attack by German forces on the Allies in 1944, pushing them back into Belgium **2** *humor* an attempt to lose weight or prevent oneself from becoming fatter

battle roy·al /ˌ·· '··/ *n fml or lit* a fierce battle or struggle

bat·tle·ship /'bætl-ʃɪp/ *n* the largest kind of warship, with the biggest guns and heaviest armour

bat·ty /'bæti/ *adj infml* slightly mad; CRAZY or ECCENTRIC —**battiness** *n* [U]

bau·ble /'bɔːbəl/ *n often derog* **1** a cheap jewel **2** *BrE* a decoration that looks like a small ball and is used to decorate a Christmas tree

Bau·haus /'baʊhaʊs/ a school in Germany in the 1920s which taught ARCHITECTURE. The school influenced many modern ARCHITECTS with its use of steel and glass and its belief that the use of a building should determine its form.

baud /bɔːd/ *n* **baud** *tech* a measure of the speed at which information is sent to or from a computer, e.g. through a telephone line. One baud equals one BIT of information per second

baulk /bɔːk, bɔːlk/ *n, v BrE for* BALK[1,2]

Baum /baʊm/, **L Frank** (1856–1919) an American writer known for his children's book *The Wizard of Oz*

baux·ite /'bɔːksaɪt/ *n* [U] the ORE from which ALUMINIUM is made

Ba·va·ri·a /bə'veəriə/ a PROVINCE in SE Germany, whose German name is **Bayern**; capital Munich —**rian** *n, adj*

bawd /bɔːd/ *n old use or lit* a woman who keeps a house of PROSTITUTES[2]

bawd·y /'bɔːdi/ *adj* about sex in a rude funny way: *bawdy jokes* —**ily** *adv* —**iness** *n* [U]

bawl /bɔːl/ *v* **1** [I;T (OUT)] to shout in a loud rough voice: *He bawled at me|bawled for his dinner.* | *The captain bawled (out) an order.* **2** [I] to cry noisily: *I couldn't sleep because the baby wouldn't stop bawling.*
  bawl sbdy. ↔ out *phr v* [T] *AmE infml* to speak to angrily; REPRIMAND: *She bawled me out for being late.*

bay[1] /beɪ/ *n* (*often cap. as part of a name*) a wide opening along a coast; part of the sea or of a large lake enclosed in a curve of the land: *The village overlooks a quiet little bay.* | *Botany Bay in Australia* | *the Bay of Biscay*

bay[2] also **bay tree** /'· ·/— *n* a tree like the LAUREL, whose sweet-smelling leaves can be used in cooking: *Add a* **bay leaf** *to the soup.*

bay[3] *n* **1** any of the parts into which a large room or building is divided down the sides by walls, shelves, etc.: *In the library, the books on history are all kept in one bay.* | *There's a loading bay at the back of the warehouse.* | *a parking bay in a multi-storey car park* **2** a side track on a railway station —see also BAY WINDOW, SICKBAY

bay[4] *v* [I] **1** to make repeatedly the long deep cry of a HOUND (=a large hunting dog) **2 bay** (*BrE*)/**bark** (*AmE*) **(at) the moon** to make a great effort to do something worthless

bay[5] *n* [S] **1** the long deep cry of a HOUND **2 hold/keep at bay** to keep (an enemy or something unwanted) some distance away: *He kept me at bay with a long knife.* | (fig.) *We managed to hold our creditors at bay by borrowing some more money from the bank.*

bay[6] *n, adj* (a horse whose colour is) reddish brown

Bay·ern Mu·nich /ˌbaɪən 'mjuːnɪkǁˌbaɪərn-/ a German football team

Bay·eux Tap·es·try /ˌbaɪɜː 'tæpəstriǁbaɪˌuː-/ [*the*] an 11th or 12th century TAPESTRY in Bayeux, N France, which shows pictures that tell the story of the Norman Conquest of England

Bay·kal , **Baikal** /baɪkæl/ a very large lake in Siberia, the 6th largest freshwater lake in the world

Bay of Bis·cay /ˌbeɪ əv ˈbɪskeɪ/ [the] a BAY between the W coast of France and the N coast of Spain, well-known for its very bad weather

Bay of Pigs /ˌ•· ˈ•/ [the] a BAY on the S coast of Cuba. In 1961 a group of Cuban EXILEs, supported by the US, landed in the Bay of Pigs, in an attempt to end the rule of Fidel Castro. The invasion failed and all of the invading (INVADE) army were either taken prisoner or killed. This event is usu. called the **Bay of Pigs Invasion**. −see also CUBAN MISSILE CRISIS

bay·o·net¹ /ˈbeɪən‸t, -net/ n a long knife fixed to the end of a soldier's gun (RIFLE)

bayonet² v [T] to drive a bayonet into (a person)

bay·ou /ˈbaɪuː‖ˈbaɪəʊ/ n (esp. in the SE US) a body of water with a slow current and many water plants

Bay·reuth /baɪˈrɔɪt/ a city in Bavaria, Germany, known for its important Wagner music FESTIVALs

bay win·dow /ˌ•· ˈ•·/ n a window built outwards from the wall, often three-sided, and built up from the ground − compare BOW WINDOW

ba·zaar /bəˈzɑːʳ/ n **1** (in English-speaking countries) a sale to collect money for some good purpose: *a church/hospital bazaar* **2** (in Eastern countries) a marketplace or a group of shops

ba·zoo·ka /bəˈzuːkə/ n a long light gun that rests on the shoulder when fired and is used esp. against TANKs (2)

BBC /ˌbiː biː ˈsiː◂/ n [the] British Broadcasting Corporation; the British radio and television broadcasting company that is paid for by the state, not by advertisers: *She works for the BBC.* | *It's on BBC tonight.* −compare ITV

BBC 1 /ˌbiː biː siː ˈwʌn/ the first of the two BBC television channels (CHANNEL¹ (4)), which broadcasts news and general entertainment programmes: *Did you see that film on BBC 1 last night?* −compare BBC 2, ITV, CHANNEL 4

BBC 2 /ˌbiː biː siː ˈtuː/ the second of the two BBC television channels (CHANNEL¹ (4)), which broadcasts esp. programmes concerning the arts and educational subjects: *a new documentary series on BBC 2* −compare BBC 1, ITV, CHANNEL 4

BBC Eng·lish /ˌ•·· ˈ•·/ n [U] a standard form of English pronunciation, aimed at by many speakers of the language in Britain and in other parts of the world, used not only within the BBC but also in teaching English in many parts of the world −see also OXFORD ENGLISH, RECEIVED PRONUNCIATION

BBC World Serv·ice /ˌ•·· ˌ•· ˈ•·/ also **World Service** [the] a division of the BBC which broadcasts radio programmes, esp. news, to many different parts of the world

BB gun /ˈbiː biː gʌn/ n AmE an air-powered RIFLE which shoots small round metal balls (**BB**s). In the US, particularly in country areas, young boys are often given BB guns so that they can learn how to shoot. BB guns can kill small animals such as birds and mice, and people are sometimes hurt by them in accidents. BB guns are rarely used by adults.

bbq n AmE abbrev. for BARBECUE

BC¹ /ˌbiː ˈsiː/ abbrev. for: before (the birth of) Christ: *Rome was founded in 753 BC.* −compare AD, BCE, CE

▷ USAGE Some people think that the abbreviations BC and AD have unnecessary religious associations and they have begun to use BCE instead of BC, and CE instead of AD. All of these abbreviations are used with numbers which indicate a number of years either before or after the birth of Jesus Christ.◁

BC² abbrev. for BRITISH COLUMBIA

BCCI /ˌbiː biː siː siː ˈaɪ/ Bank of Credit and Commerce International; an international bank which failed in 1991, causing a financial SCANDAL and also causing many savers and small businesses in many countries to lose the money that they had invested (INVEST) with the bank

BCE /ˌbiː biː siː ˈiː/ abbrev. for before common era −see BC (USAGE)

be¹ /bi/ strong /biː/ [see TABLE 6] v [auxiliary verb] **1** [+v-ing] (used to form the progressive tenses of verbs): *Don't disturb me while I'm working.* | *She was reading when he called.* | *They've been asking a lot of*

questions. | *When will you be having dinner?* (=when is it arranged?) | *He's always causing trouble.* **2** [+v-ed] a (used to form the passive voice of verbs): *Smoking is not permitted.* | *I was told about it yesterday.* | *The house is being painted.* | *She has been invited to the party.* | *The flames could be seen several miles away.* | *The police should have been informed about this.* **b** old use (used instead of **have** to form the perfect tenses of some verbs): *Christ is risen from the dead.* (=has risen) **3** [+to-v] usu. fml **a** (expresses an order or rule): *All prisoners are to be* (=must be) *in bed by 10 o'clock.* | *Visitors are to leave when the bell rings.* | *You are not to smoke here.* **b** (shows arrangements for the future): *We are to be married in June.* | *We were to have gone away last week, but I was ill.* **c** (shows what should happen): *Whatever am I to tell her* (=what should/can I tell her) *when she finds out?* | *He is more to be* (=should be more) *pitied than blamed.* **d** (shows what cannot or could not happen): *We looked and looked, but the ring was nowhere to be found.* **e** (shows what had to happen or did happen): *This discovery was to have a major effect on the treatment of heart disease.* **f** (used in conditional sentences that show a situation that does not or could not exist): *If I were to do that/Were I to do that, what would you say?* −see also BEEN

be² v **1** [L] (shows that someone or something is the same as the subject): [+n] *January is the first month of the year.* | *It's me.* | *Lack of money is our biggest problem.* | *If I were you, I shouldn't do it.* [+to-v/v-ing] *The difficulty is to know what to do/knowing what to do.* [+(that)] *The fact is (that) you know too much.* | *The biggest problem was that we didn't have enough time.* **2** [I+adv/prep] (shows position or time): *Where is he?* | *He's upstairs/at home/in the office.* | *How long has she been here?* | *The book is on the table.* | *The concert was last night.* | *The party is* (=will happen) *on Saturday.* **3** [L] **a** (shows that someone or something belongs to a group or has a quality): *She's a doctor.* | *She wants to be* (=become) *a doctor when she leaves school.* | *Snow is white.* | *Horses are animals.* | *These shoes are mine.* | *We were hungry.* | *I'm not ready.* | *Be careful!* | *It's hot today.* | *It's as if we'd never even started.* | *A knife is for cutting with.* (=that is its purpose) **b** (in short phrases or questions): *It's cold, isn't it?* | *He isn't leaving, is he?* | *"That's not your coat!" "Yes it is!"* **4** [L] (used after **there** to show that something exists): *There's a hole in your trousers.* −see THERE (USAGE) **5 be that as it may** even if that is true; in spite of that −see also BEEN

be³ v [I] **1** to exist: *Whatever is, is right.* **2** (in the INFINITIVE) to remain untroubled: *If the baby's sleeping, let her be.* −see also BEEN **3 to be or not to be, that is the question** quote a phrase from Shakespeare's play *Hamlet*, probably the most famous line from all his plays. People sometimes use parts of the phrase humorously, when a decision must be made.

beach¹ /biːtʃ/ n **1** a shore of the sea or a lake covered by sand or small stones: *They went down to the beach for a swim.* | *There are several beautiful sandy beaches along that stretch of the coast.* −see SHORE (USAGE) and see extra information on page 632 **2 we shall fight on the beaches** quote part of a famous speech made by Winston Churchill during the Second World War

beach² v [T] to run or drive (a boat) onto the shore: *to beach our canoe* − ~**ed** adj : *a beached whale*

beach ball /ˈ•· •/ n a large light ball, filled with air, for use at the beach

Beach Boys /ˈ•· •/, **The** an American popular music group with an easily recognizable smooth style of singing together, which was formed in 1961 and whose songs are still popular. Many of their songs were about young people in California enjoying themselves by surfing (SURF) and swimming in the sea, having parties, and driving fast cars.

beach bug·gy /ˈ•· ˌ•·/ also **dune buggy**− n a motor vehicle with very large tyres for use on sand beaches

beach·chair /ˈbiːtʃ-tʃeəʳ/ n AmE for DECKCHAIR

beach·comb·er /ˈbiːtʃˌkəʊməʳ/ n **1** a person who searches along a beach for useful or saleable things **2** a long rolling wave coming in from the ocean

Beachcomber the name used by John Cameron Morton (1893−1979) for his regular humorous writing in the British newspaper the Daily Express between 1924 and 1975

beach·head /ˈbiːtʃhed/ n an area on the shore of an enemy's land that has been taken by force and on which an army may be landed —compare BRIDGEHEAD

beach·wear /'biːtʃweəʳ/ n [U] clothing for the beach

Beach·y Head /ˌbiːtʃi 'hed/ an area of land with very high cliffs on the coast of SE England

bea·con /'biːkən/ n 1 a guiding or warning fire on a hill, tower, or pole 2 a tall object or a light on or near the shore, acting as a guide or warning to sailors 3 (in Britain) a BELISHA BEACON 4 a RADIO BEACON 5 a flashing light to warn airmen of heights or to guide them at an airport 6 esp. lit someone or something that provides guidance or sets a high standard to be followed

bead /biːd/ n 1 a small ball of glass or other material with a hole through it for threading on string or wire: She was wearing a string of green beads round her neck. | The sheikh sat there fingering his **worry beads**. (=a string of beads which are supposed to calm one when played with) | a bead curtain | (fig.) beads of sweat on his face 2 **draw a bead (on)** to take aim (at) when shooting 3 **tell/say one's beads** lit or old use to say one's prayers with a ROSARY — **~ed** adj : a beaded headdress | a face beaded with sweat

bead·ing /'biːdɪŋ/ n [C;U] a long narrow patterned piece of wood used for decorating walls, furniture, etc.

bea·dle /'biːdl/ n 1 an officer who in former times helped a priest in keeping order in church, in giving money to the poor, etc. 2 (in some British universities) a uniformed officer who may lead university processions, help to keep order, etc.

Beadle, Jer·e·my /'dʒerəmi/ (1948–) an English television presenter known esp. for his very cheerful manner and his programmes in which people are put into amusing or embarrassing situations

bead·y /'biːdi/ adj often humor (esp. of an eye) small, round, and shining, like a bead: **Keep your beady eyes off** my cigarettes. (=stop looking at them as if you want to steal them)

bea·gle /'biːgəl/ n a smooth-haired dog (a kind of HOUND) with short legs and large ears, sometimes used in the hunting of HARES

Beagle, HMS the ship on which Charles Darwin travelled to South America to study the plants and animals there

bea·gling /'biːglɪŋ/ n [U] (in Britain) the sport of hunting HARES with beagles

beak¹ /biːk/ n 1 the hard horny mouth of a bird, a TURTLE, etc. —see picture at BIRD 2 anything pointed and sticking out like this, such as **a** a person's hooked nose **b** the pointed front end of an ancient warship

beak² n BrE old-fash sl 1 a judge in a lower court of law; MAGISTRATE 2 a schoolmaster

bea·ker /'biːkəʳ/ n 1 esp. BrE a drinking cup with a wide mouth and usu. no handle 2 a small glass cup shaped for pouring, as used in a chemical LABORATORY —see picture at LABORATORY 3 [(of)] also **bea·ker·ful** /-fʊl/— the amount that a beaker will hold: a beaker of coffee

be-all and end-all /ˌ· · · '· ·/ n [the+S (of)] the most important thing; the whole purpose of something

beam¹ /biːm/ n 1 a large long heavy piece of wood, esp. used as part of the structure of a building 2 the bar from which scales for weighing hang —see also **broad in the beam** (BROAD¹ (9))

beam² n 1 a line of light shining out from some bright object: the bright beam of the car's headlights | a moonbeam | a laser beam 2 radio waves sent out along a narrow path in one direction only, often to guide aircraft 3 a bright look or smile: "How nice to see you!" she said, with a beam of welcome. 4 BrE **off beam** infml incorrect; mistaken: We tried to guess the price, but we were way off beam. (=a long way from the true figure)

beam³ v 1 [I] (of the sun or other shining objects) to send out light (and heat) 2 [I;T] to smile brightly and happily: He beamed (a cheerful welcome) as he opened the door. 3 [T+obj+adv/prep] to send out (radio or television signals) in a certain direction, using special equipment: The news was beamed to East Africa by satellite. 4 **Beam me up, Scotty** a phrase used in the television SCIENCE FICTION SERIES Star Trek, as a command to make someone disappear and then reappear in the spacecraft. The phrase is often used humorously now when someone wants to escape quickly from a difficult or embarrassing situation. —see also STAR TREK

beam-ends /ˌ· '·‖'· ·/ n BrE **on one's beam-ends** sl (of a person or a business) almost without any money left: We're on our beam-ends!

bean /biːn/ n 1 a seed of any of various upright climbing plants, esp. one that can be used as food. In Britain and the US, beans are often eaten by people who are VEGETARIANs (=eat no meat) or people interested in eating healthy foods. —see also BAKED BEANS 2 a plant that produces beans 3 a POD containing beans, which grows on a bean plant and is used when young as food: green beans | runner beans —see also BROAD BEAN, FRENCH BEAN 4 a seed of certain other plants, from which food or drink can be made: coffee beans 5 esp. BrE (usu. in negatives) infml the smallest possible amount of money: I haven't a bean, so I can't pay you. | It's not worth a bean. 6 **full of beans** infml full of life and eagerness 7 **not know beans** AmE infml to know nothing (about a subject): He doesn't know beans about geography. 8 **old bean** BrE old-fash sl (used to address a friend): Have a look at this, old bean! —see also **spill the beans** (SPILL¹) and see picture at VEGETABLE

bean·bag /'biːnbæg/ n 1 a sewn cloth bag filled with beans, used as a child's toy 2 a very large CUSHION filled with small pieces of POLYSTYRENE, used as a piece of furniture for sitting on

bean curd /'· ·/ n [U] TOFU

Bea·no /'biːnəʊ/, **The** a popular British weekly COMIC for children, with amusing stories and jokes

bean·pole /'biːnpəʊl/ n humor a person who is very tall and very thin

bean·sprout /'biːnspraʊt/ n a bean which has grown a small SHOOT² (1), eaten in SALADS, Chinese food, etc.

bears

grizzly bear

koala bear

polar bear

bear¹ /beəʳ/ n 1 (pl. **bears** or **bear**) a usu. large heavy animal with thick rough fur, that eats flesh and also fruit and insects: a brown bear | a polar bear 2 a person who sells business shares or goods in expectation of a fall in prices —compare BULL¹ (3) 3 a rough, bad-mannered, bad-tempered man 4 **a bear with a sore head** a person who is very bad-tempered and does not seem to want the company of other people —see also GREAT BEAR, TEDDY BEAR

bear² v **bore** /bɔːʳ/, **borne** /bɔːn‖bɔːrn/ 1 [T+obj+adv/prep] fml or lit to carry from one place to another; carry away; CONVEY: The sound of music was borne on the wind. | He came bearing gifts for all the family. 2 [T] to support (a weight or load); hold up: I doubt if that chair will bear your weight. | a load-bearing wall | (fig.) The captain of the ship bears a heavy responsibility. | (fig.) All the costs of the repairs will be borne (=paid) by our company. 3 [T] to have or show (a mark or characteristic): He was attacked by a shark years ago, and his leg still bears the scars. | This letter bears no signature. | What she says **bears no relation to** (=is very different from) the truth. | The baby **bears no resemblance to** its father. (=doesn't look like him) | His latest film **bears witness to** (=is proof of) his versatility. 4 [T] to suffer or accept (something unpleasant) without complaining; ENDURE: She bore the pain with great courage. | There's nothing we can do about it, so we'll just have to **grin and bear it**.

[+*v-ing*] *I can't bear* (=greatly dislike) *being kept waiting.* [+*to-v*] *I couldn't bear to listen any longer, so I left the room.* —see USAGE **5** [T] *usu. fml* to give birth to: *She bore/has borne three children.* [+*obj(i)+obj(d)*] *She bore him a daughter.* (=he was the father) | *a woman of child-bearing age* —see BORN¹ (USAGE) **6** [I;T]. to produce (a crop or fruit): *The tree is bearing a lot of apples this year.* | (fig.) *Her efforts to stage the production* **bore fruit** *– the play was an overnight success.* **7** [I+*adv/prep*] to move in the stated direction: *Cross the field, bear left, and you'll soon reach the village.* **8** [T *usu. in negatives*] to be suitable for; allow: *Such weak arguments won't bear serious examination.* [+*v-ing*] *His words don't bear repeating.* | *The consequences simply* **don't bear thinking about.** (=are too terrible to think about) **9** [T] *usu. fml* to keep (a feeling towards someone) in one's mind: *to bear love for/hatred against somebody* | *Although they treated her badly she doesn't* **bear a grudge** *against them.* [+*obj(i)+obj(d)*] *She doesn't bear them a grudge.* **10** [T+*obj+adv/prep*] *fml* to behave or hold (oneself) in a stated way; COMPORT: *She bore herself with great dignity.* **11 bring something to bear (on)** to direct something, e.g. force or persuasion (on); EXERT: *The government brought pressure to bear on the company to settle its dispute with the workers.* **12 bear in mind** to remember to consider; take account of: *Admittedly she didn't make a very good job of it, but you must bear in mind that she was ill at the time.* | *Bear me in mind if you are thinking of buying tickets for that play.*

▷ USAGE Compare **abide, bear, endure, stand,** and **tolerate.** 1 **Abide, bear, stand,** and **endure** are all used with "can" in questions and with NEGATIVE words to express great dislike, but **endure** is *usu.* used only about something really serious: *I can't* **abide/bear/stand** *black coffee.* | *I can't* **endure** *talking to people who are racists.* 2 **Bear, endure,** and **stand** are also used for great physical hardship; **endure** suggests pain that lasts for a long time: *He* **bore/stood** *the pain as long as he could.* | *She had* **endured** *great pain for a number of years.* 3 **Tolerate** is used of people or behaviour, but not of suffering: *I won't* **tolerate** *your rudeness.*◁

bear down *phr v* **1** [T] (**bear** sbdy./sthg. ↔ **down**) *fml* to defeat; OVERWHELM: *His determined efforts at last bore down all opposition.* | *borne down by poverty and deprivation* **2** [I] to use all one's strength and effort: *The driver bore down with all his strength to control the car when the wheels slipped.*

bear down on/upon sbdy./sthg. *phr v* [T] to come towards forcefully and threateningly, esp. at high speed: *The enemy ship bore down on our small boat.* | *As soon as she saw him enter the room she bore down on him and insisted that he join her for dinner.*

bear on/upon sthg. *phr v* [T] to have some connection with: *How does your news bear on this case?* —see also BEARING (2)

bear sthg. ↔ **out** *phr v* [T] to support the truth of: *The prisoner's story was borne out by his wife.* | *If you tell them what happened, I'll bear you out.*

bear up *phr v* [I] to show courage or strength by continuing in spite of difficulties: *She bore up bravely under her continual misfortunes.* | *Bear up! The news isn't so bad.*

bear with sbdy./sthg. *phr v* [T] to show patience towards; PUT **up with:** *You must bear with his bad temper; he's very ill.* | *If you'll just bear with me for a couple of minutes I'll be able to give you an answer.*

bear·a·ble /ˈbeərəbəl/ *adj* that can be borne or suffered; TOLERABLE: *The pain was just bearable.* | *His increase in salary made life more bearable.* —opposite **unbearable** —**bly** *adv*

bear claw /ˈ· ·/ *n AmE* a fruit-filled pastry with parallel cuts in the top that look like CLAWS (1)

beard¹ /bɪəd‖bɪərd/ *n* **1** hair on the face below the mouth, often including the jaws, chin, and neck: *Men and goats have beards.* | *He has/wears a beard.* | *He's growing a beard.* —compare MOUSTACHE, WHISKERS

▶CULTURAL NOTE In Britain and the US beards have no social or religious significance. Men choose to have a beard if they consider it fashionable or attractive. In stories and films, men who are old and WISE are often shown with beards. Beards are also sometimes associated (ASSOCIATE) with people who have LIBERAL opinions: *The Liberal Party*

has been trying to get rid of the beards and sandals image.◀

2 long hairs on a plant, as on BARLEY – – **ed** *adj* : *a tall, bearded man* – – **less** *adj*

beard² *v* [T] **1** *esp. BrE* to oppose or deal with (someone) confidently or disrespectfully; CONFRONT: *She bearded the committee and demanded an explanation.* **2 beard the lion in his den** *lit* to face someone confidently on their own ground: *He's in his office, so let's beard the lion in his den now.*

Beard, James (1903–) an American writer of newspaper articles on food and of cookbooks

Beards·ley /ˈbɪədzli‖ˈbɪər-, **Au·brey** /ˈɔːbri/ (1872–98) an English ILLUSTRATOR of many books, whose pictures are *usu.* in black and white and appear flat and stylized (STYLIZE)

bear·er /ˈbeərəʳ/ *n* **1** (*often in comb.*) *fml* a person who bears or carries something: *a bearer of bad news* | *the flagbearer* | *a pallbearer at a funeral* **2** *fml* a person who holds a note or cheque for the payment of money to himself/herself: *The banknote says "payable to the bearer on demand".* **3** *esp. IndE & PakE* a male servant

bearer bond /ˈ·· ˌ·/ *n* a BOND¹ (3) that is not recorded as belonging to a particular person and is therefore considered to belong to whoever holds it

bear gar·den /ˈ· ˌ··/ *n* a place where people are making a lot of noise and behaving in a rough way: *Shut up for a minute! It's like a bear garden in here!*

bear hug /ˈ· ·/ *n infml* a rough tight EMBRACE

bear·ing /ˈbeərɪŋ/ *n* **1** [S;U] the way a person holds their body or behaves; DEPORTMENT: *an upright, proud bearing* **2** [S;U (**on**)] connection with or influence on something: *What you have said has no bearing on the subject.* **3** [C] *tech* the part of a machine in which a turning rod is held, or which turns on a fixed rod —see also BALL BEARING **4** [C] *tech* a direction or angle as shown by a COMPASS: *to take a compass bearing* | (fig.) *In all this mass of details I'm afraid I've rather* **lost my bearings.** (=become confused)

bear·ish /ˈbeərɪʃ/ *adj* **1** rude; rough; bad-tempered **2** *tech* marked by, expecting, or tending to cause falling prices —opposite **bullish** —see also BEAR¹ (2) – –**ly** *adv* – **ness** *n* [U]

bear·skin /ˈbeəˌskɪn‖ˈbeər-/ *n* **1** [C;U] the skin of a bear: *a bearskin rug* **2** [C] a tall black fur cap worn on ceremonial occasions by certain British soldiers

beast /biːst/ *n* **1** *esp. lit* an animal, esp. a four-footed one **2** *derog* a person (or sometimes a thing) that one does not like; BRUTE: *Her husband was a real beast.* | *a beast of a job* | *You beast!*

beast·ly /ˈbiːstli/ *adj infml* very unpleasant; nasty: *a beastly person/habit* | *beastly weather* | *I've had a beastly cold.* —**beastly** *adv* : *It's beastly cold today.* —**liness** *n* [U]

beast of bur·den /ˌ· · ˈ··/ *n fml or lit* an animal, such as a horse or DONKEY, which carries things

beat¹ /biːt/ *v* **beat, beaten** /ˈbiːtn/ *or* **beat 1** [I+*adv/prep*;T] to hit again and again esp. with a stick or other hard instrument: *His father beat him for being disobedient.* | *to beat a drum* | *The rain was beating against the windows.* | *The firefighters beat back the flames.* | *The mechanic beat out the dent in the car.* (=removed it by beating) | *The police beat the door down in order to get into the house.* | *waves beating against the shore* | (fig.) *The sun beat down (on them) all day.* **2** [T (UP)] to mix with regular movements of a fork, spoon, etc.: *Beat (up) the egg whites until they become stiff.* **3** [I;T] to move regularly: *The bird beat its wings rapidly.* | *You can hear its heart beating.* **4** [T] to defeat; do better than: *She beat me at tennis.* | *She's hoping to beat the world record.* | *The beaten finalists were given silver medals.* | **It beats me** (=I can't understand) *how he can have done it.* | *That strange story beats everything (I have ever heard)!* | **You can't beat** (=there is nothing better than) *a good film.* —see WIN (USAGE) **5** [T (**to**)] to reach a place or succeed in doing something before (someone else): *We left early to beat the rush-hour traffic.* | *We were hoping to get there first, but they beat us to it.* **6 beat about the bush,** also **beat around the bush** *AmE*— to delay talking about the most important part of a subject: *I wish you'd stop beating about the bush and tell me what you really want.* **7 beat a path** to come rushing in large numbers: *If you* *invent a cheaper way of doing it, people will* **beat a path to your door.** (=will be very eager to buy it from you) **8 beat a retreat** to go away quickly so as to avoid something unpleasant: *When they saw the teacher coming, they beat a (hasty) retreat.* **9 Beat it!** *sl* Go away at once! **10 beat one's brains out** *infml* to spend a lot of time thinking or worrying about something: *I've been beating my brains out trying to think what to do about my elderly mother.* **11 beat one's breast** *lit* to show (too) great grief **12 beat someone hollow** *infml* to defeat someone completely, esp. in a game or competition **13 beat someone's brains out** *infml* to beat someone very hard, esp. on the head **14 beat the heat** *AmE infml* to try to become cooler: *We're going swimming in the lake to beat the heat.* **15 beat the pants off someone** *infml* to defeat someone completely, e.g. in a game or competition **16 beat the rap** *AmE infml* to escape criminal charges or punishment: *The police got him for illegal possession, but he beat the rap.* **17 beat time** to make regular movements or noises by which the speed of music can be measured **18 Can you beat that/it!** *sl* Have you ever seen/heard anything as strange or surprising as that! **19 if you can't beat 'em, join 'em** *infml* if you cannot win in a situation, it is better to join the other side and gain whatever advantages you can **20 to beat the band** *AmE infml* in large amounts or with great force: *It's raining to beat the band.* —see also BEATEN, BEATING, **beat one's head against a brick wall** (HEAD[1])

beat sbdy. ↔ **down** *phr v* [T (to)] *infml* to persuade (someone) to reduce a price: *He wanted £10 for the dress, but I beat him down (to £8.50).*

beat off [T] (**beat** sbdy./sthg. ↔ **off**) *phr v* [T] **1** to prevent (an attack or attacker) from succeeding; drive back; REPULSE: *The police beat off the demonstrators to let the President's car through.* | *The company managed to beat off an attempted takeover.* **2** *AmE taboo sl* [I] to MASTURBATE **3** *AmE taboo sl* [T] (**beat** sbdy. ↔ **off**) to MASTURBATE (a male)

beat sthg. ↔ **out** *phr v* [T] **1** to sound by beating: *The drums beat out a rhythm.* | *The drummer beat out the rhythm on the drums.* **2** to put out (a fire) by beating

beat sbdy. ↔ **up** *phr v* [T] *infml* to wound (someone) severely by hitting: *The boys robbed the old man and beat him up.* | *He claimed that he had been beaten up by the police.*

beat² *n* **1** a single stroke or blow, as part of a group: *one beat of the drum every 60 seconds* | *a heartbeat* **2** [usu. sing.] a regular sound produced (as if) by repeated beating: *the beat of marching feet* **3** [usu. sing.] regular STRESS[1] (4) in music or poetry: *music with a strong beat* | *Every member of the band must follow the beat.* **4** the usual path followed by someone on duty, esp. a policeman

beat³ *adj* [F] *infml* very tired: *I'm (dead) beat after all that work!*

beat·en /'biːtn/ *adj* [A] **1** (of metal) shaped by beating with a hammer: *The doors of the palace were of beaten gold.* **2** (of a path, track, etc.) given shape by the feet of those who pass along it: *We followed a well-beaten path through the forest.* **3 off the beaten track/path** not well-known; not often visited: *Let's go somewhere off the beaten track this summer.*

beat·er /'biːtə²/ *n* **1** (*often in comb.*) someone or something which beats: *an egg beater* | *a carpet beater* | *a wife beater* **2** (esp. in Britain) a person who drives wild birds or animals towards the guns of those waiting to shoot them **3** *AmE* an old car in poor condition

Beat Gen·e·ra·tion /'· ··,··/ [the] the group of young people in the 1950s including the writers Jack Kerouac and Allen Ginsberg, who refused to accept the values of Western society, and showed this by refusing to work, keeping no material possessions, and wearing their own style of clothes —see also Allen GINSBERG

be·a·tif·ic /ˌbɪəˈtɪfɪk/ *adj* giving or showing great joy, peace, or blessedness: *a beatific smile on the holy man's face* — ~**ally** /kli/ *adv*

be·at·i·fy /biˈætɪfaɪ/ *v* [T] (in the Roman Catholic Church) to declare (a dead person) officially blessed and holy —**fication** /biˌætɪfɪˈkeɪʃən/ *n* [C;U]

beat·ing /'biːtɪŋ/ *n* **1** [C;U] an act of giving repeated blows, usu. for punishment: *He was given a severe beating for lying to his father.* **2** [C] a defeat, esp. in a game or competition: *The home side got/took quite a beating.*

be·at·i·tude /biˈætɪtjuːd‖-tuːd/ *n* [U] *fml or lit* a state of great happiness or blessedness

Be·at·i·tudes /biˈætɪtjuːdz‖-tuːdz/ *n* [the+P] the statements about those who are blessed made by Jesus in the Bible (Matthew 5:3–12)

Beat·les /'biːtlz/, **The** a British popular music group who made their first record in 1962 and became probably the most famous and successful group ever. When they separated in 1970, each member of the group continued to work in popular music. —see also George HARRISON, John LENNON, Paul MCCARTNEY, Ringo STARR and see colour picture on page 554

beat·nik /'biːtnɪk/ *n* in the late 1950s and early 1960s, a person who showed opposition to the moral standards and ways of life of ordinary society. People often think of beatniks as young people with long hair and dirty clothes.

Bea·ton /'biːtn/, **Sir Ce·cil** /'sesəl/ (1904–80) an English photographer and clothing, theatre, and film DESIGNER, known esp. for his pictures of famous and wealthy people

Bea·trice¹ /'bɪətrɪs/, **Princess** (1988–) the older daughter of the Duke and Duchess of York

Beatrice² the main female character in the *Divine Comedy* by Dante, who guides him through Paradise

Beat·ty /'biːti/, **Warren** (1937–) an American actor who has appeared in many films but is most often talked about for being extremely attractive to women – see picture at BONNIE AND CLYDE

beat-up /'· ·/ *adj AmE infml* in bad condition: *a beat-up old car*

beau /bəʊ/ *n* **beaux** /bəʊz/ *or* **beaus** *old use or lit* **1** a fashionable well-dressed man **2** a woman's admirer or lover

Beau·jo·lais /'bəʊʒəleɪ‖ˌbəʊʒəˈleɪ/ *n* [U] a type of French red wine

Beau·jo·lais nou·veau /ˌbəʊʒəleɪ nuːˈvəʊ‖ˌbəʊʒəˌleɪ-/ *n* [U] the first bottles from the year's production of Beaujolais wine. Competitions are held to see who can be first to bring the new wine to Britain.

beau monde /ˌbəʊ ˈmɔːnd‖-ˈmɑːnd/ *n* [the] *Fr* the world of high society and fashion

beaut¹ /bjuːt/ *n AmE & AustrE infml* someone or something that is very good (or bad); BEAUTY (3): *That black eye is a real beaut!*

beaut² *adj AustrE infml* (of things) nice; good; MARVELLOUS: *The food/weather was beaut.*

beau·te·ous /'bjuːtiəs/ *adj poet* beautiful: *"It is a beauteous evening, calm and free."* (Wordsworth) — ~**ly** *adv*

beau·ti·cian /bjuːˈtɪʃən/ *n* a person who gives beauty treatments to skin, hair, etc.

beau·ti·ful /'bjuːtɪfəl/ *adj* **1** having beauty; giving great pleasure to the mind or senses: *a beautiful girl/lake/sunset* **2** *infml* very good: *The soup was really beautiful.* —see also **small is beautiful** (SMALL¹) — ~**ly** *adv* : *a beautifully written novel*

▷ USAGE 1 **Beautiful** is a much stronger word to describe a person's appearance than **pretty, handsome, good-looking,** or **attractive.** 2 **Beautiful** and **pretty** can be used of women, children, and things, but not usu. of men: *a beautiful girl/house* | *a pretty child/picture.* **Handsome** is usu. used of men, but a **handsome** woman is **good-looking** in a strong, healthy way. **Good-looking** can be used of men and women, but not usu. of things. **Attractive** can be used of men, women, and things: *an attractive young man* | *an attractive pattern.* —see also LOVELY (USAGE)◁

beautiful peo·ple /ˌ··· '··/ *n* [P] *AmE* rich, usu. famous people: *The beautiful people all spend their summers at Martha's Vineyard.*

beau·ti·fy /'bjuːtɪfaɪ/ *v* [T] to make beautiful

beau·ty /'bjuːti/ *n* **1** [U] the qualities in someone or something that give pleasure to the senses or lift up the mind or spirit: *a woman/a poem of great beauty* | *enchanted by the beauty of the scenery* **2** [C] someone (usu. female) or something beautiful: *His mother was a great beauty.* | *the beauties of our city* **3** [C] *infml* someone or something very good (or bad); a perfect example: *That apple is a real beauty.* | *That black eye you got in the fight is a beauty!* **4** [the (of)] the advantage (of something); a particularly good quality that makes something special or valuable: *The beauty (of my idea) is that it would cost so little!* **5 a thing of beauty is a joy for ever** *quote* a phrase from a poem by John Keats **6 Beauty is in the eye of the beholder** *saying* different people have different opinions about what is beautiful **7 Beauty is only skin deep** *saying* a person may be attractive, but they may also be an unpleasant person underneath

Beauty and the Beast /ˌ··· ·ˈ·/ a French fairy story about a beautiful young girl who has to live with an ugly, half-human creature (the Beast) to repay a favour he did her father. She finally agrees to marry him, at which point the SPELL is broken and he changes into a HANDSOME PRINCE.

beauty con·test /ˈ·· ˌ··/ *n* a competition for young women in which their appearance, and sometimes other qualities, are compared and judged. Beauty contests are popular in Britain and the US, but many people, esp. FEMINISTs, disapprove of the idea that women should be judged by how attractive they are. —see also BEAUTY QUEEN

beauty mark /ˈ·· ˌ·/ *n AmE* for BEAUTY SPOT (2)

beauty par·lour /ˈ·· ˌ··/ also **beauty sal·on** /ˈ·· ˌ··‖ˈ·· ˌ·/, **beauty shop** /ˈ·· ·/ *AmE*— *n* a place where women are given beauty treatments for the face, hair, etc.

beauty queen /ˈ·· ·/ *n* the winner of a competition in which women are judged for their beauty

beauty sleep /ˈ·· ·/ *n* [U] *usu. humor* sleep during the early part of the night, believed to be the best for beauty

beauty spot /ˈ·· ·/ *n* **1** a place known for the beauty of its scenery **2** ‖also **beauty mark** *AmE* a dark-coloured mark on the skin

Beau·voir /ˈbəʊvwɑːr‖bəʊvˈwɑːr/, **Si·mone de** /sɪˈməʊn də/ (1908–86) a French writer known esp. for her belief in EXISTENTIALISM and in a political role for women. Her works include *The Second Sex* and *The Mandarins*.

bea·ver[1] /ˈbiːvər/ *n* **1** [C] a water and land animal of the rat family with a broad flat tail and valuable fur. Beavers build DAMs across streams and are supposed to work very hard. **2** [U] the skin of this animal: *a beaver coat* —see also EAGER and see picture at RODENT BEAVER

beaver[2] *v*
  beaver away *phr v* [I (**at**)] *infml, esp. BrE* to work hard, esp. at a desk job: *We watched him beavering away at his complicated calculations.*

Bea·ver·brook /ˈbiːvəbrʊk‖-vər-/, **Lord** (1879–1964) a very successful British newspaper owner and politician born in Canada, the holder of several high offices in the government and owner of the Daily Express and other newspapers

be·bop /ˈbiːbɒp‖-bɑːp/ *n* [U] BOP[3]

be·calmed /bɪˈkɑːmd‖-ˈkɑːmd, -ˈkɑːlmd/ *adj* (of a sailing ship) unable to move because there is no wind

be·cause /bɪˈkɒz, bɪˈkəz‖bɪˈkɔːz, bɪˈkəz/ *conj* **1** for the reason that: *I do it because I like it.* | *She got the job because she was the best candidate.* | *"Why can't I go?" "Because you're too young."* **2 because of** by reason of; as a result of: *I came back because of the rain.* —see REASON (USAGE) **3 because it's there** *quote* a phrase originally used by the mountain climber George Mallory when asked to explain why he wanted to climb Mount Everest, and now sometimes used humorously as an answer when someone is asked why they want to do something very difficult or dangerous

Be·cher's Brook /ˌbiːtʃəz ˈbrʊk‖-tʃərz-/ a very difficult jump in the British Grand National horse race, at which many horses fall

Bech·et /ˈbeʃeɪ/, **Sid·ney** /ˈsɪdni/ (1897–1959) an American JAZZ musician who played the SAXOPHONE and CLARINET

beck[1] /bek/ *n* **at someone's/one's beck and call** always ready to do anything someone/one asks

beck[2] *n NEngE* a stream, esp. a small hill stream

Bec·ker /ˈbekər/, **Bor·is** /ˈbɒrɪs‖ˈbɔː-/ (1967–) a German tennis player, the youngest man to win the SINGLES competition at Wimbledon, at the age of 17

Bec·ket /ˈbekɪt/, **Saint Thomas à** (1118–70) an English SAINT and MARTYR. As ARCHBISHOP of Canterbury, he quarrelled with King Henry II. Henry is reported to have said of Becket, "Who will rid me of this turbulent priest?", and as a result Becket was murdered in Canterbury Cathedral.

Bec·kett /ˈbekɪt/, **Sam·u·el** /ˈsæmjuəl/ (1906–89) an Irish writer of plays, books, and poetry, who lived in France and is best known for his play *Waiting for Godot*

beck·on /ˈbekən/ *v* [I (**to**);T] to call, order, or signal with a movement of the head, hand, etc.: *I could see her beckoning (to) me from the other side of the room.* | *She beckoned me to follow her.* | *He beckoned with his finger and the child came running.* | *He stood waiting until the policeman beckoned him on.* | (fig.) *I'd like to stay — but work beckons, you know!*

be·come /bɪˈkʌm/ *v* **became** /bɪˈkeɪm/, **become 1** [L] to begin or come to be: *He became king at the age of 17.* | *After the death of her father she became the richest woman in the world.* | *The weather became warmer.* | *He soon became acclimatized to the warmer weather.* | *These constant delays are becoming a bit of a bore.* | *She became increasingly anxious about her husband's strange behaviour.* | *He withdrew from the competition when it became clear that he stood no chance of winning.* **2** [T] *fml* to be right or suitable to; BEFIT: *This sort of behaviour hardly becomes a person in your position.*
  become of sbdy./sthg. *phr v* [T] to happen to, often in a bad way: *I don't know what will become of us if the company goes bankrupt.* | *Whatever became of that nice girl you used to share a flat with?*

▷ USAGE **Become** can be used of people and things and with most types of adjective: *Mary* **became** *angry/famous.* | *The sky* **became** *cloudy.* | *It* **became** *clear that he was lying.* With adjectives of colour, **turn** can be used: *The leaves are* **turning** *brown*, or **go** (informally, or if the change in colour is not long-lasting; **go** is nonstandard in American English when used in this way). Compare: *His skin had* **turned/gone** *(infml) brown from the weeks he spent working in the sun.* | *His face* **went** *red when they made fun of him.* **Go** can also be used to show changes (usu. for the worse) in expressions like: *He* **went** *mad/blind/deaf/bald.* | *The meat's* **gone** *bad.* ◁

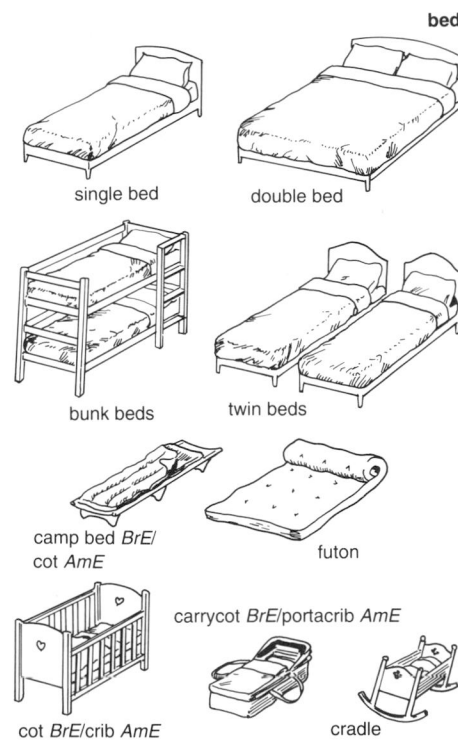

beds

single bed

double bed

bunk beds

twin beds

camp bed *BrE*/
cot *AmE*

futon

carrycot *BrE*/portacrib *AmE*

cot *BrE*/crib *AmE*

cradle

be·com·ing /bɪˈkʌmɪŋ/ *adj fml* **1** *apprec* (of colour, clothes, etc.) looking very good on the wearer: *Blue always looks very becoming on her.* **2** proper or suitable; APPROPRIATE: *His laughter was not very becoming on such a solemn occasion.* —opposite **unbecoming** — ~**ly** *adv*

bec·que·rel /ˌbekəˈrel/ *n* a unit used for measuring levels of RADIOACTIVITY

bed[1] /bed/ *n* **1** [C;U] a piece of furniture for sleeping on: *a room with two beds* | *I like reading in bed.* | *a comfortable bed for the night* | *a 40-bed hospital* (=with beds for 40 people) | *It's time for bed.* (=time to go to sleep) | *It's time those children went to bed.* | *You look ill, young man: bed is the place for you!* | *He helped me to* **make the bed**. (=make it ready for sleeping in) | *He tried to get her to* **go to bed with** *him.* (=have sexual relations with him) | *He* **took to his bed**. (=went to bed and stayed there because of illness) **2** [C] a surface that forms the base or bottom of something: *the bed of a river* | *the seabed* | *The hut rests on a bed of cement.* **3** [C] a piece of ground prepared for plants; a FLOWERBED **4** [C] a band of rock lying above or below others; STRATUM: *In this part of the country you can see the rock beds clearly, one on top of the other.* **5 be brought to bed of** *lit or old use* to give birth to (a child) **6 get out of bed on the wrong side** *infml* || also **get up on the wrong side of the bed** *AmE infml* to be in a bad temper **7 you've made your bed and you must lie on it** *saying* you must accept the bad results of your actions —see also BED OF ROSES

bed[2] *v* **-dd-** [T] **1** [+obj+adv/prep] to fix on a base (or beneath the surface); EMBED: *The machine is bedded in cement.* **2** [T (OUT)] to plant in a bed or beds: *These young plants will soon be ready for bedding (out) in the border.* **3** *old-fash* to persuade (a woman) to have sexual relations with one
bed down *phr v* **1** [T] (**bed** sbdy./sthg. ↔ **down**) to make (a person or animal) comfortable for the night **2** [I] to make oneself comfortable for the night: *I'll bed down on these chairs.*

bed and board /ˌ·· ·ˈ·/ *BrE* || **room and board** *AmE n* [U] food and a place to sleep

bed and break·fast /ˌ·· ·ˈ··/ also **b and b**— *n* [C;U] (a private house or small hotel that provides) a place to sleep for the night and breakfast the next morning for a fixed price

be·daub /bɪˈdɔːb/ *v* [T (with)] *fml* to make dirty with something wet and sticky; SMEAR[2]: *a wall bedaubed with mud*

bed bath /ˈ· ·/ *n* a thorough, whole body wash given by nurses, etc. to someone who is unable to leave their bed

bed·bug /ˈbedbʌg/ also **bug**— *n* a wingless blood-sucking insect that lives in houses and esp. beds

bed·clothes /ˈbedkləʊðz, -kləʊz/ *n* [P] the sheets, covers, etc. on a bed —compare BED LINEN

bed·ding /ˈbedɪŋ/ *n* [U] **1** bedclothes **2** materials on which an animal can sleep: *This straw will make good bedding for the animals.*

bedding plant /ˈ·· ·/ *n* a plant, often with flowers, that is planted out into a garden in the spring and that only lasts for one summer

bed·dy-bye /ˈbedi baɪ/ *AmE* || **bye-byes** *BrE— n* time for beddy-bye (used by or to children) time to go to bed and to sleep

Bede /biːd/, **The Venerable** (673–735) an English SCHOLAR and HISTORIAN

be·deck /bɪˈdek/ *v* [T (in, with)] *fml or lit* to hang decorations, jewels, flowers, etc. on; DECK out: *The cars were all bedecked with flowers for the ceremony.*

be·dev·il /bɪˈdevəl/ *v* **-ll-** *BrE* || **-l-** *AmE* [T] to continually cause trouble and difficulty for someone or something: *The whole project has been bedevilled by arguments over the plans.* — ~ **ment** *n* [U]

be·dewed /bɪˈdjuːd‖bɪˈduːd/ *adj* [F (with)] *lit* made wet as with drops of water: *cheeks bedewed with tears*

bed·fel·low /ˈbedˌfeləʊ/ *n* **1** a person who shares a bed **2** a close companion or partner, esp. in business or politics: *The two old rivals made* **strange bedfellows** (=unexpected partners) *when they agreed to work together against the government.*

Bed·ford /ˈbedfəd‖-fərd/ a town in the S of England, where the local government for Bedfordshire is based

Bed·ford·shire /ˈbedfədʃəʳ‖-fərd-/ a COUNTY in S England, whose main town is Bedford

be·dimmed /bɪˈdɪmd/ *adj* [F (with)] *lit* made less able to see or understand clearly: *eyes bedimmed with age*

bed·lam /ˈbedləm/ *n* **1** [S;U] *infml* a wild untidy noisy place or activity: *If I leave the children on their own it's*

absolute bedlam by the time I get back. **2** [C] *old use* a hospital for mad people

bed lin·en /ˈ· ˌ··/ *n* the sheets and PILLOWCASEs for a bed —compare BEDCLOTHES

bed of ros·es /ˌ·· ·ˈ··/ *n* [S] a happy comfortable state: *Life isn't always a bed of roses, you know.*

bed·ou·in /ˈbeduɪn/ *n* **bedouin** or **bedouins** (*often cap.*) a wandering Arab of the desert

bed·pan /ˈbedpæn/ *n* a low wide container for body waste, used by a person who is unable to get out of bed — compare CHAMBER POT, POTTY[2]

bed·post /ˈbedpəʊst/ *n* one of the main supports at the four corners of an old-fashioned bed —see also **between you, me, and the bedpost** (BETWEEN[1] (5))

be·drag·gled /bɪˈdrægəld/ *adj* wet and LIMP or muddy (as if) after being out in the rain: *a bedraggled appearance* | *She looked rather bedraggled.*

bed·rid·den /ˈbedˌrɪdn/ *adj* unable to get out of bed because of illness or old age: *He's bedridden with flu.*

bed·rock /ˈbedrɒk‖-rɑːk/ *n* [U] **1** the main stretch of solid rock in the ground supporting all the soil above it **2** the main facts or principles on which a belief, activity, etc. rests: *Let's* **get down to bedrock**, *and find out the truth.* | *the bedrock cost of running the business*

bed·roll /ˈbedrəʊl/ *n* *AmE* covers, esp. BLANKETs (thick woollen covers), rolled together to be carried easily and used for sleeping outdoors, esp. formerly: *The cowboy strapped his bedroll behind the saddle.*

bed·room[1] /ˈbedrʊm, -ruːm/ *n* a room for sleeping in: *The children's bedroom is on the top floor.* | *a hotel with 230 bedrooms*

bedroom[2] *adj* [A] about or suggesting sexual relations: *bedroom scenes in a film*

bed·side /ˈbedsaɪd/ *n* the side of a bed: *He has been called to the bedside of his sick father.* | *a bedside lamp*

bedside man·ner /ˌ·· ·ˈ··/ *n* a calm, gentle way of talking to sick people, used by doctors in order to show people that they do not need to worry

bed·sit·ter /ˌ·· ·ˈ··/ also **bed-sit·ting room** /ˌ·· ·ˈ·· ·/ *fml*, **bed-sit** /ˈ· ˌ·/ *infml— n BrE* a room used for both living and sleeping in. Bed-sitters are cheap to rent, and so are usu. rented by young, single people who have little money. —see HOUSE (USAGE)

bed·sore /ˈbedsɔːʳ/ *n* a sore place on a person's skin, caused by having to lie in bed for a long time

bed·spread /ˈbedspred/ *n* a decorative cloth cover for a bed

bed·stead /ˈbedsted/ *n* the main framework (wooden or metal) of a bed

bed·time /ˈbedtaɪm/ *n* [C;U] the right time for going to bed: *It's long past your bedtime, children!* | *a bedtime story*

bed wet·ter /ˈ· ˌ··/ *n* someone, esp. a child, who passes water in his sleep: *Our son was a bed wetter till he was 11.* —**bed-wetting** *n* [U]

bee /biː/ *n* **1** a stinging insect that makes sweet HONEY, lives in large social groups, and is supposed to be very busy —see picture at WASP **2** *AmE infml* a meeting of women for work: *a sewing bee* **3** a friendly competition: *a spelling bee* **4** ˈ**bee in one's bonnet** *infml* a fixed idea about something; OBSESSION: *He's got a bee in his bonnet about health foods.* **5 the bee's knees** *BrE infml* the best person or thing at an activity, in a place, etc.: *John think's he's the bee's knees around here but there are better students in the class.*

Beeb /biːb/ [*the*] *infml* the BBC

beech /biːtʃ/ *n* [C;U] (the wood of) a large forest tree with a smooth grey trunk, spreading branches, and dark green or copper-coloured leaves

Bee·cham /ˈbiːtʃəm/, **Sir Thomas** (1897–1961) an English CONDUCTOR who established the London Philharmonic Orchestra in 1932 and the Royal Philharmonic Orchestra in 1946

Beecham's pow·ders /ˌ·· ·ˈ··/ *n* [P] *tdmk* a British medicine in the form of a powder which is mixed with water and taken for headaches, colds, or FLU

Bee·ching /ˈbiːtʃɪŋ/, **Lord** (1913–85) the English chairman of the British Railways Board who was responsible for the **Beeching Plan**, which led to the closing of many small railway lines in Britain

beef[1] /biːf/ n 1 [U] the meat of farm cattle. ROAST beef with YORKSHIRE PUDDING is a TRADITIONAL British Sunday LUNCH: *beef steak | roast beef | a beef farmer* —see MEAT (USAGE) 2 [U] *infml* the power of the muscles: *Come on, put some beef into the job!* 3 [C] *infml* a complaint: *My main beef is that it went on too long.*

beef[2] v [I (about)] *infml often derog* to complain, esp. repeatedly: *Stop beefing (about your pay) and do some work!*
beef sthg./sbdy. ↔ **up** *phr v* [T] *infml* to strengthen or improve: *It's quite a good story but it needs beefing up a bit before we can publish it.*

beef·bur·ger /ˈbiːfbɜːgəʳ‖-bɜːr-/ n esp. BrE a HAMBURGER

beef·cake /ˈbiːfkeɪk/ n [U] *infml* (photographs of) strong attractive men with large muscles —compare CHEESECAKE (2)

Beef·eat·er /ˈbiːfˌiːtəʳ/ n a soldier who wears a special old-fashioned uniform and acts as a ceremonial guard in the Tower of London

beef tea /ˌ· ˈ·/ n [U] a drink made from beef juice, often given formerly to sick people

beef Wel·ling·ton /ˌ· ˈ···/ n [U] a piece of BEEF (= meat from a cow) covered with PÂTÉ DE FOIE GRAS and cooked in a pastry case

beef·y /ˈbiːfi/ adj *infml* (of a person) big, strong, and perhaps fat; HEFTY

Bee Gees /ˈbiː ˌdʒiːz/, **The** a highly successful British popular music group of three brothers, best known for their songs (which they also wrote) for the film *Saturday Night Fever*

bee·hive /ˈbiːhaɪv/ n 1 a HIVE[1] (1) 2 a women's HAIRSTYLE in which the hair is piled high on the head: *She wore her hair in a beehive.*

bee·line /ˈbiːlaɪn/ n **make a beeline for** *infml* to go quickly and directly towards: *The children ignored all the other food and made a beeline for the cakes.*

Be·el·ze·bub /biˈelzɪbʌb/ a devil, esp. Satan

been /biːn, bɪn‖bɪn/ 1 *past participle of* BE: *They've been photographed.* 2 (to have) gone and come back from: *Have you ever been to India?* 3 BrE (to have) arrived and left: *The postman hasn't been yet.* —see GO[3][4] (USAGE)

beep /biːp/ n the sound of a car horn —**beep** v [I;T] : *He sat out front in his car and beeped his horn for her to come out. | All night long the traffic kept him awake − horns beeping, tyres squealing, car doors slamming.*

beep·er /ˈbiːpəʳ/ n AmE BLEEPER

beer /bɪəʳ/ n 1 [C;U] (a glass of) an alcoholic drink made from MALT and made bitter with hops (HOP[3]): *a pint of beer | Would you like a (glass of) beer? | They brew several excellent beers in this district.*

▶CULTURAL NOTE Many different varieties of beer are sold in British pubs, e.g. **mild, bitter, lager, stout**. People usu. ask for a beer of a certain type or by the name of the company that produces the beer: *Half a bitter, please. | Two pints of Guinness.* In the US, people generally use the word "beer" when asking for or offering a beer: *Two beers, please.* Most beer sold in the US is LAGER (= pale-coloured beer), and it is always drunk very cold.◀

2 [U] (*in comb.*) any of several kinds of drink, usu. non-alcoholic, made from roots or plants: *ginger beer | root beer* 3 **I'm only here for the beer** a phrase originally used in a British advertisement for a particular kind of beer, now used humorously to mean "I am not here to offer support or because I am interested but because there is free drink" 4 **not all beer and skittles** BrE *infml* not just full of pleasure and enjoyment: *An actor's life isn't all beer and skittles.* —see also SMALL BEER and see picture at GLASS —**beery** adj : *unpleasant beery breath*

Beer·bohm /ˈbɪəbəʊm‖ˈbɪər-/, **Sir Max** /mæks/ (1872−1956) a British humorous writer

beer tent /ˈ· ·/ n a large tent in which beer and other alcoholic drinks can be bought at an outdoor event

bees·wax /ˈbiːzwæks/ n [U] 1 a fatty substance (WAX) made by bees, used for making furniture polish, candles, etc. 2 **none of your beeswax** esp. AmE *infml* not concerning you at all

beet /biːt/ n [C;U] 1 also **sugar beet**− a root vegetable from which sugar is obtained —see also SUGAR 2 AmE a BEETROOT 3 **red as a beet** AmE *infml* very red in the

face: *He turned red as a beet when I found the letter.*

Beet·ho·ven /ˈbeɪthəʊvən/, **Lud·wig van** /ˈlʊdvɪg væn/ (1770−1827) a German COMPOSER, one of the best known and most admired composers of all time, who continued writing music after he became unable to hear at the age of 30. Among the most famous of his many works are the *Fifth Symphony* and the *Emperor Concerto.*

bee·tle[1] /ˈbiːtl/ n any of many kinds of insect with hard wing coverings —see picture at INSECT

beetle[2] v [I+adv/prep] BrE *sl* (of people) to go quickly, esp. as if trying not to be noticed: *I saw him beetling off/away early last night.*

Beetle n *tdmk* a small car made by Volkswagen which has a high, rounded top

Bee·ton /ˈbiːtn/, **Mrs** (1836−65) an English cookery writer, best known for her *Book of Household Management*

beet·root /ˈbiːtruːt/ BrE ‖ **beet** AmE− n -root *or* -roots [C;U] a plant with a large round red root, cooked and eaten as a vegetable: *beetroot salad | She turned as red as a beetroot when they laughed at her.*

be·fall /bɪˈfɔːl/ v -fell /ˈfel/, -fallen /ˈfɔːlən/ [I;T] *fml* (usu. of something bad) to happen to, esp. as if by fate: *Some misfortune must have befallen them.*

be·fit /bɪˈfɪt/ v -tt- [T] *fml* to be proper or suitable to: *He always travels first class, as befits a person in his position.| a sober suit befitting the occasion* − ~**tingly** adv

be·fore[1] /bɪˈfɔːʳ/ prep 1 earlier than: *before 1937 | He got there before me. | The new road will be completed before the end of the year. | the day before yesterday* (=two days ago) *| I usu. take a bath before having my breakfast.* 2 at an earlier point in an order than; ahead of: *Your name comes before mine in the list.* 3 for the consideration of: *The proposal was put before the planning committee.* 4 *fml or lit* in front of: *The priest stood before the altar. | The great plain stretched out before them.* 5 in a more important position than: *I've always put quality before quantity.* − see LAST[1] (USAGE)

before[2] adv 1 at an earlier time; already; formerly: *Haven't I seen you before? | I thought he'd take it easy after the accident, but he carries on driving like a maniac, as before. | We had met on the Saturday before.* (compare *We met last Saturday.*) —see AGO (USAGE) 2 *becoming rare* in advance; ahead

before[3] conj 1 earlier than the time when: *Say goodbye before you go. | It will be some time before we know the full results.* 2 more willingly than; rather than: *He will die before he tells them what they want to know.* 3 if not; or else; otherwise: *Get out before I call the police.*

be·fore·hand /bɪˈfɔːhænd‖-ˈfɔːr-/ adv before something else happens; in advance: *We knew they were coming, so we bought some food beforehand.*

be·friend /bɪˈfrend/ v [T] *fml* to act as a friend to (esp. someone who is younger, or needs help): *They befriended me when I first arrived in London as a student.*

beg /beg/ v -gg- 1 [I (for);T] to ask (esp. for food, money, etc.) in a way which shows little pride or self-respect: *He lives by begging. | He begged (for) money (from the people in the street). | a begging letter* 2 [I;T (of, for)] to ask (for) with great eagerness or anxiety: *to beg a favour (of someone) | to beg (for) forgiveness | She begged and begged until I said yes.* [+to-v] *He begged to be allowed to go.* [+that] *He begged that he (should) be sent home.* [+obj+to-v] *She begged me not to tell her parents.* 3 [T] (in certain phrases) to request politely: **I beg your pardon.** (=I am sorry.) [+to-v] **I beg to differ.** (=I don't agree with you.) 4 [I] (of a dog) to sit up with its front legs held against its chest 5 **beg the question** to take as true something that is not yet proved 6 BrE **going begging** able to be got or used; AVAILABLE: *Those cakes are going begging if anyone would like them.*
beg off *phr v* [I] to excuse (oneself) from doing something one had agreed to do: *Jane has just begged off   can you take her place in the team?*

be·get /bɪˈget/ v **begot** /bɪˈgɒt‖bɪˈgɑːt/ *or* (*bibl*) **begat** /bɪˈgæt/, **begotten** /bɪˈgɒtn‖bɪˈgɑːtn/ [T] esp. bibl *or old use* to become the father of: "*Abraham begat* (=begot) *Isaac.*" (The Bible, Matthew 1:2) | (*fig.*) *Hunger begets* (=produces) *crime.*

beg·gar[1] /ˈbegəʳ/ n 1 a person who lives by begging 2 *infml* any person, esp. a man or boy: *He's a cheerful little beggar! | So you're off to San Francisco tomorrow, you*

lucky beggar! 3 beggars can't be choosers *saying* people in need must accept what they can get, without worrying about the quality

beg·gar² /ˈbegə/ v [T] **1** *fml* to make very poor: *They were beggared by trying to pay for their children's education.* **2 beggar (all) description** *BrE lit* to be beyond the powers of language to describe: *The valley was so beautiful as to beggar description.*

beg·gar·ly /ˈbegəli‖-ərli/ *adj* much too little in amount; MEAGRE: *to earn a beggarly salary* —**·liness** n [U]

beggar-my-neigh·bour /ˌ‥ · ‥/ n [U] a card game in which the aim is to obtain all one's opponents' cards, leaving them with none

Beggar's Op·e·ra /ˌ‥ ·ˈ‥·/ [*the*] an OPERA by John Gay, first produced in 1728, which takes place in and around Newgate prison in London, and has as one of its main characters a HIGHWAYMAN called Macheath

beg·gar·y /ˈbegəri/ n [U] the state of being very poor: *They were reduced to beggary by the failure of their farm.*

be·gin /bɪˈgɪn/ v **began** /bɪˈgæn/, **begun** /bɪˈgʌn/ [I;T] **1** to do or be the first part of (a process or activity); make a start (on): *I'll begin whenever you're ready.* | *Work on the new bridge will begin next month.* | *She curled up in bed and began her book.* | *The book began with the death of a reporter.* | *We'll begin by dancing|with a story|at the beginning.* [+to-v] *It began to rain.* | *Even his greatest admirers are beginning to wonder if he is too old for the job.* | *I couldn't (even) begin to explain.* (=It's quite impossible to explain.) [+v-ing] *She began learning English five years ago.* | *We can't possibly go –* **to begin with** (=the first reason is) *it's too cold, and besides, we have no money.* —see START (USAGE) **2** to (cause to) come into existence: *The war began in 1939.* | *She began a club for bird-watchers.*

Be·gin /ˈbeɪgɪn/, **Me·na·chem** /məˈnɑːkɨm/ (1913–92) an Israeli politician and PRIME MINISTER from 1977 to 1983. In 1979 he signed a peace TREATY with President Sadat of Egypt which was known as the Camp David agreement.

be·gin·ner /bɪˈgɪnə/ n a person who is just beginning to do or learn something: *I scored three goals the first time I played, but they put it down to* **beginner's luck.** (=unusual success at the start which is not expected to last) —compare STARTER

be·gin·ning /bɪˈgɪnɪŋ/ n [C;U] **1** the point at which something begins; start; origin: *at the beginning of the month* | *She knows the subject from beginning to end.* (=completely) —see PREFACE (USAGE) **2 In the beginning was the Word** the first words of St John's Gospel in the Bible **3 the beginning of the end** the point at which something good starts to come to an end or be less good

be·gone /bɪˈgɒn‖bɪˈgɔːn/ v [I *usu. imperative*] *poet* to go away at once: *Begone with you!*

be·go·ni·a /bɨˈgəʊniə/ n a type of tropical plant with bright yellow, pink, red, or white flowers

be·got /bɪˈgɒt‖bɪˈgɑːt/ *past tense of* BEGET

be·got·ten /bɪˈgɒtn‖bɪˈgɑːtn/ *past participle of* BEGET

be·grudge /bɪˈgrʌdʒ/ also **grudge**— v [T] to give or allow (something) unwillingly, esp. because it is unwanted or undeserved: *She begrudged every minute taken from her work.* [+v-ing] *I begrudge spending so much money on train fares.* [+obj(i)+obj(d)] *We shouldn't begrudge him his success.*

be·guile /bɪˈgaɪl/ v [T] **1** to charm or attract: *a beguiling smile* **2** [(AWAY, **by, with**)] *BrE* to cause (time) to pass esp. in a pleasant way: *We beguiled (away) the time by telling jokes|with a bottle of wine and some good music.* **3** [(**into**)] to deceive; cheat: *I was beguiled by his flattery into trusting him.* – –**ment** n [U]

be·gum /ˈbeɪgəm, ˈbiː-/ n (*often cap.*) (in India and Pakistan) a Muslim lady of high rank; often used as a title of respect for any married woman

be·gun /bɪˈgʌn/ *past participle of* BEGIN

be·half /bɪˈhɑːf‖bɪˈhæf/ n **on behalf of** also **in behalf of** *AmE*— for, in the interests of, or as the representative of (someone else): *On behalf of everyone here, I'd like to thank our special guest for his entertaining speech.* | *The President can't be here today, so I'm going to speak on his behalf.*

Be·han /ˈbiːən/, **Bren·dan** /ˈbrendən/ (1923–64) an Irish

writer who wrote about his experience of being in prison for IRA activities in plays such as *The Quare Fellow* (1954) and in his AUTOBIOGRAPHY *Borstal Boy*

be·have /bɪˈheɪv/ v **1** [I+adv/prep] to act in a particular way: *She's been behaving rather oddly.* | *Quantum mechanics is the branch of physics which studies the way atoms behave.* | *My car has been behaving well since it was repaired.* **2** [I;T] to act in a socially acceptable or polite way: *Behave (yourself)!* | *a well-behaved|badly-behaved child*

be·hav·iour *BrE* ‖ **-ior** *AmE* /bɪˈheɪvjə/ n [U] **1** way of behaving **2 be on one's best behaviour** to be very polite; show one's best manners – ~ **al** *adj* : *behavioural science* – ~ **ally** *adv*

be·hav·iour·is·m *BrE* ‖ **-ior-** *AmE* /bɪˈheɪvjərɪzəm/ n [U] *tech* the idea that the scientific study of the mind should be based only on outward behaviour and physical states, not on people's reports of their thoughts and feelings —**ist** n

be·head /bɪˈhed/ v [T] to cut off the head of, esp. as a punishment; DECAPITATE

Be·he·moth /bɨˈhiːmɒθ‖-mɑːθ/ an extremely large, MYTHICAL creature mentioned in the Bible, whose name is now used to describe something very big: *five warships, including two 64,000-ton behemoths* —see also LEVIATHAN

be·hest /bɪˈhest/ n [S] *fml* an urgent request or command: *at the behest of his mother*

be·hind¹ /bɪˈhaɪnd/ prep **1** at or towards the back of: *She ran out from behind a tree.* | (fig.) *I wonder what's behind* (=what is the real reason for) *his sudden change of plan.* | (fig.) *Now you can put all these worries behind you.* (=forget them) —opposite **in front of** (FRONT¹) **2** lower than, in position or quality; below: *We're three points behind the team in first place.* | *He's always behind the rest of his class in mathematics.* | *The trains are running* **behind schedule.** (=later than the proper time) —opposite **ahead of** (AHEAD) **3** in support of; encouraging: *We're (right) behind you all the way!* —see also **behind someone's back** (BACK¹ (10)), **behind the scenes** (SCENE), **behind the times** (TIME¹), **behind closed doors** (DOOR)

behind² adv **1** at or towards the back: *a house with a garden behind* | *The motorcyclists came first, with the President's car following close behind.* —compare **in front** (FRONT¹) **2** in the place where something or someone was before: *I can't unlock the car because I've left the keys behind.* | *They went for a walk but I stayed behind to look after the baby.* **3** [(**with, in**)] late; slow; BEHINDHAND: *I'm a month behind with the rent.* (=I should have paid it a month ago.)

behind³ n *euph sl* the part of the body that a person sits on; BUTTOCKS: *I gave him a kick in the behind.*

be·hind·hand /bɪˈhaɪndhænd/ adv [(**with, in**)] *rather fml* late or slow in doing something, paying something, etc.: *We're a month behindhand with the rent.*

be·hold /bɪˈhəʊld/ v **beheld** /bɪˈheld/ [T] *esp. lit or old use* to see; look at: *They beheld the great city of Babylon.* —see also LO AND BEHOLD – ~ **er** n

be·hold·en /bɪˈhəʊldən/ adj [F (**to**)] having to feel grateful or having a duty (to): *I like to do things for myself and not feel beholden to anyone else.*

be·hove /bɪˈhəʊv‖bɪˈhuːv/ also **be·hoove** /bɪˈhuːv/ *AmE*— v it **behooves one to** it is right and necessary to: *It would behoove you to work harder if you want to succeed here.*

Bei·der·becke /ˈbaɪdəbek‖-dər-/, **Bix** /bɪks/ (1903–31) an American JAZZ musician who played the piano and CORNET and was one of the few white musicians to influence the early development of jazz

beige /beɪʒ/ adj pale dull yellowish brown —**beige** n [U]

Bei·jing /ˌbeɪˈdʒɪŋ/ the capital city of the People's Republic of China; old English name **Peking**

be·ing¹ /ˈbiːɪŋ/ n **1** [U] the state of existing: *When did the universe first* **come into being?** | *This rule was brought into being because the old law was obsolete.* **2** [C] a living thing, esp. a person: *a human being* | *strange beings from outer space* | *the Supreme Being* (=God) | *sentient being* (=a being with a mind) **3** [U] the central qualities or nature of a thing, esp. a living thing: *The news shook me to the very roots of my being.*

being² *present participle of* BE: *They're being photographed.* | *All being well* (=if everything goes well), *we* *should arrive by tomorrow.* —see also **for the time being** (TIME¹ (28))

Bei·rut /beɪˈruːt/ the capital city of Lebanon. Once an important centre of business and finance in the Middle East, it was badly damaged during the long CIVIL WAR in the 1970s and '80s.

Be·kaa Val·ley /bɪˌkɑː ˈvæli/ a 100-mile-long valley in Lebanon and Syria, an important line of travel for which many wars have been fought

be·la·bour *BrE* ‖ **-bor** *AmE* /bɪˈleɪbəʳ/ *v* [T (with)] *old use* to beat severely

be·lat·ed /bɪˈleɪtɪd/ *adj* delayed; happening or arriving (too) late: *a belated apology/birthday card* – ~ **ly** *adv*: *The letter arrived belatedly, when the wedding was over.*

be·lay /bɪˈleɪ/ *v* [I;T] *tech* (on ships) to fix (a rope) by winding under and over in the shape of the figure 8 on to a special hook (a **belaying pin**)

belch /beltʃ/ *v* **1** [I] (of a person) to pass gas noisily from the stomach through the mouth **2** [T (OUT)] to throw out with force or in large quantities: *factory chimneys belching (out) smoke* —**belch** *n*: *He gave a loud belch.*

be·lea·guer /bɪˈliːgəʳ/ *v* [T *usu. pass.*] *fml* **1** to surround with an army so as to prevent escape; BESIEGE: *a beleaguered city* **2** to worry and annoy continuously; HARASS: *beleaguered parents*

Bel·fast /ˌbelˈfɑːst◂, ˈbelfɑːst‖ˈbelfæst/ the capital city of Northern Ireland. Belfast is often mentioned in the newspapers because of the bombs and shootings there —see also TROUBLES —and see colour map on page 818

bel·fry /ˈbelfri/ *n* a tower for a bell, esp. on a church —see picture at CHURCH, and see also **be/have bats in the belfry** (BAT³ (2))

Bel·gian /ˈbeldʒən/ *n, adj* (a person who comes from, or whose parents come) from Belgium: *Belgian chocolate | the Belgian foreign minister*

Bel·gium /ˈbeldʒəm/ a country in NW Europe; capital Brussels; population 9,932,000 (1989)

Bel·grade /belˈgreɪd/ the capital city of Yugoslavia and Serbia

Bel·gra·no Af·fair /belˈgrɑːnəʊ əˌfeəʳ/ [*the*] a political disagreement about the British Government's order to sink an Argentinian ship called the *General Belgrano* during the Falklands War of 1982.

Bel·gra·vi·a /belˈgreɪviə/ an expensive part of W central London where there are many foreign embassies (EMBASSY)

be·lie /bɪˈlaɪ/ *v* [T] *fml* **1** to give a false idea of: *Her smile belied her true feelings of displeasure.* **2** to show (hopes, promises, etc.) to be false or mistaken: *The poor sales of the product belied our high hopes for it.*

be·lief /bɪˈliːf/ *n* **1** [S;U (in)] the feeling that something is true or that something really exists: *(a) belief in God* [+*that*] *It's my belief that* (=I believe that) *her death was not an accident. She started taking money from her employer, in the mistaken belief that she would not be discovered. | His story is* **beyond belief.** (=too strange to be believed) —compare DISBELIEF, UNBELIEF **2** [S;U (in)] a feeling that someone or something is good or can be depended on; trust or confidence: *The failure of the operation has* **shaken my belief** (=weakened my trust) *in doctors.* **3** [C] an idea which is considered true, often one which is part of a system of ideas: *religious/political beliefs* —see also **to the best of one's belief** (BEST³ (10))

be·lie·va·ble /bɪˈliːvəbəl/ *adj* that can be believed —see also UNBELIEVABLE —**bly** *adv*

be·lieve /bɪˈliːv/ *v* [*not in progressive forms*] **1** [T] to consider to be true, honest, or real: *You can't believe anything she says. | The police didn't believe him/his account of the accident. | I asked my boss for a month's holiday and,* **believe it or not,** *she agreed! | "He says he's given up smoking."* **"Don't you believe it** – *I saw him having a cigarette only ten minutes ago!"* [+(*that*)] *It's hard to believe that she's only 25. | I can't believe* (=I'm extremely surprised) *he's getting married after all these years. | She said I needed a face-lift* – **would/can you believe it!** (=expresses surprise or shock) | *He tore up the contract and stormed out* – **I could hardly believe my eyes!** (=I was extremely surprised. —see CAN (USAGE), DISBELIEVE (USAGE), and see also **make believe** (MAKE¹) **2** [T] to hold as an opinion; think; suppose: [+(*that*)] *I believe*

they're getting married. | "Has he arrived yet?" "I believe so." | According to the poll, 65% of the public believes the President's economic policies are right. [+*obj*+*to-v*] *The banks are widely believed to be planning a cut in interest rates. | The jury believed her to be innocent.* **3** [I] to have a firm religious faith

believe in sbdy./sthg. *phr v* [T] **1** to think that (something) exists: *Do you believe in fairies/magic?* **2** to have faith or trust in: *Christians believe in Jesus. | I don't believe in astrology.* **3** to have confidence in the value of: *I don't believe in all these so-called health foods.* [+*v-ing*] *He believes in taking plenty of exercise.*

be·liev·er /bɪˈliːvəʳ/ *n* **1** a person who has faith, esp. religious faith —opposite **unbeliever 2** [+*in*] a person who believes in (something or perhaps someone): *I'm a great believer in fresh air as a cure for illness.*

Be·li·sha bea·con /bəˌliːʃə ˈbiːkən/ also **beacon**— *n* (in Britain) a flashing orange light on a post that marks a street crossing place (a ZEBRA CROSSING) for walkers

Belisha beacon

be·lit·tle /bɪˈlɪtl/ *v* [T] *fml* to cause to seem small or unimportant; DISPARAGE: *Don't belittle yourself/your efforts.*

Be·lize /bəˈliːz/ a country in Central America on the Caribbean Sea, which was a British COLONY until its independence in 1981; capital Belmopan; population 178,000 (1989)

bell /bel/ *n* **1** a round hollow metal object, usu. open-ended which makes a ringing sound when struck, or an electrical instrument which makes a similar sound: *church bells | a bicycle bell | a doorbell* —see picture at BICYCLE

► CULTURAL NOTE Many Christian churches have bells, and these are rung on Sundays, to tell people that the church service is about to begin. They are also rung, often making pleasant tunes, when people are getting married in a church. A single bell is rung repeatedly to show that someone has died. ◄

2 [*usu. sing.*] the sound of a bell, esp. as a signal or warning: *the dinner bell* **3** something shaped like a bell, hollow and widening towards the end: *the bell of a flower/of a musical instrument* —see picture at BRASS **4 Ask not for whom the bell tolls, it tolls for thee** *quote* a slightly changed phrase from a work by John Donne, used when saying that every person should feel involved in the misfortunes of others **5 give someone a bell** *BrE infml* to telephone someone —see also DIVING BELL, **ring a bell** (RING³), **as sound as a bell** (SOUND³)

Bell, Al·ex·an·der Gra·ham /ˌæhlɪgˈzɑːndəʳ ˈgreɪəm‖ -ˈzæn-/ (1847–1922) a Scottish scientist and inventor who lived in the US, best known for inventing the telephone in 1876. He also started the Bell Telephone Company.

bel·la·don·na /ˌbeləˈdɒnə‖-ˈdɑːnə/ *n* [U] **1** DEADLY NIGHTSHADE **2** a drug, used in medicine, obtained from this plant

Bel·la·my /ˈbeləmi/, **David** (1933–) an English scientist who often appears on British television and is known for his knowledge of plants and concern about the protection of the natural world

bell-bot·toms /ˈ· ˌ··/ *n* [P] trousers with legs that become wider at the bottom. Bell-bottoms were very fashionable in the 1960s, but are not considered fashionable now. —see PAIR (USAGE)

bell·boy /ˈbelbɔɪ/ also **bell·hop** /ˈbelhɒp‖-hɑːp/ *AmE* — *n* a messenger or PORTER in a hotel or club

belle /bel/ *n* a popular and attractive girl or woman: *the belle of the ball* (=the prettiest girl at the dance)

Belle Dame Sans Mer·ci /ˌbel ˌdɑːm sɑːn meəˈsi‖-meəʳ-/, **La** the title of one of the best known poems of John Keats which describes a KNIGHT who falls in love with a beautiful, magical woman

belles-let·tres /ˌbel ˈletrə/ *n* [U] *Fr* literature that is of value for its beauty rather than for its practical importance

bel·li·cose /ˈbelɪkəʊs/ *adj fml* warlike; ready to quarrel or fight —**-cosity** /ˌbelɪˈkɒsꬼtiǁ-ˈkɑːs-/ *n* [U]

bel·lig·er·ent¹ /bꬼˈlɪdʒərənt/ *adj* **1** angry and ready to fight; AGGRESSIVE: *a belligerent person/attitude* —compare PUGNACIOUS **2** [A] *tech* (esp. of a country) at war —**-ency, -ence** *n* [U]

belligerent² *n tech* a person or country that is at war

Bel·li·ni /beˈliːni/, **Ja·co·po** /ˈjækəpəʊǁˈjɑː-/ (?1400–?1470) a Venetian painter. His two sons **Gentile Bellini** (?1429–1507) and **Giovanni Bellini** (?1430–1516) were also painters and trained by him.

bell jar /ˈ· ·/ *n* a large bottle made of thick glass, used to protect something inside it, or in scientific EXPERIMENTS —see picture at LABORATORY

Bell La·bor·a·to·ries /ˈ· ·,····ǁ·ˌ·····/ **Bell Labs** /ˈ· ˌ·/ *infml* a group of laboratories (LABORATORY) in the US where scientists have made many important discoveries and developments in science and TECHNOLOGY. It is thought quite difficult to get a job there, and a mark of great success for any scientist who does.

Bel·loc /ˈbelɒkǁ-ɑːk/, **Hi·laire** /hɪˈleəʳ/ (1870–1953) an English writer best known for his humorous poems

bel·low /ˈbeləʊ/ *v* **1** [I] to make the loud deep hollow sound typical of a BULL **2** [I (**with**);T (**out**)] to shout (something) in a deep voice: *to bellow with pain/bellow out orders* —**bellow** *n*

Bellow, Saul /ˈsɔːl/ (1915–) an American writer, born in Canada, who won the Nobel Prize for literature in 1976. His many well-known NOVELs include *The Adventures of Augie March* and *Herzog*.

bel·lows /ˈbeləʊz/ *n* **bellows** [C+*sing./pl. v*] an instrument used for supplying a stream of air (e.g. to make a fire burn more quickly or to make an organ produce sound) —see PAIR (USAGE)

bell pep·per /ˈ· ˌ··/ *n AmE for* PEPPER¹ (2)

Bell's /belz/ *n* [U] *tdmk* a kind of popular Scottish WHISKY

bel·ly¹ /ˈbeli/ *n* **1** *infml* **a** the part of a person's or animal's body, between the chest and the legs, which contains the stomach, INTESTINES, etc.; ABDOMEN **b** the stomach: *a full belly* —see picture at HORSE **2** a surface or object curved or round like this part of the body: *the belly of the plane/of a violin* **3** **-bellied** /belid/ having a belly of the stated type: *pot-bellied*

belly² *v*
  belly out *phr v* [I;T (=**belly** sthg. ↔ **out**)] to (cause to) swell or become full: *The wind bellied out the sail.* | *The sail bellied out in the wind.*

bel·ly·ache¹ /ˈbeli-eɪk/ *n* **1** [C;U] an ache in the belly **2** [C] *sl, often derog* a complaint, esp. about something unimportant: *I'm sick of listening to your bellyaches.*

bellyache² *v* [I (**about**)] *sl, often derog* to complain repeatedly, esp. about something unimportant: *Stop bellyaching and get on with the job!*

belly but·ton /ˈ·· ˌ··/ *n infml* a small mark or sunken place in the middle of the stomach; NAVEL

belly dance /ˈ·· ·/ *n* a dance of Eastern origin, performed by a woman using movements of the belly and HIPs —**~dancer** *n*

belly flop /ˈ·· ·/ *n infml* a DIVE (=an act of jumping head first into water), in which the front of the body falls flat against the water

bel·ly·ful /ˈbelifʊl/ *n* [S (**of**)] *infml* an amount that is more than one can bear: *I've had a bellyful of your complaints.*

belly-land·ing /ˈ·· ˌ··/ *n infml* an act of landing a plane without use of the landing equipment

belly laugh /ˈ·· ·/ *n infml* a deep full laugh, as if coming from the belly

Bel·mont Stakes /ˌbelmɒnt ˈsteɪksǁ-mɑːnt-/ [*the*] a race for three-year-old horses held in the state of New York —see also TRIPLE CROWN

be·long /bɪˈlɒŋǁbɪˈlɔːŋ/ *v* [I+*adv/prep*] to be in the right place or situation: *That chair belongs in the other room.* | *I don't really feel I belong here.* | *"Does this book belong here?" "No, it belongs with the dictionaries on the top shelf."* | *Put it back where it belongs.*
  belong to sbdy./sthg. *phr v* [T *no pass.*] **1** to be the property of: *That dictionary belongs to me.* | (fig.) *The credit for this success belongs to the President.* **2** to be a member of, or be connected with: *What party do you belong to?*

be·long·ings /bɪˈlɒŋɪŋzǁbɪˈlɔːŋ-/ *n* [P] those things which belong to one, which are one's property: *She lost all her belongings in the fire.*

Bel·o·rus·sia /ˌbeləʊˈrʌʃə/ also **Byelorussia**— a country in E Europe bordered by Poland, Latvia, Lithuania, Russia, and Ukraine; capital Minsk; population 10,200,000 (1989)

be·lov·ed /bɪˈlʌvꬼd/ *n, adj* (a person who is) dearly loved: *beloved by/of her friends* | *His beloved wife died.* | (*usu. humor.*) *It was a gift from my beloved.* (=from my wife, husband, etc.) —see LOVE (USAGE); see also **dearly beloved** (DEARLY (3))

be·low¹ /bɪˈləʊ/ *adv* **1** in a lower place, on a lower level, or at a lower position: *I live on the fifth floor; she lives on the floor below.* | *We looked down from the mountain to the valley below.* | *officers of the rank of captain and below* | *children of seven and below* (=younger) —opposite **above** —compare BENEATH¹, UNDERNEATH¹ **2** under the surface: *The captain told the sailors to go below.* (=to a lower DECK of the ship) **3** on a later page or lower on the same page: *See p.85 below.* | *The information below was compiled by our correspondent.* —opposite **above 4** *lit* on Earth rather than in heaven: *"My words fly up, my thoughts remain below. Words without thoughts never to heaven go."* (Shakespeare, *Hamlet*) **5** *infml* (of a temperature) lower than zero: *working in temperatures of 20° below.*

below² *prep* in a lower place than or on a lower level than: *a skirt that reaches to below the knee* | *a mile below the village* | *just below the surface of the water* | *children below the age of seven* (=younger than seven) | *A captain is below a general.* (=lower in rank) | *His work is well below* (=much less than) *average.* | *families living below the official poverty line* | *Industrial production is still* **way below** (=very much lower than) *its 1982 level.* —see UNDER (USAGE); compare BENEATH², UNDER¹

Bel·sen /ˈbelsən/ a CONCENTRATION CAMP in N Germany during the Second World War near a village of the same name

belt¹ /belt/ *n* **1** a band worn around the waist, to support clothing, as a decoration, etc.: *a leather belt* **2** a circular band of leather or other material used for driving a machine or for moving things from one place to another (e.g. in an industrial process) —see also FAN BELT, CONVEYER BELT **3** (*often cap.*) an area that has a particular quality or part: *the stockbroker belt* | *the Corn/Cotton Belt* (=where corn/cotton is the chief crop) —see also BIBLE BELT, COMMUTER BELT, GREEN BELT **4** *infml* an act of hitting someone hard; powerful blow **5 below the belt** *infml* unkind in an unfair way: *That remark was a bit below the belt.* | *an unfair remark that hit him below the belt* **6 under one's belt** achieved or finished: *Once you have a degree under your belt, you'll find it easier to get a job.* —see also BLACK BELT, LIFE BELT, SEAT BELT, **tighten one's belt** (TIGHTEN)

belt² *v* **1** [T (**up**)] to fasten with a belt: *She belted (up) her raincoat.* **2** [T] to hit (as if) with a belt; THRASH: *He gave the boy a real belting.* **3** [T] *infml* to hit very hard, esp. with the hand: *I belted him in the eye.* | *The tennis player belted the ball right out of the court.* **4** [I+*adv/prep*] *sl, esp. BrE* to travel fast: *belting along/down the motorway*
  belt sthg. ↔ **out** *phr v* [T] *infml* to sing loudly: *to belt out a song*
  belt up *phr v* [I *usu. imperative*] *BrE sl* to stop talking or making a noise: *If you don't belt up I'll throw you out.*

Bel·tane /ˈbelteɪn/ *n* an ancient celebration on May 1st when fires were built (**Beltane fires**) and the cattle brought to them to guard against illness in the coming year

belt·ed /ˈbeltꬼd/ *adj* provided with a belt: *a belted raincoat*

belt·way /ˈbeltweɪ/ *n AmE for* RING ROAD

Be·lu·shi /bəˈluːʃi/, **John** (1949–82) an American actor and COMEDIAN, best known for the television programme *Saturday Night Live* and films such as *National Lampoon's Animal House* and *The Blues Brothers*. He died of taking too many drugs.

be·moan /bɪˈməʊn/ *v* [T] *fml* to express sorrow or disappointment because of: *He bemoaned his bitter fate.* | *She bemoaned the lack of money for her new project.*

be·mused /bɪˈmjuːzd/ *adj* unable to think or understand properly; confused: *a bemused expression* | *bemused by/ with all the questions*

ben /ben/ n ScotE (often cap. as part of a name) a mountain or hill: Ben Nevis

bench¹ /bentʃ/ n 1 [C] a long usu. wooden seat for two or more people, esp. one used outdoors: a park bench 2 [the] a judge or the seat where a judge sits in court: to speak from the bench | The bench declared... 3 [the+sing./pl. v] judges as a group: What does/do the bench feel about this? | He retired from the bench in 1982. 4 [C] a long heavy worktable: a carpenter's bench 5 a seat on which members of a sports team sit when they are not playing: The manager was shouting instructions from the bench.

bench² v [T] AmE to remove from a game for a short period because of breaking the rules or because of poor performance: Mr Morris benched me for taking food into the playground. | Hershiser may be benched for the next few games because of shoulder problems.

Bench·ley /'bentʃli/, **Rob·ert Charles** /'rɒbət tʃɑːlz‖'rɑːbərt tʃɑːrlz/ (1889–1945) a humorous American writer, EDITOR, theatre critic and actor who worked on the magazines Vanity Fair and The New Yorker

bench mark /'·· ·/ n 1 a mark made on something fixed at a point of known height, from which heights and distances can be measured, esp. in surveying (SURVEY¹ (3)) 2 something which can be used as a standard by which other things are judged or measured: The new salary deal for railway workers will be a bench mark for pay settlements in the public sector. | The new software package establishes several benchmarks for other spreadsheet manufacturers.

bend¹ /bend/ v bent /bent/ 1 [T] to force into a curve, angle, or sloping position, away from a straight or upright position: to bend the wire | to bend one's head in worship | an old woman who was bent down with age | He pleaded with her on bended knee. (=kneeling) | (fig.) I think we can bend the rules (=let them be broken slightly) on this occasion. 2 [I] to have or take on a curved shape or sloping position: This wire bends easily. | The branches bent in the wind. | I bent down to pick up the box from the floor. | (fig.) They refused to bend to the hijackers' demands. | I talked to her for an hour but I couldn't get her to bend (=change her mind). 3 [T+obj+adv/prep] to direct (one's efforts): She bent her mind to the job. 4 **bend over backwards** to make every possible effort to be helpful 5 **bend someone's ear** infml to talk to someone, esp. about something that is worrying one —see also BENT

bend² n 1 a curved part, esp. in a road or stream: a bend in the road/river 2 an act of bending: forward bends to stretch the spine 3 **around/round the bend** infml, often humor mad: This pink wallpaper would drive/send me around/round the bend. | That old man next door must be/have gone round the bend — he's been cutting the grass with a pair of scissors!

bend·er /'bendər/ n [S] infml a wild period of uncontrolled drinking: After he got his exam results, he went on a bender for two days.

bends /bendz/ n [the+sing./pl. v] a painful and occasionally fatal condition caused by gas in the tubes through which blood flows, suffered esp. by deep-sea DIVERS who come to the surface too quickly

be·neath¹ /bɪ'niːθ/ adv fml 1 in or to a lower position; below: We looked down from the plane at the fields spread out beneath. 2 directly under; UNDERNEATH —see UNDER (USAGE); compare BELOW¹

beneath² prep 1 fml in or to a lower position than; below; directly under, esp. so as to be covered or sheltered by: The ship sank beneath the waves. | a village beneath the hills | to feel the sand beneath one's feet 2 lower than in rank, social position, etc.: She was very contemptuous of those beneath her. 3 not suitable to; not worthy of: Such behaviour is beneath you/beneath contempt. —see UNDER (USAGE), and compare BELOW²

ben·e·dic·tine /ˌbenɪ'dɪktiːn◁/ n [U] (often cap.) a strong alcoholic drink (LIQUEUR) first made by members of the Benedictine order, usu. drunk from a small glass after a meal

Ben·e·dic·tine /ˌbenɪ'dɪktɪn◁/ n a member of a Christian religious order of MONKS obeying the rules of Saint Benedict

ben·e·dic·tion /ˌbenɪ'dɪkʃən/ n (a prayer or religious service giving) a blessing

ben·e·fac·tion /ˌbenɪ'fækʃən/ n fml 1 [U] doing good or giving money for a good purpose 2 [C] money so given

ben·e·fac·tor /'benɪˌfæktər/ **ben·e·fac·tress** /-trəs/fem.— n a person who does good or who gives money for a good purpose —compare MALEFACTOR

ben·e·fice /'benɪfɪs/ n the pay and position of the Christian priest of a PARISH

be·nef·i·cent /bɪ'nefɪsənt/ adj fml doing good; kind or generous —**cence** n [U] — **-ly** adv

ben·e·fi·cial /ˌbenɪ'fɪʃəl◁/ adj [(to)] (esp. of an action or event) producing favourable effects or useful results: His holiday has had a beneficial effect. | The fall in prices will be beneficial to small businesses. — **~ly** adv

ben·e·fi·cia·ry /ˌbenɪ'fɪʃəri‖-'fɪʃieri/ n [(of)] the receiver of a benefit or advantage, esp. of money or property: People on high incomes will be the main beneficiaries of these changes in the tax laws. | His eldest son was named in his will as the chief beneficiary. (=who would receive his property when he died)

ben·e·fit¹ /'benɪfɪt/ n 1 [U] anything that brings help, advantage, or profit; She has had the benefit of a first-class education. | For the benefit of those people who arrived late, I'll just go over the plan again. | My holiday wasn't of much benefit to me. | Let's give this new plan the **benefit of the doubt**. (=the right to favourable consideration until we know whether it is good or bad) 2 [C; U] in Britain, the general money provided by the government to people who need it, esp. to those who are sick or unemployed: Are you entitled to unemployment benefit? | child/housing benefit 3 [C] an event, esp. a theatrical performance, to raise money for some person or special purpose: a benefit for old actors | a benefit concert to raise money for the famine victims | a benefit match/year for a veteran player 4 [U] AmE for RELIEF (3) —see also CHILD BENEFIT, FRINGE BENEFIT

benefit² v 1 [T] (esp. of an action or event) to be useful, profitable, or helpful to: It's an expensive investment but it will benefit the company in the long run. 2 [I (from)] to gain advantage; receive benefit (as a result of something): I can see the advantage of this for you, but how will I benefit? | Who is most likely to benefit from/by the old lady's death? | These small businesses have benefited greatly from the fall in interest rates.

benefit of cler·gy /ˌ··· ·····/ n [U] old use the special rights of priests in the law

Benefits A·gen·cy /'··· ·····/ n [the] a British government organization which pays money to people who are unemployed, old, or ill —see also DEPARTMENT OF SOCIAL SECURITY

Be·ne·lux /'benɪlʌks/ n also **Benelux coun·tries** /'··· ····/, **Low Countries**— the countries of Belgium, the Netherlands, and Luxembourg considered as a group

Ben·et·ton /'benɪtən/ one of a group of shops selling JUMPERS and other clothes

be·nev·o·lent /bɪ'nevələnt/ adj having or showing a wish to do good and help others —compare MALEVOLENT —**lence** n [U] — **~ly** adv

Ben·gal /ˌben'gɔːl◁/ the NE part of the Indian SUBCONTINENT which is divided between India and Bangladesh

Ben·ga·li /ben'gɔːli/ n 1 [C] a person who comes from, or whose parents come from Bengal 2 [U] the language spoken by the people of Bangladesh or West Bengal in India

Ben-Gu·ri·on /ben 'guəriən/, **David** (1886–1973) an Israeli politician who led the Zionist movement to establish a Jewish state and was Israel's first PRIME MINISTER

Ben Hur /ˌben 'hɜːr/ an HISTORICAL NOVEL by Lewis Wallace set in the time of Jesus Christ. It was made into a film in 1959, in which Charlton Heston played the main character. —see picture at Charlton HESTON

Ben·i·dorm /'benɪdɔːm‖-ɔːrm/ a town on the Spanish Mediterranean coast visited by tourists from many European countries and popular with British people as a place to go on a PACKAGE HOLIDAY

be·night·ed /bɪ'naɪtɪd/ adj lit completely without knowledge or understanding, esp. of moral principles: benighted minds — **~ly** adv

be·nign /bɪ'naɪn/ adj 1 rather fml kind and gentle: a benign nature/smile 2 med (of a disease) not dangerous to life; not MALIGNANT (2): a benign tumour

— — ly _adv_ : _to smile benignly_ **— ~ ity** /bɪˈnɪɡnₐti/ _n_ [U] _fml_

Be·nin /beˈniːn‖bəˈnɪn/, **the People's Republic of** a country in W Africa which was a French COLONY called Dahomey until independence in 1960; capital Porto Novo; population 4,591,000 (1989)

Ben·je·did /ˌbenʒəˈdiːd/, **Chad·li** /ˈtʃædli/ (1929–) the president of Algeria from 1979 until 1992, when he left office after his party won little support in elections

Benn /ben/, **Tony** (1925–) a British politician who was a member of the Labour governments under Harold Wilson and James Callaghan, and is known for his strong left-wing opinions. His full name is **Anthony Wedgwood Benn**, and he was born with the title of **Viscount Stansgate**, but gave up his title so that he could be a member of the House of Commons.

Bennet, Arnold (1867–1931) an English writer best known for his NOVELS about the five POTTERY towns in the Midlands

Ben·nett /ˈbenₐt/, **Al·an** /ˈælən/ (1934–) a British writer and actor from the N of England, best known for his many humorous television plays

Ben·nett, Lou·ise /luːˈiːz/ (1929–) a Jamaican poet and actress

Ben Ne·vis /ben ˈnevₐs/ a mountain in Scotland which is the highest mountain in Britain (1343 m) —compare SCAFELL PIKE and see colour map on page 818

Ben·ny /ˈbeni/, **Jack** (1894–1974) an American COMEDIAN who started in the theatre and later had his own very popular radio and television shows. He pretended to be a MEAN person and many of his jokes were about this.

Ben·son and Hedg·es /ˌbensən ənd ˈhedʒₐz/ _tdmk_ (a British company which makes) a kind of cigarette: _A packet of Benson and Hedges, please._

bent[1] /bent/ _past tense and participle of_ BEND: _a piece of bent wire_

bent[2] _adj_ **1** _BrE sl_ dishonest, esp. by allowing oneself to be influenced by money or gifts (BRIBES): _a bent copper_ (=policeman) —opposite **straight 2** [F+_on/upon_] with one's mind set; completely determined: _She's bent on a career on the stage/bent on becoming an actress._ **3** _oldfash derog_ HOMOSEXUAL

bent[3] _n_ [(for)] a natural tendency or special natural skill (in): _He has a bent for art/an artistic bent._

Ben·tham /ˈbenθəm/, **Jer·e·my** /ˈdʒerəmi/ (1748–1832) an English PHILOSOPHER (1) who supported the idea that one should act according to what would do the most good for the most people

Ben·tine /ˈbentiːn/, **Mi·chael** /ˈmaɪkəl/ (1921–) an English COMEDY (2) performer of the 1950s, '60s and '70s, first with the Goons and later in his own television programmes

Bent·ley /ˈbentli/ _n tdmk_ a very expensive British car often driven by DIPLOMATs and politicians

Bent·sen /ˈbentsən/, **Lloyd** (1921–) a US Senator who became Secretry of the Treasury under President Clinton in 1993

be·numbed /bɪˈnʌmd/ _adj_ having all sense of feeling taken away, esp. by cold

Ben·ze·drine /ˈbenzₐdriːn/ _n_ [U] _tdmk_ a variety of the drug AMPHETAMINE

ben·zene /ˈbenziːn, benˈziːn/ also **ben·zol** /ˈbenzɒl‖-zəl/ — _n_ [U] a colourless liquid (C_6H_6) which is obtained chiefly from coal. Benzene burns quickly and is used to make certain types of engine run, and in making various chemical products. —see picture at DIAGRAM

ben·zine /ˈbenziːn, benˈziːn/ _n_ [U] a mixture of liquids obtained from PETROLEUM that burns quickly and is used to make certain types of engine run, and for cleaning

Be·o·wulf /ˈbeɪəʊwʊlf/ a very old (eighth century) EPIC (=long poem) about the adventures and fortunes of Beowulf

be·queath /bɪˈkwiːð, bɪˈkwiːθ/ _v_ [T (to)] _fml_ to give to others after death: _Her collection of paintings was bequeathed to the National Gallery when she died._ [+_obj(i)_+_obj(d)_] _His father bequeathed him a fortune._

be·quest /bɪˈkwest/ _n fml_ money or property that is bequeathed: _a bequest of £5000 to his daughter_

be·rate /bɪˈreɪt/ _v_ [T (for)] _fml_ to speak to angrily because of a fault; REBUKE

Ber·ber /ˈbɜːbəʳ‖ˈbɜːr-/ _n_ **1** [C] one of the people of NW Africa who lived there before the Arab CONQUESTs of the 7th century. Berbers live today mainly in Morocco, Algeria, and Tunisia. **2** [U] one of the languages of these people

be·reave /bɪˈriːv/ _v_ bereaved _or_ bereft /bɪˈreft/ [T (of)] _usu. pass._] _fml_ to take away, esp. by death: _He was bereaved (of his wife)._ | _bereft of all hope_

▷ USAGE **Bereaved** is used only of someone who has lost a close relative or friend through death: _He was bereaved (of his wife)._ **Bereft** is very formal, and is usu. used in poetry or with abstract nouns: _He was bereft of all hope/ideas/emotion/comfort/etc._◁

be·reaved /bɪˈriːvd/ _adj, n_ bereaved _fml_ (someone) whose close relative has just died: _a bereaved mother_ | _The bereaved was/were grief-stricken._

be·reave·ment /bɪˈriːvmənt/ _n_ [C;U] the state or an occasion of having been bereaved: _saddened by illness and bereavement_ | _a series of bereavements_

be·ret /ˈbereɪ‖bəˈreɪ/ _n_ a round usu. woollen cap with a tight headband and a soft full flat top

Ber·ge·rac /ˈbɜːʒəræk‖ˈbɜːr-/, **Cy·ra·no de** /ˈsɪrənəʊ də, sɪˈrɑːnəʊ-/ (1619–55) a French writer and soldier known for fighting DUELS and for his very large nose. His name is well known as the title of a play about him by Edmond Rostand.

Berg·man[1] /ˈbɜːɡmən‖ˈbɜːr-/, **Ing·mar** /ˈɪŋmɑːʳ/ (1918–) a Swedish film maker, whose films include _The Seventh Seal_ and _Fanny and Alexander_

Bergman[2], **In·grid** /ˈɪŋɡrɪd/ (1915–82) a Swedish actress who went to Hollywood in 1939 and became an international film star. She appeared with Humphrey Bogart in the film _Casablanca._ –see colour picture on page 685

ber·i·ber·i /ˌberiˈberi/ _n_ [U] a disease of the nerves caused by lack of VITAMIN B

Be·ring Strait /ˌbeərɪŋ ˈstreɪt‖ˌbɪər-/ [_the_] a narrow CHANNEL between Asia and N America connecting the **Bering Sea** with the Arctic Ocean

berk , burk /bɜːk‖bɜːrk/ _n BrE sl_ a fool: _You might have told me it was a formal affair – I felt a right berk in jeans and tee-shirt._

Berke·ley /ˈbɜːkli‖ˈbɜːr-/ a city in the San Francisco Bay area of California where part of the University of California is based. Berkeley was a centre of student protest during the 1960s.

Berke·ley Square /ˌbɑːkli ˈskweəʳ‖ˌbɑːr-/ a square in London known in the 17th and 18th centuries as the home of many famous people including Robert Walpole and Clive of India

Berk·shire /ˈbɑːkʃəʳ‖ˈbɑːr-/ a COUNTY in the S of England

Ber·lin /ˌbɜːˈlɪn◂‖ˌbɜːr-/ a city in N Germany which was divided into East and West from 1945 until 1990 when the German Democratic Republic (East Germany) and the Federal Republic of Germany (West Germany) were reunited

Berlin, Ir·ving /ˈɜːvɪŋ‖ˈɜːr-/ (1888–1989) an American songwriter who wrote many successful popular songs including _Alexander's Ragtime Band_ and _White Christmas_ and also many stage and film musicals

Berlin Wall /ˌ·· ˈ·/ [_the_] a wall built in Berlin in 1961 to divide East and West Berlin, and pulled down in 1989. The wall was built by Soviet-controlled East Germany to stop people escaping from East to West. The scenes of ordinary people pulling down the Wall were seen on television around the world and the event became a symbol of freedom. —see colour picture on page 752

Ber·li·oz /ˈbeəliəʊz‖ˈbeər-/, **Lou·is Hec·tor** /ˈluːiː ˈhektəʳ/ (1803–69) a French COMPOSER and CONDUCTOR

Ber·litz /ˈbɜːlɪts‖ˈbɜːr-/ _tdmk_ a company which has schools for teaching foreign languages in many cities in Europe and North America

Ber·mu·da /bəˈmjuːdə‖bər-/ a self-governing British COLONY consisting of a group of islands in the W Atlantic Ocean

Bermuda shorts /·ˌ·· ˈ·/ , also **Bermudas**— _n_ [P] knee-length SHORTS, usu. made of thin cotton material

Bermuda Tri·an·gle /·ˌ·· ˈ···/ [_the_] an area in the Atlantic Ocean between Bermuda, Florida, and Puerto Rico where many ships and aircraft are supposed to have mysteriously disappeared with no wrecks ever found

Ber·na·dette see SAINT BERNADETTE

Bern·hardt /ˈbɜːnhɑːt‖ˈbɜːrnhɑːrt/, **Sa·rah** /ˈseərə/ (1844–1923) a famous French ACTRESS, thought of by many people as one of the best actresses ever

Ber·ni lnn /ˌbɜːni ˈɪn‖ˌbɜːr-/ n one of a group of restaurants in Britain providing meals for families at fairly low prices

Bern·stein /ˈbɜːnstaɪn, -stiːn‖ˈbɜːrn-/, **Leon·ard** /ˈlenəd‖-ərd/ (1918–90) an American CONDUCTOR, COMPOSER, and piano player, famous for his popular musicals which include *West Side Story*

berries

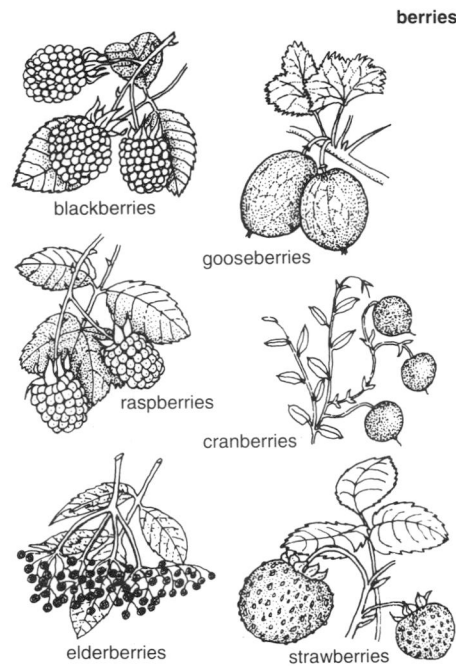

blackberries

gooseberries

raspberries

cranberries

elderberries   strawberries

ber·ry /ˈberi/ n (*often in comb.*) a small soft fruit, usu. with seeds: *to pick berries* | *blackberry jam* | *a strawberry*

Berry, Chuck (1926–) an American popular music singer, GUITARIST and songwriter who influenced the Beatles, the Rolling Stones, and others

ber·serk /bɜːˈsɜːk, bə-‖bɜːrˈsɜːrk, ˈbɜːrsɜːrk/ adj [F] mad with violent anger: *My husband will* **go berserk** *if he finds you here.*

berth¹ /bɜːθ‖bɜːrθ/ n 1 a place where a ship can stop and be tied up, as in a HARBOUR 2 a sleeping place in a ship or train; BUNK 3 *old-fash, BrE infml* a job 4 **give someone/something a wide berth** *infml* to stay at a safe distance from someone or something dangerous or unpleasant

berth² v [I;T] to come or bring into a berth: *The captain berthed his ship at midday.*

Ber·to·luc·ci /ˌbɜːtəʊˈluːtʃi‖ˌbɜːr-/, **Ber·nar·do** /bəˈnɑːdəʊ‖bərˈnɑːr-/ (1940–) an Italian film director whose films include *Last Tango in Paris*

Ber·wick·shire /ˈberɪkʃər/ a former COUNTY in SE Scotland, now part of the Borders REGION

ber·yl /ˈberɪl/ n [C;U] a usu. green precious stone

be·seech /bɪˈsiːtʃ/ v besought /bɪˈsɔːt/ or beseeched [T (of)] *fml or lit* to ask eagerly and anxiously: *to beseech a favour* [+obj+to-v] *I beseech you to go.*

be·seem /bɪˈsiːm/ v [T] *fml or old use* to be suitable or proper for

be·set /bɪˈset/ v beset; *present participle* besetting [T (by, with)] to trouble from all directions; attack continuously: *I was beset by doubts.* | *The plan was beset with difficulties from the beginning.* | *Laziness is my* besetting sin. (=the one that most often influences me)

be·side /bɪˈsaɪd/ prep 1 at or close to the side of; next to: *sitting beside the driver* | *a town beside the sea* 2 compared with: *This year's sales figures don't look very good beside last year's results.* 3 **beside oneself (with)** almost mad (with anger, excitement, etc.): *He was beside himself with joy when he heard he had passed the exam.* 4 **beside the point** having nothing to do with the main point or question: *Her age is beside the point: the question is, can she do the job?* —see BESIDES (USAGE)

be·sides¹ /bɪˈsaɪdz/ adv in addition; also: *I don't want to go; besides, I'm too tired.* | *This is my best suit; I have two others besides.*

besides² prep as well as; in addition to: *There were three other people at the meeting besides Mr Day.* | *Besides being a professional pianist, he is also a keen amateur singer.*

▷ USAGE Compare **besides** and **except. Besides** means "as well as"; *Ten of us passed* **besides** *John.* (=John passed too); **except** means "but not" or "leaving out": *All of us passed* **except** *John.* (=John did not pass)◁

be·siege /bɪˈsiːdʒ/ v [T] 1 to surround (a town, castle, etc.) with armed forces so as to prevent the people inside from getting out 2 to press all round in a crowd: *Worried relatives besieged the airline office, waiting for news of the crash.* 3 [(with)] to trouble or annoy continuously; HARASS: *We were besieged with doubts/with requests for help.*

be·smear /bɪˈsmɪər/ v [T (with)] to cover with dirty, sticky, or oily marks: *hands besmeared with dirt*

be·smirch /bɪˈsmɜːtʃ‖-ɜːrtʃ/ v [T] *fml* to damage (a person or their character) in the opinion of others

be·som /ˈbiːzəm/ n a brush made of sticks tied together on a long handle; BROOM (1)

be·sot·ted /bɪˈsɒtɪd‖bɪˈsɑː-/ adj [F (with)] made foolish or unable to behave sensibly by strong drink or powerful feeling: *besotted with drink/love/power*

be·sought /bɪˈsɔːt/ *past tense & participle of* BESEECH

be·spat·tered /bɪˈspætəd‖-ərd/ adj [(with)] marked all over with drops of liquid; spattered (SPATTER): *The windscreen of the car was so bespattered with dirt that it was difficult to see through it.*

be·speak /bɪˈspiːk/ v bespoke /bɪˈspəʊk/, bespoken /bɪˈspəʊkən/ [T] *fml* to show; be a sign of: *The efficiency of the organization bespoke careful planning.*

be·spec·ta·cled /bɪˈspektəkəld/ adj *fml or humor* wearing glasses

be·spoke /bɪˈspəʊk/ adj esp. BrE (of clothes) specially made to someone's measurements; MADE-TO-MEASURE — compare **off the peg** (PEG¹)

best¹ /best/ adj (*superlative of* GOOD) 1 the highest in quality, skill, or effectiveness; the most good: *the best tennis player in the world* | *the best man I ever knew* | *She's my best friend.* | *This has been the company's best year ever.* | *What's the best way to get there?* —see also SECOND BEST 2 **the best part of** most of: *I haven't seen her for the best part of a month.* 3 **the best things in life are free** an old saying

best² adv (*superlative of* WELL) 1 in the best way: *The one who does best will get the prize.* 2 to the greatest degree; most: *Tuesday would suit me best.* | *You can't argue with him — he always thinks he knows best.* | *She chose the more expensive one,* **for reasons best known to herself.** (=she knows why, but no one else does) | *one of our best-loved national monuments* 3 BrE **as best one can** as well as one can: *Do it as best you can.* 4 **had best** ought to; had better (BETTER²)

best³ n best 1 [the] the greatest degree of good: *Only the best is good enough for her.* | *We all want the best for our children.* | *We can't go to Spain, but perhaps it's* **all for the best.** (=it's a good thing really) | *$75 is the best* (=the most) *I can offer you.* | *10.3 seconds is my* **personal best** (=the fastest I have ever run) *in the hundred yard dash.* 4 **All the best!** (used when saying goodbye) I wish you success and happiness! **5 at best** in the most favourable conditions or according to the most favourable judgment: *This is, at best, only a temporary solution.* | *His answers were at best evasive* (=this is the most favourable thing that can be said about them), *at worst downright misleading.* **6 have/get the best of** *infml* to win or succeed at/in: *When we exchanged rooms I got the best of the bargain, because her old room was nicer.* **7 make the best of** to do as well as one can with (a thing or situation that is unsatisfactory): *We must try to make the best of things until we can afford a bigger house.* **8 make the best of a bad job** to accept, esp. in a cheerful way, bad or unsatisfactory conditions and do the best one can in the situation **9 the best of both worlds/of all possible worlds** the advantages of two different situations/of every possible situation, esp. without their disadvantages: *He lives on a farm and works in a big city, so he has the best of both worlds.* **10 to the best of one's knowledge/belief/ability** as far as one knows/believes/is able: *I will do the work to the best of my ability.* —see also **six of the best** (SIX)

best⁴ *v* [T] *old use in BrE, not unusual in AmE* to defeat: *After a long struggle, we bested them.*

Best, George (1946–) a footballer from Northern Ireland who played for Manchester United in the 1960s and is considered to be one of the greatest players ever. His career was short, and it is known that he has had a drink problem.

best be·fore date /ₗ · ·ˈ· ·ˌ/ *n* a date stamped onto food and drink containers, showing the date before which the product should be eaten or drunk: *There's no best before date on these beans.*

best friend /ₗ· ˈ·/ *n* **1** the special friend that a child likes most: *Who's your best friend, Jimmy?* **2 best friends** very friendly, esp. after an argument: *They're best friends again now.*

bes·ti·al /ˈbestɪəl‖ˈbestʃəl/ *adj* **1** of or like an animal **2** (of human beings and their behaviour) very cruel or inhuman; BRUTAL: *bestial cruelty* – ~ly *adv*

bes·ti·al·i·ty /ˌbestiˈælˌti‖ˌbestʃi-/ *n* [U] **1** *derog* the state of being bestial **2** sexual relations between a human being and an animal

bes·ti·ar·y /ˈbestiəri‖ˈbestʃieri/ *n* a book (esp. of the Middle Ages in Europe) with information about animals that is intended to amuse people or to teach moral lessons

be·stir /bɪˈstɜːʳ/ *v* -rr- [T] *fml* to cause (oneself) to move quickly or become active: *We must bestir ourselves (to finish the job).*

best man /ₗ· ˈ·/ *n* a man who helps the BRIDEGROOM at a marriage ceremony —compare BRIDESMAID, FLOWER GIRL, MATRON OF HONOUR, PAGE BOY and see also extra information on page 1406

be·stow /bɪˈstəʊ/ *v* [T (**on, upon**)] *fml* to give: *Several gifts were bestowed on the royal visitors.* – ~al *n* [U]

be·strew /bɪˈstruː/ *v* **bestrewed, bestrewn** /bɪˈstruːn/ or **bestrewed** [T] *lit* **1** to lie scattered over: *Flowers bestrewed the grave of the dead soldier.* **2** [(**with**)] to scatter things over (a surface); STREW: *They bestrewed the grave with flowers.*

be·stride /bɪˈstraɪd/ *v* **bestrode** /bɪˈstrəʊd/, **bestridden** /bɪˈstrɪdn/ [T] *fml* to sit or stand on or over (a thing) with legs apart; STRADDLE: *to bestride a horse/a fence*

best-sel·ler /ₗ· ˈ··/ *n* **1** something (esp. a book) that sells in very large numbers **2** a writer or performer whose work sells very well —**ling** *adj*: *a best-selling novelist*

bet¹ /bet/ *n* **1** [(**on**)] an agreement to risk money on the result of a future event, by which the person who guesses wrongly gives the money to the other person: *We had/We made a bet on the outcome of the next election.* | *to place a bet (with a bookmaker)* | *to win/lose a bet* **2** a sum of money risked in this way: *a £5 bet* **3** a future result that is expected: [+*that*] *My bet* (=my opinion) *is that she'll be well known in a few years' time.* | *It's a safe bet* (=certain) *that she'll turn up drunk tonight.* | *He may be very charming, but he's a bad bet for marriage.* (=he will not be a good husband) **4** *infml* a plan of action: *Your best bet is to say nothing about it.* —see also **hedge one's bets** (HEDGE²)

bet² *v* **bet** or **betted**; *present participle* **betting 1** [I;T (**on**)] to risk (money) on the result of a future event: *I bet (£5) on a horse called Silver Star, but it came in last!* [+*obj(i) +obj(d)+(that)*] *I'll bet you £5 that you can't do it.* **2** [T

(+*obj*)+*that*] to state confidently (what will happen or has happened); PREDICT: *I/I'll bet that it will rain tomorrow/ I/I'll bet it rains tomorrow.* | *I bet you she won't agree.* | *If there's any hard work to be done, you can bet he won't come.* | *I'll bet you didn't think I'd be back so soon.* **3 bet one's boots/bottom dollar/shirt/ass** *infml* to be certain: *You can bet your boots that she'll be late again.* **4 You bet** *sl* You can be sure; certainly: *"Will you tell her?" "You bet (I will)".*

be·ta /ˈbiːtə‖ˈbeɪtə/ *n* the second letter (B, β) of the Greek alphabet, sometimes used in Britain as a mark for better than average work by a student

be·take /bɪˈteɪk/ *v* **betook** /bɪˈtʊk/, **betaken** /bɪˈteɪkən/ **betake oneself** *lit* to go: *He betook himself to the palace to see the king.*

be·tel /ˈbiːtl/ *n* [U] a leaf which is wrapped round pieces of bitter red nut (**betel nut**) and other things, and is chewed (CHEW) by people in India and Southeast Asia because it has some of the effects of a drug

bête-noire /ˌbet ˈnwɑːʳ/ *n* **bêtes-noires** /ˌbet ˈnwɑːz‖-ɑːrz/ the person or thing one dislikes most

Beth·a·ny /ˈbeθəni/ a village near Jerusalem and the Mount of Olives, in which general area a number of the important events of the New Testament took place

beth·el /ˈbeθəl/ *n* **1** *esp. BrE* a place of worship for Christian Nonconformists **2** *esp. AmE* (*often cap.*) a place of worship for sailors

be·think /bɪˈθɪŋk/ *v* **bethought** /bɪˈθɔːt/ **bethink oneself of** *lit or old use* to think about; consider: *You should bethink yourself of your duty, my lord!*

Beth·le·hem /ˈbeθlɪhem/ a town on the W Bank of the River Jordan, near Jerusalem, thought to be where Jesus Christ was born —see also O LITTLE TOWN OF BETHLEHEM

be·tide /bɪˈtaɪd/ *v* [I] *lit* **1** to happen: *We shall remain friends whatever may betide.* **2 Woe betide you/him/them, etc.** *esp. lit or humor* You/He/They, etc. will be in trouble: *Woe betide them if they're late!*

be·times /bɪˈtaɪmz/ *adv lit* early; in good time

Be·tje·man /ˈbetʃmən/, **Sir John** (1906–84) an English poet who became Poet Laureate in 1972. He is known for his humorous poems about English social life and for his interest in Victorian and Edwardian ARCHITECTURE, esp. railways.

be·to·ken /bɪˈtəʊkən/ *v* [T] *fml* to be a sign of: *black clouds that betoken a storm*

be·tray /bɪˈtreɪ/ *v* [T (**to**)] **1** to be disloyal or unfaithful to: *To betray one's friends/one's principles* **2** to hand over to the power of an enemy by disloyalty: *The resistance group was betrayed (to the government) by one of its own members.* **3** to give away or make known (esp. a secret): *He betrayed the plans to enemy agents.* **4** to be a sign of (something one would like to hide); show the real feelings or intentions of: *Her trembling hands betrayed her nervousness (to him).* [+*wh*-] *Her expression betrayed how angry she really was.* | *He tried to seem angry, but his smile betrayed him.* – ~**er** *n*

be·tray·al /bɪˈtreɪəl/ *n* [C;U] (an example of) the act of betraying: *a betrayal of my principles*

be·troth /bɪˈtrəʊð, bɪˈtrəʊθ/ *v* [T (**to**)] *old use* to promise to marry or give in marriage: *Her father betrothed her to him at an early age.* | *a betrothed couple* | *He kissed his betrothed.* (=the woman he was betrothed to) – ~**al** *n* [C;U]: *to celebrate their betrothal*

bet·ter¹ /ˈbetəʳ/ *adj* **1** (*comparative of* GOOD) higher in quality, skill, or effectiveness; more good: *Their house is better than ours.* | *The sales figures are better than expected.* | *I'm worse at sums than Jean, but better at history.* | *I know a better way to do it.* | *He's no better than* (=almost as bad as) *a thief.* | *You'll feel all the better for a breath of fresh air.* **2** [F] (*comparative of* WELL) **a** improved in health: *I'm feeling a little better today.* **b** completely well again after an illness: *Now that he's better he can play football again.* **3 be better than one's word** to do more than one has promised **4 Better luck next time!** (said to encourage someone who has done badly this time in an examination, race, competition, etc.) **5 for better or for worse** a phrase from the Christian marriage service. The people getting married promise to love each other "for better or for worse" (=if things are good or bad). **6 no better than she should be** *old-fash euph infml* of low sexual morals **7 one's better half** *infml* _humor_ one's wife or husband   **8 the better part of** more than half: _I haven't seen him for the better part of a month!_ —compare WORSE[1]

better[2] _adv_ (_comparative of_ WELL)   **1** in a better way: _It works better if you put a bit of oil in._ | _He swims better than he used to._ | _You would **do better**_ (=it would be better/wiser) _to get some professional advice._   **2** to a greater degree: _She knows the story better than I do._ | _She got the job because she was better qualified than the others._ | _He has written several novels, but he is better known for his plays._   **3 go one better (than)** _infml_ to do better (than): _That was a good story, but I can go one better._   **4 had better** ought to; should: _You'd better go home now._ | _We'd better not tell him._ | _"I won't forget again, I promise."_ _"You'd better not!"_ —compare WORSE[3]

▷ USAGE 1 **Had better** is one of the most common expressions in conversation when giving firm advice about what a person _should_ or _ought to_ do, esp. to avoid some problem, unpleasantness or danger: _You'd better leave now before you cause any more trouble._ | _You'd better give me your telephone number in case someone wants to contact you._ A difference between **had better** on the one hand, and **should** and **ought to** on the other, is that **had better** is only used to talk about present or future time, but **should** and **ought to** can also talk about the past. We can say _You should have called me before you left._ | _She ought to have told her mother she was pregnant._ **Had better** can't be used in this way. 2 **Had better** is not used to compare two courses of action. Instead we use expressions like **It would be better to, You'd be better to,** or **Your best plan would be to**: _"Do you think I should fly directly to Australia or break my journey in Hong Kong?" "It would be better to/You'd be better to/Your best plan would be to spend a few days in Hong Kong. There are so many things to see there."_◁

better[3] _n_ [_the_]   **1** a person or thing that is better: _Which is the better of these two cars?_ | _There's been **a change for the better**_ (=an improvement) _in his health._   **2 for better or (for) worse** whatever happens; whether one likes it or not   **3 get the better of** to defeat (someone) or deal successfully with (a difficulty): _I wouldn't argue with her if I were you — she'll get the better of you!_ —see also BETTERS; compare WORSE[2]

better[4] _v fml_   **1** [I;T] to (cause to) improve: _a policy aimed at bettering the lot of the poorest nations_ —compare WORSEN   **2** [T] to go beyond in quality; SURPASS: _This year's results are unlikely to be bettered._   **3 better oneself:** to earn more money   **b** to educate oneself — **~ ment** _n_ [U]

better half /ₗ·· '·/ _n infml, humor_ one's husband or wife: _Hello, George! Where's your better half?_

Better Homes and Gar·dens /ₗ··· ·· · '··/ a US magazine with pictures and articles about making one's home very pleasant and pretty

betting shop /'·· ·/ _n_ a place where the business of taking BETS[1] on horse races and other competitions is carried on. Betting shops are found in towns and cities in Britain.

bet·ters /'betəz‖-ərz/ _n_ [P] people of higher rank or greater worth (than someone): _to be polite to one's **elders and betters**_

Bet·ty Ford Clin·ic /ₗbeti ₗfɔːrd 'klɪnɪk‖-fɔːrd-/ [_the_] a hospital-like institution in California where rich and often famous people go for treatment of drug and alcohol ADDICTION. It is named after Betty Ford (1918–   ), wife of former president Gerald Ford.

be·tween[1] /bɪ'twiːn/ _prep_   **1 a** in or into the space or time that separates: _standing between Sue and Brian_ | _It happened between five and six o'clock in the morning._ | _between five and six miles away_ | _You shouldn't eat between meals._ | _I hope nothing ever **comes between us.**_ (=separates us)   **b** in the range that separates (two things or amounts): _It will cost between 8 and 10 million dollars._   **2** (showing connection): _a regular air service between London and Paris_ | _a friendship between Sue and Brian_ | _talks between the management and the unions_ | _co-operation between the two companies_   **3** (showing division or sharing between two or more): _Divide it between the children._ | _a choice between two possibilities_ | _What's the difference between spaghetti and noodles?_ | _a quarrel between Sue and Brian_ | _a football match between Manchester United and Liverpool_ | _They all did the job between_

them. | _Between us, we collected £17._ | _Between cooking, writing, and running the farm, she was very busy._   **4 between a rock and a hard place** _AmE infml_ in a situation where both of two possible choices seem undesirable   **5 between you and me** also **between you, me, and the gatepost/bedpost, between ourselves**— _infml_ without anyone else knowing; privately: _Between you and me, (I think) he's rather stupid._   **6 in between** at some point (e.g. in space or time) between: _I'm not sure where it is, but it's somewhere in between New York and Chicago._ | _She did a university degree and a teacher's training course, with a year off in between (the two)._

▷ USAGE Compare **among** and **between.** When you are talking about only two things (or people) use **between:** _He divided the money **between** the two children._ If you are talking about a group of three or more things (or people) use **among:** _He divided the money **among** the three children._ | _The mountains were hidden **among** the clouds._◁

between[2] _adv_ in or into a space or period of time that is between: _I ate breakfast and dinner but nothing **(in) between.**_ —see also **few and far between** (FEW)

be·twixt /bɪ'twɪkst/ also **twixt**— _prep, adv old use or poet_ between: _not a sailor nor a soldier but something **betwixt and between**_ (=partly one and partly the other)

Bev·an /'bevən/, **A·neu·rin** /ə'naɪərₗn/ (Nye /naɪ/) (1897–1960) a British Labour politician from Wales, known for his excellent speeches. As Minister of Health (1945–51), he helped to establish the National Health Service.

bev·el[1] /'bevəl/ _n_   **1** a sloping edge or surface that does not form a right angle, usu. along the edge of wood or glass   **2** an instrument for making such a sloping edge or surface

bevel[2] _v_ **-ll-** _BrE_ ‖ **-l-** _AmE_ [T] to make a bevel on (e.g. a piece of wood) —**bevelled** _adj_ : _a bevelled mirror_

bev·er·age /'bevərɪdʒ/ _n fml_ a liquid for drinking, esp. one that is not water or medicine: _alcoholic beverages_ | _hot beverages_ (=tea, coffee, etc.)

Bev·e·ridge /'bevərɪdʒ/, **William** (1879–1963) a British ECONOMIST, writer, and ACADEMIC best known for his **Beveridge Report** (1942) in which he put forward the idea that the state should look after people from the time they are born until they die. This led to the setting up of the WELFARE STATE in Britain.

Bev·er·ley /'bevəli‖-vər-/ a market town in Humberside, E England, where the local government for Humberside is based

Bev·er·ly Hills /ₗbevəli 'hɪlz‖-vər-/ an expensive part of Los Angeles, California where many famous film stars live

Beverly Hill·bil·lies /ₗ··· '···/, **The** a popular American television programme of the 1960s and 1970s in which a poor family discover oil on their land, become rich, and move to Beverly Hills

Bev·in /'bevₗn/, **Er·nest** /'ɜːnₗst‖'ɜːr-/ (1881–1951) a British politician and TRADE UNION leader who established the Transport and General Workers' Union (TGWU), became chairman of the TUC, and as Foreign Secretary in the Labour government after the Second World War helped to form NATO

bev·y /'bevi/ _n_ [C+_sing./pl. v_]   **1** a large group or collection, esp. of girls or women: _a bevy of beauties_   **2** a group of certain kinds of birds, esp. QUAIL   **3** _dial sl_ an alcoholic drink

be·wail /bɪ'weɪl/ _v_ [T] _fml_ to express deep sorrow for or disappointment about, sometimes by crying tears

be·ware /bɪ'weər/ _v_ [I (**of**);T+_wh-; obj_] (used, with no change of form, in giving or reporting warnings) to be very careful: _Beware of the dog._ | _Beware how you handle this dangerous substance._

be·wigged /bɪ'wɪgd/ _adj lit or humor_ wearing a WIG

be·wil·der /bɪ'wɪldər/ _v_ [T] to confuse, esp. by the presence of many different things at the same time: _Big city traffic bewilders me._ | _a bewildering mass of details_ | _a bewildered look_ — **~ ment** _n_ [U]: _Imagine my bewilderment when she said that!_

be·witch /bɪ'wɪtʃ/ _v_ [T]   **1** to have a magic effect on; put under one's power by magic   **2** to charm as if by magic: _a bewitching smile_

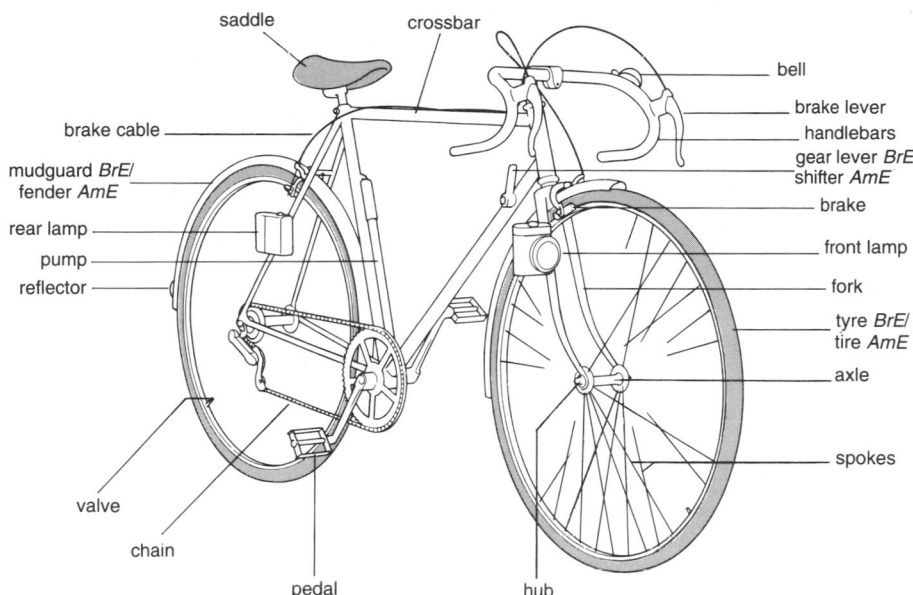

Labels on diagram: saddle, crossbar, bell, brake lever, handlebars, gear lever *BrE*/ shifter *AmE*, brake cable, mudguard *BrE*/ fender *AmE*, brake, rear lamp, front lamp, pump, fork, reflector, tyre *BrE*/ tire *AmE*, axle, spokes, valve, chain, pedal, hub

be·yond¹ /bɪˈjɒnd‖bɪˈjɑːnd/ *adv* on or to the further side; further: *They crossed the mountains and travelled to the valleys beyond.* | (fig.) *to prepare for the changes of the 1990s and beyond*

beyond² *prep* **1** on or to the further side of: *What lies beyond the mountains?* **2** (later than; past; after: *Don't stay there beyond midnight.* | *The new law extends this ban beyond 1988.* **3** more or greater than (an amount or limit): *The level of inflation has gone beyond 10%.* | *people who continue to work beyond the normal retirement age* **4** outside the range or limits of: *The switch on the wall was beyond the baby's reach.* | *The town had changed beyond recognition.* (=so much that it could not be recognized) | *His guilt has been established* **beyond reasonable doubt.** (=with certainty) | *It's* **beyond belief** (=impossible to believe) *that anyone could be so stupid.* | *success* **beyond our wildest dreams** (=far better than we could have expected) | *It's* **beyond me** (=too hard for me to understand) *why she married him.* **5** besides; except for: *I own nothing beyond the clothes on my back.* | *I can't tell you anything beyond what you know already.*

beyond³ *n* [*the*] (*often cap.*) life after death; HEREAFTER²: *What can we know of the beyond?* —see also BACK OF BEYOND

be·zique /bəˈziːk/ *n* [U] a card game for two or four players, played with 64 cards

BFA /ˌbiːef ˈeɪ/ *n* Bachelor of Fine Arts; a degree given by some American universities for studies in art, music, and acting

BFI /ˌbiː ef ˈaɪ/ [*the*] British Film Institute; a British organization begun in 1933 to encourage film making and use, which includes the National Film Theatre

Bhag·a·vad-Gi·ta /ˌbʌɡəvəd ˈɡiːtə‖ˌbɑːɡəvɑːd-/ [*the*] the best known book of the Hindu religion

bha·ji , **bhajee** /ˈbɑːdʒi/ *n* a SPICY (=strongly tasting and smelling) Indian vegetable cake fried in BATTER (=a liquid mixture of flour, egg, and milk or water): *mushroom/onion bhaji*

bhang /bæŋ/ *n* [U] a not very strong form of the drug CANNABIS used in India —compare HASHISH, MARIJUANA

Bho·pal /bəʊˈpɑːl/ a city in the N of India, where in 1984 over 2000 people died after poisonous gas escaped from a factory owned by Union Carbide, an American-owned company

BHS /ˌbiː eɪtʃ ˈes/ BRITISH HOME STORES

Bhu·tan /buːˈtɑːn/ a country in the Himalayas, E Asia, bordered by India, Tibet, and Sikkim; population 1,483,000 (1989)

Bhut·to /ˈbuːtəʊ/, **Zul·fi·kar Al·i** /ˈzʊlfɪkɑːʳ ˈæli‖-ˈɑːli/ (1928–79) a Pakistani politician who was president (1971–73) and then PRIME MINISTER (1973–77) of Pakistan. He was overthrown (OVERTHROW) in a military COUP in 1977 and executed (EXECUTE) in 1979. His daughter **Benazir Bhutto** (1953–) was prime minister from 1988 to 1990.

bi- see WORD FORMATION

BIA /ˌbiː aɪ ˈeɪ/ *n* BUREAU OF INDIAN AFFAIRS

bi·an·nu·al /baɪˈænjuəl/ *adj* happening twice each year —compare BIENNIAL

Biar·ritz /ˌbiəˈrɪts‖ˌbiːə-/ a town in SW France, popular as a holiday RESORT for rich and famous people

bi·as¹ /ˈbaɪəs/ *n* [C;U] **1** a tendency to be in favour of or against something or someone without knowing enough to be able to judge fairly; PREJUDICE¹: *They complained of bias in the way the news media reported the story* | *an anti-government bias* **2** a tendency of mind: *Her scientific bias showed itself in early childhood.* **3 on the bias** on the CROSS¹ (13); diagonally (DIAGONAL): *cloth cut on the bias* (=cut at an angle to the WEAVE, not parallel to it)

bias² *v* **-s-** *or* **-ss-** [T *often pass.*] to cause to form fixed opinions for or against something without enough information to judge fairly; PREJUDICE²: *The fact that she was a woman biased some members of the committee against her.* | *The judge was biased in favour of the second candidate, who was educated at the same college as himself.* | *biased reporting*

bias bind·ing /ˌ·· ˈ··/ *n* [U] cloth in the form of a narrow band, cut on the bias, for use when sewing curved edges or corners

bi·ath·lon /baɪˈæθlən/ *n* a sporting competition in which the competitors take part in skiing (SKI) across country and RIFLE shooting —compare DECATHLON, PENTATHLON

bib /bɪb/ *n* **1** a piece of cloth or plastic tied under a child's chin to protect its clothes when eating **2** the upper part of an APRON or DUNGAREES, above the waistline **3 one's best bib and tucker** *infml* one's best clothes

bib o·ver·alls /ˈ·· ˌ···/ *n* [P] *AmE* another name for OVERALLS (2) —see picture at OVERALL

Bi·ble /ˈbaɪbəl/ *n* [C;*the*] **1** (a copy of) the holy book of the Christians, consisting of the OLD TESTAMENT and the NEW TESTAMENT. In courts of law, people sometimes hold a Bible and swear that they will tell the truth: *The service*

included some readings from the Bible. | (fig.) *This book has always been a bible for medical students.* —see colour picture on page 424 **2** (a copy of) the holy book of the Jews; the OLD TESTAMENT

Bible Belt /ˈ·· ·/ [*the*] an area in the S of the US known for its very religious people who follow the teachings of the Bible very exactly

bible school /ˈ·· ·/ also **vacation bible school** *n AmE* (in the US) (a school, often in a church building, where there is) a set of daily activities for children, usu. for a week or more of the summer holidays, during which children have some religious education, but mostly play and learn CRAFTS: *Jennifer's in bible school this week.*

bible thump·er /ˈ·· ·/ *AmE infml humor or derog* a person who tries to attract people to Christianity in a loud and unpleasant way, usu. by warning them of terrible things that will happen to them if they do not become Christians

bib·li·cal /ˈbɪblɪkəl/ *adj* (*sometimes cap.*) of, like, or about the Bible, esp. the AUTHORIZED VERSION (=English translation of 1611): *to write English in a biblical style*

bib·li·og·ra·pher /ˌbɪbliˈɒɡrəfəʳ‖-ˈɑːɡ-/ *n* a person who makes a bibliography

bib·li·og·ra·phy /ˌbɪbliˈɒɡrəfi‖-ˈɑːɡ-/ *n* a list of writings on a subject, esp. a list of all the written materials used in the preparation of a book or article, usu. appearing at the end

bib·li·o·phile /ˈbɪbliəfaɪl/ *n* a person who loves books

bib·u·lous /ˈbɪbjʊləs/ *adj humor or pomp* liking to drink too much alcohol

Bic /bɪk/ *n tdmk* a simple, inexpensive type of BALLPOINT pen

bi·cam·er·al leg·is·la·ture /baɪˌkæmərəl ˈledʒɪsleɪtʃəʳ, -lətʃəʳ/ *n* a law-making body consisting of two parts, like the Senate and the House of Representatives which make up the US Congress

bi·car·bon·ate /baɪˈkɑːbənɪt, -bəneɪt‖-ˈkɑːr-/ also **bicarbonate of so·da** /·ˌ··· · ˈ··/, **sodium bicarbonate, baking soda, bi·carb** /ˈbaɪkɑːb ‖ -kɑːrb/*infml*— *n* [U] a chemical substance used esp. in baking and taken with water as a medicine

bi·cen·te·na·ry /ˌbaɪsenˈtiːnəri‖-ˈtenəri, -ˈsentəneri/ *esp. BrE* ‖ **bi·cen·ten·ni·al** /ˌbaɪsenˈteniəl/ *esp. AmE*— *n* the day or year exactly 200 years after a particular event: *This year is the bicentenary of the school's foundation.* | *The bicentennial of the American Revolution* —**bicentenary** *adj* : *bicentenary celebrations*

bi·ceps /ˈbaɪseps/ *n* biceps [C+*sing.*/*pl. v*] the large muscle on the front of the upper arm

bick·er /ˈbɪkəʳ/ *v* [I (**about, over, with**)] to quarrel, esp. about unimportant matters: *The two children were always bickering (with each other) (over/about their toys).*

bi·cy·cle¹ /ˈbaɪsɪkəl/ also **cycle, bike** *infml*— *n* a two-wheeled vehicle which one rides by pushing its PEDALS with the feet. It has recently become fashionable among people concerned about the ENVIRONMENT to travel by bicycle because bicycles do not cause any POLLUTION: *She goes to work on her bicycle/by bicycle.*

▷ USAGE You **ride (on)** a bicycle or a horse. At the beginning of your journey you **get on(to)** it or (*fml*) **mount** it. At the end of your journey you **get off** it or (*fml*) **dismount (from** it). —see also DRIVE (USAGE), STEER (USAGE), TRANSPORT (USAGE)◁

bicycle² also **cycle, bike** *infml*— *v* [I+*adv/prep*] to travel by bicycle —**bicyclist** *n*

bicycle shed /ˈ··· ·/, also **bike shed** *n esp. BrE* a building where bicycles can be kept for a time under shelter, esp. at a school or factory. In Britain, people sometimes make jokes about young people smoking cigarettes or having their first sexual experiences behind the school bicycle sheds.

bid¹ /bɪd/ *v* bid; *present participle* bidding [I;T] **1** [(**for**)] to offer to pay (a price) for goods or to charge (a price) for one's work or services: *He bid (£10) for an old book at the auction.* | *What am I bid for this old book?* (=What price will people offer me for it?) | *Several companies are bidding for the contract to build the bridge.* **2** (in playing cards) to make a BID² (3): *Have you bid yet?* | *I bid two hearts.* — ~ **der** *n*

bid² *n* **1** [(**for**)] an offer to pay a certain price at a sale, esp. at an AUCTION: *a bid of £5 for the old book* **2** [(**for**)] an offer to do some work at a certain price; TENDER³: *Bids for building the bridge were invited from British and American firms.* | *Have they put in a bid for the contract?* **3** (a chance or turn to make) a declaration of the number of TRICKS (=games) a cardplayer says he/she intends to win: *a bid of two hearts* | *It's your bid now, Peter.* **4** [(**for**)] an attempt to get, win, or attract: *He made a bid for freedom by climbing over the wall.* | *a bid for power* | *a rescue bid* [+*to-v*] *They brought in new tax laws in a bid to restore their popularity.*

bid³ *v* **bade** /bæd, beɪd/ *or* **bid, bidden** /ˈbɪdn/ *or* **bid; present participle bidding** [T] *old use or lit* **1** to say or wish (a greeting or goodbye to someone): [+*obj*(i)+*obj*(d)] *He bade me good morning as he passed.* **2** [+*obj*+*to-v*] to order or tell (someone to do something): *She bade him enter.* | *Do as you are bidden.* **3** [(**to**)] to invite: *guests bidden to a wedding* **4** **bid fair (to do something)** to seem likely (to do something): *This agreement bids fair to establish a lasting peace.* — ~ **der** *n*

bid·da·ble /ˈbɪdəbəl/ *adj esp. BrE* (of a person) easily influenced or controlled

bid·ding /ˈbɪdɪŋ/ *n* [U] order; command (esp. in the phrases **at someone's bidding, do someone's bidding**)

bide /baɪd/ *v* **bide one's time** to wait, usu. for a long time, until the right moment: *I'm planning to change my job, but I'm just biding my time until the right opportunity comes up.*

bi·det /ˈbiːdeɪ‖biˈdeɪ/ *n* a kind of small low bath across which one sits to wash the lower parts of the body, used esp. in France

bi·en·ni·al /baɪˈeniəl/ *adj* **1** (of an event) happening once every two years **2** (of a plant) living for two years and producing flowers and seed in the second year —compare ANNUAL, BIANNUAL — ~ **ly** *adv*

bier /bɪəʳ/ *n* a movable frame like a table, sometimes with wheels, for supporting a dead body or COFFIN, or for taking it to the grave

Bierce /bɪəs‖bɪərs/, **Am·brose** /ˈæmbrəʊz/ (1842–?1914) an American writer known for his short stories, who disappeared in Mexico and was never found

biff /bɪf/ *v* [T] *BrE sl* to hit with a quick hard blow: *He biffed me on the chin!* —**biff** *n*

bi·fo·cals /baɪˈfəʊkəlz‖ˈbaɪfəʊ-/ *n* [P] glasses for the eyes with an upper part made for looking at distant objects, and a lower part made for reading —see PAIR (USAGE) —**bifocal** *adj*

bi·fur·cate /ˈbaɪfəkeɪt‖-ər-/ *v* [I] *fml* (of roads, branches, rivers, etc.) to divide into two branches or parts; FORK² (2) —**-cation** /ˌbaɪfəˈkeɪʃən‖-fər-/ *n* [C;U]

big /bɪɡ/ *adj* **-gg-** **1** of more than average size, weight, amount, force, importance, etc.: *a big box* | *a big field* | *a big increase in prices* | *the biggest hotel in New York* | *How big is it?* | *no bigger than a pin* | *That child is big for his age.* | *The big question is what to do next.* | *a big landowner* (=who owns a lot of land) | (fig.) *big-hearted* (=generous) | *Don't cry: you're a big girl now.* | *The big day has come at last!* | *The big advantage of this system is that it is easy to use.* | *John's a big spender.* (=spends money freely) | *You should go into merchant banking — that's where the big money is.* (=that is where high wages can be earned) | *a big eater* | *his big* (=older) *sister/brother* **2** *infml* very popular and successful, esp. in sports and the entertainment business: *Frank Sinatra is very big in Las Vegas.* **3** [F+**with**] *old use* (of a woman) PREGNANT: *big with child* **4** **be big of** to be generous of: *It was big of him to lend you his car.* **5** **have a big mouth** to talk too much, esp. to give away secrets: *Be careful what you say to her — she's got a big mouth.* **6** **have big ideas** *infml* to have plans or aims to do something important or to become important **7** **the bigger they come, the harder they fall** *saying* the more important someone is and the more power that they have, the worse it is for them when they lose power **8** **too big for one's boots** *infml* believing oneself to be more important than one really is —see also **think big** (THINK¹) — ~ **ness** *n* [U]

▷ USAGE Compare **big, large,** and **great**. **1 Big** and **large** are both common when talking about actual size, though **large** is slightly more formal: *That shirt doesn't fit me; it's too big/large.* **2 Great** means "famous" or "important" when used of people: *He's a great man.* When used of things, **great** (*lit*) means "very large and impressive": *The* **great** *ship sailed into the harbour.* 3 **Great** (not **big** or **large**) can be used with uncountable nouns: *She showed* **great** *courage.* 4 Notice that **large** (not **big**) is usu. used in the expressions *a* **large** *amount|number|quantity.*◁

big·a·my /ˈbɪgəmi/ *n* [U] the state of being married to two people at the same time. Bigamy is a crime in Britain and the US. —compare MONOGAMY, POLYGAMY —**mist** *n* —**mous** *adj* —**mously** *adv*

Big Ap·ple /ˌ· ˈ··/ [*the*] *AmE* a popular name for New York City: *He went to the Big Apple to make his fortune.*

big bad wolf /ˌ· ·ˈ·/ [*the*] *often cap.* an evil WOLF who appears in various stories, trying to frighten, hurt, or eat other characters. The name is often used to describe something or someone that takes on this character: *"We are not the big bad wolf of the chemical industry," said a spokesman, yesterday.* —see picture at LITTLE RED RIDING HOOD

Big Band /ˌ· ˈ·/ *n* a kind of musical band most popular in the 1940s which had a leader, many WIND INSTRUMENTS, and sometimes a singer. The style of music was known as the **Big Band Sound**. Big Band leaders included Tommy Dorsey, Benny Goodman, and Glenn Miller: *the Big Band sound of the forties*

Big Bang /ˌ· ˈ·/ the name given to the changes in the system and rules of the London STOCK EXCHANGE which came into effect on December 27th 1986: *By October 1987, a year after Big Bang, the inflated City salaries were slipping.*

big bang theo·ry /ˌ· ˈ· ˌ··/ *n* [*the*] *tech* the idea that the universe began with the explosion of a single mass of material and that the pieces are still flying apart — compare STEADY STATE THEORY

Big Ben /ˌ· ˈ·/ the large bell in the clock tower of the Houses of Parliament in Westminster, London. The sound of Big Ben striking is well known to all British people and the tower of Big Ben is often used as a SYMBOL of London or Britain. —see colour map on page 817

Big Bird /ˌ· ˈ·/ a character from the American television programme *Sesame Street*, who is a very large yellow bird that acts like a child

big board /ˌ· ·/ *n* [*the*] *AmE* (the electronic sign showing changing share prices at) the New York Stock Exchange

Big Broth·er /ˌ· ˈ··/ a character in the book *Nineteen Eighty Four* by George Orwell. In the story, Big Brother is the head of the state and although he is not seen in person there are pictures of him everywhere with the message "Big Brother is watching you". The expression is now used to describe a leader of an organization or a government that has complete power, allows no freedom, and keeps a close watch on people's activities.

big bucks /ˌ· ˈ·/ *n* [P] *AmE infml* a lot of money: *She's earning big bucks now.*

big busi·ness /ˌ· ˈ··/ *n* [U] very large companies as a group, esp. in connection with their power and influence in politics and economic matters: *What's good for big business isn't always good for the man on the street.*

big cat /ˌ· ˈ·/ *n not tech* a large member of the cat family, such as a lion or tiger

big cheese /ˌ· ˈ·/ *n infml humor* a very important person in an organization, institution, etc.: *So you're the big cheese around here, are you?*

Big Dad·dy /ˌ· ˈ··/ (1936–) a popular wrestler (WRESTLE (1)) whose real name is **Shirley Crabtree**, known for his large size, fair hair, and humorous activities in the ring

big day /ˌ· ˈ·/ *n* [sing] a wedding day: *Are you looking forward to your big day?*

big deal /ˌ· ˈ·/ *n, interj* [S] *sl* (showing that one considers something unimportant): *"Be careful how you speak to him. He's the company president." "Big deal!"* | *What's the big deal?*

Big Dip·per /ˌ· ˈ··/ *n* 1 [C] (*sometimes not caps.*) *BrE* a ROLLER COASTER 2 [*the*] the group of stars called the PLOUGH

Big Ears /ˈ· ·/ a character in the *Noddy* children's stories, Noddy's best friend, who has large ears, a white beard, and looks like a garden GNOME (2) —see picture at NODDY

Big Eight /ˌ· ˈ·/ *n* [U] a CONFERENCE (group) of eight college FOOTBALL (2) teams from the American MIDWEST

big end /ˌ· ˈ·/ *n BrE tech* the part of a connecting rod in a car engine which joins onto the CRANK: *I think your big end's gone.*

Big·foot /ˈbɪgfʊt/ *n* -**foots** a large hairy man-like animal which some people claim to have seen in the northwest US but which cannot be proved to exist. Stories about Bigfoot are very popular in American TABLOID newspapers.

Big Four /ˌ· ˈ·/ [*the* + P] the four countries considered to be the main world powers, namely the US, UK, the former USSR and China

big game /ˌ· ˈ·/ *n* [U] the largest wild animals hunted for sport, such as lions and elephants. Big-game hunting used to be considered an adventure, but now many people disapprove of it because so many animals have been killed and there are only small numbers of some kinds (SPECIES) left: *a big-game hunter*

big·gie /ˈbɪgi/ *n infml* someone or something very large, important, or well-known: *Have you heard their new record? I think it's going to be a biggie.*

Big·gles /ˈbɪgəlz/ a character in stories by Captain W E Johns. Biggles is a fighter pilot in the First World War, known for his flying skills, daring, and ability to remain calm under enemy fire, and was very popular with British schoolboys for many years: *Biggles-style flying gear*

Big Daddy

Big Ben

Biggles

big gov·ern·ment /ˈ· ˌ···/ *n* [C;U] *AmE derog* a government which becomes involved in many parts of people's lives in order to help them take care of themselves. People who do not think WELFARE (=financial help for poor people) is a good idea, or who think that there are too many government programmes for disadvantaged people, often talk about big government to describe the kind of government that provides too many of these kinds of services.

Biggs /bɪgz/, **Ron·ald** /ˈrɒnld‖ˈrɑː-/ (**Ron·nie** /ˈrɒni‖ ˈrɑː-/) (1929–) a famous British train robber who took part in the Great Train Robbery and who escaped to Brazil

big gun /ˌ· ˈ·/ *n AmE sl* an important person who can influence events

big·head /ˈbɪghed/ *n infml* someone who has too high an opinion of their own importance

big-heart·ed /ˌ· ˈ··◂/ *adj* kind and loving: *She'd give you the coat off her back she's so big-hearted.*

big cats

leopard

mane

jaguar

lynx

lion

cheetah

tiger

cougar

big·horn /ˈbɪɡhɔːn‖-hɔːrn/ also **bighorn sheep** /ˌ·· ˈ·/ n a wild sheep with long, curved horns which lives in the Rocky Mountains in the US

bight /baɪt/ n **1** a curve in a coast larger than, or curving less than, a BAY¹ **2** a LOOP made in the middle of a rope

Big League /ˌ· ˈ·/ n AmE infml MAJOR LEAGUE —compare LITTLE LEAGUE

Big Mac /ˌ· ˈ·/ n tdmk a HAMBURGER made by McDonalds which has two pieces of meat, cheese, LETTUCE and other foods on a BUN (round bread)

Big Man on Cam·pus /ˌ· ˌ· ˈ··/ also **BMOC** n AmE infml a popular, important male student at a university, such as an ATHLETE or the president of the student's union

big name /ˌ· ˈ·/ n infml an important or well-known person or group: They've lined up quite a few big names for the concert.

big noise /ˌ· ˈ·/ a BIG SHOT

big·ot /ˈbɪɡət/ n someone who thinks unreasonably that their own strong opinion is correct, esp. about matters of religion, race, or politics — ~ed adj : bigoted people/ opinions

big·ot·ry /ˈbɪɡətri/ n [U] behaviour or beliefs typical of a bigot

big screen /ˌ· ˈ·◂/ n [the] (film made for) the cinema, as opposed to television: Her career took off when she transferred her talents to the big screen.

big shot /ˌ· ˈ·/ n a person of great importance or influence: talking to some big shot in the advertising business

big stick /ˌ· ˈ·/ n [the] the threat of using military or political force to get what one wants

Big Ten /ˌ· ˈ·/ also **Big 10** n [the] a group of ten midwestern US universities who compete with each other in sports. These teams are generally thought to be the best in college sports, and their players often go on to join professional teams —compare PAC TEN

Big Three /ˌ· ˈ·/ n [the] AmE General Motors, Ford, and Chrysler, which are the three largest American car makers: The Big Three have all announced incentives to boost flagging auto sales.

big-tick·et /ˈ· ··/ adj AmE infml expensive: big-ticket items such as refrigerators and stereos

big time /ˈ· ˌ·/ n [the] infml the highest level of importance or success (e.g. in sports or the entertainment business): She was fairly successful as an actress, but never really hit (=reached) the big time —compare SMALL-TIME —**bigtime** /ˈ· ·/ adj : a big-time gangster —**big-timer** n

big toe /ˌ· ˈ·/ n the largest toe on the inside of the foot — see picture at FOOT

big top /ˌ· ˈ·/ n a very large tent used by a CIRCUS (=a show with performing animals, people, etc.)

big wheel /ˌ· ˈ·/ n **1** BrE ‖ also **ferris wheel** esp. AmE— a machine used in amusement parks, consisting of a large upright wheel carrying seats which remain HORIZONTAL as the wheel turns round **2** a BIG SHOT

big·wig /ˈbɪɡwɪɡ/ n humor or derog sl a person with a high position in an organization

bi·jou /ˈbiːʒuː/ adj [A] (esp. of a building) small and pretty: The estate agent described this little house as a desirable bijou residence.

bike /baɪk/ n infml **1** a two-wheeled vehicle; BICYCLE **2** AmE infml MOTORCYCLE **3** get on your bike BrE infml to go out and make an effort to find a job. The phrase is connected esp. with the former British politician Norman Tebbit. —**bike** v [I+adv/prep]

bik·er /ˈbaɪkəʳ/ n **1** someone who rides a MOTORBIKE esp. one of a group often wearing black leather bearing the name of the group and/or other words and SYMBOLs —see also HELLS ANGEL **2** someone who rides a BICYCLE

bi·ki·ni /bɪˈkiːni/ n a small two-piece bathing suit for women

Bi·ko /ˈbiːkəʊ/, **Steve** /stiːv/ (1946–77) a black South African leader who died while being held by the police. His death made him into a MARTYR for black South Africans.

bi·la·bi·al /baɪˈleɪbiəl/ n, adj tech (a consonant sound such as /b/) made using both lips

bi·lat·er·al /baɪˈlætərəl/ adj concerning or including two groups or nations: a bilateral agreement on arms control —compare MULTILATERAL, UNILATERAL — ~ly adv

bil·ber·ry /ˈbɪlbəri‖-ˌberi/ also **whortleberry** — n (the blueblack fruit of) a low bushy plant growing on hillsides and in high woods in Northern Europe —compare BLUEBERRY

bile /baɪl/ n [U] **1** a bitter green-brown liquid formed in the LIVER, which helps in the DIGESTION of fats **2** fml bad temper and bitterness

bilge /bɪldʒ/ n **1** [C] the broad bottom of a ship **2** [U] dirty water in the bottom of a ship **3** [U] old-fash sl foolish talk: Don't give me that bilge!

bi·lin·gual /baɪˈlɪŋgwəl/ adj **1** of, containing, or expressed in two languages: a bilingual French-English dictionary **2** able to speak two languages equally well: a bilingual secretary

bilingual² *n* a person who is able to speak two languages equally well —compare MONOLINGUAL

bil·i·ous /ˈbɪlɪəs/ *adj* **1** sick from having too much bile in the body: *Fatty food makes some people bilious.* **2** bad-tempered; IRASCIBLE – ~**ness** *n* [U]

bilk /bɪlk/ *v* [T (**out of**)] to cheat (someone), esp. causing them to lose money; SWINDLE

Bil·ko /ˈbɪlkəʊ/, **Sergeant** the main character in a humorous television programme about an American army camp. Bilko is an army officer, played by Phil Silvers, who talks very fast and loves playing cards and finding ways to make money.

bill¹ /bɪl/ *n* **1** [(**for**)] a list of things bought, used, eaten, etc., showing the total amount that must be paid: *Could we have the bill please?* | *Have you paid the bill yet?* | *The bill for the repairs came to £650.* **2** a written plan for a new law, which is brought to parliament for it to consider: *a debate in Parliament on the government's new transport Bill*

▶ CULTURAL NOTE In the British parliament a bill is usu. produced by the Government, read out ("the First Reading"), and discussed in the House of Commons. After the Second Reading a special committee examines it in detail. This period is called the committee stage. It is followed by the report stage when there is more discussion. After the Third Reading it goes to the House of Lords, which sometimes sends it back with suggested changes. Finally, it receives the Royal Assent (= is signed by the Queen) and becomes law. In the US a bill is usually produced by one or more members of Congress. Its introduction to the House or Senate is called the "first reading". The bill is given to a special committee for study, and then is discussed and voted on by either the House or the Senate, depending on where it was first introduced. If the bill passes, it goes to the side of Congress which has not yet seen it for more study and another vote. After Congress as a whole has approved the bill, it goes to the President, who may either sign it to become law or VETO (disapprove) it. ◀

3 *AmE* a piece of paper money; NOTE¹ (4): *a five-dollar bill* **4** a printed notice: *Stick No Bills* (a public warning on a wall, fence, etc.) **5 the (old) bill** *BrE infml* the police —see also BILL OF FARE/HEALTH/ LADING/RIGHTS/SALE, **fit the bill** (FIT¹), **foot the bill** (FOOT²), **top the bill** (TOP³)

bill² *v* [T] **1** [(**for**)] *esp. tech* to send a bill to: *I can't pay now: please bill me for it later.* **2** [(**as**) usu. pass.] to advertise in printed notices: *It's been billed as the race of the year.* [+obj+to-v] *He's billed to appear as Hamlet.* | (fig.) *The following election is being billed* (=generally described) *as the most important in 30 years.*

bill³ *n* **1** *tech* the beak of a bird **2** *BrE* (*usu. cap. as part of a place name*) a long narrow piece of land sticking out into the sea: *Portland Bill*

bill⁴ *v* **bill and coo** *infml* (of lovers) to kiss and speak softly to each other

Bill and Ben the Flow·er·pot Men /ˌ· · ˌ· · ˈ··· ˌ·/ see FLOWERPOT MEN

bill·board /ˈbɪlbɔːd‖-bɔːrd/ *n AmE for* HOARDING (2)

bil·let¹ /ˈbɪlɪt/ *n* a house (usu. a private home) where soldiers are put to live for a while

billet² *v* [T (**on**)] to provide (a soldier) with a billet: *The captain billeted his men on old Mrs Smith.* (=in Mrs Smith's house)

bil·let-doux /ˌbɪleɪ ˈduː/ *n* billets-doux /ˌbɪleɪ ˈduːz/ *Fr, humor or lit* a love letter

bill·fold /ˈbɪlfəʊld/ *n AmE for* WALLET (1)

bill·hook /ˈbɪlhʊk/ *n* a tool consisting of a blade with a hooked point and a handle, used esp. for cutting off branches of trees and cutting up wood for fires

bil·liards /ˈbɪljədz‖-ərdz/ *n* [U] any of several games played on a cloth-covered table (a **billiard table**) with balls which are knocked with CUEs (=long sticks) against each other or into pockets at the corners and sides of the table —see also POOL, SNOOKER —**billiard** *adj* [A] : *billiard balls*

Bil·lings·gate /ˈbɪlɪŋzɡeɪt/ *n* a large fish market in E London

bil·lion /ˈbɪljən/ *determiner, n, pron* **billion** *or* **billions** **1** (the number) one thousand million; 1,000,000,000; 10^9 **2** *BrE old use* (the number) one million million; 1,000,000,000,000; 10^{12} – ~**th** *determiner, n, pron, adv*

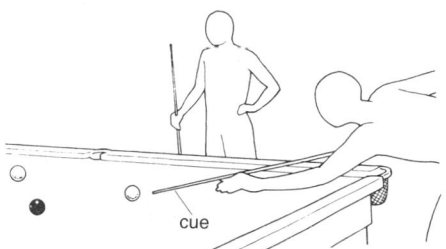

cue

bil·lion·aire /ˌbɪljəˈneər/ *n* a person whose money, property, etc. is worth one billion dollars, pounds, etc.

bill of ex·change /ˌ· · ·ˈ·/ also **promissory note** *AmE— n tech* a promise, which must by law be fulfilled, to repay a debt to someone on a fixed date

bill of fare /ˌ· · ˈ·/ *n* **bills of fare** *old-fash* a list of dishes to be served in a restaurant; MENU

bill of goods /ˌ· · ˈ·/ *n* [U] *AmE infml* **sell someone a bill of goods** deceive; cheat: *The roofers sold me a bill of goods when they fixed the roof; it leaks even worse than it did before.*

bill of health /ˌ· · ·ˈ·/ *n* **a clean bill of health** a favourable report on the health of a person or the satisfactory condition of a machine, organization etc.: *The school was given a clean bill of health by the inspector.*

bill of lad·ing /ˌ· · ˈ··/ *n* **bills of lading** *n tech* an official document stating that goods to be shipped have been received, and giving the conditions under which they will be carried

bill of rights /ˌ· · ˈ·/ *n* **bills of rights** (*usu. caps.*) a written statement of the most important rights of the citizens of a country

Bill of Rights [*the*] a document, part of the US Constitution, which LISTS the rights of US citizens, such as freedom of speech, freedom of religion, the right to trial by JURY, etc. Originally there were ten rights listed (ten AMENDMENTS), but over the years several more have been added. The US Supreme Court often deals with cases that are thought to involve in some way a right listed in the Bill of Rights, so they are said to deal with **Constitutional** subjects or questions. —See also FIFTH AMENDMENT, FIRST AMENDMENT

bill of sale /ˌ· · ˈ·/ *n* **bills of sale** an official written statement that something has been sold by one person to another

bil·low¹ /ˈbɪləʊ/ *n* [*usu. pl.*] **1** *lit* a wave, esp. a very large one **2** a rolling mass (as of flame or mist) like a large wave: *billows of smoke* – ~**y** *adj*

billow² *v* [I] **1** to rise and roll in waves **2** [(OUT)] to swell out as a sail does: *billowing skirts*

bill pos·ter /ˈ· ˌ··/ also **bill sticker** *n* a person who puts up advertising POSTERs, either as a job or (if unofficially) against the law

bil·ly /ˈbɪli/ also **bil·ly·can** /ˈbɪlikæn/ *BrE & AustrE— n* a tin pot for cooking or boiling water when camping

billy club /ˈ··· ·/ also **nightstick** *n AmE* a short stick carried by a police officer

billy goat /ˈ·· ·/ *n* (used esp. by or to children) a male goat —compare NANNY GOAT

Billy Li·ar /ˌ·· ˈ··/ the title of a popular humorous play first produced in London in 1960

billy-o /ˈ·· ·/ *n* **like billy-o** *BrE old-fash sl* a lot; very strongly, fast, or fiercely: *to run like billy-o*

Billy the Kid /ˌ·· ·ˈ·/ (1859–81) an American criminal (OUTLAW) who was hunted and finally shot. Billy the Kid is the subject of many stories and films.

bil·tong /ˈbɪltɒŋ‖-tɔːŋ/ *n* [U] *S AfrE* meat dried in the sun

bim·bo /ˈbɪmbəʊ/ *n infml* an attractive but unintelligent young woman, esp. one who has a sexual relationship with a politician or other public figure: *He's been seen with some blonde bimbo at nightclubs around town, and his wife is furious.*

bi·month·ly /baɪˈmʌnθli/ adv, adj appearing or happening **a** every two months: a bimonthly magazine **b** twice a month

bin¹ /bɪn/ n (often in comb.) **1** a large storage container, e.g. for grain or coal **2** BrE a wide-mouthed container (esp. one with a lid) used in the home for bread, flour, etc., or for waste: a bread bin | a rubbish bin —see also DUSTBIN, LITTER BIN, LOONY BIN

bin² v **-nn-** [T] BrE to put into a container for things to be thrown away: "What shall I do with this letter?" "Just bin it."

bi·na·ry /ˈbaɪnəri/ adj tech **1** consisting of two things or parts; double **2** (of a system of counting) using the two numbers, 0 and 1, as a base. The **binary system** is used in computers because the two numbers, 0 and 1, can be represented by an electrical signal that is either off or on.

bind¹ /baɪnd/ v **bound** /baʊnd/ **1** [T] usu. fml or lit to tie together, esp. with rope: Bind the prisoner's arms. | The hostages were bound hand and foot. (=tied by their hands and feet) | Bind the prisoner to her chair. | (fig.) shared commercial interests that bind the two companies together | (fig.) We feel bound together by our past experiences. **2** [T (UP)] to tie up firmly: She bound (up) her hair. | to bind up a wound with bandages **3** [T] to fasten (a book) together and enclose it in a cover **4** [T] to strengthen or decorate with a border of material: to bind the edges of a rug **5** [I;T (TOGETHER)] to (cause to) stick together in a mass: This flour mixture isn't wet enough to bind properly. | The rain will help to bind the earth (together). **6** [T] fml to cause to obey, esp. by a law or a solemn promise; have a duty (to): I am bound by my promise. [+obj+to-v] They bound him to remain silent — see also BOUND
   bind sbdy. **over** phr v [T] BrE law to order (someone) to cause no more trouble under threat of legal punishment: The two young offenders were bound over to keep the peace for 18 months.

bind² n [S] infml an annoying or difficult situation: Their refusal to sign the contract has put us in a bit of a bind. —see also DOUBLE BIND

bind·er /ˈbaɪndəʳ/ n **1** [C] a machine or person that binds, esp. books: Your book is still at the binder's. **2** [C] a usu. removable cover, esp. for holding sheets of paper, magazines, etc. —see also RING BINDER **3** [C;U] a substance that makes things stick together **4** [C] AmE an agreement involving a payment of money (DEPOSIT) by someone to show that they intend to buy some property

bind·ing¹ /ˈbaɪndɪŋ/ n **1** [C] a book cover: The binding of this book is torn. **2** [U] material sewn or stuck along the edge of something, such as a dress, for strength or decoration

binding² adj (of something written) having the power to demand obedience (e.g. to a law) or fulfilment (e.g. of a promise): a binding agreement | The contract is binding on everyone who signed it.

bind·weed /ˈbaɪndwiːd/ n [U] a plant which curls itself round other plants; wild CONVOLVULUS

binge /bɪndʒ/ n **1** infml a period of drinking, wild behaviour, etc.: They went on a binge and didn't get back until three in the morning! **2** tech a period of eating a very large amount of food, done by someone suffering from an EATING DISORDER —compare BINGE, JAG

bin·go /ˈbɪŋɡəʊ/ n, interj **1** [U] a game played for money or prizes, in which numbers chosen by chance are called out and players cross out these numbers if they appear on their own cards. The first player to cross out all the numbers on his or her card shouts out "Bingo!" or "House!" In Britain, bingo is generally thought of as a game played by working-class women in the evening. In the US, it is usu. played by older people and games are often run by the Catholic Church or on Native American lands (RESERVATIONS). Bingo is illegal in some American states because it is considered to be gambling (GAMBLE). **2** infml (an expression of pleasure at a sudden successful result): Bingo! That will make a great photo!

bin-lin·er /ˈ· ˌ··/ n BrE a plastic bag which is placed inside a DUSTBIN and used to collect waste

bin-man /ˈbɪnmæn/ n **-men** /men/ BrE infml one of the men who come to people's houses to empty their DUSTBINS

bi·noc·u·lars /bɪˈnɒkjʊ̆ləz, baɪ-ˈnɑːkjʊ̆lərz/ n [P] a pair of glasses like short TELESCOPEs for both eyes, used for

looking at distant objects: I watched the horse-race through my binoculars. —see PAIR (USAGE) —**binocular** adj

binocular vi·sion /·,··· ˈ··/ n [U] tech the ability to FOCUS both eyes on one object, possessed by humans, monkeys, and some birds

bi·no·mi·al /baɪˈnəʊmiəl/ n, adj tech (an expression) consisting of two numbers, letters, etc., connected by the sign + or the sign − (like a+b or x−7)

bio- see WORD FORMATION

bi·o·chem·is·try /ˌbaɪəʊˈkemɪ̆stri/ n [U] (the scientific study of) the chemistry of living things

bi·o·de·gra·da·ble /ˌbaɪəʊdɪˈɡreɪdəbəl/ n tech, usu. apprec able to be broken down into harmless products by the natural action of living things (e.g. bacteria): biodegradable packaging

bi·o·feed·back /ˌbaɪəʊˈfiːdbæk/ n [U] a method of learning to consciously control usu. unconscious physical tension, by using an electronic machine to measure this tension (such as blood pressure) and watching which of various mental and physical exercises are successful at reducing it

bi·og·ra·pher /baɪˈɒɡrəfəʳ‖-ˈɑːɡ-/ n a writer of biography: Dr Johnson's famous biographer, James Boswell

bi·og·ra·phy /baɪˈɒɡrəfi‖-ˈɑːɡ-/ n **1** [C] an account of a person's life written by someone else: Boswell wrote a famous biography of Dr Johnson. **2** [U] this branch of literature —compare AUTOBIOGRAPHY —**phical,** /ˌbaɪəˈɡræfɪkəl◂/ —**phic** adj —**phically** /kli/ adv

biological clock /·,···· ˈ·/ also **body clock** n [S] the system in plants, animals, and humans which controls some types of behaviour. In animals, this includes sleeping, eating, and biological events such as the MENSTRUAL CYCLE in females. Women sometimes talk about being conscious of their biological clock when they realise that they will soon be too old to have children.

biological con·trol /·,···· ·ˈ·/ n [U] the control of PESTs (=usu. small animals or insects which harm or destroy food supplies) by biological means (e.g. by the introduction of something harmless to humans and crops which eats, lives on, or competes against the pest)

biological war·fare /·,···· ˈ··/ also **germ warfare** — n [U] methods of fighting a war in which living things such as BACTERIA are used to poison, spread disease, damage crops, etc. —compare CHEMICAL WARFARE

bi·ol·o·gy /baɪˈɒlədʒi‖-ˈɑːl-/ n [U] **1** the scientific study of living things: She has a degree in biology. | a biology lesson **2** the scientific laws of the life of a certain type of living thing: the biology of bacteria —**gist** n —**gical** /ˌbaɪəˈlɒdʒɪkəl◂‖-ˈlɑː-/ adj —**gically** /kli/ adv : Biologically speaking, they're plants.

bi·o·mass /ˈbaɪəʊmæs/ n [U] tech matter from dead or living plants or animals; organic matter, esp. when burned to provide heat: cow dung, wood, and other biomass fuels

bi·on·ic /baɪˈɒnɪk‖-ˈɑːn-/ adj infml having greater than human powers (such as speed, strength, etc.)

bi·o·phys·ics /ˌbaɪəʊˈfɪzɪks/ n [U] the science concerned with the study of matter and natural forces in living things

bi·o·pic /ˈbaɪəʊˌpɪk/ n a film that tells the story of someone's life: a biopic about Gandhi

bi·op·sy /ˈbaɪɒpsi‖-ɑːp-/ n the removal of cells, liquids, etc., from the body of a sick person to discover the nature of the disease or to find out which parts of the body are infected

bi·o·rhyth·ms /ˈbaɪəʊˌrɪðəmz/ n [P] the supposed regular increases and decreases in the activity of the living processes of a person or animal, that are believed to influence behaviour and feelings

bi·o·sphere /ˈbaɪəsfɪəʳ/ n [the] tech the part of the world in which life can exist

bi·o·tech·nol·o·gy /ˌbaɪəʊtekˈnɒlədʒi‖-ˈnɑː-/ n [U] **1** the use in science and industry of living things such as cells and bacteria to make drugs and chemicals, destroy waste matter, etc. **2** AmE ERGONOMICS

bi·par·ti·san /ˌbaɪpaːtɪ̆ˈzæn‖baɪˈpɑːrtɪ̆zən/ adj of or representing two political parties: a bipartisan committee | The new law has bipartisan support.

bi·par·tite /baɪˈpɑːtaɪt‖-ˈpɑːr-/ adj **1** having two parts: a

bipartite leaf **2** agreed upon or shared by two groups: *a bipartite treaty* —compare TRIPARTITE

bi·ped /'baɪped/ *n tech* a two-legged animal —compare QUADRUPED

bi·plane /'baɪpleɪn/ *n* an aircraft, esp. of a type built in the early 20th century, with two sets of wings, one above the other —compare MONOPLANE

birch¹ /bɜːtʃ‖bɜːrtʃ/ *n* **1** [C;U] (wood from) a tree, common in northern countries, with a smooth BARK and thin branches —see also SILVER BIRCH **2** [C;*the*] a stick made from birch wood, used for punishing. The birch is still available as a punishment on the Isle of Man, but nowhere else in Britain or the US. Some older people in Britain would like to "bring back the birch" for football HOOLIGANS and VANDALS.

birch² *v* [T] to whip or hit, esp. with a birch, as a punishment

birds

swallow
robin
sparrow

thrush
pigeon
woodpecker

beak
breast
wing
claw
pheasant
kingfisher
tail feather

bird /bɜːd‖bɜːrd/ *n* **1** a creature with wings and feathers which can usu. fly in the air **2** *BrE sl, becoming old-fash* a young woman (usu. considered offensive to women): *Who was that bird I saw you with last night?* **3** *old-fash infml* a person, esp. one who is odd or remarkable: *He's a strange old bird.* **4** *saying* **a bird in the hand (is worth two in the bush)** something you already have or are sure of getting (is better than something else which you may not get in the end) **5** **birds of a feather** *infml* people of the same kind (often bad): *I'm not surprised those two are such friends; they're birds of a feather!* **6** **do bird** *BrE sl* to spend a period of time in prison **7** **for the birds** *AmE infml* silly; not practical or sensible **8** **give someone the bird** *infml, esp. BrE* to make rude noises to show disapproval of someone: *The crowd gave him the bird.* **9** **(strictly) for the birds** *sl, esp. AmE* worthless; silly **10** **the bird has flown** *infml* the person needed or wanted has gone away or escaped **11** **the birds and bees** *euph or humor* the facts about sex, esp. as told to children; FACTS OF LIFE: *He knows all about the birds and the bees.* —see also EARLY BIRD, WATER BIRD, **eat like a bird** (EAT (7)), **kill two birds with one stone** (KILL¹)

Bird, Lar·ry /'læri/ (1956–) an American BASKETBALL player

bird·bath /'bɜːdbɑːθ‖'bɜːrdbæθ/ *n* a small, usu. round bath that is not very deep and is put in a garden for birds to bathe in

bird-brained /'· ·/ *adj infml* stupid; silly

bird dog /'· ·/ *n AmE for* GUNDOG

bird·ie¹ /'bɜːdi‖'bɜːrdi/ *n* **1** (used to or by children) a little bird **2** (in GOLF) a SCORE of one stroke less than PAR on a hole **3** *AmE* SHUTTLECOCK **4** **watch the birdie** *humor* a phrase said by someone who is just about to take a photograph —compare **say cheese** (CHEESE)

bir·die² *v* [T] (in GOLF) to play (a hole) in one stroke under PAR

bird·lime /'bɜːdlaɪm‖'bɜːr-/ *also* **lime**— *n* [U] a sticky substance spread on branches to catch small birds

bird of par·a·dise /ˌ· · '···/ *n* a brightly coloured bird of the New Guinea area

bird of pas·sage /ˌ· · '··/ *n* **1** a bird that flies from one country or area to another, according to the season **2** *BrE infml* a person who never stays in one place very long

bird of prey /ˌ· · '·/ *n* a bird that kills other birds and small animals for food

bird·seed /'bɜːdsiːd‖'bɜːrd-/ *n* [U] a mixture of small seeds for feeding caged birds

Bird's /bɜːdz‖bɜːrdz/ *n tdmk* a type of CUSTARD powder (–powder which is mixed with milk and sugar and heated to make custard) made by General Foods Ltd.

Bird's Eye /'· ·/ *tdmk* the name of a company producing a range of FROZEN food products (esp. fish) which are known for quality. The products are advertised by Captain Bird's Eye, a cheerful old sea captain.

bird's-eye view /ˌ· · '·/ *n* l(**of**) a view seen from above or from the sky: *a marvellous bird's-eye view of the whole city*

bird·song /'bɜːdsɒŋ‖'bɜːrdsɔːŋ/ *n* [U] the musical noises made by birds

bird-watch·er /'· ˌ··/ *n* a person who watches wild birds in their natural surroundings, and tries to recognize different types

bi·ret·ta /bə'retə/ *n* a square cap worn esp. by Roman Catholic priests

bir·i·a·ni , byriani /ˌbɪri'ɑːni/ *n* [U] a hot, tasty, Indian, rice dish mixed with meat, fish, vegetables, etc.

Bir·ken·au /'bɜːkənaʊ‖'bɜːr-/ *also* **Auschwitz II** a Nazi death camp (a form of CONCENTRATION CAMP whose purpose was purely to kill people) for Jews in Poland during the Second World War

Bir·ken·head /'bɜːkənhed‖'bɜːr-/ a town on Merseyside, NW England, connected to Liverpool by road and railway TUNNELS¹ under the river

Bir·kens·tocks /'bɜːkənstɒks‖'bɜːrkənstɑːks/ *n tdmk* a leather SANDAL (=a shoe open at the toes and heel) with a broad, flat bottom. Many people connect Birkenstocks in their minds with people who are more interested in comfort than fashion, eat health foods, and want a simpler life style.

Bir·ming·ham /'bɜːmɪŋəm‖'bɜːr-/ **1** an industrial city in the West Midlands of England, the second largest in Britain. In the past, Birmingham was known for being a dirty, industrial city, but now it is becoming more popular, esp. as a centre of music and the arts —see colour map on page 818 **2** a city in Alabama in the US. During the 1960s and the Civil Rights movement, Birmingham was a place where relations between blacks and whites were very tense and often resulted in extreme violence. There were many protests in Birmingham over the way blacks were treated. Some of these protests were violent, as in the race RIOTS of 1963, and others were non-violent, such as the protests led by Martin Luther King, Jr. —see colour map on pages 1374-5

Birmingham Six /ˌ··· '·/ *n* [*the*+P] six Irishmen who were found guilty of putting IRA bombs in two Birmingham PUBs in 1974, killing 21 people. The men were sent to prison for life, but always said that they were innocent, and were freed in 1991, after new facts were considered about the way the police had acted. Along with other cases, this case has raised questions in Britain about police questioning of people they have caught for a crime, and about the way mistakes in justice are put right —compare GUILDFORD FOUR, MAGUIRE SEVEN, TOTTENHAM THREE

Bir·nam Wood /ˌbɜːnəm 'wʊd‖ˌbɜːr-/ the wood near **Birnam** in Perthshire, Scotland. In Shakespeare's play *Macbeth*, Macbeth is told that he will only be defeated when Birnam Wood comes to Dunsinane. Later, his enemy's army comes through Birnam Wood and each soldier cuts a large branch to hide himself, so that when the army moves on it looks as if the wood is moving. Macbeth is defeated and killed.

bi·ro /ˈbaɪərəʊ/ n **biros** BrE tdmk a BALLPOINT: written with a biro|in biro

birth /bɜːθ‖bɜːrθ/ n **1** [C;U] the act, time, or process of being born, of coming into the world out of the body of a female parent: the birth of a child | The father was present at the birth. | Last year there were more births than deaths. | The baby weighed eight pounds at birth. | She **gave birth to** a fine healthy baby. | (fig.) the birth of a new nation|political party —compare DEATH (1) —see also DATE OF BIRTH **2** [U] family origin: of noble birth | She is French by birth.

birth con·trol /ˈ· ·ˌ·/ n [U] the practice of limiting, by any of various methods, the number of children born; CON-TRACEPTION: to practise birth control | a birth control clinic

birth·day /ˈbɜːdeɪ‖ˈbɜːr-/ n **1** a day which is an exact year or number of years after one was born: my 21st birthday | a birthday party | Happy birthday to you! —compare ANNIVERSARY

▶ CULTURAL NOTE People, esp. children, often celebrate their birthdays with a **birthday party** where people play games, sometimes wear special paper hats, eat **birthday cake**, and sing a special song called Happy Birthday to you. People are usu. given presents and **birthday cards** on their birthday.◀

2 in one's birthday suit infml humor having no clothes on; NAKED

Birthday Hon·ours /ˌ·· ˌ·/ n [P] the titles and other AWARDS[2] given to public figures and deserving people by the Queen on her official birthday

birth·mark /ˈbɜːθmɑːk‖ˈbɜːrθmɑːrk/ n a usu. red or brown mark on the skin at birth

birth pa·rent /ˈ· ˌ··/ n the mother who actually gave birth to one, or one's natural father; used in comparison with other sorts of parents, such as ADOPTIVE, SURROGATE, FOSTER, etc.

birth·place /ˈbɜːθpleɪs‖ˈbɜːr-/ n [usu. sing.] the place where someone was born: Stratford-upon-Avon was Shakespeare's birthplace. | (fig.) Cooperstown, New York, is said to be the birthplace of baseball.

birth·rate /ˈbɜːθreɪt‖ˈbɜːr-/ n the number of births for every 100 or every 1000 people in a particular year in a particular place: a birthrate of three per 100 | a rapidly increasing birthrate —compare DEATH RATE

birth·right /ˈbɜːθraɪt‖ˈbɜːr-/ n [usu. sing.] a right or set of rights that belongs to someone because of the family or nation they come from: Freedom is our birthright.

birth·stone /ˈbɜːθstəʊn‖ˈbɜːrθ-/ n the valuable stone which is connected with the month of the year in which one was born: If you were born in July, then your birthstone is a ruby.

Birt·whis·tle /ˈbɜːtwɪsəl‖ˈbɜːrt-/, **Sir Harrison** (1934–) an English COMPOSER known for his modern music for voices and instruments, including Tragoedia and Ring a Dumb Carillon

bir·y·a·ni /ˌbɪriˈɑːni/ see BIRIANI

Bis·cay /ˈbɪskeɪ/, **Bay of** a part of the Atlantic Ocean running down the W coast of France to the N coast of Spain, known for its dangerous weather

bis·cuit /ˈbɪskɪt/ n **1** [C] BrE ‖ **cookie** AmE— a flat thin dry cake, sweetened or unsweetened, usu. sold in packets or tins: We had coffee and biscuits. **2** [C] AmE for SCONE **3** [U] a light yellowish brown colour **4** [U] tech cups, plates, etc., made of baked clay, after their first heating in the fire but before the GLAZE is put on **5 take the biscuit** BrE sl to be the best/worst thing one has ever seen or heard of: This latest excuse of his really takes the biscuit!

bi·sect /baɪˈsekt‖ˈbaɪsekt/ v [T] tech to divide into two usu. equal parts — ~ **ion** /baɪˈsekʃən‖ˈbaɪsek-/ n [U]

bi·sex·u·al /baɪˈsekʃuəl/ adj **1** possessing qualities of both sexes: a bisexual plant **2** sexually attracted to people of both sexes —compare HETEROSEXUAL, HOMOSEXUAL, LES-BIAN —**bisexual** n — ~ **ly** adv — ~ **ity** /baɪˌsekʃuˈælɨti/ n [U]

bish·op /ˈbɪʃəp/ n **1** (often cap.) (in some branches of the Christian church) a high-ranking priest in charge of all

the churches and priests in a large area (a DIOCESE): Bishop Desmond Tutu | the Bishop of Durham **2** (in CHESS) a piece that can be moved any number of squares from one corner towards the opposite corner—see picture at CHESS; see also **as the actress said to the bishop** (ACTRESS)

bish·op·ric /ˈbɪʃəprɪk/ n the position of a bishop, or the area (DIOCESE) that a bishop is in charge of

Bis·marck /ˈbɪzmɑːk‖-mɑːrk/, **Ot·to von** /ˈɒtəʊ vɒn‖ˈɑːtəʊ vɑːn/ (1815–98) a German politician, very popular in his time, who became CHANCELLOR of the German EMPIRE

bis·muth /ˈbɪzməθ/ n [U] a grey-white metal that is a simple substance (ELEMENT), is easily broken, and is used in medicine

bi·son /ˈbaɪsən/ also **buffalo**— n **bison** or **bisons** a large wild animal like a cow formerly common in Europe and N America, with a very large head and shoulders covered with hair

bisque /bɪsk/ n [U] thick cream soup, esp. made from SHELLFISH: lobster bisque

Bis·quick /ˈbɪskwɪk/ n [U] tdmk a mixture of flour and other substances needed to make PANCAKES, WAFFLES, or BIS-CUITS (2), sold in the US

Bis·to /ˈbɪstəʊ/ n [U] tdmk a British make of GRAVY (1) in powder form, known esp. for its advertising phrase "Aah! Bisto!", and the children used in its advertisements, called the **Bisto Kids**

bis·tro /ˈbiːstrəʊ/ n **-tros** a small BAR[1] (3) or restaurant; esp. one that is fashionable and popular

bit¹ /bɪt/ n **1** [C (of)] a small piece or amount: The floor was covered in bits of paper|bits of broken glass. —see picture at PIECE **2** [C (of)] esp. BrE any part or piece of something larger: Who would like the last bit of cake? | I liked the bit when the shark suddenly appeared behind the boat — that was the best bit in the whole film. **3** [S+of] esp. BrE a certain amount; some: a bit of bad news | I'm going to do a bit of Christmas shopping. | There's been a bit of trouble at the office. | I did a bit of teaching before I became a writer. **4** [S] a short time: I'm going out for a bit. **5** [C] infml a BrE a small coin, esp. one worth three or six old pence: a sixpenny bit b AmE 12½ cents: I wouldn't give you **two bits** (=25 cents) for that old book! —see also TWO-BIT **6 a bit** infml to some degree; rather: I'm a bit tired. | We need a bit more time. | Your article is a bit (too) long for our paper. | Could you turn the radio down a bit, please. | He's a bit of a bore. (=he's rather BOR-ING) | I wasn't a bit worried. (=I wasn't worried at all) | She's not a bit like her sister. —see MORE (USAGE) **7 a bit much** also **a bit thick** — esp. BrE more than is acceptable or fair; unreasonable: I think it's a bit much that she expects us to work at weekends. **8 bit by bit** also a **bit at a time**— infml gradually; little by little **9 bits and pieces/bobs** infml small things of various kinds: Let me get my bits and pieces together. **10 do one's bit** BrE infml to do one's share of work that needs to be done: We'll soon get it finished if we all do our bit. **11 every bit as** infml just as: She's every bit as clever as her sister. **12 to bits** into small pieces: The bridge was blown to bits by the explosion. | (fig.) My nerves have gone (all) to bits lately. —see also BIT OF FLUFF, BIT PART

▷ USAGE Use **a bit** before adjectives: I'm a (little) tired. Use **a bit of** before nouns: a bit of money | a bit of a problem.◁

bit² n **1** a metal bar, part of a BRIDLE, that is put in the mouth of a horse and used for controlling its movements —see picture at HORSE **2** the sharp part of a tool for cutting or making holes: a drill bit **3 champ/chafe at the bit** to be restless and difficult to control because of being impatient to do something —compare **straining at the leash** (STRAIN¹) **4 take the bit between one's teeth** to make a serious and determined effort to deal with something difficult or unpleasant

bit³ n tech the smallest unit of information that can be used by a computer: a 16-bit processor —compare BYTE

bit⁴ past tense of BITE

bitch¹ /bɪtʃ/ n **1** a female dog **2** derog a woman, esp. when unkind or bad-tempered: You bitch! —see also SON-OF-A-BITCH

bitch² v [I (about)] sl **1** to complain continually: I wish you'd stop bitching. **2** to make nasty or hurtful remarks about other people

bitch·en /ˈbɪtʃən/ adj AmE sl good: *That's a bitchen car.*

bitch·y /ˈbɪtʃi/ adj nasty and hurtful towards other people: *She's really bitchy.* | *a bitchy remark* —**ily** adv —**iness** n [U]

bite¹ /baɪt/ v bit /bɪt/, bitten /ˈbɪtn/ 1 [I;T] to cut, crush, or seize (something) with the teeth or to attack (someone or something) with the teeth: *Be careful. My dog bites.* | *The boy bit into the piece of cake.* | *He bit a large piece out of it.* | *Their dog bit me on the leg* | *bit a hole in my trousers.* | *Do your children bite their fingernails?* 2 [I;T] (of insects and snakes) to make a hole in the skin (of) and draw blood: *The mosquitoes are really biting this evening!* | (fig., infml) *You've been in a bad mood all day —* **what's biting you?** (=what is wrong?) 3 [I] (of fish) to accept food on a fisherman's hook and so get caught: *I've been sitting here for hours but the fish just aren't biting today.* | (fig.) *I hoped she would be interested in my plan, but she didn't bite.* (=express any interest) 4 [I] to take hold of something firmly; GRIP: *The ice on the road was so hard that the tyres wouldn't bite.* 5 [I] to have the intended, usu. unpleasant, effect: *The new higher taxes are really beginning to bite.* 6 **be bitten with** infml to develop (a strong desire for something or a strong, almost uncontrollable interest in something): *Ever since he was 16 years old, he's been bitten with a love of motorcycles.* 7 **bite off more than one can chew** infml to attempt more than one can deal with or succeed in finishing: *I told him he would be biting off more than he could chew if he tried to rebuild the house himself.* 8 **bite one's tongue** to make a great effort to stop oneself saying what one really feels 9 **bite someone's head off** infml to speak to or answer someone rudely and angrily: *I only asked you what time it was — there's no need to bite my head off!* 10 **bite the bullet** infml to suffer bravely something very unpleasant 11 **bite the dust** infml to be killed or defeated or come to an unsuccessful end: *The project bit the dust when the new management came in.* 12 **bite the hand that feeds one** to harm someone who has treated one well 13 **once bitten, twice shy** saying if you have failed at something or been hurt by it once, you will be more careful next time

bite sth. ↔ **back** phr v [T] infml to prevent oneself from saying (something that would cause offence or something that is supposed to be secret): *Peter was about to tell the secret, but he bit his words back.*

bite² n 1 [C] an act of biting or a piece removed by biting: *The cat gave its owner a playful bite.* | *I took a bite out of the apple.* | *Cut the meat into bite-sized pieces.* 2 [S] infml something to eat: *I haven't had a bite (to eat) all day.* 3 [C;U] a wound made by biting: *My face is covered with insect bites!* | *He was taken to the hospital to be treated for snake bite.* 4 [C] an act of taking food from a fisherman's hook (by a fish): *Sometimes I sit for hours without getting a bite.* 5 [S;U] sharpness or bitterness: *This cheese has no flavour: I like cheese with more bite in it.* | *a political satire without much bite to it* 6 **another/a second bite at the cherry** BrE a second chance to do or get something one wants

bit·ing /ˈbaɪtɪŋ/ adj sharply painful to the body or mind: *a cold and biting wind* | *biting remarks* — ~ **ly** adv : *a bitingly cold wind*

bit of fluff /ˌ· · ˈ·/ n BrE old-fash sl a young woman, esp. one who is sexually attractive

bit part /ˈ· ·/ n a small, unimportant character played by an actor in a play or film

bit·ten /ˈbɪtn/ past participle of BITE

bit·ter¹ /ˈbɪtə r/ adj 1 having a sharp, biting taste, like beer or black coffee without sugar —compare SWEET¹ (1), SOUR¹ (1) 2 (of cold, wind, etc.) very sharp and biting; HARSH: *It's really bitter out there today.* 3 causing pain or grief; hard to accept: *the bitter truth* | *It was a bitter disappointment/a bitter blow when we found out they had been cheating us all along.* | *I must warn you — and I speak from bitter experience — not to do business with those people.* 4 filled with or caused by hate, anger, unfulfilled expectation, or other unpleasant feelings: *bitter enemies* | *bitter tears* | *bitter opposition to the government's policies* | *He's still very bitter about the way she treated him.* 5 **a bitter pill (to swallow)** something very unpleasant that one has to accept: *The defeat was a bitter pill to swallow.* 6 **to the bitter end** infml to the end in spite of all unpleasant difficulties; until no more

effort is possible: *to struggle on to the bitter end* — ~ **ly** adv : *bitterly cold* | *bitterly disappointing* — ~ **ness** n [U]

bitter² n [U] BrE bitter beer: *A pint of bitter, please.* —see also BITTERS

bit·tern /ˈbɪtən‖-ərn/ n **bitterns** or **bittern** a brown European waterbird with long legs which makes a deep hollow low sound

bit·ters /ˈbɪtəz‖-ərz/ n [U+sing./pl. v] a bitter usu. alcoholic mixture of plant products for mixing into drinks

bit·ter·sweet /ˌbɪtəˈswiːt◂‖-tər-/ adj 1 pleasant, but mixed with sadness: *bittersweet memories of childhood* 2 of or being a type of chocolate made with very little sugar

bit·ty /ˈbɪti/ adj BrE infml, often derog consisting of or containing little bits or unconnected parts: *I thought the film was rather bitty.* —**tiness** n [U]

bi·tu·men /ˈbɪtʃʊmɪn‖bɪˈtuː-/ n [U] any of various sticky substances (such as ASPHALT or TAR), used esp. in roadmaking —**minous** /bɪˈtjuːmɪnəs‖bɪˈtuː-/ adj

bi·valve /ˈbaɪvælv/ n tech any SHELLFISH with two shells joined together, such as an OYSTER

biv·ou·ac¹ /ˈbɪvu-æk/ n a camp without tents

bivouac² v **-ck-** [I] to spend the night in the open without tents: *The climbers bivouacked halfway up the mountain.*

biv·vy bag /ˈbɪvi bæg/ also **bivouac bag** /ˈ··· ˌ·/ fml— n a small tent with no poles for one person

bi·week·ly /baɪˈwiːkli/ adv, adj appearing or happening **a** every two weeks; FORTNIGHTLY: *a biweekly magazine* **b** twice a week; SEMIWEEKLY

bi·zarre /bɪˈzɑːr/ adj noticeably odd or strange: *his bizarre appearance/behaviour* | *This is one of the most bizarre murder cases we have ever dealt with.* — ~ **ly** adv

BL /ˌbiːˈel/ BRITISH LEYLAND

blab /blæb/ v **-bb-** [I] infml to tell a secret, esp. about criminal activity, sometimes unintentionally

blab·ber /ˈblæbər/ v [I (ON)] infml to talk foolishly or too much: *I wish she'd stop blabbering (on) about her boyfriends.*

blab·ber·mouth /ˈblæbəmaʊθ‖-ər-/ n derog sl a person who tells secrets by talking too much

black¹ /blæk/ adj 1 of the colour of night; completely without light: *black shoes* | *black clouds* | *her thick black hair* | (fig.) *Go wash your hands — they're black!* (=very dirty) 2 **a** (of a person) of a dark-skinned race, esp. of the Negro race: *a black American* **b** of or for black people: *black Africa* | *He's trying to win the black vote.* —see USAGE; compare WHITE¹ (3) 3 (of coffee) without milk or cream: *I'll have my coffee black, please.* —opposite **white** 4 very bad, threatening, or hopeless: *According to the latest sales figures, things look very black for us.* | *black despair* | *She painted a black picture of the company's prospects.* —see also BLACK COMEDY, BLACK HUMOUR 5 full of anger, hate, or evil: *He gave me a black look.* | (lit) *a black-hearted villain* | (lit) *his black deeds* 6 esp. BrE not approved of, or not to be handled, by members of a trade union during a STRIKE: *a black cargo* | *black labour* 7 **any colour so long as it's black** quote a phrase used by Henry Ford when he was asked what colours were available for a particular kind of car 8 **not as black as one is painted** not as bad as people say one is —see also BLACKLY, BLACK AND WHITE, PITCH BLACK — ~ **ness** n [U]

▷ USAGE Compare **black**, **coloured**, and **Negro**. **Black** is the word which is preferred by many black people. **Coloured** and, esp., **Negro** are now considered by many black people to be offensive. In the US, many black people prefer to be called **African-Americans** in formal situations such as in newspapers or government statements.◁

black² n 1 [U] the colour that is black; the darkest colour: *After her husband died, she dressed in black for a year.* | *Put some more black (=black colouring) round your eyes.*

▶ CULTURAL NOTE Black is often thought of as the colour of evil and death. People wear black clothes to show grief at a person's death.◀

2 [C] a person of a dark-skinned race: *There were both blacks and whites at the meeting.* 3 **in the black** having money in a bank account: *Our account is (nicely) in the black this month.* —opposite **in the red**

black³ v [T] 1 to make black: *to black shoes* | *to black* someone's eye by hitting them **2** *BrE* (esp. of a trade union) to refuse to work with (goods, a company, etc.): *They've blacked his ships because he refuses to recognize the union.*

black out *v* **1** [T](**black** sthg. ↔ **out**) to darken so that no light is seen: *During the war the cities were all blacked out.* | *The whole country was blacked out because of the power strike.* **2** [I] to lose consciousness; faint: *After the accident he blacked out and couldn't remember what happened.* **3** [T](**black** sthg. ↔ **out**) prevent (news or information) from becoming publicly known; SUP-PRESS: *They blacked out all reports of the anti-government demonstration.* | (fig.) *He blacked the terrible accident out of his mind.* —see also BLACKOUT

Black, Cil·la /ˈsɪlə/ (1943–) an English popular music singer and entertainer from Liverpool, successful as a singer in the 1960s, now best known in Britain as the presenter of the television show *Blind Date*

black·a·moor /ˈblækəmʊəʳ/ *n old use or humor, derog* a black person, esp. a man

black and blue /ˌ· · ˈ·◂/ *adj* (having the skin) darkly dis-coloured as the result of being hit, esp. repeatedly; bruised (BRUISE): *After the fight, he was black and blue all over.*

Black and Tans /ˌ· · ˈ·/ *n* [the +P] a British government military force named after the colours of their uniforms, formed to oppose the Irish organization Sinn Fein (1918–20)

black and white /ˌ· · ˈ·◂/ *n* [U] **1** the showing of pictures in black, white, and grey, without additional colours: *an old film in black and white* | *a black-and-white television* **2** *usu. derog* a too simple way of explaining events, in which people or things are regarded as either completely good or completely bad: *She sees the situation very much in black and white terms, but in fact it's much more com-plicated than that.* **3 in black and white** in writing: *I want this agreement in black and white.*

black art /ˌ· ˈ·/ also **black arts** *pl.*– *n* [the] BLACK MAGIC

black·ball /ˈblækbɔːl/ *v* [T] to vote against (a person who wants to join a club)

Black Beau·ty /ˌ· ˈ··/ the name of a horse, the central character of a book of the same name, by Anna Sewell, written in 1877, and later filmed and made into a televi-sion programme

black belt /ˈ· ˌ·/ *n* (a person who holds) a high rank in the practice of certain types of Eastern self-defence, esp. JUDO and KARATE —compare DAN

black·ber·ry /ˈblækbəri‖-beri/ *n* the black or purple berry of a type of BRAMBLE: *blackberry jam* —see picture at BERRY — ~**ing** *n* [U]: *to go blackberrying* (=picking blackberries)

black·bird /ˈblækbɜːd‖-bɜːrd/ *n* a common European and American bird of which the male is completely black

black·board /ˈblækbɔːd‖-bɔːrd/ also **chalkboard** *AmE*– *n* a dark smooth surface (usu. black or green) used esp. in schools for writing or drawing on, usu. with chalk —compare WHITEBOARD

black box /ˌ· ˈ·/ *n* a FLIGHT RECORDER

Black·burn /ˈblækbɜːn‖-bɜːrn/ a town in Lancashire, NW England, known for its engineering and making of TEXTILES

black com·e·dy /ˌ· ˈ···/ *n* [C;U] (an amusing play, story, etc. based on) BLACK HUMOUR

Black Coun·try /ˈ· ˌ··/ [the] an industrial area in the West Midlands of England

black cow /ˌ· ˈ·/ *n* also **root beer float** *AmE old-fash* a drink made with ice cream and ROOT BEER: *Two black cows, please.*

black·cur·rant /ˌblækˈkʌrənt◂‖-ˈkɜːr-/ *n* a European garden fruit with small round blue-black berries: *blackcurrant jelly*

Black Death /ˌ· ˈ·/ *n* [the] the illness (probably BUBONIC PLAGUE) that killed large numbers of people in Europe and Asia in the 14th century. In Britain the Black Death is connected with the men who went round the streets to collect the dead bodies calling out "Bring out your dead!".

black e·con·o·my /ˌ· ·ˈ···/ *n* [the] business activity that is

carried on unofficially, esp. in order to avoid taxation: *the recent growth in the black economy* —compare BLACK MARKET

black·en /ˈblækən/ *v* [I;T] to make or become black or dark: *The sky blackened as the rainclouds approached.* | *The smoke had blackened the white walls of the kitchen.* | (fig.) *false accusations that blackened her good name*

black En·glish /ˌ· ˈ··/ *n* [U] the variety of English that is spoken by some black Americans and by some black British people in the US

black eye /ˌ· ˈ·/ *n* darkness of the skin round the eye as a result of being hit: *If he says that again I'll give him a black eye.*

black-eyed pea /ˌ· · ˈ·/ also **cowpea, black-eyed bean** *BrE*– *n AmE* (a plant which produces) a small bean with a black spot on it

black·face /ˈblækfeɪs/ *n* [U] a colouring of a white person's face so that they look black, used formerly by some en-tertainers, esp. in VAUDEVILLE: *Al Jolson used to appear in blackface when he sang "Mammy".*

Black·foot /ˈblækfʊt/ *n* [C; the+P] -**foot** or -**feet** (a member of) a Native American people living mainly in Montana and Alberta who were famous for their horses —see also NATIVE AMERICAN (CULTURAL NOTE)

Black For·est /ˌ· ˈ···◂/ **1** [the] an area of SW Germany popular for holidays **2** *n* [C;U] a cake (GATEAU) made of chocolate, black cherries (CHERRY), and cream

Black Forest gateau

black·guard /ˈblægɑːd, -əd‖-ərd, -ɑːrd/ *n old use or humor* a man of completely dis-honourable character; SCOUNDREL: *You blackguard!*

black·head /ˈblækhed/ *n* a small spot on the skin with a black centre

Black Hills /ˌ· ˈ·/ [the] a RANGE¹ (6) of hills in South Dakota where Mount Rushmore was carved

black hole /ˌ· ˈ·/ *n* **1** *tech* an area in outer space into which everything near it, including light itself, is pulled **2** a place which seems to pull something, esp. money, into it **3** a crowded enclosed space with too little room or air

Black Hole of Cal·cut·ta /ˌ· · ˌ· · ˈ··/ [the] a small room used as a prison in Calcutta, India. In 1756, 146 British people were put into the room, and most of them died in one night.

black hu·mour /ˌ· ˈ··/ *n* [U] humour dealing with the un-pleasant side of human life —see also BLACK COMEDY

black ice /ˌ· ˈ·/ *n* [U] hard slippery ice that does not appear different from the surface of the road it covers: *Black ice made the roads extremely dangerous.*

black·ing /ˈblækɪŋ/ *n* [U] a substance, such as a very thick liquid or polish, that is put on an object to make it black

black·ish /ˈblækɪʃ/ *adj* slightly black

black·jack /ˈblækdʒæk/ *n* **1** [U] also **pontoon** *BrE* ‖ **twenty-one** *AmE*– a card game, usu. played for money **2** [C] *AmE for* COSH¹ **3** [C] *AmE for* TRUNCHEON

black lead /ˌblæk ˈled/ *n* [U] a black mineral substance, GRAPHITE

black·leg /ˈblækleg/ *n BrE derog* someone who continues to work when their fellow workers are on STRIKE; SCAB (3) —compare STRIKEBREAKER —**blackleg** *v* [I] -**gg**-

black·list /ˈblækˌlɪst/ *n* a list of people, groups, countries, etc., who are disapproved of for some reason and are to be avoided or punished in some way: *He was on a black-list because of his sporting connections with South Africa.*

▶CULTURAL NOTE In the US during the 1940s and '50s, during the McCarthy period, many people in the film indus-try were put on an unofficial blacklist and could not get work because they were thought to be or admitted being COM-MUNISTS. —see also McCARTHYISM —**blacklist** *v* [T]: *black-listed for non-payment of debts*◀

black lung /ˈ· ˌ·/ *n* [U] *AmE* a lung disease of people who work in coal mines, caused by breathing in coal dust over a long period of time —compare SILICOSIS

black·ly /ˈblækli/ *adv* angrily or threateningly

black mag·ic /ˌ· ˈ··/ n [U] magic believed to be done with the help of evil spirits and used for evil purposes — compare WHITE MAGIC

Black Magic tdmk the name of a kind of plain chocolates sold in Britain in a black box

black·mail /ˈblækmeɪl/ n [U] **1** the practice of obtaining money or advantage by threatening to make known unpleasant facts about a person or group —compare HUSH MONEY **2** the influencing of someone's actions by threats, causing anxiety, etc.: *He accused his mother of using emotional blackmail to stop him leaving home.* —**blackmail** v [T (**into**)]: *Don't think you can blackmail me (into doing that).* — ~ **er** n

Black Ma·ri·a /ˌblæk məˈraɪə/ BrE ‖ usu. **police wagon**, **paddy wagon** AmE— n sl a vehicle used by the police to carry prisoners

black mar·ket /ˌ· ˈ··◂/ n [S] the buying and selling of goods, foreign money, etc., when such trade is not legal: *They bought dollars on the black market.* | *black-market butter* | *There's quite a big black market in foreign currency.* —compare BLACK ECONOMY

black mar·ket·eer /ˌ· ···ˈ·/ n a person who sells things on the black market

Black Mass /ˌ· ˈ·/ n a ceremony in which worshippers of the devil use forms like those of Christian worship

Black Mon·day /ˌ· ˈ··/ Monday 19 October 1987, the day on which share prices on STOCK EXCHANGES (1) all over the word fell suddenly and steeply

Black·more /ˈblækmɔːʳ/, **R D** (1825–1890) an English writer best known for his book *Lorna Doone*, a historical story which takes place on Exmoor, in Devon

Black Mus·lim /ˌ· ˈ··/ n a member of a group of black people who believe in the religion of Islam and want the establishment of a separate black society

black·out /ˈblækaʊt/ n **1** a period of darkness ordered by the government during wartime or caused by a failure of the electric power supply **2** a loss of consciousness for a short time: *She had a blackout after the accident and couldn't remember what had happened.* **3** a sudden turning off of stage lighting during a play **4** an intentional prevention of the reporting of certain facts: *The government imposed a news blackout on all information about the accident at the nuclear power station.* —see also BLACK out

Black Pan·thers /ˌ· ˈ··/ also **Black Panther Par·ty** /ˌ· ˈ·· ˌ··/ fml— a group of American black people in the 1960s and '70s who supported violent ways of obtaining changes in the law and better treatment for black people

black pep·per /ˌ· ˈ··/ n [U] PEPPER made from crushed seeds from which the dark outer covering has not been removed

Black·pool /ˈblækpuːl/ a town on the NW coast of England, a popular place for people, esp. WORKING-CLASS people, to go for the day or for a holiday. Blackpool is famous for its TOWER (the **Blackpool Tower**) and ILLUMINATIONS (=attractive coloured lights). It also has an important CONFERENCE centre. —see colour map on page 818

black pow·er /ˌ· ˈ··/ n [U] (*often cap.*) (a political movement in favour of) the belief that in any country black people should have a share of political and ECONOMIC power which is in accordance with the number of black people in that country

Black Prince /ˌ· ˈ·/, **Edward the** (1330–76) the oldest son of King Edward III of England, who wore black ARMOUR (1) in battle

black pud·ding /ˌ· ˈ··/ n [C;U] BrE a kind of thick dark-coloured SAUSAGE, made of animal blood and fat, and grain. It is usu. cut into SLICES and cooked in fat. Black pudding is connected in people's minds with the N of England, where it is popular, esp. with WORKING-CLASS people.

Black Rod /ˌ· ˈ·/ the name of the official who goes to the House of Commons to bring the members to the House of Lords for the Queen's speech at the opening of the British Parliament every year

Black Sea /ˌ· ˈ·/ [the] a large sea in SE Europe, connected to the Mediterranean by the Dardanelles and the Bosporus

black sheep /ˌ· ˈ·/ n **black sheep** someone who is thought by other members of their group to be a failure or to have brought shame on the group: *the black sheep of the family*

Black·shirt /ˈblækʃɜːt‖-ʃɜːrt/ n a member of a FASCIST organization having a black shirt as part of its uniform (from the Italian Fascist Party before the Second World War, whose members wore black shirts)

black·smith /ˈblæksmɪθ/ also **smith**— n a metalworker who makes and repairs things made of iron, esp. horseshoes

black spot /ˈ· ·/ n esp. BrE **1** a part of a road where many accidents have happened **2** any place or area of serious trouble or difficulties: *The city is one of Britain's worst unemployment black spots.*

black·strap mo·las·ses /ˌblækstræp məˈlæsᵻz/ n [U] AmE a very dark MOLASSES (thick liquid produced from sugar plants) from which most of the sugar has been removed

black-tie /ˌ· ˈ·◂/ adj (of parties and other social occasions) at which people wear EVENING DRESS (a DINNER JACKET and a black BOW TIE for men): *a black-tie dinner-dance* —see picture at EVENING DRESS, and compare WHITE-TIE

black·top /ˈblæktɒp‖-tɑːp/ n AmE **1** the black substance used to cover roads, car parks, playgrounds, etc.; TARMAC **2** the area covered by this substance: *The children were playing kickball on the blacktop.*

Black Watch /ˌ· ˈ·/ [the] the common name for the Royal Highland Regiment, a REGIMENT (=large division of men) in the British army

black·wa·ter fe·ver /ˌblækwɔːtə ˈfiːvəʳ‖-wɔːtər-, -wɑː-/ n [U] a very severe form of the disease MALARIA, esp. in W Africa

black wid·ow /ˌ· ˈ··/ n a very poisonous type of SPIDER

blad·der /ˈblædəʳ/ n **1** a bag of skin inside the body of a person or animal, in which waste liquid collects before it is passed out **2** a bag of skin, leather, or rubber (such as the rubber bag inside a football) which can be filled with air or liquid

blade /bleɪd/ n **1** the flat cutting part of a knife, sword, etc.: *The blade needs sharpening.* | *a packet of razor blades* —see pictures at RAZOR, SWORD, and TOOL **2** the flat wide part of an OAR, a PROPELLER, a BAT, etc. **3** a long flat leaf of grass or a grasslike plant: *a blade of wheat* **4** old-fash an amusing irresponsible man —see also SHOULDER BLADE

blah¹ /blɑː/ adj AmE infml dull; colourless; without strong taste: *a blah stew of vegetables* | *The inside of the house was pretty blah.* (=the decoration was uninteresting)

blah² n [U] **1** BrE sl empty talk; nonsense: *the usual blah about everybody working harder* **2** **blah, blah, blah** (used to show that more was said but that it was uninteresting) and so on: *He talked about boats and sailing blah, blah, blah.*

Blair /bleəʳ/, **Li·o·nel** /ˈlaɪənəl/ (1934–) an English dancer and choreographer (CHOREOGRAPH), born in Canada, now known as a television personality

Blake /bleɪk/, **William** (1757–1827) an English poet and artist whose best known collections of poems are *Songs of Innocence* and *Songs of Experience*

blame¹ /bleɪm/ v [T] **1** to consider (someone or something) responsible for (something bad): *Don't blame me if it doesn't work — it's not my fault.* [+obj+on] *They blamed the failure of the talks on the Russians.* [+obj+for] *They blamed the Russians for the failure of the talks.* | *They blamed the rise in oil prices for the big increase in inflation.* | *If he fails the exam he's only got himself to blame.* (=it is his fault and no one else's) **2** to find fault with: *Critics blamed the documentary for its one-sided presentation of the situation.* | *"She's left her husband." "I don't blame her* (=I quite understand her feelings/agree with her action), *after the way he treated her."* **3 be to blame (for)** to be at fault or be guilty (of): *The children were not to blame for the accident.*

blame² n [U (**for**)] responsibility for something bad: *The judge laid/put the blame for the accident on the driver of the car.* | *We were ready to take/bear the blame for what had happened.* | *It is the job of the committee to discover the cause of the accident, not to apportion blame.*

blame·less /ˈbleɪmləs/ adj free from guilt or blame; INNOCENT: *a blameless life* — ~ **ly** adv — ~ **ness** n [U]

blame·wor·thy /ˈbleɪmˌwɜːði‖-ɜːr-/ adj fml deserving blame or disapproval: *blameworthy behaviour* —**thiness** n [U]

blanch /blɑːntʃ‖blæntʃ/ v 1 [T] to make (a plant or plant product) colourless by keeping it out of the light: *blanched celery* 2 [I] to become white or pale with fear, cold, etc.: *He blanched with shock.* 3 [T] to put (a fruit or vegetable) into very hot water for a short time, esp. in order to remove the skin more easily: *blanched almonds in a cake|Blanch the peaches and remove the skins before slicing them into the jar.*

blanc·mange /bləˈmɒnʒ, -ˈmɒndʒ‖-ˈmɑː-/ n [C;U] a sweet dish consisting of a cold solid mixture of CORNFLOUR, sugar, milk, and other sweet foods

bland /blænd/ adj 1 (of food) without much taste: *This soup is too bland for me.* 2 (of people or their behaviour) showing no strong feelings or opinions or other noticeable qualities, esp. so as to avoid causing trouble or giving offence: *the radio station's bland coverage of the election campaign* – –**ly** adv – –**ness** n [U]

blan·dish·ments /ˈblændɪʃmənts/ n [P] FLATTERY intended to persuade or influence a person, esp. to do something wrong: *She resisted his blandishments.*

blank¹ /blæŋk/ adj 1 without writing, print, or other marks: *a blank page | Please write your name in the blank space at the top of the page. | If you press this key the screen will go blank. | a blank cassette* (=with nothing recorded on it) 2 empty or expressionless; without understanding or interest: *I tried to explain, but he just gave me a blank look. | My mind went completely blank and I forgot what I was supposed to be doing.* – –**ly** adv – –**ness** n [U]

blank² n 1 an empty space: *Fill in all the blanks on the form.* | (fig.) *When I tried to remember his name, my mind was a complete blank.* 2 a BLANK CARTRIDGE –see also **draw a blank** (DRAW¹)

blank car·tridge /ˌ· ˈ··/ n a CARTRIDGE that contains an explosive but no bullet

blank cheque BrE ‖ **blank check** AmE /ˌ· ˈ·/ n 1 a cheque signed and given to someone to write in whatever amount they want to receive 2 *infml* complete freedom to take whatever action one believes to be necessary to gain a result; CARTE BLANCHE: [+to-v] *She was given a blank cheque to get the company back on its feet.*

blan·ket¹ /ˈblæŋkɪt/ n 1 a thick usu. woollen covering used esp. on beds 2 [(of)] a thick covering: *The valley was covered with a blanket of mist/snow.* –see also WET BLANKET

blanket² v [T (with)] usu. pass.] to cover as if with a blanket: *The country was blanketed with snow.*

blanket³ adj [A] including all cases, classes, or possible events; unlimited: *a blanket rule | a blanket ban on smoking throughout the building*

blankety-blank /ˌblæŋkˌti ˈblæŋk◂/ adj [A] AmE euph infml for DAMN¹: *The blankety-blank key is stuck!*

blank verse /ˌ· ˈ·/ n [U] poetry that does not RHYME: *Most of Shakespeare's plays are written in blank verse.*

blare /bleəʳ/ v [I;T (OUT)] (of a horn or other loud sound-producing instrument) to produce (sounds) loudly and unpleasantly: *The radio blared out (the news). | blaring car horns/sirens* –**blare** n [S] : *the blare of a brass band*

blar·ney /ˈblɑːni‖-ɑːr-/ n [U] infml pleasant talk intended to persuade or deceive; FLATTERY

Blarney Stone /ˈ·· ˌ·/ [the] a stone in the wall of Blarney Castle in Ireland, which is supposed to bring good luck and skill in FLATTERY to people who kiss it

bla·sé /ˈblɑːzeɪ‖blɑːˈzeɪ/ adj seeming not to be concerned, worried, or excited about something or about things in general: *The pop star is very blasé about money now.*

blas·pheme /blæsˈfiːm/ v [I (against);T] to speak without respect for or use bad language about (God or religious matters): *blaspheming (against) God* – –**phemer** n

blas·phe·my /ˈblæsfɪmi/ n [C;U (against)] (an example of) disrespectful or bad language about God or holy things: *Their conversation was full of blasphemies. | What you're saying is blasphemy!*

▶ CULTURAL NOTE In Britain it is against the law to produce books or films which contain blasphemy against the Christian religion. Many people now think that this law is out of date and should either be got rid of, or changed to cover other religions in Britain. –compare SACRILEGE –**mous** adj : *a blasphemous suggestion* –**mously** adv◀

blast¹ /blɑːst‖blæst/ n 1 [C] a sudden strong movement of wind or air: *the icy blast(s) of the north wind* 2 [C] an explosion: *Police say that the blast occurred at 3 p.m.* 3 [U] the very powerful rush of air caused by an explosion, esp. by a NUCLEAR explosion: *Enormous numbers of people would be killed by blast.* 4 [C] the loud sound of a brass musical instrument: *He blew several loud blasts on his horn.* 5 AmE infml an enjoyable party with many guests: *a beer blast* 6 [U;a] AmE infml an enjoyable and exciting experience: *We had a blast at the fair. | The bicycle trip was a real blast.* 7 **(at) full blast** as hard or as fast as possible; at full power: *We're working (at) full blast to complete the order before the holidays. | a car going at full blast down the motorway*

blast² v 1 [I;T+obj+adv/prep] to break up (esp. rock) by explosions: *The road is closed because of blasting.* | *to blast away the face of the rock | They're blasting a tunnel through the mountain.* 2 [T] to attack with explosives: *The planes blasted the port.* 3 [T] lit to cause to dry up and die, esp. by great heat or cold, or by lightning: *Every green thing was blasted by the icy breath of winter. | a blasted oak* (=struck by lightning) | (fig.) *The news blasted* (=destroyed) *our hopes.* 4 [I;T] (used to express annoyance) DAMN: *Blast you! | Oh, blast! | Get that blasted dog out of here!*

blast off phr v [I] (of a spacecraft) to leave the ground; take off –see also BLAST-OFF

blast fur·nace /ˈ· ˌ··/ n a very tall steel container in which iron is separated from iron ORE by the action of heat and air blown through at great pressure

blast-off /ˈ· ·/ n [U] the moment when a spacecraft takes off; TAKEOFF: *ten seconds to blast-off* –see also BLAST **off**

bla·tant /ˈbleɪtənt/ adj shameless; offensively noticeable: *his blatant disregard for the law | blatant disobedience/discrimination* – –**ly** adv –**tancy** n [U]

blath·er /ˈblæðəʳ/ n BLETHER

blaze¹ /bleɪz/ n 1 [S] (the sudden sharp shooting up of) a bright flame: *The fire burned slowly at first, but soon burst into a blaze.* | (fig.) *In a blaze of anger she shouted at them.* 2 [C] a big dangerous fire: *The firemen were unable to control the blaze.* 3 [S (of)] a bright show (of lights, colours, etc.): *The garden was a blaze of reds and yellows.* | (fig.) *The new car was launched in a blaze of publicity.* [S (of)] a rapid continuous firing of a gun: *a blaze of machinegun fire* –see also ABLAZE, BLAZES

blaze² v 1 [I] to (begin to) burn with a bright flame: *A wood fire was blazing (away) in the hearth, but there was no other light in the room. | They fled from the blazing house.* | (fig.) *eyes blazing with anger* | (fig.) *Lights were blazing in every room.* | (fig.) *a blazing row* 2 [I (AWAY)] to fire guns rapidly and continuously: *blazing away at the enemy* 3 [T+obj+adv/prep; usu. pass.] to make (news) widely known: *The news was blazed in great headlines across the tops of the daily papers.* 4 **blaze a trail: a** to make marks along a TRAIL (=path) for others to follow **b** to lead the way, esp. in some new development or activity: *The company has blazed a trail with its innovative use of robots in manufacturing.*

blaze³ n a white mark, esp. one down the front of a horse's nose

blaz·er /ˈbleɪzəʳ/ n a loose-fitting JACKET sometimes with the special sign of a school, club, etc. on it: *a school blazer*

blaz·es /ˈbleɪzɪz/ n old-fash infml (used for adding force to expressions of extreme annoyance): *Go to blazes! | What the blazes do you think you're doing?*

bla·zon /ˈbleɪzən/ n a COAT OF ARMS

blazon² v [T] 1 [(OUT, FORTH)] to declare loudly and publicly 2 [(on, with)] to EMBLAZON

bleach¹ /bliːtʃ/ v [T] to cause to become white or pale, esp. by means of chemicals or by the action of sunlight: *to bleach handkerchiefs | hair bleached by the sun*

bleach² n [U] a chemical used in bleaching: *My shirt was so dirty that I had to use bleach on it.*

bleach·ers /ˈbliːtʃəz‖-ərz/ n [the+P] AmE cheap unroofed seats arranged in rows of different heights and used for watching a sport: *sitting in the bleachers on a hot summer day*

bleak /bliːk/ adj 1 cold and cheerless: *a bleak January day, with a cold wind and grey skies | a bleak hillside struck by the full force of the east wind | They showed me into a bleak waiting room with plain walls and a few* *uncomfortable-looking chairs.* —see also IN THE BLEAK MID-WINTER **2** not hopeful or encouraging; DEPRESSING: *The company's prospects look pretty bleak.* | *The outlook for borrowers is bleak, as interest rates are certain to rise.* —~ly *adv*

Bleak House /ˌ·ˈ·/ the title of a book by Charles Dickens, written in 1852–53

blear·y /ˈblɪəri/ *adj* (esp. of eyes) red and unable to see well because of tiredness, tears, etc.: *A bad cold has made him bleary-eyed.* —·ily *adv*: *He crawled blearily out of bed.* —·iness *n* [U]

Bleas·dale /ˈbliːzdeɪl/, **Al·an** /ˈælən/ (1946–) an English writer of plays for television and theatre, best known for his television SERIES *Boys from the Blackstuff* and *GBH*

bleat¹ /bliːt/ *v* [I] **1** to make the sound of a sheep, goat, or CALF **2** *infml* to complain, esp. in a weak, shaking voice; WHINE: *As usual, the opposition are bleating about unfair coverage by the media.*

bleat² *n* [usu. sing.] the sound made by a sheep, goat, or CALF

bleed /bliːd/ *v* **bled** /bled/ **1** [I] to lose blood: *Your nose is bleeding.* | *He lay on the floor, bleeding profusely.* | (fig.)**My heart bleeds for** (=I feel very sorry for) *those poor children.* **2** [T] *infml* to make (someone) pay too much money; EXTORT money from: *He bled them for every penny they'd got.* | *They* **bled us white** (*BrE*) **'bled us dry** (*AmE*) (=took all our money). **3** [T] to draw blood from, as doctors did in former times to treat diseases **4** [T] to draw off liquid or air from (a machine or apparatus) in order to make it work properly: *to bleed the radiators in a central heating system* | *to bleed the brakes on a car*

bleed·er /ˈbliːdəʳ/ *n* **1** *BrE sl* a person one does not like: *I told that bleeder not to come here again!* **2** *BrE sl* any person: *You lucky bleeder!* **3** *AmE infml* HEMOPHILIAC

bleed·ing /ˈbliːdɪŋ/ *adj* [A] *BrE sl* (used for giving force to an expression, esp. of annoyance) BLOODY²: *What a bleeding waste of time!*

bleeding heart lib·e·ral /ˌ··· ·ˈ···/ also **bleeding heart**— *n AmE derog* a person who wants to help other people, esp. socially and politically, but who is not very practical and sometimes behaves as though they were better than the people they are trying to help

bleep¹ /bliːp/ *n* a high, usu. repeated, sound sent out by a machine to attract someone's attention —compare BLIP

bleep² *v* **1** [I] to send out bleeps **2** [T] *BrE infml* to call (someone) using a bleeper: *They're bleeping you, doctor.* **3** [T (OUT)] *infml* to prevent (a word or words) from being heard on television or radio with bleeps: *The obscene words in the song were bleeped (out).*

bleep·er /ˈbliːpəʳ/ *BrE* ‖ **beeper, pager** *AmE*— *n* a small machine which can be carried in a pocket, fastened to clothing, etc. and which bleeps when the attention of the person wearing it is needed

blem·ish¹ /ˈblemɪʃ/ *v* [T] to spoil the beauty or perfection of: *His reputation was blemished by a newspaper article alleging he'd evaded his taxes.* —see also UNBLEMISHED

blemish² *n* something that spoils perfection: *The wine glasses were sold at half price because of blemishes in the crystal.*

blench /blentʃ/ *v* [I] to make a sudden movement in fear; RECOIL

blend¹ /blend/ *v* **1** [T] to mix together thoroughly, esp. so that the different parts can no longer be separated: *Blend the sugar, flour, and eggs (together).* | *Blend the flour into the eggs and sugar.* —see MIX(USAGE) **2** [T] to produce (tea, coffee, WHISKY, etc.) out of a mixture of several varieties: *blended whisky* **3** [I (IN, into, with)] to become combined, esp. so as to produce a pleasing effect; HARMONIZE: *Their voices blend well with each other.* | *These houses seem to blend into the countryside.* | *The house blends in well with its surroundings.*

blend² *n* something produced by blending: *a good blend of coffee* | *His speech to the staff was a judicious blend of optimism and caution.*

blend·er /ˈblendəʳ/ also **liquidizer** *BrE*— *n* a small electric machine used in the kitchen for making solid foods into soups, juices, etc. —see picture at KITCHEN

Blen·heim Pal·ace /ˌblenɪm ˈpælɪs/ a large country house in Oxfordshire owned by the Marlborough family, opened to the public at certain times

bless /bles/ *v* **blessed** *or* **blest** /blest/ [T] **1** to ask God's favour or protection for: *The priest blessed the new ship.* **2** to make or call holy: *The priest blessed the bread and wine.* | *Bless the name of the Lord!* **3** *old-fash* (in expressions of good-humoured surprise): *Bless me! He's won again!* | *Well, I'm blessed!* —compare DAMN⁴ (2) **4 be blessed with** to be lucky enough to have: *I've always been blessed with good health.* **5 Bless you!** (used when someone has sneezed (SNEEZE))

bless·ed /ˈblesɪd/ *adj* **1** holy; favoured by God: *the* **Blessed Virgin** (=the mother of Christ) | *Blessed are the peacemakers.* **2** [A] bringing happiness; desirable: *a few moments of blessed silence* **3** [A] *infml* (used to give force to expressions of annoyance): *It pours with rain every blessed time I go out.* —~ly *adv* —~ness *n* [U]

bless·ing /ˈblesɪŋ/ *n* **1** [C (**on, upon**)] an act of asking or receiving God's favour, help, or protection: *The blessing of the Lord be upon you all.* | *to ask a blessing* (=say a prayer of thanks to God) *before a meal* **2** [C] a gift from God or anything that brings happiness or good fortune: *When you feel sad,* **count your blessings.** (=remember how lucky you are) | *It was a blessing that no one was injured.* | *This rain will be a blessing for the farmers.* **3** [U] *infml* approval or encouragement: *The government has given its blessing to the new plan.* | *Do you think this was done with the President's blessing?* **4 a blessing in disguise** something that seems unpleasant but is really a good thing after all: *The storm was a blessing in disguise because it kept us at home when you phoned.* —see also MIXED BLESSING

bleth·er /ˈbleðəʳ/ also **blather**— *v* [I (ON)] *esp. ScotE & NEngE* to talk for a long time, esp. foolishly or untruthfully; CHATTER —**blether** *n* [C;U]

blew /bluː/ *v* past tense of BLOW

Bligh /blaɪ/, **Captain William** (1754–?1817) a British naval officer who was in command of the ship *HMS Bounty* when the men mutinied (MUTINY) —see also MUTINY ON THE BOUNTY

blight¹ /blaɪt/ *n* **1** [U] a disease of plants that results in the drying up and dying of the diseased parts **2** [C] something that causes annoyance, unhappiness, or destruction: *The accident* **cast a blight** *on our happiness.* **3** [U] a condition of ugliness, disorder, and decay: *the growing problem of inner-city blight*

blight² *v* [T] to infect or spoil with blight: *blighted fruit trees* | (fig.) *Her life was blighted by ill health.* | *blighted hopes*

blight·er /ˈblaɪtəʳ/ *n BrE old-fash sl* **1** a person, esp. a man, one does not like: *I told that blighter not to come here again!* **2** any person: *You lucky blighter!* | *Poor little blighter!*

bli·mey /ˈblaɪmi/ *interj BrE sl* (used for expressing surprise)

blimp /blɪmp/ *n* a small AIRSHIP

Blimp *n* see COLONEL BLIMP

blind¹ /blaɪnd/ *adj* **1** unable to see: *blind from birth* | *blind in one eye* [also *n, the*+P] *a special library service for the blind* —see BLIND² (USAGE), and see also COLOUR-BLIND **2** [A] intended for blind people: *a blind school* **3** [F (**to**)] unable or unwilling to recognize or understand (something bad): *They seem to be blind to the possible consequences of this policy.* | *He is blind to her faults.* **4** without thought, judgment, or reason: *blind haste|anger* | *in a blind panic* | *blind faith| loyalty* **5** operating without purpose or human control: *the blind forces of nature* **6** done wholly by using instruments within an aircraft and without looking outside: *blind flying* | *flying blind* | *a blind landing* **7** at or in which it is difficult to see: *a dangerous blind corner|turning* **8** [A] *BrE sl* (used to add force to an expression) slightest: *I tried to warn her, but*

blinds

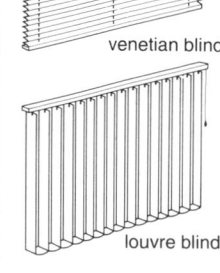

roller blind

venetian blind

louvre blind

she didn't take a blind bit of notice. | *It doesn't make a blind bit of difference.* **9 (as) blind as a bat** *infml* having difficulty in seeing: *I'm as blind as a bat without my glasses.* **10 (a case of) the blind leading the blind** people with little information advising people with even less **11 turn a blind eye (to)** to pretend not to see or notice (something, esp. something illegal): *You shouldn't really drink here, but I'm willing to turn a blind eye (to it).* —see also **effing and blinding** (EFF), and compare **turn a deaf ear to** (DEAF) — **~ly** *adv* — **~ness** *n* [U]

blind² *v* [T] **1** to make unable to see, either for a time or for ever: *The glare of the headlights blinded me for a moment.* | *blinded by the smoke* | *The soldier was blinded in battle.* | *blinded in one eye* | *a blinding flash of light* **2** [(to)] to make unable to notice or understand; take away the good sense or judgment of: *His determination blinded him to all the difficulties.* | *blinded by emotion* **3 blind with science** to confuse or fill with admiration by a show of detailed or specialist knowledge

▷ USAGE **Blinded** and **deafened** are used when we mention a particular event in which a person becomes blind or deaf: *He was blinded by dust/blinded in the war.* | *The music was so loud I was nearly deafened.* For describing a state use the adjectives **blind, deaf**: *He became blind.* | *a deaf child.*◁

blind³ *n* **1** also **window shade** *AmE*— a piece of cloth or other material, which can usu. be rolled or folded up for covering a window —see picture at KITCHEN, and see also ROLLER BLIND, VENETIAN BLIND **2** a way of hiding the truth by giving a false idea: *His newspaper job was only a blind for his real business, which was receiving stolen goods.* **3** *esp. AmE* a hidden place from which to watch animals, esp. when hunting; HIDE³

blind al·ley /ˌ· ˈ··/ *n* a little narrow street with no way out at the other end: *trapped in a blind alley* | (fig.) *We tried one idea after another, but they all seemed to be blind alleys.*

blind date /ˌ· ˈ·/ *n infml* a social meeting (DATE) between a boy and a girl who have not met before

Blind Date the title of a popular British television programme in which Cilla Black introduces people who choose an unseen partner for a blind date according to their answers to three less than serious questions. The two people usu. go away for a weekend together and then give an account of their experiences on a later programme.

blind drunk /ˌ· ˈ·/ *adj* [F] *BrE sl* extremely drunk

blind·ers /ˈblaɪndəz‖-ərz/ *n* [P] *AmE for* BLINKERS

blind·fold¹ /ˈblaɪndfəʊld/ *n* a piece of cloth that covers the eyes to prevent seeing

blindfold² *v* [T] to put a blindfold on: *The prisoner was blindfolded.*

blindfold³ *BrE* ‖ **blindfolded** *AmE*— *adv* with a blindfold over one's eyes: *I could do it blindfold.*

blind man's buff /ˌ· · ˈ·/ also **blindman's bluff** *AmE*— *n* [U] a children's game in which one child, whose eyes are covered with a blindfold, tries to catch the others

blind spot /ˈ· ·/ *n* **1** the point in the eye where the nerve enters, which is not sensitive to light **2** a place or an area that cannot be seen easily, esp. the part of the road slightly behind and to the side of the driver of a car **3** something that one is unable and perhaps unwilling to understand: *I have a blind spot where computers are concerned.*

blink¹ /blɪŋk/ *v* **1** [I;T] to shut and open (the eyes) quickly, once or several times: *She blinked (her eyes) as the bright light shone on her.* | *He blinked away his tears.* | (fig.) *She didn't even blink* (=show any surprise) *when I told her how much it would cost.* **2** [I] (of distant lights) to (seem to) go rapidly on and off: *As the ship drew near to port, we could see the lights blinking in the darkness.* **3** [I+at,T] to refuse to recognize or think about (something unpleasant): *It's no use blinking (at) the fact that unemployment is still rising.* **4** [I;T] *AmE for* WINK¹ (2)

blink² *n* **1** an act of blinking **2 on the blink** *infml* (of machinery) not working properly: *The radio's on the blink again.*

blink·ered /ˈblɪŋkəd‖-ərd/ *adj* **1** (of a horse) wearing blinkers **2** *derog* showing an inability to understand or accept anything beyond one's own familiar ideas, customs, beliefs, etc.: *blinkered opinions* | *She's so blinkered!*

blink·ers /ˈblɪŋkəz‖-ərz/ *n* [P] **1** also **blinders** *AmE*— a pair of flat pieces of leather fixed beside a horse's eyes to prevent it seeing objects on either side: (fig.) *David has blinkers on when it comes to politics.* **2** *AmE for* WINKERS

blink·ing /ˈblɪŋkɪŋ/ *adj* [A] *BrE euph infml for* BLOODY²: *Don't be such a blinking fool!*

blintze, blintze, blintz /blɪnts/ *n AmE* a thin flat breadlike cake made in Jewish cooking and rolled around cheese or fruit

blip /blɪp/ *n* **1** a very short sound produced by a machine, such as a RADAR apparatus or a machine that measures a sick person's heartbeat —compare BLEEP **2** an image produced by a RADAR apparatus **3** a short pause in a process, usu. caused by a small problem

bliss /blɪs/ *n* [U] complete happiness: *a young couple in married bliss* | *It's sheer bliss to be able to spend the day in bed.* — **~ful** *adj* — **~fully** *adv*: *blissfully happy* | *The passengers carried on drinking and dancing, blissfully unaware of the impending disaster.*

blis·ter¹ /ˈblɪstəʳ/ *n* **1** a thin watery swelling under the skin, caused by rubbing, burning, etc.: *These new shoes have given me blisters.* **2** a similar swelling on the surface of things such as painted wood or a rubber TYRE

blister² *v* [I;T] to (cause to) form blisters: *When I play tennis my hands blister from holding the racquet.* | *The heat blistered the paint on the building.*

blis·ter·ing /ˈblɪstərɪŋ/ *adj* **1** very hot: *the blistering heat of the desert* **2** full of anger and severe disapproval; SCATHING: *a blistering attack on the government* — **~ly** *adv*: *blisteringly hot*

blister pack /ˈ·· ·/ also **bubble pack** *n* a packet for small products with a clear plastic front fixed to a thick paper backing

blithe /blaɪð‖blaɪð, blaɪθ/ also **blithe·some** /-səm‖-lit— *adj* sometimes derog (esp. of a person's behaviour) happy and unworried: *a blithe lack of concern* — **~ly** *adv* : *They blithely carried on chatting, ignoring the customers who were waiting to be served.*

blith·er·ing /ˈblɪðərɪŋ/ *adj* [A] *sl* stupid; talking nonsense: *You blithering idiot!*

blitz¹ /blɪts/ *n* **1** also **blitz·krieg** /ˈblɪtskriːg/ a (period of) sudden heavy attack, esp. from the air **2** [(on)] *infml* a period of great activity for some special purpose: *an advertising blitz* | *Let's have a blitz on all these letters that need answering.*

blitz² *v* [T] to make blitz attacks on: *London was badly blitzed in 1940.*

Blitz [*the*] the repeated bombing of cities in Britain, esp. London, by the German airforce in 1940 and 1941: *The sound of the explosions reminded him of the Blitz.*

▶ CULTURAL NOTE When British people think of the Blitz, they often think of how people had to crowd together in places of safety, esp. the London Underground, during the bombing. If someone says that a situation is "just like the Blitz", they usu. mean that the situation involves a lot of loud noises and bright lights or that the situation is dangerous and involves people being forced together and helping one another. ◀

Blix·en /ˈblɪksən/, **Baroness Kar·en** /ˈkærən/ (1885–1962) a Danish writer (under the name **Isak Dinesen**) who wrote books in English and is best known for her filmed book *Out of Africa*

bliz·zard /ˈblɪzəd‖-ərd/ *n* a long severe snowstorm —see RAIN (USAGE)

bloat·ed /ˈbləʊtɪd/ *adj* unpleasantly swollen: *the bloated body of a drowned dog* | *I felt absolutely bloated after our Christmas dinner.* | (fig.) *a bloated estimate of the cost*

bloat·er /ˈbləʊtəʳ/ *n* a large fat fish (esp. a HERRING) that has been treated with salt and smoke

blob /blɒb‖blɑːb/ *n* [(of)] a drop or small round mass: *a blob of paint on the floor*

bloc /blɒk‖blɑːk/ *n* [C+sing./pl. v] a group of people (esp. politicians), political parties, or nations that act together: *the Communist bloc* —see also EN BLOC; compare BLOCK

block¹ /blɒk‖blɑːk/ *n* **1** [C (of)] a solid usu. straight-sided mass or piece of hard material such as wood or stone: *a block of ice* | *The floor was made of wooden blocks.* —see picture at PIECE **2** [C] *esp. BrE* a large building divided into separate parts: *a block of flats* | *an office block* —see picture at HOUSE, and see also TOWER BLOCK　**3** [C] *esp. AmE* (the distance along one of the sides of) a building or group of buildings built between two streets: *The office is four blocks from here.* | *We live on the same block.*　**4** [C] (**of**) a quantity of things considered as a single unit: *a block of seats in a theatre* | *a block of shares in a business*　**5** [C *usu. sing.*] something that stops movement or activity: *a block in the water pipe* | *I seem to have* **a mental block** *about computers.* (=I can't understand them at all.) | *a novelist suffering from* **writer's block** (=feeling unable to write) —see also ROADBLOCK　**6** [*the*] the large piece of wood, with a hollow for the neck, on which people's heads were cut off as a punishment in former times　**7** [C] a piece of wood or metal with words or line drawings cut into the surface of it, for printing　**8** [C] *tech* a physical unit of stored information on a MAGNETIC TAPE or DISK: *How big are the blocks on this tape?* —compare BLOC; see also BLOCK AND TACKLE, BLOCK LETTERS, STUMBLING BLOCK, **chip off the old block** (CHIP¹), **knock someone's block off** (KNOCK¹ (7))

block² *v* [T]　**1** to prevent movement through: *Something's blocking the pipe.* | *a blocked pipe* | *The road was blocked by a big truck.* | *My nose is all blocked up and I can't breathe.* | *The police have blocked off the road where the bomb was found.*　**2** [(OFF)] to shut off from view: *The trees outside the window block (off) the sun.*　**3** to prevent from happening, advancing, or succeeding: *One of the directors blocked her appointment.* | *The legislation was blocked by the House of Lords.*　**4** *tech* to limit the use of (a particular nation's money): *blocked currency*
　　block sthg. ↔ **in/out** *phr v* [T] to make a quick drawing showing the general idea of: *I've blocked in/out a rough plan of the campus.*

block·ade¹ /blɒˈkeɪd‖blɑː-/ *n* the surrounding of a place by warships or soldiers to prevent people or goods from coming in or going out: *They are threatening to impose a blockade on the country.* | *to* **run a blockade** (=get through it) | *to* **raise/lift a blockade** (=end it) —compare EMBARGO¹

blockade² *v* [T] to put under a blockade: *The ships blockaded the harbour.*

block·age /ˈblɒkɪdʒ‖ˈblɑː-/ *n*　**1** something that causes a block; OBSTRUCTION: *There's a blockage in the pipe somewhere.*　**2** a state of being blocked: *The strike has caused a blockage in food supplies.*

block and tack·le /ˌ· · ˈ··/ *n* [C;U] an arrangement of wheels and ropes for lifting heavy things: *We moved the fallen tree with (a) block and tackle.*

block·bust·er /ˈblɒkˌbʌstəʳ‖ˈblɑːk-/ *n*　**1** *infml* something very effective or remarkable, esp. a very successful film or book: *The new James Bond picture is a real blockbuster.*　**2** an extremely powerful bomb

block·head /ˈblɒkhed‖ˈblɑːk-/ *n infml* an extremely stupid person

block·house /ˈblɒkhaʊs‖ˈblɑːk-/ *n* **-houses** /ˌhaʊzɪz/ a small fort used as a shelter from enemy gunfire or for watching dangerous operations (such as powerful explosions)

block let·ters /ˌ· ˈ··/ also **block cap·i·tals** /ˌ· ˈ···/— *n* [P] the writing of words with each letter formed separately and written in its CAPITAL (=big) form. It is usual to write in block letters when completing official forms: *Please write your name in block letters.*

block par·ty /ˈ· ˌ··/ *n AmE* a party held in the street for all the people living on that block

block vote /ˌ· ˈ·/ *n* a single vote that is made by a representative of a large group, such as a trade union, and is regarded as representing the votes of all the members of the group

Bloc Qué·bé·cois /ˌblɒk keɪbeˈkwɑː‖ˌblɑːk-/ a political party in Canada which wants the PROVINCE of Quebec to be a separate country

Bloem·fon·tein /ˈbluːmfənteɪn‖-fɑːn-/ a city in South Africa, capital of Orange Free State

bloke /bləʊk/ *n BrE infml* a man

blond /blɒnd‖blɑːnd/ *adj*　**1** (of hair) light-coloured (usu. yellowish)　**2** also **blonde** *fem.*— having light-coloured usu. yellowish hair and light skin —compare BRUNETTE

blonde /blɒnd‖blɑːnd/ *n* a woman or girl with light-coloured, usu. yellowish hair. People sometimes use the phrase "Gentlemen prefer blondes", which is the title of a book by Anita Loos. —see also DUMB BLONDE

Blon·del /blɒnˈdel‖blɑːn-/, **Nic·o·las Fran·çois** /ˈnɪkələs ˈfrɑːnswɑː/ (1618–86) a French military engineer and builder, known for the arch of Porte St Denis in Paris

Blon·die /ˈblɒndi‖ˈblɑːn-/ the main character in a daily US COMIC STRIP of the same name. Blondie is a HOUSEWIFE who always gets an advantage over her husband Dagwood, usu. by using old-fashioned FEMININE tricks. For many people she is a STEREOTYPE.

Blon·din /ˈblɒndɪn‖blɑːnˈdæn/, **Charles** (1824–97) a French ACROBAT whose real name was **Jean François Gravelet**, known for crossing Niagara Falls several times by walking across on a rope

blood¹ /blʌd/ *n*　**1** [U] the red liquid which flows through the body: *The knife was covered in blood.* | *It was a serious cut and she lost a lot of blood.* | *The way they treat their children* **makes my blood boil.** (=makes me very angry) | *The sound of footsteps in the dark* **made his blood run cold.** (=frightened him) | *He's under police protection because he knows the rest of the gang* **are after his blood.** (=hate him/want to harm him physically) | (*lit*) *The invading army* **spilled the blood** *of our people.* (=killed them)　**2** [U] family relationship: *a woman of noble blood* | *princes* **of the blood** (*royal*) (=of the royal family) | *Both her parents are actors so acting* **is/runs in her blood.**　**3** [U] strong esp. unpleasant feeling; temper: *Her* **blood is up.** (=She is very angry.)　**4** [C] *old use* a fashionable young man: *young bloods drinking and shouting in the street*　**5 Blood is thicker than water** *saying* Family relationships are stronger or more important than relationships with other people　**6 blood, sweat, and tears** *quote* a slightly changed phrase from a speech made by Winston Churchill in 1940. He said that all he could offer the British government and people was "blood, toil, tears, and sweat."　**7 get blood from/out of a stone** to try to get something, esp. money, from a person, group, etc., that is unwilling to give it: *Getting my boss to agree to a pay rise is like getting blood from a stone.*　**8 in cold blood** cruelly and on purpose: *They killed the old man in cold blood!* —see also COLD-BLOODED　**9 -blooded** /blʌdɪd/having a certain kind of blood, or a certain character: *warm-blooded animals* —see also BAD BLOOD, BLUE BLOOD, FLESH AND BLOOD, NEW BLOOD, RED BLOOD CELL

blood² *v* [T *often pass.*]　**1** *BrE* to give (someone) a first experience of a new activity; INITIATE　**2** to give (a hunting dog) its first taste of blood

blood-and-thun·der /ˌ· · ˈ··/ *adj* [A] *BrE* (of a film, story, etc.) full of exciting action and meaningless violence

blood bank /ˈ· ·/ *n* a store of human blood for use in hospital treatment

blood·bath /ˈblʌdbɑːθ‖-bæθ/ *n* the killing at one time of many people; MASSACRE

blood broth·er /ˌ· ˈ··/ *n* one of two or more men who have promised loyalty to one another, during a ceremony in which their blood is mixed together

blood count /ˈ· ·/ *n* a medical examination of a person's blood to see if it contains all the right substances in the right amounts

blood-cur·dling /ˈblʌd ˌkɜːdlɪŋ‖-ɜːr-/ *adj* extremely frightening; HORRIFYING: *bloodcurdling cries/stories*

blood do·nor /ˈ· ˌ··/ *n* a person who gives some of their blood for use in the treatment of other people who are wounded or ill. In Britain and the US, blood donors are not paid for giving blood.

blood feud /ˈ· ·/ *n* a long-lasting quarrel between people or families, with murders or physical harm on both sides

blood group /ˈ· ·/ also **blood type**— *n* any of the four classes into which human blood can be separated according to the presence or absence in it of certain substances. The blood groups are called A, B, AB, and O.

blood heat /ˈ· ·/ *n* [U] a temperature about that of the human body; about 37°C

blood·hound /ˈblʌdhaʊnd/ *n*　**1** a large hunting dog with a very sharp sense of smell, used for tracking people or animals　**2** *infml* a DETECTIVE

blood·less /ˈblʌdlɪs/ *adj*　**1** without killing or violence: *a bloodless victory/coup*　**2** lacking in human feeling; lifeless: *bloodless statistics* —compare BLOODY¹　**— ~ly** *adv* — **~ness** *n* [U]

blood·let·ting /ˈblʌdˌletɪŋ/ n [U] **1** killing; BLOODSHED **2** the former medical practice of treating sick people by removing some of their blood

blood lust /ˈ· ·/ n [C;U] a strong desire to kill or wound

blood·mo·bile /ˈblʌdmə‖ˌbiːl/ n AmE a special vehicle with equipment to take blood from people who are giving their blood for the treatment of others

blood mon·ey /ˈ· ˌ··/ n [U] **1** money paid for murdering or for helping murderers **2** money paid to the family of a murdered person

blood plas·ma /ˈ· ˌ··/ n [U] PLASMA

blood poi·son·ing /ˈ· ˌ···/ also **septicaemia** tech— n [U] a serious condition in which an infection spreads from a small area of the body through the blood

blood pres·sure /ˈ· ˌ··/ n [C;U] the measurable force with which blood travels through the body: He suffers from high blood pressure.

blood red /ˌ· ˈ·◄/ adj red like blood: a blood red sunset

blood re·la·tion /ˈ· ·ˌ··/ n a person related by birth rather than by marriage

blood·shed /ˈblʌdʃed/ n [U] the flowing of blood or killing of people, usu. in fighting; SLAUGHTER: To prevent further bloodshed, the two sides agreed to a truce.

blood·shot /ˈblʌdʃɒt‖-ʃɑːt/ adj (of the eyes) having the white part coloured red: His eyes were bloodshot from too much drinking.

blood sport /ˈ· ·/ n [usu. pl.] derog the hunting and killing of birds and animals for pleasure: The group campaigns against all blood sports, especially foxhunting.

blood·stain /ˈblʌdsteɪn/ n a mark or spot of blood: There were bloodstains on the floor where they had been fighting. — ~ed adj : bloodstained clothing

blood·stock /ˈblʌdstɒk‖-stɑːk/ n [U] horses that have been bred for racing: a bloodstock auction

blood·stream /ˈblʌdstriːm/ n [(the)] the blood as it flows round the body: The drug is injected directly into the bloodstream.

blood·suck·er /ˈblʌdˌsʌkəʳ/ n **1** any creature, such as an insect or LEECH, that bites and then sucks blood from the wound **2** derog infml a person who uses other people for his/her own advantage, esp. to get money from them

blood·thirst·y /ˈblʌdˌθɜːstiǁ-ɜːr-/ adj **1** taking pleasure in killing and violence; eager for BLOODSHED **2** dealing with killing and violence: a bloodthirsty movie —**ily** adv —**iness** n

blood trans·fu·sion /ˈ· ·ˌ··/ n [C;U] the process of putting blood from one person into another person's bloodstream, usu. after an accident or illness

blood type /ˈ· ·/ n a BLOOD GROUP

blood ves·sel /ˈ· ˌ··/ n any of the tubes of various sizes through which blood flows in the body —see picture at TEETH

blood·y¹ /ˈblʌdi/ adj **1** bleeding or covered with blood: a bloody nose **2** with a lot of wounding and killing: a bloody battle —compare BLOODLESS —**ily** adv —**iness** n [U]

bloody² adj, adv [A] esp. BrE infml, not polite **1** (used for giving force to an expression or judgment): Don't be such a bloody fool! | It's bloody marvellous! | Bloody hell! **2** (used as an almost meaningless addition to angry speech): I got my bloody foot caught in the bloody chair, didn't I? | "Will you lend me £10?" "Not bloody likely!" (=certainly not!)

bloody ma·ry /ˌ·· ˈ··/ n a drink made by mixing VODKA and TOMATO juice

Bloody Mary see MARY I

bloody-mind·ed /ˌ·· ˈ··◄/ adj BrE infml opposing the wishes of others unreasonably and on purpose; intentionally unhelpful and OBSTINATE — ~**ness** n [U]

Bloody Sun·day /ˌ·· ˈ··/ Sunday, January 30th 1972 when British soldiers killed 13 people in Northern Ireland while trying to end a march against the British government's policy of INTERNMENT (=putting people in prison without a trial if they were thought to be involved with the IRA)

bloom¹ /bluːm/ n **1** [C] apprec a flower: What beautiful blooms! | The roses are **in (full) bloom**. (=flowering) **2** [S;U] a covering of fine powder on ripe GRAPES, PLUMS, etc.

3 [the+of] esp. lit the best or most favourable time of: in the bloom of youth | the first bloom of love

bloom² v [I] **1** to produce flowers, come into flower, or be in flower: The roses are blooming. **2** [usu. in progressive forms] to be in a healthy growing state; FLOURISH: The children are blooming. —compare BLOSSOM²

bloom·er /ˈbluːməʳ/ n **1** BrE humor sl a stupid mistake: I made a terrible bloomer. **2** BrE a loaf of bread which is baked at the bottom of the OVEN and has lines marked on the top

bloom·ers /ˈbluːməz‖-ərz/ n [P] **1** a woman's garment of short loose trousers gathered at the knee, worn in Europe and America in the late 19th century **2** infml for KNICKERS —see PAIR (USAGE)

bloom·ing /ˈbluːmɪŋ, ˈbluːmʌn/ adj, adv [A] esp. BrE (used for giving force to an expression): It's blooming ridiculous!

Bloo·ming·dale's /ˈbluːmɪŋdeɪlz/ n a large DEPARTMENT STORE in New York City. It sells many different kinds of goods but is known esp. for selling expensive clothes.

Blooms·bu·ry /ˈbluːmzbəri/ an area in Camden in the centre of London

Bloomsbury Group /ˈ··· ˌ·/ [the] a group of artists and writers who lived and met each other regularly in Bloomsbury in the early part of the 20th century. The most famous member of the group was Virginia Woolf.

bloop·er /ˈbluːpəʳ/ n AmE humor sl a stupid mistake

blos·som¹ /ˈblɒsəm‖ˈblɑː-/ n **1** [C] the flower of a tree or bush, esp. one that produces fruit: apple blossoms **2** [U] the mass of such flowers on a single plant, tree, or bush: a tree covered in blossom | pear trees **in blossom** (=blossoming) | cherry blossom

blossom² v [I] **1** (of a plant, esp. a tree or bush that produces fruit) to produce flowers: The apple trees are blossoming. **2** [(OUT)] to develop in a pleasing or favourable way: a blossoming friendship | Jane is blossoming (out) into a beautiful girl. | He used to be very quiet, but he's really **blossomed out** (=become cheerful and wanting to talk) since he came to live here. —compare BLOOM²

blot¹ /blɒt‖blɑːt/ n [(on)] **1** a spot or mark, esp. of ink, that spoils or makes dirty: a blot of ink on the paper | (fig.) That hideous building is a real blot on the landscape. (=it spoils the surroundings) **2** a fault or shameful action, esp. by someone usu. of good character: a blot on one's character **3** blot on one's escutcheon BrE lit or humor something shameful that spoils one's good record

blot² v -tt- [T] **1** to make blots on: She blotted the paper with ink spots. **2** to dry with blotting paper **3** blot one's copybook infml to spoil one's good record: She had a clean driving licence until she blotted her copybook by speeding.

blot sthg. ↔ **out** phr v [T] to make (something) difficult or impossible to see; cover; hide: The mist blotted out the sun.

blotch /blɒtʃ‖blɑːtʃ/ n a large irregular spot or mark on the skin, one's clothes, etc.: a blotch of ink on my dress — ~**y** adj : blotchy skin

blot·ter /ˈblɒtəʳ‖ˈblɑː-/ n **1** a large piece of blotting paper against which writing paper can be pressed to dry the ink **2** AmE a book where records are written every day, before the information is stored elsewhere (often in the phrase **police blotter**)

blotting pa·per /ˈ··· ˌ··/ n [U] special thick soft paper used to dry wet ink on paper after writing

blot·to /ˈblɒtəʊ‖ˈblɑː-/ adj [F] BrE sl extremely drunk

blouse /blaʊz‖blaʊs/ n blouses /ˈblaʊzɪz‖ˈblaʊs-/ a garment for women, similar to a shirt, reaching from the neck to the waist or below: She was wearing a black skirt and a white blouse.

blow¹ /bləʊ/ v blew /bluː/, blown /bləʊn/ **1** [I] to send out a strong current of air: The wind is blowing hard tonight.| She blew on her coffee to cool it down. **2** [I+adv/prep; T+obj+adv/prep] to move by the force of a current of air: The wind blew my hat off. | flags blowing in the wind | I shut the window to stop my papers blowing about. | I blew the dust off the book. | A sudden draught blew the door shut. | The force of the explosion blew the car into the air. | Several trees were blown down in the storm. **3** [I;T] to (cause to) sound by blowing: to *blow a trumpet* | *The horn blew loudly.* **4** [T] to make or give shape to (glass) by blowing: *to blow glass* | *He blew a beautiful glass animal.* **5** [I;T] **a** (of an electrical FUSE) to suddenly stop working because a part has melted: *The iron's not working — the fuse must have blown.* **b** to cause (a fuse) to do this **6** [T] *sl* to lose (a favourable chance) as the result of foolishness; BUNGLE: *We've blown our chances of getting the contract.* | *I've blown it!* **7** [T (on)] *sl* to spend (money) freely or wastefully: *They blew about £5000 on a holiday.* **8** [I] *sl* to leave suddenly and quickly: *Let's blow before they catch us!* **9** [T] *BrE euph sl* for DAMN: *Blow it! I've missed my train.* | *Well, I'll be blowed! He's won again!* | *Well, blow me (down)!* **10 blow hot and cold (about)** *infml* to be changeable in one's opinions, esp. by seeming sometimes interested and at other times not interested in a plan **11 blow one's lines** to make a mistake when speaking in a play **12 blow one's nose** to clean the nose by forcing a sudden current of air through it into a handkerchief **13 blow one's own trumpet/horn** *infml., usu. derog* to praise oneself: *She's very good at blowing her own trumpet.* **14 blow one's top/stack** *sl* to explode with anger, lose one's temper **15 blow someone a kiss** to kiss one's hand and then wave or blow over it towards the person one would like to receive the kiss **16 blow someone's brains out** *infml* to kill someone by a shot through the head **17 blow someone's mind** *sl* to fill someone with wonder; AMAZE —see also MIND-BLOWING **18 blow something sky-high** to destroy something completely with an explosion: (fig.) *The new evidence blew the suspect's alibi sky-high.* **19 blow the gaff** *BrE old-fash* to let something secret become known **20 blow the whistle on** *sl* to cause something undesirable to stop, esp. by bringing it to the attention of the public: *It's about time someone blew the whistle on his dishonest practices.* **21 blow town** *AmE sl* to leave a town suddenly **22 There she blows!** (supposed to be said on a WHALE-hunting ship by the first person who sees a WHALE)

blow sbdy.↔**away** *phr v* [T] *AmE sl* to kill by shooting with a gun

blow in *phr v* [I] **1** *infml* to arrive, often unexpectedly: *Jim has just blown in: we weren't expecting him until Tuesday.* **2** *tech* (of an oil well) to start producing

blow off *phr v* [T (**blow** sthg./sbdy. **off**)] *AmE sl* to treat something or someone as unimportant; to not pay attention to: *He blew off his tests without a thought for the future.* | *Mom wanted me to stay in and study but I blew her off.*

blow out *phr v* **1** [I;T (=**blow** sthg. ↔ **out**)] to (cause to) stop burning by blowing: *I blew the candle out.* **2** [I] (esp. of a TYRE) to burst: *The tyre blew out as I was driving to work.* —see also BLOWOUT

blow over *phr v* [I] **1** (of bad weather) to stop blowing; come to an end: *The storm has blown over.* **2** to be forgotten or no longer important: *It caused a scandal at the time, but the whole thing blew over in a few weeks.*

blow up *phr v* **1** [I;T (=**blow** sthg. ↔ **up**)] to (cause to) explode or be destroyed by exploding: *to blow up a bridge* | *The plane blew up in midair.* | (fig.) *Her father blew up (=was very angry) when she came home at 3 o'clock in the morning.* **2** [I;T (=**blow** sthg. ↔ **up**)] to (cause to) become firm by filling with air: *We've got a rubber boat that blows up.* | *Be sure to blow up the tyres before you set off.* **3** [T] (**blow** sthg. ↔ **up**) to make (a photograph) larger **4** [T] (**blow** sthg. ↔ **up**) to cause (something) to appear more serious or important than it really is; EXAGGERATE: *It was just a minor disagreement but it was blown up out of all proportion by the media.* **5** [I] (of bad weather) to begin to develop or arrive: *There's a storm blowing up.* | (fig.) *Our old argument has blown up again.* —see also BLOW-UP

blow² *n* **1** [C] an act or example of blowing: *Give your nose a good blow.* **2** [S] *infml* a strong wind or windy storm

blow³ *n* **1** a hard stroke with the open or closed hand or with a weapon: *a blow on the head* | *The children came to blows with each other.* (=started fighting) | (fig.) **They struck a blow** *for freedom by assassinating the colonial governor.* **2** [(**to**)] (an action or event that has) a bad effect on one's confidence, hopes, likelihood of SUCCESS, etc.: *Being beaten by a younger man came as/was a big blow to his pride.* | *The sudden rise in oil prices has* **dealt a (serious) blow** *to the company's chances of recovery.* **3** a shock or misfortune: *It was a great blow to her when her mother died.* —see also BODY BLOW, DEATHBLOW

blow-by-blow /ˌ· · ˈ·◄/ *adj* [A] with full details; describing all the events in the order in which they happened: *I want a* **blow-by-blow account** *of the match/the meeting.*

blow-dry /ˈ· ·/ *v* [T] to dry and usu. give a shape to (hair) with an electric dryer held in the hand —**blow-dry** *n* : *a cut and blow-dry* —**blow-dryer** *n* : *My blow-dryer broke, I need a new one.*

blow·er /ˈbləʊəʳ/ *n* **1** [C] a machine that blows: *to use a snow blower to clear snow from the roads* **2** [the] *BrE sl* the telephone: *Get on the blower to him at once!* —see also GLASSBLOWER

blow·fly /ˈbləʊflaɪ/ *n* a fly that lays its eggs esp. on meat or in wounds

blow·hard /ˈbləʊhɑːd‖-hɑːrd/ *n AmE infml* someone who has too high an opinion of himself/herself; BRAGGART

blow·hole /ˈbləʊhəʊl/ *n* **1** a hole in the surface of ice to which water animals (such as SEALs) come to breathe **2** a NOSTRIL in the top of the head of a WHALE

blow job /ˈ· ·/ *n taboo sl* for FELLATIO

blow·lamp /ˈbləʊlæmp/ *esp. BrE* ‖ **blow·torch** /-tɔːtʃ‖-tɔːrtʃ/*esp. AmE* — *n* a lamp or gas-pipe from which a mixture of gas and air is blown out under pressure to give a small very hot flame, used esp. for burning off paint

blown /bləʊn/ *past participle of* BLOW

blow·out /ˈbləʊaʊt/ *n* **1** a sudden bursting of a TYRE: *We had a blowout and crashed the car.* **2** *sl* a very big meal —see also BLOW¹ **out**

blow·pipe /ˈbləʊpaɪp/ also **blow·gun** /-gʌn/— *n* a tube for blowing small stones, poisoned ARROWs, or DARTs, used as a weapon

blow·torch /ˈ· ·/ *n esp. AmE* a blow-lamp

blow·up /ˈ· ·/ *n* **1** [(**of**)] a photographic ENLARGEMENT: *Look at this blow-up of the child's face.* **2** a sudden moment of anger —see also BLOW **up**

blow·y /ˈbləʊi/ *adj infml* windy: *a blowy day*

blow·zy , **blowsy** /ˈblaʊzi/ *adj* (of a woman) fat, dirty, red-faced, and untidily dressed

BLT /ˌbiː el ˈtiː/ *n AmE infml* bacon, lettuce, and tomato; a sandwich made with these foods

blub·ber¹ /ˈblʌbəʳ/ *n* [U] the fat of sea animals, esp. WHALEs, from which oil is obtained

blubber² *v old-fash, usu. derog* **1** [I] to WEEP (=cry tears) noisily: *I wish you'd stop blubbering! I can't hear what you're saying.* **2** [T (OUT)] to say while crying in this way: *He blubbered out a pathetic apology.*

blud·geon¹ /ˈblʌdʒən/ *n* a heavy-headed stick used as a weapon

bludgeon² *v* [T] to hit (someone) repeatedly with something heavy: *They bludgeoned him to death.*

　　bludgeon sbdy. **into** sthg. *phr v* [T] to force (someone) to do (something) by threats or repeated arguments: *They bludgeoned him into submission/into letting them borrow the car.*

blue¹ /bluː/ *adj* **1** of the colour of the clear sky or of the deep sea on a fine day: *She wore a dark blue dress.* | *He painted the door blue.* | *an ambulance with its blue lights flashing* | *Your hands are* **blue with cold.**

▶CULTURAL NOTE Blue is often thought of as a male colour. Boy babies are sometimes given blue clothes and girl babies, pink.◀

2 [F] *infml* sad and without hope; DEPRESSED: *I'm feeling rather blue today.* **3** *infml* concerned with sex; rather improper; RISQUE: *Some of her jokes were a bit blue.* —see also BLUE FILM **4 till one is blue in the face** unsuccessfully for ever: *You can call that dog till you're blue in the face but he'll never come.* — ~**ness** *n* [U]

blue² *n* **1** [C;U] the colour that is blue: *dressed in blue* | *A light blue would be a nice colour for the curtains.* | *The room was painted in various shades of blue.* **2** [C] *BrE* (*usu. cap.*) (a title given to) a person who has represented Oxford or Cambridge University in a sport: *He's a rugger Blue.* **3** [C] *AustrE sl* a fight **4** *AmE* (*usu. cap.*) (a member of) the army in the US Civil War which fought for the US to remain whole and against slavery (the UNION army): *The Blue and the Gray* —see also GRAY **5 out of the blue** unexpectedly: *John arrived completely out of the blue.* —see also BLACK AND BLUE, BLUES, NAVY BLUE, PRUSSIAN BLUE, ROYAL BLUE, SKY-BLUE, TRUE-BLUE, **bolt from the blue** (BOLT¹ (6))

blue ba·by /ˈ ˌ··/ n a baby whose skin is slightly blue when it is born because there is something wrong with its heart

Blue·beard /ˈbluːbɪəd‖-bɪərd/ a wicked character in old European stories who married and killed one wife after another

blue·bell /ˈbluːbel/ n a blue bell-shaped flower, esp. the wild HYACINTH

blue·ber·ry /ˈbluːbəri‖-beri/ n (the blue-black fruit of) a low bushy plant growing in N America —compare BILBERRY

blue·bird /ˈbluːbɜːd‖-bɜːrd/ n a small blue singing bird of N America

Blue Birds /ˈ ˌ·/ (in the US) a division of the Camp Fire club for younger girls and boys

blue-black /ˌ·ˈ··/ adj very dark blue

blue blood /ˌ· ˈ·‖ˈ· ·/ n [U] the quality of being a nobleman or noblewoman by birth: *Members of noble families are said to have blue blood in their veins.* —**blue-blooded** /ˌ· ˈ···/ adj

blue book /ˈ· ·/ n **1** an official report printed by the British Government, usu. the report of a committee — compare GREEN PAPER, WHITE PAPER **2** a book of paper with a blue cover which is used in American colleges for writing answers to examination questions

blue·bot·tle /ˈbluːˌbɒtl‖-ˌbɑːtl/ n a large blue fly; the meat fly or BLOWFLY

blue cheese /ˌ· ˈ·/ n [C;U] (a) cheese marked with blue lines of decay

blue chip /ˌ· ˈ·/ n, adj (an industrial share) that is expensive and in which people have confidence: *We only deal with blue chip companies.*

blue-col·lar /ˌ· ˈ···/ adj [A] of or concerning workers who do hard or dirty work with their hands: *blue-collar workers* | *a blue-collar union* —compare PINK-COLLAR, WHITE-COLLAR

Blue Cross /ˌ· ˈ·/ an American medical insurance company

Blue Dan·ube /ˌbluː ˈdænjuːb/, **The** the title of an extremely popular WALTZ written by the younger Johann Strauss in 1866

blue-eyed boy /ˌ·· ˈ·/ n infml, esp. BrE, usu. derog someone's favourite (male) person: *Smith is the boss's blue-eyed boy at the moment.*

blue film /ˌ· ˈ·/ also **blue movie**— n a film about sex; a pornographic film (PORNOGRAPHY) —see also BLUE¹ (3)

blue·fish /ˈbluːˌfɪʃ/ n **bluefish** a sea fish with a bluish colour which is caught for sport and food off the coast of N America

blue·grass /ˈbluːɡrɑːs‖-ɡræs/ n [U] **1** a kind of lively music from the Southern US, played on instruments with strings such as the GUITAR, VIOLIN, and BANJO, and usu. without an AMPLIFIER to make it louder: *a bluegrass band/concert* **2** a type of grass found in N America, esp. in Kentucky, which is known as "the Bluegrass State"

blue gum /ˈ· ·/ n an Australian tree of the EUCALYPTUS family

blue jay /ˈ· ·/ n a common N American bird with a blue back and a growth of big blue feathers on its head

blue jeans /ˈ· ·/ n [P] AmE for JEANS

blue law /ˈ· ·/ n AmE infml a law to control sexual morals, the drinking of alcohol, working on Sundays, etc.

blue moon /ˌ· ˈ·/ **once in a blue moon** infml not very often: *We only clean the car once in a blue moon.*

blue mo·vie /ˌ· ˈ···/ n AmE for BLUE FILM

blue mur·der /ˌ· ˈ···/ n **scream/shout blue murder** infml to complain very loudly: *When the doctor stuck the needle into her arm, the child screamed blue murder.*

Blue Nile /ˌ· ˈ·/ one of the two main rivers which join together to form the River Nile proper, the other being the White Nile

Blue Nun /ˌ· ˈ·/ [U] tdmk a type of quite sweet white wine which is made in the Rheinhessen area of Germany for EXPORT to the UK; it is popular and not very expensive

blue-pen·cil /ˌ· ˈ···/ v [T] infml old-fash to cross out anything offensive from (a piece of writing); CENSOR²: *to blue-pencil (the dirty words in) a play*

blue pe·ter /ˌ· ˈ···/ n [(the+)S] (sometimes cap.) a blue flag with a white square in the middle, flown on a ship to show it is ready to leave port

Blue Peter a popular British television programme for children. *Blue Peter* is well known, by both adults and children, for supporting children's activities, showing them how to do and make useful things, and encouraging them to raise money for people in need: *a Blue Peter appeal* | *a Blue Peter badge*

blue·print /ˈbluːˌprɪnt/ n a photographic copy of a plan for making a machine or building a house or other structure: *the blueprints of a new engine* | (fig.) *The report is a blueprint for the reform of the nation's tax system.*

blue rib·bon /ˌ· ˈ···/ n AmE a small blue piece of cloth given as first prize to the winner of a competition –see picture at ROSETTE —**blue-ribbon** adj : *a blue-ribbon recipe* (a prize-winning or very good recipe)

blue rinse /ˌ· ˈ··/ n a slight blue colouring of the hair, thought typical of old CONSERVATIVE¹ (1) ladies— —**blue-rinsed** adj : *the blue-rinsed hordes who form the backbone of Tory support*

blues /bluːz/ n **blues** **1** [C;the+sing./pl. v] (a song in) a slow, sad style of music originally from the Southern US: *The blues was/were first performed by the black people of New Orleans.* | *a well-known blues singer* | *Play us a blues.* —see also RHYTHM AND BLUES **2** [the] infml the state of being sad; a feeling of deep unhappiness: *a sudden attack of the blues*

Blues and Roy·als /ˌ· ˈ···/ [the] a REGIMENT (=large division of men) in the British army

Blues Broth·ers /ˈ· ˌ···/, **The** an American film with Dan Ackroyd and John Belushi, about 2 blues musicians — see colour picture on page 553

blue-sky /ˈ· ·/ adj [A] AmE done in order to test ideas, rather than for any particular practical purpose: *blue-sky research*

blue-stock·ing /ˈbluːˌstɒkɪŋ‖-ˌstɑː-/ n derog old-fash a woman who is thought to be too highly educated

bluff¹ /blʌf/ v **1** [I;T (into)] to try to frighten or persuade (someone) by pretending to be stronger, cleverer, braver, etc., than one actually is: *The terrorists say they'll blow up the plane if their demands are not met, but the police think they're only bluffing.* | *He bluffed the police into thinking that his gun was loaded.* **2** **bluff it out** infml to escape trouble by continuing a deception: *George, here comes my husband; do you think we can bluff it out?* **3** **bluff one's way out** (of) to get out of (a difficult situation) by bluffing

bluff² n [S;U] the action of bluffing: *She threatened to sack me, but it's all (a) bluff.* —see also DOUBLE BLUFF, **call someone's bluff** (CALL¹ (15))

bluff³ adj (of a person or manner) rough, cheerful, and direct, perhaps without considering the feelings of others; HEARTY: *He has a kind heart in spite of his bluff manner.* — ~ly adv — ~ness n [U]

bluff⁴ n a high steep bank or cliff: *They sat on a bluff and watched the sea.*

blu·ish /ˈbluːɪʃ/ adj slightly blue

blun·der¹ /ˈblʌndəʳ/ n a stupid unnecessary mistake: *I made an awful blunder — switched off his computer while he was working on it.*

blunder² v [I] **1** to make a blunder **2** [+adv/prep] to move awkwardly or unsteadily, as if blind: *He blundered through the dark forest.* **3** someone had blundered quote a phrase from the poem *The Charge of the Light Brigade* by Tennyson —see also CHARGE OF THE LIGHT BRIGADE — ~er n

blun·der·buss /ˈblʌndəbʌs‖-ər-/ n a type of gun used in former times, which has a barrel with a wide mouth and fires a quantity of small SHOT¹ (5) for a short distance

blunt¹ /blʌnt/ adj **1** (of a knife, pencil, etc.) not sharp: *My pencil's blunt — can I borrow your sharpener?* **2** speaking roughly and plainly, without trying to be polite or to hide unpleasant facts: *a blunt man* | *To be quite blunt, I think the government has made a complete mess of things.* — ~ly adv : *To put it bluntly, I think your chances of passing the exam are almost non-existent.* — ~ness n [U]

blunt² v [T] to make less sharp or forceful: *The bad weather has rather blunted their enthusiasm for going camping.*

Blunt, Anthony (1907–83) a British-born SPY for the Soviet Union, who worked as an art HISTORIAN and at one time worked for the Queen. His activities as a spy were only made public in 1979, when his KNIGHTHOOD was taken away from him —see also Guy BURGESS, Donald MACLEAN, and Kim PHILBY

blur¹ /blɜːʳ/ n [S] something whose shape is not clearly seen: *The houses appeared as a blur in the mist.* | (fig.) *My memory of the accident is only a blur.*

blur² v -rr- [T] **1** to make (something) difficult to see or see through clearly: *Tears blurred my eyes.* | *windows blurred with rain* | *a very blurred photograph* **2** to make less clear or noticeable: *The newspaper report deliberately blurs the distinction between the union's members and its leadership.*

blurb /blɜːb‖blɜːrb/ n **1** a short description of the contents of a book, printed on the cover or in advertisements **2** *infml* printed information, often in JARGON, which is produced by officials to provide details of something, esp. for people who may not know much about it: *estate agents' blurb* | *I can't be bothered to read all the blurb!*

blurt /blɜːt‖blɜːrt/ v
   blurt sthg. ↔ **out** phr v [T] to say suddenly and without thinking, esp. from nervousness or excitement: *Peter blurted out the news.*

blush¹ /blʌʃ/ v [I] to become red in the face, from shame or because people are looking at one: *He blushed (with embarrassment) when the girls whistled at him in the street.* | *It made me blush when the teacher told everyone how good my work was.* | *Here comes the blushing* **bride.**| (fig.) *When I see the prices that tourists are charged, it makes me blush.* (=I feel ashamed) | *I blush to think of the things I did when I was younger.* − ~**ingly** adv

blush² n **1** a case of blushing: *His remark brought a blush to my cheeks.* | *You shouldn't say such nice things about me* − **spare my blushes!** (=don't make me blush) **2 at first blush** *fml* or *lit* at the first sight: *It seemed a good idea at first blush, but its drawbacks soon became apparent.*

blush·er /ˈblʌʃəʳ/ n [C;U] (a container of) a cream or powder for colouring the cheeks

blus·ter¹ /ˈblʌstəʳ/ v [I] **1** to speak loudly and roughly, in a noisy or BOASTFUL way **2** (of wind) to blow roughly − ~**er** n

bluster² n [U] **1** noisy or BOASTFUL talk **2** the noise of rough wind or waves: *the bluster of the storm*

blus·ter·y /ˈblʌstəri/ adj (of weather) rough, windy, and violent: *a blustery winter day*

blvd written abbrev. for: BOULEVARD

Bly·ton /ˈblaɪtn/, **E·nid** /ˈiːnɪd/ (1897−1978) an English writer of books for children, who invented the characters of **Noddy**, the **Famous Five**, and the **Secret Seven**. Her books are very popular with children, but they have sometimes been criticized for SEXISM and RACISM.

BM¹ /ˌbiː ˈem/ abbrev. for: BRITISH MUSEUM

BM² n Bachelor of Medicine; the lowest level of medical degree

BMA /ˌbiː em ˈeɪ/ [the] British Medical Association; a TRADE UNION for British medical doctors

BMOC /ˌbiː em əʊ ˈsiː/ n AmE abbrev. for BIG MAN ON CAMPUS

B-mov·ie /ˈbiː ˌmuːvi/ n a cheaply-made cinema film not considered to be of very good quality

BMW /ˌbiː em ˈdʌbljuː/ n tdmk a high quality, expensive German car, generally considered to be PRESTIGIOUS and usu. driven by people who are successful in business

BMX /ˌbiː em ˈeks/ n [U] bicycle motocross; the sport of riding a bicycle, usu. a special bicycle with a strong frame and small wheels, over a course on rough ground: *a BMX bike*

B'nai B'rith /bəˌneɪ ˈbrɪθ/ an organization of Jewish people which aims to help Jews and others have better social and educational opportunities (OPPORTUNITY)

BNFL /ˌbiː en ef ˈel/ British Nuclear Fuels Limited; the company responsible for Britain's NUCLEAR power industry

BO /ˌbiː ˈəʊ/ n [U] body odour; an unpleasant smell from a person's body, usu. caused by SWEAT

bo·a¹ /ˈbəʊə/ also **boa con·stric·tor** /ˈ·· ·ˌ···/− n a large non-poisonous South American snake, that kills animals or people by crushing them

boa² also **feather boa**− n a long snake-shaped garment (a kind of STOLE) made of feathers, worn round a woman's neck esp. in former times

Bo·a·di·ce·a /ˌbəʊədɪˈsiːə/ see BOUDICCA

boar /bɔːʳ/ n **1** a male pig that is not castrated (CASTRATE) and is kept for breeding −compare HOG¹ (1, 2), SOW² **2** a WILD BOAR

board¹ /bɔːd‖bɔːrd/ n **1** [C] a long thin flat piece of cut wood; PLANK −see also FLOORBOARD **2** [C] (often in comb.) a flat piece of hard material used for a particular purpose: *Pin the list up on the board.* (=the NOTICE BOARD) | *Put the bread on the board* (=the BREADBOARD) *before cutting it.*| *The teacher wrote a sum on the board.* (=the BLACKBOARD or WHITEBOARD) | *I want to play chess but I can't find the board.* (=the CHESSBOARD) **3** [U] (the cost of) meals: *I pay £30 a week for board and lodging/bed and board.* −see also BED AND BOARD, HALF BOARD, FULL BOARD; compare LODGINGS **4** [C+sing./pl. v] **a** an official body or group that has responsibility for a particular organization or activity: *the school's board of governors* | *a board of advisers/examiners* | *the English Tourist Board* **b** also **board of directors**− a committee of the directors of a company, which is responsible for the management of the company: *Mary is the only woman on the board (of directors).* | *The board is/are meeting tomorrow.* | *We'll need the approval of the board before we can do that.* **5 go by the board** (of plans, arrangements, etc.) to be no longer possible or practical: *We had intended to get a new car, but that's gone by the board now that I've lost my job.* **6 on board** in or on (a ship or public vehicle): *go/get on board the train/the aircraft/the ship* | *As soon as I'm on board I always feel sick.* −see BOAT (USAGE), PLANE (USAGE); compare ABOARD **7 take on board** to fully understand or accept: *The management's offer shows that they have not really taken on board the union's demands.* −see also BOARDS, ABOVEBOARD, ACROSS-THE-BOARD, BIG BOARD, DRAWING BOARD, **sweep the board** (SWEEP¹)

board² v **1** [T (OVER, UP)] to cover with boards: *a boarded floor* | *Board the windows up.* **2** [T] to get into (a ship or public vehicle); go on board: *The hijackers boarded the plane at Heathrow Airport.* **3** [I+adv/prep;T] to get or supply meals and lodging for payment: *She arranged to board some students from the university.* | *I'm boarding with a friend/at a friend's house.*
   board sbdy./sthg. ↔ **out** phr v [T] to arrange for (a person or animal) to live and get food away from home: *We'll have to board the cat out while we're on holiday.*

board·er /ˈbɔːdəʳ‖ˈbɔːr-/ n **1** a pupil at a BOARDING SCHOOL **2** a person who pays to live and receive meals at another person's house; LODGER: *to take in boarders* **3** (in old naval fighting) a man who jumps onto an enemy ship: *Stand by to repel boarders!*

board game /ˈ· ·/ n any game played on a specially made board of wood, card, or stiff paper, e.g. CHESS, Monopoly, etc.

board·ing /ˈbɔːdɪŋ‖ˈbɔːr-/ n [U] boards laid side by side: *The windows were covered with boarding.*

boarding card /ˈ·· ·/ n an official card to be given up when one enters an aircraft

board·ing·house /ˈbɔːdɪŋhaʊs‖ˈbɔːr-/ n -houses /ˌhaʊzɪz/ a private lodging house, not a hotel, that supplies meals

boardinghouse reach /ˌ··· ·ˈ·/ n [U] AmE infml the practice of reaching across the dinner table for what one wants, rather than asking for it to be passed to one

boarding school /ˈ·· ·/ n [C;U] a school at which pupils live as well as study. Most British PUBLIC SCHOOLs are boarding schools: *a small country boarding school* | *two daughters at boarding school* −compare DAY SCHOOL (1)

Board of Ed·u·ca·tion /ˌ· · ··ˈ··/ n a group of people elected in each American COUNTY to make decisions on matters of education: *The Board of Education has supported busing as a method of desegregating city schools.*

board·room /ˈbɔːdruːm, -rʊm‖ˈbɔːrd-/ n a room in which the directors of a company hold meetings: *Nervous muttering is being heard in boardrooms all over the country.* −see also BOARD¹ (4b)

boards /bɔːdz‖bɔːrdz/ n **1** [P] tech the covers of a book: *a book in cloth boards* **2** [the+P] old use or pomp the theatre; the stage: *He's been on the boards* (=been an actor) *all his life.*

board·walk /ˈbɔːdwɔːk‖ˈbɔːrd-/ n a footpath often made of boards, usu. beside the sea

boast¹ /bəʊst/ v 1 [I (**about, of**);T+*that;obj*] *derog* to talk or state with unpleasant or unreasonable pride: *He's always boasting about his children|about how clever his children are.* | *Don't believe her; she's just boasting.* | *He boasted that he could speak six languages fluently.* 2 [T *not in progressive forms*] *not derog* (not of people) to have or contain (something that is unusual or a cause of reasonable pride): *The new computer boasts a number of ingenious features.*

boast² n 1 *derog* an act of boasting 2 *not derog* a cause for being proud: *It is one of their* **proudest boasts** *that they have halved the death rate from typhoid.*

boast·er /ˈbəʊstəʳ/ n *derog* someone who tends to boast

boast·ful /ˈbəʊstfəl/ adj *derog* (of a person or their words) full of self-praise – –**ly** adv – –**ness** n [U]

boat¹ /bəʊt/ n 1 (*often in comb.*) a small open vehicle for travelling across water: *a small fishing|sailing|rowing boat* | *a police patrol boat* | *We'll cross the river by boat|in a boat.* | *We had to* **take to the boats** (=get into the ship's lifeboats) *because the ship was sinking.* –see also FLYING BOAT, NARROW BOAT, and see picture at YACHT 2 *infml* any ship: *Are you going to America by boat or by air?* 3 (*usu. in comb.*) a boat-shaped dish for serving liquid food at meals: *a sauceboat* | *a gravy boat* –see picture at JUG; see also **miss the boat** (MISS¹), **push the boat out** (PUSH¹), **rock the boat** (ROCK¹), **in the same boat** (SAME¹)
▷ USAGE 1 Boats are usu. smaller than ships but the word can be used informally of a large passenger ship: *There were over 2000 passengers on the* **ship/boat.** 2 When you are in control of a **boat,** you **row** a rowing boat, **sail** a sailing boat, and **sail** or **pilot** other kinds of boat. When you direct the course of a boat you **steer** or **pilot** it. As a passenger you travel **by** boat, or **on** a particular boat. At the beginning of your journey you **get in(to)** a very small boat but with a bigger boat you **get on(to)** it, **go on board** or (*fml*) **embark.** At the end of your journey you **get out of** a very small boat, but with a larger boat you **get off** it or (*fml*) **disembark.** –see also DRIVE¹ (USAGE), TRANSPORT (USAGE), VESSEL (USAGE)◁

boat² v [I] to use a small boat for pleasure: *Let's go boating on the lake.*

boat·er /ˈbəʊtəʳ/ n 1 a stiff hat made of STRAW. Boaters are often thought of in connection with rich young men at university in Britain in the early part of the 20th century. 2 a person in a boat, esp. a boat used for pleasure: *boaters enjoying the lake on a Sunday afternoon*

boat hook /ˈ· ·/ n a long pole with an iron hook on the end, used to pull or push a small boat

boat·house /ˈbəʊthaʊs/ n -**houses** /ˌhaʊzₐz/ a small building by the water in which boats are kept

boat·man /ˈbəʊtmən/ n -**men** /mən/ a man who has small boats for hire, or who rows or sails small boats for pay

boat peo·ple /ˈ· ˌ··/ n [P] people who escape from bad conditions in their country in small boats, hoping to find safety in other countries. Since the late 1970s, many boat people have left Vietnam in this way.

Boat Race /ˈ· ·/ [*the*] (in Britain) a rowing race on the River Thames, held every year between teams from Oxford University and Cambridge University. The Boat Race is a popular national event and is shown on television.

Boat Show /ˈ· ·/ [*the*] an EXHIBITION of boats which takes place every year at Earls Court in London

boat·swain , bosun /ˈbəʊsən/ n a chief seaman on a ship, who calls the men to work and looks after the boats, ropes, and other equipment: *Are we ready to sail, boatswain?*

boat train /ˈ· ·/ n a train that takes people to or from ships in port

bob¹ /bɒb‖bɑːb/ v -**bb**- 1 [I+*adv/prep*;T+*obj+adv/prep*] to (cause) to move up or down quickly or repeatedly: *The small boat was bobbing on the rough water of the lake.* | *a little bird bobbing its head up and down* 2 [T] (of a woman, esp. in former times) to make a CURTSY quickly 3 **bob for apples** to try to pick up apples floating in water using only one's mouth and not one's hands. It is done esp. at Hallowe'en parties for children. –**bob** n
bob up *phr* v [I] to appear or reappear quickly or

suddenly: *If you try to sink an apple in water it keeps bobbing up to the surface.* | *I haven't seen him around for a while, but I'm sure he'll bob up again soon.*

bob² n **bob** *infml old-fash* a former British coin, the SHILLING (=5p): *It'll cost you ten bob.*

bob³ v -**bb**- [T] to cut (a woman's hair) so as to be hanging loosely to shoulder-length or shorter: *to have one's hair bobbed* –**bob** n : *to wear one's hair in a bob*

Bob n **Bob's your uncle!** /ˌ· · ˈ···/ *BrE* (used for showing satisfaction that a way of doing something has been found): *If the picture goes, just bang the television a few times, and Bob's your uncle!* (=the picture will come back)

Bob-a-Job Week /ˌ· · ˈ· ˌ·/ the week of the year during which members of the Scout movement in Britain raise money by doing work for anyone who requests their help, originally at one SHILLING (1) or BOB² (five new pence) per job

bob·bin /ˈbɒb‿ɪn‖ˈbɑː-/ n a small round stick or tube on which thread is wound, as in a sewing machine – compare REEL

bob·ble¹ /ˈbɒbəl‖ˈbɑː-/ n *BrE* a small, often FLUFFY, ball (of wool, etc.) used for decoration: *cushions with bobbles on them* | *a bobble hat* (=with a bobble on its top)

bobble² v [T] *AmE* to drop or handle something awkwardly, esp. a ball; FUMBLE(2): *The shortstop bobbled the ball and the runner was home.*

bob·by /ˈbɒbi‖ˈbɑːbi/ n *BrE infml, becoming rare* a policeman: *The Council wants more bobbies on the beat.* –see picture at POLICEMAN

bobby pin /ˈ·· ·/ n *AmE for* HAIRGRIP –see picture at PIN

bobby socks ,bobby sox /ˈ·· ˌ·/ n [P] *AmE* girls' socks reaching above the ankle and with the tops turned over. They were fashionable in the 1950s, esp. worn with SADDLE SHOES and wide, full skirts.

bobby sox·er /ˈbɒbi ˌsɒksəʳ‖ ˈbɑːbi ˌsɑː-/ n *AmE old-fash* a young girl between the ages of about 13 and 18, esp. during the 1950s

bobby soxer

bob·cat /ˈbɒbkæt‖ˈbɑːb-/ n a wild cat of N America

bobs /bɒbz‖bɑːbz/ n see **bits and bobs** (BIT¹)

bob·sleigh /ˈbɒbsleɪ‖ˈbɑːb-/ also **bob·sled** /-sled/– n a small vehicle that runs over snow on metal blades, built for racing down an ice-covered track and having a movable front part to control direction –**bobsleigh** v [I]

bob·tail /ˈbɒbteɪl‖ˈbɑːb-/ n (a horse or dog with) a tail cut short – –**ed** adj

Boc·cac·ci·o /bɒˈkɑːtʃiəʊ‖bəʊ-/, **Gio·van·ni** /dʒəʊˈvɑːni/ (1313–75) an Italian writer best known for a collection of stories called *The Decameron*

Boche /bɒʃ‖bɑːʃ/ n [*the* + P] *derog sl* a word used in Britain for the Germans, esp. German soldiers, during the First and Second World Wars

bod /bɒd‖bɑːd/ n *infml* 1 *BrE* a person: *He's a bit of an odd bod.* 2 a person's body: *He has a great bod!*

bode¹ /bəʊd/ v **bode well/ill (for)** *esp. lit* to be a good/bad sign for the future (for): *These early sales figures bode well for the success of the book.*

bode² *past tense of* BIDE

bod·e·ga /bəʊˈdiːɡə‖-ˈdeɪ-/ n *AmE* a small food store in a city neighbourhood, operated by Spanish-speaking people

bod·ice /ˈbɒd‿ɪs‖ˈbɑː-/ n 1 the part of a woman's dress above the waist 2 *old use* a woman's undergarment; CORSET

bodice-rip·per /ˈ·· ˌ··/ n *usu. derog* a book with a romantic story usu. set in the past, containing violent love scenes

bod·i·ly¹ /ˈbɒd‿ɪli‖ˈbɑː-/ adj [A] of the human body; PHYSICAL: *bodily comforts* | *bodily functions* | *The police charged him with* **grievous bodily harm.**

bodily² *adv* taking hold of the whole body (or whole thing): *Her son wouldn't move, so she picked him up bodily and carried him to bed.*

bod·kin /ˈbɒdkɪn‖ˈbɑːd-/ n a long thick needle without a point

Bod·lei·an Li·bra·ry /ˌbɒdliən ˈlaɪbrəri‖ˌbɑːdliən ˈlaɪbreri/ [*the*] the university library of Oxford University, which holds many of the country's oldest and most famous books and papers

bod·y /ˈbɒdi‖ˈbɑːdi/ n **1** [C] **a** the whole physical structure of a person or animal as opposed to the mind or soul: *Her body was covered from head to toe in painful red spots.* | *The murderer buried the body of his victim.* **b** this without the head or limbs: *He had a wound on his leg and two more on his body.* **2** [*the* (**of**)] the main or largest part of something: *We sat in the body of the hall.* | *Should this information go in the main body of the text, or in the notes at the end?* **3** [C (**of**)] a large amount: *a body of information* | *The oceans are large bodies of water.* | *There is now a substantial body of opinion that opposes this law.* (=many people oppose it) **4** [C] (*sometimes cap.*) a number of people who do something together in a planned way: *The House of Representatives is an elected body*|*a legislative body.* | *the governing body of the college* | *a fine body of men* | *They marched* **in a body/in one body** (=all together) *to the headmaster's office.* **5** [C] *tech* an object; piece of matter: *the speed at which a falling body travels* | *The sun, moon, and stars are* **heavenly bodies.** | *a* **foreign body** (=something that should not be there) *in one's eye* **6** [C] the frame and outer covering of a car: *The factory produces car bodies, but does not make the engines.* **7** [U] a full strong quality: *I like a wine with plenty of body.* | *This conditioner will give your hair more body.* **8** [C] *old-fash infml* a person, usu. a woman: *Mrs Jones was a dear old body.* **9 keep body and soul together** to have enough money, food, etc., to live on: *She hardly eats enough to keep body and soul together.* **10 over my/ his/her dead body** (used to show one's determination that something will not happen) not if I/he/she/etc. can prevent it: *You'll come into this house over my dead body.* **11 -bodied** /bɒdid‖bɑː-/ having the stated kind of body: *big-bodied* | *a wide-bodied jet* —see also ABLE-BODIED, FULL-BODIED

▷ USAGE One's **figure** is the shape of one's **body**, considered with regard to whether the shape is pleasing or attractive, or whether it suits a particular style of clothes: *She has an excellent* **figure. Body** would formerly have been considered impolite here, but is now becoming acceptable. **Figure** is usu. used of women. For both men and women we can use **build**: *a man/woman of small/heavy* **build.**◁

body bag /ˈ··· ·/ n AmE a large bag in which the dead body of a soldier is carried away from the scene of a crime, an accident or a battle: *Large numbers of body bags coming back from the war would lower support for US action.*

body blow /ˈ··· ·/ n **1** (in BOXING) a usu. heavy blow that strikes one's opponent between the neck and the waist **2** [(**to**)] a serious loss, disappointment, or defeat: *His injury was a body blow to our chances of winning the match.*

bod·y-build·er /ˈbɒdibɪldəʳ‖ˈbɑː-/ n a person, usu. a man, who does a lot of hard physical exercises, often using heavy weights, in order to develop big muscles. Bodybuilding has become a very popular sport. **bodybuilding** n [U]

body clock /ˈ··· ·/ n see BIOLOGICAL CLOCK

bod·y·guard /ˈbɒdigɑːd‖ˈbɑːdigɑːrd/ n **1** a man whose job is to guard an important person: *The Queen's bodyguards stopped a man who was carrying a gun.* **2** [+*sing.*/*pl. v*] a group of men with this job: *The President's bodyguard is/are waiting in the hall.*

body lan·guage /ˈ··· ˌ··/ n [U] the use of bodily movements and signs as a way of expressing one's feelings or intentions without using words

body pol·i·tic /ˌ··· ˈ···/ n [*the*] *fml* the people of a nation forming a state under the control of a single government

body pop·ping /ˈ··· ˌ··/ n [U] a young people's type of dancing popular from the 1980s, with movements intended to make the dancer appear to move like a ROBOT

body search /ˈ··· ˌ·/ n a detailed examination of a person for hidden items (e.g. drugs or weapons) **body-search** v [T] : *She was body-searched at the airport.*

Body Shop /ˈ··· ·/ one of a group of shops started in Britain and selling a wide range of women's and men's TOILETRIES and COSMETICS at low prices. The Body Shop is

known for only selling products which have not been tested on animals and for working to save the environment.

body snatch·er /ˈ·· ˌ··/ n (in former times) a person who dug up dead bodies and sold them to doctors for scientific study

body stock·ing /ˈ·· ˌ··/ n a closely-fitting garment in one piece that covers the body and often the arms and legs

bod·y·work /ˈbɒdiwɜːk‖ˈbɑːdiwɜːrk/ n [U] the main outside structure of a motor vehicle, as opposed to the engine, wheels, etc.: *The engine works well, but there is a lot of rust in the bodywork.*

Boe·ing /ˈbəʊɪŋ/ an American company which makes aircraft

Boer /bɔːʳ, bʊəʳ/ n, adj (a member) of the white people of South Africa who came there from Holland —see also AFRIKAANS

Boer War /ˌ·ˈ·/ also **South African War** [*the*] (1899–1902) a war in South Africa in which the British army successfully fought against the Boer REPUBLICs of the Transvaal and the Orange Free State to gain political rights there

bof·fin /ˈbɒfɪn‖ˈbɑː-/ n **1** BrE old-fash infml a scientist **2** BrE infml a clever person

Bo·fors gun /ˈbəʊfəz ɡʌn‖-fɔːrz-/ n a gun with two BARRELs (3), used against aircraft, named after **Bofors** in Sweden where it was first made

bog¹ /bɒɡ‖bɑːɡ, bɔːɡ/ n **1** [C;U] (an area of) soft wet ground, consisting of decaying vegetable matter, into which the feet sink **2** [C] BrE sl a TOILET — ~**gy** adj : *boggy ground*

bog² v -gg-

 bog down phr v [I;T(=**bog** sthg./sbdy. ↔ **down**)] usu. pass.] to (cause to) sink and become stuck (as if) in a bog: *The car got bogged down in the mud.* | (fig.) *The talks with the staff bogged down on the question of working hours.* | (fig.) *Let's try not to get too bogged down in these detailed points.*

Bo·garde /ˈbəʊɡɑːd‖-ɡɑːrd/, **Sir Dirk** (1920–) an English actor who has appeared in many films including *The Damned* and *Death in Venice*

Bo·gart /ˈbəʊɡɑːt‖-ɡɑːrt/, **Hum·phrey** /ˈhʌmfri/ (1899–1957) an American film actor whose films include *The Maltese Falcon*, *Casablanca*, and *The African Queen* —see colour pictures on pages 228 and 685

bo·gey /ˈbəʊɡi/ n **1** also **bogey man** /ˈ·· ˌ·/, **boogeyman**— (used by children or to threaten them) an imaginary evil spirit: *The bogey man's coming to get you!* **2** a cause of fear, esp. an imaginary one **3** (in GOLF) a number of hits of the ball which is one more than PAR (the number of hits usu. taken)

bog·gle /ˈbɒɡəl‖ˈbɑː-/ v [I (**at**)] **1** to pause before taking any action, esp. owing to fear or surprise; HESITATE: *I rather boggled at having to pay £30 for the tickets.* **2** to be very surprised, shocked, or overwhelmed (OVERWHELM): **The mind boggles** *at the amount of research yet to be done.* —see also MIND-BOGGLING

bogie¹, **bogey**, **bogy** /ˈbəʊɡi/ n **1** BrE a set of four or six wheels set in a frame under a railway engine or carriage, that make it able to go round curves **2** a small light cart (TROLLEY) **3** (in GOLF) a SCORE of one stroke over PAR on a hole

bogie² v [T] (in GOLF) to play (a hole) in one stroke over PAR

Bog·nor Re·gis /ˌbɒɡnə ˈriːdʒɪs‖ˌbɑːɡnər-/ also **Bognor** a town on the S coast of England, popular with tourists, esp. older British people

Bog·o·tá /ˌbɒɡəˈtɑː‖ˌbəʊ-/ the capital city of Colombia, built on a high PLATEAU in the Andes

bog roll /ˈ·· ·/ n [C;U] BrE sl (a roll of) TOILET PAPER

bo·gus /ˈbəʊɡəs/ adj derog pretended; intentionally false: *The reporter could not get to see the minister, so she made up a completely bogus interview with him.*

bo·he·mi·an /bəʊˈhiːmiən, bə-/ n, adj becoming rare (a person) that does not follow the accepted practices, customs, and standards of social behaviour: *Many writers, artists, and musicians are thought to be bohemians/to lead bohemian lives.*

boil¹ /bɔɪl/ v [I;T] **1 a** to cause (a liquid or its container) to reach the temperature at which liquid changes into a gas: *Peter boiled the kettle.* | *I'm boiling the soup.* **b** (of a liquid or its container) to reach this temperature: *Is the milk/the kettle boiling yet?* | (fig.) *boiling with rage* | *The way these newspapers print such blatant lies* **makes my blood boil.** (=makes me extremely angry) **2** to cook in water at 100°C: *Boil the potatoes for 20 minutes.* | *The potatoes have been boiling (away) for 20 minutes.* | *Shall I boil you an egg?* | *boiled eggs* | (fig.) *a* **boiling hot** (=extremely hot) *day* **3 boil dry** to (cause to) become dry because the liquid has changed into gas by boiling: *Don't let the pan/the vegetables boil dry.* –see COOK (USAGE); see also HARD-BOILED, SOFT-BOILED

boil away *phr v* [I] to be reduced to nothing (as if) by boiling: *The water had all boiled away and the pan was burned.*

boil down *phr v* [I;T (=**boil** sthg. ↔ **down**)] to reduce in quantity by boiling: *Put plenty of spinach in the pan because it boils down (to almost nothing).* | (fig.) *Try to boil the report down (to the main points).*

boil down to sthg. *phr v* [I] *infml* (of a statement, situation, argument, etc.) to be or mean, leaving out the unnecessary parts: *It's a long report, but it really boils down to a demand for higher safety standards.*

boil over *phr v* [I] (of a liquid) to swell as it boils, and flow over the sides of a container: *Turn off the gas; the milk is boiling over.* | (fig.) *The argument boiled over into open war.*

boil up *phr v* [I] (of troubles) to develop and reach a dangerous level: *Trouble was boiling up in the Middle East.*

boil² *n* [S] an act or state of boiling: *Give the sheets a good boil to get them white.* | *The milk has nearly* **come to the boil.** | **Bring it to the boil,** *then turn down the heat.* | *to go/take* **off the boil** | (fig.) *Try to keep them interested in the deal — we don't want them to go* **off the boil.** (=lose interest)

boil³ *n* a painful infected swelling under the skin

boiled sweet /ˈ· ·/ *n BrE* a hard, small sweet which often tastes of fruit

boil·er /ˈbɔɪlər/ *n* a container for boiling water, e.g. in a steam engine, or to provide heating in a house –see also DOUBLE BOILER, POTBOILER

boiler suit /ˈ·· ·/ also **coveralls** *AmE*– *n* [C;U] a garment made in one piece, worn for dirty work; OVERALLS –see picture at OVERALL, and compare DUNGAREES

boiling point /ˈ··· ·/ *n* **1** the temperature at which a liquid boils: *Oil has a low boiling point.* –compare FREEZING POINT **2** the point at which high excitement, anger, etc., develops into action: *Relations between the two countries have almost reached boiling point.*

bois·ter·ous /ˈbɔɪstərəs/ *adj* **1** (of a person or behaviour) noisily cheerful and rough: *Her sons are nice boys, but rather boisterous.* **2** (of weather) wild and rough – –**ly** *adv* – –**ness** *n* [U]

Bo·lan /ˈbəʊlən/, **Marc** /mɑːk/mɑːrk/ (1947–77) a British singer and song writer, known esp. as the main singer of the band Tyrannosaurus Rex (T. Rex), who died young in a London car crash

bold /bəʊld/ *adj* **1** (of a person or behaviour) brave, confident, and adventurous; not afraid to take risks: *The council today announced its bold new plans for the city centre.* | *He's a bold thinker, with lots of original ideas.* **2** *derog* (of a person or behaviour) without respect or shame; INSOLENT: *She's a bold child.* | *He sat there* (**as**) **bold as brass** (=extremely boldly) *and refused to leave.* **3** (of the appearance of something) strongly marked; clearly formed: *the bold shape of the cliffs* | *a drawing done in a few bold lines* **4** [*no comp.*] (of print) in boldface: *The headwords in this dictionary are printed in bold type.* **5** *be/make* **(so) bold (as) to** *fml or humor* (esp. in social matters) to dare to: *That's a very unusual dress you're wearing, if I might make so bold (as to say so).* – –**ly** *adv* – –**ness** *n* [U]

bold·face /ˈbəʊldfeɪs/ *n* [U] (in printing) thick black letters

bold·faced /ˌbəʊldˈfeɪst◀/ *adj* **1** without respect or shame; BOLD (2) **2** [*no comp.*] (of print) in boldface

bold·ly /ˈbəʊldli/ **to boldly go where no man has gone before** a phrase from the television SERIES *Star Trek*, describing the idea of discovering new and exciting places. The phrase is also one of the most famous examples of a SPLIT INFINITIVE, which is considered by some people to be bad English. –see also STAR TREK

bole /bəʊl/ *n* the TRUNK (=the main stem) of a tree

bo·le·ro¹ /bəˈleərəʊ/ *n* -**ros** (a piece of music written for) a Spanish dance

bol·e·ro² /ˈbɒlərəʊ/bəˈleərəʊ/ *n* -**ros** a (woman's) short JACKET, open at the front and usu. not reaching the waist

Bo·leyn /bəˈlɪn/, **Anne** (1507–36) an English queen, the second wife of King Henry VIII, who had her head cut off for supposedly having affairs with her brother and others

Bo·liv·i·a /bəˈlɪviə/ a country in W South America, one of its only two countries having no coast; capital La Paz; population 7,193,000 (1989) –**Bolivian** *n, adj*

boll /bəʊl/ *n* the seed case of the cotton plant

bol·lard /ˈbɒləd, -lɑːd/ˈbɑːlərd/ *n* a short thick post **a** *BrE* at the end of streets closed to cars so that they may not enter **b** *BrE* in the middle of a street, where walkers wait **c** on a ship or beside the water, for tying ships' ropes to

bol·locks¹ /ˈbɒləks/ˈbɑː-/ *n, interj BrE taboo sl* **1** [P] TESTICLES **2** [U] *derog* complete nonsense

bollocks² *v*

bollocks sthg. ↔ **up** *BrE* || **bol·lix** sthg. ↔ **up** *AmE* /ˈbɒlɪks/ˈbɑː-/– *phr v* [T] *taboo sl* to spoil; BUNGLE – **bollocks-up** /ˈ·· ·/ *n*

boll wee·vil /ˌ· ˈ··/ *n* an insect that attacks the cotton plant

bo·lo·gna /bəˈləʊni/ *n* [U] *AmE* a popular SAUSAGE made of BEEF, VEAL, and PORK, commonly served in sandwiches (SANDWICH). Children often take bologna sandwiches to school.

Bo·lo·gna /bəˈləʊnjə/ the capital city of Emilia-Romagna in N central Italy at the foot of the Apennines

Bol·o·gnese /ˌbɒləˈneɪz◀/ˌbəʊləˈnjeɪz/ *adj* **1** of or from Bologna in Italy **2** cooked in the Bolognese way esp. in a sauce with MINCE (=very small pieces of meat): *spaghetti bolognese* | *a bolognese sauce*

bo·lo·ney , baloney /bəˈləʊni/ *n* [U] *sl* foolish talk; nonsense: *That's a lot of boloney.*

bo·lo tie /ˈbəʊləʊ ˌtaɪ/ also **string tie** *n AmE* a string worn around the neck with ends hanging down the front of a shirt, held together by a decorative object and worn usu. by men in the western US

Bol·she·vik /ˈbɒlʃ↓vɪk/ˈbəʊl-/ *n, adj* **1** (a supporter) of the system of government introduced in the USSR in 1917 **2** *derog* (a) COMMUNIST –**vism** *n* [U]

Bol·shoi Bal·let /ˌbɒlʃɔɪ ˈbæleɪ/ˌbəʊlʃɔɪ bæˈleɪ/ [*the*] the most famous school and theatre of BALLET in the former USSR, based in Moscow

bol·shy , bolshie /ˈbɒlʃi/ˈbəʊlʃi/ *adj BrE infml derog* unhelpful or unwilling and tending to argue: *I asked her to do some typing but she's being a bit bolshy about it.*

bol·ster¹ /ˈbəʊlstər/ *n* a large long PILLOW that goes across the head of a bed under the other pillows

bolster² *v* [T (UP)] to support, strengthen, or increase: *These price cuts are sure to bolster demand for their products.* | *to bolster up someone's pride*

bolt¹ /bəʊlt/ *n* **1** a screw with no point, which fastens through a piece of metal (NUT (2)) to hold things together **2** a metal bar that slides across to fasten a door or window **3** a short heavy ARROW to be fired from a CROSSBOW **4** a flash of lightning; THUNDERBOLT **5** a large quantity of rolled cloth **6 bolt from the blue** something unexpected and unpleasant: *His sudden death came as a bolt from the blue.* –see also NUTS AND BOLTS, **have shot one's bolt** (SHOOT¹)

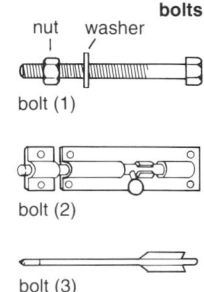

bolts

nut   washer

bolt (1)

bolt (2)

bolt (3)

bolt² *v* **1** [I] to move fast or run away suddenly: *My horse bolted and threw me in the mud.* | *The thief bolted when he saw the policeman.* **2** [T (DOWN)] to eat very quickly: *She bolted (down) her breakfast.* **3** [I;T] to (cause to) fasten with a bolt: *She bolted the door.* | *This door bolts on the inside.* | *These two metal parts bolt together; this one bolts onto that one.* | *Let me out! I'm bolted in.* **4** [T] *AmE, becoming rare* to break away from (a political party): *He bolted the Republicans.*

bolt³ *n* [S] an act of suddenly running away: *The prisoner* **made a bolt for** (=towards) *the door.*

bolt⁴ *adv* **bolt upright** straight and stiffly: *He made the children sit bolt upright.*

bolt·hole /ˈbəʊlthəʊl/ *BrE n* a place to which one can escape

Bol·ton /ˈbəʊltən/ a town in Greater Manchester, NW England, known for its wool and cotton industries and aircraft engineering

bomb¹ /bɒm‖baːm/ *n* **1** [C] a hollow metal container filled with explosive, or with other chemicals of a stated type or effect: *They planted a bomb in the post office.* | *Enemy aircraft dropped bombs on the city.* | *A* **time bomb** *explodes some time after it is placed in position.* | *The crowd threw petrol bombs at the police.* — see also LETTER BOMB **2** [*the*] the NUCLEAR bomb, or nuclear weapons in general, considered from a political

bomb

point of view. The phrase "ban the bomb" was used by people opposing the use of nuclear weapons, esp. in the 1960s: *At that stage, China did not yet have the bomb.* **3** **(go) like a bomb** *BrE infml* (to go) very well: *My new car goes like a bomb.* **4** **spend/cost a bomb** *BrE infml* to spend/cost a lot of money

bomb² *v* **1** [I;T] to attack with bombs, esp. by dropping them from aircraft **2** [I+*adv/prep*] *infml* to move quickly: *He came bombing along the road towards them.* **3** [I (OUT)] *AmE infml* to fail: *"How did he do on the last test?" "He bombed."*

bom·bard /bɒmˈbaːd‖baːmˈbaːrd/ *v* [T (**with**)] **1** to keep attacking heavily (as if) with gunfire: *The warships bombarded the port.* | *The speaker was bombarded with questions.* **2** *tech* to direct a stream of fast-moving PARTICLES at (an atom)

bom·bar·dier /ˌbɒmbəˈdɪəʳ‖ˌbaːmbər-/ *n* **1** the person on a military aircraft who drops the bombs **2** a soldier with a low rank in the Royal Artillery (=part of the British army)

bom·bard·ment /bɒmˈbaːdmənt‖baːmˈbaːrd/ *n* [C *usu. sing.*;U] (an) attack with big guns: *aerial bombardment*

bom·bast /ˈbɒmbæst‖ˈbaːm-/ *n* [U] *derog* important-sounding insincere words with little meaning — ~**ic** /bɒmˈbæstɪk‖baːm-/ *adj* : *a bombastic person/speech* — ~**ically** /kli/ *adv*

Bom·bay /ˌbɒmˈbeɪ‖ˌbaːm-/ a city and former state in W central India, the city being the largest in the country and now the capital of Maharashtra state

Bom·bay duck /ˌ·· ˈ·/ *n* [U] a food dish consisting of dried and salted fish, with a very strong taste

bomb dis·pos·al squad /ˌ·· ·ˈ··· ˌ·/ *n* a team of people whose job it is to make safe bombs which have been discovered, and prevent them from exploding

bomb·er /ˈbɒməʳ‖ˈbaː-/ *n* **1** an aircraft that carries and drops bombs —compare FIGHTER (2) **2** a person who throws or places bombs

bomber jack·et /ˈ·· ˌ··/ *n* a warm leather JACKET worn by American and British PILOTS during the Second World War. Jackets like these are seen by some people as fashionable.

bombing cam·paign /ˈ·· ·ˌ·/ *n* a number of bomb attacks by the same organization over a short period of time, often aimed at the general public rather than at anything particular and usu. done by TERRORISTS

bomb·proof /ˈbɒmpruːf‖ˈbaːm-/ *adj* giving protection against bombs: *a bombproof shelter*

bomb scare /ˈ· ·/ also **bomb threat** *AmE*— *n* a warning that a bomb has been planted in a certain place and is about to explode: *The station was closed because of a bomb scare.*

bomb·shell /ˈbɒmʃel‖ˈbaːm-/ *n* [*usu. sing.*] *infml* **1** a great and usu. unpleasant surprise: *The news of their divorce came as a bombshell to us.* **2** *old-fash* an extremely attractive woman: (esp. in the phrase **a blonde bombshell**)

bomb shel·ter /ˈ· ˌ··/ *n* a room or building, usu. underground, which is built to protect people from the effects of a bomb, esp. a NUCLEAR bomb. In the 1950s and 1960s, people in the US were encouraged to build bomb shelters for their families because people were afraid of war with the Soviet Union.

bomb-site /ˈbɒmsaɪt‖ˈbaːm-/ *n* an open space in a town, where a bomb has destroyed all the buildings

bo·na fi·de /ˌbəʊnə ˈfaɪdi◂‖ˈbəʊnə faɪd/ *adj, adv* real(ly); sincere(ly): *The hotel car park is only for bona fide guests.* (=for people actually staying at the hotel)

bona fi·des /ˌbəʊnə ˈfaɪdiz/ *n* [P] *fml or law* sincerity; honest intentions

bo·nan·za /bəˈnænzə, bəʊ-/ *n esp. AmE* something very profitable: *The film was a box-office bonanza.*

Bonanza a long-running US television programme which was set in the Wild West. Its main characters were three men who lived with their father on a RANCH (=large cattle farm).

bon·bon /ˈbɒnbɒn‖ˈbaːnbaːn/ *n* a sweet made of chocolate with a soft filling

bond¹ /bɒnd‖baːnd/ *n* **1** [C *often pl.*] something that unites two or more people or groups, such as a shared feeling or interest: *There's a close bond between them.* | *two countries that are linked by bonds of friendship* **2** [C] a written agreement or promise with the force of law: *to enter into a bond with someone* | (*pomp*) *His* **word is (as good as) his bond.** (=His spoken promise can be completely trusted.) **3** [C] an official paper promising to pay a sum of money to the person who holds it, esp. one by which a government or company borrows money from the public with the promise of paying it back with interest at a fixed time: *4½% National Savings bonds* —see also BEARER BOND, ZERO COUPON BOND **4** [S] a state of being stuck together: *This new glue makes a firmer bond.* **5** **in/out of bond** (of goods brought into a country) in/out of a bonded WAREHOUSE: *You can buy the whisky in bond or duty-paid* —see also BONDS

bond² *v* **1** [I;T (TOGETHER, **to**)] to (cause to) stick together, e.g. with glue: *bonded wood* **2** [I] *AmE* to develop strong and lasting feelings for someone, esp. between a mother and her new baby, or a father and his new baby: *Parents should have plenty of time with their new baby to allow bonding to occur* **3** [T] to put (goods) into a bonded WAREHOUSE

Bond, James a character in books by the English writer Ian Fleming. James Bond is a daring and attractive SECRET AGENT who works for the British Government and has the number 007. Many of the James Bond stories have been made into popular adventure films which are known for the exciting STUNTS and beautiful women.

bond·age /ˈbɒndɪdʒ‖ˈbaːn-/ *n* **1** *esp. lit* the condition of being a slave, or any state which seems like this; SERVITUDE: *in bondage to a cruel master* **2** sex involving the physical RESTRAINT of a partner

bonded ware·house /ˌ·· ˈ··/ *n* an official store for goods that are brought into a country and on which tax has not yet been paid

bond·hold·er /ˈbɒnd ˌhəʊldəʳ‖ˈbaːnd-/ *n* someone who holds government or industrial bonds

Bon·di Beach /ˌbɒndaɪ ˈbiːtʃ‖ˌbaːn-/ a very popular BEACH in an area of Sydney, Australia, often thought of in connection with surfing (SURF²) and attractive young women

bonds /bɒndz‖baːndz/ *n* [P] *lit* chains, ropes, etc., used for tying up a prisoner: *to escape from one's bonds*

Bond Street /ˈ· ·/ a street in London famous for its expensive shops

bone¹ /bəʊn/ *n* **1** [C] any of the various hard parts which make up the frame of a human or animal body, which protect the organs within, and round which are the flesh and skin: *He broke a bone in his leg and the doctor set it.* | *The dog was chewing/gnawing a bone.* | *a jawbone* | *She's very attractive; she's got* **good bone structure.** (=in her face) | *Put the fishbones on the side of the plate.* —see also SKELETON¹, and see picture at TEETH **2** [U] the hard substance from which these parts are formed: *The archaeologists found fragments of bone in the burial chamber.* | *a knife with a bone handle* **3** **bone of contention** something that causes argument: *The island has been a bone of contention between our two countries for years.* **4**

chilled/frozen to the bone *infml* feeling cold right through the body **5 close to/near the bone** slightly rude or improper; INDECENT or stating the truth in a cruel way: *Some of his jokes were rather close to the bone.* **6 cut something to the bone** to reduce (costs, services, etc.) as much as possible: *The bus service has been cut to the bone.* **7 have a 'bone to pick with** to have something to complain about to: *I've got a bone to pick with you. Why have you been spreading these rumours about me?* **8 make no bones about (doing) something** to feel no doubt or shame about (doing) something: *She makes no bones about her prejudice against them.* **9 not make old bones** *old-fash* not to live to be old **10 -boned** /bəʊnd/ having bones of the stated kind: *big-boned* —see also BARE BONES, FUNNY BONE, **feel in one's bones** (FEEL¹), **skin and bones** (SKIN¹) — ~**less** *adj*

bone² *v* [T] **1** to take the bones out of: *Will you bone the fish for me?* | *boned meat* **2** to stiffen (a garment) with pieces of bone
  bone up *phr v* [I (**for, on**)] *infml* to study hard, esp. for a special purpose: *You'd better bone up on the traffic rules if you want to pass your driving test.*

bone chi·na /ˌ· ˈ··◄/ *n* [U] (cups, plates, etc., made of) fine white clay mixed with crushed animals' bones; a kind of PORCELAIN. Bone china is considered to be a high quality material and things made from it are generally quite expensive.

bone-dry /ˌ· ˈ·◄/ *adj infml* perfectly dry

bone·head /ˈbəʊnhed/ *n sl* a stupid person — ~**ed** /ˌbəʊnˈhedˌd/ *adj*

bone-i·dle /ˌ· ˈ··◄/ also **bone-lazy**— *adj* extremely lazy

bone mar·row /ˈ· ˌ··/ *n* MARROW (1)

bone meal /ˈ· ·/ *n* [U] crushed bones, used for improving the soil

bone-shak·er /ˈbəʊnˌʃeɪkəʳ/ *n infml, often humor* an uncomfortable shaky old vehicle, esp. a bicycle

bon·fire /ˈbɒnfaɪəʳ‖ˈbɑːn-/ *n* a large fire made in the open air, either for pleasure or to burn unwanted things: *to build a bonfire* —see colour picture on page 1211

Bonfire Night /ˈ·· ˌ·/ *BrE* GUY FAWKES NIGHT

bon·go /ˈbɒŋgəʊ‖ˈbɑːŋ-/ also **bongo drum** /ˈ··· ·/— *n* -gos or -goes either of a pair of small drums played with the hands

bon·ho·mie /ˈbɒnəmi‖ˌbɑːnəˈmiː/ *n* [U] *Fr* cheerfulness; easy friendliness: *a spirit of bonhomie* | *his irritating bonhomie*

Bon·ing·ton /ˈbɒnɪŋtən‖ˈbɑːn-/, Chris /krɪs/ (1934–) an English MOUNTAINEER who was a member of the first British team to successfully climb the SW face of Mount Everest

bonk¹ /bɒŋk‖bɑːŋk/ *v* **1** [T] *infml* to hit, usu. not very hard: *He bonked me on the head with the end of the ladder.* **2** [I(AWAY);T] *BrE sl* to have sex (with)

bonk² *n* **1** *infml* an act of hitting someone; hit **2** *BrE sl humor* an act of having sex

bon·kers /ˈbɒŋkəz‖ˈbɑːŋkərz/ *adj* [F] *BrE sl humor* mad: *The noise is driving me bonkers!*

bon mot /ˌbɒn ˈməʊ‖ˌbəʊn-/ *n* **bons mots** /ˌbɒn ˈməʊz‖ˌbəʊn-/ *Fr* a clever saying or remark

Bonn /bɒn‖bɑːn/ the capital city of the Federal Republic of Germany from 1949 until 1990

bon·net /ˈbɒnɪt‖ˈbɑː-/ *n* **1** a round head-covering tied under the chin, and often with a BRIM (=a piece in front) that shades the face, worn by babies and, esp. in former times, by women **2** *BrE* ‖ **hood** *AmE*— a metal lid over the front of a car: *to look under the bonnet* —see pictures at CAR and at ENGINE **3** a soft flat cap worn by men, esp. soldiers, in Scotland — see also **bee in one's bonnet** (BEE)

Bon·nie and Clyde /ˌbɒni ənd ˈklaɪd‖ˌbɑː-/ Clyde Barrow and Bonnie Parker, a team of two young ROBBERS in the US who stole money from banks and businesses in Texas,

Oklahoma, New Mexico, and Missouri in the 1930s and were the subject of a popular film made in 1967

Bon·nie Prince Char·lie /ˌ·· · ˈ··/ see Charles STUART

bon·ny /ˈbɒni‖ˈbɑːni/ *adj apprec, esp. ScotE* **1** pretty and healthy: *a bonny baby* **2** [A] fine or skilful: *a bonny fighter* —**nily** *adv*

bon·sai /ˈbɒnsaɪ, ˈbəʊn-‖ˈbɑːnsaɪ, ˌbəʊn-/ *n* **bonsai** [C;U] (the art of growing) a plant in a small pot that is prevented from reaching its natural size, esp. a tree

bo·nus /ˈbəʊnəs/ *n* **1** an additional payment beyond what is usual, necessary, or expected, such as a share of the profits paid to those who work for a business: *The staff got a Christmas bonus|a productivity bonus* | *a cost of living bonus paid to workers because of rising prices* | *A* **no-claims bonus** (*BrE*) *is a reduction allowed in the cost of motor insurance when no claim has been made during previous years.* **2** [*usu. sing.*] *infml* anything pleasant in addition to what is expected: *We like our new house, and it's a real bonus that my mother lives so near.*

bon vi·vant /ˌbɒn viːˈvɒnt‖ˌbɑːn viːˈvɑːnt/ also **bon viv·eur** /-viːˈvɜːʳ/ *esp. BrE*— *n* a person who likes good wine and food and cheerful companions

bon·y /ˈbəʊni/ *adj* **1** very thin so that the bones can be seen: *her bony hand* **2** (of food) full of bones: *bony fish*

bon·zer /ˈbɒnzəʳ‖ˈbɑːn-/ *adj AustrE old-fash sl* good; nice; fine: *a bonzer new car*

Bon·zo /ˈbɒnzəʊ‖ˈbɑːn-/ a name thought of as a typical name for a dog although very few dogs in fact have this name

boo¹ /buː/ *interj, n* **boos** **1** a shout of disapproval or strong disagreement: *A loud boo came from the back of the hall.* **2** (a word) usu. shouted very suddenly at someone, often a child, to give them a sudden fright): *Boo! Scared you!* **3 can't/couldn't say boo to a goose** *infml* to be easily frightened; lack courage

boo² *v* [I;T] to express disapproval (of) or strong disagreement (with), esp. by shouting "boo": *The crowd booed (the speaker).* | *They booed him off the stage.* | *The audience started booing and hissing when the actor forgot his lines.*

boob¹ /buːb/ *esp. BrE* ‖ **boo-boo** /ˈbuːbuː/ *esp. AmE*— *n infml* a silly mistake

boob² *v infml, esp. BrE* [I] to make a silly mistake: *I've boobed again.*

boobs /buːbz/ *n* [P] *infml* a woman's breasts

boob tube /ˈ· ·/ *n* **1** *infml* a woman's short garment for the upper body made of stretchy material **2** [*the*] *AmE humor infml* television

boo·by /ˈbuːbi/ also **boob** *AmE*— *n infml* a foolish person

booby hatch /ˈ·· ˌ·/ *n sl, esp. AmE for* MENTAL HOSPITAL

booby prize /ˈ·· ·/ *n* a prize given (often as a joke) for the worst performance in a competition

booby trap /ˈ·· ·/ *n* **1** a hidden bomb which explodes when a harmless-looking object is touched **2** any harmless trap used for surprising someone, esp. as a joke: *He put a bag of flour on top of the door as a booby trap.* —**booby-trap** *v* [T] **-pp-**

boo·gey·man /ˈbuːgimæn/ *n* -**men** /men/ see BOGEY (1)

boo·gie /ˈbuːgi/ *v esp. AmE* to dance to boogie-woogie music or to ROCK or similar music

boo·gie-woo·gie /ˌbuːgi ˈwuːgi/ *n* [U] a style of BLUES (1) piano playing, with the left hand continuously repeating the same phrase while the right hand provides the tune or MELODY (2)

boo·hoo /ˌbuː ˈhuː/ *interj* (a word meant to be like the sound of loud childish crying) —**boo-hoo** *v* [I]

book¹ /bʊk/ *n* **1** (a written work in the form of) a set of printed pages fastened together inside a cover, as a thing to be read: *She's writing a book on/about her travels in China.* | *They bought me a book for my birthday.* | *Have you read that book yet?* | *This book was first published in 1978.* | *a history book* | *a book of poems* | *Jane Austen's "Persuasion" is one of the* **set books** *for this year's English exam.* **2** a set of sheets of paper fastened together inside a cover, as a thing to be written in: *an exercise book* | *a rent book* (=in which a record of rent payments is kept) | *an autograph book* **3** any collection of things fastened together, esp. one with its own covers: *a book of stamps/tickets/matches* | *a cheque book* **4** one of the

Warren Beatty and Faye Dunaway in *Bonnie and Clyde*

main divisions of a larger written work, such as a long poem or the Bible **5** the words of a light musical play —compare LIBRETTO **6 according to/by the book** according to the established rules rather than using one's own ideas or methods: *It's safer to go by the book/to do everything strictly by the book.* **7 bring someone to book** to force someone to give an explanation, or to be punished: *He was finally brought to book for fiddling the accounts.* **8 in one's book** according to one's own opinion or way of doing things: *In my book this is not the way to handle it.* **9 make (a) book on** to offer to receive and pay out money on the results of a competition or a race —see also BOOKS, CLOSED BOOK, COFFEE-TABLE BOOK, GOOD BOOK, **throw the book at** (THROW[1] (24)) **10 one for the books** *AmE infml* an unusual event: *John's cleaned his room — that's one for the books!*

book² *v* **1** [I;T (UP)] to arrange in advance to have (something); RESERVE: *to book seats on a plane/a table in a restaurant* | *I'm afraid these seats are already booked.* | *You'll have to book (up) well in advance if you want to see that show.* | *She booked a band to play at the reception.* | *He was booked on the early flight* (=had a seat booked on it) *but had to go later because of a problem at the office.* **2** [T] *infml* to enter charges against, esp. in the police records: *She was booked on a charge of speeding.* **3** [T] to write the name of (a RUGBY or football player) in a book for breaking the rules: *The referee booked both players.*

book in *phr v* **1** [T (=**book** sbdy. **in**)] to book a room for (oneself or someone else) at a hotel: *I've booked you in at the Grand Hotel.* **2** [I] to report one's arrival at a hotel desk, an airport, etc.; CHECK **in**: *We booked in at 3 o'clock.*

book sthg. ↔ **up** *phr v* [T *usu. pass.*] to keep (all the seats, rooms in a hotel, service, etc.) for people who have made arrangements in advance: *I'm sorry, the hotel is (fully) booked up.* | *That singer is always booked up for a year ahead.*

book·a·ble /ˈbʊkəbəl/ *adj* that can be booked in advance: *All seats for the show are bookable.*

book·bind·ing /ˈbʊkˌbaɪndɪŋ/ *n* [U] the art of fastening the pages of books together and enclosing them in covers —**er** *n*

book·case /ˈbʊk-keɪs/ *n* a piece of furniture containing shelves to hold books —see picture at LIVING ROOM

book club /ˈ· ·/ *n* a club that offers books cheaply to its members

book·end /ˈbʊkend/ *n* [*usu. pl.*] either of a pair of supports to hold up a row of books

Book·er Prize /ˈbʊkə ˌpraɪz/–kər–/ *n* [*the*] an important prize for literature which is given every year for the best full-length NOVEL in English written by a citizen of Britain or the Commonwealth: *a Booker Prize-winning author*

book·ie /ˈbʊki/ *n infml* a BOOKMAKER

book·ing /ˈbʊkɪŋ/ *n* [C;U] **1** a case or the act of making a formal arrangement or promise to give a performance, provide a service, etc.: *She has bookings for several concerts.* **2** *esp. BrE* a case or the act of booking a seat, hotel room, etc.; RESERVATION: *All bookings must be made by post.* | *She bought a ticket at the booking office/from the booking clerk.* **3** a case or the act of booking (BOOK[2] (2)): *There were five bookings in the match.*

book·ish /ˈbʊkɪʃ/ *adj often derog* **1** fond of books and reading; STUDIOUS **2** showing more interest in ideas from books than in practical experience —~**ness** *n* [U]

book·keep·ing /ˈbʊkˌkiːpɪŋ/ *n* [U] the act or skill of keeping the accounts of a business company or other organization —**er** *n*

book·let /ˈbʊklət/ *n* a small book, usu. with a paper cover; PAMPHLET: *I picked up a free booklet on tooth care at the dentist's.*

book·mak·er /ˈbʊkˌmeɪkər/ *esp. BrE*, also **book·ie** *infml*, **turf accountant** *BrE fml*— *n* a person whose job is to take money (BETS) risked on the results of competitions, esp. horse races

book·mark /ˈbʊkmɑːk/–mɑːrk/ also **book·mark·er** /ˈbʊkmɑːkə/–mɑːr-/— *n* something, such as a piece of RIBBON or leather, put between the pages of a book to mark a place in it

book·mo·bile /ˈbʊkməbiːl/ *n AmE for* MOBILE LIBRARY

Book of Com·mon Prayer /ˌ· · ˌ· ·ˈ·/ [*the*] the book which is used by the minister and the CONGREGATION in services in the Church of England and in the Episcopal church in the US. A modern Book of Common Prayer, called *The Alternative Service Book*, has been in use since 1980.

book·plate /ˈbʊkpleɪt/ *n* an often decorative piece of paper stuck in a book to show who owns it

books /bʊks/ *n* [P] **1** written records of business accounts, names, etc.: *Their books show a profit.* | *He was sacked for* **cooking the books.** (=stealing money by making changes in the accounts) **2 in someone's good/bad books** *infml* in favour/disfavour with someone

book·sell·er /ˈbʊkˌselər/ *n* a person who sells books to the public

book·shop /ˈbʊkʃɒp/–ʃɑːp/ *esp. BrE* || **book·store** /-stɔːr/ *esp. AmE*— *n* a shop where books are sold —compare LIBRARY (1)

book·stall /ˈbʊkstɔːl/ *n* a table or small shop open at the front, where books, magazines, etc., are shown for sale

book to·ken /ˈ· ˌ··/ *n BrE* a gift card for a certain value that can be exchanged for books at a bookshop: *a £5 book token*

book·worm /ˈbʊkwɜːm/–wɜːrm/ *n* a person who is very fond, perhaps too fond, of reading and study

boom¹ /buːm/ *v* **1** [I;T (OUT)] to make (with) a deep hollow sound: *The guns boomed.* | *a loud booming voice* | *The foghorn boomed out its warning.* **2** [I] to grow rapidly in activity, value, or importance: *Business is booming.*

boom² *n* **1** a booming sound or cry: *The new aircraft creates a* **sonic boom.** **2** a (period of) rapid growth or increase: *There's been a boom in exports this year.* | *the postwar baby boom* | *The big tax cuts fuelled a consumer boom.* | *a* **boom town** (=where wealth and population are growing very fast)

boom³ *n* **1** a long pole **a** on a boat, to which a sail is fastened **b** used as part of an apparatus for loading and unloading **c** on the end of which a camera or MICROPHONE can be moved about —see picture at YACHT **2** a heavy chain fixed across a river to stop things (esp. logs) floating down or prevent ships sailing up

boom box /ˈ· ·/ *n AmE infml* a GHETTO BLASTER

boo·mer·ang¹ /ˈbuːməræŋ/ *n* a curved stick which makes a circle and comes back when thrown, used by Australian ABORIGINES as a hunting weapon

boomerang² *v* [I (**on**)] (of a plan) to cause sudden unexpected harm to the person who made it; have the opposite result to what was intended; BACKFIRE: *His plan to reduce the number of workers boomeranged (on him), and he lost his own job.*

boon /buːn/ *n* **1** [*usu. sing.*] *fml* something very helpful or useful: *The radio is a great boon to the blind.* **2** *old use* a favour: *to ask a boon of someone*

boon com·pan·ion /ˌ· ·ˈ··/ *n* [*usu. pl.*] a good, close friend

boon·docks /ˈbuːndɒks/–dɑːks/ also **boon·ies** /ˈbuːniz/ *n* [*the*+P] *AmE infml humor* a rough country area far from any town, where few people live

Boone /buːn/**, Daniel** (1734–1820) an American PIONEER who explored and settled Kentucky. He is usually pictured with a hat made of RACCOON skin and is a popular HERO.

boor /bʊər/ *n* a rude insensitive person, esp. a man —~**ish** *adj* —~**ishly** *adv* —~**ishness** *n* [U]: *She was revolted by his utter boorishness.*

boost¹ /buːst/ *v* [T] **1** [(UP)] to lift by pushing up from below: *If you boost me up, I can just reach the window.* **2** to increase; raise: *These changes will help to boost share prices/profits/demand.* | *plans to boost production by 30% next year* **3** to help to advance or improve; encourage: *We need a holiday to boost our spirits.* | *She's always trying to boost his ego by telling him how clever he is.* **4** *infml, esp. AmE* to help or favour the interests of, esp. by speech and writing; PLUG[2] (2): *a special promotion to boost their new product*

boost² *n* [*usu. sing.*] **1** a push upwards **2** an increase or improvement: *This has given share prices a big boost.* **3** an act that brings help or encouragement: *That holiday has given her spirits a boost.* | *an ego-boost*

boost·er /ˈbuːstər/ *n* **1** a person or machine that boosts: *When the boosters have helped to lift a space station into orbit, they separate from it and return to Earth.* **2** an additional amount of a drug, to strengthen the effect of some of the same drug that was given earlier: *This* injection will protect you against the disease, but after six months you'll need a booster. **3** infml, esp. AmE a person who is very much in favour of something or someone

boot¹ /buːt/ n **1** [C usu. pl.] a covering of leather or rubber for the foot and ankle, usu. heavier and thicker than a shoe: He laced up his boots. | army boots | a pair of football boots —see picture at SHOE, and see also WELLINGTON **2** [C] BrE ‖ **trunk** AmE— an enclosed space at the back of a car for bags and boxes —see picture at CAR **3** [C usu. sing.] infml a kick with the foot **4** [the] sl the taking away of someone's job by an employer; DISMISSAL; SACK¹ (2): They gave her the boot for continually being late. | She got the boot. **5 put the boot in** sl, esp. BrE to kick someone hard, usu. when they are already on the ground **6 the boot is on the other foot** infml the situation has changed to the opposite of what it was before —see also BOOTS, **too big for one's boots** (BIG), **die with one's boots on** (DIE¹)

boot² v [T+obj+adv/prep] infml **1** to kick: He booted the ball across the field. **2** [T] AmE for CLAMP² (2): Watch out! They're booting cars today.
boot sbdy. ↔ **out** phr v [T] infml to send away rudely and sometimes with force, esp. from a job: They booted him out for being drunk at work.

boot³ n tech the action of loading an OPERATING SYSTEM for a computer from a DISK into the computer's memory — **boot** v [T (UP)]

boot⁴ n **to boot** old use or humor (often of something unpleasant) besides; in addition: He is dishonest, and a coward to boot.

boot·black /ˈbuːtblæk/ n rare a person who cleans and polishes shoes, esp. in the street for money

boot camp /ˈ· ·/ n a training camp for people who have just joined the US navy, army, or Marine Corps

boot·ed /ˈbuːtᵻd/ adj having boots of a stated type: black-booted soldiers

boot·ee /ˈbuːtiː, buːˈtiː/ n [usu. pl.] a baby's woollen boot

booth /buːð‖buːθ/ n **1** (at a market or FAIR³) a tent or small building where goods are sold or games are played **2** a small enclosed place for one person: a telephone booth | a voting booth | a listening booth in a record shop **3** a partly enclosed place in a restaurant with a table between two long seats

Booth /buːθ/, **John Wilkes** /dʒɒn wɪlks‖dʒɑːn-/ (1838–65) the man who shot and killed US President Abraham Lincoln

Booth /buːð/, **William** (1829–1912) a British religious leader who established the Salvation Army in 1878

Booth·royd /ˈbuːθrɔɪd/, **Bet·ty** /ˈbeti/ (1929–   ) a British Labour politician who became Deputy Speaker of the House of Commons in 1987, and in 1992 was elected as the first woman Speaker of the House of Commons

boot·lace /ˈbuːtleɪs/ n [usu. pl.] a LACE¹ (2) for boots

boot·leg /ˈbuːtleg/ v **-gg-** [I;T] to make, carry, or sell (esp. alcoholic drink) illegally. In the US, bootlegging is often connected with the time of PROHIBITION (1920–33), when alcohol was forbidden except for medicinal or religious purposes. —**bootleg** adj : bootleg records/whisky – ~ **ger** n

boot·less /ˈbuːtləs/ adj lit bringing no advantage/useless: bootless care

boots /buːts/ n boots BrE old use a male hotel servant who cleans shoes and carries bags

Boots one of a group of CHEMIST's shops found in most towns in Britain, which also sells articles for babies, photographic supplies, and some food items

boot sale /ˈ· ·/ BrE also **boot fair, car boot sale** BrE ‖ **garage sale** or **yard sale** AmE n a sale in a car park, school, or other open space, where a number of people sell things, esp. SECOND-HAND things, from the BOOTS of their cars. In the US, garage or yard sales are held in and around the garage or YARD (–garden) of the seller.

boot·straps /ˈbuːtstræps/ n **haul/pull oneself up by one's own bootstraps** infml improve oneself or one's situation by one's own efforts, without help from anyone else

boot·y /ˈbuːti/ n [U] esp. lit goods stolen by thieves or taken by a victorious army: to share out/divide up the booty

booze¹ /buːz/ v [I] sl to drink alcohol, esp. too much alcohol: He's out boozing with his friends.

booze² n [U] sl alcoholic drink

booz·er /ˈbuːzəʳ/ n sl **1** a person who boozes often **2** BrE a PUB

booze-up /ˈ· ·/ n BrE sl an occasion, for example a party, when a lot of alcohol is drunk

booz·y /ˈbuːzi/ adj showing signs of heavy drinking of alcohol: a boozy party/old man —**ily** adv —**iness** n [U]

bop¹ /bɒp‖bɑːp/ v **-pp-** [T] infml to hit with the hand or something held in the hand —**bop** n : a bop on the head

bop² **-pp-** [I] infml, esp BrE to dance in an informal way, esp. to popular music in a DISCO: bopping (around) to the latest hits —**bop** n : Shall we have a bop?

bop³ also **bebop**— n [U] a type of JAZZ music developed in the 1940s, which typically has difficult instrumental parts and complicated RHYTHMS

Bo Peep /bəʊ ˈpiːp/ also **Little Bo Peep**— a character from a children's NURSERY RHYME. Bo Peep is a young girl who looks after sheep, but in the nursery rhyme she has lost her sheep and cannot find them.

Bop·hu·that·swa·na /ˌbɒpuːtatˈswɑːnə‖ˌbəʊ-/ an area of South Africa which is a HOMELAND for the Bantu people

Bor·deaux /bɔːˈdəʊ‖bɔːr-/ n **1** [U] white or red wine of the Bordeaux area of France **2** a port and city in the Bordeaux area of SW France

bor·del·lo /bɔːˈdeləʊ‖bɔːr-/ n **-los** esp. lit a BROTHEL

bor·der¹ /ˈbɔːdəʳ‖ˈbɔːr-/ n **1** an edge running around or along something, often having a decorative purpose: a white handkerchief with a blue border | a border of flowers round the lawn **2** [(between, with)] (land near) the dividing line between two countries: soldiers guarding the border | to cross the border into Spain | within our borders | a town in eastern France, near the border with Germany | a border town/area/dispute **3 north of the border** BrE in Scotland: Let's now look at the election campaign north of the border.

border² v [T] **1** to form a border to: fields bordered by woods **2** to share a border with: France borders Germany along parts of the Rhine. **3** [(with)] to provide with a border, esp. for decoration: to border a skirt with lace
border on/upon sthg. phr v [T] to be very much like; VERGE on: strange behaviour that borders on madness

Border one of the British television companies controlled by the ITC, transmitting (TRANSMIT) programmes to Northern England and Scotland —see also BORDERS

bor·der·land /ˈbɔːdəlænd‖ˈbɔːrdər-/ n **1** [C] land at or near the border of two countries **2** [S] a condition between two other conditions and like each of them in certain ways: the borderland between sleeping and waking

bor·der·line /ˈbɔːdəlaɪn‖ˈbɔːrdər-/ n (**between**)) **1** [C usu. sing.] (a line marking) a border: the borderline between France and Germany on the map **2** [S] an uncertain dividing line between two (opposite) conditions: the borderline between genius and madness/between passing and failing the exam | Ann will certainly pass the exam, but Susan is a borderline case. (=may or may not pass)

Bor·ders /ˈbɔːdəz‖ˈbɔːrdərz/ [the+P] a REGION in Scotland close to the border with England, known for its low, rolling hills

bore¹ /bɔːʳ/ past tense of BEAR²

bore² n **1** [C] derog a dull uninteresting person whom other people quickly become tired of, esp. one who talks continually or repeatedly in an uninteresting way: She's become an awful bore since she got married to him. | Don't mention computers — he's a real bore on the subject. | a crashing bore **2** [S] infml, esp BrE something which is rather unpleasant or annoying; NUISANCE: It's a bore having to go out again on a cold night like this.

bore³ v [T] to make (someone) tired or uninterested, esp. by continual dull talk: He bored us all by talking for hours about his new car. | (sl) That guy really **bores the pants off** me.

bore⁴ v [I+adv/prep, T] to make a round hole or passage (in something): This machine can bore through solid rock. | Worms have bored into the wood. | to bore a hole/a well | (fig.) to bore one's way through a crowd of people

bore⁵ n **1** (often in comb.) a measurement of the size of a hole, esp. of the width of the inside of a gun barrel or pipe: a 12-bore shotgun | a small-bore rifle **2** also **borehole**— a hole made by boring, esp. for oil, water, etc.

bore⁶ n a very large wave caused by a movement of the sea running up a narrow river: a tidal bore

bored /bɔːd‖bɔːrd/ adj [(**with**)] tired and uninterested: *She's bored with her job.* | *a bored expression on her face* | *I was* **bored stiff/bored to death/bored to tears** *by their trivial conversation.*

bore·dom /ˈbɔːdəm‖ˈbɔːr-/ n [U] the state of being bored: *She made no attempt to conceal her boredom.*

bore·hole /ˈbɔːhəʊl‖ˈbɔːr-/ n a BORE⁵ (2)

bor·er /ˈbɔːrəʳ/ n a person, tool, or insect that makes round holes

Borg /bɔːg‖bɔːrg/, **Bjorn** /bjɔːn‖bjɔːrn/ (1956–) a Swedish tennis player who won the men's SINGLES title at Wimbledon five times in a row between 1976 and 1980

Bor·ges /ˈbɔːhes‖ˈbɔːr-/, **Jor·ge Lu·is** /ˈhɔːheɪ luˈiːs‖ ˈhɔːr-/ (1899–1986) an Argentinian poet and writer of short stories

bor·ing /ˈbɔːrɪŋ/ adj dull or uninteresting; TEDIOUS: *a boring job/film/person* | *The lecture was* **deadly boring.** (=extremely boring) — ~ **ly** adv : *boringly predictable*

Bor·mann /ˈbɔːmən‖ˈbɔːr-/, **Martin** (1900–?45) a German Nazi political leader, one of Hitler's closest advisers, whose SKELETON¹ (1) was discovered in 1972

born¹ /bɔːn‖bɔːrn/ past participle of BEAR²

▷ USAGE This is one of the two past participles of **bear** when it means "to give birth to". Compare *He was* **born** *in 1950* and *She has* **borne** *(fml) three children.*◁

born² adj [no comp.] **1** [F] brought into existence by or as if by birth: *Shakespeare was born in 1564.* | *The baby was born at 8 o'clock.* | *Don't try and tell me any lies; I wasn't born yesterday, you know!* | *He's a countryman* **born and bred** (=was born and grew up in the country), *so he doesn't like big cities.* | *The people won their independence, and a new nation was born.* | *He spoke with a cynicism born of bitter experience.* **2** [F] from or by birth; originally: *He was born French, but applied for Canadian citizenship when he grew up.* **3** having a stated quality from or as if from birth: *a born leader/writer* | *He was born lucky.* [F+to-v] *She was born to succeed.* (=it was always clear that she would do so) **4** **born with a silver** **'spoon in one's mouth** having money and social advantages from birth **5** **in all my born days** *infml* in all my life **6** **there's one born every minute** a phrase used when saying that someone has acted very foolishly **7** **-born** born in the stated way: *American-born* | *first-born* | *still-born* (=born dead) —see also UNBORN, **to the manner born** (MANNER)

born-a·gain /ˌ· ·ˈ·/ adj having accepted a particular religion, esp. EVANGELICAL Christianity, often through a deep spiritual experience:*a born-again Christian* | (fig.) *a born-again non-smoker/jogger*

▶ CULTURAL NOTE People who have had bad experiences often become born-again Christians and they believe their new faith in Christ helps them to start a new life. Born-again Christians are usu. open about their beliefs and like to talk about their faith. In the US they are known for being active in the MORAL MAJORITY, in FUNDAMENTALISM, and in EVANGELICAL churches.◀

borne /bɔːn‖bɔːrn/ **1** past participle of BEAR² —see BORN¹ (USAGE) **2** **borne in on/upon** brought firmly to the consciousness of: *Slowly it was borne in on the citizens that the enemy had surrounded them.* **3** **-borne** carried as stated: *waterborne diseases* | *Some plants have wind-borne seeds.*

Bor·ne·o /ˈbɔːniəʊ‖ˈbɔːr-/ the largest island in the Malay Archipelago in SE Asia

Bor·o·din /ˈbɒrədɪn‖ˈbɔːrədiːn/, **Al·ex·an·der** /ˌælɪgˈzɑːn dəʳ‖-ˈzæn-/ (1833–87) a Russian COMPOSER whose most famous work is his OPERA *Prince Igor*

bo·rough /ˈbʌrə‖-rəʊ/ n (*sometimes cap.*) a town, or a division of a large town, with some powers of local government: *the Borough of Brooklyn*

borough coun·cil /ˌ·· ˈ··/ n esp. *BrE* the organization responsible for local government in a borough

bor·row /ˈbɒrəʊ‖ˈbɑː-, ˈbɔː-/ v [I;T (**from**)] **1** to take or receive (something) from another person, usu. with that person's permission, and with the understanding that it will be returned after a certain time: *He borrowed a car from a friend for a few days.* | *Can I borrow your pen for a moment?* | *They borrowed heavily from the bank to start their new business.* | *She could not pay back all the money she had borrowed.* —compare LEND, LOAN² **2** to take or

copy (esp. ideas, words, etc.) and use them as one's own: *English has borrowed (words) from many languages.* — see also **live on borrowed time** (LIVE¹) **3 borrow trouble** *AmE infml* to worry unnecessarily

bor·row·er /ˈbɒrəʊəʳ‖ˈbɑː-, ˈbɔː-/ n **1** a person who borrows (something) **2** **neither a borrower nor a lender be** *quote* a phrase from the play *Hamlet* by Shakespeare

bor·row·ing /ˈbɒrəʊɪŋ‖ˈbɑː-, ˈbɔː-/ n a word or phrase which has been borrowed by one language from another: *English has many borrowings from French.* —see also LOANWORD

borrowing pow·ers /ˈ··· ˌ··/ n [P] the amount of money a company is allowed by its own regulations to borrow

borscht , borshcht /bɔːʃt‖bɔːrʃt/ also **borsch** /bɔːʃ‖bɔːrʃ/— n [U] a BEETROOT soup often served with sour cream

bor·stal /ˈbɔːstl‖ˈbɔːr-/ n [C;U] *BrE* (*often cap.*) a prison school for young criminals between the ages of 16 and 21: *He was sent to borstal for stealing.*

bor·zoi /ˈbɔːzɔɪ‖ˈbɔːrzɔɪ/ n a large long-haired hunting dog originally from Russia

Bosch /bɒʃ‖bɑːʃ/, **Hie·ron·y·mus** /haɪəˈrɒnɪməs‖-ˈrɑː-/ (?1450–1516) a Flemish painter known for his strange and GROTESQUE paintings, esp. *The Garden of Earthly Delights*

bosh /bɒʃ‖bɑːʃ/ n, interj [U] *infml, esp. BrE* foolish talk; nonsense

Bos·ni·a /ˈbɒzniə‖ˈbɑːz-/ an area of Yugoslavia, which together with Herzegovina formed the republic of Bosnia-Herzegovina until the country began to break up into independent units in the early 1990s

Bos·ni·a-Her·ze·go·vi·na /ˌbɒzniə ˌhɜːtsəgəˈviːnə‖ˌbɑːzniə ˌheərts-/ (since 1990) a country in SE Europe bordered by Croatia, Serbia, and Montenegro; capital Sarajevo; population 4,440,000 (1988)

bos·om /ˈbʊzəm/ n [*usu. sing.*] *esp. lit* **1** the front of the human chest, esp. the female breasts, or the part of a garment covering this: *She held the child to her bosom.* | *She carried the letter in the bosom of her dress.* **2** this part considered as the centre of feelings: *Her bosom was torn by sorrow.* | *a bosom friend/buddy* (=a very close friend) | *He spent his last years* **in the bosom of** (=living in a close relationship with) *his family.* —compare BREAST¹

bos·om·y /ˈbʊzəmi/ adj *infml* having large breasts: *a bosomy actress* —compare BUXOM

Bos·por·us /ˈbɒspərəs‖ˈbɑːs-/ also **Bos·pho·rus** /ˈbɒs pərəs, -fərəs‖ˈbɑːs-/ [*the*] the stretch of sea which separates European and Asian Turkey, and connects the Black Sea with the Sea of Marmara

boss¹ /bɒs‖bɔːs/ n *infml* **1** a person who is in charge of workers; an employer or manager: *He asked the boss/his boss for more money.* | *Who's (the) boss here?* (=Who's in charge?) | (fig.) *You can't let the children just do what they like — you've got to* **show them who's boss!** —see FATHER¹ (USAGE) **2** *esp. AmE, usu. derog* a political party chief, esp. one who controls a local party organization

boss² v [T (ABOUT, AROUND)] *infml* to give orders (to), esp. in an unpleasant way: *Tom likes to boss younger children about.*

boss³ adj *AmE, sl* excellent or fashionable: *a boss suit* | *a boss car*

boss⁴ n a round decoration which stands out from the surface of something, e.g. on a shield or the inside of a church roof

boss⁵ **make a boss shot (at)** *BrE old-fash sl* to make a first, probably not very good, attempt (at)

BOSS /bɒs‖bɔːs/ Bureau for State Security; the South African organization responsible for collecting information about other countries and for the safety of the state

bos·sa no·va /ˌbɒsə ˈnəʊvə‖ˌbɑːs-/ n [*the*] a dance which came from Brazil and is like the SAMBA

boss-eyed /ˈ· ·/ adj *BrE sl* for CROSS-EYED

boss·y /ˈbɒsi‖ˈbɔːsi/ adj *infml* too fond of giving orders: *a bossy person/manner* | *She's an old* **bossy-boots.** (=is very bossy) —**iness** n [U]

Bos·ton /ˈbɒstən‖ˈbɔːs-/ a city in Massachusetts, on the Atlantic coast of the US. Boston is historically important and usu. follows older, established ways of thinking and behaving. The city has many colleges and universities. – see colour map on pages 1374-5

Boston Globe /ˌ··ˈ·/ [*the*] an important American newspaper sold esp. in New England – see also extra information on page 896

Boston Mas·sa·cre /ˌ··ˈ···/ [*the*] violence between American COLONISTS and the British army in 1770, that resulted when a crowd of angry Boston townspeople, who were against the presence of the British army, threatened a British soldier. Other soldiers fired into the crowd, killing five people. This was one of the events leading up to the AMERICAN REVOLUTIONARY WAR.

Boston Pops /ˌ··ˈ·/ [*the*] an ORCHESTRA (=group of musicians) from Boston, Massachusetts best known for its performances and recordings of popular CLASSICAL music, and connected with Arthur Fiedler, who led it for many years

Boston Tea Par·ty /ˌ··ˈ·ˌ··/ [*the*] a protest in Boston in 1773 against the British tax on tea, when tea was thrown from British ships into the water – see colour picture on page 1015

▶ CULTURAL NOTE The SLOGAN of the American colonists at the time was, "No taxation without representation!", meaning that the colonies should either have fair representation in the British Parliament, or should be independent. Three years later, the DECLARATION OF INDEPENDENCE was signed. ◀

bo·sun /ˈbəʊsən/ *n* a BOATSWAIN

Bos·well /ˈbɒzwəl‖ˈbɑːz-/, **James** (1740–95) a Scottish lawyer and writer, most famous for his BIOGRAPHY of Samuel Johnson

Bos·worth Field /ˌbɒzwəθ ˈfiːld‖ˌbɑːzwərθ-/ the place where the final battle of the Wars of the Roses was fought in 1485, where Richard III was defeated by Henry Tudor – see also WARS OF THE ROSES

bo·tan·i·cal /bəˈtænɪkəl/ *adj* [A] of or related to plants or botany: *a beautiful* **botanical garden** *with plants from all over the world* | *botanical drugs* (=obtained from plants) – **~ly** /kli/ *adv*

bot·a·nize also **-nise** *BrE* /ˈbɒtənaɪz‖ˈbɑː-/ *v* [I] to study plant life and collect examples of plants

bot·a·ny /ˈbɒtəni‖ˈbɑː-/ *n* [U] the scientific study of plants – **-nist** *n*

Botany Bay /ˌ···ˈ·/ **1** an INLET in SE Australia, visited by Captain James Cook in 1770 **2** an area in New South Wales, Australia, where British prisoners were sent to live in the 19th century

botch /bɒtʃ‖bɑːtʃ/ *v* [T (UP)] *infml* to do (something) badly, esp. to repair (something) badly through carelessness or lack of skill: *I'm afraid I've rather botched (up) the dinner tonight.* | *a botched job* – **botch, botch-up** /ˈ· ·/ *n* : *I've made a botch/botch-up of repairing the car.* – **~ er** *n* – **~y** *adj* : *a botchy job*

both /bəʊθ/ *predeterminer, determiner, pron* **1** the two together; the one as well as the other: *Both her parents are doctors.* | *Both of them are doctors.* | *They are both doctors.* | *Both sides are keen to reach an agreement.* | *She and her husband both like dancing.* | *"I don't know which to buy." "Why not buy both (of them)?" "I can afford one, but not both."* | *They both started speaking together.* **2 both ... and ...** not only ... but also ... : *We visited both New York and London.* | *He spoke with both kindness and understanding.* | *both in Holland and in Denmark* | *both then and now* | *She both speaks and writes Swahili.*

▷ USAGE 1 You can use **both** or **both of** before nouns with a determiner (such as *the, those, his*): *I like* **both (of)** *the paintings.* | **Both (of)** *their children are grown up.* 2 **Both** (but not **both of**) can be used before nouns without a determiner: *I like* **both** *paintings.* | **Both** *paintings are by the same artist.* 3 **Both of** is used before personal pronouns: **Both of** *them speak French.* | *I'd like* **both of** *you to come.* You can also put **both** after the pronoun with the same meaning: *They* **both** *speak French.* | *I'd like them* **both** *to come.* – see also EACH (USAGE)◁

Bo·tha /ˈbəʊtə/, **P W** (1916–) the PRIME MINISTER of the Republic of South Africa from 1978 until 1984 and president from 1984 until 1989

Bo·tham /ˈbəʊθəm/, **I·an** /ˈiːən/ (1955–) a very successful English cricket player, who has ability in many cricketing skills

both·er¹ /ˈbɒðəʳ‖ˈbɑː-/ *v* **1** [T] to cause trouble, worry, or annoyance to (someone) esp. repeatedly or continually, in little ways: *I'm busy: don't bother me just now.* | *What bothers me most is the fact that he seems to take no interest in his work.* | *His old injury still bothers him* (=gives him pain) *a bit.* | *Will it bother you if I turn the radio on?* | (*polite*) *I'm* **sorry to bother you,** *but can you tell me the time?* | *Don't* **bother yourself/bother your head** (=worry) *about all these details.* | *You're looking rather* **hot and bothered** – *what's the matter?* | *I* **can't be bothered** (=am unwilling to take the trouble) *to look for it just now.* **2** [I (**with, about**)] to cause inconvenience to oneself; trouble oneself: *Don't bother with/about it.* [+*to-v*] *You needn't bother to lock the door.* | *I sent them an invitation, but they didn't even bother to reply.* [+*v-ing*] *Don't bother locking the door.* | *Goodbye* – *and don't bother coming back!* (=I don't want you to come back) **3** [I;T *imperative*] *esp. BrE* (used for adding force to expressions of displeasure): *Bother! I've missed my train!* | *Bother the lot of you! Go away!*

bother² *n* **1** [S;U] (a) trouble, inconvenience, or anxiety (usu. caused by small matters and lasting a short time): *We had a bit of bother finding our way here.* | *"I don't want to be a bother (to you), but could I stay here tonight?" "Certainly. It's no bother at all."* **2** [U] *BrE infml* fighting or public disorder: *There was a spot of bother here today.* | *The gang have gone out* **looking for bother.** (=to make trouble)

both·er·a·tion /ˌbɒðəˈreɪʃən‖ˌbɑː-/ *interj old-fash, esp BrE* (used for expressing slight annoyance): *Botheration* – *I've dropped my glasses.*

both·er·some /ˈbɒðəsəm‖ˈbɑːðər-/ *adj* causing bother: *bothersome demands/people*

Bot·swa·na /bɒtˈswɑːnə‖bɑːt-/ a country in central S Africa; capital Gaborone; population 1,256,000 (1989)

Bot·ti·cel·li /ˌbɒtɪˈtʃeli‖ˌbɑː-/, **San·dro** /ˈsændrəʊ/ (?1444–1510) an Italian painter of the RENAISSANCE, best known for *Primavera* and *The Birth of Venus*

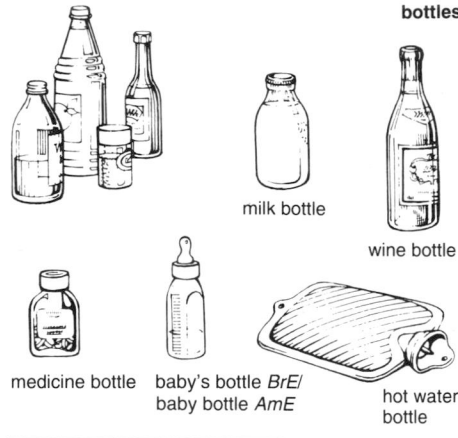

bottles

milk bottle

wine bottle

medicine bottle

baby's bottle *BrE*/ baby bottle *AmE*

hot water bottle

see also pictures at **decanter** and **flask**

bot·tle¹ /ˈbɒtl‖ˈbɑːtl/ *n* **1** [C] a container for liquids, usu. made of glass or plastic, with a rather narrow neck or mouth, and usu. no handle: *an empty milk bottle* | *to unscrew the top of a bottle* | *to uncork a wine bottle* | (*infml*) *Why don't we crack open another bottle of champagne?* **2** [C (**of**)] also **bot·tle·ful** /-fʊl/– the quantity held by a bottle: *We drank a whole bottle/two bottlefuls of wine!* **3** [*the*] alcoholic drink: *He* **hit the bottle** *when he lost his job.* | *She gave up for a while, but she's back* **on the bottle** *again now.* **4** [C *usu. sing.*] milk in bottles used in place of mother's milk: *to give the baby its bottle* **5** [U] *BrE sl* courage; daring; NERVE: *You have to hand it to her* – *she's got (a lot of) bottle.*

bottle² *v* [T] **1** to put into bottles: *a machine for bottling wine* **2** to preserve (fruit, etc.) in bottles

bottle out *phr v* [I(**of**)] *BrE sl* to refuse to do something because one is afraid

bottle sthg. ↔ **up** *phr v* [T] to control (feelings) in an unhealthy way: *Tell us what's worrying you — don't bottle it up!*

bottle bank /ˈ·· ·/ *n BrE* a container in the street into which people can put empty bottles, so that the glass can be reused

bottle-feed /ˈ·· ·/ *v* **-fed** /fed/ [T] to feed (a baby or baby animal) with a bottle, rather than with the breast — ~**ing** *n* [U]

bottle green /ˌ·· ˈ·◁/ *adj* very dark green —**bottle green** *n* [U]

bot·tle·neck /ˈbɒtlnek‖ˈbɑː-/ *n* a narrow part of a road which slows down traffic: (fig.) *a bottleneck in production*

bottle o·pen·er /ˈ·· ˌ··/ *n* a small metal instrument, used to open bottles, esp. beer bottles, with metal lids

bottle tan /ˈ·· ˌ·/ *n AmE infml* a TAN² (2) (=a brown colour of the skin) which is obtained by applying a special liquid to the skin, rather than by the action of the sun alone: *She's too busy to go to the beach so she has a bottle tan.* —**bottle tan** *v* [I] : *She's too busy to go to the beach so she's bottle tanning.*

bot·tom¹ /ˈbɒtəm‖ˈbɑː-/ *n* **1** [*the* (of)] the lowest part of something: *I eventually found the keys at the bottom of my bag.* | *at the bottom of the page/list* | *It's on the third line from the bottom of the page.* | *The body was found at the bottom of a deserted mine shaft.* | *The bottom floor of a building.* | *The police searched the house* **from top to bottom.** | (fig.) *She thanked them* **from the bottom of her heart.** (=very sincerely) **2** [C (of)] the base on which something stands: *The wet bottoms of the glasses made marks on the table.* | *to pack the bottles bottom up* (=upside down) **3** [C] the part of the body on which one sits; BUTTOCKS: *to smack a child's bottom* **4** [*the*;U] the ground under the sea, a lake, or a river: *They sent the enemy ship to the bottom (of the sea).* | *This part is too deep for swimming: I can't touch bottom.* | *the river-bottom.* **5** [*the*;U] the least important, least valuable, or least favourable part of anything; the lowest level: *He is always at the bottom of the class.* | *He started life* **at the bottom (of the ladder),** *and worked his way up.* | *They bought their house when prices were at* **rock bottom.** | *Sheffield United are at the bottom of League Division One.* **6** [*the* (of)] the far end: *I'll walk with you to the bottom of the road.* | (*BrE*) *We grow vegetables at the bottom of our garden.* **7** [*the*+of] the starting point; cause or origin: *Who is at the bottom of all this trouble? I intend to* **get to the bottom of it.** (=find out the cause) **8** [(in) U] the lowest GEAR of a motor vehicle **9** [C] also **bottoms** *pl.*— the lower part of a two-piece garment: *pyjama bottoms* **10** [C] *naut* the part of a ship below the water **11** *AmE* the second half of an INNING: *It's the bottom of the seventh and the score is tied 3-all* **12 at bottom** really; in spite of appearances: *He pretends to be very tough, but he's a kind man at bottom.* **13 Bottoms** 'up! *infml, esp. humor* Empty your glasses! Finish your drinks! **14 the bottom has fallen out of the market** prices and demand for products have fallen to a very low level **15 -bottomed** /bɒtəmd‖bɑː-/having the stated kind of bottom: *round-bottomed glasses* | *a fat-bottomed woman* —see also **bet one's bottom dollar** (BET²), **knock the bottom out of** (KNOCK¹ (9)); compare TOP¹

bottom² *v*

bottom out *phr v* [I] to reach the lowest point before rising again: *The price of oil bottomed out at $12 a barrel and has now started to rise again.*

Bottom a COMIC character in Shakespeare's play *A Midsummer Night's Dream*, who is turned into an ASS

bottom drawer /ˌ·· ˈ·/ *BrE* ‖ **hope chest** *AmE*— *n* [*usu. sing.*] *old use infml* the clothes, sheets, and other things needed for starting a home which a girl collects before getting married —compare TOP DRAWER

bot·tom·less /ˈbɒtəmləs‖ˈbɑː-/ *adj* with no bottom or limit; very deep: *a bottomless well* | (fig.) *The bank's chairman said that giving loans to that country was like pouring money into a* **bottomless pit.**

bottom line /ˌ·· ˈ·/ *n* [*the*] **1** the amount of money shown (as profit or loss) at the bottom of a set of accounts **2** the most important result in the end, esp. with regard to money; OUTCOME: *If we make all the changes I am proposing, the bottom line is that the company will save £50,000.*

bot·u·lis·m /ˈbɒtʃʊlɪzəm‖ˈbɑː-/ *n* [U] serious food poisoning caused by bacteria in preserved meat and vegetables

Bou·dic·ca /ˈbuːðɪkə‖buːˈdɪkə/ , also **Boadicea**— (died AD 60) the Queen of the Iceni people of eastern Britain, who led them in battle against the Romans. In pictures, Boudicca is usu. shown driving a CHARIOT.

bou·doir /ˈbuːdwɑːʳ/ *n* (esp. in former times) a woman's dressing room, bedroom, or private sitting room

bouf·fant /ˈbuːfɒn, -fɒnt‖buːˈfɑːnt/ *adj* (of hair or a piece of clothing) puffed out (PUFF **out**)

bou·gain·vil·le·a , **-laea** /ˌbuːgənˈvɪliə/ *n* a climbing plant with large red and purple flowers which grows in hot countries

bough /baʊ/ *n esp. lit* a main branch of a tree

bought /bɔːt/ *past tense & participle of* BUY¹

bouil·la·baisse /ˌbuːjəˈbes‖-ˈbeɪs/ *n* [C;U] a strong-tasting STEW made from fish

bouil·lon /ˈbuːjɒn‖-jɑːn/ *n* [C;U] a clear soup made by boiling meat and vegetables in water

boul·der /ˈbəʊldəʳ/ *n* a large stone or mass of rock

boules /buːl/ *n* [U] an outdoor game played esp. in France, in which one tries to throw or roll a big usu. metal ball as near as possible to a small ball (the JACK)

boule·vard /ˈbuːlvɑːd‖ˈbuːləvɑːrd, ˈbʊ-/ (*written abbrev.* **blvd**) *n* (part of the name of) a broad street in a town, sometimes having trees on each side: *Sunset Boulevard*

Bou·lez /ˈbuːlez‖buːˈlez/, **Pi·erre** /piˈeəʳ/ (1925–) a French COMPOSER and CONDUCTOR known for his modern music

Bou·logne /bʊˈlɔɪn‖-ˈləʊn/ a city on the NE coast of France, known for being one of the ports where ferries (FERRY¹) from Dover arrive when crossing the English Channel

bounce¹ /baʊns/ *v* **1** [I;T] **a** (of a ball) to spring back or up again after hitting a surface; REBOUND: *The ball hit the wall and bounced off it.* **b** to cause (a ball) to do this: *to bounce a ball against a wall* | (fig.) *The message is sent across the Atlantic by bouncing radio waves off a satellite* **2** [I+adv/prep;T+obj+adv/prep] to move with a springing movement, often suddenly or noisily: *She bounced into the room.* | *I bounced the baby on my knee.* **3** [I] (of a cheque) to be returned by a bank as worthless —compare DISHONOUR² (2)

bounce back *phr v* [I] to return to one's former strong or active state, after a failure or misfortune

bounce² *n* **1** [C] an act of bouncing **2** [U] the quality of bouncing well **3** [U] *infml* liveliness; VIGOUR

bounc·er /ˈbaʊnsəʳ/ *n* **1** *infml* a strong man employed, esp. at a club or restaurant, to throw out unwelcome customers **2** (in cricket) a fast ball that passes or hits the BATSMAN at above chest height after it bounces (BOUNCE)

bounc·ing /ˈbaʊnsɪŋ/ *adj* [A] *apprec* (esp. of babies) healthy and active

bouncing bomb /ˌ·· ˈ·/ *n* a bomb developed by Barnes Wallis (1887–1979). Bouncing bombs were used during the Second World War against the Germans by the Royal Air Force Dambusters Squadron. —see also DAM BUSTERS

bounc·y /ˈbaʊnsi/ *adj* **1** full of life and confidence, and eager for action: *a bouncy person/manner* **2** that bounces well: *a bouncy ball* —**ily** *adv* —**iness** *n* [U]

bound¹ /baʊnd/ *past tense & participle of* BIND¹: *The prisoner was bound to a stake and shot.*

bound² *adj* **1** [F+to-v] very likely; certain: *It's bound to rain soon.* | *In a group as big as this, you are bound to get occasional disagreements.* **2** [F+to-v] having a duty, legally or morally, to do something: *The priest was bound by his position to withhold the information from the* *police.* | *She thinks it's a crazy idea, and* **I'm bound to say** *I agree with her.* | *You are not legally bound to answer these questions.* **3** [(**in**)] (of a book) fastened within covers: *a cloth-bound volume* | *a Bible bound in leather* **4** *tech* (in grammar) always found in combination with another form: *"Un-" and "-er" are* **bound forms** *in the words "unknown" and "speaker".* –opposite **free 5 bound up in** very busy with or interested in; PREOCCUPIED: *She is bound up in her own problems.* **6 bound up with** dependent on; connected with: *His future is closely bound up with that of the company.* **7 I'll be bound** *old-fash infml* I'm quite certain

bound³ *n* a jump or LEAP: *With one bound, he was over the wall.* | (fig.) *Jill's making excellent progress; she's coming along* **in leaps and bounds.** –see also BOUNDS

bound⁴ *v* [I+*adv/prep*] **1** to move along quickly by jumping or leaping (LEAP) movements: *The dog bounded away/down the hill.* **2** to spring or BOUNCE back from a surface

bound⁵ *adj* [(**for**)] going to or intending to go to: *bound for home* | *homeward-bound* | *We boarded a plane bound for New York.*

bound⁶ *v* [T *usu. pass.*] to mark or form the boundaries or limits of: *The US is bounded in/on the north by Canada and in/on the south by Mexico.* –see also BOUNDS

bound·a·ry /ˈbaʊndəri/ *n* **1** [(**between**)] the dividing line, esp. between two areas of land: *A river forms the boundary (line) between the two countries.* **2** the outer limit of anything: *The boundaries of human knowledge are constantly being extended.* **3** (in cricket) the outer limit of the playing area, often marked by a rope **4** (in cricket) a shot that sends the ball across the boundary giving 4 or 6 points

bound·en /ˈbaʊndən/ *adj* [A] *fml, becoming rare* necessary; OBLIGATORY (in the phrase **bounden duty**)

bound·er /ˈbaʊndəʳ/ *n BrE old use sl* a dishonourable man who does not behave in a socially acceptable way; CAD

bound·less /ˈbaʊndləs/ *adj* without limits: *boundless wealth/imagination* – ~ **ly** *adv* – ~ **ness** *n* [U]

bounds /baʊndz/ *n* [P] the furthest limits or edges of something; the limits beyond which it is impossible or undesirable to go: *You must keep your spending within bounds.* | *His greed for power* **knows no bounds.** | *The pub was* **out of bounds** (=forbidden) *to the schoolboys.* | *It is* **not beyond the bounds of possibility** (=it is possible, though perhaps unlikely) *that he is telling the truth.*

boun·te·ous /ˈbaʊntiəs/ *adj fml or lit* giving or given freely; generous: *bounteous gifts* – ~ **ly** *adv* – ~ **ness** *n* [U]

boun·ti·ful /ˈbaʊntɪfəl/ *adj fml or lit* generous; in large quantities: *a bountiful supply*

boun·ty /ˈbaʊnti/ *n* **1** [C] money paid by a government, esp. formerly, for some special reason (e.g. as a reward for joining the army or catching a criminal) **2** [U] *esp. lit* generosity

Bounty *n tdmk* a kind of chocolate bar containing COCONUT, sold in Britain

Bounty, The also **HMS Bounty**– the name of a British naval ship famous for being the scene of a MUTINY in 1789 in the Pacific ocean and the subject of several films – see also Captain William BLIGH, MUTINY ON THE BOUNTY

bou·quet /bəʊˈkeɪ, buː-/ *n* **1** [C] a bunch of flowers given, usu. to a woman, on a special occasion, e.g. her birthday, or to say thank you for something: *At the end of the concert, the singer was presented with a bouquet of roses.* **2** [C] a bunch of flowers carried by a BRIDE –see also extra information on page 1406 **3** [C;U] the smell of wine: *a rich bouquet*

bou·quet gar·ni /ˌbuːkeɪ ˈɡɑːni‖ˌbuːkeɪ ɡɑːˈniː/ *n* a small bunch of fresh or dried HERBS in a small cloth bag which is used in cooking and removed before the dish is served

bour·bon /ˈbɜːbən‖ˈbɜːr-/ *n* [U] a type of American WHISKEY made from MAIZE, MALT, and RYE, named after Bourbon County in the state of Kentucky

bour·bon bis·cuit /ˌbuəbən ˈbɪskɪt‖ˌbɜːr-/ *n* (*often cap.*) *BrE* a chocolate BISCUIT consisting of two halves with chocolate cream in the middle

bour·geois¹ /ˈbʊəʒwɑː‖buərˈʒwɑː/ *adj old-fash* **1** belonging to or typical of the MIDDLE CLASS **2** *derog* too interested in material possessions and one's social position

bourgeois² *n* **bourgeois** *often derog* a member of the

MIDDLE CLASS, esp. one who is too interested in material possessions and social position

bour·geoi·sie /ˌbuəʒwɑːˈziː‖ˌbuər-/ *n* [*the+sing./pl. v*] *old-fash* the MIDDLE CLASS –compare PROLETARIAT

bourn¹ /bɔːn‖bɔːrn/ *n old use* (now used mainly in place names) a small stream

bourn² *n old use or lit* a limit; border: *". . . death/The undiscovered country from whose bourn/No traveller returns. . ."* (Shakespeare, *Hamlet*)

Bourne·mouth /ˈbɔːnməθ‖ˈbɔːrn-/ a town on the S coast of England where people go on holiday, also known for being a CONFERENCE centre and popular RETIREMENT place

bour·sin /ˈbuəsæn‖buərˈsæn/ *n* [U] *tdmk* a soft creamy French cheese made with GARLIC and HERBS

Bourn·ville /ˈbɔːnvɪl‖ˈbɔːrn-/ *n* [U] *tdmk* a kind of dark chocolate made by Cadbury's

bout /baʊt/ *n* **1** [(**of**)] a short period of great activity: *one of his intermittent bouts of drinking* **2** [(**of**)] an attack of illness: *a bout of flu* **3** a BOXING match

bou·tique /buːˈtiːk/ *n* a small shop, or a department of a larger shop, selling up-to-date clothes and other fashionable personal articles, esp. for young people or women

bou·ton·ni·ere /buːˌtɒniˈeəʳ‖buːtnˈɪər/ *n AmE* for BUTTONHOLE¹(2)

Bou·tros-Gha·li /ˌbuːtrɒs ˈɡɑːliː‖-trəʊs-/, **Dr Boutros** (1923–) the SECRETARY-GENERAL to the UN from 1991

bo·vine /ˈbəʊvaɪn/ *adj* of or like a cow or OX, esp. in being slow-thinking and slow-moving

Bov·ril /ˈbɒvrɪl‖ˈbaːv-/ *n* [U] *tdmk* a dark brown substance made from the meat of a cow, which is used in Britain to make a drink, or added to foods when cooking

bov·ver /ˈbɒvəʳ‖ˈbaː-/ *n* [U] *BrE old-fash sl* violence or threatening behaviour, esp. by groups of young men: *a bovver boy* | *bovver boots*

bow¹ /baʊ/ *v* **1** [I (DOWN, **before, to**)] to bend the upper part of the body forward, as a way of showing respect, admitting defeat, etc.: *He bowed (down) to/before the Queen.* | *Muslims bow to Mecca when they pray.* **2** [T (DOWN)] to bend (one's head) forward: *He bowed his head in shame/stood with his head bowed in shame.* **3 bow and scrape** *usu. derog* to behave to someone with too much politeness and obedience

bow down *phr v* [I (**to**)] *esp. lit* to admit defeat and agree to obey: *We shall never bow down to our enemies.*

bow out *phr v* [I (**of**)] to give up a position or stop taking part in something; WITHDRAW: *The chairman will be bowing out next year, and one of the younger directors will take over.*

bow to sbdy./sthg. *phr v* [T] **1** to accept or obey, esp. unwillingly: *to bow to someone's judgment/greater experience* | *I'm not at all happy about it, but I suppose I'll have to bow to the inevitable.* **2 bow to no one** to claim the highest place for oneself: *I bow to no one in my admiration for her work, but I have some doubts about this latest idea of hers.*

bow² /baʊ/ *n* **1** an act of bending forward the head or the upper part of the body, esp. to show respect: *He gave a deep/low bow.* –compare CURTSY **2 take a bow** to come on stage to receive praise (APPLAUSE) at the end of a performance

bow³ /bəʊ/ *n* **1** a weapon for shooting ARROWS consisting of a long thin piece of wood held in a curve by a tight string –see also CROSSBOW, and see picture at LONGBOW **2** a long thin piece of wood with a tight string fastened along it, used for playing musical instruments that have strings **3** a knot formed by doubling a string or cord into two curved pieces, and used for decoration in the hair, in tying shoes, etc.: *She tied the ribbon in a tight/loose bow.* –see also BOW WINDOW, **a second string to one's bow** (STRING¹)

bow⁴ /bəʊ/ *v tech* **1** [I] to bend or curve **2** [T+*obj+adv/ prep*] to play (a piece of music) on a musical instrument with a BOW³ (2)

bow⁵ /baʊ/ also **bows** *pl.*– *n* the front part of a ship –see picture at YACHT; see also **a shot across the bows** (SHOT¹), and compare STERN²

Bow Bells /ˌbəʊ ˈbelz/ the church bells of St Mary-le-Bow in London. It is said that a person born within the sound of (=able to hear) Bow Bells is a true Londoner, or Cockney –see also COCKNEY

bowd·ler·ize also **-ise** *BrE* /ˈbaʊdləraɪz/ v [T] *usu. derog* to remove (from a book, play, etc.) those parts considered rude or shocking: *a bowdlerized edition of Shakespeare*

bow·els /ˈbaʊəlz/ n [P] **1** also **bowel**– a system of pipes from the stomach which carries the waste matter out of the body; the SMALL INTESTINE and LARGE INTESTINE **2** [+of] the deepest inner part of something (esp. in the phrase **the bowels of the earth**) –**bowel** adj [A] : *a bowel disorder*

bow·er /ˈbaʊəʳ/ n **1** a pleasant shaded place under trees **2** *old use or lit* a BOUDOIR

Bow Group /ˈbəʊ gruːp/ [*the*] a centre-right political group inside the Conservative Party that tries to influence government action

Bo·wie /ˈbəʊi/, **David** (1947–   ) an English songwriter and singer of popular music, who has also acted in plays and films –see colour picture on page 554

bowl¹ /bəʊl/ n **1** (*often in comb.*) a deep round container open at the top, esp. one deeper than a BASIN, for holding liquids, flowers, etc.: *a soup bowl | cereal bowl | sugar bowl | a fruit bowl | a glass bowl* **2** [(of)] also **bowl·ful** /-fʊl/– the amount a bowl will hold: *a bowl of fruit/rice* **3** anything in the shape of a bowl: *the bowl of a tobacco pipe/of a spoon/of a toilet* **4 a bowl of cherries** a very pleasant thing, usu. in the phrase **life isn't just a bowl of cherries**

bowl² v **1** [I;T] **a** (in BOWLS or BOWLING) to roll (a ball) along a surface at the top, **b** (in cricket) to throw (a ball) at the BATSMAN **2** [T (OUT)] (in cricket) to force (a BATSMAN) to leave the field by hitting the WICKET behind him with a ball: *He bowled me (out) with the very first ball!*
   bowl along phr v [I] to move smoothly and quickly along: *The car bowled along at 90 mph.*
   bowl sbdy. ↔ **over** phr v [T] **1** to knock down by running: *Someone ran round the corner and nearly bowled me over.* **2** [usu. pass.] to give a great, esp. pleasant, surprise to: *I was really bowled over by the news.*

bowl³ n **1** a ball for rolling in the game of BOWLS **2** an act of rolling the ball in BOWLS or BOWLING

bow-leg·ged /ˌbəʊˈleg‿d◂, -ˈlegd◂‖ˈbəʊleg‿d, -legd/ adj (esp. of a person) having the legs curving outwards at the knee

bowl·er¹ /ˈbəʊləʳ/ n a person who BOWLs² , esp. in cricket –see picture at CRICKET

bowler² also **bowler hat** /ˌ··ˈ·/BrE ‖ **derby** AmE– n a man's round hard hat, usu. black, worn esp. by men who work in the City of London. Bowler hats are not often worn now and are thought of as being old-fashioned, but they still appear in humorous drawings and advertisements which show the typical Englishman: *the bowler hat brigade* –see picture at HAT

bowl game /ˈ· ·/ n (in FOOTBALL (2)) a match played as a special event, sometimes to determine the best team in a group of (usu. college) teams: *Many bowl games are played around Christmas and New Year's Day.*

bowl·ing /ˈbəʊlɪŋ/ also **tenpin bowling**– n [U] an indoor game in which a large heavy ball is rolled along a wooden track in an attempt to knock down bottle-shaped wooden objects –compare BOWLS

bowling al·ley /ˈ·· ˌ··/ n a place for rolling the ball in BOWLING, or SKITTLES

bowling ball /ˈ·· ·/ n the heavy ball used in bowling, which contains holes for fingers and thumb

bowling green /ˈ·· ·/ n an area of short smooth grass for playing BOWLS

bowls /bəʊlz/ n [U] an outdoor game played on grass in which one tries to roll a big ball as near as possible to the JACK (a small ball). Bowls is usu. played by older people –compare BOWLING

bow·man /ˈbəʊmən/ n **-men** /mən/ old use an ARCHER

bow·shot /ˈbəʊʃɒt/-ʃɑːt/ n [usu. sing.] esp. lit the distance from the place where an ARROW is fired, to the place where it lands

bow·sprit /ˈbəʊˌsprɪt‖ˈbaʊ-, ˈbəʊ-/ n a pole sticking out from the front of a ship (BOW⁵), to which ropes from the sails are fastened

Bow Street /ˈbəʊ striːt/ a street in London where there is a police court: *He was remanded in custody until 28 June by Bow Street Magistrates.*

Bow Street run·ner /ˌ·· · ˈ···/ n a member of the first police force in London, set up in 1748

bow tie /ˌbəʊ ˈtaɪ/ n a short TIE fastened at the front with a knot in the shape of a BOW³ (3), worn esp. on formal occasions: *a bow tie affair*

bow win·dow /ˌbəʊ ˈwɪndəʊ/ n a window built outwards from the wall in a curve –compare BAY WINDOW

bow-wow /ˌbaʊˈwaʊ/ ‖also **arf** or **woof** AmE interj (a word meant to be like the sound a dog makes)

box¹ /bɒks‖bɑːks/ n **1** [C] (*often in comb.*) a container for solid objects or substances, usu. with stiff straight sides and often with a lid: *a wooden/cardboard box | a tool box | a shoebox | a box of matches/tissues* **2** [C (of)] the amount a box will hold: *We ate a whole box of chocolates.* **3** [C] a small room or enclosed space:*a telephone box | the witness box in a law-court | the signal box on a railway line* **4** [C] a small enclosed space with seats in a theatre, separate from the main seating area: *the royal box* –see picture at THEATRE **5** [C] an apparatus used by cricketers to protect the male sex organs **6** [*the*] *sl* television: *What's on the box tonight?* **7** [C] a PO BOX **8 open the box** a phrase from a British television game show of the 1950s. In the game, a person had to choose between accepting an amount of money and opening a special box that might contain more money or a special prize, or might contain nothing at all. –see also BLACK BOX, CHRISTMAS BOX, MUSICAL BOX, WINDOW BOX

box² v [T] **1** to put in a box or boxes: *a boxed set of books by the same author* **2 box the compass: a** to name all 32 points of the COMPASS in their correct order **b** to change course completely; do the opposite of what was done at the beginning
   box sbdy./sthg. ↔ **in/up** phr v [T often pass.] to enclose in a small space; CONFINE: *She feels very boxed in/up in that tiny flat.*

box³ v [I (with, against); T] **1** to fight (someone) with the FISTS (=closed hands), esp. as a sport –compare WRESTLE **2 box someone's ears** infml to hit someone on the ears with the hands, esp. as a punishment

box⁴ n **give/get a box on the ears** infml to hit/be hit on the ears

box⁵ n **1** [C;U] a small tree that keeps its dark stiff leaves during the winter, often planted in rows as a wall or fence: *a box hedge* **2** [U] also **boxwood**– the hard wood of this tree

Box and Cox /ˌ·· · ˈ·/ adj, adv BrE old-fash infml sharing something by taking turns

box·car /ˈbɒkskɑːʳ‖ˈbɑːks-/ n AmE a roofed railway carriage that carries goods

box end wrench /ˌ·· · ˈ·/ n AmE for RING SPANNER –see picture at TOOL

box·er /ˈbɒksəʳ‖ˈbɑːk-/ n **1** a person who boxes, esp. professionally **2** a large short-haired dog, usu. light brown in colour

boxer shorts /ˈ·· ˌ·/ n [P] underclothes for men, covering the lower part of the body and the top part of the leg and made of thin material, usu. cotton –see PAIR (USAGE)

box·ing /ˈbɒksɪŋ‖ˈbɑːk-/ n [U] the sport of fighting with the FISTS (=closed hands): *a boxing match* –see REFEREE (USAGE) –see picture at GLOVE

Boxing Day /ˈ·· ·/ n BrE [C;U] a public holiday in England and Wales, on the first day after Christmas Day that is not a Sunday

box junc·tion /ˈ· ˌ··/ n BrE a road JUNCTION with a pattern of crossed yellow lines to warn drivers not to enter the area until the way out is clear of traffic

box num·ber /ˈ· ˌ··/ n ‖ also **post office box**, –**PO Box** a number used as a mailing address, esp. in replying to newspaper advertisements

box of·fice /ˈ· ˌ··/ n a place in a theatre, cinema, concert hall, etc., where tickets are sold: *Let's meet at the box office.* | *The play got bad reviews, but in box-office terms it was a great success.* (=it was popular and therefore profitable)

box·room /ˈbɒksrʊm, -ruːm‖ˈbɑːks-/ n BrE a small room in a house where SUITCASEs, furniture, etc., are stored

box·wood /ˈbɒkswʊd‖ˈbɑːks-/ n [U] BOX⁵ (2)

boy[1] /bɔɪ/ n 1 a young male person: *Our new baby is a boy.* | *"Come here, boy!" shouted the old man.* | *There's a new boy in our class at school.* | *a boy actor* —see CHILD (USAGE) 2 a son, esp. a young one: *My little boy hates sausages.* | *We've got two boys and one girl.* 3 (*often in comb.*) a boy or man working at a particular job: *a cowboy* | *a delivery-boy* | *an office boy* 4 *infml, esp. AmE* a male person of any age from a particular place: *The people are proud of the local boy who became president.* 5 *becoming rare* (now considered offensive) a male servant of any age 6 *old-fash or humor* (used in forming phrases for addressing men): *Thank you, my boy|dear boy|old boy.* 7 **boys will be boys** *saying* it is in the character of boys to do rough and dangerous things 8 **what are little boys made of?** a line from a NURSERY RHYME (=an old song or poem for children). The answer is "slugs and snails and puppy dogs' tails". —see also **what are little girls made of?** (GIRL) —see also BOYS, BLUE-EYED BOY, OLD BOY, PRINCIPAL BOY, WHIPPING BOY, WIDE BOY

boy[2] *interj infml, esp. AmE* (expressing excitement): *Boy, what a game!*

boy·cott /ˈbɔɪkɒt‖-kɑːt/ v [T] to refuse to do business with, attend, or take part in, as a way of showing disapproval and opposition: *They're boycotting the shop because the people there are on strike.* | *to boycott a meeting* —**boycott** n : *to declare a boycott*

Boycott, Geof·frey /ˈdʒefri/ (1940–) an English cricketer, born in Yorkshire, who is known for the many RUNs he has made in TEST cricket

boy·friend /ˈbɔɪfrend/ n 1 a frequent or regular male friend of a girl or woman, to whom she is not married. The word is used esp. when talking about the relationships of young people. Older people usu. prefer to use the word "partner" or "friend". 2 *euph* a male lover

Boy George /ˌ· ˈ·/ (1961–) a British popular music singer who became successful with the group Culture Club in the early 1980s. He often dresses like a woman, and wears heavy makeup.

boy·hood /ˈbɔɪhʊd/ n [C *usu. sing.*;U] the state or time of being a young boy —see also CHILDHOOD, GIRLHOOD

boy·ish /ˈbɔɪ-ɪʃ/ adj *often apprec* of or like a boy, esp. in appearance: *his boyish charm* | *her boyish figure* – **~ly** adv – **~ness** n [U]

Boyne /bɔɪn/, **Battle of the** the battle on the banks of the river Boyne in the Irish Republic where William III defeated James II in 1690, finally destroying Stuart chances of claiming the country

boys /bɔɪz/ n [*the*+P] *infml* a man's male friends; a group of men: *to spend a night out with the boys*

Boys' Bri·gade /ˌ· ·ˌ·/ [*the*] an organization which was set up in Britain in 1883 to encourage boys to develop team spirit and responsible behaviour

boy scout /ˌ· ˈ·‖ˈ· ·/ n a SCOUT[1] (1a)

an American   a British
boy scout   boy scout

boy·sen·ber·ry /ˈbɔɪzənbəri‖-beri/ n a fruit similar to BLACKBERRY

Boys' Own /ˌ· ˈ·◂/ adj (used to describe men) doing brave, exciting things, like a HERO in an adventure story. The **Boys' Own Paper** was a boys' magazine sold in the late 19th century and early 20th century in Britain which contained adventure stories: *He has been called a swashbuckling Boys' Own hero.* | *His background is the stuff of boys' own papers.*

Boy Won·der /ˌ· ˈ··/ see ROBIN

bo·zo /ˈbəʊzəʊ/ n -zos *sl, esp. AmE* a person who is stupid or foolish, or who behaves like a CLOWN

BP /ˌbiː ˈpiː/ 1 British Petroleum; a British company producing petrol and chemicals 2 British Pharmacopeia; a book listing drugs with their uses, etc., as approved by the British medical bodies

BPhil /ˌbiː ˈfɪl/ n Bachelor of Philosophy; (a title for someone who has) a degree gained after study at an institution of further education, e.g. a university

B.P.O.E. *written abbrev. for* The Benevolent and Protective Order of Elks —see ELKS

Br *written abbrev. for:* 1 BROTHER[1] (2) in a religious society: *Br Maurice* 2 British

BR /ˌbiː ˈɑːr/ *abbrev. for* BRITISH RAIL

bra /brɑː/ also **brassiere** *fml* — n a woman's close-fitting undergarment worn to support the breasts. In the 1960s many women who supported the WOMEN'S LIBERATION movement burnt their bras as a protest.

brace[1] /breɪs/ n 1 something used or worn for supporting, stiffening, or fastening 2 a wire frame worn inside the mouth, usu. by children, to make their teeth straight 3 either of a pair of signs { } used for connecting information printed on more than one line —compare BRACKET[1] (2) 4 (*pl.* **brace**) [(of)] (esp. in hunting or shooting) two of a kind; a pair: *three brace of pheasants* —see also BRACES

brace[2] v [T] 1 to make stronger, esp. by supporting with a brace: *We had to brace the walls when we put the new roof on.* 2 [(for)] to prepare (oneself) for something unpleasant or difficult: *Brace yourself for a shock!* | *The country is bracing itself for the threatened enemy invasion.*

brace and bit /ˌ· · ˈ·/ n a simple hand tool used for making holes in wood

brace·let /ˈbreɪslɪt/ n a band or ring worn round the wrist or arm as a decoration: *a gold bracelet* —compare BANGLE

brac·es /ˈbreɪsɪz/ *BrE* ‖ **suspenders** *AmE*— n [P] a pair of elastic cloth bands worn over the shoulders by men to hold up trousers —see PAIR (USAGE)

brac·ing /ˈbreɪsɪŋ/ adj *apprec* (esp. of air) fresh and health-giving; invigorating (INVIGORATE): *a bracing sea breeze* | *a bracing climate*

brack·en /ˈbrækən/ n [U] a plant (a kind of FERN) which commonly grows in woods, on hills, etc., and becomes a rich red-brown in autumn

brack·et[1] /ˈbrækɪt/ n 1 a structure of metal, wood, or plastic, often in the shape of a right angle, fixed to a wall to support something, such as a shelf or lamp 2 [*usu. pl.*] a also **square bracket**— either of the pair of signs [ ] used for enclosing a piece of information: *to put something in brackets* b also **angle bracket**— either of the pair of signs ⟨ ⟩ used for enclosing a piece of information c also **round bracket**— either of the pair of signs ( ); PARENTHESIS — compare BRACE[1] (3); see picture at PUNCTUATION MARK 3 a group or class fixed according to certain upper and lower limits: *a big tax cut for people in the upper income bracket* | *The party is popular with the 18–25 age bracket.*

bracket[2] v [T] 1 [(OFF)] to enclose in brackets 2 [(TOGETHER, **with**)] to regard, perhaps wrongly, as belonging to the same group or type: *In his article, the peace protesters were unfairly bracketed with the football hooligans.*

brack·ish /ˈbrækɪʃ/ adj (of water) not pure; a little salty – **~ness** n [U]

Brack·nell[1] /ˈbræknəl/ a town in Berkshire, in S England

Bracknell[2], **Lady** a character in the play *The Importance of Being Earnest* by Oscar Wilde, remembered esp. for using the phrase "A handbag!"

brad·awl /ˈbrædɔːl/ n a small tool with a sharp point for making holes

Brad·bu·ry, Mal·colm /ˈbrædbəri/, /ˈmælkəm/ (1932–) an English writer, known for his humorous books about life in universities, in particular— *The History Man*

Brad·bu·ry, Ray /ˈbrædbəri‖-beri, -bəri/ (1920–) an American writer of SCIENCE FICTION whose stories include *Fahrenheit 451* and *The Halloween Tree*

Brad·ford /ˈbrædfəd‖-fərd/ an industrial city in the N of England which is a centre of the woollen industry and where many Asian people now live

Brad·ford and Bing·ley /ˌbrædfəd ənd ˈbɪŋli‖-fərd/ [*the*] a British BUILDING SOCIETY, branches of which are found in many towns and cities in Britain

Brad·man, Sir Don·ald /ˈbrædmən/, /ˈdɒnəld‖ˈdɑː-/ (1908–) an Australian cricketer, one of the best batsmen (BATSMAN) ever to have played

Bra·dy Bunch /ˈbreɪdi ˌbʌntʃ/, **The** an American television programme of the 1960s and 1970s about a large family. Some people talk about the Brady Bunch as an example of an impossibly good family with few real problems: *The family across the street seemed like the Brady Bunch at first, but we soon learned that there were all sorts of tensions underneath.*

brae /breɪ/ *n ScotE* a hillside; slope

brag /bræg/ *v* **-gg-** [I (**about, of**); T+*that; obj*] *derog* to talk too proudly about oneself, one's possessions, etc.; BOAST: *Don't brag! | She bragged about her connections in the film world. | Untidy work is nothing to brag about. | The boys bragged that they had committed several burglaries.*

Bragg /bræg/, **Mel·vyn** /ˈmelvɪn/ (1939–   ) an English writer and broadcaster known for arts programmes such as *The South Bank Show* on television. Much of his writing is set in the Lake District.

brag·ga·do·ci·o /ˌbrægəˈdəʊʃiəʊ/ *n* [U] *esp. lit or humor* noisy bragging

brag·gart /ˈbrægət/ *n becoming rare* a person who brags a lot

Brah·man /ˈbrɑːmən/ also **Brah·min** /ˈbrɑːmɪn/— *n* a Hindu of the highest rank in the Hindu CASTE system

Brah·ma·pu·tra /ˌbrɑːməˈpuːtrə/ a river in S Asia

Brahms /brɑːmz/, **Jo·han·nes** /jəʊˈhænəs/ (1833–97) a German writer of music known for his symphonies (SYM·PHONY) and CONCERTOS

Brahms and Liszt /ˌ· · ˈ·/ *adj* [F] *BrE sl for* DRUNK

braid¹ /breɪd/ *esp. AmE* ‖ **plait** *esp. BrE*— *v* [T] to twist together three or more lengths of (hair, thread, etc.) to form a ropelike length

braid² *n* **1** [U] threads of silk, gold, etc., twisted to form a narrow decorative border for material: *gold braid for a naval officer's uniform* **2** [C *often pl.*] *esp. AmE* ‖ **plait** *esp. BrE*— a length of hair formed by twisting together three or more lengths

braille /breɪl/ *n* [U] (*sometimes cap.*) a form of printing with raised round marks which blind people can read by touching

brain¹ /breɪn/ *n* **1** [C] the organ of the body in the upper part of the head, which controls thought, feeling, and physical activity: *The brain is the centre of higher nervous activity. | He suffered severe brain damage as a result of the accident.* **2** [C;U] also **brains** *pl.*— the ability to think clearly, quickly, and well; INTELLIGENCE: *a good brain | She's certainly got a brain/plenty of brains. | He hasn't got much (of a) brain. | It takes brains to think of something like that!* **3** [C] also **brains** *pl.*— *infml* a person with a very good mind: *Some of the best brains in the country are working on this project. | His partner was the brains behind the venture.* **4 have something on the brain** *infml* to think about something continually: *I've got that song on the brain today. | He seems to have sex on the brain!* **5 -brained** /breɪnd/ having a brain of the stated type: *bird-brained* (=silly) | *scatterbrained* (=careless and unthinking) —see also **beat one's brains out** (BEAT¹ (10)), **blow someone's brains out** (BLOW¹ (16)), **rack one's brains** (RACK²)

brain² *v* [T] *infml* to hit (someone) very hard on the head, esp. so as to break their SKULL

brain·child /ˈbreɪntʃaɪld/ *n* [S] *infml* someone's idea or invention, esp. if successful: *This festival was the brainchild of the local mayor.*

brain dam·age /ˈ· ˌ··/ *n* [U] any INJURY or damage to the brain, which may be either temporary or permanent: *She suffered brain damage in the car crash. | irreversible brain damage* **brain-damaged** *adj* : *severely brain-damaged | born brain-damaged*

brain dead /ˈ· ·/ *adj* [no comp.] **1** *med* in a state in which brain death has happened: *She was pronounced brain dead on Sunday.* **2** *infml, derog* (of a person) stupid; slow to understand: *a television film for the brain dead*

brain death /ˈ· ·/ *n* [U] *med* the failure of a person's breathing and other actions of the body because of brain damage, even though the heart may continue to beat when the body is on a life-supporting machine

brain drain /ˈ· ·/ *n* a movement of large numbers of highly-skilled or professional people from the country where they were trained to other countries where they can earn more money

brain·less /ˈbreɪnləs/ *adj* silly; stupid — ~**ly** *adv*

brain·storm /ˈbreɪnstɔːm‖-stɔːrm/ *n infml* **1** *BrE* a sudden

disorder of the mind or change from sensible behaviour, lasting only a short time: *I had a brainstorm and forgot to sign any of the cheques.* **2** *AmE for* BRAINWAVE

brain·stor·ming /ˈbreɪnstɔːmɪŋ‖-ɔːr-/ *n* [U] *esp. AmE* a method of finding answers to problems in which all the members of a group think very quickly of as many ideas as they can

brains trust /ˈ· ·/ *BrE* ‖ **brain trust** *AmE*— *n* [C+*sing./pl. v*] a group of people with special knowledge and experience who answer questions or give advice

brain sur·geon /ˈ· ˌ··/ *n* a doctor who operates on the human brain. Brain surgeons are thought of as very well-educated, clever, and skilful people: *She's doing alright at school, but she'll never be a brain surgeon.*

brain·teas·er /ˈbreɪntiːzəʳ/ *n* a problem to exercise the mind, esp. one that is to be answered for pleasure; PUZZLE

brain·wash /ˈbreɪnwɒʃ‖-wɔːʃ, -wɑːʃ/ *v* [T (**into**)] *derog* to cause (someone) to change their beliefs and ideas, by a system of forceful continuous persuading: *to brainwash political prisoners | (infml) Don't let those television advertisements brainwash you into buying that soap.* — ~**ing** *n* [U]

brain·wave /ˈbreɪnweɪv/ *n* **1** *infml* ‖ also **brainstorm** *AmE* a sudden clever idea: *I've just had a brainwave. Here's what we should do!* **2** [*usu. pl.*] *tech* an electrical force that is produced by the brain and can be measured

brain·y /ˈbreɪni/ *adj infml* clever; INTELLIGENT —see CLEVER (USAGE) —**iness** *n* [U]

braise /breɪz/ *v* [T] to cook (meat or vegetables) slowly in fat and a little liquid in a covered dish: *braised celery* —see COOK (USAGE)

braising steak /ˈ·· ·/ *n* [U] cow meat that is cheaper and lower in quality than steak, usu. used in small pieces and cooked in liquid to make it tender

brake¹ /breɪk/ *n* an apparatus for reducing movement of a vehicle and bringing it to a stop, esp. by means of pressure on the wheels: *emergency brakes | to step hard on the brake | (fig.) The rise in interest rates acted as a brake on expenditure.* —see pictures at BICYCLE and CAR, and see also DISC BRAKES

brake² *v* [I;T] to (cause to) slow or stop by using a brake: *She braked suddenly to avoid the dog.*

brake³ *n* an area of rough or wet land with many low-growing wild bushes and plants

brake light /ˈ· ·/ *n* a usu. red light at the back of a vehicle, which lights up when the driver presses the brake

brake shoe /ˈ· ·/ *n* either of a pair of curved plates next to the wheel of a vehicle that may be pressed against it to stop it or slow it down

bram·ble /ˈbræmbəl/ *n* a common wild prickly bush of the rose family, esp. the wild BLACKBERRY

Bram·ley /ˈbræmli/ *n* a type of green apple with a firm, juicy flesh, used for cooking

bran /bræn/ *n* [U] the crushed skin of wheat and other grain separated from the flour. It is believed that bran is healthy, because it contains a lot of FIBRE, and some people like to add it to their breakfast CEREAL.

branch¹ /brɑːntʃ‖bræntʃ/ *n* **1** an armlike stem growing from the trunk of a tree or from another such stem: *monkeys swinging from the branches | an overhanging branch* **2** [(**of**)] a separate and usu. less important part of something larger: *a branch of a river | a branch line on a railway network* **3** [(**of**)] a part or division of a large organization, group, area of knowledge, etc.: *Psychiatry is a branch of medicine. | The bank has branches all over the country. | He's the chairman of the local branch of the union.*

branch² *v* [I] to form or become divided into branches: *Turn right where the road branches.*

branch off *phr v* [I (**from**)] to leave a main road, an established course of action, etc.: *They branched off from the main road and turned down a country lane.*

branch out *phr v* [I (**into**)] to add to the range of one's interests or activities: *The bookshop has decided to branch out into selling records and tapes.*

brand¹ /brænd/ *n* **1** [(**of**)] a class of goods which is the product of a particular company or producer: *What is your favourite brand of cigarettes? | The* **brand name** *of this soap is "Flower". | This type of coffee is the* **brand leader.** (=the brand that is sold in the largest quantities) |

(fig.) *He has his own brand* (=special kind) *of humour.* —see MAKE (USAGE) **2** a mark made, esp. by burning, usu. to show the owner of something: *These cattle have my brand on them.* **3** *lit* a piece of burnt or burning wood **4** *poet* a sword

brand² *v* [T] **1** to mark (something) by or as if by burning, esp. to show who owns it: *The cattle are branded with the farmer's initials.* | (fig.) *His unhappy childhood has branded him for life.* (=had a lasting effect on his character) **2** [(as)] to give a lasting bad name to; STIGMATIZE: *It's unfair to brand all football supporters as troublemakers.* [+obj+n] *The press branded him a liar.*

bran·dish /'brændɪʃ/ *v* [T] to shake or wave (something, esp. a weapon) about, often in a threatening way: *He brandished a newspaper at me and said, "Have you seen the news?"*

brand name /'· ˌ·/ *n* a TRADE NAME

brand-new /ˌ· '·◄/ *adj* new and completely unused: *Be careful with that record — it's brand-new!* | *a brand-new car*

Bran·do /'brændəʊ, **Mar·lon** /'mɑːlɒn‖'mɑːrlən/ (1924–) an American actor whose films include *A Streetcar Named Desire, On the Waterfront*, and *The Godfather* — see picture at The GODFATHER

Brands Hatch /ˌ· '·/ a motor-racing CIRCUIT (1) in Kent, England

Brandt /brænt/, **Wil·ly** /'vɪli/ (1913–) a West German politician, and Chancellor from 1969 to 1974

bran·dy /'brændi/ *n* [C;U] (a glass of) a strong alcoholic drink made from wine, also called COGNAC —see picture at GLASS

brandy but·ter /ˌ·· '··/ *n* [U] a sweet mixture of butter, sugar, and brandy, usu. eaten with CHRISTMAS PUDDING or MINCE PIES

brandy snap /'·· ·/ *n* a sweet, thin BISCUIT in the shape of a tube, sometimes filled with cream

Bran·son /'brænsən/, **Richard** (1950–) an English ENTREPRENEUR famous first for his record company, **Virgin**, and later for his international AIRLINE

Bran·ston Pick·le /ˌbrænstən 'pɪkəl/ *n* [U] *tdmk* a popular type of CHUTNEY made by Crosse & Blackwell; there are different FLAVOURS of Branston Pickle

bran tub /'· ·/ *n BrE* a TUB (=large round open container) filled with bran and containing small presents. Children pay a small amount of money and can then put their hand into the bran tub to find a surprise present.

Braque /brɑːk/, **Georges** /ʒɔːʒ‖ʒɔːrʒ/ (1882–1963) a French painter who worked with Picasso and was one of those who started the movement known as CUBISM

brash /bræʃ/ *adj derog* **1** showing a disrespectful or showy self-confidence: *a loud, brash young man* | *The new part of the city, with its brash and vulgar buildings* **2** hasty and too confident, esp. from lack of experience; RASH — ~**ly** *adv* – – **ness** *n* [U]

Bra·sil·i·a /brə'zɪliə/ the capital city of Brazil

brass /brɑːs‖bræs/ *n* **1** [U] a very hard bright yellow metal, a mixture of COPPER and ZINC **2** [*the+sing.|pl. v*] (the players of) the set of musical instruments in an ORCHESTRA or band that are made of brass and are played by blowing: *The brass is|are too loud.* —compare WOODWIND **3** [C] (esp. in Britain) a flat piece of brass with an ENGRAVING on it, fixed to the floor or wall of a church in memory of a dead person: *to go* **brass rubbing** (=to make copies of brasses with paper and CRAYONS) **4** [U] *infml* unashamed self-confidence; NERVE: *How did she have the brass to do that?* **5** [U] *sl, esp. NEngE* money **6** [*the + sing.|pl.v*] *AmE infml for* TOP BRASS **7 get down to brass tacks** *infml* to come to the important facts or business

brass band /ˌ· '·/ *n* a band consisting mostly of brass musical instruments. When British people think of brass bands, they often think of the industrial towns of the North of England, where brass bands are very popular. In the US, brass bands are popular with older people, and are often part of street processions.

brassed off /ˌbrɑːst 'ɒf‖ˌbræst 'ɔːf/ *adj* [F (**with**)] *BrE sl* tired and annoyed; FED UP

bras·se·rie /'bræsəri‖ˌbræsə'riː/ *n Fr, BrE* a restaurant, esp. one that is informal and fairly cheap, and serves French food —see RESTAURANT (CULTURAL NOTE)

brass hat /ˌ· '·/ *n sl* a military officer of high rank

bras·si·ere /'bræzɪəʳ‖brə'zɪər/ *n fml* a BRA

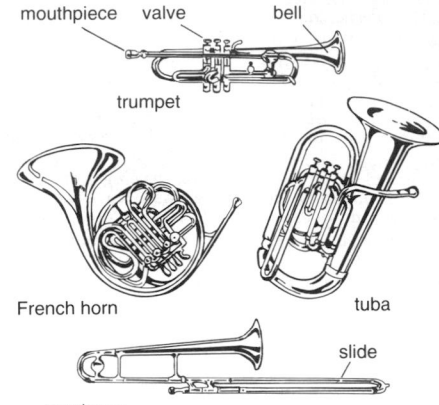

mouthpiece   valve   bell

trumpet

French horn   tuba

                                         slide

trombone

brass knuck·les /ˌ· '··/ *n* [P] *AmE for* KNUCKLE-DUSTER

brass-mon·key /ˌ· '··/ *adj infml* (of weather) very cold (from the *taboo sl* expression "cold enough to freeze the balls off a brass monkey")

Brass·o /'brɑːsəʊ‖'bræ-/ *n* [U] *tdmk* a type of polish made by Reckitt & Colman Ltd. and used for polishing BRASS

brass tacks /ˌ· '·/ *n* **get down to brass tacks** *infml* to come to the really important facts or business

brass·y /'brɑːsi‖'bræsi/ *adj* **1** like brass in colour **2** like brass musical instruments in sound **3** (*usu. derog*, esp. of a woman) loud and self-confident in manner

brat /bræt/ *n derog* a child, esp. a bad-mannered one

brat·pack /'brætpæk/ *n* [*the*] a group of successful and fashionable young actors, writers, performers, etc.: *a member of the Hollywood bratpack* | *the literary bratpack*

brat·wurst /'brætwɜːst‖-wɜːrst/ *n* [U] *Ger* a SAUSAGE made with PORK, for cooking in hot oil

Braun /brɔːn/, **Carol Moseley** (1947–) a CIVIL SERVANT who, in 1992, became the first black woman to be elected to the US Senate, representing Illinois

Braun, E·va /'eɪvə/ (1910–45) a German Nazi who married Adolf Hitler in 1945 and then killed herself at the same time as he did

bra·va·do /brə'vɑːdəʊ/ *n* [U] the act of intentionally showing one's courage or confidence, esp. in a way that is unnecessarily dangerous: *It was an act of sheer bravado.*

brave¹ /breɪv/ *adj* **1** courageous, fearless, and ready to suffer danger or pain: *brave soldiers* | *a brave attempt to recapture the city from the enemy* | *Be brave — we'll soon have your tooth out.* | *It was very brave of you to stand up and speak in front of all those people.* [also *n, the*+P] *Today we remember the brave who died in the last war.* **2** [A] *old use* fine; EXCELLENT: *a brave new world* **3 brave new world** a phrase from *The Tempest* by Shakespeare and the title of a NOVEL by Aldous Huxley – – **ly** *adv* – – **ry** /'breɪvəri/ *n* [U]: *bravery in the face of terrible danger*

brave² *v* [T] to face or risk facing (danger, pain, or trouble) without showing fear: *He braved his parents' displeasure by marrying her.* | *We decided to brave the storm and try to walk home.*

brave³ *n* a young Native American WARRIOR (=fighting man)

Brave New World /ˌ· · '·/ a book written in 1932 by Aldous Huxley which imagined a future where humans are produced and controlled to serve society without freedom of their own. The phrase is now used to describe any real or imaginary society that is similar to this.

bra·vo /'brɑːvəʊ, brɑː'vəʊ/ *interj, n* **-vos** (a shout of joy because someone, esp. a performer, has done well)

bra·vu·ra /brə'vjʊərə/ *n* [U] **1** a show of great skill in performing **2** a show of great courage or daring

brawl /brɔːl/ *n* a noisy quarrel or fight, esp. one in which several people take part, and often in a public place – **brawl** *v* [I] – – **er** *n*

brawn /brɔ:n/ *n* [U] **1** human muscle; MUSCULAR strength: *He's got more brawn than brains.* (=he's strong, but not very clever) **2** *BrE* ‖ **headcheese** *AmE*— (pieces of) meat from the head of a pig, boiled and pressed in a pot with jelly

brawn·y /'brɔ:ni/ *adj* strong; MUSCULAR: *brawny arms* —**iness** *n* [U]

bray /breɪ/ *v* [I] to make the sound that a DONKEY makes: (fig.) *He brayed with laughter.* —**bray** *n*

bra·zen¹ /'breɪzən/ *adj* **1** without shame; IMMODEST: *a brazen lie* | *brazen cheek* | *a* **brazen hussy 2** [A] *lit* of or like brass, esp. in producing a hard loud sound as brass does when struck — **~ly** *adv*

brazen² *v* **brazen it out** to face trouble or blame with unashamed confidence, as if one has done nothing wrong

bra·zi·er /'breɪziəʳ‖-ʒər/ *n* a container for burning coals

Bra·zil /brə'zɪl/ a country in E South America, the largest Latin American country; capital Brasilia; population 147,404,000 (1989) —**ian** *n, adj*

Brazil², **An·ge·la** /'ændʒələ/ (1868–1947) an English writer of stories about schoolgirl life

Brazil nut /·'· ·/ *n* **1** a S American tree whose seeds are eaten as nuts **2** the nut of this tree —see picture at NUT

Braz·za·ville /'bræzəvɪl/ the capital city of the Republic of the Congo, in Africa

breach¹ /bri:tʃ/ *n* **1** [C;U (of)] an act of breaking, disobeying, or not fulfilling a law, promise, or duty: *This new decision represents a breach of our original agreement.* | *She was sued for breach of contract.* | *These working practices are* **in breach of** *section 22 of the safety regulations.* | *He was arrested for a* **breach of the peace.** (=fighting in public) | *His* **breach of confidence** (=telling of secrets) *was condemned by his colleagues.* **2** [C] an opening, esp. one made in a wall by attackers: *a breach in the castle walls* | (fig.) *When I was ill she stepped into/threw herself into the breach and did my work as well as her own.* | (fig.) *The incident caused an irreparable breach between the two countries.* (=broke their friendship) **3 once more unto the breach dear friends, once more** *quote* a phrase from the play *Henry V* by Shakespeare, used by the king when encouraging his soldiers to fight again — see colour picture on page 1146

breach² *v* [T] **1** to break an opening in **2** to break (a promise, agreement, etc.): *to breach one's contract*

bread /bred/ *n* [U] **1** a common food made of baked flour: *a loaf of bread* | *bread and butter/jam/cheese* (=bread spread with butter/JAM/cheese) | *white/brown/wholemeal bread* **2** food considered as a means of staying alive: *to earn one's (daily) bread as a labourer* **3** *old-fash sl* money **4 bread and butter** *infml* one's way of earning money to live on; LIVELIHOOD: *I don't write just for fun — it's my bread and butter.* —see also BREAD-AND-BUTTER **5 take the bread out of someone's mouth** *infml* to make it impossible for someone to earn money, esp. by taking their work away **6 Man cannot live by bread alone** *saying from the Bible* the needs of a person's spirit must be looked after as well as those of their body. The phrase is now often used in a humorous way: *I know we're trying to save money, but man cannot live by baked beans alone.* —see also FRENCH BREAD, SLICED BREAD, **break bread with** (BREAK¹ (15)), **know which side one's bread is buttered** (KNOW¹)

bread-and-but·ter /ₐ· · '··◄/ *adj* [A] **1** concerned with the things that are necessary for life: *bread-and-butter political issues such as jobs and housing* **2** sent as thanks for being treated well as someone's guest (esp. in the phrase **a bread-and-butter letter**)

bread-and-but·ter pud·ding /ₐ· · ₐ· '··/ *n* [U] a sweet dish made from bread, dried fruit, milk, and eggs, baked in an OVEN. Bread-and-butter pudding is an old-fashioned British DESSERT.

bread·bas·ket /'bred₁bɑ:skɪt‖-₁bæ-/ *n* [(the)] **1** an important area for grain production: *The Ukraine is the breadbasket of the Soviet Union.* **2** *old-fash sl* the stomach: *Hit him in the breadbasket, Maxie!*

bread bin /'· ·/ *BrE* ‖ **bread box** *AmE n* a container for keeping bread in, so that it stays fresh

bread·board /'bredbɔ:d‖-bɔ:rd/ *n* a wooden board on which to cut a loaf of bread into SLICES (=thin pieces) —see picture at KITCHEN

bread·crumb /'bredkrʌm/ *n* [usu. pl.] a very small bit of bread: *Coat the fish with breadcrumbs, then fry it in a little oil.*

bread·fruit /'bredfru:t/ *n* [C;U] (a tropical tree that bears) a round fruit that looks and feels like bread when baked

bread·line /'bredlaɪn/ *n* **on the breadline** extremely poor

bread sauce /ₐ· '·/ *n BrE* [U] a mixture of milk, bread, onion, and SPICEs, usu. served with chicken or TURKEY

breadth /bredθ, bretθ/ *n* **1** [C;U] *fml* (the) distance from one side of something to the other; width: *What is the breadth of this river?* | *Its breadth is 16 metres.* | *It is 16 metres in breadth.* —compare LENGTH (1) **2** [U] the fact or quality of including many things or people; wide range; SCOPE: *His book shows the great breadth of his learning.* | *It is important to remember the breadth of their support in the country.* **3** [U] willingness to consider opinions, customs, etc. that are different from one's own; openness: *breadth of mind/opinions*

breadth·ways /'bredθweɪz, 'bretθ-/ also **breadth·wise** /-waɪz/— *adj, adv* in the direction of the breadth; with the broad side nearest the viewer: *files stored breadthways on a shelf*

bread·win·ner /'bred₁wɪnəʳ/ *n* a person in a family whose wages provide what the family needs to live on: *My mother was the breadwinner in our family.* | *They both work, but he is the main breadwinner* (=he earns the most money).

break¹ /breɪk/ *v* **broke** /brəʊk/, **broken** /'brəʊkən/ **1** [I;T] to (cause to) separate into parts suddenly or violently, but not by cutting or tearing: *I dropped my cup and it broke.* | *The rope broke when they were climbing it.* | *Stones hit the window and it broke into several pieces.* | *Someone has broken this chair.* | *He has broken his leg/broken a bone in his leg.* | *to break a branch off a tree* | *A large piece of ice broke away from the main mass.* | *You'll* **break your neck** (=kill yourself by falling, etc.) *if you aren't careful!* | *The floor was covered in bits of broken glass.* **2** [I;T] to (cause to) become unusable by damage to one or more parts: *I broke my watch when I fell over.* | *The typewriter is broken and will have to be repaired.* **3** [T] to split into smaller units; divide: *to break a £10 note* **4** [I] (of a wave) to curl over and fall apart as it comes in to the shore: *waves breaking on the beach/against the rocks* **5** [I+adj/adv/prep;T] to force a way into, out of, or through, esp. with sudden violence: *The invaders broke through the enemy line* | *With a great effort, the prisoner broke loose/broke free and ran off.* | *The river broke its banks and flooded the city.* | *a plane that can break the sound barrier* **6** [T] to make an opening in the surface of: *The dog scratched me but didn't break the skin.* | *to break the soil* **7** [I;T] to (cause to) come to an end: *A sudden cry broke the silence.* | *to break an electric circuit* | *The cold weather broke at the end of March.* | *We hope that this new offer will break the deadlock.* | *The visit was* **broken short** *because there was talk of war.* **8** [I;T] to interrupt (an activity): *We broke our journey to Rome at Venice.* | *The bushes will break his fall.* | *Let's break for lunch and start again afterwards.* | *The children started shouting and broke my train of thought.* **9** [I;T] to (cause to) fail, be destroyed, or suffer a complete loss of effectiveness, often as a result of a long process: *After years of working too hard, his health finally broke.* | *The prolonged bombardment broke the enemy's spirit/resistance.* | *The government brought in the army to break the strike.* | *I'm trying to break the smoking habit.* | *The prisoner may break under continuous questioning.* | *This scandal could break him politically.* | *The separation will* **make or break** *their relationship.* **10** [I;T] to win (a game) in tennis from the opponent who began it **11** [T] to fail to fulfil (an agreement), keep (a promise), or obey (a law); not act in accordance with: *to break the law/break the rules/a promise* | *He has broken his word.* (=not kept his promise) | *She had to break an appointment with the lawyer to take her son to hospital.* **12** [T] to do better than: *The runner broke the world record for the mile.* —see also RECORD-BREAKING **13** [I;T] to (cause to) come suddenly into being or notice: *The birds begin to sing as day breaks.* | *The storm broke.* | *The news broke.* | *Break the news to him gently.* **14** [T] to discover the secret of: *We finally broke the enemy's code.* **15** [I] (of the voice) to change suddenly in level, loudness, etc.: *His voice broke when he was 15 years old.* | *a voice breaking with emotion* **16 break bread with** *pomp* to eat a meal with **17 break**

camp to pack up tents and other equipment and leave a camp **18 break cover** (of an animal) to run out from a hiding place **19 break new/fresh ground** to do something new, esp. to make new discoveries **20 break one's back** ‖ *also* **break one's ass** *AmE*— to work very hard or too hard; make every possible effort: *They were breaking their backs trying to keep the deadline.* **21 break someone's heart** to make someone extremely sad: *It breaks my heart to see him working so hard for nothing.* | *She broke her father's heart by marrying John.* —see also HEARTBREAKING, HEARTBROKEN **22 break step** to stop marching together with a regular beat **23 break the back of** *infml* finish the main or the worst part of: *If we start early, we can break the back of the journey before it gets hot.* **24 break the bank: a** to win all the money, e.g. at a game of cards **b** *infml* to take all one's money: *Come on; it only costs £5 — that won't break the bank!* **25 break the ice** *infml* to remove feelings of awkwardness or nervousness, esp. between people who do not know each other, e.g. at the beginning of a party **26 break wind** *euph* to let out gases from the bowels. —see also **keep/break ranks** (RANK¹)

▷ USAGE Compare **break, tear, cut, smash, crack,** and **burst.** You cannot **break** soft things like cloth or paper, but you can **tear** them, which means "pull apart so as to leave rough edges", or **cut** them, which means "divide by using a sharp edge": *He* **tore** *the letter into pieces.* | *I* **cut** *the cake with a knife.* Things made of glass or CHINA may **break** (or **be/get broken**) or **smash,** which means "break suddenly into small pieces": *The dish* **smashed** *on the floor.* **Crack** means "break without the parts becoming separated": *You've* **cracked** *the window, but luckily you haven't* **broken** *it.* **Burst** means "break suddenly by pressure from inside": *She blew up the paper bag until it* **burst.**◁

break away *phr v* [I (**from**)] **1** to escape, esp. with a sudden violent effort: *The prisoner broke away from the two policemen who were holding him.* **2** to end one's connection with a group, organization, way of thinking, etc.: *This extremist faction broke away from the main party in 1979.* | *an innovative musician who broke away from the classical tradition* —see also BREAKAWAY

break down *phr v* **1** [T] (**break** sthg. ↔ **down**) to destroy, knock to the ground, or reduce to pieces: *The police broke the door down.* | *The old cars were broken down for their metal and parts.* **2** [I;T] (=**break** sthg. ↔ **down**)] to (cause to) be defeated, or lose effectiveness: *I tried to break down her opposition to our plan.* | *His resistance broke down.* | *This agreement will break down the barriers to free trade.* **3** [I] (esp. of machinery) to stop working; fail: *The car broke down.* **4** [I] to come to an unsuccessful end: *The peace talks broke down without any agreement being reached.* **5** [I] to lose control of one's feelings: *Peter broke down and wept when his mother died.* **6** [I;T] (=**break** sthg. ↔ **down**)] to (cause to) separate into different kinds or divide into types: *Chemicals in the body break our food down into useful substances.* | *The figures must be broken down into several categories.* —see also BREAKDOWN

break even *phr v* [I] to make neither a loss nor a profit in doing business —see also BREAKEVEN

break in *phr v* **1** [I] to enter a building by force: *They broke in through an upstairs window and stole some jewellery.* —see also BREAK-IN **2** [I (**on, upon**)] to interrupt: *She broke in with some suggestions of her own.* | *The sudden banging at the door broke in on the silence/on my thoughts.* **3** [T] (**break** sthg./sbdy. ↔ **in**) to make (a person or animal) used to something new: *Young horses have to be broken in.* (=taught to obey) | *A week in the new office should be enough to break you in.* **4** [T] (**break** sthg. ↔ **in**) to wear (new shoes or boots) to make them lose their stiffness and become comfortable

break into sthg. *phr v* [T] **1** to enter by force: *to break into a house and commit a burglary* **2** to begin suddenly: *to break into song/laughter/cheers* | *The horse broke into a gallop.* **3** to use part of, unwillingly: *We'll have to break into our savings.*

break sbdy. **of** sthg. *phr v* [T] to cure of (a bad habit): *Doctors are trying to break him of his dependence on the drug.*

break off *phr v* [I;T (=**break** sthg. ↔ **off**)] **1** to (cause to) end, esp. suddenly: *The two countries have broken off diplomatic relations (with each other).* | *The talks broke off without any solution being reached.* | *We broke off*

(work) for a cup of coffee. **2** to (cause to) become separated from the main part by breaking or being broken: *A branch broke off (the tree) in the wind.* | *I broke off a piece of chocolate and gave it to the little boy.*

break out *phr v* [I] **1** (of an undesirable condition) to begin suddenly and often violently: *War/Fighting/Panic/A fire broke out.* **2** [(**in**)] to suddenly become covered (esp. with spots on the skin): *The allergy caused him to break out in spots/a rash.* | *I broke out in a cold sweat when I realized there was a burglar downstairs.* **3** [(**of**)] to escape (from): *to break out of prison* —see also BREAKOUT, OUTBREAK

break through *phr v* **1** [I;T (=**break through** sthg.)] to force a way through: *At last sun broke through (the clouds).* | *to break through the enemy's defences* **2** [I] to make a new advance or discovery, esp. after dealing successfully with problems and difficulties: *Scientists hope to break through soon in their search for a cure for this type of cancer.* —see also BREAKTHROUGH

break up *phr v* **1** [I;T (=**break** sthg. ↔ **up**)] to (cause to) become separated into smaller pieces: *The frost will break up the soil.* | *The ship broke up on the rocks.* | *We are putting some illustrations in the book in order to break up the text.* **2** [I;T (=**break** sthg. ↔ **up**)] to come or bring to an end, esp. by separating: *Their marriage broke up.* | *The police broke up the fight.* | *The conference broke up without reaching any agreement.* **3** [I] to stop being together; separate or go in different directions: *What will happen to the children if Jim and Mary break up?* | *The crowd broke up.* **4** [I] *BrE* (of a school or pupil) to begin the holidays: *When does your school break up?* | *We broke up on Tuesday.* **5** [T] (**break** sbdy. ↔ **up**) *AmE* to amuse greatly: *His account of the meeting really broke me up.* —see also BREAKUP

break with sbdy./sthg. *phr v* [T] to end a friendship or connection with: *to break with one's former friends/with old ideas*

break² *n* **1** an act of breaking or a condition produced (as if) by breaking: *a break in the clouds* | *a break in an electrical circuit* | *The break with her husband was painful, but she thought it was for the best.* | *You'll have to* **make the break** *sometime if you want to get away from this town.* **2** a pause for rest between activities: *a coffee break* | *to take/have a weekend break* | *We've worked 24 hours* **without a break.** (=continuously) **3** [(**from, in, with**)] a change from the usual pattern or custom: *The queen's decision to send her children to ordinary schools was a break from/with tradition.* | *a break in the weather* **4** *infml* a chance (esp. to make things better); piece of good luck: *Give him a break and he'll succeed.* | *He's had a good year with several big/lucky breaks.* **5** an escape, esp. from prison **6** (in cricket) a change of direction of the ball on first hitting the ground **7** (in the game of BILLIARDS) the number of points made by one player during one turn at hitting the balls **8** (in tennis) a case of winning a game from the opponent who began it: *She needs a break of serve now.* | *two break points* **9 break of day** *lit for* DAYBREAK **10 make a break for it** *infml* to try to escape by running away

break·age /ˈbreɪkɪdʒ/ *n* [C;U] **1** (the causing of) a broken place, part, or object: *a breakage in the gas pipes* **2** (the cost of) damage caused by breaking things: *Any breakages will be paid for by the company that is transporting the goods.*

break·a·way /ˈbreɪkəweɪ/ *n* **1** a person or thing that breaks away **2** an act or example of breaking away (e.g. from a group or custom) —see also BREAK **away** —**breakaway** *adj* [A] : *A breakaway faction within the movement has formed a new terrorist group.* | *breakaway republics seeking independence from the Soviet Union*

break·dance /ˈbreɪkdɑːns‖-dæns/ *v* [I] to perform a style of dancing to ROCK music, in which the dancers often spin round on their heads or shoulders or perform other difficult, ACROBATIC moves **breakdancing** *n* **breakdancer** *n*

break·down /ˈbreɪkdaʊn/ *n* **1** a sudden failure in operation or effectiveness: *Our car had a breakdown on the road.* | *a breakdown of talks between the staff and the management* | *a complete breakdown of law and order* **2** [(**of**)] a division by types or into smaller groups, esp. for the purpose of explanation: *I'd like a breakdown of these figures, please.* —see also BREAK **down,** NERVOUS BREAKDOWN

breakdown truck /ˈ·· ˌ·/ also **breakdown lor·ry** /ˈ·· ˌ··/ BrE ‖ **towtruck** AmE— n a TRUCK fitted with apparatus for lifting and pulling along motor vehicles which have broken down —see picture at TRUCK

break·er /ˈbreɪkəʳ/ n **1** a large wave with a white top that rolls onto the shore **2** a user of a CB radio **3** -**breaker** a person or thing that breaks something: law-breakers

break·e·ven /ˌbreɪkˈiːvən◂/ n [U] a level of business activity at which a company makes neither a loss nor a profit: After two difficult years, the company hopes to reach breakeven this year, and to be in profit next year. —see also BREAK **even**

break·fast /ˈbrekfəst/ n [C;U] the first meal of the day: We usually have breakfast at 7 o'clock. | It happened at/during breakfast. | She likes eggs for breakfast. | a working breakfast (=at which business is talked about) —see also COOKED BREAKFAST, DOG'S BREAKFAST, ENGLISH BREAKFAST, WEDDING BREAKFAST —**breakfast** v [I (**on**)] : We breakfasted early (on eggs and coffee).

breakfast ce·re·al /ˈ·· ˌ···/ n [C;U] CEREAL (2)

breakfast tel·e·vi·sion /ˌ·· ˈ····, ˌ·· ··ˈ··/ n [U] television programmes which are broadcast in the early part of the morning, usu. a mixture of news, sport, and conversation

break·in /ˈ· ·/ n the entering of a building illegally and by force: a break-in at the bank —see also BREAK **in**

breaking and en·ter·ing /ˌ··· · ˈ···/ n [U] the crime of entering a house by force

break·neck /ˈbreɪknek/ adj [A] very fast and dangerous: driving at breakneck speed

break·out /ˈbreɪkaʊt/ n a violent or forceful escape from an enclosed space or a difficult situation, esp. an escape from prison, usu. by several prisoners at once —see also BREAK **out**

break·through /ˈbreɪkθruː/ n (the making of) an important advance or discovery, often after earlier failures: a major breakthrough in the treatment of cancer | The negotiators have achieved/made a dramatic breakthrough in the arms control talks. —see also BREAK **through**

break·up /ˈbreɪkʌp/ n [(of) usu. sing.] n **1** a coming to an end, esp. of a relationship or association: the breakup of a marriage/of an alliance **2** a division into smaller parts: the breakup of the large farms —see also BREAK **up**, BREAKDOWN

break·wa·ter /ˈbreɪkˌwɔːtəʳ‖-ˌwɔː-, -ˌwɑː-/ n a thick wall built out into the sea to lessen the force of the waves

bream /briːm/ n **bream** or **breams** a kind of freshwater fish, or a similar saltwater fish (**sea bream**)

Bream, Ju·li·an /ˈdʒuːliən/ (1933–) an English musician known for his GUITAR and LUTE playing

breast¹ /brest/ n **1** either of the two parts of a woman's body that produce milk: a baby at its mother's breast/at the breast | a breast cancer screening service —compare CHEST (1) **2** the upper front part of the body between the neck and the stomach, esp. in birds or animals: a bird with an orange breast | the breast pocket of a jacket | They had chicken breasts for lunch. —see picture at BIRD **3** lit the part of the body where the feelings are supposed to be: a troubled breast —compare BOSOM (2), HEART (2) **4** **make a clean breast of** to tell the whole truth about (something bad that one has done); admit to: His guilty conscience forced him to make a clean breast of everything. —see also **beat one's breast** (BEAT¹ (11))

breast² v [T] fml or lit to meet and push aside with one's chest: The winner of the race breasted the tape. | (fig.) The ship breasted the waves.

breast·bone /ˈbrestbəʊn/ also **sternum** med— n the upright bone in the front of the chest, to which the top seven pairs of RIBS are connected —see picture at SKELETON

breast-feed /ˈ· ·/ v -**fed** /fed/ [I;T] (of a woman) to feed (a baby) with milk from the breast, not from a bottle: breast-fed babies —compare NURSE² (3), SUCKLE

breast·plate /ˈbrestpleɪt/ n a piece of armour worn to protect the chest

breast pock·et /ˌ·· ˈ··/ n an outside pocket on a shirt or JACKET over the breast, usu. used for a handkerchief or pens

breast·stroke /ˈbrest-strəʊk/ n [(the) S;U] a way of swimming on one's front, by pushing the arms in front of the head through the water while drawing the knees

forwards and outwards and then sweeping them back while kicking backwards and outwards

breast·work /ˈbrestwɜːk‖-wɜːrk/ n a defensive earth wall, usu. built as high as a man's chest

breath /breθ/ n **1** [U] air taken into and breathed out of the lungs: I was out of breath/short of breath after running for the bus. | She paused for a few moments to get her breath (back). | Tooth decay often causes bad breath. (=breath that smells bad) | He fiercely criticized her speech, scarcely even pausing for breath/to draw breath between successive points. | Remember to hold your **breath** (=take no air in) when you dive into the water. | (fig.) All Europe held its breath (=waited anxiously) to see who would win the election. | (infml) He said he'd come as soon as he could, but he's so unreliable, I shouldn't **hold your breath**. | (lit) The new leader vowed to fight for the rights of his people as long as he had breath. (=until he died) **2** [C] a single act of breathing air in and out once: He took a deep breath and then dived into the water. | (fig.) Let's go out for a **breath of (fresh) air**. | She claimed not to like the place, but **in the next breath** (=the next moment) said she was taking her holiday there. | He cursed them with his last/dying breath. (=at the last moment of his life) **3** [S+of] a slight sign of (something); SUGGESTION: There's a breath of spring in the air today. | the breath of scandal **4** **take someone's ˈbreath away** to make someone unable to speak from surprise, pleasure, or shock: His sheer rudeness took my breath away. —see also BREATHTAKING **5** **under one's breath** in a low voice or a whisper —see also **with bated breath** (BATED), **catch one's breath** (CATCH¹), **waste one's breath** (WASTE²)

breath·a·lyse BrE‖-**lyze** AmE /ˈbreθəl-aɪz/ v [T] infml to test (a driver) with a breathalyser

breath·a·lys·er BrE ‖ **Breathalyzer** AmE tdmk /ˈbreθəl-aɪzəʳ/, also **drunkometer** AmE infml —n an apparatus used by the police to measure the amount of alcohol that the driver of a car has drunk. In many countries it is illegal to drive after you have drunk more than a legal limit of alcohol.

breathe /briːð/ v **1** [I;T (IN, OUT)] to take (air, gas, etc.) into the lungs and send it out again: Fish cannot breathe out of water. | The doctor told me to breathe in deeply (=take air in) and then breathe out. | He became ill after breathing (in) coal dust for many years. | They walked through the forest breathing (in) the scent of pines. | She moved to another seat to get away from the man opposite, who was breathing alcohol/tobacco fumes all over her. | (lit) I'll remember this day as long as I breathe. (=until I die) | breathing apparatus/equipment for deep sea divers **2** [T] to say softly; whisper: He breathed words of love into her ear. | She **breathed a sigh of relief** when she heard she had passed the exam. | Don't **breathe a word of it** to anyone. (=Don't tell anyone about it.) **3** [T (**into**)] to give or send out as if by breathing: His enthusiasm **breathed new life into** the department. | (fig.) She really **breathes fire** when she gets angry! **4** [I] (of flowers, wine, etc.) to take in air or feel the effects of air: Open the wine so that it can breathe before we drink it. | The shoes have leather soles, so your feet can breathe. **5** **breathe again** to feel calm after feeling anxious: He's gone; you can breathe (freely) again. **6** **breathe down someone's neck** infml to keep too close a watch on someone: I can't work properly with you breathing down my neck all the time. **7** **breathe one's last** fml or euph to die —**breathing** n [U] —see also **heavy breathing**

breath·er /ˈbriːðəʳ/ n infml a short pause for a rest: We've been working quite a long time now: let's have/take a breather. —see also **heavy breather**

breathing space /ˈ·· ·/ n [S;U] (a) short period when one is free from work, worry, pressure, etc.: They gave her a breathing space of two weeks before she had to pay back the debt.

breath·less /ˈbreθləs/ adj **1** breathing heavily or with difficulty: By the time I got to the top I was completely breathless. **2** causing one to stop breathing or breathe with difficulty: a breathless silence during the exciting last game of the tennis match | breathless haste/hurry **3** with no wind: a hot and breathless afternoon — ~**ly** adv — ~**ness** n [U]

breath·tak·ing /ˈbreθˌteɪkɪŋ/ adj **1** very exciting: a breathtaking finish to the race **2** very surprising or shocking; causing ASTONISHMENT: *breathtaking beauty/stupidity/rudeness* – – ~ **ly** *adv* : *breathtakingly beautiful*

breath test /'· ,·/ *n* a test made with a BREATHALYSER: *The breath test showed him to be over the limit.* (=having drunk too much alcohol to drive a car)

breath·y /'breθi/ *adj* (esp. of the voice) with noticeable noise of breath: *the breathy sound of the flute* —**ily** *adv* —**iness** *n* [U]

Brecht /brekt, brext/, **Ber·tolt** /'bɜːtəʊlt‖'bɜːr-/ (1898–1956) a German writer of plays and poetry, best known for his plays *The Threepenny Opera, The Caucasian Chalk Circle,* and *Mother Courage*

Brec·on Bea·cons /ˌbrekən 'biːkənz/ [the+P] a mountainous area and national park between South and Mid Wales, popular with walkers

breech /briːtʃ/ *n* the back end of the barrel of a gun, into which the SHOT¹ (5) or bullet is put

breech birth /'· ,·/ also **breech de·liv·er·y** /'· ·,···/ *n* a birth in which the baby is turned feet first or sideways rather than head first

breech·es ‖ also **britches** AmE /'brɪtʃɪz/ *n* [P] **1** short trousers fastened at or below the knee: *riding breeches* **2** now usu. humor trousers —see PAIR (USAGE)

breed¹ /briːd/ *v* **bred** /bred/ **1** [I] (of animals) to produce young: *Some animals will not breed if they are kept in cages.* | (fig., *derog*) *Those people breed like rabbits.* (=have a lot of children) **2** [T] to keep (animals or plants) for the purpose of producing and developing young animals or new plants: *He breeds tropical fish.* | *They've bred a new variety of rose with larger flowers.* | *The winning horse was bred in Ireland.* —see also CROSSBRED² **3** [T] to cause (an undesirable condition or feeling) to develop; produce: *Flies and dirt breed disease.* | *All this uncertainty breeds insecurity.* | *They oppose corporal punishment because they believe that violence breeds violence.* —see also WELL-BRED

breed² *n* [C (**of**)+*sing./pl. v*] a kind or class of animal or plant usu. developed under human influence: *a strong breed of dog* | *a new breed of rose* | (fig.) *the first of a new breed of satellites* | (fig.) *Traditional printworkers could soon be a* **dying breed** (=no longer exist) *because of new technology.* —see also CROSSBRED¹

breed·er /'briːdər/ *n* a person who breeds animals or plants

breed·ing /'briːdɪŋ/ *n* [U] **1** the producing of young by animals or plants: *the breeding season* **2** the business of keeping animals or plants for the purpose of obtaining new and better kinds, or young for sale: *cattle-breeding* | *selective breeding* | *a horse-breeding farm* **3** training in good manners, as shown by a person's social behaviour: *a person of breeding*

breeding-ground /'··· ·/ *n* [(**of**)] **1** a place where the young, esp. of wild animals or birds, are produced: *Sea cliffs are the breeding-ground of many seabirds.* **2** a place where something bad can develop freely: *Dirt is the breeding-ground of disease.* | *These overcrowded slums are a breeding-ground of crime.*

breeze¹ /briːz/ *n* **1** [C] a light gentle wind: *The flags flapped gently in the breeze.* —see WIND (USAGE) **2** [S] *sl, esp. AmE* something easily done: *Learning English is a breeze!* —see also shoot the breeze (SHOOT¹)

breeze² *v* [I+*adv/prep*] *infml* to move or go quickly and in a carelessly confident way: *He just breezed in, poured himself a drink, and breezed out again.* | *She breezed along, smiling at everyone.* | *She simply breezed through the exam.* (=passed it easily)

breeze-block /'briːzblɒk‖-blɑːk/ BrE ‖ **cinderblock** AmE *n* a light brick for building, made of cement and CINDERS

breez·y /'briːzi/ *adj* **1** of or having fairly strong breezes: *It's breezy today, so the clothes we washed will dry quickly.* **2** quick, cheerful, and light-hearted in manner: *She looked very bright and breezy in her yellow sundress.* | *a breezy personality* —**ily** *adv* —**iness** *n* [U]

Bren gun /'bren gʌn/ *n* a light MACHINEGUN

Bren·ner Pass /ˌbrenə 'pɑːs‖-nər 'pæs/ [the] a mountain PASS over the Alps between Austria and Italy

Brent /brent/ a BOROUGH of London

Brer Rab·bit /ˌbreə 'ræbɪt‖ˌbreər-/ the main character in the children's stories by Uncle Remus, from the South of the US. Brer Rabbit is remembered for always

escaping trouble at the last minute, usu. by running into "the brier patch" (=bushes full of sharp THORNS).

breth·ren /'breðrən/ *n* [P] (used as a form of address to people in church or in speaking of the members of a profession, association, or religious group) brothers: *dearly beloved brethren*

Breu·ghel /'brɔʊgəl/ see BRUEGEL

breve /briːv/ *n* a long musical note, with a time value twice as long as a SEMIBREVE —see picture at NOTATION

bre·vi·a·ry /'briːviəri, 'breː-‖-ieri/ *n* a book used in the Roman Catholic Church, containing the prayers to be said on each day by priests

brev·i·ty /'brevɪti/ *n* [U] *fml* **1** shortness in time: *the brevity of life* **2** expression in few words; the quality of being CONCISE: *the brevity of her speech*

brew¹ /bruː/ *v* **1** [T] to make (beer) **2** [I;T (**UP**)] **a** to mix (tea or coffee) with hot water and prepare for drinking **b** (of tea or coffee) to become ready for drinking: *Don't pour the tea yet — it's still brewing.* **3** [T (**UP**)] to prepare (esp. something bad); PLOT: *I'm sure he's brewing trouble.* **4** [I] (esp. of something bad) to be in preparation or ready to happen; develop: *It looks as if a storm is brewing.* | *The children have been whispering about something — I'm sure there's mischief brewing.*

brew² *n* the amount or kind of liquid brewed: *a strong brew of tea* —see also HOME BREW

brew·er /'bruːər/ *n* a person or company that makes beer

Brew·er's /'bruːəz‖-ərz/ also **Brewer's Dic·tion·a·ry of Phrase and Fa·ble** /ˌ·· ,····· · ,· · '··/ a dictionary of phrases and stories, that first came out in 1870. *Brewer's Dictionary of 20th century Phrase and Fable* now includes political events, film stars, famous murders, etc.

brew·er·y /'bruːəri/ *n* a place where beer is made

Brezh·nev /'breznef/, **Le·o·nid** /'liːənɪd/ (1906–82) the leader of the Soviet Union from 1977 to 1982

bri·ar /'braɪər/ *n* **1** [C] a tobacco pipe made from the root of a BRIER **2** [C;U] a BRIER

bribe¹ /braɪb/ *v* [T (**with**)] to influence the behaviour or judgment of (esp. someone in a position of power or trust) unfairly or illegally by offering them favours or gifts: *She was charged with attempting to bribe a police officer.* | *I bribed him into giving me the documents.* | *He bribed his way onto the committee.* [+*obj*+*to-v*] *They tried to bribe the judge to acquit them.* | (fig.) *The child was bribed with a piece of cake to go to bed quietly.*

bribe² *n* something, esp. money, offered or given in bribing: *The policeman was accused of taking/accepting bribes.*

brib·er·y /'braɪbəri/ *n* [U] the giving or taking of bribes: *charges of bribery and corruption*

bric-a-brac /'brɪk ə ˌbræk/ *n* [U] small objects of various kinds, kept for decoration and sometimes valued because they are old, unusual, or rare: *The house was cluttered with a lot of worthless bric-a-brac.*

brick¹ /brɪk/ *n* **1** [C;U] (a hard RECTANGULAR piece of) baked clay used for building: *a brick wall* | *He built his own house, brick by brick.* | *brick-red* (=brownish red) *trousers* **2** [C] something in the shape of a brick: *a brick of ice cream* **3** [C] *esp. BrE* a small building block as a child's toy **4** [C] *BrE old-fash infml* a very nice dependable person; good friend **5 make bricks without straw** to do a job without the necessary materials —see also **drop a brick** (DROP²), **bang one's head against a brick wall** (HEAD¹), **like a ton of bricks** (TON)

brick² *v*

brick sthg. ↔ **up/in** *phr v* [T] to fill or enclose completely with bricks: *All the windows were bricked up.* | *He murdered his wife, and bricked up her body in the kitchen.*

brick·bat /'brɪkbæt/ *n* a piece of something hard like a brick, esp. when thrown in anger: (fig.) *The minister got a lot of parliamentary brickbats* (=was attacked in words) *for his handling of the affair.*

brick·lay·er /'brɪkˌleɪər/ also **brick·ie** /'brɪki/ BrE *infml*— *n* a workman who builds walls, etc. with bricks —**laying** *n* [U]

brick·work /'brɪkwɜːk‖-wɜːrk/ *n* [U] building work in which bricks are used: *decorative brickwork round the windows* | *There are some cracks in the brickwork.*

brick·yard /ˈbrɪkjɑːd‖-jɑːrd/ also **brick·field** /ˈbrɪkfiːld/ BrE— n a place where bricks are made

brid·al /ˈbraɪdl/ adj of a bride or the marriage ceremony: *a bridal dress* | *the bridal couple*

bride /braɪd/ n a woman about to be married, just married, or recently married: *The bride wore a beautiful white dress.* | *his bride of one year* (=whom he married one year ago) —see also extra information on page 1406

bride·groom /ˈbraɪdgruːm, -grʊm/ also **groom** — n a man about to be married, or just married —see also extra information on page 1406

Brides·head Re·vis·it·ed /ˌbraɪdzhed riːˈvɪzɪtɪd/ a book by Evelyn Waugh, written in 1945, which was filmed for television in 1980. The story of a rich family in war-time based in a large country house suggested a pleasant idea of the past to many people in Britain.

brides·maid /ˈbraɪdzmeɪd/ n **1** an unmarried girl who helps the bride at a marriage ceremony —compare BEST MAN, FLOWER GIRL, MATRON OF HONOUR, PAGEBOY and see also extra information on page 1406 **2 be always the bridesmaid and never the bride** to be someone who is never the centre of attention and never wins anything

bride-to-be /ˌ· · ˈ·/ n brides-to-be a woman who is soon going to be a bride

bridge¹ /brɪdʒ/ n **1** a structure that carries a road or railway over a valley, river, etc.: *How many bridges are there across the River Thames?* | *the Golden Gate Bridge in San Francisco* | *a road bridge over a railway line* | (fig.) *The training programme is seen as a bridge between school and work.* **2** the raised part of a ship on which the captain and other officers stand when on duty **3** the bony upper part of the nose, between the eyes **4** the part of a pair of glasses that rests on the bridge of the nose —see picture at GLASSES **5** a small movable part of a stringed musical instrument, used for keeping the strings stretched **6** a small piece of metal for keeping artificial teeth in place, fastened to the natural teeth —see also **build bridges** (BUILD¹), **burn one's bridges** (BURN¹ (12)), **Don't cross your bridges before you come/get to them** (CROSS²), **water under the bridge** (WATER¹)

bridge² v [T] to build a bridge across: *to bridge a river* | (fig.) *These tax reforms are an attempt to* **bridge the gap** *between the rich and poor.*

bridge³ n [U] a card game for four players developed from the game of WHIST: *Make up a four for bridge at Sally's.* | *a bridge club* —see also CONTRACT BRIDGE

bridge·head /ˈbrɪdʒhed/ n **1** a strong position far forward in enemy land from which an attack will be made **2** a position well forward, from which further advances can be made: *This discovery will be a bridgehead for further advances in computer science.* —compare BEACHHEAD

bridge·work /ˈbrɪdʒwɜːk‖-wɜːrk/ n [U] esp. AmE the BRIDGES¹ (6) in a person's mouth

bridging loan /ˈ·· ˌ·/ n money lent by a bank for a short time to help a borrower to buy something, esp. a new property, before they have sold something else, esp. an old property

bri·dle¹ /ˈbraɪdl/ n leather bands put on a horse's head to control its movements —see picture at HORSE

bridle² v **1** [T] to put a bridle on: *to bridle a pony* | (fig.) *Learn to bridle* (=control) *your tongue.* (=to be careful in what you say) —see also UNBRIDLED **2** [I (at)] to express anger or displeasure, sometimes by making a proud upward movement of the head: *I asked her to do it, but she bridled at the suggestion.*

bridle path /ˈ·· ·/ n a path made esp. for horse riding, but not for vehicles

Brie /briː/ n [U] a soft French cheese

brief¹ /briːf/ adj **1** short, esp. in time: *a brief visit/letter* | *Please be brief* (=say it in a few words) *because I'm in a hurry.* | *The fans only got a brief glimpse of their idol at the airport.* | *His remarks were brief and to the point.* (=short and expressing his meaning exactly) | *a brief swimsuit* (=covering only a small part of the body) **2 in brief** in as few words as possible: *the news in brief* — ~**ly** adv : *The President stopped off briefly in London on his way to Geneva.* | *Briefly, I think we should accept their offer.*

brief² n **1** a short spoken or written statement giving facts or arguments about a law case **2** esp. BrE the

instructions about someone's duties: *The new minister's brief is to ensure that the water supply is improved.* **3** BrE **hold no brief for** to not support or be in favour of: *I hold no brief for the policies of this government, but on this occasion I think they're right.* —see also BRIEFS

brief³ v [T (on)] to give (someone) necessary instructions or information, in order to prepare them for an activity: *to brief astronauts before their mission* | *to brief reporters on the new legislation* | *The President was briefed by his advisers before the interview.* —compare DEBRIEF

brief·case /ˈbriːfkeɪs/ n a flat, often leather case for papers, esp. one that opens at the top. When people think of briefcases, they typically think of businessmen. —compare ATTACHE CASE

Brief En·coun·ter /ˌ· ·ˈ··/ a film by David Lean made in 1945, from a play by Noël Coward. It is an English love story, of a housewife and a doctor, who fall in love but then decide to separate. It is remembered esp. for the ROMANTIC scenes in a railway station and is known for its realism and artistic filming. —see colour picture on page 685

brief·ing /ˈbriːfɪŋ/ n [C;U] an act of giving necessary instructions or information: *Before the meeting, let me give you a quick briefing.*

briefs /briːfs/ n [P] UNDERPANTS or KNICKERS. This is the word used esp. by people who make or sell underpants or knickers: *a pair of briefs* | *bikini briefs* —see PAIR (USAGE)

brier, briar /braɪəʳ/ n [C;U] a wild bush covered with sharp THORNS, esp. the wild rose bush

Bri·ers /ˈbraɪəz‖-ərz/, **Richard** (1934–) an English actor known esp. for his part in the British television COMEDY SERIES of the 1970s, *The Good Life*

brig /brɪg/ n **1** a ship with two MASTs and large square sails **2** AmE infml a military prison

bri·gade /brɪˈgeɪd/ n [C+sing./pl. v] **1** a part of an army, of about 5000 soldiers **2** an organization formed to carry out certain duties: *the Fire Brigade*

brig·a·dier /ˌbrɪgəˈdɪəʳ◂/ n a military rank —see TABLE 3

brigadier-gen·eral /ˌ··· ˈ··/ n a military rank —see TABLE 3

brig·and /ˈbrɪgənd/ n fml or lit an armed thief, one of a band of thieves living esp. in mountains; BANDIT

brig·an·tine /ˈbrɪgəntiːn/ n a ship like a BRIG, but with fewer sails

bright /braɪt/ adj **1** giving out or throwing back light very strongly; full of light; shining: *bright sunlight* | *The weather forecast said it would be mostly cloudy with a few bright intervals.* | *She longed for the* **bright lights** (=interesting and exciting activity) *of the big city* | (fig.) *one of the brightest moments in our country's history* | (fig.) *It's rather a dull film — the only bright spots are the dancing scenes.* **2** (of a colour) strong, clear, and easily seen: *bright red* **3** full of life; cheerful; happy: *Her face was bright with happiness.* | *bright eyes* **4** clever; quick at learning: *a bright child/idea* | *She should do well — she's very bright.* | (infml) *That child is* **as bright as a button.** (=very clever and full of life) —see also CLEVER (USAGE) **5** showing hope or signs of future success: *You have a bright future ahead of you!* | *The long-term prospects for this industry are beginning to look brighter.* —see also ALL THINGS BRIGHT AND BEAUTIFUL, **look on the bright side (of things)** (LOOK¹) — ~**ly** adv : *shining/ smiling brightly* — ~**ness** n [U]

Bright, John (1811–89) a British Liberal politician who was in favour of free trade and led the Anti-Corn Law League

bright·en /ˈbraɪtn/ v [I;T (UP)] to (cause to) become bright: *She brightened (up) when we reached the hotel.* | *These new curtains will brighten (up) the room.*

bright-eyed and bush·y-tailed /ˌ· ˈ·· ˌ·· ˈ·/ adj infml working well and quickly, and full of new ideas

Bright·on /ˈbraɪtn/ a town on the S coast of England which is a popular place for people to go to for a holiday, esp. people who live in London. It also has an important CONFERENCE centre. —see colour map on page 818

brights /braɪts/ n [P] AmE infml car HEADLIGHTS which are on as brightly as possible: *Do you have your brights on?*

bright spark /ˌ·ˈ·/ n BrE infml, esp. humor or derog a clever or cheerful person

brill /brɪl/ adj infml, esp. BrE very good; BRILLIANT¹ (2); used only by younger people

bril·liant¹ /ˈbrɪljənt/ adj **1** very bright, splendid, or showy in appearance: *The sun shone in a brilliant blue sky.* | *brilliant colours* **2** causing great admiration or satisfaction because a very clever: *a brilliant idea|invention|scientist* **b** highly skilled; extremely good: *a brilliant speaker* | *a technically brilliant performance* –see CLEVER (USAGE) – ~ly adv –-**liance, -liancy** n [U] : *her brilliance as an engineer*

brilliant² n tech a precious stone cut with many surfaces to make it shine

bril·lian·tine /ˈbrɪljəntiːn/ n [U] an oily mixture for making men's hair shine and stay in place. It has not been used much since the 1950s except by older men.

Bril·lo pad /ˈbrɪləʊ ˌpæd/ n tdmk a type of pan SCOURER, made of a ball of wire filled with soap, made by Johnson Wax Ltd and used for cleaning pans

brim¹ /brɪm/ n **1** the top edge of a cup, bowl, etc., esp. with regard to how full it is: *The glass was full to the brim.* **2** the bottom part of a hat which turns outwards to give shade or protection against rain: *You can wear the hat with the brim turned up or down.* **3** -**brimmed** /brɪmd/ having the stated kind of BRIM¹ (2): *a broad-brimmed hat*

brim² v -mm- [I (**with**)] to be full to the brim: *His eyes brimmed with tears.*
  brim over phr v [I (**with**)] **1** to become full and begin to overflow: *Turn off the taps – the sink is brimming over.* **2** to express a lot of (a good feeling): *brimming over with self-confidence|happiness*

brim·ful, -full /ˈbrɪmˌfʊl/ adj [F (**of, with**)] full to the brim; overflowing (OVERFLOW)

brim·stone /ˈbrɪmstəʊn, -stən/ n [U] esp. old use the chemical SULPHUR –see also **fire and brimstone** (FIRE)

brin·dled /ˈbrɪndld/ adj (esp. of cows, dogs, and cats) brown with marks or bands of another colour

brine /braɪn/ n **1** [U] water containing a lot of salt, used for preserving food **2** [the+S] lit or humor the sea –see also BRINY –**brINy** adj

bring /brɪŋ/ v brought /brɔːt/ [T] **1** to come with, carry, or lead (to or towards): *Bring your friend to the party.* | *She brought some toys for the children.* | *The defendant was brought before the judge.* | *The new manager started last week, bringing with him plenty of new ideas.* [+obj(i)+obj(d)] *Bring me the book.* –see USAGE **2** to cause or lead to: *The minister's speech brought an angry reaction from his opponents.* | *The long drought brought great hardship for the farmers.* [+obj(i)+obj(d)] *The play's success brought her great satisfaction.* **3** to cause to come (to a particular place, condition, or course of action): *His sad letter brought many offers of help.* [+obj+adv|prep] *It was their interest in photography that brought them together.* | *The gas is brought ashore by a pipeline.* | *That brings the total to £200.* | *The sight brought tears to our eyes.* | *What brings you here today?* (=what is your reason for coming?) | *It was my secretary who brought the matter to my attention|notice.* | *Put the milk in a pan and bring it to the boil.* | *The company was* **brought into being** (=started) *last year.* | *The fraudulent behaviour of a few individuals has brought the whole profession into disrepute.* | *A walkout by factory workers has brought production to a standstill.* | *A few extra classes will be all that is needed to bring her up to the standard of the rest of the class.* | *She brought the meeting to an end|close as it was getting late.* [+obj+v-ing] *Her screams brought the neighbours running.* [+obj+to-v] *I* **couldn't bring myself** to *tell her the bad news.* (=couldn't bear to tell her) **4** to be sold for: *This old car will bring about £10.* [+obj(i)+obj(d)] *The pictures he sells bring him £12,000 a year.* **5** [(**against**)] law to make officially: *Do you think they'll bring charges (against him)?* | *to bring a libel action*
  ▷ USAGE **Bring, take, fetch,** and **carry** are all used to talk about movement of something along with a person, caused by that person. **Bring** suggests movement of something towards the speaker or the place where the speaker is: **Bring** *that book here.* | *They came to my party and* **brought** *me a present.* **Take** suggests movement of something to another place: **Take** *your*

umbrella when you go out. | *We went to her party and* **took** *her a present.* **Fetch** means "go and get something and bring it back": *Please* **fetch** *the scissors from the kitchen.* **Fetch** is not often used in American English. Instead, **get** or **go and get** are used for this meaning: **Get** *the sheets from the cupboard.* | *Will you* **go and get** *some eggs at the store?* **Carry** does not give any idea as to the direction of movement, but suggests support with the arms or body: *They* **carried** *the body down the mountain.* | *She* **carried** *the bag on her back.*◁

bring sthg. ↔ **about** phr v [T] to cause to happen: *Science has brought about many changes in our lives.* | *The increase in business activity was brought about by the fall in oil prices.*

bring sbdy. **around/round** phr v [T] **1** [(to)] also **bring over**– to persuade into a change of opinion: *I'm sure we'll be able to bring him around to our point of view.* **2** also **bring to**– to cause to regain consciousness: *She opened all the windows in the hope of bringing him round.*

bring sbdy./sthg. ↔ **back** phr v [T] **1** to cause to return: *All library books must be brought back before June 20.* | *If I go with you in your car, will you be able to bring me back?* | *Even if the Republicans abolish the tax, the Democrats would be sure to bring it back.* [+obj(i)+obj(d)] *Bring us back our books, please.* **2** to obtain and return with: *He brought some beautiful carpets back from Iran.* [+obj(i)+obj(d)] *When you go to the post office, will you bring me back some stamps|bring me some stamps back|bring some stamps back for me?* **3** to cause to return to the mind: *Hearing the song brought back happy memories.* | *Seeing her again brought it all back.*

bring sbdy./sthg. ↔ **down** phr v [T] **1** to cause to fall or come down: *The pilot brought the plane down gently.* | *He brought the bird down with one shot.* | *The good harvest brought down the price of strawberries.* | *Don't try to bring me down* (=to lower my behaviour) *to your level.* **2** sl to discourage or disappoint –see also **bring the house down** (HOUSE¹)

bring sthg. ↔ **down on** sbdy. phr v [T] to cause (something bad) to happen to: *His reckless spending brought down disaster on his whole family.*

bring forth sbdy./sthg. phr v [T] old use to produce, esp. give birth to: *"Bring forth men children only."* (Shakespeare, *Macbeth*)

bring sthg. ↔ **forward** phr v [T] **1** to introduce or produce for examination; show: *A plan was brought forward to allow workers to share in the profits.* | *Can you bring forward any proof of your story?* **2** also **put forward**– to bring (something in the future) nearer to the present time: *The election will be brought forward from July to June.* **3** (in BOOKKEEPING) to move (the total at the bottom of the last page) to the top of a list of figures, before adding in the figures on the new page

bring sbdy./sthg. ↔ **in** phr v [T] **1** to cause to come in; introduce: *to bring in a bill in Parliament* | *They brought experienced people in to help.* | *The policeman brought in* (=to the police station) *two boys he had caught stealing.* | *Everyone who is going to work on the project should be brought in on it* (=should take part in it) *from the planning stage.* **2** to produce as profit or income; earn: *The sale brought in over £200.* | *She's bringing in £250 a week.* **3** to give (a decision) in court: *The jury brought in a verdict of guilty.*

bring sthg. ↔ **off** phr v [T] to succeed in doing (something difficult): *to bring off a big business deal*

bring sthg. ↔ **on** phr v [T] **1** to cause or result in (an undesirable condition or situation): *Her fever was brought on by going out in the rain.* | *The crisis in our industry was brought on by intense competition from foreign producers.* **2** to cause to develop or improve: *This warm weather should bring on the crops.* | *A month in London will bring on your English.*

bring sthg. **on/upon** sbdy. phr v [T] to cause (something unpleasant) to happen to: *You've brought the trouble on yourself.*

bring sbdy./sthg. ↔ **out** phr v [T] **1** to present (a new product) to the public; introduce for sale: *They're bringing out a new model of the car next year.* | *A special issue of the magazine was brought out to commemorate the occasion.* **2** to cause to be seen; make clear: *The increased responsibility brought out her best qualities.* | *That friend of his seems to* **bring out the worst in him.** **3** also **draw out**– to help (someone) feel less nervous or awkward in the company of others: *Mary is very shy: try to bring her out at the party.* **4** esp. BrE to cause (workers) to go on

STRIKE[2] (1): *They've threatened to bring the men out if their demands aren't met.*

bring sbdy. **out in** *phr v* [T] *BrE* to cause to suffer the stated skin condition: *Eating a lot of cheese always brings me out in spots.* | *Strawberries bring him out in a rash.*

bring sbdy. ↔ **round** *phr v* [T] to BRING **around**

bring sbdy. **through** (sthg.) *phr v* [T] to cause to come successfully through (a difficult or dangerous situation): *The doctor brought him through (a serious illness).* | *The people's courage brought them through (the war).* —see also PULL **through** (1)

bring sbdy./sthg. ↔ **up** *phr v* [T] **1** to educate and care for (a child) until grown-up: *to bring up children* | *well/badly brought up* | *She was brought up to believe that money is the most important thing in life.* **2** to mention or bring to attention (a subject): *Don't bring up that embarrassing topic.* —compare COME **up** (1) **3** *esp. BrE* to VOMIT (one's food): *He brought up his dinner.* **4 bring someone up short** to cause to stop suddenly: *I was about to enter the room, when I was brought up short by a note on the door.* —see also **bring up the rear** (REAR[1])

bring-and-buy sale /ˌ·· '· ˌ·/ also **bring-and-buy** /ˌ·· '·/ — *n BrE* a sale, usu. to raise money for a CHARITY, where people bring goods to be sold and buy goods brought by other people

bringing-up /ˌ·· '·/ *n* [U] *AmE* the act of educating and caring for a child until it is an adult: *She had a terrible bringing-up.*

brink /brɪŋk/ *n* [the+S (of)] **1** an edge, e.g. at the top of a cliff or a river: *They stood on the brink of the Grand Canyon.* **2** as far as one can go without actually being in a condition or situation; VERGE: *His failures brought him to the brink of* (=dangerously near) *ruin.* | *a rare animal on the brink of extinction*

brink·man·ship /'brɪŋkmənʃɪp/ *BrE* ‖ **brinks·man·ship** /'brɪŋksmən-/ *AmE* — *n* [U] *infml* the art of trying to gain an advantage by going to the limit of safety, esp. in international politics, before stopping

brin·y /'braɪni/ *n* [the+S] *lit or humor* the sea

bri·oche /'briːɒʃ, briː'əʊʃ‖briː'əʊʃ, -'ɔːʃ/ *n* a small cake made with a lot of eggs and butter

bri·quette /brɪ'ket/ *n* coal dust pressed into a block for burning in a fireplace

Bris·bane /'brɪzbən/ a port and the capital city of Queensland state in the E of Australia, the third largest city in the country

brisk /brɪsk/ *adj* **1** quick and active: *a brisk walker/walk* | *a brisk manner* | *ice-cream vendors doing brisk business during the heat wave* **2** (esp. of wind and air) pleasantly cold and strong — ~ **ly** *adv* — ~ **ness** *n* [U]

bris·ket /'brɪskɪt/ *n* [U] meat from an animal's chest

bris·tle[1] /'brɪsəl/ *n* [C;U] (a) short stiff hair: *His chin was covered with bristles.* | *The brush is made of animal bristle(s).*

bristle[2] *v* [I (UP, at, with)] (of an animal's hair or fur) to stand up stiffly (e.g. because of anger, distrust, etc.): *The dog's hair bristled (up) when the visitors came to the door.* | (fig.) *They bristled (with anger) at his denigrating description of their activities.*

   bristle with sthg. *phr v* to have plenty of (esp. something unpleasant or unattractive); be full of: *The streets bristled with armed guards after the latest terrorist attack.*

bris·tly /'brɪsli/ *adj* **1** like or full of bristles: *a bristly chin* **2** difficult to deal with because easily angered or annoyed

Bris·tol /'brɪstl/ an industrial city and international port in the SW of England, where the local government for Avon is based. The Clifton Suspension Bridge is in Bristol. —see colour map on page 818

Bristol Chan·nel /ˌ·· '··/ *n* [the] an area of water between S Wales and SW England which goes from the Atlantic Ocean to the mouth of the Severn River

Bristol Cream /ˌ·· '·/ *n* [U] *tdmk* a type of very sweet SHERRY which is made by Harvey's; it is one of the best known types of sherry in the UK

Brit /brɪt/ *n infml* a British person: *The Brits are always complaining about the food.*

Brit·ain /'brɪtn/ Great Britain or the UK —see UK (USAGE); see also BATTLE OF BRITAIN

Bri·tan·nia /brɪ'tænjə/ **1** a female figure representing Britain, formerly shown on some coins. Britannia is usu.

shown sitting down, wearing a HELMET, and holding a TRIDENT. There is a popular PATRIOTIC song called *Rule Britannia.* —compare JOHN BULL **2** a British BUILDING SOCIETY, branches of which are found in many towns and cities in Britain

Britannia

Britannia Roy·al Na·val Col·lege /·ˌ·· ·· '·· ˌ··/ see ROYAL NAVAL COLLEGE

britch·es /'brɪtʃɪz/ *n* [P] *AmE for* BREECHES

Brit·ish /'brɪtɪʃ/ *adj* of Britain (or the British Commonwealth): *a British citizen/passport* | *the British government* | *I'm German, but my husband is British.* | *to speak British English* [also *n*, *the*+P] *The British drink a lot of tea.* —see UK (USAGE)

▶ CULTURAL NOTE British people are often thought to be RESERVED (= quiet and not showing their feelings) and to "keep a stiff upper lip" (= to accept bad luck or unpleasant events without appearing upset). British people are also thought to use UNDERSTATEMENT (= to talk in a way which makes things seem less serious or important than they really are). ◄

British A·cad·e·my /ˌ·· ·'···/ [the] a society begun in 1901 to encourage the study of language, literature, PHILOSOPHY, economics, etc.

British Ae·ro·space /ˌbrɪtɪʃ 'eərəʊspeɪs/ the largest British company producing CIVIL and military aircraft, MISSILES, and space systems. British Aerospace was formed in 1978 from various famous aircraft companies and was owned by the state, but in 1985 it became a private company.

British Air·ways /ˌ·· '··/ the largest British AIRLINE

British Ar·my of the Rhine /ˌ·· ·'· ·· '·/ [the] the British forces in W Germany since the Second World War as part of NATO's defence against the former USSR

British Board of Film Cen·sors /ˌ·· ·' · '· ·'·/ [the] a group of people in Britain who watch all films that are produced and decide whether they are suitable for children, e.g. whether they contain a lot of sex and violence. They give a CERTIFICATE to each film, which shows whether the film is suitable for all children (U), for children who have an adult with them (PG), for children over 12 years old (12), for children over 15 years old (15), or suitable for adults only (18). They can decide that the film should not be shown at all in Britain.

British-born /ˌ·· '·◄/ *adj* born in Britain: *a British-born Australian*

British Broad·cast·ing Corporation /ˌ·· '·····'··/ *n* [the] the BBC

British Cal·e·do·ni·an /ˌbrɪtɪʃ kælɪ'dəʊniən/ a former British AIRLINE company

British Coal /ˌ·· '·/ a British company which is the main producer of coal in Britain

British Co·lum·bi·a /ˌ·· ·'···/ (*abbrev.* **BC**) a PROVINCE in W Canada, bordering on the Pacific Ocean

British Com·mon·wealth /ˌ·· '····/ see COMMONWEALTH

British Coun·cil /ˌ·· '·/ [the+*sing./pl.v*] an organization representing Britain's interests abroad. It employs teachers of English and supports educational visits between Britain and other countries, and also libraries, ARTS events and EXHIBITIONs.

British Em·pire /ˌ·· '··/ [the] the group of countries formerly connected with and controlled by Great Britain, which was at its largest at the time of the First World War, when it included 25 per cent of the world's area

Brit·ish·er /ˈbrɪtɪʃərʲ/ n AmE a person who comes from, or whose parents come from Britain

British Film In·sti·tute /ˌ··· ˈ· ˌ···/ [the] a British organization which encourages film making and manages the National Film Theatre

British Gas /ˌ··· ˈ·/ a British company dealing in the production and selling of natural gas. It used to be a government-owned company but became a private company in 1986.

British Home Stores /ˌ··· ˈ· ·/ (abbrev. BHS) a group of large shops, with branches in many British towns, selling mainly clothes but also lighting, food, etc.

British Isles /ˌ··· ˈ·/ n [the+P] the group of islands made up of Great Britain, Ireland, and the smaller islands around them, such as the Channel Islands and the Isle of Man —see UK (USAGE)

British Le·gion /ˌ··· ˈ···/ also **Royal British Legion**— [the] a British organization which helps people who have been in the armed forces and their families. The British Legion collects money by selling poppies (POPPY) for Poppy Day.

British Ley·land /ˌbrɪtɪʃ ˈleɪlənd/ (abbrev. BL) a British company that makes cars

British Li·bra·ry /ˌ··· ˈ···/ n [the] the national library of Britain, based in London and Yorkshire, which receives a copy of every book produced in Britain

British Li·ons /ˌ··· ˈ···/ n [the+P] the Rugby Union team chosen from players from England, Scotland, Wales, and Ireland to play in international matches

British Mid·land /ˌbrɪtɪʃ ˈmɪdlənd/ a British AIRLINE company which has flights to many towns and cities within Britain

British Mu·se·um /ˌ··· ·ˈ··/ [the] (the building in London containing) Britain's most important collection of ancient art, writings, coins, drawings, etc. —see colour map on page 817

British Nu·cle·ar Fuels /ˌ··· ˌ··· ˈ·/ a British government-owned company which produces NUCLEAR FUEL

British O·pen /ˌ··· ˈ···/ also **the Open**— [the] an important British GOLF competition held every year in Prestwick, Scotland, for PROFESSIONAL and AMATEUR players

British Rail /ˌ··· ˈ·/ (abbrev. BR)— the national railway of Britain, formerly called British Railways

British Steel /ˌ··· ˈ·/ a British company mainly involved in the production of different types of steel

British Sum·mer Time /ˌ··· ˈ·· ·/ (abbrev. BST) n [U] time shown on clocks that is one hour ahead of Greenwich Mean Time, used in Britain from late March to late October —compare DAYLIGHT SAVING TIME

British Tel·e·com·mu·ni·cations Plc /ˌ··· ·······ˈ·· ··ˌ·/ (abbrev. BT) the largest telephone and TELECOMMUNICATIONS company in Britain

the symbol for **British Telecom**

British West In·dies /ˌ··· · ˈ···/ n [the+P] the former name for a group of states in the Caribbean Sea that are members of the Commonwealth, including the Bahamas, Barbados, Jamaica, Trinidad and Tobago, the Leeward Islands, and the Windward Islands

Brit·on /ˈbrɪtn/ n usu. fml a British person: the ancient Britons | The report said there were three Britons on the crashed plane.

Brit·tan /ˈbrɪtn/, **Sir Le·on** /ˈliːən/ (1939–) a British Conservative politician who was Secretary for Trade and Industry in 1985–86 but resigned (RESIGN) over his involvement in the **Westland affair**. In 1988 he became a European Commissioner.

Brit·tan·y /ˈbrɪtəni/ a REGION of NW France, a PENINSULA between the Bay of Biscay and the English Channel

Brit·ten /ˈbrɪtn/, **Ben·ja·min** /ˈbendʒəmɪn/ (1913–76) an English COMPOSER of music mainly for voices, including the OPERAs Peter Grimes and Billy Budd

bri·ttle¹ /ˈbrɪtl/ adj 1 hard but easily broken: brittle glass | (fig.) a brittle friendship 2 lacking warmth or depth of feeling: brittle humour

brittle² n [U] a mixture of nuts, butter, and sugar made into a hard sweet: peanut brittle

Brit·vic /ˈbrɪtvɪk/ n tdmk a company which makes soft (=not alcoholic) drinks, used esp. for mixing with spirits

Brix·ton /ˈbrɪkstən/ an area of S London, with a large black community. In 1981 Brixton was the scene of serious fighting (RIOTS) involving discontented young people, esp. black people and the police.

bro /brəʊ/ n AmE, infml (short for) brother; used esp. by black Americans

broach /brəʊtʃ/ v [T] 1 [(to)] to introduce as a subject of conversation; start to talk about (something difficult or likely to cause argument): At last he broached the subject of the new contract to them. 2 tech to open (an unopened bottle or barrel)

B-road /ˈbiː rəʊd/ n in Britain, a less important country road (often shown in yellow on maps) with the letter B before its number

broad¹ /brɔːd/ adj 1 large, or larger than usual, when measured from side to side; wide: broad shoulders | a broad river | a broad smile —compare NARROW¹ (1) 2 [after n] (after an expression of measurement) in width; across: four metres broad 3 stretching out far and wide; EXTENSIVE: broad plains | a sports centre catering for a broad range of activities | a broad-spectrum antibiotic (=one that has effect on a wide range of infections) | a policy that enjoys broad popular support (=is supported by most people) 4 not limited in thought, ideas, etc.: the broad sweep of the writer's imagination | Her taste in literature is very broad. —see also BROADMINDED 5 [A] not particular or detailed; general: Just give me a broad outline of the plan. 6 [A] full and clear; plain; open: The burglars broke into the house in broad daylight. | a broad hint 7 (of a way of speaking) strongly marked; showing clearly where the speaker comes from: He spoke broad Scots. | a broad Texas accent 8 (e.g. of jokes) rather rude, esp. about sexual matters; not acceptable in polite society: broad comedy/humour 9 broad in the beam infml having large HIPS; rather fat; more often used of women 10 It's as broad as it's long esp. BrE It does not matter which of two things or courses of action one chooses, because neither is clearly better than the other: It's cheaper by bus, but the train is a lot quicker, so it's as broad as it's long. —see WIDE (USAGE) — ~ly adv : Broadly (speaking), I agree with you. | Her job is broadly similar to mine. — ~ness n [U]

broad² n 1 [usu. pl.] (usu. cap. as part of a name) an open area of water formed where a river broadens out, esp. in eastern England: the Norfolk Broads 2 AmE derog sl a woman

broad·band /ˈbrɔːdbænd/ adj tech a system of sending radio signals which allows several messages to be sent at the same time

broad bean /ˌ· ˈ·ǁˌ· ·/ also **fava bean** AmE— n a large flat pale green bean

broad brush /ˌ· ˈ·/ n [S] a way of talking about only the main features of something.: He painted the situation with a broad brush. (=explained it only generally, not giving many details) **broadbrush** /ˈbrɔːdbrʌʃ/ adj : a broadbrush strategy for increasing sales

broad·cast¹ /ˈbrɔːdkɑːstǁ-kæst/ n an act of sending sound and/or pictures by radio or television: a live broadcast of the football game | a television/radio news broadcast

broadcast² v broadcast 1 [I;T] to send out (radio or television PROGRAMMES): The BBC broadcasts to all parts of the world. | The concert is being broadcast live. 2 [T] to make widely known: He broadcast the news to all his friends. — ~er n — ~ing n [U]

Broadcasting Com·plaints Com·mis·sion /ˌ··· ·ˈ· ·ˌ··/ [the] a group of people who look at and deal with complaints about radio or television programmes in Britain

Broadcasting House /ˌ··· ˈ·/ the central office of the BBC

Broadcasting Stan·dards Coun·cil /ˌ··· ˈ·· ˌ··/ [the] in Britain, a group of people who watch television and radio programmes, and decide whether they contain too much sex or violence or are offensive or unsuitable in any way

broad·cloth /ˈbrɔːdklɒθǁ-klɔːθ/ n [U] thick woollen cloth of very good quality

broad·en /ˈbrɔːdn/ v [I;T (OUT)] to make or become broader: The river broadens (out) at this point. | Travel broadens the mind. | His parents hoped the course would broaden his horizons. —compare WIDEN

broad gauge /ˈ· ·/ n a size of railway track of more than standard width

broad jump /ˈ· ·/ n [the] AmE for LONG JUMP

broad·loom /ˈbrɔːdluːm/ n [U] tech a CARPET that is woven in a wide piece, esp. in one single colour

broad·mind·ed /ˌbrɔːdˈmaɪndɪd◂/ adj apprec willing to respect the opinions and behaviour of other people, even if very different from one's own —opposite **narrow-minded** – – ly adv – ~ness n [U]

Broad·moor /ˈbrɔːdmɔːʳ/ a special hospital in Britain for criminals who are considered to be very dangerous because they are mentally ill

Broads /brɔːdz/ [the] the Norfolk Broads —see NORFOLK

broad·sheet /ˈbrɔːdʃiːt/ n something (such as a newspaper or advertisement) printed on a large sheet of paper

broad·side /ˈbrɔːdsaɪd/ n 1 a forceful spoken or written attack: She delivered a withering broadside against the committee's decision. 2 the firing of all the guns on one side of a ship at the same time 3 **broadside on** BrE ‖ **broadside** AmE sideways: The truck hit the car broadside on.

broad·sword /ˈbrɔːdsɔːd‖-sɔːrd/ n old use or lit a heavy sword with a broad flat blade, esp. one held and swung with both hands

Broad·wa·ter Farm Es·tate /ˌbrɔːdwɔːtə ˌfɑːm ɪˈsteɪt‖-wɔːrtər ˌfɑːrm-, -wɑː-/ a place in N London in which a police officer was killed in 1985, when there was serious fighting (RIOTS) involving discontented young people and the police. Three people, called the Tottenham Three were sent to prison for the murder but were later freed when they were found to be innocent. —see also TOTTENHAM THREE

Broad·way /ˈbrɔːdweɪ/ a street in New York City where there are many theatres and which has given its name to that city's theatre industry: a Broadway musical | The show will open on Broadway next month. —see also OFF-BROADWAY, and see colour map on pages 1374-5

bro·cade[1] /brəˈkeɪd‖brəʊ-/ n [U] decorative cloth with a raised pattern of gold or silver threads

brocade[2] v [T] to decorate (cloth) with a raised pattern: a brocaded waistcoat

broc·co·li /ˈbrɒkəli‖ˈbrɑː-/ n a vegetable whose young green or purple flower heads are eaten

bro·chure /ˈbrəʊʃəʳ, -ʃʊəʳ‖brəʊˈʃʊər/ n a book, often with pictures and of various sizes with a thin paper cover, esp. one giving instructions or details of a service: a holiday brochure | an advertising brochure

brogue[1] /brəʊg/ n [usu. pl.] a strong thick shoe with a pattern made in the leather —see PAIR (USAGE)

brogue[2] n [usu. sing.] a way of speaking, esp. the way in which the Irish speak English

broil /brɔɪl/ v 1 [T] AmE for GRILL —see COOK (USAGE) 2 [I;T] to (cause to) be very hot or too hot: It's really broiling (hot) today! | I'm broiling in this hot sun!

broil·er /ˈbrɔɪləʳ/ n 1 a young small chicken bred to be cooked by broiling 2 infml a very hot day: Yesterday was a real broiler! 3 AmE for GRILL[2] (1) —see COOK (USAGE) and see picture at PAN

broke[1] /brəʊk/ past tense of BREAK[1]

broke[2] adj [F] infml completely without money: I'm **flat broke/stony broke** (BrE). | His firm has gone broke.

bro·ken[1] /ˈbrəʊkən/ past participle of BREAK[1]: The window was broken by a ball. | a broken window

broken[2] adj 1 damaged, spoilt, or made useless by breaking: Be careful of the broken glass. | a broken clock/peg | a **broken-down** car (=in a state of disrepair) 2 not fulfilled; disregarded: a broken promise/agreement 3 discontinuous; interrupted: a broken journey/night's sleep | broken clouds 4 made weak or discouraged, esp. by misfortune, ill-health, etc.: a broken man (=without hope or confidence) | a broken spirit | a broken heart 5 [A] destroyed by the separation of a husband and wife: a broken marriage 6 (of a language other than one's own) imperfectly spoken or written: I managed to explain it to them in my broken French. – – ly adv – ~ness n [U]

broken-heart·ed /ˌ·· ˈ···◂/ adj HEARTBROKEN – – ly adv

broken home /ˌ·· ˈ·/ n a home that is showing the effect of a husband and wife separating, e.g. by lack of money or other family problems: children from broken homes |

He came from a broken home but is now a successful footballer.

bro·ker /ˈbrəʊkəʳ/ n a person who does business for another, e.g. in buying and selling business shares or foreign money: an insurance broker | a commodity broker —see also POWER BROKER

bro·ker·age /ˈbrəʊkərɪdʒ/ n [U] 1 the (place of) business of a broker: a brokerage firm/house 2 the sum of money charged by a broker

brol·ly /ˈbrɒli‖ˈbrɑːli/ n BrE infml for UMBRELLA

bro·mide /ˈbrəʊmaɪd/ n 1 [C;U] a chemical compound used in medicine to calm excitement 2 [C] fml rare a statement or idea without newness or freshness; PLATITUDE 3 [C] tech a photograph on specially treated paper used for printing: the bromides of a book

bron·chi·al /ˈbrɒŋkiəl‖ˈbrɑːŋ-/ adj of the bronchial tubes: bronchial pneumonia

bronchial tube /ˈ··· ˌ·/ n [usu. pl.] any of the branches or divisions of the bronchus —see picture at RESPIRATORY

bron·chi·tis /brɒŋˈkaɪtəs‖brɑːŋ-/ n [U] an illness (INFLAMMATION) of the bronchial tubes that brings a cough and blocks up the nose —**tic** /ˈkɪtɪk/ adj: a bronchitic cough

bron·chus /ˈbrɒŋkəs‖ˈbrɑːŋ-/ n pl **-chi** /kaɪ/ either of the two branches connecting the WINDPIPE (=breath tube) with the lungs

bron·co /ˈbrɒŋkəʊ‖ˈbrɑːŋ-/ n **-cos** a wild or half-wild horse of the western US

Bron·të /ˈbrɒnti, -teɪ‖ˈbrɑːn-/, **Anne** (1820–49) an English writer, the sister of Charlotte and Emily, best known for her NOVEL Tenant of Wildfell Hall

Bron·të, Char·lotte /ˈʃɑːlət‖ˈʃɑːr-/ (1816–55) an English writer, the sister of Anne and Emily, best known for her NOVEL Jane Eyre

Bron·të, Em·i·ly /ˈeməli/ (1818–48) an English writer, the sister of Anne and Charlotte, best known for her NOVEL Wuthering Heights

bron·to·sau·rus /ˌbrɒntəˈsɔːrəs‖ˌbrɑːn-/ n **-ri** /raɪ/ a very large four-footed plant-eating DINOSAUR

Bronx /brɒŋks‖brɑːŋks/ [the] a COUNTY, and one of the five BOROUGHS, of New York City. The Bronx is a poor area of New York, but contains the ZOO and Yankee Stadium (=the place where a BASEBALL team plays): a tough Bronx kid The South Bronx is known for drug dealers, violence and crime —see colour map on pages 1374-5

Bronx cheer /ˌ· ˈ·/ n AmE sl a rude sound made by putting one's tongue out and blowing; RASPBERRY (2)

bronze[1] /brɒnz‖brɑːnz/ n 1 [U] (the dark reddish-brown colour of) a hard metal made mainly of copper and tin: a bronze statue 2 [C] a work of art made of bronze: many fine bronzes in this collection

bronze[2] v [T] to give the appearance or colour of bronze to: bronzed by the sun

Bronze Age /ˈ· ·/ n [the] the time when bronze was used for making tools, weapons, etc. before iron was known, about 4000–6000 years ago —compare IRON AGE, STONE AGE

bronze med·al /ˌ· ˈ··/ also **bronze**— n a usu. round flat piece of bronze given to the person who comes third in a race or competition: She won the bronze medal in the women's 100 metres.

brooch /brəʊtʃ/ also **pin** AmE— n a small decorative object worn on women's clothes, fastened on with a pin — compare BADGE and see picture at PIN

brood[1] /bruːd/ n [C+sing./pl. v] 1 a family of young creatures, esp. birds: a brood of ducklings 2 infml the children of one family: She brought the whole brood with her.

brood[2] v [I] 1 [(over, about)] to spend time thinking anxiously or sadly about something; worry or PONDER: Don't just sit there brooding (over your problems) – do something! | He brooded for several days over what she had said. 2 [(over)] to hang closely: Dark clouds were brooding over the city. – – er n

brood[3] adj [A] tech kept for giving birth to young: a brood mare

brood·y /ˈbruːdi/ adj 1 (of a mother bird) wanting to sit on her eggs: (fig.) Anne always gets broody when she sees a baby. (=she wants one of her own) 2 [F] sad and silent because of self-pity, unhappy thoughts, etc. —**ily** adv —**iness** n [U]

brook¹ /brʊk/ n a small stream

brook² v [T *usu. in negatives*] *fml* to allow or accept without complaining; TOLERATE: *He would brook no interruptions from his listeners.*

Brooke /brʊk/, **Ru·pert** /ˈruːpət‖-pərt/ (1887–1915) an English poet known for his ROMANTIC war poems including *The Old Vicarage, Grantchester* and *The Great Lover.* He fought in the First World War, dying of blood-poisoning on the Greek island of Skyros.

Brooke Bond /ˌ· ˈ·/ n *tdmk* a company which makes food products and is best known for making different types of tea, including PG Tips and Brooke Bond Special

Brook·ings In·sti·tu·tion /ˈbrʊkɪŋz ɪnstɪˌtjuːʃən‖-ˌtuː-/ [the] an American organization in Washington, DC, which looks into political and economic problems

Brook·lyn /ˈbrʊklɪn/ an industrial and international port area of New York City, and one of its five BOROUGHs. People of several races live in Brooklyn and there is often RACIAL violence there. —see colour map on pages 1374-5

Brooklyn Bridge /ˌ·· ˈ·/ [the] a bridge connecting Brooklyn with Manhattan. In the US there is an old joke that IMMIGRANTS could be sold the Brooklyn Bridge because they did not know the well known buildings and customs of the city. So "being sold the Brooklyn Bridge" has come to mean being fooled in a business deal: *Did they sell you the Brooklyn Bridge?* —see colour map on pages 1374-5

Brooks /brʊks/, **Garth** /ɡɑːθ‖ɡɑrθ/ (1956-   ) an American singer of country and popular music

Brook·side /ˈbrʊksaɪd/ a television SOAP OPERA set in Liverpool, shown on Channel 4 in Britain since 1982. It is the most popular programme on Channel 4 and deals with many serious subjects in the lives of its characters.

broom /bruːm, brʊm/ n **1** [C] a large sweeping brush, usu. with a long handle —see also NEW BROOM, and see picture at BRUSH **2** [U] a large bushy plant with yellow flowers that grows on waste land

broom·stick /ˈbruːmˌstɪk, ˈbrʊm-/ n a broom. In children's stories WITCHes fly through the air on broomsticks

Bros. /brɒs‖brɔːs/ *written abbrev. for:* Brothers (in the name of a company): *Jones Bros.*

broth /brɒθ‖brɔːθ/ n [U] soup in which meat, fish, rice, or vegetables have been cooked. Broth is often given to people who are ill because it is easily eaten: *chicken broth* —see also **too many cooks spoil the broth** (COOK²), SCOTCH BROTH

broth·el /ˈbrɒθəl‖ˈbrɑː-, ˈbrɔː-/ n a house of PROSTITUTEs, where sex can be had for money

broth·er¹ /ˈbrʌðəʳ/ n **1** a male relative with the same parents: *John and Peter are brothers.* | *John is Peter's elder/younger brother.* | *Mary has five brothers and a sister.* **2** (*pl. often* **brethren**) a male member of a religious group, esp. a MONK: *a community of Christian brothers* | *Brother John* **3** a male member of the same group or nationality, or one who shares the same interests; often used of and by men who are active in a TRADE UNION: *a brother doctor* | *We must all stand together, brothers!* **4** **brothers in arms** soldiers who have fought together in a war **5 Am I my brother's keeper?** *saying* the affairs of other people are not my responsibility —see also BIG BROTHER, BLOOD BROTHER

brother² *interj esp.* AmE (an expression of slight annoyance and/or surprise): *Oh, brother!*

Brother, can you spare a dime? /ˌ··· · · · , · · ˈ·/ the title of a song written about the Depression of the 1930s in the US. In the song, a man who had been rich and respected before the Depression asks people to give him money, as he is now poor. The song has come to represent the sadness and lack of money during the Depression.

broth·er·hood /ˈbrʌðəhʊd‖-ər-/ n **1** [C+*sing./pl. v*] a society of men living a religious life **2** [U] a condition or feeling of friendliness and companionship, which is the result of shared interests, activities, etc. **3** [C+*sing./pl. v; usu. sing.*] the whole body of people in a stated business or profession: *the medical brotherhood*

brother-in-law /ˈ·· , ·/ n **brothers-in-law** *or* **brother-in-laws 1** the brother of one's husband or wife **2** the husband of one's sister **3** the husband of the sister of one's husband or wife

broth·er·ly /ˈbrʌðəli‖-ər-/ adj typical of a (loving) brother: *brotherly advice* —**-liness** n [U]

Brothers Grimm /ˌ·· ˈ·/ [the] see GRIMM

brough·am /ˈbruːəm/ n a light closed carriage with four wheels, pulled by one horse and used in former times

brought /brɔːt/ *past tense & participle of* BRING

brou·ha·ha /ˈbruːhɑːhɑː‖bruːˈhɑːhɑː/ n [U] *old use or pomp* disorderly or unnecessary noise and activity; COMMOTION

brow /braʊ/ n **1** [C *usu. pl.*] an EYEBROW **2** [C] the FOREHEAD **3** [*the*+S (of)] the upper part of a slope: *We reached the brow of the hill.* —see also **knit one's brows** (KNIT)

brow·beat /ˈbraʊbiːt/ v **-beat, -beaten** /biːtn/ [T (**into**)] to frighten or force to obey with threatening looks or words: *They browbeat him into signing the document.*

brown¹ /braʊn/ adj of the colour of earth, wood, or coffee: *brown shoes/eyes/bread* | *She's very brown* (=from being out in the sun) *after her holiday.* —**brown** n [C;U]: *dressed in brown* | *a light/dark brown*

brown² v [I;T] to (cause to) become browner: *browned by the sun* | *First brown the meat in hot fat.*

Brown, Capability (1716–83) an English gardener, whose work included planning many large and famous gardens of English country houses and castles

Brown, Charlie a character from the American COMIC STRIP *Peanuts* by Charles Schultz. Charlie Brown is not very confident and does not have many friends and is usu. unlucky. He has a dog called Snoopy.

Charlie Brown

Brown, James (1933-   ) an American popular music singer, songwriter, and musician, considered one of the greatest SOUL singers ever and known for his exciting stage performances

Brown, Jim /dʒɪm/ (1936-   ) an American FOOTBALL (2) player who set a record for making TOUCHDOWNs and later became an actor

Brown, John (1800–59) an American ABOLITIONIST (=someone who worked to end slavery) who tried to use violence to end slavery.

Charlie Brown © 1950

With followers, he took over a government weapons establishment at **Harper's Ferry**, Virginia. He was caught and hanged for TREASON. Many people felt that he was a MARTYR (=someone who dies for a just or holy cause), and during the CIVIL WAR, a song called *John Brown's Body* became popular in the North. The song is still well-known and contains the words:
> *John Brown's body lies a-mouldering in the grave,*
> *But his soul goes marching on.*

Brown, Murphy see MURPHY BROWN

brown-bag /ˌ· ˈ·/ v [I] AmE to bring one's LUNCH to work, usu. in a brown paper bag: *I'm brown-bagging this week.*

browned-off /ˌ· ˈ·/ adj [F (**with**)] BrE *infml* annoyed and discouraged; FED UP: *I got browned-off with waiting and went home.*

brown goods /ˈ· ·/ n [P] BrE electrical goods bought to provide entertainment, such as TVs, home computers, etc. —compare WHITE GOODS

brown·ie /ˈbraʊni/ n **1** a friendly little FAIRY **2** AmE a chocolate cake usu. with nuts in it —see also BROWNIES

Brownie point /ˈ·· , ·/ n [*usu. pl.*] *infml* a mark of notice and approval for something good that one has done (from the special points, called Brownie points, that are given to Brownies for doing something good or well): *He tried to gain some Brownie points by doing the washing-up.*

Brown·ies /ˈbraʊniz/ ‖ also **Brownie Guides** /ˈ·· , ·/ BrE— n [*the*+P] **1** (in Britain) a division of the GUIDES¹ (5) for younger girls **2** (in the US) a division of the Girl Scouts (SCOUT¹ (1)) for younger girls —compare CUB SCOUT

Brow·ning /ˈbraʊnɪŋ/, **E·liz·a·beth Bar·rett** /ɪˈlɪzəbəθ ˈbærət/ (1806–61) an English poet who married the poet Robert Browning in 1846

Browning, Rob·ert /ˈrɒbət‖ˈrɑːbərt/ (1812–89) an English poet, married to Elizabeth Barrett Browning, whose poems include *The Ring and The Book* and *Home Thoughts from Abroad*

brown·ish /ˈbraʊnɪʃ/ *adj* slightly brown

brown-nose /ˈ· ·/ *n AmE sl* someone who tries to win favour by insincere means: *Ted's a real brown-nose.* – **brown-nose** *v* [I;T] : *brown-nosing around the boss*

brown-out /ˈbraʊnaʊt/ *n AmE* a cut in power to some but not all electric lights in an area

brown owl /ˌ· ˈ·/ *n* (*usu. caps*) a woman leader of a group of BROWNIE GUIDES: *Ask Brown Owl if we can go.*

brown pa·per /ˌ· ˈ··/ *n* [U] a strong, brown-coloured kind of paper, used for wrapping parcels

brown rice /ˌ· ˈ·/ *n* [U] unpolished rice which still has its outer covering, which is considered to be more healthy than white rice

brown·stone /ˈbraʊnstəʊn/ *n* a house with a front of soft reddish-brown stone, common in New York City —see colour picture on page 161

Brown v. Board of Ed·u·ca·tion of To·pe·ka /ˌbraʊn vɜːsəs ˌbɔːd əv edjuˌkeɪʃən əv təˈpiːkə‖-vɜːrsəs ˌbɔːrd əv edʒə-/ also **Brown vs Board** /ˌ· ·· ˈ·/, **Brown De·ci·sion** /ˈ· ·ˌ··/ *n* [U] *law* (the court case which resulted in) a decision by the American SUPREME COURT in 1954 that it was no longer necessary for black people to attend separate schools from white people. The decision led to taking some children by bus to different schools in order to mix blacks and whites. —see also CIVIL RIGHTS MOVEMENT, PLESSY v. FERGUSON, SEGREGATION

browse /braʊz/ *v* [I] **1** [(**through**)] to look through or read parts of a book, magazine, etc. without any clear purpose, esp. for enjoyment: *to browse through|among someone's books* | *I spent hours browsing in the bookshop.* **2** to feed on young plants, grass, etc.: *cows browsing in the fields* –**browse** *n* [S (**through**)] : *I had a browse through the books on her shelf.*

Bru·beck /ˈbruːbek/, **Dave** /deɪv/ (1920–) an American JAZZ musician, piano player, and COMPOSER

Bruce /bruːs/, **Rob·ert** /ˈrɒbət‖ˈrɑːbərt/ (**the**) (1274–1329) the King of Scotland from 1307 till his death. Scotland was recognized as independent under him in 1328. The story that most people know about Robert the Bruce is that he watched a SPIDER showing determination, which encouraged him to do the same.

Bruce, Len·ny /ˈleni/ (1926–66) an American COMEDIAN who is usu. remembered for using very rough language and making jokes about things that people do not usu. joke about

bru·cel·lo·sis /ˌbruːsɪˈləʊsɪs/ *n* [U] a serious disease of people and cattle, caused by a bacterium

Brue·gel , **Brueghel** or **Breughel** /ˈbrɔɪgɫ/, **Pie·ter** /ˈpiːtəʳ/ (about 1525–69) a Flemish painter of LANDSCAPES and ordinary people, also known as **Bruegel the Elder**. His sons **Pieter (Bruegel the Younger)** and **Jan** were also painters.

Bruges /bruːʒ/ a city in NW Belgium, the capital of W Flanders PROVINCE, with many old buildings and notable art collections. Its Flemish name is **Brugge**.

Bruges Group /ˈ· ˌ·/ [*the*] a group of Conservative members of parliament who want to prevent Britain giving too much power to the European Community

bruise¹ /bruːz/ *n* a mark caused by a blow or fall, resulting in discolouring of the skin of a human, animal, or fruit but not breaking of the skin: *It was a bad accident, but she escaped with minor cuts and bruises.*

bruise² *v* **1** [T] to cause a bruise on: *She fell and bruised her knee.* | *a bruised apple* | (fig.) *bruised feelings|pride* **2** [I] to show a bruise: *Her skin bruises easily.*

bruis·er /ˈbruːzəʳ/ *n infml* a big rough strong man

bruit /bruːt/ *v*
　　bruit sthg. ↔ **abroad/about** *phr v* [T+*that*] *fml or pomp* to spread (news) everywhere: *It's been bruited abroad that you're going to get married.*

Brum /brʌm/ *BrE infml* Birmingham

Brum·mell /ˈbrʌməl/, **Beau** (1778–1840) an English DANDY¹ (=a man who takes extreme care over the way he dresses), a friend of George IV before he became king

Brum·mie¹ /ˈbrʌmi/ *n BrE infml sometimes derog* a name used for someone from Birmingham

Brummie² *adj BrE infml* having an ACCENT¹ (1) typical of Birmingham

brunch /brʌntʃ/ *n* [C;U] *infml, esp. AmE* a meal, usu. taken in the middle of the morning, that combines a late breakfast and an early LUNCH

Brunei /bruːˈnaɪ, ˈbruːnaɪ/ a SULTANATE in NW Borneo which is under British protection and became an independent member of the Commonwealth in 1984; capital Bandar Seri Begawan; population 249,000 (1989)

Bru·nel /bruːˈnel/, **Is·am·bard King·dom** /ˈɪzəmbɑːd ˈkɪndəm‖-bɑːrd-/ (1806–59) an English engineer famous for his railway engines, bridges, and iron ships

bru·nette ‖ also **brunet** *AmE* /bruːˈnet/ *n* a woman of a fair-skinned race with dark hair —compare BLOND (2)

Bru·no /ˈbruːnəʊ/, **Frank** (1961–) an English BOXER and former British, European, and Commonwealth heavyweight champion

brunt /brʌnt/ *n* [*the*+S (**of**)] the main or most damaging part of (an attack): *The brunt of her argument was directed at the trade union leader.* | *I had to* **bear the brunt of** *his anger.*

brushes

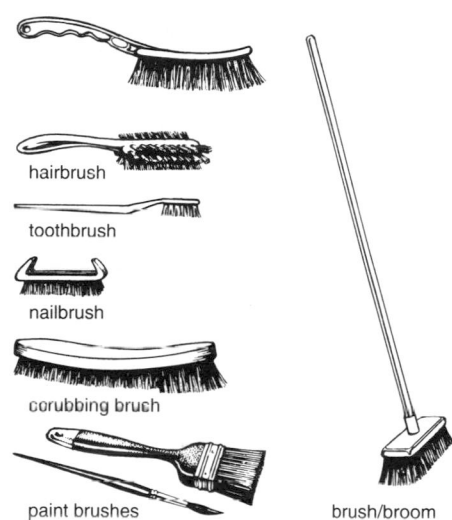

hairbrush

toothbrush

nailbrush

scrubbing brush

paint brushes

brush/broom

brush¹ /brʌʃ/ *n* **1** (*often in comb.*) an instrument for cleaning, smoothing, or painting, made from lengths of sticks, stiff hair, nylon, etc., fixed to a handle: *a clothesbrush* | *a toothbrush* | *a hairbrush* | *a paintbrush* | *a hairbrush*.] an act of brushing: *I'll just give my coat|hair a quick brush.* **3** [*usu. sing.*] a quick light touch: *He felt the brush of her silk dress against him as she passed.* **4** [(**with**)] a short usu. unpleasant meeting or argument with someone; ENCOUNTER: *I had a brush with the law.* (=with the police) **5** *tech* the tail of a fox —see also **tarred with the same brush** (TAR²)

brush² *v* **1** [T] to clean or smooth with a brush: *to brush one's coat|the floor|one's teeth|one's hair* **2** [T+*obj*+*adv*/ *prep*] to remove (as if) with a brush: *to brush away a fly with one's hand* | *to brush crumbs off the table* | *to brush one's coat clean* | *to brush someone|oneself down* (=to clean someone's|one's clothes with a brush) **3** [I+*adv*/*prep*;T] to touch against lightly or carelessly in passing: *The light wind gently brushed his cheek.* | *He brushed past the reporters without making any comment.* —see SWEEP (USAGE)
　　brush sbdy./sthg. ↔ **aside** *phr v* [T] to refuse to pay attention to; DISREGARD: *to brush difficulties|opposition| objections aside*
　　brush sbdy. **off** *phr v* [T] to refuse to listen to, talk to, or accept the friendship of: *The President brushed off their pleas for him to reconsider his decision.* —see also BRUSH-OFF

brush (sthg. ↔) **up** *phr v* [I+on;T] to improve one's knowledge of (something known but partly forgotten) by study: *I must brush up (on) my French before I go to Paris.* —**brush-up** /'· ·/ *n*

brush³ *n* [U] **1** small branches broken off from trees or bushes **2** (land covered by) small rough trees and bushes

Brush, Basil a PUPPET formerly on children's television in Britain. He looks like a FOX, dresses like an English country gentleman, and tells foolish jokes ending them with the words "Boom-boom" and a funny laugh.

brush-off /'· ·/ *n* [*the*+S] *infml* a clear refusal to be friendly or to listen; rude dismissal: *I wanted to speak to her, but she* **gave me the brush-off.** —see also BRUSH² off

brush·wood /'brʌʃwʊd/ *n* [U] BRUSH³ (1)

brush·work /'brʌʃwɜːk‖-wɜːrk/ *n* [U] the method of putting on paint with a brush, esp. the characteristic style of an ARTIST in doing this: *vigorous brushwork*

brusque /bruːsk, brʊsk‖brʌsk/ *adj* quick and rather impolite; CURT: *a brusque person/manner/refusal* — ~**ly** *adv* — ~**ness** *n* [U]

Brus·sels /'brʌsəlz/ the capital city of Belgium, in the centre of the country, and the place from which the business of the European Community and NATO is run: *Why is it that the British tend to be so fearful of Brussels?*

brus·sels sprout /ˌ··· '·/ also **sprout**— *n* [*usu. pl.*] (*often cap.* B) a vegetable that is a small tight round bunch of leaves like a very small CABBAGE, and grows in groups on the sides of a high stem

bru·tal /'bruːtl/ *adj* showing a complete lack of kind or sensitive human feelings; very cruel or severe: *brutal violations of human rights | a brutal attack/attacker | a brutal dictatorship | the brutal* (=unpleasantly correct) *truth* — ~**ly** *adv* — ~**ity** /bruːˈtælˌti/ *n* [C;U] : *the brutality/ brutalities of war*

bru·tal·ize also **-ise** *BrE* /'bruːtəl-aɪz/ *v* [T] **1** to make brutal or unfeeling: *people who have been brutalized by poverty and disease* **2** to treat brutally: *He brutalized the children.* —**ization** /ˌbruːtəl-aɪˈzeɪʃən‖-lə-/ *n* [U]

brute¹ /bruːt/ *n* **1** *sometimes humor* a rough, cruel, insensitive person, esp. a man: *an unfeeling brute | a great brute of a man | You brute!* **2** *sometimes derog* an animal, esp. a large one: *Does that great brute of yours bite? | The horse broke its leg when it fell and the poor brute had to be destroyed.*

brute² *adj* [A *no comp.*] like (that of) an animal in being unreasonable, cruel, or very strong: *brute force/strength*

Bru·te /'bruːteɪ/ **Et tu, Brute?** (=and you, Brutus?) *quote* a phrase from Shakespeare's play *Julius Caesar,* used by Caesar when he realizes that even his good friend Brutus has betrayed (BETRAY) him and is going to kill him —see also JULIUS CAESAR and colour picture on page 1146

brut·ish /'bruːtɪʃ/ *adj derog* typical of animals rather than people: *brutish ignorance* — ~**ly** *adv*

Bru·tus /'bruːtəs/, **Mar·cus** /'mɑːkəs‖'mɑːr-/ (85?–42 BC) a Roman politician who was the chief member of the PLOT to murder Julius Caesar —see also **Et tu, Brute?** (BRUTE)

Bry·ant /'braɪənt/, **Paul "Bear"** (1913–83) an American college FOOTBALL (2) COACH (teacher) who set a record for winning the most games

Bryce Can·yon Na·tion·al Park /ˌbraɪs ˌkænjən ˌnæʃənəl 'pɑːk‖-'pɑːrk/ *n* a large park in the US state of Utah, known for its scenery of unusually shaped and coloured rock

Bryl·creem /'brɪlkriːm/ *n* [U] *tdmk* a type of oil used on hair, usu. by men, to make it smooth. It was popular esp. in the 1950s and 1960s but is now thought old-fashioned. —**Brylcreem** *v* : *Brylcreemed hair*

Bryn·ner /'brɪnərʳ/, **Yul** /juːl/ (1915–85) an American actor known esp. for having no hair. He played the King in *The King and I* on stage and on film, and was the leader in *The Magnificent Seven.*

Yul Brynner

BS /ˌbiː 'es◂/ **1** British Standard; used in the numbers of

standards drawn up by the BSI: *This product conforms to BS 2001.* **2** *AmE for* BSc

BSc /ˌbiː es 'siː/ ‖usu. **BS** *AmE*— *abbrev. for:* Bachelor of Science; (a title for someone who has) a first university degree in a science subject: *He has a BSc. | Mary Jones, BSc* —compare BA

BSE /ˌbiː es 'iː/ *n* [U] bovine spongiform encephalitis; a technical name for MAD COW DISEASE

BSI /ˌbiː es 'aɪ/ [*the*] British Standards Institution; an organization which sets standards for units of measurement, clothes sizes, etc., and safety standards for electrical and other goods used in Britain

B-side /'biː saɪd/ *n* the less important side of a record (of music, etc.)

BSkyB /ˌbiː skaɪ 'biː/ a SATELLITE television company, sometimes also known as **Sky**

BST /ˌbiː es 'tiː/ **1** *abbrev. for* BRITISH SUMMER TIME **2** bovine somatotropin; a HORMONE which is fed to cows to increase the amount of milk they give. The use of BST has been criticized because the effects of the hormone on humans over a long period of time are not known.

BT /ˌbiː 'tiː/ *abbrev. for* BRITISH TELECOM

BTA /ˌbiː tiː 'eɪ/ [*the*] British Tourist Authority; an organization which brings British tourism to the notice of people abroad

BTU /ˌbiː tiː 'juː/ *n tech* British thermal unit; the amount of heat needed to raise one pound of water by one degree FAHRENHEIT —compare CALORIE

bub /bʌb/ *n AmE sl* BUDDY (2)

bub·ble¹ /'bʌbəl/ *n* **1** a hollow ball of air or gas in a liquid (or sometimes in a solid): *When water boils, bubbles rise to the surface. | The children amused themselves by blowing bubbles with the soap solution. | She examined the crystal carefully for bubbles.* —compare FOAM¹ (1) **2** something which is unsteady, risky, or unlikely to last: *the bubble of real-estate speculation | News of the defeat quickly* **burst the bubble** *of our self-confidence.*

bubble² *v* [I+*adv/prep*] **1** to form, produce, or rise as bubbles: *The gas bubbled to the surface of the water.* **2** [(AWAY)] to make the sound of bubbles rising in liquid: *We could hear the pot bubbling (away) quietly on the fire.* **3** [(OVER)] to be full of life, high spirits, happiness, etc.: *She was bubbling over with happiness and enthusiasm.| bubbling wit* **4** *AmE for* BURBLE

bubble and squeak /ˌ··· '·/ *n* [U] *BrE* potatoes and CABBAGE that have already been cooked and are then cooked together in fat

bubble bath /'·· ·/ *n* [C;U] a soap which makes BUBBLES in the water of a bath

bubble gum /'·· ·/ *n* [U] CHEWING GUM that can be blown into bubbles. In American English it is esp. connected with young children: *a magazine aimed at the bubble-gum set*

bubble pack /'·· ·/ *n* a BLISTER PACK

bub·bly¹ /'bʌbli/ *adj* **1** full of bubbles **2** full of life and high spirits; VIVACIOUS: *a bubbly personality*

bubbly² *n* [U] *old-fash infml for* CHAMPAGNE

bu·bon·ic plague /bjuːˌbɒnɪk 'pleɪg‖buːˌbɑː-/ *n* [U] a disease (common in former times) that spreads quickly from rats to people, produces swellings under the arms and elsewhere, and usu. causes death —see also BLACK DEATH

buc·ca·neer /ˌbʌkəˈnɪərʳ/ *n* a sea-robber; PIRATE

Buch·an /'bʌkən/, **John** (1875–1940) a Scottish writer, best known for his popular adventure NOVELs such as *The Thirty-nine Steps*

Bu·chan·an /bjuːˈkænən/, **James** (1791–1868) the 15th president of the US (1857–61)

Bu·cha·rest /ˌbuːkəˈrest‖'buːkərest/ the capital and largest city of Romania

Bu·chen·wald /'buːkənvæld‖-wɔːld/ a CONCENTRATION CAMP near Weimar in SW Germany during the Second World War

Buch·wald /'bʌkwɔːld/, **Art** (1925–) an American writer known esp. for his humorous newspaper articles on political subjects

buck¹ /bʌk/ *n* **1** (*pl.* **bucks** *or* **buck**) **doe** *fem.*— [C] the male of certain animals, esp. the deer, the rat, and the rabbit

—compare DOE   **2** (*pl.* **bucks** *or* **buck**) [C] an ANTELOPE **3** [*the*] *infml* responsibility for making a decision: *I don't know enough about it to decide, so I'll* **pass the buck** *to you.* | **"The Buck Stops Here"** (sign on the American president Harry S Truman's desk)   **4** [C] *infml, esp. AmE* a dollar: *600 bucks* | *to make a quick|fast buck* (=make money quickly and usu. easily)   **5** [C] *old use infml* a fine well-dressed young man in early 19th-century England: *Regency bucks*

buck² *v*   **1** [I] (esp. of a horse) to jump up with all four feet off the ground —compare REAR²(2)   **2** [T (OFF)] (esp. of a horse) to throw off (a rider) by doing this: *The wild horse bucked its first rider (off).*   **3** [I] *AmE* (esp. of a car or truck) to move in a sharp, up-and-down way: *The car bucked and stalled.*   **4** [T] *infml* to oppose in a direct manner; RESIST: *It's no use trying to* **buck the system.** | *The growth of the company has bucked the recessionary trend in the industry.*

   buck up *phr v infml*   **1** [T] (**buck** sthg. ↔ **up**) *BrE* to try to improve: *You'd better* **buck up your ideas** (=improve your behaviour, work harder, etc.) *if you want to pass that exam.*   **2** [I] *BrE* to hurry up: *If you don't buck up we'll be late.*   **3** [I;T (=**buck** sbdy. **up**)] to (cause to) become happier or more cheerful; CHEER up: *Buck up! Lots of people fail their driving test first time.* —see also BUCKED

Buck, Pearl (1892–1973) an American writer who lived most of her life until 1931 in China, and wrote several NOVELs about that country

buck·board /ˈbʌkbɔːd‖-bɔːrd/ *n* (esp. in the US in the 19th century) a light four-wheeled vehicle pulled by a horse

bucked /bʌkt/ *adj* [F (**by, at**)] *BrE infml* made more cheerful; pleased: *We were bucked by|at the good news.*

buck·et¹ /ˈbʌkɪt/ *n*   **1** an open metal, plastic, or wooden container with a handle for carrying liquids. Young children on a holiday by the sea in Britain and the US often have a **bucket and spade** *BrE*|**sand pail** *AmE* for building sandcastles.   **2** [(**of**)] also **buck·et·ful** /-fʊl/— the quantity held by a bucket: *She poured a bucket|two bucketfuls of water over me.* | (fig.) *The rain came down* **in buckets.** (=it rained very hard) —see also **kick the bucket** (KICK¹ (11))   **3 a drop in the bucket** a small amount which is not enough: *The money budgeted is a drop in the bucket compared to what is needed.*

bucket² *v* [I]   **1** [(DOWN)] *BrE infml* to rain very hard: *It's been|The rain's been bucketing down all day.*   **2** [+*adv*/*prep*] to move very roughly and irregularly: *The car bucketed down the steep road.*

bucket seat /ˈ·· ·/ *n* a round-backed separate seat for one person in a car, esp. a racing or sports car, or aircraft

bucket shop /ˈ·· ·/ *n infml, esp. BrE* a business that obtains large quantities of tickets for air travel and sells them to the public at a low price

Buck·ing·ham Pa·lace /ˌbʌkɪŋəm ˈpæləs/ also **the Palace**— the official home of the British royal family in London, containing almost 600 rooms: *Buckingham Palace today gave details of the Queen's forthcoming visit to Australia.* —see colour map on page 817

Buck·ing·ham·shire /ˈbʌkɪŋəmʃəʳ/ a COUNTY in central S England

buck·le¹ /ˈbʌkəl/ *n* a metal fastener used for joining the two ends of a belt or STRAP, for fastening a shoe, bag, etc., or for decoration —see picture at FASTENER

buckle² *v* [I;T]   **1** [(ON, UP, TOGETHER)] to (cause to) fasten with a buckle: *He buckled (up) his belt tightly.* | *The two ends buckle (together) at the back.* | *He buckled on his sword.* | *She buckled herself into her seat.* —opposite **unbuckle**   **2** to (cause to) become bent or wavy through heat, pressure, etc.: *The accident buckled the wheel of my bicycle.* | *The wheel buckled.* | (fig.) *to buckle under the attack and run away*

   buckle down *phr v* [I (**to**)] to begin to work seriously (at): *to buckle down to work|to writing the book*

   buckle to *phr v* [I] *BrE* to begin to work seriously: *If we all buckle to, we'll soon get the job done.*

buck·ler /ˈbʌkləʳ/ *n esp. lit* a small circular shield with a raised centre

buck na·ked /ˌ· ˈ··/ *adj AmE, infml* (of a person) completely NAKED

buck·ram /ˈbʌkrəm/ *n* [U] stiff cloth used, esp. in former times, for covering books, stiffening clothes, etc.

buck's fizz /ˌ· ˈ·/ *n* [C;U] (a glass of) a mixture of CHAMPAGNE and orange juice

Bucks Fizz /ˌ· ˈ·/ an English musical group formed in 1981 who played popular music and won the Eurovision Song Contest with the song *Making Your Mind Up*

buck·shee /ˌbʌkˈʃiː◂/ *adj, adv BrE old-fash sl* free; without payment

buck·shot /ˈbʌkʃɒt‖-ʃɑːt/ *n* [U] middle-sized lead shot used esp. for hunting

buck·skin /ˈbʌkˌskɪn/ *n* [U] strong soft yellowish leather made from the skin of a deer or goat

buck·tooth /ˌbʌkˈtuːθ◂/ *n* -**teeth** /ˈtiːθ/ [*usu. pl.*] a large front tooth that sticks out

buck·wheat /ˈbʌkwiːt/ *n* [U] small black grain often used as food for hens, and for making PANCAKEs

bu·col·ic /bjuːˈkɒlɪk‖-ˈkɑː-/ *adj lit* of or concerning the country and country people: *bucolic dances* — ~ **ally** /kli/ *adv*

bud¹ /bʌd/ *n* a young tightly rolled-up flower or leaf before it opens: *daffodil buds* | *rose buds* | *The new buds appear in the spring.* | *The magnolia has* **come into bud.** | *The roses are* **in bud.** —see also TASTE BUD, **nip in the bud** (NIP¹)

bud² *v* -**dd-** [I] to produce buds —see also BUDDING

bud³ *n sl, esp. AmE* BUDDY (2)

Bu·da·pest /ˌbjuːdəˈpest◂‖ˈbuːdəpest/ the capital and largest city of Hungary, on the Danube river

Bud·dha /ˈbʊdə‖ˈbʊ-, ˈbuː-/ **the Buddha**   **1** (563?–?483 BC) the title given to Gautama Siddhartha, a wealthy man from N India who gave up all his possessions and family to teach the ideas on which the religion of Buddhism is based   **2** a STATUE or picture of the Buddha

Bud·dhis·m /ˈbʊdɪzəm‖ˈbʊ-, ˈbuː-/ *n* [U] a religion of east and central Asia growing out of the teaching of Buddha that one must become free of human desires in order to escape from suffering. Followers of Buddhism believe that one is born again after death, and whether the next life is better or worse depends on how good one is in the present —see also NIRVANA —**Buddhist** *n, adj* : *a Buddhist monk*

a Buddhist temple

bud·ding /ˈbʌdɪŋ/ *adj* [A *no comp.*] beginning to develop or become successful: *a budding poet*

bud·dy /ˈbʌdi/ *n*   **1** *infml* a companion; partner: *He's my buddy.* | *We're good buddies.*   **2** *sl, esp. AmE* (used as a form of address to a man, often in anger): *Get out of my way, buddy!*   **3** a VOLUNTEER who acts as a friend and helper to a person with AIDS

buddy sys·tem /ˈ·· ˌ··/ *n AmE* an arrangement in which one person is paired with another to help each other, esp. to keep each other safe: *The camp uses a buddy system for swimmers in the lake.*

budge /bʌdʒ/ *v* [I;T] to (cause to) move a little: *We tried to lift the rock but it wouldn't budge|we couldn't budge it.* | (fig.) *She wouldn't budge from her opinions.*

bud·ger·i·gar /ˈbʌdʒərɪgɑːʳ/ also **bud·gie** /ˈbʌdʒi/ *infml*— *n* a small bright-coloured bird of Australian origin, often kept as a caged bird

bud·get¹ /ˈbʌdʒɪt/ *n*   **1** a plan of how to spend money, esp. during a particular period or for a particular purpose, taking account of what one will earn or receive and of what one will probably have to spend: *a family|weekly budget* | *The sales director is preparing the company's advertising budget for 1989.* | *It is important to* **balance one's budget.** (=make sure that no more money is being spent than is being earned) | *The new road was completed two months early and well* **within/below budget.** (=for less than the planned cost)   **2** (*sometimes cap.*) an official statement made usu. once a year that gives details of what a government plans to spend, how it intends to collect the money needed, and so how much tax people will have to pay: *The President is seeking approval from*

Congress for his budget. | *The Chancellor will present his budget to Parliament tomorrow.* −see also BUDGET DAY **3** the amount of money stated in either type of plan: *Our research budget for this year is £10,000.* | *more cuts in the education budget − ~ary adj*

budget² *v* [I (**for**);T] to make plans for the careful use of (money, time, etc.) in a way that will bring most advantage: *She budgeted for* (=planned to save enough money for) *a holiday/buying a new car.* | *She has so many commitments she has to budget her time very carefully.*

budget³ *adj* [A] not needing a lot of money; cheap: *a budget holiday*

Budget Day /ˈ·· ·/ the day in March or April when the British Chancellor of the Exchequer makes the Budget speech in parliament. The Chancellor goes to parliament carrying the speech in a special red case. The speech is broadcast, and ordinary people take great interest in its effect on such things as the price of petrol, cigarettes, and alcohol.

Bud·wei·ser /ˈbʌdwaɪzəʳ/ also **Bud** *infml*− *n tdmk* a kind of American beer

Bue·nos Ai·res /ˌbweɪnɒs ˈaɪriz||ˌbweɪnəs-/ the capital city of Argentina, an important international port and one of the largest cities in South America

buff¹ /bʌf/ *adj, n* [U] **1** (of) a pale yellowish-brown colour: *a buff envelope* **2** a soft leather of this colour made from cowskin: *a buff jacket* **3 in the buff** *old-fash infml* with no clothes on

buff² *v* [T (**UP**)] to polish (metal) with something soft

buff³ *n infml* a person who is very interested in and knows a lot about the stated subject: *a film buff* | *a wine buff*

buf·fa·lo /ˈbʌfələʊ/ *n* -**loes**, -**los**, *or* -**lo 1** a large Asian and African animal of the cattle family, with long flattish curved horns −see also WATER BUFFALO **2** also **bison**− a large wild cowlike animal formerly common in Europe and N America, with a very large head and shoulders covered with hair. In the US in the late 1800s and early 1900s buffaloes were hunted for their skins to make **buffalo robes** and were almost made EXTINCT. The smaller numbers of buffalo made life more difficult for the Native Americans, who ate buffalo meat, and this worsened the disagreement between the Native Americans and white men.

Buffalo Bill

Buffalo Bill /ˌ··· ˈ·/ (1846–1917) a SCOUT (=information gatherer) for the US army, and also a buffalo hunter who toured with his own show in peacetime, "Buffalo Bill's Wild West Show". His real name was **William Cody**.

buff·er¹ /ˈbʌfəʳ/ *n* **1** a spring put on the front and back of a railway engine or carriage to take the shock when it is connected to another carriage or hits the end of the track **2** a person or thing that protects someone or something or lessens a shock: *A little money can be a useful buffer in time of need.* **3 a** a place in a computer's memory to store information temporarily **b** a quantity of information stored in such a place

buffer² *v* [T] to act as a buffer to

buffer³ *n BrE infml* a foolish but perhaps likeable old man (esp. in the phrase **old buffer**)

buffer state /ˈ·· ·/ also **buffer**− *n* a smaller peaceful country between two larger ones, that reduces the likelihood of war between them

buffer stock /ˈ·· ·/ *n* [*often pl.*] a store of goods which is

bought or collected up when supplies are plentiful, and which is sold or given out when supplies are less plentiful

buffer zone /ˈ·· ·/ *n* a NEUTRAL area separating opposing forces or groups

buf·fet¹ /ˈbʌfɪt/ *v* [T *often pass.*] to strike forcefully or repeatedly: *We were buffeted by the wind and the rain.* | *We were buffeted about* (=thrown from side to side) *during the rough boat trip.* −**buffet** *n*

buf·fet² /ˈbʊfeɪ||bəˈfeɪ/ *n* **1** (a place where one can get) a meal consisting usu. of cold food, which people serve for themselves and eat standing up or sitting down nearby **2** *AmE* a SIDEBOARD

buffet car /ˈ·· ·||·ˈ· ·/ *n* a carriage in a train where one can get drinks and light meals

buf·foon /bəˈfuːn/ *n* a very stupid person, esp. one who is rough and noisy − − ~**ery** *n* [U]

bug¹ /bʌg/ *n* **1** [C] *esp. AmE* any small insect: *The sacks of rice were swarming with bugs.* **2** [C] *infml* a small living thing causing disease; GERM: *I'm not feeling well: I must have picked up a bug somewhere.* | *There's a nasty bug going around.* **3** [C] a BEDBUG **4** [C] *sl* an apparatus for listening secretly to other people's conversations: *The police searched the courtroom for bugs.* **5** [C] *infml* a fault or difficulty in a machine, system, computer PROGRAM, etc.: *to iron out all the bugs from the new process* −see also DEBUG **6** [*the*+S] *infml* an eager but sometimes not lasting interest in the stated thing: *bitten by the travel bug* | *the photography bug*

bug² *v* -**gg**- [T] *sl* **1** to fit with a secret listening apparatus: *The police have bugged his office.* **2** to annoy; IRRITATE: *It really bugs me when people come around without telephoning first.*

bug·a·boo /ˈbʌgəbuː/ *n* -**boos** *infml, esp. AmE* an imaginary cause of fear: *childish bugaboos*

bug·bear /ˈbʌgbeəʳ/ *n* something that causes anxiety or concern, perhaps without reason: *the bugbear of rising prices*

bug-eyed /ˌ·ˈ·◄/ *adj* having eyes that stick out or BULGE, e.g. because of lack of sleep

bug·ger¹ /ˈbʌgəʳ/ *n sl, esp. BrE* **1** *taboo* an offensive or disagreeable person **2** *taboo* a SODOMITE **3** a person or animal: *The poor bugger broke his leg skiing.* | *You lucky buggers!* | *The cheeky little bugger!* **4** something that causes a lot of trouble or difficulty: *That job's a real bugger!* | *a bugger of a job*

bugger² *v* [T] *BrE* **1** *taboo or law* to be guilty of SODOMY **2** *sl* (used for adding force to expressions of displeasure or surprise): *Bugger it! I've missed my train!* | *Bugger the lot of you!* | *Well bugger me−he's done it!*
bugger about *phr v BrE taboo sl* **1** [I (**with**)] to behave in a silly or foolish way **2** [T] (**bugger** sbdy. **about**) to cause difficulties to: *I wish the tax office would stop buggering me about.*
bugger off *phr v* [I *usu. imperative*] *BrE taboo sl* to go away: *He told me to bugger off!*
bugger sthg. ↔ **up** *phr v* [T] *BrE taboo sl* to spoil; ruin: *Losing our luggage really buggered up our holiday.*

bugger all /ˌ·· ˈ·◄/ *n* [U] *BrE taboo sl* nothing: *Like it or not, there's bugger all we can do about it.*

bug·gered /ˈbʌgəd||-əʳd/ *adj* [F] *BrE taboo sl* **1** extremely tired **2** very surprised or shocked: *Well, I'm buggered!*

bug·ger·y /ˈbʌgəri/ *n* [U] *BrE taboo or law for* SODOMY

bug·gy /ˈbʌgi/ *n* **1** *BrE* a light folding PUSHCHAIR with small wheels **2** a light carriage pulled by one horse **3** also **baby buggy** − *AmE for* PRAM

bug·house /ˈbʌghaʊs/ *n AmE sl, old fash* MENTAL HOSPITAL

bu·gle /ˈbjuːgəl/ *n* a brass musical instrument, played by blowing, like a TRUMPET but shorter, used esp. for army calls −−**gler** *n*

Bugs Bun·ny /ˌ·ˈ··/ a CARTOON rabbit who likes CARROTS and often uses the phrase "What's up, Doc?"

Bu·ick /ˈbjuːɪk/ *n tdmk* an American car made by General Motors

build¹ /bɪld/ *v* **built** /bɪlt/ [I;T] **1** to make (a structure) by putting pieces together; CONSTRUCT: *That house is built of brick(s).* | *They're building (new houses) in that area now.* | *to build roads/bridges/computers/aircraft* | *These birds build their nests out of straw.* [+obj(i)+obj(d)] *He* *built me a model ship out of wood.* [+obj+**for**] *He built a model ship for me.* **2** [(UP)] to (cause to) develop; form: *Hard work builds (up) character.* | *The queue of people waiting for tickets is building fast.* | *to build a relationship|a business* | *efforts to build confidence between the two sides* **3 build bridges** to try to establish a connection or friendly relationship, esp. between opposing groups or ideas **4 -built** formed in a stated way: *a brick-built house* | *a well-built man*

build sthg. ↔ **in/into** sthg. *phr v* [T *usu. pass.*] **1** to make so as to be a fixed part, usu. of a room: *These cupboards are built in/built into the walls.* **2** to cause to be a part of something which cannot be separated or removed from it: *The rate of pay was built into her contract.* —see also BUILT-IN

build on *phr v* [T *often pass.*] **1** (**build** sthg. ↔ **on**) to make as an additional building: *This part of the hospital was built on later.* **2** (**build on** sthg.) to use as a base for further development: *In the new job she'll be able to build on her previous experience in marketing.* **3** also **build upon**— (**build** sthg. **on** sthg.) to base on: *The company's success is built on its very popular home computers.| His argument is built on facts.* **4** (**build on** sthg.) to depend on; BANK **on**

build up *phr v* **1** [I;T (**build** sthg. ↔ **up**)] to (cause to) increase, develop, or become gradually larger: *to build up one's strength again after an illness* | *The clouds are building up.* | *He has built up a good business over the years.* | *Traffic going out of the city is already building up.* **2** [T] (**build** sbdy./sthg. ↔ **up**) to praise so as to influence the opinion of others; PROMOTE (3): *The singer has been built up into a great success.* —see also BUILDUP, BUILT-UP

build² *n* [C;U] shape and size, esp. of the human body: *a powerful build* | *My brother and I are of the same build.* —see BODY (USAGE)

build·er /'bɪldəʳ/ *n* **1** ‖ also **building contractor** *AmE*— a person whose job is building things, esp. houses: *a firm of local builders* **2** (*in comb.*) something that helps to form or develop a quality or condition: *Hard work is a great character-builder.*

builders' mer·chant /'··· ˌ··/ *n BrE* a person who owns or works in a place (**builders' merchant's**) where building materials such as bricks, cement, sand, etc. are sold

build·ing /'bɪldɪŋ/ *n* **1** [C] a structure, with a roof and walls, that is intended to stay in one place and not to be taken down again: *Houses and churches are buildings.* | *The World Trade Center is one of the world's tallest buildings.* **2** [U] the process or business of making buildings: *the building industry*

building block /'·· ·/ *n* **1** blocks of wood or plastic used by young children to play games, esp. by placing one on top of another **2** (fig.) any of the pieces out of which something is built: *Atoms are the building blocks of the universe.*

building con·tract·or /'·· ·ˌ··/ *n* a builder (1)

building site /'··· ·/ *n* a piece of ground where a building is being built

building so·ci·e·ty /'·· ·ˌ···/ *BrE* ‖ **savings and loan association** *AmE*— *n* a business organization into which people pay money in order to save it and gain interest, and which lends money to people who want to buy houses

build-up /'bɪld-ʌp/ *n* **1** [(**of, in**)] a process of increasing: *the buildup of our military forces|of traffic on the road|of tension in the region* **2** favourable public attention or praise in advance: *Despite the big buildup, the play was a flop.* —see also BUILD **up**

built-in /ˌ· '·◄/ *adj* forming a part of something that cannot be separated from it: *a built-in disadvantage of the system* | *a built-in cupboard* —see also BUILD **in**

built-up /ˌ· '·◄/ *adj* covered with buildings: *a built-up area*

bulb /bʌlb/ *n* **1** a round root of certain plants: *a tulip bulb* **2** any object of this shape, esp. (the glass part of) an electric lamp that gives out light: *a 100-watt light bulb* | *the bulb of a thermometer*

bul·bous /'bʌlbəs/ *adj often derog* shaped like a bulb; fat and round: *a bulbous nose*

Bul·ga·ri·a /bʌl'geəriə/ a country in SE Europe, bordered by the Black Sea, Romania, Yugoslavia, and Greece; capital Sofia; population 9,004,000 (1989) —**rian** *n, adj*

bulge¹ /bʌldʒ/ *n* **1** a swelling of a surface caused by pressure from inside or below: *The apple made a bulge in his pocket.* **2** a sudden unusual increase in quantity, which does not last: *The bulge in the birthrate after the war made more schools necessary.* **bulgy** *adj* **bulginess** *n* [U]

bulge² *v* [I (**with, OUT**)] to swell or curve outwards: *His stomach bulged (out).* | *His pockets were bulging with presents.* | (fig.) *a bulging bank account* (=with a lot of money in it)

Bulge see BATTLE OF THE BULGE

bul·gur /'bʌlgəʳ/ *n* [U] a form of wheat which has been cooked, cracked, and dried

bu·lim·i·a /bjuː'lɪmiə/ *n* [U] *tech* an illness in which there is a great and uncontrollable desire to eat. It is most often young women who suffer from it and they usu. VOMIT after eating too much in order not to gain weight. —see EATING DISORDER

bulk¹ /bʌlk/ *n* **1** [U] largeness of size, shape, or mass: *It was difficult to move, not because of its weight but because of its bulk.* **2** [C] an unusually large, fat, or shapeless body: *The elephant lowered its great bulk.* **3** [*the*+S (**of**)] the main or largest part: *The bulk of the work has already been done.* | *The publishing sector provided the bulk of the company's profits.* **4 in bulk** in large quantities and not packed in separate containers: *to buy/sell in bulk* | *a tanker carrying milk in bulk*

bulk² *adj* [A] (of buying and selling) in large quantities: *a bulk purchase of grain* | *a bulk order*

bulk³ *v* **bulk large** to appear important or play an important part: *The threat of economic crisis is beginning to bulk large in the government's thinking.*

bulk (sthg. ↔) **out** also **bulk up**— *phr v* [I;T] to (cause to) swell or to be or seem thicker or fuller: *She uses gel to bulk her hair out.*

bulk·head /'bʌlkhed/ *n* [*often pl.*] a wall which divides a ship, TUNNEL, spacecraft, etc. into separate parts, so that, if one part is damaged, water or air will not pass through

bulk mail /ˌ· '·/ *n* [U] *AmE* the sending of letters, esp. advertisements, to many people for a smaller charge than usual

bulk·y /'bʌlki/ *adj* **1** having bulk, esp. if large of its kind or rather fat: *a bulky parcel* **2** having great size or mass in comparison with weight: *a bulky woollen sweater* —**ily** *adv* —**iness** *n* [U]

bull

bull¹ /bʊl/ *n* **1** the adult male form of cattle, supposed to be fierce and hard to control, kept on farms to be the parent of young cattle: (fig.) *a great bull of a man* (=big and strong) —compare BULLOCK; see also BELLOW **2** the male of certain other large land or sea animals: *a bull elephant* —compare COW¹ (2) **3** a person who buys business shares or goods in expectation of a price rise or who acts to cause such a rise: *a bull market* (=in which prices are rising) —compare BEAR¹ (2) **4** *infml for* BULL'S-EYE (1) **5 a bull in a 'china shop** *infml* a rough and careless person in a place where skill and care are needed: *He's like a bull in a china shop, always knocking things over.* **6 take the bull by the horns** *infml* to face difficulties fearlessly and with determination

bull² *n* an official letter from the POPE (=the head of the Roman Catholic Church)

bull³ *n, interj* [U] *sl* foolish talk; nonsense: *That's a load/lot of bull!* —see also **shoot the bull** (SHOOT¹)

Bull, John see JOHN BULL

bull·dog /'buldɒg‖-dɔːg/ n a fierce dog of English origin with a short neck and short thick legs set far apart, often regarded as having great determination. The bulldog is sometimes used as a SYMBOL of the British character.

bulldog clip /'··· ·/ BrE‖**elephant clip** AmE n a small metal apparatus with a spring, used like a PAPER CLIP

Bulldog Drum·mond /ˌbuldɒg 'drʌmənd‖-dɔːg-/ a character, Hugh "Bulldog" Drummond, in stories by Sapper (Herman McNeile, 1888–1937). He was an ugly but likeable British ex-army officer chasing Carl Peterson, an international criminal.

bull·doze /'buldəuz/ v [T] **1** to force (objects, earth, etc.) out of the way with a bulldozer in order to form a level surface: to bulldoze the ground before building **2** [+obj+adv/prep] to force insensitively, without regard for the feelings or opinions of others: Despite public opposition, he bulldozed his plan through Parliament. | They bulldozed her into agreeing.

bull·doz·er /'buldəuzəʳ/ n a powerful machine used for pushing heavy objects, earth, etc., out of the way when a level surface is needed

bul·let /'bulɪt/ n a type of shot fired from a fairly small gun, usu. longer than it is broad and with a rounded or pointed end: The bodies of the hostages were found riddled with bullets. | Police fired rubber bullets into the crowd. | a bullet wound | A bullet-proof car/vest stops bullets from passing through it. —see picture at GUN; see also **bite the bullet** (BITE¹ (10)), and compare SHELL¹ (2), SHOT¹ (5)

bullet-head·ed /ˌ··· '···◄/ adj derog (esp. of a person) having a small round head

bul·le·tin /'bulət̩n/ n **1** a short usu. official notice or news report intended to be made public without delay: Here is the latest bulletin about the President's health. | to read a news bulletin on television **2** a short printed newspaper, esp. one produced by an organization or club: the company's quarterly bulletin

bulletin board /'··· ·/ n esp. AmE for NOTICE BOARD

bull·fight /'bulfaɪt/ n a form of public entertainment in Spain, Portugal, and Latin America, in which men ceremonially excite, fight, and often kill bulls. Many people now think that bullfights are cruel for the animals. —~er n —~ing n [U]

bull·finch /'bulˌfɪntʃ/ n a small European songbird with a bright reddish breast and a strong rounded beak

bull·frog /'bulfrɒg‖-frɑːg, -frɔːg/ n a large-headed American FROG that makes a loud noise (CROAK²)

bull-head·ed /ˌbul'hedɪd◄/ adj often derog (of a person) going determinedly but stupidly or thoughtlessly after what one wants —~ly adv —~ness n [U]

bull·horn /'bulhɔːn‖-hɔːrn/ n AmE an instrument shaped like a widening tube which is powered electrically and held to the mouth to make the sound of a voice louder —compare MEGAPHONE

bul·lion /'buljən/ n [U] bars of gold or silver: gold bullion

bul·lish /'bulɪʃ/ adj **1** tech marked by, tending to cause, or hopeful of rising prices (as in a STOCK EXCHANGE): There was a bullish trend in the market. —opposite **bearish 2** showing confidence about the future; full of OPTIMISM: He is very bullish about the prospects for his business. —~ly adv —~ness n [U]

bull·necked /ˌbul'nekt◄/ adj (of a person) with a short and very thick neck

bul·lock /'bulək/ n a male animal of the cattle family which cannot breed; OX (1) —compare BULL¹, HEIFER, STEER²

bull pen /'· ˌ·/ n **1** the area in a BASEBALL field which is used by PITCHERS² to get ready to play **2** the PITCHERS² of a BASEBALL team: The Dodgers have a strong bull pen.

bull·ring /'bulˌrɪŋ/ n an ARENA where BULLFIGHTS are held, surrounded by rows of seats

Bull Run /'· ˌ·/ the place in NE Virginia in the US where there were two important battles in the American Civil War which the Union forces lost to Confederate forces. Many men were killed or hurt in these battles.

bull ses·sion /'· ˌ··/ n AmE infml a time when a group of people get together to talk

bull's-eye /'· ·/ n **1** also **bull** infml— the circular centre of a TARGET that people try to hit when shooting or playing DARTS: to score a bull's-eye (=hit this centre) | (fig.)

Your last remark really hit the bull's-eye: it was exactly right. **2** BrE a large hard round sweet tasting of PEPPERMINT

bull·shit¹ /'bulˌʃɪt/ n, interj [U] taboo sl foolish talk; nonsense

bullshit² v -tt- [I;T] taboo sl to talk nonsense, esp. confidently in order to deceive, persuade, or get admiration

bull ter·ri·er /ˌ· '···/ n a short-haired dog of English origin which is a mixture of BULLDOG and TERRIER, bred for fighting —see also PIT BULL TERRIER

bul·ly¹ /'buli/ n a person, esp. a schoolboy or schoolgirl, who hurts or intentionally frightens weaker people

bully² v [T (into)] to act like a bully towards, often with the intention of forcing someone to do something: He bullies all the other little boys in the playground. | I wanted to stay at home but they bullied me into going.

bully off phr v [I] to start a game of HOCKEY —**bully-off** /'··· ·/ n

bully³ adj bully for you/him, etc. humor sl (used to express approval, often insincerely, of what someone has done)

bully beef /'··· ·/ n [U] BrE CORNED BEEF, esp. as used in the army

bul·ly·boy /'bulibɔɪ/ n BrE infml a rough man who behaves in a threatening way: Bullyboy tactics won't work on me— I'm not scared.

bul·rush , bullrush /'bulrʌʃ/ also **cattail** AmE— n a tall grasslike waterside plant

bul·wark /'bulwək‖-wərk/ n **1** [often pl.] a strong wall built for defence, often made of earth: (fig.) Our people's support is a bulwark against the enemy. **2** also **bulwarks** pl.— the wall round the edge of a ship

bum¹ /bʌm/ n sl, esp. BrE the part of the body on which a person sits; BUTTOCKS

bum² n AmE & AustrE derog sl **1** [C] a wandering person who lives by begging; TRAMP² **2** [the+S] AustrE the life of wandering and begging: John lost his job and went on **the bum**. **3** [C] someone who spends a lot of time on the stated activity or amusement: a beach bum **4** [C] someone who is considered worthless, lazy, or unable to do their job

bum³ v -mm- [T (off)] sl to get by begging; SCROUNGE: Can I bum a cigarette (off you)?

bum around/about phr v sl **1** [I] to spend time lazily without any clear purpose: I didn't do anything last summer; I just bummed around. **2** [I;T (for)] to spend time travelling for amusement: He's been bumming around (on) the continent for a few months.

bum⁴ adj [A] sl bad or worthless: He gave me some bum advice about buying a car.

bum·ble /'bʌmbəl/ v [I] sl **1** [(ON, about)] esp. BrE to speak so that the words are hard to hear clearly: He kept bumbling on about his operation, but I didn't really understand all the details. **2** [(ABOUT, AROUND)] to move or behave in an awkward or unskilful way: bumbling incompetence

bum·ble·bee /'bʌmbəlbiː/ n a large hairy bee which makes a loud noise when flying

bumf, bumph /bʌmf/ n [U] BrE derog sl written material, often printed information or advertisements, that is uninteresting, unnecessary, or unwanted

bum·mer /'bʌməʳ/ n infml an unpleasant experience which makes one sad: It was a real bummer standing in line for so long and still not getting tickets to the concert.

bump¹ /bʌmp/ v **1** [I+adv/prep;T] to hit or knock against (something, esp. something solid and heavy) with force or violence: The car bumped the tree. | The ball bumped down the stairs. | The two cars bumped into each other. | I bumped my knee against/on the table. **2** [I+adv/prep] to move along in an uneven way, like a wheeled vehicle going over bumps: The cart bumped along the track. | (fig.) The circulation of the magazine has been bumping along for some time at around 30,000. **3** things that go **bump in the night** humor GHOSTS, MONSTERS, etc. that make strange noises at night

bump into sbdy. phr v [T] infml to meet by chance: I bumped into an old college friend in the restaurant.

bump sbdy. ↔ **off** phr v [T] sl to kill; murder

bump sthg. ↔ **up** phr v [T] infml to increase, esp. to a desired level: *You need a good result to bump up your average.* | *to bump up production/the price*

bump² *n* **1** (the sound of) a sudden forceful blow, like something heavy hitting a hard surface: *We heard a bump in the next room.* | *He fell off the bed and landed on the floor with a bump.* **2** a raised round swelling, often caused by a blow: *a bump on his knee* **3** a raised uneven area on a surface: *She had to drive slowly because of the bumps in the road.*

bump·er¹ /ˈbʌmpəʳ/ *n* **1** a bar fixed on the front or back of a car to protect the car when it knocks against anything: *The traffic was* **bumper-to-bumper** (=very close together) *all the way home.* —see picture at CAR **2** *AmE for* BUFFER¹ (1)

bumper² *adj* [A] of unusually large size or amount: *a bumper crop/harvest/edition/pay increase*

bumper³ *n old use* a full cup or glass: *a bumper of ale*

bumper car /ˈ··· ·/ *n* [*usu. pl*] *esp. AmE* a small electric car which people drive while trying to hit other cars in an enclosed space in an AMUSEMENT PARK

bumper stick·er /ˈ·· ˌ··/ *n AmE* a small sign on the bumper¹ (1) of a car, with a humorous, political, or religious message —compare CAR STICKER

bump·kin /ˈbʌmpkɪn/ **country bumpkin** *n derog infml* an awkward foolish person from the country (rather than the city)

bump·tious /ˈbʌmpʃəs/ *adj derog* noisily showing one's high opinion of oneself; CONCEITED: *a bumptious young man* | *her bumptious manner* — **~ly** *adv* — **~ness** *n* [U]

bump·y /ˈbʌmpi/ *adj* with many BUMPS² (3); uneven: *a bumpy ride* | (fig.) *I think we've got a* **bumpy road** (a period of difficulties) *ahead of us.* —**·ily** *adv* —**·iness** *n* [U]

bun /bʌn/ *n* **1** *BrE* a small round sweet cake **2** *AmE* a small round kind of bread, usu. plain but sometimes sweetened **3** a mass of hair twisted and fastened into a tight round shape at the back of the head: *She wears her hair in a bun.* **4** **have a ˈbun in the oven** *old-fash humor* to be PREGNANT

bunch¹ /bʌntʃ/ *n* [(of)] **1** a number of things (usu. small and of the same kind) fastened, held, or growing together at one point: *a bunch of flowers/grapes/keys* | *The little girl wears her hair in bunches.* (=tied at each side of the back of the head) **2** [+*sing./pl. v*] *infml* a group: *A bunch of girls was/were sitting on the grass.* | *My students are quite a nice bunch.* | *My friend John is the pick/the best of the bunch.* **3 a bunch of fives** *BrE sl* an act of hitting someone with one's closed hand; PUNCH

bunch² *v* [I;T (UP, TOGETHER)] to (cause to) form into one or more bunches or close groups: *The captain told the players not to bunch (up) together, but to spread out over the field.* | *This cloth bunches up.* (=tends to gather into folds) | *Traffic often bunches on the big highways.* | *The children were all bunched together in the corner of the room.*

bund /bʌnd/ *n BrE* a high man-made bank of earth built to hide something such as ugly industrial buildings, to limit noise from a MOTORWAY, or to protect from enemy attack

Bun·des·bank /ˈbʊndəzˌbæŋk/ [*the*] the German central bank

bun·dle¹ /ˈbʌndl/ *n* **1** [C (of)] a number of articles tied, fastened, or held together, usu. across the middle: *a bundle of sticks* | *She tied up her few belongings into a bundle.* **2** [S] *sl* a large sum of money: *He must have made a bundle out of selling that house.* **3** *infml* **a bundle of** in a state of: *I'm so anxious I'm just* **a bundle of nerves.** (=extremely nervous) | *She's not exactly a* **bundle of fun/laughs.** (=not at all amusing to be with)

bundle² *v* **1** [I+*adv/prep*;T+*obj+adv/prep*] to (cause to) move or hurry in a rather quick and rough manner: *They arrested a man on the street and bundled him into a police car.* | *They bundled the children off to school.* | *We all bundled into the taxi.* **2** [T+*obj+adv/prep*] to put together or store hastily and untidily: *She bundled her clothes into a bag.*

bundle (sbdy.) **up** *phr v* [I;T] to dress warmly: *She bundled (herself) up in several warm sweaters before going out into the freezing cold.*

Bundt pan /ˈbʌnt pæn/ *n tdmk* a ring-like baking pan with high sides and a hole in the middle, used for baking

cakes: *Pour the batter into a greased Bundt pan.* | *a Bundt cake* (a cake baked in a Bundt pan)

bung¹ /bʌŋ/ *n* a round piece of rubber, wood, or other material used to close the hole in a container —see picture at STOPPER

bung² *v* [T] *BrE infml* to put, push, or throw, esp. roughly: *He picked up a stone and bunged it over the fence.* [+*obj(i)+obj(d)*] *Bung me a cigarette, will you?*

bung sthg. ↔ **up** *phr v* [T *often pass.*] *BrE infml* to block; stop up: *to bung up a hole* | *My nose is bunged up with a cold.*

bun·ga·low /ˈbʌŋgələʊ/ *n* **1** *BrE* a house which is all on ground level. In Britain, many old people live in bungalows. **2** *AmE* a small house which is usu. all on ground level —see HOUSE (USAGE), and see picture at HOUSE

bung·hole /ˈbʌŋhəʊl/ *n* a hole for emptying or filling a barrel

bun·gle /ˈbʌŋgəl/ *v* [T] to do badly; BOTCH: *to bungle a job* —**bungle** *n* —**bungler** *n*

bun·ion /ˈbʌnjən/ *n* a painful red swelling on the first joint of the big toe

bunk¹ /bʌŋk/ *n* **1** a narrow bed that is usu. fixed to the wall (as on a ship or train) **2** also **bunk bed** /ˈ· ·/— either of a pair of beds that are placed one above the other —see picture at BED

bunk² *v* [I+*adv/prep*, esp. DOWN] *infml* to sleep; have one's sleeping-place: *She bunked (down) with some friends/on a sofa for the night.*

bunk³ *n* [U] *sl* nonsense; BUNKUM: *That's a load of bunk.*

bunk⁴ *n* **do a bunk** *BrE sl* to run away; leave, esp. when one should not

bunk⁵ *v*

bunk off *phr v* [I] *BrE sl* **1** to leave in a hurry or when one should not **2** to stay away from school without permission; play TRUANT

bun·ker /ˈbʌŋkəʳ/ *n* **1** a place for storing coal, esp. on a ship or outside a house **2** a strongly built shelter for soldiers, esp. one built mainly underground with openings for guns **3** *BrE* ‖ **trap, sand trap** *AmE*— (in GOLF) a place dug out and filled with sand, from which it is hard to hit the ball —see picture at GOLF

Bunker, Ar·chie /ˈɑːtʃi‖ˈɑːr-/ a character in the popular American television programme of the 1970s, *All in the Family.* He was working class and very PREJUDICED (=he did not like people different from himself).

bunk·house /ˈbʌŋkhaʊs/ *n* **-houses** /ˌhaʊzɪz/ a building where workers sleep, for those who have to live at their place of work

bun·kum /ˈbʌŋkəm/ *n* [U] *sl* foolish talk; nonsense

bunk-up /ˈ· ·/ *n* [*usu. sing.*] *BrE infml* a push up from below to help someone climbing: *I want to have a look over the wall — can you give me a bunk-up?*

bun·ny /ˈbʌni/ also **bunny rab·bit** /ˈ·· ˌ··/— *n* (used esp. by or to children) a rabbit

bunny girl /ˈ·· ·/ *n* a waitress, esp. in a night club, who wears a special COSTUME with long ears and a furry tail like a rabbit's

Bun·sen burn·er /ˌbʌnsən ˈbɜːnəʳ‖-ɜːr-/ also **Bunsen**— *n* a gas apparatus that produces a hot smokeless flame for use in practical scientific work —see picture at LABORATORY

bunt /bʌnt/ *n* a deliberately short hit in the game of BASEBALL —**bunt** *v* [I] : *He bunted toward third base.*

Bun·ter /ˈbʌntəʳ/, **Billy** the main character in children's stories by Frank Richards about a British PUBLIC SCHOOL. Bunter is a fat, stupid boy with glasses who loves eating and is always getting into trouble: *a Billy Bunterish fellow*

bun·ting /ˈbʌntɪŋ/ *n* [U] small paper or cloth flags, tied together on a string and used as decorations for special occasions

Bun·ty /ˈbʌnti/ a British COMIC (=magazine for children) which is intended for young girls

Buñ·u·el /ˈbuːnjuel/, **Lu·is** /luːˈiːs/ (1900–83) a Spanish film director known for his dreamlike images and humorous attacks on the Catholic church and middle-class moral values. His films include *Le Charme Discrèt De La Bourgeoisie* and *Cet Obscur Objet Du Désir.*

Bun·yan /ˈbʌnjən/, **John** (1628–88) an English PREACHER who wrote *The Pilgrim's Progress* while he was in prison for his beliefs

Bunyan, Paul /pɔːl/ according to old stories, a GIANT LUMBERJACK (=someone whose job is cutting down trees) from the north woods of the US and Canada who travelled with a blue OX named Babe

buoy[1] /bɔɪ‖ˈbuːi, bɔɪ/ *n* a floating object fastened to the bottom of the sea, e.g. to show ships where there are rocks —see also LIFE BUOY

buoy[2] *v* [T (UP) *usu. pass.*] **1** to keep floating: *buoyed by the water* **2** to support; keep high: *profits buoyed (up) by a steady increase in demand* **3** to raise the spirits of; make confident: *They were buoyed up by hopes of success.*

buoy·an·cy /ˈbɔɪənsi‖ˈbɔɪənsi, ˈbuːjənsi/ *n* [U] **1** the tendency of an object to float, or to rise when pushed down into a liquid: *the buoyancy of light wood* **2** the power of a liquid to make an object float: *the buoyancy of water* **3** the ability to recover quickly from disappointment, bad news, etc. **4** the ability, e.g. of prices or business activity, to remain or return quickly to a high level after a period of difficulty: *the buoyancy of the American market*

buoy·ant /ˈbɔɪənt‖ˈbɔɪənt, ˈbuːjənt/ *adj* showing buoyancy: *Cork is a very buoyant material.* | *a buoyant mood* | *buoyant economy/stockmarket* — ~ **ly** *adv*

BUPA /ˈbuːpə, ˈbjuː-/ British United Provident Association; a company which sells private health insurance and runs its own hospitals outside the National Health Service: *Are you in (=insured by) BUPA?*

bur /bɜːʳ/ *n* a BURR[2]

Bur·ber·ry /ˈbɜːbəri‖ˈbɜːrbəri, -beri/ *n tdmk* an expensive kind of RAINCOAT, made from a special cloth with the same name

bur·ble /ˈbɜːbəl‖ˈbɜːr-/ also **bubble** *AmE*— *v* **1** [I] to make a sound like a stream flowing over stones **2** [I (ON, AWAY);T] to talk or say quickly but foolishly or in a way that is hard to hear clearly: *He would burble on/burble away for hours about his stamp collection.* | *She quickly burbled her thanks and left the room.*

burbs /bɜːbz‖bɜːrbz/ *n* [*the*] *AmE infml* for SUBURBS: *I know, you'll just get married and live in the burbs like everybody else!*

bur·den[1] /ˈbɜːdn‖-ɜːr-/ *n fml* **1** [C] something that is carried; a load: *a heavy burden* —see also BEAST OF BURDEN **2** [C] a heavy duty or responsibility which is hard to bear: *divorced parents who have to bear/carry the burden of maintaining two households* | *People on high incomes face a huge tax burden.* | *the burdens of high office* **3** [*the*+S (of)] the main subject or point: *The burden of his complaint was that…*

burden[2] *v* [T (**with**)] to load or trouble: *I will not burden you with a lengthy account of what happened.* | *burdened with heavy taxation* —see also UNBURDEN

burden of proof /ˌ··· ˈ·/ *n* [*the*+S] the duty or responsibility of proving something: *The burden of proof lies with the person who makes the charge.*

bur·den·some /ˈbɜːdnsəm‖ˈbɜːr-/ *adj fml* causing or being a burden; ONEROUS: *burdensome duties*

bu·reau /ˈbjʊərəʊ/ *n* **bureaux** /ˈbjʊərəʊz/ **1** *BrE* a large desk or writing-table with a wooden cover which shuts or slides over the top to close it **2** *AmE for* CHEST OF DRAWERS **3** an office or organization that collects and/or provides facts: *an information bureau* **4** *esp. AmE* a division of a government department

bu·reauc·ra·cy /bjʊəˈrɒkrəsi, -ˈrɑː-/ *n usu. derog* **1** [S] a group of government, business, or other officials who are appointed rather than elected: *the Civil Service bureaucracy* **2** [C;U] (a system of) government by such officials **3** [U] a system of doing things officially which is annoyingly and unnecessarily difficult to understand or deal with and usu. ineffective: *the company bureaucracy*

bu·reau·crat /ˈbjʊərəkræt/ *n usu. derog* a member of a bureaucracy

bu·reau·crat·ic /ˌbjʊərəˈkrætɪk◄/ *adj usu. derog* of or like a bureaucracy or a bureaucrat: *bureaucratic rules* | *In this company you have to go through complex bureaucratic procedures just to get a new pencil.* — ~ **ally** /kli/ *adv*

bureau de change /ˌbjʊərəʊ də ˈʃɒndʒ‖-ˈʃɑːndʒ/ *n Fr* an office or shop where people can change foreign money into local money or change local money into foreign money

Bureau of In·di·an Af·fairs /ˌ··· ˌ···· ·ˈ·/ also **BIA**— *n* [*the*] a US government organization which is concerned with the WELFARE and education of Native Americans and with other legal matters concerning RESERVATIONS (areas set aside for Native Americans to live on)

bur·geon /ˈbɜːdʒən‖ˈbɜːr-/ *v* [I] *fml* to grow or develop quickly: *the burgeoning home computer industry*

burg·er /ˈbɜːgəʳ‖ˈbɜːr-/ *n* **1** a round flat cake mainly of meat, often contained in a bread roll; a HAMBURGER **2** **-burger: a** a HAMBURGER in which the meat is covered with the stated substance: *a cheeseburger* **b** something like a HAMBURGER, but made of a different substance: *a nutburger/a soyaburger*

burger bar /ˈ··· ·/ *BrE n* a type of restaurant selling burgers, where food is ordered from a bar

Burger King /ˈ··· ˌ·/ *n* a restaurant in the US and some other countries which serves FAST FOOD, esp. HAMBURGERS

bur·gess /ˈbɜːdʒᵻs‖ˈbɜːr-/ *n old use or pomp* a free man of a city or country, having the right to elect representatives to the government

Burgess, Anthony (1917–93) a English writer and CRITIC, best known for his NOVELS *A Clockwork Orange* and *Earthly Powers*

Burgess, Guy (1911–63) an Englishman who was a SPY for the former Soviet Union and escaped there in 1951 —see also Anthony BLUNT, Donald MACLEAN, Kim PHILBY

burgh /ˈbʌrə‖bɜːrg, ˈbʌrəʊ/ *n ScotE for* BOROUGH

bur·gher /ˈbɜːgəʳ‖ˈbɜːr-/ *n often humor* a person who lives in a particular town: *Their wild behaviour outraged the respectable burghers of Oxford.*

bur·glar /ˈbɜːgləʳ‖ˈbɜːr-/ *n* a thief who breaks into houses, shops, etc. with the intention of stealing, esp. during the night. Humorous drawings of burglars show them wearing striped (STRIPE) jumpers and carrying a large bag marked SWAG (=things they have stolen) —see also CAT BURGLAR; compare HOUSEBREAKER, ROBBER, THIEF

burglar

burglar a·larm /ˈ··· ·ˌ·/ *n* an apparatus that makes a loud warning noise, or operates a warning system at a police station, etc., when a thief breaks into a building

bur·glar·ize /ˈbɜːgləraɪz‖ˈbɜːr-/ *v AmE for* BURGLE

bur·glar·y /ˈbɜːgləri‖ˈbɜːr-/ *n* [C;U] (an example of) the crime of entering a building (esp. a home) by force with the intention of stealing

bur·gle /ˈbɜːgəl‖ˈbɜːr-/ also **burglarize** *AmE*— *v* [T] to break into a building and steal from (it or the people in it): *Their house was burgled while they were away on holiday.*

Bur·gun·dy /ˈbɜːgəndi‖ˈbɜːr-/ *n* [U] white or red wine of the Burgundy area of France

bur·i·al /ˈberiəl/ *n* [C;U] the act or ceremony of putting a dead body into a grave: *a burial site/ground*

burk /bɜːk‖bɜːrk/ *n* a BERK

Burke /bɜːk‖bɜːrk/, **Ed·mund** /ˈedmənd/ (1729–97) a British Whig politician, born in Dublin, Ireland. He wrote many works of political THEORY and was also a great speaker.

Burke's Peer·age /ˌ· ˈ···/ *n* a book which lists the names and details of all the families with titles in Britain: *Look them up in Burke's Peerage.*

Bur·ki·na Fa·so /bʊəˌkiːnə ˈfæsəʊ‖bʊər-/ *n* a country in W Africa, N of Côte d'Ivoire; capital Ouagadougou; population 8,763,000 (1989). The former name of the country was **Upper Volta.**

bur·lap /ˈbɜːlæp‖bɜːr-/ *n* [U] *AmE for* HESSIAN

bur·lesque[1] /bɜːˈlesk‖bɜːr-/ *n* **1** [C;U] speech, acting, or writing in which a serious subject is made to seem foolish or an unimportant subject is treated solemnly as a joke: *a burlesque of a famous poem* **2** [U] (formerly in

the US) VARIETY (4), usu. including STRIPTEASE

burlesque² v [T] to cause to appear amusing by means of burlesque: *to burlesque a writer/a poem*

bur·ly /ˈbɜːli‖ˈbɜːrli/ adj (of a person) strongly and heavily built: *a big burly construction worker* —**-liness** n [U]

Bur·ma /ˈbɜːmə‖ˈbɜːr-/ the former name of MYANMAR

Burma Road /ˌ··ˈ·/ n a road leading from the country formerly called Burma to China which was used during the Second World War to supply Allied forces in China

burn¹ /bɜːn‖bɜːrn/ v **burnt** /bɜːnt‖bɜːrnt/ or **burned** **1** [I] (esp. of wood, coal, paper, etc.) to give out heat, light, and gases: *Is the fire still burning?* | *This type of coal does not burn very easily.* | *a burning match* **2** [I;T] to (cause to) be on fire, esp. to destroy or be destroyed by fire: *The house is burning — call the fire brigade!* | *I burnt all his old letters.* | *The house was* **burnt to ashes/burnt to the ground.** (=completely destroyed by fire) | *Joan of Arc was* **burnt at the stake.** (=killed by burning) | (fig.) *That £100 is burning a hole in his pocket.* (=he wants to spend it) **3** [I;T] to (cause to) be hurt or damaged, by fire or heat: *I've burnt my hand.* | *The toast has burnt.* | *burnt by the sun* | *You burnt a hole in my skirt with your cigarette.* **4** [I] to produce light; shine: *a light burning in the window* **5** [T] to use for power, heating, or lighting: *lamps that burn oil* | *a coal-burning ship* **6** [T] (of a chemical) to damage or destroy; CORRODE: *The technician's overalls were burnt by acid.* **7** [I] to produce or experience an unpleasant hot feeling: *I'm afraid the ointment will burn a bit.* | *My ears were burning after being out in the cold wind.* **8** [I (with) esp. in progressive forms] to experience a very strong feeling: *burning with anger/desire* [+to-v] *She is burning to tell you the news.* **9** [I+adv/prep] to travel at high speed: *We burned up the motorway.* | *supersonic planes burning through the stratosphere* **10** [T] to lose a lot of money, esp. in a business deal: *A lot of people got burned buying junk bonds.* **11** [T] to lose confidence in another person because they have done something to hurt you: *He's been burned in his relationships with women before.* **12 burn one's boats/bridges** infml to destroy all means of going back, so that one must go forward **13 burn one's fingers** also **get one's ¹fingers burnt**— infml to suffer the unpleasant results of a foolish action: *George got his fingers badly burnt when the firm went out of business.* **14 burn the candle at both ends** infml to work or be active from very early until very late; use up all one's strength by trying to do too many different things; get too little rest **15 burn the midnight oil** infml to work or study until late at night

▷ USAGE In British English the past tense and participle **burned** is usu. only used when the verb is intransitive: *The fire* **burned** *brightly.* | *The love of freedom* **burned** *in their hearts.* Compare: *I've* **burnt** *my hand.* | *He* **burnt** *her letters.* In American English **burned** is used both when the verb is intransitive and when it is transitive and **burnt** is not used very much.◁

burn away phr v [I;T (=**burn** sthg. ↔ **away**)] to destroy or be destroyed by burning; make or become less or nothing as a result of fire: *The pile of paper burnt away to nothing.*

burn down phr v **1** [I;T (=**burn** sthg. ↔ **down**)] to destroy (usu. a building) or be destroyed by fire: *The building (was) burnt down and only ashes were left.* **2** [I] also **burn low**— (esp. of a fire) to flame less brightly or strongly as the coal, wood, etc., is used up —compare BURN out, BURN up

burn sthg. ↔ off phr v [T] to destroy by burning: *His hair was burnt off.* | *The farmers are burning off the stubble from the fields.*

burn out phr v **1** [T usu. pass.] (**burn** sthg. **out**) to make hollow by fire: *The building was burnt out and only the walls remained.* | *the burnt-out shell of a building* —compare BURN down, BURN up **2** [I;T (=**burn** sthg. **out**)] to stop (itself) burning because there is nothing left to burn: *That small fire can be left to burn (itself) out.* **3** [I;T (=**burn** sthg. **out**)] to (cause to) stop working through damage caused by heat: *The engine has/is burnt out.* **4** [T] (**burn** sbdy. **out**) to ruin one's health and stop being active through too much work, pressure, alcohol, etc: *You'll burn yourself out if you work so hard.* | *a burnt-out poet* **5** [I] (of a ROCKET, JET, etc.) to use up all its FUEL and stop operating —see also BURNOUT

burn up phr v **1** [I] to flame more brightly or strongly:

Put some more wood on the fire to make it burn up. **2** [I;T (=**burn** sthg. ↔ **up**)] to destroy or be destroyed completely by fire or great heat: *All the wood has been burnt up.* | *The rocket burnt up when it re-entered the earth's atmosphere.* —compare BURN **down**, BURN **out** **3** [T] (**burn** sbdy. ↔ **up**) sl to fill (someone's) mind completely; OBSESS: *He was burnt up with jealousy.* **4** [T] (**burn** sbdy. ↔ **up**) to make angry: *They way he treats her really burns me up.*

burn² n **1** a hurt place or mark produced (as if) by burning: *She was treated for/She suffered severe burns.* | *rope burns* | *a burn on the surface of the table* | *first-degree burns* **2** an act of firing the motors of a spacecraft: *a short burn*

burn³ n esp. ScotE a small stream

burn·er /ˈbɜːnəʳ‖ˈbɜːr-/ n **1** (often in comb.) a person or thing that burns, esp. the part of a cooker, heater, etc., that produces flames: *a two-burner stove* **2 put something on the back burner** to delay dealing with something until a later time —see also BUNSEN BURNER; see COOK (USAGE)

Bur·nett /bɜːˈnet, ˈbɜːnət‖-ɜːr-/, **Fran·ces Hodg·son** /ˈfrɑːnsəs ˈhɒdʒsən‖ˈfrænsəs ˈhɑːdʒ-/ (1849–1924) an American writer best known for her children's books *Little Lord Fauntleroy* and *The Secret Garden*

burn·ing /ˈbɜːnɪŋ‖ˈbɜːr-/ adj [A] **1** on fire: *a burning house* | (fig.) *burning cheeks* (=cheeks that are hot and red) | (fig.) *a burning* (=very strong) *interest in science* | (fig.) *a burning ambition* **2** producing a sensation of great heat or fire: *a burning fever* | *a burning sensation on the tongue* | *burning sands* **3** very important and urgent: *Mass unemployment is one of the* **burning questions/issues** *of our time.* **4 the boy stood on the burning deck** quote a well-known phrase from a poem by Felicia Hemans

bur·nish /ˈbɜːnɪʃ‖ˈbɜːr-/ v [T] to polish (esp. metal), usu. with something hard and smooth: *burnished brass*

Burn·ley /ˈbɜːnli‖ˈbɜːrn-/ a town in Lancashire, in the N of England, formerly famous for its cotton industry

bur·nous , **burnouse** ‖ also **burnoose** AmE— /bɜːˈnuːs‖bɜːr-/ n a long one-piece loose outer garment worn by Arabs, with a soft covering for the head, neck, and shoulders

burn·out /ˈbɜːnaʊt‖ˈbɜːr-/ n [C;U] **1** the moment when the engine of a ROCKET or JET uses up all its FUEL and stops operating **2** a state in which one's health has been ruined by too much work, pressure, etc.

Burns /bɜːnz‖bɜːrnz/, **George** (1896–) an American COMEDIAN and actor who was popular in VAUDEVILLE, on the radio, and on television, esp. when he was performing with his wife, Gracie Allen. He is known for his CIGAR and his talks to the people watching.

George Burns

Burns, Rob·ert /ˈrɒbət‖ˈrɑːb-ərt/ (1759–96) a Scottish poet who wrote, in Scots DIALECT, hundreds of songs and poems, mainly on country life, love, and national pride. He is regarded as Scotland's national poet and his birthday is celebrated in many countries of the world each year on 25 January, **Burns Night.**

burnt /bɜːnt‖bɜːrnt/ past tense & participle of BURN² —see BURN¹ (USAGE)

burnt of·fer·ing /ˌ· ˈ···/ n **1** something (usu. a plant or animal) which is burnt as an offering to a god **2** humor food that has been accidentally burnt during cooking

burp /bɜːp‖bɜːrp/ v infml **1** [I] to BELCH **2** [T] to help (a baby) to get rid of stomach gas, esp. by rubbing or gently striking the back —**burp** n

burr¹ /bɜːʳ/ n [S] **1** a long loud sound of humming (HUM¹): *the burr of a sewing machine* **2** a way of pronouncing English with a strong "r"-sound: *She speaks with a soft rural burr.*

burr² , **bur** n a seed-container of certain plants, covered with PRICKLES which make it stick onto clothes

Bur·rell Col·lec·tion /ˈbʌrəl kəˌlekʃən‖ˈbɜːr-/ [the] an art collection in Glasgow, given to the city by Sir William Burrell

bur·ri·to /bəˈriːtəʊ/ n -tos a type of hot SANDWICH made with a TORTILLA which is folded around meat or beans and cheese

bur·ro /ˈbʊrəʊ‖ˈbɜːrəʊ/ n -ros esp. AmE a DONKEY, usu. a small one

Bur·roughs /ˈbʌrəʊz‖ˈbɜː-/, **Ed·gar Rice** /ˈedɡəʳ raɪs/ (1875–1950) an American writer, best known for the Tarzan stories

bur·row¹ /ˈbʌrəʊ‖ˈbɜːrəʊ/ n a hole in the ground made by an animal, esp. a rabbit, as a place to live in

burrow² v **1** [I+adv/prep;T] to make or move by digging: *The rabbits burrowed into the hillside/under the fence.* | *to burrow a hole* | *They burrowed their way under the hill.* **2** [T+obj+adv/prep] to move or press as if looking for warmth, safety, or love: *She burrowed her head into my shoulder.* **3** [I+adv/prep] to search for something as if by digging: *She burrowed into her pocket for a handkerchief.* | *What are you burrowing around in my drawer for?*

bur·sar /ˈbɜːsəʳ‖ˈbɜːr-/ n esp. BrE a person in a college or school who is responsible for the accounts, buildings, etc.

bur·sa·ry /ˈbɜːsəri‖ˈbɜːr-/ n esp. BrE **1** a bursar's office **2** a SCHOLARSHIP (1)

burst¹ /bɜːst‖bɜːrst/ v **burst 1** [I;T] to (cause to) break open or break apart suddenly and violently, usu. as a result of pressure from within and often causing the contents to become widely scattered: *We drove over some glass and one of our tyres burst.* | *After ten days of rain the river burst its banks and flooded the valley.* | *to burst a balloon* | (fig.) *You'll burst if you eat any more of that cake.* | (fig.) *The storm burst* (=suddenly started) *and we all got wet.* | (fig.) *I felt as if my heart would burst (with grief/joy).* —see BREAK (USAGE) and see also **fit to burst** (FIT² (5)) **2** [I+adv/prep;T+obj+adv/prep] to (cause to) come into the stated condition suddenly and often violently: *He burst free (from the chains).* | *The police burst through the door/came bursting into the room.* | *In spring the young flowers burst open.* **3** [I (**with**) only in progressive forms] to be so full as to be almost breaking open: *The town is bursting with tourists.* [+to-v] *She's bursting to tell you the news.* | *The bus was full to bursting point.* | (fig.) *bursting with pride/joy* **4 burst at the seams** to be extremely and usu. uncomfortably full: *I've had so much to eat that I'm bursting at the seams.* | *There were so many people that the hall was bursting at the seams.*

    burst in on/upon sbdy./sthg. phr v [T] to interrupt suddenly and usu. noisily: *They burst in on me while I was working.* | *to burst in on someone's thoughts*

    burst into sthg. phr v [T] **1** to begin suddenly to make (a sound with the voice), esp. when laughing, crying, or singing: *to burst into tears* (=start crying) | *to burst into song/laughter* **2 burst into flames** to begin burning suddenly and uncontrollably

    burst out phr v **1** [I+v-ing] to begin suddenly (to use the voice without speaking): *They burst out laughing/crying.* **2** [T] to say suddenly and with strong feeling: *"I don't believe it!" she burst out angrily.* —see also OUTBURST

burst² n **1** an act or result of bursting: *a burst in the water pipes* **2** [(**of**)] a sudden short period of great activity, loud noise, strong feeling; outbreak: *a burst of laughter/thunder/applause/machinegun fire* | *With a final burst of speed she overtook the leading runner and won the race.*

bur·then /ˈbɜːðən‖ˈbɜːr-/ n, v old use for BURDEN

bur·ton /ˈbɜːtn‖ˈbɜːrtn/ n (often cap.) **gone for a burton** BrE sl lost, broken, or killed: *The radio's gone for a burton.*

Burton, Richard (1925–84) a Welsh film and theatre actor, regarded as one of the best of his time. He was married twice to Elizabeth Taylor, and the marriages attracted almost as much attention as his acting.

Bu·run·di /bʊˈrʊndi/ a country in E central Africa, bordered by Rwanda, Tanzania, Lake Tanganyika, and Zaïre; capital Bujumbura; population 5,302,000 (1989) —**dian** n, adj

bur·y /ˈberi/ v [T] **1** to put (a dead body) into a grave: *Both my grandparents were buried here.* | (fig.) *to bury an old quarrel* **2** [(**in**)] to hide or cover over, esp. with earth: *The dog has buried a bone.* | *buried treasure* | *The climbers were buried under an avalanche of rocks.* | (fig.) *The true facts are buried in a secret government report.* | *She*

was sitting with her head buried in a newspaper. | (fig.) *He buried his hands in his pockets.* | *buried in thought* **3 bury the hatchet** to become friends again after a quarrel —see also **bury one's head in the sand** (HEAD¹)

Bur·y·at·skay·a /bʊəriˈɑːtskaɪə/ a republic of N Mongolia; capital Ulan Ude

Bury My Heart at Wound·ed Knee /ˌ··· ·ˌ·· ·ˌ·· ˈ·/ a book by Dee Brown which tells the story of the American West in a way that is sympathetic to the Native Americans

bus¹ /bʌs/ n a large passenger-carrying motor vehicle, esp. one which carries the public for payment: *to go by bus* | *I saw him on the bus.* | *London's famous double-decker buses* | *yellow school buses* | *to get/catch/miss the bus* | *to pay one's bus fare* | *There is no bus service* (=buses do not run) *to our village.* —see also DATA BUS

buses

a London bus

  ▷ USAGE You can **travel by** bus, but you **travel** or **ride in** or **on** a particular bus. At the beginning of your journey you **get on(to)** the bus and at the end of your journey you **get off** (it), **get out of** it, or **alight** (fml) (**from** it). —see also DRIVE (USAGE), STEER (USAGE), TRANSPORT (USAGE)◁

bus² v -ss-, -s- **1** [T] to take by bus, esp. (in the US) to carry (pupils) by bus to a school in a different area, where the pupils are of a different race. This may be done to mix the races at a school where otherwise only black or white children would attend. —see also BROWN v. BOARD OF EDUCATION OF TOPEKA **2** [T] AmE to take away dirty dishes from the tables in a restaurant: *a job bussing tables* —**bussing, busing** n [U]

a Greyhound bus

bus boy /ˈ· ·/ n AmE a person employed to help a waiter in a restaurant by taking away used dishes

bus·by /ˈbʌzbi/ n **1** a small fur hat worn by certain British soldiers **2** infml for BEARSKIN (2)

Busby, Sir Matt (1909–94) an English football team manager. He was the manager of the Manchester United team when several members were killed in the Munich air crash in 1958. His team was known as **Busby's babes** or the **Busby babes.**

bush /bʊʃ/ n **1** [C] a low woody plant, smaller than a tree and with many stems: *a rose bush* **2** [the+S] uncleared wild country, esp. in Australia or Africa —see also **beat about the bush** (BEAT¹ (6)), **a bird in the hand is worth two in the bush** (BIRD (4))

Bush, George (1924–) 41st president of the US (1989–92). Before the 1992 election Bush was often described as being a WIMP (=a weak person) but people stopped saying this after Operation Desert Storm. Before the election in 1988, Bush promised that he would not raise taxes by saying "Read my lips; no new taxes," but he did later raise some taxes. —see colour picture on page 950

bush·ba·by /ˈbʊʃˌbeɪbi/ n a small African animal with large eyes and ears, a long tail, and long back legs with which to jump

bushed /bʊʃt/ adj [F] esp. AmE infml very tired

bush·el /ˈbʊʃəl/ n a unit of CAPACITY, esp. for measuring grain, vegetables, and fruit —see also **hide one's light under a bushel** (HIDE), see TABLE 2

Bush House /ˌ· ˈ·/ the building in London from which the BBC World Service broadcasts radio programmes abroad

bush league /ˈ· ·ˌ·/ adj AmE unprofessional or badly done (from a name for the MINOR LEAGUEs in BASEBALL, in which the players have not yet reached professional standards): *His work is still strictly bush league.*

Bush·man /ˈbʊʃmən/ n -men /mən/ **1** a member of a race of NOMADIC people of southern Africa **2** not cap. one who lives in the Australian bush

bush·ran·ger /ˈbʊʃˌreɪndʒəʳ/ n **1** someone who lives in an uncultivated, or forested area with a small population away from civilization **2** a criminal living in such an area

bush tel·e·graph /ˌ· '···/ n [U] BrE humor the fast spreading of information by unofficial means: *The news spread through the whole school by bush telegraph.*

bush·whack /ˈbʊʃwæk/ v [I;T] AmE to push or cut one's way through trees or bushes: *Tom bushwhacked a trail ahead of us.*

bush·whack·er /ˈbʊʃwækəʳ/ n AmE someone who makes a path through thick woods esp. GUERRILLAs or others who fight in or attack from woods or rough land **bush-whacking** n [U]

bush·y /ˈbʊʃi/ adj (of hair) growing thickly: *a bushy beard/tail* —**iness** n [U]

bus·i·ly /ˈbɪzɪli/ adv see BUSY¹

busi·ness /ˈbɪznɪs/ n **1** [U] the activity of buying and selling goods and services; COMMERCE: *She wants to go into business when she leaves college.* | *It's a pleasure to do business with you.* | *He set up in business as a property developer.* | *I'm here on business.* (=for work and not for pleasure) | *the oil/insurance business* (the branch of business concerned with oil/insurance) | *He may be a friend, but business is business* (=is a serious matter) *and he's not the man for the job.* | *a business lunch* | *Our business hours are from 9 to 5.* **2** [U] the amount or value of trade being done: *"How's business?" "Business is booming."* (=doing very well) | *They are now doing almost twice as much business as they were last year.* | *They advertised their services to* **drum up business.** (=increase it) **3** [C] a particular money-earning activity or place, such as a shop or factory: *to start up a new business* | *He runs a small business in the town.* | *a profitable business* **4** [U] one's responsibility or concern: *A teacher's business is to help children learn.* | *What I do with my money is* **none of your business.** (=does not concern you) | *I wish you would* **mind your own business.** (=not pay attention to things that do not concern you) | *You* **had no business** (=no right) *to meddle/meddling in my affairs.* **5** [S] an affair or matter: *I don't understand this business.* | *Let's get down to the main business of the meeting.* (=the matter to be considered) | *a strange business* | *Investing in shares can be quite a risky business.* **6** [U] tech (in the theatre) things done by an actor apart from speaking, such as movements of the hands, the look on the face, etc.: *stage business* **7 business as usual** a phrase, sometimes written on a sign, meaning that a shop or other business is working normally (NORMAL) even though it is having difficulties, e.g. there has been a fire **8 business before pleasure** saying you should do your work first and then enjoy yourself afterwards **9 get down to business** to start dealing with the most important matter or subject: *We'd better stop chatting and get down to business.* **10** like **'nobody's/no one's business** infml, usu. apprec very fast or very well: *He can play the piano like nobody's business.* **11 not in the business of** not having the aim or purpose of: *This government is not in the business of cutting taxes simply in order to help the rich.* **12 out of business** no longer able to operate as a business: *These big increases in rents could put a lot of small shops out of business.* —see also BIG BUSINESS, FUNNY BUSINESS, MONKEY BUSINESS, SHOW BUSINESS, **mean business** (MEAN²)

business card /ˈ··· ˌ·/ also **card**— n a card given and received by business people stating the owner's name, position, company, and address —compare VISITING CARD

business class /ˈ··· ·/ also **club class** AmE— n [U] (on an aircraft) the travelling conditions which are better and dearer than TOURIST CLASS but worse and cheaper than FIRST CLASS: *I always travel business class.* | *a business-class ticket*

business end /ˈ··· ·/ n [the+S (of)] infml the end of something, such as a tool or weapon, that performs the job for which the thing is made: *the business end of a gun* (=the barrel)

Business Ex·pan·sion Scheme /ˌ··· ·'·· ·/ n a system in Britain of giving tax allowances on money used in small new businesses

busi·ness·like /ˈbɪznɪs-laɪk/ adj having qualities that bring success in business, esp. an effective and practical way of working: *a businesslike person/manner* | *The talks were frank and businesslike.*

busi·ness lunch /ˈ··· ˌ·/ n a meal at which people discuss

business, esp. when one person is trying to persuade another to buy or sell something

busi·ness·man /ˈbɪznɪsˌmæn/, **busi·ness·wom·an** /-ˌwʊmən/ fem.— n -**men** /mən/ **1** a person who works in business, esp. as an owner, director, or top manager of a company: *a successful young businessman* | *a small businessman* (=one who runs a small business) **2** a person who has the qualities necessary to be successful in business: *I'm not much of a businessman.* —see also SMALL BUSINESSMAN

business park /ˈ·· ˌ·/ n an area where a lot of companies and businesses have buildings

business rep·ly mail /ˌ··· ·ˈ· ˌ·/ n AmE for FREEPOST

business stud·ies /ˈ·· ˌ·/ n [P] a course of study at a school or college covering economic and financial subjects

business suit /ˈ·· ˌ·/ n AmE for LOUNGE SUIT

busk /bʌsk/ v [I] BrE infml to play music in the street or other public place in order to earn money — ~ **er** n

bus lane /ˈ· ·/ n a part of a wide road, marked for the use of buses only: *We shouldn't really drive up here, it's the bus lane.*

bus·man's hol·i·day /ˌbʌsmənz ˈhɒlɪdi‖-ˈhɑːlɪˌdeɪ/ n [usu. sing.] a holiday spent in doing one's usual work: *The painter spent a busman's holiday painting his own house.*

bus pass /ˈ·· ·/ n a special ticket given to old people, schoolchildren, etc. in Britain which allows them to travel free on buses

bus ser·vice /ˈ· ˌ··/ n the operation of buses in a particular area

bus shel·ter /ˈ· ˌ··/ n a small building, sometimes without walls, which keeps the rain off people who are waiting for a bus

bus sta·tion /ˈ· ˌ··/ n (the buildings at) a place where buses start and finish their journeys, and where passengers can get on and off

bus stop /ˈ· ·/ n a fixed place at the side of a road where buses stop for passengers: *waiting at the bus stop*

bust¹ /bʌst/ n **1** a piece of SCULPTURE showing a person's head, shoulders, and upper chest: *a bust of Beethoven* — compare STATUETTE **2** euph a woman's breasts; BOSOM **3** a measurement round a woman's breasts and back: *Do you have this dress in a bigger bust size?*

bust² v busted or bust [T] **1** infml to break: *I bust(ed) my watch this morning.* | *They busted the door down.* **2** AmE infml to burst: *a busted balloon* | *The pipes will bust under that pressure.* **3** sl (of the police) **a** to charge with an offence, esp. one connected with drugs; ARREST: *He was busted for possession of cocaine.* **b** to enter (someone's house) without warning to look for something illegal, esp. drugs; visit on a RAID¹ (2) **4** infml, esp. AmE to lower (a military person) in rank; DEMOTE **5** -**buster** infml a person who breaks up or destroys the stated thing: *a crimebuster* (= who catches criminals) **6 bust a gut** sl **a** to make a great effort (to do something): *I nearly bust a gut finishing that work on time.* **b** to laugh very hard: *I thought I'd bust a gut when he fell off the wall.* **7** (somewhere or something) **or bust** usu. humor a phrase used when saying that one will make a great effort to go somewhere or do something or fail completely: *San Francisco or bust!* | *I'll do it by Wednesday or bust.*

▷ USAGE In American English the past tense and participle **busted** is used more often than **bust.**◁

bust up phr v infml **1** [I] (esp. of a relationship or partnership) to separate: *They bust up after six years of marriage.* **2** [I] to laugh very hard: *We busted up laughing.* **3** [T] (bust sthg. ↔ up) AmE to damage or spoil: *The travel company's failure bust up their holiday.* —see also BUST-UP

bust³ n sl **1** a police ARREST² or RAID¹: *Several big dealers have been rounded up in a major drugs bust.*

bust⁴ adj infml **1** broken: *My watch is bust.* **2** AmE a complete failure **3 go bust** (of a business) to fail; go BANKRUPT: *I'm not surprised he went bust, considering the sort of risks he was taking.*

bus·ter /ˈbʌstəʳ/ n sl, esp. AmE, often derog (used as a form of address to a man): *Come here, buster!*

bus·tle¹ /ˈbʌsəl/ v [I] to be busily active, often with much noise: *She is always bustling about the house.* | *a bustling market town* | *a town bustling with activity* —**bustle** n [S

(of)] : *I enjoy the* **hustle and bustle of** *life in a big city.*

bustle² *n* a frame worn for holding out the back part of a woman's skirt in former times

bust-up /'··-/ *n sl* **1** a noisy quarrel **2** a coming to an end of a relationship or partnership; BREAKUP: *the bust-up of their marriage* —see also BUST **up**

bust·y /'bʌsti/ *adj infml* (of a woman) having large breasts

bus·y¹ /'bizi/ *adj* **1** having a lot of work to do; actively working or doing things: *She's rather busy now and can't see you until later.* | *busy with some important work* | *a busy man* | *All this filing will keep you busy for the rest of the morning.* [+*v-ing*] *I was too busy working to notice the time.* **2** full of work or activity: *a busy day|town* | *one of the busiest airports in the world* **3** *esp. AmE* (of telephones) in use; ENGAGED: *I'm sorry, the line is busy.* —see TELEPHONE (USAGE) **4** *derog* too full of small details: *This wallpaper's too busy for our bedroom, don't you think?* **5** **as busy as a bee/as bees** very busy —**·ily** *adv*: *busily working* | *The new government is busily changing all the laws made by its predecessors.*

busy² *v* [T (**with**)] to keep (oneself) busy: *To forget his troubles, he busied himself with answering letters|in his garden.*

bus·y·bod·y /'bizi,bɒdi‖-,bɑːdi/ *n derog* a person who takes too much interest in other people's affairs

busy Liz·zie /,bizi 'lizi/ *n BrE* a popular POT PLANT which grows close to the soil, spreads quickly, and has usu. pink flowers

busy sig·nal /'·· ,··/ *AmE* ‖ **engaged tone** *BrE*— *n* the sound one hears when the number one is calling on the telephone is already in use

but¹ /bət; *strong* bʌt/ *conj* **1** against what might be expected; in spite of this: *The situation looked desperate, but they didn't give up hope.* | *They are poor but proud.* | *It was cheap, but it goes quite well.* **2** yet at the same time; on the other hand: *It wasn't cheap, but it's very good.* | *These changes will cost quite a lot, but they will save us money in the long run.* | *an expensive but immensely useful book* | *It has some limitations,* **but then (again)** *what do you expect from a £100 computer?* **3** rather; instead: *They own not one but three houses!* | *The purpose of the scheme is not to help the employers but to provide work for young people.* **4** except that; however: *He would have won easily, but he fell and broke his leg.* | *I would like to go, but I'm too busy.* | *We were coming to see you, but it rained (so we didn't).* | *We had no alternative but to dismiss her.* | *There's no doubt|no question but (that) he's guilty.* | (*lit*) *There was not a man but had tears in his eyes.* (=they all had tears in their eyes) | **But for** (=without) *your help I'd be stranded.* **5** (used to express surprise, disagreement, or other strong feeling: *But how wonderful!* | *But that's outrageous!* **6** (used to give force to a statement): *It'll be the event of the year — everyone, but everyone, is coming.* **7** (used to change the subject) anyway: *But now to the main question...*

but² *prep* **1** other than; except: *There's no one here but me.* | *You can come any day but Thursday.* | *This car has been nothing but trouble!* | *Who but George would do such a thing?* | *What can we do but sit and wait?* **2** **the last/next but one/two/three** *esp. BrE* one/two/three etc. from the last/next: *His house is the last but one in this street.* —see also **all but** (ALL²)

▷ USAGE Compare **but, except,** and **save.** In this sentence we can use all three: *We're all here* **but/except/save** (*fml*) *Mary.* But in this sentence but cannot be used: *The window is never opened* **except/save** *in summer.* Use **but** only after words like *no, all, nobody, anywhere, everything,* or after question-words like *who?, where?, what?* **But** is usually followed by a noun or pronoun: *Who else* **but** *John would have played a trick like that?* | *They gave a toy to everyone* **but** *me.*◁

but³ *adv* **1** *esp. lit* only; just: *He is still but a child!* | *We can but try.* **2** *AmE sl* (used to add force): *Go there but fast!* | *They're rich, but I mean rich!*

but⁴ /bʌt/ *n* **(There are) no buts about it** *infml* (There is) no doubt about it or argument against it —see also **ifs and buts** (IF²)

bu·tane /'bjuːteɪn/ *n* [U] a natural gas used for cooking, heating, and lighting

butch /bʊtʃ/ *adj derog* (of a woman) showing a lot of male

tendencies; sometimes used as an offensive word to describe LESBIANS

Butch Cas·si·dy and The Sun·dance Kid /,bʊtʃ ,kæsɪdi ənd ðə 'sʌndɑːns ,kɪd‖-,dæns-/ a film made in 1969 with Robert Redford and Paul Newman, about two American BANDITS who were hunted and finally died in a SHOOT-OUT

Robert Redford and Paul Newman in *Butch Cassidy and The Sundance Kid*

butch·er¹ /'bʊtʃəʳ/ *n* **1** a person who owns or works in a shop (**butcher's**) which sells meat: *I bought some lamb at the butcher's.* **2** a person who causes suffering or death cruelly and unnecessarily

butcher² *v* [T] **1** to kill (animals) and prepare them for sale as food **2** to kill (esp. large numbers of people) bloodily or unnecessarily —see KILL (USAGE) **3** *infml* to spoil through carelessness or lack of skill: *That hairdresser really butchered my hair — it looks awful.*

butch·er·y /'bʊtʃəri/ *n* [U] **1** the preparation of meat for sale **2** cruel and unnecessary killing of human beings

Bute /bjuːt/ **1** an island off the coast of SW Scotland **2** a former COUNTY of W Scotland, including the islands of Arran and Bute, now part of Strathclyde REGION

Bu·the·lez·i /,buːtə'leɪzi/, **Chief Man·go·su·thu Gat·sha** /'mæŋɡəʊ,suːtuː 'ɡætʃə/ (1928–) the South African leader of the Zulu Inkatha movement

but·ler /'bʌtləʳ/ *n* (esp. formerly) the chief male servant of a house, in charge of the others. In Britain, the STEREOTYPE of a butler is of a very calm, EFFICIENT, polite man who has no sense of humour and never appears to be shocked or surprised by anything. People sometimes make jokes about the fact that, in old British DETECTIVE stories in which someone is murdered, it is often the butler who is found to be the murderer.

butler

Butler, Rhett /ret/ the main male character in the film *Gone With the Wind,* played by Clark Gable —see colour picture on page 685

But·lins /'bʌtlɪnz/ a group of British holiday camps, established by Billy Butlin (1899–1980). Everything is provided within these camps at a reasonable price and they are popular esp. with families and working-class people: *We always go to Butlins for our holidays.* —see also PONTINS

butt¹ /bʌt/ *v* [I;T] to strike or push against (someone or something) with the head or horns: *butting its head against the wall* —**butt** *n* : *The goat gave me a butt in the stomach!*

butt in *phr v* [I (**on**)] *sl, often derog* to interrupt, usu. by speaking: *Stop butting in (on our conversation)!*

butt² *n* [(**of, for**)] a person or thing that people make fun of: *Poor John was the butt of/for all their jokes.*

butt³ *n* **1** a large, thick, or bottom end of something: *a rifle butt* | *a cigarette butt* (=the last unsmoked end) **2** *sl*

American Homes

a mobile home

an apartment building

a brownstone

a house in New England

a ranch house

row houses

a bungalow

suburban semi-detached houses

a council house

a housing estate

a thatched cottage

a tower block

terraced houses

part of the body on which a person sits: *Get off your butt and do some work!*

butt⁴ *n* a large barrel for liquids

butte /bjuːt/ *n AmE* a hill which stands on its own and has steep sides and a flat top

but·ter¹ /ˈbʌtəʳ/ *n* [U] **1** fairly solid yellow fat made from milk or cream and spread on bread, used in cooking, etc.: *a butter dish* —compare SOFT MARGARINE **2** **Butter wouldn't melt in his/her mouth** *infml* He/She pretends to be kind, harmless, sincere, etc. but is not really so — ~**y** *adj* : *a buttery taste* | *buttery fingers*

butter² *v* [T] to spread butter on: *to butter a slice of bread* **butter** sbdy. ↔ **up** *phr v* [T] *infml* to praise (someone) too much with the hope of gaining something in return; FLATTER

butter bean /ˈ·· ·/ *n* [*usu. pl.*] a large pale yellow bean, often sold in its dried form

but·ter·cream /ˈbʌtəkriːm‖-ər-/ *n* a soft creamy spread made with butter and sugar and used inside or on top of cakes: *buttercream icing/filling*

but·ter·cup /ˈbʌtəkʌp‖-ər-/ *n* a common small yellow wild flower which often grows in fields —see picture at FLOWER

but·ter·fin·gers /ˈbʌtəˌfɪŋgəz‖ˈbʌtərˌfɪŋgərz/ *n* **butterfingers** *infml* someone who often drops things they are carrying or trying to catch

but·ter·fly /ˈbʌtəflaɪ‖-ər-/ *n* **1** [C] a type of insect with large often beautifully-coloured wings, which develops from a CATERPILLAR —compare MOTH (1), and see picture at METAMORPHOSIS **2** [C] someone who seems to be only interested in pleasure: *a social butterfly* **3** [(*the*) S] a way of swimming on one's front, moving the arms together over one's head while kicking the feet up and down together **4** **have butterflies (in one's stomach)** *infml* to feel very nervous before doing something

but·ter·milk /ˈbʌtəˌmɪlk‖-ər-/ *n* [U] the liquid that remains after butter is made from milk

butter moun·tain /ˈ·· ˌ··/ *n* [*the*] the large SURPLUS of butter which has been built up by the countries of the EC

but·ter·scotch /ˈbʌtəskɒtʃ‖-ərskɑːtʃ/ *n* [U] a sweet food made from sugar and butter boiled together

but·tock /ˈbʌtək/ *n* [*usu. pl.*] either of the two fleshy parts of the body on which a person sits

but·ton¹ /ˈbʌtn/ *n* **1** a small usu. circular fastener, made of plastic, bone, metal, etc., which is fixed to one part of a garment and passed through a hole in another part in order to join the two parts together: *One of the buttons has come off my shirt.* | *Will you help me do up* (=fasten) *my buttons?* | (fig.) *a button nose* (–a small broad flattish nose) sits—see picture at FASTENER **2** also **push button**— a button-like object that is pressed to start a machine: *I pressed the button, and the bell rang.* | *Push this button to call the elevator.* **3** *AmE* a small metal or plastic BADGE: *He had buttons all over his lapels.* **4** **on the button** *sl, esp. AmE* exactly right or on time —see also BUTTONS, PUSH-BUTTON, **bright as a button** (BRIGHT)

button² *v* [I;T (UP)] to (cause to) close or fasten with buttons: *Button (up) your coat — it's cold outside.* | *My dress buttons at the back.* **button up** *phr v* **1** [I] *sl* to keep quiet; SHUT up: *Button up, will you — I'm trying to get on with some work!* **2** [T] (**button** sthg. ↔ **up**) *infml* to complete successfully: *The new contract is all buttoned up now.*

button-down /ˈ·· ·/ *adj* [A] having the ends (of a collar) fastened to the garment with buttons: *a button-down collar/shirt*

but·ton·hole¹ /ˈbʌtnhəʊl/ *n* **1** a hole for a button to be put through to fasten a shirt, coat, etc. **2** *BrE*‖**boutonniere** *AmE* a flower to wear in a buttonhole or pinned to one's coat or dress: *wearing a rose as a buttonhole*

buttonhole² *v* [T] to stop (someone) and force them to join in a conversation: *She buttonholed me in the corridor and asked me about my plans.*

but·tons /ˈbʌtnz/ *n old-fash for* BELLBOY

Buttons a character in the PANTOMIME *Cinderella*. He is Cinderella's friend.

button-through /ˈ·· ·/ *BrE n* (of a piece of clothing) fastened (FASTEN) from the top to the bottom with buttons: *a button-through skirt/dress*

but·tress¹ /ˈbʌtrəs/ *n* a solid structure built against a wall as a support —see also FLYING BUTTRESS

buttress² *v* [T (UP, with)] to support or strengthen (as if) with a buttress: *Buttressed by its past profits, the company stayed in business through a difficult period.*

but·ty /ˈbʌti/ *n BrE dial for* SANDWICH

bux·om /ˈbʌksəm/ *adj apprec* (of a woman) attractively fat and healthy-looking, esp. having large breasts: *a buxom barmaid* —compare BOSOMY

buy¹ /baɪ/ *v* **bought** /bɔːt/ **1** [I;T] to obtain (something) by paying money: *We bought the house for £75,000.* | *Whether you are buying or selling, our prices are the best in town!* | *I'll buy the drinks.* [+obj(i)+obj(d)] *Let me buy you a drink.* [+obj+for] *Let me buy a drink for you.* | *We bought it from/(infml) off our neighbours.* [+obj+adj] *I bought my car cheap/secondhand.* | *I bought it for a song.* (=at a very small price) | *A pound doesn't buy as much now as it did ten years ago.* | (fig.) *They bought peace with their freedom.* —opposite **sell 2** [T] *sl* to accept; be willing to believe: *The police will never buy that story!* **3 buy it** *AmE infml* to die, esp. as the result of an accident: *He fell off a cliff and bought it.* **4 buy time** *infml* to delay an action or decision in order to give oneself more time: *I tried to buy time by telling them their cheque was in the post.*
buy sthg. ↔ **in** *phr v* [T] *BrE* to buy (a supply of something) in case of future need
buy into sthg. *phr v* [T] *AmE infml* to believe (an idea): *I could never buy into that Scientology stuff.*
buy sbdy. ↔ **off** *phr v* [T] to pay money to (someone) in order to persuade them not to cause trouble or carry out a threat; BRIBE
buy sbdy./sthg. ↔ **out** *phr v* [T] **1** to gain control of (a business) by buying all the shares and business rights of (other people in the business): *to buy out a business* | *He bought his partner out.* —see also BUYOUT **2** [(**of**)] to gain (someone's) freedom, esp. formerly from the armed forces or slavery by paying money: *to buy oneself out (of the army)*
buy sthg. ↔ **up** *phr v* [T] to buy all the supplies of: *All the available building land has been bought up by property developers.*

buy² *n infml* something bought, esp. something of value at a low price: *It's a good buy at that price!* | *That dress was a bad buy — I've only worn it once.*

buy·er /ˈbaɪəʳ/ *n* a person who buys, esp. professionally for a company or large shop: *a buyer for Harrods* —compare SELLER (1)

buyer's mar·ket /ˌ·· ˈ··, ˈ·· ˌ··/ *n* [S] a situation in which goods are plentiful, buyers have a lot of choice, and prices tend to be low —compare SELLER'S MARKET

buy·out /ˈbaɪaʊt/ *n* a situation in which a person or group gains control of a company by buying all or most of its shares: *a management buyout* (=by which the managers of a company gain control of it) —see also BUY **out**

buzz¹ /bʌz/ *v* **1** [I] to make the continuous sound that bees make; HUM: *the buzzing of the bees* | (fig.) *The crowd/room buzzed with excitement.* **2** [I (**for**);T] to call (someone) by using a buzzer: *She buzzed (for) her secretary.* **3** [T] *infml* to fly low and fast over: *Planes buzzed the crowd as a warning.*
buzz off *phr v* [I *usu. imperative*] *sl* to go away: *Buzz off and stop bothering me!*

buzz² *n* **1** [C] a buzzing sound **2** [S] *infml* a telephone call: *I'll just give him a buzz.* **3** also **buzz cut** *AmE infml* a CREW CUT

buz·zard /ˈbʌzəd‖-ərd/ *n* **1** *BrE* a large bird (a kind of HAWK) that kills and eats other creatures **2** *AmE* a large black bird (a kind of VULTURE) that eats dead flesh

buzz·er /ˈbʌzəʳ/ *n* (the sound of) an electric signalling apparatus that buzzes: *Come in when you hear the buzzer.*

buzz saw /ˈ· ·/ *n AmE for* CIRCULAR SAW

buzz·word /ˈbʌzwɜːd‖-wɜːrd/ *n sometimes derog* a word or phrase related to a specialized subject, which is thought to express something important but is often hard to understand: *the latest computer buzzword*

BWI /ˌbiː dʌbəljuː ˈaɪ/ Baltimore-Washington International Airport; a large airport between Baltimore, Maryland and Washington, DC

by¹ /baɪ/ *prep* **1** (used, esp. with a passive verb, to show the person or thing that performs an action or causes a result): *I was attacked by a dog.* | *The building was designed by a famous architect.* | *Our crops were destroyed by the storm.* | *The plan is opposed by most of the members.* | *a request by the police for more public cooperation* | *We are all alarmed by the rise in violent crime.* | *We were held up by a traffic jam.* —see WITH (USAGE) **2** through the use or means of: *to travel by car|bus|train* | *Send it by air mail.* | *You can reserve the tickets by phone.* | *It's not fair to judge people by their appearance.* | *I know her by sight.* (=I know what she looks like.) [+*v-ing*] *They put out the fire by pouring water on it.* | *She earns her living by selling insurance.* **3** passing through or along: *They came in by the back door.* | *It's quicker if you go by the main road.* **4** near; beside: *standing by the window* | *Sit by me.* | *I always have|keep a spare set by me.* (=close enough to reach easily) **5** past: *He walked|passed by me without noticing me.* | *I go by the house every day.* **6** (used to show the name of the person who wrote a book, directed a film, made a work of art, etc.): *a play by Shakespeare* | *Jaws – a film by Steven Spielberg based on the novel by Peter Benchley* **7** not later than; before: *Be here by four o'clock.* | *Will you finish it by tomorrow?* | *By the time the doctor arrived the patient had died.* | *By 1995 the population will have risen to over 20 million.* **8** in accordance with: *to play by the rules* | *Profits were £6 million, but by their standards this is quite a bad result.* **9** to the amount or degree of: *The price of oil fell by a further $2 a barrel.* | *They overcharged me by £3.* | *It's better by far.* (=much better) **10** (used to show the part taken, held, etc.): *He led her by the hand.* | *I grabbed the hammer by the handle.* **11** (in expressions of strong feeling and solemn promises): *By God he's done it!* | *to swear by heaven* **12** (in measurements and numbers): *a room 15 feet by 20 feet* | *to divide 10 by 5* | *to multiply 10 by 5* **13** (used to show a rate or quantity): *paid by the hour* | *You can buy them singly or by the dozen.* **14** (used to show the size of units or groups that follow each other): *little by little* | *The animals went in two by two.* | *day by day* **15** during: *Cats sleep by day and hunt by night.* **16** with regard to: *a doctor by profession* | *French by birth* | *It's alright by me if you go.* **17** (used without **a** or **the**) as a result of: *I did it by mistake|by accident.* | *better by design* **18** having (the stated person or animal) as a father: *She had two children by her first husband.* **19 (all) by oneself** (completely) alone: *He was sitting by himself.* | *I did it all by myself!*

by² *adv* **1** past: *He walked by without noticing me.* | *A lot of time has gone by since then.* **2** near: *some people standing by* **3** away or aside for future use: *Try to put|keep a bit of money by for the holidays.* **4** *esp. AmE* at or to another's home: *Stop by|Come by for a drink after work.* **5 by and by** *esp. lit or old-fash* before long; soon: *You will forget him by and by.* **6 by and large** on the whole; in general: *By and large, your plan is a good one.* **7 by the by** (used when talking about a subject of secondary importance); INCIDENTALLY: *I was doing some shopping yesterday, by the by, when I saw Mrs Jones...*

by- see WORD FORMATION

bye¹ /baɪ/ also **bye-bye** /ˌ·ˈ·‖ˈ··/— *interj infml* goodbye

bye² *n* (in cricket) a run made off a ball that the hitter (BATSMAN) did not touch

bye³ *n* a situation in a sporting competition in which a player or a team does not have to play against another team until the next round of the competition: *Our volleyball team has three byes this season.*

bye-byes /ˈbaɪbaɪz/ *esp. BrE*‖**beddy-bye** *AmE*— *n* **go to bye-byes** (used by or to children) to go to sleep

by·e·lec·tion , bye-election /ˈ· ·ˌ··/ *n esp. BrE* a special election held between regular elections to fill a position whose former holder has left it or died

By·el·o·rus·sia /biˌeləʊˈrʌʃə/ *n* see BELORUSSIA

by·gone¹ /ˈbaɪɡɒn‖-ɡɔːn/ *adj* [A *no comp.*] gone by; past; former: *in bygone days* | *relics of a bygone era*

bygone² *n* **1** a bygone object or machine no longer in use **2 let bygones be bygones** *infml* to forget and forgive past quarrels

By·graves /ˈbaɪɡreɪvz/, **Max** /mæks/ (1922–) an English singer and entertainer who used to appear in a television SERIES called *Singalongamax* and is popular esp. with older people in Britain

by·law /ˈbaɪlɔː/ *n* **1** *BrE* a special law or rule made not by a national government, but by a local council, a railway, etc. **2** *AmE* a rule made by an organization for governing its own affairs – see also extra information on page 568

by-line /ˈ· ·/ *n* a line at the beginning of a newspaper or magazine article giving the writer's name

BYOB /ˌbiː ɔːˌ əʊ ˈbiː/ (used on a party invitation, encouraging someone to bring some drink to the party with them) Bring Your Own Bottle or Bring Your Own Booze

by·pass¹ /ˈbaɪpɑːs‖-pæs/ *n* **1** a road that passes round the side of a town or other busy area: *Take the bypass to avoid the traffic in the town centre.* **2** *tech* an apparatus for sending a flow of gas, liquid, etc., round, instead of through, something else: *He's had heart bypass surgery.* (=directing blood through new blood tubes outside the heart)

bypass² *v* [T] to avoid, esp. by going round: *If we bypass the town we'll miss the rush hour traffic.* | *I bypassed the usual complaints procedure by writing directly to the owner of the company.*

by·play /ˈbaɪpleɪ/ *n* [U] action of less importance going on at the same time as the main action, esp. in a play

by-prod·uct /ˈ· ˌ··/ *n* [(**of**)] **1** something additional that is produced during the making of something else: *Silver is often obtained as a by-product during the separation of lead from rock.* **2** an additional result, sometimes unexpected or unintended —compare END PRODUCT

Byrds /bɜːdz‖ˈbɜːrdz/, **The** an American popular music group, successful in the 1960s

byre /baɪəʳ/ *n BrE old-fash* a farm building for cattle; COWSHED

Byron /ˈbaɪərən/, **Lord** (1788–1824) an English writer of ROMANTIC and SATIRICAL poetry, best known for poems such as *Childe Harold's Pilgrimage* and *Don Juan*. He is also remembered for his romantic life which included many famous love affairs and for his death of fever in Greece while fighting against the Turks for Greek independence.

by·stand·er /ˈbaɪˌstændəʳ/ *n* a person standing near, but not taking part in, what is happening; ONLOOKER: *The police asked some of the bystanders about the accident.* | *I wasn't involved in the fight – I'm just an* **innocent bystander.**

byte /baɪt/ *n tech* a unit of computer information equal to eight BITS³ —compare BIT³

by·way /ˈbaɪweɪ/ also **by·road** /ˈbaɪrəʊd/— *n* a small road or path which is not much used or known: *the highways and byways of Britain* | (fig.) *the byways* (=less well-known parts) *of English literature*

by·word /ˈbaɪwɜːd‖-wɜːrd/ *n* [(**for**)] (the name of) a person, place, or thing that is regarded as representing some quality: *The dictator's name had become a byword for cruelty and injustice.*

by·zan·tine /baɪˈzæntaɪn, -tiːn, bɪ-‖ˈbɪzəntiːn, -taɪn/ *adj fml, often derog* secret, indirect, and difficult to understand; very COMPLICATED: *the byzantine complexity of our tax laws*

By·zan·tine *adj* of or concerning the ancient city of Byzantium or the EMPIRE of which it was the centre. Constantine the Great was responsible for the establishment of the Byzantine empire, which is said to date from the setting up in 330 AD of the city of Constantinople, on the place where Byzantium had formerly stood: *Byzantine art|architecture|music*

By·zan·ti·um /bɪˈzæntiəm, baɪ-‖-ˈzænʃiəm/ an ancient city, centre of the Byzantine Empire. The city was renamed **Constantinople** by Constantine the Great, and is now called **Istanbul**.

C

C, c /siː/ **C's, c's** or **Cs, cs** **1** the third letter of the English alphabet **2** the ROMAN NUMERAL (=number) for 100 **3** a mark given to a student's work to show that it is of average standard —see also GRADE¹ (3)

c written abbrev. for **1** also **ca**— CIRCA (=about): born c 1830 **2** CUBIC **3** CENTIMETRE(s) **4** (in a small circle) COPYRIGHT

C¹ **1** a note in Western music; the musical KEY¹ (4) based on this note **2** a mark given to a student's work, showing the third level of quality (in US schools, average work): a C student

C² written abbrev. for: CELSIUS (=CENTIGRADE): Water boils at 100°C.

C2 /ˌsiː ˈtuː/ n BrE tech a WORKING CLASS person; used by companies, political parties, etc. when trying to persuade working class people to buy their products, vote for them, etc.: trying to capture the C2 vote

C4 written abbrev. for CHANNEL 4

CA written abbrev. for CALIFORNIA

CAA /ˌsiː eɪ ˈeɪ/ [the] Civil Aviation Authority; an organization which is in charge of aircraft companies and air ROUTEs in Britain

cab /kæb/ n **1** a taxi: Shall we walk or take a cab|go by cab?—see picture at TAXI **2** the part of a bus, railway engine, etc., in which the driver sits or stands **3** (in former times) a horse-drawn carriage for one

CAB /ˌsiː eɪ ˈbiː/ n abbrev. for: CITIZENS' ADVICE BUREAU

ca·bal /kə'bæl/ n [C+sing./pl. v] derog a small group of people who make secret plans for (esp. political) action

ca·ba·la cabbala, cabala /kə'bɑːlə/ also **kabala, kabbala, kabbalah** n **1** [U] a system of Jewish belief based on getting hidden meanings from the Old Testament and other writings, e.g. to see into the future **2** [C] an old, mysterious, or secret art or subject —**cabalism** /'kæbəlɪzəm/ n [U] —**cabalistic** /ˌkæbə'lɪstɪk◂/ adj

cab·a·ret /'kæbəreɪ‖ˌkæbə'reɪ/ n [C;U] (a) performance of popular music and dancing while guests in a restaurant have a meal, usu. at night —see picture at Liza MINELLI

cab·bage /'kæbɪdʒ/ n **1** [C;U] a large round vegetable with thick green leaves used (usu. cooked) as food —compare LETTUCE, and see picture at VEGETABLE **2** [C] BrE infml a derog an inactive person who takes no interest in anything **b vegetable** AmE someone who has lost the ability to think, move, etc. as a result of illness, brain damage, etc.

Cabbage Patch doll /ˈ··· ˌ·/ n tdmk a type of doll which looks like a fat child. Cabbage Patch dolls are all slightly different from one another.

cab·by , cab·bie /'kæbi/ also **cab·driv·er** /'kæbˌdraɪvəʳ/ esp. AmE— n infml a taxi driver. In Britain, cabbies, esp. **London cabbies**, are famous for talking a lot to their passengers and expressing strong opinions, esp. about politics.

ca·ber /'keɪbəʳ/ n a long heavy wooden pole used in Scotland in a sports competition (**tossing the caber**) in which the pole is thrown into the air as a test of strength

Cab·er·net Sau·vi·gnon /ˌkæbəneɪ səʊviːnˈjɒn ‖ ˌkæbərneɪ səʊviːnˈjəʊn/ n [U] **1** a type of GRAPE grown for wine **2** a popular red wine produced in various parts of the world

cab·in /'kæbɪn/ n **1** a room on a ship usu. used for sleeping **2** the small enclosed space at the front of an aircraft in which the pilot sits **3** a small roughly built usu. wooden house: They lived in a little log cabin in the mountains.

cabin boy /'·· ·/ n a boy who is a servant on a ship

cabin class /'·· ·/ n [U] (on a ship) the travelling conditions which are better and dearer than TOURIST CLASS but worse and cheaper than FIRST CLASS: I always travel cabin class.| a cabin-class ticket

cabin cruis·er /'·· ˌ··/ n a large motor boat with one or more cabins

cab·i·net /'kæbˌɪnˌɪt/ n **1** a piece of furniture, with shelves and drawers or doors, used for storing or showing things: a filing cabinet | a medicine cabinet | I keep my collection of old china in the cabinet. —compare CUPBOARD **2** [+sing./pl. v] (often cap.) (in various countries) the most important ministers of the government, who meet as a group to make decisions or to advise the head of the government: The cabinet meets|meet tomorrow to discuss this problem. | This will be discussed in cabinet (=in a meeting of the cabinet) next week.

▶CULTURAL NOTE In Britain the cabinet has about 20 members who are chosen by the Prime Minister. In the US the members of the cabinet are chosen by the President, but they are not chosen from among the members of the government. ◀

cabinet-mak·er /'··· ˌ··/ n a maker or repairer of fine furniture

Cabinet Min·is·ter /ˌ··· '···/ n a government minister who is a member of the Cabinet

Cabinet re·shuf·fle /ˌ··· ·'··/ n a change in the members of the British Cabinet, decided by the Prime Minister, in which some members are given different jobs, some members lose their job, and new members are brought in

cabin fe·ver /'·· ˌ··/ n [U] AmE a condition that results from one being forced to spend too much time indoors, esp. in winter because of bad weather. Sufferers become very bad-tempered and may behave strangely.

ca·ble¹ /'keɪbəl/ n **1** [C;U] (a length of) thick strong usu. metal rope used on ships, to support bridges, etc. **2** [C] a set of wires which carry telephone messages, television signals, etc.: an underwater telephone cable | a cable connecting a printer to a computer **3** [C] also **ca·ble·gram** /-ˌgræm/ fml— a TELEGRAM **4** [U] also **cable stitch** /'·· ·/— a twisted and knotted pattern of thread, used in knitting (KNIT) **5** [U] CABLE TELEVISION

cable² v [I;T] to send (something) or tell (someone) by TELEGRAM: We cabled the news to London. [+obj(i)+obj(d)] She cabled him some money.

Cable and Wire·less /ˌ··· '··/ n a former British TELECOMMUNICATIONS company now owned by Mercury Communications

cable car /'·· ·/ n **1** a vehicle which is supported in the air and pulled by a continuous cable, used for carrying people to the tops of mountains or other steep slopes **2** a vehicle used in cities, esp. in San Francisco, California, which is pulled by a continuously moving underground cable

cable rail·way /'·· ˌ··/ n a railway along which vehicles are pulled by a continuous cable driven by a motor, used esp. where there are very steep slopes

cable tel·e·vi·sion /ˌ·· '····, ˌ·· ··'··/ also **cable TV** /ˌ·· ·'·/, **cable**— n [U] a system of broadcasting television by cable, usu. paid for by the user, and giving the user a choice of more CHANNELs to watch than the usual channels which every television receives. It is also used in areas where the television picture would otherwise not be very good. In the US, different cable television companies operate in different areas, sometimes offering a large number of different channels for a monthly charge. —compare SATELLITE TELEVISION

ca·boo·dle /kə'buːdl/ n **the whole caboodle** also **kit and caboodle** esp. AmE sl the whole lot; everything

ca·boose /kə'buːs/ n AmE for GUARD'S VAN

Cab·ot /'kæbət/, **John** (died 1498) an Italian EXPLORER who reached the coast of N America in 1497

cab rank /'· ·/ also **cabstand** n for TAXI RANK

Ca·bri·ni /kæ'briːni/, **Mother Fran·ces Xa·vi·er** /'frɑːnsˌs 'zeɪviəʳ‖ 'fræn-/ (1850–1909) an Italian-born American NUN who became the first American to be named a SAINT (=holy person) by the Catholic Church. Many churches and other institutions are named after her.

cab·ri·o·let /'kæbriəleɪ‖ˌkæbriə'leɪ/ n a CONVERTIBLE 2

cab·stand /'kæbstænd/ n esp. AmE for TAXI RANK

ca·cao /kə'kaʊ/ n [C] (the tropical tree which produces) a seed from which COCOA and chocolate are made

cac·cia·to·re /ˌkætʃə'tɔːri‖ˌkɑːtʃ-/ adj [after n] AmE (of meat) cooked with TOMATOes, MUSHROOMs, and HERBs: chicken cacciatore

cache /kæʃ/ n [(of)] a secret store of things, or the place where they are hidden: *Police discovered a cache of weapons in the terrorists' hide-out.*

cach·et /'kæʃeɪ‖kæ'ʃeɪ/ n [U] something that brings respect; PRESTIGE: *He gets a lot of cachet from having such a famous sister.*

cack-hand·ed /ˌkæk 'hændɪd◂/ adj BrE infml awkward and unskilful; CLUMSY

cack·le[1] /'kækəl/ v [I] **1** to make the noise a hen makes, esp. after laying an egg **2** to laugh or talk unpleasantly with henlike sounds: *old ladies cackling over the latest scandal* —**ler** n

cackle[2] n **1** the sound of cackling, esp. a short high laugh: *cackles of amusement* **2 cut the cackle** BrE sl to stop talking when important action needs to be taken

ca·coph·o·ny /kəˈkɒfəni‖kəˈkɑː-/ n [S] an unpleasant mixture of loud sounds —**nous** adj

cac·tus /'kæktəs/ n -**tuses** or -**ti** /taɪ/ a desert plant protected by sharp points (PRICKLES), with thick fleshy stems and leaves

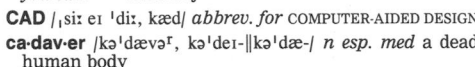

cactuses

cad /kæd/ n old-fash derog a man who behaves dishonourably: *You cheated, you cad!* — **~ dish** adj

CAD /ˌsiː eɪ ˈdiː, kæd/ abbrev. for COMPUTER-AIDED DESIGN

ca·dav·er /kəˈdævəʳ, kəˈdeɪ-‖kəˈdæ-/ n esp. med a dead human body

ca·dav·er·ous /kəˈdævərəs/ n fml looking like a dead body; very pale; thin and unhealthy: *his hollow cadaverous cheeks*

Cad·bu·ry /'kædbəri/ n tdmk [U] a British company which makes chocolate: *Cadbury's Dairy Milk chocolate*

CAD/CAM /'kædkæm/ n [U] computer-aided design and manufacture; the use of computers to plan and make industrial products

cad·die also **caddy** /'kædi/ n a person who carries GOLF CLUBs for someone else who is playing —see picture at GOLF —**caddie** v [I (for)]

cad·dy /'kædi/ n **1** a TEA CADDY **2** caddie

ca·dence /'keɪdəns/ n **1 a** a regular beat of sound; RHYTHM **b** a set of CHORDs at the end of a phrase of music **2** the rise and fall of the human voice, esp. in reading poetry

ca·den·za /kəˈdenzə/ n tech a part of a piece of music, esp. a CONCERTO, that is very decorative and is played by a single musician

Cad·er Id·ris /ˌkædər ˈɪdrɪs‖ˌkɑː-/ a mountain RIDGE in W Wales

ca·det /kəˈdet/ n **1** a person being trained to become an officer in one of the armed forces or the police **2** a member of a cadet corps

cadet corps /·'· ·/ n **cadet corps** [C+sing./pl. v] an organization which gives simple military training to pupils in some British schools

cadge /kædʒ/ v [I;T (from, off, for)] infml derog to get or try to get (something) by asking, esp. taking advantage of other people's generosity: *He's always cadging cigarettes (from/off me).* | *a dog cadging for scraps* — **cadger** n

Cadillac

Cad·il·lac /'kædɪlæk, -dəl-/ n tdmk a large American car, generally thought of as a quality car for richer people

cad·mi·um /'kædmiəm/ n [U] a soft bluish white metal that is a simple substance (ELEMENT)

ca·dre /'kɑːdəʳ, -drə, 'keɪdəʳ‖ 'kædri, 'kɑːdrə/ n **1** [+sing./pl. v] an inner group of highly trained and active people in a political party or military force **2** a member of such a group

Caer·nar·von, **Caernarfon** /kəˈnɑːvən‖kɑːrˈnɑːr-/ a small

holiday town on the coast of NW Wales. The INVESTITURE of Prince Charles took place at Caernarvon castle in 1969.

Caer·phil·ly /kəˈfɪli‖kɑːr-/ n [U] a type of white, not strong-tasting cheese originally made in Caerphilly, S Wales

Cae·sar, **Ju·li·us** /'siːzəʳ/, /'dʒuːliəs/ (100–44 BC) a Roman political leader, GENERAL, and historian. Most people think of Julius Caesar as a DICTATOR who was killed by his friend Brutus and whose story is told in Shakespeare's play *Julius Caesar*. —see also JULIUS CAESAR

cae·sar·e·an, **ce-**, **-ian** /sɪˈzeəriən/ also **caesarean sec·tion** /·ˌ··· '··/, **C-section** fml— n an operation in which a woman's body is cut open to allow a baby to be taken out, when an ordinary birth may be difficult: *Our first baby was born by caesarean.*

Caesar sal·ad /'·· ˌ··/ n a cold dish made with LETTUCE and cooked eggs

cae·su·ra /sɪˈzjʊərə‖sɪˈʒʊərə, sɪˈzʊərə/ n a pause in the middle of a line of poetry

caf·e, **café** /'kæfeɪ‖kæˈfeɪ, kə-/ n a small restaurant where light meals and drinks (in Britain only nonalcoholic drinks) are served. Cafes are used by people looking for a cheap meal or drink or somewhere to pass some time —compare RESTAURANT, COFFEE SHOP

caf·e·te·ri·a /ˌkæfɪˈtɪəriə/ n a restaurant where people collect their own food and drink and carry it to the tables, often in a shop, factory, college, etc. —compare CANTEEN

caf·e·tiere /ˌkæfəˈtjeəʳ/ n a special pot for making coffee. It has a metal FILTER which pushes the coffee GROUNDs to the bottom of the pot

caf·feine /'kæfiːn‖kæˈfiːn/ n [U] a drug found in coffee and tea, which acts as a STIMULANT (=something which makes people feel more active). Too much caffeine is now generally considered to be a bad thing and there has been an increase in caffeine-free drinks.

caf·tan, **kaftan** /'kæftæn‖kæfˈtæn/ n a long loose garment, usu. of cotton or silk, worn in the Near and Middle East. Caftans were very popular in Britain in the 1960s and 70s, esp. with HIPPIEs.

cage[1] /keɪdʒ/ n **1** an enclosure made of wires or bars in which animals or birds are kept or carried: *a bird cage* | *a tiger in its cage at the zoo* **2** an apparatus for raising and lowering people and equipment in a mine

cage[2] v [T] to put into a cage: *caged birds* | (fig.) *Mothers of young children often feel* **caged in** *staying at home all day.*

cag·ey /'keɪdʒi/ adj infml unwilling to talk freely or provide information; WARY: *She's very cagey about her past life.* —**ily** adv —**iness** n [U]

Cag·ney, **James** /'kægni/ (1904–86) an American film actor, best known for playing GANGSTERs and for the line "You dirty rat", which he is supposed to have said in one of his films

ca·goule /kəˈguːl/ n BrE a long light waterproof coat with a protective cover for the head, like a thin ANORAK

ca·hoots /kəˈhuːts/ n **in cahoots (with)** sl in partnership (with), usu. for a dishonest purpose: *The bank robbers and the police were in cahoots.* | *The bank robbers were in cahoots with the police.*

Cain /keɪn/ in the Bible, the eldest son of Adam and Eve, who killed his brother Abel out of jealousy — see also **raise Cain** (RAISE[1] (14))

Caine, **Sir Mi·chael** /keɪn/, /'maɪkəl/ (1933–) an English film actor well-known internationally and noted for his COCKNEY (=from London) ACCENT

ca·ique /kɑːˈiːk/ n a small boat used in the E Mediterranean

cairn /keən‖keərn/ n a pile of stones set up, esp. on mountain tops, to mark a place or remind people of someone or something

Cairn·gorms /'keəngɔːmz‖ 'keərngɔːrmz/ [the + P] a group of mountains in Scotland popular for walking, climbing, and skiing (SKI 2)

Cairns /keənz‖keərnz/ a city and port on the NE coast of Australia in the state of Queensland

Cai·ro /'kaɪərəʊ/ the capital city of Egypt, on the River Nile in the N of the country. Cairo is an important centre of business and government with many MUSEUMs, universities, and historic buildings. —see picture at DELTA

cais·son /ˈkeɪsən, kəˈsuːn‖ˈkeɪsɑːn, -sən/ n **1** also **cofferdam, coffer**– a large box filled with air, which allows people to work under water, e.g. when building bridges **2** a large box, usu. on two wheels, for carrying ᴀᴍ MUNITION

Caith·ness /ˈkeɪθnes/ a former COUNTY in NE Scotland, now part of Highland REGION

ca·jole /kəˈdʒəʊl/ v [I;T (**into, out of**)] to persuade by praise or false promises; COAX: *His technique is to cajole his staff rather than threaten them.* | *She's always cajoling people into doing things for her.*

Ca·jun /ˈkeɪdʒən/ n a member of the people living in S Louisiana, US, who are descended from French-Canadians. Cajuns have their own language, which is related to French, and they are also known for their music and their cooking, which is SPICY and uses esp. seafood. – **Cajun** adj : *Cajun music*/food –see also GUMBO and compare SOUL FOOD

cake¹ /keɪk/ n **1** [C;U] (a piece of) a soft food made by baking a sweet mixture of flour, eggs, sugar, etc.: *to bake a cake* | *a chocolate cake* | *a birthday cake* | *Would you like some cake*/*a slice of cake?* –compare BISCUIT; see also CHRISTMAS CAKE, CUP CAKE, MADEIRA CAKE **2** [C] (*often in comb.*) a flat shaped piece of something, esp. food: *a potato cake* | *a fishcake* | *a cake of soap* **3** [*the*+S] the total amount, esp. of money or goods, that is to be shared among everyone: *The people of the Third World want a bigger slice of the cake.* **4 have one's cake and eat it (too)** *infml* to have the advantages of something without the disadvantages that go with it: *You spend all your money on beer and then complain about being poor, but you can't have your cake and eat it, you know.* –see also PIECE OF CAKE **5 let them eat cake** a phrase which is believed to have been said by Marie Antoinette just before the French Revolution, when told that the poor people were hungry because they had no bread **6 take the cake** *AmE infml* to be more foolish or silly than anything else: *I've heard some pretty dumb ideas, but that takes the cake.*

cake² v **1** [T (**with**)] to cover thickly: *Her shoes were caked with mud.* **2** [I] to form a hard mass when dry: *Cheap lipstick always cakes.*

cake fork /ˈ· ·/ n a fork with one PRONG wider than the others and shaped like a small knife

cake tin /ˈ· ·/ *BrE* ‖ **cake pan** *AmE* ‖ a metal container for holding a cake while it is being baked

cal·a·bash /ˈkæləbæʃ/ n (a tropical American tree with) a large hard fruit whose shell can be dried and used as a bowl

cal·a·boose /ˌkæləˈbuːs‖ˈkæləbuːs/ n *AmE rare* a small prison

cal·a·brese /ˈkæləbriːs/ n *BrE* BROCCOLI

Cal·ais /ˈkæleɪ‖kæˈleɪ/ an industrial city and port in NW France, used esp. as a port for ferries (FERRY) from Dover, England

cal·a·mine lo·tion /ˌkæləmaɪn ˈləʊʃən/ n [U] a pink liquid used esp. to cool skin that has been burnt by the sun and to reduce pain or itching (ITCH)

ca·lam·i·ty /kəˈlæməti/ n a sudden terrible event causing great loss and suffering: *It would be a calamity for these people if the rains failed yet again.* –**-tous** adj : *a calamitous flood* –**-tously** adv

Calamity Jane /·ˌ··· ˈ·/ (about 1852–1903) an American from the time of the WILD WEST, remembered for her skill in shooting guns and her adventures as a rider for the PONY EXPRESS –see also Wild Bill HICKOK

cal·ci·fy /ˈkælsɪfaɪ/ v [I;T] to (cause to) become hard by the addition of LIME

cal·ci·um /ˈkælsiəm/ n [U] a silver-white metal that is a simple substance (ELEMENT) and is found in bones, teeth, and chalk

cal·cu·late /ˈkælkjʊleɪt/ v [I;T] **1** to find out or make a firm guess about (esp. an amount), esp. by using numbers: *They use a computer to calculate the cost of wages as a percentage of the company's income.* | *The government has to calculate the likely effects on revenues of a big drop in the oil price.* [+(that)] *The experts calculate that the market for these computers will expand by 200% in the next three years.* [+wh-] *The scientists calculated when the*

spacecraft would reach the moon. –see also INCALCULABLE **2 be calculated to (do something)** to be planned with the intention of (producing a particular result): *The new regulations are deliberately calculated to make cheating impossible.* | *The new system is hardly calculated to* (=is unlikely to) *make life easier!*

calculate on sthg. *phr v* [T] to depend on (something happening): [+obj/v-ing] *We calculated on an early start*/*on making an early start.* [+obj+v-ing] *Don't calculate on him agreeing with you.*

cal·cu·lat·ed /ˈkælkjʊleɪtɪd/ adj intentionally planned to gain a particular result: *a calculated threat* | *I took a calculated risk when I bought those shares.* –see also CALCULATE (2) – **~ly** adv

cal·cu·lat·ing /ˈkælkjʊleɪtɪŋ/ adj usu. derog making careful plans with the intention of bringing advantage to oneself, without considering the effects on other people: *a cold, calculating criminal*

cal·cu·la·tion /ˌkælkjʊˈleɪʃən/ n **1** [C;U] the act or result of calculating: *These calculations are based on the latest statistics.* **2** [U] care in planning, esp. for one's own advantage: *He lied with cold calculation.*

cal·cu·la·tor /ˈkælkjʊleɪtəʳ/ n a small machine which can perform calculations, such as adding and multiplying: *a pocket calculator* –see picture at MATHEMATICS

cal·cu·lus /ˈkælkjʊləs/ n -li /laɪ/ or -luses **1** [U] (in MATHEMATICS) a system for making calculations about quantities which are continually changing, such as the speed of a falling stone or the slope of a curved line –see also DIFFERENTIAL CALCULUS, INTEGRAL CALCULUS **2** [C] *med* a stone of chalky matter which sometimes forms in the body

Cal·cut·ta /kælˈkʌtə/ a city and port in east India on the Hooghly River and capital of West Bengal state. Calcutta is often thought of as a place with many very poor people. –see also BLACK HOLE OF CALCUTTA

Cal·der /ˈkɔːldəʳ/, **Al·ex·an·der** /ˌælɪgˈzaːndəʳ‖-ˈzæn-/ (1898–1976) an American SCULPTOR best known for his large outdoor works of art found in many cities, and his large MOBILES

cal·dron /ˈkɔːldrən/ n *AmE for* CAULDRON

Cal·e·do·ni·a /ˌkælɪˈdəʊniə/ *poet* originally the Roman name for northern Britain, now a name for Scotland, used mainly in names of companies –**Caledonian** /ˌkælɪˈdəʊniən/ adj

Caledonian Ca·nal /ˌ····· ·ˈ·/ [*the*] an artificial stretch of water in Scotland joining the Atlantic with the North Sea through a line of LOCHS (=lakes)

cal·en·dar /ˈkælɪndəʳ/ n **1** a printed table that lists the days, weeks, and months of the year: *a wall*/*desk calendar* | *According to the calendar my birthday falls on a Sunday this year.* | *a calendar watch* (=one which shows the date) **2** a system by which the year is divided into parts, and its beginning, end, and total length are fixed –see also GREGORIAN CALENDAR, HEGIRA CALENDAR **3** a list of important events in the year of a particular organization: *The presidential elections are the highlight of next year's political calendar.* | *According to the university calendar your examinations will be in June.* **4** *AmE for* DIARY (2)

calendar month /ˌ··· ˈ·/ n a month measured according to the CALENDAR (2), esp. one of the 12 months of the modern European system: *From January 1st to February 1st is one calendar month.* –compare LUNAR MONTH

calendar year /ˌ··· ˈ·/ n a YEAR (2)

cal·en·der /ˈkælɪndəʳ/ n *tech* a machine for rolling, pressing, and smoothing paper, cloth, etc.

calf¹ /kɑːf‖kæf/ n **calves** /kɑːvz‖kævz/ **1** [C] the young of the cow or of some other large animals such as the elephant –see MEAT (USAGE) **2** [U] calfskin: *a book bound in calf* **3 in calf** (of a cow) PREGNANT –see also **kill the fatted calf** (KILL¹ (5))

calf² n **calves** the fleshy back part of the human leg between the knee and the ankle

calf love /ˈ· ·/ n [U] PUPPY LOVE

calf·skin /ˈkɑːfˌskɪn‖ˈkæf-/ n [U] leather made from the skin of the calf: *calfskin boots*

Cal·gar·y /ˈkælgəri/ a city in S Alberta, Canada, on the Bow and Elbow rivers, which is an important centre for the oil and gas industries

Cal·i·ban /'kælɪ̯bæn/ a character in Shakespeare's play *The Tempest*, a half-human slave

cal·i·brate /'kælɪ̯breɪt/ v [T] to mark degrees and dividing points on (the scale of a measuring instrument)

cal·i·bra·tion /ˌkælɪ̯'breɪʃən/ n a set of degrees or measurement marks

cal·i·bre also **-ber** *AmE* /'kælɪ̯bəʳ/ n **1** [S;U] the level of quality, excellence, or ability of something or someone: *This work is of (a) very high calibre.* **2** [C] **a** the inside size (DIAMETER) of a tube or gun **b** the size of a bullet

cal·i·co¹ /'kælɪkəʊ/ n [U] a heavy cotton cloth

calico² *adj AmE* (of a cat or other animal) having three colours, usu. in spots of black and reddish-brown on white

Cal·i·for·ni·a /ˌkælɪ̯'fɔːniə‖-'fɔːrnjə/ *written abbrev.* **CA** a state in the SW of the US, whose major cities include Los Angeles and San Francisco. Disneyland and Hollywood are both in California. California is usu. thought of as a sunny place where young, healthy-looking people live and where new and unusual ideas are first put into practice – see colour map on pages 1374-5

Ca·lig·u·la /kə'lɪgjŭlə/ (AD 12–41) a Roman EMPEROR famous for being mad and cruel

cal·i·pers /'kælɪ̯pəz‖-əʳz/ n [P] *AmE for* CALLIPERS

ca·liph , khalif /'keɪlɪ̯f/ n (*often cap.*) a Muslim ruler: *the caliph of Baghdad*

ca·li·phate , khalifate /'keɪlɪ̯feɪt/ n the country or period of rule of a caliph

cal·is·then·ics /ˌkælɪ̯s'θenɪks/ n *AmE* CALLISTHENICS

calk /kɔːk/ v [T] to CAULK

call¹ /kɔːl/ v **1** [I;T (OUT)] to speak or say in a loud clear voice; shout: *The teacher called (out) the names of everyone in the class.* | *"Stop," he called out.* | *The frightened child called (out) for help.* | *The fishermen called to the men on the shore.* | *I've been calling for five minutes; why don't they come?* **2** [T] to ask or order (someone) to come by speaking loudly, sending an order or message, etc.; SUMMON: *Mother is calling me.* | *He called me over to his desk.* | *She has been called to give evidence to the inquiry.* | *The minister called the union leaders to a meeting.* | *Call a doctor!* | *If you don't get out I'll call the police.* | *I must go now* – **duty calls!** **3** [I;T] to (try to) speak to by telephone: *I called him this morning but he was out.* | *The office called to find out where you were.* –see TELEPHONE (USAGE) **4** [I (**at, in, on, for**)] *esp. BrE* a to make a short visit to someone: *Let's call (in) on John for ten minutes.* | *You were out when we called.* | *He called to collect the money.* | *Do you think we should call at Bob's while we're in London?* **b** (esp. of people selling things) to make regular visits: *The milkman calls every day.* **5** [T] to cause to happen by making an official declaration: *The prime minister called an election.* | *The union leaders are calling a strike.* **6** [T+obj+n] to name: *We'll call the baby Jean.* | *She's called Karina.* | *What do you call your dog?* (=what is its name?) **7** [T+obj+n|adj] to say or consider that (someone or something) is (something): *She called me stupid.* | *Are you calling me a liar?* | *I don't call Russian a hard language.* | *How can you still call yourself my friend after what you did?* | *Did you hear what he called me?* | *I don't know what I owe you, but let's call it £5.* | *I paid for the meal and you paid for the tickets, so let's* **call it quits.** (=agree that we don't owe each other anything) **8** [T] to waken (someone): *Please call me at 7 o'clock.* **9** [I (**to**);T] (of an animal) to make the usual cry (to another animal): *The birds are calling (each other).* **10** [I;T] (in card games) **a** *BrE* to BID¹ (2): *Who called last?* | *What did she call?* **b** to say what will be TRUMPS² **c** to demand to see other players' cards (in POKER) **11 call a spade a spade** *infml* to speak the plain truth without being delicate or sensitive **12 call collect** *AmE*‖**reverse the charges** *BrE*– to make a telephone call to be paid for by the person who receives it **13 call it a day** *infml* to stop work or an activity: *It's getting pretty late – let's call it a day.* **14 call one's shot** *AmE sl* to state exactly what one intends to do **15 call someone's bluff** to tell someone who claims to be or know something, or who is threatening to do something, to prove his/her claims or to do what he/she threatens to do: *When he threatened to dismiss me*

I called his bluff. **16 call someone to the colors** *AmE lit* to ask someone to serve in the armed forces, esp. during a war **17 call someone to order** to order someone to obey the rules of a formal meeting: *The chairman called the hecklers to order‖called the meeting to order.* **18 call something into question** to raise doubts about something: *I'm afraid that this incident calls into question his suitability for the job.* **19 call the tune/shots** *infml* to be in a position to give orders, decide what will happen, etc. **20 call to mind** to remember: *I'm sure I know that man, although I can't call to mind where I've met him.* –see also SO-CALLED **21 don't call 'us, we'll call 'you** a phrase used humorously to someone after they have just given a poor performance of acting or singing (from the phrase that is believed to be used by a DIRECTOR at the end of an unsuccessful AUDITION)

call back *phr v* **1** [I] *BrE* to pay another visit: *The salesman will call back later.* **2** [I;T (=call sbdy. back)] to return a telephone call: *Will you call me back later?* – see also CALL¹ (3); see TELEPHONE (USAGE)

call by *phr v* [I] *infml BrE* to visit when passing: *I'll call by at the shop on my way home.*

call sbdy./sthg. ↔ down *phr v* [T] **1** [(**on**)] to ask for something to come down (as if) from heaven; INVOKE: *The priest called down God's anger on the people.* **2** *AmE infml* to speak to angrily; REPRIMAND: *He called me down for the way I spoke to the teacher.*

call for sbdy./sthg. *phr v* [T] **1** to demand: *to call for the waiter‖the bill* | *The opposition have called for an immediate inquiry into the behaviour of the police.* **2** to need or deserve: *That remark was not called for.* (=was nasty or unfair) | *This sort of work calls for a lot of patience.* | *You're getting married? This calls for a celebration!* –see also UNCALLED-FOR **3** *BrE* to go and get (someone) from their house, office, etc.; collect: *I'll call for you at 9 o'clock.*

call sthg. ↔ forth *phr v* [T] *fml* to cause (esp. a quality) to appear to be used; EVOKE

call sbdy./sthg. ↔ in *phr v* [T] **1** to ask to come to help: *Call the doctor in.* **2** to request the return of: *The makers have called in some cars with dangerous faults.* | *to call in a loan* (=ask for it to be repaid)

call sthg. ↔ off *phr v* [T] **1** to cause (a planned event) not to take place: *The football match was called off because of the snow.* **2** to order (an activity) to be stopped: *After three days of searching the police chief called off the hunt for the escaped prisoner.* **3** to order to keep away: *Call off your dog – it's attacking me!*

call on/upon sbdy./sthg. *phr v* [T] **1** to pay a short visit to: *We can call on Mary tomorrow.* **2** [+obj+to-v] *fml* to ask (someone) to do something, esp. formally: *The congress has called on the President to answer these charges.* | *I now call on the best man to make a speech.* **3** to need to use: *to call on all one's strength*

call sbdy. ↔ out *phr v* [T] **1** to officially order (esp. a group) to come together in order to provide help: *The Government had to call out the army to restore order.* **2** *esp. BrE* to order to go on STRIKE: *The miners' leader called out his men.*

call up *phr v* **1** [I;T (=**call sbdy. ↔ up**)] *esp. AmE* to telephone: *I'll call you up this evening.* **2** [T] (**call sbdy. ↔ up**) to order (someone) to join the armed forces; DRAFT: *He was called up in 1917.* –see also CONSCRIPT¹ **3** [T] (**call sbdy./sthg. ↔ up**) to bring back; cause to come back: *This song calls up memories of my childhood.* | *The magician says he can call up the spirits of the dead.*

call² n 1 [C] a shout or cry: *We heard a call for help.* | *This bird has a very distinctive call.* | *Give me a call when you're ready to leave.* **2** [C (**for**)] a request or command for someone to do something or go somewhere: *The minister waited for a call to the palace.* | *Most of the staff ignored the union's strike call and went into work.* | *The finance minister has rejected calls from businessmen for lower interest rates.* [+to-v] *There have been calls for the government to release the detainees.* | (fig.) *He felt the call of the sea.* (=its attraction) **3** [C] an attempt to speak to someone by telephone: *I have a call for you from London.* | *I have a few calls to make.* | *Ask her to return my call when she gets home, please.* **4** [C(**on**)] a short visit, esp. of an official or professional kind: *The doctor is out on a call.* | *The President is making‖paying a call on the king.* **5** [C;U (**for, on**)] a demand or need: *We don't stock men's hats – there isn't much call for them nowadays.* | *She has so many calls on her time that it is almost impossible to see her.* [+to-v] *You have no call to say that!* **6** [C]

BrE (in card games) a BID² (3) or a player's turn to bid: *Whose call is it?* **7** [C] (in sports and games) the decision of an UMPIRE OR REFEREE **8** [C] an act of waking someone: *He asked the hotel clerk for a seven o'clock call.* **9** [C] an instrument used by hunters, which makes a sound like the cry of a bird or animal in order to attract it: *a duck call* **10** [C] the right to buy a certain quantity of something, e.g. shares, at a fixed price within a given time – compare PUT² **11 on call** not working but ready to work if needed: *The nurse is on call tonight.* **12 within call** near enough to hear a call –see also CALL OF NATURE, CURTAIN CALL, PORT OF CALL

Cal·lag·han /ˈkæləhən, -hæn/, **Sir James** (**Jim** /dʒɪm/) (1912–) a British Labour politician and PRIME MINISTER from 1976 to 1979

cal·la·net·ics /ˌkæləˈnetɪks/ *n* [U + *sing.|pl. v*] *tdmk* physical exercises intended to develop healthy and strong bodies without developing big muscles

Maria Callas

Cal·las /ˈkæləs/, **Ma·ri·a** /məˈriːə/ (1923–77) an American OPERA singer born of Greek parents, known for her powerful performances

call box /ˈ· ·/ also **phone booth, phone box, telephone booth, telephone box**– *n BrE* a small hut or enclosure containing a public telephone –see TELEPHONE (USAGE)

call·er /ˈkɔːlər/ *n* **1** a person who makes a short visit: *John's a regular caller here.* **2** a person making a telephone call, esp. as addressed by the OPERATOR: *I'm sorry, caller, the number's engaged.* | *An anonymous caller warned the police about the bomb on the train.* **3** a person who calls out numbers in a game (such as BINGO) **4** *AmE* a person who calls out the steps for a SQUARE DANCE

call girl /ˈ· ·/ *n* a woman PROSTITUTE who makes her arrangements by telephone

cal·lig·ra·phy /kəˈlɪɡrəfi/ *n* [U] (the art of producing) beautiful writing by hand **–pher, -phist** *n*

call-in /ˈ· ·/ *n AmE for* PHONE-IN

call·ing /ˈkɔːlɪŋ/ *n* **1** a strong urge or feeling of duty to do a particular kind of work; VOCATION **2** *fml* a person's profession or trade

cal·li·pers also **calipers** *AmE* /ˈkælɪpəz‖-ərz/ [P] **1** an instrument consisting of two legs fixed together at one end, used for measuring thickness, the distance between two surfaces, and inner width (DIAMETER) –see PAIR (USAGE) **2** *BrE* metal supports fixed to the legs to help a person with weak legs to walk

cal·lis·then·ics , calisthenics /ˌkælɪsˈθenɪks/ *n* [U+*sing.*| pl. v] physical exercises intended to develop healthy, strong, and beautiful bodies **–ic** *adj* [A]

call let·ters /ˈ· ˌ··/ *n* [P] *AmE* see CALL SIGN

call num·ber /ˈ· ˌ··/ *n AmE* The number written on a library book that tells what part of the library it is kept in

call of na·ture /ˌ· · ˈ··/ *n euph* a need to pass liquid or solid waste matter from the body

call op·tion /ˈ· ˌ··/ *n tech* the right to buy a fixed number of SHARES² (2) at a particular price within a set period of time

cal·lous /ˈkæləs/ *adj* **1** unkind; without sympathy for the sufferings of other people: *his callous disregard for the safety of his workers* **2** *med* (of the skin) hard and thick –compare CALLUS **– ~ ly** *adv* **– ~ ness** *n* [U]

call-out /ˈ· ·/ *n BrE* an action of calling e.g. a service engineer to come and do a job in one's house: *Do you have a call-out charge as well as a charge for labour?* | *A £30 call-out fee*

cal·low /ˈkæləʊ/ *adj derog* (of a person or behaviour) young and without experience; IMMATURE: *a callow youth*

call sign /ˈ· ·/ also **call letters** *AmE*– *n* a name, made up of letters and numbers, given to people operating radios, or to radio stations, to prove who they are

call-up /ˈ· ·/ *BrE*‖**draft** *AmE*– *n* an order to serve in the armed forces: *He got his call-up papers in July.* –see also CALL **up** (2)

cal·lus /ˈkæləs/ also **cal·los·i·ty** /kəˈlɒsɪti‖kəˈlɑː-/– *n* an area of thick hard skin: *calluses on his hands* –compare CALLOUS

calm¹ /kɑːm‖kɑːm, kɑːlm/ *adj* **1** free from excitement, nervous activity, or strong feeling; quiet and untroubled: *The police chief advised his men to stay|keep calm and not lose their tempers.* | *a calm manner* | *After yesterday's fighting on the border, the situation is now fairly calm again.* **2 a** (of weather) not windy: *After the storm it was calm.* **b** (of water) not rough; smooth; still: *The sea was calm.* **– ~ ly** *adv* **– ~ ness** *n* [U]

calm² *n* [S;U] **1** peace and quiet; absence of excitement or nervous activity: *working in the calm of the library* **2** an absence of wind or rough weather; stillness: *the calm after the storm*

calm³ *v* [T] to make calm: *She calmed the baby by giving him some milk.* | *This announcement will calm the fears of conservationists.*
   calm down *phr v* [I;T (=**calm** sbdy. ↔ **down**)] to make or become calm: *Calm down – there's nothing to worry about!* | *We tried to calm him down, but he kept shouting and swearing.*

cal·or gas /ˈkælə gæs‖-lər-/ *n* [U] *BrE tdmk* (*sometimes cap.*) a type of gas (BUTANE) sold in metal containers for use where there is no gas supply: *When we camp we usually cook with Calor gas.*

cal·o·rie /ˈkæləri/ *n* **1** a measure used to show the amount of heat or ENERGY (3) that a food will produce. When people are trying to lose weight by avoiding certain foods, they sometimes say that they are **counting their calories** or **watching their calories**: *One thin piece of bread has 90 calories.* | *a calorie-controlled diet* **2** a unit of heat –compare BTU

cal·o·rif·ic /ˌkæləˈrɪfɪk◂/ *adj* **1** *tech* heat-producing: *This coal has a high calorific value.* **2** *infml* (of food) tending to make one fat: *That chocolate cake looks very calorific.*

ca·lum·ni·ate /kəˈlʌmni-eɪt/ *v* [T] *fml* to speak calumnies about (someone); SLANDER

cal·um·ny /ˈkæləmni/ *n* [C;U (**against**)] *fml* (the act of making) an incorrect and unjust report about a person with the intention of destroying the good opinion that other people have of him/her

cal·va·ry /ˈkælvəri/ *n* a model which represents the death of Christ (CRUCIFIXION)

Calvary the Roman name for the place near Jerusalem where Christ died by being crucified (CRUCIFY)

calve /kɑːv‖kæv/ *v* [I] to give birth to a CALF: *The cow calved yesterday.*

calves /kɑːvz‖kævz/ *pl. of* CALF

Cal·vin /ˈkælvɪn/, **John** (1509–64) a French Protestant THEOLOGIAN (=person who studied religion) involved in the REFORMATION and known for the severity of his system

Cal·vin·ism /ˈkælvɪnɪzəm/ *n* [U] the Christian religious teachings of John Calvin based on the idea that events on Earth are controlled by God and cannot be changed by Man

cal·vin·ist /ˈkælvɪnɪst/ *adj* **1** of or following Calvinism **2** also **Cal·vin·ist·ic** /ˌkælvɪˈnɪstɪk◂/– *infml, often derog* having severe moral standards and tending to disapprove of pleasure; PURITANICAL: *She had a strict Calvinist upbringing.* **– Calvinist** *n*

ca·lyp·so /kəˈlɪpsəʊ/ *n* **-sos** *or* **-soes** a West Indian song based on a subject of interest in the news, often played by a STEEL BAND

ca·lyx /ˈkælɪks, ˈkeɪ-/ *n* **calyces** /ˈkælɪsiːz, ˈkeɪ-‖**

ˈkeɪ-/ *or* **calyxes** *tech* a ring of leaves (SEPALS) which protects a flower before it opens and later supports the opened flower

cam /kæm/ *n* a wheel or part of a wheel shaped to change circular movement into backwards-and-forwards movement

ca·ma·ra·de·rie /ˌkæməˈrɑːdəri‖-ˈræ-, -ˈrɑː-/ *n* [U] the friendliness and goodwill shown to each other by friends, esp. people who spend time together at work, in the army, etc.

Ca·margue /kæˈmɑːg‖-ˈmɑːrg/ an area in S France at the DELTA of the River Rhône. It is a national park well-known for the richness of its animal life, esp. birds.

Cam·ay /ˈkæmeɪ/ *n tdmk* a type of soap made by Procter & Gamble Limited; it is thought to be good for the skin

cam·ber /ˈkæmbər/ *n* [C;U] a slight upward curve towards the centre of a road or other surface, which causes water to run off to the side

Cam·bo·di·a /kæmˈbəʊdiə/ a country in SE Asia between Thailand and Vietnam; former name Kampuchea; capital Phnom Penh; population 2,055,000 (1989)

Cam·bri·an Moun·tains /ˌkæmbriən ˈmaʊntₙnz/ *n* [*the* + P] a group of mountains running from N to S across the middle of Wales

cam·bric /ˈkeɪmbrɪk/ *n* [U] a fine white cloth of cotton or LINEN

Cam·bridge /ˈkeɪmbrɪdʒ/ **1** a city in E England on the River Cam, famous for its old university. The local government for Cambridgeshire is based in Cambridge. —see colour map on page 818 **2** a city in E Massachusetts, US, across the Charles River from Boston where Harvard University is

Cambridge Cer·tif·i·cate /ˌ·· ·ˈ···/ [*the*] the short name for either of two examinations in English as a foreign language run by an examinations board of Cambridge University. The lower examination's official name is the First Certificate in English, and the higher is called the Certificate of Proficiency in English.

Cam·bridge·shire /ˈkeɪmbrɪdʒʃər/ a COUNTY in E England whose main town is Cambridge

Cambridge U·ni·ver·si·ty /ˌ··· ··ˈ···/ one of the oldest and most highly regarded British universities. Students must pass a special examination before they are accepted by the university, and the students who go there often come from PUBLIC SCHOOLS. —see also OXFORD UNIVERSITY and see OXBRIDGE (CULTURAL NOTE)

cam·cor·der /ˈkæmkɔːdər‖-kɔːr-/ *n* a VIDEO camera and recorder in one machine, which can be carried around

Cam·den /ˈkæmdən/ a BOROUGH in N London which is a fashionable place to live

came /keɪm/ *past tense of* COME

cam·el /ˈkæməl/ *n* either of two large long-necked animals used for riding or carrying goods in desert countries: **a** also **dromedary**– the Arabian camel with one large HUMP on its back **b** the **Bactrian camel** from Asia with two large HUMPs on its back —see also **the straw that breaks the camel's back** (STRAW)

cam·el·hair /ˈkæməlheər/ *n* [U] **1** a thick yellowish brown cloth made from a mixture of types of wool, usu. used for making coats **2** fine hair used in making paint-brushes

ca·mel·li·a /kəˈmiːliə/ *n* (a bush with) a large sweet-smelling flower like a rose

Cam·e·lot /ˈkæməlɒt‖-lɑːt/ the place of King Arthur's court, thought of as a wonderful magical place —see ARTHURIAN LEGEND

cam·em·bert /ˈkæməmbeər/ *n* [C;U] (a circular piece of) a French cheese with a greyish-white outside and a soft yellowish inside

cam·e·o /ˈkæmi-əʊ/ *n* **-eos** **1** (a piece of jewellery consisting of) a raised shape or figure on the background of a small fine flat stone of a different colour: *a cameo brooch* **2** a short piece of writing or acting, esp. a small part in a film or play acted by a well-known actor

cam·e·ra /ˈkæmərə/ *n* **1** an apparatus for taking still or moving photographs **2** the part of the equipment used

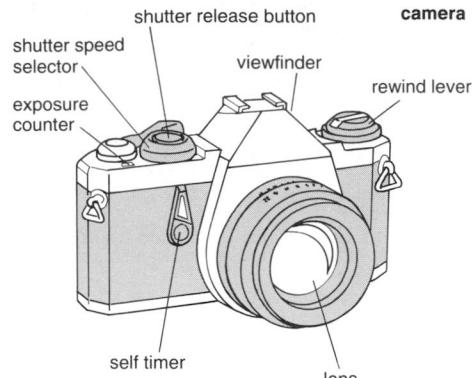

shutter release button **camera**
shutter speed selector
viewfinder
rewind lever
exposure counter
self timer
lens

for making television pictures which changes images into electrical signals **3 in camera** (esp. of a law case) held in secret; privately: *The case involved official secrets, so it was held in camera.*

cam·e·ra·man /ˈkæmərəmən/ *n* **-men** /mən/ a person who operates a camera for films or television

camera-shy /ˈ··· ·/ *adj* (of a person) not liking to be photographed

Cam·e·roon , Cameroun /ˌkæməˈruːn/ a country in W Africa in the Gulf of Guinea; capital Yaoundé; population 11,540,000 (1989) — ~**ian** *n, adj*

cam·i·knick·ers /ˈkæmi ˌnɪkəz‖-ərz/ *n* [P] *BrE* a woman's undergarment worn esp. in former times combining camisole and KNICKERS. Cami-knickers are becoming popular again and are considered to be more sexy than other underclothes. —see PAIR (USAGE)

cam·i·sole /ˈkæmₕsəʊl/ *n* a short undergarment worn esp. formerly by women on the top half of the body

cam·o·mile , chamomile /ˈkæməmaɪl/ *n* [C;U] a plant whose small sweet-smelling white and yellow flowers have medicinal qualities: *camomile tea*

cam·ou·flage[1] /ˈkæməflɑːʒ/ *n* [C;U] **1** the way that the colour or shape of something can make it difficult to see in its surroundings: *Many animals have a natural camouflage which hides them from their enemies.* **2** the use of branches, paints, nets, smoke, etc. to hide something, esp. a military object: *The soldiers covered their helmets with leaves as camouflage.*

camouflage[2] *v* [T] to hide by using camouflage: *The soldiers camouflaged the guns with branches of trees.*

camp[1] /kæmp/ *n* **1** [C;U] a place where people live in tents or huts, usu. for a short time: *We pitched our camp* (=put it in position) *near the mountaintop.* | *We'll soon be back in camp.* | *Let's go back to camp; it's getting dark.* | *Tomorrow we'll have to* **break camp.** (=take up the tents and put them away) | *When we went to the coast we stayed in a* **holiday camp.** —see also DAY CAMP **2** [C] (*usu. in comb.*) a place where people live in tents or huts, often unwillingly and for a long time: *a labour camp* | *a refugee camp* | *a military training camp* —see also CONCENTRATION CAMP, PRISON CAMP **3** [C+*sing.*/*pl. v*] a group of people or organizations who share the same ideas or principles, esp. in politics: *This is the policy favoured by the pro-nuclear camp.* | *The party divided into two separate camps on the issue.*

camp[2] *v* [I] to set up a camp or live in a camp: *The hunters camped near the river.* | *We go camping every summer.* | *a shop that sells camping equipment*

camp out *phr v* [I] **1** to sleep outdoors **2** *infml, esp. BrE* to live in uncomfortable conditions for a short time: *We'll just have to camp out until all our furniture arrives.*

camp up *phr v* **camp it up** *infml* to act or behave in a funny unnatural way, with too much movement of the hands and too much expression in the voice; OVERACT

camp[3] *adj infml* **1** (of a man) behaving or looking like a woman, esp. in an intentional way: *camp mannerisms* **2** so unreal, unnatural, or pretended, etc., as to be amusing **3** HOMOSEXUAL

cam·paign¹ /kæmˈpeɪn/ n **1** a connected set of military actions forming a separate part of a war **2** a connected set of actions intended to obtain a particular result, esp. in politics or business: *She fought a successful election campaign.* | *an advertising campaign* | *The government has launched a campaign against smoking.* | *He is a campaign coordinator for a well-known charity.*

campaign² v [I (**for**, **against**)] to lead, take part in, or go on a campaign: *Joan is campaigning for women's right to equal pay.* — ~**er** n

Campaign for Nu·cle·ar Dis·ar·ma·ment /··· ···· ·····/ also **CND**— [*the*] a British organization, esp. well known in the 1960s, which protests against the making and the use of NUCLEAR WEAPONS —see also ALDERMASTON

cam·pa·ni·le /ˌkæmpəˈniːli/ n a high bell tower which stands separately from any other building

cam·pa·nol·o·gy /ˌkæmpəˈnɒlədʒi‖-ˈnɑː-/ n [U] the art of ringing bells —**gist** n

Cam·pa·ri /kæmˈpɑːri/ n [C;U] tdmk a bitter red alcoholic drink often drunk before a meal

camp bed /ˌ· ˈ·‖ˈ· ·/ BrE ‖ usu. **cot** AmE— n a light bed which folds flat and is easily carried —see picture at BED

Camp·bell /ˈkæmbəl/, **Ben Nighthorse** /ben ˈnaɪthɔːs‖-hɔːrs/ a Democratic politician who in 1992 became the first Native American elected to the US Senate, representing Colorado

Campbell Soup Com·pa·ny /ˌ··· ˈ· ˌ···/ tdmk a food company known esp. for its soup: *Campbell's tomato soup*

Camp Da·vid /ˌ· ˈ···/ a place in Maryland, US where the president goes to relax. Most people remember it as the place where the 1979 peace TREATY (=agreement) between Israel and Egypt was signed.

camp·er /ˈkæmpəʳ/ n **1** a person who camps **2** AmE a contained room fitted onto a PICK-UP (2) big enough to live in when on holiday, having cooking equipment and beds in it —compare CARAVAN (2)

camp·fire /ˈkæmpfaɪəʳ/ n a wood fire made in the open air by campers

Camp Fire /ˈ· ·/ an American organization for girls and, since 1975, boys, in which they learn practical and social skills, and sometimes go camping (CAMP²)

camp fol·low·er /ˈ· ˌ···/ n **1** often derog a follower or supporter (e.g. of a political plan, party, or leader) who is not actually a member of the main group **2** (esp. formerly) a person (esp. a PROSTITUTE) who is not a soldier but who follows the army from place to place to provide services

camp·ground /ˈkæmpgraʊnd/ n esp. AmE an area in which people may camp

cam·phor /ˈkæmfəʳ/ n [U] a strong-smelling white substance with various medical and industrial uses, which is also used to keep insects away

camping gas /ˈ··· ·/ BrE n gas, usu. in a small, CYLINDRICAL container, used to produce light and heat for cooking when camping

camp rob·ber /ˈ· ˌ··/ n an American bird which seems unafraid of people and often flies away with food and other things that attract it

camp·site /ˈkæmpsaɪt/ n **1** esp. BrE a place, such as a field, used for camping in **2** AmE a place, often within a campground, for one group, family, or person to camp in

camp·stool /ˈkæmpstuːl/ n AmE a small folding seat with no back

cam·pus /ˈkæmpəs/ n [C;U] the grounds and buildings of a university or college: *The new library was built in the centre of the campus.* | *a campus university* (=one in which all the buildings are in the same area, often outside a town) | *Do you live* **on campus** *or in the town?*

CAMRA /ˈkæmrə/ Campaign for Real Ale; an organization in Britain which encourages the sale and drinking of beer made in the old way, and supports PUBs which sell it

cam·shaft /ˈkæmʃɑːft‖-ʃæft/ n a rod to which a CAM is fastened

Ca·mus /kæˈmjuː/, **Al·bert** /ˈælbeəʳ/ (1913–60) a French writer and thinker who wrote about the meaningless nature of human life

can¹ /kən; strong kæn/ v [modal+to-v] 3rd person sing. **can**, negative short form **can't 1** to be able to: *He's so tall he can touch the ceiling.* | *This machine can perform two million calculations per second.* | *I can't remember where I* put it. | *They have everything that money can buy.* | *Can you lift this box?* | *The police still haven't found her, but they're doing all they can.* **2** (used to show what is possible or likely): *I'm sure we can settle this problem.* | *I am confident that a solution can be found.* | *There can be no doubt that he is guilty.* | *The word "bank" can be used in several different ways|can have several different meanings.* | *Can he still be alive after all this time?* **3** to know how to: *She can speak French.* **4** to be allowed to or have permission to; may: *You can't play football here.* | *"Can we go home now, please?" "No, you can't."* | *You can't pick the ball up in football.* (=it is against the rules) **5** [usu. in questions or negatives] to allow oneself to: *She's left her husband, but can you blame her after the way he treated her?* | *It's a very kind offer, but I really can't accept it.* **6** to have to; must: *If you won't keep quiet you can get out!* **7** (used when asking someone to do something, give something, etc.): *Can you help me to lift it, please?* | *Can I have one of your cigarettes?* —compare COULD (5) **8** (used esp. in expressions of surprise) may perhaps: *What can it possibly be?* | *You can't be serious!* | *Whatever can they want?* **9** (used to show what sometimes happens): *It can get quite cold here at night.* | *He can be quite annoying sometimes.* **10** (used with verbs expressing actions of the five senses and of the mind): *I can see|hear you easily from here.* | *I can't understand him when he speaks so fast.* | *You can imagine how annoyed she was!* —see also CANNOT, CAN'T, COULD

▷ USAGE 1 Except in formal writing, **can** is now more common than **may** to express "permission": *You can go now.* It is also used to express permission for the future: *You can borrow my car tomorrow.* 2 **Can** expresses present ability: *I can swim now.* To express future ability use **will be able**: *I'll be able to play the Beethoven violin concerto if I practise for long enough.* For past ability see COULD (USAGE). 3 **Can** is not usually used to express the idea of "perhaps" (uncertainty). Instead, we use **may**, **might**, or (less commonly) **could**: *The road may/might/could be blocked.* (=Perhaps the road is blocked.) But **can** is used to ask questions about possibility: *Can this be true?* (=I am surprised) and to say that something is impossible: *This can't be true.* 4 **Can** is often used with verbs that concern the mind and the senses, such as *believe, feel, hear, see*: *I'm looking at this photograph; I can see some famous people in it.* —see also COULD (USAGE), MIGHT (USAGE), NOT (USAGE), SEE (USAGE)◁

can² /kæn/ n **1** [C] a closed metal container in which foods are preserved without air; TIN¹ (2): *He opened a can of beans|of beer.* **2** [C] a usu. round metal container with an open top or removable lid and sometimes with handles, used for holding milk, oil, waste, ashes, etc.: *a petrol can* **3** [C (**of**)] also **can·ful** /-fʊl/— the contents of a can **4** [the+S] sl a prison **b** AmE a TOILET **5 in the can** infml (of films) completed and ready for showing **6 can of worms** a very difficult situation which was hidden before: *The court case has opened up a real* **can of worms.** —see also **carry the can** (CARRY)

can³ /kæn/ v **-nn-** [T] to preserve (food) by putting it in a closed metal or glass container without air: *The fish is canned in this factory.* | *canned fruit* —see also CANNED, CANNING

can⁴ /kæn/ v **-nn-** [T] AmE infml **1** to dismiss from a job; SACK **2** to stop: *Can the noise, I'm on the telephone.*

Ca·na /ˈkeɪnə/ the ancient town of Galilee in the Bible, where Jesus performed his first MIRACLE when he changed water into wine at a wedding

Ca·naan /ˈkeɪnən/ the name for ancient Palestine and, in the Bible, the land promised to the Israelites by God — see also PROMISED LAND

Can·a·da /ˈkænədə/ a country in North America and a member of the Commonwealth; capital Ottawa; population 26, 219,000 (1989). Canada is one of the world's largest countries and rich in natural RESOURCES. English and French are the official languages. —**dian** /kəˈneɪdiən/ n, adj

Canadian ba·con /·ˌ··· ˈ··/ n [U] AmE BACON with little fat in it

ca·nal /kəˈnæl/ n an artificial stretch of water dug in the ground **a** to allow ships or boats to travel along it: *The Panama canal joins two oceans.* | *The coal is delivered by canal.* **b** to bring water to or remove water from an area:

Canals have been built to irrigate the desert. —compare CHANNEL¹ (1); see also ALIMENTARY CANAL

canal boat /·ˈ· ·/ *n* a long narrow boat for use on a canal

Can·a·let·to /ˌkænəˈletəʊ‖-nəlˈetəʊ/, **An·to·ni·o** /ænˈtəʊniəʊ/ (1697–1768) a Venetian painter known esp. for his paintings of Venice —see colour picture on page 1016

can·a·lize also **-lise** *BrE* /ˈkænəl-aɪz/ *v* [T] **1** to deepen, straighten, or widen (a river), usu. to stop flooding **2** [(into)] to direct (a variety of actions) to one particular purpose: *The company intends to canalize all its efforts into improving its image with the public.* —**lization** /ˌkænəl-aɪˈzeɪʃən‖-nəl-ə-/ *n* [U]

can·a·pé /ˈkænəpeɪ‖-pi, -peɪ/ *n* a small piece of bread spread with cheese, fish, or meat and usu. served with drinks at a party

ca·nard /kæˈnɑːd‖kəˈnɑːrd/ *n Fr* a false report or piece of news

ca·nar·y /kəˈneəri/ *n* a small yellow bird often kept as a pet for its singing

Ca·na·ry Is·lands /·ˈ· ˌ·/ also **Canaries** [*the*+P] a group of islands belonging to Spain near NW Africa which are popular with British people for a holiday in the sun

Canary Wharf /·ˌ·· ˈ·/ part of the Docklands development in E London. The Canary Wharf Tower is the tallest building in Britain.

ca·nas·ta /kəˈnæstə/ *n* [U] a card game in which two sets (PACKs) of cards are used

Can·ber·ra /ˈkæbərə/ the capital city of Australia

cancan

can·can /ˈkænkæn/ *n* (esp. in France in the 19th century) a fast dance performed on stage in which women kick their legs high and shake their long skirts

can·cel /ˈkænsəl/ *v* **-ll-** *BrE* ‖ **-l-** *AmE* [T] **1** to give up (a planned activity, event, etc.); state or decide that (something) will not happen: *She cancelled her trip to New York as she felt ill.* | *The match had to be cancelled owing to the bad weather.* | *We regret to announce that the 10.30 train to Glasgow has been cancelled.* —compare POSTPONE **2** to destroy the force, effectiveness, or value of: *I've cancelled my subscription to the magazine.* | *to cancel a cheque/postage stamp* (=by drawing a line through it)
cancel sthg. ↔ **out** *phr v* [T] to match exactly and so take away the effect of; balance: *The losses of our overseas section cancel out the profits made by the company at home.* | *The two factors cancel each other out.*

can·cel·la·tion /ˌkænsəˈleɪʃən/ *n* **1** [C;U] (an example of) the act of cancelling: *The cancellation of the order for planes led to the closure of the factory.* | *The flight is fully booked, but if there are any cancellations we will let you know.* **2** [C] the mark used when cancelling something, such as a postage stamp

can·cer /ˈkænsər/ *n* [C;U] (a serious medical condition caused by) a diseased growth in the body, which may cause death. Cancer is a common cause of death in Western countries and is a disease that people are very frightened of getting: *lung cancer* | *He's got a cancer in his throat.* | *cancer of the breast* | (fig.) *Violence is the cancer* (=the spreading evil) *of modern society.* —compare CANKER; see also CARCINOGENIC — ~ **ous** *adj* : *a cancerous growth*

Cancer *n* **1** [U] the fourth sign of the ZODIAC, represented by a CRAB (=a sea animal) —see ZODIAC (USAGE) and see picture at ZODIAC **2** [C] a person born between June 22 and July 22 —see also **Tropic of Cancer** (TROPIC)

C & A /ˌsiː ənd ˈeɪ/ *n* one of a group of large shops in Britain, known esp. for selling inexpensive clothes

can·de·la·brum /ˌkændɪ̯ˈlɑːbrəm/ *n* **-brums** *or* **-bra** /brə/ a decorative holder for several candles or lamps —compare CANDLESTICK

can·did /ˈkændɪ̯d/ *adj* open, honest, and sincere in manner; directly truthful, even when telling the truth is unwelcome: *I would like your candid opinion of these proposals.* | *To be quite candid, I don't like your hairstyle.* —see also CANDOUR — ~ **ly** *adv* : *She talked quite candidly about her unhappy marriage.*

can·di·da /ˈkændɪ̯də/ *n* [U] a type of FUNGUS (2) from the Candida group esp. candida albicans which causes THRUSH (2)

can·di·da·cy /ˈkændɪ̯dəsi/ also **can·di·da·ture** /ˈkændɪ̯dətʃər/ *esp. BrE*— *n* [C;U] the fact of being a candidate, esp. for a political office: *He announced his candidacy for the next presidential election.*

can·di·date /ˈkændɪ̯dət, -deɪt, -dɪ̯t/ *n* **1** [(**for**)] a person who wants to be chosen for a job or elected to a position, or whom other people have suggested as a suitable person for such a job or position: *They are interviewing candidates for the job of sales manager.* | *a parliamentary candidate* **2** *esp. BrE* a person taking an examination —see also extra information on page 412

Candid Cam·e·ra /ˌ·· ˈ···/ *n* a television programme of the 1950s and 1960s, both in Britain and the US, in which ordinary people were secretly filmed in amusing, difficult, or embarrassing situations. Although the programme is no longer on the television, people still sometimes use the phrase, "Smile – you're on Candid Camera!" which was always used to tell people that they were being filmed.

Can·dide /kɒnˈdiːd‖kɑːn-/ a book written in 1759 by the French PHILOSOPHER Voltaire about a young man, Candide, who has little knowledge of the world and cannot recognize evil. He travels around and has many unusual adventures which show him the wickedness of the world.

can·died /ˈkændid/ *adj* [A] covered with shiny sugar: *candied fruit*

can·dle /ˈkændl/ *n* **1** a usu. round stick of WAX containing a length of string (WICK) which gives light when it burns **2 can't hold/is not fit to hold a candle to** *infml* to be not nearly as good as: *No one can hold a candle to him when it comes to playing the guitar.* **3 Out, out brief candle!** *quote* a phrase from Shakespeare's play *Macbeth*, said by Macbeth when he is talking about how short and meaningless our lives are —see also ROMAN CANDLE, **burn the candle at both ends** (BURN¹)

can·dle·light /ˈkændl-laɪt/ *n* [U] the light produced by candles. Candlelight is thought to be ROMANTIC and to encourage interest between the sexes: *We dined by candlelight.*

candle-lit /ˈ··· ·/ *adj* lit by candles: *a candle-lit dinner for two*

Can·dle·mas /ˈkændlməs/ February 2nd, kept as a special religious day to remember the presentation of Christ in the temple and the making pure of the Virgin Mary

can·dle·stick /ˈkændl-stɪk/ *n* a holder for usu. one candle —compare CANDELABRUM

can·dle·wick /ˈkændl-wɪk/ *n* [U] cloth with a decorative pattern made of rows of raised short threads separated from other rows by bare material: *a candlewick bedspread*

can·dour *BrE* ‖ **-dor** *AmE* /ˈkændər/ *n* [U] the quality of being sincerely honest and truthful (CANDID)

C & W /ˌsiː ənd ˈdʌbəljuː/ *n abbrev. for* COUNTRY AND WESTERN

candy /ˈkændi/ *n* [U;C] *esp. AmE* (a shaped piece of) various types of boiled sugar, sweets, or chocolate: *Eating all that candy will rot your teeth!* | *Is there a candy machine here somewhere?* —compare SWEET¹ (1)

candy ap·ple /ˈ·· ˌ··/ *n AmE for* TOFFEE APPLE

candy bar /ˈ·· ·/ *n AmE* a bar covered with chocolate and filled with a variety of different sweets: *What's your favorite candy bar?*

can·dy·floss /ˈkændiflɒs‖-flɑːs, -flɔːs/ *BrE* ‖ **cotton candy** *AmE*— *n* [U] fine sticky often coloured sugar threads eaten as a sweet and usu. on a stick. Candyfloss is connected with CARNIVALs, FAIRs, and AMUSEMENT PARKs and in Britain it is also sold in seaside towns, and people often eat it when they are on holiday.

can·dy-striped /ˈ·· ˌ·/ adj (esp. of cloth) having narrow coloured lines on a white background: a candy-striped blouse

candy strip·er /ˈ·· ˌ··/ n AmE a girl who does VOLUNTARY (=without pay) work in a hospital

cane¹ /keɪn/ n 1 [C] the hard smooth thin often hollow stem of certain plants (tall grasses such as BAMBOO) —see also SUGARCANE 2 [C] a long thin stick used by schoolteachers, esp. in the past, to beat children as a punishment for bad behaviour: The teacher gave him the cane (=hit him with a cane) for fighting in school. 3 [U] lengths of cane used as a material for making furniture: cane chairs 4 [C] a length of cane used for supporting weak plants, for helping weak people to walk: a walking cane 5 [C] the woody stem of certain fruit-picking plants: raspberry canes

cane² v [T] esp. BrE 1 to punish (someone) by hitting them with a cane: a campaign to abolish caning in schools 2 (esp. in newspapers) to defeat completely; TROUNCE: England were caned by France in last night's game.

ca·nine /ˈkeɪnaɪn, ˈkæ-‖ˈkeɪ-/ adj, n tech (of, for, or typical of) a dog or related animal

canine tooth /ˈ·· ·/ n any of four sharp pointed teeth in the human mouth —compare INCISOR, and see picture at TEETH

can·is·ter /ˈkænɪstər/ n 1 a usu. metal container for holding a dry substance, such as tea —see picture at CONTAINER 2 a small container which bursts and scatters its contents when thrown or fired from a gun: a canister of teargas

can·ker /ˈkæŋkər/ n [C;U] (an area of) soreness caused by a disease which attacks the wood of trees and the flesh (esp. the mouth and ears) of animals and people: Our cat has a canker in its ear. | (fig.) Violence is the canker (=spreading evil) in our society. —compare CANCER — ~ous adj

can·na·bis /ˈkænəbɪs/ also **dope, grass, pot** sl— n [U] the drug produced from a particular type of HEMP plant (**Indian hemp**), sometimes smoked in cigarettes to give a feeling of pleasure, leading to sleepiness. Using and selling cannabis is against the law in most Western countries. —compare BHANG, HASHISH, MARIJUANA

canned /kænd/ adj 1 (of food) preserved in a tin: canned beans 2 usu. derog recorded in advance and having an unoriginal or artificial quality: canned music in the airport lounge | canned laughter on a TV comedy show 3 [F] sl drunk

can·nel·lo·ni /ˌkænɪˈləʊni/ n [U] small quantities of meat or cheese, each with a covering of PASTA

can·ne·ry /ˈkænəri/ n a factory where food is put in tins

Cannes /kæn/ a fashionable seaside holiday town in the S of France where an important international FILM FESTIVAL is held

can·ni·bal /ˈkænɪbəl/ n 1 a person who eats human flesh

▶CULTURAL NOTE Many people are familiar with an old STEREOTYPE of cannibals, which show them as black African men with bones through their noses and wearing grass skirts. In the drawings, they are usu. waving their spears as they dance round a fire on which they are cooking an EXPLORER or a MISSIONARY.◀

2 an animal which eats the flesh of other animals of the same kind: Some fish are cannibals. — ~ism n [U] — ~istic /ˌkænɪbəˈlɪstɪk◀/ adj

can·ni·bal·ize also **-ise** BrE /ˈkænɪbəlaɪz/ v [T] to take (a machine) to pieces to use the parts in other machines: He cannibalized his old car to repair the new one.

can·ning /ˈkænɪŋ/ n [U] AmE the preserving of food by storing it in tins or JARS, esp. at home: These tomatoes will be good for canning. | I'm out of canning jars.

can·non¹ /ˈkænən/ n cannons or cannon a large powerful gun, often fixed to the ground or onto a two-wheeled carriage or, in modern times, fixed to an aircraft: a 15th century cannon | fighter planes armed with cannon —see also WATER CANNON, and see picture at GUN

cannon² v [I+adv/prep] to hit or knock forcefully, esp. by accident: She came running round the corner, cannoned into me, and knocked me over.

can·non·ade /ˌkænəˈneɪd/ n continuous heavy firing by large guns

can·non·ball /ˈkænənbɔːl/ n a heavy iron ball fired from an old type of cannon

cannon fod·der /ˈ·· ˌ··/ n [U] ordinary soldiers thought of as nothing but military material to be used without regard for their lives

can·not /ˈkænət, -nɒt‖-nɑːt/ fml 1 can not: Mr Smith is sorry that he cannot accept your kind invitation to dinner. —compare CAN'T; see CAN (USAGE), MUST (USAGE) 2 **cannot but** fml or pomp must: One cannot but admire her even if one may not like her.

can·ny /ˈkæni/ adj 1 clever, careful, and not easily deceived, esp. in money matters; SHREWD 2 N E EngE nice; good: a canny lass —**nily** adv

ca·noe¹ /kəˈnuː/ n a long light narrow boat, pointed at both ends, and moved by a PADDLE held in the hands: to paddle a canoe | We crossed the lake by canoe. —see also **paddle one's own canoe** (PADDLE² (5))

canoe² v canoed, present participle canoeing [I] to travel by canoe — ~ist n

ca·no·la /kəˈnəʊlə/ n [U] AmE 1 RAPE³ 2 oil from the seeds of RAPE³, used in cooking

can·on¹ /ˈkænən/ n 1 an established law of the Christian church 2 fml a generally accepted standard of behaviour or thought: His attack on her honesty offends against the canons of good taste. 3 an official list of writings that are recognized as being truly the work of a certain writer or as being part of a larger collection of writings: This poem is now accepted as belonging to the Shakespearian canon.

canon² n a Christian priest with special duties in a CATHEDRAL

Canon tdmk a Japanese company that makes cameras, PHOTOCOPIERS, etc.

ca·non·i·cal /kəˈnɒnɪkəl‖kəˈnɑː-/ adj 1 according to CANON LAW 2 belonging to a CANON¹ (3)

can·on·ize also **-ise** BrE /ˈkænənaɪz/ v [T] (esp. in the Roman Catholic Church) to declare (a dead person) officially a SAINT: Joan of Arc was canonized in 1920. —**ization** /ˌkænənaɪˈzeɪʃən, -nə-‖-nəˈzeɪ-/ n [C;U]

canon law /ˌ·· ·/ n [U] the body of established law of the Christian church —compare CIVIL LAW, COMMON LAW, CRIMINAL LAW

ca·noo·dle /kəˈnuːdl/ v [I] BrE old-fash infml (of a man and a woman) to hold each other lovingly; CUDDLE: canoodling in the back of the cinema

can o·pen·er /ˈ· ˌ··/ n esp. AmE TIN OPENER —see picture at KITCHEN

can·o·py /ˈkænəpi/ n 1 a cover fixed above a baby's PRAM to protect the baby from the sun 2 a decorative cover usu. of cloth fixed above a bed or seat or carried on posts above a person on ceremonial occasions: (fig.) a canopy of branches 3 the enclosure over the front part (COCKPIT) of a plane

canst /kənst; strong kænst/ thou canst old use or bibl (when talking to one person) you can

cant¹ /kænt/ n [U] 1 derog insincere talk, esp. about moral or religious principles, intended to make oneself seem better than one is: He pretends he cares about unemployment, but that's just politician's cant. 2 special words used by a particular group of people, esp. to keep the meaning secret from others: thieves' cant

cant² v [I;T] (OVER) BrE to (cause to) slope or lean: The boat began to cant (over).

cant³ n a sloping surface or angle

can't /kɑːnt‖kænt/ short for: 1 can not: I can't understand what this means. | You can swim, can't you? —compare CANNOT; see CAN (USAGE), MUST (USAGE) 2 (used as the opposite of **must**, to say that something is impossible or unlikely): They can't have gone out because the light's on. (compare They must have gone out, because the light's not on.) —compare MUST¹ (2)

Can·tab /ˈkæntæb/ abbrev. for (used esp. after the title of a degree) of Cambridge University: Jane Smith, MA Cantab

can·ta·loup also **-loupe** AmE /ˈkæntəluːp‖-ləʊp/ n [C;U] a type of MELON with a hard green or yellow skin and juicy reddish-yellow flesh

can·tan·ker·ous /kænˈtæŋkərəs/ adj infml bad-tempered; quarrelsome: a cantankerous old man − ~ly adv − ~ness n [U]

can·ta·ta /kænˈtɑːtə, kən-‖kən-/ n a musical work, usu. with a religious subject, which includes singing by single performers and by a CHORUS (group of singers). It is shorter than an ORATORIO. −compare ORATORIO

can·teen /kænˈtiːn/ n 1 esp. BrE a place in a factory, school, military camp, etc., where meals are provided, usu. quite cheaply: lunch in the works canteen −compare CAFETERIA 2 a small container in which water or other drink is carried, esp. by soldiers or travellers 3 BrE (a case containing) a set of knives, forks, and spoons (CUTLERY)

can·ter¹ /ˈkæntəʳ/ n 1 [S] the movement of a horse which is faster than a TROT but slower than a GALLOP: We set off at a canter. 2 [C] a ride at this speed: I'm going for a canter round the field.

canter² v [I;T] to (cause to) move at the speed of a canter −compare GALLOP², TROT² (1)

Can·ter·bu·ry /ˈkæntəbəri‖-tərberi/ a small city in SE England, famous for its CATHEDRAL, which is the chief church of the Church of England. The Archbishop of Canterbury is the head of the Church of England.

Canterbury Tales /ˌ·ˌ···· ˈ·/, The a long poem written by Geoffrey Chaucer in the 14th century, which includes a set of stories told by PILGRIMS on their way to Canterbury. The stories are famous esp. for their BAWDY humour. − see also WIFE OF BATH

can·ti·cle /ˈkæntɪkəl/ n a short religious song usu. taken from the Bible

can·ti·le·ver /ˈkæntɬliːvəʳ‖-tl-iːvər/ n an armlike beam standing out from an upright supporting post or wall and used for supporting a shelf, either end of a bridge (a **cantilever bridge**), etc.

can·to /ˈkæntəʊ/ n -tos any of the main divisions of a long poem

can·ton /ˈkæntɒn, kænˈtɒn‖ˈkæntən, -tɑːn/ n a small political division of certain countries, esp. of Switzerland or France

Can·ton /ˌkænˈtɒn‖-ˈtɑːn/ the old name for GUANGZHOU − ~ **Cantonese** adj

Can·ton·ese /ˌkæntəˈniːz◂/ n a Chinese language spoken in and around Guangzhou, formerly called **Canton**, in SE China. Cantonese is also spoken in Hong Kong and by most overseas Chinese in California and London − compare MANDARIN

can·tor /ˈkæntəʳ, -tɔːʳ/ n 1 the man who leads the people in prayer and who sings the music in a Jewish religious service 2 the leader of a CHOIR (=group of singers) in a church

Ca·nuck /kəˈnʌk/ n AmE infml a Canadian, esp. one whose first language is French

Ca·nute /kəˈnjuːt‖-ˈnuːt/ (995?−1035) a Danish king of England whose followers thought that he could stop the sea rising by ordering it back, but he showed them that it was impossible. People sometimes mention Canute and the waves when they are talking about how impossible it is to stop something from happening.

can·vas /ˈkænvəs/ n 1 [U] strong rough cloth used for tents, sails, bags, etc.: a canvas bag | We spent the night **under canvas.** (=in a tent) 2 [C] (a piece of this used for) an oil painting: The artist showed me her canvases. (=completed paintings)

can·vass¹ /ˈkænvəs/ v 1 [I;T (for)] a to try to find out opinions, win political support, or get orders for goods, by going from place to place in (an area) and talking to (people): The party claims to have canvassed over 70% of the votes. | An army of salespeople canvassed the country to promote the new product. | I'm canvassing (for the Republicans) tonight. b to try to find out (opinions) or win (support or orders) in this way: I've been canvassing the views of our members about the proposed changes. −see colour picture on page 950 2 [T] to examine or talk about in detail: This suggestion is being widely canvassed as a possible solution to the dispute. − ~er n

canvass² n the act of canvassing: a door-to-door/house-to-house canvass

can·yon /ˈkænjən/ n a deep narrow steep-sided valley usu. with a river flowing through −see VALLEY (USAGE)

cap¹ /kæp/ n 1 a soft flat covering for the head that has a curved part sticking out at the front (a PEAK or VISOR) and is worn esp. as part of a uniform: an officer's cap − see picture at HAT

▶CULTURAL NOTE In Britain caps are sometimes worn by schoolboys as part of their school uniform. Cloth caps are thought of as typical working-class men's hats, but upper-class men often wear cloth caps in the country. In the US BASEBALL players, and the people who support each team, wear caps with the team's MASCOT on them. Caps are also popular in the US with people who work in the sun, such as farmers.◀

2 a head-covering which is a sign of one's position, profession, membership of a team or club, etc.: a nurse's cap | a cricketer's cap 3 any of several kinds of tight-fitting head-covering: a swimming cap | a shower cap − see also STOCKING CAP 4 (sometimes in comb.) a protective covering for the end or top of an object: Put the cap back on the bottle. | (fig.) a cap of snow on the hilltop − see also ICE CAP, TOE and CAP 5 an upper limit, e.g. on an amount of money that can be spent or borrowed; CEILING (2) 6 also **Dutch cap, diaphragm**− a round usu. rubber object fitted inside a woman's VAGINA to allow her to have sex without having children −see also CONTRACEPTIVE 7 a small paper container holding enough explosive to cause a very small explosion, usu. used in toy guns 8 **cap and gown** AmE the customary clothes worn for GRADUATION from a HIGHSCHOOL or university, consisting of a long black GOWN and a cap with a flat, square top 9 a head-covering given to a player chosen for a special team, esp. a national one, in cricket, football, RUGBY, etc.: Next week Shilton gets his 100th cap for England. 10 **cap in hand** in a respectful and HUMBLE way: to go cap in hand to the government for money 11 **set one's cap at** old-fash infml (of a woman) to try to attract (a man) esp. with the intention of marriage − see also **a feather in someone's cap** (FEATHER¹), **put on one's thinking cap** (THINKING¹)

cap² v -pp- [T] 1 to cover the top of: cloud-capped mountains | cap an oil well 2 to improve on (what someone has said or done): He capped my story with an even funnier one. | Cap that if you can! | His car was stolen, his wife left him, and **to cap it all** (=in addition to everything else) he lost his job! 3 also **charge-cap** (of central government in Britain) to punish (a LOCAL AUTHORITY) by giving them less money than they expected because they have spent more than a certain amount 4 to choose for a team: He's been capped for England at cricket.

cap. caps. written abbrev. for: a capital letter

CAP /ˌsiː eɪ ˈpiː/ n [the] abbrev. for: COMMON AGRICULTURAL POLICY

ca·pa·bil·i·ty /ˌkeɪpəˈbɪlɬti/ n [C;U (for, as)] the fact or quality of being capable, or a way in which someone or something is capable: No one doubts her capability for the job. | The engineer explained the plane's technical capabilities | a computer with a good graphics capability

ca·pa·ble /ˈkeɪpəbəl/ adj 1 [F+of] able; having the power, skill, or other qualities needed (to do something): The company was not capable of handling such a large order. | She's capable of murder when she loses her temper! 2 skilful and effective, esp. in practical matters: a very capable doctor/manager/driver 3 [F+of] able (to be); ready for; SUSCEPTIBLE: That remark is capable of being (=could be) misunderstood. | The new design is capable of improvement. −opposite **incapable** −-bly adv

ca·pa·cious /kəˈpeɪʃəs/ adj fml able to hold or contain a lot: a capacious bottle/suitcase − ~ly adv − ~ness n [U]

ca·pac·i·tor /kəˈpæsɬtəʳ/ n an apparatus that collects and stores electricity, as in a television set

ca·pac·i·ty /kəˈpæsɬti/ n 1 [S;U] a the amount that something can hold or contain: The fuel tank has a capacity of 12 gallons. | The seating capacity of this theatre is 500. | The hall was filled to capacity. (=completely full) | The game was watched by a capacity crowd. b the amount that something, esp. a factory, can produce: This factory has a productive capacity of 200 cars a week. | working at full capacity | There is a lot of **surplus/excess capacity** in *the steel industry.* (=more can be produced than is actually needed) **2** [C;U (**for**)] ability or power: *He has a great capacity for enjoying himself.* [+*to-v*] *Her capacity to remember facts is remarkable.* | *Watching the interview, one could see that he had not lost his capacity for evasion.* **3** [C] a particular position or duty; ROLE: *I'm speaking in my capacity as minister of trade.* | *She is employed by them in an advisory capacity.*

ca·pa·ri·son /kəˈpærɪsən/ *n* (esp. in former times) a decorative cloth covering for a horse (and rider) —**caparison** *v* [T]

cape[1] /keɪp/ *n* a loose outer garment (or part of a garment) without SLEEVEs, fastened at the neck and hanging from the shoulders: *A bicycle cape will protect you in wet weather.* | *a coat with a cape collar* —compare CLOAK[1] (1)

cape[2] *n* (*often cap. as part of a name*) a piece of land standing out into the sea: *the Cape of Good Hope* | *Cape Cod*

Cape Ca·nav·er·al /ˌkeɪp kəˈnævərəl/ the place in Florida, US, formerly called **Cape Kennedy**, from which ROCKETs are sent into space – see colour maps on pages 1374–5

Cape Cod /ˌ· ˈ·/ a CAPE[2] off Massachusetts popular with tourists, and also the place where boats to Martha's Vineyard and Nantucket go from

Cape Col·o·ny /ˌ· ˈ···/ a former name (until 1910) for CAPE PROVINCE

Cape Col·oured /ˌ· ˈ··/ also **Coloured**– *n* in South Africa, a name used to describe a person of mixed black and white race

Cape Hat·te·ras /ˌkeɪp ˈhætərəs/ a CAPE[2] off North Carolina, popular with tourists but also well known for the many ships that have been wrecked there

Cape Horn /ˌ· ˈ·/ the extreme end of South America, known for its very bad weather and dangerous ocean currents

Cape Ken·ne·dy /ˌ· ˈ···/ another name (1963–73) for **Cape Canaveral**

Cape of Good Hope /ˌ· · · ˈ·/ [*the*] a mountainous PENINSULA that sticks out into the sea at the S end of South Africa

Cape Prov·ince /ˌ· ˈ··/ a PROVINCE in the S of South Africa. Its full name is **Cape of Good Hope Province**, and it was formerly called **Cape Colony**.

ca·per[1] /ˈkeɪpər/ *v* [I (ABOUT)] *esp. lit* to jump about in a happy playful manner: *The lambs were capering (about) in the fields.*

caper[2] *n* **1** *esp. lit* a playful jumping movement: *children dancing and cutting capers* (=jumping about) **2** *sl* an activity, esp. a dishonest or illegal one

caper[3] *n* a small dark-green flower BUD used for giving a special sourish taste to food

Cape Town /ˈ· ·/ a large city in South Africa near the Cape of Good Hope

Cape Verde /ˌkeɪp ˈvɜːd‖-ˈvɜːrd/ a country made up of a group of islands in the Atlantic Ocean, W of Senegal; capital Praia; population 369,000 (1989)

ca·pil·la·ry /kəˈpɪləri‖ˈkæpəleri/ *n* a very fine hairlike tube, such as one of the smaller blood tubes in the body

capillary at·trac·tion /ˌ·····‖ ·‖ ˈ···· ·ˌ··/ *n* [U] *tech* the force which causes a liquid to rise up a narrow tube, e.g. water rising from the roots of a tree to the branches

cap·i·tal[1] /ˈkæpɪtl/ *n* **1** [C] a town which is the centre of government of a country or other political unit: *Paris is the capital of France.* | *What is the capital of California?* | (fig.) *Hollywood is the capital of the movie industry.* | *Can you name all the state capitals?* **2** [S;U] wealth, esp. money used to produce more wealth or for starting a business: *You need a lot of capital to start up a new newspaper.* | *The company was started with a capital of £10,000.* | *a successful firm that offers investors a high return on capital* | *They have a* **working capital** (=money that can be used in the course of business activity) *of £20,000.* | *What we need now is a big injection of capital.* —see also VENTURE CAPITAL **3** [C] a letter in its large form, esp. one at the beginning of a word; a capital letter: *The word DICTIONARY is printed here in capitals.* —compare LOWER CASE; see also UPPER CASE **4 make capital (out) of** to use to one's advantage: *The opposition parties are sure to make political capital out of the government's difficulties.*

capital[2] *adj* **1** [A] punishable by death: *Murder can be a capital offence.* —see also CAPITAL PUNISHMENT **2** [A] (of a letter) written or printed in its large form (such as A, B, C rather than a, b, c) —compare LOWER CASE **3** [A] of or concerning capital in the form of money or property: *a big programme of capital investment to modernize the railways* **4** *old-fash* excellent: *a capital dinner* | *That's capital!*

capital[3] *n* the top part of a COLUMN (1)

capital as·sets /ˌ··· ˈ··/ *n* [P] the machines, buildings, and other property belonging to a company

capital ex·pen·di·ture /ˌ··· ·ˈ···/ *n* [U] the buying of machinery and other long lasting ASSETs which will be used in the production process of a company over a long period of time

capital gains /ˌ··· ˈ·/ *n* [P] profits made by selling possessions

capital gains tax /ˌ··· ˈ· ·/ *n* a tax paid on profits made by selling possessions. For example, if someone buys a building, uses it for business, then sells it again, they must pay capital gains tax on the profit that they make from the sale.

capital goods /ˈ··· ·ˌ·/ *n* [P] goods such as machines which are made for the purpose of producing other goods — compare CONSUMER GOODS

capital-in·ten·sive /ˌ··· ·ˈ··◄/ *adj* (of an industry) needing a lot of CAPITAL[1] (2) compared to its other needs, such as workers —compare LABOUR-INTENSIVE

cap·i·tal·is·m /ˈkæpɪtl-ɪzəm/ *n* [U] a system of production and trade based on the private ownership of wealth, free buying and selling, and little industrial activity by the government —compare COMMUNISM, SOCIALISM

cap·i·tal·ist[1] /ˈkæpɪtl-ɪst/ *n often derog* **1** a person who supports capitalism **2** a person who owns or controls much wealth (CAPITAL) and esp. who lends it to businesses, banks, etc., to produce more wealth

capitalist[2] also **cap·i·tal·is·tic** /ˌkæpɪtl-ˈɪstɪk◄/— *adj* **1** *often derog* owning or controlling a large amount of wealth: *the capitalist class* **2** practising or supporting capitalism: *the capitalist countries of the West* | *a capitalist economy* | *the capitalist press* (=newspapers)

cap·i·tal·ize also **-ise** *BrE* /ˈkæpɪtl-aɪz/ *v* [T] **1** to write with a CAPITAL[2] (2) letter **2** to supply money to (a firm) to allow it to operate: *The bank has promised to capitalize our new business.* | *The company is seriously under-capitalized.* (=does not have enough capital to operate effectively) **3** [(**at**)] *tech* to calculate the value of (a business), based on the value of its shares or its earnings —**ization** /ˌkæpɪtl-aɪˈzeɪʃən‖-əˈzeɪ-/ *n* [S;U] : (*a*) *capitalization of £50 million*
    capitalize on sthg. *phr v* [T] to use to one's advantage: *She capitalized on his mistake and won the game.*

capital lev·y /ˌ··· ˈ··/ *n BrE* a tax on private or industrial wealth (CAPITAL) paid to the government, usu. in addition to income tax

capital pun·ish·ment /ˌ··· ˈ···/ *n* [U] punishment by death according to law; the death PENALTY
    ▶ CULTURAL NOTE Capital punishment is no longer used in Britain, but it is regularly discussed in parliament. Some people would like to see it reintroduced for all murderers, some for TERRORISTs, and some for those who kill policemen. Several US states use capital punishment and carry it out by a variety of methods including the electric chair, poisonous gas, and INJECTION of poison. ◀

Capital Ra·di·o /ˌ··· ˈ···/ a radio station in London which plays popular music and has advertisements

capital trans·fer tax /ˌ··· ˈ·· ·ˌ·/ *n* [C;U] (*often cap.*) *BrE* a tax paid when one receives money, either as a gift or when someone dies

cap·i·ta·tion /ˌkæpɪˈteɪʃən/ *n* a tax paid or payment made at the same fixed amount for each person

Cap·i·tol /ˈkæpɪtl/ [*the*] the building in Washington where the US Congress meets, or a similar building for each particular state of the US

Cap·i·tol Hill /ˌkæpɪtl ˈhɪl/ the part of the US government which is concerned with law; the US Congress (from Capitol Hill in Washington, DC, where the law buildings are): *The President's attempt to get Congress to vote in the new bill did not go down well on Capitol Hill.*

ca·pit·u·late /kəˈpɪtʃ\u{}leɪt/ v [I (to)] **1** to accept defeat, usu. on agreed conditions; SURRENDER **2** to accept or agree, often unwillingly; stop opposing: *He finally capitulated and allowed his daughter to go on holiday with her friends.* —**lation** /kəˌpɪtʃ\u{}ˈleɪʃən/ n [C;U]

ca·pon /ˈkeɪpən‖-pɑːn, -pən/ n a male chicken with its sex organs removed to make it grow big and fat for eating

Ca·pone /kəˈpəʊn, ˈæl/ (1899–1947) an American GANGSTER (=a criminal) who was the leader of ORGANIZED CRIME in Chicago from 1925 to 1931

Al Capone

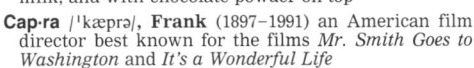

Ca·po·te /kəˈpəʊti/, **Truman** (1924–84) an American writer best known for his true accounts of unusual crimes, such as *In Cold Blood*

cap·puc·ci·no /ˌkæpʊˈtʃiːnəʊ‖ˌkɑː-/ n [C;U] (a cupful of) Italian coffee made with hot milk, and with chocolate powder on top

Cap·ra /ˈkæprə/, **Frank** (1897–1991) an American film director best known for the films *Mr. Smith Goes to Washington* and *It's a Wonderful Life*

Ca·pri /kəˈpriː/ an Italian island near the city of Naples and popular with tourists

ca·price /kəˈpriːs/ n **1** [C;U] (a) sudden often foolish change of mind or behaviour, usu. without any real cause; sudden wish to have or do something; WHIM: *the caprices of spoilt children*/(fig.) *of the weather* **2** [U] a tendency to have caprices

ca·pri·cious /kəˈprɪʃəs/ adj changing often, esp. suddenly and without good reason; not dependable; FICKLE: *He's so capricious.* | *We can't go camping while the weather is so capricious.* — **~ly** adv — **~ness** n [U]

Cap·ri·corn /ˈkæprɪkɔːn‖-ɔːrn/ n **1** [U] the tenth sign of the ZODIAC, represented by a goat —see ZODIAC (USAGE) and see picture at ZODIAC **2** [C] a person born between December 23 and January 20 —see also **Tropic of Capricorn** (TROPIC)

cap·si·cum /ˈkæpsɪkəm/ n [C;U] *tech for* PEPPER¹ (2)

cap·size /kæpˈsaɪz‖ˈkæpsaɪz/ v [I;T] (esp. of a boat) to turn over: *The boat capsized in the storm, but luckily it didn't sink.*

cap·stan /ˈkæpstən/ n **1** a round drum-shaped machine turned by hand or some other type of power in order to wind up a rope that pulls or raises heavy objects, such as a ship's ANCHOR **2** the bar that goes round and round to drive the TAPE in a TAPE RECORDER

cap·sule /ˈkæpsjuːl‖-səl/ n **1** an outer covering containing a measured amount of medicine, the whole of which is swallowed —see picture at PILL **2** the part of a spacecraft in which the pilots live and work and from which the engine is separated when the TAKEOFF is completed

cap·tain¹ /ˈkæptɪn/ n **1** a rank in the navy, army, or US Air Force or Marines —see also GROUP CAPTAIN; see TABLE 3 and see picture at RANK **2** the person in command of a ship or aircraft: *Are we ready to sail, Captain?* - see FATHER (USAGE) **3** the leader of a team or group: *She's (the) captain of the school hockey team.* (fig.) *a captain of industry* (e.g. the owner of an important company)

captain² v [T] to be captain of; command; lead

Captain Bob /ˌ·· ˈ·/ see Robert MAXWELL

Captain Cook see Captain James COOK

Captain Hook /ˌ·· ˈ·/ a PIRATE with a metal hook instead of one hand, who appears in the story *Peter Pan* by J M Barrie —see also PETER PAN and see colour picture on page 619

Captain Kan·ga·roo /ˌ·· ··ˈ·/ an American television programme for children which began in 1953 and continued into the 1960s and 1970s. Captain Kangaroo was the main character and the other well-known character from the programme was Mr. Green Jeans.

cap·tion /ˈkæpʃən/ n words printed above or below a picture, newspaper article, etc., to say what it is about or

give further information: *The caption under the photo said "The President greets the Japanese delegation."*

cap·tious /ˈkæpʃəs/ adj *fml* too ready to find fault; too CRITICAL: *a captious old lady, difficult to please* — **~ly** adv — **~ness** n [U]

cap·ti·vate /ˈkæptɪ\u{}veɪt/ v [T] to charm, excite, and attract: *The dancer quickly captivated her audience.* | *Venice's captivating beauty* —**vation** /ˌkæptɪ\u{}ˈveɪʃən/ n [U]

cap·tive¹ /ˈkæptɪv/ adj **1** held as a prisoner, esp. in war: *We were held captive for three months.* **2** not allowed to move about freely; imprisoned: *captive animals* | *a captive balloon* (=one tied to the ground by a rope) | *As we were travelling in his car, we were a captive audience for his boring stories.*

captive² n a person held as a prisoner, esp. in war

cap·tiv·i·ty /kæpˈtɪv\u{}ti/ n [U] the state of being captive: *Many animals do not breed well in captivity.* | *The hostages were released from captivity.*

cap·tor /ˈkæptər/ n usu. *fml* a person who has captured someone or something: *I soon escaped from my captors.*

cap·ture¹ /ˈkæptʃər/ v [T] **1** to take (a person or animal) prisoner: *She was captured trying to escape from the country.* | (fig.) *Their daring escape has captured the imagination of the whole country.* (=filled everyone with interest and admiration) **2** to take control of (something) by force from an enemy; win; gain: *to capture a castle* | (fig.) *They captured over 60% of the votes*/*a large share of the market.* **3** to preserve in an unchanging form on film, in words, etc.: *I captured my baby daughter's first smile on film.* | *In his book he tried to capture* (=describe) *the beauty of Venice.* **4** *tech* to put into a form that can be used by a computer: *The data is captured by means of an optical scanner.*

capture² n **1** [U] the act of taking by force or of being taken by force: *He was released yesterday, six months after his capture by the terrorists.* **2** [C] something that has been taken, caught, or won by force

Cap·u·lets and Mon·ta·gues /ˌkæpjʊ\u{}ləts ənd ˈmɒntəɡjuːz‖-ˈmɑːn-/ [the] the two families of the lovers Romeo and Juliet in Shakespeare's play. The families were enemies, which is why Romeo and Juliet's marriage had to be secret.

car /kɑːr/ n **1** also **motorcar** *BrE fml* ‖ **automobile** *AmE fml*– a road vehicle with usu. four wheels which is driven by a motor and used as a means of travel for a small number of people: *She goes to work by car.* | *a car factory* | *You can't park your car here.* | *a garage that sells new and used cars* | *a car accident* **2** (*esp. in comb.*) a railway carriage: *This train has a restaurant car*/*a sleeping car.* **3** any small vehicle in which people or goods are carried, e.g. as part of a LIFT, BALLOON, AIRSHIP, etc. —see also CABLE CAR, STREETCAR

▷ USAGE When you are in control of a **car** you **drive** it, and when you direct its course you **steer** it: *She got into the car and **drove** (it) home.* | *She **steered** (the car) carefully through the narrow gap.* As a passenger you **travel by** car, but **travel in** or **ride in** a particular car. At the beginning of your journey you **get into** it and at the end you **get out of** it. —see also DRIVE (USAGE), STEER (USAGE), TRANSPORT (USAGE)◁

Ca·rac·as /kəˈrækəs‖-ˈrɑː-/ the capital of Venezuela

ca·rafe /kəˈræf, kəˈrɑːf/ n (the amount contained in) a bottle with a wide neck for serving wine or water at meals —see picture at FLASK

car a·larm /ˈ· ·ˌ·/ n an apparatus that makes a loud warning noise when somebody tries to break into a car

car·a·mel /ˈkærəməl, -mel/ n **1** [U] burnt sugar used for giving food a special taste and colour —see also CREME CARAMEL **2** [C;U] (a piece of) sticky boiled sugar containing this and eaten as a sweet

car·a·pace /ˈkærəpeɪs/ n a protective hard shell on the outside of certain animals, such as CRABS or TORTOISES

car·at also **karat** *AmE* /ˈkærət/ n **1** a division on the scale of measurement for the purity of gold: *an 18-carat gold ring* **2** a division (equal to 200 MILLIGRAMS) on the scale of measurement for the weight of jewels

car·a·van /ˈkærəvæn/ n **1** *BrE* ‖ **trailer** *AmE*– a vehicle which can be pulled by a car, which contains cooking and sleeping equipment, and in which people live (often

car

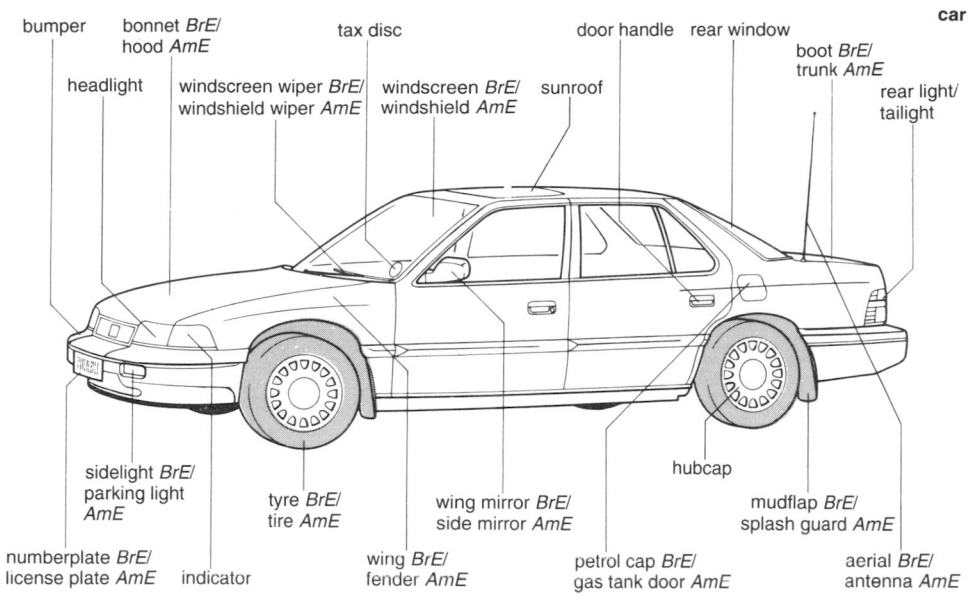

- bumper
- bonnet *BrE*/ hood *AmE*
- tax disc
- door handle
- rear window
- boot *BrE*/ trunk *AmE*
- headlight
- windscreen wiper *BrE*/ windshield wiper *AmE*
- windscreen *BrE*/ windshield *AmE*
- sunroof
- rear light/ taillight
- sidelight *BrE*/ parking light *AmE*
- tyre *BrE*/ tire *AmE*
- wing mirror *BrE*/ side mirror *AmE*
- hubcap
- mudflap *BrE*/ splash guard *AmE*
- numberplate *BrE*/ license plate *AmE*
- indicator
- wing *BrE*/ fender *AmE*
- petrol cap *BrE*/ gas tank door *AmE*
- aerial *BrE*/ antenna *AmE*

the interior of a car

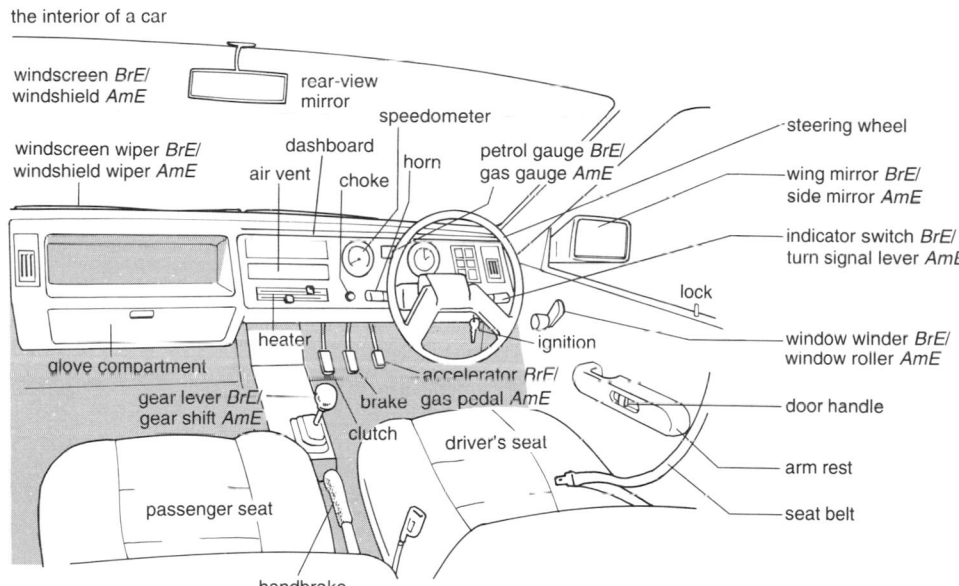

- windscreen *BrE*/ windshield *AmE*
- rear-view mirror
- speedometer
- steering wheel
- windscreen wiper *BrE*/ windshield wiper *AmE*
- dashboard
- air vent
- choke
- horn
- petrol gauge *BrE*/ gas gauge *AmE*
- wing mirror *BrE*/ side mirror *AmE*
- indicator switch *BrE*/ turn signal lever *AmE*
- lock
- heater
- glove compartment
- gear lever *BrE*/ gear shift *AmE*
- accelerator *BrE*/ gas pedal *AmE*
- brake
- clutch
- driver's seat
- ignition
- window winder *BrE*/ window roller *AmE*
- door handle
- arm rest
- seat belt
- passenger seat
- handbrake

on a **caravan site** *BrE* ‖ **trailer park** *AmE*) or travel, usu. for holidays —compare CAMPER (2) **2** *BrE* ‖ **wagon** *AmE*— a covered horse-drawn cart in which people such as gipsies (GIPSY) live or travel **3** [+*sing./pl. v*] (esp. in former times) a group of people with vehicles or animals travelling together for protection through unfriendly esp. desert areas: *a caravan of merchants*

car·a·van·ning /ˈkærəvænɪŋ/ *n* [U] *BrE* the practice of taking holidays in a caravan

car·a·van·se·rai /ˌkærəˈvænsəraɪ/ *n* (in Asian countries) a simple hotel with a large courtyard where CARAVANS (3) stop for the night

car·a·way /ˈkærəweɪ/ *n* a plant whose small strong-tasting seeds are used for giving a special taste to food: *bread with caraway seeds in it*

car·bine /ˈkɑːbaɪn‖ˈkɑːr-/ *n* a short light RIFLE (=kind of gun)

car·bo·hy·drate /ˌkɑːbəʊˈhaɪdreɪt, -drɨt‖ˌkɑːr-/ *n* **1** [C;U] *tech* any of several substances, such as sugar, which consist of oxygen, HYDROGEN, and CARBON, and which provide the body with heat and power (ENERGY) **2** [C *usu. pl.*] *infml* foods such as rice, PASTA, bread, and potatoes which contain carbohydrates. In the 1950s and 60s people worried about carbohydrates making them fat, but now they are more concerned about milk fat, fat meat, and sugar.

car·bol·ic /kɑːˈbɒlɪk‖kɑːrˈbɑːlɪk/ *adj* coming from carbon, esp. in the form of COAL TAR: *carbolic soap*

car bomb /ˈ· ˌ·/ *n* a bomb placed in a car, esp. by TERRORISTS: *a car bomb attack on an army barracks in Ulster*

car bomb·ing /ˈ· ˌ··/ *n* [C;U] (a case of) the use of a car bomb, esp. in attacks by TERRORISTS

car·bon /ˈkɑːbən‖ˈkɑːr-/ *n* **1** [U] a simple substance (ELEMENT) found in a pure form as diamonds, GRAPHITE, etc., or in an impure form as coal, petrol, etc. **2** [C;U] CARBON PAPER **3** [C] a CARBON COPY

carbon 14 /ˌkɑːbən fɔːˈtiːn◂‖ˌkɑːrbən fɔːr-/ n [U] tech the special form of carbon used in carbon dating

car·bon·at·ed /ˈkɑːbəneɪtɪ̯d‖ˈkɑːr-/ adj (esp. of a drink) containing CARBON DIOXIDE, which produces small BUBBLES

carbon cop·y /ˌ·· ˈ··/ n **1** also **carbon**— a copy, esp. of something typed, made using CARBON PAPER **2** [(of)] a person or thing that is very similar to another: *He's a carbon copy of his father.* | *This robbery is a carbon copy of one that took place last year.*

carbon dat·ing /ˌ·· ˈ··/ BrE ‖ **radioactive dating** AmE n [U] a method of scientifically calculating the age of an old object by measuring the amount of a special form of carbon in it

carbon di·ox·ide /ˌ·· ·ˈ··/ n [U] the gas produced when animals breathe out, when carbon is burned in air, or when animal or vegetable matter decays. Carbon dioxide is a GREENHOUSE GAS —compare CARBON MONOXIDE

car·bon·if·er·ous /ˌkɑːbəˈnɪfərəs◂‖ˌkɑːr-/ adj producing or containing carbon or coal: *carboniferous rocks*

car·bon·ize also **-ise** BrE /ˈkɑːbənaɪz‖ˈkɑːr-/ v [I;T] to (cause to) change into carbon by burning without air

carbon mo·nox·ide /ˌ·· ·ˈ··/ n [U] a poisonous gas produced when carbon (esp. petrol) burns in a small amount of air. People are becoming worried about the amount of carbon monoxide being produced because it is a GREENHOUSE GAS and too much of it will increase the temperature of the earth. —compare CARBON DIOXIDE

carbon pa·per /ˈ·· ˌ··/ also **carbon**— n [C;U] (a sheet of) thin paper with a coat of dark colouring substance on one side, used between sheets of writing to make copies

car·bon tet·ra·chlo·ride /ˌkɑːbən tetrəˈklɔːraɪd‖ˌkɑːr-/ n [U] a colourless liquid used for cleaning dirty marks off clothes

car boot sale

car boot sale /ˌ·ˈ· ·/ n BrE BOOT SALE

car·boy /ˈkɑːbɔɪ‖ˈkɑːr-/ n a large often green glass, metal, or plastic round bottle, often protected by a special covering, used for holding usu. dangerous chemical liquids

car·bun·cle /ˈkɑːbʌŋkəl‖ˈkɑːr-/ n **1** a large painful BOIL (=swelling under the skin) **2** an ugly addition to something. The word is sometimes used in Britain to describe a new building in a modern style that spoils the appearance of the older buildings around it (from a speech by Prince Charles in which he described a planned new part of the National Gallery as like a "monstrous carbuncle" on the face of an old friend) **3** a red jewel, esp. a GARNET

car·bu·ret·tor BrE ‖ **-retor** AmE /ˌkɑːbjʊ̈ˈretəʳ, -bə-‖ ˈkɑːrbəreɪtəʳ/ n an apparatus, esp. used in car engines, for mixing the necessary amounts of air and petrol to produce the explosive gas which burns in the engine to provide power —see pictures at CAR and ENGINE

car·cass also **-case** BrE /ˈkɑːkəs‖ˈkɑːr-/ n **1** the body of a dead animal, esp. one which is ready to be cut up as meat **2** the decaying remains of something, such as a car or a ship: *Divers have found the carcass of a wrecked ship 100 miles from the coast.* **3** derog sl the body of a dead or living person

car·cin·o·gen /kɑːˈsɪnədʒən‖kɑːr-/ n med a carcinogenic substance

car·cin·o·genic /ˌkɑːsɪnəˈdʒenɪk◂‖ˌkɑːr-/ adj med causing CANCER: *carcinogenic cleaning materials*

card¹ /kɑːd‖kɑːrd/ n **1** [C] also **playing card** fml— any of a set of 52 small sheets of stiffened paper marked to show their number and the class (SUIT) they belong to, and used for various games: *The players were dealt six cards each.* | *a pack of cards* | *a card table* | *to shuffle the cards* (=mix them up) —see also COURT CARD; see CARDS (USAGE) **2** [C] (often in comb.) a small sheet of stiffened paper (or plastic), usu. with information printed on it and having various uses: *a bank card* | *a membership card* | *Let me give you my business card.* —see also CASH CARD,

CHARGE CARD, CHEQUE CARD, CREDIT CARD, VISITING CARD **3** [C] a also **greeting card** a piece of stiffened paper usu. with a picture on the front and a message inside, sent to a person by post on special occasions, such as on a birthday or at Christmas: *a birthday card* | *I sent her a get-well card when she was in hospital.* **b** a POSTCARD —see also CHRISTMAS CARD **4** [U] stiffened paper; cardboard **5** [C] old-fash infml an entertaining and amusing person; WAG: *John's a real card; he always makes me laugh.* **6** [C] something, such as a very effective argument or course of action, which gives one an advantage and which one keeps (often secretly) until the right moment: *Things look bad for them, but they still* **have a few cards up their sleeve.** (=ready to be used) | *Then she* **played her best/strongest/trump card** *and threatened to resign.* | *The union can't win — the company* **holds all the cards.** —see also CARDS

card² n tech an instrument that is similar to a comb and is used for combing, cleaning, and preparing wool, cotton, etc., for spinning —**card** v [I;T]

car·da·mom /ˈkɑːdəməm‖ˈkɑːr-/ n [C;U] (one of) the seeds of an Asian fruit, used for giving a special taste to food, esp. in Indian and Middle Eastern cooking

card·board¹ /ˈkɑːdbɔːd‖ˈkɑːrdbɔːrd/ n [U] a stiff usu. brownish or greyish material like thick paper, used for making boxes, the backs of books, etc.: *a pad of paper with a sheet of cardboard at the back*

cardboard² adj **1** made from cardboard: *a cardboard box* **2** derog unreal; unnatural: *Her new book is full of cardboard characters.* —compare WOODEN (2)

cardboard city /ˌ·· ˈ··/ n an area where people with no homes sleep on the streets, often using cardboard boxes to keep warm; in Britain, used esp. of an area in Waterloo, London: *A bid to stop homeless kids ending up in London's cardboard cities will be launched this week.*

card-car·ry·ing /ˈ· ˌ···/ adj [A] being a full member of an organization, esp. a political one: *a card-carrying member of the Labour party*

card cat·a·log /ˈ· ˌ···/ see CARD INDEX

card·hold·er /ˈkɑːdhəʊldəʳ‖ˈkɑːrd-/ n a person who has the use of a card, esp. a CREDIT CARD: *Cardholders are advised to note down their PIN number and keep it in a safe place.*

cardi- see WORD FORMATION

car·di·ac /ˈkɑːdi-æk‖ˈkɑːr-/ adj [A] med connected with the heart or with heart disease: *cardiac disease* | *cardiac failure/arrest* (=stopping of the heart)

Car·diff /ˈkɑːdɪf‖ˈkɑːr-/ the capital and main port of Wales. Cardiff is an industrial city which also has a castle, cathedral, university, and an important RUGBY ground, **Cardiff Arms Park.** —see colour map on page 818

car·di·gan /ˈkɑːdɪgən‖ˈkɑːr-/ n a short knitted (KNIT) woollen coat with SLEEVES, usu. fastened at the front with buttons —compare SWEATER

Car·din /ˈkɑːdæn‖kɑːrˈdæn/, **Pi·erre** /piˈeəʳ/ (1922–) a French DESIGNER of clothes esp. for men

car·di·nal¹ /ˈkɑːdənəl‖ˈkɑːr-/ n **1** a priest with one of the highest ranks of the Roman Catholic Church **2** a N American bird (FINCH) of which the male is bright red in colour

cardinal² adj fml most important; chief: *a cardinal error/sin* | *This is one of the cardinal rules of mountain climbing.*

cardinal³ also **cardinal number**— n any of the numbers 1, 2, 3, etc. that show quantity rather than order — compare ORDINAL²

cardinal point /ˌ··· ˈ·/ n COMPASS POINT¹ (12)

cardinal sin /ˌ··· ˈ·/ n (in the Christian religion) one of the seven deadly SINs; pride, LUST, ENVY, anger, COVETOUSNESS, GLUTTONY, and SLOTH

cardinal vir·tue /ˌ··· ˈ··/ n a quality in a person that is highly respected and valued, esp. PRUDENCE, JUSTICE, TEMPERANCE, and FORTITUDE

card in·dex /ˈ· ˌ··/ BrE ‖ **card catalog** AmE— n (a box containing) a number of cards each carrying a particular piece of information and arranged in order, as in a library

car·di·o·pul·mo·na·ry re·sus·ci·ta·tion /ˌkɑːdiəʊpʊlmənəri rɪˌsʌsɪ̯ˈteɪʃən‖ˌkɑːrdiəʊpʊlməneri-/ see CPR

card phone /'· ·/ n BrE a public telephone which you can use only when you put in a special plastic card called a PHONECARD

card·punch /'kɑːdpʌntʃ‖'kɑːrd-/ BrE ‖ **keypunch** AmE— n a machine that puts information onto cards in such a way that computers can read and understand it, used esp. formerly

cards /kɑːdz‖kɑːrdz/ n [P] **1** games played with CARDS (1); card playing: Let's play cards/have a game of cards. | He always cheats at cards. **2** get/be given one's cards BrE infml to be dismissed from one's job **3** lay/put one's **cards on the table** to be completely open and honest about one's position, plans, etc. **4** on the cards BrE ‖ **in the cards** AmE— infml probable: They say another price increase is on the cards. | It's on the cards that she'll be offered the job. **5** play/hold one's cards close to **one's chest** to keep one's actions or intentions secret — see also HOUSE OF CARDS, play one's cards right/**properly** (PLAY)

cards

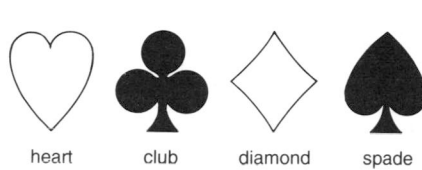

heart   club   diamond   spade

▷ USAGE The cards used in card games come in two red **suits, hearts** and **diamonds;** and two black ones, **clubs** and **spades.** Each **suit** has nine cards numbered two to ten, and also an **ace,** a **king,** a **queen,** and a **jack** or **knave.** We say the king of hearts | the jack of clubs | the queen of diamonds | the ace of spades | the ten of hearts.◁

card·sharp /'kɑːdʃɑːp‖'kɑːrdʃɑːrp/ also **card-sharp·er** /'· ¸··/— n a person who plays cards dishonestly to make money

card vote /'· ·/ n BrE a vote at a TRADE UNION meeting in which each representative's vote counts as a vote by all the people represented

care¹ /keər/ n **1** [U] the process of looking after and giving attention to someone who needs it, such as a sick or old person: Our health service provides high standards of medical care. | These disabled children need special care. | After the accident he was rushed to the hospital's **intensive care unit.** | The article offers advice on skin and hair care. —see also COMMUNITY CARE, DAY CARE **2** [U] the responsibility for protecting or looking after someone, dealing with a problem or difficulty, etc.; charge; SUPERVISION: Who will **take care of** the dog while we're away? | (BrE) The little boy's parents couldn't look after him, so he's been **taken into care.** (=into a home run by the government or local council) | Don't worry about your flight reservation – it's all been taken care of. **3** [C;U] (something that causes) worry, sorrow or uncertainty; anxiety: free from care | all the cares of the world (=very many worries) | She hasn't a care in the world. (=she has no worries at all) **4** [U] serious attention and effort: Try to do your work with a bit more care. **5** [U] carefulness in avoiding harm, damage, etc.; CAUTION: Cross the road with care. | **Take care** (=be careful) not to drop the glass.| He was charged with driving **without due care and attention.** **6** [C] esp. fml a person or thing for which one is responsible; object of one's special attention **7 care of** also c/o— (used when addressing letters to mean) at the address of: John Smith, care of Mary Jones, 14 High Street **8 Have a care!** old-fash Be more careful! —see CARE² (USAGE) **9 Take care!** (used as a way of saying goodbye, esp. to family and friends)

care² v [not in progressive forms] **1** [I (about); T+wh-; obj] to be worried, anxious, or concerned (about); mind: When his dog died Allan didn't seem to care at all. | The only thing he cares about is money. | I really care whether we win or lose. | **As if I cared** whether he comes or not! (=it doesn't matter to me at all) | I **couldn't care less** what you think! | We could be starving **for all they care.** (=they don't care at all) —see also CARING **2** [T+to-v;obj] (esp. in polite suggestions) to like; want: Would you care

to wait here, sir, until the manager can see you?

▷ USAGE Compare **care (about), care for** and **take care of. 1** To **care about** something is to think it is important: She doesn't **care about** money. | I don't **care (about)** what people think. **2** To **care for** means "to like" in negative sentences and questions: I don't really **care for** red wine. It also means (rather literary) "to look after": Who will **care for** me when I am old? **3** To **take care of** means "to look after": We will **take care of** you when you are old. | She asked her secretary to **take care of** the travel arrangements.◁

care for sbdy./sthg. phr v [T] **1** to nurse or attend (esp. someone old or sick); look after: She cared for her father in his dying years. | I am glad to see that you are being well cared for. **2** [usu. in questions and negatives] to like: I don't really care for tea; I like coffee better. | Would you care for (=do you want to have) a drink?

CARE /keər/ Cooperative for American Relief to Everywhere; an American organization that sends food, clothing and medicine in special boxes (CARE packages) to places around the world where they are needed. People often use **CARE package** informally to talk about nice things that their families or friends send to them: My mother sent me a CARE package with homemade cookies in it.

ca·reen /kə'riːn/ v [I+adv/prep] esp. AmE to go forward rapidly while making sudden movements from side to side; LURCH: As the bus careened down the hill, the passengers were thrown roughly from side to side. —compare CAREER³

ca·reer¹ /kə'rɪər/ n **1** a job or profession for which one is trained and which one intends to follow for part or the whole of one's life: a career in banking | a change of career | He's very career-minded. (=keen to do well in his job) **2** (a part of) the general course of a person's working life: She spent most of her career working in Edinburgh. | her outstanding political career —see JOB (USAGE)

career² adj [A] professional; regarding one's job as a career for a long period: He's a career soldier/diplomat; it's the only job he's ever done.

career³ v [I+adv/prep] to go at full speed; rush wildly: The car careered uncontrollably down the hill and into a tree. —compare CAREEN

career break /·'· ¸·/ n a period in which a person decides to leave their job for a while, usu. in order to do something else, but with the intention of going back to work again. Many women decide to take a career break when they have children.

career girl /·'· ¸·/ also **career wom·an** /·'· ¸··/— n a woman whose career is very important to her, so that, for example, she chooses to continue working rather than stopping in order to bring up children

ca·reer·ist /kə'rɪərɪst/ n usu. derog someone who puts success in their profession before all other things, such as friends or family, and may be willing to act unfairly to gain advancement —**-ism** n [U]

careers ad·vice /·'· ¸·/ also **careers guid·ance** /·'· ¸··/— n [U] in Britain, help and information given, usu. by a specially trained person, to help people decide what job they want to do and how they can achieve it. This help is usu. given at school or at a careers office and is free.

careers ad·vi·sor /·'· ¸··/ also **careers of·fic·er** /·'· ¸···/— n in Britain, a specially trained person whose job is to help other people decide what job they want to do and to give help and information about education, TRAINING, and careers

careers of·fice /·'· ¸··/ n in Britain, a place where people can go for help and advice about education, TRAINING, and careers. The careers office does not have information about particular jobs which are available, only general information about what you should do if you want to be a doctor, secretary, teacher, etc. Most towns have a careers office which provides a free service, mainly for young people who have just left school. —see also JOB CENTRE

career struc·ture /·'· ¸··/ n the organization of a career or profession in such a way that a person starting in it can in future expect to have opportunities to do more difficult work, take more responsibility, and earn more money: The company offers a good career structure with the possibility of rapid promotion.

care-free /ˈkeəfriː‖ˈkeər-/ adj free from anxiety; having no worries or problems: *After finishing our exams we all felt happy and carefree.*

care-ful /ˈkeəfəl‖ˈkeər-/ adj **1** [(with)] taking care (with the intention of avoiding loss or danger); CAUTIOUS: *a careful driver* | *You should be more careful with your money.* [+v-ing] *Be careful crossing the road.* (=when you cross the road) [+to-v] *I was careful not to say anything about this to the boss.* [+(that)] *Be careful (that) you don't fall off the ladder.* [+wh-] *Be careful how you carry those glasses.* **2** showing attention to details; thorough: *a careful worker* | *After careful consideration, we've decided to accept their offer.* — ~ly adv : *Hold this glass carefully; I don't want it broken.* | *a carefully planned operation* — ~ness [U]

care la·bel /ˈ·ˌ·/ n a small piece of cloth with cleaning instructions on it sewn inside a piece of clothing

care-less /ˈkeələs‖ˈkeər-/ adj **1** not taking enough care; inattentive: *He's a very careless driver; he never thinks about what he's doing.* | *It was very careless of you to lose the documents.* **2** done without care: *This is careless work. Do it again!* **3** free from care or worry; UNCONCERNED: *She's very careless with money.* (=she spends too much) | *a careless attitude* | (fig.) *careless charm* (=natural charm) — ~ly adv — ~ness n [U]

car·er /ˈkeərər/ n esp. BrE someone who stays at home and looks after a person who is old or ill

ca·ress¹ /kəˈres/ n a light loving touch or kiss

caress² v [T] to give a caress to: *She caressed his cheek lovingly.* | (fig.) *a picturesque fishing village, caressed by gentle breezes*

car·et /ˈkærət/ n tech the mark ⋀ or ⋏ used in writing and printing to show where something is to be added

care·tak·er /ˈkeəˌteɪkər‖ˈkeər-/ n **1** also **janitor** esp. AmE & ScotE — a person employed to look after a school or other usu. large public building and to be responsible for small repairs, cleaning, etc. **2** a person who looks after a house or land when the owner is absent **3** esp. AmE a person who provides care, such as a parent, teacher, or nurse

caretaker gov·ern·ment /ˈ··· ˌ··/ n a government which holds office for a usu. short period between the end of one government and the appointment of a new government

care-worn /ˈkeəwɔːn‖ˈkeərwɔːrn/ n showing the effects of grief, worry, or anxiety: *the careworn face of the mother of a large poor family*

car·fare /ˈkɑːfeər‖ˈkɑːr-/ n [U] AmE the money (FARE) that a passenger is charged for travelling in a bus, train, etc., within a town or city: *How much is the carfare to get downtown?*

car·go /ˈkɑːgəʊ‖ˈkɑːr-/ n -goes or -gos [C;U] (one load of) the goods (FREIGHT) carried by a ship, plane, or vehicle: *We sailed from Newcastle with a cargo of coal.* | *cargo vessel/plane*

car·hop /ˈkɑːhɒp‖ˈkɑːrhɑːp/ n AmE infml a waiter or waitress at a DRIVE-IN restaurant

Car·ib·be·an¹ /ˌkærɪˈbiːən◂‖ [the]* **1** the islands in the Caribbean Sea **2** the area around the Caribbean Sea

caricature

portrait   caricature

Caribbean² adj of or near the Caribbean Sea or the islands there. Most black British people are of Caribbean origin.

Caribbean Sea /ˌ···· ˈ·/ **Caribbean**— [the] the sea between Central America, South America, and the Caribbean islands

car·i·bou /ˈkærɪbuː/ n -bous or -bou a N American REINDEER

car·i·ca·ture¹ /ˈkærɪkətʃʊər/ n [C;U] (the art of making) a representation of someone, esp. in a drawing or painting or in literature, by which parts of their character or appearance are made more noticeable, odd, or amusing than they really are: *Newspapers often contain caricatures of well-known politicians.* | *a master of caricature.* | (fig., derog) *It was a caricature of a trial.* (=a very unjust trial)

caricature² v [T] to represent in caricature —**-turist** n

car·ies /ˈkeəriz/ n [U] med decay of the bones and esp. teeth: *dental caries*

car·ill·on /ˈkærɪljən, kəˈrɪ-‖ˈkærəljɑːn, -lən/ n (a tune played on) a set of bells, often in a tower, sounded by hammers controlled from a row of keys as on a piano KEYBOARD. Carillons are common in churches and public buildings in Belgium and Holland.

car·ing /ˈkeərɪŋ/ adj providing care and support, esp. to people who need to be looked after: *the caring professions, such as nursing and social work* | *Is the government seen by the voters as a caring government?*

car·jack·ing /ˈkɑːdʒækɪŋ‖ˈkɑːr-/ n [U,C] AmE an act of stealing a car by using force or violence towards the driver: *There have been three carjackings in the city this week.* | *Legislators have been urged to make carjacking a separate crime.*

Car·ling Black La·bel /ˌkɑːlɪŋ blæk ˈleɪbəl‖ˌkɑːr-/ n [U] tdmk a make of British LAGER, known esp. for advertisements in which someone else says "I bet he drinks Carling Black Label!"

Car·lisle /kɑːˈlaɪl‖kɑːr-/ a city in NW England, where the local government for Cumbria is based

Carls·berg /ˈkɑːlzbɜːg‖ˈkɑːrlzbɜːrg/ n [C;U] tdmk a well-known make of beer (LAGER)

Carl·ton Club /ˈkɑːltən ˌklʌb‖ˈkɑːrl-/ [the] (in Britain) a gentleman's CLUB¹ (3) which has a strong association with the Conservative Party

Car·lyle /kɑːˈlaɪl‖kɑːr-/, **Thom·as** /ˈtɒməs‖ˈtɑː-/ (1795–1881) a Scottish writer on political and social subjects, who was in favour of strong government

Car·men /ˈkɑːmen‖ˈkɑːrmən/ an OPERA by the French COMPOSER Bizet, first produced in 1875

car·mine /ˈkɑːmɪn, -maɪn‖ˈkɑːr-/ adj deep purplish red —**carmine**

Car·na·by Street /ˈkɑːnəbi ˌstriːt‖ˈkɑːr-/ a street in London, world-famous in the 1960s for its shops selling fashionable clothes for young people

car·nage /ˈkɑːnɪdʒ‖ˈkɑːr-/ n [U] the killing and wounding of large numbers of people or animals; SLAUGHTER: *The battlefield was a scene of terrible carnage.*

car·nal /ˈkɑːnl‖ˈkɑːrnl/ adj [A] fml, usu. derog concerning sexual desires: *carnal desires/pleasures*

car·na·tion /kɑːˈneɪʃən‖kɑːr-/ n (a small garden plant with) a sweet-smelling white, pink, or red flower. It is usual for the men taking part in an English wedding and the close members of the two families to wear a single carnation pinned to their jackets or dresses.

car·ne /ˈkɑːni‖ˈkɑːr-/ n see CHILLI (3)

Car·ne·gie /kɑːˈneɪgi‖kɑːr-/, **Andrew** (1835–1919) an American industrialist and PHILANTHROPIST, who made a lot of money in the steel industry and gave most of it away before he died. Some money went to start the many public libraries around the US which bear his name, and also to Carnegie Hall.

Car·ne·gie /ˈkɑːnəgi‖ˈkɑːr-/, **Dale** the writer of *How to Win Friends and Influence People*, a book read esp. by people who want to be successful in business. A **Dale Carnegie Course**, based on ideas in the book, gives people a chance to learn and practise skills to help them to achieve their professional and personal aims.

Carnegie Hall /ˌ··· ˈ·/ a large concert hall in New York, considered by people in the arts to be the most PRESTIGIOUS place to perform in the US

car·ne·li·an /kɑːˈniːliən‖kɑːr-/ n a CORNELIAN

car·ney also **carnie**— /ˈkɑːni‖ˈkɑːr-/ n AmE a person who works in a CARNIVAL (2); such people are often gypsies (GYPSY) and are not well respected, esp. by the people in towns visited by the carnival

car·ni·val /ˈkɑːnɪvəl‖ˈkɑːr-/ n **1** [C;U] (an occasion or period of) public enjoyment and merrymaking, with eating, dancing, drinking, and often processions and shows, held esp. in Roman Catholic countries in the weeks before Lent: *carnival time in Rio de Janeiro.*

▶CULTURAL NOTE Seaside towns in Britain often have a carnival in the summer, and an attractive young woman is chosen to be the **carnival queen.**◀

2 *AmE for* FUNFAIR **3** *AmE* a celebration usually held yearly by a school in which students make and operate the amusements

car·ni·vore /ˈkɑːnɪˌvɔːʳ‖ˈkɑːr-/ *n* a flesh-eating animal: *Lions are carnivores; rabbits are not.* —compare HERBIVORE, OMNIVORE —**·vorous** /kɑːˈnɪvərəs‖kɑːr-/ *adj*

car·ob /ˈkærəb/ *n* (the beanlike fruit of) a Mediterranean tree, used instead of chocolate by people who think it is more healthy: *carob cake* (=made using carob bean flour)

car·ol¹ /ˈkærəl/ also **Christmas carol**— *n* a religious song of joy and praise sung at Christmas. There are many well-known carols, including *O Come all ye Faithful*, *Silent Night*, and *O Little Town of Bethlehem.* —see also extra information on page 215

carol² *v* **-ll-** *BrE* **-l-** *AmE* [I] to sing carols
　carol away *phr v* [I] *BrE* to sing very cheerfully

Car·o·lin·gi·an /ˌkærəˈlɪndʒiən◂/ *adj* of or living in the period when Charlemagne ruled much of Western Europe

carol ser·vice /ˈ·· ˌ··/ *n* a religious service in which Christmas carols are sung. In the Church of England the service is often the **Service of Nine Lessons** (=readings from the Bible) **and Carols**. The readings are about the birth of Jesus. The most famous carol service is the one broadcast on Christmas Eve by the choir of King's College Chapel, Cambridge, and called the **Festival of Nine Lessons and Carols**.

carol singers

carol sing·er /ˈ·· ˌ··/ *n* a person who sings carols

carol·sing·ing /ˈ·· ˌ··/also **car·ol·ing**/ˈkærəlɪŋ/ */esp.AmE* *n* [U] the practice of singing Christmas carols. At Christmas time groups of people sing carols, both indoors and outdoors, in places such as shopping centres, railway stations, and public squares. They usually collect money for a good cause, for example homeless people. Sometimes carol singers, esp. children, go along the streets from house to house, singing in front of each house and asking for money. In the US carol singers are sometimes invited into people's houses for a drink of COCOA (2) and a biscuit.

ca·rouse /kəˈraʊz/ *v* [I] *lit* to drink a lot and be noisily merry together —**·rousal** *n* [C;U]

car·ou·sel, **carr·** /ˌkærəˈsel/ *n* **1** *AmE for* MERRY-GO-ROUND **2** a circular moving belt on which bags, cases, etc., from a plane are placed for collection by passengers **3** a circular piece of equipment into which one puts the SLIDES (=small pieces of film in frames) for showing on one kind of SLIDE PROJECTOR (=machine for showing slides)

carp¹ /kɑːp‖kɑːrp/ *v* [I (ON, about, at)] *derog infml* to find fault and complain continuously and unnecessarily: *carping criticism* | *I wish you'd stop carping (on) about the way I dress.*

carp² *n* **carp** or **carps** a large FRESHWATER fish that lives in lakes, pools, and slow-moving rivers and can be eaten. Carp is not commonly eaten in Britain or the US, where it is regarded as unclean because it feeds at the bottom of rivers.

car park /ˈ· ·/ *n esp. BrE* **1 parking lot** *AmE*— an open space where cars and other vehicles may be parked, sometimes for a small payment **2 parking garage** *AmE*— an enclosed building used for this purpose: *I parked on the third floor of a multistorey car park.* (=one with many floors) —see PARKING (USAGE)

car·pen·ter /ˈkɑːpɪntəʳ‖ˈkɑːr-/ *n* a person who is skilled at making and repairing wooden objects, esp. one who does this as a job —compare JOINER (1)

car·pen·try /ˈkɑːpɪntri‖ˈkɑːr-/ *n* [U] the art or work of a carpenter —compare JOINERY

car·pet¹ /ˈkɑːpɪt‖ˈkɑːr-/ *n* **1** [C;U] (a shaped piece of) heavy woven often woollen material for covering floors or stairs. Many homes have carpets from wall to wall (=**fitted carpets** *BrE* ‖ **wall-to-wall carpet** *AmE*) in all the main rooms, and a stair carpet going up the stairs: *a beautiful Persian carpet* | *a stair carpet* | *some bits of old carpet* —compare RUG —see picture at LIVING ROOM **2** [C (**of**)] anything which covers the ground like this: *a carpet of flowers/snow* —see also MAGIC CARPET, RED CARPET, **sweep something under the carpet** (SWEEP¹)

carpet² *v* [T] **1** to cover (as if) with a carpet: *a carpeted waiting room* **2** *infml, esp. BrE* to blame for bad work, foolish behaviour, etc.; REPRIMAND: *He was carpeted by the boss for failing to win the contract.*

car·pet·bag·ger /ˈkɑːpɪtˌbægəʳ‖ˈkɑːr-/ *n derog* a person from one area who tries to take an active part in the political life of another area, esp., in the US, a Northerner who was politically active in the South in the 1860s and 1870s in order to gain from the situation rather than to help people in the South

carpet bomb /ˈ·· ˌ·/ *v* [T] to drop many bombs over (a small area), so that nearly everything in that area is destroyed: *Planes carpet bombed Dresden in World War II and the city was devastated.*

car·pet·ing /ˈkɑːpɪtɪŋ‖ˈkɑːr-/ *n* [U] heavy woven material for making carpets

carpet slip·per /ˈ·· ˌ··/ *n* a SLIPPER

carpet sweep·er /ˈ·· ˌ··/ *n* a nonelectric machine for sweeping carpets —compare VACUUM CLEANER

car phone /ˈ· ·/ *n* a telephone for use in a car

car pool /ˈ· ·/ *n* **1** an agreement made by a number of car owners to take turns driving each other to work, school, etc. **2** *esp. BrE* a number of cars owned by a company or other organization for the use of its members

car·port /ˈkɑːpɔːt‖ˈkɑːrpɔːrt/ *n* a shelter for a car, with only a roof and one or two sides, often built against a side of a house —compare GARAGE¹ (1)

Car·raun·too·hill /ˌkærənˈtuːəl/ a mountain in the SW of the Republic of Ireland

car·rel /ˈkærəl/ *n AmE* a small enclosed space for studying in a library

car·riage /ˈkærɪdʒ/ *n* **1** [C] a wheeled vehicle, esp. a private horse-drawn vehicle —see also PRAM **2** [C] *BrE* ‖ **car** *AmE*— a railway passenger vehicle: *I'll be sitting in the third carriage from the front of the train.* **3** [U] *BrE* (the cost of) the moving of goods from one place to another: *The price includes carriage.* | *to send goods* **carriage forward** (=with the cost of moving them to be paid by the receiver) | *to send goods* **carriage paid/free** (=with the cost already paid by the sender) **4** [C] a wheeled support for moving a heavy object, esp. a gun **5** [C] a movable part of a machine: *The carriage of a typewriter holds and moves the paper.* —see picture at TYPEWRITER **6** [S;U] *fml* the way a person holds and moves their head and body; DEPORTMENT

carriage clock /ˈ·· ˌ·/ *n BrE* a small clock in a BRASS case, usu. with glass front, back, and sides, with a handle on top —see picture at CLOCK

car·riage·way /ˈkærɪdʒweɪ/ *n BrE* the part of a road's surface on which vehicles travel —see also DUAL CARRIAGEWAY

car·ri·er /ˈkæriəʳ/ *n* **1** *BrE* a carrier bag **2** a person or thing that carries, esp. a business that carries goods or passengers from one place to another for payment: *This airline is one of America's biggest international carriers.* **3** *med* a person or thing that passes diseases to others without actually suffering from the disease **4** a military vehicle or ship which carries soldiers, planes, weapons, etc., esp. an AIRCRAFT CARRIER: *an armoured personnel carrier* **5** a usu. metal frame fixed to a vehicle (e.g. a bicycle) to hold bags, goods, etc.

carrier bag /'··· ·/ also **carrier** *BrE* ‖ **shopping bag** *AmE— n esp. BrE* a strong paper or plastic bag with handles into which goods are placed in a shop so that the customer can take them away

carrier pi·geon /'··· ,··/ also **homing pigeon**— *n* a PIGEON (a type of bird) that has been trained to carry messages from one place to another

Car·ring·ton /'kærɪŋtən/, **Lord (Peter)** (1919–) a British Conservative politician, who held the positions of DEFENCE SECRETARY and FOREIGN SECRETARY, helping Zimbabwe to become independent. He resigned (RESIGN) during the Falklands war, and was SECRETARY-GENERAL of NATO from 1984 to 1988.

car·ri·on /'kæriən/ *n* [U] dead and decaying flesh: *Some birds feed on carrion.*

Car·roll /'kærəl/, **Lewis** (1832–98) an English writer who wrote two well-known children's stories, *Alice's Adventures in Wonderland* and *Through the Looking Glass.* His real name was **Charles Dodgson.**

car·rot /'kærət/ *n* **1** [C;U] (a plant with) a long thick orange pointed root eaten as a vegetable. People sometimes say that carrots help one to see in the dark if one eats a lot of them: *Have some more carrots.* | *carrot soup* | *We grow carrots in our garden.* —see picture at VEGETABLE **2** [C] *infml* a promised reward or advantage for doing something, esp. offered as a way of persuading someone (from the idea that one can encourage a DONKEY to move by putting a carrot in front of it): *They are trying to persuade the staff to accept the new machinery by* **dangling** (=offering) **the carrot** *of higher pay.* | *Their method of negotiating is a combination of* **the carrot and the stick.** (=promises and threats)

carrot-top /'··· ·/ *n infml* a person with red hair

car·rot·y /'kærəti/ *adj* (esp. of the hair) orange in colour

car·ry[1] /'kæri/ *v* **1** [T] to have or hold in one's arms, on one's back, etc., while moving: *She carried her baby on her back.* | *I carried the books in a strong paper bag.* | *We lifted the piano and carried it down the stairs.* —see BRING (USAGE) **2** [T] to act as the means by which (a person or thing) is moved from one place to another; TRANSPORT; CONVEY: *The railway system carries over 25% of the country's goods traffic.* | *Pipes carry oil across the desert.* | *The little boat was carried out to sea on the tide.* | (fig.) *Her outstanding ability carried her right to the top of her profession.* | *He ran out of the burning building* **as fast as his legs would carry him.** **3** [T] to pass from one person to another; spread: *Many serious diseases are carried by insects.* **4** [T] to be able to support the weight of (something) without moving or breaking: *These two pillars carry the whole roof.* **5** [T] to have with one or on one's body: *The police in Britain don't usually carry guns.*| *This is a dangerous area, so don't carry too much cash on you.* **6** [T *no pass.*] *fml* to move or hold (oneself) in a certain way: *They carry themselves like soldiers.* **7** [T] **a** to support or keep in operation, esp. by providing money: *Can the company afford to carry its loss-making overseas section until business improves?* **b** *tech* to support with food: *This field can carry up to ten cows.* **8** [T] to print or broadcast; contain: *All the newspapers carried articles about the pop star's marriage.* | *This radio station does not carry any advertising.* **9** [T] to keep a supply of (goods) for sale; STOCK[3]: *The store carries a good range of sports equipment.* **10** [T] to have as a usual or necessary part or result: *All our products carry a 12-month guarantee.* | *The plan carries with it the risk of losing popular support.* | *This is a serious crime and carries a long jail sentence.* | *Her opinions* **carry (a lot of) weight** *with me.* (=influence me greatly) **11** [I] to be able to reach a certain distance: *We couldn't hear her at the back of the hall because her voice doesn't carry (very well).* | *How far does this gun carry?* (=how far will it fire?) **12** [T *usu. pass.*] to give approval to (esp. a law or plan), esp. by voting: *The motion was carried by 310 votes to 306.* | *I declare the motion carried.* **13** [T *no pass.*] to win the sympathy, support, or agreement of: *The government carried most of the country and won the election.* **14** [I;T] to put (a number) into the next upright row to the left when doing addition: *To add 9 and 5 you write down 4 and carry 1.* **15** [T] to succeed in not showing the bad effects of:

He carries his age very well. | *He can't carry his drink.* (=can't drink much alcohol without getting drunk) **16** **carry all/everything before one** to be completely successful; win a complete victory **17 carry a torch for** to be in love with (esp. someone who does not return the love) **18 carry a tune** to sing correctly: *He couldn't carry a tune in a bucket!* **19 carry** something **too far** to do something for too long or to too great a degree: *She carried the joke too far.* **20 carry the can** *BrE infml* to take the blame; be responsible **21 carry the day** to win; be completely successful —see also CASH AND CARRY

carry away *phr v* [T *usu. pass.*] to fill with strong feeling or excitement, esp. so as to cause unreasonable behaviour: *Marsha got so carried away when arguing with her husband that she hit him.* | *I got rather carried away at the clothes sale and spent far too much money.*

carry sthg. **↔ forward/over** *phr v* [T] (when adding up accounts) to move (a total) from the bottom of an upright row of figures to the next page for further addition

carry sthg. **↔ off** *phr v* [T] **1** to perform or do (a part, action, duty, etc.) easily and successfully: *She carried off her part in the plan with no difficulty.* | *It's a risky venture and I'm not sure they'll be able to carry it off.* **2** to win (a prize, honour, etc.): *Jean carried off all the prizes.*

carry on *phr v* **1** [I (**with**)];T (=**carry on** sthg.)) to continue, esp. in spite of an interruption or difficulties: *We can carry on our discussion after lunch.* | *Carry on with your work.* [+*v-ing*] *Even after the music started they carried on talking.* **2** [I] *infml* to behave in a foolish, excited, or anxious manner: *You should have heard her carrying on when we told her the news!* | *I wish you'd stop carrying on* (=complaining) *about it.* **3** [I (**with**)] *infml* to have a love affair, esp an improper one: *Did you know she's been carrying on with the milkman?* —see also CARRYING-ON, CARRY-ON

carry sthg. **↔ out** *phr v* [T] **1** to perform or complete; CONDUCT: *Our planes carried out a bombing raid on enemy targets.* | *They are carrying out urgent repairs.* | *An investigation into the cause of the crash will be carried out by the Department of Transport.* **2** to fulfil (a promise, duty, etc.): *They have failed to carry out their obligations/their orders.* | *to carry out a threat* —see also CARRYOUT

carry over sthg **↔** *phr v* [T] to CARRY **forward** —see also CARRY-OVER

carry through *phr v* **1** [T] (**carry** sbdy. **through** (sthg.)) to help (someone) to continue in an effective way during (an illness, difficult period, etc.); SUSTAIN: *His strong determination carried him through (his illness).* **2** [T] (**carry** sthg. **↔ through**) to bring to a successful end; ACCOMPLISH: *Despite powerful opposition, they managed to carry their reforms through.*

carry[2] *n* [C;U] the distance an object will travel or has travelled after being fired, thrown, or hit: *a golf drive with a carry of 300 yards*

car·ry·all /'kæri-ɔːl/ *n esp. AmE* a large usu. soft bag or case; HOLDALL

car·ry·cot /'kærikɒt‖-kɑːt/ *esp.BrE* also **portacrib** *AmE tdmk— n* a small boxlike container with handles in which a baby lies and can be carried —see picture at BED

carrying charge /'··· ,·/ *n esp. AmE* money added to the price of things bought by INSTALLMENT PLAN

carrying-on /,··· '·/ also **carryings-on** *pl.— n* [U] *infml* **1** foolish, excited, or immoral behaviour: *The police were called in to investigate the scandalous carryings-on.* **2** the activity of one person having an improper love affair with another —see also CARRY **on**

carry-on /'··· ·/ *n* [S] *infml*, *esp. BrE* a piece of silly usu. annoying behaviour; FUSS —see also CARRY **on**

Carry On films /,·· '·· ,·/ *n* one of a group of British COMEDY films made esp. in the 1960s and 70s and full of rude jokes about sex and bodily processes. The films have titles like *Carry On Nurse* and *Carry On Columbus* —see colour picture on page 553

car·ry·out /'kæri-aʊt/ *adj*, *n AmE & ScotE* for TAKE-AWAY

carry-o·ver /'··· ,··/ *n* [*usu. sing.*] **1** a total that is carried forward (CARRY **forward**) **2** [(**from**)] something that is left from an earlier time or situation; REMNANT: *These regulations are a carry-over from restrictions that were imposed during wartime.* —see also CARRY **over**

car·sick /'kɑː,sɪk‖'kɑːr-/ *adj* sick because of the movement of a car — **~ness** *n* [U]

Car·son¹ /ˈkɑːsən‖ˈkɑːr-/, **Chris·to·pher,** /ˈkrɪstəfər/ (Kit) (1809–68) an American fur trapper who guided many trips in the Rocky Mountains and took thousands of Native Americans as prisoners. Carson City in the US is named after him.

Car·son², **John·ny** /ˈdʒɒni‖ ˈdʒɑː-/ (1925–   ) an American COMEDIAN and television performer who presented *The Tonight Show* from 1962 to 1992. Carson was always introduced with the words "Here's Johnny!" and then gave a long speech which was funny and often about current events, esp. political ones.

Johnny Carson

Car·son³, **Ra·chel** /ˈreɪtʃəl/ (1907–64) an American scientist who was very concerned about the effects of POLLUTION on the environment. Her book *Silent Spring* brought attention to the use of dangerous chemicals in farming.

Car·son⁴, **Violet** (1905–83) an English actress probably best remembered as the character Ena Sharples in the long-running television SERIES *Coronation Street* —see also Ena SHARPLES

car stick·er /ˈ· ˌ··/ n a piece of paper or plastic made to stick on a car window; car stickers usually have advertisements, jokes, or opinions on them —compare BUMPER STICKER

cart¹ /kɑːt‖kɑːrt/ n **1** a two-wheeled or four-wheeled vehicle pulled by an animal, esp. a horse, or pulled or pushed by hand, and used in farming or for carrying goods —see also APPLE CART **2 in the cart** sl, esp. BrE in an awkward or difficult position **3 put the cart before the horse** to do or put things in the wrong order: *You're putting the cart before the horse by buying all this furniture before you've got the house.* **4** AmE for TROLLEY

cart² v [T] **1** to carry (as if) in a cart: *Cart all this rubble away.* **2** [+obj+adv/prep] infml to take or remove, often disrespectfully, carelessly, or using force: *The demonstrators were carted off to jail by the police.* | *She carts the kids around with her wherever she goes.*

car tax /ˈ· ˌ·/ n [C;U] ROAD TAX

carte blanche /ˌkɑːt ˈblɑːnʃ‖ˌkɑːrt-/ n [U] full freedom, esp. to make decisions or spend money: [+to-v] *I was given carte blanche to reorganize the department.*

car·tel /kɑːˈtel‖kɑːr-/ n often derog a group of independent, often international companies who agree to fix prices to limit competition so that they can increase their profits. In Britain and the US it is illegal to form a cartel.

cart·er /ˈkɑːtər‖ˈkɑːr-/ BrE old use n a person whose job is driving carts

Carter, Jimmy (1924–   ) the president of the US from 1977 to 1981. Carter helped Egypt and Israel form a peace treaty which is usu. called the **Camp David agreement.** Before becoming president he helped run his family's business, a PEANUT farm, and was the governor of Georgia.

Car·thage /ˈkɑːθɪdʒ‖ˈkɑːr-/ an ancient city on the N coast of Africa, near the modern city of Tunis

Barbara Cartland

cart·horse /ˈkɑːthɔːs‖ ˈkɑːrthɔːrs/ n a large powerful horse, esp. used for heavy work and pulling carts

Car·ti·er /ˈkɑːtieɪ‖ˈkɑːr-/ a fashionable jewellery shop with branches in large cities in many countries, well-known for its very expensive watches: *a Cartier watch*

car·ti·lage /ˈkɑːtɪlɪdʒ‖ˈkɑːr-təlɪdʒ/ n [C;U] (a piece of) strong elastic substance found instead of bone in young animals and, esp. round the joints, in older animals —compare GRISTLE —**laginous** /ˌkɑːtɪˈlædʒənəs◄‖ˌkɑːrtəlˈæ-/ adj

Cart·land /ˈkɑːtlənd‖ˈkɑːrt-/, **Dame Bar·ba·ra** /ˈbɑːbərə‖ ˈbɑːr-/ (1904–   ) a very popular English writer who has written hundreds of NOVELs about love and ROMANCE: *He could have come straight out of the pages of a Barbara Cartland novel.*

cart·load /ˈkɑːtləʊd‖ˈkɑːrt-/ n the quantity that a cart can hold: *by the cartload* (=in great numbers)

car·tog·ra·phy /kɑːˈtɒgrəfi‖kɑːrˈtɑː-/ n [U] the science or art of making maps —**·pher** n

car·ton /ˈkɑːtn‖ˈkɑːrtn/ n **1** a box made from stiff paper (CARDBOARD) or plastic, used for holding goods: *a carton of cream* **2** AmE (often comb.) a container holding a certain amount or number of goods: *carton of cigarettes* (=10 packs of 20 cigarettes) | *milk carton/carton of milk*

cartoon

"Why do you always bring that elephant gun when we go out?"

car·toon /kɑːˈtuːn‖kɑːr-/ n **1** a humorous drawing, often dealing in a clever and amusing way with something of interest in the news, usu. with a CAPTION —compare COMIC STRIP **2** also **animated cartoon**– a cinema film made by photographing a set of drawings **3** a drawing used as a model for a painting or other work of art —**~ist** n

car·tridge /ˈkɑːtrɪdʒ‖ˈkɑːr-/ n **1** a metal, paper, or plastic tube containing explosive and a bullet for use in a gun **2** (in a record player) a small case containing the needle (STYLUS) that picks up sound signals from a record **3** a container holding recorded MAGNETIC TAPE used esp. with a TAPE RECORDER —compare CASSETTE (1)

cartridge pa·per /ˈ·· ˌ··/ n [U] BrE strong thick white or near-white paper for drawing on

cart track /ˈ· ·/ n a narrow road with a rough surface, usu. on a farm

car trans·por·ter /ˈ· ·ˌ··/ n a railway vehicle or large LORRY which is built to carry a number of usu. new cars to the place where they will be sold

cart·wheel /ˈkɑːtwiːl‖ˈkɑːrt-/ n a circular movement in which a person turns over by putting their hands on the ground and moving their legs sideways in the air: *Jean learned to turn cartwheels at school.* —compare SOMERSAULT —**cartwheel** v [I]

Cart·wright /ˈkɑːtraɪt‖ˈkɑːr-/, **Ed·mund** /ˈedmənd/ (1743–1823) an English inventor of machines used in weaving and the woollen industry

Ca·ru·so /kəˈruːsəʊ/, **En·ri·co** /enˈriːkəʊ/ (1873–1921) an Italian OPERA singer who was very popular among ordinary people

carve /kɑːv‖kɑːrv/ v **1** [T] to cut (usu. wood or stone) into a special shape or make (something) by cutting wood or stone: *He carved the wood into the shape of a bird.* | *They carved their initials on the tree.* | *The statue is carved out of marble.* —compare SCULPTURE (2) **2** [I;T] to cut (cooked meat) into pieces or cut (pieces) from cooked meat, esp. at a meal: *Shall I carve you another slice of turkey?* **3** [T (OUT)] to make or gain (esp. a position or advantage) by long effort: *She has carved (out) a career for herself/a niche for herself as a comic actress.*

▷ USAGE You can **carve** wood or stone **into** a shape; **carve (out)** a shape **from, in,** or **out of** wood or stone; or **carve** words, etc., **on** a wooden or stone surface.◁
carve sbdy./sthg. ↔ **up** phr v [T] **1** usu. derog to

divide, esp. in a way favourable to oneself: *They carved up the profits between themselves.* **2** sl to wound (someone) with a knife **3** BrE sl (of a motorist) to go past (another vehicle) and drive in front of it too soon

carv·er /ˈkɑːvəʳ‖ˈkɑːr-/ n **1** a person who carves **2** a CARVING KNIFE

Carver, George Washington (1864–1943) an American inventor, born of slave parents, and remembered for discovering many uses for the PEANUT and sweet potato

car·ve·ry /ˈkɑːvəri‖ˈkɑːr-/ n (part of) a restaurant that mainly serves roasted (ROAST) meats

carve-up /ˈ· ·/ n the division of something between people, usu. to their advantage: *the carve-up of Germany after the Second World War*

carv·ing /ˈkɑːvɪŋ‖ˈkɑːr-/ n **1** [C] something made by carving **2** [U] the work, art, or skill of a carver

carving fork /ˈ·· ·/ n a large fork used to hold meat in place for cutting with a carving knife

carving knife /ˈ·· ·/ n a long sharp knife used for cutting up large pieces of meat

car wash /ˈ· ·/ n a special piece of equipment into which one drives one's car for it to be washed

car·y·at·id /ˌkæriˈætɪd/ n tech a PILLAR (=support for a building) shaped like a clothed female figure

Cas·a·blan·ca /ˌkæsəˈblæŋkə‖ˌkɑːsəˈblɑː-/ **1** the largest city in Morocco, on the Atlantic coast **2** an American ROMANTIC film made in 1942 with Humphrey Bogart and Ingrid Bergman. The story takes place in the city of Casablanca. —see picture on page 685

Cas·a·no·va /ˌkæsəˈnəʊvə/ n infml, often derog a man who has (or claims to have) a lot of female lovers (from **Giacomo Casanova** (1725–98), an Italian man famous because he claimed to have had sex with very many women)

cas·bah /ˈkæzbɑː/ n an ancient walled (usually Arab) city

cas·cade¹ /kæˈskeɪd/ n **1** a steep high usu. small waterfall, esp. one part of a bigger waterfall **2** anything that seems to pour or flow downwards: *Her hair fell over her shoulders in a cascade of curls.*

cascade² v [I+adv/prep] to fall or pour in quantity: *rainwater cascading down the window*

Cascade Range /·ˈ· ˌ·/ [the] a chain of mountains in the W of the US, stretching from N California to British Columbia

case¹ /keɪs/ n **1** [C] a particular occasion or situation, esp. as it concerns or influences a particular person: *Jane's bad results were partly due to illness, but in the case of John/in John's case, no such excuse is possible.* | *They may not offer me much money.* **In that case** (=if that happens) *I won't take the job.* | *There will be no big pay increases this year, as has been the case in previous years.* | *I'm not supposed to let anyone in, but I'll make an exception* **in your case.** **2** [C] an example: *It is simply not the case* (=not true) *that educational standards have fallen.* | *Several cases of fever have been reported.* | *The company are losing some of their best people because of the low salaries – the resignation of the sales director is* **a case in point.** (=a clear or typical example) | *House prices have gone up by over 10%, in some cases by almost 20%.* | *We don't really want to sell the car, but* **it's a case of** *having to.* (=we have no choice) | *The government's by-election defeat is* **a classic case of** *mid-term unpopularity.* **3** [C] a set of events needing inquiry or action by the police or a similar body: *a case of robbery with violence* | *Police are working on/investigating the case.* **4** [C] a question to be decided in a court of law: *My case against the local council will be heard* (=judged) *today.* | *He sued the newspaper for libel, but lost the case.* **5** [C (for, against) usu. sing.] all the facts and arguments that support the opinions or claims of one side in a disagreement, legal question, etc.: *the case for the defence* | *a key piece of evidence in the prosecution's case* | *The police have a clear case against the prisoner.* | *She* **made out a good case** *for* (=gave good arguments for) *lowering our prices.* | *The case for the opposition will be put* (=explained) *by Mr Steel.* **6** [C;U] (in grammar) (changes in) the form of a word (esp. of a noun, adjective, or PRONOUN) showing its relationship with other words in a sentence: *"Me" is the object case of "I". | "Mine" is the possessive case of "I".* —see also LOWER CASE, UPPER CASE **7** [C] a person hav-

ing medical treatment or being dealt with by the police, someone doing SOCIAL WORK, etc.: *The doctor has several cases to see this morning.* | *a hopeless case* **b** a person who is difficult to deal with: *I don't know what to do about him, he's a real case.* —see also BASKET CASE, NUT CASE **8 in any case** no matter what happens: *The cost may be lower than we first thought, but in any case it will still be quite substantial.* **9 in case of** if or when (something) happens: *In case of fire, ring the bell.* **10 (just) in case a** so as to be safe if (something happens): *Take your coat in case it rains/(just) in case it should rain.* | *I'll cook plenty of potatoes just in case (they decide to stay for dinner).* **b** esp. AmE if: *In case they're late, we can always sit in the bar.*

case² n **1** a large box or container, in which goods can be stored or moved: *a packing case* | *a case of whisky* (=12 bottles) | *The porter will carry your cases* (=SUITCASES) *up to your room.* —see picture at CONTAINER **2** a box, piece of furniture, or other container for holding and protecting something: *a jewel case* | *a bookcase* | *a pillowcase* —see also LOWER CASE, UPPER CASE

case³ v [T] sl to examine, esp. with the intention of robbing: *The thief was casing the joint.* (=examining the place he intended to rob)

case his·tory /ˈ· ·ˌ··/ n a record of the past history of someone suffering from an illness, social difficulties, etc.

case·load /ˈkeɪsləʊd/ n the group of cases¹ (7a) that a doctor, SOCIAL WORKER, etc. deals with regularly: *My caseload is really high* (=I have a lot of cases to deal with).

case·ment win·dow /ˌkeɪsmənt ˈwɪndəʊ/ also **casement**— n a window that opens like a door, by means of HINGES along one side —compare SASH WINDOW

case stud·y /ˈ· ˌ··/ n a detailed study of a person or group, esp. in order to learn about their social development and relationship with other people in society

case·work /ˈkeɪswɜːk‖-wɜːrk/ n [U] SOCIAL WORK concerned with direct consideration of the problems of a particular person, family, etc. – – er n

cash¹ /kæʃ/ n [U] **1** money in the form of coins and notes, rather than cheques, CREDIT CARDS, etc.: *to pay in cash* | *I haven't any cash on me – can I pay by cheque?* | *We don't accept cheques – we only take* **hard cash** (=notes and coins)/*you have to pay* **cash down.** (=at once) **2** infml money in any form: *The company are a bit short of cash at the moment.* | *3* **cash on delivery** see COD —see also PETTY CASH; see MONEY (USAGE)

cash² v [T] to exchange (a cheque or other order to pay) for cash: *Can you cash these traveller's cheques for me?* | *Where can I get this cashed?*
  cash in phr v **1** [I (on)] to take full advantage or profit (from): *The company cashed in on its rival's difficulties by doubling production.* **2** [T] to exchange (documents, etc.) for cash: *When are you going to cash in those certificates?* | *He cashed in his chips at the end of the game.*

Cash, John·ny /ˈdʒɒni‖ˈdʒɑː-/ (1932–) an American COUNTRY AND WESTERN singer, known for songs such as *I Walk the Line* and *A Boy Named Sue*

cash and car·ry /ˌ· · ˈ··/ n [often the] a shop where goods are sold at low prices if they are bought in large quantities, paid for at once, and taken away by the buyer

cash·book /ˈkæʃbʊk/ n a book in which a record is kept of money received and paid out

cash card /ˈ· ·/ n a special plastic card used for obtaining money from a cash dispenser

cash crop /ˈ· ·/ n a crop grown for sale rather than for use by the grower —compare CATCH CROP, SUBSISTENCE CROP

cash desk /ˈ· ·/ n the desk in a shop where payments are made

cash dis·count /ˌ· ˈ··/ n an amount by which the seller reduces the price when the buyer pays with notes or coins and not by cheque or CREDIT CARD

cash dis·pens·er /ˈ· ·ˌ··/ also **ATM**— n esp. BrE a machine, esp. one placed outside a bank, from which customers can obtain money at any time by putting in a cash card and pressing numbered keys to give a special number

ca·shew /ˈkæʃuː, kəˈʃuː/ n (a tropical American tree that produces) a small curved nut —see picture at NUT

cash flow /ˈ· ·/ n [S;U] the flow of money into a business (as income) and out of a business (for wages, materials, etc.): *Despite difficult trading conditions, the company has maintained a healthy/positive cash flow this year.* | *cash-flow problems/crisis*

cash·ier¹ /kæ'ʃɪər/ n a person in charge of money and payments in a bank, hotel, shop, etc.

cash·ier² /kæ'ʃɪər, kə-/ v [T] to dismiss (esp. an officer) with dishonour from service in the armed forces

cash-in-hand /ˌ·'··ˈ·◄/ adj (of a payment for services, etc.) given to somebody in the form of CASH so that there is no document as a record of the payment. People sometimes prefer to be paid this way as a way of avoiding paying tax: *a cash-in-hand payment* | *I'd rather have the money cash-in-hand.*

cash·less /'kæʃləs/ adj done or operating without the use of money in any physical form: *a cashless transaction, by which money is transferred automatically from the buyer's account to the seller's* | *So many people have credit cards that we are nearly a* **cashless society.**

cash ma·chine /'·· ·ˌ·/ n a CASH DISPENSER

cash·mere /'kæʃmɪər‖'kæʒ-, 'kæʃ-/ n [U] fine soft wool, made from a type of long-haired goat, used for making expensive clothes: *a cashmere sweater*

cash·point /'kæʃpɔɪnt/ n BrE a CASH DISPENSER: *a cashpoint card*

cash reg·is·ter /'·· ˌ···/ n a business machine used in shops for calculating and recording the amount of each sale and the money received, and sometimes for giving change

cas·ing /'keɪsɪŋ/ n a protective covering, such as the outer rubber covering of a car TYRE: *This wire has a rubber casing.*

ca·si·no /kə'siːnəʊ/ n -nos a place where people play cards or other games for money. In the US casinos are legal only in Atlantic City, New Jersey, and in the state of Nevada. Monte Carlo in S France is known internationally for its casino.

casino

cask /kɑːsk‖kæsk/ n (the amount contained in) a barrel-shaped container, esp. a fairly small one, for holding and storing liquids: *a cask of sherry*

Casio /'kæziəʊ/ tdmk a Japanese company making watches, calculators etc.

cas·ket /'kɑːskɪt‖'kæs-/ n 1 a small usu. decorated box for holding jewels, letters, and other valuable things 2 *esp. AmE for* COFFIN

Cas·pi·an Sea /ˌkæspiən 'siː/ [the] a large salt-water lake between SE Europe and Asia

casque /kɑːsk‖kæsk/ n lit or old use a soldier's metal protective HELMET, worn in former times

Cas·san·dra /kə'sændrə/ the daughter of Priam who, in an old Greek story, was not believed when she said that his kingdom of Troy would be seized by the enemy. Someone can be described as a Cassandra if they warn others of future misfortunes but are not believed.

Cas·satt /kə'sæt/, **Mary** (1845–1926) an American painter who worked mostly in France with the Impressionists

cas·sa·va /kə'sɑːvə/ also **manioc**— n [C;U] (flour made from the thick fleshy roots of) a tropical plant

cas·se·role /'kæsərəʊl/ n 1 [C] a deep usu. covered dish in which food can be cooked and served: *a heavy iron casserole* — see picture at PAN 2 [C;U] the food cooked in this: *(a) beef casserole*

cas·sette /kə'set/ n 1 a container holding MAGNETIC TAPE, which can be fitted into a TAPE RECORDER or VIDEO — compare CARTRIDGE (3) 2 a container for photographic film which can be fitted complete into a camera

cassette play·er /·'·· ˌ···/ n a TAPE RECORDER

cassette re·cord·er /·'·· ·ˌ···/ n a TAPE RECORDER

cassette tape /·'·· ˌ·/ n a cassette (1)

cas·sock /'kæsək/ n a long, heavy garment, worn by some priests and by people helping at religious services

cast¹ /kɑːst‖kæst/ v cast [T] 1 esp. lit or old use to throw or drop: *The fishermen cast their nets into the sea.* | *The*

wicked king cast his enemies into prison. | (fig.) *The witch* **cast a spell** *on the prince and turned him into a frog.* 2 [+obj+adv/prep] to throw off; remove; get rid of SHED: *Every year the snake casts off its skin.* | *to cast aside one's doubts/inhibitions/former friends* 3 to turn or direct: *The evening sun cast long shadows (across the garden).* | *She cast a glance in his direction.* | *So far, the police investigation has not* **cast any light on** *her disappearance.* (=has not helped to explain it) | *Would you just* **cast an eye over** (=look through quickly) *this letter before I put it in the post?* | *These incidents must* **cast doubt on** *his suitability for government office.* 4 [(as, in)] to give an acting part to (a person) or choose actors for (a play): *The director cast me as a mad scientist.* | *Who is casting this play?* 5 to make (a vote) in an election: *The TV news showed the vice-president casting his vote.* 6 to make (an object) by pouring (hot metal or plastic) into a shaped container (MOULD): *to cast bronze* | *to cast a statue* 7 to calculate (a HOROSCOPE) 8 **cast one's net wide** to spread one's efforts in all directions when trying to find someone or something: *If we want the best person for the job, we must cast our net as wide as possible by advertising in all the papers.* —see also **the die is cast** (DIE²) 9 **cast pearls before swine** to say useful or nice things to people who cannot appreciate them

cast about/around for sthg. *phr v* [T *no pass.*] to search or look for in all directions

cast sbdy. ↔ **away** *phr v* [T *usu. pass.*] to leave somewhere as the result of a shipwreck: *We were cast away on an island without food or water.* —see also CASTAWAY

cast sbdy. ↔ **down** *phr v* [T *usu. pass.*] to make sad or disappointed

cast (sthg.) ↔ **off** *phr v* [I;T] 1 a (of a boat or ship) to be set free on the water by a rope being untied b to set (a boat or ship) free by untying a rope 2 to finish making a piece of KNITTING by removing (stitches) from the needle in such a way that the garment does not come undone

cast (sthg.) ↔ **on** *phr v* [I;T] to start a piece of KNITTING by putting (the first stitches) onto a needle

cast sbdy./sthg. ↔ **out** *phr v* [T (**of**)] *esp. lit or old use* to drive out or away; EXPEL —see also OUTCAST

cast² n 1 [C+sing./pl. v] the actors in a play, film, etc.: *The cast is/are waiting on the stage.* | *The film has a strong cast that includes several famous names.* 2 [C] an act of throwing something, esp. a fishing line 3 [C] a hard stiff protective covering for holding a broken bone in place while it gets better. People with an arm or leg in a cast often get their friends to write their names or a message on the cast: *He's got his leg in a* **plaster cast.** | *Do you want to sign my cast?* 4 [C] an object made by being cast (CAST¹ (6)) in a specially shaped container (MOULD): *plaster casts of the statues* 5 [C] a small pile of earth thrown out of the ground by worms when they make a hole 6 [S] *fml* appearance, type, or character: *the noble cast of his features* | *a philosophical cast of mind*

cas·ta·nets /ˌkæstə'nets/ n [P] a musical instrument made from two round pieces of hard wood, plastic, etc., fastened to the thumb by a string and played by being knocked together by the other fingers. Castanets are thought to be typical of southern Spain and Mexico.

cast·a·way /'kɑːstəweɪ‖'kæst-/ n a person who escapes from a shipwreck and reaches the shore of a strange country or lonely island. The most famous castaway in English literature is Robinson Crusoe. —see also CAST **away**

caste /kɑːst‖kæst/ n [C;U] (any of the groups in) the system by which Indian society is divided up into different classes, according to the principles of Hinduism

cas·tel·lat·ed /'kæstəˌleɪtɪd/ adj tech (of a building) having defences like a castle; made to look like a castle

cast·er, **-or** /'kɑːstər‖'kæs-/ n 1 a small metal or plastic wheel fixed to the base of a piece of furniture so that it can be easily moved 2 BrE ‖ **shaker** AmE a container with small holes in the top from which sugar, salt, etc., may be evenly spread over foods

caster sug·ar, **castor sugar** /'·· ˌ··/ BrE ‖ **granulated sugar** AmE n [U] very fine white sugar usu. used in cooking —compare GRANULATED

cas·ti·gate /'kæstɪˌgeɪt/ v [T] fml 1 to punish or speak to severely 2 to express strong disapproval of (a person, behaviour, or ideas) —**-gation** /ˌkæstɪ'geɪʃən/ n [U]

cast·ing /ˈkɑːstɪŋ‖ˈkæstɪŋ/ n **1** [C] an object shaped by being CAST¹ (6) **2** [U] the process of choosing actors for a play or film

casting vote /ˌ·ˈ· ˈ·/ n [usu. sing.] a deciding vote (usu. belonging to the person in charge of a meeting, committee, etc.) used when both sides have an equal number of votes

cast-i·ron /ˌ·ˈ·◄/ adj **1** made of cast iron **2** infml **a** strong or insensitive: She has a cast-iron stomach and can eat anything. **b** impossible to question or doubt: a cast-iron excuse

cast iron n [U] a hard but easily breakable type of iron

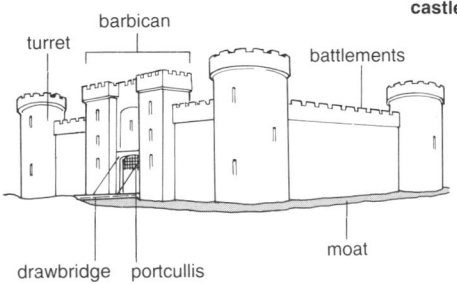

castle

turret — barbican — battlements

drawbridge — portcullis — moat

cas·tle¹ /ˈkɑːsəl‖ˈkæ-/ n **1** a large strongly-built building or set of buildings made in former times as a safe place that could easily be defended against attack: Windsor Castle **2** also **rook**— a powerful CHESS piece —see picture at CHESS **3** castles in the air plans, hopes, desires, etc., that will probably not become realities; DAYDREAMS

Castle How·ard /ˌkɑːsəl ˈhaʊəd‖ˌkæsəl ˈhaʊərd/ a STATELY HOME in Yorkshire

Cas·tle·maine XXXX /ˌkɑːsəlmeɪn ˌfɔːr ˈeks‖ˌkæ-/ n [U] tdmk a kind of Australian LAGER

cast-off /ˈ· ·/ adj [A] (esp. of clothes) unwanted by the original owner and thrown away —**castoff** /ˈkɑːstɒf‖ˈkæstɔːf/ n [usu. pl.] : She gave her castoffs to her younger sister. —see also HAND-ME-DOWN

cast·or /ˈkɑːstəʳ‖ˈkæs-/ n a CASTER

Cas·tor and Pol·lux /ˌkɑːstər ənd ˈpɒləks‖ˌkæstər ənd ˈpɑː-/ in CLASSICAL MYTHOLOGY, TWIN (=born together) brothers and famous fighters. The arrangement of stars known as Gemini or the Heavenly Twins is supposed to be named after them.

castor oil /ˌ·· ˈ·◄/ n [U] a thick yellowish medicinal oil made from the **castor-oil plant** and used esp. as a LAXATIVE. Many people who are now adults were given castor oil regularly as children and remember it for its unpleasant taste.

castor sug·ar /ˈ·· ˌ·/ n [U] CASTER SUGAR

cas·trate /kæˈstreɪt‖ˈkæstreɪt/ v [T] **1** to remove all or part of the sex organs of (a male animal or person) **2** to make (a man) lose his sense of being male —**-tration** /kæˈstreɪʃən/ n [U]

Cas·tro /ˈkæstrəʊ/, **Fi·del** /fɪˈdel/ (1927–) the leader of the COMMUNIST REVOLUTION, now President of Cuba

Cas·trol /ˈkæstrɒl‖-trəʊl/ a British company which produces motor oil

cas·u·al /ˈkæʒuəl/ adj **1** showing or feeling little interest: His casual manner/attitude annoyed her. | She tried to sound casual, but her excitement was obvious. **2** without a clear aim, plan, or intention; not serious or thorough: I took a casual glance at the article. | not a real lecture, just a few casual remarks **3** (of clothes) intended for informal situations or occasions: casual shoes **4** [A] a esp. BrE (of workers) employed for a short period of time: They employ casual labour to pick the fruit. **b** doing something only on some occasions but not regularly: casual readers of the paper | casual users of the library service **5** now rare resulting from chance: a casual meeting — ~ ly adv : casually dressed — ~ ness n [U]

casual sex /ˌ··· ˈ·/ n [U] the act of sex without the thought of forming a lasting relationship

cas·u·al·ty /ˈkæʒuəlti/ n **1** [C] a person hurt in an accident or killed or wounded in battle: There were ten serious casualties in the train crash. | Their army suffered heavy casualties. (=many of the soldiers were killed or wounded) | She read through the casualty list anxiously. **2** [C] a person or thing that has suffered loss or destruction as a result of a particular event: The new school was never finished: it was a casualty of the recent spending cuts. **3** [U] BrE ‖ **emergency room** AmE a place in a hospital where people hurt in accidents are taken for treatment: They rushed her to casualty but she was dead on arrival.

cas·u·ist /ˈkæʒuˌɪst/ n fml derog a person skilled in casuistry —**-istic** /ˌkæʒuˈɪstɪk◄/, **-istical** adj —**-istically** /kli/ adv

cas·u·is·try /ˈkæʒuˌɪstri/ n [U] fml, often derog false but clever use of arguments and reasoning, esp. when dealing with cases of conscience, law, or right and wrong behaviour

ca·sus bel·li /ˌkɑːsəs ˈbeli, ˌkeɪsəs ˈbelaɪ/ n casus belli tech Lat an event or political action which directly causes a declaration of war

cat /kæt/ n **1** a small four-legged animal with soft fur and sharp CLAWS, often kept as a pet or for catching mice and rats. A young cat is called a **kitten**. —see also MANX CAT, MIAOW, PURR

▶ CULTURAL NOTE People think that cats' favourite foods are milk or cream, and fish. Cats are often said to have nine lives, meaning that they often narrowly escape death. In Britain, some people believe that black cats bring good luck, but in the US they are thought to bring bad luck. ◀

2 an animal related to this, such as the lion or tiger — see also BIG CAT **3** BrE derog a mean unpleasant woman **4** a CAT-O'-NINE-TAILS **5** AmE **Cat got your tongue?** (used to TEASE someone when they are expected to speak and do not) **6** let the cat out of the bag infml to tell a secret, esp. unintentionally **7** like a cat on hot bricks BrE ‖ like a cat on a hot tin roof AmE— infml very nervous or anxious and unable to keep still or keep one's attention on one thing **8** play cat and mouse with to continually nearly catch (someone), and then allow them to escape; TEASE **9** BrE put/set the cat among the pigeons to cause trouble, esp. by doing or saying something that is unexpected or excites strong feeling **10** when the cat's away, the mice will play saying when the person in authority is away, the other people will enjoy themselves —see also CAT-AND-DOG, FAT CAT, **rain cats and dogs** (RAIN²), **not enough room to swing a cat** (ROOM¹ (6))

cat·a·clysm /ˈkætəklɪzəm/ n fml a violent and sudden event or change, esp. a serious flood or EARTHQUAKE — ~ **ic** /ˌkætəˈklɪzmɪk◄/ adj

cat·a·comb /ˈkætəkuːm‖-kəʊm/ n [usu. pl.] an underground burial place made up of many passages and rooms

cat·a·falque /ˈkætəfælk/ n a decorated raised stage on which a dead body may be placed before an official funeral

cat·a·lep·sy /ˈkætəlepsi/ n [U] med an illness in which a person can no longer control movement of their body, and their limbs either become stiff as in death or else remain in whatever position they are placed —**-tic** /ˌkætəˈleptɪk◄/ adj

cat·a·logue¹ also **-log** AmE /ˈkætəlɒg‖-lɔːg, -lɑːg/ n a list of places, names, objects, goods, etc. (often with information about them) put in a special order so that they can be found easily: Look in the catalogue to see whether the library has this book. | (fig.) the latest addition to the catalogue of terrorist crimes | I saw some slacks I like in the Sears catalog.

cat·a·logue² also **-log** AmE v [T] **1** to make a catalogue of (goods, objects, etc.) or list in a catalogue

ca·tal·y·sis /kəˈtæləsɪs/ n [U] the process of quickening a chemical activity by adding a catalyst

cat·a·lyst /ˈkætəlˌɪst/ n **1** a substance which, without itself changing, quickens chemical processes **2** a person, thing, or event that causes changes to happen, but without taking part in those changes: The First World War served as a catalyst for major social changes in Europe. —**-lytic** /ˌkætəlˈɪtɪk◄/ adj

catalytic con·ver·ter /ˌ·ˌ··· ·ˈ···/ n a piece of equipment fitted to the EXHAUST PIPE of a car that reduces the amount of poisonous gas sent out into the air when the engine is running

cat·a·ma·ran /ˌkætəməˈræn/ n a boat with a flat surface (DECK) supported by two narrow parallel HULLs (=floating surfaces), like two boats fastened together

cat-and-dog /ˌ· · ˈ·/ adj [A] infml full of quarrels and arguments: In the early years of their marriage they had led a cat-and-dog existence|life.

cat·a·pult[1] /ˈkætəpʌlt/ n 1 BrE ‖ slingshot AmE– a small Y-shaped stick with a rubber band fastened between the forks, used by children to shoot small stones 2 a machine for throwing heavy stones, balls, etc., used in former times as a weapon for breaking down defensive walls

catapult[2] v [T+obj+adv|prep] to fire (as if) from a catapult: The attackers catapulted stones against the town wall. | The car stopped suddenly and I was catapulted through the windscreen. | (fig.) She was catapulted to stardom by the success of her first record.

cat·a·ract /ˈkætərækt/ n 1 a large waterfall 2 med a disease of the eye in which the LENS becomes clouded and causes a gradual loss of sight

ca·tarrh /kəˈtɑːr/ n [U] a flow of thick liquid, esp. in the nose and throat, which causes a feeling of discomfort, as when one has a cold: He suffers from chronic catarrh. — ~ al adj

ca·tas·tro·phe /kəˈtæstrəfi/ n a sudden, unexpected, and terrible event that causes great suffering, misfortune, or ruin: The flood was a major catastrophe, causing heavy loss of life. | (fig.) The party could be heading for catastrophe in the election. —**-phic** /ˌkætəˈstrɒfɪk◂|-ˈstrɑː-/ adj —**-phically** /kli/ adv : the catastrophic consequences of a war

cat·a·ton·ic /ˌkætəˈtɒnɪk◂|-ˈtɑː-/ adj suffering from or being CATALEPSY: a catatonic trance

cat bur·glar /ˈ· ˌ··/ n a thief who enters and leaves a building by climbing up walls, pipes, etc.

cat·call /ˈkætkɔːl/ n a loud whistle or cry expressing disapproval or displeasure, made at events like theatre performances and sports matches —**catcall** v [I]

catch[1] /kætʃ/ v caught /kɔːt/ 1 [T] to get hold of and stop (a moving object): I threw the ball, and the dog caught it in his mouth. 2 [T] to trap, esp. after chasing or hunting; CAPTURE: The cat caught a mouse. | to catch a fish in a net | They drove off after the thieves but couldn't catch them. | The police are confident that the murderer will be caught. 3 [T] to discover suddenly and by surprise (esp. someone who is doing something wrong): I caught him in the act (of reading my diary). [+obj+v-ing] The police caught him stealing a car. | You won't catch me mending his socks for him! (=I'll never do that) | The thieves were caught red-handed. (=were found while actually stealing) | (fig.) This kind of cancer can be cured, provided it is caught early. (=if its existence is discovered at an early stage) 4 [T] to be in time for: We had to run fast in order to catch the train. | If you post the letter now, you'll just catch the last collection. | If we go home now, we might just catch the 10 o'clock news. —opposite **miss** 5 [T] to get (an illness); become infected with: to catch a cold 6 [I;T] to (cause to) become hooked, held, fastened, or stuck: My skirt caught in the door|got caught in the door. | I caught my dress on a nail. | I got my finger caught in the wire fence. | (fig.) The company is caught between the need to invest more money and the need to keep costs as low as possible. 7 [T] to attract (esp. interest or attention): The unusual panelling on the walls caught our attention. | The idea caught her imagination. | I'd like another drink; try to catch the waiter's eye. (=look at him to attract his attention) 8 [T not in progressive forms] to get or notice for a moment: I suddenly caught sight of her in the crowd. | The fans waited at the airport, hoping to catch a glimpse of their idol as he passed through. | Try to catch a bit of sleep on the journey. 9 [T not in progressive forms] to hear clearly and/or understand: I didn't quite catch your last point — could you say it again? | What did she say? I didn't catch it. 10 [T] to give a good representation of (a quality) in a picture, piece of writing, etc.: The novel catches the mood of pre-war Britain very well. | The photograph catches her smile perfectly. 11 [I] to start to burn: The wind was so strong that the fire caught quickly. —see FIRE (USAGE) 12 [T (OUT) often pass.] (in cricket) to end (a player's) turn to BAT by taking and holding a ball hit off the BAT before it touches the ground 13 [T+obj+adv|prep] to hit (a person or animal); strike: I

caught him on the chin with a heavy punch. 14 act as CATCHER in baseball: Who's catching for the Yankees today? 15 **catch as catch can** to survive in a bad situation by doing whatever you can: It's been catch as catch can for him ever since he lost his job. 16 **catch fire** to start burning 17 **catch it** infml to be in trouble for doing something wrong: We'll really catch it from the teacher if we're late again. 18 **catch one's breath: a** to stop breathing for a moment from surprise, fear, shock, etc.: The news was so unexpected I caught my breath from shock. **b** to return to one's usual rate of breathing after hard physical effort: Let me sit down for a moment while I catch my breath.

catch at sthg. phr v [T] to try to take or hold: A drowning man will catch at anything, even a straw.

catch on phr v [I] 1 to become popular or fashionable: It was a popular style in Britain, but it never really caught on in America. 2 [(to)] to begin to understand: It was a long time before the police caught on to what he was really doing.

catch sbdy. ↔ **out** phr v [T (in)] BrE to show (someone) to be doing something wrong or making a mistake: The prosecuting lawyer tried to catch the witness out by clever questioning.

catch up phr v 1 [I (with);T (=catch sbdy.|sthg. up)] to come up from behind and reach the same point or level as: You walk on and I'll catch up with you later|(esp. BrE) I'll catch you up later. | At the moment our technology is more advanced than theirs, but they are catching up (with us) fast. 2 [I (on)] to do what needs to be done in order to come up to date: I have to catch up on my work tonight, so I can't come out. | I've been away from school for two weeks, so I've got a lot of catching up to do. 3 **caught up in** included in, often against one's wishes; INVOLVED in: The government got caught up in a bitter dispute between the miners and their employers.

catch[2] n 1 [C] an act of seizing and holding something thrown or hit, esp. a ball: a good catch 2 [C] (the amount of) something caught: The boat brought back a big catch of fish. | (infml) Her husband was a good catch — he's rich and attractive. 3 [C] a hook or other apparatus for fastening something or holding it shut: The catch on this door is broken. —see also SAFETY CATCH 4 [C] infml a hidden problem or difficulty; SNAG: That house is extremely cheap; there must be a catch in|to it somewhere! | The salary is fantastic, but the catch is that you have to spend six months of the year in the Antarctic. —see also CATCH-22 5 [U] a simple game in which two or more people throw a ball to each other: Let's play catch.

catch-22 /kætʃ twenti ˈtuː/ n [U] (often cap.) a situation from which one is prevented from escaping by something that is part of the situation itself (from the title of a book by Joseph Heller about the experiences of an American airforce pilot): I can't get a job unless I belong to the union, and I can't join the union until I've got a job — it's a case of catch-22|it's a catch-22 situation!

catch-all[1] /ˈ· ··/ n AmE something used to hold or catch various small items, such as a bag or a drawer

catch-all[2] adj [A] intended to include or take account of all types, situations, or possibilities: a vague catch-all clause in the contract to protect the rights of the author

catch crop /ˈ· ··/ n a quick-growing vegetable crop planted between two rows of another crop to use soil not otherwise used —compare CASH CROP

catch·er /ˈkætʃər/ n in BASEBALL, the defensive player who stands behind the BATTER —see picture at BASEBALL

Catcher in the Rye /ˌ··· · ˈ·/, **The** a book by American author J. D. Salinger (1919–) published (PUBLISH) in 1951, about a young man, Holden CAULFIELD, who runs away from school and goes to New York. The book was esp. popular with young people, with its descriptions of ADOLESCENT life.

catch·ing /ˈkætʃɪŋ/ adj [F] infml (of a disease) infectious

catch·ment ar·e·a /ˈkætʃmənt ˌeərɪə/ n 1 the area from which a lake or river gets its water 2 the area from which a school gets its pupils, a hospital gets its patients, etc.

catch·pen·ny /ˈkætʃˌpeni/ adj [A] derog cheap and worthless, but made to appear attractive

catch·phrase /ˈkætʃfreɪz/ n a phrase, often with little meaning, which becomes fashionable and widely used for a time

catch·word /ˈkætʃwɜːd‖-wɜːrd/ n a word or phrase repeated so regularly that it becomes representative of a political party, newspaper, etc.; SLOGAN

catch·y /ˈkætʃi/ adj (of a tune or song) easy to remember: *a catchy song* —**ily** adv

cat·e·chis·m /ˈkætɬˌkɪzəm/ n a set of questions and answers, often in the form of a small book, used for religious instruction in some branches of the Christian church —**chist** n

cat·e·chize ‖ also **-chise** BrE /ˈkætɬkaɪz/ v [T] to teach (someone) religion by a process of question and answer

cat·e·gor·i·cal /ˌkætɬˈɡɒrɪkəl◄‖-ˈɡɔː-, -ˈɡɑː-/ adj unconditional; made without any doubt in the mind of the speaker or writer: *a categorical statement/assurance* | *The government has issued a categorical denial of this rumour.* — ~ ly /kli/ adv : *He categorically denied having seen it.*

cat·e·go·rize also **-rise** BrE /ˈkætɬɡəraɪz/ v [T (as)] to put in a category; CLASSIFY: *His politics are fairly left-wing, but he doesn't like to be categorized as a socialist.* | *Her writing is very individual — it's difficult to categorize.* —**rization** /ˌkætɬɡəraɪˈzeɪʃən‖-rə-/ n [C;U]

cat·e·go·ry /ˈkætɬɡəri‖-ɡɔːri/ n a division or class in a system for dividing objects into groups according to their nature or type: *The voters fall into three main categories: Republicans, Democrats, and "Don't Knows".*

ca·ter /ˈkeɪtər/ v [I;T] to provide and serve food and drinks, usu. for payment, at a public or private party rather than in a restaurant: *Who's catering at your daughter's wedding/(esp. AmE) Who's catering your daughter's wedding?* —see also SELF CATERING — ~ **er** n : *a firm of caterers*
cater for sbdy./sthg. phr v [T] to provide what is needed or wanted by: *a holiday company that caters mainly for young people* | *Our newspapers try to cater for all opinions.*
cater to sbdy./sthg. phr v [T] to try to satisfy (desires or needs, esp. of a bad kind): *Those newspapers cater to the lowest tastes.* | *She refused to cater to his ridiculous demands.*

cat·er·pil·lar /ˈkætəˌpɪlər‖-tər-/ n 1 a small long many-legged wormlike creature (LARVA of the BUTTERFLY and other insects) which feeds on the leaves of plants —see picture at METAMORPHOSIS 2 also **caterpillar track** /ˈ···· ˌ·/ — an endless chain of metal plates fastened over the wheels of a heavy vehicle, such as a TANK¹(2)

caterpillar trac·tor /ˌ···· ˈ··/ n a large heavy vehicle which moves along on a CATERPILLAR (2) and is used for farm work, road repair, or building work

cat·er·waul /ˈkætəwɔːl‖-tər-/ v [I] to make a loud unpleasant catlike sound —**caterwaul** n [S]

cat·gut /ˈkætɡʌt/ n [U] strong cord made from the INTESTINES of animals, esp. sheep, and used for the strings of musical instruments

ca·thar·sis /kəˈθɑːsɬs, kæ-‖kəˈθɑːr-/ n -ses /siːz/ fml or tech [C;U] the process by which strong and perhaps dangerous feelings are allowed to be experienced, e.g. under the influence of music or DRAMA, so that they lose their power —**tic** adj : *Watching tragic drama is supposed to have a cathartic effect on people.*

ca·the·dral /kəˈθiːdrəl/ n the chief church of a Christian DIOCESE (=an area with a BISHOP), usu. a very large, beautifully decorated stone structure: *Durham Cathedral* | *a cathedral city* (=one which has a cathedral)

Cath·er /ˈkæðər/, **Wil·la** /ˈwɪlə/ (1873–1947) an American writer who grew up in Nebraska when it was first being settled. Her books include *O Pioneers!* and *My Antonia*.

Cath·e·rine of Ar·a·gon /ˌkæθərɬn əv ˈærəɡən‖-ɡɑːn/ also **Catharine, Katherine** (1485–1536) the first wife of King Henry VIII of England

Catherine the Great /ˌ···· · ˈ·/ (1729–96) the Empress of Russia from 1762, also called **Catherine II**

catherine wheel /ˈ··· ·/ n a circular FIREWORK that is pinned to an upright surface and turns round when set on fire

cath·e·ter /ˈkæθɬtər/ n a thin tube that is put into passages in the body, used esp. for putting in or taking out liquids

cath·ode /ˈkæθəʊd/ also **negative pole**— n tech the part of an electrical instrument (such as a BATTERY) from which ELECTRONS leave, often a rod or wire represented by the sign [−] —compare ANODE

cathode ray tube /ˌ··· ˈ· ·/ n a glass instrument in which streams of ELECTRONS from the CATHODE (**cathode rays**) are directed onto a flat surface where they give out light, as in a television

cath·o·lic /ˈkæθəlɪk/ adj fml (esp. of likings and interests) general; including many different things; broad: *catholic opinions/tastes* — ~ **ity** /ˌkæθəˈlɪsɬti/ n [U]

Catholic adj, n (a member) of the Roman Catholic Church: *Catholic schools* | *Is he (a) Catholic or (a) Protestant?* — ~ **ism** /kəˈθɒlɬsɪzəm‖kəˈθɑː-/ n [U]

cat house /ˈ· ·/ n AmE old-fash a BROTHEL

cat·kin /ˈkætkɪn/ n esp BrE a stringlike bunch of soft small furry flowers that grows on certain trees such as the WILLOW or BIRCH

cat lit·ter /ˈ· ˌ··/ n [U] a special substance (LITTER¹ (3b)) on which house cats can empty their bowels

cat·nap /ˈkætnæp/ n infml a very short light sleep

cat·nip /ˈkætnɪp/ n [U] a HERB whose smell is very attractive to cats

cat-o'-nine-tails /ˌkæt ə ˈnaɪn ˌteɪlz/ also **cat**— n a whip of nine knotted cords fastened to a handle, used formerly for punishing people

CAT scan /ˈkæt skæn/ also **CT scan** n med an image of the body made by X-RAYS with an advanced machine that can make a picture of a CROSS-SECTION of the body. CAT scans can be used to discover whether a disease such as CANCER is present.

cat's cra·dle /ˌ· ˈ··/ n [U] a children's game played with string wound round the fingers and passed from one finger to another to make various shapes

cat's eye /ˈ· ·/ n 1 a small object fixed in the middle of a road which shines when lit by car lights in the dark 2 a valuable stone which REFLECTS a narrow band of light

Cat·skill Moun·tains /ˌkætskɪl ˈmaʊntɬnz/ [the+pl] mountains in the southeast of the US state of New York, which are part of the Appalachian mountain range

cat's paw /ˈ· ·/ n infml someone who does unpleasant or dangerous jobs on the orders of another person; TOOL¹ (3)

cat·suit /ˈkætsuːt, -sjuːt‖-suːt/ n a tightly fitting garment, worn esp. by women, consisting of a combined top and trousers

cat·sup /ˈkætsəp/ n [U] esp. AmE KETCHUP

cat's whis·kers /ˌ· ˈ··/ infml **be the cat's whiskers** to be an excellent person or thing: *My new calculator really is the cat's whiskers!*

cat·tail /ˈkæt-teɪl/ n AmE ‖ **bulrush** BrE— a tall, grasslike plant with a thick brown top, which grows near water

cat·ter·y /ˈkætəri/ n BrE a place where cats are looked after or bred

cat·tle /ˈkætl/ n [P] cows and BULLs, esp. as kept on farms for meat or milk: *He has twenty (head of) cattle on his farm.* | *The cattle are in the shed.*

cattle grid /ˈ··· ·/ **cattle guard** AmE— n a set of poles placed over a hole in a road, which cars can go across but animals cannot

cat·tle·man /ˈkætlmən/ **cat·tlewom·an** /ˈkætlwʊmən/ fem.— n -men /mən/ a man who looks after cattle

cattle mar·ket /ˈ··· ˌ··/ n a place where cattle are bought and sold: (fig.) *The Miss World contest is just a cattle market.*

cattle truck /ˈ··· ˌ·/ n BrE a railway vehicle or a LORRY made to carry cattle

cat·ty /ˈkæti/ adj infml derog showing a desire to hurt or harm someone, esp. in a way that is not openly or directly expressed; MALICIOUS: *She often makes catty remarks about her stepmother.* —**tily** adv —**tiness** n [U]

catty-cor·ner /ˈ··· ˌ··/ adv AmE for KITTY-CORNER

Ca·tul·lus /kəˈtʌləs/, **Gai·us Va·ler·i·us** /ˈɡaɪəs vəˈlɪəriəs/ (about 84–54 BC) a Roman poet

cat·walk /ˈkætwɔːk/ n a narrow raised footway, esp. along a bridge or round a large machine, or sticking out into a room for MODELs to walk on in a fashion show

Cau·ca·si·an /kɔːˈkeɪziən‖-ˈkeɪʒən/ adj 1 of the white race of man, according to physical features 2 of the Caucasus, its people, or languages —**Caucasian** n

Cau·ca·sus /ˈkɔːkəsəs/ [the] 1 mountains in S Europe between the Black Sea and the Caspian Sea, containing Mount Elbrus, Europe's highest mountain 2 a region of S Europe, also called **Caucasia** between the Black Sea and the Caspian Sea

cau·cus /ˈkɔːkəs/ n [C+*sing.*/*pl. v*] (a meeting of) a group of people in a political party, who come together to decide on political plans or to choose people who will represent the party in an election —see also extra information on page 412

cau·dal /ˈkɔːdl/ adj tech of or at the tail or tail-end of the body — ~**ly** adv

caught /kɔːt/ past tense & participle of CATCH

caul·dron , cal· /ˈkɔːldrən/ n old use or lit a large round open metal pot for boiling liquids over a fire. In stories, WITCHes use cauldrons to make harmful substances.

Caul·field /ˈkɔːlfiːld/, **Hol·den** /ˈhəʊldən/ The main character in the novel *The Catcher in the Rye* by J D Salinger. As a TEENAGER he experiences many of the difficulties associated with that time of life.

cau·li·flow·er /ˈkɒlɪˌflaʊəʳ‖ˈkɔː-, ˈkɑː-/ n [C;U] (the white part, cooked and eaten as food, of) a garden vegetable with green leaves around a large firm white head of un-developed flowers —see picture at VEGETABLE

cauliflower ear /ˌ···· ˈ·/ n an ear which is damaged and an odd shape as a result of a blow to the head, esp. while boxing

caulk , calk /kɔːk/ v [T] to block up (cracks, esp. in a ship) with oily or sticky WATERPROOF material

caus·al /ˈkɔːzəl/ adj fml having or showing the relationship of cause and effect: *They denied that there was any causal connection/link between unemployment and crime.* — ~**ly** adv

cau·sal·i·ty /kɔːˈzælɪti/ n [U] fml the relationship between a cause and its effect; principle that events have causes

cau·sa·tion /kɔːˈzeɪʃən/ n [U] fml **1** the action of causing something **2** the relationship of cause and effect; causality

caus·a·tive /ˈkɔːzətɪv/ adj fml **1** acting as a cause; produc-ing an effect: *one of several causative factors in the com-pany's failure* **2** tech (of a verb or verb form) showing that the subject of the verb is the cause of an action or state — ~**ly** adv

cause[1] /kɔːz/ n **1** [C (**of**)] something which produces an effect; a person, thing, or event that makes something happen: *Ice on the road was the cause of the accident.* | *In our view, the* **root cause**/**underlying cause** *of the crime problem* (=the most important cause from which all others come) *is poverty and unemployment.* | *He is the cause of all my unhappiness.* **2** [U] something that pro-vides a satisfactory reason for an action; JUSTIFICATION; GROUNDS: *Don't complain without (good) cause.* | *to show cause* (=give a good reason) *for dismissing a worker* | *The patient's condition is* **giving cause for concern**. **3** [C] a principle, aim, or movement that is strongly celebrated or supported: *her lifelong devotion to the cause of women's rights* | *collecting money for good causes such as famine relief* **4** [C] law the reason for action in a court of law; a matter over which a person takes legal action **5 make common cause (with)** fml to take action together for a particular purpose: *We made common cause with neigh-bouring countries against the invaders.* —see also LOST CAUSE; see REASON (USAGE)

cause[2] v [T] to lead to or to be the cause of: *What caused the accident?* | *They have been charged with causing criminal damage.* [+obj+to-v] *His illness caused him to miss the game.* [+obj(i)+obj(d)] *This car has caused me a lot of trouble.* | *Her irresponsible behaviour has caused a great deal of anxiety to/for her family.* | *They believe inflation is caused by big wage increases.*

▷ USAGE Compare **cause**, **make**, and **let**. **Cause** with an object can be formal or informal: *Cigarettes may* **cause** *cancer.* | *Why do you always* **cause** *trouble?* **Cause** with an object and infinitive with *to* is formal: *The earthquake* **caused** *several buildings to collapse.* **Make** when used with a verb has a similar meaning, but is more common in conversation, and is followed by an object and an infinitive without *to*: *It's a sad film; it'll* **make** *you cry.* **Let** (=allow) can be formal or infor-mal. It is usually followed by an object and infinitive without *to*: *The valve* **lets** *water enter the pump.* | *Let me go!*◁

cause cé·lè·bre /ˌkəʊz seˈlebrə, ˌkɔːz-/ n **causes célèbres**

(*same pronunciation*) Fr **1** an event which attracts a lot of usu. unfavourable attention **2** a case in a court of law that receives a lot of public interest

cause·way /ˈkɔːzweɪ/ n a raised road or path, esp. across wet ground or water

caus·tic /ˈkɔːstɪk/ adj **1** able to burn or destroy by chemi-cal action; CORROSIVE: *caustic soda* **2** (esp. of remarks) showing strong dislike or disapproval and intended to hurt; bitter: *John's always making caustic comments about your work.* | *caustic satire/wit* — ~**ally** /kli/ adv

cau·ter·ize also **-ise** BrE /ˈkɔːtəraɪz/ v [T] med to burn (a wound, snake bite, etc.) with a very hot iron or caustic substance to destroy infection

cau·tion[1] /ˈkɔːʃən/ n **1** [U] the quality of using great care and attention, esp. in order to avoid danger: *Open the box with caution.* | *You must exercise great caution when oper-ating the machine.* | *Their claims should be treated with extreme caution.* (=not accepted or believed without care-ful thought) **2** [C] a spoken warning usu. given by a policeman, judge, etc., when a person has broken the law or done something wrong but when the crime is not seri-ous: *I'll let you off with a caution this time.* **3** [S] old-fash a person or thing that causes amusement

caution[2] v [T] **1** [(**about, against**)] to warn against pos-sible danger: *She cautioned the child against talking to strange men.* [+that] *The director cautioned that these changes could lead to job losses.* [+obj+that] (law) *The policeman said, "I must caution you that anything you say may be used against you (at your trial)."* **2** [(**for, about**)] BrE law to warn officially about something bad already done, often with the threat of future punishment for doing it again: *The policeman cautioned me for speeding.*

cau·tion·ar·y /ˈkɔːʃənəri‖-neri/ adj fml or humor giving ad-vice or a warning: *a* **cautionary tale** (=story) *about a boy who had been seriously injured while playing near the railway line*

cau·tious /ˈkɔːʃəs/ adj [(**about, of, with**)] using or show-ing caution; careful to avoid risks; PRUDENT: *a cautious approach to dealing with the problem* | *cautious with money* | *The bank is very cautious about lending money.* | *a very cautious driver* | *cautious optimism* — ~**ly** adv : *She opened the door cautiously so as not to wake the baby.* | *These suggestions were cautiously welcomed by the com-mittee.* — ~**ness** n [U]

cav·al·cade /ˌkævəlˈkeɪd, ˈkævəlkeɪd/ n [C+*sing.*/*pl. v*] a ceremonial procession of riders, vehicles, etc.

cav·a·lier /ˌkævəˈlɪəʳ◂/ adj thoughtless and disrespect-ful; OFFHAND: *I'm annoyed at your cavalier attitude towards this serious matter* | *a cavalier manner*

Cavalier n **1** (*usu. cap.*) a sup-porter of the King against Parliament in the English Civil War in the 17th cen-tury. The Cavaliers fought against the ROUNDHEADS **2** tdmk a medium-sized British car made by Vauxhall

cav·al·ry /ˈkævəlri/ n [(the)] U+*sing.*/*pl. v*] **1** (esp. in for-mer times) soldiers who fight on horseback: *The cavalry was/were advanc-ing.* | *cavalry officers*

Cavalier

▶ CULTURAL NOTE In old Western films, the US Cavalry often arrives just in time to save people from being hurt or killed, and people sometimes say "the cavalry is on its way" when someone is coming to help or rescue another person. ◀

2 a branch of a modern army that uses armoured vehi-cles —compare INFANTRY

cav·al·ry·man /ˈkævəlrimən/ n **-men** /mən/ (esp. in former times) a soldier who fights on horseback

cave[1] /keɪv/ n a deep natural hollow place, either under-ground, with an opening to the surface, or in the side of a cliff or hill

cave[2] v

  cave in phr v [I] **1** (of a roof or the covering over a hollow place) to fall in or down **2** [(to)] *infml, often derog.* to give up opposition, esp. as a result of pressure or persuasion; YIELD: *They refused to cave in to the terrorists' demands.* —**cave-in** /¹· ·/ *n* : *a cave-in at the mine*

ca·ve·at /¹keɪviæt, ¹kæv-/ *n* [(**against**)] *fml* a statement or warning intended to prevent misunderstanding: *The evidence looks convincing but there is one important caveat – namely, that it all comes from the same unreliable source.*

caveat emp·tor /ˌkeɪviæt ¹emptɔː ͬ, ˌkæv-/ *n* [U] *Lat* a warning principle in buying and selling that responsibility for the quality of goods must be taken by the buyer. It means "buyer beware".

cave·man /¹keɪvmæn/ *n* -**men** /men/ **1** a person who lived in a cave in very ancient times. The STEREOTYPE of a caveman is of a man with long hair and beard, wearing an animal's skin round his body, carrying a piece of wood as a weapon, and pulling his wife along behind him by her hair. **2** *infml* a man who acts in a rough violent manner

caveman

Cav·en·dish /¹kævəndɪʃ/, **Henry** (1731–1810) an English scientist who discovered HYDROGEN and the arrangement of chemicals that make up water

cav·ern /¹kævən‖-ərn/ *n* a large cave

cav·ern·ous /¹kævənəs‖-ərnəs/ *adj* (of a space or hole) very large and deep: *The lion opened its cavernous mouth.* | *a cavernous hall* – –**ly** *adv*

cav·i·ar , -are /¹kæviɑː ͬ/ *n* [U] **1** the very expensive ROE (=salted eggs) of various large fish, esp. the STURGEON, eaten as food. Caviar is a special food for most people, but is thought to be typical of the life style of the very rich. **2 caviar to the general** *BrE lit or humor* something liked and understood only by a person of sensitivity and good education

cav·il /¹kævəl/ *v* -**ll** *BrE* ‖ -**l** *-AmE* [I (**at**)] to find fault in an annoying and unnecessary way – –**ler** *n*

cav·i·ty /¹kævᵻti/ *n fml or tech* a hole or hollow space in a solid mass: *a cavity in a tooth* | *in a wall*

cavity wall /¹··· ·/ *n* a wall consisting of two walls with a narrow space between them, used in buildings to keep out noise, cold, etc.: *cavity wall insulation* (=material placed inside the cavity wall, to help keep heat inside a building)

ca·vort /kə¹vɔːt‖-ɔːrt/ *v* [I] *infml* (esp. of a person) to jump or dance about noisily; CAPER

caw /kɔː/ *v* [I] to make the loud rough cry of various large birds such as CROWs —**caw** *n*

Cax·ton /¹kækstən/, **William** (about 1422–91) the first person in England to print books and other documents

cay·enne pep·per /ˌkeɪen ¹pepə ͬ/ also **cayenne** /ˌkeɪ¹en◂/ *n* [U] (a powder made from) a PEPPER¹ (2) with long thin very hot-tasting red fruit

Cay·man Is·lands /¹keɪmən ˌaɪləndz/ a group of three islands in the Caribbean Sea, NW of Jamaica

CB /ˌsiː ¹biː◂/ *n* [U] Citizens' Band; a radio on which people can speak to each other over short distances. In the US, long-distance TRUCK drivers often have CBs, which they use to speak to other drivers, both socially and to avoid the police. Users of CBs often give themselves NICKNAMEs.

CBC /ˌsiː biː ¹siː/ Canadian Broadcasting Corporation; a television company that is supported by the Canadian government

CBE /ˌsiː biː ¹iː/ *n* Commander of the British Empire; an award given to people for services to the country

CBI /ˌsiː biː ¹aɪ/ [*the*] Confederation of British Industry; an organization which helps in the development and growth of British industry, and exchanges information and ideas with the government

CBS /ˌsiː biː ¹es/ Columbia Broadcasting System; one of the national television companies which broadcast all over the US: *a CBS news reporter*

cc *abbrev. for:* **1** CUBIC CENTIMETRE: *a 200 cc engine* **2** CUBIC CAPACITY

CCITT /ˌsiː siː ˌaɪ tiː ¹tiː/ Comité Consultatif Internationale de Télégraphique et Téléphonique; an international organization with its main offices in Geneva. Its members represent the telephone companies and authorities from countries around the world, and they decide standards for all kinds of telephone, TELECOMMUNICATIONS, and computer equipment.

CCTV *written abbrev. for:* CLOSED CIRCUIT TELEVISION

CD /ˌsiː ¹diː/ *n* **1** a COMPACT DISC **2** a CERTIFICATE OF DEPOSIT **3** Corps Diplomatique; the letters CD on the back of a car show that it is used by a DIPLOMAT

CDC /ˌsiː diː ¹siː/ CENTERS FOR DISEASE CONTROL

CDP /ˌsiː diː ¹piː/ *n AmE* Census Designated Place; an area that is not legally considered a single city, but looks like one and is called by one name, esp. by the people who live there: *Carney CDP, Maryland*

CD-ROM /ˌsiː diː ¹rɒm‖-¹rɑːm/ *n* compact disc read-only memory; a COMPACT DISC on which very large quantities of information can be stored for use by a computer. Unlike the information on a FLOPPY DISK, the information on a CD-ROM cannot be changed or removed.

CDT¹ /ˌsiː diː ¹tiː/ *n* [U] *BrE* Craft, Design, and Technology; a practical subject, involving the designing and making of things in metal, wood, etc., studied in many British schools and colleges

CDT² *abbrev for* CENTRAL DAYLIGHT TIME

CE /ˌsiː ¹iː/ *abbrev. for:* common era —see BC (USAGE)

cease¹ /siːs/ *v* [I;T] *fml* to stop (esp. an activity or state): *It rained all day without ceasing.* | *Cease fire!* (=Stop shooting!) [+*to-v*] *As from the end of the month, this regulation will cease to have effect.* [+*v-ing*] *The company has ceased trading in this part of the world.* —see also **wonders will never cease** (WONDER² (7))

cease² *n* **without cease** *fml* continuously; without ceasing —see also CEASELESS

cease-fire /¹· ·/ *n* an agreement to stop fighting for a certain period, esp. so that a more lasting peace agreement can be established: *to negotiate a cease-fire* – compare ARMISTICE, TRUCE

cease·less /¹siːsləs/ *adj fml* unending; continuous; without ceasing: *ceaseless activity* – –**ly** *adv* : *She practised ceaselessly.*

Ceau·çes·cu /tʃaʊ¹ʃeskuː/, **Nic·o·lae** /¹nɪkəlaɪ/ (1918–89) a president of Romania, who became increasingly unpopular and dependent on his secret police for his position until he was removed from power and EXECUTEd

ce·dar /¹siːdə ͬ/ *n* **1** [C] a tall EVERGREEN tree **2** [U] also **ce·dar·wood** /¹siːdəwʊd‖-ər-/– the hard reddish sweet-smelling wood of this tree used for making pencils, decorative boxes, furniture, etc.

cede /siːd/ *v* [T (**to**)] *fml* to give (usu. land or a right) to another country or person, esp. after losing a war: *By the terms of the treaty, a third of their territory was ceded to France.* —see also CESSION

ce·dil·la /sᵻ¹dɪlə/ *n* (when writing certain languages) a mark put under a letter (as with ç in French) to show that it has a special sound

Cee·fax /¹siːfæks/ *tdmk* an information service without sound provided by the BBC for paying customers on a special television CHANNEL

CEGB /ˌsiː iː dʒiː ¹biː/ [*the*] Central Electricity Generating Board; the organization which supplied electricity in England and Wales before 1990. In 1990 the industry was divided into four companies, Power Gen, National Power, National Grid, and Nuclear Electric, two of which were sold to private buyers.

cei·lidh /¹keɪli/ *n* an evening entertainment in Scotland and Ireland which includes singing, dancing, and story telling

cei·ling /ˈsiːlɪŋ/ n 1 the inner surface of the top of a room —compare ROOF¹ (1) 2 [(on)] a usu. official upper limit on prices, wages, rents, etc.: *The government set/imposed a ceiling on imports of foreign cars.* 3 tech height above ground: *a low cloud ceiling | The plane has an operational ceiling of 50,000 feet.* —see also GLASS CEILING

cel·e·brate /ˈselɪbreɪt/ v 1 [I;T] to mark (an event or special occasion) by enjoying yourself, publicly or privately: *We celebrated (her birthday) with a party/by going out to a restaurant. | These good results have given us something to celebrate.* 2 [T] fml to praise in writing, speech, etc.: *poems that celebrate the joys of love* 3 [T] to perform a religious ceremony, esp. the Christian Mass solemnly and officially

cel·e·brat·ed /ˈselɪbreɪtɪd/ adj [(as, for)] well-known; famous: *a celebrated writer/legal trial | Venice is celebrated for its beautiful buildings.*

cel·e·bra·tion /ˌselɪˈbreɪʃən/ n 1 [U] the act of celebrating 2 [C] an occasion of celebrating, such as a party: *the new country's independence celebrations*

ce·leb·ri·ty /sɪˈlebrɪti/ n 1 [C] a famous person, esp. in the business of entertainment: *to interview celebrities on television* 2 [U] fml the state of being famous; fame

ce·ler·i·ty /sɪˈlerɪti/ n [U] fml speed; quickness

cel·e·ry /ˈseləri/ n [U] (the bunched greenish-white stems of) a small plant eaten cooked or uncooked as a vegetable: *He dug up a **head of celery**. | She ate a **stick of celery**. | celery soup* —see picture at VEGETABLE

ce·les·ti·al /sɪˈlestiəl‖-tʃəl/ adj fml of the sky or heaven: *The sun, the stars, and the moon are celestial bodies. | Angels are celestial beings.*

cel·i·bate /ˈselɪbɪt/ n, adj (a person, esp. a priest or NUN, who is) unmarried and not taking part in sexual activity, esp. as the result of a religious promise —compare CHASTE (1) —**-bacy** n [U]: *a vow (=promise) of celibacy*

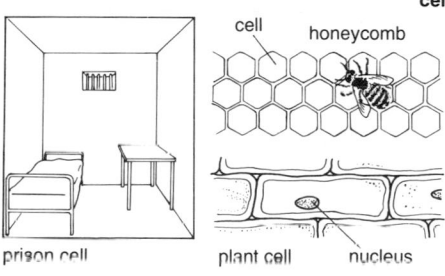

cell

cell   honeycomb

prison cell   plant cell   nucleus

cell /sel/ n 1 a small room a in a prison for one person or a small number of people b in a MONASTERY or CONVENT for one person 2 a very small division of living matter, with one centre of activity (NUCLEUS (2)), able alone or with others to perform all the operations necessary for life —see also RED BLOOD CELL 3 one of a number of small parts belonging to a larger structure, esp. one of the divisions of a HONEYCOMB 4 an apparatus for making a current of electricity by chemical action 5 [+sing./ pl. v] a small group of people operating secretly as part of a larger, usu. political organization: *a terrorist cell* 6 **-celled** /seld/ having the stated number or type of cells: *single-celled organisms*

cel·lar /ˈselər/ n 1 an underground room, usu. without windows and used for storing goods: *a coal cellar* 2 a store of wine belonging to a person, restaurant, etc.

cel·lar·age /ˈselərɪdʒ/ n [U] 1 the amount of cellar space 2 the charge for storing something in a cellar

cell di·vi·sion /ˈ· ·ˌ··/ n [C;U] (an act of) the process by which plant and animal cells increase their numbers — see also MEIOSIS, MITOSIS

cel·list /ˈtʃelɪst/ also **violoncellist** fml— n a person who plays the cello

cel·lo /ˈtʃeləʊ/ also **violoncello** fml— n -los a stringed musical instrument, like the VIOLIN and VIOLA but larger and producing a deeper sound

Cel·lo·phane /ˈseləfeɪn/ n [U] tdmk thin transparent material used for wrapping goods, esp. food

cell·phone /ˈselfəʊn/ n a cellular telephone

cel·lu·lar /ˈseljʊlər/ adj 1 consisting of CELLS (3) 2 (of cloth) loosely woven: *cellular blankets* 3 having many holes; POROUS: *cellular rock* 4 using a network of radio stations to pass on signals: *She has a cellular telephone in her car.*

cel·lu·lite /ˈseljʊlaɪt/ n [U] fat which gathers just below the skin on a person's, esp. a woman's, body and gives the skin a slightly lumpy appearance. Cellulite is considered very unattractive and is supposed to be difficult to get rid of.

cel·lu·loid /ˈseljʊlɔɪd/ n [U] tdmk 1 a plastic substance made mainly from CELLULOSE (2) and formerly used for making photographic film 2 **on celluloid** on cinema film: *Her marvellous acting talent is preserved on celluloid.*

cel·lu·lose /ˈseljʊləʊs/ n [U] 1 the material from which the cell walls of plants are made, used in making paper, plastic, many artificial materials, etc. 2 also **cellulose ac·e·tate** /ˌ···ˈ····/ tech— a plastic material used for many industrial purposes, esp. making photographic films or explosives

Cel·si·us /ˈselsiəs/ also **centigrade**— (abbrev. C) adj, n (of or in) a scale of temperature in which water freezes at 0° and boils at 100°: *Is it measured in Fahrenheit or Celsius? | a celsius thermometer | [after n] a temperature of 12° Celsius*

▶CULTURAL NOTE In Britain, temperatures are often given in Celsius and Fahrenheit, since many older people are not used to the Celsius scale. In the US, temperatures are still given in Fahrenheit.◀

Celt /kelt, selt/ n a member of an ancient group of people who were living in Britain before the arrival of the Romans and whose various CULTURES and languages are still found esp. in parts of Scotland, Wales, and Ireland, where many people are descended from Celts 2 any member of related groups who settled in areas of Europe and Asia centuries ago

Cel·tic¹ /ˈkeltɪk, ˈseltɪk/ adj of (the languages of) the Celts

Cel·tic² /ˈseltɪk/ a Scottish football team based in Glasgow. There is much competition between Celtic and Rangers, the other main Glasgow football team.

ce·ment¹ /sɪˈment/ n [U] 1 a grey powder, made from LIME and clay, which becomes hard like stone after being mixed with water and allowed to dry, used in building to join bricks together and in making CONCRETE 2 a thick sticky hard-drying ADHESIVE used for filling holes, as in the teeth, or for joining things together

cement² v [T] 1 [(TOGETHER)] to join or make firm (as if) with cement: *Our holiday together cemented our friendship.* 2 [(OVER)] to cover with cement

cement mix·er /ˈ·ˈ ˌ··/ also **concrete mixer**— n a machine shaped like a drum which turns round and round, in which cement, sand, and water are mixed to make CONCRETE

cem·e·tery /ˈsemɪtri‖-teri/ n a piece of ground, usu. not belonging to a church, in which dead people are buried. In Britain, people used to be buried in CHURCHYARDs, but now most people who are buried are buried in cemeteries —compare CHURCHYARD, GRAVEYARD

cen·o·taph /ˈsenətɑːf‖-tæf/ n a MONUMENT built as a lasting reminder of dead people who are buried somewhere else, esp. those killed in war. In Britain, "The Cenotaph" means the one in Whitehall, London, where the Remembrance Day ceremony is held.

cen·sor¹ /ˈsensər/ n 1 an official who examines books, films, etc., or (esp. in war or in a prison) private letters, with the power to remove anything offensive or (in war) helpful to the enemy: *Parts of this film have been banned by the censor.* 2 (in ancient Rome) an official whose duties included taking the CENSUS and watching and controlling public morals 3 tech (in PSYCHOLOGY) something which prevents unacceptable memories, ideas, and wishes from coming into one's consciousness

censor² v [T] to examine (books, films, letters, etc.) as a censor: *to censor the prisoners' letters*

cen·so·ri·ous /senˈsɔːriəs/ adj fml always looking for mistakes and faults; eager to censure; severely CRITICAL: *censorious people/behaviour* — **~ly** adv — **~ness** n [U]

cen·sor·ship /ˈsensəʃɪp‖-ər-/ n [U] the work of a censor; act or system of censoring: *the censorship of the press|of television programmes*

cen·sure¹ /ˈsenʃərˈ/ n [U] *fml* the act of expressing strong disapproval; severe CRITICISM: *The opposition passed a vote of censure on the government.*

censure² v [T] *fml* to express strong disapproval of (someone or their behaviour); judge severely and unfavourably: *The policeman was officially censured for his handling of the incident.*

cen·sus /ˈsensəs/ n **censuses** **1** an official counting of a country's total population, with other important information about the people. In Britain and the US there is usu. a census every ten years. **2** an official counting of something for governmental planning: *a traffic census*

cent /sent/ n (a coin equal to) 0·01 of any of certain units of money, such as the dollar; PENNY —compare NICKEL, DIME, QUARTER (4)

cent- see WORD FORMATION

cen·taur /ˈsentɔːrˈ/ n in CLASSICAL MYTHOLOGY, a creature with the head, chest, and arms of a man and the body and legs of a horse

cen·ta·vo /senˈtɑːvəʊ/ n **-vos** (a coin equal to) 0.01 of the standard unit of money in various Spanish-speaking and Portuguese-speaking countries

cen·te·nar·i·an /ˌsentɪˈneəriən/ n a person who is (more than) 100 years old

cen·te·na·ry /senˈtiːnəri‖-ˈte-, ˈsentəneri/ n [(of)] the day or year exactly 100 years after a particular event

cen·ten·ni·al /senˈteniəl/ n *AmE* a centenary

cen·ter /ˈsentərˈ/ n, v *AmE for* CENTRE

Centers for Dis·ease Con·trol /ˌ··· ·ˈ· ·ˌ·/ *(abbrev* CDC) [the] a US government-supported organization in Atlanta, Georgia, that works to prevent and control the spread of infectious diseases, and studies ways to improve the health of Americans

cen·ti·grade /ˈsentɨgreɪd/ *adj, n (often cap.)* CELSIUS: *a centigrade thermometer*

cen·ti·gram, -gramme /ˈsentɨgræm/ n a unit for measuring weight —see TABLE 2

cen·time /ˈsɒntiːm‖ˈsɑːn-/ n (a coin equal to) 0·01 of any of certain units of money, such as the FRANC

cen·ti·me·tre *BrE* ‖ **-ter** *AmE* /ˈsentɨˌmiːtərˈ/ *(written abbrev.* **c** or **cm**) n unit for measuring length —see TABLE 2

cen·ti·pede /ˈsentɨpiːd/ n a small wormlike creature with many legs

cen·tral /ˈsentrəl/ *adj* **1** [A *no comp.*] at or forming the centre of a place, object or system: *the central plains of North America | a city in central Asia | Computer terminals in various parts of the country are linked up to a central database.* **2** conveniently near the centre; easily reached: *Our house is very central for the shops and theatres. | The company is moving from its central location to new offices in the suburbs.* **3** [(to)] of the greatest importance; main: *The central aim of this government is social equality. | She played a central role in the negotiations. | His sudden disappearance was central to the plot of the book.* — ~**ly** *adv* : *a centrally located office | a centrally heated house* (=with central heating) *| a centrally planed economy* (=one using central planning)

Central **1** a REGION in central Scotland, including the town of Stirling **2** one of the British television companies controlled by the ITC TRANSMITTING programmes to central England, esp. the Midlands

Central Af·ri·can Re·pub·lic /ˌ··· ˌ··· ·ˈ···/ [the] a country in central Africa; capital Bangui; population 2,841,000 (1989)

Central A·mer·i·ca /ˌ··· ·ˈ···/ a narrow piece of land joining North and South America, and consisting of Belize, Guatemala, Honduras, El Salvador, Nicaragua, Costa Rica, and Panama

central bank /ˌ··· ·ˈ·/ n a state-owned bank which controls the amount of money available and the general banking systems in a country, and influences interest rates. In Britain the central bank is the Bank of England. In the US it is the Federal Reserve Bank.

Central Belt /ˌ··· ·ˈ·/ [the] the industrial area in Scotland between Glasgow and Edinburgh

Central Crim·i·nal Court /ˌ··· ˈ··· ˌ·/ [the] see OLD BAILEY

Central Day·light Time /ˌ··· ˈ·· ·/ *abbrev.* **CDT** — n [U] *AmE* the time used in the summer months in the Central TIME ZONE of the US

central gov·ern·ment /ˌ··· ˈ···/ n [C;U] the government of the country as a whole from a political centre, as opposed to local government

central heat·ing /ˌ··· ˈ··/ n [U] a system of heating buildings in which heat is produced and controlled at a single point and carried by pipes to the various parts of the building by hot air or water. Many private houses in Britain and the US have central heating.

Central In·tel·li·gence A·gen·cy /ˌ··· ·ˈ··· ˌ···/ see CIA

cen·tral·is·m /ˈsentrəlɪzəm/ n [U] the practice of or principle of bringing something under the control of the central body of an organization, such as a political or educational system

cen·tral·ize also **-ise** *BrE* /ˈsentrəlaɪz/ v [T] to bring under central control: *The process of economic planning has been centralized.* —see also DECENTRALIZE —**-ization** /ˌsentrəlaɪˈzeɪʃən‖-trələ-/ n [U]

central lock·ing /ˌ··· ˈ··/ n [U] a system of operating the locks on a vehicle by one door only; the others then lock or unlock at the same time: *My new car has central locking.*

Central Mosque /ˌ··· ·ˈ·/ [the] the main Muslim place of worship in Britain, in Regents Park, London

central nerv·ous sys·tem /ˌ··· ˈ·· ˌ··/ n the part of the NERVOUS SYSTEM which consists of the brain and the SPINAL CORD

Central Of·fice /ˌ··· ˈ··/ [the] the central office of the Conservative Party in Britain

Central Of·fice of In·for·ma·tion /ˌ··· ˌ··· ··· ˈ··/ [the] a British government organization which prepares and publishes (PUBLISH) information about Britain

Central Park /ˌ··· ·ˈ·/ the main city park in New York City. It is a popular place for New Yorkers but also known to be a dangerous place to go at night. —see colour map on page 1376

central plan·ning /ˌ··· ·ˈ··/ n [U] the system of arranging the economic situation esp. of a COMMUNIST country by means of orders from a central government

Central Pow·ers /ˌ··· ·ˈ··/ [the + P] Austria-Hungary, Germany, Bulgaria, and Turkey, the countries that opposed the Allies in the First World War

central pro·ces·sing u·nit /ˌ··· ·ˈ··· ˌ··/ *(abbrev.* CPU) n the most important controlling part of a computer system where the main operations are performed —see also MICROPROCESSOR, and see picture at COMPUTER

central res·er·va·tion /ˌ··· ··· ·ˈ··/ n *BrE* ‖ **median strip** *AmE* — a thin area of land running down the middle of a large road, to keep traffic apart

Central Stan·dard Time /ˌ··· ˈ·· ·/ also **Central Time**, *abbrev.* **CST** — n [U] *AmE* the time used for Autumn to Spring in the Central Time Zone of the US

cen·tre¹ *BrE* ‖ **-ter** *AmE* /ˈsentərˈ/ n **1** [C (**of**)] a middle part or point; point equally distant from all sides; the exact middle, esp. the point around which a circle is drawn: *Although London is Britain's capital it is not at the centre of the country. | I like chocolates with soft centres. | the high cost of land in the centre of the city* —see also DEAD CENTRE **2** [C] **a** the main or most active area in relation to a particular activity: *Hong Kong is a major banking and financial centre. | the centre of the shipbuilding industry* **b** a place or building intended for a stated activity: *a sports|leisure centre | a youth training centre | the World Trade Center in New York* —see also CONFERENCE CENTRE, DETENTION CENTRE, JOB CENTRE **3** [C] an area where a large number of people live: *The missiles are aimed at military targets, not at urban centres|centres of population.* **4** [the+S] a middle position, in politics, not supporting EXTREME¹ (3) ideas; a MODERATE¹ (3) political position: *Political parties often move to the centre just before an election. | Her political views are slightly left of centre.* **5** [C] (in games like football) a player who plays in or near the middle of the field —compare BACK¹ (6), FORWARD⁵; see also COST CENTRE, MUSIC CENTRE; see MIDDLE (USAGE)

centre² *BrE* ‖ **-ter** *AmE* v [T] to place in or at the centre: *to centre a picture on the wall*

centre (sthg.) **on/upon/round/around** sbdy./sthg. *phr*

cereals

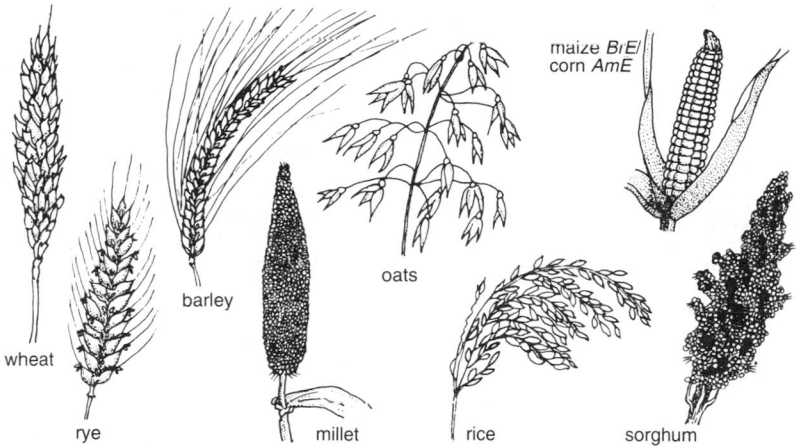

maize *BrE*/
corn *AmE*

oats

barley

wheat

rye   millet   rice   sorghum

v [T *usu. pass.*] to (cause to) have as a main subject or area of concern: *The dispute centres on the question of over-time pay.* | *Our thoughts were centred on the girl who had died.* | *His interests are centred round his family.*

centre court /ˌ·· ˌ·/ (*often cap.*) the main tennis court at WIMBLEDON, where the best players play their matches in front of seated crowds: *Navratilova is on centre court at 2.00.*

cen·tre·fold -terfold *AmE* /ˈsentəfəʊld ‖ -tər-/ *n* (a picture covering all of) the two facing pages in the middle of a magazine. The word is esp. used to describe a picture of a young woman with no clothes on, photographed in a position which is intended to be sexually exciting.

centre for·ward /ˌ·· ˈ··/ *n becoming rare* (in football) an attacking player who plays in the centre of the field

centre of grav·i·ty /ˌ·· ˈ··/ *n* that point in any object on which it will balance

centre par·ty /ˈ·· ˌ··/ *n* a political party which is seen as having a MODERATE¹ (3) political position

cen·tre·piece -terpiece *AmE* /ˈsentəpiːs‖-ər-/ *n*   **1** a decoration, esp. an arrangement of flowers, placed in the middle of a table   **2** [(of)] the most noticeable, attractive, or important part of a larger whole: *These tax cuts are the centrepiece of their economic programme.*

centre stage /ˌ·· ˈ·/ *n* [U] the place or person to which everyone's attention is drawn

cen·tri·fu·gal /ˌsentrɪˈfjuːɡəl◂, senˈtrɪfjʊɡəl‖senˈtrɪfjʊɡəl/ *adj tech* tending to move in a direction away from the centre: *centrifugal force* —opposite **centripetal**

cen·tri·fuge /ˈsentrɪfjuːdʒ/ *n* an apparatus for spinning a container round very quickly so that the heavier liquids and any solids are forced to the outer edge or bottom of the container

cen·trip·e·tal /senˈtrɪpɪtl/ *adj tech* tending to move in a direction towards the centre: *centripetal force* —opposite **centrifugal**

cen·trist /ˈsentrɪst/ *n, adj* (of) a person who supports the CENTRE¹ (4) in politics; MODERATE

cen·tu·ri·on /ˌsenˈtʃʊəriən‖-ˈtʊə-/ *n* an army officer of ancient Rome, commanding a company of about 100 soldiers

cen·tu·ry /ˈsentʃəri/ *n*   **1** a period of 100 years   **2** (*sometimes cap.*) any of the 100-year periods counted forwards or backwards from the supposed year of Christ's birth: *The period 1900 –1999 is the twentieth century.* | *There have been two World Wars during this century.* (=since 1900) | *He was born at the turn of the century.* (=about 1900)   **3** 100 runs made by one cricket player in one INNINGS: *He made/scored a century.*

CEO /ˌsiː iː ˈəʊ/ *n esp. AmE*   **1** Chief Executive Officer; the person in charge of a large company: *She was appointed CEO in March.*   **2** the President of the US

ce·phal·ic /sɪˈfælɪk/ *adj* [A] *tech* of or connected with the head

ce·ram·ics /sɪˈræmɪks/ *n*   **1** [U] the making of pots, TILES, etc., by shaping pieces of clay and baking them until they are hard   **2** [P] articles produced in this way: *an exhibition of ceramics and sculpture* —**ceramic** *adj* : *ceramic tiles in the bathroom*

Cer·be·rus /ˈsɜːbərəs‖ˈsɜːr-/ *n* in CLASSICAL MYTHOLOGY, the three-headed dog who guarded the entrance to Hades

ce·re·al /ˈsɪəriəl/ *n*   **1** [C] a plant grown to produce grain for food, such as wheat, rice, etc.: *Oats and barley are cereals.* | *cereal crops*   **2** [C;U] a food made from grain. In Britain and the US cereals such as CORNFLAKES are often eaten for breakfast.

cer·e·bel·lum /ˌserɪˈbeləm/ *n med* a part of the brain below the cerebrum, concerned with controlling movements of the body

cer·e·bral /ˈserɪbrəl‖səˈriː-, ˈserɪ-/ *adj*   **1** [*no comp.*] *med* of or connected with the brain: *a cerebral hemorrhage*   **2** *esp. fml or humor* using or needing effort of the mind rather than the feelings; (too) INTELLECTUAL: *a rather cerebral person/film* — –~ly *adv*

cerebral pal·sy /ˌ··· ˈ··‖·ˌ·· ˈ··, ˌ··· ˈ··/ *n* [U] a disease caused by damage to the brain before or during birth. People with cerebral palsy have difficulty in controlling their muscles and in speaking   see also CONDUCTIVE EDUCATION

cer·e·bra·tion /ˌserɪˈbreɪʃən/ *n* [U] *fml or humor* the working of the brain; the act of thinking

cer·e·brum /səˈriːbrəm/ *n* **-brums** *or* **-bra** /brə/ *med* the front part of the brain, concerned with thought and decision

cer·e·mo·ni·al /ˌserɪˈməʊniəl◂/ *adj* marked by or done according to ceremony: *the President's ceremonial duties* — ~ly *adv*

ceremonial² *n* [C;U] (a) special ceremony for a particular event: *religious ceremonial*

cer·e·mo·ni·ous /ˌserɪˈməʊniəs◂/ *adj* paying great attention to ceremony and formal behaviour; extremely formal or polite —see also UNCEREMONIOUS — – ~ly *adv* — – ~ness *n* [U]

cer·e·mo·ny /ˈserɪməni‖-məʊni/ *n*   **1** [C] a special formal, solemn, and long-established action or set of actions used for marking an important social or religious event: *a wedding ceremony* | *The new graduates receive their degrees at a special ceremony.* —see also MASTER OF CEREMONIES   **2** [U] the special order and formal behaviour demanded by custom on particular occasions: *The queen was crowned with due ceremony.* —see also **stand on ceremony** (STAND¹ (24))

ce·rise /səˈriːz‖səˈriːs, -ˈriːz/ *adj* clear pinkish red in colour —**cerise** *n* [U]

cert¹ /sɜːt‖sɜːrt/ *n* [*usu. sing.*] *BrE infml* a certainty; something considered certain to happen or succeed: *It's a (dead) cert that this horse will win the race.*

cert² *written abbrev. for:* CERTIFICATE

cer·tain¹ /ˈsɜːtn‖ˈsɜːrtn/ *adj*   **1** proved beyond all doubt to

exist or to be true; clearly known: *There is no certain cure
for this illness.* | *It's almost certain (that) they're dead by
now.* | *It's not certain when he lived.* **2** [F (**about, of**)] (of
people) completely confident about the truth of something; having no doubt; sure: *She was quite certain
(about/of it).* [+(*that*)] *I'm almost certain (that) she saw me
yesterday.* [+*wh-*] *We're not certain where he lives.* **3** sure
(to happen); so likely that there can be no real doubt: *The
army marched off to face certain death.* [F+*to-v*] *She's cer-
tain to find out/to pass the exam.* | *It's certain (that) the
price of gold will go up.* | *It now looks certain that the game
will be postponed.* **4 for certain** without doubt: *I know
for certain that he's in there, but he won't answer me.* **5
make certain** to do something so as to be sure: *Make cer-
tain (that) you know what time the train goes.* | *We went
to the theatre early and made certain we all got seats/made
certain of getting seats.* —see SURE (USAGE)

certain² *determiner* **1** of a particular but not clearly
described type; quantity, degree, etc.: *There are certain
reasons why this information cannot be made public.* | *It's
not a beautiful building, but it has a certain charm.* |
*When the water reaches a certain level, the pump switches
itself off.* **2** named but not known: *A certain Ms Jones
phoned you today.* **3** some but not a lot: *He makes a cer-
tain profit from his business but he'll never be rich.* | *I
agree with you to a certain extent, but...*

certain³ *pron* [+*of*] *fml* certain ones; some but not all: *Certain of these questions have never been answered.*

cer·tain·ly /ˈsɜːtnli‖ˈsɜːr-/ *adv* without doubt; of course: *He
certainly works very hard.* | *"Will you help me?" "Cer-
tainly (I will)."* | *"Shall I drive?" "Certainly not!"*

▷ USAGE Compare **certainly** and **definitely**. **1
Definitely** is used to give strength to a statement: *He's
definitely the best player in the team.* **Certainly** is
often used when there is some doubt left in the
speaker's mind: *It's **certainly** very beautiful, but it's
far too expensive.* Sometimes the doubts are not expressed openly but only suggested: *"He's a brilliant student, isn't he?" "Well, he **certainly** works very hard."*
(=but I do not agree that he is brilliant) **2 Definitely**
is more common than **certainly** in reply to a request
for information: *"Is he good at his job?" "Oh yes,
definitely."* **3 Certainly** (like *of course*) but not
definitely can be used in reply to a request: *"Can you
help me with my homework?" "Yes, **certainly."*** —see
also SURELY (USAGE)◁

cer·tain·ty /ˈsɜːtnti‖ˈsɜːr-/ *n* **1** [C] also **cert** *BrE infml—*
something that is certain to be true or certain to happen:
It's a dead (=complete) *certainty that this horse will win
the race.* | *I know for a certainty that the company has been
bought up.* **2** [(**with**) U] the state of being certain; freedom from doubt: *I can't say with (any) certainty what my
plans are.*

cer·ti·fi·a·ble /ˈsɜːtɪˌfaɪəbəl‖ˈsɜːr-/ *adj* that can or should be
certified (CERTIFY), esp. as being mad

cer·tif·i·cate /səˈtɪfɪkət‖sər-/ *n* a DOCUMENT (=official paper)
giving a statement made by an official person that a fact
or facts are true: *a birth/marriage/death certificate* | *a cer-
tificate of health*

cer·tif·i·cat·ed /səˈtɪfɪkeɪtɪd‖sər-/ *adj esp. BrE* having successfully completed a course of training for a profession:
a certificated nurse

certificate of de·pos·it /·ˌ···· · ·ˈ·ˌ·/ *n* a document proving
that its owner has placed a specific sum of money in a
bank, and that the bank has agreed to pay a specific rate
of INTEREST

Certificate of Pre-Vo·ca·tion·al Ed·u·ca·tion /·ˌ··· · · ·ˌ···
··ˈ·ˌ·/ (*abbrev.* **CPVE**) *n* an examination taken by pupils
in Britain who want to stay on at school after taking their
GCSE, to prepare for a VOCATIONAL course or for work,
rather than for A-level or AS-level examinations

certified mail /ˌ···· ·ˈ·/ *n* [U] *AmE* mail sent by RECORDED
DELIVERY

certified milk /ˌ···· ·ˈ·/ *n* [U] *AmE for* ATTESTED MILK

certified pub·lic ac·coun·tant /ˌ···· ·ˌ··· ·ˈ··/ *n AmE for* CHAR-
TERED ACCOUNTANT

cer·ti·fy /ˈsɜːtɪˌfaɪ‖ˈsɜːr-/ *v* [T] **1** to declare that (something)
is correct or true, esp. after some kind of test: *The bank
certified my accounts.* [+*obj+adj*] *The doctor certified the
prisoner insane.* [+*that*] *I certify that I witnessed the sign-*

ing of this document. **2** to give a CERTIFICATE to (someone) declaring successful completion of a course of training for a profession: *a certified teacher* **3** to declare
officially to be mad

cer·ti·tude /ˈsɜːtɪˌtjuːd‖ˈsɜːrtɪˌtuːd/ *n* [U] *fml* the state of being
or feeling certain; freedom from doubt

ce·ru·le·an /səˈruːliən/ *adj tech or lit* deep blue, like a clear
sky

Cer·van·tes /sɜːˈvæntɪz‖sɜːr-/, **Mi·guel de** /mɪˈgwel də/
(1547–1616) a Spanish writer, best known for the NOVEL
Don Quixote

cer·vi·cal /ˈsɜːvɪkəl, səˈvaɪkəl‖ˈsɜːrvɪkəl/ *adj med* of a neck
or cervix: *cervical vertebrae* | *cervical cancer*

cervical smear ‖ **Pap smear** *AmE* — /ˌ··· ·ˈ·, ·ˌ··· ·ˈ·‖ˌ··· ·ˈ·/
n a test for CANCER of the cervix. Women are advised to
have this test regularly.

cer·vix /ˈsɜːvɪks‖ˈsɜːr-/ *n* -**vices** /vɪsiːz/ *or* -**vixes** *med* the
narrow necklike opening into the WOMB

ce·sar·e·an /sɪˈzeəriən/ *n* a CAESAREAN

ces·sa·tion /seˈseɪʃən/ *n* [C;U (**of**)] *fml* a short pause or a
stop: *a cessation of hostilities* (=fighting with an enemy) |
a momentary cessation of breathing

ces·sion /ˈseʃən/ *n* [C;U] *fml* (an example of) the giving of
land, property, or rights —see also CEDE

cess·pit /ˈsesˌpɪt/ also **cess·pool** /ˈsesˌpuːl/ — *n* an underground container or hole, in which waste from a building, esp. body waste (SEWAGE), is collected

ce·ta·ce·an /sɪˈteɪʃən/ *adj, n tech* (of) a fishlike MAMMAL
(=an animal which feeds its young on milk) which lives
in water, such as a WHALE

Cey·lon /sɪˈlɒn‖-ˈlɑːn/ the former name for SRI LANKA

Ce·zanne /sɪˈzæn‖seɪˈzɑːn/, **Paul** /pɒl/ (1839–1906) a
French painter who influenced the development of
CUBISM and ABSTRACT art

cf *written abbrev. for:* compare

CFC /ˌsiː ef ˈsiː/ also **chlorofluorocarbon**— *n* a gas used
in FRIDGES and AEROSOL cans, now believed to be responsible for damaging the OZONE LAYER. Many products now
avoid using CFCs and usu. have **"CFC-free"** written on
them.

Chab·lis /ˈʃæbliː‖ʃæˈbliː/ *n* [C;U] a very dry white wine
produced in N Burgundy, France

cha-cha /ˈtʃɑː tʃɑː/ also **cha-cha-cha** /ˌ·· ·ˈ·/— *n* -**chas** a fast
spirited dance of South American origin

Chad /tʃæd/ a country in N central Africa; capital
Ndjamena; population 5,538,000 (1989)

chafe /tʃeɪf/ *v* **1** [I;T] to (cause to) become sore or worn
by rubbing: *Her new shoes chafed her feet.* **2** [T] to make
(part of the body) warm by rubbing **3** [I (**at, under**)] to
become or be impatient or annoyed: *They are beginning
to chafe at/under these restrictions.* —see also **chafe at the
bit** (BIT²)

chaff¹ /tʃɑːf‖tʃæf/ *n* [U] **1** the HUSKS (=outer seed covers)
separated from grain before it is used as food **2** dried
grasses and plant stems used as food for farm animals
—see also **the wheat from the chaff** (WHEAT)

chaff² *v* [T] *old-fash infml* to make fun of (someone) in a
friendly way

chaff³ *n* [U] *old-fash infml* friendly joking; BANTER

chaf·finch /ˈtʃæfɪntʃ/ *n* a small bird with a cheerful song,
common in Europe

chafing dish /ˈ··· ·/ *n* ‖ also **fondue** *AmE* — a container with
a heater under it, used for cooking or keeping food warm,
esp. at the table

Cha·gall /ʃæˈgæl/, **Marc** /mɑːk‖mɑːrk/ (1887–1985) a Russian artist who lived in France and painted in bright
colours

chag·rin¹ /ˈʃæɡrɪn‖ʃəˈɡrɪn/ *n* [U] *fml* annoyance and disappointment, caused by failure or unfulfilled hopes:
Much **to his chagrin**, *he was not offered the job.*

chagrin² *v* [T] to cause to feel chagrin; disappoint greatly

chain¹ /tʃeɪn/ *n* **1** [C;U] (a length of) usu. metal rings, connected to or fitted into one another, used for fastening,
supporting, decorating, etc.: *The bridge was supported
by heavy iron chains hanging from two towers.* | *The
Mayoress wore her **chain of office.*** (=her official chain) |

She always wears a gold chain round her neck. —see picture at BICYCLE **2** [C **(of)**] **a** a number of connected things: *a mountain chain* | *a chain of events* **b** a number of shops, hotels, etc. under the same ownership or management: *a well-known chain of fast-food restaurants* —see also CHAIN STORE, FOOD CHAIN **3** [C] a number of people who are all buying houses from one another, so that each sale is dependent on the previous one: *I should be able to buy the house pretty quickly, since I'm not in a chain.* **4** [C] an old measurement of length —see TABLE 2   **5 in chains** kept in prison or as a slave

chain² v [T+obj+adv/prep] to limit the freedom of (someone or something) (as if) with a chain: *The dogs were chained up for the night.* | *The kidnappers chained the girl's hands and feet together.* | *With a sick husband, she's chained to the house all day.*

chain gang /ˈ· ·/ n [C+sing./pl. v] a group of prisoners chained together for work outside their prison.

chain let·ter /ˈ· ˌ··/ n a letter sent to several people who are asked to send copies to several more people. Chain letters are meant to bring luck or sometimes great wealth, if you are asked to send money to people on a list.

chain mail /ˈ· ·/ also **chain ar·mour** /ˈ· ˌ··/— n [U] armour made by joining small metal rings together into a protective garment, used esp. in former times

chain re·ac·tion /ˌ· ·ˈ··/ n a number of related events or chemical changes, each of which causes the next

chain saw /ˈ· ·/ n a SAW made up of a circular chain fitted with teeth and driven by a motor —compare CIRCULAR SAW; and see picture at SAW and at TOOL

chain-smoke /ˈ· ·/ v [I;T] to smoke (cigarettes) continually, esp. lighting each new one from the previous one —**smoker** n

chain stitch /ˈ· ·/ n [C;U] a way of sewing in which each new stitch is pulled through the last one

chain store /ˈ· ·/ also **multiple store** esp. BrE— n (any of) a group of usu. large shops of the same kind owned by one organization —see also CHAIN¹ (2)

chairs

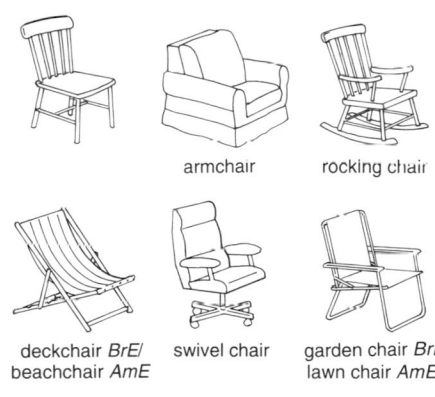

armchair   rocking chair

deckchair BrE/   swivel chair   garden chair BrE/
beachchair AmE   lawn chair AmE

wheelchair   high chair

chair¹ /tʃeəʳ/ n **1** [C] a piece of furniture for one person to sit on, which usually has a back, a seat, four legs, and sometimes arms: *sitting on a chair at her desk* | *sitting in a comfortable chair watching TV* —see also ARMCHAIR, BATH CHAIR, DECKCHAIR, HIGH CHAIR, WHEELCHAIR **2** [C *usu. sing.*] (the office, position, or official seat of) a CHAIRPERSON, esp. one in charge of a meeting: *Please address your remarks to the chair.* | *Who will be* **in the chair** *at tomorrow's meeting?* | *She's the chair of the housing committee.* —see CHAIRPERSON **3** [C **(of)**] the position of PROFESSOR:

She holds a chair of chemistry in the university. **4** [the+S] infml (esp. in the US) the punishment of death by means of an ELECTRIC CHAIR **5** [C] old use for SEDAN CHAIR

chair² v [T] **1** to be CHAIRPERSON of (a meeting): *The commission of inquiry was chaired by a well-known judge.* **2** BrE to lift up and carry (someone), as a sign of admiration: *When he won the race his supporters chaired him round the field.*

chair lift /ˈ· ·/ n an apparatus which carries people up and down steep slopes in chairs that hang from a moving wire

chair·man /ˈtʃeəmən‖ˈtʃeər-/ n -men /mən/ **1** a chairperson, esp. a male one: *He was elected chairman of the education committee.* —see PERSON (USAGE) **2** the head, usu. male, of a large organization or company: *The chairman of British Rail/American Airlines* **3** (in former times) a man employed to help carry a SEDAN CHAIR

chair·man·ship /ˈtʃeəmənʃɪp‖ˈtʃeər-/ n [usu. sing.] the rank, position, or period in office of a chairman: *a commission of inquiry under the chairmanship of a well-known judge*

chair·per·son /ˈtʃeəˌpɜːsən‖ˈtʃeərˌpɜːrsən/ n a person who is in charge of a meeting or who directs the work of a committee or organization —see PERSON (USAGE)

chair·wom·an /ˈtʃeəˌwʊmən‖ˈtʃeər-/ n -women /ˌwɪmɪn/ a female chairperson

chaise /ʃeɪz/ n **1** a light two-wheeled or four-wheeled carriage, used in former times, pulled by one horse **2** AmE a CHAISE LONGUE

chaise longue /ˌʃeɪz ˈlɒŋ‖-ˈlɔːŋ/ n chaises longues or chaise longues (same pronunciation) Fr **1** a COUCH, with an arm at only one end, on which one can sit and stretch out one's legs **2** AmE a long chair for sitting back in

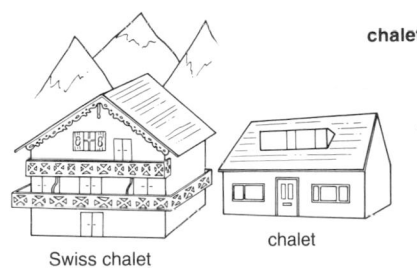

chalets

Swiss chalet   chalet

chal·et /ˈʃæleɪ‖ʃæˈleɪ/ n **1** a usu. wooden house or hut with a steeply sloping roof, esp. common in Switzerland **2** esp BrE a small house (BUNGALOW) or hut, esp. in a holiday camp —compare LODGE² (3)

chalet par·ty /ˈ··· ˌ··‖·ˈ· ˌ··/ n BrE a skiing (SKI) holiday during which a number of people, esp. young, single and wealthy people, stay in a chalet. The travel company employs others to do the cooking and cleaning.

chal·ice /ˈtʃælɪs/ n a gold or silver decorated cup, used esp. to hold wine in Christian religious services

chalk¹ /tʃɔːk/ n **1** [U] a soft white or grey rock (LIMESTONE) originally formed in ancient times from the shells of very small sea animals: *chalk hills* | *Some plants will not grow on chalk.* **2** [C;U] (a piece of) this substance, white or coloured, used for writing or drawing: *The teacher wrote on the blackboard with a piece of chalk.* | *a box of coloured chalks* **3 as different as chalk and cheese** BrE infml completely unlike each other

chalk² v [T **(on, up)**] to write, mark, or draw with chalk: *to chalk (up) political slogans on walls*
    chalk sthg. ↔ **out** phr v [T] to describe in a general way, in words or with drawings: *The general chalked out his plan of attack.*
    chalk sthg. ↔ **up** phr v [T] infml **1** to succeed in getting (esp. points in a game): *Our team has chalked up another victory.* **2** [(**to, against**)] to charge to, or record on, someone's account or one's own account: *Chalk up the drinks to me.* | *Anything you do wrong will be chalked up against you.*

chalk·board /ˈtʃɔːkbɔːd‖-bɔːrd/ n AmE for BLACKBOARD

chalk·y /ˈtʃɔːki/ adj of or like (white) chalk: *chalky soil* | *the chalky whiteness of his face* —**iness** n [U]

chal·lenge¹ /'tʃælᵻndʒ/ v [T] **1** [(to)] to invite (someone) to compete against one in a fight, match, etc.: *I challenged him to a game of tennis.* [+obj+to-v] *I challenge you to race me across the lake.* —compare DARE¹ (2) **2** to question the rightness, legality, etc., of; DISPUTE: *She challenged the authority of the court.* | *Traditional female roles are constantly being challenged by contemporary feminists.* **3** to test the abilities of (a person or thing); STIMULATE: *I only like to study something if it really challenges me.* [+obj+to-v] *The difficulty of putting our ideas into practice challenged us to find a new method.* **4** to stop and demand official proof of the name and intentions of (someone): *The sentry challenged the stranger.* **5** *law* to declare that one will not accept (a JUROR) before the beginning of a case —**lenger** *n*

challenge² *n* **1** [C] an invitation to compete in a fight, match, etc.: *a challenge to a game of tennis* | *The president faces a challenge to his leadership from his deputy.* [+to-v] *He accepted his friend's challenge to swim across the river.* **2** [C] a questioning of the rightness, legality, etc., of something: *This new report represents a challenge to the accepted version of events.* **3** [C;U] (something with) the quality of testing strength, skill, or ability: *One of the biggest challenges facing the present government is that of creating new jobs and new industries.* | *I'm looking for a job with a bit more challenge.* **4** [C] a demand to stop and give proof of one's name, intentions, etc.: *The stranger was met with the challenge "Who goes there?"* **5** [C] *law* a statement that one will not accept a JUROR, made before the beginning of a case

chal·lenged /'tʃælᵻndʒd/ *adj AmE euph* DISABLED, esp. in the stated way: [also *n*, *the*+P] *special facilities for the visually challenged* (=blind people, or those who cannot see well)

Chal·len·ger /'tʃælᵻndʒəʳ/ an American space SHUTTLE¹ (2) which exploded after TAKEOFF on one of its flights in 1986, killing all the people inside. The terrible accident was watched on television by many people and shocked the whole of the US.

chal·leng·ing /'tʃælᵻndʒɪŋ/ *adj* needing the full use of one's abilities and effort; difficult, but in an interesting way: *a challenging problem* | *She finds her new job very challenging.*

cham·ber /'tʃeɪmbəʳ/ *n* **1** *old use* a room, esp. a bedroom **2** (the hall used for meetings of) a usu. elected lawmaking body: *In Britain the upper chamber of Parliament is the House of Lords, the lower the House of Commons.* **3** [*often pl.*] a room set aside for a special purpose: *Cases not dealt with in court are sometimes heard in the judge's chambers.* **4** an enclosed space, esp. in a body or machine: *The heart has four chambers.* | *burial chambers* —see picture at GUN

cham·ber·lain /'tʃeɪmbəlᵻn‖-bər-/ *n* an important official who manages the affairs of a king's or nobleman's court with regard to cleaning, cooking, buying food, etc.

Chamberlain

Chamberlain, Nev·ille /'nevᵻl/ (1869–1940) a British Conservative politician and PRIME MINISTER at the beginning of the Second World War. He is generally thought to have been wrong to make an agreement with Hitler in Munich in 1938 and is remembered for using the phrase "Peace in our time". —see also MUNICH AGREEMENT

Chamberlain, Wilt (1936–) an American BASKETBALL player, known as **Wilt the Stilt** because of his height (2.16 metres). He set several records for the number of points he won.

cham·ber·maid /'tʃeɪmbəmeɪd‖-ər-/ *n* a female servant employed to clean and tidy bedrooms, esp. in a hotel

chamber mu·sic /'··‚··/ *n* [U] music written for a small group of instruments and suitable for performance in a private home or small hall

chamber of com·merce /ˌ··· · '··/ *n* [C+*sing./pl. v*] a group of businessmen, esp. in a particular town or area, working together for the purpose of improving trade

chamber of hor·rors /ˌ··· · '··/ *n* a place in which very unpleasant or frightening objects can be seen, esp. the room which shows models of famous criminals and murders in Madame Tussaud's MUSEUM of WAXWORKS in London

chamber or·ches·tra /'·· ‚···/ *n* [C+*sing./pl. v*] a small group of musicians, usu. with one player for each instrumental part

chamber pot /'·· ·/ *n* a round container for liquid and solid body waste, usu. used in the bedroom and kept under the bed. Chamber pots are now usually used only by the old or sick. —compare BEDPAN, POTTY²

cha·me·le·on /kə'miːliən/ *n* **1** a small LIZARD that can change its colour to match its surroundings **2** someone who changes their behaviour, ideas, etc., to suit the situation

cham·ois¹ /'ʃæmwɑː/ *n* **chamois** /'ʃæmwɑːz/ a small wild goatlike animal from the mountains of Europe and SW Asia

cham·ois² /'ʃæmi/ also **chamois leath·er** /'·· ‚··/, **cham·my** /'ʃæmi/, **shammy**— *n* **chamois** /'ʃæmiz/ [C;U] (a piece of) soft leather prepared from the skin of chamois, sheep, or goats and used for cleaning and polishing

cham·o·mile /'kæməmaɪl/ *n* [C;U] CAMOMILE

champ¹ /tʃæmp/ also **chomp**— *v* [I (**on, at**); T] (of a horse) to bite noisily: *The horse is champing (at) his hay.* —see also **champ at the bit** (BIT²)

champ² *n infml for* CHAMPION¹ (1)

cham·pagne /ʃæm'peɪn/ also **cham·pers** /'ʃæmpəz‖-ərz/ *BrE infml*— *n* [U] an expensive (French) white wine containing a lot of BUBBLES, usu. drunk on special occasions. Champagne used to be drunk only by the very rich, but now a lot of people occasionally drink it: *a champagne reception* (=at which champagne is served) —see also SPARKLING WINE

cham·pi·on¹ /'tʃæmpiən/ *n* **1** also **champ** *infml*— a person or animal that has won a competition of skill, strength, etc., esp. a sporting competition: *a tennis champion* | *the world chess champion* | *the* **reigning** *heavyweight boxing* **champion** (=the champion at the present time) | *a champion racehorse* **2** [(**of**)] a person who fights for, supports strongly, or defends a principle, movement, person, etc.: *a champion of women's rights/of the poor*

champion² *v* [T]+ to fight for, support strongly, or defend (a principle, movement, person, etc.): *He has championed numerous causes connected with civil liberties.*

champion³ *adj, adv N EngE infml* very good or well: *"How do you feel?" "Champion, thanks!"*

cham·pi·on·ship /'tʃæmpiənʃɪp/ *n* **1** [C] also **championships** *pl.*— a competition held to find the champion: *The championship will be held tomorrow.* | *the European basketball championship* **2** [C] the position, title, rank, or period of being champion: *I don't think this new boxer can take the championship from him.* **3** [U (**of**)] the act of championing: *The party is well known for its championship of women's rights.*

Champs E·ly·sées /ˌʃɒnz e'liːzeɪ‖ˌʃɑːnz ˌeɪliː'zeɪ/ [*the*] an important street in Paris which leads up to the Arc de Triomphe (a national MONUMENT)

chance¹ /tʃɑːns‖tʃæns/ *n* **1** [U] the force that seems to make things happen without cause or reason, and that cannot be controlled or influenced by humans; luck; good or bad fortune: *Chance plays an important part in many card games.* | *It happened quite* **by chance.** | *Have you got a spare stamp* **by any chance?** **2** [C;U (**of**)] (a) possibility; (degree of) likelihood that something will happen, esp. something desirable: *You'd have more chance of catching the train if you got a bus to the station instead of walking.* | *The withdrawal of the American from the competition has greatly increased the Italian's chances of success.* [+(*that*)] *There's some chance/a good chance that she'll be released without being charged.* | *There's* **an outside chance** (=a small chance) *that he'll win.* | *She pinned her hopes on the chance of getting the part.* | *The theatre was almost fully booked, but he went* **on the off chance** (=because of the unlikely possibility) *of getting a ticket.* | *You don't* **stand a chance** *of winning the case.* (=there is no likelihood that you will) | *I think I'm* **in with a chance** *of winning this competition.* | *Is there any chance of/What are the chances of getting an interview with her?* |

Not a chance|No chance! (=certainly not) | *(infml)*
Chances are (=it is likely) *she's already heard the news.* |
I'd say she's got about **a fifty-fifty chance** *of passing.* (=it
is equally likely that she will pass as that she will fail)|
It was a **chance in a million** *that he should have broken
his leg on that particular day.* (=he was extremely unlucky)   **3** [C **(of)**] a situation that is favourable for a particular purpose; OPPORTUNITY: *I never miss a chance of
playing football.* [+to-v] *He had no chance to apologize.* |
*The long spell of dry weather gave us a chance to paint
the house.* | *Those poor children haven't got a* **chance in
life.** | *If I give you a* **second chance** *will you promise to
be good?* | *You should accept — you may never get another
chance.* | *The offer of a free trip round the world is* **the
chance of a lifetime.**   **4** [C; U **(of)**] (a) risk: *The rope
might break, but that's a chance we'll have to take!* |
There's always an element of chance (=some risk) *in buy-
ing stocks and shares.* | *Let's find another place to park — I
don't want to* **take the chance** *of getting a fine.*

▷ USAGE Compare **chance, opportunity,** and **occasion.** 1 Both **chance** and **opportunity** can mean "a
time suitable for doing something you want to do": *I'll
have a* **chance|**an **opportunity** *to visit the Louvre when
I'm in Paris.* 2 You can use **chance,** but not **opportunity,** to talk about possibility alone: *There is a* **chance**
(=a possibility) *that I'll see him.* 3 An **occasion** is either
a moment when something happens: *I was punished
by the teacher on several* **occasions** or a reason: *I did
not wish to go to Paris, and had no* **occasion** *(fml) to
go.* (=no reason to go)◁

chance² *v* [*not in progressive forms*]   **1** [T] *fml* to take a
chance with; risk: *to chance all one's money on a game
of cards*   **2** [I+to-v; it+I+that] *fml* to take place by chance;
happen by accident: *She chanced to be in the park when
I was there.* | *It chanced that we were both travelling on
the same plane.*   **3** **chance it/chance one's luck/chance
one's arm** *infml* to take a chance of succeeding, even
though failure is possible: *The police may catch us, but
we'll just have to chance it/chance our luck.*
    chance on/upon sbdy./sthg. *phr v* [T] to meet or find
by chance: *She chanced on some valuable documents
when she was cleaning out the attic.*

chance³ *adj* [Λ *no comp.*] accidental; unplanned: *a chance
meeting*

chan·cel /ˈtʃɑːnsəl‖ˈtʃæn-/ *n* the eastern part of a church,
where the priests and CHOIR (=singers) usu. sit —see picture at CHURCH

chan·cel·ler·y /ˈtʃɑːnsələri‖ˈtʃæn-/ *n*   **1** the building in
which a chancellor has his offices   **2** [+*sing./pl. v*] the
officials who work in a chancellor's office   **3** also
chancery— the offices of an official representative (AM
BASSADOR or CONSUL) of a foreign country

chan·cel·lor /ˈtʃɑːnsələr‖ˈtʃæn-/ *n*   **1** (*often cap.*) **a** a state
or legal official of high rank: *The most important judge
in Britain is the* **Lord Chancellor.** **b** (in some countries)
the chief minister: *Herr Willy Brandt, the former West
German chancellor*   **2** see CHANCELLOR OF THE EXCHEQUER
  3 the official head of various universities —compare VICE-
CHANCELLOR

**Chancellor of the
Ex·cheq·uer** /ₗ··· ··· ·|··/ also
Chancellor— *n* the British
government minister in
charge of taxes and government spending. The work of
the Chancellor of the Exchequer is the same as that of
the Finance Minister in
many other countries. —see
also BUDGET¹ (2), BUDGET DAY

**Chancellor of
the Exchequer**

chan·ce·ry /ˈtʃɑːnsəri‖ˈtʃæn-/
n   **1** (in Britain) the Lord
Chancellor's division of the
High Court of Justice   **2** an
office for the collection and safe-keeping of official papers
  3 a CHANCELLERY (3)

chan·cy /ˈtʃɑːnsi‖ˈtʃænsi/ *adj infml* risky; of uncertain
result: *That was a chancy thing to do; you could have been
killed.* | *We may be able to get tickets but it's a bit chancy.*
—**iness** *n* [U]

chan·de·lier /ₗʃændəˈlɪər/ *n* a usu. large branched decorative holder for candles or electric lights, usu. hanging

from the CEILING

chand·ler /ˈtʃɑːndlər‖ˈtʃæn-/ *n old use* a person who makes
or sells candles —see also SHIP'S CHANDLER

Chandler, Ray·mond /ˈreɪmənd/ (1888–1959) an American
writer whose most famous character was the PRIVATE
DETECTIVE Philip Marlowe

Cha·nel /ʃəˈnel/, **Co·co** /ˈkəʊkəʊ/ (1883–1971) a French
fashion designer (DESIGN) known esp. for her 'little black
dress' as well as other clothing and PERFUMEs *like*
Chanel No. 5

change¹ /tʃeɪndʒ/ *v*   **1** [I;T **(from, to)**] to make or become
different; give, or begin to have, a different form, nature,
or character: *In autumn the leaves change from green to
brown.* | *Don't start moving until the traffic lights change
(to green).* | *She's changed a lot since I last saw her.* | *His
attitudes have changed little despite the events of the last
few years.* | *They've changed the time of our lesson.* | *The
discovery of oil there has changed the whole character of
the area.* | *the rapidly-changing world of micro technol-
ogy*   **2** [T **(for)**] to give, take, or put something in place
of (something else, usu. of the same kind); exchange: *Her
new dress didn't fit so she took it back to the shop and
changed it (for another).* | *She changed her books at the
library.* | *He's changed jobs/changed his job.* (=got a new
job) | *The teams changed sides/changed over/changed
round* (=each went to the opposite side) *at half time.* |
Let's change the subject. (=talk about something else) |
I wouldn't **change places** *with her for anything.* (=I
wouldn't like to be in her situation.) | *The room looks
much better now you've changed it round/changed things
round.* (-moved the furniture, etc., into different positions)   **3** [I **(into, out of**); T] to put (different clothes) on
oneself: *I'm just going to change out of this suit/change
into something more comfortable.* | *Can you wait five
minutes while I change (my dress)?*   **4** [T] **a** to put (fresh
clothes or coverings) on a baby, child, bed, etc.: *to change
the sheets/change a baby's nappy* **b** to put fresh clothes
or coverings on (a baby, child, bed, etc.): *I'm just going
to change the baby.*   **5** [T **(for, into)**] to give (money) in
exchange for money of a different type: *Where can I
change my English money for/into dollars?* | *Can you
change a pound?* (=give me CHANGE² (5) for it)   **6** [I;T] to
leave and enter (different vehicles) in order to continue
a journey: *To get to Manchester, you'll have to change
(trains) at Birmingham.*   **7** [I (UP, DOWN, **into, to**)] ‖also
shift *AmE*— to put the engine of a vehicle into a higher
or lower GEAR¹ (1), usu. in order to go faster or slower:
Change into second gear when you go up the hill. | *Change
down before going up the hill and then change up at the
top.*   **8** **change gear(s)** ‖also **shift gear(s)** *AmE*— to
make a change in speed and power by putting the engine
of a vehicle into a different GEAR¹ (3): *Change gear at the
bottom of the hill.* | (fig.) *He began his speech quite for-
mally, but then changed gear and told some jokes.*   **9**
change hands to go from the ownership of one person
to another: *This house has changed hands three times in
the last two years.*   **10** **change one's mind** to form a new
opinion or wish: *I used to think she was clever but I've
changed my mind.* | *I wish you'd stop changing your mind.*
  11 **change one's spots** (*usu. in negatives*) to change one's
character, habits, or way of life   **12** **change one's tune**
to change one's opinion, decision, etc., and so act in a
different way: *He said he would never speak to me again
but he'll soon change his tune.*   **13** **change step** (when
marching in a group) to move from keeping time with
one foot to keeping time with the other —compare
EXCHANGE
    change into *phr v* [T]   **1** (**change into** sbdy./sthg.) to
become (something different): *When the prince kissed the
cat it changed into a beautiful princess.*   **2** (**change**
sbdy./sthg. **into** sbdy./sthg.) to cause to become (something different): *You can't change iron into gold.*
    change over *phr v* [I **(from, to)**] to make a complete
change: *In 1971 Britain changed over from pounds, shillings, and pence to the new decimal currency.* —see also
CHANGEOVER

change² *n*   **1** [C;U **(in, of)**] (an example of) the act or result
of changing: *a sudden change in the weather* | *the pace
of technological change* | *Many old people find it difficult
to cope with change.* | *If we are to avoid defeat we need a
change of leadership/a change in tactics.* | *There's been a
change for the better in her health.* (=it has improved) |
We've made a lot of changes since you were last here. | *The*

government has proposed major changes in the laws relating to immigration. | The extraordinary experience brought about a complete change in her outlook. | She's had a **change of heart** (=change of opinion) *about leaving the company.* **2** [C *usu. sing.*] something different, esp. something done for variety and excitement: *Let's go to a restaurant* **for a change.** | *You should take a holiday — you need a change (from work).* | *"The train arrived on time today." "That* **makes a change!***"* (=that is different from what usually happens) **3** [C (**of**)] something new and fresh used in place of something else: *He took a* **change of clothes** *with him, because he was going to stay until the next day.* | *This car needs an oil change.* **4** [U] the money that is returned to someone when the amount they have given is more than the cost of the goods being bought: *If it cost 25 pence and you gave her a pound you should get 75 pence change.* **5** [U] **a** coins of low value: *How much have you got in change?* | *He emptied the* **loose change** *out of his pockets.* **b** [(**for**)] money in low-value coins or notes exchanged for a coin or note of higher value: *Can you give me change for a 50-pence piece?* —see also SMALL CHANGE; see MONEY (USAGE) **6** [*the*+S] *infml for* CHANGE OF LIFE **7 get no/small change out of someone** *infml* to get no/little help from someone —see also **ring the changes** (RING³)

change·a·ble /ˈtʃeɪndʒəbəl/ *adj* likely to change; often changing: *changeable weather* | *a changeable temper* **—bly** *adv* **—bility** /ˌtʃeɪndʒəˈbɪlɨti/, **— ~ness** /ˈtʃeɪndʒ-əbəlnɨs/ *n* [U]

change·less /ˈtʃeɪndʒləs/ *adj fml* unchanging; without change: *changeless blue skies* **— ~ly** *adv*

change·ling /ˈtʃeɪndʒlɪŋ/ *n* a baby secretly exchanged for another, esp. a stupid ugly child left in place of a beautiful clever one, supposedly by fairies (FAIRY (1))

change of life /ˌ· · ·ˈ·/ also **change—** *n* [*the*+S] the MENOPAUSE

change·o·ver /ˈtʃeɪndʒˌəʊvəʳ/ *n* a change from one activity or system of working to another: *Britain's changeover to decimal money was in 1971.* —see also CHANGE **over**

change ring·ing /ˈ· ˌ··/ *n* [U] the art of ringing a set of bells (e.g. in a church tower) in continually varying order

Changing of the Guard /ˌ··· · ˈ·/ [*the*] a ceremony regularly held outside Buckingham Palace, in which guards in red uniforms and black hats (BEARSKINS) replace others. The Changing of the Guard is a popular tourist attraction.

changing room /ˈ·· ·/ ‖ **locker room** *AmE* — *n* a room where people change clothes, esp. for sport, and which usu. contains SHOWERS, LOCKERS, etc.

chan·nel¹ /ˈtʃænl/ *n* **1** a narrow sea passage connecting two seas —compare CANAL **2** the deepest part of a river, HARBOUR, or sea passage: *Ships must follow the channel into the port.* **3** a way, course, or passage for liquids: *There's a channel in the middle of the old street to help rainwater flow away.* **4** (the shows broadcast on) a particular television station: *Turn to the other channel — I don't like this show.* | *We watched the news on Channel 4.* **5** also **channels** *pl.—* any course or system by which information travels, requests are dealt with, etc.: *You should go through the official channels if you want a government grant.* | *The information was received through intelligence channels.* **6** a way, course, or direction of thought or action: *He needs a new channel for his energy.*

channel² *v* **-ll-** *BrE* ‖ **-l-** *AmE* [T (**into**)] **1** to direct towards a particular purpose: *I decided to channel my energies into something useful.* | *The famine relief money was channelled through volunteer groups.* **2** to form a CHANNEL¹ (3) in, or take in a CHANNEL¹ (3): *to channel (water into) the desert* **3 a** to act as a MEDIUM³ by speaking for the spirits of the dead **b** to allow the power of God to flow through one's body or hands to make other people well or healthy again

Channel [*the*] the ENGLISH CHANNEL

Channel 4 /ˌtʃænl ˈfɔːʳ/ one of Britain's four main television stations, which is supported by advertising and the various ITV stations, and broadcasts programmes intended for people whose interests are shared with relatively small numbers of others —compare BBC 1, BBC 2, ITV

chan·nel·ing /ˈtʃænəl-ɪŋ/ *n AmE* [U] The receiving of messages from people or beings who are not present or seen

on the earth. It is not widely believed in or practised. **—lor, -ler** *n*

Channel Is·lands /ˈ·· ˌ··‖ˌ·· ˈ··/ [*the* + P] a group of British islands in the English Channel near the coast of France. The main islands are Jersey, Guernsey, Alderney, and Sark.

channel-surf /ˈ·· ˌ·/ also **channel-hop** *v* [I] *AmE sl* to watch television, quickly changing from one CHANNEL¹(4) to another, not watching any programme for a very long time

Channel Tun·nel /ˌ·· ˈ··/ [*the*] an underground passage which is being built below the English Channel to take trains travelling between England and France

chant¹ /tʃɑːnt‖tʃænt/ *v* [I;T] **1** to sing (words) to a chant: *a choir chanting in church* **2** to repeat (words) continuously in time: *The crowd chanted slogans*

chant² *n* **1** a regularly repeated tune, often with many words sung on one note, esp. used in religious services: *a Hindu chant* —see also GREGORIAN CHANT **2** words continuously repeated in time: *The crowd's chant was "More jobs! More money!"*

Chau·tau·qua /ʃəˈtɔːkwə, tʃə-/ also **Chautauqua So·ci·e·ty** /ˌ·ˈ·· ·ˌ···/— an organization begun in the US in the late 19th century that provided religious education informally combined with entertainment and music, often in summer outdoor settings. The organization no longer exists but its name is sometimes used in connection with modern attempts to provide similar experiences.

chan·try chap·el /ˈtʃɑːntri ˌtʃæpəl‖ˈtʃæn-/ *n* a CHAPEL (=a small church or part of a church) paid for by someone so that priests can pray for his or her soul there after death

chan·ty ‖also **-tey** *AmE* /ˈʃænti/ *n* a SHANTY²

Cha·nu·kah /ˈhɑːnŋ̊kə‖ˈkɑːnəkə, ˈhɑː-/ a Jewish holiday; HANUKKAH

cha·os /ˈkeɪ-ɒs‖-ɑːs/ *n* [U] **1** a state of complete and thorough disorder and confusion: *The failure of the electricity supplies created utter/complete chaos in the city.* | *The country was plunged into chaos following the President's assassination.* **2** *poet* the state of the universe before there was any order

cha·ot·ic /keɪˈɒtɪk‖-ˈɑːtɪk/ *adj* in a state of complete disorder and confusion: *The city traffic was chaotic.* **— ~ally** /kli/ *adv*

chap¹ /tʃæp/ *n infml, esp. BrE* a man or boy; a word now sounding rather old-fashioned or upper-class: *a decent sort of chap* —see also CHAPS

chap² *v* **-pp-** [I;T] to (cause to) become sore, rough, and cracked: *chapped hands/lips*

chap·ar·ral /ˌtʃæpəˌræl, ˌtʃæ-/ *n* [U] *AmE* land on which many plants, esp. small oaks, grow close together, found esp. in the SW US

chap·el¹ /ˈtʃæpəl/ *n* **1** [C] a place, such as a small church, a room in a hospital, prison, etc. (but not a PARISH church), used for Christian worship **2** [C] a room or area in a church with its own ALTAR, used esp. for private prayer and small religious services **3** [C] **a** (esp. in England and Wales) a place of Christian worship used by NONCONFORMISTS (=those who do not belong to the established state church or the Roman Catholic Church) **b** (in Scotland) a Roman Catholic church **4** [U] the religious services held in such places: *He goes to chapel every Sunday night.* | *I'll meet you after chapel.* **5** [C+*sing./pl. v*] a branch of a union in jobs such as printing and JOURNALISM: *The chapel has/have voted to go back to work.* | *a chapel meeting*

chapel² *adj* [F] *BrE old-fash* (esp. in England and Wales) NONCONFORMIST: *He's chapel but his wife's a member of the Church of England.* —compare CHURCH²

chapel of rest /ˌ··· · ˈ·/ *n* **chapels of rest** a place where bodies are kept before being buried

chap·er·on¹ , **-one** /ˈʃæpərəʊn/ *n* (esp. formerly) an older person (usu. a woman) who goes with a young unmarried woman in public and is responsible for her behaviour

chaperon² , **-one** *v* [T] to act as a chaperon to

chap·lain /ˈtʃæplɨn/ *n* a priest or other religious minister responsible for the religious needs of a club, a part of the armed forces, a hospital, etc.: *the prison/school chaplain* —see PRIEST (USAGE)

chap·lain·cy /'tʃæpl̩nsi/ n the position of a chaplain or the building where a chaplain works

chap·let /'tʃæpl̩t/ n esp. lit a decorative band of flowers worn on the head

Chap·lin /'tʃæpl̩n/, **Charlie** (1889–1977) an English film actor and director who worked mainly in the US in silent black and white COMEDY films, in which he usu. played a TRAMP with a small black MOUSTACHE and a BOWLER hat, who walked with the backs of his feet together and the toes pointing outwards – see picture on page 553

Chap·pa·quid·dick /ˌtʃæpə'kwɪdɪk/ an island off the coast of Massachusetts in the US, connected by a bridge to Martha's Vineyard. In 1969 Edward Kennedy was involved in a car accident there in which a woman died. People often mention Chappaquiddick as a reason for Kennedy not becoming a CANDIDATE for the American presidency.

chaps /tʃæps, ʃæps/ n [P] protective leather covers worn over trousers, esp. when riding a horse

Chap Stick /'· ·/ n tdmk a small stick of a wax-like substance used to protect and heal chapped (CHAP²) lips

chap·ter /'tʃæptər/ n **1** any of the main divisions of a book or long article, usu. having a number or title: You have to wait till the last chapter to find out who the murderer was. | This subject is dealt with in Chapter 5. | (fig.) The Civil War was a sad chapter in American history. | (fig.) This is the latest chapter in a bitter dispute. **2** [+sing./pl. v] (a general meeting of) all the priests connected with a CATHEDRAL **3** esp. AmE a local branch of a society, club, etc.

Chapter 11 /ˌtʃæptər ɪ'levən/ a part of the US BANKRUPTCY laws that allows a company in financial difficulty to reorganize itself so that it will not be forced to close down: Our competitor has filed for Chapter 11 | Chapter 11 proceedings

chapter and verse /ˌ··· '·/ n [U] the exact details of where to find a piece of information: When the interviewer asked her to justify her statement, she quoted chapter and verse.

chapter house /'·· ·/ n a building or room where the priests connected with a CATHEDRAL meet

chapter of ac·ci·dents /ˌ··· '···/ n [S] BrE a number of unfortunate events coming one after another

char¹ /tʃɑːr/ v **-rr-** [I;T] to (cause to) become black by burning: There was nothing left of the house but a few charred remains.

char² v **-rr-** [I] BrE old-fash to work as a cleaner in a house, office, public building, etc.

char³ n BrE old-fash a CHARWOMAN

char⁴ n [U] BrE old-fash sl tea: a cup of char

char·a·banc /'ʃærəbæŋ/ n BrE old-fash a large comfortable bus used for pleasure trips

char·ac·ter /'kærəktər/ n **1** [C;U] the combination of qualities which make a particular person, thing, place, etc., different from others; nature: The twins look alike but have very different characters. | A tendency not to show emotions is supposed to be part of the British national character. | a man of good character | When they pulled down the old houses in the centre of the town, the whole character of the place was changed. | I can't understand why she did that – it's quite out of character. (=not at all typical of her behaviour) —compare CHARACTERISTIC², PERSONALITY(1) **2** [U] a combination of qualities that are regarded as valuable or admirable, such as high principles, honesty, etc.: a woman of great character | a nice old house with a lot of character **3** [C] a person in a book, play, etc.: It's a good story, but I find some of the characters rather unconvincing. **4** [C] the opinion that other people have about a person; REPUTATION: a newspaper story that blackened (=damaged) his character | The defendant is a man of previous good character. (=does not have a criminal record) **5** [C] infml **a** a person: She's a strange character. | (derog) Some character just walked up and stole my bag. **b** an odd or humorous person: She's a real character|quite a character – she has us in fits of laughter. | a well-known **character actor** (=one who often plays odd or humorous people) **6** [C] a letter, mark, or sign used in writing or printing: a notice printed in Chinese characters | The characters on my typewriter are too small. | Our new printer operates at 60 characters per

second. **7** [C usu. sing.] fml official position; CAPACITY: He was there in his character as a town official. **8** [C] old-fash, esp. BrE a usu. written statement of a person's abilities; REFERENCE: My employer gave me a good character.

character as·sas·si·na·tion /ˈ··· ···,··/ n [C;U] a cruel and usu. unjust attack on someone's character, esp. in print

char·ac·ter·is·tic¹ /ˌkærəktə'rɪstɪk◄/ adj [(of)] typical; representing a person's or thing's usual character: With characteristic generosity, he offered to buy tickets for all of us. | the characteristic taste of Italian wine | It's characteristic of her that she never complained. –opposite **uncharacteristic** – **ally** /kli/ adv : She gave a characteristically outspoken interview.

characteristic² n [(of)] a special and easily recognized quality of someone or something; ATTRIBUTE: Good planning is one of the characteristics of a successful business. –compare CHARACTER (1)

char·ac·ter·i·za·tion /ˌkærəktəraɪ'zeɪʃən‖-tərə-/ n [C;U (as)] (an example of) the act or skill of characterizing: The film's characterization of the explorer as selfish and untrustworthy is totally false. | She writes exciting stories, but her characterization is weak.

char·ac·ter·ize also **-ise** BrE /'kærəktəraɪz/ v [T] **1** to be characteristic of: An interest in people's deepest feelings characterizes all her writings. | The education system there is characterized by an emphasis on success in exams. **2** [(as)] to describe the character of; PORTRAY: Opponents of the law have characterized it as an attack on free speech.| The hero of the book is characterized as a person of very strong principles.

char·ac·ter·less /'kærəktələs‖-tər-/ adj derog not having a strong character; ordinary: characterless modern houses

cha·rade /ʃə'rɑːd‖ʃə'reɪd/ n something which is easily seen to be false or foolish: The trial was a mere charade; the verdict of guilty had already been decided.

cha·rades /ʃə'rɑːdz‖ʃə'reɪdz/ n [U] a game in which words are acted by players, often part (SYLLABLE) by part, until other players can guess the whole word. Charades is played at parties by adults or children.

char·broil /'tʃɑːbrɔɪl ‖ 'tʃɑːr-/ v [I;T] AmE to cook over a very hot charcoal fire: He charbroiled the steaks on the barbecue. **–ed** adj : charbroiled steaks

char·coal /'tʃɑːkəʊl‖'tʃɑːr-/ n [U] (pieces of) the black substance made by burning wood in a closed container with little air, used in sticks for drawing with or sometimes as FUEL: a sketch drawn in charcoal | a charcoal drawing | charcoal stoves

chard /tʃɑːd‖tʃɑːrd/ also **Swiss chard**– n [U] a vegetable with large juicy leaves and stems

Char·don·nay /ˌʃɔːdə'neɪ ‖ ˌʃɑːr-/ n [U] **1** a type of GRAPE grown for wine **2** a popular white wine originally from Burgundy and now produced in various parts of the world

charge¹ /tʃɑːdʒ‖tʃɑːrdʒ/ v **1** [I;T (for)] to ask in payment: How much do you charge for a double room? | They charge a heavy tax on imported wine. | This shop doesn't charge for delivery. [+obj(i)+obj(d)] They tried to charge me £80 for a room for a night! **2** [T (to)] **a** to record (the cost of something) to someone's debt: Charge the purchases to my account. **b** AmE to buy something with a CREDIT CARD: "Can you afford that dress?" "No, but I'll charge it." **3** [I (at);T] to rush (as if) in an attack: Suddenly the wild animal charged (at) us. | The children charged into the playground. **4** [T (with)] to bring an esp. criminal charge against; ACCUSE: He was charged with the robbery|with stealing the jewels. | A man has been charged in connection with the murder. **5** [T+that; obj] to declare openly (that something is wrong): The shareholders charged that the directors had withheld vital information. **6** [T+obj+to-v/with] fml to instruct or command; give as a duty or responsibility: She charged me to look after|with looking after her son. **7** [T (with)] **a** to load (a gun) **b** old use to fill (a glass): Charge your glasses with wine. **8** [I;T] to (cause to) take in and store electricity: to charge up a car battery | If the red light comes on, it means the battery isn't charging.

charge² n **1** [C;U (for)] the price asked or paid for goods or a service: The admission charge is £5. | interest charges | a 10% service charge | Is there any charge for having the goods delivered? (=does it cost anything) |

What are the charges in this hotel? | *The faulty part was replaced* **free of charge.** | (*BrE*) *She hadn't got the correct coins for the phone box, so she had to* **reverse the charges.** (=get the receiver of the call to pay for it) —see COST (USAGE) **2** [U (**of**)] a position of care, control, or responsibility for a person, group, organization, etc.: *I'd like to speak to the person* **in charge.** | *I had to go to a conference so I left my deputy* **in charge.** | *Student nurses should not be left alone* **in charge of** *hospital wards.* | *She* **took charge of** *the family business when her father died.*| *The company is* **in/under my charge** *while the director is away.* | (*fml*) *He has charge of the children while his wife is at work.* **3** [C] *fml* a person (esp. a child) or thing for which one is responsible: *I became my uncle's charge* (=legally in his care) *after my father's death.* | *It was a hot day so the playgroup leader bought some ice cream for his little charges.* **4** [C (**against, of**)] an official statement saying that someone is responsible for a crime; AC-CUSATION: *He was arrested* **on a charge of** *murder.* | *The police* **brought a charge** (*of murder*) *against him.* | *She faces two charges of theft.* (=will have to reply to them in a court of law) | *The police have examined all the facts, and have decided not to* **press/prefer charges** *against him.* (=not to officially charge him) **5** [C] a written or spoken statement blaming someone for doing something undesirable or morally wrong; ALLEGATION: *The President tried to* **counter the charge** (=reply to it and prove it to be false) *that his budget favoured the rich.* | *This policy leaves him* **open to charges of** (=likely to be blamed for) *favouring the rich.* **6** [C] a rushing forceful attack by soldiers, wild animals, etc. **7** [C] an amount of explosive to be fired at one time **8** [C;U] **a** (a quantity of) electricity put into a BATTERY or other electrical apparatus: *The battery is* **on charge.** (=is having a charge put into it) **b** power or force, esp. of feelings: *the strong emotional charge of the book* | (*sl*) *They seem to get quite* **a charge** (=a lot of excitement) *out of playing this dangerous game.* **9** a property of matter considered positive or negative from which comes a determination of how strong an electrical force can be between two PARTICLES with this property **10** [C+*to-v*] *fml* an order; command: *The old servant fulfilled his master's charge to care for the children.*

charge·a·ble /ˈtʃɑːdʒəbəl‖-ɑːr-/ *adj* **1** [F (**to**)] (of costs) that can or must be paid by someone: *These debts are chargeable to me/my account.* **2** [(**with**)] that can be charged, blamed, or held responsible: *a chargeable offence*

charge ac·count /ˈ· ·ˌ·/ *n AmE for* CREDIT ACCOUNT

charge-cap /ˈ· ·/ *v* [T] see CAP² (3)

charge card /ˈ· ·/ *n* a small esp. plastic card, usu. provided by a particular shop, which allows one to obtain goods there, the cost being charged to one's account and paid later: *a Harrods charge card* —compare CHEQUE CARD, CREDIT CARD, DEBIT CARD

charged /tʃɑːdʒd‖ tʃɑːrdʒd/ *adj* causing strong feelings or much argument: *Whether changes should be made in the voting system is a highly charged political question.* | *an emotionally charged atmosphere*

char·gé d'af·faires /ˌʃɑːʒeɪ dæˈfeəʳ‖ˌʃɑːr-/ *n* **chargés d'affaires** (*same pronunciation*) *Fr* an official who acts as a representative of his/her government during the absence of the AMBASSADOR or in a country to which no AM-BASSADOR has been appointed

charge hand /ˈ· ·/ *n BrE* a worker whose position is just below that of a FOREMAN

charge nurse /ˈ· ·/ *n BrE* a nurse in charge of a hospital ward, esp. when a man —compare SISTER (4)

Charge of the Light Bri·gade /ˌ· · · ˈ· ·ˌ·/ [*the*] an unsuccessful attack made by British soldiers riding horses during the Crimean War, in which many British soldiers were killed because they were sent into a valley which was heavily defended by Russian CANNONs. Alfred Lord Tennyson described this battle in his poem *The Charge of the Light Brigade*, which has many well-known lines, including:
> *Half a league, half a league,*
> *Half a league onward.*
> *All in the valley of Death*
> *Rode the six hundred.*
—see colour picture on page 1015

charg·er¹ /ˈtʃɑːdʒəʳ‖-ɑːr-/ *n old use or lit* a soldier's horse

charger² *n old use* a large flat plate for carrying and serving food

charge sheet /ˈ· ·/ *n* a record kept in a police station of charges made and people to be tried in court

Char·ing Cross /ˌtʃærɪŋ ˈkrɒs◂‖ˈ-krɔːs◂/ one of the main line railway stations in London —see colour map on page 817

Charing Cross Road /ˌ··· ˈ·/ a street in central London, famous for its bookshops

char·i·ot /ˈtʃæriət/ *n* a two-wheeled horse-drawn vehicle with no seats, used in ancient times in battles and races

char·i·o·teer /ˌtʃæriəˈtɪəʳ/ *n* the driver of a chariot

Chariots of Fire /ˌ···· · ˈ·/ a film made in Britain in 1981. It was based on the story of two runners in the 1924 Olympics, and was about love for one's country and a sense of honour. It won several Academy Awards.

cha·ris·ma /kəˈrɪzmə/ *n* **1** [U] the strong personal charm or power to attract that makes a person able to have great influence over people or win their admiration; MAG-NETISM (2): *He could never be a film star; he's got no charisma.* | *a political leader of great charisma* **2** [C] *tech* a power, e.g. of curing diseases, given to a person by the favour of God — ~ **tic** /ˌkærɪzˈmætɪk◂/ *adj* : *a charismatic leader*

charismatic move·ment /ˌ···ˈ·· ˌ··/ *n* [(*the*)] (*often cap.*) groups of worshippers within the Christian church who give particular importance to praying as a group and to speaking by the direct influence of God

char·i·ta·ble /ˈtʃærɪtəbəl/ *adj* **1** kind and generous, esp. in giving help to the poor **2** kind and sympathetic in judging others: *I know he made a mistake, but let's be charitable – he was tired at the time.* | *Even on the most charitable analysis, it has not been a great success so far.* —opposite **uncharitable** **3** [A *no comp.*] concerned with giving help to the poor: *a charitable institution* | *charitable donations* —**bly** *adv*

char·i·ty /ˈtʃærɪti/ *n* **1** [U] (money or help given because of) kindness and generosity towards people who are poor, sick, in difficulties, etc.: *She gave the old woman some shoes* **out of** (=because of) *charity.* | *The victims of the disaster lived on charity until they could make new lives for themselves.* | *a charity performance given by international entertainers to raise money for famine relief* | *They make regular donations to charity.* **2** [C] an organization that helps people who are poor, sick, in difficulties, etc. A **registered charity** is allowed to raise money without paying taxes. Typical charities to which people give money are those which help blind people, sick children, or people in the Third World: *a housing charity* | *The flood victims received money and clothes from several charities.* | *The Red Cross is an international charity.* | *a charity school* (=one where poor children used to be taught free) **3** [U] sympathy and kindness shown when judging others: *They showed little charity towards their former leader after his election defeat.* **4 charity begins at home** *saying* one must give help to or take care of one's own family, people of one's own country, etc. before other people

charity card /ˈ···· ·/ *n* **1** a Christmas card sold to raise money for a charity **2** also **affinity card**– a type of CREDIT CARD given out by a bank or BUILDING SOCIETY. Every time the card is used, the bank or building society gives a small sum of money to a particular charity. —compare CHEQUE CARD

Charity Com·mis·sion /ˈ···· ·ˌ··/ [*the*] an organization in Britain that keeps a list of charities and controls how they are run — ~ **er** *n*

charity shop /ˈ··· ˌ·/ *n* a shop which sells esp. SECOND-HAND goods to raise money for a charity: *He gave his walking boots to the local charity shop.*

char·la·dy /ˈtʃɑːˌleɪdi‖ˈtʃɑːr-/ *n* a CHARWOMAN

char·la·tan /ˈʃɑːlətən‖ˈʃɑːr-/ *n* a person who deceives others by falsely claiming to have a special knowledge or skill, esp. in medicine: *He's not a doctor, he's a charlatan; he knows nothing about medicine.* —compare QUACK² (1)

Char·le·magne /ˈʃɑːləmeɪn‖ˈʃɑːr-/ (742–814) the first European EMPEROR since Roman times, whose court was in what we now know as France

Charles /tʃɑːlz‖tʃɑːrlz/, **Prince** (1948–) the first son of Queen Elizabeth II and next in line to the British THRONE. His title is the **Prince of Wales**. He married Lady Diana Spencer in St Paul's Cathedral in 1901, and they have two sons, Prince William and Prince Harry. Charles and Diana separated in 1992. Prince Charles is known esp. for his interest in ARCHITECTURE and the environment, and he has made speeches about both these subjects which have caused much discussion and disagreement. –see also Princess DIANA

Charles I /ˌtʃɑːlz ðə ˈfɜːst‖ˌtʃɑːrlz ðə ˈfɜːrst/ (1600–49) a king of England, Scotland, and Ireland, who was executed (EXECUTE) after the English Civil War when parliament stopped supporting him

Charles II /ˌtʃɑːlz ðə ˈsekənd‖ˌtʃɑːr-/ (1630–85) a king of England, Scotland, and Ireland, who was the son of Charles I, and who became king after the English Civil War

Charles, Ray (1930–) an American popular music singer, songwriter, and pianist, blind since childhood, who became successful in the 1960s and still performs today

Charles de Gaulle Air·port /ˌʃɑːl də ɡəʊl ˈeəpɔːt‖ˌʃɑːrl də ɡɔːl ˈeərpɔːrt/ also **Charles de Gaulle**– the main Paris airport

Charles·ton /ˈtʃɑːlstən‖-ɑːr-/ n [the+S] a quick lively dance, popular in the 1920s

Charleston a city in S Carolina in the US –see colour map on page 1374·5

char·ley horse /ˌtʃɑːli ˈhɔːs ‖ ˌtʃɑːrli ˈhɔːrs/ n AmE infml a sudden pain in a large muscle, such as the leg or arm muscles, caused by the muscle contracting (CONTRACT³ (1)) after hard exercise: *"I have a charley horse in my thigh,"* he groaned.

Char·ley's Aunt /ˌtʃɑːliz ˈɑːnt‖ˌtʃɑːrliz ˈænt/ a very popular FARCE (=silly, humorous play) by Brandon Thomas (1856–1914) about a man who dresses up as an old lady and pretends to be the aunt of a friend of his

char·lie /ˈtʃɑːli‖-ɑːr-/ n BrE infml (often cap.) a fool: *I felt a real/proper charlie when I dropped all the plates.*

Charlie and the Choco·late Fac·to·ry /ˌ··· · ˈ·· ˌ···/ a well-known children's story by Roald Dahl about a poor boy who wins the chance to tour a magical chocolate factory

Charlie Brown /ˌ·· ˈ·/ see Charlie BROWN

Charl·ton /ˈtʃɑːltən‖ˈtʃɑːr-/, **Bobby** (1937–) an English footballer who played for Manchester United. His brother JACK CHARLTON (1935–) played for Leeds United, and they both played for England in the winning 1966 World Cup team. Bobby Charlton is considered to be one of the best British footballers of all time.

charm¹ /tʃɑːm‖tʃɑːrm/ n 1 [C;U] the power or ability to please, attract, or delight: *This lovely old town has a charm you couldn't find in a big city.* | *a man of great charm* | *When she discovered how rich he was, she really* **turned on the charm.** (=started using her charm) 2 [C] an act, expression, or phrase believed to have magical powers; SPELL³ 3 [C] an object worn on a chain or BRACELET to keep away evil or bring good luck; lucky charms include hearts and horseshoes 4 **like a charm** perfectly; with complete success: *My little plan* **worked like a charm.**

charm² v [T] 1 [(into)] to delight, attract, or influence by charm: *The child charms everyone (into doing what she wants).* | *She was charmed by Venice.* 2 to control (as if) by magic: *charm snakes* | *It seemed as if he had a* **charmed life** (=protected by magic); *nothing bad ever happened to him.*

charm·er /ˈtʃɑːməʳ‖-ɑːr-/ n 1 someone who charms others 2 someone who charms animals –see also SNAKE CHARMER

charm·ing /ˈtʃɑːmɪŋ‖-ɑːr-/ adj very pleasing; delightful: *What a charming young man!* | *charming manners* | *a charming smile/city/garden/story* – **~ly** adv

Charming, Prince see PRINCE CHARMING

charm school /ˈ· ˌ·/ n AmE a school where young people were sometimes sent to learn how to behave in polite society. Charm schools are now rare.

char·nel house /ˈtʃɑːnl haʊs‖ˈtʃɑːr-/ n lit a place where the bodies and bones of dead people are stored

Cha·ron /ˈkeərən/ in CLASSICAL MYTHOLOGY, the boatman who took the souls of the dead across the river Styx to Hades

charts

graph

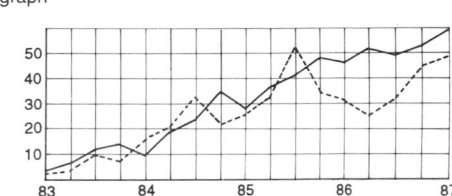

bar chart

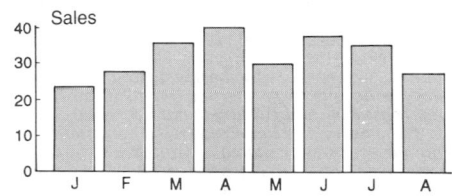

pie chart

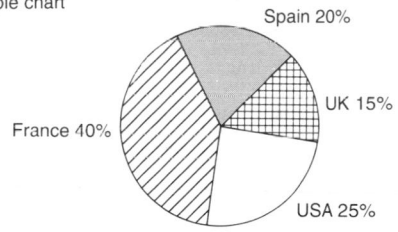

chart¹ /tʃɑːt‖tʃɑːrt/ n 1 (a sheet of paper with) information written or drawn in the form of a picture, GRAPH, etc., usu. with the intention of making it easy to understand: *a sales chart* | *a weather chart* 2 a map, esp. a detailed map of a sea area 3 [usu. pl.] a list, produced weekly, of the most popular records: *That song has been* **in the charts** *for weeks.* | *her recent* **chart-topping** *single* –see also BAR CHART, FLOWCHART, PIE CHART

chart² v [T] to make a map or chart of; show or record on a chart: *to chart the sea area between France and Britain* | (fig.) *The book charts her rise to fame as an actress.* –see also UNCHARTED

char·ter¹ /ˈtʃɑːtəʳ‖-ɑːr-/ n 1 [C] BrE a signed statement from a ruler, government, etc., giving rights, freedoms, etc., to the people, an organization, or a person: *The rights of our citizens are governed by charter.* | (fig., derog) *This new law amounts to a tax evader's charter.* (=allows people to escape paying taxes) –see also CITIZEN'S CHARTER 2 [C] a statement of the principles, duties, and purposes of an organization: *These principles are embodied in the UN charter.* 3 [U] the practice of hiring or renting cars, buses, planes, etc., for special use: *They have yachts available for charter.*

charter² v [T] 1 to give a charter to, or establish by means of a charter 2 to hire or rent out (a plane, train, bus, etc.) for a special use: *a chartered plane/ship/flight* –see HIRE (USAGE)

Charter 77 /ˌtʃɑːtə sevənti ˈsevən ‖ ˌtʃɑːrtər-/ an organization in Czechoslovakia, established in 1977 to protect and improve CIVIL LIBERTY

charter flight /ˈ··· ·/ n a low cost journey in a plane on which all seats have been reserved (RESERVE¹) in advance by travel companies for their customers –compare SCHEDULED FLIGHT

chartered ac·coun·tant /ˌ··· ·ˈ··/ BrE ‖ **certified public accountant** AmE– n an ACCOUNTANT who has successfully completed his/her training –see also ACCOUNTANT

Char·ter·house /ˈtʃɑːtəhaʊs‖ˈtʃɑːrtər-/ also **Charterhouse**

School /ˌ·⋯ ˈ·/ a top British PUBLIC SCHOOL for boys in Surrey, S England

charter mem·ber /ˌ·⋯ ˈ··/ n esp. AmE an original member of a society or organization

Char·treuse /ʃɑːˈtrɜːz‖ʃɑːˈtruːz/ n [U] tdmk a strong sweet green or yellow French alcoholic drink made with HERBS, usu. drunk from a small glass after a meal

char·wom·an /ˈtʃɑːˌwʊmən‖ˈtʃɑːr-/ also **charlady, char**— n **charwomen** /-ˌwɪmɪn/ old-fash, esp. BrE a woman who works as a cleaner in a house, office, or public building

char·y /ˈtʃeəri/ adj [F (of)] fml unwilling to take risks; CAUTIOUS: You should be chary of investing any money in such a risky venture. —**ily** adv

Cha·ryb·dis /kəˈrɪbdɪs/ see SCYLLA AND CHARYBDIS

chase¹ /tʃeɪs/ v **1** [I (after);T] to follow rapidly in order to catch: The cat chased the mouse but couldn't catch it. | Chase after Ann and ask her to get some eggs while she's at the shops. | (fig.) He's always chasing (after) the girls. (=trying to attract them) | (fig.) We had 200 applicants chasing (=trying to get) 3 jobs! **2** [T+obj+adv/prep] to make (someone) leave by chasing them; drive away: The dog ran out into the garden and chased the birds away.| She chased the children out of the kitchen. **3** [I+adv/prep] to rush; hurry: I've chased all round the building looking for you. | The children are always chasing in and out/chasing about (the house). **4** [T (UP)] to make inquiries about (something) or talk to (someone) in order to find information or get something done: The police have been trying to chase (up) the dead man's sister, but they have no idea where she lives. | Those books I ordered still haven't come − I'll have to chase the manager about them. **5 chase the dragon** sl to take the drug HEROIN, esp. by putting it into the blood with a needle

chase² n **1** [C] an act of chasing someone or something: There was a long chase before the criminal was caught.| There was an exciting car chase in the film. **2** [the+S] fml the sport of hunting esp. foxes: the thrill of the chase **3** [C] (often cap. as part of a name) an area of land set aside for the breeding of wild animals for hunting and shooting: Cannock Chase **4 give chase** rather fml to chase something or someone: The old lady saw the thief running up the street and gave chase on her bicycle. —see also PAPER CHASE, WILD-GOOSE CHASE

chase³ v [T] tech to decorate (metal) by marking it with a tool without a cutting edge: chased silver

Chase, Chev·y /ˈtʃevi/ (1943–) an American COMEDIAN who appears on television and in films

Chase Man·hat·tan Bank /ˌ·⋯ˌ·· ˈ·/ the third largest bank in the US, with its main offices in New York City

chas·er /ˈtʃeɪsər/ n a weaker alcoholic drink drunk after a stronger one, or a stronger alcoholic drink drunk after a weaker one: After drinking a pint of beer he had a whisky as a chaser.

chas·m /ˈkæzəm/ n a very deep crack or opening in the surface of the earth or ice: (fig.) There was a (deep) political chasm between the two countries which nearly led to war.

chas·sis /ˈʃæsi/ n chassis /ˈʃæsiz/ **1** the frame on which the body and working parts of a vehicle are fastened or built **2** the landing apparatus of a plane

chaste /tʃeɪst/ adj **1** apprec not taking part in sexual activity, esp. immoral sexual activity —compare CELIBATE; see also CHASTITY **2** MODEST (3) **3** pomp (esp. of a style of writing) simple; not too highly decorated − ~**ly** adv

chas·ten /ˈtʃeɪsən/ v [T] to make (someone) want to improve their behaviour as a result of punishment or suffering: He was rather chastened by the accident, which had happened because he was driving too fast. | a chastening experience

chas·tise /tʃæˈstaɪz/ v [T] fml to punish or blame severely, esp. by beating − ~**ment** n [C;U]

chas·ti·ty /ˈtʃæstɪti/ n [U] **1** (esp. of young women) the condition of being sexually chaste and of having a very pure and INNOCENT attitude to sex: Chastity before marriage is still demanded in some societies. **2** euph for VIRGINITY

chastity belt /ˈ⋯ · / n a special belt with a lock worn by some women in former times and intended to prevent them from having sexual relations

chas·u·ble /ˈtʃæzjʊbəl/ n a loose-fitting garment without

arms, worn by some Christian priests at religious services, esp. the Mass

chat¹ /tʃæt/ v -tt- [I (about, AWAY, ON)] infml to talk in a friendly informal manner: She chatted with most of the guests at the party. | The two friends sat in a corner and chatted (away) about the weather/about what they had been doing since they last met.

chat sbdy. ↔ up phr v [T] BrE infml to talk to (esp. someone of the opposite sex) in a friendly way in order to begin a relationship, persuade them to do something, etc.: The local boys chat up all the foreign girls in the tourist season. | If you chat him up a bit he might lend it to you.

chat² n infml [C;U (about, with)] (a) friendly informal conversation: I had a chat (about that) with Mary. | There's too much chat in this office! —see also CHAT SHOW

chât·eau , **chat-** /ˈʃætəʊ‖ʃæˈtəʊ/ n -teaus or -teaux /ˈʃætəʊz‖ʃæˈtəʊz/ a castle or large country house in France. The châteaux, esp. those along the Loire, are esp. popular with tourists.

chat·e·laine /ˈʃætl-eɪn/ n **1** the female owner, or wife of the owner, of a large country house or castle **2** (in former times) a set of chains fastened to a woman's belt for carrying keys, etc.

chat·line /ˈtʃætlaɪn/ n a British telephone service which people call to have a conversation with others who have called the same service. After public concern that some young people call chatlines a lot and leave their parents with very high bills, chatlines were closed down in Britain in 1992.

chat show /ˈ· ·/ BrE ‖ **talk show** AmE— n a radio or television show on which well-known people talk to each other and are asked questions. The presenters of chat shows often become extremely famous themselves: a chat-show host

chat·tel /ˈtʃætl/ n law an article of movable property (esp. in the phrase **goods and chattels**): (fig.) He treats his wife as if she were just a chattel. (=a piece of his property)

chat·ter¹ /ˈtʃætər/ v [I] **1** [(about, AWAY, ON)] (of people) to talk quickly, continuously, and for a long time, usu. about something unimportant: The teacher told the children to stop chattering in class. | chattering on about his new car **2** [(AWAY)] (of certain animals and birds) to make rapid speechlike sounds: The monkeys were chattering away in the trees. **3** (of the teeth) to knock together repeatedly, esp. through cold or fear: I was so cold my teeth were chattering. − ~**er** n

chatter² n [U] **1** rapid informal unimportant conversation **2** a rapid knocking sound made by teeth, machines, etc., or the rapid speechlike sounds made by certain animals and birds: the chatter of the enemy's guns

chat·ter·box /ˈtʃætəbɒks‖-tərbaːks/ n infml a person who talks a lot, esp. about things that are unimportant

chattering class·es /ˈ⋯ ˌ··/ n [the +P] BrE people who are very interested in news and CURRENT AFFAIRS, esp. broadcasters and people who write for the newspapers

Chatterley, Lady see LADY CHATTERLEY

chat·ty /ˈtʃæti/ adj infml **1** fond of talking or chatting: He's a friendly, chatty sort of person. **2** having the style of informal conversation: a chatty letter

chat-up line /ˈ· · ˌ·/ BrE‖usu. **line** AmE— n something that someone, esp. a man, says in order to try to start a relationship with someone they are interested in sexually, esp. the first time they meet. Certain chat-up lines are felt to have been used so often that they are now only used jokingly, for example "Do you come here often?" and "Haven't we met somewhere before?"

Chau·cer /ˈtʃɔːsər/, **Geoff·rey** /ˈdʒefri/ (about 1340–1400) an English writer best known for his long poem The Canterbury Tales, in which members of a group of PILGRIMs tell each other stories, many of which are BAWDY and humorous

chauf·feur /ˈʃəʊfər, ʃəʊˈfɜːr/ **chauffeuse** /ʃəʊˈfɜːz ‖ -ɜːrz/ fem.— n a person employed to drive a car for someone else −**chauffeur** v [I;T (AROUND, ABOUT)] : (fig.) Your mother shouldn't waste her time chauffeuring you around; you'll have to learn to drive yourself!

chau·vin·is·m /ˈʃəʊvɪnɪzəm/ n [U] **1** very great and often unthinking admiration for one's country; proud and unreasonable belief that one's country is politically, morally, and militarily, better than all others **2** unreasonable belief that the sex to which one belongs is better than the other sex: *When she tried to become an engineer, she came up against* (=was faced by) *a lot of male chauvinism.*

chau·vin·ist /ˈʃəʊvɪnɪst/ *n, adj* (a person or organization) feeling, showing, or based on chauvinism: *a chauvinist foreign policy* | *Her husband's such a chauvinist that he tries to tell her how to vote.* —see also MALE CHAUVINIST — ~ **ic** /ˌʃəʊvɪˈnɪstɪk◂/ *adj* — ~ **ically** /kli/ *adv*

Chá·vez /ˈtʃɑːves/, **Ce·sar** /seɪˈzɑːr/ (1927–) a Mexican-American labour ACTIVIST who organized the United Farm Workers' Union for people who pick fruit and vegetables and often must move around to find work. He led successful BOYCOTTS of some products to help win better wages and protection from harmful chemicals for workers.

cheap¹ /tʃiːp/ *adj* **1** low in price and good value for money; INEXPENSIVE: *Fresh vegetables are very cheap in the summer.* | *Bread is cheap in this shop because they bake it themselves.* | *This is the cheapest restaurant in town.* (=it charges the lowest prices) | *Houses like that* **don't come cheap.** (=are expensive) | *She got those trousers* **on the cheap** (=at a very low price) *at the market.* | *(derog) The industry is maintained by the* **cheap labour** (=work done for low pay) *of immigrant workers.* **2** low in price and of little value or low quality: *Her shoes looked* **cheap and nasty** *to me.* | (fig.) *A hundred years ago human life was held a lot cheaper than it is today.* (=was considered to have little value) **3** (of behaviour) offensively unpleasant and showing a lack of principles or sincere feelings; VULGAR: *I hate his kind of cheap humour.* | *cheap emotion* | *cheap thrills* | *I felt very cheap* (=ashamed) *because I'd lied to my friend.* **4** *AmE infml* not liking to spend money; STINGY **5 cheap and cheerful** *infml* (esp. of decorations, etc.) looking cheap, but not ashamed of it — ~ **ly** *adv* — ~ **ness** *n* [U]

cheap² *adv* at a very low price: *I was very lucky to get it so cheap.*

cheap·en /ˈtʃiːpən/ *v* **1** [I;T] to (cause to) become cheaper in price or value: *The dollar's increase in value has cheapened imports.* **2** [T] to make (esp. oneself) seem less good or honourable; DEGRADE: *Don't cheapen yourself by getting involved in their shady deals.*

cheap-jack /ˈ· ·/ *adj* [A] *BrE* **1** cheap and worthless; SHODDY **2** producing or selling cheap worthless goods

cheap·skate /ˈtʃiːpskeɪt/ *n derog* a person who spends or gives very unwillingly

cheat¹ /tʃiːt/ *v* **1** [I (at)] to behave in a dishonest or deceitful way in order to win an advantage, esp. in a game: *He always cheats at cards.* | *Any student caught cheating will be disqualified from the exam.* **2** [T (of, out of)] to take from (someone) deceitfully: *They cheated the old woman (out) of her money by making her sign a document she didn't understand.* **3** [T] *lit* to avoid or escape as if by deception: *The swimmers cheated death in the stormy seas.* **4** [I (on)] *infml* to be sexually unfaithful (to): *They've only just got married, and already she's started cheating (on him)!*

cheat² *n* **1** a person who cheats; dishonest person: *I saw you drop that card, you cheat!* **2** *rare* an example of cheating or dishonesty

check¹ /tʃek/ *n* **1** [C (on)] an examination or INSPECTION, e.g. to make certain that something is correct or in good condition: *an airport security check* | *a check on the quality of all goods leaving the factory* | *They gave the car a thorough check before setting out on their journey.* | *The police are* **running a check** *on everyone who was at the party.* (=finding information about them) | *I don't think I've got a copy of the report, but I'll have a check through my files.* | *You'll have to* **keep a check** *on the oil — there's a leak in the tank.* —see also CHECKUP, SPOT CHECK **2** [C] a standard against which something can be tested or examined: *She glanced through his lecture notes as a check that she had noted down all the important information.* **3** [S (on); U] (a means of) the prevention of movement or development; RESTRAINT: *The river acted as a check on the army's advance.* | *We've kept the disease in check for a year now.* | *You must put a check on your spending.* | *The police tried to* **hold** *the angry crowd* **in check.** **4** [C] **a** *AmE for* CHEQUE **b** *AmE for* TICK¹ (2) **5** [C] a ticket or

object for claiming something; RECEIPT: *I've lost the check for my coat.* **6** [C] *AmE & ScotE* a bill at a restaurant **7** [C;U] a pattern of squares, esp. on cloth: *a red and white check tablecloth* —see also CHECKED **8** [U] (in CHESS) the position of the king when under direct attack from an opponent's piece(s): *He put her in check with his knight.* —see also CHECKMATE, RAIN CHECK

check² *v* **1** [I (**for, on,** UP);T] to test, examine, or mark to see if something is correct, true, in good condition, etc.: *Their bags were checked by security guards as they entered the building.* | *She read the letter through before sending it, checking for spelling mistakes.* | *She checked through the letter before sending it.* | *"Is the baby asleep?" "I'll just go and check (up)."* | *The police are checking up on what the man told them.* | *She asked her surveyor to check the floorboards for dry rot.* | *Before you send the letter, check with Bill* (=ask him) *to see if the address is right.* [+*that/wh*-] *I must just check that the potatoes are cooked/whether the potatoes are cooked.* **2** [T] to find out and note: *She checked the temperature every morning before leaving home.* **3** [T] to stop, control, or hold back; RESTRAIN: *More police have been recruited in an attempt to check the increase in crime.* | *A change of wind checked the fire.* —see also UNCHECKED **4** [T] (in CHESS) to move one's pieces so as to put the opponent's king) under direct attack **5** [T] *AmE for* TICK¹ (2) **6** [T] **a** *AmE* to leave or accept (something) to be looked after: *They checked their coats before taking their seats in the theatre.* **b** [(IN)] to leave or accept (LUGGAGE) to be taken somewhere, esp. by air: *He checked (in) his bags.* | *His baggage was checked through to Bangkok.* —see also CROSS-CHECK, DOUBLE-CHECK

check in *phr v* **1** [I (**at, to**)] to report one's arrival at a hotel desk, an airport, etc.: *He checked in at the hotel under a false name.* | *You must check in (at the airport) an hour before your plane leaves.* —compare CHECK **out** (1) **2** [T] (**check sthg. ↔ in**) *esp. AmE* to have the return of (an article) recorded: *I'm just going to check in these books at the library.* —see also CHECK² (6b), CHECK-IN

check sthg. ↔ **off** *phr v* [T] to mark (e.g. names or items in a list) as having been dealt with

check out *phr v* **1** [I (**of**)] to leave a hotel after paying the bill —compare CHECK **in 2** [I;T (=**check** sthg. ↔ **out**)] *infml* **a** to find out whether (something) is true by making inquiries: *The police are still checking out his story/his alibi.* **b** to be found to be true after inquiries have been made: *How does his story check out with the facts?* **3** [T] (**check** sthg. ↔ **out**) *infml, esp. AmE* to examine (something) in order to learn the qualities of: *Have you checked out that new Thai restaurant?* | *boys checking out the other team's cheerleaders* **4** [T] (**check** sthg. ↔ **out**) *esp. AmE* to have the removal of (an article) recorded: *to check a book out (of a library)* —see also CHECKOUT

check sthg. ↔ **over** *phr v* [T] to examine (something) in order to make sure it is correct: *Please check this work over and correct any mistakes.*

check·book /ˈtʃekbʊk/ *n AmE for a* CHEQUEBOOK

check card /ˈ· ·/ also **check guar·an·tee card** /ˌ· ··ˈ· ·/— *n AmE for a* CHEQUE CARD

checked /tʃekt/ *adj* having a pattern of squares: *checked curtains* —compare CHEQUERED; see also CHECK¹ (7), and see picture at PATTERN

Check·er /ˈtʃekər/, **Chubby** (1941–) an American singer popular esp. in the 1960s, whose most famous song is *The Twist*

check·ered /ˈtʃekəd‖-ərd/ *adj AmE for* CHEQUERED

check·ers /ˈtʃekəz‖-ərz/ *n* [U] *AmE for* DRAUGHTS

check-in /ˈ· ·/ *n* [C;U] (a place for) the reporting of one's arrival at a hotel desk, airport, etc.: *The airline boasts superior service from reservations through check-in to baggage handling.* | *a check-in counter* —see also CHECK **in**

checking ac·count /ˈ· · ·ˌ·/ *n AmE* a bank account which usu. earns little or no interest and from which money can be taken out at any time by cheque; CURRENT ACCOUNT — compare DEPOSIT ACCOUNT

check·list /ˈtʃekˌlɪst/ *n* [(**of**)] a complete list, e.g. of checks to be made, things to be done, etc.: *The crew of the aircraft went through the safety checklist before takeoff.*

check·mate¹ /ˈtʃekmeɪt/ *n* [C;U] **1** (in CHESS) the position of a king at the end of a game when under direct attack, from which escape is impossible **2** (a) complete defeat —compare STALEMATE

checkmate² *v* [T] **1** (in CHESS) to defeat (the opponent's king and therefore the opponent) with a checkmate: *She checkmated my king|checkmated me in six moves.* **2** to stop; completely defeat

check-out /'tʃek-aʊt/ *n* **1** [C] a desk in a self-service shop where one pays for goods. The sum owed is calculated by a CASHIER who then takes the money. **2** [C;U] the time at which a guest must leave a hotel room or be charged for another day: *Checkout is at midday in this hotel.* | *checkout time* —see also CHECK out

check-point /'tʃekpɔɪnt/ *n* a place, esp. on a border, where an examination of people, goods, etc., is made

Checkpoint Char-lie /ˌ·· '··/ the best-known checkpoint in the Berlin Wall between what was formerly East and West Germany

check-room /'tʃek-rʊm, -ruːm/ *n esp. AmE for* **1** LEFT LUGGAGE OFFICE **2** a CLOAKROOM

checks and bal-anc-es /ˌ·· '···/ *n* [P] limits put on a group, esp. a part of a government, by stating that another group has the power to change or VETO (disapprove) the first group's actions or decisions: *A system of checks and balances was built into the US government.*

check-up /'tʃek-ʌp/ *n infml* a general medical examination, usu. taken regularly, to test one's state of health and discover any disease at an early stage: *to have an annual checkup* —compare PHYSICAL

ched-dar /'tʃedəʳ/ *n* [U] (*often cap.*) a hard smooth usu. yellowish cheese, probably the most popular cheese in Britain and the US: *a mild|mature cheddar*

Cheddar Gorge /ˌ·· '·/ a deep valley in the Mendip Hills, SW England, famous for its CAVES

Cheech and Chong /ˌtʃiːtʃ ənd 'tʃʊŋ‖-'tʃɔːŋ/ two American COMEDIANS who were popular in the 1970s, esp. with younger people who used drugs

cheek¹ /tʃiːk/ *n* **1** [C] the fleshy part of the face below the eye, esp. in humans: *He kissed her on the cheek.* —see picture at HEAD **2** [U] *BrE infml* disrespectful rude behaviour: *What a cheek!* | *Well, of all the cheek!* [+to-v] *He had the cheek to say that I was late.* **3** [C] *infml* either of the two soft fleshy parts at the back lower end of the body, esp. in human beings; BUTTOCK **4 cheek by jowl (with)** very close together or closely connected: *It was incongruous to see a bishop sitting there cheek by jowl with the Communist leader.* **5 turn the other cheek** to take no action against someone who has hurt or harmed one **6 -cheeked** /tʃiːkt/ having cheeks of the stated kind: *rosy-cheeked children* —see also **tongue in cheek** (TONGUE(10))

cheek² *v* [T] *BrE infml* to speak or behave rudely or disrespectfully towards: *She was sent to the headmistress for cheeking the other teachers.*

cheek-bone /'tʃiːkbəʊn/ *n* [*usu. pl.*] the bone above the cheek, just below the eyes

cheek-y /'tʃiːki/ *adj BrE* ‖ **sassy** *AmE* — disrespectful, esp. towards someone older such as one's teacher or parents; rude; IMPUDENT: *a cheeky remark|little boy* —see IMPOLITE (USAGE) —**ily** *adv* —**iness** *n* [U]

cheep /tʃiːp/ *v* [I] to make the weak high noise made by young birds —**cheep** *n*

cheer¹ /tʃɪəʳ/ *n* **1** [C] a shout of praise, approval, or encouragement: *I heard the cheers of the crowd, and I knew our team was winning.*

▶ CULTURAL NOTE If someone **gives a cheer** it usu. means that they shout "Hurray!" or "Hurrah!", to show their approval of something. Sometimes someone will call for **three cheers** for someone. Then they will usu. say "Hip hip..." and the other people present will shout "Hurray!", three times altogether. ◀

2 [U] *fml or lit* a feeling of happiness and confidence; good spirits: *After the long hard winter, the feeling of spring in the air filled her with cheer.* | *The general's speech gave cheer to his anxious troops.* **3** [U] *lit or old-fash* eating, drinking, and being merry: *Christmas cheer* —see also CHEERS

cheer² *v* **1** [I] to shout in praise, approval, or support: *The crowd cheered as the teams arrived.* **2** [T (ON)] to encourage by cheering: *The crowd cheered their favourite rider (on).* **3** [T] to give encouragement or hope to: *The*

trapped miners were cheered when they heard the rescue party. | *cheering news*

cheer up also **buck up**— *phr v infml* **1** [I;T (=cheer sbdy. **up**)] to (cause to) become happier, more cheerful: *Cheer up! The news isn't too bad.* | *He took her to the ballet to cheer her up.* **2 Cheer up! It might never happen** *infml* (said to someone who looks very thoughtful and unhappy, for no reason that one can see)

cheer-ful /'tʃɪəfəl‖-'tʃɪər-/ *adj* **1** happy and lively; in good spirits: *a cheerful person|grin* **2** bright and pleasant; likely to cause happy feelings: *cheerful music|wallpaper* | *high street boutiques selling cheap and cheerful clothes* **3** pleasantly willing: *his cheerful compliance with our requests* —see also **cheap and cheerful** (CHEAP¹) — ~**ly** *adv* — ~**ness** *n* [U] : *singing cheerfully* | *She cheerfully admitted her mistake.*

cheer-i-o /ˌtʃɪəri'əʊ/ *interj BrE infml* goodbye

Cheer-i-os /ˌtʃɪəri'əʊz/ *n* [P] *tdmk* a popular American breakfast CEREAL containing OATS

cheer-lead-er /'tʃɪəˌliːdəʳ‖-'tʃɪər-/ *n* (esp. in the US) a person who calls for and directs cheering, e.g. at a football game, using certain agreed cheers and dance-like movements. In the US, every HIGH SCHOOL has a team of cheerleaders (usu. girls), chosen for their attractive appearance, confidence, and ability to jump and perform dance-like movements. Professional sports teams also have cheerleaders, who are highly paid and are often highly skilled dancers; the **Dallas Cowboys** (a football team) are famous for their cheerleaders.

cheer-less /'tʃɪələs‖-'tʃɪər-/ *adj* dull; without comfort or happiness; saddening: *a cheerless rainy day* — ~**ly** *adv* — ~**ness** *n* [U]

cheers /tʃɪəz‖tʃɪərz/ *interj* **1** used for expressing good wishes when drinking with someone, esp. when taking the first mouthful of a new drink. (People raise their glasses towards each other and sometimes move them together to touch each other, when they say 'cheers'.) **2** *BrE infml* goodbye **3** *BrE infml* thank you

Cheers an amusing American television programme set in a bar called Cheers in Boston —see colour picture on page 686

cheer-y /'tʃɪəri/ *adj* bright; cheerful: *a cheery greeting* —**ily** *adv* —**iness** *n* [U]

cheese /tʃiːz/ *n* **1** [C;U] (a) soft or firm solid food made from milk: *cheese made from the milk of cows, sheep, or goats* | *English cheeses* | *Will you grate some cheese to sprinkle over the pasta?* | *a wine and cheese party* **2 say cheese** (a phrase said by someone who is just about to take a photograph to make people smile): *Come on, everyone, say cheese!* —see also BIG CHEESE, BLUE CHEESE, CREAM CHEESE —compare **watch the birdie** (BIRDIE)

cheese-bur-ger /'tʃiːzbɜːgəʳ‖-ɜːr-/ *n* a HAMBURGER cooked with a piece of cheese on top of the meat

cheese-cake /'tʃiːzkeɪk/ *n* **1** [C;U] a cake in a sweet pastry case, made from a mixture containing soft cheese **2** [U] *old-fash infml* photographs of pretty women with few clothes on —compare BEEFCAKE

cheese-cloth /'tʃiːzklɒθ‖-klɔːθ/ *n* [U] thin cotton cloth used for putting round some kinds of cheeses, and sometimes for making clothes

cheesed off /ˌtʃiːzd 'ɒf‖-'ɔːf/ *adj* [(with)] *BrE sl* thoroughly tired of something; having lost all interest; FED UP: *I'm cheesed off (with this job).*

cheese-par-ing /'tʃiːzˌpeərɪŋ/ *n* [U] too great carefulness when giving or spending money — **cheeseparing** *adj* [A]: *cheeseparing little economies*

chee-tah /'tʃiːtə/ *n* a long-legged spotted African animal of the cat family, about the size of a small LEOPARD and able to run very fast —see picture at BIG CATS

Chee-ver /'tʃiːvəʳ/, **John** (1912–82) an American writer, best remembered for his short stories

chef /ʃef/ *n* a skilled usu. male cook, esp. the chief cook in a hotel or restaurant. The STEREOTYPE of a chef is of a man who wears a white coat or APRON and a tall white hat, and who becomes upset or angry easily, esp. if his cooking goes wrong: *a pastry chef* —compare COOK²

chef d'oeu-vre /ˌʃeɪ 'dɜːvrə‖-'dɜːvrə, -'dɜːrv/ *n* **chefs d'oeuvre** (*same pronunciation*) *Fr fml* the best piece of work by a painter, writer, etc.; MASTERPIECE

Che Gue·va·ra /ˌtʃeɪ ɡəˈvɑːrə/ (1926–67) an Argentine REVOLUTIONARY (=supporter of anti-government forces). He helped Fidel Castro come to power in Cuba and was killed by GUERRILLAS in Bolivia.

Chek·hov , **Chekov** /ˈtʃekɒf‖-ɔːf/, **An·ton Pav·lo·vich** /ˈænton ˈpævlɒvɪtʃ‖-ɑːn ˈpɑːv-/ (1860–1904) a Russian writer of plays and short stories, best known for his plays *The Seagull*, *Uncle Vanya*, and *The Cherry Orchard* ∼**ian** /tʃeˈkəʊviən/ *adj*

Chelms·ford /ˈtʃelmzfəd‖-fərd/ a town in Essex, England, where the local government for that COUNTY is based

Chel·sea /ˈtʃelsi/ an area of London known for its expensive housing and fashionable shops

Chelsea bun /ˌ·· ˈ·/ *n* a small, round, sweet cake with dried fruit in it

Chelsea Flow·er Show /ˌ··· ˈ··· [*the*] a large flower show which takes place in London in May every year and is visited by people from all over Britain

Chelsea pen·sion·er /ˌ·· ˈ···/ *n* an old or sick person who was once a soldier in the British army and who now lives in a special hospital in Chelsea

Chel·ten·ham /ˈtʃeltənəm/ a town in W England which is famous for its horse racing, its SPA and its PUBLIC SCHOOLS

Chel·ten·ham Gold Cup /ˌ··· ˌ· ˈ·/ [*the*] a horse race which is run once a year at Cheltenham, England

Cheltenham La·dies' Col·lege /ˌ··· ˈ·· ˌ·/ *n* a PUBLIC SCHOOL for girls in Cheltenham, started in 1853

chem·i·cal /ˈkemɪkəl/ *adj* of, connected with, used in, or made by chemistry: *A chemical reaction occurs if you put zinc into sulphuric acid.* | *a chemical solution* | *chemical engineering* − ∼ **ly** /kli/ *adv*

chemical² *n* a substance used in or produced by chemistry; any of the ELEMENTS or the compounds formed from them: *toxic/organic chemicals*

chemical re·ac·tion /ˌ··· ·ˈ··/ *n* a process in which the atoms of substances mix and arrange themselves differently to form new substances, without using or making heat: *Pour this solution into that one, and a chemical reaction will take place.* −compare NUCLEAR REACTION

chemical war·fare /ˌ··· ·ˈ·/ *n* [U] methods of fighting a war in which CHEMICAL WEAPONS are used −compare BIOLOGICAL WARFARE

chemical weap·on /ˌ··· ˈ··/ *n* [*usu. pl*] a weapon in war which uses non-explosive chemicals e.g. poisonous gas: *An agreement has been reached to ban the use of all chemical weapons.*

che·mise /ʃəˈmiːz/ *n* a woman's simple dress that hangs straight from the shoulder

chem·ist /ˈkemɪst/ *n* 1 a scientist who specializes in chemistry 2 also **pharmacist** *BrE or fml AmE*− *BrE* a skilled person who owns or runs a shop where medicines are sold (a **chemist's**). TOILETRIES are also usu. sold there.: *The chemist made up my prescription immediately.* −see also DRUGSTORE, PHARMACY

chem·is·try /ˈkemɪstri/ *n* [U] 1 the science which studies the substances (ELEMENTS) which make up the Earth, universe, and living things, how these substances combine with each other, and how they behave under different conditions 2 the chemical structure and behaviour of a particular substance: *the chemistry of lead* 3 the physical CONSTITUTION of someone: *It's part of my chemistry to need a warm climate.* 4 the feeling between two people, esp. who are attracted to each other, which cannot be explained by reason or science: *The chemistry was right between us.* | *I couldn't help falling in love − it was chemistry.*

chemistry set /ˈ··· ˌ·/ *n* a box containing the necessary chemicals and equipment for usu. young people to practise chemistry at home: *Mum bought me a chemistry set for my birthday!*

chem·o·ther·a·py /ˌkiːməʊˈθerəpi, ˌke-/ *n* [U] the use of chemical substances to treat and control certain diseases, esp. CANCER. It usu. has unpleasant SIDE EFFECTS, for example, sickness and loss of hair on the patient's head: *She is having/undergoing a course of chemotherapy.* −**peutic** /ˌkiːməʊˈθerəˈpjuːtɪk, ˌke-/, **-peutical** *adj* −**peutically** /kli/ *adv*

che·nille /ʃəˈniːl/ *n* [U] (cloth made from) twisted thread with a soft smooth brush-like surface, used for dresses,

curtains, etc.: *a chenille bedspread*

cheque *BrE* ‖ **check** *AmE* /tʃek/ *n* 1 a specially printed sheet of paper supplied by a bank on which an order can be written 2 a written order to a bank to pay a certain sum of money from one's bank account to oneself or to another person. It is usu. made on a CHEQUE (1): *I'd like to pay by cheque, please, rather than in cash.* | *She wrote me a cheque.* | *If the banks are closed you can* **cash a cheque** (=use a cheque to get cash) *at the Post Office.* | *We can't issue the tickets for your flight until your cheque has been cleared.* (=the money has been paid from your bank account) −compare DRAFT¹ (2); see also BLANK CHEQUE, TRAVELLER'S CHEQUE

cheque·book /ˈtʃekbʊk/ *BrE* ‖ **checkbook** *AmE*− *n* a set of CHEQUES (1) bound together in a small book. When a cheque is removed, a small piece of paper (a **cheque stub**) remains, on which one can write details of who the cheque was paid to, how much it was for, etc.

chequebook jour·nal·is·m /ˌ·· ˈ····/ *n* [U] low-quality writing esp. connected with TABLOID newspapers, who pay large amounts of money for details of famous people's private lives, and print shocking and sensational stories about them

cheque card /ˈ· ·/ also **banker's card, cheque guarantee card** /ˌ· ··ˈ · ˌ·/ *n* a card given by a bank to those who have an account with it, which promises that the bank will pay out the money written on their cheques up to a certain amount, usu. between £50 and £250: *I'm afraid we can't accept/take a cheque without a cheque card.* −compare CHARGE CARD, CHARITY CARD, CREDIT CARD, DEBIT CARD

chequ·ered *BrE* ‖ **checkered** *AmE* /ˈtʃekəd‖-ərd/ *adj* 1 covered with a pattern of differently coloured squares −compare CHECKED 2 (esp. of a person's past life) varied; with many changes of fortune: *He'd had a chequered past but was now determined to be successful.* | *a chequered career/history*

chequered flag /ˌ·· ˈ·/ *n* [*the*] a flag covered with black and white squares, used to signal the start and finish of a motor race

chequ·ers /ˈtʃekəz‖-ərz/ *n* see CHINESE CHEQUERS

Chequers the official country house of the British Prime Minister, NW of London

Cher /ʃeər/ (1946–) an American singer and actress who has performed in many films

Cher·bourg /ˈʃeəbʊəg‖ˈʃeərbʊərg/ a city and port in NW France, where many ferries (FERRY¹) from England go to

cher·ish /ˈtʃerɪʃ/ *v* [T] *fml* 1 to care for tenderly; love: *The old man cherished the girl as if she were his daughter.* | *his most cherished possession* 2 to keep (hope, love, or other deep feelings) firmly in mind: *I cherish the hope that he will come back.* | *cherished memories*

Cher·nen·ko /tʃɜːˈnjeŋkəʊ‖tʃɜːr-/, **Kon·stan·tin** /ˈkɒnstəntiːn‖ˈkɑːn-/ (1911–85) a Soviet politician, President 1984–85 and leader of the Communist Party

Cher·no·byl /tʃɜːˈnəʊbəl‖tʃər-/ a place in the former USSR where in 1986 an explosion at a NUCLEAR power station caused deaths and illnesses locally as well as POLLUTION over wide areas of Europe: *the Chernobyl disaster* | *We believe Koeberg could never become a Chernobyl.*

Cher·o·kee /ˈtʃerəkiː/ *n* [C;*the*+P] (a member of) a Native American people from the US states of North Carolina and Tennessee. The Cherokee had a form of government similar to that of the US which was called the **Cherokee Nation**. Many Cherokee died on the **Trail of Tears**, when they were forced to leave their lands and go to Indian Territory in what is now Oklahoma. −see also NATIVE AMERICAN (CULTURAL NOTE)

che·root /ʃəˈruːt/ *n* a CIGAR with both ends cut square

cher·ry /ˈtʃeri/ *n* 1 [C] a small soft fleshy red, yellow, or black round fruit with one hard seed in the middle: *a cherry tart* | *cherry red* (=a bright red) −see picture at FRUIT 2 [C;U] (the wood of) the tree on which this fruit grows: *a cherry orchard* 3 [C *usu. sing.*] *sl* the state of being without sexual experience; VIRGINITY (esp. in the phrase **lose one's cherry**) 4 **the cherry on the cake** also **the cherry on the top**− something else that is pleasant to have, in addition to what is expected: *The videos are primarily made to entertain people. If they learn something, it's the cherry on the top.* **another/a second**

bite at the cherry (BITE² (6)); **bowl of cherries** (BOWL¹ (4))

Cherry Or·chard /'·· ¡··/, **The** a play by Anton Chekhov about the changes for the worse suffered by the Russians who owned land and property

cher·ub /'tʃerəb/ n **1** a fat pretty usu. male child with small wings, as shown in old paintings **2** infml a charming pretty child **3** (pl. **cherubs** or **cherubim**) any of the winged ANGELs guarding the seat of God according to the Bible —compare SERAPH— ~ **ic** /tʃəˈruːbɪk/ adj — ~ **ically** /kli/ adv

cher·vil /'tʃɜːvɪl‖-'tʃɜːr-/ n [U] a strong-smelling garden plant (HERB) whose leaves are used to give a special taste to food

Ches·a·peake Bay /¡tʃesəpiːk 'beɪ/ a bay (body of water connected to the sea) on the US east coast, important for trade and shipping

Che·shire /'tʃeʃəʳ/ a COUNTY in NW England, famous for its hard cheese

Chesh·ire cat /¡·· '·/ n the cat in Lewis Carroll's children's story *Alice's Adventures in Wonderland* which disappeared slowly until only its smile remained: *She was grinning like a Cheshire cat.*

Cheshire cheese /¡·· '·/ n [U] hard, white, sourish cheese originally made in Cheshire

Cheshire Homes /'·· ¡·/ [the +P] (in Britain) places where very sick people can live and receive a lot of care and medical attention, although they are not expected to get better

Ches·il Bank /¡tʃezəl 'bæŋk/ also **Chesil Beach**— a long high bank of stones thrown up by the sea, stretching SE from the coast of Dorset, in S England, to the Isle of Portland

chess /tʃes/ n [U] a game for two players, who move their pieces in turn according to fixed rules across a board in an attempt to trap (CHECKMATE) their opponent's king. One player is described as 'black' and the other as 'white'.

chess·board /'tʃesbɔːd‖-bɔːrd/ n a square board with 64 black and white squares, each square being next to a square of a different colour, on which chess or DRAUGHTS is played

chess·man /'tʃesmæn/ also **chess piece**— n **-men** /men/ any one of the 16 black or 16 white pieces used in the game of chess: *She set up the chessmen, ready to play.*

chest /tʃest/ n **1** the upper front part of the body between the neck and the stomach, enclosing the heart and lungs: *a hairy chest* | *He's got a weak chest.* (=he gets a lot of coughs and colds) | *a sweater chest size 38* —compare BREAST¹ **2** (the amount contained in) a large strong box in which valuable objects are kept, goods packed, etc.: *a chest of tea* —see also CHEST OF DRAWERS, HOPE CHEST, TEA CHEST, and see picture at CONTAINER **3 get something off one's chest** to bring a worry out into the open by talking about it **4 -chested** /tʃestₗd/ having a chest of the stated kind: *a flat-chested woman* (=with small breasts)

chessmen

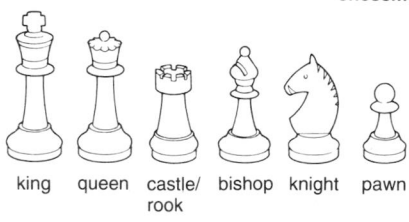

king   queen   castle/   bishop   knight   pawn
                 rook

Ches·ter /'tʃestəʳ/ a town in Cheshire in NW England, where the local government for that COUNTY is based. It has many historical buildings, and there is a wall around the old part of the town.

ches·ter·field /'tʃestəfiːld‖-ər-/ n a long seat (COUCH) with a back and sides, thickly filled out with comfortable soft material and usu. covered with leather

Ches·ter·ton /'tʃestətən‖-tər-/, **G K** (1874–1936) an English writer whose best-known stories are about Father Brown, a priest who uses his clever mind to explain or find the answer to crimes

chest·nut¹ /'tʃesnʌt/ n **1** [C] a smooth reddish-brown nut that stays enclosed in a smooth case until ripe, and can be cooked and eaten **2** [C;U] (the wood of) the tree (**chestnut tree**) on which this nut grows **3** [C;U] HORSE CHESTNUT —see picture at TREE **4** [C] a reddish-brown horse **5** [C] infml a joke or story so old and well-known that it is no longer funny or interesting: *His speeches are always full of old chestnuts.* **6 pull someone's chestnuts out of the fire** BrE infml to save someone from a difficult situation, esp. at the LAST MINUTE

chestnut² adj deep reddish-brown: *her chestnut hair*

chest of drawers /¡· · '·/ also **bureau** AmE— n a piece of furniture with several drawers, usu. used for holding clothes

chest·y /'tʃesti/ adj infml **1** esp. BrE showing or suffering from disease of the chest: *a chesty cough* | *He was a bit chesty, so I didn't send him to school.* **2** derog having large breasts —**ily** adv

che·val glass /ʃəˈvæl glɑːs‖-glæs/ n a long movable mirror in an upright frame

chev·a·lier /¡ʃevəˈlɪəʳ/ n rare a KNIGHT, esp. one who is a member of certain honourable associations: *a Chevalier of the Legion of Honour in France*

Che·val·i·er /ʃəˈvælieɪ/, **Maur·ice** /'mɒrɪs‖'mɔː-/ (1888–1972) a French actor, singer, and entertainer who appeared on stage, film, and television around the world and was known for his charm and for his easily recognizable voice, esp. when he spoke or sang in English with a French ACCENT

Chev·i·ot Hills /¡tʃeviət 'hɪlz/ also **Cheviots**— [the + P] a range of hills between England and Scotland

Chev·ro·let /ˈʃevrəleɪ‖¡ʃevrəˈleɪ/ n also **Chevy** infml – tdmk an American car. The Chevrolet is usually thought of as a large family car. Many American people have grown up with these cars, and connect them with their youth: *I remember those evenings, kissing in the back seat of the old Chevy.*

chev·ron /'ʃevrən/ n a piece of cloth in the shape V or Λ, worn on the SLEEVE of a uniform to show the wearer's rank

Chev·y /'ʃevi/ n infml a CHEVROLET

chew¹ /tʃuː/ v [I (**on**);T (**up**)] **1** to crush or keep biting with the teeth: *Chew your food well before you swallow it.* | *The dog was chewing on a bone.* | *He can't chew without his false teeth.* | *to chew tobacco* **2 chew the cud** infml to think deeply before making a decision **3 chew the fat** infml to have a long conversation about many subjects; CHAT: *We sat there drinking beer and chewing the fat until it was time to go home.* —see also **bite off more than one can chew** (BITE¹)

chew sbdy. ↔ **out** phr v [T] infml, esp. AmE to speak angrily to: *He chewed out his secretary for being late to work.*

chew sthg. ↔ **over** phr v [T] infml to think about (a question, problem, etc.): *I'll chew it over for a few days and then let you have my answer.*

chew² n **1** [S] an act of chewing **2** [C] a sweet or piece of tobacco made to be chewed but not always swallowed: *a chew of tobacco* | *a penny chew* (=a sweet bought for a small sum of money)

chewing gum /'·· ·/ also **gum**— n [U] a sticky substance usu. having a special, often sweet, taste, made to be chewed but not swallowed. Children often get rid of their chewing gum by sticking it under their chairs or desks in school, sometimes intending to chew it again later.

chew·y /'tʃuːi/ adj (of food) needing to be chewed; not very soft: *chewy meat/toffees*

Chey·enne /ʃaɪˈæn/ n [C;the+P] (a member of) a Native American people of the western plains of the US —see NATIVE AMERICAN (CULTURAL NOTE)

Chiang Kai-shek /¡tʃæŋ ¡kaɪ 'ʃek/ (1887–1975) a Chinese politician who ruled Taiwan after the Nationalist government was forced out of MAINLAND China by the Communists in 1949

Chi·an·ti /kiˈænti‖kiˈɑːnti/ n [U] a red Italian wine

Chi·an·ti·shire /kiˈæntiʃəʳ/ humor an area of Tuscany, in Italy, where many upper-class British people live or go to stay: *The Nielsens are off there, too, to Chiantishire, or Tuscany as the Italians like to call it.*

chi·a·ro·scu·ro /kɪˌɑːrəˈskʊərəʊ/ n [U] *tech* the arrangement or treatment of light and dark parts in a picture

chic /ʃiːk/ n [U] good style, esp. in one's manner or the way one dresses; a fashionable SOPHISTICATED quality: *She wears her clothes with great chic.* —**chic** *adj* : *a chic little hat* — ~ly *adv*

Chi·ca·go /ʃ³ˈkɑːgəʊ/ a large city in the US state of Illinois, beside Lake Michigan. Chicago is the third largest city in the US, and an important industrial centre. Among its many SKYSCRAPERs (=very tall buildings) is the **Sears Tower**, the tallest building in the world at 443 m. Chicago is known for its MUSEUMs, such as the **Art Institute**, and its universities, such as the **University of Chicago** and **Northwestern University**. During PROHIBITION in the 1930s, the city was known for its GANGSTERs (=criminals), esp. Al Capone. Chicago is sometimes known as **the Windy City**. —see colour map on pages 1374-5

Chicago Board of Trade /·,·· ·ˈ· · ·/ [the] an important market in Chicago, US, in which future contracts for the delivery of commodities (COMMODITY (1)) are bought and sold

Chicago Trib·une /·,·· ˈ··/ [the] a daily newspaper produced in Chicago, in the US, which is thought of as the voice of the people of the Middle West —see also extra information on page 896

chi·ca·ne·ry /ʃɪˈkeɪnəri/ n [U] deception; dishonest and deceitful practice

Chi·ca·no /tʃɪˈkɑːnəʊ/ n -nos *old-fash AmE* a US citizen from Mexico, or whose family came from Mexico: *Many Chicanos live in the Southwest of the US.*

Chich·es·ter /ˈtʃɪtʃɪstəʳ/ a town in West Sussex in England where the local government for that COUNTY is based

Chichester, Sir Francis (1901–72) an English YACHTSMAN who sailed alone round the world in 1966–67 in his boat Gipsy Moth IV

chi·chi /ˈʃiːʃiː/ *adj infml, rather derog* trying to be fashionable but appearing too showy or decorated

Chi-Chi /ˈtʃiː tʃiː/ a famous PANDA that lived in London Zoo

chick /tʃɪk/ n **1** a baby bird, esp. a chicken: *chicks cheeping for their mother* **2** *old-fash sl* a young woman. Many women find this word offensive.

chick·a·dee /ˈtʃɪkədiː/ n *AmE* **1** a small American bird **2** **My little chickadee** *AmE* a phrase used as an expression of fondness (first used by W C Fields in the film of the same name)

chick·en¹ /ˈtʃɪk³n/ n **1** [C] a common farmyard bird. A female chicken is a **hen** and a male chicken is a **cock** (*BrE*)/**rooster** (*AmE*): *He keeps chickens on his farm.* — see also CHICK, CLUCK¹ **2** [U] the meat of this bird eaten as food: *Do you like roast chicken?* | *chicken sandwiches* —see MEAT (USAGE)

▶CULTURAL NOTE In the US, soup made with chicken meat (**chicken soup**) is thought of as something that is good to eat when one is ill. ◀

3 [C] *sl* a person who lacks courage; coward: *Don't be such a chicken!* **4** [U] *infml* a children's game to test one's courage: *to play chicken* **5 one's chickens will/have come home to roost** one's bad or unwise actions will cause problems for one now **6 no (spring) chicken** *infml* no longer young —see also **count one's chickens before they're hatched** (COUNT¹)

chicken² *adj* [F] *sl* cowardly

chicken³ *v*
    chicken out *phr v* [I (**of**)] *derog sl* to decide not to do something because of being afraid: *I wanted to tell the director what I thought, but I chickened out (of it) at the last minute.*

chick·en·feed /ˈtʃɪk³nfiːd/ n [U] *sl* a small unimportant amount of money: *The bank offered to lend us £1000 but it's chickenfeed compared to what we need.*

chicken-fried steak /·,·· · ˈ·/ n [C,U] *AmE* a thin piece of BEEF coated with BREADCRUMBs and cooked in hot fat

chick·en·heart·ed /ˌtʃɪk³nˈhɑːtɪd◄‖-ɑːr-/ also **chicken-livered** *adj esp. lit* lacking courage; cowardly — ~ness *n* [U]

chicken Ki·ev /ˌ··· ˈ··/ n [U] a dish consisting of chicken breasts containing butter that has been given a special taste, esp. with GARLIC and PARSLEY

Chicken Lit·tle /ˌ··· ˈ··/ a story for children in which a chicken called Chicken Little thinks that the sky is falling and persuades many other animal friends that great danger is coming

chicken-liv·ered /ˌtʃɪk³n ˈlɪvəd◄ ‖ -vərd/ *adj AmE infml* cowardly: *You chicken-livered idiot!*

chicken pox /ˈ··· ·/ n [U] an infectious disease, caught esp. by children, which causes a slight fever and spots on the skin

chick·en·shit /ˈtʃɪk³nʃɪt/ n *AmE taboo* a person who lacks courage; COWARD

chicken wire /ˈ··· ·/ n [U] wire netting with HEXAGONAL-shaped holes used esp. for enclosing an area for chickens

chick·pea /ˈtʃɪkpiː/ n ‖ also **garbanzo**, **garbanzo bean** *AmE* (the bushy plant that produces) a seed like the common PEA but bigger, which is often eaten as food. Chick peas are the main vegetable in HUMMUS, a dish from the Middle East which is popular in the US and Britain.

chick·weed /ˈtʃɪkwiːd/ n [U] any of a large family of plants, esp. a common garden WEED with small white flowers

chic·le /ˈtʃɪkəl/ n [U] the thickened juice (GUM²) of a tropical American tree used in making CHEWING GUM

chic·o·ry /ˈtʃɪkəri/ n [U] **1** a thick-rooted European plant with blue flowers whose leaves are eaten raw as a vegetable **2** a powder made from the dried crushed roots of this plant and sometimes added to coffee to give a special taste

chide /tʃaɪd/ *v* **chided** or **chid** /tʃɪd/, **chid** or **chidden** /ˈtʃɪdn/ [I;T (**for, with**)] *fml* or *lit* to speak to (someone who has done wrong) angrily; REBUKE

chief¹ /tʃiːf/ n **1** [(**of**)] a leader, ruler, or head; the person in a group, party, organization, etc. who has the highest rank: *The Queen is chief of the armed forces by right.* | *the chief of police* (=of the police department) | *an American Indian tribal chief* **2** *old-fash infml* (used as a polite form of address by one man to another) **3 in chief** *lit* most of all; in particular **4 -in-chief** /ˌ· ·ˈ·/ having the highest rank: *In the Second World War Eisenhower was commander-in-chief of the Allied armed forces.* **5 too many chiefs and not enough Indians** *infml* too many people in charge of something, and not enough people to actually do the work

chief² *adj* [A] **1** highest in rank: *the chief clerk* | *chief priest* | *the chief political correspondent on the Washington Post* | *the chief executive of IBM* **2** most important; main: *Rice is the chief crop in this area.* | *the chief cause of crime* | *the chief thing to remember* | *the prosecution's chief witness* —see also CHIEFLY

chief con·sta·ble /ˌ· ˈ···◄/ n a British police officer in charge of the police in a large area

chief cook and bot·tle-wash·er /ˌ· ·· · ˈ·· ˌ··/ n *infml humor* a person who is in charge of an event, esp. someone who has to do a lot of small unimportant jobs to make sure it goes well: *"Is there any more wine?" "Ask my husband — he's the chief cook and bottle-washer today!"*

Chief Ex·ec·u·tive /ˌ· ·ˈ···/ n [the] *AmE* the President of the US

chief ex·ec·u·tive of·fic·er /ˌ· ·ˈ··· ˌ···/ n **1** *AmE* also **CEO** a MANAGING DIRECTOR **2** *BrE* someone in a higher position than the MANAGING DIRECTOR in a company

chief in·spect·or /ˌ· ·ˈ···◄/ n (*often caps.*) a British police officer of middle rank: *Chief Inspector Jones*

chief jus·tice /ˌ· ˈ···/ n (*often caps.*) the head judge of a court of justice, esp. (in the US) of the Supreme Court: *Chief Justice Warren E Burger* —see also extra information on page 742

chief·ly /ˈtʃiːfli/ *adv* **1** mainly; mostly but not wholly: *Bread is made chiefly of flour.* | *The accident happened chiefly as a result of carelessness.* | *The company is chiefly concerned with computer software.* **2** above all; especially: *Chiefly, I ask you to remember to write to your mother.*

chief of staff /ˌ· · ˈ·/ n **chiefs of staff** (*often caps.*) **1** a high-ranking officer in the armed forces who serves as main adviser to a commander **2** the high-ranking official who advises the leader of a service organization, or group of employees: *the White House Chief of Staff* **3** one of the JOINT CHIEFS OF STAFF

Chief Rab·bi /ˌ· ˈ··/ n [the] the main leader of the JEWISH religion in a country

chief su·per·in·ten·dent /ˌ· ····'···◄/ n (often caps.) a British police officer of high rank: Chief Superintendent Brown

chief·tain /'tʃiːftṣn/ n the leader of a tribe or similar group, esp. of a Scottish CLAN; chief − ~ship n [C;U]

Chief Whip /ˌ· '·/ [the] (in British politics) a leading member of a political party who encourages active support for the party and its ideas and makes sure that party members attend meetings and vote

chif·fon /'ʃɪfɒn‖ʃɪ'fɑːn/ n [U] a soft thin silky material used for scarves (SCARF), evening dresses, etc.: a pink chiffon nightdress

chif·fo·nier , **-fonnier** /ˌʃɪfə'nɪəʳ/ n   **1** a high CHEST OF DRAWERS; TALLBOY   **2** a low movable cupboard with a top that can be used as a side table at meals

chig·ger /'tʃɪgəʳ/ n AmE a tiny insect which lives in tall grass. Chiggers bite animals and humans and suck blood.

chi·gnon /'ʃiːnjɒn‖-jɑːn/ n Fr a knot of hair worn at the back of a woman's head

chi·hua·hua /tʃɪ'wɑːwə/ n a type of very small dog

chil·blain /'tʃɪlbleɪn/ n a red painful swelling usu. on the toes or fingers, caused by coldness and poor blood supply

child /tʃaɪld/ n **child·ren** /'tʃɪldrən/   **1** a young human being of either sex, from before birth to the completion of physical development: I've lived in this house since I was a child. | The disease is common among young children. | She's an only child. (=She has no brothers or sisters.) | (fig.) Peter's a child (=inexperienced) in money matters. −see USAGE   **2** a son or daughter of any age: They have two children; their son is a doctor and their daughter is an architect. | Will you go and collect the children from school?   **3** [(of)] someone who is very influenced by a stated person, place, or situation: We are all children of the nuclear age.   **4 children should be seen and not heard** a phrase used esp. in Victorian times to tell children to be quiet and not talk. The phrase is now used to talk about this old-fashioned idea of how children should behave.   **5 get someone/be with child** old use or bibl to make someone/be PREGNANT   **6 give me/us a child until it is seven and it is mine/ours for life** a saying believed to have been expressed first by the Jesuits −see JESUIT   **7 great/heavy with child** old use or bibl (of a woman) near the time of giving birth −see also BRAINCHILD   **8 never work with children or animals** a phrase often said by people who work in the world of acting, as children and animals are believed to be difficult to work with, and also to get all the attention and praise because they are very sweet

▷ USAGE A very young **child** under the age of about 18 months, is a **baby** or (more formally) an **infant**. A child who has just learned to walk is a **toddler**. A child up to the age of 9 or 10 is sometimes called a **little girl** or **little boy**, esp. by adults, and **girl** or **boy** can be used about anyone up to the age of about 20. However, someone aged between 13 and 19 may prefer to be called a **teenager** or a **young woman** or **young man**. Teenagers are sometimes called **young adults**, esp. where their health or social behaviour is being formally discussed. A younger teenager may also be formally called an **adolescent**, but this word often shows disapproval. A **youth** is an older, usu. male, teenager, but this word, too, usu. shows disapproval: The police arrested several youths who were fighting. To talk generally about anyone between the ages of about 10 and 25, people would usu. say simply **young people** or (more formally) **the young**. −see also GIRL (USAGE)   **2 Kid** (infml) is used both for **children**: Let's take the kids to the park, and (especially in American English) for young people: We met a group of college kids.◁

Child, Ju·li·a /'dʒuːliə/ (1912−   ) an American CHEF (=professional cook) who has taught cooking through her popular television programmes and books. Her high voice is easily recognized by many Americans.

child a·buse /'· ·ˌ·/ n [U] the act of causing deliberate physical harm, either violent or sexual, to a child, or cruelty, or lack of attention which might be harmful to a child: the current alarming increase in cases of child abuse | a helpline for victims of child abuse − ~ r n

▶ CULTURAL NOTE Child abuse appears to be a growing problem in both Britain and the US, and it is receiving a great deal of attention from the public, the MEDIA, and both governments. Action is being taken to deal with it through

social care agencies, SOCIAL WORKERs, and the police. The public, teachers, and doctors are asked to report cases where they SUSPECT child abuse. It is often found to be a child's parents, esp. the father, who are responsible, but also sometimes it can be other family members, a teacher, or another person who looks after the child. In Britain, a child is often removed from the family home while the case is examined; child abusers are usu. considered to be criminals and are often sent to prison. In the US, though child abuse is illegal, the abusers are usu. offered COUNSELLING and support, and, wherever possible, families are kept together −see also CLEVELAND◄

child·bear·ing /'tʃaɪldˌbeərɪŋ/ n [U] the process of giving birth to children: women of childbearing age

child ben·e·fit /ˌ· '···/ also **family allowance** − n [U] (in Britain) a small sum of money paid weekly by the government to every family for each child

child·birth /'tʃaɪldbɜːθ ‖ -bɜːrθ/ n [U] the act of giving birth to a child

child·care /'· ·/ n [U] ‖ also **day care** AmE − the care of young children by people who are paid to do this: Mothers thinking of returning to work will obviously want to explore the pros and cons of different childcare arrangements. | inadequate childcare provision in Britain

child·hood /'tʃaɪldhʊd/ n [C usu. sing.; U] the state or time of being a child: He had a happy childhood in the country. −see also BOYHOOD, GIRLHOOD, SECOND CHILDHOOD

childhood sweet·heart /ˌ·· '··/ n someone of the opposite sex and of about the same age as oneself whom one knew and liked very much when one was a child: The end of the movie was so romantic; he married his childhood sweetheart.

child·ish /'tʃaɪldɪʃ/ adj   **1** of or for a child: the little girl's high childish voice   **2** derog unsuitable for an adult; IMMATURE (2): a childish remark | childish behaviour | It was very childish of him to lose his temper over something so unimportant. −compare CHILDLIKE − ~ly adv − ~ness n [U]

child·less /'tʃaɪldləs/ adj having no children, esp. when one would like to have children: a childless couple − ~ness n [U]

child·like /'tʃaɪldlaɪk/ adj often apprec (typical) of a child, esp. having a natural lovable quality: childlike trust − compare CHILDISH

Child·line /'tʃaɪldlaɪn/ a British telephone HELPLINE for children to call when they are frightened or have problems they cannot discuss with people they know

child·min·der /'tʃaɪldmaɪndəʳ/ ‖ also **nanny** or **baby-sitter** AmE − n someone who is paid to look after other people's children, usu. when both parents are at work and usu. in the childminder's own home. In Britain, the local authority checks to see that the childminder's home is safe for children, that they are responsible people, etc. −compare BABY-SITTER, NANNY −**ding** n [U]

child prod·i·gy /ˌ· '···/ n an INFANT PRODIGY

child·proof /'tʃaɪldpruːf/ also **child-re·sist·ant** /'· ·ˌ·/ adj not able to be damaged, opened, worked etc. by a child: a childproof bottle (= a bottle that a child cannot break or open)

chil·dren /'tʃɪldrən/ pl of CHILD

Children in Need /ˌ·· · '·/ a British CHARITY organization which raises money on television and helps children in Britain and abroad

children of Is·rael /ˌ··· · '··/ n [P] Bibl the JEWS

children's home /'·· ˌ·/ n a house provided by the state with professional carers to look after children whose parents cannot take care of them because of e.g. illness, imprisonment, death, or the child's own difficult behaviour

child sex·u·al a·buse /ˌ· ˌ···· ·'·/ n [U] sexual harm done to children −see CHILD ABUSE (CULTURAL NOTE)

child's play /'· ·/ n [U] something very easy to do: Going on a diet is child's play compared to giving up smoking.

child sup·port /'· ·ˌ·/ n [U] AmE money that a parent, usu. a father, must pay after DIVORCE to support children who live with the other parent: The court ordered him to pay $500 a month child support.

Chil·e /'tʃɪli/ a long, narrow South American country bordered in the W by the Pacific Ocean and in the E by the

Andes; capital Santiago; population 12,961,000 (1989) —**Chilean**

chili /'tʃɪli/ n [C;U] AmE for CHILLI

chill¹ /tʃɪl/ v **1** [I;T] to (cause to) become cold, esp. without freezing: *Put the wine in the fridge to chill.* | *You must be chilled to the bone after being out on such a cold day.* **2** [T] to cause a cold feeling of fear: *His menacing eyes chilled her.* | *a chilling murder story* **3** [T] esp. lit to discourage or lower the spirits of: *Failure chilled his hopes.*
   chill out phr v [I] AmE sl to calm down or relax when one has become worried, angry, or over-excited: *Chill out! Have a beer — it's Friday!* | *Chill out, man, I didn't do it on purpose!*

chill² n **1** [C] an illness marked by coldness and shaking of the body: *Don't go out in this weather — you'll catch a chill.* **2** [S] a slightly unpleasant degree of coldness: *There was a chill in the air this morning.* —see also CHILLY **3** [S] an unpleasant sensation of coldness, esp. from fear or discouragement: *The bad news cast a chill over the meeting.* | *The thought of them finding out about it struck a chill into her heart.* **4** [S] coldness of manner; (a state of) unfriendliness: *Recent events have led to a chill in relations between the two countries.*

chill³ adj cold; chilly: *a chill wind* | (fig.) *a chill greeting*

chil·ler /'tʃɪlər/ n infml a film or book that is purposely made or written to be frightening

chil·li /'tʃɪli/ BrE ‖ also **chile, chili** AmE— n **chillies 1** [C] the very hot-tasting seed case of a kind of PEPPER plant **2** [U] also **chilli powder**— a hot red powder made from this, used for giving a special taste to food, esp. Indian, African, or Mexican food —compare PEPPER **3** [U] also **chilli con car·ne** /ˌtʃɪli kən 'kɑːni‖-'kɑːr-/— a dish of meat and beans cooked with this powder

chill·y /'tʃɪli/ adj **1** rather cold; cold enough to be uncomfortable: *It soon became chilly when the fire went out.* | *I feel chilly without a coat.* **2** unfriendly: *a chilly stare/welcome* **3** causing fear, anxiety, or discouragement: *the chilly facts* —**iness** n [S;U]

Chil·tern Hills /ˌtʃɪltən 'hɪlz‖-tərn-/ also **Chilterns**— [the + P] a range of hills in SE England

Chiltern Hun·dreds /ˌ·· '··/ n [the + P] the job of representing a particular government area in Buckinghamshire in Britain which no longer exists. Members of Parliament **apply for the Chiltern Hundreds** when they want to stop working before the next GENERAL ELECTION.

chime¹ /tʃaɪm/ n **1** the sound made (as if) by a set of bells: *The chime of the clock woke him up.* **2** [usu. pl.] a set of bells rung to produce a tune

chime² v **1** [I;T] to (cause to) ring: *The church bells chimed.* **2** [T] to show (the time) by ringing: *The clock chimed one o'clock.* **3** [I (TOGETHER, with)] infml to be in accordance or agreement: *Her views on this chime with mine.*
   chime in phr v [I (with)] infml to interrupt or join in a conversation by expressing an opinion: *He's always ready to chime in with his opinion.* | *"I want to come, too."* she chimed in.

chi·me·ra, -maera /kaɪ'mɪərə, kɪ-/ n **1** an imaginary terrible female creature, made up of parts of different animals, which breathes fire **2** a dream that can never become true; unreal fancy

chi·me·ri·cal /kaɪ'merɪkəl, kɪ-/ adj often derog imaginary; fanciful: *chimerical ideas/plans*

chim·ney /'tʃɪmni/ n **1** a hollow passage often rising above the roof of a building which allows smoke and gases to pass from a fire: *factory chimneys pouring smoke into the air* —see picture at HOUSE
   ▶ CULTURAL NOTE Santa Claus is believed to come down people's chimneys on Christmas Eve to bring them their presents. —see colour picture on page 1212◀
   2 tech a narrow passage on a rock face, up which one can climb —see picture at MOUNTAIN **3** a glass tube often wide at the centre and narrow at the top, that is put around a flame in an oil lamp

chim·ney·breast /'tʃɪmnibrest/ n esp. BrE the wall which encloses a chimney and stands out into a room —compare MANTELPIECE

chimney cor·ner /'·· ˌ··/ n a seat by the side of a large open fireplace

chim·ney·piece /'tʃɪmnipiːs/ n old-fash a wooden or brick

decorative covering fixed onto or built into the wall above and around the fire; MANTELPIECE

chim·ney·pot /'tʃɪmnipɒt‖-pɑːt/ n a short pipe made of metal or esp. EARTHENWARE (=baked clay), fixed to the top of a chimney —see picture at HOUSE

chim·ney·stack /'tʃɪmnistæk/ n **1** the tall chimney of a building such as a factory **2** BrE a group of small chimneys sticking up from a roof

chim·ney·sweep /'tʃɪmni-swiːp/ also **sweep** infml— n a person whose job is cleaning the insides of chimneys. In the past, chimney-sweeps often employed children to climb up into the chimneys, and often treated them badly. Now they use special long brushes. In Britain chimney-sweeps are believed to bring good luck, and some people will go to shake their hand, or even invite a chimney-sweep to their WEDDING, for this reason.

chim·pan·zee /ˌtʃɪmpæn'ziː, -pən-/ also **chimp** /tʃɪmp/ infml— n a dark-haired African APE (=large monkey without a tail). Chinpanzees are thought to be the most intelligent of the apes. In British ZOOs in the past chimps were often dressed in clothes, sat at tables and given food to have a **chimpanzees' tea party** for people to watch, but now this is felt to be cruel. —see picture at APE

chin /tʃɪn/ n **1** the front part of the face (esp. of a human being) below the mouth: *His chin was completely covered by his beard.* | *He punched me on the chin.* —see also DOUBLE CHIN, and see picture at HEAD **2** **(keep one's) chin up** infml to (try to) stay cheerful in a difficult situation: *He's having a pretty rough time but he seems to be keeping his chin up.* | *Chin up! Things can't get any worse!* — see also CHINLESS

chi·na /'tʃaɪnə/ n [U] **1** a hard white substance made by baking fine clay at high temperatures: *china cups* **2** also **chi·na·ware** /'tʃaɪnəweəʳ/— plates, cups, etc., made from china or a similar substance; CROCKERY: *Please put the china away carefully.* —see also BONE CHINA, **bull in a china shop** (BULL¹ (5))

China the largest country in E Asia, bordered by the former USSR and Mongolia to the N, the former USSR to the W, and Pakistan, India, Nepal, Bhutan, Myanmar, Laos, and Vietnam to the S; capital Beijing; population 1,133,692,000 (1990). China has the largest number of people of any country in the world, at over one BILLION. Chinese civilization is generally regarded as the oldest in the world. China was ruled by family dynasties (DYNASTY) until 1912 when it became a republic. In 1949 the Nationalists were defeated by the Communists and Mao Tse-tung declared China a People's Republic. —see also CHINESE, CONFUCIUS, CULTURAL REVOLUTION, GREAT LEAP FORWARD, GREAT WALL OF CHINA, LONG MARCH, MAO TSE-TUNG, MARCO POLO

China Sea /ˌ·· '·/ [the] a part of the Pacific Ocean, off the coast of China

China tea /ˌ·· '·/ n [U] a kind of tea grown in China, dried in smoke which gives it a special taste

Chi·na·town /'tʃaɪnətaʊn/ n [C;U] an area in a city where there are Chinese shops, restaurants, and clubs, and where many Chinese people live. The most famous Chinatown is in the US city of San Francisco.

chin·chil·la /ˌtʃɪn'tʃɪlə/ n [C;U] (the soft pale grey fur of) a small South American animal like a SQUIRREL with a long tail

chine /tʃaɪn/ n tech an animal's BACKBONE (=set of bones down the centre of the back) used as meat

Chi·nese /ˌtʃaɪ'niːz◀/ n **1** [the +P] people from China: *I like the Chinese.* **2** [U] the language of China. The spoken language varies widely across China but the written language is shared and understood everywhere. —see also CANTONESE, IDEOGRAM, MANDARIN **3** [C;U] infml (a restaurant serving) food of the kind eaten in China — **Chinese** adj : *I'm Chinese.* | *a Chinese vase*

Chinese cheq·uers /ˌ·· '··/ BrE ‖ **Chinese checkers** AmE— n [U] a game for two to six players in which small balls are moved from hole to hole on a board in the shape of a star

Chinese lan·tern /ˌ·· '··/ n a folding LANTERN or decoration like a lantern made of thin, usu. brightly coloured paper

Chinese medi·cine /ˌ·· '·· ‖ ·· '···/ n [U] the method of preventing and treating illness that is customarily practised in China, which uses Chinese HERBs, and may include ACUPUNCTURE. Still new to Britain and the US, this method is considered an ALTERNATIVE MEDICINE.

Chinese wall /ˌ·· ˈ·/ *n* a problem which seems too difficult to defeat

Chinese whis·pers /ˌ·· ˈ··/ *BrE* ‖ usu. **telephone** *AmE—n* [S] a game in which someone WHISPERS (= talks very quietly) a sentence into another's ear, who then whispers what has been heard to a third person and so on until the last person has been told. The last person then tells the group the sentence, which is usually completely different from the original and makes people laugh.

Chin·gach·gook /tʃɪnˈɡaːtʃɡʊk/ the Indian chief in a number of stories by James Fenimore Cooper about Native American life

chink[1] /tʃɪŋk/ *n* [(in)] **1** [C] a narrow crack or opening: *He watched the girls through a chink in the wall.* **2** [C] a narrow beam (of light) shining through such a crack: *a chink of light in the darkness of the room* **3** [C] a small but dangerous fault or weakness: *a tiny chink in his argument | She prepared for the talks very carefully, knowing that any* **chink in her armour** (=weaknesses in her defence or argument) *would be seized upon.* **4** [S] the sound of chinking (CHINK[2]): *I heard the chink of glasses next door.*

chink[2] *v* to make a high sound like that of glasses hitting each other; CLINK[1]

Chink *n taboo derog sl* a Chinese person

Chink·ie , Chinky /ˈtʃɪŋki/ *n* **1** *BrE infml* a TAKEAWAY which sells Chinese food **2** *taboo derog sl* a Chinese person

chin·less /ˈtʃɪnləs/ *adj* **1** having a chin that is small or slopes inwards **2** *BrE infml* weak and cowardly

chinless won·der /ˌ·· ˈ··/ *n BrE sl* a man from an upper-class family who appears to be rather stupid

chi·nos /ˈtʃiːnəʊz/ *n* [P] *AmE* trousers made from **chino**, a strong cotton material. They are produced in many different colours and are very popular, esp. with young men, because they are usu. inexpensive. —see PAIR (USAGE)

chin·strap /ˈtʃɪnstræp/ *n* the band round the chin, which helps to keep a HELMET in place

chintz /tʃɪnts/ *n* [U] cotton cloth printed with usu. flowery patterns, used for making curtains, furniture covers, etc.

chintz·y /ˈtʃɪntsi/ *adj* **1** made of or looking like chintz **2** *AmE infml* cheap and of low value

chin up /ˌ· ·/ also **pull up** *n AmE* an exercise in which one hangs on to a bar and pulls up one's body weight until one's chin is above the bar: *He did ten chin ups in quick succession.*

chin·wag /ˈtʃɪnwæɡ/ *n* [S] *BrE infml* an informal conversation; CHAT

chips

chips *BrE/*
French fries *AmE*

crisps *BrE/*
chips *AmE & AustrE*

chip[1] /tʃɪp/ *n* **1** a small piece broken off something: *a chip of glass/wood | chocolate chip cookies* —see picture at PIECE **2** a mark left when a small piece is broken off or knocked out of an object: *There's a chip in this cup.* **3** [usu. pl.] *BrE* ‖ **French fry** *AmE*— a long thin piece of potato cooked in deep fat: *She was frying chips. | oven-cooked chips* —see also FISH AND CHIPS

▶ CULTURAL NOTE 1 British people are known to be fond of fish and chips eaten together, but chips may be served as part of any main course or may be bought separately from a TAKEAWAY and eaten with salt and VINEGAR or tomato KETCHUP. 2 In Britain and the US many people now try to eat fewer chips because of their high fat content, which is felt to be unhealthy. There is a well-known phrase **chips with everything** which is used to describe a particular kind of poor quality British food in which everything is served with chips: *In British schools in the old days it used to be*

chips with everything, but now they have brought in the dieticians. ◀

4 [usu. pl.] also **potato chip**— *AmE & AustrE for* CRISP[1] **5** a flat plastic object (COUNTER[2] (2)) used for representing money in certain games **6** also **microchip, silicon chip**— a very small piece of SILICON containing a set of ELECTRONIC parts and their connections, which is used in computers and other machines —compare INTEGRATED CIRCUIT **7** a shot or kick in football, RUGBY, etc. in which the ball is sent into the air, esp. over an opposing player, and travels only a short distance **8** a short GOLF shot that sends the ball high in the air and onto the green **9** **a chip off the old block** *infml, often apprec* a person very like his or her mother or father in character **10** **have a 'chip on one's shoulder** *infml* to be quarrelsome or easily offended, esp. as a result of feeling unfairly treated: *He's got a chip on his shoulder about not having gone to university.* **11** **have had one's chips** *BrE infml* to have lost one's power, position, life, etc.: *I'm afraid we've had our chips — the company has gone bankrupt.* **12** **when the chips are down** *infml* when a very important point is reached at which an important decision has to be made or serious action taken: *When the chips are down, you have only yourself to depend on.* —see also BLUE CHIP

chip[2] *v* **-pp-** **1** [I;T] to (cause to) lose a small piece from the surface or edge, e.g. by breaking or dropping: *This china chips easily. | Someone's chipped my best glass. | I'm afraid I've chipped a piece out of/off this saucer.* **2** [T] *esp. BrE* to cut potatoes into small pieces ready to be cooked as CHIPS[1] (3) **3** [T] (in football, GOLF, etc.) to kick or hit (a ball) in a short, high ARC

chip away *phr v* **1** [T] (**chip** sthg. ↔ **away**) to destroy bit by bit, by breaking small pieces off: *I chipped away the damaged brick and replaced it with a new one.* **2** [I (**at**)] to (try to) break small pieces of something: *He was chipping away at the rock with a hammer.*

chip in *phr v infml* **1** [I (**with**); T+*that*] to enter a conversation between other people with an opinion: *John chipped in with a remark/chipped in that it was time to go home.* **2** [I (**with**);T (=**chip in** sthg.)] to add (one's share of money): *If everyone chips in (a pound) we could get her something really nice.*

chip·board /ˈtʃɪpbɔːd‖-bɔːrd/ *n* [U] board made from waste pieces of wood mixed with glue, used as a building material

chip·munk /ˈtʃɪpmʌŋk/ also **ground squirrel** *n* a small American animal like a SQUIRREL with a long bushy tail and black-and-white bands along its back

chip·o·la·ta /ˌtʃɪpəˈlɑːtə/ *n* a small thin SAUSAGE

chip pan /ˈ· ·/ *n* a deep pan with a wire basket inside used for cooking esp. CHIPS (= potatoes cut into usu. long thin pieces and cooked in oil)

Chip·pen·dale /ˈtʃɪpəndeɪl/ *adj, n* [U] (of or being) an 18th-century English furniture style known for its graceful shape and fine decoration: *Chippendale chairs*

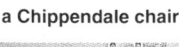

a Chippendale chair

Chip·pen·dales /ˈtʃɪpəndeɪlz/ , **The** an American group of attractive men with well-developed muscles who entertain women by performing in a show in which they remove most of their clothes

chip·per /ˈtʃɪpər/ *adj esp. AmE* cheerful and active; SPRIGHTLY

Chip·pe·wa /ˈtʃɪpəwɑː/ [C;*the +P*] (a member of) a Native American people of the US state of Michigan, also called **Ojibwa** —see NATIVE AMERICAN (CULTURAL NOTE)

chip·ping /ˈtʃɪpɪŋ/ *n* [*usu. pl.*] *esp. BrE* a small rough piece of stone used when putting new surfaces on roads, railway tracks, etc.: *loose chippings on the road*

chip·py /ˈtʃɪpi/ *n N Eng sl* a shop which sells cooked fish and CHIPS[1] (3)

chip shop /ˈ· ·/ also **chippy** *n* a shop which cooks and sells CHIPS (CHIP[1] (3)), fish, PIEs etc. which are usu. taken away to eat. Chip shops are very popular in Britain esp. when people want a quick cheap meal.

Chi·rac /ˈʃɪəræk‖ʃɪəˈrɑːk/, **Jacques** /ʒæk‖ʒɑːk/ (1932–   ) a French RIGHT-WING politician who was Prime Minister from 1974 to 1976 and 1986 to 1988

chi·ro·man·cy /ˈkaɪrəmænsi/ n [U] *tech* the art or practice of telling someone's character or their future by examining their hands; PALMISTRY

chi·rop·o·dist /kɪˈrɒpədɪst, ʃɪ-‖-ˈrɑː-/ also **podiatrist** *esp. AmE*– n a person who looks after the human foot and treats diseases of the foot —**dy** n [U]

chi·ro·prac·tic /ˈkaɪərəpræktɪk/ n [U] the method of treating back, joint, and muscle pain by feeling and pressing the bones, esp. those of the back and neck —**tor** n

chirp /tʃɜːp‖tʃɜːrp/ also **chir·rup** /ˈtʃɪrəp‖ˈtʃɪ-, ˈtʃɜː-/‖-/ v **1** [I (AWAY)] to make the short sharp sound(s) of small birds or some insects **2** [I;T (OUT)] to say or speak in a way that sounds like this —**chirp** n

chirp·y /ˈtʃɜːpi‖ˈtʃɜːrpi/ adj *infml, esp. BrE* happy and cheerful; LIGHT-HEARTED: *a chirpy little song* | *in a chirpy mood* —**ily** adv —**iness** n [U]

chis·el¹ /ˈtʃɪzəl/ n a metal tool with a sharp cutting edge at the end of a blade, used for cutting into or shaping wood, stone, etc. —see picture at TOOL

chisel² v -ll- *BrE* ‖ -l- *AmE* **1** [I;T+obj+adv/prep] to cut or shape with a chisel: *She chiselled an inscription on the marble.* | *He chiselled a hole in the door to fit a new lock.* —see also COLD CHISEL **2** [T (**out of**)] *old-fash sl* **a** to trick; deceive: *He's chiselled me out of £5!* **b** to obtain by deceit

▷ USAGE You can **chisel** wood or stone **into** a shape; **chisel (out)** a shape **from, in,** or **out of** wood or stone; or **chisel** words, etc. **on** a wooden or stone surface.◁

chis·el·ler *BrE* ‖ **-eler** *AmE* /ˈtʃɪzələr/ n *old-fash sl* a person who gets things by deceitful and unfair practices

Chis·holm /ˈtʃɪzəm/ , **Shir·ley** /ˈʃɜːli ‖ ˈʃɜːr-/ (1924–   ) an American politician, who was the first black woman to be elected to CONGRESS (1969–83)

Chisholm Trail /ˈ·· ˌ·/ n a path leading from Texas to Kansas along which cattle were driven in the late 1800s. There is an old popular song about the Chisholm Trail.

chit¹ /tʃɪt/ n a short letter, esp. a signed note showing money owed or paid: *He'd brought a chit from the manager entitling him to collect the goods.*

chit² n *old-fash infml, often derog* a spirited and usu. disrespectful young woman: *a chit of a girl*

chit·chat /ˈtʃɪt-tʃæt/ n [U] *infml* informal light conversation or GOSSIP —**chitchat** v [I] **-tt-**

chit·ter·lings /ˈtʃɪtəlɪŋz‖-ər-/ also **chit·lings** /ˈtʃɪtlɪŋz/ **chitlins**— n [P] *esp. AmE* the INTESTINES of a pig eaten as food. These are one of the foods regarded as SOUL FOOD by black people in the US.

Chit·ty Chit·ty Bang Bang /ˌtʃɪti tʃɪti ˈbæŋ bæŋ/ a film and song about a car of the same name which has a character of its own and can fly

chiv·al·rous /ˈʃɪvəlrəs/ adj (esp. of men) showing bravery, honour, generosity, and good manners, esp. to women: *A chivalrous old gentleman opened the door for her.* —~ **ly** adv

chiv·al·ry /ˈʃɪvəlri/ n [U] **1** (in the MIDDLE AGES) the beliefs or practices of noble soldiers (KNIGHTS) as a group **2** the qualities (such as bravery, honour, generosity, and kindness to the weak and poor) which this system aimed at developing **3** **the age of chivalry is dead/gone** men no longer behave in the old gentle, polite way towards women. Sometimes if a man opens a door, for example, for a lady, someone may say approvingly or jokingly, "You see, the age of chivalry is not dead."

chives /tʃaɪvz/ n [P] a plant related to the onion, with narrow grasslike leaves used for giving a special taste to food

chiv·y , chivvy /ˈtʃɪvi/ v [T (UP, ALONG)] *infml* to urge (someone) to do something or to hurry, esp. in an annoying way: *I'll have to chivy the children up/along, otherwise they'll be late for school.* [+obj +to-v] *She chivied him to help her with all the paperwork.*

Chloe , Chloë /ˈkləʊi/ see DAPHNIS AND CHLOE

chlo·ride /ˈklɔːraɪd/ n [C;U] a chemical compound that is a mixture of chlorine with another substance, often used for cleaning and disinfecting: *sodium chloride*

chlo·ri·nate /ˈklɔːrɪneɪt/ v [T] to disinfect by putting in chlorine: *Water is usually chlorinated in public swimming pools to keep it pure.* | *chlorinated water* —**nation** /ˌklɔːrɪˈneɪʃən/ n [U]

chlo·rine /ˈklɔːriːn/ n [U] a greenish-yellow strong-smelling gas that is a simple substance (ELEMENT) and is found in many chemical compounds. It is usu. added to the water in public swimming pools to help to keep it clean.

chlo·ro·fluo·ro·car·bon /ˌklɔːrəʊfluərəʊˈkɑːbən‖-ˈkɑːr-/ n see CFC

chlor·o·form¹ /ˈklɒrəfɔːm, ˈklɔː-‖ˈklɔːrəfɔːrm/ n [U] a colourless strong-smelling poisonous chemical used as an ANAESTHETIC (=a substance that makes people unable to feel anything)

chloroform² v [T] to make unconscious with chloroform: *The kidnappers tied him up and then chloroformed him.*

chlo·ro·phyll /ˈklɒrəfɪl, ˈklɔː-‖ˈklɔː-/ n [U] the green-coloured substance in the stems and leaves of plants

choc /tʃɒk‖tʃɑːk, tʃɔːk/ also **choc·cy** /ˈtʃɒki‖ˈtʃɑː-, ˈtʃɔː-/— n [*usu. pl.*] a CHOCOLATE (2): *a box of chocs*

choc·a·hol·ic /ˌtʃɒkəˈhɒlɪk‖ˌtʃɑːkəˈhɔː-, ˌtʃɔːk-/ n a CHOCOHOLIC

choc-ice /ˈ·· ·/ *BrE* ‖ **ice cream bar** *AmE* – n a brick-shaped piece of ice cream with a covering of chocolate

chock¹ /tʃɒk‖tʃɑːk/ n a shaped piece of wood placed under a door, boat, barrel, or wheel to prevent it from moving; WEDGE. When an aircraft or other vehicle is ready to start moving, people sometimes shout "Chocks away!", meaning "remove the chocks".

chock² v [T (UP)] to hold in place or support with a chock

chock-a-block /ˌtʃɒk ə ˈblɒk◂‖ˈtʃɑːk ə ˌblɑːk/ adj, adv [F (**with**)] *infml* very crowded; packed tightly: *The road was chock-a-block with cars again today.*

chock-full /ˌ·· ˈ·◂/ adj [F (**of**)] *infml* completely full: *The train was chock-full of tourists.*

choc·o·hol·ic /ˌtʃɒkəˈhɒlɪk‖ˌtʃɑːkəˈhɔː-, ˌtʃɔːk-/ also **chocaholic**— n a person who cannot control the urge to eat chocolate

choco·late¹ /ˈtʃɒklət‖ˈtʃɑːkələt, ˈtʃɔːk-/ n **1** [U] a solid sweet usu. brown substance made by crushing the cooked seeds of a tropical American tree (CACAO), eaten as a sweet: *a piece/bar of chocolate* | *chocolate cake* | *chocolate biscuits* **2** [C] also **choc, choccy** *BrE infml*— a small sweet made by covering a centre, such as a nut, with this substance: *a half-pound box of chocolates* | *liqueur chocolates* —see also CHOCOLATES **3** [C;U] (a cupful of) a drink made from hot milk or water mixed with powder made from this substance: *a mug of hot chocolate* —compare COCOA; see also MILK CHOCOLATE, PLAIN CHOCOLATE

chocolate² adj of a variable usu. brownish grey colour – **chocolate** n [U]

chocolate box¹ /ˈ··· ·/ n a colourful attractive box in which chocolates are sold

chocolate-box² adj [A] *BrE derog* pretty or SENTIMENTAL (2), in the way that pictures on a BOX OF CHOCOLATES sometimes are: *a chocolate-box scene* **chocolate-boxy, chocolate-boxey** adj : *I didn't like the cottage much – too chocolate-boxy for my taste.*

chocolate chip cook·ie /ˌ··· ·ˈ··/ n *AmE* a sweet BISCUIT containing bits of chocolate. Chocolate chip cookies are one of Americans' favourite sweets. They are often baked at home, or are freshly baked by small stores.

chocolate milk /ˌ··· ˈ·/ n [U] milk which is mixed with chocolate powder

choco·lates /ˈtʃɒkləts‖ˈtʃɑːkələts, ˈtʃɔːk-/ n [P] a box containing CHOCOLATES¹ (2): *I gave her some chocolates as a small thank-you.*

Choc·taw /ˈtʃɒktɔː‖ˈtʃɑːk-/ n [C; *the*+P] (a member of) a Native American people from the southeastern US —see NATIVE AMERICAN (CULTURAL NOTE)

choice¹ /tʃɔɪs/ n **1** [C (**between**)] an act of choosing or a chance to choose: *Candidates for the degree were offered/given a choice between a thesis and an exam.* | *I'm confident that we made a good choice/the right choice.* | *I didn't have to work all weekend – I did it* **by choice.** | *Those who come early to the sale get first choice.* | *a difficult choice* **2** [C (**for, as**)] a person or thing chosen: *He was a very good choice as chairman.* | *Italy was our*

second choice — all the flights to Greece were booked up. |
You can have whichever you want — **take your choice.**
3 [U (**between**)] the power or right to choose:
*Philosophers disagree about whether we have free
choice/freedom of choice.* | *We had no choice but to accept
the majority decision.* **4** [C (**of**)] a variety from which to
choose: *There is a wide choice of software available for
this model.* —see also CHOOSE, HOBSON'S CHOICE

choice² *adj* **1** *fml* (esp. of food) of high quality: *choice apples* **2** belonging to a standard of meat in the US, set by
the FDA: *choice steak* **3** *lit or humor* (of language) well
chosen: *She told him what she thought of him in a few
choice* (=suitably angry) *phrases.* — ~**ly** *adv* — ~**ness** *n*
[U]

choir /kwaɪə^r/ *n* **1** [+*sing./pl. v*] a group of people who sing
together, for example at school or during religious serv-
ices: *The church choir is/are singing tonight.* —see also
CHORAL SOCIETY **2** [*usu. sing.*] the part of a church where
these people sit: *The choir dates from the 14th century.*

choir·boy /ˈkwaɪəbɔɪ‖-ər-/ *n* a boy who sings in a church
choir —compare CHORISTER

▶ CULTURAL NOTE In Britain, choirboys are often shown,
esp. in humorous drawings, as being very sweet and looking like little ANGELs, but in fact having a strong sense of
MISCHIEF. ◀

choir loft /ˈ· ˌ·/ *n esp. AmE* a raised area, often at the front
of a church, where the choir sits

choir·mas·ter /ˈkwaɪəmɑːstə^r‖-ərmæ-/ *n* the director of a
choir

choir school /ˈ· ··/ *n* a school for choirboys, connected with
a church

choke¹ /tʃəʊk/ *v* **1** [I;T] to (cause to) have great difficulty
in breathing or stop breathing because of blocking of or
damage to the breathing passages: *He almost choked to
death on a fish bone.* | *She choked with laughter/fury.* |
(fig.) *plants choked by weeds* **2** [T (UP, **with**)] to fill (a
space or passage) completely, so that movement is im-
possible: *Leaves choked up the pipe.* | *The roads were
choked with traffic.* **3** [T] *tech* to use a CHOKE² (2) to
reduce the amount of air to (an engine) in order to make
starting easier
choke sthg. ↔ **back/down** *phr v* [T] to control (esp.
violent or very sad feelings) as if by holding them in the
throat: *to choke back one's anger/one's tears*
choke sbdy. ↔ **off** *phr v* [T] *infml* to stop, get rid of,
or prevent: *They'd ruthlessly choked off all opposition to
their plans.*

choke² *n* **1** the act or sound of choking **2** an apparatus
that controls the amount of air going into a car engine,
esp. to help a cold engine start: *Pull the choke out.* (=the
control button that works it) —see picture at CAR

choke·cher·ry /ˈtʃəʊkˌtʃeri/ *n* **chokecherries** *AmE* a kind
of sour CHERRY: *chokecherry jam*

choked /tʃəʊkt/ also **choked up** /ˌ· ˈ·/ *BrE— adj* [F] *sl* angry
or upset: *I was really choked to hear he'd died.* | *She
seemed choked up about it.*

chok·er /ˈtʃəʊkə^r/ *n* a NECKLACE or narrow band of decorative material worn very tightly round a woman's neck

chok·y , chokey /ˈtʃəʊki/ *n* (*the*) U] *BrE old-fash sl* prison

chol·er /ˈkɒlə^r‖ˈkɑː-/ *n* [U] *lit* anger; bad temper — ~ **ic** *adj*
— ~**ically** /kli/ *adv*

chol·e·ra /ˈkɒlərə‖ˈkɑː-/ *n* [U] an infectious disease caused
by bacteria which attacks esp. the stomach and bowels
causing severe DIARRHOEA, sickness, etc., and often leads
to death

cho·les·te·rol /kəˈlestərɒl‖-rəʊl/ *n* [U] a substance found in
all cells of the body, which helps to carry fats, and too
much of which has been said to be bad for the arteries
(ARTERY). In Britain and the US, people are now advised
to reduce the amount of cholesterol that they eat, e.g. by
eating fewer eggs and less RED MEAT: *cholesterol-free foods*
(=which contain no cholesterol)

chomp /tʃɒmp‖tʃɑːmp, tʃɔːmp/ *v* [I;T] to CHAMP¹

Chom·sky /ˈtʃɒmski‖ˈtʃɑː-/ , **No·am** /ˈnəʊəm/ (1928–) an
American PHILOSOPHER and LINGUIST (= someone who is
involved with language) who has produced many new
ideas about language

choose /tʃuːz/ *v* **chose** /tʃəʊz/, **chosen** /ˈtʃəʊzən/ **1** [I (**between, from**); T] to pick out freely, and after considera-

tion, from a number of things, possibilities, etc.: *It was
such a big menu I didn't know what to choose.* | *Have you
chosen (a hat) yet?* | *He chose his words carefully, hoping
to avoid a quarrel.* | *She's been chosen as the new club
president.* | *Anyone choosing politics as a career must face
intense competition.* | *We had to choose between leaving
early and paying for a taxi.* | *There's* **little/nothing to
choose between them.** (=they are both alike/equally
good) | *There are ten to choose from.* [+*obj(i)*+*obj(d)*] *She
chose him a book.* [+*obj*+**for**] *She chose a book for him.*
[+*obj*+*to-v*] *They chose him to represent them.* [+*wh-*] *I'll
let you choose where we should go to eat.* **2** [I;T+*to-v/that;
obj*] to decide: *Do as you choose.* (=as you want) | *They
chose to ignore her warning.* | *He chose not to go home
until later.* | *I chose that we should stay.* —see also CHOICE¹

choos·y , choosey /ˈtʃuːzi/ also **picky** *AmE— adj* (too) careful in choosing; hard to please: *Jean's very choosy about
what she eats.*

chop¹ /tʃɒp‖tʃɑːp/ *v* -**pp-** **1** [T] to cut by repeatedly hitting
with a heavy sharp-ended tool, such as an AXE: *They're
chopping wood in the forest.* | *I chopped a branch off the
tree.* **2** [I (AWAY, **at**)] to make a quick stroke or repeated
strokes with a sharp-ended tool: *I've been chopping away
(at this tree) for half an hour but it's still standing.* **3** [T]
to make or produce by doing this: *Will you chop the fire-
wood, please?* | *We had to chop a path through the forest.*
4 [T] to cut into small pieces: *Chop the onions then fry
them in the oil.* **5** [T] to hit (a ball) with a quick downward stroke **6** [T *often pass.*] *infml* to bring to an end
or reduce: *The government has chopped funding for the
arts.* | *The budget has been chopped by half.*
chop sthg. ↔ **down** *phr v* [T] to cause (esp. a tree) to
fall by chopping: *to chop down an oak tree*
chop sthg. ↔ **up** *phr v* [T] to cut into small pieces:
*Those chunks of meat are rather large — could you chop
them up a bit smaller?*

chop² *n* **1** a small piece of meat, esp. lamb or PORK, usu.
containing a bone: *We're having lamb chops for dinner.*
2 a quick short cutting blow with an AXE or similar
weapon **3** a short sharp blow, as in BOXING, KARATE, etc.
4 get the chop *BrE sl* **a** to be dismissed from work **b** to
be stopped suddenly by official action: *Our building plan
got the chop; it was too expensive.* —see also CHOPS

chop³ *v* -**pp-** [I (ABOUT)] **1** (esp. of the wind) to change
direction: (fig.) *One minute you want to go, the next you
don't — I wish you'd stop chopping about.* **2 chop and
change** *BrE* to keep changing (one's opinions, plans, activities, etc.): *I wish you wouldn't chop and change (your
plans) like this; make up your mind!* **3 chop logic** to use
arguments which seem reasonable but which are in fact
false

chop-chop /ˌ· ˈ·/ *adv, interj BrE infml* quickly; without
delay: *Chop-chop! We'll miss the bus at this rate.*

chop·house /ˈtʃɒphaʊs‖ˈtʃɑː-/ *n* -**houses** /haʊzɨz/ *esp. old
use* a restaurant specializing in STEAK and CHOPS² (1)

Cho·pin /ˈʃɒpæn‖ˈʃəʊ-/, **Fréd·é·ric** /ˈfredərɪk/ (1810–49) a
Polish COMPOSER, one of the best known and most admired composers of piano music of all time, who lived
with the writer George Sand.

chop·per /ˈtʃɒpə^r‖ˈtʃɑː-/ *n* **1** a heavy sharp-ended tool for
cutting wood or meat —see picture at AXE **2** *sl for*
HELICOPTER **3** *sl* a motorcycle with very long front FORKs
(=supports for the front wheel)

chop·pers /ˈtʃɒpəz‖ˈtʃɑːpərz/ *n* [P] *sl for* teeth

chopping board /ˈ··· ·/ also **chopping block** *n* a thick flat
piece of wood or plastic on which food is placed while
it is cut into small pieces

chop·py /ˈtʃɒpi‖ˈtʃɑːpi/ *adj* (of water) with many short
rough irregular waves —**piness** *n* [U]

chops /tʃɒps‖tʃɑːps/ *n* [P] the fleshy covering of an animal's
jaw: (fig., *derog*) *He* **licked his chops** *as he thought of all
the money he'd make on the deal.* (=looked forward
eagerly to his profit)

chop·stick /ˈtʃɒp-stɪk‖ˈtʃɑːp-/ *n* [*usu. pl.*] either of a pair
of narrow sticks held between the thumb and fingers and
used in E Asian countries for lifting food to the mouth
—see picture at STICK

Chop·sticks /ˈtʃɒpstɪks‖ˈtʃɑːp-/ a well-known simple tune
that people sometimes play on the piano, esp. when they
are BORED or thinking about something else

chop su·ey /ˌtʃɒp ˈsuːi‖ˌtʃɑːp-/ n [U] a Chinese dish made of small pieces of vegetables and meat or chicken served with rice —compare CHOW MEIN

cho·ral /ˈkɔːrəl/ adj of or sung by a CHOIR or CHORUS: a choral group | choral music

cho·rale /kɒˈrɑːl‖kəˈræl, -rɑːl/ n a HYMN (=a song of praise) to be sung in a church: a Bach chorale

choral so·ci·e·ty /ˈ·· ·ˌ··/ n a group of people who sing together and are not connected with a church

chord¹ /kɔːd‖kɔːrd/ n a combination of two or more musical notes sounded at the same time: the opening chords of a sonata —see also **strike a chord** (STRIKE¹ (16))

chord² n a straight line joining two points on a curve: a chord of a circle

chore /tʃɔːʳ/ n **1** a regular and necessary piece of work or job, esp. in a house: the daily chores of cleaning, cooking, and shopping | the administrative chores of the office **2** a piece of uninteresting, difficult, or unpleasant work: It's such a chore filling in tax forms.

chor·e·o·graph /ˈkɒriəgrɑːf, ˈkɔː-‖ˈkɔːriəgræf/ v [T] to make up or arrange the steps and dances for (a BALLET or piece of music)

choreographer /ˌkɒriˈɒgrəfəʳ, ˌkɔː-‖ˌkɔːriˈɑːg-/ n a person who choreographs a piece of music

chor·e·og·ra·phy /ˌkɒriˈɒgrəfi, ˌkɔː-‖ˌkɔːriˈɑːg-/ n [U] the art of making up or arranging dances for the stage

chor·is·ter /ˈkɒristəʳ‖ˈkɔːr-, ˈkɑːr-/ n a member of a group of people who sing together (CHOIR), esp. a boy who sings in a church —compare CHOIRBOY

chor·tle /ˈtʃɔːtl‖ˈtʃɔːrtl/ v, n [I] (to give) a laugh of pleasure and satisfaction; CHUCKLE: He chortled with delight when I told him my news.

cho·rus¹ /ˈkɔːrəs/ n **1** [C] a part of a song repeated after each VERSE (=a group of lines) of a song: The audience joined in the chorus. —compare VERSE (2) **2** [C+sing./pl. v] a group of people who sing together: the Brighton Festival Chorus **3** [C] a piece of music written to be sung by such a group **4** [C+sing./pl. v] a group of dancers, singers, or actors who play a supporting part in a film or show: The chorus is/are dressed as fairies. | She's a star, but I'm just a chorus girl. **5** [S (of)] something said by many people at one time: The election results were greeted by a chorus of groans. **6** [C] tech **a** (in ancient Greek plays) a group of actors who used poetry and music to explain or give opinions on the action of the play **b** (in Elizabethan plays) a person who makes a speech before, after, or during the play, explaining or giving opinions on the action of the play —see also DAWN CHORUS

chorus² v [T] to sing or say at the same time: The papers all chorused the praises of the president.

chose /tʃəʊz/ past tense of CHOOSE

cho·sen /ˈtʃəʊzən/ past participle of CHOOSE —see also WELL-CHOSEN

chosen peo·ple /ˌ·· ˈ··/ n [the+P] any of various peoples who believe they are chosen by God esp. the JEWS

Chou En-lai /ˌtʃəʊ en ˈlaɪ/ (1898–1976) a Chinese politician who was PRIME MINISTER of China from 1949 to 1976

chow¹ /tʃaʊ/ also **chow chow** /ˈ· ·/— n a dog with a thick coat and a blue tongue, originally bred in China

chow² n [U] sl food

chow³ v

   chow down phr v [I;T(=chow sthg. ↔ **down**)] AmE sl to eat as though one is very hungry, and showing pleasure

chow·der /ˈtʃaʊdəʳ/ n [U] a thick soup prepared from bits of fish and other sea animals (SHELLFISH), vegetables, meat, and often milk: clam chowder

chow mein /ˌtʃaʊ ˈmeɪn/ n [U] a Chinese dish made of bits of vegetables and meat or chicken mixed with NOODLES —compare CHOP SUEY

Christ¹ /kraɪst/ n **1** also **Jesus Christ, Jesus**— the man on whose life, death, and teachings Christianity is based. According to the Bible, the holy book of the Christians, Jesus was the son of God, born on Earth to the Virgin Mary. He died on a CROSS¹ (2) to save all men and women from their SINS. **2** [the] the MESSIAH (1) —see also JESUS

Christ² also **Jesus Christ, Jesus, Christ Almighty**— interj sl (used for expressing annoyance, unwelcome surprise, etc.): Christ! I've forgotten the keys! —see JESUS (USAGE), SAKE (USAGE)

Christ·church /ˈkraɪstʃɜːtʃ‖-ɜːr-/ a city in New Zealand, in the E of South Island

chris·ten /ˈkrɪsən/ v [T] **1** to make someone (esp. a baby) a member of a Christian church by the ceremony of BAPTISM and usu. the giving of a name; BAPTIZE: The baby was christened by the priest. [+obj+n] We christened our baby John. | (fig.) The ship was christened the Queen Mary. (=given this name at a ceremony) | (fig.) Party members who did not support her policies were christened (=given the NICKNAME) "Wets" by the Prime Minister. **2** infml, esp. BrE to use for the first time: Have you christened your new car yet? — ~ **ing** n [C;U]

Chris·ten·dom /ˈkrɪsəndəm/ n [U] old use **1** all Christian people in general **2** the Christian countries of the world

Chris·tian¹ /ˈkrɪstʃən, -tiən/ n **1** a person who believes in the teachings of Christ or belongs to a Christian church: When did you first become a Christian? **2** infml (used by Christians) a good person

Christian² adj **1** [no comp.] (believing in or belonging to any of the branches) of Christianity: the Christian church | Christian ideas —opposite **non-Christian 2** (often not cap.) apprec following the example of Christ; kind, generous, etc.: It wasn't very Christian of you to laugh at his tale of woe. —opposite **unchristian**

Christian³ the main character in The Pilgrim's Progress whose story tells of a religious person's journey through life

Christian Aid /ˌ·· ˈ·/ a Christian CHARITY organization which helps developing countries

Christian e·ra /ˌ·· ˈ··/ n [the+S] the system of time counted from the birth of Christ —see also AD, BC, CE

Chris·ti·an·i·ty /ˌkrɪstiˈænˌti/ n [U] the religion based on the life and teachings of Christ. Christianity began in Palestine in the first century and was spread by missionaries (MISSIONARY). In the West it later split into a number of related divisions. The three main divisions of the Christian church are the Protestant, Roman Catholic, and Eastern Orthodox Churches: He converted to Christianity in 1987. | "Love thy neighbour" is one of the basic tenets of Christianity.

Christian name /ˈ·· ·/ n (esp. in Christian countries) a person's FIRST NAME —see FIRST NAME (USAGE)

Christian Sci·ence /ˌ·· ˈ··/ n [U] a branch of Christianity started by Mary Baker Eddy in America in 1866. It includes the belief that illness is cured by means of faith. Christian Scientists do not take medicines or have SURGERY; instead, they talk with a **Christian Science Practitioner**, who helps them find a way to cure or deal with their illness according to their religion. — **~entist** n

Christian Science Mon·i·tor /ˌ·· ˈ·· ·ˌ··/ [the] a daily American newspaper which reports on matters of national and international interest —see also extra information on page 896

Chris·tie /ˈkrɪsti/, **Dame Ag·a·tha** /ˈægəθə/ (1890–1976) an English writer of popular books and plays, many of which have been made into films. Her most famous characters are the DETECTIVES Hercule Poirot and Miss Marple, and two of her best-known books are Murder on the Orient Express and Death on the Nile: an Agatha-Christie style country house murder —see also MOUSETRAP

Chris·tie's /ˈkrɪstiz/ a large AUCTION HOUSE with branches in London and New York, where valuable paintings, furniture, etc., are sold —compare SOTHEBY'S

Christ·mas /ˈkrɪsməs/ n [C;U] **1** also **Christmas Day** /ˌ·· ˈ·/— a Christian holy day held on December 25th (or in some churches January 6th) in honour of the birth of Christ, usu. kept as a public holiday: Christmas dinner | a Christmas present —see also BOXING DAY, CHRISTMAS CARD, CHRISTMAS TREE and see colour picture on page 1212 **2** the period just before and just after this: to go ski-ing at Christmas | the Christmas holidays —see also **the ghost of Christmas past** (GHOST¹ (6)), XMAS —see also extra information on page 215

Christmas bo·nus /ˌ·· ˈ··/ n an additional payment made at Christmas by the British state to all OLD AGE PENSIONERS (= women over 60 and men over 65 years of age)

Christmas box /ˈ·· ·/ n (in Britain, esp. formerly) a small gift of money to the postman, milkman, etc., to thank them for their services during the year. Very few people still give such a gift.

Christmas cake /ˈ··· ·/ n [C;U] BrE (a) heavy cake containing a lot of dried fruit and usu. having a covering of ICING (=hard sugar), made to be eaten at Christmas —compare CHRISTMAS PUDDING and see picture on page 215

Christmas card /ˈ··· ·/ n a card with a picture on it that one person sends to another at Christmas with good wishes: *I'll put him on my Christmas card list.* —see colour picture on page 1212

Christmas car·ol /ˌ··· ˈ··/ n see CAROL¹

Christmas Carol, A a book by Charles Dickens in which the characters of Scrooge, Bob Cratchit, and Tiny Tim appear

Christmas cook·ie /ˌ··· ˈ··/ n AmE a special biscuit eaten in the US at Christmas

Christmas crack·er /ˌ··· ˈ··/ n a CRACKER (3)

Christmas Day /ˌ··· ˈ·/ see CHRISTMAS (1)

Christmas din·ner /ˌ··· ˈ··/ n a meal eaten on or before Christmas Day with family or friends, typically consisting mainly of TURKEY with various different vegetables and SAUCEs, followed by CHRISTMAS PUDDING

Christmas Eve /ˌ··· ˈ·/ n [U] the day, and esp. the evening, before Christmas. Christmas Eve is not a public holiday in Britain or the US: *I always go to my parents' house on Christmas Eve.* —see also extra information on page 0000

Christmas pres·ent /ˈ··· ˌ··/ n a present given at Christmas —see colour picture on page 1212

Christmas pud·ding /ˌ··· ˈ··/ n [C;U] (in Britain) (a) heavy sweet PUDDING containing a lot of dried fruit and often covered with burning BRANDY (=a strong alcohol), served hot esp. at the end of dinner on Christmas Day —compare CHRISTMAS PUDDING

Christmas stock·ing /ˌ··· ˈ··/ also **stocking**– n a long sock hung by a fireplace or bed on Christmas Eve, into which small Christmas presents are put for children. A TANGERINE and/or a nut are often put into the stocking. Small children are told that the presents are brought by Santa Claus or Father Christmas BrE) who has climbed down the chimney during the night. —see also extra information on page 215 and colour picture on page 1212

Christ·mas·time /ˈkrɪsməstaɪm/ n [U] AmE the season when people prepare for and celebrate Christmas, from mid-December to the end of the year: *I hope to see all of my relatives at Christmastime.*

Christmas tree /ˈ··· ·/ n a PINE tree, either real or artificial, bought during the Christmas season and decorated with TINSEL, BAUBLES, FAIRY LIGHTs, etc. It usu. has a star, a fairy, or an angel on the top. A family's Christmas presents are often piled around the bottom of the tree. —see colour picture on page 1212

Chris·to /ˈkrɪstəʊ/ the name used by the American artist **Christo Jaracheff** (1935–) known for his large-scale, temporary pieces of work which change the appearance of natural or man-made objects; for example, he once wrapped a tall building in plastic

Christopher see SAINT CHRISTOPHER

Chris·to·pher /ˈkrɪstəfəʳ/, **Warren F.** (1925–) an American politician who became Secretary of State under President Clinton in 1993

Chris·to·pher Rob·in /ˌ··· ˈ··/ a small boy who is a friend of Pooh Bear in stories and poems by A A Milne

Christ's Hos·pi·tal /ˌ· ˈ···/ a school in S England where the pupils wear long dark blue coats and yellow STOCKINGS (=long socks) and which was originally built as a hospital for children with no parents

chro·mat·ic /krəʊˈmætɪk, krə-/ adj 1 of colours; coloured 2 of the musical SCALE¹ (5) **(chromatic scale** /·ˌ·ˈ·· ·/) which consists of SEMITONEs

chrome /krəʊm/ n [U] a hard ALLOY (=combination of metals) of chromium with other metals, esp. used for covering objects with a thin shiny protective metal plate: *The trimmings on the car are made of chrome.*

chrome yel·low /ˌ· ˈ··/ n [U] a bright yellow

chro·mi·um /ˈkrəʊmiəm/ n [U] a blue-white metal that is a simple substance (ELEMENT) found only in combination with other chemicals, used for covering objects with a thin shiny protective plate: *chromium-plated*

chro·mo·some /ˈkrəʊməsəʊm/ n tech a threadlike object found in all living cells, which passes on and controls the nature, character, etc., of a young plant, animal, or cell —see also X CHROMOSOME, Y CHROMOSOME

chron- see WORD FORMATION on page 0000

chron·ic /ˈkrɒnɪk/ˈkrɑː-/ adj 1 (of a disease) continual; lasting a long time: *chronic hepatitis* | (fig.) *chronic unemployment* —compare ACUTE (4) 2 [A] suffering from a disease over a long period: *a chronic alcoholic/invalid* | *chronic depression* | (fig.) *a chronic complainer* 3 BrE sl very bad; terrible: *The food was absolutely chronic!* —**ally** /kli/ adv : *chronically ill*

chronic fa·tigue syn·drome /ˌ··· ·ˈ· ˌ··/ n see M.E.

chron·i·cle¹ /ˈkrɒnɪkəl/ˈkrɑː-/ n [(of)] a record of historical events, arranged in order of time: *The Daily Chronicle* (=title of a newspaper) | (fig.) *Every time I visit my grandmother she gives me a chronicle of her complaints.*

chronicle² v [T] to make a chronicle of (events): *to chronicle the growth of a town* —**cler** n

chron·o·graph /ˈkrɒnəɡrɑːf/ˈkrɑːnəɡræf/ n tech an instrument for measuring and recording periods of time

chron·o·log·i·cal /ˌkrɒnəˈlɒdʒɪkəl/ˌkrɑːnəˈlɑː-/ adj arranged according to the order of time: *We'll talk about the causes of the war in chronological order.* — ~**ly** /kli/ adv

chro·nol·o·gy /krəˈnɒlədʒi/-ˈnɑː-/ n 1 [U] the science which measures time and gives dates to events 2 [C] a list or table arranged according to the order of time: *a chronology of the events of last year*

chro·nom·e·ter /krəˈnɒmɪtəʳ/-ˈnɑː-/ n tech a very exact clock for measuring time, esp. as used for scientific purposes

chrys·a·lis /ˈkrɪsəlɪs/ n **chrysalises** /-sɪz/ the PUPA (=an insect in its inactive stage) of a MOTH or BUTTERFLY in its hard outer shell —compare COCOON¹

chry·san·the·mum /krɪˈsænθɪməm/ n || also **mum** AmE infml – a garden plant with large brightly coloured bushy flowers —see picture at FLOWER

Chrys·ler /ˈkraɪzləʳ/ also **the Chrysler Corporation** fml tdmk one of the three largest American car makers. Their cars are usually more expensive than average American cars, and they are considered to be of better than average quality: *He drives a Chrysler Le Baron.* | *My last three cars have been Chryslers.*

Chubb /tʃʌb/ tdmk (in Britain) a safety lock on a door

chub·by /ˈtʃʌbi/ adj (esp. of children and young adults) pleasantly fat: *chubby cheeks* —see FAT (USAGE) —**biness** n [U]

chuck¹ /tʃʌk/ v [T] 1 infml to throw (something), esp. with a short movement of the arms: [+obj(i)+obj(d)] *Chuck me the ball.* [+obj+adv/prep] *Chuck the ball to me.* | *I chucked the empty packet away/chucked it in the bin.* | (fig.) *Don't make so much noise, or the driver will chuck us off (the bus).* 2 [(IN)] sl to stop or give up; leave: *He got fed up with his job and chucked it (in).* 3 **chuck someone under the chin** to touch someone gently or playfully under the chin

chuck sbdy./sthg. ↔ **out** phr v [T] infml 1 [(of)] infml to force (a person) to leave: *The owner threatened to chuck us out (of the restaurant) if we didn't stop singing.* 2 to throw away (something useless or unwanted); get rid of; DISCARD: *I'm going to chuck out these old shoes.* —**chucker-out** /ˌ··· ˈ·/ n

chuck² n 1 a gentle or loving stroke under the chin 2 **give someone the chuck/get the chuck** BrE infml to dismiss someone/be dismissed from a job or relationship

chuck³ n 1 [U] meat, esp. BEEF, from the side of an animal just above the top of the front legs: *chuck steak* 2 [C] an apparatus for holding a tool, etc., in a machine

chuck·le /ˈtʃʌkəl/ v [I] to laugh quietly: *I could hear him chuckling to himself as he read his book.* —see LAUGH¹ (USAGE) —**chuckle** n : *He gave a chuckle.*

chuck wag·on /ˈ· ˌ··/ n AmE a truck which carries and provides food for a group of people

chuffed /tʃʌft/ adj [F] BrE infml pleased or happy: *She's very chuffed about her new job.*

chug /tʃʌɡ/ v -**gg**- 1 [I+adv/prep] (of an engine or vehicle) to make, or move while making, a low repeated knocking

The nativity

Christmas is the main public holiday in Britain and the US when people spend time with their families, eat special food, and drink a lot. Christmas is a Christian festival to remember the birth of Jesus, and people often regret that it is now very 'commercial' and seen as a time of merry-making and present-giving.

Before Christmas Day

Because people give each other presents, in the days and weeks before Christmas the shops become very busy. Newspapers and television, etc. say how many shopping days there are left and people often spend a lot of money. Many people enjoy this but others feel that Christmas has become too much of a business and so has lost its meaning.

People also buy and send CHRISTMAS CARDs to their friends, usually containing the message 'Merry Christmas'. The cards often show pictures of the NATIVITY (=the birth of Christ), SANTA CLAUS, CHRISTMAS TREES, ROBINS or scenes of old-fashioned Christmases.

robin

CAROLs (=special religious songs) are sung, especially in churches. Some carols, e.g. *O Come all Ye Faithful* and *Silent Night*, are very well known. People sometimes go CAROL SINGING (CAROLing *AmE*), which means singing carols in the street, outside people's houses.

People usually decorate their houses and many people have a Christmas tree in their house which they also decorate.

Young children are told that Santa Claus will bring them presents if they are good. Children sometimes write a letter to Santa Claus telling him what presents they would like for Christmas. They hang up a STOCKING (really a sock) on Christmas Eve and Santa Claus is supposed to come down the chimney in the night and fill it with presents.

December 24th, the day before Christmas Day, is called CHRISTMAS EVE. Some people go to a special church service called MIDNIGHT MASS (in *BrE*, Christmas Eve service in *AmE*) at 12 o'clock at night. Others may have a drink with their friends.

Christmas Day

Christmas Day is a public holiday. Families usually spend the day opening their presents and eating and drinking together. The most important meal is Christmas dinner. The typical meal consists of TURKEY (=meat) with potatoes and other vegetables, e.g. CARROTs and SPROUTs. In Britain this is followed by CHRISTMAS PUDDING. Other TRADITIONAL foods in Britain include CHRISTMAS CAKE and MINCE PIES. Americans bake special biscuits called CHRISTMAS COOKIES which they eat over the Christmas season.

Christmas cake

At the start of the meal, British people often pull a CRACKER, which contains a small toy, a paper hat, and a joke.

cracker and hat

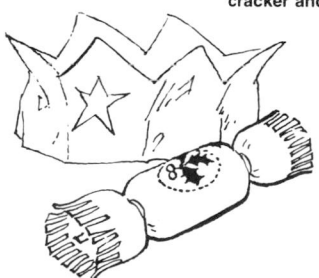

After Christmas

In Britain, the day after Christmas day is called BOXING DAY and is also a public holiday. A lot of sport takes place on Boxing Day and many people now spend time watching sport on television. In the US many stores hold special sales, where things can be bought cheaply, on the day after Christmas.

Twelve days after Christmas (TWELFTH NIGHT) is the time when people are supposed to take down their decorations and remove their Christmas trees. — see also page 1212.

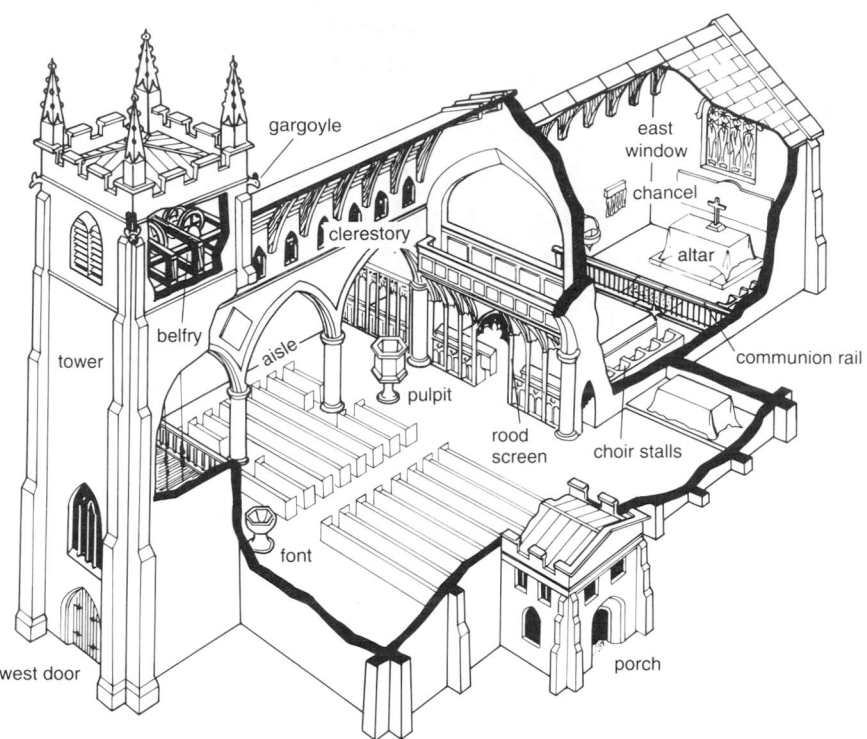

gargoyle

east window

chancel

clerestory

altar

belfry

tower

aisle

communion rail

pulpit

rood screen

choir stalls

font

west door

porch

sound: *I heard the little car chugging along/away.* | *They watched the old steam engine chugging up the hill.* **2** [T] *AmE infml* to drink quickly: *He chugged his lemonade.* —**chug** *n* [S] : *the chug of the motorboat*

chuk·ker /ˈtʃʌkəʳ/ also **chuk·ka** /-kə/— *n* one of the periods of seven minutes each into which the game of POLO is divided

chum[1] /tʃʌm/ *n esp. BrE infml* a good friend, esp. among children; a word used esp. by MIDDLE-CLASS and UPPER-CLASS adults: *his school chums*

chum[2] *v* **-mm-**
    chum up *phr v* [I (**with**)] *esp. BrE infml* to make friends: *She's chummed up with the girl in the next room.*

chum·my /ˈtʃʌmi/ *adj* [(**with**)] *esp. BrE infml* friendly

chump /tʃʌmp/ *n* **1** *infml* a fool; a word used esp. by MIDDLE-CLASS and UPPER-CLASS *people: You chump, Rodney!* **2** also **chump chop** /ˈ· ·/— *esp. BrE* a thick piece of meat with a bone through one end **3** (**go**) **off one's chump** *BrE sl* (to become) mad

chunk /tʃʌŋk/ *n* **1** [(**of**)] a thick piece or lump with a usu. irregular shape: *a chunk of coal/cake/cheese* —see picture at PIECE **2** *infml* a large part or amount: *The car repairs took quite a chunk out of her salary.*
    ▷ USAGE Compare **chunk, hunk, slice,** and **lump**. All these words are used about pieces of something, but give different ideas of size, shape and material. A **chunk** is a large, usually uneven piece of a solid material that can be cut or divided: *a chunk of meat.* **Hunk** is similar in meaning but is used especially of food that can be broken or cut off: *a hunk of bread.* A **slice** is a thin, flat, cleanly-cut piece of something, especially food: *a slice of bread/sausage/cheese.* A **lump** is a mass of a solid material, of no regular size or shape, especially one which has not been shaped by human control: *a lump of rock.* (But *a lump of sugar* is usually regular in size and shape.) —see also the picture at PIECE◁

chunk·y /ˈtʃʌŋki/ *adj* **1** short, thick, and solid **2** *infml, sometimes apprec* (of a person, esp. a man) having a broad chest and strong-looking body, and not very tall **3** (of materials, clothes, etc.) thick and heavy: *a chunky woollen sweater* | *a chunky silver bracelet* **4** (of food) containing thick solid pieces: *chunky marmalade*

Chun·nel /ˈtʃʌnl/ *n* [*the*] a popular name for the CHANNEL TUNNEL

church[1] /tʃɜːtʃ‖tʃɜːrtʃ/ *n* **1** [C] a building for public Christian worship: *Our house is opposite the Baptist church.* | *the church spire* | *a Gothic church*
    ▶ CULTURAL NOTE Many churches are very beautiful old buildings, and many people like to visit them to admire them, even if they are not Christians. —see also CATHEDRAL◀

2 [U] the religious services held in a church: *They go to church every Sunday.* | *I saw them at church/after church.* | *a church service*
    ▶ CULTURAL NOTE In Britain, few people now go to church regularly, although more people go at the special religious times of Christmas and Easter. In the US, many people still go to church regularly.◀

3 [*the*+S] the profession of the CLERGY (=priests and people employed for religious reasons): *to enter/join the church* **4** [U] religious power as compared with state power: *the separation of church and state* **5** [C] (*usu. cap.*) the organization of Christian believers, or of any of the various branches of Christianity: *the Catholic Church* | *the Church of England* —see also CHAPEL, HIGH CHURCH, LOW CHURCH —compare MEETING HOUSE

church[2] *adj* [F] *BrE old-fash* (in England and Wales) belonging to the established state church: *My uncle's church, but none of the rest of us are.* —compare CHAPEL[2]

Church Ar·my /ˈ· ·/ [*the*] a British organization of ordinary people under the authority of the CHURCH OF ENGLAND who help local officers of the church with their work in society esp. with the less fortunate —compare SALVATION ARMY

Church Com·mis·sion·ers /ˌ·· ·¹····/ [the + P] a group of people who control the buildings and money of the Church of England

church·go·er /ˈtʃɜːtʃˌgəʊəʳ‖-ɜːr-/ n a person who regularly attends public Christian worship in a church

Church House /ˌ· ·¹·/ a house in London which is the office of the GENERAL SYNOD (=council of religious officers) of the Church of England

Chur·chill /ˈtʃɜːtʃɪl‖ˈtʃɜːr-/, **Sir Win·ston** /ˈwɪnstən/ (1874–1965) an English politician who was the PRIME MINISTER of Britain during most of the Second World War. He made many famous speeches and is admired and remembered for his great leadership of the nation. He was Prime Minister again from 1951–55. He is often shown wearing a hat and smoking a large CIGAR. He made the V-SIGN(1), meaning victory —see also BATTLE OF BRITAIN, SIR WINSTON CHURCHILL and see picture on page 752 – ~**ian** /tʃɜːˈtʃɪliən‖tʃɜːr-/ adj : a stirring Churchillian speech

Winston Churchill

church·man /ˈtʃɜːtʃmən‖ˈtʃɜːrtʃ-/ n -men /mən/ a priest; CLERGYMAN

church·key /ˈtʃɜːtʃkiː‖-ɜːr-/ n AmE infml BOTTLE OPENER

Church of Eng·land /ˌ·· · ¹···◂/ n 1 [the] the state church which is established by law in England, and was separated from the Roman Catholic Church in the 16th century. Its priests can marry, and its head is the King or Queen, though it is governed by the Archbishop of Canterbury and the Archbishop of York 2 [U] also **C of E**— a member of the Church of England: Are you Church of England? —see also ANGLICAN, DISSOLUTION OF THE MONASTERIES, GENERAL SYNOD, HIGH CHURCH, LOW CHURCH

Church of Ire·land /ˌ·· · ¹···◂/ [the] an independent ANGLICAN church in the Republic of Ireland and Northern Ireland

Church of Je·sus Christ of Lat·ter-Day Saints /ˌ·· · ¹··· ·· ¹··· ·· ¹·/ [the] the MORMON church, based on the DIVINE REVELATIONS (–teachings directly from God) of Joseph Smith

Church of Scot·land /ˌ·· · ¹···◂/ n [the] the official established Presbyterian church in Scotland

church school /ˈ· ·¹·/ n in Britain a PRIMARY SCHOOL that is partly controlled by a church

church·war·den /ˌtʃɜːtʃˈwɔːdn‖ˈtʃɜːrtʃwɔːrdn/ n (in a Church of England church) either of two people who are not priests and are elected, by the people who attend a church, to be responsible for that church's property and money

church wed·ding /ˌ· ¹··/ n a wedding which takes place in a church, esp. a TRADITIONAL wedding —see also extra information on page 1406

church·yard /ˈtʃɜːtʃjɑːd‖ˈtʃɜːrtʃjɑːrd/ n a piece of ground around and belonging to a church, in which dead members of that church are buried. Not all churches have a churchyard, esp. in the US. —compare CEMETERY, GRAVEYARD

churl /tʃɜːl‖tʃɜːrl/ n old use 1 a rude person 2 a person of low social class

churl·ish /ˈtʃɜːlɪʃ‖-ɜːr-/ adj bad-tempered and rude: a churlish reply | It would be churlish to refuse such a kind offer. — ~**ly** adv — ~**ness** n [U]

churn¹ /tʃɜːn‖tʃɜːrn/ n 1 a container in which milk is shaken until it becomes butter 2 BrE a large metal container in which milk is stored or carried from the farm

churn² v 1 [T] to make (milk) into butter or make (butter) from milk using a churn 2 [I;T (UP)] to (cause to) move about violently: The ship churned the water up as it passed. | (fig.) My stomach started to churn when I

thought about my exams.
  churn sthg. ↔ **out** phr v [T] infml, often derog to produce in large amounts, by or as if by machinery: She churns out three or four new books every year.

chute /ʃuːt/ n 1 a narrow sloping passage along which something may be passed, dropped, or caused to slide: a rubbish chute 2 infml a PARACHUTE

chut·ney /ˈtʃʌtni/ n [U] a mixture of various fruits, hot-tasting seeds, and sugar, eaten with other dishes such as meat or cheese, and esp. with CURRY: mango chutney

chutz·pah /ˈhʊtspə/ n [U] apprec sl, esp. AmE disrespectful confidence; NERVE

CIA /ˌsiː aɪ ˈeɪ/ [the] the Central Intelligence Agency; the US government department that collects information about other countries, esp. in secret —compare FBI The CIA is sometimes accused of secretly influencing the affairs of other nations.

ciao /tʃaʊ/ interj It (used to say HELLO or goodbye)

ci·ca·da /sɪˈkɑːdə‖sɪˈkeɪdə, -ˈkɑː-/ n a tropical insect with large transparent wings that makes a high singing noise

cic·a·trice /ˈsɪkətrɪs/ also **cic·a·trix** /-trɪks/– n **cicatrices** /ˌsɪkəˈtraɪsiːz/ lit or med a SCAR

Ci·ce·ro /ˈsɪsərəʊ/, **Mar·cus Tul·li·us** /ˈmɑːkəs ˈtʌliəs‖ˈmɑːr-/ (106–43 BC) a Roman CONSUL who was a famous public speaker and writer

ci·ce·ro·ne /ˌsɪsəˈrəʊni, ˌtʃɪtʃə-/ n lit a guide who shows places of interest to tourists

CID /ˌsiː aɪ ˈdiː/ [the] the Criminal Investigation Department; the branch of the UK police force made up of DETECTIVES and brought in for special and serious cases. The CID used to be based at Scotland Yard near Whitehall and is now at New Scotland Yard in Westminster.

ci·der ‖also **cyder** BrE /ˈsaɪdəʳ/ n [C;U] 1 BrE (a glass of) an alcoholic drink made from apples. A lot of cider, esp. strong cider, is made in the West Country: Two glasses of cider and a beer, please. —see also SCRUMPY 2 AmE a fresh, non-alcoholic drink made from apples —see also HARD CIDER

Cider with Ro·sie /ˌsaɪdə wɪð ˈrəʊzi‖-dər-/ a book by Laurie Lee which tells the story of a young boy growing up in the country

Cid, The see EL CID

ci·gar /sɪˈgɑːʳ/ n a tube-shaped roll of uncut tobacco leaves for smoking, usu. larger and more expensive than a cigarette. Cigars are connected in people's minds with certain famous, and often rich, men, for example Winston Churchill and Groucho Marx. —see also close, but no cigar (CLOSE³)

cig·a·rette ‖also -**ret** AmE rare /ˌsɪgəˈret‖ˌsɪgəˈret, ˈsɪgəret/ also **fag** BrE infml— n a thin paper tube of finely cut tobacco for smoking: She lit her cigarette and then stubbed it out almost immediately. | a packet of cigarettes | an ashtray full of cigarette ends

cigarette card /ˌ···¹· ·◂, ¹··· ·¹/ n a card bearing a picture of e.g. a car, bird, etc. formerly found in cigarette packets and intended to be collected into sets

cigarette end /···¹· ·◂, ¹··· ·¹/ also **cigarette butt** n esp. BrE the part of a cigarette that remains when one has finished smoking it

cigarette hold·er /···¹· ·◂, ¹··· ·¹/ n a narrow tube for holding a cigarette when smoking it

cigarette light·er /···¹· ·◂, ¹··· ·¹/ n a LIGHTER¹

cigarette pa·per /···¹· ·◂, ¹··· ·¹/ n [C;U] (a piece of) thin paper used in making one's own cigarettes, including cigarettes containing MARIJUANA, an illegal substance in Britain and the US

cig·gy /ˈsɪgi/ n BrE infml a cigarette: Want a ciggy?

ci·lan·tro /sɪˈlɑːntrəʊ, -ˈlæn-/ n [U] AmE for CORIANDER

Cil·la /ˈsɪlə/ infml for Cilla BLACK

C-in-C /ˌsiː ɪn ˈsiː/ n COMMANDER IN CHIEF

cinch /sɪntʃ/ n [S] infml 1 something done easily: The exam was a cinch. 2 something certain to happen: It's an absolute cinch that this horse will win the race.

Cin·cin·nat·i /ˌsɪnsɪˈnæti◂/ a city in SW Ohio, on the Ohio river, with large manufacturing interests —see colour map on pages 1374-5

cinc·ture /ˈsɪŋktʃəʳ/ n lit a belt

cin·der /ˈsɪndəʳ/ n a very small piece of burnt or partly burnt wood, coal, etc.: *Clear out yesterday's cinders before you make the fire.* | *The cake was burnt to a cinder.* (=burnt black)

cinder block /ˈ·· ·/ n [C;U] *AmE for* BREEZE BLOCK

Cin·de·rel·la /ˌsɪndəˈrelə/ **1** *also* **Cinders** /ˈsɪndəz ‖ -derz/ *infml*— a young woman in an old FAIRY STORY who is treated like a slave by her STEPMOTHER and two ugly sisters. One day, a prince (Prince Charming) invites all the ladies in the country to a BALL (=a grand dance), but Cinderella cannot go as she has no dress. That night, her FAIRY GODMOTHER (=special magic friend) appears and says "You *shall* go to the ball!" She waves her magic WAND (=magic stick) and changes six white mice into horses, a PUMPKIN (=a large round yellow vegetable) into a COACH, and produces a beautiful dress and glass SLIP-PERs (=shoes). Cinderella goes to the ball with a warning to be home by midnight, as at midnight the magic will disappear and everything will change back. At the ball, Prince Charming falls in love with Cinderella and dances with her all the time, but hearing the clock strike midnight, she runs away, leaving one of the glass slippers. The prince searches everywhere for the girl whose foot fits the glass slipper and finally finds Cinderella and marries her. The story of Cinderella is one of the most popular subjects for British PANTOMIMEs: *A young student became a modern-day Cinderella yesterday when she married Japan's Prince Aya in an ancient ceremony.* (Daily Mail, 5.7.90) – see colour picture on page 357 **2** someone or something that receives little attention or respect, and perhaps deserves to receive more: *The care of old people seems to be the Cinderella of the social services.* | *Cambridgeshire is the Cinderella of the church world – with many beautiful buildings not on the tourist map like neighbours in Norfolk and Suffolk.*

cinder track /ˈ·· ·/ n a race track covered with fine CINDERS (= small piece of burnt wood, coal, etc.)

cine- see WORD FORMATION

cin·e·ma /ˈsɪnɪmə/ n **1** [C] *BrE* ‖ **movie theater** *AmE*— a theatre in which films are shown: *There is only one cinema in our town.* | *a new eight-screen cinema complex* **2** [the+S] *also* **pictures** *BrE infml* ‖ **movies** *esp. AmE*— a showing of a film: *Let's go to the cinema tonight.* **3** [the+S] *esp. BrE* ‖ **movies** *esp. AmE*— the art or industry of making films: *He's worked in the cinema all his life.* | *a leading figure in the Italian cinema* —see also BRITISH BOARD OF FILM CENSORS

cin·e·ma·to·gra·phy /ˌsɪnɪməˈtɒɡrəfi‖-ˈtɑː-/ n [U] *tech* the art or science of making films —**pher** n

cin·na·mon¹ /ˈsɪnəmən/ n [U] the sweet-smelling BARK (=outer covering) of a tropical Asian tree, used for giving a special taste to food: *a cinnamon stick* (=a stick-shaped rolled-up piece of this bark)

cinnamon² adj having a light yellowish-brown colour – **cinnamon** n [U]

Cin·za·no /tʃɪnˈzɑːnəʊ/ n *tdmk* a type of sweet Italian VERMOUTH, usu. drunk with a MIXER (2)

ci·pher¹ , **cypher** /ˈsaɪfəʳ/ n **1** (a system of) secret writing; CODE: *a message written in cipher* **2** a person of no importance or influence: *He's a mere cipher in the company.* **3** *lit* the number 0; zero **4** *rare* a MONOGRAM

cipher² v [T] to put a message into cipher —compare DECIPHER

cir·ca /ˈsɜːkə‖ˈsɜːr-/ (*written abbrev.* **c** *or* **ca**) prep *fml* (used esp. with dates) in about: *He was born circa 1060 and died in 1118.*

cir·ca·di·an /sɜːˈkeɪdiən‖sɜːr-/ adj [A] *tech* (esp. of changes in the body) related to a period of about 24 hours: *studying the circadian rhythms of unborn babies* | *Flying from San Francisco to Rome has upset his circadian clock, so he feels as if it was the middle of the night.*

Cir·ce /ˈsɜːsi‖ˈsɜːr-/ in CLASSICAL MYTHOLOGY, a woman who did magic and who changed people into pigs, including the friends of Odysseus

cir·cle¹ /ˈsɜːkəl‖ˈsɜːr-/ n **1** (a flat round area enclosed by) a curved line on which every point is equally distant from one fixed point inside the curve **2** something having the general shape of this curve; a ring: *a circle of trees|of chairs* | *children standing in a circle* **3** [+sing.|pl. v] *also* **circles** pl.— a group of people connected in an in-

formal way by common interests: *She has a large circle of friends.* | *In political circles there is talk of war.* | *She moves in different circles* (=has different groups of friends) *from me.* **4** an upper floor in a theatre, usu. with seats set in curved rows: *Are we going to sit in the circle or in the stalls?* —see also DRESS CIRCLE, and see picture at THEATRE **5** a process or chain of events which finishes where it began; CYCLE: *The circle of the seasons has brought us again to spring.* | *We seem to be arguing in a circle|to be going round in circles.* **6** come full circle to go through several changes or developments and end up back at the starting point: *After several years of working in a band, he has now gone back to being a solo musician, so his career has come full circle.* **7** square the circle to attempt something impossible –see also CORN CIRCLE, GREAT CIRCLE, ROUNDABOUT, VICIOUS CIRCLE

circle² v **1** [T] to draw or form a circle around: *The teacher circled the pupils' spelling mistakes in red ink.* **2** [I;T] to move or travel in a circle (around): *The plane circled (around) the airport before landing.* | *a spacecraft circling the Earth* | *The vultures were circling overhead.*

cir·clet /ˈsɜːklɪt‖ˈsɜːr-/ n a narrow round band of gold, silver, jewels, etc., worn on the head, arms, or neck as decoration, esp. formerly

cir·cuit /ˈsɜːkɪt‖ˈsɜːr-/ n **1** (movement along) a curving path that forms a complete circle round an area: *We made|did the circuit of the old city walls.* | *She ran three circuits of the track.* | *the circuit of the Earth round the sun* **2** (the places on) a regularly repeated journey from place to place made by a person or group for usu. professional purposes: *The judge is on circuit for most of the year.* (=visits different courts) | *He retired this year after over ten years on the tennis circuit.* (=places visited by professional players for important games) | *a well-known entertainer on the night club circuit.* —see also CIRCUIT COURT **3** the complete circular path of an electric current: *A break in the circuit had caused the lights to go out.* | *a circuit diagram* —see also CLOSED CIRCUIT TELEVISION, PRINTED CIRCUIT, SHORT CIRCUIT **4** a group of establishments offering the same films, plays, etc.

circuit break·er /ˈ·· ˌ··/ n *tech* a SWITCH or other apparatus which interrupts an electric current if this becomes necessary, e.g. for safety reasons

circuit court /ˈ·· ˌ·/ n a court that is held regularly at several places outside the country's main city, only at particular times of the year, when a judge visits it

cir·cu·i·tous /sɜːˈkjuːɪtəs‖sɜːr-/ adj *fml* going a long way round instead of in a straight line; not direct: *the river's circuitous course* | *a circuitous route* – ~**ly** adv

cir·cu·lar¹ /ˈsɜːkjʊləʳ‖ˈsɜːr-/ adj **1** round and usu. flat; shaped like a circle: *a circular table* **2** forming or moving in a circle: *a circular bus route* | (fig.) *a circular argument that doesn't lead anywhere*

circular² n a printed advertisement, paper, or notice given or sent to a large number of people for them to read: *There were only bills and circulars in the post this morning.*

cir·cu·lar·ize *also* -**ise** *BrE* /ˈsɜːkjʊləraɪz‖ˈsɜːr-/ v [T] to send circulars to (a group of people)

circular saw /ˌ··· ˈ·/ n a SAW² which cuts with sharp teeth on a round metal blade and is driven by a motor – compare CHAIN SAW

cir·cu·late /ˈsɜːkjʊleɪt‖ˈsɜːr-/ v [I;T] to (cause to) move or flow around in a closed system, always remaining within that system: *Blood circulates through the body.* | *Money circulates in the economy.* **2** [I;T] to (cause to) spread widely; DISSEMINATE: *The news of the enemy's defeat quickly circulated round the town.* | *A lot of false information has been circulated.* | *Rumours of a military coup began to circulate.* **3** [I] to move from person to person, esp. at a social gathering; MINGLE: *He circulated at the party, talking to lots of people.* —**latory** /ˌsɜːkjʊˈleɪtəri, ˈsɜːkjʊlətəri‖ˈsɜːrkjʊlətɔːri/ adj

circulating cap·i·tal /ˈ··· ˌ··/ n [U] see FLOATING CAPITAL

cir·cu·la·tion /ˌsɜːkjʊˈleɪʃən‖ˌsɜːr-/ n **1** [C;U] the flow of gas or liquid around a closed system, esp. the movement of blood through the body: *Bad circulation makes you feel cold.* **2** [U] the movement of something, such as news or money, from place to place or from person to person: *the circulation of rumours* | *The government has reduced the number of £5 notes in circulation.* | *These ideas have* *been in circulation for some time.* | *She's* **out of circulation** (=not taking part in social life) *at the moment because she's working for her exams.* **3** [S] the average number of copies of a newspaper, magazine, etc., that are regularly sold: *This magazine has a large circulation*|*a circulation of 400,000.* | *Our circulation will fall if we increase the price to 45p.* | *a mass-circulation newspaper* (=read by a large number of people)

circum- see WORD FORMATION

cir·cum·cise /ˈsɜːkəmsaɪz‖ˈsɜːr-/ *v* [T] **1** to cut off the skin at the end of the sex organ (=the FORESKIN) of (a male) **2** to cut off the CLITORIS of (a female)

cir·cum·ci·sion /ˌsɜːkəmˈsɪʒən‖ˌsɜːr-/ *n* [C;U] the act of circumcising, esp. of a boy baby, esp. as part of a Jewish or Muslim religious ceremony, or because it is believed to be wise for health reasons

cir·cum·fer·ence /səˈkʌmfərəns‖sər-/ *n* **1** [C;U] the length round the outside of a circle; distance round a round object: *the circumference of a wheel*|*of the Earth* | *It is 3 metres in circumference.* **2** [(*the*) S (**of**)] the line round the outside edge of a figure, object, or place of any shape; PERIPHERY —**-ential** /səˌkʌmfəˈrenʃəl‖sər-/ *adj*

cir·cum·flex /ˈsɜːkəmfleks‖ˈsɜːr-/ *adj* [A] (of an ACCENT¹ (3) put above a letter to show pronunciation) being the mark over ê —compare ACUTE (6), GRAVE³

cir·cum·lo·cu·tion /ˌsɜːkəmləˈkjuːʃən‖ˌsɜːr-/ *n* [C;U] *fml* (an example of) the use of an unnecessarily large number of words to express an idea, esp. when trying to avoid answering a difficult question directly —**-tory** /-ˈlɒkjətəri, -ləˈkjuːtəri‖-ˈlɑːkjətɔːri/ *adj*

cir·cum·nav·i·gate /ˌsɜːkəmˈnævɪɡeɪt‖ˌsɜːr-/ *v* [T] *fml* to sail completely round (the Earth, an island, etc.) —**-gation** /ˌsɜːkəmnævɪˈɡeɪʃən‖ˌsɜːr-/ *n* [C;U]

cir·cum·scribe /ˈsɜːkəmskraɪb‖ˈsɜːr-/ *v* [T] **1** [*often pass.*] *fml* to keep within narrow limits; RESTRICT: *His activities have been severely circumscribed since his illness.* **2** *tech* to draw a line round: *to circumscribe a square by drawing a circle round it* —**-scription** /ˌsɜːkəmˈskrɪpʃən‖ˌsɜːr-/ *n* [U]

cir·cum·spect /ˈsɜːkəmspekt‖ˈsɜːr-/ *adj* (of a person or action) acting or done after careful thought; CAUTIOUS: *I'm surprised he got married in such a hurry — he's usually pretty circumspect.* —**-ly** *adv* —**spection** /ˌsɜːkəmˈspekʃən‖ˌsɜːr-/ *n* [U]

cir·cum·stance /ˈsɜːkəmstæns, -stəns‖ˈsɜːr-/ *n* **1** [C *usu. pl.*] a fact, condition, or event concerned with and influencing another event, person, or course of action: *We can't judge what he did until we know all the circumstances.* | *This rule can only be waived in exceptional circumstances.* | *The level of the fine depends on the circumstances of the case.* | *They have been living* **in reduced circumstances** (=with very little money) *since she lost her job.* **2** [U] the combination of facts, conditions, or events that influence one's action, regarded as being outside one's control: *Force of circumstance compelled us to close the business.* | *a victim of circumstance* **3** [U] formal and usu. official ceremony: *the* **pomp and circumstance** *of a royal wedding* **4** **in/under no circumstances** never; whatever happens: *Under no circumstances must you leave the house.* **5** **in/under the circumstances** considering the situation at a particular time: *I wanted to leave but then my uncle died, so under the circumstances I decided to stay.* | *The result was the best that could be expected in the circumstances.*

cir·cum·stan·tial /ˌsɜːkəmˈstænʃəl◂‖ˌsɜːr-/ *adj* **1** (of information, esp. concerning a crime) based on or dealing with related circumstances, but not really proving anything; INCIDENTAL: *You can't convict him merely on* **circumstantial evidence.** **2** *fml* (of a description) containing all the details: *a circumstantial account of the visit* —**-ly** *adv*

cir·cum·vent /ˌsɜːkəmˈvent‖ˌsɜːr-/ *v* [T] to avoid or defeat (as if) by passing round, esp. as the result of cleverness: *The company opened an office abroad in order to circumvent the tax laws.* —**-vention** /-ˈvenʃən/ *n* [U]

cir·cus /ˈsɜːkəs‖ˈsɜːr-/ *n* **1** (a performance by) a travelling group of people and animals who entertain the public with acts of skill and daring. Circuses are generally considered to be entertainment for children. They include performances by CLOWNs and wild animals such as lions,

tigers, and elephants. The RINGMASTER introduces all the acts. A circus will usually stay in an area for a few days and then move on to another town. **2** the place, usu. covered with a tent, where this performance takes place, with seats round a ring in the middle **3** *BrE* a round open area where a number of streets join together: *Oxford Circus* **4** *derog* a noisy badly behaved meeting, etc. **5** (in ancient Rome) a space surrounded by seats for the public in which fights, races, etc., took place

cirque /sɜːk‖sɜːrk/ *n tech* a steep-sided bowl-shaped hollow on a mountain side, originally formed by ice —see picture at MOUNTAIN

cir·rho·sis /sɪˈrəʊsəs/ *n* [U] *med* a very serious disease of the LIVER, which often leads to death. Cirrhosis of the liver is often caused by drinking too much alcohol.

cir·rus /ˈsɪrəs/ *n* [U] light feathery white cloud very high up —compare CUMULUS, NIMBUS (1)

CIS /ˌsiː aɪ ˈes/ [*the*] the Commonwealth of Independent States; the name taken by a group of states which formerly made up most of the USSR, the largest of which is Russia

cis·sy /ˈsɪsi/ *n, adj* SISSY

Cis·ter·cian¹ /sɪˈstɜːʃən‖-ɜːr-/ *n* a member of a religious group begun at Citeaux, France in 1098 in order to follow more closely Saint Benedict's rules, which include little sleep, hard work, and no meat

Cistercian² *adj* of the religious order of Cistercians: *a Cistercian chapel*

cis·tern /ˈsɪstən‖-ərn/ *n* a container with a pipe leading in and out, used for storing water, esp. for a TOILET

cit·a·del /ˈsɪtədəl, -del/ *n* **1** a strong heavily-armed fort, usu. in, near, or above a city, built to be a last place of safety and defence in time of war **2** *fml or lit* a place where something is kept safe or kept in existence; STRONGHOLD: *the last citadel of freedom*

ci·ta·tion /saɪˈteɪʃən/ *n* **1** [C (**for**)] an official statement concerning a person's qualities or actions, esp. bravery in battle **2** [C] a short passage taken from something written or spoken; QUOTATION **3** [U] the act of citing or being cited

cite /saɪt/ *v* [T] **1** to mention, esp. as an example in a statement, argument, etc.; QUOTE: *The minister cited the latest crime figures as proof of the need for more police.* **2** to call (someone) to appear before a court of law; give a SUMMONS to. *He was cited in a divorce case.* **3** [(**for**)] *fml* to mention as worthy of praise; COMMEND: *cited for bravery in an official report*

Cit·i·bank /ˈsɪtibæŋk/ the largest bank in the US, with branches in many countries and its main offices in New York City

cit·i·zen /ˈsɪtɪzən/ *n* **1** a person who lives in a particular city or town, esp. one who has voting or other rights there **2** a person who belongs to a particular country by birth or by being naturalized (NATURALIZE), who gives loyalty to it, and expects protection from it, whether or not he/she actually lives there: *She's a British citizen but lives in India.* | *She became a US citizen after living there for several years.* —compare ALIEN² (2), NATIONAL², SUBJECT¹ (5); see also CITIZENSHIP

Citizen Kane /ˌsɪtɪzən ˈkeɪn/ a film about a man who owned several important newspapers. It was directed by Orson Welles, who also acted in it.

cit·i·zen·ry /ˈsɪtɪzənri/ *n* [U+*sing./pl. v*] *old use* all the citizens in a place

Citizens Ad·vice Bu·reau /ˌ··· ·ˈ·· ·ˌ·/ also **CAB**— *n* [*the*] (in Britain) a largely VOLUNTARY organization with branches in many towns and cities which gives free advice to members of the public who need help with legal, financial, and other problems. It gets its money from local government and from the Department of Trade and Industry.

citizen's ar·rest /ˌ··· ·ˈ·/ *n* an act by someone who is not a police officer of arresting (ARREST) a person who has done something illegal: *Peter clapped his hand on the man's shoulder and said "I am making a citizen's arrest".*

Cit·i·zens' Band /ˌ··· ˈ·◂/ *n* [U] see CB

Citizens' Char·ter /ˌ··· ˈ··/ [*the*] a statement by John Major's Conservative government of the standards of service which the public has a right to expect from

British government departments and organizations

cit·i·zen·ship /ˈsɪtɨzənʃɪp/ n [U] the rights of a citizen; state of being a citizen: *After eight years in the country he applied for citizenship.* | *Canadian citizenship*

cit·ric ac·id /ˌsɪtrɪk ˈæsɨd/ n [U] a weak acid obtained from the juice of some fruits, esp. LEMON and LIME⁴ juice

Cit·ro·ën /ˈsɪtrəʊən, ˈsɪtrən‖ ˌsɪtrəʊˈen/ *tdmk* a French company that makes cars. Citroën cars are well-known for clever and modern DE-SIGN —see also DEUX-CHEVAUX

2CV

cit·ron /ˈsɪtrən/ n **1** [C] a pale yellow thick-skinned fruit like a LEMON **2** [U] the preserved skin of this fruit, used for giving a special taste to cakes

cit·ro·nel·la /ˌsɪtrəˈnelə/ n [U] a plant similar to grass which is used to produce **citronella oil**, which smells of LE-MONs and is used to keep insects away

cit·rus¹ /ˈsɪtrəs/ also **citrus tree** /ˈ·· ·/— n any of several types of prickly trees of the orange family grown in warm countries for their juicy fruit

citrus², **citrous** *adj* [A] of citrus trees and their fruit: *citrus fruits such as oranges, lemons, and limes*

cit·y /ˈsɪti/ n **1** a large group of houses and other buildings where people live and work, usu. having a centre of entertainment and business activity. It is usu. larger and more important than a town, and in Britain it usu. has a CATHEDRAL: *an office in the city centre* | *the city of St Albans* | *Paris is the capital city of France.* —compare TOWN, VILLAGE **2** [+sing./pl. v] all the people who live in a city: *a city living in fear* —see also GARDEN CITY, INNER CITY

City also **City of Lon·don** /ˌ·· ·ˈ··/ *fml*— [the] *BrE* an area in central London which is the British centre for money matters. It measures one square mile (2.5 square kilometres). The Bank of England and the Stock Exchange are here, as well as many financial companies. Few people live in the City, but many travel there each day to work: *There are rumours in the City that the company is about to be taken over.* | *a firm of City stockbrokers* —compare WALL STREET; see also CITY GENT and see colour map on page 817

city desk /ˈ·· ·/ n *AmE* a department within a newspaper which deals with local news (=news of the city in which the newspaper is produced) rather than national or international news: *Lou Grant ran the city desk for the Herald.*

city-dwel·ler /ˈ·· ˌ··/ n a person who lives in a city

city fa·ther /ˌ·· ˈ··/ n [usu. pl.] pomp, esp. *AmE* a member of the governing body of a city

city gent /ˌ·· ˈ·/ n *BrE* a man who wears a dark or pin-stripe suit to his job in the business or government institutions of central London. When people think of city gents they have in their minds a picture of a man wearing a BOWLER HAT and carrying a black UMBRELLA, even though few people look like this today.

city gent

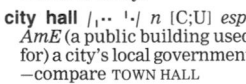

city hall /ˌ·· ˈ·/ n [C;U] esp. *AmE* (a public building used for) a city's local government —compare TOWN HALL

City of Da·vid /ˌ·· · ˈ··/ [the] *Bibl* Jerusalem

city slick·er /ˌ·· ˈ··/ n sometimes derog a person who lives and works in a city and has no experience of (the hardships of) country life: *city slickers hitting the holiday trail to a working ranch*

city-state /ˌ·· ˈ·‖ˈ·· ·, ˌ·· ˈ·/ n (esp. in former times) a city which, with the surrounding country area, forms an independent state: *Athens was one of the city-states of ancient Greece.* —compare NATION STATE

City Tech·nol·o·gy Col·lege /ˌ·· ·ˈ··· ˌ··/ also **CTC** *infml*— n a college in Britain for young people over 16 which specializes in technical education. Its money comes partly from the government and partly from industrial companies.

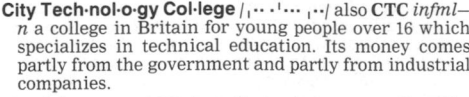

civ·et /ˈsɪvɨt/ n **1** [C] also **civet cat** /ˈ·· ·/ a small catlike animal of Asia and Africa **2** [U] a strong-smelling liquid obtained from a civet and used in making PERFUME

civ·ic /ˈsɪvɪk/ adj [A] of a city or its citizens: *The president's visit was the most important civic event of the year.* | *civic duties/pride*

civic cen·tre /ˌ·· ˈ··/ n an area in a town where there is a planned group of public buildings, e.g. local government offices, theatres, etc.

civic du·ty /ˌ·· ˈ··/ n any of the things which a citizen is expected to do, e.g. helping a police officer who asks for help

civic-mind·ed /ˌ·· ˈ··◄/ adj *AmE* favouring or supporting the interests of the COMMUNITY: *No civic-minded person would leave a wreck like that in their front yard.*

civ·ics /ˈsɪvɪks/ n [U] a social science dealing with the rights and duties of citizens, the way government works, etc.

civ·ies /ˈsɪviz/ n [P] CIVVIES

civ·il /ˈsɪvəl/ adj **1** [A no comp.] of, belonging to, or consisting of the ordinary population of citizens; not military or religious: *We were married in a civil ceremony, not in church.* | *civil strife/unrest/disorder* (=fighting between citizens) | *civil aviation* (=aircraft for ordinary citizens, rather than military aircraft) —compare CIVILIAN **2** [A no comp.] belonging to, or judged under, CIVIL LAW: *It was a civil case so he was not sent to prison.* | *a civil offence* —compare CRIMINAL¹ (1,2) **3** polite enough to be acceptable, though without being friendly; COURTEOUS: *Try to be civil to her, even if you don't like her.* | **Keep a civil tongue in your head!** (=Stop speaking rudely!) | *That's very civil of you.* (=That's very kind of you.) —see also CIVILLY

civil a·vi·a·tion /ˌ·· ··ˈ··/ n [U] the operation of aircraft for anything except military purposes: *Civil aviation has been suspended within 100 miles of the war zone.*

Civil Aviation Au·thor·i·ty /ˌ·· ··ˈ·· ·ˌ··/ also **CAA**— [the] (in Britain) an independent organization which controls the operation of AIRLINES, esp. with regard to safety

civil de·fence /ˌ·· ·ˈ·/ n [U] the protection of the ordinary population of a country against military attack by an enemy, esp. from the air

civil dis·o·be·di·ence /ˌ·· ··ˈ···/ n [U] refusal to obey laws that one thinks are unjust, esp. in a non-violent way that ones hopes will force the government to change its position. Henry David Thoreau wrote an ESSAY called *Civil Disobedience* in the mid-19th century from where many of the ideas about and reasons for this practice come. One of the most famous examples of civil disobedience was the action taken by Mahatma Gandhi in India in the early 1920s.

civil en·gi·neer·ing /ˌ·· ··ˈ··/ n [U] the planning, building, and repair of public works, such as roads, bridges, large public buildings, etc. —**civil engineer** n

ci·vil·ian /sɨˈvɪljən/ n, adj (a person) not of the armed forces: *a return to civilian government after years of military rule* | *civilian clothes* | *the shooting of innocent civilians* —compare CIVIL¹

ci·vil·i·ty /sɨˈvɪlɨti/ n [C;U] (an act of) politeness and good manners: *He greeted us with civility.* | *We exchanged a few civilities.* (=polite remarks)

civ·i·li·za·tion also **-sation** *BrE* /ˌsɪvəl-aɪˈzeɪʃən‖-vələ-ˈzeɪ-/ n **1** [U] (the people or countries that have reached) an advanced stage of human development marked by a high level of art, religion, science, and social and political organization: *the benefits of modern civilization* | *a danger that threatens the whole of civilization* —compare CULTURE **2** [C] a civilized society of a particular time or place: *the civilization of ancient China* **3** [U] *infml* life in a place which has all the comforts of the modern world: *When we get down this mountain and back to civilization, I want a hot bath!* **4** [U] the process of civilizing or of being civilized **5 the end of civilizaton as we know it** the end of the world. This phrase is used, not too seriously, esp. in films and books about situations in which the Earth is in great danger: *Will these aliens invade? Could this mean the end of civilization as we know it?*

civ·i·lize ‖ also **-lise** *BrE* /ˈsɪvəl-aɪz/ *v* [T] **1** to bring from a lower stage of development to a highly developed stage of social organization: *The Romans hoped to civilize all the tribes of ancient Europe.* **2** to cause to improve in habits and manners: *the teacher's civilizing influence on her young pupils*

civ·i·lized ‖ also **-lised** *BrE* /ˈsɪvəl-aɪzd/ *adj* **1** [*no comp.*] having a highly developed social organization; in a state of civilization. *The dictator's terrible crimes will be condemned by all civilized nations.* **2** pleasant, charming, and without roughness of manner or style: *a very civilized person* | *We spent a rather civilized evening in a quiet little wine bar.*

civil law /ˌ·· ˈ·/ *n* [U] **1** the body of law concerned with judging private quarrels between people and dealing with the rights of private citizens, rather than with criminal or military cases **2** also **Roman Law**— the body of law belonging to ancient Rome and the modern systems of law based upon it **3** the law of a particular state as opposed to other kinds of law, such as international law —compare CANON LAW, COMMON LAW, CRIMINAL LAW

civil lib·er·ty /ˌ·· ˈ···/ also **civil liberties** *pl.*— *n* [U] freedom of opinion, thought, speech, action, etc., so long as this does not harm other people —compare CIVIL RIGHTS

civil list /ˈ·· ·/ *n* [*the*+S] (in Britain) the sum of money voted yearly by Parliament to the King or Queen as head of state, and to certain other related people

civ·il·ly /ˈsɪvəl-i/ *adv* **1** politely; in a civil way: *If you can't behave civilly you'd better leave.* **2** in accordance with CIVIL LAW

civil mar·riage /ˈ·· ˌ··/ *n* (in law) a marriage performed by someone who is not a priest

civil par·ish /ˌ·· ˈ··/ *n* a PARISH (2)

civil rights /ˌ·· ˈ·/ *n* [P] the non-political rights of freedom, equality, etc., which belong to a citizen without regard to race, religion, colour, sex, etc.: *Do blacks and whites have the same civil rights in your country?* | *equal civil rights for men and women* —compare CIVIL LIBERTY; see also BILL OF RIGHTS

Civil Rights Act of 1964 /ˌsɪvəl ˌraɪts ækt əv ˌnaɪntiːn sɪksti ˈfɔːᵊ/ [*the*] an American law which says that businesses must treat people equally no matter what colour or religion they are or where they are from. This law also says that businesses such as restaurants or hotels cannot refuse to serve someone because of their colour, and that no business can refuse to hire someone for a job because of their colour. In the South, especially, many white people during the 1960s were very upset by this law and there were many times when it was broken. Many people in the US remember news reports and photographs of black people sitting down in restaurants that had once only served white people and that this caused much hate and often violence. Today feelings are not as strong but many black people still face PREJUDICE.

civil rights move·ment /ˌ·· ˈ· ˌ··/ [*the*] in the US, the attempt from 1954 onwards to get equal rights for black people, and people of any race or colour, through non-violent actions, was led esp. by Dr Martin Luther King, Jr. Several cases involving civil rights went to the US Supreme Court; the most important was BROWN v. BOARD OF EDUCATION OF TOPEKA. In 1964 a Civil Rights Act was passed making unequal treatment of races illegal, and in 1965, the government banned (BAN) the last tests and restrictions which some states had used to stop black people from voting; this gave all adults the right to vote, regardless of colour —see also CIVIL RIGHTS ACT OF 1964, JIM CROW, Martin Luther KING, SOUTH (1) (CULTURAL NOTE)

civil ser·vant /ˌ·· ˈ··/ *n* a person employed in the CIVIL SERVICE —see OFFICER (USAGE)

► CULTURAL NOTE In Britain, the STEREOTYPE of a civil servant is of someone who insists on doing everything in an official way and obeying a lot of small, unimportant rules. Civil servants are also thought of first as being rather boring men all dressed in similar grey suits, although of course there are many female civil servants. ◄

civil ser·vice /ˌ·· ˈ··/ [*the*] (*often caps.*) **1** all the various departments of the British and US national governments

except the armed forces, law courts, and religious organizations. In Britain, people enter the civil service by taking examinations in competition with other people. Civil servants are not allowed to take any active part in politics. They do not change when the government changes. In the US, most people enter through examinations, but some people receive civil service posts as a reward for political services, and so the holders of these posts change depending which party forms the government: *She works in the civil service.* **2** [+*sing./pl. v*] all the people who are employed in these departments: *The civil service get/gets longer holidays than we do.*

civil war /ˌ·· ˈ·/ *n* **1** [C;U] (a) war between opposing groups of people from the same country, fought within that country: *Civil war broke out after the President's death.* | *The country is now in a state of civil war.* **2** [*the*] also **American Civil War, the War Between the States** a war (1861–65) between the American North and South, which began when 11 southern states **rebelled** (=opposed and fought) against the US **Federal** government. These **rebel** states formed a separate government called the CONFEDERACY, and together tried to **secede** (=separate) from the UNION (=the US). The northern states (also 11 in number at that time), under the US government, formed the Union army and fought to keep the South.The war was caused mainly by the disagreement over **slavery** (=owning slaves). The South's economy depended on slavery and farming, while the North depended on industry and Northerners wanted an end to slavery. As new states in the West were joining the US, members of CONGRESS had argued over whether the new states should be allowed to have slavery, and whether the government should be allowed to forbid it. The disagreement over the balance of power between the **Federal** (=central) government and state governments was a bitter one. When President LINCOLN was elected, the southern states feared that he would **abolish** (=forbid) slavery altogether, so they **seceded from the Union**.The Confederacy's president was Jefferson DAVIS, and its army was was led by Robert E. LEE. The Union, or **Yankees**, under Lincoln, fought under the command of Ulysses S. GRANT. The South won many battles, and Lee was much admired for his military excellence, but the North had more soldiers and supplies. More than 600,000 soldiers died before the North won a victory which kept the Union (=North and South) together.During the war, Lincoln declared the slaves of the Confederacy to be free (see EMANCIPATION PROCLAMATION). After the war, slavery was abolished altogether by the 13th **Amendment** (=change) of the CONSTITUTION. The period of rebuilding the country, esp. the South, that followed the war was called RECONSTRUCTION. **3** [*the*] also **the English Civil War** —a war (1642–51) resulting from a power struggle between King Charles I and the English parliament led by Oliver Cromwell, during which the King, Charles I, was defeated and executed (EXECUTE) —see also SPANISH CIVIL WAR

civ·vies , civies /ˈsɪviz/ *n* [P] *sl* the kind of clothes ordinary people wear, as opposed to a military uniform. This word is used mainly by people in the armed forces: *an army officer in civvies*

civ·vy street /ˈsɪvi striːt/ *n* [U] *sl, now rare* life outside the armed forces. This word is used mainly by people who are or have been in the armed forces.

clack /klæk/ *v* **1** [I;T] to (cause to) make one or more quick sharp sounds: *The typewriters clacked busily.* **2** [I] *infml* to talk quickly and continuously; CHATTER: *clacking tongues* (=people talking quickly and continuously) —**clack** *n* [S] : *the incessant clack of knitting needles*

Clack·man·nan·shire /klækˈmænənʃəᵊ/ a former COUNTY in central Scotland, now part of Central REGION

Clac·ton /ˈklæktən/ also **Clacton-on-Sea** /ˌ·· · ˈ·/ *fml*— a coastal town in Essex, England

clad /klæd/ *adj* [(**in**)] *esp. lit* (*often in comb.*) covered or clothed: *She was clad all in silk and lace.* | *poorly-clad children* | *an armour-clad ship*

Clai·borne /ˈkleɪbɔːn‖-bɔːrn/, **Craig** /kreɪg/ (1920–) an American writer of cookbooks and newspaper articles on food

claim¹ /kleɪm/ *v* **1** [I (**on, for**);T] to ask for, take, or state that one should have (something to which one has a right): *Did you claim on the insurance after your car*

accident? | *Old people are entitled to claim a special heating allowance from the government.* | *If no one claims the lost umbrella, the person who found it can keep it.* | *A small terrorist group has claimed responsibility for the bombing in London.* | (fig.) *The flood claimed hundreds of lives.* **2** [T+*to-v*|(*that*); *obj*] to declare to be true; state, esp. in the face of opposition; MAINTAIN: *They claim to have discovered/claim that they have discovered a cure for the disease, but this has not yet been proved.* **3** [T] to deserve or need: *This problem claims our undivided attention.*

claim² *n* **1** [C;U (**for, on**)] a demand or request for something which one has a right to have: *The management is considering the union's pay claim.* | *When her house was burgled, she made a claim on the insurance.* | *He put in a claim for his travelling expenses.* | *He laid claim to the throne.* (=said it was his by right) **2** [C;U (**to, on**)] a right to something: *He has a rightful claim to the property; it was his mother's.* | *You may be my sister, but that doesn't mean you have any claims on me.* | *The town's claim to fame is that it has the country's oldest church.* **3** [C] a statement that something is true or real, esp. one that other people may disagree with; ASSERTION: *The government say they have reduced personal taxation, but I would dispute this claim.* [+*to-v*] *I make no claim to understand all the complexities of the matter.* [+*that*] *I don't accept the claim that they have reduced taxes.* **4** [C] something claimed, esp. an area of land or a sum of money —see also **jump a claim** (JUMP¹ (10)), **stake a claim** (STAKE²)

clai·mant /ˈkleɪmənt/ *n* [(**to**)] *fml or law* a person who asks for something, esp. money, because they think they have a right to it: *rival claimants to the throne* | *claimants of unemployment benefit*

clair·voy·ant /kleəˈvɔɪənt‖kleər-/ *n* a person who claims to be able to see what will happen in the future — **clairvoyant** *adj* : *clairvoyant powers* —**ance** *n* [U]

clam¹ /klæm/ *n* a small soft-bodied sea animal with a shell in two parts that can open and close, that lives in sand or mud and can be eaten: (fig.) *She shut up like a clam* (=stopped talking suddenly) *when they started to ask questions.*

clam² *v* -mm- *esp. AmE* **go clamming** to collect clams by digging in the sand or mud
clam up *phr v* [I] *sl* to become silent, esp. because of fear or unwillingness to give information: *She clammed up whenever I mentioned her husband.*

clam·bake /ˈklæmbeɪk/ *n esp. AmE* **1** an informal party by the sea, esp. one where clams, etc., are cooked and eaten **2** *sl* a noisy, high-spirited party or political meeting

clam·ber /ˈklæmbəʳ/ *v* [I+*adv*|*prep*] to climb using both the feet and hands and usu. with difficulty: *We clambered down the side of the cliff.* | *Tell the children to stop clambering (about) over my new furniture.*

clam·my /ˈklæmi/ *adj* unpleasantly sticky, slightly wet, and usu. cold: *clammy hands/weather* —**mily** *adv* —**miness** *n* [U]

clam·our¹ *BrE* ‖ **clamor** *AmE* /ˈklæməʳ/ *n* **1** [S] a loud continuous, usu. confused noise or shouting: *a clamour of voices/of bells* **2** [U (**for**)] a continuous strong demand or complaint made by a large number of people: *The government ignored the clamour for a public inquiry into these events.* —**orous** *adj* : *clamorous demands*

clamour² *BrE* ‖ **clamor** *AmE* *v* [I] **1** [I (**for**)] to express (a demand) continually, loudly, and strongly: *The people were clamouring for his execution.* | *The children were clamouring to be fed.* **2** to make a loud confused noise

clamp¹ /klæmp/ *n* **1** [C] an apparatus for fastening or holding things firmly together, usu. consisting of two parts that can be moved nearer together by turning a screw —see picture at LABORATORY **2** [C;*the*+S] also **wheel-clamp** *fml* ‖ **Denver boot** *AmE*— an apparatus that is fastened to the wheels of a car, etc., in order to prevent it from moving

clamp² *v* **1** [T+*obj*+*adv*|*prep*] to fasten or hold with a clamp: *Clamp the two pieces of wood together until the glue dries.* | *Clamp it onto the edge of the table.* **2** [T] also **wheelclamp** *BrE fml* ‖ **boot** *AmE*— to prevent (a car, etc.) from moving by putting a clamp on the wheels. In Britain, vehicles are usually clamped in a town because they have been parked in the wrong place. Their owners

have to pay to get them back: *Oh no! My van's been/I've been clamped again! — —er n*
clamp down *phr v* [I (**on**)] to use one's power to limit or prevent practices that are disapproved of: *The police are determined to clamp down on violence at football matches.* —see also CLAMPDOWN

clamp·down /ˈklæmpdaʊn/ *n* [(**on**)] a sudden usu. official limitation or prevention of doing or saying something: *The government has ordered a (total) clampdown on public demonstrations.* —see also CLAMP **down**

clan /klæn/ *n* [C+*sing./pl. v*] **1** (esp. in Scotland) a group of families, all originally descended from one family and all usu. having the same family name. In the past, each clan had a chief and wore cloth decorated with a particular pattern (a TARTAN): *the McIntosh clan* **2** *humor* a large family or group of related people: *The whole clan is/are coming to stay with us at Christmas.*

clan·des·tine /klænˈdestɪn/ *adj* done secretly or privately, and often against the law: *a clandestine meeting/marriage* — —**ly** *adv* — —**ness** *n* [U]

clang /klæŋ/ *v* [I;T] to (cause to) make a loud ringing sound like the sound of metal being hit —**clang** *n* [S]

clang·er /ˈklæŋəʳ/ *n BrE sl* a very noticeable mistake or unintentionally foolish remark: *She dropped a clanger when she mentioned his ex-wife.*

clan·gor ‖ also **-gour** *BrE* /ˈklæŋəʳ/ *n* [(*the*) S] *esp. lit* a sound of repeated clanging: *the clangor of the bells* — ~**ous** *adj* — —**ously** *adv*

clank /klæŋk/ *v* [I;T] to (cause to) make a short loud sound, like that of a heavy metal chain being moved —**clank** *n* [S] : *the clank of chains as the ship's anchor was lowered into the sea*

clan·nish /ˈklænɪʃ/ *adj often derog* (of a group of people) closely united and tending not to trust or welcome people from outside the group — ~**ly** *adv* — ~**ness** *n* [U]

clans·man /ˈklænzmən/ **clans·wom·an** /-ˌwʊmən/ *fem.* — *n* **-men** /mən/ a member of a CLAN

clap¹ /klæp/ *v* -pp- **1** [I;T] to bring (one's open hands) together with a quick movement and loud sound, esp. to show approval of a performance: *The audience clapped loudly/enthusiastically at the end of the play.* —see also HANDCLAP **2** [T+*obj*+**on**] to hit lightly with the open hand in a friendly manner, usu. on the back: *His boss clapped him on the back approvingly.* **3** [T+*obj*+*adv*|*prep*] *infml* to put or place, usu. quickly and effectively: *The judge clapped her in prison before she had time to explain.* | *He clapped his hand over his mouth as soon as he realized what he had said.* **4 clap eyes on** *BrE infml* to see: *I haven't clapped eyes on her for years.*

clap² *n* **1** [C] a loud explosive sound: *a clap of thunder* **2** [S] an act of clapping the hands: *Give him a clap, everyone!* **3** [S (**on**)] a light friendly hit, usu. on the back, with the open hand

clap³ *n* [*the*] *euph sl* the disease GONORRHEA

clap·board /ˈklæpbɔːd‖ˈklæbərd, ˈklæpbɔːrd/ *n* [U] *AmE for* WEATHERBOARD (1): *a clapboard house*

Clap·ham Junc·tion /ˌklæpəm ˈdʒʌŋkʃən/ a very busy railway station in SW London where a lot of people catch a train to work or change trains

clapped-out /ˌˈ·ˈ◂/ *adj infml, esp. BrE* **1** (of a thing) old and worn out: *a clapped-out old car* **2** [F] (of a person) very tired

clap·per /ˈklæpəʳ/ *n* **1** the hammer-like object inside a bell which strikes it to make it ring **2** an apparatus that makes a repeated loud noise: *Some farmers use clappers to keep birds off their crops.* —see also CLAPPERS

clap·per·board /ˈklæpəbɔːd‖-ərbɔːrd/ *n* a wooden board on which a short description of a scene to be filmed for the cinema or television is written. It is held up in front of the camera and its two connecting parts are clapped together.

clap·pers /ˈklæpəz‖-ərz/ *n* **like the clappers** *BrE infml* very fast: *to go/run like the clappers*

Clap·ton /ˈklæptən/, **Er·ic** /ˈerɪk/ (1945-) an English popular music GUITAR player, very much admired for his great skill

clap·trap /ˈklæptræp/ *n* [U] *infml* empty, insincere, or foolish talk or writing; nonsense: *He talked a lot of dangerous claptrap about the glories of war.*

claque /klæk/ n [C+sing./pl. v] a group of people hired to give support by clapping (CLAP), esp. at a political meeting

Clare[1] /kleə^r/ a COUNTY in the W of the Republic of Ireland

Clare[2], **Dr Anthony** (1942–) a British television and radio presenter who is also a PSYCHIATRIST

Clare[3], **John** (1793–1864) an English poet who wrote poems esp. about country life and went mad in 1837

Clar·ence House /ˌklærəns ˈhaʊs/ the house in London, next to St James's Palace, where Queen Elizabeth, the Queen Mother lives

clar·et[1] /ˈklærət/ n [U] **1** red wine, from the Bordeaux area of France **2** a deep purplish red colour

claret[2] adj having a deep purplish red colour

Clar·i·dge's /ˈklærɪdʒɪz/ a London hotel. Claridge's is thought to be a place where only the rich upper classes eat and stay.

clar·i·fi·ca·tion /ˌklærɪfɪˈkeɪʃən/ n [C;U] the act of clarifying or an example of something being clarified: *They asked for further clarification/for a clarification of the government's plans.*

clar·i·fy /ˈklærɪfaɪ/ v [T] **1** fml to make clearer and easier to understand, esp. by explaining and giving more details: *Will you clarify that statement?* | *When will the government clarify its position on equal pay for women?* **2** to make (a fat, esp. butter) clear and pure, esp. by gentle heating

clar·i·net /ˌklærɪˈnet/ n a musical instrument of the WOOD-WIND family, with a single REED (2) – see picture at WOODWIND

clar·i·net·tist , **-netist** /ˌklærɪˈnetɪst/ n a clarinet player

clar·i·on /ˈklærɪən/ n (the sound made by) a kind of TRUMPET used in former times: (fig.) *the clarion call* (=very clear call) *of duty*

clar·i·ty /ˈklærɪti/ n [U] clearness, esp. the quality of being easy to understand: *clarity of expression*

Clark /klɑːk‖klɑːrk/, **Dick** (1929–) the host of several television GAME SHOWS and other programmes, known esp. for *American Bandstand*. People often say that Dick Clark looks very young for his age.

Clark, Sir Ken·neth /ˈkenəθ/ (1903–83) an EXPERT on the history of art, well-known in Britain esp. for his television programme *Civilization*

Clark, Pe·tu·la /pəˈtjuːlə ‖ -ˈtuː-/ (1932–) a female British singer of popular music

Clark, William (1770–1838) an American EXPLORER –see LEWIS AND CLARK

Clarke /klɑːk‖klɑːrk/, **Arthur C.** (1917–) a British scientist and writer of SCIENCE FICTION books, probably best-known for his book *2001: A Space Odyssey* which was made into an extremely popular and successful film in 1984

Clarke, Ken·neth /ˈkenəθ/ (1940–) an important British politician of the Conservative Party

Clarks /klɑːks‖klɑːrks/ tdmk (any of the shops owned by) a British company that makes shoes, esp. noted for its good range of children's shoes in different widths: *I got Jenny some sandals in/from Clarks.*

clash[1] /klæʃ/ v **1** [I (with)] to be in opposition or come into opposition: *Police and demonstrators clashed* (=met and fought) *outside the palace.* | *This shirt clashes with my trousers.* (=the colours do not match) | *Her wedding clashed with* (=was at the same time as) *my exam so I couldn't go.* **2** [I;T (TOGETHER)] to (cause to) make a loud noise, as of two metal objects struck together: *The cymbals clashed.* | *She clashed two pans together to wake us up.*

clash[2] n **1** [C (of, between)] an example of opposition or disagreement; CONFLICT: *a border clash between two armies* | *a serious clash of opinions/interests* | *There have been angry clashes in the Senate between supporters and opponents of the President.* | *They're both very determined people, so there's rather a clash of personalities.* **2** [S] a loud metallic noise: *the clash of cymbals/swords*

Clash, The one of the most popular British PUNK music groups formed in the 1970s whose success continued even when punk went out of fashion

clasp[1] /klɑːsp‖klæsp/ n **1** a usu. metal fastener for hold-

ing together two things or two parts of one thing: *the clasp on a belt* **2** [usu. sing.] a tight firm hold, esp. by someone's hand or arms; GRIP

clasp[2] v [T] **1** to take and hold firmly with the hands or arms: *He clasped the child in his arms.* | *The two men clasped hands warmly.* **2** [+obj+adv/prep] to fasten with a clasp: *I clasped the necklace round her neck.*

▷ USAGE Compare **clasp**, **grasp**, and **grip**. **Clasp** means "to take and/or hold firmly inside your hand or arms": *The little girl was clasping a large doll.* **Grasp** means "to catch onto and hold firmly, especially with your hands": *I was able to save myself by grasping a rope.* **Grip** means "to take and keep a very tight hold of something, especially with your fingers or with a tool": *He gripped my arm in fear.*◁

clasp knife /ˈ· ·/ n a large knife whose blades fold into the handle; JACK KNIFE

class[1] /klɑːs‖klæs/ n **1** [C+sing./pl. v] also **classes** pl. – a social group whose members have the same political, social, and ECONOMIC position and rank: *the ruling class/classes* | *a member of the landowning class* –see also LOWER CLASS, MIDDLE CLASS, UPPER CLASS, WORKING CLASS **2** [U] the system of dividing society into groups with different social and political positions: *Class distinctions have become less important during the last 50 years.* –see also CLASS SYSTEM **3** [C+sing./pl. v] a group of pupils or students who are taught together: *The English class is/are reading Shakespeare.* | *We were both in the same class.* | *a class of 25 children* **4** [C] AmE a group of students who will finish studying in a particular year: *the class of 1979* **5** [C;U] a period of time during which pupils or students are taught: *What time does the next class begin?* | *She's attending evening classes in computer studies.* | *He told them off for talking in class.* **6** [C] a division of people or things according to their quality, level of performance, etc.: *What class (of degree) did you get? First, second, or third?* | *a first-class rail carriage* | *a top-class scientist/orchestra* | *Your mother's cooking is* **in a class of its own** *– it's marvellous!* –see also BUSINESS CLASS, CLUB CLASS, ECONOMY CLASS, FIRST CLASS, SECOND CLASS, TOURIST CLASS **7** [C] tech a division of animals or plants below a PHYLUM and above an ORDER[1] (15) **8** [U] infml a stylish quality, e.g. in clothes or social behaviour, that attracts admiration: *a girl with real class*

class[2] v [T (**as, among, with**)] to regard as belonging to a particular class or type; consider: *In some countries, people who disagree with the government are classed as criminals.*

class ac·tion /ˌ· ˈ···◁/ n AmE a LAWSUIT set up by a group of people for their own advantage and also for that of all others with the same complaint: *The miners with lung diseases brought a class action against the company.* – **class-action** adj : *a class-action suit*

class-con·scious /ˈ· ˌ··/ adj often derog very conscious of one's own social position and sometimes distrustful of, or unfriendly towards, people from other classes: *She's too class-conscious to be friendly with the cleaners.* – **~ness** n [U]

clas·sic[1] /ˈklæsɪk/ adj [A no comp.] **1** of the highest quality or class and esp. serving as a model, standard, or perfect representative of a particular type: *a classic horse race* | *Lewis Carroll's classic children's stories* | *This film is a classic western movie.* **2** of a very typical and well-known kind: *a classic example/case of love at first sight* | *a classic mistake* | *(infml) He didn't really say that? That's classic!* **3** simple in style and likely to remain fashionable for a long time: *a simple classic suit*

classic[2] n **1** a book, play, or other work of art that is regarded as being a very fine example of its type and having lasting importance: *Shakespeare's plays are among the great classics of English literature.* | *a modern classic* | *His production of "Dracula" is one of the classics of the pre-war cinema.* | (fig.) *That joke's a classic.* **2** a famous esp. sporting event, usu. with a long history –see also CLASSICS

clas·si·cal /ˈklæsɪkəl/ adj [no comp.] **1** connected with, belonging to, or influenced by the art, life and literature of ancient Greece and Rome: *classical authors/languages* | *a classical education* | *a building in the classical style of architecture* **2** (of music) written with serious artistic intentions and having an attraction that lasts over a long period of time: *She prefers pop music*

and jazz to classical music. | the works of several classical composers, including Bach and Mozart **3** based on or belonging to an old or established system of principles or methods, e.g. in art or science; TRADITIONAL or ORTHODOX: Classical scientific ideas about light were changed by Einstein. | How do you explain this in terms of classical Marxist theory?

classical my·thol·o·gy /ˌ··· ·'···/ n the ancient stories of the Greeks and Romans —see colour picture on page 423

classic car /ˌ·· '· / n a model of car, usu. not as old as a VINTAGE car, which is considered to be notable in some way, e.g. for its shape or its performance: The Ford Thunderbird/E-type Jaguar is a true classic car.

clas·si·cis·m /'klæsᵻsɪzəm/ n [U] **1** the principles, ideas, and style (esp. with regard to balance, regularity, and simpleness of form) of the art or literature of ancient Greece or Rome **2** (often cap.) (in art and literature, esp. in Europe in the 18th century) the quality of being simple, balanced, and controlled, not giving way to feeling, and following ancient models —compare REALISM (2), ROMANTICISM

clas·si·cist /'klæsᵻsᵻst/ n a person who studies CLASSICS

classic rock /ˌ·· '·/ n [U] ROCK MUSIC in the style of, and including, the most successful songs of the 1960s and 1970s, for example those of the Rolling Stones —compare HARD ROCK

clas·sics /'klæsɪks/ n [the+P;U] (often cap.) the languages, literature, and history of ancient Greece and Rome. Very few people study classics now, but in the past a person without knowledge of the subject was considered uneducated.

Classics Il·lus·tra·ted /ˌ·· '····/ AmE (any of) a group of COMICS² which retell well-known and important stories form literature: The Classics Illustrated version of "The Three Musketeers" | I read "Moby Dick" in Classics Illustrated.

clas·si·fi·ca·tion /ˌklæsᵻfᵻ'keɪʃən/ n **1** [U] the act or process of classifying people or things (such as plants, animals, books in libraries, etc.) into groups **2** [C] a group, division, class, or CATEGORY into which something is placed

clas·si·fied /'klæsᵻfaɪd/ adj **1** (of government, esp. military, information) officially secret **2** divided or arranged in classes

classified ad /ˌ··· '·/ also **classified, small ad** BrE ‖ also **want ad** AmE— n a usu. small advertisement placed in a newspaper by a person wishing to sell or buy something, offer or get employment, etc.: She scanned the column of classified ads.

clas·si·fy /'klæsᵻfaɪ/ v [T] to arrange (animals, plants, books, etc.) into classes; divide according to class or type

class·is·m /'klɑːsɪzəm‖'klæs-/ n [U] unfair opinions based on social class, esp. the belief that one's own class is the best —compare SEXISM —-**ist** adj

class·less /'klɑːsləs‖'klæs-/ adj **1** (of a society) not divided into social classes **2** belonging to no particular social class: a classless accent — ~ness n [U]

class·mate /'klɑːsmeɪt‖'klæs-/ n a member of the same class in a school, college, or, in the US, university: We were classmates ten years ago.

class·room /'klɑːs-rʊm, -ruːm‖'klæs-/ n a room in a school, college, etc., in which a class meets for a lesson

class strug·gle /ˌ·· '···◂/ also **class war** /ˌ·· '·◂/— n [(the) U] **1** disagreement and opposition between different classes in a society **2** (in Marxist political thought) the struggle for power carried on between the CAPITALIST class (=the owners of property, factories, etc.) and the PROLETARIAT (=the ordinary workers)

class sys·tem /'· ˌ··/ n [the] the division of society into UPPER CLASS, MIDDLE CLASS, and LOWER CLASS according to social background and professional position

class·work /'klɑːswɜːk‖'klæswɜːrk/ n [U] school work done by students in class, rather than as HOMEWORK

class·y /'klɑːsi‖'klæsi/ adj infml fashionable and of high class: one of the classiest restaurants in London

clat·ter¹ /'klætər/ v [I;T] to (cause to) make a clatter, esp. as a result of movement: The metal dish clattered down the stone stairs.

clatter² n **1** [S] a loud noise like that made by hard objects hitting each other: a clatter of dishes **2** [U] noise caused by people talking or busy activity: the busy clatter of the city

Clau·di·us /'klɔːdiəs/ (10 BC–54 AD) an EMPEROR of Rome. His name is known in Britain and the US esp. because of a television series called I, Claudius which was based on two books by Robert Graves.

clause /klɔːz/ n **1** tech (in grammar) a group of words containing a subject and FINITE verb, forming a sentence or part of a sentence, and often doing the work of a noun, adjective, or adverb. In "she came home when she was tired", she came home and when she was tired are two separate clauses. —compare PHRASE, SENTENCE; see also DEPENDENT CLAUSE, INDEPENDENT CLAUSE, PENALTY CLAUSE, RELATIVE CLAUSE, SUBORDINATE CLAUSE **2** a separate division of a written legal DOCUMENT with its own separate and complete meaning: Their contracts contain a no-strike clause.

Clause 28 /ˌklɔːz twenti 'eɪt/ part of a British law which forbids local government authorities from spending money on any activity which gives favourable treatment to HOMOSEXUALS

claus·tro·pho·bi·a /ˌklɔːstrə'fəʊbiə/ n [U] fear of being shut up in a small enclosed space —compare AGORAPHOBIA

claus·tro·pho·bic¹ /ˌklɔːstrə'fəʊbɪk/ n a person suffering from claustrophobia

claustrophobic² adj **1** suffering from claustrophobia **2** (of a space) causing claustrophobia: a claustrophobic little room

clav·i·chord /'klævᵻkɔːd ‖ -kɔːrd/ n an early musical instrument similar to a piano

clav·i·cle /'klævɪkəl/ n med for COLLARBONE —see picture at SKELETON

claw¹ /klɔː/ n **1** a sharp usu. curved nail on the toe of an animal or bird: The cat dug its claws into me. —see picture at BIRD **2** a limb of certain insects and sea animals, such as CRABs, used for attacking, catching, and holding objects —see picture at LOBSTER **3** the split curved end of some tools for pulling nails out of wood: a claw hammer **4** have/get one's claws in(to): **a** to show jealousy or strong dislike of (someone), esp. by saying unpleasant things about them **b** to try to trap, esp. in order to marry

claw² v [I (at);T] to tear, pull, take hold of, etc., (as if) with claws: The cat clawed a hole in my stocking/clawed at the leg of the table. | She clawed her way to the top of the political ladder.
  claw sthg. ↔ **back** phr v [T] **1** to get back with great difficulty or effort: Through aggressive advertising the company managed to claw back its share of the market. **2** esp. BrE (of a government) to get back (money given to the public in tax cuts) by means of increases in other forms of tax

clay /kleɪ/ n [U] heavy firm earth that is soft when wet but becomes hard when baked at a high temperature, from which bricks, pots, etc., are made —see also FEET OF CLAY — ~ **ey** /'kleɪ-i/ adj : clayey soil

Clay, Cas·si·us /'kæsiəs/ see MUHAMMAD ALI

clay·more /'kleɪmɔːʳ/ n a large sword used in former times in the Scottish Highlands

clay pi·geon /ˌ·· '··/ n a plate-shaped piece of baked clay thrown up into the air to be shot at in the sport of **clay pigeon shooting**

clean¹ /kliːn/ adj **1** free from dirt: Are your hands clean? | a spotlessly clean room | Sweep the floor clean. | I changed into a clean shirt. **2** free from bacteria or anything impure: clean drinking water | clean energy (=energy produced in a way that does not cause POLLUTION) **3** free from RADIOACTIVE FALLOUT: They say the nuclear power station here is completely clean. **4** not yet used; fresh: a clean piece of paper **5** morally or sexually pure: Don't worry about it; it's all good clean fun! | a clean joke (=one not concerned with sex) **6** not disobeying rules or laws; fair or honest: a clean fight | She has a clean record. (=is not a criminal) | a clean driving licence | All the presidential candidates fought a clean campaign. **7** having a smooth edge or surface; even; regular: a clean cut | the aircraft's clean lines | (fig.) to make a clean break with the past **8** [F] sl having no hidden weapons, illegal drugs, etc.: The police searched him but he was clean.

9 a clean bill of health a favourable report on the health of a person or the satisfactory condition of a machine, organization, etc.: *The factory was later given a clean bill of health by the inspector.* **10 come clean** *infml* to admit one's guilt or tell the (esp. unpleasant) truth: *Why don't you come clean about your involvement in all this?* —see also CLEANLY, **make a clean breast of** (BREAST¹) — ~**ness** *n* [U] : *The cleanness of his room surprised me.*

clean² *v* **1** [I;T] to (cause to) become clean, esp. by rubbing and often without water: *Your shoes need cleaning.* | *to clean one's nails/one's teeth/the windows* | *to clean marks off the table* —see also DRY-CLEAN, SPRING-CLEAN **2** [T] to cut out the inside parts of the body from (birds and animals that are to be eaten) —compare EVISCERATE ~**ing** *n*: *to do the cleaning*

▷ USAGE In order to clean a room and its contents you can **brush** any surface at any level using a brush, usually held in one hand. You can **sweep** the floor using a brush with a long handle. You can **dust** surfaces above floor level using a soft cloth. You can **scrub** any surface by rubbing it hard with a short, stiff brush using water. You can **wipe** any surface by rubbing it with a cloth, probably using some water. —see also WASH (USAGE)◁

clean sthg./sbdy. ↔ **out** *phr v* [T] **1** to make (the inside of a room, box, etc.) clean and tidy: *She cleaned out the rabbit's hutch.* **2** *infml* **a** to take all the money of: *If we have to get the car repaired, we'll be completely cleaned out.* **b** to steal everything from (a place): *The thieves cleaned out the store.*

clean up *phr v* **1** [I;T (=clean sthg. ↔ up)] to clean thoroughly and remove anything unwanted: *It's your turn to clean (the kitchen) up.* | *Clean up this mess at once!* | (fig.) *The new mayor has promised to clean up the town by getting rid of all the criminals.* **2** [I;T (=clean up sthg.)] *infml* to gain (a large amount of money) as profit: *We really cleaned up at the races today.* | *He cleaned up a fortune playing cards.* —see also CLEANUP

clean³ *n* [S] an act of cleaning: *Give the windows/your shoes a good clean.*

clean⁴ *adv* **1** completely: *I clean forgot it was her birthday.* [+adv/prep] *The bullet went clean through his arm.* | *The bank robbers* **got clean away.** (=escaped easily) **2 clean bowled** (in cricket) bowled (BOWL² (2)) by a ball which does not touch the BAT

clean-cut /ˌ· ˈ·◂/ *adj* **1** well shaped; regular: *a clean-cut hairstyle* **2** neat and clean in appearance; PRESENTABLE: *a clean-cut college boy*

clean·er /ˈkliːnəʳ/ *n* **1** a person whose job is cleaning offices, houses, etc. **2** a machine, apparatus, or substance used in cleaning

clean·er's *BrE* ‖ **cleaners** *AmE* /ˈkliːnəz‖-nərz/ *n* [(the) S] **1** a DRY CLEANER'S **2 take someone to the cleaner's** *infml* to cause someone to lose all their money or possessions, esp. by dishonesty

cleaning la·dy /ˈ·· ˌ·/ *n* a woman who works as a cleaner in a house, office, or public building: *She has a cleaning lady who comes in twice a week.*

clean-limbed /ˌ· ˈ·◂/ *adj apprec or humor* (esp. of a young man) tall, well-built, and active-looking

clean·li·ness /ˈklenlin̩s/ *n* [U] **1** habitual cleanness: *high standards of cleanliness* **2 cleanliness is next to godliness** you need to keep your body clean in order to be a good and religious person. This phrase is connected esp. with Puritan ideas about religion and behaviour. —see also PURITAN

clean·ly¹ /ˈkliːnli/ *adv* in a clean manner (esp. CLEAN¹ (4)): *The branch snapped cleanly in two.* | *The voting was split cleanly along party lines.*

clean·ly² /ˈklenli/ *adj fml* careful to keep clean; habitually clean

cleanse /klenz/ *v* [T] *fml* **1** to make (a cut, wound, or one's skin) clean or pure: *The nurse cleansed the wound before stitching it.* **2** [(of)] to make morally pure or free from guilt: *He asked God to cleanse him of his sins.*

cleans·er /ˈklenzəʳ/ *n* [C;U] a substance, such as a chemical liquid or powder, used for cleaning: *Always use a gentle cleanser to remove make-up from your face.*

clean-shav·en /ˌ· ˈ··◂/ *adj* with no hair on the lower part

of the face: *He used to have a moustache and beard, but now he's clean-shaven.*

clean sweep /ˌ· ˈ·/ *n* [*usu. sing.*] **1** a complete removal or change: *The company chairman has made a clean sweep and replaced his entire management team.* **2** a complete victory: *The race was a clean sweep for Germany — they finished first, second, and third.*

clean·up /ˈkliːnʌp/ *n* **1** [S] the act of cleaning thoroughly: *a cleanup campaign against industrial pollution* **2** [C] *sl, esp. AmE* a very large profit

clear¹ /klɪəʳ/ *adj* **1** easy to see through: *clear glass* **2** free from anything that marks or darkens: *The sun shone out of a clear sky.* (=with no clouds) | *clear eyes* | *clear skin* **3** easy to hear, read, or understand: *His voice rang out (as) clear as a bell.* | *a clear speaker* | *a clear style of writing* | *The instructions on the packet weren't very clear.* **4** able to think and understand quickly and well: *a clear thinker* | *He didn't have another drink because he wanted to keep a clear head for his interview.* **5** [(to)] impossible to doubt, question, or be mistaken about; plain; UNMISTAKABLE: *a clear case of murder* | *clear evidence of her guilt* | *They won by a clear majority.* | *It is becoming clear (to most people) that the government's policy was wrong.* [+wh-] *It is not yet clear whether we will be affected by these changes.* | *One thing I'd like to* **make** *absolutely* **clear** *is that...* | *I don't want this to happen again —* **do I make myself clear?** (shows annoyance) **6** [F (about)] feeling certain; having no doubts or uncertainty: *She seems quite clear about her plans.* [+wh-] *I'm still not quite clear how it works/which button to press.* **7** [(of)] open; free from anything that blocks or covers: *a clear view* | *The road is clear of snow now.* | *to tidy up one's papers and leave a clear desk* **8** (of time) free from (other) planned activity: *I see that next week is clear: let's meet then.* | *We have three clear weeks in which to finish the job.* **9** [(of)] free from guilt or blame; untroubled: *with a clear conscience* **10** [A;after *n*] *tech* (esp. of wages or profit) remaining after all taxes, etc., have been paid; NET³: *I get a clear £200 a week.* | *I get £200 a week clear.* —see also ALL CLEAR, CLARITY, CLEARLY, **the coast is clear** (COAST¹) — ~**ness** *n* [U]

clear² *adv* **1** in a clear manner: *The signal is coming in loud and clear.* **2** [(of)] out of the way; so as to be no longer inside or near: *She jumped clear (of the train).* | *When I get clear of* (=repay) *my debts, I'm going to go for a long holiday.* **3** [+adv/prep] completely; all the way: *You can see clear to the mountains today!* see also **steer clear of** (STEER¹)

clear³ *v* **1** [I;T (of)] to (cause to) become clear: *After the storm the sky cleared.* | *This soap should help clear your skin (of spots).* **2** [T (AWAY, from, off)] to remove (anything that blocks, covers, or prevents movement) from (a place): *I'll just clear all my papers off the table.* | *Will you clear the dinner plates away/clear the table?* | *Police cleared the crowd/cleared the area close to the explosion.* | *Snowploughs have been out clearing the roads.* | *He* **cleared his throat** *before beginning to speak.* | (fig.) *This agreement will* **clear the way** *for further talks.* **3** [T (of)] to show or declare to be free from blame or guilt: *He's been cleared of murdering the old lady.* **4** [T (with)] **a** to give or get official permission to or for: *The plans for the new road have not yet been cleared by the local council.* | *The plane took off as soon as it was cleared.* | *You can't begin the project until you've cleared it with the authorities.* **b** to satisfy all the official conditions of: *The car cleared customs and was soon across the border.* **5** [T] to pass by or over (something) without touching: *The horse easily cleared the fence.* **6** [T] to repay (a debt) in full **7** [I;T] **a** to pass (a cheque) from one bank to another through the CLEARINGHOUSE **b** (of a cheque) to pass in this way: *It will take four days for your cheque to clear.* **8** [T] *infml* to earn (more than the stated sum of money): *She clears £20,000 a year easily.* **9** [T] *tech* to discover the meaning of (a message in a secret language); DECODE **10 clear the air** to remove doubt and bad feeling by honest explanation **11 clear the decks** *infml* to get ready for action: *Let's clear the decks and start work.*

clear off *phr v* [I] *infml* to leave a place, often quickly: *Clear off before I call the police!*

clear out *phr v* **1** [I (of)] *infml* to leave, esp. a building or enclosed space, often quickly **2** [T] (**clear** sthg. ↔ **out**) **a** to collect and throw away (unwanted objects): *to clear out all one's old clothes* **b** to empty or make

clear of unwanted objects, dirt, etc.: *I wish you'd clear out your drawers – they're full of junk.* –see also CLEAROUT
clear up *phr v* **1** [T] (**clear** sthg. ↔ **up**) to find an answer to; explain: *to clear up a mystery* | *a murder case that was never cleared up* **2** [I;T] (=**clear** sthg. ↔ **up**)] to put in order; tidy up; finish: *I've got a big backlog of work to clear up by the weekend.* | *Don't expect me to clear up after you* (=tidy your things) *all the time!* **3** [I] to become less bad or come to an end: *I hope the weather clears up before Sunday.*

clear⁴ *n* **in the clear** *infml* free from danger, guilt, debt, etc.: *The police have gone so we're in the clear.*

clear·ance /ˈklɪərəns/ *n* **1** [C;U] the act of clearing or fact of being cleared (esp. CLEAR³ (2,4,7)): *Clearance of this cheque could take a week.* | *The ship sailed as soon as it got clearance.* | *a programme of slum clearance* (=getting rid of old houses) –see also CLEARANCES **2** [C;U] the distance between one object and another passing beneath or beside it: *The clearance between the bridge and the top of the bus was only ten centimetres.* **3** [U] also **security clearance**– official acceptance, esp. after some kind of examination, that a person can be depended on not to tell government secrets to an enemy: *You need clearance before you can work in this laboratory.*

clear·an·ces /ˈklɪərənsɪz/ *n* [*the* + P] the system of forcing people to leave their homes and land in Scotland in the 18th and 19th centuries to make the land clear for sheep farming. Many people left Scotland and went to Canada and the US.

clearance sale /ˈ··· ·/ *n* a time when a shop sells goods cheaply so as to get rid of as many as possible

clear-cut /ˌ·ˈ·◄/ *adj* **1** clear in shape; DISTINCT (2): *the clear-cut outline of the mountains against the sky* **2** clear in meaning; DEFINITE: *clear-cut plans for future expansion*

clear-head·ed /ˌ·ˈ··◄/ *adj* showing clear understanding; not confused: *a clear-headed decision* – **~ly** *adv* – **~ness** *n* [U]

clear·ing /ˈklɪərɪŋ/ *n* **1** [C] a usu. small area of land cleared of trees and bushes: *a clearing in the forest/jungle* **2** [U] (in Britain) the process of finding places at universities or POLYTECHNICs, used by students who have not done as well as expected in their A-level examinations. Usually, students are offered places before the results of their examinations are known, but they are only able to accept the place if their results are good enough. If their results are not good enough, they use the clearing system, in which they try to find a university or polytechnic that will accept them.

clearing bank /ˈ··· ·/ *n* (in Britain) a bank that handles the financial deals of companies and other people and is a member of the **London Bankers' Clearing House**

clear·ing-house /ˈklɪərɪŋhaʊs/ *n* -**houses** /ˌhaʊzɪz/ a place where banks exchange cheques and settle their accounts

clear·ly /ˈklɪəli‖ˈklɪərli/ *adv* **1** in a clear manner, esp. in a way that is easy to hear, read, or understand: *to explain something clearly/speak clearly* | *The bottle was clearly labelled.* **2** undoubtedly; plainly: *That's clearly a mistake.* | *Clearly, there will have to be an inquiry about this.*

clear·out /ˈklɪəraʊt/ *n* [S] *infml, esp. BrE* an act of clearing something out (CLEAR **out**): *We gave the house a good clearout today.*

clear-sight·ed /ˌ·ˈ··◄/ *adj* **1** able to see clearly **2** able to make good judgments about the future – **~ly** *adv* – **~ness** *n* [U]

clear·way /ˈklɪəweɪ‖ˈklɪər-/ *n esp. BrE* a stretch of road which is not a MOTORWAY but on which cars can only stop when in difficulties

cleat /kliːt/ *n* **1** [*usu. pl.*] any of several pieces of rubber, iron, etc., fastened to the SOLE (=the bottom) of a shoe to prevent slipping **2** a small bar with two short arms around which ropes can be tied, esp. on a ship

cleav·age /ˈkliːvɪdʒ/ *n* **1** [C;U] a break caused by splitting; division: *a sharp cleavage in society between rich and poor* **2** [C] the space between a woman's breasts, esp. that which can be seen when she is wearing a low-cut dress

cleave /kliːv/ *v* **cleaved** *or* **cleft** /kleft/ *or* **clove** /kləʊv/, **cleaved** *or* **cleft** *or* **cloven** /ˈkləʊvən/ [T+*obj*+*adv/prep*] *lit or old use* to divide or separate by a cutting blow
cleave to sbdy./sthg. *phr v* **cleaved to** *or* **clove to** [T] *lit or old use* **1** to remain loyal or faithful to (a person, belief, custom, etc.) **2** to stick to (something else)

cleav·er /ˈkliːvər/ *n* a heavy tool, used esp. by BUTCHERs for cutting up large pieces of meat –see picture at AXE

Cleese /kliːz/, **John** (1939–) an English actor who usu. plays humorous parts. He is unusually tall and is best known for playing men who behave in very strange and amusing ways, esp. in the television SERIES *Monty Python's Flying Circus* and as the hotel owner Basil Fawlty in the television series *Fawlty Towers* –see colour picture on page 686

John Cleese

Clee·thorpes /ˈkliːθɔːps‖-θɔːrps/ a coastal town in Humberside in England

clef /klef/ *n* a sign put at the beginning of a line of written music to show the PITCH of the notes: *a treble/bass clef*

cleft¹ /kleft/ *n* a crack, opening, or split: *a cleft in the rocks*

cleft² *past tense & participle of* CLEAVE

cleft pal·ate /ˌ· ˈ··/ *n* an unnatural split in the roof of the mouth, with which people are sometimes born and which causes difficulty in speaking

cleft stick /ˌ· ˈ·/ *n BrE* (**caught**) **in a cleft stick** (caught) in an awkward position from which it is difficult to escape or in which it is difficult to make a decision

clem·a·tis /ˈklemətɪs, klɪˈmeɪtɪs/ *n* [U] a climbing plant with white, yellow, pink, or purple flowers

clem·en·cy /ˈklemənsi/ *n* [U] *fml* **1** willingness not to punish or to punish less severely: *an appeal for clemency* **2** mildness (MILD), esp. of the weather

Clem·ens /ˈklemənz/, **Sam·u·el Lang·horne** /ˈsæmjuəl ˈlæŋhɔːn‖-hɔːrn/ the real name of Mark TWAIN

clem·ent /ˈklemənt/ *adj* **1** *fml* (esp. of the weather) not severe; MILD **2** *lit* showing sympathy in deciding punishments; MERCIFUL: *a clement judge* – **~ly** *adv*

clem·en·tine /ˈkleməntiːn, -taɪn/ *n* a kind of small, sweet orange

Clem·en·tine /ˈkleməntaɪn/ an old popular song about a girl who drowns. It is usually sung in a humorous, rather than a serious way:
Oh my darling, oh my darling,
Oh my darling, Clementine;
Thou art lost and gone forever,
Dreadful sorry, Clementine.

clench /klentʃ/ *v* [T] to close or hold tightly in a way that shows determination or anger: *She clenched her teeth and refused to move.* | *He clenched his fists threateningly.* – **clench** *n*

Cleopatra

Cle·o·pat·ra /ˌkliːəˈpætrə◄/ (69–30 BC) a Queen of Egypt famous for her beauty and for having killed herself by holding an ASP (=a small snake) to her breast. Shakespeare wrote the play *Antony and Cleopatra* about her relationship with the Roman general Mark Antony.

Cleopatra's Nee·dle /ˌ···· ˈ··/ one of two OBELISKs (=tall, pointed pieces of stone) originally from Egypt. One stands on the Embankment in London, and one in Central Park, New York.

clere·sto·ry /ˈklɪəstəri‖ˈklɪərˌstɔːri/ *n* the upper part of the wall of a large church, which has windows in it and rises

A Norman church

A Tudor manor house

An Elizabethan House

An American colonial mansion

Georgian houses

Victorian terraced house

Modern American architecture

Greta Garbo

Marilyn Monroe

Humphrey Bogart

James Dean

Elizabeth Taylor

Richard Gere

Meryl Streep

Sean Connery

Michelle Pfeiffer

Robert de Niro

Jane Fonda

Dustin Hoffman

Jack Nicholson

above the lower roofs —see picture at CHURCH

cler·gy /ˈklɜːdʒi‖-ɜːr-/ n [(the) P] (esp. in the Christian church) the people who are members of the priesthood and who are allowed to perform religious services

cler·gy·man /ˈklɜːdʒimən‖-ɜːr-/ n -men /mən/ a member of the clergy; priest —see PRIEST (USAGE)

cler·ic /ˈklerɪk/ n a clergyman

cler·i·cal /ˈklerɪkəl/ adj [no comp.] **1** of or concerning someone who works in an office: clerical work | a clerical error **2** of or concerning the clergy: wearing a clerical collar – –ly /kli/ adv

cler·i·hew /ˈklerɪhjuː/ n a four-lined humorous poem about a well-known person

clerk¹ /klɑːk‖klɜːrk/ n **1** also **clerical worker**— a person employed to keep records or accounts, or to do general office work: a filing clerk **2** an official in charge of the records of a court, town council, etc. —see also TOWN CLERK **3** also **salesclerk**— AmE a person who works in a shop selling things **4** law a priest; clergyman —see OFFICER (USAGE)

clerk² v [I] infml, esp. AmE to act or work as a clerk

clerk of works /ˌ· · ˈ·/ n BrE the person in charge of building operations in a particular place

Cleve·land¹ /ˈkliːvlənd/ **1** a COUNTY in NE England. In 1987 there was a lot of public concern in Britain when some children in Cleveland were taken away from their parents by the SOCIAL SERVICES because doctors and SOCIAL WORKERS believed that the children were being abused (ABUSE) by their parents. It was later found that most of the children had not been abused, and this led many people to question the methods used by the doctors and social workers. **2** a city in the US state of Ohio. Many Americans use Cleveland as an example of a city which is not very nice and rather dull. —see colour map on page 1374-5

Cleveland², **Gro·ver** /ˈɡrəʊvər/ (1837–1908) the 22nd and 24th president of the US

clev·er /ˈklevər/ adj **1** quick at learning and understanding; having or showing a quick, able, and effective mind; INTELLIGENT: the cleverest girl in the class | a clever idea **2** skilful in using the hands or body: clever with his hands/at making things **3** infml effective and easy to use or handle: What a clever little device! **4** infml derog having a quick mind but without seriousness, good judgment, or sincerity: a clever lawyer's tricks | Don't try and get clever with me! **5 too clever by half** infml, esp. BrE too sure of one's cleverness, in a way that offends people – –ly adv – –ness n [U]

▷ USAGE In Britain, **bright** and **smart** (which is sometimes derogatory) are informal words for **clever**: She's one of the brightest in the class. | He tries too hard to be smart. But in the US, **clever** is often derogatory and smart and bright are used more often and approvingly: the smartest boy in school | She's very bright. In both countries **quick** is an informal word meaning bright and able to learn fast: Her children are very quick. **Brainy** (infml) means very bright, often at academic work, but sometimes suggests that someone is rather odd and does not have a very good social life: a brainy professor who's hopeless at parties. **Brilliant** is a very strong word meaning extremely bright: He's a brilliant mathematician. —see also GENIUS (USAGE), INTELLIGENT (USAGE)◁

clever clogs /ˈ· · ·/ n BrE infml (an expression used to someone when they have just made what they think is a very clever remark or suggestion): "Put it on the other way up." – "I tried that an hour ago. Come on, clever clogs, you can do better than that!"

clever dick /ˈ· · ·/ n infml, esp. BrE someone who annoys others by trying to sound clever

clew /kluː/ n tech (a metal circle fastened to) the lower corner of a ship's sail

Cli·burn /ˈklaɪbɜːn‖-bɜːrn/, **Van** (1934–) an American piano player of classical music

cli·ché /ˈkliːʃeɪ‖kliːˈʃeɪ/ n derog an expression or idea used so often that it has lost much of its expressive force: I know it's a bit of a cliché, but she means everything to me. —compare PLATITUDE —**clichéd** adj: a clichéd remark

click¹ /klɪk/ n **1** a slight short sound: The key turned with

a click. | the click of heels as she ran down the stairs **2** tech a sound made, as in some African languages, by pressing the tongue against the teeth or the roof of the mouth and then moving it rapidly away

click² v **1** [T] to strike or move with a click: She clicked her fingers in time to the music. | The soldier clicked his heels together. **2** [I] to make a click, esp. as a result of movement: The bolt clicked into place. | The door clicked shut. **3** [I (with)] infml to suddenly become clear or be understood: It suddenly clicked that we had been talking about two completely different people. **4** [I (with)] infml to be a success: a film that really clicked (with the public) | John and Anne clicked (with each other) as soon as they met. —see also **click into place** (PLACE¹ (13))

cli·ent /ˈklaɪənt/ n **1** a person who gets help and advice from a professional person, e.g. a lawyer **2** a person who buys goods or services: She's one of my most valued clients. | a prostitute's clients —see CUSTOMER (USAGE)

cli·en·tele /ˌkliːənˈtel‖ˌklaɪənˈtel, ˌkliː-/ n [C+sing./pl. v] often pomp those who use the services of a business, shop, professional person, etc.: Our clientele has/have always favoured quality rather than quantity. | a very select clientele

client state /ˌ· · ˈ◂/ n [(of)] a country which is dependent upon the support and protection of another larger and more powerful country —compare SATELLITE (3)

cliff /klɪf/ n a high very steep face of rock, ice, etc., esp. on a coast: climbers clinging to the cliff face —see also WHITE CLIFFS OF DOVER

Cliff infml for Cliff RICHARD

Cliff, Jimmy (1948–) an internationally famous Jamaican singer-songwriter of REGGAE music

cliff-hang·er /ˈklɪfˌhæŋər/ n infml **1** a competition or fight of which the result is in doubt until the very end: The election was a real cliffhanger. **2** (esp. on the radio and on television) a play or story of adventure, performed in parts which each end with an exciting moment of uncertainty about what will happen next

Cliff's Notes /ˌ· · ˈ·/ in the US, a small book which makes a short general statement of the main points of a work of literature, and explains it. Students sometimes read them instead of reading the works of literature themselves —see also CRIB²

Clift /klɪft/, **Montgomery** (1920–66) an American theatre and film actor well-known for his good looks and for acting ROMANTIC parts

Clif·ton Su·spen·sion Bridge /ˌklɪftən səˈspenʃən ˌbrɪdʒ/ [the] a very high SUSPENSION BRIDGE over the River Avon in Bristol

cli·mac·ter·ic /klaɪˈmæktərɪk, ˌklaɪmækˈterɪk/ n a point in life when important changes take place in the human body, such as the MENOPAUSE

cli·mac·tic /klaɪˈmæktɪk/ adj of or forming a CLIMAX: a climactic car chase —compare CLIMATIC

cli·mate /ˈklaɪmət/ n **1** the average weather conditions at a particular place over a period of years: a tropical climate —compare WEATHER¹ **2** the general feelings or opinions of a group of people at a particular time: the present political climate | a climate of unrest

cli·mat·ic /klaɪˈmætɪk/ adj of climate: climatic conditions —compare CLIMACTIC – –ally /kli/ adv

cli·ma·tol·o·gy /ˌklaɪməˈtɒlədʒi‖-ˈtɑː-/ n [U] the science that studies climate

cli·max¹ /ˈklaɪmæks/ n **1** the most exciting, important, or effective part in a story, experience, set of events, etc., which usu. comes near the end: The climax of the film is a brilliant car chase. | The election campaign reached its climax last night, with a televised debate between the two candidates. —see also ANTICLIMAX **2** the highest point of sexual pleasure; ORGASM

climax² v [I (in)] to come to a climax: a life of service to the nation, climaxing in her appointment as President

climb¹ /klaɪm/ n **1** [T] to go up towards the top of: They climbed the hill. | The little train climbed the mountainside slowly. **2** [I] to rise or slope upwards continuously: The plane/the road climbed steeply. | The sun climbed steadily in the sky. | The value of imports has climbed (=increased) sharply in the past year. | (fig.) He climbed to power slowly but surely. **3** [I;T] to go up, through, into, or out of, etc., usu. moving from a lower to a higher position, by using the hands and feet: *to climb a ladder/a tree* | *The old lady climbs (up) the stairs with difficulty.* | *She climbed into the lifeboat/onto the table/out of the window.* | *We climbed down the side of the cliff.* **4** [I (**up**);T] (of a plant) to grow upwards along (a supporting surface): *I have several climbing plants in the garden.* **5** [I+**into**, **out of**] *infml* to get into or out of clothing quickly or with effort: *The firemen climbed into their uniforms.* **6 go climbing** to climb hills or mountains as a sport: *We went climbing in the Alps last year.*

climb down *phr v* [I] *infml* to admit that one has been wrong or has made a mistake esp. so as to make a difficult situation easier —**climb-down** /'· ·/ *n* : *His last-minute climb-down saved the country from war.*

climb² *n* [*usu. sing.*] **1** an act of climbing or a journey made by climbing: *The climb down was even harder than the climb up.* | *the minister's climb to power* **2** a place to be climbed; very steep slope: *There was a steep climb on the road out of town.*

climb·er /'klaɪmə^r/ *n* a person or thing that climbs: *This plant is a good climber.* | *a famous mountain climber*

climb·ing frame /'·· ,·/ *BrE* ‖ **jungle gym, monkey bars** *AmE*— *n* a large frame made of bars for children to climb on

climb·ing i·ron /'·· ,·/ *n* [*usu. pl.*] a CRAMPON

clime /klaɪm/ *n poet for* CLIMATE: *sunny southern climes*

clinch¹ /klɪntʃ/ *v* **1** [T] *infml* to settle (a business matter or an agreement) firmly: *The two businessmen clinched the deal quickly.* | *The offer of more money clinched it for her and she accepted the job.* **2** [I] (of two people) to hold each other tightly with the arms, esp. when fighting **3** [T] to fix (a nail) in place by bending the point over

clinch² *n* [S] the position of two people when holding each other tightly with the arms: *The two fighters/lovers were locked in a clinch.*

clinch·er /'klɪntʃə^r/ *n infml* a last point, fact, or remark which decides an argument

cline /klaɪn/ *n tech* (esp. in grammar) something that changes gradually, like a slope rather than like stairs; CONTINUUM

Cline, Patsy (1932–63) an American popular music singer who died in an air crash. A film based on her life was called *Sweet Dreams*, which was also the title of one of her songs.

cling /klɪŋ/ *v* **clung** /klʌŋ/ [I (**to**)] **1** to hold tightly; refuse to go or let go; stick firmly: *His wet shirt clung to his body.* | *The smell of cigarette smoke tends to cling.* | *They clung to one another for comfort.* | (fig.) *She still clings to the belief that her son is alive.* **2** to stay very near; remain too close, esp. because of lack of confidence: *a little child who clings to his mother*

cling·film /'klɪŋfɪlm/ *esp. BrE* ‖ **plastic wrap, Saran wrap** *AmE tdmk*— *n* [U] a thin transparent plastic put round foods to keep them fresh

clin·ic /'klɪnɪk/ *n* **1 a** *esp. BrE* a building or part of a hospital where usu. specialized medical treatment and advice is given to OUTPATIENTS: *a family-planning clinic* | *the ear, nose, and throat clinic* **b** *AmE* a building, often a part of a hospital, where treatment is given at a lower cost or free **2** an occasion when treatment is given at a clinic: *Is the clinic being held today?* —compare SURGERY (2) **3** a group of doctors who work together and share the same offices: *Go to Dr Jones' clinic.* **4** an occasion in a hospital when medical students are taught by watching the treatment of sick people **5** a meeting held by a skilled or professional person to which people bring their problems: *an MP's weekly clinic for his constituents*

clin·i·cal /'klɪnɪkəl/ *adj* **1** of or connected with a clinic or hospital **2** [A] (of medical teaching) given in a hospital and using sick people as examples: *clinical training* | *clinical medicine* **3** appearing not to be influenced by personal feelings; cold; DETACHED: *his clinical attitude towards his divorce* — ~**ly** /kli/ *adv*

clinical ther·mom·e·ter /'··· ·'···/ *n tech* a THERMOMETER for measuring the temperature of the human body

clink¹ /klɪŋk/ *v* [I;T] to (cause to) make a slight high sound like that of pieces of glass lightly hitting each other: *They clinked their glasses together to toast the bride and groom.* —**clink** *n* [S] : *the clink of glasses*

clink² *n* [*the*+S] *sl* prison: *He's in the clink.*

clink·er /'klɪŋkə^r/ *n* [C;U] (a lump of) the partly burnt matter left after coal has been burned; (a piece of) SLAG

clinker-built /,·· '·◂/ *adj tech* (of a boat or ship) made from boards or plates whose bottom edges cover the top edges of the next lower boards or plates

Clin·ton /'klɪntən/, **Hil·lary Rod·ham** /'hɪləri 'rɒdəm‖'rɑː-/ (1947–) the wife of President Bill Clinton, who was named by him in 1993 to be in charge of changing the US health care system

Clinton, William J. (Bill) (1946–) the 42nd president of the US (1992–). During the 1992 election campaign, newspapers questioned whether he had tried to avoid serving in the Vietnam War, but Clinton attracted voters with his thorough plans for what he would do as president and his concern for ordinary people's problems. — see colour picture on page 950

clip¹ /klɪp/ *n* **1** (*often in comb.*) any of various kinds of small plastic or metal objects used for holding things tightly together or in place: *Fasten these bills together with a paper clip, please.* | *a tie clip* | *a hair clip* **2** a container in or fastened to a gun, from which bullets can be rapidly passed into the gun for firing

clip² *v* -**pp**- [I+*adv/prep*;T+*obj*+*adv/prep*] to (cause to) fasten onto something with a clip: *Do your earrings clip on?* | *Clip these sheets of paper together/onto this board.*

clip³ *v* -**pp**- [T] **1** to cut with scissors or another sharp instrument, esp. in order to make shorter or neater: *I must clip the hedge.* | *We clipped 50 sheep today.* (=cut off their wool) | *The guard on the train clipped our tickets.* **2** [+*obj*+*adv/prep*] *infml* to hit with a short quick blow: *She clipped him round the ear.* **3 clip someone's wings** to prevent someone from being as active or powerful as before

clip⁴ *n* **1** [C] an act of clipping (CLIP³ (1)): *Give the hedge a clip.* **2** [C] something clipped, such as **a** a short piece of a longer film: *They showed a clip from her new film on TV last night.* **b** *tech* the quantity of wool cut from a FLOCK (a group) of sheep at one time **c** *esp. AmE* a newspaper CUTTING **3** [C] *infml* a short quick blow: *I gave him a clip on the ear.* **4** [S] *infml* a fast speed: *We moved off at a good clip.*

clip·board /'klɪpbɔːd‖-bɔːrd/ *n* a small board with a clip at the top so that sheets of writing paper can be held firmly in place

clip joint /'· ·/ *n derog sl* a dishonest business, esp. a restaurant or NIGHTCLUB, that regularly charges too much

clip-on /'· ·/ *adj* [A] that can be fastened to something with a clip: *clip-on earrings* | *a clip-on tie*

clipped /klɪpt/ *adj* **1** (of a way of speaking) with words pronounced quickly and rather sharply **2** *tech* (of a word) shortened by having a part left out: *"Ad" is a clipped form of "advertisement".*

clip·per /'klɪpə^r/ *n* a fast sailing ship used in former times, esp. for travelling long distances —see picture at SAIL

clip·pers /'klɪpəz‖-ərz/ *n* [P] (*often in comb.*) a tool with two blades used for cutting the nails or hair, and also for HEDGES, wire, etc. —see PAIR (USAGE)

clip·pie /'klɪpi/ *n BrE old-fash sl* a person, esp. a woman, employed to take the passengers' payments on a bus

clip·ping /'klɪpɪŋ/ *n* a piece cut off or out of something: *nail clippings* | *grass clippings* | (*esp. AmE*) *a newspaper clipping*

clique /kliːk/ *n* [C+*sing./pl. v*] *derog* a closely united usu. small group of people who do not allow others easily to join their group

cli·quish /'kliːkɪʃ/ also **cli·quey** /'kliːki/— *adj derog* of or like a clique; EXCLUSIVE — ~**ness** *n* [U]

clit·o·ris /'klɪtərᵻs/ *n* a small organ at the front of the VULVA that is a centre of sexual sensation in women —**ral** *adj*

Clive of In·di·a /,klaɪv əv 'ɪndiə/ (1725–74) a British soldier and STATESMAN (= someone with a large part in the government of a state) who broke French power in India, became governor of Bengal state and improved British management there. The British typically see him as a ROMANTIC figure in Arabic dress who saved the Bengalis from their own leader.

Cllr *BrE abbrev. for* COUNCILLOR

Clo *abbrev. for* CLOSE⁵ (2) (used in street names)

cloak¹ /kləʊk/ *n* **1** a loose outer garment, usu. without SLEEVEs, which is fastened under the throat, covers most of the body, and is sometimes worn instead of a coat —compare CAPE¹ **2** something which covers, hides, or keeps secret: *His friendly behaviour was a cloak for his evil intentions.*

cloak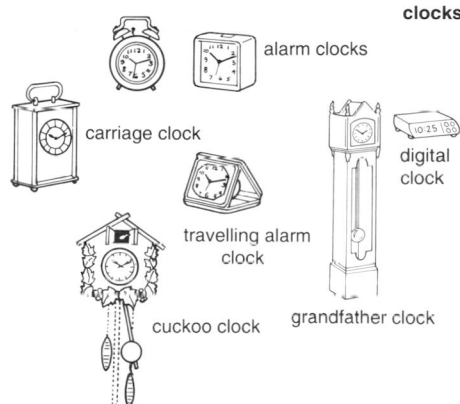

cloak

cloak² *v* [T (**with, in**)] to cover, hide, or keep secret (ideas, facts, intentions, etc.): *cloaked in secrecy|mystery*

cloak-and-dag·ger /ˌ··ˈ···/ *adj* [A] full of exciting mystery and secrecy: *He had been involved in cloak-and-dagger operations for the secret services.*

cloak·room /ˈkləʊkrʊm, -ruːm/ *n* **1** also **checkroom, coatroom, coat check** *AmE* – a room, e.g. in a theatre, where hats, coats, etc., can be left for a short time **2** *euph, esp. BrE* a TOILET, esp. in a public building

clob·ber¹ /ˈklɒbəʳ‖ˈklɑː-/ *v* [T] *sl* **1** to strike or attack severely and repeatedly: *I'll clobber you if you don't do what you're told.* | *The government's going to clobber the unions if they won't agree.* **2** to defeat completely: *They were absolutely clobbered in last night's game.*

clobber² *n* [U] *sl, esp. BrE* **1** the belongings that one carries around with one: *my fishing clobber* **2** *old-fash* clothes

cloche /klɒʃ‖kləʊʃ/ *n* **1** a glass or transparent plastic cover put over young plants to protect them **2** a close-fitting bell-shaped woman's hat, popular esp. in the 1920s

clocks

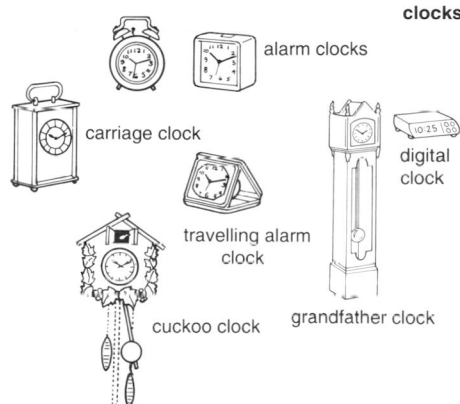

alarm clocks

carriage clock

digital clock

travelling alarm clock

cuckoo clock

grandfather clock

clock¹ /klɒk‖klɑːk/ *n* **1** [C] an instrument for measuring and showing time that is not worn on the body: *The clock in the living room is (running) a few minutes fast|slow.* | *The clock struck one.* | *I set my alarm clock for 6.30.* | *We met under the Town Hall clock.* | *the face|hands of a clock* | *a digital clock* —see USAGE **2** [*the*+S] *infml* **a** a MILEOMETER: *a car with 10,000 miles on the clock* **b** a SPEEDOMETER **3 against the clock: a** under pressure, in order to complete something before a certain time: *We're working against the clock to finish the report by Friday.* **b** (in sport, etc.) timed by a STOPWATCH: *The jump-off will be against the clock.* **4 around/round the clock** all day and all night without stopping: *We worked around the clock to finish the job.* —see also ROUND-THE-CLOCK **5 put the clock back** ‖ also **set the clock back** *AmE:* **a** (in countries which officially change the time at the beginning of winter and summer) to change the time shown on a clock to a time one or two hours earlier **b** to set aside modern laws, ideas, practices, etc., and return to those of an earlier period: *The government's plans for education will put the clock back 20 years.* **6 put the clock on/forward** also **set the clock ahead** *AmE*– (in countries which officially change the time at the beginning

of winter and summer) to change the time shown on a clock to a time one or two hours later: *In Britain they put the clock on an hour in spring.* —see also BRITISH SUMMER TIME, DAYLIGHT SAVING TIME **7 watch the clock** *derog* to think continually of how soon the day's work will end: *a bad worker who's always watching the clock* | *a clockwatcher* —see also O'CLOCK, BIOLOGICAL CLOCK, 24 HOUR CLOCK, CLOCK-WATCHING

▷ USAGE If a **clock** or **watch** says 11.50 at 12 o'clock, then it is (10 minutes) **slow;** if it says 12.05, it is (5 minutes) **fast.** If it gets faster every day it **gains** (time); if it gets slower every day it **loses** (time). When you put it to the right time you **set** it: *I set my watch by the radio.* (=by listening to the radio time signal) —see also O'CLOCK (USAGE), TIME⁴ (USAGE), TO¹ (USAGE)◁

clock² *v* [T] **1** to record the time taken by (someone) to do (something), using a STOPWATCH: *She was clocked at 59 seconds for the first lap.* **2** *infml* to show or record on a SPEEDOMETER, MILEOMETER, etc.: *We clocked 100 mph down the motorway.* **3** *BrE sl* to hit (someone) **4** *BrE sl* to see

clock in/on *phr v* [I] **1** to record the time when one arrives at work, usu. on a special card. People who have to clock in when they arrive at work are usu. BLUE-COLLAR workers. **2** to arrive at work: *We usually clock in at 9 o'clock.*

clock out/off *phr v* [I] **1** to record the time when one leaves work, usu. on a special card. People who have to clock out when they leave work are usu. BLUE-COLLAR workers. **2** to leave work

clock up *sthg. phr v* [T] *infml* **1** to record (a distance travelled, a speed reached, points won, etc.): *We clocked up 1000 miles coming here.* **2** to succeed in getting; gain: *The team has clocked up six victories since the season began.*

clock³ *n* a decorative pattern on the side of a sock or STOCKING

clock-ra·di·o /ˌ·ˈ···/ *n* a RADIO ALARM

clock tow·er /ˈ· ˌ··/ *n* a usu. four-sided tower often forming part of a building, such as a church, and with a clock on each of the sides, near the top

clock-watch·ing /ˈ· ˌ··/ *n* [U] the act of watching the time very carefully when one is at work because one is waiting to go home —see also **watch the clock** (CLOCK¹)

clock·wise /ˈklɒk-waɪz‖ˈklɑːk-/ *adj, adv* in the direction in which the hands of a clock move: *Turn the lid clockwise if you want to fasten it tightly.* | *a clockwise movement of the lid* —opposite **anticlockwise** *BrE,* **counterclockwise** *AmE*

clock·work /ˈklɒk-wɜːk‖ˈklɑːk-wɜːrk/ *n* [U] **1** machinery that can usu. be wound up with a key, and that is used esp. in clocks and toys: *The children played with their clockwork trains.* **2 like clockwork** smoothly and without trouble: *The arrangements went ahead like clockwork.* **3 regular as clockwork** in a completely regular way: *He visits us every Friday, regular as clockwork.*

Clockwork Or·ange /ˌ··ˈ···/, **A** a book by Anthony Burgess, later made into a film, about an imaginary future in which there is a lot of violence and a government with very strong power over people

clod /klɒd‖klɑːd/ *n* **1** a lump or mass, esp. of clay or earth —see picture at PIECE **2** *infml* a stupid person; fool

clod·dish /ˈklɒdɪʃ‖ˈklɑːd-/ *adj infml* like a CLOD (2): *cloddish ignorance* — **~ly** *adv* — **~ness** *n* [U]

clod·hop·per /ˈklɒdˌhɒpəʳ‖ˈklɑːdˌhɑː-/ *n* **1** an awkward person with rough manners **2** [*usu. pl.*] *humor* a big heavy strong shoe

clog¹ /klɒg‖klɑːg/ *n* **1** [*usu. pl.*] a kind of shoe that either has a thick wooden bottom (SOLE) or is completely made from one piece of wood —see PAIR (USAGE), and see picture at SHOE **2** something that makes movement or action difficult, esp. a heavy block of wood fastened to an animal's leg to stop it wandering —see also CLEVER CLOGS

clog² *v* **-gg-** [I;T (UP, **with**)] to (cause to) become blocked or filled so that movement or activity is very difficult: *The pipe's clogged with grease.* | *The road to the airport is clogged with traffic.* | *Don't clog your memory (up) with useless information.*

clog dance /ˈ· ·/ *n* a kind of COUNTRY DANCE in which the dancers wear clogs

cloi·son·né /klwɑ:ˈzɒneɪ‖ˌklɔɪzənˈeɪ/ n [U] decorative work in which different colours of ENAMEL (=a glasslike substance often used for covering metal) are kept apart by thin metal bands

clois·ter[1] /ˈklɔɪstəʳ/ n **1** [C] also **cloisters** pl.— a covered passage which has open archways on one side facing into an open square garden or courtyard, and which usu. forms part of a church, college, MONASTERY, or CONVENT **2** [the+S] (the peaceful life of) a CONVENT or MONASTERY

cloister[2] v [T] to shut (esp. oneself) away from the world in or as if in a CONVENT or MONASTERY: a scientist who cloisters himself in his laboratory | He had led a cloistered existence and had little experience of ordinary life.

clone /kləʊn/ n **1** tech the descendant of a single plant or animal, produced nonsexually from any one cell, and with exactly the same form as the parent **2** infml a person or thing that seems to be a copy of someone or something else: He's got no originality – he's just a David Bowie clone. —compare IDENTIKIT, LOOK-A-LIKE **3** a microcomputer (=a small computer) that can use SOFTWARE that is really made for another company's computers: The new computer is yet another IBM clone. **clone** v [T]

clop /klɒp‖klɑːp/ v -pp- [I (along)] to move making a sound like horses' hooves (HOOF) hitting a hard surface —**clop** n [S]

close[1] /kləʊz/ v **1** [I;T] to (cause to) shut: Close the windows/the gate. | Close your eyes and go to sleep. | The door closed behind me as I went out. **2** [I;T] to (cause to) stop being open to the public: What time does the bank/the park close? | The shop closes for lunch. **3** [I;T (DOWN)] to (cause to) stop operating or providing services, esp. without the intention of starting again: The firm has decided to close (down) its London branch. | Hundreds of jobs were lost when the factory closed. | They may be forced to close the local hospital. **4** [I;T] to come to an end or bring to an end: The conference closed with a short speech by the organizer. | to close one's account with a bank | He scored a goal in the closing minutes of the game. **5** [T] to settle (a matter); come to an agreement about: The question is now closed and there will be no further discussion. | She was promoted after **closing a deal** worth £2 million. —see also CLOSING **6** [I;T] to (cause to) come together: His arms closed tightly round her. | That wound will soon close (up). **7** [I+adv/prep] (of business shares, CURRENCY, etc.) to be worth a particular amount at the end of a day's trading, e.g. on the STOCK EXCHANGE: The pound closed at $1.49 last night. | The company's shares closed down/closed lower after heavy selling. —see OPEN (USAGE)

close (sthg. ↔) **down** phr v [I;T] **a** (of a radio or television station) to stop broadcasting at the end of the day **b** to cause (a radio or television station) to stop broadcasting at the end of the day —see also CLOSE[1] (2), CLOSEDOWN

close in phr v [I (on, upon)] to surround gradually and usu. from all sides, esp. in a threatening way: The people were trapped when the enemy army began to close in (on them). | (fig.) Night is closing in.

close (sthg. ↔) **out** phr v [I;T] AmE (of a business) to try to get rid of (all one's goods) by selling them at reduced prices

close (sbdy./sthg. ↔) **up** phr v [I;T] to (cause to) come nearer each other or draw together: Close up the ranks! | The cut on her arm soon closed up.

close with sbdy./sthg. phr v [T] **1** BrE to agree with (someone) or to (something): The businessman quickly closed with the offer/closed with the inspector. **2** lit to begin to fight: The two armies closed with each other.

close[2] /kləʊs/ adj **1** [(to)] near; not far away in space or time: The church is close to the shops. | He was shot at close range. | The exams are getting very close/are getting **too close for comfort**; I must do some work for them. | Her parents live **close at hand**. | (fig.) The question of women's rights is a subject close to her heart. **2** near in relationship, friendship, or degree of connection: He's a close relative/one of my closest friends. | She and her mother have always been very close. | He has close links with terrorist groups. | Sources close to the government are predicting an election. **3 a** tight; with little or no space: close stitches | You need a magnifying glass to read such close print. **b** very near to the surface: The barber gave him a close shave. —see also CLOSE SHAVE **4** thorough and

careful: We kept a **close watch** on the prisoners. | After close questioning, the police released the suspect. | His work does not bear close inspection/scrutiny. | We'll have to keep a **close eye** on his work from now on. **5** not very different from an original: He bears a close resemblance to his father. | a close translation **6** without fresh air, and perhaps too warm; STUFFY: It's very close in here; open the window. **7** (esp. of a competition) decided by a very small difference: The election results were very close. | a close finish/match —compare NARROW[1] (3) **8** tech (in PHONETICS, of a vowel) pronounced with little space above the tongue —opposite open **9** [F (about)] infml secretive: She's always been very close about her past life. **10** [F (with)] infml not generous; STINGY: close with money **11 at close quarters** very near or near together: The witness had not seen the man at close quarters. —see NEAR (USAGE) – ~ly adv : a closely guarded secret – ~ness n [U]

close[3] /kləʊs/ adv **1** near: Don't come too close! | Although he came very close, he did not win the race. [+adv/prep] They live close by. | We live close to the church. | They sat close together. | She followed close behind. **2 close, but no cigar** AmE (said when someone has done something that was almost, but not quite, effective, right, or successful) **3 close on** (esp. before numbers) almost: It happened close on 50 years ago. | Close on 90 people came. **4 close to: a** almost; nearly: The cost was close to $1 million. | He came close to losing his temper. **b** (ˌkləʊz ˈtuː) from very close: He looks much older when you see him close to. **5 close to home** near the (usu. unpleasant) truth: Everyone felt uncomfortable because his remarks were a little too close to home. **6** esp. BrE **(sail) close to the wind** (to be) near to dishonesty or improper behaviour

close[4] /kləʊz/ n [S] fml the end of an activity or of a period of time: at the close of play/of the 19th century | As the evening came/drew **to a close**, the guests went home. | The chairman brought the meeting **to a close**.

close[5] /kləʊs/ n **1** an enclosed area or space, esp. the area around a CATHEDRAL (=a large important church); courtyard **2 a** BrE a road closed at one end **b** esp. ScotE a narrow passage leading off a street to an enclosed area or shared stairs for a block of flats

close call /ˌkləʊs ˈkɔːl/ n infml a CLOSE SHAVE

close-cropped /ˌkləʊs ˈkrɒpt◄‖-ˈkrɑːpt◄/ adj (of the hair) cut very short

closed /kləʊzd/ adj **1** [(to)] (esp. of a shop or public place) not open to the public: The shop is closed on Thursdays. | The gardens are closed to visitors in winter. | a club with a closed membership (=open only to a special few) | The inquiry was held **behind closed doors**. **2** not allowing influences from outside: a closed society | It's no use arguing with him; he's got a closed mind. **3** [A] tech complete in itself; forming a unit that allows no additions: a closed system | a closed set

closed book /ˌ · ˈ ·/ n [S] infml **1** [(to)] something of which one knows or understands nothing: Computers are a closed book to me. **2** something which is completed or finished with

closed cir·cuit tel·e·vi·sion /ˌ · ˌ ··· ˈ····, ˌ · ˌ ··· ··ˈ··/ also **CCTV** abbrev. n [U] a system used to protect shops, banks, etc., by using cameras to send pictures to a number of television sets: This building is protected by closed circuit television.

closed-loop re·cy·cling sys·tem /ˌ · · · ˈ· · ˌ ··/ n a method of providing people who are living in a SPACE STATION with around 5 kilograms of fresh water each every day by reusing all the waste liquids on board

close·down /ˈkləʊzdaʊn/ n **1** [C] (in a factory, business, etc.) a general stopping of work; SHUTDOWN **2** [C;U] esp. BrE the end of a period of broadcasting —see also CLOSE down

closed pri·ma·ry /ˌ · ˈ···/ n an election in the US in which voters may vote only for CANDIDATES (=people who are trying to get political office) of the party to which they belong, in order to choose who will represent the party in the final election. Most states hold closed primaries so that Democrats choose the Democratic NOMINEE and Republicans the Republican one. —compare OPEN PRIMARY

closed sea·son /ˌ · ˈ··/ n AmE for CLOSE SEASON

closed shop /ˌ· ˈ·◂/ n a place of work where all the workers must belong to a particular TRADE UNION. In the 1960s and 1970s there were a lot of closed shops in Britain and in the US, but in the 1980s the power of trade unions was reduced by the government and now there are not so many.

Close En·count·ers of the Third Kind /ˌ· ·ˌ··· · ˌ· ˈ·/ a 1977 American SCIENCE FICTION film directed by Steven Spielberg which has meetings with ALIENS (an encounter of the third kind) as its subject

close·fist·ed /ˌkləʊsˈfɪstɟd◂/ adj infml not generous with money; STINGY

close-grained /ˌkləʊs ˈgreɪnd◂/ adj (of wood) having a fine natural pattern (GRAIN (4)), esp. having narrow yearly rings

close-hauled /ˌkləʊs ˈhɔːld◂/ adj tech (of a sailing ship) having the sails arranged to sail as near directly into the wind as possible

close-knit /ˌkləʊs ˈnɪt◂/ also **close·ly-knit** /ˌ·· ˈ·◂/— adj tightly connected or united by social, political, or religious beliefs and activities: a close-knit family/community

close·out /ˈkləʊzaʊt/ n AmE an occasion when a business tries to get rid of all its goods by selling them at reduced prices —see also CLOSE out

close sea·son /ˈkləʊs ˌsiːzən/ also **closed season** AmE— n 1 the period of each year when certain animals, birds, or fish may not by law be killed for sport: the close season for fishing —opposite open season 2 BrE the summer period when football teams do not play any important matches

close-set /ˌkləʊs ˈset◂/ adj set close together: close-set eyes

close shave /ˌkləʊs ˈʃeɪv/ also **close call**— n infml a situation in which something dangerous or very unpleasant is only just avoided: That was a close shave — that car nearly hit us!

clos·et[1] /ˈklɒzɟt‖ˈklɑː-, ˈklɔː-/ n 1 esp. AmE a cupboard built into the wall of a room and going from the floor to the CEILING —compare CUPBOARD 2 now rare a small room for private thought or prayer 3 old use a TOILET —see also WC 4 **come out of the closet** to declare oneself openly as a HOMOSEXUAL —see also **skeleton in the closet** (SKELETON)

closet[2] adj [A] not publicly admitted; secret: a closet communist/homosexual/admirer of the president

closet[3] v [T (TOGETHER, with) often pass.] to enclose (esp. oneself) in a private room: They're closeted (together) in her office. | He spent over an hour closeted with the bank manager.

close thing /ˌkləʊs ˈθɪŋ/ n [S] infml 1 a CLOSE SHAVE: That was a close thing! We nearly hit the other car! 2 a game, election, risk taken, etc., which comes close to failing before it succeeds

close-up /ˈkləʊs ʌp/ n a photograph taken from very near: a close-up of her face | a picture of her face in close-up

clos·ing /ˈkləʊzɪŋ/ AmE | **completion** BrE— n [C;U] the final step in buying and selling a house or other property: Our closing is next Friday. | I was amazed at all the closing costs that no one had mentioned before.

closing pri·ces /ˈ·· ˌ··/ n [P] the buying and selling prices of STOCKS[1] (3) and SHARES[1] (2) when the STOCK EXCHANGE finishes business for the day —see also CLOSE[1] (7)

closing time /ˈ·· ·/ n [C;U] BrE the time, fixed by law, at which a PUB must close and stop serving drinks

clo·sure /ˈkləʊʒəʳ/ n [C;U] (an example of) the act of closing, esp. of a business or organization which has to stop operating: Lack of money forced the closure of the company. | They are campaigning against hospital closures.

clot[1] /klɒt‖klɑːt/ n 1 a half-solid mass or lump, usu. formed from a liquid, esp. blood: a blood clot in his leg 2 sl, esp. BrE a stupid person; fool

clot[2] v -tt- [I;T] to (cause to) form into clots: a drug to prevent the blood from clotting —see also CLOTTED CREAM

cloth /klɒθ‖klɔːθ/ n **cloths** /klɒθs‖klɔːðz, klɔːθs/ 1 [U] material made from wool, cotton, nylon, etc., by weaving, and used for making garments, coverings, etc.: I need several metres of cloth to make a long dress. 2 [C] (often in comb.) a piece of this used for a special purpose: Clean the windows with a soft/damp cloth. | a dishcloth | a

tablecloth —see CLOTHES (USAGE) 3 [the+S] fml or humor the profession of being a priest: a man of the cloth (=a priest)

cloth cap /ˌ· ˈ·/ also **flat cap**—  **cloth cap**
n a soft flat woollen cap with a stiff pointed piece at the front. The cloth cap is sometimes used to represent the idea of the WORKING CLASS in Britain.

clothe /kləʊð/ v [T] 1 to cover with clothes or provide clothes for: They have to work hard to feed and clothe their large family. | Her partially-clothed body was found in a wood. 2 lit to cover (something) as if with clothing: Mist clothed the hills. —see also CLAD

clothes /kləʊðz, kləʊz/ n [P] garments, such as trousers, dresses, shirts, and socks, that are worn to cover the body: Put on your school clothes. | football clothes | a clothes brush —see also PLAIN-CLOTHES

▷ USAGE Compare **clothes, cloth, material, clothing, garment,** and **dress. Clothes** is the usual word for things we wear: She's got some beautiful **clothes.** | **Clothes** are made from various kinds of **cloth** or **material,** such as wool or cotton: How much **cloth/material** will I need to make a pair of trousers? **Clothing** [U] is a more formal word for **clothes.** A **garment** [C] (rather formal) is a single article of **clothing.** A **dress** [C] is a kind of outer **garment** worn by women: What a pretty **dress** she's wearing!, but in certain expressions **dress** [U] is a particular type of **clothing:** The men had to wear formal evening **dress** to go to the company dinner. —see also DRESS (USAGE)◁

clothes bas·ket /ˈ· ˌ··/ n a large plastic basket for holding clothes ready for drying or ironing

clothes brush /ˈ· ·/ n a brush for removing FLUFF, dust, mud, etc. from clothes esp. coats, JACKETS, etc.

clothes hang·er /ˈ· ˌ··/ n a HANGER

clothes·horse /ˈkləʊðzhɔːs, ˈkləʊz-‖-hɔːrs/ n 1 a frame on which clothes are hung to dry, usu. indoors 2 infml, derog, esp. AmE a person who is very interested in clothes

clothes·line /ˈkləʊðzlaɪn, ˈkləʊz-/ n a rope or cord on which clothes are hung to dry, usu. outdoors

clothes peg /ˈ· ·/ BrE ‖ **clothes·pin** /ˈkləʊðzˌpɪn, ˈkləʊz-/ AmE— n a small wooden or plastic instrument for holding wet washed clothes on a clothesline to dry —see picture at PEG

▶CULTURAL NOTE If there is a bad smell, people sometimes joke about putting a clothes peg on their nose so that they will not be able to smell it.◀

cloth·i·er /ˈkləʊðiəʳ/ n fml, becoming rare a person who makes or sells men's clothes or material for clothes

cloth·ing /ˈkləʊðɪŋ/ n [U] esp. fml the garments, such as trousers, dresses, shirts, etc., worn together on different parts of the body: an article of clothing | The staff at the chemical plant wear protective clothing. | food, clothing, and shelter | a clothing manufacturer —see also **wolf in sheep's clothing** (WOLF[1]); see CLOTHES (USAGE)

clotted cream /ˌ· ·ˈ·/ n [U] thick cream made esp. in SW England by slowly heating milk and taking the cream from the top

clo·ture /ˈkləʊtʃəʳ/ n (in US government) a way of ending argument over a BILL[2] and forcing a vote on it: Senator Bradley tried to force cloture on the housing bill.

cloud[1] /klaʊd/ n 1 [C;U] a white or grey mass floating in the sky in various shapes, which is formed from very small drops of water: dark threatening storm clouds | fluffy white clouds | There's more cloud today than yesterday. 2 [C (of)] a mass of dust, smoke, etc., which floats weightlessly in the air: a cloud of smoke | a factory chimney emitting clouds of toxic gas | a mushroom cloud following a nuclear explosion 3 [C (of)] a large number of small things moving in a mass; SWARM: a cloud of mosquitoes 4 [C] something that threatens or that causes unhappiness or anxiety: The clouds of war were gathering. | I'm sorry to cast a cloud over the party, but there's been some bad news. | They're very happy now, but I'm afraid there's a cloud on the horizon; he has to go into the army soon. **5 I wandered lonely as a cloud** *quote* a phrase from a poem by William Wordsworth about daffodils —see DAFFODIL **6 under a cloud** out of favour or regarded with distrust: *He left his job under a cloud.* **7 up in the clouds** lost in private thoughts; in a DAYDREAM —see also **have one's head in the clouds** (HEAD¹ (30))

cloud² *v* **1** [I (OVER);T] to (cause to) become covered with clouds: *The sky clouded over and it started to rain.* | *The thick mist clouded the mountain tops.* | (fig.) *His face suddenly clouded over.* (=he began to look worried or upset) **2** [I;T (UP)] to (cause to) become less clear or transparent: *The steam has clouded the windows up.* | *You'll cloud the beer if you shake the barrel.* **3** [T] to make uncertain, unclear, or confused: *Age clouded his memory.* | *That's a separate argument and it will only cloud the issue.* **4** [T] to spoil: *The news of the accident clouded the whole day for them.*

cloud·bank /ˈklaʊdbæŋk/ *n* a thick mass of low cloud

cloud·burst /ˈklaʊdbɜːst‖-ɜːr-/ *n* a sudden very heavy fall of rain

cloud-capped /ˈ· ·/ *adj lit* (of mountains, hills, etc.) having the top surrounded by clouds

cloud-cuck·oo-land /ˌ· ˈ··· ·/ *n* [U] *derog, esp. BrE* (sometimes caps.) an imaginary place of unreal dreams and impossible perfection: *One of Mr Gyngell's employees said last night: "If he really thinks people rushing into work at 3 a.m. are going to start thinking positively about anything, he's living in cloud-cuckoo-land".*

cloud·less /ˈklaʊdləs/ *adj* without clouds; clear: *a cloudless sky/day*

cloud nine /ˌ· ˈ·/ *n* **on cloud nine** *infml, esp. AmE* very happy: *He was on cloud nine after his wife had the baby.*

cloud seed·ing /ˈ· ˌ··/ *n* [U] a way of causing it to rain or snow by dropping chemicals into clouds from an aircraft

cloud·y /ˈklaʊdi/ *adj* **1** full of clouds; OVERCAST: *a cloudy day/sky* **2** not clear or transparent: *cloudy beer* | *a cloudy recollection of the accident* —**iness** *n* [U]

Clough /klʌf/, **Bri·an** /ˈbraɪən/ (1936–) an English footballer and manager

Clou·seau /ˈkluːzəʊ‖kluːˈzəʊ/, **Inspector Jacques** /ʒæk‖ ʒɑːk/ a humorous character played by actor Peter Sellers in the Pink Panther films. He is a French policeman, always very serious, often wrong, and often causing accidents.

clout¹ /klaʊt/ *n sl* **1** [C] a hard blow or knock given with the hand or something held in the hand **2** [U] influence, esp. political influence: *Its massive export earnings give the company a lot of clout with the government.* **3** [C *often pl.*] *NEngE* an article of clothing

clout² *v* [T] *sl* to hit hard with the hand or something held in the hand

clove¹ /kləʊv/ *n* the dried flower of a tropical Asian plant, usu. used whole for giving a special taste to food

clove² *n* any of the small BULBs into which a larger bulb can be divided: *a clove of garlic*

clove³ *past tense of* CLEAVE

clove hitch /ˈ· ·, ˌ· ˈ·/ *n* a knot used for fastening a rope around a bar

clo·ven /ˈkləʊvən/ *past participle of* CLEAVE

cloven hoof /ˌ·· ˈ·/ *n* an animal's foot which is divided into two parts, like the foot of a cow or sheep

clo·ver /ˈkləʊvəʳ/ *n* [U] **1** a small usu. three-leafed plant with pink, purple, or white flowers, often grown as food for cattle **2 in clover** *infml* living in comfort and having plenty of money: *We'll be in clover if you get that job.* —see also FOUR-LEAVED CLOVER

clo·ver·leaf /ˈkləʊvəliːf‖-vər-/ *n* **-leafs** *or* **-leaves** /liːvz/ **1** the leaf of a clover plant **2** the network of curved roads which connect two very important roads (esp. MOTORWAYS) where they cross each other

clown¹ /klaʊn/ *n* **1** an entertainer, esp. in the CIRCUS, who wears funny clothes and special MAKE-UP, often with a large red painted smile, and tries to make people laugh by jokes, tricks, or actions. It is often said that people who are clowns are really rather sad people, underneath all their cheerful make-up and acting. —see picture at COSTUME **2** *derog* a fool, esp. someone who continually behaves in a silly way; BUFFOON: *The teacher wondered which kid would be the* **class clown** *(esp. AmE) this year.*

clown² *v* [I (ABOUT, AROUND)] *derog* to act stupidly; play the fool: *Will you children stop clowning and eat up your dinner!*

clown

clown·ish /ˈklaʊnɪʃ/ *adj derog* of or like a CLOWN¹ (2): *clownish behaviour* — **~ly** *adv* — **~ness** *n* [U]

cloy /klɔɪ/ *v* [I] *fml* to become unpleasant through too much sweetness or through being taken in too great a quantity: *Chocolates start to cloy if you eat too many.* | *a love story of cloying sentimentality*

cloze test /ˈkləʊz test/ *n BrE* a test used in teaching, where the student must supply the missing words in a short piece of writing

club¹ /klʌb/ *n* **1** [+*sing./pl. v*] an organization consisting of people who join together for a certain purpose, esp. sport or amusement: *an active member of the school's chess club* | *He joined the local stamp club.* | *The tennis club has/have organized a dance.* | (fig.) *countries that belong to the nuclear club* —see also COUNTRY CLUB, GOLF CLUB **2 a** a building where a club meets **b** a NIGHTCLUB **3** an association of people, usu. upper-class men or men connected with the Establishment, who like to meet together to relax and discuss things. The club usu. owns a building where members can eat, drink, and sometimes sleep. New members pay to join or are elected (ELECT) by other members. **4** a thick heavy stick, used as a weapon: *to brandish a club* **5** a specially shaped stick for hitting a ball in certain sports: *a golf club* —see picture at GOLF **6 a** a black three-leafed figure printed on a playing card **b** a card belonging to the SUIT (=set) of cards that have one or more of these figures printed on them: *I have four clubs in my hand.* | *the seven/king of clubs* —see CARDS (USAGE) and see picture at CARDS **7 in the club** *infml, esp. BrE* expecting a baby; PREGNANT **8 Join the club!** (said when other people are in the same situation): *"I've got a bad cold." "Join the club." (=I've got one, too)*

club² *v* **-bb-** [T] to beat or hit hard (as if) with a CLUB¹ (5): *He was clubbed to death with the butt of a gun.* — **club together** *phr v* [I] to share the cost of something with others: *We clubbed together to buy her a present.*

club·ba·ble /ˈklʌbəbəl/ *adj, BrE old-fash* likely to be a popular member of a club; SOCIABLE

club·bing /ˈklʌbɪŋ/ *n* [U] *BrE* the visiting of NIGHTCLUBS: *She* **goes clubbing** *(=visits nightclubs) every night.*

club class /ˈ· ·/ *n* BUSINESS CLASS

club·foot /ˈklʌbfʊt/ *n* [C;U] (the condition of having) a badly-shaped foot twisted out of position from birth — **~ed** /ˌklʌbˈfʊtɪd◂/ *adj*

club·house /ˈklʌbhaʊs/ *n* **-houses** /haʊzɪz/ a building where a club meets, esp. one used by a sports group

club·land /ˈklʌblænd/ *n* [U] the part of London around St James's, where most of the famous clubs are found

Club Med /ˌklʌb ˈmed/ also **Club Méd·i·ter·ra·née** /ˌklʌb mediteræˈneɪ/ *fml* — a company which sells holidays to specially-built villages in various parts of the world, esp. aimed at people in the higher social groups

club sand·wich /ˌ· ˈ···/ *n esp. AmE* three pieces of bread with cold food between them (such as cold meat and SALAD), to be eaten with the hands

club so·da /ˌ· ˈ··/ *n AmE for* SODA WATER

Inspector Clouseau

cluck[1] /klʌk/ n 1 (a sound like) the low short noise that a hen makes when calling her CHICKs (baby hens) or sitting on her eggs 2 *AmE sl* a stupid person or one who has behaved in a stupid way: *You can be a real* **dumb cluck** *sometimes.*

cluck[2] v 1 [I] to make a cluck 2 [I (**over**); T] to express (a feeling) by making a sound like this: *She clucked her disapproval.* | *The old lady clucked over her grandchildren, feeding them everything they liked.*

clue[1] /kluː/ n 1 [(**to**)] something, such as an object or a piece of information, that helps to find an answer to a question, difficulty, or mystery: *Police have still found no clues as to the whereabouts of the missing woman.* | *I'll never guess the answer – give me another clue!* 2 **not have a clue** *infml* a to know nothing (about something): "*Do you know the time of the next train?*" "*I haven't a clue.*" | *She hasn't a clue about computers.* b to be stupid or lacking in skill: *That new clerk hasn't a clue – it's taken him all afternoon just to file three letters!* 3 a question or information about a word the answer to which will complete one part of a CROSSWORD

clue[2] v
clue sbdy. **in** *phr v* [T] *infml* to provide with the latest facts, news, etc.: *I don't know what's been going on – could you clue me in?*
clue sbdy. **up** *phr v* [T (**about, on**)] *infml* to cause (esp. oneself) to become well-informed about something: *You'd better clue yourself up a bit before you go for the interview!*

Clue·do /ˈkluːdəʊ/ *BrE tdmk*‖**Clue** *AmE tdmk*– n [U] a board game in which each player becomes a certain character in a murder story and tries to discover which character is the murderer, which instrument was used in the murder, and which room in a house it was done in

clued-up /ˌ· ˈ·/ *adj infml* knowing a lot about something: *She's very clued up about the new pay scheme.*

clue·less /ˈkluːləs/ *adj infml, esp. BrE* helpless, stupid, or IGNORANT: *I'm completely clueless about cricket.*

clump[1] /klʌmp/ n 1 [C (**of**)] a group of trees, bushes, plants, etc., growing together: *a little clump of reeds* 2 [C (**of**)] a heavy solid lump or mass of something, such as soil or mud: *sticky clumps of earth on his boots* 3 [S] a heavy slow sound, such as that made by slow footsteps

clump[2] v 1 [I+*adv/prep*] to walk with slow heavy noisy footsteps: *She clumps around/about in her heavy boots.* 2 [I;T (TOGETHER)] to (cause) to gather into or form a clump

clum·sy /ˈklʌmzi/ *adj* 1 awkward and ungraceful in movement or action; without skill or grace: *He's too clumsy to be a good dancer.* | *You clumsy oaf! You've knocked over my coffee!* 2 unskilful in handling people; without TACT: *a clumsy attempt to apologize* 3 difficult to handle or control; UNWIELDY –**sily** *adv* –**siness** n [U]

clung /klʌŋ/ *past tense & past participle of* CLING

clunk /klʌŋk/ n the dull sound of something heavy, esp. metal, hitting something else

clunk-click /ˌ· ˈ·/ n (in Britain) a word that is sometimes used to remind people to fasten their SEAT BELTs in cars. It comes from a well-known old television advertisement which told people to **clunk-click, every trip.**

clunk·er /ˈklʌŋkəʳ/ n *AmE infml* an old machine, esp. a car, that works very badly and will probably not be useful for much longer

clunk·y /ˈklʌŋki/ *adj AmE infml* large or heavy and awkward: *clunky shoes/furniture*

clus·ter[1] /ˈklʌstəʳ/ n 1 [(**of**)] a number of things of the same kind growing or being close together in a group: *a cluster of bees/of stars* | *a small cluster of older buildings in the modern city centre* 2 a small metal BADGE fixed to a soldier's RIBBON (2) as an added sign of honour

cluster[2] v [I;T (TOGETHER)] to (cause to) gather or grow in one or more clusters: *The men clustered together for warmth/clustered round the notice board.* | *Most of the foreign embassies are clustered in this area.*

cluster bomb /ˈ·· ˌ·/ n a bomb that sends out a number of smaller bombs when it explodes –**cluster-bomb** v [T]

clutch[1] /klʌtʃ/ v 1 [T] to hold tightly: *The mother clutched her baby in her arms.* 2 [I (**at**)] to try to hold or seize: *He clutched desperately at the branch as he fell.* 3 **clutch at straws** to be prepared to try anything to get oneself out of a difficulty

clutch[2] n 1 (the PEDAL that operates) an apparatus, esp. in a car, which allows working parts of machinery to be connected or disconnected smoothly: *Take your foot off the clutch after changing gear.* –see picture at CAR 2 [*usu. sing.*] an act of clutching or the fingers and hands in the act of clutching; GRIP: 3 *AmE* a CLUTCH BAG –see also CLUTCHES

clutch[3] n [(**of**)] (the chickens born from) a number of eggs laid by one bird at one time: *a clutch of eggs* | (fig.) *a clutch of new trainees*

clutch bag /ˈ· ·/ n a type of HANDBAG that is carried in the hand rather than with a STRAP. It is usu. used by women when they are going out somewhere special in the evening.

clutch·es /ˈklʌtʃɪz/ n [P] control or power: *in the clutches of the enemy* | *She fell into the clutches of that awful man!*

clut·ter[1] /ˈklʌtəʳ/ v [T (**up, with**)] to make untidy or confused, esp. by filling with useless or unwanted things: *The room was cluttered (up) with toys.* | *His mind's cluttered with useless information.*

clutter[2] n [S;U] (a collection of) things scattered about in a disorderly fashion: *a desk full of clutter* | *Her room is always in a clutter.* (=untidy)

Clw·yd /ˈkluːɪd/ a COUNTY in N Wales

Clyde[1] /klaɪd/ [*the*] a large river which goes through Glasgow

Clyde[2] see BONNIE AND CLYDE

Clydes·dale /ˌklaɪdzdeɪl ˈbæŋk/ [*the*] one of the main banks in Scotland. Like other Scottish banks it prints its own banknotes.

Clyde·side /ˈklaɪdsaɪd/ the towns between Glasgow and Greenock on the river Clyde in Scotland where many famous shipbuilding firms were established in the past

cm *written abbrev. for* CENTIMETRE(s)

CND /ˌsiː en ˈdiː/ the CAMPAIGN FOR NUCLEAR DISARMAMENT; a British organization that opposes the use of NUCLEAR weapons: *a big CND demonstration*

CND

CNN /ˌsiː en ˈen/ Cable News Network; an American CABLE television station that only broadcasts news

c/o /ˌsiː ˈəʊ ·/ *abbrev. for:* care of; (esp. used when writing addresses) to be held or looked after by: *Send it to John Hammond c/o Dorothy Smith.*

Co[1] *written abbrev. for* COUNTY[1]: *Sunderland, Co Durham*

Co[2] /kəʊ/ *abbrev. for* COMPANY (1): *James Smith & Co*

CO *written abbrev. for* COLORADO

C.O. /ˌsiː ˈəʊ·/ n Commanding Officer; a person in the armed forces who holds a position above others

co- see WORD FORMATION

coach[1] /kəʊtʃ/ n 1 *BrE* ‖ **bus** *AmE*– a comfortable bus used for long-distance travel or touring: *We went to Switzerland by coach.* | *This hotel welcomes coach parties.* (=groups of people travelling in coaches) 2 also **carriage** *BrE* ‖ **car** *AmE*– a railway passenger carriage 3 a person **a** who trains sportsmen and sportswomen for games, competitions, etc.: *a football/baseball coach* **b** who is employed privately to train a student for an examination: *a mathematics coach* 4 *AmE* the cheapest class of seats in a plane or train: *Do you want coach or first-class?* 5 a large enclosed four-wheeled horse-drawn carriage, used esp. in former times or in official ceremonies: *a coach and four* (=four horses) | *the royal coach* – see also **drive a coach and horses through** (DRIVE[1])

coach[2] v [I;T (**for, in**)] to train or teach, esp. not in a place of formal education; give instruction or advice to (a person or a group of people): *I coach people for English exams.* | *She coaches me in French.* | *to do some private coaching* –see TEACH (USAGE)

Coach and Hors·es /ˌ· · ˈ··/ [*the*] (in Britain) a very common name for a PUB: *We had a pint in the Coach and Horses.*

coach·build·er /ˈkəʊtʃˌbɪldəʳ/ n *BrE* a skilled worker who builds the bodies of motor vehicles, railway carriages, etc.

coach·man /ˈkəʊtʃmən/ n -men /mən/ a person employed to drive a horse-drawn coach

coach sta·tion /ˈ· ˌ··/ n BrE (the building or buildings at) a place where a COACH(1) starts and finishes its journey and where passengers can get on and off

coach·work /ˈkəʊtʃwɜːk‖-wɜːrk/ n [U] BrE the outside body of a car

co·ad·ju·tor /kəʊˈædʒʊtər‖ˌkəʊəˈdʒuːtər, kəʊˈædʒʊtər/ n fml a helper; ASSISTANT

co·ag·u·late /kəʊˈægjʊleɪt/ v [I;T] to (cause to) change from a liquid into a solid state, esp. by chemical action: *Blood coagulates when it meets air.* —**-lation** /kəʊˌægjʊˈleɪʃən/ n [U]

coal¹ /kəʊl/ n 1 [U] a black or brownish-black mineral which is dug from the earth, which can be burnt to give heat, and from which gas and many other products can be made: *a sack/lump of coal | a coal fire | a coal miner* 2 [C] a burning piece of coal; EMBER: *A coal fell from the fire and burned the rug.* 3 **carry/take coals to Newcastle** infml to take goods to a place where they are plentiful already —see also COKE¹, **haul over the coals** (HAUL¹)

coal² v 1 [T] to supply (a ship, railway engine, etc.) with coal 2 [I] (of ships, engines, etc.) to take in coal

coal·bun·ker /ˈkəʊlˌbʌŋkər/ n a container or small building where coal is stored

coal cel·lar /ˈ· ˌ··/ n AmE for COAL HOLE

co·a·lesce /ˌkəʊəˈles/ v [I] fml or tech to grow together so as to form one group, body, mass, etc.; MERGE —**-lescence** n [U]

coal·face /ˈkəʊlfeɪs/ n 1 [C] the part of a coalmine from which coal is actually cut 2 [the+S] esp. BrE the place where a particular job is actually done, not just talked about: *new methods that can be used by teachers working at the coalface* (=in the classroom)

coal·field /ˈkəʊlfiːld/ n an area where there is a lot of coal under the ground

coal gas /ˈ· ·/ n [U] gas produced by burning coal, used esp. for lighting and heating —compare NATURAL GAS

coal·hole /ˈkəʊlhəʊl/ BrE ‖ **coal cellar** AmE — n a small usu. underground room where coal is stored

coal·house /ˈkəʊlhaʊs/ n -houses /haʊzɪz/ a small building where coal is stored

Coal·ite /ˈkəʊlaɪt/ n [U] tdmk a smokeless substance similar to coal for burning on fires esp. in the many areas of Britain where people are not allowed to burn coal

co·a·li·tion /ˌkəʊəˈlɪʃən◂/ n a union of separate political parties for a special purpose (esp. to form a government), usu. for a limited period of time: *to form a coalition | a coalition government* —see also extra information on page 412

coal·man /ˈkəʊlmæn/ n -men /men/ a man who delivers coal to people's houses

coal·mine /ˈkəʊlmaɪn/ n a mine from which coal is dug

coal·scut·tle /ˈkəʊlˌskʌtl/ also **scuttle**— n a bucket in which coal is carried and from which it can be poured —see picture at FIREPLACE

coal tar /ˈ· ·/ n [U] a thick black sticky liquid made by heating coal without air, from which many drugs and chemical products may be obtained

coarse /kɔːs‖kɔːrs/ adj 1 not fine or smooth; lumpy or rough: *coarse sand | a coarse woollen cloth* 2 lacking grace, education, or sensitivity; CRUDE; VULGAR: *coarse behaviour | a coarse joke* — **~ly** adv — **~ness** n [U]

coarse fish·ing /ˌ· ˈ··/ n [U] BrE the sport of trying to catch fish that are not TROUT or SALMON in lakes or rivers

coars·en /ˈkɔːsən‖ˈkɔːr-/ v [I;T] to (cause to) become coarse

coast¹ /kəʊst/ n 1 [the+S;C] the land on or close to the edge of the sea: *The ship sank three miles off the French coast. | a hotel on the coast | the southern and eastern coasts of Britain* —see SHORE (USAGE) 2 [C] esp. AmE an act of coasting down a hill 3 **the coast is/was clear** infml all danger has/had gone: *As soon as the coast was clear the two thieves made their getaway.*

coast² v 1 [I (along, down, ALONG)] to keep moving, esp. down a hill, without using any effort or power: *The children were coasting along on their bicycles/coasting down the slope. | (fig.) She coasted through her exams.* —

compare FREEWHEEL 2 [I;T] AmE SLEDGE² (2)

coast·al /ˈkəʊstl/ adj [A no comp.] on or near the coast: *a coastal resort | coastal waters | coastal fishing*

coast·er /ˈkəʊstər/ n 1 a ship which sails from port to port along a coast 2 a small round mat placed under a bottle, glass, etc., to protect a table top or other surface —see also ROLLER COASTER

coaster brake /ˈ·· ·/ n AmE a BRAKE on a bicycle which is worked by moving the PEDALs backwards

coast·guard /ˈkəʊstɡɑːd‖-ɡɑːrd/ n 1 [the+S+sing./pl. v] (often caps.) a naval or police organization that watches from the coast for ships in danger and attempts to prevent unlawful activity at sea 2 [C] a member of this organization

coast·line /ˈkəʊstlaɪn/ n the shape of a coast, esp. as seen from the sea or on a map: *a rocky coastline*

coat¹ /kəʊt/ n 1 an outer garment with long SLEEVES, often fastened at the front with buttons and usu. covering the body down to the knees, worn esp. to keep warm or for protection: *a warm winter coat | a fur coat | a raincoat | a scientist in a white coat* —see also MORNING COAT, and see pictures at LABORATORY and at OVERALL 2 BrE oldfash or AmE a JACKET 3 an animal's fur, wool, or hair: *The dog's coat was shiny and healthy-looking.* 4 [(of)] a covering spread over a surface: *a coat of paint/of dust* 5 **-coated** /kəʊtɪd/ having the stated kind of coat: *a curly-coated dog | a chocolate-coated biscuit* —see also **cut one's coat according to one's cloth** (CUT¹)

coat² v [T (in, with)] to cover with a COAT¹ (4): *to coat a cake with chocolate | The table was coated in/with dust.*

coat check /ˈ· ·/ n AmE for a CLOAKROOM

coat hang·er /ˈ· ˌ··/ n a HANGER

coat·ing /ˈkəʊtɪŋ/ n 1 [C (of)] a covering on or over a surface: *a cake with a coating of chocolate | electric wire with a plastic coating* 2 [U] cloth from which coats are made

coat of arms /ˌ· · ˈ·/ n coats of arms a set of patterns or pictures, usu. painted on a shield or shield-like shape, used by a noble family, town council, university, etc., as their special sign —see also HERALDRY

coat of arms

coat of many col·ours /ˌ· · ˌ·· ˈ··/ [the] the coat which, according to the Bible, Jacob made for his favourite son, Joseph —see also JOSEPH

coat·room /ˈkəʊtrʊm, -ruːm/ n AmE for a CLOAKROOM

coat tails /ˈ· ·/ n [P] 1 the long divided piece of material which hangs down from the back of a man's TAILCOAT 2 **on someone's coat tails** esp. AmE (esp. in politics) using the help or influence of someone else: *He was voted into the Assembly on Davidson's coat tails.*

coax /kəʊks/ v [T] 1 [(into, out of)] to persuade (someone) by gentle kindness, patience, or FLATTERY: *The children had to be coaxed into going to school. [+to-v] She coaxed him to take her to the theatre. | (fig.) to coax a wire through a hole* 2 [+obj+adv/prep] to get (something) by gently persuading: *I coaxed a smile from the little girl.* — **~ingly** adv

cob /kɒb‖kɑːb/ n 1 a CORNCOB —see also CORN ON THE COB 2 a male SWAN 3 a strong short-legged type of horse 4 a type of large nut, esp. one from the HAZEL tree

co·balt /ˈkəʊbɔːlt/ n [U] a shiny silver-white metal that is an ELEMENT (=a simple substance), used in blue colouring materials and in making metals

Cobb /kɒb‖kɑːb/, **Ty** /taɪ/ (1886–1961) a BASEBALL player who established a record of 4000 hits

cob·ber /ˈkɒbər‖ˈkɑː-/ n AustrE & NZE, infml a friend; MATE

cob·ble /ˈkɒbəl‖ˈkɑː-/ v [T] 1 [(TOGETHER)] to make or put together quickly and roughly: *We cobbled together a proposal to put before the committee.* 2 rare to repair (shoes)

cob·bled /ˈkɒbəld‖ˈkɑː-/ adj (of a road) covered with cobblestones

Cob·bleigh /ˈkɒbli‖ˈkɑː-/ **old Uncle Tom Cobbleigh and**

all a line from an old British song about a large group of people who do things together. The people are all listed by name, and the list ends with the words "old Uncle Tom Cobbleigh and all". The phrase is now used to say that every possible person was present or involved in something.

cob·bler¹ /ˈkɒblər‖ˈkɑː-/ *n* **1** a person who makes or repairs shoes **2** *AmE* a cooked fruit dish with a sweet bread-like topping: *peach cobbler*

cobbler² *n* a sweet dish made with cooked fruit with a sweet, bread-like covering: *peach cobbler*

cob·blers /ˈkɒbləz‖ˈkɑːblərz/ *n* [U] *BrE sl* foolish talk; nonsense: *I've never heard such a load of old cobblers in my whole life!*

cob·ble·stone /ˈkɒbəlstəʊn‖ˈkɑː-/ also **cobble—** *n* [usu. pl.] a naturally rounded stone, used for covering the surface of roads in former times

Cob·den /ˈkɒbdən‖ˈkɑː-/, **Richard** (1804–65) a British Liberal politician who helped to start the Anti-Corn Law League and believed in FREE TRADE

co·bra /ˈkəʊbrə/ *n* an African or Asian poisonous snake that can spread the skin of its neck to make itself look bigger —see picture at SNAKE

cob·web /ˈkɒbweb‖ˈkɑːb-/ also **spiderweb** *AmE—* *n* **1** a very fine network of sticky threads made by a SPIDER to catch insects —see picture at SPIDER **2 blow/brush the cobwebs away** *infml* to make oneself feel fresher and more active with air and exercise: *Let's go for a walk and blow the cobwebs away.* — ~**by** *adj*

co·ca /ˈkəʊkə/ *n* [U] a South American bush. Cocaine is produced from its leaves.

Co·ca-Co·la /ˌkəʊkə ˈkəʊlə/ also **Coke, coke—** *n* [C;U] *tdmk* (a small bottle, can, or glass of) a sweet non-alcoholic CARBONATED drink of American origin

Coca-Cola

co·caine /kəʊˈkeɪn/ *n* [U] also **coke** *sl—* a drug used for preventing pain in medical operations which is now often taken illegally for pleasure. It is usu. in the form of a white powder which is sniffed (SNIFF¹) into the nose. One can become dependent on it. Cocaine is expensive and is sometimes used by wealthy, fashionable people —see also CRACK²

coc·cyx /ˈkɒksɪks‖ˈkɑːk-/ *n* **coccyxes** *or* **coccyges** /kɒkˈsaɪdʒiːz‖ˈkɑːksɹ̩-/ *med* a small bone shaped like a TRIANGLE at the bottom of the BACKBONE in humans —see picture at SKELETON

coch·i·neal /ˌkɒtʃɹ̩ˈniːl‖ˌkɑː-/ *n* [U] a bright red substance made from the dried body of a tropical American insect and used for colouring food

Co·chise /kəʊˈtʃiːs/ (about 1815–74) a leader of the APACHES. He gave the US government a lot of trouble in the 1860s, until in 1871 his people were given a RESERVATION (3) on their own land.

coch·le·a /ˈkɒkliə‖ˈkɑː-/ *n* **-leas** *or* **-leae** /-li-iː/ *med* a SPIRAL-shaped tube like part of the inner ear

Coch·ran /ˈkɒkrən‖ˈkɑː-/, **Ed·die** /ˈedi/ (1938–60) an American popular music singer and GUITAR player whose best-known song is *Summertime Blues*

cock¹ /kɒk‖kɑːk/ *n* **1** [C] also **rooster** *esp. AmE—* a fully-grown male chicken: *The cock crowed at dawn.* —see also COCK-A-DOODLE-DOO, COCKEREL

▶ CULTURAL NOTE In Britain in former times men used to make two cocks fight each other, usu. until one of them was killed, and BET² (1) on which one would win. ◀

2 [C] (*often in comb.*) a fully-grown male of any bird: *a cock robin* **3** [C] a TAP, VALVE, etc., for controlling the flow of liquid in a pipe; STOPCOCK **4** [C] the hammer of a gun **5** [C] a small pile of HAY **6** [U] *BrE sl* foolish talk; nonsense **7** [C] *BrE sl* (used as a friendly form of address by men to men, esp. in London and Northern England) **8** [C] *taboo sl for* PENIS **9 cock of the walk** *infml, often derog* someone who is (or thinks he is) the most power-

ful or influential person among a group **10 live like 'fighting cocks** *infml, esp. BrE* to live very well, esp. eating very good food —see also HALF COCK

cock² *v* **1** [I;T (UP)] **a** (of parts of the body) to stand up: *The horse's ears cocked.* **b** to cause (parts of the body) to stand up: *The dog cocked its hind leg and urinated.* **2** [T] to set (the hammer of a gun) in the position ready for firing: *to cock a pistol* **3** [T] to cause (a hat) to slope slightly; TILT **4 cock a snook (at)** *BrE infml* to show open disrespect (for): *The artist cocked a snook at the critics by exhibiting an empty frame.*
cock sthg. ↔ **up** *phr v* [T] *BrE sl* to spoil or ruin (arrangements, plans, etc.): *He's furious — his secretary's cocked up his travelling schedule.* —see also COCK-UP

cock·ade /kɒˈkeɪd‖ˈkɑː-/ *n* a decorative knot of material worn on a hat as a sign of rank, membership, etc.

cock-a-doo-dle-doo /ˌkɒk ə ˌduːdl ˈduː‖ˌkɑːk-/ *n* **-doos** the loud long cry made by a COCK¹ (1)

cock-a-hoop /ˌkɒk ə ˈhuːp‖ˌkɑːk-/ *adj* [F] *infml* **1** [(**about, at**)] very happy and pleased: *He was cock-a-hoop about his new job.* **2** in disorder; very untidy

cock-a-leek·ie /ˌkɒk ə ˈliːki‖ˌkɑːk-/ *n* [U] *BrE* soup made from boiled chicken and vegetables, esp. LEEKs

cock·a·ma·mie /ˌkɒkəˈmeɪmi◄‖ˌkɑːk-/ *adj AmE infml* foolish or nonsensical; RIDICULOUS: *He told us this cock-amamie story about getting lost just around the corner.*

cock-and-bull sto·ry /ˌ· · ˈ· ‖ˌ· ˌ·/ *n infml* a foolish improbable story told as if it were true: *She came out with some cock-and-bull story about being delayed by a camel in the road.*

cock·a·too /ˌkɒkəˈtuː‖ˈkɑːkətuː/ *n* **-toos** *or* **-too** an Australian bird (a type of PARROT) with a CREST (=a lot of large feathers) on the top of its head

cock·a·trice /ˈkɒkətraɪs‖ˈkɑːk-/ *n* the Greek name for a BASILISK

cock·chaf·er /ˈkɒktʃeɪfər‖ˈkɑːk-/ *n* a European BEETLE (=a type of insect) which attacks trees and plants

cock·crow /ˈkɒk-krəʊ‖ˈkɑːk-/ *n* [U] *lit* sunrise

cocked hat /ˌ· ˈ·/ *n* **1** a three-cornered hat with turned-up edges, worn in former times or with special uniforms **2 knock someone/something into a cocked hat** *infml* to defeat or spoil completely: *He'll knock all the other competitors into a cocked hat.* | *Her refusal knocked all my plans into a cocked hat.*

cock·e·rel /ˈkɒkərəl‖ˈkɑː-/ *n* a young COCK¹ (1)

cock·er span·iel /ˌkɒkə ˈspænjəl‖ˌkɑːkər-/ also **cocker—** *n* a short-legged dog with long ears and a silky coat

cock·eyed /ˌkɒkˈaɪd◄‖ˌkɑːk-/ *adj sl* **1** turned or twisted to one side; CROOKED; ASKEW **2** foolish, esp. based on false ideas or beliefs; stupid: *cockeyed notions*

cock·fight /ˈkɒkfaɪt‖ˈkɑːk-/ *n* a fight between COCKS¹ (1), watched as a sport — ~**ing** *n* [U]

cock·horse /ˌkɒkˈhɔːs‖ˈkɑːkhɔːrs/ *BrE‖***hobbyhorse** *AmE—* *n rare* a stick with a model horse's head fastened to the top, which children pretend to ride. This is a well-known word because of the NURSERY RHYME (=old song or poem for children) which begins
Ride a cockhorse to Banbury Cross,
To see a fine lady upon a white horse...

cock·le /ˈkɒkəl‖ˈkɑː-/ *n* **1** a common European soft-bodied SHELLFISH used for food. In Britain they are often thought of in connection with MUSSELs, as there is a famous song about "selling cockles and mussels alive, alive-oh". **2 warm the cockles of one's/the heart** to make one feel happy and satisfied: *To hear her talk about her little boy would warm the cockles of your heart.*

cock·le·shell /ˈkɒkəlʃel‖ˈkɑː-/ *n* **1** the heart-shaped shell of the cockle **2** *lit* a small light boat

Cock·ney /ˈkɒkni‖ˈkɑːkni/ *n* **1** [C] a person from the East End of London, usu. someone who is WORKING CLASS and who speaks with a strong ACCENT. Only someone born near enough to hear Bow Bells, the bells of a church in the City of London, is considered to be a true Cockney. **2** [U] the way of speaking English that is typical of Cockneys: *to speak broad Cockney* | *a Cockney accent* —see also RHYMING SLANG

cock·pit /ˈkɒkˌpɪt‖ˈkɑːk-/ *n* **1** the part of a plane, small boat, or racing car in which the pilot or driver sits —see pictures at AIRLINER and YACHT **2** a small enclosed space where COCKFIGHTs take place: (fig.) *The Middle East has been the cockpit of modern history.* **3** (in former times) a space on the lower floor (DECK) of a warship for the treatment of people wounded in battle

cock·roach /'kɒk-rəʊtʃ‖'kɑːk-/ also **roach** *AmE infml*— *n* a large black insect which lives esp. in old or dirty houses —see picture at INSECT

cocks·comb /'kɒks-kəʊm‖'kɑːks-/ *n* **1** the COMB[1] (4) on the head of a male chicken **2** also **coxcomb**— *lit* the cap of a JESTER

cock·sure /ˌkɒk'ʃʊəʳ‖ˌkɑːk-/ *adj infml* too self-confident; offensively sure of oneself

cock·tail /'kɒkteɪl‖'kɑːk-/ *n* **1** [C] a mixed alcoholic drink, usu. drunk at parties or special occasions and served before the main meal **2** [C;U] a mixture of small pieces of certain foods, usu. served cold in a glass and eaten at the beginning of a meal: *a seafood/prawn cocktail* **3** [C;U] a mixture of small pieces of fruit, usu. eaten at the end of a meal: *a tin of fruit cocktail* —see also MOLOTOV COCKTAIL

cocktail lounge /'·· ·/ *n* a public room in a hotel, club, etc., where alcoholic drinks can be bought

cocktail par·ty /'·· ˌ··/ *n* a party for which one usu. dresses formally and at which there is no dancing. Alcoholic drinks are served, and there is usu. something light to eat, such as QUICHE or CANAPÉs. Cocktail parties are thought of as an UPPER-CLASS activity for fashionable people, or they may be held at a formal public occasion, e.g. before a PRESS CONFERENCE or at the LAUNCH of a new book.

Cocktail Party, The a play by T S Eliot

cocktail stick /'·· ·/ *n* a small pointed stick on which small pieces of food, e.g. squares of cheese, can be served

cocktail wait·ress /'·· ˌ··/ *n AmE* a woman who serves drinks to people sitting at tables in a BAR[1] (3a)

cock·up /'·· ·/ *n BrE sl* something that has been done badly or put into complete disorder: *She made a complete cockup of the arrangements.* —see also COCK **up**

cock·y /'kɒki‖'kɑːki/ *adj infml* self-confident in an unpleasant way; COCKSURE —**iness** *n*

co·coa /'kəʊkəʊ/ *n* **1** [U] an unsweetened brown powder made by crushing the cooked seeds of a tropical tree (CACAO) and removing some of the fat, used for giving the taste of chocolate to foods and drinks **2** [C;U] (a cupful of) a drink made from hot milk or water mixed with this powder, often drunk at bedtime, esp. by children: *a mug of cocoa* —compare CHOCOLATE[1]

co·co·nut /'kəʊkənʌt/ *n* **1** [C] the very large brown hardshelled nut-like fruit of a tall tropical tree (**coconut palm**), with white flesh and a hollow centre filled with juice (**coconut milk**) **2** [U] the flesh of this seed eaten raw or used in cooking: *shredded coconut | coconut oil*

coconut mat·ting /ˌ···· '··/ *n* [U] a type of hard rough matting made from the material on the outside of a COCONUT and made into e.g. DOORMATS (= a mat on which to clean one's shoes before entering a house)

coconut shy /'···· ˌ·/ *n* (in Britain) a game at a FAIR[3] (1), in which people throw balls at coconuts to win a prize by knocking them off posts

co·coon[1] /kə'kuːn/ *n* a protective case of silky threads in which some kinds of PUPA (=an insect in its inactive stage) are enclosed —compare CHRYSALIS

cocoon[2] *v* [T (**from, against**)] to keep in a protective covering: (fig.) *He was cocooned against real hardship by his family's wealth.*

Co·co the Clown /ˌkəʊkəʊ ðə 'klaʊn/ (1900–74) a Russianborn CLOWN, one of the greatest CIRCUS performers ever, who was well known in Britain esp. in the 1950s

Coc·teau /'kɒktəʊ‖ˌkɑːk'təʊ/, **Jean** /ʒɒn‖ʒɑːn/ (1889–1963) a French writer and filmmaker known for his Surrealism, whose work includes the film *Orphée* and the play *La Machine Infernale*

cod /kɒd‖kɑːd/ also **cod·fish** /'kɒd-fɪʃ‖'kɑːd-/— *n cod or* **cods** [C;U] (the white flesh, used as food, of) a large N Atlantic sea fish: *fishing for cod | cod fillets/steaks*

COD /ˌsiː əʊ 'diː/ *abbrev. for:* **1** cash on delivery; a situation in which a customer receiving goods pays the person handing them over: *to send a parcel COD* **2** *AmE* collect on delivery

co·da /'kəʊdə/ *n* **1** a usu. independent passage that ends a piece of music **2** a partly independent passage that ends a work of literature

cod·dle /'kɒdl‖'kɑːdl/ *v* [T] **1** to MOLLYCODDLE **2** to cook (esp. an egg) slowly in water just below boiling point: *coddled eggs*

code[1] /kəʊd/ *n* **1** a system of words, letters, numbers, etc., used instead of ordinary writing, esp. to keep messages secret: *a message written in code | a computer code | We've* **broken/cracked their code!** (=learnt how to read it) **2** a system of signals used instead of letters and numbers in a message that is to be broadcast, sent by TELEGRAPH, etc.: *a telegraphic code* —see also MORSE CODE **3** also **dialling code** *BrE* ‖ **area code** *AmE*— part of a telephone number that represents a particular town or country and is used before the number of the person or organization one wishes to call: *What's the code for Aberdeen?* **4** a collection of established social customs: *an accepted code of conduct/moral code* **5** a collection of laws or rules: *the Napoleonic Code* —see also GENETIC CODE, MACHINE CODE, POSTCODE, ZIP CODE

code[2] also **encode** *fml*— *v* [T] to translate into a CODE[1] (1,2): *a coded message* —opposite **decode**

code book /'· ·/ *n BrE* a small book listing the telephone numbers (codes) one needs to ring to connect with a certain town or country: *Have you seen the code book?*

co·deine /'kəʊdiːn/ *n* [U] a drug made from OPIUM, used as a pain-killing medicine

code name[1] /'· ·/ *n* a name which few people know or understand given to e.g. a military plan of action, a computer PROGRAM, a new technical development, etc. in order to keep the subject secret from other people: *Philip O'Donnell, code name Doc, was the perfect spy.*

code name[2] *v* [T] to give a code name to (sbdy or sthg): *We'll code name this project "Midnight."*

code of prac·tice /ˌ· · '··/ *n* codes of practice a set of rules which are not law but describe the attitudes and actions of an industry, an organization, or a group of people involved in a common activity: *The insurers' code of practice requires the client to be given a week in which to change his mind.*

co·dex /'kəʊdeks/ *n* **codices** /'kəʊdɪˌsiːz/ *tech* an ancient book written by hand

cod·ger /'kɒdʒəʳ‖'kɑː-/ *n infml derog or humor* an old man (esp. in the phrase **old codger**)

cod·i·cil /'kəʊdɪˌsɪl‖'kɑːdɪsəl, -sɪl/ *n law* a later addition to a WILL (=an official paper stating who is to have one's possessions after one's death)

co·di·fy /'kəʊdɪˌfaɪ‖'kɑː-/ *v* [T] to arrange (esp. laws) into a CODE[1] (5) or system —**fication** /ˌkəʊdɪfɨ'keɪʃən‖ˌkɑː-/ *n* [C;U]

cod-liver oil /ˌ· ·· '·◂/ *n* [U] oil from the LIVER (=an organ of the body) of the COD, which is full of useful VITAMINs. Cod-liver oil used to be regularly given to children until the 1940s and 1950s. Many children hated it because of its unpleasant taste.

cod·piece /'kɒdpiːs‖'kɑːd-/ *n* a sometimes decorated bag used formerly to cover the opening in the front of men's tight-fitting trousers

cods·wal·lop /'kɒdzwɒləp‖'kɑːdzwɑː-/ *n* [U] *BrE old-fash sl* nonsense

cod war /'· ·/ *n* any of three arguments between Britain and Iceland in 1958, 1972–73, and 1975–76, about Iceland's decision to limit the amount of cod that British boats could catch in the sea around Iceland

Co·dy /'kəʊdi/, **Wil·liam Fred·e·rick** /'wɪljəm 'fredərɪk/ the real name of BUFFALO BILL

Coe /kəʊ/, **Se·bas·ti·an** /sɨ'bæstiən‖-tʃən/ (1956–) an English middle-distance runner who broke several world records and won GOLD MEDALs in the Olympic Games in 1980 and 1984. In 1990 he left sport to go into politics and became a Member of Parliament in 1992.

co·ed[1] /ˌkəʊ'ed◂‖'kəʊed/ *adj infml* (of education, a school, etc.) coeducational: *It used to be a single-sex school but it's gone coed.*

coed[2] *n old-fash AmE infml* a female student in a college open to both sexes

co·ed·u·ca·tion /ˌkəʊedjʊ'keɪʃən‖-dʒə-/ *n* [U] the system of educating boys and girls together in the same buildings and classes − ~ **al** adj

co·ef·fi·cient /ˌkəʊɪˈfɪʃənt/ n tech **1** the number by which a VARIABLE² is multiplied: *In 8pz the coefficient of pz is 8.* **2** a number that measures some quality or process: *The* **coefficient of expansion** *shows the amount by which a substance expands for a particular change of temperature.*

co·e·qual /ˌkəʊˈiːkwəl/ n fml any of two or more people who are equal with one another in rank, ability, power, etc. −**coequal** adj [(with)] − ~ **ly** adv

co·erce /kəʊˈɜːs‖-ˈɜːrs/ v [T] fml **1** [(**into**)] to make (an unwilling person or group) do something, by force, threats, etc.; COMPEL: *The defendant claimed he had been coerced into making a confession.* **2** [often pass.] to keep (a person, group, or activity) under control by using force, threats of punishment, etc.; REPRESS

co·er·cion /kəʊˈɜːʃən‖-ˈɜːrʒən/ n [U] fml the act of coercing or fact of being coerced: *They won the election through a mixture of bribery and coercion.* | *He said he had made the confession under coercion.*

co·er·cive /kəʊˈɜːsɪv‖-ˈɜːr/ adj fml using force; strong enough to coerce: *to use coercive measures/methods* − ~ **ly** adv − ~ **ness** n [U]

co·e·val /kəʊˈiːvəl/ n, adj [(with)] lit (a person) of the same age

co·ex·ist /ˌkəʊɪgˈzɪst/ v [I (with)] to exist together at the same time, esp. peacefully: *Can the President coexist with a hostile Congress?*

co·ex·ist·ence /ˌkəʊɪgˈzɪstəns/ n [U (with)] (esp. of countries with opposed political systems) the state of peacefully existing together −**ent** adj

C of E /ˌsiː əv ˈiː/ abbrev. for: CHURCH OF ENGLAND (2): *"What religion are you?" "C of E".*

cof·fee /ˈkɒfi‖ˈkɔːfi, ˈkɑːfi/ n **1** [U] a brown powder made by crushing the berries (**coffee beans**) of a tropical tree: *Brazil exports a lot of coffee.* | *to grind the coffee in a coffee mill* **2** [C;U] (a cupful of) a hot drink made from this powder, to which milk is often added: *Would you like some coffee/a cup of coffee?* | *I never drink instant coffee, only real coffee.* | *One black coffee and one white* (=with milk), *please.* | *a coffee-coloured dress* −see also IRISH COFFEE

▶CULTURAL NOTE In the US, many people drink coffee with their breakfast and feel that they must have some or the day has not begun well. ◀

coffee bar /ˈ·· ·/ n BrE a place where light meals, cakes, and non-alcoholic drinks are served − compare COFFEE SHOP

coffee break /ˈ·· ·/ n esp. AmE a short pause from work in the middle of the morning or afternoon for a drink, a rest, etc.

cof·fee·cake /ˈkɒfikeɪk‖ˈkɔː-, ˈkɑː-/ n AmE a sweet breadlike cake usually eaten as a SNACK with a cup of coffee

coffee house /ˈ·· ·/ n (esp. in Central Europe and formerly in England) a place where non-alcoholic drinks, cakes, and light meals are served, often used by fashionable people as an informal meeting place −compare COFFEE SHOP

coffee klatch , coffee klatsch /ˈkɒfi klætʃ‖ˈkɔː-, ˈkɑː-/ n AmE a social occasion when a group of people, usu. women, meet each other to talk and drink coffee

coffee ma·chine /ˈ·· ·ˌ·/ n a DRINKS MACHINE

Cof·fee·mate /ˈkɒfimeɪt ‖ ˈkɔː-, ˈkɑː-/ n [U] tdmk a powdered substance added to coffee instead of cream or milk

coffee morn·ing /ˈ·· ˌ··/ n BrE a social occasion when a group of people, usu. women, meet at the home of one of the group to talk and drink coffee. Often the people pay for the coffee, and the money collected is given to a church or CHARITY.

cof·fee·pot /ˈkɒfipɒt‖ˈkɔːfipɑːt, ˈkɑː-/ n a container in which coffee is made or served −see picture at POT

coffee shop /ˈ·· ·/ n **1** esp. AmE a small restaurant, often in a hotel, that serves drinks and simple inexpensive meals −compare CAFE, COFFEE BAR **2** a shop that sells various kinds of coffee

coffee ta·ble /ˈ·· ˌ··/ n a low table, usu. used in a LIVING ROOM −see picture at LIVING ROOM

coffee-table book /ˈ·· ·· ˌ·/ n often derog a large expensive book with a lot of pictures in it, which is intended to look attractive rather than to give a lot of serious information

cof·fer /ˈkɒfər‖ˈkɔː-, ˈkɑː-/ n a large strong chest for holding money, jewels, or other valuable objects: (fig.) *The government's coffers are almost empty.* (=they have no money)

cof·fer·dam /ˈkɒfədæm‖ˈkɔːfər-, ˈkɑː-/ also **coffer−** n a CAISSON

cof·fin /ˈkɒfɪn‖ˈkɔː-, ˈkɑː-/ also **casket** esp. AmE− n the box in which a dead person is buried or burnt −see also **nail in someone's coffin** (NAIL¹ (3))

cog /kɒg‖kɑːg/ n **1** any of the teeth round the edge of a wheel (**cogwheel**) that cause it to move or be moved by another wheel: *the cogs in a car's gear wheels* **2** a COGWHEEL **3** infml an unimportant person in a large business or organization: *I'm just a cog in the machine of a big insurance company.*

co·gent /ˈkəʊdʒənt/ adj fml (esp. of reasons or arguments) tending to persuade or to produce belief; CONVINCING: *cogent arguments in favour of the proposal* − ~ **ly** adv −**gency** n [U]

cog·i·tate /ˈkɒdʒɪteɪt‖ˈkɑː-/ v [I (**about, on, upon**)] fml or humor to think carefully and seriously about something; PONDER −**tation** /ˌkɒdʒɪˈteɪʃən‖ˌkɑːdʒə-/ n [C;U]

cog·i·to er·go sum /ˌkɒgɪtəʊ ɜːgəʊ ˈsʊm‖ˌkəʊ-, -ɜːr-/ see DESCARTES

co·gnac /ˈkɒnjæk‖ˈkəʊ-, ˈkɑː-/ n [C;U] (a glass of) BRANDY (=a fine strong alcoholic drink) made in France

cog·nate¹ /ˈkɒgneɪt‖ˈkɑːg-/ adj [(with)] fml or tech related in origin or qualities: *Italian and Spanish are cognate languages.*

cognate² n fml or tech someone or something related in origin or sharing some qualities with another person or thing, esp. a word in one language that is similar to one in another language and has the same origin

cog·ni·tion /kɒgˈnɪʃən‖kɑːg-/ n [U] fml or tech the act or experience of knowing, including consciousness of things and judgment about them: *in full cognition of the facts*

cog·ni·tive /ˈkɒgnətɪv‖ˈkɑːg-/ adj fml or tech of or about cognition: *cognitive psychology/learning* − ~ **ly** adv

cog·ni·zance , -sance /ˈkɒgnɪzəns‖ˈkɑːg-/ n **take cognizance of** fml or law to take notice of; take into consideration: *The judge has taken cognizance of the new facts in your case.*

cog·ni·zant , -sant /ˈkɒgnɪzənt‖ˈkɑːg-/ adj [F+of] fml or law having knowledge or information; AWARE: *The judge said he was not fully cognizant of the facts in the case.*

cog·no·men /kɒgˈnəʊmən‖kɑːg-, ˈkɒgnə-/ n **1** pomp a descriptive NICKNAME, such as "the Great" in "Frederick the Great" **2** tech a person's SURNAME (=family name), esp. in ancient Rome

co·gno·scen·ti /ˌkɒnjəʊˈʃenti‖ˌkɑːnjə-/ n [(the) P] people who have, or claim to have, special knowledge of or experience in fashion, art, food, etc.; CONNOISSEURS

cog·wheel /ˈkɒg-wiːl‖ˈkɑːg-/ also **cog−** n a wheel with teeth round the edge that can move or be moved by another wheel of the same type −see picture at COG

co·hab·it /ˌkəʊˈhæbɪt/ v [I (with)] fml (of unmarried people) to live together as though married: *Ann and Peter have been cohabiting/Ann has been cohabiting with Peter for years.* − ~ **ation** /kəʊˌhæbɪˈteɪʃən/ n [U]

Co·han /ˈkəʊhæn/, **George M.** (1878−1942) an American actor, PLAYWRIGHT, and songwriter, best known for the songs *I'm a Yankee Doodle Dandy, You're a Grand Old Flag,* and *Give My Regards to Broadway.* A film and a musical have been made about his life.

Co·hen /ˈkəʊɪn/, **Leonard** (1934−) a Canadian FOLK singer esp. popular in the 1960s

co·here /kəʊˈhɪər/ v [I] fml **1** to stick together; be united: *to make two surfaces cohere* **2** to be reasonably and naturally connected, esp. in thought; show coherence: *an argument that simply fails to cohere*

co·her·ence /kəʊˈhɪərəns/ also **co·her·en·cy** /-rənsi/− n [U] natural or reasonable connection; an orderly relationship between parts, esp. in speech, writing, or argument; CONSISTENCY

co·her·ent /kəʊˈhɪərənt/ adj (esp. of speech, writing, or argument) naturally or reasonably connected and therefore easy to understand; showing coherence; CONSISTENT: *to construct a coherent argument* | *They seem to have no coherent plan for saving the company.* —opposite **incoherent** — ~**ly** *adv*

co·he·sion /kəʊˈhiːʒən/ *n* [U] **1** the act or state of sticking together tightly: *We need greater cohesion in the party if we're going to win the next election.* **2** *tech* close relationship, based on grammar or meaning, between different parts of a sentence or between one sentence and another —**sive** /ˈhiːsɪv/ *adj* : *cohesive forces in society* | *a cohesive group* —**sively** *adv* —**siveness** *n* [U]

Cohn-Ben·dit /ˌkəʊn ˈbendɪt/, **Dan·ny** /ˈdæni/ (1945–) a leader of a LEFT-WING political movement in France in the 1960s

co·hort /ˈkəʊhɔːt‖-hɔːrt/ *n* **1** [+*sing./pl. v*] *tech* any group of people who share some common quality, esp. those of the same age, in a study of the population **2** [+*sing./pl. v*] (in the ancient Roman army) a group of between 300 and 600 soldiers under one commander **3** *often derog, esp. AmE* a companion; ASSOCIATE: *the mayor and his disreputable cohorts*

COHSE /ˈkəʊzi/ the Confederation of Health Service Employees; the British TRADE UNION for nurses and other medical workers

COI /ˌsiː əʊ ˈaɪ/ [*the*] the Central Office of Information; the office of the British government which produces information for the general public and others

coif /kɔɪf/ *n* a close-fitting cap covering the top, sides, and back of the head, worn by some NUNS (=members of female religious groups)

coif·feur /kwɒˈfɜːʳ/ *n fml or pomp* a HAIRDRESSER

coif·fure /kwɒˈfjʊəʳ‖kwɑː-/ *n fml* a way of arranging or wearing the hair; HAIRSTYLE —**fured** *adj*

coil¹ /kɔɪl/ *v* [I+*adv/prep*;T (UP)] to (cause to) wind or twist round and round to form a ring or SPIRAL: *The snake coiled around the tree/coiled itself into a ball.* | *a coiled spring*

coil² *n* **1** a connected set of rings or twists into which a rope, wire, length of hair, etc., can be wound; continuous circular shape made by winding: *a coil of rope* | *her heavy coil of hair* **2** *tech* an electrical apparatus made by winding wire into a continuous circular shape, used for carrying an electric current —see picture at ENGINE **3** a coil of metal or plastic which is fitted inside the UTERUS (=the child-bearing organ of a woman) to prevent her from having children; IUD

Coim·bra /ˈkwɪmbrə/ a city in W central Portugal, formerly the capital. It is famous for having the country's oldest university.

coin¹ /kɔɪn/ *n* **1** a piece of metal, usu. flat and round, made by a government for use as money: *I changed a £5 note/a $5 bill because I needed some coins for the ticket machine.* | *He paid me in coin.* | *Let's* **toss/flip a coin** *to decide who should go first — do you want heads or tails?*

▶CULTURAL NOTE People sometimes bite a coin, usu. jokingly, to see if it is GENUINE.◀

2 pay someone in their own coin *esp. BrE fml* to treat someone in the same (bad) way as they have treated others **3 the other side of the coin** the other or opposite side of an argument, situation, etc.: *These workers earn a lot more than us, but the other side of the coin is that their job is much more dangerous.*

coin² *v* [T] **1** to make (coins) from metal **2** to invent (a word or phrase): *Who coined the word "nuke"?* **3 coin money** also **coin it**— *BrE infml* to earn a lot of money very quickly: *That restaurant must be coining money — it's always full.* **4 to coin a phrase** *humor* (used for excusing oneself when one has used a very well-known and ordinary phrase): *Many hands make light work, to coin a phrase.* — ~ *er n*

coin·age /ˈkɔɪnɪdʒ/ *n* **1** [U] the system of coins used in a country: *decimal coinage* **2** [C] a word or phrase recently invented: *The word "nuke" is a fairly recent coinage.* **3** [U] **a** the act of making coins **b** the act of inventing new words or phrases

co·in·cide /ˌkəʊɪnˈsaɪd/ *v* [I (with)] **1** to happen at the same time or during the same period: *Her holidays don't coincide with mine.* | *The Queen's visit has been planned*

to coincide with the school's 200th anniversary. **2** (of ideas, opinions, etc.) to be in agreement: *Our interests happened to coincide.*

co·in·ci·dence /kəʊˈɪnsɪdəns/ *n* **1** [C;U] (an example of) the happening by chance at the same time or place of two or more events which are similar or related: *What a coincidence that I was in London at the same time as you!* | *By* **sheer coincidence**/*By a curious coincidence, my husband and I have the same birthday.* | *It is no coincidence that his car was seen near the bank at the time of the robbery.* **2** [U] *fml* the condition or fact of coinciding: *coincidence of opinions*

co·in·ci·dent /kəʊˈɪnsɪdənt/ *adj* **1** [(with)] *tech or fml* existing or happening in the same position and time **2** *fml* being in complete agreement

co·in·ci·den·tal /kəʊˌɪnsɪˈdentl/ *adj* resulting from a coincidence: *It was purely coincidental that we were travelling on the same plane.* — ~ **ly** *adv* : *Coincidentally, he and I were on the same plane.*

Coin·treau /ˈkwɒntrəʊ‖kwɑːnˈtrəʊ/ *n* [U] *tdmk* a strong colourless alcoholic drink, tasting of oranges, usu. drunk from a small glass after a meal

coir /kɔɪəʳ/ *n* [U] the rough hair outer covering of the COCONUT, used for making ropes, mats, etc.

co·i·tus /ˈkɔɪtəs, med ˈkəʊ.tɪ̱əs/ also **co·i·tion** /kəʊˈɪʃən/— *n* [U] *med or fml* the act of sex; SEXUAL INTERCOURSE —**coital** /ˈkɔɪtl, med ˈkəʊ.tl/ *adj*

coitus in·ter·rup·tus /ˌkɔɪtəs ɪntəˈrʌptəs, med ˌkəʊ.tɪ̱-/ *n* [U] *fml* the practice of taking the man's sex organ out of the woman's sex organ before ejaculating (EJACULATE), to prevent the woman having a baby

coke¹ /kəʊk/ *n* [U] the solid substance that remains after gas has been removed from coal by heating, which is burnt as a FUEL

coke² *n* **1** [C;U] also **Coke**— *tdmk for* COCA-COLA **2** [U] *sl for* COCAINE

col /kɒl‖kɑːl/ *n* a low place between two high points in a mountain range; mountain PASS² (5) —see picture at MOUNTAIN

col. *written abbrev. for:* COLONEL

co·la /ˈkəʊlə/ *n* [C;U] (a glass of) a non-alcoholic sweet CARBONATED dark-coloured drink: *Two colas, please.* | *What kind of cola is this?* —see also DIET COLA

COLA /ˈkəʊlə/ *n* cost of living adjustment; in the US, a way of increasing wages or SOCIAL SECURITY payments to keep up with INFLATION

col·an·der /ˈkʌləndəʳ, ˈkɒ-‖ˈkʌ-, ˈkɑː-/ also **cullender**— *n* a metal or plastic bowl with many small holes in the bottom, used for separating liquid from food: *Strain the peas in the colander.*

Col·ches·ter /ˈkəʊltʃɪstəʳ‖-tʃes-/ a town in SE England. It was the Roman capital of Britain .

cold¹ /kəʊld/ *adj* **1** having a low or lower than usual temperature; not warm: *cold water* | *a cold wind* | *It's a cold day for July, isn't it?* | *It's getting cold — let's shut the window.* | *I'm (feeling) cold; I should have put a coat on.* | *My coffee has gone cold.* | *My toes are as cold as ice.* | *(fig.) She went cold with fear when she heard the footsteps outside her door.* —opposite **hot 2 a** not cheerful or friendly: *a cold handshake/greeting* | *She seemed rather cold towards the visitors.* **b** not influenced by feeling: *a cold calculating murderer* | *a cold evaluation of the facts* | *The prospect of another party* **left her cold.** (=she was not excited or pleased about it) —see also COOL, FROSTY **3** (of food) cooked but not eaten hot: *cold meat* | *Shall I heat up the pies or shall we eat them cold?* **4** [F] (esp. in children's games) still a long way from finding a hidden object, the answer, etc.: *You're getting colder.* —compare HOT¹ (11), WARM¹ (7) **5** [F] *infml* unconscious, esp. as the result of a severe blow to the head: *I knocked him cold with one blow.* | *She's* **out cold.** —see also **in cold blood** (BLOOD¹), **blow hot and cold** (BLOW¹), **pour cold water over/on** (POUR) — ~ **ly** *adv* : *"Good morning," she said coldly.* | *coldly analytical* — ~ **ness** *n* [U]

▷ USAGE Compare **cold** and **cool**, **hot** and **warm**. **Cold** suggests a lower temperature than **cool**, perhaps uncomfortably low: *cold weather*. **Cool** often suggests a pleasantly low temperature: *a nice cool breeze* | *a lovely cool room* (said when you are hot). In the same way,

hot suggests a higher temperature than **warm**, or a temperature which would not be comfortable for a long period. **Warm** often suggests a pleasantly high temperature: *The handle is too* **hot** *to touch.* | *I've caught a cold, so I'm going to take a quick* **hot** *bath and go to bed.* | *I could lie in a* **warm** *bath for hours.* | *a lovely* **warm** *room* (said when you are cold).◁

cold² *n* **1** [(*the*) U] the absence of heat; low temperature or cold weather: *Don't go out in the cold without a coat!* | *The machine is designed to work in extremes of heat or cold.* **2** [C;U] an illness, esp. of the nose and/or throat, which causes headaches, coughing, slight fever, and general discomfort: *I've got a bad cold.* | *He caught (a)* **cold** *in the storm yesterday.* **3 come in from the cold** to become accepted or recognized, esp. by a powerful group of people (from the title of a book by John Le Carré, *The Spy Who Came in from the Cold*) **4 feed a cold and starve a fever** *saying* a phrase stating an old belief that if you have a cold you should eat a lot to get better, but if you have a FEVER (=your body is hot because of illness) you should eat nothing **5 (out) in the cold** *infml* not considered or not taking part: *He was left out in the cold at school because he didn't like sports.* —see also COMMON COLD, **catch one's death of cold** (CATCH¹)

cold³ *adv* completely; thoroughly: *When he asked her to marry him she turned him down cold.* | *He stopped cold when he heard a noise behind him.*

cold-blood·ed /ˌ· '···◁/ *adj* **1** [*no comp.*] having a body temperature that changes according to the temperature of the surroundings: *Snakes are cold-blooded.* —compare WARM-BLOODED **2** showing complete lack of feeling; cruel: *a cold-blooded murder* **3** *infml* very sensitive to cold — ~**ly** *adv* — ~**ness** *n* [U]

cold call /ˌ· '·/ *n* a telephone call made to a number found in the telephone book or on a list in order to try to sell something to the person who answers.

cold chis·el /ˌ· '···/ *n* a CHISEL (=a strong narrow sharp-ended steel tool) for cutting cold metal

cold com·fort /ˌ· '···/ *n* [U] something that does not give comfort; no CONSOLATION: *It's cold comfort to know that your disease is a common one when you are ill.*

Cold Comfort Farm /ˌ· · '·/ a humorous NOVEL by **Stella Gibbons** about a lonely farm where the people are very strange and the life is very hard

cold cream /'· ·/ *n* [U] a thick white sweet-smelling oily cream for cleaning and smoothing the skin

cold cuts /'· ·/ *n* [P] *esp. AmE* thinly cut pieces of various types of cold meat

cold feet /ˌ· '·/ *n* [P] *infml* loss of courage or confidence, esp. just before doing something that is planned (esp. in the phrases **get/have cold feet**): *They got cold feet at the last minute and refused to sign the contract.*

cold fish /ˌ· '·/ *n* an unfriendly person who deals with others in a cold way

cold frame /'· ·/ *n* a small glass-covered frame for protecting young plants

cold front /ˌ· '·‖'· ·/ *n* the advancing edge of a cold mass of air

cold fu·sion /ˌ· '···/ *n* [U] NUCLEAR FUSION taking place at room temperature using ordinary chemicals. It is widely believed by scientists not to be possible, and has not been satisfactorily proved.

cold-heart·ed /ˌ· '···◁/ *adj* unkind; showing no sympathy: *a cold-hearted refusal to help* —compare WARM-HEARTED — ~**ly** *adv* — ~**ness** *n* [U]

Col·ditz /'kəʊldɪts/ a town in Germany that is famous for its castle, which was used as a prisoner-of-war camp in the Second World War and from which many escapes were attempted, a few successfully.

cold shoul·der /ˌ· '···/ *n* [*the*+S] *infml* intentionally cold unsympathetic treatment (esp. in the phrases **give/get the cold shoulder**): *After he left his wife for a younger woman, his friends all gave him the cold shoulder.* —**cold-shoulder** /· '···/ *v* [T]

cold show·er /ˌ· '···/ *n* an act of washing the body under cold running water. People often say jokingly that a man needs a cold shower if he is sexually excited, because it is thought that a cold shower will calm him down.

cold snap /'· ·/ also **cold spell** *AmE* — *n* a sudden short period of very cold weather

cold sore /'· ·/ *n* a sore on the lips or inside the mouth, that often comes with a cold or fever —see also HERPES

cold steel /ˌ· '·/ *n* [U] *lit* a fighting weapon such as a knife or sword, rather than a gun

cold stor·age /ˌ· '···/ *n* [U] **1** storage (e.g. of food) in a cold place in order to keep things fresh or in good condition **2** the condition of being put aside for future action: *We'll put the plan into cold storage until we can find some more money.*

cold store /'· ˌ·/ *n* a cold usu. REFRIGERATEd room for keeping food, fur, etc. in

Cold·stream Guards /ˌkəʊldstriːm 'ɡɑːdz‖-'ɡɑːrdz/ [*the*] one of the most famous REGIMENTS (=divisions of men) in the British army, formed more than three hundred years ago

cold sweat /ˌ· '·/ *n* [S] a state in which one SWEATs and feels cold at the same time, because of fear or nervousness: *to break out in a cold sweat*

cold tur·key /ˌ· '···/ *n* [U] *sl* **1** (the unpleasant sick feeling caused by) the sudden stopping of the use of a drug by an ADDICT (=someone who is dependent on a drug) **2 go cold turkey** to stop the use of a drug suddenly: *When I gave up smoking I went cold turkey.*

cold war /ˌ· '·/ *n* a state of severe political struggle between countries with opposed political systems, who attack each other in various political ways without actually fighting

Cold War [*the*] the political struggle between the US and the Soviet Union after the Second World War, which was most severe in the 1950s but in the 1970s gave way to DÉTENTE. By late 1991 it was considered to be over.

Cole /kəʊl/, **Nat King** /næt kɪŋ/ (1917–65) an American singer known for his soft, smooth voice. He had most success with his recordings of popular love songs, e.g. *When I Fall in Love.*

Cole, Old King a character in a NURSERY RHYME (=an old song or poem for children):
Old King Cole was a merry old soul,
And a merry old soul was he .....

Cole·man /'kəʊlmən/, **Or·nette** /ɔː'net‖ɔːr-/ (1930–) an American JAZZ musician and COMPOSER known for his SAXOPHONE playing

Cole·man·balls /'kəʊlmənbɔːlz/ *n* [P] *BrE derog humor* the foolish things sometimes said by sports COMMENTATORs, esp. when they are excited. The term was first used by the humorous magazine *Private Eye* about **David Coleman**, a well-known sports commentator on British television.

Co·le·ridge /'kəʊlərɪdʒ/, **Sam·u·el Tay·lor** /'sæmjuəl 'teɪləʳ/ (1772–1834) an English poet and CRITIC, best-known for his poems *The Rime of the Ancient Mariner* and *Kubla Khan.* He took drugs, including OPIUM, for many years. He and William Wordsworth were the leaders of the Romantic movement in England —see also ANCIENT MARINER

cole·slaw /'kəʊlslɔː/ *n* [U] finely cut uncooked CABBAGE (=a leafy vegetable) in a DRESSING eaten as a SALAD

Col·ette /kɒ'let‖kəʊ-/ (1873–1954) a French writer best-known for her NOVELS *Chéri* and *Gigi*

co·ley /'kəʊli/ *n* **coley** *or* **coleys** [C;U] (the white flesh, used as food, of) a large North Atlantic sea fish

Col·gate /'kəʊlɡeɪt/ *n tdmk* a type of TOOTHPASTE made by Colgate-Palmolive Limited

col·ic /'kɒlɪk‖'kɑː-/ *n* [(*the*) U] a severe pain in the stomach and bowels, esp. of babies

col·ick·y /'kɒliki‖'kɑː-/ *adj* like colic or suffering from colic: *a colicky baby*

Col·i·se·um /ˌkɒlɪ'siːəm‖ˌkɑː-/ see COLOSSEUM

co·li·tis /kə'laɪtɪs/ *n* [U] swelling of the COLON (=part of the bowels) causing severe discomfort

col·lab·o·rate /kə'læbəreɪt/ *v* [I] **1** [(with, in)] to work together or with someone else, esp. for a special purpose; COOPERATE: *The police and the army collaborated (in catching the terrorists).* | *Our company is collaborating with a German firm in designing a new computer.* [+to-v] *The two organizations collaborated to ensure the disease was wiped out.* **2** [(with)] *derog* to help an enemy country which has taken control of one's own: *Anyone who had collaborated (with the enemy) was shot.* —**rator** *n*

—**-ration** /kə‚læbə'reɪʃən/ n [U (**with, between**)] : *The two companies are working in close collaboration (with each other).* | *shot for collaboration with the enemy* —**rative** /kə'læbərətɪv‖-bəreɪtɪv/ adj : *a collaborative venture*

col·lab·o·ra·tion·ist /kə‚læbə'reɪʃən-₁st/ n derog a person who helps an enemy that has taken control of a country —**ism** n [U]

col·lage /'kɒlɑːʒ‖kə'lɑːʒ/ n 1 [C] a picture made by sticking various materials or objects onto a surface 2 [U] the art of making such pictures

col·la·gen /'kɒlədʒən‖'kɑː-/ n [U] a PROTEIN in the cells of the body that is not easily weakened

col·lapse¹ /kə'læps/ v 1 [I] to fall down or inwards suddenly as a result of pressure or loss of strength or support: *The bridge collapsed under the weight of the train.* 2 [I] to fall helpless or unconscious: *He collapsed at the end of the long race.* | (fig.) *The children collapsed with laughter when their father fell in the river.* 3 [I] to fail suddenly and completely; break down: *The company collapsed in its first year of trading.* | *All opposition to the government collapsed in the face of the threat of war.* | *He felt as if his whole world had collapsed (about him) when his children were killed in a car crash.* 4 [I; T] to fold into a shape that takes up less space: *This table collapses, so I can store it easily when I'm not using it.* | *Collapse the table and put it away.* 5 [I;T] med a (of a lung or BLOOD VESSEL) to fall into a flattened mass b to cause (a lung or blood vessel) to fall into a flattened mass: *The doctors had to collapse her right lung to save her life.*

collapse² n 1 [U] (an example of) the act of collapsing: *The storm caused the collapse of the roof.* | *The collapse of the peace talks led to renewed fighting.* | *The country's economy is on the verge of collapse.* 2 [C;U] (an example of) the sudden and complete loss of strength and/or will: *a state of near/utter collapse* | *He suffered from a nervous collapse.*

col·lap·si·ble /kə'læps₁bəl/ adj that can be collapsed for easy storing: *a collapsible bicycle*

col·lar¹ /'kɒlər‖'kɑː-/ n 1 the part of a shirt, dress, or coat, that stands up or folds down round the neck: *a tight collar* | *What size (of) collar is this shirt?* | *a coat with a fur collar* 2 a band put round an animal's neck: *Where are the dog's collar and lead?* 3 a round leather object put round the shoulders of a horse to help it pull a vehicle 4 tech a coloured marking round an animal's neck 5 any of various ring-like machine parts 6 **hot under the collar** angry or excited: *He got hot under the collar when he realised they were criticising his report.* —see also BLUE-COLLAR, DOG COLLAR, WHITE-COLLAR

collar² v [T] infml to seize; catch and hold: *The police collared him as he was getting on the boat.* | (fig.) *He was collared by some journalists as he left his office.*

col·lar·bone /'kɒləbəʊn‖'kɑːlər-/ also **clavicle** med— n either of a pair of bones joining the RIBS to the front of the shoulders —see picture at SKELETON

col·lards /'kɒlədz‖'kɑːlərdz/ **collard greens** /₁·· '·/— n [P] a vegetable with green leaves, cooked and eaten as food, esp. in the southern US

collar stud /'·· ·/ n a small buttonlike object for fastening a collar to a shirt

col·late /kə'leɪt/ v [T] 1 fml to examine and compare (copies of books, notes, etc.) carefully in order to find the differences between them: *to collate two ancient manuscripts* 2 tech to arrange (the sheets) of (a book) in the proper order before they are bound together

col·lat·e·ral¹ /kə'lætərəl/ n [S;U] tech valuable property promised to a lender if one is unable to repay a debt; SECURITY (4): *He used/put up/offered his house as (a) collateral for the loan.*

collateral² adj fml or tech 1 additional, but with less importance; SECONDARY: *A collateral aim of the government's industrial strategy is to increase employment.* | *The bombs were aimed at military targets but there was some collateral damage to civilian areas.* 2 descended from the same person but through different sons or daughters: *Cousins are collateral relatives but brothers are directly related.* 3 of or being COLLATERAL¹

col·la·tion /kə'leɪʃən/ n fml 1 [U] the act of collating 2 [C] a usu. cold light meal: *a cold collation after the funeral*

col·league /'kɒliːg‖'kɑː-/ n someone who works in the same place, office, etc. as oneself, esp. in a profession: *May I introduce one of my colleagues at the bank?* | *She and I are colleagues.* —compare WORKMATE

col·lect¹ /kə'lekt/ v 1 [I;T (UP)] to come or bring together in one place so as to form a group or mass; gather: *Collect (up) the books and put them in a pile on my desk.* | *A crowd of people collected to watch the procession.* | *The department collects information on political extremists.* 2 [T] to gather (objects) over a long period of time, as a HOBBY, for study, etc.: *John collects foreign coins.* 3 [T] to come to take away: *He collected the children from school.* | *She collected her skirt from the cleaner's.* 4 [I (**for**);T] to ask for or obtain payment of (money, taxes, rent, etc.): *The government is trying to improve the way it collects taxes.* | *We're collecting (money) for the famine victims.* 5 [T] to get control of (oneself, one's senses or feelings, etc.): *I tried to collect my thoughts but I was too excited.* —see GATHER (USAGE)

col·lect² /'kɒlɪkt, -lekt‖'kɑː-/ n a short prayer read near the beginning of certain Christian religious services

collect³ /kə'lekt/ adj, adv AmE to be paid for by the receiver: *a collect phone call* | *Call me collect as soon as you get home.* | *I sent you the books collect.*

col·lect·able¹ /kə'lektəbəl/ adj fashionable to buy and keep, esp. because of being likely to increase in value: *Thirties' pottery figures are very collectable just now.*

collectable² n AmE an object to be put in a collection, esp. something made for that purpose or which is old or rare: *That record is a collectable.*

col·lect·ed /kə'lekt₁d/ adj having control of oneself, one's thoughts, senses, etc.; calm: *How can you stay so* **cool, calm, and collected** *after an argument?* — ~ly adv

col·lec·tion /kə'lekʃən/ n 1 [U] the act or process of collecting: *The local council is responsible for the collection of domestic waste.* | *He made arrangements for the collection of his baggage from the airport.* 2 [C (**of**)] a set of things of the same type that have been collected: *a wealthy family with a magnificent art collection* | *I'll add it to my stamp collection.* | *Her new book is a collection of short stories.* 3 [C] an act of collecting money e.g. at a religious service: *to take round the collection plate in church* | *to organize a collection for charity* | *His workmates held/made a collection for his leaving party.* 4 [C (**of**) usu. sing.] a group, pile, etc., that has gathered together: *a collection of dust in the corner* | *an unusual collection of people at the party* 5 [C] esp. BrE the emptying of a letterbox by a postman: *What time is the next collection?* —see also COLLECTOR

col·lec·tive¹ /kə'lektɪv/ adj of or shared by a number of people or groups of people considered as one or acting as one: *the collective opinion of the governments of Western Europe* | *collective ownership/leadership* — ~ly adv : *We were collectively responsible for the accident.*

collective² n a group of people working together for their shared advantage, esp. a business owned and controlled by the people who work in it

collective bar·gain·ing /·‚·· '···/ n [U] discussions between employers and employees in order to reach agreement on wages, working conditions, etc.

collective farm /·‚·· '·/ n (esp. in Communist countries) a large farm made by joining a number of small farms together, owned by the state, and controlled by the farm workers

collective noun /·‚·· '·/ n tech (in grammar) a noun, such as "committee" or "family", that is the name of a group of people or things considered as a unit. In the singular a collective noun can be followed either by a singular verb or (esp. in British English) by a plural verb, so in this dictionary collective nouns are marked [+sing./pl. v].

collective re·spon·si·bil·i·ty /·‚·· ···'···/ n [U] responsibility shared equally by a group of people: *Society has a collective responsibility to ensure the elderly are cared for.*

col·lec·tor /kə'lektər/ n (often in comb.) 1 a person employed to collect taxes, tickets, debts, etc.: *a rent collector* 2 a person who collects stamps, coins, etc., as a HOBBY: *a stamp collector*

collector's i·tem /·'·· ‚··/ n an object of interest to COLLECTORS (2) because of its beauty or rarity

col·leen /'kɒliːn, kɒ'liːn‖kɑː'liːn, 'kɑːliːn/ n IrE a girl

col·lege /ˈkɒlɪdʒ‖ˈkɑː-/ *n* **1** [C;U] a place where people go for more advanced education after school, esp. in a particular subject or professional skill: *a teacher(s') training college* | *an agricultural college* | *He's at law college|art college.* | *She started college last year.* | *my college scarf* —see also SIXTH FORM COLLEGE; see THE (USAGE) **2** [C] (esp. in Britain) a body of teachers and students forming a separate part of certain universities: *a member of one of the Oxford colleges* | *King's College Cambridge* **3** [C;U] *AmE* a school for higher education giving a BACHELOR'S DEGREE and possibly a MASTER'S degree and DOCTORATE —see also JUNIOR COLLEGE and see also extra information on page 408 **4** [C] (in Britain) any of certain large schools **5** [C] the building or buildings used by any of these educational organizations: *The college is next to the station.* **6** [C+*sing.|pl. v*] the teachers and students of a college considered as a whole **7** [C] a body of people with a (stated) common profession, purpose, duty, or right: *She's a member of the Royal College of Nursing.* | *the electoral college*

college boards /ˈ·· ˌ·/ *n* [P] a set of examinations which students must take in order to enter an American college or university. They include the SAT.

College of Arms /ˌ··· ˈ·/ also **College of Her·alds** /ˌ··· ˈ··|— [the]* the organization which decides on the coats of arms (COAT OF ARMS) of British families and institutions

col·le·gi·ate /kəˈliːdʒiət/ *adj* **1** of or belonging to a college or college students: *collegiate sports* | *a collegiate theatre* **2** having COLLEGES (2): *a collegiate university*

collegiate church /·ˌ··· ˈ·/ *n* a Christian church (not a CATHEDRAL) with more than one regular priest or MINISTER

col·lide /kəˈlaɪd/ *v* [I (**with**)] **1** to crash violently: *The two planes collided (with each other) in midair.* **2** to come into disagreement; be opposed: *The President collided with Congress over his budget plans.* —see also COLLISION

col·lie /ˈkɒli‖ˈkɑːli/ *n* a large long-haired dog used for looking after sheep or kept as a pet —see picture at DOG

col·li·er /ˈkɒliər‖ˈkɑː-/ *n esp. BrE* **1** *fml or old-fash* a person employed to cut coal in a mine; coal MINER **2** a ship for carrying coal

col·lie·ry /ˈkɒljəri‖ˈkɑːl-/ *n esp. BrE* a COALMINE and the buildings, machinery, etc., connected with it

Col·lins /ˈkɒlɪnz‖ˈkɑː-/, **Jack·ie** (1941–) an English writer of popular NOVELs, esp. about the lives of rich and fashionable people, e.g. in Hollywood. She is the sister of Joan Collins.

Collins, Joan /dʒəʊn/ (1933–) an English actress who has appeared in many films, and is known esp. for playing the part of Alexis Carrington in the American television SOAP OPERA *Dynasty*. She is the sister of Jackie Collins.

Collins, Ju·dy /ˈdʒuːdi/ (1939–) an American popular music singer whose best-known songs are *Amazing Grace* and *Send in the Clowns*.

Collins, Mi·chael /ˈmaɪkəl/ (1890–1922) an Irish NATIONALIST and Sinn Fein member who took part in the Easter Rising in Dublin in 1916

Collins, Phil /fɪl/ (1951–) an English popular music singer, songwriter, and drummer

Collins, Wil·kie /ˈwɪlki/ (1824–89) an English writer of many NOVELs, esp. known for *The Moonstone*, considered to be the first English mystery novel, and *The Woman in White*

col·li·sion /kəˈlɪʒən/ *n* [C;U (**between, with**)] (an example of) the act of colliding (COLLIDE): *Three people were killed in a head-on collision between a bus and a car.* | *a collision of principles|interests*

collision course /·ˈ·· ˌ·/ *n* [(**with**)] a course (of movement or action) likely to end in collision: *The employers' organization is on a collision course with the unions.*

col·lo·cate /ˈkɒləkeɪt‖ˈkɑː-/ *v* [I (**with**)] *tech* (of words) to go together or with another word in a way which sounds natural: *"Strong" collocates with "coffee" but "powerful" does not.* | *The words "strong" and "coffee" collocate.*

col·lo·ca·tion /ˌkɒləˈkeɪʃən‖ˌkɑː-/ *n tech* **1** [U] the way in which some words regularly collocate with others **2** [C] a habitual combination of words which sounds natural: *"Strong coffee" is a typical collocation in English but "powerful coffee" is not.*

col·loid /ˈkɒlɔɪd‖ˈkɑː-/ *n tech* a mixture of substances in which one substance is thoroughly spread, but not dissolved (DISSOLVE) in another —compare SOLUTION (2), SUSPENSION

col·lo·qui·al /kəˈləʊkwiəl/ *adj* (of words, phrases, style, etc.) of or suitable for ordinary, informal, or familiar conversation; not formal or special to literature: *"I'm going nuts" is a colloquial expression.* — ~ly *adv*

col·lo·qui·al·is·m /kəˈləʊkwiəlɪzəm/ *n* an expression used in, or suitable for, ordinary, informal, or familiar conversation: *"Nuts" meaning "mad" is a colloquialism.*

col·lo·quy /ˈkɒləkwi‖ˈkɑː-/ *n* [(**with, between**)] *fml or old* use a formal conversation

col·lude /kəˈluːd/ *v* [I (**with**)] *fml or law* to act together or with someone else in collusion: *He is accused of colluding with the terrorists to supply them with explosives.*

col·lu·sion /kəˈluːʒən/ *n* [U (**between, with**)] *esp. fml or law* secret agreement between two or more people with the intention of cheating or deceiving others: *One of the employees acted in collusion with the bank robbers.* —**sive** /ˈluːsɪv/ *adj*

col·ly·wob·bles /ˈkɒliˌwɒbəlz‖ˈkɑːliˌwɑː-/ *n* [*the*+P] *BrE infml* a slight stomach-ache usu. caused by nervousness: *The thought of my driving test gives me the collywobbles.*

Col·man's /ˈkəʊlmənz/, **Colman's of Nor·wich** /ˌ··· ˈ··/ *n tdmk* a company which makes different types of MUSTARD; it is best known for its yellow English mustard

co·logne /kəˈləʊn/ also **eau de cologne**— *n* [U] a sweet-smelling liquid used to make one feel fresh and smell pleasant; light PERFUME

Cologne a city in Germany on the river Rhine. It is a port and an industrial centre. It was heavily bombed during the Second World War.

Co·lom·bi·a /kəˈlɒmbiə‖-ˈlʌm-/ a country in NW South America which has coastline on both the Pacific Ocean and the Caribbean Sea; capital Bogotá; population 31,193,000 (1989). —**bian** *n, adj*
▶ CULTURAL NOTE COCAINE is produced illegally in Colombia and the country has difficulties controlling the drug trade.◀

Co·lom·bo /kəˈlʌmbəʊ/ the capital city and main port of Sri Lanka

co·lon¹ /ˈkəʊlən/ *n med* the LARGE INTESTINE (=the lower part of the bowels) in which food changes into solid waste matter and passes into the RECTUM

colon² *n* the sign (:) used in writing and printing to introduce an explanation, example, QUOTATION, etc. —compare SEMICOLON and see picture at PUNCTUATION MARK

colo·nel /ˈkɜːnl‖ˈkɜːr-/ *n* an army or airforce rank —see TABLE 3

Colonel Blimp /ˌ·· ˈ·/ also **Blimp**— *n BrE derog* an old man with old-fashioned and very CONSERVATIVE political ideas, who has an unreasonably high opinion of his own importance

Colonel Bo·gey /ˌ·· ˈ·/ a military march written by Major F.J. Ricketts

Colonel San·ders /ˌkɜːnl ˈsɑːndəz‖ˌkɜːrnl ˈsændərz/ the name of the man who developed the RECIPE for the fried chicken sold by the FAST-FOOD restaurant called **Colonel Sanders' Kentucky Fried Chicken**. His name is often used instead of the whole name of the restaurant. He is shown in advertisements as an older Southern American gentleman because fried chicken is a special dish of the South of the US.

co·lo·ni·al¹ /kəˈləʊniəl/ *adj* **1** [no comp.] of or having colonies (COLONY): *Britain was once a major colonial power.* | *The people of Africa have successfully fought against colonial rule.* **2** [no comp.] (often cap.) connected with or made in America when it was a British COLONY: *colonial furniture* | *a beautiful old colonial house near Boston* **3** describing a style of 18th and early 19th century building in the US that was influenced by Georgian and old Greek and Roman buildings —see colour picture on page 227 **4** *infml derog* typical of a COLONIAL²: *a colonial mentality*

colonial² *n* a person who is living or has lived in a COLONY but is not a member of the original population. The STEREOTYPE of a colonial is of an UPPER-CLASS older person (if a man, with a MOUSTACHE), who has strong RIGHT-WING opinions.

co·lo·ni·al·is·m /kə'ləʊniəlizəm/ *n* [U] *now often derog* the principle or practice of having colonies (COLONY) abroad: *British colonialism led to the establishment of a large empire.* —compare IMPERIALISM, NEOCOLONIALISM

co·lo·ni·al·ist /kə'ləʊniəlɪst/ *n, adj* (a supporter) of colonialism: *a nation with colonialist ambitions*

col·o·nist /'kɒlənɪst‖'kɑː-/ *n* a person who settled in a new colony soon after it was established: *the American colonists of the 17th century*

col·o·nize also **-nise** *BrE* /'kɒlənaɪz‖'kɑː-/ *v* [T] to establish a colony in (a country, area, etc.): *The British first colonized Australia in the 18th century.* —**nizer** *n* —**nization** /ˌkɒlənaɪ'zeɪʃən‖ˌkɑːlənə-/ *n* [U] : *the colonization of Africa*

col·on·nade /ˌkɒlə'neɪd‖ˌkɑː-/ *n* a row of COLUMNS (=upright stone posts) usu. supporting a roof or row of arches —**naded** *adj*

col·o·ny /'kɒləni‖'kɑː-/ *n* **1** a country or area under the political control of a distant country: *a former French colony in Africa* —see also CROWN COLONY, DOMINION (2), PROTECTORATE **2 a** (the area settled by) a group of people who leave their own country to live in another place and usu. remain citizens of their own country **b** *AmE* one of the 13 settlements in the US which formed the original United States: *Connecticut was one of the 13 original colonies.* **3** [+*sing.*/*pl. v*] a group of people from the same country or with the same interests, profession, etc., living together: *the French colony in Saigon* | *an artists' colony* | *a nudist colony* **4** [+*sing.*/*pl. v*] a group of the same kind of animals or plants living or growing together: *a colony of ants*/*bacteria*

col·or /'kʌlər/ *AmE for* COLOUR

Col·o·ra·do /ˌkɒlə'rɑːdəʊ◂‖ˌkɑːlə'ræ-/ *written abbrev.* **CO—** a mountainous state in the Western US, whose capital city is Denver. It is popular with Americans for both winter and summer holidays. —see colour map on pages 1374-5

col·o·ra·do bee·tle /ˌ·····¹··/ also **potato beetle—** *n* a small black and yellow insect that attacks potato plants

Colorado Riv·er /ˌ·····¹··/ a large river in the US which flows through several states and the Grand Canyon —see colour map on pages 1374-5

col·o·ra·tion /ˌkʌlə'reɪʃən/ *n* [U] arrangement of colours; colouring

col·o·ra·tu·ra /ˌkɒlərə'tʊərə, -'tjʊ-‖ˌkʌ-/ *n* **1** [U] fast difficult musical passages in singing **2** [C] a woman, esp. a SOPRANO, who sings such music

color line /'·· ·/ *n AmE for* COLOUR BAR

co·los·sal /kə'lɒsəl‖kə'lɑː-/ *adj* extremely large: *It requires government spending on a colossal scale.* | *a colossal building* — **~ly** *adv*

Col·os·se·um /ˌkɒlə'siːəm‖ˌkɑːl-/ , **Coliseum** [*the*] the AMPHITHEATRE in Rome built in the first century AD and now one of the most famous of all Roman remains

co·los·sus /kə'lɒsəs‖kə'lɑː-/ *n* **-suses** *or* **-si** /-saɪ/ a person or thing of great size or importance: *an intellectual colossus like Leonardo* | *The book makes clear that even when he was being wrong, Freud bestrides all his contemporaries like a colossus.*

Colossus of Rhodes /·ˌ·· · '·/ [*the*] a famous STATUE of Apollo which, according to the old story, stood with one leg on either side of the entrance to the island of Rhodes, and ships passed underneath it. It was one of the Seven Wonders of the World, and was destroyed by an EARTHQUAKE.

col·our¹ *BrE* ‖ **color** *AmE* /'kʌlər/ *n* **1** [U] the quality in objects which allows the eyes to see the difference between (for example) a red flower and a blue flower when both are the same size and shape: *The book has illustrations in colour.* | *These insects can change colour.* | *a colour television* **2** [C] red, blue, green, black, brown, yellow, white, etc.: *"What colour is the paint you bought?" "It's red."* | *"What colour did you paint the door?" "I painted it red."* **3** [S;U] the general appearance of a person's skin, esp. as this shows the state of their health: *He lost colour* (=became pale) *during his illness.* | *The fever gave her a* **high colour.** (=a lot of colour) | *The cold wind*

brought colour to her cheeks. (=made them red) **4** [C] the colour of a person's skin showing which race they belong to: *people of all colours* (=black, brown, white, etc.) —see also COLOURED **5** [U] details or behaviour of a place, thing, or person, that interest the mind or eye and excite the imagination; character: *She loved the life, noise, and colour of the market.* | *The lecturer told a few jokes and anecdotes* **to add colour to** *his talk.* —see also LOCAL COLOUR **6 give**/**lend colour to** to make (something, esp. something unusual) appear likely or true: *Her wet hair lent colour to her claim that she had fallen into the lake.* **7 off colour** *infml* not in good health: *You look a little off colour today.* **8 see the colour of someone's money** *infml* to have clear proof that someone has enough money to pay: *I don't trust him to pay us — I want to see the colour of his money first.* —see also COLOURS, OFF COLOUR, PRIMARY COLOUR

colour² *BrE* ‖ **color** *AmE—* *v* **1** [T] to cause (something) to have colour, esp. with a CRAYON or pencil rather than a brush: *The little boy coloured the picture.* [+*obj*+*adj*] *She colours her hair red.* **2** [I] to take on colour or change colour: *The leaves have already started to colour; it will soon be winter.* | *He coloured with embarrassment.* **3** [T] to give a special effect or feeling to (a person, event, etc.); influence in a personal way: *Personal feelings coloured his judgment.* | *a highly-coloured account of his difficulties* **colour** sthg. **↔ in** *phr v* [T] to put colour into (an area or shape): *The child coloured in the houses, but left the sky white.*

colour bar /'·· ·/ also **color line** *AmE— n* the set of laws or social customs in some places which prevents people of different colours from mixing freely

colour-blind /'·· ·/ *adj* unable to see the difference between (certain) colours: *He's red*/*green colour-blind.* —**colour blindness** /'·· ˌ··/ *n* [U]

colour code /'·· ·/ *v* [T] to mark (several similar items) with different colours so as to make it easy to see the difference between them: *The tickets were colour-coded according to price.*

col·oured¹ *BrE* ‖ **colored** *AmE* /'kʌləd‖-ərd/ *adj* **1** having colour, esp. as opposed to white, or black and white: *coloured sheets* | *coloured photographs* **2** (*in comb.*) having the stated colour: *She wore a cream-coloured*/*multi-coloured dress.* | *brightly-coloured tropical birds* **3** (now usu. considered offensive to black people) belonging to a dark-skinned race; black —see BLACK (USAGE)

col·oured² *BrE* ‖ **colored** *AmE— n derog* **1** [*usu. pl.*] (now usu. considered offensive to black people) a person belonging to a dark-skinned race **2** (*often cap.*) a CAPE COLOURED

col·our·fast *BrE* ‖ **colorfast** *AmE* /'kʌləfɑːst‖'kʌlərfæst/ *adj* having colour which will not change or come out in water: *Don't put that shirt in with the rest of the washing — it's not colourfast.* — **~ness** *n* [U]

col·our·ful *BrE* ‖ **colorful** *AmE* /'kʌləfəl‖-lər-/ *adj* **1** brightly coloured; full of colour: *a bird with colourful wings* **2** exciting the senses or imagination; rich in expressive variety or detail: *a colourful period of history* | *a colourful character* | *his colourful career as an international journalist*

col·our·ing *BrE* ‖ **coloring** *AmE* /'kʌlərɪŋ/ *n* **1** [C;U] a substance used for giving a special colour to another substance, esp. food; DYE: *These tinned beans contain no artificial colouring.* **2** [U] (healthy or ill appearance as shown by) skin colour; COMPLEXION: *People always think I'm ill because of my colouring.*

col·our·ize also **-ise** *BrE* ‖ **colorize** *AmE* /'kʌləraɪz/ *v* [I;T] to add colour to (an old film that was made in black and white): *talk of colorizing Casablanca*

col·our·less *BrE* ‖ **colorless** *AmE* /'kʌlələs‖'kʌlər-/ *adj* **1** without colour: *Water is a colourless liquid.* **2** dull; lacking variety, interest, strong personal character, etc.: *a rather colourless person*/*town* | *a colourless existence* **3** having less than usual colour; pale — **~ly** *adv* — **~ness** *n* [U]

col·ours *BrE* ‖ **colors** *AmE* /'kʌləz‖-ərz/ *n* [P] **1** a special sign, cap, BADGE, etc., worn as a sign of one's club, school, team, etc.: (*BrE*) *He won his colours* (=was chosen for the team) *for football this year.* **2** the official flag of a country, ship, part of the army, etc.: *the regimental colours* **3 one's true colours** one's real (esp. unpleasant) character, esp. when seen for the first time: *I liked him at first, but now he's shown his true colours|I've seen him in his true colours.* —see also FLYING COLOURS, **sail under false colours** (SAIL[7])

colour scheme /ˈ·· ·/ *n* the arrangement of colours in a room, painting, etc.: *an original|interesting colour scheme*

colour sup·ple·ment /ˈ·· ˌ···/ also **colour supp** /ˈkʌlə ˌsʌp ‖ -lər-/ *infml— n BrE* a magazine printed in colour and given free with a newspaper, esp. a Sunday newspaper

colt /kəʊlt/ *n* a young male horse —compare FILLY

Colt *n tdmk* a kind of PISTOL

colt·ish /ˈkəʊltɪʃ/ *adj often derog* playful and lively, esp. in an awkward uncontrolled way — ~**ly** *adv* — ~**ness** *n* [U]

Col·trane /kɒlˈtreɪn‖kəʊl-/, **John** (1926–67) an American JAZZ musician who played the SAXOPHONE. He had a great influence on modern jazz.

Co·lum·bi·a /kəˈlʌmbiə/ see DISTRICT OF COLUMBIA

Columbia Pic·tures /·ˌ··· ˈ···/ also **Columbia** an American film company which produces films for cinema and television

Columbia U·ni·ver·si·ty /·ˌ···· ··ˈ···/ a well-respected private university in New York City, known esp. for its school of JOURNALISM

col·um·bine /ˈkɒləmbaɪn‖ˈkɑː-/ *n* a plant with bright downward-hanging flowers

Columbine in PANTOMIME, the woman Harlequin loves

Co·lum·bo /kəˈlʌmbəʊ/ an American television SERIES in which the main character, Lieutenant Columbo, is a DETECTIVE in the Los Angeles police department. He is known for always wearing a dirty old raincoat.

Co·lum·bus /kəˈlʌmbəs/ the capital city of the state of Ohio in the US

Columbus, Chris·to·pher /ˈkrɪstəfəʳ/ (1451–1506) the Italian NAVIGATOR who was the first European to discover America in 1492, though he mistakenly thought he had found Asia. Many British people are familiar with the RHYME: *In fourteen hundred and ninety two Columbus sailed the ocean blue.* —see colour picture on page 1015

Columbus Day /·ˈ·· ˌ·/ an American public holiday held on October 12 to honour Christopher Columbus

column

column

col·umn /ˈkɒləm‖ˈkɑː-/ *n* **1** a tall solid upright stone post used in a building as a support or decoration or standing alone as a MONUMENT: *a graceful Ionic column* **2** [(**of**)] anything similar to a column in shape, appearance, or use: *a column of smoke | to add up a column of figures* **3** [+*sing.|pl. v*] **a** a large number of rows of people, vehicles, etc., following one behind the other: *a column of soldiers* **b** a long line of ships one behind the other **4** one of two or more divisions of a page, lying side by side and separated from each other by a narrow space, in which lines of print are arranged: *There are two columns on each page of this dictionary.* —see also PERSONAL COLUMN **5** an article by a particular writer or on a particular subject, that regularly appears in a newspaper or magazine: *his weekly column in the "New York Times" | the gossip column* —see also FIFTH COLUMN

col·umn·ist /ˈkɒləmɪst, -ləmnɪst‖ˈkɑː-/ *n* a person who writes a newspaper or magazine COLUMN (5)

co·ma /ˈkəʊmə/ *n* a state of long unnatural deep unconsciousness, from which it is difficult to wake up, caused by disease, poison, a severe blow to the head, etc.: *She*

went into a coma after swallowing a whole bottle of sleeping pills.* —see also COMATOSE

Co·man·che /kəˈmæntʃi/ *n* [C; *the* + P] (a member of) a Native American people who lived in a large area of the SW of the US from the 18th century and were excellent horsemen and fierce fighters —see NATIVE AMERICAN (CULTURAL NOTE)

Com·a·neci /kɒməˈnetʃ‖kəʊməˈniːtʃ/, **Na·di·a** /ˈnɑːdiə/ (1961–) a Romanian GYMNAST who won three GOLD MEDALs in the 1976 Olympic Games

co·ma·tose /ˈkəʊmətəʊs/ *adj* **1** *tech* in a coma; deeply unconscious **2** *infml* inactive and sleepy; TORPID: *feeling a bit comatose after dinner*

comb[1] /kəʊm/ *n* **1** [C] **a** an object used for tidying, arranging, or straightening the hair usu. consisting of a piece of plastic, metal, bone, etc. with a row of thin teeth **b** an object like this in shape that is worn in a woman's hair as a decoration **2** [C] an object like a comb used for straightening and cleaning wool, cotton, etc. **3** [S] an act of combing: *Your hair needs a good comb.* **4** [C] the red growth of flesh on top of the head of a COCK (=a fully-grown male chicken) **5** [C] a HONEYCOMB—see also FINE-TOOTH COMB

comb[2] *v* [T] **1** to tidy, arrange, or straighten (esp. the hair) with a comb: *Comb your hair before you go out.* **2** [(**for**)] to search (a place) thoroughly: *The police combed the woods for the missing boy.*

comb out *sbdy.|sthg. phr v* [T (**from**)] *infml* **1** to find and get rid of (unnecessary people or things): *to reduce costs by combing out unnecessary staff* **2** to remove (twists or KNOTs) from (hair) by combing: *She combed out the knots in the cat's long fur.* —**comb-out** /ˈ· ·/ *n* [S] *infml*: *a comb-out of clerical staff*

comb *written abbrev. for:* **1** combination **2** combined

com·bat[1] /ˈkɒmbæt‖ˈkɑːm-/ *n* [C;U (**with, between, against**)] (a) struggle between opposing people or armies: *These troops have very little experience of actual combat. | killed in combat | The knight challenged his enemy to* **single combat**. (=a fight between only two people) | *The two men were* **locked in mortal combat**. (=fighting until the death of one of them) | (fig.) *the combat between good and evil | a combat plane*

com·bat[2] /ˈkɒmbæt, kəmˈbæt‖kəmˈbæt, ˈkɑːmbæt/ *v* -**tt**- *BrE* ‖ -**t**- *or* -**tt**- *AmE*— [T] *fml* to fight or struggle against; try to defeat: *The police are now using computers to help combat crime. | new government strategies to combat inflation|drug abuse*

com·ba·tant /ˈkɒmbətənt‖kəmˈbætənt/ *n* a person taking a direct part in fighting: *In the last war as many noncombatants as combatants were killed.* —see also NON-COMBATANT

combat fa·tigue /ˈ·· ·ˌ·/ *n* [U] *tech* BATTLE FATIGUE

com·ba·tive /ˈkɒmbətɪv‖kəmˈbætɪv/ *adj sometimes derog* ready and eager to fight or argue: *a combative spokesman for right-wing policies* — ~**ly** *adv*

comb·er /ˈkəʊməʳ/ *n* **1** a person or machine that combs wool, cotton, etc. **2** a long curling wave

com·bi·na·tion /ˌkɒmbɪˈneɪʃən‖ˌkɑːm-/ *n* **1** [U] the act of combining or state of being combined: *The two writers worked well in combination.* **2** [C(**of**)] a result of combining; a number of separate things or people that are combined to form a single unit or whole: *An alloy is a combination of two or more different metals. | A combination of high interest rates and falling demand forced the company to close. | Her expression was a combination of guilt and dismay. | Working as a team, the singer and the songwriter proved to be a* **winning combination**. **3** [C] the numbers or letters needed to open a COMBINATION LOCK: *You can't open the safe unless you know the combination.* **4** [C] any of the sets of a stated number of things that can be chosen from a group where their order does not matter: *The three possible combinations of two letters chosen from ABC are AB, BC, and AC.* —compare PERMUTATION; see also COMBINATIONS

combination lock /·ˈ·· ·/ *n* a lock which can only be opened when its control is turned in accordance with a special list of numbers or letters

com·bi·na·tions /ˌkɒmbɪˈneɪʃənz‖ˌkɑːm-/ also **coms** /kɒmz‖kɑːmz/ *BrE infml* ‖ **union suit** *AmE*— *n* [P] a one-piece usu. woollen undergarment that covers the whole body, worn esp. formerly —see PAIR (USAGE)

com·bine[1] /kəmˈbaɪn/ v **1** [I;T (**with**)] to join together, to form a single unit or whole; unite: *The two countries combined against their common enemy.* | *The three parties combined to form a coalition government.* | *Let's combine my scientific knowledge and your business skills and start a company.* | *The combined effect of low profits and high inflation proved fatal to the company.* | *Low profits, combined with high inflation, proved fatal.* **2** [T (**with**)] to have or do at the same time: *They combined their holiday with a visit to their relatives.* | *to combine business with pleasure* —see MIX (USAGE)

com·bine[2] /ˈkɒmbaɪn‖ˈkɑːm-/ n **1** [+sing.|pl. v] a group of people, businesses, etc., joined or acting together: *A large industrial combine is|are reopening the factory.* **2** also **combine harvester** /ˌ·· ˈ···/— a machine that REAPS (=cuts), THRESHEs (=separates the seed from the stem), and cleans grain

combining form /·'·· ·/ n tech a form of a word that cannot stand alone, but is used with other words to build new ones: *The combining form "Afro-", meaning "African", combines with "American" to make "Afro-American".*

com·bo /ˈkɒmbəʊ‖ˈkɑːm-/ n **-bos** [C+sing.|pl. v] infml a small band that plays JAZZ or dance music

com·bus·ti·ble[1] /kəmˈbʌstɪbəl/ adj **1** that can catch fire and burn easily: *Petrol is highly combustible.* —opposite **incombustible** **2** (of a person) easily excited or annoyed

combustible[2] n a combustible substance

com·bus·tion /kəmˈbʌstʃən/ n [U] **1** the process of catching fire and burning **2** tech the chemical activity, usu. in the presence of oxygen, that produces light and heat —see also INTERNAL-COMBUSTION ENGINE

come[1] /kʌm/ v **came** /keɪm/, **come** ■ to move or travel **1** [I+adv/prep] to move towards the speaker or a particular place: *Come here and look at this.* | *"How did you get here?" "We came by train."* | *He came towards me|through the door.* | *The police came to his rescue.* | *Could you come and see me tomorrow?* | *What time are you coming back?* | *My parents are coming for dinner|coming to have dinner with us.* | *Would you like to come to the concert with me?* [+v-ing] *The little girl came running to her mother for sympathy.* | *A man comes to clean the windows every Friday.* —compare GO[1] **2** [I+adv/prep] to reach a particular point or place by travelling (over a distance): *They've come hundreds of miles to be here tonight.* | (fig.) *Computer technology has come a long way since the 1970* ■ to arrive at or be in a place or position **3** [I] to arrive, esp. as expected or in the usual course of events: *I've been waiting for hours and he still hasn't come!* | *Christmas is coming soon.* | *The time has come for us to make a decision.* | *We come now to the main business of the meeting.* | *The news came as a great shock to him.* | *The bill could hardly have come at a worse time.* (=this was a very bad time for it to come) | *I'm very busy, but come the new year* (=when the new year arrives) *I'll have more free time.* | *If I don't have the correct tools for the job, I use whatever* **comes to hand.** (=is within reach) | *I never plan ahead; I just take life as it comes.* **4** [I+adv/prep] to reach: *The water came (up) to my neck.* | *Her hair comes (down) to her waist.* **5** [I+adv/prep] to be in a particular place or position in order: *The address should come above the date.* | *Monday comes after Sunday.* | *Your family should always come before* (=be more important than) *your job.* | *She came first in the exam.* (=got the highest marks) ■ to pass into another state **6** [I+adv/prep] to arrive at or pass into a particular state or position: *The general came to power in a military coup.* | *The new law comes into effect next month.* | *The government is coming under increasing pressure to change its policies.* | *The new battleship is expected to come into service in 1991.* | *When will this case come to trial|to court?* | *The car skidded off the road and came to rest in a field.* —see also COME **into,** COME **to 7** [L+adj] to become: *The buttons on my coat came undone.* | *His dream of winning a gold medal has come true.* | *Don't worry — it'll all* **come (out) right** *in the end.* —see also COME **apart,** COME **away,** COME **off;** see BECOME (USAGE) **8** [I+to-v] to begin as a result of time or experience: *In time you may come to like it here.* | *This is the kind of behaviour we have come to expect of him.* other meanings **9** [(**from**)]

to happen: *No good will come from all this.* [+to-v] *How did Jean come to be invited to this party?* | (lit) *And so it came to pass* (=happened) *that they were married.* | **Come what may** (=whatever happens), *I'm determined to do it.* | (infml) **How come** (=how did it happen that) *he didn't find out?* **10** [I+adv/prep;+adj] to be offered, produced, sold, etc.: *Shoes come in many shapes and sizes.* | *The car comes complete with a radio and sunroof.* | *Houses like that don't come cheap.* **11** [I] sl to have an ORGASM ■ fixed phrases **12 Come again?** infml What did you say? **13 come and go** to pass or disappear quickly; change: *Fashions come and go but this type of dress is always popular.* | *I've got so much to do* **I don't know whether I'm coming or going.** (=used to express hurried and disordered activity) **14 come clean** infml to admit to guilt or mistake: *Congressmen in the banking scandal decided to come clean before the electorate.* **15 come it (with|over)** sl, esp. BrE to behave with rude disrespect towards someone **16 come to that** infml (used when one wants to add something to a remark) actually; in fact: *I haven't seen her for weeks ... or her parents, come to that.* **17 come to think of it** infml (used when one wants to add something one has just thought of) when one begins to consider that: *... and he sent me a lovely present. Come to think of it, I must write to thank him.* **18 come up and see me sometime** a phrase which is believed to have been said by Mae West as an invitation to a man to come and visit her, with the suggestion that she found him sexually attractive. The phrase is often used humorously now. **19 don't come the** ... BrE infml don't act the part of or pretend to be: *Don't come the grand lady with me!* **20 Do you come here often?** see CHAT-UP LINE **21 I came, I saw, I conquered** quote a phrase from the writings of Julius Caesar describing how he went to Britain and defeated it. The phrase is often used now, with the words slightly changed: *He came, he fought, he conquered...but Mickey Rourke had better not tear up his Equity card, despite winning his first professional boxing bout.* —see also **veni, vidi, vici** (VENI) **22 years|weeks|days, etc., to come** in the future: *The effects of the drought will be felt for years to come.* | *She was to remember his warning in the days to come.* —see also COMING, **come clean** (CLEAN[1]), **come in from the cold** (COLD[2]), **come a cropper** (CROPPER[2]), **come unstuck** (UN-STUCK) ■ phrasal verbs

come about phr v [I] **1** to happen esp. in a way that seems impossible to prevent: *How did this situation come about?* [it+I+that] *Can you explain how it came about that you were an hour late?* **2** (of a ship) to change direction

come across phr v **1** [T no pass.] (**come across** sthg.|sbdy.) to meet, find, or discover, esp. by chance: *She came across some old letters in the course of her search.* —compare RUN **across 2** [I] to be effective and well received: *Your speech came across very well.*

come across as sbdy.|sthg. phr v [T] to seem to be: *She came across as a very sophisticated woman.* [+v-ing] *He came across as being rather nervous.*

come across with sthg. phr v [T no pass.] infml to provide (money or information) when needed

come along phr v [I] **1** also **come on**— **a** to advance, develop, or improve, esp. in health: *How's your English coming along?* **b** to improve in health: *Mother's coming along nicely, thank you.* **2** to appear or arrive by chance: *I got the job because I came along at the right time.* | *Take any opportunity that comes along.* **3** also **come on**— to follow: *You go now; I'll come along later.* **4 Come along!** esp. BrE | also **come on! a** Make an effort! Try harder!: *Come along, someone must know the answer to my question.* **b** Hurry up!: *Come along — we're late!*

come apart phr v [I] to break into pieces without the use of force: *I picked up the old book and it just came apart in my hands.* | (fig.) *The government's whole industrial strategy is* **coming apart at the seams.**

come around phr v [I] esp. AmE for COME **round**

come at sbdy.|sthg. phr v [T no pass.] **1** also **come for** sbdy.|sthg.— to advance towards in a threatening manner: *She came at me with a knife.* **2** infml to reach a knowledge or understanding of: *It was a long time before we came at the truth.*

come away phr v [I (**from**)] to become disconnected without being forced: *I only touched the handle and it came away (from the door) in my hand.*

come back phr v [I] **1** [(**to**)] to return to memory: *It's all coming back to me now!* **2** [(**IN**)] to become fashionable or popular again: *Do you think long dresses will ever come back (in)?* **3** [(**at, with**)] to reply in a forceful, often unkind way; RETORT —see also COMEBACK

come between sbdy./sthg. *phr v* [T *no pass.*] to interrupt or cause trouble between: *John lets nothing come between himself and his work.* | *We mustn't let this silly quarrel come between us.*

come by sthg. *phr v* [T] to obtain or receive; come to have: *Jobs are hard to come by with so many people out of work.* | *That's a nasty bruise – how did you come by it?*

come down *phr v* [I] **1** to fall to a lower level: *The price of oil has come down dramatically.* | *Since Julia lost her job, she's really come down in the world.* (=fallen to a lower standard of living) | *John came down in my opinion* (=lost my respect) *after his bad behaviour.* **2** [(to)] to be passed on from one period of history to another: *This story has come down to us from ancient times.* **3** [(from)] *sl* to stop feeling the effects of a drug that influences the mind **4** [(from)] *BrE* to leave a university after a period of study **5 come down in favour of/on the side of** to decide to support, esp. after long thought: *The court came down on the side of the unions.* **6 come down to earth (with a bump)** to return to reality: *He was daydreaming, but he came down to earth with a bump when the teacher twisted his ear.* —see also COMEDOWN

come down on sbdy./sthg. *phr v* [T *no pass.*] **1** to punish or speak to with severe disapproval: *The courts are going to come down more heavily on young criminals.* **2** [(for)] to demand forcefully: *The bank came down on us for immediate payment.*

come down to sthg. *phr v* [T *no pass.*] to mean or be equal to in fact; BOIL **down to**: *What it comes down to is a choice between cutting wages or reducing the number of staff.*

come down with sthg. *phr v* [T *no pass.*] *infml* to catch (an infectious illness): *I think I'm coming down with a cold.*

come forward *phr v* [I] to offer oneself to fill a position, give help to the police, etc.: *Only two people have come forward for election to the committee.* | *No one has come forward with any information about the murder.*

come from sthg. *phr v* [T *no pass.*] to have as a place or point of origin: *I come from Newcastle but I've spent most of my life in London.* | *Milk comes from cows.* | *The passage she quoted comes from Shakespeare.* | *Where's that noise coming from?*

come in *phr v* [I] **1** to arrive or be received: *Reports are coming in of a major earthquake in Mexico.* | *There's very little money coming in at present.* **2** to become necessary or important, esp. in a plan: *I also need someone to persuade my parents that it's a good idea – that's where you come in.* **3** to become fashionable: *When did the short skirt first come in?* —opposite **go out** **4** (of the sea) to rise: *The tide's coming in so don't stay on the sand too long.* opposite **go out** **5** [+*adv*] to finish in the stated place in a race or competition: *My horse came in third/last.* **6 come in useful/handy** to be useful: *This string may come in useful one day, so don't throw it away.* —see also **come in from the cold** (COLD[2]), **when one's ship comes in** (SHIP[1])

come in for sthg. *phr v* [T *no pass.*] to be given (esp. blame, disapproval, etc.); receive: *The police came in for a lot of criticism over their handling of the strike.*

come into sthg. *phr v* [T] **1** to receive (a sum of money) after someone's death; INHERIT: *He came into a fortune when his mother died.* **2** to begin to be in (a particular state): *to come into fashion* | *to come into existence* | *The town came into sight/view as we turned the corner.* —see also COME[1] (9) **3 come into one's own** to show one's true worth or abilities: *On bad roads, this tough little car really comes into its own.*

come of sthg. *phr v* [T *no pass.*] **1** to result from: *I doubt if any good will come of these peace initiatives.* [+*v*-*ing*] *The car crashed into a tree – that's what comes of buying cheap tyres!* **2** to be descended from: *She comes of/from a farming family.* **3 come of age** to reach an age (usu. 18 or 21) when one is considered by law to be responsible for oneself and for obedience to the law —see also COMING OF AGE

come off *phr v* **1** [I;T (=**come off** sthg.)] to become unfastened or disconnected (from): *A button came off as I was climbing over the wall.* | *The hook came off the wall when I hung up my coat.* | *Does the lid come off or is it fixed?* **2** [I] to take place; happen: *The wedding came off as planned.* **3** [I] to succeed; have the intended effect:

It was a clever joke but it didn't quite come off. **4** [I+*adv*] to finish in the stated way; have the stated degree of success: *She came off rather badly in the debate.* **5 Come off it!** *infml* Stop lying or pretending!: *Now come off it – I never said that!*

come on *phr v* [I] **1** to start or appear: *I can feel a headache coming on.* | *There is a storm coming on.* | *What time does that programme come on?* [+*to*-*v*] (*esp. BrE*) *It came on to rain.* **2** to COME **along** (1, 3) **3 Come on!: a** Try harder! Make an effort!: *Come on, Liverpool!* **b** Hurry up! **c** Cheer up! **d** You know what you just said is not right: *"It'll take at least two hours to do this!" "Oh, come on! I could do it in 20 minutes!"* —see also COME-ON

come out *phr v* [I] **1** to appear: *The stars came out as soon as it was dark.* | *When will her new book come out?* (=be offered for sale) **2** to become clear or publicly known, esp. after being kept secret: *At last the truth has come out.* | *It eventually came out that he had been stealing money from his employers.* **3** (of colour, a mark, etc.) to be removed, esp. by washing; disappear: *I've washed this shirt twice and the ink still hasn't come out.* **4** [+*adv*/*prep*] to declare oneself publicly, esp. to be in favour of or against a plan, belief, etc.: *The committee has come out strongly against any change in the law.* | *Most of the speakers came out in favour of/in support of these proposals.* **5** [+*adv*/*prep*] to finish in the stated way or position: *The answer to the sum came out wrong/right.* | *In a series of safety tests, this was the car that came out on top.* **6** (of a photograph) to be successfully developed (DEVELOP): *Our holiday photos didn't come out.* **7** to declare oneself openly (e.g. to one's family and friends) to be a HOMOSEXUAL **8** *BrE* to refuse to work; STRIKE: *The teachers are coming out in support of their pay claim.* **9** becoming rare (of a young lady of the upper classes) to be formally introduced in upper-class society, usu. at a dance: *Amanda is coming out next spring.* | *debutantes at a coming out party*

come out in sthg. *phr v* [T *no pass.*] to become partly covered by (marks caused by an illness or disease): *Jean has come out in spots so she's staying in bed.* —see also OUTCOME

come out with sthg. *phr v* [T *no pass.*] *infml* to say, esp. suddenly or unexpectedly: *John came out with a really stupid remark.*

come over *phr v* **1** [I (**to, from**)] to come after travelling a long distance: *When did you first come over to England?* **2** [I] to make a short informal visit: *Come over and see us sometime.* **3** [I] to be effective and well received; COME **across**: *Your talk came over very well.* **4** [I (**to**)] to change sides or opinions, esp. so as to join the speaker's side **5** [T (=**come over** sbdy.) *no pass.*] (of a sudden strong feeling) to take hold of (someone) suddenly and strangely: *A feeling of faintness came over me, so I had to lie down.* | (*humor*) *What's come over him? He's quite polite today!* (=this is very unusual) **6** [L+*adj*] *infml, esp. BrE* (esp. followed by adjectives of feeling or illness) to become: *I suddenly came over a bit queasy, so I had to lie down.*

come round *BrE*||**come around** *AmE*– *phr v* [I] **1** also **come to**– to regain consciousness **2** [(to)] to change sides or opinions: *He'll soon come round to our way of thinking.* **3** to happen as usual: *Christmas will soon be coming round again.* **4** to become calmer after being in a bad temper: *Leave him alone and he'll soon come round.* **5** to make a short informal visit to someone who lives nearby

come through *phr v* **1** [I] (esp. of news, results, etc.) to become publicly known: *Have your examination results come through yet?* | *News has just come through that the man has been injured.* **2** [I;T (=**come through** (sthg.)) *no pass.*] to continue to live or exist after (a difficult or dangerous event or situation); SURVIVE: *The driver had lost so much blood that he was lucky to come through (the operation).*

come to sbdy./sthg. *phr v* **1** [T *no pass.*] to arrive at a particular state or position: *At last the war came to an end.* | *It has come to my attention/my notice that some money is missing.* | *We came to the conclusion that she was telling the truth.* | *I'll come straight to the point – when do you want the money?* | *All this sex and violence on the TV – what is the world coming to?* (=shows disapproval and anxiety) —see also COME[1] (9) **2** [T] to amount to: *The bill came to £5.50.* **3** [T+*obj*/*v*-*ing*; *no pass.*] to concern: *When it comes to politics/to repairing cars I know nothing.* **4** [T *no pass.*] to enter the mind, esp. suddenly: *I* *can't remember her name now — it'll come to me later.* **5 come to oneself: a** to regain self-control **b** to regain consciousness **6 have something coming to one** to receive (something deserved, esp. something bad): *He thinks he's got away with it, but he's got a big surprise coming to him!* —see also **come to grief** (GRIEF), **come to grips with** (GRIP²), **come to heel** (HEEL¹), **come to life** (LIFE)

come under sthg. *phr v* [T *no pass.*] **1** to be governed or controlled by: *This comes under the jurisdiction of the Education Secretary.* **2** to be able to be found below or after (a key word, HEADING, etc.): *What section does this come under?* —see also COME¹ (9), **come under the hammer** (HAMMER¹)

come up *phr v* [I] **1** to come to attention or consideration: *Your question came up at the meeting.* —compare BRING **up** (2) **2** to happen in the course of time, esp. unexpectedly: *I'll let you know if anything comes up.* | *I'll be late home — something's just come up at work.* **3** to come near, esp. by walking; APPROACH: *He came up and asked me if I knew the time.* **4 come up in the world** to reach a higher standard of living or social class

come up against sthg./sbdy. *phr v* [T *no pass.*] to meet (usu. a difficulty or opposition); ENCOUNTER: *They came up against a number of unexpected problems.*

come upon sbdy./sthg. *phr v* [T *no pass.*] to COME across (1)

come up to sthg. *phr v* [T] to equal: *Your recent work hasn't come up to your usual high standards.*

come up with sthg. *phr v* [T *no pass.*] *infml* to think of (a plan, reply, etc.); produce: *The airline has come up with a novel solution to the problem of jet-lag.*

come² *interj* (an expression of not very strong disapproval): *Come, come! You can't expect me to believe that!*

come·back /ˈkʌmbæk/ *n* [*usu. sing.*] **1** a return to a former position of strength, importance, or high position, after a period of absence: *The old actor made/staged a successful comeback after twenty years.* **2** a clever quick reply; RETORT —see also COME **back**

Com·e·con /ˈkɒmɪkɒn‖ˈkɑːmɪkɑːn/ [*the*] the Council for Mutual Economic Assistance; an organization of Communist countries, whose aim was to encourage trade and friendly relations among its members. It broke up in 1991.

Come Danc·ing /ˌ· ˈ··/ a British television programme in which COUPLEs and teams compete in a BALLROOM DANCING competition

co·me·di·an /kəˈmiːdiən/ **co·me·di·enne** /kəˌmiːdiˈen/ *fem.— n* **1** a person, esp. a professional entertainer, who tells jokes or does amusing things to make people laugh **2** an actor who plays funny parts in plays or films

come·down /ˈkʌmdaʊn/ *n* [*usu. sing.*] *infml* **1** a fall in importance, rank, or respect: *She used to have a big car, so she finds it a bit of a comedown to have to go everywhere by bus.* **2** an ANTICLIMAX: *After such a wonderful holiday it was rather a comedown to have to start work again.* —see also COME **down**

com·e·dy /ˈkɒmɪdi‖ˈkɑː-/ *n* [C;U] a (type of) funny play, film, or other work in which the story and characters are amusing and which ends happily: *Shakespeare's comedies* | *Do you prefer comedy or tragedy?* | *a comedy show on TV* **2** [U] the amusing quality of something; HUMOUR: *At last he saw the comedy of the situation and laughed.* —see also BLACK COMEDY, LOW COMEDY, SITUATION COMEDY

Comedy of Er·rors /ˌ··· ·ˈ··/, **The** an amusing play by Shakespeare involving two sets of TWINS (= children born to the same mother at the same time) which leads to mistakes (errors) and misunderstandings

comedy of man·ners /ˌ··· ·ˈ··/ *n* a comedy that provides amusement by making the behaviour and fashions of a particular group look foolish

come-hith·er /ˌ· ˈ··/ *adj* [A] *infml* sexually inviting: *come-hither eyes* | *a come-hither look*

come·ly /ˈkʌmli/ *adj lit* attractive; having a pleasing appearance: *a comely young woman* —**liness** *n* [U]

come-on /ˈ· ·/ *n* **1** *infml, esp. AmE* an attraction to persuade people to buy particular goods **2 give someone the come-on** *sl* (esp. of a woman) to behave in a sexually exciting way towards: *She gave me the come-on as soon as her husband was out of the room.* —see also COME **on**

com·er /ˈkʌmər/ *n infml* **1** (*often in comb.*) a person who comes or arrives: *a latecomer at the party* | *newcomers to our town* | *serving drinks to all comers* **2** *esp. AmE* a person who appears to be very successful or likely to succeed

co·mes·ti·ble /kəˈmestɪbəl/ *n* [*usu. pl.*] *fml or humor* something to be eaten as food

com·et /ˈkɒmɪt‖ˈkɑː-/ *n* an object in space that moves round the sun in a long ELLIPTICAL path and has a very bright head and a long tail. The most well-known comet is Halley's comet.

come-up·pance /ˌkʌm ˈʌpəns/ *n* [*usu. sing.*] *infml* a well-deserved punishment or misfortune; one's DESERTS: *He'll get his come-uppance one of these days.*

com·fit /ˈkʌmfɪt/ *n old use* a sweet covered in sugar with a fruit or nut centre

com·fort¹ /ˈkʌmfət‖-ərt/ *n* **1** [U] the state of being free from anxiety, pain, or suffering, and of having all one's physical needs satisfied: *to live in comfort* **2** [C] something that satisfies one's physical needs: *all the comforts of modern civilization* **3** [C;U] (a person or thing that gives) strength, hope, or sympathy for an unhappy person: *My husband was a great comfort to me when our son was ill.* | *The priest spoke a few words of comfort to the dying man.* | *We can take comfort from the fact that the situation is not actually getting worse.* | *to offer someone a crumb* (= a very small bit) *of comfort* **4 tidings of comfort and joy** a phrase from a CAROL (a religious song sung at Christmas) —see also COLD COMFORT, CREATURE COMFORTS, DISCOMFORT —**-less** *adj fml*: *a grey, comfortless day*

comfort² *v* [T] to give COMFORT¹ (3) to: *I tried to comfort Jean after her mother's death.* | *comforting words* —**ingly** *adv*

Comfort *n* [U] *tdmk* a type of FABRIC CONDITIONER made by Lever Brothers Limited

com·for·ta·ble /ˈkʌmftəbəl, ˈkʌmfət-‖ˈkʌmfərt-, ˈkʌmft-/ *adj* **1** providing comfort: *a comfortable chair/room/pair of shoes/income* | *They still have a comfortable lead over their rivals.* **2** feeling comfort, esp. not experiencing (too much) pain, grief, anxiety, etc.: *The doctor said that mother was comfortable after her operation.* | *Are you comfortable on that hard stool?* | *I won't be comfortable until I know what happened.* **3** having enough money to be free of worry; not poor: *We're not rich but we're fairly comfortable.* —see also UNCOMFORTABLE —**bly** *adv*: *comfortably ensconced in an armchair*

comfortably off /ˌ··· ·ˈ·/ *adj* [F] fairly rich

com·fort·er /ˈkʌmfətər‖-fər-/ *n* **1** a person who gives comfort **2** *old use* a length of usu. woollen cloth worn around the neck to keep it warm; SCARF **3** *AmE for* QUILT —see also JOB'S COMFORTER

comfort sta·tion /ˈ··· ˌ··/ *n AmE euph for* PUBLIC CONVENIENCE

com·fy /ˈkʌmfi/ *adj infml* comfortable: *a comfy chair*

com·ic¹ /ˈkɒmɪk‖ˈkɑː-/ *adj* **1** causing laughter; humorous: *a comic performance* **2** [A *no comp.*] of COMEDY: *a comic actress/writer* —compare TRAGIC

comic² *n* **1** *also* **comic book** *AmE*— a magazine for children containing COMIC STRIPs. Famous comics include *The Beano* and *The Dandy* (in Britain) and *Marvel* comic books (in the US): *comic-book heroes such as Superman and Batman* **2** a person who is funny, esp. a professional COMEDIAN: *a stand-up comic* —see also COMICS

com·i·cal /ˈkɒmɪkəl‖ˈkɑː-/ *adj* funny, esp. in an odd or unexpected way: *a comical hat* —**-ly** /kli/ *adv*

comic op·e·ra /ˌ··· ·ˈ··/ *n* an OPERA with an amusing story, speaking as well as singing, and usu. a happy ending

Comic Re·lief /ˌ··· ·ˈ·/ a British CHARITY organization set up and run by a group of professional COMEDIANs to raise money for poor and disadvantaged people in the world, esp. Africa. It collects money on one day a year, when people are encouraged to telephone a special television programme and promise an amount of money and to wear amusing red noses in support of the charity. Some people also buy red noses to put on the front of their cars.

com·ics /ˈkɒmɪks‖ˈkɑː-/ *also* **funnies**— *n* [*the*+P] *esp. AmE* the part of a newspaper containing COMIC STRIPs. On Sundays, American newspapers usu. include a separate section of comics, in colour: *I always read the comics before the political news.*

comic strip /ˈ··· ·/ also **strip cartoon** BrE— n a set of drawings telling a short story, often with words showing the speech of the characters in the pictures —compare CARTOON

com·ing¹ /ˈkʌmɪŋ/ n 1 [S] arrival: With the coming of winter the days get shorter. 2 **comings and goings** infml acts of arriving and leaving: We watched the comings and goings of the guests from our bedroom window.

coming² adj [A] 1 that is coming or will come: during the coming months 2 infml likely to succeed: a coming young man —see also UP-AND-COMING

coming of age /ˌ··· ·ˈ·/ n [usu. sing.] the 18th birthday of a person, when they become legally an adult. At 18 British people are allowed to vote in elections, get married without the permission of their parents, and buy and drink alcohol in a PUB. In the US, either the 18th or 21st birthday might be thought of as a coming of age; at 18 people are allowed to vote and get married, but in many states you cannot buy alcohol until you are 21. —see also **come of age** (COME of)

com·i·ty /ˈkɒmɟti‖ˈkɑː-/ n [C;U] fml rare (a society built on) friendly polite behaviour

comity of na·tions /ˌ··· · ˈ··/ n [U] law the respect and friendship shown by countries for each other, esp. as regards each other's laws, customs, and systems of government

com·ma /ˈkɒmə‖ˈkɑːmə/ n the mark (,) used in writing and printing for showing a short pause —see also INVERTED COMMA and see picture at PUNCTUATION MARK

com·mand¹ /kəˈmɑːnd‖kəˈmænd/ v 1 [T] to tell (someone) to do something, with the right to be obeyed; formally order, esp. as a military leader: Do as I command (you). [+obj+to-v] The general commanded his men to attack the city. [+that] He commanded that we (should) attack at once. —see ORDER (USAGE) 2 [I;T] to be in a position of control (over), esp. as a military leader: General Carter commands the Parachute Regiment. | He is not fit to command. 3 [T] to deserve and get: to command respect | She can command a high fee for her services. | His paintings command a high price these days. | The proposals command wide support in Congress. 4 [T] to control (a place) from above: This hill fort commands the whole valley. | (fig.) The house commands (=looks down on) a fine view of the sea. 5 [T] fml to be able to use; have at one's service: The company commands considerable resources.

command² n 1 [C] an order: Fire on my command/when I give the command. 2 [U] the right to command; control: The army is under the king's direct command. | Who is the officer in command? | to **take command** of an army/a situation | the army's command structure 3 [C+sing./pl. v] a a military unit under separate control: pilots of the Southern Air Command b a group of officers or officials who give orders: the German High Command 4 [S;U] the ability to control and use: He has a good command of French/an impressive command of the details. 5 [C] an instruction to a computer to perform a particular operation: a sequence of commands

com·man·dant /ˌkɒmənˈdænt‖ˈkɑːməndænt/ n the chief officer in charge of a military organization: the commandant of a prison camp

command e·con·o·my /·ˈ·· ·,···/ n an economic system in which production levels are controlled by a central authority

com·man·deer /ˌkɒmənˈdɪəʳ‖ˌkɑː-/ v [T] to take (private property) for military use, without needing permission or giving payment: The soldiers commandeered the house and used it for/as offices.

com·mand·er /kəˈmɑːndəʳ‖kəˈmæn-/ n 1 the officer of any rank who is in charge of a group of soldiers 2 a naval rank – see TABLE 3 and see picture at RANK 3 a British police officer of high rank

commander in chief /·,··· · ˈ·/ n an officer in control of all the armed forces of a country, area, etc.: The Queen is commander in chief of the British armed forces.

com·mand·ing /kəˈmɑːndɪŋ‖kəˈmæn-/ adj 1 [A no comp.] having command; in charge: Who's your commanding officer? 2 [A] looking down from above: The castle has a commanding position on a steep hill. | (fig.) The Republicans now have a commanding lead in the opinion polls. 3 producing respect and obedience; AUTHORITATIVE: a

commanding voice/appearance

com·mand·ment /kəˈmɑːndmənt‖kəˈmænd-/ n 1 (often cap.) any of the TEN COMMANDMENTS: to keep the commandments 2 lit a command

command mod·ule /·ˈ· ,··/ n tech the part of a space vehicle from which operations are controlled

com·man·do /kəˈmɑːndəʊ‖kəˈmæn-/ n -dos or -does 1 (a member of) a small fighting force specially trained for making quick attacks into enemy areas 2 **the Commandoes** a unit of the British Royal Marines who secretly land in enemy country, usu. from the sea, to prepare the way for the main army. They are generally thought of as being strong and TOUGH (=able to bear the most difficult conditions).

command per·form·ance /·,·· ·ˈ··/ n a special performance at a theatre given at the request of the head of state

command post /·ˈ·· ,·/ n (in the military) the place from which a commander and his officers direct operations

com·me·di·a dell'ar·te /kɒˌmeɪdiə del ˈɑːteɪ‖kə-, -ˈɑːrti/ It a popular form of COMEDY in Italy from the 16th to 18th century, which used speeches invented by the actors as they acted and MASKs and which had great influence on European theatre

comme il faut /ˌkɒm iːl ˈfəʊ‖ˌkɑːm-/ adj [F] Fr according to correct or established social standards: You can't wear those old trousers for the wedding – it's absolutely not comme il faut.

com·mem·o·rate /kəˈmeməreɪt/ v [T] 1 to give honour to the memory of, esp. by a public ceremony: a festival commemorating the 400th anniversary of the birth of Shakespeare 2 to be in memory of: This statue commemorates those who died in the war. —**ration** /kəˌmeməˈreɪʃ*ə*n/ n [U (of)] : A religious service will be held in commemoration of those who died in the war. —**rative** /kəˈmem*ə*rətɪv/ adj : a commemorative service/stamp

com·mence /kəˈmens/ v [I;T] fml or pomp to begin; start: If everyone has arrived, the meeting may now commence. | We may now commence the meeting. [+to-v/v-ing] Having said he would not make a long speech, he commenced to do/commenced doing exactly that. —see START (USAGE)

com·mence·ment /kəˈmensmənt/ n 1 [C;U (of)] fml the act of commencing; beginning 2 [C] AmE a ceremony at which university, college, or high school students are given their degrees or DIPLOMAs. At a commencement all the students wear special ROBEs and caps, and there are usually several speeches, including one by the VALEDICTORIAN of the class.

com·mend /kəˈmend/ v [T] fml 1 [(for)] to speak favourably of; express one's approval of or admiration for: She was highly commended for her organizational skills. | The new grammar book has much to commend it. 2 [(to)] to put (esp. oneself) into the care or charge of someone else; ENTRUST: The dying man commended his soul/himself to God.

com·men·da·ble /kəˈmendəb*ə*l/ adj worthy of praise: commendable efforts —**bly** adv

com·men·da·tion /ˌkɒmənˈdeɪʃ*ə*n‖ˌkɑː-/ n 1 [C (for)] an official prize or honour given for a special quality: a commendation for bravery 2 [U] fml praise; approval

com·men·su·rate /kəˈmenʃ*ə*rɟt/ adj [(with)] fml 1 equal in size, quality, or length of time; EQUIVALENT 2 suitable; APPROPRIATE: The salary will be commensurate with your age and experience.

com·ment¹ /ˈkɒment‖ˈkɑː-/ n [C;U (about, on)] 1 (a) written or spoken opinion, explanation, or judgment made about an event, person, situation, etc.: He made several unfavourable comments about their candidate. | Some of her criticisms are unreasonable, but most of what she says is **fair comment**. 2 **no comment** a phrase used by people in public life to newspaper reporters when they do not want to say anything about a subject: "Could you confirm the rumours of your resignation, Mr Baker?"–"No comment!"

comment² v [I (on, upon); T+that;obj] to make a comment; give an opinion: The minister refused/declined to comment on the rumours of his resignation. | Jean commented that it was a better play than usual, and I agreed.

com·men·ta·ry /ˈkɒment*ə*ri‖ˈkɑːmənteri/ n [(on)] 1 [C] a written collection of opinions, explanations, judgments, etc., on a book, event, person, etc. 2 [C;U] (a) spoken description (with opinions and explanations) that is broadcast with, and at the same time as, an event, occasion, football match, etc.: *a commentary on the baseball game on TV* | (fig.) *We couldn't see Tom, but Sally gave us* **a running commentary** *on what he was doing.*

com·men·ta·tor /ˈkɒmənteɪtəʳ‖ˈkɑː-/ *n* a broadcaster who gives a commentary, e.g. on a sports match: *a football commentator* —**commentate** *v* [I (**on**)]

com·merce /ˈkɒmɜːs‖ˈkɑːmɜːrs/ *n* [U] **1** the buying and selling of goods and services; trade: *international commerce* **2** *old use* exchange of ideas, opinions, or feelings **3** *old use* SEXUAL INTERCOURSE —see also CHAMBER OF COMMERCE

com·mer·cial¹ /kəˈmɜːʃəl‖-ɜːr-/ *adj* **1** [*no comp.*] of, related to, or used in commerce: *a commercial venture* | *commercial vehicles* | *commercial art and design* (=for advertising, etc.) **2** [A *no comp.*] producing or likely to produce profit: *The film was highly praised, but was not a commercial success.* | *Oil has been found in commercial quantities in the North Sea.* | *Do these discoveries have any commercial value/applications?* **3** *derog* (of records, books, etc.) produced in order to make money, rather than for art: *His new record is much too commercial.* **4** [*no comp.*] (of television or radio) paid for by charges made for advertising — ~**ly** *adv* : *The new drug is not yet commercially available.*

commercial² *n* an advertisement on television or radio

commercial bank /ˌ·'·· ˌ·/ *n* a bank which accepts DEPOSIT ACCOUNTS, which the customer can close without giving warning, and which makes INVESTMENTS for a short time only

commercial break /ˌ·,·· '·/ also **break** *infml—n* a pause for advertisements during a television or radio programme

Commercial Court /ˌ·'·· ˌ·/ [*the*] a British court which hears cases concerning the movement of goods, insurance, banking, etc.

com·mer·cial·is·m /kəˈmɜːʃəlɪzəm‖-ɜːr-/ *n* [U] *often derog* the principles, methods, and practices of commerce, esp. those concerned only with making profits

com·mer·cial·ize also **-ise** *BrE* /kəˈmɜːʃəlaɪz‖-ɜːr-/ *v* [T] *often derog* to make (something) too commercial, esp. to treat with regard to, rather than of religion, art, etc.: *Do you agree that Christmas is too commercialized these days?* —**ization** /kəˌmɜːʃəlaɪˈzeɪʃən‖kəˌmɜːrʃələ-/ *n* [U]

commercial pa·per /ˌ·,·· '··/ *n* [U] *AmE tech* documents that record debts which must be paid after a short time. These are bought and sold, usu. between companies, at a DISCOUNT of their full value, as a way of getting money immediately: *They raised $50,000 yesterday selling commercial paper.*

commercial ra·di·o /ˌ·,·· '···/ *n* [U] (in Britain) local radio stations whose money comes from advertising and which are controlled by the IBA (= Independent Broadcasting Authority) —see also COMMERCIAL TELEVISION, IBA

commercial sub·jects /ˌ·'·· ˌ··/ *n old-fash for* BUSINESS STUDIES

commercial tel·e·vi·sion /ˌ·,·· '····, ·,·· ··'··/ *n* [U] (in Britain) independent television companies whose money comes from advertising not from the government and which in Britain are controlled by the IBA —see also COMMERCIAL RADIO, IBA

commercial trav·el·ler /ˌ·,·· '···/ *n BrE old-fash for* SALES REPRESENTATIVE

com·mie , Commie /ˈkɒmi‖ˈkɑː-/ *n derog sl, esp. AmE for* COMMUNIST

com·mis·e·rate /kəˈmɪzəreɪt/ *v*
  commiserate with sbdy. *phr v* [T (**on**, **over**)] to feel or express sympathy for (a person), esp. over something not very serious: *I commiserated with my friend after he failed his driving test.*

com·mis·e·ra·tion /kəˌmɪzəˈreɪʃən/ *n* [C;U (**on**)] *usu. pl.* (an expression of) sympathy for the (esp. not very serious) misfortune of another person: *Please give her my commiserations on failing her exam.* —compare CONDOLENCE

com·mis·sar /ˌkɒmɪˈsɑːʳ‖ˌkɑː-/ *n* (in the Soviet Union) **1** the official title of a government minister until 1946 **2** an official responsible for political education, esp. in the armed forces

com·mis·sar·i·at /ˌkɒmɪˈseəriət‖ˌkɑː-/ *n tech* [C+*sing./pl.*

v;U] (a department dealing with) the supply of provisions to an army

com·mis·sa·ry /ˈkɒmɪˌsəri‖ˈkɑːmɪˌseri/ *n* **1** an officer with duties in the commissariat **2** *esp. AmE* a place where soldiers or people employed by a firm, esp. a film company, can buy and eat food

com·mis·sion¹ /kəˈmɪʃən/ *n* **1** [C;U (**on**)] (an amount of) money, usu. related to the value of goods sold, paid to the person who sold them: *He gets a 10% commission on everything he sells.* | *There is a salary of £10,000, plus the opportunity to earn commission.* | *You have to pay a 25p commission on each cheque you cash.* **2** [C] a special job, duty, or power, given to a person or group of people: *Does that artist take/accept commissions?* [+*to-v*] *The commission to build the new theatre was given to a well-known architect.* **3** [C+*sing./pl. v*] (*often cap.*) a group of people specially appointed at a high level to do certain work, esp. to find out facts and write a report: *The government has set up a commission to suggest improvements in the educational system.* | *The commission has/have recommended the abolition of the examination.* | *a* **Royal Commission** *on gambling* **4** [C] (an official paper appointing someone to) any of several high ranks in the armed forces: *He's got his commission and is now a lieutenant.* **5** [U (**of**)] *fml or law* the act of committing (COMMIT) a crime: *the commission of murder by a person or persons unknown* **6** **in/out of commission** (of a ship, machine, etc.) ready/not ready for active use —see also HIGH COMMISSION

commission² *v* [T] **1** to give a COMMISSION¹ (2,4) to: [+*obj+to-v*] *He has been commissioned to paint a picture of the queen.* **2** to place a special order for, or appoint someone to do (something): *The king commissioned a portrait of the queen.* | *This inquiry was commissioned by the previous government.*

Commission for Ra·cial E·qual·i·ty /·,·· ·· ,·· ·'···/ [*the*] a British government organization established in 1976 to make sure that people of all races are treated fairly and equally by employers, schools, etc.

com·mis·sion·aire /kəˌmɪʃəˈneəʳ/ *n esp. BrE* a uniformed attendant at the entrance to a cinema, theatre, hotel, etc.

commissioned of·fic·er /·,·· '····/ *adj* a middle-ranking or high-ranking officer in the armed forces —compare NCO

com·mis·sion·er /kəˈmɪʃənəʳ/ *n* (*often cap.*) **1** an official in charge of a particular government department in some countries: *Commissioner Addo is responsible for education.* **2** a member of a COMMISSION¹ (3): *The* **Commissioners of Inland Revenue** *control British national taxes.* **3** the head of the police department in some places in the US: *Report directly to the Commissioner.* —see also CHURCH COMMISSIONERS, HIGH COMMISSIONER

commissioner for oaths /·,··· ·'·/ *n esp. BrE* a lawyer who has the legal power to witness an OATH made by someone who is making a formal legal statement

com·mit /kəˈmɪt/ *v* -**tt**- [T] **1** to do (something wrong or illegal): *to commit a crime/a sin/suicide/murder* **2** [(**to**)] to promise (esp. oneself, one's property, etc.) to a certain cause, position, opinion, or course of action: *The government has committed itself to improving health education/has committed considerable resources to improving the rail system.* | *The director has been asked to state the company's position, but so far he has refused/declined to commit himself (on this issue).* —see also COMMITTED **3** [(**to**)] to order (someone) to be put somewhere, esp. in prison or in a MENTAL HOSPITAL: *He was found guilty and committed (to prison).* **4** [(**to**)] *fml* to put into a particular place or state, e.g. in order to be kept for future use or to be got rid of: *The body was committed to the flames.* (=was burnt) | *to commit something to memory* (=to memorize it) | *She committed the facts to writing/to paper.* (=wrote them down)

com·mit·ment /kəˈmɪtmənt/ *n* [C;U (**to**)] **1** a responsibility or promise to follow certain beliefs or a certain course of action: *As members of the alliance, we must honour our defence commitments.* | *Come and look round our shop without commitment to buy anything.* | *I'm afraid I can't come, owing to other/prior commitments.* | *I don't want to get married because I don't want any commitments.* | *The general has repeated/stressed his commitment to holding elections as soon as possible.* **2** the state of being committed; deeply-felt loyalty to a particular aim, belief, etc.: *The company's success this year would not have been possible without the commitment and dedication of the staff.*

a deep commitment to feminist principles

com·mit·tal /kə'mɪtl/ *n* [C;U (**to**)] (an example of) the act of sending a person to prison or to a MENTAL HOSPITAL

com·mit·ted /kə'mɪtᵻd/ *adj* [(**to**)] **1** giving one's whole loyalty to a particular aim, job, or way of life: *a committed nurse/Christian/teacher* | *She's very committed to her job/to helping those who are homeless.* **2** [F] having made a firm promise or statement of intention: *The government is firmly committed to (maintaining) its nuclear energy programme, and is very unlikely to change its policy.*

com·mit·tee /kə'mɪti/ *n* [C+*sing./pl. v*] a group of people chosen, esp. by and from a larger group, to do a particular job or for special duties: *He's on the committee that controls council spending/on the finance committee.* | *to hold/attend a committee meeting* | *They've set up a committee to examine the question of park facilities.* —see also SELECT COMMITTEE

com·mit·tee·man /kə'mɪtimæn/ **-wom·an** /ˌwʊmən/ *fem.—n* **-men** /men/ a member of a committee

committee stage /·'·· ·/ *n law* (in either house of the British Parliament) the stage between the second and third consideration (READING) of a suggested law (BILL), when it is closely examined by a small committee

com·mode /kə'məʊd/ *n* **1** a piece of bedroom furniture like a chair with a CHAMBER POT under it **2** *old use* a piece of furniture containing drawers or shelves

com·mo·di·ous /kə'məʊdiəs/ *adj lit or fml* having plenty of space: *a commodious house* – **-ly** *adv*

com·mod·i·ty /kə'mɒdᵻti/kə'mɑː-/ *n* **1** an article of trade or COMMERCE, esp. a mineral or farm product: *The country is heavily dependent on its exports of agricultural commodities.* | *There have been big rises in commodity prices, especially copper and tin.* | *commodity brokers* **2** *fml* a thing of use or value: *Tact is a valuable commodity.*

commodity mar·ket /·'··· ˌ··/ *n* a place where raw materials such as coffee, sugar, wool, wheat, etc., are bought and sold in large quantities. The main commodity market in Britain is the **London Commodity Exchange** and in the US it is the **Chicago Board of Trade.**

com·mo·dore /'kɒmədɔːʳ/'kɑː-/ *n* **1** a naval rank —see TABLE 3 **2** the captain in charge of a FLEET (=a group) of MERCHANT ships (=ships carrying goods, materials, etc.) **3** the president of a club for people who go sailing

com·mon¹ /'kɒmən/'kɑː-/ *adj* **1** found or happening often and in many places; usual: *Rabbits and foxes are common in Britain.* | *a common occurrence* | *a common failing among teachers* | *one of the commonest/most common causes of heart disease* | *It is now very common for women to hold managerial jobs.* —compare RARE¹ (1), SCARCE¹ (1) **2** [A *no comp.*] of no special quality or rank; of the ordinary type: *Common salt is very cheap.* | *How will these changes affect* **the common man?** (=ordinary people) | *He didn't even have the* **common** *courtesy to reply to her letter.* —see also COMMON COLD **3** [A;F+**to**; *no comp.*] a belonging to or shared equally by two or more; united; JOINT: *united by their common desire to win their country's independence* | *to* **make common cause** (=join together) *against an enemy* | *This useful feature is common to both these computers.* (=they both have it) | *When it comes to politics my mother and I are on* **common ground.** (=we have the same opinions) **b** of or belonging to society as a whole; general: *The government says it is acting for the* **common good.** | *It's* **common knowledge** *among politicians that an election will be called soon.* | *This forest is* **common land.** | *Their latest system is by* **common consent** (=as everyone agrees) *the best personal computer on the market.* **4** *esp. BrE derog* rough in manner or appearance and (regarded as being) of low social class; VULGAR: *He's so common.* | *a common-looking woman* | *She's* **as common as muck** (=extremely common). **5** [A *no comp.*] *tech* having the same relationship to two or more quantities: *5 is a common factor of 10 and 20.* —see also BOOK OF COMMON PRAYER, COMMONLY – **– ~ ness** *n* [U]

common² *n* **1** an area of grassland with no fences which people in general are free to use: *Every Saturday Jean went riding on the village common.* **2** **in common** shared with someone else: *John and I have nothing in common.* (=no shared interests, qualities, etc.) | *In com-*

mon with most young people he hates getting up in the morning. **3** **out of the common** *fml* unusual —see also COMMONS

Common Ag·ri·cul·tu·ral Pol·i·cy /ˌ·· ··'··· ˌ··/ also **CAP—** [*the*] the system of support for farmers used by the EC

common car·ri·er /ˌ·· '··/ *n AmE* **1** a CARRIER (1) **2** a company that provides telephone or other TELECOMMUNICATIONS lines in exchange for payment

com·mon·al·ty /'kɒmənəlti/'kɑː-/ *n* [*the*+S+*sing./pl. v*] *fml* the common people; ordinary citizens

common cold /ˌ·· '·/ *n* [*the*] *tech for* COLD² (2)

Common Cold U·nit /ˌ·· '· ˌ··/ [*the*] (in Britain) a place where a group of scientists worked until 1991 to try to find a cure for COLDS² (2)

common de·nom·i·na·tor /ˌ·· ·'····/ *n* **1** *tech* a number which can be divided exactly by the lower number in a set of FRACTIONS **2** a quality or belief shared by all the members of a group: *There is one common denominator in these very different schemes – namely, that they are all aimed at reducing pollution.*

Common En·trance Ex·am·i·na·tion /ˌ·· '·· ···ˌ··/ [*the*] an examination taken in PREPARATORY SCHOOLs by children, usu. boys between the ages of 12 and 14, in order to be able to go to a British PUBLIC SCHOOL

com·mon·er /'kɒmənəʳ/'kɑː-/ *n* a person who is not a member of a noble family: *The princess married a commoner.*

common frac·tion /ˌ·· '··/ *n esp. AmE for* VULGAR FRACTION

common ground /ˌ·· '·/ *n* [U] a familiar subject of interest, argument, etc. which both or all people agree on: *Both parties refused to enter common ground and the meeting ended in disaster.*

com·mon·hold /'kɒmənhəʊld/'kɑː-/ *adj, adv, n tech* (having) a shared FREEHOLD between the owners of different properties within the same building. Commonhold is being introduced in England and Wales to give more rights to people who own FLATs in a building owned by someone else. —compare FREEHOLD

common land /ˌ·· '·/ *n* [U] (in Britain) land which is owned by no one and cannot be fenced, and is available for everyone to use

common-law /'·· ·/ *adj* [A] according or related to common law: *common-law penalties*

common law /ˌ·· '·/ *n* [(*the*) U] **1** the body of law originating in England and the modern systems of law based upon it —compare CANON LAW, CIVIL LAW, CRIMINAL LAW **2** the unwritten law, esp. of England, based on custom and court decisions rather than on laws made by Parliament —compare STATUTE LAW

common-law hus·band /ˌ·· '··/ *n* a man who lives with a woman as if he was her husband

common-law mar·riage /ˌ·· '··/ *n* a union between a man and a woman who live together and agree to call themselves husband and wife without the performance of a marriage ceremony

common-law wife /ˌ·· · '·/ *n* a woman who lives with a man as if she was his wife

com·mon·ly /'kɒmənli/'kɑː-/ *adv* **1** usually or generally: *It was commonly believed/thought that he was a spy.* | *a commonly used fertilizer* —compare UNCOMMONLY **2** *derog* in a COMMON¹ (4) manner

Common Mar·ket /ˌ·· '··/ [*the*] *old-fash* the EC

common noun /ˌ·· '·◄/ *n* (in grammar) a noun that is not the name of a single particular person, place, or thing: *"Book" and "sugar" are common nouns.* —compare PROPER NOUN

common-or-gar·den /ˌ·· · '··◄/ *adj* [A] *infml, esp. BrE* ordinary: *a common-or-garden sewing machine which doesn't do any fancy stitching*

com·mon·place¹ /'kɒmənpleɪs/'kɑː-/ *adj* ordinary; not regarded as special or unusual: *Heart transplant operations are becoming fairly commonplace.*

commonplace² *n* a well-known remark with little meaning or interest: *We exchanged a few commonplaces about our work and the weather.* —compare PLATITUDE

common room /'·· ·/ *n esp. BrE* a room in a school or college for the use of teachers and/or students when they are not teaching or studying

com·mons /'kɒmənz‖'kɑː-/ n 1 [the+P] old use the ordinary people as opposed to their rulers or people of noble birth 2 [U] BrE lit or pomp meals provided for a large group of people, e.g. at a college: They kept us **on short commons**. (=didn't give us enough to eat)

Commons n [the+S+sing./pl. v] the HOUSE OF COMMONS

common sense /ˌ‥ '‥◂/ n [U] practical good sense and judgment gained from experience, rather than special knowledge from school or study: Although she's not very academic she's got plenty of common sense. —see also SENSIBLE —**commonsense** adj [A]: a commonsense approach to the problem

com·mon·weal /'kɒmənwiːl‖'kɑː-/ n [the+S] lit or pomp the general good of all the people living in a country

com·mon·wealth /'kɒmənwelθ‖'kɑː-/ n tech, fml, or lit a country or state

Commonwealth n 1 [the] also **British Commonwealth** esp. old use, **Commonwealth of Na·tions** /ˌ‥‥ '‥/ fml—an organization of about 50 independent states which were formerly parts of the British Empire, established to encourage trade and friendly relations among its members. The Queen is the head of the Commonwealth: representatives of Canada, Australia, New Zealand, Kenya, Jamaica, and other Commonwealth countries 2 [C] the official title of **a** some states of the United States, such as Virginia and Kentucky **b** some countries or states which are made up of an official association with other states, such as Australia, Puerto Rico, etc.: The Commonwealth of Puerto Rico 3 [the] (the period of rule over) England from 1649 to 1660, esp. under Cromwell: Theatres were closed during the Commonwealth.

Commonwealth Day /ˌ‥‥ ˌ‥/ see EMPIRE DAY

Commonwealth Games /ˌ‥‥ '‥/ [the] a sports event in which the member countries of the Commonwealth compete in various sports, held every four years in one of the competing countries

Commonwealth of In·de·pen·dent States /ˌ‥‥ ‥ ˌ‥‥ '‥/ see CIS

com·mo·tion /kə'məʊʃən/ n [C;U] (an example of) noisy and excited movement or activity: "What's all the commotion about?" asked the angry teacher. | The announcement of the new higher taxes caused quite a commotion in Parliament.

com·mu·nal /'kɒmjʊ̩nəl, kə'mjuːnl‖'kɑː-/ adj 1 shared or used by all the members of a group: communal ownership of property | We organized the cleaning on a communal basis. | a communal television room in a hotel 2 tech of, related to, or based on racial, religious, or language groups: communal riots in India

com·mune¹ /'kɒmjuːn‖'kɑː-, kə'mjuːn/ n 1 [+sing./pl. v] **a** a group of people who work as a team, esp. in farming, and usu. give what they produce to the state **b** a group of people who live together, though not belonging to the same family, and who share their lives and possessions. In Britain and the US in the 1960s many HIPPIEs lived in communes: He ran away from home and joined a commune. 2 the smallest division of local government in some countries, such as France and Belgium

com·mune² /kə'mjuːn/ v [I (**with**)] lit to exchange thoughts or feelings: I often walk by the sea to commune with nature.

com·mu·ni·ca·ble /kə'mjuːnɪkəbəl/ adj fml (esp. of thoughts, ideas, illnesses, etc.) that can be (easily) passed from one person to another —**bly** adv

com·mu·ni·cant /kə'mjuːnɪ̩kənt/ n (in the Christian church) a person who receives COMMUNION

com·mu·ni·cate /kə'mjuːnɪ̩keɪt/ v 1 [T (**to**)] to make (opinions, feelings, information, etc.) known or understood by others, e.g. by speech, writing, or bodily movements: Our teacher communicates his ideas very clearly. | The Prime Minister has communicated his displeasure to the American ambassador. 2 [I (**with**)] to share or exchange opinions, feelings, information, etc.: He's a shy boy who can't communicate very well. | Deaf people use sign language to communicate. | Bats communicate (with each other) by making high-pitched noises. 3 [T (**to**)] tech to pass on (a disease, heat, etc.): Some diseases are easily communicated. 4 [I (**with**)] fml (esp. of rooms) to join; be connected: communicating bedrooms 5 [I] (in the Christian church) to receive COMMUNION

com·mu·ni·ca·tion /kəˌmjuːnɪ̩'keɪʃən/ n 1 [U] the act or process of communicating: Communication with Europe was difficult during the postal strike. | Radio is an important means of communication. | We are in radio communication with the spacecraft. | communication links/technology 2 [C] fml something communicated; a message, letter, etc.: He received a communication from the solicitors telling him that his uncle had died. —see also COMMUNICATIONS

communication cord /ˌ‥‥ˌ'‥ ˌ‥/ n BrE a chain which a passenger can pull to stop a train in an EMERGENCY (=a sudden dangerous situation). There is a punishment of a FINE³ for pulling it at any other time.

com·mu·ni·ca·tions /kəˌmjuːnɪ̩'keɪʃənz/ n [P (**with**)] the various ways of travelling, moving goods and people, and sending information, between places; connections by means of roads, railways, radio, telephones, etc.: Moscow has excellent communications with all parts of the Soviet Union. | communications networks/systems | The new satellite has improved communications between Europe and the US.

communication skills /ˌ‥‥ˌ'‥ ˌ/ n [P] the ability to present your ideas clearly in speech and writing. Good communication skills are considered by employers to be a valuable personal characteristic and are often requested in job advertisements: The Chairman wants all our managers to take a course in communication skills this year.

communications sat·el·lite /ˌ‥‥ˌ'‥ ˌ‥‥/ also **communication satellite** n a man-made object in space which goes around the Earth sending radio, television, and telephone signals around the world

com·mu·ni·ca·tive /kə'mjuːnɪ̩kətɪv‖-keɪtɪv/ adj 1 very willing to talk or give information: You're not very communicative this morning; is anything the matter? —opposite **uncommunicative** 2 related to communication: communicative ability

com·mu·nion /kə'mjuːnjən/ n 1 [U (**between, with**)] fml or lit the sharing or exchange of deep thoughts, ideas, and feelings, esp. of a religious kind: communion with nature | a mystical communion between man and God | Through the long hours of the night he held communion with (=talked seriously and deeply with) the condemned man. 2 [C+sing./pl. v] a group of people or religious organizations having the same religious beliefs; DENOMINATION: He belongs to the Anglican communion.

Communion also **Holy Communion**— n [U] the Christian ceremony in which bread and wine are shared as a sign of Christ's body and blood in order to remember him. The Communion ceremony repeats the actions of Christ at the Last Supper: The communicants came up to take/receive Communion from the priest. (=by eating the bread and drinking the wine) —compare MASS, EUCHARIST; see also CONSUBSTANTIATION

com·mu·ni·qué /kə'mjuːnɪ̩keɪ‖kəˌmjuːnɪ̩'keɪ/ n an official report or declaration, usu. to the public or newspapers: The palace has issued a communiqué denying the paper's allegations.

com·mu·nis·m /'kɒmjʊ̩nɪzəm‖'kɑː-/ n [U] (the belief in) a social and political system in which the means of production are owned and controlled by the state or the people as a whole, and the goods and wealth produced are shared according to the principle "from each according to his ability, to each according to his needs" —compare CAPITALISM, SOCIALISM

Communism n [U] the system of government in which a single party controls the means of production, with the aim of establishing a classless society according to the principles of communism: Chinese Communism —compare CAPITALISM; see also MARXISM, MARXISM-LENINISM

▶ CULTURAL NOTE Most British and American people associate Communism esp. with the Soviet Union and many people in both countries fear Communism. This was esp. true in the US during the 1950s and 1960s, when the Cold War was at its height. —see also McCARTHYISM◀

com·mu·nist /'kɒmjʊ̩nɪst‖'kɑː-/ adj, n (of) a person favouring the principles of communism — ~ **ic** /ˌkɒmjʊ̩'nɪstɪk◂‖ ˌkɑː-/ adj

Communist n a person believing that Communism is the best possible form of society: She's a Communist. | Chinese Communists

▶CULTURAL NOTE In the US, especially in the 1950s and 1960s, many people disapproved of Communists and considered American Communists to be disloyal to their country. **Commie, Red,** and **Pinko** became derogatory terms for Communists. The word Communist is still sometimes used to mean anyone whose political ideas are LEFT WING. —see also HUAC, Joseph McCARTHY, McCARTHYISM **Communist** adj : Communist ideas | the Communist Revolution◀

Communist bloc /ˈ···· ₁·/ [the] the group of Communist countries, esp. in Eastern Europe, which supported and formed ALLIANCEs with the USSR

Communist Man·i·fes·to /₁··· ·· ˈ···/, **The** a book by Karl Marx and Friedrich Engels which set out all the basic principles of Communism. It was first published (PUBLISH) in 1848.

Communist Par·ty /ˈ···· ₁·/, **the** [+ sing./pl. v] a political party, also known as **the Communists**, which follows the principles of MARXISM-LENINISM.

com·mu·ni·ty /kəˈmjuːnₐti/ n **1** [C+sing./pl. v] a group of people living together and/or united by shared interests, religion, nationality, etc.: the Polish community in Britain | The President met leaders of the black community during his visit to Chicago. | rural communities | the academic community | This terrorist attack has been condemned by the entire **international community.** (=by all the countries of the world) **2** [the+S] the public; people in general: The job of a politician is to serve the (whole) community. | community singing (=singing in which all present may take part) —see SOCIETY (USAGE) **3** [U (**of**)] shared possession: community of property/companies | The two men were united by **community of interests.** (=by having the same aims and needs) **4** [C] tech a group of plants or animals living together in the same surroundings, dependent on each other for the means of existence

Community [the] infml for the EC

community care /·₁··· ·ˈ·/ n [U] help from the SOCIAL SERVICES for people who would once have had to live in institutions, e.g. mentally ill people, so that they can live in their own homes in the local community. This is a recent British government idea, and there is some concern that not all these people will be able to manage without the special care of the people who worked at the institution.

community cen·tre /·ˈ··· ₁·/ n a building where people from a certain area or group can meet for social, educational, or other purposes

community chan·nel /·ˈ··· ₁··/ also **public access channel** n a television CHANNEL provided by most CABLE television companies (in the US) which enables people served by the company to broadcast their own programmes or other information

community charge /·ˈ··· ₁·/ [the] (in Britain) the official name of a local tax introduced by the Conservative Party. It began to be collected in Scotland in 1989 and in England and Wales in 1990. It was based on each adult person paying the same amount, and replaced the RATEs (=a local tax based on property). It was usu. known as the POLL TAX. It was generally unpopular, e.g. because a poor family in one house might have to pay a lot more than quite a rich single person living next door. After a lot of trouble, and some RIOTs, the Conservative government announced in 1990 that the community charge would be replaced in 1993 by the COUNCIL TAX.

community chest /·ˈ··· ·/ n **1** esp. AmE an amount of money collected by the people and businesses of an area to help people in need **2** a square on which one can land in the board game Monopoly

community col·lege /·ˈ··· ₁··/ also **junior college** n [C;U] (in the US) a COLLEGE (3) which is generally attended by students who live at home rather than at the college, and which is usu. cheaper than other colleges because it usu. is partly paid for by the local government. Working people often attend community colleges to improve their QUALIFICATIONs. Also, students who are not accepted to the college of their choice because of poor examination results often attend their community college; after achieving better examination results there, they may **transfer** to a better college where they can finish a BACHELOR's degree.

community coun·cil /·₁··· ·ˈ··/ n **1** a form of local govern-

ment in Wales **2** a local advisory body in Scotland with no political authority

community home /·ˈ··· ₁·/ n (in Britain) a special school for young people who have broken the law. They live and receive training there. It replaces the old APPROVED SCHOOL and REMAND HOME —see also REFORMATORY

community po·lic·ing /·₁··· ·ˈ··/ n [U] a system for preventing crime and encouraging good relations between the police and the public, by having the same policemen working in a particular area so that the people in that area know and trust them

community prop·er·ty /·ˈ··· ₁···/ n [U] law (in the US) property such as houses or land, etc., bought by either a husband or wife but considered to be owned by both

community ser·vice /·₁··· ·ˈ··/ n [U] **1** VOLUNTARY WORK done to help other people within the local COMMUNITY: Her care of the retired people in the home is an outstanding example of community service. **2** a punishment given by a court for certain less important crimes, according to which an offender must do socially useful work, e.g. repairing old people's homes or helping HANDICAPPED children, instead of going to prison: a sentence of 100 hours of community service

com·mu·ta·ble /kəˈmjuːtəbəl/ adj that can be commuted (COMMUTE[1] (2,3))

com·mu·ta·tion /₁kɒmjᵿˈteɪʃən‖₁kɑː-/ n **1** [C;U (**from, to**)] (a) reduction in a punishment: The court ordered the commutation of his sentence from death to life imprisonment. **2** [U (**into, for**)] fml the act of exchanging one thing for another **3** [C] tech a payment of one sort made instead of an equal payment of another sort

commutation tick·et /₁··· ·ˈ··/ n AmE a ticket sold at a reduced price by a railway or bus company for a fixed number of trips between two places during a fixed period of time —compare SEASON TICKET

com·mu·ta·tive /kəˈmjuːtətɪv‖ˈkɑːmjəteɪtɪv/ adj tech not depending on the order in which an operation is carried out: Addition is commutative, but subtraction is not.

com·mu·ta·tor /ˈkɒmjᵿteɪtəʳ‖ˈkɑː-/ n tech an apparatus used in electric motors, machines, etc., for changing the direction of flow of an electric current

com·mute¹ /kəˈmjuːt/ v **1** [I (**between, from, to**)] to travel regularly a long distance between one's home and work, esp. by train or car. Many people in Britain now commute to work, esp. into London. In the US, people have to commute in most of the large cities. People who commute are usu. WHITE-COLLAR workers: She commutes from Cambridge to London/between Cambridge and London every day. | a suburb within easy commuting distance of the city - see also COMMUTER **2** [T (**from, to**)] to make (a punishment) less severe: His sentence was commuted from death to life imprisonment. **3** [T (**into, for**)] to ex change (one thing, esp. one kind of payment) for another: He commuted his pension into/for a lump sum. —see also COMMUTABLE, COMMUTATION

commute² n infml the trip made in commuting. It's a long commute from New York to Boston.

commuters

com·mut·er /kəˈmjuːtəʳ/ n a person who commutes to work every day: a crowded commuter train

▶CULTURAL NOTE In Britain, the image of the typical commuter is of someone in SMART clothes who works in an office, is RESPECTABLE and CONSERVATIVE, and who sits and reads a newspaper on the train and does not talk to anyone else. In the US people often think of commuters in connection with TRAFFIC JAMs because most people commute in their cars.◀

commuter belt /·ˈ··ˈ··/ *n* an area around a large town from which many people commute to work every day. (In Britain, this is mostly used of the area around London.)

Co·mo /ˈkəʊməʊ/, **Perry** (1912–   ) an American popular music singer of usu. ROMANTIC songs, popular esp. with older people

com·pact¹ /kəmˈpækt, ˈkɒmpækt‖kəmˈpækt/ *adj* **1** firmly and closely packed together; DENSE: *The trees grew in a compact mass.* **2** small but cleverly made or arranged; fitting neatly into a small space: *a compact office/camera* **3** expressed in few words; CONCISE: *a compact statement* – – **ly** *adv* – –**ness** *n* [U]

com·pact² /ˈkɒmpækt‖ˈkɑːm-/ *n* **1** a small flat container for a woman's FACE POWDER, a POWDER PUFF, and a mirror **2** also **compact car** /ₜ·· ˈ·/– *AmE* a small car

compact³ *n fml* an agreement between two or more people, countries, etc.: *banking compacts* [+to-v] *They made a compact never to speak about the matter again.*

com·pact⁴ /kəmˈpækt/ *v* [T] to press together firmly and closely: *a compacted mass of snow*

compact disc player

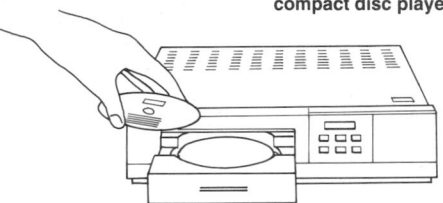

compact disc , compact disk /ₜ·· ˈ· ₜ·/ also **CD**– *n* a small circular piece of hard plastic on which high-quality recorded sound or large quantities of information can be stored. In Britain and the US, it has largely replaced the RECORD² (4).

compact disc player, compact disk player /·ˈ· ˈ· ₜ·/ also **CD player** – *n* a piece of equipment which can turn the information stored on a COMPACT DISC back into the original sounds, music, etc.: *a portable compact disc player*

com·pan·ion /kəmˈpænjən/ *n* **1** *esp. lit* a person who goes somewhere with or spends time with another, either because of friendship or by chance: *a close companion* | *a travelling companion* | *My fellow prisoners made/were good companions* | (fig.) *The fear of being discovered was his constant companion.* (=He was continuously afraid of being discovered.) –compare COMRADE, PARTNER **2** (esp. formerly) a person, usu. a woman, paid to live with another (often older or ill) person: *The old lady's companion always drives the car.* –compare PARTNER **3** [(to)] either of a pair or set of things; one thing that matches another: *I used to have a companion to that vase, but I broke it.* | *a companion volume* **4** (usu. in titles) a book which explains how to do something; HANDBOOK: *the Motorist's Companion*

com·pan·io·na·ble /kəmˈpænjənəbəl/ *adj* friendly; showing a friendly relationship: *a companionable evening together playing cards* | *a companionable silence* (=comfortable even though no one spoke) –**bly** *adv*

Companion of Hon·our /·ₜ··· ·ˈ··/ also **CH** [*the*] a British AWARD given by the king or queen to someone who has performed a special service of national importance: *What did she do to get the Companion of Honour?* –compare ORDER OF MERIT

com·pan·ion·ship /kəmˈpænjənʃɪp/ *n* [U] the relationship of companions; friendly company: *He missed the companionship he'd enjoyed in the navy.*

com·pan·ion·way /kəmˈpænjənweɪ/ *n* the steps leading from the one DECK (=floor) of a ship to another –compare GANGPLANK

com·pa·ny /ˈkʌmpəni/ *n* **1** [C+*sing./pl. v*] an organization made up of people who work together for purposes of business or trade: *a pharmaceutical company* | *insurance companies* | *to form a new company* | *a private/ public/state-owned company* | *Which company do you work for?* | *My company sells farm machinery.* | (in names) *Robinson and Company* –see also HOLDING COMPANY, PUBLIC COMPANY **2** [C+*sing./pl. v*] a group of entertainers who work together: *a theatre/dance company* | *The Royal Shakespeare Company* **3** [U] the presence of another person; companionship: *Would you like some company?* | *I was grateful for Jean's company on the long journey up to Edinburgh.* **4** [U+*sing./pl. v*] companions; the people with whom a person spends time: *pleasant company* | *The people at this party are really boring* – **present company excepted,** *of course!* (=I don't include you) **5** [U] one or more guests: *No, you can't go out tonight; we're expecting company.* | *You should never swear in company.* (=when guests are present) **6** [C+*sing./pl. v*] **a** a group of about 120 soldiers, usu. part of a REGIMENT or BATTALION **b** officers and men of a ship **7 be good/bad company** to be a good/bad person to be with: *John's rather depressed; he's not very good company at the moment.* **8 be in good company** *humor* to be in the same (usu. difficult) situation as another person: *"Why are we going to France? I can't speak a word of French." "Don't worry, you're in good company – neither can I!"* **9 keep someone company** to be, go, remain, etc. with someone; provide companionship: *If you're going out for a walk, I'll come along and keep you company.* **10 two's company, three's a crowd** *saying* two people can spend time happily together, but if there are more than two this may be a problem. The phrase is used esp. about two people who are sexually attracted to each other not wanting a third person to spoil the amount of attention they can give to each other. –see also **part company** (PART²)

company car /ₜ··· ˈ·/ *n* a car which is provided for a person by their employer, either because they have to travel in order to do their job or because they have an important job and the car is a kind of reward. It is available for their private use. In Britain a company car is seen as a STATUS SYMBOL by many people: *a salary of £25,000 plus a company car*

company law /ₜ··· ˈ·/ *n* [U] the area of law that concerns how businesses operate and what their responsibilities to each other, to customers, and to governments are

company sec·re·ta·ry /ₜ··· ˈ··../ *n esp. BrE* a high-ranking member of a business company who deals with accounts, legal matters, etc.

com·pa·ra·ble /ˈkɒmpərəbəl‖ˈkɑːm-/ *adj* [(with, to)] **1** similar; that can be compared; EQUIVALENT: *A comparable car would cost far more abroad.* | *a system for ensuring that people doing comparable jobs receive comparable rates of pay* **2** deserving to be compared: *His poetry isn't bad, but it's hardly comparable with Shakespeare's!* –see also INCOMPARABLE –**bly** *adv* – –**bility** /ₜkɒmpərəˈbɪlₜti‖ₜkɑːm-/ *n* [U] : *a system of public pay comparability*

com·par·a·tive¹ /kəmˈpærətɪv/ *adj* [*no comp.*] **1** (of the form of an adjective or adverb) expressing an increase in quality, quantity, or degree: *"Bigger" is the comparative form of "big".* | *"More comfortable" is the comparative form of "comfortable".* | *"Worse" is the comparative form of "bad", and also of "badly".* –compare POSITIVE¹ (5), SUPERLATIVE¹ (1) **2** measured or judged by a comparison which is not stated: *the comparative wealth of the south of England* (=its wealth compared with the rest of the country) | *He's a comparative newcomer to television.* (=He has been on television before, but not often.) | *a comparative stranger* **3** based on or making a comparison: *a comparative study of European languages* | *a collection of comparative statistical data about different countries*

comparative² also **comparative degree** /·ₜ··· ·ˈ·/– *n* [*the*+S] the form of an adjective or adverb that shows some increase in quality, quantity, or degree: *"Bigger" is the comparative of "big".* | *"More comfortable" is the comparative of "comfortable".*

com·par·a·tive·ly /kəmˈpærətɪvli/ *adv* **1** when compared with others; rather: *Man is a comparatively new creature on the face of the earth.* | *Comparatively speaking, these aircraft are quite cheap.* **2** in a COMPARATIVE¹ (3) way: *two languages to study comparatively*

com·pare¹ /kəmˈpeəʳ/ *v* **1** [T (to, with)] to examine or judge (one thing) in relation to another thing in order to show the points of similarity or difference: *The report compares the different types of home computer currently available.* | *I compared the copy with the original, and/but there wasn't much difference.* | *Compare our prices!* (=with those of other shops, which are higher) | *Our staff turnover is low compared with other companies.* | *Compared to a student grant the pay is quite good.* **2** [T] to show a similarity between (one thing and another): *It's impossible to compare London and New York/to compare the two cities; they're quite different.* **3** [I (**with**)] to be worthy of comparison: *1983 was an excellent year for wine – I'm afraid this year's doesn't compare.* (=is not nearly so good) | *Life/living in a town can't compare with life/living in the country.* (=life in the country is much better) | *She was pleased to discover that her work compared favourably with her older sister's.* **4 compare notes** *infml* to talk about each other's experiences and opinions of something: *We've been comparing notes on our trips to India.* **5 Shall I compare thee to a summer's day?** *quote* a phrase from a poem from Shakespeare, describing how beautiful a particular woman was

▷ USAGE **Compare** can be followed by **to** or **with**: *London is large,* **compared to/with** *Paris.* **Compare to** is often used when showing that two things are alike: *The poet* **compares** *the woman he loves* **to** *a rose.* (=says she is like a rose) **Compare with** is often used when looking at the ways in which two things are like and unlike each other: *If we* **compare** *French schools* **with** *British schools, we find there are many differences.*◁

compare² *n* **beyond/without compare** *esp. lit* to a very high degree: *beauty/beautiful beyond compare*

com·pa·ri·son /kəm'pærɪsən/ *n* **1** [U (**with**)] the act of comparing: *By comparison with London, Paris is small.* | *The driver's injuries were trivial in comparison with those suffered by his passenger.* | *My garden doesn't stand/bear comparison with his.* (=his garden is much nicer) **2** [C (**between, with**)] a statement of the points of similarity and difference between two things: *He drew* (=made) **a comparison** *between* (=compared) *religion and superstition.* **3** [U (**between**)] similarity: *There is* **no comparison** *between frozen and fresh fish.* (=fresh fish is better) **4** [U] *tech* (in grammar) the changing of the form of an adverb or adjective to show the three degrees of POSITIVE, COMPARATIVE, and SUPERLATIVE

com·part·ment /kəm'pɑːtmənt‖-ɑːr-/ *n* any of the parts into which an enclosed space, e.g. a railway carriage or box, is divided: *We sat in a second-class compartment.* | *the ice compartment in a fridge* –see also GLOVE COMPARTMENT, and see picture at CAR

com·part·men·tal·ize also **-ise** *BrE* /ˌkɒmpɑːt'mentl-aɪz‖kəm-pɑːrt-/ *v* [T] to divide into separate compartments, divisions, etc.; CATEGORIZE: *compartmentalized information* **–ization** /ˌkɒmpɑːt-mentl-aɪ'zeɪʃən‖ kəm-pɑːrt-mentl-ə'zeɪʃən/ *n* [U]

com·pass /'kʌmpəs/ *n* **1** an instrument for showing direction, consisting of a freely moving pointer which always turns to the MAGNETIC NORTH –see INSTRUMENT (USAGE) **2** also **compasses** *pl.* – a V-shaped instrument used for drawing circles, measuring distances on maps, etc.: *a pair of compasses* –see picture at MATHEMATICS **3** [*usu. sing.*] *fml* an area or range of interest, activity, etc.; SCOPE: *Finance is not within the compass of this department.* –see also **box the compass** (BOX²)

com·pas·sion /kəm'pæʃən/ *n* [U (**for, on**)] sympathy for the sufferings of others, causing a desire to help them: *She felt/had/showed great compassion for the sick children.*

com·pas·sion·ate /kəm'pæʃənət/ *adj* [(**towards**)] feeling or showing compassion – ~ **ly** *adv*

compassionate leave /·ˌ··· '·/ *n* [U] special permission to leave work or military service for a short time for personal reasons, e.g. the death of a relative: *The soldier was given compassionate leave to attend his mother's funeral.*

compassion fa·tigue /·'·· ·ˌ·/ *n* [U] the state of being tired of being sympathetic esp. to the problems of less fortunate people or animals, caused by hearing and/or seeing too much about the problem: *I think I must have compassion fatigue. I just can't get interested in this programme.*

compass point /'·· ·/ *n* any of the 32 marks on a COMPASS, showing direction

com·pat·i·bil·i·ty /kəmˌpætɪ'bɪlɪti/ *n* [U (**with**)] the ability

to exist together or to be used together

com·pat·i·ble¹ /kəm'pætɪbəl/ *adj* [(**with**)] **1** able to exist or live together: *Their marriage ended because they were simply not compatible.* | *compatible blood groups* | *This project is not compatible with the company's long-term plans.* –opposite **incompatible** **2** able to be used together or with (another thing): *Is your computer compatible with the Lotus spreadsheet program?* [after *n*] *Is this software Apple Macintosh compatible?* –**bly** *adv*

compatible² *n* a piece of equipment, such as a computer or a computer PROGRAM, that can be used with the stated other type of equipment: *a computer workshop for those who have just acquired an IBM compatible* | *MS-DOS is the operating system used by IBM personal computers and their compatibles such as Amstrad 1512.*

com·pat·ri·ot /kəm'pætriət‖-'peɪt-/ *n fml* a person who was born in or is a citizen of the same country as another: *He tried to avoid spending too much time with his compatriots when he lived abroad.*

com·peer /'kɒmpɪəʳ‖'kɑːm-/ *n fml or old use* a person of equal rank, esp. a companion

com·pel /kəm'pel/ *v* **-ll-** [T] **1** [+*obj*+*to*-*v*] to make (a person or thing) do something, by force, moral persuasion, or orders that must be obeyed: *Employees are compelled to join the company's pension plan after a year's service.* | *His conscience compelled him to admit his part in the affair.* **2** *fml* to cause (a feeling, event, etc.) to exist or happen, as if by force: *Lack of funds for the campaign compelled his withdrawal.* | *a degree of political skill that compels our admiration* –compare IMPEL; see also COMPULSION

com·pel·ling /kəm'pelɪŋ/ *adj* **1** that holds one's attention, esp. by being exciting: *a compelling adventure story* **2** that compels one to do something: *I have no compelling reasons to refuse.* | *compelling arguments for accepting this proposal* – ~ **ly** *adv*

com·pen·di·ous /kəm'pendiəs/ *adj fml* (of books, etc.) giving information in a short but complete form – ~ **ly** *adv*

com·pen·di·um /kəm'pendiəm/ *n* **-diums** or **-dia** /diə/ [(**of**)] *fml* (a book containing) a short but detailed and complete account of facts, a subject, etc.: *a compendium of useful information*

com·pen·sate /'kɒmpənseɪt‖'kɑːm-/ *v* **1** [T (**for**)] to provide with a suitable payment for some loss, damage, inconvenience, etc.: *Many firms compensate their workers if they are injured at work.* **2** [I (**for**)] to act as a balance (for); remove the bad effect (of): *Her intelligence more than compensates for her lack of experience.* | *Nothing can compensate for losing my husband.* –**satory** /ˌkɒmpən'seɪtəri‖kəm'pensəˌtɔːri/ *adj* : *compensatory payments*

com·pen·sa·tion /ˌkɒmpən'seɪʃən‖ˌkɑːm-/ *n* [S;U (**for**)] something (esp. money) given as a way of compensating: *The union is seeking compensation for two factory workers who were dismissed last week.* | *The travel agents offered them £200 in compensation for their lost holiday.* | *a compensation claim* –compare CONSOLATION, RECOMPENSE

com·pere¹ /'kɒmpeəʳ‖'kɑːm-/ *n BrE* a person who introduces the various acts in a television stage show or other presentation

compere² *v* [I;T] *BrE* to act as the compere of (a television or stage show)

com·pete /kəm'piːt/ *v* [I (**with, against, for**)] to try to win something in competition with someone else: *to compete with/against a rival company* | *She and her sister are always competing for attention.* | *The government has to reconcile the competing demands for tax cuts and higher public spending.* [+*to*-*v*] *Several advertising agencies are competing to get the contract.* –see also COMPETITION, COMPETITOR

com·pe·tence /'kɒmpətəns‖'kɑːm-/ also **com·pe·ten·cy** /-tənsi/ *rare– n* **1** [U] ability to do what is needed; skill: *I'm only worried about his attitude to the job; his competence (as a designer) is not in question.* –opposite **incompetence** **2** [U] *tech* **a** the powers of a court of law: *The case is beyond this court's competence.* **b** the qualities necessary for a person to be admitted to a court of law (e.g. as a witness), such as having the right citizenship **3** [S] *lit or old use* enough money to live on comfortably

com·pe·tent /'kɒmpətənt‖'kɑːm-/ *adj* **1** having the ability or skill to do something: *a competent swimmer* | *My secretary is perfectly competent, but she doesn't have much initiative.* [+ to-v] *His French seems quite good to me, but then I'm not really competent to judge.* —opposite **incompetent** **2** showing competence; satisfactory: *He did a competent job.* **3** [F] having the legal power to deal with something: [+to-v] *This court is not competent to hear your case.* — ~ ly *adv*

com·pe·ti·tion /ˌkɒmpəˈtɪʃən‖ˌkɑːm-/ *n* **1** [C] a test of strength, skill, ability, etc.: *to go in for|enter a competition* | *a crossword competition* [+to-v] *a competition to find a designer for the new airport building* **2** [U (**with, between, for**)] the act of competing; the struggle between several people or groups to win something or gain an advantage; RIVALRY: *There was intense|keen|fierce competition between the journalists to get the story.* | *He was in* **competition with** *some world-class runners, so he did well to win the race.* | *The two products|companies are in* **direct competition.** (=are|produce similar products at similar prices) | *They believe that competition in business benefits the consumer.* **3** [U] the (other) competitors: *Anyone wanting to enter the computer business faces tough competition.* | *It's important in business to keep a careful watch on the competition.* | *They had to keep their prices low because of foreign competition.*

com·pet·i·tive /kəmˈpetɪtɪv/ *adj* **1** of, based on, or decided by competition: *the competitive nature of private industry* | *competitive sports* **2** liking to compete: *Jane's got a very competitive nature.* **3** (of a price, product, or producer) able to compete because it is at least as good, cheap, etc. as the competitors: *I always shop at that supermarket; its prices are very competitive.* | *Because of the high exchange rate, our products have lost their* **competitive edge.** (=their ability to compete successfully) — ~ ly *adv* — ~ ness *n* [U]

com·pet·i·tor /kəmˈpetɪtəʳ/ *n* a person, team, firm, product, etc., competing with another or others; RIVAL: *There were ten competitors in the race.* | *We lost the contract to our competitors.*

com·pi·la·tion /ˌkɒmpəˈleɪʃən‖ˌkɑːm-/ *n* **1** [U] the act or process of compiling **2** [C] a report, collection of writings, etc., that has been compiled

com·pile /kəmˈpaɪl/ *v* [T] to make (a report, a book, etc.) from facts and information found in various places: *It takes years of work to compile a dictionary.*

com·pil·er /kəmˈpaɪləʳ/ *n* **1** a person who compiles information for a report, a book, etc. **2** *tech* a PROGRAM which translates a computer language (such as BASIC) which is understood by the PROGRAMMER into a language (such as MACHINE CODE) which is understood by the computer

com·pla·cen·cy /kəmˈpleɪsənsi/ also **com·pla·cence** /-səns/— *n* [U] *usu. derog* a feeling of satisfaction with oneself or with a situation, esp. without good reason: *The state of the economy is increasingly desperate; I can see no justification for the government's complacency.*

com·pla·cent /kəmˈpleɪsənt/ *adj* [(**about**)] *usu. derog* pleased or satisfied with oneself or with a situation, often unreasonably; not worrying, even though one perhaps should be: *After so many wins we grew|got complacent and thought we'd never lose — so of course we lost the next match!* | *a complacent smile* — ~ ly *adv* : *"I'm bound to get promoted", he said complacently.*

com·plain /kəmˈpleɪn/ *v* [I (**about, to**);T+*that*; *obj*] to express feelings of annoyance, dissatisfaction, unhappiness, etc.; say in an annoyed, unhappy, dissatisfied way: *Mary is always complaining.* | *Our neighbour said that if we made any more noise he'd complain (about us) to the police.* | *He complained that the room was too hot.* | *They complained bitterly about the injustice of the system.* — ~ **er** *n* — ~ **ing** *adj* — ~ **ingly** *adv*
  complain of sthg. *phr v* [T] to say that one has (a pain, illness, etc.): *He went to the doctor complaining of difficulty in breathing.*

com·plain·ant /kəmˈpleɪnənt/ *n law* a person who makes a complaint in a court of law; PLAINTIFF

com·plaint /kəmˈpleɪnt/ *n* **1** [C (**about, against**)] a statement or cause of annoyance, dissatisfaction, unhappiness, pain, etc.: *to make a complaint* | *The pupils made a list of their complaints about school meals.* | *The police received several complaints about the noise from our party.* | *the hospital's complaints procedure* (=system for

dealing with complaints by patients) | *"How are you?" "No complaints, thanks."* (=I'm all right) **2** [U (**about**)] the act of complaining: *There's been widespread complaint about the selection procedure.* | *If your neighbours are too noisy then you have* **cause for complaint.** (=a good reason to complain) **3** [C] an illness, esp. in the stated part of the body: *a rare liver complaint* **4 lodge a complaint (against, with)** *fml or law* to complain formally (about, to): *Our neighbours lodged a complaint against us with the police|with the housing authorities.*

com·plai·sance /kəmˈpleɪzəns/ *n* [U] *fml* willingness to do what pleases others

com·plai·sant /kəmˈpleɪzənt/ *adj fml* willing to please others; ready to agree — ~ ly *adv*

Com·pleat An·gler /kəmˌpliːt ˈæŋgləʳ/, **The** a 17th century book by Izaak Walton which told all about fishing and is still sometimes read today

com·ple·ment¹ /ˈkɒmpləmənt‖ˈkɑːm-/ *n* **1** [(**to**)] something which, when added to something else, completes it or makes it perfect: *A fine wine is a complement to a good meal.* **2** the number or quantity needed to make something complete: *At last the English department has its* **full complement** of *teachers.* (=has all the teachers it needs) **3** (in grammar) a word or phrase (esp. a noun or adjective) that follows a verb and describes the subject of the verb: *In "John is cold" and "John became chairman", "cold" and "chairman" are complements.*

com·ple·ment² /ˈkɒmpləment‖ˈkɑːm-/ *v* [T] to make (something) complete or perfect; supply what is lacking in (something): *This wine complements the food perfectly.* | *Our local bus and rail services complement each other very well.* —compare COMPLIMENT

com·ple·men·ta·ry /ˌkɒmpləˈmentəri◂‖ˌkɑːm-/ *adj* **1** making something complete; supplying what is lacking or needed for completion **2** *tech* (of a pair of angles) making up 90° together —compare SUPPLEMENTARY (2)

complementary col·ours /ˌ····· ˈ··/ *n* [P] colours which when mixed make white or grey

complementary medi·cine /ˌ····· ˈ··/ *n* ALTERNATIVE MEDICINE when used to COMPLEMENT (=help) standard medical treatment —see also ALTERNATIVE MEDICINE; compare WESTERN MEDICINE —see also extra information on page 829

com·plete¹ /kəmˈpliːt/ *adj* **1** having all necessary, usual, or wanted parts; lacking nothing: *Is this pack of cards complete?* | *a complete wordprocessing system, with a computer, screen, and printer* | *John's birthday did not seem complete without his father there.* | *the complete gardener's kit* (=everything a good gardener needs) —opposite **incomplete 2** [F] finished; ended: *When will work on the new railway be complete?* **3** total; thorough: *His resignation came as a complete surprise to his staff.* | *in complete control of the situation* | *I made a complete fool of myself.* | *Our humiliation was complete* **4** [F+**with**] fully or additionally supplied: *We bought the house complete with furniture.* — ~ **ness** *n* [U]

complete² *v* [T] **1** to make (something) whole or perfect by adding what is missing: *I need one more stamp to complete my collection.* | *Seeing the family all together again completed her happiness.* **2** to finish; bring to an end (esp. something that takes a long time): *When will work be completed on the new road?* | *He completed the book with a chapter on the practical applications of his theory.* | *She has just completed an 18-month jail sentence.*

com·plete·ly /kəmˈpliːtli/ *adv* totally; in every way: *The operation was completely successful.* | *Is the work completely finished?* | *I completely forgot about it*

com·ple·tion /kəmˈpliːʃən/ *n* [U] **1** the act of completing something: *Completion of this bridge is expected in 1990.* | *We were paid* **on completion** of *the work.* (=when we finished it) | *The completion date is April 10th.* **2** the state of being complete: *The new road is near completion.*

com·plex¹ /ˈkɒmpleks‖ˌkɑːmˈpleks◂/ *adj* **1** difficult to understand, explain, or deal with; not clear or simple: *a complex problem|issue for which there is no simple solution* | *complex bureaucratic procedures* **2** consisting of many closely connected parts: *a complex network of roads connecting Glasgow and Edinburgh* | *complex machines* **3** *tech* (of a word or sentence) consisting of a main part and one or more other parts: *"Childish" is a complex word* consisting of a main part, *"child"*, and the suffix, *"-ish"*. | *"If it rains, I won't go" is a complex sentence with a main clause, "I won't go", and another clause, "If it rains".* —compare COMPOUND² (2), SIMPLE (3)

com·plex² /'kɒmpleks‖'kɑːm-/ n **1** a system consisting of a large number of closely related parts: *a shopping/sports complex* (=an area containing everything needed for shopping/sport) | *a complex of welfare regulations* **2** [(**about**)] a group of unconscious confused wishes, fears, feelings, etc., which influence a person's behaviour, esp. for the worse: *He's got a persecution complex* —see also INFERIORITY COMPLEX, OEDIPUS COMPLEX, SUPERIORITY COMPLEX

com·plex·ion /kəm'plekʃən/ n **1** the natural colour and appearance of the skin, esp. of the face: *a good/healthy/dark/fair/pale complexion* **2** [*usu. sing.*] a general character or nature: *This information puts a (whole) new complexion on the situation.* (=completely changes it) | *governments of various political complexions*

com·plex·i·ty /kəm'pleksɨti/ n [C;U (**of**)] (an example of) the state of being COMPLEX¹ (1,2): *the complexities of the tax laws* | *a political problem of great complexity*

com·pli·ance /kəm'plaɪəns/ n [U (**with**)] *fml* **1** obedience to a rule, agreement, demand, etc.: *Compliance with the law is expected of all citizens.* **2** the tendency to agree (too) willingly to other people's wishes or demands: *His compliance with everything we suggest makes it hard to know what he really feels.* —see also COMPLY

com·pli·ant /kəm'plaɪənt/ adj readily acting in accordance with a rule, order, the wishes of others, etc. —see also COMPLY — ~ **ly** adv

com·pli·cate /'kɒmplɨkeɪt‖'kɑːm-/ v [T] **1** to make (something) difficult to understand or deal with: *There are six candidates and, to complicate matters still further, every voter has four votes!* | *Plans for the release of political prisoners were complicated by a fresh outbreak of terrorist activity.* —compare SIMPLIFY **2** [*often pass.*] to make (a situation, esp. an illness) worse: *a serious disease complicated by an additional bacterial infection*

com·pli·cat·ed /'kɒmplɨkeɪtɨd‖'kɑːm-/ adj **1** difficult to understand or deal with: *a complicated legal problem.* | *It's rather complicated to explain, but I'll try.* **2** consisting of many closely related or connected parts: *a complicated machine* — ~ **ly** adv — ~ **ness** n [U]

com·pli·ca·tion /ˌkɒmplɨ'keɪʃən‖ˌkɑːm-/ n **1** something that makes a situation, process, etc, more complicated: *The car ran out of petrol, and as a further complication I had no money!* | *the complications of the plot* **2** a new illness that happens during the course of another illness, making treatment more difficult: *The doctors were sure they could cure the patient, but when complications set in they lost hope.*

com·plic·i·ty /kəm'plɪsɨti/ n [U (**in**)] *fml* the act of taking part with another person in some wrong action, esp. a crime: *He denied complicity in the murder.* —see also ACCOMPLICE

com·pli·ment¹ /'kɒmplɨmənt‖'kɑːm-/ n [(**on**)] an expression of praise, admiration, or respect: *He was showered with compliments on his excellent performance.* | *They paid her the compliment of making her an honorary member.* | *She said how nice my dress was, so I returned the compliment and said I liked hers.* —see also COMPLIMENTS, **fish for compliments** (FISH² (4))

com·pli·ment² /'kɒmplɨment‖'kɑːm-/ v [T (**on**)] to praise with a compliment: *John complimented Jean (on her new dress).* | *I must compliment you on the way you handled the meeting.* —compare COMPLEMENT, FLATTER (1)

com·pli·men·ta·ry /ˌkɒmplɨ'mentəri◂‖ˌkɑːm-/ adj **1** expressing admiration, praise, respect, etc.: *complimentary remarks* | *My boss was very complimentary about my work.* —opposite **uncomplimentary** **2** [*no comp.*] given free as a favour or out of respect: *complimentary tickets for the theatre*

com·pli·ments /'kɒmplɨmənts‖'kɑːm-/ n [P] good wishes: *That was an excellent dinner — my compliments to the chef!*

compliment slip /'··· ˌ·/ n a piece of paper with a company's name and address on it which is sent out with other papers, etc., instead of a proper letter —compare COVERING LETTER

com·pline , **-plin** /'kɒmplɨn‖'kɑːm-/ n [U] *tech (often cap.)* (esp. in the Roman Catholic Church) the last religious service held in the evening —compare EVENSONG, VESPERS

com·ply /kəm'plaɪ/ v [I (**with**)] *fml* to act in accordance with a demand, rule, etc.: *He reluctantly complied with their wishes.* | *The factory was closed for failing to comply with government safety regulations.* —see also COMPLIANCE

com·po·nent /kəm'pəʊnənt/ n any of the parts that together make a whole machine or system: *the components/component parts of a camera* | *Revenues from oil are the biggest single component in the country's income.* —compare CONSTITUENT¹ (2)

com·port /kəm'pɔːt‖-ɔːrt/ v [T+obj+adv/prep] *fml, often pomp* to behave (oneself) in the stated way: *She comported herself well.*

com·port·ment /kəm'pɔːtmənt‖-ɔːr-/ n [U] *fml, often pomp* behaviour; manner

com·pose /kəm'pəʊz/ v **1** [I;T] to write or produce (music, poetry, etc.): *to compose a symphony/(fml) a letter* | *This piece of music was composed for the piano.* —see also COMPOSER, COMPOSITION **2** [T] to make (esp. oneself) calm, quiet, etc.: *Jean was nervous at first but soon composed herself.* | *She remained perfectly composed throughout the trial.* —see also COMPOSURE **3** *fml* to settle (a point of disagreement): *The two leaders soon composed their differences and became friends.* **4** [T] *tech* (in printing) to form (words, sentences, pages, etc.) ready for printing —see also COMPOSITOR **5 be composed of** to be formed from (the stated parts): *Water is composed of hydrogen and oxygen.* —see also DECOMPOSE; see COMPRISE (USAGE)

com·pos·er /kəm'pəʊzəʳ/ n a person who writes music: *Beethoven, Mozart, and all the great classical composers* —compare MUSICIAN

com·pos·ite /'kɒmpəzɨt‖kɑːm'pɑː-/ n **1** something made up of different parts or materials **2** *AmE for* IDENTIKIT —**composite** adj [A] : *a composite picture*

com·po·si·tion /ˌkɒmpə'zɪʃən‖ˌkɑːm-/ n **1** [U] the act of composing music, poetry, etc.: *He played a piece of music of his own composition.* (=which he had composed) **2** [C] a piece of music or art, or a poem: *This is one of Bach's later compositions.* **3** [C;U (**of**)] (the arrangement of) the various parts from which something is made up: *scientific instruments for analyzing the chemical composition of plants* | *changes in the composition of the committee as a result of the election* **4** [C] an ESSAY (=a short piece of writing) done as an educational exercise **5** [U] *tech* the arrangement of or process of arranging words, sentences, pages, etc., for printing

com·pos·i·tor /kəm'pɒzɨtəʳ‖-'pɑː-/ n a person who arranges words, sentences, pages, etc., ready for printing

com·pos men·tis /ˌkɒmpəs 'mentɨs‖ˌkɑːm-/ adj [F] *esp. law* able to think clearly and be responsible for one's actions —opposite **non compos mentis**

com·post¹ /'kɒmpɒst‖'kɑːmpəʊst/ n [U] a mixture of decayed plant matter, such as grass or leaves, used for making the soil richer

compost² v [T] to put compost on or make compost from

compost heap /'·· ·/ n a place, usu. in a garden, where plant matter is piled up to make compost

com·po·sure /kəm'pəʊʒəʳ/ n [U] calmness; a steady unworried manner or state of mind: *Keep calm: don't lose your composure!* —see also COMPOSE (2)

com·pote /'kɒmpɒt, -pəʊt‖'kɑːmpəʊt/ n [C;U] fruit cooked in sweetened water and usu. eaten cold

com·pound¹ /'kɒmpaʊnd‖'kɑːm-/ n **1** a combination of two or more parts, substances, etc., esp. a chemical substance consisting of at least two different simple substances (ELEMENTS) combined so as to have qualities different from those of the substances from which it is made: *Sulphur dioxide (SO_2) is a compound made from sulphur and oxygen.* | *natural compounds* —compare MIXTURE (1) **2** a compound word

compound² adj **1** (of a single whole) consisting of two or more parts, substances, etc.: *an insect's compound eye* | *a compound leaf* (=made of several small leaves joined to one stem) **2** *tech* (of a word or sentence) consisting of two or more main parts: *"Childcare" is a compound*

word consisting of the two main parts "child" and "care". —compare COMPLEX¹ (3), SIMPLE (3)

com·pound³ /kəm'paʊnd/ v [T] **1** [often pass.] to make worse by adding to or increasing; EXACERBATE: *Our difficulties were compounded by the language barrier.* | *to compound an error* **2** [(from, of)] to make (a substance or quality) by combining parts: *The medicine was compounded from several drugs.* **3** [(into)] to combine (parts) to form a whole: *He compounded the drugs into a medicine.*

com·pound⁴ /'kɒmpaʊnd‖'kɑːm-/ n an area enclosed by a wall, fence, etc., containing a group of buildings: *a factory/prison compound*

compound frac·ture /ˌ‥ '‥/ n med a break or crack in a bone which causes it to cut through the surrounding flesh, making an open wound —compare SIMPLE FRACTURE

compound in·terest /ˌ‥ '‥/ n [U] interest calculated both on the original sum of money lent or borrowed and on the unpaid interest already earned or charged —compare SIMPLE INTEREST

com·pre·hend /ˌkɒmprɪ'hend‖ˌkɑːm-/ v [not in progressive forms] fml **1** [I;T] to understand: *The child read the story but did not comprehend its full meaning.* **2** [T] to include: *The park comprehends all the land on the other side of the river.*

com·pre·hen·si·ble /ˌkɒmprɪ'hensˌbəl‖ˌkɑːm-/ adj [(to)] fml that can be understood: *a long, scarcely comprehensible report written in official language* | *This document is comprehensible only to lawyers.* —opposite **incomprehensible** —**·bly** adv —**·bility** /ˌkɒmprɪhensˌ'bɪlˌti‖ˌkɑːm-/ n [U]

com·pre·hen·sion /ˌkɒmprɪ'henʃən‖ˌkɑːm-/ n [U (of)] fml the act of understanding or ability to understand: *How he managed it is beyond my comprehension* (=I cannot understand it). | *The teacher set the class a comprehension test.* (=to test the students' ability to understand written or spoken language)

com·pre·hen·sive¹ /ˌkɒmprɪ'hensɪv‖ˌkɑːm-/ adj **1** thorough; broad; including a lot or everything: *a newspaper that provides comprehensive coverage of world affairs* | *a comprehensive knowledge of his subject* | *comprehensive insurance* **2** [no comp.] BrE (of education) teaching pupils of all abilities in the same school: *the controversy over comprehensive education in the sixties* – **~ ly** adv

comprehensive² also **comprehensive school** /ˌ‥·'‥· ·/— n (in Britain) a school for pupils over the age of 11 which teaches children of all abilities.

► CULTURAL NOTE The **comprehensive system** was introduced in 1965 and largely replaced the old system of GRAMMAR SCHOOLs and SECONDARY MODERNs, which took pupils depending on whether they had passed or failed an exam called the ELEVEN-PLUS. There was great public argument about the change. Some people were afraid that the standard of education in Britain would fall. Others felt strongly that it was unfair to separate children out at the age of 11. Over 80% of British pupils now attend comprehensive schools. Although in most parts of Britain there is now no examination at 11, children are often put in groups according to their level of ability at a comprehensive: *I considered public school for my son, but in the end decided to send him to the local comprehensive.* —compare GRAMMAR SCHOOL, PUBLIC SCHOOL, SECONDARY MODERN ◄

com·press¹ /kəm'pres/ v [T (into)] **1** to force (a substance) into less space; press together: *compressed air* **2** to put (thoughts, ideas, etc.) into fewer words: *He compressed his report into three pages.* — **~ible** adj : *a compressible gas* — **~ion** /'preʃən/ n [U] : *a compression chamber*

com·press² /'kɒmpres‖'kɑːm-/ n a small thick mass of cloth pressed to part of the body, esp. to stop bleeding or swelling, reduce fever, etc.: *She applied a cold compress to his sprained ankle.*

com·pres·sor /kəm'presᵊr/ n a part of a machine, for compressing gas or air

com·prise /kəm'praɪz/ v [not in progressive forms] **1** [L+n] to consist of (parts): *The United Kingdom comprises England, Wales, Scotland, and Northern Ireland.* | *a commission of inquiry comprising three eminent judges and three members of the public.* **2** [T] (of parts) to form: *Fifteen separate republics comprise the Soviet Union.*

▷ USAGE Compare **comprise, compose, consist of, constitute,** and **include**: *The United Kingdom consists of/is composed of/comprises England, Wales, Scotland, and Northern Ireland.* (=these are all the parts that together form it) | *England, Wales, Scotland, and Northern Ireland* **constitute/comprise** (=together form) *the United Kingdom.* | *The United Kingdom* **includes** *Northern Ireland and Wales.* (=these are two of the parts that together form the United Kingdom, but there are others) **Be comprised of** is sometimes used in the sense of '**consists of**': *A chess set is comprised of 32 chessmen,* but some people consider this use to be incorrect.◁

com·pro·mise¹ /'kɒmprəmaɪz‖'kɑːm-/ n [C;U (between)] (an act of) settling an argument or difference of opinion by each side agreeing to some of the demands of the other; an agreement reached in this way that is acceptable to both sides: *Progress has been made towards a political compromise between the two nations.* | *He asked £1500 for his old car, but I thought it was only worth £1000. We finally reached/arrived at a compromise and I paid £1250.* | *Both sides are determined to get what they want, and there seems to be no possiblity of compromise.*

compromise² v **1** [I (on)] to make a compromise: *He asked more than I was willing to pay, so we compromised on a price.* **2** [T] to put into a dishonourable position; bring shame to: *They refused to compromise their principles by doing a deal with the terrorists.* | *The minister was compromised by his association with the prostitute.*

com·pro·mis·ing /'kɒmprəmaɪzɪŋ‖'kɑːm-/ adj [A] dishonourable and making one feel very ashamed: *You have put me in a very compromising position.* | *She found some compromising photographs in his wallet.*

Comp·ton /'kʌmptən/, **Den·is** /'denˌs/ (1918–) an English cricketer and footballer

comp·trol·ler /kən'trəʊləᵊr, kəmp-/ n fml (an official title for) a CONTROLLER (2)

com·pul·sion /kəm'pʌlʃən/ n **1** [U] force or influence that makes a person do something: [+to-v] *You are under no compulsion to tell me, but it will be better for you if you do.* —see also COMPEL **2** [C] a strong desire, usu. an unreasonable one, that is difficult to control: [+to-v] *She felt a sudden compulsion to hit him.*

com·pul·sive /kəm'pʌlsɪv/ adj **1** resulting from a compulsion; very difficult to stop or control: *a compulsive need to succeed* | *compulsive eating* **2** suffering from one or more compulsions: *a compulsive gambler* – **~ ly** adv – **~ ness** n [U]

compulsive shop·per /·ˌ· '‥/ a SPENDAHOLIC

com·pul·so·ry /kəm'pʌlsəri/ adj which must be done by law, by orders, etc.; OBLIGATORY: *Education is compulsory for all children in Britain between the ages of 5 and 16.* | *a campaign to make the wearing of car seat belts compulsory* —compare VOLUNTARY¹ (1) —**rily** adv

com·punc·tion /kəm'pʌŋkʃən/ n [U usu. in questions and negatives] an awkward feeling of guilt that stops one doing something: *She didn't have the slightest compunction about telling me a lie.*

com·pu·ta·tion /ˌkɒmpjʊ'teɪʃən‖ˌkɑː-/ also **computations** pl.– n [C;U] fml (the result of) calculating: *According to my computation(s), the bank should pay me £100 interest.*

com·pute /kəm'pjuːt/ v [I;T] fml to calculate (a result, answer, sum, etc.)

com·put·er /kəm'pjuːtəʳ/ n an electronic machine that can be supplied with a PROGRAM (=plan of operations) and can store and recall information, and perform various processes on it. A computer is now a standard piece of office equipment, often used by all members of STAFF, esp. as a WORD PROCESSOR: *We use a computer to do our accounts.* | *a home/personal computer* | *the most up-to-date computer software* | *a new computer-controlled heating system* | *I sent the sample for computer analysis.* —see also MAINFRAME, MICROCOMPUTER, MINICOMPUTER, PERSONAL COMPUTER, WORD PROCESSOR

computer-aid·ed de·sign /·ˌ· ··· '·ˌ·/ also **CAD** – n [U] the use of COMPUTER GRAPHICS in industry as part of the process of planning how to make such things as cars, aircraft, buildings, and electronic equipment: *a computer-aided design system*

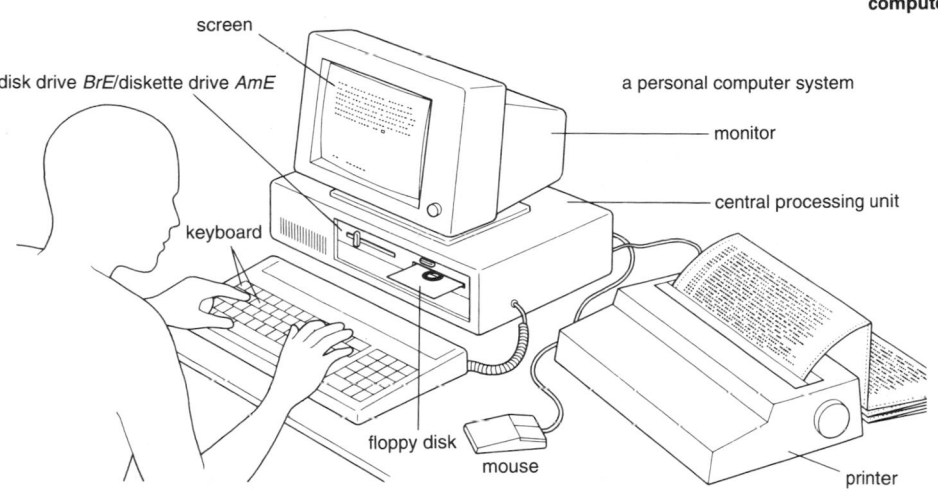

screen

disk drive *BrE*/diskette drive *AmE*

a personal computer system

monitor

central processing unit

keyboard

floppy disk

mouse

printer

computer dat·ing a·gen·cy /·,·· '·· ,···/ *n* a DATING AGENCY that uses computers to find partners for people

computer game /·'·· ,·/ *n* a game played on a computer, often in which the player takes part in an imaginary story and tries to destroy enemies or save people from danger

computer graph·ics /·,·· '··/ *n* [P] information in the form of images which can be stored, changed, or OUTPUT by a computer. As well as being used in industry, computer graphics are thought by some people to be a modern art form.

computer hack·er /·,·· '··/ *n* [C] see HACKER

com·put·er·ize also **-ise** *BrE* /kəm'pjuːtəraɪz/ *v* [I;T] to use or begin to use a computer to control (an operation, system, etc.): *The firm has decided to computerize its wages department.* | *Our firm computerized years ago!* | *computerized criminal records* **—ization** /kəm,pjuːtərɑɪ'zeɪʃən‖-rə-/ *n* [U]

computer mo·del·ling /·,·· '···/ *n* [U] the building of a picture of an object on a computer so that it can be looked at from any angle. It is esp. used in the planning of such things as cars, buildings, etc., and when information collected by other machines, e.g. in outer space, is needed in a form that people can see.

computer pro·gram·mer /·,·· '···/ *n* a person whose job is to PROGRAM²(1) computers

computer sci·ence /·,·· '··/ *n* [U] the study of computers and what they can do, often as a main subject: *a computer science major/degree* | *She studied computer science at Cornell.*

computer vi·rus /·,·· '··/ *n* a PROGRAM (=plan of operations) secretly introduced into a computer which makes copies of itself and often damages other programs on the computer, including the OPERATING SYSTEM. They are introduced by electronic VANDALs or e.g. by a worker who has some reason to be angry with the company, and begin to operate at a particular signal, e.g. a name or a date.

com·put·ing /kəm'pjuːtɪŋ/ *n* [U] the act or job of working with computers

com·rade /'kɒmrɪd, -reɪd‖'kɑːmræd/ *n* **1** *fml* a close companion, esp. a person who shares difficult work or danger: *his comrades in the navy* —compare COMPANION, PARTNER **2** (esp. used as a title in Communist countries or among LEFT-WING groups) a fellow member of a union, political party, etc.: *Comrades, please support this motion.*| *Comrade Gorbachev* — **~ly** *adj*

comrade in arms /,·· '·/ *n* **comrades in arms** (in the military) someone who fights on the same side as oneself: *(fig) We're comrades in arms on the local council.*

com·rade·ship /'kɒmrɪdʃɪp, -reɪd-‖'kɑːmræd-/ *n* [U] *fml* companionship; friendship

coms /kɒmz‖kɑːmz/ *n* [P] *infml for* **1** COMBINATIONS **2** COMMUNICATIONS

con¹ /kɒn‖kɑːn/ *v* -**nn**- [T (**into, out of**)] *infml* **1** to trick (a trusting person), usu. in order to make money: *I'm afraid you've been conned.* | *They've conned me out of £5!* **2** to persuade, esp. by deceit: *He conned me into doing all his work for him.*

con² *n infml* a trick, esp. a CONFIDENCE TRICK —see also MOD CON, PROS AND CONS

con³ *n sl* a prisoner; CONVICT —see also EX-CON

con⁴ *v* -**nn**- [T] *old use* to study or examine (something) very carefully in order to learn it

Con *written abbrev. for:* CONSERVATIVE PARTY

Co·nan Doyle /,kəʊnən 'dɔɪl/, **Sir Arthur** (1859–1930) a British doctor and writer who wrote stories about the famous DETECTIVE Sherlock Holmes —see also Sherlock HOLMES, HOUND OF THE BASKERVILLES

con·art·ist /'· ··/ *n infml* someone who tricks or deceives people in a criminal way, usu. in order to get money from them

conc *written abbrev. for* CONCESSIONARY

con·cat·e·nate /kɒn'kætɪneɪt‖kɑːn-/ *v* [T] *fml or tech* to join together as in a chain **—nation** /kɒn,kætɪ'neɪʃən‖kɑːn-/ *n* [C;U] : *a concatenation of events* (=a set of events coming one after the other)

con·cave /,kɒn'keɪv◂, kən-‖,kɑːn'keɪv◂, kən-/ *adj* curved inwards, like the inside surface of a hollow ball: *a concave mirror* —opposite **convex**

con·cav·i·ty /kɒn'kævɪti/ *n fml* **1** [U] the state of being concave **2** [C] a concave place or shape

con·ceal /kən'siːl/ *v* [T (**from**)] *rather fml* to hide; keep from being seen or known: *He concealed his feelings/his debts from his wife.* | *He was found to be carrying a concealed weapon.* | *She tried to conceal how she felt.*

con·ceal·ment /kən'siːlmənt/ *n* [U] *fml* **1** the act of concealing: *Concealment of evidence is a criminal offence.* **2** the state of being concealed: *The criminals stayed in concealment* (=hidden) *until the police had passed.*

con·cede /kən'siːd/ *v* [T] **1** to admit as true, correct, or proper, often unwillingly: *The government conceded defeat as soon as the election results were known.* [+*that*] *I'm willing to concede that he's a good runner, but I still think I can beat him.* | *I concede that particular point, but I still think you're wrong.* **2** [(**to**)] to give as a right or PRIVILEGE: *After the First World War Germany conceded a lot of land (to her neighbours).* **3** to allow by accident; used esp. in newspapers: *Despite conceding a goal in the first five minutes, the Cowboys went on to win the game.* —see also CONCESSION

con·ceit /kən'siːt/ *n* **1** [U] also **con·ceit·ed·ness** /kən'siːtɪdnɪs/— too high an opinion of one's own abilities, value, importance, etc. **2** [C] *tech* an unusual, cleverly expressed, but not very serious comparison, esp. in poetry: *the use of conceits in Elizabethan poetry*

con·ceit·ed /kən'siːtɪd/ *adj* having too high an opinion of oneself; extremely proud of oneself or pleased with oneself: *I don't want to sound conceited, but I think my new book might be a best-seller.* — ~**ly** *adv*

con·cei·va·ble /kən'siːvəbəl/ *adj* that can be believed; imaginable: *It is just conceivable that he'll win, but it's very unlikely really.* | *What conceivable reason could they have for doing such a crazy thing?* —opposite **inconceivable** —**bly** *adv*

con·ceive /kən'siːv/ *v* **1** [T] to form an idea of; think of; imagine: *Scientists first conceived the idea of the atomic bomb in the 1930s.* [+*wh*-] *I can't conceive why you told her.* (=I don't understand, because it was not a sensible thing to do) —see PERCEIVE (USAGE) **2** [I;T] *esp. tech or bibl* to become PREGNANT with (a child): *The baby was conceived in March and born in December.* | (fig.) *He conceived a violent hatred of his captors.* —see also CONCEPTION
conceive of sthg. *phr v* [T (**as**)] to think of; imagine: *In ancient times the world was conceived of as flat.* [+*v*-ing] *It's difficult to conceive of living without electricity.* —see also CONCEPTION

con·cen·trate¹ /'kɒnsəntreɪt‖'kɑːn-/ *v* **1** [I;T (**on, upon**)] to direct (one's thoughts, efforts, attention, etc.) towards a particular activity or purpose: *I can't concentrate (on my work) when I'm hungry.* | *The terrorists concentrated their activities on the main supply routes.* | *This year the company has concentrated on improving its efficiency.* **2** [I+*adv*/*prep*;T+*obj*+*adv*/*prep*] to (cause to) come together in or around one place: *Industrial development is being concentrated in the south of the country.* | *The crowds concentrated round the palace.* **3** [T] *tech* to make (esp. a liquid) stronger by removing some of the water from it

concentrate² *n* [C;U] a concentrated material or liquid: *orange juice concentrate*

con·cen·trat·ed /'kɒnsəntreɪtɪd‖'kɑːn-/ *adj* **1** increased in strength by the removal of liquid or the addition of more of a substance: *concentrated orange juice* **2** [A] showing concentration and determination: *He has made a concentrated effort to improve his work.* | *a concentrated mind*

con·cen·tra·tion /ˌkɒnsən'treɪʃən‖ˌkɑːn-/ *n* **1** [U] the direction of attention towards a single thing, idea, subject, etc.: *Her work as a simultaneous translator requires strong powers of concentration.* | *I lost my concentration and nearly drove into a bridge* | *poor concentration* **2** [C;U] a close gathering: *There is a concentration of industry in the south of the country.* | *the increasing concentration of power in central government* **3** [S] *tech* the measure of the amount of a substance contained in a liquid: *a high concentration of sulphuric acid*

concentration camp /ˌ··'·· ·/ *n* a large enclosed area where political prisoners or people considered as threats to the state are imprisoned. During the Second World War the Nazis sent many millions of people, esp. Jews, to concentration camps, where more than six million people were killed: *Both his parents died in the concentration camps.* —see also AUSCHWITZ, HOLOCAUST

con·cen·tric /kən'sentrɪk/ *adj* [(**with**)] *tech* having the same centre: *concentric circles*

con·cept /'kɒnsept‖'kɑːn-/ *n* [(**of**)] a thought, idea, or principle; NOTION: *It is difficult to grasp the concept of infinite space.*

con·cep·tion /kən'sepʃən/ *n* **1** [C;U (**of**)] (a) general understanding; idea: *He's got a pretty strange conception of friendship.* | *You've no conception of what it was like to be there.* **2** [U] the act of forming an idea, plan, etc.: *The conception of the book took five minutes, but writing it took a year.* **3** [C;U] *tech* the starting of a new life by the union of a male and a female sex cell

con·cep·tu·al /kən'septʃuəl/ *adj fml* of or based on the formation of concepts: *the conceptual framework of the play* — ~**ly** *adv*

conceptual art /·ˌ···'·/ *n* [U] *tech* art in which the artist intends to describe an idea rather than make an art object

con·cep·tu·al·ize also **-ise** *BrE* /kən'septʃuəlaɪz/ *v* [I;T] to form a concept (of)

con·cern¹ /kən'sɜːn‖-'sɜːrn/ *v* [T *not usu. in progressive forms*]

1 [*no pass.*] to be about: *This article concerns a man who was wrongly imprisoned.* **2** to be of importance or interest to; have an effect on: *These problems concern all of us.* | *This regulation doesn't concern you, so don't worry about it.* | **To whom it may concern** ... (=the beginning of a letter that anyone may read) **3** [(**about, with**)] to worry or interest (esp. oneself): *It isn't your problem — don't concern yourself with it.*

concern² *n* **1** [C] a matter that is of interest or importance to someone: *"I'm only worried about your school work,"* said the teacher. *"Your private life isn't my concern."* | *a policy that fails to address* (=deal with) *the concerns of ethnic minorities* | *How much money I earn is none of your concern*/*is no concern of yours.* **2** [C;U (**for, about**)] worry; anxiety: *There is no cause for concern; your son's accident was not too serious.* | *a matter of considerable public concern* | *a teacher's concern for his students* | *The report expressed serious*/*grave concern about the doctor's competence.* **3** [C] a business company; ENTERPRISE: *It was two years before the business was a going concern.* (=a successful operation) | *The restaurant is a family concern.*

con·cerned /kən'sɜːnd‖-'sɜːr-/ *adj* **1** [(**about, for**)] anxious; worried: *He has never been very concerned about what other people think of him.* | *The children's mother was very concerned for their safety when they didn't come back from school at the usual time.* | *Concerned parents approached the school about the problem.* —see NERVOUS (USAGE) **2** [F (**for**)] having an active personal interest; SOLICITOUS: *I am concerned for their happiness.* [+*to-v*/*that*] *She's most concerned to solve this problem*/*that this problem should be solved.* —see also UNCONCERNED **3** [F (**in**);after *n*] having something to do with; taking part: *Everyone who was concerned in the affair regrets it very much.* | *I have enjoyed my visit very much, and would like to thank all (the people) concerned.* | *I'll pass on your comments to the people concerned.* **4 as far as I'm**/**you're, etc., concerned** to the degree that it has an influence on or matters to me/you, etc.: *As far as we're concerned you can go whenever you want.* (=We don't mind when you go.) | *As far as I'm concerned* (=in my opinion) *the whole idea is crazy.* **5 be concerned with** to be about: *This story is concerned with a Russian family in the 19th century.* **6 where something is concerned** in matters that have an effect on something: *Where money is concerned, I always try to be very careful.*

con·cern·ed·ly /kən'sɜːnɪdli‖-'sɜːr-/ *adv* in a concerned way

con·cern·ing /kən'sɜːnɪŋ‖-'sɜːr-/ *prep rather fml* about; with regard to; in connection with: *Concerning your request, I am pleased to inform you that* ... | *Police are anxious to hear any information concerning his whereabouts.*

con·cert /'kɒnsət‖'kɑːnsərt/ *n* **1** a performance given by a number of musicians: *to attend a concert of Vivaldi's music* | *record crowds at Elton John's concert on Saturday* | *tickets for a pop concert* —compare RECITAL (1) **2 in concert: a** *fml* working together; in agreement: *The various governments decided to act in concert over this matter.* **b** playing or singing at a concert: *We went to see Cliff Richard in concert at the Palladium.*

con·cert·ed /kən'sɜːtɪd‖-'sɜːr-/ *adj* planned or done together by agreement; combined: *The European governments made a concerted effort to stop drug smuggling.* — ~**ly** *adv*

con·cert·go·er /'kɒnsət̬ˌgəʊəʳ‖'kɑːnsərt-/ *n* a person who often goes to concerts

concert grand /ˌ··'·/ *n* a piano of the largest size, played esp. at concerts

concert hall /'·· ·/ *n* a large public building where esp. concerts are performed

con·cer·ti·na¹ /ˌkɒnsə'tiːnə‖ˌkɑːnsər-/ *n* a small musical instrument of the ACCORDION family, held and played in the hands by pressing in from each side

concertina² *v* **-naed, -naing** [I] *BrE infml* (of a vehicle) to become pressed together like a concertina as the result of a crash: *The lorry concertinaed when it hit the wall.*

con·cert·mas·ter /'kɒnsət̬ˌmɑːstəʳ‖'kɑːnsərtˌmæs-/ *n AmE for* LEADER (3)

con·cer·to /kən'tʃɜːtəʊ‖-'tʃertəʊ/ *n* **-tos** a piece of music for one or more SOLO instruments and ORCHESTRA

concert pitch /'·· ˌ·/ *n* [U] **1** *tech* the PITCH (=the degree of highness or lowness of sound) used as the standard for all musical instruments **2 at concert pitch (for)** *BrE* in a state of complete, and perhaps anxious, readiness and fitness: *After all the briefing sessions at head office, our sales team is at concert pitch.*

con·ces·sion /kənˈseʃən/ n **1** [C] a point, right, etc., given or allowed, esp. unwillingly or after a disagreement: *She wouldn't let her son have a motorbike, but as a concession she offered to give him some money towards a car.* | *The President pledged never to make concessions to terrorists.* —see also CONCEDE **2** [U] *fml* the act of giving or allowing something as a right: *The law includes special concessions for certain religious groups.* **3** [C] a right given by a government, an owner of land, etc., to perform some type of business activity in a place or property belonging to the giver of the right: *oil concessions in the North Sea* [+*to-v*] *He's won a concession to sell food in the town hall* **4** [C] *BrE infml* a person who is given a concessionary price: *Admission £2. Concessions £1.* —see also CONCESSIONS

con·ces·sion·aire /kənˌseʃəˈneəʳ/ n *infml* someone who has been given a CONCESSION (3)

con·ces·sion·ar·y /kənˈseʃənəri‖-neri/ adj *BrE* **1** given as a concession **2** *BrE* (of the price of something) specially reduced. Concessionary prices are given to certain groups of people with little money, e.g. PENSIONERS and students, for various things, e.g. travel or entry to a theatre or cinema.

con·ces·sions /kənˈseʃənz/ n [P] *AmE* the goods available from a CONCESSION STAND

concession stand /·ˈ·· ˌ·/ n *AmE* a small business that sells food and drinks or SOUVENIRS at a sporting event, cinema, theatre, or tourist attraction: *You can get hot dogs at the concession stand over there.*

concessive clause /kənˌsesɪv ˈklɔːz/ n a CLAUSE, often introduced by *although*, which shows willingness to CONCEDE (=to admit) a point that goes against the main argument of a sentence: *The sentence "Although it's old, it still works well", begins with a concessive clause.*

conch /kɒntʃ, kɒŋk‖-/ n (the large twisted shell of) a SNAIL-like tropical sea animal

con·chie , **conchy** /ˈkɒnʃi‖ˈkɑːn-/ n *derog, esp. BrE* a CONSCIENTIOUS OBJECTOR

con·chol·o·gy /kɒŋˈkɒlədʒi‖kɑːŋˈkɑː-/ n [U] *tech* the scientific study of shells and the animals that live in them —gist *n*

con·ci·erge /ˌkɒnsiˈeəʒ‖ˌkɑːnsiˈeəʒ/ n *Fr* **1** (esp. in France) a person who looks after the entrance to a block of flats **2** *esp. AmE* a person working in a hotel who looks after the special needs of guests

con·cil·i·ate /kənˈsɪlieɪt/ v [T] *fml* to win the support or friendly feelings of (someone), removing the anger or distrust they felt before —ator *n*

con·cil·i·a·tion /kənˌsɪliˈeɪʃən/ n [U] the act or process of conciliating: *The government ignored the union's attempts at conciliation.*

conciliation ser·vice /·ˌ··ˈ·· ˌ··/ n *BrE* an organization which tries to bring about agreement between the opposite sides when there is an industrial disagreement: *The conciliation service failed to resolve the dispute between management and the union.* —see also ACAS

con·cil·i·a·to·ry /kənˈsɪliətəri‖-tɔːri/ adj trying to conciliate or intended to conciliate: *a conciliatory gesture/attitude*

con·cise /kənˈsaɪs/ adj short and clear; expressing a lot in a few words: *a concise explanation/book/speaker* — ~ly *adv*

con·ci·sion /kənˈsɪʒən/ also **con·cise·ness** /kənˈsaɪsnəs/— n [U] the quality of being concise: *the clarity and concision of his account*

con·clave /ˈkɒŋkleɪv‖ˈkɑːn-/ n [C **(of)**+*sing./pl. v*] a private, secret meeting: *A conclave of cardinals was held to elect the new Pope.* | *The ministers sat/met* **in conclave** *to consider the matter.*

con·clude /kənˈkluːd/ v *rather fml* **1** [I;T **(by, with)**] to (cause to) come to an end: *We concluded the meeting at 8 o'clock with a prayer/by saying a prayer.* **2** [T+*that*; *obj; not in progressive forms*] to come to believe after consideration of known facts; reach a decision or judgment (that): *The inquiry concluded that the accident had been caused*

by human error. **3** [T **(with)**] to arrange or settle (something), often after long talking or argument: *to conclude an agreement/a sale*

con·clu·sion /kənˈkluːʒən/ n **1** [C] a judgment or decision reached after consideration: *These are the report's main conclusions.* | *What conclusions did you come to/draw/reach?* [+*that*] *She came to the conclusion that he had forgotten.* | *Be careful not to* **jump to conclusions.** (=form a judgment too quickly) **2** [C] the end; closing part: *I found the conclusion of his book very interesting.* | **In conclusion** (=as the last thing), *I should like to say how much I have enjoyed myself.* **3** [U **(of)**] the arrangement or settlement of something, such as a business deal: *the conclusion of a peace treaty* —see also FOREGONE CONCLUSION

con·clu·sive /kənˈkluːsɪv/ adj putting an end to doubt or uncertainty: *a conclusive argument* | *conclusive evidence* | *proof that he was the murderer* —opposite **inconclusive** — ~ly *adv* : *This proves conclusively that she was telling the truth.*

con·coct /kənˈkɒkt‖-ˈkɑːkt/ v [T] **1** to make (something) by mixing or combining parts: *Jean concocted a splendid meal from the leftovers.* **2** to invent (something false) so as to deceive: *John concocted an elaborate excuse for being late.*

con·coc·tion /kənˈkɒkʃən‖-ˈkɑːk-/ n something concocted: *They gave me a very strange concoction to drink.*

con·com·i·tant¹ /kənˈkɒmɪtənt‖-ˈkɑː-/ adj [**(with)**] *fml* existing or happening together with something else: *war with all its concomitant sufferings* — ~ly *adv*

concomitant² n [**(of)**] *fml* something that often or naturally goes with something else: *Deafness is a frequent concomitant of old age.*

con·cord /ˈkɒŋkɔːd‖ˈkɑːŋkɔːrd/ n [U] **1** *fml* friendly relationship; peace and agreement: *These neighbouring states had lived in concord for centuries.* —compare DISCORD **2** *tech* (in grammar) agreement between words, esp. between a verb and the subject of a sentence

con·cord·ance /kənˈkɔːdəns‖-ɔːr-/ n *tech* an alphabetical list of all the words used in a book or collection of books by one writer, with information about where they can be found and usu. about how they are used: *a Shakespeare concordance*

con·cor·dant /kənˈkɔːdənt‖-ɔːr-/ adj [**(with)**] *fml* being in agreement or of the same regular pattern

con·cor·dat /kɒnˈkɔːdæt‖kɑːnˈkɔːr-/ n *tech* an agreement between separate groups, esp. between the church and a state on religious matters

Concorde

Con·corde /ˈkɒŋkɔːd‖ˈkɑːŋkɔːrd/ a passenger aircraft with a long pointed front. It is the fastest of all passenger aircraft and flies at twice the speed of sound. Since 1976, both British Airways and Air France have offered passenger flights on Concorde, which are expensive but considered to be PRESTIGIOUS: *He likes to travel in style, so he's going on Concorde.*

con·course /ˈkɒŋkɔːs‖ˈkɑːŋkɔːrs/ n **1** a hall or open place where passages or roads meet and crowds of people can gather: *the airport concourse* **2** an act of coming or happening together: *a large concourse of people*

con·crete¹ /ˈkɒŋkriːt‖kɑːnˈkriːt/ adj **1** existing as something real or solid, rather than as an idea or something imagined in the mind: *A car is a concrete object, but speed is not.* | (fig.) *I need something a bit more concrete than an apology from you — how about some compensation?* | *The word "car" is a concrete noun.* —compare ABSTRACT¹ (1) **2** particular as opposed to general; clear; DEFINITE:

Have you got any concrete proposals as to what we should do? | *There's no concrete evidence of their guilt.* **3** made of concrete: *a concrete floor* − ~**ly** *adv*

con·crete² /ˈkɒŋkriːt‖ˈkɑːn-/ *n* [U] a building material made by mixing sand, very small stones, cement, and water: *reinforced concrete*

concrete³ *v* [T] to cover (a path, wall, etc.) with concrete: *They'd had their garden concreted over.*

concrete jun·gle /ˌ·· ˈ···/ *n* an unpleasant city area full of big ugly buildings and with no open spaces

concrete mix·er /ˈ·· ˌ··/ *n* a CEMENT MIXER

con·cu·bi·nage /kɒnˈkjuːbᵻnᵻdʒ‖kɑːn-/ *n* [U] *fml or tech* the practice of living together as husband and wife without being married

con·cu·bine /ˈkɒŋkjᵿbaɪn‖ˈkɑːŋ-/ *n* a woman who lives with and has sex with, but is not married to, an Eastern ruler: *The king had four wives and twenty concubines.*

con·cu·pis·cence /kɒnˈkjuːpᵻsəns‖kɑːn-/ *n* [U] *fml* sexual desire; LUST —**cent** *adj*

con·cur /kənˈkɜːʳ/ *v* -**rr**- [I] *fml* **1** [(with)] to agree; have the same opinion: *The two judges concurred (with one another) on the ruling.* **2** to happen at the same time; COINCIDE: [+*to-v*] *Everything concurred to produce the desired effect.*

con·cur·rence /kənˈkʌrəns‖-ˈkɜːr-/ *n fml* **1** [U] an agreement of opinion **2** [C (of)] an example of actions, events, etc., happening at the same time: *an interesting concurrence of events*

con·cur·rent /kənˈkʌrənt‖-ˈkɜːr-/ *adj* [(with)] **1** existing or happening at the same time: *He is serving two concurrent prison sentences.* (=two sentences intended to run at the same time) **2** *fml* in agreement: *My opinions are concurrent with yours.* − ~**ly** *adv* : *Three of his plays are running concurrently on Broadway.*

con·cuss /kənˈkʌs/ *v* [T *often pass.*] *esp. BrE* to cause concussion to: *The driver of the crashed car was badly concussed.*

con·cus·sion /kənˈkʌʃən/ *n* [U] damage to the brain (usu. not long-lasting) caused by a heavy blow, shock, or violent shaking: *The little boy fell out of a window and was taken to hospital suffering from concussion.*

con·demn /kənˈdem/ *v* [T] **1** [(as)] to express very strong disapproval of (someone or something): *Most people would condemn violence of any sort.* | *The law has been condemned by its opponents as an attack on personal liberty.* **2** [(to)] to state the punishment for (a guilty person), esp. a punishment of death or long imprisonment: *The prisoner was condemned to death.* | *the condemned man* [+*obj+to-v*] *The judge condemned her to spend six years in prison.* **3** [(to)] to force into an unhappy state or situation: *His bad leg condemned him to a wheelchair.* | *Her shyness condemned her to a life of loneliness.* **4** [(as)] to declare (something) officially unfit for use: *Although this house is condemned (as unfit), an old lady still lives here.* **5** to show the guilt of (a person): *His nervousness condemned him.*

con·dem·na·tion /ˌkɒndəmˈneɪʃən, -dem-‖ˌkɑːn-/ *n* [C;U (of)] (an example of) the act of condemning: *Condemnations of the terrorist bombing came from all over the world.* | *The congressmen were unanimous in their condemnation.*

condemned cell /·ˌ· ˈ·, ·ˈ· ·/ *n BrE* a room where prisoners who are to be punished by death are kept −see also DEATH ROW

con·den·sa·tion /ˌkɒndenˈseɪʃən, -dən-‖ˌkɑːn-/ *n* **1** [U (of)] *tech* the change from a gas to a liquid or, sometimes, to a solid: *the condensation of steam into water* **2** [U] small drops of liquid or solid formed in this way, esp. drops of water formed when steam becomes cool: *There was a lot of condensation on the windows.* **3** [C;U (of)] (an example or result of) the act of making something shorter

con·dense /kənˈdens/ *v* **1** [I;T] **a** (of a gas) to become liquid, or sometimes solid, esp. by becoming cooler **b** to cause (a gas) to do this **2** [T] to make (a liquid) thicker by removing some of the water: *condensed soup* **3** [T] to reduce (esp. something written) to a smaller or shortened form: *a condensed report*

condensed milk /·ˌ· ˈ·/ *BrE* ‖ **sweetened condensed milk** *AmE*— *n* [U] sweetened milk which is thickened by

taking away some of the water, and is usu. sold in tins −compare EVAPORATED MILK

con·dens·er /kənˈdensəʳ/ *n* **1** an apparatus that makes a gas change into a liquid **2** a CAPACITOR (=a machine for storing electricity, esp. in a car engine)

con·de·scend /ˌkɒndɪˈsend‖ˌkɑːn-/ *v* [I] **1** [+*to-v*] *usu. humor or derog* to do something unsuited to one's high social or professional position: *The managing director condescended to have lunch with us in the canteen.* **2** [(to)] *derog* to behave as though one is better or more important than others: *Mrs Harris is always so condescending − who does she think she is!* —**scension** /ˈsenʃən/ *n* [U]

con·dig·n /kənˈdaɪn/ *adj fml* (esp. of punishment) both severe and well deserved − ~**ly** *adv*

con·di·ment /ˈkɒndᵻmənt‖ˈkɑːn-/ *n fml* a powder or liquid used for giving a special taste to food: *Salt, ketchup, and pepper are condiments.*

con·di·tion¹ /kənˈdɪʃən/ *n* **1** [C (of)] a state of being or existence: *The astronauts soon got used to the condition of weightlessness.* | *(old use) people of every condition* (=every position in society) **2** [U] a state of general health, fitness, or readiness for use: *His car has been well maintained and is in excellent condition.* | *Archaeologists have discovered some ancient jewellery in almost perfect condition.* | *a neglected house in poor condition* | *Her condition is improving.* (=She is getting well again.) | *Sit still! You're in no condition to do anything.* | *He's out of condition because he never takes any exercise.* **3** [C (for, of)] something that is stated as necessary in order for something else to happen or exist: *They set|laid down strict conditions for letting us use their information.* | *The allies insist on free elections as a condition of their continued support.* | *Under the conditions of the agreement, the job must be completed by the end of the month.* [+*that*] *She will join us on one condition: that we divide all the profits equally.* | *I'll come on condition (that)* (=only if) *John is invited too.* −see also CONDITIONAL **4** [C] an illness of the stated kind or body part: *He has a heart condition.* **5** **on no condition** *BrE* never; in no situation: *This equipment should on no condition be used by untrained staff.* −see also CONDITIONS

condition² *v* [T] **1** to have a controlling or deciding effect on; DETERMINE: *What I can buy is conditioned by the amount I earn.* **2** [+*obj+to-v*] *tech or derog* to train to behave in a certain way in certain conditions: *Most people are conditioned to believe what they read in the papers.* −see also CONDITIONING **3** to put into good health or a good state for work or use: *Your dog looks very well conditioned.* | *a shampoo that conditions the hair* −see also AIR-CONDITIONING, CONDITIONER

con·di·tion·al¹ /kənˈdɪʃənəl/ *adj* [*no comp.*] **1** [(on, upon)] depending on a certain condition or conditions: *His agreement to buy our house was conditional on our leaving all the furniture in it.* | *a conditional acceptance* − opposite **unconditional** **2** (in grammar) expressing a condition or supposition: *A conditional clause often begins with the words "if" or "unless".* − ~**ly** *adv*

conditional² *n* (in grammar) a conditional form, esp. a sentence or CLAUSE

conditional dis·charge /·ˌ·ˌ··· ˈ···/ *n* a judgment made by a court which means that a person who has carried out a small crime is allowed to go without punishment as long as they obey certain conditions set by the court: *He was lucky to get a conditional discharge.* −compare SUSPENDED SENTENCE

conditioned re·flex /·ˌ·· ˈ···/ also **conditioned re·sponse** /·ˌ·· ·ˈ·/— *n tech* a REFLEX (=a movement which one has no power to prevent) that is developed as the result of repeated treatment or training: *a conditioned response to a stimulus*

con·di·tion·er /kənˈdɪʃənəʳ/ *n* [C;U] **1** a liquid put onto hair after washing to make it softer **2** also **fabric conditioner**— a liquid in which clothes, etc., are rinsed (RINSE) after being washed, to make them softer

con·di·tion·ing /kənˈdɪʃənɪŋ/ *n* [U] the process by which people or animals are trained to behave in a certain way in certain conditions −see also AIR-CONDITIONING

con·di·tions /kənˈdɪʃənz/ *n* [P] the situation at a particular place or surrounding facts and events; CIRCUMSTANCES:

The union has striven to improve our working conditions. | Under present conditions we cannot possibly increase our pay offer. | The fog and ice made driving conditions very bad. | What are housing conditions like in East London? | Conditions in the famine area have been described as "desperate".

▷ USAGE Compare **conditions** and **situation.** They can both mean "state of affairs; circumstances": *We are studying the economic* **conditions/situation** *in several developing countries.* **Conditions** here suggests matters which affect daily life such as food, work, and houses. **Situation** suggests more general matters such as government planning and FINANCE. **Conditions** often describes something that has stayed the same for some time, but **situation** may suggest a recent change: *weather conditions of the Arctic winter | the political situation in Eastern Europe*◁

con·do /ˈkɒndəʊ‖ˈkɑːn-/ *n AmE for* CONDOMINIUM

con·dole /kənˈdəʊl/ *v*
  condole with sbdy. *phr v* [T **(on, over)**] to express condolences to

con·do·lence /kənˈdəʊləns/ *n* [C *often pl*; U **(on)**] (an expression of) sympathy for someone who has experienced great sorrow, misfortune, etc.: *Please accept my condolences on your mother's death. | a letter of condolence —* compare COMMISERATION

con·dom /ˈkɒndəm‖ˈkɑː-, ˈkʌn-/ *also* **sheath, prophylactic** *esp. AmE— n* a covering, usu. of rubber, worn over the male sex organ during sex, used as a means of BIRTH CONTROL and protection against disease: *Oh no! The condom's split/burst.*

▶CULTURAL NOTE Since the appearance of the disease AIDS people have been encouraged to use condoms as a means of practising SAFE SEX and protecting themselves against AIDS and other diseases. Condoms can be bought at a CHEMIST's shop, or sometimes from a VENDING MACHINE, e.g. in the toilets in a bar or PUB. People often joke about men being embarrassed to ask for condoms in a shop, esp. if the assistant is a woman. There are various generally-known names for a condom which include a **French letter**, a **rubber**, (*BrE*) a **Durex**, and (*BrE old-fash*) a **Johnny**. The expression **a packet of three** is also sometimes used, meaning "a packet of condoms".◀

con·do·min·i·um /ˌkɒndəˈmɪniəm‖ˌkɑːn-/ *n* **1** [C] *AmE also* **condo** (a flat in) a block of flats of which each one is owned by the people living in it —see picture at HOUSE **2** [C;U] rule of a country by two or more other states acting together: *a country ruled in this way: the English-French condominium of the New Hebrides*

con·done /kənˈdəʊn/ *v* [T] to forgive (wrong behaviour); regard (a wrong action) as harmless or acceptable: *I cannot condone the use of violence under any circumstances.*

con·dor /ˈkɒndɔːʳ‖ˈkɑːndər, -dɔːr/ *n* a very large American VULTURE (=a bird that feeds on dead bodies)

con·duce /kənˈdjuːs‖-ˈduːs/ *v*
  conduce to/towards sthg. *phr v* [T] *fml* to help to produce; be conducive to

con·du·cive /kənˈdjuːsɪv‖-ˈduː-/ *adj* [F+to] *rather fml* likely to produce; helping (an esp. desirable result) to happen: *The atmosphere in the conference room was hardly conducive to frank and friendly discussions. | The friendly tone of the meeting seemed conducive to finding a solution to the problem. — ~ness n* [U **(to)**]

con·duct¹ /kənˈdʌkt/ *v* **1** [T] to go with and guide or lead: *The guide conducted us round the castle. | We went on a* **conducted tour** *of the cathedral.* **2** [T] to carry out or direct: *The business is conducted from small offices in the City. | The company conducted a survey to find out local reaction to the leisure centre. | The government is to conduct an inquiry into the incident.* **3** [T+obj+adv/prep] *fml* to behave (oneself): *I think he conducted himself admirably, considering the difficult circumstances.* **4** [I;T] to direct the playing of (musicians or a musical work) **5** [T] to act as the path for (electricity, heat, etc.): *Plastic and rubber won't conduct electricity, but copper will. —* see also CONDUCTOR

con·duct² /ˈkɒndʌkt, -dəkt‖ˈkɑːn-/ *n* [U] **1** *fml* behaviour: *The reporter was accused of unethical/unprofessional conduct. | a prize for good conduct* **2** [(**of**)] direction of the

course of (a business, activity, etc.): *dissatisfaction with the conduct of the war/the negotiations*

con·duc·tion /kənˈdʌkʃən/ *n* [U] the passage of electricity along wires, water through pipes, etc.

con·duc·tive /kənˈdʌktɪv/ *adj tech* able to conduct electricity, heat, etc.: *Copper is a very conductive metal. —***tivity** /ˌkɒndʌkˈtɪvẓti‖ˌkɑːn-/ *n* [U] : *the high conductivity of copper*

conductive ed·u·ca·tion /·ˌ··· ··ˈ··/ *n* a system for teaching children with CEREBRAL PALSY to use their minds and bodies as much as they possibly can. It was developed in Hungary by Dr Andras Peto.

con·duc·tor /kənˈdʌktəʳ/ *n* **1** a person who directs the playing of a group of musicians, usu. by waving a BATON (1) **2** something that acts as a path for electricity, heat, etc.: *Wood is a poor conductor of heat.* —see also LIGHTNING CONDUCTOR **3** a person employed to collect payments from passengers on a public vehicle. Conductors on buses are now quite rare in Britain and the US; it is more usual to buy a ticket before travelling or to pay the DRIVER of the vehicle. **4** *esp. AmE* the guard on a train

conductor rail /·ˈ·· ·/ ‖ usu. **third rail, live rail** *AmE n tech* the RAIL¹(2) from which electricity is passed to an electric railway engine

con·duct·ress /kənˈdʌktrẓs/ *n old-fash* a female CONDUCTOR (3)

con·duit /ˈkɒndɪt, ˈkɒndjuẓt‖ˈkɑːnduẓt/ *n* a pipe or passage for carrying water, gas, a set of electric wires, etc.: (fig.) *a foreign-registered company serving as a conduit for money flowing out of the country*

cone¹ /kəʊn/ *n* **1** a solid figure with a round base and a point at the top —see also CONIC, CONICAL **2** a hollow or solid object shaped like this: *The police put those cones in the road as warning signs.* **3** the fruit of a PINE or FIR tree —see also CONIFER and see picture at TREE **4** *also* **cornet** *BrE—* a thin pastry container for ICE CREAM, pointed at one end, to be eaten together with its contents

cone² *v*
  cone sthg. ↔ **off** *phr v* [T] to close (a road or part of a road) to traffic by putting a row of CONES (2) across or along it

cone·head /ˈkəʊnhed/ *n AmE humor* an imaginary person from another world who has a head shaped like a cone but otherwise looks like a human. Coneheads know very little about human life and customs and are always surprised by them. Coneheads were created by performers on the American television programme *Saturday Night Live.*

Con·e·sto·ga /ˌkɒnẓˈstəʊgə‖ˌkɑːn-/ *also* **Conestoga wag·on** /·ˈ·· ˌ··/ ‖—*n* a COVERED WAGON

co·ney /ˈkəʊnɪ/ *n* a rabbit, CONY

Coney Is·land /ˌ·· ˈ··/ an area of Brooklyn, New York, famous for its amusement park and BEACH

con·fab·u·late /kənˈfæbjẓleɪt/ *v* [I **(with)**] *pomp* to talk together

con·fab·u·la·tion /kənˌfæbjẓˈleɪʃən/ *also* **con·fab** /ˈkɒnfæb ‖ˈkɑːn-/*infml— n pomp* a private conversation: *Let's have a short confab about it before we decide.*

con·fec·tion /kənˈfekʃən/ *n fml* a sweet-tasting dish

con·fec·tion·er /kənˈfekʃənəʳ/ *n* a person who makes or sells sweets, ice cream, cakes, etc.

confectioner's sug·ar /·ˈ··· ˌ··/ *n* [U] *AmE for* ICING SUGAR

con·fec·tion·e·ry /kənˈfekʃənərɪ/ *n* **1** [U] sweets, ice cream, cakes, etc. **2** [C] a confectioner's shop

con·fed·e·ra·cy /kənˈfedərəsɪ/ *n* [C+*sing./pl. v*] a union of people, parties, or states, esp. for political purposes or trade

Confederacy *also* **Confederate States** /·ˌ··· ·ˈ·/— [*the*] the southern states that fought and lost against the northern states (the UNION) in the American Civil War, under the leadership of Jefferson Davis and General Robert E. Lee —see also CIVIL WAR (2)

con·fed·e·rate¹ /kənˈfedərẓt/ *adj* (*sometimes cap.*) belonging to a confederacy or to the Confederacy: *the Confederate Army/States*

confederate² *n* **1** *derog* a person who shares in a crime; ACCOMPLICE **2** a member of a confederacy **3** (*often cap.*)

AmE derog a person who (today) shares the political views and aims of the Confederacy

con·fed·er·ate³ /kən'fedəreɪt/ v [I;T] to (cause to) combine in a confederacy

Confederate flag /kən,fedər's̩t 'flæg/ [*the*] the flag of the Confederacy. Today it is still used, esp. by some American southerners, to show support for the Confederacy and is generally thought to stand for RACISM against blacks, and WHITE SUPREMACY

con·fed·e·ra·tion /kən,fedə'reɪʃən/ n a confederacy

Confederation of Brit·ish In·dus·try /···,·· · ,·· '···/ [*the*] *fml for* the CBI

con·fer /kən'fɜː^r/ v -rr- *fml* 1 [I (**with**)] to talk together; compare opinions: *The minister is still conferring with his advisers.* 2 [T (**on, upon**)] to give (a title, honour, favour, etc.): *An honorary degree was conferred on him by the university.* — ~ ment n [C;U]

con·fe·rence /'kɒnfərəns‖'kɑːn-/ n [(**on**)] 1 a formal meeting, e.g. between people who share the same business interests or belong to the same political party, which is held so that opinions and ideas can be exchanged: *My boss attended a conference on plastics last weekend.* | *The Historical Association/Labour Party are holding their annual conference next week.* | *The manager cannot see you now; she is* **in conference**. (=having a business meeting) —see also PRESS CONFERENCE 2 *esp. AmE* in a group of teams which play against each other; LEAGUE: *College football has two main conferences, the* PAC TEN and the Big Ten.

conference cen·tre /'··· ,·/ n a building with office equipment which can be hired by companies as a place for holding meetings, EXHIBITIONs, and other business events

conference ta·ble /'··· ,·/ n a large table in an office where meetings are held

con·fess /kən'fes/ v 1 [I;T (**to**)] to admit (a fault, crime, or something wrong that one has done): *The prisoner has confessed (her crime/to the murder).* [+v-ing] *He confessed (to) leaving the cigarette on the chair.* [+(that)] *Jean confessed (that) she'd eaten all the cakes.* | *I* **have to/must confess** *I didn't believe him at first.* [+obj+adj] (*fml*) *The police have confessed themselves (to be) completely puzzled by this strange crime.* 2 [I;T (**to**)] *tech* to tell (one's faults) to a priest or to God: *to confess one's sins*

► CULTURAL NOTE Many Christian people, esp. Roman Catholics, believe that their faults will be forgiven if they confess them and do PENANCE for them —see also CONFESSION (2) ◄

3 [T] *tech* (of a priest) to hear the CONFESSION (2) of (a person)

con·fessed /kən'fest/ *adj* [A] not secret; having admitted it: *Mrs Jones is a (self-)confessed alcoholic.* | *a confessed criminal* — ~ ly /'fes,s̩dli/ *adv*

con·fes·sion /kən'feʃən/ n 1 [C;U] (an example of) the act of admitting one's crimes, faults, etc.: *I've got a confession to make — I scraped your car when I was parking mine.* | *He wrote and signed a full confession of his guilt.* | *To reintroduce the tax would be a confession of failure by the government.* | (*humor*) *"I haven't brushed my teeth today." "What a confession!"* 2 [C;U] (an example of) the act of telling one's faults to a priest privately, e.g. in the confessional

► CULTURAL NOTE A Roman Catholic is meant to do this at least once a year. The Catholic priest can give the person a PENANCE, e.g. to say a particular prayer a certain number of times, and ABSOLUTION (= forgiveness for their SINs). The priest must never tell anyone anything that the person tells him as part of their confession, even if the person has hurt or killed someone. ◄

3 [U] a religious service at which people admit their faults to God 4 [C (**of**)] *fml* (esp. in religion) a declaration of belief: *a confession of faith* 5 [C+*sing./pl.* v] *tech* a religious group (usu. Christian) with its own organization and a shared system of belief

con·fes·sion·al /kən'feʃənəl/ n a place in a church (usu. an enclosed place) where the priest hears people make their CONFESSION (2): *the secrets of the confessional*

con·fes·sor /kən'fesə^r/ n *tech* the priest to whom someone regularly makes their CONFESSION (2)

con·fet·ti /kən'feti/ n [U] small pieces of coloured paper thrown over the BRIDE and BRIDEGROOM after a wedding,

esp. as they come out of a church or thrown at other occasions where people celebrate: *Their friends showered them with confetti.*

con·fi·dant /'kɒnf,s̩dænt, ,kɒnf,s̩'dænt, -'dɑːnt‖'kɑːnf,s̩dænt/ **confidante** (*same pronunciation*) *fem.* — n a person to whom one tells one's secrets or with whom one talks about personal matters

con·fide /kən'faɪd/ v [T (**to**)] to tell (information, personal matters, etc.) secretly to a person one trusts: *"I don't really like my brother," she confided.* [+that] *He confided (to me) that he had spent five years in prison.*
 confide in sbdy. *phr v* [T] to talk freely to (someone), esp. about personal matters, and be confident that one's secrets will be kept: *Alan felt he could confide in his brother.*

con·fi·dence /'kɒnf,s̩dəns‖'kɑːn-/ n 1 [U (**in**)] a calm unworried feeling or manner based on a strong belief in one's abilities; SELF-ASSURANCE: *She's a good student but she lacks confidence (in herself).* | *The company is looking forward with confidence to the next five years.* 2 [U (**in**)] a strong belief in the ability of a person, plan, etc., to do what is needed effectively and successfully: *We have every confidence in your ability.* | *The government failed to win public confidence in its plan for economic recovery.* | *After another poor performance, the company's management has now lost the confidence of its shareholders.* | *The opposition parties have* **tabled a motion of no confidence** *BrE* ‖ **taken a vote of no confidence** *AmE in the government*. (=stated that they do not trust the government's ability to do its job) —see also VOTE OF CONFIDENCE 3 [U] faith; complete trust: *Little Johnny used to be very shy and withdrawn with adults, but I have won his confidence now.* | *I'm telling you this* **in confidence**. (=as a secret) | *She* **took him into her confidence** *and told him the whole truth.* 4 [C] a secret; a personal matter told secretly to someone else: *The girls exchanged confidences about their boyfriends.*

confidence-build·ing /'··· ,·/ *adj* (of an action, speech, etc.) that increases confidence: *This introduction course will be of value to anyone without prior experience of computing, serving as a confidence-building preparation prior to further training.*

confidence man /'··· ,·/ n a CONMAN

confidence trick /'··· ,·/ also **con** *infml* — n a dishonest trick played on a trusting person in order to get their money

con·fi·dent /'kɒnf,s̩dənt‖'kɑːn-/ *adj* [(**of**)] feeling or showing confidence: *a confident smile* | *a confident prediction that business would improve* | *We are confident of success.* [F+(that)] *We are confident that next year's profits will be much higher.* —see also SELF-CONFIDENT — ~ ly *adv*

con·fi·den·tial /,kɒnf,s̩'denʃəl◄ ,kɑːn-/ *adj* 1 spoken or written in secret and intended to be kept secret: *This information is strictly confidential.* | *a confidential naval report on the failure of equipment* | *Please keep what I am about to tell you confidential.* 2 trusted with private matters: *a confidential secretary* 3 showing full trust: *a confidential voice/look* — ~ ly : *She leaned over to me confidentially.* | *Confidentially, between you and me, I think he's going to resign.* — ~ ity /,kɒnf,s̩denʃi'æls̩ti‖,kɑːn-/ n [U] : *to respect someone's confidentiality*

con·fid·ing /kən'faɪdɪŋ/ *adj fml* trustful: *her confiding nature* — ~ ly *adv*

con·fig·u·ra·tion /kən,fɪgjʉ'reɪʃən/ n 1 *fml or tech* the arrangement of the parts of something; shape or LAYOUT: *the configuration of pistons in an engine* 2 *tech* the combination of HARDWARE equipment needed to run a computer system

con·fine /kən'faɪn/ v [T (**to**)] 1 to keep within limits; RESTRICT: *Please confine yourself/your remarks to the subject under discussion.* | *The police cadet's duties were confined to taking statements from women and children.* 2 to shut or keep in a small or enclosed space: *Any soldier who deserts his post will be confined to quarters.* 3 [*usu. pass.*] *med* to put (a woman who is about to give birth to a baby) in bed

con·fine·ment /kən'faɪnmənt/ n 1 [U (**to**)] the act of confining or state of being confined —see also SOLITARY CONFINEMENT 2 [C;U] *tech* an act of giving birth to a child: *This is her third confinement.*

con·fines /'kɒnfaɪnz‖'kɑːn-/ *n* [P (**of**)] limits or borders: *within the confines of one country | beyond the confines of human knowledge*

con·firm /kən'fɜːm‖-ɜːrm/ *v* [T]   **1** to give support or certainty to (a fact, belief, statement, etc.), e.g. by providing more proof or by stating that something is true or correct: *He said he would accept the job, so we have asked him to confirm his acceptance in writing. | The expression on her face confirmed our worst fears. | This new evidence confirms (me in) my opinion that they are lying. | The President refused to either confirm or deny this rumour.* [+*that*] *The announcement confirmed that the election would take place on June 20th.* [+*wh-*] *a note asking us to confirm when we would be arriving*   **2** to give formal approval to (a person, agreement, position, etc.); agree to; RATIFY: *When do you think the President will confirm you in office?*   **3** *tech* to admit (a person) to full membership of the Christian church: *I was confirmed when I was 12.*

con·fir·ma·tion /ˌkɒnfə'meɪʃən‖ˌkɑːnfər-/ *n* [C;U]   **1** [(**of**)] something that confirms: *a letter in confirmation of a hotel reservation | confirmation of my suspicions | There has still been no official confirmation of the report.*   **2** *tech* a religious service in which a person is made a full member of the Christian church

confirmation hear·ing /·‥'·· ‚·‥/ *n* a special meeting of US SENATORS that examines someone appointed to high office by the president, and decides if they are suitable for the job

con·firmed /kən'fɜːmd‖-ɜːr-/ *adj* [A] firmly settled in a particular way of life or way of thinking: *a confirmed bachelor*

con·fis·cate /'kɒnfɪ̩skeɪt‖'kɑːn-/ *v* [T (**from**)] to take (private property) away from someone esp. with the official right to do so, usu. as a punishment: *The teacher confiscated my radio because I was playing it in the classroom.* —**cation** /ˌkɒnfɪ̩'skeɪʃən‖ˌkɑːn-/ *n* [C;U] : *the confiscation of pornographic material by the police*

con·fis·ca·to·ry /'kɒnfɪ̩skeɪtəri, kən'fɪskətəri‖kən'fɪskətɔːri/ *adj fml*   **1** that confiscates: *the confiscatory powers of customs officials*   **2** taking away too much: *confiscatory taxes*

con·fla·gra·tion /ˌkɒnflə'greɪʃən‖ˌkɑːn-/ *n fml* a very large fire that destroys much property, esp. buildings or forests

con·flate /kən'fleɪt/ *v* [T] *fml* to bring (parts) together to form a single whole; combine —**flation** /'fleɪʃən/ *n* [C;U]

con·flict[1] /'kɒnflɪkt‖'kɑːn-/ *n* [C,U (**between**)]   **1** a state of disagreement or argument between opposing groups or opposing ideas or principles; opposition: *The two parties have been in conflict since the election. | The governor's refusal to apply the law brought him into conflict with the federal government. | the conflict between religion and science*   **2** (a) war or battle; struggle: *This is a serious dispute, and could lead to armed conflict.*   **3** never in the field of human conflict was so much owed by so many to so few *quote* part of a speech made to the British Parliament in 1940 by Winston Churchill about the Battle of Britain and the bravery of the Royal Air Force —see also BATTLE OF BRITAIN

con·flict[2] /kən'flɪkt/ *v* [I (**with**)] to be in opposition; disagree: *Do British immigration laws conflict with any international laws? | conflicting opinions/advice/evidence*

conflict of in·terest /ˌ·· '·· / *n* conflicts of interest [(**between**)] a conflict between two of someone's different areas of activity, so that it becomes difficult to continue being involved in both of them. It is usu. experienced by someone who holds a responsible or public position: *There is a growing conflict of interest between her position as a politician and her business activities.*

con·flu·ence /'kɒnfluəns‖'kɑːn-/ *n* [(**of**)] *fml* the place where two or more rivers flow together: *the confluence of the Rhine and the Mosel | (fig.) a confluence of ideas*

con·form /kən'fɔːm‖-ɔːrm/ *v* [I (**to**)]   **1** to obey or be in accordance with established rules: *You must either conform to the rules or leave the school. | This piece of equipment does not conform to the official safety standards.*   **2** to behave in accordance with generally accepted ideas or customs; behave like most other people: *There is great pressure on schoolchildren to conform.* —see also CONFORMIST — ~ **er** *n* — ~ **ance** *n* [U (**with**, **to**)] : *The equipment is not in conformance with the official safety standards.*

con·for·ma·ble /kən'fɔːməbəl‖-ɔːr-/ *adj* [F+**to**] *fml* acting

in agreement; suitable: *We trust that the arrangements we have made are conformable to your wishes.* — **bly** *adv*

con·for·ma·tion /ˌkɒnfɔː'meɪʃən‖ˌkɑːnfɔːr-/ *n* [C;U] *fml or tech* the way something is formed; shape

con·form·ist /kən'fɔːmɪ̩st‖-ɔːr-/ *adj, n usu. derog* (of) a person who conforms to the established rules, values, and customs of society —opposite **nonconformist**

con·for·mi·ty /kən'fɔːmɪ̩ti‖-ɔːr-/ *n* [U (**with**, **to**)] *fml* agreement with established rules, customs, etc.: *to behave in* conformity with *the law/your beliefs*

con·found /kən'faʊnd/ *v* [T]   **1** to confuse and surprise by being unexpected: *The extraordinary election results confounded the government. | He gave a marvellous performance that completely confounded his critics.*   **2** *old use* to defeat (an enemy, plan, etc.)   **3** [(**with**)] *fml* to mix up in one's mind; CONFUSE (2)   **4** Confound it/him/them, etc. *old-fash infml* DAMN it/him/them, etc.

con·found·ed /kən'faʊndɪ̩d/ *adj* [A] *old-fash infml* (used to express annoyance): *that confounded boy/dog | a confounded idiot/nuisance* — ~ **ly** *adv*

con·fra·ter·ni·ty /ˌkɒnfrə'tɜːnɪ̩ti‖ˌkɑːnfrə'tɜːr-/ *n* [C+*sing./pl. v*] a group of people, esp. of religious people who are not priests, who work together for some good purpose

con·frère /'kɒnfreəʳ‖'kɑːn-/ *n Fr pomp* a companion, esp. a person who shares in one's job

con·front /kən'frʌnt/ *v* [T]   **1** to face bravely or threateningly: *The actress was confronted by a large group of reporters as she left the stage door. | They have confronted the problem of terrorism with great determination.*   **2** to be faced with and have to deal with: *I prepared answers for the questions I expected to confront in the interview.*   **confront sbdy. with sthg.** *phr v* [T] to force to deal with or accept the truth of; bring face to face with: *When the police confronted her with the evidence, she admitted that she was guilty.*

con·fron·ta·tion /ˌkɒnfrən'teɪʃən‖ˌkɑːn-/ *n* [C;U (**with**)] (an example of) the act of confronting, esp. a situation or manner marked by open opposition: *We cannot risk (another) confrontation with the union.*

con·fron·ta·tion·al /ˌkɒnfrən'teɪʃənəl‖ˌkɑːn-/ *adj* intentionally causing or likely to cause confrontation; PROVOCATIVE: *a confrontational policy | a confrontational style of government*

Con·fu·cian·is·m /kən'fjuːʃənɪzəm/ *n* [U] a Chinese way of thought which teaches that one should be loyal to one's family, friends, and rulers and treat others as one would like to be treated. Confucianism was developed from the ideas of Confucius. —**Confucian** *adj*

Con·fu·cius /kən'fjuːʃəs/ (about 551 to 479 BC) a Chinese PHILOSOPHER who encouraged justice and peace and who taught social and moral principles which became a part of Chinese civilization. In Britain and the US, people sometimes pretend to give a QUOTE from Confucius as a joke, when they are pretending to give someone wise advice, usu. starting "Confucius he say…" or "Confucius says…"

con·fuse /kən'fjuːz/ *v* [T]   **1** to cause to be mixed up in the mind; BEWILDER: *Don't give me so much information — you're confusing me. | Waking up in strange surroundings confused her. | (fig.) The chess player confused the computer by making some irrational moves halfway through the game.*   **2** [(**with**)] to mix up in one's mind; be unable to tell the difference between (esp. similar people or things): *I'm always confusing John and/with Paul — which one is John?*   **3** to put into disorder; make less clear, more difficult to deal with: *That argument's completely irrelevant — you're confusing the issue.*

con·fused /kən'fjuːzd/ *adj*   **1** mixed up in one's mind: *The little girl was very confused by all the noise and activity. | He gets confused easily.*   **2** in disorder; not able to be separated easily: *a confused babble of voices* — ~ **ly** /-'fjuːzɪ̩dli/ *adv*

con·fus·ing /kən'fjuːzɪŋ/ *adj* making one feel confused: *The instructions were so confusing I couldn't understand them. | a confusing array of instruments* — ~ **ly** *adv*

con·fu·sion /kən'fjuːʒən/ *n* [U]   **1** the state of being mixed up or mistaken: *There was some confusion as to whether we had won or lost. | To avoid confusion, the teams wore different colours. | Conflicting reports have led to widespread public confusion over the government's* *intentions.* **2** the act of confusing; mixing up: *Confusion of) between the crow and the rook is quite common.* (i.e. because they are so similar) **3** a state of great disorder: *The party is in complete confusion after its election defeat.* | *a scene of panic and confusion*

con·fute /kən'fjuːt/ *v* [T] *fml* to prove (a person or argument) to be completely wrong —**futation** /ˌkɒnfjuː'teɪʃən‖ˌkɑːn-/ *n* [C;U]

con·ga /'kɒŋgə‖'kɑːŋgə/ *n* (the music for) a fast Latin American dance, in which the dancers form a long winding chain (a **conga line**). People sometimes **do the conga** at informal parties, esp. when they have drunk a lot of alcohol.

con·gé /'kɒnʒeɪ‖kɔːn'ʒeɪ, 'kɑːnʒeɪ/ *n Fr pomp* **1** formal and respectful DEPARTURE **2 give someone their congé** *fml* to dismiss someone suddenly from one's presence or favour

con·geal /kən'dʒiːl/ *v* [I;T] to become or cause (a liquid) to become thick or solid: *The soup had congealed by the time we returned.* | *congealed blood*

con·ge·ni·al /kən'dʒiːniəl/ *adj* pleasant; in agreement with one's tastes and nature: *congenial work/weather/companions* | *I find him very congenial.* — ~**ly** *adv*

con·gen·i·tal /kən'dʒenᵻtl/ *adj med* (of diseases) existing at or from one's birth: *a congenital defect* | (fig.) *a congenital liar* (=person who always lies) — ~**ly** *adv* : *congenitally deaf*

con·ger eel /ˌkɒŋgər 'iːl‖ˌkɑːn-/ also **conger**— *n* a large rather fierce snakelike sea fish

con·ges·ted /kən'dʒestᵻd/ *adj* **1** (of a street, city, narrow place, etc.) very full or blocked, esp. because of traffic: *Oxford Street is always very congested.* **2** *med* (of a blood tube or part of the body) very full of liquid: *His lungs seem to be congested, doctor.* —**tion** /'dʒestʃən/ *n* [U] : *traffic congestion* | *congestion of the lungs*

con·glom·e·rate /kən'glɒmərᵻt‖-'glɑː-/ *n* **1** a large business organization consisting of different companies that produce goods of very different kinds: *a multinational conglomerate* **2** *esp. tech* a mass of various materials gathered together, esp. a rock consisting of small stones held together by clay

con·glom·e·ra·tion /kən,glɒmə'reɪʃən‖-,glɑː-/ *n* [(of)] *fml* a collection or mass of many different things gathered together: *It's not really a theory, just a confused conglomeration of ideas.*

Con·go /'kɒŋgəʊ‖'kɑːŋ-/ [the] **1** also **People's Republic of Congo** *fml* —a country in W Central Africa; capital Brazzaville; population 1,941,000 (1989) **2** the name informally used for a central African country called at different times **Congo Free State**, the **Belgian Congo**, and the **Democratic Republic of Congo**. Since 1971 it has been known as Zaïre; capital Kinshasa; population 34,491,000 (1989) **3** the former name of the second longest African river, in 1971 renamed the Zaïre — ~**lese** /ˌkɒŋgə'liːz◂ ‖ ˌkɑːŋ-/ *adj*

con·grats /kən'græts/ *interj infml* congratulations

con·grat·u·late /kən'grætʃᵿleɪt/ *v* [T (**on**)] **1** to express one's pleasure, praise, or admiration for (someone) because of a happy event or something successfully done: *We congratulated her on the birth of her daughter/on having come first in her exams.* **2** to have pleasure and pride in (oneself) for something successfully done: *She congratulated herself on having thought of such a good idea.* —**lation** /kən,grætʃᵿ'leɪʃən/ *n* [U]

con·grat·u·la·tions /kən,grætʃᵿ'leɪʃənz/ *interj, n* [P (**on**)] an expression used when one is congratulating someone on their success, luck, etc. People usu. offer someone their congratulations, or say the word "Congratulations", when someone has won a prize, passed a test, got married, had a baby, etc., or when someone has just announced that they are going to get married or have a baby: *"I've just passed my driving test!" "Congratulations!"* | *Congratulations on winning the race/on your marriage!* | *Please give her/pass on my congratulations when you see her.* | *There you are, Kevin! I hear congratulations are in order. Well done!*

con·grat·u·la·to·ry /kən,grætʃᵿ'leɪtəri‖-'grætʃᵿlətɔːri/ *adj* that congratulates: *a congratulatory letter/telegram* | *congratulatory remarks*

con·gre·gate /'kɒŋgrᵻgeɪt‖'kɑːŋ-/ *v* [I] to come together in

a large group: *The crowds congregated in the town square to hear the President speak.*

con·gre·ga·tion /ˌkɒŋgrᵻ'geɪʃən‖ˌkɑːŋ-/ *n* [C+*sing./pl. v*] a group of people gathered together, esp. in a church, for religious worship: *The congregation knelt to pray.* | *a member of the congregation* —see ATTEND (USAGE)

Con·gre·ga·tion·al /ˌkɒŋgrᵻ'geɪʃənəl◂‖ˌkɑːŋ-/ *adj* of Congregationalism: *the Congregational church*

Con·gre·ga·tion·al·is·m /ˌkɒŋgrᵻ'geɪʃənəlɪzəm‖ˌkɑːŋ-/ *n* [U] a Protestant branch of the Christian church in which each local church governs its own affairs —**ist** *n*

con·gress /'kɒŋgres‖'kɑːŋgrᵻs/ *n* [C+*sing./pl. v*] **1** a formal meeting of representatives of societies, countries, etc., to exchange information and opinions: *the Congress of Vienna* | *a medical congress* | *The matter will be discussed in congress tomorrow.* **2** the elected law-making body of certain countries

Congress the law-making body of the US, consisting of the Senate and the House of Representatives: *She has been elected/has been returned to Congress.* | *Congress has approved the new education budget.* | *The President has lost the support of Congress.* —see also extra information on page 568

▶ CULTURAL NOTE Congress decides whether a BILL (= a suggested law) becomes a law. If the Senate and the House of Representatives both agree to a bill, the President is asked to agree. The President can say no to (VETO) the bill, but Congress can still make it a law if two-thirds of the members of each house agree. —compare HOUSE OF REPRESENTATIVES, SENATE; see also CONGRESSMAN, CONTINENTAL CONGRESS◀

con·gres·sion·al /kən'greʃənəl/ *adj* [A] (*often cap.*) of a congress, esp. the US Congress: *congressional hearings/elections* | *a congressional committee*

Congressional Med·al of Hon·or /·ˌ··· ·ˌ·· ·ˈ··/ also **Medal of Honor** *infml*— [the] the highest military honour in the US, which is given to soldiers who show special courage

Congressional Rec·ord /·ˌ··· ·ˈ··/ [the] the printed record of all the official business of the US Congress, which records everything that is said and the results of votes —compare HANSARD

con·gress·man /'kɒŋgrᵻsmən‖'kɑːŋ-/ **con·gress·wo·man** /-ˌwʊmən/*fem.*— *n* -**men** /mən/ (*often cap.*) a member of a congress, esp. of the US House of Representatives: *on the advice of my Congressman* | *an interview with Congresswoman Anne Harding* —see also extra information on page 568

Congress of Vi·en·na /·ˌ·· · ·ˈ··/ [the] a meeting of representatives from various European countries in 1814 and 1815 to plan the reorganization of Europe after the defeat of Napoleon I

Congress Par·ty /'·· ˌ··/, **the** an important political party in India

con·gru·ent /'kɒŋgruənt‖'kɑːŋ-/ *adj* **1** [(**with**)] *tech* (of figures in GEOMETRY) having the same size and shape as another or each other: *congruent triangles* **2** [(**with**)] *fml* CONGRUOUS — ~**ly** *adv* —**ence** *n* [U]

con·gru·i·ty /kən'gruːᵻti/ *n* [(**between**)] *fml* **1** [U] the state of being alike **2** [C *usu. pl.*] a point of agreement

con·gru·ous /'kɒŋgruəs‖'kɑːŋ-/ also **congruent** /-ənt/— *adj* [(**with**)] *fml* fitting; suitable: *behaviour congruous with his rank* —opposite INCONGRUOUS

con·ic /'kɒnɪk‖'kɑː-/ *adj tech* of or shaped like a CONE (1)

con·i·cal /'kɒnɪkəl‖'kɑː-/ *adj* of or shaped like a CONE (1): *huts with conical roofs* — ~**ly** /kli/ *adv*

conic sec·tion /·ˌ·· ·ˈ··/ *n* a shape made from a CONE by passing an imaginary flat surface through it. This is an important idea in GEOMETRY.

co·ni·fer /'kəʊnᵻfəʳ, 'kɒ-‖'kɑː-/ *n* a tree on which CONES (3) grow and which is usu. EVERGREEN (=does not lose its leaves in winter). Many conifers have economic value because they are used for TIMBER.

co·nif·er·ous /kə'nɪfərəs‖kəʊ-, kə-/ *adj* of or being a conifer: *coniferous trees* —compare DECIDUOUS (1); see also EVERGREEN

conj *written abbrev. for:* CONJUNCTION

con·jec·ture¹ /kən'dʒektʃəʳ/ *n* [C;U] *fml* (the forming of) a guess, opinion, or judgment based on incomplete or uncertain information: *The Senator didn't know the facts; what he said was pure conjecture.* | *Whether or not the President knew will always be a matter for conjecture.* (=we will never know) —**tural** *adj*

con·jec·ture² *v* [I;T+*that;obj*] *fml* to form a conjecture; guess: *The general conjectured that the enemy only had about five days' supply of food left.*

con·join /kən'dʒɔɪn/ *v* [I;T] *fml or tech* to (cause to) join together or unite for a common purpose

con·joint /kən'dʒɔɪnt/ *adj fml* joined together; united; combined — —**ly** *adv*

con·ju·gal /'kɒndʒʊɡəl‖'kɑːn-/ *adj* [A] *fml* of marriage; CONNUBIAL: *the conjugal bed*

conjugal rights /₁··· ¹·/ *n* [P] the right of having SEXUAL INTERCOURSE with one's husband or wife: *He demanded his conjugal rights.*
▶ CULTURAL NOTE In Britain, a man formerly had the legal right to have sex with his wife, and he could not be found guilty of raping (RAPE) his wife. This law was changed in 1991.◀

con·ju·gate /'kɒndʒʊɡeɪt‖'kɑːn-/ *v tech* **1** [I] (of a verb) to have different grammatical forms to show number, person, tense, etc.: *The verb "to go" conjugates irregularly.* **2** [T] to list or state the different grammatical forms of (a verb) that show number, person, tense, etc.: *Can you conjugate "to have" in the present tense?* —compare DECLINE¹ (4), INFLECT (1)

con·ju·ga·tion /₁kɒndʒʊ'ɡeɪʃən‖₁kɑːn-/ *n tech* **1** [C] (in some languages) a class of verbs that conjugate in the same way: *There are four conjugations in Latin but also many irregular verbs.* **2** the way that a particular verb conjugates: *The verb "to be" has an irregular conjugation.* —compare DECLENSION

con·junc·tion /kən'dʒʌŋkʃən/ *n* **1** [C] a word such as "but", "and", or "while" that connects parts of sentences, phrases, or CLAUSES **2** [C;U] *fml* (a) combination of qualities, groups, or events: *The army is acting* **in conjunction with** (=in combination with) *the police in the hunt for the terrorists.* **3** [U] *tech* the meeting or passing of two stars, PLANETs, etc. in the same division of the ZODIAC: *This month Mars and Venus are* **in conjunction.**

con·junc·tive /kən'dʒʌŋktɪv/ also **con·junct** /'kɒndʒʌŋkt, kən'dʌŋkt‖/— *n, adj tech* (a word) joining phrases together: *a conjunctive adverb*

con·junc·ti·vi·tis /kən₁dʒʌŋktɪ'vaɪtɪs/ ‖ also **pinkeye** *AmE* — *n* [U] *med* a painful disease of the eye, with redness and swelling. It is very infectious.

con·junc·ture /kən'dʒʌŋktʃəʳ/ *n* [(of)] *fml* a combination of events or situations, usu. producing difficulties

con·jure¹ /'kʌndʒəʳ‖'kɑːn-, 'kʌn-/ *v* **1** [T+*obj*+*prep*] to cause to appear (as if) by magic: *The magician conjured a rabbit out of his hat.* **2** [I] to do clever tricks which seem magical, esp. by very quick movement of the hands: *Paul's very good at conjuring.* **3** **a name to conjure with** *BrE* the name of **a** a very influential or important person or thing **b** a very difficult or strange-sounding, and usu. long, name
conjure sthg. ↔ **up** *phr v* [T] **1** to bring into the mind or cause to be remembered; EVOKE: *This place conjures up vivid memories.* **2** to cause to appear (as if) by magic: *Jean can conjure up a good meal in half an hour.*

con·jure² /kən'dʒʊəʳ/ *v* [T+*obj*+*to-v*] *old use* to ask (someone) solemnly to do something: *He conjured them with his dying breath to look after his children.*

con·jur·er, -or /'kʌndʒərəʳ‖'kɑːn-, 'kʌn-/ *esp. BrE* ‖ usu.

conjurer

magician *AmE n* a person, esp. a professional entertainer, who does CONJURING TRICKS to amuse others, esp. producing objects or small animals, esp. rabbits, from a TOP HAT or other places. They sometimes use a MAGIC WAND. In Britain, conjurers are often hired to entertain children at birthday parties.

conjuring trick /¹··· ₁·/ *n* a clever trick which seems magical, esp. one that involves very quick movement of the hands

conk¹ /kɒŋk‖kɑːŋk, kɔːŋk/ *n BrE sl, usu. humor* a nose

conk² *v* [T] *sl* to hit (someone), esp. on the head with a heavy blow
conk out *phr v sl* **1** [I] to fail suddenly; break down: *Our car conked out on the way home.* **2** [I] *AmE* to (go to) sleep, often suddenly or when very tired: *I conked out for three hours when I got home from work* **3** [T(**conk** sbdy. ↔ out)] *AmE* to knock unconscious; KNOCK OUT

con·ker /'kɒŋkəʳ‖'kɑːŋ-/ *n esp. BrE* the shiny brown nutlike seed of the HORSE CHESTNUT tree —see also CONKERS; —see picture at TREE

con·kers /'kɒŋkəz‖'kɑːŋkərz/ *n* [U] (esp. in Britain) a children's game in which one person swings a conker on a piece of string in an attempt to break an opponent's conker. The conkers are given numbers depending on how many other conkers they have defeated. Children sometimes bake their conkers in the OVEN or soak them in VINEGAR to make them harder.

con·man /'kɒnmæn‖'kɑːn-/ also **confidence man**— *n* -**men** /men/ a person who performs CONFIDENCE TRICKs to get money from people in a dishonest way

con·nect /kə'nekt/ *v* **1** [T (UP)] to join (one object, place, etc.) to another by means of something that comes in between the two; unite: *This railway line connects London and Edinburgh.* | *The plumber connected (up) all the pipes and turned on the tap.* **2** [T (**with**) *often pass.*] to consider as being related; ASSOCIATE: *The woman's face was familiar, but I didn't immediately connect her with the girl who used to live next door to me.* | *The police are connecting this incident with last week's terrorist bombing.* (=they believe there is a connection between the two events) **3** [T (**to**)] to join by telephone: *Operator, you've connected me to the wrong person again!* **4** [T (UP, **to**)] to join (a machine) to an electricity or other power supply: *Make sure it's connected (up) properly before you switch on at the mains.* | *Has the phone/electricity been connected yet?* | *These terminals are connected to our mainframe computer.* **5** [I (**with, to**)] (of trains, buses, etc.) to be planned so that passengers can change from one to the other: *This flight connects with a flight for Paris.* | *connecting flights*

con·nect·ed /kə'nektɪd/ *adj* **1** [(**with**)] joined or related: *a series of connected events* | *problems connected with alcoholism* —opposite **unconnected** **2** having social, professional, or business relationships of the stated kind: *He's* **well connected** (=knows powerful or influential people) *in political circles.* **3** joined electrically or telephonically: *a connected terminal* | *Are the telephones connected?* —opposite **disconnected** **4** [(**with**)] related by birth or marriage: *Most European royal families are connected (with each other).*

Con·nec·tic·ut /kə'netɪkət/ *written abbrev.* **CT**— a state in the NE United States. It was one of the 13 original colonies (COLONY) of Britain.–see colour maps on page 1374-5

connecting rod /·¹·· ·/ *n* a rod that joins two moving parts, esp. one connecting the PISTON to the CRANKSHAFT in the engine of a motor vehicle

con·nec·tion /kə'nekʃən/ also **connexion** *BrE*— *n* **1** [C;U (**between, with**)] (an example of) the state of being connected; relationship: *There's a strong connection between smoking and heart disease.* | *Is there any connection between these two crimes?* | *The company has connections with a number of American firms.* | *His career was ruined because of his connections with the Mafia/his Mafia connections.* **2** [C] something that connects: *This town has very good road and railway connections with the coast.* | *I phoned Andy, but we had such a bad connection that we gave up trying to talk.* | *The radio won't work because of a faulty/loose connection.* (=a wire out of its correct place) **3** [U (**to, with**)] the act of connecting: *The connection of the pipes to the main water supply only took a few minutes.* **4** [C] a plane, train, bus, etc., planned to take passengers arriving by another one: *There are connections at Paris*

for all European capitals. | *If we're late we'll miss our connection.* **5** [C *usu. pl.*] *sometimes derog* a social, professional, or business person with whom one has a working relationship: *He'll get the job — he has all the right connections.* | *connections in high places* **6** [C *usu. pl.*] a person connected to others by a family relationship: *She's English but has Irish connections.* **7 in connection with** with regard to: *In connection with your request of March 18th we are sorry to tell you. . .* | *The police are interviewing two men in connection with the jewel robbery.* **8 in this connection** *fml* while we are mentioning this; in this CONTEXT: *In this connection, I would like to say that* ...

con·nec·tive /kə'nektɪv/ *n, adj fml or tech* **1** (a word) joining phrases, parts of sentences, etc.; CONJUNCTION: *"And" is a frequent connective in English.* **2** (something) joining things together: *The surgeon cut through connective tissue to expose the bone.*

Con·ne·ry /'kɒnəri‖'kɑːn-/, **Sean** /ʃɔːn/ (1930–) a Scottish film actor. He is famous esp. for playing the character of James Bond in several films, such as *Dr No*, and *From Russia With Love.* —see colour picture on page 228

con·ne·xion /kə'nekʃən/ *n BrE* CONNECTION

con·ning tow·er /'·· ,··/ *n tech* a heavily armoured raised place on a warship or on top of a SUBMARINE (=underwater ship)

con·nip·tion /kə'nɪpʃən/ also **conniption fit** /·'·· ,·/ — *n AmE infml humor* an attack of great anger or of being upset, often about something not very important. It is usually said of another person, not of oneself: *Your mother's going to have a conniption when she finds out you took her car.*

con·niv·ance /kə'naɪvəns/ *n* [U (**at, with**)] the act of conniving: *They could not have escaped without the connivance of the guards.*

con·nive /kə'naɪv/ *v* [I (**with**)] to work together secretly for some wrong or illegal purpose; CONSPIRE: [+*to-v*] *The two students connived (with each other) to cheat in the examination.*
connive at sthg. *phr v* [T] *BrE* to make no attempt to stop (something wrong): *The young policeman connived at the man's escape because he felt sorry for him.*

con·nois·seur /ˌkɒnə'sɜːʳ‖ˌkɑː-/ *n* [(**of**)] *apprec* a person who has a good knowledge and understanding of subjects such as art or music, and whose judgments are respected: *a connoisseur of fine wines/antique furniture* | *Ask Julia; she's something of a connoisseur of modern art.*

Con·nol·ly /'kɒnəli‖'kɑː-/, **Billy** (1942–) a Scottish COMEDIAN from Glasgow, known for having long hair and a beard, and telling rude stories and jokes in a strong Scottish ACCENT

Con·nors /'kɒnəz‖'kɑːnərz/, **Jimmy** (1952–) an American tennis player who won at Wimbledon in 1974

con·no·ta·tion /ˌkɒnə'teɪʃən‖ˌkɑː-/ *n* (any of) the feelings or ideas that are suggested by a word, rather than the actual meaning of the word: *The word "armchair" has connotations of comfort and relaxation.* —compare DENOTATION —**tative** /'kɒnəteɪtɪv‖'kɑːn-, kə'nəʊtətɪv/ *adj*

con·note /kə'nəʊt/ *v* [T] *esp. tech* (of a word) to suggest (feelings or ideas) in addition to the actual meaning: *The word "plump" connotes cheerfulness.* —compare DENOTE

con·nu·bi·al /kə'njuːbiəl‖-'nuː-/ *adj* [A] *fml* of marriage; CONJUGAL: *living in a state of connubial bliss*

con·quer /'kɒŋkəʳ‖'kɑːŋ-/ *v* **1** [I;T] to take (land) by force; win (land) by war: *The Normans conquered England in 1066.* | *a conquering army* | *a conquered city* **2** [I;T] to defeat (an enemy); be victorious over (an enemy): *The Zulus conquered all the neighbouring tribes.* **3** [T] to gain control over (something unfriendly or difficult): *After many attempts to climb it, the mountain was finally conquered in 1985.* | *She conquered her fear and picked up the enormous spider.* | *efforts to conquer inflation* **4** [T] *lit* to succeed in gaining the praise and attention of: *The painter went to Paris intending to conquer the artistic world.* —see also **I came, I saw, I conquered** (COME (21)) **– – or** *n*

con·quest /'kɒŋkwest‖'kɑːŋ-/ *n* **1** [U (**of**)] the act of conquering: *the Norman Conquest* | *the conquest of space* **2** [C] something conquered, esp. land gained in war: *French conquests in Asia* **3** [C] *often humor* a person (usu. of the

opposite sex) whose admiration or love has been won: *She's one of his numerous conquests.*

con·quis·ta·dor /kɒn'kwɪstədɔːʳ‖kɑːn'kiː-/ *n* **-dores** /kɒnˌkwɪstə'dɔːreɪz‖kɑːnˌkiː-/ *or* **-dors** (*often cap.*) any of the Spanish conquerors of Mexico and Peru in the 16th century

Con·rad /'kɒnræd‖'kɑːn-/, **Joseph** (1857–1924) a British NOVELIST of Polish origin. His books, which include *Heart of Darkness, Lord Jim* and *Nostromo,* were about foreign settings, sea life, and how it feels to be an outsider.

Con·rail , ConRail /'kɒnreɪl‖'kɑːn-/ a system of FREIGHT railways in the US, set up under loose government control —compare AMTRAK

Con·ran /'kɒnrən‖'kɑːn-/, **Ter·ence** /'terəns/ (1931–) an English DESIGNER and businessman, best-known for establishing Habitat, where he sold a popular range of furniture, etc.

con·san·guin·i·ty /ˌkɒnsæŋ'gwɪnɪti‖ˌkɑːn-/ *n* [U] *fml* relationship by birth: *People are not allowed to marry within certain degrees of consanguinity.*

con·science /'kɒnʃəns‖'kɑːn-/ *n* [C;U] **1** an inner sense that is conscious of the moral rightness or wrongness of one's behaviour or intentions, and makes one know whether one is doing right or wrong: *Be guided by your conscience.* | *I had a bad/guilty conscience about not telling her the truth.* | *I haven't done anything wrong — I've got a clear conscience.* | *She has no conscience (at all) about cheating.* (=does not feel at all guilty about it) | *I can't advise you what to do — it's a matter of conscience.* (=of your own moral judgment) | *The dog's sad look at the front door pricked her conscience* (=made her feel guilty) *and she took him out for a walk.* | *The pictures of the famine stirred the public conscience.* | *a prisoner of conscience* (=someone who is in prison for esp. political or religious beliefs) **2 always let your conscience be your guide** a phrase known esp. from a cheerful song in the Disney CARTOON film *Pinnochio* **3 in all conscience** *fml* being fair and reasonable: *I couldn't in all conscience shut him out on such a wet night.* **4 on one's conscience** making one feel guilty: *It's on my conscience that I didn't pay you for the tickets last week.* —see CONSCIOUS (USAGE)

conscience clause /'·· ,·/ *n* a part of a law that says that the law need not be obeyed by people whose consciences will not allow them to obey it

conscience mon·ey /'·· ,··/ *n* [U] money paid, usu. secretly, because of something bad one has done in order to satisfy one's guilty conscience

conscience-strick·en /'·· ,··/ also **conscience-smitten**— *adj* very sorry for having done something wrong

con·sci·en·tious /ˌkɒnʃi'enʃəs◂‖ˌkɑːn-/ *adj* showing great care, attention, or seriousness of purpose: *a conscientious worker* | *a conscientious piece of work* —see CONSCIOUS (USAGE) **– – ly** *adv* **– – ness** *n* [U]

conscientious ob·jec·tor /ˌ····· ·'··/ *n* a person who refuses to serve in the armed forces because of moral or religious beliefs. Although conscientious objectors are officially recognized in Britain and the US, proof is necessary for both governments that a person is really a conscientious objector, e.g. because they belong to a particular religious or PACIFIST organization. During the First World War and the Second World War many conscientious objectors were put in prison in Britain and the US because they could not prove that they belonged to one of these organizations. —see also DRAFT DODGER, VIETNAM WAR — **conscientious objection** *n* [U]

con·scious /'kɒnʃəs‖'kɑːn-/ *adj* **1** [F] having all one's senses working and able to understand what is happening; not in a sleeplike state: *He is badly hurt but still conscious.* | *She was barely conscious.* **2** [F (**of**)] knowing, understanding, or recognizing something; AWARE: *We suddenly became conscious of a sharp increase in the temperature.* | *He wasn't conscious of having offended her.* [+*that*] *I was conscious that he was ill at ease, despite his efforts at conversation.* **3** [A] intentional: *a conscious decision/effort* **4** (*in comb.*) thinking about or very concerned with the stated thing: *a bargain-conscious shopper* | *money-conscious* | *media-conscious politicians* —see also SELF-CONSCIOUS **– – ly** *adv*

▷ USAGE The opposite of **conscious** is **unconscious**: *He's still* **unconscious/He's not conscious** *yet after the accident.* | *I was* **conscious/unconscious** *of her presence.* In PSYCHOLOGY, **conscious** is compared with **subconscious** or **unconscious**: *the* **conscious/subconscious/unconscious** *(mind)* | *a(n)* **conscious/subconscious/unconscious** *dislike.* None of these words should be confused with **conscientious**, which is related in meaning to **conscience**.◁

con·scious·ness /'kɒnʃəsnɨs‖'kɑːn-/ n **1** [U] the condition of being awake and able to understand what is happening: *David lost consciousness at eight o'clock and died a few hours later.* | *When will she regain consciousness?* **2** [U] the ideas, feelings, opinions, etc., held by a person or a group of people about the stated thing: *The experience helped to change her social/political consciousness* **3** [S;U (of)] a state or quality of knowing or feeling something; awareness (AWARE): *a consciousness of danger* [+*that*] *a consciousness that someone else was in the dark room —* see also STREAM OF CONSCIOUSNESS

consciousness rais·ing /'··· ˌ··/ n [U] the process of increasing people's understanding of, and concern about, a moral, social, or political matter: *Deaths from heart disease had risen by so much that the Health Education Council immediately embarked upon a consciousness-raising exercise.*

cons·cript[1] /kən'skrɪpt/ ‖ also **draft** *AmE—* v [T (**into**)] to make (someone) serve in one of the armed forces by law: *My sons were conscripted (into the navy/for military service) in the last war.* —compare RECRUIT[2] (2)

con·script[2] /'kɒnskrɪpt‖'kɑːn-/ also **draftee** *AmE—* n a person made to serve in one of the armed forces by law — compare RECRUIT[1]

con·scrip·tion /kən'skrɪpʃən/ n [U] the practice of making people serve in one of the armed forces by law —see also NATIONAL SERVICE

con·se·crate /'kɒnsɨkreɪt‖'kɑːn-/ v [T] **1** to declare as holy in a special ceremony: *to consecrate a new church* | *consecrated bread and wine* | *to be buried in consecrated ground* **2** [(**to**)] *fml* to set apart solemnly for a particular purpose: *He consecrated his life to helping the poor.* —**cration** /ˌkɒnsɨ'kreɪʃən‖ˌkɑːn-/ n [U] : *the consecration of a new bishop*

con·sec·u·tive /kən'sekjˀtɪv/ adj following in regular unbroken order: *The numbers 4, 5, 6 are consecutive.* | *It's been raining for five consecutive days.* — ~**ly** adv

con·sen·sus /kən'sensəs/ n [usu. sing.] a general agreement; the opinion of most of the people in a group: *What is the (general) consensus of opinion, gentlemen?* | *Can we reach a consensus on this issue?* | *the decline of consensus politics in Britain* | *He's not really in touch with consensus reality* (=what most people agree is real).

con·sent[1] /kən'sent/ v [I (**to**)] *rather fml* to give one's permission or agreement (to a course of action): *Her father reluctantly consented to the marriage.* —see also ASSENT, DISSENT

consent[2] n [U (**to**)] *rather fml* **1** agreement or permission: *My father will never give his consent to our marriage.* | *There is,* **by general/common consent** (=as most people agree), *a serious unemployment problem.* | *The car had been taken without the owner's consent.* —see also AGE OF CONSENT **2 with one consent** *old use* with complete agreement

consenting ad·ult /·ˌ·· '··, ·ˌ·· ·'·/ n *esp. law* an adult who is willing to take part in sexual, esp. HOMOSEXUAL, acts with another adult. Most kinds of sexual activity are legal only if the people involved are consenting adults. —see also AGE OF CONSENT

con·se·quence /'kɒnsɨkwəns‖'kɑːnsɨkwens/ n **1** [C (**of**)] something that follows from an action or set of conditions; result: *The high level of unemployment has produced harmful social consequences.* | *The safety procedures had been ignored, with disastrous consequences.* | *You made the wrong decision, and now you must* **take the consequences.** (=accept the bad things that happen as a result) | **As a/In consequence** *of your laziness and rudeness, I am forced to dismiss you.* **2** [U (**to**)] *fml* importance: *It's of little/no consequence to me.*

Con·se·quen·ces /'kɒsɨkwənsɨz‖'kɑːnsɨkwen-/ n [P +*sing.v*] a game played by a group of people, in which a story is written by means of each person adding a sentence without knowing the sentences already written. The stories usu. involve famous people or friends in unlikely humorous or rude situations and the last sentence of the story begins "And the consequence was…"

con·se·quent /'kɒnsɨkwənt‖'kɑːn-/ adj [(**to, on**)] following as a result: *Competition in the market has led to goods being produced cheaply and a consequent deterioration in quality.* | *(fml) Severe flooding was consequent on the heavy rains.* —compare SUBSEQUENT; see also CONSEQUENTLY

con·se·quen·tial /ˌkɒnsɨ'kwenʃəl◂‖ˌkɑːn-/ adj fml **1** important; SIGNIFICANT: *a consequential decision* —opposite **inconsequential 2** thinking oneself very important; SELF-IMPORTANT: *a bustling consequential little man* **3** consequent

con·se·quent·ly /'kɒnsɨkwəntli‖'kɑːnsɨkwen-/ adv as a result; therefore: *Much of our knowledge and consequently much of our appreciation of his work is based on one biography.* | *The bank refused to help the company; consequently, it went bankrupt.*

con·ser·van·cy /kən'sɜːvənsi‖-ɜːr-/ n *BrE* **1** [+*sing./pl. v*] a group of officials who control and protect an area of land, a river, etc.: *the Thames Conservancy* **2** CONSERVATION (2)

con·ser·va·tion /ˌkɒnsə'veɪʃən‖ˌkɑːnsər-/ n [U (**of**)] **1** the act of keeping something from being wasted or lost: *conservation of energy/momentum* | *a renewed appeal for the careful conservation of water supplies* **2** the careful preservation and protection of natural things, such as animals, forests, rivers, and plants, to prevent them being spoiled, wasted, or lost for ever. Conservation has become a very important subject in politics: *wildlife conservation* | *conservation measures* —see also CONSERVE[1]

conservation a·re·a /·ˌ···'·· ˌ···/ n an area usu. of a town or city with special ARCHITECTURAL or historic interest where the local authority carefully controls building and development work in order to protect the area. There are thousands of conservation areas in Britain.

con·ser·va·tion·ist /ˌkɒnsə'veɪʃənɨst‖ˌkɑːnsər-/ n an active supporter of CONSERVATION (2), esp. one who is not in favour of new buildings or new roads if they will cause damage to the natural world: *The plans to build a big road through the forest were cancelled due to pressure from conservationists/from the conservationist lobby.* (=groups of people interested in conservation) —**ism** n [U]

con·ser·va·tis·m /kən'sɜːvətɨzəm‖-ɜːr-/ n [U] **1** dislike of change, esp. sudden change: *people's innate conservatism in matters of language* **2** (*often cap.*) the (political) belief that the established order of society should be kept as it is for as long as possible and that any change should be gradual. In Britain, conservatism is usually thought of in connection with the Conservative Party. In the US, it is usually thought of in connection with the Republican Party.

con·ser·va·tive[1] /kən'sɜːvətɪv‖-ɜːr-/ adj **1** liking old and established ways, not liking change, esp. sudden change: *a very conservative attitude to education* **2** not very modern in style, taste, manners, etc.; TRADITIONAL: *a very conservative suit/hairstyle* **3** careful; intentionally kept rather low: *At a* **conservative estimate,** *the holiday will cost £300.* (=it will probably cost more) — ~**ly** adv

conservative[2] n a CONSERVATIVE (1,2) person: *Aunt Mary's a real conservative. She's totally opposed to women going out to work.*

Conservative also **Tory—** n, adj (a member) of the Conservative Party: *Conservative policies* | *the Conservative Member of Parliament for Eastbourne* | *The council consists of eight Labour members, five Liberals, and two Conservatives.*

Conservative Par·ty /·ˌ··· ˌ··/, **the** also **Tory Party—** [+*sing./pl. v*] one of the three main British political parties, also known as **the Conservatives** or **the Tories.** It is RIGHT-WING, tending to be opposed to great or sudden changes in the established order of society. It is against state control of industry. The Conservative Party has formed the government in Britain since 1979.: *He's a paid-up member of the Conservative Party.* | *The Conservatives have been in power for 13 years.*

con·ser·va·toire /kən'sɜːvətwɑːʳ‖-ɜːr-/ *BrE* ‖ **conservatory**

AmE — *n* a school where people are trained in music or acting

con·ser·va·to·ry /kən'sɜːvətəri‖-'sɜːrvətɔːri/ *n* **1** a glass-enclosed area, sometimes forming part of a house, where plants are grown. People also build conservatories to add more space to their houses, and to make a pleasant place to sit in the sun. **2** *esp. AmE for* CONSERVATOIRE

con·serve¹ /kən'sɜːv‖-ɜːrv/ *v* [T] to keep from being wasted, damaged, lost, or destroyed; preserve: *Conserve your energy — you'll need it!* | *We must conserve our forests and woodlands for future generations.* | *various methods of conserving electricity*

con·serve² /'kɒnsɜːv‖'kɑːnsɜːrv/ *n* [C *often pl.*;U] *fml* fruit preserved by cooking in sugar; JAM

con·sid·er /kən'sɪdəʳ/ *v* **1** [I;T] to think about, esp. in order to make a decision; examine: *He paused to consider the situation.* | *Your suggestions will be carefully considered.* [+*v-ing*] *I'm considering changing my job.* (=I may change it) [+*wh-*] *We've decided to move but are still considering where to go to.* **2** [T] to take into account: *Before you decide to leave your job, consider the effect it will have on your family.* [+*that*] *If you consider that she's only been studying English for six months, she speaks it very well. Have you considered how difficult it is for the new students?* —see also CONSIDERING **3** [T+*obj*+*n/adj*] to think of in the stated way; regard as: *I consider it a great honour/I consider myself greatly honoured to be invited to join the committee.* | *Do you consider her suitable for the job?* | *A further increase in interest rate is now considered unlikely.* **4 Consider it done.** (a phrase used to tell someone who asks you to do something for them that you will be happy to help them): | *"Could you possibly type this out for me?" "Consider it done!"* **5 be considering one's position** *euph* to be thinking about whether one should RESIGN from one's job

con·sid·e·ra·ble /kən'sɪdərəbəl/ *adj* fairly large or great; of an amount or degree that must be taken seriously: *A considerable number of people object to the government's attitude to immigration.* | *She has considerable influence with the President.* | *at considerable expense* —compare INCONSIDERABLE

con·sid·e·ra·bly /kən'sɪdərəbli/ *adv* much; a great deal: *It's considerably colder today than it was yesterday.*

con·sid·er·ate /kən'sɪdərɪt/ *adj* [(**towards, to**)] *apprec* thoughtful of the wishes, needs, or feelings of others: *Your children are always very considerate towards old people.* | *It was very considerate of you to let us know you were going to be late.* —opposite **inconsiderate** — ~**ly** *adv* — ~**ness** *n* [U] : *I appreciate your considerateness in telling me about it.*

con·sid·e·ra·tion /kənˌsɪdə'reɪʃən/ *n* **1** [U (**for**)] thoughtful attention to or care for the wishes, needs, or feelings of others: *John never showed any consideration for his mother's feelings.* | *The name of the murdered woman has not been released, out of consideration for her parents.* **2** [U (**for, to**)] careful thought; thoughtful attention: *We shall give your request our fullest consideration.* | *After due/long consideration, I have decided to recommend him for the post.* | *She is one of three actresses under consideration for the part.* **3** [C] a fact to be considered when making a decision: *Time is an important consideration.*| *Political rather than economic considerations influenced the location of the new factory.* **4** [C *usu. sing.*] *fml* a payment for a service; reward: *For a small consideration, my friend will help you move your belongings to your new house.* **5 in consideration of** *fml* in return for; because of: *a small payment in consideration of their services* **6 on no consideration** *fml* never; whatever happens: *On no consideration must you leave the patient unattended.* **7 take something into consideration** to remember something when making a judgment or decision: *Your teachers will take your recent illness into consideration when they mark your exams.* | *Taking everything into consideration, the result is better than I expected.*

con·sid·ered /kən'sɪdəd‖-ərd/ *adj* **1** [A] reached after careful thought: *"What do you think of this painting?" "It's complete rubbish." "Oh, I see. That's your* **considered opinion**, *is it?"* **2** [after *adv*] *fml* thought of in the stated usu. good way: *Her paintings are well considered abroad.*| *a very highly considered General* **3 all things considered** when one considers everything that might have produced a different result: *The ground was muddy, and*

she hadn't run for a month, so her speed was really quite good, all things considered.

con·sid·er·ing¹ /kən'sɪdərɪŋ/ *prep, conj* if one takes into account the rather surprising fact (of): *Considering the strength of the opposition, we did very well to score two goals.* [+*that*|*wh-*] *He did very well in his exams considering that he had studied so little/considering how little he had studied.*

considering² *adv* (*in end position only*) *infml* when one considers everything that might have produced a different result: *Yes, her speed was quite good, considering.*

con·sign /kən'saɪn/ *v* [T] **1** [(**to**)] to send (something) to a person or place for sale: *The goods were consigned to you by railway.* **2** [+*obj*+*prep*] *fml* to put into the care or control of someone else: *The captured rebels were consigned to the dungeons.* | (*humor*) *"Where's her letter?" "I signed it to the wastepaper basket."*

con·sign·ee /ˌkɒnsaɪ'niː, -sɪ-‖ˌkɑːn-/ *n tech* the person to whom something is delivered

con·sign·ment /kən'saɪnmənt/ *n* **1** [C (**of**)+*sing.*|*pl. v*] a quantity of goods consigned together: *The last consignment of bananas was bad.* **2** [U] the act of consigning **3 on consignment** sent to a person or shop that pays only for what is sold and returns what is unsold: *to order/send/ship goods on consignment*

con·sign·or , -**er** /kən'saɪnəʳ/ *n tech* a person who consigns goods

con·sist /kən'sɪst/ *v*
consist in sthg. *phr v* [T *not in progressive forms*] *fml* to have as a base; depend on: *The beauty of Venice consists largely in the style of its ancient buildings.*
consist of sthg. *phr v* [T *not in progressive forms*] to be made up of: *The United Kingdom consists of Great Britain and Northern Ireland.* | *a cargo of supplies, consisting mainly of food and medicines* —see COMPRISE (USAGE)

con·sis·ten·cy /kən'sɪstənsi/ *also* **con·sis·tence** /-əns/*rare*— *n* **1** [U] the state of always keeping to the same principles or course of action: *Your behaviour lacks consistency — you say one thing and do another!* —opposite **inconsistency** **2** [C;U] the degree of firmness, stiffness, or thickness: *First mix the butter and sugar to the consistency of thick cream.*

con·sis·tent /kən'sɪstənt/ *adj* **1** (of a person, behaviour, beliefs, etc.) continually keeping to the same principles or course of action; having a regular pattern: *the defendant's consistent denial of the charges* | *The last five years have seen a consistent improvement in the country's economy.* | *a consistent advocate/supporter of penal reform* **2** [(**with**)] in agreement or accordance: *a consistent argument* | *This statement is not consistent with what you said earlier.* | *This development is consistent with the company's aims of reducing its costs.* —opposite **inconsistent** — ~**ly** *adv* : *I'm fed up with your attitude — it's been consistently negative from the very beginning.*

con·so·la·tion /ˌkɒnsə'leɪʃən‖ˌkɑːn-/ *n* [C;U] (a person or thing that gives) comfort during a time of sadness or disappointment: *You boys were a great consolation to me when your father died.* | *I'm sorry I forgot your present: it's not much consolation, I know, but here's your card.* —compare COMPENSATION, RECOMPENSE

consolation prize /ˌ·· '·· ·/ *n* a prize given to someone who has not won a competition, esp. to someone who has come second: *The runners-up each received a T-shirt as a consolation prize.*

con·sol·a·to·ry /kən'sɒlətəri, -'səʊlə-‖-'səʊlətɔːri, -'sɑː-/ *adj fml* intended to console

con·sole¹ /kən'səʊl/ *v* [T (**with**)] to give comfort or sympathy to (someone) in times of disappointment or sadness: *We tried to console her when her dog died.* | *Console yourself with the thought that it might have been worse!* —see also INCONSOLABLE

con·sole² /'kɒnsəʊl‖'kɑːn-/ *n* a flat surface containing the controls for a machine, piece of electrical equipment, ORGAN (4), etc.: *a computer console*

con·sol·i·date /kən'sɒlɪdeɪt‖-'sɑː-/ *v* [I;T] **1** to (cause to) become stronger and firmer: *We've made a good start; now it's time to consolidate.* (=make sure we keep our good position) | *His successful negotiations with the Americans helped him to consolidate his position in the government.* | *The company has consolidated its hold on* *the market.* **2** [(into)] to (cause to) combine into fewer or one; MERGE: *Several local businesses have recently consolidated to form a single large company.* | *a consolidated school district* —**dation** /kənˌsɒlɪ̩ˈdeɪʃən||-̩sɑː-/ *n* [C;U]: *the consolidation of the three firms*

consolidated fund /ˌ·ˌ··· ˈ·/ *n* [*the*+S] *tech* (in Britain) money collected from taxation in order to pay the interest on the national debt

con·sols /kənˈsɒlz||-ˈsɑːlz/ *n* [P] *tech* British government BONDs which earn interest and are repayable on demand

con·som·mé /kənˈsɒmeɪ, ˈkɒnsəmeɪ||̩kɑːnsəˈmeɪ/ *n* [U] clear soup made from meat and/or vegetables

con·so·nance /ˈkɒnsənəns||ˈkɑːn-/ *n* **1** [U (**with**)] *fml* agreement among parts **2** [C;U] *tech* a pleasant-sounding combination of musical notes; HARMONY — opposite **dissonance**

con·so·nant[1] /ˈkɒnsənənt||ˈkɑːn-/ *n* **1** any of the speech sounds made by partly or completely stopping the flow of air as it goes through the mouth **2** a letter representing a consonant sound; any of the letters of the English alphabet except a, e, i, o, u

consonant[2] *adj* **1** [(**with, to**)] in agreement; CONSISTENT: *This policy is scarcely consonant with the government's declared aims.* **2** *tech* having musical consonance —opposite **dissonant**

con·sort[1] /ˈkɒnsɔːt||ˈkɑːnsɔːrt/ *n* a wife or husband, esp. of a ruler —see also PRINCE CONSORT, QUEEN CONSORT

consort[2] *n fml* **1** a group of musicians who perform music of former times, or the group of old-fashioned instruments they use: *a consort of viols* **2 in consort** (**with**) together (with): *He ruled in consort with his father.*

con·sort[3] /kənˈsɔːt||-ɔːrt/ *v*
consort together *phr v* [I] *often derog* to consort with each other: *Thieves often consort together.*
consort with sbdy. *phr v* [T] *often derog* to spend time in the company of (esp. bad people): *to consort with criminals*

con·sor·ti·um /kənˈsɔːtiəm||-ɔːr-/ *n* **-tiums** *or* **-tia** /tiə/ a combination of several companies, banks, etc., for a common purpose: *The new aircraft was developed by a European consortium.*

con·spec·tus /kənˈspektəs/ *n* [(**of**)] *fml* a short report, a set of tables, etc., giving a general view of a subject

con·spic·u·ous /kənˈspɪkjuəs/ *adj* [(**for**)] noticeable; attracting attention; easily seen: *a conspicuous high-rise office block* | *He was conspicuous for his bravery.* | *You were* **conspicuous by your absence** *yesterday.* (=people noticed you were not present) —opposite **inconspicuous** — **~ly** *adv* — **~ness** *n* [U]

conspicuous con·sump·tion /ˌ·ˌ··· ·ˈ··/ *n* [U] wasteful spending intended to attract attention and show one's wealth and high social position, esp. done by people who have recently become wealthy and want other people to know it

con·spir·a·cy /kənˈspɪrəsi/ *n* [C;U] a secret plan by two or more people to do something against the law: *a fraud conspiracy* [+*to-v*] *a conspiracy to smuggle drugs into the country* | *The men were found guilty of conspiracy to murder.* —see also CONSPIRATOR

conspiracy of si·lence /ˌ·ˌ··· ·ˈ··/ *n* **conspiracies of silence** a secret agreement to keep silent about something bad, esp. for selfish reasons

conspiracy theo·ry /·ˈ·· ··· ·ˈ·/ *n* [S] an explanation of an event based on the belief that it was caused by a group of powerful people acting and planning it in secret: *the conspiracy theory explanation of President Kennedy's assassination*

con·spi·ra·tor /kənˈspɪrətər/ *n* a person who takes part in a conspiracy

con·spi·ra·to·ri·al /kənˌspɪrəˈtɔːriəl/ *adj* of or suggesting a conspiracy or a conspirator: *a conspiratorial gathering* | *a conspiratorial glance/wink* — **~ly** *adv*

con·spire /kənˈspaɪər/ *v* [I+*to-v*] **1** [(**with, TOGETHER**)] to plan (something bad) together secretly; take part in a conspiracy: *The criminals conspired (together/with each other) to rob a bank.* **2** (of events) to combine or work together, esp. with bad results: *Events conspired to produce great difficulties for the government.*

con·sta·ble /ˈkʌnstəbəl||ˈkɑːn-/ *n* **1** a British police officer of the lowest rank: *Send Constable Timms.* | *Please could you help me, Constable?* —see also PATROLMAN (1), P.C., W.P.C., OFFICER (3) **2** *tech* the governor of a royal castle **3** *tech* (in former times) an important official in a royal or noble HOUSEHOLD

Constable, John (1776–1837) an English painter known esp. for his paintings and drawings of Suffolk scenery, esp. *The Haywain*, which is one of the most famous British paintings —see colour picture on page 1016

con·stab·u·la·ry /kənˈstæbjʊləri||-leri/ *n* [C+*sing./pl. v*] *esp. BrE* the police force of a particular area or country —see also PATROL (5)

con·stan·cy /ˈkɒnstənsi||ˈkɑːn-/ *n* [U] *fml* **1** freedom from change: *constancy of purpose/of temperature* **2** faithfulness; loyalty: *constancy between husband and wife*

con·stant[1] /ˈkɒnstənt||ˈkɑːn-/ *adj* **1** fixed or unchanging; INVARIABLE: *He drove at a constant speed.* | *A thermostat keeps the temperature constant.* **2** continually happening or repeated; regular: *constant arguments* | *The machinery requires constant maintenance.* | *under constant attack in the newspapers* **3** *lit* loyal; faithful: *a constant friend* — **~ly** *adv*

constant[2] *n tech* something, esp. a number or quantity, that never varies —compare VARIABLE[2]

Con·stan·tine the Great /ˌkɒnstəntaɪn ðə ˈɡreɪt||ˌkɑːn-/ (274–337 AD) the first Christian ruler of the Roman Empire, also known as **Constantine I**. He was responsible for the establishment of the Byzantine Empire, and set up its most important city, Constantinople, in 330 AD.

Con·stan·ti·no·ple /ˌkɒnstæntɪ̩ˈnəʊpəl||ˌkɑːn-/ the city on the Bosphorus which was the capital of the Byzantine Empire for seven centuries from 330 AD onwards, when it was set up by Constantine the Great on the place where Byzantium had formerly stood. Later it was the capital of Turkey. It is now called Istanbul.

con·stel·la·tion /ˌkɒnstɪ̩ˈleɪʃən||ˌkɑːn-/ *n* **1** a number of stars seen from the Earth as a group and often having a name (e.g. the Great Bear) **2** [(**of**)] *lit* a group or gathering, esp. an admired one: *a constellation of famous television performers*

con·ster·na·tion /ˌkɒnstəˈneɪʃən||ˌkɑːnstər-/ *n* [U] *rather fml* great shock and worry or fear; DISMAY: *He was filled with consternation to hear that his friend was so ill.* | *To his consternation, he realized that he had left his chequebook at home.* | *She found, to her utter/total consternation, that she was pregnant.*

con·sti·pa·tion /ˌkɒnstɪ̩ˈpeɪʃən||ˌkɑːn-/ *n* [U] the condition of being unable to empty the bowels frequently enough and/or effectively: *"I've got terrible constipation, mum." "Take a laxative."* —**ted** /ˈkɒnstɪpeɪtɪd||ˈkɑːn-/ *adj* : *You'll get constipated if you never eat fruit.*

con·sti·tu·en·cy /kənˈstɪtʃuənsi/ *n* **1** any of the areas of a country that elect a representative to a parliament: *I must protest at the siting of the new missile base in my constituency.* | *Our MP doesn't even live in this constituency.* **2** [+*sing./pl. v*] the voters living in such an area: *The constituency is/are voting tomorrow.* —compare WARD[1] (2) **3** any group that supports or is likely to support a politician or party: *Big business is his most important constituency.* —see also extra information on page 0000

con·sti·tu·ent[1] /kənˈstɪtʃuənt/ *n* **1** a voter; member of a constituency: *The minister's constituents feel that he does not spend enough time dealing with their problems.* **2** any of the parts that make up a whole: *the constituents of gunpowder/cement* —compare COMPONENT

constituent[2] *adj* [A] being one of the parts that make a whole: *the constituent parts of an atom* | *The EC and its constituent members*

constituent as·sem·bly /·ˌ··· ·ˈ··/ *BrE* ‖ **constitutional convention** *AmE* — *n* (*often caps.*) a body of representatives elected to establish or change the constitution of a country

con·sti·tute /ˈkɒnstɪtjuːt||ˈkɑːnstɪ̩tuːt/ *v fml* **1** [L *not in progressive forms*] to form or make up; be: *the 50 states that constitute the USA* | *Your attitude constitutes a direct challenge to my authority.* —see COMPRISE (USAGE) **2** [T] to formally establish or appoint: *Governments should be constituted by the will of the people.*

con·sti·tu·tion /ˌkɒnstɪ̩ˈtjuːʃən||ˌkɑːnstɪ̩ˈtuː-/ *n* **1** [C] (*often cap.*) the system of laws and principles according to which a country or an organization is governed. Although the constitution of most countries is written down, the British constitution is not: *a proposal to amend* (=change) *the club's constitution.* —see also CONSTITUTION OF THE UNITED STATES **2** [C] the general condition of a person's body or mind: *an old man with a weak constitution* **3** [C (of)] *fml* the way in which something is put together: *objections to the constitution of the committee* **4** [U (of)] the act of establishing, making, or setting up — see also extra information on page 568

con·sti·tu·tion·al[1] /ˌkɒnstɪˈtjuːʃənəl◂‖ˌkɑːnstɪˈtuː-/ *adj* **1** allowed or limited by a political constitution: *There are severe constitutional constraints on the power of the British monarchy.* | *a constitutional government* | *constitutional rights* | *The government can't refuse to hold a by-election — it's not constitutional.* —opposite **unconstitutional**; also CONSTITUTIONAL MONARCHY; see CONSTITUTIONALITY (CULTURAL NOTE) **2** of a political constitution: *a constitutional crisis* **3** of a person's constitution: *a constitutional weakness of the chest* —see also CONSTITUTIONALLY

constitutional[2] *n old-fash* a walk taken to keep oneself healthy

constitutional con·ven·tion /ˌ······ ·ˈ··/ *n AmE* a body of representatives elected to establish or change the constitution of a country: CONSTITUENT ASSEMBLY

Constitutional Convention [*the*] the meeting of representatives in 1787 in Philadelphia that led to the writing of the Constitution of the United States of America

con·sti·tu·tion·al·is·m /ˌkɒnstɪˈtjuːʃənəlɪzəm‖ˌkɑːnstɪˈtuː-/ *n* [U] the belief that a government should be based on established laws and principles —**ist** *n*

con·sti·tu·tion·al·i·ty /ˌkɒnstɪˌtjuːʃəˈnælɪti‖ˌkɑːnstɪˌtuː-/ *n* [U] the quality of being in agreement with a CONSTITUTION (1): *The senator questioned the constitutionality of the proposed law.*

▶ CULTURAL NOTE In the US all laws that come into effect must be in agreement with the Constitution of the United States, whether they are passed at the local, state, or FEDERAL (=national) level. If someone thinks a law is **unconstitutional**, they can ask for a judgment about the law in the courts. A law, or any decision based on it, cannot remain in force if it is found by a court to be **unconstitutional**. Questions which come before the Supreme Court (=the highest court in the US) are always about the **constitutionality** of laws or of legal actions. Americans respect their Constitution very highly because it protects their political freedoms.◀

con·sti·tu·tion·al·ly /ˌkɒnstɪˈtjuːʃənəli‖ˌkɑːnstɪˈtuː-/ *adv* **1** in accordance with a political constitution: *The government must always act constitutionally.* **2** in accordance with a person's constitution: *Margaret is constitutionally incapable of modifying her opinions.*

constitutional mon·ar·chy /ˌ······ ·ˈ··/ *n* a state ruled by a king or queen, in which the powers of the ruler are restricted to those allowed by the CONSTITUTION and laws of the country —compare ABSOLUTE MONARCHY

Constitution of the U·nit·ed States /··ˌ·· · · ·ˌ·· ·ˈ·/ also **Constitution** [*the*] the highest law of the government of the US, consisting of seven ARTICLEs and 25 AMENDMENTs (=a change to the original) which were written down in 1787 and officially came into use in 1789. The Constitution of the US sets out how the government should be formed and what the rights of States and individuals are. When it was first written the rights of individuals were not included, but in 1791 ten AMENDMENTs (additions) known as the Bill of Rights were added. Most Americans would recognize the PREAMBLE (beginning statement) of the Constitution, which reads, "We the people of the United States, in order to form a more perfect union, establish justice, insure domestic tranquility, provide for the common defense, promote the general welfare, and secure the blessings of liberty to ourselves and our posterity, do ordain and establish this Constitution for the United States of America."

con·strain /kənˈstreɪn/ *v* [T] *fml* to hold back, or force into an unwanted action, by limiting one's freedom to act or choose: *Our research has been constrained by lack of cash.* [+*obj+to-v*] *I felt constrained to do what he told me.*

con·strained /kənˈstreɪnd/ *adj* awkward; unnatural: *a constrained manner/smile* — ~**ly** /nᵻdli/ *adv*

con·straint /kənˈstreɪnt/ *n fml* **1** [C (on)] something that limits one's freedom of action; RESTRICTION: *legal/financial constraints on the company's activities* | (*tech*) *constraints on the rules of grammar* **2** [U] a forced or unnatural manner, hiding one's natural feelings and behaviour: *The children showed unusual constraint in the presence of the new teacher.* **3** [U] the threat or use of force as a strong influence on one's actions; COMPULSION: *We obeyed, but under constraint.*

con·strict /kənˈstrɪkt/ *v* [T] *fml* to make narrower, smaller, or tighter: *The tight collar constricted his neck/his breathing.* —compare RESTRICT — ~**ion** /ˈstrɪkʃən/ *n* [C;U] : (*a*) *constriction of the blood vessels* — ~**ive** /ˈstrɪktɪv/ *adj*

con·stric·tor /kənˈstrɪktəʳ/ *n tech* **1** a muscle that reduces or increases the size of an organ in the body **2** a snake, such as a BOA, that kills animals by winding itself round them and crushing them

con·struct[1] /kənˈstrʌkt/ *v* [T] **1** [(**from, of, out of**)] to build; make by putting together or combining parts: *to construct a bridge/a sentence/an argument* **2** *tech* to draw (a GEOMETRIC figure) using suitable instruments: *Construct a square on this line.* — ~**or** *n*

con·struct[2] /ˈkɒnstrʌkt‖ˈkɑːn-/ *n tech* an idea formed in the mind by combining pieces of information; CONCEPT: *theoretical constructs*

con·struc·tion /kənˈstrʌkʃən/ *n* **1** [U] the work of building; building industry: *He works in construction/in the construction industry.* | *construction workers* **2** [U] the act or process of constructing: *There are two new hotels* **under construction.** (=being built) | *a lucrative contract for the construction of four new power stations.* | *A chair is an object of simple construction.* **3** [C] something constructed, esp. a building: *a peculiarly shaped construction* **4** [C] *tech* the arrangement and relationship of words in a phrase or sentence: *A learner's dictionary should give both the meanings of words and examples of the constructions in which they are used.* **5** [C] a meaning or explanation given to a statement, action, etc.; INTERPRETATION: *Please don't* **put the wrong construction on** *his odd behaviour.* — ~**al** *adj*

con·struc·tive /kənˈstrʌktɪv/ *adj* (esp. of a statement or remark) useful; helping to improve or develop something: *a very constructive attitude/suggestion* | *constructive criticism* (=telling you how to improve) —compare DESTRUCTIVE (2) — ~**ly** *adv* — ~**ness** *n* [U]

con·strue /kənˈstruː/ *v* [T] **1** [+*obj+adv/prep*] *fml* to place a particular meaning on (a statement, action, etc.); understand or explain in a particular way: *They construed her silence as meaning that she agreed.* | *I think my remarks have been wrongly construed.* —see also MISCONSTRUE **2** *tech* to explain the relationship of words in (a sentence), esp. when translating Latin or Greek

con·sub·stan·ti·a·tion /ˌkɒnsəbstænʃiˈeɪʃən‖ˌkɑːn-/ *n* [U] *tech* the belief that the body and blood of Christ are present together with the bread and wine offered by the priest during Communion (=a Christian religious service) —compare TRANSUBSTANTIATION

con·sul /ˈkɒnsəl‖ˈkɑːn-/ *n* **1** a person appointed by a government to protect and help its citizens and its interests in trade in a foreign city —compare AMBASSADOR, HIGH COMMISSIONER **2** either of the two chief public officials of the ancient Roman republic, each elected for one year — ~**ar** /ˈkɒnsjᵿləʳ‖ˈkɑːnsələr/ *adj* : *the consular office/section of the embassy* — ~**ship** *n* [C;U]

con·su·late /ˈkɒnsjᵿlᵻt‖ˈkɑːnsəlᵻt/ *n* **1** the official building in which a CONSUL (1) lives or works **2** the rank or period of office of a consul

con·sult /kənˈsʌlt/ *v* [T] to go to (a book, a person with special knowledge, etc.) for information, advice, etc.: *to consult a dictionary* | *Have you consulted a doctor about your rash?* | *Why was I not consulted before you made the decision?* | *to consult a lawyer*
  consult with sbdy. *phr v* [T *pass. rare*] to exchange opinions, information, etc., with: *Before we can accept the management's offer we must consult with the workers again.*

con·sul·tant /kənˈsʌltənt/ *n* **1** [(**to**)] a person who gives specialist professional advice to others: *a consultant to a software firm* | *an industrial relations consultant* | *a firm of consultants* **2** *esp. BrE* ‖ **specialist** *AmE* a high ranking hospital doctor who gives specialist advice.

Usually a person goes to an ordinary doctor first, and is then sent to a consultant. —**tancy** *n* : *He was appointed to a lucrative consultancy.*

con·sul·ta·tion /ˌkɒnsəlˈteɪʃən/ˌkɑːn-/ *n* **1** [C (**on, about**) *often pl.*] a meeting held to exchange opinions and ideas, esp. so that a decision can be made: *We held a hurried consultation on the stairs outside her room.* | *After consultations with his military advisers, the President decided to declare war.* **2** [U (**with**)] the act or process of consulting: *Implementation of the proposed changes would require consultation with teachers and parents.* | *We made the decision* **in consultation with** *the union members.*

con·sul·ta·tive /kənˈsʌltətɪv/ *adj* that can give advice or make suggestions; ADVISORY: *a consultative committee*

con·sult·ing /kənˈsʌltɪŋ/ *adj* [A] **1** providing specialist or professional advice: *a consulting lawyer* **2** of or for consultation or a consultant: *a doctor's consulting room*

con·su·ma·bles /kənˈsjuːməbəlz/‖-ˈsuː-/ *n* [P] food or provisions that can be consumed

con·sume /kənˈsjuːm/‖-ˈsuːm/ *v* [T] *fml* **1** to eat or drink, esp. eagerly or in large amounts **2** to use up (time, money, goods, etc.): *Arguing about details consumed many hours of the committee's valuable time.* | *a* **time-consuming** *process* | *Furnaces consume fuel.* | *a growing gap between what the country produces and what it consumes* —see also CONSUMPTION **3** (of a fire) to destroy: *The fire soon consumed the wooden buildings.* **4** [*often pass.*] to fill the thoughts or feelings of continuously, esp. in a damaging way: *She was consumed with guilt/jealousy.* —see also CONSUMING

con·sum·er /kənˈsjuːməʳ/‖-ˈsuː-/ *n* a person who buys and uses goods and services: *The price increases were passed on by the firm to the consumers.* | *a consumer advice and protection centre* | *consumer surveys*

Consumer Coun·cil /·ˈ·· ˌ·ˈ·/ [*the*] an independent public body in Britain which between 1963 and 1971 performed a similar service to the Consumers' Association in protecting the rights of consumers

consumer dur·a·bles /ˌ·ˌ·· ˈ···/ *BrE* ‖ **durable goods** *AmE*— *n* [P] large articles that are only bought infrequently, such as cars, beds, or televisions (as opposed to something bought regularly, such as food or clothes)

consumer goods /·ˈ·· ˌ·/ *n* [P] goods such as food, clothing, and equipment used in the home —compare CAPITAL GOODS

con·sum·er·ism /kənˈsjuːmərɪzəm/‖-ˈsuː-/ *n* [U] **1** the idea or belief that buying as many goods as possible is desirable for a person or society **2** support for the interests of consumers, e.g. in making sure that prices are not too high, that the quality of goods is satisfactory, etc.

consumer price in·dex /ˌ·ˌ·· ˈ· ˌ·ˈ·/ *n* *AmE* a list of figures available from the government each month that show what ordinary people must pay for various goods and services, and how much these prices have gone up or down in relation to previous figures —compare RETAIL PRICE INDEX

consumer pro·tec·tion /ˌ·ˌ·· ·ˈ··/ *n* [U] actions by government, business, and private groups to protect people who buy things from being physically hurt, cheated, or treated unfairly in any way

consumer re·search /ˌ·ˌ·· ·ˈ·, ·ˌ·· ˈ··/ *n* [U] the study of what people who buy goods and services want, like, and buy, in order to test the market for a new product. This is often done by someone questioning people in shops, or visiting them at home: *After extensive consumer research the new product was launched.*

Consumer Re·ports /·ˌ·· ·ˈ·/ an American magazine which tests and reports on the quality of consumer products. It accepts no advertising and the information it provides is highly respected as being dependable —compare WHICH?

Consumers' As·so·ci·a·tion /·ˈ·· ···ˌ·ˈ·/ [*the*] a British organization that looks after the interests of CONSUMERS, esp. by testing products and services available, in order to suggest the best ones to buy, and that also fights for the rights of consumers generally —see also WHICH?

consumer so·ci·e·ty /·ˈ·· ·ˌ···/ *n* a society in which the production of consumer goods and the satisfaction of human wants are seen to be very important: *We live in a consumer society.*

consumer ter·ror·is·m /·ˌ·· ˈ···/ *n* [U] the deliberate spoiling of food or other products on sale to the public, in order either to obtain money from the company which sells the product or to protest against something the company is doing. An example of this in 1989 involved objects, such as broken glass and pins, being put into baby food in Britain in order to BLACKMAIL the food company: *The government said it would not give way to consumer terrorism.* | *a campaign of consumer terrorism* —**ist** *n*

con·sum·ing /kənˈsjuːmɪŋ/‖-ˈsuː-/ *adj* [A] (of feelings, etc.) very strong and having a controlling influence: *It was her consuming ambition to become an architect.* | *a consuming interest/passion*

con·sum·mate¹ /kənˈsʌmɨt/ *adj* [A *no comp.*] *fml* **1** perfect; complete: *He won the race with consummate ease.* | *consummate happiness/skill* **2** highly skilled: *a consummate liar/politician* —**ly** *adv*

con·sum·mate² /ˈkɒnsəmeɪt‖ˈkɑːn-/ *v* [T] *fml* **1** to make (a marriage) complete by having sex. In English and American law a marriage is legal after the wedding, but it is not considered complete until sex has taken place, and it can be declared NULL AND VOID if one partner cannot or will not consummate the marriage in this way. **2** to finish or perfect; complete: *His happiness was consummated when she agreed to spend the day with him.* | *to consummate a business deal*

con·sum·ma·tion /ˌkɒnsəˈmeɪʃən‖ˌkɑːn-/ *n* **1** [C (**of**) *usu. sing.*] the point at which something is made complete or perfect: *the consummation of ten years' work* **2** [U] the act of consummating a marriage

con·sump·tion /kənˈsʌmpʃən/ *n* **1** [S;U (**of**)] the act of consuming or an amount consumed (CONSUME): *Consumption of oil has declined in recent years.* | *The food was declared unfit for human consumption.* | *The car's fuel consumption is very high.* | *There's too great a consumption of alcohol in Britain.* —see also CONSPICUOUS CONSUMPTION **2** [U] *old use* TUBERCULOSIS of the lungs (=a serious disease): *She died from/of consumption.*

con·sump·tive /kənˈsʌmptɪv/ *n, adj old use* (a person) suffering from TUBERCULOSIS of the lungs

cont *written abbrev. for:* **1** containing **2** contents **3** CONTINENT¹ **4** continued

con·tact¹ /ˈkɒntækt‖ˈkɑːn-/ *n* **1** [U (**with**)] the act or state of touching or coming together: *His drill* **came into contact with** *an electric cable, and he was nearly electrocuted.* | *Have the children been in contact with the disease?* | *They avoided* **eye contact** (=avoided looking directly at each other) *all evening.* **2** [U (**with**)] the state of having a connection or exchanging information or ideas with someone else; COMMUNICATION: *Until recently, this remote tribe had little contact with the outside world.* | *Have you been* **in contact with** *your solicitor recently?* | *We* **made contact with** *the ship by radio.* | *Are you in radio contact with the climbers?* | *I've lost contact with George in the last few months.* (=I have not seen him, telephoned him, had a letter from him, etc.) **3** [C] *infml* a social, professional, or business connection; a person who knows who can help one: *I've got a useful contact in the tax office.* | *Ask Henry — he's got the right contacts/some good contacts.* **4** [C] an electrical part that can be moved to touch another part in order to complete an electrical CIRCUIT **5** [C] *infml for* CONTACT LENS

contact² *v* [T] to reach (someone) by message, telephone, etc.: *Have you contacted the child's parents?* | *For further information, contact your local agent.*

contact³ *adj* [A] caused or made active by touch: *contact poisons/explosives* | *He doesn't like playing* **contact sports**. (=sports which involve physical contact with other players)

contact der·ma·ti·tis /ˌ·· ···ˈ··/ *n* [U] a painful condition of the skin caused by direct contact with a substance, esp. a chemical, which makes the skin react by becoming red and swollen

contact lens /ˈ·· ·/ also **lens, contact** *infml*— *n* [*often pl.*] a small plastic LENS shaped to fit closely over the centre of the eye to improve the eyesight, or sometimes to change the colour of the eyes: *hard/soft contact lenses* —see PAIR (USAGE)

contact print /ˈ·· ·/ *n tech* a photographic print made by putting an exposed film into direct contact with paper or film and allowing light to reach it

con·ta·gion /kən'teɪdʒən/ n fml **1** [C;U] the act of spreading a disease by touch, or a disease spread in this way —compare INFECTION **2** [C (**of**)] a harmful influence that spreads from person to person: *a contagion of fear*

con·ta·gious /kən'teɪdʒəs/ adj **1** (of a disease) that can be passed from one person to another by touch: *Measles is highly contagious.* | (fig.) *contagious laughter|enthusiasm* —compare INFECTIOUS **2** (of a person) having a contagious disease − ∼ly adv − ∼ness n [U]

con·tain /kən'teɪn/ v [T not in progressive forms] **1** to hold; have within itself or as a part: *That box contains old letters.* | *Beer contains alcohol.* | *This book contains all the information you need.* | *The bill contained several new clauses.* | *a file containing classified information* –see also CONTENTS **2** to hold back; keep under control or within limits: *Try to contain your enthusiasm|anger!* | *She couldn't contain herself any longer − she simply had to tell him the good news.* | *Doctors are struggling to contain the epidemic.* –see also SELF-CONTAINED **3** tech to surround (esp. an angle): *How big is the angle contained by these two sides?*

con·tain·er /kən'teɪnər/ n **1** a box, barrel, bottle, or any other object used for holding something: *Can you find some kind of container for these buttons?* **2** tech a very large usu. metal box in which goods are packed to make it easy to lift or move them, e.g. onto a ship or road vehicle: *a cargo container* | *a container port* (=port that handles ships that carry containers)

con·tain·er·ize also **-ise** BrE /kən'teɪnəraɪz/ v [T] tech **1** to pack (goods) in CONTAINERS (2) **2** to change (a place) so that CONTAINERs (2) can be used there: *plans to containerize the port* –**ization** /kən,teɪnəraɪ'zeɪʃən‖-rə-/ n [U]

con·tain·ment /kən'teɪnmənt/ n [U] **1** the act of containing (CONTAIN (2)) something: *the containment of an epidemic|of crowd violence at soccer matches* **2** the use of political means other than war to prevent an unfriendly state from becoming more powerful

con·tam·i·nant /kən'tæmɪnənt/ n something that contaminates

con·tam·i·nate /kən'tæmɪneɪt/ v [T] to make impure or bad by mixing in impure, dirty, or poisonous matter: *Large areas of land have been contaminated by the leakage from the nuclear reactor.* | *contaminated food|drugs* | (fig.) *Our students are being contaminated by his extreme right-wing ideas!* –**nator** n –**nation** /kən,tæmɪ'neɪʃən/ n [U]: *radioactive contamination*

con·tan·go /kən'tæŋgəʊ/ n **-gos** BrE tech a sum of money which someone buying SHARES¹ (2) pays to the seller in order to delay delivery until a later date —compare BACK-WARDATION

contd written abbrev. for: continued

con·tem·plate /'kɒntəmpleɪt‖'kɑːn-/ v **1** [I;T] to think (about) deeply and thoughtfully, esp. when considering a possible course of action or future event: *The doctor contemplated the difficult operation he had to perform.* | *The possibility of war is too horrifying to contemplate!* | *He refuses to contemplate change.* [+v-ing] *The government has contemplated reforming the entire tax system.* | (infml) *I hope your mother isn't contemplating coming to stay with us!* **2** [T] fml to look at quietly and solemnly: *to contemplate a beautiful sunset* **3 contemplate one's navel** humor to think deeply; used esp. when one is not doing anything very much

con·tem·pla·tion /,kɒntəm'pleɪʃən‖,kɑːn-/ n [U (**of**)] **1** the act of thinking deeply and quietly; deep thought: *She seemed lost in contemplation.* | *The monks spent an hour in contemplation each morning.* **2** fml the act of looking at something quietly and solemnly —**plative** /kən'templətɪv, 'kɒntəmpleɪtɪv‖kən-, 'kɑːntem-/ adj : *He has a quiet, contemplative nature.*

con·tem·po·ra·ne·ous /kən,tempə'reɪniəs/ adj [(**with**)] fml existing or happening during the same period of time; CONTEMPORARY (2) − ∼ly adv –**neity** /kən,tempərə'niːɪti/ n [U]

con·tem·po·ra·ry¹ /kən'tempərəri, -pəri‖-pəreri/ adj **1** modern; belonging to the present time: *contemporary dress|art|morals* | *a contemporary building* **2** [(**with**)] of or belonging to the same (stated) time: *Beethoven was contemporary with Napoleon.* | *Contemporary reports of*

---

past events are often more interesting than modern historians' view of them. –see NEW (USAGE)

contemporary² n a person living at the same time or of the same age as another: *John is a contemporary of mine;* *we were at school together.* | *Beethoven and Napoleon were contemporaries.*

con·tempt /kən'tempt/ n [U] **1** [(**for**)] a total lack of respect; the feeling that someone or something is completely worthless, unimportant, or undesirable; DISDAIN: *Take no notice of them − treat them with the contempt they deserve.* | *His contempt for most of his fellow politicians is clearly expressed in his book.* | *He is completely* **beneath contempt**. (=not even worth the effort of feeling contempt) | *I hold those fools in (utter) contempt.* –compare DISDAIN¹ **2** [(**of**)] disobedience of or disrespect towards a judge, court of law, etc: *He was charged with* **contempt of court**. | *He was found in contempt of the order.*

con·temp·ti·ble /kən'temptəbəl/ adj deserving to be treated with contempt; DESPICABLE: *That was a contemptible trick to play on a friend!* | *an absolutely contemptible little man* –**bly** adv

con·temp·tu·ous /kən'temptʃuəs/ adj [(**of**)] showing contempt: *He gave a contemptuous laugh.* | *Contemptuous of danger, he rushed back into the burning building.* − ∼ly adv : *She tossed her head contemptuously.*

con·tend /kən'tend/ v **1** [I (**against, for, with**)] to compete or struggle against difficulties: *They are contending for the championship.* | *I've got enough problems to contend with, without your interference!* **2** [T+that;obj] fml to claim; say or state strongly: *The police contended that the man was in the area at the time of the robbery.* –see also CONTENTION

con·tend·er /kən'tendər/ n [(**for**)] (esp. in sports) a person who takes part in a competition: *a serious contender for the championship* | *a leading contender to succeed the prime minister*

con·tent¹ /kən'tent/ adj [F (**with**)] satisfied; happy; not wanting more than one has: *content with life* [+to-v] *John seems content to sit in front of the television all night.* | (derog) **Not content with** *having overthrown the government, the military dictator imprisoned all his opponents.* –see also CONTENTED

content² v [T] **1** to make happy or satisfied **2 content oneself with** to limit oneself to, and be satisfied with: *As he had to drive home after the party, he contented himself with two glasses of beer.*

content³ n [U] lit CONTENTMENT –opposite **discontent**; see also **to one's heart's content** (HEART)

con·tent⁴ /'kɒntent‖'kɑːn-/ n **1** [U] the subject matter, esp. the ideas, of a book, speech, etc.: *I like the style of his writing but I don't like the content.* **2** [S] the amount of the stated substance contained in something: *the lead content of paint* | *food with a high fat content* –compare CONTENTS

con·tent·ed /kən'tentəd/ adj satisfied; quietly happy: *contented cows* | *a contented smile* − ∼ly adv

con·ten·tion /kən'tenʃən/ n fml **1** [C] a point of view that one argues in favour of; ASSERTION: *I strongly oppose that contention.* [+that] *It is my contention that the plan would never have been successful.* –see also **bone of contention** (BONE) **2** [U (**against, for, with, between**)] arguing, competing, or struggling between people: *The pay increase is the key point of contention.* | *This issue is no longer* **in contention**.(=being argued about) | *Losing three matches in a row has put them out of contention for the championship title.* (=they are no longer able to win it)

con·ten·tious /kən'tenʃəs/ adj fml **1** likely to cause argument; CONTROVERSIAL: *a contentious issue|decision* **2** (of a person) fond of arguing − ∼ly adv − ∼ness n [U]

con·tent·ment /kən'tentmənt/ n [U] quiet happiness; satisfaction: *The cat purred in obvious contentment.* | *the contentment of a well-fed baby*

con·tents /'kɒntents‖'kɑːn-/ n [P] **1** [(**of**)] that which is contained in something: *He drank the contents of the bottle.* | *The police emptied her bag and examined the contents.* | *The Prime Minister declined to go into details on the contents of his talks with the Chancellor.* **2** a list in a book saying what the book contains: *Look at the contents (page) before you buy the book.* | *the table of contents* –compare CONTENT

con·test¹ /ˈkɒntest‖ˈkɑːn-/ n **1** a struggle or fight to gain control or advantage: *the contest for leadership of the party* **2** a competition, esp. one judged by a group of specially chosen judges: *a beauty contest*

con·test² /kənˈtest/ v [T] *fml* **1** to compete for; fight for: *How many people are contesting the seat on the council?* | *a fiercely contested takeover bid* **2** to argue about the rightness of: *I intend to contest the judge's decision in another court.* | *Her husband has filed for divorce and she's contesting it.*

con·tes·tant /kənˈtestənt/ n someone competing in a contest: *Tonight's lucky contestants have already been selected from the audience.*

con·text /ˈkɒntekst‖ˈkɑːn-/ n **1** the parts of a piece of writing, a speech, etc. which surround a word or passage and which influence or help to explain its meaning: *In some contexts "mad" means "foolish", in some "angry", and in others "insane".* | *He was furious that the papers had quoted his remarks completely* **out of context**. **2** the surrounding conditions in which something takes place: *Look at your own job in the wider context of the whole department.* | *The report should be considered within its social context.*

con·tex·tu·al /kənˈtekstʃuəl/ adj of or according to the context: *This word has a special contextual meaning here.* – ~**ly** adv

con·tex·tu·al·ize also **-ise** BrE /kənˈtekstʃuəlaɪz/ v [T] to put into context **--ization** /kənˌtekstʃuəlaɪˈzeɪʃən‖-lə-/ n [U]

Con·ti /ˈkɒnti‖ˈkɑːn-/, **Tom** (1945–) a Scottish stage and film actor whose films include *Merry Christmas, Mr Lawrence* and *Shirley Valentine*

con·ti·board /ˈkɒntibɔːd‖ˈkɑːntibɔːrd/ n [U] *tdmk* (*often cap.*) a type of board covered in MELAMINE and used for shelves

con·ti·gu·i·ty /ˌkɒntɪˈɡjuːɪti‖ˌkɑːn-/ also **con·tig·u·ous·ness** /kənˈtɪɡjuəsnɪs/— n [U (**to, with**)] *fml* nearness; the state of being contiguous

con·tig·u·ous /kənˈtɪɡjuəs/ adj [(**to, with**)] *fml* **1** touching; next (to); having a shared border: *England is the only country contiguous to/with Wales.* **2** next to or near in time or order: *contiguous events* – ~**ly** adv

con·ti·nent¹ /ˈkɒntɪnənt‖ˈkɑːn-/ n any of the seven main large masses of land on the Earth: *the European continent* | *the continents of Africa and Asia*

continent² adj *fml* able to control oneself, esp. a one's bowels and BLADDER **b** *old use* one's sexual desires – opposite **incontinent** **--nence** n [U]

Continent [*the*] Western Europe not including the British Isles: *He's gone for a holiday on the Continent – Italy, I think.*

▷ USAGE When Americans speak of **Europe** they usually mean both Britain and the **Continent**: *We're going to* **Europe** *this summer.* British speakers who are going, for example, to France or Spain might say: *We're going to the* **Continent**.◁

con·ti·nen·tal¹ /ˌkɒntɪˈnentl◀‖ˌkɑːn-/ adj **1** (typical) of a very large mass of land: *a continental climate* | *continental waters* (=the sea round a continent) **2** (of food, ideas, behaviour, etc.) thought to be typical of other European countries, esp. France and Italy. People often use **continental** to describe things they admire and want to copy, such as particular types of food or types of behaviour: *continental food* | *The cafe has tables outside on the pavement – it looks very continental.* **3** [A] (*often cap.*) *AmE* of or in the North American continent: *The continental United States does not include Hawaii.*

continental² n **1** *old-fash* a person who comes from Europe, but not one from the British Isles **2 not worth a continental** *AmE infml* worthless

continental break·fast /ˌ···ˈ··/ n a light breakfast usu. consisting of CROISSANTS or bread rolls, butter, JAM, and coffee, typically eaten in various European countries – compare ENGLISH BREAKFAST

Continental Con·gress /ˌ····ˈ··/ [*the*] the law-making body that governed the 13 colonies (COLONY) that later formed the US. It passed the Declaration of Independence.

continental day /ˌ····ˈ·/ n [*the*+U] a school working day, common in Europe but not in Britain, which does not include an hour for a meal but starts and finishes early so that the children can do sports, music, and other activi-

ties in the afternoons. There has been some discussion about introducing this in Britain, because it means that in winter children can go home more safely, while it is still light.

Continental Di·vide /ˌ···· ·ˈ·/ also **Great Divide**– [*the*] the chain of high mountains running from North to South in North America. They divide the rivers which flow into the Pacific Ocean from those which flow into the Atlantic Ocean or the Gulf of Mexico.

continental drift /ˌ···· ˈ·/ n [U] *tech* the very slow movement of the CONTINENTS across the surface of the Earth

continental quilt /ˌ···· ˈ·/ n BrE for DUVET

continental shelf /ˌ···· ˈ·/ n a plain under the sea forming the edge of a CONTINENT, typically ending in a very steep slope to the ocean's depths

con·tin·gen·cy /kənˈtɪndʒənsi/ n a future event that may or may not happen, esp. one that would cause problems if it did happen; possibility: *We must be prepared for every contingency.* | *We have* **contingency plans** *ready in case there is a flood.* | *contingency reserves*

contingency fee /·ˈ···· ,·/ n (in the US) the amount of money that a lawyer will collect only if the person he/she is advising wins in court. It is usually a PERCENTAGE of the total amount that the court decides on.

con·tin·gent¹ /kənˈtɪndʒənt/ adj *fml* **1** [F+**on, upon**] dependent on something uncertain or in the future: *The company's future is contingent on the outcome of the trial.* **2** happening by chance; accidental – ~**ly** adv

contingent² n **1** a group of soldiers, ships, etc., gathered together to help a larger force: *The army has been strengthened by a large contingent of foreign soldiers.* **2** [+*sing./pl. v*] *infml* a representative group forming part of a large gathering: *Have the Scottish contingent arrived at the meeting yet?*

con·tin·u·al /kənˈtɪnjuəl/ adj **1** [A] *often derog* repeated often and over a long period; regular; frequent: *continual demands for improved working conditions* | *continual interruptions* **2** continuing without interruption or break: *They lived in continual fear.* – ~**ly** adv

▷ USAGE Compare **continual** and **continuous**. **Continual** usually describes actions (often annoying or undesirable actions) which are repeated over a period of time: *Stop that* **continual** *hammering.* | *I'm tired of the way he* **continually** *complains about everything.* **Continuous** describes things and events which continue without interruption: *The trees formed a* **continuous** *line on the horizon.* | *The plane landed after flying* **continuously** *for 16 hours.*◁

con·tin·u·ance /kənˈtɪnjuəns/ n [S;U] *fml* the state or act of continuing: *Continuance of the war will mean shortages of food.*

con·tin·u·a·tion /kənˌtɪnjuˈeɪʃən/ n [(**of**)] **1** [U] the act of continuing: *How can you support the continuation of trade relations with such a country?* **2** [C] something which continues from something else: *The Baltic Sea is a continuation of the North Sea.*

con·tin·ue /kənˈtɪnjuː/ v **1** [I (**with**);T] to (cause to) go on over a long period or space, without stopping or being interrupted; carry on: *The fighting continued for a week.* | *The road continues for another five miles.* | *If sales continue at their present rate, we will make record profits this year.* | *How long can they continue (with) this damaging strike?* [+*to-v*] *Although they were obviously getting angry, he continued to stare at them.* | *Despite having new owners, the company will continue to be run by its present management.* [+*v-ing*] *He continued writing his diaries until he died.* | *The dollar remained high because of the continued strength of the US economy.* **2** [I;T] to (cause to) start again after an interruption: *After a short break the game continued.* | *The story will be continued next week.* [+*v-ing*] *Are you going to continue gardening after dinner?* **3** [I+*adv/prep*] to remain in a place, state, or condition; stay: *She will continue as spokeswoman for the organization.* **4** [I;T] to say also; go on to say, esp. after an interruption: *The politician continued by saying that he thought taxes should be lowered.* | *"And so",* *she continued, "the fight for equality must go on."* –see also CONTINUAL, CONTINUOUS, DISCONTINUE

continuing ed·u·ca·tion /·ˌ···· ··ˈ··/ n [U] education provided for adults outside the formal educational system, usu. by means of classes that are held in the evening; ADULT EDUCATION —compare FURTHER EDUCATION

con·ti·nu·i·ty /ˌkɒnt₃ˈnjuːₔti‖ˌkɑːntₔˈnuː-/ n [U]   **1** [(**in, between**)] uninterrupted connection; the fact or quality of being continuous: *There's no continuity between the three parts of the book.*   **2** *tech* the arrangement of the parts of a film, broadcast, etc., to give the appearance of continuous action   **3** *tech* the music, words, etc., that connect the parts of a broadcast, film, etc.

continuity an·nounc·er /··ˈ··· ·ₔ·/ n the person responsible for giving the listeners or viewers information between the programmes on radio or television

continuity girl /··ˈ··· ·/ **continuity man** *masc.— n* the person responsible for the CONTINUITY (2) of a film

con·tin·u·o /kənˈtɪnjuˌəʊ/ also **figured bass**— *n* -**os** (in music, esp. of the 17th and 18th centuries) a musical part consisting of a set of low notes with figures showing the higher notes (CHORDS) to be played with them

con·tin·u·ous /kənˈtɪnjuəs/ *adj* continuing without interruption; unbroken: *The brain needs a continuous supply of blood.* | *The government is under continuous pressure to reform the parliamentary system.* | *a continuous line of cars/rise in the population* | *that printer uses continuous paper* (=connected sheets of folded pages) —see CONTINUAL (USAGE) — ~ly *adv*

continuous as·sess·ment /·ˌ··· ·ˈ··/ n [U] the system of judging the quality of a student's work at every stage of a course, rather than only in exams at the end of the course. This is an important part of the GCSE courses which are now taught in British schools: *"What proportion of your degree course was continuous assessment?" "Sixty per cent."*

con·tin·u·um /kənˈtɪnjuəm/ n -**uums** or -**ua** / juə/ *fml or tech*   **1** something which is without parts and the same from beginning to end: *the continuum of time* | *the space/time continuum*   **2** something that changes gradually and without sudden breaks: *a continuum from the lowest to the highest forms of life*

con·tort /kənˈtɔːt‖-ɔːrt/ v [I;T (**with**)] to (cause to) twist violently out of shape: *Her face was contorted with anger/with pain.* | *trees with contorted branches*

con·tor·tion /kənˈtɔːʃən‖-ɔːr-/ n   **1** [U] the act of contorting or being contorted: *the contortion of the body caused by certain kinds of poison*   **2** [C] a twisted position or movement: *the contortions of a snake*

con·tor·tion·ist /kənˈtɔːʃənₔst‖-ɔːr-/ n someone, esp. a professional entertainer, who can twist their body into unnatural shapes and positions: (fig.) *Watch out for Sally in an argument — she's a bit of a verbal contortionist!*

con·tour¹ /ˈkɒntʊəʳ‖ˈkɑːn-/ n   **1** also **contours** *pl.*— the shape of the outer edges of an area: *the irregular contours of the British coastline*   **2** also **contour line** /ˈ·· ·/— a line drawn on a map to show the limits of the areas at or above a certain height above sea level: *the 500 foot contour* | *a contour map*

contour² v [T] *tech*   **1** to build (a road) along the contours of a hill   **2** to show the contours of (an area) on a map

contour³ *adj* [A] following the contours of the land: *contour farming/ploughing*

con·tra /ˈkɒntrə‖ˈkɑːn-/ n [*usu. pl.*]   **1** (*often cap.*) a member of a military organization which fought the Nicaraguan government in the 1980s: *the Contra rebels* —see also IRANGATE   **2** someone who opposes another, usu. in a political sense: *Tory contras opposed to Heseltine*

contra- see WORD FORMATION

con·tra·band /ˈkɒntrəbænd‖ˈkɑːn-/ *adj, n* [U] (of or being) goods which it is not legal to bring into a country: *Customs officials seized several tons of contraband cigarettes.* | *to trade in contraband*

con·tra·bass /ˌkɒntrəˈbeɪs‖ˌkɑːn-/ n a DOUBLE BASS

con·tra·cep·tion /ˌkɒntrəˈsepʃ ə n‖ˌkɑːn-/ n [U] the act or practice of preventing sex from resulting in the birth of a child, and/or the methods for doing this; BIRTH CONTROL: *Most doctors give advice on contraception.* | *Which method/form of contraception do you use?*

▶ CULTURAL NOTE In Western countries, contraception is widely accepted and used, but the Catholic church is opposed to its use, and believes only in using the RHYTHM METHOD as a means of BIRTH CONTROL. ◀

con·tra·cep·tive /ˌkɒntrəˈseptɪv‖ˌkɑːn-/ n a drug, object, or method used as a means of preventing an act of sex from resulting in the woman becoming PREGNANT. Contraceptives are usu. obtained from a doctor, except for the CONDOM, which can be bought, e.g. at a CHEMIST's shop: *The percentage of married couples using contraceptives is very high in this country.* —see also CAP¹ (6), CONDOM, IUD, PILL, SPERMICIDE; see CONDOM (CULTURAL NOTE) — **contraceptive** *adj* [A] : *contraceptive advice/pills*

con·tract¹ /ˈkɒntrækt‖ˈkɑːn-/ n   **1** a formal written agreement, having the force of law, between two or more people or groups: *a building contract* | *According to the terms of your contract (of employment) you must give three months' notice if you intend to leave.* | *The company has won a valuable contract for the construction of a dam.* | *Is the contract binding (on us)?* [+to-v] *Our shop has entered into/made a contract with a clothing firm to buy 100 coats a week.* | *If you don't deliver the goods by Friday we will be breaking the contract/in breach of contract.* — see also CONTRACT³ (2), CONTRACTOR, CONTRACTUAL   **2** a signed paper on which the conditions of such an agreement are written: *a draft contract* | *to draw up a contract* | *to sign a contract*   **3** an agreement (spoken rather than written) in the card game BRIDGE, to win a certain number of TRICKS: *a contract of four spades* | *They made the contract.*   **4** *sl* an agreement to kill a particular person, esp. for money; used mainly by criminals: *There was a contract out on him.*

contract² v
   contract in *phr v* [I (**to**)] *esp. BrE* to agree or promise, esp. officially, to take part
   contract out *phr v*   **1** *esp. BrE* [I (**of**)] to agree or promise, esp. officially, not to take part: *to contract out of a pension scheme*   **2** [T] (**contract** sthg. ↔ **out**) ‖ also **farm** sthg. ↔ **out** *AmE*— (of a company, organization, etc.) to arrange by formal agreement to have (a job, services, etc.) done by another company: *Many councils are contracting out services such as garbage collection to private companies as a way of cutting costs.*

con·tract³ /kənˈtrækt/ v   **1** [I;T] to (cause to) become smaller, narrower, or shorter: *Metal contracts as it becomes cool.* | *In conversational English "is not" often contracts to "isn't".* —see also CONTRACTION   **2** [I;T] to arrange by formal agreement: *to contract an alliance* [+to-v] *The firm contracted to build the new railway within the year.* | *Our shop contracted with a local clothing firm for 100 coats a week.*   **3** [T] *fml* to get or begin to have (something bad, esp. an illness): *My son's contracted pneumonia.* | *to contract a debt/a bad habit*

contract bridge /ˌ·· ·/ n [U] a form of the card game BRIDGE, in which the partnership playing the HAND¹ (4b) make a CONTRACT¹ (3) (=say how many TRICKS¹ (5) they will try to win) and any additional tricks are recorded separately —compare AUCTION BRIDGE

con·trac·tile /kənˈtræktaɪl‖-tl/ also **con·trac·ti·ble** /kənˈtræktₔbəl/— *adj tech* (esp. of a muscle) that can become smaller: *The heart is a highly contractile organ.*

con·trac·tion /kənˈtrækʃən/ n   **1** [U] the process of contracting: *the contraction of metal as it cools*   **2** [C (**of**)] a shortened form of a word or words: *"Haven't" is a contraction of "have not".*   **3** [C] *tech* a very strong and often painful tightening of a muscle, esp. of the muscles around the WOMB during the process of birth: *Come into the hospital when there is a five minute space between (your) contractions.*

con·trac·tion·a·ry /kənˈtrækʃ ə nəri‖-ʃəneri/ *adj* showing or causing contraction, and esp. causing a reduction in business activity: *the contractionary influences of the Chancellor's policy* —opposite **expansionary**

con·trac·tor /kənˈtræktəʳ‖ˈkɑːntræk-/ n a person or company that contracts to do work or provide supplies in large amounts, esp. to provide building materials or workers for building jobs

con·trac·tu·al /kənˈtræktʃuəl/ *adj* of or agreed in a contract: *a contractual duty to give three months' notice of your intention to leave* | *contractual obligations* — ~ly *adv* : *contractually binding*

con·tra·dict /ˌkɒntrəˈdɪkt‖ˌkɑːn-/ v   **1** [I;T] to say that (a person, opinion, something written or spoken, etc.) is wrong or untruthful: *If you contradict me once more, you're fired!* | *Don't contradict your father!*   **2** [T] (of a statement, action, fact, etc.) to be opposite in nature or character to (another one); disagree with: *Their alibis contradict each other.* (=if one is true, the other must be false)

con·tra·dic·tion /ˌkɒntrəˈdɪkʃən‖ˌkɑːn-/ n **1** [C] a statement, action, or fact that contradicts another or itself: *It is a contradiction to say you support the government but would not vote for it in an election.* | *The prosecution quickly pointed out the contradictions in the defendant's testimony.* | *"Married bachelor" is* **a contradiction in terms.** (=an impossible combination of words) **2** [C;U (between)] direct opposition between things compared; disagreement: *Your behaviour is* **in (direct) contradiction** to *your principles.* | *There's no contradiction between the Prime Minister's views and my own.* **3** [U] the act of contradicting or being contradicted: *I think I can say, without fear of contradiction, that this is of vital importance for all of us.*

con·tra·dic·to·ry /ˌkɒntrəˈdɪktəri‖ˌkɑːn-/ adj [(to)] contradicting; not in agreement: *contradictory reports/ desires/advice* —see also SELF-CONTRADICTORY

con·tra·dis·tinc·tion /ˌkɒntrədɪˈstɪŋkʃən‖ˌkɑːn-/ n **in contradistinction to** fml as opposed to; rather than; in CONTRAST to: *plants in contradistinction to animals*

con·tra·flow /ˈkɒntrəfləʊ‖ˈkɑːn-/ n esp. BrE an arrangement on a large road by which traffic going in both directions uses only one side of the road, e.g. because the other side is being repaired: *A temporary contraflow is in force on the motorway.*

con·trail /ˈkɒntreɪl‖ˈkɑːn-/ also **vapour trail** n tech a line of white steam made in the sky by planes flying at a great height

con·tra·in·di·ca·tion /ˌkɒntrəˌɪndɪˈkeɪʃən‖ˌkɑːn-/ n tech a physical sign or condition which makes it inadvisable to take or continue taking a medicine: *High blood pressure is a contraindication for this drug.* —**cated** /-ˈɪndʒkeɪtʃd/ adj

con·tral·to /kənˈtræltəʊ/ n -tos ALTO¹ (2)

con·trap·tion /kənˈtræpʃən/ n infml, usu. derog a strange-looking machine or piece of equipment: *I don't understand how this contraption works.* | *That's a curious contraption; what's it for?*

con·tra·pun·tal /ˌkɒntrəˈpʌntl◂‖ˌkɑːn-/ adj of or using musical COUNTERPOINT — ~ **ly** adv

con·tra·ri·wise /ˈkɒntrəriwaɪz, kənˈtreəri-‖ˈkɑːntreri-/ adv old-fash or humor in the opposite way or direction; conversely (CONVERSE)

con·tra·ry¹ /ˈkɒntrəri‖ˈkɑːntreri/ n **1** [the+S] fml the opposite: *They say he is guilty, but I believe the contrary.* **2** **on the contrary** (used for expressing strong opposition or disagreement with what has just been said) not at all; no: *"I hear you are enjoying your new job." "On the contrary, I find it rather dull."* **3** **to the contrary** to the opposite effect; differently: *If you don't hear (anything) to the contrary I'll meet you at seven o'clock tonight.* | *You may be right; there's no evidence to the contrary.*

▷ USAGE Compare **on the contrary, on the other hand, in contrast.** Use **on the contrary** to show complete disagreement with what has just been said: *"Does it rain a lot in the desert?" "On the contrary, it hardly ever rains."* Use **on the other hand** when adding a new and different fact to a statement: *It rarely rains in the desert, but* **on the other hand** *it rains a lot in the coastal areas.* Use **in contrast** to show the (surprising) difference between two very different facts: *It is hot in the desert in the day, but* **in contrast** *it's very cold at night.*◁

contrary² adj **1** [(to)] completely different or wholly opposed: *contrary opinions/opinions contrary to mine* | *Contrary to* (=against) *all our advice, he gave up his job.* **2** fml (of weather conditions) unfavourable; ADVERSE: *Our sailing boat was delayed by contrary winds.*

con·trar·y³ /kənˈtreəri/ adj (of a person) tending to go against the wishes of others; difficult to deal with or work with; OBSTINATE: *Don't be so contrary!* —**ily** adv —**iness** n [U]

con·trast¹ /ˈkɒntrɑːst‖ˈkɑːntræst/ n **1** [U (with, to)] the comparison of objects or situations that are dissimilar, esp. to show differences: **In contrast with/to** *your belief that we will fail, I am confident that we will succeed.* | *The coastal areas have mild winters, but* **by contrast** *the cen-*

tral plains become extremely cold. —see CONTRARY (USAGE) **2** [C;U (between)] (a) difference between people or things that are compared: *Such a contrast between brother and sister is surprising.* | *This artist uses contrast* (=between light and dark, or different colours) *skilfully.* | *The contrast between this year's high profits and last year's big losses is really quite striking.* **3** [C (to, for)] something noticeably different from something else: *The black furnishings provide an interesting contrast to the white walls.* **4** [the+U] the degree of difference between the light and dark parts of a photograph or of a television picture: *Can you adjust the contrast please?*

con·trast² /kənˈtrɑːst‖-ˈtræst/ v [(with)] **1** [T] to compare (two things or people) so that differences are made clear: *In her speech she contrasted the government's optimistic promises with its dismal achievements.* **2** [I] to show a difference when compared: *His behaviour contrasts unfavourably with his principles.* | *sharply contrasting attitudes*

con·tra·vene /ˌkɒntrəˈviːn‖ˌkɑːn-/ v [T] fml to act in opposition to; break (a law, rule, custom, etc.): *to contravene the parking regulations* —**vention** /ˈvenʃən/ n [C;U] : *to act in contravention of the law* | *in direct contravention of my instructions* | *repeated contraventions of the rules*

con·tre·temps /ˈkɒntrətɒŋ‖ˈkɑːntrətaːn/ n -temps /tɒŋz‖taːnz/ Fr, often humor an unlucky and unexpected event, esp. a socially uncomfortable one: *There was a slight contretemps when both his girlfriends arrived together.*

con·trib·ute /kənˈtrɪbjuːt/ v **1** [I;T (to, towards)] to join with others in giving (money, help, etc.): *I contributed (a pound) towards Jane's leaving present.* **2** [I (to)] to help in causing a situation, event, or condition: *Various factors contributed to his downfall.* | *This advertising campaign has contributed significantly to the success of the new car.* | *She didn't contribute anything to the discussion.* **3** [I;T (to)] to write and send (a written article) to a magazine, newspaper, etc.: *She regularly contributes to the college magazine.*

con·tri·bu·tion /ˌkɒntrɪˈbjuːʃən‖ˌkɑːn-/ n **1** [C;U (to, towards)] the act of contributing or something contributed: *Chekhov's contribution to Russian literature* | *He has made an important contribution to the company's success.* **2** [C] an amount of money given to a cause, CHARITY, etc.: *All contributions, however small, will be greatly appreciated.* **3** [C usu. pl.] a regular payment, esp. to the state, to pay for something such as a PENSION, etc.: *Are you up-to-date with your National Insurance contributions?*

con·trib·u·tor /kənˈtrɪbjʊtər/ n [(to)] a person who contributes: *a regular contributor to our magazine*

con·trib·u·to·ry /kənˈtrɪbjʊtəri‖-tɔːri/ adj **1** [A] helping to bring about a result: *His heavy smoking was a contributory cause of his early death.* **2** (of a PENSION or insurance plan) paid for by the workers as well as by the employer —opposite **noncontributory**

contributory neg·li·gence /ˌ· ····· ˈ···/ n [U] law failure to take enough care to avoid or prevent an accident, leading to being held partly responsible in law for any damage, loss, etc., caused: *He drove the car with worn tyres, so he was found guilty of contributory negligence when it skidded across the road and injured two pedestrians.*

con·trite /ˈkɒntraɪt‖ˈkɑːn-/ adj old use or lit feeling or showing guilt or sorrow for one's actions: *a contrite apology* — ~ **ly** adv —**trition** /kənˈtrɪʃən/ n [U]

con·triv·ance /kənˈtraɪvəns/ n fml **1** [C] something contrived, esp. a machine or apparatus: *a clever new contrivance for milking cows* **2** [C usu. pl.] a clever, often deceitful, plan; SCHEME **3** [U (of)] the act of contriving or ability to invent

con·trive /kənˈtraɪv/ v [T] **1** to cause (something) to happen in accordance with one's plans or in spite of difficulty: *She somehow contrived a meeting with the Queen.* [+to-v] *After a lot of difficulty I contrived to attract the President's attention.* **2** to make or invent in a clever way, esp. because of a sudden need: *She contrived a party dress from an old piece of material.* | *I'm sure you'll contrive some way of dealing with the situation.*

con·trived /kənˈtraɪvd/ adj unnatural and forced: *I quite liked the story, but I thought the ending was rather contrived.*

con·trol¹ /kən'trəʊl/ v -ll- [T] **1** to have a directing influence over; fix or limit the amount, degree, or rate of; REGULATE: *The pressure of steam in the engine is controlled by this button.* | *Try to control yourself/your temper!* | *officially controlled prices* | *computer-controlled production* **2** to have power over; rule: *At that time the Romans controlled a vast empire.* | *a bad teacher who couldn't control his class* | *state-controlled media* | *The government has a controlling stake in this company.* (=owns more than 50% of it) **3** *tech* to test (esp. a scientific study) by comparison with a chosen standard: *a controlled experiment*

control² n **1** [U (**of, over**)] the power to command, influence, or direct: *Which party has control of the Congress?* | *George took/gained control of the business after his father died.* | *I lost control (of myself) and hit him.* | *You have no control over that dog.* | *in full control of the situation* | *The Vice-President is now* **in control**. (=in command or in charge) | *The government has been overthrown and the country is now* **in/under the control of** *the military.* | *The car went* **out of control** *and crashed.* —see also SELF-CONTROL **2** [C;U (**of, over**)] (a method or system used for) the fixing or limiting of the amount, degree, or rate of an activity; act of controlling: *The government has imposed strict controls on/over the import of luxury goods.* | *wage/price controls* | *an arms control agreement between the superpowers* | *tough methods of crowd-control* **3** [C] also **controls** *pl.*— the place from which, or means by which, a machine, system, etc., is controlled: *The co-pilot is at the controls/at the* **control panel**. | *the* **control tower** *of an airport* | *passport control* | *the volume control of a radio/TV* —see also REMOTE CONTROL **4** [U+*sing./pl. v*] the people who are in control of an activity or operation: *ground control* (=at an airport) | *air-traffic control* | *Mission control has/have lost contact with the space shuttle.* **5** [C] *tech* something used as a standard against which the results of a (scientific) study can be measured: *We used the new fertilizer on 100 plants and compared their growth with that of a* **control group** *of plants that had not been treated.* **6** [C] *tech* (in SPIRITUALISM) the dead person who guides a MEDIUM **7 under control** working properly, esp. after being in a dangerous or confused state; controlled in the correct way: *It took the new teacher months to bring her class under control.* | *Don't worry — everything is under control.* | *They soon brought/had the fire under control.* —see also BIRTH CONTROL

control freak /·'· ‚·/ n *AmE derog sl* a person who cannot prevent himself/herself from trying to control situations and other people

controlled school /·'·· ‚·/ n a British VOLUNTARY school for which the local education authority is financially responsible, and whose managers do not have control over religious education —compare AIDED SCHOOL, VOLUNTARY SCHOOL

con·trol·ler /kən'trəʊlə^r/ n **1** a person who directs something: *air-traffic controllers* **2** also **comptroller** *fml*— a government official responsible for money matters

con·tro·ver·sial /ˌkɒntrə'vɜːʃəl◂|ˌkɑːntrə'vɜːrʃəl◂/ adj causing much argument or disagreement: *a controversial speech/decision/politician/book* — ~ **ly** adv

con·tro·ver·sy /'kɒntrəvɜːsi, kən'trɒvəsi|'kɑːntrəvɜːrsi/ n [C;U (**about, over**)] (a) fierce argument or disagreement about something, esp. one that is carried on in public over a long period: *The lie detector tests have been the subject of much controversy.* | *recent controversies surrounding his appointment to the Cabinet*

con·tu·ma·cious /ˌkɒntjʊ'meɪʃəs|ˌkɑːntə-/ adj fml unreasonably disobedient, esp. to an order made by a court — ~ **ly** adv —**macy** /'kɒntjʊməsi|'kɑːntə-/ n [U]

con·tu·me·li·ous /ˌkɒntjʊ'miːliəs|ˌkɑːntə-/ adj disrespectfully rude and offensive — ~ **ly** adv

con·tume·ly /'kɒntjuːmli, -tjʊmɪli|kən'tuːmᵊli/ n [C;U] fml (an example of) disrespectful and offensive behaviour or language

con·tuse /kən'tjuːz|-'tuːz/ v [T] med for BRUISE

con·tu·sion /kən'tjuːʒən|-'tuː-/ n [C;U] med a BRUISE or bruising

co·nun·drum /kə'nʌndrəm/ n **1** a trick question asked for fun; RIDDLE **2** a confusing and difficult problem

con·ur·ba·tion /ˌkɒnɜː'beɪʃən|ˌkɑːnɜːr-/ n a group of towns that have spread and joined together to form an area of high population often with a large city as its centre

con·va·lesce /ˌkɒnvə'les|ˌkɑːn-/ v [I] to spend time getting well after an illness: *He was sent to a nursing home in the country to convalesce.*

con·va·les·cence /ˌkɒnvə'lesəns|ˌkɑːn-/ n [S;U] the length of time a person spends getting well after an illness: *a long (period of) convalescence*

con·va·les·cent /ˌkɒnvə'lesənt◂ ‖ ˌkɑːn-/ adj, n (for or being) a person spending time getting well after an illness: *She's still a convalescent.* | *a convalescent nursing home*

con·vec·tion /kən'vekʃən/ n [U] the movement in a gas or liquid caused by warm gas or liquid rising and cold gas or liquid sinking: *a convection heater* | *Warm air rises by convection.*

con·vec·tor /kən'vektə^r/ n a heating apparatus in which air becomes hot by passing over hot surfaces and then moves about an enclosed space, room, etc., by convection

con·vene /kən'viːn/ v fml **1** [I] (of a group of people, a committee, etc.) to meet; come together, esp. for a formal meeting: *The President's foreign policy advisers convened for an emergency session.* **2** [T] to call (a group of people, committee, etc.) to meet: *He's convened (a meeting of) the council to discuss the campaign.*

con·ven·er , -or /kən'viːnə^r/ n esp. BrE a member of a committee, etc., whose duty is to call meetings

con·ve·ni·ence /kən'viːniəns/ n **1** [U] the quality of being convenient; suitableness for a particular purpose, situation, etc.: *We bought this house for its convenience: it's very near the shops and there is a good transport service.* | *For the sake of convenience, the library books are separated into different categories.* **2** [C] an apparatus, service, etc., which gives comfort or advantage to its user: *This house has all the latest conveniences.* **3** [U] fml personal comfort or advantage: *He thinks only of his own convenience.* | *Please come* **at your (earliest) convenience**. (=as soon as it is convenient for you) | *The arrangement suits his convenience very well.* | *Theirs was a* **marriage of convenience**. (=they married for convenience, and not because they were in love) **4** [C] BrE a PUBLIC CONVENIENCE —see also FLAG OF CONVENIENCE; see TOILET (USAGE)

convenience food /·'··· ‚·/ n [C;U] food which is easy to prepare and can be used at any time, e.g. tinned or frozen food

convenience food store /·'··· ‚· ‚·/ also **convenience store**— n *AmE for* CORNER SHOP

con·ve·ni·ent /kən'viːniənt/ adj **1** [(**for, to**)] suited to one's needs or to the situation; not causing any difficulty: *Will three o'clock be convenient for you?* | *I'm afraid this isn't a very convenient moment to see you.* | *They met in a mutually convenient place.* (=suited to both their needs) | *For the government, the transport strike is politically convenient because it distracts people's attention from wider problems.* **2** [(**for**)] near; easy to reach: *Our house is very convenient for the shops.* —opposite **inconvenient** — ~ **ly** adv : *conveniently situated in a quiet suburb*

con·vent /'kɒnvənt|'kɑːnvent/ n a building or set of buildings in which NUNS live: *She entered a convent* (=began to live there) *at the age of 16.* —compare MONASTERY; see also CONVENT SCHOOL

con·ven·ti·cle /kən'ventɪkəl/ n (in England in former times) a building used for a secret meeting of NONCONFORMISTS (=Christians in disagreement with the established state religion)

con·ven·tion /kən'venʃən/ n **1** [C;U] (an example of) generally accepted practice, esp. with regard to social behaviour: *It is a matter of convention that businessmen should wear suits.* | *the conventions of the modern novel* | *a long-standing convention* —see HABIT (USAGE) **2** [C] (a meeting of) a group of people gathered together with a shared purpose: *a teachers' convention*

▶ CULTURAL NOTE In the US, national conventions for the two political parties are held every four years in order to choose who will fight for the job of president and VICE-PRESIDENT against the other party's CANDIDATE. The parties also decide what their general policies (POLICY) will be: *We attended the national Democratic Convention in New York.*◀

3 [C] a formal agreement esp. between countries on something that is important to them all: *The countries all agreed to sign the convention.* | *the Geneva Convention* — compare PACT, TREATY (1)

con·ven·tion·al /kən'venʃənəl/ *adj* **1** *often derog* following accepted customs and standards, sometimes too closely and without originality: *I'm afraid I'm rather conventional in my tastes.* | *After a few conventional opening remarks, he made a brilliant speech.* | *More and more people are turning away from conventional Western medicine to alternative methods of treatment.* | *conventional clothes/opinions* —opposite **unconventional 2** (of a weapon, etc.) not NUCLEAR: *conventional weapons/warfare* — ~ **ly** *adv* — ~ **ity** /kən,venʃə'næl₅ti/ *n* [C;U]

conventional ov·en /·'··· ,·/ *n* an ordinary OVEN, not a MICROWAVE: *This will take 3 minutes in a microwave or 25 minutes in a conventional oven.*

convent school /'·· ,·/ *n* a school, esp. one for girls, that is run by Catholic NUNS and often has severe rules of behaviour that must be obeyed

con·verge /kən'vɜːdʒ‖-ɜːr-/ *v* I **(on)** (of two or more things) to come together towards the same point: *The roads converge just before the station.* | *The two armies converged on the enemy capital.* | *Our interests appear to converge at this point.* —compare DIVERGE — **-vergence** *n* [C;U] — **-vergent** *adj* : *convergent lines*

con·ver·sant /kən'vɜːsənt‖-ɜːr-/ *adj* **1** [F+with] *fml* familiar; having knowledge of: *Before you start to play the game you should make sure you're conversant with the rules.* | *Are you conversant with the facts of the case?* **2** [(in)] *AmE* able to hold a conversation: *He's conversant in French but not really fluent.* | *a conversant speaker of Russian*

con·ver·sa·tion /,kɒnvə'seɪʃən‖,kɑːnvər-/ *n* [C;U] (an) informal talk in which people exchange news, feelings, and thoughts: *a telephone conversation* | *to have/hold a conversation* | *It's impossible to carry on a conversation with all this noise in the background.* | *This is a private conversation; don't interrupt!* | *In today's programme, three well-known artists are* **in conversation with** (=talking to) *the President of the Academy.*

con·ver·sa·tion·al /,kɒnvə'seɪʃənəl◄‖,kɑːnvər-/ *adj* (of a word, phrase, or style) commonly used in conversation: *Business letters are not usually written in conversational style.* | *classes in conversational French* — ~ **ly** *adv*

con·ver·sa·tion·al·ist /,kɒnvə'seɪʃənəl₅st‖,kɑːnvər-/ *n* a person whose conversation is clever and interesting

conversation piece /·'·· ,·/ *n* something, e.g. an interesting object, that provides a subject for conversation. It is often said in a joking way of objects which seem very strange or ugly.

con·ver·sa·zi·o·ne /,kɒnvəsætsi'əʊni‖,kɑːnvərsɑː-/ *n* **-ones** *or* **-oni** /'əʊni/ *It, fml* a meeting for conversation about art, literature, science, etc.

con·verse¹ /kən'vɜːs‖-ɜːrs/ *v* I **(on, about, with)**] *fml* to talk informally; have a conversation: *It's difficult to converse rationally with people who hold extremist views.*

con·verse² /'kɒnvɜːs‖kən'vɜːrs/ *adj* [A] *fml* (of opinions, beliefs, or statements) opposite; CONTRARY²: *I hold the converse opinion.*

con·verse³ /'kɒnvɜːs‖'kɑːnvɜːrs/ *n* **1** [*the* (**of**)] a fact, word, statement, etc., that is the opposite of another: *"Buyer" is the converse of "seller".* **2** [*the* (**of**)] *tech* (in LOGIC) a statement made by changing the order of some of the words in another statement: *"It's windy but not wet" is the converse of "It's wet but not windy".* **3** [U] *old use for* CONVERSATION

con·verse·ly /kən'vɜːsli, 'kɒnvɜːsli‖kən'vɜːrsli, 'kɑːnvɜːrsli/ *adv* on the other hand; taking the opposite point of view: *this newspaper story could damage their reputation; conversely, it will give them a lot of free publicity.*

con·ver·sion /kən'vɜːʃən‖-'vɜːrʒən/ *n* **1** [C;U (**of, from, into, to**)] the act or process of converting; a change from one purpose, system, etc., to another: *the conversion of kilometres into miles/steam into power* | *conversion from coal to gas heating* | *a company that does house conversions* (=changing large houses into several smaller units) **2** [C (**from, to**)] a change in which a person accepts a new religion, belief, etc., completely: *her conversion to Islam/Christianity* | *His sudden conversion to the anti-*

nuclear movement may make the voters suspicious. | *to undergo a conversion* | *a deathbed conversion* (=one made just before death) **3** [C;U] *tech* (in RUGBY and American football) the act of kicking the ball over the bar of the GOAL to gain additional points after a TRY²(2) or TOUCHDOWN (3)

con·vert¹ /kən'vɜːt‖-ɜːrt/ *v* **1** [I;T (**to, into**)] to (cause to) change into another form, substance, or state, or from one purpose, system, etc., to another: *Coal can be converted to gas.* | *This sofa converts into a bed.* | *to convert pounds into dollars* | *They live in a converted barn.* (=a BARN changed into a house) **2** [I;T (**from, to**)] to (persuade to) accept a particular religion, belief, etc.: *He was converted to Christianity after visiting Jerusalem.* | *Anne has converted to Catholicism.* | (fig.) *My daughter has finally converted me to pop music.* (=persuaded me to like it) **3** [T] *tech* (in RUGBY and American football) to complete (a TRY²(2) or TOUCHDOWN) by kicking the ball over the bar of the GOAL: *You score two points for converting a try.* —see also CONVERSION

con·vert² /'kɒnvɜːt‖'kɑːnvɜːrt/ *n* [(**to**)] a person who has been persuaded to accept a particular religion, political belief, etc.: *a convert to Christianity* | *She's a recent convert to the idea of a European defence policy.*

con·vert·er /kən'vɜːtə'‖-ɜːr-/ *n tech* **1** a machine that converts things, esp. a FURNACE in which steel is made by blowing air through melted iron **2** also **convertor**— an apparatus that changes the form or direction of something, esp. one that changes the form in which information is written so that it can be accepted by a computer

con·ver·ti·ble¹ /kən'vɜːt₅bəl‖-ɜːr-/ *adj* **1** [(**into**)] that can be converted: *This bed is easily convertible into a sofa.* **2** (of a car) having a roof that can be folded back —see picture at CAR **3** [(**into**)] **a** (of some financial arrangements) that can be changed into something else: *a convertible life insurance policy* | *convertible bonds* (=which can be exchanged for SHARES¹ (2)) **b** (of a type of money) that can be freely exchanged for other types of money: *The dollar is a convertible currency, but the rouble is not.* — **-bility** /kən,vɜːt₅'bɪl₅ti‖-ɜːr-/ *n* [U]

convertible² *n esp. AmE* a car with a roof that can be folded back —see also CABRIOLET

con·vex /,kɒn'veks◄, kən-‖,kɑːn'veks◄, kən/ *adj* curved outwards, like the surface of the eye: *a convex mirror/lens* —opposite **concave** — ~ **ly** *adv* — ~ **ity** /kən'veks₅ti/ *n* [C;U]

con·vey /kən'veɪ/ *v* [T] **1** [(**from, to**)] *rather fml* to take or carry from one place to another: *Your luggage will be conveyed by helicopter from the airport to your hotel.* **2** [(**to**)] to make (feelings, ideas, thoughts, etc.) known: *Our government's anger was conveyed to their ambassador.* | *His music conveys a sense of optimism. He tried to convey how he felt.* **3** [(**to**)] *law* to give the rights to (land or property) to someone

con·vey·ance /kən'veɪəns/ *n* **1** [U] the act of conveying: *the conveyance of goods by road* **2** [C] *fml* a vehicle: *a public conveyance* **3** [C] *law* an official paper that CONVEYS (3) the right to land or property

con·vey·anc·ing /kən'veɪənsɪŋ/ *n* [U] the act or process of dealing with all the documents necessary for passing the ownership of property from one person to another: *When I sold my last house, I was so fed up with lawyers that I did all my own conveyancing.*

con·vey·er, -or /kən'veɪə'/ *n* **1** someone or something that conveys: *the conveyer of good news* **2** a CONVEYER BELT

conveyer belt /·'·· ,·/ *n* an endless moving belt that carries objects from one place to another, e.g. in a factory so that someone can do the same operation on many different objects: *He took his suitcase off the conveyer belt at the airport.* | (fig., derog) *the conveyer belt mentality of most modern artists* —see also CAROUSEL

con·vict¹ /kən'vɪkt/ *v* [T (**of**) *usu. pass.*] to prove or declare that (someone) is guilty of a crime after a trial in a court: *They were convicted of murder.* | *a convicted rapist* —opposite **acquit**

con·vict² /'kɒnvɪkt‖'kɑːn-/ *n* a person who has been found guilty of a crime and sent to prison, esp. for a long time. If a man is said to look like a convict, it usu. means that his hair is cut extremely short: *an escaped convict*

con·vic·tion /kən'vɪkʃən/ *n* [C;U] **1** the act of convicting or being convicted of a crime: *This was her third*

conviction for stealing. | *His conviction caused rioting in the streets.* | *They had no previous convictions.* —opposite **acquittal** **2** (a) very firm and sincere belief: *She's a woman of strong convictions.* | *He said he wasn't frightened, but his voice lacked conviction/didn't carry conviction.* (=he didn't sound as if he believed what he was saying) | *a conviction politician* (=whose beliefs tend not to change) [+*that*] *She had a firm conviction that she was always right.*

con·vince /kən'vɪns/ v [T (of)] to make (someone) completely certain about something; persuade: *We finally convinced them of our innocence.* [+*obj*+(*that*)] *They failed to convince the directors that their proposals would work.* | *I'm convinced that she is telling the truth.* | *a convinced Christian* (=sure of his/her faith)

con·vinc·ing /kən'vɪnsɪŋ/ adj **1** able to convince: *a convincing speaker/speech* —opposite **unconvincing** **2** certain; clear: *a convincing victory* (=a win by a large number of points) | *They won by a convincing margin.* – ~ly adv

con·viv·i·al /kən'vɪviəl/ adj pleasantly merry and friendly: *convivial companions* | *a very convivial atmosphere* – ~ly adv – ~ity /kən,vɪvi'æl.ti/ n [U]

con·vo·ca·tion /ˌkɒnvə'keɪʃən/ʃˌkɑːn-/ n **1** [U] the act of calling people together for a meeting **2** [C+*sing./pl. v*] an organization of church officials, or of members of certain universities, that holds formal meetings **3** the name for GRADUATION(1) at some American universities

con·voke /kən'vəʊk/ v [T] *fml* to call together for a meeting: *to convoke Parliament*

con·vo·lut·ed /'kɒnvəluːtɪd/ʃ'kɑːn-/ adj **1** *fml* twisted; curved: *sheep with convoluted horns* **2** difficult to understand; COMPLICATED, esp. without good reason: *convoluted arguments* – ~ly adv

con·vo·lu·tion /ˌkɒnvə'luːʃən/ʃˌkɑːn-/ n [*usu. pl.*] *fml* a fold, twist, or the act of folding or twisting: *a snake's convolutions* | (fig.) *to follow the convolutions of her argument/of the story*

con·vol·vu·lus /kən'vɒlvjʊləs/ʃ-'vɑːl-/ n [C;U] a climbing plant, such as the MORNING GLORY

con·voy[1] /'kɒnvɔɪ/ʃ'kɑːn-/ n [C+*sing./pl. v*] **1** a group of ships or vehicles travelling together, esp. for protection: *Convoys of lorries took food to the disaster area.* | *Cars should cross the desert in convoy in case there is a breakdown.* **2** a protecting force of armed ships, vehicles, soldiers, etc.; ESCORT: *The weapons were sent under convoy because of the danger of enemy attack.* | *a naval convoy*

convoy[2] v [T] (of an armed ship, vehicle, soldiers, etc.) to go with and protect (a group of ships, vehicles, etc.)

con·vulse /kən'vʌls/ v [T (with)] to shake violently, in or as if in convulsions: *We were convulsed with laughter.*

con·vul·sion /kən'vʌlʃən/ n [*usu. pl.*] a number of sudden violent uncontrollable shaking movements caused esp. by illness: *He couldn't breathe because he sometimes had convulsions.* | (fig.) *We were all in convulsions of laughter.*

con·vul·sive /kən'vʌlsɪv/ adj "being, having, or producing a convulsion: *a convulsive movement of the muscles* – ~ly adv

co·ny, **coney** /'kəʊni/ n **1** [C] *AmE nonstandard* a rabbit **2** [U] rabbit fur as used in making fur coats

coo /kuː/ v [I] **1** to make (a sound like) the low soft cry of a DOVE or PIGEON **2** to make soft loving noises: *They all cooed over the new baby.* —see also **bill and coo** (BILL[4]) –**coo** n

cook[1] /kʊk/ v **1** [I;T] to prepare (food) for eating by using heat; make (a dish): *There are various ways of cooking rice.* | *Do you want your vegetables cooked or raw?* | *I learnt how to cook at school.* [+*obj(i)*+*obj(d)*] *She cooked us a marvellous dinner.* **2** [I] (of food) to be prepared in this way: *Make sure the meat cooks for at least an hour.* **3** [T] *infml* to change (facts, numbers, etc.) dishonestly for one's own advantage; FALSIFY: *She was sacked for* **cooking the books.** (=stealing money by making changes in the accounts) —compare CREATIVE ACCOUNTING **4 cook someone's goose** to get someone into serious trouble: *I could mention where he really was at the weekend to his wife — that'd cook his goose!*
▷ USAGE A modern gas or electric **cooker** (**stove** *AmE*) usually has three parts: the **oven**, the **grill** (**broiler**

AmE), and the **burners** or **hotplates** on top. The **oven** is used for **baking** bread and cakes, or **roasting** a large piece of meat. The **grill** is an apparatus for cooking by direct heat and can be used, for example, for **grilling** (**broiling** *AmE*) meat or **toasting** bread (making it hard and brown). The gas **burners** or electric **hotplates** can be used for **boiling** food in a pot with water, for **stewing** food (=cooking food slowly in liquid to make a **stew**) or for **frying** (=cooking food in hot fat or oil). **Simmering** is very gentle slow boiling. **Steaming** is cooking food in water but in an inner container so that the water does not directly touch the food. **Braising**, used usually of meat, means cooking slowly in a covered pot with a little fat and water.◁
cook sthg. ↔ **up** *phr v* [T] *infml* to invent falsely; CONCOCT: *They cooked up some excuse about an accident, but no-one believed them.*

cook[2] n **1** a person who prepares and cooks food: *John's a cook in a hotel.* | *My mother is a really good cook.* –compare CHEF **2 too many cooks spoil the broth** *saying* if too many people are trying to do the same job at the same time, they will not do it successfully —see also CHIEF COOK AND BOTTLE-WASHER

Cook, Captain James (1728–79) an English EXPLORER of the coasts of Australia and New Zealand. He claimed the E coast of Australia for Britain. He also discovered several islands in the Pacific, including Hawaii, where he was killed.

Cook, Peter (1937–) an English COMEDIAN, known esp. for his DRY[1] (9) humour and for his television partnership with Dudley Moore

Cook, Thomas (1808–92) an English TRAVEL AGENT who started a business in 1841 which grew into one of the largest in the world —see also THOMAS COOK

cook·book /'kʊkbʊk/ n *esp. AmE* a book on how to prepare and cook food; COOKERY BOOK

cook-chill /ˌ· '·◁/ v [T] *BrE* to preserve (food) by cooking it and then keeping it at a low temperature until it is needed, when it is reheated. This process is used in hospitals and also for READY MEALs stored in shops, and there has been some concern that food produced in this way may not be safe to eat when heating instructions are not followed very carefully.

Cooke, Al·is·tair /'æl.ɪsteəʳ/ (1908–) an American radio and TV broadcaster, born in England. He is known particularly for his long-running radio SERIES, *Letter from America*, which describes American life and people to the British, and also for his frequent appearances on American television.

cooked break·fast /ˌ· '··/ n (in Britain) a breakfast consisting of cooked food, usu. including eggs, often together with BACON, SAUSAGEs, or TOMATOEs. It is usu. followed by TOAST and tea or coffee.

cook·er /'kʊkəʳ/ n **1** *esp. BrE* ‖ **stove** *esp. AmE*— an apparatus on which food is cooked —see COOK (USAGE), and see picture at KITCHEN **2** *BrE* a fruit, esp. an apple, suitable for cooking

cook·e·ry /'kʊkəri/ *esp. BrE*‖*usu.* **cooking** *AmE*— n [U] the art or skill of cooking: *cookery lessons* | *He's an expert on Indian cookery.*

cookery book /'··· ,·/ also **cookbook** *esp. AmE*— n a book on how to prepare and cook food

cook·house /'kʊkhaʊs/ n -**houses** /ˌhaʊz.ɪz/ *old-fash* a kitchen in the open air, where food is cooked in a camp

cook·ie /'kʊki/ n **1** also **biscuit** *BrE* ‖ **cooky** *AmE*— *esp. AmE* a flat thin dry cake, sweetened or unsweetened, usu. sold in packets or tins: *We had cookies and coffee.* | *chocolate-chip cookies* **2** *ScotE for* BUN (1) **3** also **cooky**— *AmE sl* a person of a particular type: *a smart/tough cookie* **4 that's the way the cookie crumbles** *humor* that's how things are and one must accept them (used when something unfortunate, unpleasant, etc., has just happened)

cookie cut·ter /'·· ,··/ n *AmE* an instrument which cuts flat cookies into special shapes before baking: (fig.) *cookie-cutter houses lined the street* (=all the houses looked alike).

Cookie Mon·ster /'··· ,··/ [*the*] a character from the television programme *Sesame Street* who appears whenever there are cookies around and eats them all

cookie sheet /'·· ·/ n AmE for BAKING SHEET

cook·ing /'kʊkɪŋ/ adj [A] suitable for or used in cooking: *cooking sherry | cooking oil*

cooking ap·ple /'·· ,··/ n an apple that one eats cooked — compare EATING APPLE

cooking oil /'·· ·/ n [U] oil from plants, such as SUNFLOWERS or OLIVES, used in cooking, esp. frying (FRY)

cook·out /'kʊk-aʊt/ n infml, esp. AmE a meal cooked and eaten outdoors

Cook·son /'kʊksən/, **Cath·e·rine** /'kæθərɪ̧n/ (1906–) an English writer of historical stories, mostly set in the NE of England. She is extremely popular, esp. among female readers.

cooky /'kʊki/ n esp. AmE a COOKIE (1, 3)

cool¹ /kuːl/ adj **1** neither warm nor very cold; pleasantly cold: *a cool day | A cool breeze blew off the sea. | a nice cool beer | As it was a hot day, she wore a cool dress.* —see COLD (USAGE) **2** calm and not easily excited: *If you hear the fire bell, keep cool and don't panic. | We need someone with a cool head.* (=who doesn't get too excited) **3** [(towards)] lacking warm feelings; not as friendly as usual: *He seemed rather cool towards me today — I wonder if I've offended him. | The president was given a cool reception when he visited London.* **4** disrespectful in a calmly self-confident way: *And then, as cool as you like, he picked up the contract and tore it in half. | Well, he certainly is a cool customer* (=someone who is calm in a disrespectful or admired way), *and no mistake!* **5** [A] infml (used to give force to an expression, esp. to large amounts of money): *He earns a cool half million a year.* **6** sl very good: *You look real(ly) cool in that new dress.* — ~ish adj — ~ly /'kuːl-li/ adv — ~ness n [U]

cool² v [I;T (DOWN)] **1** to (cause to) become cool: *We opened the windows to cool the room. | a water-cooled/air-cooled engine | Let your tea cool (down) a little before you drink it. | (fig.) Their initial enthusiasm soon cooled.* — compare WARM² **2 cool it** infml **a** keep calm; calm down!: *Come on, you guys, cool it!* **b** to reduce the speed of an operation or the pressure on someone else: *They know we're keen to get the contract now, so I think we should cool it for a bit.* **3 cool one's heels** to be forced to wait: *He kept them cooling their heels for an hour outside his door.*

cool down phr v [I;T (=cool sbdy. **down**)] to (cause to) become calmer and less excited: *It took me a long time to cool down after the argument. | I tried to cool her down but she was too angry.*

cool³ n **1** [the+S] a temperature that is pleasantly cold: *the cool of the evening* **2 keep/lose one's cool** sl to keep/lose one's calmness and self control

cool⁴ adv **play it cool** to behave in a calm and unexcited way; not lose one's temper: *They expected us to be angry, but we had decided to play it cool.*

coo·lant /'kuːlənt/ n [C;U] tech a liquid used for cooling down part of a machine or apparatus that gets hot —see picture at ENGINE

cool·box /'kuːlbɒks||-bɑːks/ also **cool·bag** /-bæg/ ‖ **cooler** AmE— a container which is specially made to keep food and drink cool and fresh, for use on PICNICs. It is usu. made of plastic and has one or more containers for ice.

cool·er /'kuːləʳ/ n **1** [C] a container in which something is cooled or kept cool: *a wine cooler* **2** [C] AmE for a COOLBOX **3** AmE infml a machine which provides AIR CONDITIONING: *Turn on the cooler, it's hot in here.* **4** [the+S] sl prison

cool-head·ed /,· '···◁/ adj calm; not easily excited: *a cool-headed person/decision*

Coo·lidge /'kuːlɪdʒ/, **Calvin** (1872–1933) the President of the US from 1923 to 1929

coo·lie /'kuːli/ n (esp. in India and some parts of the Far East) an unskilled worker paid extremely low wages: *He treats her like a coolie — she works for next to nothing and never gets a day off.*

cooling-off pe·ri·od /,·· '· ,··/ n **1** a period before a planned STRIKE² when unions and employers have a chance to reach an agreement **2** a period after the signing of some types of sales agreement, when one can change one's mind about buying something: *a thirty-day cooling-off period.*

cooling sys·tem /'·· ,··/ n a system for decreasing or keeping low the temperature of e.g. an engine by means of air, a liquid, or a gas: *The power station was shut down after a fault was detected in the cooling system.*

coon /kuːn/ n **1** taboo derog sl a black person (considered extremely offensive) **2** AmE infml for RACCOON

co-op /'kəʊ-ɒp||'kɑːp/ n (often cap.) infml **1** abbrev. for COOPERATIVE² : *My friends and I belong to a local co-op.* **2** (in Britain) **a** an organization of people with similar aims (the **Co-operative Society**) which owns a group of shops. All profits from their sales are given back in one way or another to the members of the society. **b** [C] a shop owned by this society

coop¹ /kuːp/ n a cage for small animals, esp. hens

coop² v

coop sbdy./sthg ↔ **up** phr v [T (in) usu. pass.] to shut into a small space; CONFINE: *cooped up in a tiny room/in prison*

coo·per /'kuːpəʳ/ n a person who makes barrels

Cooper, Gar·y /'gæri/ (1901–62) an American actor who often played strong, silent heroes (HERO), for example in the film *High Noon*

Cooper, Henry (1934–) an English BOXER who held the British HEAVYWEIGHT title from 1959, losing it to Joe Bugner in 1971. He also fought Muhammed Ali for the world title, but lost.

Cooper, James Fen·i·more /dʒeɪmz 'fenɪmɔːʳ/ (1789–1851) an American NOVELIST who wrote books of adventure about life in the US, including *The Deerslayer* and *Last of the Mohicans*

Cooper, Tommy (1921–84) a British COMEDIAN, known esp. for wearing a FEZ (=a red hat), for getting his magic tricks wrong, and for his CATCHPHRASE, "Just like that!"

Tommy Cooper

co·op·e·rate, co-operate /kəʊ-'ɒpəreɪt||-'ɑːp-/ v [I (**with, in**)] to work or act together for a shared purpose: *They'll get the job finished much more quickly if they all cooperate. | The British cooperated with the French in designing the satellite.* [+to-v] *Several countries cooperated to build the new plane.* —**rator** n

co·op·e·ra·tion, co-operation /kəʊˌɒpə'reɪʃən||-ˌɑːp-/ n [U (**with**)] **1** the act of working together for a shared purpose: *This film was produced in cooperation with Australian TV.* **2** willingness to work together; help: *I need your cooperation in this matter. | The union decided on a policy of non-cooperation with the management.*

co·op·e·ra·tive¹ /kəʊ'ɒpərətɪv||-'ɑːp-/ adj **1** willing to cooperate; helpful: *The management would like to thank the staff for being so cooperative.* —opposite **uncooperative** **2** [no comp.] made, done, or operated by people working together: *a cooperative farm/venture* —see also CO-OP — ~ly adv

cooperative² also **co-op** n a COOPERATIVE¹ (2) firm, farm, shop, etc., esp. one that is owned and run by all the people who work in it: *a housing/farm cooperative | We decided to set up a cooperative.*

Coo·pers and Ly·brand De·loitte /,kuːpəz ənd ,laɪbrænd dᵻ̧'lɔɪt||-pərz-/ an international ACCOUNTANCY firm

Coo·pers·town /'kuːpəztaʊn||-pərz-/ n a town in the State of New York which has the Baseball Hall of Fame (a building which has sports equipment and information about famous BASEBALL players spread out for public view): *A number of players are being admitted to Cooperstown this year.*

co-opt /ˌkəʊ 'ɒpt||-'ɑːpt/ v [T (**into, onto**)] (of a committee or similar group) to choose, but not elect (someone) as a member by the votes of all the existing members. Sometimes a person who is co-opted is at first not willing to be a member: *I was co-opted onto the board of directors.*

co·or·di·nate¹ /kəʊˈɔːdɪneɪt‖-ˈɔːr-/ v [T] to make (people or things) work together, so as to increase effectiveness: *She's a beautiful dancer: all her movements are perfectly coordinated.* | *We used a computer to coordinate the marketing campaign.* | *a well-coordinated response to the enemy attack*

co·or·di·nate² /kəʊˈɔːdɪnɪt‖-ˈɔːr-/ n tech one of a set of numbers and/or letters that give the exact position of a point on a map, computer SCREEN, etc. —see also COORDINATES

coordinate³ adj [A] tech 1 equal in importance or rank; not SUBORDINATE: *coordinate clauses in a sentence, joined by "and"* 2 of or based on COORDINATES² — **~ly** adv

co·or·di·nates /kəʊˈɔːdɪnɪts‖-ˈɔːr-/ n [P] separate women's clothes that are intended to be worn together because the colours match

co·or·di·na·tion /kəʊˌɔːdɪˈneɪʃən‖-ˌɔːr-/ n [U] 1 [(of)] the act of coordinating (COORDINATE¹): *careful coordination of our research efforts* 2 the way in which muscles work together when performing a movement: *Dancers need good coordination|a good sense of coordination.*

Coors /kʊəz‖kʊərz/ n tdmk a kind of beer made by an American company

coot /kuːt/ n a small dark grey water bird with a short beak

coo·ties /ˈkuːtiz/ n AmE infml disease producing bacteria or bodylice (LOUSE), believed to be caught by touching a person or thing; used esp. by children: *"Sit next to your sister — she doesn't have cooties, you know."*

cop¹ /kɒp‖kɑːp/ n infml a policeman or policewoman: *My father's a cop.* | *a cop car* | *little boys playing* **cops and robbers** —see also COP SHOP

cop² v -pp- [T] sl 1 BrE to catch (someone doing something wrong) 2 **cop it** BrE to be in serious trouble: *You'll really cop it if they catch you smoking again!* 3 **Cop that!** BrE Look at that! 4 **cop a plea** AmE to agree to say one is guilty of a CHARGE² (4) so that one can get a reduced punishment: *The police got him for homicide but he copped a plea and got away with 90 days.*
   cop out phr v [I (**of, on**)] sl, often derog to avoid the responsibility of making a difficult decision or acting according to one's principles: *Don't try to cop out (of it) by telling me you're too busy!* —see also COP OUT

cop³ n BrE sl 1 **a fair cop** a fair or just ARREST. This phrase is supposedly used by criminals when they have been caught, but it has been used so often that it is now really only a joke. 2 **not much cop** not very good: *This film isn't much cop.*

Co·pa·ca·ban·a /ˌkəʊpəkəˈbænə/ a fashionable BEACH in Rio de Janeiro where many young people go

cope¹ /kəʊp/ v [I (**with**)] to deal successfully with a difficult situation: *The factory coped very well with the sudden increase in demand.* | *With three small children, she just couldn't cope on her own.*

cope² n a long loose article of clothing worn by priests on special occasions

Co·pen·ha·gen /ˌkəʊpənˈheɪgən◀‖ˈkəʊpənheɪgən/ the capital city of Denmark. It is a port and industrial centre in the east of the country. There is a well-known old popular song which contains the phrase "Wonderful, wonderful Copenhagen".

Copenhagen, Battle of [the] a naval battle between the British and the Danish in 1801. The British navy under Lord Nelson had received orders to leave the area because Danish ships were approaching. Nelson put his TELESCOPE to his blind eye and said "I see no ships". His ships remained where they were, and in the battle that followed the Danes were defeated.

Co·per·ni·can sys·tem /kəʊˈpɜːnɪkən ˌsɪstɪm‖-ɜːr-/ [the] the idea, first suggested by Copernicus, that the Earth and the other PLANETS in our SOLAR SYSTEM travel round the Sun —compare PTOLEMAIC SYSTEM

Co·per·nic·us /kəʊˈpɜːnɪkəs‖-ˈpɜːr-/, **Nicholas** (1473–1543), a Polish ASTRONOMER (=person who studies the stars), known for the Copernican system

cop·i·er /ˈkɒpiəʳ‖ˈkɑː-/ n a machine for making photographic copies; PHOTOCOPIER

co·pi·lot /ˈkəʊˌpaɪlət/ n a pilot who shares the control of a plane with the main pilot

cop·ing /ˈkəʊpɪŋ/ n the top row of stone or brick on a wall

or roof: *The wall was attractively topped off with some* **coping stones**.

co·pi·ous /ˈkəʊpiəs/ adj plentiful; ABUNDANT: *copious tears* | *copious quantities of food* — **~ly** adv

Cop·land /ˈkəʊplənd/, **Aaron** (1900–1990) an American COMPOSER of popular classical music

cop-out /ˈ· ·/ n an occasion when one tries to avoid the responsibility of making a difficult decision or acting according to one's principles: *She said she was going to tell him what he could do with his job, but in the end she just kept her mouth shut. What a cop-out!*

cop·per¹ /ˈkɒpəʳ‖ˈkɑː-/ n 1 [U] a soft reddish metal that is a simple substance (ELEMENT), is easily shaped, and allows heat and electricity to pass through it easily: *copper pipes* | *copper wires* | *The chemical symbol for copper is "Cu".* 2 [C] BrE infml, becoming rare a coin of low value made of copper or BRONZE: *He had only a few coppers in his pocket.* 3 [U] a reddish-brown colour: *copper hair* — **~y** adj

copper² n infml a policeman or policewoman

copper beech /ˌ·· ˈ·/ n a large tree with purple- or copper-coloured leaves

copper-bot·tomed /ˌ·· ˈ···◀/ adj 1 having copper on the bottom: *a copper-bottomed saucepan* 2 BrE infml safe in every way; completely without risk: *a copper-bottomed investment*

Cop·per·field /ˈkɒpəfiːld‖ˈkɑːpər-/, **David** see DAVID COPPERFIELD

cop·per·head /ˈkɒpəhed‖ˈkɑːpər-/ n a large copper-coloured poisonous snake found in the eastern US

cop·per·plate /ˈkɒpəpleɪt‖ˈkɑːpər-/ n [U] neat, regular curving, old-fashioned handwriting, usu. with all the letters of a word joined together: *The invitation was written in fine copperplate handwriting.*

cop·pice /ˈkɒpɪs‖ˈkɑː-/ n a small wood of trees or bushes, esp. one that is specially managed to provide wood for fencing etc.

Cop·po·la /ˈkɒpələ‖ˈkɑː-/, **Francis Ford** (1939–) an American film director best known for the films *The Godfather* and *Apocalypse Now*

cop·ra /ˈkɒprə‖ˈkɑːprə/ n [U] the dried flesh of the COCONUT, from which oil is pressed for making soap

copse /kɒps‖kɑːps/ n a small wood of trees or bushes

cop shop /ˈ· ·/ n BrE infml a POLICE STATION

Cop·tic /ˈkɒptɪk‖ˈkɑːp-/ adj of the Coptic Church, or the language used in its religious services

Coptic Church /ˌ·· ˈ·/ [the] a branch of the Christian church based in Ethiopia and Egypt

cop·u·la /ˈkɒpjʊlə‖ˈkɑːp-/ n tech (in grammar) a special type of verb which connects the subject of a sentence with the COMPLEMENT. In this dictionary copulas are marked [L]: *In the sentence "The house seems big", "seems" is a copula.*

cop·u·late /ˈkɒpjʊleɪt‖ˈkɑːp-/ v [I (**with**)] fml to have sex. This word is usu. used either about animals, or in a disapproving way, to show that the sex has little emotional feeling. — **-lation** /ˌkɒpjʊˈleɪʃən‖ˌkɑːp-/ n [U]

cop·u·la·tive /ˈkɒpjʊlətɪv‖ˈkɑːpjʊleɪ-/ adj, n tech (describing) a word or word group that connects other words or word groups: *a* **copulative conjunction** *such as "and"*

cop·y¹ /ˈkɒpi‖ˈkɑːpi/ n 1 [C (**of**)] a thing made to be exactly like another: *I sent the letter, but kept a copy for my files.* | *It's not a genuine Michelangelo—it's only a copy.* | *The secretary made a copy of the document.* 2 [C (**of**)] a single example of a magazine, book, newspaper, etc.: *Did you get your copy of The Times today?* | *This book has already sold over a million copies.* 3 [U] tech written material to be printed: *All copy must be typewritten and sent to the editor by Monday morning.* | *a copy editor* | *clever advertising copy* | *I know it's a very sad story, but my editor thinks it's good copy.* (=interesting news) —see also FAIR COPY, HARD COPY, SOFT COPY

copy² v 1 [T] to make a copy of: *Would you copy this letter for me, please?* 2 [T] to follow (someone or something) as a standard or pattern; IMITATE: *Street fashion tends to copy the clothes produced by the big Paris designers.* 3 [I;T (**from, off**)] derog to cheat by writing (exactly the same thing) as someone else: *Their answers are exactly the same—one of them must have copied from the other.*

copy sthg. ↔ **out** *phr v* [T] to write (something) exactly as written elsewhere: *I copied out her notes into my notebook.*

cop·y·book¹ /ˈkɒpibʊk‖ˈkɑː-/ *n* a book containing examples of good handwriting, formerly used in schools as a standard for pupils learning to write —see also **blot one's copybook** (BLOT²)

copybook² *adj* [A] *BrE* completely suitable or correct: *a copybook answer*

cop·y·cat /ˈkɒpikæt‖ˈkɑː-/ *n derog infml* a person who copies other people's behaviour, dress, manners, work, etc., in a completely unoriginal way: *Don't be such a copycat!* | *a copycat crime/killing* (=similar to a famous crime that another person has done)

Cop·y·dex /ˈkɒpideks‖ˈkɑː-/ *n* [U] *tdmk* an ADHESIVE (=sthg. that sticks or causes sticking) made by a British company of the same name

cop·y·ist /ˈkɒpi-ɟst‖ˈkɑː-/ *n* a person who makes written copies

cop·y·right /ˈkɒpiraɪt‖ˈkɑː-/ *n* [C;U] the right in law to be the only producer or seller of a book, play, film or record for a fixed period of time: *Who holds/owns the copyright for/on the book: you, or the publisher?* | *Copying this videocassette without permission would be a breach/infringement of copyright.*

cop·y·writ·er /ˈkɒpiraɪtəʳ‖ˈkɑː-/ *n* a person who writes the words for advertisements

coq au vin /ˌkɒk əʊ ˈvæn‖ˌkəʊk-/ *n* [U] a dish of chicken cooked in red wine with BACON, MUSHROOMs, and onions

coq·ue·try /ˈkɒkɟtri‖ˈkəʊ-/ *n* [C;U] a behaviour typical of a coquette

co·quette /kəʊˈket, kɒ-‖ˈkəʊ-/ *n* a woman who tries to attract the admiration of men without having sincere feelings for them; a woman who FLIRTS —**quettish** *adj* —**quettishly** *adv*

cor·a·cle /ˈkɒrəkəl‖ˈkɔː-, ˈkɑː-/ *n* a small light round boat, built like a basket, sometimes used by fishermen on Irish and Welsh lakes

cor·al¹ /ˈkɒrəl‖ˈkɔː-, ˈkɑː-/ *n* [U] a white, pink, or reddish stonelike substance formed from the bones of very small sea animals. It is often used for making jewellery: *a coral island* | *a coral necklace* | *The ship was wrecked on a coral reef.*

coral² *adj* having a pink or reddish orange colour: *coral lipstick*

Coral (in Britain) one of a group of BETTING SHOPS

coral reef /ˌ··ˈ·/ *n* **coral reefs** a mass of LIMESTONE (=a type of hard rock) formed by coral and/or other living things in warm, SHALLOW sea water and known for its beautiful colours —see also GREAT BARRIER REEF

cor an·glais /ˌkɔːr ˈɒŋgleɪ‖-ɔːŋˈgleɪ/ also **English horn** *AmE*— *n* **cors anglais** (*same pronunciation*) *Fr* a musical instrument of the WOODWIND family, like a large OBOE

cor·bel /ˈkɔːbəl‖ˈkɔːr-/ *n tech* a piece of stone or wood built out from a wall as a support for a beam or other heavy object

Cor·bett /ˈkɔːbɟt‖ˈkɔːr-/, **Ron·nie** /ˈrɒni‖ˈrɑː-/ (1930–) a Scottish actor and COMEDIAN known esp. for his part in the British television programme *The Two Ronnies*, in which he performed with Ronnie Barker

cor bli·mey /ˌkɔː ˈblaɪmi‖ˌkɔːr-/ also **blimey**— *interj BrE old-fash sl* (used for showing surprise)

Corbusier see LE CORBUSIER

cord¹ /kɔːd‖kɔːrd/ *n* **1** [C;U] (a piece of) thick string or thin rope: *I tied the suitcase shut with a piece of cord.* **2** [C;U] (a piece of) wire with a protective covering, for connecting electrical equipment to a supply of electricity **3** [U] CORDUROY: *a cord skirt* —see also CORDS, COMMUNICATION CORD, CORDLESS, SPINAL CORD, UMBILICAL CORD, VOCAL CORDS

cord² *n AmE* a quantity of FIREWOOD (=wood cut for burning in a fire): *We go through about three cords of wood in the winter.*

cord³ *v* [T] to tie, bind, or connect with cord: *a corded bundle of hay*

cord·age /ˈkɔːdɪdʒ‖ˈkɔːr-/ *n* [U] rope or cord in general, esp. on a ship

cor·di·al¹ /ˈkɔːdiəl‖ˈkɔːrdʒəl/ *n* [U] fruit juice which is added to water and drunk: *lemon cordial*

cordial² *adj fml* warmly and friendly, but quite formal and polite: *a cordial smile/welcome/reception* — ~ **ity** /ˌkɔːdiˈælɟti‖ˌkɔːrdʒiˈæ-, ˌkɔːrˈdʒæ-/ *n* [U]

cor·di·al·ly /ˈkɔːdiəli‖ˈkɔːrdʒəli/ *adv fml* **1** in a cordial manner: *You are cordially invited to the wedding.* **2** dislike/hate **cordially** to dislike/hate very strongly

cor·dite /ˈkɔːdaɪt‖ˈkɔːr-/ *n* [U] *tech* smokeless explosive powder

cord·less /ˈkɔːdləs‖ˈkɔːrd-/ *adj.* not connected with wires to a supply of electricity: *a cordless phone* | *Is your iron cordless?*

cor·don¹ /ˈkɔːdn‖ˈkɔːrdn/ *n* **1** a line of police, military vehicles, etc., placed round an area to protect or enclose it: *The police immediately put/threw a cordon round the accident to keep people away.* **2** *tech* a fruit tree with its branches cut so that it grows as a single stem, esp. flat against a wall

cordon² *v*

cordon sthg. ↔ **off** *phr v* [T] to surround (an area) with a line of police, military vehicles, etc.: *The demonstrators couldn't reach the embassy because the whole area was cordoned off.*

cor·don bleu /ˌkɔːdɒŋ ˈblɜː‖ˌkɔːrdɑːn ˈbluː/ *adj* [A] *Fr* of or practising cooking at the highest standard: *She's a real cordon bleu cook!* | *a course in cordon bleu cookery*

cordon san·i·taire /ˌkɔːdn sænɪˈteəʳ‖ˌkɔːr-/ also **sanitary cordon** *n Fr* a guarded line between infected and uninfected areas to prevent the spread of of the infection: *A cordon sanitaire has been placed around the infected towns.* | (fig.) *The school believes it is drawing a cordon sanitaire around the minds of its pupils.* **2** a line of small states not fighting or supporting either side which separates two enemy powers or two powers which, if combined, may threaten other states: *The Allies created a cordon sanitaire of buffer-states to cut Communism off from Europe.*

cords /kɔːdz‖kɔːrdz/ also **cor·du·roys** /ˈkɔːdʒɟrɔɪz, -djɟ-‖ˈkɔːrdə-/— *n* [P] *infml* trousers made from corduroy: *a pair of cords*

cor·du·roy /ˈkɔːdʒɟrɔɪ, -djɟ-‖ˈkɔːrdə-/ *n* [U] thick strong cotton cloth with thin raised lines on it, used for making outer clothing: *a corduroy jacket*

corduroy road /ˌ··· ˈ·/ *n* (esp. in the US) a rough road made from logs laid side by side

core¹ /kɔːʳ/ *n* **1** the hard central part of certain fruits that contains the seeds: *I ate the apple, and threw the core away.* **2** [(of) *usu. sing.*] the most important or central part of anything: *The Earth has a molten core.* | *The belief in free enterprise is at the core of their political thinking.* | *the core of the problem* **3** *tech* **a** a bar of MAGNETIC metal used in an electric motor to provide a path for the magnetic field **b** a ring-shaped piece of MAGNETIC material used in computer memories **4 to the core** thoroughly; completely: *She's American to the core.* | *The system is rotten to the core.* (=thoroughly bad) —see also HARD CORE

core² *v* [T] to remove the core from (a fruit)

co·re·li·gion·ist /ˌkəʊrɟˈlɪdʒənɟst/ *n* a member of the same religion

cor·er /ˈkɔːrəʳ/ *n* a specially shaped knife for coring apples

co·re·spon·dent /ˌkəʊrɟˈspɒndənt‖-ˈspɑːn-/ *n law* a person charged with ADULTERY (=sex outside marriage) with the wife or husband of a person wanting a DIVORCE (=an end to the marriage) —compare CORRESPONDENT, RESPONDENT

core time /ˈ·· ·/ *n* [U] *BrE* the period during the middle part of the day when an office or other place of work that operates FLEXITIME expects all its people to be working

Cor·fu /ˌkɔːˈfuː‖ˈkɔːrfuː/ a Greek island NW of mainland Greece which is a popular tourist place

cor·gi /ˈkɔːgi‖ˈkɔːrgi/ *n* **corgis** a small dog with short legs and a pointed nose. British people think of corgis in connection with the British royal family, as the Queen keeps some as pets.

co·ri·an·der /ˌkɒriˈændəʳ‖ˌkɔː-/ also **cilantro** *AmE* — *n* [U] the strong-tasting leaves or seeds of a small plant, used for giving a special taste to esp. Asian and Mexican food

Co·rin·thi·an /kəˈrɪnθɪən/ adj of, like, or typical of the most richly decorated style of ancient Greek building: *Corinthian columns have the leaves of plants, made in stone, around their bell-shaped tops.* —compare DORIC, IONIC

cork¹ /kɔːk‖kɔːrk/ n **1** [U] the light springy BARK (=the outer covering) of the **cork oak** (=a tree from Southern Europe and North Africa): *cork tiles on the floor | a cork mat | Cork always floats.* **2** [C] a round piece of this material, or something of the same shape made of rubber or plastic, fixed into the neck of a bottle to close it tightly: *I couldn't get the cork out of the wine bottle — I didn't have a corkscrew.*

cork² v [T (UP)] to close the neck of (a bottle or similar container) tightly with a cork —opposite **uncork**
cork sthg. ↔ **up** phr v [T] infml to keep (esp. feelings) unexpressed; SUPPRESS: *corked-up emotions*

Cork 1 the largest COUNTY in the Irish Republic **2** the second largest city in the Irish Republic

cork·age /ˈkɔːkɪdʒ‖ˈkɔːr-/ n [U] the charge made by a hotel or restaurant for allowing people to drink wine which they have brought with them

corked /kɔːkt‖kɔːrkt/ adj (of wine) tasting bad because of a decaying cork

cork·er /ˈkɔːkəʳ‖ˈkɔːr-/ n old-fash infml a very interesting, noticeable, or excellent person or thing; used esp. by UPPER-CLASS people —**corking** adj

cork·screw¹ /ˈkɔːkskruː‖ˈkɔːrk-/ n an apparatus of twisted metal with a handle, used for pulling CORKS¹ (2) out of bottles —see picture at SCREW

corkscrew² adj [A] shaped like a corkscrew; SPIRAL

corm /kɔːm‖kɔːrm/ n tech the thick underground stem of certain plants, from which the flowers and leaves grow in the spring

cor·mo·rant /ˈkɔːmərənt‖ˈkɔːr-/ n a large black fish-eating seabird with a long neck and a beak like a hook —see picture at WATER BIRD

corn¹ /kɔːn‖kɔːrn/ n [U] **1** BrE (the seed of) any of various types of grain plants, such as BARLEY, OATS, and esp. wheat: *a field of ripe corn* —see picture at CEREAL **2** esp. AmE & AustrE for: **a** MAIZE **b** SWEET CORN —see also INDIAN CORN

corn² n a painful area of thick hard skin on the foot, usu. on or near a toe. Corns are mainly thought of as an old person's problem: *Don't step on my corns. | a corn plaster* —see also **tread on someone's corns** (TREAD¹ (7))

corn·ball /ˈkɔːnbɔːl‖ˈkɔːrn-/ n [U] AmE infml a story or joke that is CORNY: *"We just watched the three stooges: what cornball!" | The movie was all cornball.*

Corn Belt /ˈ· ·/ [the] the area of the middle West US in which most corn (=MAIZE) is grown, esp. Iowa, Illinois, and Indiana as well as parts of other states

corn bread /ˈ· ·/ n [U] (esp. in the US) bread made from CORNMEAL

corn chip /ˈ· ·/ n AmE crushed corn formed into a bite-sized flat piece and fried (FRY), often eaten as a SNACK, esp. with a DIP² (3)

corn cir·cle /ˈ· ˌ··/ also **crop circle**— n any of a variety of patterns that began appearing in the fields of farms in England and some other European countries in the late 1980s and the 1990s. No one has offered a completely satisfactory explanation of where the corn circles come from, and some people think they are the work of beings from outside the Earth.

corn·cob /ˈkɔːnkɒb‖ˈkɔːrnkɑːb/ also **cob**— n the woody central part of an ear of CORN¹ (2). PIPES¹ (2) are sometimes made from corncobs, and in the US **corncob pipes** are thought of as being used by poor people who live in country areas.

corn·crake /ˈkɔːnkreɪk‖ˈkɔːrn-/ n a European bird with a loud sharp cry

corn dog /ˈ· ·/ n AmE a FRANKFURTER covered in CORN¹ (2) meal, fried (FRY), and usu. served on a stick. Corn dogs are usu. eaten at outdoor shows or sporting events rather than at home.

corn dol·ly /ˈ· ˌ··/ n a figure made from STRAW, used for decoration. Corn dollies were originally made in many societies to give thanks for the HARVEST and to wish luck for the next year's crop.

cor·ne·a /ˈkɔːnɪə‖ˈkɔːr-/ n a strong transparent protective covering on the front outer surface of the eye —see picture at EYE - -·**neal** adj

corn dolly

corned beef /ˌkɔːnd ˈbiːf ‖ ˌkɔːrnd-/ n [U] **1** also **bully beef** BrE a kind of pressed cooked BEEF in tins, which is cheap to buy and is sometimes thought of as typical army food **2** AmE beef which has been completely covered in salt water and SPICES to preserve it. It has a dark pink colour when cooked and a taste different from ordinary beef: *corned beef and cabbage*

Cor·neille /kɔːˈneɪ‖kɔːr-/, **Pi·erre** /piˈeəʳ/ (1606–84) a French poet and writer of plays

cor·ne·li·an /kɔːˈniːlɪən‖kɔːr-/ also **carnelian**— n a reddish, reddish-brown, or white stone used in jewellery

Cor·nell /kɔːˈnel‖kɔːr-/ an important American university in Ithaca, New York

cor·ner¹ /ˈkɔːnəʳ‖ˈkɔːr-/ n **1** [(of)] (the inside or outside of) the point at which two lines, edges, surfaces, roads, etc., meet: *I hit my knee on the corner of the table. | The number's in the top left-hand corner of the page. | There's a telephone at the corner of the street. | Out of the corner of my eye, I saw them sneaking out of the room. | They live* **just round the corner.** (=very near) | (fig.) *Politicians are always telling us that better times are just round the corner.* (=coming soon) | (fig.) *The company has been through a bad period but I think we've now* **turned the corner.** (=the situation is improving) —see also CORNER SHOP **2** [(of)] a part of the world, esp. a distant one: *People came from* **all four corners of the world** (=from every country) *to see the Olympic Games. | They live in a remote corner of England.* **3** a difficult or threatening position from which it is difficult to escape: *They've forced me into a corner: I'm going to have to give them what they want. | The champion's in a* **tight corner** *here: it looks as if he's going to lose the game.* **4** also **corner kick** /ˈ·· ·/— (in football) a kick taken from the corner of the field: *They scored from a corner.* **5** [(on) usu. sing.] a position of complete control over the supply of certain goods: *They're trying to establish a corner on the silver market.* **6 corner of a foreign field** a phrase from a poem by Rupert Brooke —see also ENGLAND **7 -cornered** /kɔːnəd‖kɔːrnərd/having the stated number or kind of corners: *a three-cornered hat* | (fig.) *The election was a three-cornered fight.* (=with three parties competing against each other) —see also HOLE-AND-CORNER, **cut corners** (CUT¹ (23))

cor·ner² v **1** [T] to force (a person or animal) into a difficult or threatening position: *He fought like a cornered animal.* **2** [T] to gain control of (the supply of certain goods): *They're buying all the wheat they can get hold of, because they're trying to* **corner the market**. **3** [I] (of a vehicle, driver, etc.) to turn a corner: *My car corners well even in wet weather.*

corner shop /ˈ·· ·/ BrE ‖ **convenience food store** AmE — n a small shop, usu. but not always on a corner, which may sell almost any small items, such as food, cigarettes, alcohol, and other things needed every day. Many also now have VIDEO-TAPES. In Britain many of these shops have been bought by families of Indian or Pakistani origin. In the US they are more likely to be part of a REGIONAL or national group of shops. Corner shops are usu. open for longer hours than other shops.

corner shop

cor·ner·stone /ˈkɔːnəstəʊn‖ˈkɔːrnər-/ n [(of)] **1** a stone set at one of the bottom corners of a building, often put in place at a special ceremony: *The mayor laid the cornerstone of the new library.* **2** something of first importance, on which everything else is based: *Wage control is the* *cornerstone of the government's economic policy.* — compare FOUNDATION STONE

cor·net /'kɔːnɪt‖kɔːr'net/ n **1** a small brass musical instrument like a TRUMPET **2** *BrE for* CONE (4)

Cor·net·to /kɔː'netəʊ ‖ kɔːr-/ n *tdmk* a type of ICE CREAM made by Wall's and consisting of a CORNET (2) filled with ice cream, chocolate and nuts; there are different FLAVOURS of Cornetto

corn ex·change /'· · ·ˌ·/ n a place where corn is, or was formerly, bought and sold

corn·flakes /'kɔːnfleɪks‖'kɔːrn-/ n [P] small flat pieces of crushed CORN[1] (2), eaten usu. at breakfast with milk and sugar. It is a standard breakfast food in both Britain and the US.

corn·flour /'kɔːnflaʊə\r‖'kɔːrn-/ *BrE* ‖ **cornstarch** *AmE*— n [U] fine white flour made from crushed CORN[1] (2), rice, or other grain, used in cooking to thicken liquids

corn·flow·er /'kɔːnflaʊə\r‖'kɔːrn-/ n a small wild European plant sometimes grown in gardens for its blue flowers: *cornflower-blue eyes*

cor·nice /'kɔːnɪs‖'kɔːr-/ n a decorative border at the top edge of the front of a building or PILLAR or round the top inside edges of the walls in a room

cor·niche /kɔː'niːʃ‖kɔːr-/ n a road built along a coast

corn·i·ly /'kɔːnɪli‖'kɔːr-/ adv in a CORNY way

corn·i·ness /'kɔːninɪs‖'kɔːr-/ n the condition of being CORNY

Corn·ing Ware /'kɔːnɪŋ weə\r‖'kɔːr-/ n [U] *tdmk* a popular kind of American glass, usually white in colour, which does not break when heated or dropped. It is used for pots, pans, and baking dishes.

Cor·nish /'kɔːnɪʃ‖'kɔːr-/ adj of Cornwall or its language

Cornish pas·ty /ˌ·· '··/ n (in Britain) a folded piece of pastry baked with meat and potatoes in it, usu. for one person to eat

Corn Laws /'· ˌ·/ [*the* + P] (in Britain in the 19th century) laws controlling the price of foreign corn, making it much higher than that produced at home. This protected British farmers from competition and hurt the ordinary people, and after much protest the laws were changed in 1846 — see also ANTI-CORN-LAW LEAGUE

corn liq·uor /'· ˌ·/ *also* **corn whiskey**— n [U] *AmE* a kind of WHISKY (alcoholic drink) made from CORN[1] (2)

corn·meal /'kɔːnmiːl‖'kɔːrn-/ n [U] flour made from MAIZE. It is usually yellow in colour and is used to make CORN BREAD and many other foods.

corn on the cob /ˌ· · · '·/ n the woody central part of an ear of CORN[1] (2) and the eatable pieces of corn which grow in rows along it. It is popular with British people as a first course in a meal. In the US it is eaten with the main part of the meal as a vegetable, and is often eaten on the Fourth of July.

corn pone /'kɔːn pəʊn‖'kɔːrn / n [U] a kind of bread made from CORN[1] (2), eaten esp. in the South

corn·row /'kɔːnrəʊ ‖ 'kɔːrn-/ n a hairstyle worn esp. by people of West Indian and West African origin in which the hair is put into small tight PLAITS in lines along the head

corn·starch /'kɔːnstɑːtʃ‖'kɔːrnstɑːrtʃ/ n *AmE for* CORNFLOUR

corn syr·up /'· ˌ··/ n [U] *AmE* a very sweet, thick liquid (SYRUP) made from CORN[1] (2) and used in cooking: *Add a tablespoon of light corn syrup.*

cor·nu·co·pi·a /ˌkɔːnjʊ'kəʊpiə‖ˌkɔːrnə-/ *also* **horn of plenty**— n a horn-shaped decorative container full of fruit, flowers, grain, etc., used as a SYMBOL of having plenty of everything: *After she reached the White House, the First Lady would wear only American designers in public, a decision which opened a cornucopia for Nancy. During her eight years there, she would accept designer goods worth more than $1 m.*

Corn·wall /'kɔːnwɔːl, -wəl‖'kɔːrn-/ a COUNTY in the extreme SW of England which is a popular tourist area. It includes the Isles of Scilly. It is also well-known for having a lot of tin mines in the past. —see also CORNISH and see colour map on page 818

Corn·wal·lis /kɔːn'wɒlɪs‖kɔːrn'wɑː-/, **Charles** (1738–1805) a British soldier who led the British forces in the War of American Independence. He was later Governor General of India.

corn·y /'kɔːni‖'kɔːrni/ adj infml having no original, interesting, or exciting qualities; too simple, old-fashioned, and familiar: *a corny joke/story* —see also CORNILY

co·rol·la·ry /kə'rɒləri‖'kɔːrəleri, 'kɑː-/ n fml something, such as a statement or course of action, that naturally follows from something else: *The government wants to spend more on defence: but the corollary of that argument is that they want to spend less on everything else.*

co·ro·na /kə'rəʊnə/ n **-nas** or **-nae** /niː/ the shining circle of light seen round the sun when the moon passes in front of it in an ECLIPSE

cor·o·na·ry[1] /'kɒrənəri‖'kɔːrəneri, 'kɑː-/ adj med of the heart: *coronary heart disease*

coronary[2] *also* **coronary throm·bo·sis** /ˌ···· ·'··/ fml —**-ses**— n infml the stopping of the blood supply to the heart, causing a HEART ATTACK: *He had/suffered a massive coronary and died instantly.* —compare STROKE[2] (3)

cor·o·na·tion /ˌkɒrə'neɪʃən‖ˌkɔː-, ˌkɑː-/ n the ceremony at which a king or queen is crowned. In Britain, this is held in Westminster Abbey. The occasion at which the present king or queen was crowned (which in the case of Queen Elizabeth II took place in 1953) is known as **the Coronation**. —see colour picture on page 752

Coronation Street /ˌ··'·· ·/ one of the most popular and longest running British television programmes ever, first broadcast in 1960. It is a SOAP OPERA set in Lancashire in the N of England and tells of events in the lives of the working class people who live in a street named Coronation Street. Some of its best-known characters have been Elsie Tanner, Ena Sharples, Bet Lynch, and Ken Barlow. —see colour picture on page 686

cor·o·ner /'kɒrənə\r‖'kɔː-, 'kɑː-/ n a public official who holds inquiries into the cause of a person's death, esp. if the death is not clearly the result of natural causes — see also INQUEST

cor·o·net /'kɒrənɪt‖ˌkɔːrə'net, ˌkɑː-/ n **1** a small crown usu. worn by princes or members of noble families **2** any crownlike decoration for the head: *a coronet of flowers*

corp /kɔːp‖kɔːrp/ abbrev. for: **1** CORPORATION **2** CORPORAL[2]

cor·po·ra /'kɔːpərə‖'kɔːr-/ pl. of CORPUS

cor·po·ral[1] /'kɔːpərəl‖'kɔːr-/ adj [A] fml of the body; physical

corporal[2] n an army or air force rank —see TABLE 3, p B3

corporal pun·ish·ment /ˌ··· '···/ n [U] hitting people as a way of punishing them, esp. in schools, with a CANE or a leather belt. Corporal punishment is illegal in the US and now, since 1986, in Britain, too. In British schools in the past, boys used to be punished like this much more than girls. They were hit either on their hand or on their BOTTOM[1] (3).

cor·po·rate /'kɔːpərɪt‖'kɔːr-/ adj **1** of, belonging to, or shared by all the members of a group; COLLECTIVE: *corporate responsibility* **2** [A] of or belonging to a corporation: *The company is concerned about its* **corporate image.** (—that is, it is regarded by the public) | *The bank has both individual and corporate customers.* | *a key feature of our long-term corporate planning* **3** [A] forming a single body: *The university is a corporate body formed from several different colleges.* —**-ly** adv

corporate hos·pi·tal·i·ty /ˌ···· ··'···/ n [U] the entertaining of its customers by a company, by giving them special meals, drinks, etc., in pleasant surroundings, e.g. at a theatre or at a sporting event

cor·po·ra·tion /ˌkɔːpə'reɪʃən‖ˌkɔːr-/ n [C+*sing/pl. v*] **1** a group of people who are permitted by law to act as a single unit, esp. for purposes of business, with rights and duties separate from those of its members: *Mary works for a large American corporation.* | *a multinational corporation.* | *the British Broadcasting Corporation* **2** *BrE* a town COUNCIL: *The corporation has/have closed the road.*

corporation tax /ˌ···'·· ˌ·/ n [U] a tax paid by all companies in Britain and the US

cor·po·re·al /kɔː'pɔːriəl‖kɔːr-/ adj fml **1** of or for the body as opposed to the spirit: *corporeal needs such as food* **2** that can be touched; material; physical — **~ly** adv

corps /kɔː\r/ n corps /kɔːz‖kɔːrz/ [C+*sing./pl. v*] **1** *(often cap.)* a trained army group with special duties and responsibilities: *the medical corps* **2** *(often cap.)* a branch of the army equal in size to two DIVISIONS **3** a group of people united in the same activity: *the president's press corps*

corps de bal·let /ˌkɔː də ˈbæleɪ‖ˌkɔːr də bæˈleɪ, -ˈbæleɪ/ *n* [C+*sing.|pl. v*] *Fr* BALLET (3)

corpse /kɔːps‖kɔːrps/ *n* a dead body, esp. of a person. This word is either used formally, e.g. by police officers or doctors, or in plays and stories about murders. A more usual expression would be simply 'a body'.

cor·pu·lent /ˈkɔːpjʊlənt‖ˈkɔːr-/ *adj euph* (of a person) very fat —**lence** *n* [U]

cor·pus /ˈkɔːpəs‖ˈkɔːr-/ *n* **corpora** /ˈkɔːpərə‖ˈkɔːr-/ or **corpuses** a collection **a** of all the writings of a special kind, or by a certain person: *the corpus of Shakespeare's works* **b** of material or information for study: *The dictionary is based on a corpus of 10,000,000 words taken from books and newspapers in English.*

Corpus Chris·ti /ˌkɔːpəs ˈkrɪsti ‖ ˌkɔːr-/ a city in SE Texas on the Gulf of Mexico – see colour map on pages 1374-5

Cor·pus Christi, Feast of [*the*] a celebration in the ROMAN CATHOLIC church when the BLESSED SACRAMENT (=bread made holy) is carried in PROCESSION. Corpus Christi is Latin for "Body of Christ", the words the priest says to each person when he gives out the holy bread in the church service.

cor·pus·cle /ˈkɔːpəsəl, kɔːˈpʌ-‖ˈkɔːrpə-/ *n* any of the red or white cells in the blood

cor·ral[1] /kɒˈrɑːl, kə-‖kəˈræl/ *n* an enclosed area, esp. in N America, where cattle, horses, etc., are kept

corral[2] *v* -ll- [T] to drive (animals) into a corral: (fig.) *They corralled the protesters and kept them away from the President's car.*

cor·rect[1] /kəˈrekt/ *adj* **1** based on or in accordance with the truth or the facts; right; without mistakes: *a correct answer* | *correct spelling* | *If these predictions turn out to be correct, the company is going to have a very good year.* **2** following approved or established standards of manners, action, etc.: *correct behaviour* | *Make sure that these papers are processed according to the correct procedures.* | *His behaviour in public is always terribly correct: I wonder if he ever makes a joke.* —opposite **incorrect** — ~**ly** *adv* — ~**ness** *n* [U]

correct[2] *v* [T] **1** to make or set right: *Correct my pronunciation if it's wrong.* | *These spectacles will correct her eyesight defect.* | *They issued a new statement correcting the errors that had appeared in the earlier one.* **2** (of a teacher) to show the mistakes in: *I've been correcting the kids' homework for hours.* **3** *old-fash* to punish in order to improve the behaviour of

cor·rec·tion /kəˈrekʃən/ *n* **1** [U] the act of correcting **2** [C] a change that corrects something: *Teachers usually make corrections in red ink.* **3** [U] *old-fash* punishment: *They sent him to a* **house of correction**. (=a prison)

correctional fa·cil·i·ty /·ˈ··· ·,··/ *n AmE tech or euph* prison

correction fluid /·ˈ·· ,··/ also **correcting fluid**— *n* [U] a special white liquid in a bottle or a pen which is put over a written mistake so that one can write in that place again

cor·rec·ti·tude /kəˈrektɪtjuːd‖-tuːd/ *n* [U] *fml or pomp* correctness of behaviour

cor·rec·tive /kəˈrektɪv/ *adj, n fml* (something) intended to correct: *corrective measures|treatment* — ~**ly** *adv*

cor·rel·ate[1] /ˈkɒrɪleɪt‖ˈkɔː-, ˈkɑː-/ *v* [I;T (**with**)] to (show to) have a close shared relationship or connection of cause and effect: *They are trying to find out if these behaviour patterns correlate with particular changes in diet.* | *Smoking and lung cancer are closely correlated.*

cor·rel·ate[2] /ˈkɒrɪlɪt‖ˈkɔː-, ˈkɑː-/ *n* either of two things that correlate with each other

cor·re·la·tion /ˌkɒrɪˈleɪʃən‖ˌkɔː-, ˌkɑː-/ *n* **1** [C (**between**)] a shared relationship or connection of cause and effect: *a high correlation between unemployment and crime* **2** [U (**of**)] *fml* the act of correlating

cor·rel·a·tive /kəˈrelətɪv/ *adj, n* **1** *fml* (any of two or more things that are) naturally related **2** *tech* (either of two words) regularly used together but rarely used next to each other: *"Either" and "or" are* **correlative conjunctions.**

cor·re·spond /ˌkɒrɪˈspɒnd‖ˌkɔːrɪˈspɑːnd, ˌkɑː-/ *v* [I] **1** [(**with, to**)] to be in agreement; match; be CONSISTENT (with) or EQUIVALENT (to): *The problem is that what she says doesn't correspond with what she does.* | *The contents of the box must correspond to the description on the label.* **2** [(**with**)] to exchange letters regularly. This word is used of personal letters but is more formal than saying that people wrote to each other: *Janet and Bob corresponded (with each other) for many years.*

cor·re·spon·dence /ˌkɒrɪˈspɒndəns‖ˌkɔːrɪˈspɑːn-, ˌkɑː-/ *n* [S;U (**between, with**)] **1** the act of exchanging letters **2** the letters exchanged between people: *The library bought all the correspondence between Queen Victoria and her daughters.* **3** a state or case of corresponding; agreement between particular things

correspondence course /·ˈ·· ·,·/ *n* a set of lessons, often leading to a degree, in which the student works at home and receives lessons by mail: *I'm doing|taking a correspondence course in business studies.*

cor·re·spon·dent[1] /ˌkɒrɪˈspɒndənt‖ˌkɔːrɪˈspɑːn-, ˌkɑː-/ *n* **1** a person with whom another person exchanges letters regularly **2** someone employed by a newspaper, television, etc., to report news from a particular area or on a particular subject: *a war correspondent* | *Here is a report from our environment correspondent.* —compare CORESPONDENT

correspondent[2] *adj* [(**with**)] *fml* in agreement; matching; corresponding: *The election result was correspondent with the government's wishes in the matter.*

cor·re·spon·ding /ˌkɒrɪˈspɒndɪŋ◀‖ˌkɔːrɪˈspɑːn-, ˌkɑː-/ *adj* [A] matching or related: *There has been a decline in the value of the pound and a corresponding increase in the strength of the dollar.* | *Profits for the first three months are 50% higher than in the corresponding period of last year.* — ~**ly** *adv*

cor·ri·dor /ˈkɒrɪdɔː‖ˈkɔːrɪdər, ˈkɑː-/ *n* **1** a passage, esp. between two rows of rooms: *Room 101 is at the end of the corridor.* | *a corridor train* | (fig.) *the* **corridors of power** (=the places where government decisions are made) **2** a narrow piece of land (or air space) that passes through a foreign country: *the Polish Corridor (to the sea)* —see also NORTHEAST CORRIDOR

cor·ri·gen·dum /ˌkɒrɪˈdʒendəm‖ˌkɔː-, ˌkɑː-/ *n* -**da** /də/ *tech* something (to be) made correct, esp. in a printed book

cor·rob·o·rate /kəˈrɒbəreɪt‖kəˈrɑː-/ *v* [T] to support or strengthen (a statement, opinion, idea, etc.) by fresh information or proof: *Someone who saw the accident corroborated the driver's statement.* —**rator** *n* —**ration** /kəˌrɒbəˈreɪʃən‖kə,rɑː-/ *n* [U] —**rative** /kəˈrɒbərətɪv‖ kəˈrɑːbəreɪtɪv/ *adj*: *corroborative evidence*

cor·rode /kəˈrəʊd/ *v* [I;T (AWAY)] to (cause to) become worn away or be gradually destroyed, esp. by chemical action over a long period: *Water corrodes metal.* | *The machine doesn't work because the electrical contacts have corroded.* —compare ERODE

cor·ro·sion /kəˈrəʊʒən/ *n* [U] **1** the process of corroding: *If any of the acid leaks it may cause corrosion.* | (fig.) *the corrosion of moral standards* **2** a substance, such as RUST, produced by this process: *corrosion on the car body*

cor·ro·sive /kəˈrəʊsɪv/ *adj* **1** able to corrode: *Danger! Corrosive material!* —opposite **noncorrosive** **2** gradually weakening or destroying society, a person's feelings, etc.: *the corrosive influence of mass unemployment* | *corrosive feelings of bitterness* **3** (of language) very fierce: *a corrosive attack on the government* — ~**ly** *adv* — ~**ness** *n* [U]

cor·ru·gated /ˈkɒrəgeɪtɪd‖ˈkɔː-, ˈkɑː-/ *adj* formed in rows of wavelike folds: *Sheets of* **corrugated iron** *are often used for roofs and fences.* | (fig.) *a corrugated brow*

cor·ru·ga·tion /ˌkɒrəˈgeɪʃən‖ˌkɔː-, ˌkɑː-/ *n* a fold in a corrugated surface

cor·rupt[1] /kəˈrʌpt/ *adj* **1** practising or marked by the dishonest and improper use of one's power or position, e.g. to make money illegally: *a corrupt judge* | *corrupt officials in the passport office* | *the corrupt use of public money* **2** morally wicked: *corrupt pornographic writings* **3** containing mistakes; different from the original: *a corrupt text* — ~**ly** *adv* — ~**ness** *n* [U]

corrupt[2] *v* [T] **1** to cause to become morally bad; change from good to bad: *Do you think young people are corrupted by big city life?* | *corrupted by power* **2** to change the original form of (a language, set of teachings, etc.) in a bad way: *Has English been corrupted by the introduction of foreign words?* —see also **power tends to corrupt**...(POWER¹ (13)) — **~ible** *adj* — **~ibility** /kəˌrʌptɬˈbɪlɬti/ *n* [U]

cor·rup·tion /kəˈrʌpʃən/ *n* **1** [U] the act or process of corrupting **2** [U] **a** dishonesty, esp. by people in positions of power: *The new military rulers said that the previous government had been* **riddled with** (=full of) **corruption. b** immoral behaviour; being corrupt: *the corruption of the ancient Roman court* **3** [C (**of**) *usu. sing.*] a form of something, such as a word, that is changed from its correct or original form: *The word "Thursday" is a corruption of Thor's Day.*

cor·sage /kɔːˈsɑːʒ‖kɔːr-/ *n* a small bunch of flowers worn by a woman at the neck or waist, usu. only on very formal occasions —compare NOSEGAY

cor·sair /ˈkɔːseəʳ‖ˈkɔːr-/ *n* a PIRATE or pirate ship from N Africa that used to stop and rob ships in former times

corse /kɔːs‖kɔːrs/ *n old use or poet for* CORPSE

corse·let /ˈkɔːslɬt‖ˈkɔːr-/ *n* a piece of armour worn in former times on the upper part of the body, but not usu. covering the arms

cor·set /ˈkɔːsɬt‖ˈkɔːr-/ also **corsets** *pl.*— *BrE* ‖ **girdle** *AmE* — *n* a very tight-fitting article of UNDERWEAR worn, esp. by women, to give shape to the waist and HIPs. Corsets are now worn only by older women. — **~ed** *adj*

Cor·si·ca /ˈkɔːsɪkə‖ˈkɔːr-/ a large island in the Mediterranean Sea belonging to France. It is very mountainous. —**can** *adj, n* : *Napoleon was a Corsican.* | *Corsican wines*

cor·tege , **-tège** /kɔːˈteɪʒ‖kɔːrˈteʒ/ *n fml* a procession following the dead body at a funeral, usu. the funeral of a very important person

Cor·tés /ˈkɔːtez‖kɔːrˈtez/, **Her·nán** /hɜːˈnæn‖hɜːr-/ or **Her·nan·do** /hɜːˈnændəʊ‖hɜːr-/ (1485–1547) a Spanish adventurer who conquered (CONQUER) the Aztec Empire in Mexico

cor·tex /ˈkɔːteks‖ˈkɔːr-/ *n* **-tices** /tɬsiːz/ *tech* the outer covering of something, esp. of the brain —**-tical** /ˈkɔːtɪkəl‖ˈkɔːr-/ *adj*

cor·ti·sone /ˈkɔːtɬzəʊn‖ˈkɔːrtɬsəʊn/ *n* [U] a powerful substance used esp. in treating RHEUMATIC diseases

co·run·dum /kəˈrʌndəm/ *n* [U] a very hard mineral used in powder form for polishing and sharpening tools

cor·us·cate /ˈkɒrəskeɪt‖ˈkɔː-, ˈkɑː-/ *v* [I] *fml* to flash; SPARKLE: *a coruscating jewel* | (fig.) *coruscating wit* —**-cation** /ˌkɒrəˈskeɪʃən‖ˌkɔː-, ˌkɑː-/ *n* [U]

cor·vette /kɔːˈvet‖kɔːr-/ *n tech* a small fast warship used for protecting other ships from attack

cos³ /kɒz/ *conj nonstandard* becauoe ooo aloo COS LETTUCE

cos² /kɒs‖kɑːs/ *abbrev. for:* COSINE

Co·sa Nos·tra /ˌkəʊzə ˈnɒstrə‖ˌkəʊsə ˈnəʊs-/ the US branch of the MAFIA

Cos·by /ˈkɒzbi‖ˈkɑːz-/, **Bill** (1937–) an American actor and COMEDIAN known esp. for the television SERIES *The Cosby Show* in the 1980s and for being the first black person to get an important role in a regular television series in the 1960s

Bill Cosby

Cosby Show /ˈ·· ˌ·/, **The** an American television COMEDY SERIES about a black American family —see colour picture on page 686

Co·sell /ˈkəʊsel/, **How·ard** /ˈhaʊəd‖-ərd/ (1920–) an American sports COMMENTATOR (=someone who tells people about a sports game as it is happening) who used to cover most football games on television. Cosell talked a lot and had strong opinions.

cosh¹ /kɒʃ‖kɑːʃ/ *BrE* ‖ **blackjack, sap** *AmE*— *n infml* a short heavy metal pipe or filled rubber tube used as a weapon: *They were arrested for possession of two guns and a cosh.*

cosh² *v* [T] *infml, esp. BrE* to hit with a cosh

Co·si fan tut·te /ˌkəʊsi fæn ˈtʊti‖ˌkəʊˌsiː fɑːn ˈtʊteɪ/ an OPERA by Mozart

co·sig·na·to·ry /ˌkəʊˈsɪgnətəri‖ -tɔːri/ *n fml* a person signing together with others, often for an organization, country, etc.: *Britain, France, and Germany were all cosignatories of/to the agreement.*

co·si·ly /ˈkəʊzɬli/ *adv* in a COSY¹ way

co·si·ness /ˈkəʊzinɬs/ *n* [U] the condition of being COSY¹

co·sine /ˈkəʊsaɪn/ *n tech* the FRACTION (1) calculated for an angle by dividing the length of the side next to it in a RIGHT-ANGLED TRIANGLE by the length of the side opposite the right angle —compare SINE, TANGENT

cos let·tuce /ˌkɒs ˈletɬs‖ˌkɑːs-, ˌkəʊs-/ *BrE* ‖ **romaine lettuce** *esp. AmE*— *n* a LETTUCE with long leaves

cos·met·ic¹ /kɒzˈmetɪk‖kɑːz-/ *n* [*usu. pl.*] any substance, such as a face-cream or body-powder, that is intended to make the skin or hair more beautiful: *They sell lipstick, hair gel, and a whole range of other cosmetics.* | *the cosmetics industry* | *cruelty-free cosmetics* —see also MAKE-UP (1)

cosmetic² *adj* **1** [A] intended to make the skin or hair more beautiful: *a cosmetic cream* **2** *derog* dealing only with the outside appearance rather than the central part of something; SUPERFICIAL: *These changes in the law are purely cosmetic and do nothing to deal with the real problem.* | *a few cosmetic repairs to the house*

cos·me·ti·cian /ˌkɒzməˈtɪʃən‖ˌkɑːz-/ *n* a person professionally trained in the use of cosmetics

cosmetic sur·ge·ry /·ˌ·· ˈ···/ *n* [U] medical operations performed to change a person's appearance, e.g. to improve the shape of their nose or to enlarge their breasts. This is becoming increasingly popular in Britain, although less so than in the US, and people are more open about having this kind of surgery, but it is expensive and still seen as a sign of VANITY by most people —compare PLASTIC SURGERY

cos·mic /ˈkɒzmɪk‖ˈkɑːz-/ *adj* of or found in space or the universe: *Planets were formed out of cosmic dust.* | (fig.) *a scandal of cosmic* (=extremely large) *proportions* —**~ally** /kli/ *adv*

cosmic ray /ˌ·· ˈ·/ *n* [*usu. pl.*] a stream of RADIATION reaching the Earth from outer space

Cos·mo /ˈkɒzməʊ‖ˈkɑː-/ *infml for* COSMOPOLITAN magazine

cos·mog·o·ny /kɒzˈmɒgəni‖kɑːzˈmɑː-/ *n* [C;U] *fml* (a set of ideas about) the origin of the universe: *primitive cosmogonies*

cos·mol·o·gy /kɒzˈmɒlədʒi‖kɑːzˈmɑː-/ *n* [U] the science of the origin and structure of the universe, esp. as studied in ASTRONOMY

cos·mo·naut /ˈkɒzmənɔːt‖ˈkɑːzmənɔːt, -nɑːt/ *n* a Soviet ASTRONAUT

cos·mo·pol·i·tan¹ /ˌkɒzməˈpɒlɬtən◂ ‖ˌkɑːzməˈpɑː-/ *adj* **1** consisting of people from many different parts of the world: *London is a very cosmopolitan city* **2** (of a person, belief, opinion, etc.) not narrow-minded; showing wide experience of different people and places: *She has a very cosmopolitan outlook on life.* **3** *tech* (of an animal or plant) existing in most parts of the world

cosmopolitan² *n usu. apprec* a person who has travelled widely and feels equally at home everywhere

Cosmopolitan also **Cosmo** *infml*— a monthly magazine for women produced in both Britain and the US in different VERSIONs. In Britain it has an image which is intended to attract the more modern, young, independent, and COSMOPOLITAN¹ (2) reader. In the US it is very often criticized by FEMINISTs for being old-fashioned in its views of women and men.

cos·mos /ˈkɒzmɒs‖ˈkɑːzməs/ *n* [*the*+S] the whole universe considered as an ordered system

Cosmos a British travel company known for arranging bus tours and reasonably-priced holidays abroad

Cos·sack /ˈkɒsæk‖ˈkɑːs-/ *n* a member of a people who lived on the plains of S Russia and the Ukraine, famous for their skill in riding horses, their fierce fighting, and their characteristic way of dancing with the knees bent, the body low, and the arms folded in front of the body. A small number still exist. —**Cossack** *adj*

cos·set /ˈkɒsᵻt‖ˈkɑː-/ v -tt- [T] to pay a great deal of attention to making (a person) comfortable and happy; PAMPER: *These farmers have been cosseted for years by generous government subsidies.*

cost[1] /kɒst‖kɔːst/ n 1 [C] the amount of money paid or needed for buying, doing, or producing something: *the high cost of renting a house in central London* | *The students are given £150 a year to cover the cost of books and stationery.* | *High production costs lead to high prices in the shops.* | *The cost of policing the demonstration will be met/borne by the local council.* | *The dealer said he would sell me the car* **at cost.** (=at the same price he paid) 2 [C;U] something needed, given, or lost, in order to obtain something: *He saved the children from the fire at the cost of his own life.* (=but he died) | *We must avoid war* **at all costs/whatever the cost.** (=it is extremely important to avoid war) 3 **to one's cost** from one's own unpleasant experience: *As I learned to my cost when I was ill in New York, you should always take out medical insurance before you go abroad.* —see also COSTS, **count the cost** (COUNT[1]); see COST[2] (USAGE)

cost[2] v cost 1 [L (+obj)+n] to have (an amount of money) as a price: *a powerful new computer costing over $10,000* | *"How much do these shoes cost?" "They cost £30."* | *It's costing me a small fortune* (=a lot) *to send the children on holiday.* | *Champagne* **costs the earth.** (=is very expensive) | *High unemployment* **costs** *the government billions of pounds in lost taxes.* | (fig.) *The mistake cost him his job.* 2 [T *no pass.*] *infml* to be expensive for (someone): *It will cost you to go by train; why not go by bus?* 3 [T] (*past tense & participle* **costed**) to calculate the price to be charged for (a job, someone's time, etc.): *The builder costed the job at £150.* 4 **cost an arm and a leg** to have a very high or too high price

▷ USAGE Compare **price, cost,** and **charge.** When talking about the money needed to buy a particular object, the usual word is **price:** *What is the* **price** *of this watch?* **Cost** (*n*) is like **price,** but is used less for objects, and more **a** for services: *the* **cost** *of having the house painted* **b** for general things: *the* **cost** *of living* | *the* **cost** *of food.* The amount of money you pay for something is what it **costs** (*v*) you: *How much did this watch* **cost** *you?* The person who is selling goods or services to you **charges** you for them: *How much did he* **charge** *you for repairing the car?* **Charge** (*n*) means "a sum of money demanded, especially for allowing someone to do something": *There will be a small* **charge** *for admission to the museum.*◁

Cos·ta /ˈkɒstə‖ˈkəʊs-/ n BrE humor (used, esp. in newspapers, when describing a place on the coast that has particular characteristics): *the Costa del crime* | *Costa del Rip-off*

Costa Bra·va /ˌkɒstə ˈbrɑːvə‖ˌkəʊs-/ [the] the part of the Mediterranean coast in E Spain. It is a popular place for young British people to go on holiday as it is possible to go there very cheaply.

Costa del Sol /ˌkɒstə del ˈsɒl‖ˌkəʊstə del ˈsəʊl/ [the] the part of the Mediterranean coast in S Spain. It is a popular place for British people to go on holiday, but also people often think of the Costa del Sol as a place where successful criminals go to live.

co-star[1] /ˈkəʊ stɑːʳ/ n a famous actor or actress who appears together with another famous actor or actress in a film or play

co-star[2] v -rr- 1 [I (with)] to appear as a co-star: *It's the first time she's co-starred with Robert Redford.* 2 [T] (of a film or play) to have as co-stars: *"Gone with the Wind", the classic movie co-starring Vivien Leigh and Clark Gable*

Cos·ta Ri·ca /ˌkɒstə ˈriːkə‖ˌkəʊ-/ a country in Central America; capital San José; population 2,922,000 (1989) — **-can** n, adj

cost/ben·e·fit a·nal·y·sis /ˌ· ˈ··· ·ˌ···/ n a system of determining a course of action by examining various possibilities with regard to what they will cost and what BENEFIT they will bring. The course of action which will bring the greatest benefit at the smallest cost is seen as the most desirable.

cost cen·tre /ˈ· ˌ··/ n a part of a business, such as a department or a group of people or machines, for which costs can be worked out and controlled

cost-ef·fec·tive /ˈ· ·ˌ··/ adj bringing the best possible profits or advantages for the lowest possible cost: *They discovered that it was more cost-effective to import the engines from Spain than to manufacture them here.* — ~ly adv — ~ness n [U]

Cos·tel·lo /kɒˈsteləʊ‖kɑː-/, **El·vis** /ˈelvᵻs/ (1954–) a British popular music singer and songwriter, whose best-known song is *Oliver's Army*

cos·ter·mon·ger /ˈkɒstəˌmʌŋgəʳ‖ˈkɑːstərˌmɑːŋ-, -ˌmʌŋ-/ also **coster** /ˈkɒstəʳ‖ˈkɑː-/— n BrE a person who sells fruit and vegetables from a cart in the street, esp. in London

cost·ing /ˈkɒstɪŋ‖ˈkɔːs-/ n [U] the process of measuring and looking at the cost of a business activity, product, department, etc.

cost·ive /ˈkɒstɪv‖ˈkɑː-/ adj rare suffering from or causing CONSTIPATION

cost·ly /ˈkɒstli‖ˈkɔːstli/ adj 1 rather fml costing a lot of money, esp. when this is regarded as unreasonable or unnecessary: *Selling your house can be a costly and time-consuming business.* | *a costly delay* 2 gained or won at a great loss: *the costliest war in our history* (=with greatest loss of life) —**liness** n [U]

Cost·ner /ˈkɒstnəʳ‖ˈkɑː-/, **Kev·in** /ˈkevᵻn/ (1955–) an American actor and DIRECTOR whose films include *Dances with Wolves, Robin Hood: Prince of Thieves,* and *JFK*

cost of liv·ing /ˌ· · ˈ··/ n [(the) S] the cost of buying the goods and services one needs to live at an average standard of comfort: *The cost of living has gone up 5% in the last year, so we asked for a wage increase of 7%.* —compare STANDARD OF LIVING

cost-of-liv·ing in·dex /ˌ· · ˈ·· ˌ··/ n a number based on rising and/or falling prices of goods, services, etc. usu. over a year, which shows whether the cost of living has gone up or down. Since the Second World War many employers and unions have agreed to use it as a guideline for wage deals. Other payments such as SOCIAL SECURITY and some PENSIONS are also based on it. —compare RETAIL PRICE INDEX

cost-plus /ˌ· ˈ·/ n a method of agreeing on a selling price in which an agreed rate of profit is added to the cost price **cost-plus** /ˌ· ˈ·◂/ adj : *cost-plus pricing*

cost price /ˌ· ˈ·◂/ also **cost** esp. AmE— n [U] the price a shopkeeper pays for an article, which is less than the price the buyer pays the shopkeeper (**the retail price**): *The employees of the store are allowed to buy furniture at cost price/at cost.*

costs /kɒsts‖kɔːsts/ n [P] the cost of taking a matter to a court of law, esp. as ordered to be paid by the side that lost the case to the side that won it: *She won the case and was awarded costs.*

costume

national costume/dress | period costume/dress | a clown's costume

cos·tume /ˈkɒstjuːm‖ˈkɑːstuːm/ n 1 [C;U] the clothes typical of a certain period, country, or profession, esp. as worn in plays: *They are all dressed in national costume.* | *actors in 18th-century costumes* | *a costume drama* (=one in which clothes from a former period are worn) 2 [C] BrE a SWIMMING COSTUME 3 [C] old-fash a woman's suit

costume jew·elle·ry /ˈ·· ˌ···/ n [U] expensive-looking jewellery made from cheap materials

cos·tu·mi·er /kɒˈstjuːmiəʳ‖kɑːˈstuː-/ n a person who makes or deals in costumes, esp. for plays

co·sy[1] /'kəʊzi/ *esp. BrE* ‖ **cozy** *AmE adj* **1** *apprec* warm, comfortable and protected from unpleasantness: *a cosy little house* | *The room had a nice cosy feel.* **2** *sometimes derog* based on or showing a close relationship, perhaps with a dishonest purpose: *cosy deals between the union leaders and the company management* —see also COSILY

cosy[2] *n* a covering put over a teapot to keep the contents warm: *a tea cosy*

cot /kɒt‖kɑːt/ *n* **1** *BrE* ‖ **crib** *AmE*— a small bed for a young child, usu. with high movable sides so that the child cannot fall out **2** *AmE for* CAMP BED —see picture at BED

co·tan·gent /kəʊˈtændʒənt/ *n tech* the FRACTION calculated for an angle by dividing the length of the sides next and opposite to it in a right-angled TRIANGLE

cot death /'· ˌ·/ *BrE* ‖ **crib death** *AmE*— *n* an unexpected and usu. unexplainable death of a baby that had been healthy. It is now officially called SUDDEN INFANT DEATH SYNDROME.

Côte d'A·zur /ˌkəʊt dæˈzjʊəʳ‖-dəˈzʊər/ [*the*] an area of the coast in SE France, part of the Riviera, containing many popular places for holidays, e.g. Nice and Cannes. It is considered by British people to be a SOPHISTICATED place.

Côte d'I·voire /ˌkəʊt diːˈvwɑːʳ/ a country on the coast of Guinea, W Africa; capital Abidjan; population 12,098,000 (1989)

Côte d'Or /ˌkəʊt ˈdɔːʳ/ [*the*] an area in central France, near Dijon, from which the wine called Burgundy comes

co·te·rie /'kəʊtəri/ *n* [C+*sing.*|*pl. v*] *fml* a close group of people with shared interests, tastes, etc. It is sometimes difficult to be admitted to a coterie because they do not easily accept new members: *a small coterie of artists* | *Mrs Thatcher went to the hotel for lunch with her personal coterie.*

co·ter·mi·nous /kəʊˈtɜːmɪnəs‖-ɜːr-/ *adj* [(with)] *fml* sharing the same border: *England is coterminous with Wales.* — ~ly *adv*

co·til·lion /kəˈtɪljən/ *n* a dance of 18th-century French origin

Cots·wolds /'kɒtswəʊldz‖'kɑːts-/ *n* [*the*+P] (the area containing) a range of hills in the SW of England. It is a pretty area, much visited by tourists, where many of the local houses are made from **Cotswold stone** (=stone taken from the hills).

cottage

a typical English cottage

cot·tage /'kɒtɪdʒ‖'kɑː-/ *n* **1** a small house, esp. an old one in the country. These are often thought of in a very ROMANTIC way as being COSY and safe, and having a thatched roof (THATCH[1]) and roses round the door: *They dreamed of buying a little cottage in the country.* —see HOUSE (USAGE) **2** *BrE sl* a place, such as a PUBLIC CONVENIENCE, where COTTAGING takes place

cottage cheese /ˌ·· '·‖'·· ·/ *n* [U] soft lumpy white cheese made from sour milk. It is fairly low in fat and often eaten by people trying to lose weight.

cottage hos·pi·tal /ˌ·· '···/ *n BrE* a small hospital, usu. in a country area

cottage in·dus·try /ˌ·· '···/ *n* an industry whose labour force consists of people working at home with their own tools or machinery: *Hand-knitting sweaters has become a cottage industry in some parts of Scotland.*

cottage loaf /ˌ·· '·/ *n* a loaf of bread made in two round pieces with the smaller one stuck on top of the larger one

cottage pie /ˌ·· '·/ *n* [U] SHEPHERD'S PIE

cot·tag·er /'kɒtɪdʒəʳ‖'kɑː-/ *n BrE* **1** *rare* a person who lives in a country COTTAGE **2** *sl* a man who wants to have sex with other men in a public place

cot·tag·ing /'kɒtɪdʒɪŋ‖'kɑː-/ *n* [U] *BrE sl* the practice of looking for male HOMOSEXUAL partners in public TOILETS, which is illegal in Britain

a reel of cotton

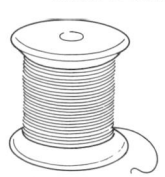

cot·ton[1] /'kɒtn‖'kɑːtn/ *n* [U] **1** a tall plant grown in warm areas for the soft white hair that surrounds its seeds **2** (thread or cloth made from) the hair of this plant: *a reel of red cotton* | *a cool white cotton shirt* | *Cotton is more comfortable to wear than nylon.* **3** *AmE for* COTTON WOOL

cotton[2] *v*
  cotton on *phr v* [I (**to**)] *infml* to begin to understand; REALIZE: *He'd been speaking for half an hour before I cottoned on (to what he meant)!*

Cotton Belt /'·· ·/ [*the*] the area across the S of the US from Texas to the E coast, in which cotton is grown

Cotton Bowl /'·· ·/ [*the*] a college football CHAMPIONSHIP game played every year in Dallas, Texas and put on television in the US

cotton bud /'·· ·/ *BrE* ‖ **Q-tip** *AmE tdmk*— *n* a short plastic stick with a small amount of cotton wool at each end, used for cleaning ears or other places that are hard to reach, e.g. on machinery

cotton can·dy /ˌ·· '··/ *n* [U] *AmE for* CANDYFLOSS

cotton gin /'·· ·/ *n* a machine that separates seeds, etc. from cotton

cotton-pick·ing /'·· ˌ··/ *adj* [A] *AmE infml* (used to give force to an expression of annoyance): *Mind your own cotton-picking business!*

cotton reel /'·· ·/ *BrE* ‖ **spool** *AmE*— *n* a plastic or wooden object on which COTTON[1] (2) is wound, for use in sewing

cot·ton·tail /'kɒtnteɪl‖'kɑːtn-/ *n* a small American rabbit with a white tail

cot·ton·wood /'kɒtnwʊd‖'kɑːtn-/ *n* [C;U] (the wood from) a N American broad-leafed tree which drops seeds that look like cotton in the early summer

cotton wool /ˌ·· '·/ *BrE* ‖ **cotton** *AmE*— *n* [U] a soft mass of cotton used for cleaning wounds, etc.: *Put a pad of cotton wool over the cut.* | *She used a piece of cotton wool to clean off her make-up.* | (fig.) *cotton wool clouds* | (fig.) *She wrapped her children up in cotton wool to protect them from the realities of life.*

couch[1] /kaʊtʃ/ *n* **1** a long comfortable piece of furniture, usu. with a back and arms, on which more than one person can sit, or a person can lie; SOFA: *Lie down on the couch if you're feeling ill.* | *the psychiatrist's couch* —see picture at LIVING ROOM **2** *lit* a bed

couch[2] *v* **be couched in** *fml* (of a statement, letter, etc.) to be expressed in the stated way: *His refusal was couched in rather unfriendly terms.*

cou·chette /kuːˈʃet/ *n* **1** a narrow shelf-like folding bed on which a person can sleep on a train **2** a comfortable seat on a night boat or train —compare SLEEPING CAR

couch grass /'kuːtʃ grɑːs, 'kaʊtʃ-‖-græs/ *n* [U] a rough grass with long creeping roots

couch potato

couch po·ta·to /'· ·ˌ··/ *n infml derog* a person who takes little or no exercise, but spends most of their time sitting around, esp. watching television

cou·gar /'kuːgəʳ/ also **mountain lion, puma, panther**— *n* **-gars** *or* **-gar** a large powerful brown wild cat from the mountainous areas of Western North America and South America —see picture at BIG CATS

cough¹ /kɒf‖kɔːf/ v **1** [I] to push air out from the throat suddenly, with a short rough sound, esp. because of discomfort in the throat during a cold or other infection: *You're coughing a lot – I think you smoke too much.* **2** [T (UP)] to clear (something) from the throat by doing this: *We knew she was seriously ill when she started to cough (up) blood.* **3** [I] to make a sound like a cough: *The engine coughed once or twice, but wouldn't start.*
cough (sthg. ↔) **up** phr v [I;T] sl to produce (esp. money or information) unwillingly: *Dad coughed up (£100) for our holiday.*

cough² n **1** [C] an act or sound of coughing: *She gave a nervous cough.* **2** [S] a (medical) condition marked by frequent or repeated coughing: *John had a bad cough all last week.* –see also WHOOPING COUGH

cough sweet /'· ·/ BrE also **cough drop**– n a MEDICATED sweet used for making a sore throat feel better

cough syr·up /'· ˌ··/ n [U] a usu. sweet MEDICATED liquid used to help prevent coughing

could /kəd; strong kʊd/ v 3rd person sing. **could**, negative short form **couldn't** /'kʊdnt/ [modal+to-v] **1** (describes **can** in the past): *I could run very fast when I was a schoolgirl.* | *I couldn't get the tickets yesterday.* **2** (used instead of **can** to describe what someone has said, asked, etc.): *He said we could smoke.* (His actual words were "You can smoke.") | *She asked whether she could go home.* **3** (used to show what is or might be possible, but without real force or certainty): *This new project could create 5000 new jobs.* | *It could be weeks before we know the full cost of the accident.* | *The government could do a lot more to help small businesses.* | *In my view, this accident could have been prevented.* | *We couldn't have picked a worse day for the picnic – it rained nonstop.* | *I could have kicked him* (=I wanted to) *when he said that.* **4** (in CLAUSES expressing purpose) might; would be able to: *He turned his face away so that I couldn't see the tears.* **5** (used to make a request): *Could you put this case on the shelf for me, please?* –compare CAN¹ (7): Tentativeness and Requests **6** (used to suggest a possible or desirable course of action): *If she's not at home, you could try phoning her at the office.* **7** (shows annoyance) *You could be a bit more careful!* | *You could have told me you were going to be late.* –compare MIGHT (4); see NOT (USAGE) and

▷ USAGE **1** When talking about the past, **could** can be used when we want only to say that someone had the ability or power: *She could play the piano when she was five.* To express the idea of having the ability to do something and then doing it, you can use **manage to** (="try, then succeed") or **be able to** (more formal): *I managed to/was able to get the tickets I wanted* (=I could and I *did*). Succeed in, which is followed by *v-ing*, has the same meaning but is rather formal: *He succeeded in passing the examination.* But you can use **could not** to express the idea of "lack of success": *I couldn't/was unable to* (more formal) *find the person I was looking for.* **2** Could (past tense **could have**) can be used like **may** and **might** (past tenses **may have** and **might have**) to express the idea of "perhaps" (uncertainty), but is less common: *He may/might/could be on his way now.* (=perhaps he is coming) | *He may/might/could have been delayed.* (=Perhaps he has been delayed.) –see also CAN (USAGE), MIGHT (USAGE)◁

couldst /kʊdst/ v **thou couldst** old use or bibl (when talking to one person) you could

cou·lee /'kuːli, -lei/ n AmE a small valley with steep sides that was created by water running through it but is now usu. dry: *Cattle are grazing down in the coulee.*

coun·cil /'kaʊnsəl/ n [C+sing./pl. v] **1** a group of people appointed or elected to make laws, rules, or decisions, or to give advice: *The Council of Ministers is the real power in the EC.* | *The matter was debated in the Security Council of the United Nations.* | (fig.) *The neighbours held a council of war to decide what to do about the problem of litter louts.* **2** esp. BrE the organization responsible for local government in a town, COUNTY, etc., often consisting of elected representatives and full-time non-elected employees: *The council have told us to cut down the trees.* | *We discussed this matter in council.* (=at a council meeting) | *Council meetings are held in the council chamber.* | *She's on the council.* (=is an elected member of it) | *She works for the council.* (=is a paid employee of the council) – see also extra information on page 568

▷ USAGE The British use **council** to refer to their local government authority. It is less common in the US, where the system of local government varies from state to state, and Americans must usually be more specific and say e.g. **city council, town council, county council.**◁

council es·tate /'··· ·ˌ·/ n BrE a piece of land on which houses have been built by the local council. They are rented to people for a small amount of money –see also COUNCIL HOUSE

Council for the Pro·tec·tion of Ru·ral En·gland /ˌ··· ··· ˌ·· ·ˌ·· '··/ also **CPRE**– [the] an association which aims to keep the countryside in England from being destroyed by farmers or DEVELOPERS

council house /'·· ·/ n (in Britain) a house or flat (**council flat**) owned by the local town or COUNTY council, for which the family living in it pays rent: *As an unmarried mother, you will be near the top of the list for a council house.* –see colour picture on page 162

▶CULTURAL NOTE Council houses are usu. plain in appearance and are cheap to rent. They are typically lived in by working class people. Recently, people living in council houses have had the chance to buy the house if they have enough money.◀

coun·cil·lor BrE ‖ **councilor** AmE– /'kaʊnsələʳ/ n a member of a council: *You should complain to your local councillor.*

coun·cil·man /'kaʊnsəlmən/ **coun·cil·wo·man** /-wʊmən/ fem.– n -**men** /mən/ AmE a member of a council

Council of Eu·rope /ˌ··· · '··/ [the] an organization which has over 20 European countries as its members. Set up in 1949, it is based in Strasbourg. Members are encouraged to help one another in matters of law, politics, and CULTURE, and to settle arguments in its European Court of Human Rights –compare EC

council of war /ˌ··· · '·/ n a discussion about how to meet danger, opposition, a problem, etc. or to plan some joint action: *The bosses are having a council of war right now to try to avoid total collapse.*

council tax /'·· ˌ·/ n a British local government tax related to the value of people's houses. It replaces the very unpopular POLL TAX in 1993.

coun·sel¹ /'kaʊnsəl/ n counsel **1** [C] law a lawyer (in Britain a BARRISTER) acting for someone in a court of law: *The judge asked counsel for the defence to explain.* | *Both parties were represented by counsel.* (=both people had lawyers) **2** [U] fml or lit advice: *The king took counsel from the assembled nobles.* **3 keep one's own counsel** to keep one's plans, opinions, or intentions secret

counsel² v -ll- BrE ‖ -l- AmE [T] **1** fml to advise as a suitable course of action: *They counselled patience/caution.*[+obj+to-v] *She counselled them not to accept his explanation.* **2** to give advice and support to (esp. someone experiencing difficulty): *The unit was set up to counsel people with alcohol problems.* | *a counselling service for new students*

coun·sel·lor BrE ‖ **counselor** AmE /'kaʊnsələʳ/ n **1** someone who is paid to listen to people's problems and provide support and advice: *Have you thought of seeing a counsellor?* –see also MARRIAGE GUIDANCE COUNSELLOR **2** esp. AmE a lawyer

count¹ /kaʊnt/ v **1** [I (UP, to)] to say or name the numbers in order, one by one or by groups: *children learning to count* | *Count (up) to twenty and then open your eyes.* **2** [T] to name or take note of (all the units belonging to a group) one by one in order to find the whole number in the group; total: *Have you counted the money yet?* | *We counted the passengers and found that two were missing.* [+wh-] *The machine automatically counts how many people have used it.* **3** [T] to include when finding a total: *There are six people in my family, counting my parents.* **4** [T+obj+n/adj/prep] to consider or regard in the stated way: *After the accident they counted themselves lucky to be alive.* | *Pavlova is counted among the greatest dancers of the century.* **5** [I not in progressive forms] to have value, force, influence, or importance: *It is not what you say but what you do that counts.* | *She's the only person that really counts around here.* (=the only important person) | *For tax purposes this counts as* (=is officially regarded as) *unearned income.* | *In business, a strong* *personality often counts for more* (=is more valuable or important) *than formal training.* | *That goal doesn't count, the player was out of bounds.* | *In light of your actions, your words* **count for nothing**. (=have no value at all) **6** ...**but who's counting?** (used to say that the number of something received or achieved does not matter to one, although this suggests that it really does): *"He scored seven goals." "Eight, actually, but who's counting?"* | *"That's all of them then — about 30 each." "32, I made it, but then who's counting?"* **7** **count one's chickens before they're hatched** to make plans depending on something advantageous which has not yet happened **8** **count sheep** to imagine one is counting sheep, with the eyes closed. British people are advised to count sheep as a way of falling asleep. **9** **count the cost: a** to understand or suffer the bad effects of something done **b** to consider all risks before making a decision or doing something

count down *phr v* [I] to count backwards in seconds to zero, esp. before sending a spacecraft into space — see also COUNTDOWN

count sbdy. **in** *phr v* [T] *infml* to include, esp. in a planned activity: *If you're planning a trip to London count me in.* — opposite **count out**

count on/upon sbdy./sthg. *phr v* [T] **1** to depend on: *You can count on me: I'll help you.* | *She can always be counted on for support.* [+v-ing] *We're counting on winning this contract.* [+obj+v-ing] *You can't count on the weather being fine.* [+obj+to+v] *You can count on him to come.* **2** to expect; take into account: [+(obj)+v-ing] *I didn't count on arriving so early/on John arriving so early.*

count sbdy./sthg. ↔ **out** *phr v* [T] **1** to put down one by one while counting: *He counted out ten £5 notes.* **2** to declare (a BOXER who fails to get up from the floor after ten seconds) to be the loser of a fight: *Tyson was counted out in the tenth round.* **3** *infml* to decide not to include; EXCLUDE: *If you're playing football in this weather you can count me out.* — opposite **count in**

count² *n* **1** an act of counting or total reached by counting: *The vote was so close that we had to have several counts.* | *The number of students was 523 at the last count.* **2** any of a number of crimes of which a person is thought to be guilty: *The prisoner was found not guilty on all counts.* | (fig.) *This policy has failed on several counts.* (=in several different ways) **3** **keep/lose count** to know/fail to know the exact number: *I've lost count of how many times I've seen this programme.* (=because I've seen it so often) **4** **out for the count** (in BOXING) to be unconscious for a period of ten counted seconds: (fig.) *Don't try to wake George — he's out for the count.* (=fast asleep)

count³ *n* (*often cap.*) a European nobleman with a rank similar to that of a British EARL — compare COUNTESS

count·a·ble /ˈkaʊntəbəl/ *adj* that can be counted: *A* **countable noun** *can also be called a* **count noun** *and is often marked* [C] *in this dictionary.* — opposite **uncountable**

Count Basie see BASIE, **Count**

count·down /ˈkaʊntdaʊn/ *n* an act of counting backwards in seconds to zero: *a ten-second countdown before the spacecraft takes off* — see also COUNT **down**⁸

coun·te·nance¹ /ˈkaʊntⁱnəns/ *n fml* **1** [C] the appearance or expression of a person's face: *a fierce/angry countenance* **2** [U] support or approval: *Terrorists will get no countenance here.*

countenance² *v* [T] *fml* to give support or approval to; regard as acceptable; SANCTION: *We have said several times that we will never countenance violence.* [+v-ing] *The government will not countenance giving in to blackmail.*

coun·ter¹ /ˈkaʊntəʳ/ *n* **1** a narrow table or flat surface at which customers are served in a shop, bank, restaurant, etc.: *I'm sorry, this counter is closed now.* **2** also **countertop** *AmE* for WORKTOP **3** **over the counter** (when buying drugs) without a doctor's PRESCRIPTION: *You can buy antibiotics over the counter in this country.* **4** **under the counter** privately, secretly, and often illegally: *You can buy alcohol under the counter there, but it's risky and expensive.*

counter² *n* **1** a person or esp. an electrical apparatus that counts: *Set the counter to zero and you'll know where the recording starts.* — see also GEIGER COUNTER **2** a small flat object used in some table games, e.g. instead of money or to mark one's place on a board

counter³ *v* [I;T] to move or act in order to oppose or defend oneself against (something): *They moved two destroyers into the area to counter the threat from the enemy battleship.* | *They were accused of wasting public money, but they countered (this charge) with the claim that they had wide public support.* | *new measures that are aimed at countering the rise in violent crime*

counter⁴ *adj, adv* [F+to] (in a manner or direction that is) opposed or opposite: *He acted counter to all advice.* | *behaviour that* **runs counter to** *international law*

counter⁵ *n* something that is opposed or can be used to oppose something else: *The new missiles will be useful as* **a bargaining counter** (=a means of gaining an advantage) *in the arms control talks.*

counter- see WORD FORMATION

coun·ter·act /ˌkaʊntərˈækt/ *v* [T] to reduce or oppose the effect of (something) by opposite action: *The drug counteracts the effects of the poison.* — ~ **ion** /ˈækʃən/ *n* [C;U]

coun·ter·at·tack¹ /ˈkaʊntərətæk/ *n* an attack made to stop, oppose, or return an enemy attack

counterattack² *v* [I;T] to make a counterattack (on) — ~ **er** *n*

coun·ter·at·trac·tion /ˌkaʊntərəˈtrækʃən/ *n* an attraction that competes with another

coun·ter·bal·ance¹ /ˈkaʊntəˌbæləns‖-tər-/ *n* a weight or force that acts as a balance for another weight or force

coun·ter·bal·ance² /ˌkaʊntəˈbæləns‖-tər-/ *v* [T] to oppose or balance with an equal weight or force: *The elevator is counterbalanced by a heavy weight that moves in the opposite direction.* | (fig.) *Its usefulness fails to counterbalance its considerable expense.*

coun·ter·blast /ˈkaʊntəblɑːst‖-tərblæst/ *n* (e.g. in newspapers) a violent or angry reply: *Her speech brought a quick counterblast from the opposition leader.*

coun·ter·claim /ˈkaʊntəkleɪm‖-tər-/ *n* an opposing claim, esp. in law

coun·ter·clock·wise /ˌkaʊntəˈklɒkwaɪz‖-tərˈklɑːk-/ *adj, adv AmE* for ANTICLOCKWISE

coun·ter·es·pi·o·nage /ˌkaʊntərˈespiənɑːʒ, -nɪdʒ/ also **coun·ter·in·tel·li·gence** /ˌkaʊntərɪnˈtelⁱdʒəns/— *n* [U] secret police work directed towards uncovering and opposing enemy ESPIONAGE

coun·ter·feit¹ /ˈkaʊntəfɪt‖-tər-/ *v* [T] to make an exact copy of (something) in order to deceive: *They had been counterfeiting £5 notes.* — ~ **er** *n*

counterfeit² *adj* made exactly like something real in order to deceive: *counterfeit money/passports* | (fig.) *counterfeit sympathy*

coun·ter·foil /ˈkaʊntəfɔɪl‖-tər-/ *n esp. BrE* a part of a cheque, money order, etc., kept by the sender as a record, STUB

coun·ter·in·sur·gen·cy /ˌkaʊntərɪnˈsɜːdʒənsi‖-ɜːr-/ *n* [U] military activity against INSURGENTS

coun·ter·mand /ˌkaʊntəˈmɑːnd, ˈkaʊntəmɑːnd‖ˌkaʊntərˈmænd/ *v* [T] to declare (an order or command already given) ineffective, often by giving a different order: *The sergeant's order was countermanded by a superior officer.*

coun·ter·mea·sure /ˈkaʊntəmeʒəʳ‖-tər-/ *n* [*often pl.*] an action taken to oppose another action or situation: *government countermeasures against terrorism*

coun·ter·of·fen·sive /ˈkaʊntərəfensɪv/ *n* a large-scale attack made to oppose or return an enemy attack: *The speech marked the start of our counteroffensive against the military government.*

coun·ter·pane /ˈkaʊntəpeɪn‖-ər-/ *n BrE* a top covering for a bed; BEDSPREAD

coun·ter·part /ˈkaʊntəpɑːt‖-ərpɑːrt/ *n* a person or thing that has the same purpose or does the same job as another in a different system: *The Minister of Defence is meeting his American counterpart in Washington today.* — compare OPPOSITE NUMBER

coun·ter·point /ˈkaʊntəpɔɪnt‖-ər-/ *n* **1** [U] the combining of two or more tunes so that they can be played together as a single whole **2** [C] a tune added to another in this way

coun·ter·poise /ˈkaʊntəpɔɪz‖-ər-/ *v, n* COUNTERBALANCE¹,²

coun·ter·pro·duc·tive /ˌkaʊntəprəˈdʌktɪv◂‖-tər-/ *adj* tending to work against a desired aim; having an opposite effect from the one intended: *These hardline measures proved counterproductive, as they simply increased opposition to the government.*

counter·rev·o·lu·tion /ˌ··· ··ˈ·· / n [C;U] political or military opposition to a REVOLUTION or to a government established by revolution — ~**ary** *adj, n* : *counter-revolutionary forces*

coun·ter·sign¹ /ˈkaʊntəsaɪn‖-ər-/ v [T] to sign (a paper already signed by someone else): *When you have signed the agreement, it will be countersigned by one of the directors.*

countersign² *n BrE* a PASSWORD

coun·ter·sink /ˈkaʊntəsɪŋk‖-ər-/ v **-sank** /sæŋk/, **-sunk** /sʌŋk/ [T] *tech* to fit (a screw) into an enlarged hole so that its head fits level with the surface

coun·ter·ten·or /ˌkaʊntəˈtenər‖ˈkaʊntərˌtenər/ n (a male singer with) a high voice; ALTO (1)

coun·ter·vail·ing /ˌkaʊntəˈveɪlɪŋ◂ ‖ -ər-/ adj [A] acting with equal force but opposite effect: *He had to admit that the countervailing argument was equally as strong as his own.*

coun·tess /ˈkaʊntɪs/ n a woman who holds the rank of EARL or COUNT either for herself or because she is the wife of an earl or count —compare COUNT³

coun·ting·house /ˈkaʊntɪŋhaʊs/ n **-houses** /ˌhaʊzɪz/ (in former times) a business office where accounts and money were kept

count·less /ˈkaʊntləs/ adj very many; too many to be counted: *countless reasons against it*

count noun /ˈ· ·/ n *tech* a noun that has both singular and plural forms and that can be used with numbers and words such as **many**, **few**, etc., or with **a** or **an**. In this dictionary, count nouns are often marked [C]. —compare UNCOUNTABLE

coun·tri·fied /ˈkʌntrɪfaɪd/ adj *often derog* of or like the country or country people; UNSOPHISTICATED

coun·try¹ /ˈkʌntri/ n **1** [C] an area of land that is a nation, esp. considered together with its population, political organization, industry, etc.: *Portugal is a smaller country than Spain.* | *England is my native country.* (=the country where I was born) | *The best farmland is in the north of the country.* | *The company has branches in 15 countries.* | *the world's major oil-producing countries* | *Bulgaria used to be a socialist country.* | *Several countries were represented at the conference.* —compare NATION (1); see also MOTHER COUNTRY; see FOLK (USAGE) **2** [*the*] the land outside cities or towns; land used for farming or left unused: *We're going to have a day in the country tomorrow.* —see also CROSS-COUNTRY **3** [U] land with a special nature or character: *good farming country* | *This is foxhunting country.* (=an area where people hunt foxes) **4 go to the country** *esp. BrE* (of a government) to have a GENERAL ELECTION: *If they're defeated in Parliament the government will go to the country.* **5 your country needs you** a phrase used on a British POSTER during the First World War to persuade people to join the army

country² adj [A] of, in, or from the COUNTRY¹ (2): *country life* | *country sports* | *a country house*

country and west·ern /ˌ··· · ˈ··/ also **country music, C&W**— n [U] popular music in the style of the southern and western US. Its centre is Nashville in Tennessee: *She sings in a country and western band.*

country bump·kin /ˌ··· ˈ··/ n see BUMPKIN

country club /ˈ··· ·/ n a sports and social club, usually with land in the country. The members of a country club usu. have to be quite rich to afford to belong to it.

Country Code /ˈ··· ˌ·/ [*the*] *BrE* a collection of advice for people who visit the British countryside on how to behave when in the country, e.g. to close all gates, keep dogs under control, etc.: *Always follow the Country Code.*

country cous·in /ˌ··· ˈ··/ n *derog* a simple inexperienced person who is confused by busy city life —see also BUMPKIN

country dance /ˌ··· ˈ·‖ˈ··· ·/ n any of several dances for several pairs of dancers arranged in rows or circles — **country dancing** n [U]

country house /ˌ··· ˈ·/ n *BrE* a large house in the country, often of historical interest, which the public can pay to see around. The house's owners sometimes do not live

in it, or it may be owned by an organization such as the National Trust —see also STATELY HOME

Country Life /ˌ··· ˈ·/ a British monthly magazine which writes about life in the COUNTRY¹ (2), the natural world and gardening. *Country Life* is connected in people's minds with wealthy people who live in the country or own land in the country.

coun·try·man /ˈkʌntrimən/ **coun·try·wom·an** /-ˌwʊmən/ *fem.*— n **-men** /mən/ **1** a person from one's own country; COMPATRIOT: *He was unpopular with his (fellow) countrymen.* **2** a person living in the country (=not in a town) or having country ways

country mu·sic /ˈ·· ˌ··/ n [U] COUNTRY AND WESTERN

country seat /ˌ··· ˈ·/ n the country house of a rich landowner

coun·try·side /ˈkʌntrisaɪd/ n [(*the*) U] land outside the cities and towns, used for farming or left unused; country areas: *Modern agriculture is spoiling our beautiful countryside.*

Countryside Com·mis·sion /ˈ··· ·ˌ··/ [*the*] a British organization which aims to CONSERVE and improve the countryside, and provides facilities (FACILITY) for the public, such as PATHWAYS and national parks

coun·ty¹ /ˈkaʊnti/ n **1** (in Britain) a unit of local government in England, Wales, and Northern Ireland. There are 46 counties in England and 6 in Wales. Each is governed by an elected group of people, a COUNTY COUNCIL, and within each county there are usu. several DISTRICT COUNCILs, and in some areas also PARISH COUNCILs. Northern Ireland has simply 26 district councils, and Scotland has a different system of local government. Many counties have names that end in 'shire', e.g. Hertfordshire, Lancashire, Cheshire. They each have their own character and are connected with different things in the British mind, e.g. Devon is connected with holidays and cream, and Kent with HOPS³. —compare REGION **2** (in the US) the largest unit below the level of a state: *Orange County in California* —compare PROVINCE

county² adj *BrE old-fash* belonging to or typical of the wealthy landowning classes in Britain. Many people think of county people as speaking with very upper-class ACCENTS and wearing clothes which are expensive and of good quality, but not fashionable or modern.

county cham·pi·on·ship /ˌ··· ˈ·····/ [*the*] a British cricket competition in which teams representing English counties play against each other —see also CRICKET

county coun·cil /ˌ··· ˈ··/ n [C+*sing./pl. v*] (in Britain) a body of people elected to govern a county

county court /ˌ··· ˈ·/ n a local court of law in Britain or some US states which deals with small cases. In Britain county courts are used for CIVIL cases, not for criminal cases, but in the US they are used for both. —see also extra information on page 742

county crick·et /ˌ··· ˈ··/ n [U] cricket played in England between teams each representing an English county —see also CRICKET

county fair /ˌ··· ˈ·/ n *AmE* a fair usu. held each year in a particular county with competitions to choose the best entries in different categories, e.g. farm animals, sewing projects, cooking, etc. County fairs also usu. have musical entertainments, rides on special machines, and games of skill.

county town /ˌ··· ˈ·/ *BrE* ‖ **county seat** *AmE*— n the town where the local government of a COUNTY¹ is based

coup /kuː/ n **1** a clever move or action that obtains the desired result: *Getting the contract was quite a coup|a notable coup.* | *He pulled off* (=made) *a real coup by getting the first interview with the new minister.* **2** a coup d'état

coup de grâce /ˌkuː də ˈɡrɑːs/ n [S] *Fr* a blow or shot which kills: *to give|receive the coup de grace* | (fig.) *The publicity caused by his connection with gangsters was the coup de grâce to his election campaign.*

coup d'é·tat /ˌkuː deɪ ˈtɑː‖-deˈtɑː/ also **coup**— n **coups d'état** (*same pronunciation*) a sudden violent seizing of state power by a small group that has not been elected

cou·pé /ˈkuːpeɪ‖kuːˈpeɪ/ also **coupe** /kuːp/— n an enclosed car with two doors and a sloping back

cou·ple¹ /ˈkʌpəl/ n **1** [C (**of**)] two things related in some way; two things of the same kind: *I found a couple of socks in the bedroom but they don't make a pair.* **2** [C+*sing.|pl. v*] two people who live or spend time together, esp. a husband and wife: *young married couples | They're a nice couple.* **3** [S (**of**)] *infml* a few; several; a small number: *I'll be back in a couple of minutes. | I'll just have a couple of drinks.*

▷ USAGE Compare **pair** and **couple**: A **pair** is a set of two things which are not usually used separately. These may be two things which are not joined together, such as *shoes*, or something made in two parts, such as *trousers*: *a* **pair** *of socks | a* **pair** *of scissors.* Any two things of the same kind can be spoken of as a **couple**: *I saw a* **couple** *of cats in the garden. | Could you lend me a* **couple** *of pounds?* —see also PAIR (USAGE)◁

couple² *v* **1** [T (**to**, TOGETHER)] to join together; connect: *They coupled the carriages of the train together.* —opposite **uncouple** **2** [I (**with**)] (esp. of animals) to unite sexually; MATE

couple sthg. **with** sthg. *phr v* [T *usu. pass.*] to join (one thing or set of things) to (another): *A reputation for quality, coupled with very competitive prices, has made these cars very popular.*

coup·let /ˈkʌplɪt/ *n* two lines of poetry, one following the other, that are of equal length: *rhyming couplets* — compare TRIPLET; see also HEROIC COUPLET

coup·ling /ˈkʌplɪŋ/ *n* something that connects two things, esp. two railway carriages

cou·pon /ˈkuːpɒn‖-pɑːn/ *n* **1** a ticket that shows the right of the holder to receive some payment, service, etc.; VOUCHER: *Tear off this coupon and use it to get 25p off your next jar of coffee. | a 50-cents-off coupon for mayonnaise* **2** a printed form on which goods can be ordered, an ENQUIRY made, a competition entered, etc.: *To take advantage of our special offer, simply fill in the coupon and send it to us.*

cour·age /ˈkʌrɪdʒ‖ˈkɜːr-/ *n* [U] **1** the quality that makes a person able to control fear in the face of danger, pain, misfortune, etc.; bravery: *She showed remarkable courage when she heard the bad news. | a man of great courage | I didn't have the courage to tell him.* **2 have the courage of one's (own) convictions** to be brave enough to do or say what one thinks is right **3 take one's courage in both hands** to gather enough courage to do something that needs a lot of bravery —see also DUTCH COURAGE

Courage *tdmk* a British company that makes and sells beer in shops and its own PUBS

cou·ra·geous /kəˈreɪdʒəs/ *adj* brave; showing courage: *a courageous action|person | It was courageous of you to say what you did.* — **~ly** *adv* — **~ness** *n* [U]

cour·gette /kʊəˈʒet/‖kʊr-/ *BrE* ‖ **zucchini** *AmE*— *n* a small green MARROW (=long vegetable with a dark green skin) eaten cooked as a vegetable or raw in SALADs —see picture at VEGETABLE

cou·ri·er¹ /ˈkʊriər/ *n* **1** a person or company that is employed to carry messages or other official papers, esp. of an urgent or official kind: *We sent the contract to Tokyo by courier.* **2** someone who goes with and looks after travellers on a tour

courier² *v* [T(**to**)] to send with a COURIER¹ (1)

course¹ /kɔːs‖kɔːrs/ *n* **1** the path along which something moves; direction of movement taken by someone or something: *the course of a river | The plane changed course to avoid the storm. | The ship was blown off course.|* (fig.) *a politician attempting to* **steer a middle course** *between conservatism and reform |* (fig.) *The company is* **on course** *to achieve its profit targets.* **2** [(**of**) *usu. sing.*] continuous movement from one point to another in space or time: *The enemy should be defeated* **in the course of** (=during) *the year. | During the course of the next few minutes we will be serving tea and biscuits.* **3** the usual, natural, or established pattern or process by which something happens or is done: *He has committed a crime and now the law must take its course. | They decided to let the illness* **run its course.** *| He is charged with attempting to* **pervert the course of** *justice.* (=to prevent the law from operating properly) **4** a plan of action: *Their police officers carry guns, and ours may soon have to adopt a similar course. | Your best* **course of action** *is to try to forget about her.* **5** an area of land or water on which a race is held or certain types of sport played: *a golf*

course | a race course —see also ASSAULT COURSE **6** [(**in**)] a set of lessons or studies: *a course of lectures | a four-year history course | to take|do a course in car maintenance* —see also COURSE BOOK, CRASH COURSE **7** [(**of**)] *esp. BrE* actions, a set of events of a planned and fixed number, esp. for the purpose of medical treatment: *a course of drugs|anti-rabies injections* **8** any of the different parts of a meal: *We had a three-course dinner: chicken soup, roast beef, and ice-cream.* **9** a continuous level line of bricks, stone, etc., all along a wall —see also DAMP COURSE **10 in due course** without too much delay; at the right time **11 in the course of time** when enough time has passed **12 in the ordinary/normal course of events/things** usually; in the way things ordinarily happen: *In the ordinary course of events they'd be here by now; the plane must be late.* **13 of course** also **course** *infml*—a certainly; NATURALLY (3): *Of course I'll give you your money back. | "Were you glad to leave?" "Of course not!"* **b** (often followed by **but** and used as a way of introducing a point of doubt or disagreement) I agree (that): *Of course you must make a profit, but not if it involves exploiting people. | Of course these figures may not be completely accurate, but I think we should take them very seriously.* —see also MATTER OF COURSE, **stay the course** (STAY¹)

▷ USAGE **Of course** (=certainly) is a polite way of agreeing and showing willingness to help, in reply to requests such as *Can you help me?* and *May I borrow this book?* But **of course** is not polite in reply to a question asking for information: *"Do many students study English at your school?" "Yes, they do|Yes, the majority."* The reply **of course** here would suggest "this fact is so obvious that you ought to know it".◁

course² *v* **1** [I+*adv|prep*] *esp. lit* (of liquid) to flow rapidly: *Tears coursed down his cheeks.* **2** [I;T] *BrE* to chase (a rabbit or HARE) with dogs as a sport: *to go coursing*

course book /ˈ· ·/ *n BrE* a book giving information, esp. information that develops slightly every lesson, that is used regularly during a whole set of lessons, e.g. during a whole TERM or year —compare TEXT BOOK

court¹ /kɔːt‖kɔːrt/ *n* **1** [C;U] a room or building in which law cases are heard and judged: *Silence in court! | Her case will be heard in the High Court. | The case was* **settled out of court.** (=without having to be heard by a judge) *| an out-of-court settlement* —see also COURT OF APPEAL, COURTROOM, OATH **2** [(*the*) U] the people, esp. law officers and members of the JURY, who are gathered together in a court to hear and judge a law case: *The court stood when the judge entered. | The defendant told the court that he had never seen the woman before.* —see also CONTEMPT **3** [C;U] (a part of) an area specially prepared and marked for various ball games, such as tennis: *a squash/badminton court | Are the players on court yet?* —see picture at TENNIS **4** [C] *(often cap. as part of a name)* **a** a short street surrounded by buildings on three sides: *They lived in Westbury Court.* **b** *esp. BrE* a block of flats **c** also **courtyard**— an open space wholly or partly surrounded by buildings, esp. next to or inside a castle, large house, etc. **5** [C;U] the official home of a king or queen: *the Court of Versailles | He is well-known at court|in court circles. | The newspaper's court correspondent* (=a reporter who deals with news concerning the royal family) **6** [C+*sing.|pl. v*] the king or queen with his/her family and the officials, noblemen, servants, etc., who attend him/her: *the Moroccan court* **7 pay court to** *old-fash* to COURT² (2) **8 rule something|someone out of court** to prevent a person, matter, or subject from being considered by a court of law **9 take someone to court** to start an action in law against someone —see also **the ball is in your court** (BALL¹ (10))

court² *v* **1** [T] to pay attention to (an important or influential person) in order to gain favour, advantage, approval, etc.: *He's courting the farmers because he needs their votes in the election.* **2** [T] to try to obtain (a desired state): *The teacher tried to court popularity by giving his students very little work.* **3** [T] to risk (something bad), often foolishly or thoughtlessly: *to court danger|arrest|disaster* **4** [I;T] *old-fash* **a** (of a man) to visit and pay attention to (a woman he hopes to marry): *John courted Mary for years.* **b** (of a man and woman) to be in a relationship that may lead to marriage: *a* **courting couple**

Cour·tauld In·sti·tute /ˈkɔːtəʊld ˌɪnstɪtjuːt‖ˈkɔːr-, -tuːt/ [*the*] an art GALLERY in London, esp. known for its collection of Impressionist and post-Impressionist paintings

court card /ˈ· ·/ *BrE* ‖**face card** *AmE*— *n* the king, queen, or JACK in a set of playing cards

cour·te·ous /ˈkɜːtiəs‖ˈkɜːr-/ *adj* polite and kind; showing good manners and respect for others —opposite **discourteous** − ~**ly** *adv* − ~**ness** *n* [U]

cour·te·san /ˌkɔːtɪˈzæn‖ˈkɔːrtɪzən/ *n* (esp. in former times) a woman who takes payment for sex from noble and socially important people; a high-class PROSTITUTE

cour·te·sy /ˈkɜːtɪsi‖ˈkɜːr-/ *n* **1** [U] polite behaviour; good manners: *I really think you should tell her you've given the job to someone else; it's a matter of* **common courtesy**. (=accepted politeness) —opposite **discourtesy 2** [C] a polite or kind action or expression **3 (by) courtesy of** by the permission or generosity of (someone), usu. without payment: *This picture appears in the exhibition by courtesy of the National Art Collection.*

courtesy ti·tle /ˈ··· ˌ·· / *n* a title given (e.g. to certain relatives of British PEERs) by polite custom and not held by legal right

court·house /ˈkɔːthaʊs‖ˈkɔːrt-/ *n* **-houses** /ˌhaʊzɪz/ *esp. AmE* a building containing courts of law

court·ier /ˈkɔːtɪəʳ‖ˈkɔːr-/ *n* (in former times) a noble who attended at the court of a king or other ruler

court·ly /ˈkɔːtli‖ˈkɔːrtli/ *adj* graceful and polite in manners: *courtly behaviour* −**-liness** *n* [U]

court-mar·tial[1] /ˌ·ˈ··‖ˈ· ˌ··/ *n* **courts-martial** *or* **court martials 1** a military court of officers appointed to try people for offences against military law: *He was tried by court-martial.* **2** a trial before such a court

court-martial[2] *v* **-ll-** *BrE* ‖ **-l-** *AmE* [T] to try (someone) in a court-martial

Court of Ap·peal /ˌ· · ·ˈ·/ also **Appeal Court**— [*the*] (in Britian) the highest court to which one may take a criminal or CIVIL case apart from the House of Lords —see also extra information on page 742

Court of Appeals /ˌ· · ·ˈ·/ also **Appellate Court**— [*the*] (in the US) a court which examines FEDERAL cases that have been brought to them by people unsatisfied with the decision of a lower court. There are 12 of these courts in the US, each dealing with cases in a particular area of the country. —see also extra information on page 742

court of in·quir·y /ˌ· · ·ˈ··‖ˌ· · ·ˈ···/ *n* **courts of inquiry** *esp. BrE* a body of people appointed to find out the facts or causes of a particular event, esp. an accident: *The government set up a court of inquiry to investigate the causes of the air disaster.* —compare GRAND JURY

court of law /ˌ· · ·ˈ·/ *n* **courts of law** a COURT[1] (1 and 2)

Court of St James' /ˌ· · ·ˈ·/ [*the*] **1** the court of the British king or queen **2 to the Court of St James'** *fml* to Britain: *the new American ambassador to the Court of St James'*

Court of Ses·sion /ˌ· · ·ˈ··/ [*the*] the highest CIVIL court in Scotland

court or·der /ˌ· · ·ˈ··/ *n* an order given by a court of law that someone must do or not do something

court re·port·er /ˌ· · ·ˈ··/ *n* a person who records, on a special machine similar to a TYPEWRITER, everything that is said in a court during a case

court·room /ˈkɔːtruːm, -rʊm‖ˈkɔːrt-/ *n* the room in which a TRIAL is held

court·ship /ˈkɔːt-ʃɪp‖ˈkɔːrt-/ *n* **1** [C;U] (the length of time taken by) the act of courting (COURT[2] (2)) **2** [U] special behaviour, dancing, etc. used by animals to attract each other before mating (MATE): *unusual courtship displays*

court shoe /ˈ· ·/ *BrE* ‖ **high heel, heel** *AmE*— *n* a type of plain shoe with middle sized heels and no fastenings— see picture at SHOE

court·yard /ˈkɔːtjɑːd‖ˈkɔːrtjɑːrd/ *n* a COURT[1] (4c)

cous·cous /ˈkuːskuːs/ *n* [U] a North African dish, made of specially prepared crushed wheat cooked in steam and served with cooked meat (esp. lamb) and vegetables

cous·in /ˈkʌzən/ *n* **1** also **first cousin**— the child of one's uncle or aunt: *These are my cousins, Tom and Liz.* —see also COUSIN GERMAN, FIRST COUSIN, KISSING COUSIN, and SECOND COUSIN **2** a related person or thing: *He's a distant cousin of mine.* | *the people of Spain and their cousins in South America*

Cous·teau /kuːˈstəʊ/, **Jacques** /ʒæk‖ʒɑːk/ (1910−) a

French EXPLORER of the sea, writer, broadcaster, and maker of films about life under water. He also invented SCUBA equipment.

cou·ture /kuːˈtjʊəʳ‖-ˈtʊər/ also **haute couture**— *n* [U] the business of making and selling fashionable women's clothes —**-turier** /kuːˈtjʊərieɪ‖-ˈtʊəriər/ *n*

cove[1] /kəʊv/ *n* a small sheltered opening in the coastline; small BAY[1]

cove[2] *n BrE old-fash sl* a man

cov·en /ˈkʌvən/ *n* [C+*sing.*/*pl. v*] a gathering of witches (WITCH)

cov·e·nant[1] /ˈkʌvənənt/ *n* **1** a formal solemn agreement between two or more people or groups **2** *BrE* a DEED OF COVENANT

covenant[2] *v* [T] to promise in writing by a covenant; PLEDGE: *I covenanted (to pay/that I would pay) £50 a year to help rebuild the college.*

Cov·ent Gar·den /ˌkɒvənt ˈgɑːdn‖ˌkʌvənt ˈgɑːr-/ **1** an area of London once famous for its fruit and vegetable market, now replaced by expensive but popular shops, eating places, etc. —see colour map on page 817 **2** another name for the Royal Opera House, which is next to the place where Covent Garden market used to be

Covent Garden

Cov·en·try /ˈkʌvəntri, ˈkɒv-‖ˈkʌv-, ˈkɑːv-/ **1** an industrial city in the centre of England. Its present CATHEDRAL replaces one that was left in ruins when Coventry was badly bombed in the Second World War. **2 send someone to Coventry** (of a group of people) to refuse to speak to someone as a sign of disapproval or as a punishment; OSTRACIZE

cov·er[1] /ˈkʌvəʳ/ *v* **1** [T (OVER, with)] to place something upon or over (something) in order to protect or hide it: *We covered the body with a sheet.* | *Cover the food with a cloth.* | *The noise was so loud that she covered her ears with her hands.* **2** [T] to be or lie on or over the surface of (something); spread over (something): *The furniture was covered in/with dust.* | *The water kept rising till it almost covered our heads.* **3** [T] to fill (an area); EXTEND over: *The city covers 25 square miles.* **4** [T] to complete (a distance) by travelling: *We aimed to cover 400 miles before nightfall.* | (fig.) *After 25 lessons we had only covered half the course.* **5** [T] to deal with or take into account: *The book covers the period from 1870 to 1914.* | *The rights of part-time workers are not covered by these regulations.* **6** [T] to report the details of (an event) for a newspaper, TV station, etc.: *She covered the Ethiopian famine for CBS news.* **7** [T] to be enough money for: *Will £10 cover the cost of the damage?* **8** [T (**against**)] to protect from loss; insure: *Are you covered against fire?* **9** [T] **a** to protect (a person) by aiming a gun at an enemy: *The sheriff walked into the street while his deputy covered him from an upstairs window.* **b** to keep a gun aimed at (someone): *The policeman covered the suspect while I searched him.* **10** [T] to watch (a building, area, etc.) for possible trouble: *The police have got all the roads out of town covered.* **11** [T] (in sport) **a** to watch and stay close to (an opponent) **b** to defend (an area or position) against attack by the other team: *Cover the goalmouth, Pat!* | *Who's covering second base?* **12** [I (**for**)] to take responsibility in place of someone who is absent: *John's ill today, so Jean's covering for him.* **13 cover (all) one's bases** *AmE* to know one's weak points (in an argument, plan, etc.) and be prepared to defend them: *I don't think you've covered all your bases in this merger proposal.*

cover sthg. ↔ **up** *phr v* **1** [T] to prevent from being noticed or becoming publicly known: *He tried to cover up his nervousness.* | *The newspapers printed the story before the government could cover it up.* —see also COVER-UP **2** [I] *infml* to cover the body: *Women in Muslim countries cover up when they go out.* | *If you don't cover up you'll catch cold!*

cover up for sbdy. *phr v* [T] *infml* to hide something wrong or dishonourable in order to save (another person) from punishment, blame, etc.

cover² n **1** [C] something that protects or encloses by covering, esp. a piece of material, lid, or top: *an engine cover* | *a cushion cover* | *a manhole cover* | *Put another cover on the bed if you get cold.* **2** [C] the outer front or back page of a magazine or book: *I only bought the book because of its cover.* | *She read the book* **from cover to cover.** (=from beginning to end) **3** [U] shelter or protection: *The soldiers had no cover from the enemy guns.* | *When it started raining, we* **took cover** (=sheltered) *under a tree.* | *They escaped* **under cover of** *darkness.* | *The union provided safety cover* (=did necessary safety work) *for the mine during the strike.* — see also **break cover** (BREAK¹) **4** [U (**against**)] insurance against loss, damage, etc.: *We've got full cover against fire and theft.* **5** [S;U] something that hides or keeps something secret: *Their travel business is just a cover for a drug-smuggling operation.* **6** [C] *tech* a place for one person set at a table with a knife, fork, etc. **7** [U] *tech* the plant life of an area **8** **under plain/separate cover** in a plain/separate envelope —see also FIRST DAY COVER

cov·er·age /ˈkʌvərɪdʒ/ n [U] **1** the amount of time and space given by television, a newspaper, etc., to a particular subject or event: *The wedding got massive media coverage.* | *The president's visit got blanket coverage.* (=coverage in newspapers, on the radio, on television, etc.) **2** the amount of protection given by insurance; risks covered by insurance

cov·er·alls /ˈkʌvərɔːlz/ n [P] *AmE* a BOILER SUIT

cover charge /ˈ·· ·/ n a charge made by a restaurant in addition to the cost of the food and drinks or the cost of service

covered wag·on /ˌ·· ˈ··/ also **Conestoga, Conestoga wagon**— n a large horse-drawn vehicle with rounded cloth-covered top, in which settlers crossed N America in the WILD WEST —see colour picture on page 358

cover girl /ˈ·· ·/ n a young attractive woman whose photograph is on the cover of a magazine: *her cover girl looks*

cov·er·ing /ˈkʌvərɪŋ/ n something that covers or hides: *a light covering of snow*

covering let·ter /ˌ··· ˈ··/ *BrE* ‖ **cover letter** /ˈ·· ˌ··/ *AmE*— n a letter or note containing an explanation or additional information, sent with a parcel or another letter — compare COMPLIMENT SLIP

cov·er·let /ˈkʌvələt‖-vər-/ n a BEDSPREAD

cover note /ˈ·· ·/ n esp. BrE a document giving insurance cover to someone while their insurance POLICY is being prepared

cover sto·ry /ˈ·· ˌ··/ n a story to go with the picture on the cover of a magazine

cov·ert¹ /ˈkʌvət, ˈkəʊvɜːt‖ˈkəʊvərt/ adj secret or hidden; not openly shown or admitted: *covert dislike* | *covert activity by the CIA to undermine their government* —opposite **overt** — **~ly** adv

cov·ert² /ˈkʌvət‖-ərt/ n a thick growth of bushes and small trees in which animals can hide

cover-up /ˈ·· ·/ n [(**for**)] an attempt to prevent something dishonourable or criminal from becoming publicly known —see also COVER **up**

cov·et /ˈkʌvɪt/ v [T] esp. bibl or humor to desire eagerly (esp. something belonging to another person): *He won the coveted Lawson Award.* (=which everyone wants to win)

cov·et·ous /ˈkʌvɪtəs/ adj derog too eager for wealth or property or for someone else's possessions — **~ly** adv

cov·et·ous·ness /ˈkʌvɪtəsnɪs/ n [U] the state of being covetous. Covetousness is one of the Seven Deadly Sins —see also SEVEN DEADLY SINS

cov·ey /ˈkʌvi/ n a small group of PARTRIDGEs, GROUSE, or other birds

cow¹ /kaʊ/ n **1** a fully-grown female type of cattle, kept on farms, esp. to provide milk. In stories, cows are often named Daisy or Buttercup: *Bring the cows in for milking.* | *A young cow is called a calf.* | *a herd of 25 cows* — see also FRIESIAN, JERSEY (2), MOO; see MEAT (USAGE) **2** the female of certain other large sea and land animals: *a cow elephant* —compare BULL¹ (2), HEIFER **3** derog sl a woman: *You silly cow!* **4** **have a cow** infml humor, esp. AmE to react to something by becoming very excited,

angry, or emotional, and to express one's emotions, for example by shouting: *My mom had a cow last night because we didn't come home until midnight.* | *Okay, okay! Don't have a cow!* **5** **How now, brown cow?** a phrase used in Britain in the past to teach people to speak in a socially acceptable way, rather than with a regional ACCENT **6** **till the** ˈ**cows come home** infml for a very long time, possibly for ever: *You can sit there till the cows come home, but I don't think she'll turn up.* —see also SACRED COW

cow² v [T] to bring under control by violence or threats: *The people were cowed by the execution of their leaders.*

Cow & Gate /ˌ·· ˈ·/ n tdmk a company which makes food and milk products for babies

cow·ard /ˈkaʊəd‖-ərd/ n derog a person who is afraid to face danger, pain, or hardship; person who shows fear in a dishonourable way: *I'm afraid I'm something of a coward when it comes to snakes.* | *You snivelling little coward!*

Coward, Sir No·ël /ˈnəʊəl/ (1899–1973) an English actor and writer of plays and songs. He is remembered esp. for his comedies (COMEDY), including *Private Lives* and *Blithe Spirit* and for his unusual personality and WIT.

Noël Coward

cow·ard·ice /ˈkaʊədɪs‖-ər-/ also **cow·ard·li·ness** /ˈkaʊədlɪnɪs‖-ərd-/— n [U] derog lack of courage: *He was accused of cowardice in the face of the enemy.*
▶CULTURAL NOTE The colour yellow is connected in people's minds with cowardice —see also YELLOW¹ (3)◀

cow·ard·ly /ˈkaʊədli‖-ər-/ adj derog typical of a coward; showing a dishonourable lack of courage: *cowardly behaviour*

cow·bell /ˈkaʊbel/ n a bell hung from the neck of a cow so that the cow can be easily found

cow·boy /ˈkaʊbɔɪ/ n **1** also **cowhand, cowpoke** infml— a person employed to look after cattle, esp. on horseback in N America: *cowboy boots* —see also COWBOYS AND INDIANS
▶CULTURAL NOTE The idea that most people have of cowboys comes from cowboy films and is not very realistic. People think of cowboys as wearing special clothes such as STETSONs and long boots, and they think of cowboys as being honest but rough, independent, and strong. People sometimes compare American men to cowboys if they have a very independent job and behave in a very MASCULINE way: *The American engineers on the Kuwait oil operation are modern-day, tobacco-chewing cowboys with hard hats instead of Stetsons.* —see also WESTERN◀
2 BrE sl someone who is careless and dishonest in business: *a firm of cowboy builders*

cowboy film /ˈ·· ˌ·/ BrE ‖ **cowboy movie** AmE — n infml a WESTERN²

cowboy hat /ˈ·· ˌ·/ n a STETSON —see picture at HAT

cowboys and In·di·ans /ˌ·· ˈ···/ n [P + sing. v] a game played by children who act the parts of cowboys and Native Americans (Indians) as they have seen them in films (WESTERNs): *Let's play cowboys and Indians.* | *Cowboys and Indians is their favourite game.*

cow·catch·er /ˈkaʊˌkætʃəʳ/ n a strong metal frame on the front of a railway engine used to push objects off the track

Cow·drey /ˈkaʊdri/, **Col·in** /ˈkɒlɪn‖ˈkɑː-/ (1932–) an English cricket player who was captain of the England team. He was known as an excellent BATSMAN.

cow·er /ˈkaʊəʳ/ v [I (DOWN)] to bend low and move back because of fear or shame; CRINGE: *The dog cowered when its master shouted at it.* | *We found the kidnapped children cowering in a corner.*

Cowes /kaʊz/ an English seaport, holiday town, and sailing centre on the Isle of Wight. Every year there is a REGATTA (=boat racing event) here, known as **Cowes**

Week. It is considered to be one of the most important sporting and social events of the year.

cow·girl /ˈkaʊgɜːl‖-gɜːrl/ n a female person employed to look after cattle, esp. on horseback in N America

cow·hand /ˈkaʊhænd/ n a person employed to look after cattle; a COWBOY, cowgirl, or cowherd

cow·herd /ˈkaʊhɜːd‖-hɜːrd/ n a person employed to look after cows and milk them

cow·hide /ˈkaʊhaɪd/ n [C;U] (a) skin of a cow, with or without the hair on it

cowl /kaʊl/ n 1 a loose head covering (a HOOD) for the whole of the head except the face, worn esp. by MONKs 2 a metal chimney-top cover that is moved by the wind to allow smoke to escape 3 a cover for an engine; cowling

cow·lick /ˈkaʊˌlɪk/ n esp. AmE a small mass of hair that stands up from the head

cowl·ing /ˈkaʊlɪŋ/ also **cowl**— n a removable metal cover for an aircraft engine —see picture at AIRCRAFT

cowl neck /ˌˈ ˈ/ also **cowl neck·line** /ˌˈ ˈ‖—/— n the neck of an article of clothing which falls in folds at the front

cow·man /ˈkaʊmən/ n -men /mən/ 1 BrE a man employed to look after cows; COWHERD 2 AmE a man who owns a RANCH (=land on which cows are raised)

co-work·er /ˌkəʊ ˈwɜːkəʳ‖ˈkəʊ ˌwɜːrkər/ n a fellow-worker

cow·pat /ˈkaʊpæt/ BrE ‖ **cow chip, cow·pat·ty** /ˈkaʊpæti/ AmE— n euph a flat lump of cow DUNG

cow·poke /ˈkaʊpəʊk/ n AmE infml a COWBOY

cow·pox /ˈkaʊpɒks‖-pɑːks/ n [U] a disease of the cow which, when given to humans, protects them against SMALLPOX

cow·punch·er /ˈkaʊpʌntʃəʳ/ n AmE infml a COWBOY

cow·rie , cowry /ˈkaʊri/ n a shiny brightly-marked tropical shell, formerly used as money in parts of Africa and Asia

cow·shed /ˈkaʊʃed/ also **cow·house** /-haʊs/— n a building to which cows are taken to be milked or in which they live in winter

cow·slip /ˈkaʊˌslɪp/ n a small European wild plant of the PRIMROSE family which has sweet-smelling yellow flowers

cox /kɒks‖kɑːks/ also **cox·swain** /ˈkɒksən, -sweɪn‖ˈkɑːk-/ fml— n a person who guides and controls a rowing boat, esp. in races —see also BOX AND COX —**cox** v [I;T]

cox·comb /ˈkɒkskəʊm‖ˈkɑːks-/ n 1 old use a foolish man who spends too much time and money on his clothes and appearance 2 a COCKSCOMB (2)

Cox's /ˈkɒksɪz‖ˈkɑːk-/ n a popular English apple for eating, with an orange-yellow skin

coy /kɔɪ/ adj showing a (pretended) lack of self-confidence, esp. in order to attract interest or to avoid dealing with something difficult: She gave him a coy smile. | Don't be so coy — I know you'd like to do the job really. — **-ly** adv — **-ness** n [U]

coy·ote /ˈkɔɪ-əʊt, kɔɪˈəʊti‖ˈkaɪ-əʊt, kaɪˈəʊti/ n a small WOLF that lives in western N America and Mexico

coy·pu /ˈkɔɪpuː/ n -pus or -pu a large water rat of S America, kept on fur farms for its valuable fur called NUTRIA

coz·en /ˈkʌzən/ v [T] old use to trick; deceive

co·zy /ˈkəʊzi/ adj AmE for COSY —**-zily** adv —**-ziness** n [U]

CP /ˌsiː ˈpiː/ abbrev. for: COMMUNIST PARTY

CPA /ˌsiː piː ˈeɪ/ also **certified public accountant**— n AmE for CHARTERED ACCOUNTANT

CPR /ˌsiː piː ˈɑːʳ/ n [U] cardiopulmonary resuscitation; the act of breathing into someone's mouth and pressing repeatedly on their chest or their heart to make them breathe again after an accident or some other damage to themselves —compare ARTIFICIAL RESPIRATION

CPRE /ˌsiː piː ɑːr ˈiː/ [the] abbrev. for COUNCIL FOR THE PROTECTION OF RURAL ENGLAND

CPS /ˌsiː piː ˈes/ [the] abbrev. for CROWN PROSECUTION SERVICE

CPU /ˌsiː piː ˈjuː/ n CENTRAL PROCESSING UNIT

CPVE /ˌsiː piː viː ˈiː/ abbrev. for CERTIFICATE OF PRE-VOCATIONAL EDUCATION

crab¹ /kræb/ n 1 [C] a sea animal with a flattened shell-

covered body and five pairs of legs, of which the front pair are large powerful PINCERS 2 [U] the flesh of this animal cooked as food: crab salad —see also CRABS

crab

crab² v -bb- [I (about)] infml to complain in a bad-tempered way; GRUMBLE

crab ap·ple /ˈ· ˌ··/ also **crab**— n (the tree that produces) a small sour apple, often used to make jelly

crab·bed /ˈkræbɪd/ adj 1 BrE (of writing) difficult to read because the letters are too close together 2 old-fash crabby — **-ly** adv — **-ness** n [U]

crab·by /ˈkræbi/ adj infml bad-tempered; IRRITABLE

crab·grass /ˈkræbgrɑːs‖-græs/ n [U] a type of rough grass that grows easily in LAWNs and is difficult to get rid of

crabs /kræbz/ n [(the) P] the condition of having a kind of LOUSE (**crab louse**) in the hair around the sexual organs

crab·wise /ˈkræbwaɪz/ also **crab·ways** /-weɪz/— adv sideways, esp. in an awkward manner

crack¹ /kræk/ v 1 [I;T] to (cause to) break without dividing into separate parts; split: Don't pour hot water into the glass or it will crack. | The window was cracked but not broken. —see BREAK (USAGE) 2 [I;T (OPEN)] to (cause to) break open: to crack nuts | I cracked two eggs into a frying-pan. 3 [I;T] to (cause to) make a sudden loud sharp sound: The whip cracked threateningly. 4 [I] (of a person's voice) to change suddenly in level, loudness, etc.: His voice cracked with emotion. 5 [I;T] to (cause to) hit with a sudden hard blow: The boy fell and cracked his head against the wall. 6 [I (UP)] to lose control or effectiveness as a result of difficulties or pressure; fail: The whole political system is beginning to crack up. | The prisoner is refusing to give information, but he may crack under torture. 7 [T] infml to make (a joke) 8 [T] to discover the secret of (a CODE¹ (1)) 9 [T] infml to open (a bottle) for drinking 10 crack a smile AmE infml to smile, esp. after being upset or angry 11 crack open the books AmE infml to begin studying 12 cracked up to be infml generally believed to be or regarded as being: This pub isn't all it's cracked up to be – the beer's terrible. 13 get cracking‖also get weaving BrE— infml a to start working hard at something b to go or leave quickly

crack down phr v [I (on)] to take strong and severe action to deal with something bad: The police are cracking down on illegal gambling. —see also CRACKDOWN

crack on phr v BrE infml [I (with)] to continue working very hard (on something)

crack up phr v infml 1 [I] to suffer a sudden and complete loss of physical or esp. mental strength and ability: Now, where did I put those papers this time? I think I must be cracking up! —see also CRACKUP 2 [I] to laugh: We cracked up when he did his George Bush imitation. 3 [T(**crack** sbdy. ↔ **up**)] to cause to laugh: She really cracks me up with her bored housewife jokes.

crack² n 1 a line of division caused by splitting; very thin mark or opening caused by breaking, but not into separate parts: There's a crack in this cup|in the window.| Small cracks were found in the aircraft's wings. | (fig.) The door was opened just a crack. 2 a loud sharp sound: a crack of thunder | the crack of a pistol 3 a sudden sharp blow esp. caused accidentally: I got a nasty crack on the head when I went through that low door 4 [(at usu. sing.)] infml an attempt: I've never done this before, but I'll have a crack (at it). 5 [(about)] a clever quick joke or remark: He's always making cracks about my big feet. 6 a sudden change in the level or loudness of the voice 7 at the crack of dawn very early in the morning 8 the crack of doom old-fash, often humor the end of the world 9 a fair crack of the whip BrE infml a fair chance of doing something —see also paper over the cracks (PAPER²)

crack³ adj [A] of very high quality or skill: a crack commando unit | a crack shot|marksman (=someone who always hits what they shoot at)

crack⁴ n [U] sl an extremely pure form of the drug COCAINE, which is illegally taken for pleasure. It is an ADDICTIVE drug and is a big social problem in some countries, esp. the US.

crack·brained /ˈkrækbreɪnd/ *adj* foolish; CRAZY: *a crack-brained idea*

crack·down /ˈkrækdaʊn/ *n* [(on)] action taken to stop or discourage a bad activity: *a crackdown on drunken driving* —see also CRACK **down**

cracked /krækt/ *adj* [F] *infml* foolish; slightly mad

crack·er /ˈkrækəʳ/ *n* **1** a small thin unsweetened BISCUIT; a CREAM CRACKER or SODA CRACKER: *I'm not really hungry — I'll just have some crackers and cheese.* **2** a FIRE-CRACKER **3** (in Britain) a tube of brightly coloured paper which makes a harmless exploding sound when pulled apart, usu. containing a small gift and a joke. Crackers are used esp. at parties, Christmas dinner, etc. —see also extra information and picture on page 215 **4** *BrE infml* someone or something that is very good; used esp. of a very attractive woman **5** *AmE derog* a poor white person from the American South

Crack·er·jack /ˈkrædədʒæk‖-kər-/ a popular British children's television programme of the 1960s which gave Crackerjack pencils as prizes to children and always began with the words: "It's Friday, it's five to five, and it's Crackerjack!"

Cracker Jack /ˈ··· ·/ *n* [U] *tdmk* sweetened POPCORN that is sold in a small box with a prize inside. It is very popular with children in America.

crack·ers /ˈkrækəz‖-ərz/ *adj* [F] *BrE infml* (of a person) mad: *I'm not going to lend him money — do you think I'm crackers?*

crack·ing /ˈkrækɪŋ/ *adj* [A] very fast or good

crack·le /ˈkrækəl/ *v* [I;T] to (cause to) make small sharp repeated sounds: *The fire crackled.* | *Why is the radio crackling so much?* | (fig.) *The crowd crackled with excitement.* —**crackle** *n* [S] : *the crackle of dry twigs under our feet* —**crackly** *adj*

crack·ling /ˈkræklɪŋ/ *n* [U] **1** the sound of something that crackles: *the crackling of the fire* **2** the hard easily broken brown skin of cooked PORK

crack·pot /ˈkrækpɒt‖-pɑːt/ *adj, n infml, often humor* (typical of) a person with very strange or mad ideas: *The man's a complete crackpot.* | *another of his crackpot ideas*

cracks·man /ˈkræksmən/ *n* -**men** /mən/ *old-fash* a person who steals things by opening SAFES²

crack-up /ˈkræk-ʌp/ *n infml* a sudden failure or loss of control of the mind and feelings; BREAKDOWN

Crad·dock /ˈkrædək/, **Fanny** (1910–) an English cook who wrote many books on cookery and appeared on television with her husband showing people how to make different dishes

cra·dle¹ /ˈkreɪdl/ *n* **1** [C] a small bed for a baby, esp. one made so that it can be moved gently from side to side: *She was rocking the cradle.* —see picture at BED **2** [C (**of**) usu. sing.] the place where something began; place of origin: *Ancient Greece was the cradle of Western European culture.* **3** [the+S] the earliest years of one's life: *to live in the same village* **from the cradle to the grave** (=all through one's life) | *In future, people will place more importance on the* **cradle-to-grave** *lifetime of products.* **4** [C] *BrE* ‖ **scaffold** *AmE*— a frame for supporting something being built or repaired, or for doing certain jobs: *Window cleaners are pulled up and down tall buildings on cradles.* —see also CAT'S CRADLE

cradle² *v* [T] to hold gently as if in a cradle: *John cradled the baby in his arms.*

cradle-snatch /ˈ··· ·/ *v* [I] *infml* to have a sexual relationship with someone who is a lot younger than oneself: *I hear you're going out with Jack's daughter—there you go, cradle-snatching again! —~er n*

craft¹ /krɑːft‖kræft/ *n* **1** [C] (a job or trade needing) skill, esp. with one's hands: *the ancient craft of making stained-glass windows | the jeweller's craft | traditional village crafts* **2** [C] all the members of a particular trade or profession as a group **3** [U] skill in deceiving people; GUILE: *He used a certain amount of craft to make the sale.*

craft² *n* craft **1** a boat or ship: *The harbour was full of pleasure craft.* **2** an aircraft or spacecraft

craft³ *v* [T often pass.] *esp. AmE* to make using skill, esp. by hand: *a carefully crafted belt | a beautifully crafted film*

-craft see WORD FORMATION

crafts·man /ˈkrɑːftsmən‖ˈkræ-/ **crafts·wo·man** /-ˌwʊmən/*fem.* — *n* -**men** /mən/ a person who is skilled in a CRAFT¹: *furniture made by the finest craftsmen* — ~**ship** *n* [U]

craft·y /ˈkrɑːfti‖ˈkræf-/ *adj* cleverly deceitful; CUNNING: *a crafty idea/politician* —**ily** *adv* —**iness** *n* [U]

crag /kræg/ *n* a high steep rough rock or mass of rocks

crag·gy /ˈkrægi/ *adj* steep and rough; having many crags: *craggy hills* | (fig.) *his craggy face* (=attractive in a rough way)

cram /kræm/ *v* -**mm**- **1** [T+obj+adv/prep] to force into a small space; STUFF: *to cram people into a railway carriage* | *hungry children cramming food down their throats* | *a busy programme, with three meetings crammed into one morning* **2** [T (**with**)] to fill (something) too full: *The box was crammed with letters.* | *A huge crowd of people crammed the stadium to watch the game.* **3 a** [I (**for**)] to prepare oneself for an examination by studying very hard and quickly **b** [T] to prepare (someone) for an examination in this way

Cram, Steve /stiːv/ (1960–) an English runner who broke three world records in 1985

cram-full /ˌ·ˈ·◂/ *adj* [F (**of**)] *infml* very full

cram·mer /ˈkræməʳ/ *n old-fash, usu. infml* a special school or book that prepares people quickly for an examination. It is generally thought that students who need a crammer are either lazy or not very clever.

cramp¹ /kræmp/ *n* [C (*esp. AmE*);U (*esp. BrE*)] severe pain from the sudden tightening of a muscle, which makes movement difficult: *The swimmer suddenly got cramp/got a cramp and had to be lifted from the water.* —see also CRAMPS

cramp² *v* [T] **1** to limit or prevent the movement, growth, or development of; RESTRICT: *Her education was cramped by her lack of money.* **2** to fasten tightly with a CRAMP³ **3 cramp someone's style** *infml* to prevent someone from doing as well as they could, or as they wish, usu. simply by being near them: *I'll leave you alone with Jenny—I wouldn't want to cramp your style!*

cramp³ *n* **1** also **cramp i·ron** /ˈ· ··/— a metal bar bent at both ends used for holding together pieces of wood, metal, etc. **2** a CLAMP¹

cramped /kræmpt/ *adj* **1** [(**for**)] limited in space: *a cramped little office | cramped living conditions | We're a bit cramped for space in this little house.* **2** (of writing) written too closely together

cram·pon /ˈkræmpən/ *n* [usu. pl.] also **climbing iron**— a metal frame with sharp points (SPIKES) underneath, fastened to the bottom of boots to make climbing less difficult, esp. on ice

cramps /kræmps/ *n* [P] sharp pains in the stomach, esp. (*AmE*) the pains women often experience during MEN-STRUATION

cran·ber·ry /ˈkrænbəri‖-beri/ *n* a small red sour-tasting berry, used esp. to make a sweet thick liquid to be eaten with certain meats. **Cranberry sauce** is often served with turkey at Thanksgiving in the US. —see picture at BERRY

crane¹ /kreɪn/ *n* **1** a machine for lifting and moving heavy objects by means of a very strong rope or wire fastened to a long movable arm: *We used a crane to lift the piano into the theatre.* **2** a tall waterbird with very long legs and neck

crane² *v* [I;T] to stretch out (one's neck) to get a better view: *Jane craned her neck to look for her mother in the crowd.* | *The children at the back craned forward to see what was happening.*

Crane, Ich·a·bod /ˈɪkəbɒd ‖ -bɑːd/ a character in the short story *The Legend of Sleepy Hollow* by Washington Irving

crane fly /ˈ· ·/ *n fml* an insect with very long legs; DADDY LONGLEGS

cra·ni·um /ˈkreɪniəm/ *n* -**niums** *or* -**nia** /niə/ *med* the bony framework of the human or animal head; part of the SKULL that covers the brain —**al** *adj*

crank¹ /kræŋk/ *n* **1** an apparatus, such as a handle fixed at right angles to a rod, for changing movement in a straight line into circular movement **2** *infml, often humor* a person with very unusual and strongly-held ideas, often concerning food and health, esp. ideas that other people think are very foolish: *She's a real crank; she only eats brown rice and nuts.* **3** *AmE infml* a bad-tempered person; GROUCH

crank² *v* [T(UP)] to cause to move by turning a crank: *to crank an engine*
  crank sthg. ↔ **out** *phr v* [T] *infml, esp. AmE* to produce in large amounts, as if by machinery: *He cranks out detective stories at the rate of three or four a year.*

crank·shaft /ˈkræŋkʃɑːft‖-ʃæft/ *n* a rod that turns or is driven by a crank, esp. in a car engine

crank·y /ˈkræŋki/ *adj infml* **1** *BrE* very strange; odd; ECCENTRIC: *a cranky old man* | *cranky ideas* **2** (of a machine or apparatus) unsteady; shaky; in need of repair **3** *AmE* bad-tempered: *a cranky baby/old lady*

Cran·mer /ˈkrænməʳ/, **Thomas** (1489–1556) an English churchman and Archbishop of Canterbury who supported Henry VIII and was put to death by Mary I, by burning

cran·ny /ˈkræni/ *n esp. humor or lit* a small narrow opening in a wall, rock, etc.; small crack: *a mouse hiding in a cranny in the stone wall* —see also **nooks and crannies** (NOOK) —**-nied** *adj*

crap¹ /kræp/ *n taboo sl* **1** [U] solid waste matter passed from the bowels **2** [S] an act of passing waste matter from the bowels: *to have a crap* **3** [U] something worthless or unwanted that does not deserve serious attention: *His speech was just a load of (old) crap.* | *Clear all this crap off the table.* —see also CRAPS

crap² *v* **-pp-** [I] *taboo sl* to pass waste matter from the bowels
  crap out *phr v* [I] *AmE* **1** to lose at CRAPS **2** *infml* to stop working and become unusable: *My car crapped out this morning; I had to take the bus to work.*

crape /kreɪp/ *n* [U] **1** CREPE (1) **2** black material worn as a sign of grief at someone's death. People do not usu. wear crape now, although many people do wear black clothes when they go to a funeral.

crap·py /ˈkræpi/ *adj sl* of very low quality: *a crappy idea*

craps /kræps/ *n* [U] an American game played with two DICE for money: *Let's* **shoot craps.** (=play this game) –
  crap *n* [A] : *a crap player*

crash¹ /kræʃ/ *v* **1** [I;T] to (cause to) have a sudden, violent, and noisy accident: *The car crashed into a tree and burst into flames.* | *John crashed his car last night.* | *The plane crashed shortly after take-off.* **2** [I+adv/prep] to move violently and noisily: *The angry elephant crashed through the forest.* **3** [I;T] to (cause to) fall or hit a surface noisily and violently, esp. breaking into pieces: *She crashed the plates angrily down on the table.* | *big waves crashing against the rocks* **4** [I] to make a sudden loud noise: *The thunder/drums crashed dramatically.* **5** [I;T] (in COMPUTERS) to (cause to) fail so that no further work can be done: *The computer/We crashed at ten this morning and haven't been up since.* **6** [I] (of a business or an organization concerned with money) to fail suddenly; COLLAPSE: *The New York Stock Exchange crashed in 1929.* **7** [T] *infml for* GATECRASH **8** [I (OUT)] *sl* to spend the night; sleep: *Can I crash on your floor tonight?* **9** [I] *AmE sl* to COME **down** (3) (=stop feeling the effects of a drug) in a very unpleasant way: *They really crashed on that acid they took.*

crash² *n* **1** a violent vehicle accident: *There was a serious car/train/plane crash this morning.* **2** a sudden loud noise made e.g. by a violent blow, fall, break, etc.: *a crash of thunder* | *the crash of breaking glass* **3** a sudden usu. unexpected and unexplained failure of a computer or computer system **4** a sudden severe business failure: *No one was prepared for the crash.* **5** **the Crash of 1929** also **the Great Crash** the failure of the New York Stock Exchange in 1929 that was the beginning of a severe world DEPRESSION

crash³ *adj* [A] needing great effort to reach the desired results quickly: *He wanted to lose weight so he went on a* **crash diet.** | *a crash programme of railway modernization*

crash⁴ *adv* [+adv/prep] with a crash: *The chandelier landed crash on the floor.*

crash bar·ri·er /ˈ· ˌ··/ *n* a strong fence or wall built to keep vehicles and/or people apart where there is a possibility of an accident: *crash barriers down the middle of the motorway* —compare CRUSH BARRIER

crash course /ˈ· ·/ *n* a course of lessons intended to teach a skill, language, etc., quickly: *I'm taking a crash course in French.*

crash-dive /ˈ· ·/ *v* [I] (of a SUBMARINE) to sink quickly to a great depth —**crash dive** *n*

crash hel·met /ˈ· ˌ··/ *n* a very strong protective head covering (HELMET) worn by racing car drivers, motorcycle riders, etc. In Britain and in most US states it is illegal to ride a motorcycle without wearing a crash helmet – see picture at HELMET

crash·ing /ˈkræʃɪŋ/ *adj* [A] *infml* (of something bad) very great; complete (esp. in the phrase **a crashing bore**)

crash-land /ˈ· ·/ *v* [I;T] to crash or cause (a plane) to crash in a controlled way so that as little damage as possible is done —**crash landing** /ˌ· ˈ··/ *n*

crass /kræs/ *adj fml* showing great stupidity and a complete lack of feeling or respect for others: *crass behaviour/ignorance/insensitivity* – ~**ly** *adv* – ~**ness** *n* [U]

Crat·chit /ˈkrætʃɪt/, **Bob** a character in Dickens' book *A Christmas Carol* who is very poor and has a young son who is very ill, but whose goodness and honesty finally get their reward

crate¹ /kreɪt/ *n* **1** a box or frame, esp. made of wood, for storing or carrying fruit, bottles, etc.: *a milk crate* **2** [(of)] also **crate·ful** /-ful/– the amount that a crate contains: *We sold ten crates of lemonade in two hours.* **3** *old-fash infml*, a very old car or plane

crate² *v* [T (UP)] to pack into a crate

cra·ter /ˈkreɪtəʳ/ *n* **1** the round bowl-shaped mouth of a VOLCANO **2** a round hole in a surface formed by an explosion, falling METEOR, etc.: *a bomb crater* | *craters on the moon*

cra·vat /krəˈvæt/ *BrE* ‖ **ascot** *AmE*– *n* a wide piece of material loosely folded and worn round the neck by men. It is generally thought of as a piece of clothing worn by upper-class people, esp. when wearing informal clothes —compare TIE¹ (1)

crave /kreɪv/ *v* **1** [I (for, after); T] to have a very strong almost uncontrollable desire for (something, esp. something bad): *I was craving for a cigarette.* | *He craved stardom.* **2** [T] *fml or pomp* to ask seriously for: *May I crave your attention?*

cra·ven /ˈkreɪvən/ *adj fml derog* completely lacking courage; COWARDLY – ~**ly** *adv* – ~**ness** *n* [U]

crav·ing /ˈkreɪvɪŋ/ *n* [(for)] a very strong, almost uncontrollable desire: *a craving for sweets* [+to-v] *a craving to have a cigarette* —see DESIRE² (USAGE)
  ▶ CULTURAL NOTE If a woman says she has a craving for something, people often joke that she must be PREGNANT (=going to have a baby), as cravings, esp. for odd or unusual things, are thought of in this connection.◀

craw·dad /ˈkrɔːdæd/ also **craw·fish** /ˈkrɔːfɪʃ/ *n AmE infml* CRAYFISH

Craw·ford /ˈkrɔːfəd‖-fərd/, **Joan** /dʒəʊn/ (1908–77) an American film actress who generally played strong women and who was one of America's top actresses; her daughter wrote a book about her that criticized her strongly.

Crawford, Mi·chael /ˈmaɪkəl/ (1942–) an English actor and entertainer, known esp. for his television SERIES *Some Mothers Do 'Ave 'Em*

crawl¹ /krɔːl/ *v* [I] **1** to move slowly with the body close to the ground, or on the hands and knees: *The baby crawled across the room.* | *There's an insect crawling down your sleeve.* | *(fig.) The traffic crawled along at ten miles an hour.* **2** [(with)] to be completely covered by insects, worms, etc.: *The kitchen was crawling with ants.* | *(fig.) The town was crawling with police.* **3** [(to)] *infml derog* to try to win the favour of someone in a powerful position by being too nice to them: *She got her job by crawling to the chief engineer.*

crawl² *n* **1** [S] a very slow movement or speed: *traffic moving at a crawl* **2** [(the)] S;U] a rapid way of swimming while lying on one's stomach, moving first one arm and then the other over one's head —see also PUB-CRAWL

crawl·er /ˈkrɔːləʳ/ *n* **1** *derog sl* a person who tries to win the favour of someone in a powerful position by being too nice to them; SYCOPHANT **2** something that goes slowly, esp. a heavy vehicle —see also CRAWLERS, KERB CRAWLER, NIGHT CRAWLER

crawler lane /ˈ·· ˌ·/ n BrE a part of a road, esp. a MOTOR-WAY, for slow vehicles

crawl·ers /ˈkrɔːləz‖-ərz/ n [P] ROMPERS

cray·fish /ˈkreɪˌfɪʃ/ also **crawdad, crawfish**– n -**fish** or -**fishes** [C;U] (the flesh of) a small LOBSTER-like animal that lives in rivers and streams –see picture at LOBSTER

cray·on¹ /ˈkreɪən, -ɒn‖-ɑːn, -ən/ n a stick of coloured WAX or CHALK used for writing or drawing, esp. on paper: *children's crayons | a packet of crayons*

crayon² v [I;T] to draw with a crayon

craze /kreɪz/ n [(for)] a very popular fashion that usu. only lasts for a very short time: *This computer game is the latest craze among the young in Japan.*

crazed /kreɪzd/ adj [(with)] driven mad or made extremely angry: *a crazed expression | He was crazed with grief.*

cra·zy /ˈkreɪzi/ adj infml 1 mad; foolish; INSANE: *You're crazy to go out in this weather. | a crazy idea | This noise is driving me crazy. | He has a crazy sister in the state asylum.* 2 [F+about] wildly excited; very keen or interested: *You know I'm crazy about you. | She's just crazy about dancing.* 3 **a crazy mixed-up kid** infml humor a young person who feels confused and uncertain what to do in life 4 **like crazy** wildly and very actively: *to work like crazy* —·**zily** adv —·**ziness** n [U]

crazy bone /ˈ·· ·/ n AmE for FUNNY BONE

Crazy Gang /ˈ·· ˌ·/, **The** a group of British COMEDIANS (=a man who makes people laugh) who performed jokes and songs on stage during the 1930s

crazy golf /ˌ·· ˈ·/ n [U] a game like GOLF in which players hit the ball through various silly and amusing OBSTA-CLES. Crazy golf courses are mainly found in SEASIDE towns in Britain.

Crazy Horse /ˌ·· ˈ·/ (1842–77) a Native American chief of the Sioux, who together with Sitting Bull defeated General Custer and his army in a famous battle at Little Bighorn

crazy pav·ing /ˌ·· ˈ··/ n [U] esp. BrE irregular pieces of stone fitted together to make a path or flat place

crazy quilt /ˌ·· ˈ·/ n AmE a QUILT made from small irregularly shaped pieces of cloth sewn together

creak /kriːk/ v [I] to make the sound of a badly-oiled door when it opens: *The floorboards in the old house creaked noisily. | creaking with age* (fig.) *The tax system is creaking under its increasingly heavy workload.* —**creak** n

creak·y /ˈkriːki/ adj that creaks: *a creaky old chair* —·**ily** adv —·**iness** n [U]

cream¹ /kriːm/ n 1 [U] the thick yellowish-white liquid that rises to the top of milk. Cream is thought of as very nice but unhealthy so it is kept for special occasions: *Have some cream in your coffee. | At the dairy they skim the cream off the milk. | strawberries and cream* –see also DOUBLE CREAM, SINGLE CREAM, SOUR CREAM 2 [C;U] a food containing this or a similar soft smooth substance: *chocolate creams | cream of chicken soup* 3 [C;U] a mixture made thick and soft like cream: *face cream* (=to soften one's skin) *| cream cleaner* (=for cleaning the kitchen, bathroom, etc.) *| Put some of this cream on that burn.* –see also COLD CREAM 4 [the (of)] the best part: *The wedding was attended by the cream of New York society. | Naturally, our personnel department selects only* **the cream of the crop.** (=the best people)

cream² adj yellowish-white: *a cream dress/suit* —**cream** n [U]

cream³ v [T] 1 to make into a thick soft mixture: *Cream the butter and sugar together. | creamed potatoes* 2 to take cream from the surface of (milk) 3 sl, esp. AmE to defeat completely

cream sbdy./sthg. ↔ **off** phr v [T] to remove (the best): *We cream off the best athletes and put them in a special squad. | The private bus companies will cream off the most profitable routes from the state-run bus service.*

cream out phr v [I] AmE infml to fall or go off course, esp. when skiing (SKI²)

cream cheese /ˌ· ˈ·‖ˈ· ·/ n [U] soft white smooth cheese made from milk and sometimes cream

cream crack·er /ˌ· ˈ··/ n also **cracker** infml– BrE a light, unsweetened BISCUIT often eaten with cheese

cream·er /ˈkriːmər/ n a small JUG for holding cream

cream·e·ry /ˈkriːməri/ n a place where milk, butter, cream, and cheese are produced or sold; DAIRY

cream of tar·tar /ˌ·· · ˈ··/ n [U] TARTAR¹ (3)

cream of wheat /ˌ·· · ˈ·/ n [C;U] tdmk (often cap.) (a bowl of) a hot CEREAL (2) made from finely crushed WHEAT

cream puff /ˈ· ˈ·/ n a light hollow pastry filled with whipped cream or CUSTARD

cream tea /ˌ· ˈ·/ n (in Britain) a light meal taken in the early afternoon consisting of small cakes (SCONES), jam, and cream usu. also with a pot of tea. It is considered to be typically English and is often something people have when on holiday: *a Devon cream tea*

cream·y /ˈkriːmi/ adj 1 containing cream: *creamy milk* 2 thick, soft, and smooth like cream: *a rich creamy liquid | creamy soap* —·**iness** n [U]

crease¹ /kriːs/ n 1 a line made on cloth, paper, etc., by folding, crushing, or pressing: *You've got a crease in your dress where you've been sitting. | He had razor-sharp creases in his trousers.* (=the trousers were very carefully pressed) 2 a line marked on the ground to show special areas or positions in certain games, esp. cricket –see picture at CRICKET

crease² v 1 [I;T] to make a line or lines appear on (a garment, paper, cloth, etc.) by folding, crushing, or pressing: *She wanted to wear her black dress but it was too creased. | a material that creases easily | His brow was creased in concentration.* (=he was thinking hard) 2 [T (UP)] BrE infml to cause to laugh a lot: *I was creased up with laughter.*

cre·ate /kriˈeɪt/ v 1 [T] to cause (something new) to exist; produce (something new): *Some people believe God created the world. | The project will create up to 60 new jobs. | to create a stir/a sensation* (=to cause great surprise and interest) *| The regulations are so complicated they will only create confusion. | This decision creates a dangerous precedent.* 2 [T+obj+n] to appoint (someone) to a special rank or position: *He was created Prince of Wales in a formal ceremony.* 3 [I] BrE infml to be noisily angry: *He really created when he found I'd broken the window!*

cre·a·tion /kriˈeɪʃən/ n 1 [U (of)] the act of creating: *a report proposing the creation of an independent Scottish parliament | a job-creation scheme* 2 [C] something created; something produced by human invention or imagination: *an artist's creations | the latest creations* (=fashionable clothes, etc.) *from Paris* 3 [U] the whole universe: *Are we the only thinking species in the whole of creation? | (AmE) I've looked all over creation for my glasses and I can't find them anywhere.*

Creation [the] (in the Christian religion) God's act of creating the Universe, the Earth, and all living things on Earth. The story of the Creation is told in the book of Genesis in the Bible.

▶ CULTURAL NOTE According to the Bible story, God made the Universe, the Earth, and all the animals. He then made Adam, the first man, out of dust, and Eve, the first woman, from one of Adam's RIBS. This took God six days, and on the seventh day he rested. –see also FALL ◀

cre·a·tion·is·m /kriˈeɪʃənɪzəm/ n [U] the belief that God created the universe in the way described in the Bible –see also CREATION SCIENCE —·**ist** n : *Creationists don't believe in Darwinian evolution.*

creation sci·ence /·ˈ·· ˌ··/ n [U] an attempt to give a scientific explanation to Creation, as described in the Bible, by people who do not accept the idea of EVOLUTION

cre·a·tive /kriˈeɪtɪv/ adj apprec 1 producing new and original ideas and things; imaginative and inventive: *creative thinking | a very creative musician* 2 resulting from newness of thought or expression: *his creative designs for the new college building* —~**ly** adv

creative ac·count·ing /·ˌ·· · ˈ··/ n [U] (in business) the art of changing accounts to achieve a more desirable set of figures in a way that is misleading but not illegal

cre·a·tiv·i·ty /ˌkriːeɪˈtɪvəti/ also **cre·a·tive·ness** /kriˈeɪtɪvnəs/— n [U] apprec the ability to produce new and original ideas and things; imagination and inventiveness: *an education system that lets children use their creativity*

cre·a·tor /kriˈeɪtər/ a person who CREATES (1)

Creator n [the] God

crea·ture /'kriːtʃəʳ/ n **1** a living being of any kind, but not a plant; an animal, bird, fish, etc.: *The crocodile is a strange-looking creature.* | *creatures from outer space* **2** (often used in expressions of feeling, esp. sympathy) a person of the stated kind: *The poor creature had no home, family, or friends.* | *He is* **a creature of habit.** (=a person with very fixed habits) **3** [(of)] a person whose rank or position is dependent on total obedience to another: *a creature of the military government* **4 all creatures great and small** *quote* the second line of a HYMN —see also ALL THINGS BRIGHT AND BEAUTIFUL

creature com·forts /ˌ·· '··/ n [P] food, clothes, warmth and other things that increase physical comfort

crèche /kreʃ‖kreʃ,kreɪʃ/ n **1** *BrE* ‖ **day-care center, nursery** *AmE*— a place, e.g. provided at a place of work, where babies and small children are cared for while their parents work. Crèches are sometimes provided at sports centres and events such as CONFERENCEs, but they are still quite rare —compare NURSERY (1), PLAYGROUP **2** *AmE for* CRIB¹ (3)

Cre·da /'kriːdə/ *tdmk* a British company that makes electrical goods for the home, e.g. cookers

cre·dence /'kriːdəns/ n [U] *fml* acceptance as true; belief: *The public does not* **give much credence to** *the government's promises.*

cre·den·tials /krɪ'denʃəlz/ n [P] **1** a letter or other written proof of a person's position, good character, etc.: *The new ambassador presented his credentials to the court.* **2** anything that proves a person's abilities, qualities, or suitability: *Both candidates for the job have excellent credentials.* | *The new finance minister has very sound credentials as an economist.*

cred·i·bil·i·ty /ˌkredɪ'bɪlɪti/ n [U] the quality of deserving belief and trust; being credible: *If we don't keep our promises, we'll* **lose credibility** *with the public.* | *The Chernobyl accident has undermined/damaged the credibility of the nuclear power industry.* —see also STREET-CREDIBILITY

credibility gap /ˌ··'··· ·/ n the difference between what someone, esp. a politician, says and what they really mean or do

cred·i·ble /'kredɪbəl/ adj deserving to be believed, trusted, or taken seriously: *a credible story* | *a barely* (=only just) *credible excuse* | *a credible defence policy* —see also INCREDIBLE **—bly** *adv*

cred·it¹ /'kredɪt/ n **1** [U] a system of buying goods or services and paying for them later. People generally use this system to buy large or expensive things such as furniture or electrical goods which they want immediately, but sometimes find difficult to pay for at once. Businesses like the system because it encourages people to spend or borrow money: *If you can't afford to pay cash, buy the furniture* **on credit.** | *six months' credit* | *This shop gives/offers interest-free credit.* —compare HIRE PURCHASE **2** [U] the quality of being likely to repay debts and being trusted in money matters: *Her credit is good.* —see also CREDIT RATING **3** [U] (the amount of) money in a person's bank account, as at a bank: *My account is* **in credit.** (=there is money in it) —compare DEBIT¹ (2) **4** [U] belief or trust in the truth or rightness of something: *Do you place any credit in the government's story?* | *The theory is gaining credit* (=becoming more popular) *with economists.* **5** [U (**for**)] public approval or praise given to someone because of something they have done: *She was given no credit for her invention.* | *The government is trying to claim the full credit for the fall in prices.* **6** [C (**to**) *usu. sing.*] a cause of honour: *You're a credit to your team.* | *Our armed forces* **do us credit.** (=are a credit to us) —opposite **discredit 7** [C] (esp. in the US) a completed unit of a student's work that forms part of a course, esp. at a university: *She hasn't enough credits to get her degree.* **8 to someone's credit: a** in someone's favour; in a way that brings honour to someone: *The King, to his great credit, opposed the establishment of a military government.* **b** to/in someone's name; belonging to or done by someone: *She's not yet 30, but already has five books to her credit!* (=she has written five books) —see also CREDITS, LETTER OF CREDIT

credit² v [T *not in progressive forms*] **1** *esp. BrE* to accept as true; believe: *Their claim/statement is rather hard to credit.* | (shows surprise) *Well, would you credit it — he's actually arrived on time!* **2** [(**to**)] to add to an account:

The money/cheque has been credited to your account. —compare DEBIT²

credit sbdy. with sthg. *phr v* [T] to accept that (someone) has (a quality) or is responsible for (an action); give credit to: *I credit him with a certain amount of sense.* | *She is credited with having saved the company from bankruptcy.*

cred·i·ta·ble /'kredɪtəbəl/ adj deserving praise or approval: *a creditable attempt to establish peace* | *a very creditable achievement* —opposite **discreditable —bly** *adv*

credit ac·count /ˈ·· ·ˌ·/ *BrE* ‖ **charge account** *AmE*— n an account with a shop which allows one to take goods at once and pay for them later

credit card /ˈ·· ·/ n a small plastic card which is used instead of money to pay for goods and services from shops, travel companies, petrol stations, etc. The cost is charged to one's account and paid later: *Do you take credit cards?* | *We accept all major credit cards.* | *an alarming rise in credit card fraud* —compare CHARGE CARD, CHEQUE CARD, DEBIT CARD

credit con·trol /ˈ·· ·ˌ·/ n [U] *tech* a business department which decides how much CREDIT a new customer can have, and tries to make sure that money owed to the company is paid at the right time

credit crunch /ˈ·· ˌ·/ n CREDIT SQUEEZE

credit lim·it /ˈ·· ˌ··/ n the most money that a customer can spend on credit, or that a person is allowed to borrow from a CREDIT CARD company, etc.: *a credit limit of £250*

credit note /ˈ·· ·/ *BrE* ‖ also **credit voucher** *AmE*— n a note given by a shop when goods have been returned, allowing one to buy other goods of the same value: *I'm afraid we don't give cash refunds, but you can have a credit note.*

cred·i·tor /'kredɪtəʳ/ n a person or organization to whom money is owed —compare DEBTOR

credit rat·ing /ˈ·· ˌ··/ n an opinion about how likely a person or business is to repay their debts. Credit ratings of a business are based on the company's value and performance, and are determined by other companies who specialize in finding this information. Credit ratings for people are determined by rather secretive companies who look at how a person has handled debt in the past.

cred·its /'kredɪts/ also **credit ti·tles** /ˈ·· ˌ··/ *fml*— n [P] the names of the actors and other people responsible for a cinema or television show, which appear in a list at the beginning or end

credit squeeze /ˈ·· ·/ also **credit crunch**— n a period during which the government makes the borrowing of money difficult, usu. in an effort to reduce spending and increase saving

credit trans·fer /ˈ·· ˌ··/ n [C;U] a way of moving money to a different bank account without using a cheque, e.g. by STANDING ORDER

credit u·nion /ˈ·· ˌ··/ n (esp. in the US) a COOPERATIVE (2) that operates like a bank for its members and lends them money at low rates of interest. Credit unions are often formed by the employees of a large company, or members of some other large organization.

credit vouch·er /ˈ·· ˌ··/ n *AmE for* CREDIT NOTE

cred·it·wor·thy /'kredɪtˌwɜːði‖-wɜːr-/ adj likely to pay debts; having a good CREDIT RATING: *Creditworthy customers may buy on account.* **—thiness** n [U]

cre·do /'kriːdəʊ, 'kreɪ-/ n **-dos** a formal statement of beliefs; CREED

cred·u·lous /'kredjʊləs‖-dʒə-/ adj too willing to believe, esp. without being given real proof **— ·ly** *adv* **— ·ness, credulity** /krɪ'djuːlɪti‖-'duː-/ n [U] : *a far-fetched story that would stretch the credulity even of a child*

Cree /kriː/ n [U;C] (a member of) a TRIBE of Native Americans who live mainly in Canada and northern Montana —see NATIVE AMERICAN (CULTURAL NOTE)

creed /kriːd/ n **1** a system of beliefs or principles: *the Socialist creed* | *people of every colour and creed* (=esp. religion). **2** a formal statement of religious belief, esp. as said at certain church services

creek /kriːk/ n **1** *BrE* a long narrow body of water reaching from the sea, a lake, etc., into the land **2** *AmE* a small narrow stream **3 up the creek (without a paddle)** *infml* in trouble: *I was really up the creek when I lost my keys.*

Creek n [C;the+P] (a member of) a TRIBE of Native Americans formerly living in Georgia and Alabama —see also NATIVE AMERICAN (CULTURAL NOTE)

creel /kriːl/ n a basket for carrying fish

creep¹ /kriːp/ v crept /krept/ [I] **1** [+adv/prep] to move slowly, quietly, and carefully, esp. so as not to attract attention: *We crept upstairs so as not to wake the baby.* | *The cat was creeping silently towards the mouse.* | (fig.) *Old age is creeping up on me.* | (fig.) *The newspaper's circulation has crept up from 800,000 to almost a million* (fig.) *Mistakes start to creep in when you work too hard.* **2** to move with the body close to the ground: *The dog crept under the car to hide.* | *creeping insects* **3** to grow along the ground or a surface: *a creeping plant* **4** (of the skin) to have an unpleasant sensation, as if worms, insects, etc., are moving over it: *I hated that horror film — it really made my flesh creep.* —see also CREEPS

creep² n **1** [C] sl an unpleasant person, esp. one who tries to win the favour of people of higher rank, esp. by praising them insincerely **2** [U] tech the slow movement of loose soil, rocks, etc. —see also CREEPS

creep·er /ˈkriːpəʳ/ n a plant which climbs up trees and walls or grows along the ground

creep·ers /ˈkriːpəz‖-ərz/ n [P] BrE shoes with thick rubber bottoms. They are also known as **brothel creepers** and were esp. fashionable in the 1950s when they were worn esp. by TEDDY BOYS.

creeps /kriːps/ n [the+P] infml an unpleasant sensation of fear: *The old castle gives me the creeps.* —see also CREEP¹ (4)

creep·y /ˈkriːpi/ adj infml causing or feeling an unpleasant sensation of fear: *a creepy story/old house* —**ily** adv —**iness** n [U]

creepy-crawl·y /ˌ·· ˈ·-/ n infml, esp. BrE a creeping insect

cre·mate /krɪˈmeɪt‖ˈkriːmeɪt/ v [T] to burn (the body of a dead person) at a funeral ceremony. In the past, most people used to be buried in the ground when they died, but now many people choose to be cremated instead. —see also ASHES —**mation** /krɪˈmeɪʃən/ n [C;U]

crem·a·to·ri·um /ˌkreməˈtɔːriəm‖ˌkriː-/ also **crem·a·to·ry** /ˈkremətəri‖ˈkriːmətɔːri/ esp. AmE— n -**iums** or -**ia** /iə/ a building in which the bodies of dead people are cremated

crème car·a·mel /ˌkrem ˈkærəməl, -mel/ n a sweet, yellowish-coloured food made from milk, eggs, and sugar which goes brown during cooking and forms a liquid on the outside when removed from its container

crème de la crème /ˌkrem də laː ˈkrem/ [the] Fr the best, most experienced, most intelligent people

Crème de Menthe /ˌkrem də ˈmɒnθ‖-ˈmaːnt/ n [U] a strong thick sweet green alcoholic drink, tasting of PEPPERMINT, usu. drunk from a small glass after a meal

Cre·mo·ra /krɪˈmɔːrə/ n [U] tdmk a powdered substance added to coffee instead of cream or milk

cren·el·lat·ed BrE ‖ **crenelated** AmE /ˈkrenəl-eɪtɪd/ adj tech protected by BATTLEMENTS: *a crenellated castle*

cre·ole /ˈkriːəʊl/ n (often cap.) **1** [C;U] an American or West Indian language, formed by the combination of a European language with one or more other languages — compare PIDGIN (1) **2** [C] a person descended from both Europeans and Africans **3** [C] a white person born in the West Indies or parts of Spanish America, or descended from the original French settlers in the southern US **4** [U] food prepared in the hot strong-tasting style of the southern US: *shrimp creole* —**creole** adj

cre·o·sote¹ /ˈkriːəsəʊt/ n [U] a thick brown strong-smelling oily liquid used for preserving wood

creosote² v [T] to paint with creosote

crepe , **crêpe** /kreɪp/ n **1** [U] also **crape**— light soft thin cloth, with a finely lined and folded surface, made from cotton, silk, wool, etc. **2** [U] also **crepe rub·ber** /ˌ· ˈ·-/ — tightly pressed rubber used esp. for making the bottoms of shoes: *crepe-soled shoes* **3** [C] a very thin PANCAKE (1) **4** [U] CREPE PAPER

crepe pa·per /ˌ· ˈ·-‖ˈ· ˌ·-/ also **crepe**— n [U] thin brightly coloured paper with a finely lined and folded surface, esp. used for making decorations

crêpes su·zette , **crepes suzette** /ˌkreɪp suːˈzet/ n [P] a dish of thin PANCAKEs with a thick orange liquid, served with

a strong alcoholic drink, esp. BRANDY or CURAÇAO, which is often lit to make a flame at the table

crept /krept/ past tense & participle of CREEP

cre·pus·cu·lar /krɪˈpʌskjʊləʳ/ adj **1** lit of the time when day is changing into night or night into day; not bright; faint **2** tech (of an animal) active only during this time

cre·scen·do¹ /krɪˈʃendəʊ/ n -**dos** **1** a piece of music which gradually becomes very loud —opposite **diminuendo** **2** infml a point of greatest excitement or urgency: *The demands for an election rose to a crescendo.*

crescendo² adj (of a piece of music) gradually becoming louder

cres·cent /ˈkresənt/ n **1** the curved shape of the moon during its first and last quarters, when it forms less than half a circle **2** something shaped like this, such as a curved row of houses or curved street: *an oriental crescent-shaped sword* **3** (often cap.) this shape as a sign of the Muslim religion: *medieval wars between Cross (=Christianity) and Crescent (=Islam)* —see also RED CRESCENT

crescent roll /ˈ·· ˌ·/ n AmE for CROISSANT

crescent wrench /ˈ·· ˌ·/ n AmE a spanner with parts that can be moved to hold things of different sizes —see picture at TOOL

cress /kres/ n [U] a very small plant whose sharp-tasting leaves are eaten raw: *a salad of mustard and cress* — see also WATERCRESS

Cres·si·da /ˈkresɪdə/ also **Cres·seid** /ˈkresɪd/— see TROILUS AND CRESSIDA

crest /krest/ n **1** a showy growth of feathers on top of a bird's head **2** a decoration like this worn, esp. in former times, on top of soldiers' HELMETS **3** [(of)usu. sing.] the top or highest point of something, esp. of a hill or a wave: *The path follows the crest of the hill for several miles.* | *The President is currently riding the crest of a wave of popularity.* (=is very popular at the present time) **4** a special picture used as a personal mark on letters, envelopes, etc., or above the shield on a COAT OF ARMS

Cres·ta Run /ˈkrestə ˌrʌn/ [the] a deep, steep path with twists in it cut into the ice each year at St Moritz in Switzerland, for riding TOBOGGANS down

crest·ed /ˈkrestɪd/ adj having a crest: *crested writing paper* | *a crested grebe* (=type of bird with a crest)

crest·fal·len /ˈkrest.fɔːlən/ adj disappointed and sad; having lost one's self-confidence

Crete /kriːt/ an island in SE Greece in the E Mediterranean Sea. It is a popular tourist place. —**Cretan** adj

cret·in /ˈkretɪn‖ˈkriːtn/ n **1** taboo sl an extremely stupid person; an extremely offensive word **2** med a person whose development of mind and body has stopped in early childhood — —**ous** adj

cret·onne /kreˈtɒn, ˈkretɒn‖ˈkriːtaːn, krɪˈtaːn/ n [U] heavy printed cotton cloth, used for curtains, etc.

cre·vasse /krɪˈvæs/ n a deep open crack, esp. in thick ice: *The dog fell into the crevasse.* —see picture at MOUNTAIN

crev·ice /ˈkrevɪs/ n a narrow crack or opening, esp. in rock

crew¹ /kruː/ n [C+sing./pl. v] **1 a** all the people working on a ship, plane, spacecraft, etc.: *The plane crashed, killing all its passengers and crew.* **b** all these people except the officers: *The crew is/are waiting for instructions from the captain.* **2** a group of people working together: *a train track repair crew* | *the camera crew on a movie set* —see also GROUND CREW **3** a rowing team **4** infml a group or collection of people: *We're a happy crew in our office.* | *His friends are rather a motley crew.* (=a strange or unusual mixture of people)

crew² v [I;T] to act as a crew member on (a boat)

crew³ old use past tense of CROW

crew cut /ˈ· ·/ also **buzz** AmE— n a very closely cut style of hair

Crewe /kruː/ a town in Cheshire, NW England, which is an important railway centre

crew·el·work /ˈkruːəlˌwɜːk‖-wɜːrk/ n [U] EMBROIDERY using thick thread made from wool

crew·man /ˈkruːmən/ n -**men** /mən/ a member of a CREW¹ (1, 2, and 3): *Mr Pod shared the boat with six crewmen.*

crew neck /ˈ· ·/ n a plain round neck on a jumper — compare V-NECK

▶ Cricket

Cricket is a very popular sport in Britain, played mainly in the summer. Professional cricket is controlled by the MCC (the Marylebone Cricket Club). The main competition is the COUNTY CHAMPIONSHIP, in which the 18 county cricket clubs play against one another during the season. Each match takes 3–4 days to complete.

The other form of cricket is called LIMITED OVERS (or ONE-DAY) cricket, in which matches are completed in a day. There is a limited-overs championship, played on Sundays. There are also two KNOCKOUT competitions, the finals of which are played at the Lord's Cricket ground in London.

International cricket matches are called TEST MATCHes (or TESTs) and can take 5 days to complete. They are played between the following teams: Australia, England, India, New Zealand, Pakistan, South Africa, Sri Lanka, and the West Indies. When England and Australia play test matches against one another, they are said to be playing for the ASHES.

Many people consider cricket to be England's national game and to be typical of a style of behaviour thought to be very English which includes above all a sense of honour and fairness. It is traditionally played by men and boys and although there are some women's teams, including a national one, the most important cricket club in England (the MCC) voted in 1991 not to accept women members. – see REFEREE (USAGE).

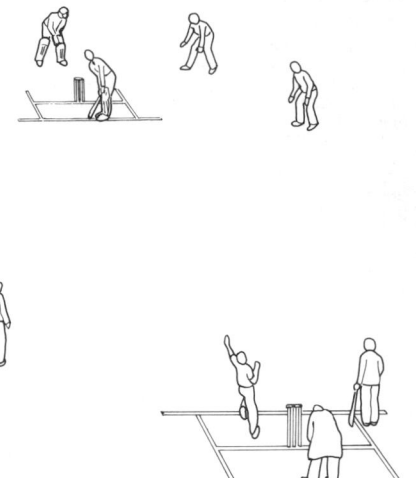

crib¹ /krɪb/ n **1** [C] esp. AmE a bed for a baby or young child; COT –see picture at BED **2** [C] an open box or wooden frame holding food for animals; MANGER: a corn crib **3** [C] BrE ‖ **crèche** AmE– a model of the scene of Jesus' birth, often placed in churches and homes at Christmas. It consists of all or most of the following: in the centre, a CRIB¹ (2) containing the baby Jesus surrounded by Mary and Joseph, SHEPHERDs with their sheep, three kings with presents, and an OX and an ASS. Above the scene is the star which signalled the birth of Jesus. –see picture on page 1212 **4** [C] infml **a** something copied dishonestly from someone else's work, esp. at school **b** also **trot** AmE– a book supplying a translation or giving answers to questions, often used dishonestly by students **5** [U] infml the game of cribbage **6** [C] the four cards set aside for the dealer to use in cribbage

crib² v **-bb-** [I;T (**from, off**)] infml to copy (something) dishonestly from someone else: I didn't know the answers so I cribbed them off Jean.

crib·bage /ˈkrɪbɪdʒ/ also **crib** infml– n [U] a card game in which points are shown by putting small pieces of wood in holes in a small board (**cribbage board**)

Crib·bins /ˈkrɪbⁱnz/, **Ber·nard** /ˈbɜːnəd‖ˈbɜːrnərd/ (1928–) an English theatre, film, and television actor, known esp. for acting COMIC parts

crib death /ˈ· ·/ n AmE for: COT DEATH

crick¹ /krɪk/ n [(**in**)] a sudden painful stiffening of the muscles, esp. in the back or the neck, making movement difficult: a crick in my neck

crick² v [T] to produce a crick in: She cricked her neck playing tennis.

crick·et¹ /ˈkrɪkⁱt/ n [U] **1** an outdoor game, popular in Britain, played in summer with a small ball covered with red leather, a BAT, and WICKETs, by two teams of 11 players each, usu. dressed all in white. One team tries to get RUNs² (10) while the other team FIELDs –see colour picture on page 884. **2** **not cricket** BrE old-fash or humor (of an action) unfair or not honourable: It would have been easy to cheat, but it wouldn't have been cricket.

cricket² n a small brown insect, the male of which makes loud short noises by rubbing its leathery wings together

crick·et·er /ˈkrɪkⁱtəʳ/ n a person who plays cricket

cried /kraɪd/ past tense & participle of CRY

cri·er /ˈkraɪəʳ/ n a TOWN CRIER

cries /kraɪz/ 3rd person sing. present tense of CRY

cri·key /ˈkraɪki/ interj BrE sl (an expression of surprise)

crime /kraɪm/ n **1** [C] an offence which is punishable by law: the crime of arson | Drug-smuggling is a serious crime. | bank robbers and other people who **commit** violent crimes | They say that murderers always return to *the* **scene of the crime**. **2** [U] illegal activity in general: It is the job of the police to prevent crime. | The latest crime statistics show a worrying rise in violent crime. | a crime wave (=situation in which there is a lot of crime) **3** [C] a bad, immoral, or dishonourable act: She committed the unforgivable crime of voting against her own party in the defence debate. **4** [S] infml a shame; pity: It's a crime that this food should be wasted. **5** **crime doesn't pay** saying people who COMMIT crimes will not become rich, but will be caught and punished –compare SIN; see also OR-GANIZED CRIME, WAR CRIME

crime a·gainst hu·man·i·ty /ˌ· ··· ·ˈ···/ n an extremely serious crime such as causing the deaths of large numbers of people, esp. directed against a population of whom most or all have done nothing to their AGGRESSOR

Cri·me·a /kraɪˈmiːə/ [the] a PENINSULA of the Ukraine in the Black Sea. The Crimean War was fought here.

Crime and Pun·ish·ment /ˌ· · ·ˈ···/ the best-known book of the Russian writer Dostoyevsky, which was also made into a film

Crimean War /·ˌ· ·ˈ·/ [the] (1853–56) a war in which Russia fought against Turkey, Britain, France, and Sardinia, begun because of an argument over the holy places in Palestine and ending with the fall of the Russian base of Sevastopol. It is remembered as an extremely bloody war, for the new nursing ideas of Florence Nightingale, and for a British military operation which failed badly, known as the Charge of the Light Brigade.

crime of pas·sion /ˌ· · ·ˈ···/ n a crime, usu. murder, resulting from sexual jealousy and popularly believed to often be punished more lightly by a judge

Crime·watch /ˈkraɪmwɒtʃ‖-wɑːtʃ, -wɔːtʃ/ a British television programme which gives details of crimes which have not been explained and asks the viewing public to telephone or go to the police if they can help with information

crim·i·nal¹ /ˈkrɪmⁱnəl/ adj **1** being a crime: a criminal offence (=a serious offence, esp. one that you could be sent to prison for) | criminal behaviour/tendencies **2** [A no comp.] of crime or its punishment: Does he have a criminal record? | Her attorney advised her to institute criminal proceedings against her employers. –compare CIVIL (2) **3** infml very wrong: a criminal waste of money – ~ **ly** adv

criminal² n a person who is guilty of crime: Prison is a place for punishing criminals. | Putting these young men into prison alongside **hardened criminals** (men who have been guilty of many crimes) is the surest way to make them reoffend.

criminal dam·age /ˌ·ⁱ ·ˈ·/ n the offence of deliberately damaging or destroying the property of another person

crim·i·nal·ize /ˈkrɪmɟnəlˌaɪz/ v [T] to cause to become a criminal **-ization** /ˌkrɪmɟnəl-aɪˈzeɪʃən‖-nələ-/ n [U]

criminal law /ˌ‥ ˈ‥/ n [U] the law concerning crimes and their punishments: *She's an expert in criminal law.* −compare CANON LAW, CIVIL LAW, COMMON LAW and see also extra information on page 742

crim·i·nol·o·gy /ˌkrɪmɟˈnɒlədʒi‖-ˈnɑː-/ n [U] the scientific study of crime and criminals **--gist** n

crimp[1] /krɪmp/ v [T] to press (esp. hair) into small regular folds

crimp[2] n infml, esp. AmE something that spoils or limits: *The thought of that meeting has really put a crimp in my day!*

crim·plene /ˈkrɪmpliːn/ n [U] tdmk a type of artificially-made material used for clothes, which tends not to develop CREASES when it is folded or crushed. Crimplene was very popular and fashionable in the 1960s, but most fashion-conscious people would not wear it now.

crim·son[1] /ˈkrɪmzən/ adj having a deep purplish red colour: *a crimson sky* | *She turned crimson with embarrassment.* **−crimson** n

crimson[2] v [I;T] to (cause to) become crimson: *His face crimsoned when he saw her watching him.*

cringe /krɪndʒ/ v [I] **1** to bend and move back, esp. from fear; COWER: *The dog cringed when it saw my stick.* **2** [(before, to)] to behave without self-respect towards someone in a more important or powerful position: *He always cringes before|to the boss.* **3** [(at)] infml to have a very uncomfortable feeling of shame or dislike: *I cringed with embarrassment when my father was rude to my teacher.*

crin·kle[1] /ˈkrɪŋkəl/ v [I;T] to (cause to) become covered with fine lines or folds, e.g. by pressing or crushing: *My clothes were all crinkled when I got them out of the case.* | *to crinkle one's nose in disgust*

crinkle[2] n a fold or line made e.g. by crushing cloth or paper −compare WRINKLE[1] (1)

crin·kly /ˈkrɪŋkli/ adj **1** having many crinkles **2** (of hair) curly **--kliness** n [U]

crin·o·line /ˈkrɪnəlɟn/ n a woman's stiff undergarment worn in former times to support a full skirt

cripes /kraɪps/ interj sl, esp. BrE (an expression of surprise)

Crip·pen /ˈkrɪpɟn/, **Doctor** (1862–1910) an American doctor who is well-known because he murdered his wife in a particularly BRUTAL way while living in England. He was given the DEATH SENTENCE.

crip·ple[1] /ˈkrɪpəl/ n someone who is unable to use one or more of their limbs properly, esp. the legs (usu. considered offensive to disabled people) −see also DISABLED

cripple[2] v [T] **1** to hurt or wound (a person) so that use of one or more of the limbs is made difficult or impossible: *The accident crippled him for life.* | *a crippling blow* **2** infml to damage or weaken seriously: *The country was crippled by the war.* | *the company's crippling debts*

Cris·co /ˈkrɪskəʊ/ n [U] tdmk a kind of oily substance used in solid or liquid form in cooking in the US: *Fry the meat in a little Crisco.*

cri·sis /ˈkraɪsɟs/ n **-ses** /siːz/ **1** a point or moment of great danger, difficulty, or uncertainty: *The sudden rise in oil prices led to an economic crisis.* | *The present housing crisis* (=severe shortage of housing) *is the result of years of neglect.* | *Relations between the two countries have reached crisis point.* **2** the time in a serious illness at which there is a sudden change for better or worse

Crisis at Christ·mas /ˌ‥ · ˈ‥/ n now officially called **Crisis** (in Britain) an organization which gives food, clothing, and a place to sleep to poor and homeless people in large cities, esp. in the weeks before Christmas, usu. using an empty building to do this work in

crisis line /ˈ‥ ·/ also **hotline**− n AmE a telephone service which offers free help to people who think themselves to be in a particular crisis: *a crisis line for the parents of missing children* −compare HELPLINE

crisis man·age·ment /ˈ‥ ˌ‥·/ n [U] the art or process of keeping a situation of great danger or uncertainty under control: *Once news of the redundancies leaks out, your job will become largely an exercise in crisis management.*

crisis of con·fi·dence /ˌ‥ · ˈ‥·/ n **-ses of confidence** a

point when confidence in a plan, person, company etc. becomes very weak: *The crisis of confidence in the party led to its leader's downfall.*

crisp[1] /krɪsp/ also **potato crisp** BrE‖**potato chip** AmE & AustrE− n a thin piece of potato cooked in very hot fat, dried, and sold in packets; crisps are generally considered to be not a very healthy food: *I'll have a pint of beer and a packet of crisps, please.* −see picture at CHIP

crisp[2] adj **1** hard; dry; easily broken: *crisp pastry* | *crisp bacon* **2** firm and fresh, as if recently made or grown: *a crisp apple* | *crisp vegetables* | *a crisp new five-pound note|five-dollar bill* **3** (of the air, weather, etc.) cold, dry, and fresh: *a crisp winter day* **4** (of style, manners, etc.) quick and confident; showing no doubts or slowness; BRISK: *a crisp reply|performance* **5** (of hair) tightly curled **− ~ly** adv **− ~ness** n [U]

crisp[3] v [I;T (UP)] to (cause to) become crisp, esp. by cooking or heating

Crisp, Quen·tin /ˈkwentɟn/ (1908–) a British-born writer, performer, and CRITIC, who lives in the US. He is known for his books which include *The Naked Civil Servant* and *How to Have a Lifestyle*, and for his unusual opinions and way of life

crisp·bread /ˈkrɪspbred/ n a dry unsweetened BISCUIT made from grain, often eaten by people wanting to lose weight, in place of bread, or by those who consider it to be a healthy food

crisp·y /ˈkrɪspi/ adj infml CRISP[2] (1, 2) **--iness** n [U]

criss·cross /ˈkrɪskrɒs‖-krɔːs/ n a pattern made by crossing a lot of straight lines; network of lines: *a crisscross design* **crisscross** v [I;T]: *railway lines crisscrossing the map*

cri·te·ri·on /kraɪˈtɪəriən/ n **-ria** /riə/ or **-rions** an established standard or principle, on which a judgment or decision is based: *What criteria do you use to judge a good wine?* | *Our proposal failed to meet the criteria established by the government, so they gave us no money.*

crit·ic /ˈkrɪtɪk/ n **1** a person who gives judgments about the good and bad qualities of something, esp. art, music, films, etc., esp. someone who does this as a job: *She's the music critic for "The Times".* **2** a person who dislikes and expresses strong disapproval of something or someone: *an outspoken critic of the government's defence policy* | *It's easy to be an* **armchair critic.** (=do nothing oneself but express disapproval of others)

crit·i·cal /ˈkrɪtɪkəl/ adj **1** of or being a moment of great danger, difficulty, or uncertainty, when a sudden change to a better or worse condition is likely; of or being a CRISIS. *a critical stage in his illness|in the negotiations* | *a matter of critical importance* | *We arrived at the critical moment.* | *The next two weeks will be critical (for the company).* **2** providing a careful judgment of the good and bad qualities of something: *a critical analysis|assessment of the government's record* | *critical writings* | *Her new book received* **critical acclaim.** (=was praised by the critics) | *It was a critical success* (=critics liked it) *but the public gave the thumbs down.* **3** [(of)] finding fault; judging severely: *Why are you so critical of everything I wear?* **− ~ly** /kli/ adv

critical mass /ˌ‥ ˈ‥/ n [C;U] (in science) the amount of a substance necessary for an atomic CHAIN REACTION to take place: (fig.) *The party never reached the critical mass; everyone sat around the whole evening looking uncomfortable.*

critical path a·nal·y·sis /ˌ‥ ‥ ·ˈ‥·‥/ n a method of planning a large piece of work so that there will be few delays and the cost will be as low as possible

crit·i·cis·m /ˈkrɪtɟsɪzəm/ n [C;U] **1** (an) unfavourable judgment or expression of disapproval: *Criticism doesn't worry me.* | *This decision has come in for* (=received) *a great deal of criticism.* **2** (an example of) the forming and expressing of judgments about the good or bad qualities of anything, esp. artistic work; work of a critic: *literary criticism*

crit·i·cize ‖ also **-cise** BrE /ˈkrɪtɟsaɪz/ v [I;T] **1** [(for)] to judge with disapproval; point out the faults of: *The report strongly criticizes the police for failing to deal with this problem.* **2** to make judgments about the good and bad points of: *It's hard to criticize one's own work.*

cri·tique /krɪˈtiːk/ *n* an article, book, etc., criticizing something, such as the work of a writer

crit·ter /ˈkrɪtəʳ/ *n AmE infml* a creature

croak¹ /krəʊk/ *v* **1** [I] to make a deep low noise such as a FROG makes **2** [I;T] to speak with a rough voice as if one has a sore throat **3** [I] *sl* to die

croak² *n* a croaking noise

Cro·at /ˈkrəʊæt/ *n* **1** [C] someone who is from or whose parents are from Croatia: *I think he's a Croat.* **2** [U] one of the languages of Croatia: *Do you speak Croat?*

Cro·a·tia /krəʊˈeɪʃə/ a country in SE Europe bordered by Slovenia and Hungary in N, by the Adriatic Sea in W, and Serbia and Bosnia in E; capital Zagreb; population 4,680,000 (1988) **—·tian** *adj*

cro·chet¹ /ˈkrəʊʃeɪ‖krəʊˈʃeɪ/ *n* [U] (examples of) the art of making clothes, tablecloths, etc., with a special hooked needle (**crochet-hook**)

crochet² *v* [I;T] to make by means of crochet: *to crochet a shawl* —compare KNIT (1)

crock¹ /krɒk‖krɑːk/ *n* a clay pot

crock² *n infml* **1** *esp. BrE* an old car **2** a weak old person: *We old crocks can't run like you.*

Crock·er /ˈkrɒkəʳ‖ˈkrɑː-/, **Bet·ty** /ˈbeti/ *tdmk* a name made up by a food company in the US for use on its products and cookbooks: *a Betty Crocker cake mix | Betty Crocker's International Cookbook*

crock·e·ry /ˈkrɒkəri‖ˈkrɑː-/ *esp. BrE* ‖ **earthenware** *esp. AmE*— *n* [U] cups, plates, etc., made from baked clay

Davy Crockett

Crock·ett /ˈkrɒkɪt‖ˈkrɑː-/, **Da·vy** /ˈdeɪvi/ (1786–1836) an American FRONTIERSMAN and politician who died defending the Alamo. In the popular imagination Davy Crockett wears a leather shirt and trousers and a hat made from animal skins, and carries a long gun for hunting in the forests. He is also known for his humour. A well-known popular song describes him as "king of the wild frontier".

crock of gold /ˌ· · ˈ·/ *n* a pot of gold which is supposed to be found at the end of a RAINBOW (=an arch with seven colours in the sky)

croc·o·dile /ˈkrɒkədaɪl‖ˈkrɑː-/ *n* **-diles** *or* **-dile** **1** [C] a large REPTILE that lives on land and in lakes and rivers in the hot wet parts of the world. It has a long hard-skinned body and a long mouth with many teeth. —compare ALLIGATOR **2** [U] the skin of this animal used as leather: *crocodile shoes* **3** [C] *BrE* a line of people, esp. schoolchildren, walking in pairs **4 in a while, croco·dile** see ALLIGATOR

crocodile

Crocodile Dun·dee /ˌ··· ·ˈ·/ a funny American film about an Australian CROCODILE hunter of the same name who goes to New York

crocodile tears /ˈkrɒkədaɪl ˌtɪəz‖ˈkrɑːkədaɪl ˌtɪərz/ *n* [P] insincere tears or other insincere signs of sorrow or sympathy

cro·cus /ˈkrəʊkəs/ *n* a small low-growing plant with a single purple, yellow, or white flower which opens in early spring —see picture at FLOWER

Croe·sus /ˈkriːsəs/ (ruled 560–546 BC) a king of W Asia Minor who became extremely wealthy

croft /krɒft‖krɔːft/ *n BrE* a very small farm, esp. in Scotland

Croft *n tdmk* a company which makes several different types of SHERRY

croft·er /ˈkrɒftəʳ‖ˈkrɔːf-/ *n BrE* a person who lives and works on a croft

crois·sant /ˈkrwɑːsɒŋ‖krwɑːˈsɑːnt/ ‖ also **crescent roll** *AmE*— *n* a piece of breadlike baked pastry, shaped like a CRESCENT, and usu. eaten with coffee at breakfast. This is generally thought of as the type of breakfast one eats in France, although it is also popular with those who are familiar with it through travelling.

Cro-Ma·gnon /krəʊ ˈmænjɒn ‖ -ˈmægnən/ *n* an early type of human being who lived in Europe from around 60,000 BC to 10,000 BC

crom·lech /ˈkrɒmlek‖ˈkrɑːm-/ *n tech* **1** a circle of upright stones built in ancient times in Britain and France **2** a DOLMEN

Cromp·ton /ˈkrɒmptən‖ˈkrɑː-/, **Rich·mal** /ˈrɪtʃməl/ (1890–1969) an English writer. She wrote the famous SERIES of children's books of which the first is *Just William*.

Oliver Cromwell with roundhead soldiers

Crom·well /ˈkrɒmwel‖ˈkrɑː-/, **Ol·i·ver** /ˈɒlɪvəʳ ‖ ˈɑː-/ (1599–1658) an English general, politician, and PURITAN. He was leader of the Parliamentarian army against King Charles I in the Civil War and became Lord Protector of England after the king's EXECUTION —see also CIVIL WAR (3)

Cromwell, Thomas (about 1485–1540) an English lawyer and politician who helped to make the English church independent of Rome, helping King Henry VIII stop the operations of certain religious institutions in England. He was executed (EXECUTE) by Henry VIII. —see also DISSOLUTION OF THE MONASTERIES

Cromwell Road /ˌ·· ˈ·/ a very long road in London which goes from the Victoria and Albert Museum to Earl's Court Road, along which there are many famous and interesting buildings

crone /krəʊn/ *n derog* an old woman, esp. one who is ugly or nasty

Cron·kite /ˈkrɒŋkaɪt‖ˈkrɑː-/, **Wal·ter** /ˈwɒltəʳ ‖ ˈwɔːl-/ (1916–) an American television news reporter and ANCHOR (3) until 1980. Cronkite's opinions were respected and trusted by many Americans.

Cro·nus /ˈkrəʊnəs/ , **Cro·nos** /ˈkrəʊnɒs‖-nɑːs/ also **Kronos**— in Greek MYTHOLOGY, a son of Uranus who became ruler of the world (Roman name Saturn)

cro·ny /ˈkrəʊni/ *n infml, sometimes derog* a friend or companion, esp. of a person in a position of power: *The mayor's always doing favours for his cronies.*

crook¹ /krʊk/ *n* **1** *infml* a very dishonest person, esp. a criminal: *That second-hand car dealer is nothing but a crook – his cars are either stolen or unsafe to drive.* **2** a bend or curve: *She carried the parcel in the crook of her arm.* **3** a long stick or tool with a curved end: *a shepherd's crook* —see also **by hook or by crook** (HOOK¹); see picture at STICK

crook² *v* [T] to bend: *He crooked his finger, signalling me to follow him.*

crook³ *adj AustrE infml* **1** sick; ill: *I'm feeling a bit crook today.* **2** (of things) nasty; bad: *The food was crook.*

crook·ed /'krʊkɪd/ adj 1 not straight; twisted; bent: *a crooked street* 2 *infml* dishonest: *a crooked politician* — ~**ly** adv — ~**ness** n [U]

croon /kruːn/ v [I;T] 1 to sing (usu. old slow popular songs) with feeling: *He crooned into the microphone.* 2 to sing gently in a low soft voice: *She crooned a lullaby.*

croon·er /'kruːnər/ n *old use or humor* an entertainer who croons. A famous example is Bing Crosby, sometimes called "the old crooner" in an AFFECTIONATE way.

crop¹ /krɒp‖krɑːp/ n 1 [*often pl.*] a plant or plant product such as grain, fruit, or vegetables grown by a farmer: *Wheat is a widely grown crop in Britain and North America.* | *The heavy rain did a lot of damage to the crops.* —see also CASH CROP, CATCH CROP, SUBSISTENCE CROP 2 the amount of such a product that is grown and gathered in a single season or place: *We've had the biggest wheat crop ever this year.* | *a record crop of apples* | (fig.) *this year's crop of new students* 3 a baglike part of a bird's throat where food is stored 4 a short riding whip 5 [*usu. sing.*] hair cut very short: *I don't think a crop suits her — it makes her look like a prisoner.*

crop² v **-pp-** 1 [T] (of an animal) to bite off and eat the tops of (plants): *The sheep cropped the grass.* 2 [T] to cut (a person's hair or a horse's tail) short 3 [I+adv] (of a plant) to produce a crop: *The potatoes have cropped well this year.*

crop out/up phr v [I] (of rocks, etc.) to show above the surface of the ground —see also OUTCROP

crop up phr v [I] *infml* to happen or appear unexpectedly: *Something has cropped up at work so I'll be late home tonight.*

crop cir·cle /'· ˌ··/ n a CORN CIRCLE

crop·per¹ /'krɒpər‖'krɑː-/ n a person or thing that crops

cropper² n BrE **come a cropper** sl a to fall heavily b to fail completely

crop spray·ing /'· ˌ··/ also **crop dusting**— n [U] the spreading of insect-killing chemical powders and liquids over crops, esp. from a low-flying plane

cro·quet /'krəʊkeɪ, -ki‖krəʊ'keɪ/ n [U] a game played on grass in which players knock wooden balls through HOOPS (=small metal arches) with a MALLET (=long-handled wooden hammer). Croquet was popular formerly in Britain, but is quite unusual nowadays except in some parks or gardens. Many people believe that it is played only by UPPER-CLASS people. In the US croquet is often played by children in their own garden.

cro·quette /krəʊ'ket/ n a small rounded mass of crushed meat, fish, potato, etc., covered with egg and BREAD-CRUMBS and cooked in deep fat

crore /krɔːʳ/ n **crore** or **crores** IndE & PakE ten million; 100 LAKHS: *crores of/six crore of rupees*

Cros·by /'krɒzbi‖'krɔː-/, **Bing** /bɪŋ/ (1904–77) an American singer and film actor, esp. famous for his style of singing and the COMEDY films he made with Bob Hope. His most famous song is called *White Christmas.*

cro·sier , **crozier** /'krəʊʒəʳ, ˈziəʳ/ n a long stick with a decorative curved end, carried by a BISHOP

cross¹ /krɒs‖krɔːs/ n 1 a mark (x or +) often used a as a sign of where something is or should be b as a sign that something is incorrect c as the signature of a person who cannot write 2 an upright post with a bar crossing it near the top, on which people were tied or nailed and left to die as a punishment in ancient times: *Christ's death on the cross* 3 (*often cap.*) this shape as the sign of the Christian faith (because Christians believe that Jesus Christ was killed on a cross): *Jesus hanging on the Cross* | *medieval wars between Cross and Crescent* (=the Christian and Muslim religions) —see also CROSS² (6) 4 any object, structure, or picture in this shape, used for decoration or worn as a sign of the Christian faith: *She wore a small gold cross on a chain.* | *a wooden cross on his grave* —see also CRUCIFIX, MALTESE CROSS 5 a decoration of this shape worn as an honour (a MEDAL), esp. for military bravery: *He won the George Cross during the war.* 6 [(between)] a mixture of two different things or qualities: *The taste is a cross between coffee and chocolate.* — see also CROSS² (4) 7 a cause of sorrow or suffering which tests one's patience or goodness: *Everyone* **has a cross to bear** *in life.* —see also RED CROSS, **the sign of the cross** (SIGN¹ (9))

cross² v 1 [I;T] to go, pass, or reach across (something): *The soldiers took three days to cross the desert.* | *a railway line that crosses the country from coast to coast* | *Make sure there's no traffic before you cross (the road).* 2 [I;T] to place, lie, or pass across each other: *I'll meet you where the path crosses the main road.* | *Jean crossed her arms.* —see also CROSSED 3 [I;T] to pass in opposite directions: *I got your letter the day after I sent mine: they must have crossed in the post.* 4 [T (with)] to cause (an animal or plant) to breed with one of another kind: *This flower has been produced by crossing several different varieties.* —see also CROSS¹ (6), CROSSBREED 5 [T] (in Britain) to draw two lines across (a cheque) to show that it must be paid into a bank account —compare OPEN¹ (10) 6 [T] to make a hand movement down and across (oneself) as a religious act: *She crossed herself as she left the church.* 7 [I;T] (in football, HOCKEY, etc.) to kick or pass (the ball) across the field 8 [T] to oppose the plans or wishes of: *Anne hates being crossed, so don't argue with her.* —see also DOUBLE-CROSS 8 **cross my heart (and hope to die)** *infml* (used when making a promise): *I didn't do it, cross my heart!* **cross one's mind** to come into one's thoughts: *It didn't even cross my mind that he would be upset.* 11 **cross someone's palm (with silver)** to give money to someone, esp. so that they will tell you what is going to happen to you in the future 12 **cross swords with** to argue or openly disagree with: *This isn't the first time he has crossed swords with the party leader.* 13 **cross the Rubicon** to make a decision or take an action that cannot later be changed (from the action taken by Julius Caesar in crossing the river Rubicon into Italy in 49 BC, against the orders of the Roman Senate) 14 **not to cross your bridges before you come/get to them** not to waste time thinking about difficulties which may never happen —see also **dot one's i's and cross one's t's** (DOT²), **keep one's fingers crossed** (FINGER¹ (8))

cross sbdy./sthg. **off** (sthg.) phr v [T] to remove (from) by drawing a line through: *If you can't come, cross your name off (the list).*

cross sthg. ↔ **out** phr v [T] to draw a line through (writing): *Cross that out and write it again.*

cross over phr v [I (to)] 1 BrE *euph* to die 2 AmE (of an entertainer) to find success in a field other than the one that one has established one's fame in: *She crossed over (to the pop charts) with her latest hit single.* —see also CROSSOVER

cross³ adj [(with)] angry; bad-tempered: *Dad was really cross with me when I broke the window.* — ~**ly** adv = ~**ness** n [U]

cross- see WORD FORMATION

Cross and Black·well /ˌkrɒs ənd 'blækwəl ‖ ˌkrɔːs-/ n tdmk a company which makes many different types of food product, sold esp. in tins and bottles

cross·bar /'krɒsbɑːʳ‖'krɔːs-/ n 1 a bar joining two upright posts, esp. two GOALPOSTS: *They've* **hit the crossbar** (=nearly got a GOAL) *several times.* 2 the bar between the seat and the HANDLEBARS on a bicycle —see picture at BICYCLE

cross·bench·es /'krɒsˌbentʃ‿z‖'krɔːs-/ n [P] seats in both houses of the British parliament for members who do not belong to the official government or opposition parties —**-er** n

crossbones n see SKULL AND CROSSBONES

cross·bow /'krɒsbəʊ‖'krɔːs-/ n a powerful weapon combining a BOW³ and a gun, used esp. in former times: *to fire a crossbow bolt*

cross·breed¹ /'krɒsbriːd‖'krɔːs-/ v [I;T] a to cause (an animal or plant) to breed with one of another breed b (of an animal or plant) to breed with one of another breed —compare INTERBREED —**-bred** /bred/ adj : *crossbred sheep*

crossbreed² n an animal or plant which is a mixture of breeds —compare INTERBREED

cross-Chan·nel /ˌ· '···◂/ adj passing across the English CHANNEL: *Heavy storms caused difficulties for cross-channel traffic.* | *a cross-Channel ferry*

cross·check /ˌkrɒs'tʃek‖ˌkrɔːs-/ v [T] to make certain of the correctness of (a calculation, statement, etc.), e.g. by using a different method of calculation —**cross-check** n

cross-coun·try /ˌ· '···◂/ adj, adv across the fields or open country: *cross-country skiing/running*

cross-country² *n* [C;U] a race run not on a track but across open country and fields

cross-cul·tu·ral /ˌ· ˈ···◄/ *adj* belonging to or involving different CULTURES or comparison between them: *cross-cultural event/studies*

cross-cur·rent /ˈkrɒsˌkʌrənt‖ˈkrɔːskɜːr-/ *n* a current in the sea, a river, etc., moving across the general direction of the main current

cross-dress·ing /ˌ· ˈ··/ *n* [U] the practice of wearing the clothes of the opposite sex, esp. for sexual pleasure —**er** *n*

crossed /krɒst‖krɔːst/ *adj* (of a telephone line) connected by mistake to two or more telephones

crossed cheque /ˌ· ˈ·/ *n BrE* (in Britain) a cheque which has two lines across it, showing that it must be paid into a bank account

cross-ex·am·ine /ˌ· ·ˈ···/ also **cross-question**— *v* [T] to question (esp. a witness) very closely, usu. in order to compare the answers with other answers given before —**ination** /ˌ· ···ˈ··/ *n* [C;U] —**iner** /ˌ· ·ˈ···/ *n*

cross-eyed /ˌ· ˈ◄‖ˈ· ·/ *adj* having the eyes looking in towards the nose

cross-fer·ti·lize also **-lise** *BrE* /ˌ· ˈ···/ *v* [T] **1** to FERTILIZE by adding male sex cells from one plant to female sex cells from another **2** [*often pass.*] to influence with ideas from different areas: *Europe has been cross-fertilized by contact with many other societies.* —**lization** /ˌ· ···ˈ··/ *n* [U]

cross·fire /ˈkrɒsfaɪər‖ˈkrɔːs-/ *n* [U] one or more lines of gunfire firing across a particular point: *When the terrorists fought the police, several onlookers were caught in the crossfire.*

cross-grained /ˌ· ˈ·◄/ *adj* **1** (of wood) having the GRAIN (4) running across rather than along it **2** *infml* difficult to please; ARGUMENTATIVE

cross-hatch·ing /ˈ· ˌ··/ *n* [U] lines drawn across part of a picture to show that something is made of different material or to produce the effect of shade

cross·ing /ˈkrɒsɪŋ‖ˈkrɔː-/ *n* **1** a place at which a road, river, border, etc., can be crossed —see also LEVEL CROSSING, PEDESTRIAN CROSSING and see picture at ZEBRA **2** a place where two lines, tracks, etc., cross **3** a journey across the sea: *Did you have a rough crossing?*

cross-legged

He sat with his legs crossed.

He sat cross-legged.

cross-legged /ˌkrɒs ˈlegd◄‖ˌkrɔːs ˈleg᷂d◄/ *adj, adv* having the knees wide apart and ankles crossed: *He was sitting cross-legged on the floor.*

cross·o·ver /ˈkrɒsəʊvər‖ˈkrɔːs-/ *n AmE* an act or occasion of an entertainer who is popular in one field finding successes in another: *a crossover from television to movies* | *a crossover hit/artist* —see also CROSS OVER (2)

crossover pri·ma·ry /ˈ··· ˌ··/ *n AmE* an OPEN PRIMARY

cross-patch /ˈkrɒspætʃ‖ˈkrɔːs-/ *n humor sl* a bad-tempered person

cross·piece /ˈkrɒspiːs‖ˈkrɔːs-/ *n* a piece of anything lying across something else

cross-ply /ˈkrɒsplaɪ‖ˈkrɔːs-/ *adj* (of a motor tyre) made stronger by cords pulled tightly across each other inside the rubber —compare RADIAL² —**crossply** *n*

cross-pur·pos·es /ˌ· ˈ···/ *n* **at cross-purposes** (of two people) misunderstanding each other; actually talking about different things, but believing they are talking about the same thing: *It was several minutes before we realized we were talking at cross-purposes.*

cross-ques·tion /ˌ· ˈ··/ *v* [T] to CROSS-EXAMINE — ~**er** *n*

cross-re·fer /ˌ· ·ˈ·/ *v* [I;T (**from, to**)] to direct (the reader) from one place in a book to another place in the same book: *In this dictionary capital letters are used to cross-refer (you) from one word to another.*

cross-ref·erence /ˌ· ˈ··‖ˈ· ˌ··/ *n* a note directing the reader from one place in a book to another place in the same book: *In this dictionary cross-references are shown in capital letters.*

cross·roads /ˈkrɒsrəʊdz‖ˈkrɔːs-/ *n* **crossroads** **1** a place where two or more roads cross **2** a point at which an important decision must be taken: *It was a crossroads in my life.* | *a crossroads decision*

cross-sec·tion /ˈ· ˌ··/ *n* **1** (a drawing of) a surface made by cutting across something at right angles to its length: *a cross-section of a worm/of a plant stem* —see picture at TEETH **2** a part or group that is typical or representative of the whole: *The researchers interviewed a cross-section of the American public.*

cross-stitch /ˈ· ·/ *n* [C;U] (decorative sewing which uses) a stitch like an X made by crossing one stitch over another

cross street /ˈ· ·/ *n AmE* a street that crosses another street. This word is used esp. when giving directions: *I live on Vanowen Blvd and the nearest cross streets are Lindley and Etiwanda.*

cross talk /ˈ· ·/ *n* [U] **1** *BrE* rapid exchange of clever remarks, esp. between two actors **2** interruption of a radio or telephone conversation by unwanted signals from elsewhere

cross·tree /ˈkrɒs-triː‖ˈkrɔːs-/ *n tech* either of two beams fastened across the top of a ship's MAST

cross·walk /ˈkrɒswɔːk‖ˈkrɔːs-/ *n AmE for* PEDESTRIAN CROSSING

cross·wind /ˈkrɒsˌwɪnd‖ˈkrɔːs-/ *n* a wind blowing across the line of flight of a plane, direction of movement of traffic, etc.

cross·wise /ˈkrɒsˌwaɪz‖ˈkrɔːs-/ *adj, adv* crossing something or each other: *logs laid crosswise on the floor*

crossword

CROSSWORD

across down

cross·word /ˈkrɒsˌwɜːd‖ˈkrɔːsˌwɜːrd/ also **crossword puz·zle** /ˈ··· ˌ··/— *n* a printed game in which words are fitted into a pattern of numbered squares in answer to numbered CLUES (=questions or information about the necessary word) in such a way that words can be read across as well as down when the pattern is completed. Crosswords are very popular in Britain and the US and are found in many different newspapers and magazines. People who can finish difficult ones quickly are often thought to be very clever: *She does the Times crossword before breakfast.*

crotch /krɒtʃ‖krɑːtʃ/ *n* **1** also **crutch**— **a** the place between the tops of the legs of the human body **b** the place where the legs of a pair of trousers, etc., join: *These jeans are too tight in the crotch.* —see picture at HUMAN **2** the place where a branch separates from a tree

crotch·et /ˈkrɒtʃᵻt‖ˈkrɑː-/ *BrE* ‖ **quarter note** *AmE* — *n* a musical note with a time value a quarter as long as a SEMIBREVE —see picture at NOTATION

crotch·et·y /ˈkrɒtʃᵻti‖ˈkrɑː-/ *adj infml* (esp. of someone old) bad-tempered; liking to argue and complain

crouch /kraʊtʃ/ *v* [I (DOWN)] to lower the body closer to the ground by bending the knees: *He crouched down to stroke the dog.* | *The cat crouched, ready to spring at the bird.* —compare SQUAT¹ (1)

croup¹ /kruːp/ n [U] *med* a disease of the throat, esp. in children, that makes breathing difficult and causes coughing

croup² n the fleshy part above the back legs of certain animals, esp. the horse

crou·pi·er /ˈkruːpɪə^r/ n a person employed to collect and pay out money at a place where games are played for money, e.g. a CASINO

crou·ton /ˈkruːtɒn‖-tɑːn/ n [*usu. pl.*] a small square of bread cooked in fat and served in soup

crow¹ /krəʊ/ n **1** a large shiny black bird with a loud cry **2 as the ¹crow flies** in a straight line: *We're two kilometres from town as the crow flies, but nearly five by road.* —see also CROW'S FOOT, CROW'S NEST, **eat crow** (EAT (5))

crow² v [I] **1** to make the loud high cry of a COCK: *It was dawn, and I could hear a cock crowing somewhere.* **2** [(about, over)] *infml derog* to express pride openly, esp. when taking pleasure from someone else's misfortune: *They were crowing over their defeated opponents, little knowing that it would be their turn to lose next time.* **3** (esp. of a baby) to make wordless sounds of happiness

crow³ n [S] **1** the loud high cry of a COCK: *He gave a triumphant crow.* —see also COCK-A-DOODLE-DOO **2** a wordless sound of happiness as made by babies

Crow¹ n (a member of) a Native American tribe who now live in southern Montana —see NATIVE AMERICAN (CULTURAL NOTE)

Crow², Jim see JIM CROW

crow·bar /ˈkrəʊbɑː^r/ n an iron bar used to raise heavy objects off the ground, to force open a box, etc.

crowd¹ /kraʊd/ n **1** [C+*sing.*/*pl. v*] a large number of people gathered together: *A big crowd soon gathered at the scene of the accident.* | *There were crowds of people at the theatre.* | *a football crowd* **2** [C] *infml* a particular social group: *I don't spend much time with the college crowd.* **3** [C] a large number of things in disorder: *a crowd of books and papers on his desk* **4** [*the*] people in general, esp. when thought of as easily influenced or lacking original ideas: *I do what I like; I don't go with*/*follow the crowd.* —see also **two's company, three's a crowd** (COMPANY)

crowd² v **1** [I+*adv*/*prep*] (esp. of people) to come together in large numbers: *People crowded round the scene of the accident.* | *They all crowded into the cinema.* **2** [T] (esp. of people) to fill: *Shoppers crowded the streets.* | *The beach was crowded with holidaymakers.* **3** [T+*obj*+*adv*/*prep*] to press tightly into a small space: *He crowded his large family into the taxi.* **4** [T] *infml* to push or put pressure on in a threatening way: *Don't crowd her — give her some space!* | *They're crowding me with their unreasonable demands.*
  crowd sbdy./**sthg. out** *phr v* to keep out because of lack of space: *The big firms are trying to crowd our small business out of the market.*

crowd·ed /ˈkraʊdɪd/ adj **1** completely full; filled with a crowd: *a very crowded bus*/*street* **2** uncomfortably close together: *We'll be a bit crowded in that tiny room.* —**~ness** n [U]

crowd·ed out /ₗ·· ˈ·ₗ/ adj [F] *infml, esp. BrE* very full; PACKED-OUT: *The cinema was crowded out.*

crown¹ /kraʊn/ n **1** [C] a decorative covering for the head, usu. made of gold and jewels, worn by a king or queen as a sign of royal power **2** [C] **a** an object in this shape **b** a representation of this shape: *a printed crown on an official envelope* **c** a piece of metal in this shape for wearing, e.g. on a uniform, as a mark of office, rank, etc. **d** a sign in this shape used with numbers, usu. from one to five, in a system to judge standards or quality: *The English Tourist Board gives this hotel three crowns.* **3** [*the*] (*usu. cap.*) the governing power of a kingdom: *land belonging to the Crown* **4** [*the*] **a** the position of king or queen: *rival claimants to the crown* **b** a CHAMPIONSHIP title: *He won the heavyweight boxing crown in 1985.* **5** [C] the top or highest part of something, e.g. of the head, a hat, or a mountain: *the crown of a hill* **6** [C] **a** an old British coin worth 25 pence **b** any of several units of money in certain European countries: *Swedish*/*Czechoslovak crowns* —see also HALF A CROWN **7** [C] (an artificial covering for) the part of a tooth above the GUM —see picture at TEETH

crown² v [T] **1** to place a crown solemnly on the head of (a person) as a sign of royal power or of victory: *to crown a beauty queen* [+*obj*+n] *They crowned him king of Portugal.* —see also CORONATION **2** to cover the top of (something): *Mist crowned the mountain.* **3** to complete in a way that is suitable or deserved: *Success has crowned her years of effort.* **4** to put a protective covering on (a tooth) **5** *sl* to hit (someone) on the head: *Be quiet or I'll crown you!* **6 to crown it all** to make (one's) good or bad fortune complete: *My house burnt down, my car was stolen, and to crown it all I lost my job.* —see also CROWNING

crown col·o·ny /ₗ· ˈ··ₗ/ n (*often caps.*) a British COLONY ruled by a governor appointed by the British government

Crown Court /ₗ· ˈ·/ [C;U] part of the Supreme Court of England and Wales which hears serious criminal cases and APPEALS¹ (3) from a Magistrates' Court —see also extra information on page 742

Crown Der·by /ₗ· ˈ··/ n [U] a type of fine PORCELAIN made in the city of Derby, England

crowned head /ₗ· ˈ·/ n a king or queen: *All the crowned heads of Europe were at the funeral.*

crown·ing /ˈkraʊnɪŋ/ adj of more importance or value than anything else; above all other things: *Her crowning ambition was to become a famous writer.* | *the president's crowning achievement*

crown jew·els /ₗ· ˈ··/ n [P] (*often caps.*) the crowns, swords, jewels, etc., worn by a king or queen on important state occasions. The British Crown Jewels can be seen in the Tower of London. They are often used as a SYMBOL of something which is so valuable that it cannot be given a price.

crown of thorns /ₗ· ˈ·/ n (*sometimes cap. C and T*) a crown of small, sharp, pointed THORNS which, according to the Bible, was placed on Jesus Christ's head when he was crucified (CRUCIFY)

crown prince /ₗ· ˈ·◂/ n (*often cap.*) the man who has the legal right to be king after the death of the present ruler: *Crown Prince George*

crown prin·cess /ₗ· ·ˈ·◂‖ₗ· ˈ··◂/ n (*often cap.*) **1** the woman who has the legal right to be ruling queen after the death of the present ruler **2** the wife of a crown prince

Crown Pro·se·cu·tion Ser·vice /ₗ· ··ˈ·· ˌ··/ also **CPS**— n [*the*] the government organization in England and Wales which is responsible for bringing legal charges against criminals —compare DISTRICT ATTORNEY

crow's foot /ˈ· ·/ n *crow's feet* [*usu. pl.*] a WRINKLE at the corner of a person's eye, sometimes thought of as a sign of age or lack of sleep

crow's nest /ˈ· ·/ n a small box or shelter near the top of a ship's MAST, from which a person can watch for danger, land, etc.

Crow·ther /ˈkraʊðə^r/, **Les·lie** /ˈlezli/ (1933–) an English actor and COMEDIAN and one of the first presenters of the children's television programme, *Crackerjack*

Croy·don /ˈkrɔɪdn/ a BOROUGH of S London

cro·zier /ˈkrəʊʒə^r, -zɪə^r/ n a CROSIER

CRT /ₗsiː ɑː ˈtiː‖-ɑːr-/ n *abbrev. for* CATHODE RAY TUBE

cru·cial /ˈkruːʃəl/ adj **1** [(to, for)] of deciding importance: *a crucial moment in the negotiations* | *The success of this experiment is crucial to the project as a whole.* **2** *sl* excellent — **~ly** adv

cru·ci·ble /ˈkruːsɪbəl/ n **1** a container in which metals or other substances are heated to very high temperatures **2** *esp. lit* a severe test: *to pass through the crucible of war*

cru·ci·fix /ˈkruːsɪfɪks/ n a CROSS¹ (4) with a figure of Christ on it

cru·ci·fix·ion /ₗkruːsɪˈfɪkʃən/ n **1** [C;U] (an example of) the act of crucifying **2** [C] (*often cap.*) a picture or other representation of the Crucifixion

Crucifixion [*the*] the death of Jesus Christ by being nailed to a cross and left to die. In pictures of the Crucifixion Jesus is shown with a CROWN OF THORNS on his head. —see also RESURRECTION

cru·ci·form /ˈkruːsɪfɔːm‖-fɔːrm/ adj *fml* cross-shaped

cru·ci·fy /ˈkruːsɪfaɪ/ v [T] **1** to kill (someone) by nailing or tying them to a CROSS¹ (3) and leaving them to die. Christians believe that Jesus Christ was crucified. **2** to be very cruel and unpleasant to, esp. publicly: *If they find out the truth about the boss, the staff will crucify him!* — see also CRUCIFIXION

crud /krʌd/ *n* [U] *infml, esp. AmE* dirt, or an unpleasant substance: *I've got crud under my fingernails from working in the garden.* | *Did you clean out that crud from behind the stove yet?* — ~ **dy** *adj* : *Those jeans are really cruddy — why don't you wash them?*

crude¹ /kruːd/ *adj* **1** in a raw or natural state; untreated: *crude oil* | *crude rubber* **2** lacking grace, education, or sensitive feeling; VULGAR: *crude jokes* | *Don't be so crude!* **3** not skilfully made or properly finished: *a crude shelter in the forest* | *The painting was a crude forgery.* | *a crude* (=not very exact) *estimate of the cost* — ~ **ly** *adv*

crude² also **crude oil** /ˌ· ·ˈ·/ — *n* [U] untreated oil: *1000 barrels of crude*

cru·di·tés /ˈkruːdɪteɪ/ *n* [P] pieces of raw vegetables served before a meal, often with a DIP² (3)

cru·di·ty /ˈkruːdɪti/ *n* **1** [U] also **crude·ness** /ˈkruːdn̩s/ — the quality of being crude: *the crudity of their building methods* **2** [C] *fml* a crude act, remark, etc.

cru·el /ˈkruːəl/ *adj* **1** [(to)] liking to cause pain and suffering; enjoying the pain of others; very unkind: *a cruel and sadistic murderer* | *Don't be cruel to animals, Sammy.* | *cruel remarks* **2** painful; causing suffering: *a cruel disappointment/wind* | *The death of their daughter was a cruel blow.* **3 be cruel to be kind** to do something now that seems to be cruel to someone in order to help them in a more general way — ~ **ly** *adv*

Cru·el·la de Vil /kruˌelə də ˈvɪl/ an evil woman in a children's book and Walt Disney film called *The Hundred and One Dalmatians* who wants to harm the dogs in the story: *Jade's mother has cast me as some kind of Cruella de Vil — charged me with sabotaging Jade's university career.*

cru·el·ty /ˈkruːəlti/ *n* **1** [U] the quality of being cruel: *cruelty to animals* **2** [C] a cruel act, remark, etc.: *the cruelties of war*

cruelty-free /ˌ··· ˈ·◂/ *adj* (of COSMETICs) that have not been tested on animals: *our wide range of cruelty-free products*

cru·et /ˈkruːɪt/ *n* **1** (a holder for) a set of containers for pepper, salt, oil, etc., for use at meals **2** any one of these containers, esp. a small glass bottle for oil or VINEGAR

Cruft's /krʌfts/ (in Britain) a short name for **Cruft's Dog Show**, a competition held every year to judge which is the finest animal in the country for each breed of dog

cruise¹ /kruːz/ *v* **1** [I] to sail in an unhurried way, esp. for pleasure: *to go cruising in the Mediterranean* — see also CRUISE² **2** [I] (of a car, plane, etc.) to move at a fast but steady speed on a long journey: *cruising along at 100 kilometres an hour* **3** [I;T] *sl* to look in (public places) for a sexual partner, esp. one of the same sex

cruise² *n* a sea voyage for pleasure, esp. one on a large ship and lasting for several days or weeks. This type of holiday is usually expensive and many people think that only rich people go on cruises: *They went on a cruise to Tenerife.*

Cruise, Tom (1962–) an American actor who has played leading film parts since the early 1980s, e.g. in *Top Gun* and *Cocktail*. He is esp. popular with women.

cruise con·trol /ˈ· ·ˌ·/ *n tech* an apparatus fitted to a motor vehicle, esp. a car, which keeps it running at a steady speed which can be chosen by the driver

cruise lin·er /ˈ· ·ˌ·/ *n* a large ship specially built for cruises

cruise mis·sile /ˈ· ·ˌ·/ *n* (*sometimes cap.*) a GUIDED MISSILE (=an explosive weapon guided by electrical means) that flies fairly slowly and close to the ground and has a RADAR system for examining the ground

▶ CULTURAL NOTE There was a great deal of PROTEST in the 1980s over the introduction of US cruise missiles into Britain. Protest camps were set up at Greenham Common, and at Molesworth in Cambridgeshire. ◀

cruis·er /ˈkruːzər/ *n* **1** a large fast warship **2** a CABIN CRUISER **3** *AmE* a police car

crul·ler /ˈkrʌlər/ *n AmE* a light ring-shaped cake (DOUGHNUT) made from two twisted pieces joined together: *Half a dozen crullers, please.*

crumb /krʌm/ *n* **1** a very small piece of dry food, esp. bread

or cake: *Brush the crumbs off the table.* | (fig.) *crumbs of information/of comfort* —see picture at PIECE **2** *AmE sl* a worthless person —see also CRUMBS

crum·ble¹ /ˈkrʌmbəl/ *v* **1** [I;T] to (cause to) break into very small pieces: *He crumbled the bread in his fingers.* **2** [I] to weaken; decay; become ruined: *a crumbling church* | *Our hopes crumbled when the business went bankrupt.* | *Opposition to the new law soon crumbled.*

crumble² *n esp. BrE* ‖ **crisp** *AmE*— [C;U] (a cooked dish of sweetened fruit covered with) a dry mixture of flour, fat, and sugar: *apple crumble*

crum·bly /ˈkrʌmbli/ *adj* easily crumbled: *crumbly biscuits*

crumbs /krʌmz/ *interj BrE sl* (an expression of surprise or slight annoyance) This is a rather old-fashioned expression which you might find in stories about schoolchildren.

crum·my /ˈkrʌmi/ *adj sl* **1** of poor quality; worthless: *a crummy book* | *What a crummy idea!* **2** rather ill: *He felt pretty crummy.*

crum·pet /ˈkrʌmpɪt/ *n* **1** [C] (esp. in Britain) a small round breadlike cake with holes in one side, eaten hot with butter —compare MUFFIN **2** [U] *BrE sl* women, considered as sexual objects (considered extremely offensive to women): *She's a nice bit of crumpet!*

crum·ple /ˈkrʌmpəl/ *v* **1** [I;T (UP)] to (cause to) become full of irregular folds by pressing, crushing, etc.: *a crumpled dress/suit/newspaper* | *The front of the car crumpled when it hit the wall.* | (fig.) *His face crumpled and he started to cry.* **2** [I (UP)] *infml* to lose the strength or will to fight: *The enemy forces crumpled under the bombardment.*

crumple zone /ˈ··· ·/ *n tech* a part of the body of a motor vehicle which crumples more easily than the rest of the vehicle if hit in an accident, and so protects the people in the vehicle by absorbing (ABSORB) the IMPACT

crunch¹ /krʌntʃ/ *v* **1** [I (on);T] to crush (food) noisily with the teeth: *The dog was crunching (on) a bone.* **2** [I] to make a noise like the sound of something being crushed: *Our feet crunched on the frozen snow.* | *The stones crunched under the car tyres.* —see also NUMBER CRUNCHING — ~ **y** *adj*

crunch² *n* **1** [S] a crunching sound: *I heard a loud crunch as the truck ran into the wall.* **2** [*the*] *infml* a difficult moment when something important must be decided: *They're against our plan now but* **when/if it comes to the crunch** *they'll support us.*

Crunch·ie /ˈkrʌntʃi/ *n tdmk* a type of chocolate bar made by Cadbury's

cru·sade¹ /kruːˈseɪd/ *n* **1** (*usu. cap.*) any of the Christian wars to win back Palestine from the Muslims in the 11th, 12th, and 13th centuries, led by European kings and lords **2** [(against, for)] a united effort for the defence or advancement of an idea, principle, etc.: *I think he's running a one-man crusade against cigarette smoking.* | *a crusade for women's rights* — **sader** *n*

crusade² *v* [I (against, for)] to take part in a crusade: *to crusade against nuclear weapons* | *a crusading young politician* — **sader** *n*

cruse /kruːz/ *n bibl or old use* a small pot or JAR for oil, wine, etc.

crush¹ /krʌʃ/ *v* **1** [T] to press with great force so as to break, damage, or destroy the natural shape or condition: *Don't crush the box, there are eggs inside!* | *The tree fell on top of the car and crushed it.* **2** [T] to break into a powder by pressure: *This machine crushes wheat grain to make flour.* **3** [I+adv/prep] to move in large numbers through or into a small space: *The people crushed through the gates.* **4** [T] to destroy completely, esp. by the use of great force: *The military government has ruthlessly crushed all opposition.* | *a crushing defeat* | (fig.) *He was crushed/His hopes were crushed by the chairman's remark.*

crush² *n* **1** [S] uncomfortable pressure caused by a large crowd of people filling a small space: *There was such a crush on the train that I could hardly breathe.* **2** [U] a drink made by crushing fruit and adding water: *orange crush* —compare SQUASH² (3) **3** [C (on)] *infml* a strong but short-lived feeling of love for someone, like that often experienced by a TEENAGER; an INFATUATION: *Did you* **have a crush on** *one of the teachers when you were at school?*

crush bar·ri·er /ˈ· ˌ···/ n a fence used to keep back crowds at football matches, processions, etc. —compare CRASH BARRIER

Crusoe, Robinson see ROBINSON CRUSOE

crust /krʌst/ n [C;U] **1** (a piece of) the hard usu. brown outer surface of baked bread **2** the baked pastry on a PIE **3** a hard outer covering, as of earth or snow: *a thin crust of ice on the aeroplane's wing* —see also UPPER CRUST

crus·ta·cean /krʌˈsteɪʃən/ n any of a group of animals with a hard outer shell that are closely related to the insects: *Lobsters, crabs, and shrimps are crustaceans.* — **crustacean** adj

crust·y /ˈkrʌsti/ adj **1** having a hard well-baked crust: *a crusty loaf* **2** bad-tempered; SURLY: *a crusty old soldier* —**ily** adv —**iness** n [U]

crutch /krʌtʃ/ n **1** a stick with a piece that fits under the arm, for supporting a person who has difficulty in walking: *When she broke her leg she had to walk on crutches.* **2** something that provides support or a help: *Her religion was a crutch to her when John died.* **3** CROTCH (1)

crux /krʌks/ n [the] the central or most important part of a problem: *The crux of the matter is ...*

Cruyff /ˈkrɔɪf/, **Jo·hann** /ˈjəʊhæn ‖ jəʊˈhɑːn/ (1947–) a Dutch footballer who was European Footballer of the Year in 1973 and 1974 and later became manager of Barcelona football club

cry¹ /kraɪ/ v **1** [I;T] to produce (tears) from the eyes as a sign of sorrow: *She cried bitterly when she heard the news of her friend's death.* | *a sad love story that made me cry* | *The baby was crying for milk.* (=because he was hungry)| *to cry oneself to sleep* (=cry till one falls asleep) | *to cry tears of disappointment* —compare WEEP (1)

▶CULTURAL NOTE In Britain and the US, crying is not thought to be typical of or suitable to a man, though it has always been considered understandable in certain circumstances, e.g. at a FUNERAL or when done by a young boy. It is gradually becoming more acceptable generally, but people still often think of a man who cries as EFFEMINATE and laugh unkindly at him. This is esp. true of young men, who might call him a **wimp** or a **pansy**, or (esp. if he is young) a **sissy** or a **crybaby**.◀

2 [I (OUT)] to make loud sounds expressing fear, pain, surprise, or some other feeling: *He cried out with pain when he burnt his fingers.* **3** [I (for);T (OUT)] to call loudly; shout: *She cried out for help.* | *"Help!" he cried, as he fell into the water.* **4** [I] to make the natural sound of certain animals and birds: *Can you hear the seagulls crying?* **5** [T] old use to make known publicly by shouting: *to cry the news* **6 cry for the moon** BrE infml to demand something impossible **7 cry one's eyes/heart out** to cry very sadly and usu. for a long time: *When his dog died he cried his eyes out.* **8 cry over spilt milk** to waste time being sorry about something which cannot now be changed: *It's no use crying over spilt milk — we've got to decide what to do next.* **9 cry wolf** to call for help unnecessarily, risking the possibility that people will not believe that you need help later when you really do (from Aesop's story of a boy who was guarding sheep. He kept shouting "Wolf!" even though there was no wolf there, because he found his work boring, so that when a WOLF really did come, no one believed him.): *A spokesman for the Theatre Campaign said: "No longer can the government say we are crying wolf. Cuts have gone so deep that we are now reduced to shutting theatres for a time."* **10 for crying out loud** sl (used to give strength to a demand, request, etc.): *For crying out loud shut that door!*

cry sthg. ↔ down phr v [T] BrE to express an unfavourable opinion of

cry off phr v [I] BrE to say one will not fulfil a promise or agreement: *He tried to cry off at the last minute, but we held him to his promise.*

cry out against sthg. phr v [T pass. rare] to express loudly one's strong disapproval of: *The villagers cried out against the building of a motorway which would cut right through the village.*

cry out for sthg. phr v [T no pass.] to be in great need of; demand urgently: *The country is crying out for rain.*

cry² n **1** [C (of)] any loud sound expressing fear, pain, or other strong feeling: *a cry of anger|pain|fear|delight* **2** [C (for)] a loud call; shout: *There was a loud cry from the direction of the woodshed.* | *a cry of "Stop, thief!"* **3** [S] a period of crying: *You'll feel better after you've had*

a (good) cry. **4** [C] the natural sound made by certain animals or birds: *the warning cry of a mother bird to her chicks* **5** [C] a call to action: *a battle cry* (=to show or encourage bravery in a battle) | *The demand for tax cuts is the party's favourite* **rallying cry.** (=used to encourage support) —see also WAR CRY **6 in full cry** BrE (of a group of dogs) making loud noises as they hunt an animal: (fig.) *At the meeting, the parents were in full cry, demanding further government spending on schools.* —see also HUE AND CRY, **a far cry** (FAR²)

cry·ba·by /ˈkraɪˌbeɪbi/ n derog a person, esp. a child, who cries too often

cry for help /ˌ· · ˈ·/ n [S] (used of a DESPERATE (3) action, esp. an attempt at SUICIDE) an attempt to get some help and attention from other people, rather than to hurt oneself or anyone else: *I think she took the pills knowing her mother would find her in time; it was just a cry for help.*

cry·ing /ˈkraɪ-ɪŋ/ adj [A] infml (of something bad) that demands urgent attention: *The state of the roads is a* **crying shame.**

cry·o·gen·ics /ˌkraɪəˈdʒenɪks/ n the science of very low temperature

cry·on·ics /kraɪˈɒnɪks‖-ˈɑː-/ n the process of freezing a body in liquid NITROGEN at the moment of its death. People who pay for their bodies to be frozen like this hope that at some future time doctors will be able to bring them back to life.

crypt /krɪpt/ n a room under a church, often used in the past as a BURIAL place

cryp·tic /ˈkrɪptɪk/ adj secret or mysterious; difficult to understand, sometimes intentionally: *a cryptic message* | *a cryptic comment|remark* (=with hidden meaning) —compare ELLIPTICAL (3) — **~ally** /kli/ adv

crypto- see WORD FORMATION

cryp·to·gra·phy /krɪpˈtɒgrəfi‖-ˈtɑː-/ n [U] the study of secret writing and CODES —**pher** n —**phic** /ˌkrɪptəˈgræfɪk◀/ adj —**phically** /kli/ adv

crys·tal /ˈkrɪstl/ n **1** [C;U] (a shaped piece of) a natural mineral that is either transparent, looking like ice, or is only slightly coloured **2** [U] colourless glass of very high quality: *a crystal wine glass* | *a crystal chandelier* **3** [C] a small regular shape with its surfaces in an even arrangement, formed naturally by a substance when it becomes solid: *crystals of salt* | *copper sulphate crystals* **4** [C] AmE the transparent cover over the face of a clock or watch

crys·tal ball /ˌ··ˈ·/ n a ball of crystal or glass used by FORTUNE-TELLERS to look into the future: (fig.) *He's an expert but not even his crystal ball can tell us how the stockmarket will change.* —see picture at FORTUNE TELLER

crystal clear /ˌ·· ˈ·/ adj very clearly stated or understood; allowing no possibility of doubt: *I'd like to make it crystal clear that I do not agree with these proposals.*

crystal gaz·ing /ˈ·· ˌ··/ n [U] the practice of looking into a ball of crystal or glass in an attempt to see the future: (fig.) *The article contained some firm predictions, but also a lot of crystal gazing.* (=guessing about the future) —**er** n

crys·tal·line /ˈkrɪstəlaɪn, -liːn‖-lən/ adj **1** of or like crystal; very clear; transparent: *a crystalline mountain stream* **2** made of CRYSTALs (3): *crystalline rocks*

crys·tal·lize also **-lise** BrE /ˈkrɪstəlaɪz/ v **1** [I;T] to (cause to) form CRYSTALs (3): *The liquid will crystallize at 50°C.* **2** [I;T] to (cause to) become clear and fixed in form: *a number of related ideas that gradually crystallized into a practical plan* **3** [T] to preserve (fruit) by covering with sugar: *crystallized cherries* —**lization** /ˌkrɪstəlaɪˈzeɪʃən‖-lə-/ n [C]

Crystal Pal·ace /ˌ·· ˈ··/ [the] a building mainly of glass and iron, built in Hyde Park, London to contain the Great Exhibition of 1851. The Crystal Palace was destroyed by fire in 1936, but the name *Crystal Palace* is now used by an ATHLETICS ground and a football team.

crystal set /ˈ·· ·/ n a simple radio receiver of an old-fashioned kind

Cry, the Be·lov·ed Coun·try /ˈ· · ·ˌ·· ˌ··/ the title of a book by Alan Paton about life in South Africa after the Second World War

CSE /ˌsiː es ˈiː/ n Certificate of Secondary Education; an examination in any of a range of subjects, at a lower level than the GCE, taken (until 1988) in British schools by pupils aged 15 or over: *She left school with three CSEs and five O levels.* —compare GCSE

C-sec·tion /ˈ· ˌ·/ *n infml* a CAESAREAN

C-SPAN /ˈ· ˌ·/ a US CABLE television station which broadcasts the US Congress and the meetings of its various committees

CS gas /ˌsiː es ˈɡæs/ *n* [U] TEAR GAS

CST /ˌsiː es ˈtiː/ *abbrev. for* CENTRAL STANDARD TIME

CT *written abbrev. for* CONNECTICUT

CTC /ˌsiː tiː ˈsiː/ *n infml for* CITY TECHNOLOGY COLLEGE

cu *written abbrev. for:* CUBIC

cub /kʌb/ *n* **1** the young of various meat-eating wild animals, such as the lion, bear, etc.: *a fox and her cubs | lion cubs* **2** (*often cap.*) a member of the CUB SCOUTS **3** a young and inexperienced person: *a cub reporter on a newspaper*

Cu·ba /ˈkjuːbə/ the largest island in the West Indies. Cuba has been a republic since 1960, under the leadership of Fidel Castro; capital Havana —**Cuban** *n, adj* —see also Fidel CASTRO

▶ CULTURAL NOTE There are many Cuban REFUGEEs in the US; some came when the former government fell in 1959 and many others as BOAT PEOPLE in the 1980s. Most of them live in Florida. The present Communist government of Cuba is viewed very negatively by most Americans. ◀

Cuban mis·sile cri·sis /ˌ··· ˈ··· ˌ··/ [*the*] a dangerous situation which developed in 1962 when the Soviet Union began to build bases for NUCLEAR MISSILEs in Cuba. US President John F. Kennedy complained and stopped ships from going to Cuba, and the Soviet Union agreed to remove the bases —see also BAY OF PIGS

cub·by·hole /ˈkʌbihəʊl/ *n* a small enclosed space, sometimes used either as a room or a cupboard: *She works in a little cubbyhole at the end of the corridor.*

cube¹ /kjuːb/ *n* **1** a solid object with six equal square sides: *a sugar cube | The box was cube-shaped.* **2** the number made by multiplying a number by itself twice: *The cube of 3 is 27.* (3×3×3=27)

cube² *v* [T] **1** to multiply a number by itself twice: *3 cubed* (written 3³) *is 27.* **2** to cut (something) into cubes: DICE² (1)

cube root /ˌ· ·ˈ·/ /ˈ· ·/ *n* the number which when multiplied by itself twice equals a particular number: *If 3 is the cube root of 27* (written 3√27), *then 3×3×3=27.*

cu·bic /ˈkjuːbɪk/ *adj* being a measurement of space when the length of something is multiplied by its width and height: *a cubic centimetre* (often written as *cc*) *| a cubic metre|inch|foot | "What's the cubic capacity (=size) of this engine?" "2000 cc."*

cu·bi·cal /ˈkjuːbɪkəl/ *also* **cubic**—*adj* having the shape of a cube

cu·bi·cle /ˈkjuːbɪkəl/ *n* a very small division of a larger room, such as one used for dressing or undressing in at a swimming pool, or studying in a library

cub·is·m /ˈkjuːbɪzəm/ *n* [U] (*often cap.*) a 20th century art style in which the subject matter is represented by GEOMETRIC shapes. Picasso and Braque are the most famous artists connected with Cubism. —**ist** *n*

cu·bit /ˈkjuːbɪt/ *n bibl* an ancient unit of length equal to the length of the arm between the wrist and the elbow

Cub Scout /ˈ· ˌ·/ *also* **cub** *n* a member of a division of the SCOUTS for younger boys: *My little brother is in the Cub Scouts.* —compare BROWNIES

Trembling Woman
by Picasso

cubism

cuck·old¹ /ˈkʌkəld, ˈkʌkəʊld‖-kəld/ *n humor or derog, now rare* a man whose wife has had sex with another man since their marriage

cuckold² *v* [T] *humor or derog, now rare* (of a wife, or of another man) to make (the husband) into a cuckold

cuck·oo¹ /ˈkʊkuː‖ˈkuːkuː, ˈkʊ-/ *n* **-oos** a grey European bird that lays its eggs in other birds' nests for them to HATCH and has a call that sounds like its name

cuckoo² *adj sl* mad; foolish: *You're cuckoo!*

cuckoo clock /ˈ··· ·/ *n* a wall clock with a wooden bird inside that comes out to tell each hour with the call of a cuckoo —see picture at CLOCK

cu·cum·ber /ˈkjuːkʌmbəʳ/ *n* [C;U] a long thin round vegetable with a dark green skin and light green watery flesh, usu. cut in pieces and eaten raw —see picture at VEGETABLE

▶ CULTURAL NOTE Cucumber sandwiches are often thought of as very GENTEEL or English UPPER-CLASS. ◀

cud /kʌd/ *n* [U] food that has been swallowed and brought up again to the mouth from the first stomach of certain animals which have four stomachs, such as the cow, for further eating: *cows in the meadow* **chewing the cud** —see also **chew the cud** (CHEW¹)

cud·dle¹ /ˈkʌdl/ *v* [I;T] to hold (someone, something, or each other) lovingly and closely in the arms: *The little girl cuddled her pet dog. | Susie and John were cuddling in the cinema.*

  cuddle up *phr v* [I (**to**, TOGETHER)] to lie close and comfortably (together): *The children cuddled up to each other in bed.*

cuddle² *n* [S] an act of cuddling: *My little daughter came to me for a cuddle. | Give me a cuddle, mummy.*

cud·dle·some /ˈkʌdlsəm/ *adj* cuddly

cud·dly /ˈkʌdli/ *adj* lovable; suitable for cuddling: *a cuddly little baby*

cud·gel¹ /ˈkʌdʒəl/ *n* **1** a short thick heavy stick or similar object used as a weapon, esp. one that has a rough surface; short heavy CLUB¹ (4) **2 take up the cudgels (for)** *BrE* to begin to take part in an argument or struggle, esp. in support of a person, principle, etc.: *He took up the cudgels on behalf of the political prisoners.*

cudgel² *v* **-ll-** *BrE* ‖ **-l-** *AmE* [T] to beat with a cudgel: (fig.) *We* **cudgelled our brains** (=forced ourselves to think hard) *trying to remember the lost address.*

cue¹ /kjuː/ *n* **1** (esp. in a play) a word, phrase, or action that is the signal for the next person to speak or act: *The actor missed his cue and came onto the stage late.* **2** an action, event, etc., that provides a signal for something to be done or a standard that can be copied: *I wasn't sure what to do, so I* **took my cue** *from the person sitting next to me. | The fall in interest rates may be a cue for an upturn in consumer spending. | He shows up* (**right**) **on cue** (=exactly as expected) *every evening at suppertime.*

cue² *v*

  cue sbdy. **in** *phr v* [T] to give (someone) a sign to be ready to do something: *The studio manager will cue you in when it's your turn to sing.*

cue³ *n* a long straight wooden stick used for pushing the ball in games such as BILLIARDS and SNOOKER: *She chalked her cue again.* —see picture at BILLIARDS

cue ball /ˈ· ·/ *n* **1** the ball which a player hits with a CUE³ in order to make other balls move in a game such as BILLIARDS **2** *AmE humor sl* a BALD person

cuff¹ /kʌf/ *n* **1** the end of a SLEEVE (=the arm of a garment) **2** *AmE for* TURN-UP (1): *trouser cuffs* **3 off the cuff** without preparation or consideration: *I'm afraid I can't answer your question off the cuff. | an off-the-cuff remark|estimate* —see also HANDCUFFS

cuff² *v* [T] to hit lightly with the open hand: *She cuffed the boy on the side of the head and pushed him into the car.* —**cuff** *n* : *He gave his son a cuff round the ear.*

cuff link /ˈ· ·/ *n* [usu. pl.] an object like two connected buttons used to fasten a shirt cuff through two BUTTONHOLEs —see PAIR¹ (USAGE)

cuffs /kʌfs/ *n* [P] *infml for* HANDCUFFS

cui·rass /kwɪˈræs/ *n* a piece of armour covering the upper half of the body but not the arms

cui·sine /kwɪˈziːn/ *n* [U] **1** a style of cooking: *French cuisine* **2** food that has been prepared: *When in Naples, try the excellent local cuisine.*

cul-de-sac /ˈkʌl də ˌsæk, ˈkʊl-‖ˌkʌl də ˈsæk, ˌkʊl-/ *n* a street with only one way in or out; BLIND ALLEY

cul·i·na·ry /ˈkʌlɪnəri‖ˈkʌlɪneri, ˈkjuːl-/ *adj fml* connected with or used in the kitchen or cooking: *culinary herbs*

cull¹ /kʌl/ v **1** [I;T] to kill the weakest or unwanted members of (a group of animals): *Every year the seals are culled to prevent their population from increasing.* **2** [T] *fml* to choose or collect (esp. information) from among others: *The facts were culled from various sources.*

cull² n **1** an act of culling: *a seal cull* **2** something found worthless as a result of culling: *Those potatoes over there are culls.*

cul·len·der /ˈkʌlɪndəʳ/ n a COLANDER

Cul·lod·en /kəˈlɒdn‖-ˈlɑː-/ (the place of) a battle in Scotland in 1746, in which the Jacobite army under Charles Edward Stuart ("Bonnie Prince Charlie") was severely defeated by the **Duke of Cumberland**, second son of King George the Second —see also **Charles Edward** STUART

cul·mi·nate /ˈkʌlmɪneɪt/ v
  culminate in sthg. *phr* v [T] to reach the highest point, degree, or stage of development in; end in: *Their years of work culminated in the discovery of a cure.* | *a series of minor clashes culminating in full-scale war*

cul·mi·na·tion /ˌkʌlmɪˈneɪʃən/ n [the (of)] the last and highest point, when this is reached after a long period of effort or development; CLIMAX: *The discovery was the culmination of his life's work.*

cu·lottes /kjuːˈlɒts‖kjʊˈlɑːts/ n [P] women's short trousers shaped to look like a skirt —see PAIR (USAGE)

cul·pa·ble /ˈkʌlpəbəl/ *adj fml* deserving blame: *culpable negligence* —**bly** *adv* —**bility** /ˌkʌlpəˈbɪlɪti/ n [U]

cul·prit /ˈkʌlprɪt/ n the person guilty of a crime or responsible for a problem: *Someone was breaking windows, but we soon caught the culprit.* | (fig.) *Our prices are rising too quickly, and high production costs are the main culprit.*

cult /kʌlt/ n **1** (the group of people that follow) a system of worship, esp. one that is different from the usual and established forms of religion in a particular society, for example, the Moonies **2** a particular fashion or style, e.g. in art, music, or writing, that is followed with great interest and keenness by a fairly small group: *His music has become something of a cult.* | *Her books aren't bestsellers, but they have a certain cult following.* | *a cult movie* | *The Morris Minor convertible is rather a cult car in Britain.* —see also PERSONALITY CULT

cul·ti·va·ble /ˈkʌltɪvəbəl/ *adj* that can be cultivated

cul·ti·vate /ˈkʌltɪveɪt/ v [T] **1** to prepare (land) for the growing of crops **2** to plant, grow, and raise (a crop) by preparing the soil, providing water, etc. **3** to improve or develop (the mind, a feeling, etc.) by careful attention, training, or study: *to cultivate a knowledge of music* **4** to pay special and friendly attention to (someone that one regards as useful): *John always tries to cultivate people who might be able to help him professionally.*

cul·ti·vat·ed /ˈkʌltɪveɪtɪd/ *adj* **1** showing good education, manners, etc.; CULTURED: *a cultivated audience* **2** (of land) used for growing crops —opposite uncultivated

cul·ti·va·tion /ˌkʌltɪˈveɪʃən/ n [U] the process of cultivating: *to bring new land under cultivation* | *the cultivation of cotton*

cul·ti·va·tor /ˈkʌltɪveɪtəʳ/ n **1** a tool or machine for loosening earth, destroying unwanted plants, etc. **2** a person who cultivates, e.g. a farmer

cul·tu·ral /ˈkʌltʃərəl/ *adj* of or related to culture: *concerts, plays, and other cultural events* | *the cultural diversity of the United States* —~ly *adv*

cultural lit·e·ra·cy /ˌ··· ·····/ n [U] *tdmk* a good general knowledge of the CULTURE (1) of a society, esp. a knowledge of the history, literature, art, politics, GEOGRAPHY, science, religion, and FOLKLORE which form a part of that culture, and the knowledge of which is generally shared by the people of that society. The phrase was made famous by the book, *Cultural Literacy*, written by the American E.D. Hirsh, Jr. *et al*: *Immigrants often lack cultural literacy of their new country.*

Cultural Rev·o·lu·tion /ˌ···· ··ˈ··/ n [the] a mass movement in China begun by Mao Zedong in 1966 to renew the basic institutions of the country. The Cultural Revolution was marked by violence against educated people.

cul·ture /ˈkʌltʃəʳ/ n **1** [C;U] the customs, beliefs, art, music, and all the other products of human thought made

by a particular group of people at a particular time: *ancient Greek culture* | *a tribal culture* | *pop culture* | *the* **culture gap** (=difference in culture) *between Britain and France* —compare CIVILIZATION; see also SUBCULTURE **2** [U] artistic and other activity of the mind, and the works produced by this: *Paris is a good city for people who are interested in culture.* | *a woman of culture and taste* **3** [U] the practice of raising animals and growing plants: *bee culture* —see also AGRICULTURE, HORTICULTURE **4** [C;U] (a group of bacteria produced by) the growing of bacteria for scientific use

Culture Club /ˈ··· ·/ a British popular music group, known esp. for their lead singer Boy George. One of their most successful records was *Karma Chameleon* in 1983.

cul·tured /ˈkʌltʃəd‖-ərd/ *adj* **1** having or showing good education, manners, and esp. an interest in art, music, literature, etc.: *cultured minds that like good books and paintings* —opposite uncultured **2** caused to grow by artificial means: *a cultured virus* | *cultured pearls*

culture shock /ˈ··· ·/ n [U] the feeling of shock or of being disorientated (DISORIENTATE) which someone has when they experience a different and unfamiliar culture

culture vul·ture /ˈ·· ˌ·/ n *humor, sometimes derog* a person who is very interested in CULTURE (2) and knows a lot about it, although perhaps they do not make much effort to make judgments about it: *She moved to London, where she suddenly turned into a real culture vulture.*

cul·vert /ˈkʌlvət‖-ərt/ n a pipe for waste water that passes under a road, railway line, etc.

cum /kʊm, kʌm/ *prep* (used when one thing, place, event, etc., has two purposes or natures) combined with; together with: *a kitchen-cum-bathroom* (=both in one room) | *a lunch-cum-business meeting* —see also CUM LAUDE

cum·ber /ˈkʌmbəʳ/ v [T (with)] *rare* to ENCUMBER

cum·ber·some /ˈkʌmbəsəm‖-bər-/ also **cum·brous** /-brəs/ *rare*— *adj* heavy and awkward to carry, wear, etc.: *a cumbersome parcel/uniform* | (fig.) *the firm's cumbersome salary system*

Cum·bri·a /ˈkʌmbriə/ a COUNTY of NW England (since 1974), made up mostly of the old counties of **Cumberland** and **Westmorland**. It contains the beautiful Lake District National Park. —**brian** *adj*

cum·in /ˈkʌmɪn/ n [U] a plant whose pleasant-smelling seeds are used in cooking and medicine

cum lau·de /kʌm ˈlɔːdi, kʊm-, -ˈlaʊdeɪ‖kʊm ˈlaʊdi/ *adj, adv* [F] *Latin* with praise; recognition given by some American universities of special achievement: *She graduated cum laude from Harvard.* —compare HONOURS (2), MAGNA CUM LAUDE, SUMMA CUM LAUDE; see also DEGREE

cum·mer·bund /ˈkʌməbʌnd‖-ər-/ n a broad belt of cloth worn round a man's waist, esp. as part of formal evening dress

Cum·mings /ˈkʌmɪŋz/, **E E** (1894–1962) an American poet who is best remembered for the unusual ways in which he arranged the words and letters in his poems e.g. *Spring is like a perhaps hand*, and *anyone lived in a pretty how town*. He always wrote his name in small letters.

cum·quat /ˈkʌmkwɒt‖-kwɑːt/ n KUMQUAT

cu·mu·la·tive /ˈkjuːmjʊlətɪv‖-leɪtɪv/ also **accumulative**— *adj* increasing steadily in amount or degree by one addition after another: *cumulative interest payable on a debt* | *cumulative damage to the environment* – ~ly *adv*: *Cumulatively, the effects of the drug are disastrous.*

cu·mu·lus /ˈkjuːmjʊləs/ n [U] thick white feathery cloud with a flat base —compare CIRRUS, NIMBUS (1)

Cu·nard /kjuːˈnɑːd‖-ˈnɑːrd/ a company which has operated many famous passenger ships, including the QE2

cu·nei·form /ˈkjuːnɪfɔːm, ˈkjuːni-ˌfɔːm‖kjuːˈnɪəfɔːrm/ *adj, n* [U] (of or written in) the letters used in writing by the peoples of ancient Mesopotamia. From being drawings of objects and being written from top to bottom, they developed into signs for words and SYLLABLES and began to be written from left to right.

cun·ni·lin·gus /ˌkʌnɪˈlɪŋgəs/ n [U] the practice of touching the female sex organs with the lips and tongue in order to give sexual pleasure —compare FELLATIO

cun·ning¹ /ˈkʌnɪŋ/ *adj* **1** clever in deceiving; SLY: *as cunning as a fox* | *a cunning trick/person* **2** *infml rare*, esp.

AmE attractive; CUTE: _a cunning little girl_ **3** _old use_ skilful: _cunning hands_ – –**ly** _adv_

cunning² _n_ [U] **1** cleverness in deceiving; GUILE: _She showed considerable cunning in the way she avoided answering the question._ **2** _old use_ skill

cunt /kʌnt/ _n taboo_ **1** VAGINA **2** _sl, esp. BrE_ a very unpleasant or stupid person

cup¹ /kʌp/ _n_ **1** [C] a small round container, usu. with a handle, from which liquids are drunk, esp. hot liquids such as tea or coffee: _a cup and saucer_ | _a chipped cup_ – compare MUG¹ (1) **2** [C] also **cup·ful** /-fʊl/– **a** the amount a cup will hold: _Would you like a cup of coffee?_ | _two cupfuls of sugar_ **b** an exact measure of quantity used in cooking, equal to 0.3 British pints (0.5 American pints) or 0.28 litres **3** [C] something shaped like a cup: _the cup of a flower_ | _bra cups_ **4** [C] (a specially shaped usu. silver container given as a prize in) a competition, esp. in sport: _We won the cup for the first time this year._| _She's been picked to play in the Wightman Cup._ **5** [C;U] a mixed alcoholic drink: _cider cup_ **6** _AmE for_ HOLE¹ (5) – see picture at GOLF **7 in one's cups** _old-fash euph_ drunk **8 my cup runneth over** _phrase from the Bible_ I am extremely happy and contented **9 one's cup of tea** the sort of thing one likes: _Jazz isn't really my cup of tea – I prefer disco music._

cup² _v_ **-pp-** [T] to form (the hands) into the shape of a cup: _He cupped his hands and I poured some water into them._| _She cupped her hands round the mug of hot coffee._

Cup [_the_] _infml for_ FA CUP

cup·bear·er /ˈkʌpˌbeərəʳ/ _n_ an official in a royal or noble court who serves wine on special occasions

cup·board /ˈkʌbəd‖-ərd/ _n_ a piece of furniture with doors, or a set of shelves with doors, where clothes, plates, food, etc., can be stored: _The sugar's in the cupboard._ | _Put your shirts in the airing cupboard._ –compare CABINET, CLOSET; see picture at KITCHEN

cupboard love /ˈ·· ·/ _n_ [U] love shown only for the purpose of gaining a reward, e.g. by a pet hoping for food

cup cake /ˈ· ·/ _n_ a small round cake baked in a cup-shaped container

cup fi·nal /ˈ· ˌ··/ _n BrE_ (esp. in football) the last match to decide the winning team in a competition –compare CUP TIE

Cup Final [_the_] (in Britain) the final of the FA Cup, played every year at Wembley

Cu·pid /ˈkjuːpɪd/ _n_ **1** the Roman god of sexual love, i.e. love between a man and a woman, represented in art as a beautiful winged boy carrying a BOW³ and ARROWS. It was said that when one of his arrows hit a person, that person would immediately fall in love with someone: _After years apart, Joan and Malcolm were reunited – by their Cupid daughter, Linda._ | _She had planned to use Mr Parnell to further her husband's career, but Cupid's dart struck._ **2 play Cupid (to someone)** to arrange for two people to fall in love: _The US Navy is playing Cupid to dolphins, encouraging them to mate._

cu·pid·i·ty /kjuːˈpɪdɪti/ _n_ [U] _fml derog_ very great desire, esp. for money and property; GREED

cu·po·la /ˈkjuːpələ/ _n_ a small DOME on top of a building

cup·pa /ˈkʌpə/ _n_ [usu. sing.] _BrE infml_ a cup of tea: _I'm dying for a cuppa._

cu·pric /ˈkjuːprɪk/ _adj tech_ containing copper

cup tie /ˈ· ·/ _n BrE_ (esp. in football) a match between two teams competing in a competition –compare CUP FINAL

cur /kɜːʳ/ _n old use or humor_ **1** a fierce dog, esp. a MONGREL **2** a worthless unpleasant person

cu·ra·ble /ˈkjʊərəbəl/ _adj_ (of a disease) that can be cured – opposite **incurable** —**bly** _adv_

cu·ra·çao /ˈkjʊərəsəʊ, ˌkjʊərəˈsəʊ/ _n_ [U] a strong thick sweet alcoholic drink, tasting of oranges, usu. drunk from a small glass after a meal

cu·rate /ˈkjʊərɪt/ _n_ a priest of the lowest rank, appointed to help the priest of a PARISH

curate's egg /ˌ·· ˈ·/ _n_ [S] _BrE_ something that has both good and bad parts: _The play was rather like the curate's egg, and the good parts of it were excellent._

cu·ra·tive /ˈkjʊərətɪv/ _n, adj_ (something) that cures an illness: _the curative powers of a new drug/the town's special water_

cu·ra·tor /kjʊˈreɪtəʳ/ _n_ the person in charge of a MUSEUM, library, etc. – –**ship** _n_

curb¹ /kɜːb‖kɜːrb/ _n_ **1** a controlling influence; CHECK: _Keep a curb on your temper._ **2** _AmE for_ KERB –see picture at HOUSE **3** a length of chain or leather passing under a horse's jaw and fastened to the BIT²

curb² _v_ [T] to control (something undesirable, such as strong feelings, wasteful spending, etc.); RESTRAIN: _to curb one's extravagance/enthusiasm_ | _new efforts to curb drug trafficking_

curd /kɜːd‖kɜːrd/ also **curds** _pl._ – _n_ [U] the thick soft almost solid substance that separates from milk when it becomes sour, eaten as food or used for making cheese – compare WHEY; see also LEMON CURD

curd cheese /ˌ· ˈ· ‖ ˈ· ·/ _n_ [U] a smooth sharp-tasting soft cheese made from the curds of milk

cur·dle /ˈkɜːdl‖ˈkɜːrdl/ _v_ [I;T] to (cause to) form into curd; (cause to) thicken: (fig.) _Their screams_ **made my blood curdle** _with terror._ –see also BLOODCURDLING

cure¹ /kjʊəʳ/ _v_ [T] **1** [(of)] to bring health to (a person) in place of disease or illness: _When I left hospital I was completely cured._ | _This medicine will cure you of your cough._ | (fig.) _A spell in the army will cure him of his laziness!_ –compare TREAT¹ (4) **2** to make (a disease, illness, etc.) go completely away, esp. by medical treatment: _The only way to cure backache is to rest._ | (fig.) _government action to cure unemployment_ –compare HEAL; see TREAT (USAGE) **3** to preserve (food, skin, tobacco, etc.) by drying it, hanging it in smoke, covering it with salt, etc.: _The tobacco leaves are cured in wood-smoke._

cure² _n_ **1** [(for)] a medicine that cures an illness, disease, etc.: _There is still no cure for the common cold._ | (fig.) _a cure for inflation/unemployment_ **2** a return to health after illness: _The new treatment effected a miraculous cure._ **3** a course of medical treatment: _to take the cure for alcoholism_ –see also REST CURE

cu·ré /ˈkjʊəreɪ‖kjʊˈreɪ/ _n_ a PARISH priest in France

cure-all /ˈ· ·/ _n_ something that can cure any illness, deal with any problem, etc.; PANACEA

cu·ret·tage /kjʊəˈretɪdʒ‖ˌkjʊərəˈtɑːʒ/ _n_ [U] the removal of diseased flesh and skin from the body (e.g. from inside the WOMB) with a special medical instrument (**curette**)

cur·few /ˈkɜːfjuː‖ˈkɜːr-/ _n_ **1** [C] a rule that all people should remain indoors at stated times: _to impose a curfew_ | _a curfew from midnight to 8 o'clock in the morning_ **2** [U] the time during which people must be indoors according to this rule: _We mustn't go out during curfew._

cu·ri·a /ˈkjʊəriə/ _n_ **-iae** /i-iː/ [_the_] (_often cap._) the POPE and the officials helping him in the government of the Roman Catholic Church

Cu·rie /ˈkjʊəri/, **Ma·rie** /ˈmɑːri‖məˈriː/ (1867–1934) a famous French PHYSICIST, born in Poland, who with her husband Pierre discovered POLONIUM and RADIUM, and added to what was known about RADIOACTIVITY

cu·ri·o /ˈkjʊəriəʊ/ _n_ **-ios** a usu. small object, valuable because of its age, rarity, or beauty

cu·ri·os·i·ty /ˌkjʊəriˈɒsəti‖-ˈɑːs-/ _n_ **1** [S;U] the desire to know or learn: _There was (an) intense curiosity about their wedding plans._ [+to-v] _We were_ **burning with curiosity** _to know what had happened._ **2** [C] a strange or rare object, custom, etc.: _This old map is quite a curiosity._ **3 curiosity killed the cat** _saying_ (a phrase used to someone to tell them not to be so INQUISITIVE)

cu·ri·ous /ˈkjʊəriəs/ _adj_ **1** [(as to, about)] eager to know or learn, esp. about something unfamiliar or mysterious; INQUISITIVE: _I'm curious about/as to what happened._ | _The tourists were surrounded by curious children._ [+to-v] _We were curious to know where she'd gone._ –opposite **incurious 2** odd or unusual, esp. in a way that is hard to explain: _a curious noise/state of affairs_ | _It's curious that she left without saying goodbye._ **3 curiouser and curiouser** _quote_ a phrase from _Alice's Adventures in Wonderland_ by Lewis Carroll, used by Alice when she suddenly grew very tall. People remember it because we would usu. say that something was _even more curious_, not _curiouser_, and so it is often used humorously –see also ALICE IN WONDERLAND – –**ly** _adv_ : _She watched curiously as I opened the box._ | _Curiously (enough), we had met before._

curl¹ /kɜːl‖kɜːrl/ _n_ **1** a small hanging mass of hair in a curving shape. Curls are often noticed and remarked on by people in Britain and the US, and many people curl their hair artificially, e.g. using curlers or CURLING TONGS, or by having a PERM¹: *a little boy with beautiful blonde curls* —compare WAVE² (5); see also CURLY **2** something with the shape of a curl: *A curl of smoke rose from her cigarette.* | (fig.) *a curl of the lip* (=showing SCORN)

curl² *v* [I;T (UP)] **1** to twist into or form a curl or curls: *I don't like my hair straight so I'm going to have it curled.*| *The dying leaves became brown and curled up.* | *Smoke curled* (=moved in a SPIRAL) *out of the chimney.* **2** to (cause to) go in a winding direction: *The climbing plant curled round the trunk of the tree.*
　curl up *phr v* [I] to lie comfortably with the arms and legs drawn close to the body: *She curled up in front of the fire with a book.*

curl·er /ˈkɜːᵊr|ˈkɜːr-/ *n* [*often pl.*] an object around which hair is twisted to make it curl. In old books and films, women are often shown wearing their curlers at bedtime or in the early morning, and not wanting anyone, esp. a man they do not know, to see them like this. In Britain curlers are thought of as being worn mostly by WORKING-CLASS women, and women shown in curlers are often smoking a cigarette and in a rather untidy home environment. —see picture at ROLL

cur·lew /ˈkɜːlju:|ˈkɜːrlu:/ *n* a long-legged brownish water bird with a long curved beak

cur·li·cue , **curlycue** /ˈkɜːlɪkju:|ˈkɜːr-/ *n* a decorative twisted pattern, such as one made with a pen

curl·ing /ˈkɜːlɪŋ|ˈkɜːr-/ *n* [U] a Scottish and Canadian winter sport played by sliding flat heavy stones (**curling stones**) over ice towards a mark called the **tee**

curling tongs /ˈ·· ͵·/ also **curling i·ron(s)** /ˈ·· ͵··/ *n* [*pl.*] a piece of electrical equipment which is heated and has a handle joined to a metal rod (around which the hair is wound) and another long piece of metal to keep the hair in place until a curl is formed

curl·y /ˈkɜːli|ˈkɜːrli/ *adj* having curls or tending to curl: *curly hair* —**iness** *n* [U]

cur·mud·geon /kɜːˈmʌdʒən|ˈkɜːr-/ *n old use or humor* a bad-tempered old person — ~ **ly** *adj*

cur·rant /ˈkʌrənt|ˈkɜːr-/ *n* **1** a small dried seedless GRAPE, esp. used in baking cakes: *currant buns* **2** (*esp. in comb.*) the small black, red, or white juicy fruit that grows in bunches on certain bushes: *a redcurrant* | *a blackcurrant*

cur·ren·cy /ˈkʌrənsi|ˈkɜːr-/ *n* **1** [C;U] the particular type of money in use in a country: *the different currencies of Europe* | *the proposed single European currency* | *The British teachers in China were paid in local currency.* (=in the money of China) | *currency dealers* —see also HARD CURRENCY, SINGLE CURRENCY **2** [U] *fml* the state of being generally believed or accepted: *Reports about the president's illness are gaining currency among foreign journalists.*

cur·rent¹ /ˈkʌrənt|ˈkɜːr-/ *adj* **1** belonging to the present time; of the present day: *They are expecting profits of over $2 million in the current year.* | *the current issue of "The New Yorker"* | *This word is no longer in current use.* —see NEW (USAGE) **2** *tech* (of money) officially acceptable as currency: — ~ **ly** *adv* : *The rate of inflation currently stands at 7%.*

current² *n* **1** [C] a continuously moving mass of liquid or gas, esp. one flowing through slower-moving liquid or gas: *The current is strongest in the middle of the river.* | *currents of hot air* | (fig.) *the current of public opinion* **2** [C;U] the flow of electricity past a fixed point: *This button switches the current on.* —see also ALTERNATING CURRENT, DIRECT CURRENT

current ac·count /ˈ·· ͵·͵·/ *BrE* ||**checking account** *AmE*— *n* a bank account from which usu. earns little or no interest and from which money can be taken out at any time by cheque —compare DEPOSIT ACCOUNT

current af·fairs /͵·· ·ˈ·/ also **current events** *n* [*pl.*] important things that are happening in the world at the present time —**current affairs** *adj* : *a current affairs programme/class*

current as·sets /͵·· ˈ··/ *n* [P] ASSETS such as STOCK, money in the form of coins or notes, and debts owed, which change quickly in the course of day-to-day business

current li·a·bil·i·ties /͵·· ··ˈ···/ *n* [P] money which is owed to a business and is expected to be paid within 12 months

cur·ric·u·lum /kəˈrɪkjŭləm/ *n* **-la** /lə/ *or* **-lums** a course of study offered in a school, college, etc.: *Has computer studies been introduced into the school curriculum?* —compare SYLLABUS, TIMETABLE¹ (2)

curriculum vi·tae /kə͵rɪkjŭləm ˈviːtaɪ/ *n* **curriculum vitaes** *or* **curricula vitae** /-kjŭlə-/ [*usu. sing.*] *fml* a short written account of a person's education and past employment; CV —see also JOB (CULTURAL NOTE)

Cur·rie /ˈkʌri|ˈkɜː-/**, Ed·wi·na** /edˈwiːnə/ (1946–) a British Conservative politician and former minister for health. In December 1988 she made a speech in which she claimed that most British eggs were infected by SALMONELLA. There was much protest about her speech, and she resigned from her job as junior Health Minister later in the month.

Cur·ri·er and Ives /͵kʌriər ənd ˈaɪvz|͵kɜː-/ *adj* typical of a style of American art, named after the two men who invented it. It shows scenes from daily life in 19th century America.

cur·ry¹ /ˈkʌri|ˈkɜːri/ *n* [C;U] a type of food from India and other parts of S Asia, consisting of meat, vegetables, etc., cooked in a thick often hot-tasting liquid and usu. eaten with rice or special bread: *I like hot curries.* | *a (plate of) chicken curry with rice*
　▶CULTURAL NOTE British people often make jokes about curry upsetting your stomach so that you keep going to the toilet. ◀

curry² *v* [T *usu. pass.*] to make (meat, vegetables, etc.) into a curry: *curried chicken* | *curried eggs*

curry³ *v* [T] **1** to rub and clean (a horse) with a special comb (**currycomb**) **2 curry favour** to try to win attention by insincere means: *to curry favour with one's teacher*

curry pow·der /ˈ·· ͵··/ *n* [U] a mixture of hot SPICES (=strong-tasting dried vegetable parts) crushed into a fine powder, used in cooking

curse¹ /kɜːs|kɜːrs/ *v* **1** [T] to express a wish that great misfortune will happen to (someone), esp. by calling on magical powers: *The witchdoctor cursed me, and my children and grandchildren too.* | *She cursed him for ruining her life.* —opposite **bless 2** [I;T] to swear (at): *She cursed the car when it refused to start.* **3 be cursed with** to suffer misfortune or great harm because of: *She was cursed with a stammer all her life.*

curse² *n* **1** [C (**on**)] a word or sentence asking God, heaven, etc., to make something evil or harmful happen to someone or something. In Western countries people do not generally believe that curses can work: *an ancient and powerful curse* | *Our tribe is under a curse.* | *The witch doctor put a curse on him.* | *to utter a curse* **2** [C (**to**)] a cause of trouble, harm, etc.: *Foxes can be a curse to farmers.* **3** [C] a word or words used in swearing; word or words expressing anger, hate, etc.: *She gave a couple of curses and then got up again.* **4** [the] *euph sl* (a time of) menstruating (MENSTRUATE): *She's got the curse.*

curs·ed /ˈkɜːsɪd|ˈkɜːr-/ also **curst** /kɜːst|kɜːrst/— *adj* [A] *old-fash infml* hateful; annoying: *I wish that cursed dog would be quiet.* — ~ **ly** *adv*

cur·sive /ˈkɜːsɪv|ˈkɜːr-/ *adj* (of writing) written in a flowing rounded style with the letters joined together; in the style of handwriting rather than printing — ~ **ly** *adv*

cur·sor /ˈkɜːsəʳ|ˈkɜːr-/ *n* a mark or a small light which can be moved around a SCREEN¹ (4) connected to a computer, in order to do operations at a particular position

cur·so·ry /ˈkɜːsəri|ˈkɜːr-/ *adj* (of work, reading, etc.) quick and not thorough; done without attention to details: *Even a cursory glance at the report showed that it was full of mistakes.* —**rily** *adv*

curt /kɜːt|kɜːrt/ *adj* (of a person, his/her manner, etc.) saying too little to be polite; BLUNT¹ (2): *a curt reply/manner* — ~ **ly** *adv* — ~ **ness** *n* [U]

cur·tail /kɜːˈteɪl|kɜːr-/ *v* [T] *fml* to reduce in degree or effect; limit: *Owing to the war, the government's public health programme had to be severely curtailed.* — ~ **ment** *n* [C;U]

cur·tain¹ /ˈkɜːtn|ˈkɜːrtn/ *n* **1** a piece of hanging cloth that can be pulled across to cover a window or door, to divide a room, etc.: *velvet curtains* | *It's getting dark — I'd better* **draw the curtains.** (=pull them across the window) | (fig.) *The castle was hidden behind a thick curtain of smoke.* —see picture at LIVING ROOM **2** a sheet of heavy material that can be lowered across the front of a stage in a theatre: *As the curtain rises, a dead body is seen on the stage.* **3 curtain up** (the time of) the raising of the curtain in the theatre —see also CURTAINS, DRAPES, IRON CURTAIN, SAFETY CURTAIN —see picture at THEATRE

curtain² *v* [T] to provide with a curtain

   curtain sthg. ↔ **off** *phr v* [T] to separate or divide off with a curtain: *One of the beds in the hospital ward was curtained off.*

curtain call /'·· ·/ *n* the appearance of actors at the end of a performance for APPLAUSE: *She took seven curtain calls.*

curtain hook /'·· ·/ *n* a small plastic or metal hook which is joined to the back of the top of a curtain and also to a curtain ring: *There are twenty rings and only fourteen curtain hooks.*

curtain rail /'·· ·/ *n* a length of plastic or metal placed at the top of a window, from which curtains hang and along which they may be pulled: *The sooner the curtain rail goes up the sooner we can have a bit of privacy.*

curtain rais·er /'·· ‚··/ *n* a short play acted before the main play: (fig.) *This project is a curtain raiser for a much bigger programme of research.*

curtain ring /'·· ·/ *n* a plastic, metal or wooden ring which connects with a curtain hook and moves along the curtain rail or rod: *I want some plastic curtain rings for the shower curtain.*

curtain rod /'·· ·/ *n* a rod placed at the top of a window or door bearing rings which can move freely along its length and from which a curtain hangs

cur·tains /'kɜːtnz‖'kɜːr-/ *n* [P] *sl* the end, esp. of a person's life: *If your work doesn't improve it will be curtains for you.* (=you'll be dismissed)

curt·sy, -sey /'kɜːtsi‖'kɜːr-/ *n* a woman's act of respect to a person of higher rank, esp. to a member of a royal family, done by bending the knees and lowering the head and shoulders —compare BOW² (1) —**curtsy** *v* [I]

cur·va·ceous , -cious /kɜː'veɪʃəs‖kɜːr-/ *adj infml, often humor* (of a woman) having a pleasingly well developed figure, with attractive curves — ~**ly** *adv*

cur·va·ture /'kɜːvətʃər‖'kɜːr-/ *n* [C;U] **1** the state of being curved or the degree to which something is curved: *the curvature of the Earth's surface* **2** *med* (an) unnatural curving of a body part, usu. causing pain or illness: *curvature of the spine*

curve¹ /kɜːv‖kɜːrv/ *n* **1** a line of which no part is straight and which contains no angles; a rounded bend: *a curve in the road|the river* **2** also **curve ball** /'· ·/ *—* (in BASEBALL) a throw in which the ball spins so that it curves unexpectedly and is difficult to hit: (fig.) *The reporter* **threw** *the politician* **a curve** *by asking him an unexpected question.*

curve² *v* [I;T] to (cause to) bend in the shape of a curve: *The road curved to the right.*

Cush·ing /'kʊʃɪŋ/, **Peter** (1913–) an English actor known esp. for acting in HORROR FILMS (=films that frighten) and for playing the part of Sherlock Holmes in the film *The Hound of the Baskervilles.*

cush·ion¹ /'kʊʃən/ *n* **1** a bag filled with a soft substance on which a person can lie, sit, or rest comfortably: *He lay on the sofa with a cushion under his head.* —compare PILLOW¹ (1); see picture at LIVING ROOM **2** something like this in shape or purpose: *Hovercrafts ride on a cushion of air.* **3** the soft rubber border on the inside edge of a table used in the game of BILLIARDS

cushion² *v* [T] **1** to reduce the force or (unpleasant) effects of: *Nothing can cushion the shock of the tragedy.* | *The training programme helps to cushion the effects of unemployment.* **2** [(against)] to protect from hardship or sudden change: *He was cushioned against inflation by his government pension.* **3** [*usu. pass.*] to provide with cushions: *a cushioned seat*

cush·y /'kʊʃi/ *adj infml* **1** (of a job, style of life, etc.) needing little effort; easy, esp. in a way that makes other people jealous **2 a cushy number** an easy job: *You've landed yourself a cushy little number here, Tom!* —**iness** *n* [U]

cusp /kʌsp/ *n tech* **1** the point formed by two curves meeting: *the cusp of the moon in its first quarter* **2** the time represented by the end of one sign of the ZODIAC and the beginning of the next: *I was born* **on the cusp** *(of Capricorn and Aquarius).*

cus·pi·dor /'kʌsp‚dɔːr/ *n AmE for* SPITTOON

cuss¹ /kʌs/ *n sl* **1** a curse **2** a person of the stated, usu. unpleasant kind: *an irritable old cuss*

cuss² *v* [I;T] *sl* to curse

cuss box /'· ·/ *n AmE* SWEAR BOX

cuss·ed /'kʌs‚d/ *adj sl* **1** too unwilling to change one's opinions, actions, etc., even when they are clearly mistaken; OBSTINATE **2** *rare* hateful or annoying; CURSED — ~**ly** *adv* — ~**ness** *n* [U]

cus·tard /'kʌstəd‖-ərd/ *n* **1** [U] *esp. BrE* a yellow liquid for pouring over sweet foods, made of sweetened milk thickened with eggs and flour, or made with a dry mixture of these sold as **custard powder**: *apple pie and hot custard* **2** [C;U] a soft usu. baked mixture of sweetened milk and eggs: *a caramel custard*

custard cream /‚·· '·/ *n BrE* a sweet BISCUIT filled with a mixture tasting of custard

custard pie /‚·· '·/ *n* a flat pastry case that contains custard, or something intended to look like custard, that is thrown at someone. The throwing of custard pies at people is typical of SLAPSTICK humour, both on stage and in films, and many people consider it to be funny.

Cus·ter /'kʌstər/, **General George Armstrong** (1839–76) a US Army officer who first became famous in the American Civil War. He was later killed, with all the men under his command, by Sioux Native Americans, led by Crazy Horse and Sitting Bull, at the Little Bighorn River in Montana in a battle known as **Custer's Last Stand**.

cus·to·di·al /kʌ'stəʊdiəl/ *adj* of or connected with custody, esp. of criminals: *The offender was too young to be given a custodial sentence.* (=a period in prison)

cus·to·di·an /kʌ'stəʊdiən/ *n* **1** a person in charge of a public building; keeper of a library, castle, etc. This word is often the official title for such a person: *the custodian of the royal library* **2** *fml* a person with custody over someone or something: (fig.) *politicians who set themselves up as custodians of public morality* — ~**ship** *n* [U]

cus·to·dy /'kʌstədi/ *n* [U] **1** [(of)] the act or right of looking after someone and making decisions about their education, medical treatment, etc., esp. when this right is given in a court of law: *After his divorce, the father was* **awarded/granted** (=given) **custody** *of the children.* | *a terrible custody battle between the two parents* **2** [(in, into)] the state of being guarded, esp. by the police: *The man has now been taken into custody.* (=he is being kept in a police prison before going in front of a judge) | *She was* **held in** *police* **custody** *for six hours.* —see also PROTECTIVE CUSTODY

cus·tom /'kʌstəm/ *n* **1** [C;U] (an) established and habitual practice, esp. of a religious or social kind, that is typical of a particular group of people: *a tribal custom hundreds of years old* | *Social customs vary greatly from country to country.* **2** [C] the habitual practice of a person: *It was his custom to get up early and have a cold bath.* —see HABIT (USAGE) **3** [U] *BrE* ‖ **patronage** *AmE* regular support given to a shop by those who buy its goods or services: *We lost a lot of custom when the new supermarket opened.* —see also CUSTOMS

custom and prac·tice /‚·· · '··/ *n* [U] (in law) an established practice which by long continuance has earned the force of a law or right esp. the established practice of a particular profession, society, area etc.

cus·tom·a·ry /'kʌstəməri‖-meri/ *adj fml* established by custom; usual or habitual: *It is customary to wear formal clothes on these occasions.* | *"I hate it," he said, with his customary candour.* — -**rily** /mər‚li‖‚kʌstə'mer‚li/ *adv*

custom-built /‚·· '·◂/ *adj* (of a car, machine, etc.) made especially for one person or group of people

cus·tom·er /'kʌstəmər/ *n* **1** a person or organization that buys goods or services from a shop, business, etc., esp. regularly: *The new shop across the road has taken away most of my customers.* | *This company is one of the Post Office's biggest customers.* | *The new sugar-free drinks were produced in response to customer demand.* | *a valued*

customer —compare PATRON **2** *sl* a person of the stated kind: *an odd customer* | *She's rather a tricky customer to do business with.* **3 the customer is always right** one should always show respect to the customers, even if they are being very unreasonable or unpleasant; a phrase that is believed to be used by people who work in shops

▷ USAGE When people go out to buy things in shops, they are **shoppers:** *a busy street full of* **shoppers.** When people buy things from a particular shop, they are that shop's **customers:** *Mrs Low can't come to the telephone — she's serving a* **customer.** If you are paying for professional services, e.g. from a lawyer or a bank, you are a **client**, but in the case of medical services you are a **patient.** If you are staying in a hotel, you are a **guest.** If you are using transportation services you are a **passenger**, though increasingly **customer** is also used in this sense.◁

cus·tom·ize also **-ise** *BrE* /ˈkʌstəmaɪz/ *v* [T] to make, build, or change especially for one person

custom-made /ˌ·· ˈ·◂/ *adj* (of an article of clothing, pair of shoes, etc.) made specially for one person or group of people

cus·toms /ˈkʌstəmz/ *n* [P] **1** (*often cap.*) a place where travellers' belongings can be searched when leaving or entering a country, esp. to see if they are trying to SMUGGLE anything into the country: *As soon as I'd got through customs I jumped into a taxi.* | *When you go through Customs, go straight through the 'Nothing to declare' channel, the green one.* **2** taxes paid on goods entering or leaving a country: *Have you paid* **customs duty** *on this camera?* **3** (*often cap.*) the government organization established to collect these taxes —compare EXCISE[1]

customs and ex·cise /ˌ··· · ˈ··/ *n* (*often caps.*) the part of the British taxation system which collects INDIRECT taxes; these are CUSTOMS (2), EXCISE, and VAT. Direct taxes (taxes on people's income) are collected by the Inland Revenue.

customs of·fic·er /ˈ·· ˌ···/ also **customs of·fi·cial** /ˈ·· ·ˌ··/— *n* a government official whose job it is to make sure that customs duties are paid on goods entering a country, and that illegal goods are not brought into the country. In films, books, etc., customs officers usually ask "Have you anything to declare?": *A customs officer checked our luggage at the port.* | *Customs officers seized a quarter of a million pounds' worth of heroin.*

cut[1] /kʌt/ *v* **cut,** *present participle* **cutting** to do something using a sharp edge or instrument **1** [I;T] to make a narrow opening in (something) with a sharp edge or instrument, accidentally or on purpose: *Be careful not to cut your fingers on the broken glass.* | *I cut myself/my face when I was shaving.* | *We had to cut through the car door to free the trapped man.* **2** [T+obj+adv/prep] to remove from the main part of something with a sharp instrument: *I cut the picture out of the newspaper.* | *Cut the rind off the cheese.* | *The surgeon cut away the diseased tissue from the patient's lungs.* | (fig.) *Some scenes have been cut from the film.* **3** [T (UP)] to divide or separate with a sharp edge or instrument: *The boys cut the cake in two and ate half each.* **4** [T] to make by using a sharp instrument: *to cut a hole in a piece of cloth* | *We cut our way through the forest.* | *I cut myself free/loose with my axe.* **5** [I+adv] to be able to be separated, divided, or marked with a sharp instrument: *A freshly baked loaf doesn't cut easily.* —see BREAK (USAGE) to make something smaller or shorter **6** [T] to shorten with a sharp instrument **a** in order to improve the appearance: *to cut the grass/one's fingernails* | *I'm having my hair cut tomorrow.* (=someone will cut it for me) **b** before gathering a crop: *to cut the corn* **7** [T] to make less in size, amount, value, etc.; reduce: *The company has cut the workforce by half.* (=reduced the number of workers to half its former level) | *The new machinery was introduced in an effort to cut labour costs.* | *Your speech is too long — it needs cutting.* **8** [T] to put (a film or recording) into completed form by rearranging it, removing unwanted parts, etc.; EDIT to stop or interrupt something **9** [T (OFF)] to interrupt a supply of gas, electricity, etc.): *The electricity was cut (off) for two hours yesterday.* **10** [I] to stop photographing a scene when making a film: *"Cut!" shouted the director.* other meanings **11** [T] to grow (a tooth): *Our baby's just cutting her first teeth so she cries a lot.* **12** [T] to hurt the feelings of, esp. by saying something nasty: *His joke cut me deeply.* | *a cutting remark* **13** [T] *infml*

to be intentionally absent from (a class, school, etc.): *to cut a lecture* **14** [I;T] to divide (a pile of playing cards) in two before starting to play **15** [T] to cross: *The line AC is cut by line PQ at point Z.* | *A path had been worn in the grass where people had* **cut the corner.** (=gone across instead of round the edge) **16** [T] (in some sports, such as GOLF or cricket) to make (a ball) spin by hitting it with a downward movement **17** [T] *infml* to make (a RECORD[2] (5)): *They cut their first single in 1992.* fixed phrases **18** [I (**with**)] to DILUTE; weaken the purity of: *The heroin was cut with powdered milk.* **19 cut a figure** *old-fash* to be impressive because of one's appearance: *Sir Giles cut quite a figure* (=looked very fine) *at the ball last night.* **20 cut and run** *sl, rather old-fash* to escape by running **21 cut a swath through** to destroy the main part of: *The storm cut a swath through the town.* **22 cut both/two ways** (of an action) to have disadvantages as well as advantages for both people or both sides **23 cut corners** to do something in a less than perfect way in order to save time, money, etc. **24 cut it fine** to leave oneself very little time, money, etc., to do what is needed **25 cut no ice/not much ice (with)** to have little or no effect or influence (on someone), esp. to fail to impress (someone): *Your empty promises won't cut any ice with her.* **26 cut one's coat according to one's cloth** *BrE* to avoid spending more than one earns **27 cut one's losses** to stop taking part in a failing business, firm, etc., before one loses too much money **28 cut one's teeth on/in (something)** to gain one's first experience from doing (something) **29 cut someone (dead)** to refuse to recognize someone one knows, in order to be rude: *I saw Jane in town today but she cut me dead.* **30 cut someone some slack** to give someone a little freedom to do as they wish **31 cut something short** to bring something to an end suddenly and before the proper time: *The accident forced them to cut their holiday short/to cut short their holiday.* | *Well,* **to cut a long story short** (=without telling you all the details), *we finally reached London at four in the morning.* **32 cut the ground from under/beneath someone's feet** to destroy someone's chances of success by taking their ideas or acting before them: *They cut the ground from under my feet by printing a story on the same subject the week before mine.* **33 cut up rough** *BrE infml* to become (violently) angry: *When the policewoman stopped the car, its driver cut up rough and tried to hit her.* phrasal verbs

cut across sthg. *phr v* [T] **1** to take a shorter way across (a field, corner, etc.) **2** to go beyond or across the limits of: *a new political grouping that cuts across party lines*

cut back *phr v* **1** [T] (**cut** sthg. ↔ **back**) to cut (a plant) close to the stem; PRUNE[2] (2) **2** [I (**on**);T (=**cut** sthg. ↔ **back**)] to reduce (an amount spent, produced, etc.): *We oppose any plans to cut back (on) the education budget.* —see also CUTBACK

cut down *phr v* **1** [T] (**cut** sthg. ↔ **down**) to bring down by cutting: *to cut down a tree* **2** [T] (**cut** sbdy. ↔ **down**) to knock down, wound, or kill (someone), esp. in a cruel and unjust way: *Several soldiers were cut down by the machine-gun fire.* | *He was cut down in his* **prime.** (=killed at the best time of life) **3** [I (**on**);T (=**cut** sthg. ↔ **down**)] to reduce (an amount done, eaten, etc.): *I haven't given up drinking but I'm cutting down.* | *The doctor told me to cut down (on) smoking.* **4** [T] (**cut** sthg. ↔ **down**) to reduce the length of (a piece of clothing): *If you cut down these trousers they'll fit your daughter.* **5 cut someone down to size** *infml* to show someone to be less good or important than they think they are

cut in *phr v infml* **1** [I (**on**)] to interrupt someone who is talking: *I'm sorry to cut in on your conversation, but...* **2** [I (**on**)] to drive into a space between cars in a dangerous way: *You nearly caused a crash by cutting in (on me) like that!* **3** [I (**on**)] (of a machine) to begin to operate when needed: *The temperature rose, and the fridge suddenly cut in.* **4** [I (**on**)] to stop two people dancing in order to replace one of them **5** [T(**cut** sbdy. ↔ **in**)] to include (someone) in a profitable situation: *If you'll work on Sunday I'll cut you in for half the take.*

cut off *phr v* [T] (**cut** sbdy./sthg. ↔ **off**) **1** to separate by cutting; SEVER: *Her little finger was cut off in an accident at the factory.* **2** to disconnect or discontinue: *We were cut off in the middle of our conversation.* (=the telephone was disconnected) | *They had their electricity cut off because they didn't pay the bill.* | *The President decided to cut off foreign aid to these countries.* **3** to block off or surround so that further movement out or in is impossible: *The soldiers were cut off from the main part of the army.* | (fig.) *Mary felt cut off from her friends when she moved.* **4** to take away from (a person) the right to have one's property when one is dead; DISINHERIT: *If you marry that man I'll* **cut you off without a penny!** (=leave you with no money) **5 cut off one's nose to spite one's face** to take action, because one is angry, that results in damage to oneself —see also CUTOFF

cut out *phr v* **1** [T (of)] (**cut** sthg. ↔ **out**) to remove by cutting: *She cut the advertisement out of the newspaper.* **2** [T] (**cut** sthg. ↔ **out**) to make by cutting: *to cut out a dress* **3** [T] (**cut** sthg. ↔ **out**) *infml* to leave out; stop (esp. a harmful activity): *I must cut out cigarettes/going to bed late.* | *I like your article, but would you cut out the reference to the Kennedys?* **4** [I] (of a machine) to stop suddenly: *The engine keeps cutting out when I go up hills.* **5 cut it/that out** *infml* to stop it: *The children were fighting so their mother told them to cut it out or go to bed.* **6 cut out for something/to do something** (usu. in negatives) naturally well suited for something: *I'm just not cut out for city life.* **7 have one's work cut out (for one)** *infml* to have a lot of work to do: *They'll have their work cut out if they want to build the dam in six months.* —see also CUTOUT

cut up *phr v* [T] (=**cut** sbdy./sthg. ↔ **up**) **1** to cut into little pieces: *a machine for cutting up vegetables* **2** [usu. pass.] *infml* to make very sad and upset: *Alice was really cut up when her friend died.* **3** [I] *AmE infml* to misbehave in a way that is wild and difficult to control: *The students started cutting up as soon as the teacher left the room.* —see also CUTUP

cut² *n* **1** the result of cutting; an opening or wound: *a cut in the cloth* | *How did you get that cut on your hand?* **2** a something obtained by cutting, esp. a piece of meat: *cuts of fresh lamb* —see also COLD CUTS **b** esp. *AmE* a CUTTING (3) **3** [(in)] a planned reduction in size, amount, etc.: *Congress is strongly opposed to cuts in military spending/public services.* | *tax cuts* **4** [(of)] *infml* a share: *to take a 50% cut of the profits* **5** the act of cutting (=dividing) a pile of playing cards in two before starting to play **6** the style in which clothes are made or a person's hair is shaped: *the cut of a suit* | *a fashionable cut* **7** a quick sharp stroke in cricket, tennis, etc. **8** material left out of a written or filmed work: *The author/producer agreed to all the cuts we made.* **9** the process or product of editing (EDIT) a film: *The director insisted on overseeing the final cut.* **10 a cut above** *infml* noticeably better than; of higher quality or rank than: *She thinks she's a cut above other people.* **11 the cut of someone's jib** *BrE infml, old-fash* someone's manner or appearance: *I don't like the cut of his jib.* **12 the unkindest cut (of all)** *quote* a slightly changed phrase from Shakespeare's play *Julius Ceasar.* It concerns the knife wound given to Caesar by Brutus, whom Caesar had thought was his friend. This expression is now used, esp. in newspapers, about almost any type of cut. People also often change it to **the kindest cut (of all)**: *The title of the documentary was "Caesarian Birth — The Unkindest Cut?"* —see also SHORT CUT

cut-and-dried /ˌ··· ˈ·◂/ also **cut-and-dry**— *adj* already settled and unlikely to be changed: *a cut-and-dried argument* | *The result of the election is fairly cut-and-dried.* | *There is no cut-and-dried solution to the problem.*

cut and thrust /ˌ··· ˈ·/ *n* [the (of)] *esp. BrE* the methods of arguing or behaving that are typical of any activity that tests skill and ability: *the cut and thrust of parliamentary debate*

cut·a·way¹ /ˈkʌtəweɪ/ *adj* [A] (of a plan, drawing, model, etc.) having or showing parts cut away or absent, to allow the inside to be seen: *Here is a cutaway drawing of a power-generating wind turbine.*

cutaway² *n* a TAILCOAT

cut·back /ˈkʌtbæk/ *n* a planned decrease; reduction to an earlier rate: *more cutbacks in public expenditure* —see also CUT **back**

cute /kjuːt/ *adj* **1** (esp. of something or someone small) attractive in an amusing or interesting way: *What a cute little baby!* | *He's the cutest boy in our school.* **2** *sometimes derog* (too) clever; SHREWD: *Be careful with him — he's a cute operator.* — ~**ly** *adv* — ~**ness** *n* [U]

cut glass /ˌ· ˈ·◂/ *n* [U] glass (esp. bowls or VASES) with

patterns cut on it: *a cut-glass bowl* | *My grandmother collects cut glass.*

cu·ti·cle /ˈkjuːtɪkəl/ *n* an outer covering of hard skin, esp. round the lower edges of the fingernails and toenails — see picture at HAND

cu·tie /ˈkjuːti/ *n AmE infml* a pretty little child, esp. a girl: *Isn't she a cutie!*

cut·lass /ˈkʌtləs/ *n* a short sword with a slightly curved blade, as used formerly in the navy or by a PIRATE —see picture at SWORD

cut·ler /ˈkʌtləʳ/ *n* a person who makes or sells knives, etc.

cut·le·ry /ˈkʌtləri/ also **flatware, silverware** *AmE*— *n* [U] knives, forks, spoons, and other instruments used for eating: *a set of cutlery*

cut·let /ˈkʌtlɪt/ *n* **1** a small piece of meat for one person, cut with a bone connected to it: *lamb cutlets* **2** a flat CROQUETTE: *vegetarian cutlets*

cut·off /ˈkʌtɒf‖-ɔːf/ *n* **1** a fixed limit or stopping point: *The machine will stop when it reaches its cutoff point.* (=when it has worked enough) **2** an apparatus for stopping or controlling the flow of water, gas, etc. in a pipe —see also CUTOFFS, CUT **off**

cut·offs /ˈkʌtɒfs‖-ɔːfs/ *n* [P] *esp. AmE* shorts made by cutting off the legs of JEANS or trousers —see PAIR (USAGE)

cut·out /ˈkʌtaʊt/ *n* **1** something that interrupts or disconnects an electric CIRCUIT when a current that is too heavy is passing through: *a cutout switch/fuse* **2** a figure cut out of wood or paper: *a cardboard cutout of George Bush* —see also CUT **out**

cut-price /ˌ· ˈ·◂/ *adj* [A] **1** also **cut rate**— sold at a price or rate below the standard charge; cheap: *cut-price food/petrol* | *Large industrial users can buy cut-rate electricity.* **2** (of a shop) selling goods at reduced prices: *a cut-price garage*

cut·purse /ˈkʌtpɜːs‖-pɜːrs/ *n old use* a PICKPOCKET

cut·ter /ˈkʌtəʳ/ *n* **1 a** a small fast boat belonging to a larger ship, esp. used for moving supplies or passengers to and from the land **b** a lightly armed government ship used for preventing smuggling (SMUGGLE) **2** (often in comb.) an instrument used for cutting: *a pair of wire-cutters* **3** a worker whose job is cutting cloth, glass, stone, metal, etc.

cut·throat¹ /ˈkʌtθrəʊt/ *adj* very fierce, cruel, or unprincipled: *cutthroat competition in business*

cutthroat² *n* **1** esp. *old use* a murderer; fierce criminal **2** also **cutthroat ra·zor** /ˌ·· ˈ··/— an old-fashioned type of RAZOR with a very sharp open blade

cut·ting¹ /ˈkʌtɪŋ/ *n* **1** a stem, leaf, etc., that is cut from a plant and put in soil or water to form roots and grow into a new plant: *Do you mind if I take a cutting from this plant?* **2** *BrE*‖**clipping** *AmE*— an article, photograph, etc., that is cut out from a newspaper or magazine: *a cutting from an old newspaper* | *a cuttings file/library for use by researchers* **3** also **cut** *AmE*— something produced by cutting, esp. a passage cut through a hill for a road or railway

cutting² *adj* bitter or severe; causing pain: *a cutting east wind* (=strong and cold) | *a cutting remark* (=unpleasant and unkind) — ~**ly** *adv*

cutting edge /ˌ·· ˈ·/ *n* [S;U] **1** the quality of sharp directness, esp. in speaking or writing **2** the most advanced position, where important action is taken: *This new model is at the cutting edge of computer technology.*

cutting room /ˈ·· ·/ *n* **1** a room where a film is cut and the final form prepared **2 on the cutting room floor** *infml* useless, worthless, unwanted: *I suppose I'll be on the cutting room floor when they announce the redundancies.*

cut·tle·fish /ˈkʌtl̩fɪʃ/ *n* **cuttlefish** a sea animal like a SQUID with a hard body and ten arms (TENTACLEs) that puts out a black inky liquid when attacked

Cut·ty Sark /ˌkʌti ˈsɑːk‖-ˈsɑːrk/ [the] a CLIPPER (=fast sailing ship) built in 1869. It carried tea from China to England quickly, racing against similar ships. The Cutty Sark is now preserved at Greenwich, London.

cut·up /ˈkʌtʌp/ *n AmE* a person who entertains others by behaving in an amusing way —see also CUT **up**

Cuz·co /ˈkʊskəʊ/ a city in southern Peru, once the most

important city of the Inca people, with many palaces and temples. Much of ancient Cuzco was destroyed by the Spanish in 1533.

CV, cv /ˌsiː ˈviː/ also **curriculum vitae** *fml, esp. BrE* ‖ **résumé** *esp. AmE— n* a short written account of a person's education and past employment, used esp. when they are looking for a new job — see also JOB (CULTURAL NOTE)

C&W /ˌsiː ənd ˈdʌbəljuː/ *n* [U] *abbrev. for* COUNTRY AND WESTERN

cwm /kuːm/ *n* a short valley in Wales

cwt *written abbrev. for:* HUNDREDWEIGHT

cy·an /ˈsaɪən‖ˈsaɪ-æn, -ən/ *adj* deep greenish blue —**cyan** *n* [U]

cy·a·nide /ˈsaɪənaɪd/ *n* [U] a very strong poison: *Their spies are instructed to swallow cyanide capsules if they are caught.*

cy·ber·net·ics /ˌsaɪbəˈnetɪks‖-bər-/ *n* [U] the scientific study of the way in which information is moved about and controlled in machines, the brain, and the nervous system —**ic** *adj* —**ically** /kli/ *adv*

cy·borg /ˈsaɪbɔːg‖-bɔːrg/ *n* a man-like creature that is partly human and partly machine

Cyc·la·des /ˈsɪklədiːz/ [*the*+P] a group of Greek islands in the Aegean Sea, including Naxos and Paros

cy·cla·mate /ˈsɪkləmeɪt/ *n* [C;U] any of various artificial sweeteners, used (esp. formerly) by people trying to avoid sugar

cyc·la·men /ˈsɪkləmən/ *n* **cyclamen** a plant of the PRIMROSE family, with white, purple, pink, or red flowers

cy·cle[1] /ˈsaɪkəl/ *n* **1** a number of related events happening in a regularly repeated order: *the cycle of the seasons* | *the seemingly endless cycle of violence in this troubled part of the world* —see also LIFE CYCLE **2** the period of time needed for this to be completed: *a 50-minute cycle* **3** a group of songs, poems, etc., connected with some central event or person

cycle[2] *n* a bicycle: *My cycle's been stolen.* —see BICYCLE (USAGE)

cycle[3] *v* [I+*adv/prep*] to travel by bicycle: *Do you cycle to work?* | *He goes cycling every weekend.*

cy·clic /ˈsaɪklɪk/ also **cy·cli·cal** /-klɪkəl/— *adj fml* happening in cycles: *cyclical changes in the level of business activity* — ~ **ally** /kli/ *adv*

cy·clist /ˈsaɪklɪst/ *n* **1** a person riding a bicycle: *I overtook a group of cyclists.* | *a cyclist's helmet* **2** a person who is able to ride a bicycle: *I'm not much of a cyclist* (=I am not good at riding a bicycle), *I'm afraid.*

cy·clo·cross /ˈsaɪkləʊ ˌkrɒs‖-ˌkrɔːs/ *n* [U] the sport of racing bicycles over rough ground, usu. including carrying the bicycle up and down steep slopes. Cyclo-cross bicycles are lighter and have much narrower wheels than MOUNTAIN BIKES.

cy·clone /ˈsaɪkləʊn/ *n* a very violent tropical wind or storm moving very rapidly in a circle round a calm central area —compare HURRICANE, TYPHOON; see also ANTICYCLONE; see STORM (USAGE)

cy·clops /ˈsaɪklɒps‖-klɑːps/ *n* a GIANT in ancient Greek stories who only had one eye, in the middle of his forehead

cy·clo·style /ˈsaɪkləstaɪl/ *BrE* ‖ **mimeograph** *AmE— v* [T] to make (a document, etc.) cheaply using a special apparatus that makes a STENCIL from which copies are made: *a cyclostyled newsletter*

cy·clo·tron /ˈsaɪklətrɒn‖-trɑːn/ *n* a piece of equipment used by scientists to find out about the nature of matter. It makes small pieces of atoms called PARTICLES travel in a circular path at an increasingly high speed —compare LINEAR ACCELERATOR

cy·der /ˈsaɪdər/ *n BrE* CIDER

cyg·net /ˈsɪɡnɪt/ *n* a young SWAN

cyl·in·der /ˈsɪlɪndər/ *n* **1** a hollow or solid shape with a circular base and straight sides **2** an object or container shaped like this, esp. a hollow metal tube: *a cylinder of oxygen* **3** the tube within which a PISTON moves backwards and forwards in an engine or piece of machinery: *an engine with four/six cylinders* | *brake cylinders* —see picture at ENGINE

cy·lin·dri·cal /sɪˈlɪndrɪkəl/ *adj* in the shape of a cylinder: *Beer cans are cylindrical.* — ~ **ly** /kli/ *adv*

cym·bal /ˈsɪmbəl/ *n* either of a pair of round thin metal plates that are struck together to make a loud ringing noise, used in music: *a clash of cymbals* —see picture at PERCUSSION — ~ **ist** *n*

Cym·ru /ˈkʌmri/ the Welsh name for Wales

cyn·ic /ˈsɪnɪk/ *n sometimes derog* someone who thinks that people tend to act only in their own interests, and who always has a low opinion (sometimes unfairly) of people's reasons for doing things: *"I'm sure she's only pretending to be ill, to get people's sympathy." "Honestly, Sue, you're such a cynic!"* — ~ **ism** /ˈsɪnsɪzəm/ *n* [U] : *appalled by the cynicism of the government's proposals*

cyn·i·cal /ˈsɪnɪkəl/ *adj sometimes derog* like or typical of a cynic: *cynical remarks/behaviour* | *She was very cynical about the press conference and said the president was only there to boost his popularity.* — ~ **ly** /kli/ *adv*

cy·no·sure /ˈsaɪnəʃʊər, ˈsɪn-‖ˈsaɪnəʃʊər/ *n fml or pomp* a person or thing that is a centre of attention or interest

cy·pher /ˈsaɪfər/ *n, v* CIPHER

cy·press /ˈsaɪprɪs/ *n* a tree with dark green leaves and hard wood. It does not lose its leaves in winter.

Cy·prus /ˈsaɪprəs/ an island in the E Mediterranean, S of Turkey; capital Nicosia; population 694,000 (1989) — **Cypriot** /ˈsɪpriət/ *adj, n*

Cy·ril·lic /sɪˈrɪlɪk/ *adj, n* [U] (written in or being) the alphabet used for Russian, Bulgarian, various other Slavonic languages, Mongolian, etc.

cyst /sɪst/ *n* an enclosed hollow growth in or on the body, containing liquid matter: *She had an operation to remove a cyst.* | *a benign/malignant cyst*

cys·tic fi·bro·sis /ˌsɪstɪk faɪˈbrəʊsɪs/ *n* [U] a long-lasting serious disease that some people are born with which damages the GLANDS of the body. It sometimes results in early death.

cyst·i·tis /sɪˈstaɪtɪs/ *n* [U] a disease of the BLADDER, esp. of women, in which water must be passed frequently from the body, often with pain and difficulty

cy·tol·o·gy /saɪˈtɒlədʒi‖-ˈtɑː-/ *n* [U] the scientific study of cells — **gist** *n*

Cy Young A·ward /ˌsaɪ ˈjʌŋ əˌwɔːd ‖ -əˈwɔːrd/ [*the*] a prize given every year to the most successful PITCHER (=the person who throws the ball) in the big LEAGUES of American BASEBALL

czar /zɑːr/ *n* a TSAR

cza·ri·na /zɑːˈriːnə/ *n* a TSARINA

Czech /tʃek/ also **Czech·o·slo·vak** /ˌtʃekəˈsləʊvæk◂/, **Czech·o·slo·vak·i·an** /ˌtʃekəsləʊˈvækiən, -ˈvɑː-/— *adj, n* (a person) who is, or whose parents are, from Czechoslovakia

Czech·o·slo·vak·i·a /ˌtʃekəsləʊˈvækiə, -ˈvɑː-/ a country in central Europe, bordering on Austria, Germany, Hungary, Poland, and the former USSR; capital Prague; population 15,639,000 (1989). From after the Second World War until 1989, Czechoslovakia was a Communist state under the influence of the USSR. It now consists of two independent republics: the Czech Republic; capital Prague; population 10,400,000 (1990) and Slovakia; capital Bratislava; population 5,300,000 (1990).

D

D, d /diː/ **D's, d's** or **Ds, ds** 1 the fourth letter of the English alphabet 2 the ROMAN NUMERAL (number) for 500

d written abbrev. for: died: d 1937

D 1 a note in Western music; the musical KEY¹ (4) based on this note 2 a mark given to a student's work, showing that it is of a very low standard —see also GRADE¹ (3); see also D AND C, D-DAY, D-NOTICE

-'d short for: 1 would: I asked if she'd go. (=if she would go) 2 had: I asked if she'd gone. (=if she had gone) 3 infml (in questions after **where, what, when,** etc.) did: Where'd he go? (=Where did he go?) —compare 'S¹ (3)

d' short for: (infml) do: D'you like it?

DA /ˌdiː ˈeɪ/ n DISTRICT ATTORNEY

dab¹ /dæb/ n 1 a slight or light touch: He made a few dabs at the fence with the paintbrush but it didn't really have much effect. 2 infml a small quantity of a soft or liquid substance: a dab of paint/of butter 3 a DAB HAND —see also DABS

dab² v **-bb-** 1 [I (at);T] to touch lightly or gently, usu. several times: She dabbed (at) the wound with a wet cloth. 2 [T (on)] to cover with light quick strokes and usu. carelessly and incompletely: She dabbed some cream on her face.

dab·ble /ˈdæbəl/ v 1 [I (at, in)] sometimes derog to work at or study something without serious intentions: to dabble in politics | I've dabbled in sculpture a bit. 2 [T (in)] to move (one's hands, feet, etc.) playfully about in water: She dabbled her toes in the river. **--bler** n

dab hand /ˌ· ˈ·/ also **dab—** n [(at)] BrE infml a person who is very good at something: She's a dab hand at sailing.

dabs /dæbz/ n [P] BrE sl for FINGERPRINTS

Dac·ca /ˈdækə/ DHAKA

dacha /ˈdætʃə‖ˈdɑː-/ n a Russian country house or COTTAGE

Dach·au /ˈdækaʊ, ˈdæx-‖ˈdɑː-/ n a CONCENTRATION CAMP near the town of Dachau in S Germany in which many Jews and other prisoners were killed during the Second World War: His whole family was sent to Dachau.

dachs·hund /ˈdækshʊnd, -sənd/ also **sausage dog** BrE infml— n a small dog with short legs and a long body —see picture at DOG

Dac·ron /ˈdækrɒn‖ˈdeɪkrɑːn/ n tdmk a kind of cloth made from man-made materials. In the US, clothes made from this material are considered unfashionable by many young people: a Dacron polyester sportshirt

dac·tyl /ˈdæktɪl‖-tl/ n tech a measure of poetry consisting of one strong (or long) beat followed by two weak (or short) beats, as in "carefully" — — ic /dækˈtɪlɪk/ adj, n

dad /dæd/ n infml father: What are you doing, Dad? | I'll have to ask my mum and dad. —see FATHER (USAGE)

Da·da·is·m /ˈdɑːdɑː-ɪzəm/ also **Da·da** /ˈdɑːdɑː/— n [U] an early 20th-century movement in art and literature which was a violent reaction against previous ideas about art and writing, and was particularly concerned with producing unexpected, strange images which give a feeling of unreality. Dadaism was one of the main influences upon Surrealism. — — ist, — istic adj

Daddies sauce /ˌ·· ˈ·/ n tdmk a type of SAUCE made by HP Foods Limited for adding FLAVOUR to food just before it is eaten

▶CULTURAL NOTE Daddies Sauce is usu. eaten by people at home; it is not usu. offered in restaurants or on grand occasions.◀

dad·dy /ˈdædi/ n (used esp. by or to young children) father: Daddy's home! | That's my daddy. —compare MUMMY¹; see also SUGAR DADDY; see FATHER (USAGE)

daddy long·legs /ˌdædi ˈlɒŋlegz‖-ˈlɔːŋ-/ n **daddy longlegs** 1 also **crane fly** fml— BrE a flying insect with long legs 2 AmE an insect with long legs that is similar to a SPIDER

Daddy War·bucks /ˌdædi ˈwɔːbʌks ‖ -ˈwɔːr-/ an American

COMIC STRIP character. He is a very rich businessman and takes care of a young girl, Little Orphan Annie.

da·do /ˈdeɪdəʊ/ n **-does** the lower part of a wall in a room that is decorated differently, e.g. with different-coloured paint, from the upper part

Dad's Ar·my /ˌ· ˈ··/ a British television comedy programme about a group of old soldiers who were part of the Home Guard, defending a small southern English town during the Second World War —see also HOME GUARD

Dae·da·lus /ˈdiːdəl-əs‖ˈded-/ in CLASSICAL MYTHOLOGY, a great inventor who made the Labyrinth and was the father of Icarus

dae·mon /ˈdiːmən/ n lit 1 (in ancient Greek stories) a being like a spirit, halfway between gods and humans 2 a spirit that fills a person with the power to think, do, or make new things —compare DEMON — ~ ic /dɪˈmɒnɪk‖ -ˈmɑː-/ adj : a daemonic laugh — ~ ically /kli/ adv

daf·fo·dil /ˈdæfədɪl/ also **daff** /dæf/ infml— n a very common bell-shaped pale yellow flower of early spring —see picture at FLOWER

▶CULTURAL NOTE 1 The daffodil is one of the plants which has an association with Wales. Some Welsh people wear a daffodil pinned to their coat on Saint David's Day (1st March). 2 There is a very well-known poem by William Wordsworth which British people often quote when talking about daffodils. It begins:
I wandered lonely as a cloud
That floats on high o'er vales and hills,
When all at once I saw a crowd,
A host, of golden daffodils.◀

Daf·fy Duck /ˌdæfi ˈdʌk/ a CARTOON character who does silly things and who mispronounces his 's' sounds when he speaks

daft /dɑːft‖dæft/ adj infml, esp. BrE silly; foolish: a daft idea | What a daft thing to say! | Don't be so daft! — ~ ly adv — ~ ness n [U]

dag·ger /ˈdægəʳ/ n 1 a short pointed knife used as a weapon, esp. formerly: He sheathed his dagger again. 2 also **obelisk—** a sign (†) used in printing to draw the reader's attention to something 3 **at daggers drawn (with someone)** in a state of open dislike and readiness to fight (with someone) 4 **Is this a dagger which I see before me?** quote a line from Shakespeare's play Macbeth, said by Macbeth when he is preparing to murder the king. He imagines a dagger with blood on it in the air in front of him. 5 **look daggers at** to look angrily at; GLARE at —see also CLOAK-AND-DAGGER

da·go /ˈdeɪɡəʊ/ n **-gos** or **-goes** derog taboo a person, esp. a man, from Spain, Portugal, or Italy

da·guer·reo·type /dəˈgerəʊtaɪp‖-rə-/ n [C;U] a kind of early photograph

Dag·wood /ˈdægwʊd/ (in the US) a COMIC STRIP character who is married to the character **Blondie**. He is known for being lazy.

Dagwood sand·wich /ˈ·· ˌ··/ n AmE a very large SANDWICH with many different kinds of meat and cheese in it

Dahl /dɑːl/, **Ro·ald** /ˈrəʊəld/ (1916–90) a popular British writer, esp. of children's books which often combine frightening things with humour —see also CHARLIE AND THE CHOCOLATE FACTORY

dah·li·a /ˈdeɪliə‖ˈdæliə/ n a big brightly coloured garden flower with a lot of pointed PETALS

Dail /dɔɪl, daɪl/ also **Dail Ei·reann** /ˌdɔɪl ˈeərən, ˌdaɪl-‖ -ˈeɪrən/ fml— [the] the lower house of the Irish parliament

dai·lies /ˈdeɪliz/ n [P] 1 DAILY PAPERS 2 AmE for RUSHES

dai·ly¹ /ˈdeɪli/ adj, adv every day (or every working day): my daily journey to work | She goes there twice daily. | a daily newspaper | She gets paid daily. | She is paid on a daily basis.

daily² n 1 [usu. pl.] a DAILY PAPER 2 also **daily help** /ˌ·· ˈ·/— infml, esp. BrE someone, esp. a woman, who comes to clean a house daily but does not live there

daily bread /ˌ·· ˈ·/ n [U] infml 1 food, money, and other things necessary for life (esp. in the phrase **earn one's daily bread**) 2 **Give us this day our daily bread** quote a phrase from the Lord's Prayer, asking God to provide food each day

daily doub·le /ˌ·· '··/ n AmE a single BET on the results of two horse or dog races in a row

Daily Ex·press /ˌ·· ·'·/ also **Express**– [the] a popular national daily newspaper in Britain. It is a TABLOID –see also extra information on page 896

Daily Mail /ˌ·· '·/ also **Mail**– [the] a popular national daily newspaper in Britain. It is a TABLOID –see also extra information on page 896

Daily Mir·ror /ˌ·· '··/ also **Mirror**– [the] a popular national daily newspaper in Britain. It is a TABLOID –see also extra information on page 896

daily pa·per /ˌ·· '··/ n also **daily** infml –a newspaper printed and sold every day except Sunday –see also SUNDAY PAPER; see also extra information on page 896

Daily Tel·e·graph /ˌ·· '··/ also **Telegraph**– [the] a national daily newspaper in Britain. It is a QUALITY PAPER –see also extra information on page 896

Daim·ler /'deɪmlə'/ tdmk a company which makes cars, esp. a famous large, comfortable, and expensive car called a Daimler. British people think of Daimlers as being driven typically by very rich, older, upper-class people.

dain·ty¹ /'deɪnti/ adj **1** small, pretty, and delicate: a dainty child/dress/movement **2** not easy to please, esp. about food; FASTIDIOUS: a dainty eater –**-tily** adv –**-tiness** n [U]

dainty² n an especially nice small piece of food, esp. a little cake

dai·qui·ri /'daɪkˌri, 'dæk-/ n a sweet alcoholic drink made of RUM and esp. LEMON or LIME juice

dair·y /'deəri/ n **1** a place on a farm where milk is kept and butter and cheese are made **2** a company which makes or sells mostly milk and dairy products: Altadena Dairies makes most of the yogurt sold there.

dairy cat·tle /'·· ˌ··/ n [P] cattle kept for milk rather than for meat

dairy farm /'·· ·/ n a farm that produces milk, and sometimes butter and cheese – ~ **er** n

dair·y·maid /'deərimeɪd/ also **milkmaid**– n old use a woman who works in a DAIRY (1)

dair·y·man /'deərimən‖-mən, -mæn/ n **-men** /mən/ a man who works in a DAIRY (1) or runs a DAIRY FARM

dairy prod·uce /'·· ˌ··/ n [U] milk and things made from milk, such as butter and cheese. Many people in Britain and the US believe that too much dairy produce makes people fat and is bad for them.

dairy prod·ucts /'·· ˌ··/ n [P] DAIRY PRODUCE

Dairy Queen /'·· ˌ·/ also **DQ**– n tdmk an American FAST-FOOD restaurant which sells ice cream and other foods. Dairy Queen is a popular place for TEENAGERS to go

da·is /'deɪɪs, deɪs/ n [usu. sing.] a raised part of the floor at one end of a hall or meeting room, for speakers or other important people

dai·sy /'deɪzi/ n **1** a very common flower, which is white around a yellow centre and grows among grass. People think of daisies as simple and ordinary, but attractive and fresh: The lawn was covered in daisies. –see picture at FLOWER **2 push up the daisies** BrE humor to be dead and buried –see DEAD¹

daisy chain /'·· ·/ n BrE a string of daisies joined together using their STALKs to make a circle to wear round the neck or wrist, usu. made by children

dai·sy wheel print·er /'·· · ˌ··/ n a kind of PRINTER (3) with a part called a **daisy wheel** that moves to press letters onto the paper and consists of a piece of metal shaped like a large daisy, having a different letter of the alphabet at the end of each "PETAL". A daisy wheel printer produces good quality print like the print from a TYPEWRITER, and some typewriters also have a daisy wheel –see also DOT MATRIX PRINTER, GOLF BALL (2), and LASER PRINTER

Dak·ar /'dækɑː' ‖ dəkɑːr/ [the] an important seaport and economic centre in Senegal, W Africa

Da·ko·tas /də'kəʊtəz/ [the+P] the US states of North Dakota and South Dakota

Da·lai La·ma /ˌdælaɪ 'lɑːmə‖ˌdɑː-/ also **Grand Lama** /ˌ· '··/– [the] the head of the Tibetan Buddhist religion. He has lived outside Tibet since the Chinese took control of it in 1950 and leads the movement for an independent Tibet.

dale /deɪl/ n N EngE or poet a valley –see also DALES

dalek

da·lek /'dɑːlek/ n (often cap.) a frightening creature with a metal body, from a British children's television SERIES called Dr Who. Daleks talk in a strange voice that does not rise or fall, like the voice of a a machine. When they are going to kill someone, they say "Exterminate!" –see also DR WHO

Dales /deɪlz/ also **Yorkshire Dales** n [the+P] an area of hills and valleys in the N of England, popular with tourists

Daley, Arthur see ARTHUR DALEY

Dal·glish /dæl'gliːʃ/, **Ken·ny** /'keni/ (1951–) a skilful Scottish footballer and manager who played for Glasgow Celtic and Liverpool, which he also managed

Da·li /'dɑːli/, **Sal·va·dor**
/'sælvədɔː'/ (1904–89) a Spanish Surrealist painter known for his strange life and habits. He had a long thin MOUSTACHE.

Salvador Dali

Dal·las /'dæləs/ **1** a city in Texas in the US. It is a centre for business and industry and is esp. famous for its rich oil businesses. It is also remembered as the place where John F Kennedy was shot in 1963. –see colour map on page 1374 5 **2** an American television SERIES which became very popular in many parts of the world. Dallas is about a wealthy family called the Ewings who own an oil company and live on a very big RANCH called Southfork. The people in Dallas have exciting lifestyles and are only interested in power, money, and sex. –see also JR

Dallas Cow·boys /ˌ·· '··/, **The** a leading AMERICAN FOOTBALL team from Dallas, Texas

dal·li·ance /'dæliəns/ n [U] old-fash the act of dallying with someone; FLIRTATION

dal·ly /'dæli/ v [I (ABOUT, over)] to be slow or waste time: Don't dally about or we'll be late. | They dallied over their food for a while.
    dally with sbdy./sthg. phr v [T] **1** to consider (an idea), but not very seriously; TOY with: He often dallies with the idea of setting himself up in business. **2** old-fash to seem to want to start a love relationship with (someone), but without serious intentions

Dal·ma·tia /dæl'meɪʃə/ an area of Croatia on the E coast on the Adriatic Sea

Dal·ma·tian /dæl'meɪʃən/ n (usu. cap.) a type of large short-haired dog that is white with black spots. There is a famous children's book called The Hundred and One Dalmatians. –see picture at DOG

dam¹ /dæm/ n a wall or bank built across a river to keep back water, esp. to make a RESERVOIR: the Aswan Dam in Egypt | The village was swept away when the dam burst.| The beavers had built a new dam across the stream. –compare DIKE¹ (1)

dam² v **-mm-** [T (UP)] to keep back by means of a dam: to dam (up) the water/the river
    dam sthg. ↔ **up** phr v [T] to control (a feeling, esp. of anger or annoyance) in an unhealthy way; SUPPRESS: to dam up one's resentment

dam³ n the mother of a four-legged animal, esp. a horse –compare SIRE¹ (1)

dam

dam·age[1] /'dæmɪdʒ/ n 1 [U (to)] the process of spoiling the condition or quality of something and the harm or loss that results: *The flood caused serious damage to the crops.* | *This will do a lot of damage to her political reputation.* | *He suffered* **brain damage** *in the car accident.* 2 *[the] infml* the price, esp. of something done for you: *What's the damage?*

damage[2] v [T] to cause damage to: *to damage someone's reputation* | *The building was severely damaged by the explosion.* | *Smoking can damage your health.* | *The incident had a damaging effect on East-West relations.*

damage lim·i·ta·tion ex·er·cise /ˌ···ˈ··/ n an attempt to limit the damage to something, esp. one's REPUTATION or CREDIBILITY, as much as possible: *Since news of its involvement in the scandal was leaked, the Government has been engaged in a damage limitation exercise.*

dam·ag·es /'dæmɪdʒz/ n [P] *law* money that a person is ordered by a court to pay to another person for causing damage or for unfairly writing bad things about them so that other people will have a low opinion of them: *She sued him for libel, and the court ordered him to pay her damages of £1500.* | *The court awarded her £1500 in damages.*

Da·mas·cus /də'mæskəs/ 1 the capital of Syria 2 **road to Damascus** the way one suddenly comes to believe something of great importance in one's life (from a story in the Bible in which St Paul was travelling to Damascus to stop Christianity there when a light blinded him, and he heard the voice of God and became a Christian): *The experience of meeting people who had no homes and no food, but were still sure of their beliefs, was her road to Damascus.*

dam·ask[1] /'dæməsk/ n [U] a kind of cloth with a pattern woven into it, used in the past by very rich people for clothes and curtains. Now it is used for covering furniture, and for white tablecloths for formal occasions.

damask[2] *adj* 1 made of damask: *a damask tablecloth* 2 *poet* pink: *her damask cheek*

Dam Bust·ers /ˈ·ˌ··/, **The** a British second world war film about Dr Barnes Wallis's BOUNCING BOMB (=a bomb which springs up again after hitting a surface) which destroyed DAMs (=a wall to keep back water) on the Ruhr river in Germany. The music from the film is particularly remembered.

dame /deɪm/ n 1 *AmE old-fash sl* (esp. said by men) a woman. There is a famous song from the musical *South Pacific* called *There is nothing like a dame.* 2 (*sometimes cap.*) in Britain, the part of an ugly old woman in a PANTOMIME, acted by a man

Dame *n* (the title of) a woman who has been given a DBE (British rank of honour): *Dame Ellen Terry was a famous actress.* | *When was she made a Dame?* —compare KNIGHT

Dame Ed·na /deɪm 'ednə/ also **Dame Edna Ev·er·age** /-ˌednə 'evərɪdʒ/ an amusing female character who wears wildly unusual clothes and glasses and who thinks she is amusing, attractive, and intelligent. She was invented and played by the Australian COMEDIAN Barry Humphries. —see also Barry HUMPHRIES and colour picture on page 553

dam·mit /'dæmɪt/ *interj* 1 (an expression of annoyance): *Will you hurry up, dammit!* 2 **as near as dammit** almost, though possibly a few less: *"How many were*

there?" "A hundred." "Really?" "Well, as near as dammit."

damn[1] /dæm/ *adj, adv* [A] *sl* 1 also **damned, goddamn**— (used for giving force to an expression, good or bad): *a damn fool* | *You were damn lucky the police didn't catch you.* | *Don't lie to me — you knew damn well what was happening.* —see also DARN[2] 2 **damn all** *BrE* nothing: *He's the meanest person I know — you'll get damn all out of him.*

damn[2] also **damnation**— *interj sl* (an expression of annoyance or disappointment): *Damn! I've forgotten the key* —see also DARN[2], DASH[1] (4)

damn[3] *n infml* [S *usu. in negatives*] even the smallest amount: *I don't* **care/give a damn** *what he does.* | *His promise isn't* **worth a damn.**

damn[4] *v* [T] 1 (esp. of God) to send to punishment without end after death —see also DAMNED[1] (1), [2] 2 (often used in CURSES[1] (2)): *Damn it!* | *Damn you!* —compare BLESS[1] (3) 3 to declare to be bad or worthless: *The play was damned by all the critics.* —see also DAMNED[1] (4) 4 to cause to fail completely; ruin: *He damned himself with one stupid remark.* 5 **damn someone/something with faint praise** to praise someone or something only slightly, in a way that suggests that one really dis approves

dam·na·ble /'dæmnəbəl/ *adj old-fash* very bad; APPALLING: *This damnable weather!* —**bly** *adv infml*

dam·na·tion[1] /dæm'neɪʃən/ *n* [U] 1 the act of damning or state of being damned: *condemned to eternal damnation in Hell* 2 **in damnation** *old-fash sl* (used for giving strength to an expression of anger): *What in damnation do you mean by that?*

damnation[2] *interj sl* (an expression of annoyance or disappointment): *Oh no! I've forgotten the key. Hell and damnation!*

damned[1] /dæmd/ *adj* 1 sent by God to punishment without end after death: *They will be eternally damned* 2 *infml* (used for giving force to an expression, good or bad; used esp. by UPPER-CLASS people): *It's a damned nuisance.* | *damned bad luck* 3 **Well, I'm damned/I'll be damned!** *infml* (a strong way of saying) I'm very sur prised! 4 **damned if she does and damned if she doesn't** *infml* people will find fault with her whatever course of action she chooses

damned[2] *n [the+P]* in the Christian and Muslim religions, people who have behaved so immorally that after death they are sent to Hell to be punished for ever

damned·est[1] /'dæmdɪst/ *n* **do one's damnedest** *infml* to do everything possible: *She's doing her damnedest to pass the exam.*

damnedest[2] *adj [the+A] infml, esp. AmE* the most unusual, surprising, etc.: *Isn't that the damnedest thing you've ever heard?*

damn·ing /'dæmɪŋ/ *adj* likely to lead to ruin or failure: *We found some* **damning evidence** *that implicated both of them.*

Damocles see SWORD OF DAMOCLES

damp[1] /dæmp/ *adj* rather wet, often in an unpleasant way: *damp grass* | *damp clothes* | *The tenants complained to their landlord about the damp walls in the bedroom.* | *an unhealthy damp climate* | *Use a damp cloth to clean the table.* — ~**ish** *adj* — ~**ly** *adv*

▷ USAGE Compare **damp, humid,** and **moist. Damp** is often used in a bad sense: *I can't wear these socks; they're* **damp. Moist** is used especially of food and parts of the body, and has a good sense (=not too dry): *a rich,* **moist** *cake* | **moist** *eyes/lips.* **Humid** is a more scientific word usually used of climate or weather: *It was hot and* **humid** *in the jungle.*◁

damp[2] also **damp·ness** /'dæmpnɪs/— *n* [U] slight wetness: *There's a patch of damp on my bedroom wall.* —see also RISING DAMP

damp[3] *v* [T] 1 to wet slightly; dampen: *Damp the dress before you iron it.* 2 to make (a stringed musical instru ment) sound less loudly, e.g. by using a DAMPER (3)

damp sthg. ↔ **down** also **dampen** sthg. ↔ **down**— *phr v* [T] 1 to make (a fire) burn more slowly, often by covering it with ash 2 to control and reduce

RESTRAIN (2): *They were too keen at first and we had to damp down their enthusiasm.*

damp course /ˈ· ·/ also **damp-proof course** /ˈ· · ˌ·/— *n BrE* a thickness of material in a wall to prevent RISING DAMP (=wetness coming up through the bricks)

damp·en /ˈdæmpən/ *v* [T] **1** to make damp: *The rain hardly dampened the ground.* **2** to reduce the strength of (feelings, esp. of happiness or keenness): *It was an unpleasant event and it dampened our spirits for a while.*

damp·er /ˈdæmpəʳ/ *n* **1** an influence that makes people feel sad or discouraged: *The accident* **put a damper on our party.** **2** a metal plate, door, etc., that can be moved to control the amount of air that reaches a burning fire and make it burn more or less brightly **3** an apparatus that stops the shaking of a piano string

damp squib /ˌ· ˈ·/ *n BrE infml* something which is intended to be exciting, effective, etc., but which fails and disappoints

dam·sel /ˈdæmzəl/ *n* **1** *lit* a young unmarried woman, esp. one of noble birth **2 damsel in distress** *humor* a woman who is in a difficult situation from which a man can save her (from old stories in which a damsel is often held as a prisoner and is saved by a young KNIGHT, humorously known as a **knight in shining armour**): *"Thank you very much." "Not at all, madam. Always happy to help a damsel in distress."* —see picture at KNIGHT

dam·son /ˈdæmzən/ *n* (the small acid purple fruit of) a kind of PLUM tree: *damson jam*

dan /dæn/ *n* a level of skill in a MARTIAL ART, higher than a BLACK BELT: *He's a first dan in judo.* —compare BLACK BELT

dance¹ /dɑːns‖dæns/ *v* **1** [I] to move the feet and body in a way that matches the speed or movements of music: *She loves to dance.* | *They danced all night to the music of the band.* | *Would you like to dance with me?*

▶ CULTURAL NOTE Many young people in Britain and the US go to DISCOS and NIGHT CLUBS to dance, esp. on Saturday nights. They usu. dance in pairs of one man and one woman. For many young people this is a good way to meet people of the opposite sex. Some DANCEs (3) are held at which older people can dance older dances. Companies and clubs may hold a dance on a special occasion such as Christmas. ◀

2 [T] to perform (a type of dance): *We danced the waltz.* **3** [T+*obj*+*adv*/*prep*] to cause to dance: *She danced the baby round the room.* **4** [I] to move quickly up and down, or about: *The branches of the trees danced in the breeze.* | *The figures on the computer screen danced up and down in front of my eyes.* (=I couldn't read them properly) **5 dance attendance on/upon someone** *BrE* to pay someone a lot of attention, get everything they might need, etc., showing that one is very keen to please them **6 dance to someone's tune** to do what someone wants without asking questions, in a way that shows complete obedience —**dancer** *n* : *Is he a good dancer?* | *She's a dancer on the stage.* | *folk dancers*

dance² *n* **1** [C] an act of dancing: *Let's have one more dance before we go home.* | *She did a little dance of excitement.* | *to play dance music* **2** [C] (the name of) a particular set of movements performed to music: *The waltz is a beautiful dance.* | *a traditional tribal dance* **3** [C] a social meeting or party for dancing, esp. older-style dancing rather than DISCO dancing: *They're giving/holding a dance on New Year's Eve.* **4** [C] a piece of music for dancing: *The band played a slow dance.* **5** (*the*) U] (*sometimes cap.*) the art of dancing, esp. BALLET dancing —see also COUNTRY DANCE, SONG AND DANCE, SQUARE DANCE, **lead someone a dance** (LEAD¹ (10))

dance-band /ˈ· ·/ *n* a group of musicians (a band) who play music for dancing to —**dance-band** *adj* : *a dance-band singer*

dance floor /ˈ· ·/ *n* **1** a special floor for dancing on **2 on the dance floor** at dancing: *She's wonderful on the dance floor.*

dance hall /ˈ· ·/ *n* a large public room where people pay to go and dance. Dance halls are rather old-fashioned now and are connected in people's minds with dancing before the 1960s. Many older-style dances, where people WALTZ, etc., are now held in hotels. Most young people who like dancing go to DISCOS or NIGHT CLUBS.

Dance of Death /ˌ· · ˈ·/ also **danse macabre** [*the*] an imagined dance danced by people as they are led to their death, either by their own SKELETON (=body consisting only of bones) or by a skeleton representing death. In the Middle Ages painters, writers, and musicians used the Dance of Death to express the idea that all people are equal in death, and that death can come to anyone at any time, so people should behave morally in order always to be ready to be judged by God.

dance of the sev·en veils /ˌ· · · ˌ·· ˈ·/ *n* a sexy Eastern dance (known to most Westerners through old films) in which a woman slowly removes seven long pieces of thin material (the veils) from her body as she dances

dance stu·di·o /ˈ· ·ˌ··/ *n* a large room usu. with mirrors on the walls and bars to hold onto where people learn or practise dancing

danc·ing girl /ˈ·· ˌ·/ *n* a professional woman dancer in a place of popular entertainment, or in the Middle East, esp. in the past. People sometimes use the expression **Bring on the dancing girls**, meaning "Let's add some (more) excitement to this occasion!"

Dan Dare /ˌ· ˈ·/ the main character in a number of adventure stories in the British boys' COMIC² (1) *Eagle*. He is the keen young captain of a space ship, and his main enemy is the Mekon: *The man destined to be Britain's first astronaut hasn't got the Dan Dare look.*

D and C /ˌdiː ənd ˈsiː/ *n* a hospital operation to clean the inside of a woman's WOMB

dan·de·li·on /ˈdændⁱlaɪən/ *n* a common small wild brightyellow flower whose seeds travel long distances on the wind —see picture at FLOWER

dandelion clock /ˈ···· ˌ·/ *n BrE* a soft round mass of white seeds of the dandelion on a STALK. Children in Britain often blow the seeds into the air and pretend that they can tell what time it is by the number of times they need to blow to remove them all.

dan·der /ˈdændəʳ/ *n* **get one's/someone's dander up** *oldfash infml* to make oneself/someone angry: *Her stubborn attitude really got my dander up.*

dan·di·fied /ˈdændⁱfaɪd/ *adj often derog* dressed like a dandy: *a dandified person/appearance*

dan·dle /ˈdændl/ *v* [T] to move (a baby or small child) up and down on one's arms or on one's knee in play

dan·druff /ˈdændrəf, -drʌf/ *n* [U] a common medical condition in which bits of dead skin form on the head and can be seen in the hair and on one's clothes

dan·dy¹ /ˈdændi/ *n becoming rare* a man who spends a lot of time and money on his clothing and personal appearance

dandy² *adj old-fash infml. esp. AmE* very good: *a dandy idea*

Dandy, The a popular British children's COMIC² (1)

Dane /deɪn/ *n* **1** a person who is from or whose parents are from Denmark **2** a VIKING —see also DANISH, GREAT DANE

dan·ger /ˈdeɪndʒəʳ/ *n* **1** [U (of, to)] the possibility of harm or loss: *The red flag means "Danger!"* | *a danger signal* | *a place where children can play without danger* | *The patient's life is in danger.* | *The operation was a success and she is now out of danger.* | *He is in (great/real) danger of losing his job.* | *Climbing mountains is fraught with* (=full of) *danger.* **2** [C (of, to)] a case or cause of danger: *the dangers of smoking* | *This narrow bridge is a danger to traffic.* | *Violent criminals like that are a danger to society.*

danger list /ˈ·· ·/ *n* **1 on the danger list** so ill that death is possible **2 off the danger list** no longer so ill that death is possible

danger mon·ey /ˈ·· ˌ··/ *n* [U] additional pay for dangerous work

dan·ger·ous /ˈdeɪndʒərəs/ *adj* able to or likely to cause danger: *a dangerous drug/animal/criminal* | *It's dangerous to go too near the edge of the cliff.* | *The situation is potentially very dangerous.* — ~**ly** *adv* : *He was driving dangerously.* | *She is dangerously ill.*

dan·gle /ˈdæŋgəl/ *v* **1** [I;T] to (cause to) hang or swing loosely: *keys dangling from a chain* | *He sat on the edge of the table dangling his legs.* **2** [T+*obj*+*prep*] to offer as an attraction: *They might do the job if you dangle a bonus in front of them.*

Dan·iel /'dænjəl/ according to the Bible, a Jew who lived before the time of Christ. He was taken prisoner by Nebuchadnezzar and put into a lions' DEN, but the lions did not kill him because God protected him. He told the people who had taken him prisoner about bad things which God would do to them in the future, including the fall of their city, Babylon. His story is told in one of the books of the Bible called "Daniel". —see also **in the lion's den** (LION)

Dan·iels /'dænjəlz/, **Paul** (1938–) an English entertainer who makes people laugh and performs magic tricks on television: *The Paul Daniels Magic Show*

Da·nish¹ /'deɪnɪʃ/ *adj* of Denmark, its people, or their language: *I'm Danish.* | *the Danish economy*

Danish² *n* **1** [U] the language of Denmark **2** [S] a DAN-ISH PASTRY

Danish blue /ˌ·· '·/ *n* [U] a kind of cheese with blue marks in it made in Denmark

Danish pas·try /ˌ·· '··/ also **Danish** ‖ also **sweet roll** *AmE*— *n* a sweet cake made of rich light pastry

dank /dæŋk/ *adj* unpleasantly wet and usu. cold: *an old house with a dark, dank cellar* | *The prison was cold and dank.* — ~**ness** *n* [U]

Dank·worth /'dæŋkwəθ‖-wərθ/, **John** (1927–) a British writer of JAZZ music, leader of a group of musicians, and SAXOPHONE player

danse ma·ca·bre /ˌdɑːns məˈkɑːbrə, -bɑːr/ *n Fr for* DANCE OF DEATH

Dan·te /'dænti, -teɪ‖'dɑːnteɪ/ (1265–1321) an Italian poet who is known esp. for *The Divine Comedy*, a long poem about a journey through HELL, PURGATORY, and HEAVEN

Dante's In·fer·no /ˌ··· ·'··/ the first part of Dante's *The Divine Comedy*, about Hell. This phrase is sometimes used to describe a terrible scene of destruction, darkness, fire, etc.: *South of Kuwait City is Dante's Inferno, where hundreds of oil fires are still burning.*

Dan·ton /'dæntɒn‖-tən/, **Georges Jacques** /ʒɔːʒ ʒæk‖ʒɔːrʒ ʒɑːk/ (1759–94) a leader of the French Revolution

Dan·ube /'dænjuːb/ [*the*] a long and important European river. It rises in the Black Forest in Germany and flows through Vienna in Austria, Budapest in Hungary, and through Romania and the former USSR, and finally into the Black Sea.

Dan·zig /'dæntsɪg/ the old German name for Gdansk, now in Poland

Daph·ne /'dæfni/ in GREEK MYTHOLOGY a woman loved by Apollo. When he chased her, she prayed to the goddess of the earth to save her and was changed into a LAUREL tree.

Daph·nis and Chlo·e , Daphnis and Chloë /ˌdæfnɪs ənd 'kləʊi/ an early Greek love story which tells of the love and adventures of a boy and a girl found and looked after by SHEPHERDs until they both discover their rich parents and get married

dap·per /'dæpər/ *adj* **1** (esp. of small men) very neat in appearance and quick in movements: *a dapper little salesman in a business suit* **2** *infml* nicely dressed

dap·pled /'dæpəld/ *adj* marked with cloudy roundish spots of colour, or of sun and shadow: *a dappled horse* | *the dappled shade of a tree*

dapple-grey /ˌ·· '·◂/ *n, adj* (a horse that is) grey with spots of darker grey

DAR /ˌdiː eɪ 'ɑːr/ *abbrev. for* DAUGHTERS OF THE AMERICAN REVOLUTION

Dar·by and Joan /ˌdɑːbi ən 'dʒəʊn‖ˌdɑːrbi-/ *n* [P] *BrE* **1** *infml* a happily married and quite old husband and wife: *Katherine Hepburn's romance with Spencer Tracy was the love of a lifetime – Romeo and Juliet stuff that grew into Darby and Joan.* **2 Darby and Joan club** a social club for old people

Dar·da·nelles /ˌdɑːdə'nelz‖ˌdɑːrdn'elz/ [*the*+P] the long narrow piece of sea connecting the Mediterranean and the Sea of Marmara between European Turkey and Asian Turkey, and the first part of the way into the Black Sea. In ancient times it was known as the Hellespont. In 1915, during the First World War, the British attacked the Dardanelles in order to get arms to Russia, but the attack failed.

dare¹ /deər/ *v* **1** [I+*to-v*/*to-v*; *not usu. in progressive forms*] to be brave enough or rude enough (to do something dangerous, difficult, or unpleasant): *How dare you accuse me of lying!* | *That is as much as I dare tell you.* | *We all knew she was wrong, but none of us dared (to) tell her.* | *I daren't tell you any more, because it's highly confidential.* | *The government would never dare (to) increase taxes so soon before the election.* —see NOT (USAGE) **2** [T+*obj*-*to-v*] to try to persuade (someone) to do something dangerous as a way of proving their bravery; CHALLENGE: *I dared her to jump.* | *They dared me to spend a night in the graveyard.* **3** [T] *fml* to be brave enough to face: *He dared the anger of the entire family.* **4 who dares wins** the official MOTTO (1) of the SAS

dare² *n* an invitation to do something dangerous as a way of proving one's bravery; CHALLENGE: *She jumped off the bridge for a dare.*

Dare, Dan see DAN DARE

dare·dev·il /'deədevəl‖'deər-/ *n* a person who is prepared to take dangerous risks, esp. in a very careless way: *a daredevil motorcyclist*

daren't /deənt‖deərnt/ *BrE short for:* dare not: *I daren't ask him.*

dare·say /ˌdeə'seɪ◂‖'deərseɪ/ *v* **I daresay** *esp. BrE* I suppose (that); perhaps: *I daresay you're right.*

Dar-es-Sa·laam /ˌdɑːr es sə'lɑːm/ the former capital of Tanzania and its main port, on the Indian Ocean. It is also the main port for Zambia.

Dar·in /'dær₁n/, **Bobby** (1936–73) an American popular music singer who had many successful songs in the 1960s including *Dream Lover*

dar·ing¹ /'deərɪŋ/ *adj* showing bravery and a willingness to take risks: *a daring rescue attempt* | *a daring escape from prison* | *a daring crime* | *a daring film* (=unusual and perhaps shocking) — ~**ly** *adv* : *a film that's daringly different*

daring² *n* [U] adventurous bravery or willingness to take risks: *a person/a plan of great daring*

Dar·jee·ling /dɑː'dʒiːlɪŋ‖dɑːr-/ **1** a city in the north of India **2** a high-quality tea from the north of India

dark¹ /dɑːk‖dɑːrk/ *adj* **1** partly or completely without light: *too dark to read* | *In winter it gets dark here early.* | *a dark room* | *a dark, badly-lit street* —opposite **light 2** tending towards black: *a dark green dress*

► CULTURAL NOTE Dark suits are usu. worn by businessmen and by other men on formal occasions, e.g. at FUNERALS. ◄

3 having brown or black hair **4** having a skin which is browner than usual for a white person **5** having a brown or black skin **6** sad; without much hope; GLOOMY: *dark days ahead* | *Don't always look on the dark side of things.* **7** having an evil or threatening quality; SINISTER: *There's a dark side to his character.* | *She gave me a dark look.* | *He had an obsession with dark forces.* **8** secret; hidden: *Keep it dark–don't tell anybody!* —see also tall, dark, and handsome (TALL) — ~**ly** *adv*: *"We'll see," he said darkly,* – ~ **ness** *n* [U]

dark² *n* **1** [*the*] the absence of light; darkness: *Can cats see in the dark?* | *Some children are afraid of the dark.* **2** [U] the time of day when there is no light: *We don't go out after dark.* | *Make sure you get home before dark.* **3 in the dark** without knowledge; in a state of IGNORANCE: *They kept the public in the dark about the new missiles.* —see also **a shot in the dark** (SHOT¹)

Dark Ag·es /'· ˌ··/ *n* [*the*+P] the period in European history from about AD 476 (the fall of Rome) to about AD 1000. It is generally regarded as a time when society was not very developed in art, education, literature, etc.: *"I lost her job because she was pregnant." "What? I thought we'd moved out of the Dark Ages!"*

Dark Con·ti·nent /ˌ· '···/ [*the*] the name given to Africa by Europeans in the 19th century

dark·en /'dɑːkən‖'dɑːr-/ *v* [I;T] **1** to (cause to) become dark: *The sky darkened as the storm began.* | *Darken the green paint by adding black.* | *As he read the report his face darkened with anger.* —compare LIGHTEN¹ **2 Never darken my door/these doors again!** *humor or pomp* Don't come back here again!

dark glas·ses /ˌ· ˈ··/ n [pl.] GLASSES with dark glass to reduce the amount of light that enters the eyes, worn in strong sunshine

dark horse /ˌ· ˈ·/ n **1** BrE a person who tends to keep their activities, feelings, or intentions secret, and who may have unexpected qualities or abilities: *I never know what he's thinking — he's such a dark horse.* **2** AmE (esp. in politics) a person in a competition about whom little is known and who surprises others by winning: *Tsongas was the dark horse of the Democratic candidates.*

dark meat /ˈ· ˌ·/ n [U] the darker meat from some parts of a cooked bird, such as that on the leg

dark·room /ˈdɑːkruːm, -rʊm‖ˈdɑːrk-/ n a dark room in which photographs can be developed

dark Sa·tan·ic mills /ˌ· ·ˌ·· ˈ·/ a phrase from William Blake's HYMN *Jerusalem*, used to suggest the unpleasant appearance and poor working conditions of the industrial buildings in the north of England in the past: *I was invited back to my old school, set among the once dark Satanic mills of Oldham in Lancashire.*

dark·y , darkey, darkie /ˈdɑːki‖ˈdɑːrki/ n taboo derog a black man or woman (considered extremely offensive)

dar·ling[1] /ˈdɑːlɪŋ‖ˈdɑːr-/ n **1** (used when speaking to someone you love or to a member of your family): *Hurry up, darling, or we'll be late.*

▶CULTURAL NOTE 1 People of all classes may call someone of the opposite sex **darling** when they are in love. Many people habitually call their husbands, wives, and children **darling**. Older people use **dear** to members of their families, but it is not usu. used by younger people. Some people also call their husbands, wives, and children **sweetheart**, or (in Britain, esp. in the north of England) **love**, or (esp. in the US) **honey** or **sweetie**. However, many people in both countries do not usu. use any of these words, but call members of their families by their names or NICK-NAMEs. 2 People often joke about actors (of both sexes) and male HOMOSEXUALs calling all their friends **darling**.◀

2 (used informally as a friendly form of address, esp. by or to a woman; said e.g. by a person working in a shop or restaurant): *What can I get you, darling?* **3** a person who is very lovable or much liked: *My granddaughter is a little darling. | He used to be the darling of the Establishment until he fell from power.*

darling[2] adj [A] **1** dearly loved: *my darling husband/wife/daughter* **2** infml (used esp. by women) charming; very nice: *What a darling little house!*

Darling, Grace (1815–42) an Englishwoman whose father looked after a LIGHTHOUSE. She is remembered by British people because she bravely rowed out in a storm with her father to save nine people after their ship had sunk.

Darling Buds of May /ˌ·· ·ˌ· ˈ·/, **The** an amusing British television programme about the Larkin family which looks back in time to country life in the south of England, based on a number of books by H.E. Bates

Dar·ling·ton /ˈdɑːlɪŋtən‖ˈdɑːr-/ a town in NE England known esp. for its connection with the railway industry

darn[1] /dɑːn‖dɑːrn/ v [I;T] to repair (a hole in cloth or a garment with a hole in it) by weaving threads through and across: *to darn a sock/the hole in a sock* —**darn** n

darn[2] adj, adv, interj euph for DAMN[1,2]

darn·ing /ˈdɑːnɪŋ‖ˈdɑːr-/ n [U] **1** the work of darning **2** clothes to be darned: *a basket of darning*

Dar·row /ˈdærəʊ/, **Clar·ence** /ˈklærəns/ (1857–1938) an American lawyer who is most famous for defending a teacher who was taken to court for teaching his students about EVOLUTION and Darwinism —see also SCOPES TRIAL

dart[1] /dɑːt‖dɑːrt/ n **1** [C] a small sharp-pointed object to be thrown, shot, etc., esp. one used as a weapon or in games: *a poisoned dart* —see also DARTS **2** [S] a quick sudden movement in a particular direction: *The prisoner made a dart for the door.* **3** [C] a fold sewn into a garment to make it fit better

dart[2] v **1** [I+adv/prep] to move suddenly and quickly: *He darted towards the door/across the road. | The fish darted under the rock.* **2** [T+obj+adv/prep] to throw or send out suddenly and quickly: *The snake darted out its tongue. | He darted an angry look at me.*

d'Ar·tag·nan /dɑːˈtænjən‖ˌdɑːrtənˈjɑːn/ a character from the book *The Three Musketeers* by Alexandre Dumas —see also THREE MUSKETEERS

dart·board /ˈdɑːtbɔːd‖ˈdɑːrtbɔːrd/ n a circular board at which darts are thrown in games

Dart·ford Tun·nel /ˌdɑːtfəd ˈtʌnl‖ˌdɑːrtfərd-/ [the] a road which goes under the River Thames at Dartford, E of London, and connects the two halves of the M25, the road that goes all the way round London

Darth Va·der /ˌdɑːθ ˈveɪdər‖ˌdɑːrθ-/ a frightening and evil character in the film *Star Wars* —see also STAR WARS and see colour picture on page 685

Dart·moor /ˈdɑːtmɔːr, -mʊər‖ˈdɑːrt-/ **1** a large wild open hilly area of great natural beauty in Devon in SW England. Dartmoor is one of the ten National Parks in England and Wales. **2** Dartmoor Prison, a prison where dangerous criminals are kept. It is a long way from other places, and is thought to be very difficult to escape from.

Dartmoor po·ny /ˌ·· ˈ··/ n a small horse of the kind that live wild on Dartmoor

Dart·mouth /ˈdɑːtməθ‖ˈdɑːrt-/ a port in Devon, England. Many British naval officers are trained at the **Royal Naval College** there.

darts /dɑːts‖dɑːrts/ n [U] any of several games in which DARTS[1] (1) are thrown at a circular board (a DARTBOARD): *They were playing darts in the bar.*

▶CULTURAL NOTE Many people think of darts as a game played by working class men in PUBs and working men's clubs.◀

Dar·win /ˈdɑːwᵻn‖ˈdɑːr-/ a city on the N coast of Australia and the chief port for that area

Darwin, Charles (1809–82) a world-famous English scientist. As a young man he spent five years on the HMS Beagle, visiting many places in S America, including the Galapagos Islands. His studies led him to the important scientific idea that plant and animal forms change over long periods of time through the workings of NATURAL SELECTION. He wrote about this idea in his book *The Origin of Species*, which caused a lot of fierce argument and disagreement when it was first printed in 1859 because it did not agree with the account of the Creation in the Bible. His ideas and THEORY OF EVOLUTION are now very widely accepted. —**ian** ‖ adj

Dar·win·is·m /ˈdɑːwᵻnɪzəm‖ˈdɑːr-/ n [S;U] the scientific idea that animals and plants have their present forms because of the working of NATURAL SELECTION (the idea that only those most suited to their conditions live, while the others die) —**ist** n, adj

dash[1] /dæʃ/ v **1** [I+adv/prep] to run quickly, esp. when hurrying: *He dashed across the street/up the stairs. | They've been dashing about all day. | I must dash (off) — I've got to catch a train.* —see RUN (USAGE) **2** [I+prep; T+obj+prep] to (cause to) strike violently, often resulting in damage or destruction: *The waves dashed (the boat) against the rocks. | In her fury, she dashed all the plates to the floor.* **3** [T] to put an end to (esp. hopes): *The injury dashed his hopes of running in the Olympics.* **4** [T] BrE euph for DAMN[2]: *Dash it all, I've lost again!*

dash sthg. ↔ **off** phr v [T] to write or draw quickly and without serious attention: *to dash off a letter*

dash[2] n **1** [S] a sudden quick run: *The prisoners made a dash for freedom.* **2** [C usu. sing.] a short race for runners; SPRINT[2] (2): *the 100-yard dash* **3** [C (of)] a small amount of something mixed with or added to something else: *a dash of pepper/colour* —see picture at PIECE **4** [C] a mark (—) used in writing and printing: *The dash is longer than the hyphen.* —compare HYPHEN **5** [U] a combination of bravery, style, and self-confidence; PANACHE **6** [(the) S] the sound of liquid hitting something: *the dash of the waves against the side of the ship* **7** [C] a long sound or flash of light used in sending messages by Morse Code —compare DOT[1] (2) **8** [C] esp. AmE a dashboard **9 cut a dash** to make people admire you because of your appearance and style

dash·board /ˈdæʃbɔːd‖-bɔːrd/ also **dash** esp. AmE— n the instrument board in a car —see picture at CAR

dashed /dæʃt/ adj [A] BrE old-fash euph for DAMN[1] (1): *That dashed cat! He's here again!*

dash·ing /ˈdæʃɪŋ/ adj having style and self-confidence: *a dashing young officer* —**~ ly** adv

dast·ard·ly /ˈdæstədli‖-ərd-/ adj old-fash behaving like a coward and a BULLY

DAT /ˌdiː eɪ ˈtiː/ n [U] digital audio tape, used to record sounds as a set of coded (CODE²) numbers, giving better quality results than other methods

da·ta /ˈdeɪtə, ˈdɑːtə/ n [P;U] **1** facts; information: *We can't tell you the results of the survey until we have looked at all the data.* **2** information in a form that can be processed by and stored in a computer system: *We use a keyboard to input the data.*

▷ USAGE Although it is plural in its Latin form, **data** is now coming to be used as an uncountable noun: *These* **data** *are very interesting.* | *This* **data** *is very interesting.* Some people still do not like this uncountable use of the word.◁

da·ta·base /ˈdeɪtəbeɪs/ also **data bank** /ˈ·· ·/— n a large collection of data that is stored in a computer system in such a way that it can easily be found by a computer user

database man·age·ment sys·tem /ˌ··· ˈ··· ˌ··/ n a system used in a computer that organizes the arrangement of data in a database and controls entry to, the putting in of, and the taking out of that data

data bus /ˈ·· ·/ n tech an electrical path along which data flows between different parts of a computer system

data pen /ˈ·· ˌ·/ n a type of pen which "reads" the coded (CODE) product information on a packet, tin, etc. and gives the price, name and type of product, etc.

Da·ta·post /ˈdeɪtəpəʊst/ tdmk (in Britain) a Royal Mail service for urgent parcels, letters, etc.: *Send these parcels (by) Datapost, please.*

data pro·cess·ing /ˌ·· ˈ···/ n [U] the use of data by computers

Data Pro·tec·tion Act /ˌ··· ·ˈ·· ˌ·/ [the] a British law, effective since 1987, that protects people against the misuse of information about them stored on computers, and makes it necessary for people who hold personal information on computers to REGISTER with an authority

date¹ /deɪt/ n **1** a stated point in time shown by one or more of the following: the number of the day, the month, and the year (but not usu. by the month alone): *The date on the coin is 1921.* | *"What's the date today?" "It's the third of August."* | *They agreed to discuss the details of the contract* **at a later date**. (=at some time in the future) | *The* **closing date** *for this competition* (=the date after which entries will not be accepted) *is December 31st, 1993.* **2** a fixed arrangement to meet at a particular time and place: *The two leaders have not yet* **set a date** *for their next meeting.* *The sixth is OK? Well, let's make that a date then.* **3** infml **a** a planned social meeting between a man and woman, or boy and girl: *Does your mother let you go out on dates?* —see also BLIND DATE **b** esp. AmE a person with whom one has this sort of arrangement: *Of course you can bring your date to the party.* —see also DATE² (5), DOUBLE DATE

▶CULTURAL NOTE It is quite important for many TEENAGERS in the US and Britain to have a boyfriend or girlfriend, i.e. a friend of the opposite sex. The first date is often considered an important occasion, and an important part of becoming an adult. On a date, a boy and girl may go to the cinema, to a restaurant, or to a dance, etc., and on some dates a boy and girl may expect to hold hands, kiss, and hold each other.◀

4 to date fml until today; yet: *We made our offer four weeks ago but we have not had a reply to date.* — see also OUT-OF-DATE, UP-TO-DATE

date² v **1** [T] to guess or decide the date of: *The archaeologists have dated the building to about 250 BC.* **2** [T] to write the date on: *The leaked document was dated June 11th.* **3** [I] to begin to seem unfashionable; become DATED: *His songs are so good that they have hardly dated at all.* **4** [T] to show clearly the age of: *He's got a big collection of Beatles records, so that dates him rather!* **5** [I;T] infml, esp. AmE to go on or have a DATE¹ (3) with (someone or each other): *She's been dating him for months but it's still not very serious.* | *They've been dating (each other) since April.* —see also BLIND DATE —**datable, dateable** adj
    date back to sthg. also **date from** sthg.— phr v [T no pass.] to have lasted or existed since: *This church dates back to 1173.* | *The custom dates from the time when men wore swords.*

date³ n a small fruit with a long stone inside, which grows on a tree (**date palm**) in hot dry countries and turns brown and sweet as it dries: *pressed dates*

dat·ed /ˈdeɪtɪd/ adj clearly belonging to a former time; old-fashioned; OUTMODED: *It was a good film when it came out, but it looks rather dated now.*

Da·tel /ˈdeɪtel/ tdmk in Britain, a system for sending information from one computer to another by telephone. Bank computers, for example, use Datel at night.

date·line /ˈdeɪtlaɪn/ n **1** INTERNATIONAL DATE LINE **2** a line in a newspaper article that gives its date and place of origin

Dateline n tdmk a very large British DATING AGENCY that uses computers to find partners for people

date·mark /ˈ·· ·/ n [U] a mark showing the date esp. a letter (**date-letter**) stamped on gold or silver PLATE¹ (5) showing the date when the object was made: *The date-mark on this teapot shows it to be about a hundred years old.* —**date-mark** v [T]

date of birth /ˌ·· ·ˈ·/ n the date on which someone was born: *Give full personal details, including date of birth.* | *Date of birth: 2.4.72.*

date rape /ˈ·· ·/ n [C;U] the RAPE of a woman by a man that she knows and usu. that she has spent the evening with socially: *Date rape is an under-reported crime on many campuses.*

date stamp /ˈ·· ·/ n **1** a stamp with letters and numbers that can be changed according to the date one wants for recording the date one sends or receives a letter, pays a bill, etc. **2** the mark made by such a stamp —**date stamp** v [T]

dating a·gen·cy /ˈ·· ˌ···/ n an organization which brings together people who want to meet others, usu. for the purpose of forming a social and sexual relationship, sometimes leading to marriage. People pay for this service and fill in a form giving details about themselves and the kind of person they would like to meet, or sometimes make a VIDEO of themselves —see also COMPUTER DATING AGENCY

da·tive /ˈdeɪtɪv/ n tech a particular form of a noun in certain languages, such as Latin and German, which shows that the noun is the INDIRECT OBJECT of a verb —**dative** adj

Dat·sun /ˈdætsən/ tdmk a Japanese company that makes cars

daub¹ /dɔːb/ v **1** [T] to cover with something soft and sticky: [+obj+with] *His clothes were daubed with mud and oil.* | *to daub the wall with paint* [+obj+on] *She daubed paint on the wall.* —see SPREAD (USAGE) **2** [I] infml to paint pictures without much skill

daub² n **1** [U] mud or clay for making walls —see also WATTLE AND DAUB **2** [C] a small bit of a soft or sticky substance: *a daub of paint/of butter* **3** [C] a badly painted picture

daugh·ter /ˈdɔːtəʳ/ n **1** someone's female child: *They have two daughters and a son.* | *a present for their baby daughter* | *Our daughter is getting married on Saturday.* **2** something thought of as a daughter: *French is a daughter (language) of Latin.*

daughter-in-law /ˈ··· ·/ n daughters-in-law, daughter-in-laws the wife of one's son. In the West the daughter-in-law does not usu. become so much part of her husband's family as she does in some other societies. —compare SON-IN-LAW

daugh·ter·ly /ˈdɔːtəliǁ-tərˈ-/ adj fml having the qualities of a good daughter. This is an uncommon word that most people would avoid using: *daughterly concern for her parents*

Daughters of the A·mer·i·can Rev·o·lu·tion /ˌ··· ·· ·ˌ··· ·ˈ··/ also **DAR**— n [the+P] a society for American women whose families have been in America since the AMERICAN REVOLUTIONARY WAR. The society generally supports NATIONALISTIC and RIGHT-WING ideas.

daunt /dɔːnt/ v [T often pass.] **1** to cause to lose courage or determination; DISHEARTEN: *He didn't seem daunted by the difficulties facing him.* | *The examination questions were rather daunting.* —see also UNDAUNTED **2** nothing daunted fml not discouraged by difficulties: *The rockface looked very steep but, nothing daunted, he started climbing.*

daunt·less /ˈdɔːntləs/ adj esp. lit not easily discouraged; fearless: *dauntless fighters* — ~ **ly** adv

dau·phin /ˈdəʊfæn‖ˈdɔːfən/ n (often cap.) the oldest son of the king of France in former times

dav·en·port /ˈdævənpɔːt‖-pɔːrt/ n AmE a large SOFA, often one which can be changed into a bed

Da·vid /ˈdeɪvɪd/ **1** a famous STATUE of a man, made in MARBLE by Michelangelo. It is thought of as one of the best examples of the human form in art. —see picture at MICHELANGELO **2** see SAINT DAVID

David, Elizabeth (1914–92) an English cookery writer known esp. for writing about French and Mediterranean food

David, King (died about 962 BC) a king of Israel before the time of Christ. His story is told in the Bible and he is said to have written some of the Psalms. His friendship with **Jonathan**, the son of **Saul**, the first king of Israel, is used as an example of the most loyal friendship possible between two people. When David was just a boy he killed the GIANT Goliath with a stone from his SLING² (3), and this has led to the names **David** and **Goliath** being used when people want to describe someone small and weak trying to defeat someone very strong: *For years Lech Walesa was a David fighting Goliaths.* –see colour picture on page 424

David Cop·per·field /ˌdeɪvɪd ˈkɒpəfiːld ‖ -ˈkɑːpər-/ a NOVEL by Charles Dickens describing the life of a boy called David Copperfield in Victorian England. Many well-known characters appear in it, among them Mr Micawber and Uriah Heep.

Da·vies /ˈdeɪvɪs/, **Sir Peter Maxwell** (1934–) an English COMPOSER (=writer of music)

da Vin·ci /də ˈvɪntʃi/, **Le·o·nar·do** /ˌliːəˈnɑːdəʊ ‖ -ɑːr-/ (1452–1519) a great Italian painter of the Renaissance. Among his most famous works are *The Last Supper* and the *Mona Lisa*. He is also famous for his cleverness and his strong interest in science. Sometimes he is known just as Leonardo. —see colour picture on page 1016

Da·vis /ˈdeɪvɪs/, **An·ge·la** /ˈændʒᵻlə/ (1944–) a black American woman who is active in LEFT-WING politics

Davis, Bet·te /ˈbeti/ (1908–89) an American film character actress whose working life in films covered over 50 years. She was known for her powerful, DRAMATIC performances.

Davis, Sir Col·in /ˈkɒlᵻn‖ˈkɑː-/ (1927–) a well-known British CONDUCTOR (=a person who directs the playing of a group of musicians)

Davis, Jefferson (1808–89) the president of the Confederate states during the American Civil War —see also CIVIL WAR (2)

Davis, Joe /dʒəʊ/ (1901–78) an English SNOOKER player who was world CHAMPION for 20 years

Davis, Miles /maɪlz/ (1926–91) an American TRUMPET player and JAZZ band leader

Davis, Steve /stiːv/ (1958–) an English SNOOKER player who won three world titles in the 1980s and who is known for his calm, quiet play

Davis Cup /ˌ·· ˈ·/ [the] an important international men's tennis competition

dav·it /ˈdævᵻt, ˈdeɪvᵻt/ n either of a pair of long curved poles that swing out over the side of a ship for lowering boats, etc.

Da·vy Jones's lock·er /ˌdeɪvi dʒəʊnzᵻz ˈlɒkər‖-ˈlɑːkər/ infml humor the bottom of the sea, esp. as a place where people lie dead

daw·dle /ˈdɔːdl/ v [I] infml to waste time; move or do something very slowly: *He dawdled all morning/all the way to school.* | *The children dawdled over their food.* —**dler** n

Dawes Plan /ˈdɔːz ˌplæn/ [the] a plan thought up by Charles G. Dawes, an American banker, to help Germany pay its REPARATIONS (=a payment for damage) to other countries after the First World War

Daw·kins /ˈdɔːkɪnz/, **Richard** (1941–) a British scientist who has studied the behaviour of animals and written about animal behaviour and EVOLUTION. He is known esp. for his book *The Selfish Gene.*

dawn¹ /dɔːn/ n **1** [C;U] also **daybreak**— the time of day when light first appears; the first appearance of light in the sky before the sun rises: *The postman has to get up before dawn every day.* | *the stillness of a summer dawn* |

We drove all night and arrived just as **dawn was breaking.** —compare DUSK **2** [the (of)] the beginning or first appearance of a new period, idea, feeling, etc.: *the dawn of civilization/of hope/of the new technology* **3** at **(the) break of dawn** at the first light of day

dawn² v [I] (of the day, morning, etc.) to begin to grow light just before the sun rises: *The morning dawned fresh and clear after the storm.*
    dawn on/upon sbdy. phr v [T no pass.] to become known by: *It suddenly/gradually dawned on me that I'd caught the wrong train.*

dawn cho·rus /ˌ·ˈ··/ n [often the] loud singing by many different birds together at dawn

dawn raid /ˌ·ˈ·/ n an early morning attack or police action: (fig.) *a dawn raid on the ailing company's shares*

Daw·son /ˈdɔːsən/, **Les** /lez/ (1934–93) a popular English COMEDIAN who has often appeared on television and is known esp. for telling jokes about his MOTHER-IN-LAW

day /deɪ/ n **1** [C] a period of 24 hours: *There are seven days in a week.* | *the day before yesterday* | *the day after tomorrow* | *the last day of our vacation* | *Christmas Day was a Wednesday last year.* —see also DAYS; see USAGE

► CULTURAL NOTE Different days of the week have different activities connected with them. Many people joke about disliking **Monday** morning, when the working week begins. In Britain, **Wednesday** or **Thursday** may be EARLY CLOSING DAY in a small town, when many of the shops shut for the afternoon. **Friday** is the day that many non-professional workers get paid. It is also the last working day before the weekend, and people often feel very glad when Friday comes. People may go out for a meal or dancing on Friday night. **Saturday** is also a busy shopping day. Most people do not work on Saturday. It is also a day for doing jobs at home, such as cleaning the car. In the afternoon there are sports events such as football matches, and in the evening people often go out, for a meal, or dancing, or to a friend's house for dinner. **Sunday** is the day when Christians go to church; the main SERVICE¹ (6) is in the morning. Other people may have a LIE-IN (= stay in bed late). The Sunday papers are larger than the daily ones and some people spend a long time reading them. In Britain many people follow the custom of a Sunday lunch consisting of ROAST meat and vegetables followed by a PUDDING. People may visit relatives or friends, or go out somewhere in the car.◄

2 [C;U] the time between sunrise and sunset: *Call me in the evening as I'm usually out during the day.* | *It rained all day and all night.* **3** [C] a period of work within a 24-hour period: *She works an eight-hour day and a five-day week.* | *She's paid by the day.* | *Did you have a good day at the office?* –see also WORKING DAY **4** [C] also **days** pl.— a particular period or point of time: *Young people have a lot of freedom* **these days/in this day and age.** (=now) | *In the days before the war/In those days/In my day* (=in the past), *things were different.* | **Some day/One day** (=at some time in the future) *we'll take a trip to China.* —see also DAYS¹ **5** [S] a period of success or fame: **In her day**, *she was a very well-known singer.* | *He used to be a very good actor, but I'm afraid he's* **had his day** now. (=he is no longer good or popular) **6** [the] lit a struggle, battle, or competition: *to lose/win the day* **7 by day** during the day (esp. when compared with **by night**): *He works in an office by day and drives a taxi by night.* —see also DAYS² **8 day after day/day in day out** continuously for many days: *It went on raining day after day.* **9 day and night** all the time: *noisy neighbours who play their radio day and night* **10 from day to day/day by day** each day; as time goes on: *The situation changes from day to day.* **11 from one day to the next** two days in a row: *I never know her plans from one day to the next.* **12 go ahead/on, make my day** a phrase made famous by an American film by Clint Eastwood, when he was carrying a gun and inviting his enemy to make a move so that he would have a reason to shoot him **13 have a nice day** a phrase used, esp. in the US, when saying goodbye to someone during the day **14 make someone's day** infml to make someone very pleased and happy: *It made her day when her grandchildren came to see her.* **15 the other day** in the recent past: *I saw your friend the other day.* **16 to the day** (of time) exactly: *We left Spain one year ago to the day.* (=exactly one year ago) **17 to this day** until now: *I haven't told him the whole story to this day!* —see also DAYS, **in all my born days**

(BORN²), **call it a day** (CALL¹), **at the end of the day** (END¹)

▷ USAGE If today is Wednesday, then Monday was **the day before yesterday** and Friday will be **the day after tomorrow**.◁

Day¹, Dor·is /'dɔːɹ̣s‖'dɔː-/ (1924–   ) an American singer and actress who has appeared in many films and on television and was esp. popular in the 1950s. Her appearance and her image are thought to be pure, healthy, and home-loving.

Day², Sir Robin (1923–   ) an English broadcaster and writer. He is famous for his INTERVIEWS of politicians, in which he asks them very sharp and thorough questions in a very determined way. He often wears a BOW TIE with spots on it.

Sir Robin Day

Day·an /daɪ'jɑːn‖dɑː-/, **Mosh·e** /'mɒʃeɪ‖'məʊ-/ (1915–81) a soldier who was the Foreign Minister of Israel from 1977 to 1979, remembered abroad esp. because he wore a PATCH (5) over one eye

day·boy /'deɪbɔɪ/ n esp. BrE a boy who is a DAY PUPIL

day·break /'deɪbreɪk/ n [U] DAWN¹ (1)

day camp /'· ·/ n AmE a place where children can go during the day on school holidays to do various activities such as sports or CRAFTS: *There will be several day camps in the park from July 6 for children aged 6 to 16.*

day care /'· ·/ also **daycare**– n [U] **1** (in Britain) the care of people who cannot look after themselves during the day, by paid workers . **2** (in the US) the care of children during the day whose parents are both working –**daycare** adj [A] : *day-care centres*

day·dream /'deɪdriːm/ n a pleasant dreamlike set of thoughts while one is awake, often drawing attention away from present surroundings: *a daydream about being a rock star* –**daydream** v [I] : *Sorry, I wasn't listening – I was daydreaming.* –~**er** n

day·girl /'deɪgɜːl‖-gɜːrl/ n esp. BrE a girl who is a DAY PUPIL

day·glo , day·glo /'deɪgləʊ/ adj [A] tdmk of a bright orange, green, yellow, or pink colour that seems to give out light (GLOW) in the daytime: *dayglo socks/paint*

day·light /'deɪlaɪt/ n [U] **1** the light of day: *We'll keep on driving while there's still daylight.* | *the daylight hours* **2** the very beginning of the day; DAWN **3** **see daylight** to begin to understand something: *I thought about the problem for days before I began to see daylight.* –see also DAYLIGHTS

daylight rob·ber·y /ˌ·· '···/ n [U] infml the act of charging far too much money for something: *£2.50 for a cup of coffee? It's daylight robbery!*

day·lights /'deɪlaɪts/ n [P] infml life; consciousness: *I'll beat/knock the (living) daylights out of you if you do that again.* (=strike or beat you very severely) | *That spider scared the (living) daylights out of me.* (=frightened me very much)

daylight sav·ing time /ˌ·· '·· ·/ also **daylight savings time, daylight time** /'·· ˌ·/ – n [U] (in the US) time shown on clocks that is one hour ahead of the standard time, used during the summer –compare BRITISH SUMMER TIME

day nur·se·ry /'· ˌ···/ n a NURSERY (1)

Day of A·tone·ment /ˌ·· · '···/ [the] a Jewish holiday on which Jews do not eat but pray for forgiveness for the things they have done wrong (SINs) during the past year. It is also known as Yom Kippur.

day off /ˌ· '·/ n **days off** a day when one does not go to work and one has a day's holiday: *I work on Saturdays, so I get Mondays as my day off.* | *My boss keeps asking me to go in on my day off.*

day of judg·ment /ˌ· · '···/ [the] (often cap.) JUDGMENT DAY

day of reck·on·ing /ˌ· · '···/ n [the] a time when the results of past mistakes are felt, or when past offences are punished

Day of the Jack·al /ˌ· ·· '··/, **The** a film (based on the book of the same name by the English writer, Frederick Forsyth) about a professional killer attempting to murder the then French president General de Gaulle

day out /ˌ· '·/ n days out a day when one goes somewhere for the whole day, in order to enjoy oneself: *We haven't had a day out for ages.*

day pu·pil /'· ˌ··/ n esp. BrE a pupil who lives at home but goes to a school where some of the pupils live. The pupils who live in the school usu. regard day pupils as less important.

day re·lease course /ˌ· ·'· ·/ n BrE an educational course attended by workers who are allowed to leave their work on certain days; they are said to be **on day release**

day re·turn /ˌ· ·'·/ n BrE a ticket for travel to the place you are going to and back again on the same day. Day returns are usu. cheaper if you do not travel at the busiest time in the morning, when everyone is going to work.

day·room /'deɪruːm, -rʊm/ n a public room for reading, writing, and amusement in schools, military camps, hospitals, etc.

days¹ /deɪz/ n [P] **1** one's life: *He began his days in the island of Corsica, but went on to become Emperor of France.* **2** **his/her/its days are numbered** someone or something cannot live or continue much longer: *Your days of slaving over a hot stove are numbered; the microwave is now taking over in a big way.*

days² adv esp. AmE by day repeatedly; during any day: *She works days.*

day school /'· ·/ n **1** [C;U] a school whose pupils attend only during the day, returning home at night and at weekends –compare BOARDING SCHOOL **2** [C] a special course of lessons, talks, etc., given on a single day

day·time /'deɪtaɪm/ n [(the) U] the time between sunrise and sunset; DAY (2): *I can't sleep in the daytime.* | *daytime flights* –opposite **nighttime**

day-to-day /ˌ· · '·◂/ adj [A] **1** happening as a regular part of life: *the day-to-day routine* | *life's day-to-day problems* –compare EVERYDAY **2** planning for one day at a time with little thought for the future: *Since his wife died he's been living a day-to-day existence.*

Day·to·na Beach /deɪˌtəʊnə 'biːtʃ/ a city in the US state of Florida where a famous car race is held

day trip /'· ·/ n BrE a visit to somewhere, usu. by bus or train, just for pleasure and only lasting one day: *They're going on a day trip to Blackpool.*

day-trip·per /'· ˌ··/ also **tripper**– n esp. BrE, often derog a person on a pleasure trip to somewhere, which only lasts one day: *I hate Yarmouth at this time of year. You can't move for all the day-trippers.*

Daz /dæz/ n [U] tdmk a type of WASHING POWDER made by Procter and Gamble Limited

daze¹ /deɪz/ v [T often pass.] to make unable to think or feel clearly, esp. by a shock or blow; STUPEFY: *After the accident Jean was dazed.* | *The news left us dazed.* –~**dly** /'deɪzɣdli/ adv

daze² n **in a daze** in a dazed condition

daz·zle /'dæzəl/ v [T] **1** to make unable to see because of a sudden very strong light shining in the eyes: *The lights of the car dazzled me.* **2** to fill with wonder or admiration: *She was dazzled by her sudden success* | *a dazzling display of skill.* –**dazzle** n [S] : *The theatre was a dazzle of bright lights.*

DBE /ˌdiː biː 'iː/ n Dame Commander of the (Order of the) British Empire; a title given in Britain to a woman as an honour because she has done something of national importance. A woman who has a DBE can use the title **Dame** instead of **Mrs, Miss**, or **Ms**: *She was awarded a DBE in 1992.*

dbl abbrev. for. DOUBLE (1)

DBMS /ˌdiː biː em 'es/ n database management system; a set of computer PROGRAMs which controls and makes easier the use of information stored on a computer

DBS /ˌdiː biː 'es/ n [U] direct broadcasting by SATELLITE; a way of broadcasting many different television programmes to people's houses. To receive these programmes, people have to buy a special part for their television set and a receiving dish for the outside of their house.

DC /ˌdiː ˈsiː◂/ abbrev. for: **1** DIRECT CURRENT —compare AC **2** District of Columbia (the area of the US containing its capital): Washington, DC —see also WASHINGTON DC **3** Detective Constable; the lowest rank in the British police force's PLAIN-CLOTHES division

DCC /ˌdiː siː ˈsiː/ abbrev. for: DIGITAL COMPACT CASSETTE

DCD /ˌdiː siː ˈdiː/ abbrev. for: DIGITAL COMPACT DISC

DD /ˌdiː ˈdiː/ abbrev. for: DIRECT DEBIT

D-day /ˈdiː ·ˌ/ n **1** 6th June, 1944; in the Second World War, the day the ALLIES landed in France to begin the spread of their forces through Europe, under the command of General Eisenhower. It is remembered for its military organization, willingness to work effectively together, and success. **2** a day on which an important operation or planned action is to begin: So, today is D-day, then?

DDS /ˌdiː diː ˈes/ n AmE Doctor of Dental Surgery; (a title for someone who has qualified (QUALIFY) to be) a DENTIST

DDT /ˌdiː diː ˈtiː/ n [U] a chemical that kills insects. DDT was used on food crops all over the world until it was discovered that it remains in the crops and can harm people.

DE written abbrev. for DELAWARE

de- see WORD FORMATION

DEA /ˌdiː iː ˈeɪ/ n abbrev. for DRUG ENFORCEMENT ADMINISTRATION

dea·con /ˈdiːkən/ n (in various Christian churches) a religious official who is directly below a priest in rank

dead¹ /ded/ adj [no comp.] **1** no longer alive: I'm afraid he's dead. | a dead man|cat|leaf | Two of the terrorists were shot dead (=shot and killed) by the police. —compare INANIMATE; see also DECEASED¹, DEPARTED(2) **2** no longer in use, operation, or existence: a dead language | dead ideas —compare LIVING¹ (2) **3** without the necessary power to work properly: dead matches | a dead battery | The telephone went dead in the middle of our conversation. —compare LIVE² (3,4) **4** [A] complete: a dead stop | dead silence | a dead loss (=a completely useless person or thing) **5** without life, movement, or activity: dead rocks and stones | The whole place seems dead. **6** [F] unable to feel; NUMB: It's so cold that my fingers have gone dead. **7** (of a ball in some sports) out of PLAY¹ (8) **8** (of sounds and colours) dull; not clear or bright **9 dead as a doornail** infml completely dead **10 dead to the world** very deeply asleep or unconscious —see also DEATH, **flog a dead horse** (FLOG) — ~ness n [U]

dead² n [P often the] people who have died: The dead are thought to number more than 400. | Because of the continued fighting, families have been unable to bury their dead. | the resurrection of the dead —see also DECEASED², DEPARTED(2)

dead³ adv **1** suddenly and completely: The train stopped dead. **2** [ı adj] infml completely: dead certain | dead tired **3** [ı adv/prep] infml directly: dead ahead | His shot was dead on target.

dead⁴ n **in the dead of night/winter** in the quietest or least active period of the night or winter

dead-and-a·live /ˌ· · ·ˈ·/ n BrE (of a place, person, or activity) uninteresting; dull

dead beat /ˌ· ˈ·◂/ adj infml completely tired

dead·beat /ˈdedbiːt/ n sl **1** a lazy aimless person **2** AmE infml someone who avoids paying their debts

dead cen·tre /ˌ· ˈ·/ n [the] (in) the exact centre: Aim for the dead centre.

dead duck /ˌ· ˈ·/ n infml a plan, idea, etc., that has failed or is likely to fail

dead·en /ˈdedn/ v [T] to cause to lose strength, feeling, brightness, etc.: This drug will deaden the pain. | The thick walls of the shelter deadened the noise of the bombing.

dead end /ˌ· ˈ·◂/ n **1** an end (esp. of a street) with no way out **2** a position or situation beyond which movement or development is impossible: We've come to a dead end in our efforts to reach an agreement.

dead-end job /ˌ· · ˈ·/ n a boring job, often needing little skill or ability, which does not lead to other more exciting jobs

dead ground /ˌ· ˈ·/ n [U] ground through which one can move without being seen by the enemy, e.g. because of the way the ground slopes

dead·head¹ /ˈdedhed/ n AmE **1** a person who rides on a train, bus, etc., without buying a ticket **2** a car, bus, TRUCK, or train which is empty when it is moved

deadhead² v [I] AmE to drive a train, bus, or TRUCK without passengers or goods: I'm going to deadhead home as soon as I unload these potatoes.

dead heat /ˌ· ˈ·/ n a race in which two or more competitors finish at exactly the same time

dead let·ter /ˌ· ˈ·/ n **1** a letter that cannot be either delivered or returned to the sender **2** a law or rule that still exists but that people no longer obey

dead·line /ˈdedlaɪn/ n a date or time before which something must be done or completed: Next Tuesday is the deadline for sending in your application. | I'm working to a deadline. (=My work must be finished by a certain time.) | Can you meet the deadline? (=finish in time)

dead·lock /ˈdedlɒk‖-lɑːk/ n [C;U] a position in which a disagreement cannot be settled; STALEMATE: The talks about arms control have reached (a) complete deadlock. | Will the new proposal break (=end) the deadlock? —dead·lock v [I;T] —deadlocked adj : the deadlocked Vietnam peace talks

deadlock n [C,U] a position in which…break (=end) the deadlock

dead loss /ˌ· ˈ·/ n sl a complete waste; something or someone that is completely useless: He won't know, he's a dead loss at maths.

dead·ly /ˈdedli/ adj **1** likely to cause death: a deadly poison|weapon **2** aiming to kill or destroy: deadly enemies **3** [A] complete or total: He said it in deadly earnest. (=completely seriously) | deadly accuracy **4** [A] like death in appearance: deadly paleness **5** infml very uninteresting; dull: a deadly party|bore —-liness n [U]

deadly² adv **1** very (in phrases like **deadly serious, deadly dull, deadly boring**) **2** like death: deadly pale

deadly night·shade /ˌdedli ˈnaɪtʃeɪd/ also **belladonna**— n [C;U] a poisonous European plant from which the drug BELLADONNA is obtained

deadly sin /ˌ·· ˈ·/ n a MORTAL SIN —see also SEVEN DEADLY SINS

dead-man's float /ˌ· · ˈ·/ n [S] AmE the act of staying on the surface of water with one's face in the water and one's arms and legs out to one's sides: The first thing you'll learn in your swimming class is the dead-man's float.

dead march /ˈ· ·/ n a piece of solemn slow marching music for a funeral

dead·pan /ˈdedpæn/ adj, adv infml with no show of feeling, esp. when telling jokes as if they were serious: deadpan humour | She played her part completely deadpan.

dead par·rot sketch /ˌ· ˈ·· ˌ·/ n [the] the most famous SKETCH¹ (3) from the humorous British television programme Monty Python's Flying Circus. It is about a man who goes into a pet shop to complain about his dead parrot. People sometimes describe someone who has completely failed or been completely defeated as "a dead parrot". —see also MONTY PYTHON

dead reck·on·ing /ˌ· ˈ···/ n [U] the mapping of the position of a ship or aircraft without looking at the sun, moon, or stars —compare RECKONING

dead ring·er /ˌ· ˈ··/ n [+for] infml someone who looks very like someone else: You're a dead ringer for my brother.

Dead Sea /ˌ· ˈ·◂/ n [the] a very large lake in the Middle East. It is well-known firstly because the water is very salty and people float on it very easily, and secondly because of the discovery near it of the Dead Sea Scrolls.

Dead Sea Scrolls /ˌ· · ˈ·/ n [the+P] ancient Jewish religious writings written or copied around the time of Christ and found near the Dead Sea between 1947 and 1956

dead weight /ˌ· ˈ·/ n something which is very heavy to carry, esp. because it is alive but unable to move its body, e.g. because it is unconscious

dead wood /ˌ· ˈ·/ BrE ‖ **dead·wood** /ˈdedwʊd/ AmE — n [U] people or things that are useless or no longer needed: The problem with that company is that it's got too much dead wood. | There's quite a bit of dead wood in the report, so it should be easy to shorten it.

deaf¹ /def/ adj **1** unable to hear at all or to hear well: Look, he's got a hearing aid — he's deaf. | sign language for deaf *people | Speak up; I'm rather deaf.* **2** [F (**to**)] unwilling to hear or listen: *She was deaf to all my requests.* **3 turn a deaf ear to** to be unwilling to hear or listen to: *My parents turned a deaf ear to my requests for money.* —compare **turn a blind eye to** (BLIND¹); —see BLIND² (USAGE) —~**ness** *n* [U]

deaf² *n* [P often *the*] people who are deaf: *a special school for the deaf | the profoundly deaf*

deaf-aid /'··/ *n BrE infml for* HEARING AID

deaf-and-dumb /,··'·◄/ *adj* deaf and unable to speak — **deaf-and-dumb** *n AmE*

deaf·en /'defən/ *v* [T] to make deaf, esp. for a short time: *We were deafened by the noise. | deafening* (=very loud) *music* —see BLIND² (USAGE)

deaf-mute /,·'·||'··/ *n, adj fml* (a person who is) deaf and unable to speak

deal¹ /di:l/ *v* **dealt** /delt/ **1** [I;T (**to**, OUT)] to give out (playing cards) to players in a game: *It's my turn to deal. | to deal (out) the cards | I dealt three cards to each player.* [+*obj(i)+obj(d)*] *He dealt me three cards.* **2** [T (**to**, OUT)] to give, esp. as a share of something: *I dealt out two biscuits to each of the children.* **3** [T] *esp. lit or old use* to strike (a blow): [+ *obj(i) + obj(d)*] *She* **dealt him a blow** *on the head.* **4** [I;T] *sl* to buy and sell (illegal drugs)
   deal in sthg. *phr v* [T *usu. not pass.*] to buy and sell; trade in: *She deals in men's clothing.*
   deal with sbdy./sthg. *phr v* [T] **1** to take action about; TACKLE: *effective measures to deal with drug smuggling | All complaints will be dealt with by the manager. | It was a difficult situation, but she dealt with it effectively.* **2** to be about; have as a subject: *The book deals with the troubles in Ireland.* **3** to do business, esp. trade, with: *I've dealt with this store/person/company for 20 years.*

deal² *n* **1** [C] an agreement or arrangement, esp. in business or politics, esp. one that is to the advantage of both sides: *The car company has* **done** (*BrE*)/**made** (*AmE*) **a deal** *with a Polish firm to supply engines in exchange for wheels. | The prosecution lawyers offered to do a deal with the defence in order to get the man convicted. | Do we have a deal?* **2** [S] a particular type of treatment that is given or received: *They promised to give the nurses a better deal* (=more money, etc.) *if they were elected. | We have been getting* **a rough/raw deal.** (=unfair treatment) —see also NEW DEAL **3** [S (**of**)] a quantity or degree, usu. large: *We have spent* **a great deal of** *money on the new hospital. | You will have to work* **a good deal** *faster.* —see MORE (USAGE) **4** [C] the process of giving out cards to players in a card game: *Whose deal is it?* —see also DEALER (2) **5 it's a deal** I agree to the arrangement you have just suggested: *"I want sixty dollars for it." "I'll give you forty." "Fifty." "OK, it's a deal."* —see also BIG DEAL

deal³ *n* [U] *esp. BrE* FIR or PINE wood used for making things: *a deal table*

deal·er /'di:lə^r/ *n* **1** a person in a stated type of business: *a used-car dealer | a drug dealer* —see also DOUBLE-DEALER **2** a person who deals playing cards

deal·er·ship /'di:ləʃɪp||-lər-/ *n* a place that deals in the stated product: *There's a Rover dealership in Riverhead.*

deal·ing /'di:lɪŋ/ *n* [U] methods of business or personal relations: *I believe in* **plain dealing.** (=honest methods, esp. in business)

deal·ings /'di:lɪŋz/ *n* [P] personal or business relations: *I've had some dealings with him, but I don't know him very well.*

dean /di:n/ *n* (*sometimes cap.*) **1** (esp. in the Anglican Church) a high-ranking priest in charge of several priests or church divisions **2** (in some universities) a person in charge of a division of study, or in charge of students and their behaviour, or, in the US, in charge of a part of the administration

Dean, James (1931–55) an American film actor who played young men opposed to authority. He died in a car crash. His most famous film was *Rebel Without a Cause*, and many people think of him as representing youthful REBELLION. —see colour picture on page 228

dean·e·ry /'di:nəri/ *n* the area controlled by a DEAN (1) or the office of a dean

Dean's List /'· ,·/ *n* [*the*] in the US, a list of students in a college or university who have reached a high standard in their work

dear¹ /dɪə^r/ *adj* **1** much loved: *He's my dearest friend.* **2** [A] (*usu. cap.*) (used at the beginning of a letter): *Dear Jane | Dear Sir* **3** [F+**to**] precious; of the greatest importance: *His family is very dear to him.* **4** *esp. BrE* expensive: *It's too dear: I can't afford it.* —~**ness** *n* [U]

dear² *n* **1** (*esp. BrE*) a person who is loved or lovable: *Be a dear and make me some tea.* **2 a** (used when speaking to someone you love or to a member of your family): *Did you have a good day at work, dear?* **b** (used informally as a friendly form of address, esp. by or to a woman; said e.g. by a person working in a shop or restaurant): *That will be fifty pence please, dear.* —see DARLING¹ (CULTURAL NOTE)

dear³ *interj* (used for expressing surprise, sorrow, slight anger, discouragement): *Oh dear! I've spilled my coffee. | "My mother is ill again." "Dear! Dear! I'm sorry to hear that." | Dear me! I'm going to be late!*

dear⁴ *adv* **cost someone dear** to result in a lot of suffering and trouble: *Her decision to marry him cost her dear.*

Dear Ab·by /,dɪər 'æbi/ *n tdmk* an American newspaper COLUMN written by Abigail Van Buren which prints letters from readers asking for advice along with answers —see AGONY AUNT, Ann LANDERS

dear·est /'dɪərᵻst/ *n often pomp* (used for speaking to someone) a much-loved person: *The flowers are for you, (my) dearest.* —see also **nearest and dearest** (NEAR¹)

Dear John let·ter /,·· '· ,··/ *n* a letter to a man from his wife or girlfriend which tells him that she no longer loves him

dear·ie /'dɪəri/ *n* DEARY

dear·ly /'dɪəli||'dɪərli/ *adv* **1** with strong feeling, esp. of love: *I would dearly love to go back to Scotland. | He loves his wife dearly.* **2** at a terrible cost in time, effort, pain, etc.: *He paid dearly for his mistake.* **3 dearly beloved** dear people; used by a priest talking to his CONGREGATION: *Dearly beloved, we have come together in the sight of God...*

dearth /dɜ:θ||dɜ:rθ/ *n* [S+**of**] *fml* a lack (of); SHORTAGE

dear·y /'dɪəri/ also **dearie**— *n old-fash infml* (used when speaking to someone) DEAR²

death /deθ/ *n* **1** [C;U] the end of life; time or manner of dying: *He remained in good health right up to his death. | His mother's sudden death was a great shock to him. | Drunken driving causes thousands of deaths every year. | Did she die a natural death, or was she murdered? | The judge sentenced him to death by hanging.* —compare BIRTH; see also DECEASE, DEMISE **2** [U] the state of being dead: *as still/cold as death | Hundreds of animals were burned* **to death** *in the forest fire.* —compare LIFE (3) **3** [C (**of**)] the cause of loss of life (often in the phrase **be the death of**): *Drinking will be the death of him. | If you go out without a coat, you'll* **catch your death of cold.** —see also DEADLY **4** [S;U] destruction or disappearance: *a defeat that meant the death of all my hopes | Death to imperialism!* **5** [U] (*usu. cap.*) the destroyer of life, usu. represented as a SKELETON: *a picture of Death wearing a black cloak and holding a sickle* **6 at death's door** *esp. humor* very ill, and likely to die: *Anyone would think he was at death's door, the way he's complaining, but he's only got a bit of a cold!* **7 like death warmed up** *BrE* || also **like death warmed over** *AmE– infml* very ill or tired: *Ever since I caught this cold, I've been feeling like death warmed up.* **8 in at the death** present at the death of a hunted animal or at the defeat of a person, plan, etc. **9 nothing is certain but death and taxes** *quote* a slightly changed phrase from a piece of writing by Benjamin Franklin **10 put to death** to kill, esp. with official permission: *The prisoners were all put to death.* **11 till death us do part** *BrE* || **till us do us part** *AmE quote* a phrase from the Christian marriage service. The two people getting married promise that they will stay together and love each other "till death us do part" (=until one of them dies). **12 to death** beyond all acceptable limits: *I am sick to death of their complaints. | Your mother will be worried to death about you.* —see also KISS OF DEATH, **do to death** (DO²)

death·bed /'deθbed/ *n* [*usu. sing.*] the bed on which someone dies: *He forgave them* **on his deathbed.** *| a deathbed repentance/conversion*

death·blow /'deθbləʊ/ *n* [*usu. sing.*] an act or event that destroys or ends: *His refusal to help us* **dealt a deathblow to** *our plans.*

death camp /'· ·/ n a CONCENTRATION CAMP, esp. one of the German camps of the Second World War

death cer·tif·i·cate /'· ·,···/ n a legal document signed by a doctor stating the fact and usu. the cause of someone's death. In Britain and the US a person may not be legally buried without a death certificate.

death du·ties /'· ·,··/ BrE ‖**death tax** /'· ·/ AmE– n [P] money that had to be paid to a government as a tax on property that had been left to a person when the original owner had died. This tax is now called INHERITANCE TAX and sometimes also ESTATE TAX in the US.

Death in Ven·ice /ₗ· · · '··/ a book by Thomas Mann, later made into a film, in which the HERO, a successful writer, comes to love a beautiful Polish boy and cannot make himself leave Venice, even though there is CHOLERA there. The cholera finally kills him. People sometimes make jokes, esp. about Venice, using this phrase.

death·less /'deθləs/ adj unforgettable; IMMORTAL (used jokingly about things which are exactly the opposite): the Inland Revenue's usual deathless prose – ~ **ly** adv

death·like /'deθlaɪk/ adj like death or like that of death: a deathlike puleness/silence

death·ly /'deθli/ adj, adv like death: a deathly cold body | a deathly silence/hush

death mask /'· ·/ n a copy of a dead person's face made by pressing a soft material (e.g. PLASTER OF PARIS) over the face

Death of a Sales·man /ₗ· · · '··/ a play of the late 1940s by Arthur Miller in which Willy Loman, the main character, kills himself after he loses his job

death pen·al·ty /'· ,··/ also **death sen·tence** /'· ,··/ [the] punishment by death –see CAPITAL PUNISHMENT (CULTURAL NOTE)

death rate /'· ·/ n the number of deaths for every 100 or 1000 people in a particular year in a particular place –compare BIRTHRATE

death rat·tle /'· ,··/ n an unusual noise sometimes heard from the throat of a dying person

death row /ₗdeθ 'rəυ/ n [U] esp. AmE the part of a prison in which those prisoners are kept who will be punished by death: convicted murderers waiting on death row

death's-head /'· ·/ n a human SKULL representing death

death squad /'· ·/ n [C + sing /pl n] a group of people who travel around killing political opponents, often acting on the orders of a political party. Death squads are usu. thought of as working in countries where DEMOCRACY does not exist or is not very strong.

death toll /'· ·/ n the number of people who died in a particular way or because of a particular event: The death toll from the earthquake is approaching two hundred.

death trap /'· ·/ n infml something very dangerous to life: That old boat is a real death trap.

Death Val·ley /ₗ· '··/ a DESERT area in the US states of Nevada and California. It is one of the hottest places in the world, and many PIONEERS died trying to cross Death Valley.

death war·rant /'· ,··/ n a written official order to kill (EXECUTE) someone

death·watch bee·tle /'deθwɒtʃ ₗbiːtl ‖ -waːtʃ-, -wɔːtʃ-/ n an insect that causes serious damage to old buildings by digging into the wood

death wish /'· ·/ n [S] a conscious or unconscious desire for death

deb /deb/ n infml for DEBUTANTE

de·ba·cle also **débâcle** BrE /deɪ'baːkəl, dɪ-/ n a badly organized event which is a complete failure: Our high school sports day was a complete débâcle.

de·bar /dɪ'baːʳ/ v
debar sbdy. **from** sthg. phr v **-rr-** [T+obj/v-ing] to officially prevent from: Until recently, people who did not own property were debarred from jury service/from serving on juries in Britain. –compare DISBAR

de·bark /dɪ'baːrk‖-aːrk/ v [I] becoming rare **1** to take the outside off (a tree) **2** to DISEMBARK – ~ **ation** /ₗdiːbaːr'keɪʃən‖-aːr-/ n [C;U]

de·base /dɪ'beɪs/ v [T] **1** to reduce in quality or value or in the opinion of others; DEGRADE: The word "situation" is so overused that it has become rather debased. **2** to lower the real value of (coins) by making them with less valuable metal: to debase the currency **3** **debase the coinage** to make people have a lower opinion of something: It's no use lowering the standard for university entry. It's just debasing the coinage. – ~ **ment** n [C;U]

de·ba·ta·ble /dɪ'beɪtəbəl/ adj **1** doubtful; perhaps not true; questionable: a debatable statement | It's debatable whether this policy has caused unemployment. **2** claimed by more than one country: a debatable border area

de·bate¹ /dɪ'beɪt/ n **1** [C] a meeting, esp. in public, in which a question is talked about by at least two people or groups, each expressing a different opinion: There was a long debate in Parliament on the question of capital punishment. | a heated debate **2** [C usu. sing.;U] the process of talking about a question in detail; DISCUSSION: After much debate, the committee voted to close the school. | How to solve this problem is still a matter for debate. | the current debate on inner-city crime (=this is a subject that people generally are now talking about)

debate² v **1** [I;T] to hold a debate about (something), usu. in an attempt to reach a decision: They debated for over an hour on the merits of the different systems. | The Senate will debate the subject of tax increases. [+wh-] They debated whether to accept the management's proposals. **2** [T] to consider in one's own mind the arguments for and against something: I debated the idea in my mind. [+wh-] She debated whether to accept their offer. – **bater** n **5**: a skilled debater

de·bauch¹ /dɪ'bɔːtʃ‖dɪ'bɔːtʃ, dɪ'baːtʃ/ v [T usu. pass.] to cause to behave badly, esp. in relation to sex and alcohol: debauched young men

debauch² n an occasion of wild behaviour, esp. in relation to sex and alcohol; wild party or ORGY

de·bauch·ee /ₗdebɔː'tʃiː, -'ʃiː‖dɪ,bɔː'tʃiː, dɪ,baː-/ n derog a debauched person

de·bauch·e·ry /dɪ'bɔːtʃəri‖dɪ'bɔː-, dɪ'baː-/ n [U] wild behaviour, esp. in relation to sex and alcohol: a life of total debauchery

de Beau·voir, Si·mone /də 'bəυvwaːʳ‖-,bəυ'vwaːr/ /siː'məυn/ (1908–86) a French writer, thought by some to be the mother of FEMINIST writing and whose name is often connected to that of Jean-Paul Sartre

Deb·en·hams /'debənəmz/ n [C;U] one of a group of large shops in Britain, selling mainly clothes and goods for the house

de·ben·ture /dɪ'bentʃəʳ/ n **1** BrE an official paper that is sold by a business company and represents a debt on which the company must pay the buyer a fixed rate of interest; BOND¹ (3) **2** AmE a BOND¹ (3) which is not guaranteed (GUARANTEE) by the property of the company that sells it

de·bil·i·tate /dɪ'bɪlₐteɪt/ v [T] to make weak, esp. through heat, illness, or hunger: a debilitating disease | We were all debilitated by the extreme heat.

de·bil·i·ty /dɪ'bɪlₐti/ n [U] fml weakness, esp. as the result of disease

deb·it¹ /'debₐt/ n **1** a record in a book of accounts of money spent or owed **2** a charge against a bank account –compare CREDIT¹ (3); see also DIRECT DEBIT

debit² v [T] **1** [(against)] to record (an amount of money taken from an account): Debit £10 against Mr Smith/Mr Smith's account. **2** [(with)] to charge with money owed: Debit Mr Smith/Mr Smith's account with £10. –compare CREDIT² (2)

debit card /'·· ·/ n a small plastic card which is used instead of money or a CHEQUE to pay for goods and services from shops, garages, etc. The cost is taken directly from the user's bank account. Debit cards can also be used to obtain money from CASH DISPENSERS. –compare CHARGE CARD, CHEQUE CARD, CREDIT CARD; see also SWITCH

debit note /'·· ·/ n a document informing a buyer that his or her bank account has been debited with the amount shown on the note, usu. because the buyer was charged too little originally

deb·o·nair /ₗdebə'neəʳ◂/ adj apprec, becoming rare (usu. of men) cheerful, charming, and fashionably dressed: a debonair manner/young man

de Bo·no /də 'bəυnəυ/, **Dr Edward** (1933–) a Maltese-born British doctor who invented the idea of LATERAL THINKING

de·bouch /dɪ'baʊtʃ, -'buːʃ/ v [I+adv/prep] esp. tech (esp. of a river) to come out from a narrow place (such as a valley) into a broader place: *The river debouches into a wide plain.* | (fig.) *a football crowd debouching from a row of buses*

De·brett's /də'brets/ also **Debrett**— n **1** a book which is a guide to the members of the British royal family and the people of the highest social class **2** a company which produces books about correct social behaviour

de·brief /ˌdiː'briːf/ v [T] to officially get information from (someone such as a SPY, ASTRONAUT, or HOSTAGE) after completion of a job, trip, or escape from an enemy country —compare BRIEF³

deb·ris /'debriː, 'deɪ-‖də'briː, deɪ-/ n [U] the remains of something, usu. something large such as a building, that has been broken to pieces or destroyed; ruins: *After the bombing/the earthquake there was a lot of debris everywhere.*

debt /det/ n **1** [C] something owed to someone else: *a debt of £10* | *to pay one's debts* | (fig.) *We owe you a debt of gratitude for your help.* **2** [U] the state of owing; the duty of repaying something: *I'm heavily in debt at the moment, but hope to be out of debt when I get paid.* | *I'll always be in debt to you for your help.* | *If we spend more than our income we'll* **run into debt**. (=begin to owe money) —see also BAD DEBT, NATIONAL DEBT

▶CULTURAL NOTE In the past, people were often rather ashamed of getting into debt, but now it is considered quite normal to owe money on one's CREDIT CARD, on a HIRE PURCHASE deal, etc. People sometimes talk of a 'buy now, pay later' mentality.◀

debt col·lect·or /'· ·ˌ··/ n someone who is employed to collect debts: *Look out of the window and see if that's the debt collector at the door.*

debt of hon·our /ˌ· · '··/ n a debt that one ought to pay even though the law does not force one to

debt·or /'detər/ n a person, group, or organization that owes money: *debtor nations* —compare CREDITOR

de·bug /ˌdiː'bʌg/ v -gg- [T] infml **1** to search for and remove the BUGS (=faults) in (a computer PROGRAM) **2** to remove the BUGS (=secret listening apparatus) from (a room or building)

de·bunk /ˌdiː'bʌŋk/ v [T] infml to point out the true facts about (people, ideas, etc. that have received too much praise): *Their version of events was once widely believed, but now it's been thoroughly debunked. — –er n*

De·bus·sy /də'bjuːsi, -'buː-‖ˌdeɪbjuː'siː/, **Claude** /kləʊd/ (1862–1918) a French COMPOSER (=writer of music), one of the first to try to make images and show feelings through the quality of the sounds rather than through the patterns of the notes

de·but /'deɪbjuː, 'debjuː‖deɪ'bjuː, dɪ-/ n a first public appearance: *The singer made his debut as Mozart's Don Giovanni.*

deb·u·tante /'debjʊtɑːnt/ also **deb** infml— n a young UPPERCLASS woman who attends certain special parties, dances, and other social events as a way of being formally introduced to upper-class society

DEC /dek/ Digital Equipment Corporation; the world's second largest maker of computers, with main offices in the US and branches in many countries

Dec. written abbrev. for: December

dec·ade /'dekeɪd, de'keɪd/ n a period of ten years: *Prices have risen steadily during the past decade.* | *a movement which grew in the early decades of this century*

dec·a·dence /'dekədəns/ n [U] **1** a fall to a lower or worse level, e.g. of morality, civilization, or art, from a former higher or better level **2** a state of having low standards of behaviour or morality

dec·a·dent /'dekədənt/ adj marked by decadence; in a state of DECLINE, esp. morally: *the last decadent years of the Roman Empire* | *How decadent to stay in bed all day!* – ~ly adv

de·caf /'diːkæf/ adj,n [U] abbrev. for: decaffeinated (coffee or, rarely, tea)

de·caf·fei·na·ted /diː'kæfₛneɪtₛd/ adj with the CAFFEINE (=a

drug which makes you feel more active) removed. Some people drink decaffeinated coffee, tea, or COLA because ordinary coffee or tea excites their mind and they feel unwell or cannot sleep, and some drink it because they think ordinary tea and coffee are bad for the heart.

de·cal /'diːkæl, 'de-‖diː'kæl, 'dekəl/ n esp. AmE for TRANSFER² (3)

Dec·a·logue /'dekəlɒg‖-lɔːg, -lɑːg/ [the] tech the Ten Commandments

De·cam·e·ron /dɪ'kæmərən/ [the] a group of amusing stories, often about sex, by the great Italian writer Boccaccio. Written in the middle of the 14th century this work had a great influence on English literature.

de·camp /dɪ'kæmp/ v [I] infml to leave a place quickly and usu. in secret: *The lodger has decamped without paying his bill.*

de·cant /dɪ'kænt/ v [T] **1** to pour (liquid, esp. wine) from one container into another **2** infml to move (people) from one living or working place into another

de·cant·er /dɪ'kæntər/ n a container (usu. of glass and decorated) for holding alcoholic drinks, esp. wine, before they are poured into glasses. It is used for decorative effect and, in the case of wine, to improve the taste.

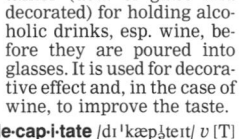 

decanter

de·cap·i·tate /dɪ'kæpₛteɪt/ v [T] to cut off the head of, esp. as a punishment; BEHEAD —-tation /dɪˌkæpₛ'teɪʃən/ n [C;U]

de·cath·lon /dɪ'kæθlɒn‖-lɑːn, -lən/ n a competition in ATHLETICS in which the competitors have to take part in ten separate events: *The decathlon includes the 100 metres sprint, the long jump, and the javelin.* —compare PENTATHLON, BIATHLON

de·cay¹ /dɪ'keɪ/ v **1** [I;T] to (cause to) go through chemical changes which cause destruction: *Sugar can decay the teeth.* | *decayed wood* **2** [I] to fall to a lower or worse state; lose health, power, activity, etc.; DECLINE: *Perhaps all nations decay in the course of time.* | *a decaying urban area*

decay² n [U] **1** the process or state of decaying: *The empty house has* **fallen into decay**. | *The wood has been specially treated to be resistant to decay.* **2** the decayed parts of the teeth: *The dentist used a drill to remove the decay.*

Dec·ca /'dekə/ a large company which produces music recordings and entertainment equipment such as televisions, etc.

de·cease /dɪ'siːs/ n [U] fml or law death: *Upon your decease the house will pass to your wife.*

de·ceased¹ /dɪ'siːst/ adj fml, euph, or law (of people) no longer living, esp. recently dead

deceased² n **deceased** [the] fml, euph, or law the dead person; a word used esp. by policemen, lawyers, and UNDERTAKERS: *The deceased left a large sum of money to his wife.* | *The deceased were both killed with the same knife.*

de·ceit /dɪ'siːt/ n **1** [U] the quality of being dishonest **2** [C] a trick; DECEPTION (2)

de·ceit·ful /dɪ'siːtfəl/ adj tending to deceive; dishonest – ~ly adv – ~ness n [U]

de·ceive /dɪ'siːv/ v [T (into)] to cause (someone) to accept as true or good what is false or bad, usu. for a dishonest purpose: *He deceived me — he lied about the money.* | *They deceived her into signing the papers.* | *Unless my eyes deceive me, that's the vice-president sitting over there.* | *You're just deceiving yourself if you carry on believing that she loves you.* —-ceiver n

de·cel·e·rate /ˌdiː'seləreɪt/ v [I;T] tech to (cause to) go slower, esp. in a vehicle: *to decelerate when approaching a corner* —opposite accelerate —-ration /ˌdiːseləˈreɪʃən/ n [U]

De·cem·ber /dɪ'sembər/ (written abbrev. **Dec.**) n [C;U] the 12th and last month of the year, between November and January. December 25th is Christmas Day. In Britain and the northern parts of the US, December, January, and February are the winter months. The temperature is low and there may be snow and ice: *It happened on December the tenth/on the tenth of December/(AmE) on December tenth.* | *This office opened in December 1991.* | *She started work here last December/the December before last.*

de·cen·cies /ˈdiːsənsiz/ n observe the decencies *becoming rare* to behave in accordance with socially accepted standards of behaviour

de·cen·cy /ˈdiːsənsi/ n [U] the quality of being decent: *I know you didn't like him, but at least* **have the decency to** *go to his funeral!*

de·cent /ˈdiːsənt/ adj **1** proper; socially acceptable; not causing shame or shock to others: *decent behaviour | Those tight trousers of yours aren't very decent!* —opposite **indecent** **2** good enough; ADEQUATE: *a decent wage/standard of living | You can get quite a decent meal there without spending too much.* **3** *infml* nice; kind: *It was very decent of you to drive me to the station.* – ~**ly** adv

de·cen·tral·ize also **-ise** BrE /ˌdiːˈsentrəlaɪz/ v [I;T] **a** to move (government, a business, etc.) from one central place or office to several different smaller ones **b** (of government, a business, etc.) to move in this way —see also CENTRALIZE —**-ization** /ˌdiːsentrəlaɪˈzeɪʃən‖-lə-/ n [U]

de·cep·tion /dɪˈsepʃən/ n **1** [U] the act of deceiving **2** [C] something that deceives; a trick

de·cep·tive /dɪˈseptɪv/ adj tending or intended to deceive; misleading: *She seems to have plenty of confidence, but appearances are sometimes deceptive.* – ~**ly** adv: *The salesman made it look deceptively simple.* – ~**ness** n [U]

dec·i·bel /ˈdesɪbel, -bəl/ n tech a measure of the loudness of sound

dec·i·bels /ˈdesɪbelz, -bəlz/ n [P] *infml humor* noise

de·cide /dɪˈsaɪd/ v **1** [I (**on**);T] to make a choice or judgment about (a course of action), esp. in a way that ends uncertainty or disagreement; reach a decision about: *I don't know which one to take — I'll let you decide. | We've decided on Paris* (=that we will go to Paris) *for our next holiday. | After long discussion they decided in favour of the younger candidate. | What has the committee decided?* [+wh-] *We couldn't decide which one to buy/whether to buy the red one or the blue one.* [+to-v/(that)] *She's decided to say no/that she will say no. | The court has decided for/decided in favour of the defendant.* (=passed a judgment in the DEFENDANT's favour) **2** [T] to cause to make a choice; make (someone) decide: *Your words have decided me.* [+obj+to-v] *What was it that finally decided you to give up your job?* **3** [T] to bring to a clear or certain end: *A goal in the last minute decided the match. | The chairperson has the* **deciding vote.**

de·cid·ed /dɪˈsaɪdɪd/ adj **1** very clear and easily seen or understood; UNQUESTIONABLE: *a decided change for the better* **2** having or showing no doubt; sure of oneself: *a man of very decided opinions* —see also UNDECIDED

de·cid·ed·ly /dɪˈsaɪdɪdli/ adv fml **1** in a very DECIDED (2) manner: *He spoke so decidedly that none of us dared question him.* **2** without doubt; clearly: *The company's prospects look decidedly gloomy.*

de·cid·u·ous /dɪˈsɪdʒuəs/ adj tech **1** having leaves that fall off in autumn: *deciduous trees* —opposite **evergreen** — compare CONIFEROUS **2** falling off seasonally or at a certain stage of development of life: *a child's deciduous teeth*

dec·i·mal¹ /ˈdesɪməl/ adj **1** based on the number 10: *decimal currency* | go **decimal** to start using a DECIMAL SYSTEM, e.g. of COINAGE: *Britain went decimal in 1971.* – ~**ly** adv

decimal² also **decimal frac·tion** /ˌ··· ˈ··/– n a PROPER FRACTION expressed by a system of counting based on the number ten. The first number following the dot in a decimal represents TENTHs, the second HUNDREDTHs, the third THOUSANDTHs, etc. So for example, the fraction 25/100 is written 0·25 as a decimal. —compare INTEGER, VULGAR FRACTION

dec·i·mal·ize also **-ise** BrE /ˈdesɪməlaɪz‖ˈdesəmə-/ v [I;T] to change to a decimal system of money, measurements, etc. —**-ization** /ˌdesɪməlaɪˈzeɪʃən‖ˌdesəmələ-/ n [U]

decimal point /ˌ··· ˈ·/ n the dot at the left of a DECIMAL²: *That's 10·6* (=ten point six), *not 106; you've forgotten the decimal point!*

decimal sys·tem /ˈ··· ˌ··/ n a system of counting based on the number ten

dec·i·mate /ˈdesɪmeɪt/ v [T] to destroy a large part of: *Disease decimated the population.* —**mation** /ˌdesɪˈmeɪʃən/ n [U]

de·ci·pher /dɪˈsaɪfəʳ/ v [T] to read or find the meaning of

(something difficult or secret, esp. a CODE): *I can't decipher his handwriting.* —compare CIPHER²; see also INDECIPHERABLE

de·ci·sion /dɪˈsɪʒən/ n **1** [C;U] (a) choice or judgment; (an) act of deciding: [+ to-v] *Who made the decision to go there? | Whose decision was it? | The judge will give his decision tomorrow. | The committee expects to come to/reach/make a decision soon. | a bad decision | Decision is difficult in these cases.* **2** [U] the quality of being able to make choices or judgments quickly and to act on them with firmness; RESOLUTION —opposite **indecision** **3** **Decisions! Decisions!** a phrase used humorously when making an unimportant decision

de·ci·sive /dɪˈsaɪsɪv/ adj **1** showing determination and firmness; RESOLUTE: *You'll have to be more decisive if you want to do well in business.* **2** leading to a clear result; putting an end to doubt: *They won the war after a decisive battle.* **3** unquestionable: *a decisive advantage* — opposite **indecisive** – ~**ly** adv – ~**ness** n [U]

deck¹ /dek/ n **1** a floor built across a ship over all or part of its length: *Let's go up on deck and sit in the sunshine. | Our cabin is on the lower deck.* —see picture at YACHT **2** a floor or level of a bus that has more than one **3** *esp. AmE* a set of playing cards; PACK¹ (3): *She cut the deck.* **4** *AmE* a roofless raised wooden entrance built out from the back or side of a house —compare PATIO, PORCH **5 on deck** *AmE* (esp. in BASEBALL) ready to be the next person who BATS² (2) **6 -decker** /ˈdekəʳ/ having a stated number of floors, levels, or thicknesses: *a double-decker bus | a three-decker sandwich* —see also TAPE DECK, **clear the decks** (CLEAR³), **hit the deck** (HIT¹ (10))

deck² v **1** [T (OUT)] to decorate, esp. with colourful or pretty things: [+ obj + **in**] *The street was decked out in flags for the royal wedding.* [+ obj + **with**] *The Christmas tree was decked with gifts.* **2** [T] *AmE sl* to knock (someone) down: *He made me mad so I decked him.*

deck·chair /ˈdektʃeəʳ/ n a folding chair with a long seat made of cloth (usu. brightly coloured CANVAS), used out of doors. They are used esp. on beaches: *sitting on deckchairs on the beach* —see picture at CHAIR

deck·hand /ˈdekhænd/ n a man or boy who does unskilled work on a ship

deck ten·nis /ˈ· ˌ··/ n [U] a game, played esp. on a ship, in which the players throw a rubber ring over a net stretched across the DECK¹

de·claim /dɪˈkleɪm/ v [I;T] *fml, sometimes derog* to speak loudly and clearly about (something), often using pauses and hand movements to increase the effect of the words: *She was declaiming against the waste of the taxpayers' money.*

dec·la·ma·tion /ˌdekləˈmeɪʃən/ n fml, sometimes derog [C;U] the act or art of declaiming —**-tory** /dɪˈklæmətəri‖-tɔːri/ adj

dec·la·ra·tion /ˌdekləˈreɪʃən/ n **1** [C;U] the act of declaring: *These events led to the declaration of war.* **2** [C] a statement giving official information: *Please make a written declaration of all the goods you bought abroad.*

Declaration of In·de·pen·dence /·····, ··· ·ˈ··/ n also **American Declaration of Independence** esp. BrE— [the] the document that declared the freedom of the original 13 American colonies (COLONY) from British rule.

▶CULTURAL NOTE Written mostly by Thomas Jefferson and signed by members of the Congress, the Declaration of Independence is one of the great political documents of the western world, and was one of the first official statements by a government that "all men are created (CREATE) equal", that they have "certain INALIENABLE rights, that among these are life, LIBERTY, and the PURSUIT OF HAPPINESS". Its ADOPTION (= formal acceptance) on the Fourth of July 1776 is now celebrated as Independence Day, a public holiday in the US —see also CONTINENTAL CONGRESS, FOURTH OF JULY◀

de·clar·a·tive /dɪˈklærətɪv/ adj tech (esp. in grammar) making a statement or having the form of a statement: *a declarative sentence* —compare IMPERATIVE, INTERROGATIVE

de·clare /dɪˈkleəʳ/ v **1** [T] to make known publicly or officially, according to rules, custom, etc.: *Britain declared* **war on** *Germany in 1914.* [+obj+n/adj] *Jones was declared the winner of the fight. | I now declare this*

meeting open. | *The medical examiner declared me fit.* **2** [T] to state or show with great force so that there is no doubt about the meaning: *He declared his loyalty to the government*|*his total opposition to the plan.* [+(that)] *She declared (that) she knew nothing about the robbery.* [+obj+n|adj] *She declared herself (to be) a supporter of the cause.* | *The police declared themselves (to be) completely puzzled by the lack of evidence.* **3** [T] to make a full statement of (property for which tax may be owed to the government): *The customs officer asked me if I had anything to declare.* **4** [I] (of the captain of a cricket team) to end the team's INNINGS before all its members have been put out **5** [I;T] (in a card game) to say which type of card will be played as TRUMPS **6 I declare!** *old-fash* (an expression of slight surprise or slight anger) **7 I have nothing to declare but my genius** *quote* a phrase which is believed to have been used by Oscar Wilde, the Irish writer, when going through CUSTOMS —**clarable** *adj* : *Have you any declarable goods?* —**claratory** /dɪˈklærətəri‖-tɔːri/ *adj*
  declare against sbdy./sthg. *phr v* [T] to state one's opposition to
  declare for sbdy./sthg. *phr v* [T] to state one's support for

de·clared /dɪˈkleəd‖-ˈkleərd/ *adj* openly admitted as: *a declared supporter of the government* | *It's their declared intention to increase taxes.*

de·clas·si·fy /diːˈklæsɪ̱faɪ/ *v* [T] to declare (esp. political and military information) to be no longer secret —**fication** /ˌdiːklæsɪ̱fɪˈkeɪʃ*ə*n/ *n* [U]

de·clen·sion /dɪˈklenʃ*ə*n/ *n tech* (in some languages) a class of nouns and/or adjectives that DECLINE¹ (4) in the same way: *There are five declensions in Latin.* —compare CONJUGATION

dec·li·na·tion /ˌdeklɪ̱ˈneɪʃ*ə*n/ *n* **1** *tech* the angle of a COMPASS needle, east or west, from true north: *a declination of 15 degrees* **2** *rare* a formal refusal

de·cline¹ /dɪˈklaɪn/ *v* **1** [I] to go from a better to a worse position, or from higher to lower; DETERIORATE: *His influence declined as he grew older.* | *the government's declining popularity* | *Do you think standards of morality have declined in recent years?* | *The old lady wants to spend her declining years by the sea.* **2** [I] *fml or lit* to slope downwards: *About two miles east, the land begins to decline towards the river.* **3** [I;T] to refuse (a request or offer), usu. politely; express unwillingness: *We asked them to come to our party, but they declined (the invitation).* [+to-v] *The official at first declined to make a statement, but later she agreed.* —see REFUSE (USAGE) **4** [I;T] *tech* **a** (of a noun, PRONOUN, or adjective) to have different grammatical forms according to its position or purpose in a sentence **b** to list or state the different grammatical forms of (a noun, PRONOUN, or adjective) —compare CONJUGATE, INFLECT

decline² *n* [C *usu. sing.*;U] a period or process of declining; movement to a lower or worse position: *There has been a sharp decline in profits this year.* | *The birthrate is* **on the decline**. (=getting lower)

Decline and Fall of the Ro·man Em·pire /·ˌ· · ˌ· · · · · · ‖· ˈ···/, **The** a serious historical work in a number of books written by Edward Gibbon. Its full title is *History of the Decline and Fall of the Roman Empire.*

de·cliv·i·ty /dɪˈklɪvɪ̱ti/ *n fml or tech* a downward slope —compare ACCLIVITY

de·coc·tion /dɪˈkɒkʃ*ə*n‖-ˈkɑːk-/ *n fml* a liquid obtained by boiling something for a long time in water

de·code /ˌdiːˈkəʊd/ *v* [T] to discover the meaning of (something written in a CODE): *We decoded the enemy's telegram.*

dé·colle·tage /ˌdeɪkɒlˈtɑːʒ‖ˌdeɪˌkɑːləˈtɑːʒ/ *n* **1** the parts of a woman's body, esp. the breasts, which show when she wears a very low-cut dress **2** a top edge of a woman's dress that is cut very low to show part of the shoulders, chest, and breasts

dé·col·leté /deɪˈkɒlteɪ‖ˌdeɪˌkɑːləˈteɪ/ *adj* (esp. of a dress) leaving uncovered part of the shoulders, chest, and breasts

de·col·o·nize also **-nise** *BrE* /ˌdiːˈkɒlənaɪz‖-ˈkɑː-/ *v* [T] to give political independence to (a former COLONY) —**nization** /ˌdiːkɒlənaɪˈzeɪʃ*ə*n‖-kɑːlənə-/ *n* [U]

de·com·pose /ˌdiːkəmˈpəʊz/ *v* [I;T] **1** to (cause to) decay: *decomposed vegetable matter* **2** to (cause to) break up and separate into simple parts: *to decompose a chemical compound* —**position** /ˌdiːkɒmpəˈzɪʃ*ə*n‖-kɑːm-/ *n* [U]

de·com·press /ˌdiːkəmˈpres/ *v* [T] to reduce the pressure of air on — ~ **ion** /ˈpreʃ*ə*n/ *n* [U] : *decompression sickness* | *Deep-sea divers get back to normal air pressure by going through a* **decompression chamber.**

de·con·gest·ant /ˌdiːkənˈdʒestənt/ *n* a medicine that reduces swelling and blocking, esp. in the nose

de·con·tam·i·nate /ˌdiːkənˈtæmɪ̱neɪt/ *v* [T] to remove dangerous (e.g. RADIOACTIVE) substances from —**nation** /ˌtæmɪ̱ˈneɪʃ*ə*n/ *n* [U]

de·con·trol /ˌdiːkənˈtrəʊl/ *v* **-ll-** [T] to end control of: *to decontrol prices*

dé·cor /ˈdeɪkɔːʳ‖ˈdeɪˈkɔːr/ *n* [C;U] the decorative furnishing and arranging of a place, esp. a room, house, or stage: *It's a good restaurant, but I don't really like the décor.*

dec·o·rate /ˈdekəreɪt/ *v* **1** [T (with)] to provide with something that is added because it is attractive or beautiful, and not because it is necessary: *The streets were decorated with flags.* | *to decorate a cake with icing* **2** [I;T] to paint or put paper, etc., on the walls of a house: *How much will it cost to decorate the kitchen?* | *We spent the weekend decorating.* **3** [T (for)] to give (someone) an official mark of honour, such as a MEDAL: *They were decorated for outstanding bravery.*

▷ USAGE **Decorate, adorn, embellish,** and **garnish** all mean "to add something to, so as to make more attractive". **Decorate** is usually used of places and buildings: *The children* **decorated** *the house for Christmas.* **Adorn** (rather *fml or lit*) is usually used of people: *She* **adorned** *herself with jewels.* **Embellish** often has a figurative meaning: *He* **embellished** *the story to make it more amusing.* **Garnish** is most often used of cooking: *a fried fish* **garnished** *with pieces of tomato.*◁

dec·o·ra·tion /ˌdekəˈreɪʃ*ə*n/ *n* **1** [U] the act or art of decorating **2** [C *often pl.*] something that decorates; ORNAMENT: *Christmas decorations* **3** [C] something given as a sign of honour, esp. a military MEDAL

dec·o·ra·tive /ˈdekərətɪv‖ˈdekərə-, ˈdekəreɪ-/ *adj* used for decorating; ORNAMENTAL: *a decorative gold table* — ~ **ly** *adv*

dec·o·ra·tor /ˈdekəreɪtəʳ/ *n* **1** a person who paints houses inside and out: *I can't come and see you this week — I've got the decorators in.* **2** an INTERIOR DECORATOR

dec·o·rous /ˈdekərəs/ *adj fml* (of appearance or behaviour) correct; showing proper respect for the manners and customs of society — ~ **ly** *adv*

de·co·rum /dɪˈkɔːrəm/ *n* [U] correct and respectful behaviour or appearance; PROPRIETY; a word used mainly by older people: *I hope you will behave with suitable decorum at the funeral.*

de·coy¹ /ˈdiːkɔɪ/ *n* **1** a person or thing that is used for tricking someone or getting them into a dangerous position; a word used esp. in police or military operations **2** a model of a bird that is used for attracting wild birds within range of guns: *a decoy duck*

de·coy² /dɪˈkɔɪ/ *v* [T (into)] to deceive (a person) into a position of danger: *They decoyed him into a dark street, where they robbed him.*

de·crease¹ /dɪˈkriːs/ *v* [I;T] to (cause to) become less in size, amount, strength, or quality; reduce: *Our sales are decreasing.* | *They are making further efforts to decrease military spending.* —opposite **increase**

de·crease² /ˈdiːkriːs/ *n* **1** [C;U] the process of decreasing **2** [C (in)] an amount by which something decreases: *a 6% decrease in his income*

de·cree¹ /dɪˈkriː/ *n* **1** an official command or decision that has the force of law, esp. one made by a king, a military government, etc.: *to issue a decree* [+that] *a decree that political activity should be restricted* | *to forbid it* **by decree** **2** *esp. AmE* a judgment of certain types in a court of law

de·cree² *v* [T] to order or judge officially, with the force of law: *to decree an end to the fighting* [+that] *They have decreed that the fighting should end.* [+obj+adj] *The committee decreed the film unsuitable for children.*

decree ab·so·lute /·ˌ· · ˈ···/ *n* **decrees absolute** *BrE law* an order by a court that officially ends the marriage of two people, each of whom is then free to marry again: *My decree absolute comes through next week.* —see also DECREE NISI

decree ni·si /dɪˌkriː ˈnaɪsaɪ/ *n* **decrees nisi** *BrE law* an order by a court that a marriage will be ended at a certain future time (usu. after six weeks) if there is no good reason why it should not end, e.g. both people have changed their mind —see also DECREE ABSOLUTE

de·crep·it /dɪˈkrepɪt/ *adj* weak and in bad condition from old age or hard use: *a decrepit old man/old chair*

de·crep·i·tude /dɪˈkrepɪtjuːd‖-tuːd/ *n* [U] *fml* the quality of being decrepit

de·cry /dɪˈkraɪ/ *v* [T] *fml* to speak disapprovingly of; say bad things about (esp. something dangerous to the public): *to decry the violence of modern films*

ded·i·cate /ˈdedɪkeɪt/ *v* [T] to give to a holy purpose, often with a solemn ceremony: *The new church will be dedicated on Sunday.*
　　dedicate sbdy./sthg. **to** sbdy./sthg. *phr v* [T] **1** to give completely to (a particular cause, purpose, or action); DEVOTE **to**: *The doctor dedicated her life/herself to finding a cure.* **2** to declare (a book, performance, etc.) to be in honour of (a person): *He dedicated his first book to his mother.*

ded·i·cat·ed /ˈdedɪkeɪtɪd/ *adj* **1** [(to)] (esp. of people) very interested in or working very hard for an idea, purpose, etc.; COMMITTED: *She's very dedicated to her work.* | *a dedicated doctor* | *This organization is dedicated to overthrowing democracy.* **2** [no comp.] *tech* (esp. of a computer or a computer PROGRAM) intended to be used for one particular purpose: *a dedicated word-processor* – ~ly *adv*

ded·i·ca·tion /ˌdedɪˈkeɪʃən/ *n* **1** [C;U] the act of dedicating **2** [C;U] the quality of being dedicated, esp. in an unselfish way: *They worked with great dedication to find a cure for cancer.* **3** [C] the words used in dedicating a book or performance to someone

de·duce /dɪˈdjuːs‖dɪˈduːs/ *v* [T (from)] *fml* to reach a decision or judgment about (a fact or situation) by using one's knowledge or reason; INFER: *What did Darwin deduce from the presence of these species in the Galapagos?* [+that] *The police deduced that the murder had been committed by a woman.* —see also DEDUCTION, DEDUCTIVE –-ducible *adj*

de·duct /dɪˈdʌkt/ *v* [T (from)] to take away (an amount, a part) from a total; subtract: *Your cost of the breakages will be deducted from your pay.* —compare SUBTRACT – ~ible *adj* : *Your expenses are deductible from tax.*

de·duc·tion /dɪˈdʌkʃən/ *n* [C;U] **1** (an example or result of) a process of reasoning using general rules or principles to form a judgment about a particular fact or situation: *We worked out the answer by deduction.* | *What deductions have you made from that, Watson?* [+that] *Her deduction that he was now dead was correct.* —compare INDUCTION (6) **2** the process of deducting or an amount which is deducted: *Your gross salary will be £900 a month, which works out at about £650 after all deductions.*

de·duc·tive /dɪˈdʌktɪv/ *adj* using deduction; reasoning from a general idea or set of facts to a particular idea or facts: *the deductive process* | *deductive reasoning* —compare INDUCTIVE – ~ly *adv*

deed /diːd/ *n* **1** *esp. lit or old use* something done on purpose; an action: *to do good deeds* | *to be honourable in word and deed* | *the murderer's evil deeds* **2** *law* a written and signed paper that is an official record of an agreement, esp. an agreement concerning who owns property —see also TITLE DEED

deed of cov·e·nant /ˌ· · ˈ···/ *n* **deeds of covenant** a legal agreement in Britain in which a person promises to pay a fixed sum to another person or organization, e.g. a CHARITY, regularly for an agreed period of time. Tax does not have to be paid on deeds of covenant.

deed poll /ˈ· ·/ *n* **deed polls** *or* **deeds poll** *law* (esp. in Britain) a legal deed signed by one person only, esp. when changing one's name: *I've changed my name by deed poll.*

dee·jay /ˌdiːˈdʒeɪ, ˈdiːdʒeɪ/ *n* a DISC JOCKEY

deem /diːm/ *v* [T *not in progressive forms*] *fml* to consider; have the opinion; judge: [+obj+n/adj] *We would deem it an honour if the minister agreed to meet us.* | *It was deemed advisable to keep the affair secret.* [+that] *They*

deemed that he was no longer capable of managing his own affairs.

deep¹ /diːp/ *adj* **1** going far down from the top: *a deep hole in the ground* | *The river is very deep here.* [after *n*] *a mine two kilometres deep* | *ankle-deep in mud* **2** going far in from the outside or the front edge: *a deep wound* | *deep borders of red silk* | *a house deep in the forest* [after *n*] *a shelf 30 centimetres deep* (=30 centimetres from front to back) *and 120 metres long* | *cars parked three deep* **3** coming from or reaching very low in the chest: *He took a deep breath, filling his lungs with clean air at last.* —compare SHALLOW¹ (3) **4** near the outer limits of the playing area: *a hit into the deep field* **5** (of a colour) strong and dark: *The sky was deep blue.* —compare LIGHT³ (2), PALE¹ (2) **6** (of a sound) low: *a deep voice* | *a deep sigh* **7** (of feelings or conditions) strong and unlikely to change; extreme; INTENSE: *deep feelings* | *a deep sleep* | *a deep sense of gratitude* | *a deep distrust of lawyers* | *a deep disorder of the mind* **8** seriously bad or damaging: *in deep trouble/dishonour* **9** understanding difficult matters thoroughly; wise: *a deep mind/thinker* **10** difficult to understand; mysterious: *deep scientific principles* | *a deep person* | *a deep dark secret* **11** go off (at) the ˈdeep end *sl* to lose one's temper suddenly, violently, and unreasonably **12** in/into deep water *infml* in/into serious trouble **13** thrown in at the ˈdeep end *infml* having to begin with the most difficult part of a job —see also DEPTH, DEPTHS – ~ly *adv* : *We are deeply grateful for your support.* | *His remarks were deeply offensive/embarrassing.* – ~ness *n* [U]

deep² *adv* [+adv/prep] **1** to a great depth; deeply: *He pushed his stick deep (down) into the mud.* | *We're deep in debt.* | *She was deep in thought and didn't hear the phone ringing.* **2** far along in time; late: *They danced deep into the night.* **3 deep down** in one's true nature; in fact rather than appearance: *She may seem rather unfriendly, but deep down she's very nice.*

deep³ *n* [the] *poet* the sea

deep·en /ˈdiːpən/ *v* [I;T] to make or become deeper or more extreme: *to deepen a well* | *deepening shadows* | *The crisis deepened.*

deep freeze /ˌ· ˈ·‖ˈ· ·/ *n* an apparatus for keeping food at very low temperatures; FREEZER

deep fry /ˈ· ·/ *v* [T] to FRY (food) completely under the surface of oil or fat

deep-laid /ˌ· ˈ·◂/ *adj* planned in secret: *a deep-laid scheme*

deep-root·ed /ˌ· ˈ···◂/ *also* **deeply rooted** /ˌ·· ˈ···◂/– *adj* strongly fixed in one's nature, esp. for a long time; INGRAINED: *For some people, smoking is a deep-rooted habit.*

deep-sea div·ing /ˌ· · ˈ··/ *n* [U] the sport or activity of going down under the sea at a distance from the shore usu. from a boat and usu. with breathing equipment: *We did some deep-sea diving while we were on holiday.* —**deep-sea diver** *n*

deep-seat·ed /ˌ· ˈ···◂/ *adj* (esp. of feelings) existing far below the surface: *a deep-seated sorrow*

Deep South /ˌ· ˈ·/ [the] the part of the southeastern US which lies farthest south, esp. the parts of Alabama, Georgia, Louisiana, and Mississippi which are farthest south; used esp. in talking about politics or history —see also SOUTH (1)

▶ CULTURAL NOTE States in the Deep South are often considered to have populations which are more RACIST than other states because the economy of Southern states was based on SLAVERY before the Civil War. These states still have large black populations. People from the Deep South are also considered to be more CONSERVATIVE, and the FUNDAMENTALIST churches have strong support there. Americans sometimes use Deep South in a way that shows their dislike of or lack of respect for something from there. —see also SOUTH (1) (CULTURAL NOTE)◀

deep throat /ˌ· ˈ·/ *n* *AmE infml* a secret giver of information

deer /dɪər/ *n* **deer** a grass-eating animal that is able to run very fast. The males usu. have wide branching horns (ANTLERS). A young deer is called a **fawn**. Deer are thought of as being gentle and TIMID animals. There is a famous Disney film about a young deer called *Bambi.* —see also RED DEER, REINDEER

deer·stalk·er /ˈdɪəstɔːkər‖ˈdɪər-/ *n* a kind of soft hat with

deer

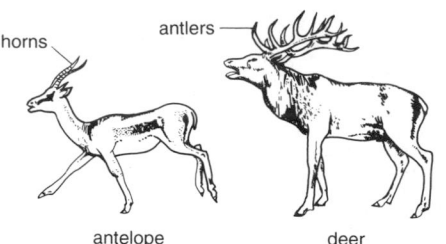

horns antlers

antelope   deer

ear-coverings that can be worn up or down. Many people connect the deerstalker with Sherlock Holmes.

de·es·ca·late /ˌdiːˈeskəleɪt/ v [I;T] to (cause to) decrease in force, range, or rate; used esp. in connection with military actions: *to de-escalate the bombing/the tensions in the region* —**-lation** /ˌdiːeskəˈleɪʃən/ n [U]

de·face /dɪˈfeɪs/ v [T] to spoil the surface or appearance of, e.g. by writing or making marks: *to deface a monument/an inscription* — ~**ment** n [U]

de fac·to /ˌdeɪ ˈfæktəʊ‖ˌdiː-, ˌdeɪ-/ adj, adv Lat fml in actual fact, though not perhaps justly or according to law: *a de facto state of war* —compare DE JURE, IPSO FACTO

de·fame /dɪˈfeɪm/ v [T] fml to damage the good opinion held about (a person or group), usu. unfairly, by writing or saying something bad about them; LIBEL or SLANDER someone —**famatory** /dɪˈfæmətəri‖-ˌtɔːri/ adj : *defamatory remarks* —**famation** /ˌdefəˈmeɪʃən/ n [U] : *to sue a newspaper for defamation of character*

de·fault¹ /dɪˈfɔːlt/ v [I] to fail to fulfil a contract, agreement, or duty, esp. **a** [(on)] to fail to pay a debt: *He defaulted on his payments for support of the child.* **b** to fail to take part in a competition — ~**er** n

default² n **1** [U] failure to do something that is demanded by duty or law, such as paying one's debts or appearing at the proper time in a court of law **2** [U] failure to take part in a competition: *She won* **by default**, *because her opponent refused to play.* **3** [C] a particular way that a computer system will perform an operation, except if the user gives it different instructions **4 in default of** because of the absence or lack of

de·feat¹ /dɪˈfiːt/ v [T] **1** to win a victory over, e.g. in a war, competition, or game; beat: *After a long campaign, the Duke of Wellington's army defeated Napoleon.* | *The English team was defeated by three goals to one.* | *The Opposition's motion was heavily defeated in Congress.* | (fig.) *I've tried to understand your idea, but I'm afraid it defeats me.* —see WIN (USAGE) **2** to cause to fail; FRUSTRATE (2): *It was lack of money, not of effort, that defeated their plan.* —see also SELF-DEFEATING

defeat² n **1** [C;U] (an example of) being defeated: *The government has suffered a serious defeat.* | *They remained dignified in defeat.* | *After several defeats, the team is now doing well again.* **2** [U] the act of defeating: *the defeat of our enemies* —opposite **victory**

de·feat·is·m /dɪˈfiːtɪzəm/ n [U] derog the practice of thinking or talking in a way that shows an expectation of being unsuccessful —**-ist** n, adj : *Don't be such a defeatist!* | *a defeatist attitude*

def·e·cate /ˈdefɪkeɪt/ v [I] fml to pass waste matter from the bowels —**-cation** /ˌdefɪˈkeɪʃən/ n [U]

de·fect¹ /ˈdiːfekt, dɪˈfekt/ n something missing or imperfect; fault: *Before they leave the factory, all the cars are carefully tested for defects.* | *a hearing defect*

de·fect² /dɪˈfekt/ v [I (from, to)] to desert a political party, group, or country, esp. in order to join an opposing one: *She defected to the West.* — ~**or** n : *political defectors* — ~**ion** /ˈfekʃən/ n [C;U] : *several defections from the Labour Party* | *What caused his defection?*

de·fec·tive /dɪˈfektɪv/ adj **1** not working properly; faulty: *defective machinery/hearing* **2** (of a person) well below the average, esp. in mind —see also MENTAL DEFECTIVE **3** tech lacking one or more of the usual forms of grammar: *"Must" and "can" are defective verbs.* — ~**ly** adv — ~**ness** n [U]

de·fence¹ BrE ‖usu. **defense** AmE /dɪˈfens/ n **1** [U] the act or process of defending: *the defence of one's country* | *the art of self-defence* | *He spoke* **in defence of** *justice/the government's record.* —see also CIVIL DEFENCE, SELF DEFENCE **2** [C;U] means, methods, or things used in defending: *government spending on defence* | *The defences of the city are strong.* | *She caught him when his defences were down.* | *Trees are a defence against the wind.* | *Good strong locks are the best defence against burglars.* **3** [C usu. sing.] arguments used in defending oneself, esp. in a court of law: *The prisoner's defence was rather weak.* | *She said, in her defence, that she had not seen the "No Parking" sign.* **4** [the+S+sing./pl. v] the defendant in a court case together with his/her lawyer or lawyers: *The defence have/has asked for an adjournment.* —compare PROSECUTION (2) — ~**less** adj

defence² BrE ‖usu. **defense** AmE /dɪˈfens‖ˈdiːfens/ n **1** [C+sing./pl. v] the part of a team that tries to defend its own GOAL in a match **2** [C] a set of moves or methods used in defending, esp. in CHESS: *Her defence crumbled.*

defence mech·a·nis·m /·ˈ· ˌ····/ n **1** a process in the brain which makes one forget about things that are difficult or painful to accept **2** a reaction by the body to fight illness: *These glands in your neck have come up as a defence mechanism to fight the infection in your mouth.*

de·fend /dɪˈfend/ v **1** [T (against, from)] to keep safe from harm; protect against attack: *The country cannot be defended against a nuclear attack.* | *When the dog came towards me I picked up a stick to defend myself.* | *The union said they would take action to defend their members' jobs.* **2** [I;T] (in sports) to protect (a position) so as to keep an opponent from advancing, making points, or winning: *They defended (their goal) with great skill.* **3** [T] to act as a lawyer for (the person who has been charged) —compare PROSECUTE (2) **4** [T] to use arguments to support, protect, or show the rightness of; JUSTIFY: *How can you defend the killing of animals for scientific research?* —see also DEFENCE, DEFENSIVE — ~**er** n

de·fen·dant /dɪˈfendənt/ n a person against whom a charge is brought in a court of law. In Britain and the US a defendant is considered to be INNOCENT until the police and the lawyers have proved his/her guilt to the JURY beyond all reasonable doubt. —compare PLAINTIFF

de·fend·er /dɪˈfendəʳ/ n (in sports) one of the players who tries to defend his or her team's GOAL in a match

Defender of the Faith /·ˌ· ·· · ˈ·/ a title used by all kings and queens of England since Henry VIII, who was given it by the Pope at that time for writing a paper attacking the ideas of Martin Luther

defense v AmE for DEFENCE¹,²

de·fen·si·ble /dɪˈfensɪbəl/ adj that can be defended: *a defensible fortress/position* | *His behaviour was perfectly defensible.* —**bly** adv

de·fen·sive¹ /dɪˈfensɪv/ adj **1** that defends; used or intended for defence: *defensive weapons/tactics* | *a defensive position/alliance* —opposite **offensive 2** sometimes derog (of a person or behaviour) seeming to expect disapproval or attack: *She became very defensive when I asked her how much the car had cost.* — ~**ly** adv — ~**ness** n [U]

defensive² n **on the defensive** sometimes derog prepared for disapproval or attack, because one is expecting it

de·fer /dɪˈfɜːʳ/ v **-rr-** [T] to delay until a later date; POSTPONE: *Let's defer the decision for a few weeks.* | *His military service was deferred until he finished college.* — ~**ment** n [C;U]

defer to sbdy./sthg. phr v **-rr-** [T] humor or fml to agree to accept the opinion or decision of (someone), esp. because of respect: *I'll be happy to defer to your advice/to your greater experience in these matters.*

def·er·ence /ˈdefərəns/ n [U] fml regard for the wishes, opinions, etc., of another person, because of one's respect or love for them, or because of the other person's higher position or greater power: *We treated her advice with* **due deference**. | *They were married in church,* **out of/in deference to** *their parents' wishes.* —**-ential** /ˌdefəˈrenʃəl/ adj —**-entially** adv

de·fi·ance /dɪˈfaɪəns/ n [U] defiant behaviour or a defiant manner; open disobedience: *She acted* **in defiance of** *my orders/of the law.* | *He slammed the door in a spirit of defiance.*

de·fi·ant /dɪˈfaɪənt/ adj openly and fearlessly refusing to obey, esp. in a way that shows no respect: *a defiant child/attitude* | *With a last defiant gesture, they sang a revolutionary song as they were led away to prison.* — ~ **ly** adv

de·fi·cien·cy /dɪˈfɪʃənsi/ n [C;U] (a case of) the quality of being deficient; lack: *vitamin deficiency* | *The deficiencies in the system soon became obvious.*

deficiency dis·ease /·ˈ··· ·ˌ·/ n [C;U] (a) disease caused by a lack of one or more food substances necessary for health

de·fi·cient /dɪˈfɪʃənt/ adj [(in)] having none or not enough (of); lacking (in); INADEQUATE: *food deficient in iron* | *a deficient supply of water* | *deficient in skill* — ~ **ly** adv

def·i·cit /ˈdefɪsɪt/ n the amount by which something is less than what is needed, esp. the amount by which money that goes out is more than money that comes in: *The directors have reported a deficit of £2.5 million.*

▶ CULTURAL NOTE In the US, the country's BUDGET deficit is an important political issue.◀

de·file[1] /dɪˈfaɪl/ v [T] fml to destroy the pureness of: *The animals defiled the water.* | *disgusting video films that defile the minds of the young* — **filer** n — ~ **ment** n [U]

de·file[2] /dɪˈfaɪl, ˈdiːfaɪl/ n a narrow passage, esp. through mountains

de·fine /dɪˈfaɪn/ v [T] **1** to give the meaning of (a word or idea); describe exactly: *Some words are hard to define because they have many different uses.* **2** to explain the exact qualities, limits, duties, etc., of: *The powers of the President are defined in the constitution.* | *This book attempts to define the position of the national government in local affairs.* **3** to show the edge or shape of: *I saw a clearly defined shape outside the window.* **4** [(as)] to show the nature of; CHARACTERIZE: *What defines us as human?*

def·i·nite /ˈdefɪnɪt, ˈdefənɪt/ adj clearly known, seen, or stated; without any uncertainty: *So you're coming on Tuesday, after all; that's definite now, is it?* | *Adding the cushions has made a definite improvement to the room.* | *We must set definite standards for our students.* | *He was very definite about it.* —see also DEFINITELY; INDEFINITE

definite ar·ti·cle /ˌ··· ˈ···/ n **1** (in English) the word "the" **2** (in other languages) a word used like "the" —compare INDEFINITE ARTICLE; see also ARTICLE[1] (4)

def·i·nite·ly /ˈdefɪnɪtli, ˈdefənɪtli/ adv **1** without doubt; clearly: *That was definitely the best play I've seen all year.* | *She is definitely coming/definitely not coming.* | *"Is she coming?" "Definitely!"* | *"Do you smoke?" "Definitely not!"* **2** in a definite way: *He explained his intentions very definitely.* —see CERTAINLY (USAGE)

def·i·ni·tion /ˌdefɪˈnɪʃən/ n **1** [C] an exact statement of the meaning, nature, or limits of something, esp. of a word or phrase: *the definitions in a dictionary* | *An English person is British by definition.* (=it is part of the meaning of being "English") **2** [U] clearness of shape, colour, or sound: *This photograph lacks definition.*

de·fin·i·tive /dɪˈfɪnɪtɪv/ adj **1** providing a last decision that cannot be questioned or changed; CONCLUSIVE: *a definitive decision by the Supreme Court* **2** that cannot be improved as a treatment of a particular subject: *She's written the definitive life of Lord Byron.* —compare AUTHORITATIVE — ~ **ly** adv

de·flate /ˌdiːˈfleɪt, dɪ-/ v **1** [I;T] to (cause to) become smaller by losing air or gas: *to deflate a balloon* **2** [T] to take away the pride or self-confidence of (someone), esp. suddenly: *One sharp remark is enough to deflate him.* **3** [I;T] to reduce the supply of money (of) or lower the level of prices (of); a word used in economics or financial planning: *to deflate the national economy*

de·fla·tion /ˌdiːˈfleɪʃən, dɪ-/ n [U] **1** the act of deflating or process of being deflated **2** (in ECONOMICS) a decrease in the amount of money being used in a country, esp. as a result of government decisions, leading to less demand for goods, less industrial activity, and usu. intended to or likely to cause lower prices —compare INFLATION, REFLATION

de·fla·tion·a·ry /ˌdiːˈfleɪʃənəri, dɪ-ˈ-neri/ also **disinflationary** — adj (in ECONOMICS) producing deflation of money or prices: *deflationary policies/wage settlements*

de·flect /dɪˈflekt/ v [I;T (**from**)] to (cause to) turn from a straight course or fixed direction, esp. after hitting something: *The bullet deflected when it hit the tree.* | *One of their forwards deflected the ball into the goal.* | (fig.) *to deflect someone from their purpose* | (fig.) *a politician trying to deflect criticism by changing the subject*

de·flec·tion /dɪˈflekʃən/ n [C;U] **1** a turning aside; turning off course: *the deflection of the bullet by the tree* **2** (the amount of) a movement away from 0 by the pointer, needle, etc., of a measuring instrument: *a deflection of 30°*

de·flow·er /ˌdiːˈflaʊəʳ, dɪ-/ v [T] esp. lit to have sex with (a woman who has not had sex before)

De·foe /dɪˈfəʊ/, **Daniel** (1660–1731) an English writer, whose most famous NOVELs are *Robinson Crusoe* and *Moll Flanders*

de·fog /diːˈfɒg‖-ˈfɑːg, -ˈfɔːg/ v **-gg-** AmE for DEMIST

de·fo·li·ant /ˌdiːˈfəʊliənt, dɪ-/ n [C;U] (a) chemical substance used on plants to make their leaves drop off early

de·fo·li·ate /ˌdiːˈfəʊlieɪt, dɪ-/ v [T] to use defoliant on — **ation** /ˌfəʊliˈeɪʃən/ n [U]

de·for·est /diːˈfɒrɪst‖-ˈfɔː-, -ˈfɑː-/ v [T] to clear (an area) of forest or trees: *More and more of the country is being deforested.*

de·for·es·ta·tion /diːˌfɒrɪˈsteɪʃən‖-ˌfɔː-, -ˌfɑː-/ n [U] the action of clearing an area of forest or trees: *The deforestation of South America is of worldwide concern.*

de·form /dɪˈfɔːm‖-ɔːrm/ v [T] to change the usual shape of (something), esp. so as to spoil its appearance or usefulness: *a face deformed by disease/anger* | *He was born with a severely deformed foot.* | *Heat deforms plastics.*

de·for·ma·tion /ˌdiːfɔːˈmeɪʃən‖-ɔːr-/ n **1** [U] the action of deforming or process of being deformed: *the deformation of a solid object by pressure* **2** [C;U] (a) change of shape, esp. for the worse

de·for·mi·ty /dɪˈfɔːmɪti‖-ɔːr-/ n [C;U] (an) imperfection of the body, esp. one that can be seen: *Lack of essential minerals can cause deformity in unborn children.*

de·fraud /dɪˈfrɔːd/ v [T (**of**)] to deceive so as to get or keep something wrongly and usu. not legally: *She defrauded her employers of thousands of dollars.*

de·fray /dɪˈfreɪ/ v [T] fml to provide for the payment of; pay: *The company will defray the cost of the trip/all your expenses.*

de·frock /ˌdiːˈfrɒk‖-ˈfrɑːk/ also **unfrock**– v [T] to remove (a priest) from his position as a punishment for behaviour or beliefs that are disapproved of

de·frost /ˌdiːˈfrɒst‖-ˈfrɔːst/ v **1** [I;T] to remove ice from; unfreeze: *to defrost a refrigerator* | *Don't let the meat defrost too quickly.* **2** [T] AmE for DEMIST — — **er** n

deft /deft/ adj effortlessly skilful; ADROIT: *deft fingers* | *a deft performance* — ~ **ly** adv — ~ **ness** n [U]

de·funct /dɪˈfʌŋkt/ adj fml or humor no longer living, existing, or having effect: *The scheme for building a new airport seems to be completely defunct now.*

de·fuse /ˌdiːˈfjuːz/ v [T] **1** to remove the FUSE[1] from (something explosive) in order to prevent an explosion: *to defuse a bomb* **2** to make less dangerous or harmful: *to defuse a dangerous situation*

de·fy /dɪˈfaɪ/ v [T] **1** to show no fear of nor respect for; openly disobey; refuse to obey: *The child defied his parents and went to the cinema after school.* | *They defied their party leader and voted against his plan.* | (fig.) *The acrobat seemed to defy the law of gravity.* **2** [+obj+to-v] to ask (someone), very strongly, to do something considered impossible: *I defy you to produce any evidence that supports your claim.* **3** to make impossible or unsuccessful: *The untidiness of the room defies description.* | *The disease has so far defied all attempts to find a cure.*

De·gas /ˈdeɪɡɑː‖dəˈɡɑː/, **Ed·gar** /ˈedɡəʳ/ (1834–1917) a French Impressionist artist, famous particularly for his paintings of women dancing, of CAFE life, and of racing scenes

de Gaulle /də ˈɡəʊl‖-ˈɡɔːl/, **General Charles** (1890–1970) a French general and politician who is well-known for his determination to free his country from Nazi rule during the Second World War. He was the President of France between 1959 and 1969.

de·gen·e·rate[1] /dɪ'dʒenərɪt/ adj having become worse in character, quality, etc., in comparison with a former state: a degenerate species | the last degenerate member of a noble family —**racy** n [U]

de·gen·e·rate[2] n a degenerate person, esp. one whose sexual behaviour is regarded as unacceptable

de·gen·e·rate[3] /dɪ'dʒenəreɪt/ v [I (into)] 1 to pass from a higher to a lower type or condition: The wide paved road degenerated into a narrow bumpy track. | The argument soon degenerated into a brawl. 2 to sink into a low state of mind or morals —**ration** /dɪˌdʒenə'reɪʃən/ n [U] : the degeneration of moral standards|of a bodily organ —**rative** /dɪ'dʒenərətɪv/ adj : a degenerative disease of the heart

de·grade /dɪ'greɪd/ v 1 [T] to cause to lose self-respect or the good opinion of other people; DEBASE: It was very degrading to be punished in front of the whole class. | Don't degrade yourself by answering him. 2 [I;T] tech to (cause to) change from a higher to a lower kind of living matter, or from a compound chemical to a simpler one —see also BIODEGRADABLE —**gradation** /ˌdegrə'deɪʃən/ n [C;U]

de·gree /dɪ'griː/ n 1 [C] tech any of various units of measure, esp. of temperature or angles: Water freezes at 32 degrees Fahrenheit (32°F) or 0 degrees Celsius (0°C). | an angle of 90 degrees (90°) | The city lies at a latitude of 30 degrees North (30° N). 2 [C;U] a point on an imaginary line used for measuring or comparing qualities, feelings, abilities, etc.: The children have different degrees of ability. | To what degree can they be trusted? | They can be trusted to some|a certain degree. | They cannot be trusted in the slightest degree. | The minister expressed a degree of (=a certain amount of) optimism about the state of the economy. | She is getting better by degrees, but it will be some time before she is completely well. 3 [C (in)] a title given by a university or certain colleges to a student who has completed a course of study successfully: To do the job, you must have a degree in chemistry|a chemistry degree.

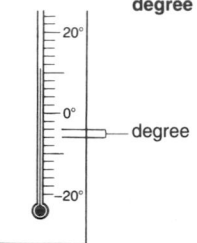

degree
degree

▶CULTURAL NOTE 1 In England and Wales and in the US first degrees include a BA for arts subjects and a BSc BrE‖BS AmE for science and SOCIAL SCIENCE. Higher degrees include an MA or an MSc BrE‖MS AmE and a PhD. In Scotland degree courses last four years instead of three, and an MA or an MSc is a first degree. In the US one can also earn an AA degree for two years study in a JUNIOR COLLEGE, but this is a lower degree than a BA. 2 In Britain, students can GRADUATE[3] with an ordinary degree or an HONOURS DEGREE, which is better. The highest level of honours degree is called a **first** or a first class degree, and very few students get this. The next best level is called a **second** or a second class degree, and this is split into a higher level, called a **two-one**, and a lower level, a **two-two**. The lowest level is a **third** or a third class degree. In the US, very good students graduate **summa cum laude** or **magna cum laude**, or simply **cum laude**; the people who get these honours would be in about the top 10% of graduates.◀

4 [U] old use a rank in society: a lady of high degree **5 to a degree: a** partly; not very much: I think that's true to a degree, but the situation is not quite so simple. **b** very much indeed: She's untidy to a degree — her papers are all over the floor! —see also SECOND DEGREE, THIRD DEGREE

de Hav·il·land /də 'hævɪlənd/, **O·liv·i·a** /ə'lɪvɪə/ (1916–   ) an American actress known for her beauty who made a lot of films and won two important prizes

de·hu·man·ize also **-ise** BrE /ˌdiː'hjuːmənaɪz/ v [T] to remove the human qualities from: The prisoners had been dehumanized by disease and ill treatment. —**ization** /ˌdiːhjuːmənaɪ'zeɪʃən‖-mənə-/ n [U]

de·hy·drate /ˌdiːhaɪ'dreɪt‖diː'haɪdreɪt/ v 1 [T] to dry completely; remove all the water from: to dehydrate milk to make milk powder | dehydrated vegetables 2 [I] to lose water from the body: People can very quickly dehydrate in the desert. —**dration** /ˌdiːhaɪ'dreɪʃən/ n [U]

de·ice /ˌdiː'aɪs/ v [T] to make free of ice; remove ice from

de·i·fy /'diːɪfaɪ, 'deɪ-/ v [T] to make a god of; treat as an object of worship: In some ancient societies kings were deified. | (fig.) to deify money —**fication** /ˌdiːɪfɪ'keɪʃən, ˌdeɪ-/ n [U]

Deigh·ton /'deɪtn/, **Len** /len/ (1929–   ) an English THRILLER writer

deign /deɪn/ v [T+to-v;obj;usu. in negatives] often derog to think that something is worthy of one's attention: The students sent their suggestions to the principal but he didn't even deign to reply.

de·is·m /'diːɪzəm, 'deɪ-/ n [U] the belief in a God whose existence can be proved by looking at the world he made rather than by considering some message he personally gave to humans —compare THEISM —**ist** n

de·i·ty /'diːɪti, 'deɪ-/ n a god or goddess: the deities of ancient Greece

Deity n [the] fml God

dé·jà vu /ˌdeɪʒɑː 'vjuː, -'vuː/ n [U] Fr the feeling of remembering something that in fact one is experiencing for the first time: As she stepped into the room she had a strong feeling|sense of déjà vu.

de·jec·ted /dɪ'dʒektɪd/ adj having or showing low spirits; seeming sad or disappointed: a dejected look|person — ~ **ly** adv —**tion** /'dʒekʃən/ n [U]

de ju·re /ˌdiː 'dʒuːəri, ˌdeɪ 'dʒuːəreɪ/ adj, adv Lat by legal right, though not necessarily in fact: the de jure ruler — compare DE FACTO

dek·ko /'dekəʊ/ n **have a dekko (at)** BrE sl to have a look (at)

de Klerk /də 'klɜːk‖-'klɜːrk/, **FW** (1936–   ) a South African politician and president since 1989. While he was in power the black leader Nelson Mandela came out of prison, after 27 years, and gradually many of the laws which had set up the system of APARTHEID (=the separation of blacks and whites) were officially ended.

de Koo·ning /də 'kuːnɪŋ/, **Wil·lem** /'wɪləm/ (1904–   ) a Dutch-born American painter of ABSTRACTS[2]

De La Mare /də lɑː 'meəʳ/, **Wal·ter** /'wɔːltəʳ/ (1873–1956) an English writer remembered esp. for his poems

Del·a·ware /'deləweəʳ/ written abbrev. **DE**— [the] a state in the eastern US. It was one of the 13 original colonies (COLONY). Except for Rhode Island, it is the smallest state. —see colour map on page 1374-5

de·lay[1] /dɪ'leɪ/ v 1 [T] to move to a later time; DEFER: We decided to delay our holiday until next month. | The long-delayed meeting at last took place on Monday. [+v-ing] They delayed publishing the report until after the election. 2 [T] to cause to be late: Our plane was delayed by fog. 3 [I] to move or take action slowly, esp. on purpose: They're trying to delay until help arrives. | Don't delay: send off your application today!

delay[2] n 1 [U] the act of delaying or the state of being delayed: Do it without delay! | Incoming flights will be subject to delay because of the fog. | After much delay, the results of the exam were published. 2 [C] an example of being delayed: Heavy traffic is causing serious delays on all routes to the coast. 3 [C] the time during which something or someone is delayed: Delays of up to two hours were reported on all roads this morning.

Del Boy /'del bɔɪ/ the NICKNAME of **Derek Trotter**, a character in the British television programme Only Fools and Horses who sells things and is known for not being completely honest, but who is a cheerful, pleasant man

de·lec·ta·ble /dɪ'lektəbəl/ adj very pleasing; delightful: What delectable food you cook! —**bly** adv

de·lec·ta·tion /ˌdiːlek'teɪʃən/ n [U] fml or humor enjoyment, pleasure, or amusement

del·e·gate[1] /'delɪgɪt/ n a person who has been elected or appointed to speak, vote, or take decisions for a group, such as a representative at a meeting: She was our delegate at the party conference.

del·e·gate[2] /'delɪgeɪt/ v 1 [I;T (to)] to give (part of one's power, rights, etc.) to someone else for a certain time: Part of the art of management is knowing when to delegate. | I have delegated my command to Captain Roberts. 2 [T] to appoint as a representative or to do a particular job: [+obj+to-v] *I've been delegated to organize the weekly meetings.*

del·e·ga·tion /ˌdelɪˈgeɪʃən/ n **1** [U] the act of delegating or the state of being delegated **2** [C | sing./pl. v] a group of delegates: *The French delegation is/are just arriving at the conference.*

de·lete /dɪˈliːt/ v [T (**from**)] to take, rub, or cut out (esp. written words): *Delete his name from the list of members.*

del·e·ter·i·ous /ˌdelɪˈtɪəriəs◂/ adj fml harmful to the mind or body; INJURIOUS: *the deleterious effects of being exposed to radiation* — ~ **ly** adv

de·le·tion /dɪˈliːʃən/ n **1** [U] the act of deleting or the state of being deleted **2** [C] a word, letter, etc. that has been deleted

Del·hi /ˈdeli/ an area and city in India. The city of Delhi was India's capital until 1857 —see also NEW DELHI

del·i /ˈdeli/ infml abbrev. for: DELICATESSEN

de·lib·e·rate¹ /dɪˈlɪbərət/ adj **1** (esp. of something bad) done on purpose or as a result of careful planning; intentional: *The car crash wasn't an accident; it was a deliberate attempt to kill him! | a deliberate insult* **2** (of speech, thought, or movement) slow; unhurried: *The old man stood up in a very deliberate way and left the room.* — ~ **ly** adv : *She deliberately ignored me when I passed her in the street.* — ~ **ness** n [U]

de·lib·e·rate² /dɪˈlɪbəreɪt/ v [I (**on**, **upon**, **about**);T] fml to consider carefully, often in formal meetings with other people: *The cabinet are still deliberating (the question).* [+wh-] *The committee deliberated whether to approve our proposal.*

de·lib·e·ra·tion /dɪˌlɪbəˈreɪʃən/ n fml **1** [C often pl.;U] careful consideration; thorough examination of a matter: *After much deliberation, we found that nothing could be done. | Our deliberations failed to produce a decision.* **2** [U] the quality of being slow and unhurried in speech, thought, or movement

de·lib·e·ra·tive /dɪˈlɪbərətɪv‖-bəreɪtɪv/ adj for the purpose of deliberating: *Parliament is a deliberative assembly.*

del·i·ca·cy /ˈdelɪkəsi/ n **1** [U] the quality of being delicate **2** [C] something good to eat that is considered rare or expensive: *Caviar is a great delicacy.*

del·i·cate /ˈdelɪkət/ adj **1** needing careful handling, esp. because easily broken or damaged; FRAGILE: *Be careful with those wine glasses — they're very delicate.* **2** easily made ill: *a very delicate child* **3** finely made in a way that shows great skill: *a delicate piece of workmanship* **4** needing careful or sensitive treatment in order to avoid failure or trouble: *a delicate situation/subject | The negotiations are at a very delicate stage.* **5** (of a taste, smell, etc.) pleasing but not strong and perhaps not easy to recognize: *a delicate flavour/smell* **6** quick to show or feel the effect or presence of something; sensitive: *a delicate instrument that can record even very slight changes in the temperature* —see also INDELICATE — ~ **ly** adv

del·i·cates /ˈdelɪkəts/ n [P] clothes which are made from delicate materials and must be washed gently

del·i·ca·tes·sen /ˌdelɪkəˈtesən/ n a shop that sells unusual and often expensive foods, esp. foods that are cooked and ready to eat. In the US, many delicatessens also sell sandwiches (SANDWICH¹) and some have tables at which to eat. Many delicatessens also sell only KOSHER food: *I bought some salami from the delicatessen.*

de·li·cious /dɪˈlɪʃəs/ adj **1** pleasing to the senses of taste or smell: *What a delicious apple! | a delicious smell of cooking | Thank you for a delicious meal, Mrs Atkins.* **2** giving great pleasure or amusement; delightful: *a delicious joke* — ~ **ly** adv — ~ **ness** n [U]

de·light¹ /dɪˈlaɪt/ n **1** [U] a great pleasure and satisfaction; joy: *I read your new book with real delight. | She takes* **delight in** (=enjoys) *teasing her sister.* **2** [C] something or someone that gives great pleasure: *Your new book/little dog is a real delight! | to savour* (=enjoy) *the delights of London's night life* —see also TURKISH DELIGHT

delight² v [T] to cause (someone) great satisfaction, enjoyment, or joy: *a book that is certain to delight | She delighted the audience with her jokes about the president.* **delight in** sthg. phr v [T no pass.] to take great pleasure in (esp. something unpleasant): *He delights in scandal.* [+v-ing] *They seem to delight in keeping everyone else waiting.*

de·light·ed /dɪˈlaɪtɪd/ adj [(**by**, **with**)] very pleased or satisfied: *We were delighted by/with the response to our advertisement.* [F+to-v] *Thanks for your invitation — I'd be delighted to come!* [F (*that*)] *We're delighted that you'll be able to come.*

de·light·ful /dɪˈlaɪtfəl/ adj very pleasing: *a delightful holiday/child/little house* — ~ **ly** adv

De·li·lah /dɪˈlaɪlə/ a woman in the Bible who persuaded Samson to tell her his secret, that his hair was the origin of his strength. She then had it cut it off to weaken him.

de·lim·it /dɪˈlɪmɪt/ v [T] fml to fix the limits of: *to delimit the powers of various officials* — ~ **ation** /dɪˌlɪmɪˈteɪʃən/ n [U]

de·lin·e·ate /dɪˈlɪnieɪt/ v [T] fml to show by drawing or describing —**-ation** /dɪˌlɪniˈeɪʃən/ n [U]

de·lin·quen·cy /dɪˈlɪŋkwənsi/ n **1** [U] behaviour, esp. by young people, that is not in accordance with accepted social standards or with the law. Acts of delinquency would include fighting, damaging property, stealing cars for a short time for pleasure, and writing on walls in public places. **2** [C] fml an offence against the law or accepted social standards

de·lin·quent¹ /dɪˈlɪŋkwənt/ adj **1** having broken a law, esp. one which is not very serious; having a tendency to break the law or to do socially unacceptable things: *delinquent youths/behaviour* **2** tech (of debts, accounts, etc.) not having been paid in time

delinquent² n a person, esp. a young person, who is delinquent: *a juvenile* (=young) *delinquent*

del·i·ques·cent /ˌdelɪˈkwesənt◂/ adj fml or tech taking up water from the air and so becoming liquid, as salt does in wet weather —**-cence** n [U]

de·lir·i·ous /dɪˈlɪriəs/ adj in an excited dreamy state, esp. caused by illness: *During the fever he became delirious and said some strange things. | delirious with joy* — ~ **ly** adv : *deliriously happy*

de·lir·i·um /dɪˈlɪriəm/ n **1** [C;U] an excited dreamy state in serious illness **2** [S] a very excited state: *a delirium of joy* —see also DELIRIOUS

delirium tre·mens /dɪˌlɪriəm ˈtremənz‖-ˈtriː-/ n [U] fml for D T's

De·li·us /ˈdiːliəs/, **Fred·e·rick** /ˈfredərɪk/ (1862–1934) an English COMPOSER (=writer) of classical music, known for his works for both voices and instruments

de·liv·er /dɪˈlɪvər/ v **1** [I;T (**to**)] to take (goods, letters, etc.) to people's houses or places of work: *Letters are delivered every day. | Yes, we deliver newspapers. | Will you deliver, or do I have to come to the shop to collect the goods?* **2** [T+obj+prep] to send or aim (a blow, kick, etc.) to the intended place: *She delivered a hard kick to his knee.* **3** [T] to speak or read aloud to people listening: *to deliver a lecture/a speech* **4** [T] **a** to help in the birth of: *The doctor delivered her baby.* **b** to help in giving birth: *The doctor delivered the woman (of twin boys).* **5** [T (**from**)] fml to set free; RESCUE: *They prayed to God to deliver them from danger.* **6** [I (**on**);T] to fulfil (a promise or hope) or produce (something promised or hoped for): *Do you think the government will deliver on their election promises/deliver the promised tax cuts?* **7** [T] esp. AmE to bring (votes, influence, etc.) to the support of a political movement, a person trying to get elected, etc.: *The Democrats are hoping she will deliver the black vote.* (=persuade black people to vote for them) **8 deliver the goods** sl to DELIVER (6) —see also **stand and deliver** (STAND¹ (21)) — ~ **er** n

deliver sthg. **up** phr v [T (UP) often pass.] to put into (someone else's) possession: *The town was delivered (up) to the enemy.*

de·liv·er·ance /dɪˈlɪvərəns/ n [U (**from**)] fml the act of saving from harm or danger, or the state of being saved: *deliverance from slavery*

de·liv·er·y /dɪˈlɪvəri/ n **1** [C;U (**to**)] the act of taking or giving something to someone, or the things taken or given: *The next postal delivery is at 2 o'clock. | The company has just* **taken delivery of** (=received) *a new computer system. | a delivery van* **2** [C] the birth of a child: *The mother had an easy delivery.* **3** [C;U] the manner or style of speaking in public: *a good/fast/slow delivery* **4** [C] (in cricket) an act or style of throwing a ball: *He was*

eventually bowled by an excellent delivery from Frazer.

de·liv·er·y·man /dɪˈlɪvərimən/ n -men /mən/ a man who delivers goods to people who have bought or ordered them, usu. locally

delivery note /·ˈ··· ·/ n tech a document sent with goods to show that they have been delivered

delivery room /·ˈ··· ·/ n a room in a hospital in which women give birth

dell /del/ n lit a small valley with grass and trees

De·loitte /dʒˈlɔɪt/ a British ACCOUNTANCY firm, now joined with another company to form Coopers and Lybrand Deloitte

De·lors /dəˈlɔːr/, **Jacques** /ʒækˈʒɑːk/ (1925–ɪ) a French politician and the president of the European Commission

de·louse /ˌdiːˈlaʊs/ v [T] to remove LICE (pl. of LOUSE) or similar creatures from (a person, clothes, etc.)

Del·phic or·a·cle /ˌdelfɪk ˈɒrəkəl ‖ -ˈɔː-, -ˈɑː-/ [the] the temple in the town of Delphi in ancient Greece where a priestess answered questions with words thought to be from the god Apollo.

del·phin·i·um /delˈfɪniəm/ also **larkspur**– n an upright branching plant with usu. blue flowers growing all the way up its long stems

del·ta /ˈdeltə/ n **1** the fourth letter (Δ, δ) of the Greek alphabet **2** an area of low land shaped like a Δ where a river divides into branches towards the sea: *the Nile Delta in Egypt*

delta

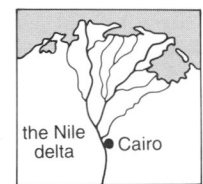

the Nile delta ● Cairo

Delta Force /ˈ·· ˌ·/ an American military group which is mainly responsible for rescue operations and special forces work –compare SAS

de·lude /dɪˈluːd/ v [T (into)] to mislead the mind or judgment of; deceive: *You're just deluding yourself if you think she still loves you.* | *He deluded everyone into following him.* –see also DELUSION

del·uge¹ /ˈdeljuːdʒ/ n a great flood or a very heavy rain: (fig.) *a deluge of questions*

deluge² v [T] **1** fml to cover with a great flood of water **2** [(with) usu. pass.] to cover or fill with a great flood of things; INUNDATE: *The minister was completely deluged with questions/insults.*

de·lu·sion /dɪˈluːʒən/ n **1** [U] the act of deluding or the state of being deluded **2** [C] a false belief, esp. if strongly held: *to suffer from* **delusions of grandeur** (=the belief that one is extremely important, powerful, etc.) [+that] *He is* **under the delusion** *that he is Napoleon.* –see ILLUSION (USAGE)

de·lu·sive /dɪˈluːsɪv/ also **de·lu·so·ry** /-səri/– adj likely to delude; misleading: *a delusive act/belief* – –ly adv

de luxe also **deluxe** /dʒ ˈlʌks‖-ˈlʊks/ adj of especially high quality: *The car's price is very reasonable; of course, the de luxe model costs a lot more.*

delve /delv/ v [I] **1** [(into)] to search deeply: *He delved into the family archives looking for the facts.* **2** poet or old use to dig

Dem /dem/ abbrev for: a Democrat b Democratic

de·mag·ne·tize also **-tise** BrE /ˌdiːˈmægnətaɪz/ v [T] **1** to take away the MAGNETIC qualities of **2** tech to remove sounds from (a MAGNETIC TAPE) **—-tization** /ˌdiːmægnətaɪˈzeɪʃən‖-nətə-/ n [U]

dem·a·gogue also **-gog** AmE /ˈdeməgɒg‖-gɑː/ n derog a leader who tries to gain, or has gained, power by exciting people's feelings rather than by reasoned argument **—-gogic** /ˌdeməˈgɒgɪk◄‖-ˈgɑː-/ adj **—-gogically** /kli/ adv **—-goguery** /ˈdeməgɒgəri ‖ -gɑːg-/ n [U]

de·mand¹ /dɪˈmɑːnd‖dɪˈmænd/ n **1** [C (for)] an act of demanding; claim: *The management has refused to agree to our demand for a 6% pay rise.* | *This work* **makes great demands** *on my time.* (=takes up a lot of my time) | *Do you think they will give in to the terrorists' demands?* – see REQUEST² (USAGE) **2** [S;U (for)] the desire of people for particular goods or services; the ability and willingness of people to pay for them: *There's not much*

demand for houses of this sort. | *These developments have created a great demand for home computers.* | *Her books are in great demand at the moment.* –see also SUPPLY AND DEMAND

demand² v [T] **1** to ask for firmly and not be willing to accept a refusal; claim as if by right: *I demand an apology/an explanation!* [+to-v] *She demanded to speak to the manager.* [+that] *The opposition have demanded that all the facts (should) be made public.* **2** to need urgently: *This work demands your immediate attention.* **3** [(of)] to need (effort, hard work, etc.) in order to be successful; REQUIRE: *Work of this nature demands many personal sacrifices/demands a great deal of those who embark on it.*

de·mand·ing /dɪˈmɑːndɪŋ‖dɪˈmænd-/ adj needing a lot of attention and effort: *A new baby and a new job can be equally demanding.*

demand-side /·ˈ· ·/ adj [A] of or being an economic POLICY that places a lot of importance on DEMAND¹ (2) and using things up –compare SUPPLY-SIDE

de·mar·cate /ˈdiːmɑːkeɪt‖dɪˈmɑːr-/ v [T] to mark the limits of: *to demarcate a frontier*

de·mar·ca·tion /ˌdiːmɑːˈkeɪʃən‖-ɑːr-/ n [U] limitation; separation: *a row of trees on the line of demarcation between the two pieces of land*

demarcation dis·pute /·ˌ··ˈ··· ·ˌ·/ n a disagreement between different trade unions about which jobs should be done by the members of each union

de·mean /dɪˈmiːn/ v [T] fml to cause (oneself) to lose one's sense of personal pride: *Don't demean yourself by answering him.* | *It was very demeaning to have to ask his permission for everything I wanted to do.*

de·mea·nour BrE‖**-nor** AmE /dɪˈmiːnər/ n fml behaviour towards others; outward manner: *She has a cheerful and friendly demeanour.*

de·men·ted /dɪˈmentᵻd/ adj mad; of unbalanced mind – –ly adv

de·men·tia /dɪˈmenʃə, -ʃiə‖-tʃə/ n [U] tech decay of the mind, esp. leading to madness. ALZHEIMER'S DISEASE is a well-known cause of dementia.

dem·e·ra·ra sug·ar /ˌdeməreərə ˈʃʊgər/ n [U] rough brown sugar, usu. from the West Indies

de·mer·it /diːˈmerᵻt/ n fml **1** a fault; bad quality: *We discussed the merits and demerits of her research proposal.* –compare MERIT¹ **2** AmE a mark against someone for something wrong they have done, esp. at school: *The teacher gave him three demerits and extra homework for coming in late.*

de·mesne /dɪˈmeɪn/ n fml or law the land round a great house; land owned by and for the use of a lord or king

dem·i·god /ˈdemigɒd‖-gɑːd/ **dem·i·god·dess** /-dʒᵻs/fem.– n (in ancient stories) someone greater than a human but less than a god

dem·i·john /ˈdemidʒɒn‖-dʒɑːn/ n a large narrow-necked bottle, often with small handles, holding from about 5 to 45 litres

de·mil·i·ta·rize also **-rise** BrE /ˌdiːˈmɪlᵻtəraɪz/ v [T] to take away the military character of; prevent (esp. a border area) from being used for military purposes: *a demilitarized zone* **—-rization** /ˌdiːmɪlᵻtəraɪˈzeɪʃən‖-tərə-/ n [U]

De Mille /də ˈmɪl/, **Ag·nes** /ˈægnᵻs/ (1908–ɪ) an American dancer and CHOREOGRAPHER who planned the dances for several Broadway musicals e.g. *Oklahoma!,* as well as for some BALLETS

De Mille, Cec·il B. /ˈsesᵻl biː/ (1881–1959) an American film producer and director. Cecil B. De Mille helped to form the popular image of a film director as someone who uses a MEGAPHONE and makes actors do exactly as he wants: *a Cecil B. De Mille epic with a cast of thousands*

de·mise /dɪˈmaɪz/ n [U] law or euph death: *Upon his demise the title will pass to his son.* | (fig.) *the demise of a famous newspaper*

de·mist /ˌdiːˈmɪst/ BrE‖**defog, defrost** AmE– v [T] to remove steam from (the windows of a car) by means of heat or warm air – –er n

dem·o /ˈdeməʊ/ n demos infml **1** abbrev. for DEMONSTRATION **2** AmE a recording sent to record companies in order to show the skill of a new singer or music group: *They receive dozens of demo tapes every week.*

de·mob¹ /diːˈmɒb‖-ˈmɑːb/ v **-bb-** [T] BrE infml to demobilize

demob² n [U] BrE infml demobilization

de·mo·bi·lize also **-lise** BrE /diːˈməʊbɪlaɪz/ [I;T often pass.] fml to send home the members of (an armed force), usu. at the end of a war; allow to leave military service —see also MOBILIZE (2) —**-lization** /dɪˌməʊbɪlaɪˈzeɪʃən‖-bələ-/ n [U]

de·moc·ra·cy /dɪˈmɒkrəsi‖dɪˈmɑː-/ n **1** [U] government by the people, or by elected representatives of the people. Democracy was first developed in Ancient Greece: *The military government promised to restore democracy within one year.* —compare ARISTOCRACY (3) **2** [C] a country governed by its people or their representatives **3** [U] social equality and the right to take part in decision-making: *industrial democracy*

dem·o·crat /ˈdeməkræt/ n a person who believes in or works for democracy

Democrat n **1** a member or supporter of the Democratic Party of the US —compare REPUBLICAN **2** (in Britain) infml for a LIBERAL DEMOCRAT

dem·o·crat·ic /ˌdeməˈkrætɪk◄/ adj **1** of or favouring democracy: *democratic ideals | a democratic country* **2** believing in or practising the principle of equality: *The company is run on democratic lines, and all the staff are involved in making decisions.* —opposite **undemocratic** —**-ally** /kli/ adv : *the democratically-elected government*

Democratic adj of or supporting the DEMOCRATIC PARTY —compare REPUBLICAN¹

Democratic Par·ty /ˌ···ˈ···, ˌ···/, **the** one of the two main political parties of the US, also known as **the Democrats**. The Democratic Party's policies (POLICY) are more LIBERAL¹ (2) than those of the Republican Party —compare REPUBLICAN PARTY

de·moc·ra·tize also BrE **-tise** /dɪˈmɒkrətaɪz‖dɪˈmɑː-/ v [T] to make democratic or more democratic: *to democratize the union's decision-making processes* —**-tization** /dɪˌmɒkrətaɪˈzeɪʃən‖dɪˌmɑːkrətə-/ n [U]

dé·mo·dé /ˌdeɪˈməʊdeɪ‖ˌdeɪməʊˈdeɪ/ adj no longer in fashion: *démodé clothes/ideas*

de·mog·ra·phy /dɪˈmɒɡrəfi‖-ˈmɑː-/ n [U] the statistical (STATISTICS) study of human population —**-pher** n —**-phic** /ˌdeməˈɡræfɪk◄, ˌdiː-/ adj : *changing demographic trends*

de·mol·ish /dɪˈmɒlɪʃ‖dɪˈmɑː-/ v [T] **1** to destroy (esp. a large structure); pull or tear down: *They're going to demolish that old factory.* | (fig.) *We've demolished all her arguments.* **2** infml to eat up hungrily: *to demolish two big platefuls of chicken*

dem·o·li·tion /ˌdeməˈlɪʃən◄/ n [C;U] (an example of) the act of demolishing

demolition der·by /ˌ···· ˈ··/ n AmE a kind of car race in which the drivers try to hit other cars to knock them out of the competition

de·mon /ˈdiːmən/ n **1** an evil spirit: (fig.) *That child is a little demon.* **2** infml a person with unusual strength, skill, etc.: *a demon for work | a demon card-player* —compare DAEMON

de·mon·e·tize also **-tise** BrE /diːˈmʌnɪtaɪz‖diːˈmɑː-/ v [T] to stop using (esp. a coin or note) as a standard of money

de·mo·ni·a·cal /ˌdiːməˈnaɪəkəl◄/ also **de·mon·ni·ac** /dɪˈməʊniæk/— adj of or like a demon: *demoniacal cruelty* —**-ly** /kli/ adv

de·mon·ic /dɪˈmɒnɪk‖dɪˈmɑː-/ adj by a demon or being a demon: *demonic possession* (=being controlled by an evil spirit) | *a demonic spirit* —**-ally** /kli/ adv

de·mon·stra·ble /dɪˈmɒnstrəbəl, ˈdemən-‖dɪˈmɑːn-/ adj fml that can be clearly proved or shown to be true: *a demonstrable fact* —**-bly** adv : *But that idea is demonstrably false!* —**-bility** /dɪˌmɒnstrəˈbɪlɪti‖dɪˌmɑːn-/ n [U]

dem·on·strate /ˈdemənstreɪt/ v **1** [T] to prove or make clear (a fact), esp. by reasoning or providing examples: *His last remark demonstrates his total ignorance of the subject.* [+that] *Galileo demonstrated that objects of different weights fall at the same speed.* **2** [T] to show or describe clearly: *The first-aid instructor demonstrated the correct way to bandage a wound.* [+wh-] *I will now demonstrate how the machine works.* **3** [T] to show the value or use of (esp. a machine), esp. to a possible buyer: *to demonstrate a new kitchen gadget* **4** [I (against)] to take part

in a public show of strong feeling or opinion, often with marching, big signs, etc.: *They demonstrated against the government's nuclear policy.* —see also DEMONSTRATOR

dem·on·stra·tion /ˌdemənˈstreɪʃən/ also **demo** infml— n **1** [C;U] an act of showing or proving something: *She gave us a demonstration of the machine to show how it worked.* | *Can I have a demonstration of what it does?* **2** [C] a public show of strong feeling or opinion, often with marching, big signs, etc. Many people connect demonstrations with students, esp. LEFT-WING students. There were a lot of demonstrations during the 1960s, some of them violent: *to hold/stage a demonstration against cuts in welfare spending | We're going on/taking part in a CND demonstration this afternoon. | Police used tear gas to break up the demonstration.* —compare RALLY² (1)

de·mon·stra·tive /dɪˈmɒnstrətɪv‖dɪˈmɑːn-/ adj **1** showing feelings openly: *He's not very demonstrative.* —opposite **undemonstrative 2** [(of)] fml showing or proving something: *The report is demonstrative of the government's concern about this matter.* — **-ly** adv

demonstrative pro·noun /·ˌ··· ˈ··/ also **demonstrative**— n tech a PRONOUN that points out the person or thing that is meant and separates it from others: *"This", "that", "these", and "those" are all demonstrative pronouns.*

dem·on·stra·tor /ˈdemənstreɪtər/ n **1** a person who takes part in a public demonstration: *The demonstrators claim they were attacked by the police.* **2** a person who demonstrates something **3** (esp. in British universities) a person who helps science students with their practical work

de·mor·al·ize also **-ise** BrE /dɪˈmɒrəlaɪz‖dɪˈmɔː-, dɪˈmɑː-/ [T] to lessen or destroy the courage and confidence of: *After months of inactivity, the army was completely demoralized. | a series of demoralizing failures* —**-ization** /dɪˌmɒrəlaɪˈzeɪʃən‖dɪˌmɔːrələ-, dɪˌmɑː-/ n [U]

de·mote /dɪˈməʊt/ v [T] to lower in rank or position —opposite **promote** —**-motion** /dɪˈməʊʃən/ n [C;U]

de·mot·ic /dɪˈmɒtɪk‖dɪˈmɑː-/ adj fml (of a form of language, esp. Modern Greek) used by the ordinary people

de·mo·ti·vate /diːˈməʊtɪveɪt/ v [T] to take away from (a person) their eagerness to do their job or the satisfaction they get from doing their job —**-vation** /ˌdiːməʊtɪˈveɪʃən/ n [U]

Demp·sey /ˈdempsi/, **Jack** (1895–1983) a famous American BOXER who held the HEAVYWEIGHT title from 1926 to 1926

de·mur¹ /dɪˈmɜːr/ v **-rr-** [I (at)] fml to make clear, by words or actions, one's opposition to or disapproval of a plan, suggestion, etc.: *They demurred at the idea of working on Sunday.*

demur² n **without demur** fml with no sign of disagreement or disapproval

de·mure /dɪˈmjʊər/ adj **1** (esp. of a woman or child) quiet, serious, and not trying to draw attention to oneself: *a demure young lady* **2** pretending to be like this — **-ly** adv — **-ness** n [U]

de·mys·ti·fy /ˌdiːˈmɪstɪfaɪ/ v [T] to make (something) less mysterious or less difficult to understand: *a book attempting to demystify the whole subject of computers.* —**-fication** /ˌdiːmɪstɪfɪˈkeɪʃən/ n [U]

den /den/ n **1** the home of a usu. large fierce wild animal, such as a lion **2** a centre of secret, esp. illegal, activity: *a den of thieves | an opium den | a den of iniquity* **3** infml a small comfortable quiet room in a house, where a person, usu. a man, can be alone: *Father's in his den.* **4** AmE a group of CUB SCOUTS

De·na·li /dəˈnɑːli/ a mountain in **Denali National Park** in central Alaska which is the highest point in North America. It was formerly called Mount McKinley.

de·na·tion·al·ize also **-ise** BrE /diːˈnæʃənəlaɪz/ v [T] to remove from state ownership; PRIVATIZE —**-ization** /ˌdiːnæʃənəlaɪˈzeɪʃən‖-nələ-/ n [C;U]

Dench /dentʃ/, **Dame Ju·di** /ˈdʒuːdi/ (1934–) one of Britain's finest classical actresses in the theatre, the cinema, and on television

den·gue fe·ver /ˈdeŋɡi ˌfiːvər/ n [U] a serious infectious illness which is carried by mosquitoes (MOSQUITO) in hot countries

Deng Xiao·ping /ˌdʌŋ ˌʃaʊˈpɪŋ/ (1904–) a Chinese Communist leader who has been in and out of power but has had great influence in important positions since the late 1970s

de·ni·al /dɪ'naɪəl/ n [C;U] **1** the act or an example of saying that something is not true; act of denying (DENY): *The government has issued a firm denial of this rumour.* **2** the act or an example of refusing to give or do something: *a denial of justice*

de·ni·er¹ /dɪ'naɪəʳ/ n a person who denies (DENY) something

den·i·er² /'deniəʳ/ n a measure of the fineness of the threads of silk, nylon, etc. Lower numbers mean finer threads: *15-denier tights*

den·i·grate /'denɪˌgreɪt/ v [T] *fml* to declare to be not very good or not important; DISPARAGE —**gration** /ˌdenɪˈgreɪʃən/ n [U]

den·im /'denɪm/ n [U] a strong cotton cloth used esp. for making JEANS

den·ims /'denɪmz/ n [P] trousers made of denim; JEANS: *a pair of blue denims*

De Ni·ro /də 'nɪərəʊ/, **Rob·ert** /'rɒbət‖'rɑːbərt/ (1945–) an American actor known esp. for his parts in the films *Taxi Driver* and *The Deer Hunter* —see colour picture on page 228

den·i·zen /'denɪzən/ n [(of)] *lit or humor* an animal, plant, or person, that lives or is found in a particular place: *denizens of the deep* (=sea creatures)

Den·mark /'denmɑːk‖-mɑːrk/ a small country in northern Europe bordering on Germany and surrounded on three sides by the sea; capital Copenhagen; population 5,132,000 (1989) —see also DANISH

den moth·er /'· ˌ··/ n *AmE* a woman who leads a group of CUB SCOUTS

Den·ning /'denɪŋ/, **Lord** (1899–) an English judge who held some of the highest legal positions, for 20 years being Master of the Rolls. He was in charge of many important cases, and has often given judgments or opinions which have caused a lot of public argument or disagreement.

Den·nis the Men·ace /ˌdenɪs ðə 'menɪs/ n a character from the British COMIC *The Beano.* He is a little boy with untidy hair, a red and black STRIPED jumper, and a wicked GRIN who is always getting into trouble: *They look so cheeky – like a trio of Dennis the Menaces. And at bedtime Jimmy, Ben, and Tommy Carpenter certainly live up to their image.*

de·nom·i·nate /dɪ'nɒmɪneɪt‖dɪ'nɑː-/ v [T+obj+n] *fml or pomp* to give a name to; call; DESIGNATE

de·nom·i·na·tion /dɪˌnɒmɪˈneɪʃən‖dɪˌnɑː-/ n **1** a religious group that is part of a larger religious body: *The service was attended by Christians of all denominations.* **2** a standard of value: *coins of many denominations/of low denominations* **3** *fml* a name, esp. for a class or type

de·nom·i·na·tion·al /dɪˌnɒmɪˈneɪʃənəl‖dɪˌnɑː-/ adj of, controlled by, or being a religious denomination: *a denominational school* —see also INTERDENOMINATIONAL

de·nom·i·na·tor /dɪ'nɒmɪneɪtəʳ‖dɪ'nɑː-/ n the number below the line in a FRACTION: *4 is the denominator in ¼.* —compare NUMERATOR; see also COMMON DENOMINATOR

de·no·ta·tion /ˌdiːnəʊˈteɪʃən/ n esp. *tech* the thing that is actually named or described by a word, rather than the feelings or ideas that are suggested by the word —compare CONNOTATION —**tive** /dɪ'nəʊtətɪv‖'diːnəʊteɪtɪv, dɪ'nəʊtə-/ adj

de·note /dɪ'nəʊt/ v [T] **1** to be a name of; mean: *The word "lion" denotes a certain kind of wild animal.* **2** to be a mark or sign of: *A smile often denotes pleasure.* [+that] *The sign "=" denotes that two things are equal.* —compare CONNOTE

de·noue·ment /deɪ'nuːmɒŋ‖ˌdeɪnuː'mɑːŋ/ n the end of a story when everything is explained

de·nounce /dɪ'naʊns/ v [T (as)] to express strong disapproval of, esp. publicly; CONDEMN: *The minister's action was denounced in all the newspapers.* | *She was denounced as a traitor.*

dense /dens/ adj **1** closely packed or crowded together: *a dense crowd* | *dense trees/traffic* **2** difficult to see through: *a dense mist* **3** stupid; slow to understand: *One or two of the students are a bit dense.* — ~ **ly** adv : *a densely populated area* — ~ **ness** n [U]

den·si·ty /'densɪti/ n **1** [U] **a** the quality of being DENSE

(1,2): *the density of the crowd/of the mist* **b** the degree to which a space or area is filled: *population density* | *low-density housing* (=a small number of houses in a large area) **2** [C;U] *tech* the relation of the amount of matter (the mass) to the space into which the matter is packed (its VOLUME (2)): *the density of a gas* **3** [C;U] *tech* the amount of information that can be stored per unit of space on a MAGNETIC TAPE or DISK: *Are these high- or low-density disks?* | *The density of this tape is 6250 bpi.* (=bits per inch)

dent¹ /dent/ n a small hollow place in the surface of something man-made, which is the result of pressure or of being hit: *a dent in the side of my car* | (fig.) *The holiday has made a big dent in our savings.*

dent² v [T] to make a dent in: *I'm afraid I've dented the car.*

den·tal¹ /'dentl/ adj of or related to the teeth: *dental decay*

dental² n, adj *tech* (a speech sound) made by putting the end of the tongue against the upper front teeth

dental floss /ˌ·· '·/ n [U] a type of thread usu. covered in WAX and used for cleaning between the teeth

dental hy·gie·nist /ˌ·· '···, ˌ·· ·'··/ n a HYGIENIST

dental plate /ˌ·· '·/ n a PLATE¹ (5a)

dental sur·geon /ˌ·· '··/ ‖ usu. **oral surgeon** *AmE*— n *fml* a dentist

den·tine /'dentiːn/ *BrE* ‖ **den·tin** /'dentɪn/*AmE*— n [U] a hard substance that forms the main part of the tooth —see picture at TEETH

den·tist /'dentɪst/ n a person who has been professionally trained to treat the teeth. In Britain and the US, people usu. go to see their dentist every six months when they are children (and in Britain this is paid for by the state), although often they go less frequently as adults. Many people, esp. older people, connect the dentist's with pain, and some actually fear going there: *I have to go to the dentist/to the dentist's this morning.* —compare ORAL SURGEON; —see also DENTAL¹, ORTHODONTIST

den·tis·try /'dentɪstri/ n [U] the work of a dentist

den·ture /'dentʃəʳ/ n *fml* a PLATE¹ (5b) into which false teeth are fixed

den·tures /'dentʃəz‖-ərz/ n [P] FALSE TEETH

de·nude /dɪ'njuːd‖dɪ'nuːd/ v [T (of)] *fml* to completely remove the (natural) protective covering from: *Wind and rain had denuded the mountainside of soil.*

de·nun·ci·a·tion /dɪˌnʌnsiˈeɪʃən/ n [C;U] (an example of) the act of denouncing (DENOUNCE): *The President issued a tough denunciation of terrorism.*

Den·ver /'denvəʳ/ the capital city of Colorado, a mountainous state of the US. It is called the **Mile-High City** because it is one mile above sea level. —see colour map on page 1374–5

Denver, John (1943–) an American singer and writer of popular music. His many famous songs include *Annie's song* and *Rocky Mountain High.*

Denver boot /ˌ·· '·/ n *infml for* WHEEL CLAMP

de·ny /dɪ'naɪ/ v [T] **1** to declare untrue; refuse to accept as a fact: *The minister has strenuously denied these allegations.* | *She denies any involvement in the robbery.* [+v-ing/that] *The accused man denies ever having met her/denies that he has ever met her.* [+obj+to-v] (*fml*) *Do you deny this to be your writing?* | **There's no denying that** (=it's very clear that) *this will be a serious blow to the government.* —compare AFFIRM, ADMIT **2** to refuse to give or allow: *Permission to enter was denied.* [+obj(i)+obj(d)] *I was denied the chance of going to university when my parents' business collapsed and they lost everything they owned.* **3** to refuse to allow (oneself) too much pleasure: *We denied ourselves for years, until we'd finished paying for the house.* **4** *fml* to disclaim connection with or responsibility for; DISOWN: *He has denied his country and his principles!* —see also DENIAL, DENIER¹

de·o·do·rant /diː'əʊdərənt/ n [C;U] a chemical substance that destroys or hides unpleasant smells, esp. those of the human body: *a roll-on deodorant* —compare ANTIPERSPIRANT

de·o·do·rize also **-rise** *BrE* /diː'əʊdəraɪz/ v [T] to remove or hide the unpleasant smell of

dep *written abbrev. for:* **a** DEPART **b** DEPARTURE —compare ARR (2)

de·part /dɪˈpɑːt‖-ɑːrt/ v **1** [I (from)] *fml or lit* to leave; go away, esp. when starting a journey: *The train to Edinburgh will depart from platform 6 in five minutes.* – compare ARRIVE (1) **2 depart this life** *euph* to die; used esp. on GRAVESTONES
depart from sthg. *phr v* [T] to turn away from or stop following (a usual or former course of action, way of thinking, etc.): *We departed from our normal practice of holding the meetings in public.* –see also DEPARTURE (2)

de·part·ed /dɪˈpɑːtɪd‖-ɑːr-/ adj **1** gone for ever: *to remember one's departed youth* **2** *euph* dead; a word used esp. by priests and older people: *our dear departed father* [also *n, the +C, pl.* **departed**] *Let us pray for all the faithful departed.*

de·part·ment /dɪˈpɑːtmənt‖-ɑːr-/ (*written abbrev.* **dept**) n **1** [C+*sing./pl.* v] any of the important divisions or branches of a government, business, college, etc.: *The History Department is/are using this room.* | *the toy department of a large store* | *She's the head of the firm's personnel department.* | *He's a senior executive at the Department of Transport/at the State Department.* **2** [C] (in various countries) a political division rather like a COUNTY in Britain or a state in the US **3** [S] *infml* an activity or subject which is the special responsibility of a particular person: *I'm not going to repair the clock – that's your department.* – ~al /ˌdiːpɑːtˈmentl◂‖-ɑːr-/ adj: *a departmental meeting*

Department of Ed·u·ca·tion and Sci·ence /ˌ·ˌ··· ··ˌ·· ˈ··/ also **DES**– [*the*] the British government department responsible for educational planning and decisions in England and Wales –compare SED

Department of Em·ploy·ment /ˌ·ˌ··· ·ˈ··/ [*the*] the government department in Britain which is responsible for all areas to do with employment, such as new laws and programmes on TRAINING, HEALTH AND SAFETY, EQUAL OPPORTUNITIES, etc.

Department of Health /ˌ·ˌ··· ˈ·/ [*the*] the government in Britain which is responsible for health and the National Health Service

Department of Health and Hu·man Ser·vi·ces /ˌ·ˌ··· ˌ·· ˌ·· ˈ···/ [*the*] the American government department which is responsible for programmes concerning health, WELFARE (=aid to poor people), and SOCIAL SECURITY. Before 1979, it was called the Department of Health, Education, and Welfare.

Department of Jus·tice /ˌ·ˌ··· ˈ··/ [*the*] a department of the US government, headed by the Attorney General, which advises the government, writes laws, and represents the government in court

Department of La·bor /ˌ·ˌ··· ˈ··/ [*the*] the American government department concerned with how workers are treated by employers. It examines subjects such as fair wages, safety, and the number of hours worked each week

Department of Mo·tor Ve·hic·les /ˌ·ˌ··· ˈ·· ˌ···/ DMV

Department of So·cial Se·cu·ri·ty /ˌ·ˌ··· ˌ·· ·ˈ···/ [*the*] see DSS

Department of State /ˌ·ˌ··· ˈ·/ [*the*] the department of the American government which manages FOREIGN POLICY (=one country's relationships with the others)

Department of the En·vi·ron·ment /ˌ·ˌ··· ··ˈ···/ also **DOE**– [*the*] the British government department concerned with planning, REGIONAL development, local government (including local government taxes) and protection of the countryside and old buildings

Department of the In·te·ri·or /ˌ·ˌ··· ··ˈ···/ [*the*] an American government department with responsibility for protecting natural RESOURCES (=the land and water and the things in them, such as trees, MINERALS, animals, fish, etc.) The head of this department is called the Secretary of the Interior.

Department of Trade and In·dus·try /ˌ·ˌ··· ˌ·· ˈ···/ also **DTI**– [*the*] the British government department concerned with trade and industry

department store /ˌ·ˈ·· ·/ n a large shop divided into departments, in each of which a different type of goods is sold. Among the most famous department stores are, in Britain, Harrods, Debenhams, and John Lewis, and in the US, Macy's, Bloomingdales, and Marshall Field.

de·par·ture /dɪˈpɑːtʃəʳ‖-ɑːr-/ n **1** [C;U] an act of departing: *There are several departures a day for New York.* | *What is the departure time of the flight to New York?* | (*fml*) *It is time to* **take our departure.** (=to leave) | (fig.) *his*

sudden departure from the political scene **2** [C (**from**)] a change from a usual or former course of action, etc.; DIVERGENCE: *The new policy represents a complete departure from their previous position.* | *This is a new departure for the company.*

departure lounge /·ˈ··· ˌ·/ n the area at an airport where people wait until their flights are ready to leave. They can eat or drink, buy certain things, change money, etc., while they are waiting.

de·pend /dɪˈpend/ v **1** [*it+*T+*wh-*] to vary according to; be decided by: *You can buy them in all sizes – it depends how much you're prepared to spend.* **2 That (all) depends/It all depends** That/It has not yet been decided
depend on/upon sbdy./sthg. *phr v* [T] **1** to trust (usu. a person); have confidence in: *You can't depend on John – he nearly always arrives late.* [+*obj+to-v/v-ing*] *We're depending on you to finish the job/on you finishing the job by Friday.* | *They'll be here soon,* **depend upon** it. (=you can be sure) **2** to be supported by, esp. with money; need for one's support: *The organization depends on the government for most of its income.* | *The country depends heavily on its tourist trade.* **3** [*not in progressive forms*] to vary according to; be decided by: *The price of the shares will depend on the number of people who want to buy them.* [+*wh-*] *The amount you pay depends on where you live.*

de·pen·da·ble /dɪˈpendəbəl/ adj able to be trusted; RELIABLE: *She won't forget – she's very dependable.* | *a dependable source of income* —**bly** adv —**bility** /dɪˌpendəˈbɪlˌti/ n [U]

de·pen·dant , **-dent** /dɪˈpendənt/ n a person who depends on someone else for food, clothing, money, etc. A person's dependants are usu. their husband or wife and any children under 18: *Please state your name, age, and the number of dependants you have.*

de·pen·dence /dɪˈpendəns/ n [U (**on, upon**)] **1** the state of being dependent; inability to exist or operate without the help or support of someone or something else: *We need to reduce our dependence on oil as a source of energy.* –see also INDEPENDENCE **2** trust; RELIANCE: *I always place/put a lot of dependence on what she says.* **3** the need to have certain drugs regularly, esp. dangerous ones; ADDICTION

de·pen·den·cy /dɪˈpendənsi/ n a country controlled by another

de·pen·dent /dɪˈpendənt/ adj **1** [(**on**)] needing the help or support of someone or something else: *a dependent child* | *The country is heavily dependent on foreign aid/on its oil exports.* –see also INDEPENDENT **2** [F+**on**] that will be decided by: *The size of the crowd is largely dependent on the weather.*

dependent clause /·ˌ··· ˈ·/ also **subordinate clause**– n *tech* (in grammar) a CLAUSE which cannot stand by itself, but can help to make a sentence when it is part of, or joined to, an INDEPENDENT CLAUSE: *"When I came" is a dependent clause in the two sentences "When I came, she had left" and "She wants to know when I came".*

de·pict /dɪˈpɪkt/ v [T (**as**)] *fml* to represent or show in or as if in a picture: *This painting depicts the birth of Venus.* | *The book depicts her as a rather unpleasant character.* –compare PICTURE[2] (2) —**piction** /dɪˈpɪkʃən/ n [C;U]

de·pil·a·to·ry /dɪˈpɪlətəriː‖-tɔːriː/ n, adj (a substance) that gets rid of unwanted hair, esp. on the human body

de·plete /dɪˈpliːt/ v [T] *fml* to lessen greatly in amount, contents, etc.: *The seamen's strike has seriously depleted the country's stocks of food.* —**pletion** /dɪˈpliːʃən/ n [U]

de·plor·a·ble /dɪˈplɔːrəbəl/ adj very bad; deserving severe disapproval; a fairly formal word rarely used by young people in spoken English: *The condition of this room is deplorable.* | *a deplorable waste of the taxpayers' money* —**bly** adv : *She behaved deplorably.*

de·plore /dɪˈplɔːʳ/ v [T *not in progressive forms*] *fml* to feel or express sorrow and usu. severe disapproval for: *One must deplore their violent behaviour.*

de·ploy /dɪˈplɔɪ/ v [T] to spread out or arrange for effective action, esp. for military action: *The general deployed his forces.* | *We will have to deploy all our resources to win this election.* – ~**ment** n [U]

de Pom·pa·dour /də ˈpɒmpədʊəʳ‖-ˈpɑːmpədɔːr/, **Madame** (1721–64) the MISTRESS of King Louis XV of France. She had a lot of influence over politics from 1745 until her death.

de·pop·u·late /ˌdiːˈpɒpjʊ̆leɪt‖-ˈpɑːp-/ v [T usu. pass.] to reduce greatly the population of (an area) —**lation** /ˌdiːpɒpjʊ̆ˈleɪʃən‖-pɑːp-/ n [U]

de·port[1] /dɪˈpɔːt‖-ɔːrt/ v [T] to send (someone who is not a citizen) out of the country, e.g. because they have broken the law or do not have a legal right to stay — ~**ation** /ˌdiːpɔːˈteɪʃən‖-ɔːr-/ n [C;U] : to issue a deportation order

deport[2] v [T] fml to behave (oneself); CONDUCT (3) (oneself)

de·por·tee /ˌdiːpɔːˈtiː‖-ɔːr-/ n a person who has been deported or who is to be deported

de·port·ment /dɪˈpɔːtmənt‖-ɔːr-/ n [U] fml 1 esp. BrE the way a person, esp. a young lady, stands and walks 2 esp. AmE the way a person, esp. a young lady, behaves in the company of others

de·pose /dɪˈpəʊz/ v [T] 1 to remove from a position of power, esp. from that of ruler: The head of state was deposed by the army. 2 law to state (information) solemnly in a court of law —see also DEPOSITION

de·pos·it[1] /dɪˈpɒzɪ̆t‖dɪˈpɑː-/ v [T] 1 [+ obj + adv/prep] to put or set down, usu. in a stated place: Where can I deposit this load of sand? | She deposited her shopping on the table/deposited herself in the nearest chair. 2 to let fall (fine substances) and leave lying: As the river slows down it deposits rich soil at its bends. | Every surface was covered in dust deposited by the desert winds. 3 to place in a bank or SAFE[2]: You can deposit your valuables in the hotel safe. —see also DEPOSITOR, SAFE-DEPOSIT BOX 4 to pay (money) that will be returned later if certain conditions are kept: Tenants are usually required to deposit £100 with the agent, in case of damage or default.

deposit[2] n 1 [C;U] a matter that has been deposited in rock by a natural process: There are rich deposits of gold in those hills. b matter that has been deposited by liquid: salt deposits | too much deposit in a bottle of wine 2 [C] an act of placing money in a bank or SAFE[2]: I'd like to make a deposit please. | a deposit box 3 [C usu. sing.] the first part of a payment for goods or service, as a sign that the payment will be completed: The hotel requires a deposit for all advance bookings. | We put down a deposit on a new car today. —compare DOWN PAYMENT 4 [C usu. sing.] money paid at the beginning of a business agreement, to be held in case the agreement is not kept: You may have to pay a deposit to open an electricity account, but if you pay your bills promptly they won't keep it. | When you return the bottle we'll return your deposit. | to put down a deposit of £100 on a new car

deposit ac·count /·ˈ·· ·ˌ·/ n esp. BrE a bank account which earns interest and from which money can usu. be taken out only if advance notice is given —compare CHECKING ACCOUNT, CURRENT ACCOUNT, SAVINGS ACCOUNT

dep·o·si·tion /ˌdepəˈzɪʃən, ˌdiː-/ n 1 [U] the act of deposing (DEPOSE) someone from a position of power 2 [C;U] law (the act of making) a solemn statement to a court of law

de·pos·i·tor /dɪˈpɒzɪ̆tər‖dɪˈpɑː-/ n a person who DEPOSITs money in a bank account

de·pos·i·to·ry /dɪˈpɒzɪ̆təri‖dɪˈpɑːzɪ̆tɔːri/ n a person or place that keeps things safely stored

dep·ot /ˈdepəʊ‖ˈdiːpəʊ/ n 1 a storehouse for goods 2 a place where military stores are kept, and where new soldiers are trained 3 a AmE a railway station or bus station, esp. a small one b a place where buses are kept and repaired; a bus garage

de·prave /dɪˈpreɪv/ v [T] to make evil in character: The judge described the rapist as a vicious and depraved man. | Do you believe that these films are likely to **deprave and corrupt** young people? —**pravation** /ˌdeprəˈveɪʃən/ n [U] —**pravity** /dɪˈprævɪ̆ti/ n [C;U]

dep·re·cate /ˈdeprɪ̆keɪt/ v [T not in progressive forms] fml to express disapproval of (an action, etc.); DEPLORE: We strongly deprecate the use of violence by the strikers. —**catingly** adv —**cation** /ˌdeprɪ̆ˈkeɪʃən/ n [U]

dep·re·ca·to·ry /ˈdeprɪ̆keɪtəri‖-kətɔːri/ adj 1 trying to prevent disapproval; APOLOGETIC: He admitted his mistake with a deprecatory smile. 2 expressing disapproval; deprecating

de·pre·ci·ate /dɪˈpriːʃieɪt/ v 1 [I] to fall in value: The car's value will depreciate by about £2000 in the first year. —opposite **appreciate** 2 [T] fml to represent as of little value; DENIGRATE: We must not depreciate the work she

has done. —**ation** /dɪˌpriːʃiˈeɪʃən/ n [U]

de·pre·ci·a·to·ry /dɪˈpriːʃiətəri‖-ʃətɔːri/ adj tending to DEPRECIATE (2): depreciatory remarks

dep·re·da·tion /ˌdeprɪ̆ˈdeɪʃən/ n [usu. pl.] fml an act of destroying or ruining: Not a single village escaped the depredations of war.

de·press /dɪˈpres/ v [T] 1 to cause to feel sad and without hope; discourage: The thought of having to take the exam again depressed me. 2 to make less active or strong; cause to sink: The threat of war has depressed business activity. 3 fml to press down: Depress this button to rewind the tape.

de·pressed /dɪˈprest/ adj 1 a low in spirits; sad and without hope b suffering from DEPRESSION: You look rather depressed. | She's very depressed about her exam results at the moment. | He's been depressed for several months now. 2 suffering from low levels of business activity, unemployment, etc.: depressed areas of the country 3 flattened, esp. with the central part lower than the edges

de·press·ing /dɪˈpresɪŋ/ adj causing sadness or discouragement; GLOOMY: depressing news | What a depressing film! — ~**ly** adv

de·pres·sion /dɪˈpreʃən/ n 1 [C;U] a a feeling of sadness and hopelessness b a mental disorder during which people suffer from great sadness, unnatural tiredness and unwillingness to do anything, difficulty in thinking, etc.: He suffers from acute depression. 2 [C] a long period of seriously reduced business activity and high unemployment —compare RECESSION; see also GREAT DEPRESSION 3 [C] a part of a surface which is lower than the other parts: The rain collected in several depressions on the ground. 4 [C] tech an area where the pressure of the air is low in the centre and higher towards the outside: A depression over the Atlantic usually brings bad weather in Britain.

Depression [the] see GREAT DEPRESSION

dep·ri·va·tion /ˌdeprɪ̆ˈveɪʃən/ n 1 [U] the act of depriving or state of being deprived 2 [C] a lack or loss: The refugees suffered terrible deprivations.

de·prive /dɪˈpraɪv/ v
deprive sbdy. **of** sthg. phr v [T] to take away from; prevent from using or having (something thought to be necessary or a right): This law will deprive us of our most basic rights. | The railways have been deprived of the money they need for modernization.

de·prived /dɪˈpraɪvd/ adj without the food, money, and comfortable living conditions considered necessary for a reasonable life in Western society: deprived children | a deprived childhood

de·pro·gram /ˌdiːˈprəʊɡræm/ v AmE [T] to bring (a person) back to an earlier way of thinking, esp. after they have been persuaded strongly and continuously into following and obeying a religious CULT

dept , Dept written abbrev. for: DEPARTMENT

depth /depθ/ n [C usu. sing.;U] 1 the state or degree of being deep: What is the depth of this lake? | We dived to a depth of 30 feet. 2 the quality of being deep in feeling, understanding, etc.: They underestimated the depth of public feeling on this issue. 3 **out of/beyond one's depth: a** in water that is deeper than one's height **b** beyond one's ability to understand: I'm out of my depth in this argument. 4 **in depth** /ˌ· ˈ·◄/going beneath the surface appearance of things; done with great thoroughness: We studied the situation in depth. | an in-depth study —see also DEPTHS

depth charge /ˈ· ˌ·/ also **depth bomb** n a bomb that explodes at a certain depth under water, used for attacking SUBMARINES

depths /depθs/ n [the+P] the deepest, most central, or worst part of something: in the depths of the ocean | in the depths of winter/of despair | According to the latest opinion polls, the government has **plumbed new depths** (=reached a new low level) of unpopularity.

dep·u·ta·tion /ˌdepjʊ̆ˈteɪʃən/ n [C+sing./pl. v] a group of people who are sent somewhere (e.g. to a meeting) as representatives of a larger group: A deputation from the railwaymen's union has/have gone to have talks with the Prime Minister.

de·pute /dɪˈpjuːt/ v [T + obj + to-v] fml to appoint (someone) to do something instead of oneself: *I've been deputed to take charge of the shop while she's away at the conference.*

de·pute sthg. **to** sbdy. *phr v* [T] *fml* to give (part of one's job) to (someone else); DELEGATE to: *She's deputed the running of the shop to me while she's away at the conference.*

dep·u·tize also **-tise** *BrE* /ˈdepjᵿtaɪz/ *v* [I (**for**)] to act as a deputy: *Who's going to deputize for you when you're on holiday?*

dep·u·ty /ˈdepjᵿti/ *n* **1** a person, esp. one who is next in rank to the person in command, who has the power to take charge when the leading person is away: *John will be my deputy while I am away.* | *the deputy-headmistress of the school* **2** a member of the lower house of parliament in certain countries, such as France **3** (in the US) a person who has been appointed to help a SHERIFF

de·rail /ˌdiːˈreɪl, dɪ-/ *v* [T] to cause (a train) to run off the railway line: *The 9.45 from Penzance was derailed by rocks placed on the line.* | (fig.) *right-wing elements determined to derail the peace process* — ~ **ment** *n* [C;U]

de·ranged /dɪˈreɪndʒd/ *adj* completely unbalanced in the mind; INSANE: *a deranged mind* | *He's totally deranged.* —**rangement** *n* [C;U]

der·by /ˈdɑːbi‖ˈdɜːrbi/ *n* **1** *AmE for* BOWLER² **2** *esp. AmE* a race which any competitor can enter: *a bicycle derby* **3** (in football and other sports) a match between two teams based in the same area: *the Manchester derby* (=between Manchester United and Manchester City)

Derby a city in Derbyshire. It is known for its industries, which include engineering and CHINA —see also CROWN DERBY

Derby, the a very important yearly horse race held at Epsom in England in May or June, on a day which is known as **Derby Day** —see also KENTUCKY DERBY

Der·by·shire /ˈdɑːbiʃər‖ˈdɜːr-/ a COUNTY in central England

de·reg·u·late /ˌdiːˈregjᵿleɪt/ *v* [T] to remove government rules and controls from (certain types of business activity) —**lation** /ˌdiːregjᵿˈleɪʃən/ *n* [U] : *the deregulation of air fares*

Der·ek /ˈderᵻk/, **Bo** /bəʊ/ (1957–) an American actress, known for her beauty, who played the part of a perfect woman in the film *10*

der·e·lict¹ /ˈderᵻlɪkt/ *adj* (esp. of a building) not used or lived in, and falling into decay or ruin: *a derelict old house*

derelict² *n fml* a person, esp. an ALCOHOLIC, who has no home or legal means of support; VAGRANT: *Many derelicts in the city live on the streets.*

der·e·lic·tion /ˌderᵻˈlɪkʃən/ *n* **1** [C;U] *fml* failure to do what one should do: *The policeman was accused of* **dereliction of duty**. **2** [U] the state of being derelict

de·ride /dɪˈraɪd/ *v* [T] *fml* to laugh at or make fun of (something considered worthless); RIDICULE —see also DERISION

de ri·gueur /də riːˈgɜːr/ *adj* [F] *Fr* proper and necessary according to fashion or custom: *That sort of hat is de rigueur at a formal wedding.*

de·ri·sion /dɪˈrɪʒən/ *n* [U] the act of deriding, esp. by unkind laughter: *They greeted his suggestion with shouts of derision.*

de·ri·sive /dɪˈraɪsɪv/ also **derisory** — *adj* showing derision: *derisive laughter* — ~ **ly** *adv*

de·ri·so·ry /dɪˈraɪsəri/ *adj* **1** so useless, ineffective, or small that it cannot be taken seriously; deserving derision: *They described the latest pay offer as "derisory".* **2** showing derision —**rily** *adv*

der·i·va·tion /ˌderᵻˈveɪʃən/ *n* **1** [C;U] the point or origin from which something comes: *What is the derivation of this word?* **2** [U] the process of deriving

de·riv·a·tive¹ /dɪˈrɪvətɪv/ *adj usu. derog* not original or new because of copying or showing the influence of others: *a very derivative style of painting/writing.* — ~ **ly** *adv*

derivative² *n* [(**of**)] something that is based on or formed from something else of the same type: *French is a derivative of Latin.* | *Heroin is a derivative of morphine.*

de·rive /dɪˈraɪv/ *v*

    derive from *phr v* [T] **1** (=**derive** sthg. **from** sbdy./sthg.) to obtain (esp. something non-material) from: *He derives a lot of pleasure from meeting new people.* | *This word is derived from Latin.* **2** (=**derive from** sthg.) to come from; have as an origin: *The word "deride" derives*

from Latin. | *His power derives mainly from his popularity with the army.* —see also DERIVATION —**derivable** *adj*

der·ma·ti·tis /ˌdɜːməˈtaɪtᵻs‖ˌdɜːr-/ *n* [U] a disease of the skin, marked by redness, swelling, and pain —see also CONTACT DERMATITIS

der·ma·tol·o·gy /ˌdɜːməˈtɒlədʒi‖ˌdɜːrməˈtɑː-/ *n* [U] the scientific study of the skin, esp. of its diseases and their treatment —**gist** *n*

de·rog·ate /ˈderəgeɪt/ *v*

    derogate from sthg. *phr v* [T] *fml* to lessen (a valuable quality, a right, etc.); DETRACT **from**

de·rog·a·to·ry /dɪˈrɒgətəri‖dɪˈrɑːgətɔːri/ *adj fml* showing or causing dislike or lack of respect. Derogatory words and phrases are marked *derog* in this dictionary: *He made derogatory remarks about the government's economic policy.* —**rily** /dɪˈrɒgətərᵻli‖dɪˌrɑːgəˈtɔːrᵻli/ *adv*

der·rick /ˈderᵻk/ *n* **1** a CRANE for lifting and moving heavy weights, for example into or out of a ship **2** a tower built over an oil well to raise and lower the DRILL

der·ring-do /ˌderɪŋ ˈduː/ *n* [U] *old use or humor* courageous action without thought of danger

Der·ry /ˈderi/ **1** a COUNTY in Northern Ireland, known for its farming **2** *infml for* LONDONDERRY

derv /dɜːv‖dɜːrv/ *n* [U] *BrE tdmk* an oil product used in DIESEL ENGINES

der·vish /ˈdɜːvɪʃ‖ˈdɜːr-/ *n* a member of any of a number of Muslim religious groups. Some dervishes are famous for dancing, spinning around, and shouting loudly as religious practices; they are known as **whirling dervishes**.

DES /ˌdiː iː ˈes/ [*the*] the Department of Education and Science; the British government department responsible for educational planning and decisions in England and Wales —compare SED

de·sal·i·nate /diːˈsælᵻneɪt/ *v* [T] to remove salt from (esp. sea water) so that it can be used at home and in factories —**nation** /diːˌsælᵻˈneɪʃən/ *n* [U]

de·scale /ˌdiːˈskeɪl/ *v* [T] to remove unwanted chalky matter (SCALE² (2)) from the inside of: *This kettle needs to be descaled.*

des·cant /ˈdeskænt/ *n* [C;U] **1** music sung or played at the same time as the main music and usu. higher **2** high music; SOPRANO or TREBLE³ (2)

Des·cartes /ˈdeɪkɑːt‖deɪˈkɑːrt/, **Re·né** /rəˈneɪ/ (1596–1650) a French MATHEMATICIAN and PHILOSOPHER, famous for his saying "cogito ergo sum" (=I think, therefore I am)

de·scend /dɪˈsend/ *v* [I;T] *rather fml* to come, fall, or sink from a higher to a lower level; go down: *The sun descended behind the hills.* | *The Queen descended the stairs.* | *I want to talk about all these points in descending order of importance.* opposite **ascend** —see also DESCENT

    descend on/upon sbdy./sthg. *phr v* [T] **1** (of a group of people) to attack: *Armed thieves descended on the helpless travellers.* **2** to arrive, esp. in large numbers, to visit or stay with, often unexpectedly: *The whole family descended on us at Christmas.*

    descend to sthg. *phr v* [T+*obj/v-ing*] to lower oneself to (a dishonourable or unpleasant level of behaviour): *I didn't expect him to descend to personal abuse/to abusing me personally.*

de·scen·dant /dɪˈsendənt/ *n* [(**of**)] a person (or animal) that has another as grandfather or grandmother, great-grandfather, etc.: *He is a descendant of Queen Victoria.* —compare ANCESTOR

de·scend·ed /dɪˈsendᵻd/ *adj* [F+**from**] having the stated person or animal as grandfather or grandmother, great-grandfather, etc. Some people are very proud of the people they are descended from: *She claims to be descended from George Washington.*

de·scent /dɪˈsent/ *n* **1 a** [C;U] the process of going down: *We watched anxiously (during) her descent from the tree.* | (fig.) *his descent into a life of crime* **b** [C] an easy; downward slope, path, etc.: *a steep descent* —opposite **ascent** **2** [U] family origins of the stated type: *She is of German descent.* **3** [S;U] a sudden and esp. unwelcome visit or attack: *the annual descent on the city of thousands of tourists*

de·scribe /dɪˈskraɪb/ *v* [T] **1** [(**as**)] to say what something is like; give a picture of in words: *The police asked me to*

describe the two men. [+*wh-*] *Try to describe exactly how it happened.* | *The seller described it as a vintage car, but I'd call it an old wreck.* **2** *fml or tech* to draw or move in the shape of: *to describe a circle within a square* | *The falling star described a long curve in the sky.* —see also DESCRIPTION

de·scrip·tion /dɪˈskrɪpʃən/ n **1** [C;U] (the act of giving) a statement or account that describes: *The police have issued a detailed description of the missing woman.* | *This book gives a good description of life on a farm.* **2** [C] a sort or kind: *The hall was packed with people of every description/all descriptions.* | *I think it's a bird of some description.* **3 beyond description** (used to add force to what one is saying): *The play was boring beyond description.*

de·scrip·tive /dɪˈskrɪptɪv/ adj **1** that describes: *descriptive writing* | *a descriptive passage in a novel* **2** [*no comp.*] *tech* describing how a language is used: *a descriptive grammar of English* —compare PRESCRIPTIVE (1) — ~**ly** adv — ~**ness** n [U]

de·scry /dɪˈskraɪ/ v [T *not in progressive forms*] *lit* to notice or see (esp. something distant)

Des·de·mo·na /ˌdezdɪˈməʊnə/ the wife of Othello in Shakespeare's play *Othello*, who was killed by her husband who thought she was having sexual relations with another man

des·e·crate /ˈdesɪkreɪt/ v [T] to use (something holy) for purposes which are not holy: *to desecrate a church by using it as a stable* —**cration** /ˌdesɪˈkreɪʃən/ n [S;U]

de·seg·re·gate /diːˈsegrɪgeɪt/ v [T] to end racial or sexual SEGREGATION in (e.g. a school). In the US desegregation of schools was a big political and legal problem, esp. in the 1950s and 1960s —see also BUS² (1) —**gation** /diːˌsegrɪˈgeɪʃən/ n [U]

de·se·lect /ˌdiːsɪˈlekt/ v [T] to refuse to choose (a person) for a job, place in a team, etc. that they have previously done or had

de·sen·si·tize also **-tise** *BrE* /diːˈsensɪtaɪz/ v [T] to make less sensitive to light, pain, etc.: *to desensitize photographic material* | *I think children are becoming desensitized to violence through watching too much on TV.* —**tization** /diːˌsensɪtaɪˈzeɪʃən/-tə-/ n [U]

des·ert¹ /ˈdezət/ n **1** a large sandy piece of land where there is very little rain and usu. not much plant life: *the Sahara Desert* | *a hot desert wind* **2** a place that is cheerless and without activity: *a cultural desert* —see also DESERTS

de·sert² /dɪˈzɜːt/ v **1** [T] to leave empty or leave completely: *The guard deserted his post.* | *the silent deserted streets of the city at night* **2** [T] to leave at a difficult time or in a cruel way, esp. with the intention of not returning; ABANDON: *The baby's mother deserted him soon after giving birth.* | *All my friends have deserted me!* | (fig.) *When he had to speak his confidence suddenly deserted him.* **3** [I (**from**)] to leave military service without permission

de·sert·er /dɪˈzɜːtəʳ/ n a person who leaves military service without permission: *Deserters were shot without mercy.*

de·ser·tion /dɪˈzɜːʃən/ n [C;U] (an example of) the act of leaving one's duty, one's family, or military service without permission, esp. with the intention of never returning: *After two years he divorced his wife on the grounds of her desertion.*

desert is·land /ˌ··· ˈ··/ n a small tropical island a long way from other land and with no one living there. Desert islands are thought of as being rather ROMANTIC (2) places, with sun, warm seas, and plenty of food and water available, perfect places to escape from the worries and responsibilities of ordinary life.

Desert Is·land Discs /ˌ··· ˌ·· ˈ·/ a programme on BBC Radio 4 in which famous people talk about their lives and choose the eight records they would like to take with them if they were stuck on a desert island. They also choose one book (not the Bible or Shakespeare, as these are already on the island) and one LUXURY object.

Desert Or·chid /ˌ··· ˈ···/ one of Britain's finest racehorses, who won many famous races in the 1980s

Desert Rats /ˌ··· ˈ·/ [*the*] a group of British soldiers who

fought in North Africa in the Second World War, and in the Gulf War in 1991 using TANKS (2).

de·serts /dɪˈzɜːts/-ˈzɜːrts/ n [P] what someone deserves, esp. if bad: *He eventually got his just deserts.*

Desert Shield see OPERATION DESERT SHIELD

Desert Storm see OPERATION DESERT STORM

de·serve /dɪˈzɜːv/-ˈzɜːrv/ v [T *not in progressive forms*] **1** to have earned by one's actions or character; be worthy of: *You've been working all morning — you deserve a rest.* [+*to-v*] *She deserved to win/to be punished.* **2 deserve well/ill of** *fml* to deserve to be treated well/badly by

de·serv·ed·ly /dɪˈzɜːvɪdli/-ˈzɜːr-/ adv rightly: *She's made a lot of money, and deservedly so.* —opposite **undeservedly**

de·serv·ing /dɪˈzɜːvɪŋ/-ˈzɜːr-/ adj worthy of support or help: *to give money to deserving causes such as children's charities* [F+**of**] *He is deserving of the highest praise for his conduct during the hijack.* — ~**ly** adv

dés·ha·bil·lé /ˌdeɪzæˈbiːeɪ/ *BrE* ‖ also **dishabille** *AmE*— n [U] the state of being only partly dressed. This word is usu. used of a woman, often with the suggestion that she is deliberately trying to excite a man: *She came to the door in (a state of) déshabillé.*

des·ic·cant /ˈdesɪkənt/ n *tech* a chemical substance that makes things dry

des·ic·cate /ˈdesɪkeɪt/ v [T] *fml* to dry, esp. as a way of preserving: *desiccated coconut*

de·sid·e·ra·tum /dɪˌzɪdəˈreɪtəm, -ˈrɑː-, dɪˌsɪ-/ n **-ta** /tə/ *fml* something desired as necessary

de·sign¹ /dɪˈzaɪn/ v **1** [I;T] to make a drawing or pattern of (something that will be made or built); develop and draw the plans for: *to design (dresses) for a famous shop* | *Who designed the Sydney Opera House?* **2** [T *often pass.*] to plan or develop for a certain purpose or use: *a book designed mainly for use in colleges* [+*obj*+*to-v*] *The building has been specially designed to provide easy access for people in wheelchairs.* —see also DESIGNER¹

design² n **1** [C] a drawing or pattern showing how something is to be made: *Have you seen the latest designs for the new library?* **2** [U] also **designing**— the art of making such drawings or patterns: *a course in dress design* **3** [U] the arrangement of the parts in any man-made product, such as a machine or a work of art, as this influences the product's practical usefulness, artistic quality, etc.: *The success of this car shows the importance of good design in helping to sell the product.* **4** [C] a decorative pattern, esp. one that is not repeated: *a carpet with a floral design in the centre* — see picture **5** [C] a plan in the mind; SCHEME **6 by design** as a result of purposeful planning; intentionally: *She arrived just as we were leaving, but whether this was by accident or by design I'm not sure.* —see also DESIGNEDLY, DESIGNS

des·ig·nate¹ /ˈdezɪgneɪt/ v [T] **1** to choose or name for a particular job or purpose: [+ *obj* + **as**/n] *The Town Hall has been designated (as) an emergency feeding centre in the event of an enemy attack.* [+*obj*+*to-v*] *She has been designated to take over the position of party chairman.* **2** *fml* to point out or call by a special name: *These crosses on the drawing designate all the possible entrances to the castle.*

des·ig·nate² /ˈdezɪgnət, -neɪt/ adj [after n] *fml* chosen for an office but not yet officially placed in it: *the minister designate*

designated hit·ter /ˌ····· ˈ··/ also **dh**— n (in the game of BASEBALL) a BATTER who replaces the PITCHER when it is his turn to hit. The rule allowing a designated hitter is used in the American LEAGUE but not in the National LEAGUE.

des·ig·na·tion /ˌdezɪgˈneɪʃən/ n **1** [U (**of, as**)] the act of designating **2** [C] *fml* a name or title: *Her official designation is Research Editor.*

de·sign·ed·ly /dɪˈzaɪnɪdli/ adv on purpose; intentionally

de·sign·er¹ /dɪˈzaɪnəʳ/ n a person who makes plans or patterns, esp. professionally: *a designer of aircraft engines* | *a dress designer*

designer² adj [A] **1** made by and usu. carrying the name of a well-known designer: *designer jeans/sheets* **2** *often humor or derog* intended to make the user appear extremely fashionable: *designer stubble/socialism* **3** changed by GENETIC ENGINEERING: *a designer virus*

designer drug /ˌ·ˈ·· ˌ·/ *n* a drug that is produced artificially that has effects similar to those of illegal drugs such as COCAINE or HEROIN, but is not illegal itself

de·sign·ing¹ /dɪˈzaɪnɪŋ/ *adj derog* intending to deceive; cleverly dishonest: *a designing woman who's only after your money*

designing² *n* [U] DESIGN² (2)

de·signs /dɪˈzaɪnz/ *n* [P (on, upon)] clever and dishonest plans, esp. to get possession of something: *He has de-signs on your money/your job.*

de·sir·a·ble /dɪˈzaɪərəbəl/ *adj* **1** worth having, doing, or desiring: *a desirable house* | *For this job it is desirable to know something/desirable that you know something about medicine.* —compare UNDESIRABLE **2** causing sex-ual desire: *a beautiful and desirable woman* —**bly** *adv* —**bility** /dɪˌzaɪərəˈbɪlɪti/ *n* [U]

de·sire¹ /dɪˈzaɪəʳ/ *v* [T *not in progressive forms*] *fml* **1** to wish, want, or hope for, very much: *We all desire happi-ness.* [+to-v/that] *The Queen desires to see you at once/that you (should) come at once.* [+obj+to-v] *She desires you to come at once.* | *The standard of cooking here leaves a lot to be desired.* (=is not very satisfactory) —compare WANT, WISH **2** to wish to have sexual relations with

desire² *n* **1** [C;U (for)] a strong hope or wish: *The two leaders spoke of their desire for improved relations.* [+to-v/that] *He expressed a desire to see the papers/that the papers should be made public.* | *We must take into account the desires of our members.* **2** [C;U (for)] a strong wish for sexual relations with **3** [C *usu. sing.*] something or someone that is desired: *What is your greatest desire/your heart's desire?*

▷ USAGE You can have a **desire** for anything: *a desire for success* | *a desire to attend the meeting.* **Appetite** is used for things of the body, especially food: *The baby has a good/healthy appetite.* (=likes eating) A **crav-ing** is a strong desire, especially for things which are thought to be bad: *a craving for cigarettes.* **Lust** is a very strong and usually derogatory word: *the lust for power/sex.*◁

de·sir·ous /dɪˈzaɪərəs/ *adj* [F+of] *fml* feeling a desire; hav-ing a strong wish:*desirous of wealth/fame*

de·sist /dɪˈzɪst, dɪˈsɪst/ *v* [I (from)] *fml* to stop doing; not do any more: *The judge told the man to desist from threatening his wife.*

desk /desk/ *n* **1** a piece of furniture rather like a table, often with drawers, at which one reads, writes, or does business **2** a place, e.g. in an airport or hotel, where in-formation is provided, questions are answered, etc.: *the airport information desk* | *Leave your key at the reception desk.* | *(AmE) a desk clerk in a hotel*

de·skill /ˌ·ˈ·/ *v* [T] **1** to remove or reduce the skill in (a job), usu. by changing to machinery **2** to prevent (a wor-ker) from using skill through changes in the patterns or processes of making something

desk·top pub·lish·ing /ˌdesktɒp ˈpʌblɪʃɪŋ‖-tɑːrp-/ also **DTP**— *n* [U] using a small computer in offices and similar places to DESIGN and write papers, advertisements, books, maga-zines, etc., until they are ready for printing, sometimes using only one person or very few people: *The availabil-ity of reasonably-priced computers and laser printers has made the use of desktop publishing packages a reality.*

desk·work /ˈdeskwɜːk‖-wɜːrk/ *n* [U] *often derog* office work; work done at a desk

des·o·late¹ /ˈdesələt/ *adj* **1** (of a place) sad and without peo-ple or comfort: *a desolate old house* **2** (of a person) very sad through loss of hope, friends, etc. —see ALONE (USAGE) —**ly** *adv* —**lation** /ˌdesəˈleɪʃən/ *n* [U]

des·o·late² /ˈdesəleɪt/ *v* [T *usu. pass.*] to make desolate: *She was desolated by the death of her husband.* | *desolated streets*

de So·to /də ˈsəʊtəʊ/, **Her·nan·do** /həˈnændəʊ ‖ hər-/ **Fer·nan·do** /fəˈnændəʊ, fər-/ (?1500–42) a Spanish EX-PLORER who discovered the Mississippi River

de·spair¹ /dɪˈspeəʳ/ *v* [I (of)] to lose all hope or confidence: *Don't despair: things will get better soon!* | *I despair of ever passing my driving test!* | *She received the news with a despairing sigh.* —~ **ingly** *adv*

despair² *n* [U] **1** complete loss of hope or confidence: *Defeat after defeat filled us with despair/drove us into the*

depths of despair. **2** [(of)] something that causes this feeling: *He is the despair of his teacher because he refuses to study.*

de·spatch /dɪˈspætʃ/ *n, v* DISPATCH

de·spatch·es /dɪˈspætʃɪz/ *n* DISPATCHES

des·pe·ra·do /ˌdespəˈrɑːdəʊ/ *n* **-does** *or* **-dos** a violent crimi-nal who fears no danger

des·per·ate /ˈdespərɪt/ *adj* **1** ready for any wild act and not caring about danger, esp. because of loss of hope; RECKLESS: *a desperate criminal* **2** [F (for)] suffering ex-treme need, anxiety, or loss of hope: *She's desperate for work/for money.* [+to-v] *They're desperate to escape.* **3** (of an action) full of risk or danger; done as a last attempt and with little hope of success: *a last desperate attempt to save the company* | *desperate measures* **4** (of a situa-tion) extremely difficult and dangerous; GRAVE: *The country is in a desperate state.* | *a desperate shortage of food* —~ **ly** *adv* : *He glanced around desperately.* | *I'm desperately sorry.*

Desperate Dan /ˌ··· ˈ·/ a very large COWBOY with an equally large APPETITE. He is a character in the British children's COMIC¹ (2) *The Dandy.*

Desperately Seek·ing Su·san /ˌdespərtli ˌsiːkɪŋ ˈsuːzən/ an American film in which the popular music singer Madonna acted the part of a young woman called Susan

des·per·a·tion /ˌdespəˈreɪʃən/ *n* [U] the state of being desperate: *He kicked at the door in desperation.*

des·pic·a·ble /dɪˈspɪkəbəl, ˈdespɪ-/ *adj* deserving to be despised; CONTEMPTIBLE: *despicable behaviour/cowards* —**bly** *adv*

de·spise /dɪˈspaɪz/ *v* [T *not in progressive forms*] to regard as worthless, bad, or completely without good qualities; feel extreme dislike and disrespect for

de·spite /dɪˈspaɪt/ *prep fml* in spite of; not prevented by: *He came to the meeting despite his illness.* (=though he was ill) | *Demand for these cars is high, despite their high price.*

de·spoil /dɪˈspɔɪl/ *v* [T (of)] *fml or lit* to steal from using force, esp. in time of war; PLUNDER: *The victorious army despoiled the city of all its treasures.*

de·spon·dent /dɪˈspɒndənt‖dɪˈspɑːn-/ *adj* [(about, at)] com-pletely without hope and courage; feeling that no im-provement is possible: *She's become very despondent about her prospects of getting another job.* —~ **ly** *adv* —**dency** *n* [U]

des·pot /ˈdespɒt, -ət‖ˈdespət, -ɑːt/ *n* a person who has all the power of government and uses it unjustly and cruelly; TYRANT: *She rules her family like a real despot.* —~ **ic** /dɪˈspɒtɪk, de ‖ˈspɑː-/ *adj* —**ically** /kli/ *adv*

des·pot·is·m /ˈdespɒtɪzəm/ *n* [U] rule by a despot

des·res /ˌdez ˈrez/ *n BrE infml* desirable RESIDENCE; a house that has desirable qualities; used mainly in house adver-tisements

des·sert /dɪˈzɜːt‖-ɜːrt/ *n* [C;U] (a) sweet food served after the main part of a meal

des·sert·spoon /dɪˈzɜːtspuːn‖-ɜːrt-/ *n esp. BrE* **1** a spoon between the sizes of a TEASPOON and TABLESPOON, used for eating dessert **2** also **des·sert·spoon·ful** /-fʊl/(*pl.* **spoonfuls, -spoonsful**)— the amount held by a dessert-spoon, equal to about two TEASPOONS —see pictures at PLACE SETTING and SPOON

dessert wine /·ˈ· ·/ *n* [C;U] a sweet wine served with des-sert or between meals

de·sta·bil·ize also **-ise** *BrE* /diːˈsteɪbəlaɪz/ *v* [T] to make less firm or steady, esp. politically: *a deliberate attempt to destabilize the economy of a rival country* —**ization** /diːˌsteɪbəlaɪˈzeɪʃən‖-bələ-/ *n* [U]

des·ti·na·tion /ˌdestɪˈneɪʃən/ *n* a place to which someone is going or to which something is sent, esp. at the end of a long journey: *The parcel was sent to the wrong desti-nation.* | *We eventually arrived at our destination.*

des·tined /ˈdestɪnd/ *adj* **1** [(for)] intended, esp. by fate, for some special purpose: *destined for an acting career* [F+to-v] *They were destined (by fate) never to see each other again.* | *Medicine is her destined profession.* **2** [F (for)] having as a destination: *a ship destined for America*

des·ti·ny /ˈdestɪni/ *n* **1** [C] fate; what must happen and can-not be changed or controlled: *It was the great man's des-tiny to lead his country to freedom.* **2** [U] (*often cap.*) the power that decides the course of events, thought of as a person or a force: *Destiny is sometimes cruel.*

des·ti·tute /ˈdestɪtjuːt‖-tuːt/ adj **1** without food, clothing, shelter, etc., or the money to buy them; extremely poor **2** [F+of] fml lacking in; completely without: *She was destitute of human feeling.* —**tution** /ˌdestɪˈtjuːʃən‖-ˈtuː-/ n [U]

de·stroy /dɪˈstrɔɪ/ v [T] **1** to damage (something) so severely that it cannot be repaired; put an end to the existence of; ruin: *The fire destroyed most of the building.* | *All hopes of a peaceful settlement were destroyed by his speech.* **2** euph to kill (an animal), esp. one that is sick or badly hurt —see also DESTRUCTION

de·stroy·er /dɪˈstrɔɪəʳ/ n **1** a person who destroys **2** a small fast warship

de·struc·tion /dɪˈstrʌkʃən/ n [U] **1** the act of destroying or state of being destroyed: *the destruction of the South American rain forests* | *The enemy bombs caused widespread destruction.* **2** fml something that destroys: *Drink was her destruction.*

de·struc·tive /dɪˈstrʌktɪv/ adj **1** causing destruction: *a destructive storm* | *Small children can be very destructive.* **2** tending to find fault and point out what is wrong without suggesting improvements: *destructive criticism* —compare CONSTRUCTIVE — ~ **ly** adv — ~ **ness** n [U]

des·ul·to·ry /ˈdesəltəri, ˈdez-‖-tɔːri/ adj fml not having a particular plan or purpose: *a desultory conversation* —**rily** /ˈdesəltərɪli, ˈdez-‖ˌdesəlˈtɔːrɪli, ˌdez-/ adv

de·tach /dɪˈtætʃ/ v [T (**from**)] to separate from a larger mass or group and usu. without violence or damage: *You can detach the handle by undoing this screw.* | *The general detached a small force to go and guard the palace.* —compare ATTACH — ~ **able** adj : *a detachable handle*

de·tached /dɪˈtætʃt/ adj **1** [no comp.] esp. BrE (of a house) not connected on any side with any other building. Many British people think that a detached house is the best type of house to have —compare SEMIDETACHED **2** not showing much personal feeling: *She has a very detached attitude to her divorce.* | *a detached observer*

de·tach·ment /dɪˈtætʃmənt/ n **1** [U] the act of detaching **2** [U] the state of being DETACHED (2): *to adopt an attitude of complete detachment* **3** [C+sing./pl. v] a group, esp. of soldiers, sent from the main group on special duty: *A detachment of troops was/were ordered to surround the airport.*

de·tail¹ /ˈdiːteɪl‖dɪˈteɪl/ n **1** [C] a single point or fact about something: *Everything in her story is correct down to the smallest detail.* | *The full details of the agreement have not yet been made public.* | *If you're interested in the job, I'll send you all the details.* **2** [U] such single parts considered together: *He has a good eye for detail and notices almost everything.* | *The colour in that picture is very good, but there's too much detail.* | *She described the accident* **in (great) detail.** (=giving all the details) | *Well, without* **going into detail** (=I won't tell you all the details) *we've managed to find a suitable house.* **3** [C+sing./pl. v] a small working party of soldiers or sailors — ~ **ed** adj : *a detailed account of his work*

detail² v [T] **1** to appoint (esp. soldiers) to do some special duty: [+obj+to-v] *He detailed three soldiers to look for water.* **2** to give a full list of: *Could you detail all your expenses on this form?*

de·tain /dɪˈteɪn/ v [T] **1** to prevent (a person) from leaving for a certain time: *The police have detained two men for questioning at the police station.* —see also DETENTION **2** to delay: *This matter isn't very important, and shouldn't detain us very long.*

de·tain·ee /ˌdiːteɪˈniː/ n a person detained officially, esp. for political reasons, often in a camp rather than a prison

de·tas·sel /diːˈtæsəl/ v [I;T] AmE to remove (the flowering part) from a male CORN plant in order to prevent it from breeding: *Those fields have to be detasseled this week.* | *a summer job detasseling corn*

de·tect /dɪˈtekt/ v [T] to find out; notice or discover: *Small quantities of poison were detected in the dead man's stomach.* | *I detected a note of annoyance in his voice.* — ~ **able** adj

de·tec·tion /dɪˈtekʃən/ n [U] the act or work of detecting: *His crime escaped detection* (=was not found out) *for many years.*

de·tec·tive /dɪˈtektɪv/ n **1** a policeman whose job is to find out information that will lead to criminals being caught. Detectives usu. wear ordinary clothes, not uniforms: *Several plain-clothes detectives were also sent to the scene of the crime.* —see also CID, STORE DETECTIVE **2** a person who tries to find out information about something, esp. a crime, for someone else, and who is usu. paid by that person. There are many famous detectives in FICTION, among them Sherlock Holmes, Hercule Poirot, and Perry Mason — see also PRIVATE DETECTIVE

detective

detective nov·el /·ˈ·· ˌ··/ n a DETECTIVE STORY in the form of a book

detective sto·ry /·ˈ·· ˌ··/ n a story in which there is usually a murder and a detective trying to find out who the murderer is and why it happened

de·tec·tor /dɪˈtektəʳ/ n any instrument for finding out the presence of something: *a metal detector* —see also LIE DETECTOR

dé·tente /ˈdeɪtɒnt, deɪˈtɒnt‖-ɑːnt/ n [C;U] (a state of) calmer political relations between countries which are unfriendly towards each other

de·ten·tion /dɪˈtenʃən/ n [C;U] **1** the act of detaining someone (DETAIN), esp. someone who is believed to be guilty of a crime, or the state of being detained: *the detention of terrorists without trial* | *They were released from detention without being charged.* **2** the state of being kept in school after school hours as a punishment, usu. for disobeying a school rule: *He was kept in detention for talking during class.* | *I've had three detentions this semester.*

detention cen·tre /·ˈ·· ˌ··/ BrE‖**detention home** AmE— n a place where young people who have committed crimes go for short periods for training in obedience and self-control if they are too young to go to prison

de·ter /dɪˈtɜːʳ/ v -**rr**- [T (**from**)] to prevent from acting, esp. by the threat of something unpleasant: *We need severe punishments to deter people from dealing in drugs.* —see also DETERRENT

de·ter·gent /dɪˈtɜːdʒənt‖-ɜːr-/ n [C;U] something, esp. chemical product without soap in it, used for cleaning clothing, dishes, etc. Many detergents are now considered bad for the environment.

de·te·ri·o·rate /dɪˈtɪəriəreɪt/ v [I] to become worse: *his deteriorating health* | *Relations between the superpowers have deteriorated sharply in recent weeks.* —**ration** /dɪˌtɪəriəˈreɪʃən/ n [U]

de·ter·mi·nant /dɪˈtɜːmɪnənt‖-ɜːr-/ n fml something that decides, fixes, settles, or limits: *Is cost or reliability the main determinant in choosing a new car?*

de·ter·mi·na·tion /dɪˌtɜːmɪˈneɪʃən‖-ɜːr-/ n [U] **1** the ability to make firm decisions and act in accordance with them; strong will to succeed: *a woman of great determination who always gets what she wants* **2** [+to-v] firm intention: *The police chief spoke of his determination to catch the killers.* **3** the finding of the exact position or nature of something: *the determination of the cause of his death* —see also SELF-DETERMINATION

de·ter·mine /dɪˈtɜːmɪn‖-ɜːr-/ v [T] fml **1** to (cause to) form a firm intention or decision: [+to-v/that] *We determined to go at once/that we would go at once.* [+obj+to-v] *Her encouragement determined me to carry on with the work.* [T+that; obj] *The court determined that the man was guilty of assault.* **2** to fix or find out exactly, e.g. by making calculations, collecting information, etc.: *to determine the position of a star/the cause of the accident* [+wh-] *We should first try to determine how much it is going to cost.* **3** to have a controlling influence on; have a direct and important effect on: *The amount of rainfall determines the size of the crop.* | *The size of the crop is determined by the amount of rainfall.*

de·ter·mined /dɪ'tɜːmɪnd‖-ɜːr-/ adj having a strong will; RESOLUTE: *a very determined woman who always gets what she wants* [F+to-v] *I am determined to go and nothing will stop me.*

de·ter·min·er /dɪ'tɜːmɪnə^r‖-ɜːr-/ n tech a word that limits the meaning of a noun and comes before adjectives that describe the same noun: *In the phrases "his new car" and "that green coat", the words "his" and "that" are determiners.*

de·ter·min·is·m /dɪ'tɜːmɪnɪzəm‖-ɜːr-/ n [U] the belief that acts and events are settled by earlier causes and nothing can be done to change them or prevent them —**·tic** /dɪˌtɜːmɪ'nɪstɪk◀-ɜːr-/ adj : *deterministic beliefs*

de·ter·rent /dɪ'terənt‖-'tɜːr-/ n, adj (something) that DETERS: *Do you think the threat of punishment has a deterrent effect?* | *Some people claim that we only have small wars because of the nuclear deterrent.* (=the threat of atomic war, which prevents countries from fighting) —**·rence** n [U]

de·test /dɪ'test/ v [T not in progressive forms] to hate very much: *I detest people who tell lies.* | *She detests having to talk to people at parties.* — ~ **able** adj : *a detestable child* — ~ **ably** adv — ~ **ation** /ˌdiːte'steɪʃən/ n [U]

de·throne /dɪ'θrəʊn/ v [T] to remove (a king or queen) from power — ~ **ment** n [U]

det·o·nate /'detəneɪt/ v [I;T] to (cause to) explode by means of a special apparatus: *They detonated the bomb and destroyed the bridge.*

det·o·na·tion /ˌdetə'neɪʃən/ n [C;U] (the noise of) an explosion

det·o·na·tor /'detəneɪtə^r/ n a piece of equipment used to detonate something explosive

de·tour /'diːtʊə^r/ n a way round something to avoid a traffic problem or to visit something in a different place: *They made a detour to avoid the town centre.*

de·tract /dɪ'trækt/ v
detract from sthg. *phr v* [T not in progressive forms] to take something of value away from; cause to be or seem less valuable: *All the decoration detracts from the beauty of the building's shape.* | *I don't want to detract from their achievement in winning the cup, but the fact is that their opponents were very weak.* —compare ADD to

de·trac·tion /dɪ'trækʃən/ n [U (**from**)] something which detracts: *To say that his work is strongly influenced by earlier film-makers is no detraction (from its value).*

de·trac·tor /dɪ'træktə^r/ n a person who says bad things about someone or something in order to make him/her/it seem less good or valuable: *Her detractors say she does not really understand ordinary people.*

de·train /ˌdiː'treɪn/ v [I] AmE fml to get off a railway train

det·ri·ment /'detrɪmənt/ n fml [U (**to**)] the condition of suffering harm or damage: *Do you think the government can carry out these policies without detriment to its popularity?* | *He smoked a lot,* **to the detriment of** *his health.* — ~ **al** /ˌdetrɪ'mentl◀/ adj [(**to**)] : *a decision that may be detrimental to the company's future* — ~ **ally** adv

de·tri·tus /dɪ'traɪtəs/ n [U] tech loose material produced by something breaking up or being rubbed away

De·troit /dɪ'trɔɪt/ a city in SE Michigan in the US, on the Detroit river. It is famous for its (now troubled) car industry, and its music industry —see colour map on pages 1374-5

▶CULTURAL NOTE There are so many car factories in Detroit that Americans often just say "Detroit" when they mean car companies. Because of economic problems, Detroit has become a fairly poor area.◀

de trop /də 'trəʊ/ adj [F] Fr pomp too much or too many; not needed: *I thought the last part of her speech was rather de trop.*

Det·tol /'detɒl, -tl‖-tl/ n [U] tdmk a liquid for killing GERMs, used esp. in the treatment of cuts, stings, spots etc.

deuce /djuːs‖duːs/ n **1** [U] (in tennis) 40–40; 40 points to each player. After deuce has been reached, one of the players must then get two points in a row to win the game —see also ADVANTAGE (3) **2** a playing card or throw of the DICE worth two points **3** [(*the*) S] old-fash euph sl (used for adding force to an expression) the devil: *What the deuce happened?* | *We had the deuce of a time finding their house.*

deuc·ed /'djuːsɪd, djuːst‖'duː-/ adj, adv [A] old-fash euph sl very bad(ly); unfortunate(ly); DAMNED: *You seem to be in a deuced hurry.* | *This bag is deuced heavy!* — ~ **ly** adv

de·us ex mach·in·a /ˌdeɪʊs eks 'mækɪnə ‖ -'mɑː-/ n Lat **1** (in early Greek and Roman theatre) a god brought onto the stage to decide the end of the play **2** any unlikely or artificial way of doing something which is used suddenly or at the last minute to end a problem: *The author produces a perfect deus ex machina in the form of the woman's long lost twin who cures all her problems in about two pages.*

Deutsch·mark /'dɔɪtʃmɑːk‖-mɑːrk/ also **Deutsch·e Mark** /ˌdɔɪtʃə 'mɑːk‖-'mɑːrk/, **mark—** n the standard unit of money in Germany. The Deutschmark is regarded as an extremely STABLE type of money.

deux-che·vaux /ˌdɜː ʃə'vəʊ ‖ ˌduː-/ also **2CV** n Fr a small French car which is becoming more popular in Britain, esp. with young MIDDLE-CLASS people

de Val·ois /də 'vælwɑː/, **Dame Ni·nette** /niː'net/ (1898–   ) an Irish BALLET dancer and manager who helped develop the style and content of British ballet and whose original ballet company is now the Royal Ballet

de·val·u·a·tion /diːˌvæljuˈeɪʃən/ n [C;U] a reduction in the value of something, esp. in the official exchange value of money: *A further devaluation of the pound may be necessary to improve our balance of payments.*

de·val·ue /diː'væljuː/ v **1** [I;T] to reduce the exchange value of (money): *We had to devalue (our currency) last year.* —compare REVALUE (2) **2** [T] to make (e.g. a person or action) seem less valuable or important: *Let's not devalue his work unjustly.*

dev·a·state /'devəsteɪt/ v [T] to destroy completely (a city, area of land, etc.) so that nothing useful or valuable remains: *The fire devastated the city.* | *The country's coffee crop was devastated by the floods.* | (fig.) *We were devastated by the awful news.* —**·station** /ˌdevə'steɪʃən/ n [U]

dev·a·stat·ing /'devəsteɪtɪŋ/ adj **1** destroying completely: *a devastating storm* | (fig.) *a devastating argument against our plan* **2** infml very good, attractive, etc.; IRRESISTIBLE: *You look devastating in that new dress.* | *his devastating charm* — ~ **ly** adv

de·vel·op /dɪ'veləp/ v **1** [I;T (**from**, **into**)] to come or bring gradually to a larger, more complete, or more advanced state; (cause to) grow or increase: *In less than ten years, it develops from a seed into a full-grown tree.* | *They do exercises to develop their muscles.* | *From small beginnings it has developed into a big multinational company.* **2** [T] to study, think out, or talk about in detail; ELABORATE: *I'd like to develop this idea a little more fully before I go on to my next point.* **3** [T] to bring out the full possibilities of (esp. land or natural substances): *to develop the natural resources of a country* (=by searching for minerals, etc.) | *The council are planning to develop the area to the west of the town centre.* (=by building new houses, offices, roads, etc. there) —see also DEVELOPER **4** [I] fml to begin to be seen or become active: *Trouble is developing in the cities.* **5** [T] fml to come to have gradually; ACQUIRE: *She has developed an interest in international affairs.* | *The baby seems to have developed a cold.* **6** [I;T] (in photography) to (cause to) appear on a film or photographic paper: *Our holiday photos haven't been developed yet.* | *These photographs haven't developed very well.*

de·vel·op·er /dɪ'veləpə^r/ n **1** [C] a person who hopes to make a profit from building on land, improving buildings, etc. **2** [C;U] a chemical substance used for developing photographs

developing coun·try /·ˌ··· '··/ also **developing nation—** n euph a poor country that is trying to build up its industry and improve the living conditions of its people

de·vel·op·ment /dɪ'veləpmənt/ n **1** [U (**from**, **into**)] the act of developing or the process of being developed: *the development of a seed into a plant* | *This was an important stage in the country's development.* **2** [C (**from**, **of**)] a result of developing: *This new rose is a development from a very old kind of rose.* **3** [C] a new event or piece of news: *Have you heard about the latest development in the murder trial?* | *The use of computers in business is a fairly recent development.* **4** [C] a developed piece of land, esp.

one that has houses built on it: *to live in a new* **housing development** — ~ **al** /dɪˌveləpˈmentl◂/ *adv*

development ar·e·a /·ˈ··· ˌ···/ *n BrE* an area of high unemployment, to which the government encourages new industries to come

de·vi·ant /ˈdiːviənt/ also **de·vi·ate** /-ɬt/ *AmE*— *adj* (of a person's behaviour) different from what is socially acceptable in Britain, the US, and many other countries: *sexually deviant behaviour* | *Deviant children need help.* —**ance** *n* [U] —**deviant** *n*

de·vi·ate /ˈdiːvieɪt/ *v* [I (*from*)] to be different or move away from a usual or accepted standard of behaviour: *She never deviates from her regular habits.* | *On this occasion the plane deviated from its usual flight path.*

de·vi·a·tion /ˌdiːviˈeɪʃən/ *n* **1** [C;U (*from*)] (a) noticeable difference from what is expected, esp. from accepted standards of behaviour: *sexual deviation* | *a slight deviation from the original plan* **2** [C] *tech* a measurable difference from a standard, esp. **a** the difference between the MAGNETIC NORTH (=to which the COMPASS needle points) and true north **b** (in STATISTICS) the difference between a measure and the average of all the measures

de·vi·a·tion·ist /ˌdiːviˈeɪʃənɬst/ *n derog* a person who disagrees about some points of a system of political beliefs —**ism** *n* [U]

de·vice /dɪˈvaɪs/ *n* **1** a piece of equipment intended for a particular purpose: *a device for varying the speed of a camera's shutter* | *The missile has a heat-seeking device which enables it to find its target.* —see MACHINE (USAGE) **2** a plan, esp. for a rather dishonest purpose: *a device for avoiding income tax* **3** a special phrase intended to produce a particular effect in a work of literature: *a rhetorical device* **4** *euph* a bomb or other explosive weapon: *an incendiary device* **5** *tech* a drawing or picture used by a noble family as their special sign: *the device on his shield* **6 leave someone to their own devices** to leave someone alone, without help

dev·il¹ /ˈdevəl/ *n* **1** [*the*] (*usu. cap.*) the most powerful evil spirit in Christianity; Satan. The Devil is usually shown in pictures as a man-like creature, usually red in colour, with two small horns coming out of his head and a small, pointed beard. He usually has a FORKED tail and CLOVEN HOOFS. In his hand he holds a long fork with three points. The Devil is thought of as living in Hell and ruling over the people there. —see also HELL **2** [C] an evil spirit: *spending eternity tormented by devils* **3** [C] an evil person: *My son can be a little devil at times!* **4** [C] *infml humor* a high-spirited person who is ready for adventure: *Go on,* **be a devil** *and have another cream cake!* **5** [C] *infml* (in expressions of strong feeling) a person: *You lucky devil!* | *The poor devils have been stuck at the airport for three days.* **6** [(*the*) *sl* (used to give force to various expressions, esp. of displeasure): *We had a devil of a job trying to persuade her.* | *What the devil happened?* **7 between the devil and the deep (blue) sea** *infml* facing two choices, both of which are unpleasant **8 Devil take the hindmost** You must make sure of your own success and not worry about other people **9 give the devil his due** to be fair even to a bad person **10 go to the devil a** to be ruined **b** to go away at once: *"I want $100 from you today."* *"Go to the devil!"* **11 like the devil** *infml* with great speed, force, etc.: *We ran like the devil.* **12 The devil finds work for idle hands to do** If people are not kept busy, they may do something that they should not be doing **13 the 'devil to pay** *sl* a great deal of trouble: *There'll be the devil to pay if we're caught inside the building.* **14 the devil you know** also **better the devil you know**— an expression used to give one's opinion that it is better to stay with someone who is not very dependable than to find someone else, who you may later find is

devil

exactly the same or worse: *I'm not happy about dealing with his company, but it's a case of the devil you know.*.. **15 The 'devil you will/won't, he can/can't,** etc. *old-fash sl* (used as a rude reply showing strong disagreement): *"John says he'll leave early today."* *"The devil he will!"* —see also **play the devil with** (PLAY² (22)), **talk of the devil** (TALK¹ (12))

devil² *v* **-ll-** *BrE* ‖ **-l-** *AmE* [T] **1** *BrE* to cook in a very hot-tasting thick liquid: *devilled chicken/eggs* **2** *AmE* to add a hot SPICE to a food which has been cut up very fine

dev·il·ish /ˈdevəlɪʃ/ *adj* very bad or very difficult: *devilish schemes* | *a devilish problem to solve* — ~ **ness** *n* [U]

dev·il·ish·ly /ˈdevəlɪʃli/ also **devilish**— *adv infml* (showing displeasure) very; a word used esp. by upper-class people: *It was devilish(ly) hard work climbing the mountain.*

devil-may-care /ˌ··· ˈ·◂/ *adj* cheerful, careless, and wild in behaviour; RECKLESS

dev·il·ment /ˈdevəlmənt/ also **dev·il·ry** /-ri/ ‖ also **deviltry** *AmE*— *n* [U] (a piece of) wild or bad behaviour that usu. causes trouble: *That child is always busy with some devilment or other.*

devil's ad·vo·cate /ˌ··· ˈ···/ *n* a person who continually questions a plan, idea, etc., even though they may not disagree with it, in order to test how good it is: *He wouldn't join in the argument, but just played devil's advocate.*

devil's-food cake /ˈ··· ˌ·/ *n* [C;U] *AmE* a kind of rich chocolate cake

Devil's Is·land /ˌ·· ˈ··/ an island off the coast of French Guiana which became well known for its use as a prison for criminals who had been given sentences of hard labour

dev·il·try /ˈdevəltri/ *n AmE for* DEVILMENT

de·vi·ous /ˈdiːviəs/ *adj* **1** not going in the straightest way: *a devious route* **2** *derog* not direct and not completely honest: *He's very devious.* | *She used devious means to gain power.* — ~ **ly** *adv* — ~ **ness** *n* [U]

de·vise /dɪˈvaɪz/ *v* [T] **1** to plan or invent, esp. cleverly: *They devised a plan for getting the jewels out of the country.* **2 devise and bequeath** *law* to BEQUEATH

de·vi·tal·ize also **-ise** *BrE* /ˌdiːˈvaɪtl-aɪz/ *v* [T] to take the strength or power from —compare REVITALIZE —**ization** /diːˌvaɪtl-aɪˈzeɪʃən‖-əˈzeɪ-/ *n* [U]

de·void /dɪˈvɔɪd/ *adj* [F+*of*] *fml* empty (of); lacking (in): *This house is totally devoid of furniture.* | *He is devoid of human feeling!*

de·vo·lu·tion /ˌdiːvəˈluːʃən/ *n* [U] the giving of governmental or personal power to a person or group at a lower or more local level. Some people in Scotland and Wales would like devolution from the British government: *the devolution lobby* —see also HOME RULE — ~ **ist** *n, adj*

de·volve /dɪˈvɒlv‖dɪˈvɑːlv/ *v*

devolve on/upon sbdy. *phr v* [T *no pass.*] (of power, work, etc.) to be passed to (a person or group at a lower level): *While the President is ill, most of his work will devolve on his deputy.*

devolve to sbdy. *phr v* [T *no pass.*] *law* (of land, goods, etc.) to become the property of (someone) on the death of the owner: *The house will devolve to his daughter.*

Dev·on /ˈdevən/ a COUNTY in SW England noted for its natural beauty. Many British people think of cream, CIDER, and holidays in connection with Devon

de·vote /dɪˈvəʊt/ *v*

devote sthg. **to** sbdy./sthg. *phr v* [T] to set apart for; give completely to: *He has devoted his life to helping blind people.* | *I don't think we should devote any more time to this question.* | *Several pages of the paper were devoted to an account of the election.*

de·vot·ed /dɪˈvəʊtɬd/ *adj* [(*to*)] showing great fondness or loyalty; caring a great deal: *a devoted father/friend* | *He is very devoted to his wife.* | *devoted to music/football* | *Most of our meetings were devoted to discussing the housing problem.* — ~ **ly** *adv*

dev·o·tee /ˌdevəˈtiː/ *n* **1** [(*of*)] a person who has great admiration for, or interest in, someone or something: *a devotee of Bach* (=Bach's music)/*football* **2** a very religious person: *The temple was full of devotees praying.*

de·vo·tion /dɪˈvəʊʃən/ *n* **1** [U (*to*)] great fondness or loyalty **2** the act of devoting or the condition of being devoted to something **3** attention to religion; devoutness (DEVOUT) —see also DEVOTIONS

de·vo·tion·al /dɪˈvəʊʃənəl/ adj about or used in religious devotions: devotional literature

de·vo·tions /dɪˈvəʊʃənz/ n [P] religious acts, esp. prayers

de·vour /dɪˈvaʊəʳ/ v [T] **1** to eat hungrily and in large quantities, so that nothing remains: The lion devoured the deer. | (fig.) She devoured the new book. **2** [usu. pass.] (of a feeling) to possess (a person); completely take up the attention of: He was devoured by hatred/jealousy.

de·vout /dɪˈvaʊt/ adj **1** (of people) seriously concerned with religion; PIOUS: a devout Hindu/Catholic **2** [A] felt very deeply; sincere: It is my devout hope that he will never come back. — ~ly adv — ~ness n [U]

dew /djuː‖duː/ n [U] the small drops of water which form on cold surfaces during the night

dew·drop /ˈdjuːdrɒp‖ˈduːdrɑːp/ n a drop of dew, or something that looks like one

Dew·ey dec·i·mal sys·tem /ˌdjuːi ˈdesɪməl ˌsɪstɪm‖ˌduːi-/ also **Dewey decimal clas·si·fi·ca·tion** /ˌ‥‥ ‥‥‥ ˌ‥‥ˌ‥/— [the] a way of putting library books in order by giving decimal numbers to books of different types. It was thought of by **Melvil Dewey** (1851–1931), an American LIBRARIAN.

dew·lap /ˈdjuːlæp‖ˈduː-/ n a hanging fold of loose skin under the throat of a cow, dog, etc.

dew·pond /ˈdjuːpɒnd‖ˈduːpɑːnd/ esp. BrE a small hollow, usu. man-made, in which dew collects

dew·y /ˈdjuːi‖ˈduːi/ adj wet with, or as if with, dew —**ily** adv —**iness** n [U]

dewy-eyed /ˌ‥ ˈ‥◂/ adj **1** having eyes that are slightly wet with tears **2** too willing to believe and trust because of inexperience

dex·ter·i·ty /dekˈsterɪti/ n [U] apprec quick cleverness and skill, esp. in the use of the hands: the dexterity with which he plays the piano

dex·ter·ous /ˈdekstərəs/ also **dex·trous** /ˈdekstrəs/— adj apprec having dexterity; ADROIT: She untied the knots with dexterous fingers. — ~ly adv

dex·trose /ˈdekstrəʊz, -strəʊs/ n [U] a form of sugar (GLUCOSE) found in many sweet fruits

DFW /ˌdiː ef ˈdʌbəljuː/ Dallas-Fort Worth International Airport; a very large American airport that serves the area around Dallas and Fort Worth, Texas: a short stopover at DFW

dh /ˌdiː ˈeɪtʃ/ n a DESIGNATED HITTER

Dhak·a /ˈdækə/ the capital of Bangladesh, an industrial city

dho·ti /ˈdəʊti/ n a garment worn on the lower part of the body by some Hindu men, consisting of a cloth that goes round the waist and between the legs

dhow /daʊ/ n an Arab ship with one large sail, used for trade round the coasts

DHSS /ˌdiː eɪtʃ es ˈes/ [the] the Department of Health and Social Security; the former name of the Department of Social Security —see DSS

Di /daɪ/, **Princess** infml for DIANA¹

DI /ˌdiː ˈaɪ/ n Detective Inspector; a middle rank in the British police force's PLAIN-CLOTHES division

di·a·be·tes /ˌdaɪəˈbiːtiːz, -tɪs/ n [U] a disease in which there is too much sugar in the blood. Some people with diabetes have to INJECT a substance called INSULIN every day. Others may be able to control it by eating the correct foods. Without insulin, the sufferer may go into a COMA and die.

di·a·bet·ic /ˌdaɪəˈbetɪk◂/ adj, n (typical of or suitable for) a person suffering from diabetes: She's diabetic/She's a diabetic. | diabetic jam (=made for diabetics)

di·a·bol·i·cal /ˌdaɪəˈbɒlɪkəl ‖ -ˈbɑː-/ also **diabolic** rare— adj **1** very cruel and evil: What a diabolical plan! **2** infml, esp. BrE extremely unpleasant or of very low quality: His French/Her cooking is diabolical. | I've been waiting for this train for 45 minutes. It's really diabolical! — ~ly /kli/ adv

di·a·crit·ic /ˌdaɪəˈkrɪtɪk/ n a mark placed over, under, or through, a letter, to show a sound value different from that of the same letter without the mark, frequently used in some languages, e.g. in Arabic — ~al adj: diacritical marks

di·a·dem /ˈdaɪədem/ n lit a crown of jewels, flowers, etc.: her royal diadem

di·ae·re·sis , di·e- /daɪˈɪərɪsɪs, -ˈe-‖-ˈe-/ n -ses /siːz/ a sign (ü) placed over the second of two vowels to show that it is pronounced separately from the first —compare UMLAUT

Di·ag·hi·lev /diˈægɪlef/, **Ser·gei Pav·lo·vich** /sɜːˈgeɪ ˈpævləvɪtʃ ‖ sɜːr-/ (1872–1929) a Russian who arranged for Russian Art and Music to be seen both at home and abroad and who had his own dance company, the famous Ballet Russe

di·ag·nose /ˈdaɪəgnəʊz‖-nəʊs/ v [T (as)] to discover the nature of (a disease or fault) by making a careful examination: The doctor diagnosed my illness (as a rare bone disease). | to diagnose the fault in an engine

di·ag·no·sis /ˌdaɪəgˈnəʊsɪs/ n -ses /siːz/ [C;U (of)] (a judgment which is the result of) the act of diagnosing: Diagnosis is one of the most important parts of the doctor's work. | The two doctors made/gave different diagnoses of my disease. | What was the doctor's diagnosis? —compare PROGNOSIS (1)

di·ag·nos·tic /ˌdaɪəgˈnɒstɪk◂‖-ˈnɑː-/ adj of or for diagnosing: a diagnostic test

di·ag·o·nal /daɪˈægənəl/ adj **1** (of a straight line) joining two opposite corners of a square or other four-sided flat figure: Draw a diagonal line to divide the square into two triangles. **2** (of a line) following a sloping direction: a cloth with a diagonal pattern —**diagonal** n : The two diagonals of a square cross in the centre. — ~ly adv : The path goes diagonally across the field.

diagrams

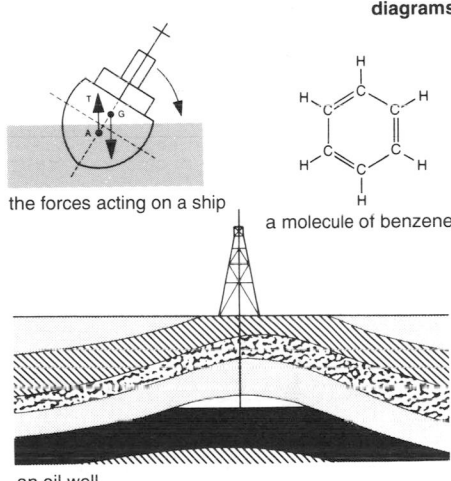

the forces acting on a ship

a molecule of benzene

an oil well

see also pictures at **chart** and **plan**

di·a·gram /ˈdaɪəgræm/ n a plan or figure drawn to explain a machine, idea, etc.; drawing which shows how something works rather than what it actually looks like: a diagram of a railway system | The book uses simple diagrams to explain the rules of chess. — ~**matic** /ˌdaɪəgrəˈmætɪk◂/ adj : a diagrammatic representation of a molecule — ~**matically** /kli/ adv

dial¹ /daɪəl/ n **1** the face of an instrument, such as a clock, showing measurements by means of a pointer and figures —see also SUNDIAL **2** a wheel on a telephone with numbered holes for the fingers, which is moved round when one makes a telephone call. This type of telephone is now rarely found in Britain and the US, as now PUSH-BUTTON telephones are mostly used.

dial² v -ll- BrE ‖-l- AmE [I;T] to make a telephone call (to) by using a dial or similar apparatus, e.g. the set of PUSH BUTTONS on a modern telephone: How do I dial Paris? | Put in the money before dialling. —see TELEPHONE (USAGE)

di·a·lect /ˈdaɪəlekt/ n [C;U] a variety of a language, spoken in one part of a country, which is different in some words or grammar from other forms of the same language: *Kurdish has three major dialects.* | *a poem written in a Scottish dialect* —compare ACCENT¹ (1) – ~**al** /ˌdaɪə'lektɪk◂/ *adj* – ~**ally** *adv*

di·a·lec·tic /ˌdaɪə'lektɪk/ also **dialectics**– *n* [U] *tech* the art or method of arguing and examining ideas so as to reach the truth, according to certain rules of question and answer that were developed by Socrates, Plato, and Hegel – ~**al** *adj* –**tician** /ˌdaɪəlek'tɪʃ*ə*n/ *n*

dialling code /'··· ·/ *BrE* ‖ **area code** *AmE*– *n* a telephone CODE¹ (3)

dialling tone /'··· ·/ *BrE* ‖**dial tone** /'·· ·/*AmE*– *n* the sound made by a telephone receiver to show that one may now dial the number that one wants

di·a·logue *BrE*‖**-log** *AmE* /'daɪəlɒg‖-lɔːg, -lɑːg/ *n* [C;U] **1** (a) written conversation in a book or play: *a short dialogue between Hamlet and the grave-digger* | *He's not very good at writing dialogue.* **2** (an) exchange of ideas and opinions, esp. between two countries, groups, etc., whose positions are opposed: *At last there can be (a) reasonable dialogue between our two governments.* —compare MONOLOGUE (2)

di·al·y·sis /daɪ'æljsjs/ *n* [U] *tech* a process by which solid substances can be separated from liquid, used esp. for making pure the blood of people whose KIDNEYs do not work properly

di·am·e·ter /daɪ'æmjtər/ *n* **1** (the length of) a straight line going from one side of a circle to the other side, passing through the centre of the circle: *The diameter of the circle is six centimetres.* | *The circle is six centimetres in diameter.* —compare RADIUS **2** *tech* a measurement of how many times bigger an object looks, when seen through a microscope or MAGNIFYING GLASS: *This microscope magnifies 20 diameters.*

di·a·met·ri·cally /ˌdaɪə'metrɪkli/ *adv* completely and directly (opposed or opposite): *My ideas are diametrically opposed to* (=completely different from) *hers.*

di·a·mond /'daɪəmənd/ *n* **1** [C;U] a very hard valuable precious stone, usually colourless, which is used in jewellery and for cutting things: *and industrial diamond* | *a diamond mine*

▶CULTURAL NOTE In Britain and the US, a diamond ring is often given by a man to a woman to show that they are ENGAGED. In connection with this custom, people often mention the sayings **diamonds are forever**, which is best known from the title of a James Bond book by Ian Fleming, and **diamonds are a girl's best friend**, which is a song title from the MUSICAL show of Anita Loos's book *Gentlemen Prefer Blondes.* —see also CARBON, ROUGH DIAMOND◀

2 [C] a figure with four straight sides of equal length that stands on one of its points **3** [C] **a** this figure printed in red on a playing card **b** a card belonging to the SUIT (=set) of cards that have one or more of these figures printed on it: *the four|queen of diamonds* | *I've only got four diamonds in my hand.* —see CARDS (USAGE) and see picture at CARDS **4** [C] (in BASEBALL) **a** the area of the field inside the four BASES² (6) **b** the whole playing field —see picture at BASEBALL

Diamond, Neil /niːl/ (1941–   ) an American popular music singer and writer of songs

diamond in the rough /ˌ···· ·'·/ *n AmE for* ROUGH DIAMOND

diamond ju·bi·lee /ˌ··· '···/ *n* the date that is exactly 60 years after the date of some important personal event, esp. of becoming a king or queen —compare GOLDEN JUBILEE, SILVER JUBILEE

diamond wed·ding /ˌ··· '··/ also **diamond wedding an·ni·ver·sa·ry** /ˌ··· '·· ··,···/ ‖ also **diamond anniversary** /ˌ··· ·'···/ *AmE*– *n* the date that is exactly 60 years after the date of a wedding —compare GOLDEN WEDDING, SILVER WEDDING

Di·an·a¹ /daɪ'ænə/, (1961–   ) the wife of Prince Charles and the mother of Prince William and Prince Henry. Charles and Diana separated in 1992. Diana is well-known for being very attractive, very WELL-GROOMED, and very FEMININE. She is usu. called **the Princess of Wales** or **Princess Diana** in news broadcasts, etc., or sometimes **Diana**, esp. if Prince Charles has just been mentioned but her official title is **Diana, Princess of Wales**. **Princess Di** and **Di** are only used by people talking informally about her or by TABLOID newspapers —see also Prince CHARLES

Diana² in Roman MYTHOLOGY, the goddess of the hunt and the moon. She was the sister of Apollo. (Her Greek name was Artemis.)

di·a·per /'daɪəpər‖'daɪpər/ *n* **1** [C] *AmE for* NAPPY **2** [U] (fine cotton or LINEN cloth with) a pattern of straight lines which cross each other so as to form small DIAMOND (2) shapes

di·aph·a·nous /daɪ'æfənəs/ *adj* (esp. of cloth) so fine and thin that it can be seen through

di·a·phragm /'daɪəfræm/ *n* **1 a** the muscle that separates the lungs from the stomach **b** the front part of the chest above the waist **2** any thin plate or piece of stretched material which makes or is moved by sound: *The diaphragm of a telephone is moved by the sound of the voice.* **3** a CAP¹ (6) **4** the group of small plates lying one above the other which control the amount of light entering a camera

di·a·rist /'daɪərjst/ *n* the writer of a DIARY (1): *Samuel Pepys was a famous English diarist of the 17th century.*

di·ar·rhoe·a, **-rhe·a** /ˌdaɪə'rɪə/ *n* [U] an illness in which the bowels are emptied too often and in too liquid a form. People from the US and the West often suffer from diarrhoea when they go to other countries, because of the change in their food, water, etc., and they sometimes joke about this, saying they had **the runs**, **the trots**, **Delhi belly** (esp. in India), **Montezuma's revenge** (esp. in S America), etc.

di·a·ry /'daɪəri/ *n* **1** (a book containing) a daily record of the events in a person's life. A diary is considered to be very personal, and reading someone else's diary without their permission is strongly disapproved of: *a lockable diary* | *Did you* **keep a diary** (=write a diary) *while you were travelling in Europe?* | *Her diary entry for 12th March reads simply "Saw him again."* —see also DIARIST; see JOURNAL (USAGE) **2** *BrE*‖**calendar** *AmE*– a book with marked separate spaces for each day of the year, in which one may write down things to be done in the future: *"Can you come on Wednesday?" "I'll just look in my diary to see if I'm free."* | *He made a note of the date in his diary.*

Diary of a No·bod·y /ˌ··· · · '···/, **The** a book written in 1892 by two brothers, George and Weedon Grossmith, which covers 15 months of the life of Charles Pooter in the early 1890s and remains popular today

Di·as·po·ra /daɪ'æspərə/ also **Dispersion**– [*the*] (the Jews living in) the various countries outside ancient Palestine or modern Israel in which Jews are scattered: *the people|the countries of the Diaspora*

di·a·ton·ic scale /ˌdaɪətɒnɪk 'skeɪl‖-tɑː-/ [*the*] a set of eight musical notes using a fixed pattern of spaces (INTERVALs) between the notes

di·a·tribe /'daɪətraɪb/ *n* [(against)] *fml* a long violent attack in speech or writing

dib·ble¹ /'dɪbəl/ also **dib·ber** /'dɪbər/– *n* a small pointed hand tool which is used to make holes in the earth for small plants

dibble² *v* [T] **1** to plant (seeds or plants) with a dibble **2** to make holes in (the earth) with a dibble

dibs /dɪbz/ *n AmE infml* **have dibs on something** to claim something as yours: *I've got dibs on playing second base.*

dice¹ /daɪs/ *n* **dice 1** [C] a small six-sided block of wood, plastic, etc., with a different number of spots from 1 to 6 on the various sides, used in games of chance: *to throw|cast the dice* | *a pair of dice* | *A dice|One of the dice has rolled under the table.* **2** [U] any game of chance which is played with these: *to play dice* **3 no dice** *infml*, *esp. AmE* **a** no use: *It was no dice.* **b** (used to show refusal): *"Will you just ask her for us?" – "No dice."*

dice

▷ USAGE The old singular form **die** is now rare, esp. in British English except in the saying **The die is cast** (=the decision or action has been taken and cannot now be changed).◁

dice² *v* **1** [T] to cut (food) into small square pieces: *The meat should be finely diced.* | *diced carrots* **2** [I (for)] to play dice with someone, for money, possessions, etc.:

They spent their time drinking and dicing. **3 dice with
death** to take a great risk
dice sthg. ↔ **away** *phr v* [T] to lose (money or possessions) by playing dice: *He diced away all his money.*
dic·ey /ˈdaɪsi/ *adj infml, esp. BrE* risky and uncertain
di·chot·o·my /daɪˈkɒtəmi‖-ˈkɑː-/ *n* [(**between**)] *fml* a division into two esp. opposite parts or groups: *the growing
dichotomy between the opponents and supporters of
nuclear weapons*
dick /dɪk/ *n* **1** *taboo sl for* PENIS **2** *AmE old-fash sl* a PRI-
VATE DETECTIVE —see also CLEVER DICK, SPOTTED DICK
Dick and Jane /ˌ· · ·ˈ·/ two characters in American schoolbooks which teach children to read. Schoolbooks with
stories about Dick and Jane are not used as much as they
were in the 1950s and 1960s, because the stories are considered rather dull and because Dick and Jane are seen
to represent only white, MIDDLE-CLASS values and a style
of life which many Americans no longer share.
dick·ens /ˈdɪkᵻnz/ *n* **the dickens** *euph infml, esp. BrE* (used
for adding force to an expression) the devil:
What/Who/Where the dickens is that?
Dickens, Charles (1812–70) an English NOVELIST, considered by many to be the greatest one of all. His many
famous books describe life in Victorian England and
show how hard it was, esp. for the poor and for children.
They include *The Pickwick Papers, Oliver Twist, A
Christmas Carol, David Copperfield, Great Expectations,*
and *A Tale of Two Cities.*
Dic·ken·si·an /dɪˈkenziən/ *adj* suggesting Charles Dickens
or his writings, e.g. **a** the old-fashioned, unpleasant dirt-
iness of Victorian England: *Most deputies work two to an
office in a space of Dickensian grimness.* **b** the cheerfulness of Victorian amusements and customs: *a real Dickensian Christmas*
dick·er /ˈdɪkəʳ/ *v* [I (**for, with**)] *infml* to argue about the
price for something one wants to buy; HAGGLE
dick·head /ˈdɪkhed/ *n taboo sl* a complete fool. This word
is mostly used only by young people, and is a very strong
word which is offensive to some people.
Dick·in·son /ˈdɪkɪnsən/, **Em·i·ly** /ˈeməli/ (1830–86) an
American poet who is sometimes called "The Belle of
Amherst". She is also known for being a RECLUSE for the
last 25 years of her life.
dick·y¹ /ˈdɪki/ *adj BrE infml* weak; likely to break or go
wrong: *My father has a dicky heart. | Be careful up there!
The ladder's a bit dicky.*
dicky² *n* **1** also **dickey** *AmE—* a false shirt-front **2** *esp.
BrE* a small third seat at the back of an old-fashioned two-
seat car
dick·y·bird /ˈdɪkibɜːd‖-bɜːrd/ *n esp. BrE* **1** (used esp. by or
to children) any small bird **2** [*usu. in negatives*] *sl* a
word; anything: *We haven't heard a dickybird from them
since they moved house.*
dic·ta /ˈdɪktə/ *pl of* DICTUM
Dic·ta·phone /ˈdɪktəfəʊn/ *n tdmk* an office machine into
which one can dictate
dic·tate¹ /dɪkˈteɪt‖ˈdɪkteɪt/ *v* **1** [I;T (**to**)] to say (words) for
someone else to write down or for a machine to record:
*He can't type so he dictates everything. | She dictated a let-
ter to her secretary.* **2** [T (**to**)] to state (demands, conditions, etc.) with the power to make them happen: *We're
now in a position to dictate our own demands (to the
management).* [+*wh-*] *We can dictate how the money will
be spent.* **3** [T] to have a controlling influence on; DETER-
MINE: *The amount of money available will dictate the type
of computer we buy.*
dictate to sbdy. *phr v* [T *usu. in negatives*] to give
orders to, esp. with an unreasonable show of power: *I re-
fuse to be dictated to! | We can't dictate to them how
they should spend their money.*
dic·tate² /ˈdɪkteɪt/ *n* [*usu. pl.*] an order which should be
obeyed, esp. one that comes from one's own mind: *to fol-
low/obey the dictates of your own conscience*
dic·ta·tion /dɪkˈteɪʃən/ *n* **1** [U] the act of dictating or of
writing down what is dictated: *a secretary* **taking dic-
tation** | *Dictation makes my throat sore.* **2** [C] a piece
of writing that is dictated to test one's ability to hear and
write a foreign language correctly: *The teacher gave us
two French dictations today.*

dic·ta·tor /dɪkˈteɪtəʳ‖ˈdɪkteɪtər/ *n often derog* a ruler who
has complete power over a country, esp. if the power has
been gained by force
dic·ta·to·ri·al /ˌdɪktəˈtɔːriəl◂/ *adj usu. derog* (of people or behaviour) of or like a dictator; TYRANNICAL: *a dictatorial
ruler* | *dictatorial power* | *Don't be so dictatorial!* — ~ **ly**
adv
dic·ta·tor·ship /dɪkˈteɪtəʃɪp‖-ˈteɪtər-/ *n* **1** [C;U] (the period
of) government by a dictator **2** [C] a country ruled by
a dictator
dic·tion /ˈdɪkʃən/ *n* [U] **1** the way in which a person
pronounces words: *Actors need training in diction.* **2** the
choice of words and phrases to express meaning: *poetic
diction* (=the use of special words in poetry)
dic·tion·a·ry /ˈdɪkʃənəri‖-neri/ *n* **1** a book that gives a list
of words in alphabetical order, with their meanings in
the same or another language and usu. their pronuncia-
tions: *This book is a dictionary.* | *a German-English dic-
tionary* **2** a book like this that deals with words and
phrases concerning a special subject: *a science diction-
ary* | *a dictionary of place names* —compare GLOSSARY,
THESAURUS
Dictionary of Na·tion·al Bi·og·ra·phy /ˌ·····ˌ·····ˈ····/, **The**
also **DNB** (*abbrev.*) a book containing the life stories of
all important British people from early times to today
dic·tum /ˈdɪktəm/ *n* -**ta** /-tə/ *or* -**tums** a formal statement of
opinion, esp. made by a judge in court —see also OBITER
DICTUM
did /dɪd/ *past tense of* DO —see NOT (USAGE)
di·dac·tic /daɪˈdæktɪk, dᵻ-/ *adj fml* **1** (of speech or writing) intended to teach, esp. to teach a moral lesson: *didac-
tic poetry* **2** *derog* (of a person) too eager to teach or give
instructions — ~ **ally** /kli/ *adv*
did·dle /ˈdɪdl/ *v* [T (**out of**)] *infml* to get something from
(someone) by dishonest means; cheat
did·dums /ˈdɪdəmz/ *interj BrE* (a word used to a child to
show that one is sorry that they are upset)
Did·dy·man /ˈdɪdimæn/ [*the+P*] -**men** /men/ a group of little people who appear in television and stage shows with
the COMEDIAN Ken Dodd, singing a song which includes
the words "We are the Diddymen who live in Knotty
Ash"
did·ger·i·doo /ˌdɪdʒəriˈduː/ *n* didgeridoos a long WOOD-
WIND instrument played by the Australian Aborigines,
which has become well-known in Britain because the
COMEDIAN and entertainer Rolf Harris played it
Did·i·on /ˈdɪdiən/, **Joan** (1934–) an American writer best
known for *A Book of Common Prayer*
did·n't /ˈdɪdnt/ *short for:* did not: *You saw him, didn't you?*
Di·do /ˈdaɪdəʊ/ in Roman MYTHOLOGY, the queen of Carthage. She killed herself rather than marry the king of
Libya, although Virgil in his *Aeneid* makes her kill herself because Aeneas leaves her.
didst /dɪdst/ **thou didst** *old use or bibl* (when talking to one
person) you did
die¹ /daɪ/ *v* **died**, *present participle* **dying** /ˈdaɪ-ɪŋ/ **1** [I
(**of**);L] (of people, animals, and plants) to stop living; be-
come dead: *She's very ill and I'm afraid she's dying.* | *He
died in his sleep.* (=while he was sleeping) | *Three
hundred people died in the air crash.* | *She died of cancer/of
hunger.* | (fig.) *His secret died with him.* (=was lost when
he died) | (fig.) *My love for you will never die.* | *He died
happy.* | *She died a rich woman.* | *to die by one's own hand*
(=kill oneself) | *It was her* **dying wish** (=a wish made as
she was dying) *to be buried next to her husband.* —see
DEAD¹ (CULTURAL NOTE) **2** [I] (of a machine) to stop
operating suddenly: *The engine spluttered a few times,
then died.* | *The phone just* **died on me** *while I was in the
middle of a conversation.* **3** **be dying for/to** *infml* to
have a great wish for/to: *I'm dying for a cigarette.* | *We're
all dying to hear what happened.* **4** **die a** ... **death** to die
in a particular way: *They died a horrible death.* **5** **die
hard** (of old beliefs, customs, etc.) to take a long time to
disappear —see also DIEHARD **6** **die in one's bed** to die
quietly at home of old age or illness rather than because
of an accident, in war, etc. **7** **die (the death) of a thousand cuts** to be killed or destroyed very slowly, as if
bleeding to death through many small wounds: *Immediate action is needed before legal and advice services die of*

a thousand cuts. **8 die with one's boots on** to die while still working or fighting **9 never say die** never admit that you have been defeated and are unable to do something; a phrase used to encourage someone and make them more cheerful: *"I've got no chance, then." "Come on, now, never say die! We still haven't tried asking your father."* **10 to one's dying day** as long as one lives: *I'll remember that awful sight to my dying day.* —see also **do or die** (DO²)
　die away *phr v* [I] (esp. of sound, wind, light) to become gradually less and less and finally stop
　die back *phr v* [I] (of a plant) to die but remain alive in the roots
　die down *phr v* [I] (of physical qualities and feelings) to become less strong or violent; SUBSIDE (3): *The fire/The wind is dying down.* | *The excitement soon died down.*
　die off *phr v* [I] (of a group of living things) to die one by one: *As she got older and older, her relatives all died off.*
　die out *phr v* [I] (of families, races, customs, and ideas) to disappear completely; become EXTINCT: *The practice of children working in factories has nearly died out.*

die² *n* **1** a metal block used for shaping metal, plastic, etc. **2** *old or AmE singular of* DICE¹ (1) **3 The die is cast** the decision or action has been taken and cannot now be changed —see DICE (USAGE)

die-cast·ing /ˈ· ˌ··/ *n* [C;U] (something made by) the process of making metal objects by forcing (not pouring) the liquid metal under pressure into a MOULD (=a hollow container)

die·hard /ˈdaɪhɑːd‖-hɑːrd/ *n* a person who opposes change and refuses to accept new ideas even when they are good: *a diehard conservative* | *It's no good asking him to join the union; he's a real diehard.* —see also **die hard** (DIE¹)

Di·eppe /diˈep/ a port in N France. FERRY¹ services operate from here to Newhaven in England.

di·e·re·sis /ˌdaɪˈɪərↄsɪ̣s, -ˈe-‖-ˈe-/ *n* **-ses** /siːz/ DIAERESIS

die·sel /ˈdiːzↄl/ also **diesel fu·el** /ˈ·· ˌ··/, **diesel oil** /ˈ··ˌ·/— *n* **1** [U] a type of heavy oil used instead of petrol, etc. in DIESEL ENGINES **2** [C] *infml, esp. AmE* a vehicle driven by diesel

diesel en·gine /ˈ·· ˌ··/ *n* an engine that burns diesel instead of petrol, often used for buses, trains, and goods vehicles. More cars are also beginning to have diesel engines now, as diesel is a cheaper and less wasteful FUEL than petrol. It is also safer if there is an accident, and causes less POLLUTION.

di·et¹ /ˈdaɪↄt/ *n* **1** [C;U] the sort of food and drink usually taken by a person or group: *A balanced diet and regular exercise are both important for health.* | *The poor people in Ireland used to live on a diet of potatoes.*
　▶CULTURAL NOTE In recent years, people in both Britain and the US have become concerned with eating a more healthy diet. This generally means eating more FIBRE, less fat, less salt, and less sugar.◀
　2 [C] a limited list of food and drink that a person is allowed, e.g. one that is controlled for medical reasons: *The doctor ordered him to* **go on a diet** *to lose weight.* | *a high-fibre diet* | *a low-fat diet* | *I'm finding it impossible to stick to my diet.*
　▶CULTURAL NOTE Some British and American people, particularly young women, go on diets to lose weight and make themselves SLIM and therefore, they think, more attractive. Other people, esp. people who do not do this to themselves, often joke about them eating just LETTUCE leaves, CARROTS, etc. Every year many new books appear containing the latest fashionable diet plans.◀

diet² *v* [I] to eat according to a special diet, esp. in order to become thinner and so more attractive: *No sugar in my coffee, please; I'm dieting.* —see also DIETER

diet³ *n* **1** a meeting to talk about political or church matters **2** (*often cap.*) (in certain countries) a parliament

di·e·ta·ry /ˈdaɪↄtↄri‖-teri/ *adj* of or concerning diet: *religious dietary rules*

dietary fi·bre /ˌ··ˈ··/ *n fml for* FIBRE (2)

diet co·la /ˈ·· ˌ·/ *n* a CARBONATED dark-coloured DIET DRINK

diet drink /ˈ·· ˌ·/ *n* a non-alcoholic drink, usu. CARBONATED, which contains very few CALORIES, drunk esp. by people who do not want to put on any weight

di·et·er /ˈdaɪↄtↄr/ *n* a person who diets or is dieting

di·e·tet·ics /ˌdaɪↄˈtetɪks/ *n* [U] the science of diet and its effects on health —**dietetic** /ˌdaɪↄˈtetɪk◀/ *adj* : *dietetic studies*

di·e·ti·cian, -tian /ˌdaɪↄˈtɪʃↄn/ *n* a person trained in dietetics

Die·trich /ˈdiːtrɪk, -ɪx/, **Mar·le-**   Marlene Dietrich
·ne /mɑːˈleɪnↄ‖mɑːr-/ (1904–
92) an American actress and
night club performer, born
in Germany who usu. played
the part of an extremely sexually attractive woman. She
is best remembered for her
part in the film *Blue Angel*.

Dieu et mon droit /ˌdjɜː eɪ mɒn ˈdrwɑː‖ˌdjʊ eɪ mɑːn ˈdwɑː/ *Fr* God and my right; the phrase belonging to the British royal family's COAT OF ARMS

dif·fer /ˈdɪfↄr/ *v* [I] **1** [(**from, in**)] to be dissimilar in nature, character, type, etc.; be different: *Their house differs from mine in having no garage.* | *The two squares differ in colour but not in size.* **2** [(**with, about, on, over**)] (of people) to have an opposite opinion; disagree: *The two sides in the dispute still differ (with each other) over the question of pay.* | *You can't persuade me to change my mind about this – we'll just have to* **agree to differ.** (=accept that we have different opinions) **3 I beg to differ** *fml* I disagree with you

dif·fe·rence /ˈdɪfↄrↄns/ *n* [(**between**)] **1** [C] a way of being dissimilar; something that makes one thing different from another: *There are many differences between living in a city and living in the country.* **2** [S;U] the fact of being different, or an amount by which one thing is different from another: *There's a big difference between understanding a language and being able to speak it.* | *I can't see much difference between these two books.* | *The difference in price was only £10 so we decided to take the plane.* | *It doesn't* **make any difference/the slightest difference** *to me whether you go or stay.* (=I don't care at all) | *When you're learning to drive, having a good teacher* **makes a big difference/makes all the difference.** (=has a noticeable or valuable effect) **3** [C *often pl.*] a slight disagreement: *They've settled their differences and are friends again.* | *They had* **a difference of opinion** *over who should drive, but Sue won in the end.* —see also **split the difference** (SPLIT¹)

dif·fe·rent /ˈdɪfↄrↄnt/ *adj* **1** [(**from, than, to**)] unlike; not the same or of the same kind: *Mary and Jane are quite different (from each other/to each other).* | *She looks different with her hair short.* **2** separate; other; DISTINCT: *This is a different car from the one I drove yesterday.* | *Their three children all go to different schools.* (=they do not all go to the same one) | *I've started using a different* (=another) *brand.* | *We make this dress in three different colours.* **3** various; several: *Different members of the party complimented her on her speech.* **4** *infml, sometimes derog* unusual; special: *"What do you think of our new carpet?" "Well, it's certainly different."* **5 and now for something completely different** *quote* a phrase regularly used in the British television programme *Monty Python's Flying Circus.* It is now used to suggest that something very strange and funny is about to happen —see also MONTY PYTHON – **~ ly** *adv*
　▷USAGE 1 Teachers prefer **different(ly) from,** but **different(ly) to** *BrE* and **different(ly) than** *AmE* are also commonly used. 2 Compare **different** and **various.** Both mean "not the same" but **various** is used about several things which are not the same: *The minister gave* **various** *reasons* (=a number of different reasons) *for the government's decision.* | *This time the minister gave* **different** *reasons* (=not the same as last time) *for the government's decision.*◁

dif·fe·ren·tial¹ /ˌdɪfↄˈrenʃↄl◀/ *n* **1** an amount or degree of difference between things, esp. difference in wages between people doing jobs of different types in the same industry or profession: *The management are keen to maintain existing pay differentials.* **2** a DIFFERENTIAL GEAR

differential² *adj* based on or depending on a difference: *differential rates of pay/tax according to one's income*

differential cal·cu·lus /ˌ··· ˈ···/ n [(the) U] (in MATHEMATICS) a way of measuring the speed at which an object is moving at a particular moment; one of the two ways of making calculations about quantities which are continually changing —compare INTEGRAL CALCULUS

differential gear /ˌ··· ˈ·/ n an arrangement of GEARs that allows one back wheel of a car to turn faster than the other when the car goes round a corner

dif·fe·ren·ti·ate /ˌdɪfəˈrenʃieɪt/ v 1 [I (**between**);T (**from**)] to see or express a difference (between); DISTINGUISH or DISCRIMINATE: *This company does not differentiate between men and women — everyone is paid at the same rate.* | *Can you differentiate this kind of rose from the others?* 2 [T (**from**)] (of a quality) to make different by its presence: *What differentiates these two products?* | *Its unusual nesting habits differentiate this bird from others.* —**·ation** /ˌdɪfərenʃiˈeɪʃən/ n [C;U]

dif·fi·cult /ˈdɪfɪkəlt/ adj 1 needing a lot of effort, skill, etc.; hard to do, make, understand, or deal with; not easy: *English is difficult* | *is a difficult language.* | *a difficult exam* [+to-v] *It was a difficult choice to make.* | *It was difficult (for us) to decide which one to buy.* 2 (of people) hard to deal with; not easy to please or persuade; OBSTINATE: *a difficult child* | *She's just being difficult.* 3 full of problems; causing unhappiness, anxiety, etc.: *The educational system has been going through a difficult time owing to cuts in public expenditure.* | *His angry employees did their best to* **make life difficult** *for him.* (=cause problems for him) —see UNEASY (USAGE)

dif·fi·cul·ty /ˈdɪfɪkəlti/ n 1 [U (**in**)] the fact or quality of being difficult; trouble: *She had great difficulty in understanding him.* | *His English was very bad and he spoke with difficulty.* | *We managed to finish it without much* | *any difficulty.* 2 [C often pl.] something difficult; a situation or problem that causes trouble: *He's having financial difficulties.* | *When sales slowed down, the company* **got into difficulties**.

dif·fi·dent /ˈdɪfɪdənt/ adj [(**about**)] 1 lacking a belief in one's own qualities and abilities, and therefore unwilling to speak or act with confidence: *He is rather diffident about expressing his opinions.* 2 RESERVED[1] — **~ly** adv —**dence** n [U]

dif·fract /dɪˈfrækt/ v [T] tech to break up (a beam of light) into the SPECTRUM (=a number of dark and light or coloured bands) — **~ion** /dɪˈfrækʃən/ n [U]

dif·fuse[1] /dɪˈfjuːz/ v [I;T] fml to (cause to) spread out freely in all directions; DISPERSE: *to diffuse knowledge* | *a smell* | *a feeling of happiness* —**·fusion** /dɪˈfjuːʒən/ n [U] : *Clouds cause the diffusion of light from the sun.*

dif·fuse[2] /dɪˈfjuːs/ adj fml 1 diffused: *Direct light is better for reading than diffuse light.* 2 derog using too many words and not keeping to the point: *a diffuse speech* | *writer* — **~ly** adv — **~ness** n [U]

dig[1] /dɪɡ/ v **dug** /dʌɡ/; present participle **digging** 1 [I;T] to break up and move (earth), esp. using a spade: *to dig the garden* | *The dog has been digging in that corner for an hour.* | *to dig for gold* (=look for it by digging) 2 [I; T] to make (a hole) by taking away the earth: *to dig a hole* | *We shall have to dig under the river* | *through the mountain to lay this pipe.* | *The prisoners escaped by digging an underground tunnel.* —see also DIGGER, DIGGINGS 3 [T] to uncover (esp. root vegetables) by taking away the earth: *to dig potatoes* 4 [T] old-fash sl to like and understand; APPRECIATE: *I really dig the way she sings.* 5 **dig for victory** a phrase used in Britain during the Second World War to encourage people to grow their own fruit and vegetables in order to help Britain win the war 6 **dig one's own grave** to cause one's own failure, ruin, or death: *You're just digging your own grave if you go on smoking so heavily.* 7 **dig someone in the ribs** to touch someone with one's elbow, esp. to share a joke

dig in phr v 1 [T] (**dig** sthg. **↔ in**) to mix (something) into the soil by digging: *to dig in some fertilizer* | *dig some fertilizer into the soil* 2 [I;T (=**dig** sbdy. **in**)] to make a protective place for (oneself) by digging: *The soldiers were ordered to dig (themselves) in.* 3 [T] (**dig** sbdy. **in**) infml to establish (oneself) in a position; get (oneself) firmly settled: *I like my new job but I haven't had time to dig myself in yet.* | *I'm well dug in now.* 4 [I] infml to help oneself to food and start eating; TUCK **in**: *Here's your breakfast, so dig in!* 5 **dig one's heels in** infml to refuse to change one's mind or do what others want

dig into phr v [T] 1 (**dig** sthg. **into** sbdy./sthg.) to push into: *to dig a fork into the meat* 2 (**dig into** sthg.) to examine thoroughly: *The police are digging into all the old files connected with this case.*

dig sthg. **↔ out** phr v [T (**of**)] 1 to get out by digging; free from being buried: *to dig the car out of the snow* 2 to find by searching: *I dug out these old trousers to give to the boy.* | *By careful questioning they managed to dig out the information they were looking for.*

dig sthg. **↔ up** phr v [T] 1 to find or take out of the ground by digging: *We dug up the rose bushes and planted some cabbages.* 2 to find (something hidden or forgotten) by careful searching; UNEARTH: *Her political opponents dug up a scandal from her past.*

dig[2] n infml 1 a quick push; POKE: *John's falling asleep — just give him a dig!* | (fig.) *That last remark was a dig at me.* (=made in order to annoy me) 2 a process of digging up an ancient place, town, or building so that it can be studied by students of ancient times: *to go on an archaeological dig* —see also DIGS

di·gest[1] /daɪˈdʒest, dɪ-/ v 1 [I;T] to (cause to) be changed after eating into a form that the body can use: *Mary can't digest fat.* | *Cheese doesn't digest easily.* 2 [T] to think about and understand the meaning or importance of; ASSIMILATE (2): *It took me some time to digest what I had heard.* —compare INGEST — **~ible** adj

di·gest[2] /ˈdaɪdʒest/ n a short account of a piece of writing which gives the most important facts: *a digest of Roman laws*

di·ges·tion /daɪˈdʒestʃən, dɪ-/ n [C;U] the act of digesting or the ability to digest food: *He has a good* | *weak digestion.* | *This rich food is bad for your digestion.* —compare INDIGESTION

di·ges·tive /daɪˈdʒestɪv, dɪ-/ adj [A] connected with or helping in the digesting of food: *the digestive processes* | *the human digestive system*

digestive bis·cuit /·ˌ·· ˈ··/ n (in Britain) a type of plain slightly sweet BISCUIT, sometimes eaten with cheese

dig·ger /ˈdɪɡə[r]/ n a person or machine that digs

dig·gings /ˈdɪɡɪŋz/ n [P] 1 a place where people dig for metal, esp. gold 2 old-fash for DIGS

di·git /ˈdɪdʒ⅄t/ n 1 any of the numbers from 0 to 9: *The number 2001 contains four digits.* 2 fml a finger or toe

di·gi·tal /ˈdɪdʒ⅄tl/ adj 1 of or based on a system in which information is represented in the form of changing electrical signals: *a high-quality digital sound recording* 2 showing quantity in the form of numbers, rather than as a point on a scale, etc.: *a digital watch* | *a digital reading* 3 fml of the fingers and toes — **~ly** adv

digital au·di·o tape /ˌ··· ˈ··· ˌ·/ n [U] see DAT

digital clock /ˌ··· ˈ·/ n a clock which shows the time as a line of numbers usu. on the 24 hour system instead of having two hands point to the numbers —see picture at CLOCK

digital com·pact cas·sette /ˌ···· ˌ··· ·ˈ·/ also **DCC** (abbrev.). **digital cassette** /ˌ···· ·ˈ·/ n a container holding sound that has been digitally recorded

digital com·pact cas·sette play·er /ˌ···· ˌ··· ·ˈ· ˌ··/ **digital cassette player** /ˌ···· ·ˈ· ˌ··/ n a machine for playing digital compact cassettes

digital com·pact disc /ˌ···· ˌ·· ˈ·/ n a COMPACT DISC on which sound is recorded in the form of changing electrical signals (digitally)

digital com·put·er /ˌ···· ·ˈ··/ n a type of computer, now the most common type, that performs operations by using a BINARY system —compare ANALOGUE COMPUTER

digital re·cord·ing /ˌ···· ·ˈ··/ n 1 (the act of) recording using a system of numbers instead of sound waves 2 a recording made in this way

di·gi·tize also **-tise** BrE /ˈdɪdʒ⅄taɪz/ v [T] to put (information) into a digital form —**tizer** n —**tization** /ˌdɪdʒ⅄taɪˈzeɪʃən‖-tə-/ n [U]

dig·ni·fied /ˈdɪɡn⅄faɪd/ adj having or showing dignity: *a dignified manner* | *a dignified old man* —opposite **undignified**

dig·ni·fy /ˈdɪɡn⅄faɪ/ v [T (**by, with**)] to give dignity or importance to (esp. something that does not deserve it): *Don't try to dignify those few hairs on your face by calling them a beard!*

dig·ni·ta·ry /ˈdɪgnɪˌtəri‖-teri/ n fml a person holding a high position, esp. in public life: *Many of the local dignitaries attended the funeral.*

dig·ni·ty /ˈdɪgnɪti/ n 1 [U] calmness, formality, and seriousness of manner or style: *The dignity of the occasion was spoilt when she fell down the steps.* 2 [U] goodness and nobleness of character, of a kind that makes people feel respect and admiration: *an old lady of great dignity* 3 [C] a high position, rank, or title 4 **beneath one's dignity** below one's standard of social or moral behaviour —see also INDIGNITY, **stand on one's dignity** (STAND¹ (26))

di·graph /ˈdaɪgrɑːf‖-græf/ n tech a pair of letters that represent one sound, such as *"ea"* in *"head"* and *"ph"* in *"phrase"*

di·gress /daɪˈgres/ v [I (**from**)] fml (of a writer or speaker) to turn aside from the main subject or line of argument and talk about something else: *I'll tell you a funny story, if I may digress (from my subject) for a moment.* — ~**ion** /ˈgreʃən/ n [C;U (**from**)] : *several long digressions (from the subject) in this chapter*

digs /dɪgz/ n [P] BrE infml one or more rented furnished rooms; LODGINGS: *When his family left London, Tom moved into digs.*

Di·jon /ˈdiːʒɒn‖diːˈʒɑːn/ a city in E central France with food and drink industries, famous esp. for its MUSTARD

dike¹ , dyke /daɪk/ n 1 a wall or bank built to keep back water and prevent flooding. In an old story, a little Dutch boy saved his area from being flooded by putting his finger in a hole in a dike to stop the water coming through: *The government's policy is a bit like sticking your finger in the dike when the hole's already quite big.* —compare DAM¹ 2 esp. BrE a narrow passage dug to carry water away; DITCH 3 ScotE a wall, esp. round a field

dike² , dyke n sl, usu. derog a woman who is sexually attracted to other women; LESBIAN

dik·tat /dɪkˈtæt/ n often derog 1 [C] an order forced on people by a ruler or a country which has beaten them in a war 2 [U] the practice of giving such orders: *government by diktat*

di·lap·i·dat·ed /dɪˈlæpɪ̦deɪtɪd/ adj (of things) in bad condition because of age or lack of care; falling to pieces: *a dilapidated old car/castle*

di·lap·i·da·tion /dɪˌlæpɪˈdeɪʃən/ n [U] the state of being dilapidated

di·lap·i·da·tions /dɪˌlæpɪˈdeɪʃənz/ n [P] BrE law the money that one must pay for damage done to a furnished house that one has been renting

di·late /daɪˈleɪt/ v [I;T] a (of parts of the body, esp. the eyes) to become wider or further open by stretching: *Her eyes dilated with terror.* b to cause to become wider or further open: *The cat dilated its eyes.* —**lation** /daɪˈleɪʃən/ n [U] **dilate on/upon** sthg. phr v [T] fml to speak or write at length on (a subject)

dil·a·to·ry /ˈdɪlətəri‖-tɔːri/ adj fml (of people or their behaviour) slow in action; showing a tendency to delay: *I must apologize for being so dilatory in replying to your letter.*

dil·do /ˈdɪldəʊ/ n -**dos** an object shaped like a PENIS (=male sex organ) that can be placed inside a woman's VAGINA for sexual pleasure

di·lem·ma /dɪˈlemə, daɪ-/ n a situation in which one has to make a difficult choice between two courses of action, both perhaps equally undesirable: *She was in a dilemma as to whether to stay at school or get a job.* | *Their offer has put me in a bit of a dilemma.* —see also **on the horns of a dilemma** (HORN)

dil·et·tan·te /ˌdɪlɪˈtænti‖-ˈtɑːnti/ n -**tes** or -**ti** /ti/ usu. derog a person who studies or has an interest in some activity, such as an art or branch of knowledge, but does not take it very seriously —compare AMATEUR —**dilettante** adj

dil·i·gence /ˈdɪlɪ̦dʒəns/ n 1 [U] the quality of being diligent 2 [C] (in former times) a public carriage pulled by horses

dil·i·gent /ˈdɪlɪ̦dʒənt/ adj (of people or their behaviour) hardworking; showing steady careful effort: *He's not especially clever, but he's a diligent worker and should do well in the examinations.* | *Diligent police inquiries even-*

tually turned up some clues. — ~**ly** adv

dill /dɪl/ n [U] a plant whose seeds are used to give a rather sharp taste to food

Dil·lin·ger /ˈdɪlɪndʒər/, **John** (1903–34) an American bank robber and murderer who terrorized the Midwest. He was declared Public Enemy Number One by the FBI in 1925 and was shot dead by FBI men in Chicago as he was leaving a theatre.

Dil·lon's /ˈdɪlənz/ one of a group of British bookshops

dill pick·le /ˌ· ˈ··/ n a CUCUMBER which has been preserved whole, often served with SANDWICHes. Thin pieces of dill pickle are called **dill slices**.

dil·ly /ˈdɪli/ n AmE infml something exciting or remarkable: *a dilly of a rollercoaster*

dil·ly-dal·ly /ˈdɪliˌdæli/ v [I] infml to waste time, esp. by being unable to make up one's mind or by stopping often in the middle of doing something

di·lute¹ /daɪˈluːt/ v [T (**with**)] to make (a liquid) weaker and thinner by mixing another liquid with it: *I diluted the paint with a little oil.* | *Dilute the orange juice with six parts of water.* | (fig.) *The President's influence has been further diluted* (=reduced) *by the election of fifteen new senators from the opposition party.* —**lution** /ˈluːʃən/ n [C;U (**with**)] : *the illegal dilution of beer* | *a dilution of one part of anti-freeze to two parts of water*

di·lute² /ˌdaɪˈluːt◂/ adj that has been diluted: *dilute sulphuric acid*

dim¹ /dɪm/ adj 1 (of a light) not bright: *The light is too dim for me to read easily.* | (fig.) *Prospects for any early settlement of the dispute are dim.* (=are not good) 2 not easy to see; INDISTINCT: *the dim shape of a large building in the mist* 3 (of the eyes) not able to see clearly: *The old man's eyesight was dim.* 4 infml, esp. BrE slow to learn or understand; stupid 5 not clear in the mind: *a dim awareness that something was wrong* 6 **take a dim view of** infml to regard with disapproval — ~**ly** adv : *dimly aware of a slight tapping sound* — ~**ness** n [U]

dim² v -**mm**- 1 [I;T] to make or become dim: *The lights in the theatre began to dim.* | *The smoke dimmed his eyes.* 2 [T] AmE ‖ **dip** BrE– to change (the HEADLIGHTS of a car) so that they are less bright: *Dim your lights, there's a car coming.*

Di Mag·gi·o /də ˈmædʒiəʊ/, **Joe** /dʒəʊ/ (1914–) an American BASEBALL player who played for the New York Yankees team and was considered to be one of the greatest players of all time. He was the second husband of Marilyn Monroe.

Dim·ble·by /ˈdɪmbəlbi/, **Richard** (1913–65) an English broadcaster famous for his reporting of important public events such as the CORONATION of Queen Elizabeth and the funeral of Winston Churchill. He had a very recognizable voice and a serious style of speaking.

dime /daɪm/ n 1 a coin of the US and Canada, worth ten cents or one tenth of a dollar —compare CENT 2 **a dime a dozen** AmE infml not at all unusual or valuable —see also **ten a penny** (TEN)

dime nov·el /ˈ· ˌ··/ n AmE a small, cheap book containing a very eventful story, esp. one printed in the late 1800s and early 1900s

di·men·sion /daɪˈmenʃən, dɪ-/ n 1 a measurement in any one direction, esp. as used for establishing the position of something in space: *Length is one dimension, and breadth is another.* | *Time is sometimes called the* **fourth dimension**. 2 a particular side or part of a problem, subject, etc.; ASPECT: *There is another dimension to this problem which you haven't considered.* 3 -**dimensional** /daɪˈmenʃənəl, dɪ-/ having the stated number of dimensions: *three-dimensional objects* —see also THREE-D

di·men·sions /daɪˈmenʃənz, dɪ-/ n [P (**of**)] (measurements of) size: *What are the dimensions of this room?* (=its height, length, and width) | (fig.) *a problem of enormous dimensions*

dime store /ˈ· ·/ also **five-and-dime** n AmE FIVE-AND-TEN

di·min·ish /dɪˈmɪnɪʃ/ v 1 [I;T] to (cause to) become or seem smaller: *His illness diminished his strength.* | *the government's diminishing popularity* 2 [T] to cause to seem less important or valuable

diminished re·spon·si·bil·i·ty /·ˌ· ··· ˈ···/ n [U] law (in judging a person who has killed someone) limitation of criminal responsibility for the killing because of disorder or illness of the mind

diminishing re·turns /·ˌ···· ·ˈ·ˌ/ n [P] *tech* a rate of profit that beyond a certain point stops increasing in relation to the increase of work or effort: *the law of diminishing returns* | (fig.) *The more I do for my son the less he thanks me — it's a case of diminishing returns.*

di·min·u·en·do /dɪˌmɪnjuˈendəʊ/ n, adj, adv -dos (a piece of music) getting softer —opposite **crescendo**

dim·i·nu·tion /ˌdɪmɪˈnjuːʃən‖-ˈnuː-/ n [C;U] *fml* a case or the state of diminishing or being diminished: *a diminution in income*

di·min·u·tive¹ /dɪˈmɪnjɵtɪv/ adj *fml* very small, and sometimes also lovable

diminutive² n a word formed by adding a diminutive suffix: *The word "duckling" is a diminutive, formed from "duck".*

diminutive suf·fix /·ˌ···· ˈ··/ n *tech* an ending which is added to a word to express smallness: *A duckling is a small duck, and "-ling" is a diminutive suffix.*

dim·i·ty /ˈdɪmɵti/ n [U] *rare* strong cotton cloth with a raised pattern

dim·mer /ˈdɪməʳ/ also **dimmer switch** /ˈ·· ˌ·/ n a piece of equipment for controlling the brightness of an electric light

dim·ple /ˈdɪmpəl/ n *apprec* a small hollow place on the skin, esp. one formed in the cheek when a person smiles. Dimples are usu. considered attractive.

dim sum /ˌ· ˈ·/ n [P;U] any of various Chinese foods typically consisting of small pieces of meat or vegetables wrapped in rice or a kind of light bread and cooked in steam or hot oil; a popular lunchtime meal

dim·wit /ˈdɪmwɪt/ n *infml* a stupid person: *Don't sit on the butter, (you) dimwit!* —**dim-witted** /ˌ·ˈ···◂/ adj

din¹ /dɪn/ n *derog* a loud, continuous, confused, and unpleasant noise: *to* **kick up** (=make) **a din**

din² v -nn- [I] (of a sound) to be heard loudly and unpleasantly (esp. in the phrase **din in someone's ears**): (fig.) *What she said about me was dinning in my ears all night.*
din sthg. **into** sbdy. *phr v* [T] *infml* to repeat (something, such as a fact or lesson) forcefully over and over again to (someone) as a way of making them remember: *I ought to remember that rule. I had it dinned into me often enough at school.*

di·nar /ˈdiːnɑːʳ‖dɪˈnɑːr, ˈdiːnɑːr/ n a unit of money used in the former Yugoslavia and in several Muslim countries

dine /daɪn/ v [I] *fml* to eat dinner: *We dined at the Ritz.* —see also **wine and dine** (WINE²)
dine off/on sthg. *phr v* [T *pass. rare*] to eat (food, esp. special or expensive food) for dinner: *to dine on lobster and strawberries*
dine out *phr v* [I] to eat dinner away from home, esp. in a restaurant
dine out on sthg. *phr v* [T *pass. rare*] to talk about (an interesting experience one has had or interesting information one knows) in order to attract attention or admiration: *Ever since he met Paul McCartney at a party, he's been dining out on the story.*

Dine, Jim /dʒɪm/ (1935–) an American painter well-known as a leader of the POP ART movement

American diner

din·er /ˈdaɪnəʳ/ n 1 a person who dines, esp. in a restaurant 2 *AmE* a (style of) restaurant which is typically American, esp. common in country areas. Diners are very informal, cheap, and popular with families, for breakfast, LUNCH, and dinner. Customers sit in BOOTHS (3) of VINYL, or may sit at the bar for their meal. Waitresses wear a uniform and a white APRON, and offer country-style meals such as soup, HAM, mashed (MASH) potatoes and GRAVY, and ice-cream sodas, as well as the usual HAMBURGERs, HOT DOGs, and SANDWICHes. 3 *AmE* for DINING CAR

Diners Card /ˈ··· ·/ also **Diner's Club Card** /ˈ··· ˌ·/ n *tdmk* the name of a type of CHARGE CARD

Din·e·sen /ˈdɪnɪsən/, **I·sak** /ˈaɪzək/ *tdmk* (1885–1962) a Danish writer who wrote many books in English. Her real name was Karen Blixen and one of her most famous books was *Out of Africa*, which was made into a film.

di·nette /daɪˈnet/ n *AmE* 1 a small dining area which is usually in or near the kitchen: *We haven't got a dining room, only a dinette.* 2 also **dinette set** a table and matching chairs used when people have meals. A dinette is cheaper than a DINING TABLE and chairs, but not as nice.

ding-a-ling /ˈdɪŋ ə lɪŋ/ n *AmE infml* a stupid, confused person

ding·bat /ˈdɪŋbæt/ n *AmE infml* a stupid, confused person, especially a woman

ding-dong /ˌdɪŋˈdɒŋ◂‖ˈdɪŋdɔːŋ/ adj, n 1 [A;U] (like) the noise made by a bell: *the loud dingdong of the church bells* 2 [A;S] *BrE infml* (being) a noisy fight or argument: *They were having a real dingdong/a dingdong argument.*

dinghies

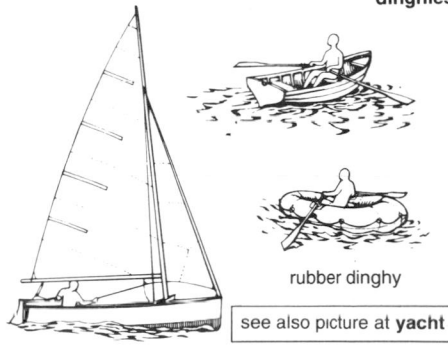

rubber dinghy

see also picture at **yacht**

din·ghy /ˈdɪŋgi, ˈdɪŋi/ n 1 a small open sailing boat used esp. for racing —compare YACHT 2 a small open boat, used for pleasure or for taking people between a ship and the shore —see also RUBBER DINGHY

din·gle /ˈdɪŋgəl/ n *old-fash* a small wooded valley

din·go /ˈdɪŋgəʊ/ n -goes an Australian wild dog

din·gy /ˈdɪndʒi/ adj (of things and places) dirty and dull or dark in colour; DRAB: *a dingy street* | *The curtains are getting rather dingy.* —**gily** adv : *She was dingily dressed in an old brown suit.* —**giness** n [U]

dining car /ˈ··· ·/ also **restaurant car** n a carriage on a train where meals are served

dining room /ˈ·· ·/ n a room where meals are eaten in a house, hotel, etc.

dining ta·ble /ˈ·· ˌ··/ n a table esp. for having meals on: *She spread her books on the dining table and settled down to study.* —compare DINNER TABLE

Din·kins /ˈdɪŋkɪnz/, **David** (1927–) an American Democrat politician, the first black MAYOR of New York City (from January 1990)

din·kum /ˈdɪŋkəm/ adj see FAIR DINKUM

din·ky¹ /ˈdɪŋki/ adj 1 *BrE old-fash* small and charming: *Look at that dinky little spoon!* 2 *AmE derog* small and unimportant: *a dinky little room/hotel* 3 with no children and with both husband and wife working so that there are two incomes; from the first letters of "double income, no kids (yet)": *a dinky couple/household*

dinky² n *infml* Double Income No Kids Yet; one of two young married people in professional jobs who do not yet have children and who are both earning quite a lot of money: *highly processed, value-added "recipe" dishes aimed at the "dinky" market*

Dinky , also **Dinky toy** n **Dinkys** tdmk a small toy vehicle popular since the 1940s and 1950s

din·ner /ˈdɪnəʳ/ n 1 [C;U] the main meal of the day, eaten either at midday or in the evening: *What time do you have dinner?* | *I was cooking the dinner when the phone rang.* | *It happened at/during dinner.* | *We're having fish for dinner.* | *The children have to pay for their school dinners.* (=midday meal provided by the school) | *It's dinner time!* —see also TV DINNER **2** [C] a formal occasion in the evening when this meal is eaten: *The firm are giving/holding a dinner in honour of her retirement.*

▷ USAGE If **dinner** is at midday, the evening meal is called **tea** or **supper**. If **dinner** is in the evening, the midday meal is called **lunch**. In Britain, people use these words differently depending on which part of the country they come from and on their social class. In the US, people also use these words differently depending on which part of the country they come from; **dinner** is usually eaten in the evening except for special occasions: *Christmas dinner.* Some people use either **supper** or **dinner** to mean the evening meal. **Tea** is not used in American English.◁

3 eat one's dinners to complete the process of becoming a BARRISTER. In order to become a barrister in England, a person must study and pass exams, but must also belong to the INNS OF COURT and must eat a certain number of dinners in them: *He read for the Bar, but failed to eat his dinners.* **4 more**...**than you've had hot dinners** very very many; used particularly when someone is praising a person for their great experience: *She's nursed more babies than you've had hot dinners.*

dinner bell /ˈ·· ·/ n a bell rung (e.g. in school) to let people know that dinner is ready

dinner dance /ˈ·· ·/ n a social evening which includes a formal dinner and has music for dancing to: *the company's annual dinner dance*

dinner jack·et /ˈ·· ˌ··/ also **tuxedo** AmE— (abbrev. is **DJ**) n **1** a man's black or white JACKET for very formal evening occasions —see picture at EVENING DRESS **2** a complete suit of clothes including a dinner jacket, black trousers, a white shirt, and black BOW TIE —compare TAILS (2)

dinner la·dy /ˈ·· ˌ··/ n BrE a woman who serves meals to children in a school

dinner par·ty /ˈ·· ˌ··/ n a social event in which people are invited to a person's house for an evening meal: *Let's have a dinner party for your birthday.*

dinner ser·vice /ˈ·· ˌ··/ also **dinner set** /ˈ·· ·/ n a complete set of plates and dishes for dinner

dinner ta·ble /ˈ·· ·/ n [the] the occasion when people are having dinner: *I wish you wouldn't talk about these nasty subjects at the dinner table.* —compare DINING TABLE

di·no·saur /ˈdaɪnəsɔːʳ/ n **1** any of several types of extremely large REPTILES that lived in very ancient times and disappeared suddenly **2** something very large and old-fashioned that no longer works well or effectively: *one of the dinosaurs of the computer industry*

dint /dɪnt/ n **by dint of** by means of: *She reached the top by dint of great effort.*

di·o·cese /ˈdaɪəsɪs/ n (in the Anglican and Roman Catholic churches) the area under the control of a BISHOP —**-cesan** /daɪˈɒsɪsən‖-ˈɑː-/ adj [A]

Di·o·ge·nes /daɪˈɒdʒɪniːz‖-ˈɑː-/ (about 412–323 BC) a Greek thinker who believed that a good life is a simple life and tried to show this by living in a BARREL. He is also famous for walking the streets looking for 'an honest man'.

Di·o·ny·sus /ˌdaɪəˈnaɪsəs/ in CLASSICAL MYTHOLOGY, the god of wine. A **Dionysian** occasion is one where people get drunk.

Di·or /ˈdiːɔːʳ‖diːˈɔːr/, **Christian 1** (1905–57) a French fashion DESIGNER who made very expensive clothes for rich people. His famous collection of clothes in 1947 was called the New Look. **2** tdmk his company's make of expensive clothes and PERFUME

di·ox·ide /daɪˈɒksaɪd‖-ˈɑːk-/ n [C;U] a chemical compound containing two atoms of oxygen to every atom of another ELEMENT

di·ox·in /daɪˈɒksɪn‖-ˈɑːk-/ n [U] a powerful chemical used for killing plants. Adults and unborn babies have been poisoned and killed by dioxin in industrial accidents and through its use as a chemical weapon —see AGENT ORANGE

dip¹ /dɪp/ v -pp- **1** [T (**in, into**)] to put in a liquid for a moment: *I dipped my pen in the ink.* | *She dipped her hand into the water.* **2** [I;T] to (cause to) drop slightly: *The sun dipped below the western sea.* | *The road dips just around the corner.* | *You should dip your headlights when you meet another car at night.* | *driving through the city on dipped headlights.* **3** [T] to pass (animals) through a bath containing a chemical that kills insects: *to dip sheep*

dip into sthg. phr v [T] **1** to read or study for a short time and without much attention: *I haven't read the report properly—I've only dipped into it.* **2** to put one's hand into (a place) and take something out: *She kept dipping into the bag of sweets.* **3** to use (money that has been saved): *The company had to dip into a reserve fund to pay for all the new equipment.*

dip² n **1** [C] infml a quick swim in the sea, a lake, etc.: *I'm just going for a dip/to have a dip.* **2** [C] a slight drop to a lower level: *a sudden dip in the road* | *an unexpected dip in profits* **3** [U] a thick liquid mixture into which food, such as vegetable pieces, can be dipped, esp. at parties: *cheese/avocado dip* **4** [C;U] (a special liquid for) the process of dipping animals **5** [C] AmE sl a stupid or silly person —see also LUCKY DIP

Dip. written abbrev. for: DIPLOMA

diph·ther·i·a /dɪfˈθɪəriə, dɪp-/ n [U] a serious infectious disease of the throat which makes breathing difficult, now rare in developed countries with child health care programmes

diph·thong /ˈdɪfθɒŋ, ˈdɪp-‖-θɔːŋ/ n tech **1** a compound vowel sound made by pronouncing two vowels quickly one after the other: *The vowel sound in "my" is a diphthong.* —compare MONOPHTHONG **2** a DIGRAPH

di·plo·ma /dɪˈpləʊmə/ n [(in)] an official paper showing that a person has successfully finished a course of study or passed an examination: *She has a diploma in education/a high school diploma.*

di·plo·ma·cy /dɪˈpləʊməsi/ n [U] **1** the art and practice of establishing and continuing relations between nations **2** skill at dealing with people and getting them to agree; TACT: *He needed all his diplomacy to settle their quarrel.* —see also GUNBOAT DIPLOMACY

dip·lo·mat /ˈdɪpləmæt/ n **1** a person who is employed to represent one country in another, such as an AMBASSADOR **2** a person who is skilled in DIPLOMACY (2)

dip·lo·mat·ic /ˌdɪpləˈmætɪk◀/ adj **1** [A no comp.] concerning diplomacy or diplomats: *the diplomatic service* | *They can't be prosecuted for this offence—they have diplomatic immunity.* (=special rights belonging to diplomats) **2** apprec skilled in dealing with people; showing TACT: *Try to be diplomatic when you refuse her invitation.* —opposite **undiplomatic** (for 2) — ~ **ally** /kli/ adv : *She handled the situation very diplomatically.*

diplomatic corps /··ˈ·· ˌ·/ n pl. **-corps** all the diplomats working in a country

diplomatic re·la·tions /ˌ··ˈ···· ·ˈ··/ n [P (**with**)] the arrangement between two countries that each keep representatives at an EMBASSY in the other country: *Following this incident, the United States* **broke off diplomatic relations** *with Iran.*

Diplomatic Ser·vice /··ˈ·· ˌ··/ [the] a division of the British Civil Service which employs the people who work in British embassies (EMBASSY) abroad

di·plo·ma·tist /dɪˈpləʊmətɪst/ n a diplomat

dip·per /ˈdɪpəʳ/ n **1** a big spoon for taking up liquid out of a container **2** a small bird that feeds on the bottom of streams

Dipper also **Big Dipper** n [the] esp. AmE a group of stars, the PLOUGH

dip·py /ˈdɪpi/ adj esp. AmE infml crazy or foolish: *She's gone clean dippy.*

dip·so·ma·ni·a /ˌdɪpsəˈmeɪniə/ n [U] an uncontrollable desire for alcoholic drinks

dip·so·ma·ni·ac /ˌdɪpsəˈmeɪniæk/ n a person suffering from dipsomania

dip·stick /ˈdɪpˌstɪk/ n **1** a stick for measuring the depth of liquid in a container, esp. the amount of oil in a car's

For the full story see Cinderella

Cinderella has to stay at home and sweep the floor

while her ugly sisters put on their best clothes and get ready to go to the ball (a very special dance).

Her fairy godmother appears and says "ou shall go to the ball".

She uses magic to change a pumpkin and mice into…

… a coach and horses so that Cinderella can go to the ball.

Then she gives her a beautiful dress to wear.

Prince Charming falls in love with Cinderella

but she has to leave the ball by midnight.

She leaves her glass slipper behind.

There was much fighting and a lot of crime in the Wild West because there was no government. Cowboys often fought each other in gunfights in the street, outlaws committed crimes such as robbing trains, and cowboys also fought against Indians (Native Americans). When the cowboys made peace with the Indians, the Indians, sometimes with the cowboys, sat and smoked a peace pipe.

gunfighter

covered wagon

outlaws

tepee

Indian
(Native American)

engine —see picture at ENGINE **2** *BrE sl* a fool, stupid person

dip-switch /ˈdɪpˌswɪtʃ/ *n BrE* an instrument in a car for lowering the beam of the HEADLIGHTS

dip-tych /ˈdɪptɪk/ *n tech* a picture made in two parts which can close like the covers of a book —compare TRIPTYCH

dire /daɪəʳ/ *adj* **1** (of needs and dangers) very great; extreme; terrible: *in dire need of food* | *The company is in dire straits.* (=in a seriously difficult position) **2** [A] causing great fear for the future: *dire warnings/predictions*

di-rect¹ /dɪˈrekt, ˌdaɪˈrekt◂/ *v* [T] **1** [+obj+adv/prep] to turn or aim (attention, remarks, movement, activity, etc.) in the stated direction: *This warning is directed at you.* | *Please direct your complaints to the manager.* | *We directed our steps homewards.* | *civil unrest directed against the white community* | *Most of the money will be directed towards medical research.* **2** to control and be in charge of (an activity or situation); manage: *He directed the building of the new bridge.* | *A policewoman stood in the middle of the road, directing the traffic.* **3** *fml* to order, esp. officially; command: [+obj+to-v] *The judge directed the jury to find the prisoner guilty.* [+that] *The general directed that his men should retreat.* —see ORDER (USAGE) **4** to be the person who instructs the actors in (a film or play); be the DIRECTOR (2) of: *Who directed that new Italian film?* **5** [(to)] to tell (someone) the way to a place: *I'm lost. Can you direct me to Times Square?* —see LEAD (USAGE)

direct² *adj* **1** straight; going from one point to another without turning aside: *Which is the most direct route to London?* | *a direct flight from London to Los Angeles* (=without stopping) **2** [no comp.] without any other person, reason, etc. coming between: *Unemployment has increased as a direct result of government policies.* (=and for no other reason) | *The organization was investigated at the direct request of the President.* **3** (of people and their manner) honest, easily understood and not attempting to deceive: *He refused to give a direct answer to my question.* | *She's always very direct, so you know exactly what she's thinking* **4** [A] exact: *He's the direct opposite of his brother.* **5** [A no comp.] (of family relationships) passing in a straight line from parent to child: *She's a direct descendant of the poet Wordsworth.* —see also DIRECTLY — ~**ness** *n* [U]

direct³ *adv* in a straight line; without stopping or turning aside: *The next flight doesn't go direct to Rome. It goes by way of Paris.*

direct cur-rent /ˌ·ˈ··/ *n* [U] a flow of electricity that moves in one direction only —compare ALTERNATING CURRENT

direct deb-it /ˌ·ˈ··/ *esp. BrE‖***automatic payment** *AmE— n* [C,U] an order to a bank to pay money from one's account to another named account at regular times: *Please cancel all my direct debits.* | *If you wish to pay by direct debit, please complete the mandate below.* —compare STANDING ORDER

direct de-pos-it /ˌ·ˈ···/ *n* [U] *AmE* a common method of paying a person's wages directly into their bank account, so that neither a cheque nor money in the form of coins and notes is used. The employee receives instead a piece of paper with information about how much has been paid into the account.

direct dial /ˌ·ˈ·/ *n* [U] a system by which telephone users in a large building can get the telephone line they want themselves, and do not have to ask a special worker (=SWITCHBOARD OPERATOR) to get it for them: *All bedrooms feature private bathrooms, satellite TV, in-house movie channel, direct dial telephone, etc.*

direct dis-course /ˌ·ˈ···/ *n* [U] *AmE for* DIRECT SPEECH

direct free kick /ˌ·ˌ·ˈ·/ *n* (in football) a FREE KICK given to one team, from which a direct shot at GOAL can be made —compare INDIRECT FREE KICK, PENALTY KICK

direct grant school /ˌ··ˈ·ˌ·/ *n* a British GRAMMAR SCHOOL which receives money directly from the central government and not from local government like most other SECONDARY SCHOOLS

di-rec-tion /dɪˈrekʃən, daɪ-/ *n* **1** [C;U] the point or position towards which a person or thing moves, faces, or is aimed: *She drove off in the direction of London.* (=towards London) | *Stones were flying about in every*

direction. | *Which direction does the house face?* | *She has a good* **sense of direction** *and never gets lost.* | (fig.) *Their economic policy is moving in the direction of* (=tending towards) *retrenchment.* | (fig.) *His greatest problem is that he lacks direction/has no* **sense of direction.** (=he does not know what he wants to do with his life, job, etc.) | (fig.) *The law on women's rights is still unsatisfactory, but this new change is* **a step in the right direction.** **2** [U] control or management: *The investigation was carried out* **under the direction of** *a senior police officer.* —see also DIRECTIONS

di-rec-tion-al /dɪˈrekʃənəl, daɪ-/ *adj* connected with direction in space; suitable for finding out where radio signals come from (esp. in the phrase **directional aerial**)

direction find-er /ˈ··· ˌ···/ *n* a piece of equipment for finding out where radio signals are coming from

di-rec-tions /dɪˈrekʃənz, daɪ-/ *n* [P] instructions on what to do, how to do something, or how to get from one place to another: *Follow the directions on the packet.* | *We asked a policeman and he gave us directions to Buckingham Palace.*

di-rec-tive /dɪˈrektɪv, daɪ-/ *n* an official order or instruction: *The management has issued a new directive about the use of company cars.*

di-rect-ly¹ /dɪˈrektli, daɪ-/ *adv* **1** in a direct manner: *She answered me very directly and openly.* [+adv/prep] *We live directly opposite the church.* | *to buy goods directly from the manufacturers* **2** *BrE* **a** at once: *Answer me directly!* **b** *infml* very soon: *He should be here directly if you don't mind waiting.*

directly² *conj BrE infml* as soon as: *I came directly I got your message.*

direct mail /ˌ·ˈ·/ *n* [U] advertisements which are sent through the post to many people: *a public relations company offering everything from lobbying and management consulting to research, direct-mail campaigns, and traditional public relations*

direct meth-od /ˌ·ˈ··, ˌ·ˈ···/ *n* a method of teaching a foreign language without using the student's own language

direct ob-ject /ˌ·ˈ··, ˌ·ˈ···/ *n tech* the noun, noun phrase, or PRONOUN that is needed to complete the meaning of a statement with a TRANSITIVE verb: *In "I saw Mary", "Mary" is the direct object. In "I gave Mary the money", "the money" is the direct object.* —compare INDIRECT OBJECT

film director

di-rec-tor /dɪˈrektəʳ, daɪ-/ *n* **1** a member of the group of top managers who run a company: *She's on the board of directors.* **2** a person who directs a play or film, instructing the actors, cameramen, etc. —compare PRODUCER (2) **3** anyone who directs an organization or activity: *the President's budget director*

di-rec-tor-ate /dɪˈrektərɪt, daɪ-/ *n* **1** [+sing./pl. v] a board of directors of a company **2** a directorship

Director-Gen-e-ral /ˌ·ˌ·ˈ···/ (abbrev. **DG**) [the] the head of the BBC: *Lord Chancellor Kilmuir was asked by the Director-General of the BBC whether serving judges would be willing to speak on the radio about great judges of the past.*

Director of Pub-lic Pros-e-cu-tions /ˌ·ˌ··· ·ˌ··ˈ···/ (abbrev. **DPP**) [the] the British government lawyer who decides in certain doubtful cases whether a person should be tried by a court of law

Director of Stud-ies /ˌ·ˌ··· ˈ··/ *n* a teacher in a British university or language school who is in charge of the organization of the students' study programmes

di·rec·tor·ship /dʒ'rektəʃɪp, daɪ-‖-ər-/ n (the period of holding) the position of a company director: *As well as being a politician, he holds several directorships.*

di·rec·to·ry /daɪ'rektəri, dʒ-/ n a book or list of names, facts, etc., usu. arranged in alphabetical order: *The telephone directory gives people's names, addresses, and telephone numbers.* –see TELEPHONE (USAGE)

directory en·qui·ries /·ˌ···ˈ··/ n [+ *sing./pl v*] the service on the main British telephone network which one rings to ask for a number one does not know, giving the name and address of the person or company concerned –compare INFORMATION (2)

direct pri·ma·ry /·ˌ· ˈ···/ n AmE an election in which people choose from several CANDIDATES of one political party who they want to run against the candidate from the other political party

direct rule /·ˌ· ˈ·/ n [U] direct government of Northern Ireland by the UK parliament which in 1972, after violence in Northern Ireland, replaced rule by the Northern Ireland government

direct speech /·ˌ· ˈ·, ˌ·· ˈ·/ BrE ‖ **direct discourse** AmE– n [U] *tech* the style used to report someone's actual words. This is done by repeating the words without any changes in grammar, e.g. *"I don't want to go," said Julia.* –compare INDIRECT SPEECH

direct tax /·ˌ· ˈ·/ n [C;U] (a) tax, such as income tax, which is actually collected from the person who pays it, rather than on the sale of goods or services –opposite **indirect tax** – ~ation /·ˌ· ·ˈ··/ n [U]

dire·ful /'daɪəfəl‖'daɪər-/ adj lit threatening or producing terrible effects – ~ly adv

Dire Straits /ˌ· ˈ·/ a British popular music group successful since the 1980s

dirge /dɜːdʒ‖dɜːrdʒ/ n 1 a slow sad song sung over a dead person 2 derog any slow sad song or piece of music

dir·i·gi·ble /'dɪrɪdʒəbəl, dʒ'rɪ-/ n a large aircraft filled with gas which can be guided; AIRSHIP

dirk /dɜːk‖dɜːrk/ n a short sword used in Scotland in former times; a kind of DAGGER

dirn·dl /'dɜːndl‖'dɜːr-/ n 1 a wide skirt that is gathered at the waist 2 a dress with wide skirt that has a tight waist and with a close-fitting upper part, as originally worn in Austria. Such dresses were fashionable in the 1950s.

dirt /dɜːt‖dɜːrt/ n [U] 1 any unclean substance, such as mud or dust: *She washed the dirt off the kitchen floor/off the child's knees.* | *Take off your boots before you tread any more dirt into the carpet.* 2 soil; loose earth: *The children were outside playing happily in the dirt.* 3 unpleasant or immoral talk or writing about sex 4 infml nasty talk about people; SCANDAL: *Her political career was ruined when the papers dug up some dirt about her past.* –see also **treat someone like dirt** (TREAT¹)

dirt bike /'· ˌ·/ n a small MOTORCYCLE for young people, usu. not ridden on the streets

dirt cheap /ˌ· ˈ·◄/ adj, adv infml extremely cheap: *This dress was dirt cheap.* | *I got it dirt cheap.*

dirt farm·er /'· ˌ··/ n AmE a farmer who earns his living by farming his own land, esp. without hired help

dirt poor /ˌ· ˈ·/ adj AmE infml very poor; having very little money

dirt road /ˈ· ·/ n a road of hard earth

dirt track /ˈ· ·/ n a track used for some types of motorcycle races

dirt·y¹ /'dɜːti‖'dɜːr-/ adj 1 not clean; covered or marked with dirt, or likely to make dirt: *dirty hands/clothes* | *Put the dirty dishes* (=plates, cups, etc.) *in the sink.* | *Repairing cars is a dirty job.* 2 (of thoughts or words) concerned with sex in an unpleasant way: *They sat drinking and telling dirty jokes.* | *He took his secretary away for a dirty weekend.* 3 infml unpleasant: *The fishermen won't go out on such a dirty night.* | *She gave me a* **dirty look.** (=looked at me with disapproval) | *"Empire" is a* **dirty word** *these days.* (=people disapprove of the idea) 4 not fair: *a dirty fighter* 5 **do the dirty on** BrE infml to treat in an unfair or dishonest way 6 **dirty pool** unfair acts: *He plays dirty pool – don't trust him.* –see also **wash one's dirty linen (in public)** (WASH¹ (7)) **–ily** adv

dirty² v [I;T] to make or become dirty: *You'll dirty your hands if you touch that machine.*

Dirty Den /ˌ··ˈ·/ a character, Dennis Watts, from the British television programme *Eastenders*, whose activities were not always honest

dirty great /'··· ·/ adj BrE sl extremely big: *We suddenly saw this dirty great truck coming towards us.*

dirty mac bri·gade /ˌ··· ˈ· ·ˌ·/ [the] BrE infml derog a collective word for men with an unhealthy interest in sex. A typical image is of a man in a long, dirty coat who either reads PORNOGRAPHIC magazines or makes improper advances towards women, including flashing (FLASH): *It's a widely held opinion that it's the dirty mac brigade who are chiefly responsible for obscene telephone calls.*

dirty old man /ˌ··· ˈ·/ n a usu. middle-aged man who has an unhealthy interest in sex, esp. one who continually tries to establish sexual relationships with much younger women or children

dirty trick /ˌ··· ˈ·/ n an unkind dishonest way of treating someone: *He ordered the drinks and then left me to pay. That was a dirty trick, wasn't it?*

dirty tricks /ˌ··· ˈ·/ n [P] secret dishonest or illegal activity, including crimes such as murder, performed for a government or other political group. The group of people who do it are sometimes called informally the **dirty tricks brigade**.

dirty week·end /ˌ··· ·ˈ·‖ˌ·· ˈ···/ n a weekend when a man and a woman who are not married to each other go away together to have sex: *He's gone off with the boss's wife for a dirty weekend in Brighton.*

dirty work /'·· ·/ n [U] 1 unpleasant work that no one wants to do: *She left it to me to call them they were sacked— she always gets me to do her dirty work for her.* 2 infml dishonest behaviour: *There's been some dirty work with the club accounts, and some money is missing.*

dis- see WORD FORMATION

dis·a·bil·i·ty /ˌdɪsə'bɪlʒti/ n 1 [U] the state of being disabled: *She gets a* **disability pension** *from the government.* 2 [C] something that disables; a HANDICAP: *Blindness is a very serious disability.*

dis·a·ble /dɪs'eɪbəl/ v [T] 1 [often pass.] to make (a person) unable to use his/her body properly: *a disabled soldier* | *He was disabled in the war. He lost his left arm.* | *a disabling disease* 2 to cause (e.g. a machine) to be no longer able to operate 3 [(from)] fml to take away (from a person) a power or right; DISQUALIFY: *He is disabled from voting.* – ~ment n [C;U]

dis·a·bled /dɪs'eɪbəld/ n [the+P] people who are physically disabled: *The theatre has very good access for the disabled.*

dis·a·buse /ˌdɪsə'bjuːz/ v [T (of)] fml to free (a person) from a wrong belief: *I must disabuse you of that idea.*

dis·ad·van·tage /ˌdɪsəd'vɑːntɪdʒ‖-'væn-/ n [C;U] an unfavourable condition or quality that makes a person or thing less successful or effective than others: *One of the main disadvantages of the system is that it uses very large amounts of fuel.* | *If you don't speak good English, you'll be at a* **big disadvantage** *when you try to get a job.* | *Her height will be very much* **to** her **disadvantage** *if she wants to be a dancer.*

dis·ad·van·taged /ˌdɪsəd'vɑːntɪdʒd‖-'væn-/ adj (of a person) suffering from a disadvantage, esp. with regard to one's social position, family background, etc.: *disadvantaged students from the poorest homes*

dis·ad·van·ta·geous /ˌdɪsædvən'teɪdʒəs, -væn-/ adj [(to)] causing or being a disadvantage – ~ly adv

dis·af·fect·ed /ˌdɪsə'fektʒd◄/ adj [(towards)] dissatisfied and lacking loyalty, esp. political loyalty: *Some of the government's most loyal supporters are now becoming disaffected.* **--fection** /'fekʃən/ n [U] : *There's growing disaffection among the more moderate members of the party.*

dis·af·fil·i·ate /ˌdɪsə'fɪlieɪt/ v [I;T (from)] (of a person or organization) to break one's connection with an organization –compare AFFILIATE

dis·af·for·est /ˌdɪsə'fɒrʒst‖-'fɔː-, -'fɑː-/ also **disforest** BrE v [T] DEFOREST – ~ation /ˌdɪsəfɒrʒ'steɪʃən‖-fɔː-, -fɑː-/ n [U]

dis·a·gree /ˌdɪsə'griː/ v [I (with)] 1 (of people) to have different opinions; quarrel slightly: *Bill and I often* *disagree but we're good friends.* | *I strongly disagree with the last speaker.* | *We disagreed over what should be done.* **2** (of statements, reports, etc.) to be different (from each other); fail to CORRESPOND: *These two reports of the accident disagree on a number of points.*

 disagree with sbdy. *phr v* [T *no pass.*] (of food or weather) to have a bad effect on; make ill: *Chocolate always disagrees with me.*

dis·a·gree·a·ble /ˌdɪsəˈɡriːəbəl/ *adj* **1** unpleasant; not what one likes or enjoys: *a disagreeable job* **2** (of people) bad-tempered and unfriendly: *Stop being so disagreeable!* —**bly** *adv* – –**ness** *n* [U]

dis·a·gree·ment /ˌdɪsəˈɡriːmənt/ *n* **1** [C;U] the fact or a case of disagreeing: *Bill and I have been having a few disagreements lately.* | *I am in total disagreement with you over this.* **2** [U (**between**)] lack of similarity (between statements, reports, etc.): *There is considerable disagreement between these two estimates of the cost.*

dis·al·low /ˌdɪsəˈlaʊ/ *v* [T] *fml* to refuse officially to recognize or allow: *to disallow a goal/a claim*

dis·ap·pear /ˌdɪsəˈpɪər/ *v* [I] **1** to go out of sight: *The sun disappeared behind a cloud.* **2** to stop existing; come to an end: *These beautiful birds are fast disappearing.* **3** to leave or become lost, esp. suddenly or without explanation: *By the time the police arrived the gang had disappeared.* | *My keys have disappeared off the table.* | *Several top-secret files have mysteriously disappeared.* – –**ance** *n* [C;U] : *Her disappearance was very worrying.*

dis·ap·point /ˌdɪsəˈpɔɪnt/ *v* [T] **1** to fail to fulfil the hopes of (a person): *I'm sorry to disappoint you, but I can't come after all.* **2** to prevent the fulfilment of (a plan or hope); FRUSTRATE: *to disappoint someone's hopes*

dis·ap·point·ed /ˌdɪsəˈpɔɪntɪd◂/ *adj* **1** [(**about, at, in, with**)] (of a person) unhappy at not seeing hopes come true: *Since he lost the election he's a disappointed man.* | *She was very/deeply disappointed about/at losing the race.* | *My parents will be disappointed in/with me if I fail the exam.* [F+to-*v*] *I was disappointed to hear that they weren't coming.* [F+(*that*)] *I'm disappointed (that) you're not coming.* **2** (of a plan or hope) defeated; not fulfilled: *disappointed hopes* – –**ly** *adv*

dis·ap·point·ing /ˌdɪsəˈpɔɪntɪŋ◂/ *adj* making one unhappy at not seeing hopes come true: *What disappointing news!* | *Your exam marks are rather disappointing. I expected you to do better.* | *disappointing profit figures* – –**ly** *adv*

dis·ap·point·ment /ˌdɪsəˈpɔɪntmənt/ *n* **1** [U] the state of being disappointed: **To my great disappointment,** *she wasn't on the train.* (=this made me disappointed) **2** [C] someone or something disappointing: *Our son has been a disappointment to us.* | *The film was a bit of a disappointment. We expected it to be much better.*

dis·ap·pro·ba·tion /ˌdɪsæprəˈbeɪʃən/ *n* [U] *fml* disapproval, esp. of something immoral

dis·ap·prov·al /ˌdɪsəˈpruːvəl/ *n* [U] the state of disapproving: *He spoke with disapproval of your behaviour.* | *She shook her head in disapproval.* (=as a sign of disapproval) | *She gave up her job, greatly* **to my disapproval.** (=making me disapprove)

dis·ap·prove /ˌdɪsəˈpruːv/ *v* **1** [I (**of**)] to have an unfavourable opinion of someone or something, esp. for moral reasons: *He disapproves of mothers going out to work. In fact, he disapproves very strongly.* **2** [T] to refuse to agree officially to: *Congress disapproved the legislation.* —**provingly** *adv*

dis·arm /dɪsˈɑːm/ *v* **1** [T] to take the weapons away from: *The police disarmed the criminal.* **2** [I] (esp. of a country) to reduce the size and strength of its armed forces —compare REARM **3** [T] *apprec* to gain the trust or favour of, esp. through friendliness: *We didn't trust him at first, but his charming manner completely disarmed us.* | *a disarming smile*

dis·ar·ma·ment /dɪsˈɑːməmənt/|-ˈɑːr-/ *n* [U] the act or principle of reducing or giving up weapons by a government. In Britain, many supporters of NUCLEAR disarmament are members of CND: *a lifelong supporter of* **nuclear disarmament** —compare ARMAMENT (3), REARMAMENT

dis·ar·range /ˌdɪsəˈreɪndʒ/ *v* [T] *fml* to upset the arrangement of; make untidy – –**ment** *n* [U]

dis·ar·ray /ˌdɪsəˈreɪ/ *n* [U] *fml* the state of disorder: *She*

rushed out of the burning house with her clothes in disarray. | (fig.) *This latest internal row has thrown the government into complete disarray.*

dis·as·so·ci·ate /ˌdɪsəˈsəʊʃieɪt, -sieɪt/ *v* [T (**from**)] to DISSOCIATE

di·sas·ter /dɪˈzɑːstər‖dɪˈzæ-/ *n* [C;U] **1** (a) sudden serious misfortune causing great suffering and damage: *The flood was a terrible disaster. Hundreds of people died.* | *The crash was the worst air disaster* (=crash of a plane) *this year.* | *Everything was going well, and then suddenly* **disaster struck.** (=something terrible happened) **2** *infml* (a) complete failure: *The party was an absolute disaster—the guests all got drunk and started fighting with each other.*

disaster ar·e·a /·ˈ·· ˌ···/ ‖ also **distressed area** *AmE*— *n* a place which has suffered a lot of damage because of a disaster such as a flood. In the US, if the governor or the president says that a place is a disaster area, it is then allowed to receive money from the state or FEDERAL government to build again: *The area has been declared a disaster area.*

di·sas·trous /dɪˈzɑːstrəs‖dɪˈzæ-/ *adj* very bad; being or causing a disaster: *a disastrous mistake/marriage/failure* | *The new system has had a disastrous effect on productivity.* – –**ly** *adv*

dis·a·vow /ˌdɪsəˈvaʊ/ *v* [T] *fml* to refuse to admit that one has (knowledge, a connection, etc.): *She disavowed all responsibility for their actions.* | *He disavowed any intention to deceive the public.* – –**al** *n* [C;U]

dis·band /dɪsˈbænd/ *v* [I;T] to break up and separate: *The club has disbanded.* | *The officers disbanded the club.* – –**ment** *n* [U]

dis·bar /dɪsˈbɑːr/ *v* -**rr**- [T *often pass.*] to make (a lawyer) leave the BAR or the legal profession —compare DEBAR – **ment** *n* [U]

dis·be·lief /ˌdɪsbɪˈliːf/ *n* [U] lack of belief that something is true or that something really exists: *He shook his head in disbelief.* —compare UNBELIEF, BELIEF

dis·be·lieve /ˌdɪsbɪˈliːv/ *v* [I (**in**);T] to refuse to believe (a statement or person): *I see no reason to disbelieve what he says.* —**liever** *n* — compare UNBELIEVER

 ▷ USAGE **Disbelieve** is a strong and rather formal word which suggests that there are good reasons for not accepting something (especially a story or statement) as true. It is not the usual opposite of **believe.** People say: *I don't* **believe** *you.* | *I don't* **believe** *in letting children do whatever they like.*◁

dis·burse /dɪsˈbɜːs‖ -ɜːrs/ *v* [T] *fml* to pay out (money) esp. from a sum saved or collected for a purpose – – **ment** *n* [C;U] : *the disbursement of £20* | *to make several small disbursements*

disc *BrE* ‖ **disk** *AmE* /dɪsk/ *n* **1** something round and flat, or looking flat: *the disc of the full moon* **2** a record for playing on a RECORD PLAYER —see also COMPACT DISC **3** a flat piece of CARTILAGE (=strong bendable material) between the bones of one's back: *The pain was caused by a slipped disc.* **4** a DISK (2) in a computer system

dis·card¹ /dɪsˈkɑːd‖-ɑːrd/ *v* **1** [T] to get rid of as useless: *to discard an old coat/one's old friends* **2** [I;T] (in card games) to give up (unwanted cards): *to discard the Queen of Hearts* | *You've got to discard before you can pick up another card.*

dis·card² /ˈdɪskɑːd‖-ɑːrd/ *n* a card discarded in a card game

disc brakes /ˈ· ·/ *n* [P] BRAKES (=apparatus for stopping the wheels of a vehicle) which work by the pressure of a pair of discs against another one in the centre of a car wheel

di·scern /dɪˈsɜːn‖-ɜːrn/ *v* [T *not in progressive forms*] to see, notice, or understand, esp. with difficulty; PERCEIVE: *I could just discern the shape of a horse in the mist.* [+*that*] *I soon discerned that the man was lying.* [+*wh*-] *It was difficult to discern which of them was telling the truth.* – –**ible** *adj* : *There is still no discernible improvement in the economic situation.* – –**ibly** *adv*

di·scern·ing /dɪˈsɜːnɪŋ‖-ɜːr-/ *adj apprec* showing an ability to make good judgments, esp. in matters of style, fashion, beauty, etc.: *The paper has a discerning readership.* | *a fashionable clothes shop for the discerning young man*

di·scern·ment /dɪˈsɜːnmənt‖-ɜːr-/ n [U] apprec the quality of being discerning: He showed great discernment in his choice of wine.

dis·charge¹ /dɪsˈtʃɑːdʒ‖-ɑːr-/ v usu. fml **1** [T (from)] to allow or tell (a person) to go: The judge discharged the prisoner. | Although she was still ill, she discharged herself from hospital. | He was discharged from the army. **2** [I+adv/prep;T] to send, pour, or let out (gas, liquid, etc.): The chimney discharges smoke. | The River Rhine discharges (itself) into the North Sea. **3** [T] to perform (a duty or promise) properly **4** [T] to pay (a debt) completely **5** [T] to unload: to discharge the ship/the cargo | The aircraft discharged its passengers. **6** [T (**at, into**)] to fire or shoot (a gun, ARROW, etc.) **7** [I] (of a wound) to send out PUS (=infected liquid matter) **8** [I;T] **a** (of a piece of electrical equipment) to send out electricity or lose stored electrical power **b** to cause the removal of electricity or of stored electrical power from

dis·charge² /dɪsˈtʃɑːdʒ, ˈdɪstʃɑːdʒ‖-ɑːr-/ n usu. fml **1** [U] the action of discharging: the discharge of one's debts/of one's duty/of smoke from a chimney | After my discharge from the army I went into business. **2** [C;U] something that is discharged: a discharge of electricity | The fish in the river were poisoned by discharge from the chemical factory.

discharged bank·rupt /·ₐˌ··/ n a BANKRUPT (=someone who is unable to pay their debts) who has obeyed the orders of the court and is now free to do business again

disc har·row /ˈ·ₐˌ··/ n a machine with a set of DISCs on a frame, which is rolled over the ground to break it up so that crops can be planted

di·sci·ple /dɪˈsaɪpəl/ n **1** a follower of any great teacher (esp. of a religious teacher): Martin Luther King considered himself a disciple of Gandhi. **2** (often cap.) in the Christian religion, one of the first followers of Christ, esp. an APOSTLE: the 12 disciples

di·sci·ple·ship /dɪˈsaɪpəlʃɪp/ n [U] the state or time of being a disciple

dis·ci·pli·nar·i·an /ˌdɪsɪplɪˈneəriən/ n a person who can make people obey orders or who believes in firm discipline: a strict disciplinarian

dis·ci·pli·na·ry /ˈdɪsɪplɪnəri, ˌdɪsɪˈplɪ-‖ˈdɪsɪplɪneri/ adj connected with punishment or the encouragement of obedience: The college authorities took disciplinary action against the protesting students. | She was dismissed in accordance with the company's usual disciplinary procedures.

dis·ci·pline¹ /ˈdɪsɪplɪn/ n **1** [C;U] (a method of) training to produce obedience and self-control: school/military discipline | Learning poetry is a good discipline for the memory. —see also SELF-DISCIPLINE **2** [U] a state of order and control gained as a result of this training: The teacher can't keep discipline in her classroom. **3** [U] punishment that is intended to produce obedience: That child needs discipline! **4** [C] a branch of learning studied at a university: an academic discipline

discipline² v [T] **1** to train or develop, esp. in obedience and self-control: They never make any attempt to discipline their children. | a disciplined army | I've disciplined myself to do two hours of exercises every day. **2** to punish for the purpose of keeping order and control: The offenders will be severely disciplined.

disc jock·ey /ˈ·ₐˌ··/ n **1** a broadcaster who introduces records of popular music on a radio or television show, and talks in an entertaining way between records **2** someone hired to introduce and play records at a party

dis·claim /dɪsˈkleɪm/ v [T] to state that one does not have or accept; DENY: He disclaimed all responsibility for the accident. [+v-ing] She disclaims being involved in the affair.

dis·claim·er /dɪsˈkleɪmər/ n a statement which disclaims: to issue/publish a disclaimer

dis·close /dɪsˈkləʊz/ v [T] **1** to make known (esp. something that has been kept secret) publicly: The judge asked the reporters not to disclose the name of the murder victim. [+that] She disclosed that she had been in prison. **2** to show by uncovering: The curtain opened, disclosing an empty stage.

dis·clo·sure /dɪsˈkləʊʒər/ n **1** [U] the act of disclosing: the unauthorized disclosure of state secrets **2** [C] a fact, esp.

a secret fact, which is disclosed: In the course of the trial a number of sensational disclosures were made.

dis·co /ˈdɪskəʊ/ also **discotheque** fml— n -cos **1** a club where people dance to recorded popular music **2** a social occasion at which people dance to recorded popular music: the Friday night disco in the church hall —see DANCE¹ (1) (CULTURAL NOTE)

disco danc·ing /ˈ··ˌ··/ n [U] dancing to modern recorded popular music

dis·col·o·ra·tion /dɪsˌkʌləˈreɪʃən/ n **1** [U] the act of discolouring or the process of being discoloured **2** [C] a discoloured place; a mark or STAIN

dis·col·our BrE ‖ **discolor** AmE /dɪsˈkʌlər/ v [I;T] to (cause to) change colour and look worse: teeth discoloured by years of smoking

dis·com·bob·u·late /ˌdɪskəmˈbɒbjʊleɪt‖-ˈbɑː-/ v [T] AmE infml to confuse or upset: The stress of moving house is discombobulating her.

dis·com·fit /dɪsˈkʌmfɪt/ v [T] fml to make (someone) feel rather annoyed and uncomfortable; EMBARRASS slightly: She hadn't done anything, so she was rather discomfited when he thanked her for her valuable help.

dis·com·fi·ture /dɪsˈkʌmfɪtʃər/ n [U] the act of discomfiting or state of being discomfited

dis·com·fort /dɪsˈkʌmfət‖-ərt/ n **1** [U] lack of comfort; the state of being uncomfortable: The wound isn't serious, but may cause some discomfort. **2** [C] something that makes one uncomfortable: the discomforts of travel **3** [U] slight anxiety or shame: She turned red with discomfort when the teacher called out her name.

dis·com·mode /ˌdɪskəˈməʊd/ v [T] fml to cause difficulty for; INCOMMODE

dis·com·pose /ˌdɪskəmˈpəʊz/ v [T] fml to make (someone) lose control and become worried —**posure** /ˈpəʊʒər/ n [U]

dis·con·cert /ˌdɪskənˈsɜːt‖-ɜːrt/ v [T often pass.] to make (someone) feel doubt and anxiety; PERTURB: Their parents were disconcerted by their silence. | It was rather disconcerting to find that someone had been opening my letters. — —**ingly** adv : The baby is disconcertingly like Mr Jones.

dis·con·nect /ˌdɪskəˈnekt/ v [T] **1** [(from)] to undo the connection of (esp. a public supply, e.g. electricity, telephone wires, etc.): They've disconnected our phone because we didn't pay the bill. | to disconnect a waterpipe from the mains supply **2** to break the telephone connection between (two people): I think we've been disconnected, operator — will you try the number again, please? — —**ion** /ˈnekʃən/ n [C;U]

dis·con·nect·ed /ˌdɪskəˈnektɪd◂/ adj (esp. of thoughts and ideas) having no connection: a few disconnected remarks — —**ly** adv

dis·con·so·late /dɪsˈkɒnsəlɪt‖-ˈkɑːn-/ adj hopelessly sad, esp. at the loss of something: She is disconsolate about/at/over the death of her cat. — —**ly** adv

dis·con·tent¹ /ˌdɪskənˈtent/ also **dis·con·tent·ment** /-mənt/— n [U (with)] lack of satisfaction; restless unhappiness: growing discontent among the young unemployed —opposite content(ment)

discontent² v [T] to make (someone) discontented

dis·con·tent·ed /ˌdɪskənˈtentɪd◂/ adj [(with)] dissatisfied and restlessly unhappy: She has a discontented look, as if she never enjoys life. | He's discontented with his job. | discontented customers — —**ly** adv

dis·con·tin·ue /ˌdɪskənˈtɪnjuː/ v [T] rather fml to stop or end; no longer continue (esp. something that has existed or happened regularly or for a long time): The bus service has been discontinued. | discontinued software | The shop is having a sale of discontinued lines. (=products that are no longer being produced) —**uance** n [U]

dis·con·ti·nu·i·ty /ˌdɪskɒntɪˈnjuːɪti‖-kɑːntɪˈnuː-/ n **1** [U] the quality of not being continuous **2** [C (**between**)] fml a breaking or space; GAP

dis·con·tin·u·ous /ˌdɪskənˈtɪnjuəs/ adj not continuous in space or time: This is a discontinuous line - - - - . — —**ly** adv

dis·cord /ˈdɪskɔːd‖-ɔːrd/ n **1** [U] fml disagreement between people: marital discord **2** [C;U] (a) lack of agreement heard when musical notes are played which do not sound pleasant together —compare CONCORD, HARMONY

dis·cord·ant /dɪsˈkɔːdənt‖-ɔːr-/ *adj* in a state of discord: *discordant opinions/sounds* — ~ **ly** *adv*

dis·co·theque /ˈdɪskətek, ˌdɪskəˈtek/ *n fml for* DISCO

dis·count¹ /ˈdɪskaʊnt/ *n* **1** a reduction made in the cost of buying goods: *The staff at the shop get a discount of ten per cent.* | *We can give you a small discount.* | *a discount retailer/rate* —compare REBATE **2 at a discount: a** below the usual price **b** *fml* not valuable or wanted: *Honesty seems to be rather at a discount today.*

dis·count² /dɪsˈkaʊnt‖ˈdɪskaʊnt/ *v* [T] to regard (a story, piece of news, suggestion, etc.) as unimportant or unlikely to be true or valuable: *Experts have discounted the possibility of a second earthquake in the area.*

dis·coun·te·nance /dɪsˈkaʊntɪnəns/ *v* [T] *fml* to look with disfavour on (behaviour) and try to prevent it

discount rate /ˈ·· ·/ *n AmE* the rate of interest which the Federal Reserve Bank charges American banks that borrow from it —compare BASE RATE, PRIME RATE

discount store /ˈ··· ·/ also **discount house** *n* a shop where goods are sold below the price suggested by the makers

dis·cour·age /dɪsˈkʌrɪdʒ‖-ˈkɜːr-/ *v* [T] **1** to take away courage, confidence, or hope from: *If you fail your driving test the first time, don't let it discourage you/don't be discouraged.* | *a very discouraging result* **2** to prevent or try to prevent (an action), either by showing disapproval or by putting difficulties in the way: *We discourage smoking in this school.* | *The political instability of the region has discouraged investment by big companies.* **3** [(**from**)] to make (someone) unwilling to do something, esp. because of the threat of something unpleasant; DETER: *The bad weather discouraged people from attending the parade.* —opposite **encourage** —**agingly** *adv*

dis·cour·age·ment /dɪsˈkʌrɪdʒmənt‖-ˈkɜːr-/ *n* **1** [U] the action of discouraging or fact of being discouraged **2** [C] something that discourages

dis·course¹ /ˈdɪskɔːs‖-ɔːrs/ *n fml* **1** [C (**on, upon**)] a serious speech or piece of writing about a particular subject: *The priest delivered a long discourse on/upon the evils of adultery.* **2** [U] serious conversation: *They passed the hours in learned discourse.* **3** [U] connected language in speech or writing: *to analyse the structure of scientific discourse*

dis·course² /dɪsˈkɔːs‖-ɔːrs/ *v*
discourse upon/on sthg. *phr v* [T] *fml* to make a long formal speech about: *She discoursed at length upon/on the relationship between crime and environment.*

dis·cour·te·ous /dɪsˈkɜːtiəs‖-ɜːr-/ *adj fml* (of people or their behaviour) not polite; showing bad manners; rude: *It was discourteous of you not to thank him.* — ~ **ly** *adv* — ~ **ness** *n* [U]

dis·cour·te·sy /dɪsˈkɜːtəsi‖-ɜːr-/ *n* [C;U] *fml* (an act of) discourteousness: *You showed great discourtesy by not asking him to sit down.*

dis·cov·er /dɪsˈkʌvəʳ/ *v* [T] **1** to find (something that already existed but was not known about before): *Columbus discovered America in 1492.* | *Scientists have discovered a new virus.* —see INVENT (USAGE) **2** to find out (a fact, the answer to a question or problem, etc.): *We soon discovered the truth.* | *Police have discovered a bomb factory at a country house.* [+wh-] *Did you ever discover who sent you the flowers?* | *We never discovered how to open the box.* [+(that)] *Scientists have now discovered that this disease is carried by rats.* — ~ **er** *n*

dis·cov·e·ry /dɪsˈkʌvəri/ *n* **1** [U] the event of discovering: *The country became very rich following the discovery of oil.* **2** [C] a fact or thing that has been discovered: *The archaeologists have made a number of important discoveries.*

Discovery [*the*] the ship in which Captain Scott and Sir Ernest Shackleton went to the Antarctic in 1900–04. It is now kept as a MUSEUM on the river Tay in Dundee, where it was built.

disc park·ing /ˈ· ˌ··/ *n* [U] parking in a car park or on a street which is only permitted to drivers whose cars show a special disc which they have bought

dis·cred·it¹ /dɪsˈkredɪt/ *v* [T] **1** to cause people to lack faith in; stop people believing in or having respect for: *The idea that the sun goes round the Earth has long been dis-*credited. | *Much of his work has been discredited because we now know that he used false information.* | *a deliberate attempt to discredit the government* **2** to refuse to believe in: *One should discredit a good deal of what is printed in newspapers.* —see also CREDIT

discredit² *n* **1** [U] loss of belief, trust, or the good opinion of others: *Their behaviour has brought discredit on English football.* | *I know several things to* **her discredit.** (=bad things about her) **2** [S+to] someone or something that brings shame or loss of respect; a DISGRACE: *That boy is a discredit to his family.*

dis·cred·i·ta·ble /dɪsˈkredɪtəbəl/ *adj* (of behaviour) causing discredit; SHAMEFUL —**bly** *adv*

di·screet /dɪˈskriːt/ *adj* (of people or their behaviour) careful and sensible, esp. in what one chooses not to say; careful to avoid causing difficulty or discomfort, esp. in social situations: *a discreet silence* | *It wasn't very discreet of you to ring me up at the office.* —opposite **indiscreet**; compare DISCRETE — ~ **ly** *adv*

di·screp·an·cy /dɪˈskrepənsi/ *n* [C;U (**between, in**)] difference; lack of agreement or similarity: *There is some discrepancy between their two descriptions.* | *How do you explain these discrepancies in the accounts?*

di·screte /dɪˈskriːt/ *adj esp. tech or fml* separate; DISTINCT: *The picture consisted of a lot of discrete spots of colour.* —compare DISCREET — ~ **ly** *adv* — ~ **ness** *n* [U]

di·scre·tion /dɪˈskreʃən/ *n* [U] **1** the quality of being discreet: *You can trust her to keep your secret — she's* **the soul of discretion.** (=very discreet) **2** the right or ability to decide what is most suitable to be done: *I won't tell you what time to leave — you're old enough to use your own discretion.* | *The hours of the meetings will be fixed at the chairperson's discretion.* (=according to the chairperson's decision) **3 Discretion is the better part of valour** It is better to be careful than to take risks

di·scre·tion·a·ry /dɪˈskreʃənəri‖-neri/ *adj fml* not governed by fixed rules but left to someone's decision: *discretionary powers* | *a discretionary grant of money*

di·scrim·i·nate /dɪˈskrɪmɪneɪt/ *v* **1** [I (**between**);T (**from**)] to see or make a difference between things or people; DISTINGUISH: *Death does not discriminate. It comes to everyone.* | *You must learn to discriminate between facts and opinions/to discriminate facts from opinions.* **2** [I (**against, in favour of**)] *usu. derog* to unfairly treat one person or group worse or better than others: *This new law discriminates against lower-paid workers.*

di·scrim·i·nat·ing /dɪˈskrɪmɪneɪtɪŋ/ *adj apprec* showing an ability to see a difference, esp. in value, between two things, people, etc.; showing good judgment, esp. in matters of taste: *discriminating filmgoers*

di·scrim·i·na·tion /dɪˌskrɪmɪˈneɪʃən/ *n* [U] **1** [(**against, in favour of**)] *often derog* the act or system of treating different groups or people in different ways, esp. unfairly. In Britain and the US, there are laws against discrimination according to race, religion, or sex: *discrimination against women* | *racial discrimination* **2** *apprec* the quality of being discriminating: *man of discrimination* —see also POSITIVE DISCRIMINATION, REVERSE DISCRIMINATION

di·scrim·i·na·to·ry /dɪˈskrɪmɪnətəri‖-tɔːri/ *adj often derog* showing or based on discrimination: *discriminatory immigration laws*

di·scur·sive /dɪˈskɜːsɪv‖-ɜːr-/ *adj* (of a person, words, or writing) passing from one subject or idea to another in an informal way, without any clear plan: *to write in a discursive style* — ~ **ly** *adv* — ~ **ness** *n* [U]

di·scus /ˈdɪskəs/ *n* a heavy plate-shaped object, now usu. made of wood or plastic, which is thrown as far as possible as a sport

di·scuss /dɪˈskʌs/ *v* [T (**with**)] to consider (something) by talking or writing about it from several points of view: *She discussed her plans with her mother.* | *The chairman refused to discuss the rumours that the company was in difficulties.* | *The second chapter discusses different approaches to the treatment of cancer.* [+wh-] *We discussed what to do and where we should go.*

di·scus·sion /dɪˈskʌʃən/ *n* [C;U] a case of or the action of discussing: *to have/hold a discussion about our future plans* | *to settle the matter with as little discussion as possible* | *The question of school books will* **come up for**

discussion *at today's meeting.* | *We haven't made a decision about the new factory yet — the subject is still* **under discussion.** (=being discussed)

dis·dain¹ /dɪsˈdeɪn/ *n* [U] *fml* complete lack of respect; the feeling that someone or something is worthless or not important enough to deserve one's attention —compare CONTEMPT (1)

disdain² *v* [T *not in progressive forms*] *fml* **1** to regard with disdain: *They disdained our offers of help.* **2** [+*to-v*] to refuse to do something because of pride: *She disdained to answer his rude remarks.*

dis·dain·ful /dɪsˈdeɪnfəl/ *adj* [(**of, towards**)] showing disdain: *a disdainful smile* — *–ly adv*

dis·ease /dɪˈziːz/ *n* [C;U] (an) illness or unhealthy condition caused by infection, a disorder, etc., but not by an accident: *a serious disease of the liver* | *an infectious disease* | *a blood/brain disease* | *a rare plant disease* | *to contract* (=begin to have) *a disease* | *Many diseases are/Some disease is caused by bacteria.* | (fig.) *diseases of the mind/of society* —**diseased** *adj*: *a diseased bone/plant* | (fig.) *a diseased imagination* —see also HEART DISEASE, SOCIAL DISEASE

▷ USAGE Though **illness** and **disease** are often used in the same way, **illness** is really a state, or length of time, of being unwell, which may be caused by a **disease**. It is **diseases** that can be caught and passed on if they are infectious, and that are the subjects of medical study: *Several children are away from school because of illness.* | *a rare heart disease*◁

dis·em·bark /ˌdɪsɪmˈbɑːk‖-ɑːrk/ *also* **debark** *v* [I;T (**from**)] **a** (of people) to go on shore from a ship **b** to put (people or goods) on shore —opposite **embark** —see BOAT (USAGE) — ~**ation** /ˌdɪsembɑːˈkeɪʃən‖-ɑːr-/ *n* [U]

dis·em·bod·ied /ˌdɪsɪmˈbɒdɪd◂ ‖ -ˈbɑː-/ *adj* [A *no comp.*] **1** (of a soul) existing without a body: *the disembodied spirits of the dead* **2** (of a sound) coming from someone who cannot be seen: *Disembodied voices could be heard in the darkness.*

dis·em·bowel /ˌdɪsɪmˈbaʊəl/ *v* -ll- *BrE* ‖ -l- *AmE* [T] to take out the bowels of ~**ment** *n* [U]

dis·en·chant·ed /ˌdɪsɪnˈtʃɑːntɪd‖-ˈtʃænt-/ *adj* [(**with**)] (of a person) having lost one's belief in the value of something: *disenchanted with my job* —**chantment** *n* [U]

dis·en·fran·chise /ˌdɪsɪnˈfræntʃaɪz/ *v* [T] to take away the right to vote from (a person) —opposite **enfranchise** — ~**ment** /-tʃɪzmənt‖-tʃaɪz-/ *n* [U]

dis·en·gage /ˌdɪsɪnˈgeɪdʒ/ *v* [I;T (**from**)] **1 a** (esp. of parts of a machine) to come loose and separate **b** to loosen and separate: *Disengage the gears when you park the car.* **2** (of soldiers, ships, etc.) to stop fighting: *The two sides disengaged (themselves) after suffering heavy losses.* — ~**ment** *n* [U (**from**)]

dis·en·tan·gle /ˌdɪsɪnˈtæŋgəl/ *v* [T] **1** to remove knots from (rope, hair, etc.) and straighten it out **2** [(**from**)] to free from a position that is difficult to escape from; EXTRICATE: *I finally managed to disentangle myself from the barbed wire/from an unhappy relationship.* **3** [(**from**)] to separate from a confused condition, esp. to find out by doing this: *How can I disentangle the truth from all these lies?* — ~**ment** *n* [U]

dis·e·qui·lib·ri·um /ˌdɪsekwɪˈlɪbrɪəm, ˌdɪsiː-/ *n* [U] *fml* the loss or lack of EQUILIBRIUM (=balance)

dis·es·tab·lish /ˌdɪsɪˈstæblɪʃ/ *v* [T] to take away the official position from (a national church such as the Church of England) — ~**ment** *n* [U]

dis·fa·vour *BrE* ‖ **-vor** *AmE* /dɪsˈfeɪvər/ *n* [U] *fml* **1** dislike and disapproval: *The proposal is regarded with extreme disfavour by most doctors.* **2** [(**with**)] the state of being disliked or disapproved of: *John seems to be in disfavour/have fallen into disfavour with the boss.* —see also FAVOUR

dis·fig·ure /dɪsˈfɪgər‖-ˈfɪgjər/ *v* [T] to spoil the beauty of: *a street disfigured by ugly buildings* | *He was disfigured for life by the burns he received in the accident.* — ~**ment** *n* [C;U]

dis·for·est /dɪsˈfɒrɪst‖-ˈfɔː-, -ˈfɑː-/ *v* [T] to DEFOREST — ~**ation** /-ˌfɒrɪˈsteɪʃən‖-ˌfɔː-, -ˌfɑː-/ *n* [U]

dis·fran·chise /dɪsˈfræntʃaɪz/ *v* [T] to DISENFRANCHISE — ~**ment** /-tʃɪz-‖-tʃaɪz-/ *n* [U]

dis·gorge /dɪsˈgɔːdʒ‖-ɔːr-/ *v* **1** [T] to bring up from the stomach through the mouth: *The dog disgorged the bone it had swallowed.* | (fig.) *chimneys disgorging smoke* **2** [T] *infml* to give up (something stolen): *They persuaded him to disgorge the missing documents.* **3** [I+*adv/prep*;T] (of a river) to flow out; pour out (its water): *The Mississippi disgorges (its waters) into the Gulf of Mexico.*

dis·grace¹ /dɪsˈgreɪs/ *n* [S;U (**to**)] (a cause of) shame or loss of honour and respect: *His actions brought disgrace on the whole family.* | *Harry's* **in disgrace** (=regarded with disapproval) *because of the way he behaved at the party.* | *Doctors like that are a disgrace to their profession.* | *That old dress of yours is a disgrace.* | *The condition of these old buildings is a national disgrace.*

disgrace² *v* [T] **1** to bring shame and dishonour on; be a disgrace to: *You disgraced yourself last night by drinking too much.* **2** [*usu. pass.*] to cause (a public person) to be out of favour; DISCREDIT: *The corrupt official was publicly disgraced.*

dis·grace·ful /dɪsˈgreɪsfəl/ *adj* bringing or deserving disgrace: *disgraceful behaviour* — *–ly adv* : *disgracefully dirty streets*

dis·grun·tled /dɪsˈgrʌntld/ *adj* [(**at, with**)] annoyed and disappointed, esp. because of not getting what one wants

dis·guise¹ /dɪsˈgaɪz/ *v* [T] **1** [(**as**)] to change the usual appearance or character of (someone or something), in order to hide the truth: *He escaped by disguising himself as a security guard.* | *She disguised her voice when she phoned the newspaper.* **2** to hide (the real and usu. unpleasant state of things): *There's no disguising the fact/It is impossible to disguise the fact that business is bad.* | *He couldn't disguise his disappointment.*

disguise² *n* [C;U] something that is worn to hide who one really is: *The thief wore a false beard and glasses as a disguise.* | *a clever disguise* | *She crossed the border* **in disguise.** (=wearing a disguise) | (fig.) *His opinions are just imperialism* **in disguise.** —see also **a blessing in disguise** (BLESSING (4))

dis·gust¹ /dɪsˈgʌst, dɪz-/ *n* [U (**at**)] a strong and often sick feeling of dislike caused by an unpleasant sight, sound, or smell, or by behaviour that one strongly disapproves of: *The sight of rotting bodies filled him with disgust.* | *I left the room in disgust (at their conversation).*

disgust² *v* [T *not in progressive forms*] to cause a feeling of disgust in: *Your habits disgust me.* | *I'm completely disgusted at/with the way my wife has treated him.*

Disgusted, Tun·bridge Wells /·,····,·· ·/ *also* **Disgusted of Tunbridge Wells** /·,·· ·,·· ·/ *BrE humor* an amusing name for an imaginary MIDDLE-CLASS person from the town of Tunbridge Wells in S England, who writes strong letters of complaint to newspapers, esp. about things in modern behaviour or modern life which they find shocking or disgusting —see also TUNBRIDGE WELLS

dis·gust·ing /dɪsˈgʌstɪŋ, dɪz-/ *adj* **1** causing a feeling of disgust: *What a disgusting smell!* | *disgusting food/behaviour* **2** *infml* very unpleasant or bad; AWFUL: *I think it's disgusting the way the government keeps putting up taxes.* ~**ly** *adv*: *disgustingly smelly feet* | *They're disgustingly rich.*

dish¹ /dɪʃ/ *n* **1 a** a large flat often round or OVAL container, sometimes with a lid, from which food is put onto people's plates: *a serving dish* | *a vegetable dish* —compare BOWL; see also DISHES **b** *also* **dishful** /-fʊl/— the amount a dish will hold: *two dishes/dishfuls of potatoes* **2** *AmE* any plate or bowl **3** food cooked or prepared in a particular way: *an unusual dish of fish cooked in a wine sauce with chestnuts* —see also SIDE DISH **4** any object shaped like a dish, e.g. the large REFLECTOR of a radio TELESCOPE —see also SATELLITE DISH **5** *infml* a sexually attractive person (may be considered offensive to women): *She's quite a dish, isn't she?* —see also DISHY

dish² *v* [T] *old-fash infml, esp. BrE* to cause the failure of (a person or his/her hopes)
 dish sthg. ↔ **out** *phr v* [T] *infml* **1** to serve out to several people; HAND out: *He dished out the soup.* | *He likes dishing out advice.* **2** **dish it out** to punish or express disapproval of someone, esp. thoughtlessly or unjustly
 dish (sthg. ↔) **up** *phr v* [I;T] to put (the food for a meal) into dishes, ready to be eaten: *Would you help me dish up (the vegetables/the dinner).*

dis·ha·bille /ˌdɪsəˈbiːl/ n AmE for DESHABILLE

dis·har·mo·ny /dɪsˈhɑːməni‖-ɑːr-/ n [U] disagreement; lack of HARMONY —**nious** /ˌdɪshɑːˈməʊniəs◂ ‖ -ɑːr-/ adj

dish·cloth /ˈdɪʃklɒθ‖-klɔːθ/ n a cloth for washing dishes

dis·heart·en /dɪsˈhɑːtn‖-ɑːr-/ n [T] to cause to lose hope and confidence; discourage: *Don't be disheartened.* | *disheartening news* — **~ingly** adv — **~ment** n [C;U]

dish·es /ˈdɪʃɪz/ n [P] all the dishes, plates, cups, knives, forks, etc., that have been used for a meal: *Let's wash/do the dishes.*

di·shev·elled also **-eled** AmE /dɪˈʃevəld/ adj (of a person or their appearance, esp. the hair) very untidy

dish·ful /ˈdɪʃfʊl/ n a DISH[1] (2)

dis·hon·est /dɪsˈɒnɪst‖-ˈɑː-/ adj (of a person or their behaviour) not honest; tending to cheat or deceive: *a dishonest politician* | *to get money by dishonest means* | *It was very dishonest of you to lie to them about your qualifications.* — **~ly** adv

dis·hon·est·y /dɪsˈɒnɪsti‖-ˈɑː-/ n [U] being dishonest; lack of honesty: *The report was a mixture of half-truth and downright dishonesty.*

dis·hon·our¹ BrE ‖ **-or** AmE /dɪsˈɒnəʳ‖-ˈɑː-/ n [S(to);U] fml (something or someone that causes) loss of honour: *His desertion from the army was a dishonour to his family/ brought dishonour on his family.*

dishonour² BrE ‖ **-or** AmE v [T] **1** to bring dishonour to; DISGRACE **2** (of a bank) to refuse to pay out money on (a cheque) —compare BOUNCE[1] (3)

dis·hon·ou·ra·ble BrE ‖ **-orable** AmE /dɪsˈɒnərəbəl‖ -ˈɑː-/ adj (esp. of behaviour) not honourable; SHAMEFUL: *a dishonourable action* —**bly** adv

dishonourable dis·charge /ˌ·ˈ····ˈ··/ n [C;U] (a case of) being made to leave the army with dishonour because one has behaved in an unacceptable way

dish·pan /ˈdɪʃpæn/ n AmE a large bowl put into a sink in which one washes dishes: *Mom always puts on moisturizer to prevent* **dishpan hands** (=dry hands caused by washing dishes)

dish tow·el /ˈ· ˌ·/ n esp. AmE a cloth for drying dishes; TEA TOWEL —see picture at KITCHEN

dish·wash·er /ˈdɪʃˌwɒʃəʳ‖-ˌwɔː-, -ˌwɑː-/ also **dish·wash·ing ma·chine** /ˈdɪʃwɒʃɪŋ məˌʃiːn‖-wɔː-, -wɑː-/ — n **1** a machine that washes DISHES. Although they are becoming more common, it is still considered a LUXURY to own a dishwasher. —see picture at KITCHEN **2** a person who washes DISHES

dishwashing liq·uid /ˈdɪʃwɒʃɪŋ ˌlɪkwᵻd‖-wɔː-, -wɑː-/ n [U] AmE WASHING-UP LIQUID

dish·wa·ter /ˈdɪʃˌwɔːtəʳ‖-ˌwɔː-, -ˌwɑː-/ n [U] often derog water in which dirty dishes have been washed: *This tea tastes like dishwater.*

dishwater blond /ˌ···ˈ·/ n [C;U] AmE infml (a person with) hair of a dull light brown colour

dish·y /ˈdɪʃi/ adj infml (of a person) having sexual charm: *Have you met her dishy husband?* —see also DISH[1] (5)

dis·il·lu·sion /ˌdɪsᵻˈluːʒən/ v [T] to free from an ILLUSION (=a wrong idea); tell or show the (esp. unpleasant) truth to: *I hate to disillusion you, but his real reason for helping you was that he was after your money.* — **~ment, disillusion** n [U]

dis·il·lu·sioned /ˌdɪsᵻˈluːʒənd/ adj [(at, about, with)] feeling bitter and unhappy as a result of having learned the unpleasant truth about someone or something, esp. that one formerly admired or respected: *He's very disillusioned with the present government/at the government's handling of the economy.*

dis·in·cen·tive /ˌdɪsᵻnˈsentɪv/ n [(to)] a practice, system, etc., that discourages action or effort; something that fails to provide an INCENTIVE: *This tax will be a disincentive to industrial development.*

dis·in·cli·na·tion /ˌdɪsɪnkləˈneɪʃən/ n [S;U (for, towards)] (a) lack of willingness: [+to-v] *She has shown a marked disinclination to do anything to help us.*

dis·in·clined /ˌdɪsɪnˈklaɪnd/ adj [F+to-v] unwilling; RELUCTANT: *I'm disinclined to lend him any more money.* —see also INCLINED

dis·in·fect /ˌdɪsɪnˈfekt/ v [T] to clean (things and places)

with a chemical that can destroy bacteria: *to disinfect a wound/the toilet* —see also INFECT — **~ion** /ˈfekʃən/ n [U]

dis·in·fec·tant /ˌdɪsɪnˈfektənt/ n [C;U] a chemical used to destroy bacteria

dis·in·fla·tion·a·ry /ˌdɪsɪnˈfleɪʃənəri‖-neri/ adj DEFLATIONARY

dis·in·for·ma·tion /ˌdɪsɪnfəˈmeɪʃən ‖ -fər-/ n [U] false information spread intentionally to give people mistaken ideas, esp. in political situations

dis·in·gen·u·ous /ˌdɪsɪnˈdʒenjuəs/ adj (of a person or behaviour) not open or sincere; slightly dishonest and untruthful: *The car salesman was rather disingenuous, giving the impression that the car used very little fuel.* —compare INGENUOUS — **~ly** adv — **~ness** n [U]

dis·in·her·it /ˌdɪsɪnˈherᵻt/ v [T] to take away from (usu. one's own child) the legal right to receive (INHERIT) one's property after one's death — **~ance** n [U]

dis·in·te·grate /dɪsˈɪntᵻgreɪt/ v [I;T] to break up into small pieces: *The box was so old it just disintegrated when I picked it up.* | (fig.) *The project disintegrated owing to lack of financial backing.* —**gration** /dɪsˌɪntᵻˈgreɪʃən/ n [U]

dis·in·ter /ˌdɪsɪnˈtɜːʳ/ v -rr- [T often pass.] fml to dig up (esp. a body from a grave) —opposite inter — **~ment** n [C;U]

dis·in·terest·ed /dɪsˈɪntrᵻstᵻd/ adj **1** willing or able to act fairly because one is not influenced by personal advantage; OBJECTIVE: *As a disinterested observer, who do you think is right?* **2** [(in)] infml not caring; uninterested: *She seems completely disinterested (in her work).* — **~ly** adv — **~ness** n [U]

▷ USAGE Compare **disinterested** and **uninterested**: *The argument should be settled by someone who is* **disinterested**. (=who will not gain personally by deciding in favour of one side or the other) | *I'm completely* **uninterested** *in football.* (=I do not find football at all interesting.)◁

dis·in·vest·ment /ˌdɪsɪnˈvestmənt/ BrE also **divestment** AmE— n [U] the act of taking one's money out of a place or business in which one has previously invested (INVEST) it

dis·joint·ed /dɪsˈdʒɔɪntᵻd/ adj (of words or ideas) not well connected; not following in reasonable order: *She gave a rather disjointed account of the incident.* — **~ly** adv — **~ness** n [U]

dis·junc·tive /dɪsˈdʒʌŋktɪv/ adj tech (of a CONJUNCTION) expressing a choice or opposition between two ideas: *"Or" is disjunctive/is a disjunctive conjunction, but "and" is not.*

disk /dɪsk/ n AmE **1** for DISC **2** also **disc**– a flat circular piece of plastic used for storing computer information —see also FLOPPY DISK

disk drive /ˈ· ·/ n a piece of electrical equipment used for passing information to and from a DISK (2) —see picture at COMPUTER

dis·kette /dɪsˈket‖ˈdɪsket/ n a small FLOPPY DISK —see picture at COMPUTER

dis·like¹ /dɪsˈlaɪk/ v [T not in progressive forms] to consider unpleasant; not to like: *I dislike big cities.* | *Why do you dislike her so much?* [+v-ing] *I dislike having to get up early.*

dis·like² /ˌdɪsˈlaɪk◂/ n [C;U (of, for)] (a) feeling of disliking: *to have a dislike of/for cats* | *She took an immediate dislike to him.* (=began to dislike him at once) | *We all have our* **likes and dislikes**. (=things we like and things we dislike)

dis·lo·cate /ˈdɪsləkeɪt‖-ləʊ-/ v [T] **1** to put (a bone) out of its proper place: *I dislocated my shoulder when I was playing tennis.* | *a dislocated shoulder* **2** to put (plans, business, machinery, etc.) into disorder; DISRUPT

dis·lo·ca·tion /ˌdɪsləˈkeɪʃən‖-ləʊ-/ n [C;U] (a case of) being dislocated: *people suffering from dislocations and broken bones* | *The storm caused considerable dislocation of air traffic.*

dis·lodge /dɪsˈlɒdʒ‖-ˈlɑːdʒ/ v [T (from)] to force or knock out of a position: *The coughing dislodged the fishbone from his throat.* —see also LODGE — **~ment** n [U]

dis·loy·al /dɪsˈlɔɪəl/ adj [(to)] not loyal; UNFAITHFUL: *disloyal behaviour* | *disloyal to the king* — **~ly** adv — **~ty** n [C;U (to)]

dis·mal /ˈdɪzməl/ adj expressing or causing sadness; lacking hope or happiness; GLOOMY: a dismal song | dismal weather | a dismal failure | The future looks pretty dismal. – ~ly adv

dis·man·tle /dɪsˈmæntl/ v 1 [I;T] a to take (a machine or article) apart b to be able to be taken to pieces: This engine dismantles easily. 2 [T] to bring to an end (a system, arrangement, etc.), esp. by gradual stages: The new government set about dismantling their predecessors' legislation. – ~ment n [U]

dis·mast /dɪsˈmɑːst‖-ˈmæst/ v [T] to take away the MASTS (=poles which carry the sails) from (a ship)

dis·may[1] /dɪsˈmeɪ/ v [T] to fill with dismay: We were dismayed by|at the cost.

dismay[2] n [U] a strong feeling of fear, anxiety, and hopelessness: They listened in|with dismay to the news. | They were filled with dismay by the outcome of the trial. | **To their dismay**, the door was locked.

dis·mem·ber /dɪsˈmembər/ v [T] to cut or tear (a body) apart, limb from limb: The young man's dismembered body was found in a box. – ~ment n [U]

dis·miss /dɪsˈmɪs/ v [T] 1 [(from)] to refuse to consider (a subject or idea) seriously: He just laughed, and dismissed the idea as impossible. 2 [(from)] fml to remove from a job; SACK[2]: If you're late again you'll be dismissed (from your job). 3 [(from)] to send away or allow to go: The teacher dismissed the class early. 4 (of a judge) to stop (a court case) before a result is reached: The judge dismissed all the charges against Smith, saying "Case dismissed!" 5 (in cricket) to end the INNINGS of (a player or team)

dis·miss·al /dɪsˈmɪsəl/ n [C;U] an act of dismissing or case of being dismissed: She's suing the company for unfair dismissal.

dis·miss·ive /dɪsˈmɪsɪv/ adj [(of)] considering a person, idea, etc. to be not worthy of attention or respect: He might have been less dismissive of their talents if he could have seen their latest achievements.

dis·mount /dɪsˈmaʊnt/ v 1 [I (from)] to get off a horse, bicycle, etc. –see BICYCLE (USAGE) 2 [T] to take down (esp. a gun) from its base or support

Dis·ney /ˈdɪzni/, **Walt** /wɔːlt/ (1901–66) an American film producer, esp. of ANIMATED CARTOONs, such as Donald Duck, Mickey Mouse, and Bambi. He also produced nature documentaries (DOCUMENTARY) and adventure films, all of which are very popular with children: Disney films

Dis·ney·land /ˈdɪznilænd/ tdmk a very large amusement park which opened in 1955 in California in the US. The rides and shows are based on Disney characters and a whole imaginary world has been made: Fruit bats crossed the circle of the moon, the final touch of Disneyland magic. | The SS constructed Disneyland castles as headquarters for the German leaders. –see also EURODISNEY and see colour map on page 1374–5

Disney World /ˌ· ·/ officially called the **Walt Disney World** tdmk a very large amusement park opened in 1971 in Florida, featuring many of the characters from Disney films. Both Disneyland and Disney World are popular holiday places for British tourists, esp. those with children. –see also EURODISNEY

dis·o·be·di·ent /ˌdɪsəˈbiːdiənt, ˌdɪsəʊ-/ adj [(to)] (esp. of a child) failing or refusing to obey: a disobedient child | He was disobedient to his mother. | It was very disobedient of you to stay out so late. –see also CIVIL DISOBEDIENCE – ~ly adv –ence n [U (to)]

dis·o·bey /ˌdɪsəˈbeɪ, ˌdɪsəʊ-/ v [I;T] to fail to obey: Don't dare to disobey! | to disobey the rules | He disobeyed his mother and went to the party.

dis·o·blige /ˌdɪsəˈblaɪdʒ/ v [T] fml to go against the wishes of; cause inconvenience to: It was very disobliging of her to refuse to help. –**bligingly** adv

dis·or·der[1] /dɪsˈɔːdər‖-ˈɔːr-/ n 1 [U] lack of order; confusion; DISARRAY: The house was in a state of complete disorder because of the young children. 2 [C;U] (a) violent public expression of political dissatisfaction: public disorder because of the tax increases 3 [C;U] (a) failure of part of the body (or mind) to work properly: suffering from (a) stomach disorder | a rare nervous disorder

disorder[2] v [T] to put into DISORDER[1] (1,3): a disordered (=ill) mind|brain

dis·or·der·ly /dɪsˈɔːdəli‖-ˈɔːrdər-/ adj 1 untidy; completely lacking organization or order: a disorderly room 2 causing trouble, noise, or violence in public; UNRULY: disorderly conduct|youths | They were arrested for being **drunk and disorderly**. –**liness** n [U]

disorderly house /·ˌ··· ˈ·/ n law, esp. BrE a place where women can be hired for sexual pleasure; BROTHEL

dis·or·gan·ized also **-ised** BrE /dɪsˈɔːgənaɪzd‖-ˈɔːr-/ adj (esp. of arrangements, systems, etc.) in a state of disorder; lacking organization: The company's accounts are rather disorganized. | I've been a bit disorganized about answering my letters. –**ization** /dɪsˌɔːgənaɪˈzeɪʃən‖-ˌɔːrgənə-/ n [U]

dis·o·ri·en·tate /dɪsˈɔːriənteɪt/ BrE ‖ **dis·o·ri·ent** /-riənt/ v [T usu. pass.] to cause (someone) to lose the sense of direction: I'm completely disorientated – which direction are we heading in? | (fig.) His mother's death really disorientated him. –**tation** /dɪsˌɔːriənˈteɪʃən/ n [U]

dis·own /dɪsˈəʊn/ v [T not in progressive forms] to refuse to accept as one's own; say that one has no connection with: The organization disowned him when he was arrested for fraud.

dis·par·age /dɪˈspærɪdʒ/ v [T] to speak about without respect; make (someone or something) sound of little value or importance: He tends to disparage the efforts of conservationists. | disparaging remarks –**agingly** adv – ~ment n [C;U]

dis·pa·rate /ˈdɪspərət/ adj fml (of two or more things) completely different; impossible to compare in their qualities: Chalk and cheese are disparate substances. – ~ly adv

dis·par·i·ty /dɪˈspærəti/ n [C;U (**between, in, of**)] fml (an example of) being completely different or unequal: There is (a) considerable disparity in the rates of pay for men and women. –see also PARITY

dis·pas·sion·ate /dɪsˈpæʃənət/ adj usu. apprec (of a person or behaviour) calm and fair and not easily influenced by personal feelings –see also PASSIONATE – ~ly adv – ~ness n [U]

di·spatch[1], **despatch** /dɪˈspætʃ/ v [T] 1 [(to)] to send to a place or for a particular purpose: to dispatch letters|invitations | A messenger was dispatched to take the news to the soldiers at the front. 2 infml to finish (esp. food) quickly: We soon dispatched the chocolate cake. 3 euph to kill, usu. officially and according to plan

dispatch[2], **despatch** n 1 [C] a message carried by a government official, or sent to a newspaper by one of its writers: to send|carry a dispatch from Rome to London 2 [U] fml speed and effectiveness: She did the job with great dispatch. 3 [U] the act of dispatching –see also DISPATCHES

dispatch box /·ˈ··/ n 1 [C] a box for official papers 2 [the] a box on a central table in the British House of Commons, next to which the most important members of parliament stand to make speeches

di·spatch·es, despatches /dɪˈspætʃɪz/ n [P] official reports sent to a government to describe a battle: He was **mentioned in dispatches** for his bravery.

dispatch rid·er /·ˈ·ˌ··/ n a messenger, on horseback or motorcycle, who carries dispatches. Many people think of dispatch riders in connection with war and passing important information to other army groups at great speed and often at great personal danger.

di·spel /dɪˈspel/ v -ll- [T] to drive away (as if) by scattering: The sun soon dispelled the mist. | Her reassuring words dispelled our doubts|fears.

di·spen·sa·ble /dɪˈspensəbəl/ adj not necessary; that can be dispensed with –opposite **indispensable**

di·spen·sa·ry /dɪˈspensəri/ n a place where medicines are dispensed and where medical attention is given, esp. in a hospital or school –compare PHARMACY (1)

dis·pen·sa·tion /ˌdɪspenˈseɪʃən, -pen-/ n 1 [C;U] (a case of) permission to disobey a general rule or break a promise, often in a religious context. A dispensation from the Church allows people to be free from a law or promise, such as marriage: Their marriage was annulled by a special dispensation from the Church. 2 [U] fml the act of dispensing: the dispensation of justice 3 [C] fml a particular religious system, esp. considered as controlling human affairs during a period: during the Christian dispensation

di·spense /dɪ'spens/ v [T] **1** [(to)] to give out to a number of people: *A judge dispenses justice.* | *This machine dispenses coffee.* | *to dispense favours* **2** to mix and give out (esp. medicines available only on PRESCRIPTION from a doctor)
dispense with sbdy./sthg. *phr v* [T] **1** to do without or manage to exist without: *We shall have to dispense with the car. We can't afford it.* **2** to make unnecessary: *The new computer system will dispense with the need for keeping files.*

di·spens·er /dɪ'spensə^r/ n **1** a person who dispenses medicines **2** a machine or container from which something can be obtained, e.g. by pushing or by pressing a handle: *a soap dispenser in a public toilet* | *a drinks dispenser* | *a cash dispenser outside a bank*

dispensing chem·ist /·,·· '··/ n (in Britain) a person who both sells medicines and is trained to dispense them

di·sper·sal /dɪ'spɜːsəl‖-ɜːr-/ n [U] the act of dispersing or the fact of being dispersed: *After the dispersal of the crowd, five people were found to be hurt.*

di·sperse /dɪ'spɜːs‖-ɜːrs/ v **1** [I;T] to (cause to) scatter or spread in different directions, so as to be no longer present: *After school the children dispersed to their homes.* | *The wind dispersed the clouds.* | *Police used tear gas to disperse the crowd.* **2** [T] to place at different points: *Groups of police were dispersed all along the street where the Queen was to pass.*

di·sper·sion /dɪ'spɜːʃən‖dɪ'spɜːrʒən/ n [U] *tech* dispersal: *the dispersion of light by a prism*

Dispersion n [the] the DIASPORA

di·spir·ited /dɪ'spɪrᵻtᵻd/ adj lit discouraged; without hope; in low spirits − −ly adv

dis·place /dɪs'pleɪs/ v [T] **1** to force out of the usual place: *He displaced a bone in his knee while playing football.* | *The indigenous population was soon displaced by the settlers.* **2** to take the place of (as if) by pushing out; SUPPLANT

displaced per·son /·,· '··/ n a person who has been forced to leave his or her country because of war or PERSECUTION; a REFUGEE

dis·place·ment /dɪs'pleɪsmənt/ n **1** [U] the act of displacing or process of being displaced **2** [S] *tech* the weight of water pushed aside by a ship or floating object

displacement ac·tiv·i·ty /·'··· ·,···/ n [C;U] an activity which replaces someone's usual or expected behaviour, e.g. when the expected behaviour is prevented. The person may not realize the connection between the two: *Obsessively cleaning the house was probably a displacement activity for telling her husband what she really felt.*

di·splay¹ /dɪ'spleɪ/ v [T] **1** to arrange or spread out for public view: *to display fruit in a shop window* **2** *rather fml* to show (esp. a feeling or quality): *She displayed great self-control when they told her the news.*

display² n [C;U] an act of displaying something, or something that is displayed: *a fireworks display* | *The goods were on display in the shop window.* | *a fine display of fruit* | *an impressive display of skill* | *a sudden display of temper*

dis·please /dɪs'pliːz/ v [T] *fml* to cause displeasure to; annoy: *The old lady was most displeased with/by/at the children's noisy behaviour.*

dis·plea·sure /dɪs'pleʒə^r/ n [U] *fml* angry dislike, annoyance, or disapproval: *I incurred her displeasure by refusing the invitation.*

dis·port /dɪ'spɔːt‖-ɔːrt/ v [I;T] *fml* to amuse (oneself) actively

dis·po·sa·ble /dɪ'spəʊzəbəl/ adj intended to be used once or for a short time and then thrown away: *disposable paper cups* | *a disposable cigarette lighter*

disposable in·come /·,··· '··/ n [U] the amount of money left from someone's income when they have paid their tax, their bills, and paid for necessary things like food and housing

dis·pos·al /dɪ'spəʊzəl/ n [U] **1** the act of getting rid of something; removal: *waste disposal* | *a team of bomb disposal experts* **2** *fml* the way that people or things are arranged: *the disposal of troops along the frontier* **3** at someone's disposal able to be used freely by someone: *During their visit I put my car at their disposal.* | *We will*
use all the means at our disposal to solve this dispute. **4** *AmE for* GARBAGE DISPOSAL

dis·pose /dɪ'spəʊz/ v [T+obj+adv/prep] *fml* to put in place; arrange: *to dispose one's books on the shelves*
dispose of sthg. *phr v* [T] to get rid of or destroy: *The murderer was unable to dispose of the body.* | *I can dispose of your argument quite easily.*
dispose sbdy. **to/towards** sthg. *phr v* [T] *fml* to give a feeling of the stated type towards: *The defendant's youth disposed the judge to leniency.* **3** [F + to] having a feeling of the stated type towards: *He was favourably/unfavourably disposed to the proposal.*

dis·posed /dɪ'spəʊzd/ adj fml **1** [F+to-v] willing: *After the way she treated me, I didn't feel disposed to help her.* −see also INDISPOSED, WELL-DISPOSED **2** [F+to] having a tendency: *She is disposed to sudden bouts of depression.*

dis·po·si·tion /,dɪspə'zɪʃən/ n **1** [C] a particular tendency of character, behaviour, etc.; nature; TEMPERAMENT: *He has a cheerful disposition.* **2** [C;U] *fml* (an) arrangement: *the disposition of the troops on the battlefield* **3** [C;U] *law* an act of formally giving property to someone

dis·pos·sess /,dɪspə'zes/ v [T (of)] *fml* to take property away from: *The rebel leaders were dispossessed of all their property.* | *fighting for the rights of the dispossessed* (=people who have lost all their property or possessions) − −ion /·'zeʃən/ n [U]

Dis·prin /'dɪsprᵻn/ n [C;U] *tdmk* a type of PAINKILLER made by Reckitt and Colman Limited; Disprin is not a very strong painkiller and it is used by people in their homes. Disprin PILLS are usu. dissolved (DISSOLVE) in water and then drunk.

dis·proof /dɪs'pruːf/ n [U (of)] *fml* the act of disproving or something (such as a fact) that disproves

dis·pro·por·tion /,dɪsprə'pɔːʃən‖-ɔːr-/ n [S;U (between)] a lack of PROPORTION; lack of proper relation between the parts: *a disproportion between their wealth and our poverty*

dis·pro·por·tion·ate /,dɪsprə'pɔːʃənᵻt‖-ɔːr-/ adj [(to)] not in proper PROPORTION; too much or too little in relation to something else: *We spend a disproportionate amount of our income on rent.* | *The reaction of the police was disproportionate to the threat that the rioters presented.* − −ly adv

dis·prove /dɪs'pruːv/ v [T] to prove (something) to be false

di·spu·ta·ble /dɪ'spjuːtəbəl, 'dɪspjᵻ-/ adj not necessarily true; able to be questioned; DEBATABLE −opposite **indisputable** −−bly adv

dis·pu·ta·tion /,dɪspjᵻ'teɪʃən/ n old use a speech or argument, esp. a formal one made according to certain rules of reasoning

dis·pu·ta·tious /,dɪspjᵻ'teɪʃəs/ adj fml tending to argue; ARGUMENTATIVE − −ly adv

di·spute¹ /dɪ'spjuːt/ v **1** [I;T (about, over, with)] to argue (about something), esp. angrily and for a long period: *The two governments disputed (over) the ownership of the territory.* | *The question was hotly disputed in the Senate.* **2** [T] to disagree about or question the truth or correctness of: *I dispute the minister's figures − the true cost of the project is much higher.* | *"There are hundreds of cases." "I would dispute that."* **3** [T] to struggle in order to gain or keep, esp. in war: *The defending army disputed every inch of ground.*

dispute² /dɪ'spjuːt, 'dɪspjuːt/ n [C;U (about, with, over)] (an) argument or quarrel, esp. an official one between one group or organization and another: *a pay dispute* | *a prolonged legal dispute over the ownership of the land* | *The miners were in dispute with their employers over pay.* | *She is beyond all dispute/without dispute* (=undoubtedly) *the best chemist in the firm.* | *This question is still in/under dispute.* (=being argued about) | *They claim to provide the best service in the business, but I think that's open to dispute.* (=can be questioned)

disputed ter·ri·to·ry /·,·· '····/ n [C;U] (an area of) land claimed by two or more states: *the disputed territory of Nagorno Karabakh*

dis·qual·i·fi·ca·tion /dɪs,kwɒlᵻfᵻ'keɪʃən‖-,kwɑː-/ n **1** [U] the act of disqualifying or process of being disqualified: *Any attempt at cheating will result in immediate disqualification.* **2** [C (for)] something that disqualifies

dis·qual·i·fy /dɪs'kwɒlᵻfaɪ‖-'kwɑː-/ v [T (for, from)] to make or declare unfit, unsuitable, or unable to do something: *His youth/His criminal record disqualified him for the job/from getting the job.* | *Three of the athletes were disqualified for taking drugs.* | *to be disqualified from driving/from holding public office*

dis·qui·et /dɪs'kwaɪət/ v [T] *fml* to make anxious: *a disquieting remark*

disquiet² n [U] anxiety and dissatisfaction

dis·qui·si·tion /ˌdɪskwɪ'zɪʃən/ n [(on, about)] *fml* a long (perhaps too long) speech or written report

Dis·rae·li /dɪz'reɪli/, **Ben·ja·min** /'bendʒəmᵻn/ (1804–81) an English politician and writer of Jewish origin. He was PRIME MINISTER in 1868 and from 1874 to 1880.

dis·re·gard¹ /ˌdɪsrɪ'gɑːd‖-ɑːrd/ v [T] to pay no attention to; treat as unimportant or unworthy of notice: *She completely disregarded all our objections.*

disregard² n [U (for, of)] lack of proper attention to or respect for someone or something; NEGLECT: *The government has shown a total disregard for the needs of the poor.* | *reckless disregard of passenger safety*

dis·re·pair /ˌdɪsrɪ'peəʳ/ n [U] the state of needing repair; bad condition: *The old houses had* **fallen into disrepair.**

dis·re·pu·ta·ble /dɪs'repjᵿtəbəl/ *adj* having a bad character; having or deserving a bad REPUTATION: *disreputable people/behaviour* | *a disreputable gambling club* —opposite **reputable** —**bly** *adv* — ~**ness** n [U]

dis·re·pute /ˌdɪsrɪ'pjuːt/ n [U] loss or lack of people's good opinion; bad REPUTE: *The hotel* **fell into disrepute** *after the shooting incident.* | *This pointless prosecution has* **brought** *the law* **into disrepute.**

dis·re·spect /ˌdɪsrɪ'spekt/ n [U] lack of respect or politeness — ~**ful** *adj* — ~**fully** *adv*

dis·robe /dɪs'rəʊb/ v [I] *fml* to take off (esp. ceremonial outer) clothing: *After the trial, the judge disrobed and left the court.*

dis·rupt /dɪs'rʌpt/ v [T] to bring or throw into disorder: *An accident has disrupted railway services into and out of the city.* | *A crowd of protesters disrupted the meeting.* — ~**ion** /'rʌpʃən/ n [C;U] : *The strike has caused widespread disruption of transport services.* — ~**ive** /'rʌptɪv/ *adj* : *He has a disruptive influence on the other children.* — ~**ively** *adv*

dis·sat·is·fac·tion /dɪˌsætᵻs'fækʃən, ˌdɪsˌsæ-/ n [U (at, with)] lack of satisfaction; displeasure: *her dissatisfaction at his late arrival*

dis·sat·is·fied /dɪˈsætᵻsfaɪd, ˌdɪsˈsæ-/ *adj* [(with)] feeling or showing dissatisfaction; not satisfied: *dissatisfied customers* | *He seemed dissatisfied with my explanation.*

dis·sat·is·fy /dɪ'sætᵻsfaɪ, ˌdɪs'sæ-/ v [T] to fail to satisfy; displease

dis·sect /dɪ'sekt, daɪ-/ v [T] **1** to cut up (esp. the body of a plant or animal) so as to study the shape and relationship of the parts, as medical students do: *to dissect a frog* **2** to study very carefully, esp. so as to find the faults: *The lawyers dissected his claim to the title.*

dis·sec·tion /dɪ'sekʃən, daɪ-/ n **1** [C;U] (an example of) the act of dissecting or process of being dissected **2** [C] a part of an animal or plant that has been dissected

dis·sem·ble /dɪ'sembəl/ v [I;T] *fml* to hide (one's true feelings, intentions, etc.) — ~**bler** n

dis·sem·i·nate /dɪ'semᵻneɪt/ v [T] *fml* to spread (news, ideas, etc.) widely —**nation** /dɪˌsemᵻ'neɪʃən/ n [U] : *the dissemination of information*

dis·sen·sion /dɪ'senʃən/ n [C;U (among, between)] (a) disagreement, esp. leading to argument: *His words caused a great deal of dissension among his followers.*

dis·sent¹ /dɪ'sent/ n **1** [U] refusal to agree, esp. with an opinion that is held by most people; difference of opinion: *The proposal was approved with little dissent.* | *I must express my strong dissent.* —opposite **assent** —see also CONSENT **2** [C] *esp. AmE* a judge's opinion, especially that of a SUPREME COURT judge, which does not agree with that of most of the other judges of a law case **3** [U] *now rare* religious separation from the Church of England

dis·sent² v [I (from)] to express disagreement, esp. with an opinion that is held by most people: *Only one member of the committee dissented from the final report.* | *The motion was passed with only one or two* **dissenting voices.**

dis·sent·er /dɪ'sentəʳ/ n **1** a person who dissents **2** (*often*

cap.) a member of a church that has become separate from the Church of England (from Protestant dissenters in the 16th century who refused to accept the DOCTRINE of the established church); NONCONFORMIST

dis·ser·ta·tion /ˌdɪsə'teɪʃən‖ˌdɪsər-/ n [(on)] a long usu. written treatment of a subject, esp. one written for a higher university degree —compare THESIS

dis·ser·vice /dɪ'sɜːvᵻs, ˌdɪs'sɜː-‖-'ɜːr-/ n [S;U (to)] harm or a harmful action: *You have done a serious disservice to your country by selling military secrets to our enemies.*

dis·si·dent /'dɪsᵻdənt/ n a person who openly and often strongly disagrees with an opinion, a group, or a government. Typically, dissidents are people who oppose cruel and unjust political systems and who are persecuted (PERSECUTE) for their opinions: *political dissidents* —**dissident** *adj* —**dence** n [U]

dis·sim·i·lar /dɪ'sɪmᵻləʳ, dɪs'sɪ-/ *adj* [(to)] (*often in negatives*) unlike; not similar: *The two writers are not dissimilar in style.* — ~**ly** *adv* — ~**ity** /dɪˌsɪmᵻ'lærᵻti, dɪsˌsɪ-/ n [C;U]

dis·sim·u·late /dɪ'sɪmjᵿleɪt/ v [I;T] *fml* to hide (one's true feelings); DISSEMBLE —**lation** /dɪˌsɪmjᵿ'leɪʃən/ n [C;U]

dis·si·pate /'dɪsᵻpeɪt/ v **1** [I;T] to (cause to) disappear or scatter: *The crowd soon dissipated when the police arrived.* **2** [T] to spend, waste, or use up foolishly; SQUANDER: *He dissipated his large fortune in a few years of heavy spending.*

dis·si·pat·ed /'dɪsᵻpeɪtᵻd/ *adj* (typical of a person) who wastes his/her life in search of foolish or dangerous pleasure: *dissipated habits/young men*

dis·si·pa·tion /ˌdɪsᵻ'peɪʃən/ n [U] **1** the act of causing something to be scattered or wasted: *the dissipation of our valuable oil reserves* **2** the continual search for foolish or dangerous pleasure: *a life of dissipation*

dis·so·ci·ate /dɪ'səʊʃieɪt, -sieɪt/ *also* **disassociate**— v [T (from)] to regard as, or cause to be, separate or unconnected: *Can the private and public lives of a politician ever be dissociated?* | *You can't dissociate yourself from the actions of your colleagues in the union.* —**ation** /dɪˌsəʊʃi'eɪʃən, -si'eɪʃən/ n [U]

dis·so·lute /'dɪsəluːt/ *adj* (typical of a person) who leads a bad or immoral life — ~**ly** *adv* — ~**ness** n [U]

dis·so·lu·tion /ˌdɪsə'luːʃən/ n **1** [U] the ending or breaking up of an association, group, marriage, etc.: *the dissolution of Parliament before a general election* **2** [U] decay, esp. death: *the dissolution of the Roman Empire* **3** [C] *AmE law* a DIVORCE

Dissolution of the Mon·as·ter·ies /···ˌ···ˈ···‖···ˌ···ˈ···ˌ/ [*the*] the destruction of the monasteries (MONASTERY) by soldiers of the English King Henry VIII in 1539 after he became Head of the English Church and broke with the Church of Rome

dis·solve /dɪ'zɒlv‖dɪ'zɑːlv/ v **1** [I;T] to make or become liquid by putting into liquid: *Sugar dissolves in water.* | *Dissolve the tablets in warm water.* **2** [I;T] **a** to cause (an association, group, etc.) to end or break up: *The military government dissolved the country's parliament and suspended all political activity.* **b** (of an association, group, etc.) to end or break up **3** [I+in/into] to lose one's self-control under the influence of strong feeling: *to dissolve in tears/laughter* **4** [I] to disappear; FADE *away*: *Opposition to the idea gradually dissolved.* | *The vision dissolved before her eyes.* —see also DISSOLUTION

dis·so·nance /'dɪsənəns/ n **1** [C;U] (a) combination of musical notes which do not sound pleasant when heard together; DISCORD (2) **2** [S;U] a lack of agreement in beliefs, or between beliefs and actions —**nant** *adj* : *dissonant opinions*

dis·suade /dɪ'sweɪd/ v [T (from)] to advise (someone) against doing something; persuade not to: *I tried to dissuade her (from getting married).* —see also PERSUADE —**suasion** /dɪ'sweɪʒən/ n [U]

dis·taff /'dɪstɑːf‖'dɪstæf/ n **1** the stick from which the thread is pulled in hand spinning **2 on the distaff side** on the woman's side of the family

dis·tance¹ /'dɪstəns/ n **1** [C;U (to, from, between)] (the amount of) separation in space or time; the amount of space or time between two points or events: *What is the distance between London and Glasgow/from London to Glasgow?* | *The school is some distance* (=quite far) *away.* |

My office is within (easy) walking distance of the station. | *The dog looked dangerous, so I decided to* **keep my distance.** (=stay far enough away from it) | *I can hardly remember him at this distance of in time.* | *These planes can cover long distances in a very short time.* | *My office is* **within spitting distance of** (=very near) *Westminster.* —see also LONG DISTANCE, MIDDLE DISTANCE **2** [(the) S] a distant point or place: *You can see the ancient ruins in the distance.* | *It looks quite nice from a distance, but when you get close you can see that it's pretty awful.* | *The pyramids are visible at a distance of several kilometres.* **3** [C;U] social separation or coldness in personal relations: *There has been a great distance between us since our quarrel.* | *My father always* **kept me at a distance.** (=refused to become too friendly with me)

distance² *v* [T (**from**)] to separate (esp. oneself), esp. in the mind or feelings: *to distance oneself from the actions of one's government*

distance learn·ing /'·· ,··/ *n* [U] *BrE* the study of a subject by students who do not attend classes but use, for example, television, computers, and local teachers —see also OPEN COLLEGE, OPEN UNIVERSITY

dis·tant /'dɪstənt/ *adj* **1** [(from)] separate in space or time; far off: *distant lands* | *the distant sound of a bell* | *in the* **dim and distant past** | *We hope to go there in the* **not-too-distant future.** (= fairly soon but not very soon) [after *n*] *30 miles distant (from the village)* **2** not very closely related: *a distant connection between two ideas* | *The two boys are distant relations.* **3** showing lack of friendliness; RESERVED: *a distant manner*

dis·tant·ly /'dɪstəntli/ *adv* **1** not closely: *Those two people ideas are distantly related.* **2** in a manner that shows inattention, social separation, or lack of friendliness: *She looked at me distantly.*

dis·taste /dɪs'teɪst/ *n* [S;U (**for**)] a not very strong feeling of dislike, esp. of something unpleasant, unattractive, or offensive: *She looked at his shabby clothes with distaste.* | *a distaste for town life*

dis·taste·ful /dɪs'teɪstfəl/ *adj* [(to)] unpleasant; disagreeable; causing distaste: *a rather distasteful duty* | *a distasteful joke* —see TASTELESS (USAGE) — ~ **ly** *adv* — ~ **ness** *n* [U]

dis·tem·per¹ /dɪ'stempər/ *n* [U] *esp. BrE* paint used in the past for walls and other surfaces and which can be made thinner by mixing with water —**distemper** *v* [T] : *to distemper the walls*

distemper² *n* [U] an infectious disease of animals, esp. dogs, causing fever, disordered breathing, and general weakness

dis·tem·pered /dɪ'stempəd‖-ərd/ *adj lit or old use* mad: *a distempered mind*

dis·tend /dɪ'stend/ *v* [I;T] *fml* to (cause to) swell because of pressure from inside: *His stomach was distended because of lack of food.* —**tension** /dɪ'stenʃən/ *n* [U]

dis·til usu. **-till** *AmE* /dɪ'stɪl/ *v* **-ll-** [T] **1 a** to make (a liquid) into gas and then make the gas into liquid: *Water can be made pure by distilling it.* | *distilled water* **b** to make (alcoholic drinks) by this method: *Brandy is distilled from wine.* **2** to take and separate the most important parts of (a book, a subject, etc.): *The televised interview was distilled from 16 hours of film.* — ~ **lation** /ˌdɪstɪ'leɪʃən/ *n* [C;U]

dis·til·ler /dɪ'stɪlər/ *n* a person or company that distils, esp. one that produces strong alcoholic drink

dis·til·le·ry /dɪ'stɪləri/ *n* a factory or business firm where alcoholic drinks are produced by distilling: *a whisky distillery*

dis·tinct /dɪ'stɪŋkt/ *adj* **1** [(from)] clearly different or separate: *Those two ideas are quite distinct (from each other).* | *The party split into two distinct groups.* | *The rule only applies to nationals of the country,* **as distinct from** *foreign visitors.* **2** clearly seen, heard, understood, etc.; noticeable: *a distinct smell of burning* | *There's a distinct possibility that she'll be appointed as a director.* — ~ **ly** *adv* : *I distinctly* (=clearly) *remember telling you to come.* — ~ **ness** *n* [U]

▷ USAGE Anything clearly noticed is **distinct:** *There's a* **distinct** *smell of beer in this room.* A thing or quality that is clearly different from others of its kind is **distinctive,** or **distinct** from: *Beer has a very* **distinc-**

tive *smell. It's quite* **distinct** *from the smell of wine.*◁

dis·tinc·tion /dɪ'stɪŋkʃən/ *n* **1** [C;U (**between**)] the fact of being distinct; clear difference: *I can't see any distinction between these two cases.* | *It's important to* **draw a distinction** *between the policies of the leaders and the views of their supporters.* | *a rather* **fine distinction** (=one that is difficult to notice) **2** [S;U] the quality of being unusually good; excellence: *a writer of real distinction* **3** [C] a special mark of honour, fame, or excellence: *These are the highest distinctions that have ever been given by our government.* | *She got a distinction in her chemistry exam.* | *This country* **enjoys the dubious distinction** *of having the highest rate of inflation in the world.*

dis·tinc·tive /dɪ'stɪŋktɪv/ *adj* clearly marking a person or thing as different from others: *She has a very distinctive way of walking.* | *a distinctive flavour* —see DISTINCT (USAGE) — ~ **ly** *adv* — ~ **ness** *n* [U]

dis·tin·guish /dɪ'stɪŋgwɪʃ/ *v* **1** [T *not in progressive forms*] to see, hear, or notice as being separate or distinct; recognize clearly: *I can distinguish them by their uniforms.* | *Can you distinguish the different buildings at such a distance?* **2** [I (**between**);T (**from**) *not in progressive forms*] to recognize differences (between): *It's important to distinguish between compound interest and simple interest.* | *Small children can't distinguish right from wrong.* **3** [T *not in progressive forms*] *fml* to make different: *Elephants are distinguished by their long trunks.* **4 distinguish oneself** to behave or perform noticeably well: *She distinguished herself in the debate.*

dis·tin·guish·a·ble /dɪ'stɪŋgwɪʃəbəl/ *adj* that can be clearly or easily distinguished: *A black object is not easily distinguishable on a dark night.* | *Those two objects ideas are not easily distinguishable (from each other).* —opposite **indistinguishable**

dis·tin·guished /dɪ'stɪŋgwɪʃt/ *adj* [(for)] having excellent quality or great fame and respect: *a distinguished performance politician* | *distinguished for his scientific achievements* | *a distinguished-looking old man* —opposite **undistinguished** —see FAMOUS (USAGE)

dis·tort /dɪ'stɔːt‖-ɔːrt/ *v* [T] **1** to give a false or dishonest account of; twist out of the true meaning: *Stop distorting what I've said.* | *The newspapers gave a distorted account of what had happened.* **2** to twist out of a natural, usual, or original shape or condition: *a face distorted by with anger* | *a radio that distorts sound* — ~ **ion** /dɪ'stɔːʃən‖-ɔːr-/ *n* [C;U]

dis·tract /dɪ'strækt/ *v* [T (**from**)] to take (a person's attention) off something, esp. for a short time: *She was distracted (from her work) by the noise outside.* | *a distracting influence* | *The celebrations distracted public attention from the government's problems.*

dis·tract·ed /dɪ'stræktɪd/ *adj* [(with)] very anxious and unable to think clearly because one is troubled about many things: *a distracted look* | *distracted with worry about her daughter* — ~ **ly** *adv*

dis·trac·tion /dɪ'strækʃən/ *n* **1** [C] something or someone that distracts, esp. an amusement: *There are too many distractions here to work properly.* **2** [U] an anxious confused state of mind: *The child's continual crying* **drove me to distraction.** | *She loves him* **to distraction. 3** [U] distracting or being distracted: *Let's invite her to the disco — she needs distraction.*

dis·train /dɪ'streɪn/ *v* [I (**upon**)] *law* to take goods from someone in order to force payment of a debt

dis·trait /dɪ'streɪ/ *adj Fr* not paying close attention to one's surroundings, esp. because of worry; distracted

dis·traught /dɪ'strɔːt/ *adj* [(with)] very anxious and troubled almost to the point of madness: *distraught with grief worry*

dis·tress¹ /dɪ'stres/ *n* [U] **1** great suffering of the mind or body; pain or great discomfort: *The sick man showed signs of distress.* | *Your thoughtless behaviour has caused us all a great deal of distress.* **2** suffering caused by lack of money: *a company in financial distress* **3** a state of danger or great difficulty: *Send out a* **distress signal.** *The ship is sinking.* | *a* **damsel in distress**

distress² *v* [T *often pass.*] to cause distress to: *We were distressed to find that the children had not returned.*

dis·tressed /dɪ'strest/ *adj BrE euph* **1** poor; IMPOVERISHED: *distressed gentlefolk circumstances area* **2** (of furniture) treated to look old and well used in an attractive way

dis·tress·ing /dɪˈstresɪŋ/ also **dis·tress·ful** /dɪˈstresfəl/— adj causing distress: *distressing news* − ∼ly adv

dis·trib·ute /dɪˈstrɪbjuːt/ v [T] **1** [(to, among)] to divide and give out among several people, places, etc: *to distribute the prizes to|among the winners | distributing leaflets to the crowd* **2** [(over)] to spread out through an area: *This new machine distributes seed evenly and quickly (over the whole field).* | *This species of plant is widely distributed.* (=is found in many different areas) **3** to supply (goods) in a particular area, esp. to shops

dis·tri·bu·tion /ˌdɪstrəˈbjuːʃən/ n **1** [C;U] the act of dividing and giving out among several people, places, etc.: *the distribution of prizes | The newspaper is having distribution problems in the north of the country.* **2** [S;U] the position or arrangement of (members of a group) in space or time: *The distribution of these animals has changed in the last century.* **3** [S;U] the sharing out of profits by a company among its SHAREHOLDERS − ∼al adj

dis·trib·u·tive /dɪˈstrɪbjʊtɪv/ adj [A no comp.] **1** distributing; connected with distribution: *the distributive trades of transport and marketing* **2** tech (of a word) concerning each single member of a group: *Distributive words in English include "each", "every", "either", and "neither".* − ∼ly adv

dis·trib·u·tor /dɪˈstrɪbjʊtər/ n **1** a person or organization that distributes goods: *The company is the local distributor for Volkswagen spare parts.* **2** an instrument which sends electric current in the right order to each SPARK PLUG in a car engine −see picture at ENGINE

dis·trict /ˈdɪstrɪkt/ n **1** a fixed division of a country, a city, etc., made for various official purposes: *a postal district* **2** an area with a special and particular quality, or of a particular kind: *the Lake District in northern England | a poor district in a city* −see AREA (USAGE)

district at·tor·ney /ˌ·· ·ˈ···/ n (often caps.) AmE in the US, the state official who is responsible for bringing legal charges against criminals in a particular area −compare CROWN PROSECUTION SERVICE

district coun·cil /ˌ·· ˈ··/ n in Britain, a government authority elected by the people living in an area , which deals with local services, such as housing, RUBBISH COLLECTION, and PLANNING PERMISSION: *On May 2nd you will have the chance to elect a new District Council to serve you for the next four years.*

district court /ˌ·· ˈ·/ n in the US, the court where law cases are first heard −see also extra information on page 742

district nurse /ˌ·· ˈ·/ n in Britain, a nurse, employed by a local authority, who visits and treats people in their own homes −compare HEALTH VISITOR

District of Co·lum·bi·a /ˌ·· · ·ˈ···/ also **the District** (abbrev. **DC**) [the] Washington, D.C.; a special FEDERAL area in the E of the US which includes Washington, the capital

district vis·it·or /ˌ·· ˈ···/ n in Britain, a church worker who visits people who are sick, old, or in need of help in an area

dis·trust¹ /dɪsˈtrʌst/ v [T] to lack trust or confidence in; have little faith in: *He distrusts banks, so he keeps his money at home.*

distrust² n [S;U (of)] lack of trust: *deep distrust between the former enemies | I have a distrust of aeroplanes.* − ∼ful adj − ∼fully adv − ∼fulness n [U]

dis·turb /dɪˈstɜːb‖-ɜːrb/ v [T] **1** to interrupt (esp. a person who is working) or break the sleep of: *I'm sorry to disturb you, but could you tell me how this machine works? | Did the cats disturb you in the night?* **2** to make (someone) anxiously dissatisfied; worry: *We were rather disturbed by the way the government tried to cover up the truth. | a disturbing new development in the dispute between the two countries* **3** to change the usual or natural condition of: *A light wind disturbed the surface of the water.* **4** disturb the peace law to cause public disorder

dis·turb·ance /dɪˈstɜːbəns‖-ɜːr-/ n [C;U] **1** an act of disturbing or the state of being disturbed: *They were charged by the police with causing a disturbance.* (=making a lot of noise and possibly fighting) **2** something that disturbs: *The noise of traffic is a continual disturbance.*

dis·turbed /dɪˈstɜːbd‖-ɜːr-/ adj ill or seriously upset in the mind or the feelings: *emotionally disturbed children*

dis·u·nite /ˌdɪsjuːˈnaɪt/ v [T] to cause disunity in

dis·u·ni·ty /dɪsˈjuːnɪti/ n [U] lack of UNITY, esp. with disagreement and quarrelling; DISSENSION

dis·use /dɪsˈjuːs/ n [U] the state of no longer being used: *an old law that has fallen into disuse*

dis·used /ˌdɪsˈjuːzd◂/ adj no longer used: *a disused mine|railway line*

di·syl·lab·ic /ˌdaɪsɪˈlæbɪk, ˌdɪ-/ adj tech (of a word) having two SYLLABLES

ditch¹ /dɪtʃ/ n a V- or U-shaped passage cut into the ground, esp. for water to flow through: *a drainage ditch by the side of the road* −see also LAST-DITCH

ditch² v [T] sl to get rid of; leave suddenly; ABANDON: *She got bored with her boyfriend and ditched him. | He promised to drive us to London but he ditched us 50 miles away. | I think we'd better ditch the last part. It's too long.*

dith·er¹ /ˈdɪðər/ v [I (about)] infml to behave nervously and uncertainly because one cannot decide: *For God's sake stop dithering and make up your mind!*

dither² n [S] infml a state of nervous inability to make decisions: *I'm all in a dither about the concert.*

di·tran·si·tive /ˌdaɪˈtrænsətɪv, -zə-/ adj tech (of a verb) that must take both an INDIRECT OBJECT and a DIRECT OBJECT. Ditransitive verbs are marked [T +obj(i)+obj(d)] in this dictionary: *The verb "give" is ditransitive in the sentence "She gave me the book".* −compare INTRANSITIVE, TRANSITIVE −**ditransitive** n

dit·to /ˈdɪtəʊ/ n -tos **1** a mark ( ) used to show that a word, which is usu. directly above the mark, e.g. in a list, is repeated; a sign meaning "the same":
one black pencil at 12p
" blue " " 15p
(=one black pencil at 12p, one blue pencil at 15p) **2** infml (I think) the same: *"I'm really annoyed about this." "Ditto."* (=I am, too) **3** AmE a PHOTOCOPY

dit·ty /ˈdɪti/ n often humor a short simple song

di·u·ret·ic /ˌdaɪjʊˈretɪk/ n, adj (a medicine or food) that increases the flow of URINE

di·ur·nal /daɪˈɜːnəl‖-ˈɜːr-/ adj fml or tech (esp. in the study of the sun, stars, etc.) taking one day; daily: *the diurnal rotation of the Earth* − ∼ly adv

di·van /dɪˈvæn‖ˈdaɪvæn/ n **1** a long soft seat or bed (**divan bed**) on a base, usu. without back or arms **2** (often cap.) (in former times) a state council room in some Eastern countries, esp. Turkey

dive¹ /daɪv/ v dived also dove /dəʊv/AmE− [I] **1** [(IN, off, from, into)] to throw oneself head first into water: *The girl dived into the swimming pool. | The bird dived into the water to catch the fish.* −see also SKIN DIVE **2** [(DOWN, for)] to go under the surface of the water: *They are diving for gold from the Spanish wreck. | a diving suit* (=a special suit worn by people who dive) **3** [+adv|prep] to move quickly on land or in air, downwards, head first, or out of sight: *The rabbit dived into its hole. | He dived into the doorway|under the table so they wouldn't see him. | The engines failed and the plane dived to the ground. | He dived into* (=put his hands into) *the bag and brought out two red apples.*
dive in phr v [I] to start doing something quickly and eagerly: *We all dived in and helped ourselves to the food.*

dive² n **1** an act of diving: *a graceful dive into the pool | When the shots sounded in the street, we made a dive for the nearest doorway.* **2** infml a not very respectable place for meeting, drinking, etc.: *a low dive* **3 take a dive** sl to agree to lose a match dishonestly, esp. a BOXING match

dive-bomb /ˈ· ·/ v [I;T] (of a plane) to dive and then bomb: *to dive-bomb a crowd of people* − ∼er n

div·er /ˈdaɪvər/ n a person who dives, esp. one who works at the bottom of the sea in special clothing with a supply of air

di·verge /daɪˈvɜːdʒ, də-‖-ˈɜːr-/ v [I (from)] to separate and go on in different directions: *This is where our opinions diverge (from each other).*

di·ver·gence /daɪˈvɜːdʒəns, də-‖-ˈɜːr-/ n [C;U] (an example of) the action or amount of diverging −**-gent** adj : *divergent opinions* −**-gently** adv

di·vers /ˈdaɪvəz‖-ərz/ adj [A] old use or humor many different: *Divers persons were present, of all stations in life.*

di·verse /daɪˈvɜːs‖dəˈvɜːrs, daɪ-/ adj different (from each other); showing variety: *many diverse interests | The* programme deals with subjects as diverse as pop music and ancient Greek drama. − ~**ly** adv

di·ver·si·fy /daɪ'vɜːsɪfaɪ‖dʒ'vɜːr-, daɪ-/ v **1** [I;T] to make or become different in form, quality, aims, or activities; vary **2** [I (**into**)] (of a business) to change to producing more and different products in order to make a business larger or to protect it if the market for certain products fails: *Because of over-production of dairy products, dairy farmers in Europe are being encouraged to diversify into non-agricultural uses of land, such as golf courses.* | *Our factory is trying to diversify (its range of products).* (=to make a large number of different products) | *a publishing company that is now diversifying into the software market* —**fication** /daɪ,vɜːsɪfɪ'keɪʃən‖dʒ,vɜːr-, daɪ-/ n [U]

di·ver·sion /daɪ'vɜːʃən, dʒ-‖-'ɜːrʒən/ n **1** [C;U] a turning aside from a main or usual course, activity, or use: *the diversion of a river to supply water to the farms* | *a traffic diversion due to an accident on the main road* **2** [C] something that turns someone's attention away from something else that one does not wish to be noticed: *I think your last argument was a diversion to make us forget the main point.* | *The bank robbers* created a diversion *to distract the attention of the police.* **3** [C] something that amuses people: *Big cities have lots of cinemas and other diversions.*

di·ver·sion·a·ry /daɪ'vɜːʃənəri, dʒ-‖-'ɜːrʒəneri/ adj intended to form a diversion from the most important operation or main point: *diversionary tactics*

di·ver·si·ty /daɪ'vɜːsɪti, dʒ-‖-'ɜːr-/ n [S;U (**of**)] the condition of being different or having differences; variety: *a considerable diversity of opinion on this issue* | *the cultural diversity of the United States*

di·vert /daɪ'vɜːt, dʒ-‖-'ɜːrt/ v [T] **1** [(**from, to**)] to cause to turn aside or change from one use or direction to another: *They diverted the river to supply water to the town.* | *diverted traffic* | *to divert additional government resources to the inner cities* **2** [(**from**)] to turn (a person, attention, criticism, etc.) away from something; DISTRACT: *The outbreak of fighting in the North has diverted public attention away from other national problems.* **3** fml to amuse: *a new game to divert the children* | *a diverting game*

di·vest /daɪ'vest, dʒ-/ v
  divest sbdy. **of** sthg. phr v [T] fml **1** to take away (the official position, special rights, property, etc.) of: *They divested the king of all his power.* **2** to take off (the ceremonial clothes) of **3** to cause (oneself) to get rid of (esp. business operations or false ideas): *The American conglomerate GIO is to divest itself of its oil interests.* | *to divest oneself of pride*

di·vest·ment /daɪ'vestmənt/ also **di·ves·ti·ture** /daɪ'vestʃtʃər‖-tʃuər/− n [U] AmE for DISINVESTMENT

di·vide¹ /dʒ'vaɪd/ v **1** [I;T (**into, from, between**)] to separate into two or more parts or groups: *The class divided into three groups when we went on our outing.* | *Divide this line into 20 equal parts.* | *Divide it in half.* | *The country is divided into 12 provinces.* | *A low wall divides our garden from our neighbour's garden.* | *He divides his time between working and looking after the children.* **2** [T (**UP, between, among, with**)] to separate and give out or share: *The prize money will be divided up|will be equally divided between|among the three winners.* | *Divide the cake with your sister.* **3** [I;T (**by, into**)] to find out how many times one number contains or is contained in another number: *Divide 15 by 3* | *15 divided by 3 is 5.* | *3 divides into 15 5 times.* —compare MULTIPLY **4** [T] to be an important cause of disagreement between; separate into opposing groups: *The issue of education policy divided the party.* | *The opposition groups are hopelessly divided.* | *a clear* dividing line *between those for and those against the motion* **5** [I] tech to vote by separating into groups: *Parliament divided on the question, and the Government won narrowly.*

divide² n **1** [(**between**)] fml a difference; lack of sameness or UNITY: *the divide between two political systems* | *the North-South divide* **2** tech a line of high land that rises between two different river systems; WATERSHED —see CONTINENTAL DIVIDE **3** euph the great divide a death (from separating the dead from the living): *He has crossed the great divide.* **b** the most important difference: *The*

great divide between the upper and lower town is the quality of the shops.

divided high·way /·,·· '··/ n AmE for DUAL CARRIAGEWAY

div·i·dend /'dɪvɪdənd, -dend/ n **1** that part of the money made by a business, which is divided among those who own shares in the business, usu. twice a year: *The company declared a large dividend at the end of the year.* **2** tech a number to be divided by another number − compare DIVISOR **3** **pay dividends** to produce an advantage, esp. as a result of earlier action: *Their decision five years ago to computerize the company is now paying (handsome) dividends.*

di·vid·er /dɪ'vaɪdər/ n a stiff card that sticks out and is used to separate two sets of pages in a FILE

di·vid·ers /dʒ'vaɪdəz‖-ərz/ n [P] an instrument for measuring or marking off lines, angles, etc. −see PAIR (USAGE), and see picture at MATHEMATICS

div·i·na·tion /,dɪvʒ'neɪʃən/ n [U] the act or skill of telling the unknown or the future, usu. by reading certain events as signs from God

di·vine¹ /dʒ'vaɪn/ adj **1** [no comp.] of, connected with or being God or a god: *divine worship* | *to attend* divine service (=an act of worship in church) **2** infml old-fash (used esp. by women) extremely good; WONDERFUL: *The meal was simply divine!* − ~**ly** adv

divine² v **1** [T] fml or lit to discover or guess (something unknown) by or as if by magic: [+obj|wh-] *At last I divined the truth|divined what she meant.* **2** [I (**for**);T] also **dowse**− to (try to) find underground water or minerals with a special Y-shaped stick (**divining rod/dowsing rod**) that is believed to point towards them. People who do this claim that it works, but many other people do not believe it because it cannot be tested or proved scientifically: *He divined (for) water on my farm.*

divine³ n now rare a priest, esp. of the Christian religion

Divine Com·e·dy /·,· '···/ [the] a poem written by Dante at the beginning of the 14th century telling of his SYMBOLIC journey to God through Hell (the **Inferno**), Purgatory, and Paradise, with Beatrice the woman he loves and who saves him −see also DANTE

Divine Of·fice /·,· '··/ [the] the fixed forms of prayer and ceremony for daily worship used by Roman Catholic priests

di·vin·er /dʒ'vaɪnər/ also **dowser** n a person who divines for underground water or minerals

divine right /·,· '·/ also **divine right of kings** /·,· ,· · '·/ n [S;U] the idea that a king receives his right to rule directly from God and not from the people: *the divine right of kings* | (fig.) *You seem to think you have a divine right to open my mail.*

diving bell /'·· ·/ n a bell-shaped metal container in which people can work under water

div·ing-board /'daɪvɪŋbɔːd‖-bɔːrd/ n a board fixed at one end, esp. high off the ground, off which people DIVE into the water −compare SPRINGBOARD

di·vin·i·ty /dʒ'vɪnʃti/ n **1** [U] the quality or state of being DIVINE¹ (1) **2** [C] (often cap.) a god or goddess **3** [U] the study of God and religious beliefs; THEOLOGY

Divinity n [the] God

divinity school /·'··· ,·/ n AmE for THEOLOGICAL COLLEGE

di·vis·i·ble /dʒ'vɪzʒbəl/ adj [(**by, into**)] that can be divided: *15 is divisible by 3.* −opposite indivisible

di·vi·sion /dʒ'vɪʒən/ n **1** [U (**between, among, into**)] separation or sharing: *the division of responsibility among the teachers* **2** [C+sing.|pl. v] one of the parts or groups into which a whole is divided: *She works in the company's export division.* | *a naval division* (=a group of ships that fight together) | *Wolverhampton Wanderers are in the 1st Division.* **3** [C (**between**)] something that divides or separates: *The river forms the division between the old and new parts of the city.* | *deep political divisions between the two groups* **4** [U (**between**)] disagreement between the members of a group; DISSENSION **5** [U] the process of finding out how many times one number or quantity is contained in another: *The children are learning to do division.* | **division sign** (÷) −compare MULTIPLICATION; see also LONG DIVISION **6** [C] tech a vote in the British parliament in which all those in favour ('aye') go to one place and all those against ('no') go to another:

to force a division | *the* **division bell** (=bell rung to tell members there will be a division)

division lob·by /·ˈ·· ˌ··/ *n* (in Britain) either of the two places to which a Member of Parliament goes to vote for or against something in a DIVISION (6)

division of la·bour /·ˌ··· · ˈ··/ *n* |(*the*) U| a system in which each member of a group specializes in a different type of work

di·vi·sive /dɪˈvaɪsɪv/ *adj* tending to make people argue amongst themselves; causing DISUNITY: *a divisive policy/issue* — ~**ly** *adv* — ~**ness** *n* |U|

di·vi·sor /dɪˈvaɪzəʳ/ *n tech* the number by which another number is divided: *When 15 is divided by 3, the number 3 is the divisor.* —compare DIVIDEND (2)

di·vorce¹ /dɪˈvɔːs‖-ɔːrs/ *n* **1** |C;U| (a case of) the official ending of a marriage, esp. as declared by a court of law: *Their marriage ended in divorce.* | *She wants to get a divorce.* | *an increase in the number of divorces*

▶CULTURAL NOTE Divorce is legal in Britain, though not in Ireland, and can be given for an IRRETRIEVABLE BREAK-DOWN (=failure) of a marriage. This can be caused by ADULTERY, cruelty, or DESERTION and since 1969, when the Divorce Reform Act took effect, by two years separation. In the US divorce is also legal, though different states may have different laws about it. In most states one may get a divorce for the same reasons as in Britain, usually after at least one year's separation, and in some states one can get a NO-FAULT divorce (=one that does not blame either person). In both Britain and the US, the court decides which parent should have CUSTODY of the children, how the property is to be divided, and whether one partner, usu. the husband, should pay money (*BrE* MAINTENANCE *AmE* CHILD SUPPORT or ALIMONY) towards the living costs of the other and/or children —compare SEPARATION◀

2 |C (**between**)| a separation: *a growing divorce between workers and management*

divorce² *v* **1** |I;T| to officially end a marriage between/to (a husband and wife): *They're getting divorced.* | *She divorced him after years of unhappiness.* | *a divorced woman* **2** |T (**from**)| to separate completely: *It is difficult to divorce politics from sport.* | *Some of his ideas are completely divorced from reality.*

▷USAGE If Tom and Jill are married but intend to end their marriage we can say *Tom and Jill are getting* **divorced.** If we are talking mainly about Jill we can say *Jill is getting a* **divorce/getting divorced (from** *Tom).* But if Jill is taking action in law against Tom to end the marriage we can say *Jill is* **divorcing** *Tom.* —see also MARRY (USAGE)◁

di·vor·cée /dɪˈvɔːsiː‖dɪˌvɔːrˈseɪ, -ˈsiː/ **di·vor·cé** /dɪˈvɔːsiː, -seɪ‖-ɔːr-/ *masc.* — *n old fash* a woman whose marriage has ended in divorce —compare WIDOW

di·vulge /daɪˈvʌldʒ, dɪ-/ *v* |T (**to**)| *fml* to tell or make known (what has been secret); REVEAL: *Who divulged our plans (to the press)?* [+*that*] *The doctor divulged that the President had been ill for some time before he died.* [+*wh*-] *They refused to divulge where they had hidden the money.* —**vulgence** *n* |U|

div·vy /ˈdɪvi/ *v* |T (UP)| *sl* to divide: *a conspiracy to divvy up the market between them*

Di·wa·li, Dewali, Divali /dɪˈwɑːli/ an important HINDU religious celebration held in October or November marked by special food, gifts, and the lighting of lamps

Dix·ie /ˈdɪksi/ *AmE infml* **1** the Southern states of the US, esp. the south-eastern states where slaves were owned before the war between the States (the Civil War). There is a well-known popular song called *Dixie* written in 1859 by Daniel D Emmett.

dix·ie·land /ˈdɪksilænd/ *n* |U| old-style (TRADITIONAL) JAZZ played with a two-beat RHYTHM by a small band and often including a part played by just one instrument, originally from the southern states of the US

Dix·on of Dock Green /ˌdɪksən əv ˌdɒk ˈɡriːn‖-ˌdɑːrk-/ *n* a former long-running British television programme in which Sergeant Dixon was a London policeman, played by Jack Warner, at the Dock Green police station. Each programme began with Sergeant Dixon saying "evenin' all". For many people, Sergeant Dixon is the typical British "friendly bobby" (=friendly policeman), always ready to help people and always completely honest.

People sometimes mention him when saying that modern policemen are not always like him: *For people who have grown up with the Dixon of Dock Green image of the police, these allegations of police brutality and dishonesty will have come as quite a shock.*

Dix·ons /ˈdɪksənz/ (in Britain) one of a group of shops which sell electrical, electronic, and photographic equipment

DIY /ˌdiː aɪ ˈwaɪ/ *n* |U| *esp. BrE, abbrev. for*: do-it-yourself; the practice of doing repairs, painting the house, etc. oneself, instead of paying workmen: *a DIY shop* | *a DIY fanatic*

▶CULTURAL NOTE DIY is a very popular free time activity in Britain. Special shops, such as B & Q and Payless, sell everything needed for DIY.◀

diz·zy /ˈdɪzi/ *adj* **1** having an unpleasant feeling of loss of balance and confusion, as if things are going round and round: *They danced round in circles until they were dizzy.* | *Climbing ladders makes me dizzy.* **2** [A] causing this feeling: *looking down from a* **dizzy height** | (fig.) *She rose to the dizzy height* (=important position) *of vice-president.* **3** *infml, esp. AmE* careless and forgetful: *A dizzy blonde works at the front desk.* —**zily** *adv* —**ziness** *n* |U|

DJ /ˌdiː ˈdʒeɪ◀/ *n abbrev.* **1** *for*: DISC JOCKEY **2** *for*: DINNER JACKET

Dja·kar·ta /dʒəˈkɑːtə‖-ɑːr-/ see JAKARTA

Dji·bou·ti /dʒɪˈbuːti/ a country in NE Africa, formerly a French COLONY; capital Djibouti; population 510,000 (1989)

djinn /dʒɪn/ *n* a GENIE

DMV /ˌdiː em ˈviː/ [*the*] the Department of Motor Vehicles; in many US states, the government department for taxing and licensing (LICENSE) drivers, cars, and other vehicles

DNA /ˌdiː en ˈeɪ◀/ *n* |U| *tech* deoxyribonucleic acid; the acid which carries GENETIC information in a cell

DNA pro·fil·ing /ˌ··· ˈ···/ *n* |U| the practice of using information from DNA in blood, SEMEN, or other body liquids found at the scene of a crime to discover who the criminal is **DNA profile** *n*

DNB /ˌdiː en ˈbiː/ the DICTIONARY OF NATIONAL BIOGRAPHY

D-no·tice /ˈ· ˌ··/ *n* (in Britain) an official request to a newspaper that certain information shall not be made public, for reasons of national safety

do¹ /duː/ *v* **did** /dɪd/, **done** /dʌn/; *3rd person sing. present* **does** /dəz/; *strong* dʌz/ [*auxiliary verb*] **1** [+*to-v*] (a used with another verb, esp. to form questions or negatives): *Do you like my new car?* | *He didn't answer.* | *Where do you live?* | *Doesn't he look funny?* | *Don't just stand there watching!* | (*esp. BrE*) *Don't let's stop.* (compare *Let's not stop.*) | *Why don't you come for the weekend?* (=Please come!) | *Not only did I see him, but I spoke to him.* | *Little does he know* (=he is unconscious of the fact) *that the police are watching him.* **b** (used to strengthen or support another verb): *Do be careful!* | *"Why didn't you tell me?"* *"I did tell you."* | *He owns, or did own, a Rolls Royce.* — see NOT(USAGE) **2** [I] (used instead of another verb): *She likes it, and so do I.* | *"Would you like to join us?"* *"I don't mind if I do."* (=yes please) | *He speaks English better than he did.* (=better than he used to speak it) | *"You stepped on my toe." "No, I didn't!"* | *She writes novels, doesn't she?* (=I think she writes novels.) | (*esp. BrE*) *She writes novels, does she?* (=I am asking) | *"You left the door open." "So I did!"* (=you are right) | (*fml*) *"Will you write to her?" "I have already done so."* | (*BrE*) *"Will she come?"* *"She may do."* | *"You ought to phone your mother." "I already have done."* **3** [T] (used instead of another verb): *"What are you doing?" "I'm cooking." | What he does is (to) teach.* **4** *What . . . doing* (often expressing disapproval) Why?: *What is that book doing on the floor?* (=Why is it there?) | *What was that man doing in your room?*

do² *v* **1** [T] to perform the actions that are necessary in order to complete (something) or bring it into a desired state: *to do a sum/a crossword/one's homework/exercises* | *I'll do the cooking/the cleaning.* | *Have you done* (=cleaned) *your teeth?* | *to do one's hair* (=arrange it) | *They do fish* (=cook it) *very well in this restaurant.* | *to* *do repairs* | *to do* (=study) *science at school* | *This car can do 80 miles an hour.* | *It's a pleasure to do business with you.* | *We did everything we could to help him.* | *Don't do anything stupid.* | *We* **did our best** *to help him.* | *There's nothing more to do|to be done.* | *What do you do (for a living)?* (=What is your work?) | *All we can do now is wait.* —see MAKE (USAGE) **2** [T] (used in certain expressions): *He's only* **doing his duty.** | *You* **did right** *to tell me what they were doing.* [+obj(i)+obj(d)] *That won't* **do (you)** any **harm.** | *The medicine will* **do you good.** | *The photograph doesn't* **do her justice.** | *Will you* **do me a favour?** | *Will you* **do us the honour** *of coming to dinner?* **3** [I+well, badly, etc.] to advance or perform successfully or unsuccessfully; PROGRESS: *The children are doing well at their new school.* | *I hope you'll do better in future.* | *The company always does badly at this time of year.* | *How are you doing in the new job?* **4** [*not in progressive forms*] **a** [I (for)] to be enough or suitable: *Will £5 do?* | *That'll do nicely.* | *This little bed will do for the baby.* | *You needn't use milk — water will do.* | *That will do! Stop!* **b** [T] to be enough or suitable for (someone): *Will £5 do you?* | *I suppose this coat will have to do me for another year.* **5** [I+adv|prep] to behave in a stated way: *Do as you're told.* | *You did well to get here so quickly.* **6** [T] *infml, esp. BrE* (of people) **a** to cheat: *I'm afraid he's done you on that sale! You've been done.* **b** to punish; hurt: *If you say that again, I'll do you!* **7** [T] *infml* to visit (a place) and see everything interesting in it: *Can we do Oxford in three days?* **8** [T] to perform as or copy the manner of; IMPERSONATE: *He does Ronald Reagan very well.* **9** [I *only in progressive forms*] *infml* to happen: *What's doing at your place tonight?* | *There's nothing doing in this town at night.* **10 do or die** *fml* to succeed or die; do everything possible to succeed **1 do time** *infml* to be in prison **12 do to death** to kill: (fig.) *That joke has been done to death by being repeated so often.* **13 I do** the answer to a question in the marriage service "Do you take this woman/man to be your lawful wedded wife/husband?", by which one agrees formally to be married: *She couldn't wait to walk up the aisle and say "I do".* **14 do well by** to treat well **15** *BrE* **up and doing** *infml* out of bed and active: *He's up and doing by five o'clock in the morning!* —see also **do one's bit** (BIT¹), **how do you do** (HOW), **nothing doing** (NOTHING), **do (someone) proud** (PROUD)

do away with sbdy./sthg. *phr v* [T] **1** to cause to end; ABOLISH: *The government did away with free school meals.* **2** also **make away with—** *infml* to kill or murder (someone or oneself)

do sbdy. ↔ **down** *phr v* [T] *BrE infml* **1** to cheat **2** to try to make someone, esp. someone who is not present, seem unimportant, worthless, etc.

do for sbdy./sthg. *phr v* [T] **1** *BrE infml* to keep house or do cleaning for **2** *BrE sl* to kill; murder **3 What will you do for (something)?** What arrangements will you make for (something)?: *What will you do for food when you are camping?* —see also **done for** (DONE²)

do in *phr v* [T] **1** (do sbdy. ↔ **in**) *sl* to kill: *They did her in with an axe!* **2** (**do** sbdy. **in**) *infml* to tire completely: *That long walk really did me in!*

do sthg. ↔ **out** *phr v* [T] *infml, esp. BrE* to clean thoroughly: *I'll do out the living room.*

do sbdy. **out of** sthg. *phr v* [T *often pass.*] *infml* to cause to lose by cheating: *I've been done out of my rights.*

do over *phr v* [T] **1** (**do** sthg. ↔ **over**) to repaint (a room, wall, etc.) **2** (**do** sthg. **over**) *AmE* to do or make again: *Your work is full of mistakes; you'd better do it over.* **3** (**do** sbdy. ↔ **over**) *BrE sl* to attack and wound

do up *phr v* **1** [I;T (=**do** sthg. ↔ **up**)] to fasten or tie: *Do up your buttons|my dress|this knot.* | *This skirt does up at the back.* —see OPEN (USAGE) **2** [T] (**do** sthg. ↔ **up**) to repair or redecorate: *They did up an old house and sold it for a big profit.* **3** [T] (**do** sbdy. **up**) to make (oneself) more beautiful: *Mary has done herself up for the party.*

do with sthg. *phr v* [T] **1** [*no pass.*] (usu. after **could**) to need or want: *I could do with a cup of tea.* | *This room could do with a good clean.* **2** [*no pass.*] *BrE infml* (with negatives) to allow; accept or experience willingly: *I can't do with|I can't be doing with all this loud music.* **3** [*no pass.*] to cause (oneself) to spend time doing: *The boys didn't know what to do with themselves when school ended.* **4** (in questions with **what**) to take action with regard to: *"What have you done with my pen?" "I've put it away."* | *"What shall we do with the children?" "Take*

---

them out to the park." **5 have|be to do with** to have a connection with: *Her job has|is to do with telephones.* **6 have|be something|nothing|anything|a lot, etc., to do with** to have some|no|any|a lot of, etc., connection with: *Her job has nothing to do with telephones.* | *Don't have anything to do with him — he's completely untrustworthy.* | *What he does at home is nothing to do with* (=does not concern) *his teacher.* **7 What is someone doing with..?** Why has someone got (something): *What were you doing with my diary just now?* —see also DONE² (1)

▷ USAGE Compare **do with** and **do to**. *What have you done with my book?* means "Where is it?" but *What have you done to my book?* suggests that you have damaged it.◁

do without (sbdy./sthg.) *phr v* [I;T] to manage to live or continue satisfactorily without: *I haven't enough money to buy a car, so I'll just have to do without (one).* | (shows annoyance) *I can do without* (=would rather not have) *your sarcastic comments, thank you!*

do³ *n* **dos** *or* **do's** /duːz/ *infml* **1** *esp. BrE* a big party: *After the wedding there was a big do at the Savoy.* **2 dos and don'ts** rules of behaviour: *the dos and don'ts of working in an office*

do⁴ , doh /dəʊ/ *n* [S;U] the first or eighth note in the SOL-FA musical scale

DOA /ˌdiː əʊ ˈeɪ/ *adj* [F] *abbrev. for:* dead on arrival, usu. used in hospitals

d.o.b. /ˌdiː əʊ ˈbiː/ *n abbrev. for:* date of birth

Dob·bin /ˈdɒbɪn‖ˈdɑː-/ a popular name esp. in Britain for a farm horse or a quiet, slow horse

Do·ber·mann pin·scher /ˌdəʊbəmən ˈpɪnʃər‖-bər-/ *n* a middle-sized fierce-looking dog of German origin, often used as a guard dog —see picture at DOG

doc /dɒk‖dɑːk/ *n infml* a doctor: *Good morning, doc!*

do·cent /dəʊˈsent/ *n AmE* a person, often unpaid, who guides others through MUSEUMs, parks, and other attractions

do·cile /ˈdəʊsaɪl‖ˈdɑːsəl/ *adj* quiet and easily controlled, managed, or influenced; SUBMISSIVE: *a docile child|horse* **—cility** /dəʊˈsɪlɪti‖dɑː-/ *n* [U]

dock¹ /dɒk‖dɑːk/ *n* **1** [C] a place where ships are loaded and unloaded, or repaired: *the docks of London* —see also DRY DOCK **2** [*the*+S] the place in a court of law where the prisoner stands —see colour picture on page 751 **3 in dock** *BrE* away being repaired: *My car's in dock this week.*

dock² *v* [I;T (**at**)] to (cause to) sail into, or remain at, a dock: *The ship docked at Portsmouth.* | *We'll be docking in about half an hour.*

dock³ *v* [T] **1** to cut off the end of, cut short: *docking a horse's tail* **2** to take away (esp. money) from (something else, esp. wages): *If you're late for work again your wages will be docked.* | *to dock £5 from someone's wages*

dock⁴ *n* [C;U] a common plant with broad leaves (**dock leaves**) that grows by the roadside in Britain and other northern countries. Many people use dock leaves to rub on their skin if they get stung by a NETTLE

dock·er /ˈdɒkər‖ˈdɑː-/ also **longshoreman** *AmE—* *n* a person who works at a dock, loading and unloading ships

dock·et¹ /ˈdɒkɪt‖ˈdɑː-/ *n* **1** *fml or tech, esp. BrE* a list or piece of paper describing the contents of something, giving information about its use, etc. **2** *AmE law* **a** a list stating the causes for a trial in court **b** a list of cases that are to come before a particular court

docket² *v* [T] *fml or tech, esp. BrE* to describe in a docket: *to docket a parcel of goods*

Dock Green see DIXON OF DOCK GREEN

dock·land /ˈdɒklənd, -lænd‖ˈdɑː-/ also **docklands** *pl.—* *n* [U] the area around the docks in a large port: *London's dockland by the Thames* | *dockland development*

Dock·lands /ˈdɒkləndz‖ˈdɑːk-/ a new development of houses and offices in E London, along the river Thames, formerly a poor area. It includes the Canary Wharf tower, also known as the DS. Tower, which is the tallest building in Europe. **The Docklands Light Railway** connects the area to the City of London, and there is a Docklands airport. Docklands is thought of as representing the new society which the Conservative government of the 1980s wanted to build. However, it has also been criticized for encouraging rich people, esp. YUPPIES, to move into the area and forcing local people to leave because the houses are too expensive for them.

dock·side /ˈdɒksaɪd/ ‖ /ˈdɑːk-/ n [the] the area beside a dock: goods delivered to the dockside

dock·yard /ˈdɒkjɑːd/ ‖ /ˈdɑːkjɑːrd/ n a place where ships are built or repaired; SHIPYARD

Doc Mar·tens /ˌdɒk ˈmɑːt̬nz/ ‖ /ˌdɑːk ˈmɑːrtnz/ n [P] tdmk see DR MARTENS

doc·tor¹ /ˈdɒktər/ ‖ /ˈdɑːk-/ n   **1** a person whose profession is to attend to and treat sick people: She wants to be a doctor when she leaves school. | You should see/consult a doctor about your earache. | Doctor Smith will see you now. | Good morning, doctor. | You'd better go to the doctor/to the doctor's about your toe. —see also FLYING DOCTOR   **2** a person holding one of the highest degrees given by a university, such as a PHD   **3** AmE (used when speaking to or about a DENTIST): My dentist is called Doctor Steen.   **4** infml a person whose job is to repair the stated thing: a radio/bicycle doctor   **5 Is there a doctor in the house?** a phrase which theatre managers are supposed to use if a member of the public is taken ill in the theatre and needs a doctor   **6 under the doctor (for)** BrE infml being treated by a doctor (for) —see FATHER (USAGE)

doctor

▷ USAGE In Britain, medical doctors are called **doctor** but SURGEONS and DENTISTS are called Mr, Miss, Mrs, or Ms followed by their family name. In the US, dentists, medical doctors, and surgeons are called doctor. In both countries holders of a PhD are entitled to be called doctor but rarely use the title outside universities. The title is usu. written **Dr.**◁

doctor² v [T] infml   **1** derog to change, esp. in a dishonest way: They were charged with doctoring the election results. | It was discovered that the accounts had been doctored.   **2** euph, esp. BrE to make (esp. an animal) unable to breed by removing its sex organs; NEUTER²: The cat has been doctored.   **3** rare to give medical treatment to

doc·tor·al /ˈdɒktərəl/ ‖ /ˈdɑːk-/ adj [A] of or related to the university degree of DOCTOR¹ (2): a doctoral degree/thesis

doc·tor·ate /ˈdɒktərət/ ‖ /ˈdɑːk-/ n the university degree of a DOCTOR¹ (2)

Doctor of Phi·los·o·phy /ˌ· · ·ˈ· ·/ n fml for PHD

Doctor Ruth /ˌdɒktə ˈruːθ/ ‖ /ˌdɑːktər-/ (1928–) an American SEXOLOGIST (=a person who studies and works in the field of sex) who is well-known for speaking openly about sex on radio and television

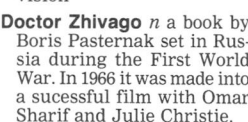

Dr. Ruth Westheimer

Doctor Zhivago n a book by Boris Pasternak set in Russia during the First World War. In 1966 it was made into a successful film with Omar Sharif and Julie Christie.

doc·tri·naire /ˌdɒktrɪˈneər/ ‖ /ˌdɑːk-/ adj derog believing in, or trying to put into action, a system of ideas without considering the practical difficulties: a doctrinaire socialist

doc·trine /ˈdɒktrɪn/ ‖ /ˈdɑːk-/ n [C;U] a principle or set of principles (esp. of a religious or political kind) that is taught: religious doctrine | the doctrines of the Catholic Church [+that] They still cling to the doctrine that high wages cause unemployment. —see also INDOCTRINATE —**trinal** /dɒkˈtraɪnəl/ ‖ /ˈdɑːktrɪnəl/ adj : doctrinal differences between two churches

doc·u·dra·ma /ˈdɒkjuˌdrɑːmə/ ‖ /ˈdɑːkjʊˌdrɑːmə, -ˌdræmə/ n AmE a film, usually for television, which presents a true story as a play

doc·u·ment¹ /ˈdɒkjʉmənt/ ‖ /ˈdɑːk-/ n a paper that provides information, esp. of an official kind: Let me see all the legal documents concerning the sale of this land. | top-secret military documents

document² /ˈdɒkjʉment/ ‖ /ˈdɑːk-/ v [T] to prove or record with documents: The history of this area is very well documented.

doc·u·men·ta·ry¹ /ˌdɒkjʉˈmentəri/ ‖ /ˌdɑːk-/ adj [A]   **1** related to or consisting of documents: documentary proof/evidence   **2** providing facts and information, rather than telling a story: documentary films —compare FEATURE FILM

documentary² n [(on, about)] a film or television or radio broadcast that presents facts: We watched a documentary about gold miners in South Africa. —compare FEATURE FILM

doc·u·men·ta·tion /ˌdɒkjʉmənˈteɪʃən, -men-/ ‖ /ˌdɑːk-/ n [U] proof in the form of documents: Their claim to own the land is not supported by proper documentation.

DOD /ˌdiː əʊ ˈdiː/ abbrev. for the US Department of Defense

Dodd /dɒd/ ‖ /dɑːd/, **Ken** (1927–) an English COMEDIAN from Liverpool who created the DIDDYMEN and is known for his **tickling stick**, a special stick for tickling (TICKLE) people

dod·der /ˈdɒdər/ ‖ /ˈdɑː-/ v [I] infml (of a person) to behave or walk weakly and shakily, usu. from age — ~ **er** n

dod·der·ing /ˈdɒdərɪŋ/ ‖ /ˈdɑː-/ also **dod·der·y** /-dəri/— adj infml (of a person) weak, shaky, and slow, usu. from age — ~ **ly** adv

dod·dle /ˈdɒdl/ ‖ /ˈdɑːdl/ n [usu. sing.] BrE infml something that is very easy: That driving test was a real doddle.

dodge¹ /dɒdʒ/ ‖ /dɑːdʒ/ v   **1** [I;T] to avoid (something) by moving suddenly aside: He dodged the falling rock and escaped unhurt. | She dodged past me.   **2** [T] infml to avoid (a responsibility, duty, etc.) by a trick or in some dishonest way; EVADE: She somehow managed to dodge all the difficult questions. —**dodger** n : a tax dodger —see also DRAFT DODGER

dodge² n infml a clever way of avoiding something or of deceiving or tricking someone: a tax dodge

Dodge tdmk an American car made by Chrysler: He drives a Dodge Dart.

dodge·ball /ˈdɒdʒbɔːl/ ‖ /ˈdɑːdʒ-/ n [U] a game played by American children in which the object is to avoid being hit by a large rubber ball thrown by the opposing players

Dodge City /ˌ· ˈ···/ a city in Kansas in the US

▶ CULTURAL NOTE In the 19th century Dodge City was a place where many people came to drink and play cards. People did not obey the law, and there were often shootings on the street: Nobody wants to live in some kind of Dodge City with bullets flying all over the place. ◀

dodg·ems /ˈdɒdʒəmz/ ‖ /ˈdɑː-/ also **bumper cars** n [the+P] infml a form of entertainment at FUNFAIRs or other places of public amusement in which people try to drive small electric cars (**dodgem cars**) in an enclosed space, often intentionally hitting other cars

dodg·y /ˈdɒdʒi/ ‖ /ˈdɑː-/ adj infml, esp. BrE   **1** not safe; risky; dangerous: a dodgy plan | Don't sit on that chair. It's a bit dodgy.   **2** dishonest and not to be trusted: a dodgy person/business

do·do /ˈdəʊdəʊ/ n **dodos** or **dodoes**   **1** a large bird that could not fly and that no longer exists: (fig.) Fashions change fast, and this year's winner may be a dodo next year.   **2 (as) dead as a dodo** infml completely dead or forgotten about   **3** AmE a stupid person

DOE /ˌdiː əʊ ˈiː/ [the]   **1** abbrev. for: DEPARTMENT OF THE ENVIRONMENT   **2** for: Department of Energy, an American government department

doe /dəʊ/ n the female of certain animals, esp. the deer, the rabbit, and the rat —compare BUCK¹ (1)

do·er /ˈduːər/ n infml a person who does things or is active: an evil-doer | She's a doer, not just a thinker.

does /dəz; strong dʌz/ 3rd person singular present of DO¹,² —see NOTE (USAGE)

does·n't /ˈdʌzənt/ short for: does not: It doesn't matter. | Doesn't he live in the house next to yours?

doff /dɒf/ ‖ /dɑːf, dɔːf/ v [T] old use or pomp to take off (esp. one's hat): He doffed his cap to the old lady. —opposite **don**

dogs

poodle   pekinese   dachshund

spaniel   collie   greyhound

Alsatian esp. *BrE*/
German shepherd
esp. *AmE*   Afghan   Labrador

Dalmatian   Dobermann pinscher   Old English sheepdog

pit bull terrier   Yorkshire terrier   rottweiler   Jack Russell

dog¹ /dɒg‖dɔːg/ *n* **1** a common four-legged animal, esp. any of the many varieties kept by humans as companions or for hunting, working, guarding, etc. A young dog is called a **puppy**: *a guard dog | Our dog's a mongrel. | I could hear the neighbours' dog barking.*

▶ CULTURAL NOTE Dogs are very popular and very common in Britain and the US. They are treated as members of the family, and esp. in Britain are paid a great deal of attention. In Britain, there are often stories about dogs in the newspapers. People sometimes talk about dogs as **man's best friend**. However, worry is growing about the health risk from dogs' EXCREMENT in towns, and about people keeping fierce dogs that can injure or kill people. ◀

2 a male dog or the male of certain animals like it, esp. the fox and the WOLF — see also BITCH¹ **3** *infml* a person of the stated kind: *He's a dirty dog. | You lucky dog!* **4** *AmE sl* **a** a failure or a disappointment: *The party was a real dog.* **b** a very unattractive woman (This would be very offensive to any woman who heard it, and would usu. only be used by a man to other men.) **5 a dog in the manger** someone who does not want others to use or enjoy something even though they themselves do not need or want it **6 dog eat dog** a hard struggle to continue to exist, with people competing fiercely against each other: *It's dog eat dog in the business world.* **7 dressed up like a dog's dinner** *BrE infml* dressed in fine clothes which one thinks very splendid, but which other people consider rather silly **8 every dog has its day** *saying* every person, no matter how unpleasant they are, has their period of success **9 let sleeping dogs lie** *infml* not to interrupt or trouble a person, situation, etc. when this is likely to cause problems or disorder **10 not have a 'dog's chance** *infml* to have no chance at all **11 put on the dog** *AmE infml* to pretend to be more wealthy or knowledgeable than one really is: *He was really putting on the dog to try to impress her.* **12 treat someone like a dog** *infml* to treat someone very badly — see also DOGS, HOT DOG, TOP DOG **13 you can't teach an old dog new tricks** *saying* someone who is old and fixed in their

ways cannot learn new ideas or new ways of doing things — see also **(a case of) the tail wagging the dog** (TAIL)

dog² *v* **-gg-** |T *often pass.*| (esp. of problems, difficulties, etc.) to follow closely like a dog; PURSUE: *We were dogged by bad luck throughout the journey.*

dog bis·cuit /'· ₁··/ *n* a small dry hard piece of baked bread-like food for dogs

dog·cart /'dɒgkɑːt‖'dɔːgkɑːrt/ *n* **1** a two-wheeled vehicle, pulled by a horse, with two seats across the vehicle, back to back **2** a small cart to be pulled by a large dog

dog·catch·er /'dɒg₁kætʃəʳ‖'dɔːg-/ *n* an official of a town whose duty it is to catch wandering dogs and take them off the streets

dog col·lar /'· ₁··/ *n* **1** a neckband for a dog, onto which a LEAD² (4) can be fastened **2** *infml* a priest's round white collar, stiff and fastened at the back

dog days /'· ·/ *n* |(the) P| *(often caps.) esp. lit* the hottest days of the year: *the dog days of summer*

doge /dəʊdʒ/ *n* the highest government official in Venice and in Genoa in former times

dog-eared /'· ·/ *adj* (esp. of books and papers) having the corners of the pages bent down with use

dog-end /'· ·/ *n infml, esp. BrE* **1** a cigarette end **2** something left over and not considered of value

dog·fight /'dɒgfaɪt‖'dɔːg-/ *n* **1** a fight between dogs, or any cruel uncontrolled fight without proper rules **2** a fight between armed aircraft

dog·fish /'dɒg₁fɪʃ‖'dɔːg-/ *n* a kind of small SHARK

dog·ged /'dɒg₄d‖'dɔː-/ *adj* (of a person or their behaviour) refusing to give up in the face of difficulty or opposition; TENACIOUS: *dogged perseverance* — ~**ly** *adv* — ~**ness** *n* [U]

Dog·ger Bank /₁dɒgə 'bæŋk‖₁dɔːgər-/ an area in the North Sea off the Yorkshire coast, known for its fishing ground

dog·ge·rel /'dɒgərəl‖'dɔː-, 'dɑː-/ *n* [U] silly and worthless poetry that is often not intended to be serious

dog·go /'dɒgəʊ‖'dɔː-/ *adv* **lie doggo** *old-fash sl* to lie or hide quietly without moving or making a noise; remain in hiding

dog·gone /'dɒgɒn‖'dɔːgɔːn/ *v* [T] *AmE euph sl* DAMN⁴: *Doggone it, I've lost again!* — **doggone, -goned** *adj* |A| : *That doggoned cat has upset the milk!*

dog·gy , **doggie** /'dɒgi‖'dɔːgi/ *n* (used esp. to or by children) a dog

doggy bag, doggie bag /'·· ·/ *n esp. AmE* a small bag provided by a restaurant for taking home food that remains uneaten after a meal. The amount of food provided in restaurants is usu. much greater in the US than in Britain, and it is considered quite acceptable to take some of it home.

dog·house /'dɒghaʊs‖'dɔːg-/ *n* **in the doghouse** *infml* in a state of disfavour or shame

do·gie /'dəʊgi/ *n AmE* a motherless CALF (=baby cow) in a group of cattle

dog·leg /'dɒgleg‖'dɔːg-/ *n* a sharp bend in a road, a racetrack, or esp. part of a GOLF course

dog·ma /'dɒgmə‖'dɔːgmə, 'dɑːgmə/ *n* [C;U] *often derog* an important belief or set of beliefs that people are expected to accept without reasoning: *Catholic dogma | Marxist dogma*

dog·mat·ic /dɒg'mætɪk‖dɔːg-, dɑːg-/ *adj usu. derog* holding one's beliefs very strongly and expecting other people to accept them without question: *a dogmatic person/manner | He's very dogmatic about the right way to bring up children.* — ~**ally** /kli/ *adv*

dog·ma·tis·m /'dɒgmətɪzəm‖'dɔːg-, 'dɑːg-/ *n* [U] *usu. derog* the quality of being dogmatic — **-tist** *n*

do-good·er /₁· '··‖'· ₁··/ *n usu. derog* a person who tries to help people who have problems, but may be impractical or ineffective

dog pad·dle /'· ₁··/ also **dog·gy paddle** /'·· ₁··/ *n* |(the) S| *infml* a simple swimming stroke in which the legs are kicked while the arms make short quick movements up and down in the water like the front legs of a swimming dog

dogs /dɒgz‖dɔːgz/ *n* **1** |the+P| a sports event at which dogs (esp. GREYHOUNDS) race and money is won or lost: *a night out at the dogs* **2** [P] *humor sl* feet: *I've walked so much*

today that my dogs are really killing me. **3** [P] also **fire-dogs, andirons** supports for burning logs in a fireplace **4 go to the dogs** to become ruined, esp. to change from a better to a worse moral condition: *"This country's going to the dogs!" said the old man.*

dogs·bod·y /ˈdɒgzˌbɒdi‖ˈdɔːgzˌbɑːdi/ n BrE infml a person in a low-ranking position who has to do the least interesting work: *I'm just the dogsbody in this office.*

dog's dinner /ˌ· ˈ··/ also **dog's breakfast** n [S] BrE derog sl something badly or untidily done: *I don't know who designed this course, but it's a real dog's dinner.*

dog sled /ˈ· ˌ·/ n a small carriage pulled by dogs over snow, used especially in Alaska and the northern part of Canada

dog's life /ˈ· ˌ·/ n [S] an unhappy dull existence

dog tag /ˈ· ˌ·/ n AmE infml a small piece of metal on which a soldier's name, blood type, and number are written, worn round his neck

dog-tired /ˌ· ˈ·◄/ adj infml extremely tired

dog·trot /ˈdɒgtrɒt‖ˈdɔːgtrɑːt/ n [usu. sing.] a way of moving along that is faster than walking but slower than running

dog war·den /ˈ· ˌ··/ n (in Britain) an official worker whose job is to collect dogs which are out without their owners, and make sure that people do not take dogs into areas where they are not allowed: *I suggest that the council employ Dog Wardens to patrol the beach.*

dog·wood /ˈdɒgwʊd‖ˈdɔːg-/ n [C;U] a kind of flowering tree or bush from North America

doh /dəʊ/ n DO⁴

DOH /ˌdiː əʊ ˈeɪtʃ/ [the] abbrev. for: DEPARTMENT OF HEALTH

doi·ly , doyley, doyly /ˈdɔɪli/ n a decorative piece of cloth or paper used under a dish or under cakes on a plate

do·ing /ˈduːɪŋ/ n **1** [C;U] something that one causes to happen; an act: *This must be your doing.* (=I think you did this.) **2** [U] hard work: *The job will take a lot of doing.*

do·ings /ˈduːɪŋz/ n doings BrE infml any small thing, esp. something whose name one has forgotten or does not know: *Put this little doings on the table.*

do-it-your·self /ˌ· · ·ˈ·/ n [U] see DIY – ~ **er** n : *She's a great do-it-yourselfer.*

Dol·by /ˈdɒlbi‖ˈdɔːl-, ˈdəʊl-/ n [U] tdmk a system for reducing unwanted noise on sound recordings: *in Dolby stereo*

dol·drums /ˈdɒldrəmz‖ˈdəʊl-, ˈdɑːl-, ˈdɔːl-/ n [the+P] **1** an area on the ocean where ships cannot move because there is no wind **2 in the doldrums** infml **a** in an unhappy state of mind **b** in a state of inactivity: *The motor trade is really in the doldrums.*

dole¹ /dəʊl/ n **1** [U] money that is given by the government to people who are unemployed: *My dole cheque should arrive tomorrow.* **2 go/be on the dole** BrE infml to start to receive money from the government because one is unemployed: *I've been on the dole for six months.*

dole² v

dole sthg. ↔ **out** phr v [T (to)] to give (esp. money or food in small shares); DISTRIBUTE: *She doled out the money.* | *I doled out food to all the children.*

dole·ful /ˈdəʊlfəl/ adj causing or expressing unhappiness or low spirits: *a doleful glance/experience* – ~ **ly** adv – ~ **ness** n [U]

dole queue /ˈ· ·/ n all the people who are unemployed: *Labour plan to invest in the public sector in order to expand the economy and shorten the dole queues.*

Do·lit·tle /ˈduːlɪtl/, **Dr** a man in children's stories who gets on well with animals and can talk their language by Hugh Lofting

doll¹ /dɒl‖dɑːl, dɔːl/ n **1** a small figure of a person used esp. as a child's toy. Dolls are thought of as toys for girls, but boys also play with them, esp. **action man** dolls dressed as soldiers **2** infml usu. derog a pretty but silly young woman who pays too much attention to her clothes and appearance **3** sl (may be considered offensive to women) a young girl or woman, esp. an attractive or charming one: *My granddaughter is a little doll.* **4** AmE sl a very nice person: *"OK, I'll lend you $20." "You're a doll, Bill!"*

doll² v

doll sbdy. ↔ **up** phr v [T often pass.] infml to dress (someone or oneself) prettily: *all dolled up to go to a*

party | (fig.) *He dolled up the report to make it sound more impressive.*

dol·lar /ˈdɒləʳ‖ˈdɑː-/ n **1** [C usu. sing.] a standard of money, as used in the US, Canada, Australia, New Zealand, Hong Kong, Zimbabwe, and some other countries. It is worth 100 cents and its sign is $. **2** [C] a piece of paper, a coin, etc., of this value **3** [the] the value of US money in relation to the money of other countries: *the rising/falling dollar* – see also **bet one's bottom dollar** (BET³), **feel/look like a million dollars** (MILLION)

dollar di·plo·ma·cy /ˌ··· ·ˈ···/ n [U] the use of financial threats by a country to increase its political power in another country

dollars-and-cents /ˌ··· ·ˈ·/ adj AmE considered from a practical or financial point of view: *It's an interesting idea but from a dollars-and-cents point of view it just won't work.*

dol·lop /ˈdɒləp‖ˈdɑː-/ n [(of)] infml **1** a shapeless mass: *a dollop of clay/mashed potato* **2** a spoonful, esp. of food

doll's house /ˈ· ˌ·/ BrE‖**doll·house** /ˈdɒlhaʊs‖ˈdɑːl-, ˈdɔːl-/ AmE– n -**houses** /ˌhaʊzɪz/ **1** a child's toy house in which small dolls, toy furniture, etc., can be put **2** a very small house

dol·ly /ˈdɒli‖ˈdɑːli, ˈdɔːli/ n **1** (used esp. by and to children) a child's doll **2** tech a flat frame on wheels for moving heavy objects, such as television or cinema cameras

dolly bird /ˈ··· ·/ also **dolly** n BrE infml, old-fash, usu. derog a pretty young woman, esp. one wearing fashionable clothes and not considered very intelligent

dol·men /ˈdɒlmen, -mən‖ˈdəʊlmən, ˈdɑːl-, ˈdɑːl-/ also **cromlech** n tech a group of upright stones supporting a large flat piece of stone, built in ancient times in Britain and France. The most famous example in Britain is Stonehenge.

dol·our BrE ‖ **-or** AmE /ˈdɒləʳ‖ˈdəʊ-/ n [U] poet great sorrow –**orous** adj –**orously** adv

dolphin

porpoise

dolphin

dol·phin /ˈdɒlfɪn‖ˈdɑːl-, ˈdɔːl-/ n a sea animal two to three metres long, which swims about in groups, going over and under the surface of the water in curves. Dolphins are known to be very clever and friendly to humans.

dol·phi·na·ri·um /ˌdɒlfɪˈneəriəm‖ˌdɑːl-, ˌdɔːl-/ n a pool, sometimes with transparent walls, where dolphins are kept and the public can see them

dolt /dəʊlt/ n old-fash, derog a slow-thinking foolish person: *Don't drop it, you dolt!* – ~ **ish** adj – ~ **ishly** adv

do·main /dəˈmeɪn, dəʊ-/ n **1** an area of activity, interest, or knowledge; REALM: *This problem lies outside the domain of medical science.* **2** esp. old use the land owned or controlled by one person, a government, etc.

dome /dəʊm/ n **1** a rounded roof on a building or room **2** something of this shape: *the blue dome of the sky* | *the pink dome of his bald head*

domed /dəʊmd/ adj (often in comb.) covered with or shaped like a dome

Domes·day Book, Doomsday Book /ˈduːmzdeɪ bʊk/ [the] a record of all the lands of England, showing their size, value, ownership, etc., made in 1086 on the orders of William the Conqueror. The Domesday Book has been very valuable in the study of English history.

do·mes·tic¹ /dəˈmestɪk/ adj **1** of or in the house or home: *domestic electrical goods* **2** concerning the family or private life: *Her domestic problems are beginning to affect her work.* **3** enjoying home duties and pleasures: *In spite of being a successful career woman, she's basically very domestic.* **4** of or within a particular country; not foreign or international: *the government's domestic policies* | *domestic flights* – ~ **ally** /kli/ adv

domestic² n a servant who works in a house

domestic an·i·mal /·‚·· '··‚/ n an animal that is not wild but is kept in a house or on a farm

do·mes·ti·cate /dəˈmestɨkeɪt/ v [T] **1** to make (an animal) able to live with people and work for them, esp. on a farm or as a pet: *Cows were domesticated to provide us with milk.* —compare TAME² (1) **2** [*usu. pass.*] to cause to enjoy living at home and doing jobs around the house: *Their son is very domesticated and often does the cooking.* —**cation** /dəˌmestɨˈkeɪʃən/ n [U]

do·mes·tic·i·ty /ˌdəʊmesˈtɪsɨti/ n [U] (a liking for) home or family life: *a scene of happy domesticity*

domestic sci·ence /·‚·· '··/ also **housecraft** BrE, also **home economics** n [U] the study of the skills of housekeeping, such as cooking and sewing. It is taught as a subject in many British and American schools, esp. to girls

domestic ser·vice /·‚·· '··/ n [U] (esp. in former times) the work of a servant in a house. In Britain it is no longer common for people to have servants living in their houses, although many people employ other people to help them clean their house for a few hours each week. —see also CLEANER, CLEANING LADY, SERVANT

domestic vi·o·lence /·‚·· '··/ n [U] violence that takes place in the home, usu. between a husband and wife: *the bad old days when the police didn't think that domestic violence counted as a crime*

Do·mes·tos /dəˈmestɒs ‖ -əʊs/ n [U] tdmk a type of BLEACH made by Lever Brothers Limited used in the home to kill GERMs, clean up dirt and remove nasty smells

dom·i·cile /ˈdɒmɨsaɪl‖ˈdɑː-, ˈdəʊ-/ n fml or law a person's home; the place where a person lives or is considered to live for official purposes: *His last known domicile was 10 New Street, Cambridge.*

dom·i·ciled /ˈdɒmɨsaɪld‖ˈdɑː-, ˈdəʊ-/ adj [F+adv/prep] fml or law having one's domicile: *He does some work in the Middle East but is domiciled in Britain for tax purposes.*

dom·i·cil·i·a·ry /ˌdɒmɨˈsɪliəri‖ˌdɑːmɨˈsɪlieri, ˌdəʊ-/ adj [A] fml or law of, to, or at someone's home: *The health inspectors spend 50% of their time on domiciliary visits.*

dom·i·nance /ˈdɒmɨnəns‖ˈdɑː-/ n [U] the fact or position of dominating; importance, power, or controlling influence: *Our dominance of the market is seriously threatened by this new product.* —compare DOMINATION

dom·i·nant¹ /ˈdɒmɨnənt‖ˈdɑː-/ adj **1** most noticeable or important: *Blue is the dominant colour in his later paintings.* | *Peace was the dominant theme of the conference.* **2** high and easily seen: *The Town Hall was built in a dominant position on a hill.* **3** stronger than the other parts of a system or group: *The right hand is dominant in most people.* | *a dominant group in society* **4** tending to dominate other people: *a dominant personality* **5** tech (of groups of physical qualities passed on from parent to child) able to appear in the child even if only in the GENES of one parent: *Brown eyes are dominant and blue eyes are recessive.*

dominant² n [(the) S] the fifth note of a musical scale of eight notes —compare TONIC² (3)

dom·i·nate /ˈdɒmɨneɪt‖ˈdɑː-/ v [I;T] **1** to have or exercise control or power (over): *The committee works well together, although sometimes the chairman tends to dominate.* **2** to have the most important place or position (in): *The team has dominated international football for years.* | *The great cathedral dominates the centre of the city.* | *The election campaign was dominated by the issue of unemployment.*

dom·i·na·tion /ˌdɒmɨˈneɪʃən‖ˌdɑː-/ n [U] the act of dominating or the state of being dominated: *After the leader died, rival parties struggled for domination of the community.* —compare DOMINANCE

dom·i·neer /ˌdɒmɨˈnɪər‖ˌdɑː-/ v [I (over)] usu. derog to try to control other people, usu. without any consideration of their feelings or wishes: *a domineering personality*

Do·min·go /dəˈmɪŋɡəʊ/, **Pla·ci·do** /ˈplæsɨdəʊ/ (1941–) a Spanish OPERA singer who has played leading TENOR parts in operas in many countries since 1962 and is considered to be one of the best opera singers in the world

Dom·i·ni·ca /ˌdɒmɨˈniːkə‖ˌdɑː-/ the Commonwealth of Dominica, an island in the West Indies which has been a member of the COMMONWEALTH (1) since 1978; chief town Roseau; population 81,000 (1989) —**can** n, adj

Do·min·i·can /dəˈmɪnɪkən/ adj, n (a member) of a Christian religious group established by St Dominic in 1215, who lead a holy life according to a particular set of religious rules

Do·min·i·can Re·pub·lic /dəˌmɪnɪkən rɪˈpʌblɨk/ [the] a country in the West Indies on the island of Hispaniola, which it shares with Haiti; capital Santo Domingo; population 7,019,000 (1989)

do·min·ion /dəˈmɪnjən/ n **1** [U (over)] esp. lit the power or right to rule: *Alexander the Great held dominion over a vast area.* **2** [C] the land(s) held in complete control by one person, ruler, or government: *the king's dominion(s)*

Dominion Day /·'·· ‚·/ a national holiday in Canada, in memory of the beginning of the Dominion of Canada in 1867

Do·min·ions /dəˈmɪnjənz/ n [the+P] countries including Australia, New Zealand, and Canada, which belonged to the British Empire, ruled themselves, and had the same king or queen as Britain

dom·i·no /ˈdɒmɨnəʊ‖ˈdɑː-/ n **-noes** one of a set of small flat pieces of wood, plastic, etc., with a different number of spots on each, used for playing a game (**dominoes**)

Domino, Fats /fæts/ (1928–) an American popular music singer, songwriter, and PIANIST who made many very successful records in the 1950s. He was a leading figure in the development of ROCK 'N' ROLL.

domino ef·fect /'··· ·‚·/ n [(the) S] (usu. in politics) a situation in which one event or action causes similar (usu. undesirable) actions to happen one after another, in the way that a row of standing dominoes will fall over one after another if one of them is pushed —compare KNOCK-ON

domino theo·ry /'··· ‚··/ n [U] the idea that if one country becomes Communist, then other countries in that area will also become Communist

don¹ /dɒn‖dɑːn/ n BrE a university teacher, esp. at Oxford and Cambridge

don² v **-nn-** [T] old use or pomp to put on (clothing and hats) —opposite **doff**

Don n (used in Spanish speaking countries as a polite title before a man's first name): *Don Miguel*

Don [the] a river in SW Russia

Don·a·hue /ˈdɒnəhjuː‖ˈdɑːn-/, **Phil** /fɪl/ (1935–) the host of a popular American talk show

Don·ald Duck /ˌdɒnəld ˈdʌk‖ˌdɑː-/ a character, based on a duck, in the CARTOONs of Walt Disney. Donald Duck was one of the first Disney characters and is now recognized as a SYMBOL of Disney. —compare MICKEY MOUSE¹

do·nate /dəʊˈneɪt‖ˈdəʊneɪt/ v [I,T (to)] to make a gift of (something), esp. for a good purpose: *Last year he donated £1000 to cancer research.* —see also DONOR

do·na·tion /dəʊˈneɪʃən/ n [C;U (to)] the act of donating or something donated: *We are collecting donations for the relief fund.* | *They made a generous donation to charity.* | *The hospital receives a good deal of money in donations.*

Don·cas·ter /ˈdɒŋkəstər‖ˈdɑːŋkæs-/ an industrial town in S Yorkshire in the north of England, which is known for its race course where the **St. Leger** race is held every year

done¹ /dʌn/ past participle of DO¹‚²

done² adj [F no comp.] **1** [(with)] finished: *The job's nearly done.* | *When you are done, give us a call.* | *The affair's now* **over** *and* **done with.** (=completely ended) **2** also **done for** /'··/, **done in** /‚· '··/ – very tired: *I feel completely done in!* **3** cooked enough to eat: *Are the potatoes done yet?* **4** socially acceptable: *It's not done to call the teachers by their first names.* | *It's* **the done thing** *to serve champagne at weddings.* **5 Done!** Agreed! I accept!: *"I'll give you £5 for it." "Done!"* —see also **be hard done by** (HARD² (3))

Don·e·gal /ˌdɒnɨˈɡɔːl‖ˌdɑː-/ a COUNTY in the NW of the Republic of Ireland

Don Gio·van·ni /ˌdɒn dʒəʊˈvɑːni‖ˌdɑːn-/ n infml **1** a DON JUAN **2** an OPERA by Mozart

Don Ju·an /ˌdɒn ˈhwɑːn, -ˈwɑːn, -ˈdʒuːən‖ˌdɑːn-/ n infml a man who is a great lover; LADY-KILLER (from an old Spanish story in which Don Juan SEDUCES a young girl and kills her father, but ends up in HELL): *He thinks he's a bit of a Don Juan.*

don·key /ˈdɒŋki‖ˈdɑːŋki/ *n* **1** a grey or brown animal like a horse, but smaller and with longer ears; ASS¹: *a photograph of Susan having a donkey ride at the seaside.*
▶CULTURAL NOTE Donkeys are thought to be STUBBORN, which means that they are determined to do what they want and it is difficult to make them do anything else. At the seaside and at some outdoor shows or entertainments, etc. in Britain, children can have donkey rides.◀
2 a foolish slow-thinking person

donkey der·by /ˈ·· ˌ··/ *n* a race on donkeys done for amusement, e.g. at a village FETE or on a BEACH

donkey jack·et /ˈ·· ˌ··/ *n BrE* a thick coat, usu. very dark blue, reaching down to the top of the legs, and usu. with a piece of leather or plastic across the shoulders. Donkey jackets are usu. worn by people with outdoor jobs, such as LABOURERS.

donkey's years /ˈ·· ·/ *n* [U] *BrE sl* a very long time: *That was donkey's years ago.* | *I haven't seen him for donkey's years.*

don·key·work /ˈdɒŋkiwɜːk‖ˈdɑːŋkiwɜːrk/ *n* [U] *infml, esp. BrE* the hard uninteresting part of a piece of work: *Why do I always have to do the donkeywork?*

Donne /dʌn/, **John** (1571 or 72–1631) an English religious and love poet, the greatest of the writers of METAPHYSICAL poetry, in which strong feeling and clever reason are combined

don·nish /ˈdɒnɪʃ‖ˈdɑːnɪʃ/ *adj esp. BrE* typical of a university DON, esp. in being more interested in ideas than in real life; BOOKISH – ~**ly** *adv*

do·nor /ˈdəʊnəʳ/ *n* **1** a person who gives or DONATES something **2** (*often in comb.*) someone who gives part of their body to be put into someone else for medical purposes: *a blood/kidney donor*

donor card /ˈ·· ·/ *n* a card carried by people who agree that when they die parts of their body, such as their eyes or KIDNEYS, can be used by doctors, e.g. by being put into the body of another person

Don·o·van /ˈdɒnəvən‖ˈdɑː-/, **Ja·son** /ˈdʒeɪsən/ (1968–) an Australian singer and actor who, with Kylie Minogue, appeared in the Australian television SOAP OPERA "Neighbours", and then went on to become a successful singer. He is popular esp. with young TEENAGERS and considered good-looking and attractive in a healthy, homely way.

Don Quix·ote /ˌdɒn ˈkwɪksət, -kiˈhəʊti‖ˌdɑːn-/ a character in the book *Don Quixote de la Mancha* by Miguel de Cervantes. Don Quixote is an IDEALIST who is prepared to fight for what he believes in, but he often misunderstands things or makes foolish mistakes. For example, he is remembered esp. for **tilting at windmills**, attacking WINDMILLS because he thought they were dangerous MONSTERS.

don't /dəʊnt/ *short for:* **1** do not: *Don't worry!* | *You know him, don't you?* –see also **dos and don'ts** (DO³) **2** *nonstandard, esp. AmE* does not: *She don't like it.*

do·nut /ˈdəʊnʌt/ *n AmE* DOUGHNUT

doo·dah /ˈduːdɑː/ *BrE* ‖ **doo·dad** /ˈduːdæd/ *AmE– n infml*, often *humor* a small object whose name one has forgotten or does not know; THINGAMAJIG; WHATSIT: *Pass us that doodah, will you?* | *What's this little doodad?* | *Have you got the doodad that goes with this?* –see also DOOHICKEY, WHATCHAMACALLIT

doo·dle /ˈduːdl/ *v* [I] to draw lines, figures, etc., while thinking about something else: *I always doodle when I'm making phone calls.* –**doodle** *n* : *His notebook was covered in doodles.*

doo·dle·bug /ˈduːdlbʌg/ *n* a V-1

doo·hick·ey /ˈduːhɪki/ *n AmE infml, humor* a small object whose name one has forgotten or does not know; a small bit of machinery: *Press this button and twist that doohickey to turn it on.*

Doo·lit·tle /ˈduːlɪtl/, **E·li·za** /ɪˈlaɪzə/ a character in Shaw's play *Pygmalion*. Eliza is a working class London flower seller who is taught by Professor Henry Higgins to speak and behave like a rich lady. –see also PYGMALION

doom¹ /duːm/ *n* [C *usu. sing.*;U] **1** a terrible fate; unavoidable destruction or death: *to meet one's doom* | *to go to one's doom* **2 doom and gloom** *infml* sad and discouraging thoughts; hopelessness: *The new economic forecast is full of doom and gloom.*

doom² *v* [T (**to**) *usu. pass.*] to cause to suffer something unavoidable and terrible, such as death or destruction: *The plan was doomed (to failure) from the start.* | *We saw the doomed aircraft just before it crashed.* [+*obj+to-v*] *They were doomed to die.*

Dooms·day /ˈduːmzdeɪ/ **1** the last day of the world's existence **2 till Doomsday** *infml* forever: *You'll be stuck in this job till Doomsday unless you get some better qualifications.*

Doomsday Book /ˈ·· ·/ [*the*] DOMESDAY BOOK

Doones·bu·ry /ˈduːnzbəri/ an American COMIC STRIP by Gary Trudeau which shows the foolishness of American politics and ways of life in an amusing way

door /dɔːʳ/ *n* **1** a movable flat or panelled (PANEL²) surface that opens and closes the entrance to a building, room, vehicle, or piece of furniture: *to open/shut the door* | *I can hear someone knocking at the door.* | *the cupboard door/kitchen door/car door* | *If you can't get in the front door, go to the back door.* | *Will you* **answer the door?** (=open it to let someone in) | *Goodbye, Mr Carter – my secretary will show you to the door.* (=take you to the main door) | *When he became drunk and aggressive his host* **showed him the door.** (=made it clear he was not welcome and should leave) | (fig.)*This agreement opens the door to/shuts the door on improved relations between our two countries.* | (fig.) *Discussions have been going on* **behind closed doors.** (=in secret) —compare GATE (1) **2** an opening for a door; DOORWAY: *She came through the door.* **3** (in certain fixed phrases) a house or building: *My sister lives only two doors away/a few doors away.* | *Our house is* **next door** *to the paper shop.* | *The journey takes about six hours* (**from**) **door to door.** | *We went from door to door collecting money for charity.* **4 be on the door** to have some duty at the entrance to a theatre, club, etc., such as collecting tickets **5 lay something at someone's door** to blame something on someone **6 out of doors** in the open air; OUTDOORS **7 shut the door in someone's face** to refuse to listen to or deal with someone: *We offered the management a compromise but they just shut the door in our face.* –see also BACK DOOR, FRONT DOOR, NEXT DOOR, **at death's door** (DEATH)

door·bell /ˈdɔːbel‖ˈdɔːr-/ *n* a bell that visitors to a house can ring for attention

door·keep·er /ˈdɔːˌkiːpəʳ‖ˈdɔːr-/ *n* a person who guards the main door of a large building and lets people in and out —compare DOORMAN

door·knob /ˈdɔːnɒb‖ˈdɔːrnɑːb/ *n* a usu. round handle on a door to open it with

door·knock·er /ˈdɔːnɒkəʳ‖ˈdɔːrˌnɑːkər/ *n* a metal instrument fixed to a door and used by visitors for knocking at it

door·man /ˈdɔːmæn, -mən‖ˈdɔːr-/ *n* **-men** /men, mən/ a man in a hotel, theatre, etc., who watches the door, helps people to find taxis, sometimes lets people in and out, and usu. wears a uniform —compare DOORKEEPER

door·mat /ˈdɔːmæt‖ˈdɔːr-/ *n* a mat placed in front of or inside a door for cleaning one's shoes on: (fig.) *She's been treated like a doormat by that family of hers all her life.* (=they have never considered her feelings or needs and she has never complained)

door·nail /ˈdɔːneɪl‖ˈdɔːr-/ *n* see **dead as a doornail** (DEAD¹)

door·plate /ˈdɔːpleɪt‖ˈdɔːr-/ *n* a flat piece of metal, usu. brass, fixed to a door and bearing a name, esp. the name of the person living or working inside –see also NAMEPLATE

door prize /ˈ· ·/ *n AmE* a prize given to someone who has drawn or paid for a winning ticket at a show, dance, or party, esp. if the purpose of the draw is to raise money for CHARITY

door·step /ˈdɔːstep‖ˈdɔːr-/ *n* **1** a step in front of an outer door **2** *BrE sl* a very thick piece of bread cut from a loaf **3 on one's doorstep** very near to where one lives or is staying: *"Is the lake far from your hotel?" "No, it's right on our doorstep!"*

door·step·ping /ˈdɔːˌstepɪŋ‖ˈdɔːr-/ *n, adj* [A;U] *BrE derog* (the practice of) causing people inconvenience in private in order to find things to write about them in newspapers: *doorstepping journalists*

door·stop /'dɔːstɒp‖'dɔːrstɑːp/ *BrE* ‖ also **door·stop·per** /-stɒpəʳ‖-stɑː-/— *n* an apparatus for holding a door open or preventing it from opening too far

door-to-door sales·man /ˌ··· '··/ *n* a sales person who visits people in their homes, without invitation, to try to sell them something and who is often very clever at persuading people to buy things they do not need. In Britain, the image that many people have of a door-to-door salesman is of someone who uses lies and tricks in order to sell things, the most popular trick being to put one foot inside the open door of a house so that the person who lives there cannot close the door and has to listen to the salesman. This kind of selling is common for home improvements e.g. DOUBLE-GLAZING, and also ENCYCLOPEDIAS.

door·way /'dɔːweɪ‖'dɔːr-/ *n* an opening for a door into a building or room (not into a piece of furniture): *She stood in the doorway, unable to decide whether to go in.*

dope¹ /dəʊp/ *n* **1** [U] *infml* an ILLEGAL drug, esp. MARIJUANA: *He was arrested for selling dope.* | *a dope dealer* (=someone who sells drugs) **2** [C] *infml* a stupid person **3** [U (on)] *old-fash sl* information, esp. from someone who can be trusted: *Give me all the dope on the new teacher.* **4** [U] *old-fash* any thick liquid used for making machines run easily

dope² *v* [T (UP)] *infml* to give a drug to (a person) or put a drug in (food or drink), esp. in order to make someone sleepy: *They doped his drink and then robbed the house while he lay unconscious.* | *The horse was disqualified from the race because it had been doped.*

dop·ey , **dopy** /'dəʊpi/ *adj* **1** *infml* dull and inactive in the mind and feelings as if from alcohol or a drug; not fully awake: *Lack of sleep can make you feel dopey.* **2** *sl* stupid

Dopey one of the seven DWARFS in the Walt Disney film *Snow White*. He is not very clever.

dop·pel·gäng·er /'dɒpəlgæŋəʳ, -geŋ-‖'dɑː-/ *n Ger* the spirit of a living person seen as the person's double; a WRAITH

Dop·pler ef·fect /'dɒplər ɪˌfekt‖'dɑː-/ *n* [the] *tech* a noticed change in the frequency of sound or light waves produced by a moving object, caused by a change of speed or direction in relation to the person listening to the object. The effect can be noted e.g. when the sound of a SIREN (=noise made by a fire engine) becomes lower as it passes by. —see also RED SHIFT

Dor·ches·ter /'dɔːtʃɪstəʳ‖'dɔːrtʃes-/ a market town in Dorset, S England, known for its connections with the writer Thomas Hardy, who was born nearby. The local government of Dorset is based there.

Dorchester [the] a large, expensive hotel in London

Dor·dogne /dɔː'dɔɪn‖dɔːr'dəʊn / [the] an area in SW France around the River Dordogne which is popular with British tourists

Do·ri·an Gray /ˌdɔːriən 'greɪ/ the main character from Oscar Wilde's story *The Picture of Dorian Gray* in which Dorian's PORTRAIT (=a painting of a person) is physically marked with the signs of the bad life he is living while Dorian remains young and good-looking until his death. When he dies, he and the portrait change faces and the truth becomes known.

Dor·ic /'dɒrɪk‖'dɔː-, 'dɑː-/ *adj* of, like, or typical of the oldest and simplest style of ancient Greek building: *a Doric pillar* —compare CORINTHIAN, IONIC

Do·ri·tos /də'riːtəʊz/ *n tdmk* (a packet of) a type of CORN CHIP that tastes slightly hot

dork /dɔːk‖dɔːrk/ *n AmE sl* a person who is considered stupid because they behave strangely or wear odd clothes: *He didn't get the joke. What a dork!* – – **y** *adj* : *a dorky grin*

dor·mant /'dɔːmənt‖'dɔːr-/ *adj* inactive, esp. not actually growing or producing typical effects: *These bulbs remain dormant for a period of time, before becoming active again under the earth during winter.* | *a dormant volcano* (fig.) *The report lay dormant for two years while the company tried to find additional finances to implement its suggestions.*

dor·mer /'dɔːməʳ‖'dɔːr-/ also **dormer win·dow** /'·· ˌ··/ *n* a window built upright in a sloping roof

dor·mi·to·ry¹ /'dɔːmɪtəri‖'dɔːrmɪtɔːri/ also **dorm** /dɔːm‖dɔːrm/*infml*— *n* **1** a large room for sleeping in, containing a number of beds; usu. in a BOARDING SCHOOL or YOUTH HOSTEL: *The girls planned a midnight feast in*

the dormitory. **2** *AmE* a building in a college or university, where students live and sleep; HALL OF RESIDENCE

dormitory² *adj* [A] *esp. BrE* ‖ **bedroom** *AmE*— (of a place) from which people travel to work in the city every day: *a dormitory town/suburb*

dor·mo·bile /'dɔːməbiːl‖'dɔːr-/ also **camper van** *BrE* ‖ **camper** *AmE n tdmk* a vehicle big enough to live in when on holiday, having cooking equipment and beds in the back part

dor·mouse /'dɔːmaʊs‖'dɔːr-/ *n* **-mice** /maɪs/ a small European woodland animal with a long furry tail that looks rather like a SQUIRREL. In Lewis Carroll's children's book *Alice's Adventures in Wonderland* one of the characters is a dormouse. It is always very sleepy. —see colour picture on page 619

Dor·o·thy Per·kins /ˌdɒrəθi 'pɜːkɪnz‖ˌdɔːrəθi 'pɜːr-/ *n* one of a group of shops in Britain which sells women's clothes at quite low prices: *There's a Dorothy Perkins just off Broad Street.*

Dors /dɔːz‖dɔːrz/, **Diana** (1931–84) a popular English film and television actress thought of as very sexy when young

dor·sal /'dɔːsəl‖'dɔːr-/ *adj* [A] *tech* of, on, or near the back, esp. of an animal: *the dorsal fin of a shark*

Dor·set /'dɔːsɪt‖'dɔːr-/ a COUNTY in SW England on the Channel coast; ADMINISTRATIVE capital Dorchester

do·ry /'dɔːri/ *n* a flat-bottomed rowing boat used for fishing

DOS /dɒs‖dɑːs/ *abbrev. for:* disk operating system, the SOFTWARE which is loaded into a computer to instruct it to operate

dos·age /'dəʊsɪdʒ/ *n fml* [usu. sing.] the amount of a dose: *a dosage of one tablet three times a day for seven days*

dose¹ /dəʊs/ *n* **1** [(of)] a measured amount (of a medicine) given or to be taken at one time: *Take one dose of this cough syrup three times a day.* | (fig.) *In the accident, the workers received a heavy dose of radiation.* **2** [(of)] a period of experiencing something unpleasant: *a bad dose of flu* **3** *sl* a case of GONORRHEA **4 like a dose of salts** *BrE infml* very quickly and easily: *This new dishwasher will get through all the dirty dishes like a dose of salts.*

dose² *v* [T (UP, with)] *often derog* to give medicine to: *She dosed up the children with cough syrup.*

dosh /dɒʃ‖dɑːʃ/ *n* [U] *BrE sl* money: *Have you got any dosh?*

do-si-do /ˌdəʊ siː 'dəʊ/ *n* an action in a COUNTRY DANCE in which partners pass each other back to back

doss¹ /dɒs‖dɑːs/ *n* [S] *sl, esp. BrE* a short sleep: *to have a doss*

doss² *v*

doss down *phr v* [I] *sl, esp. BrE* to lie down to sleep, esp. not in a proper bed or one's usual place: *It was too late to go home, so I dossed down on their floor.*

doss·er /'dɒsəʳ‖'dɑː-/ *n sl, esp. BrE* a homeless person who sleeps in a variety of places; TRAMP

doss·house /'dɒshaʊs‖'dɑːs-/ *n* **-houses** /haʊzˌɪz/ *sl, esp. BrE* a cheap lodging house, esp. one for short stays

dos·si·er /'dɒsieɪ‖'dɔːsjeɪ, 'dɑː-/ *n* a set of papers containing detailed information on a person or subject; FILE: *The secret police keep dossiers on all opponents of the government.*

dost /dʌst/ thou **dost** *old use or bibl* you do

Dos·toy·ev·sky , **Dostoevsky**, **Dostoevski** /ˌdɒstɔɪ'efski ‖ ˌdɑːstə'yef-/, **Fe·od·or Mi·khail·o·vich** /'fiːədɔːʳ mɪ'kaɪləvɪtʃ/ (1821–81) a Russian writer who wrote many NOVELS about human thought and behaviour and who spent many years in a prison camp in Siberia because of his political beliefs. He is considered to be a very important figure in world literature and his novels include *Crime and Punishment* and *The Brothers Karamazov.*

dot¹ /dɒt‖dɑːt/ *n* **1** a small round mark or spot: *Put a dot over the letter i.* | *He watched the train until it was only a dot in the distance.* | *Her blouse was black with white dots on it.* **2** a short sound or flash of light used in sending messages by MORSE CODE —compare DASH² (7) **3 on the dot** *infml* at the exact point in time: *The three o'clock train arrived on the dot.* | *It arrived on the dot of three o'clock.* —see also YEAR DOT

dot² *v* **-tt-** [T] **1** to mark with a dot: *to dot a j* | *a dotted minim* **2** [often pass.] to cover (as if) with dots: *a lake*

dotted with little boats | The company now has over 20 stores dotted about the country. **3** *infml* **to dot one's/the i's and cross one's/the t's** to be extremely careful in a slightly annoying way: *This new textbook is supposed to be for advanced students but it really dots the i's and crosses the t's.* —see also DOTTED LINE

do·tage /ˈdəʊtɪdʒ/ *n* **in one's dotage** weak in one's mind because of old age

dote /dəʊt/ *v*
     dote on/upon sbdy. *phr v* [T] to show great fondness for, esp. in a way that seems foolish: *He dotes on his youngest son.*

doth /dʌθ/ *old use or bibl* does

dot·ing /ˈdəʊtɪŋ/ *adj* [A] extremely fond, esp. foolishly so: *a doting husband who thinks his wife can do no wrong* − −**ly** *adv*

dot-ma·trix print·er /ˌ·· ·· ˌ··/ *n* a printing machine that forms characters from dots printed by needles in a single unit

dotted line /ˌ·· ˈ·/ *n* **1** a line of dots on paper, usu. one on which something is to be written, such as one's name or the answer to a question: *On this map paths are shown by dotted lines.* **2** **sign on the dotted line** *infml* to agree to something unconditionally, esp. by signing an official paper

dot·ty /ˈdɒti‖ˈdɑːti/ *adj infml* weak-minded; slightly mad: *My aunt has gone a bit dotty in her old age.*

dou·ble /ˈdʌbəl/ *adj* **1** consisting of two similar or combined parts; two together: *double doors | a double lock on the door | The word "better" has a double "t" in the middle. | a double murder (=in which two people are killed at the same time) | a double-page advertisement in a magazine | The company received a double blow when it lost two big orders in one week. | a double gin (=two measures of GIN) —compare SINGLE¹ (2)* **2** made for two people: *a double bed | a double room in a hotel* **3** having two different uses or qualities; DUAL: *a double meaning | This switch has a double purpose. | The teacher was accused of applying* **double standards.** (=of treating one group differently from another) **4** deceiving; seeming to be one thing while actually being another: *to lead a double life* —see also DOUBLE-DEALER **5** (of a flower) having more than the usual number of PETALS: *a double daffodil* —see also DOUBLY −**double** *adv*: *a piece of cloth folded double | When you drink too much you sometimes see double. | He was almost* **bent double** *with age.* (=having a very bent back)

double² *n* **1** [C;U] something that is twice the size, quantity, value, or strength of something else: *I paid only £2 for this old book and a dealer offered me double (=£4) for it. | "Would you like a whisky?" "I'll have a double, please."* (=a double measure) **2** [C] a person who looks very much like another: *He is my double, though we are not related.* **3** [C] an actor or actress who takes the place of another in a film for some special, esp. dangerous, purpose **4** [C] a BET (=act of risking money) on two races, with any money won on the first being risked on the second: *He won the daily double.* **5** [C] (in the card game of BRIDGE) an act of doubling (DOUBLE⁴ (3)) **6** [C] (in the game of DARTS) a throw of the dart that hits a point between the two outer circles on the board, and has twice the usual value **7** in BASEBALL, a hit which allows the BATTER³ to reach second base **8** **at/on the double** very quickly and without any delay: *The soldiers marched off at the double. | I phoned him as it was an emergency, and he came round at the double.* **9** **double or quits** *BrE* ‖ **double or nothing** *AmE* the decision (in a game where money is risked, such as DICE) to risk winning twice the amount one has already won, or losing it all —see also DOUBLES

double³ *predeterminer* twice: *I bought double the amount of milk. | His weight is double what it was ten years ago. | Her income is double the national average.*

double⁴ *v* **1** [I;T] to make, be, or become twice as great or as many: *Sales doubled in five years. | The house has doubled in value since I bought it. | They doubled their output with the new machine.* **2** [T (BACK, OVER)] to fold in half: *Double this blanket and put it over the baby.* **3** [I] (in the card game of BRIDGE) to make twice as much as what the opponents will lose if they lose, or win if they win **4** [I] (in BASEBALL) to hit the ball so as to allow the

BATTER³ to run to second base: *Garvey doubled to left field.*
     double as sbdy./sthg. *phr v* [T] to have a second use, job, or purpose as: *This chair doubles as a bed. | In the play, Mary is playing the part of the dancer but also doubles as the mother.*
     double back *phr v* [I] to turn suddenly and sharply back; return along the same path: *He started running towards the street but suddenly doubled back to the house.*
     double up *phr v* **1** [I;T (=double sbdy. ↔ up)] **a** (of a person) to bend at the waist, usu. with pain or laughter: *They all doubled up with laughter.* **b** to cause to do this: *He was doubled up with pain.* **2** [I (with)] to share a bedroom: *When the guests came, she doubled up with her sister.*

double-act /ˈ·· ·/ *n* two COMEDIANs who work and perform together

double a·gent /ˌ·· ˈ··/ *n* someone who is employed by the government of one country to find out secret information about an enemy country while pretending to work in the same way for that enemy country —compare SPY² (1)

double-bar·relled *BrE* ‖ **-reled** *AmE*− /ˌ·· ˈ··◁/ *adj* **1** (of a gun) having two barrels fixed side by side **2** *BrE infml* (of family names) having two parts, as in *Smith-Fortescue: A double-barrelled name is thought to show that someone is of high social class.* **3** *AmE* having two purposes: *a double-barreled plan* **4** *AmE* being very strong or forceful: *a double-barreled attack*

double bass /ˌdʌbəl ˈbeɪs/ also **bass** *n* the largest and deepest instrument of the VIOLIN family

double bed /ˌ·· ˈ·/ *n* a bed in which two people can sleep together —see picture at BED

double bill /ˌ·· ˈ·/ also **double feature** *n* a cinema or theatre performance in which two main films or plays are shown

double bind /ˌ·· ˈ·/ *n* a situation in which any choice a person makes will have unpleasant results

double-blind /ˌ·· ˈ··◁/ *adj tech* (of an EXPERIMENT or study comparing two or more groups) in which neither the experimenters nor the people being studied know which people are being given the new drug, etc. and which are not: *In a double-blind study, the researchers gave a placebo drink or a little bit of alcohol to a small group of volunteers.*

double bluff /ˌ·· ˈ·/ *n* an attempt to deceive someone by telling them the truth in the hope that they will think one is lying —see also BLUFF

double boil·er /ˌ·· ˈ··/ *n* [C] a piece of equipment for cooking food which consists of two pans that fit together, the lower pan having water in it

double-breast·ed /ˌ·· ˈ··◁/ *adj* (esp. of a coat or JACKET) made so that one side of the front is brought across the other side of the front with a double row of buttons — compare SINGLE-BREASTED and see picture at SUIT

double-check /ˌ·· ˈ·/ *v* [I;T] to examine (something) twice or again for exactness or quality: *These figures must be double-checked before the report is published.*

double chin /ˌ·· ˈ·/ *n* a fold of loose skin between the face and neck that looks like a second chin

double cream /ˌ·· ˈ·/ *n* [U] *BrE* very thick cream —compare SINGLE CREAM

double-cross /ˌ·· ˈ·/ *v* [T] *sl* to cheat (esp. someone with whom one has already agreed to do something dishonest): *One of the thieves double-crossed the others by hiding the stolen jewels.* −**double cross** *n* − −**er** *n*

double date /ˌ·· ˈ·/ *n infml, esp. AmE* a social meeting in which two couples go out together −**double-date** *v* [I (with)] : *Let's double-date (with Joanne and Jerry).*

double-deal·er /ˌ·· ˈ··/ *n infml* a dishonest deceiving person −**-ing** *n* [U]

double-deck·er /ˌ·· ˈ··◁/ *n* **1** **double-decker bus** /ˌ·· ·· ˈ·/ a bus with two levels, the typical British bus —compare SINGLE-DECKER **2** a SANDWICH made with three pieces of bread leaving two spaces that are filled with food

double-dip¹ /ˌ·· ˈ·/ *n AmE* an ice cream CONE with two balls of ice cream

double-dip² *v* [I] *AmE* to collect pay or money from two places at once, usu. in a way that is not legal or not approved of, such as receiving WELFARE while working

double-dutch /ˌ·· ˈ·/ *n* [U] **1** *humor* speech or writing that one cannot understand; nonsense: *Their conversation about computers was all double-dutch to me!* **2** *AmE* a game of jumping over two long ropes which are quickly passed one after the other beneath the jumper's feet and over the head: *Most girls know eight or ten rhymes to go with double dutch.*

double-edged /ˌ·· ˈ·◂/ *adj* **1** having two cutting edges **2** having two quite different purposes or meanings: *a spy with a double-edged mission* | *a double-edged remark/compliment*

double en·ten·dre /ˌduːblɒnˈtɒndrə‖-blɑːnˈtɑːn-/ *n Fr* a word or phrase that may be understood in two different ways, one of which is usu. sexual

double fault /ˌ·· ˈ·/ *n* (in games like tennis) two mistakes in a player's SERVICE[1] (9), which may lose a point

double fea·ture /ˌ·· ˈ··/ *n* DOUBLE BILL

double fig·ures /ˌ·· ˈ··/ *n* [P] the numbers 10 to 99: *I don't know how many people work there, but it's well into double figures.*

double first /ˌ·· ˈ·/ *n* (in Britain) two first-class university degrees obtained at the same time. People have to be very clever to achieve this: *a brilliant research doctor with a double first from Cambridge*

double-glaz·ing /ˌ·· ˈ··/ *n* [U] *esp. BrE* glass on a window or door in two separate sheets with a space in between them. Double-glazing salesmen are known for putting a lot of pressure on people to buy their product: *The double-glazing keeps in the heat and keeps out the noise.* – **double-glaze** *v* [T]

Double Glouces·ter /ˌ·· ˈ··/ *n* [U] a popular British cheese

doub·le-head·er /ˌdʌbəlˈhedəʳ/ *n* two games of BASEBALL played one after the other

double in·dem·ni·ty /ˌ·· ·ˈ···/ [U] *AmE law* a feature of a life insurance POLICY that allows for twice the amount of money to be paid if the insured person dies in a particular way, such as an accident: *a double indemnity clause*

double jeop·ar·dy /ˌ·· ˈ···/ *n esp. AmE law* the action of making a person face a trial twice for the same offence. This is forbidden in American law except in special situations.

double-joint·ed /ˌ·· ˈ··◂/ *adj* having joints that allow movement (esp. of the fingers) backwards as well as forwards: *He's double-jointed.* | *a double-jointed elbow*

double-park /ˌ·· ˈ·/ *v* [I;T] to park (a vehicle) on a road beside another vehicle already parked. It is ILLEGAL in Britain and the US.

double play /ˈ·· ·/ *n* in BASEBALL, the action of putting out two runners by throwing the ball quickly from one BASE to the next

double-quick /ˌ·· ˈ·◂/ *adj, adv infml* very quick(ly): *Get the doctor double-quick – the baby's swallowed a pin!*

double room /ˌ·· ˈ·/ *n* a room in a hotel, etc. in which two people can sleep: *Have you got a double room for one night, please?*

doub·les /ˈdʌbəlz/ *n* **doubles** a match, esp. of tennis, played between two pairs of players: *the men's/women's doubles at Wimbledon* –compare SINGLES; see also MIXED DOUBLES

double stan·dard /ˌ·· ˈ··/ *n* a rule, principle, judgment, etc. which is more severe for one set of people, situation, etc. than another, esp. the rules of sexual behaviour which are more severe for women than for men

doub·let /ˈdʌblɪ̈t/ *n* a tight-fitting article of clothing for men, worn on the upper half of the body in Europe from about 1400 to the middle 1600s: *doublet and hose*

double take /ˌ·· ˈ·/ *n infml* a quick but delayed movement of surprise usu. made for humorous effect (used esp. in the phrase **do a double take**)

double-talk /ˈ·· ·/ *n* [U] *infml* language that appears to be serious or sincere but may have more than one meaning or be a mixture of sense and nonsense –**double-talk** *v* [I;T] : *You can't double-talk your way out of this!* – ~**er** *n*

double·think /ˈdʌbəlˌθɪŋk/ *n* [U] *derog* belief in two opposing ideas at the same time

double time /ˌ·· ˈ·/ *n* [U] **1** double wages paid to people who work at weekends or on public holidays as a reward for working on days when most people do not want to work –compare **time and a half** (TIME[1] (42)) **2** *AmE* a slow run, done esp. by people in the army

double vi·sion /ˌ·· ˈ··/ *n* [U] (the state of) seeing two of everything after e.g. a knock on the head or too much alcohol

double wham·my /ˌdʌbəl ˈwæmi/ *n infml* a combination of two bad things which come together: *the double whammy of more taxes and higher prices*

double whis·key /ˌ·· ˈ··/ also **large whiskey** *n* **-whiskies** two measures of whiskey from a bottle in a bar, PUB, etc.: *a double whiskey and soda/coke*

double yel·low lines /ˌ·· ·· ˈ·/, **double yellows** /ˌ·· ˈ··/ *n* [P] two yellow lines painted on the side of a road next to the PAVEMENT to show that cars cannot be parked there –compare SINGLE YELLOW LINE

dou·bloon /dʌˈbluːn/ *n* a former gold coin of Spain and Spanish America

doub·ly /ˈdʌbli/ *adv* **1** to twice the degree: *to make doubly sure* | *You've got to be doubly careful when you're driving in fog.* **2** in two ways or for two reasons: *You are doubly mistaken.*

doubt[1] /daʊt/ *v* [T *not in progressive forms*] **1** to be uncertain about; not trust or have confidence in: *I doubt his honesty.* | *She did exactly what she promised – I'm sorry I ever doubted her.* | *I've always doubted the value of this approach to education.* **2** to consider unlikely: *We may have it ready by tomorrow, but I very much doubt it.* [+*that*] *I doubt that she will get the job.* (=I don't think she will) [+**if/whether**] *I doubt if/whether we will make a profit out of it.* (=I don't think we will) – ~**er** *n*

▷ USAGE In negative statements **doubt** is followed by *that*: *I don't* **doubt** (=I am certain) *that he's telling the truth.* In other statements **doubt** is often followed by *if* or *that*, though some people feel *whether* is the only correct form here: *I* **doubt** *whether he's telling the truth.* (=I do not believe he is telling the truth.)◁

doubt[2] *n* **1** [C;U (**about**)] (a feeling of) uncertainty of belief or opinion; lack of confidence or trust: *troubled by religious doubt/doubts* [+*wh-*] | *There's some doubt whether John will come on time.* | *I've no doubt who did it.* | [+(*that*)] *There's no doubt that he'll come.* | *He's quite sure that the business will do well, but I still* **have my doubts (about it).** | *It was* **without doubt** (=certainly) *the most successful film of the year.* **2** [U] a state of uncertainty: *The whole matter is still* **in (some) doubt.** | *Her guilt has been established* **beyond reasonable doubt/beyond the shadow of a doubt.** | *His ability has never been in doubt – the question is whether he is prepared to work hard.* **3 no doubt** almost certainly; very probably: *No doubt he was just trying to help.* | *The court will no doubt deal severely with the criminals.* | *"John will probably be late, won't he?" "No doubt."* –see also **benefit of the doubt** (BENEFIT[1])

▷ USAGE 1 **Doubt** is followed by *that* after *no* or *not*. Compare *There is no* **doubt** *that he is guilty* and *It seems to me that there is some* **doubt** *(as to) whether he is guilty.* 2 **No doubt** and (more formal) **doubtless** can be used simply to mean "I think" or "I agree": **No doubt** *you'll be at the party tonight* (=I expect you'll be there). But **without doubt** and **undoubtedly** express a stronger sense of knowing the real truth: *There will* **undoubtedly** (=certainly) *be trouble with the unions if she is dismissed.*◁

doubt·ful /ˈdaʊtfəl/ *adj* **1** [(**about**)] (of a person) full of doubt; uncertain; unconfident: *He says he can do it, but I'm rather doubtful (about it).* [F+**if, whether**] *I'm doubtful whether she will agree to this.* **2** causing doubt or uncertainty; open to question: *It's doubtful that he ever found out about it.* | *The story he gave the police is very doubtful.* **3** not settled or decided: *The future is too doubtful for us to make plans.* **4** not probable; unlikely: *It is doubtful that we can get the engine working before morning.* **5** probably worthless or dishonest; QUESTIONABLE: *a doubtful advantage* | *This document looks a bit doubtful – let's show it to a lawyer.* | *a promise of doubtful value* | *There's a rather* **doubtful character** *watching our house.* – ~**ly** *adv*

Doubting Thom·as /ˌ·· ˈ··/ *n humor* a person who tends to express doubt and does not easily believe things (from the story in the Bible of the follower of Jesus called Thomas who did not believe that Jesus had risen from the dead until he saw proof of it): *a Doubting Thomas who thought that the doctors had no chance of making him well again*

doubt·less /ˈdaʊtləs/ *adv* **1** very probably: *It will doubtless rain on the day of the garden party.* **2** without doubt; certainly: *They have doubtless planned a counter-attack.* —see DOUBT² (USAGE)

douche /duːʃ/ *n* (an instrument for forcing) a stream of water into or onto any part of the body to wash it, esp. for medical reasons

dough /dəʊ/ *n* [U] **1** flour mixed with water ready for baking **2** *sl* money

dough·boy /ˈdəʊbɔɪ/ *n AmE infml* an American soldier during the FIRST WORLD WAR

dough·nut¹ ‖also **donut** *AmE* /ˈdəʊnʌt/ *n* a small round often ring-shaped cake cooked in hot fat and covered with sugar: *a jam doughnut*

doughnut² *v* [I;T] to gather closely round (a person who is being filmed) in order to appear in the film with them — ~ **doughnutting** *n* [U]

dough·ty /ˈdaʊti/ *adj old use or humor* full of courage and determination

dough·y /ˈdəʊi/ *adj* **1** (of bread, cake, etc.) not cooked enough; soft or too soft **2** (of human skin) unhealthily pale; PASTY

Doug·las¹ /ˈdʌɡləs/ the capital of the Isle of Man

Douglas², Kirk (1916–) an American film actor known for playing the HERO in films such as *Spartacus*

Douglas³, Mi·chael /ˈmaɪkəl/ an American film actor, son of Kirk Douglas, known for his part in the films *Fatal Attraction* and *Romancing the Stone*

Doug·lass /ˈdʌɡləs/, **Fred·e·rick** /ˈfredərɪk/ (1817–95) a former slave who worked to get rid of the slave system and wrote the story of his own life

Doun·reay /ˈduːnreɪ, duːnˈreɪ/ a town in Scotland where there was a NUCLEAR power station until 1977

dour /dʊəʳ ˈdaʊə/ *adj* cold and unsmiling in one's nature or manner; cheerless; GLOOMY: *a dour character/expression* — ~ **ly** *adv*

douse , dowse /daʊs/ *v* [T (**with, in**)] to put into liquid (esp. water) or throw water over: *to douse a fire* | *I doused the cloths in disinfectant.*

dove¹ /dʌv/ *n* **1** a kind of PIGEON, a soft-voiced bird often used as a sign of peace and freedom from anything seen as wrong: *A pair of doves were cooing* (=making their gentle noise) *in a tree outside the window.* Doves are sometimes mentioned when people are talking about loving behaviour or life-long faithfulness between a man and a woman: *Gentle as a dove came the sound of her voice.*| *They were cuddling up to each other like a pair of doves.* **2** (in politics) a person in favour of peace and COMPROMISE —opposite **hawk**; see picture at HAWK

dove² /dəʊv/ *esp. AmE a past tense of* DIVE

dove·cote /ˈdʌvkəʊt, -kɒt‖-kəʊt, -kɑːt/ also **-cot** /-kɒt‖-kɑːt/ *n* a house built for doves to live in

Do·ver /ˈdəʊvəʳ/ a town in SE England on the Channel coast which is known as a port from which ships travel to and from France carrying passengers and goods. The port at Dover is below some high cliffs which can be seen from a distance and English people say that the first sight of **the white cliffs of Dover** is a sign that one is near home again after travelling. —see also WHITE CLIFFS OF DOVER and —see colour map on page 818

dove·tail¹ /ˈdʌvteɪl/ *n* a join formed in wood with a shaped piece sticking out at the end of one piece fitting closely into a cut-out place in the other piece

dovetail² *v* **1** [T (TOGETHER)] to join (wood) by means of dovetails **2** [I;T (**with, into**)] to (cause to) fit skilfully or perfectly together: *I dovetailed my holiday arrangements with Joyce's so that there would always be one of us to run the shop.*

dow·a·ger /ˈdaʊədʒəʳ/ *n* **1** *infml* a grand-looking rich old lady **2** a woman of high social class who has land or a title from her dead husband: *a dowager duchess*

dow·dy /ˈdaʊdi/ *adj* **1** (esp. of a woman) dressed in a dull and unattractive way **2** (of clothes) uninteresting and old-fashioned; not stylish: (fig.) *an attempt to jazz up the company's rather dowdy image* —**dily** *adv* —**diness** *n* [U]

Dow Jones /ˌdaʊ ˈdʒəʊnz◂/ also **Dow Jones Average** /ˌ· ˈ···/, **Dow Jones In·dex** /ˌ· · ˈ··/— *n* [*the*] a daily list of the relative prices of shares on the American STOCK EXCHANGE, based on the daily average prices of 30 industrial shares. The prices listed by Dow Jones are thought to show how the American STOCK MARKET in general is performing. —compare FINANCIAL TIMES INDEX

down¹ /daʊn/ *adv* **1** from above towards a lower place or position; to the floor, the ground, or the bottom: *The man bent down to kiss the child.* | *It gets cold quickly when the sun goes down.* | *The boy fell down and hurt himself.* | *The old lady was knocked down by a car.* | *She came down from her bedroom.* | *The telephone wires were blown down by the storm.* | *Put the cup down on the table.* | *We looked down at the sea from the top of the cliffs.* **2** in a low or lower than usual place or level: *down at the bottom of the sea* | *The river is down.* | *The telephone wires are down.*| *It's very early, and no one is down* (=downstairs) *yet.* **3** from standing to sitting, or sitting to lying: *Please sit down.* | *You may feel better if you go and lie down.* **4** in or into the body as a result of swallowing: *Can't you get the medicine down?* | *She's been very sick and she can't keep her food down.* **5** in or towards the south: *He's flying down to London from Scotland.* | *They live down south.* —compare UP¹ (4) **6** *BrE* away from a university, e.g. at the end of a course of study: *When is John coming down from Oxford/Harvard?* | *He was sent down* (=dismissed from the university) *for taking drugs.* **7** along; away from the person speaking: *Will you walk down to the library with me?* **8** (with verbs of fixing or fastening) firmly or tightly: *Have you stuck down the back of the envelope?* | *They closed the lid and nailed it down.* **9** on paper; in writing: *"Did you write/copy/mark/put down the telephone number?" "I have it down somewhere."* | *Please put my name down on the list.* | *I see she's down* (on the programme) *to give a talk about the marketing department.* **10** at or towards a lower level, e.g. of price or quantity: *Production has gone down this year.* (=we have produced less) | *This year's profits are well down on* (=when compared with) *last year's.* | *They wanted to charge £5000 for the car, but we managed to get them down/get the price down to £4500.* | *Everyone in the company, from the Managing Director down, will have to take a pay cut.* | *We're down to our last $5.* (=this is all the money we have left) **11** in or towards a lower or worse condition: *The military government had kept the people down for many years.* | *That family has certainly* **come down in the world.** (=moved to a lower social level) **12** (showing less noise, activity, strength, etc.): *Let the fire burn down.* | *Can you quieten the children down?* | *I wish you would turn the radio down* (=lower) *a bit.* | *They shouted the speaker down.* (=made him stop talking) **13** from the past: *These jewels have been passed/handed down in our family from mother to daughter for 300 years.* **14** into a smaller, lower, thinner, weaker, etc., state: *Boil it down.* | *This whisky's been watered down.* | *The heels of his shoes had worn down.* | *He got his report down to only three pages.* **15** (of money) to be paid at once in CASH: *You can buy this washing machine for $60 down and $10 a week for a year.* **16** to the moment of catching, getting, or discovering: *The men hunted the lion down.* | *The police ran the thief down.* | *We never succeeded in tracking that rumour down.* (=finding out where it came from) **17** from top to bottom: *He washed/hosed the car down.* **18 down to: a** to and including a lower degree or position in a set: *Everyone uses the firm's canteen, from the chairman down to the boy who sweeps the floors.* **b** the responsibility or fault of: *It's down to Tom whether he decides to pay.* | *The failure of the project is really down to bad management.* **19 down 'under** *infml* in or to Australia or New Zealand **20 down with** ill with: *Jane has gone/come down with a cold/with flu.* **21 Down with** … (a shout used to show opposition) I/We don't want … : *Down with the government!* compare UP (16)

down² *adj* **1** [F] sad; in low spirits; DEPRESSED: *He was very down after losing his job.* **2** [A] directed or going down: *the down escalator/train* (=from London or any central place) **3** [F] behind an opponent (by): *He was down (by) two sets to one, but went on to win the tennis match.* **4** [F] *infml* finished; already dealt with: *eight down and two to go* **5** [F] *tech* (of computer systems) not in operation: *The computer is down now but should be back up in an hour.* — opposite **up** **6 down for** entered on the list for (a race, school, etc.): *What subjects are you down for this term?* **7 down on** *infml* having and expressing a low opinion of: *Don't be so down on him.* —see also **be down on one's luck** (LUCK)

down³ *prep* **1** to or in a lower place in; downwards by way of: *We ran down the hill.* | *The water poured down the pipe.* | *The bathroom is down those stairs.* **2** along; to or at the far end of: *He looked down the barrel of the gun.* | *They live just down the road.* **3** in the direction of the current of: *to go down the river* **4** *BrE nonstandard* to; down to: *I'm just going down the shops.*

down⁴ *n* **1** (in FOOTBALL (2)) any of the four plays during which the team which has the ball tries to move it ten yards or more along the field towards the GOAL: *It's third down and five yards to go (the team is making its third attempt to move the ball and has to move it five more yards to reach ten yards).* **2 have a down on someone** *infml* to have a low opinion of someone; dislike them — see also DOWNS, UPS AND DOWNS

down⁵ *v* [T] **1** to knock or force to the ground: *The boxer downed his opponent in the third round.* **2** to swallow quickly (esp. a liquid): *He downed his coffee and left.* **3** *AmE* to defeat: *Our baseball team easily downed the opposition.* **4 down tools** to stop working, esp. suddenly and because one is unhappy or dissatisfied about something —compare STRIKE¹ (7), ² (1)

down⁶ *n* [U] fine soft feathers or hair, as on a young bird or a baby's head − −**y** *adj*

Down a former COUNTY of Northern Ireland

down- see WORD FORMATION

down-and-out /₁· · ¹·◀/ *n, adj* **down-and-outs** *infml* (a person who is) suffering from lack of money, work, home, etc., and unable to change the situation

down-at-heel /₁· · ¹·◀/ *adj* (of a person) dressed in old worn-out clothes whose condition suggests lack of money

down·beat /ˈdaʊnbiːt/ *adj infml* not showing strong, eager, or hopeful feelings; RESTRAINED —compare UPBEAT

down·cast /ˈdaʊnkɑːst‖-kæst/ *adj* **1** sad and discouraged; DEJECTED: *I felt a bit downcast when I failed my exam.* **2** directed downwards: *with downcast eyes*

down·court /ˈdaʊn₁kɔːt‖-₁kɔːrt/ *adv, adj* in BASKETBALL, towards or in the side of the court in which a player can get a GOAL (**make a basket**): *Magic moves the ball downcourt, passing it to Byron Scott.*

down·er /ˈdaʊnəʳ/ *n sl* **1** a drug that reduces the activity of the mind and body —compare UPPER² **2** an experience, person, or situation that causes sadness or discouragement: *He's a real downer − he never does anything but complain.* **3 be on a downer** *infml* to be feeling low in spirits: *She's on a bit of a downer at the moment. She split up with her boyfriend a couple of weeks ago.*

down·fall /ˈdaʊnfɔːl/ *n* (something that causes) a sudden fall from a high position; ruin: *Drink and gambling brought about his downfall|were his downfall.* | *The scandal led to the downfall of the government.*

down·grade /ˈdaʊngreɪd, ₁daʊnˈgreɪd‖ˈdaʊngreɪd/ *v* [T (**to**)] **1** to give a lower position to (an employed person) or lower level to (a job): *She was downgraded to assistant manager.* —opposite **upgrade** **2** *AmE* to make something seem unimportant: *The mayor downgraded the citizens' complaints, saying that other factors had to be considered first.*

down·heart·ed /₁daʊnˈhɑːtɪd◀‖-ɑːr-/ *adj* in low spirits; sad; DESPONDENT − −**ly** *adv*

down·hill /₁daʊnˈhɪl◀/ *adj, adv* **1** (sloping or going) towards the bottom of a hill: *running downhill* | *downhill skiing* [after *n*] *the path downhill* **2** *infml* (becoming) easier, esp. after a period of effort or difficulty: *The hardest part of the work is over − it's all downhill from now on.* **3 go downhill** to move towards a lower or worse state or level: *His work has been going downhill recently.*

Dow·ning Street /ˈdaʊnɪŋ striːt/ the government of Great Britain (from the name of the street in London which contains the official houses of the British **Prime Minister** (Number 10) and the **Chancellor of the Exchequer**, and the **British Foreign and Commonwealth Office**): *talks between Dublin and Downing Street* | *Mr Major's first months in Downing Street (=as PRIME MINISTER)* | *Downing Street reported a drop in the*

number of unemployed. −see also NUMBER TEN and see colour picture on page 950

down·light·er /ˈdaʊnlaɪtəʳ/ *n* a light placed at a high level and directed downwards −compare UPLIGHTER

down·load /daʊnˈləʊd/ *v* [T] to move (information or PROGRAMS) from one computer system to another

down·mar·ket /₁· ¹···◀/ *adj* being or using goods produced to meet the demand of the lower social groups −compare UP-MARKET

down pay·ment /₁· ¹··/ *n* a part of the full price paid at the time of buying something, with the rest to be paid later: *They saved up enough to make a down payment on a new lounge suite.* −compare DEPOSIT² (3)

down·play /₁daʊnˈpleɪ/ *v* [T] to make (something) seem less important than it really is; PLAY **down**: *Most of the newspaper reports downplayed the significance of this accident.*

down·pour /ˈdaʊnpɔːʳ/ *n* a heavy fall of rain −see RAIN (USAGE)

down·right¹ /ˈdaʊnraɪt/ *adv infml* (esp. of something bad) thoroughly; completely: *She wasn't just unfriendly, she was downright rude.*

downright² *adj* [A] *infml* **1** (esp. of something bad) thorough; complete: *a downright cheat* | *His comment was a downright insult.* **2** plain; direct; FORTHRIGHT: *a downright kind of man who says just what he thinks*

downs /daʊnz/ *n* [P] *BrE* (*often cap. as part of a name*) low rounded grassy hills, esp. chalk hills, as in the south of England: *the North/South Downs*

down·side /ˈdaʊnsaɪd/ *adj* (esp. in business) showing an expectation or likelihood of loss, disadvantage, or failure: *downside estimate of future sales* —opposite **upside** − **downside** *n* [S] : *The downside of the project is that some jobs will be lost.*

down·spout /ˈdaʊnspaʊt/ also **drainspout** *n AmE for* DRAINPIPE (2)

Down's syn·drome /ˈ· ₁··/ also **mongolism** *now usu. taboo*− *n* [U] a condition which results in a baby being born with lower than average mental ability and having sloping eyes, a low forehead, and broad hands with short fingers. Down's syndrome is usu. caused by an additional CHROMOSOME being present in a baby. A mother is more likely to have a baby with Down's syndrome if she is over 35 years old.

down·stage /₁daʊnˈsteɪdʒ◀/ *adj, adv* towards or at the front of a theatrical stage: *The actor came downstage.* | *A battle was being acted downstage.* | *downstage action* − opposite **upstage**

down·stairs /₁daʊnˈsteəz◀‖-eərz◀/ *adv* on or to a lower floor and esp. the main or ground floor of a house: *to come downstairs* | *Is anyone downstairs?* −compare UPSTAIRS −**downstairs** *adj* [A] : *a downstairs bedroom* − **downstairs** *n* : *We haven't painted the downstairs yet.*

down·stream /₁daʊnˈstriːm◀/ *adj, adv* (moving) with the current, towards the mouth of a river, stream, etc.: *The boat drifted downstream.* —opposite **upstream**

down·time /ˈdaʊntaɪm/ *n* [U] **1** the time during which a machine, esp. a computer, is not operating **2** *AmE* time when a person is not working, esp. when they are resting or relaxing: *Everybody needs their downtime after a hard day's work.*

down-to-earth /₁· · ¹·◀/ *adj apprec* practical and honest: *a down-to-earth approach to health care* | *She's very down-to-earth and will tell you what she really thinks.*

down·town¹ /₁daʊnˈtaʊn◀/ *adj, adv esp. AmE* to, towards, or in the business section of a town or city: *to go downtown* | *downtown restaurants/offices* —compare UPTOWN, MIDTOWN

downtown² /ˈdaʊntaʊn/ *n AmE* the business center of a town or city: *City Hall has recently passed a proposal to improve street lighting in the city's downtown.*

down·trod·den /ˈdaʊn₁trɒdn‖-₁trɑː-/ *adj esp. lit* treated badly or without respect by those in positions of power: *downtrodden workers*

down·turn /ˈdaʊntɜːn‖-tɜːrn/ *n* [(**in**)] a (usu. unwelcome) lessening of business activity, production, etc.: *A downturn in shipbuilding orders has meant the laying-off of hundreds of workers.* −opposite **upturn**

down un·der /₁· ¹··/ *adv humor infml* in Australia or New

Zealand: *Conserving water is part of everyday life down under and most Australians re-use their domestic water in the garden.*

down·ward /ˈdaʊnwəd‖-wərd/ *adj* [A] going down: *a downward movement of the head* | *the downward trend of share prices* | (fig.) *the downward path to ruin* —opposite **upward**

down·wards /ˈdaʊnwədz‖-wərdz/ also **downward** *AmE— adv* **1** towards a lower level or position: *He looked downwards to avoid my eyes.* | *Everyone in the company had to take a pay cut, from the chairman downwards.* **2** with a particular side towards the ground or floor: *He lay face downwards.* —opposite **upwards** **3** from an earlier time: *downwards through the years*

down·wind /ˌdaʊnˈwɪnd◂/ *adj, adv* in the direction that the wind is moving

dow·ry /ˈdaʊəri/ *n* the property and money that a woman brings to her husband in marriage

dowse¹ /daʊs/ *v* [T] to DOUSE

dowse² /daʊz/ *v* [I] to DIVINE² (2)

dow·ser /ˈdaʊzəʳ/ *n* a DIVINER

doy·en /ˈdɔɪən/ **doy·enne** /dɔɪˈen/ *fem.— n* the oldest, longest-serving, or most experienced member of a group: *He was the doyen of sports commentators.*

Doyle, Sir Arthur Conan see CONAN DOYLE

doy·ley , doyly /ˈdɔɪli/ *n* a DOILY

doz. *n written abbrev. for* DOZEN

doze /dəʊz/ *v* [I] to sleep lightly or for a short time: *Grandfather was dozing in front of the television.* —**doze** *n* : *to have a little doze*
  doze off also **drop off, nod off** *phr v* [I] to fall into a light sleep unintentionally: *The lecture was so boring that I dozed off in the middle of it.*

doz·en /ˈdʌzən/ *determiner, n* **dozen** or **dozens** **1** a group of 12: *a dozen eggs* | *These eggs are 40p a half dozen.* (=40p for six) – see TABLE 1 **2 dozens (and dozens) of** *infml* lots (and lots) of; very many: *I've been there dozens of times.* – see also BAKER'S DOZEN, **nineteen to the dozen** (NINETEEN)

doz·y /ˈdəʊzi/ *adj* **1** sleepy: *a dozy feeling/afternoon* **2** *BrE infml* stupid; slow in understanding: *a dozy boy* —**ily** *adv* —**iness** *n* [U]

DP /ˌdiː ˈpiː/ *abbrev. for* DATA PROCESSING: *the DP department*

D Phil /ˌdiː ˈfɪl/ *n* a PHD

DPP /ˌdiː piː ˈpiː/ *n* [the] *abbrev. for* DIRECTOR OF PUBLIC PROSECUTIONS

DQ /ˌdiː ˈkjuː/ *AmE infml abbrev. for* DAIRY QUEEN

Dr *written abbrev. for:* Doctor

drab¹ /dræb/ *adj* uninteresting; lacking brightness or colour; cheerless: *a drab green dress* | *Nothing ever brightened their drab lives.* —~**ly** *adv* —**ness** *n* [U]

drab² *n old use derog* a dirty, untidy, and perhaps immoral woman

Drab·ble /ˈdræbəl/, **Margaret** (1939–) an English NOVELIST who is best known for her books about middle class women in modern life

drabs /dræbz/ *n* see DRIBS

drachm /dræm/ *n* a DRAM (1)

drach·ma /ˈdrækmə/ *n* -**mas** or -**mae** /miː/ **1** the standard of money of modern Greece **2** an ancient Greek silver coin and weight

dra·co·ni·an /drəˈkəʊniən/ *adj* very severe or cruel; HARSH: *draconian measures/legislation to deal with the problem of street crime*

Drac·u·la /ˈdrækj�lə/ a frightening VAMPIRE who has FANGS (=long teeth) and wears a black CAPE and has become a well-known character in HORROR films and books (from the story of Count Dracula, written by the Irishman Bram Stoker in 1897): *He's got horrible sticky-out teeth. He looks just like Dracula.* —see also VAMPIRE

Dracula

draft¹ /drɑːft‖dræft/ *n* **1** [C] the first rough and incomplete form of something written, drawn, or planned: *I've made a first draft of my speech for Friday, but it still needs a lot of work.* | *a draft proposal for a new law* | *a plan still only in draft form* **2** [C] a written order for money to be paid by a bank, esp. from one bank to another: *a draft drawn on the Glasgow branch of our bank for £50* | *to get money from Paris to Rome by (bank) draft —* compare CHEQUE **3 a** [*the*] *AmE for* CONSCRIPTION **b** [(*the*) U] *esp. AmE* a group of people chosen by CONSCRIPTION **4** [C] *AmE for* DRAUGHT **5** a system in some American sports in which PROFESSIONAL teams pick college players for their teams: *He's likely to be the number one draft choice for the Washington Redskins.*

draft² *v* [T] **1** to make a draft of: *to draft a letter to the bank manager* **2** [(into)] *AmE for* CONSCRIPT¹

draft board /ˈ· ˌ·/ *n AmE* the committee which decides who will be drafted into the armed forces

draft dod·ger /ˈ· ˌ··/ *n AmE* a person who deliberately and illegally takes action to avoid military CONSCRIPTION —see also VIETNAM WAR, compare CONSCIENTIOUS OBJECTOR

draft·ee /drɑːˈftiː‖dræfˈtiː/ *n AmE for* CONSCRIPT²

drafts·man /ˈdrɑːftsmən‖ˈdræfts-/ **drafts·wom·an** /-wʊmən/ *fem.— n* -**men** /mən/ **1** a person who puts a suggested law or a new law into proper words **2** *AmE for* DRAUGHTSMAN (1) **3** *esp. AmE for* DRAUGHTSMAN (2)

draft·y /ˈdrɑːfti‖ˈdræfti/ *adj AmE for* DRAUGHTY

drag¹ /dræg/ *v* -**gg-** **1** [T] to pull (something heavy) along with great effort: *dragging a great branch along* | *The protesters were dragged away by the police.* | (fig.) *Why must you drag me out to a concert on a cold night like this?* **2** [I (ALONG)] to move along while touching the ground: *The bottom of her long dress dragged (along) in the dust.* **3** [I] to move along too slowly or with difficulty: *He dragged behind the others.* | *The play dragged a bit in the third act.* **4** [T (**for**)] to look for something by pulling a heavy net along the bottom of (water): *They're dragging the river for the body of the missing girl.* **5 drag one's feet/heels** *infml* to act intentionally in a slow or ineffective way
  drag sbdy. ↔ **down** *phr v* [T] to cause to feel ill or low in spirits: *His unhappy marriage seems to be dragging him down.*
  drag sthg. ↔ **in** *phr v* [T] to introduce (something or someone unconnected with the main subject): *John and Mary were having an argument and I got dragged in.* | *He's always dragging politics into his conversation.*
  drag on *phr v* [I] to continue for an unreasonable length of time: *The meeting dragged on for hours.* | *Their unhappy marriage dragged on because of family pressures.*
  drag out *phr v* [I;T (=**drag** sthg. ↔ **out**)] to (cause to) last an unnecessarily long time: *They dragged out the meeting with long speeches.*
  drag sbdy./sthg. ↔ **up** *phr v* [T] *infml* **1** to draw attention to (a usu. unpleasant subject or event that has been generally forgotten about) unnecessarily: *The newspapers keep dragging up the mistake he made ten years ago.* **2** *BrE* to bring up (a child) badly, esp. without good manners

drag² *n* **1** [C;U] the action or an act of dragging **2** [C (**on, upon**)] something or someone that makes it harder to advance towards a desired end: *He felt that his family was a drag on his success.* **3** [S] *sl* something or someone that is unexciting and uninteresting: *The party was a drag, so we left early.* | *Don't be such a drag!* | *"We've got all these envelopes to address." "What a drag!"* **4** [C] *sl* an act of breathing in cigarette smoke: *He took a long drag on his cigar.* **5** [U] *sl* the clothing of one sex worn by the other: *in drag* | *a drag act* (=a performance in which a man is dressed as a woman or a woman as a man) | *a drag queen* **6** [S;U] the force of the air that acts against the forward movement of an aircraft or vehicle **7** [C *usu. sing.*] *AmE sl* a street or road: *the main drag*

drag·gled /ˈdrægəld/ *adj* BEDRAGGLED

drag·gy /ˈdrægi/ *adj infml* unpleasantly dull

drag·net /ˈdrægnet/ *n* **1** a net that is pulled along the bottom of a river or lake, to bring up anything that may lie there **2** a system of connected actions and methods for catching criminals

Dragnet an American television show which was based

on the activities of the Los Angeles police. The main character, Joe Friday, is famous for saying "Just the facts, m'am."

drag·o·man /ˈdrægəmən, -gəʊ-/ n **-mans** (in some countries of the Middle East, esp. formerly) a person who is a guide and translator

dragon

drag·on /ˈdrægən/ n **1** a large imaginary animal with wings and the power to breathe out fire **2** infml a fierce bad-tempered old woman: *We were really frightened of the maths teacher. She was a real dragon.* —see also **chase the dragon** (CHASE¹ (5))

drag·on·fly /ˈdrægənflaɪ/ n a large brightly-coloured insect with a long thin body and large thin wings —see picture at INSECT

dra·goon¹ /drəˈguːn/ n a member of a European army group formerly consisting of heavily armed soldiers on horseback

dragoon² v
  dragoon sbdy. **into** sthg. phr v [T] to force into doing something by violent measures, threats, or other pressures: (fig.) *I was dragooned into helping with the children's party.*

drag queen /ˈ· ˌ·/ n a HOMOSEXUAL man who dresses as a woman

drag race /ˈ· ˌ·/ n AmE a short car race which is won by the car which can ACCELERATE fastest from being stopped. Many TEENAGERs enter drag races illegally, often in stolen cars.

drag·ster /ˈdrægstər/ n a car used in DRAG racing which is long, narrow, and low to the ground

drain¹ /dreɪn/ v [I;T] **1** [(AWAY, OFF, OUT)] to (cause to) flow off gradually or completely: *to drain all the oil from/out of the engine | Boil the vegetables for 20 minutes then drain off the water. | The rainwater drained off/away. | (fig.) These children drain my energy! | (fig.) This country is being drained of its best doctors. | (fig.) The old lady's strength is draining away.* **2** [(OFF, of)] to (cause to) become gradually dry, as water or other liquid is removed: *to drain a field/a flooded mine | Let the wet glasses drain a bit before you dry them up. | She was so afraid/angry that her face was drained of blood. | She drained her glass* (=drank all the contents) *and asked for more water. | (fig.) I feel drained of emotion.*

drain² n **1** [C] (the GRATING over) a means of draining, such as a ditch or underground pipe that carries waste water away: *The drains overflowed after the heavy rain. | Don't pour those tea leaves down the drain — you'll block the sink.* —see picture at HOUSE **2** [S (on)] something that empties or uses up: *All this spending is a drain on my savings.* **3** **down the drain** infml wasted; brought to nothing: *The results of years of work went down the drain.* —see also BRAIN DRAIN, **laugh like a drain** (LAUGH¹ (7))

drain·age /ˈdreɪnɪdʒ/ n [U] a system or means for draining, such as a pipe or ditch: *This soil has good drainage. | drainage channels*

draining board /ˈ·· ·/ n a slightly sloping board with GROOVEs in the surface, on which wet dishes are placed after washing so that the water will run off them —see picture at KITCHEN

drain·pipe /ˈdreɪnpaɪp/ n **1** a pipe that carries waste water away from buildings **2** also **downspout, drainspout** AmE— a pipe that carries rain water from the roof of a building into a DRAIN —see picture at HOUSE

drainpipe trou·sers /ˈ·· ˈ··/ n [P] BrE infml tight-fitting trousers with narrow legs, esp. as worn in Britain in the 1950s by TEDDY BOYS

drake /dreɪk/ n a male duck —see also DUCKS AND DRAKES

Sir Francis Drake

Drake, Sir Francis (1540–96) an English NAVIGATOR who was the first Englishman to sail around the world and who led the English navy to victory against the Spanish Armada. There is a popular belief that Drake was very calm when he first saw the ships of the Spanish Armada and completed the game of BOWLS he was playing in Plymouth before preparing to fight.

dragster

dram /dræm/ n **1** also **drachm**— a small unit of weight or of liquid – see TABLE 2 **2** infml a small alcoholic drink, usu. WHISKY. This word is usu. used in speech rather than writing and its use in the Scottish expression "a wee dram" is widely known.

dra·ma /ˈdrɑːmə‖ˈdrɑːmə, ˈdræmə/ n **1** [C] a piece of writing to be performed by actors; play for the theatre, television, radio, etc. **2** [U] plays considered as a form of literature: *the themes of contemporary British drama | the drama of Shakespeare* **3** [C;U] an exciting and unusual situation or set of events: *Their holidays are always full of drama. | There was high drama at the airport when news of the hijack came through.*

dra·mat·ic /drəˈmætɪk/ adj **1** [no comp.] connected with drama or the theatre: *a dramatic production* **2** exciting and unusual, like something that could happen in a drama: *his dramatic escape from the prison camp | The conversation stopped when she made her dramatic entrance. | He made a dramatic recovery.* —**~ally** /kli/ adv

dramatic i·ron·y /ˌ·ˌ·· ˈ···/ n [U] a method used in drama by which the people watching the play can see a different meaning in the words spoken because they know information which the characters in the play do not know

dra·mat·ics /drəˈmætɪks/ n **1** [U] the study or practice of theatrical skills such as acting **2** [P] often derog behaviour that shows too much feeling; HISTRIONICS

dram·a·tis per·so·nae /ˌdræmətɪs pɜːˈsəʊnaɪ, pəˈsəʊniː‖ -pərˈsəʊni/ n [(the) P] Lat the characters or actors in a play

dram·a·tist /ˈdræmətɪst/ n a writer of plays, esp. serious ones; PLAYWRIGHT

dram·a·tize also **-tise** BrE /ˈdræmətaɪz/ v **1** [T] to change (a book, report, etc.) so that it can be performed as a play: *He's dramatizing his novel for television.* **2** [I;T] derog to present (something) in a (too) dramatic way: *Don't dramatize (the events) — just give us the facts!* —**-tization** /ˌdræmətaɪˈzeɪʃən‖-mətə-/ n [C;U]

Dram·bu·ie /dræmˈbjuːi/ n [U] tdmk a strong alcoholic drink made with WHISKY, usu. drunk in a small glass after a meal

drank /dræŋk/ past tense of DRINK¹

drape¹ /dreɪp/ v [T] **1** to cover or decorate (as if) with folds of cloth: [+obj+**over, round**] *They draped the flag over/round the coffin.* [+obj+**in, with**] *They draped the coffin in/with the flag.* **2** [(**over, (a)round**)] to cause to hang loosely and carelessly: *He draped his legs over the arm of the chair.* —see SPREAD (USAGE)

drape² *n* [*usu. sing.*] the way cloth is arranged or clothing is cut —see also DRAPES

drap·er /ˈdreɪpər/ *n BrE, becoming rare* a person who sells cloth, curtains, sewing materials, etc.

drap·er·y /ˈdreɪpəri/ *n* **1** [U] *BrE* ‖ **dry goods** *AmE*— the trade of or goods sold by a draper: *the drapery department of the store* **2** [C;U] cloth arranged in folds: *a photograph taken against a background of drapery*

drapes /dreɪps/ also **drap·er·ies** /ˈdreɪpəriz/ *n* [P] *AmE* curtains, esp. long, thick curtains

dras·tic /ˈdræstɪk/ *adj* strong, sudden, and often violent and severe: *Drastic measures/changes are needed to improve the performance of the company.* —~**ally** /kli/ *adv* : *His work has changed drastically since his illness.*

drat /dræt/ *v* -**tt**- [T] *old-fash sl* (used to show annoyance) DAMN: *Drat it! I forgot my keys!* | *Drat!* | *Drat you! You're ten minutes late!* | *Stop that dratted noise!*

draught¹ usu. **draft** *AmE* /drɑːft‖dræft/ *n* **1** a current of cold air flowing through a room: *You'll catch cold if you sit in a draught.* **2** the flow of air to a fire: *to increase the draught to a furnace* **3** an act of swallowing liquid or the amount of liquid swallowed at one time: *She took a long draught of cider.* **4** *esp. lit* a liquid for drinking, esp. a medicine: *a sleeping draught* **5** the depth of water needed by a ship so that it will not touch bottom: *a small boat with a very shallow draught* **6** *BrE* ‖ **checker** *AmE*— a small round piece used in playing the game of draughts **7 on draught** (of beer, etc.) served by being drawn from a large container such as a barrel: *The pub has several good beers on draught.*

draught² usu. **draft** *AmE* — *adj* [A] **1** (of animals) used for pulling loads: *a draught horse* **2** (of beer, etc.) on draught: *I asked for draught beer, not bottled beer.*

draughts /drɑːfts‖dræfts/ *BrE* ‖ **checkers** *AmE*— *n* [U] a game played by two people, each with 12 round pieces, on a board of 64 squares (**draughtboard** *BrE* ‖ **checkerboard** *AmE*)

draughts·man *esp. BrE* ‖ **drafts-** *esp. AmE* /ˈdrɑːfts mən‖ˈdræfts-/ **draughts·wom·an** /-ˌwʊmən/ *fem.*— *n* -**men** /mən/ **1** a person who makes drawings of all the parts of a new building or machine that is being planned **2** a person who draws well

draughty /ˈdrɑːfti‖ˈdræfti/ *adj* with cold currents of air blowing through: *a draughty bedroom*

Dra·vid·i·an /drəˈvɪdiən/ *n* belonging to a group of related languages spoken in S India and N Sri Lanka: *Tamil is a Dravidian language.*

draw¹ /drɔː/ *v* **drew** /druː/, **drawn** /drɔːn/ **1** [I;T] to make (pictures), or make a picture of (something), with a pencil or pen: *Jane draws very well.* | *to draw a line/a map* | *He drew a portrait/his house.* | *Draw a circle and write your name in it.* | (fig.) *Shakespeare draws his characters well.* —compare WRITE¹ (1) **2** [T] to cause to come, go, or move by pulling: *The horse drew the cart up the hill.* | *a plough drawn by oxen* | *to draw the curtains* (=to open or close them by pulling) | *She drew the doctor aside* (=led him to a place where private conversation was possible) *to discuss her mother's health.* | (fig.) *Don't let yourself get drawn into their argument.* **3** [T (OUT)] to take or pull out: *to draw water from the well* | *to draw a nail/a tooth* | *He suddenly drew a knife/a gun (out of his pocket) and threatened me with it.* | *I drew (out) £100 from my bank account today.* | *He dodged, but the knife nicked him and* **drew blood** *from his arm.* **4** [T] to receive or earn; be given: *to draw a winning card/number* | *They draw their wages every Friday.* **5** [T] **a** to cause to come; attract: *I feel drawn towards him.* | *The play is drawing big crowds.* | *Her shouts* **drew the attention of** *the police.* **b** [+ *obj* + *adv/prep*] to gather or obtain from the stated place or person: *The party draws most of its support from the industrial areas.* | *They drew courage from his example.* **6** [I+*adv/prep*] *esp. lit* to move or go steadily or gradually: *Winter is drawing near.* | *The car drew ahead of the others.* | *The bus drew in (to the side of the road) to let the car past.* | *The train drew into/out of the station.* | *Her life was drawing to an end.* | (fig.) *The two political parties are drawing further apart.* **7** [I;T] to end (a game, competition, etc.) without either side winning: *They drew (the match) five all.* (=five points each) | *a drawn game* —compare TIE¹ (5) **8** [T] to take (breath) in: *She drew a deep breath and then continued.* | *They stopped to* **draw**

breath (=to slow down their breathing) *at the top of the hill.* | (fig.) *I didn't have time to draw breath* (=I was very busy) *this morning.* **9** [I] to produce or allow a current of air, esp. to make a fire burn better: *The chimney isn't drawing very well.* **10** [T] to get or form by the use of reason or information: *to draw a comparison* | *What conclusion did you draw from their statement?* | *It's important to draw a distinction between the two ideas.* **11** [T] to remove the bowels from: *to draw a chicken* **12** [T (**on**)] to use for taking money out of a bank: *to draw a cheque on one's bank account* **13** [T] *tech* (of a ship) to need (a stated depth of water) in order to float: *The boat draws a metre of water.* **14** [T] to bend (a BOW³) by pulling back the string, ready to shoot an ARROW **15 draw a blank** *infml* to be unsuccessful, esp. in an attempt to find information or the answer to a problem **16 draw the line (at)** to fix a limit beyond which one will not do or agree to (something): *Of course I want to help you, but I draw the line at lying.* —see also **at daggers drawn** (DAGGER (3)), **draw a veil over something** (VEIL¹ (3))

draw back *phr v* [I (**from**)] **1** to move oneself away: *The crowd drew back in terror as the building crashed to the ground.* **2** to be unwilling to consider or agree to something: *The firm drew back from making an immediate commitment.* —see also DRAWBACK

draw for sthg. *phr v* [T+*obj/wh-*] to choose or make a decision by picking one of a number of objects, marked pieces of paper, etc.; draw LOTS for: *Let's draw for the right to go first/for who will go first.*

draw in *phr v* [I] to have fewer hours of daylight; close in: *In autumn the days begin to draw in.* —opposite **draw out** —see also **draw in one's horns** (HORN)

draw sthg. ↔ **off** *phr v* [T] to allow to flow out: *to draw off some water from the radiator*

draw on *phr v* **1** [I] to come near in time; APPROACH: *Winter is drawing on.* **2** [T] (**draw on** sbdy./sthg.) to make use of a supply of (esp. money): *I'll have to draw on my savings to pay for the repairs.* | *A writer has to draw on his imagination and experience.* **3** [T] (**draw on** sthg.) to breathe in smoke from: *He drew on his pipe/cigarette.*

draw out *phr v* **1** [T] (**draw** sthg. ↔ **out**) to cause to stretch in time, perhaps unnecessarily; PROLONG: *The question and answer session drew the meeting out for a further two hours.* | *a long-drawn-out debate* **2** [I] to have more hours of daylight: *The days are drawing out now that it's spring.* —opposite **draw in 3** [T] (**draw** sbdy. ↔ **out**) to make (someone) feel more willing to speak freely or openly; BRING **out**: *She's very shy but he managed to draw her out.*

draw up *phr v* **1** [T] (**draw** sthg. ↔ **up**) to prepare and usu. put into written form; DRAFT: *to draw up a plan/a contract/a list of candidates* **2** [I] (of a vehicle) to arrive at a certain point and stop: *The car drew up (at the gate) and three men got out.* **3** [T *often pass.*] (**draw** sbdy. ↔ **up**) to place in prepared order: *The soldiers were drawn up outside the palace.* **4 draw oneself up** to make oneself stand straight, often proudly: *He drew himself up to his full height.*

draw² *n* **1** a result with neither side winning: *The game ended in a draw.* **2** the choosing of winning tickets in a LOTTERY: *He picked a winning number on the first draw.* | *He won and I lost:* **that's the luck of the draw.** —compare RAFFLE¹ **3** a person, thing, or event that attracts esp. a paying public: *The new singer is a big draw.* **4 quick/fast on the draw** *infml* quick at pulling out a hand gun: (fig.) *When she was interviewed, she was very quick on the draw.* (=quick at answering questions)

draw·back /ˈdrɔːbæk/ *n* a difficulty or disadvantage; something that can cause trouble: *The only drawback of the plan is that it costs too much.* | *The high cost is a major drawback.* —see also DRAW **back**

draw·bridge /ˈdrɔːˌbrɪdʒ/ *n* (in former times) a bridge that can be pulled up to let ships pass, to protect a castle from attack, etc.

drawer¹ /drɔːʳ/ *n* a sliding boxlike container with an open top used for storing clothes, STATIONERY, etc., which fits into a table, desk, cupboard, or CHEST OF DRAWERS and which is opened by pulling out and closed by pushing in: *The paper is in my desk drawer.* —see also BOTTOM DRAWER, TOP DRAWER, and see picture at KITCHEN

draw·er² /ˈdrɔːəʳ/ *n* a person who draws

drawers /drɔːz‖drɔːrz/ *n* [P] *old use for* KNICKERS —see PAIR (USAGE)

draw·ing /ˈdrɔːɪŋ/ n **1** [U] the art of making pictures or representing objects, plans, etc. with a pen or pencil **2** [C] a picture made by drawing: *a drawing of a cat* —see also LINE DRAWING

drawing board /ˈ·· ·/ n **1** a flat piece of wood on which paper is laid to draw on; used esp. by artists and GRAPHIC DESIGNERS **2** **go back to the drawing board** *infml* to start again after one's first attempt has failed

drawing pin /ˈ·· ·/ *BrE* ‖ **thumbtack** *AmE*— n a short pin with a broad flat head, used esp. for putting notices on boards or walls —see picture at PIN

drawing room /ˈ·· ·/ n **1** *fml for* LIVING ROOM. Many British upper class families use this word to describe the main room in their home. —compare SITTING ROOM, FRONT ROOM **2** *AmE* a private room in a railway train, in which three people can sleep

drawl /drɔːl/ v [I;T] (OUT) to speak or say slowly, with vowels greatly lengthened —**drawl** n : *She speaks with a Southern drawl.*

drawn¹ /drɔːn/ *past participle of* DRAW¹

drawn² adj **1** (esp. of the face) changed as if by pulling or stretching: *a face drawn with sorrow/exhaustion* **2** (of games, competitions, etc.) ended with neither side winning: *a drawn match*

draw·string /ˈdrɔːˌstrɪŋ/ n [*often pl.*] a string or cord that can be pulled tighter or looser to tie up bags, etc.

dray /dreɪ/ n a flat four-wheeled cart for carrying heavy loads, esp. barrels of beer

Dr. Bar·nar·do's /ˌdɒktə bəˈnɑːdəʊz‖ˌdɑːktər bərˈnɑːr-/ see BARNARDO HOMES

dread¹ /dred/ v [T] to feel great fear or anxiety about: *I'm just dreading this exam.* [+*to-v*] **I dread to think** *what will happen if she finds out.* [+*v-ing*] *She dreaded having to meet his parents.* [+(*that*)] *He dreaded that his parents would find out.* | *the dreaded day*

dread² n [S;U (*of*)] (a) great fear or anxiety: *They* **live in dread of** *being caught.*

dread³ adj [A] *lit* causing great fear or anxiety: *God's dread judgment*

dread·ful /ˈdredfəl/ adj **1** causing great fear or anxiety; terrible: *the dreadful news of the accident* | *in dreadful pain* **2** *infml* very unpleasant or unenjoyable: *bad: What a dreadful noise!* | *The play last night was just dreadful.* —see also PENNY DREADFUL —~**ness** n [U]

dread·ful·ly /ˈdredfəli/ adv *infml* extremely; used before words with unpleasant meanings: *I'm dreadfully sorry.* | *She looks dreadfully tired.*

dread·locks /ˈdredlɒks‖-lɑːks/ n [P] a hairstyle consisting of thick lengths of twisted hair, often worn by male RASTAFARIANS or by young people who consider it to be a fashionable style: *a young Rasta man with dreadlocks*

dread·nought /ˈdrednɔːt/ n a type of BATTLESHIP used at the beginning of the 20th century

dream¹ /driːm/ n **1** a group of related thoughts, images, or feelings experienced during sleep: *I had a strange dream about my mother last night.* **2** a group of thoughts, images, or feelings like these, experienced when the mind is not completely under conscious control; DAYDREAM **3** [*usu. sing.*] a state of mind in which one does not pay much attention to the real world: *John* **lives in a dream. 4** something that one thinks about and hopes for; ASPIRATION: *It was his dream to sail his boat around the world.* | *The band's record was successful* **beyond their wildest dreams.** (=more successful than they had hoped or expected) | *Meeting the princess was (like)* **a dream come true. 5** *infml* a very beautiful, excellent, or enjoyable thing or person: *Their new house is a real dream.* | *The car goes like a dream.* **6 I have a dream**...*quote* the first words of a speech by Martin Luther King, in which he expressed his hopes for the future of black people —see also Martin Luther KING

dream² v dreamed *or* dreamt /dremt/ [I (*of, about*); T+*obj* (*that*)] **1** to have (a dream) (about something): *Do you dream at night?* | *"What did you dream about?"* *"I dreamt (that) I was flying to the moon."* **2** to imagine (something): *I never said that! You must have been dreaming/You may have dreamt that.* | *I never dreamt that such a thing could happen!* **3 not dream of** *infml* not consider; not be able to, esp. for moral reasons: *I wouldn't dream of letting the children do that!*

dream *sthg.* ↔ **away** *phr* v [T] to spend (time) in dreaming or inactivity: *to dream away the hours*

dream *sthg.* ↔ **up** *phr* v [T] *sl, often derog* to invent (esp. something unusual or silly): *They can always dream up some new excuse for the train arriving late.*

dream·boat /ˈdriːmbəʊt/ n *sl* **1** a very attractive person of the opposite sex **2** *BrE* someone who knows he or she is attractive and is proud of it

dream·er /ˈdriːməʳ/ n **1** a person who dreams **2** a person who has impractical ideas or plans **3** a person who is not very good at what they are doing because they are always thinking about something else

dream·ing /ˈdriːmɪŋ/ also **dream·time** /ˈdriːmtaɪm/ n [U] the time, according to old Australian Aborigine stories, when the first ANCESTORs were created

dreaming spires /ˌ·· ˈ·/ n [P] *quote* a phrase from a poem by Matthew Arnold, which people use to suggest the beauty of Oxford, the English university town

dream·land /ˈdriːmlænd/ n **1** [C;U] a beautiful and happy place that exists only in one's imagination —compare NEVER-NEVER LAND **2** sleep: *He's off to dreamland.*

dream·less /ˈdriːmləs/ adj (of sleep) without dreams; peaceful —~**ly** adv

dream·like /ˈdriːmlaɪk/ adj as in a dream; unreal

dreamt /dremt/ *past participle of* DREAM²

dream tick·et /ˈ· ˌ··/ n [C *usu. S*] a perfect combination of two people, esp. in an election

dream world /ˈ· ·/ n a world of impractical or unreal ideas. People are often said **to live in a dream world** if they have hopes or expectations which are unlikely to come true: *If you think there won't be any more wars, you're living in a dream world.*

dream·y /ˈdriːmi/ adj **1** (of a person) living more in the imagination than in the real world **2** peaceful and beautiful; not clear, sharp, or exact: *soft dreamy music* | *The misty scene had a dreamy quality about it.* **3** *sl* wonderful; desirable; beautiful: *Isn't that dress dreamy!* —**ily** adv —**iness** n [U]

drear /drɪəʳ/ adj *poet* dreary

drear·y /ˈdrɪəri/ adj **1** sad or cheerless; GLOOMY: *a dreary November day, cold and without sunshine* **2** *infml* dull; uninteresting: *Addressing envelopes is dreary work.* —**ily** adv —**iness** n [U]

dredge¹ /dredʒ/ v [I;T (*for*)] to use a dredger in, on, or for (something): *They are dredging (the lake) for the dead body.* | *Can we dredge the harbour to make it deeper?*

dredge *sthg.* ↔ **up** *phr* v [T] **1** to bring to the surface of water, esp. using a dredger **2** *infml* to bring to notice (something unpleasant from the past that has been forgotten about): *to dredge up an old quarrel/an old scandal*

dredge² v [T] to cover (food) lightly by scattering (something powdery) over it: *to dredge a fish with flour* | *cakes dredged in icing sugar* —see SPREAD (USAGE)

dredg·er /ˈdredʒəʳ/ also **dredge** n a machine or ship used for digging or sucking up mud and sand from the bottom of a river, etc.

Dred Scott Case /ˌdred ˈskɒt ˌkeɪs‖-ˈskɑːt-/ also **Dred Scott de·ci·sion** /ˌ· ˈ· ·ˌ··/ n a decision by the US SUPREME COURT in 1857 that a black person could not be a US citizen and thus could not bring a LAWSUIT (=a legal case against someone) in a US court

▶ CULTURAL NOTE The case was brought to the Supreme Court by a slave named Dred Scott, who claimed that because he had once lived in a state which did not allow slavery he should be a free man and not a slave. As well as declaring that Scott could not be a citizen, the CHIEF JUSTICE said that CONGRESS could not disallow slavery in any state. The decision made Congress, ABOLITIONISTs, and many other people very angry and was one of the major causes of the CIVIL WAR. ◄

Dreft /dreft/ n [U] *tdmk* a type of WASHING POWDER made by Procter & Gamble Limited

dregs /dregz/ n [P] small pieces of solid material that sink to the bottom of a liquid and are thrown away: *coffee dregs* | (fig.) *Murderers and drug dealers are* **the dregs** (=most worthless part) **of society.** —compare LEES

Drei·ser /ˈdraɪsəʳ/, **The·o·dore** /ˈθiːədɔːʳ/ (1871–1945) an American writer who wrote *Sister Carrie* and *An American Tragedy*

drench /drentʃ/ v [T (**to, with**) often pass.] to make (usu. people, animals, or clothes) thoroughly wet: *I went out without my umbrella and got drenched to the skin!* | *a drenching rain* | *drenched in/with sweat* —see also SUN-DRENCHED

Dres·den /ˈdrezdən/ a city in E Germany known for its CHINA industry, and for being destroyed by bombing in 1945. When people want to give an idea of something delicate and beautiful but easily damaged they sometimes mention a Dresden SHEPHERDESS (a china model of a girl who looks after sheep)

dress¹ /dres/ v **1** [I;T] to put clothes on (oneself or someone else): *I'll be ready in a moment; I'm just dressing/getting dressed.* | *Could you dress the baby for me?* —see USAGE **2** [I;T often pass.; not in progressive forms] to provide (oneself or someone else) with clothes of the stated type: *She dresses well on very little money.* | *He was neatly/informally/immaculately dressed.* | *an old lady dressed in black* | *They were* **dressed in their Sunday best.** (=best clothes) | *She went to the party dressed as a nun.* **3** [I] to put on formal clothes for the evening: *You are expected to dress for dinner in this hotel.* **4** [T] to make or choose clothes for: *The princess is dressed by a famous dress designer.* **5** [T] to clean and put medicine and a protective covering on (a wound) **6** [T] to prepare for use, esp. to prepare for cooking or eating: *He dressed the salad with oil and vinegar.* | *to dress birds for the market* (=clean them and remove the feathers) | *(tech) to dress the ground for planting, by spreading fertilizer* | *(tech) dressed* (=cut and shaped) *stones for building* **7** [T] **a** to arrange (the hair) by combing, brushing, curling, etc. **b** to arrange goods to be shown publicly in (e.g. a shop window) **8** [I;T] *tech* to form or cause (soldiers) to form a straight line: *Officer, dress those men to the right!* | *Soldiers, dress right!* **9 dressed (up) to kill** *infml* wearing very bright fashionable clothes **10 dressed (up) to the nines** *infml* wearing one's best and most formal clothes **11 all dressed up and nowhere to go** *humor* a phrase used when someone seems dressed in their best clothes for no clear reason

▷ USAGE Compare **dress, put on,** and **wear.** You can **put on** any article of clothing: *She* **put on** *a woolly scarf before she went out.* When you **put on** all your clothes you can say **dress** (rather literary) or **get dressed:** *I got up and* **put on** *my clothes/***dressed***/got dressed.* **Wear** means "to have (clothes) on" and is usually used to describe someone's habits or appearance: *She always* **wears** *black.* | *I'll be* **wearing** *a red coat.* Here you can also use **dress in** and **be dressed in:** *She always* **dresses in black.** | *I'll be* **dressed in** *a red coat.*◁

dress sbdy. ↔ **down** *phr v* [T] to attack angrily in words (someone who has done something wrong); TELL off —**dressing-down** /ˌ·ˈ·/ n : *The naughty children got a good dressing-down.*

dress up *phr v* **1** [I (**as, in**)] (usu. of children) to wear someone else's clothes for fun and pretence: *to dress up as an astronaut* | *The little girl likes dressing up (in her mother's clothes).* **2** [I] to put on formal clothes or one's best clothes: *Don't bother to dress up for the party.* | *She's* **all dressed up and nowhere to go.** (an old saying) **3** [T (**as, in**)] (**dress** sbdy./sthg. ↔ **up**) to make (something or someone) seem different or more attractive: *He dressed the facts up to make them more interesting.*

dress² n **1** [C] an article of clothing for a woman or girl, with or without SLEEVES, that covers the body from shoulder to knee or below —compare SKIRT¹ (1) **2** [U] (*in comb.*) clothing of the stated kind: *national dress* | *actors wearing period dress* (=the clothes of another age) | *Do we have to wear* **evening dress** *for this party?* —see also FULL DRESS, MORNING DRESS; see CLOTHES (USAGE)

dress³ adj [A no comp.] **1** of or used for a dress: *dress material* **2** (of clothing) suitable for a formal occasion: *a dress shirt/suit* **3** (of an occasion) at which formal or special clothes are worn —see also DRESS CIRCLE, DRESS REHEARSAL

dres·sage /ˈdresɑːʒ‖drəˈsɑːʒ/ n [U] the performance by a trained horse of various actions as a result of slight movements by the rider

dress cir·cle /ˈ· ˌ··/ n the first or lowest curved row of raised seats in a theatre

dress·er /ˈdresər/ n **1** *esp. BrE* a piece of furniture for holding dishes and other articles used in eating, with open shelves above and cupboards below **2** *AmE* a CHEST OF DRAWERS, used esp. for clothing, often with a mirror on top **3** a person who looks after clothes in the theatre and helps actors to dress **4** someone who dresses in the stated way: *a fashionable/snappy/sloppy dresser*

dress·ing /ˈdresɪŋ/ n **1** [U] the act of a person who dresses: *Dressing is difficult for her since her accident.* **2** [C] material used to cover a wound: *to put on a clean dressing* **3** [C;U] a usu. liquid mixture for adding to a dish, esp. a SALAD: *a* **French dressing 4** [U] *AmE for* STUFFING (2) —see also SALAD DRESSING, WINDOW DRESSING

dressing gown /ˈ·· ·/ ‖**bathrobe** *AmE*— n esp. BrE a garment rather like a long loose coat, worn indoors when a person is not fully dressed, esp. after getting up in the morning —see also BATHROBE

dressing room /ˈ·· ·/ n a room used for dressing, esp. in a theatre

dressing ta·ble /ˈ·· ˌ··/ also **vanity table** *AmE*— n a low table with a mirror, usu. in a bedroom, at which one sits to arrange one's hair, etc.

dress·mak·er /ˈdresˌmeɪkər/ n a person, usu. a woman, who makes clothes according to customers' specific requests. Few people now have their clothes made by dressmakers as it is much more expensive than buying them OFF-THE-PEG (ready-made). —**making** n [U]

dress re·hears·al /ˈ· ·ˌ··/ n the last REHEARSAL (=practice performance) of a play when the actors wear the special clothes prepared for public performance of the play

dress sense /ˈ· ˌ·/ n [U] a knowledge of or skill with clothes; an ability to make oneself attractive and presentable: *She's got no/a good dress sense.*

dress·y /ˈdresi/ adj **1** (of clothes) for formal, not ordinary, wear **2** *sometimes derog* (of a person) fashionable in dress

drew /druː/ past tense of DRAW¹

Drew, Nan·cy /ˈnænsi/ a character in children's books who is a DETECTIVE and finds the answer to mysteries (MYSTERY⁴). The popular set of books is by Carolyn Keene, the American writer.

Drey·fus /ˈdreɪfəs/, **Al·fred** /ˈælfrɪd/ (1859–1935) a French army officer who was wrongly charged in 1893 with giving defence secrets to Germany, and sent to prison. Attempts to have him declared not guilty and freed failed because of anti-Jewish feeling and the power of the army. The **Dreyfus Affair** split the whole of French society. In 1906 Dreyfus was finally declared not guilty.

drib·ble¹ /ˈdrɪbəl/ v **1** [I] ‖ usu. **drool** *AmE* —to let the natural liquid (SALIVA) flow out slowly from the mouth: *The baby is dribbling. Can you wipe his mouth?* **2** [I;T] **a** (of a liquid, esp. saliva, or a powdery solid) to flow out in drops: *water dribbling from the pipe* **b** to allow to do this: *This artist works by dribbling paint straight from the tube.* **3** [I;T] (in ball games) to move (the ball) by a number of short kicks, strokes, or BOUNCES

dribble² n **1** a small thin flow; TRICKLE **2** an act of dribbling a ball

drib·let /ˈdrɪblɪt/ n a very small unimportant amount: *to pay the money in driblets*

dribs /drɪbz/ n **dribs and drabs** *infml* small unimportant amounts: *They're paying me back in dribs and drabs.*

dried /draɪd/ past tense & participle of DRY²: *dried milk/flowers* —see also CUT-AND-DRIED

dried fruit /ˌ· ˈ·/ n [C,U] fruit dried either industrially or in the sun and used in cooking or eaten in its dried state

dried milk /ˌ· ˈ·/ also **powdered milk**— n [U] milk which has been made with a powder by having the water taken out of it

dri·er /ˈdraɪər/ n a DRYER

drift¹ /drɪft/ v **1** [I] to float or be driven along by wind, waves, or currents: *They drifted out to sea.* | *(fig.) She just drifts aimlessly from job to job.* | *(fig.) They had been married for a long time but gradually* **drifted apart** *until they separated.* | *(fig.) The conversation drifted from one subject to another.* **2** [I;T] to (cause to) pile up under the force of the wind or water: *The snow was drifting in great piles against the house.* | *leaves drifted by the wind*

drift² n **1** [C] a mass of something, such as snow or sand, blown together by wind: *a drift of dead leaves* | *a snowdrift* **2** [C;U] a general tendency or movement: *the drift*

drive

of young people from the country to the city | *We must stop this drift towards war.* **3** [S] the general meaning; GIST: *I'm sorry. I can't quite catch the drift of what you're saying.*

drift·er /ˈdrɪftər/ n **1** *often derog* a person who travels or moves about aimlessly or who has no aim in life **2** a fishing boat that uses a floating net (a **driftnet**)

drift·wood /ˈdrɪftwʊd/ n [U] wood floating on water and often washed onto the shore: *After the storm they made a fire from the driftwood on the beach.*

drill¹ /drɪl/ n **1** [C] a tool or machine for making holes: *a road drill* | *a dentist's drill* **2** [C;U] (a piece of) training and instruction in a subject or for a purpose, esp. by means of repeating and following exact orders: *The soldiers do rifle drill in the mornings.* | *a* **fire drill** (=practice in dealing with fire in a building) | *a grammar drill for students of English* **3** [the] BrE infml the correct way of doing something effectively; PROCEDURE: *What's the drill for getting money after four o'clock?*

drill² v **1** [I;T] to use a drill on (something): *to drill for oil* | *to drill someone's teeth* | *The workmen are drilling (in) the road.* **2** [T] to make with a drill or use a drill on: *to drill a hole in the wall* | *to drill an old filling out of a tooth* **3** [I;T] **a** to train (soldiers) in military movements **b** to practise military movements under instruction **4** [T] **a** [(in)] to instruct and exercise (students) by the repeating of words, actions, etc.: *drilling the class in the use of the past tense* **b** [+obj+IN, into] to teach (facts) in this way: *She drilled it into the children that they must say "Thank you" to their hostess.*

drills

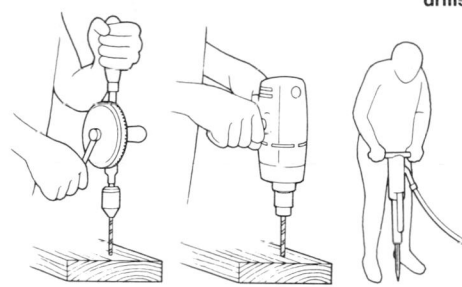

hand drill   electric drill   pneumatic drill

drill³ n **1** a machine for planting seeds in rows **2** a row of seeds planted in this way

drill⁴ n [U] a type of strong cotton cloth: *drill trousers*

dri·ly /ˈdraɪli/ adv see DRY¹

drink¹ /drɪŋk/ v **drank** /dræŋk/, **drunk** /drʌŋk/ **1** [I;T (UP)] to move (liquid) from the mouth down the throat; swallow: *Drink (up) your tea before it gets cold.* **2** [I] to use alcohol, esp. habitually or too much: *He doesn't smoke or drink.* | *You shouldn't* **drink and drive.** (=drive a car after drinking alcohol) | *He* **drinks like a fish.** (=drinks a lot of alcohol) | *I only* **drink socially.** (=only drink at parties, social occasions, etc.)

▶CULTURAL NOTE To drink a reasonable amount of alcohol is thought to be acceptable in British and American society, but to drink so much or so often that you are not in control is seen as medically and socially unwise. ◀

3 [I (to);T] to have an alcoholic drink in order to wish someone success, health, etc.: *Let's drink to your success in your new job!* | *We* **drank a toast** *to the bride and groom.* —see also HEALTH (3) **4** [T+obj+adv/prep] to bring to a stated condition by drinking alcohol: *He drank himself into unconsciousness.* | *He drank his troubles away.* **5** **drink someone under the table** infml to drink much more alcohol than someone without becoming drunk

drink sthg. ↔ **in** phr v [T] to receive through the senses, esp. eagerly: *They drank in the sights and sounds of the city.*

drink² n [C;U] **1** (an amount of) a liquid suitable for drinking: *Would you like a drink of water?* | *Have you any soft drinks?* (=non-alcoholic cold drinks) **2** (a glass, measure, etc. of) alcohol for drinking: *Have another drink!* | *There's no drink in the house.* | *The continual quarrelling* **drove her to drink.** (=made her begin to drink a lot of

alcohol) | *He has a drink problem.* (=he habitually drinks too much) | *Don't forget we're invited to the Willises for drinks Sunday lunchtime.* —see also DRINKS PARTY, HARD DRINK

drin·ka·ble /ˈdrɪŋkəbəl/ adj suitable or safe for drinking

drink-driv·ing /ˌ· ˈ··/ BrE ‖ **drunk driving** AmE— n [U] the act of driving while under the influence of alcohol: *Although more breath tests for drink driving were given, the number of positive results dropped.* —see also MADD — **drink-driver** ‖ **drunk driver** n

▶CULTURAL NOTE This is against the law in Britain and the US, and taken very seriously by the police and also by the public now, although many people used to think it less serious. Some drivers believe that no alcohol should be drunk at all, but others think that a small amount is acceptable and will not affect their skill on the road. There is a lot of publicity, esp. at Christmas every year, to persuade people not to drink and drive, and relatives of those killed or hurt by drink-drivers have argued that punishments should be more severe. ◀

drink·er /ˈdrɪŋkər/ n a person who drinks alcohol, esp. too much: *a* **hard drinker**

drinking foun·tain /ˈ·· ˌ··/ n an apparatus, usu. in a public place, that provides water for drinking

drinking-up time /ˌ· ˈ· ˌ·/ n [U] in Britain, a period of time allowed in a place where alcoholic drinks are sold, for people to finish their drinks after the official closing time

drinking wa·ter /ˈ·· ˌ··/ n [U] water that is pure enough for people to drink

drinks ma·chine /ˈ· ··ˌ·/ also **coffee machine** n a machine which makes and serves hot drinks when one puts in money

drinks par·ty /ˈ· ˌ··/ BrE‖**cocktail party** AmE— n a party at which alcohol is the main thing offered. Middle or upper class people might invite their neighbours for drinks at midday on a Saturday or Sunday. Drinks parties are often quite large: *a farewell drinks party for one of my colleagues*

drip¹ /drɪp/ v **-pp-** **1** [I (DOWN);T] to fall or let fall in drops: *Water is dripping (down) from the roof.* | *The roof is dripping water.* **2** [I] to produce small drops of liquid: *a dripping tap*

drip with sthg. phr v [T] to be very full of or covered with: *The woman was dripping with expensive jewels.*

drip² n **1** [S] the action or sound of falling in drops: *All night I heard the drip drip drip of the water.* **2** [C] a piece of medical equipment used for putting liquid from a tube directly into a patient's bloodstream: *The patient was put on a drip after her operation.* **3** [C] sl an uninteresting unconfident person without a strong character

drip-dry /ˌ· ˈ·◄/ adj (of clothing) that will dry smooth and needs no ironing after being hung while it is wet: *a drip-dry shirt* —**drip-dry** v [I;T]

drip·ping¹ /ˈdrɪpɪŋ/ also **drippings** pl. AmE n [U] the fat that has come from meat during cooking. Some people think that dripping is very tasty and have childhood memories of eating bread and dripping. Other people think it is unhealthy and unpleasant and would not want to eat it at all.

dripping² adj, adv very wet: *I'm absolutely dripping!* | *a* **dripping wet** *towel*

drive¹ /draɪv/ v **drove** /drəʊv/, **driven** /ˈdrɪvən/ **1** [I;T] to move or travel in (a vehicle with more than two wheels) while guiding and controlling it: *to drive a car/train/ bus* | *Shall we stop for lunch or shall we drive on?* (=continue driving) | *They drove to the station.* | *He loaded the van and drove off.* | *I'm learning to drive.* —compare RIDE¹ (1) **2** [T+obj+adv/prep] to take (someone) in a vehicle: *Can you drive me to the station?* **3** [T+obj+adv/prep] to force to go: *The farmer was driving his cattle along the road.* | *The bad weather has driven the tourists away.* | *The firemen were driven back by the flames.* | *The shortage of bread will probably drive prices up.* **4** [T] to provide the power for: *The engines drive the ship.* **5** [T+obj+adv/ prep] to force to go somewhere by hitting: *to drive the nail into/through the wood* **6** [T+obj+adv/prep] to produce by opening a way: *to drive a tunnel through a mountain/under a river* **7** [T] to force (someone) into a usu. unpleasant condition or undesirable course of action: *[+obj+adv/prep] Continual failure drove him to despair/to*

drink. | *That noise is driving me out of my mind.*
[+obj+adj] *The pain nearly drove her mad.* [+obj+to-v]
Poverty and hunger drove them to steal. **8** [I] (esp. of rain)
to move along with great force: *driving rain* **9 drive a
coach and horses through** (to destroy an argument,
case, etc.): *The new evidence drove a coach and horses
through the case against them.* **10 drive a hard bargain**
to get an agreement very much in one's own favour **11
drive something home (to)** to make something unmistakably clear (to): *The accident at the factory really
drove home (to us) the point that safety regulations must
be observed.*

▷ USAGE If you are in control of a car you **drive** it, if
you are in control of a ship you **pilot** it, and if you are
in control of a bicycle you **ride** it. If you direct the
course of a car, ship, or bicycle you **steer** it. But when
talking about a plane, the words **fly** and **pilot** mean
both being in control of it and directing its course: *to*
fly/pilot *an aeroplane* —see also CAR (USAGE), TRANS-
PORT (USAGE)◁

drive at sthg. *phr v* [T *no pass.*; *in progressive forms*]
infml to mean or suggest indirectly; HINT: *What are you
driving at?*

drive off *phr v* **1** [T] (**drive** sbdy./sthg. ↔ **off**) to force
away or back; REPEL: *They drove off their attackers.* **2** [I]
(in the game of GOLF) to make the first stroke

drive² *n* **1** [C] a journey in a vehicle (esp. for pleasure):
They went for a drive along the coast. **2** [C] also **drive-
way** – a road for vehicles that connects a private house
or garage with the street —see picture at HOUSE **3** [C] an
act of hitting a ball, the distance a ball is hit, or the force
with which it is hit: *to hit a long high drive to the right*
4 [C] a planned effort by a group for a particular purpose;
CAMPAIGN: *The club is having a membership drive.* (=to
get more members) | *a big anti-smoking drive* **5** [C] an
important natural human need which must be fulfilled:
*Hunger, thirst, and sex are among the strongest human
drives.* **6** [U] a forceful active quality of mind that gets
things done; INITIATIVE: *He's clever but he won't succeed
because he lacks drive.* **7** [C;U] the apparatus by which
a machine is set or kept in movement: *This car has (a)
front-wheel drive.* (=the engine turns the front wheels)
8 [C] *BrE* a competition of the stated type, esp. of a card
game: *a whist drive* —see also DISK DRIVE

drive-a-way car /ˈdraɪvəweɪ ˌkɑːʳ/ *also* **driveaway** *n AmE*
a car which its owner needs in another place. The owner
pays a **driveaway company** to move the car for him.
People who wish to travel cheaply may telephone or visit
a driveaway company and see if there is a car waiting
to be delivered to the place they want to go: *I might go
to LA next week if I can get a driveaway.* —compare **getaway car** (GETAWAY)

drive-by /ˈ·· ·/ *adj* [A] *AmE* (of a crime) done from a mov-
ing car: *a drive-by shooting* | *Drive-by murders have ter-
rorized the city.*

drive-in /ˈ·· ·/ *adj* [A] *esp. AmE* that people can use while
remaining in their cars: *a drive-in restaurant/cinema* –
drive-in *n* : *Are you coming to the drive-in tonight?*

driv-el /ˈdrɪvəl/ *v* -ll- *BrE* ‖ -l- *AmE* [I (ON)] to talk nonsense
—**drivel** *n* [U] : *Don't talk such drivel!* – –**ler** *n*

driv-en /ˈdrɪvən/ *adj* (of a person) full of a sense of urgency
about something; extremely MOTIVATED: *He's a driven
man.*

driv-er /ˈdraɪvəʳ/ *n* **1** a person who drives: *the driver of a
car* | *special insurance rates for young drivers* **2** a GOLF
CLUB (2) with a wooden head —see also SUNDAY DRIVER

driver's li-cense /ˈ·· ˌ··/ *n AmE* for DRIVING LICENCE

drive-way /ˈdraɪvweɪ/ *n* a DRIVE² (2)

driv-ing /ˈdraɪvɪŋ/ *adj* [A] **1** passing on or carrying power
or force: *a driving wheel* **2** able to produce strong or
noticeable effects; DYNAMIC: *He is the owner of the company, but his deputy is the real driving force behind it.*
3 having great force: *driving rain* **4** of or about guid-
ing and controlling vehicles, esp. cars: *a driving school* |
a driving test **5 in the 'driving seat** *infml* in charge;
in control

driving ban /ˈ·· ˌ·/ *n* an order forbidding a person to drive:
*He received a driving ban after being caught with twice
the legal amount of alcohol in his blood.*

driving li-cence /ˈ·· ˌ··/ *BrE* ‖ **driver's license** *AmE n* a

paper giving official permission to drive a motor vehicle,
obtained after success in a **driving test**.

▶CULTURAL NOTE In Britain, a driving licence can be obtained at the age of 17. In the US, the age is 15 or 16, depending on the state. Most people in Britain learn through
taking driving lessons from a private instructor, but in the
US many people learn to drive at school.◀

driving range /ˈ·· ˌ·/ *n* an open outdoor area where people
(pay to) practise hitting GOLF balls

driving test /ˈ·· ˌ·/ *n* the examination which one must pass
before one can have a driving licence and drive a vehicle on public roads

driving under the in-flu-ence /ˌ·· · · ˈ··/ ‖also **driving
while intoxicated** *AmE*– *n* [U] the crime of driving a
car after drinking too much alcohol; DRINK-DRIVING

driz-zle¹ /ˈdrɪzəl/ *v* [*it*+I] to rain in very small drops or very
lightly —see RAIN (USAGE)

drizzle² *n* [S;U] (a) fine misty rain —**-zly** *adj* : *a drizzly day*

Dr Martens /ˌ·· ˈ··/ *also* **Doc
Martens** [P] *tdmk* a make of
strong heavy-looking shoes
or boots with LACES. Dr Martens are very practical shoes
worn by people in certain
jobs, esp. policemen. They
are also worn as fashion
shoes, esp. by young people.

Dr Martens

droid /drɔɪd/ *n esp. AmE,
humor* (from SCIENCE FICTION
stories) a machine that looks
like a human; someone who
seems to be a machine be-
cause he or she shows either
no thought or no emotions:
*That place is run by a bunch
of droids. You can't talk to anyone.*

droll /drəʊl/ *adj* odd and amusing: *a droll person/expres-
sion/situation* –**drolly** /ˈdrəʊl-li/ *adv* – –**ness** *n* [U]

droll-er-y /ˈdrəʊləri/ *n* [C;U] *old-fash* (an example of) droll
humour

drom-e-da-ry /ˈdrɒmədəri‖ˈdrɑːməderi/ *n* a type of CAMEL
with one HUMP on its back

drone¹ /drəʊn/ *v* [I] to make a continuous low dull sound:
An aeroplane droned overhead.

drone on *phr v* [I (about)] to continue to speak in an
uninteresting way in a low dull voice: *He always drones
on (and on) about his problems.*

drone² *n* [(the) S] **1** a continuous dull low sound: *the distant drone of the traffic* **2 a** a fixed deep note sounded
continuously during a piece of music **b** the pipe in a set
of BAGPIPES that makes a sound like this

drone³ *n* **1** a male BEE **2** *BrE derog* a person who lives
on other people's work; PARASITE **3** *AmE* a dull person
in a dull job

dron-go /ˈdrɒŋgəʊ‖ˈdrɑːŋ-/ *n* -goes *esp. AustrE, infml* a
stupid or worthless person

drool /druːl/ *v* [I] *derog* **1** to let the natural liquid (SALIVA)
flow from the mouth, esp. because of a pleasant sight or
smell: *At the sight of the food the dog started drooling.* **2**
AmE ‖ **dribble** *BrE*– (of a baby) to let saliva flow out
slowly from the mouth **3** [(over)] to show enjoyment or
admiration in a foolish or unpleasant way: *The boys were
all drooling over a picture of a girl in a bikini.* —compare
SLOBBER

droop /druːp/ *v* [I] **1** to hang or bend downwards: *His
shoulders drooped with tiredness.* | *The flowers in the vase
drooped in the hot room.* | *a tree with drooping branches*
2 to become sad or weakened; LANGUISH: *Our spirits
drooped.* –**droop** *n* [(the) S] : *the droop of his shoulders*

drop¹ /drɒp‖drɑːp/ *v* -pp- **1** [I;T] to fall or let fall, esp. unintentionally, unexpectedly, or suddenly: *She dropped her
glasses and broke them.* | *I dropped the box on my foot.* |
The fruit dropped (down) from the tree. | *Your button has
dropped off!* | (fig.) *She dropped into a deep sleep.* (fig.)
They worked until they dropped. (=until they were com-
pletely tired) | (fig.) *Her face dropped* (=she looked
shocked or disappointed) *when she saw the bill.* **2** [I;T]
to (cause to) fall to a lower level or amount: *The price of
oil has dropped sharply/dropped to $12 a barrel.* | *He
dropped his voice to a whisper.* | *The motorist dropped his*

speed. | The wind/The temperature has dropped. **3** [T+obj+adv/prep] infml to allow (someone) to get out of a vehicle: *Drop me (off) at the corner.* **4** [T] to stop seeing, talking about, doing, or considering; give up: *Let's drop the subject.* | *When the fire alarm rang I dropped everything* (=stopped what I was doing) *and ran out of the building.* | *I'm going to drop history this year.* (=stop studying it) | *They were planning to build a tunnel there, but I think they've dropped the idea now.* **5** [T (from)] to stop including; leave out: *I've been dropped (from the football team) for next Saturday's match.* | *He often drops his "h's"* (=doesn't pronounce them) *when he talks.* **6** [I+adv] to visit unexpectedly or informally: *Drop in and see us when you're next in London!* | *Drop round one evening next week.* | *Jane dropped in on me after supper.* | *Bill dropped by this morning.* **7** [I+adv/prep] to get further away from a moving object by moving more slowly than it: *Our boat started the race well, but soon dropped off/away (from the others)/dropped behind (the others).* **8** [T] to add while talking about something else (esp. in the phrases **drop a hint/a suggestion**) —see also **let drop** (LET¹ (6)) **9** [T] infml to lose (money): *I dropped £1000 over that deal.* **10** [T] infml to knock down with a shot or blow **11** [T] (in cricket) to fail to catch a ball hit by a BATSMAN: *Gooch dropped Gatting in the second over.* **12** [T] infml to take (a drug) by mouth: *to drop acid* **13 drop a brick/clanger** BrE infml to do or say something foolish and socially uncomfortable: *He dropped a brick in front of the president by calling her "Sir".* **14 drop dead: a** infml to die suddenly **b** sl (used rudely in commands to express dislike, annoyance, etc.) **15 drop someone a line/note** to write a short letter to someone **16 drop someone/something like a hot potato** infml to quickly stop dealing with someone or something that has suddenly become unpleasant **17 drop the pilot** old-fash to get rid of a skilled or trusted helper —see also **the penny dropped/has dropped** (PENNY)
drop off phr v [I] **1** also **drop away**— to lessen in amount, value, etc.: *Interest in the game has dropped off.* | *Sales have dropped off this winter.* **2** infml to fall into a light sleep; DOZE off
drop out phr v [I] **1** [(of)] to stop attending or taking part: *He dropped out of college after only two weeks.* **2** to move away from or refuse to join ordinary society because of not agreeing with accepted practices, standards, and ways of living —see also DROPOUT

drop² n **1** [C] the amount of liquid that falls in one round mass: *a drop of oil/rain* | *a tear drop* —see picture at PIECE **2** [C] a small amount of drink: *"Would you like some more tea?" "Just a drop, please."* | *He's had a drop too much* (=of alcohol) *to drink.* | (fig.) *There isn't a drop of jealousy in her.* **3** [C] a small round sweet of the same kind: *fruit drops/chocolate drops* **4** [S] **a** a distance or fall straight down: *a long drop to the bottom of the cliff* | *a drop of nine metres* **b** a fall in amount, quality, etc.: *a big drop in the temperature* | *another drop in sales* **5** [C] esp. AmE a place where something can be dropped or left: *a mail drop* **6** [C] something that is dropped: *a drop of grain sacks from an aircraft to the hungry people* **7 a drop in the bucket/the ocean** a very small amount, esp. when compared with a larger amount which is needed or wanted: *The money we collected for the famine victims is really just a drop in the ocean.* **8 at the drop of a hat** suddenly and needing almost no excuse: *She expects me to rush over and help at the drop of a hat.* —see also DROPS
drop cloth /'· ·/ AmE ‖ **dust sheet** BrE— n a large sheet of cloth used for throwing over furniture, floors, shop goods, etc. to protect them from dust, paint, or damage
drop-dead /'· ·/ adj, adv AmEsl apprec extremely and immediately impessive: *He's handsome, but not drop-dead handsome.* | *a drop-dead evening gown*
drop goal /'· ·/ n a SCORE in the game of RUGBY made with a dropkick
drop-in /'· ·/ n (tech) a condition caused by accidentally introducing information during the movement of DATA in a computer —compare DROP-OUT (2)
drop-in cen·tre /'· · ·,··/ n an informal place where people can go for help or information and where they may meet friends and sit and talk
drop-kick /'drɒpkɪk‖'drɑːp-/ n a kick made (e.g. in the game of RUGBY) by dropping a ball and kicking it immediately
drop-kick /'· ·/ v **1** [I] to make a dropkick **2** [T] to SCORE a GOAL with a dropkick — ~ **er** n

drop·let /'drɒpl⅃t‖'drɑːp-/ n a very small drop of liquid
drop-out /'drɒpaʊt‖'drɑːp-/ n **1** someone who leaves a school or college without completing the course **2** usu. derog someone who leaves ordinary society because they do not agree with accepted practices, standards, and ways of living —see also DROP **out**
drop-out /'·· ·/ n **1** a dropkick given to the defending team in the game of RUGBY **2** (tech) a condition caused by the accidental loss of information during the movement of DATA in a computer —compare DROP-IN **3** a case of an electronic machine not working for a short time
drop·per /'drɒpəʳ‖'drɑː-/ n a short glass tube with an air-filled part (BULB) at one end, used for measuring out liquids, esp. liquid medicine, in drops
drop·pings /'drɒpɪŋz‖'drɑː-/ n [P] waste matter from the bowels of animals and birds: *bird/sheep droppings*
drops /drɒps‖drɑːps/ n [P] (often in comb.) liquid medicine to be taken drop by drop: *eyedrops* | *These drops are administered orally.*
drop scone /'· ·/ also **pancake** ScotE n a small round cake made by dropping a spoonful of BATTER onto a hot pan, which may be served for tea with butter and JAM
drop shot /'· ·/ n a delicate shot in a game such as tennis or SQUASH, in which the ball drops gently to the ground and does not rise up again very far, so that it is difficult to hit
drop·sy /'drɒpsi‖'drɑːpsi/ n [U] a gathering of liquid under the skin or in the organs because of various diseases —**-sical** adj
dross /drɒs‖drɑːs, drɔːs/ n [U] **1** waste or worthless matter **2** something that is of very poor quality: *I thought the film was utter dross!*
drought /draʊt/ n [C;U] (a long period of) dry weather when there is not enough water: *The crops failed because of the drought.*
drove¹ /drəʊv/ past tense of DRIVE¹
drove² n a group of esp. farm animals driven in a body: *a drove of cattle*
drov·er /'drəʊvəʳ/ n a person who drives cattle or sheep
droves /drəʊvz/ n [P] a crowd of people moving together: *droves of sightseers* | *The tourists came in droves.*
drown /draʊn/ v **1** [I;T] to (cause to) die by being under water and unable to breathe: *She drowned in the river.* **2** [T] to cover completely with water, esp. by a rise in the water level; SUBMERGE: *streets and houses drowned by the floods* **3** [T (with, in)] to cover thickly; SMOTHER: *drowning the bananas with cream* **4** [T (OUT)] to prevent (a sound) from being heard by making a loud noise: *The band drowned out our conversation.* **5 drown one's sorrows** to drink alcohol in an attempt to forget one's troubles
drowse /draʊz/ v [I] to be in a light sleep or pleasantly sleepy state
drow·sy /'draʊzi/ adj **1** sleepy: *The medicine may make you drowsy.* **2** making one sleepy: *a drowsy summer afternoon* **3** peacefully inactive: *a drowsy village* —**-sily** adv —**-siness** n [U] : *These pills may cause drowsiness.*
drub·bing /'drʌbɪŋ/ n infml a thorough defeat: *We gave the other team a good drubbing.*
drudge¹ /drʌdʒ/ v [I] to do hard uninteresting work
drudge² n a person who drudges
drudg·e·ry /'drʌdʒəri/ n [U] hard uninteresting work
drug¹ /drʌg/ n **1** a medicine or a substance used for making medicines: *a drug used in the treatment of cancer* **2** a substance one takes, esp. as a habit, for pleasure or excitement: *Tobacco and alcohol can be dangerous drugs.* | *a growing market for* **hard drugs** *such as heroin and cocaine* | *Is he* **on drugs**? (=Does he take ILLEGAL drugs?) | *efforts to control drug trafficking* (=the trade in illegal drugs) | *Some people argue that the use of* **soft drugs** *such as marijuana leads to the use of hard drugs.*
▶ CULTURAL NOTE Illegal drugs, esp. cannabis and LSD, became popular among young people in the 1960s and 70s. Drugs were seen as a way of examining the unconscious mind and of gaining knowledge of the rich experiences of the mind. The use of illegal drugs is now a serious problem in both Britain and the US. ◀
3 a drug on the market infml goods which no one wants to buy

drug² *v* -gg- [T] **1** to add drugs to, esp. so as to produce unconsciousness: *a drugged cup of coffee* **2** to influence with drugs or give drugs to, esp. so as to produce unconsciousness: *They drugged him to kill the pain.* | *He's* **drugged up to the eyeballs.**

drug a·buse /ˈ· ·,·/ also **drug misuse,** *BrE*— *n* [U] the use of drugs, both legal and not legal, not for medical reasons but for pleasure or because of ADDICTION: *the growing problem of drug abuse*

drug ad·dict /ˈ· ,··/ *n* a person who habitually takes drugs, e.g. HEROIN or COCAINE, to give themselves pleasure, and has become dependent on the drug to such a degree that they would be very ill if they were unable to continue taking it — ~ **ion** *n* [U] : *The singer was reported to be receiving help to overcome his drug addiction.*

drug bar·on /ˈ· ,··/ *n derog* someone who is the head of an organization which makes a lot of money from selling ILLEGAL drugs, such as NARCOTICS

drug czar /ˈ· ,·/ *n* (in America) an official appointed by the government to try and stop the trade in ILLEGAL drugs

Drug En·force·ment Ad·min·i·stra·tion /ˌ· ·ˈ·· ···,·ˈ·/ (*abbrev* DEA) an American government organization which makes sure that people and companies obey the laws about dangerous drugs. They try to catch people who bring dangerous drugs into the US and people who sell drugs within the US.

drug·get /ˈdrʌgɪt/ *n* [C;U] (a piece of) rough heavy cloth used esp. as a floor covering

drug·gie /ˈdrʌgi/ *n infml* a DRUG ADDICT or someone who often takes drugs

drug·gist /ˈdrʌgɪst/ *n AmE for* PHARMACIST (2)

drug mis·use /ˌ· ·ˈ·/ *n BrE for* DRUG ABUSE

drug push·er /ˈ· ,··/ *n* someone who sells ILLEGAL drugs such as HEROIN for profit, and encourages people to take them

drug re·ha·bil·i·ta·tion /ˌ· ····ˈ·· ,··/ ‖ also **drug re·hab** /ˌdrʌgˈriːhæb/ *AmE*— *n* [U] the process of learning to live without drugs and to fight DRUG ADDICTION. In Britain and the US, drug rehabilitation centres exist to help DRUG ADDICTS.

drug rehabilitation cen·tre /ˌ· ····ˈ·· ,··/ *n* a place where medical help is given to DRUG ADDICTS to enable them to stop taking harmful drugs such as HEROIN

drugstore

drug·store /ˈdrʌgstɔːʳ/ *n esp. AmE* a PHARMACY, esp. one which sells not only medicine, but also beauty products, school supplies, small things to eat, garden products, film, etc., and formerly, simple meals.

▶CULTURAL NOTE Drug stores as an institution do not really exist in Britain, and the British idea of them is very much a part of the American way of life as seen in films and TV programmes of the 1950s and 1960s.◀

dru·id /ˈdruːɪd/ *n* (*often cap.*) a member of the ancient Celtic priesthood of Britain, Ireland, and France, before the Christian religion

▶CULTURAL NOTE There are people today who call themselves druids. They are considered by most people to be harmless but definitely odd. They are known about esp. because of their visits to Stonehenge where they perform various religious ceremonies at important times of the year for them, such as the longest day in the middle of summer. —see also STONEHENGE, SUMMER SOLSTICE◀

drum¹ /drʌm/ *n* **1** [C] a musical instrument consisting of

a skin stretched tight over a hollow circular frame, which is played by being hit with the hand or with a stick: *the steady beat of the drum* —see picture at PERCUSSION **2** [C] something that looks like a drum, esp. a part of a machine or a large container for liquids: *an oil drum* **3** **bang/beat the drum for** to speak in eager support of

drum² *v* -mm- [I] **1** to play a drum **2** [+ *adv/prep*] to make drum-like noises, esp. by continuous beating or striking: *He drummed on the table with his fingers.* | *the rain drumming against the window*

drum sthg. into sbdy. *phr v* [T] *infml* to put (an idea, rule, etc.) firmly into (someone's mind) by continuous repeating: *She drummed it into the children that they must not cross the road alone.*

drum sbdy. out *phr v* [T (**of**)] to send away formally and in dishonour; EXPEL: *He was drummed out of the army.*

drum sthg. ↔ up *phr v* [T] *infml* to obtain by continuous effort and esp. by advertising: *Let's try to drum up some more business.* | *to drum up support/enthusiasm for a cause*

drum·beat /ˈdrʌmbiːt/ *n* a stroke on a drum or its sound

drum ma·jor /ˌ· ˈ··‖ˈ· ,··/ *n* the male leader of a band of marching musicians, esp. a military band

drum ma·jor·ette /ˌ· ··ˈ·‖ˈ· ··,·/ *n* —see MAJORETTE

drum·mer /ˈdrʌməʳ/ *n* a person who plays a drum

drum·stick /ˈdrʌmˌstɪk/ *n* **1** a stick for beating a drum **2** *infml* the lower part of the leg of a chicken or similar bird, eaten as food. These are often covered in BREADCRUMBS and cooked in hot oil, and eaten with the fingers.

drunk¹ /drʌŋk/ *past participle of* DRINK¹

drunk² *adj* [F] under the influence of alcohol: *The police charged him with being* **drunk and disorderly.** | *He got* **drunk** *on only two glasses of wine.* | *He's* **dead/blind drunk.** (=very drunk) | (fig.) *drunk with power* — compare SOBER¹ (1)

drunk³ *n often derog* a person who is (habitually) drunk

drunk·ard /ˈdrʌŋkəd‖-ərd/ *n derog* a person who is often drunk —compare ALCOHOLIC²

drunk·en /ˈdrʌŋkən/ *adj* [A] **1** drunk: *a drunken sailor* **2** resulting from or connected with too much drinking of alcohol: *a drunken sleep* | *a drunken party* — ~**ly** *adv* — ~**ness** *n* [U]

drunk·o·me·ter   /drʌˈkɒmˌtəʳ‖-ˈkɑː-/   *n*   *AmE* BREATHALYSER

Dru·ry Lane /ˌdrʊəri ˈleɪn/ a street in London famous for its theatre

Druze , Druse /druːz/ *n* [*the*] a Muslim religious group who live in the mountainous parts of Lebanon, Syria, and Israel and whose beliefs include some taken from Islam, Christianity, and Gnosticism

Dr Who /ˌ·· ˈ·/ a British children's television SERIES, started in 1963, about a character called Dr Who, who travels in time and space in a time machine (called the **Tardis**) with different companions. He fights wicked people and beings from other worlds, usu. in a non-violent way. Many adults who enjoyed the programmes as children still like to watch them, esp. the ones featuring DALEKS. —see also DALEK, TARDIS and see colour picture on page 686

dry¹ /draɪ/ *adj* **1** having no water or liquid inside or on the surface; not wet, sticky, or MOIST: *Don't put your shirt on until it's dry.* | *The soil is too dry for planting vegetables.* | *The paint isn't dry yet — be careful!* | *The well has gone dry.* | *dry skin* (=without natural liquids) | *The kettle boiled dry.* (=boiled until there was no water left) **2** without rain or wetness; lacking HUMIDITY: *a dry climate* | *a dry month* | *dry heat* —compare HUMID **3** having or producing thirst: *I always feel dry in this hot weather.* | *It's dry work digging in the sun.* **4** [A] (esp. of bread) eaten without butter, JAM, etc.: *dry toast* **5** without tears or other liquid substances from the body: *dry-eyed* (=not crying) | *a dry cough* | *By the end of the play, there wasn't* **a dry eye in the house.** (=everyone was crying) **6** (of alcoholic drinks, esp. wine) not sweet; not fruity in taste: *dry sherry* | *dry white wine* **7** no longer giving milk: *a dry cow* **8** not allowing the sale of alcoholic drink: *There are still some dry states in the US.* **9** amusing without appearing to be so; quietly IRONIC: *I like his dry humour.* **10** dull and uninteresting: *The book was* **as dry as dust.**

(=very dull) **11** *BrE infml* of or being a Conservative politician who has UNCOMPROMISING views −compare WET² (3) **12 (as) dry as a bone** *infml* perfectly dry; BONE-DRY −see also DRIP-DRY, **home and dry** (HOME² (4)) −**dryly, drily** *adv* − −**ness** *n* [U]

dry² *v* **1** [I;T (OUT, UP, OFF)] to make or become dry: *Dry your hands.* | *Hang out the washing to dry.* | *The clothes will soon dry (out) in the sun.* | *to dry (up) the dishes* | *The swimmer dried off in the hot sun.* | *She ran in after the rainstorm and dried herself off with a thick towel.* **2** [T] to preserve (esp. food) by removing liquid: *dried fruit/milk* | *dried flowers* −see also CUT-AND-DRIED
dry out *phr v* [I;T (=**dry** sbdy. **out**)] **1** to (cause to) give up dependence on alcoholic drink **2** to (cause to) become completely dry
dry up *phr v* **1** [I;T (=**dry** sthg. ↔ **up**)] to (cause to) become completely dry: *During the drought the reservoirs dried up.* | *a dried-up river bed* **2** [I] (of a supply of something) to come to an end: *Our sources of information have dried up.* **3** [I] **a** [*usu. imperative*] *sl* to stop talking or writing, or be quiet, usu. because one has forgotten what one has to say next or cannot think of anything to say **b** *infml* to forget one's words when acting in a play: *He dried up three times in the second act.*

dry·ad /ˈdraɪæd/ *n* a female spirit in ancient Greek stories who lived in a tree; wood NYMPH −compare OREAD

dry bat·te·ry /ˈ· ˌ···/ also **dry cell** /ˈ· ·/− *n* an electric BATTERY containing chemicals which are not in a liquid form

dry-clean /ˌ· ˈ·/ *v* [T] to clean (clothes, material, etc.) with chemicals instead of water

dry clean·er's /ˌ· ˈ··/ *n* a shop where clothes, curtains, etc., can be taken to be dry-cleaned

Dry·den /ˈdraɪdən/, **John** (1631−1700) an English writer of poetry and plays

dry dock /ˈ· ·/ *n* a place in which a ship is held in position while the water is pumped out, leaving the ship dry for repairs: *The ship is in dry dock being painted.*

dry·er , drier /ˈdraɪəʳ/ *n* (*often in comb.*) a machine that dries: *a hairdryer*

dry-eyed /ˌ· ˈ·◄/ *adj* (of a person) not having tears in the eyes; not crying

dry goods /ˈ· ·/ *n* [P] **1** *BrE* goods such as tobacco, drugs, tea, coffee, dried fruits, etc. **2** *AmE* goods such as clothing, cloth, sheets, curtains, and other things made from cloth: *a dry goods store/department*

dry ice /ˌ· ˈ·/ *n* [U] CARBON DIOXIDE in a solid state, used mainly to keep food and other things cold

dry land /ˌ· ˈ·/ *n* [U] land as opposed to water: *After three weeks at sea we were glad to get onto dry land again.*

dry mar ti ni /ˌ· ·ˈ··/ *n* [C;U] a (glass of an) alcoholic drink made from GIN and dry VERMOUTH. It is famous esp. for being the favourite drink of James Bond, who used to ask for *"a dry martini, shaken, not stirred"*

dry rot /ˌ· ˈ·/ *n* [U] diseased growth in wood, e.g. in wooden floors, which turns wood into powder

dry run /ˌ· ˈ·/ *n infml* a practice exercise before the actual event: *Shall we do a dry run of the presentation?* | *Both the parties are treating the local elections as a dry run for the general election.*

dry-shod /ˌ· ˈ·/ *adj, adv* [F] *old use* without getting the shoes or feet wet: *to cross the stream dry-shod*

dry-stone wall /ˌ· · ˈ·/ *n* a stone wall built without MORTAR

DSc /ˌdiː es ˈsiː/ *n* Doctor of Science; a person given this degree by a university, after a period of study in a scientific subject

DSS /ˌdiː es ˈes/ *n* [*the*] Department of Social Security; the British government department which is responsible for paying people any BENEFITS that they are allowed, e.g. FAMILY CREDIT or UNEMPLOYMENT BENEFIT

DTI /ˌdiː tiː ˈaɪ/ *n* [*the*] see DEPARTMENT OF TRADE AND INDUSTRY

DTP /ˌdiː tiː ˈpiː/ *abbrev. for*: DESKTOP PUBLISHING

D T's /ˌdiː tiːz/ also **delirium tremens** *fml*− *n* [(*the*) P] a nervous state in which a person's body, caused by habitually drinking too much alcohol shakes and they see unreal things: *He's got the DT's.*

du·al /ˈdjuːəl‖ˈduːəl/ *adj* [A] consisting of two separate

---

parts or having two parts like each other; double: *a training aircraft/a driving instructor's car with dual controls* | *a* **dual-purpose** *instrument* | *the government's dual aim of cutting taxes and increasing job opportunities* − −**ity** /djuːˈælₔti‖duː-/ *n* [U]

dual car·riage·way /ˌ·· ˈ····/ *n* *BrE‖***divided highway** *AmE*− a main road on which the traffic travelling in opposite directions is kept apart by a central band or separation of some sort

dual cit·i·zen·ship /ˌ··· ˈ····/ *n* [U] the state of being a citizen of two countries: *She got dual citizenship last year and now holds a Swiss and a British passport.*

dub¹ /dʌb/ *v* **-bb-** [T (*obj i n*] **1** (esp. in newspapers) to name humorously or descriptively: *a period of strikes and labour troubles, which the papers dubbed "the winter of discontent"* **2** *lit or old use* (of a king or queen) to make (someone) a KNIGHT by a ceremonial touch on the shoulder with a sword and by giving him the title "Sir" before his name. The man who is being dubbed kneels for the ceremony. At the end the king/queen says "Arise/Rise Sir ...." This ceremony is known from stories from the MIDDLE AGES, and is still used regularly in Britain when men are given national honours.

dub² *v* [T] **1** (into) to change the original spoken language of (a film, radio show, or television show): *a Swedish film dubbed into English* | *Is it dubbed or does it have subtitles?* **2** (*esp. BrE*) to make a record out of two or more different pieces of music or sounds mixed together

dub³ *n* [U] a West Indian style of poetry spoken to the RHYTHM of REGGAE music: *a dub poet*

Du·bai /duːˈbaɪ/ a state on the Persian Gulf, part of the United Arab Emirates

dub·bin /ˈdʌbₔn/ *n* [U] a thick oily substance used for making leather softer and to stop water going through it

Dub·ček /ˈdʊbtʃek/, **Al·ex·an·der** /ˌælɪgˈzɑːndəʳ‖-ˈzæn-/ (1921−92) a Czech politician who was the first secretary of the COMMUNIST Party in 1967 and became speaker of the Czech parliament in December 1989

du·bi·e·ty /djuːˈbaɪəti‖duː-/ *n* [U] *fml* uncertainty or doubt; dubiousness

du·bi·ous /ˈdjuːbiəs‖ˈduː-/ *adj* **1** [(**about**)] feeling doubt; undecided or uncertain: *I'm still dubious about that plan.* **2** causing doubt; of uncertain value or meaning or possibly dishonest: *a dubious suggestion* | *a plan of dubious merit* | *a rather dubious character* − −**ly** *adv* − −**ness** *n* [U]

Dub·lin /ˈdʌblₔn/ the capital city of the Republic of Ireland. Dublin is known as the home of famous Irish writers, such as Jonathan Swift, George Bernard Shaw, and James Joyce, and mentioned in songs: *"In Dublin's fair city, where girls are so pretty..."* −see colour map on page 818 − −**er** *n*

Du·bon·net /duːˈbɒneɪ, djuː-‖ˌduːbəˈneɪ/ *n* [C;U] *tdmk* a drink made from French sweet wine, often served before a meal, in a small glass

du·cal /ˈdjuːkəl‖ˈduː-/ *adj* of or like a DUKE

duc·at /ˈdʌkət/ *n* a gold coin formerly used in several countries of Europe

duch·ess /ˈdʌtʃₔs/ *n* (*often cap.*) **1** the wife of a DUKE: *the Duchess of Kent* **2** a woman of ducal rank in her own right

du·chesse po·ta·toes /djuːˌʃes pəˈteɪtəʊz/ *n* [P] potatoes which have been boiled, mixed with egg, shaped into little cakes, and then baked

Duchess of Wind·sor /ˌ··· ˈ··/ see **Wallis** SIMPSON

Duchess of York /ˌ··· ˈ·/ [*the*] a title given to Sarah Ferguson after her marriage to Prince Andrew, the Duke of York, in 1986. The Duke and Duchess of York separated in 1992.

ducks

duch·y /ˈdʌtʃi/ *n* (*often cap.*) (used esp. in names) the lands of a DUKE or duchess: *the Duchy of Cornwall*

duck¹ /dʌk/ *n* **ducks** or **duck** **1** [C] **drake** *masc.* a common swimming bird with short legs and a wide beak, either wild or kept for meat, eggs, and soft feathers. When they make a noise, they are said to QUACK: *A young duck is called a duckling.* **2** [U] the meat of this bird as food: *a plate of roast duck* —see MEAT (USAGE) **3** [C] *infml, esp. BrE* (used for addressing) a person one likes: *She's a sweet old duck.* **4** [C] (in cricket) the failure of a BATSMAN to make any runs at all **5 take to something like a duck to water** *infml* to learn or get used to something naturally and very easily —see also DUCKS, DEAD DUCK, LAME DUCK, SITTING DUCK, **like water off a duck's back** (WATER[1])

duck² *v* **1** [I;T] to lower (one's head or body) quickly, esp. so as to avoid being hit: *She had to duck (her head) to get through the low doorway.* | *He saw a policeman coming, and ducked behind a car.* **2** [T **(in)**] to push under water: *The children ducked each other in the swimming pool.* **3** [T] *infml* to try to avoid (a difficulty or unpleasant duty); DODGE: *His speech was full of generalizations, and ducked all the real issues.* **—duck** *n*
  duck out of sthg. *phr v* [T+*obj/v-ing*] *infml* to escape one's responsibility for: *Don't try to duck out of cleaning up the kitchen!*

duck³ *n* [U] a heavy strong usu. cotton cloth —see also DUCKS

duck·billed plat·y·pus /ˌdʌkˌbɪld ˈplætɪpəs/ *n* an egg-laying Australian animal with a beak like a duck's

duck-boards /ˈdʌkbɔːdz‖-bɔːrdz/ *n* [P] *BrE* narrow boards with spaces between, nailed on longer pieces of wood, for making a path over muddy ground

duck – duck – goose /ˌ· · ˈ·/ *n* [U] an American children's game usually played by a large group of children sitting in a circle, in which one player chooses another to be the GOOSE, and each tries to run the fastest around the circle

duck·ing stool /ˈ··· ·/ *n* a seat on one end of a long pole, to which bad-tempered and unpleasant women were tied in former times in order to be ducked in water as a punishment

duck·ling /ˈdʌklɪŋ/ *n* a small young duck —see also UGLY DUCKLING

ducks /dʌks/ *n* **1** [P] trousers made of DUCK³: *dressed in white ducks* —see PAIR (USAGE) **2** [S] also **ducky** *esp. BrE infml* (used to address a person in a friendly way): *How's that for you, ducks? Got enough there?*

ducks and drakes /ˌ· · ˈ·/ *n* [U] **1** a children's game in which one makes flat stones jump across the surface of water **2 play ducks and drakes with** *infml* to waste (money) wildly

duck·weed /ˈdʌkwiːd/ *n* [U] any of various plants that grow on the surface of fresh water

duck·y¹ /ˈdʌki/ *n infml* DUCKS (2)

ducky² *adj* **1** *AmE* perfect; satisfactory: *Oh, that's just ducky.* **2** *AmE* attractive in an amusing or interesting way; CUTE: *a ducky little cottage*

duct /dʌkt/ *n* **1** a thin, narrow tube in the body or in plants which carries liquids, air, etc.: *tearducts* **2** a pipe or tube for carrying liquids, air, electric power lines, etc. —see also AQUEDUCT, VIADUCT

duc·tile /ˈdʌktaɪl‖-tl/ *n* **1** (esp. of metals) able to be pressed or pulled into shape without needing to be heated **2** *lit* (of a person or behaviour) easily influenced or controlled; MALLEABLE **—-tility** /dʌkˈtɪlɪti/ *n* [U]

duct·less gland /ˌdʌktləs ˈglænd/ *n* an ENDOCRINE GLAND

dud /dʌd/ *n infml* someone or something that has little or no value or use, or that fails to serve its purpose: *Several of the fireworks were duds.* (=failed to work properly) | *She's a dud at sports.* **—dud** *adj* : *a dud light bulb*

dud cheque /ˌ· ˈ·/ *n* a cheque which is useless because the dishonest person who paid with it has no money in the account on which it is drawn

dude /djuːd‖duːd/ *n AmE sl* **1** a city man, esp. an Easterner in the West **2** a man; GUY

dude ranch /ˈ· ·/ *n* (in the US) a holiday place that offers activities, such as horse riding, typical of a RANCH (=a Western cattle farm)

dud·geon /ˈdʌdʒən/ *n* **in high dudgeon** *fml* angry and bitter because of bad treatment

due¹ /djuː‖duː/ *adj* **1** [F (**to**)] owed or owing as a debt or right: *Our grateful thanks are due to the police department for their help in the making of this film.* | *We must give*

credit where it is due. (=praise someone who deserves praise, even if unwillingly) | *Any money that is due to you will be paid before the end of the month.* **2** [A] *fml* proper, correct, or suitable: *driving with due care and attention* | *The trial was conducted with due process of law.* **3** [F] payable: *a bill due today* **4** [F] (esp. showing arrangements made in advance) expected or supposed (to happen, arrive, etc.): *The next train to London is due at 4 o'clock.* | *Her baby is due* (=will be born) *next month.* [+*to-v*] *I am due to leave quite soon now.* | [+ for] *I am due for an increase in pay soon.* **5 due to** because of; caused by: *His success is entirely due to hard work.* | *Their increase in profits is due in part to/due largely to their innovative market strategy.* | *The price of gold rose again, due partly to rumours of war.* **6 with (all) due respect** (a phrase used when a speaker does not wish to appear rude, but does want to disagree with someone or find fault with them): *I know you are an expert in your field, but with all due respect this report needs to be rewritten before it can be published.* —see also DULY

▷ USAGE Compare **due to** and **owing to**, which are similar in meaning. 1 **Due to** is used after the verb *to be*; you cannot use **owing to** in this sentence: *His absence was* due to *the storm.* 2 Some people think that **due to** should only be used after the verb *to be*, but many speakers use it after other verbs, in the same way as **owing to**: *He arrived late* due to/owing to (=because of) *the storm.*◁

due² *n* **someone's due** something that rightfully belongs or is owed to someone, esp. something non-material: *I don't like him, but,* **to give him his due,** *he's good at his job.* | *She never takes more than her due.* —see also DUES, **give the devil his due** (DEVIL[1])

due³ *adv* (before **north, south, east,** and **west**) directly; exactly: *due north (of here)*

due date /ˈ· ·/ *n* the date on which something is due to happen, e.g. an amount of money must be paid

du·el¹ /ˈdjuːəl‖ˈduːəl/ *n* a fight with hand guns or swords, arranged (esp. formerly) between two people to settle a quarrel: *to fight a duel* | (fig.) *another duel between the company and the union*

duel² *v* **-ll-** *BrE* **-l-** *AmE* [I (**with**)] to fight a duel —**duellist, dueller** *n*

du·en·na /djuˈenə‖duː-/ *n* (esp. formerly) an older woman in a Spanish-speaking or Portuguese-speaking country who watches over the daughters of a family and goes with them in public; CHAPERON

dues /djuːz‖duːz/ *n* [P] official charges or payments: *to pay union dues* | (fig.) *Agassi had lost the match, but he had done well, and had paid his dues.* —see also TAX (USAGE)

du·et /djuˈet‖duˈet/ also **duo** *n* a piece of music for two performers —compare SOLO¹ (1)

duff /dʌf/ *adj BrE infml* useless or worthless

duf·fel bag /ˈdʌfəl bæg/ *n* a bag about half a metre in length, made of strong cloth, with a round bottom and a string round the top, for carrying clothes and other belongings —compare KIT BAG

duffel coat, **duffle coat** /ˈ· · ·/ *n BrE* a loose coat made of a rough heavy woollen cloth, usu. fastened with TOGGLES (=long tubelike buttons) and often having a covering for the head joined to the neck. These coats are often worn by schoolchildren.

duffel coat

duf·fer /ˈdʌfər/ *n old-fash infml* [(**at**)] a foolish person or slow learner: *She's a duffer at games.*

Du·fy /ˈduːfiː‖duːˈfiː/, **Ra·oul** /rɑːˈuːl/ (1877–1953) a French painter known for his bright watercolour and oil paintings, esp. of horse racing and sailing scenes

dug¹ /dʌg/ *past tense & participle of* DIG¹

dug² *n esp. lit* an animal's UDDER or NIPPLE

dug·out /ˈdʌgaʊt/ *n* **1** a small light boat made by cutting out a deep hollow space in a log: *a dugout canoe* **2** a (usu. military) shelter dug in the ground with an earth roof

—compare TRENCH (2) **3** a low shelter at the side of a sportsground, esp. a BASEBALL ground, where players and team officials can sit

DUI /ˌdiː juː ˈaɪ/ n [U] DRIVING UNDER THE INFLUENCE: *The police usu. have a large number of DUI arrests on New Year's Eve.*

Du·ka·kis /duːˈkɑːkɪs/, **Mi·chael** /ˈmaɪkəl/ (1933–) an American Democrat politician who was the governor of Massachusetts from 1974–78, and also from 1982 onwards, and stood for president in 1988, losing to George Bush

duke /djuːk‖duːk/ n (*often cap.*) a nobleman of the highest rank outside the royal family: *the Duke of Norfolk* | *He became a duke on the death of his father.* —see also DUCHESS

duke·dom /ˈdjuːkdəm‖ˈduːk-/ n **1** the rank of a duke **2** the lands of a duke; DUCHY

Duke of Ed·in·burgh /ˌ· · ˈ····/ [*the*] see Prince PHILIP

Duke of Edinburgh's a·ward /ˌ· · ˌ···· ·ˈ·/ **Duke of Edinburgh's** n any of various MEDALs given to people as part of a programme suggested by the Duke of Edinburgh, in which young people take part in esp. physical activities which are useful to themselves or others, and reach a certain standard: *She's doing her Duke of Edinburgh gold at the moment. She's gone off camping in Snowdonia.*

Duke of Wel·ling·ton /ˌ· · ˈ···/ [*the*] (1769–1852) an Irish soldier and politician whose most famous victory was the defeat of Napoleon at Waterloo in 1815

Duke of West·min·ster /ˌ· · ˈ···/ [*the*] (1951–) one of the richest men in England and owner of a lot of land

Duke of Wind·sor /ˌ· · ˈ··/ see EDWARD VIII

Duke of York /ˌ· · ˈ·/ [*the*] see Prince ANDREW

dukes /djuːks‖duːks/ n [P] *sl for* FISTS: *Put your dukes up and fight!*

dul·cet /ˈdʌlsɪt/ adj *lit or humor* (esp. of sounds) sweet and calming: *She spoke in dulcet tones.*

dul·ci·mer /ˈdʌlsɪmər/ n **1** ‖ usu. **hammered dulcimer** *AmE* a European and American musical instrument with up to 100 strings, played with light hammers **2** a small stringed instrument popular in American FOLK MUSIC, rested on the player's LAP and plucked (PLUCK) with the fingers or a PICK

dull¹ /dʌl/ adj **1** (of colours or surfaces) not bright; not shining: *a dull grey* **2** not clear or sharp: *a dull knocking sound somewhere in the house* | *a dull pain* **3** (of weather, the sky, etc.) cloudy; not sunny; OVERCAST: *a dull day with showers of rain* **4** uninteresting or unexciting; BORING: *an afternoon of dull lectures* | *There's never a dull moment when John comes to stay.* (=there is always something interesting or amusing happening) **5** slow in thinking, learning, and understanding **6** (of things with edges or points) not sharp; BLUNT **7** (of trade) not active; SLUGGISH: *a dull day on the stockmarket* **8** (as) **dull as ditchwater** *infml* very uninteresting —**~y** /ˈdʌl-li/ adv —**~ness** n [U]

dull² v [T] to make dull: *Give me something to dull* (=lessen or make less sharp) *the pain.* | *Her hearing was dulled by age.*

dull·ard /ˈdʌləd‖-ərd/ n *becoming rare* a dull slow-thinking person

Dul·les /ˈdʌlɪs/ an airport serving the Washington DC area

Dulles, John Foster (1888–1959) an American secretary of state (1953–59) and representative at the United Nations (1945–49). He fought Communism and encouraged agreements for security between the US and other countries.

Dul·wich /ˈdʌlɪdʒ, -ɪtʃ/ an area in SE London with many large houses with pleasant gardens

du·ly /ˈdjuːli‖ˈduːli/ adv *fml* in a proper manner, time, or degree; as expected: *The taxi that he had ordered duly arrived, and we drove off.* | *Your suggestion has been duly noted.* | *I enclose the contract, duly signed.*

Du·mas /ˈdjuːmɑː‖duːˈmɑː/, **Al·ex·an·dre** /ˌælɪgˈzɑːndrə/ (1802–70) a French writer of stories and plays including *The Count of Monte Cristo* and *The Three Musketeers*

Du Mau·ri·er /duː ˈmɒriei, djuː-‖də-/, **Daphne** (1907–89) an English writer of NOVELs, including *Jamaica Inn* and *Rebecca*

dumb /dʌm/ adj **1** unable to speak (may be considered offensive to people who are unable to speak): *dumb animals* | *The terrible news* **struck us dumb.** [also n, the+P] *special schools for the deaf and dumb* **2** unwilling to speak; silent: *The prisoner remained dumb throughout his trial.* **3** *infml* esp. *AmE* stupid: *That was a dumb thing to say.* —**~ly** adv —**~ness** n [U]

dumb·bell /ˈdʌmbel/ n **1** [*usu. pl.*] a weight consisting of two large metal balls connected by a short bar and usu. used in pairs for exercises to strengthen the body **2** *sl, esp. AmE* a stupid person

dumb blonde /ˌ· ˈ·/ n a woman who is thought to be attractive but stupid. The woman need not actually have BLONDE hair or be dumb (=stupid) but may be called this by men or other women as a quick, offensive description. It would not be used in front of the person, but only about them: *She's just a dumb blonde.* | *She plays the dumb blonde in the film.*

dumb·found , dumfound /dʌmˈfaʊnd/ v [T] to make unable to speak because of wonder, surprise, or lack of understanding; SURPRISED: *She dumbfounded her critics by winning all the prizes.*

dumb·found·ed , dumfounded /dʌmˈfaʊndɪd/ also **dumb·struck** /ˈdʌmstrʌk/— adj [(**at, by**)] unable to speak because of shock, surprise, or lack of understanding; SURPRISE: *We were all dumbfounded at/by the news.* | *a dumbfounded silence* [+that] *I was dumbfounded that she could say such a thing.*

dum·bo /ˈdʌmbəʊ/ n *infml, esp. AmE* a stupid person: *Don't do it that way, you dumbo!*

Dumbo an elephant with large ears which is a Walt Disney film character

dumb show /ˈ· ·/ n [C;U] something performed with actions only, and without any speaking: *to tell a story in dumb show*

dumb·wait·er /ˌdʌmˈweɪtər/ n **1** a small LIFT² (2) used for moving food, plates, etc., from one level of a building (esp. a restaurant) to another **2** *BrE*‖**lazy Susan** *AmE*— a small table that turns round on a fixed base, used for serving food

Dum·fries and Gal·lo·way /dʌmˌfriːs ənd ˈgæləweɪ/ a REGION in SW Scotland, including the town of Dumfries

Dum·fries·shire /dʌmˈfriːsʃər/ a former COUNTY in S Scotland, now part of Dumfries and Galloway REGION

dum·my /ˈdʌmi/ n **1** an object made to look like and take the place of a real thing: *a dummy gun made of plastic* **2** a model of a human figure made of wood, plastic, etc. and used to make or show off clothes: *a dressmaker's dummy* **3** *BrE* ‖ **pacifier** *AmE*— a rubber TEAT for sucking, put in a baby's mouth to keep it quiet **4** *sl, esp. AmE* a stupid fool: *You dummy!* **5** (a player with) the open cards on the table in the game of BRIDGE

dummy run /ˌ·· ˈ·/ also **trial run** n a practice attempt made before the real thing; REHEARSAL: *a dummy run in preparation for the ceremony tomorrow*

dump¹ /dʌmp/ v **1** [T + obj + adv/prep] to drop or unload (something), esp. heavily or carelessly, in a rough pile: *Don't dump that sand in the middle of the path!* | *They dumped their bags on my floor and left!* | (fig.) *Some people I used to know turned up and dumped themselves on me for the weekend.* (=stayed for the weekend without being invited to do so) **2** [I;T] to get rid of (things which are not wanted, etc.) irresponsibly; ABANDON: *He dumped his old car at the side of the road.* | *No dumping here!* | (fig.) *He's just dumped his latest girlfriend.* | *That school is just a* **dumping ground** *for problem children.* **3** [T] *derog* to sell (goods) in a foreign country more cheaply than at home, esp. below the cost of production; this might happen when the products are not wanted by the country selling them, when they are below the standard considered safe or legal by the home country but thought acceptable in other parts of the world, e.g. medical supplies or other products: *The company denied dumping baby milk substitutes on Third World hospitals.* **4** [T] *tech* to move (information stored in a computer's memory) to another place of storage, such as a DISK

dump² n **1** also **tip** *BrE*— a place for dumping waste material: *the town rubbish dump* **2** (a place for) a stored supply of military materials: *an ammunition dump* **3** *derog sl* a dirty, untidy, or disorderly place: *This town's a real dump!* —see also DUMPS **4** the result of moving information stored in a computer's memory to another place, such as a DISK: *I haven't analysed this dump yet to see what the problem was.*

dump·er /'dʌmpəʳ/ also **dumper truck** /'·· ˌ·/, **dump truck** /'· ·/*AmE*— *n* a vehicle with a large movable container on the front, used for carrying and emptying heavy loads of soil, stones, etc.

dump·ling /'dʌmplɪŋ/ *n* **1** a lump of flour mixed with water, cooked by boiling in water and often served with meat or having meat inside it: *chicken and dumplings* **2** a sweet food made of pastry with fruit inside it: *apple dumplings*

dumps /dʌmps/ *n* (**down**) **in the dumps** *infml* sad; DEPRESSED

dump·ster /'dʌmpstəʳ/ *n tdmk* (*often cap.*) (in America) a large metal container for rubbish; SKIP³

dump·y /'dʌmpi/ *adj infml derog* (esp. of a person) short and fat: *a dumpy little woman* —**iness** *n* [U]

dun /dʌn/ *n* **1** [U] a brownish-grey colour that lacks brightness **2** [C] a horse of this colour —**dun** *adj*

Dun & Brad·street /ˌdʌn ənd 'brædstriːt/ an American company that sets CREDIT RATINGs for national and international businesses, based on their records of paying their debts, delivering goods, etc.

Dun·a·way /'dʌnəweɪ/, **Faye** /feɪ/ (1941–) an American actress whose films include *Bonnie and Clyde* and *Mommie Dearest*

Dun·bar·ton·shire /dʌn'bɑːtnʃəʳ‖-'bɑːr-/ a former COUNTY in central Scotland, now part of Strathclyde REGION

Dun·can /'dʌŋkən/ a character in Shakespeare's *Macbeth*, the king of Scotland who was murdered by Macbeth

Duncan, Is·a·do·ra /ˌɪzə'dɔːrə/ (1878–1927) an American dancer and teacher who had a great influence on modern dance

dunce

dunce /dʌns/ *n* a slow learner; stupid person: *the dunce of the class* | *I was a dunce at chemistry.*

dunce's cap /'·· ˌ·/ also **dunce cap** /'·· ·/, **dunce's hat** *n* a tall round pointed paper hat formerly placed on the heads of pupils at school if they were stupid or slow to learn. Hats like this are never used now, but they sometimes appear in CARTOONs, often with a large letter "D" on them.

Dun·dee /dʌn'diː/ a city in eastern Scotland with a university and a CATHEDRAL

Dundee cake /·· ˌ·/ *n* [C;U] a large British fruit cake decorated with ALMONDs on the top

dun·der·head /'dʌndəhed‖-ər-/ *n becoming rare* a stupid person

dune /djuːn‖duːn/ also **sand dune** *n* a sandhill, often long and low, piled up by the wind on the seashore or in a desert

dune bug·gy /'· ˌ··/ *n* a BEACH BUGGY

Dun·e·din /dʌn'iːdɪn/ a city on the SE coast of South Island, New Zealand

dung /dʌŋ/ *n* [U] solid waste material from the bowels of animals, esp. cows and horses; animal MANURE

dun·ga·rees /ˌdʌŋgə'riːz/ *n* [P] **1** *BrE* ‖ **overalls** *AmE* a workmen's trousers with a BIB (2) and shoulder STRAPs made of usu. blue DENIM (=heavy cotton cloth) **b** similar trousers made of any material and worn as a fashion GARMENT —compare BOILER SUIT, OVERALLS **2** *AmE* a type

of heavy JEANS usu. worn for working in—see PAIR (USAGE), and see picture at OVERALL —**dungaree** *adj* [A] : *dungaree pockets*

Dun·ge·ness /ˌdʌndʒə'nes◂/ a part of Kent, England, which sticks out into the English Channel. There are two NUCLEAR power stations there.

dun·geon /'dʌndʒən/ *n* a dark underground prison, esp. beneath a castle

Dungeons and Drag·ons /ˌ··· · '··/ *tdmk* a ROLE PLAYING game in which the players pretend to be a character who must achieve or prevent a particular situation, such as finding a magic ring: *My two sons have dozens of books on Dungeons and Dragons and play it with their friends.*

dunk /dʌŋk/ *v* [T] (**in**) *infml* **1** to dip (bread, cake, etc., which one is eating) into coffee, tea, etc.: *She always dunks her biscuits in her coffee.* **2** *AmE* to dip (something or someone) into liquid: *She dunked her friend in the swimming pool.* **3** (in BASKETBALL) to throw (the ball) into the basket from above the basket **4 dunk for apples** *AmE* ‖ **dip for apples** *BrE*, **duck for apples** *ScotE* to play a game in which players whose eyes are covered must use their teeth to pick up apples floating in water. This game is esp. popular at HALLOWE'EN parties. —**dunk** *n*

Dun·kirk /ˌdʌn'kɜːk◂‖'dʌnkɜːrk/ **1** a city and port in N France **2** the Second World War operation in which many small boats went from England to Dunkirk to bring back safely to England soldiers who had been fighting the advancing Germans: *the biggest military operation since Dunkirk*

Dunkirk spir·it /ˌ··· '··/ *n* (*the*)U) a refusal to give up in a difficult or impossible situation (from the attitude shown by those who went to Dunkirk in small boats to RESCUE soldiers fighting the Germans in the Second World War)

Dún Laogh·aire /duːn 'leərə‖dʌn-/ a port in E Ireland whose former names are Dunleary and Kingstown

Dun·lop /'dʌnlɒp ‖ -lɑːp/ *tdmk* a British company which makes TYREs for cars and other vehicles

Dun·net Head /ˌdʌnɪt 'hed/ a PROMONTORY in Scotland, the most northerly point on the Scottish mainland

Dun·sta·ble /'dʌnstəbəl/ a town in Bedfordshire, England, with motor and other industries

du·o /'djuːəʊ‖'duːəʊ/ *n* **duos** **1** a DUET **2** [+*sing.*/*pl.* *v*] *infml* a pair, esp. two singers or musicians performing together

du·o·dec·i·mal /ˌdjuːə'desɪməl‖ˌduː-/ *adj tech* concerning the number 12, esp. calculation by 12s, rather than by 10s as in the decimal system

du·o·de·num /ˌdjuːə'diːnəm‖ˌduː-/ *n* -**na** /nə/ *or* -**nums** *tech* the first part of the bowel below the stomach —**nal** /ˌdjuː'diːnl◂‖ˌduː-/ *adj* : *a duodenal ulcer*

du·o·logue /'djuːəlɒg‖'duːələːg, -lɑːg/ *n fml* a DIALOGUE between two people

dupe¹ /djuːp‖duːp/ *n* a person who is tricked or deceived by someone else

dupe² *v* [T (**into**) *often pass.*] to trick or deceive: *The salesman duped the old lady into buying a faulty dishwasher.*

du·plex /'djuːpleks‖'duː-/ *n, adj* [A] *AmE* **1** a SEMIDETACHED house —see picture at HOUSE **2** (a flat) having rooms on two floors of a building: *a duplex apartment* —compare TRIPLEX²

du·pli·cate¹ /'djuːplɪkɪt‖'duː-/ *n, adj* (something that is) exactly like another: *duplicate keys to the front door* | *If you've lost your key I can give you a duplicate.* | *This form should be filled out in duplicate.* (=two copies should be filled out)

du·pli·cate² /'djuːplɪkeɪt‖'duː-/ *v* [T] **1** to copy exactly: *Can you duplicate this key for me?* **2** to copy written, printed, or drawn material on a special machine called a duplicator: *All the members received duplicated notices of the meeting.* Duplicating has been replaced by photocopying (PHOTOCOPY²) **3** to repeat or equal: *an extraordinary feat which would be impossible to duplicate* —**cation** /ˌdjuːplɪ'keɪʃən‖ˌduː-/ *n* [U]

du·pli·ca·tor /'djuːplɪkeɪtəʳ‖'duː-/ *n* a machine that makes copies of written, printed, or drawn material. Duplicators have been mostly replaced by PHOTOCOPIERS.

du·plic·i·ty /djuː'plɪsɪti‖duː-/ *n* [U] *fml* the quality of being dishonest and deceitful

Du Pont /dju: ˈpɒnt‖du: ˈpɑːnt/ a large US chemical company, named after the family that started it, which has developed NYLON, RAYON, CELLOPHANE, and other materials

Du Pré /du: ˈpreɪ, dju:-/, **Jac·que·line** /ˈdʒækəliːn/ (1945–87) an English CELLIST who made many recordings, esp. of music by Elgar. She married Daniel Barenboim in 1967, and they played many concerts together before MULTIPLE SCLEROSIS (a serious disease) caused her to give up playing and continue her work as a teacher.

dur·a·ble /ˈdjʊərəbəl‖ˈdʊ-/ adj able to last; long-lasting: *trousers of durable material* | *a durable, easy-to-clean surface* | *a durable peace between two nations* —see also CONSUMER DURABLES --**bly** adv --**bility** /ˌdjʊərəˈbɪlˌti‖ˌdʊ-/ n [U]

Dur·a·cell /ˈdjʊərəsel ‖ ˈdʊ-/ n tdmk a company which makes batteries (BATTERY (1)) which are generally considered to last longer than most other types of battery: *I always use Duracell batteries in my radio.*

durable goods /ˈ··· ˌ·/ n [P] AmE for CONSUMER DURABLES

Du·ran Du·ran /djuˌræn djuˈræn/ a British popular music group successful in the 1980s

du·ra·tion /djuˈreɪʃən‖dʊ-/ n [U] fml the time during which something (esp. a state or feeling) exists, lasts, or continues: *an illness of short duration* | *He will be in hospital for the duration of the school year.* | *German citizens in Britain were interned for the duration.* (while the war lasted)

Dü·rer /ˈdjʊərəʳ/, **Al·brecht** /ˈælbrekt, -ext/ (1471–1528) a German artist known for his drawings and ENGRAVINGS, in particular his very detailed pictures of himself and other people

du·ress /djʊˈres‖dʊ-/ n [U] fml illegal or unfair threats; COERCION: *a promise made under duress*

dur·ex /ˈdjʊərəcks‖ˈdʊ-/ n tdmk **1** [C] BrE (often cap.) a CONDOM: *a packet of durex on the bedside table* **2** [U] AustrE SELLOTAPE

Dur·ham /ˈdʌrəm‖ˈdɜːr-/ **1** a city in NE England with a university and a CATHEDRAL. The local government for the COUNTY of Durham is based there. **2** also **County Durham** a COUNTY in NE England

dur·ing /ˈdjʊərɪŋ‖ˈdʊ-/ prep **1** all through (a length of time): *We go swimming every day during the summer.* (compare *We went swimming every day* for *three months.*) | *They lived abroad during the war.* (=while the war was happening) | *a long speech, during which he made various promises to the voters* **2** at some moment in (a length of time): *He died during the night.*

▷ USAGE Compare **during** and **for**. When you are talking about the time within which something happens use **during**: *Call me sometime during the holidays.* When you are talking about how long something lasts use **for**: *I was on the 'phone for ten minutes.* | *I went to France for two weeks during the summer.*◁

Durk·heim /ˈdɜːkhaɪm‖ˈdɜːrk-/, **E·mile** /eˈmiːl/ (1858–1917) a French sociologist (SOCIOLOGY) who helped to establish modern sociology as a scientific subject

Dur·rell /ˈdʌrəl/, **Ger·ald** /ˈdʒerəld/ (1925–) an English writer of travel books and books about the natural world, who is also known for his work as the Director of Jersey Zoo

Durrell, Lawrence (1912–90) an English poet and writer of NOVELs, including the *Alexandria Quartet*, which was set in Egypt

Dür·ren·matt /ˈdjʊərənmæt‖ˈdʊrənmɑːt/, **Frie·drich** /ˈfriːdrɪk, -ix/ (1921–90) a Swiss writer of plays, including *The Visit* and *The Physicists*

durst /dɜːst‖dɜːrst/ old use past tense of DARE: *He durst not do it.*

dusk /dʌsk/ n [U] the time when daylight is becoming less bright; darker part of TWILIGHT, esp. at night: *The street lights go on at dusk.* —compare DAWN¹ (1)

dusk·y /ˈdʌski/ adj **1** darkish; shadowy: *dusky brown* | *the dusky light of the forest* **2** old-fash lit or taboo derog having dark skin —**iness** n [U]

Düs·sel·dorf /ˈdʊsəldɔːf‖ˈdʊːsəldɔːrf/ a city in Germany on the rivers Rhine and Düssel

dust¹ /dʌst/ n **1** [U] dry powder made of extremely small grains of waste matter, esp. of the kind that settles on in-

door surfaces: *There was a layer of dust on the books before I cleaned them.* | *atmospheric dust* **2** [U] finely powdered earth: *The car raised a cloud of dust as it went down the dirt road.* | *The heat and dust of India* | *The rain soon settled/laid the dust.* (=stopped it from rising, by making the ground wet) **3** [U] fine powder made of small pieces of the stated substance: *gold dust* | *coal dust* **4** [U] lit the earthly remains of bodies once alive: *the dust of our ancestors* **5** [S] an act of dusting: *I gave the living room a quick dust.* **6 kick up/raise a dust (about)** infml to argue and shout (about) **7 when the dust has settled** infml when the confusion is over **8 dust thou art and unto dust shalt thou return** quote from the Bible people were made from dust (according to the Bible) and will become dust again when they die —see also **ashes to ashes, dust to dust** (ASH), DUSTY, **bite the dust** (BITE¹ (11))

dust² v **1** [I;T (OFF, DOWN)] to clean the dust from (esp. furniture); remove dust (from): *Don't forget to dust the shelves.* | *I dust (the room) every morning.* | *She stood up and dusted herself down.* **2** [T] **a** to cover with dust or fine powder: [+*obj*+**with**] *to dust the plants with insecticide* **b** to put (a fine powder) on a surface: [+*obj*+**over**] *to dust sugar over a cake* —see CLEAN (USAGE), SPREAD (USAGE)

dust sthg. ↔ **off** phr v [T] to prepare to use or practise again (something that has not been used for a long time): *I won't write a new lecture. I'll just dust off the one I gave last year.*

dust·bin /ˈdʌstbɪn/ BrE ‖ **ashcan, garbage can, trashcan** AmE– n a container with a lid, for holding household waste, such as empty cans and boxes, old newspapers, etc., until it can be taken away: *Wrap the vegetable peelings in newspaper and throw them in the dustbin.* —see picture at HOUSE

dustbin man /ˈ··· ˌ·/ n DUSTMAN

dust·bowl /ˈdʌstbəʊl/ n an area that suffers from DUST STORMs and long dry periods

Dust Bowl /ˈ· ·/ [the] an area in the south-central US, in such states as Oklahoma, which suffered from dust blowing from the fields in high winds during the 1930s. The dust storms made it difficult to grow anything and many farmers in that area became very poor. The problems of the Dust Bowl helped make the Great Depression worse.

dust·cart /ˈdʌstkɑːt‖ kɑːrt/ BrE ‖ **garbage truck** AmE n a large vehicle which goes from house to house to collect the contents of dustbins

dust·er /ˈdʌstəʳ/ n **1** a cloth for removing dust from furniture **2** AmE a light coat worn to protect one's clothes from dust while cleaning the house **3** AmE, infml for DUST STORM

dust jack·et /ˈ· ˌ··/ also **dust cover, jacket** n a removable paper cover of a book, often having writing or pictures describing the book

dust·man /ˈdʌstmən/ also **bin man, dustbin man** BrE ‖ **garbage man, trash man, garbage collector, sanitation worker** AmE– n **-men** /mən/ someone employed to remove waste material from DUSTBINS. There is a well-known old British popular song called *My Old Man's a Dustman*.

dust·pan /ˈdʌstpæn/ n a flat container with a handle into which household dust and other waste materials can be brushed: *I've just broken a cup — have you got a dustpan and brush?*

dust·sheet /ˈdʌst-ʃiːt/ ‖ usu. **drop cloth** AmE– n a large sheet of cloth used for throwing over furniture, shop goods, etc., in order to keep the dust off: *She covered the furniture with dustsheets before she started to paint the room.*

dust storm /ˈ· ·/ n a violent weather condition with strong winds carrying large quantities of dust

dust-up /ˈdʌst-ʌp/ n BrE sl a quarrel or esp. a fight

dust·y /ˈdʌsti/ adj **1** dry and covered or filled with dust: *a dusty room* | *In the summer the town becomes very dusty.* **2** like dust; powdery **3** (of a colour) not bright; having a shade of grey: *dusty brown/pink* **4** lacking life or interest; dry: *a dusty treatise*

Dutch¹ /dʌtʃ/ adj **1** of the people, country, or language of the Netherlands (Holland): *a Dutch painter* | *She's Dutch.*

▶CULTURAL NOTE Most people know the story of the little Dutch boy who saved his area from being flooded by putting his finger in a hole in the dike to stop the water coming through: *The government's policy is a bit like sticking your finger in the dike when the hole's already quite big.*◀

2 go Dutch (with someone) to share the cost, esp. of a meal. People use this expression particularly when a man and a woman go out together and the woman pays for herself instead of being paid for by the man: *Kate and John always go Dutch when they go out to restaurants.*

Dutch² *n* **1** [U] the language of the Netherlands **2** [*the*+P] the people of the Netherlands —see also DOUBLE-DUTCH

Dutch auc·tion /ı· ·‿·/ *n* [C;U] a public sale at which the price is gradually reduced until someone will pay it: *to sell fruit by Dutch auction*

Dutch barn /ı· ·‿·/ *n* a farm building with a curved roof on a frame that has no walls

Dutch cap /ı· ·‿·/ *n* a CAP¹ (6)

Dutch cour·age /ı· ·‿·/ *n* [U] *infml* the courage to do something that one gets from drinking alcohol

Dutch elm dis·ease /ı· ·‿·‿·/ *n* [U] a disease that attacks and kills ELM trees. An EPIDEMIC of this in the 1970s killed elm trees in many countries including Britain and the US.

Dutch·man /ˈdʌtʃmən/ *n* **-men** /mən/ **1** a man from the Netherlands **2** a piece of wood, metal, etc. used to repair bad work after something has been made **3 I'm a Dutchman** (a phrase used to show disbelief): *"I'm emigrating to Australia soon." "Sure, and I'm a Dutchman."* (=I don't believe you)

Dutch ov·en /ı· ·‿·/ *n* **1** an upright metal shield that throws the heat forward onto things baked in front of a fire **2** a brick OVEN whose walls are heated before baking things **3** a heavy iron pot with a tight-fitting lid used for cooking

Dutch Re·formed Church /ı··ı· ·‿·/ [*the*] the religion which most of the South African people who speak Afrikaans belong to. It was taken to South Africa by the Dutch settlers in the 17th century.

Dutch treat /ı· ·‿·/ *n infml* an occasion at which everyone pays their own bill —see also **go Dutch** (DUTCH¹)

Dutch un·cle /ı· ·‿·/ *n* **talk (to someone) like a Dutch uncle** to speak in an angry complaining way, showing strong disapproval, esp. to someone who has done something wrong

du·ti·a·ble /ˈdjuːtiəbl‖ˈduː-/ *adj* (of goods) on which one must pay DUTY (2)

du·ti·ful /ˈdjuːtɪfəl‖ˈduː-/ also **du·te·ous** /-tiəs/*fml*— *adj* (of people and behaviour) showing proper respect and obedience — — **ly** *adv* — ~ **ness** *n* [U]

du·ty /ˈdjuːti‖ˈduːti/ *n* [C;U] **1** something that one does either because it is part of one's job or because it is morally or legally right that one should do it: *His duties include taking letters to the post and making coffee.* | *to do one's duty as a soldier* | *I feel it's my duty to help them.* | *It's the duty of a lawyer to act in the best interests of his clients.* | *I'm* (**in**) **duty bound** (=forced by my conscience) *to visit my old aunt.* | *He writes to his ex-employer once a year but he's only* **acting out of duty.** (=not because he wants to) **2** also **duties** *pl.*— any of various types of tax: *Customs duties are paid on goods entering the country, death duties on property when the owner dies, and stamp duty when one sells a house.* **3 do duty for** (of things) to (be able to) be used instead of: *This log will do duty for a table.* **4 on/off duty** (esp. of soldiers, nurses, etc.) at/not at work: *When I'm off duty I play tennis.* | *I'm on* **night duty** (=working at night) *this week.* —see also HEAVY-DUTY; see TAX (USAGE)

duty-free /ı·· ·‿·/ *adj, adv* (of goods) allowed to come into the country without tax: *You can bring in one bottle duty-free.* | *the duty-free shop at the airport* (=which sells duty-free goods) —**duty-free** *n* : *Don't forget to buy some duty-frees.*

Du·val·i·er /duːˈvælieɪ, djuː-‖ˌduːvɑːlˈjeɪ/, **Fran·çois** /ˈfrɒnswɑː‖frɑːnˈswɑː/ (1907–71) the president of Haiti 1957–71. Known as **Papa Doc**, he ruled as a DICTATOR, with the **Tontons Macoutes** as a private force to get rid of opponents.

Duvalier, Jean-Claude /ʒɒn kləʊd‖ʒɑːn-/ (1951–) the president of Haiti 1971–86. Known as **Baby Doc**, he came

to rule after the death of his father François, and was the youngest president in the world at the age of 19.

du·vet /ˈduːveɪ, ˈdjuː-‖duːˈveɪ/ also **continental quilt** *BrE*— *n* a large bag filled with feathers or man-made material, which is placed inside a removable washable cover, and is used on a bed instead of a sheet and BLANKETs to keep one warm

DVLC /ˌdiː viː el ˈsiː/ [*the*] Driver and Vehicle Licensing Centre; the British government department responsible for collecting road tax and sending out driving LICENCEs to people when they pass their **driving test**

Dvo·řák /ˈdvɔːʒæk, ˈvɔː-‖ˈdvɔːrʒɑːk/, **An·to·nín** /ˈæntəʊniːn/ (1841–1904) a Czech COMPOSER known for his symphonies (SYMPHONY), such as the *New World Symphony*, songs, and music for VIOLIN, CELLO, and piano

dwarf¹ /dwɔːf‖dwɔːrf/ *n* **dwarfs** or **dwarves** /dwɔːvz ‖ dwɔːrvz/ **1** a person, animal, or plant of much less than the usual size: *Their second son is a dwarf.* | *a dwarf apple tree* **2** a small imaginary manlike creature

▶CULTURAL NOTE Dwarfs in European MYTHOLOGY are small, wise creatures who live in secret places, often under the ground, and have big heads and long beards. They appear in many stories, where they may be kind and helpful to humans or may be feared. People in European countries such as Germany and Norway believed in dwarfs and GIANTs even after Christianity was introduced, and many beliefs about them still exist, which have spread to Britain with fairy stories such as those told by the Brothers Grimm: *the story of Snow White and the Seven Dwarfs* —see also SEVEN DWARFS, WHITE DWARF◀

dwarf² *v* [T] **1** to make (someone or something) appear small by comparison: *The old cathedral is dwarfed by the skyscrapers that surround it.* **2** to prevent the proper growth of: *Bonsai is the art of dwarfing trees*

dwell /dwel/ *v* **dwelt** /dwelt/ or **dwelled** [I+*adv/prep*] **1** *lit or old use* to live (in a place): *to dwell in a forest|on an island* —see LIVE (USAGE) **2 -dweller** /dwelər/ a person or animal that lives in the stated place: *city-dwellers* | *cave-dwellers*

dwell on/upon sthg. *phr v* [T] to think or speak a lot about, esp. to an unhealthy or annoying degree: *Stop dwelling on your problems and do something about them!* | *The book dwells too much on the economic aspects of the problem.*

dwell·ing /ˈdwelɪŋ/ *n fml or humor* a house, flat, etc., where people live: *Welcome to my humble dwelling!*

dwelling house /ˈ·· ·/ *n esp. law* a house which is lived in rather than being used as a shop, office, etc.

DWI /ˌdiː dʌbəlˈjuː ˈaɪ/ *n* [U] *AmE* driving while intoxicated (=drunk on alcohol); used mainly by police

dwin·dle /ˈdwɪndl/ *v* [I (AWAY)] to become steadily fewer or smaller: *The number of people who live on the island is rapidly dwindling.* | *the island's dwindling population* | *Membership has dwindled to only 25.* | *Her hopes|money gradually dwindled away.*

Dyck, Sir Anthony Van see VAN DYCK

dye¹ /daɪ/ *n* [C;U] a vegetable or chemical substance, usu. in liquid form, used to change the colour of things esp. by dipping —compare PAINT¹ (2)

dye² *v* **dyes, dyed, dyeing** [T] to give a (different) colour to (something) by means of dye: *She dyes her hair.* [+*obj*+*adj*] *She dyed the dress|shoes green.* | (fig.) *Sunset dyed the sky red.* — — **r** *n*

dyed-in-the-wool /ı· · · ·‿·/ *adj often derog* impossible to change from the stated quality; UNCOMPROMISING: *Charles is a dyed-in-the-wool Republican.*

Dyf·ed /ˈdʌvᵻd/ a COUNTY in SW Wales

dy·ing /ˈdaɪ-ɪŋ/ *present participle of* DIE¹

dyke /daɪk/ *n* **1** a DIKE **2** *sl* a LESBIAN; the word used to be only *derog*, but some Lesbians themselves now use it

Dyl·an /ˈdɪlən/, **Bob** (1941–) an American singer and

Bob Dylan

writer of songs who was a great influence on popular music in the 1960s. His early songs were often protest songs, on the subjects of war and the CIVIL RIGHTS movement in America, and many young people were influenced by the words of his songs, e.g. *Blowin' In The Wind* and *The Times They Are A-Changin'*.

dy·nam·ic /daɪˈnæmɪk/ *adj* **1** *often apprec* (esp. of people) full of activity, new ideas, the will to succeed, etc.; forceful: *a dynamic young businessman | a dynamic period in history | concert pianists Katia and Marielle Labeque, known as the* **dynamic duo**,... —compare STATIC¹ (1) **2** *tech* of force or power that causes movement **3** *tech* (in grammar) being a verb that describes an action or event rather than a state, e.g. *watch* in *She is watching television* or *play* in *They are playing tennis* —compare STATIVE — ~**ally** /kli/ *adv*

dy·nam·ics¹ /daɪˈnæmɪks/ *n* [U] the science that deals with objects or matter in movement —compare KINETICS, STATICS

dynamics² *n* [P] (in music) changes of loudness

dy·na·mis·m /ˈdaɪnəmɪzəm/ *n* [U] (in a person) the quality of being dynamic

dy·na·mite¹ /ˈdaɪnəmaɪt/ *n* [U]
1 a powerful explosive used esp. in MINING **2** *infml* something or someone that will cause great shock, surprise, admiration, etc.: *That news story/That new singer is really dynamite!*

dynamite

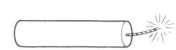

dynamite² *v* [T] to blow up with dynamite

dy·na·mo /ˈdaɪnəməʊ/ *n* **-mos** **1** a machine which turns some other kind of power into electricity: *bicycle lights powered by a dynamo* —compare GENERATOR, MAGNETO **2** *infml* an extremely energetic person

dyn·a·sty /ˈdɪnəsti‖ˈdaɪ-/ *n* a line of kings or other rulers, following one another in time and all belonging to the same family: *a dynasty of Welsh kings | the Ming dynasty in China between 1368 and 1644* —-**stic** /dɪˈnæstɪk‖daɪ-/ *adj*: *dynastic rule*

Dynasty a television SOAP OPERA made in America and also shown in Britain, known mainly for its stars, e.g. Joan Collins, and the expensive clothes worn in the programmes

d'you /djʊ, dʒə/ *short for:* (*infml*) do you: *D'you see what I mean?*

dys·en·te·ry /ˈdɪsəntəri‖-teri/ *n* [U] a painful disease of the bowels that causes them to be emptied more often than usual and to produce blood and MUCUS

dys·lex·i·a /dɪsˈleksiə/ also **word blindness**— *n* [U] *tech* a problem in reading caused by difficulty in seeing the difference between letter shapes —-**ic** *adj*

dys·pep·si·a /dɪsˈpepsiə, -ˈpepʃə/ *n* [U] difficulty in the breaking down of food in the body after it has been eaten; INDIGESTION

dys·pep·tic /dɪsˈpeptɪk/ *adj* **1** suffering from, or caused by, dyspepsia **2** bad-tempered

E

E, e /iː/ **E's, e's** *or* **Es, es** the fifth letter of the English alphabet

E[1] a note in Western music; the musical KEY[1] (4) based on this note —see also E NUMBER

E[2] *written abbrev. for:* **1** east(ern) **2** *esp. BrE* EARTH[1] (4)

each[1] /iːtʃ/ *determiner, pron* every single one of two or more things or people considered separately: *She had a cut on each foot/each of her feet.* | *They each want to do something different.* | *I cut the cake into pieces and gave one to each of the children.* | *There are four bedrooms, each with its own bathroom.* | *It costs $60 for a week, and then $10 for each additional day.*

▷ USAGE Compare **both** and **each**. **1 Both** is used for two things taken together while **each** is used for any number of things taken separately. Compare **Both** *my children* (=I have two children) *go to the same school* and **Each** *of my children* (=I have two or more children) *goes to a different school.* **2 Both** always takes a plural verb: **Both** *these books are mine.* **Each** is usually singular, except **a** after a plural subject: **Each** *has his own room.* | *They* **each** *have their own room.* | *They've* **each** *decided, haven't they?* **b** (in *BrE*) sometimes when **each of** is followed by something long and plural: **Each** *of the three young doctors in the hospital is/are specializing in a different subject.* —see also ALL[3]; see EVERY (USAGE)◁

each[2] *adv* for or to every one: *The tickets are £1 each.*

each oth·er /ˌ· ˈ··/ *also* **one another** —*pron* (*not used as the subject of a sentence*) (shows that each of two or more does something to the other(s)): *Susan and Robert kissed each other.* (=Susan kissed Robert and Robert kissed Susan.) | *They held each other's hands.* | *The students in the class told each other about their own countries.*

each way /ˌ· ˈ·◂/ *adj, adv* (of money) placed to win more money if the horse or dog on which money is risked comes first, second, or third, in a race: *an each-way bet* | *He backed Red Rum each way.*

ea·ger /ˈiːgəʳ/ *adj* [(for)] marked by strong interest or impatient desire; full of ENTHUSIASM: *She listened to the story with eager attention.* | *He is eager for success/eager for you to meet his friends.* [F+to-v] *The company is eager to expand into new markets.* [F +that] (*fml*) *I am eager that they should win.* — ~**ly** *adv* — ~**ness** *n*

eager bea·ver /ˌ· ˈ··/ *n infml* someone who is almost too eager or works too hard

ea·gle[1] /ˈiːgəl/ *n* **1** a very large strong bird with a hooked beak and very good eyesight which kills small birds and animals for food: *The bald eagle is the emblem of the US.* —compare HAWK **2** (in GOLF) a SCORE of two strokes less than PAR on a hole

eagle[2] *n* (in GOLF) (the taking of) two fewer than the suggested number of STROKES (hits) of the ball to reach the hole: *He scored an eagle on the 14th hole.*

eagle

Eagle [*the*] the title of a weekly British magazine for boys, full of picture stories of adventure, which came out during the 1950s and 60s. Its great HERO was Dan Dare.

eagle-eyed /ˌ·· ˈ·◂/ *adj* looking with very keen attention and noticing small details: *an eagle-eyed teacher* | *Peter watched eagle-eyed while Bill counted the money.*

Eagle has Land·ed /ˌ··· ˈ··/, **The** the title of a book and film about a German plan to seize Winston Churchill during the Second World War

Eagle Scout /ˈ·· ˌ·/ *n* a boy SCOUT in the US who has earned the highest rank

ea·glet /ˈiːglɪt/ *n* a young eagle

Ea·kins /ˈiːkᵻnz/, **Thomas** (1844–1916) an American

painter known for his realistic style in pictures such as *The Gross Clinic*

Ea·ling com·e·dy /ˌiːlɪŋ ˈkɒmədi‖-ˈkɑː-/ *n* one of many humorous black-and-white films made at **Ealing Studios** in London, esp. in the 1950s, which featured many famous British actors: *I really love all those Ealing comedies.*

ear[1] /ɪəʳ/ *n* **1** [C] either of the two organs by which people or animals hear, one on each side of the head: *You needn't shout into my ear like that. I can hear you perfectly well.* | *an ear infection* | *Dogs have very good ears.* (=they hear very well) **2** [S (**for**)] keen recognition of sounds, esp. in music and languages: *She's got a good ear for music.* | *Peter learned to play the piano* **by ear.** (=without written music) **3** [S] sympathetic attention: *She* **gained the ear of** *the managing director and voiced her opinion.* **4 all ears** *infml* listening eagerly: *Tell us what happened. We're all ears!* **5 go in (at) one ear and out (at) the other** *infml* (of information, orders, etc.) to have no effect because not listened to: *I told the children to go to bed, but it went in one ear and out the other, and they're still here.* **6 keep one's/an ear to the ground** to keep oneself informed of news, events, etc.: *I haven't heard of any new developments yet but I'll keep my ear to the ground.* **7 out on one's ear** *sl* suddenly thrown out of a place or esp. dismissed from a job, because of misbehaviour: *Do that one more time, and you're out on your ear!* **8 someone's ears are/must be burning** *infml* we/people have been talking (esp. unkindly) about someone **9 up to one's ears in** *infml* deep in or very busy with: *I'm up to my ears in work/in debt.* —see also get/give a thick ear (THICK[1]), bend someone's ear (BEND[1]), fall on deaf ears(FALL[1]),go/send someone off/away with a flea in his/her ear (FLEA), make a pig's ear of (PIG[1]), play it by ear (PLAY[1]), prick up one's ears (PRICK[2]), turn a deaf ear to (DEAF), wet behind the ears (WET) and see picture at HEAD

ear[2] *n* the head of a grain-producing plant, used for food: *an ear of corn/wheat*

ear·ache /ˈɪəreɪk/ *n* [C (*esp. AmE*); U (*esp. BrE*)] (a) pain in the inside part of the ear —see ACHE (USAGE)

ear·drum /ˈɪədrʌm‖ˈɪər-/ *n* a tight thin skin inside the ear, which allows one to hear sound

eared /ɪəd‖ɪərd/ *adj* (*usu. in comb.*) having ears that can be seen, or are of a particular kind: *the eared seal* | *a pink-eared rabbit* | *a sharp-eared little boy who hears everything we say* | *golden-eared corn*

ear·ful /ˈɪəful‖ˈɪər-/ *n* [S] *infml* angry or complaining talk, esp. that goes on for a long time: *If he comes here again and tries to make trouble, he'll get an earful from me!* —compare MOUTHFUL

Ear·hart /ˈeəhɑːt‖ˈeərhɑːrt/, **A·me·li·a** /əˈmiːliə/ (1898–1937) an American pilot, famous for being the first woman to fly across the Atlantic alone, and for mysteriously disappearing while on a flight across the Pacific

earl /ɜːl‖ɜːrl/ *n* a British nobleman of high rank: *the Earl of Warwick* —compare COUNT[3], COUNTESS

earl·dom /ˈɜːldəm‖ˈɜːr-/ *n* **1** the rank of an earl **2** the lands of an earl or COUNTESS

Earl Grey /ˌ· ˈ·/ *n* [U] a type of tea which has a particular taste and smell, from an oil that is used in it: *My friend always drinks Earl Grey.*

ear·li·est /ˈɜːliəst‖ˈɜːr-/ *n* **at the earliest** no earlier than, and probably later than: *The letter will reach him on Monday at the (very) earliest.* | *The meeting can't be held until October at the earliest.* —opposite **at the latest**

ear·lobe /ˈɪələub‖ˈɪər-/ *n* a LOBE (1) —see picture at HEAD

Earl's Court /ˌ· ˈ·◂/ **1** a large building in London where shows such as the motor show and other EXHIBITIONS are held, which many people visit **2** the area of W London around this building. It is an area where many young people live in BED-SITTERS, and is known for the large number of visiting Australians who stay there. It is sometimes called **Kangaroo Valley** because of this.

ear·ly /ˈɜːli‖ˈɜːrli/ *adj* **1** arriving, developing, happening, etc., before the usual, arranged, or expected time: *an early lunch* | *I was early for work today.* [after n] *The train was ten minutes early.* —compare LATE[1] **2** happening towards the beginning of the day, one's life, a period of time, etc.: *She returned in the early morning.* | *memories* *of his early childhood* | *She was born in the early 1950s.* | *a nearly motor car* (=one of the first developed) | *The new car seems to be going well, but it's still* **early days.** (=it's too early to be certain) *He must be in his early fifties.* — compare LATE¹   **3** [A *no comp.*] *fml* happening soon: *We await your early reply concerning the above request.*   **4** **early to bed, early to rise, makes a man healthy, wealthy, and wise** *saying* a phrase used, esp. by parents to their children to make them go to bed early —**liness** *n* [U]

early² *adv*   **1** before the usual, arranged, or expected time: *He always arrives early.*   **2** near the beginning of a period: *The bush was planted early in the season.* | *She's already here — she arrived earlier this week.* | *The wheel was discovered very* **early on** *in human history.* — compare LATE²

Early A·mer·i·can /ˌ‥ ˈ‥‥◂/ *n* [S] a style of furniture, cloth, or building in the US which is supposed to look like that used in the early 19th century: *We're going to redo the living room in Early American.*

early bird /ˈ‥ ˈ‥/ *n*   **1** a person who gets up or arrives early. This may be thought good or bad, depending on the habits of the speaker: *"Do you think it's too early to phone him?" "Not at all. He's a real early bird."*   **2** **(it's) the early bird (that) catches the worm** *saying* someone who does things before other people will have success

early clos·ing day /ˌ‥ ˈ‥ ‥/ also **early closing, half day closing** —*n* the day of the week, usu. Wednesday or Thursday, when some smaller British shops close early, usu. at one o'clock. It is the same day every week in any one town: *You'd better go now if you want some bread. It's early closing today.* | *"Which day is early closing day?" "It's Wednesday in Westerham and Thursday in Brasted."*

Early Day Mo·tion /ˌ‥ ˈ‥ ‥‥/ *n BrE* a suggestion formally made in writing in parliament by a member of parliament and signed by other members; members of parliament make suggestions in this way in order to find out or show how much support they get: *180 MPs have already signed the Early Day Motion tabled by Robert Parry.*

Early Learn·ing Cen·tre /ˌ‥ ˈ‥ ˌ‥/ *n* [C] one of a group of British shops which sell toys, games, books and other things for children. They are known for selling good quality toys, which are often educational, and they have a POLICY of not selling toy guns or toys which are just fashionable for a short time.

early re·tire·ment /ˌ‥ ·ˈ‥·/ *n* [U] the act of stopping work before the usual age for doing so, which is usually 60 or 65. Companies sometimes ask workers to **take early retirement** as a way of reducing their number of workers, or as a way of getting rid of a difficult worker: *He's hoping to get the offer of early retirement if the takeover goes through.*

early warn·ing sys·tem /ˌ‥ ˈ‥ ˌ‥/ *n*   **1** a network of RADAR stations called **early warning stations** which give information in advance of enemy air attack   **2** any system which gives early information about danger: *an early warning system for river pollution*

ear·mark /ˈɪəmɑːk‖ˈɪərmɑːrk/ *v* [T (**for**)] to set aside (money, time, etc.) for a particular purpose: *These funds are earmarked for famine relief.*

ear·muffs /ˈɪəmʌfs‖ˈɪər-/ *n* [P] a pair of ear coverings connected by a band over the top of the head and worn to protect a person's ears from cold —see PAIR (USAGE)

earn /ɜːn‖ɜːrn/ *v*   **1** [I;T] to get (money) by working: *He earns £20,000 a year (by writing stories).* | *He's earning a fortune as a consultant engineer.* | *How does she* **earn her living?** | *Now that you're earning, you should think about buying a house.*   **2** [T] to get (something that one deserves) because of one's qualities or actions: *He earned a lot of praise from the papers for the way he handled the strike.* | *She's earned a break after all that hard work.*   **3** [T+obj(i)+obj(d)] to cause (someone) to get; make worthy of; GAIN: *Her success in the exam earned her a place at university.* | *His skill in negotiating earned him a reputation as a shrewd tactician.* —see GAIN¹ (USAGE) — ~**er** *n*

earned in·come cred·it /ˌ‥ ˈ‥ ˌ‥/ *n* [U] (in the US) money returned to working parents who do not earn enough to support their families. It comes from tax money that is taken out of wages.

earn·er /ˈɜːnəʳ ‖ ˈɜːr-/ *n* a nice little earner *infml* something which earns a very satisfactory amount of money: *The sale of novelty trays turned out to be a nice little earner for the company.*

ear·nest¹ /ˈɜːnɪst‖ˈɜːr-/ *adj* determined and serious, esp. too serious: *We made an earnest endeavour to persuade her.* | *an earnest young man who never laughs* — ~**ly** *adv* — ~**ness** *n* [U]: *I say this* **in all earnestness.**

earnest² *n* **in earnest**: **a** seriously; in a determined way: *It soon began to snow in real earnest.* (=very hard)   **b** serious; not joking: *I'm sure he was in earnest when he said he wanted to marry her.*

earnest³ *n* [S] *fml*   **1** a part payment of money, as a sign that one will pay the full amount later; DEPOSIT² (3)   **2** [(**of**)] something which comes first to show what will come after: *The current economic slump is an earnest of the major recession to come.*

earn·ings /ˈɜːnɪŋz‖ˈɜːr-/ *n* [P]   **1** money which is earned by working: *What are your* **take-home earnings** *after tax and deductions?*   **2** money made by a company or government: *a decline in our export earnings*

earnings re·lat·ed /ˌ‥ ·ˈ‥·‥/ *adj* (of a payment or BENEFIT) related to how much someone earns: *an earnings related pension*

Earp /ɜːp‖ɜːrp/, **Wy·att** /ˈwaɪət/ (1848–1929) an American policeman of the Wild West, remembered esp. for his part in killing three men in a GUNFIGHT at the O.K. CORRAL in Tombstone, Arizona. A television programme of the 1950s and 1960s based on his life made his name familiar to many Americans.

ear·phones /ˈɪəfəʊnz‖ˈɪər-/ *n* [P]   **1** the two pieces that fit over the ears in a HEADSET, and turn electrical signals or radio waves into sound —see PAIR (USAGE)   **2** a hairstyle for women in which long hair is plaited (PLAIT) and wound in circles over the ears

ear·piece /ˈɪəpiːs‖ˈɪər-/ *n*   **1** a piece that fits into one's ear and is connected to a radio or TAPE RECORDER that one carries about, so that one can listen without other people having to listen too   **2** [*usu. pl.*] either of two pieces of a hat or cap, which cover the ears to keep them warm   **3** [*usu. pl.*] either of the two pieces of a pair of glasses which hold the glasses onto the ears —see picture at GLASSES

ear·plug /ˈɪəplʌg‖ˈɪər-/ *n* [*usu. pl.*] either of two pieces of soft material which are put into the ears to keep out water or noise —see PAIR (USAGE)

ear·ring /ˈɪəˌrɪŋ/ *n* [*often pl.*] a piece of jewellery worn on the ear —see PAIR (USAGE)

ear·shot /ˈɪəʃɒt‖ˈɪərʃɑːt/ *n* **within/out of earshot** within/beyond the distance at which a sound can be heard

ear-split·ting /ˈ‥ ·‥/ *adj* extremely loud: *an ear-splitting noise/scream*

earth¹ /ɜːθ‖ɜːrθ/ *n*   **1** [(*the*) U] (*often cap.*) the world on which we live: *They returned successfully from the moon to (the) Earth.* | *the planet Earth* —see picture at SOLAR SYSTEM   **2** [U] the surface of the Earth as opposed to the sky: *the biggest star* **on earth** (=in the world) —see LAND (USAGE)   **3** [U] soil in which plants grow: *He filled the pot with earth and planted a rose in it.*   **4** [(*the*) C *usu. sing.*] *BrE* ‖ **ground** *AmE* (an additional safety wire that makes) a connection between a piece of electrical apparatus and the ground —compare EARTH²   **5** [C] *esp. BrE* the hole where certain wild animals live, such as foxes   **6** [C] (in chemistry) an OXIDE (=chemical combination with oxygen) of certain metals: *the rare earths*   **7** **come back/down to earth** to stop dreaming and return to practical matters   **8** *BrE* **look/feel like nothing on earth** *infml* feeling or looking very strange, unhealthy, etc.: *The morning after the party he looked/felt like nothing on earth.* | *You look like nothing on earth in that ridiculous hat!*   **9** **on earth** *infml* (used for giving force to a question with **what, who,** etc.): *What on earth are you doing?* | *Who on earth told you that?*   **10** **make the earth move** *infml* to achieve the highest point of sexual pleasure: *He promised he'd make the earth move.*   **11** **did the earth move for you?** *humor* a phrase used after having sex to ask one's partner whether they felt the highest point of sexual pleasure   **12** *BrE* **run (something/someone) to earth** to find (something/someone) by searching everywhere: *After searching for him everywhere, she finally ran him to earth in the garden shed.*   **13** **earth to**

(someone) *esp. AmE, humor* a way of getting someone's attention when they are not listening or aren't understanding; based on SCIENCE-FICTION stories, in which people on different PLANETs talk to each other by radio: *Earth to Joan, earth to Joan – can you hear me, Joan?* —see also DOWN-TO-EARTH, **promise someone the earth** (PROMISE¹), **the salt of the earth** (SALT¹)

earth² *BrE* ‖ **ground** *AmE— v* [T] to connect (a piece of electrical equipment) to the ground with a wire — compare EARTH¹ (4)

earth·bound /ˈɜːθbaʊnd‖ˈɜːrθ-/ *adj* **1** unable to leave the surface of the earth **2** unable to rise above ordinary practical matters

earth·en /ˈɜːθən, -ðən‖ˈɜːr-/ *adj* made of earth or baked clay: *an earthen floor/pot*

earth·en·ware /ˈɜːθənweəʳ, -ðən-‖ˈɜːr-/ *n* [U] **1** (cups, dishes, pots, etc., made of) rather rough baked clay: *an earthenware flowerpot* —compare PORCELAIN **2** *AmE for* CROCKERY

earth·ling /ˈɜːθlɪŋ‖ˈɜːrθ-/ *n* (in SCIENCE FICTION stories) a human being, when addressed or talked about by a creature from another world: *"Take me to your leader, earthling," said the green creature from the spacecraft.*

earth·ly /ˈɜːθli‖ˈɜːrθli/ *adj* [A] **1** of this world as opposed to heaven; material: *all my earthly possessions* **2** [*usu. in questions or negatives*] *infml* possible: *There's no earthly reason for me to go.* **3** *not have an earthly* [*usu. in questions or negatives*] *BrE infml* not to have the slightest chance/hope/idea: *"Will John win the prize?" "No, he hasn't an earthly."*

earth moth·er /ˈ· ˌ··/ *n* **1** also **mother earth** —the earth, when it is believed to be the mother of life, or to have its own SPIRIT, or to be a GODDESS **2** a woman who thinks it is more important to be kind and look after other people, and to feel close to nature, than it is to worry about money, success, or her appearance. The words earth mother are often used in a disapproving way by people who think that this sort of woman is rather silly. These people disagree with what they see as her SENTIMENTAL ideas about nature and caring for people, and believe that her political opinions are too LEFT WING.

earth·quake /ˈɜːθkweɪk‖ˈɜːrθ-/ *n* a sudden shaking of the earth's surface, which may be violent enough to cause great damage: *The town was destroyed by the earthquake.*

▶ CULTURAL NOTE Britain generally does not suffer from serious earthquakes. The US, however, has a major FAULT in Northern California, and suffers serious earthquakes regularly both there and in Alaska. —see SAN ANDREAS FAULT◀

earth sci·ence /ˈ· ˌ··/ *n* any of the sciences such as GEOLOGY, METEOROLOGY, or OCEANOGRAPHY, that deal with parts of the earth and natural processes which happen there

earth·shat·ter·ing /ˈɜːθˌʃætərɪŋ‖ˈɜːrθ-/ also **earth·shak·ing** /-ˌʃeɪkɪŋ/— *adj* of the greatest importance to the whole world: *The President's assassination was an event of earthshattering importance.* | *Our trip to Dundee wasn't exactly an earthshattering event!* – ~ly *adv*

Earth shoe /ˈ· ˌ·/ *n tdmk* a shoe which is lower at the heel than at the front of the foot; Earth shoes were popular in the US in the 1970s and were worn esp. by people concerned with the environment and healthy living

Earth Sum·mit /ˈ· ˌ··/ [*the*] a large meeting held in Rio de Janeiro in 1992, where political leaders from many countries met to discuss problems that affect the whole world, esp. problems of the ENVIRONMENT

earth·ward /ˈɜːθwəd‖ˈɜːrθwərd/ *adj* towards the earth, esp. from the air or space —compare LANDWARD

earth·wards /ˈɜːθwədz‖ˈɜːrθwərdz/ *esp. BrE* ‖ usu. **earthward** *AmE— adv* towards the earth, esp. from the air or space —compare LANDWARDS

earth·work /ˈɜːθwɜːk‖ˈɜːrθwɜːrk/ *n* [*usu. pl.*] a man-made bank of earth used esp. formerly as a protection against enemy attack. Such a bank used now might be called a BUND.

earth·worm /ˈɜːθwɜːm‖ˈɜːrθwɜːrm/ *n* a common kind of long thin worm which lives in the soil

earth·y /ˈɜːθi‖ˈɜːrθi/ *adj* **1** of or like earth: *potatoes with an earthy taste* **2** concerned with things of the body

rather than with things of the mind, esp. in a way that is direct and perhaps impolite: *an earthy sense of humour* **3** *AmE, infml* practical and honest; DOWN-TO-EARTH —**iness** *n*

ear trum·pet /ˈ· ˌ··/ *n* a tube that becomes wider at one end, used in the past by people who could not hear well for making sounds louder by putting the narrow end to the ear. They are often used or shown in jokes about old people with poor hearing.

ear·wig /ˈɪəwɪg‖ˈɪər-/ *n* an insect with two curved toothlike parts on its tail, a long thin body, and several pairs of legs

ease¹ /iːz/ *n* [U] **1** the ability to do something without difficulty: *They are expected to win the election* **with ease.** | *The government is very concerned about the ease with which the terrorists got onto the plane.* **2** the state of being comfortable and without worries or problems: *Gloria is a rich woman now, and lives a life of ease.* | *He didn't feel completely* **at** (his) **ease** *in the strange surroundings.* (=he felt nervous and uncomfortable) | *Give her a drink to put her at her ease.* **3** (stand) **at ease** (used as a military command) (to stand) with one's feet apart and one's hands behind one's back —compare **at attention** (ATTENTION¹ (4)), **stand easy** (EASY²) **4 take one's ease** *fml* to rest from work or effort —see also EASY, ILL AT EASE

ease² *v* **1** [I (OFF);T] to make or become less severe: *I gave him some medicine to ease the pain.* | *The pain began to ease (off).* **2** [T] to make less anxious: *I eased her mind by telling her that the children were safe.* **3** [I] to become less troublesome or difficult: *Tensions in the region have eased a little.* **4** [T+obj+adv/prep] to move slowly and carefully into a different position: *The drawer in my desk was stuck fast, but I eased it open with a knife.* | *He eased himself slowly into the hot bath.* | (fig.) *She's never been a great success in the job, and now they're trying to* **ease her out.** (=make her leave without actually dismissing her)

ease off/up *phr v* [I] *infml* to become less active: *The rain is beginning to ease off.* | *The doctor told me to ease up a bit and stop working so hard.*

ea·sel /ˈiːzəl/ *n* a wooden frame on which one can place a picture while it is being painted. Easels were formerly used to support BLACKBOARDs and still appear in humorous drawings of classrooms.

eas·i·ly /ˈiːzɪ̣li/ *adv* **1** without difficulty: *I can easily finish it today.* **2** without doubt: *She is easily the best student in the class.*

east¹ /iːst/ (abbrev. **E**) *n* (*often cap.*) **1** [*the*;U] the direction from which the sun rises; the direction which is on the right of a person facing north: *A strange light appeared in the east.* | *It's a few kilometres to the east of London.* | *I'm lost – which way is east?* **2** [*the*] the eastern part of a country: *The rain will spread later to the east.* **3 east is east and west is west, and never the twain shall meet** *quote* a phrase from a poem by Rudyard Kipling. People sometimes say it when they want to say that people from Europe and people from Asia will never understand each other completely.

east² (abbrev. **E**) *adj* (*often cap.*) **1** in the east or facing the east: *The church's east window has beautifully coloured glass.* | *She lives in East Africa.* **2** (of a wind) coming from the east: *a cold east wind* —see NORTH² (USAGE)

east³ (abbrev. **E**) *adv* (*often cap.*) **1** towards the east: *The room faces east, so we get the morning sun.* | *The plane flew east.* | *Cleveland is (a long way) east of Chicago.* **2 back east** *AmE infml* to or in the EAST (3)

East *n* [*the*] **1** the eastern part of the world as seen from Europe, esp. Asia: *the mysteries of the East* —see also FAR EAST, MIDDLE EAST, NEAR EAST, ORIENT **2** the countries of Eastern Europe and Asia which had Communist governments: *East-West relations during the early 60s* **3** *AmE* the part of the US east of the Mississippi

East An·gli·a /ˌiːst ˈæŋgliə/ an area in E England formed by the counties (COUNTY) of Norfolk and Suffolk, and sometimes parts of other counties next to them

East Bank /ˌ· ˈ·/ [*the*] the east bank of the River Jordan —compare WEST BANK

east·bound /ˈiːstbaʊnd/ *adj* travelling or leading towards the east: *an eastbound train* | *the eastbound side of the motorway*

East Coast /ˌ· ˈ·◂/ *n* the eastern coastal states of the US, sometimes used only for those north of, and including, Washington, D.C.
▶CULTURAL NOTE The East Coast is thought of in connection with its cities, such as New York City, Boston, Philadelphia, and Washington. Americans from the WEST COAST often think of Easterners as having old-fashioned lifestyles and ideas. East Coast Americans may be more conscious of TRADITION (= old ways) because it was this area that was first settled by the Europeans. —compare WEST COAST ◀

East End /ˌ· ˈ·◂/ also **East End of Lon·don** /ˌ· · · ˈ·◂/ [the] the eastern part of central London north of the River Thames, containing much of the DOCKLANDS: *a white boxer from the East End of London* —**East Ender** *n*
▶CULTURAL NOTE It is thought of by many people as a poor, rough area, but one of great character and friendliness among the working class people who live there. It is now changing because of the introduction of new industries and very expensive housing bought by the rich. —see also COCKNEY ◀

East·End·ers /ˈiːstˈendəz‖-ərz/ a popular British television SOAP OPERA set in the East End of London in the imaginary **Albert Square**: *A couple of EastEnders stars are going to visit the children in hospital.*

Eas·ter /ˈiːstəʳ/ *n* [C;U] **1** also **Easter Sun·day** /ˌ·· ˈ··/— a Christian holy day in March or April when Christians remember the death of Christ and his return to life **2** the period just before and just after this, including GOOD FRIDAY and **Easter Monday**, when many people do not go to work: *the Easter holidays*
▶CULTURAL NOTE On GOOD FRIDAY Christians remember the death of Christ on the cross, and on **Easter Sunday** they celebrate Christ's rising from death and victory over death. Many Christians go to church on Easter Sunday even if they do not go at other times of the year.

Easter Monday is a holiday in Britain. On Easter Sunday in Britain people give presents of Easter eggs, esp. to children. For American customs, see EASTER BASKET, EASTER BUNNY. Easter is connected in people's minds with Spring, the coming to life of the earth after the winter, and such things as flowers, esp. DAFFODILS, and young animals, esp. lambs and CHICKS. In the past, people used to have new clothes at Easter and women had very decorated new hats called **Easter bonnets.** ◀

Easter bas·ket /ˈ·· ˌ··/ *n* in the US, a basket of sweets, usually JELLY BEANS, small chocolate eggs, and a chocolate Easter Bunny, left out on Easter morning to be discovered by children, who believe it is a gift from the Easter Bunny

Easter bon·net /ˌ·· ˈ··/ *n old-fash* or *humor* a BONNET (–a type of women's hat) formerly bought to wear to church at EASTER: *I see you've got your Easter bonnet on then.*

Easter bun·ny /ˌ·· ˈ··/ *n* in the US, the imaginary bunny (=rabbit) who is believed by children to deliver their Easter baskets and hide their Easter eggs on Easter morning —see colour picture on page 1211

Easter egg /ˈ·· ·/ *n* **1** *BrE* a usu. chocolate egg to be eaten at Easter, they are often given as presents, esp. to children **2** *AmE* an egg which has been coloured and perhaps decorated, usually by a child. In the US, these eggs are then hidden by the child's parents, and on Easter morning the child hunts for them, believing them to have been hidden by the Easter Bunny. —see colour picture on page 1211

Easter Is·land /ˈ·· ˌ··/ an island in the South Pacific Ocean, W of Chile. It is famous for the very large heads cut out of stone many centuries ago.

eas·ter·ly¹ /ˈiːstəli‖-ərli/ *adj* **1** towards or in the east: *We set off in an easterly direction.* **2** (of a wind) coming from the east: *a light easterly breeze*

easterly² *n* a wind coming from the east; used mainly in television and radio programmes, newspaper articles, etc. about the weather

Easter Mon·day /ˌ·· ··/ see EASTER (CULTURAL NOTE)

east·ern /ˈiːstən‖-ərn/ (abbrev. **E.**) *adj* (*often cap.*) **1** of or belonging to the east part of the world or of a country: *Eastern regions will have heavy rain today.* | *an interest in Eastern religions* (=from India, China, etc.) —see

NORTH (USAGE) **2** full of **Eastern promise** a phrase used in advertisements for Fry's Turkish Delight chocolate and now sometimes used in a joking way to describe something desirable and unusual from eastern countries

Eastern bloc /ˈ·· ˌ·/ [the] the USSR and the group of countries which used to be under its influence or control

Eastern Day·light Time /ˌ·· ˈ·· ·/ *abbrev.* **EDT** the time used in the summer months in the Eastern Time Zone of the US

East·ern·er /ˈiːstənəʳ‖-ərnər/ *n AmE* someone who lives in or comes from the eastern US

Eastern Eu·rope /ˌ·· ˈ··/ a political area of Europe consisting of Albania, Bulgaria, Czechoslovakia, Hungary, Poland, Romania, Yugoslavia, all formerly Communist countries under the influence or control of the former USSR. The area included East Germany. —**Eastern European** /ˌ·· ··ˈ··◂/ *n, adj*

east·ern·most /ˈiːstənməʊst‖-ərn-/ *adj* [no comp.] furthest east: *the easternmost part of the island*

Eastern Or·tho·dox Church /ˌ·· ·ˈ·· ·/ [the] see ORTHODOX CHURCH

Eastern Stan·dard Time /ˌ·· ˈ·· ˌ·/ *abbrev.* **EST** the time used from autumn to spring in the Eastern Time Zone of the US

Easter Ris·ing /ˌ·· ˈ··/ [the] an armed opposition to British rule in Ireland in 1916. Before the Irish stopped fighting they told the British they had established an independent Irish republic. The British later executed (EXECUTE) the leaders and refused to accept the republic.

Easter Sun·day /ˌ·· ˈ··/ see EASTER

East Eu·ro·pe·an /ˌ·· ··ˈ··◂/ *n* [C] a person from one of the countries of Eastern Europe —**East European** *adj*

East In·di·a Com·pa·ny /ˌ· ˈ··· ˌ···/ [the] any of several European companies that opened trade with India and the Far East in the 1600s. The **British East India Company** lasted the longest (to 1858) and had the most influence, eventually bringing India into the British Empire.

East Lo·thi·an /ˌ· ˈ···/ a former COUNTY in central Scotland, now part of Lothian REGION

East Ger·ma·ny /ˌ· ˈ···/ *also* **German Democratic Republic** a former republic in N central Europe which reunited with the former West Germany in 1990 **East German** — *n, adj*

East·man /ˈiːstmən/, **George** (1854–1932) an American inventor and businessman who established the **Kodak** photographic company, selling cameras that could easily be carried and film (instead of the glass plates previously used)

East Riv·er /ˌ· ˈ··/ [the] a river flowing into New York Harbor, separating Manhattan from Long Island —see colour map on page 1376

East Side /ˌ· ˈ·◂/ see LOWER EAST SIDE

East Sus·sex /ˌ· ˈ··/ a coastal COUNTY in the south of England

east·ward /ˈiːstwəd‖-wərd/ *adj* going towards the east: *in an eastward direction*

east·wards /ˈiːstwədz‖-wərdz/ also **eastward** — *adv* towards the east: *We sailed eastwards.* —see also EAST³

East-West re·la·tions /ˌ· · ·ˈ··/ *n* [P] the political relations between the former Soviet Union and other former EASTERN BLOC countries such as East Germany, Hungary, Romania, etc. (East), and the US, Britain, France, the former West Germany, etc. (West): *an improvement in East-West relations* | *a conference to discuss East-West relations*

East·wood /ˈiːstwʊd/, **Clint** /klɪnt/ (1930–) an American film actor and director best known for playing parts as a gunfighter in WESTERNs and a modern city police officer. His characters almost always have right on their side, and no fear. —see colour picture on page 685

eas·y¹ /ˈiːzi/ *adj* **1** that can be done, made, gained, etc., without great difficulty or effort; not difficult: *a very easy exam* | *The exam was easy.* | *an easy victory* | *There are no easy answers to this question.* | *[+to-v] John is easy to please|an easy person to please.* (=it is not difficult to please him) | *It's quite an easy language to learn.* | *It's* *easy for us to get to London because we live very near the station.* **2** comfortable and without worry or anxiety: *He has stopped working now, and leads a very easy life.* | *I can't go to bed* **with an easy mind** *until I know she's safe.* **3 (as) easy as pie** *infml* very easy **4 by/in easy stages** (on a journey) going only short distances at a time **5 easy on the ear/eye** *infml* nice to listen to/look at **6 I'm easy** *infml BrE* I don't mind at all: *"Would you like to go to the theatre or the cinema?" "I'm easy."* **7** *AmE, infml, derog* PROMISCUOUS: *She's easy.* —see also EASE, EASILY —**iness** *n* [U]

easy² *adv* **1** without too much effort, hurry, or anxiety: *The doctor told me to* **go easy/take things easy** *and stop working so hard.* | *Just* **take it easy** (=remain calm) *and tell us exactly what happened.* **2 easy come, easy go** *infml* what was easily gained is easily lost (used to find fault with people who spend their money freely and carelessly and do not save it) **b** (often said to show that one is not worried about losing something or freely spending money; often said humorously) **3 easier said than done** easy to talk about but difficult to do: *We've been told to increase our output, but it's easier said than done.* **4 go easy on: a** to be less severe with (someone): *Go easy on her, she's still only young.* **b** not to use too much of (something): *Go easy on the whisky if you're going to be driving!* **5 stand easy** (used as a military command) to stand more comfortably than when **at ease** (EASE¹)

easy chair /ˌ·· ˈ·/ *n* a big comfortable chair with arms

eas·y·go·ing /ˌiːziˈɡəʊɪŋ◂/ *adj* taking life easily; tending not to worry or get angry: *Our teacher is very easygoing. She doesn't mind if we turn up late.*

easy lis·te·ning /ˌ··· ˈ···/ ‖ *also* **muzak** *tdmk*, **elevator music** *AmE—n, adj* [U] (of) a relaxing type of music popular esp. with MIDDLE-AGED people

easy-pea·sy /ˌiːzi ˈpiːzi/ *adj* a children's word for **easy** or **very easy**, sometimes used by a child to say forcefully that they can do something which it has been suggested they cannot: *"You can't get over the wall." "Yes, of course I can. Easy-peasy."*

Easy Rid·er /ˌ·· ˈ··/ an American film made in 1969 about two young men who are interested in ROCK music, drugs, etc. travelling across the US on MOTORBIKES

easy street /ˈ··· ·/ *n* **on easy street** *infml* in a comfortable condition of life, with no worries about money: *Since they inherited his aunt's fortune, they've been on easy street.*

easy terms /ˌ·· ˈ·/ *n* [P] *BrE* an arrangement by which one pays for something in a number of small payments instead of all at once: *We bought the dishwasher* **on easy terms.** —see also HIRE PURCHASE

easy vir·tue /ˌ·· ˈ··/ *n* [U] *old use* **woman of easy virtue** *derog* a woman who will sleep with different men

eat /iːt/ *v* **ate** /et, eɪt‖eɪt/, **eaten** /ˈiːtn/ **1** [I;T] to take (food) in through the mouth and swallow it in order to feed the body: *You'll get ill if you don't eat.* | *Eat your dinner!* | *Tigers eat meat.* **2** [I] to have a meal: *What time do you usually eat?* | *Shall we* **eat out** *tonight?* (=in a restaurant rather than at home) **3** [I+*prep*; T+*obj*+*adv*] to use up, damage, or destroy (something), esp. by chemical action: *The acid ate away the metal.* | *The acid has eaten into/through the metal.* | (fig.) *All these bills are eating into* (=gradually using up) *our savings.* **4** [T] *infml* to cause to be annoyed or anxious: *He's been in a bad temper all day. I wonder what's eating him.* **5 eat crow** *AmE infml* to be forced to admit that one was wrong; accept what one has fought against **6 eat, drink, and be merry (for tomorrow we die)** *saying* enjoy life, because it is very short. People who say this are often criticizing people who worry about eating the right things, but do not know how to have a good time. **7 eat like a bird** *AmE* to eat very little: *No wonder she's so thin. She eats like a bird.* **8 eat one's heart out (for)** to be very unhappy (about) or have great desire (for someone or something) without talking about it: *She's eating her heart out for that boy.* **9 eat one's words** to admit to having said something wrong **10 eat out of someone's hand** *infml* to be very willing to obey or agree with someone: *They were angry at first, but she soon had them eating out of her hand.* **11 eat someone out of house and home** *infml* to eat a lot of someone else's supply of food **12 eat your heart out** *infml* (used in a humorous way to mean) you should be upset or jealous about this: *He's the new teenage idol – eat your heart out, Michael Jackson!* **13**

you are what you eat *saying* your character and your physical health are decided by the kind of food you eat —see also **eat one's dinners** (DINNER) —see also **I'll eat my hat** (HAT)

eat (sthg. ↔) **up** *phr v* [I;T] **1** to eat all of (something): *Come on, eat up. There's plenty left!* | *Be a good girl and eat up your vegetables.* | (fig.) *A big car eats up money.* **2 be eaten up with** to be completely and violently full of (a feeling): *He's eaten up with jealousy.*

eat·a·ble /ˈiːtəbəl/ *adj* (of food) in a fit condition to be eaten —compare EDIBLE

eat·er /ˈiːtəʳ/ *n* someone who eats in the stated way: *He's a big eater.* (=he eats a lot) | *The children are rather fussy eaters.*

eat·e·ry /ˈiːtəri/ *n* [C] *esp. AmE* a restaurant or other place to eat: *one of the best Knoxville eateries*

eating ap·ple /ˈ··· ˌ··/ *n* an apple that one eats raw —compare COOKING APPLE

eating dis·or·der /ˈ··· ·ˌ···/ *n* a medical condition in which patterns of eating are not those of most people, e.g. BULIMIA or ANOREXIA: *Eating disorders are usually associated with teenage girls.*

eats /iːts/ *n* [P] *infml* food, esp. when provided for other people: *You organize the drinks for the party, and I'll do the eats.*

eau de co·logne /ˌəʊ də kəˈləʊn/ *n* [U] COLOGNE

eaves /iːvz/ *n* [P] the edges of a roof which come out beyond the walls: *Birds have nested under our eaves.*

eaves·drop /ˈiːvzdrɒp‖-drɑːp/ *v* **-pp-** [I (on)] to listen secretly, to other people's conversation. In this way one often hears things which are private or secret and it is thought to be a dishonest thing to do. —compare OVERHEAR —~**per** *n*

ebb¹ /eb/ *n* **1** [*the* (*of*)] the flowing of the sea away from the shore; the going out of the TIDE: *The tide is* **on the ebb.** —compare FLOW² (2) **2 at a low ebb** in a bad or inactive state: *Relations between the two countries are at a low ebb.*

ebb² *v* [I] **1** (of the TIDE) to flow away from the shore **2** [(AWAY)] to grow less; become gradually lower or weaker: *His courage slowly ebbed away as he realized how hopeless the situation was.*

ebb tide /ˌ· ˈ·/ *n* the flow of the sea away from the shore; falling TIDE: *The ship sailed out of harbour on the ebb tide and came back on the flood tide.* —opposite **flood tide**

EBCDIC /ˈebsᵻdɪk/ *n* [U] extended binary-coded decimal-interchange code; a set of 256 characters each using 8 bits, used for exchange of information between esp. IBM computers: *All electronic submissions must be in EBCDIC.* —compare ASCII

eb·o·ny /ˈebəni/ *adj, n* [U] (having the colour of) a hard heavy black wood

Ebony an American magazine esp. for and about African Americans

e·bul·li·ent /ɪˈbʌliənt, ɪˈbʊ-/ *adj fml* full of life, happiness, and eager excitement: *She was in an ebullient mood, telling jokes and buying drinks for everyone.* —~**ly** *adv* —~**ence** *n* [U]

EBV /ˌiː biː ˈviː/ *n abbrev. for* EPSTEIN-BARR VIRUS

ec *abbrev. for:* EUROCHEQUE

EC /ˌiː ˈsiː/ [*the*] **1** the European Community; a West European political and economic organization established under the Treaty of Rome to encourage trade and friendly relations between its member countries, and to compete with other major economic powers; until recently known as the EEC

the EC flag

► CULTURAL NOTE Many people in Britain are not keen on the EC. They feel that Britain will lose its character and lose control over its own affairs by being a member. They esp. dislike the way in which EC law controls the small details of life in Britain. Britain frequently complains about the EC's programme and spending. —compare COUNCIL OF EUROPE and see also BRUSSELS◄

2 EUROPEAN COMMISSION

ec·cen·tric¹ /ɪkˈsentrɪk/ *adj* **1** behaving differently from what is usual or socially accepted, esp. in a way that is strange or amusing: *If you go to the palace in tennis shoes, they'll think you're rather eccentric.* | *eccentric behaviour.* **2** [*no comp.*] *tech* (of two or more circles) not drawn round the same centre —compare CONCENTRIC **3** [*no comp.*] *tech* not (moving) in a regular circle: *Mars, Venus, and the other planets move in eccentric orbits.* – – **ally** /kli/ *adv*

eccentric² *n* an eccentric person: *The old lady is a bit of an eccentric.*

ec·cen·tri·ci·ty /ˌeksenˈtrɪsɪti, -sən-/ *n* [C;U] (an example of) eccentric behaviour: *The English are famous for their eccentricities/eccentricity.*

Ec·cles cake /ˈekəlz keɪk/ *n BrE* a type of small cake made of pastry filled with dried fruit

ec·cle·si·as·tic /ɪˌkliːziˈæstɪk◂/ *n fml* a priest, usu. in the Christian church

ec·cle·si·as·ti·cal /ɪˌkliːziˈæstɪkəl/ also **ecclesiastic** – *adj* connected with the Christian church, esp. with its formal and established organization: *ecclesiastical history/music* – – **ly** /kli/ *adv*

ECG /ˌiː siː ˈdʒiː/ *BrE* ‖ **EKG** *AmE*– *n* **1** electrocardiograph; an apparatus that records in the form of a drawing the electrical changes that take place in the heart as it beats **2** electrocardiogram; the drawing made by an electrocardiograph: *The doctor ordered an ECG.* – compare EEG

ech·e·lon /ˈeʃəlɒn‖-lɑːn/ also **echelons** *pl.*– *n* **1** a level within an organization: *She works in the higher echelons of the Civil Service.* **2** *tech* an arrangement of ships, soldiers, planes, etc., like steps rather than in a single line. *The ships sailed past in echelon.*

ech·o¹ /ˈekəʊ/ *n* **-oes** **1** a sound sent back or repeated from a surface, e.g. from a wall or the inside of a CAVE: *She shouted "hello" and listened for the echo.* | (fig.) *In his earlier works you can hear an echo of Eliot's poetry.* (=something that seems similar to it or copied from it) **2 to the echo** *BrE old use* very loudly: *She was cheered to the echo.*

echo² *v* **-oes, -oed, -oing** **1** [I] to come back as an echo: *Their voices echoed in the big empty hall.* **2** [I (**with, to**)] (of a place) to be filled with echoes: *The room echoed with/to the sound of their happy laughter.* **3** [T] to copy or repeat, esp. in agreement: *I should like to echo the words of the previous speaker.*

é·clair /ɪˈkleəʳ, eɪ-/ *n* a small finger-shaped cake made of a special kind of pastry, with cream inside and usu. chocolate on top. Eclairs are generally thought of as being very tasty to eat but rather bad for you. They have been used in advertisements with the words "Naughty but Nice".

e·clec·tic /ɪˈklektɪk/ *adj fml* (of people, methods, ideas, etc.) not following any one particular system or set of ideas, but using parts of many different ones: *The painter's style is very eclectic.* – – **ally** /kli/ *adv* – – **ism** /tɪsɪzəm/ *n* [U]

e·clipse¹ /ɪˈklɪps/ *n* **1** [C (**of**)] the disappearance, complete or in part, of the sun's light when the moon passes between it and the Earth, or of the moon's light when the Earth passes between it and the sun: *There was a* **total/partial eclipse** *(of the sun).* | *a lunar eclipse* (=of the moon) **2** [C;U (**of**)] the loss of fame, power, success, etc.; DECLINE: *During the seventies, her acting career was* **in eclipse**.

eclipse² *v* [T *often pass.*] **1** (of the moon or Earth) to cause an eclipse of (the sun or moon): *The moon is partially eclipsed.* **2** to do or be much better than; cause to seem less important, clever, famous, etc., by comparison: *She is completely eclipsed by her sister, who is cleverer, prettier, and more amusing.*

e·clip·tic /ɪˈklɪptɪk/ *n* [*the*+S] *tech* the path along which the sun seems to move

ECO /ˌiː siː ˈəʊ/ [*the*] *abbrev.* for ENGLISH CHAMBER ORCHESTRA

e·co-friend·ly /ˈiːkəʊ ˌfrendli/ *adj* not harmful to the ENVIRONMENT: *the growing market for eco-friendly products such as biodegradable detergents and fridges which do not use CFCs* —compare GREEN¹ (1)

e·co·log·i·cal /ˌiːkəˈlɒdʒɪkəl◂‖-ˈlɑː-/ *adj* **1** of or concerning ecology or the ecology: *The destruction of these big forests could have serious ecological consequences.* **2** also

ecologically sound /ˌ··· ˈ·/ – not harming the ecology; GREEN; ECO-FRIENDLY: *an ecological washing powder* – – **gically** /kli/ *adv* : *Ecologically* (=from an ecological point of view), *the new dam has been a disaster.* | *an ecologically sound forestry management policy*

e·col·o·gy /ɪˈkɒlədʒi‖ɪˈkɑː-/ *n* [U] (the scientific study of) the pattern of relations of plants, animals, and people to each other and to their surroundings – – **gist** *n*

ec·o·nom·ic /ˌiːkəˈnɒmɪk◂, ˌɪk-‖-ˈnɑː-/ *adj* **1** [A *no comp.*] connected with trade, industry, and the management of money; of economics: *The country is in a bad economic state.* | *the government's economic policies* **2** profitable: *The airline says this route is no longer economic, so they're going to discontinue it.* | *to sell goods at an economic price* —opposite **uneconomic**

ec·o·nom·i·cal /ˌiːkəˈnɒmɪkəl, ˌɪk-‖-ˈnɑː-/ *adj* **1** using money, time, goods, etc., carefully and without waste: *It's not a very economical method of heating.* | *an economical little car that doesn't use much fuel* | *If you've got a large family, it's more economical to travel by car than by train.* | fig. **2 be economical with the truth** *humor* to lie indirectly or not to tell the whole truth: *I think most politicians learn to be economical with the truth.* | *Officially, the hospital is not going to close. But the NHS managers are being economical with the truth, for no more patients are being admitted.*

ec·o·nom·i·cally /ˌiːkəˈnɒmɪkli, ˌɪk-‖-ˈnɑː-/ *adv* **1** not wastefully: *Mary dresses very economically because she makes all her clothes herself.* **2** in a way connected with economics: *Economically (speaking), the country is in a very healthy state.* | *Is the company economically viable?*

Economic and Mon·e·ta·ry U·nion /ˌ····· · ˌ···· ˈ··/ *n* see EMU

economic cli·mate /ˌ···· ˈ··/ *n* the national or international economic situation: *We cannot afford to employ more staff in the current economic climate.*

economic growth /ˌ···· ˈ·/ *n* [U] the growth and development of a country's ECONOMY as shown in increased production and INVESTMENT, a higher standard of living, etc.

economic mi·grant /ˌ···· ˈ··/ *n* a person who leaves the town or country in which they lived, in order to find somewhere to earn a living: *Hundreds of economic migrants are arriving in the city every day.*

economic mir·a·cle /ˌ···· ˈ···/ *n* unexpected RECOVERY from a bad economic situation: *Can the Chancellor bring about an economic miracle?* | *the German post-war economic miracle*

economic ref·u·gee /ˌ···· ··ˈ·/ *n* a person who goes to live in another country wealthier than his or her own not for political reasons, but in the hope of achieving a better standard of living. Most governments do not accept this type of refugee.

ec·o·nom·ics /ˌiːkəˈnɒmɪks, ˌɪk-‖-ˈnɑː-/ *n* **1** [U] the scientific study of the way in which wealth is produced and used: *She's studying economics at college.* **2** [P] the way in which something, such as a plan or course of action, is influenced by economic considerations: *The economics of the scheme need to be looked at very carefully.* –see also MACROECONOMICS, MICROECONOMICS, HOME ECONOMICS

e·con·o·mist /ɪˈkɒnəmᵻst‖ɪˈkɑː-/ *n* a person who studies and is skilled in economics

Economist [*the*] *tdmk* a British weekly magazine which discusses current world affairs from a financial angle, read esp. by business people

e·con·o·mize also **-mise** *BrE* /ɪˈkɒnəmaɪz‖ɪˈkɑː-/ *v* [I (**on**)] to avoid waste: *We have to economize on water during the dry season.*

e·con·o·my¹ /ɪˈkɒnəmi‖ɪˈkɑː-/ *n* **1** [C] the system by which a country's wealth is produced and used: *The new oil that we have found will improve the economy/our economy.* | *Most of the countries in the region have unstable economies.* | *a capitalist economy* —see also BLACK ECONOMY, MIXED ECONOMY, MARKET ECONOMY, COMMAND ECONOMY **2** [C;U] (an example of) the careful use of money, time, effort, etc., in order to avoid waste: *to practise economy* | *We're trying to make a few economies.* | *economy of effort* | *We had an* **economy drive** (=we all tried to spend less) *in order to save money for our holiday.* | *They are able to keep their costs low because of* **economies of scale.** (=the advantages of producing something in very large quantities) | *buying cheap tyres is* **a false economy** – *they may cost a bit less, but they will wear out much more quickly.* —see also ECONOMICAL

economy² *adj* [A *no comp.*] cheap; less expensive: *Buy the large* **economy** *packet and you'll save money.*

economy class /·'··· ·ˌ·/ *n* [U] (on an aircraft) the cheapest travelling conditions: *The seats are very close together in* **economy** *class.* —compare FIRST CLASS **economy class** *adv*: *We're going to travel* **economy class.**

economy of scale /·ˌ··· · '·/ *n* a reduction in costs because of an increase in the scale of production: *Large companies often benefit from economies of scale.*

e·co·sys·tem /'iːkəʊˌsɪstᵻm/ *n* all the plants, animals, and people in an area together with their surroundings, considered from the point of view of their relationship to each other

e·co·ter·ror·is·m /'iːkəʊˌterərɪzəm/ *n* [U] the deliberate destruction of the environment, often for political reasons

ec·sta·sy /'ekstəsi/ *n* **1** [C;U] (a state of) very strong feeling, esp. of joy and happiness: *A look of ecstasy spread over his face as he swallowed the delicious oysters.* | *She was in a trancelike state of religious ecstasy.* | *The children were* **in ecstasies/went into ecstasies** *when he told them about the holiday.* **2** [U] an ILLEGAL drug used esp. by young people to give a feeling of HAPPINESS and ENERGY, particularly at NIGHTCLUBs and parties —see ACID HOUSE PARTY

ec·stat·ic /ɪk'stætɪk, ek-/ *adj* experiencing or causing great joy: *She was absolutely ecstatic when I told her the news.* — ~**ally** /kli/ *adv*

ECT /ˌiː siː 'tiː/ *n* [U] electro-convulsive therapy; ELECTRIC SHOCK THERAPY

ec·top·ic preg·nan·cy /ek,tɒpɪk 'pregnənsi‖-ˌtɑː-/ *n med* TUBAL PREGNANCY

ECU /'ekjuː‖eɪ'kuː/ *n* European Currency Unit; the official unit of money of the EC

Ec·ua·dor /'ekwədɔːʳ/ a country in South America; capital Quito; population 10,490,000 (1989) — ~**ian** /ˌekwə-'dɔːriən◂/

e·cu·men·i·cal /ˌiːkjʊ'menɪkəl◂ ‖ ˌek-/ *adj* supporting or tending towards agreement in aims and beliefs between the different branches of the Christian religion, with a hope of uniting them in one church — ~**ly** /kli/ *adv*

ec·ze·ma /'eksᵻmə‖'eksᵻmə, 'egzᵻmə, ɪg'ziːmə/ *n* [U] a red swollen condition of the skin; usu. in one or two areas of the body at a time, with dryness and itching (ITCH), and often with an unknown cause

ed. /ed/ *abbrev. for:* **1** edited **2** (*pl* eds) edition **3** (*pl* eds) editor **4** education

E·dam /'iːdæm/ *n* [U] a yellow cheese from the Netherlands made in balls covered with red WAX

ed·dy¹ /'edi/ *n* a circular movement of water, wind, dust, smoke, etc.: *The little paper boat was caught in an eddy and spun round and round in the water.*

eddy² *v* [I] (of water, wind, dust, smoke, etc.) to move round and round or in a varying direction: *The mist eddied round the old house.*

Eddy, Mary Baker (1821–1910) an American religious leader, who started the Christian Science movement in 1866

E·den /'iːdn/ also **Garden of Eden**—the garden where according to the Bible, Adam and Eve, the first human beings, lived before their disobedience to God. It is thought of as a place or state of complete happiness —see also FALL and see colour picture on page 424

Eden, Sir Anthony (1895–1977) an English Conservative politician and PRIME MINISTER (1955–57)

edge¹ /edʒ/ *n* **1** the part or place where something ends or begins or that is farthest from its centre: *Don't go too near the edge of the cliff.* | *She stood by the water's edge.* | *If you don't want it, leave it on the edge of your plate.* | *Can you stand a coin up on its edge?* | (fig.) *He felt he was on the edge of madness.* **2** the thin sharp cutting part of a blade, tool, etc.: *This knife has a very sharp edge.* **3** **have the edge on/over** to be (slightly) better than or have a (slight) advantage over: *She has the edge on the other students because she spent a year in England.* **4 on edge** nervous; EDGY: *I'm sorry if I was rude to you – I'm a bit*

on edge at the moment. **5 on the edge** *esp. AmE, infml* on the edge of madness; about to go mad: *Poor Aunt Ethel – I think she's on the edge.* | *What's wrong with me today? I must be on the edge!* **6 take the edge off** to lessen the force of: *That'll take the edge off your hunger.* **7 -edged** /edʒd/ having an edge or edges of the stated type or number: *a sharp-edged blade* | *a two-edged sword* —see also CUTTING EDGE, DOUBLE-EDGED and see picture at SERRATED

edge² *v* **1** [T (**with**)] to provide with an edge or border: *She had a white handkerchief edged with blue.* **2** [I+*adv/prep*; T+*obj*+*adv/prep*] to (cause to) move gradually, esp. with small sideways movements: *He edged (his way) towards the front of the crowd.* | *She edged her chair closer to mine.* | (fig.) *He's been running the company for years, but they're trying to edge him out now.* | (fig.) *Prices have been stable for a while, but they are beginning to edge up again now.* **3** to cut the edges of (an area of grass) with a tool that cuts into the ground, in order to make a straight line and a neat appearance: *Will you edge the lawn after I've mown it?*

edge·ways /'edʒweɪz/ also **edge·wise** /-waɪz/— *adv* sideways: *The door's so narrow you could only get this painting through edgeways.* —see also **get a word in edgeways** (WORD¹)

edg·ing /'edʒɪŋ/ *n* [C;U] something that forms an edge or border: *a white handkerchief with (a) blue edging*

edging tool /'··· ˌ·/ *n* a garden tool used for making the edges of a grass area neat by cutting into the ground

edg·y /'edʒi/ *adj infml* nervous and easily made angry: *She's been a bit edgy lately, waiting for the exam results.* —**ily** *adv*

ed·i·ble /'edᵻbəl/ *adj* fit to be eaten; suitable to be used as food: *These berries are edible but those are poisonous.* | *edible fungi* —opposite **inedible** —compare EATABLE

e·dict /'iːdɪkt/ *n* **1** an official public order made by someone in a position of power. An edict is almost always made by one person acting without taking the advice of others: *The king issued an edict forbidding the wearing of swords within the city.* **2** *esp. humor* any order or command

ed·i·fi·ca·tion /ˌedᵻfᵻ'keɪʃən/ *n* [U] *fml or humor* the improvement of the mind or character; often used in connection with something whose educational value is low in the opinion of the speaker: *Now here,* **for your edification,** *is Professor Spinks to talk about Mexican pottery.*

ed·i·fice /'edᵻfᵻs/ *n fml or pomp* a large fine building, such as a palace or church

ed·i·fy /'edᵻfaɪ/ *v* [T] *fml or humor* to improve (the mind or character of): *a most edifying lecture* —see also UN-EDIFYING

Ed·in·burgh /'edᵻnbərə/ the capital of Scotland, in the east of the country on the River Forth; a centre of business, education, the law, book production, engineering and other industries. It is also a centre of musical life, theatre, etc. and for this reason is sometimes called **the Athens of the North.** —see also EDINBURGH FESTIVAL and see colour map on page 818

Edinburgh, Duke of [*the*] —see Prince PHILIP

Edinburgh Fes·tiv·al /ˌ···· '···/ also **Edinburgh In·ter·na·tion·al Fes·ti·val of Mu·sic and Dra·ma** /ˌ···········ˌ···· · ˌ···· · '··/— [*the*] a yearly programme of musical and theatrical events, and other entertainment, taking place over about three weeks in the summer in and around Edinburgh, one of the largest of its kind anywhere. Many of the main events are performed by world-famous groups, but there are also many other events performed by people such as university students, and these are known as **the Fringe.** Many famous writers and performers have begun their professional lives at the Edinburgh Festival.

Edinburgh rock /ˌ···· '·/ *n* [U] sweets made of sugar and coloured in many different colours

Ed·i·son /'edᵻsən/**, Thom·as Al·va** /'tɒməs 'ælvə‖'tɑː-/ (1847–1931) an American inventor, most famously of the LIGHT BULB and of a way of sending electricity to distant places, but also of an early MICROPHONE, record player, and equipment for the cinema, TELEGRAPH, and telephone

ed·it /'edᵻt/ *v* [T] **1** to prepare for printing, broadcasting, etc., by deciding what shall be included or left out, putting right mistakes, etc.: *They've asked me to edit one of the volumes in their new series of Shakespeare plays.* | *to edit a computer program* | *If a film is well edited, it can add greatly to its excitement.* **2** to be the editor of (a newspaper or magazine): *He used to edit the Washington Post.*

edit sthg. ↔ **out** *phr v* [T] to remove when preparing something for printing, broadcasting, etc.: *The rude words she used were edited out before the programme was broadcast.*

e·di·tion /ɪˈdɪʃən/ *n* (any one of) a number of copies of a book, newspaper, magazine, etc., that are produced and printed at one time: *The last edition of the newspaper comes out at midnight.* | *This is the second edition of this dictionary.* | *Is there a paperback edition of this book?* | *He owns some valuable* **first editions** *of well-known authors* —compare IMPRESSION.

ed·i·tor /ˈedɪtə^r/ *n* **1** a person who edits: *an editor of educational books* | *a TV script editor* **2** a person who is in charge of a newspaper or magazine, and responsible for its organization and opinions: *the editor of the Daily Telegraph* – –**ship** *n* [U]

ed·i·to·ri·al[1] /ˌedɪˈtɔːriəl◂/ *adj* of or done by an editor: *the editorial staff* | *She's made a lot of editorial changes in their book.* – –**ly** *adv*

editorial[2] also **leader, leading article** *BrE*– *n* an article in a newspaper giving the paper's opinion on a matter, rather than reporting information. It is often written by or for the editor.

Ed·monds /ˈedməndz/, **No·el** /ˈnəʊəl/ (1948–) an English entertainer who was formerly a radio DISC JOCKEY (= someone who plays records, tapes, etc.) and now works in television mainly as a person who introduces programmes.

Ed·mon·ton /ˈedməntən/ the capital city of Alberta, W Canada, on the North Saskatchewan river

Edna, Dame see DAME EDNA

EDT /ˌiː diːˈtiː/ *abbrev. for* EASTERN DAYLIGHT TIME

ed·u·cate /ˈedjʊkeɪt‖ˈedʒə-/ *v* [T] to teach or train, esp. through formal instruction at a school or college; provide with education or instruction: *He was born in England but was educated in America.* | *a campaign to educate the public on the dangers of smoking*

ed·u·cat·ed /ˈedjʊkeɪtɪd‖ˈedʒə-/ *adj* **1** (*often in comb.*) having had an education, esp. of the stated kind or from the stated place: *self-educated* | *half-educated* | *a Harvard-educated lawyer* **2** well-trained; skilled: *She has very educated tastes.* | *an educated ear for music*

educated guess /ˌ··· ˈ·/ *n infml* a guess based on a certain amount of information, and therefore likely to be right

ed·u·ca·tion /ˌedjʊˈkeɪʃən‖ˌedʒə-/ *n* [S;U] the process by which a person's mind and character are developed through teaching, or through formal instruction at a school or college: *an institute of adult education* | *the Minister of Education* | *She completed her education in Switzerland.* | *The government is spending a lot of money on education.* —see also FURTHER EDUCATION, HIGHER EDUCATION, TEACH (USAGE) and extra information on page 408

ed·u·ca·tion·al /ˌedjʊˈkeɪʃənəl◂‖ˌedʒə-/ *adj* **1** [*no comp.*] of or for education: *He was visiting schools and other educational establishments in the area.* | *the decline of educational standards* **2** providing education and information: *It was the most educational experience I have ever had.*

ed·u·ca·tion·al·ist /ˌedjʊˈkeɪʃənəlɪst‖ˌedʒə-/ also **ed·u·ca·tion·ist** *esp. BrE* /-ʃənɪst/— *n* a specialist in education

ed·u·ca·tor /ˈedjʊkeɪtə^r‖ˈedʒə-/ *n esp. AmE* a person who educates as a profession

Edward /ˈedwəd‖-wərd/, **Prince** (1964–) the youngest son

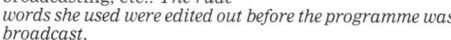

of Queen Elizabeth II of Great Britain. Prince Edward worked for a short time in the armed forces, as expected of men in the royal family, but later went to work in the theatre.

Edward I /ˌedwəd ðə ˈfɜːst‖-wərd ðə ˈfɜːrst/, **King** (1239–1307) a king of England who took part in the CRUSADES (CRUSADE[1])

Edward II /ˌedwəd ðə ˈsekənd ‖ -wərd-/, **King** (1284–1327) a king of England, the son of Edward I

Edward III /ˌedwəd ðə ˈθɜːð‖-wərd ðə ˈθɜːrd/, **King** (1312–77) a king of England who ruled during the BLACK DEATH and the start of the HUNDRED YEARS' WAR

Edward IV /ˌedwəd ðə ˈfɔːθ ‖ -wərd ðə ˈfɔːrθ/, **King** (1442–83) the king of England from 1461 to 1483

Edward V /ˌedwəd ðə ˈfɪfθ‖-wərd-/, **King** (1470–about 1483) a king of England who, with his brother, was put in prison by one of his uncles. Many people think that they were later murdered.

Edward VI /ˌedwəd ðə ˈsɪksθ ‖ -wərd-/, **King** (1537–53) the king of England from 1547 to 1553

Edward VII /ˌedwəd ðə ˈsevənθ‖-wərd-/, **King** (1841–1910) a king of Britain, the eldest son of Queen VICTORIA. When he was the Prince of Wales, before he became king, he did not take his position as the queen's son seriously, and spent his life enjoying himself at horse races, in the theatre, etc. He had many mistresses, including Lillie Langtry.

Edward VIII /ˌedwəd ði ˈeɪtθ‖-wərd-/, **King** (1894–1972) a king of Britain for only a few months, at the end of which he was forced to ABDICATE because he had decided to marry an American woman, called Mrs. Simpson, who was not of royal blood and who had been married before. They married, and lived abroad for the rest of their lives. —see also ABDICATION

Ed·ward·i·an /edˈwɔːdiən‖-ˈwɔːr-/ *n, adj* (a British person) of or living in the period of King EDWARD VII of Britain, who was king 1901–10: *Edwardian architecture* | *a famous Edwardian*

EEC /ˌiː iː ˈsiː/ [*the*] a former name for the EC

EEG /ˌiː iː ˈdʒiː/ *n* **1** electroencephalograph; an apparatus that records in the form of a drawing the electrical activity of the brain **2** electroencephalogram; the drawing made by an electroencephalograph —compare ECG

eek /iːk/ *interj infml humor* (used coming from the mouths of characters in COMIC STRIPs to express sudden fear and surprise)

eel /iːl/ *n* a long thin snake-like fish —see also CONGER EEL

e'en /iːn/ *short for:* (*poet*) EVEN[1]

Ee·ny, mee·ny, mi·ney, mo /ˌiːni ˌmiːni ˌmaɪni ˈməʊ/ the first line of a short poem which children say as a way of choosing between different possibilities when they do not know which to choose. At each beat of the poem they point to the next possibility.

EEOC /ˌiː iː əʊ ˈsiː/ *n abbrev. for:* EQUAL EMPLOYMENT OPPORTUNITY COMMISSION

e'er /eə^r/ *short for:* (*poet*) EVER

ee·rie /ˈɪəri/ *adj* causing fear because strange: *It's eerie to walk through a dark wood at night.* | *an eerie sound* —**rily** *adv* —**riness** *n* [U]

Ee·yore /ˈiːɔː^r/ a character in the Winnie the Pooh children's stories by A. A. Milne. Eeyore is a donkey who is usually sad, feeling sorry for himself, and fearing the worst thing that could happen, but who is also lovable and funny.

eff /ef/ *v BrE euph sl* **effing and blinding** using rude words; swearing: *You should have heard him effing and blinding when he hit his thumb with the hammer.*

eff off *phr v* [I] *euph sl for* FUCK off

ef·face /ɪˈfeɪs/ *v* [T] *fml* to rub out or remove the surface of: *Part of the address on the letter has been effaced.* | (*fig.*) *She could never efface the memory of* (=forget) *that awful evening.* —see also SELF-EFFACING

ef·fect[1] /ɪˈfekt/ *n* [C;U] (**on, upon**)] **1** a result or condition produced by a cause; something that happens when one thing acts on another: *One of the effects of this illness is that you lose your hair.* | *suffering from the effects of too much alcohol* | *The advertising campaign didn't have much effect on sales.* | *The disclosures had the effect of reducing the government's popularity.* **2** a result

In Britain åll children have to go to school between the ages of 5 and 16. In the US children must go to school from the age of 6 to between the ages of 14 and 16, depending on the state they live in.

Subjects

In England and Wales the subjects taught in schools are laid down by the NATIONAL CURRICULUM, which was introduced in 1988 and sets out in detail the subjects that children should study and the levels of achievement they should reach by the ages of 7, 11, 14, and 16, when they are tested.

The National Curriculum does not apply in Scotland, where each school decides what subjects it will teach.

In the US the subjects taught are decided by state and local governments.

Whereas British schools usually have prayers and religious instruction, American schools are not allowed to include prayers or to teach particular religious beliefs.

Examinations

At 16 students in England and Wales take GCSE examinations. These examinations are taken by students of all levels of ability in any of a range of subjects, and may involve a final examination, an ASSESSMENT of work done during the two year course, or both of these things. At 18 some students take A-LEVEL examinations, usually in not more than 3 subjects. It is necessary to have A-levels in order to go to a university or POLYTECHNIC.

In Scotland students take the SCE examinations. A year later, they can take examinations called HIGHERS, after which they can either go straight to a university or spend a further year at school and take the Certificate of Sixth Year Studies. In Scotland the university system is different to that in England

and Wales. Courses usually last four years rather than three, and students study a larger number of subjects as part of their degree.

In the US school examinations are not as important as they are in Britain. Students in HIGH SCHOOLs do have exams at the end of their last two years, but these final exams are considered along with the work that the students have done during the school years.

As well as exams at school, American high school students who wish to go to college also take SATs, national examinations. A student's SAT results are presented to colleges when students apply for entry, along with a record of the student's achievements at high school.

Social Events and Ceremonies

In American high schools there is a formal ceremony for GRADUATION (=completion of high school). Students wear a special CAP and GOWN and receive a DIPLOMA from the head of the school. Students often buy a class ring to wear, and a yearbook, containing pictures of their friends and teachers.

There are also special social events at American schools. Sports events are popular, and CHEERLEADERs lead the school in supporting the school team and singing the school song. At the end of their junior year, at age 17 or 18, students attend the junior-senior PROM, a very formal dance which is held in the evening. The girls wear long evening dresses and the boys wear TUXEDOs.

In Britain, there are no formal dances or social occasions associated with school life. Some schools have a SPEECH DAY at the end of the school year when prizes are given to the best students and speeches are made by the head teacher and sometimes an invited guest. However, in many British schools students and teachers organize informal dances for the older students.

class	school		age	school	class
UK				**US**	
	NURSERY SCHOOL, PLAYGROUP		3	NURSERY SCHOOL (optional)	
	or KINDERGARTEN (optional)		4		
reception class			5	KINDERGARTEN	
year 1	INFANT SCHOOL		6		first grade
year 2			7		second grade
year 3	JUNIOR SCHOOL	PRIMARY SCHOOL	8	ELEMENTARY SCHOOL	third grade
year 4			9		fourth grade
year 5			10		fifth grade
year 6			11		sixth grade
year 7			12	JUNIOR HIGH SCHOOL	seventh grade
year 8			13		eighth grade
year 9		SECONDARY SCHOOL	14		ninth grade (freshman)
year 10			15	HIGH SCHOOL	tenth grade (sophomore)
year 11			16		eleventh grade (junior)
year 12	SIXTH FORM COLLEGE		17		twelfth grade (senior)
year 13			18		freshman
first year (fresher)	UNIVERSITY or POLYTECHNIC		19	COLLEGE	sophomore
second year			20		junior
third/final year			21		senior
postgraduate	UNIVERSITY		22	GRADUATE SCHOOL	
			23		

produced on the mind or feelings; an IMPRESSION: *Her new red dress produced quite an effect on everyone.* | *Don't look at the details, consider the general effect.* | *Don't pay any attention to him — he's only doing it* **for effect.** (=to shock or surprise people) **3 in effect: a** in operation: *The old system of taxation will remain in effect until next May.* **b** in fact, although perhaps not appearing so: *Their response was in effect a refusal.* —see also EFFECTIVELY (2) **4 into effect** into operation: *A new system of taxation will come|be brought|be put into effect next May.* **5 take effect: a** to come into operation: *The new system will take effect next May.* **b** to begin to produce results: *The medicine quickly took effect.* **6 to . . . effect** *fml* with (the stated) general meaning or result: *He called me a fool, or* **words to that effect**. | *She has made an announcement* **to the effect that** *more people will lose their jobs.* | *These weapons were first used, to devastating effect* (=causing very great destruction), *in 1945.* —see also EFFECTS, GREENHOUSE EFFECT, SIDE EFFECT; see AFFECT (USAGE)

effect² *v* [T] *fml* to cause; produce: *We have tried our best to effect a reconciliation between the two parties.* —see AFFECT (USAGE)

ef·fec·tive /ɪˈfektɪv/ *adj* **1** producing the desired result: *Their efforts to improve the school have been very effective.* | *an effective treatment for hair loss* —opposite **ineffective** **2** having a pleasing effect; STRIKING: *That's rather an effective use of colour.* **3** [*no comp.*] actual; real: *Although there is a parliament, the army is in effective control of the country.* **4** [*no comp.*] in operation: *When does the new system become effective?* —compare EFFICACIOUS, EFFICIENT; see also COST-EFFECTIVE — ~ **ness** *n* [U]

ef·fec·tive·ly /ɪˈfektɪvli/ *adv* **1** in an effective way **2** in fact, although perhaps not appearing so: *Effectively, their response was a refusal.* | *Chances of a settlement were effectively wrecked by this announcement.* —see also **in effect** (EFFECT¹)

ef·fects /ɪˈfekts/ *n* [P] **1** things, such as recorded sounds, patterns of lights, man-made objects or creatures intended to seem real, that are produced to be heard or seen in a film, broadcast, or theatrical production: *He won an award for the* **special effects** *he did for this film.* —see also SOUND EFFECTS **2** *fml or law* belongings; personal property: *The deceased left no (personal) effects.*

ef·fec·tu·al /ɪˈfektʃuəl/ *adj fml* (of an action) producing the intended effect; effective: *effectual measures to combat unemployment* —opposite **ineffectual** — ~ **ly** *adv*

ef·fec·tu·ate /ɪˈfektʃueɪt/ *v* [T] *fml* to carry out successfully; effect

ef·fem·i·nate /ɪˈfemɪnət/ *adj derog* (of a man or his behaviour) having qualities that are regarded as typical of women; unmanly — ~ **ly** *adv* — ~ **nacy** *n* [U]

ef·fer·vesce /ˌefəˈves‖ˌefər-/ *v* [I] *fml or tech* (of a liquid) to have BUBBLES forming inside, usu. by chemical action. The bubbles are usu. produced quickly and in large numbers.

ef·fer·ves·cent /ˌefəˈvesənt◂‖ˌefər-/ *adj* **1** (of a liquid) effervescing **2** (of a person) full of life and excitement ~ **ly** *adv* — ~ **ence** *n* [U]

ef·fete /ɪˈfiːt‖eˈ-/ *adj fml derog* **1** weak; worn out; having lost one's original power **2** effeminate: *an effete young man* — ~ **ness** *n* [U]

ef·fi·ca·cious /ˌefɪˈkeɪʃəs◂/ *adj fml* (of a medicine, a course of action, etc.) producing the desired effect, esp. in curing an illness or dealing with a problem: *an efficacious remedy* —compare EFFECTIVE, EFFICIENT — ~ **ly** *adv*

ef·fi·ca·cy /ˈefɪkəsi/ *n* [U] *fml* the quality of being efficacious

ef·fi·cient /ɪˈfɪʃənt/ *adj* working well, quickly, and without waste: *Our efficient new machines are much cheaper to run.* | *She is a quick efficient worker.* —opposite **inefficient** —compare EFFECTIVE, EFFICACIOUS — ~ **ly** *adv* — **ciency** *n* [U]: *It would improve our efficiency if we used more up-to-date methods.*

ef·fi·gy /ˈefɪdʒi/ *n* [(of)] *fml* a likeness of a person, made of wood, paper, stone, etc.; often life size: *The protesters burnt an effigy of the Prime Minister.*

ef·flo·res·cence /ˌefləˈresəns/ *n* [U] *fml or tech* the period or action of the forming and developing of flowers on a plant

ef·flu·ent /ˈefluənt/ *n* [C *usu. pl.*;U] *tech* liquid waste, such

as chemicals or SEWAGE (human waste material), that flows out from a factory or similar place, usu. into a river or the sea: *There is a law against dangerous effluent(s) being poured into our rivers.*

ef·flux /ˈeflʌks/ *n* [U] *fml or tech* the outward flow of gas or liquid

ef·fort /ˈefət‖ˈefərt/ *n* **1** [S;U] (something that needs) the use of physical strength or power of the mind; trying hard with mind or body: *It's quite an effort to lift this heavy box.* | *It took a lot of effort to lift it.* | *We lifted it without much effort.* | *A great deal of effort has gone into this exhibition.* **2** [C] an attempt using all one's powers: *Despite all our efforts we were still beaten.* [+*to-v*] *The prisoner made no effort to escape.* (=didn't try to escape) | *Please make an effort* (=try hard) *to get there on time.* | *The company is selling off some of its buildings in an effort to save money.* **3** [C] something made or done as the result of trying: *Finishing the work in one day was a very good effort.* | *These essays of yours are very poor efforts.*

ef·fort·less /ˈefətləs‖ˈefərt-/ *adj* seeming to make or need no effort, yet very good: *She skates with such effortless grace.* — ~ **ly** *adv* — ~ **ness** *n* [U]

ef·fron·te·ry /ɪˈfrʌntəri/ *n* [U] rudeness without any sense of shame; NERVE¹ (3): [+*to-v*] *You crashed my car and now you have the effrontery to ask to borrow my bicycle.*

ef·ful·gent /ɪˈfʌldʒənt‖ɪˈfʊl-, ɪˈfʌl-/ *adj lit* shining brightly; BRILLIANT

ef·fu·sion /ɪˈfjuːʒən/ *n fml derog* an uncontrolled expression of strong feelings in speech or writing: *Her effusions of gratitude were clearly insincere.*

ef·fu·sive /ɪˈfjuːsɪv/ *adj often derog* showing (too) much feeling: *Her effusive welcome made us feel most uncomfortable.* — ~ **ly** *adv* : *He thanked them effusively.* — ~ **ness** *n* [U]

EFL /ˌiː ef ˈel/ English as a Foreign Language; English as it is taught to people who do not speak it as their first language —compare ESL, ESOL, ESP, TEFL, TESOL

EFTA /ˈeftə/ European Free Trade Association; an association of some northern and central European countries which have a common market

EFTPOS /ˈeftpɒs‖-pɑːs/ *n* Electronic Funds Transfer at Point of Sale; a system which allows people to pay for goods in shops using a DEBIT CARD or CREDIT CARD to move money electronically from their accounts. EFTPOS is becoming widely used in shops in Britain as it is a quick and convenient method of paying for things.

e.g. /ˌiː ˈdʒiː/ *abbrev.* for example: *You must avoid sweet foods, e.g. cake, chocolate, sugar, and ice cream.*

e·gal·i·tar·i·an /ɪˌɡælɪˈteəriən/ *adj often apprec* having or showing the belief that all people are equal and should have equal rights: *an egalitarian society* — ~ **ism** *n* [U]

egg¹ /eɡ/ *n* **1** [C] a rounded object with a usu. hard shell which is produced by a female bird, snake, etc., and which contains a baby animal until it has developed enough to come out: *The hen laid an egg.* | *The chick hatched out of the egg.* **2** [C;U] (the contents of) an egg, esp. one laid by a hen, when used for food: *I had a boiled egg for breakfast.* | *You've got egg all down your tie.* **3** [C] a cell produced by a woman or female animal, which joins with the male seed (SPERM) to make a baby **4 have** ¹**egg on one's face** *infml* to be made to seem foolish: *The committee's report, which describes this policy as "a total failure", has left the government with egg on its face.* **5 put all one's eggs in one basket** *infml* to depend completely on the success of one thing: *When the company she'd invested all her money in went bankrupt, she wished she hadn't put all her eggs in one basket.* —see also NEST EGG, SCOTCH EGG, **bad egg** (BAD¹)

egg² *v*

egg sbdy. **on** *phr v* [T] to encourage strongly, esp. to do something wrong: *He wouldn't have thrown that stone if the other boys hadn't egged him on.* [+*obj+to-v*] *They egged the crowd on to riot.*

egg and spoon race /ˌ· · ˈ· ·/ *n* a race between people running while balancing an egg on a spoon. The winner is the first person to complete the distance without the egg falling off the spoon. Egg and spoon races are often held at children's school SPORTS DAYS.

egg·cup /ˈeg-kʌp/ *n* a small container without a handle that holds a boiled egg so that it can be eaten

egg·head /'eghed/ *n usu. derog* a clever, highly educated person, esp. one who is impractical

egg·nog /ˌeg'nɒg‖'egnɑːg/ *n* [C;U] (a cupful of) a drink made from eggs, milk or cream, sugar, and usu. alcohol, esp. RUM, and drunk at Christmas and New Year in the US

egg·plant /'egplɑːnt‖'egplænt/ *n esp. AmE for* AUBERGINE – see picture at VEGETABLE

egg roll /ˌ·ˈ·/ *n AmE for* SPRING ROLL

egg·shell /'egʃel/ *n* **1** the usu. hard outside part of an egg **2** a type of paint with a smooth, dull finish

egg tim·er /'·ˌ··/ *n* a small two-part glass container with sand in it that runs from one part to the other in about three minutes, which is used for measuring the time when boiling eggs

e·go /'iːgəʊ, 'egəʊ/ *n* **egos** **1** one's opinion of oneself; SELF-ESTEEM: *He has an enormous ego.* (=thinks he is a very fine person) | *Is success good for one's ego?* | *to boost someone's ego by praising them* **2** *tech* (in Freudian PSYCHOLOGY) the one of the three parts of the mind that connects a person to the outside world, because it can think and act; conscious self –compare ID, SUPEREGO; see also ALTER EGO

e·go·cen·tric /ˌiːgəʊ'sentrɪk◂, ˌe-/ *adj derog* thinking only about oneself rather than about other people; selfish – **~ally** /kli/ *adv* – **~ity** /ˌiːgəʊsen'trɪsɨti, ˌe-/ *n* [U]

e·go·is·m /'iːgəʊɪzəm, 'e-/ *n* [U] **1** *derog* the quality of always thinking about oneself and about what will be best for oneself; selfishness –compare ALTRUISM, EGOTISM **2** the belief that people's moral behaviour should be based on what is most advantageous to themselves –**ist** *n* –**istic** /ˌiːgəʊ'ɪstɪk◂, ˌe-/ *adj* –**istically** /kli/ *adv*

e·go·ma·ni·a /ˌiːgəʊ'meɪniə, ˌe-/ *n esp. AmE, infml* extreme egoism (1): *Dictators often display egomania.* –**maniac** *n*

eg·o·tis·m /'iːgətɪzəm, 'e-/ *n* [U] *derog* the act of or tendency towards talking too much about oneself and believing that one is better and more important than other people –compare EGOISM (1) –**tist** *n* –**tistic** /ˌiːgə'tɪstɪk◂, ˌe-/ –**tistical** *adj* –**tistically** /kli/ *adv*

ego trip /'·· ·/ *n sl derog* an act or set of acts done mainly because it makes one feel proud of oneself: *When he's lecturing he's not really bothered about the students learning. It's just an ego trip.* | *He's on a real ego trip at the moment.*

e·gre·gious /ɪ'griːdʒəs/ *adj* [A] *fml derog* (of something bad, such as a mistake) especially and noticeably bad; BLATANT: *It was an egregious error to address the Queen as "dear".* – – **ly** *adv*

e·gress /'iːgres/ *n* [U] *fml or law* the act, power, or right of going out, esp. from a building or enclosed place – opposite **ingress**

e·gret /'iːgrɨt, -et/ *n* a fairly large long-legged water bird with long white feathers

E·gypt /'iːdʒɪpt/ a country in north-east AFRICA and the SINAI PENINSULA bordering on the Mediterranean and Red Seas; capital Cairo; population 53,080,000 (1989). Egypt is known esp. for its ANCIENT CIVILIZATION, and many people go there to see the PYRAMIDs and other remains.

E·gyp·tian /ɪ'dʒɪpʃən/ *adj* of, belonging to, or being a native of Egypt –**Egyptian** *n*

E·gyp·tol·og·y /ˌiːdʒɪp'tɒlədʒi‖-'tɑː-/ *n* the study of the buried remains and the language of Ancient Egypt: *the Egyptology Department at the British Museum* –**gist** *n*

eh /eɪ/ *interj BrE infml* (used for showing surprise or doubt, or when asking someone to agree or repeat what they have just said): *Let's have another drink, eh?* | *"I'm cold!" "Eh?" "I said I'm cold!"* –compare PARDON¹ (4)

Eich·mann /'aɪkmən, 'aɪx-/, **Ad·olf** /'ædɒlf‖'eɪdɑːlf/ (1906–62) an Austrian Nazi who was an SS official under Adolf Hitler, responsible for mass killings. He was executed (EXECUTE) after being found guilty of war crimes.

ei·der·down /'aɪdədaʊn‖-dər-/ *n* a thick warm covering for a bed filled with the soft feathers (DOWN¹) of a type of large black and white duck (**eider duck**)

Eif·fel Tow·er /ˌaɪfəl 'taʊəʳ/ [*the*] a 300-metre-high metal tower in the centre of Paris, built in 1887–89. It is often thought of as representative of Paris or France.

Ei·ger /'aɪgəʳ/ also **Eiger Moun·tain** /ˌ·· '··/– [*the*] a mountain in the ALPS in Switzerland

eight /eɪt/ *determiner, n, pron* **1** (the number) 8 – see TABLE 1 **2** [+*sing./pl. v*] a team of eight rowers in a racing boat: *The Oxford eight is/are using a new lightweight boat.* – see also PIECE OF EIGHT **3 one over the eight** *BrE infml* slightly drunk – **eighth** /eɪtθ/ *determiner, n, pron, adv*

eigh·teen /ˌeɪ'tiːn◂/ *determiner, n, pron* (the number) 18 –see TABLE 1,

▶CULTURAL NOTE People are allowed to vote at the age of 18 in the UK and in most states in the US ◀

18 – 30 hol·i·days /ˌeɪtiːn 'θɜːti ˌhɒlɨdeɪz‖-'θɜːrti ˌhɑːlɨdeɪz/ *n* [P] group holidays for people between the ages of 18 to 30, esp. people who are not married. The image that many people have of 18-30 holidays is that many of the people who go on them choose to spend their time drinking alcohol, having sex, and behaving badly.

18-wheel·er /ˌeɪtiːn 'wiːləʳ◂/ *n AmE* a very large TRUCK (=vehicle that carries goods on roads) which has 18 wheels. They are used esp. for moving goods over long distances.

eighth note /'·· ·/ *n AmE for* QUAVER¹ (2) –see picture at NOTATION

800 num·ber /eɪt'hʌndrɨd ˌnʌmbəʳ/ also **800 line, toll-free number** *n AmE* a telephone number which one can telephone without paying for the call

eight·ies /'eɪtiz/ *n* **1** [*the*] also **'80s**– the 1980s (=the years from 1980 to 1989) **2 in his/her/their eighties** aged from 80 to 89: *He must be in his eighties now.* [*the*] **3** the numbers from 81 to 89, esp. when used to measure temperature: *a hot day with temperatures in the low eighties*

86, eighty-six /ˌ·· '·/ *v* [T] *AmE sl* to stop serving esp. food at a restaurant: *86 the salmon steak – we ran out of it.*

eigh·ty /'eɪti/ *determiner, n, pron* (the number) 80 – see TABLE 1 –**tieth** /'eɪtiəθ/ *determiner, n, pron, adv*

Ein·stein /'aɪnstaɪn/, **Albert** (1879–1955) an American PHYSICIST, born in Germany, who studied the behaviour of atoms and formed the THEORY of RELATIVITY. Einstein is generally thought of as being one of the cleverest people ever born: *Go and ask Simon. He's the Einstein of the family.* | *By the time he was six he could do long division. We thought we had another Einstein on our hands.* | *You do not have to have the IQ of an Einstein to be a programmer.* | *He's no Einstein.*

Albert Einstein

Ei·re /'eərə/ the Republic of Ireland. Eire is its Irish GAELIC name. –see REPUBLIC OF IRELAND

Ei·sen·how·er /'aɪzənhaʊəʳ/, **Dwight Da·vid** /dwaɪt 'deɪvɨd/ (also called **Ike** /aɪk/ *infml*) (1890–1969) President of the US from 1953 to 1961. He was a general in the American army during the Second World War and one of the chief commanders of the forces fighting the Germans. He commanded them on **D-Day**.

Ei·sen·stein /'aɪzənstaɪn/, **Ser·gei Mi·khai·lo·vich** /'seəgeɪ mɪ'kaɪləvɪtʃ‖seər'geɪ-/ (1898–1948) a Russian film director generally thought of as one of the greatest of all time and known esp. for *Potemkin* and *Alexander Nevsky*

ei·stedd·fod /aɪ'stedfəd‖-vɑːd/ [*the*] (*often cap.*) a yearly meeting in Wales at which competitions are held for Welsh poets, singers, and musicians. It is thought to be a great honour to win a prize or title at an eisteddfod.

ei·ther¹ /'aɪðəʳ‖'iː-/ *determiner* **1** one or the other of two: *She's lived in London and Manchester, but doesn't like either city very much.* | *You can get there by plane or by boat, but either way/in either case it's very expensive.* –compare ANY¹ **2** one and the other of two; each: *He sat in the car with a policeman on either side of him.* – compare BOTH (1)

either² *pron* one or the other of two: *There's coffee or tea – you can have either.* | *Take either of the books.*

▷ USAGE When **either** and **neither** are used as pronouns and followed by a plural noun, they usually take a singular verb in formal writing: *Is* **either/neither** *of the factories in operation yet? But in speech and informal writing a plural verb is usually used: Are* **either/neither** *of the teams playing this week?*◁

either³ *conj* (used to begin a list of two or more possibilities separated by **or**): *It's either a boy or a girl. | Either say you're sorry or (else) get out. | It's either blue, red, or green – I can't remember. | She's one of those people that you either love or hate.*

▷ USAGE **Either** ... **or** and **neither** ... **nor** are usually followed by a plural pronoun and plural verb, except in formal writing: *If* **either** *David* **or** *Janet come, they will want a drink.* In formal English this would be: *If* **either** *David* **or** *Janet comes, he or she will want a drink.*◁

either⁴ *adv* [*only in negatives*] also: *I haven't read this book, and my brother hasn't either.* (=both haven't read it) | *"I can't swim!" "I can't, either!/Neither can I!"* (=I, too, am unable to swim.) —compare TOO (3)

either-or /ₗ·· ˈ·/ *adj* [A] *infml* needing or resulting in an unavoidable choice between only two possibilities: *We fight, or we surrender – it's an either-or situation.*

e·jac·u·late /ɪˈdʒækjᵿleɪt/ *v* [I;T] **1** to cause (the male seed (SPERM)) to come suddenly out from the PENIS **2** *fml* to cry out or say suddenly and shortly: *"Watch out!" he ejaculated.* —**lation** /ɪˌdʒækjᵿˈleɪʃən/ *n* [C;U]

e·ject /ɪˈdʒekt/ *v* [T (**from**)] *fml* to throw out with force: *They were making such a noise in the restaurant that the police came and ejected them.* — –**ion** /ɪˈdʒekʃən/ *n* [U]

e·jec·tor seat /·ˈ·· ˌ·/ *esp. BrE* ‖ **ejection seat** *esp. AmE*— *n* a seat which throws the pilot out and away from a plane when he or she can no longer control it and must reach the ground by PARACHUTE

eke /iːk/ *v*
eke sthg. ↔ **out** *phr v* [T (**with, by**)] **1** to cause (a small supply) to last longer by being careful or by adding something else: *She eked out her small income by cleaning other people's houses.* **2 eke out a living** to make just enough money to live on

EKG /ₗiː keɪ ˈdʒiː/ *n AmE for* ECG

el /el/ also **L** *n AmE infml* the ELEVATED RAILWAY in Chicago, US

e·lab·o·rate¹ /ɪˈlæbᵊrət/ *adj* full of detail; carefully worked out and with a large number of parts: *She made elaborate preparations for the party, and then no one came. | The curtains had an elaborate pattern of flowers. | an elaborate excuse* – –**ly** *adv* – –**ness** *n* [U]

e·lab·o·rate² /ɪˈlæbᵊreɪt/ *v* [I (**on**)] to add more detail or information: *What you've told me of your plan sounds most interesting. Would you care to elaborate (on it)?* —**ration** /ɪˌlæbᵊˈreɪʃən/ *n* [C;U]

El Al·a·mein /el ˈæləmeɪn/ a city on the north coast of Egypt

El Alamein, Battle of an important battle in 1942 during the Second World War in which Montgomery's British forces defeated Rommel's German and Italian soldiers thus ending a string of victories for Hitler

é·lan /ˈeɪlɒn‖eɪˈlɑːn/ *n* [U] *Fr* liveliness and stylishness: *She played the piano with great élan.*

e·land /ˈiːlənd/ *n* **elands** *or* **eland** a large African ANTELOPE (=deerlike animal) with horns that curve round and round

e·lapse /ɪˈlæps/ *v* [I] *fml* (of time) to pass by: *Three months have elapsed since he left home.*

e·las·tic¹ /ɪˈlæstɪk/ *adj* **1** (of material such as rubber) able to spring back into shape after being stretched or bent: *This swimming costume is made of elastic material.* **2** (esp. of plans or arrangements) able to be changed if the situation changes; not fixed: *My timetable for this week is fairly elastic.* —**ticity** /ₗiːlæsˈtɪsᵊti/ *n* [U]

elastic² *n* [U] (a piece of) elastic material, esp. rubber: *I like these skirts with elastic round the waist.*

elastic band /·ˌ·· ˈ·/ *n BrE for* RUBBER BAND

E·las·to·plast /ɪˈlæstəplɑːst‖-plæst/ *n* [C;U] *BrE tdmk* a type of usu. pink elastic material used to cover a cut or small wound; a PLASTER¹ (2)

e·lat·ed /ɪˈleɪtᵻd/ *adj* [(**at, by**)] filled with excited joy and

pride: *The elated crowd cheered and cheered. | She seemed elated at/by the news.* [F+to-v/that] *We were all elated to hear of the victory/elated that we had won.*

e·la·tion /ɪˈleɪʃən/ *n* [U] the state of being filled with excited pride and joy: *They couldn't conceal their elation.*

El·ba /ˈelbə/ an island west of Italy where NAPOLEON I was sent in 1814 after his defeat by Russia, Britain, Austria, and the other countries fighting against France

el·bow¹ /ˈelbəʊ/ *n* **1** [C] (the outer point of) a joint where the arm of a person or the FORELEG of an animal bends —see picture at HORSE **2** [C] the part of a garment which covers the elbow: *He had a patch on the elbow of his jacket.* **3** [C] something in the shape of an elbow, such as a joint in a pipe, chimney, etc. **4** [*the*+S] *BrE sl* dismissal from a relationship, one's job, etc.: *She got fed up with her boyfriend, so she gave him the elbow/he got the elbow.* **5 at one's elbow** *esp. BrE* close by and ready when needed

elbow² *v* [T+*obj*+*adv/prep*] to push with the elbows: *I tried to stop him, but he elbowed me out of the way. | She elbowed her way through the crowd.*

elbow grease /ˈ·· ·/ *n infml* hard work with the hands, esp. polishing and cleaning; often used in suggesting that one should work harder: *It's no use just passing the duster over it. It needs a bit of elbow grease.*

el·bow·room /ˈelbəʊrʊm, -ruːm/ *n* [U] space in which to move freely

El Cid /el ˈsɪd/ *Sp.* (c. 1030–99) a Spanish soldier who fought for both Christians and Moors and whose life is often seen as a perfect example of CHIVALRY, Christian values, and love of his country

el·der¹ /ˈeldəʳ/ *adj* [A *no comp.*] (of a person, esp. in a family) older, esp. the older of two; it is sometimes used because it seems politer than saying somebody is older, which they might think means they are old: *He is my elder brother. | Her elder daughter is married.* | [after *n*] *William Pitt* **the Elder** *was a British prime minister, and so was his son, William Pitt the Younger.* —compare YOUNGER

▷ USAGE Compare **elder** and **older**. **Older** is used of people or things, but **elder** is used only of people, and can never be used in comparisons: *Jane is Mary's* **elder** *sister. | Jane is* **older** *than* (not **elder** *than*) *Mary.*◁

elder² *n* **1** the older one, esp. of two people: *Which is the elder (of the two sisters)? | You should have more respect for* **your elders.** (=people who are older than you) **2** a person who holds a respected, often official position: *The village elders are always consulted on important matters like this.*

elder³ *n* a small tree with white flowers in large flat groups and black berries (**elderberries**). **Elderberry wine** and **elderflower wine** were once commonly made, esp. by country people. —see picture at BERRY

el·der·ly /ˈeldəli‖ˈeldərli/ *adj* (of a person) old: *My father is rather elderly now and can't walk very fast.* [(also *n*, *the*+P)] *We should provide better care for the elderly. |* (fig.) *Their national airline consists of three or four rather elderly planes.*

▷ USAGE **Elderly** is a polite way of saying **old.** —see OLD (CULTURAL NOTE)◁

elder states·man /ₗ·· ˈ··/ *n* an old and respected person, usu. no longer in a position of power, who is asked for advice because of his or her long experience, esp. in politics

el·dest /ˈeldᵻst/ *n, adj* (a person, esp. in a family, who is) oldest of three or more: *She has three children, and her eldest has just started school.*

El Do·ra·do, Eldorado /ₗel dəˈrɑːdəʊ/ a place of unbelievable wealth (from the land called **El Dorado** which the Spanish of the 16th century thought to exist somewhere in Central, S, or N America): *They go off to the big city thinking it's El Dorado and are quite amazed when they don't make their fortune. | the greatest natural-resources Eldorado of all – the carve-up of Antarctica's mineral wealth*

e·lect¹ /ɪˈlekt/ *v* [T] **1** [(**to**)] to choose (someone) for an official position by voting: *She has been elected to the committee. | They elected a President/elected him as President.* [+*obj*+*n*] *They elected him President.* [+*obj*+*to-v*] *They elected her to represent them on the committee.* **2** [+*to-v*;

Elections in Britain

Britain is divided into 650 political areas, known as constituencies (CONSTITUENCY) or SEATS. Each constituency is represented in the House of Commons by an MP (Member of Parliament), elected by the people in the constituency. At a GENERAL ELECTION, the people of Britain who are aged over 18 VOTE to choose who will serve in the House of Commons and which party will form the government.

The main political parties choose a CANDIDATE to fight for a seat in each constituency. So, in each constituency people usually have four or five candidates to choose from, each representing a different political party. People vote by putting a cross by the name of one of the candidates on the **ballot paper**. The person who is elected for each constituency is the one who gains the most votes within that constituency.

When voting is completed, the political party that has won the most seats is asked to form a government, and that party's leader becomes PRIME MINISTER, which means that they hold more seats than all the other parties together, and so cannot easily be defeated in votes in the House of Commons. Sometimes there is a **minority government** in which one party has more seats than any other party and can form a government, but does not have more seats than all the other parties together, so can easily be defeated in votes in the House of Commons. This situation is also called a **hung parliament**. In this situation, the ruling party may join with another party to form a **coalition** so that it can pass laws in the House of Commons. The longest time that a parliament can run is five years, but the Prime Minister has the power to **call an election** at any point within this period, usually depending on the government's opinion of whether they have a good chance of being re-elected.

Elections in the US

Congress, the central law-making body in the US, is made up of the HOUSE OF REPRESENTATIVES and the SENATE. Members of both houses are elected by the people of the state they represent. There are 435 members of the House of Representatives, called REPRESENTATIVES or CONGRESSMEN/ CONGRESSWOMEN. The number of Representatives for each state depends on the population of the state. States such as California, which has a large population, have many Representatives, while states with a low population, such as Wyoming, may have only one or two. States are divided into smaller areas called **districts**, and the people in each district elect one Representative. Elections are held for all the seats in the House of Representatives every two years.

There are 100 members of the Senate, called SENATORS, two for each state. Senators hold office for a term of six years. Every two years a third of the Senators are elected by the people.

General elections

Congressmen and Congresswomen usually belong to one of the two main political parties, but the party does not choose who runs for Congress. There is usually a primary election or CAUCUS held to decide which one of the candidates from each party will represent that party in the general election. In the general election, voters usually have a choice among candidates from the two main parties and candidates from small parties or ones who are running independently. The candidate who receives the most votes is elected.

Electing the President

Presidential elections are similar to elections for the House of Representatives and the Senate and are held every four years. Presidential candidates, who usually have experience in Congress or in state government, decide themselves if they want to run for president. Primary elections and caucuses are held in most states to help choose who will be each party's candidate in the presidential election. Primaries determine how many delegates to the party convention will vote for each candidate. The candidate with the most votes at the party convention is officially nominated (named) as that party's candidate.

Presidential elections work by a system called the ELECTORAL COLLEGE. Each state has a number of electoral college votes equal to the number of Senators and Representatives it has. The candidate who wins the most votes in a state receives all that state's electoral college votes. The candidate with the most electoral college votes wins the election and becomes the president. —see also pages 568 and 949

a ballot paper

Jane Dixon	Green	
Michael Fox	Conservative	
Robin James	Liberal Democrat	X
Sarah Wood	Labour	

obj] *fml* to decide (to do something), esp. when choosing between possible courses of action: *Employees may elect to take their pension in monthly payments or as a single lump sum.*

elect² *adj* [after *n*] *fml* chosen for or elected to a position but not yet officially placed in it: *The President elect will be installed next week.*

elect³ *n* [*the*+P] **1** people chosen by God to be saved **2** *often humor* a specially chosen and extremely important group of people: *The directors always listen to him. He's one of the elect.*

e·lec·tion /ɪˈlekʃən/ *n* [C;U] **1** (an example of) the choosing by vote of a representative to take an official (esp. political) position: *The Government has called a* **snap election.** (=decided suddenly and unexpectedly to have an election) | *The election results will be broadcast tonight.*| *Trade union representatives are chosen by election.* | *an election campaign* **2 Election Day** (in the US) the day legally chosen for national elections, which is the first Tuesday after the first Monday in November, in even years (1992, 1994, etc.) US presidents are elected every four years. In some states Election Day is a public holiday. Bars and public places selling alcoholic drinks are closed on election day during the times when people can vote. —see also BY-ELECTION, GENERAL ELECTION and extra information on page 412

e·lec·tion·eer·ing /ɪˌlekʃəˈnɪərɪŋ/ *n* [U] *sometimes derog* the work of persuading people to vote for a political party by visiting voters, making speeches, etc.

e·lec·tive /ɪˈlektɪv/ *adj fml* (of a position) for which the holder is chosen by election: *The office of President of the US is an elective one, but the position of Queen of England is not.*

e·lec·tor /ɪˈlektəʳ‖-tər, -tɔːr/ *n* **1** a person who has the right to vote in an election **2** (in the US) a member of the Electoral College

e·lec·to·ral /ɪˈlektərəl/ *adj* [A] concerning elections or electors: *Many people say the electoral system in this country should be changed.* | *guilty of electoral malpractice* | *Have you got your name on the* **electoral roll/register**? (=the official list of people who have the right to vote)

electoral col·lege /ˌ·ˈ···ˈ··/ *n* [C+*sing./pl. v*] (*often cap.*) a group of people who are given the right to elect a leader, esp. (in the US) the national body elected by the voters of each state to choose the President according to the votes of the people —see also extra information on page 412

electoral re·gis·ter /ˌ·ˈ··· ˈ··/ also **electoral roll** /ˌ·ˈ··· ˈ·/— the official list of people who have the right to vote: *Have you got your name on the electoral register?*

e·lec·to·rate /ɪˈlektərət/ *n* [C+*sing./pl. v*] all the people in a country or an area who have the right to vote

E·lec·tra com·plex /ɪˈlektrə ˌkɒmpleks‖-ˌkɑːm-/ *n* (in FREUDIAN PSYCHOLOGY) an unconscious sexual desire of a young girl for her father combined with hatred of her mother (from CLASSICAL MYTHOLOGY. After the death of her father, Electra helped her brother to kill their mother and her lover.) —compare OEDIPUS COMPLEX

e·lec·tric /ɪˈlektrɪk/ *adj* **1** [*no comp.*] worked by electricity: *an electric clock/fire* —compare ELECTRICAL, ELECTRONIC **2** [A *no comp.*] produced by, producing, or carrying electricity: *electric power* | *an electric generator* (=that makes electricity) | *an* **electric storm** (=with thunder and lightning) **3** very exciting: *The atmosphere at the concert was electric.* | *His speech had an electric effect on the crowd.*

▷ USAGE **Electric** is used **a** of things that produce electricity **b** of things directly worked or produced by electricity, especially things that might be worked by some other kind of power: *an* **electric** *generator/clock/light/shock.* **Electrical** is used of people and their work, or where the association with electric power is less direct: *an* **electrical** *engineer/*|**electrical** *apparatus/an* **electrical** *fault in the system.*◁

e·lec·tri·cal /ɪˈlektrɪkəl/ *adj* [*no comp.*] concerned with or using electricity: *electrical engineering* | *electrical apparatus* | *I think the fault is probably electrical.* —compare ELECTRONIC; see ELECTRIC (USAGE) — ~ **ly** /kli/ *adv*

electrical ap·pli·ance /ˌ·ˈ··· ·ˈ··/ *n* a machine, usu. for use in the house, which works by electricity: *ovens, fridges, and other electrical appliances*

electrical en·gi·neer /ˌ·ˈ··· ··ˈ·/ *n* a person trained in electrical engineering

electrical en·gi·neer·ing /ˌ·ˈ··· ··ˈ··ˈ/ *n* [U] a branch of engineering which develops the use of electricity in practical ways

electric blan·ket /ˌ·ˈ··· ˈ···/ *n* a double sheet of cotton, wool, or man-made material with electric wires passing through, used for making a bed warm. Electric blankets are made for use either above or beneath the body

electric chair /ˌ·ˈ··· ˈ·/ also **chair** *infml*— *n* [*the*] (punishment using) a chairlike apparatus with a supply of electricity which is used for killing certain criminals in some states of the US —see CAPITAL PUNISHMENT

electric eye /ˌ·ˈ··· ˈ·/ *n infml for* PHOTOELECTRIC CELL (2)

electric fire /ˌ·ˈ··· ˈ·/ *n* a heater which works by electricity, usu. used to heat rooms in a house. The heat comes from wires made red-hot by the electricity.

electric gui·tar /ˌ·ˈ··· ·ˈ·/ *n* a GUITAR which works by electricity and is connected to a piece of equipment which makes the sound louder. Electric guitars are esp. used in popular music.

el·ec·tri·cian /ɪˌlekˈtrɪʃən, ˌelɪk-/ *n* a person whose job is to fit and repair electrical apparatus

e·lec·tri·ci·ty /ɪˌlekˈtrɪsɨti, ˌelɪk-/ *n* [U] **1** the power which is produced by various means (e.g. by a BATTERY or GENERATOR), which is carried usu. by wires, and which provides heat and light, drives machines, etc. **2** a feeling of great excitement, esp. one that spreads through a group of people

electricity sup·ply /ˌ·ˈ·ˈ··· ·ˌ·, ·ˌ·ˈ··· ·ˌ·/ *n* the flow of electricity to a building, machine, etc.: *If you don't pay your electricity bill, your electricity supply will be cut off.*

e·lec·trics /ɪˈlektrɪks/ *n* [P] *BrE infml* the wires and other equipment that work an electrical (part of an) apparatus: *I don't know why the car won't start; perhaps it's a problem in the electrics.*

electric shock /ˌ·ˈ··· ˈ·/ *n* a shock to the body caused by electricity: *I got an electric shock when I touched that wire.*

electric shock ther·a·py /ˌ·ˈ··· ˈ· ˌ···/ also **e·lec·tro·con·vul·sive therapy** /ɪˌlektrəʊkənˌvʌlsɪv ˈθerəpi/ *n* [U] *med* the treatment of MENTAL ILLNESS (=disorders of the mind) by passing a small electric current through the brain. This is a very CONTROVERSIAL method of treatment.

e·lec·tri·fy /ɪˈlektrɨfaɪ/ *v* [T] **1** to change (something) to a system using electric power: *The national railway system has nearly all been electrified.* **2** to excite greatly: *The band gave an electrifying performance.* —**-fication** /ɪˌlektrɨfɨˈkeɪʃən/ *n* [U]

electro- see WORD FORMATION

e·lec·tro·car·di·o·gram /ɪˌlektrəʊˈkɑːdiəgræm‖-ˈkɑːr-/ *n med* —see ECG (2)

e·lec·tro·car·di·o·graph /ɪˌlektrəʊˈkɑːdiəgrɑːf‖-ˈkɑːrdiəgræf/ *n med* see ECG (1)

e·lec·tro·cute /ɪˈlektrəkjuːt/ *v* [T] to wound or kill by passing electricity through the body —**-cution** /ɪˌlektrəˈkjuːʃən/ *n* [C;U]

e·lec·trode /ɪˈlektrəʊd/ *n* either of the two points (TERMINALS) at which the current enters and leaves a BATTERY or other electrical apparatus —see also ANODE, CATHODE

e·lec·tro·en·ceph·a·lo·gram /ɪˌlektrəʊɪnˈsefələgræm, -trəʊen-/ *n med* —see EEG (2)

e·lec·tro·en·ceph·a·lo·graph /ɪˌlektrəʊɪnˈsefələgrɑːf, -trəʊen-‖-græf/ *n med* —see EEG (1)

E·lec·tro·lux /ɪˈlektrəlʌks/ *tdmk* a company which makes VACUUM CLEANERS, REFRIGERATORS, and other electrical goods: *We've bought a new Electrolux fridge.*

e·lec·trol·y·sis /ɪˌlekˈtrɒlɨsɨs, ˌelɪk-‖-ˈtrɑː-/ *n* [U] **1** the separation of a liquid into its chemical parts by passing electricity through it from an ANODE to a CATHODE **2** the destruction of hair roots by means of an electric current. Electrolysis is used to permanently remove unwanted hair on the legs, arms, and face, esp. by women: *You can have the hairs on your legs removed by electrolysis.*

e·lec·tro·lyte /ɪˈlektrəlaɪt/ *n* liquid, such as COPPER SULPHATE, which can be broken down into its chemical parts by passing electricity through it — **·lytic** /ˌlektrə'lɪtɪk◂/ adj

e·lec·tro·mag·net·is·m /ɪˌlektrəʊ'mægnᵻtɪzəm/ n [C] one of the four FUNDAMENTAL FORCES in the universe, caused by the movement and exchange of positively and negatively charged bits of matter in atoms — **~tic** /-mæg'netɪk◂/ adj

e·lec·tron /ɪ'lektrɒn‖-trɑːn/ n a very small piece of matter that moves round the NUCLEUS (=central part) of an atom and that by its movement causes an electric current in metal. It carries a negative charge (CHARGE² (8)) —see also NEUTRON, PROTON

el·ec·tron·ic /ɪˌlek'trɒnɪk, ˌelɪk'trɒnɪk◂‖-'trɑː-/ adj 1 using CHIPS, TRANSISTORS, or VALVES which have an effect on the electricity going through a piece of equipment, for example a radio, television or computer 2 using electronic equipment: *electronic warfare | electronic music | a factory that makes electronic components | I don't understand all this electronic wizardry that goes into making a computer.* —compare ELECTRIC (1), ELECTRICAL — **~ally** /kli/ adv

electronic funds trans·fer /ˌ···· '· ˌ··/ n [U] a system of moving money from one place to another very safely and quickly by computer, used internationally by banks, shops, etc.

electronic mail /ˌ···· '·/ also **e-mail**— n [U] an electronic system which joins a group of computers, allowing people to send messages to each other on their computers

el·ec·tron·ics /ɪˌlek'trɒnɪks, ˌelɪk- ‖ -'trɑː-/ n [U] the study or making of apparatus that works electronically: *She works in electronics/in the electronics industry.*

electronic tag·ging /ˌ···· '··/ n [U] a way of punishing people who have committed crimes that are not very serious. The criminal is allowed to go home, but has a special band (**electronic tag**) containing electronic equipment around their wrist or ANKLE so that the police can always know where they are

electron mi·cro·scope /·ˌ·· '···/ n a microscope which uses a beam of electrons to make very small things large enough to see

e·lec·tro·plate¹ /ɪ'lektrəʊpleɪt/ v [T] to coat (an object) thinly with metal by using ELECTROLYSIS: *Are these spoons solid silver or electroplated?* —see also EPNS

electroplate² n [U] electroplated goods

electrostatic deposition analysis n see ESDA TEST

el·e·gant /'elᵻgənt/ adj apprec 1 having the qualities of grace and beauty; stylish: *an elegant woman | elegant clothes/manners | an elegant piece of furniture* —opposite **inelegant** 2 (of an idea) pleasingly neat and simple: *an elegant piece of reasoning* — **~ly** adv —**gance** n [U]

el·e·gi·ac /ˌelᵻ'dʒaɪək/ adj fml connected with elegies, esp. expressing sorrow for something that is lost: *His description of his youth at the end of the 19th century has an elegiac quality.* — **~ally** /kli/ adv

el·e·gy /'elᵻdʒi/ n a poem or song written to show sorrow for the dead or for something lost

el·e·ment /'elᵻmənt/ n 1 [C] any of more than a hundred simple substances that consist of atoms of only one kind and that, alone or in combination, make up all substances: *Both hydrogen and oxygen are elements, but water, which is formed when they combine, is not.* 2 [S+of] (a small amount of) a quality which can be noticed: *There is an element of truth (=some truth) in what you say. | The darkness and fog gave the attackers the element of surprise. | There's always an element of risk in this sort of investment.* 3 [C] a part of a whole; COMPONENT: *Honesty is an important element in anyone's character.* 4 [C] also **elements** pl.— a particular group of people, esp. people who are regarded with disapproval, within a larger whole: *There's a rowdy element in this class that seems determined to spoil things for the rest. | lawless elements in the crowd* 5 [C] the heating part of a piece of electrical apparatus: *The element of this electric kettle has broken.* 6 [C] old use any of the four substances earth, air, fire, and water, from which (it was formerly believed) everything material was made 7 **in/out of one's element** doing/not doing what one is happiest or best at doing —see also ELEMENTS

el·e·men·tal /ˌelᵻ'mentl◂/ adj of or like a great force of nature: *The storm struck with elemental fury.* —see also ELEMENTS (1)

el·e·men·ta·ry /ˌelᵻ'mentəri◂/ adj 1 simple and easy: *The question/answer is elementary.* Many people know and use Sherlock Holmes's phrase "Elementary, my dear Watson" when someone asks them a question which seems difficult except to them. 2 concerning or introducing the first and most simple part of something, esp. of education or an area of study: *some elementary English exercises for the learner* 3 PRIMARY¹ (2)

elementary par·ti·cle /ˌ····· '···/ n tech any of the 20 or more types of small pieces of matter (including ELECTRONS, PROTONS, and NEUTRONS) which make up atoms

elementary school /··'··· ˌ·/ also **grade school, grammar school**— n AmE a school at which elementary subjects are taught for the first six years of a child's education —see also extra information on page 408

el·e·ments /'elᵻmənts/ n [the+P] 1 the weather, esp. bad weather: *Shall we brave the elements and go for a walk?* (=in spite of the bad weather) —see also ELEMENTAL 2 [(of)] the first or most simple things one has to learn about a subject: *the elements of calculus*

el·e·phant /'elᵻfənt/ n -**phants** or -**phant** a very large animal with two TUSKs (long curved teeth) and a TRUNK (long nose) with which it can pick things up. People sometimes say, "Elephants never forget", because they are believed to have very good memories: *He's got the memory of/a memory like an elephant.* —see also PINK ELEPHANT, WHITE ELEPHANT

el·e·phan·tine /ˌelᵻ'fæntaɪn◂ ‖ -tiːn/ adj often humor heavy and awkward like an elephant: *The big fat man walked with slow elephantine steps.*

el·e·vate /'elᵻveɪt/ v [T] fml 1 to make finer, higher, or more educated: *Can't you read something more elevating than these silly romantic novels? | His elevated sentiments* (=fine and noble words) *were much admired by the audience.* 2 to raise to a higher rank or position: *He was elevated to the rank of captain.*

elevated rail·way /ˌ···· '··/ n a railway which runs on a kind of continuous bridge above the streets in a town. The elevated railway in Chicago is often called the **el** or **L**.

el·e·va·tion /ˌelᵻ'veɪʃən/ n 1 [U] fml the act of elevating or the state or quality of being elevated: *His elevation to the position of First Secretary was announced yesterday. | The elevation* (=fine and noble quality) *of her style is much admired.* 2 [S] height above sea-level: *Their house is at an elevation of 2000 metres.* —compare ALTITUDE (1) 3 [C] (a drawing, esp. done by an ARCHITECT, of) a flat upright side of a building: *This drawing shows the front elevation of the house.* —compare FACADE (1), PLAN¹ (3), SECTION¹ 4 [S] the angle made with the horizon by pointing a gun, etc.: *The cannon was fired at an elevation of 60 degrees.* —compare TRAJECTORY 5 [C] fml a hill; a high place

el·e·va·tor /'elᵻveɪtəʳ/ n 1 AmE ‖ **lift** BrE— an apparatus in a building for taking people and goods from one level to another. It is like a very small room, and moves up and down to each floor.: *I took the elevator to the 14th floor.* 2 a machine consisting of a moving belt with buckets, used for raising grain and liquids, unloading ships, etc. 3 a storehouse for grain 4 a movable part in the tail of an aircraft which makes it able to climb and descend — compare AILERON

elevator mu·sic /'···· ˌ··/ also **muzak** tdmk— n [U] AmE, infml, derog a type of music played in SUPERMARKETS, etc. which is supposed to be relaxing and not stop you thinking about other things

e·lev·en /ɪ'levən/ determiner, n, pron 1 (the number) 11 — see TABLE 1 2 [+sing./pl. v] BrE a team of eleven players in football, cricket, etc.: *The school football eleven is/are playing tomorrow.* — **~th** determiner, n, pron, adv

eleven-plus /·ˌ·· '·/ n [the+S] an examination for 11-year-old children used in Britain esp. before the introduction of COMPREHENSIVE education. The result of the examination decided whether a child went to a GRAMMAR SCHOOL or a SECONDARY MODERN school.

e·lev·en·ses /ɪ'levənzᵻz/ n [U] BrE infml coffee, tea, or a light meal, which is taken at about 11 o'clock in the morning

eleventh hour /·ˌ·· '·/ n [the] the very last moment: *War, which had seemed almost certain, was averted at the eleventh hour.*

elf /elf/ n **elves** /elvz/ a small fairy with pointed ears which is said to play tricks on people

Elf *tdmk* a French company which sells petrol in Britain: *There's an Elf garage on the ring-road.*

el·fin /ˈelfɪn/ adj of or like an elf: *her delicate elfin features*

El·gar /ˈelgɑːʳ/, **Sir Edward** (1857–1934) English COMPOSER of music for both instruments and voices, perhaps most famous for his *Enigma Variations.* He wrote the music for a PATRIOTIC song *Land of Hope and Glory.*

El·gin Mar·bles /ˌelgɪn ˈmɑːbəlz‖-ˈmɑːr-/ n [the + P] SCULPTURES from the Parthenon in Greece brought to England by the Earl of Elgin in 1803 and now in the British Museum. Many people now think that Elgin had no right to bring the sculptures to Britain, and that they should be returned to Greece.

El Grec·o /ˌel ˈgrekəʊ/ (about 1541–1614) a Spanish artist famous for his religious paintings. He was called El Greco, "the Greek", because he was born in Crete.

e·li·cit /ɪˈlɪsɪt/ v [T (from)] *fml* to succeed in drawing out (facts, information, etc.) from someone, esp. after much effort: *After much questioning, he elicited the truth (from the boy).* | *Their appeal for funds didn't elicit much of a response.* — ~**ation** /ɪˌlɪsɪˈteɪʃən/ n [U]

e·lide /ɪˈlaɪd/ v [T] to leave out the sound of (a letter or part of a word) in pronunciation: *We usually elide the "d" in "Wednesday".* —**elision** /ɪˈlɪʒən/ n [C;U]

el·i·gi·ble /ˈelɪdʒɪbəl/ adj **1** [F (for)] fulfilling the necessary conditions: *Is she eligible for maternity leave?* [+*to-v*] *Anyone over the age of 18 is eligible to vote.* **2** suitable to be chosen, esp. for marriage (esp. of a man): *an eligible bachelor* —compare MARRIAGEABLE —**bility** /ˌelɪdʒɪˈbɪlɪti/ n [U]

e·lim·i·nate /ɪˈlɪmɪneɪt/ v [T] **1** [(from)] to remove or get rid of completely: *Can we ever eliminate hunger from the world?* | *Our team was eliminated (from the competition) in the first round.* | *The police have eliminated all the other suspects* (=shown that they are not guilty), *so only one now remains.* | *This new process has eliminated the need for checking the products by hand.* **2** *infml* to murder —**nation** /ɪˌlɪmɪˈneɪʃən/ n [U (from)]: *Their elimination from the competition in the first round was a great surprise.* | *The police realized, by* **a process of elimination** (=by eliminating each possibility in turn until only one was left), *that the husband must have been the murderer.*

E·lim Pen·te·cost·al Church /ˌiːlɪm pentɪˈkɒstl ˌtʃɜːtʃ‖-ˈkɔːstl ˌtʃɜːrtʃ, -ˈkɑːstl-/ [*the*] a PROTESTANT church, one of the two main PENTECOSTAL churches in Britain. Many members of the Elim Pentecostal Church are of W Indian origin.

El·i·ot /ˈeliət/, **George** (1819–80) an English woman writer (real name **Mary Ann** or **Marian Evans**), among the greatest English NOVELISTS. Her books show learning, humour, and feeling, and deal with morality. They give a detailed picture of many different people at all levels of English country society. Her most famous book was *Middlemarch.*

Eliot, T S (1888–1965) English poet and writer of plays, born in the US, who won the 1948 NOBEL PRIZE for literature. His works include *The Cocktail Party, The Waste Land,* and *The Lovesong of J. Alfred Prufrock.*

e·lite /eɪˈliːt, ɪ-/ n [C+*sing./pl.* v] often derog a group that is of higher level or rank, e.g. professionally, socially, or in ability, or that has a great deal of power or influence in relation to its size: *The army was controlled by a small elite of officers.* | *She was chosen as one of the elite squad for the Olympic Games.* | *Only the educational elite go|goes to Oxford or Cambridge.*

e·lit·is·m /eɪˈliːtɪzəm, ɪ-/ n [U] *derog* (behaviour based on) the belief that there should be elites and that they deserve power, influence, special treatment, etc.: *It's sheer elitism to restrict these privileges to the management staff.* —**ist** adj, n

e·lix·ir /ɪˈlɪksəʳ/ n [(for)] *lit* something with a magical power to cure; PANACEA: *Don't imagine that lowering inflation is an elixir for all our economic ills.* | **the elixir of life** (=sthg. giving unending life)

E·liz·a·beth I /ɪˌlɪzəbəθ ðə ˈfɜːst‖-ˈfɜːrst/, **Queen** (1533–1603) a queen of England, daughter of HENRY VIII. She never married, and is thought of as a very strong woman. While she was Queen CATHOLICS were attacked and PROTES-

TANTS looked on favourably, the Spanish ARMADA was defeated, and MARY QUEEN OF SCOTS was murdered, but England became extremely powerful under her control. She is known for saying "I know I have the body of a weak and feeble woman, but I have the heart and stomach of a King..."

Queen Elizabeth I

Elizabeth II /ɪˌlɪzəbəθ ðə ˈsekənd/, **Queen** (1926–) the queen of Britain since 1952, married to the Duke of EDINBURGH. She has four children: Prince CHARLES, Princess ANNE, Prince ANDREW and Prince EDWARD. —see colour picture on page 752

E·liz·a·be·than /ɪˌlɪzəˈbiːθən◂/ n, adj (an English person) of or living in the period of Queen Elizabeth I of England: *Elizabethan drama* | *a famous Elizabethan* —see colour picture on page 227

elk /elk/ n **elks** or **elk** a very large European and Asian deer with very big flat ANTLERS (=branching horns), similar to the N American MOOSE

Elks /elks/ also the **Benevolent and Protective Order of Elks**— *fml* an organization for men with branches around the world but mostly in small towns and cities in the US: *Is your father an Elk?*

El·ling·ton /ˈelɪŋtən/, **Duke** (1899–1974) an American JAZZ musician who was a piano player, wrote music, and was leader of his own very successful big band. His many famous arrangements include *Mood Indigo* and *Sophisticated Lady.*

el·lipse /ɪˈlɪps/ n the curved shape that is seen when one looks at a circle sideways

el·lip·sis /ɪˈlɪpsɪs/ n -**ses** /siːz/ [C;U (of)] (an example of) the leaving out of a word or words from a sentence when the meaning can be understood without them: *There is an ellipsis of "was" in the following sentence: "In the accident the child was hurt and the mother killed."* (=was killed)

el·lip·ti·cal /ɪˈlɪptɪkəl/ also **el·lip·tic** /-tɪk/— adj **1** having the shape of an ellipse: *The Earth's path round the sun is elliptical.* **2** having the quality of ellipsis **3** *fml* (of speech or writing) difficult to understand because more is meant than is actually said: *an elliptical remark* — compare CRYPTIC — ~**ly** /kli/ adv

El·lis Is·land /ˈelɪs ˌaɪlənd/ a small island off New York City which for over 50 years (1892–43) was the first place in the US to which most people hoping to enter the US were taken: *He loved the American way of life from the moment he first set foot on Ellis Island.*

elm /elm/ n [C;U] (the hard heavy wood of) any of several large tall broad-leaved trees —see also DUTCH ELM DISEASE

el·o·cu·tion /ˌeləˈkjuːʃən/ n [U] the art of good clear speaking in public, with proper attention to the control of the voice and the making of the sounds. People sometimes take elocution lessons to rid themselves of a non-standard way of speaking.

e·lon·gate /ˈiːlɒŋgeɪt‖ɪˈlɔːŋ-/ v [T] to make (something) longer (in space but not time): *This picture you've painted isn't like me — the face is too elongated.* —**gation** /ˌiːlɒŋˈgeɪʃən‖ɪˌlɔːŋ-/ n [C;U]

e·lope /ɪˈləʊp/ v [I (with)] to run away secretly with the intention of getting married, usu. without parental approval: *She eloped with her lover.* | *She and her lover eloped.* — ~**ment** n [C;U]

el·o·quent /ˈeləkwənt/ adj **1** *apprec* able to express ideas and opinions readily and well, so that the hearers are influenced: *an eloquent speaker* | *an eloquent appeal for support for the strike* **2** *fml* expressing or showing something very strongly though without words: *These ruins are an eloquent reminder of the horrors of war.* — ~**ly** adv —**quence** n [U]

El Pas·o /el ˈpæsəʊ/ a city in W Texas in the US, on the Rio Grande —see colour map on pages 1374–5

El Sal·va·dor /el ˈsælvədɔːʳ/ a country in Central America, bordering on the Pacific Ocean; capital San Salvador; population 5,207,000 (1989)

else /els/ *adv* **1** (after question words and some PRONOUNS)
a besides; also: *I've said I'm sorry. What else* (=what more) *can I say?* | *Who else* (=which other person or people) *did you see?* | *Does anyone else want to look at this book?* | *I don't know the answer. You'll have to ask someone else.*
b apart from that; otherwise; instead: *Everyone else but me* (=all the other people) *has gone to the party.* | *It's not in the cupboard. Where else could it be?* | *She was wearing someone else's coat.* (=not her own) **2 or else: a** or otherwise; or if not: *You must pay £100 or else go to prison.* | *The book must be here, or else you've lost it.* **b** (used for expressing a threat): *Do what I tell you – or else!*

else·where /els'weə^r, 'elsweə^r‖'elsweər/ *adv* at, in, from, or to another place: *tourists from France, Italy, and elsewhere* | *They were dissatisfied with this supplier, and decided to take their business elsewhere.* (=to buy from somewhere else)

Els·tree /'elstri:/ *also* **Elstree Stu·di·os** /ˌ‥ '‥‥/ – a British film-making centre in N London started in the 1920s and popularly known as the British Hollywood although without such success

ELT /ˌiː el 'tiː/ *n* [U] *esp. BrE* English Language Teaching; the teaching of the English language to people whose first language is not English —compare EFL, TESOL

El·ton /'eltən/, **Ben** (1962–) a British writer and performer of ALTERNATIVE COMEDY

e·lu·ci·date /ɪ'luːsɪˌdeɪt/ *v* [I;T] *fml* to explain or make clear (a difficulty or mystery); CLARIFY: *I don't understand; could you please elucidate?* | *Can anyone elucidate the reasons for this strange decision?* **––dation** /ɪˌluːsɪ'deɪʃən/ *n* [U] **––datory** /ɪ'luːsɪˌdeɪtəri‖-dətɔːri/ *adj : a few elucidatory comments*

e·lude /ɪ'luːd/ *v* [T] **1** to escape from, esp. by means of a trick: *The fox succeeded in eluding the hunters by running back in the opposite direction.* **2** (of a fact, answer, etc.) to be difficult for (someone) to find or remember: *I remember his face, but his name eludes me for the moment.* (=I can't remember it) | *A cure for this disease has so far eluded scientists.*

e·lu·sive /ɪ'luːsɪv/ *adj* difficult to catch, find, or remember: *I've been trying to get her on the phone, but she seems to be rather elusive.* | *Despite all their efforts, success remained elusive.* | This word is used to describe the Scarlet Pimpernel, a character in the book of the same name who helped people escape from the French Revolution and who the French government could not catch. —see also SCARLET PIMPERNEL, **they seek him here, they seek him there**… (SEEK (6)) **– –ly** *adv* **– –ness** *n* [U]

elves /elvz/ *pl. of* ELF

El·vis /'elvɪs/ *also* **Elvis the Pel·vis** /ˌ‥‥ '‥‥/— see PRESLEY, Elvis

Elvis sight·ing /'‥ ‥‥/ *n AmE* a reported appearance of the dead singer Elvis Presley. These are usu. intended as humour, though a few people seem to think that he is still alive.

El·way /'elweɪ/, **John** (1960–) an American FOOTBALL (2) player who plays the position of QUARTERBACK

E·ly /'iːli/ a country town in the east of England with a famous CATHEDRAL and market

E·lys·i·an Fields /ɪˌlɪziən 'fiːldz‖ˌɪˌlɪʒən-/ [*the*+P] Elysium

E·lys·i·um /ɪ'lɪziəm‖ɪ'lɪʒiəm, -zi-/ *also* **Elysian fields**– *lit* a place or state of great happiness (from old Greek stories where Elysium was the place where good people went after their death)

em- see WORD FORMATION

'em /əm/ *pron infml or dial for* THEM: *Tell 'em what to do.*

e·ma·ci·a·ted /ɪ'meɪʃieɪtɪd/ *adj* extremely thin from hunger or illness: *By the time the prisoners were set free, they were terribly emaciated and could hardly walk.* —see THIN¹ (USAGE) **––ation** /ɪˌmeɪsi'eɪʃən/ *n* [U]

e-mail /'iː meɪl/ *n* [U] ELECTRONIC MAIL

em·a·nate /'eməneɪt/ *v*
emanate from sthg. *phr v* [T *no pass.*] *fml* (esp. of something nonmaterial) to come (out) from; ISSUE **from**: *Strange-smelling gases emanated from holes in the ground.* | *Do you know where these rumours emanated from?* **––nation** /ˌemə'neɪʃən/ *n* [C;U]: *strange-smelling emanations*

e·man·ci·pate /ɪ'mænsɪˌpeɪt/ *v* [T (**from**)] to make free socially, politically, or legally: *She's a very emancipated woman.* (=not limited by old-fashioned ideas about the position of women) | (fig.) *This new machine will emancipate us from all the hard work we once had to do.* **––pation** /ɪˌmænsɪ'peɪʃən/ *n* [U]: *the emancipation of slaves/women*

Emancipation Proc·la·ma·tion /‥‥'‥ ‥ˌ‥‥/ [*the*] the order by US President Abraham Lincoln on January 1, 1863, which ordered the end of slavery in the CONFEDERATE states during the American CIVIL WAR. This Proclamation was intended to weaken the Confederate states. Slavery was ended altogether soon after the Civil War by the **13th Amendment** to the CONSTITUTION.

e·mas·cu·late /ɪ'mæskjʊˌleɪt/ *v* [T *often pass.*] **1** to take away all the strength and effectiveness from; weaken: *The proposed reform has been emasculated by changes made to it by parliament.* **2** *med* to take away the power of becoming a father from; CASTRATE: (fig.) *There are still some men who feel emasculated if they work for a woman.* **––lation** /ɪˌmæskjʊ'leɪʃən/ *n* [U]

em·balm /ɪm'bɑːm‖-'bɑːm, -'bɑːlm/ *v* [T] to treat (a dead body) with special chemicals, oils, etc., in order to prevent it from decaying. Dead bodies are almost always buried or cremated (CREMATE) in Western society. In the US a body must by law be embalmed before it is buried. – ~er *n*

em·bank·ment /ɪm'bæŋkmənt/ *n* **1** a wide wall of stones or earth built to keep a river from overflowing its banks or to carry a road or railway over low ground **2** a slope of earth, stone, etc., that rises from either side of a railway or road

Embankment *also* **Thames Embankment**– **1** [*the*] a road in London on the N bank of the River Thames **2** an underground (=TUBE⁴) station on the Embankment – see colour map on page 817

em·bar·go¹ /ɪm'bɑːgəʊ‖-ɑːr-/ *n* **-goes** [(**on**)] an official order forbidding trade, esp. with another country: *They've put an embargo on the supply of oil to the enemy.* | *All imports are now under an embargo.* | *They're accused of trying to break the oil embargo.* —compare BLOCKADE¹, MORATORIUM

embargo² *v* **-goes, -going, -goed** [T] to put an embargo on

em·bark /ɪm'bɑːk‖-ɑːrk/ *v* [I;T] to go, put, or take on a ship: *We embarked at Southampton and disembarked in New York a week later.* | *The ship embarked passengers and wool at an Australian port.* —see TRANSPORT¹ (USAGE) **– –ation** /ˌemboː'keɪʃən‖-bɑːr-/ *n* [C;U]
embark on/upon sthg. *phr v* [T] to start (esp. something new): *It's late in life to embark on a new career.* | *The railways are about to embark on a major programme of modernization.*

em·bar·ras de ri·chesse /ɒmˌbærɑː də riː'ʃes‖ˌɑːmbɑː-/ *n* too much of something good, e.g. wealth or many nice things to choose from, so that it is difficult to decide what to do

em·bar·rass /ɪm'bærəs/ *v* [T *often pass.*] **1** to cause to feel anxious and uncomfortable, esp. in a social situation; make SELF-CONSCIOUS: *She was embarrassed when they kept telling her how clever she was.* | *It was so embarrassing when the children started laughing in the middle of the service.* | *a series of revelations that has embarrassed the government* **2** *fml* to cause to have difficulties with money: *financially embarrassed* (=having no money, or having debts) **– –ingly** *adv* **– –ment** *n* [C;U] : *He could not hide his embarrassment.* | *That rude child is an embarrassment to her parents.* (=she embarrasses them) | *Owing to my current financial embarrassment, I cannot pay the bill.*

em·bas·sy /'embəsi/ *n* (*often cap.*) (the official building used by) a group of officials, usu. led by an AMBASSADOR, who are sent by a government to live in a foreign country for the purpose of keeping good relations with its government: *the American Embassy in Moscow* —compare LEGATION

em·bat·tled /ɪm'bætld/ *adj* **1** surrounded by enemies: *Their embattled army finally surrendered.* **2** (of a person, company, etc.) continually troubled by annoying or harmful influences: *embattled companies fighting off takeover bids*

em·bed /ɪm'bed/ *v* **-dd-** [T (**in**)] to fix (something) firmly and deeply in a mass of surrounding matter: *He couldn't move the sword; it was firmly embedded (in the rock). | The arrow embedded itself in the door.*

em·bel·lish /ɪmˈbelɪʃ/ v [T (**with**)] **1** to make more beautiful by adding decorations; ADORN: *a white hat embellished with pink roses* —see DECORATE (USAGE) **2** to make (a statement or story) more interesting by adding untrue details – ~ **ment** n [C;U]

em·ber /ˈembəʳ/ n [*usu. pl.*] a red-hot piece of wood or coal from or in a fire that is no longer burning with flames

em·bez·zle /ɪmˈbezəl/ v [I;T] to steal (money that is placed in one's care): *The clerk embezzled £1000 from the bank where she worked.* – ~ **ment** n [U] **–zler** n

em·bit·ter /ɪmˈbɪtəʳ/ v [T *often pass.*] to fill with painful or bitter feelings; make sad and angry: *He was embittered by his many disappointments.*

em·bla·zon /ɪmˈbleɪzən/ also **blazon**– v [T+*obj*+**on, with**] **1** to decorate (a shield or flag) with a COAT OF ARMS: *a flag with the family arms emblazoned on it | a flag emblazoned with the family arms* **2** to show in a very noticeable way: *The manufacturer's name is emblazoned on the packet.* –see SPREAD (USAGE)

em·blem /ˈembləm/ n [(**of**)] an object which is regarded as the sign of something, e.g. of a country, a group, or an idea: *The national emblem of England is a rose.* – compare SYMBOL (1)

em·ble·mat·ic /ˌembləˈmætɪk◄/ adj [(**of**)] acting as an emblem: *The crown is emblematic of the power of a king.* – ~ **ally** /kli/ adv

em·bod·i·ment /ɪmˈbɒdɪmənt‖ɪmˈbɑ:-/ n [(*the*) S+**of**] someone or something that represents, includes, or is very typical of something: *The new factory is the embodiment of the very latest ideas. | He is the embodiment of evil.* (=is very evil)

em·bod·y /ɪmˈbɒdi‖ɪmˈbɑ:di/ v [T (**in**)] **1** to include; INCORPORATE: *The new car embodies many improvements. | Many improvements are embodied in the new car.* **2** *fml* to express (an idea, principle, etc.) in a real or physical form that can be seen or noticed: *The country's constitution embodies the ideals of freedom and equality. | She embodies her principles in her behaviour.*

em·bold·en /ɪmˈbəʊldən/ v [T] *fml* to give (someone) greater courage or the necessary courage to do something: *The protesters were emboldened by the fact that the police were unarmed. [+obj+to-v] She smiled, and this emboldened him to speak to her.*

em·bo·lis·m /ˈembəlɪzəm/ n med (something, such as a hardened mass of blood or an amount of air, which causes) a blocking of a tube which carries blood through the body

em·bos·omed /ɪmˈbʊzəmd/ adj [F + adv/prep] poet enclosed or surrounded: *a house embosomed in trees*

em·boss /ɪmˈbɒs‖ɪmˈbɔːs, -ˈbɑːs/ v [T] **1** to make a raised pattern on the surface of (metal, paper, leather, etc.): [+obj+**with**] *The firm's paper is embossed with its name and address.* **2** to produce (an address or a decoration) in a form raised above the surface of metal, paper, leather, etc.: *The paper bore an embossed heading.* | [+obj+**on**] *The name and address of the firm are embossed on its paper.*

em·brace¹ /ɪmˈbreɪs/ v **1** [I;T] to take and hold (someone or each other) in the arms as a sign of love: *She embraced her son tenderly. | The two sisters met and embraced.* **2** [T] *fml* to include or cover: *This course of study embraces every aspect of the subject. | an all-embracing course* **3** [T] *fml* to make use of or accept eagerly: *to embrace an opportunity* **4** [T] *fml* to become a believer in: *She embraced socialism/the Muslim faith.*

embrace² n an act of embracing: *They met in a tender embrace.*

em·bra·sure /ɪmˈbreɪʒəʳ/ n an opening in the thick wall of a fort or castle that gets either wider or narrower towards the outside

em·bro·ca·tion /ˌembrəˈkeɪʃən/ n [C;U] a liquid medicine used for rubbing a part of the body that is stiff or aching from exercise; it often smells very strongly —compare LINIMENT

em·broi·der /ɪmˈbrɔɪdəʳ/ v **1** [I;T (**with**)] to make a decorative needlework picture or pattern (on or of): *She sat embroidering to pass the time. | The dress was embroidered*

with flowers/in silk thread. | *I embroidered wild flowers and birds on the cloth. | an embroidered tablecloth* **2** [T (**with**)] to improve (a story or account of events) by adding details from the imagination; EMBELLISH

em·broi·der·y /ɪmˈbrɔɪdəri/ n **1** [C;U] (something made by) embroidering: *I did an embroidery of wild flowers and birds. | She's very good at embroidery.* **2** [U] imaginary details that are added to improve a story: *Just tell me the truth without a lot of embroidery!*

em·broil /ɪmˈbrɔɪl/ v [T (**in**) *often pass.*] to cause (oneself or another) to join in an argument or other difficult situation: *John and Peter were quarrelling, but Mary refused to get embroiled (in the argument).*

em·bry·o /ˈembriəʊ/ n **-os 1** the young of a creature in its first state before birth or before coming out of an egg — compare FOETUS **2 in embryo** still developing; incomplete: *The plans are still in embryo.*

em·bry·on·ic /ˌembriˈɒnɪk◄‖-ˈɑːnɪk/ adj in an undeveloped or very early state of growth

em·cee MC /ˌemˈsiː/ n AmE infml for MASTER OF CEREMONIES **emcee** v

e·mend /ɪˈmend/ v [T] to take the mistakes out of (something written) before printing —compare AMEND (1) – ~ **ation** /ˌiːmenˈdeɪʃən/ n [C;U]

e·mer·ald /ˈemərəld/ n [C;U] (the colour of) a bright green precious stone: *a ring set with emeralds | emerald green curtains*

Emerald Isle /ˌ··· ˈ·/ [*the*] *lit or humor* Ireland, so called because of the greenness of its country areas

e·merge /ɪˈmɜːdʒ‖-ɜːr-/ v [I (**from**)] **1** to come out or appear from inside or from being hidden: *The sun emerged from behind the clouds.* | (fig.) *Several interesting new poets have emerged in recent years.* **2** to become known, esp. as a result of inquiry: *Eventually the truth of the matter emerged.* [it+I+*that*] *It later emerged that the driver of the car had been drunk.* **3** to be in a particular condition following a (usu. difficult) event or experience: *The President has emerged from this incident with his reputation intact. | After the election, the socialists emerged as the largest single party.* **4** to become an independent nation no longer ruled by another country: *Sophisticated weapons systems are being sold to emerging nations.* – **emergence** n [U] : *The 1960s saw the emergence of many new nations.*

e·mer·gen·cy /ɪˈmɜːdʒənsi‖-ɜːr-/ n an unexpected and dangerous happening which must be dealt with at once: *Ring the bell in an emergency.* (=if there is an emergency) | *an emergency exit* (=for use in an emergency) | *The rioting grew worse and the government declared a state of emergency.* | *an emergency meeting of the leadership*

emergency room /·ˈ··· ·/ n AmE for CASUALTY (3)

e·mer·gent /ɪˈmɜːdʒənt‖-ɜːr-/ adj [A] in the early stages of existence or development: *the emergent nations of Africa*

e·mer·i·tus /ɪˈmerɪtəs/ adj [A; *after n*] (*often cap.*) (of a PROFESSOR or other university teacher) no longer holding office but keeping one's title; often used after RETIREMENT: *the emeritus professor of chemistry | She is Professor Emeritus of Latin.*

Em·er·son /ˈeməsən‖-mər-/, **Ralph Wal·do** /ræltf ˈwɔːldəʊ/ (1803–82) an American poet and writer who had great influence on the religious and PHILOSOPHICAL thought of his time

em·er·y /ˈeməri/ n [U] (*usu. in comb.*) powdered CORUNDUM (=a very hard mineral) which is used for polishing things and making them smooth: *She rubbed it with **emery paper**.* (=paper with emery stuck to it) | *He filed his nails with an **emery board**.*

e·met·ic /ɪˈmetɪk/ n, adj (something, esp. medicine) eaten or drunk to cause a person to bring up food from the stomach through the mouth: *If someone drinks poison, give them an emetic at once.*

EMF /ˌiː em ˈef/ abbrev. for: EUROPEAN MONETARY FUND

EMI /ˌiː em ˈaɪ/ n a large British CORPORATION which made electrical goods and records. It is now part of Thorn-EMI.

em·i·grant /ˈemɪgrənt/ n a person who emigrates —compare IMMIGRANT; see EMIGRATE (USAGE)

em·i·grate /ˈemɪgreɪt/ v [I (**from, to**)] to leave one's own country in order to go and live in another: *Her family*

emigrated to America in the 1850s. --**gration** /ˌemɪ-ˈgreɪʃən/ n [C;U]

▷ USAGE People who **emigrate** are **emigrants** from the country that they leave, and their action is called **emigration**: *A ship full of emigrants left Liverpool for Australia*. But from the point of view of the country they enter, the same people are **immigrants**, and their action is called **immigration**: *to pass through* **Immigration** *Control at the port*. To **migrate** is to move from one country to another for a limited period; the word is used especially of birds, and the action is called **migration**: *the spring* **migration** *of the wild ducks*.◁

ém·i·gré , **emigré** /ˈemɪgreɪ/ n Fr someone who leaves their own country, usu. for political reasons: *There were many Russian émigrés living in Paris at that time*.

em·i·nence /ˈemɪnəns/ n **1** [U] the quality of being famous and of a high rank, esp. in science, the ARTS, etc.: *She achieved/won eminence as a painter/a scientist*. **2** [C] *fml* a hill or piece of high ground

Eminence n (used when speaking to, or speaking about, a CARDINAL (=a priest with a high rank in the Roman Catholic church)): *Good morning, Your Eminence*. | *Their Eminences have met to discuss the matter*.

ém·i·nence grise /ˌemɪnɒns ˈgriːz/ n **éminences grises** (*same pronunciation*) Fr someone who secretly has great influence (e.g. over a king or government) but does not hold an official position of power

em·i·nent /ˈemɪnənt/ adj (of a person) famous and admired; DISTINGUISHED: *Even the most eminent doctors could not cure him*. —compare IMMANENT, IMMINENT; —see FAMOUS (USAGE)

eminent do·main /ˌ··· ·ˈ·/ n [U] AmE law the right of the government to take away private property from a person (usu. with payment) when there is a more important public use for it. For example, the government might wish to destroy houses in the path of a new road.

em·i·nent·ly /ˈemɪnəntli/ adv fml apprec very; perfectly: *Your decision was eminently fair/sensible*.

e·mir /eˈmɪər/ also **amir**— n a Muslim ruler, esp. in Asia and parts of Africa

e·mir·ate /ˈemɪr‚t‖ɪˈmɪər‚t/ n the position, state, power, lands, etc., of an emir

em·is·sa·ry /ˈemɪsəri‖-seri/ n fml a person who is sent with an official message or to do special work, often of a secret kind

e·mis·sion /ɪˈmɪʃən/ n [C;U] fml the act of emitting or something emitted: *the sun's emission of light* | *We've been receiving powerful radio emissions from a distant star system*.

emission stan·dards /·ˈ··· ‚·ˈ·/ n [P] a set of standards such as those agreed by the EC or the US to control the levels of TOXIC (=poisonous) waste produced by motor vehicles. Most people who want to protect the environment consider the emission standards to be a good idea.

e·mit /ɪˈmɪt/ v -tt- [T] fml to send out (heat, light, smell, sound, etc.); DISCHARGE¹ (2): *The chimney emitted a cloud of smoke*. | (fig.) *John emitted a few curses*.

Em·men·ta·ler , **-thaler** /ˈeməntɑːlər/ also **Swiss cheese** ‖ **Swiss cheese** AmE— n [U] a pale yellow hard cheese of Swiss origin with large holes and a not very strong taste

Em·mer·dale /ˈemədeɪl ‖ -ər-/ a popular British television SOAP OPERA about people who live on a farm in a small Yorkshire village

Em·my /ˈemi/ also **Emmys, Emmy A·ward** /ˈ··· ‚ɪ/— n an American prize given each year to a number of people whose work of various kinds in television is excellent. It takes the form of a STATUETTE: *Sir John Gielgud has won the first Emmy Award, the highest award of American television*. —compare OSCAR

e·mol·li·ent /ɪˈmɒliənt‖ɪˈmɑː-/ n, adj fml (something, esp. a medicine) which softens the skin and reduces pain when it is sore: *This is a powerful emollient against sunburn*. | (fig.) *His emollient words calmed the situation down*.

e·mol·u·ment /ɪˈmɒljᵿmənt‖ɪˈmɑːl-/ n fml money or other form of reward received for work of a professional kind: *Emoluments connected with this position include free education for your children*. —compare SALARY, FRINGE BENEFIT

e·mo·tion /ɪˈməʊʃən/ n **1** [C] any of the strong feelings of the human spirit: *Love, hatred, and grief are emotions*. | *His speech had an effect on our emotions rather than on our reason*. **2** [U] strength of feeling; excited state of the feelings: *She described the accident in a voice shaking with emotion*. – ~**less** adj – ~**lessly** adv

e·mo·tion·al /ɪˈməʊʃənəl/ adj **1** having feelings which are strong or easily made active: *He got very emotional when we had to leave, and started to cry*. —opposite **unemotional**; see also **tired and emotional** (TIRED) **2** (of words, music, etc.) causing or intended to cause strong feeling: *I hate this slushy emotional music they play when two people kiss in a film*. **3** [no comp.] connected with one's emotions and one's ability to control them: *The child's bad behaviour is the result of emotional problems*. – ~**ly** adv : *The child is emotionally disturbed*. | *Stop behaving so emotionally!*

e·mo·tion·al·is·m /ɪˈməʊʃənəlɪzəm/ n [U] the quality of feeling or showing too much emotion, and of allowing oneself to be controlled by it

e·mo·tive /ɪˈməʊtɪv/ adj causing strong feeling: *Capital punishment* (=killing criminals) *is a very emotive issue*. – ~**ly** adv

em·pan·el , im- /ɪmˈpænl/ v -ll- BrE ‖ **-l-** AmE— [T] fml to make (a JURY (=12 people who decide in court whether the prisoner is guilty)) by choosing from a list of people who are suitable to serve on it

em·pa·thy /ˈempəθi/ n [S;U (**with**)] the ability to imagine oneself in the position of another person, and so to share and understand that person's feelings: *As a rich and privileged person she has very little empathy with the people she claims to represent*. —compare SYMPATHY

em·pe·ror /ˈempərər/ **empress** fem.— n the ruler of an empire

Emperor's New Clothes /ˌ··· · ˈ·/, **The** the title of a story by Hans Christian Anderson in which an EMPEROR is tricked into paying a lot of money for some new clothes. The clothes do not exist, but the emperor is told that they are magic clothes which cannot be seen by stupid people. Not wanting to say he cannot see them himself, the emperor wears nothing in a public PROCESSION and everyone pretends to see and admire the clothes until a child shouts, "But he doesn't have anything on!" The idea is now often used to describe situations where there is really nothing there, but nobody will say this: *The quality of the product is a bit like the emperor's new clothes— there only in the advertising*. | *Is it a masterpiece or a classic example of the Emperor's New Clothes?*

em·pha·sis /ˈemfəsɪs/ n -ses /siːz/ [C;U (**on, upon**)] special force or attention given to something to show that it is particularly important: *Our English course places/lays/puts great emphasis on conversational skills*. | *a new economic policy, with a greater emphasis on reducing inflation* | *"You're not coming, are you?" he said, with great emphasis on "you're"*. (=he said the word slowly and loudly)

em·pha·size also **-sise** BrE /ˈemfəsaɪz/ v [T] to place emphasis on: *He thumped the table with his hand to emphasize what he was saying*. [+that] *I'd like to emphasize* (=to make this point very clearly) *that we are ready to meet the management at any time*.

em·phat·ic /ɪmˈfætɪk/ adj **1** done or expressed with emphasis; forceful: *She answered with an emphatic "No"*. | *an emphatic refusal* **2** clear and undoubted: *an emphatic victory*

em·phat·i·cally /ɪmˈfætɪkli/ adv **1** in a manner that shows emphasis: *"Certainly not," she said emphatically*. **2** most certainly: *I will emphatically not give my approval for this silly scheme*.

em·phy·se·ma /ˌemfᵻˈsiːmə/ n [U] a diseased condition in which the lungs become swollen with air, causing difficulty in breathing and often preventing the proper action of the heart

em·pire /ˈempaɪər/ n **1** (*often cap.*) a group of countries all ruled by the ruler or government of one particular country. A country which is ruled from another country is often called a COLONY: *The British Empire once covered large parts of the world*. **2** (esp. in business) a large organization or group of organizations: *He started off with one small factory, and now he's the head of a huge industrial empire*. | *Her* **empire building** *activities have* *included the purchase of several smaller companies.* – compare KINGDOM

Empire¹ [*the*] the BRITISH EMPIRE

Empire² *adj* **1** of or connected with the British Empire: *He thinks he's still living in the Empire days.* **2** of or connected with the second or esp. the first French Empire and esp. connected with the style of buildings, furniture, and high-waisted women's dresses typical of that time

Empire Day /ˈ·· ·/ a day when British schoolchildren were encouraged to think about being citizens of the British Empire. It was celebrated on 24th May, Queen Victoria's birthday, from 1902 until 1958, when Commonwealth Day was introduced in its place.

Empire State Build·ing /ˌ·· ˈ·ˌ··/ , also **Empire State—** [*the*] a building in New York City which has 102 floors and was for many years the tallest in the world —see colour map on page 1376

Empire State Building

em·pir·i·cal /ɪmˈpɪrɪkəl/ *adj* guided by or based on practical experience of the world we see and feel, not by ideas out of books: *We now have empirical evidence that the moon is covered with dust.* —**cally** /kli/ *adv*

em·pir·i·cis·m /ɪmˈpɪrɪˌsɪzəm/ *n* [U] the system of working by empirical methods

em·place·ment /ɪmˈpleɪsmənt/ *n* a special position prepared for a heavy gun or other piece of usu. military equipment to stand on

em·ploy¹ /ɪmˈplɔɪ/ *v* [T] **1** [(as)] to use the services of (a person or group) to perform work in return for pay; give a job to: *The firm employs about a hundred people/employs more women than men.* | *We employ her as an adviser.* | *The new contract will enable us to employ about 50 extra people.* [+obj+to-v] *We're employing a firm of architects to design a new extension.* —see also UNEMPLOYED **2** *fml* to use: *The police had to employ force to break up the crowd.* | *This bird employs its beak as a weapon.* **3 be employed in doing something** to be busy doing something: *The children were employed in building sandcastles.*

employ² *n* [U] *fml* employment: *She has fifty workers in her employ.* (=she employs them)

em·ploy·a·ble /ɪmˈplɔɪəbəl/ *adj* (of a person) suitable to be employed —opposite **unemployable**

em·ploy·ee /ɪmˈplɔɪ-iː, ˌemplɔɪˈiː/ *n* [(of)] a person who is employed: *a government employee* | *an employee of the government* | *The company has over 50 employees.*

em·ploy·er /ɪmˈplɔɪəʳ/ *n* a person or group that employs others: *The car industry is one of our biggest employers.*

em·ploy·ment /ɪmˈplɔɪmənt/ *n* **1** [U] the state of being employed: *The number of people in employment* (=who have jobs) *has fallen.* —opposite **unemployment** **2** [U] paid work: *looking for employment* **3** [U+of] *fml* the act of using: *Do you think the employment of force was justified?* **4** [C] *fml* a useful activity: *Gardening is a pleasant employment for a Sunday afternoon.*

Employment Act /·ˈ·· ˌ·/ [*the*] a set of laws made in Britain in 1989 in order to replace old laws which were unfair to women, and to encourage equal opportunities (OPPORTUNITY) for men and women in employment

Employment Ac·tion /·ˌ·· ˈ··/ a British Government programme to give jobs for a certain period to people who have not had a job for a long time

employment a·gen·cy /·ˈ·· ˌ···/ see RECRUITMENT AGENCY

employment ex·change /·ˈ·· ·ˌ·/ *n old-fash for* JOB CENTRE

Employment Train·ing /·ˈ·· ˌ··/ also **ET—** *n* [U] a British government programme in the 1990s for training people who have been unemployed for six months or more to help them get jobs

em·po·ri·um /ɪmˈpɔːriəm/ *n* **-riums** *or* **-ria** /riə/ *fml or humor* a large shop

em·pow·er /ɪmˈpaʊəʳ/ *v* [T+obj+to-v] *fml* to give (someone) the power or legal right to do something: *The new law empowered the police to search private houses.* —compare ENABLE, ENTITLE

em·press /ˈemprɪs/ *n* **1** a female EMPEROR **2** the wife of an EMPEROR

emp·ti·ly /ˈemptɪli/ *adv* in an EMPTY¹ (2) way

emp·ty¹ /ˈempti/ *adj* **1** containing nothing: *I see your glass is empty; can I fill it up?* | *There are three empty houses in our street.* (=no one lives in them) | *I won't have my children going to school* **on an empty stomach.** (=not having eaten anything) [F + of] *At this time of night the streets are empty of traffic.* **2** *derog* (of words, actions, etc.) without sense or purpose; meaningless, unreal, or insincere: *Her protest was an empty gesture; she knew it would have no effect.* | *empty promises/threats* —**tiness** *n* [U]

empty² *v* **1** [I;T (**of**, **OUT**)] to make or become empty: *They emptied the bottle.* (=drank or poured out all that was in it) | *The police made him empty (out) his pockets.* (=remove their contents) | *The room emptied very quickly.* | *to empty a bag of its contents* **2** [T+obj+adv/prep] to put by removing from a container: *He emptied the biscuits onto the plate.* | *They emptied the rubbish into plastic bags.* **3** [I (**into**)] to send or move its contents out: *The River Nile empties* (=flows) *into the Mediterranean Sea.*

empty³ *n* [*usu. pl.*] *infml* a container that has been emptied: *She took all the empties* (=empty bottles) *back to the shop.*

empty-hand·ed /ˌ·· ˈ··◂/ *adv* bringing nothing with one, esp. because no advantage or profit has been gained: *They came back from the negotiations empty-handed.*

empty-head·ed /ˌ·· ˈ··◂/ *adj infml* foolish and silly; completely lacking the power of serious thought or feeling

EMS /ˌiː em ˈes/ *abbrev. for:* EUROPEAN MONETARY SYSTEM

e·mu /ˈiːmjuː/ *n* **emus** *or* **emu** a large Australian bird which has a long neck and long legs but cannot fly

emu

EMU /ˌiː em ˈjuː/ *n* Economic and Monetary Union; the planned system for one economic plan and the same money for all the members of the EC

em·u·late /ˈemjʉleɪt/ *v* [T] **1** to try to do as well as or better than (another person): *His ambition was to emulate his mother and become a member of parliament.* (=she had been one) **2** (of computers and electronic equipment) to perform in the same way as (a different computer or piece of equipment): *Will this terminal emulate a VT220?* —**lation** /ˌemjʉˈleɪʃən/ *n* [U (**of**)]

e·mul·si·fi·er /ɪˈmʌlsɪfaɪəʳ/ *n* something added esp. to prepared food to keep liquids and solids from separating; a kind of food ADDITIVE

e·mul·si·fy /ɪˈmʌlsɪfaɪ/ *v* [T] *tech* to make into an emulsion

e·mul·sion¹ /ɪˈmʌlʃən/ *n* [C;U] **1** a creamy mixture of liquids which do not completely unite, such as oil and water **2** the substance on the surface of a photographic film which makes it sensitive to light **3** emulsion paint

emulsion² *v* [T] *BrE infml* to paint with emulsion paint

emulsion paint /·ˈ·· ˌ·/ *n* [C;U] *BrE* paint for walls and other surfaces inside buildings in which the colour is mixed into an emulsion and which is not shiny when it dries —compare ENAMEL, GLOSS PAINT

EN /ˌiː ˈen/ *abbrev. for:* ENROLLED NURSE

en- see WORD FORMATION

en·a·ble /ɪˈneɪbəl/ *v* [T] **1** [+obj+to-v] to make able; give the power, means, or right to do something: *This bird's large wings enable it to fly very fast.* | *The fall in the value of the pound will enable us to export more goods.* | *This dictionary will enable you to understand English words.* —compare EMPOWER, ENTITLE **2** to make possible: *an expansion programme that will enable a large increase in student numbers*

en·a·bling /ɪˈneɪblɪŋ/ *adj* [A] (of a law) making something possible or giving someone special powers: *Before these changes to the constitution can be made, the necessary* **enabling legislation** *will have to be passed.*

en·act /ɪˈnækt/ v [T] **1** to make into law: *Several bills* (=plans for laws put forward for consideration) *were enacted at the end of this session of Parliament.* **2** *fml* to perform (a play or a part in a play) — –**ment** n [C;U]

e·nam·el¹ /ɪˈnæməl/ n [U] **1** a glassy substance which is melted and put onto objects made of metal, glass, or clay and then hardens to form a decoration or protection **2** a paint which is used esp. on wood to produce a very shiny surface —compare EMULSION PAINT **3** the hard smooth outer surface of the teeth —see picture at TEETH

enamel² v -**ll-** *BrE* ‖ -**l-** *AmE*– [T] to cover or decorate with ENAMEL¹ (1,2)

e·nam·el·ware /ɪˈnæməlweəʳ/ n [U] metal pots and pans for cooking which are covered with ENAMEL¹ (1)

en·am·oured *BrE* ‖ **enamored** *AmE* /ɪˈnæməd‖-ərd/ adj [F+**of, with**] very fond of; liking very much; charmed: *He's so enamoured of his own plan that he won't even consider mine.* | *I'm not very enamoured of this new scheme.*

en bloc /ɒn ˈblɒk‖ɑːn ˈblɑːk/ adv *Fr* all together as a single unit: *The whole department resigned en bloc.*

en·camp /ɪnˈkæmp/ v [I;T *usu. pass.*] to make or place in a camp: *The army encamped there for the night.* | *The soldiers were encamped on the edge of the forest.* | (fig.) *The news reporters had encamped themselves outside my house and refused to go away until I agreed to speak to them.*

en·camp·ment /ɪnˈkæmpmənt/ n a large esp. military camp

en·cap·su·late /ɪnˈkæpsjʊleɪt‖-sə-/ v [T (**in**)] to express the main points or ideas of (something) in a short form or a small space: *I think this one sentence encapsulates her whole philosophy.* —-**lation** /ɪnˌkæpsjʊˈleɪʃən‖-sə-/ n [C;U]

en·case /ɪnˈkeɪs/ v [T (**in**) *often pass.*] to cover completely: *His body was encased in armour.*

en·chain /ɪnˈtʃeɪn/ v [T] *lit* to hold (as if) in chains

en·chant /ɪnˈtʃɑːnt‖ɪnˈtʃænt/ v [T] **1** [*often pass.*] to fill with delight; charm: *He was enchanted by/with the idea.* | *an enchanting child* **2** *lit or old use* to use magic on: *a palace in an enchanted wood* —see also DISENCHANTED

en·chant·er /ɪnˈtʃɑːntəʳ‖ɪnˈtʃæn-/ n a magician

en·chant·ment /ɪnˈtʃɑːntmənt‖ɪnˈtʃænt-/ n **1** [C;U] a delightful influence or feeling of delight: *The beauty of the scene filled us with enchantment.* **2** [C] *lit or old use* a condition caused by magic powers; SPELL³

en·chant·ress /ɪnˈtʃɑːntrɪs ‖ ɪnˈtʃæn-/ n **1** a woman of great sexual charm **2** a female magician

en·chi·la·da /ˌentʃɪˈlɑːdə/ n -**das** a Mexican food consisting of a TORTILLA that is filled with small pieces of meat, or cheese, etc., rolled up, and covered with a hot-tasting SAUCE

en·cir·cle /ɪnˈsɜːkəl‖-ɜːr-/ v [T] to surround; form a circle round: *Rebel forces had encircled the airport.* | *He encircled her in his arms.* | *The house was encircled by/with trees.* — –**ment** n [U]

en·clave /ˈenkleɪv, ˈeŋ-/ n a part of a country, or a group of people of a separate race or nation, which is completely surrounded by another

en·close /ɪnˈkləʊz/ v [T] **1** [*often pass.*] to surround with a fence or wall so as to shut in: *The garden is enclosed by a high wall.* **2** to put inside an envelope, esp. in addition to something else: *I enclose a cheque for £50 (with this letter).*

en·clo·sure /ɪnˈkləʊʒəʳ/ n **1** [C] an enclosed place: *There's a special enclosure where you can look at the horses before the race starts.* **2** [C] something put in an envelope with a letter **3** [U (**of**)] the act of enclosing or state of being enclosed: *The enclosure of public land meant that ordinary people could no longer use it.*

en·code /ɪnˈkəʊd/ v [T] to put (e.g. a message) into a CODE —opposite **decode**

en·co·mi·um /ɪnˈkəʊmiəm/ n -**miums** or -**mia** /miə/ *fml* an expression of very high praise; EULOGY

en·com·pass /ɪnˈkʌmpəs/ v [T] **1** to include or be concerned with (a wide range of activities, subjects, etc.); COMPRISE: *The course encompasses the whole of English literature since 1850.* | *a large company whose activities encompass printing, publishing, and computers* **2**

fml to surround completely: *The enemy encompassed the city.* | (fig.) *Doubts and fears encompassed her.*

en·core /ˈɒŋkɔːʳ‖ˈɑːŋ-/ n *Fr* **1** (used as a call for more, by listeners who have been pleased by a performance, esp. a musical one) **2** an additional or repeated performance given esp. by a musician at the end of a performance

en·coun·ter¹ /ɪnˈkaʊntəʳ/ v [T] *fml* **1** to meet or have to deal with (something bad, esp. a danger or a difficulty); be faced with: *We encountered a lot of problems/opposition.* **2** to meet unexpectedly: *She encountered a friend on the plane.*

encounter² n [(**with**)] **1** a sudden meeting, either unexpected or dangerous: *I had a* **close encounter** *with a poisonous snake.* **2** **close encounter of the** ... **kind** humor an experience of meeting or being very close to someone or something, esp. someone or something unusual (from the title of the film *Close Encounters of the Third Kind*): *I've just had a close encounter of the parliamentary kind—I met my MP.*

en·cour·age /ɪnˈkʌrɪdʒ‖ɪnˈkɜːr-/ v [T] **1** to make (someone) feel brave enough or confident enough to do something, by giving active approval: *You should encourage her in her attempts to become a doctor, instead of being so negative about it.* [+obj+to-v] *He encouraged me to apply for the job.* **2** to give active approval to; support; FOSTER (2): *It's in companies' interests to encourage union membership.* | *In their view, the benefit system just encourages laziness.* —opposite **discourage** — –**ment** n [C;U] : *Your words were a great encouragement to me.* | *I couldn't have done it without your encouragement.*

en·cour·aged /ɪnˈkʌrɪdʒd‖ɪnˈkɜːr-/ adj [F (**at, by**)] feeling new courage, hope, and confidence: *They were encouraged at/by the news.* [+to-v] *I was encouraged to hear you'll be giving us your support.*

en·cour·ag·ing /ɪnˈkʌrɪdʒɪŋ‖ɪnˈkɜːr-/ adj causing feelings of courage, hope, and confidence: *The latest trade figures are very encouraging.* | *It's encouraging that so many young players are coming into the team.* — –**ly** adv

en·croach /ɪnˈkrəʊtʃ/ v
    encroach on/upon sthg. *phr* v [T] to take more of (something) than is right, usual, or acceptable; INTRUDE upon: *His new farm buildings encroach on his neighbour's land.* | *Be careful not to encroach on her sphere of authority.* — –**ment** n [C;U (**on, upon**)]: *I resent all these encroachments on my valuable time.*

en·crust·ed /ɪnˈkrʌstɪd/ adj [F+**with, in**] completely covered with a large amount of: *She wore a gold crown encrusted with jewels.* | *His boots were encrusted in mud.*

en·cum·ber /ɪnˈkʌmbəʳ/ v [T (**with**)] *fml* to make action or movement difficult for; weigh down: *She was encumbered with heavy suitcases/with debts.* —-**brance** n : *These heavy suitcases are a great encumbrance.*

en·cyc·lic·al /enˈsɪklɪkəl/ n a letter sent by the POPE (=the head of the ROMAN CATHOLIC church) to all Roman Catholic BISHOPS

en·cy·clo·pe·di·a , -paedia /ɪnˌsaɪkləˈpiːdiə/ n a book or set of books dealing with every branch of knowledge, or with one particular branch, usu. in alphabetical order: *A dictionary deals with words and an encyclopedia deals with facts.* | *an encyclopedia of modern science*

Encyclopaedia Bri·tan·ni·ca /ɪnsaɪkləˌpiːdiə brɪˈtænɪkə/ [the] a very large encyclopedia with many VOLUMES, generally regarded by British and American people as being an excellent place to find information

en·cy·clo·pe·dic , -paedic /ɪnˌsaɪkləˈpiːdɪk◂/ adj apprec (of knowledge, memory, etc.) wide and full, like the contents of an encyclopedia

end¹ /end/ n **1** [C (**of**)] the point at which something stops or after which it no longer exists: *A rope has two ends.* | *Which end of the box has the opening?* | *We walked to the end of the garden/the road.* | *Have you reached the end of the story?* | *I started work at the end of August.* | *a successful end to the negotiations* | *The year is* **at an end**/*has* **come to an end.** (=has finished) | *Her story was a pack of lies* **from beginning to end.** | *If he passes the exam we'll* **never hear the end of it.** (=he will never stop talking about it) **2** [C] *a little piece left over: cigarette ends* —see also ODDS AND ENDS **3** [C] also **ends** pl.— *fml* an aim or purpose: *Does the end/Do the ends justify the means?* | *He wants to buy a house, and is saving money* **to that end.** | *She will stop at nothing to achieve her ends.* **4** [C] *infml* a particular part, e.g. of a business or activity: *My partner looks after the advertising end.* | *Let's hope that they keep their end of the bargain.* **5** [C *usu. sing.*] *euph* a person's death: *His end was peaceful.* —see also STICKY END **6** [*the*+S] *infml* (used as an expression of amused or weak disapproval): *Look at your dirty hands – you really are the (absolute) end!* **7 at the end of the day** when everything is considered; this expression is now used so frequently as to be almost meaningless: *At the end of the day, it's the government's responsibility to stop this sort of thing from happening.* **8 end to end** with the points or the narrow sides touching each other: *We can provide seats for ten people if we put these two tables end to end.* **9 in the end: a** at last; FINALLY: *He tried several times to pass the exam, and in the end he succeeded.* **b** when everything is considered: *In the end, I think one must blame these children's parents.* —see LASTLY (USAGE) **10 get/have one's end away** *infml, sl* to have sex: *He'll be hoping to have his end away.* **11 keep one's end up** *infml, esp. BrE* to go on facing difficulties bravely and successfully **12 living end** *AmE, infml* (used as an expression of strong approval or disapproval): *Well – isn't that the living end!* | *She really is the living end!* **13 make (both) ends meet** *infml* to get just enough money for all one's needs: *She scarcely earns enough money to make ends meet.* **14 no end** *infml* very much; very pleasingly: *Your latest book amused me no end.* **15 no end of** *infml* an endless amount of; very great deal of: *It caused me no end of worry.* **16 on end: a** (of time) without a break; continuously: *He sat there for hours on end.* **b** upright: *We had to stand the table on end to get it through the door.* **17 put an end to** to stop from happening or existing any more: *I'm determined to put an end to all these rumours.* **18 the end (of the world) is nigh** the world is going to end very soon; a phrase written on large boards carried in the street by religious people who want to warn others to lead better lives because they will soon die and be judged by God; often used humorously —see also BIG END, DEAD END, LOOSE END, SHARP END, TAIL END, BE-ALL AND END-ALL, **thrown in at the deep end** (DEEP), **the thick end of** (THICK¹), **get the wrong end of the stick** (WRONG¹)

end² *v* [I;T] **1** to (cause to) finish; come or bring to an end: *The party ended at midnight.* | *The war ended in 1975.* | *He ended his letter with good wishes to the family.* | *The news of their marriage ended weeks of speculation.* | *The story ends on a hopeful note.* **2 end it all** *euph* to kill oneself

▷ USAGE Compare **end** and **finish**. 1 When used transitively, **finish** is much more common than **end**: *Have you finished your work yet?* When used intransitively, **finish** is more informal than **end,** but **end** is commonly used in writing: *What time did the party finish?* | *The concert ended at 10 o'clock.* | *Their holiday ended in tragedy.* 2 **End** cannot be used with a verb ending in *-ing* in sentences like this: *Have you finished reading that book I gave you?*◁

end in sthg. *phr v* [T *no pass.*] to have as a result at the end: *The battle ended in victory.* | *Their marriage ended in divorce.*

end up *phr v* [L] to be in the end (in the stated place, condition, etc.): *He ended up (as) head of the firm.* | *We set off for Newcastle but ended up in Scotland.* [+*v-ing*] *We didn't like it at first, but we ended up cheering.*

en·dan·ger /ɪnˈdeɪndʒəʳ/ *v* [T] to cause danger to: *You will endanger your health if you work so hard.* | (*law*) *He was charged with possessing explosives with intent to endanger life.*

endangered spe·cies /·,·· ˈ··/ *n* a type of animal or plant which is in danger of becoming EXTINCT (=may soon disappear from the world): *As a result of widescale land drainage, the swallow-tail butterfly has become an endangered species.*

en·dear /ɪnˈdɪəʳ/ *v*
 endear sbdy. **to** sbdy. *phr v* [T] to cause to be loved or liked by: *His kindness endeared him to everyone.* | *His habit of playing loud music at night didn't endear him to the neighbours.*

en·dear·ing /ɪnˈdɪərɪŋ/ *adj* causing feelings of love or liking: *an endearing smile* – –**ly** *adv*

en·dear·ment /ɪnˈdɪəmənt‖ɪnˈdɪər-/ *n* [C;U] (an expression of) love: *He was whispering endearments to her.*

en·deav·our¹ *BrE* ‖ **-or** *AmE* /ɪnˈdevəʳ/ *v* [I+*to-v*] *fml or*

pomp to try: *I will endeavour to pay the bill as soon as possible.*

endeavour² *BrE* ‖ **-or** *AmE* – *n* [C;U] *fml or pomp* (an) effort: *They couldn't do it, despite their* **best endeavours.** (=they tried as hard as possible) | *The climbing of Mount Everest was an outstanding example of human endeavour.* [+*to-v*] *She made no endeavour/every endeavour to help us.*

en·dem·ic /enˈdemɪk, ɪn-/ *adj* (esp. of a disease) found regularly in a particular place: *This chest disease is endemic among miners in this area.* —compare EPIDEMIC, PANDEMIC

end game /ˈ· ·/ *n* the last stage in the game of CHESS, when most of the playing pieces have been taken from the board

end·ing /ˈendɪŋ/ *n* the end of a story, film, play, or word: *Children like stories with happy endings.*

en·dive /ˈendɪv‖ˈendaɪv/ *n* [C;U] **1** *BrE* ‖ also **chicory** *AmE*– a plant with curly green leaves which are eaten raw **2** *AmE* the white inner leaves of the CHICORY plant

end·less /ˈendləs/ *adj* **1** never finishing (esp. of something unpleasant); having or seeming to have no end: *The journey seemed endless.* | *I'm fed up with your endless complaining.* **2** *tech* (of a belt, chain, etc.) circular; with the ends joined: *The machine drives an endless belt.* – –**ly** *adv*

en·do·crine gland /ˈendəʊkrɪn, ˌɡlænd, -kraɪn-/ also **duct·less gland**– *n med* an organ of the body (such as the PITUITARY and THYROID GLANDS) which pours HORMONE*s* (=substances which start up processes in the body) into the blood for them to be carried round the body

en·dorse , in- /ɪnˈdɔːs‖-ɔːrs/ *v* [T] **1** to express approval or support of (opinions, actions, a person, etc.): *The committee's report fully endorses the government's proposals.* | *When the former President endorsed her candidacy, she knew she had a good chance of being elected.* **2** to write something, esp. one's name, on the back of (esp. a cheque) **3** [*usu. pass.*] *BrE* (of a court) to write a note on (a driving LICENCE) to say that the driver has broken the law – ~**ment** *n* [C;U] : *If you get any more endorsements you won't be allowed to drive.*

en·dow /ɪnˈdaʊ/ *v* [T] to provide (a hospital, college, etc.) with a usu. large amount of money that gives a continuing income
 endow sbdy. **with** sthg. *phr v* [T *usu. pass.*] *fml* to provide with (a good quality or ability) from birth: *She is endowed with both beauty and brains.*

en·dow·ment /ɪnˈdaʊmənt/ *n* **1** [C *usu. pl.*] *fml or humor* a quality that a person has; ATTRIBUTE: *His natural endowments are somewhat limited, and scarcely fit him for this post.* **2** [U] the act of endowing **3** [C *usu. pl.*] the money that an organization receives when it has been endowed

endowment mort·gage /·ˈ· ·· ,ˈ··/ *n* a MORTGAGE (=lending of money to buy a house) which is paid back by the money gained from an endowment policy

endowment pol·i·cy /·ˈ· ·· ,····/ *n* a type of insurance agreement by which a person pays money regularly over a number of years so that an agreed amount will be paid to them at the end of that time, or to their family if they die before then

end prod·uct /ˈ· ,··/ *n* something which is produced as the result of a number of operations, esp. industrial processes: *Our raw material is oil, and our end product is nylon stockings.* —compare BY-PRODUCT

en·due /ɪnˈdjuː‖ɪnˈduː/ *v*
 endue sbdy. **with** sthg. *phr v* [T] *fml* to fill (a person) with (a good quality): *endued with a spirit of public service*

en·dur·ance /ɪnˈdjʊərəns‖ɪnˈdʊər-/ *n* [U] the power of enduring: *Long-distance races are won by the runners with the greatest endurance.* | *The course is a real test of endurance.*

en·dure /ɪnˈdjʊəʳ‖ɪnˈdʊər/ *v* **1** [T] to bear (pain, suffering, etc.) patiently or for a long time: *They endured tremendous hardship on their journey to the South Pole.* [+*to-v*/*v-ing*] *I can't endure to see/endure seeing animals suffer like that.* **2** [I] *fml* to remain alive or in existence, esp. in spite of difficulty: *We can't endure much longer in this desert without water.* | *Her fame will endure for ever.* | *enduring fame* —see BEAR (USAGE) —**durable** *adj*

end us·er /ˈ· ,··/ *n* the person who actually uses a product:

These books are sold to schools, but the end users are the students.

end·ways /ˈendweɪz/ also **end·wise** /-waɪz/esp. *AmE*— *adv* **1** with the end forward; not sideways: *The box is quite narrow when you look at it endways (on).* **2** with the ends touching each other: *Put the tables together endways.*

en·e·ma /ˈenɪmə/ *n* **1** the putting of a liquid (such as medicine) into the bowels through their lower opening (the RECTUM) **2** an amount of liquid put in like this

en·e·my /ˈenəmi/ *n* **1** a person who hates and opposes another person; one of two or more people who hate and oppose each other: *He's a ruthless businessman and he's* **made** *a lot of* **enemies.** (=a lot of people hate him) | *John and Paul are enemies.* (=of each other) | (fig.) *Abraham Lincoln was the enemy of slavery.* (=fought against it) | *She's* **her own worst enemy.** (=stupidly does things that harm herself) **2** [+*sing.|pl. v*] (the armed forces of) a country with which one is at war: *The enemy had advanced and was|were threatening our communications.* | *enemy forces|missiles*

en·er·get·ic /ˌenəˈdʒetɪk◂/-ər-/ *adj* full of energy; very active: *an energetic tennis player* | *an energetic supporter of the peace movement* − ~ **ally** /kli/ *adv*

en·er·gize also **-gise** *BrE* /ˈenədʒaɪz/-ər-/ *v* [T] esp. *tech* to give energy to: *Food energizes the body.*

en·er·gy /ˈenədʒi/-ər-/ *n* [U] **1** the quality of being full of life and action; power and ability to do a lot of work or be physically active: *Young people usually have more energy than the old.* **2** also **energies** *pl.*− the power which one can use in working: *You'll need to apply|devote all your energy|energies to this job.* | *I didn't have the energy to disagree with her.* **3** the power which can do work, such as drive machines or provide heat: *atomic|electrical energy* | *The sun's energy* (=which keeps it burning) *will last for millions of years.* | *a cheap source of energy*

en·er·vate /ˈenəveɪt/-ər-/ *v* [T] *fml* to make weak; take away energy from; DEBILITATE: *He was enervated by his long illness.* | *I find this heat very enervating.*

en·fant ter·ri·ble /ˌɒnfɒn teˈriːblə/ ǀ ˌɑːnfɑːn-/ *n* enfants terribles (*same pronunciation*) *Fr* a shocking but also often interesting and amusing person: *the enfant terrible of the British film industry*

en·fee·ble /ɪnˈfiːbəl/ *v* [T often pass.] *fml* to make weak; cause to lose strength completely: *The country was enfeebled by war, drought, and disease.* − ~ **ment** *n* [U]

En·field /ˈenfiːld/, **Harry** (1961−) an English writer and COMEDIAN who writes for and appears in many successful radio and television programmes and who invented the character Loadsamoney −see also LOADSAMONEY

en·fi·lade /ˈenfɪleɪd, -lɑːd/ *v* [T] to shoot at with gunfire directed along the length of a line of soldiers in battle − **enfilade** *n*

en·fold /ɪnˈfəʊld/ *v* [T (in)] to enclose, esp. in one's arms: *She enfolded the child lovingly in her arms.*

en·force /ɪnˈfɔːs/-ɔːrs/ *v* [T] **1** to cause (a rule or law) to be obeyed or carried out effectively: *Governments make laws and the police enforce them.* **2** [(on, upon)] to make (something) happen, esp. by threats or force; IMPOSE: *They tried to enforce agreement with their plans.* − ~ **able** *adj* −opposite **unenforceable** − ~ **ment** *n* [U] : *The police are responsible for the enforcement of the law.*

en·forced /ɪnˈfɔːst/-ɔːrst/ *adj* made to be so by the way things happened; not able to be anything else: *He was shipwrecked on an uninhabited island and spent a year in enforced solitude.*

en·fran·chise /ɪnˈfræntʃaɪz/ *v* [T] **1** to give the right to vote at elections: *When were women enfranchised in Britain?* −opposite **disenfranchise** −see also FRANCHISE², SUFFRAGE **2** to free (a slave) − ~ **ment** /-tʃɪz-ǀ-tʃaɪz-/ *n* [U]

en·gage /ɪnˈgeɪdʒ/ *v fml* **1** [T] to attract and keep (the interest and attention) of (someone): *The new toy didn't engage the child|the child's attention for long.* **2** [I (**with**);T] to (cause to) fasten onto, fit into, or lock together with another part of a machine: *This wheel engages with that wheel and turns it.* | *When the two wheels engage the smaller one will start to turn.* | *She engaged the clutch and the car moved forwards.* −opposite **disengage** **3** [I (**with**);T] to begin to fight (with): *They engaged the enemy (in battle).* | *The two fleets engaged at dawn.* −opposite

disengage **4** [T (**as**)] esp. *BrE* to arrange to employ (someone): *I've engaged a new assistant|engaged him as my new assistant.* [+obj+to-*v*] *I've engaged a man to work as your assistant.* **5** [T] esp. *BrE* to order (a room, seat, etc.) to be kept for one: *I've engaged a room at the hotel.*
  engage in *phr v* [T] *fml* **1** (**engage in** sth.) to take part in: *Politicians should not engage in business affairs that might affect their political judgment.* **2** (**engage sbdy. in** sth.) to make (someone) join with one in: *While one of the robbers engaged the guard in conversation, the others crept into the factory.*

en·ga·gé /ˌɒngæˈʒeɪ/ ǀ ˌɑːngɑː-/ *adj* [F] *Fr* actively concerned with esp. political questions

en·gaged /ɪnˈgeɪdʒd/ *adj* **1** [(to)] having agreed to marry: *Our son is engaged (to a nice young woman).* | *Edward and I are engaged|have got engaged.* | *They're engaged to be married.* **2** [F (**in, on**)] busy; spending time on doing something: *"Can you come on Monday?" "No, I'm engaged."* (=I've arranged to do something) | *Come on Monday evening if you are not* **otherwise engaged.** (=doing something else) | *The company is engaged in a legal dispute with one of its suppliers.* **3** [F] *BrE* ǁ **busy** *AmE*− (of a telephone line) in use: *Sorry! The line|number is engaged.* | *I keep getting the engaged tone.* −see TELEPHONE (USAGE) **4** [F] (of a public TOILET) in use − opposite **vacant** (for (4))

engaged tone /·'· ·/ *BrE* ǁ **busy signal** *AmE*− *n* [often *the*] the sound one hears from a telephone when the person one has rung is already on the telephone to somebody else: *I keep getting the engaged tone.*

en·gage·ment /ɪnˈgeɪdʒmənt/ *n* **1** [C] an agreement to marry: *Have you heard that John has broken off his engagement to Mary?* (=said he no longer wishes to marry her)

▶ CULTURAL NOTE It is still the custom in Britain and the US for a man and woman who are going to marry to **get engaged.** They tell their family and friends, and may put a notice in the newspaper. Sometimes they have a party. The man usually gives the woman an engagement ring. There is usually a period of time between the engagement and the wedding for the two people to save money, find somewhere to live, make wedding plans, etc., and to be sure of their decision. ◀

2 [C] an arrangement to meet someone or to do something: *I can't see you on Monday because I have a* **previous|prior engagement.** (=one made at an earlier time) **3** [C] esp. *tech* a battle: *Although it was only a short engagement, a lot of men were killed.* **4** [U] the engaging (ENGAGE (4)) of parts of a machine

engagement par·ty /·'·· ˌ·ǃ/ *n* a party to celebrate an engagement. Guests usu. take a present which will be useful to the people getting married.

engagement ring /·'·· ·/ *n* a ring, usu. containing precious stones, esp. DIAMONDs, which a man gives to a woman when they decide to marry, and which she wears on the third finger of her left hand (the one to the left of the longest finger when you are looking at the back of your left hand) −see picture at RING

en·gag·ing /ɪnˈgeɪdʒɪŋ/ *adj apprec* charming: *an engaging smile* − ~ **ly** *adv*

En·gels /ˈengəlz/, **Frie·drich** /ˈfriːdrɪk, -ɪx/ (1820−95) a German political thinker and REVOLUTIONARY (=person active in trying to change the existing social and political system) who together with Karl MARX wrote *The Communist Manifesto* and helped to begin the political system of COMMUNISM. Although Engels and Marx worked together on their ideas, many people think that Marx alone was the father of Communism.

en·gen·der /ɪnˈdʒendər/ *v* [T] *fml* to produce or be the cause of (a state, feeling, etc.): *Racial inequality engenders conflict.*

en·gine /ˈendʒɪn/ *n* **1** a piece of machinery with moving parts which changes power from steam, electricity, oil, etc., into movement: *the engine of a car* | *a jet engine* | *engine trouble* **2** also **locomotive** *fml*− a machine which pulls a railway train **3** -**engined** /endʒɪnd/−having an engine or engines of the stated kind or number: *a twin-engined aircraft* (=having two engines) | *a diesel-engined car* −see also FIRE ENGINE

engine driv·er /'·· ˌ·/ *BrE* ǁ **engineer** *AmE*− *n* someone who drives a railway engine

Atlas

Pictures of Atlas usually show him carrying the world on his shoulders.

The Medusa

The Medusa was a terrible monster with snakes instead of hair who was so ugly that people changed to stone when they looked at her. She was killed by Perseus who cut off her head.

The Trojan Horse

During the Trojan War the Greeks hid inside a big wooden horse to trick their enemies into letting them inside the city of Troy. The trick was successful and once the horse was inside the city gates the soldiers jumped out and caught the Trojans by surprise.

Neptune

Neptune was the ancient Roman god of the sea and is usually shown carrying a special kind of long fork called a trident.

Eros

Eros was the Greek god of love and is usually shown carrying a bow and arrow. He was believed to shoot people with his arrows to make them fall in love.

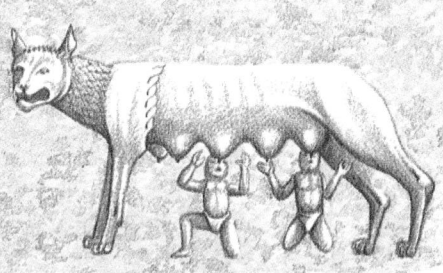

Romulus and Remus

According to legend, Romulus and Remus were twin brothers who were left by their parents to die until a wolf found them and looked after them. When they grew up they were supposed to have founded the city of Rome.

Adam and Eve in the Garden of Eden

David and Goliath
David kills Goliath, even though Goliath is much bigger and stronger than he is, and becomes a great hero.

God tells Adam and Eve that they must not eat apples from the Tree of Knowledge, but a serpent persuades Eve to take one and share it with Adam. As a punishment God makes them leave the Garden of Eden.

Moses and the Red Sea
God opens a way through the Red Sea so that Moses can lead the Israelites out of Egypt where they had been kept as slaves.

Jesus walks on the water
According to the Bible, Jesus did many things which other people could not do to show them that he was different from ordinary men.

Judas
Judas is paid thirty pieces of silver by the Roman to betray Jesus. He takes them to where Jesus is and shows them which man is Jesus by kissing h

engine

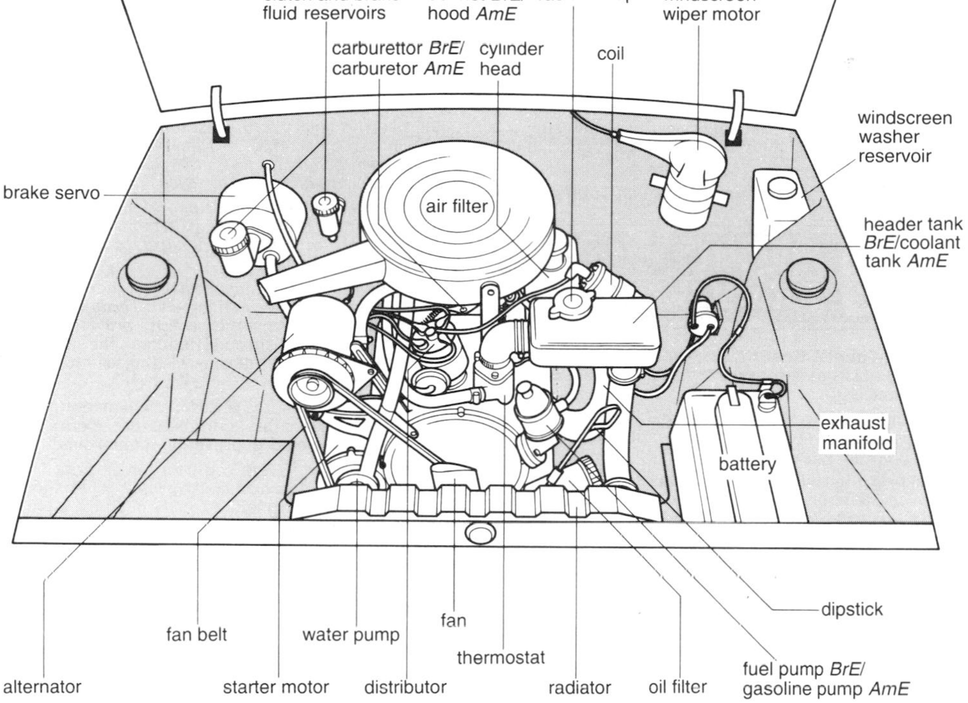

clutch and brake
fluid reservoirs

bonnet *BrE*/
hood *AmE*

radiator cap

windscreen
wiper motor

carburettor *BrE*/
carburetor *AmE*

cylinder
head

coil

windscreen
washer
reservoir

brake servo

air filter

header tank
BrE/coolant
tank *AmE*

exhaust
manifold

battery

dipstick

fan belt　　water pump　　fan　　thermostat

fuel pump *BrE*/
gasoline pump *AmE*

alternator　　starter motor　　distributor　　radiator　　oil filter

---

en·gi·neer¹ /ˌendʒɪˈnɪəʳ/ *n* **1** a person who is professionally trained to plan the making of machines, roads, bridges, electrical equipment, etc.: *an electrical/mechanical engineer* **2** a skilled person who controls an engine or engines, esp. on a ship: *the chief engineer* **3** *AmE for* ENGINE DRIVER

engineer² *v* [T] **1** to arrange or cause by clever secret planning; CONTRIVE: *He had powerful enemies who engineered his downfall.* **2** [often pass.] to plan and make as an engineer does: *This new jet engine is superbly engineered.*

en·gi·neer·ing /ˌendʒɪˈnɪərɪŋ/ *n* [U] the science or profession of an ENGINEER¹ (1): *She studied engineering at university.* | *an engineering firm* —see also CIVIL ENGINEERING

Eng·land /ˈɪŋɡlənd/ **1** the largest country in Britain; capital London —compare BRITAIN, UNITED KINGDOM and see colour map on page 818 **2 England expects that every man will do his duty** *quote* a phrase used by Lord Nelson to his men just before the Battle of Trafalgar. **3 England is a nation of shopkeepers** *quote* a phrase from a work by Napoleon Bonaparte **4 If I should die, think only this of me: That there's some corner of a foreign field That is forever England** *quote* part of the poem *The Soldier* by Rupert Brooke which is associated with a very ROMANTIC image of England **5 lie back and think of England** a phrase believed to have been used by Victorian teachers and mothers when they advised young women about what to do when their husbands had sex with them. The phrase is often used humorously now when something is happening to a person and they do not like it but have to accept it. **6 There'll always be an England** the title and first line of a PATRIOTIC song **7 this blessed plot, this earth, this realm, this England** *quote* a phrase from Shakespeare's play *Richard II* describing how beautiful England is

Eng·lish¹ /ˈɪŋɡlɪʃ/ *adj* **1 a** belonging to England, its people, etc.: *an English village* | *English history* | *My father is English, but my mother is Scottish.* **b** *infml* belonging to Britain, its people, etc. **2** of or related to English as a language: *English grammar*

English² *n* **1** [U] the language of Britain, the US, Australia, etc.: *Do you speak English?* | *She's Greek, but her*

English is excellent. | *How do you say that in English?* **2** [U] English language and literature as a subject of study: *She read* (=studied) *English at Oxford.* **3** [*the*+P] **a** the people of England: *The English are famous for liking tea.* **b** *infml* the people of Britain.

English break·fast /ˌ·· ˈ·◌/ *n* a breakfast usu. consisting of cooked BACON and eggs followed by TOAST and MARMALADE, eaten in England. When CEREAL or fruit or fruit juice and/or toast and marmalade are offered as well as bacon and eggs in a hotel, the meal is sometimes advertised as a **full English breakfast**. Although it is thought of as a typical English meal, few English people have English breakfast every day. —compare CONTINENTAL BREAKFAST

English Cham·ber Or·ches·tra /ˌ·· ˈ·◌ ˌ··◌/ [*the*] a CHAMBER ORCHESTRA based in London

English Chan·nel /ˌ·· ˈ·◌/ also **Channel** – [*the*] the piece of water between N France and S England. In order to reach the rest of Europe the British have always had to cross the Channel which makes them feel separate from the rest of Europe. With the opening of the CHANNEL TUNNEL (=a passage under the Channel), this may change. —see colour map on page 818

English Her·i·tage /ˌ·· ˈ·◌/ a British government organization which preserves places, buildings, which are important in English history, and encourages people to visit them —compare NATIONAL TRUST

English horn /ˌ·· ˈ·/ *n AmE for* COR ANGLAIS

En·glish·man /ˈɪŋɡlɪʃmən/ **En·glish·wo·man** /-ˌwʊmən/ *fem.*— *n* **-men** /mən/ **1** a British citizen born in England or of English parent(s) **2 an Englishman's home is his castle** *BrE saying* an English person's home is very important to them and they can do what they like there **3 mad dogs and Englishmen go out in the midday sun** *quote* a phrase from a song by Noël Coward

English Na·tion·al Bal·let /ˌ·· ˌ··· ˈ·◌ ‖ ˌ·· ˌ··· ·ˈ·/ [*the*] an English BALLET company which performs CLASSICAL and modern ballet

English Na·tion·al Op·er·a /ˌ·· ˌ··· ˈ··◌/ , **ENO** [(*the*)] an English OPERA company which performs operas in English at the London Coliseum

English Na·ture /ˌ·· ˈ·◌/ a British government organization responsible for the care of wild animals and plants in

England. Until 1991 the Nature Conservancy Council was responsible for this.

English Sheep·dog /ˌ·· ˈ··/ n AmE for OLD ENGLISH SHEEPDOG

English-Speak·ing U·nion /ˌ·· ·· ˈ··/ [the] an organization started in 1918 to advance the education of English-speaking people around the world. It arranges educational visits, courses, and meetings and supports English-language study to make international understanding easier.

the symbol for the English Tourist Board

English Tour·ist Board /ˌ·· ˈ·· ˌ·/ [the] an organization which exists to encourage tourists to go on holiday in England

Eng. Lit. /ˌɪŋ ˈlɪt/ abbrev. for English Literature; the study of great works of literature written in English: I've got an Eng. Lit. exam tomorrow.

en·grave /ɪnˈɡreɪv/ v [T] 1 to cut (words, pictures, etc.) on (wood, stone, or metal): [+ obj+on] His memorial was engraved on the stone. [+obj+with] The stone was engraved with his memorial. | (fig.) The terrible scene was engraved on his memory. 2 to prepare (a special plate of metal) in this way, for printing —see SPREAD (USAGE) —**graver** n

en·grav·ing /ɪnˈɡreɪvɪŋ/ n 1 [C] a picture printed from an engraved metal plate: I bought an old engraving of London Bridge. 2 [U] the art or work of an engraver

en·gross /ɪnˈɡrəʊs/ v [T (in) usu. pass.] to fill completely the time and attention of; ABSORB (2): I was so engrossed in my work that I completely forgot the time. | an engrossing book

en·gulf /ɪnˈɡʌlf/ v [T (in)] esp. lit (of the earth, the sea, etc.) to surround and swallow up: The stormy sea engulfed the small boat. | The house was engulfed in flames.

en·hance /ɪnˈhɑːns‖ɪnˈhæns/ v [T] to increase in strength or amount: Good secretarial skills should enhance your chances of getting a job. | Hopefully, the meeting will enhance the prospects of world peace. | computer-enhanced learning (=learning in which the student is helped or guided by a computer as well as by a teacher) — ~ **ment** n [C;U]

e·nig·ma /ɪˈnɪɡmə/ n a person, thing, or event that is mysterious and very hard to understand: No one could explain how the ship had suddenly disappeared — it was all a bit of an enigma. — ~ **tic** /ˌenɪɡˈmætɪk◂/ adj : an enigmatic person/smile — ~ **tically** /kli/ adv

en·join /ɪnˈdʒɔɪn/ v [T] 1 [(on)] fml to order (someone to do something or something to be done): He enjoined obedience on the soldiers. [+obj+to-v] He enjoined them to fight bravely for their country. 2 [(from)] esp. AmE to forbid; PROHIBIT

en·joy /ɪnˈdʒɔɪ/ v [T] 1 to get pleasure from (things and experiences); like: I enjoyed the film. [+v-ing] I enjoy going to the cinema. 2 fml to possess or use (something good): He has always enjoyed (=had) very good health. 3 **enjoy oneself** to be happy; experience pleasure: Did you enjoy yourself at the party? — ~ **ment** n [C;U] : I didn't get much enjoyment out of that book.

▷ USAGE In British English **enjoy** is always followed by a noun or a pronoun or by a verb with -ing: "Did you enjoy your holiday?" "Yes, I enjoyed it very much." | He enjoyed himself on holiday. | He enjoys travelling by train. Note that in American English the expression **Enjoy!** is sometimes used in informal speech with the meaning "enjoy yourself" or "have a nice time".◁

en·joy·a·ble /ɪnˈdʒɔɪəbəl/ adj (of things and experiences) giving pleasure: an enjoyable holiday —opposite **unenjoyable** —**bly** adv

en·large /ɪnˈlɑːdʒ‖-ɑːr-/ v [I;T] to (cause to) grow larger or wider: This photograph probably won't enlarge well. | The medical tests showed that he was suffering from an enlarged liver.

enlarge on/upon sthg. phr v [T] to add more length and detail to (a statement); ELABORATE: She only gave us the bare facts, so we asked her to enlarge on them.

en·large·ment /ɪnˈlɑːdʒmənt‖-ɑːr-/ n 1 [C] a photograph that has been printed in a larger size than the original: I'm sending mother an enlargement of the baby's photo. 2 [U] the act of or result of enlarging

en·light·en /ɪnˈlaɪtn/ v [T] to cause to understand deeply and clearly, esp. by making free from TRADITIONAL or false beliefs: Peter thought the world was flat until I enlightened him! | an enlightening experience

en·light·ened /ɪnˈlaɪtənd/ adj apprec showing true and deep understanding; wise, esp. in being free of false beliefs: enlightened opinions | The papers praised the judge's enlightened ruling.

en·light·en·ment /ɪnˈlaɪtənmənt/ n [U] 1 the act of enlightening or state of being enlightened: The tax laws are so complicated that only an expert can provide enlightenment. 2 (in Buddhism and Hinduism) the state of freedom from desire and suffering, leading to union with the spirit of the universe

Enlightenment n [the] the period in the 18th century in Europe, when certain thinkers taught that science and the use of reason would improve the human condition

en·list /ɪnˈlɪst/ v 1 [I;T] to (cause to) join the armed forces: He enlisted when he was 18. | We must enlist more men. 2 [I (in)] esp. BrE to join a course of study, a political group, etc., esp. by putting one's name on a list: I've enlisted in the Women's Studies course. 3 [T] to obtain (help, sympathy, etc.): They enlisted my support for the campaign to keep the hospital open. — ~ **ment** n [C;U]

enlisted man /ˌ·ˈ· ˈ·/, **enlisted wom·an** /ˌ·ˈ· ˈ··/ fem. — n AmE a person in the armed forces whose rank is below that of an officer

en·liv·en /ɪnˈlaɪvən/ v [T] to make more active, cheerful, or interesting: This otherwise dreary book is enlivened by some very amusing illustrations.

en masse /ˌɒn ˈmæs‖ˌɑːn-/ adv Fr all together; in a mass or crowd: The senior management resigned en masse.

en·mesh /ɪnˈmeʃ/ v [T (in) usu. pass.] to catch (as if) in a net: He was enmeshed in his own lies.

en·mi·ty /ˈenmɪti/ v [C;U] fml the state of being an enemy or feeling hatred for someone; HOSTILITY

En·nis·kil·len /ˌenɪsˈkɪlən/ a town in Northern Ireland where 11 people were killed by an IRA bomb on REMEMBRANCE DAY in November 1987

en·no·ble /ɪˈnəʊbəl/ v [T] 1 to make better and more honourable: Her character has been ennobled by all her sufferings. 2 to make (someone) a nobleman — ~ **ment** n [U]

en·nui /ɒnˈwiː‖ɑːn-/ n [U] Fr fml or lit tiredness and dissatisfaction caused by lack of interest and having nothing to do

E·no /ˈiːnəʊ/ also **Eno's** tdmk a powder that is mixed with water and drunk to cure stomach problems or to make the bowels empty more easily

ENO /ˌiː en ˈəʊ/ abbrev. for: the ENGLISH NATIONAL OPERA

e·nor·mi·ty /ɪˈnɔːmɪti‖-ɔːr-/ n 1 [C;U] fml (an act of) great wickedness: I don't think that even now he realizes the full enormity of his crime. 2 [U] the quality of being very great, esp. in difficulty; IMMENSITY: If I'd known the enormity of the task before I took it on, I wouldn't have attempted it.

e·nor·mous /ɪˈnɔːməs‖-ɔːr-/ adj extremely large: an enormous house/meal/amount of money — ~ **ness** n [U]

e·nor·mous·ly /ɪˈnɔːməsli‖-ɔːr-/ adv extremely: She's enormously rich. | It amused me enormously.

e·nough¹ /ɪˈnʌf/ determiner, pron [(for)] as much or as many as may be necessary: Have we got enough food? | Not enough is known about what really happened. | We have enough seats for everyone. [+to-v] She hasn't got enough to do. | Is there enough money/money enough (for us) to get a bottle of wine? | I've **had enough of** your rudeness! (=too much of it) | I've eaten **more than enough**. (=too much) | He said he would return the money, and I was fool enough/enough of a fool to believe him. (=so foolish that I believed him) | "I saw her coming out of his room with a guilty look on her face." "**Enough said**."

(=you have made your meaning clear and need not say more)

▷ USAGE 1 Enough comes after adjectives: *Are you sure he's old* **enough?** 2 **Enough** usually comes before a plural or uncountable noun: **enough** *people/money.* It can be used after the noun but this is rather formal or literary: *Ah! If only there were money* **enough** *for us to travel there!* 3 **Sufficient** has the same meaning as **enough,** but is more formal, and cannot come after a noun. —see also ADEQUATE (USAGE)◁

enough² *adv* **1** to the necessary degree: *I didn't bring a big enough bag.* | (in polite requests) *Would you be kind enough to let us know the date of your arrival?* | *Is it warm enough for you?* [+to-v] *He didn't run fast enough to catch the train.* **2** to a certain degree; quite; rather: *It's difficult enough, but it could have been worse.* | *It was natural enough that she should have been annoyed.* (=her annoyance was understandable) **3** **curiously/oddly/strangely enough** although this is CURIOUS/ODD/strange: *He's lived in France for years, but strangely enough he can't speak a word of French.* —see also **fair enough** (FAIR¹), **sure enough** (SURE²)

en·pas·sant /ˌɒn ˈpæsɒn‖ˌɑːn pɑːˈsɑːn/ *adv Fr fml* (used to introduce an additional remark, esp. about a different subject): *I would like to say en passant how useful I found your report.*

en·quire /ɪnˈkwaɪəʳ/ *v* [I;T] to INQUIRE —see ASK (USAGE)

en·qui·ry /ɪnˈkwaɪəri‖ˈɪŋkwaɪəri, ɪnˈkwaɪəri, ˈɪŋkwˌɹi/ *n* [C;U] INQUIRY

en·rage /ɪnˈreɪdʒ/ *v* [T] to make very angry; INFURIATE. *Her behaviour enraged him.* | *I was enraged to find they had disobeyed my orders.*

en·rap·ture /ɪnˈræptʃəʳ/ *v* [T] to fill with great joy or delight: *The beauty of her singing enraptured us.*

en·rich /ɪnˈrɪtʃ/ *v* [T] **1** to make rich: *The discovery of oil will enrich the nation.* **2** to improve the quality of, as by adding something: *Music can enrich your whole life.* | *This nuclear reactor works with enriched uranium.* | *a fertilizer that enriches the soil* – ~**ment** *n* [U]

en·rol *esp. BrE* ‖ **enroll** *esp. AmE* /ɪnˈrəʊl/ *v* -ll- [I;T (**as, in**)] to make (oneself or another person) officially a member of a group: *She decided to enrol in the history course at the local evening school.* – ~**ment** *n* [C;U]

Enrolled Nurse /ˌ·ˌ ˈ·/ *n* STATE ENROLLED NURSE

en route /ˌɒn ˈruːt‖ˌɑːn-/ *adv* [(**for, from, to**)] *Fr* on the way; travelling: *We were en route from London to New York.*

en·sconce /ɪnˈskɒns‖ɪnˈskɑːns/ *v* [T (**in**)] *fml or humor* to place or seat (esp. oneself) comfortably in a safe place: *He ensconced himself was ensconced in a big armchair in front of the fire*

en·sem·ble /ɒnˈsɒmbəl‖ɑːnˈsɑːm-/ *n* **1** a set of things that combine with or match each other to make a whole: *The coat, hat, and shoes make an attractive ensemble.* **2** [+sing./pl. v] a small group of musicians who regularly play together –compare ORCHESTRA **3** *tech* the quality of playing music in such a way that the notes are sounded properly together by all the players

en·shrine /ɪnˈʃraɪn/ *v* [T (**in**)] *fml* to put or keep (as if) in a SHRINE (=holy place): *These important rights are enshrined in the constitution.*

en·shroud /ɪnˈʃraʊd/ *v* [T (**in**) often pass.] *fml* to cover and hide: *Mist enshrouded the hills.* | *The hills were enshrouded in mist.*

en·sign /ˈensaɪn, -sən‖ˈensən/ *n* **1** a flag on a ship which acts as a special sign, esp. to show what nation the ship belongs to **2** an officer of the lowest rank in the US navy – see TABLE 3 **3** (in former times) an officer of the lowest rank in the British army **4** *esp. AmE* a small piece of metal or plastic with a picture or words on it, worn to show a person's rank

en·slave /ɪnˈsleɪv/ *v* [T] to make into a slave: *The captives were enslaved by the victorious army.* – ~**ment** *n* [U]

en·snare /ɪnˈsneəʳ/ *v* [T (**in, into**)] to catch (as if) in a trap: *He ensnared the old lady into giving him all her savings.*

en·sue /ɪnˈsjuː‖ɪnˈsuː/ *v* [I (**from**)] *fml* to happen afterwards, often as a result: *Serious fighting ensued.* | *Thousands were killed in the ensuing battle.*

en suite¹ /ˌɒn ˈswiːt◂‖ˌɑːn-/ *adj Fr* (of a room) leading off

another room; adjoining (ADJOIN). En suite is usu. used to describe a bathroom which is joined directly to a bedroom. It is considered to be a LUXURY to have an en suite bathroom and they are often mentioned in advertisements for hotels or houses for sale: *House for sale with four bedrooms, two with en suite bathroom.*

en suite² *n* **1** an en suite bathroom **2** a bedroom with a bathroom leading off it

en·sure *esp. BrE* ‖ **insure** *esp. AmE* /ɪnˈʃʊəʳ/ – *v* [T] to make (something) certain to happen: *a change in the law that will ensure fair treatment for people of all races* [+that] *If you want to ensure that you catch the plane, take a taxi.* [+obj(i)+obj(d)] *This medicine will ensure you* (=make certain that you get) *a good night's sleep.* —see INSURE (USAGE)

en·tail /ɪnˈteɪl/ *v* [T] **1** to make (an event or action) necessary; INVOLVE (2): *Writing a history book entails a lot of work.* **2** [(**on, upon**) *often pass.*] *law* (esp. in former times) to arrange that (one's property) will become the property of one's son or daughter or another named person after one's death, and may not be sold to anyone else: *The castle and the land are entailed on the eldest son.*

en·tan·gle /ɪnˈtæŋgəl/ *v* [T (**in, with**)] to cause to become twisted or mixed with something else: *The bird entangled itself in the net.* | *The sailor's legs got entangled with the ropes.* | (fig.) *He got himself entangled in some dishonest business dealings.* —opposite **disentangle** – compare ENTWINE, TANGLE¹

en·tan·gle·ment /ɪnˈtæŋgəlmənt/ *n* **1** [C;U] (an) act of entangling or becoming entangled: *He's had another of his entanglements with the law.* (=with the police) **2** [C *often pl.*] a fence made of BARBED WIRE, placed so as to make the advance of enemy forces difficult

En·teb·be /enˈtebi/ a town in S Uganda. It has an important international airport where in 1976 Israeli soldiers managed to free 91 passengers who were on a plane which had been hijacked (HIJACK) (= taken control of by force).

en·tente /ɒnˈtɒnt‖ɑːnˈtɑːnt/ *n Fr* a (formally declared) friendly relationship between two or more countries, which has less force than an ALLIANCE

Entente Cor·di·ale /ɒnˌtɒnt kɔːdiˈɑːl‖ɑːnˌtɑːnt kɔːr-/ *n Fr* an agreement between two or more countries (from the name of an agreement between Britain and France about foreign affairs in 1904)

en·ter /ˈentəʳ/ *v* **1** [I;T] *rather fml* to come or go in or into: *The thieves entered the building by the back door.* | *Knock before you enter.* | *Everybody stands up when the judge enters the court.* | *The talks have now entered their third week.* (=have already lasted more than two weeks) **2** [I (**for**);T] to declare one's intention of taking part (in): *Several of the world's finest runners have entered the race/entered for the race.* **3** [T (**for, in**)] to cause to take part: *She's entered her best two horses (in the race).* **4** [T] to become a member of (esp. a profession): *She entered politics/parliament at an early age.* **5** [T (**in**)] to cause to be included, in a store of information: *Is the word "yonks" entered in this dictionary?* | *To enter the data into the computer, you type it in then press the "Enter" key.* **6** [T (UP, **in**)] *fml* to write down (names, amounts of money, etc.) in a book: *You must enter the £5 you spent in the account book.* **7** [T] *fml* to make officially: *I have entered a complaint against you with the authorities.* | *The prisoner entered a plea of "not guilty".*

enter into sthg. *phr v* [T] **1** to allow oneself to share in or become part of: *He entered into the spirit of the game with great excitement.* **2** [*no pass.*] to have any important part in or influence on: *The money doesn't enter into it; it's the principle of the thing that I object to.* **3** *fml* to begin to take part in formally: *Before you enter into an agreement of this nature, you should read the contract carefully.*

enter on/upon sthg. *phr v* [T] *fml* to begin (esp. a job, a period of official duty, etc.): *The new teacher entered upon his duties in the autumn.*

en·te·ri·tis /ˌentəˈraɪtɪs/ *n* [U] a painful infection of the bowels

en·ter·prise /ˈentəpraɪz‖-ər-/ *n* **1** [C] a plan, course of action, etc., esp. one that is daring or difficult: *They have just embarked on their latest enterprise, which is to sail round the world in a very small boat.* **2** [U] willingness to take risks and do things that are difficult, new, or daring: *I admire their enterprise in trying to start up a new business.* **3** [C] an organization, esp. a business firm: *This company is one of the largest enterprises of its kind.*

▶ CULTURAL NOTE This word is often connected with the period of CONSERVATIVE government beginning in 1979, and esp. with the political ideas of Margaret Thatcher, the aims of which were to encourage people to open their own businesses and to depend less on the state. —see also FREE ENTERPRISE, PRIVATE ENTERPRISE◀

enterprise al·low·ance /ˈ··· ·ˌ··/ *n* an amount of money paid by the British government to specially chosen people who have started their own businesses after being UNEMPLOYED

Enterprise Al·low·ance Scheme /ˌ···· ·ˈ·· ·/ *n* [*the*] a British government plan established to encourage the unemployed to start their own businesses, but which has now been replaced by the Training and Enterprise Councils (TECS)

enterprise cul·ture /ˈ··· ·ˌ··/ *n* a national way of life in which the idea of starting and running private businesses is thought important —see ENTERPRISE (3)

enterprise e·con·o·my /ˈ··· ·ˌ···/ *n* an economic environment which is favourable to the establishment and development of businesses

enterprise so·ci·e·ty /ˈ··· ·ˌ···/ *n* a society which encourages people to start businesses and to look after themselves rather than expect the state to provide services

enterprise zone /ˈ··· ˌ·/ *n* (in Britain) a poor area of the country or a city in which the government tries to encourage new businesses to start up by offering them financial advantages. The idea is to bring new life to areas whose typical industries have disappeared.

en·ter·pris·ing /ˈentəpraɪzɪŋ‖-ər-/ *adj apprec* having or showing ENTERPRISE (2): *It's very enterprising of them to try and start up a business like that.* – – **ly** *adv*

en·ter·tain /ˌentəˈteɪn‖-ər-/ *v* **1** [T] to amuse and interest, esp. by a public performance; keep the attention of (people watching or listening): *The play failed to entertain its audience.* | *a very entertaining speech* **2** [I;T] to give a party (for); provide food and drink (for): *We're entertaining our neighbours this evening.* (=giving them a meal in our house) | *We don't do much entertaining.* **3** [T] *fml* to be ready and willing to think about or accept (an idea, doubt, suggestion, etc.); consider: *I wouldn't entertain such an outrageous idea.* – – **ingly** *adv*

en·ter·tain·er /ˌentəˈteɪnəʳ‖-tər-/ *n* a person who entertains professionally, e.g. by singing or telling jokes: *a popular television entertainer*

en·ter·tain·ment /ˌentəˈteɪnmənt‖-tər-/ *n* **1** [U] the act or profession of entertaining: *This law applies to theatres, cinemas, and other places of public entertainment.* | *Senior staff get an allowance for the entertainment of foreign visitors.* **2** [C;U] something, esp. a public performance, that entertains: *It's not a very serious film, but it's good entertainment.* | *this week's entertainments*

en·thral, **enthrall** *BrE* ‖ **enthrall**, **enthral** *AmE* /ɪnˈθrɔːl/ *v* **-ll-** [T] to hold the complete attention and interest of (someone) as if by magic; CAPTIVATE: *The little boy was enthralled by the soldier's stories of battles.* | *an enthralling book* – – **ingly** *adv*

en·throne /ɪnˈθrəʊn/ *v* [T] to mark the official beginning of the period of rule of (a king, queen, or BISHOP) by seating them on a THRONE (=official seat) – – **ment** *n* [C;U]

en·thuse /ɪnˈθjuːz‖ɪnˈθuːz/ *v infml* **1** [I (**about, over**)] to speak with or show enthusiasm: *She was enthusing about a film she'd just seen.* **2** [T] to cause to be enthusiastic: *a good teacher, who was always able to enthuse her students*

en·thu·si·as·m /ɪnˈθjuːziæzəm‖ɪnˈθuː-/ *n* [C;U (**for, about**)] a strong active feeling of interest and admiration: *She shows boundless enthusiasm for her work.* | *Among his many enthusiasms is a great fondness for Eastern music.* —**-astic** /ɪnˌθjuːziˈæstɪk◀ ‖ ɪnˌθuː-/ *adj* : *We explained our plans, and he was very enthusiastic (about them).* —**-astically** /kli/ *adv*

en·thu·si·ast /ɪnˈθjuːziæst‖ɪnˈθuː-/ *n* a person who is habitually full of enthusiasm, esp. for the stated thing: *a bicycling enthusiast*

en·tice /ɪnˈtaɪs/ *v* [T+*obj*+*adv*/*prep*/*to-v*] to persuade (someone) to do something (esp. something bad), by offering something pleasant: *He enticed her away from her husband.* | *The beautiful weather enticed me into the garden.* | *an enticing smell of cooking* —**ticingly** *adv* – – **ment** *n* [C;U] : *The enticements of the big city lured her away from her home and family.*

en·tire /ɪnˈtaɪəʳ/ *adj* [A] **1** with nothing left out; complete: *an entire set of Shakespeare's plays* | *She spent the entire day in bed.* **2** complete in degree; total: *I am in entire agreement with you.*

en·tire·ly /ɪnˈtaɪəli‖-ər-/ *adv* **1** completely; in every way: *I entirely agree with you.* | *We're not entirely happy about this.* (=we're rather dissatisfied) **2** only; not shared with others: *It's your fault entirely.*

en·tir·e·ty /ɪnˈtaɪərˌti/ *n* [U] *fml* completeness; wholeness: *He bought the collection in its entirety.* (=all of it)

en·ti·tle /ɪnˈtaɪtl/ *v* [T *often pass.*] **1** [(**to**)] to give (someone) the right to do something or have something: *This ticket entitles you to a free seat at the concert.* [+*obj*+*to-v*] *Only members of the company are entitled to use the facilities.* | *I think I'm entitled to know why I wasn't given the job.* (=I should be told) —compare EMPOWER, ENABLE **2** [+*obj*+*n*] to give (a title) to (a book, play, etc.): *The book is entitled "Crime And Punishment".* – – **ment** *n* [U] : *You've used up all your holiday entitlement.* (=all the days you are allowed to take)

en·ti·ty /ˈentˌti/ *n* something that has a single separate and independent existence: *After the war Germany was divided; no longer one political entity.*

en·tomb /ɪnˈtuːm/ *v* [T *often pass.*] *fml or lit* to put (as if) in a TOMB (=large grave); bury – – **ment** *n* [C;U]

en·to·mol·o·gy /ˌentəˈmɒlədʒi‖-ˈmɑː-/ *n* [U] the scientific study of insects —compare ETYMOLOGY —**-gist** /ˌentəˈmɒlədʒ̩st‖-ˈmɑː-/ —**-gical** /ˌentəməˈlɒdʒɪkəl ‖ -ˈlɑː-/ *adj, n*

en·tou·rage /ˈɒntʊrɑːʒ‖ˈɑːn-/ *n* [C+*sing./pl. v*] all the people who surround and follow an important person: *The president's entourage occupied six cars.*

en·trails /ˈentreɪlz/ *n* [P] **1** the inside parts of an animal, esp. the bowels **2** signs of what will happen in the future. In ancient times people used to kill an animal and examine its entrails as a way of knowing the future.

en·train /ɪnˈtreɪn/ *v* [I;T] *tech* to get or put into a train: *The soldiers entrained/were entrained as soon as they had come off the ship.*

en·trance¹ /ˈentrəns/ *n* **1** [C (**to**)] a gate, door, or other opening by which people enter a place: *Excuse me, where is the entrance to the cinema/the park?* —opposite **exit 2** [C] an act of entering: *She made an impressive entrance leading her two pet tigers.* | *The king doesn't make his entrance until the third scene of the play.* **3** [U] the right to enter; ADMISSION: *We were refused entrance because we weren't properly dressed.* | *a school entrance examination* (=which one must pass in order to become a pupil) | *How much is the entrance fee?*

▷ USAGE Compare **entrance** and **entry**. Both words can be used to mean the act of entering. However, **entrance** is used especially when talking about a ceremony or performance, or about the right to enter. Compare: *to make an entrance onto the stage* | *an entrance examination* | *Britain's entry into the EEC* | *"No entry"* (road sign).◁

en·trance² /ɪnˈtrɑːns‖ɪnˈtræns/ *v* [T *usu. pass.*] *apprec* to fill with great wonder and delight: *The children watched entranced as the circus animals performed.*

en·trant /ˈentrənt/ *n* [(**to**)] a person who enters a profession or a race or competition: *When did they start accepting women entrants to the civil service?* | *Entrants should send their competition forms in by the end of the month.*

en·trap /ɪnˈtræp/ *v* **-pp-** [T (**into**) *often pass.*] *fml* to catch as if in a trap; deceive or trick (into): *He was entrapped into making a confession by the clever questioning of the police.* – – **ment** *n* [U]

en·treat /ɪnˈtriːt/ *v* [T (**for**)] *fml* to beg or ask without pride very seriously; IMPLORE: *She entreated us for our help.* [+*obj*+*to-v*] *She entreated us to help her.* – – **ingly** *adv*

en·trea·ty /ɪnˈtriːti/ *n* [C;U] *fml* (an example of) entreating: *All our entreaties were in vain, and he was shot at dawn.*

en·tre·côte /ˈɒntrəkəʊt‖ˈɑːn-/ *n Fr* a high-quality cut of BEEF STEAK (= meat from cattle)

en·trée /'ɒntreɪ‖'ɑːn-/ n Fr 1 [C;U (**into**)] the right or freedom to enter or join: *His wealth gave him an|the entrée into upper-class society.* 2 [C] **a** *esp. BrE* a small meat dish, served after the fish and before the main dish in a formal dinner **b** *esp. AmE* the main dish of a meal

en·trench , **intrench** /ɪn'trentʃ/ v [T+*obj+adv/prep*] to establish (oneself) firmly in a particular place or position, so that one cannot easily be moved: *He entrenched himself behind his newspaper and refused to speak to her.* | *He's completely entrenched in his political views.* – ~ **ment** n [U]

en·trenched /ɪn'trentʃt/ adj 1 *often derog* (of rights, customs, beliefs, etc.) firmly established, often in a way that is unreasonable: *You can't shift her from her entrenched beliefs.* 2 (of a place that is being defended) protected by TRENCHes (=long deep ditches)

en·tre nous /ˌɒntrə 'nuː‖ˌɑːn-/ adv Fr between ourselves; in secret and not to be mentioned to anyone else: *I've heard – and this is strictly entre nous – that she's been promised his job when he leaves.*

en·tre·pre·neur /ˌɒntrəprə'nɜːr‖ˌɑːn-/ n a person who starts a company or arranges for a piece of work to be done, and takes business risks in the hope of making a profit – ~ **ial** adj : *entrepreneurial skills*

en·tro·py /'entrəpi/ n [U] *tech* a measure of the degree of disorder in a system, which takes into account the fact that disorder naturally increases with the passage of time **entropic** /en'trəʊpɪk, -'trɒ-‖-'trəʊ-, -'trɑː-/ adj

en·trust , **intrust** /ɪn'trʌst/ v [T] to give (someone) (something) to be responsible for: [+*obj*+**with**] *I entrusted you with the care of the child.* [+*obj*+**to**] *I entrusted the child to your care.*

en·try /'entri/ n 1 [C;U (**into**)] the act of coming or going in; ENTRANCE[1] (2): *Britain's entry into the war was not long delayed.* | *He was charged with trying to gain illegal entry into the building.* | *You mustn't drive up a street with a No Entry sign.* 2 [C] *esp. AmE* a door, gate, or passage by which one enters a place 3 [C;U] a piece of information that is written or included in a list, a book, etc.: *She made an entry in her diary to remind herself of the date.* | *The next entry in this dictionary is the word "entryism".* 4 [C] a person or thing taking part in a race or competition: *She's going to judge the entries in the children's painting competition.* | *Send in your entry forms before January 16th.* –see ENTRANCE[1] (USAGE)

en·try·is·m /'entri-ɪzəm/ n [U] *usu. derog* the practice of joining a political party in order to change its ideas and plans from inside

en·try·phone /'entrifəʊn/ n a telephone outside the door of a block of flats or offices which people use to talk to someone inside the building and to ask them to open the door and let them come in

en·try·way /'entriweɪ/ n AmE a passage by which one enters a place

en·twine /ɪn'twaɪn/ v [T (TOGETHER, **in**, **round**) *often pass.*] to twist together, round, or in: *They walked along with their fingers entwined (together).* | *The plant had entwined itself round the branches of the tree.* –compare ENTANGLE

E num·ber /'iː nʌmbər/ n a number, with the letter E in front of it, used on food containers in Britain to name particular chemicals known as FOOD ADDITIVEs that are in the food. In the US such substances are shown by their chemical names.: *For today's healthy lifestyle there's no more natural drink than tea. No artificial flavours, colours or E numbers.*

e·nu·me·rate /ɪ'njuːməreɪt‖ɪ'nuː-/ v [T] *fml* to name (things on a list) one by one: *He enumerated the reasons for his decision.* – –**ration** /ɪˌnjuːmə'reɪʃən‖ɪˌnuː-/ n [C;U]

e·nun·ci·ate /ɪ'nʌnsieɪt/ v 1 [I;T] to pronounce (words), esp. carefully and clearly; ARTICULATE: *An actor must learn to enunciate (his words) clearly.* 2 [T] *fml* to make a clear and reasoned statement about: *This theory was first enunciated by Von Kramm as long ago as 1860.* – –**ation** /ɪˌnʌnsi'eɪʃən/ n [U]

en·vel·op /ɪn'veləp/ v [T (**in**)] to wrap up or cover completely: *The building was soon enveloped in flames.* | *mountains enveloped in mist* – ~ **ment** n [U]

en·ve·lope /'envələʊp/ n 1 a flat paper container for a letter 2 [(**of**)] *fml or lit* anything that covers or surrounds: *an envelope of mist*

en·vi·a·ble /'enviəbəl/ adj 1 (of a quality, possession, etc.) very desirable: *The company has an enviable reputation for reliability.* | *It's not an enviable task, trying to get the two sides to reach an agreement.* –opposite **unenviable** 2 (of a person) making one feel ENVY – –**bly** adv

en·vi·ous /'enviəs/ adj [(**of**)] feeling or showing ENVY: *I'm very envious of your new job.* (=I wish I had a job like that.) –see JEALOUS (USAGE) – ~ **ly** adv – ~ **ness** n [U]

en·vi·ron·ment /ɪn'vaɪərənmənt/ n 1 [*the*+S] the natural conditions, such as air, water, and land, in which people, animals, and plants live: *new laws to prevent the pollution of the environment* –see also ECOLOGY 2 [C] the physical and social conditions in which people live, esp. as they influence their feelings and development: *Children need a happy home environment.* | *a well-planned modern factory that offers a pleasant working environment* –compare ENVIRONS, SURROUNDINGS – ~ **al** /ɪnˌvaɪərən'mentl◂/ adj : *The environmental effect of this new factory could be disastrous.* – ~ **ally** adv

Environmental Health Of·fi·cer /ˌ·ˌ···· '· ˌ···/ (*abbrev.* **EHO**) n a local government worker who works in the Environmental Health Service

Environmental Health Ser·vice /ˌ·ˌ···· '· ˌ·/ [*the*] a service which is provided by British local authorities (LOCAL AUTHORITY) to prevent the spread of illnesses and to provide services which keep the environment clean

en·vi·ron·men·tal·ist /ɪnˌvaɪərən'mentl-ˌst/ n a person who tries to prevent the ENVIRONMENT (2) from being spoilt – –**ism** n [U]

Environmental Pro·tec·tion A·gen·cy /ˌ·ˌ···· ·'·· ˌ···/ (*abbrev.* **EPA**) [*the*] an American government organization which works against POLLUTION

environment friend·ly /·ˌ···· '··◂/ , also **environmentally friend·ly** /···ˌ··· '··/– n not harmful to the ENVIRONMENT (2)

▶CULTURAL NOTE A recent increased interest in and understanding of the environment has resulted in a demand for products which do not harm it and which are then advertised as environment friendly.◀

environment sec·re·ta·ry /·ˌ··· ˌ····/ n a British governmental position established in the 1960s to control matters related to the environment

en·vi·rons /'envɪrənz, ɪn'vaɪərənz‖ɪn'vaɪərənz/ n [P (**of**)] *fml* the area surrounding a town: *Oxford and its environs are worth a visit.* –compare ENVIRONMENT

en·vis·age /ɪn'vɪzɪdʒ/ also **en·vi·sion** AmE /ɪn'vɪʒən/– v [T] to see in the mind as a future possibility; FORESEE: *It should be quite simple; I don't envisage any difficulty.* [+*v-ing/that*] *When do you envisage being able/that you will be able to pay me back?*

en·voy /'envɔɪ/ n a person who is sent as a representative, esp. by one government to do business with another government

en·vy[1] /'envi/ n [U (**at**, **of**, **towards**)] the feeling you have towards someone when you wish that you had their qualities or possessions: *They were full of envy/green with envy when they saw my new car.* | *Their beautiful garden is the envy of all the neighbours.* (=they all wish they had one like it) –compare JEALOUSY; see JEALOUS (USAGE), SEVEN DEADLY SINS

envy[2] v [T] to feel envy towards (someone) because of (something): *How I envy you; I wish I could make my hair curl like that.* | *I envy your ability to work so fast.* [+*obj(i)+obj(d)*] *I don't envy you your journey in this bad weather.*

en·zyme /'enzaɪm/ n a CATALYST (=a chemical substance) produced by certain living cells, which can cause chemical change in plants or animals or can make these changes happen more quickly, without being changed itself

e·on /'iːən/ n AEON

E111 /ˌiː treble 'wʌn/ n a European Community form which a person from one EC country fills in in order to obtain health care when they travel in other EC countries

E·os /'iːɒs‖-ɑːs/ see AURORA

EPA /ˌiː piː 'eɪ/ [*the*] *abbrev. for:* ENVIRONMENTAL PROTECTION AGENCY

ep·au·let , **-lette** /ˌepəˈlet/ n a decorative part on the shoulder of a uniform

epaulet

Ep·cot Cen·ter /ˈepkɒt ˌsentər‖ -kɑːt-/ [the] the Experimental Prototype Community of Tomorrow Center; a part of Walt Disney World in Orlando, Florida in the US, where visitors can see some of the machines and equipment which may be used in the future

é·pée /ˈepeɪ/ n a sharp-pointed stiff narrow sword, with a bowl-shaped guard for the hand, used in FENCING — compare FOIL³, SABRE (2)

e·phem·e·ral /ɪˈfemərəl/ adj lasting only a short time; TRANSITORY: *His success as a singer was ephemeral.* | *ephemeral fashions* — **rally** adv

ep·ic¹ /ˈepɪk/ n **1** a long poem telling the story of the deeds of gods and great men and women, or the early history of a nation: *"The Odyssey" is an epic of ancient Greece.* **2** a book, film, etc. (usu. a long one), that has some of the qualities of an epic: *a Hollywood epic about the Roman Empire*

epic² adj usu. apprec **1** (of stories, events, etc.) full of brave action and excitement, like an epic: *an account of their epic journey across the desert* **2** often humor unusually great: *To celebrate the victory, a banquet of epic proportions was held.*

ep·i·cen·tre BrE ‖ **-ter** AmE /ˈepɪˌsentər/ n tech the place on the Earth's surface which is just above the point inside the Earth where an EARTHQUAKE begins

ep·i·cure /ˈepɪkjʊər/ n a person who takes great interest in the pleasures of food and drink; GOURMET

ep·i·cu·re·an /ˌepɪkjʊˈriːən/ adj, n (being or typical of) a person who particularly enjoys the more delicate pleasures of the senses, esp. eating and drinking

Epicurean n, adj (a person) believing in or concerned with the teaching which states that pleasure is good and suffering is bad and should be avoided (It is named after the Greek thinker Epicurus (341–270 BC) who first developed this idea.) — compare STOIC, HEDONISM

ep·i·dem·ic /ˌepɪˈdemɪk◂/ n a large number of cases of the same infectious disease during a single period of time: *There has been an epidemic of cholera|a cholera epidemic in the city.* | (fig.) *There has recently been an epidemic of car stealing.* | *Violence is reaching epidemic levels in the city.* —compare ENDEMIC

ep·i·der·mis /ˌepɪˈdɜːmɪs‖-ɜːr-/ n [C;U] med the outside part of the skin

ep·i·dur·al /ˌepɪˈdjʊərəl◂‖-ˈduː-/ n med the putting of a substance into a patient's lower back with a needle to free them from pain, done e.g. to a woman who is giving birth

ep·i·glot·tis /ˌepɪˈɡlɒtɪs‖-ˈɡlɑː-/ n med a little shield at the back of the tongue, which closes to prevent food or drink from entering the lungs —see picture at RESPIRATORY

ep·i·gram /ˈepɪɡræm/ n a short clever amusing saying or poem: *My favourite epigram is "Everything I like is either illegal, immoral, or fattening".*

ep·i·gram·mat·ic /ˌepɪɡrəˈmætɪk◂/ adj expressed in a short clever amusing way: *her epigrammatic wit* — **ally** /kli/ adv

ep·i·lep·sy /ˈepɪlepsi/ n [U] an illness of the brain which causes sudden attacks of uncontrolled violent movement and loss of consciousness

ep·i·lep·tic /ˌepɪˈleptɪk◂/ adj, n (of, for, or being) a person who suffers from epilepsy: *He had an epileptic fit.* | *an epileptic child*

ep·i·logue ‖also **-log** AmE /ˈepɪlɒɡ‖-lɔːɡ, -lɑːɡ/ n **1** the last part of a piece of literature which finishes it off, esp. a speech made by one of the actors at the end of a play — compare PROLOGUE (1) **2** a short religious broadcast at the end of a day's broadcasting

E·piph·a·ny /ɪˈpɪfəni/ n [the] Feast of the Epiphany, a Christian holy day on January 6th, in memory of the coming of the three kings from the East to see the baby Jesus

e·pis·co·pa·cy /ɪˈpɪskəpəsi/ also **e·pis·co·pate** /ɪˈpɪskəpət/ —n [U] fml **1** the rank or period of office of a BISHOP (=a high official and priest of the Christian church) **2** [+sing.|pl. v] all the BISHOPS

e·pis·co·pal /ɪˈpɪskəpəl/ adj **1** fml of a BISHOP **2** (often cap.) (of a church) governed by BISHOPS (esp. in the phrase **the Episcopal Church**)

Episcopal Church /ˌ···· ˈ·/ also **Protestant Episcopal Church**— [the] a church in the US which developed from the Anglican Church (Church of England) and was established after the AMERICAN REVOLUTION. Since 1976 both men and women in the Episcopal Church have been allowed to become priests.

e·pis·co·pa·li·an /ɪˌpɪskəˈpeɪliən◂/ n, adj (often cap.) (a member) of an episcopal church

ep·i·sode /ˈepɪsəʊd/ n **1** a particular event which is separate, but also forms part of a larger whole: *It was one of the funniest episodes in my life.* **2** a single broadcast that is one of a continuous set telling a story: *In the final episode we will find out who did the murder.*

ep·i·sod·ic /ˌepɪˈsɒdɪk◂‖-ˈsɑː-/ adj (of a story, play, etc.) made up of separate and usu. loosely connected parts: *The book is written in an episodic format.* — ~ **ally** /kli/ adv

e·pis·tle /ɪˈpɪsəl/ n fml or humor a letter, esp. a long and important one

Epistle n [often pl.] any of the letters written by the first followers of Christ, in the Bible: *St Paul's Epistle to the Romans*

e·pis·to·la·ry /ɪˈpɪstələri‖-təleri/ adj fml **1** of letters or the writing of letters **2** carried on by, or in the form of, letters

ep·i·taph /ˈepɪtɑːf‖-tæf/ n a short statement about a dead person, often written on a stone above their grave

ep·i·thet /ˈepɪθet/ n fml an adjective or descriptive phrase, esp. of praise or blame, used about a person: *The king was known as Alfred the Great, but in my opinion the epithet* (="Great") *was undeserved.*

e·pit·o·me /ɪˈpɪtəmi/ n [the+S+of] a thing or person that shows the stated quality or set of qualities to a very great degree; typical example: *His behaviour was the epitome of bad manners.*

e·pit·o·mize also **-mise** BrE /ɪˈpɪtəmaɪz/ v [T] to be typical of; be an epitome of: *This strike epitomizes what is wrong with industrial relations in this country.*

e plu·ri·bus u·num /eɪ ˌplʊərəbəs ˈuːnəm/ Lat one out of many, meaning a national government consisting of many states. This phrase appears on several American coins and on the Great Seal of the United States.

EPNS /ˌiː piː en ˈes/ n, adj electro-plated nickel silver; in Britain, a mark pressed on to goods such as knives, forks, and teapots, that are covered in a thin coat of silver rather than made of solid silver

e·poch /ˈiːpɒk‖ˈepək/ n a long period of time in the history of the Earth or of human society, esp. as marked by events or developments of a particular kind: *The first flight into space marked a new epoch in the history of mankind.*

epoch-mak·ing /ˈ·· ˌ··/ adj (esp. of an event) very important, esp. because it changes the way people live: *The steam-engine was an epoch-making invention.*

e·pon·y·mous /ɪˈpɒnəməs‖ɪˈpɑː-/ adj tech (of a character in literature) being the character after whom the stated book, play, etc., is named: *Hamlet is the eponymous hero of Shakespeare's play "Hamlet".*

e·pox·y res·in /ɪˌpɒksi ˈrezɪn‖ɪˌpɑː-/ n [U] an industrially-made RESIN that is used esp. as a glue

Ep·ping For·est /ˌepɪŋ ˈfɒrɪst‖-ˈfɔː-, -ˈfɑː-/ an area of woodland open to the public, N of London. It was formerly a royal hunting ground.

Ep·som /ˈepsəm/ a town in SE England where there is a famous RACECOURSE (=where horses race). Two of the best-known races run there are the DERBY and the OAKS.

Epsom salts /ˌ··· ˈ·/ n [U;P] a bitter colourless or white powder, used medically to empty the bowels

Ep·stein-Barr vi·rus /ˌepstaɪn ˈbaɪ ˌvaɪərəs ‖ -ˈbɑːr-/ also abbrev. **EBV**— [the] a VIRUS (=something which causes infectious illnesses in the body) which causes GLANDULAR FEVER

eq·ua·ble /ˈekwəbəl/ adj **1** (of a person) of even calm temper; not easily annoyed: *I like working with Mary because* *she has such an equable nature.* **2** (of temperature) without great changes; even and regular: *Britain has quite an equable climate; it seldom gets too hot or too cold.* —compare EQUITABLE —**bly** *adv* —**bility** /ˌekwəˈbɪlɪti/ *n* [U]

e·qual¹ /ˈiːkwəl/ *adj* **1** [(in, to, with)] (of two or more) the same in size, number, value, rank, etc.: *Cut the cake into six equal pieces.* | *Women demand equal pay for equal work.* (=equal to men) | *The two squares are equal in size; this one is equal to that.* | *The diplomats chose a neutral country so that they could meet* **on equal terms.** (=with neither side having an advantage) **2** [F+to] (of a person) having enough strength, ability, etc. (for): *Bill is quite equal to* (*the task of*) *running the office.* | *She had to give a speech to 3000 people, but she proved quite equal to the situation/occasion.* (=able to deal with whatever happened) —opposite **unequal** —see also EQUALLY **3 all men are created equal** *quote* from the American DECLARATION OF INDEPENDENCE **4 all animals are equal, but some are more equal than others** *quote* from *Animal Farm* by George Orwell, meaning that, although a TOTALITARIAN SOCIALIST state may say that all people are equal, in practice its leaders have a better life than other people

equal² *n* a person who is equal (to someone else or to oneself): *We should all be equals in the eyes of the law.* | *a boss who treats her staff as equals* —see also **first among equals** (FIRST²)

equal³ *v* -**ll**- *BrE* ‖ -**l**- *AmE* [*not in progressive forms*] **1** [L] (of a size or number) to be the same as: *"x=y" means that x equals y.* | *The year's sales figures up until October equal the figures for the whole of last year.* **2** [T (in, as)] to reach the same standard as: *None of us can equal her grace as a dancer.* | *Thompson today equalled the world record for the 400 metres.* (=ran as fast as the fastest ever time) | *Their ignorance* **is only equalled by** *their stupidity.*

Equal Em·ploy·ment Op·por·tu·ni·ties Com·mis·sion /ˌ·· ·ˌ··· ··ˈ··· ·ˌ··/ also **EEOC**— [*the*] an American government office that encourages employers to make jobs available to people without consideration of their race, religion, sex, age, etc.

e·qual·i·ty /ɪˈkwɒlɪti‖ɪˈkwɑːr-/ *n* [U] the state of being equal: *They are fighting for the equality of women.* (=for women to be equal with men) | *racial equality* | *equality of opportunity*

e·qual·ize also **-ise** *BrE* /ˈiːkwəlaɪz/ *v* **1** [T] to make equal in size or numbers: *A small adjustment will equalize the temperature in the two rooms.* **2** [T] to spread out evenly all through: *Our party's policy is to try to equalize the tax burden.* **3** [I] *esp. BrE* to reach the same total of points, etc. as one's opponents in sport: *England equalized a few minutes before the end of the match.* —**ization** /ˌiːkwəlaɪˈzeɪʃən‖-lə-/ *n* [U]

e·qual·iz·er also **-iser** *BrE* /ˈiːkwəlaɪzər/ *n* **1** *esp. BrE* a GOAL, point, etc. that makes one's total equal to that of one's opponents in sport: *England scored the equalizer a few minutes before the end of the match.* **2** something which makes things equal or balanced

eq·ual·ly /ˈiːkwəli/ *adv* **1** as (much); to an equal degree: *They're both equally fit.* | *They can both run equally fast.* **2** in equal shares: *They shared the work equally between them.* **3** (comparing two ideas) at the same time and in spite of that: *We must help people to find houses outside the city, but equally, we must remember that some city people want to remain where they are.*

equal op·por·tu·ni·ties /ˌ··· ··ˈ···/ *n* [P] the same chances of employment, level of pay, and other advantages to everyone, regardless of race, colour, or sex: *We believe in equal opportunities.* | *The council is an Equal Opportunities Employer.*

Equal Op·por·tu·nit·ies Com·mis·sion /ˌ··· ··ˈ··· ·ˌ··/ also **EOC**— [*the*] a British government body established in 1975 to make sure that men and women have the same chances in education and employment, and that they are treated fairly and equally by their teachers, employers, etc.

Equal Pay Act /ˌ·· ˈ· ·/ [*the*] a law in Britain which says that men and women should get equal pay for doing equal work, and should have the same conditions of employment

▶CULTURAL NOTE The law provides for equal pay for people doing the same or similar work and for 'work of equal value' but this is difficult to prove and women's pay is still lower on average. ◀

equal rights /ˌ·· ˈ·/ *n* EQUAL OPPORTUNITIES

Equal Rights A·mend·ment /ˌ·· ˈ· ·ˌ··/ —see ERA¹

eq·ua·nim·i·ty /ˌiːkwəˈnɪmɪti, ˌekwə-/ *n* [U] *fml* calmness of mind and temper, esp in difficult situations: *He received the bad news with surprising equanimity.*

e·quate /ɪˈkweɪt/ *v* [T (**with**)] to consider or make equal: *You can't equate passing examinations and being intelligent/with being intelligent.*

equation

$$x = \frac{-b \pm \sqrt{b^2 - 4ac}}{2a}$$

e·qua·tion /ɪˈkweɪʒən/ *n* **1** [C] a statement that two quantities are equal: *In the equation 2x+1=7, what is x?* | (fig.) *Most people believe the factory would provide more jobs but* **the other side of the equation** *is the pollution it would cause.* —compare FORMULA **2** [S;U] *fml* the state of being equal or equally balanced: *There is an equation between unemployment and rising crime levels.*

e·qua·tor /ɪˈkweɪtər/ *n* [*the*+S] (*often cap.*) an imaginary line drawn round the world halfway between its most northern and southern points (POLEs): *The nearer you get to the equator, the hotter it is.* —see picture at GLOBE

eq·ua·to·ri·al /ˌekwəˈtɔːriəl◂/ *adj* **1** of or near the equator: *the equatorial rain forest* **2** very hot: *an equatorial climate*

Equatorial Guin·ea /ˌ····· ˈ··/ a country in W central Africa consisting of a MAINLAND part and several islands; population 341,000 (1989); capital Malabo

e·quer·ry /ɪˈkweri, ˈekwəri‖ˈekwəri/ *n* a male official in a royal court, who goes about with and serves the king or a member of the royal family

e·ques·tri·an /ɪˈkwestriən/ *adj* of or including the riding of horses: *I always enjoy the equestrian events at the Olympic Games.*

equi- see WORD FORMATION

e·qui·dis·tant /ˌiːkwɪˈdɪstənt◂/ *adj* [F (**from**)] equally distant: *Rome is about equidistant from Cairo and Oslo.* | *Paris, Bordeaux, and Lyons are roughly equidistant.* (=the same distance from each other)

e·qui·lat·e·ral /ˌiːkwɪˈlætərəl◂/ *adj* (of a TRIANGLE) having all three sides equal —compare ISOSCELES, SCALENE and see picture at TRIANGLE

e·qui·lib·ri·um /ˌiːkwɪˈlɪbriəm/ *n* [S;U] **1** a state of balance between opposing forces, weights, influences, etc.: *Certain ear diseases can affect one's equilibrium.* | *We must try to keep the opposing economic forces in equilibrium.* **2** balance of the mind, emotions, etc.; EQUANIMITY

e·quine /ˈekwaɪn, ˈiː-/ *adj* of or like horses: *a long, equine face*

eq·ui·noc·tial /ˌiːkwɪˈnɒkʃəl◂, ˌe-‖-ˈnɑːk-/ *adj* (at the time) of the equinox: *equinoctial gales* (=strong winds at this time)

eq·ui·nox /ˈiːkwɪnɒks, ˈe-‖-nɑːks/ *n* either of the two times in the year (about March 21 and September 22) when all places in the world have day and night of equal length: *the vernal* (=spring) *and autumnal equinoxes* —compare SUMMER SOLSTICE, WINTER SOLSTICE

e·quip /ɪˈkwɪp/ *v* [T] -**pp**- **1** [(with, for)] to provide with what is necessary for doing something: *a well-equipped/poorly-equipped hospital* | *We can't afford to equip the army properly.* (=buy weapons, uniforms, etc., for it) | *They equipped themselves with a pair of sharp axes and set off for the forest.* **2** [(for)] to make able, fit, or prepared: *Your education will equip you for your future life.* [+obj+to-v] *Having anticipated the problems, I was well equipped to deal with the situation.*

e·quip·ment /ɪˈkwɪpmənt/ *n* [U] **1** the set of things needed for a particular activity, esp. an activity of a practical or technical kind: *She set up/tested all her equipment.* | *to* *install video equipment | fire-fighting equipment | The police found bomb-making equipment in the terrorists' hideout.* **2** *fml* the process of equipping

eq·ui·ta·ble /ˈekwᵻtəbəl/ *adj* fair and just: *an equitable division of the money* | *an equitable solution to the dispute* —opposite **inequitable**; compare EQUABLE **--bly** *adv*

eq·ui·ty¹ /ˈekwᵻti/ *n* [U] **1** *fml* the quality of being equitable; fairness: *They shared the work of the house with reasonable equity.* —opposite **inequity 2** (esp. in the legal systems of English-speaking countries) the principle of justice which may be used to correct a law when that law would cause hardship in special cases **3** the total owned by a company after what it owes has been taken away from the value

equity² *n* [*usu. pl*] *tech* an ordinary SHARE (=one of the equal parts into which ownership of a company is divided), on which no fixed amount of interest is paid: *the equities market* | *equity capital/investment*

Equity 1 the British trade union of actors and actresses. Entrance to the union is extremely difficult; but without a membership card (**equity card**) an actor or actress cannot work as a professional. **2** also **Actor's Equity Association** *fml*— the American trade union for actors and actresses who work in the theatre —compare AFTRA, SAG

e·quiv·a·lent¹ /ɪˈkwɪvələnt/ *adj* [(to)] (of time, amount, value, number, etc.) same; equal: *He changed his pounds for the equivalent amount in dollars.* | *Changing his job like that is equivalent to giving him the sack.* | *There is no exactly equivalent French tense to the present perfect tense in English.* **- ~ ly** *adv* **--lence** *n* [U]

equivalent² *n* [(of, to)] something equivalent: *Some American words have no British equivalents.* | *Change this money for gold or its equivalent in dollars.* | *A company car is the equivalent of an extra £2000 a year on your salary.*

e·quiv·o·cal /ɪˈkwɪvəkəl/ *adj* **1** (of words or statements) having a double or doubtful meaning; AMBIGUOUS **2** (of behaviour or events) questionable; mysterious —opposite **unequivocal - ~ ly** /kli/ *adv*

e·quiv·o·cate /ɪˈkwɪvəkeɪt/ *v* [I] *fml* to speak in an equivocal way on purpose to deceive people: *For goodness sake, answer yes or no, but don't equivocate!* **--cation** /ɪˌkwɪvəˈkeɪʃən/ *n* [C;U]

er /ɜːʳ, əʳ/ *interj* (used when one cannot decide what to say next): *And then he — er—er — just suddenly seemed to — er — disappear!*

e·ra /ˈɪərə/ *n* **1** a set of years which is counted from a particular point in time: *The Christian era is counted from the birth of Christ.* **2** a very long period of time in the history of the Earth or of human society, esp. as marked by events or developments of a particular kind: *The era of space travel has begun.*

ERA¹ /ˌiː aːr ˈeɪ/ [*the*] *AmE* Equal Rights Amendment; a suggested change to American law, intended to give women the same legal rights as men. Although the suggested law was passed (=agreed to) by CONGRESS, not enough states agreed in time for it to become a law.

ERA² *n* earned run average; in BASEBALL, a number which represents how often a PITCHER has allowed people to hit the ball and then make a RUN¹ (10)

e·rad·i·cate /ɪˈrædᵻkeɪt/ *v* [T] to put an end to (something bad or undesirable); get rid of completely: *to eradicate crime/disease/malaria/poverty* **--cator** *n* **--cation** /ɪˌrædᵻˈkeɪʃən/ *n* [U]

e·rase /ɪˈreɪz‖ɪˈreɪs/ *v* [T] *fml* to rub out or remove (something, esp. a pencil mark): (fig.) *Nothing can erase from her mind the memory of that terrible day.*

e·ras·er /ɪˈreɪzəʳ‖-sər/ *n esp.AmE* something that is used to erase marks, esp. a piece of rubber for erasing pencil marks

e·ra·sure /ɪˈreɪʒəʳ‖-ʃər/ *n* [C;U] *fml* (a place marked by) erasing

ere /eəʳ/ *prep, conj poet or old use* before: *I shall be gone ere morning/ere you return.*

e·rect¹ /ɪˈrekt/ *adj* **1** upright; standing straight up on end, not leaning over or lying down: *She held her head erect and her back straight.* **2** *med* (of the PENIS) in a state of ERECTION (3) **- ~ ly** *adv* **- ~ ness** *n* [U]

erect² *v* [T] **1** to fix or place (a solid thing which was lying

flat) in an upright position: *They erected their tent at the edge of the field.* **2** *fml* to build or establish (a solid thing which was not there before): *This monument was erected to Queen Charlotte.* (=in honour of the memory of Queen Charlotte)

e·rec·tile /ɪˈrektaɪl‖-tl/ *adj med* (of a part of the body, esp. the PENIS) able to fill with blood, which makes the part stand upright: *erectile tissue* (=flesh)

e·rec·tion /ɪˈrekʃən/ *n* **1** [U] the erecting or building of something: *The erection of the new hospital took several years.* **2** [C] something built or erected **3** [C;U] (an example of) the state of the PENIS when upright: *to get/lose an erection*

erg /ɜːg‖ɜːrg/ *n* a unit of work or ENERGY: *It takes about 350 ergs to lift a pin one inch.*

er·go /ˈɜːgəʊ‖ˈɜːr-/ *adv Lat, sometimes humor* (used for introducing the result of a reasoned argument) therefore

er·go·nom·ics /ˌɜːgəˈnɒmɪks‖ˌɜːrgəˈnɑː-/ also **biotechnology** *AmE*— *n* [U] the study of making the right working conditions, machines, and equipment for people to work most effectively **--ic** /ˌɜːgəˈnɒmɪk◂‖ˌɜːrgəˈnɑː-/ *adj* : *an ergonomic design* **--ically** /kli/ *adv*

E·rie /ˈɪəri/, **Lake** a lake between the US and Canada. It is one of the GREAT LAKES. —see colour map on pages 1374-5

Erie Ca·nal /ˌ‧‧ ‧ˈ‧/ [*the*] an artificial waterway in the American state of New York which connects Lake Erie and the Hudson River. Built in the early 19th century, the canal allowed trade between New York City and the states of the Midwest, which led to it being the subject of popular songs.

Er·iks·son , Ericsson /ˈerɪksən/, **Leif** /liːf/ (10th or 11th century) a Norwegian who is thought to have sailed to North America around the year 1000 and so is considered by some to be the first European to discover the New World

Er·i·tre·a /ˌerᵻˈtreɪə‖-ˈtriːə/ an area in Ethiopia in NE Africa which has been in a state of FAMINE (=lack of food) and war for many years **--trean** *n, adj*

ERM /ˌiː aːr ˈem/ *abbrev.* **1** *for:* EUROPEAN EXCHANGE RATE MECHANISM **2** *for:* EXCHANGE RATE MECHANISM²

er·mine /ˈɜːmᵻn‖ˈɜːr-/ *n* **ermines** *or* **ermine 1** [U] the white winter fur of the STOAT (=a small animal), often worn, esp. formerly, by people such as kings and noblemen

▶CULTURAL NOTE Ermine has always signalled wealth, and women esp. used to dream of owning an ermine coat, but now many people are against killing animals for their fur, and fur is out of fashion. **2** [C] (the name given in winter to) a STOAT◀

Er·nie /ˈɜːni‖ˈɜːr-/ the familiar name for a computer in Britain which picks the prize-winning numbers of PREMIUM BONDS. Ernie is the short form of the man's name Ernest and comes from the first letters of the words Electronic RANDOM Number Indicating (INDICATE) Equipment.

Ernst /eənst‖eərnst/, **Max** /mæks/ (1891–76) a German-born painter, well-known for his work in the fields of DADAISM and SURREALISM

e·rode /ɪˈrəʊd/ *v* [I;T (AWAY)] to wear or be worn away gradually, esp. by the slow action of water, wind, etc.: *The coast is slowly eroding (away).* | *The sea erodes the rocks.* | (fig.) *Jealousy is eroding our friendship.*

e·ro·ge·nous /ɪˈrɒdʒənəs‖ɪˈrɑː-/ *adj tech* (of a part of the body) sexually sensitive: *The female breasts are an* **erogenous zone.**

E·ros /ˈɪərɒs‖ˈerɑːs/ **1** the god of love in ancient Greek stories, known as CUPID in Roman stories. He is represented as a beautiful winged boy carrying a BOW³ and ARROWS. **2** *n* [U] sexual love **3** a STATUE (=man-made figure) representing Love in Piccadilly Circus, London. People often meet near it. —see colour picture on page 423

e·ro·sion /ɪˈrəʊʒən/ *n* [U] the process of eroding or being eroded: *Soil erosion by rain and wind is a serious problem here.* | (fig.) *the slow erosion of royal power* **--sive** /ɪˈrəʊsɪv/ *adj*

e·rot·ic /ɪˈrɒtɪk‖ɪˈrɑː-/ *adj apprec* of, dealing with, or producing sexual love and desire: *erotic feelings* | *an erotic picture* | *an erotic sensation* **- ~ ally** /kli/ *adv*

▷ USAGE Compare **erotic, sexual,** and **sexy. Erotic** is used particularly for works of art: *an erotic film* | *some* erotic *pictures*. **Sexual** simply means "connected with or in regard to sex": *the sexual organs* | **sexual** *habits*. **Sexy** means "exciting in a sexual way": *You look very sexy in those jeans.*◁

e·rot·i·ca /ɪˈrɒtɪkə‖ɪˈrɑː-/ *n* [P] erotic books, pictures, etc.: *a collection of erotica*

e·rot·i·cis·m /ɪˈrɒtɪ̱sɪzəm‖ɪˈrɑː-/ *n* [U] the quality of being erotic

err /ɜːr/ *v* [I] **1** *fml* to make a mistake; do something wrong: *To err is human.* (old saying) | *It's better to* **err on the side of** *caution* (=to be too careful, rather than not careful enough) **2** **to err is human, to forgive, divine** *quote* a phrase from a work by Alexander Pope

er·rand /ˈerənd/ *n* a short journey made to carry a message, or to do or get something: *I'm in a hurry — I've got some errands to do.* | *I've no time to* **go on/run errands for** *him.* | *an errand of mercy* (=to get or bring help) —see also FOOL'S ERRAND

er·rant /ˈerənt/ *adj* [A] *fml or humor* wandering away from home and behaving in a bad or irresponsible way: *She went to London to bring back her errant daughter.* —see also KNIGHT-ERRANT

er·rat·ic /ɪˈrætɪk/ *adj* changeable without reason; not regular in movement or behaviour: *She's a very erratic tennis player.* (=sometimes good, sometimes bad) | *He made erratic movements with his hands.* — **~ally** /kli/ *adv*

er·ra·tum /eˈrɑːtəm/ *n* **-ta** /tə/ [*usu. pl.*] *Lat* a mistake in printing or writing, esp. one noted in a list at the beginning of a book

er·ro·ne·ous /ɪˈrəʊniəs/ *adj fml* (of a statement, belief, etc.) incorrect; mistaken: *the erroneous belief that the Earth is flat* — **~ly** *adv*

er·ror /ˈerər/ *n* **1** [C] a mistake: *There are several errors in the calculations.* | *The accident was caused by an* **error of judgment** *on the part of the pilot.* | *a programming error causing faulty readings* **2** [U] the state or quality of being wrong or mistaken: *The accident was caused by* **human error.** | *I did it in* **error.** (=by mistake) | *It's time you pointed out to him the* **error of his ways.** (=the way in which he is behaving badly) | *The computer screen showed an* **error message** *because I had typed in the wrong instructions.* —see also **trial and error** (TRIAL)

▷ USAGE **Error** is a more formal word than **mistake**: *Your homework is full of* **mistakes/errors** (*fml*). **Error** (literary) is sometimes used to suggest something that is morally wrong: *the* **errors** *of his youth*. In certain fixed phrases only one of the two words can be used: *an* **error** *of judgment* | *by* **mistake.**◁

er·satz /ˈeəzæts‖ˈeərzɑːts/ *adj derog* used instead of something else, either because of cost or because the real thing cannot be obtained; not real; artificial: *ersatz flour made from potatoes* | *ersatz coffee*

Erse /ɜːs‖ɜːrs/ *n* [U] the GAELIC language, esp. as spoken in Ireland

e·ruc·ta·tion /ˌɪˌrʌkˈteɪʃən/ *n* [C;U] *fml* (an example of) the action of belching (BELCH)

er·u·dite /ˈerʊdaɪt/ *adj fml* (of a person or book) full of learning; SCHOLARLY: *an erudite work on the history of the Roman Empire* — **~ly** *adv* —**dition** /ˌerʊˈdɪʃən/ *n* [U] : *a book that displays great erudition*

e·rupt /ɪˈrʌpt/ *v* [I] **1** (of a VOLCANO) to explode and pour out fire, LAVA, etc.: *Mount Vesuvius hasn't erupted for many years.* | (fig.) *Violence erupted in the city after the football match.* **2** [(in)] *med* (of a person or their skin) to become suddenly covered in unhealthy spots: *Her face erupted in pimples.* **3** *med* (of a tooth) to come up through the skin of the GUM¹; start to grow — **~ion** /ɪˈrʌpʃən/ *n* [C;U]: *There have been several volcanic eruptions this year.*

Er·ving /ˈɜːvɪŋ‖ˈɜːr-/ , **Ju·li·us** /ˈdʒuːliəs/ (1950–) an American BASKETBALL player often called **Dr. J**

er·y·sip·e·las /ˌerɪˈsɪpələs/ *n* [U] an infectious illness which makes the skin very red and sore

ESA /ˌiː es ˈeɪ/ [*the*] *abbrev. for* EUROPEAN SPACE AGENCY

E·sau /ˈiːsɔː/ *bibl* the son of Isaac and Rebecca and the TWIN brother of Jacob to whom he sold his BIRTHRIGHT

es·ca·late /ˈeskəleɪt/ *v* [I;T] **1** (of war) to make or become more serious by stages: *The government escalated the war by starting to bomb enemy cities.* **2** to make or become higher, greater, etc.: *The cost of living is escalating.* |

What started as a small difficulty has escalated into a major crisis. | *High unemployment has escalated violence in the cities.* | *escalating inflation* —**lation** /ˌeskəˈleɪʃən/ *n* [U]: *the escalation of hostilities* | *the recent escalation in street violence*

es·ca·la·tor /ˈeskəleɪtər/ ‖ also **moving staircase** *BrE*— *n* a set of moving stairs in an underground railway station, a large city shop, an airport, etc.

es·ca·lope /ˈeskəlɒp‖ˈskæləp/ *n BrE* a thin boneless piece of PORK, BEEF, or esp. VEAL (=meat from a young cow), cooked in hot fat

es·ca·pade /ˈeskəpeɪd/ *n* a wild, exciting, and sometimes dangerous act or adventure, esp. one that disobeys rules: *just a youthful escapade*

es·cape¹ /ɪˈskeɪp/ *v* **1** [I (**from**)] to get away e.g. from an enclosed space, a situation which prevents freedom of action, etc.; find a way out; get free: *The prisoners have escaped.* | *They managed to escape from the burning building by breaking down the door.* | *The gas was escaping from a small hole in the pipe.* | *You're just trying to escape from reality by taking all these drugs.* | *an escaped prisoner* (=one who has escaped) **2** [T] (of a person) to avoid (something dangerous or unpleasant): *She escaped death by inches when the wall collapsed.* | *We go south to escape the winter.* [+v-ing] *He narrowly* (=only just) *escaped being drowned.* | **There's no escaping the fact** (=It must be recognized) *that the government has become very unpopular.* **3** [T] (of an event, fact, etc.) to be unnoticed or forgotten by: *I'm afraid your name escapes me.* (=I've forgotten it) | *Nothing escaped his attention.*

escape² *n* **1** [C;U (**from, of**)] (an act of) escaping: *There have been several escapes from this prison recently.* | *The thief jumped into a car and* **made his escape.** | *She had a* **narrow escape** (=only just avoided danger) *when the wall nearly fell on her.* | *The explosion was caused by an escape of gas.* | *There's no escape from this place.* (=you can't get out) —see also FIRE ESCAPE **2** [S] something that frees one from unpleasant or dull reality: *I read love stories as an escape from reality.* —see also ESCAPISM

es·cap·ee /ˌeskeɪˈpiː, ɪˌskeɪˈpiː/ *n* a prisoner who has escaped from prison

es·cape·ment /ɪˈskeɪpmənt/ *n* the part of a clock or watch which controls the moving parts inside

escape ve·lo·ci·ty /·ˈ· ·,···/ *n* [S;U] the speed at which an object must move in order to get free from the pull of the Earth or another PLANET, and not fall back

es·cap·is·m /ɪˈskeɪpɪzəm/ *n* [U] *derog* activity intended to provide escape from unpleasant or dull reality: *He thinks that reading science fiction is just escapism.* —**ist** *adj, n*

es·ca·pol·o·gy /ˌeskəˈpɒlədʒi‖-ˈpɑː-/ *n* [U] the art or practice of escaping, esp. from bags, chains, etc., as a theatrical performance —**gist** *n*

e·scarp·ment /ɪˈskɑːpmənt‖-ɑːr-/ *n* a long cliff on a mountainside

es·cha·tol·o·gy /ˌeskəˈtɒlədʒi‖-ˈtɑː-/ *n* [U] (in religious, esp. Christian, teaching) the study of or set of beliefs concerned with the end of the world —**gical** /ˌeskətəˈlɒdʒɪkəl‖-ˈlɑː-/ *adj*

Esch·er /ˈeʃər/ , **Mau·rits Cor·ne·lis** /ˈmɔːrɪts kɔːˈneɪlɪs‖-kɔːr-/ (1898–1970) a Dutch artist known for works which trick the eye

es·chew /ɪsˈtʃuː/ *v* [T] *fml* to avoid habitually, esp. for moral or practical reasons: *to eschew bad company/alcoholic drinks*

Es·co·ri·al , **Escurial** /eˈskɔːriæl‖-riəl/ *n* [*the*] a set of buildings near Madrid in Spain including one of the finest churches in Europe; a palace, a famous library, and an art collection

es·cort¹ /ˈeskɔːt‖-ɔːrt/ *n* **1** [+*sing./pl. v*] one or more people, ships, cars, or aircraft, who go or travel with someone or something as a guard or as an honour: *The prisoner travelled* **under** (**police**) **escort.** (=with some police) | *an aircraft-carrier with an escort of smaller warships* **2** a social companion, esp. a man who takes a woman out for the evening **3** a man or woman who is paid to go out socially with another: *an escort agency*

e·scort² /ɪˈskɔːt‖-ɔːrt/ *v* [T (**to**)] to go with (someone) as an escort: *The queen was escorted by the directors as she toured the factory.* | *The drunken man was escorted firmly*

to the door. | *a group of motorcyclists escorting the presidential limousine*

Escort /ˈeskɔːt‖-ɔːrt/ *n tdmk* a popular middle-sized car made by Ford

es·crow /ˈeskrəʊ/ *n* [U] an object, such as a written CONTRACT or document, or money, which is held by one person while an agreement between two other people is being fulfilled

e·scutch·eon /ɪˈskʌtʃən/ *n* a ceremonial shield on which the sign (COAT OF ARMS) of a noble family is painted

Es·da test /ˈezdə test/ *n* electrostatic deposition analysis test; a scientific test used in legal cases to show in what order the pages of a document were produced. In Britain Esda tests have been used to prove that in certain important cases, the police lied about statements taken from people, or changed them later.: *Every time the Esda test was performed, it showed that Phillips's confession to the murder had not been recorded contemporaneously by the detectives*

Eskimo (Inuit)

Es·ki·mo /ˈeskəməʊ/ *n* a member of a race of people living in the icy far north of N America, Siberia, and the surrounding islands. People from this race consider the word Eskimo offensive and prefer to be called Inuits. – **Eskimo** *adj*

▶CULTURAL NOTE Many people still have an old-fashioned idea of Eskimos as living in IGLOOS (= houses made of ice), wearing furs, and fishing through holes in the ice, although modern Eskimos do not live like this.

ESL /ˌiː es ˈel/ English as a Second Language; English taught to or studied by people whose mother tongue is not English but who are living in an English-speaking country. In Britain many adults and children from Asian backgrounds take ESL lessons as well as others coming from abroad either for work purposes or as REFUGEES. –compare EFL, ESOL, ESP, TEFL, TESOL

ESOL /ˈiːsɒl‖-sɔːl/ *AmE* English for Speakers of Other Languages; a way of teaching English which attempts to recognize the importance of the speaker's first or other languages –compare EFL, ESL, ESP, TEFL, TESOL

e·soph·a·gus /ɪˈsɒfəgəs‖ɪˈsɑː-/ *n esp. AmE for* OESOPHAGUS

es·o·ter·ic /ˌesəˈterɪk◂, ˌiːsə-/ *adj* unusual, secret, or mysterious and known only by a few people, esp. INITIATES: *esoteric knowledge/practices* –**~ally** /kli/ *adv*

ESP[1] /ˌiː es ˈpiː/ *n* [U] extrasensory perception; knowledge or feelings about outside, past, or future things obtained without the use of the ordinary five senses. Many people do not believe in this kind of knowledge as it is difficult to prove its existence scientifically.

ESP[2] English for Special Purposes; English taught to people who wish to learn it for a particular limited use, e.g. reading scientific documents. It will include specialist VOCABULARY.

esp. *written abbrev. for:* especially

es·pe·cial /ɪˈspeʃəl/ *adj* [A] *fml for* SPECIAL[1] (2)

es·pe·cial·ly /ɪˈspeʃəli/ also **specially**– *adv* **1** to a particularly great degree: *"Do you like chocolate?" "Not especially."* | *an especially difficult problem* **2** in particular; above all: *Noise is unpleasant, especially when you're trying to sleep.* **3** for a particular person, purpose, etc.: *I bought it especially for you.*

Es·pe·ran·to /ˌespəˈræntəʊ/ *n* [U] an artificial language intended for international use. Although it was invented in 1877, it has not been popular or successful. Many people still do not know what Esperanto is and only a small number of people in the world speak it. –compare INTERLINGUA; see also INTERNATIONAL LANGUAGE

es·pi·o·nage /ˈespiənɑːʒ/ *n* [U] the action of spying (SPY); work of finding out secrets, esp. the political secrets of a country: *They were convicted of espionage.* | *Industrial espionage is the stealing of information about another firm's business.*

es·pla·nade /ˌespləˈneɪd ‖ ˈesplənɑːd/ *n* a level open space for walking, often beside the sea in a seaside town

ESPN /ˌiː es piː ˈen/ *n* [U] a CABLE TELEVISION station in the US which broadcasts only sports

es·pous·al /ɪˈspaʊzəl/ *n* [C;U (**of**)] *fml* the fact of giving one's support to an aim, idea, etc.: *The government's espousal of monetarism may have increased our industrial problems.*

es·pouse /ɪˈspaʊz/ *v* [T] *fml* to (decide to) support (an aim, idea, etc.): *the socialist philosophy espoused by this organization*

es·pres·so /eˈspresəʊ, ɪˈspre-/ *n* **-sos** [C;U] (a cup of) coffee made by forcing steam through crushed coffee beans. In Britain espresso coffee is chiefly found in Italian restaurants. It was esp. popular in the 1960s when young people met in coffee bars. In the US it is difficult to find it outside of large cities that may have a European influence.

es·prit /eˈspriː/ *n* [U] *Fr* liveliness and humour: *She performed the dance with great esprit.*

esprit de corps /eˌspriː də ˈkɔːʳ/ *n* [U] *Fr* loyalty among the members of a group

es·py /ɪˈspaɪ/ *v* [T] *lit* to see suddenly, usu. from a distance or unexpectedly

Esq. /ɪˈskwaɪəʳ‖ˈesk-, ɪˈskwaɪər/ also **Esquire** *rare*– *n BrE* (in the past, the usual title for a man on a letter to him, e.g. "Robert Jones, Esq."; now most people would write "Mr Robert Jones"): *The envelope is addressed to Peter Jones, Esq.*

Es·quire /ɪˈskwaɪəʳ‖ˈesk-, ɪˈskwaɪər/ an American and British men's magazine which contains features such as men's fashion, sports, etc. Esquire is meant to be read by men aged between 20 and 40. It is similar to magazines such as COSMOPOLITAN for women.

es·say[1] /ˈeseɪ/ *n* **1** a short piece of writing on a particular subject as part of a course of study: *We've got to write an essay about the war with Napoleon.* | *literary essays* **2** a short piece of literature in which a writer gives his or her thoughts on a particular subject usu. in a graceful and pleasing style **3** *fml or pomp* an attempt – **~ist** *n*

es·say[2] /eˈseɪ/ *v* [T] *fml or pomp* to make an attempt at: *When the weather improved we essayed the ascent of the mountain.*

essay ques·tion /ˈ·· ˌ··/ *n* a question in an examination paper that must have an answer in the form of an essay

es·sence /ˈesəns/ *n* **1** [(*the*)S (**of**)] the central or most important quality of a thing; the real or inner nature of a thing, by which it can be recognized or put into a class: *The essence of his religious teaching is love for all humanity.* | *the essence of the problem* **2** [C;U] something removed from a substance, usu. in the form of a liquid or jelly, having a strong smell or taste of the original substance: *essence of roses* | *vanilla essence* | *Did you use coffee essence in making this cake?* –compare EXTRACT[2] (2) **3 in essence** in its/one's nature; ESSENTIALLY: *In essence, the problem is a simple one.* **4 of the essence** *fml* very important: *We must hurry. Time is of the essence.*

es·sen·tial[1] /ɪˈsenʃəl/ *adj* **1** [(**to, for**)] completely necessary for the existence, success, etc. of something: *We can live without clothes, but food and drink are essential.* | *Good timing is essential to/for our plans.* | *It's essential that you arrive/to arrive on time.* | **Essential services** *will be maintained despite the industrial dispute.* **2** [A] most important; central; FUNDAMENTAL: *What is the essential difference between the two political systems?*

essential[2] *n* [*often pl.*] **1** something necessary: *The room was furnished with the* **bare essentials**: *a bed, a chair, and a table.* **2** something of central importance. A book which is about the most important facts in a subject is often called "The Essentials of...", e.g. "The Essentials of English Grammar"

es·sen·tial·ly /ɪˈsenʃəli/ *adv* **1** in reality, though perhaps not in appearance; BASICALLY: *She's essentially a very nice* *person.* **2** necessarily: *"Must I do it today?" "Not essentially."*

essential oil /·¦·· '·/ *n* a strong-smelling plant oil in a pure form, usu. mixed with alcohol, usu. used for PERFUME or medicine

Es·sex /'esɪks/ a COUNTY in England NE of London; ADMINISTRATIVE capital Chelmsford

Essex, David (1947–) an English popular music singer and actor

Essex, Robert Devereux, Earl of (1567–1601) a favourite of the unmarried Queen Elizabeth I of England. He fell out of favour and was put to death by Elizabeth.

Essex girl /ₗ·¦·· '·/ *n BrE infml, derog* the STEREOTYPE of a typical young woman from Essex (or the area near Essex) in SE England which is used in jokes, stories, etc. In these jokes an Essex girl is supposed to be loud, VULGAR, stupid and too willing to have sex.

Essex man /ₗ·¦·· '·/ *n BrE infml, derog* the STEREOTYPE of a typical man from Essex (or the area near Essex) in SE England which is used in jokes, stories, etc. In these jokes an Essex man is supposed to be loud, VULGAR, not well educated or honest and to have very RIGHT-WING political opinions.

Es·so /'esəʊ/ *tdmk* a large petrol company which has many petrol stations in Britain, more than any other company except Shell. In the US it is called EXXON: *"What petrol do you use?" "Well, I usually get Esso."*

est *written abbrev. for:* **1** established: *H. Perkins and Company, est 1869* **2** estimated (ESTIMATE): *population est 60,000*

EST /ₗiː es 'tiː/ *abbrev. for* EASTERN STANDARD TIME

es·tab·lish /ɪ'stæblɪʃ/ *v* [T] **1** to set up; begin; CREATE: *This company/school was established in 1850.* | *The company has established a new system for dealing with complaints.* | *This judgment will establish a precedent.* | *a long-established company* | *Frank Cooper Limited – Established 1874* **2** [(as, in)] to cause to be firmly settled or accepted in a particular state or position; put beyond doubt: *She established herself as the most powerful minister in the new government.* | *Now that he has established himself in the team, he is playing with much more confidence.* | *Her latest film has really established her reputation as a director.* | *well-established procedures* **3** to find out or make certain of (a fact, answer, etc.): *I have been unable to establish the truth of his story.* [+that] *It has been established that she was not there at the time of the crime.* [+wh-] *The police are trying to establish where he is.* **4** [usu. pass.] to make (a religion) official for a nation: *The established religion of Egypt is Islam.*

es·tab·lish·ment /ɪ'stæblɪʃmənt/ *n* **1** [U (of)] the act of establishing or state of being established: *The government must encourage the establishment of new industry.* | *The club has grown rapidly since its establishment three years ago.* **2** [C] a place run as a business or for a special purpose: *The hotel is a well-run establishment.* | *a research establishment*

Establishment *n* [the+S+sing./pl. v] **1** the powerful organizations and people who control public life and support the established order of society: *It's no good fighting the Establishment; it/they will always win in the end.* | *He's an important Establishment figure.* | *The party is basically anti-Establishment.* | *He's very Establishment.*

▶ CULTURAL NOTE In Britain, members of the Establishment are usually men who have been to PUBLIC SCHOOL and Oxford or Cambridge University and then become heads of big companies or colleges, important CIVIL SERVANTS, etc. The Establishment is generally considered to be bad and unjust by people who are not part of it. In the US, the Establishment is especially associated with people from the East Coast, especially people who have been to schools such as Harvard and Yale. ◀

2 (*sometimes not cap.*) a powerful controlling group of the stated kind: *Will the boxing Establishment allow this fight to be televised?*

es·tate /ɪ'steɪt/ *n* **1** a (large) piece of land in the country, usu. with one large house on it and one owner: *Real wine-lovers prefer wine which has been bottled on the estate.* **2** *BrE* a piece of land on which buildings (of a stated type) have all been built together in a planned way: *An industrial estate has factories on it, and a housing estate has houses on it.* | *We live on a council estate.* (=one with houses built by the local council) **3** *law* the whole of a person's property, esp. as left after death: *When her will was published, we were surprised at the size of her estate.* **4** *old use or fml* the stated rank or condition in life: *They were joined together in the holy estate of matrimony.* (=marriage) —see also FOURTH ESTATE, REAL ESTATE

estate a·gent /·'·· ₗ··/ *BrE* ‖ **real estate agent, realtor** *AmE*— *n* a person whose business is to buy, sell, or look after houses or land for people. Estate agents are generally unpopular because it is thought that they describe houses as much better than they really are, and that they charge a lot of money for very little work. —**estate agency** *n*

estate car /·'·· ·/ *BrE* ‖ **station wagon** *AmE*— *n* a private motor vehicle with a door at the back, folding or removable back seats, and a lot of room to put boxes, cases, etc., inside —compare HATCHBACK, SALOON, SPORTS CAR

estate tax /·'·· ₗ·/ *n* [U;C] *AmE* a tax on the money and possessions of a dead person, paid by the HEIRS, when the value is over a certain amount set by the government

Es·tee Lau·der /ₗesteɪ 'lɔːdər/ a company which makes PERFUME, etc.

es·teem¹ /ɪ'stiːm/ *n* [U] *fml* respect; good opinion (of a person): *a distinguished scientist who is held in (high) esteem by his colleagues* –compare ESTIMATION (2); see also SELF-ESTEEM

esteem² *v* [T] **1** *fml* to respect and admire (esp. a person) greatly: *The old teacher was much loved and esteemed.* **2** [+obj+adj/n] *fml or pomp* to consider to be (esp. something good): *His employers did not esteem him (to be) worthy of trust.* | *We would esteem it a favour if you would settle this account forthwith.*

es·thete /'iːsθiːt‖'es-/ *n AmE for* AESTHETE —**esthetic** /iːs'θetɪk‖es-/, **esthetical** *adj* —**esthetically** /kli/ *adv* —**esthetics** *n* [U]

es·ti·ma·ble /'estɪməbəl/ *adj fml apprec* (of a person or their behaviour) worthy of esteem —see also INESTIMABLE

es·ti·mate¹ /'estɪmeɪt/ *v* **1** [T (at)] to judge or calculate the nature, value, size, amount, etc., of (something), esp. roughly; form an opinion about: *We have not estimated the proper price for the contract yet.* | *The value of the painting was estimated at several thousand pounds.* [+(that)] *I estimate that we should arrive at 5.30.* | *The movie cost an estimated $25 million to make.* | *"What time is the plane due?" "Well, the estimated time of arrival is 5.20."* —see also UNDER-/OVERESTIMATE **2** [I(for)] to calculate the probable cost of doing a job, such as building or repairing something: *I asked three building firms to estimate for the repairs to the roof.* compare QUOTE¹ (3) —**mator** *n*

es·ti·mate² /'estɪmət/ *n* **1** [(of)] a calculation or judgment of the nature, value, size, amount, etc., of something: *to make an estimate* | *My estimate of the cost was about right.* | *At a rough* (=not exact) *estimate there are about 6000 people in the crowd.* [+that] *Her estimate that we would arrive at 5.30 was exactly correct.* **2** a statement of the probable cost of doing a job: *We got two or three estimates before having the roof repaired, and accepted the lowest.* —compare QUOTATION (3)

es·ti·ma·tion /ₗestɪ'meɪʃən/ *n* [U] **1** the act of estimating or forming a judgment: *This will simply lead, in our estimation, to further problems.* **2** ESTEEM¹: *He has lowered himself in my estimation.* (=I no longer have such a high opinion of him)

Es·to·ni·a /e'stəʊniə/ a country in NE Europe bordered on the W and N by the Baltic Sea, on the E by Russia, and on the S by Latvia; capital Tallinn; population 1,573,000 (1989) —**nian** *adj*

Es·to·ni·an /e'stəʊniən/ *n* **1** [C] a person who comes from or whose parents come from Estonia **2** [U] the main language spoken in Estonia

es·trange /ɪ'streɪndʒ/ *v* [T (**from**)] to cause (esp. people in a family) to become unfriendly towards each other: *The argument estranged him from his brother.* — **~ment** *n* [C;U (**from, between**)]: *The quarrel led to (a) complete estrangement (between her and her family).*

es·tranged /ɪˈstreɪndʒd/ *adj* **1** no longer living with one's husband or wife: *The couple became estranged in the early eighties.* **2** no longer friendly with: *They never see their estranged daughter.*

e·stro·gen /ˈiːstrədʒən‖ˈes-/ *n AmE for* OESTROGEN

es·tu·a·ry /ˈestʃuəri, -tʃəri/ *n* the wide lower part or mouth of a river, into which the sea enters at HIGH TIDE: *the Thames estuary*

estuary

the Thames estuary

ET[1] /ˌiː ˈtiː/ *n* a character in an extremely popular children's film of the same name which was made in 1982 by Steven Spielberg. ET is a very ugly but friendly being from outer space, famous for saying, "ET phone home." —see colour picture on page 685

ET[2] *abbrev. for* EMPLOYMENT TRAINING

ETA[1] /ˌiː tiː ˈeɪ/ *n* estimated time of arrival; the time that a vehicle, esp. a plane, is expected to arrive

ETA[2] /ˈetə/ a political organization in Spain which uses violence in its fight for a separate state for the Basque people which is independent of Spain and France

et al. /ˌet ˈæl/ *adv Lat fml* and (the) other people: *"The Human Embryo" by Brodsky, Rosenblum, et al.*

etc. also **et·cet·e·ra** /ˌetˈsetərə/— *adv Lat* and the rest; and so on: *We'd better buy tea, sugar, etc.* | *The letter says pay at once, they've warned us before, etc., etc.*

etch /etʃ/ *v* [I ;T (**on, in**)] to draw (a picture) by cutting lines on a metal plate with a needle and then using acid to eat out the lines, so that one can print from the plate: (fig.) *This terrible event is etched for ever on/in my memory.*

etch·ing /ˈetʃɪŋ/ *n* **1** a picture made by printing from an etched plate. **2 Come up and see my etchings** *humor* a phrase which, in jokes, a man says to a woman to invite her upstairs to his bedroom so that he can have sex with her

e·ter·nal /ɪˈtɜːnl‖-ɜːr-/ *adj* lasting for ever; without beginning or end: | (fig.) *I'm sick of their eternal complaints.* | (fig.) *an eternal optimist* – ~ **ly** *adv*

Eternal City /ˌ·ˈ·· ˈ··/ *poet* [*the*] Rome

eternal tri·an·gle /ˌ·ˌ·· ˈ···/ *n* [S] the difficult situation resulting from the love of two people, usu. of the same sex, for another person, usu. of the other sex: *The film tells a familiar story about an eternal triangle.*

e·ter·ni·ty /ɪˈtɜːnɪti‖-ɜːr-/ *n* **1** [U] time without end: *God will live for all eternity.* **2** [U] the state of time after death, which is said to last for ever **3** [S] a very long time which seems endless: *I was so anxious that every moment seemed an eternity.*

eternity ring /·ˈ··· ˌ·/ *n* (esp. in Britain) a special kind of ring given as a sign of love that will last forever

eth·a·nol /ˈeθənɒl, ˈiː-‖-nɒʊl/ also **ethylalcohol**– *n* [U] *tech* ALCOHOL (1)

Eth·el·red II /ˌeθəlred ðə ˈsekənd/ also **Ethelred the Un·read·y** /-ði ʌnˈredi—/ (968?–1016) an English king who lost his kingdom to the Danes

e·ther /ˈiːθər/ *n* **1** [U] a light colourless gas used formerly as an ANAESTHETIC to put people to sleep before an operation **2** [*the*+S] *old use* the air as the material through which radio waves travel **3** [*the*+S] also **aether** *old use* or *poet*– the upper air

e·the·re·al /ɪˈθɪəriəl/ *adj* **1** of unearthly lightness and very delicate; like a spirit or fairy: *The music has an ethereal quality.* | *She has an ethereal beauty.* **2** *poet* of the ETHER (2): *the blue ethereal sky* – ~ **ly** *adv*

eth·ic /ˈeθɪk/ *n* a system of moral behaviour: *the Christian ethic* | *The modern ethic seems to be to get as much money as you can without worrying how you get it.* | *the Protestant work ethic* –see also WORK ETHIC

eth·i·cal /ˈeθɪkəl/ *adj* **1** [*no comp.*] connected with ETHICS (2): *The article questions the ethical conduct of certain journalists, who are claimed to have used threats in order to obtain interviews.* | *The doctors' ethical committee decides whether it is morally right to perform certain operations.* **2** morally good or right: *I won't do it. It's not ethical.* –opposite **unethical**

eth·i·cally /ˈeθɪkli/ *adv* **1** in connection with ETHICS (2): *Ethically (speaking), I think the operation was wrong.* **2** in a morally good way: *I think he has behaved quite ethically.*

eth·ics /ˈeθɪks/ *n* **1** [U] the study of morals: *I'm doing ethics in my philosophy course.* **2** [U;P] moral rules or principles of behaviour governing a person or group: *Whether a country should have nuclear weapons or not should be a question of ethics, not of politics.* | *The psychiatrist was charged with violating professional ethics by talking about his patients.*

E·thi·o·pi·a /ˌiːθiˈəʊpiə/ a country in NE Africa bounded to the NE by the Red Sea; capital Addis Ababa; population 49,513,000 (1989). Ethiopia has been in the news because of its FAMINE (=people not getting enough to eat) and CIVIL WAR (=one group of people in the country fighting another group). —**pian** *adj*

E·thi·o·pi·an /ˌiːθiˈəʊpiən/ *n* a person who comes from or whose parents come from Ethiopia

eth·nic[1] /ˈeθnɪk/ *adj* **1** of a racial, national, or tribal group: *ethnic art/traditions* **2** interestingly unusual because typical of such a group: *This music would sound more ethnic if you played it on steel drums.*

ethnic[2] *n AmE* in Britain or the US, a person belonging to a group of a different race from the main group in the country

ethnic cleansing /ˌ·· ˈ··/ *n* [U] the process of removing a group of people from an area because of their race or religion, usu. by force, and sometimes by killing them. The word is used esp. in connection with the removal of Muslims by Serbs from some parts of Bosnia.

eth·nic·ally /ˈeθnɪkli/ *adv* in connection with a racial, national, or tribal group: *The two peoples are ethnically related.*

ethnic mi·nor·i·ty /ˌ··· ·ˈ···/ *n* a group of people of a different race from the main group in a country

ethnic pride /ˌ··· ˈ·/ *n* [U] belief in and loyalty to one's race

eth·no·cen·tric /ˌeθnəʊˈsentrɪk◂/ *adj* based on the belief that one's own race, nation, group, etc. is better and more important than others: *He has the ethnocentric idea that the Scots are the most intelligent people in the world.*

eth·nog·ra·pher /eθˈnɒɡrəfər‖eθˈnɑː-/ *n* a person who studies ethnography

eth·nog·ra·phy /eθˈnɒɡrəfi‖eθˈnɑː-/ *n* [U] the scientific description of the different races of human beings —**phic** /ˌeθnəˈɡræfɪk◂/ *adj* —**phically** /kli/ *adv*

eth·nol·o·gy /eθˈnɒlədʒi‖eθˈnɑː-/ *n* [U] the scientific study of the different races of human beings —compare ANTHROPOLOGY, SOCIOLOGY —**gist** *n* —**gical** /ˌeθnəˈlɒdʒɪkəl‖ -ˈlɑː-/ *adj* —**gically** /kli/ *adv*

e·thos /ˈiːθɒs‖ˈiːθɑːs/ *n* the set of ideas, or beliefs, or the moral attitudes of a person or group: *The company ethos is one of cooperation between all members of the firm.* | *the public school ethos*

eth·yl al·co·hol /ˌeθəl ˈælkəhɒl, ˌiːθaɪl-‖-hɔːl/ also **ethanol**– *n* [U] *tech* ordinary alcohol found in alcoholic drinks. It is also used for removing fat and oil —compare METHYL ALCOHOL

e·ti·o·lat·ed /ˈiːtiəleɪtd̬/ *adj fml* seriously weakened —**lation** /ˌiːtiəˈleɪʃən/ *n* [U]

et·i·ol·o·gy /ˌetiˈɒlədʒi, ˌiːti-‖-ˈɑːlə-/ *n* [U] *med* (the study of) the cause of disease: *What is the etiology of this condition?* (=What caused this illness?) —**gical** /ˌetiəˈlɒdʒɪkəl◂, ˌiːti-‖-ˈlɑː-/ *adj* —**gically** /kli/ *adv*

et·i·quette /ˈetɪket‖-kət/ *n* [U] the formal rules of proper (social) behaviour: *medical/professional etiquette*

▶ CULTURAL NOTE In Britain, the rules of social behaviour are not as severe as they were in the past, but there are still many rules about formal behaviour in upper-class society. People who move up in society sometimes look at etiquette books to learn how they are expected to behave. ◀

Et·na /ˈetnə/ , also **Mount Etna**– an active VOLCANO in Sicily, Italy

E·ton /ˈiːtn/ also **Eton Col·lege** /ˌ·· ˈ··/– a very expensive British PUBLIC SCHOOL (=independent school) for boys to which the upper class and leaders of society send their sons –**ian** /iːˈtəʊniən/ *n, adj*

▶CULTURAL NOTE Eton is generally considered to be the top British public school and a place which produces many of the nation's leaders. Men who have been educated at Eton are known as **Old Etonians** and many like their sons to be educated at Eton too. —see also HARROW.◀

et·y·mol·o·gy /ˌetɬˈmɒlədʒi‖-ˈmɑː-/ n 1 [U] the study of the origins, history, and changing meanings of words 2 [C] (an account of) the history of a particular word — compare entomology —**gist** n —**gical** /ˌetɬməˈlɒdʒɪkəl◂‖ -ˈlɑː-/ adj —**gically** /kli/ adv

E-type /ˈiː taɪp/ n tdmk the name of a type of fast, expensive, sports car made by Jaguar in the 1960s.

eu·ca·lyp·tus /ˌjuːkəˈlɪptəs/ n a tall tree which produces a strong-smelling oil used in medicines for treating colds

Eu·cha·rist /ˈjuːkərɬst/ n [the+S] (the holy bread and wine used in) the Christian ceremony based on Christ's last supper on Earth: to take/receive the Eucharist | The priest celebrated the Eucharist. —compare COMMUNION, MASS — ~**ic** /ˌjuːkəˈrɪstɪk◂/ adj

Eu·clid /ˈjuːklɪd/ (about 300 BC) a Greek MATHEMATICIAN who is known for the development of a system of GEOMETRY which is also called Euclid

eu·clid·e·an , -ian /juːˈklɪdiən‖juː-/ adj (often cap.) of or being the GEOMETRY (=system of describing lines, angles, surfaces, and solids) described by Euclid

eu·lo·gis·tic /ˌjuːləˈdʒɪstɪk◂/ adj fml (of a speech or piece of writing) full of eulogy: a eulogistic speech about the great achievements of the dead king — ~**ally** /kli/ adv

eu·lo·gize also **-gise** BrE /ˈjuːlədʒaɪz/ v [T] fml to make a eulogy about (usu. a person or their qualities) —**gist** n: He's just a eulogist for the government.

eu·lo·gy /ˈjuːlədʒi/ n [C;U **(on, of, to)**] fml (a speech or piece of writing containing) high praise, usu. of a person or their qualities: a eulogy to the royal family

eu·nuch /ˈjuːnək/ n a man who has been castrated (CASTRATE) (=had part of his sex organs removed), esp. one formerly employed in the women's areas of some Eastern courts: (fig.) a political eunuch (=someone who has no real political power)

eu·phe·mis·m /ˈjuːfɬmɪzəm/ n [C;U] (an example of) the use of a pleasanter, less direct name for something thought to be unpleasant: "Pass away" is a euphemism for "die".

eu·phe·mis·tic /ˌjuːfɬˈmɪstɪk◂/ adj (of a word, speech, or writing) containing or consisting of euphemisms. Euphemistic words or phrases are marked euph in this dictionary: "Ladies' room" is a euphemistic term for "toilet". — ~**ally** /kli/ adv

eu·pho·ni·ous /juːˈfəʊniəs‖juː-/ adj fml pleasant in sound

eu·pho·ni·um /juːˈfəʊniəm‖juː-/ n a musical instrument which is a kind of TUBA, made of brass and played by blowing

eu·pho·ri·a /juːˈfɔːriə‖juː-/ n [U] a feeling of extreme happiness, pride, and excitement: They were in a state of euphoria after the baby was born. —**ric** /juːˈfɔrɪk‖ juˈfɔːrɪk, -ˈfɑːr-/ adj —**rically** /kli/ adv

Eu·phra·tes /juːˈfreɪtiːz/ [the] a long river which flows from Turkey through Syria and Iraq into the Persian Gulf

Eu·ra·sian /jʊəˈreɪʒən, -ʃən/ adj 1 of Europe and Asia 2 (of a person) of mixed European and Asian birth

Eu·re·ka /jʊəˈriːkə/ interj humor used as a cry of pleasure at one's success in suddenly discovering the answer to a problem: Eureka! I've found the answer!

▶CULTURAL NOTE **Eureka** means "I've found it" in Greek, and when people say it they are conscious of its use by Archimedes, who was in his bath when he suddenly thought of a way of measuring DENSITY. —see also ARCHIMEDES◀

eu·rhyth·mics /juːˈrɪðmɪks‖juː-/ n [U;P] a system of exercising the body with music that is supposed to be good for the spirit —**mic** adj [A] : eurhythmic exercises

Eu·rip·i·des /juːˈrɪpɬdiːz/ (?480–406 BC) an ancient Greek writer of plays

Eu·ro /ˈjʊərəʊ/ adj [A] European; used esp. for new things connected with the EC: Isn't there going to be some sort of Euro scheme for it next year?

Euro- see WORD FORMATION

Euro-bash·ing /ˈ··· ˌ··/ n [U] finding fault with everything connected with the EC. Certain British MPs on the right of the Conservative Party and certain Labour MPs too are known for Euro-bashing.

Eu·ro·bond /ˈjʊərəʊbɒnd‖-bɑːnd/ n tech a financial SECURITY (5) on which the named CURRENCY is not the currency of the country in which it has been produced

Eu·ro·cheque /ˈjʊərəʊtʃek/ tdmk n a special sort of cheque which can be used for making payments from one's own bank account in most European countries

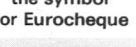
the symbol
for Eurocheque

eurocheque

Eu·ro·crat /ˈjʊərəʊkræt/ n often derog an official of the EC

Eu·ro·dis·ney /ˈjʊərəʊdɪzni/ tdmk an extremely large amusement park, run by the Walt Disney Company, just outside Paris in France. It is based on Disneyland and Disneyworld in the US.

Eu·ro·dol·lar /ˈjʊərəʊˌdɒlər‖ ˌdɑːr-/ n a US dollar which has been put into European banks to help trade and provide an international money system, because it is easy to exchange for other sorts of money

Euro MP /ˌjuːərəʊ em ˈpiː/ An a member of the European Parliament. Euro MPs are also known as MEPs.: Anita Pollock, Kingston's Euro MP, has succeeded in steering a report calling for better childcare through the European Parliament.

Eu·rope /ˈjʊərəp/ 1 one of the seven large land masses in the world (CONTINENTs). Europe lies N of the Mediterranean and goes E as far as the Ural Mountains in the USSR. —see CONTINENT (USAGE) 2 the EC: Britain's future lies in Europe. | I am sure Britain was right to **go into Europe**. (=to join the EC) 3 the mainland of the CONTINENT of Europe, not including the British Isles: With the Channel Tunnel we could travel to Europe direct. 4 **Europe from the Atlantic to the Urals** the dream of a greater undivided Europe rather than a Europe divided into opposing East and West by political differences

Eu·ro·pe·an¹ /ˌjʊərəˈpiːən◂/ adj of or from Europe: Euro pean trade

European² n 1 a person who comes from or whose parents come from Europe 2 infml a person who is keen on the idea of the EC or of closer union between European countries

European Coal and Steel Com·mu·ni·ty /ˌ····· ˌ· ˈ· ˌ····/ also **ECSC**— [the] a European Community body which gives help to the coal and steel industries

European Com·mis·sion /ˌ···· ·ˈ··/ abbrev. **EC** [the] a group of 17 members, including two British, chosen by the countries belonging to the EC to suggest plans for it, carry out the EC's decisions, and make sure its laws are kept —see also EC

European Com·mis·sion·er /ˌ···· ·ˈ···/ n a member of the European Commission

European Com·mu·ni·ty /ˌ···· ·ˈ···/ [the] the EC

European Con·ven·tion on Hu·man Rights /ˌ···· ·ˌ··· ˌ·· ˈ·/ [the] an agreement which many European countries, including Britain, have signed to show that they will respect people's rights of freedom, quality, etc. If somebody wants to ask for this convention to be obeyed, they go to the **European Human Rights Commission** in Strasbourg. If they are still not satisfied, they can take their case to the European Court of Human Rights.

European Court of Hu·man Rights /ˌ···· ˌ· ˌ·· ˈ·/ [the] the court of the Council of Europe

European Court of Jus·tice /ˌ···· ˌ· ˈ··/ [the] the court of the EC, in Luxembourg

European Cup /ˌ···· ˈ·/ [the] 1 a football competition between national teams of European countries 2 the cup given to the winner of this competition

European Cup-win·ners' Cup /ˌ···· ˈ··· ˌ·/ [the] 1 a football competition to find the best of the teams which have won the national cup finals in their own countries 2 the cup given to the winner of this competition

European Cur·ren·cy U·nit /ˌ···· ˈ··· ˌ·/ see ECU

European Ec·o·nom·ic Com·mu·ni·ty /ˌ···· ˌ···· ·ˈ···/ also **Community** [the] the EEC

European Ex·change Rate Mech·a·nis·m /ˌ···· ·ˈ· ·ˌ····/ also **ERM, exchange rate mechanism**— [the] a system for controlling the exchange rate between the money of one EC country and that of another. Britain joined the ERM in 1991 and left again in 1992.

European Free Trade As·so·ci·a·tion /ˌ···· ·· ˈ· ·ˌ····/ also **EFTA**— [the] an organization of non-EC countries which aimed to establish free trade between themselves. In 1991 it was agreed that EFTA countries should enter into an association with the EC.

European Mas·ters /ˌ···· ˈ··/ [the] an important GOLF competition held in different European countries

European Mon·e·ta·ry Sys·tem /ˌ···· ˈ···· ·ˌ··/, abbrev. EMS [the] a system established in 1979 to limit changes in exchange rates between the money of one EC country and another

European O·pen /ˌ···· ˈ··/ [the] an important GOLF competition played in Europe and open to players from all over the world: Sandy Lyle finished second in the European Open.

European Par·lia·ment /ˌ···· ˈ···/ n [the] a parliament directly elected by the people in the EC. Its powers are limited, but increasing.

European part·ners /ˌ···· ˈ··/ n [P] BrE fml our European partners the other member states of the EC

European Space A·gen·cy /ˌ···· ·· ˈ· ·ˌ··/ also abbrev. ESA— [the] an organization formed in 1975 to manage Europe's space programme

Eu·ro·scep·tic /ˈjʊərəʊ ˌskeptɪk/ n a British politician who is not in favour of Britain's membership of the EC

Eu·ro·tun·nel /ˈjʊərəʊtʌnl/ tdmk a partnership of a French company and a British company responsible for building the CHANNEL TUNNEL

Eu·ro·vi·sion Song Con·test /ˌjʊərəʊvɪʒən ˈsɒŋ ˌkɒntest‖ -ˈsɔːŋ ˌkɑːn-/ [the] a competition shown on television in which singers or groups of singers representing European countries sing specially written popular songs. The Eurovision Song Contest is very popular, but many British people, esp. young people, make jokes about it, saying that the songs are silly and not very good.

Eu·ry·di·ce /jʊəˈrɪdɪsi/ see ORPHEUS AND EURYDICE

eu·ryth·mics /juːˈrɪðmɪks‖jʊ-/ n EURHYTHMICS

Eurythmics a British POP[3] group consisting of Dave Stewart and Annie Lennox

eu·sta·chian tube /juːˈsteɪʃən ˌtjuːb‖-ˌtuːb/ n (often cap.) med either of the pair of tubes which join the ears to the throat

Eus·ton /ˈjuːstən/ one of the main line railway stations in London —see colour map on page 817

eu·tha·na·si·a /ˌjuːθəˈneɪziə‖-ˈneɪʒə/ also **mercy-killing**— n [U] tech or euph the painless killing of people who are incurably ill or very old. In Britain and the US euthanasia is illegal, but many people approve of it in certain cases, and some would like to see the law changed.

e·vac·u·ate /ɪˈvækjueɪt/ v [T] 1 to take all the people away from (a place): The village was evacuated because the army needed it. 2 [(from, to)] to move (a person) away from a place in order to protect them from danger: In the war many children were evacuated from the cities to the countryside. | After the explosion at the plastics factory the town was evacuated. 3 fml to empty (the bowels) —**ation** /ɪˌvækjuˈeɪʃən/ n [C;U]

e·vac·u·ee /ɪˌvækjuˈiː/ n a person who has been evacuated. For a British person, a typical evacuee is one of the many thousands of British children sent out of the big cities during the Second World War to live with another family in a safe place.

e·vade /ɪˈveɪd/ v [T] 1 derog to avoid (esp. a duty or responsibility), esp. using deception: Give me a direct answer, and stop evading the issue. [+v-ing] If you try to evade paying your taxes you risk going to prison. 2 to get out of the way of or escape from: She evaded her pursuers by hiding in a cave. | After his escape he evaded capture for several days. —see also EVASION

e·val·u·ate /ɪˈvæljueɪt/ v [T] to calculate or judge the value of: The school has only been open for six months, so it's hard to evaluate its success. —**ation** /ɪˌvæljuˈeɪʃən/ n [C;U]

ev·a·nes·cent /ˌevəˈnesənt◂/ adj fml soon disappearing and being forgotten —**cence** n [U]

e·van·gel·i·cal[1] /ˌiːvænˈdʒelɪkəl◂/ adj 1 (often cap.) (of certain Protestant Christian churches) believing in the importance of faith, of studying the Bible, and of persuading people to become Christians, rather than in religious ceremonies 2 sometimes derog showing (too) great eagerness in spreading one's own beliefs or ideas: They are pushing their ideas with an almost evangelical fervour. — ~ism n [U]

evangelical[2] n a person who has evangelical beliefs

e·van·ge·list /ɪˈvændʒɪlɪst/ n a person who travels from place to place and holds religious meetings in order to persuade people to become Christians —see BILLY GRAHAM —**lism** n [U] —**listic** /ɪˌvændʒɪˈlɪstɪk◂/ adj

Evangelist n any of the four writers (Matthew, Mark, Luke, and John) of the books of the Bible called the Gospels

e·van·ge·lize also **-lise** BrE /ɪˈvændʒɪlaɪz/ v [I ;T] to teach the Christian religion as an evangelist

Ev·ans /ˈevənz/, **Dame E·dith** /ˈiːdɪθ/ (1888–1976) an English actress, remembered esp. for playing the part of Lady Bracknell in the play The Importance of Being Earnest

e·vap·o·rate /ɪˈvæpəreɪt/ v [I;T] to (cause to) change into steam and disappear: The rainwater in the street soon evaporated in the warm sunshine. | (fig.) Hopes of reaching an agreement are beginning to evaporate. (=disappear) —**ration** /ɪˌvæpəˈreɪʃən/ n [U]

evaporated milk /·ˌ···· ·ˈ·/ n [U] tinned milk which is thickened by taking away some of the water, but not sweetened —compare CONDENSED MILK

e·va·sion /ɪˈveɪʒən/ n 1 [U] the act of evading (EVADE) —see also TAX EVASION 2 [C] something evasive, esp. an attempt to avoid telling the whole truth: The minister's speech was full of evasions.

e·va·sive /ɪˈveɪsɪv/ adj 1 derog not direct; trying to hide the truth: She gave an evasive answer. 2 intended to avoid being hit, seized, etc.: If the bullets start coming this way, **take evasive action.** — ~ly adv — ~ness n [U]

eve /iːv/ n 1 [U] (usu. cap.) the night or day before the stated religious day or holiday: We're giving a party on Christmas Eve. | December 31st is New Year's Eve. 2 [the+S (of)] the time just before an important event: On the eve of the election no one was confident enough to predict the result. 3 [U] poet evening

Eve in the Jewish and Christian religions and in Islam, the first woman. According to the Bible, Eve lived in the Garden of Eden with Adam, the first man: There's nothing new in such crimes. They've been going on since Eve ate the apple in the Garden of Eden. —see FALL and see colour picture on page 424

e·ven[1] /ˈiːvən/ adv 1 (used just before the surprising part of a statement, to add to its strength) which is more than might be expected: Even the younger children enjoyed the concert. (=so certainly everyone else did) | The younger children even enjoyed the concert. (=so certainly they enjoyed everything else) | He's a strict vegetarian – he doesn't even eat cheese. | She was so weak after the illness that she couldn't even walk without help. 2 (used for making comparisons stronger) still; yet: It was cold yesterday, but it's even colder today. 3 (used for adding force to an expression) (and) one might almost say; INDEED (2): He looked depressed, even suicidal. | He looked depressed, suicidal even. 4 **even as** just at the same moment as: I tried to phone her, but even as I was phoning she was leaving the building. 5 **even if** no matter if: Even if we could afford it, we wouldn't go abroad for our holidays. (=because we don't want to. Compare If we could afford it, we'd (like to) go abroad for our holidays.) 6 **even now/so/then** in spite of what has/had happened; though that is true: I explained everything, but even then he didn't understand. | It was raining, but even so we had to go out. 7 **even though** though: Even though it was raining, we had to go out.

even[2] adj 1 [(with)] flat, level, and smooth; forming a straight line: After driving on the bumpy surface, it was nice to get back onto even ground. | Cut the bushes even with the fence. (=not higher and not lower) 2 [(with)] (of things that can be measured and compared) equal: She won the first game and I won the second, so now we're *even/I'm even with her. | He cheated me, but I'll* **get even with him** *(=harm him as he has harmed me) one day! | He stands an* **even chance** *of winning.* (=it is equally likely that he will win or lose) —see also EVENS, BREAK **even 3** (of a number) that can be divided exactly by two: *2, 4, 6, 8, etc. are even numbers.* —opposite **odd 4** regular and unchanging: *travelling at an even speed | She has a very even temperament.* (=stays calm and doesn't often get angry or excited) —compare UNEVEN — ~**ly** *adv* — ~**ness** *n* [U]

even³ *v*

even out *phr v* [I;T (=**even** sthg. ↔ **out**)] to (cause to) become level or equal: *Prices have been rising very fast, but they should even out soon. | The loss of their best player has evened out the difference between the teams.*

even sthg. ↔ **up** *phr v* [T] to make equal or fairer; produce a fair balance in: *You've paid for the meal, so if I pay for the taxi that'll even things up.*

even⁴ *n* [U] *poet* evening

even field /ˌ·· ˈ·/ *n* EVEN PLAYING-FIELD

even-hand·ed /ˌ·· ˈ···◂/ *adj* giving fair and equal treatment to all sides; IMPARTIAL

eve·ning /ˈiːvnɪŋ/ *n* **1** [C;U] the end of the day and early part of the night, between sunset or the end of the day's work and bedtime: *a warm evening | on Tuesday evenings | I'll work in the evening. | an evening party |* (fig.) *People look forward to security in the evening* (=end part) *of their lives.* —compare AFTERNOON and see also EVENINGS **2** [C] entertainment of the stated type, happening in the early part of the night: *Will you come to our musical evening on Thursday?* **3 evenin' all** *quote* the phrase used by the policeman Dixon at the beginning of each programme of *Dixon of Dock Green*, an old British television programme. People sometimes say this as a joke when they meet their friends in the evening, or when they are pretending to be a policeman.

evening class /ˈ·· ·/ *n* a lesson which usu. adults attend in the evenings: *Details of evening classes are given below.*

evening dress

dinner jacket *BrE*/ tuxedo *AmE*

tails

white-tie   black tie

morning dress   evening dress

evening dress /ˈ·· ·/ *n* **1** [U] special clothes worn for formal occasions in the evening usu. a formal suit and a BOW TIE for men and a long dress for women **2** [C] a usu. long dress worn by women on such formal occasions

▶ CULTURAL NOTE People are much freer these days to wear what they like when they go out, e.g. to the theatre or a concert. Invitations and tickets for some dances, etc. ask people to wear evening dress, and one would expect to wear it, e.g., to a dance in high society, or to a dinner in honour of a visiting head of state. —compare FULL DRESS, MORNING DRESS; see also BLACK-TIE, WHITE-TIE ◀

eve·ning meal /ˌ·· ˈ·/ *n esp. BrE* the main meal of the day, usu. eaten between about 6 and 8 o'clock in the evening: *Bed, breakfast, and evening meal £22.50 | We get an evening meal when we're on the late shift.*

eve·nings /ˈiːvnɪŋz/ *adv esp. AmE* in the evening repeatedly; during any evening: *I'm always at home evenings.*

Evening Stan·dard /ˌ·· ˈ··/ also **Standard**— [*the*] a daily newspaper sold in London

evening star /ˌ·· ˈ·/ *n* [*the*] (*often cap.*) a bright PLANET, usu. Venus, seen in the western sky in the evening —compare MORNING STAR

even play·ing field /ˌ·· ˈ·· ·/ also **even field**— *n esp. BrE* a situation in which competitors can compete without any of them having unfair disadvantages. This expres-

sion is often used when people are talking about economic competition, e.g. when someone is complaining that THIRD WORLD countries do not get a fair chance.

evens /ˈiːvənz/ *esp. BrE*‖**even odds** /ˌ·· ˈ·/*esp. AmE*— *n infml* chances that are the same for and against: *The chances of her coming are about evens.* (=equally likely that she will win or won't)

e·ven·song /ˈiːvənsɒŋ‖-sɔːŋ/ *n* [U] (*often cap.*) the evening religious service in the Church of England. This service is often sung, and many British COMPOSERs have written music for it. —compare COMPLINE, MORNING PRAYER, VESPERS

e·vent /ɪˈvent/ *n* **1** [C] a happening, esp. an important, interesting, or unusual one: *The programme reviews the most important events of 1985. | The article discusses the (course of) events which led up to his resignation. | a social/sporting event* —see also HAPPY EVENT, NON-EVENT **2** [C] any of the races, competitions, etc., arranged as part of a day's sports: *The next event will be the 100 metres race.* —see also FIELD EVENT, THREE-DAY EVENT **3** [(*the*) S] (a possible) case: **In the event of** *rain* (=if it rains), *the party will be held indoors. | I'll probably see you tomorrow, but* **in any event** (=even if I don't) *I'll phone. | I don't know whether I'm going by car or by train, but* **in either event** (=whichever I do) *I'll need money.* **4 at all events** in spite of everything; at least: *She had a terrible accident, but at all events she wasn't killed.* **5 in the event** *esp. BrE* as it happened; when it actually happened: *We were afraid he would be nervous on stage, but in the event he performed beautifully.*

even-tem·pered /ˌ·· ˈ···◂/ *adj* having a calm good temper; not easily made angry; EQUABLE

e·vent·ful /ɪˈventfəl/ *adj* full of interesting or exciting events: *He's led quite an eventful life. | We've had rather an eventful day.* —opposite **uneventful** — ~**ly** *adv* — ~**ness** *n* [U]

e·ven·tide /ˈiːvəntaɪd/ *n* [(*the*) U] *poet* **1** evening: *at eventide* **2** old age: *The Eventide Rest Home, £300 per week*

e·ven·tu·al /ɪˈventʃuəl/ *adj* [A] (of an event) happening at last as a result: *The new computer system is expensive, but the eventual savings it will bring are very significant. | a research programme aimed at the eventual eradication of this disease*

e·ven·tu·al·i·ty /ɪˌventʃuˈælᵻti/ *n fml* a possible event or result, esp. an unpleasant one: *We must be prepared for all eventualities/for any eventuality. | This plan covers* (=has an answer for) *all eventualities.*

e·ven·tu·al·ly /ɪˈventʃuəli, -tʃəli/ *adv* at last; in the end: *He worked so hard that eventually he made himself ill. | After many attempts she eventually managed to get promotion.*

e·ven·tu·ate /ɪˈventʃueɪt/ *v*
eventuate in sthg. *phr v* [T] *fml or pomp* to result in; have as a result: *A rapid rise in prices soon eventuated in mass unemployment.*

ev·er /ˈevər/ *adv* **1** (used mostly in questions, negatives, comparisons, and sentences with **if**) at any time: *Nothing ever makes him angry. | "Do you ever go to concerts?" "No, never./Yes (sometimes)." | I don't remember ever seeing him before. | If you're ever in Spain, do come and see me. | "Have you ever been to Paris?" "No, never./Yes, I have." | It's colder than ever today.* (=colder than it has been before) *| That's the biggest fish I've ever seen. | I* **hardly ever** (=almost never) *go to bed after midnight. | He* **rarely, if ever,** (=probably never) *loses his temper. | The company is making ever larger* (=increasingly large) *profits. | He's a dynamic businessman, if* **ever there was** one. (=extremely dynamic) *| He's still as cheerful as ever in spite of all his disappointments. |* (*infml*) *I never ever drink coffee.* **2** (used esp. with expressions of time or in combination) always: *He came here for a holiday several years ago and he's lived here* **ever since**. *| The prince and princess got married and lived happily ever after. |* **As ever** (=as usually happens), *she refused to admit that she was wrong. | The world's ever-increasing population will cause great problems in the future. | I will love you* **for ever**. **3** (used after **how, what, when, where, who,** and **why** for giving force to a question): *What ever are you doing? | How ever shall we get there?* **4** *AmE infml* (used for strengthening EXCLAMATIONs in the form of questions): *Was he ever mad!* (=he was very angry) **5 ever and anon** *poet* from time to time **6 ever so/such** *infml,*

esp. BrE very: *It's ever so cold.* | *She's ever such a nice girl.*
7 Yours ever also **Ever yours**— *infml* (used at the end of a letter above the signature)

Ev·e·rage /ˈevərɪdʒ/, **Dame Edna** see DAME EDNA

Ev·e·rest[1] /ˈevərˌɪst, -rest/ also **Mount Everest**— the highest mountain in the world (8848 metres), in the Himalayas, on the border of Tibet and Nepal. It was first climbed by Sir Edmund Hillary and Tenzing Norgay on a British attempt in 1953.

▶ CULTURAL NOTE British people were very proud of the British team's success in climbing Everest, and esp. pleased that it was done in the year of the Queen's CORONATION. People sometimes use "Everest" to give the idea of something which is the highest achievement. ◀

Everest[2] *tdmk* a British company which supplies DOUBLE GLAZING (=glass on a window in two separate sheets with a space between them)

Ev·er·glades /ˈevəgleɪdz‖-vər-/ [*the*+P] an area of low wet tropical land in Florida in the USA covering about 5000 square miles. The Everglades, a national park, is famous for its wildlife, esp. ALLIGATORS.

ev·er·green /ˈevəgriːn‖-ər-/ *n, adj* (a tree or bush) that does not lose its leaves in winter: (fig.) *I love these evergreen tunes.* (=old ones that are still good or popular) —compare CONIFEROUS, DECIDUOUS

ev·er·last·ing /ˌevəˈlɑːstɪŋ◂‖ˌevərˈlæ-/ *adj* **1** *fml* lasting for ever; without an end: [A; after *n*] *God has promised us everlasting life*|*life everlasting after death.* **2** [A] *derog* lasting too long or happening too often: *I'm fed up with your everlasting complaints!* — **ly** *adv*

Ev·er·ly Broth·ers /ˈevəli ˌbrʌðəz‖-vərli ˌbrʌðərz/, **The** Don Everly (1937–) and Phil Everly (1939–), two American popular music singers, songwriters, and GUITAR players with a very recognizable soft style of singing together. They were successful in the 1950s and 1960s and influenced many other singers.

ev·er·more /ˌevəˈmɔːʳ‖ˌevər-/ *adv lit* for all future time: *He swore to love her (for) evermore.*

Ever Read·y /ˌ·· ˈ·· ◂/ *n tdmk* a company which makes batteries (BATTERY (1))

Ev·ert /ˈevət‖-ərt/, **Chris** /krɪs/ (1954–) an American tennis player who won Wimbledon and the US Open many times and is one of the most successful and popular women tennis players ever

Ev·er·ton /ˈevətən‖-vər-/ the name of a British football club based in Liverpool

ev·ery /ˈevri/ *determiner* **1** each (of more than two): *Every student* (=all the students) *has to take the examination.*| *Every time I see him* (=whenever I see him) *he looks miserable.* | *Eat up every (single) bit of your supper.* (=all of it) | *I enjoyed every minute of the party.* (=all of it) | *Go to bed, every one of you!* | *My new job is more interesting in every way than my old one.* | *(fml, after a* POSSESSIVE) *They believed his every word.* (=everything he said) —see USAGE **2** (of things that can be counted, esp. periods of time) once in each: *He comes to see us every day*|*every three days.* | *Change the oil in the car every 5000 miles.* **3** as much (hope, chance, reason, etc.) as possible: *There is every chance that she will succeed.* (=she probably will) | *There is every reason to believe that he is telling the truth.*| *The airline takes every possible measure to ensure the safety of its passengers.* **4 every last** *infml* every, not leaving out any: *You must pick up every last bit of paper from the floor.* **5 every now and then** also **every now and again, every so often**— from time to time; sometimes but not often: *I write to him every now and then.* **6 every other** (of things which can be counted) the 1st, 3rd, 5th, etc. or the 2nd, 4th, 6th, etc.: *Take the medicine every other day.* | *They visit us every other month.*

▷ USAGE Compare **each** and **every**. 1 **Each** before a noun takes a singular verb. You use **each** when you are thinking of the members of a group separately, or one at a time: *Each pupil was given a different book by the teacher.* **Every** always takes a singular verb. You use **every** when you are thinking of a whole group, or making general statements: *Every boy ran in the race.*| *Every child likes* (=all children like) *to get presents.* 2 **Each** can be used before *of*, or after a subject, in sentences like these: **Each** *of us wants to get a share of the money.* | *We* **each** *have a room of our own.* **Every** cannot be used in these positions.◁

ev·ery·bod·y /ˈevribɒdi‖-baːdi/ *pron* every person; everyone: *Everybody agreed it was a good idea.* | *The police told everybody to remain in their cars.* —see EVERYONE (USAGE)

ev·ery·day /ˈevrideɪ/ *adj* [A] ordinary, common, and usual: *Accidents and small injuries are an everyday occurrence in this job.* | *After the bomb it was some time before the town resumed its everyday routines.* | *Conserving water is part of* **everyday** *life in Australia.* | *The closure of the local bus service will make a great difference to their everyday lives.* —compare DAY-TO-DAY (1)

Ev·ery·man /ˈevrimæn/ *lit* a typical ordinary person (from the name of a character in a 16th century play): *The leading character is a symbol for Everyman.*

ev·ery·one /ˈevriwʌn/ *n* every person: *If everyone is ready, we'll begin.* | *They gave a prize to everyone who passed the exam.* | *I stayed at work after everyone else* (=every other person) *had gone home.* | *Has everyone brought their exercise books?* | *Everyone but John arrived on time.* (=John was late) | *The canteen's almost empty! Where is everyone?* (=the people who are usually here)

▷ USAGE 1 **Everyone, every, anyone, no one,** and **someone** (also **everybody,** etc.) always take a singular verb, but they are often followed by a plural pronoun, except in very formal speech and writing: *Has* **everyone** *finished their drinks*|*his or her drink (fml)?* | **Anyone** *can do it if they try*|*if he or she tries (fml).* | **Someone's** *left the door open, haven't they?* 2 Compare **every** one and **everyone. Everyone** (or **everybody**) can only be used of people and is never followed by "of": **Every** one means each person or thing, and is often followed by "of". **Everyone** in the class passed the exam. | There are 16 students and **every** one of them passed.◁

ev·ery·thing /ˈevriθɪŋ/ *pron* **1** (used with singular verbs) each thing; all things: *Everything is ready for the party.*| *I've forgotten everything I learnt at school.* | *They've eaten everything else.* (=all the other things) **2** the most important thing or person: *Money isn't everything.* | *Her daughter is everything to her.* **3 and everything** *infml* and so on; ETC.: *She's worried about her work and everything.* **4 everything you (ever*|*always) wanted to know about** (sthg.), **but never dared*|*were afraid (to) ask** *humor* a phrase used to advertise information; it was first used, not humorously, to advertise a book about sex: *Everything you wanted to know about getting back to work, but never dared to ask!*

ev·ery·where /ˈevriweəʳ/ ‖ also **ev·ery·place** /-pleɪs/*AmE*— *adv* (in, at, or to) every place: *I can't find it though I've looked everywhere.* | *His cats follow him everywhere he goes.* | *We must clean the house – everywhere looks so dirty!* | *It was raining hard and there were puddles everywhere.*

every which way /ˌ·· ˈ· ·/ *adv AmE infml* (with verbs of movement) in every direction, without any order: *When the police arrived, the crowd started running every which way.*

e·vict /ɪˈvɪkt/ *v* [T (**from**)] to force to leave a house or land by law: *If you don't pay your rent you'll be evicted.* — ~ **ion** /ɪˈvɪkʃən/ *n* [C;U]

ev·i·dence /ˈevɪdəns/ *n* [U] **1** [(**of, for**)] something, such as a fact, sign, or object that gives proof or reasons to believe or agree with something: *an important piece of evidence* | *When the police arrived, he had already destroyed the evidence of his guilt.* (=papers, photos, etc., proving he was guilty) | *Is there any evidence for believing the world is round?* | *The report found no evidence of damage to crops by acid rain.* [+*that*] *There was some evidence that the documents had been tampered with.* | *The documents showed evidence of having been tampered with.* [+*to-v*] *There is some*|*insufficient evidence to suggest that he was there on the night of the murder.* | *The supposed murder weapon was produced in evidence at his trial.* **2** the answers given in a court of law: *The witness gave (her) evidence in a clear firm voice.* **3 in evidence** present and able to be seen and noticed: *The police were much in evidence* (=very noticeable) *whenever the President appeared in public.* —see also QUEEN'S EVIDENCE

ev·i·dent /ˈevɪdənt/ *adj* [(**to**)] plain, easy to the senses; clear because of evidence: *Despite her evident distress, she carried on working.* [+*that*] *It's evident (to me) that they have no experience in this work.* —see also SELF EVIDENT

ev·i·dent·ly /ˈevɨdəntli/ *adv* it is proved by clear signs (that); it is plain (that): *He is evidently not well.* –compare APPARENTLY, OBVIOUSLY

e·vil[1] /ˈiːvəl/ *adj* **-ll-** *BrE*‖**-l-** *AmE* **1** *fml* not good morally; wicked; harmful: *The play is based on an evil king who lived in Saxony.* | *That woman* **has an evil tongue**. (=says bad things about people) **2** *infml* very unpleasant: *What an evil smell!* | *It was an evil night.* (=the weather was very bad) –**evilly** /ˈiːvəl-li/ *adv*

evil[2] *n* [C;U] *fml* **1** (a) great wickedness or misfortune: *We must conquer the twin evils of disease and poverty.* | *her usual speech about the evils of socialism* –see also NECESSARY EVIL **2 hear no evil, see no evil, speak no evil** a phrase used when saying that a person does not hear, see, or say any bad things. The phrase is associated with the THREE WISE MONKEYS, three monkeys who are shown sitting together with one covering its ears, one covering its eyes, and one covering its mouth. –see also THREE WISE MONKEYS

e·vil·do·er /ˌiːvəlˈduːər/ *n fml* a person who does evil. This is a word only used by serious religious people

evil eye /ˌ·· ˈ·/ *n* [*the*+S] (*sometimes caps.*) the supposed power to harm people by looking at them. In the past, it was believed that certain people had this power.

e·vince /ɪˈvɪns/ *v* [T] *fml* (of a person or their behaviour) to show (a feeling, quality, etc.) clearly; REVEAL

e·vis·ce·rate /ɪˈvɪsəreɪt/ *v* [T] *fml or tech* to cut out the bowels and other inside parts of the body from –compare CLEAN[2] (2)

E·vi·ta /eˈviːtə/ a musical show about the life of Eva Peron the wife of a former Argentinian leader. One of the most famous songs from the show is *Don't Cry For Me, Argentina*.

e·voc·a·tive /ɪˈvɒkətɪv‖ɪˈvɑː-/ *adj* [(**of**)] that produces memories and feelings: *The taste of the cakes was evocative of my childhood.* | *an evocative smell*

e·voke /ɪˈvəʊk/ *v* [T] *fml* to produce or call up (a memory or feeling, or its expression): *That old film evoked memories of my childhood.* –**evocation** /ˌevəˈkeɪʃən, ˌiːvəʊ-/ *n* [C;U]

ev·o·lu·tion /ˌiːvəˈluːʃən, ˌevə-‖ˌevə-/ *n* [U] **1** (the scientific idea of) the gradual development of the various types of plants, animals, etc., from fewer and simpler forms: *In the course of evolution, some birds have lost the power of flight.*

▶CULTURAL NOTE According to this idea man developed from other animals and is related to APES[1]. Some religions do not accept this as being true. This idea was developed by Charles Darwin, who wrote about it in his book *On the Origin of Species*. –compare CREATIONISM◀

2 gradual change and development: *the evolution of the modern motor car* | *the evolution of philosophical thought*

ev·o·lu·tion·a·ry /ˌiːvəˈluːʃənəri◂, ˌevə-‖ˌevəˈluːʃəneri◂/ *adj* of or resulting from evolution; developing gradually

e·volve /iˈvɒlv‖ɪˈvɑːlv/ *v* [I;T (**from**)] to develop gradually by a long continuous process: *Some people believe that we evolved from the apes.* | *The British political system has evolved over several centuries.* | *They evolved a new system for running the factory.* | *Language is constantly evolving.* | *folk music which evolved out of popular culture*

ewe /juː/ *n* a fully-grown female sheep –compare RAM[1] (1)

ew·er /ˈjuːər/ *n* a large wide-mouthed container used in the past for liquid, esp. water for washing with

Ew·ing /ˈjuːɪŋ/, **J R** see JR

Ew·ings /ˈjuːɪŋz/ [*the*] a rich family who own an oil company in the American television programme *Dallas* –see also DALLAS, JR

ex /eks/ *n infml* someone's former wife, husband, girlfriend, or boyfriend: *I saw your ex the other day.*

ex- see WORD FORMATION

ex·a·cer·bate /ɪɡˈzæsəbeɪt‖-ər-/ *v* [T] *fml* to make (something bad) worse; AGGRAVATE: *The drugs they gave her only exacerbated the pain.* | *The border incident exacerbated East-West tension.* –**-bation** /ɪɡˌzæsəˈbeɪʃən‖-sər-/ *n* [U]

ex·act[1] /ɪɡˈzækt/ *adj* **1** correct in every detail; completely according to fact; PRECISE: *The exact time is three minutes and 35 seconds past two.* | *It's about two o'clock – three minutes and thirty-five seconds past,* **to be exact.** | *What was the exact route that they took?* | *I don't know the exact terms of the agreement.* | *He entered the hall at the exact moment* (=at the very same time) *that the concert began.* **2** marked by thorough consideration or careful measurement of small details of fact: *You have to be very exact in this job, because a small mistake can make a big difference.* –see also EXACTLY –**~ness** *n* [U]

exact[2] *v* [T (**from**)] *fml* to demand and obtain by force, threats, etc.: *I finally managed to exact a promise from them.*

ex·act·ing /ɪɡˈzæktɪŋ/ *adj* (of a person or a piece of work) demanding much care, effort, and attention: *It was a day of exacting and tiring work.* | *exacting standards of safety* –**~ly** *adv*

ex·act·i·tude /ɪɡˈzæktɨtjuːd‖-tuːd/ *n* [U] *fml* exactness

ex·act·ly /ɪɡˈzæktli/ *adv* **1** (used with numbers and measures, and with **what, where, who,** etc.) with complete correctness: *Tell me exactly where she lives.* | *The train arrived at exactly eight o'clock.* (=neither earlier nor later) **2** (used for adding force to an expression) just; really; quite: *They were doing exactly the opposite to what I had told them.* **3** (used as a reply) quite right: *"So you believe, minister, that we must spend more on education?" "Exactly."* **4 not exactly: a** not really: *We weren't exactly driving fast.* | *He's not exactly (what you would call) stupid, but ...* **b** (as a reply) that is not altogether true: *"So you missed the meeting." "Not exactly. I got there five minutes before it finished."*

ex·ag·ge·rate /ɪɡˈzædʒəreɪt/ *v* [I;T] to say or believe more than the truth about (something); make (something) seem larger, better, worse, etc., than it really is: *The machine is very useful, but he's exaggerating when he calls it the greatest invention ever made!* | *The seriousness of the situation has been much exaggerated in the press.* | *He has an exaggerated idea of his own importance.* –**-ratedly** *adv* –**-ration** /ɪɡˌzædʒəˈreɪʃən/ *n* [C;U] : *To call it a mountain would be an exaggeration; it's more of a hill.* | *I can say without exaggeration that she's the most useful person in the company.*

ex·alt /ɪɡˈzɔːlt/ *v* [T] *fml* **1** to praise (esp. God, a person, or their qualities) highly **2** to raise (a person) to a high rank –compare EXULT

ex·al·ta·tion /ˌeɡzɔːlˈteɪʃən, ˌeksɔːl-/ *n* [U] *fml or lit* a very strong feeling of happiness, power, etc.

ex·alt·ed /ɪɡˈzɔːltɨd/ *adj* **1** (of a person or their position) of high rank: *He felt very humble in such exalted company.* **2** *fml or lit* filled with exaltation –**~ly** *adv*

ex·am /ɪɡˈzæm/ *n* **1** also **examination** *fml*– a spoken or written test of knowledge: *Did you pass your history exam?* | *When will we know the exam results?* | *She failed her exams and she's going to have to take them again.* **2** *AmE, infml* a medical examination

ex·am·i·na·tion /ɪɡˌzæmɨˈneɪʃən/ *n* **1** [C] *fml* an exam **2** [C;U] (an act of) examining: *Before we can offer you the job, you'll have to have/undergo a medical examination.* | *The examination of all the witnesses took a week.* | *The committee's proposals are still* **under examination.** (=being examined) –see also PHYSICAL[2]

examination pa·per /·ˈ···· ˌ··/ *n fml for* PAPER[1] (3)

ex·am·ine /ɪɡˈzæmɨn/ *v* [T] **1** to look at, inquire into, or consider (a person or thing) closely and carefully, in order to find out something: *The doctor examined her carefully.* | *My luggage was closely examined when I entered the country.* | *The police examined the room for fingerprints.* | *to examine accounts/evidence/economic policy* **2** [(**on**)] to ask (a person) questions in order to find out something, for example in a court of law: *The witness was examined on her relationship with the accused.* –see also CROSS-EXAMINE **3** [(**in, on**)] *fml* to test (a person's) knowledge by means of an exam: *You will be examined in French and German/on your knowledge of American history.* –**-iner** *n* : *This candidate has failed to satisfy the examiners.* (=has not passed the exam)

exam pa·per /·ˈ· ˌ··/ *n* PAPER[1] (3)

ex·am·ple /ɪɡˈzɑːmpəl‖ɪɡˈzæm-/ *n* **1** [(**of**)] something taken from a number of things of the same kind, which shows the usual quality of the rest or shows a general rule: *This church is a wonderful example/a classic example of medieval architecture.* | *You have said there are several suitable machines to do this job; can you give me any examples?* (=mention some types) **2** [(**to**)] *apprec* a person, or a person's behaviour, that is worthy of being copied: *Mary's courage is an example to us all.* **3** [(to)] a piece of behaviour or way of acting that may be copied by other people: *She arrived at the office early, to set a good example to the others.* | *He followed his brother's example by setting up a small design agency.* **4 for example** (*abbrev.* **e.g.**) here is one of the things or people just spoken of: *A lot of us want to leave now — Bill, for example/for example, Bill.* **5 make an example of someone** to punish someone so that others will be afraid to behave as they did —see also EXEMPLIFY

▷ USAGE When we ourselves are an example to be copied, we **set** *an* **example**: *Drink your milk and* set *a* good **example** *to the other children!* When we invent an example to explain what we mean we **give** *an* **example**: *She talked about large animals and* **gave** *elephants as an* **example**.◁

ex·as·pe·rate /ɪgˈzɑːspəreɪt‖ɪgˈzæ-/ v [T *usu. pass.*] to annoy or make extremely angry, esp. by testing the patience of: *I was exasperated by/at all the delays.* —**ratedly** *adv* —**ration** /ɪgˌzɑːspəˈreɪʃən‖ɪgˌzæ-/ n [U] : *In sheer exasperation, she gave the machine a kick.*

ex·as·pe·rat·ing /ɪgˈzɑːspəreɪtɪŋ‖ɪgˈzæ-/ adj extremely annoying: *He's really a most exasperating man!* —**ratingly** *adv* : *exasperatingly slow*

Ex·cal·i·bur /ekˈskælɪbəʳ/ King Arthur's sword —see ARTHURIAN LEGEND

ex ca·the·dra /ˌeks kəˈθiːdrə/ adj, adv Lat fml, often derog (of a statement or command) (made) by the official right of one's high office: *It shows contempt for the public to make these ex cathedra pronouncements without any previous discussion.*

ex·ca·vate /ˈekskəveɪt/ v [I;T] **1** to make (a hole) by digging: *They plan to excavate a large hole before putting in the foundations.* **2** to uncover (something from an earlier time under the earth) by digging: *Schliemann excavated the ancient city of Troy.* —**vation** /ˌekskəˈveɪʃən/ n [C;U] : *The excavation of the buried city took a long time.* | *archaeological excavations*

ex·ca·va·tor /ˈekskəveɪtəʳ/ n **1** also **steam shovel** *AmE*— a large machine that digs and moves earth in a bucket at the end of a long arm **2** a person who excavates

ex·ceed /ɪkˈsiːd/ v [T] **1** to be greater than: *The cost will not exceed £50.* | *The cost of the damage exceeded* (=was worse than) *our worst fears.* | *The amount of money we raised exceeded all our expectations.* (=was better than we had hoped for) **2** *derog* to do more than (what is legal, necessary, etc.): *He was fined for exceeding* (=driving faster than) *the speed limit.*

ex·ceed·ing·ly /ɪkˈsiːdɪŋli/ adv extremely; to an unusual degree: *They were exceedingly kind to me.*

ex·cel /ɪkˈsel/ v -ll- [I;T (at, in) *not in progressive forms*] *fml* to be the best or better than: *When it comes to singing, she really excels.* | *He's never excelled at games.* (=isn't very good at them) | *What a marvellous meal, Jim! You've really* **excelled yourself.** (=done even better than usual)

ex·cel·lence /ˈeksələns/ n [U] the quality of being excellent: *the excellence of her cooking*

Ex·cel·len·cy /ˈeksələnsi/ n (used as a title for speaking to or about certain people of high rank in the state, for example an AMBASSADOR, or the church): *Good morning, Your Excellency.* | *His Excellency the Spanish Ambassador*

ex·cel·lent /ˈeksələnt/ adj extremely good; of very high quality: *Your examination results are excellent.* | *They are in excellent health.* | *The food was excellent.* | *an excellent idea* — —**ly** *adv*

ex·cept¹ /ɪkˈsept/ prep not including; leaving out; but not: *Everyone was tired except John.* | *Everyone except John was tired.* | *I can take my holidays at any time except in August.* | *I know nothing about him except that he lives next door.* | *I know nothing about the accident except what I read in the paper.* | *You can't get credit except by making special arrangements with management.* —see BESIDES (USAGE), BUT² (USAGE)

except² *conj* **1** apart from: *I can do everything around the house except cook.* **2** *infml* but: *I would go, except it's too far.* **3 except for: a** apart from; with the EXCEPTION of: *Except for one old lady, the bus was empty.* | *The road was empty except for a few cars.* **b** (only before nouns and

PRONOUNS) except: *Everyone was tired except for John.* | *Except for John, everyone was tired.* **c** if it were not for; but for (BUT): *She would have left her husband years ago except for the children.*

except³ v [T (**from**)] *fml* to leave out from a number or group; not include: *You will all be punished; I can except no one.*

ex·cept·ed /ɪkˈseptɪd/ adj [after n] apart from; except for: *Everyone, John excepted, was tired.* | *John excepted, everyone was tired.* | *The people at this party are really boring* — **present company excepted,** *of course* (=not including you).

ex·cept·ing /ɪkˈseptɪŋ/ prep except: *He answered all the questions excepting the last one.* | *Dogs are not allowed in the shop,* **always excepting** *blind people's guide dogs.* (=they are allowed)

ex·cep·tion /ɪkˈsepʃən/ n [C;U(to)] **1** (a case of) excepting or being excepted: *You must answer all the questions* **without exception.** | *It's been very cold this month, but today's an exception.* | *an exception to the rule* | *We don't usually take cheques, but we'll* **make an exception** *in your case.* (=we will accept your cheque) | *This problem affects all European countries, and Britain is no exception.* **2 take exception (to)** to be offended or made angry (by): *I took the greatest exception to his rude remarks.* **3 with the exception of** except; apart from: *With the exception of John, everyone passed the exam.*

ex·cep·tio·na·ble /ɪkˈsepʃənəbəl/ adj fml likely to cause dislike or offence; OBJECTIONABLE: *That play is quite suitable for children to see; there's nothing exceptionable in it.* —opposite **unexceptionable**

ex·cep·tion·al /ɪkˈsepʃənəl/ adj usu. apprec unusual, esp. of unusually high quality, ability, etc.; being an exception: *All her children are clever, but the youngest girl is really exceptional.* (=unusually clever) | *It was an exceptional game.* | *The firemen showed exceptional bravery.* — —**ly** /ɪkˈsepʃənəli/ adv : *exceptionally honest*

ex·cerpt /ˈeksɜːpt‖-ɜːr-/ n [(**from**)] a piece taken from a book, speech, or musical work for copying, performing, etc.: *One of the Sunday newspapers is publishing excerpts from her new book.*

ex·cess¹ /ɪkˈses, ˈekses/ n [S;U (**of**)] **1** something more than is reasonable; more than a reasonable degree or amount: *There is an excess of violence in the film.* | *He drinks* **to excess.** **2** *fml* the fact of being, or an amount by which something is, greater than something else: *This year's profits were* **in excess of** (=more than) *a million pounds.*

ex·cess² /ˈekses/ adj [A] additional; more than is usual, allowed, etc.

excess bag·gage /ˌ·· ˈ··/ also **excess luggage**— n [U] a passenger's cases, bags, and boxes that are more than an AIRLINE will carry free

ex·cess·es /ɪkˈsesɪz/ n [P] actions so bad that they go beyond the limits of what is acceptable: *The government seemed unable to curb* (=limit) *the excesses of its secret police.* | *the excesses of war*

ex·ces·sive /ɪkˈsesɪv/ adj too much; too great; going beyond what is reasonable or right: *The prices at this hotel are excessive.* | *He takes an excessive interest in clothes.* — —**ly** adv

ex·change¹ /ɪksˈtʃeɪndʒ/ n **1** [C;U] (a case of) the act of exchanging: *There was an exchange of political prisoners between the two countries.* | *He gave me an apple* **in exchange for** *a piece of cake.* | *We thought we'd do an exchange. She'll come over at Easter and I'll go there in the summer.* | *We're going to do an exchange. He'll have my bike and I'll take the car.* **2** [C] a TELEPHONE EXCHANGE **3** [C] (often cap.) a place where business people meet to buy and sell goods, shares, etc.: *They sell corn at the Corn Exchange, and company shares at the Stock Exchange.* **4** [C] a short period of fighting or talking between two people or groups: *Two soldiers were wounded in the exchange.* | *I had an acrimonious exchange with the manager.* —see also FOREIGN EXCHANGE, JOB CENTRE

exchange² v [T (**for, with**)] to give and receive in return (something of the same type or equal value): *The two teams exchanged presents before the game.* | *The battery I bought is the wrong size — I wonder if the shop will exchange it?* | *The fighters exchanged blows.* (=hit each other) | *I haven't seen him for years, though we exchange* letters at Christmas. | I exchanged seats with Bill. (=I took his and he took mine) | We move into the new house as soon as we have exchanged contracts. (=the last stage of buying a house) | Where can I exchange my dollars for pounds? – ~**able** adj

Exchange and Mart /ɪksˌtʃeɪndʒ ənd ˈmɑːt‖-ˈmɑːrt/ a British weekly national newspaper in which people advertise things such as cars which they want to sell, buy, or exchange

exchange rate /·ˈ· ·/ n the rate at which the money of one country is changed for that of another: We keep an eye on local exchange rates to find out where it is cheapest to buy parts from.

exchange rate mech·a·nis·m /·ˈ· · ˌ····/ n **1** [the] EUROPEAN EXCHANGE RATE MECHANISM **2** [C] any system for controlling the exchange rate between the money of one country and that of another country

Ex·cheq·uer /ɪksˈtʃekəʳ‖ˈekstʃekər/ [the] (in Britain) the government department that is responsible for the collection of taxes and the paying out of public money. It is part of the Treasury, whose chief minister is called the **Chancellor of the Exchequer** –compare TREASURY (1)

ex·cise¹ /ˈeksaɪz/ n [U] the government tax on certain goods produced and used inside a country –compare CUSTOMS (1)

ex·cise² /ɪkˈsaɪz/ v [T] fml to remove (as if) by cutting out: The tumour was excised. –compare AMPUTATE –**cision** /ɪkˈsɪʒən/ n [C;U]

ex·ci·ta·ble /ɪkˈsaɪtəbəl/ adj usu. derog easily excited –**bility** /ɪkˌsaɪtəˈbɪlˌti/ n [U]

ex·cite /ɪkˈsaɪt/ v [T] **1** to cause to lose calmness and have strong feelings, esp. of expectation and happiness: Don't excite yourself! Relax! | The news of her arrival excited the crowd. **2** fml to cause a person or people to have (a strong feeling): The court case has excited a lot of public interest.

ex·cit·ed /ɪkˈsaɪtˌd/ adj **1** full of strong feelings of expectation and happiness; not calm: She's very excited about getting a part in the film. | The scientists are excited about the results of the experiment. | The excited children were opening their Christmas presents. | (infml) Their new record is **nothing to get excited about**. (=not very good) **2** esp. AmE, infml ready for sex – ~**ly** adv

ex·cite·ment /ɪkˈsaɪtmənt/ n **1** [U] the state or quality of being excited: He has a weak heart, and should avoid excitement. **2** [C] an exciting event: Life will seem very quiet after the excitements of our holiday.

ex·cit·ing /ɪkˈsaɪtɪŋ/ adj causing excitement: an exciting film|football match|new development –opposite **unexciting** – ~**ly** adv

ex·claim /ɪkˈskleɪm/ v [I (**at**);T] fml to speak or say loudly and suddenly, because of surprise or other strong feeling: She exclaimed in delight when she saw the presents. | He exclaimed at the size of the bill. | "Good heavens!" he exclaimed. "It's six o'clock already."

ex·cla·ma·tion /ˌekskləˈmeɪʃən/ n the word(s) expressing a sudden strong feeling: "Good heavens!" is an exclamation (of surprise).

exclamation mark /·ˈ·· ·/ BrE‖**exclamation point** AmE– n a mark (!) written after the actual words of an exclamation, as in ' "I'm hungry!" she exclaimed.' –see picture at PUNCTUATION MARK

ex·clude /ɪkˈskluːd/ v [T] **1** [(**from**)] to keep or shut out: People under 21 are excluded from (joining) the club. **2** [(**from**)] to leave out from among the rest: No one was excluded from sentry duty. (=everyone did it) –opposite **include 3** to shut out (a reason or possibility) from the mind; not consider; REJECT: We cannot exclude the possibility that his wife killed him.

ex·clud·ing /ɪkˈskluːdɪŋ/ prep not counting; not including: There were thirty people in the hotel, excluding the hotel staff. –opposite **including**

ex·clu·sion /ɪkˈskluːʒən/ n [U (**from**)] **1** the act of excluding or fact of being excluded: His exclusion from the negotiations infuriated the union. **2 to the exclusion of** so as to leave out (all other members of a group); and not: He plays golf to the exclusion of all other sports.

exclusion zone /·ˈ·· ˌ·/ n a large area which the Government does not allow people to enter, either because it is

dangerous or for defence reasons: a fifty-mile exclusion zone

ex·clu·sive¹ /ɪkˈskluːsɪv/ adj **1** that excludes people considered to be socially unsuitable and charges a lot of money: one of London's most exclusive hotels **2** [A] limited to one person, group, or organization; not shared with others: This bathroom is for the President's exclusive use. | The reporter managed to get an exclusive interview with the Prime Minister. **3 exclusive of** not taking into account; without; excluding: The hotel charges £6 a day, exclusive of meals. –opposite **inclusive of** – ~**ness** n [U]

exclusive² n a newspaper story given to or printed by only one newspaper: If you pay me £20,000, I'll give your paper the story as an exclusive. –compare SCOOP¹ (3)

ex·clu·sive·ly /ɪkˈskluːsɪvli/ adv only; and nothing/no one else: This room is exclusively for women. | He writes exclusively for the Washington Post.

ex·com·mu·ni·cate /ˌekskəˈmjuːnɪˌkeɪt/ v [T] (esp. in the Roman Catholic Church) to formally take away membership of the church from (someone) as a punishment –**cation** /ˌekskəmjuːnɪˈkeɪʃən/ n [C;U] : The Church threatened them with excommunication.

ex-con /ˌ· ˈ·/ n sl a former prisoner

ex·co·ri·ate /ɪkˈskɔːrieɪt/ v [T] fml to express a very bad opinion of (a book, play, performance, etc.): an excoriating review –**ation** /ɪkˌskɔːriˈeɪʃən/ n [C;U]

ex·cre·ment /ˈekskrˌmənt/ n [U] fml the solid waste matter passed from the body through the bowels

ex·cres·cence /ɪkˈskresəns/ n fml an ugly growth on an animal or plant: (fig.) In my opinion, the new museum extension is an excrescence.

ex·cre·ta /ɪkˈskriːtə/ n [P] fml or tech excrement or URINE (=liquid waste matter)

ex·crete /ɪkˈskriːt/ v [I;T] fml or tech (of animals and humans) to pass out (waste matter esp. FAECES) from the body: The skunk excretes a very powerful smell when it is frightened. –compare SECRETE¹

ex·cre·tion /ɪkˈskriːʃən/ n [C;U] fml or tech (the act of producing) excreta

ex·cru·ci·at·ing /ɪkˈskruːʃieɪtɪŋ/ adj (of pain) extremely bad: I've got an excruciating headache. | (fig.) an excruciating performance – ~**ly** adv

ex·cul·pate /ˈekskʌlpeɪt/ v [T (**from**)] fml to free (someone) from blame; prove that (someone) has not done something wrong; EXONERATE –**pation** /ˌekskʌlˈpeɪʃən/ n [U]

ex·cur·sion /ɪkˈskɜːʃən‖ɪkˈskɜːrʒən/ n a short journey made for pleasure, usu. by several people together: We went on a day excursion (=there and back in a day) to Blackpool. | The travel company arranges excursions round the island.

ex·cu·sa·ble /ɪkˈskjuːzəbəl/ adj (of behaviour) that can be forgiven –opposite **inexcusable** –**bly** adv

ex·cuse¹ /ɪkˈskjuːz/ v [T] **1** [(**for**)] to forgive (someone) for (a small fault): (used esp. as a polite way of saying one is sorry) Please excuse my bad handwriting. | Please excuse me for opening your letter by mistake. | She excused his interruption. **2** [usu. in questions and negatives] to make (bad behaviour) seem less bad, or harmless; JUSTIFY: I don't think this excuses the government's neglect. [+v-ing] Nothing can excuse lying to your parents. **3** [(**from**)] to free (someone) from a duty: Can I be excused from football practice today? [+obj(i)+obj(d)] (esp. BrE) I was excused football practice because I had a cold. **4** [usu. pass.] euph (said esp. by children at school) to give permission to (someone) to go to the TOILET: May I be excused, miss? **5 Excuse me: a** (a polite expression used when starting to speak to a stranger, when one wants to get past a person, or when one disagrees with something they have said) Forgive me: Excuse me, does this bus go to the station? | He pushed his way through the crowd, saying "Excuse me." | Excuse me, but you're completely wrong. **b** AmE for SORRY² : She said "Excuse me" when she stepped on my foot. **6 excuse oneself: a** to offer an excuse **b** to ask permission to be absent: He excused himself from the party. **7 Excuse 'me!** also **Excuse me for living!**– infml (said humorously or angrily when really meaning that a complaint against you is very unreasonable and about nothing) Forgive me: "You weren't very polite to your mother." "Well, excuse me – I'm not perfect!" |

"I wish you hadn't embarrassed me by telling those bad jokes." "Well, excuse me for living!"

▷ USAGE In British English, you say (**I'm**) **sorry** to a person if you accidentally touch them, or push against them, or get in their way (for example, if you step on someone's foot). You might also hear the rather old-fashioned expression **I beg your pardon.** In American English you say **Excuse me** ◁

ex·cuse² /ɪkˈskjuːs/ *n* [C;U (for)] **1** the reason, whether true or untrue, given when asking to be forgiven for absence, wrong behaviour, a fault, etc.: *His excuse for being late was that he had missed the bus.* | *Stop making excuses!* | *I know it's poor work. I can only say* **by way of excuse/in excuse** *that I was ill at the time.* **2** a reason; JUSTIFICATION: *She loves giving parties, and does so whenever she can find an excuse.*(=e.g. a birthday, ANNIVERSARY, etc.) [+*to-v*] *trying to think of an excuse to leave* **3 make one's/someone's excuses** to explain why one/someone is not doing something or for absence: *Please make my excuses at tomorrow's meeting—I've got too much work to do to come.*

▷ USAGE Compare **reason, excuse,** and **pretext**: *His* **reason** *for leaving early was that his wife was ill.* (=she really was ill) | *His* **excuse** *for leaving early was that his wife was ill.* (=he said she was ill, and this may or may not have been true) | *He left early on the* **pretext** *that his wife was ill.* (=she was not ill at all and he had another reason for leaving early) ◁

ex·di·rec·to·ry /ˌeks daɪˈrektəri, dɪ-/ *BrE*‖**unlisted** *AmE*— *adj* (of a telephone number) not in the telephone book: *I've decided to go ex-directory.* (=have my number removed from the telephone book)

▶CULTURAL NOTE People may **go ex-directory** (= have their telephone number removed from the telephone book) if they are famous and want to protect their private life, or if they have been getting annoying telephone calls.◀

ex·e·cra·ble /ˈeksɪkrəbəl/ *adj fml* extremely bad: *She has execrable manners.* —**bly** *adv*

ex·e·crate /ˈeksɪkreɪt/ *v* [T] *fml* to feel or express hatred of; curse —**cration** /ˌeksɪˈkreɪʃən/ *n* [C;U]

ex·ec·u·tant /ɪgˈzekjʊtənt/ *n fml* a performer, esp. of musical pieces

ex·e·cute /ˈeksɪkjuːt/ *v* [T] **1** to kill (someone) as a lawful punishment: *She was executed for murder.* **2** *fml* to perform or do (an order, plan, or piece of work) completely: *The plan was good, but it was badly executed.* | *The house-to-house search was executed with military precision.* **3** *fml* to perform (music, dance steps, etc.) **4** *law* to carry out the orders in (a WILL² (5))

ex·e·cu·tion /ˌeksɪˈkjuːʃən/ *n* **1** [C;U] (a case of) lawful killing as a punishment: *Executions used to be held in public.* **2** [U (**of**)] *fml* the carrying out, performance, or completion of an order, plan, or piece of work: *The idea was never put/carried into execution.* **3** [U] *fml* skill in performing music: *The musician's execution was perfect, but he played without feeling.* **4** [U (**of**)] *law* the act of carrying out the orders in a WILL² (5)

ex·e·cu·tion·er /ˌeksɪˈkjuːʃənəʳ/ *n* an official who executes criminals

ex·ec·u·tive¹ /ɪgˈzekjʊtɪv/ *adj* [A] **1** concerned with making and carrying out decisions, esp. in business: *She has been given full executive powers in this matter.* **2** having the power to carry out government decisions and laws: *The executive branch carries out the laws which have been made by the politicians.* **3** of or for EXECUTIVES² (1): *Secretaries aren't allowed to use the executive dining room.* **4** desirable and expensive because of the high quality suitable for an executive

executive² *n* **1** [C] a person in an executive position, esp. in business: *a young advertising executive* **2** [*the*+S+*sing./pl. v*] the EXECUTIVE¹ (2) branch of government —compare JUDICIARY, LEGISLATURE

executive car /·ˈ··· ˌ·/ *n* a car which is expensive but which an executive could afford and would be likely to buy

executive house /·ˈ··· ˌ·/ *n* a modern house which costs more than average, but which an executive could afford and would be likely to buy

executive hous·ing /·ˌ··· ˈ··/ *n* [U] executive houses

executive jet /·ˌ··· ˈ·/ *n* a small JET plane for the use of an important businessman or government official

executive priv·i·lege /·ˌ··· ˈ···/ *n AmE* the right of the president or another government leader to keep the records of his office secret. In the US, during Watergate, the Supreme Court ruled that there are limits to executive privilege

executive suite /·ˈ··· ˌ·/ *n* a well furnished set of rooms in an office building for the use of an important businessman or government official

ex·ec·u·tor /ɪgˈzekjʊtəʳ/ *n* a person or bank that carries out the orders in someone's WILL² (5) after that person has died: *He appointed the bank to act as his executor.* | *Her son was one of the executors.*

ex·e·ge·sis /ˌeksɪˈdʒiːsɪs/ *n* -**ses** /siːz/ [C;U] *tech* serious explanation after deep study, esp. of the Bible

ex·em·plar /ɪgˈzempləʳ, -plɑːʳ/ *n fml* a good or typical example; MODEL¹ (5)

ex·em·pla·ry /ɪgˈzempləri/ *n* **1** *apprec* suitable to be copied as an example: *Her behaviour was exemplary.* (=very good) **2** [A] *fml* intended to serve as a warning: *The heavy jail sentence was given partly as an exemplary punishment.* (=to warn other people) | **exemplary damages** (=money that the court makes someone pay as a warning not to cause damage to someone else's good name)

ex·em·pli·fy /ɪgˈzemplɪfaɪ/ *v* [T] **1** to be an example of: *Her pictures nicely exemplify the sort of painting that was being done at that period.* **2** to give an example of: *In this dictionary we often exemplify the use of a word.* —**fication** /ɪgˌzemplɪfɪˈkeɪʃən/ *n* [C;U]

ex·empt¹ /ɪgˈzempt/ *adj* [F (**from**)] freed from a duty, service, payment, etc.: *He is exempt from military service* | *tax-exempt investments*

exempt² *v* [T (**from**)] to make (someone or something) exempt: *He was exempted from military service because of bad health.* — ~**ion** /ɪgˈzempʃən/ *n* [C;U (**from**)] : *exemption from military service*

ex·er·cise¹ /ˈeksəsaɪz‖-ər-/ *n* **1** [C;U] (a) use of any part of the body or mind so as to strengthen and improve it: *If you don't take/get more exercise you'll get fat.* | *She does exercises to strengthen her voice.* **2** [C] a question or set of questions to be answered by a student for practice: *Look at Exercise 17 in your book.* **3** [C] a set of actions carried out by soldiers, naval ships, etc., in time of peace to practise fighting: *The soldiers are here for a NATO exercise.* **4** [S (**in**)] any set of actions, esp. when intended to have a particular effect: *Getting this report done in such a short time was quite a difficult exercise.* | *After the President's embarrassing remark, his staff had to stage an exercise in damage limitation.* (=try to limit the damage he had done) **5** [S; U (**of**)] *fml* the use of a (stated) power or right: *Expelling him from the club was a legitimate exercise of the committee's authority.*

exercise² *v* **1** [I;T] to (cause to) take exercise: *You're getting fat; you should exercise more.* | *She was exercising her horse in the park.* **2** [T] *fml* to use (a power, right, or quality): *The judge thought it appropriate to exercise leniency in passing sentence.* | *to exercise caution/restraint* **3** [T (**by, about**) *usu. pass.*] *fml* to trouble (a person or their mind): *I've been greatly exercised about what we ought to do.*

exercise bike /ˈ··· ˌ·/ *n* a machine like a bicycle which does not move along which people can use indoors to get exercise and be healthy

ex·ert /ɪgˈzɜːt‖-ɜːrt/ *v* [T] **1** to use (strength, skill, etc.) to gain a desired result; APPLY (2): *She couldn't open the door, even by exerting all her strength.* | *The company has been exerting pressure on me to get another qualification.* | *to exert one's influence* **2 exert oneself** to make a great effort: *She can run 100 metres in 13 seconds without unduly exerting herself.* | *He never exerts himself to help anyone.*

ex·er·tion /ɪgˈzɜːʃən‖-ɜːr-/ *n* [C;U] (a case of) exerting oneself; (an) effort: *I was really tired after all my exertions.*

Ex·e·ter /ˈeksɪtəʳ/ *n* a city in Devon in SW England, where local government for the county of Devon is based

ex·e·unt /ˈeksiʌnt/ *v pl. of* EXIT³

ex gra·tia /ˌeks ˈgreɪʃə/ *adj Lat* (of a payment) made as a favour, not because one has a legal duty to do it: *The* company refused to accept responsibility for the accident, but gave me £10,000 as an ex gratia payment.

ex·hale /eks'heɪl/ v [I;T] to breathe out (air, gas, etc.): *Breathe in deeply and then exhale slowly.* | *He lit his pipe and exhaled clouds of smoke.* —opposite **inhale** —**halation** /ˌekshə'leɪʃən/ n [U]

ex·haust¹ /ɪg'zɔːst/ v [T] **1** to tire out: *What an exhausting day!* | *I'm completely exhausted.* **2** to use up completely: *We had exhausted our supply of oxygen.* | *My patience is exhausted.* | (fig.) *We've exhausted this subject* (=finished this conversation): *let's go on to the next.* — ~**ion** /ɪg'zɔːstʃən/ n [U] : *She ran and ran until she dropped from exhaustion.* | *The mine was closed owing to exhaustion.* (=there was no more coal left)

exhaust² n **1** [C] also **exhaust pipe** /·'··/, **tail pipe** AmE— the pipe which allows unwanted gas, steam, etc., to escape from an engine or machine **2** [U] the gas or steam which escapes through this pipe

ex·haus·tive /ɪg'zɔːstɪv/ adj thorough; including all cases or possibilities: *After an exhaustive search the missing document was found.* | *exhaustive inquiries* — ~**ly** adv — ~**ness** n [U]

ex·hib·it¹ /ɪg'zɪbɪt/ v **1** [I;T] to show (something) in public: *The new cars were proudly exhibited in the showroom window.* | *She has exhibited (her paintings) in Paris.* **2** [T] fml to give a sign of (a feeling, quality, etc.); show: *The negotiating team exhibited no emotion when they heard the offer.*

exhibit² n **1** something or a set of things exhibited, esp. in a MUSEUM: *Many of the exhibits were flown here from Canada.* **2** something brought into a law court to prove the truth: *Exhibit A was the murder weapon.* **3** AmE for EXHIBITION (1)

ex·hi·bi·tion /ˌeksɪ'bɪʃən/ n **1** [(of)] a public show of objects: *an international trade exhibition* | *to put on|stage|mount an exhibition of French paintings* | *The newly discovered Greek sculpture is now on exhibition at the national museum.* | *exhibition halls* **2** [(of)] an act of exhibiting: *a disgraceful exhibition of bad temper* **3** a piece of foolish behaviour: *Get up off the floor and stop making such an exhibition of yourself.* (=behaving so foolishly)

ex·hi·bi·tion·is·m /ˌeksɪ'bɪʃənɪzəm/ n [U] often derog behaviour intended to attract attention to oneself and often to shock people. Forms of exhibitionism include taking your clothes off in public or dressing in a way that most people find very odd. —**ist** n —**istic** /ˌeksɪbɪʃə'nɪstɪk/ adj

ex·hib·i·tor /ɪg'zɪbɪtəʳ/ n a person, firm, etc., that exhibits something: *All exhibitors must remove their displays before eight o'clock.*

ex·hil·a·rate /ɪg'zɪləreɪt/ v [T] to make (someone) cheerful and excited: *I was exhilarated by my ride in the sports car.* | *This sea air is most exhilarating.* —**ratingly** adv —**ration** /ɪgˌzɪlə'reɪʃən/ n [U]

ex·hort /ɪg'zɔːt/ v [T] fml to urge or advise strongly: [+obj+to-v] *The general exhorted his men to fight bravely.* — ~**ation** /ˌeksɔː'teɪʃən‖-ɔːr-/ n [C;U] : *In spite of all my exhortations, they went ahead with the plan.*

ex·hume /ɪg'zjuːm, eks'hjuːm‖ɪg'zuːm, ɪk'sjuːm/ v [T] fml to take (a dead body) out of the grave —**humation** /ˌeksjʊ'meɪʃən/ n [C;U] : *The coroner issued an exhumation order.*

ex·i·gen·cy /'eksɪdʒənsi, ɪg'zɪ-/ also **ex·i·gence** /'eksɪdʒəns, 'egzɪ-/— n [often pl.] fml an urgent need; a difficult situation in which one must act without delay: *The exigencies of the situation demanded that we take immediate action.*

ex·i·gent /'eksɪdʒənt/ adj fml **1** needing quick action or help; urgent **2** demanding or expecting more than is reasonable from others

ex·ig·u·ous /ɪg'zɪgʊəs/ adj fml too small in amount; not enough — ~**ly** adv — ~**ness** n [U]

ex·ile¹ /'eksaɪl, 'egzaɪl/ n **1** [S;U] forced or unwanted absence from one's country, often for political reasons: *Napoleon was sent into exile.* | *He had a long exile on St Helena.* | *An opponent of the government in self-imposed exile* **2** [C] someone who has left or been forced to leave their country, esp. for political reasons or reasons connected with money: *a political exile* | *a tax exile*

exile² v [T (to)] to send (someone) into exile: *They exiled Napoleon to St Helena.* —compare BANISH

ex·ist /ɪg'zɪst/ v [I] **1** to live or be real; have been: *The technology for performing these operations already exists.* | *The Roman Empire existed for several centuries.* | *The two sides have reached a partial agreement, but several differences still exist between them.* **2** [(on)] (of a person) to continue to live, esp. with difficulty: *They're paid hardly enough to exist on.* | *She exists on tea and bread.*

ex·ist·ence /ɪg'zɪstəns/ n **1** [U] the state of existing: *Harry doesn't believe in the existence of God.* | *This law came into existence in 1918|has been in existence since 1918.* **2** [S] life; way of living: *She led|had a miserable existence.*

ex·ist·ent /ɪg'zɪstənt/ adj (still) existing: *This is the only copy of his book now existent.* —opposite **nonexistent**

ex·is·ten·tial /ˌegzɪ'stenʃəl◂/ adj related to existence or existentialism: *"There is no God" is an existential statement.*

ex·is·ten·tial·is·m /ˌegzɪ'stenʃəlɪzəm/ n [U] the modern belief and teaching of Kierkegaard, Sartre, Heidegger, etc., that people are alone in a meaningless world, that they are completely free to choose their actions, and that their actions determine their nature rather than the other way round —**ist** adj, n : *an existentialist philosopher*

ex·ist·ing /ɪg'zɪstɪŋ/ adj [A] present: *Under existing regulations, you are not allowed to bring animals into the country.* | *Human rights are not tolerated under the existing regime.*

ex·it¹ /'egzɪt, 'eksɪt/ n [(from)] **1** (often written over or on a door) a way out: *How many exits are there from this cinema?* | *a fire exit* **2** an act of leaving: *He made a quick exit when he heard the police coming.*

exit² v [I] (of a person) to go out; leave: *She exited pretty quickly when she heard him arriving.*

exit³ v pl. **exeunt** /'eksiʌnt/ [I] Lat (used as a stage direction in printed copies of plays) goes out; goes off stage: *Exit Hamlet, bearing the body of Polonius.*

▷ USAGE In stage directions, **exit** and **exeunt** come before the subject. **Exit** does not take "s" in the 3rd person singular.◁

EXIT /'egzɪt, 'eksɪt/ a British organization which aims to change the law against helping seriously ill people to die if they wish to. The organization gives advice to such people and their families. The Hemlock Society is a similar organization in the US. —see also EUTHANASIA

exit poll /'·· ˌ·/ n a process of asking people how they have voted in an election immediately after they have voted in order to discover the likely result of the election

exit vi·sa /'·· ˌ·/ n official permission (usu. in the form of a stamp in one's PASSPORT or a document) needed in some countries in order to leave the country legally

Ex·moor /'eksmʊəʳ/ a large area of open country (MOORLAND) in Devon and Somerset in SW England. Exmoor is a NATIONAL PARK and is known for its wild ponies (PONY). It is generally considered to be a beautiful area of British countryside and it is popular with holidaymakers and visitors to Britain.

Exmoor po·ny /ˌ·· '··/ n a type of PONY (=small horse) coming from the Exmoor area, with a brown coat, short ears, and large eyes

Ex·o·cet mis·sile /ˌeksəʊset 'mɪsaɪl‖-'mɪsəl/ n tdmk a type of explosive weapon that is guided by RADAR to hit distant objects or places

ex·o·dus /'eksədəs/ n [S (from)] a going out or leaving by a great number of people: *Every fine weekend there is a general exodus of cars from the city to the country.*

Exodus the second book of the Bible which tells the story of the Exodus, the journey out of Egypt to the Promised Land made by Moses and the JEWS

ex of·fi·ci·o /ˌeks ə'fɪʃiəʊ/ adj, adv Lat because of one's position: *The president is an ex officio member of the committee.* (=because he is the president)

ex·og·a·my /ek'sɒgəmi‖ek'saː-/ n [U] tech the practice of marrying outside one's own group, esp. as demanded by custom or law —**mous** adj

ex·on·e·rate /ɪg'zɒnəreɪt‖ɪg'zaː-/ v [T (from)] to free (someone) from blame; decide that (someone) is not guilty: *The report on the accident exonerates the company (from any responsibility).* —**ration** /ɪgˌzɒnə'reɪʃən‖ɪgˌzaː-/ n [U]

ex·or·bi·tant /ɪg'zɔːbɪtənt‖-ɔːr-/ adj (of costs, amounts, demands, etc.) much greater than is reasonable, usual, or expected: *The hotel charges exorbitant prices.* | *The job makes exorbitant demands upon my time.* − ~ **ly** *adv* −**tance** *n* [U]

ex·or·cis·m /ˈeksɔːsɪzəm‖-ɔːr-/ *n* [C;U] an act or the art of exorcizing −**cist** *n*

Exorcist /ˈeksɔːsɨst‖-ɔːr-/, **The** an American book which was written in the 1960s and later became a film. It tells the story of a young girl who behaves very strangely after Satan begins to live in her body.

ex·or·cize also **-cise** *BrE* /ˈeksɔːsaɪz‖-ɔːr-/ *v* [T] **1** to drive out (an evil spirit) from (a person or place) by solemn command: *They called in a priest to exorcize the ghost/the house.* **2** to get rid of (esp. a bad thought or feeling): *He could not exorcize the memory of the car crash.*

ex·ot·ic /ɪgˈzɒtɪk‖ɪgˈzɑː-/ *adj usu. apprec* excitingly different, strange, or unusual; (as if) from a distant and esp. tropical country: *exotic flowers/food/smells* | *an exotic dress* − ~ **ally** /kli/ *adv*

ex·ot·ic·a /ɪgˈzɒtɪkə‖ɪgˈzɑː-/ *n* [P] things that are excitingly different or unusual, esp. works of art, literature, etc.: *musical exotica*

ex·pand /ɪkˈspænd/ *v* **1** [I;T] to increase in size, number, VOLUME, degree, etc.; (cause to) grow larger: *Water expands when it freezes.* | *The company has expanded its operations in Scotland by building a new factory there.* | *the rapidly expanding market for computers* −opposite **contract** **2** [I (**on**);T] to make (a story, argument, etc.) more detailed by addition; ENLARGE (on): *I don't quite follow your reasoning. Can you expand (on it)?* | *You'll have to expand your argument if you want to convince me.* **3** [I] (of a person) to become more friendly and willing to talk: *He expanded a little when he had had a drink, and started to talk more freely.* − ~ **able** *adj*

ex·panse /ɪkˈspæns/ also **expanses** *pl.*− *n* [S+**of**] a wide space spreading in all directions: *We gazed out over the limitless expanse/expanses of the desert.*

ex·pan·sion /ɪkˈspænʃən/ *n* **1** [U] the act or process of expanding or being expanded: *Metals undergo expansion when heated.* | *The new factory is large, to allow room for expansion.* | *the company's expansion into new markets* **2** [C] something which has been expanded: *His book is an expansion of the play he wrote before.*

ex·pan·sion·a·ry /ɪkˈspænʃənəri‖-neri/ *adj* showing or causing expansion, esp. causing an expansion in business activity: *an expansionary monetary policy*

ex·pan·sion·is·m /ɪkˈspænʃənɪzəm/ *n* [U] *usu. derog* the intention of expanding one's land, influence, etc.: *The country's leaders were accused of territorial expansionism.* −**ist** *n, adj*

ex·pan·sive /ɪkˈspænsɪv/ *adj* **1** (of a person) friendly and willing to talk: *After she'd had a few drinks, Mary became very expansive.* **2** large and splendid − − **ly** *adv* : *"£100 each? I'll take twenty," he said expansively.* − ~ **ness** *n* [U]

ex·pat /ˌeksˈpæt/ *n infml, abbrev. for* expatriate: *The coast is crawling with expats!*

ex·pa·ti·ate /ɪkˈspeɪʃieɪt/ *v* **expatiate on/upon** sthg. *phr v* [T] *fml* to speak or write a lot or in detail about

ex·pat·ri·ate¹ /eksˈpætriət, -trieɪt‖eksˈpeɪ-/ also **expat** *infml*− *n* a person living in a foreign country

►CULTURAL NOTE This is a word used to describe someone who will never really be part of the society in the country where they live, and who is likely to return home after a certain period. Expatriates often go abroad to work for a certain length of time. British expatriates pay less tax than other British citizens. There is a STEREOTYPE of a British expatriate as living a lazy life in a sunny place and drinking a lot of GIN (= a kind of alcoholic drink) with other British expatriates.◄

ex·pat·ri·ate² /eksˈpætrieɪt‖eksˈpeɪ-/ *v* [T] *fml* to cause (a person) to leave their own country by force or legal power; EXILE −compare REPATRIATE

ex·pect /ɪkˈspekt/ *v* [T] **1** [*obj*] to think or believe (that something will happen): [+(*that*)] *I expect (that) she'll pass the exam.* [+*to-v*] *He expects to fail the exam.* [+*obj*+*to-v*] *I expect him to fail the exam.* | *We weren't expecting so many people to come to the party.* | *I* **half expected** *to see her there but maybe she was too busy to come.* | *I* **fully expected** *to see them − they come every year.* | *They are ex-*

pected *to make an announcement later on today.* | *It wasn't as hot as I expected.* (=I thought it would be hotter) | *"Will she come soon?" "I expect so/I expect not."* **2** to think or consider that (something or someone) is likely to come or happen: *"He failed his exam." "But what else did you expect?"* | *I'm expecting a letter.* | *I expect John home at six o'clock.* | *I'm expecting John at any minute now.* | *His weakness after the illness is* **(only) to be expected.** (=is quite usual) | *She's expecting a baby.* (=is PREGNANT) | *She's expecting a baby in June.* (=will give birth in June) −see also EXPECTING **3** [(**from**)] to have or express a strong wish for (something) or that (someone) will do something, with the feeling that this is reasonable or necessary: *The general expects complete obedience from his men.* [+*obj*+*to-v*] *You can't expect children to be quiet all the time.* | (in polite requests) *Patrons are expected to vacate their rooms by midday.* **4** [+(*that*); *obj*; *not in progressive forms*] *infml* to suppose; think (that something is true): *"Who broke that cup?" "I expect it was the cat."*

▷ USAGE Compare **expect, look forward to,** and **hope.** If you **expect** something, you think that it will happen: *We're* **expecting** *a visit from Bill this summer.* | *I* **expect** *the train will be late, as usual.* If you **look forward** to something, you think that it will happen, and feel happy as a result: *I'm really* **looking forward to** *the holidays.* | *I'm* **looking forward to** *meeting her.* If you **hope** for something, you want it to happen and you think there is a possibility that it might happen: *We're all* **hoping** *for fine weather.* | *I* **hope** (*that*) *the weather will be fine for the match.* −see also ANTICIPATE (USAGE), WAIT (USAGE)◁

expect sthg. **of** sbdy./sthg. *phr v* [T] to hope or think it likely that (someone or something) will be or do (something): *There's no need to give me the money; I don't expect it of you.* | *I wouldn't have expected such rudeness of her.* (=I would not have thought she would be so rude) | *Don't expect too much of his idea.* (=don't think it likely to be good)

ex·pec·tan·cy /ɪkˈspektənsi/ *n* [U] hope; the state of expecting: *We waited for the announcement in a state of happy expectancy.* −see also LIFE EXPECTANCY

ex·pec·tant /ɪkˈspektənt/ *adj* **1** waiting hopefully: *The expectant crowds waited patiently for the queen.* **2** [A *no comp.*] PREGNANT: *a clinic for* **expectant mothers** − − **ly** *adv* : *They waited expectantly.*

ex·pec·ta·tion /ˌekspekˈteɪʃən/ *n* [C;U] the act of expecting or something that is expected: *He has little expectation of passing the exam.* (=does not expect to pass) | *We thought Mary would pass, but* **against/contrary to (all) expectation(s)**, *she didn't.* | *We thought John would do well, but he has succeeded* **beyond expectation/our expectations.** | *They closed the windows* **in expectation of** (=because they expected) *rain.* | *I usually enjoy his films, but that one didn't come up to/live up to my expectations.* (=was not as good as I expected)

expectation of life /ˌ··ˌ·· · ˈ·/ *n* [C;U] LIFE EXPECTANCY

ex·pec·ting /ɪkˈspektɪŋ/ *adj* [F] *infml, euph for* PREGNANT; a word used esp. in speech: *My wife's expecting again.*

ex·pec·to·rant /ɪkˈspektərənt/ *n* a type of cough medicine that helps to get rid of PHLEGM

ex·pec·to·rate /ɪkˈspektəreɪt/ *v* [I] *tech or euph* to force liquid from the mouth; SPIT

ex·pe·di·ent¹ /ɪkˈspiːdiənt/ *adj* (of a course of action) useful or helpful for a purpose, esp. one's own purpose or advantage, although not necessarily morally correct: *She thought it expedient not to tell her mother where she had been.* −opposite **inexpedient** − − **ly** *adv* − −**ency, -ence** *n* [U] : *The government will not condemn its allies for torturing prisoners. It is a question of expediency.* (=it is not to the government's advantage to do so) | *His behaviour seems to be governed solely by expediency.*

expedient² *n* a useful plan, idea, or action, esp. one thought of in a hurry because of an urgent need: *As she had forgotten her keys, she got into the house by the simple expedient of climbing through a window.*

ex·pe·dite /ˈekspɨdaɪt/ *v* [T] *fml* to make (a plan or arrangement) go faster: *We appealed to the government to expedite the procedure for the release of the prisoners.*

ex·pe·di·tion /ˌekspɨˈdɪʃən/ *n* **1** [C+*sing./pl. v*] (the people, vehicles, etc., going on) a (long) journey for a certain purpose: *I'm sending/taking part in/going on an expedition to photograph wild animals in Africa.* | *an expedition to the North Pole* **2** [U] *fml* the quality of being expeditious

ex·pe·di·tion·a·ry /ˌekspɪˈdɪʃənəri‖-neri/ *adj* [A] of or being an army sent abroad to fight: *The British Expeditionary Force went to France in 1914.*

ex·pe·di·tious /ˌekspɪˈdɪʃəs/ *adj fml* (of people or their actions) quick and without delay − ~ **ly** *adv*

ex·pel /ɪkˈspel/ *v* **-ll-** [T (**from**)] **1** to send away by force, esp. from a country; force to leave: *After the outbreak of fighting, all foreign journalists were expelled.* **2** to dismiss officially from a school, club, etc.. People are usu. expelled for breaking the rules by behaving in a way which is completely unacceptable: *If I catch you smoking in the school grounds again, you'll be expelled.* **3** *fml* to force out from the body or a container: *She expelled the air from her lungs.* −see also EXPULSION

ex·pend /ɪkˈspend/ *v* [T (**in, on**)] to spend or use up (esp. time, care, effort, etc.): *Don't expend all your energy on such a useless job.*

ex·pen·da·ble /ɪkˈspendəbəl/ *adj* that may be used up for a purpose: *The officer regarded his soldiers as expendable.* (=did not mind if they were killed)

ex·pen·di·ture /ɪkˈspendɪtʃəʳ/ *n* [S;U (**of, on**)] spending or using up: *Government expenditure on education is rising.* −compare INCOME

ex·pense /ɪkˈspens/ *n* [S;U] **1** cost in money, time or effort: *I don't know how the government can justify the expense of the project.* | *It's too much of an expense to own a car.* | **At great expense** (=by paying a lot of money) *I was finally able to buy the painting.* | *She* **spared no expense/went to a lot of expense** (=spent a lot of money) *to make the wedding a success.* | *I don't want to put you to the expense of* (=make you pay for) *buying me dinner.* | (fig.) *He finished the job* **at the expense of** (=causing the loss of) *his health.* **2 at someone's expense: a** with someone paying the cost: *He had his book printed at his own expense.* **b** (esp. of a joke or trick) against someone, so as to make them seem silly: *He tried to be clever at my expense.* −see also EXPENSES

expense ac·count /·ˈ·ˌ·/ *n* a record of money spent in travel, hotels, etc., in the course of one's work, which will be paid by one's employer: *I'm on an expense account.* (=have the cost of food, travel, etc., paid by my employer) | *expense-account lunches*

ex·pens·es /ɪkˈspensɪz/ *n* [P] the money used or needed for a purpose, often money paid by an employer for travel costs, etc. which people have as part of their job: *Her company sent her to Paris and paid all her expenses.* | *She was sent to Paris,* **all expenses paid.** | *travelling/holiday/funeral expenses* | *I didn't pay for the train fare − it was on expenses.*

ex·pen·sive /ɪkˈspensɪv/ *adj* costing a lot of money, esp. in relation to the amount of money a buyer has or to other things of a similar kind: *Your fur coat looks expensive/must have been expensive.* | *a very expensive watch/present* | (fig.) *Letting that goal in was an expensive mistake. It cost us the championship.* − ~ **ly** *adv*

ex·pe·ri·ence¹ /ɪkˈspɪəriəns/ *n* **1** [U (**of**)] (the gaining of) knowledge or skill which comes from practice in an activity or doing something for a long time, rather than from books: *How many years' experience do you have of teaching English?* | *Don't correct him all the time − he'll learn by experience.* | *I know from my own experience how difficult this kind of work can be.* **2** [C] something that happens to one and has an effect on the mind and feelings: *Our journey by camel was quite an experience!* | *a fascinating/traumatic/humiliating experience*

experience² *v* [T] to feel, suffer, or learn by (an) experience: *For the first time, we experienced defeat.* | *I experienced great difficulty in getting a visa to leave the country.* | *Our country has experienced great changes in the last 30 years.*

ex·pe·ri·enced /ɪkˈspɪəriənst/ *adj* [(**at, in**)] often apprec having skill or knowledge as a result of much experience: *She's a very experienced traveller.* (=has travelled a lot) | *an experienced lawyer* | *She's very experienced at/in repairing cars.*

ex·per·i·en·tial /ɪkˌspɪəriˈenʃəl‖/ *adj fml* based on experience; EMPIRICAL − ~ **ly** *adv*

ex·per·i·ment¹ /ɪkˈsperɪmənt/ *n* [C (**on**);U] (a) trial made in order to learn something or prove the truth of an idea: *They did/carried out/performed an experiment on the monkey to test the new drug.* | *We hope to find the answer to this problem by experiment.* | *an economic/social experiment*

ex·per·i·ment² /ɪkˈsperɪment/ *v* [I (**on, with**)] to do an experiment: *Is it right to experiment on animals?* | *They experimented with the new materials.* | *We found the right fuel mixture by experimenting.*

ex·per·i·men·tal /ɪkˌsperɪˈmentl◂/ *adj* used for or connected with experiments: *an experimental farm* | *This version is purely experimental, but we hope to have a commercial model soon.* − ~ **ly** *adv*

ex·pe·ri·men·ta·tion /ɪkˌsperɪmenˈteɪʃən/ *n* [U] the making of experiments: *After much experimentation they discovered how to split the atom.*

ex·pert /ˈekspɜːt‖-ɜːrt/ *n, adj* [(**at, in, on**)] (a person) with special skill or knowledge which comes from experience or training: *a medical/scientific/economic expert* | *She's (an) expert at/in/on teaching small children.* | *He's expert at hiding his feelings.* | *an expert card-player* − ~ **ly** *adv* − ~ **ness** *n* [U]

ex·per·tise /ˌekspɜːˈtiːz‖-ɜːr-/ *n* [U] skill in a particular field; KNOW-HOW: *His business expertise will be of great help to us.* | *She displayed considerable expertise in bringing the horse under control.*

expert sys·tem /·ˈ·· ˈ·ˌ·/ *n* a computer system which contains information on a particular subject and is intended to find the answers to problems in a similar way to the human brain −compare ARTIFICIAL INTELLIGENCE

ex·pi·ate /ˈekspieɪt/ *v* [T] *fml* to pay for or make up for (a crime or wicked action) by accepting punishment readily and by doing something to show that one is sorry −**-ation** /ˌekspiˈeɪʃən/ *n* [U]

ex·pire /ɪkˈspaɪəʳ/ *v* [I] **1** (of something which lasts for a period of time) to come to an end; run out: *The trade agreement between the two countries will expire next year.* | *The car broke down two days after the guarantee had expired.* **2** *lit* to die

ex·pir·y /ɪkˈspaɪəri/ also **ex·pi·ra·tion** /ˌekspɪˈreɪʃən/− *n* [U] the end of something which lasts for a period of time: *What's the expiry date on the spare film?* (=date before which it will be good to use) | *The President can be elected again at/on the expiration of his first four years in office.*

ex·plain /ɪkˈspleɪn/ *v* **1** [I;T (**to**)] to make (something) clear or easy to understand, usu. by speaking or writing: *I don't understand this, but Paul will explain.* | *The lawyer explained the new law (to us).* [+wh-] *John explained how it worked with a diagram.* | *Can you explain what this word means?* [+(that)] *He couldn't see how it worked until I explained that you had to turn it on first.* **2** [T] to give or be the reason for; account for: *Can you explain your brother's behaviour?* [+wh-] *That explains why she's not here.* **3 explain oneself: a** to make one's meaning clear: *I don't understand what you're talking about. Would you explain yourself further?* **b** to give reasons for one's behaviour: *Late again, Smith? I hope you can explain yourself!*

explain sthg. ↔ **away** *phr v* [T] to avoid blame for or cause to seem unimportant by giving an explanation or excuse: *The government will find it difficult to explain away the latest unemployment figures.*

ex·pla·na·tion /ˌekspləˈneɪʃən/ *n* [C;U (**of, for**)] **1** (an act of) explaining: *She's written an explanation of how the system works.* | *He gave/offered no explanation for his absence.* **2** something that explains: *The only explanation of/for his strange behaviour is that he's been working too hard.* | *He said, in explanation of his remarks, that the newspapers hadn't quoted him fully.* [+that] *His explanation that he had been held up by the traffic didn't seem very plausible.*

ex·plan·a·to·ry /ɪkˈsplænətəri‖-tɔːri/ *adj* (of a statement, a piece of writing, etc.) intended to explain: *There are some explanatory notes at the end of the chapter.* −see also SELF-EXPLANATORY

ex·ple·tive /ɪkˈspliːtɪv‖ˈeksplətɪv/ *n* **1** *fml* an often meaningless word used for swearing, to express violent feeling; OATH or curse: *He let loose a string of expletives.* (=he said a lot of swear words) **2 expletive deleted** a swear word has been removed from a written document.

This phrase became well known at the time of WATER-GATE when written documents of the conversations of President Nixon were read aloud.

ex·pli·ca·ble /ek'splɪkəbəl/ *adj* [F] *fml* (of behaviour or events) that can be explained: *Her behaviour is explicable if you consider her youth.* —opposite **inexplicable** —**bly** *adv*

ex·pli·cate /'eksplɪ̇keɪt/ *v* [T] *fml* to explain (esp. a work of literature) in detail

ex·pli·cit /ɪk'splɪsɪ̇t/ *adj* 1 (of a statement, rule, etc.) clear and fully expressed: *I gave you explicit instructions not to tamper with the controls.* —compare IMPLICIT 2 with full details; GRAPHIC: *There are several sexually explicit scenes in the film.* — — **ly** *adv* : *They were explicitly warned not to go up the mountain at night.* — — **ness** *n* [U]

ex·plode /ɪk'spləʊd/ *v* 1 [I;T] to blow up or burst or cause (esp. a bomb or other explosive) to blow up or burst: *The bomb exploded at 10.15 pm.* | *Don't touch that parcel; it might explode!* | *The army took the bomb away to a safe place and exploded it.* 2 [I (**in, into, with**)] (of a person) to show sudden violent and usu. noisy feeling: *He exploded with/in anger.* | *The audience exploded into/with laughter.* 3 [T *often pass.*] to prove (a belief) to be wrong or mistaken: *to explode a claim/theory* | *These statistics have finally* **exploded the myth** *that women are worse drivers than men.*

ex·plod·ed /ɪk'spləʊdɪ̇d/ *adj tech* (of a drawing, model, etc.) showing the parts of something separated but in correct relationship to each other

ex·ploit¹ /ɪk'splɔɪt/ *v* [T] 1 *derog* to use (esp. a person) unfairly for one's own profit or advantage; a word used to describe the misuse of power relations, esp. by employers or strong social and political groups: *The firm exploits its workers disgracefully.* | *The world economic system exploits the developing countries in favour of the developed ones.* | *The opposition parties are sure to exploit the government's difficulties over this issue.* 2 to use or develop (a thing) fully so as to get profit: *to exploit the country's mineral resources* — — **er** *n* — — **ation** /ˌeksplɔɪ'teɪʃən/ *n* [U]

ex·ploit² /'eksplɔɪt/ *n apprec* a brave and successful act: *He performed many daring exploits, such as crossing the Atlantic Ocean in a rowing boat.*

ex·ploit·a·tive /ɪk'splɔɪtətɪv/ *adj derog* tending to exploit people

ex·plo·ra·to·ry /ɪk'splɒrətəri‖ɪk'splɔːrətɔːri/ *adj* (of an action) done in order to find out something: *The doctors carried out an exploratory operation on my stomach.* | *exploratory talks with the leaders of the strike*

ex·plore /ɪk'splɔːʳ/ *v* [T] 1 to travel into or through (a place) for the purpose of discovery: *exploring the Amazon jungle* 2 to examine (esp. a subject or question) carefully in order to find out more: *We must explore all the possibilities.* —**ploration** /ˌeksplə'reɪʃən/ *n* [C;U] : *a voyage of exploration into outer space* | *There must be a full exploration of all the possibilities before we decide.*

explorer

ex·plo·rer /ɪk'splɔːrəʳ/ *n* someone who explores, esp. a person who travels for the purpose of discovery: *a famous 19th-century explorer*

ex·plo·sion /ɪk'spləʊʒən/ *n* 1 (a loud noise caused by) an act of exploding: *When she lit the gas there was a loud explosion.* | (fig.) *Explosions of laughter could be heard coming from the classroom.* | *an explosion of anger* 2 a sudden increase in the stated thing: *How can we account for the recent* **population explosion?** | *the sudden explosion of drug abuse*

ex·plo·sive¹ /ɪk'spləʊsɪv/ *adj* 1 that can explode: *It's highly dangerous to smoke when handling explosive materials.* | (fig.) *The old man has an explosive temper.* 2 (of a subject or question) that can cause very strong feeling; very CONTROVERSIAL: *Race relations are an explosive issue.* — — **ly** *adv* — — **ness** *n* [U]

explosive² *n* an explosive substance: *Gunpowder is an explosive.* —see also HIGH EXPLOSIVE, PLASTIC EXPLOSIVE

ex·po·nent /ɪk'spəʊnənt/ *n* 1 [(**of**)] a person who expresses, supports, performs, or is an example of a stated thing: *She is one of the leading exponents of Freudian psychiatry.* 2 *tech* a sign written above and to the right of a number or letter in MATHEMATICS to show how many times that quantity is to be multiplied by itself: *In 12^3 the number 3 is the exponent; in y^n the letter n is the exponent.*

ex·po·nen·tial /ˌekspəʊ'nenʃəl◂/ *adj tech* 1 produced or expressed by multiplying a set of quantities by themselves: *an exponential growth rate* | *The population is increasing on an exponential curve.* 2 containing an EXPONENT (2): y^n *is an exponential expression.* — — **ly** *adv*

ex·port¹ /ɪk'spɔːt‖-ɔːrt/ *v* [I;T] to send (goods) out of a country for sale: *We export (goods) to over 40 different countries.* | *They sell to the home market (=trade within the country) but they don't export.* | (fig.) *Britain has exported its language to many parts of the world.* —compare IMPORT¹ — — **able** *adj* — — **er** *n* : *Switzerland is a big exporter of watches.*

ex·port² /'ekspɔːt‖-ɔːrt/ *n* 1 [U] (the business of) exporting: *The export of gold is forbidden.* | *export earnings/sales/markets* 2 [C *often pl.*] something exported: *We depend on our exports for foreign currency.* | *Wool is one of the chief exports of Australia.* | *Selling insurance overseas is Britain's largest* **invisible export.** (=means of bringing money into the country other than by selling goods) —compare IMPORT²

ex·por·ta·tion /ˌekspɔː'teɪʃən‖-ɔːr-/ *n* [U] the action of exporting: *the exportation of corn to Asia* —compare IMPORTATION

Export Cred·it Guar·an·tee De·part·ment /ˌ··· ˌ··· ··'···ˌ··/ [*the*] a British government department which protects British EXPORTERs against losses from exporting (EXPORT) goods, e.g. non-payment by the buyers, etc.

ex·port·er /ɪk'spɔːtəʳ‖-ɔːr-/ *n* a person or country that exports: *Switzerland is a big exporter of watches.* —compare IMPORTER

export li·cence /'·· ˌ··/ *n* a document from the Department of Trade and Industry in Britain, allowing someone to sell certain goods abroad, e.g. weapons or works of art

ex·pose /ɪk'spəʊz/ *v* [T] 1 [(**to**)] to uncover; leave without protection: *Keep indoors and don't expose your skin to the sun.* | (fig.) *As a nurse in the war she was exposed to many dangers.* 2 [(**to**)] to make known (a secretly guilty person or action) a word used esp. when shame is brought on a person who is well-known or well-respected: *I threatened to expose him (to the police).* 3 to uncover (a film) to the light, when taking a photograph: *The photograph is too light. It must have been over-exposed.* 4 to leave (a baby) to die of cold and hunger out of doors: *The ancient Greeks are said to have exposed their unwanted babies.* 5 **expose oneself** (of a man) to show one's sexual parts on purpose, in the hope of exciting or shocking people

ex·po·sé /ek'spəʊzeɪ‖ˌekspə'zeɪ/ *n* [(**of**)] *Fr* a public statement of the esp. shocking facts about something. Exposés are often written by newspaper or television reporters: *an exposé of government corruption*

ex·posed /ɪk'spəʊzd/ *adj* [(**to**)] not protected from attack or sheltered from bad weather: *The army was left in an exposed position.* | *an exposed hillside*

ex·po·si·tion /ˌekspə'zɪʃən/ *n* 1 [C;U] *fml* (an act of) explaining and making clear: *She gave a full exposition of the projected marketing campaign.* 2 [C] an international show (EXHIBITION) of the products of industry

ex post fac·to law /ˌeks pəʊst 'fæktəʊ ˌlɔː/ *n law* a law which makes an action a crime and then punishes people who took that action before the law was made. Laws like this are forbidden in the US.

ex·pos·tu·late /ɪkˈspɒstʃʊleɪt||-ˈspɑː-/ v [I (**with, about, on**)] *fml* to reason with someone or express disagreement, annoyance, etc., esp. in order to prevent someone from doing something: *The ambassador expostulated at some length about foreign interference in the internal affairs of her country.* --**lation** /ɪkˌspɒstʃʊˈleɪʃən||-ˌspɑː-/ n [C;U]

ex·po·sure /ɪkˈspəʊʒəʳ/ n 1 [C;U (**to**)] (a case of) being exposed (EXPOSE (1)) to the stated influence: *After only a short exposure to sunlight he began to turn red.* | *The scientists risked exposure to harmful radiation.* | (fig.) *Being a soldier entails a certain exposure to danger.* 2 [U] the effect on the body of being out in cold weather for a long time: *We nearly died of exposure on the cold mountain.* 3 [C;U (**of**)] (a case of) being exposed (EXPOSE (2)): *I threatened them with public exposure.* | *Repeated exposures of governmental corruption have appeared in the newspapers.* 4 [C] the amount of film that must be exposed (EXPOSE (3)) for one photograph: *I have three exposures left on this film.* 5 [C] the length of time that a film must be exposed (EXPOSE (3)) to take a photograph: *an exposure of 1/100 of a second* 6 [S] the direction in which a room or house faces: *My bedroom has a southern exposure.* --see also INDECENT EXPOSURE and see picture at CAMERA

ex·pound /ɪkˈspaʊnd/ v [I (**on**);T (**to**)] *fml* to give a reasoned and detailed account or explanation (of): *She expounded for some hours on her theories about Central America.* | *to expound one's views*

ex·press¹ /ɪkˈspres/ v [T] 1 to show (a feeling, opinion, or fact), esp. in words: *She expressed our surprise when I told her how much it was.* | *We expressed our thanks.* [+wh-] *I can hardly express how grateful I feel.* 2 *BrE* to send by express post: *This letter is urgent; we'd better express it.* 3 [(**from, out of**)] *fml* to press (oil, juice, etc.) out of something: *The juice is expressed from the grapes and made into wine.* 4 **express oneself** to speak or write one's thoughts or feelings: *She expresses herself in good clear English.*

express² n 1 [C] also **express train** /·ˌ· ˈ·/— a fast train: *We caught the 9.30 express to London.* 2 [U] also **express delivery** *esp. BrE*— a service given by the post office, railways, etc., for carrying things faster than usual: *Send the letter by express.*

express³ adv by express post: *Send the parcel express.*

express⁴ adj [A] 1 going or sent quickly: *an express bus* | *I sent the letter by express delivery.* 2 *fml* clearly stated or understood; particular: *It was her express wish that you should have her jewels after her death.* | *I came here with the express purpose of seeing you.* --see also EXPRESSLY

Express [the] DAILY EXPRESS

ex·pres·sion /ɪkˈspreʃən/ n 1 [C;U] (an example of) the act of expressing; showing of feelings, opinions, etc., by words or actions: *He closed his letter with expressions of grateful thanks.* | *A government should permit the free expression of political opinion.* | *She gave him the present as an expression of gratitude.* | *You should give expression to (=express) your feelings, not hide them.* | *His anger at last found expression in (=was expressed) in loud cursing.* 2 [C] a look on a person's face: *When I saw her expression I knew I was in for trouble.* | *a puzzled/confident/surprised expression* 3 [C] a word or group of words: *"In the family way" is an old-fashioned expression meaning "pregnant".* 4 [U] the quality of showing or performing with feeling: *She has a beautiful voice, but she doesn't sing with much expression.* 5 [C] *tech* (in MATHEMATICS) a sign or group of signs that represents a quantity: x^2+4 *is an expression.*

ex·pres·sion·is·m /ɪkˈspreʃənɪzəm/ n [U] (*often cap.*) a style of painting, writing, or music (esp. in Europe in the late 19th and early 20th centuries) which expresses feelings rather than describing objects and experiences -- compare IMPRESSIONISM --**ist** n, adj

ex·pres·sion·less /ɪkˈspreʃənləs/ adj (esp. of a voice or face) not showing any feeling; a word usu. used when talking about someone who is thought to be deliberately hiding their feelings: *"I'm not angry," she said, in a controlled, expressionless voice.* -- ~**ly** adv

ex·pres·sive /ɪkˈspresɪv/ adj [(**of**)] full of feeling and meaning: *She has such an expressive face.* | *A baby's cry can be expressive of hunger or pain.* -- ~**ly** adv : *He plays the piano very expressively.* -- ~**ness** n [U]

express let·ter /·ˌ· ˈ··/ *BrE*||**special delivery** *AmE*— n a letter sent by express post

ex·press·ly /ɪkˈspresli/ adv *fml* 1 clearly; in an EXPRESS⁴ (2) way: *I told you expressly to report to me every day.* 2 on purpose: *The law was passed expressly to prevent such activities.*

express post /·ˌ· ˈ·/ *BrE*||**special delivery** *AmE*— adv the system of sending mail faster than usual and at a higher cost

ex·press·way /ɪkˈspreswei/ n *AmE* a road with at least two, and as many LANEs for traffic in each direction, and without any traffic lights, so that the driver may travel on it without stopping, usu. in or near a big city

▷ USAGE NOTE Many different *AmE* words describe this kind of road. **Expressways** are often in or near big cities. **Freeways** are also often near cities, or connect them. Like expressways they do not cost anything to use. **Turnpikes** and **tollways** are usu. longer, sometimes stretching all the way across a state, and the driver must pay to use them. Some of the roads in the **Interstate Highway** (=road going from one state to another) system are tollways, others are free. **Superhighway** is used to name any of these kinds of roads.◁

ex·pro·pri·ate /ɪkˈsprəʊprieɪt/ v [T] to take away (something owned by someone else), often for public use and/or without payment: *The State expropriated all the company's oil wells during the war.* --**ator** n --**ation** /ɪkˌsprəʊpriˈeɪʃən/ n [C;U]

ex·pul·sion /ɪkˈspʌlʃən/ n [C;U (**from**)] (an act of) expelling (EXPEL) or being expelled

ex·punge /ɪkˈspʌndʒ/ v [T (**from**)] *fml* to rub out or remove (a word, name, etc.) from a list, book, etc.: *The details we wanted had been expunged from the records.*

ex·pur·gate /ˈekspəɡeɪt||-ər-/ v [T] to remove harmful or offensive parts from (a book, play, etc.): *I've only read the expurgated version of this book, which is rather boring.* --see also UNEXPURGATED --**gation** /ˌekspəˈɡeɪʃən||-ər-/ n [C;U]

ex·qui·site /ɪkˈskwɪzɪt, ˈekskwɪ-/ adj 1 very finely made or done; extremely beautiful or skilful: *exquisite manners/grace/beauty* | *an exquisite piece of jewellery* 2 (of power to feel) sensitive and delicate: *He has exquisite taste in music.* 3 *fml* (of pain or pleasure) very great -- ~**ly** adv -- ~**ness** n [U]

ex·ser·vice·man /ˌ·ˈ····/— **ex·ser·vice·wom·an** /ˌ·ˈ·· ˌ··/ *fem.*— n esp. *BrE* a person who was formerly in one of the armed forces --compare VETERAN¹ (1)

ex·tant /ɪkˈstænt/ adj *fml* (esp. of something written, painted, etc.) still existing

ex·tem·po·ra·ne·ous /ɪkˌstempəˈreɪniəs/ adj spoken or done without time for preparation; extempore -- ~**ly** adv -- ~**ness** n [U]

ex·tem·po·re /ɪkˈstempəri/ adj, adv (spoken or done) without time for thought or preparation: *an extempore speech* | *It's very hard to speak* (=make a speech) *extempore.*

ex·tem·po·rize also **-rise** *BrE* /ɪkˈstempəraɪz/ v [I] to perform extempore; AD-LIB: *One of the actresses forgot her lines and had to extemporize.* --**rization** /ɪkˌstempəraɪˈzeɪʃən||-pərə-/ n [C;U]

ex·tend /ɪkˈstend/ v 1 [I+adv/prep] (of space, land, time, etc.) to reach, stretch, or continue: *The hot weather extended into October.* | *The kingdom extended as far as the mountains/hundreds of miles in every direction.* | (fig.) *The regulations do not extend to foreign visitors.* 2 [T] to make longer or greater, esp. so as to reach a desired point: *We will eventually extend the road as far as the station.* | *They extended the railway to the next town.* | *You can extend the guarantee by paying an extra £20.* | *She arrived for an extended* (=long) *stay.* | *The company plans to extend its activities to produce videos.* 3 [T] to stretch out (a part of one's body) to the limit: *The bird landed with its wings extended.* 4 [T (**to**)] *fml* to give or offer (help, friendship, etc.) to someone: *I would like to extend a warm welcome to our visitors.* [+obj(i)+obj(d)] *The bank will extend you credit.* (=the right to borrow money) 5

[T *usu. pass.*] to cause to use all possible power: *The horse won the race easily without being fully extended.*

ex·tend·ed fam·i·ly /·,·· '···/ *n* a family unit that consists not only of parents and children but also of other close relations such as grandfathers, grandmothers, and COUSINs —compare NUCLEAR FAMILY

▶ CULTURAL NOTE Because many young people move away from where they grew up, British people do not depend on the extended family for support as much as people do in some other countries. ◀

ex·ten·sion /ɪkˈstenʃən/ *n* 1 [C;U] (an example of) the act of extending or being extended: *a further extension of the power of central government* | *the extension of the copyright laws to cover recorded material* 2 [C (**of**)] a part which is added to make something longer, wider, or larger: *We're having an extension built onto the house.* | *I planned an extension of my holiday.* | (*BrE*) *The pub's got an extension tonight.* (=it is open after usual opening hours) 3 [C] any of many telephone lines which connect various rooms or offices in a large building to the SWITCHBOARD: *My extension (number) is 45.* 4 [U] a part of a university which offers courses to people who are not full-time students: *He's taking a political science class through* UCLA *extension.* | *She's doing an* **extension course.** 5 also **extension lead** *BrE* ‖ **extension cord** *AmE*— an electrical lead which can easily be bent and which has a PLUG at one end used to connect a piece of electrical equipment to the electricity supply some distance away: *You'll need an extension lead if you want to take the lamp up into the loft.*

ex·ten·sive /ɪkˈstensɪv/ *adj* large in amount, area, or range; having an effect on or including many parts: *The storm caused extensive damage.* | *We're having extensive repairs done to the building.* | *The story received extensive coverage in the newspapers.* | *The house has extensive grounds.* − − **ly** *adv* : *She has read extensively.*

ex·tent /ɪkˈstent/ *n* 1 [U (**of**)] the length or area to which something extends: *From the moon you can see the full extent of the Sahara desert.* | (fig.) *I was surprised at the extent of his knowledge.* | *What's the extent of the damage?* (=how much damage is there) 2 [S] a stated degree: *I agree with what you say to* **some extent** (=partly)/**to a certain extent/to a large extent.** | *The temperature rose* **to such an extent** (=so much) *that the firemen had to leave the burning building.* 3 [*the*+S+**of**] the limit: *I've reached the extent of my patience.*

ex·ten·u·ate /ɪkˈstenjueɪt/ *v* [T] to lessen the seriousness of (bad behaviour) by finding excuses for it; a word used esp. in connection with criminal acts: *He stole the money, but there were* **extenuating circumstances.** (=facts that might excuse him) −−**ation** /ɪkˌstenjuˈeɪʃən/ *n* [U] : *Does the psychiatrist's report have anything to say in extenuation of her crime?* (=that might excuse it)

ex·te·ri·or¹ /ɪkˈstɪəriər/ *adj* outer; on or from the outside, esp. of a building: *the exterior walls of the prison* | *exterior paintwork* [F+**to**] *The male reproductive organs are exterior to* (=outside) *the body.* −opposite **interior**; compare EXTERNAL

ex·te·ri·or² *n* 1 the outside; the outer appearance or surface: *We're painting the exterior of the house.* | *She maintained a calm exterior, though really she was furious.* 2 a picture of an outdoor scene: *Some artists only paint exteriors.* −opposite **interior**

ex·ter·mi·nate /ɪkˈstɜːmɪneɪt‖-ɜːr-/ *v* [T] to kill (all the creatures or people in a place, or all those of a certain kind or race): *to exterminate rats/mosquitos* −−**nator** *n* −−**nation** /ɪkˌstɜːmɪˈneɪʃən‖-ɜːr-/ *n* [U]

▶ CULTURAL NOTE Many British people remember the way that the DALEKs, evil creatures from space in the television programme *Dr Who*, said "Exterminate! Exterminate!" in a level voice with no rise and fall, and they sometimes say the word in this way as a joke. ◀

ex·ter·nal /ɪkˈstɜːnl‖-ɜːr-/ *adj* 1 [(**to**)] on, of, or for the outside: *an external wound* | *This medicine is* **for external use** (=to put on the skin), *not to drink.* | *The engine is external to the boat.* | *An* **external student** *studies outside the university.* | *An* **external examination** *is arranged by people outside one's own school.* —compare EXTERIOR 2 that can be seen but is not natural or real: *He is actually very shy, despite external appearances.* (=even though he appears not to be) 3 foreign: *This newspaper doesn't*

pay enough attention to external affairs. −opposite **internal** − − **ly** *adv*

ex·ter·nal ex·am·in·er /·,·· ·'···/ *n BrE* someone who visits a place of learning to examine students, or to check the quality of examination papers and make sure that standards stay the same in similar institutions −compare INTERNAL EXAMINER

ex·ter·nal·ize also **-ise** *BrE* /ɪkˈstɜːnəlaɪz‖-ɜːr-/ *v* [T] *tech* (in PSYCHOLOGY) 1 to give outward expression to (feelings), esp. by words 2 to RATIONALIZE (1b) −−**ization** /ɪkˌstɜːnəlaɪˈzeɪʃən‖ɪkˌstɜːrnələ-/ *n* [C;U]

ex·ter·nals /ɪkˈstɜːnlz‖-ɜːr-/ *n* [P] outward forms and appearances: *You mustn't judge people by externals.*

ex·tinct /ɪkˈstɪŋkt/ *adj* 1 (of a kind of animal) no longer existing: *Dinosaurs have been extinct for millions of years.* | (fig.) *The belief in magic is almost extinct nowadays.* 2 (of a VOLCANO) no longer active

ex·tinc·tion /ɪkˈstɪŋkʃən/ *n* [U (**of**)] 1 the state of being or becoming extinct: *Is the human race threatened with complete extinction?* 2 *fml* the process of extinguishing: *the extinction of a fire/of our hopes*

ex·tin·guish /ɪkˈstɪŋgwɪʃ/ *v* [T] *fml* to put out (a light or fire): *Smoking is forbidden. Please extinguish your cigarettes.* | (fig.) *Nothing could extinguish his faith in human nature.*

ex·tin·guish·er /ɪkˈstɪŋgwɪʃər/ *n* a FIRE EXTINGUISHER

ex·tir·pate /ˈekstɜːpeɪt‖-ɜːr-/ *v* [T] *fml* to destroy (something bad) completely −−**pation** /ˌekstɜːˈpeɪʃən‖-ɜːr-/ *n* [U]

ex·tol /ɪkˈstəʊl/ *v* **-ll-** [T] *fml* to praise very highly: *He keeps extolling the merits of his new car.* | *a speech extolling the virtues of free enterprise*

ex·tort /ɪkˈstɔːt‖-ɔːrt/ *v* [T (**from**)] to obtain (something) by force or threats: *They accused him of trying to extort money with menaces.* | *He extorted a promise from her.* − − **ion** /ˈstɔːʃən‖-ɔːr-/ *n* [C;U]: *The confession was obtained by extortion.* − − **ioner**, − − **ionist** *n*

ex·tor·tion·ate /ɪkˈstɔːʃənᵻt‖-ɔːr-/ *adj derog* (of a demand, price, etc.) much too high; EXORBITANT − − **ly** *adv* : *The rent was extortionately high.*

ex·tra¹ /ˈekstrə/ *adj, adv* 1 [A] additional(ly); beyond what is usual or necessary: *I need some extra money.* | *an extra loaf of bread* | *I'm going to work extra hard.* 2 as well as the regular charge: [F] *Dinner costs £13, and wine is extra.* | *They charge extra for wine.* [after *n*] *I had to pay £3 extra.*

extra² *n* 1 something added, for which an extra charge is made: *At this hotel a hot bath is an extra.* 2 a film actor who has a very small part: *We need a thousand extras for the big crowd scene.* 3 a special EDITION (=one printing) of a newspaper: *Late evening extra!* (shouted by newspaper seller) 4 (in cricket) a run that is not scored (SCORE) by a stroke of the BAT. For example, a BYE and a NO BALL are both extras.

extra- see WORD FORMATION

ex·tract¹ /ɪkˈstrækt/ *v* [T (**from**)] 1 to pull or take out, esp. with effort or difficulty: *She had a tooth extracted.* | (fig.) *They extracted a confession from the criminal.* 2 to remove (a substance which is contained in another substance) with a machine or instrument or by chemical means: *The oil is extracted from the seeds of certain plants.*

ex·tract² /ˈekstrækt/ *n* 1 [C (**from**)] a passage of written or spoken matter that has been taken from a longer work; EXCERPT: *She read me a few extracts from his letter.* 2 [C;U (**of**)] a product obtained by extracting (EXTRACT¹ (2)): *meat extract* −compare ESSENCE (2)

ex·trac·tion /ɪkˈstrækʃən/ *n* 1 [C;U (**from**)] (an example of) the act of extracting: *Her teeth were so bad that she needed five extractions.* | *The extraction of coal from these deep mines is expensive.* 2 [U] family origin in a stated place: *He is an American of Russian extraction.* (=his family came from Russia)

ex·trac·tor /ɪkˈstræktər/ also **extractor fan** /·'·· ·/− *n* an apparatus which takes out impure or smelly air from a kitchen, factory, etc.

ex·tra·cur·ric·u·lar /ˌekstrəkəˈrɪkjələr ◀/ *adj* (esp. of activities such as sports, music, or acting) outside the regular course of work (CURRICULUM) in a school or college. These activities are usu. free, and allow students to follow their own interests while using the facilities (FACILITY) of their place of study: *extracurricular activities*

ex·tra·di·ta·ble /ˈekstrədaɪtəbəl/ *adj* (of a crime) for which a person can be extradited

ex·tra·dite /ˈekstrədaɪt/ *v* [T (**from, to**)] to send (someone who may be guilty of a crime and who has escaped to another country or state) back for trial: *The English murderer was caught by the French police and extradited to Britain.* —**-dition** /ˌekstrəˈdɪʃən/ *n* [C;U] : *Is there an ex-tradition treaty between these two countries?*

ex·tra·ju·di·cial /ˌekstrədʒuːˈdɪʃəl/ *adj* beyond or outside the ordinary powers of the law

ex·tra·mar·i·tal /ˌekstrəˈmærɪtl◂/ *adj* of a married person's sexual relationships outside marriage: *an extramarital affair*

ex·tra·mu·ral /ˌekstrəˈmjʊərəl◂/ *adj* **1** connected with a place or organization but happening or done outside it: *This hospital provides extramural care.* **2** *esp. BrE* (of a student, course, etc.) connected with a university but working or happening outside it: *I attended extramural lectures organized by the University of Birmingham.* — opposite **intramural**

ex·tra·ne·ous /ɪkˈstreɪniəs/ *adj* **1** [(**to**)] not belonging or directly connected; IRRELEVANT: *His account of the war includes a lot of extraneous details.* | *This is extraneous to the subject we were discussing.* **2** being or coming from outside: *extraneous noises|forces* — ~**ly** *adv*

extra·or·di·nar·i·ly /ɪkˌstrɔːdənərˈɪli‖ɪkˌstrɔːrdnˈerˌɪli, ˌekstrəˈɔːrdnˈerˌɪli/ *adv* **1** very strangely: *Why does he behave so extraordinarily?* **2** more than usually; extremely: *It took an extraordinarily long time.*

extra·or·di·na·ry /ɪkˈstrɔːdənəri‖ɪkˈstrɔːrdnˈeri, ˌekstrəˈɔːrdnˈeri/ *adj* **1** very strange: *What an extraordinary hat!* **2** more than what is ordinary; special: *a girl of extraordinary beauty* | *An Act was passed giving the army extraordinary powers.* **3** [A] (of an arrangement) in addition to the ordinary one(s): *There will be an extraordinary meeting next Wednesday to discuss the emergency resolution.* **4** [after *n*] *fml* (of certain officials) additional to the usual official(s); employed on a special service: *an ambassador extraordinary*

ex·trap·o·late /ɪkˈstræpəleɪt/ *v* [I;T (**from**)] **1** (in MATHEMATICS) to work out (the value of a number which depends on measurements) by filling in the other measurements beyond those already known: *We don't know the exact figure for forest damage, but we can extrapolate from the sample surveys.* **2** *a* to guess (something in the future) from facts already known: *to extrapolate future energy demands* **b** to use (facts already known) so as to form a guess about the future —**lation** /ɪkˌstræpəˈleɪʃən/ *n* [U]

ex·tra·sen·so·ry per·cep·tion /ˌekstrəˌsensəri pəˈsepʃən‖-pər-/ *n* [U] see ESP¹

ex·tra·ter·res·tri·al /ˌekstrətəˈrestriəl◂/ *adj* (coming from) outside the Earth; a word often used in SCIENCE-FICTION stories: *Does extraterrestrial life exist?*

ex·tra·ter·ri·to·ri·al /ˌekstrətərɪˌtɔːriəl◂/ *adj* **1** *fml* outside the country: *Most of Britain's former extraterritorial possessions are now independent.* **2** *tech* (of a right) free from control by local law: *An ambassador has extraterritorial rights and cannot be punished for breaking the law.*

extra time /ˌ··· ˈ·/ *n* [U] a period of usu. 30 minutes added to the end of a football match which has ended in a draw. Extra time is added in certain competitions when there needs to be a clear winner.

ex·trav·a·gant /ɪkˈstrævəgənt/ *adj derog* **1** wasteful, esp. of money: *Don't be so extravagant; spend your money more carefully.* | *an extravagant party* **2** (of ideas, behaviour, and the expression of feeling) uncontrolled; beyond what is reasonable: *He makes the most extravagant claims for his new system.* — ~**ly** *adv* —**gance** *n* [C;U] : *His latest extravagance is a handmade silk shirt.* | *complaints about the government's extravagance*

ex·trav·a·gan·za /ɪkˌstrævəˈgænzə/ *n* a very grand and expensive piece of entertainment: *Her latest musical extravaganza features fifty dancing girls and live horses on stage.*

ex·tra·vert /ˈekstrəvɜːt‖-ɜːrt/ *n* an EXTROVERT

ex·treme¹ /ɪkˈstriːm/ *adj* **1** [A *no comp.*] greatest possible; of the highest degree: *in extreme danger* | *extreme cold* | *The extreme penalty of the law in England used to be punishment by death.* **2** [A *no comp.*] furthest possible;

at the very beginning or end: *The capital is in the extreme south of the country.* | *In extreme old age people often lose their memories.* **3** *often derog* (esp. of opinions and those who hold them) going beyond the usual limits; likely to be disapproved of by most people: *His political views are rather extreme.* | *She's an extreme right-winger.* | *The government had to take extreme measures to quell the uprising.*

extreme² *n* **1** the furthest possible limit; an extreme degree: *He used to be a Communist but now he's gone to the opposite|other extreme and joined the Fascists.* | (*fml*) *She has been generous* **in the extreme.** (=very generous) | *Sometimes he eats enormous amounts and sometimes nothing. He* **goes from one extreme to the other.** **2** **go/be driven to extremes** to (be forced to) act too violently or behave in an extreme way

ex·treme·ly /ɪkˈstriːmli/ *adv* to an extreme degree; very; highly: *I'm extremely sorry|angry.*

ex·trem·is·m /ɪkˈstriːmɪzəm/ *n* [U] *usu. derog* (esp. in politics) the holding of EXTREME¹ (3) opinions —**ist** *n* : *The bomb was planted by right-wing extremists.*

ex·trem·i·ties /ɪkˈstremˌtiz/ *n* [P] *fml* **1** the farthest parts of the body, esp. the hands and feet **2** strong, sudden, and severe action: *If they don't repay the loan soon, we shall have to resort to extremities.*

ex·trem·i·ty /ɪkˈstremˌti/ *n* [S;U (**of**)] *fml* the highest degree, esp. of suffering and sorrow; (a case of) the greatest misfortune: *The poor animal was in an extremity of pain.* — see also IN EXTREMIS

ex·tri·cate /ˈekstrɪkeɪt/ *v* [T (**from**)] to set free from something that it is difficult to escape from; DISENTANGLE: *The wrecked car had to be lifted before the driver could be extricated.* | *I managed to extricate myself from the situation by telling a small lie.* —**cable** /ekˈstrɪkəbəl/ *adj* —**cation** /ˌekstrɪˈkeɪʃən/ *n* [U]

ex·tro·vert, extravert /ˈekstrəvɜːt‖-ɜːrt/ *n* **1** a person who likes to spend time in activities with other people rather than being quiet and alone **2** *infml* a cheerful confident person —compare INTROVERT

ex·tro·vert·ed, extraverted /ˈekstrəvɜːtˌd‖-vɜːr-/ *adj* being or typical of an extrovert: *extroverted behaviour* —**version** /ˌekstrəˈvɜːʃən‖-ˈvɜːrʒən/ *n* [U]

ex·trude /ɪkˈstruːd/ *v* [T (**from**)] **1** *fml* to push or force out by pressure **2** *tech* to shape (plastic or metal) in this way, by forcing through a DIE (=a block with a shaped hole in it) —**rusion** /ɪkˈstruːʒən/ *n* [C;U]

ex·u·be·rant /ɪgˈzjuːbərənt‖ɪgˈzuː-/ *adj* **1** (of people and their behaviour) overflowing with life and cheerful excitement: *exuberant high spirits* | (fig.) *His paintings were full of exuberant colour.* **2** (of plants) growing strongly and plentifully: *the exuberant growth of a tropical rain forest* — ~**ly** *adv* —**rance** *n* [U]

ex·ude /ɪgˈzjuːd‖ɪgˈzuːd/ *v* [I;T] to (cause to) flow out slowly and spread in all directions: *A sticky substance exuded from the broken branch.* | (fig.) *She exudes confidence.*

ex·ult /ɪgˈzʌlt/ *v* [I (**at, in, over**)] *fml or lit* to show great delight and pleasure, often at the defeat or failure of someone else; a word usu. used with disapproval in modern English: *The soldiers exulted at their victory|exulted over their defeated enemies.* —compare EXALT — ~**ation** /ˌegzʌlˈteɪʃən/ *n* [U] : *The climber gave a cry of exultation when he reached the mountain top.*

ex·ul·tant /ɪgˈzʌltənt/ *adj fml or lit* exulting; JUBILANT: *The exultant crowds were dancing in the streets.* — ~**ly** *adv*

Ex·xon /ˈeksɒn‖-ɑːn/ *tdmk* the largest oil company in the US, called Esso in Britain: *It's two cents lower at the Exxon station.*

Exxon Val·dez /ˌeksɒn vælˈdiːz‖-sɑːn/ [*the*] *tdmk* the ship that caused the world's largest oil problem when it was wrecked in Prince William Sound, Alaska, in 1989, and large quantities of oil poured into the sea. Exxon spent a large amount of money on cleaning up the oil, which killed birds and sea animals, but was taken to court by many owners of damaged property. —see also AMOCO CADIZ

eye¹ /aɪ/ *n* **1** the organ of the body with which one sees: *He lost an eye in an accident, and now he has a glass eye.* | *She has blue eyes.* | *an eye specialist* | *She closed her eyes and went to sleep.* —see picture at HEAD **2** also **eyes** *pl.*— the power of seeing: *My eye fell upon* (=I noticed) *an*

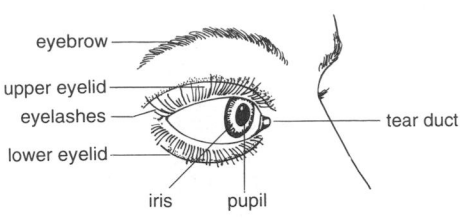

eyebrow
upper eyelid
eyelashes
lower eyelid
iris pupil
tear duct

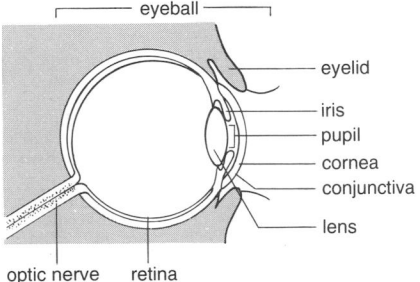

eyeball
eyelid
iris
pupil
cornea
conjunctiva
lens
optic nerve retina

interesting article in the newspaper. | She has **a (good) eye for** (=an ability to notice, judge, etc.) fashion. | **To my eye** (=in my opinion, having seen them) his paintings are just ugly daubs. | I **couldn't believe my eyes** when I saw how big it was. | She never **took her eyes off** (=stopped watching) the baby for a moment. **3** the hole in a needle through which the thread passes **4** a dark spot on a potato, from which a new plant can grow **5** the calm centre of a storm, esp. of a HURRICANE **6** a small ring-shaped or U-shaped piece of metal into which a hook fits for fastening: Her dress was fastened with hooks and eyes. —see picture at FASTENER **7 an eye for an eye** phrase from the Bible a punishment which hurts the criminal in the same way as they hurt someone else: If the state punishes a murderer by death it's an eye for an eye. **8 get/keep one's eye in** BrE (in ball games such as cricket or tennis) to get/keep, through practice, the ability to see the ball and to judge its direction **9 have eyes in the back of one's head** infml to be able to see or notice everything: How did you know I was there? You must have eyes in the back of your head. **10 (in) the eyes of** (in) the judgment or opinion of: In her father's eyes she can do no wrong. | In the eyes of (=according to) the law it is an offence, no matter how well intentioned. | The eyes of the world are upon us today. (=everyone around the world is watching) **11 keep an/one's eye on** infml to watch carefully: Please keep an eye on the baby for me. **12 keep an eye out for** infml to try to notice and remember (someone or something); be on the LOOKOUT for **13 keep one's eyes open/peeled/**(also **skinned** BrE) infml to watch carefully: The thieves kept their eyes peeled for the police. **14 make eyes at** infml to show that one finds (someone) sexually attractive by looking at them in an inviting way: He makes eyes at every girl he sees. **15 my eye!** old-fash infml (used for expressing disagreement or sometimes surprise): A diamond, my eye! That's glass. **16 one in the eye for** infml a disappointment or defeat for; a very informal expression: If we win the cup, it'll be one in the eye for that journalist — he's always said we're no good. **17 only have eyes for** to be interested only in: He only has eyes for his wife. (=he's not interested in other women) **18 under/before one's very eyes** in front of one; surprisingly in one's presence: The car blew up before our very eyes. **19 up to the eyes/one's eyes in** infml very busy with (esp. work): I can't come out today; I'm up to the eyes in work. **20 with/have an eye to** having/to have as one's purpose: She bought the house with an eye to making a quick profit out of it. **21 with half an eye** infml without looking or inquiring closely: You can see with half an eye that he and his wife are unhappy together. **22 with one's eyes open** knowing fully what the problems, difficulties, results, etc., might be: You married him with your eyes open, so don't complain

now! **23 -eyed** /aɪd/ having an eye or eyes of the stated type or number: a one-eyed dog | a blue-eyed girl **24 mine eyes have seen the glory of the coming of the Lord** quote the first line of the song Battle Hymn of the American Republic by Julia Ward Howe —see also BLACK EYE, ELECTRIC EYE, EVIL EYE, MAGIC EYE — **~less** adj

eye² v **eyeing** or **eying** [T (UP)] to look at closely or with desire: She eyed me suspiciously. | The child was eyeing the chocolate cake. | The boys stood on the corner eyeing (up) the local girls.

eye·ball¹ /ˈaɪbɔːl/ n **1** the whole of the eye, including the part hidden inside the head, which forms a more or less round ball **2 eyeball to eyeball (with)** infml face to face; facing each other, esp. in an angry or threatening way: The two politicians confronted each other eyeball to eyeball. | an eyeball-to-eyeball confrontation —see picture at EYE

eyeball² v [T] AmE sl to look directly at

eye·brow /ˈaɪbraʊ/ also **brow**— n **1** the line of hairs above each of the two human eyes: He had thick bushy eyebrows. **2 raise one's eyebrows** to show surprise or disapproval, often by moving one's eyebrows upwards: The president's insensitive comments caused a lot of eyebrows to be raised. (=shocked or annoyed many people) **3 up to one's eyebrows (in)** infml very busy (at): I can't come out — I'm up to my eyebrows (in work). —see pictures at EYE and HEAD

eyebrow pen·cil /ˈ·· ˌ··/ n [C;U] (a stick of) coloured material in a holder, used esp. by women for darkening the eyebrows

eye-catch·ing /ˈ· ˌ··/ adj unusual or attractive, so that one's attention is caught: an eye-catching advertisement — **~ly** adv

eye·ful /ˈaɪfʊl/ n [S] infml an attractive or interesting sight worth looking at: Get an eyeful of (=look at) this! | She's quite an eyeful!

eye·glass /ˈaɪɡlɑːs‖-ɡlæs/ n a glass (LENS) for one eye, the sight of which is weak; MONOCLE. It is not common now to see someone wearing an eyeglass but some people, usu. men, wore one in the past.

eye·glass·es /ˈaɪɡlɑːsɪz‖-ɡlæs-/ n [P] old use or AmE for GLASSES —see PAIR (USAGE)

eye·lash /ˈaɪlæʃ/ n any of the small hairs of which a number grow from the edge of each eyelid in humans and most hairy animals: She had long attractive eyelashes/false eyelashes. —see pictures at EYE and HEAD

eye·let /ˈaɪlɪt/ n a hole with a metal ring round it, which is placed in material such as leather or cloth so that a rope or string may be passed through it —see picture at SHOE

eye lev·el /ˈ· ˌ··/ adj of a height level with (=equal to) the height of one's eyes: Hang the picture at eye level. | an eye-level grill

eye·lid /ˈaɪlɪd/ n either of the pieces of covering skin which can move down to close each eye —see picture at EYE

eye·lin·er /ˈaɪˌlaɪnəʳ/ n [U] a usu. black substance used along the bottom edge of the top eyelid, and often also the top edge of the lower eyelid, to show up the shape of a woman's eye more clearly —compare EYE SHADOW

eye-o·pen·er /ˈ· ˌ···/ n a surprising sight, event, etc., esp. one that gives knowledge of something not known before: I knew he was strong, but it was quite an eye-opener when I saw him lift that car.

eye-patch /ˈaɪpætʃ/ n a PATCH (5)

eye pen·cil /ˈ· ˌ··/ n an EYEBROW PENCIL

eye·piece /ˈaɪpiːs/ n the glass (LENS) at the eye end of an instrument such as a microscope or TELESCOPE

eye shad·ow /ˈ· ˌ··/ n [C;U] (a container of) a coloured cream or powder used esp. by women on the eyelids to make the eyes look larger, more attractive, etc. — compare EYELINER

eye·sight /ˈaɪsaɪt/ n [U] the power of seeing: She has good/poor eyesight. | We test your eyesight before giving you a driving licence.

eye·sore /ˈaɪsɔːʳ/ n infml something ugly to look at, esp. when many people can see it. Modern buildings are sometimes described as eyesores: That new multi-storey car park is a real eyesore.

eye·tooth /ˈaɪtuːθ/ n -teeth /tiːθ/ 1 either of the two long pointed CANINE teeth (CANINE TOOTH) at the two upper corners of the mouth 2 give one's eyeteeth for/to *infml* to give up all one has in order to (get): *I'd give my eyeteeth to be able to play the piano like that.*

eye·wash /ˈaɪwɒʃ‖-wɔːʃ, -wɑːʃ/ n [U] *infml* nonsense; something said or done to deceive: *He says he's very busy, but it's all eyewash; he never does any work at all.*

eye·wit·ness /ˈaɪˌwɪtnɪs/ n [(to, of)] a person who has seen an event happen, and so is able to describe it, for example in a law court: *Were there any eyewitnesses to the crime?* | *an eyewitness account of the accident*

ey·ing /ˈaɪ-ɪŋ/ *present participle of* EYE²

eyot /eɪt, ˈeɪət/ n *BrE* a small island in a river

ey·rie, **eyry** *BrE* ‖ *usu.* **aerie** *AmE* /ˈɪəri, ˈeəri, ˈaɪəri/ n the nest of a large flesh-eating bird, esp. an EAGLE, built high in rocks or cliffs

F

F /ef/ **F's, f's** or **Fs, fs** the sixth letter of the English alphabet

F¹ **1** a note in Western music; the musical KEY¹ (4) based on this note **2** AmE a mark given to a student's work, meaning he or she has failed on a piece of work or the course: *Mark got an F in math – he'll have to do the class again.* —see GRADE 1 (3)

F² abbrev. for: FAHRENHEIT: *Water boils at 212 °F.*

fa /faː/ n [S] the fourth note in the SOL-FA musical SCALE

FA /ˌef ˈeɪ◂/ [the] Football Association; the ruling body for English football, which controls both the AMATEUR and the professional game and arranges the FA CUP —see also FOOTBALL (1) and see also extra information on page 501

FAA /ˌef eɪ ˈeɪ/ [the] abbrev. for FEDERAL AVIATION ADMINISTRATION

fab /fæb/ adj old-fash infml extremely good; FABULOUS

Fab·er·gé egg /ˌfæbəʒeɪ ˈeg‖fæbər‚ʒeɪ-/ n one of many beautiful jewelled eggs made by Peter Carl Fabergé for members of the Russian royal family. The Fabergé eggs are now very valuable.

Fa·bi·an /ˈfeɪbiən/ n, adj (a member) of the Fabian Society

Fabian So·ci·e·ty /ˈ··· ·‚···/ [the] a British organization of left-wing thinkers which was started in the late 19th century and which used to be an important influence on the Labour Party

fa·ble /ˈfeɪbəl/ n **1** [C] a short story that teaches a lesson (a MORAL) or truth, esp. a story in which animals or objects speak. Some of the best known fables were written by Aesop **2** [C] a story about great people who never actually lived; LEGEND; MYTH **3** [U] such stories considered as a group: *The course is about fable and legend in modern literature.* **4** [C] a false story or account

fa·bled /ˈfeɪbəld/ adj usu. apprec **1** spoken of or famous in fables; LEGENDARY **2** very famous

fab·ric /ˈfæbrɪk/ n **1** [C;U] (a) cloth made by threads woven together in any of various ways **2** [(the) S] the walls, roof, etc., of a building; structure: *The cost of repairing the fabric of the church was very high.* | (fig.) *The whole* **fabric of society** (=all of it and everything that holds it together) *was changed by the war.*

fab·ri·cate /ˈfæbrɪkeɪt/ v [T] to make or invent in order to deceive: *It turned out that he had fabricated the whole story.* —**cation** /ˌfæbrɪˈkeɪʃən/ n [C;U] : *The whole story was a complete fabrication.* (=a lie)

fabric con·di·tion·er /ˈ·· ·‚···/ also **conditioner‖fabric soft·en·er** /ˈ·· ‚···/ AmE— n a chemical added to water when washing clothes to make the clothes softer, usu. by softening the water

fab·u·lous /ˈfæbjʊləs/ adj **1** infml extremely good or pleasant; excellent: *It was a fabulous party!* **2** fml nearly unbelievable: *She possesses fabulous wealth.* **3** [no comp.] existing or told about in FABLES: *The dragon is a fabulous creature.*

fab·u·lous·ly /ˈfæbjʊləsli/ adv extremely (rich, great, etc.): *fabulously wealthy*

fa·cade, façade /fəˈsɑːd, fæ-/ n **1** the front of a building, esp. of a grand building —compare ELEVATION (3) **2** an appearance, esp. one that is false: *Although they put up a facade of honesty, they were involved in various criminal activities.*

face¹ /feɪs/ n **1** [C] the front part of the head from the chin to the forehead and hair: *a nice/round/spotty face* | *She had/wore a surprised expression on her face.* | *I was so ashamed that I couldn't* **look her in the face.** (=look directly at her) | (fig.) *Poverty is the unacceptable face of capitalism.* —see picture at HEAD **2** [C] a look or expression on the face: *a happy face* | *When he was told he couldn't go to the zoo he* **pulled a long face.** (=looked sad) | *Although she didn't feel very confident, she* **put on a brave face** *and accepted the challenge.* | *The children sat at the window* **making/pulling faces** (=rude or funny expressions) *at the passers-by.* **3** [C (**of**)] the front, outer, or most important surface of something: *They climbed the north face of the mountain.* | *The face of the building is covered with climbing plants.* | *the face of a clock/watch* | *They seem to have disappeared* **off the face of the earth.** (=completely) —see picture at MOUNTAIN **4** [C] the surface of a rock, either on or below the ground, from which coal, gold, diamonds, etc., are dug: *The miners work at the coal face for seven hours each day.* **5** [U] a state of being respected by others: *He was afraid of failure because he didn't want to* **lose face** *with his colleagues.* | *England* **saved (their) face** *by getting a goal in the last minute to draw the match.* —see also FACE-SAVING **6** [U] esp. BrE self-confidence or daring, esp. which is disrespectful or rude: *I don't know how you can have the face to see her after all the lies you've told.* **7** [C] a TYPEFACE **8** **face to face (with)** in or into the direct presence (of): *I've talked to him on the telephone but I've never actually met him face to face.* | *She came face to face with poverty for the first time.* **9** **in the face of** in spite of; against: *In the face of great hardship, she managed to keep her sense of humour.* **10** **on the face of it** judging by what one can see; APPARENTLY **11** **put a good/bold/brave face on something** to behave or make it appear as if things are better than they really are **12** **set one's face against** to oppose strongly **13** **to someone's face** in someone's presence; openly: *He wouldn't be so rude to her face.* **14** **-faced** /feɪst/ having a face or expression of the stated type: *red-faced* | *sad-faced* **15** **(Is this) the face that launched a thousand ships(?)** quote a phrase from a play by Christopher Marlowe describing the beauty of Helen of Troy

face² v **1** [I+adv/prep; T] to have or turn the face or front towards (something) or in a certain direction: *She turned to face the newcomer and introduced herself.* | *The house faces the park.* | *The building faces north/towards the north.* | *a sunny south-facing garden* | *A diagram appears on the facing* (=opposite) *page.* **2** [T] **a** to be in a position in which one must deal with (a problem or unpleasant situation): *Manufacturing industry faces a grim future if the government pursues its present policies.* **b** to accept or deal with (a problem or unpleasant situation), firmly and without trying to avoid it: *We'll have to face (the) facts – we simply can't afford a holiday this year.* | *He couldn't face his boss after making such a fool of himself at the meeting.* **3** [T] to need consideration or action by: *The main difficulty that faces us today is of supplying food to those in need.* **4** [T (**with**) often pass.] to cover or partly cover (esp. the front part of) with a different material: *The front of the brick house was faced with stone.* **5** **face the music** infml to meet and deal with the unpleasant results of one's actions: *He knew he'd never get away with it so he decided to face the music and give himself up to the police.*

face sthg./sbdy. **↔ out** phr v [T] to oppose or deal with bravely: *Everyone admired the way she faced out the opposition in the debate.* —compare OUT FACE

face up to sthg. phr v [T] to be brave enough to accept or deal with: *You must learn to face up to your responsibilities.*

face sbdy. **with** sthg./sbdy. phr v [T] to force to meet or deal with; bring face to face with: *When we faced her with all the evidence, she admitted the crime.*

face card /ˈ· ·/ n AmE for COURT CARD

face·cloth /ˈfeɪsklɒθ‖-klɔːθ/ also **face flan·nel** /ˈ· ‚··/ BrE‖**washcloth** AmE— n a FLANNEL¹ (2) used to wash esp. the face, hands, etc.

face cream /ˈ· ·/ n [C;U] (a) thick cream spread on the face, usu. by women, to clean or soften it, or protect it from dryness

face·less /ˈfeɪsləs/ adj usu. derog without any clear character or ordinary human feelings: *Our life is controlled by faceless bureaucrats.*

face-lift /ˈ· ‚·/ n **1** a medical operation to make the face look younger by tightening the skin: (fig.) *This room needs a face-lift. Why don't you put up some new wallpaper?*

face-off /ˈ· ·/ n AmE **1** (in ICE HOCKEY) a way of starting play by dropping the PUCK between two players of opposite teams **2** a situation in which opposing groups of people are likely to fight each other: *a face-off between police and rioters*

face pack /ˈ· ·/ n a cream that is spread over the face and then removed. It is usu. used by women to clean and improve the skin.

face pow·der /ˈ· ˌ··/ n [U] a flesh-coloured powder spread on the face, usu. by older women, to make them look or smell nice

face-sav·ing /ˈ· ˌ··/ adj which allows self-respect to be kept: *a face-saving solution to the dispute* (=by which neither side loses its self-respect) —see also FACE¹ (5) —**-er** n

fac·et /ˈfæsɪt/ n **1** any of the many flat sides of a cut jewel or precious stone **2** any of the many parts of a subject to be considered; ASPECT: *One needs to consider the various facets of the problem.*

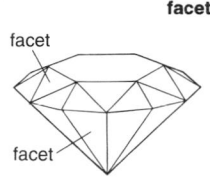
facet
facet

fa·ce·tious /fəˈsiːʃəs/ adj using or tending to use unsuitable jokes; unserious; FLIPPANT: *facetious remarks — ~ly adv — ~ness n* [U]

face-to-face /ˌ·· ˈ·◂/ adj [A] within each other's presence or sight: *a face-to-face meeting between the two leaders.*

face val·ue /ˌ· ˈ··/ n **1** [C;U] the value or cost as shown on the front of something, such as a postage stamp: *This stamp has a face value of 25 cents, but it's worth several thousand dollars nowadays.* **2** [U] the value or importance of something as it appears at first: *I was foolish enough to take his remarks at (their) face value; I should have known he was exaggerating.*

fa·cial¹ /ˈfeɪʃəl/ adj of the face: *She bears a strong facial resemblance to my sister. — ~ly adv*

facial² n a women's beauty treatment in which the skin of the face is treated with various substances and may also be massaged (MASSAGE)

fa·cile /ˈfæsaɪl‖ˈfæsəl/ adj **1** derog too easy; not deep; meaningless:*facile remarks | a facile conversation* **2** [A] fml easily done or obtained: *facile success — ~ly adv — ~ness n* [U]

fa·cil·i·tate /fəˈsɪlɪteɪt/ v [T] fml to make easy or easier; help: *The new underground railway will facilitate the journey to the airport. —-tation* /fəˌsɪlɪˈteɪʃən/ n [U]

fa·cil·i·ta·tor /fəˈsɪlɪteɪtəʳ/ n AmE a person who helps an activity to go forward but does not control it: *Joe and Ed are the facilitators of a men's encounter group.*

fa·cil·i·ties /fəˈsɪlɪtiz/ n [P] **1** things such as buildings, shops, or services that are useful or help one to do something: *The house is well situated in reach of good shopping and transport facilities. | The school has excellent sporting facilities.* **2** euph for TOILET: *Where are the facilities?*

fa·cil·i·ty /fəˈsɪlɪti/ n **1** [U (in, with)] fml ability to do or perform something easily and well: *her facility within languages* **2** [U] fml the quality of being able to be done or performed easily: *The facility of this piece of music makes it a pleasure to play.* **3** [C] an arrangement or system that makes a particular activity possible: *The computerized phone has a call-back facility. | an overdraft facility at the bank* **4** [C] a place or building used for a particular purpose or activity: *a training/research/ storage facility* **5** [C] an advantage; CONVENIENCE (2): *A free bus to the airport is a facility offered only by this hotel.*

fac·ing /ˈfeɪsɪŋ/ n [U] **1** an outer covering or surface of a wall, etc. for protection or decoration **2** additional material sewn into the edges of a garment to improve it, esp. in thickness

fac·ings /ˈfeɪsɪŋz/ n [P] the collar and parts (CUFFs) around the wrists of a garment, esp. a uniform, made in a different colour from the rest of the garment

fac·sim·i·le /fækˈsɪmɪli/ n [(of)] **1** an exact copy of a picture, piece of writing, etc.: *Many of the drawings are reproduced in facsimile in the catalogue. | a facsimile of a famous sculpture* **2** fml for a FAX

fact /fækt/ n **1** [C] something that has actually happened or is happening; something known to be or accepted as being true: *I don't want to argue about theories, just about facts. | Certain interesting facts about the moon have just been discovered. | Don't give me a long account, just tell me the plain/bare facts. [+(that)] The fact that you haven't got these qualifications doesn't necessarily mean you won't be able to enter the university. | She didn't answer my letter.* **The fact (of the matter) is** *she didn't even read it.* **2** [U] the truth; reality: *"Is this story fact or fiction?" "It's*

based on fact." **3 as a matter of fact/in (actual) fact/in point of fact** really; actually: *Officially he is in charge, but in actual fact his secretary does all the work. | He doesn't mind. In fact, he's very pleased. | "I suppose you haven't finished that report yet?" "I finished it yesterday, as a matter of fact."* —see also ACCESSORY (3), FACT OF LIFE

▷ USAGE 1 You can use **in fact** (and **as a matter of fact**) when you are giving information which adds force to something you have said: *I don't like him; in fact, I hate him. | I don't have a car.* **In fact**, *I can't drive.* 2 **As a matter of fact** (and **in fact**) are also used when you are disagreeing with something someone has said: *"You're always late for work." "No, I'm not!* **As a matter of fact** *I'm nearly always early." | "He's too old for the job." "Well, he's younger than you,* **as a matter of fact."**◁

fact-find·ing /ˈ· ˌ··/ adj [A] having as its purpose the discovery and making clear of the facts of a situation: *The government representatives went on a fact-finding mission to Africa to discover how bad the famine really was.*

fac·tion /ˈfækʃən/ n **1** [C] a group or party within a larger group that disagrees with the rest of the group or with other groups: *There are various factions within the ruling regime.* **2** [U] fml argument, disagreement, or fighting within a group or party

fac·ti·tious /fækˈtɪʃəs/ adj fml caused or produced intentionally or by human action; artificial: *A factitious demand for sugar was caused by rumours of shortage.*

fact of life /ˌ· · ˈ·/ n something that exists and that cannot (easily) be changed: *Starvation is a fact of life in many countries at the moment.* —see also FACTS OF LIFE

fac·tor /ˈfæktəʳ/ n **1** [(in)] any of the forces, conditions, or influences that act with others to bring about a result: *The president's support is an important factor in the success of the project. | the factors determining the rise in interest rates* **2** [(of)] (in MATHEMATICS) a whole number which, when multiplied by one or more whole numbers, produces a given number: *2, 3, 4, and 6 are all factors of 12.* **3** a measurement of how much a particular kind of SUNTAN OIL will protect one from the harmful effects of the sun on the skin: *a suntan oil with factor 6* **4** ScotE a person who looks after the lands of another **5** old use a person who acts or does business for another

Factor 8 /ˌfæktər ˈeɪt/ n [U] a PROTEIN that helps blood to thicken and which is given to HAEMOPHILIACS (=a person without Factor 8 in their blood). It must be checked thoroughly as some people have become infected with AIDS after receiving treatment of Factor 8.

fac·tor·ize also **-ise** BrE /ˈfæktəraɪz/ also **factor—** v [T] tech to divide into FACTORs (2) —**ization** /ˌfæktəraɪˈzeɪʃən ‖ -rə-/ n [U]

fac·to·ry /ˈfæktəri/ n a building or group of buildings where goods are made, esp. in great quantities by machines: *She works in a car factory. | factory workers*

factory farm /ˈ··· ·/ n usu. derog a farm where animals are kept in small cages and made to grow or produce eggs, milk, etc., very quickly —**factory-farm** v —**factory farming** /ˌ··· ˈ··/ n [U]

factory floor /ˌ··· ˈ·/ also **shop floor** n [the] the part of a factory where ordinary workers do their jobs, away from the management: *That decision won't go down well on the factory floor.* (=with the workers)

fac·to·tum /fækˈtəʊtəm/ n a servant who has to do all kinds of work

fact sheet /ˈ· ·/ n a piece of paper with only the most important information about something, esp. from a radio or television programme: *Our fact sheet for this week's programme contains both these recipes. Write to...*

facts of life /ˌ· · ˈ·/ n [the+P] euph the details of sex and how babies are born: *Have you told your son the facts of life yet?* —see also FACT OF LIFE

fac·tu·al /ˈfæktʃuəl/ adj based (only) on fact: *a factual account of the war — ~ly adv : factually accurate*

fac·ul·ty /ˈfækəlti/ n **1** [(of)] a natural power of the mind or body: *the faculty of hearing/memory | He has lost the use of his limbs but he is still in possession of all his faculties.* (=can think, see, hear, etc.) **2** [(for, of)] an ability or skill: *Yes, he does seem to have a faculty for making friends.* **3** (often cap.) a group of similar subject departments in a university: *The department of physics*

is in the Faculty of Science. **4** [+*sing.|pl. v*] *AmE* all the teachers and other professional workers of a school, university, or college

FA Cup /ˌef eɪ ˈkʌp/ [*the*] a football competition open to all AMATEUR and professional football teams in the FA in England and Wales, and arranged by the FA. It is the most PRESTIGIOUS football competition in England: *Liverpool won the FA Cup.* —see also FOOTBALL

fad /fæd/ *n infml, often derog* **1** an interest or activity that is followed very keenly but usu. only for a short time: *His interest in photography is only a passing fad.* | *the latest fad* **2** *esp. BrE* a set of very particular likes and dislikes. Many children have fads about certain foods: *She's a food-fad.* (=has strong ideas about what she will eat and not eat) *– ~ dish adj – ~ dishly adv –dy adj*

fad di·et /ˈ· ˌ··/ *n* a DIET of few or strange foods which is supposed to make people lose weight but which is often unsuccessful: *She has tried lots of different fad diets but she is still fat.*

fade /feɪd/ *v* **1** [I (AWAY); T] to (cause to) lose brightness, colour, strength, freshness, etc.: *Flowers soon fade when they have been cut.* | *These curtains were once bright green but the sun has faded them.* **2** [I (AWAY)] to disappear or die gradually: *The shapes faded (away) into the night.* | *Hopes of a peace settlement are now fading.*
fade in/up *phr v* [I;T (=**fade** sthg./sbdy. ↔ **in/up**)] (in film making or broadcasting) to (cause to) appear or be heard gradually: *We fade in the closing music as the hero rides off into the sunset.*
fade out *phr v* [I;T (=**fade** sthg./sbdy. ↔ **out**)] (in film making or broadcasting) to (cause to) disappear or become silent gradually: *When she started insulting everyone during the television interview they faded her out and showed an advertisement.* —**fadeout** /ˈfeɪdaʊt/ *n*

fae·ces also **feces** *AmE* /ˈfiːsiːz/– *n* [P] *fml or tech* the solid waste material passed from the bowels —**faecal** /ˈfiːkəl/ *adj*

Fae·roe Is·lands, Faroe- /ˈfeərəʊ ˌaɪləndz/ also **Faeroes, Faroes** [*the*+P] a group of islands belonging to Denmark, in the NE Atlantic

fae·ry , faerie /ˈfeəri/ *n* [U] *poet* the world or power of fairies; the imaginary world of stories —**faery** *adj*

faff /fæf/ *v*
faff about/around *phr v* [I] *BrE infml* to do unnecessary things without any organization: *Sit down and stop faffing around. I'll do it.*

fag¹ /fæg/ *n BrE sl* a cigarette

fag² *n AmE derog sl for* HOMOSEXUAL

fag³ *n infml, BrE* **1** [S] an unpleasant and tiring piece of work: *Cleaning the oven is a real fag!* **2** [C] (in certain British PUBLIC SCHOOLs) a young pupil who has to do jobs for an older pupil

fag⁴ *v* **-gg-** [I] *infml, BrE* **1** [(**for**)] (of a pupil in certain British PUBLIC SCHOOLs) to have to do jobs for an older pupil **2** [(AWAY)] to work hard

fag end /ˈ· ·/ *n infml* **1** [C] *BrE* ‖ **cigarette butt** *AmE* the last bit of a smoked and usu. no longer burning cigarette: *an ashtray full of fag ends* **2** [*the*+S+**of**] *esp. BrE* the very end or last part of something esp. when it is of lower quality or less interesting: *At the fag end of the football season the fans lose interest.*

fagged /fægd/ also **fagged out** /ˌ· ˈ·/ *adj* [F] *sl, BrE* extremely tired

fag·got also **fagot** *AmE* /ˈfægət/ *n* **1** *BrE* a ball of cut-up meat mixed with bread, which is cooked **2** *AmE derog sl for* HOMOSEXUAL **3** *BrE derog sl* an unpleasant or silly person: *"He thinks he's going to make a lot of money out of it." "Silly old faggot!"* **4** *old use* a bunch of small sticks for burning

fag-hag /ˈ· ˌ·/ *n AmE sl* a woman who likes to spend time with HOMOSEXUAL men rather than with other men

Fa·gin /ˈfeɪgɪn/ *n* a character

in the story of *Oliver Twist* by Charles Dickens. Fagin is the leader of a group of thieves and is the person who receives and sells the goods that the thieves have stolen.

Fahd ibn Ab·dul·a·ziz /ˌfɑːd ɪbən ˌæbdʊləˈziːz/, **King** (1923–) the king of Saudi Arabia since 1982

Fah·ren·heit /ˈfærənhaɪt/ *adj, n* [A;U] (of or in) a scale of temperature in which water freezes at 32° and boils at 212°: *Is it measured in Fahrenheit or Celsius?* | *a Fahrenheit thermometer* | [after *n*] *32° Fahrenheit equals 0° Celsius.* —see CELSIUS (CULTURAL NOTE)

fai·ence /faɪˈɑːns, -ˈɒns‖feɪˈɑːns/ *n* [U] cups, dishes, etc., made of baked clay decorated with a GLAZE, of European origin

fail¹ /feɪl/ *v* **1** [I; T+*to-v; obj*] to not do what is expected, wanted, or needed: *I tried to fix it but I failed.* | *If the crops fail* (=do not grow)*there will be a serious food shortage.* | *She failed miserably* (=completely) *in her attempt to persuade the committee.* | *The letter failed to arrive.* | *His secretary failed to tell him about the meeting.* | *My grandson never fails to phone me on my birthday.* (=always telephones me) | *I would be failing in my duty if I did not warn you of the dangers of your action.* **2** [I;T] to be unsuccessful in (a test or examination); not pass: *"Why did you fail (your driving test)?" "I went through a red light."* **3** [T] to judge (someone) to be unsuccessful in a test or examination: *He passed the practical exam but the teachers failed him in the written paper.* **4** [T+*to-v; obj*; *not in progressive forms*] *fml or pomp* to be unable: *I fail to see why you find it so amusing.* **5** [I] to stop operating properly, or to be unable to continue: *The rocket's engine failed a few seconds after takeoff.* | *When the price of oil doubled many businesses failed.* **6** [T] to disappoint or leave (someone), esp. at a difficult time: *Her friends failed her when she most needed them.* | *At the last moment his courage failed him and he ran away.* | *When I think of all this waste,* **words fail me.** (=it makes me so angry that I cannot find words to describe it) **7** [I] to lose strength; become weak: *The president's health is failing fast.* | *In the failing light I could hardly see the road in front of me.*

fail² *n* **1** ‖also **F** *AmE*– an unsuccessful result in a test: *"What were your results?" "A fail in history and passes in everything else."* **2 without fail** with complete certainty: *I'll bring you that book next time, without fail.*

fail·ing¹ /ˈfeɪlɪŋ/ *n* a fault, imperfection, or weakness: *That machine has one big failing: it uses too much fuel.*

failing² *prep* in the absence or failure of: *You may find her in the cafeteria, or* **failing that,** *try the library.*

fail-safe /ˈ· ·/ *adj* **1** made so that a failure in any part causes the whole machine, plan, etc., to return to a safe, usu. inactive, state: *a fail-safe device/mechanism* **2** that cannot fail: *a fail-safe plan*

fail·ure /ˈfeɪljər/ *n* **1** [U] lack of success; act of failing: *His plans ended in failure.* **2** [C] a person, attempt, or thing that fails: *As a writer, he was a complete failure.* | *She had many failures before finding the right method.* | *The party was a dismal failure.* **3** [C;U] the non-performance or non-production of something: *The drought caused crop failure.* | *She died of (a) heart failure.* [+*to-v*] *The government's failure to carry out their election pledge* **4** [C;U] inability of a business to continue, esp. through lack of money

fain /feɪn/ *adv old use* **1** with pleasure: *I would fain stay here for ever.* **2** rather; as a PREFERENCE: *They would fain be wed, but...*

faint¹ /feɪnt/ *adj* **1** weak and about to lose consciousness: *He felt faint from lack of food/faint with hunger* **2** lacking clearness, brightness, strength, etc.: *I heard a faint sound in the distance.* | *The colours became fainter and fainter as the sun sank.* | *She made a faint attempt at a smile.* | *faint memories* **3** very small; slight: *Our chances of victory are now very faint.* | (*infml*) *I haven't* **the faintest idea** *what you're talking about.* —see also **damn with faint praise** (DAMN⁴ (5)) **4 faint heart never won fair lady** *saying* you must act with courage or spirit if you want to achieve success *– ~ ly adv – ~ ness n* [U]

faint² *v* [I] to lose consciousness unexpectedly: *The young soldier fainted in the hot sun.* | *I nearly fainted when they told me the price.*

faint³ *n* an act or condition of fainting: *She fell down in a (dead) faint.*

Fagin

faint-heart·ed /ˌ· ˈ···◂/ adj lacking courage or spirit; cowardly — ~**ly** adv — ~**ness** n [U]

fair¹ /feəʳ/ adj **1** free from injustice, dishonesty, or self-interest: *a fair decision* | *You must be fair to both sides.* (=treat them both equally) | *He was late for the meeting but,* **to be fair,** *he didn't know about it until this morning.* | *It's not fair! Why should she always have first choice?* | *That was a perfectly fair tackle.* (=allowed by the rules of the game) [F+*to-v*] *I think it's fair to say that she was not to blame for the accident.* | *They've brought an adjudicator in to* **see fair play** (= make sure everyone is treated justly) *in the competition.* | *They are determined to win the election* **by fair means or foul.** (=in any way, honest or dishonest) —opposite **unfair** **2** [*no comp.*] quite good, large, etc.; reasonable: *His knowledge of the language is fair.* | *Her written work is excellent, but her practical work is only* **fair-to-middling.** | *She has a fair-sized garden.* | *I think I've got a* **fair idea** (=a reasonable understanding) *of what the job involves.* | *The builders are making good progress but they still have* **a fair way to go.** (=quite a lot more to do) **3** (having skin or hair that is) light in colour; not dark: *a fair complexion* **4** (of weather, etc.) not stormy; clear: *a fair sky* **5** favourable to a ship's course: *a fair wind* **6** *esp. old use* (of a woman) beautiful **7** [A] pleasing but not sincere: *I believed his fair promises.* **8** [A *no comp.*] *infml* (used to give force to an expression) real: *It's a fair treat to hear her sing.* **9 fair enough** *infml* all right; satisfactory — see also FAIRLY **10 with my own fair hands** *infml, humor* using my own hands **11 all's fair in love and war** *saying* in some situations any method of achieving what one wants is acceptable — ~**ness** n [U]

fair² also **fair and square** /ˌ· · ˈ·◂/ adv **1** in a just or honest manner, or according to the rules; fairly: *You must play fair (and square).* **2** straight; directly: *I hit him fair (and square) on the nose.*

fair³ n **1** *esp. BrE* a place of outdoor entertainment, with large machines to ride on and other amusements; FUN-FAIR **2** a market, esp. one held at a particular place at regular periods for selling farm produce: *a cattle fair* **3** *AmE* a yearly event at which farm products and equipment are shown and entered in competitions, and amusements are offered for people of all ages: *the De Kalb County Fair* **4** a very large show of goods, advertising, etc.: *a book fair* **5** an occasion when articles are sold and games are played to raise money for CHARITY; FETE

fair cop·y /ˌ· ˈ··/ n a clean perfect copy of a piece of writing: *My report is finished but it's very messy — I need time to make a fair copy.*

fair din·kum /feə ˈdɪŋkəm‖feər-/ adj, adv AustrE infml honest(ly); real(ly)

fair game /ˌ· ˈ·/ n [U (for)] someone or something that it is easy or reasonable to attack; an easy TARGET: *His idiotic speech was fair game for his opponents.*

fair·ground /ˈfeəgraʊnd‖ˈfeər-/ n an open space on which a FAIR³ (1) is held

fair·ing /ˈfeərɪŋ/ n a smooth rounded cover for an engine, part of a vehicle, etc., that allows the air to flow smoothly over it

fair isle /ˈ· ·/ n, adj [U] (a style of KNITTING or KNITTED GARMENT) having bands of a repeated pattern worked in several colours against a plain background (from **Fair Isle,** one of the Shetland Islands, where the style came from)

fair·ly /ˈfeəli‖ˈfeərli/ adv **1** in a manner that is free from injustice, dishonesty, or self-interest: *I felt they hadn't treated me fairly.* —opposite **unfairly** **2** to some degree; rather; quite: *Cut the meat fairly small, but not too small.* | *It's fairly hot today.* | *a fairly difficult exercise* **3** *infml* completely: *He fairly rocketed past us on his motorbike.*

▷ USAGE Compare **fairly, rather,** and **quite** when used with adjectives and adverbs. 1 Notice the word order in front of nouns: *It's a* **fairly/rather** *good book.* | *It's* **rather/quite** *a good book.* 2 **Fairly** is the least strong and **rather** the strongest of the three. Compare *It's a* **fairly** *good book* (=not too bad) and *It's a* **rather** *good book* (=I really think it's good). 3 **Rather** can sometimes have the meaning "too much": *It's* **rather** *warm in here, isn't it?* (=let's open a window) —see also QUITE (USAGE), RATHER (USAGE)◁

fair-mind·ed /ˌ· ˈ··◂‖ˈ· ˌ··/ adj apprec fair in judgment; just; giving equal treatment

fair play /ˌ· ˈ·/ n [U] **1** playing according to the rules of a game **2** *BrE* just treatment without cheating or dishonesty. British people think of themselves as putting special value on fair play. —see also CRICKET

fair sex /ˌ· ˈ·/ n [the] *old-fash* women considered as a group; GENTLE SEX

fair·way /ˈfeəweɪ‖ˈfeər-/ n the part of a GOLF COURSE along which one hits the ball in order to get to the GREEN² (2), where the hole is —see picture at GOLF

fair-weath·er /ˈ· ˌ··/ adj [A] present in times of success but absent in times of trouble (esp. in the phrase **a fair-weather friend**)

fairy

fai·ry /ˈfeəri/ n **1** a usu. small imaginary figure with magical powers and shaped like a human

▶ CULTURAL NOTE Many British children believe that fairies live at the bottom of their gardens, and British and American children believe that the TOOTH FAIRY replaces with money any teeth that come out and are put under their pillows. ◀

2 *derog* a HOMOSEXUAL man who behaves in a female way

fairy god·moth·er /ˌ·· ˈ···/ n infml a person who helps, and esp. saves, someone who is in trouble (from a story in which Cinderella, an unhappy young woman, is able to go to a BALL² only because her fairy godmother suddenly appears and magically produces a beautiful dress and a carriage to take her there) —see also CINDERELLA and see colour picture on page 357

fai·ry·land /ˈfeərilænd/ n **1** [U] the land where fairies live **2** [S] a place of delicate and magical beauty

fairy lights /ˈ·· ·/ n [P] *BrE* small coloured lights, esp. those used to decorate a Christmas tree

Fairy Liq·uid /ˌ·· ˈ··/ also **Fairy** tdmk— n [U] tdmk a kind of liquid used for washing dishes

fai·ry·tale /ˈfeəriteɪl/ adj [A] as if from a fairy tale; magical: *a fairytale castle* | *It was a fairy-tale romance.*

fairy tale /ˈ·· ·/ also **fairy sto·ry** /ˈ·· ˌ··/ n **1** a story about fairies and other magical people which always ends happily: *Our grandfather knew hundreds of fairy tales, and we always loved to hear them.* **2** a story or account that is hard to believe, esp. one intended to deceive: *Do you really expect me to believe that fairy tale?*

fait ac·com·pli /ˌfeɪt əˈkɒmpli‖-ˌækɑːmˈpliː/ n **faits accomplis** /ˌfeɪt əˈkɒmpliːz‖-ˌækɑːmˈpliːz/ something that has already happened or has been done and that cannot be changed: *They have presented us with a fait accompli; I'm afraid there's absolutely nothing we can do about it.*

faith /feɪθ/ n **1** [U (**in**)] firm belief; trust; complete confidence: *I'm sure she'll do as she promised. I've got great faith in her.* | *He still has great talent, but he has lost faith in himself.* | *an unshakeable faith in the essential goodness of human nature* **2** [U] (loyalty to one's) word of honour; promise: *I kept/broke faith with them.* | *The government has conducted the negotiations* **in good/bad faith.** (=sincerely/insincerely) —see also GOOD FAITH **3** [U (**in**)] belief and trust in God: *Had it not been for her great faith (in God), she would have given up.* **4** [C] a system of religious belief; religion: *The ceremony was attended by representatives of the Christian and Jewish faiths.* **5 faith, hope, and charity** three important good qualities in a Christian, according to Jesus Christ in the

Bible **6 O, ye of little faith** *humor* (a phrase used to find fault with someone who has just shown that they have no confidence in something or someone)

faith·ful¹ /ˈfeɪθfəl/ *adj* **1** [(to)] full of or showing loyalty: *a faithful friend* | *The dog remained faithful to his master.* **2** true to the facts or to an original: *a faithful account/copy/translation* **3** [(to)] loyal to one's (marriage) partner by having no sexual relationship with anyone else —see also FIDELITY — ~ **ness** *n* [U]

faithful² *n* **1** [*the*+P] religious people: *The faithful are gathering in the mosque to pray.* **2** [C] a loyal follower: *At election time we rely on old party faithfuls to help organize things.*

faith·ful·ly /ˈfeɪθfəl-i/ *adv* **1** with faith: *You promised faithfully that you would come.* **2** exactly: *I copied the map faithfully.* **3 Yours faithfully** *esp. BrE* (the usual polite way of ending a formal letter, when addressing someone as Sir, Madam, etc.) —see YOURS (USAGE)

faith heal·ing /ˈ· ˌ··/ *n* [U] a method of treating diseases by prayer and religious faith. Only a few people in Britain and the US practise this. —**faith healer** *n*

faith·less /ˈfeɪθləs/ *adj fml* disloyal; not deserving trust: *a faithless friend* — ~ **ly** *adv* — ~ **ness** *n* [U]

fake¹ /feɪk/ *v* **1** [T] to change (something) so that it falsely appears better, more valuable, etc.: *He faked the results of the experiment to prove his theory.* **2** [T] to copy (something) so as to deceive: *He faked my signature to get money from my bank.* —see also FORGE¹ **3** [I;T] *infml* to pretend: *She faked illness so that she did not have to go to school.* | *I thought he was really hurt but he was faking BrE‖faking it -AmE.* —see also FEIGN (1) —**faker** *n*

fake² *n* a person or thing that is not what he/she/it looks like or pretends to be; a usu. worthless copy of something, intended to deceive: *We thought it was a genuine antique, but it turned out to be a fake.* | *I thought he was a priest but after he robbed me I realized he was a fake.*

fake³ *adj* [A] made and intended to deceive: *a fake antique mirror* | *a fake laugh*

fake fur /ˌ· ˈ·/ *n* [C;U] (an article of clothing made from) man-made fur. Fake fur coats are often worn by people who do not agree with killing animals for their fur.

fa·kir /ˈfeɪkɪəʳ, ˈfæ-, fæˈkɪəʳ‖fəˈkɪər, fæ-/ *n* a wandering Hindu or Muslim holy man

fa·laf·el, felafel /fəˈlɑːfəl/ *n* a food, originally from the Middle East, which is made from crushed CHICK PEAs formed into balls and fried

fal·con /ˈfɔːlkən‖ˈfæl-/ *n* a bird that kills and eats other animals and can be trained to hunt

fal·con·er /ˈfɔːlkənəʳ‖ˈfæl-/ *n* a person who keeps, trains, or hunts with falcons

fal·con·ry /ˈfɔːlkənri‖ˈfæl-/ *n* [U] **1** the art of training falcons to hunt **2** the sport of hunting with falcons

Falk·lands /ˈfɔːlkləndz‖ˈfɔːk-/ **Falkland Is·lands** /ˈ·· ˌ··‖ ˌ·· ˈ··/ [*the*+P] a group of islands in the SW Atlantic ocean near Argentina, under British control. Known as the **Malvinas** in Argentina.

Falklands War /ˌ··· ˈ·/ [*the*] a war between Britain and Argentina in the Falkland Islands in 1982. Britain declared war after Argentina seized the Falkland Islands. The British forces recaptured the Falklands. It is sometimes thought that public support for the Conservative Party, then in power in Britain, and its leader Margaret Thatcher, increased after the Falklands War.

fall¹ /fɔːl/ *v* **fell** /fel/, **fallen** /ˈfɔːlən/ ■to move to a lower position or level **1** [I] to go down freely from a higher to a lower position or level, e.g. by losing balance or as a result of GRAVITY: *Don't walk along the top of the wall. You might fall.* [+*adv/prep*] *The ripe fruit fell from the tree.* | *Some ash fell off the end of her cigarette.* | *She's not a good rider — she keeps falling off.* | *The roof fell in.* (=sank inwards) | *The snow fell thickly, making travel difficult.* **2** [I (OVER, DOWN)] to come down from a standing position, esp. suddenly and usu. by accident: *She slipped and fell (down).* | *Five runners fell over in the mud.* | *She fell flat on her face.* | *He fell to his knees and begged forgiveness.* **3** [I] to become lower in level, degree, or quantity; drop: *Interest rates fell sharply last week.* | *The water level fell (by) three feet.* | *the falling demand for new cars* | *The temperature fell four degrees.* | *Their voices fell to a whisper.* —opposite **rise** ■shows a

change in condition: to pass into a different and often less desirable state **4** [I] *esp. fml or lit* to drop down wounded or dead, esp. in battle: *A prayer was said in memory of those who fell in the war.* —see also FALLEN² **5** [I;L] to pass, esp. suddenly or unintentionally, into a new state or condition; become: [+*adj*] *He fell ill.* | *She fell asleep.* [+*adv/prep*] *She fell into a deep sleep.* | *They fell in love.* | *The book was old and soon fell apart.* | *an old law that has fallen into disuse* [+*n*] *He fell victim to her perfume/fell prey to her charms.* **6** [I] to lose power or a high position: *The government will probably fall at the next election.* | *We must stand or fall together.* **7** [I (**to**)] to be defeated or taken by force (by): *The city fell (to the enemy).* **8** [I] (of the face) to take on a look of sadness, disappointment, shame, etc., esp. suddenly: *Her face fell when I told her the news.* ■other meanings **9** [I (**on**)] to come or happen, as if by descending: *Night fell quickly.* | *A silence fell on the room.* | *His eyes fell on* (=he suddenly saw) *the body.* | *Christmas falls on a Friday this year.* | *The stress falls on the last syllable of that word.* **10** [I+*adv/prep*] to hang loosely: *Her hair falls over her shoulders/down her back.* **11** [I+*adv/prep*] to slope downwards: *The land falls (away) towards the river.* **12** [I (**from**)] to be spoken: *A few muttered curses fell from his lips.* | *I guessed what was happening by the few remarks she let fall.* (=accidentally made) **13** [I+*prep*] to belong to a particular area of activity, responsibility, etc.: *These subjects fall under the general heading of "zoology".* | *This matter falls outside the scope of the committee's inquiry.* **14** [I] *old use* to give in to a wrong or immoral desire: *He was tempted, but did not fall.* —see also FALLEN³ ■fixed phrases **15 fall between two stools** *BrE* to be unable to decide between two courses of action and so be unsuccessful with regard to both **16 fall by the wayside** to no longer try or take part; give up, esp. because of failure or discouragement **17 fall flat** to fail to produce the desired effect or result: *His jokes fell flat.* (=nobody was amused) **18 fall foul of** to quarrel, fight, or get into trouble with: *His business methods were not entirely honest, and he soon fell foul of the law.* (=got into trouble with the police) **19 fall off one's chair** to be very surprised: *I nearly fell off my chair when I heard the news.* **20 fall on deaf ears** (of advice, warnings, requests, etc.) to be ignored or paid no attention **21 fall/land on one's feet** *infml* to be successful or fortunate, esp. after being in a difficult situation; have good luck **22 fall short (of)** to fail to reach (a desired result, standard, etc.): *The council planned to build 100 houses this year but they have fallen short of their target.* —see also **let fall**(LET¹) ■phrasal verbs

fall about *phr v* [I] *BrE, infml* to lose control of oneself (with laughter): *They fell about (laughing/with laughter) when she dropped all the eggs.*

fall back *phr v* [I] to move or turn back, esp. because someone is attacking or moving towards one: *The crowd fell back to let the policemen through.*

fall back on/upon sthg. *phr v* [T *no pass.*] to use when there is failure or lack of other means; RESORT **to**: *When I lost my job I was glad I had my savings to fall back on.*

fall behind *phr v* **1** [I;T (=**fall behind** sbdy./sthg.) *no pass.*] to become gradually further behind: *We can't afford to fall behind our competitors in using new technology.* **2** [I (**with**)] to fail to produce something at the proper time: *I'm falling behind with my work. I must try to catch up.* | *If you fall behind with the rent you may be thrown out.*

fall down *phr v* [I (**on**)] *infml* to fail or be ineffective: *Where this plan falls down is that it doesn't allow enough time for possible delays.* | *You've been falling down on the job recently. Is there anything troubling you?* —see also FALL (1,2)

fall for sthg./sbdy. *phr v* [T] **1** to be deceived by: *Don't fall for his tricks.* **2** *infml* to fall in love with, esp. suddenly: *She fell for him in a big way.*

fall in *phr v* [I;T (=**fall** sbdy. ↔ **in**)] to (cause to) take one's proper place in a military formation: *Fall in, men!* | *The captain fell the soldiers in for inspection.*

fall into sthg. *phr v* [T] **1** to begin or have by chance: *I fell into conversation with someone who said he knew you.* **2** to be divided into: *This topic falls naturally into three sections.*

fall in with sbdy./sthg. *phr v* [T] **1** *BrE* to agree with or to: *I'm quite happy to fall in with you/with your suggestion.* **2** to meet or begin to mix socially with: *Her son fell in with a bad crowd.*

fall off *phr v* [I] to become less in quality, amount, etc.»

The demand for new cars has fallen off sharply in the last 12 months.

fall on/upon sbdy./sthg. *phr v* [T] **1** to attack eagerly: *The soldiers fell on the enemy.* | (fig.) *The hungry children fell on the food.* **2 fall on hard times** to lose one's money and social position

fall out *phr v* **1** [I (**with**)] to quarrel: *Jane and Paul have fallen out (with each other) over the education of their children.* **2** [I;T (=**fall** sbdy. ↔ **out**)] to (cause to) leave one's place in a military formation: *Fall out, men!* | *The sergeant fell the squad out.* **3** [I+adv] to happen: *Let's wait and see how everything falls out.* | *As things fell out, we were right to be suspicious.*

fall through *phr v* [I] to fail to be successfully completed: *The deal fell through at the last minute.*

fall to *phr v* **1** [I;T (=**fall to** sthg.)] to begin: *The meal's all ready, kids. Fall to!* | *They fell to work with a will.* [+v-ing] *He fell to thinking about the early days and his lost friends.* **2** [T (=**fall to** sbdy.)] to be the (esp. unpleasant) duty of: *It fell to me to break the bad news to her.*

fall² *n* **1** [C (**from**)] an act of falling: *She had a bad fall and broke her hip.* | *He fell off the ladder, but some bushes broke his fall.* (=prevented him from falling very hard) —see RISE² (USAGE) **2** [C (**of**)] (the quantity of) something that has fallen: *A fall of rocks blocked the road.* | *We had a heavy fall of snow.* **3** [C (**in**)] a decrease in quantity, price, demand, degree, etc.: *We have not sold our goods because of the fall in demand.* | *a sudden fall in temperature* | *another fall in the value of the dollar* — opposite **rise** **4** [S (**of**)] the distance through which anything falls: *It's a fall of 70 metres to the foot of the cliff.* **5** [*the* | S (**of**)] the defeat or loss of power of a city, state, government, etc. *The fall of France occurred in 1940.* | *the fall of the Marcos regime in 1986* **6** [S (**from**)] (*sometimes cap.*) a change from a life of goodness, honesty, etc., to one of immorality: *a fall from grace.* **7** [(*the*) S] *AmE for* AUTUMN — see also FALLS

Fall *n* [*the* | S] the story in the Bible that tells how Adam and Eve, the first man and the first woman, disobeyed God. According to the story, God forbids Adam and Eve from eating the fruit (sometimes called "the apple") on the Tree of Knowledge in the Garden of Eden. The SERPENT (=snake) persuades Eve to taste the fruit, and then Eve gives the fruit to Adam to eat. They are ashamed of disobeying God and wear FIG leaves because they are also now ashamed of having no clothes on. When they tell God that they have eaten the fruit he sends them out of the Garden of Eden. This story is supposed to describe the way that human beings first learnt about the difference between good and evil.

fal·la·cious /fəˈleɪʃəs/ *adj fml* containing or based on false reasoning: *a fallacious argument* — **~ly** *adv*

fal·la·cy /ˈfæləsi/ *n* **1** [C] a false idea or belief: *It's a popular fallacy that success always brings happiness.* **2** [C;U] *fml* false reasoning: *I was able to show the fallacy of his argument.* —see also PATHETIC FALLACY

fall·back /ˈfɔːlbæk/ *n* something that can be used when the usual supply, method, activity, etc. fails: *If he doesn't show up for work we've got no fallback.* | *What's the fallback when the engine fails?*

fall·en¹ /ˈfɔːlən/ *past participle of* FALL: *The road was blocked by a fallen tree.*

fallen² *n* [*the*+P] *fml* those soldiers who have been killed in battle or war

fallen³ *adj old-fash* (of a woman) sexually immoral

fallen ar·ches /ˌ··ˈ··/ *n* the hollow parts on the bottom of the feet when these have become flat: *I've got fallen arches.*

fall guy /ˈ·· ·/ *n infml, esp. AmE* **1** a person who is tricked into being punished for someone else's crime; SCAPEGOAT **2** a person who is easily cheated, tricked, or made to seem a fool

fal·li·ble /ˈfælɪbəl/ *adj* able or likely to make a mistake or be wrong —opposite **infallible** —**bility** /ˌfælɪˈbɪləti/ *n* [U]

falling-out /ˌ··ˈ·/ *n* **fallings-out, falling-outs** a disagreement that may lead to a break in relations: *He had a falling-out with his sister over their parents' estate.*

falling star /ˌ··ˈ·/ *n* a SHOOTING STAR

fall line /ˈ· ·/ *n* the natural slope of a hill (e.g. one used for skiing (SKI)) straight down from top to bottom

fal·lo·pi·an tube /fəˌləʊpiən ˈtjuːb‖fəˈləʊpiən tuːb/ *n* either of the two tubes in a female through which eggs pass to the WOMB (=place inside a woman where a child grows)

fall·out /ˈfɔːlaʊt/ *n* [U] the dangerous RADIOACTIVE dust that is left in the air after a NUCLEAR explosion: *He built a fallout shelter* (=strong building to keep out fallout) *in his back garden.*

fal·low /ˈfæləʊ/ *adj* (of land) dug or ploughed (PLOUGH) but left unplanted to improve its quality: *The farmer left the land fallow for a year.*

fallow deer /ˈ·· ·/ *n* a small deer of Europe and Asia with a light brownish-yellow coat

falls /fɔːlz/ *n* [P] (used esp. in names) a place where a river makes a sudden deep drop; WATERFALL: *Niagara Falls* | *We're going to see the falls.*

Falls Road /ˌ· ˈ·/ [*the*] a street in the Catholic area of Belfast known for the violence which has taken place there

false¹ /fɔːls/ *adj* **1** not true or correct: *If you've made a false statement to the police you could be in trouble.* | *They lulled her into a false sense of security.* (=made her feel safe when really she was not) | *The criminal was travelling on a false passport.* **2** not faithful or loyal: *a false friend* **3** not real: *a false door* (=that looks like a door but does not open) | *The clown was wearing a false nose.* **4** [A] careless; unwise: *If you make one false move I'll shoot you!* — **~ly** *adv* — **~ness** *n* [U]

false² *adv* **play someone false** to deceive someone, esp. in love

false a·larm /ˌ· ·ˈ·/ *n* a warning of something bad which does not happen: *Someone shouted "Fire!", but it was a false alarm.*

false bot·tom /ˌ· ˈ··/ *n* a piece of wood, cardboard, etc., that looks like the bottom of a box or chest but which in fact hides a secret space

false dawn /ˌ· ˈ·/ *n* **1** light which appears in the sky just before DAWN **2** an expectation that something good is about to happen, but which in fact may not happen: *I fear that this ceasefire may be yet another false dawn.*

false·hood /ˈfɔːlshʊd/ *n fml* **1** [C] an untrue statement; lie **2** [U] the telling of lies; lying

false im·pris·on·ment /ˌ· ·ˈ···/ *n* [U] the putting of someone in prison for no legal reason

false pre·tenc·es /ˌ· ·ˈ··‖ˌ· ˈ···/ *n* [P] **under false pretences** using actions or appearances intended to deceive: *He obtained money from her under false pretences.*

false start /ˌ· ˈ·/ *n* an occasion in a race when a runner leaves the starting line too soon: (fig.) *After several false starts, work on the new hospital finally got under way.*

false teeth /ˌ· ˈ·/ *n* also **dentures** /fml— *n* [P] a set of artificial teeth worn by someone who has lost all or most of their natural teeth

fal·set·to /fɔːlˈsetəʊ/ *adv,n* an unnaturally high man's speaking or singing voice (with): *We really need to find a man who can sing falsetto.*

fals·ies /ˈfɔːlsiz/ *n* [P] *infml* pieces of material shaped to cover the breasts and make them seem larger

fal·si·fy /ˈfɔːlsɪfaɪ/ *v* [T] to make (something, esp. a written or printed paper) false by changing: *They suspected that he had been falsifying the accounts.* —**fication** /ˌfɔːlsɪfɪˈkeɪʃən/ *n* [C;U]

fal·si·ty /ˈfɔːlsɪti/ *n* [U] *fml* the quality of being false or untrue

Fal·staff /ˈfɔːlstɑːf‖-stæf/ a character from SHAKESPEARE's plays *Henry IV* and *Merry Wives of Windsor*, who is a fat, fun-loving, and likeable person who is not always completely honest: *In Irving's book he is a Falstaffian figure of great geniality and flamboyant tastes.*

fal·ter /ˈfɔːltəʳ/ *v* **1** [I] to walk or move unsteadily through weakness, fear, etc.: *When the sick man faltered, the nurse took his arm.* | *a baby's first faltering steps* **2** [I] to lose strength of purpose or action; HESITATE: *Don't falter in your resolve now that success is so near.* **3** [I] to lose strength or effectiveness; weaken: *The business faltered badly last year but it seems to be recovering now.* | *the president's faltering popularity* **4** [T (OUT)] to say in a weak and broken manner: *Trembling with shock, she managed to falter out a few words of thanks.* — **~ingly** *adv*

Fal·well /ˈfɔːlwel/, **Jerry** (1933–   ) an American EVANGELIST who started a religious and political group called Moral Majority, Inc. He attracted millions of followers by talking about Christianity on American television. – see also MORAL MAJORITY

fame /feɪm/ n [U] the condition of being well known and talked about; RENOWN: *She won overnight (=sudden) fame with her first novel.* | *The village's only* **claim to fame** *is that the Queen once visited it.*

famed /feɪmd/ adj [(for)] well known; famous: *This area is famed for its natural beauty.* | *Marianne Welch, daughter of famed novelist Henry Welch*

fa·mil·i·al /fəˈmɪliəl/ adj [A] fml (typical) of a family

fa·mil·i·ar¹ /fəˈmɪliər/ adj **1** [(to)] generally known, seen, or experienced; common: *St Paul's cathedral is a familiar sight (to all Londoners).* | *She looks very familiar* (=I have seen her before) *but I can't remember her name.* | *Her account of the breakdown of her marriage was a familiar story* (=typical of marriage breakdowns) *to the psychiatrist.*   **2** [F+with] having a thorough knowledge (of); CONVERSANT: *I am not really familiar with the taxation laws here.* –opposite **unfamiliar**   **3** too friendly, esp. in a way which shows lack of respect: *She told the taxi-driver not to be so familiar.*   **4** without tight control; informal: *He wrote in an easy familiar style.* –see also FAMILIARLY

familiar² n **1** also **familiar spir·it** /ˌ·ˈ··, ··ˈ··/– a spirit or devil that serves a particular person, such as a WITCH   **2** *old use* a close friend; companion: *the duke and his familiars*

fa·mil·i·ar·i·ty /fəˌmɪliˈærəti/ n **1** [U+with] thorough knowledge (of): *His familiarity with the language/the rules impressed us all.*   **2** [U] the freedom of behaviour usu. only expected in the most friendly relations: *They greeted each other with such familiarity that we thought they must be brother and sister.*   **3** [C usu. pl.] fml an act or expression of such freedom: *his unwelcome familiarities*   **4 familiarity breeds contempt** *saying* knowing a person very well leads to knowing their faults, and allows disrespect and dislike to develop

fa·mil·i·ar·ize also **-ise** BrE /fəˈmɪliəraɪz/ v [T (with)] to make (someone, esp. oneself) well informed (about): *You should familiarize yourself with the rules before you start to play the game.*

fa·mil·i·ar·ly /fəˈmɪliəli‖-liər-/ adv in an informal, easy, or friendly manner: *Charles, familiarly known as Charlie*

fam·i·ly /ˈfæməli/ n **1** [C+sing./pl. v] one's parents, grandfather and grandmother, brothers and sisters, uncles, aunts, etc.: *My family is very large/close.* | *My family are all tall.* | *The whole family came to visit us at Christmas.* | *He's a friend of the family.* | *a family gathering/occasion*   **2** [C+sing./pl. v] a group of one or usu. two adults and their children living in the same home: *Do you know the family who've just moved in next door?* | *It's a film for all the family/a family film.* (=suitable for children as well as older people) | *a single-parent family*
▶CULTURAL NOTE In Britain and the US usually only the mother, father, and children live together, not the grandparents.◀
3 [C+sing./pl. v] all those people descended from a common person (ANCESTOR): *Our family has/have lived in this house for over a hundred years.* | *a noble family*   **4** [S;U] children: *Have you any family?* | *We won't* **start a family** (=begin to have children) *until we've been married a few years.*   **5** [C] *tech* a group of related animals, plants, languages, etc.: *The cat family includes lions and tigers.* | *Spanish belongs to the same language family as Italian, both being descended from Latin.*   **6 in the ʼfamily way** *old-fash euph* going to give birth to a child; PREGNANT

family al·low·ance /ˌ··· ·ˈ··/ n [U] the old name for CHILD BENEFIT

family cir·cle /ˌ··· ˈ··/ n [(the) S] the closely related members of a family: *Don't say anything about it outside the family circle.*

Family Circle a magazine for women containing information about food, the family, health, with short stories, etc.

family cred·it /ˌ··· ˈ··/ n [U] (in Britain) money offered by the government to working parents on a low income. The amount varies according to the income and the number

of children in the family; formerly **family income supplement** –see also EARNED INCOME CREDIT

family doc·tor /ˌ··· ˈ··/ n infml for GENERAL PRACTITIONER

family in·come sup·ple·ment /ˌ··· ˈ·· ˌ··/ n [U] see FAMILY CREDIT

Family Income Sup·port /ˌ··· ˈ·· ·ˌ·/ n [U] (in Britain) money given by the government to people who are unemployed and have children

family man /ˈ··· ·/ n **1** a man with a wife and children   **2** a man who is fond of home life

family name /ˈ··· ˌ·/ n a SURNAME

family pack /ˈ··· ·/ n a large packet of food, etc. sold in shops which would be enough for a whole family: *Try and get a family pack of tissues, will you?*

family plan·ning /ˌ··· ˈ··/ n [U] the controlling of the number of children born in a family and of the time of their birth by the use of any of various CONTRACEPTIVE methods: *a family planning clinic*

Family Plan·ning As·so·ci·a·tion /ˌ··· ˈ·· ···ˌ··/ [the] a British private organization which gives free advice on family planning. The main American organization of this kind is called Planned Parenthood.

family prac·tice /ˈ··· ˌ··/ n [U] AmE a speciality in American medicine in which doctors learn to treat general health problems and problems connected with families and people of all ages –see also GENERAL PRACTICE **family practitioner** /ˈ··· ·ˌ··/ n

family tree /ˌ··· ˈ·/ n a plan or drawing showing the relationship of the members of a family, esp. one that covers a long period. In Britain and the US, many people like to spend time finding out about their family tree.

fam·ine /ˈfæmɪn/ n [C;U] (a case of) extreme lack of food for a very large number of people: *Many people die of starvation during famines every year.* | *an appeal for famine relief in Ethiopia*

fam·ished /ˈfæmɪʃt/ adj [F] infml very hungry

fa·mous /ˈfeɪməs/ adj **1** very well known, esp. for a special ability, quality, or feature: *a famous actor* | *a world-famous painting by Renoir* | *France is famous for its fine food and wine.*   **2** [A] (of an event) likely to be widely talked about or remembered; REMARKABLE: *The Labour Party may be on the verge of a famous victory.*   **3** *old-fash* very good; excellent: *famous weather for a walk*   **4 famous last words** a phrase used when someone has said something that expresses cheerfulness and certainty about the future, to warn them that they might be wrong: *"I'm sure I'll pass my driving test this time." "Famous last words."*
▷ USAGE Compare **famous, well-known, distinguished, eminent, notorious,** and **infamous**. 1 **Famous** is like **well-known** but is a stronger word and means "known over a wide area": *the doctor, the postman and other* **well-known** *people in the village* | *A* **famous** *film star has come to live in our village.* 2 **Distinguished** and **eminent** are used especially of people who are famous for serious work in science, the arts etc.: *a* **distinguished** *writer* | *an* **eminent** *surgeon.* 3 **Notorious** means "famous for something bad": *He was* **notorious** *for his evil deeds.* 4 **Infamous** (rather literary) can mean the same as **notorious** if it is followed by a noun: *an* **infamous** *criminal,* but it can also mean merely wicked or evil (not necessarily **famous**): *His crimes were* **infamous,** *but few people knew about them.*◁

Famous Five /ˌ··· ˈ·/ [the] a group of characters in children's books by Enid Blyton. The Famous Five, four children and a dog, have many adventures together.

fa·mous·ly /ˈfeɪməsli/ adv old-fash infml extremely well: *He is getting on famously at his new school.*

fan¹ /fæn/ n an instrument for making a flow of air, esp. cool air, such as an arrangement of feathers or paper in a half circle waved by hand, or a set of broad blades turned by a motor: *a paper/electric fan* | *an extractor fan in a kitchen to get rid of the smell of cooking* –see picture at ENGINE; see also **the shit will hit the fan** (SHIT)

fan² v **-nn-** **1** [T] to cause air, esp. cool air, to blow on (something) (as if) with a fan: *She fanned her face with a newspaper.* | *We fanned the fire to make it burn brighter.*   **2** [T] to cause to become more active or more serious: *This incident could* **fan the flame(s)** *of rebellion.* | *His* *rudeness fanned her irritation into anger.* **3** [I;T (OUT)] to spread in a gradually widening half circle: *The soldiers fanned out across the hillside in their search for the man.* | *She fanned the pack of cards out.*

fan³ /fæn/ *n* a very keen follower or supporter of a sport, performing art, famous person, etc.: *football fans* | *I'm one of your greatest fans.* | *She's an ardent Bruce Springsteen fan; she's joined his* **fan club.** | *That singer has to employ two people just to answer his* **fan mail.** (=letters sent to him by fans)

fan-as·sist·ed /ˌ· ·'··◂/ *adj* (of OVENs) with the heat being moved around the whole oven by a fan: *I think fan-assisted ovens dry out the food too much.*

fa·nat·ic /fə'nætɪk/ *n often derog* a person who shows very great and often unreasoning keenness for something, esp. for a religious or political belief: *The heathen temple was torn down by a crowd of religious fanatics.* | *a health food fanatic* − −**al** *adj* − −**ally** /kli/ *adv*

fa·nat·i·cis·m /fə'nætɪsɪzəm/ *n* [U] the behaviour, character, or ideas of a fanatic

fan belt /'· ·/ *n* a continuous belt driving a FAN to keep an engine cool —see picture at ENGINE

fan·ci·er /'fænsiər/ *n* (*usu. in comb.*) a person who has the stated interest, esp. someone who breeds or trains certain types of birds, dogs, plants, etc.: *a pigeon-fancier*

fan·ci·ful /'fænsɪfəl/ *adj* **1** *often derog* produced by the imagination; not based on reason or good sense: *He had some fanciful notion about crossing the Atlantic in a barrel.* **2** full of often strange decorative detail; ELABORATE: *fanciful designs* − −**ly** *adv*

fan·cy¹ /'fænsi/ *n* **1** [C (**to**)] a liking, esp. one formed without the help of reason: *I think young Peter has* **taken quite a fancy to** (−likes or is sexually attracted to) *that girl next door.* **2** [U] imagination, esp. in a free and undirected form: *She went* **wherever the/her fancy took her.** (=without a fixed or clear plan made in advance) | *The painting* **caught/took his fancy** (=he liked it), *so he bought it.* **3** [C] *fml* an opinion or idea that is not based on fact; NOTION: *Take no notice − it's just an old woman's fancy.*

fancy² *v* [T] *esp. BrE* **1** *infml* **a** to have a liking for; wish for: *I fancy a swim.* [+*v-ing*] *I don't fancy going all that way in such bad weather.* **b** to be sexually attracted to: *I really fancy that new secretary.* **2** (*usu. in imperative to express surprise, shock, etc.*) *infml* to form a picture of; imagine: *"He had no clothes on." "Fancy that!"* [+*v-ing*] *Fancy working in this heat every day!* (=How unpleasant to work in such heat!) [+*obj+v-ing*] *Fancy her saying a thing like that!* **3** to consider to be likely to do well: *I fancy Black Queen for the 4.30.* (−I think that this horse may win the 4.30 race) | *I don't* **fancy your chances** *of getting a ticket at this late stage.* (=I don't think you will be able to) **4** [+(*that*); *obj*] *fml* to believe without being certain; think: *I fancy I have met you before.* **5 a little of what you fancy does you good** the title of an old British MUSIC HALL song, now used when you are going to have or do something that is considered to be slightly wrong **6 fancy oneself** *often derog* to have a very high opinion of oneself: *You can tell from the way she parades around in her fine clothes that she really fancies herself.* | *He fancies himself (as) a good swimmer.*

fancy³ *adj* **1** decorative or brightly coloured; not ordinary; ELABORATE: *fancy cakes* | *They are too fancy for me; I prefer the plain ones.* | *It was a simple lunch − nothing fancy.* **2** *derog* (of a price) higher than is usual or reasonable: *He sells poor goods and charges fancy prices.*

fancy dress /ˌ·· '·/ *BrE*‖**masquerade** *AmE*− *n* [U] unusual or amusing clothes worn for a special occasion or party. There are different types of fancy dress. Sometimes people dress to look like a famous person from history, and sometimes look like a person with a particular job, e.g. a CLOWN or a POLICEMAN: *I went to the* **fancy-dress party/ball** *dressed as a pirate.* | *Do you know where I can get a* **fancy-dress costume?**

fancy-free /ˌ·· '·/ *adj* free to do anything or like anyone, esp. because one is not in love: *Since my divorce I've been really happy −* **footloose and fancy-free** *again!*

fancy man /'·· ·/ *n old-fash derog* a woman's lover

fancy wom·an /'·· ˌ··/ *n old-fash derog* **1** a man's lover; MISTRESS **2** a PROSTITUTE

fan·cy·work /'fænsiwɜːk‖-wɜːrk/ *n* [U] decorative sewing; EMBROIDERY

fan·dan·go /fæn'dæŋɡəʊ/ *n* **-gos** **1** [C] (the music for) a very active Spanish or South American dance **2** [U] *AmE* foolish, noisy behaviour

fan·fare /'fænfeər/ *n* a short loud ceremonial piece of usu. TRUMPET music played to introduce a person or event: *to sound a fanfare* | (*fig.*) *The dictator's secret diaries were published with due fanfare.*

fang /fæŋ/ *n* a long sharp tooth of an animal, such as a dog or a poisonous snake

fan·light /'fænlaɪt/ *BrE*‖**transom, transom window** *AmE*− *n* a small window over a door or a larger window

Fan·nie Mae /ˌfæni 'meɪ/ an American financial institution which buys and sells LOANs and MORTGAGEs to banks and other institutions, but does not deal directly with ordinary borrowers

fan·ny /'fæni/ *n* *sl* **1** *AmE* the part of the body on which one sits; BOTTOM¹ (3) **2** *BrE taboo* the outer sex organs of a woman

fan·ta·si·a /fæn'teɪziə, ˌfæntə'zɪə‖fæn'teɪʒə/ *n* **1** a piece of music that does not follow any regular style **2** a piece of music made up of a collection of well-known tunes

Fan·ta·si·a /fæn'teɪzɪə ‖ -ʒə/ a film made by the Walt Disney company in 1940 in which CARTOON characters dance to CLASSICAL (2) music

fantas·ize also **-ise** *BrE* /'fæntəsaɪz/ *v* [I (**about**); T+*that*; *obj*] to form strange or wonderful ideas in the mind: *She fantasized about winning the lottery.* | *He fantasized about meeting Marilyn Monroe.*

fan·tas·tic /fæn'tæstɪk/ *adj* **1** *infml* extremely good; wonderful: *a fantastic meal* | *You look fantastic!* **2** extremely great or large: *She won a fantastic sum of money in the casino.* **3** (of an idea, plan, etc.) too extreme or unrelated to reality to be practical or reasonable; PREPOSTEROUS: *Your proposals are utterly fantastic; we couldn't possibly afford them.* **4** odd, strange, or wild in shape, meaning, etc.; not controlled by reason: *He was troubled by fantastic dreams.* − −**ally** /kli/ *adv* : *fantastically expensive*

fan·ta·sy /'fæntəsi/ *n* **1** [U] imagination, esp. when unlimited or allowed complete freedom **2** [C;U] something produced from free imagination, whether expressed in words or not: *The whole story is a fantasy.* | *He lives in a world of fantasy.* | *sexual fantasies* **3** [U] stories about imaginary worlds which often involve magic. The characters are often searching for an object which will cause good to win over evil, and they usu. fight with swords rather than modern weapons. −compare SCIENCE FICTION

fan·zine /'fænziːn/ *n* a magazine written by and for very keen supporters of a particular performer, sports team etc. Fanzines are usu. written without official approval and are known for their strong opinions and lack of respect for people in authority.

FAO /ˌef eɪ 'əʊ/ [*the*] Food and Agriculture Organization; a part of the United Nations which aims to improve the production and DISTRIBUTION of AGRICULTURE in developing countries

far¹ /fɑːr/ *adv* **farther** /'fɑːðər‖'fɑːr-/ *or* **further** /'fɜːðər‖'fɜːr-/, **farthest** /'fɑːðɪst‖'fɑːr-/ *or* **furthest** /'fɜːðɪst‖'fɜːr-/ **1** at, to, or from a great distance; a long way: *We didn't go (very) far.* | *Have you come far?* [+*adv/prep*] *We walked far into the woods.* | *They travelled far from home.* | *How far is it to the station?* | (*fig.*) *I don't know how far* (=how much) *I should believe him.* | (*fig.*) *A pound doesn't* **go very far** (=buy much) *these days.* | (*fig.*) *She's an excellent young musician; she should* **go far.** (=be very successful in the future) | (*fig.*) *Her rudeness* **went too far.** (=she was too rude) | (*fig.*) *You're* **taking/carrying** *that joke* **too far.** (=going beyond what is acceptable) **2** [+*prep*, esp. **into**] at or to a great distance in time: *They worked far into the night.* | *We can't plan far beyond August.* | *He can see far into the future.* **3** very much: *It's far too hot in this room; open the windows.* | *Tell him to go away; I'm far, far too busy to see him.* | *The film is far better/worse than the book.* | *She is* **by far** the *best teacher.* | *She is the best teacher* **by far.** −see MORE (USAGE) **4 as/so far as** to the degree that: *I'll help you as far as I can.* | *So far as I know, they're coming by car. BrE* | *As far as I know AmE* **5 far and away** by a great deal or amount; very much: *She is far and away*

the best actress in the country. **6 far and wide** also **far and near** − everywhere: *They looked far and wide for the missing dog.* | *People came from far and near to see the Pope.* **7 far be it from me to** (used esp. to show disagreement or disapproval) I certainly would not want to: *Far be it from me to interfere in your work, but isn't this rather an impractical idea?* **8 far from: a** very much not; a long way from being; not at all: *I'm far from pleased with your behaviour.* | *She is not a good driver* − **far from it!** **b** also **so far from** − rather than; instead of; the opposite of: *(So) far from taking my advice, he went and did just what I had warned him against.* **9 in so far as** also **in as far as, insofar as** − to the degree that: *I'll help you in so far as I can.* **10 it is a far, far better thing I do than I have ever done** quote a phrase from the book *A Tale of Two Cities* by Charles Dickens, said by the main good character of the book when he is about to give his own life to save that of someone else **11 so far: a** up to the present: *He's had three wives so far.* | *"Have you met your new neighbour?" "Not so far."* **b** to a certain point, degree, distance, etc.: *When the level reaches so far, stop the flow.* | *I can only trust him so far.* | *We can extend your loan* **so far and no further.** **12 So far, so good** Things are satisfactory up to this point, at least: *We're over the wall. So far, so good. Now we've got to swim the river.* − see FARTHER² (USAGE)

▷ USAGE **Far** is usually used in questions or negatives about distance: *How far did you walk?* | *Did you walk far?* | *No, we didn't walk far.* It is also used in simple statements after *too, as* and *so*: We walked as **far** *as the river.* | *We walked much too* **far.** Compare: *We walked* **a long way**/(**far** could not be used here except in very formal or literary writing).◁

far² *adj* **farther** *or* **further, farthest** *or* **furthest 1** being a long way away: *Let's walk back to the office; it's not far.* | *In the far distance I saw a rider approaching.* | *(lit or poet) He lives in a far country.* **2** [A] also **farther**− (of one of two things) more distant: *She swam to the far side of the lake.* | *It's in a cupboard at the far end of the room.* **3** [A] (of a political position) very much to the LEFT or RIGHT; extreme: *the far left* | *a supporter of far right ideas* **4 a far cry from** completely different and often less good than: *The present economic situation is a far cry from the one predicted by the previous government.*

Far·a·day /ˈfærədeɪ/, **Mi·chael** /ˈmaɪkəl/ *n* (1791−1867) an English CHEMIST and PHYSICIST who discovered the connection between electricity and MAGNETISM and produced the first DYNAMO

far·a·way /ˈfɑːrəweɪ/ *adj* [A] **1** distant: *faraway places* **2** (of the look in a person's eyes) dreamy, as if looking at or thinking about something distant

farce /fɑːs‖fɑːrs/ *n* **1** [C] a light humorous play full of silly things happening **2** [U] the branch of theatrical writing concerned with this type of play **3** [C] an occasion or set of events that is silly and empty and pretending to be something which it is not; SHAM: *The talks with the unions were a farce, since the politicians had already made the decision.* −**farcical** *adj* −**farcically** /kli/ *adv*

fare¹ /feəʳ/ *n* **1** [C] (*often in comb.*) the price charged to carry a person by bus, train, taxi, plane, etc.: *to pay one's train fare* | *The bus company will prosecute any* **fare dodgers** (=people who try to avoid paying their fares) *it catches.* **2** [C] a paying passenger in a taxi **3** [U] anything intended to provide enjoyment, esp. food provided for a meal: *good/simple/standard fare* | *an evening of diverse musical fare* −see also BILL OF FARE

fare² *v* [I+adv] **1** to get on; succeed: *I think I fared quite well in the interview.* **2** to experience treatment in the stated way: *The unions will fare badly if the government's plan becomes law.*

Far East /ˌ· ˈ·◂/ *n* [the] the countries in Asia that are east of India, such as China, Japan, etc. −compare MIDDLE EAST, NEAR EAST −∼**ern** *adj*

fare·well /feəˈwel‖feər-/ *interj, n fml or old use* goodbye: *Farewell! I hope we meet again soon.* | *It's time to say our farewells.* | *a farewell party*

far·fetched /ˌfɑːˈfetʃt◂‖ˌfɑːr-/ *adj* too improbable to be believed or accepted: *He told us a farfetched story about the president asking for his advice.*

far-flung /ˌ· ˈ·◂/ *adj* **1** spread over a great distance: *Our*

far-flung trade connections cover the world. **2** distant; REMOTE: *in a far-flung corner of the empire*

Far From the Mad·ding Crowd /ˌfɑː frəm ðə ˌmædɪŋ ˈkraʊd‖ˌfɑːr-/ a book by Thomas Hardy about the lives of country people in mid-Victorian Dorset. The phrase is now sometimes used humorously when talking about the peace and quiet of the country.

far-gone /ˌ· ˈ·/ *adj* [F (**in**)] *infml* in an advanced state, esp. of something unpleasant such as madness, debt, or being drunk: *You're too far-gone* (=drunk) *to drive; get a taxi.*

far·i·na·ceous /ˌfærɪˈneɪʃəs◂/ *adj tech* consisting of or containing flour or STARCH: *Bread, potatoes, and pasta are all farinaceous foods.*

farm¹ /fɑːm‖fɑːrm/ *n* **1** an area of land, together with its buildings, concerned with the growing of crops or the raising of animals: *We work on the farm.* | *a sheep/dairy/fruit farm* | *a farm labourer* **2** a farmhouse −see also FACTORY FARM, FISH FARM, FUNNY FARM

farm² *v* [I;T] to use (land) for growing crops, raising animals, etc.: *We farm a hundred acres of arable land.*
   farm sthg./sbdy. ↔ **out** *phr v* [T (**on**)] to arrange for someone else to deal with (work) or take care of (children) instead of oneself: *We have more work here than we can deal with* − *can we farm some out?* | *They're always farming out their children on their relatives.*

farm belt /ˈ· ·/ *n* an area of land used for farming esp. the central plains of the US

farm·er /ˈfɑːməʳ‖ˈfɑːr-/ *n* a person who owns or manages a farm: *a sheep/coconut farmer* −see also SMALL FARMER

Farmer, Fan·nie /ˈfæni/ (1857−1915) the writer of a popular American cookbook used by many people

Farmer John /ˌ·· ˈ·/ *n tdmk* a company in the US which sells meat products such as BACON and HOT DOGS

farm·hand /ˈfɑːmhænd‖ˈfɑːrm-/ *n* a person who works on a farm; farm LABOURER

farm·house /ˈfɑːmhaʊs‖ˈfɑːrm-/ also **farm**− *n* **-houses** /haʊzɪz/ the main house on a farm, where the farmer lives

farm·ing /ˈfɑːmɪŋ‖ˈfɑːr-/ *n* [U] the practice or business of being in charge of or working on a farm: *new methods in dairy farming* −see also MIXED FARMING

farm la·bour·er /ˈ· ˈ···/ *n* a person who works on a farm, but who does not own the farm

farm·land /ˈfɑːmlænd, -lənd‖ˈfɑːrmlænd/ *n* [U] land used or suitable for farming, esp. cultivated land or PASTURE

farm·stead /ˈfɑːmsted‖ˈfɑːrm-/ *n esp. AmE* a farmhouse and its surrounding buildings

farm·yard /ˈfɑːmjɑːd‖ˈfɑːrmjɑːrd/ also **barnyard**− *n* a yard surrounded by farm buildings

Farn·bo·rough Air Show /ˌfɑːnbərə ˈeə ˌʃəʊ‖ˌfɑːrnbɔːrəʊ ˈeər-/ [the] a large international event where different types of aircraft are shown, held every two years at Farnborough, England

Fa·roes /ˈfeərəʊz/ [the] see FAEROE ISLANDS

far-off /ˌ· ˈ·◂/ *adj* distant in space or time: *in the far-off days of my youth*

far-out¹ /ˌ· ˈ·◂/ *adj* **1** *old-fash infml* very different or unusual; strange: *far-out ideas* **2** *AmE sl* extremely good; wonderful: *a far-out party*

far out² *interj AmE sl* (an expression of admiration or happiness): *Far out! Tickets to the concert!* | *You're coming to visit? Far out!*

far·ra·go /fəˈrɑːgəʊ, fəˈreɪ-/ *n* **-goes** [(**of**)] *derog* a confused collection; mixture: *The whole story was a farrago of lies and deceit.*

far-reach·ing /ˌ· ˈ···◂/ *adj* having a wide influence or effect: *The splitting of the atom had far-reaching consequences.*

far·ri·er /ˈfæriəʳ/ *n* a person, usu. a BLACKSMITH, who makes and fits shoes for horses

far·row /ˈfærəʊ/ *v* [I] *tech* (of a female pig) to give birth to a LITTER of young pigs

Farrow, Mi·a /ˈmiːə/ (1946−) an American actress who often works with Woody Allen and whose films include *Rosemary's Baby* and *Hannah and Her Sisters*

Far·si /ˈfɑːsiː‖ˈfɑːr-/ *n* [U] the Persian language of modern Iran −see PERSIAN²

Far Side /ˈ· ˌ·/, **The** a CARTOON by the American artist Gary Larson, which appears in newspapers, and is known for its wild and silly humour, often involving animals that act like people

far·sight·ed /ˌfɑːˈsaɪtɪd◀‖ˌfɑːr-/ adj **1** also **far·see·ing** /fɑːˈsiːɪŋ◀‖ fɑːr-/— apprec able to see the future effects of present actions: the government's far-sighted measures to combat the drugs problem —opposite **shortsighted 2** esp. AmE for LONGSIGHTED — ~**ly** adv — ~**ness** n [U]

fart[1] /fɑːt‖fɑːrt/ v [I] taboo to send out air from the bowels through the ANUS
fart about/around phr v [I] infml to spend time in pointless, aimless, or worthless activity

fart[2] n taboo **1** an escape of air from the bowels **2** sl a stupid and uninteresting person: He's a boring old fart.

far·ther[1] /ˈfɑːðə[r]‖ˈfɑːr-/ adv (comparative of FAR[1]) **1** at or to a greater distance or more distant point; further: Let's not walk any farther. [+adv/prep] They pushed the boat farther into the water. | They drove three miles farther down the road. | The explosion could be heard ten miles away, and even **farther afield**. (=farther away) **2** to a greater degree; further: We can't take this plan any farther (ahead) until the funding is approved.

farther[2] adj [A] (comparative of FAR[2]) more distant; FAR[2] (2): On the farther side of the street there was a row of small shops.

▷ USAGE When speaking of real places and distances you can use either **farther, farthest** or **further, furthest: farther/further** down the road | What's the **farthest/furthest** place you've ever been to? In other cases, especially with the meaning "more", "extra", "additional" **further, furthest** are usu. used: a college of **further** education | for **further** information write to the above address.◁

far·thest /ˈfɑːðəst‖ˈfɑːr-/ adj, adv (superlative of FAR) most far: Who can swim (the) farthest? [+adv/prep] Which of these cities is farthest (away) from London? —see FARTHER (USAGE)

far·thing /ˈfɑːðɪŋ‖ˈfɑːr-/ n a former British coin worth one quarter of an old PENNY

fas·cia /ˈfeɪʃə/ n **1** a long band or board on the surface of something, esp. one over a shop bearing the shop's name **2** BrE old-fash the instrument board in a car; DASHBOARD

fas·ci·nate /ˈfæsɪˌneɪt/ v [T] **1** to attract and hold the interest or attention of: Anything to do with old myths and legends fascinates me. | I was fascinated to see how skilfully the old craftsman worked. | The students were fascinated with/by his ideas. **2** to fix with the eyes so as to take away the power of movement, as a snake does with a small creature —**nation** /ˌfæsɪˈneɪʃən/ n [S;U]: Chinese art has a great fascination for me. | The beautiful woman exercised a strange fascination over him.

fas·ci·nat·ing /ˈfæsɪˌneɪtɪŋ/ adj extremely interesting and charming: a fascinating old city full of ancient buildings | I find her books quite fascinating. — ~**ly** adv

fas·cis·m /ˈfæʃɪzəm/ n [U] (often cap.) a political system in which all industrial activity is controlled by the state, no political opposition is allowed, military strength is approved of, support of one's own nation and race is strongly encouraged, and SOCIALISM is violently opposed

fas·cist /ˈfæʃɪst/ n, adj **1** (often cap.) (a supporter) of fascism **2** derog (someone) acting in a cruel, hard, rather military way which allows no (political) opposition: As the riot police advanced the students shouted, "Leave us alone, you fascist pigs!"

fash·ion[1] /ˈfæʃən/ n **1** [C;U] the way of dressing or behaving that is usual or popular at a certain time: Fashions have changed since I was a girl. | Narrow trousers are the latest fashion. | It's not the fashion to send children away to school now. | We like to keep up with fashion/with the latest fashions. | a fashion show (=of clothes) | a fashion house (=company that produces clothes) | Long hair is **out of/in fashion** (=(not) considered very modern) now. | My teenage daughter is very **fashion-conscious**. **2** [U] changing custom, esp. in women's clothing: a book about the history of fashion **3** [S] rather fml a manner; way of making or doing something: The children lined up in an orderly fashion. **4** **after a fashion** although not very well: John can speak Russian, after a fashion, but can't read it at all. **5** **-fashion** in the way of a; like a: to dress schoolboy-fashion | to eat Italian-fashion

fashion[2] v [T] (**out of, from, into**)] fml to shape or make, usu. with one's hands or with only a few tools: Taking some branches and leaves, he fashioned a simple shelter. | She fashioned the pot out of clay/fashioned the clay into a pot. | (fig.) Many influences help to fashion our children's characters.

fash·ion·a·ble /ˈfæʃənəbəl/ adj **1** (made, dressed, etc.) according to the latest fashion: a fashionable hat/woman | It's fashionable among the British to go to the south of France for their holidays. **2** of or for people of high social position or people who make or decide upon fashion: fashionable society | a fashionable restaurant | She moves in fashionable circles. (=has connections with people of high social standing) —opposite **unfashionable**; see also OLD-FASHIONED —**ably** adv : fashionably dressed

fashion plate /ˈ·· ˌ·/ n AmE sometimes derog a person who thinks it very important to dress in the latest fashion

Fass·bin·der /ˈfæsbɪndə[r]/, **Rai·ner Wer·ner** /ˈraɪnə[r] ˈwɜːnə[r]‖-ˈwɜːr-/ n (1946–82) a German writer and film director, many of whose 40 films show German life after the Second World War

fast[1] /fɑːst‖fæst/ adj **1** quick; moving or able to move quickly: a fast car | the fast train to New York (=one that travels fast and stops at few stations) | the fast growth of the oil industry | fast music | a fast runner —see FAST-NESS (USAGE) **2** taking a short time compared to other people or things: a fast journey **3** firmly fixed and unlikely to move or change: The colours aren't fast, so be careful when you wash these towels. | The label says this shirt is **colour fast**. | He made the rope fast (=tied it firmly) to the metal ring. **4** [F; after n] (of a clock) showing a time that is later than the true time: My watch is fast/is five minutes fast. **5** having or being a high photographic speed: a fast lens | a fast film **6** [A] allowing quick movement: There had been an accident in the fast lane of the highway. | a fast pitch | Cook it in a fast (=very hot) oven. **7** old-fash wanting too much pleasure and spending too much money: James belongs to a very fast set at college. **8** **fast and furious** (esp. of games and amusements) noisy and active **9** **pull a fast one (on)** infml to deceive (someone) with a trick —see also FAST-NESS, SPEED, FAST FOOD, FAST LANE

fast[2] adv **1** quickly: She drives very fast. | Their population is growing fast. **2** firmly; tightly: The car was stuck fast in the mud. **3** ahead of a correct time: The train's running five minutes fast. **4** old use close; near: a brook fast by **5** **fast asleep** sleeping deeply **6** **play fast and loose with** old-fash to treat in a selfishly careless way —see also **thick and fast** (THICK[2])

fast[3] v [I] to eat little or no food for a particular length of time, esp. for religious reasons: Muslims fast during Ramadan.

fast[4] n an act or period of fasting: Friday is a fast day | He broke his fast by drinking some milk.

fast·back /ˈfɑːstbæk‖ˈfæst-/ n AmE a car with a long sloping rear window and usu. only two doors

fast breed·er re·ac·tor /ˌ·ˈ·· ·ˈ··/ n a NUCLEAR REACTOR which produces more FISSILE material than it needs to produce electricity

fast col·oureds /ˌ·ˈ···/ n [P] BrE coloured clothes which will not lose or change colour when washed in a WASHING MACHINE

fas·ten /ˈfɑːsən‖ˈfæ-/ v [I;T] to make or become firmly fixed or closed: The bag won't fasten properly. | He fastened his coat. | Fasten your seat belts. | I fastened the pages together with a paperclip. | She fastened the notice to the board. | She fastened the loose edge down with some glue. | He fastened on his sword/fastened his sword on. | (fig.) She fastened her eyes on him. | (fig.) Don't try and fasten the blame on me. —opposite **unfasten**
fasten on/onto/upon sthg. phr v [T] to take eagerly and use; seize on: The president fastened on the idea at once.

fas·ten·er /ˈfɑːsnə[r]‖ˈfæ-/ n something that fastens things together: Could you do up the fasteners on the back of my dress, please. —see also ZIP[1] (1)

fas·ten·ing /ˈfɑːsənɪŋ‖ˈfæ-/ n something that holds things shut, esp. doors and windows

fast food /ˈ· ˌ·/ n [U] food such as HAMBURGERs and cooked chicken that is quickly and easily prepared, and sold by a restaurant to be eaten at once or taken away: a well-known chain of fast-food restaurants

fasteners

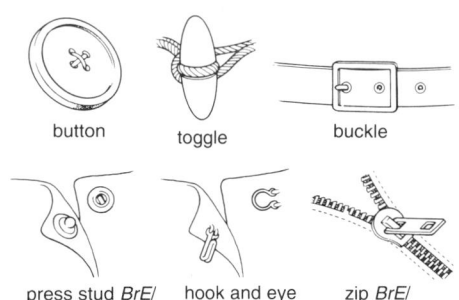

button | toggle | buckle

press stud *BrE/* | hook and eye | zip *BrE/*
snap fastener *AmE* | | zipper *AmE*

fast-for·ward /ˌ·ˈ··/ *n* [(*the*)U] a way of operating a TAPE RECORDER or VIDEO² (2) so that the TAPE is wound forward fast without being played

fas·tid·i·ous /fæˈstɪdiəs/ *adj* (typical of a person who is) extremely difficult to please or satisfy, esp. disliking anything at all dirty, unpleasant, or rough: *Jean is too fastidious to eat with her fingers.* —compare FUSSY (1) – ~**ly** *adv* – ~**ness** *n* [U]

fast lane /ˈ· ˌ·/ *n* **1** the LANE of a MOTORWAY used by vehicles travelling fast and going past other vehicles **2 life in the fast lane** a very exciting style of life: *With all her money and film-star friends, she really lives her life in the fast lane.*

fast·ness /ˈfɑːstnʲs‖ˈfæst-/ *n* **1** [U] the quality of being firm and fixed: *colour fastness* **2** [C] *esp. lit* a safe place which is hard to reach: *The rebels have withdrawn to their* **mountain fastness** *for the winter.*

▷ USAGE There is no noun formed from **fast** when it means **quick**. Use instead **speed** or **quickness**. ◁

Fast·net /ˈfɑːstnet‖ˈfæst-/ [*the*] a famous YACHTING race held every two years from the south of England up to the Fastnet Rock near Ireland

fat¹ /fæt/ *adj* **1** having (too) much fat on the body: *fat cattle* | *a fat baby* | *You'll get even fatter if you eat all those cream cakes.*

► CULTURAL NOTE In Britain and the US it is not considered attractive to be fat, and many people, esp. women, worry that they are too fat and try to lose weight. ◄

2 (of meat) containing a lot of fat: *fat bacon* —see also FATTY¹ **3** thick and well-filled: *a fat book* | (fig.) *a fat bank account* | (fig.) *The cinema industry has had a series of fat* (=profitable) *years.* **4** [A] *infml* nearly nonexistent: *A fat lot of good/of use that is!* | *a fat chance* **5 the opera isn't over till the fat lady sings** *saying* something is not finished until one particular important part has taken place – ~**ness** *n* [U]

▷ USAGE If you want to be polite about someone do not say that they are **fat. (Rather) overweight** is a more polite way of saying the same thing. **Plump** is most often used of women and children and means "slightly (and pleasantly) fat". **Chubby** (used of babies and children) also means "pleasantly fat". **Stout** means "rather fat and heavy" and **tubby** means "short and rather fat, especially in the stomach". If someone is extremely fat and unhealthy they are said to be **obese**. —see also THIN (USAGE)◁

fat² *n* **1** [U] the white or yellowish substance in the bodies of animals and human beings, esp. just under the skin, which helps to keep them warm **2** [C;U] this substance or the oily substance found in some plants, esp. seeds, when in solid or almost solid form, considered as food: *He can't eat fat.* | *He fried the potatoes in deep fat.* | *Butter is made of animal fat but some kinds of margarine are made of vegetable fats.* **3 live off/on the fat of the land** to live in great comfort with plenty to eat, without having to work very hard **4 the fat is in the fire** *infml* something has been done which will result in a lot of trouble —see also **chew the fat** (CHEW¹)

fa·tal /ˈfeɪtl/ *adj* **1** [(to, for)] causing or resulting in death: *a fatal accident/illness* | (fig.) *Marriage at this stage could*

be fatal to your career.* **2 *infml* bringing danger or ruin, or having unpleasant results: *It's fatal to stay up working late into the night; you always feel terrible next day.* —see also FATALLY

Fa·tal At·trac·tion /ˌ··· ·ˈ··/ a film with Michael Douglas and Glen Close as the main actors, in which a woman develops a dangerous OBSESSION for a married man who once had sex with her and follows him everywhere: *The court refused to order a Fatal Attraction-style pursuer to stop plaguing him.*

fa·tal·is·m /ˈfeɪtl-ɪzəm/ *n* [U] the belief that events are decided by fate and are outside human control –**ist** *n* –**istic** /ˌfeɪtlˈɪstɪk◄/ *adj* : *a fatalistic attitude to death* –**istically** /kli/ *adv*

fa·tal·i·ty /fəˈtælʲti/ *n fml* **1** [C] *tech* a violent accidental death: *It was a bad crash, but there were no fatalities.* (=no one was killed) **2** [U] the quality of being fatal: *New drugs have reduced the fatality of this disease.* | *The fatality rate on our roads has been increasing.* **3** [S] *fml* the quality of being decided by fate

fa·tal·ly /ˈfeɪtl-i/ *adv* so as to cause death, ruin, or misfortune: *fatally wounded* | *She was fatally attracted to him.*

fat cat /ˌ· ·/ *n AmE infml derog* a rich man, esp. one who smokes a CIGAR and drives a large expensive car

fat city /ˌ· ·/ *n AmE sl* **in fat city** very fortunate and very happy because of new material wealth: *If this deal goes through, we'll be in fat city!* | *Those guys are in fat city since their rent was lowered.*

fate /feɪt/ *n* **1** [U] (*often cap.*) the power or force which is supposed to be the cause of and in control of all events, in a way which is beyond human control. Fate is not an important idea in the lives of British or American people. *He expected to spend his life in Italy, but fate had decreed otherwise.* | *She wondered what fate had in store for her next.* (=what would happen to her next) **2** [C] an end or result, esp. death: *They met with a terrible fate.* **3** [S] what will or must happen to someone or something: *Your school report is important, but ultimately it's the university examiners who will decide your fate.* (=decide whether you can or cannot enter university) | *The company's fate is still uncertain.* | *The fate of the hostages depends upon the release of the political prisoners.* **4 a fate worse than death: a** something terrible or frightening: *Going out with Henry would be a fate worse than death.* **b** *old use or humor* (for a woman) the loss of VIRGINITY, esp. before marriage —see also **tempt fate** (TEMPT), DESTINY

fat·ed /ˈfeɪtʲd/ *adj* [F] caused or fixed by fate: [+*to-v*] *You and I were fated to meet.* [+*that*] *It was fated that we should meet.* —see also ILL-FATED

fate·ful /ˈfeɪtfəl/ *adj* (of a day, event, or decision) having an important (esp. bad) influence on the future: *Their fateful decision to declare war changed the course of history.* – ~**ly** *adv*

Fates /feɪts/ *n* [*the*] the three goddesses who, according to the ancient Greeks, decided the course of human life

fat farm /ˈ· ·/ *n AmE infml derog* a place where fat people go in order to lose weight. Some of these places are very expensive. They try to make people healthy through exercise, eating well, and relaxing. —compare HEALTH FARM

fat·head /ˈfæthed/ *n infml* a fool; stupid person: *Don't do that, (you) fathead!* –**headed** /ˌfæt ˈhedʲd◄/ *adj* –**headedness** *n* [U]

fa·ther¹ /ˈfɑːðəʳ/ *n* **1** a male parent of a child or animal: *the fathers and mothers of the schoolchildren* | *He became a father* (=a child of his was born) *this year.* | *My uncle has been like a father to me since my own father died.* | *Can we borrow the car, father?* | *a father of four* (=having four children) | *a father-to-be* (=soon to be a father) —see UNCLE (USAGE) **2** [+*of*] the man who began or invented (the stated thing): *Einstein is regarded by many as the father of modern scientific thought.* **3** [*usu. pl.*] a FOREFATHER: *the customs of our fathers* —see also CITY FATHER, FOUNDING FATHER **4 how's your father?** *BrE infml* sex: *How about a bit of how's your father?* – ~**less** *adj* : *a poor fatherless child*

▷ USAGE 1 We can use **father** and **mother** when addressing these people directly: *Can I borrow the car, father?* | **Mother**, *could you lend me £5?* Certain other words for jobs and ranks can also be used in this way: *Yes,* **doctor.** (in the medical meaning of the word) |

Waiter‖ | *No*, **sergeant.** —see also UNCLE (USAGE) 2 When you are addressing your **father** or **mother,** or talking about them to another member of your family, you do not use the possessive pronoun "my": *Are you all right*, **mother?** | *Has* **father** *gone out?* Outside the family it is more common to include the possessive pronoun: **(My) father** *used to take us to the seaside every year.* | **(My) mother** *will be worried if I come home late.* When talking of someone else's father or mother, use a suitable possessive pronoun: *Does* **your mother** *know you're out?* | *Where is* **his father** *now?* When talking of a male or a female parent, use articles in the normal way: *It's hard work being a* **mother.** | *Most people blamed* **the father** *for the family's problems.* 3 Compare **father, dad, daddy, mother, mum, mummy.** The ways in which sons and daughters address their parents vary from family to family. The most common forms of address are probably **mum** (*AmE* **mom**) and **dad.** In many families **mother** and **father** are used, but some families consider these terms too formal. **Mummy** (*AmE* **mommy**) and **daddy** are also commonly used, esp. by children, but by some adult sons and daughters too, esp. in upper-class families.◁

father² *v* [T] *old use or humor* (of a man) to become the father of: (fig.) *He fathered the concept of the welfare state.*
   father sthg. **on/upon** sbdy. *phr v* [T] *esp. BrE* to say or suggest that (someone) is responsible for inventing or thinking of: *Don't try and father that silly idea on me.*

Father *n* **1** (a title of respect for a priest, esp. in the Roman Catholic Church): *Father Brown is our local priest.* | *Will you have some more tea, Father?* **2** [*our*|*the*] God: *our Father in heaven*

Father Christ·mas /ˌ··ˈ··/ *BrE* see SANTA CLAUS

father fig·ure /ˈ··ˌ··/ *n* an esp. older man on whom one depends for advice, help, moral support, etc.

fa·ther·hood /ˈfɑːðəhʊd‖ ðər / *n* [U] the condition of being a father: *the responsibilities of fatherhood*

father-in-law /ˈ··· ·/ *n* **fathers-in-law** *or* **father-in-laws** the father of a person's wife or husband

Father Knows Best /ˌ··· ·ˈ·/ an American television programme of the 1950s. The programme is sometimes used as an example of the typical American family of the 1950s, with a father who went off to work and was seen as wise and able to help his children with their problems and a mother who stayed at home with the children.

fa·ther·land /ˈfɑːðəlænd‖ -ðər-/ *n* (used esp. of Germany) the country of one's birth or family origin —see also MOTHER COUNTRY

fa·ther·ly /ˈfɑːðəli‖ -ðər-/ *adj apprec* like or typical of a good father: *a fatherly old doctor* | *He gave her a fatherly kiss.* —compare PATERNAL —**liness** *n* [U]

Father of the Church /ˌ··· · ·ˈ·/ *n pl* **Fathers of the Church** one of the teachers of the early Christian church whose writings are used to answer any difficult points of faith or practice

Father's Day /ˈ·· ·/ *n* the third Sunday in June on which fathers are given cards and presents as a sign of love and to thank them for everything they do —compare MOTHER'S DAY

fath·om¹ /ˈfæðəm/ *n* a unit of measurement (6 feet or 1·8 metres) for the depth of water: *The sea is sixty fathoms deep here.* | *The boat sank in twenty fathoms.*

fathom² *v* [T (OUT)] *infml* to get at the true meaning of; come to understand: *I couldn't fathom his meaning.* [+*wh*-] *I've been trying to fathom out how to do it.*

fath·om·less /ˈfæðəmləs/ *adj esp. lit* too deep to be measured or understood; UNFATHOMABLE: *fathomless depths* | *a fathomless mystery*

fa·tigue¹ /fəˈtiːg/ *n* **1** [U] great tiredness; exhaustion (EXHAUST¹): *He was pale with fatigue after his sleepless night.* **2** [U] *tech* the tendency of a metal to break as the result of repeated bending (esp. in the phrase **metal fatigue**) **3** [C] (in the army) a job of cleaning or cooking: *fatigue duty* | *He had to spend Sunday doing fatigues.*

fatigue² *v* [T] *fml* to make tired: *He felt irritable and fatigued after the long journey.*

fa·tigues /fəˈtiːgz/ *n* [P] also **fatigue u·ni·form** /·ˈ· ˌ···/ *AmE* — army clothes worn for field duty

fat·so /ˈfætsəʊ/ *n infml derog* a fat person: *Hey, fatso – get off my car!*

fat·ted calf /ˌfætᵻd ˈkɑːf‖-ˈkæf/ see **kill the fatted calf** (KILL)

fat·ten /ˈfætn/ *v* [T (UP)] to make fatter: *The pigs are being fattened for market.* | *Have some more cake! You need fattening up a bit.* | *fattening foods*

fat·ty¹ /ˈfæti/ *adj* containing (a lot of) fat: *fatty tissue* | *She can't eat fatty meat – give her lean beef.* —**tiness** *n* [U]

fatty² also **fatso** *n infml derog* (used esp. by children) a fat person

fatty ac·id /ˌ··· ˈ··/ *n* (the chemical name for) an ORGANIC acid which a cell needs in order to process food and produce ENERGY (=the power to do work)

fat·u·ous /ˈfætʃuəs/ *adj* very silly without seeming to know it: *What a fatuous remark!* – ~**ly** *adv* —**fatuousness, fatuity** /fəˈtjuːᵻti‖fəˈtuː-/ *n* [U]

fat·wa /ˈfætwɑː/ *n* a formal legal opinion given by an islamic (ISLAM) religious authority.

fau·cet /ˈfɔːsᵻt/ *n AmE for* TAP¹ (1)

Faulk·ner /ˈfɔːlknəʳ/, **William** (1897–1962) an American writer of NOVELs about the Southern US, such as *The Sound and the Fury* and *As I Lay Dying*

fault¹ /fɔːlt/ *n* **1** a mistake or imperfection; something wrong or incorrect: *There are several faults in that page of figures.* | *A small electrical fault in the motor caused it to stop.* | **Through no fault of her own** (=not because of any mistake she made) *she lost her job.* **2** a bad or weak point, but not of a serious moral kind, in someone's character: *Your only fault is that you won't concentrate.* | *I love her for her faults as well as for her virtues.* **3** *tech* (in GEOLOGY) a crack in the Earth's surface, where one band of rock has slid against another —see EARTHQUAKE, SAN ANDREAS FAULT **4** (in games like tennis) a mistake in a SERVICE¹ (9), which may lose a point: *a double fault* **5 at fault** in the wrong: *Which of the two drivers was at fault in the car crash?* **6 be someone's fault** to be something for which someone can rightly be blamed: *"It's not our fault (that) we're late." "Whose fault is it, then?"* **7 find fault (with)** to complain (about), esp. too much or too often: *She's always finding fault with the way I do things.* **8 to a fault** (of a good quality) to an extreme degree; too much: *He's generous to a fault.* —see WRONG (USAGE)

fault² *v* **1** [T *usu. in questions or negatives*] to find a mistake or imperfection in: *It was impossible to fault her performance|her logic.* **2** [I] *tech* (of rocks) to break and form a FAULT¹ (3): *ancient faulted rocks*

fault·less /ˈfɔːltləs/ *adj apprec* without a fault; perfect: *The dancers gave an absolutely faultless performance.* – ~**ly** *adv* – ~**ness** *n* [U]

fault·y /ˈfɔːlti/ *adj* (esp. of machines, equipment, etc.) having faults; DEFECTIVE: *a faulty connection in the electrical system* | *faulty reasoning* —**ily** *adv*

faun /fɔːn/ *n* an ancient Roman god of the fields and woods, with a man's body and a goat's horns and legs —compare SATYR

fau·na /ˈfɔːnə/ *n* [C;U] all the animals living wild in a particular place or belonging to a particular age in history: *the fauna of the forest* —compare FLORA

Fauntleroy, Little Lord see LITTLE LORD FAUNTLEROY

Fau·ré /ˈfɔːreɪ‖faʊˈreɪ/, **Ga·bri·el Ur·bain** /ˈgeɪbriəl ˈʊəbæn ‖ -ʊərˈbæn/ (1845–1924) a French COMPOSER most famous for his REQUIEM

Faust /faʊst/, **Jo·hann** /ˈjəʊhæn‖-hɑːn/ also **Dr Faus·tus** /ˌdɒktə ˈfaʊstəs‖ˌdɑːktər-/— a 16th century German doctor who performed magic and is said to have sold his soul to the devil in exchange for knowledge and power. Many stories and pieces of music have been written about him.

fau·vis·m /ˈfəʊvɪzəm/ *n* a movement in painting 1905–08 using pure, bright colours and including the work of the painters Matisse and Braque

faux a·mi /ˌfəʊzæˈmiː/ *n* **faux amis** *Fr* a word in one language that looks like a word in another but has a different meaning, e.g. the French word "actuel" means "current, present-day" in English and not "actually"

faux pas /ˌfəʊ ˈpɑː, ˌfəʊ pɑː/ *n* **faux pas** /ˌfəʊ ˈpɑːz/ *Fr* a social mistake in words or behaviour; GAFFE: *He*

committed a terrible faux pas when he called the Queen "My dear".

fa·va bean /ˈfɑːvə biːn/ n AmE for BROAD BEAN

fa·vour¹ BrE|| **favor** AmE /ˈfeɪvəʳ/ n **1** [U] active approval: *He did all he could to win her favour.* | *I'm sure the president will look with favour on such a proposal.* | *The idea is beginning to gain widespread favour.* | *a movie director who seems to be* **in favour** (=popular) *with the critics just now* | *I'm afraid I'm* **out of favour** (=unpopular) *at the office at the moment.* **2** [U] unfairly generous treatment; (too much) sympathy or kindness towards one person as compared to others: *A mother shouldn't show favour to one of her children.* **3** [C] a kind act that is not forced or necessary: *As a special favour, I'll let you stay up late tonight.* | *I want to* **ask a favour** *of you; will you lend me your car?* | *Thanks a lot! I'll* **return the favour** *sometime!* | *Would you* **do me a favour** *and turn off that radio?* | *He will be in a position to dispense favours to his supporters if he is elected.* | *(fml) We would esteem* (=think) *it a great favour if you would reply at once.* **4** [C] *esp. BrE* a piece of metal (BADGE) or of coloured cloth (RIBBON) worn to show that one belongs to a particular political party, supports a particular team, etc. **5** [C] *AmE* a small gift given to guests at a party **6 in favour of: a** approving of; on the side of or in support of: *Are you in favour of workers' control of companies?* | *The committee came out in favour of* (=decided to support) *the minister's proposals.* **b** choosing instead; because of a PREFERENCE for: *He turned down a university appointment in favour of a political career.* **c** (of a cheque) payable to: *This cheque is made out in favour of the Cats Protection Society.* **7 in someone's/something's favour** to someone's/something's advantage: *The system tends to operate in favour of the wealthier classes.* | *The plan has this in its favour, that it won't cost much.* —see also FAVOURS, **curry favour** (CURRY³), **without fear or favour** (FEAR¹)

favour² BrE|| **favor** AmE– v [T] **1** to support or believe in (a plan, idea, course of action, etc.); regard with favour: *The president is believed to favour further tax cuts.* | *This is the least favoured option of all those available.* **2** to be unfairly fond of; treat (too) generously: *Parents shouldn't favour one of their children more than the others.* **3** (of conditions) to give support or advantage to; operate in favour of: *The system tends to favour those who have studied English.* **4** to look like (a relation): *She favours her mother.*
favour sbdy. **with** sthg. *phr v* [T] *fml* to give: *Kindly favour me with a reply at your earliest convenience.*

fa·vou·ra·ble BrE|| **favorable** AmE /ˈfeɪvərəbəl/ adj **1** (of a message, answer, etc.) saying what one is pleased to hear; expressing approval: *I've been hearing favourable accounts of your work.* **2** winning favour and approval: *The new manager has created a very favourable impression.* **3** [(to)] (of conditions) advantageous: *The company will lend you money on very favourable terms.* —opposite **unfavourable** —**·rably** adv : *Her book was favourably reviewed.* | *He speaks favourably of you.*

fa·voured BrE|| **favored** AmE /ˈfeɪvəd/‖-əd/ adj **1** having special advantages or desirable qualities: *a house in a favoured position* (=in attractive and convenient area) **2** receiving unfairly generous treatment: *All the best seats were reserved for favoured customers.* **3** [F+with] *fml* having an appearance of the stated kind: *She is favoured with great beauty.* | *an ill-favoured child*

fa·vou·rite¹ BrE|| **favorite** AmE /ˈfeɪvərɪt/ n **1** something or someone that is loved above all others: *I like all her books but this one is my favourite.* **2** someone who receives unfairly generous treatment: *A teacher shouldn't have favourites in the class.* **3** the one expected to win or succeed: *I put all my money on the favourite in the big horse race, but it only came in third.* | *John is favourite to get the nomination for club president.*

favourite² BrE|| **favorite** AmE– adj [A] most loved; being a favourite: *Who's your favourite writer?* | *my favourite record/movie/restaurant* | *his favourite subject of conversation* —see LOVE (USAGE)

favourite son /ˌ··· ˈ·/ n AmE a well-known person, usu. a politician, who is popular with the people in the area he comes from: *Idaho's favorite son in the primary election*

fa·vou·ri·tis·m BrE|| **favoritism** AmE /ˈfeɪvərɪtɪzəm/ n [U] *derog* the practice of giving unfairly generous treatment

to one person: *Giving that job to his friend's son was a clear case of favouritism.*

fa·vours BrE || **favors** AmE /ˈfeɪvəz‖-ərz/ n [P] *old-fash euph* a woman's agreement to sexual activity

Fawkes /fɔːks/, **Guy** (1570–1606) an English ROMAN CATHOLIC killed for his part in the secret plan to blow up the HOUSES OF PARLIAMENT in 1605. **Guy Fawkes' Night** is celebrated each year on November 5th with a BONFIRE on which the figure of a man, called a GUY¹(2), is burned, and with FIREWORKS. —see also GUY FAWKES NIGHT, GUN-POWDER PLOT

Fawl·ty /ˈfɔːlti/, **Basil** a character in a very popular British television COMEDY programme called *Fawlty Towers.* Basil Fawlty is the owner of a hotel and is known for often becoming very angry, nervous, or worried, and also for being very rude to people. The character is played by the actor John Cleese. —see colour picture on page 686

Fawlty Tow·ers /ˌ·· ˈ··/ n a funny British television programme about a hotel called Fawlty Towers, and its owner, Basil Fawlty, played by John Cleese. In the hotel, things often go wrong and the people who work there, esp. Basil Fawlty, often behave in strange ways. —see colour picture on page 686

fawn¹ /fɔːn/ n a young deer less than a year old

fawn² adj, n [U] (having) a light yellowish-brown colour

fawn³ v
fawn on/upon sbdy. *phr v* [T] **1** (esp. of a dog) to jump on, rub against, etc., as an expression of love **2** *derog* to try to gain the favour of (someone) by over-praising and being insincerely attentive: *It sickens me to see them fawning on their rich uncle.*

fax¹ /fæks/ v [T] to send (copies of printed material, letters, pictures, etc.) using a system by which the information is sent in ELECTRONIC form along a telephone line; used esp. in business: *I'll fax the menu to you in the morning.*

fax² n the printed material received or sent electronically by the fax machine: *Did you receive my fax?* | *I'm sending you a fax.* | *Send it by fax.*

fax ma·chine /ˈ· ·ˌ·/ n the machine which is used for sending or receiving faxes

fax num·ber /ˈ· ˌ··/ n the telephone number which must be used to send a fax to a particular fax machine

fay /feɪ/ n poet for FAIRY

faze /feɪz/ v [T] *infml, esp. AmE* to surprise and shock (someone) so much as to prevent speech or action: *His actions didn't faze me in the least; I expected him to behave badly.*

FBI /ˌef biː ˈaɪ/ [the] Federal Bureau of Investigation; the police department in the US that is controlled by the central government, and is particularly concerned with crimes that involve people or places in more than one state

FC /ˌef ˈsiː/ n **1** abbrev. for: FOOTBALL CLUB **2** written abbrev. for: FORESTRY COMMISSION

FCC /ˌef siː ˈsiː/ [the] see FEDERAL COMMUNICATIONS COMMISSION

FCO /ˌef siː ˈəʊ/ [the] Foreign and Commonwealth Office; the part of the British government which deals with Britain's affairs and relations with other countries. It is under the control of the **Foreign Secretary** and sends DIPLOMATs to foreign countries to represent Britain. —compare HOME OFFICE, STATE DEPARTMENT

FDA /ˌef diː ˈeɪ/ [the] Food and Drug Administration; the American government organization which decides the safety of food and drugs. The FDA decides what can legally be added to food, whether medical drugs are safe enough to be sold, and how to show information about food and drugs on the containers.

FDR /ˌef diː ˈɑːʳ/ see Franklin D. ROOSEVELT

FDIC /ˌef diː aɪ ˈsiː/ Federal Deposit Insurance Corporation an American government organization which promises the safety of money put into the named bank or institution: *Belmont National Bank, member FDIC*

FE /ˌef ˈiː/ abbrev. for: FURTHER EDUCATION

fe·al·ty /ˈfiːəlti/ n [U] (in former times) loyalty (to one's king or lord): *In return for his land he* **swore fealty** *to the king.*

fear¹ /fɪəʳ/ n **1** [C;U (of)] an unpleasant and usu. strong feeling caused by the presence or expectation of danger:

That child will do anything – she seems totally without fear. | *I have a great fear of fire|spiders.* [+*that*] *I was suddenly seized with|by the fear that they would drown.* | *My fears that he might get lost proved to be unfounded.* | *I'm* **living in (daily) fear** *of dismissal.* (=always afraid that I'll be dismissed) | **In fear and trembling** (=very much afraid) *he listened to the footsteps of the guards.* | *That loud bang* **put the fear of God into** *me.* (=frightened me very much) | *He goes* **in fear of** *his life.* (=is afraid he will be killed or die) | *The announcement that the factory would be closed confirmed our worst fears.* **2** [U (**of**)] likelihood or possibility, esp. of something bad: *"Will the children forget about lunch?" "There's no fear of that!"* **3 for fear of/that** because of anxiety about/that; in case (of): *I dare not go there for fear of him seeing me|that he will see me.* **4 No fear!** *BrE infml* (in answer to a suggestion that one should do something) Certainly not! **5** *BrE* **without fear or favour** with justice; not showing more sympathy for one side than for the other **6 the only thing we have to fear is fear itself** *quote* a phrase used by Franklin Roosevelt in his first speech as President in 1932 and now reused in other situations

fear² *v* [*not in progressive forms*] *fml* **1** [T] to be afraid of; consider or expect with feelings of fear: *She has always feared old age.* [+(*that*)] *Experts fear that there will be a new outbreak of the disease.* **2** [I (**for**)] to be afraid (for the safety of someone or something): *She feared for the little boy when she saw him at the top of the tree.* | *Never* (=do not) *fear; they will be safe.* **3 I fear** *fml or pomp* (used when giving bad news) I'm sorry that I must now say: *I fear we have missed our chance.* | *"Is there enough money?" "I fear not."* | *"Is she very ill?" "I fear so."*

fear·ful /ˈfɪəfəl‖ˈfɪər-/ *adj* **1** causing fear: *a fearful storm* **2** *pomp* very bad; (of a bad thing) very great: *What a fearful waste of time!* **3** [F (**of**)] *fml* afraid: *He was fearful of her anger.* [+(*that*)] *We were fearful that she would be angry.* – ~**ly** *adv* – ~**ness** *n* [U]

fear·less /ˈfɪələs‖ˈfɪər-/ *adj* [(**of**)] without fear; not afraid: *their fearless opposition to the junta* | *He gave them his honest opinion, fearless of the consequences.* – ~**ly** *adv* : *He gazed fearlessly at the gunman.* – ~**ness** *n* [U]

fear·some /ˈfɪəsəm‖ˈfɪər-/ *adj esp. lit or humor* causing fear; very unpleasant, esp. in appearance: *The children were a fearsome sight after their mud fight.*

fea·si·ble /ˈfiːzɪˌbəl/ *adj* able to be carried out or done; possible and reasonable: *Your plan sounds quite feasible.* | *It's simply not economically feasible to stage such a lavish production.* –compare PLAUSIBLE –**bly** *adv* –**bility** /ˌfiːzɪˈbɪlɪti/ *n* [U]: *We're having a* **feasibility study** *done to find out if the plan will work.*

feast¹ /fiːst/ *n* **1** a splendid meal, esp. a public one: *The king gave|held a feast.* | *What a marvellous meal you've given us – a real feast!* | (fig.) *a feast for the eyes* | (fig.) *a feast of music*–see also MIDNIGHT FEAST **2** a day or period of time kept in memory of a religious event: *Christmas is an important feast for Christians*–see also MOVABLE FEAST

feast² *v* [I (**on, upon**)] **1** to eat and drink very well; have a specially good meal (of): *The birds are feasting on the berries.* **2 feast one's eyes on/upon** to look at eagerly and with delight: *He feasted his eyes on the beautiful scene.*

Feast of Tab·er·nac·les /ˌ· · ˈ···/ *n* see SUKKOTH

Feast of Weeks /ˌ· · ˈ·/ *n* see SHABUOTH

feat /fiːt/ *n* an action needing strength, skill, or courage: *It was quite a feat to move that piano by yourself!* | *feats of endurance* | *a remarkable feat of engineering*

fea·ther¹ /ˈfeðəʳ/ *n* **1** any of the many parts of the covering which grows on a bird's body, each of which has a stiff rod-like piece in the middle, with soft hair-like material growing from it on each side: *an ostrich feather* | *a plume of feathers* | *a pillow stuffed with feathers* **2 a feather in someone's cap** an honour that someone can be justly proud of: *They want you to photograph the Queen? That'll be quite a feather in your cap!* **3 make the feathers/fur/sparks fly** *infml* to cause a quarrel or fight: *When Derek found Bob had damaged his bicycle, it really made the feathers fly!* –see also **birds of a feather** (BIRD), **ruffle someone's feathers** (RUFFLE¹)

feather² *v* [T] **1** [(**with**)] to put feathers on the end of (an ARROW) to act as guides in flight **2** *tech* to make (the blade of an OAR) lie flat on the surface of the water at the

end of a STROKE² (5) **3 feather one's nest** *usu. derog* to make oneself rich, esp. dishonestly, through a job in which one is trusted –see also **tar and feather** (TAR²)

feather bed /ˌ·· ˈ·/ *n* a large flat bag that is filled with feathers and used for sleeping on –compare MATTRESS

fea·ther·bed /ˈfeðəbed‖-ər-/ *v* [T] *derog* to protect by giving generous help in the form of money, tax advantages, working conditions, etc.: *Their government featherbeds its industries so that they can sell their products much more cheaply than we can.*

feather bo·a /ˌ·· ˈ··/ *n* a BOA²

fea·ther·brained /ˈfeðəbreɪnd‖-ər-/ *adj infml* very silly and thoughtless: *He was too featherbrained to think of asking for a receipt.*

feather dust·er /ˌ·· ˈ··/ *n* a long stick with a bunch of feathers fixed to one end used for removing light dust

feathered friends /ˌ·· ˈ·/ *n pl* birds, esp. in the phrase **our feathered friends**

fea·ther·weight /ˈfeðəweɪt‖-ər-/ *n* **1** a BOXER (1) heavier than a BANTAMWEIGHT but lighter than a LIGHTWEIGHT **2** someone or something of very little weight or importance: *The other two members of the committee are just featherweights.*

fea·ther·y /ˈfeðəri/ *adj* **1** covered with feathers **2** *apprec* soft and light: *feathery pastry|clouds*

fea·ture¹ /ˈfiːtʃəʳ/ *n* **1** [(**of**)] a (typical or noticeable) part or quality: *Wet weather is a feature of life in Scotland.* | *The exciting car chase was the one* **redeeming feature** *in the film.* (=the only part that made the film worth seeing) | *an essential|key feature of the plan* | *one of the regular features of the programme* | *a house with unusual architectural features* **2** any of the noticeable parts of the face: *Her mouth is her worst feature.* –see also FEATURES **3** a special long article in a newspaper or magazine: *Did you read the feature on personal computers in the New York Times?* | *a feature writer* **4** a film being shown at a cinema: *What's this week's main feature at the Odeon?*

feature² *v* **1** [T] to include as a leading performer: *This film features Dustin Hoffman (as a divorced father).* **2** [T] to advertise particularly: *We're featuring bedroom furniture this week.* **3** [I+*adv|prep*] to play an important part: *Fish features very largely in the diet of these islanders.*

feature film /ˈ·· ˌ·/ *n* a full-length cinema film with an invented story and professional actors –compare DOCUMENTARY²; see also DOUBLE FEATURE

feature-length /ˈ·· ·/ *adj* of the same length as a feature film: *a feature-length documentary*

fea·ture·less /ˈfiːtʃələs‖-tʃər-/ *adj* uninteresting, because of having no noticeable features: *a house in the middle of a featureless plain*

fea·tures /ˈfiːtʃəz‖-ərz/ *n* [P] the parts of the face: *He had regular features|Chinese features.* | *Her features were careworn.* (=showing the results of worry and age)

fe·brile /ˈfiːbraɪl‖ˈfebrəl/ *adj fml or med* of or caused by fever

Feb·ru·a·ry /ˈfebruəri, ˈfebjuri‖ˈfebjueri/ (*written abbrev.* **Feb.**) *n* [C;U] the second month of the year, between January and March: *It happened on February the tenth|on the tenth of February|(AmE) on February tenth.* | *This office opened in February 1991.* | *She started work here last February|the February before last.*

▸ CULTURAL NOTE Most people think of February as a cold, wet, perhaps snowy month. When they think of February, they may also think of SAINT VALENTINE'S DAY, which is on the 14th February. ◂

fe·ces /ˈfiːsiːz/ *n* [P] *AmE for* FAECES –**fecal** /ˈfiːkəl/ *adj*

feck·less /ˈfekləs/ *adj* worthless and without purpose or plans for the future: *That feckless brother of mine will never get a decent job.* | *His feckless behaviour landed him in court for debt.* – ~**ly** *adv* – ~**ness** *n* [U]

fec·und /ˈfekənd, ˈfiːkənd/ *adj fml* producing a lot of crops or young; FERTILE: *a fecund fruit tree* – ~**ity** /fɪˈkʌndɪˌti/ *n* [U]

fed /fed/ *past tense & participle of* FEED –see also FED UP

Fed¹ [*the*] *AmE infml* the Federal Reserve Bank

Fed² *n AmE infml* **1** (a criminal's name for) an FBI AGENT **2** *usu. derog* a person who works for a US government

AGENCY and is often seen as causing trouble in the lives of ordinary people

fed·e·ral /'fedərəl/ *adj* **1** of or being a FEDERATION: *Switzerland is a federal republic.* **2** of the central government of the US as compared with the governments of the states that form it: *Americans pay both federal taxes and state taxes.* —see also extra information on page 568

Federal A·vi·a·tion Ad·min·i·stra·tion /ˌ··· ··'··· ···,··/ also **FAA**— [*the*] an American government organization which is concerned with aircraft and airport safety

Federal Bu·reau of In·ves·ti·ga·tion /ˌ··· ˌ·· · ···'··/ [*the*] see FBI

Federal Com·mu·ni·ca·tions Com·mis·sion /ˌ··· ···'·· ·ˌ··/ also **FCC**— [*the*] an American government organization which is responsible for rules concerning broadcasting publicly or privately on radio, television, CABLE, and SATELLITE TELEVISION

federal court /ˌ··· '·/ *n* a court which hears cases that have to do with American law or the American CONSTITUTION —see also extra information on page 742

Federal Ex·press /ˌ··· ·'·/ *tdmk* an American COURIER company which operates internationally

fed·e·ral·is·m /'fedərəlɪzəm/ *n* [U] the belief in a FEDERAL system of government —**ist** *n, adj*

Federal Re·serve Bank /ˌ··· ·'· ˌ·/ [*the*] one of 12 banks each operating in a different area of the US under the authority of the Federal Reserve System

Federal Re·serve Sys·tem /ˌ··· ·'· ˌ··/ also **Fed**— [*the*] the central banking (CENTRAL BANK) system of the US. The central bank of the US is the Federal Reserve Bank.

Federal Trade Com·mis·sion /ˌ··· '· ·ˌ··/ [*the*] see FTC

fed·e·rate /'fedəreɪt/ *v* [I;T] to form or become a federation

fed·e·ra·tion /ˌfedə'reɪʃən/ *n* **1** [C] a group of states united with one government which decides foreign affairs, defence, etc., but in which each state can have its own government to decide its own affairs **2** [U] the action or result of uniting in this way: *What hopes are there for European federation?* **3** [C] a group of societies, organizations, trade unions, etc., that have come together in this way: *the Federation of British Fishing Clubs*

fe·do·ra /fɪ'dɔːrə/ *n* a man's hat made of FELT, with a BRIM all the way round and a fold on top going from back to front. Fedoras were popular in the US in former times.

fed up /ˌ· '·/ *adj* [F (**about, of, with**)] *infml* unhappy, tired, and not satisfied, esp. about something uninteresting, annoying, or time-wasting that one has had too much of: *I'm rather fed up with your complaints.* | *The management is pretty fed up with/about the union's lack of co-operation concerning new technology.* | *I'm fed up of waiting for him — I'm going home!* [+*that*] *She'll be a bit fed up that you didn't telephone.*
▷ USAGE Some people say **fed up of,** not **fed up with:** *I'm* **fed up of** *it.* But this is often considered incorrect.◁

fee /fiː/ *n* **1** a sum of money paid for professional services to a doctor, lawyer, private school, etc.: *doctor's fees* —see PAY (USAGE) **2 fee fi fo fum** /ˌfiː ˌfaɪ ˌfəʊ 'fʌm/ (**I smell the blood of an Englishman**) a phrase used by the GIANT in the fairy story of *Jack and the Beanstalk* when he thinks that he can smell Jack in his castle

fee·ble /'fiːbəl/ *adj* **1** lacking strength or force; FRAIL: *You'll find your grandfather is a lot feebler than when you last saw him.* **2** (of a joke, idea, story, etc.) weak; silly; not well thought out: *a feeble suggestion/excuse* — ~ **ness** *n* [U] —**feebly** *adv*

fee·ble·mind·ed /ˌfiːbəl'maɪndɪd◄/ *adj* **1** not clever; with less than the usual INTELLIGENCE **2** *euph* very stupid — ~ **ness** *n* [U]

feed /fiːd/ *v* **fed** /fed/ **1** [T (**on, with**)] to give food to: *We have to feed 120 guests after the wedding.* | *He's got a big family — lots of hungry mouths to feed!* | *The baby will soon learn to feed himself.* | *We feed our dogs on fresh meat.* | *She feeds the baby with a spoon.* | (fig.) *They fed the fire with logs.* | (fig.) *These little streams feed the lake.* | (fig.) *You should water this plant once a week and feed it* (=with minerals etc. needed for plant growth) *in spring and summer.* —see also FORCE-FEED, SPOON-FEED **2** [I (**on**)] (esp. of an animal or baby) to eat: *The horses were feeding quietly in the stable.* | *Cows feed on grass.* **3** [T+*obj* +*adv/prep*] to put, supply, or provide, esp. continually: *Keep feeding the wire into/through the hole.* | *You feed in*

the money here and the coffee comes out there. | *The information is fed back to the appropriate government department* | *to feed data into a computer.* **4** [T+*obj(i)*+*obj(d)*] *infml* to provide with: *We fed the spy some false information in the hope that he would pass it back to his government.* | *They tried to feed me a line* (=a false story) *about unexpected extra expenses.* **5** [T] to put coins into (a PARKING METER) continually and illegally whenever one's parking period comes to an end, in order to keep one's parking place —see also **bite the hand that feeds one** (BITE¹ (12))

feed sthg. to sthg./sbdy. *phr v* [T] to give as food to: *You'd better feed this old bread to the ducks.*

feed sbdy./sthg. ↔ **up** *BrE* ‖ **fatten up** *phr v* [T] to make (a person or animal) fatter and healthier by providing lots of good food: *That thin little boy needs feeding up.* —see also FED UP

feed² *BrE* ‖ **feeding** *AmE*— *n* **1** [C] a meal taken by an animal or baby: *How many feeds a day does the baby get?* **2** [U] food for animals: *a bag of hen feed* —see also CHICKENFEED **3** [C] the part of a machine through which the machine is supplied with power or FUEL: *There's a blockage in the petrol feed.* **4** [C] *BrE* a person who supplies a stage entertainer with lines or situations about which he/she can make jokes **5** [C] *AmE infml* a meal: *We had a pretty good feed at my uncle's yesterday.*

feed·back /'fiːdbæk/ *n* [U] **1** remarks about or in answer to an action, process, etc., passed back to the person (or machine) responsible, so that changes can be made if necessary: *The company welcomes feedback from people who use its goods.* | *There's been a lot of positive feedback on the new proposals. I asked my boss for feedback about my work.* | *The college uses feedback from students to prepare new training centres.* **2** uncontrolled noise from an electrical amplification (AMPLIFY) system

feed·bag /'fiːdbæg/ *n AmE for* NOSEBAG

feed·er /'fiːdəʳ/ *BrE*‖**eater** *AmE n* **1** a person, animal or plant that eats or takes in food in the stated way: *Little Timmy is a noisy feeder.* **2** a branch road, airline, railway line, etc., that connects with a main one

feeder school /'·· ˌ·/ *n* a school, e.g. a MIDDLE SCHOOL (2), which regularly sends pupils to a SECONDARY school in the same area

feed·ing /'fiːdɪŋ/ *AmE for* FEED²(1)

feeding bot·tle /'·· ˌ··/ *BrE*‖**baby bottle** *AmE*— *n* a bottle with a rubber cap (TEAT‖NIPPLE) from which a baby can suck liquids

feeding ground /'·· ·/ *n* a place where a group of animals or birds find food to eat

Feeding of the Five Thou·sand /ˌ··· ·· ˌ· '··/ [*the*] a story from the Bible in which Jesus fed 5000 people with five loaves of bread and two fish. 12 full baskets of food remained when the people had finished eating.

feed·lot /'fiːdlɒt ‖ -lɑːt/ *n AmE* a large enclosed area where cattle are fattened before being killed

feel¹ /fiːl/ *v* **felt** /felt/ **1** [T] to get knowledge of by touching with the fingers; handle in order to examine, test, or find out something: *Just feel the quality of the cloth!* [+*wh*-] *I can't feel where the light switch is.* | *The nurse felt the child's forehead to see if he had a fever.* **2** [T *not in progressive forms*] to experience (the touch or movement of something): *It's nice to feel the wind on your face.* | *He felt a sudden stab of pain in his chest.* [+*obj*+*v-ing*] *I can feel a pin sticking into me.* | *She felt her heart beating faster.* [+*obj*+*to-v*] *I felt something touch my foot.* | *He felt her hand tense up in his.* **3** [L+*adj*; I+*adv*] to experience (a condition of the mind or body); be consciously: *"Are you feeling better?" "Yes, I feel fine now."* | *Do you feel hungry yet?* | *She felt cold/cheated/happy.* | *I feel sure that's him!* | *I feel a hundred.* (=years old) | *I felt as if/as though* (=it seemed to me that) *I was going to faint.* **4** [I+*adv/prep*] to search with the fingers rather than the eyes: *She felt (around) in her bag for a pencil.* **5** [L+*adj*; I+*adv/prep*] to give or produce the stated sensation; seem: *Your hands feel cold.* | *It feels cold in this room.* | *How does it feel to be a famous writer?* | *It feels as if/as though there's something sticking out of the mattress.* | *What's this in my pocket? It feels like a nut.* **6** [L+*adj*; I+*adv*] to give one the stated sensation: *My feet feel cold.* | *My leg feels as if it's broken.* **7** [T *not in progressive forms*] to suffer because of (a state or event): *Old people tend to feel the cold quite badly.* **8** [L+*n*] to think or believe oneself to be: *I* felt such a fool when I realized what I'd done. **9** [T] to have as an opinion; believe, esp. not as a result of reasoning: *What do you feel about this idea?* [+(*that*)] *I can't help feeling (that) you haven't been completely honest with me.* | *The company feels that this is not a good time to invest a large amount of money.* [+*obj*+*n*|*adj*] (*fml*) *She felt herself (to be) unwanted there.* **10** [T] to have knowledge or consciousness of, but not as the result of reasoning; SENSE: [+(*that*)] *She instinctively felt that there was someone else in the room*|*that someone was following her.* **11 feel free to do something** (*often imperative*) to consider oneself welcome to do something: *Please feel (completely) free to make suggestions.* **12 feel in one's bones** to believe strongly (that something is true or will happen), though without proof: *She's going to phone tonight! I can feel it in my bones.* **13 feel like** to have a wish for; want: *I don't feel like dancing now.* | *Do you feel like a cup of coffee?* **14 feel one's way: a** to move carefully (as if) in the dark: *They felt their way down the dark passage.* **b** to act slowly and carefully: *He hasn't been in the job long and he's still feeling his way.*

feel for sbdy. *phr v* [T] to be sorry for; be unhappy about the suffering of; feel sympathy for: *I really feel for the parents of that boy who was killed in the crash.*

feel sbdy. ↔ **out** *phr v* [T] *AmE infml* to get (someone's) opinions or feelings, e.g. by asking questions: *Have you felt out your parents about using the cabin?*

feel sbdy. ↔ **up** *phr v* [T] *sl* to touch (a woman) sexually, usu. without permission. Feeling somebody up is likely to cause great offence.

feel² *n* [S] **1** the sensation caused by feeling something: *I like the feel of this cloth; it has a warm woolly feel.* **2** *infml, esp. BrE* an act of feeling: *Your neck looks swollen — let me have a feel.* **3 get the feel of** to become used to: *You'll soon get the feel of the new job*|*car.*

feel·er /ˈfiːləʳ/ *n* **1** one of the two thread-like parts on the front of an insect's head, with which it touches things **2 put out feelers** to make a suggestion as a test of what others will think or do: *I'm putting out feelers to see if she'd like to come and work for us.*

feelers

feelers

feel·ing¹ /ˈfiːlɪŋ/ *n* **1** [C | of] a consciousness (of something felt in the mind or body): *a feeling of shame*|*danger*|*thirst*|*pleasure*|*relief* | *feelings of shame*|*doubt* **2** [C;U] a belief or opinion, esp. one that is not based on reason: *There's considerable division of feeling* (=different opinions) *over the issue.* [+ (*that*)] *I have a feeling we're being followed.* | *There seems to be a general feeling that the election will be in June.* | *I don't really know what to think — I've got very mixed feelings on the subject.* **3** [U] the power to feel; sensation: *He lost all feeling in his toes.* **4** [U] excitement of mind, esp. in a bad sense: *The new working hours caused*|*aroused a lot of bad*|*ill feeling at the factory.* **5** [U (for)] sympathy and understanding: *She plays the piano with great feeling.* | *You have no feeling for the beauty of nature.* —see also FEELINGS

feeling² *adj* [A] showing strong feelings: *She gave him a feeling look.* — ~ **ly** *adv* : *"I hate him," she said feelingly.*

feel·ings /ˈfiːlɪŋz/ *n* [P] the part of a person's nature that feels, compared to the part that thinks; sensations of joy, sorrow, hate, etc.: *maternal*|*nationalist*|*antagonistic feelings* | *She has very strong feelings on this subject.* | *You'll hurt his feelings* (=make him unhappy) *if you forget his birthday.* | *I'm very sorry I offended you —* **no hard feelings?** (=I hope you will forgive me)

fee-pay·ing /ˈ· ͵··/ *adj* **1** that pays FEES: *a fee-paying student*|*client* **2** that charges FEES: *a fee-paying school*

feet /fiːt/ *pl. of* FOOT —see also COLD FEET, ITCHY FEET

feet of clay /͵· · ˈ·/ *n* [P] a hidden weakness, usu. of morals or principles: *They eventually realized that the leader they so admired had feet of clay.*

feign /feɪn/ *v* [T] **1** *fml* to pretend to have or be; put on a false air of: *He feigned death to escape capture.* | *a feigned illness* **2** *old use* to invent (an excuse, reason, etc.)

feint¹ /feɪnt/ *n* a false attack or blow, made to draw the enemy's attention away from the real danger

feint² *v* [I] to make a feint, esp. by pretending to hit with one hand and then using the other: *The boxer feinted with his left, and then landed a heavy punch with his right.*

feist·y /ˈfaɪsti/ *adj AmE infml, often apprec* excited and keen to quarrel; COMBATIVE

fe·la·fel /fəˈlɑːfəl/ *n* FALAFEL

feld·spar /ˈfeldspɑːʳ/ also **felspar** — *n* [U] a type of white or light red stone

fe·li·ci·tate /fɪˈlɪsɪteɪt/ *v* [T (on, upon)] *pomp or humor* to CONGRATULATE —**·tations** /fɪ͵lɪsɪˈteɪʃənz/ *n* [P]

fe·li·ci·tous /fɪˈlɪsɪtəs/ *adj fml* (of a word or remark) suitable and well-chosen — ~ **ly** *adv* — ~ **ness** *n* [U]

fe·li·ci·ty /fɪˈlɪsɪti/ *n fml* **1** [U] happiness **2** [C;U] (an example of) the quality of being felicitous

fe·line /ˈfiːlaɪn/ *adj, n* (of or like) a member of the cat family: *Lions and tigers are felines.* | *There is a feline grace about the way she moves.*

Fe·lix the Cat /͵fiːlɪks ðə ˈkæt/ a CARTOON character for children, a black and white cat

fell¹ /fel/ *past tense of* FALL

fell² *v* [T] **1** to cut down (a tree) **2** to knock down (a person): *He felled his opponent in the first round.*

fell³ also **fells** *pl.* — *n NEngE* **1** high wild rocky country **2** a hill or mountain

fell⁴ *adj* [A] **1** *lit* evil, dangerous, and terrible: *a fell disease* **2 at**|**in one fell swoop** *infml* all at once: *The gambler lost his money, his car, and his home at one fell swoop.*

fel·la·ti·o /fəˈleɪʃiəʊ/ *n* [U] *fml* the practice of touching the male sex organ with the lips and tongue in order to give sexual pleasure —compare CUNNILINGUS

fel·ler /ˈfeləʳ/ also **fel·la** /ˈfelə/ *n infml* a FELLOW¹ (1, 4)

Fel·li·ni /feˈliːni/, **Fed·e·ri·co** /͵fedəˈriːkəʊ/ (1920–93) an Italian film director whose films include *La Dolce Vita*

fel·low¹ /ˈfeləʊ/ *n* **1** *infml* a man: *See if those fellows want some beer.* | *How are you, old fellow?* **2** [(of)] *BrE* a member of a society connected with some branch of learning or of certain university colleges: *a Fellow of the Royal Society* | *She's a fellow of Girton College.* **3** (*often in comb.*) someone with whom one shares a (stated) activity or spends time in a (stated) place: *She and I were schoolfellows.* (=were at school together) **4** *infml, esp. BrE* a boyfriend

fellow² *adj* [A] another (of two or more things or people like oneself): *one's fellow travellers*|*prisoners*|*students* | *It's nice to meet a fellow jazz fan.*

fellow feel·ing /͵·· ˈ··/ *n* [S;U (for, with)] understanding and sympathy for someone who is like or has had similar experiences as oneself: *I have a lot of*|*a certain fellow feeling with her because she's a migrant like me.*

fel·low·man, fellow-man /͵feləʊˈmæn/ *n* -**men** /ˈmen/ [S] human beings considered as a group: *charitable organizations which aim to help their fellowman*

fel·low·ship /ˈfeləʊʃɪp/ *n* **1** [C] a group or society of people with a shared interest, esp. a group of Christians who meet together regularly to worship **2** [U] the condition of being friends through sharing or doing something together; companionship: *There was a strong feeling of fellowship amongst the members of the team.* **3** [C] *BrE* the position of a fellow of a college **4** [C] the money given to GRADUATES to allow them to continue their studies at an advanced level **5** [C] a group of officials who decide who is to receive this money

fellow trav·el·ler /͵·· ˈ···/ *n* **1** someone who is travelling with you **2** *usu. derog* someone who is sympathetic to the aims of the Communist Party without being actually a member **3** someone who shares an idea or system of ideas which is believed in by only a small group of people: *During the mid-1980s several people were mentioned as Supreme Court nominees, along with such fellow travelers as Robert Bork.*

fells /felz/ *n* [P] FELL³

fel·on /ˈfelən/ *n* **1** *law* a criminal guilty of felony **2** a WHITLOW

fel·o·ny /ˈfeləni/ *n* [C;U] *law* (a) serious crime such as murder or armed robbery: *guilty of felony* | *felony charges* —compare MISDEMEANOUR —**·nious** /fɪˈləʊniəs/ *adj*

fel·spar /ˈfelspɑːʳ/ *n* [U] FELDSPAR

felt¹ /felt/ *past tense & participle of* FEEL

felt² n [U] thick firm cloth made of wool, hair, or fur that has been pressed flat: *a felt hat*

felt-tip pen /ˌ· · ˈ·/ also **felt-tipped pen, felt tip** /ˈ· ·/— n a pen with a small piece of felt at the end instead of a NIB

fem. *written abbrev. for:* FEMININE

fe·male¹ /ˈfiːmeɪl/ adj **1** (typical) of the sex that gives birth to young: *a female elephant* | *We only employ female workers.* | *the female form* **2** (of a plant or flower) producing fruit **3** *tech* having a hole made to receive a part that fits into it: *a female plug* — ~**ness** n [U]

female² n **1** a female person or animal: *The female sat on the eggs while the male bird brought food.* **2** *often derog* a woman: *Some idiotic female asked me to sign an anti-government petition today.* **3 the female of the species is more deadly than the male** *quote* a phrase from a poem by Rudyard Kipling, often used when saying how cruel women are

▷ USAGE **Female** and **male** are used as nouns and adjectives to show what sex a creature is. They are the usual words to use about animals: *a* **male**/**female** *elephant* | *The* **females** *are often more aggressive than the* **males**. They are the right words to use when you are completing forms: *Sex:* **male**/**female**, but otherwise are not usually used about people. It is offensive to call a woman *a* **female**. —see also FEMININE (USAGE)◁

fem·i·nine /ˈfemɪnɪn/ adj **1** of or having the qualities considered womanly, e.g. gentleness and prettiness: *a room decorated in feminine pinks and pastels* | *He has a rather feminine voice.* **2** *tech* (in grammar) for or belonging to the class of words that usu. includes most of the words for females: *"Actress" is the feminine form of "actor".* | *The word for "door" is feminine in German.* | *a feminine ending* —compare MASCULINE, NEUTER

▷ USAGE Compare **male**/**female** and **masculine**/**feminine**. **Female** and **male** are used to show what sex a creature is: *a* **male** *chimpanzee*. They are also used when talking about things which relate to one sex or the other: *The* **female** *voice tends to be higher than the* **male** *voice.* | *the* **male**/**female** *body.* **Feminine** and **masculine** are used only of people, to describe qualities which are supposed to be typical of one or other sex: *He has delicate* **feminine** *hands.* | *He is a very* **masculine** *sort of person.* | *She has a deep* **masculine** *voice.*◁

fem·i·nin·i·ty /ˌfemɪˈnɪnɪti/ n [U] *usu. apprec* the quality of being FEMININE (1), esp. when considered attractive to men

fem·i·nis·m /ˈfemɪnɪzəm/ n [U] (activity in support of) the principle that women should have the same rights and chances as men —-**nist** adj, n : *the feminist movement* | *feminist issues|fiction* | *an ardent feminist*

▶ CULTURAL NOTE The feminist or women's MOVEMENT in Britain and the US has tried to change the present system to give women equality with men, esp. in the areas of jobs and pay. Women's chances for education and jobs have improved since feminism began, but some people think that feminists do not like men or are LESBIANS. Many women today still want the same rights and chances as men but also want to keep some of the typical roles expected of women, such as staying at home to take care of children.◀

femme fa·tale /ˌfæm fəˈtɑːl/ |ˌfem-/ n *Fr* **femmes fatales** *(same pronunciation)* a woman who attracts men, esp. into dangerous situations, by her mysterious charm

fe·mur /ˈfiːməʳ/ n **femurs** or **femora** /ˈfemərə/ *med* the long bone in the upper part of the leg —see picture at SKELETON —**femoral** /ˈfemərəl/ adj

fen /fen/ n an area of low wet land, esp. in E England —see also FENS

fence¹ /fens/ n **1** an upright structure like a wall, but made of posts of wood or metal joined together by boards of wood or wire, dividing two areas of land: *They were talking across the garden fence.* | *a picket fence* —compare WALL, and see picture at HOUSE **2** *sl* someone who buys and sells stolen goods **3 on/off the fence** in/not in a situation where one avoids taking sides in an argument, in order to see where one's own advantage lies: *Stop sitting on the fence and say what you really think!* | *Why don't you come down off the fence and commit yourself for once?* —see also **mend (one's) fences** (MEND¹)

fence² v **1** [I] to fight with a long thin sword as a sport **2** [I (**for**)] to try to gain an advantage over an opponent who is doing the same: *The two racing drivers fenced for a chance to gain the lead.* **3** [T (AROUND)] to put a fence round: *The tree was fenced around with wire.*

fence sth./sbdy. ↔ **in** phr v [T] **1** to surround or close in (an area) with a fence, esp. to protect what is inside: *We fenced in the garden to keep the sheep out.* **2** to keep in by surrounding with a fence: *Why don't you fence your sheep in?* | (fig.) *I like being at home with the baby, but sometimes I feel very fenced in.*

fence sth. ↔ **off** phr v [T] to separate or shut out (an area) with a fence: *We fenced off the lake in case the children should fall in.*

fenc·er /ˈfensəʳ/ n someone who fences as a sport

fenc·ing /ˈfensɪŋ/ n [U] **1** the sport of fighting with a long thin sword **2** (material for making) fences: *Has the fencing been delivered to the site?* | *The camp was surrounded by wire fencing.*

fend /fend/ v **fend for oneself** to look after oneself: *I've had to fend for myself since I was 14.*

fend sth. ↔ **off** phr v [T] to push away; act to avoid: *She fended off their blows with her arms.* | *He fended off the difficult questions.*

fend·er /ˈfendəʳ/ n **1** a low metal wall round an open fireplace, to stop the coal from falling out **2** *AmE* for a WING¹ (4) (=a guard over the wheel of a car) —see picture at CAR **b** MUDGUARD —see picture at BICYCLE **3** an object such as a mass of rope, an old tyre, a lump of wood, etc., that hangs over the side of a boat to protect it from damage by other boats or when coming to land

fender-bend·er /ˈ·· ˌ··/ n *AmE infml* a car accident in which no people are hurt and there is only slight damage to cars: *Traffic was held up because of a fender-bender on the expressway.*

fen·nel /ˈfenl/ n [U] a plant with yellow flowers whose root can be eaten and whose leaves and seeds are used for giving a special taste to food

Fens /fenz/ [*the*] an area of flat land in E England which used to be partly covered by the sea and now produces good crops

fe·nu·greek /ˈfenjʊˌɡriːk/ n [U] an Asian plant whose seeds are used for giving a special taste to food, esp. in Indian cooking

fer·al /ˈferəl, ˈfɪərəl/ adj [no comp.] *tech* (of an animal) wild, esp. after living with people and later escaping: *feral cats|pigeons*

Fer·di·nand and Is·a·bel·la /ˌfɜːdɪnænd ənd ˌɪzəˈbelə‖ ˌfɜːr-/ Ferdinand (1452–1516), Spanish ruler with his wife Isabella I of Castile (1451–1504) also known as the **Catholic Monarchs**

Fer·gie /ˈfɜːɡi‖ˈfɜːr-/ the name used in popular newspapers for Sarah Ferguson, the Duchess of York

Fer·gu·son /ˈfɜːɡəsən‖ˈfɜːr-/, **Sa·rah** /ˈseərə/ (1959–) Sarah Ferguson, who married Prince Andrew in 1986 and has two daughters, Princess Beatrice (1988–) and Princess Eugenie (1990–). Her official title became the **Duchess of York**, although she was sometimes called **Fergie** in the popular newspapers. In 1992 it was officially stated that she and Prince Andrew were going to separate.

Fer·man·agh /fəˈmænə‖fər-/ a former COUNTY in the SW of Northern Ireland, now a local government DISTRICT

fer·ment¹ /fəˈment‖fər-/ v [I;T] **1** to (cause to) change chemically and become filled with gas by the action of certain living substances such as YEAST, esp. in such a way that sugar turns to alcohol: *The wine is beginning to ferment.* | *Cider is fermented apple juice.* **2** to be in or cause (a state of political trouble and excitement): *His speeches fermented trouble among the workforce* — ~**ation** /ˌfɜːmenˈteɪʃən‖ˌfɜːrmən-/ n [U]

fer·ment² /ˈfɜːment‖ˈfɜːr-/ n [U] (the condition of) trouble and excitement, esp. of a political kind; UNREST: *The whole country was in a state of ferment.*

Fer·mi /ˈfɜːmi‖ˈfɜːr-/, **En·ri·co** /enˈriːkəʊ/ (1901–54) an Italian-born American scientist who won a NOBEL PRIZE and helped build the first NUCLEAR REACTOR

fern /fɜːn‖fɜːrn/ n a green plant with feathery shaped leaves and no flowers —**ferny** adj

fe·ro·cious /fəˈrəʊʃəs/ adj
fierce, cruel, and violent: a
ferocious lion | a ferocious at-
tack | (fig.) The heat is fero-
cious today. — —ly adv —
~ness n [U]

fern

fe·ro·ci·ty /fəˈrɒsɨti‖fəˈrɑː-/ n
[U] ferociousness

Fer·ra·ri /fəˈrɑːri/ n tdmk a car
made by the Italian company
Ferrari, famous for its speed
and quality both as a road
car and a racing car

Fer·ra·ro /fəˈrɑːrəʊ/, **Ger·al·dine** /ˈdʒerəldiːn/ (1935–) an
American Democrat politician. In 1984 she became the
first woman in the US to be the vice-presidential (VICE-
PRESIDENT) CANDIDATE from one of the two main parties.

fer·ret¹ /ˈferɨt/ n **1** a small fierce European animal of the
WEASEL family with a pointed nose, which catches rats
and rabbits by going into their holes **2** someone who
searches with great activity, esp. habitually

ferret² v [I] **1** [+adv/prep] infml to search by pushing
things about: I've been ferreting about/around in my desk
for that missing letter. **2** to hunt rats and rabbits with
ferrets
ferret sthg. ↔ **out** phr v [T] infml to discover (something) by searching: At last I managed to ferret out the
truth.

Fer·ri·er /ˈferiər/, **Kath·leen** /ˈkæθliːn/ (1912–53) an English
concert singer known both in Europe and the US

ferr·is wheel /ˈferɨs ˌwiːl/ n esp. AmE for BIG WHEEL (1)

fer·ro·con·crete /ˌferəʊˈkɒŋkriːt‖-ˈkɑːŋ-, -kɑːŋˈkriːt/ n [U]
REINFORCED CONCRETE

fer·rous /ˈferəs/ adj tech related to or containing iron: fer-
rous metals

fer·rule /ˈferuːl, ˈferəl‖ˈferəl/ n a metal band or cap that is
put on the end of a thin stick or tube

fer·ry¹ /ˈferi/ also **fer·ry·boat** /ˈferibəʊt/— n a boat that goes
across a river or any other esp. narrow stretch of water,
carrying people and things: You can cross the river by
ferry. | a car ferry | When does the next ferry leave?

ferry² v [T+obj+adv/prep] to carry (as if) on a ferry: The
boatman ferried them across the river. | Every day I ferry
the children to and from school in my car.

fer·ry·man /ˈferimən/ n **-men** /mən/ a person who guides a
ferry across water

fer·tile /ˈfɜːtaɪl‖ˈfɜːrtl/ adj **1** producing many young,
fruits, or seeds: Some fish are very fertile: they lay thousands of eggs. **2** (of land) which produces or can produce
good crops: fertile soil **3** [no comp.] (of living things) able
to produce young or fruit: Are these eggs fertile? **4** (of
a person's mind) inventive; full of suggestions, ideas, etc.:
a fertile imagination —opposite **infertile**; compare BAR-
REN, STERILE —**-tility** /fɜːˈtɪlɨti‖fɜːr-/ n [U]: Margaret
wants a child so she's taking special drugs to increase her
fertility. | a fertility symbol

Fertile Cres·cent /ˌ··· ˈ··/ [the] an area of the MIDDLE EAST
around the rivers Tigris and Euphrates, where many
very old CIVILIZATIONs were based. The Fertile Crescent
includes parts of Israel, Lebanon, Jordan, and Iraq.

fer·ti·lize also **-lise** BrE /ˈfɜːtɨlaɪz‖ˈfɜːrtl-aɪz/ v [T] **1** to start
the development of young (in a female creature or plant)
by sexual or other means: Bees fertilize the flowers. **2** to
put fertilizer on (land) —see also CROSS-FERTILIZE
—**lization** /ˌfɜːtɨlaɪˈzeɪʃən‖ˌfɜːrtələ-/ n [U] : Keep the eggs
in a warm place after fertilization.

fer·ti·liz·er /ˈfɜːtɨlaɪzər‖ˈfɜːrtl-aɪzər/ n [C;U] a natural or
chemical substance that is put on the land to make crops
grow better: Animal manure makes a good fertilizer. | ar-
tificial fertilizers

fer·vent /ˈfɜːvənt‖ˈfɜːr-/ adj being, having, or showing deep
sincere feelings: a fervent desire to win | a fervent nation-
alist — ~ly adv : He fervently begged us not to go. —**vency**
n [U]

fer·vid /ˈfɜːvɨd‖ˈfɜːr-/ adj fml showing too strong feeling;
IMPASSIONED: his fervid support for capital punishment —
~ly adv

fer·vour BrE ‖ **fervor** AmE /ˈfɜːvər‖ˈfɜːr-/ n [U] the qual-

ity of being ferv[...]
ary fervour

fess /fes/
  fess up phr v [...]
responsibility; CO[...]
dow when I told h[...]
fess up! Who ate [...]

fes·ter /ˈfestər/ v [I] [...]
and diseased: (fig.)[...]
fester daily, until [...]

fes·ti·val /ˈfestɨvəl/ n [...]
of a religious even[...]
gious ceremonies, [...]
of the Christian chu[...]
(often cap.) a group[...]
mances held usu. [...]
Cannes Film Festiva[...] ....gh restival | a pop
festival

Festival Hall /ˌ··· ˈ·/ also **Royal Festival Hall**— [the] a
large concert hall on the SOUTH BANK of the River Thames
in London, built in 1951

Festival of Nine Les·sons and Car·ols /ˌ··· ·ˌ· ˌ··· ˈ··/ n
a service held just before Christmas in some Christian
churches containing readings from the Bible and
Christmas CAROLs —see also CAROL SERVICE

fes·tive /ˈfestɪv/ adj of or suitable for a FESTIVAL (1): The
Christmas period is often called the **festive season**. | (lit
or humor) They all sat round the **festive board**. (=table
spread with a FEAST) | a festive occasion

fes·tiv·i·ty /feˈstɪvɨti/ n [U] **1** happiness and festive activity
2 also **festivities** pl. – a festive event: Don't stay in here
on your own; come next door and join the festivities. |
Christmas festivities

fes·toon¹ /feˈstuːn/ n a chain of flowers, leaves, RIBBONs,
etc., hung up in a curve between two points as a
decoration

festoon² v [T (**with**)] to decorate with festoons: The hall
was festooned with flowers.

fet·a /ˈfetə/ n [U] a kind of white, salty cheese made from
sheep's or goat's milk

fe·tal /ˈfiːtl/ adj AmE foetal (FOETUS)

fetch /fetʃ/ v [T] **1** to go and get from another place and
bring back: Run and fetch the doctor! [+obj(i)+obj(d)]
Could you fetch me a clean shirt from my bedroom? **2** to
be sold for: The house should fetch a high price/at least
£80,000. **3** [+obj(i)+obj(d)] esp. BrE infml to strike with
(a blow, kick, etc.): I fetched him a clip round the ear. **4**
rare to breathe (esp. a deep breath or SIGH) **5 fetch and
carry (for)** to do small jobs (for someone), as if one was
a servant: You can't expect me to fetch and carry for you
all day! —see BRING (USAGE)
  fetch up phr v [I+adv/prep] BrE infml to arrive; end
up, esp. without planning: I fell asleep on the train and
fetched up in Glasgow.

fetch·ing /ˈfetʃɪŋ/ adj old-fash infml attractive or pleasing
in appearance: a fetching outfit — ~ly adv

a village fete

fete¹, **fête** /feɪt, fet/ n **1** BrE a day of public enjoyment
and entertainment, held usu. out of doors in villages in
summer. Often money is collected for a special purpose
by selling cakes, JAM, home made woollen clothes, etc.
and by providing tea, and games for the children: Our

fete [right margin, partial]
village is holding a f[...]
of the new hall. **2** [...]
Prom Night is th[...]

fête², **fête** v [...]
with publi[...]
the loca[...]

fe·tid /[...]
fe[...]

...*e to raise money for the building* ...*mE* a celebration or entertainment: ...*fete of the year for high school students.*

...*usu. pass.*] to show honour to (someone) ...parties and ceremonies: *After it won the cup,* ...*football team was feted everywhere it went.*

...iːt∫d‖'fetʃd/ *adj* smelling extremely bad; FOUL: *the* ...*d odour of the decomposing corpses*

et·ish /'fetɪʃ, 'fiː-/ *n* **1** an object that is worshipped as a god by people in some undeveloped societies, and is thought to have magic power **2** something to which one pays an unreasonable amount of attention or which one admires to a foolish degree: *Make sure you clean your room before he comes; he has a fetish about/makes a fetish of tidiness.* **3** *tech* (in PSYCHOLOGY) an object whose presence is necessary for sexual satisfaction

fet·ish·is·m /'fetɪʃɪzəm, 'fiː-/ *n* [U] **1** the practice of worshipping fetishes **2** unreasonable attention to or admiration for something **3** *tech* (in PSYCHOLOGY) the practice of having a fetish —**·ist** *n* —**·istic** /ˌfetɪˈʃɪstɪk◂, ˌfiː-/ *adj*

fet·lock /'fetlɒk‖-lɑːk/ *n* the back part of a horse's leg near the foot, that has longer hairs on it than the upper part —see picture at HORSE

fet·ter¹ /'fetər/ *n* **1** a chain for the foot of a prisoner **2** also **fetters** *pl.* — something that prevents freedom of movement or action: *He longed to escape from the fetters of an unhappy marriage.*

fetter² *v* [T (to)] to tie or prevent from moving (as if) with fetters: *fettered by responsibility* —see also UNFETTERED

fet·tle /'fetl/ *n* [U] *BrE infml* (the stated) condition of health, strength, confidence, etc.: *I've been a bit ill recently, but I'm in fine fettle now.* | *Your lawn looks in good fettle.*

fet·tu·ci·ne , **fettucini** /ˌfetʊ'tʃiːni/ *n* [U] flat, thin PASTA in the shape of long bands

fe·tus /'fiːtəs/ *n* a FOETUS

feud¹ /fjuːd/ *n* a state of strong dislike and/or violence which continues over some time as a result of a quarrel, usu. between two people, families, etc.: *a bitter feud over territory* —compare VENDETTA

feud² *v* [I (with)] (esp. of two families) to keep up the memory of a quarrel by violent acts; carry on a feud: *They spend their time feuding with their neighbours.*

feud·al /'fjuːdl/ *adj* **1** [A *no comp.*] of, according to, or being the system by which people held land and received protection in return for giving work or military help, as practised in Western Europe from about the 9th to the 15th century: *the feudal system* | *their feudal lord* **2** *infml* (of behaviour or a relationship) like that which existed between lords and their servants in feudal times: *It seems a bit feudal to call him "sir".*

feu·dal·is·m /'fjuːdl-ɪzəm/ *n* [U] the feudal system

fe·ver /'fiːvər/ *n* [S;U] **1** (a medical condition caused by) an illness in which the sufferer suddenly develops a very high temperature: *Flu is an infectious disease characterized by fever, aches and pains, and exhaustion.* | *She has a very high fever.* | *The fever will soon go down/abate.* —see also HAY FEVER, SCARLET FEVER, YELLOW FEVER **2** [(of)] an extremely excited state: *He was in a fever of impatience waiting for her to come.* | *Football fever gripped the town when the local team reached the cup final.* | *Our excitement rose to* **fever pitch** (=to the highest degree) *as the great day approached.* | *The school is in a* **fever heat** *of excitement as the playoff approaches.*

fever blis·ter /'·· ˌ··/ *n AmE* COLD SORE

fe·vered /'fiːvəd‖-ərd/ *adj* [A] **1** hot, (as if) when suffering from fever: *She wiped his* **fevered brow**. **2** too excited: *These lurid stories are merely a product of his fevered imagination.*

fe·ver·ish /'fiːvərɪʃ/ *adj* **1** having or showing a slight fever: *You're a bit feverish; you should go to bed.* **2** caused by fever: *a feverish dream* **3** extremely active or excited: *They worked with feverish haste to finish the job.* — ~ **ly** *adv*

few /fjuː/ *determiner, pron, n* [P] **1** (used without a to show the smallness of a number) not many; not enough: *She has few friends.* | *I have very few (chocolates) left.* | *So few (people) came that we had to cancel the meeting.* | *Few of the children noticed the time passing.* | *Few understand*

his complicated theories. | *There are so few that I can't give you one.* (compare *There is so little that I can't give you any.*) | *I have too few chances to enjoy myself.* (compare *I have too little time …*) | *It was an enormous ship; There were no fewer than* (=at least) *a thousand cars on it!* | *Which of you has the fewest mistakes* —compare LITTLE³ (1), PLENTY¹ **2** [*no comp.*] (used with **a** or **the**) a small number (of), but at least some: *She bought a few eggs and a little milk.* | *There are only a very few* (=not many) *left.* | *Let's invite a few friends to come with us.* | *Here are a few more stamps for your collection.* | *Can you stay a few days longer?* | *I'm keeping the few that remain for tomorrow.* | *John was among the few who really understood it.* | *She's been abroad for the last few years.* | *I may be a few minutes late.* | *Everyone was there* – *Tim, Paul, Jenny, Mandy, to* **name but a few**. | *She didn't invite me to her wedding, but my boss was one of* **the chosen few**. (=the few people to be invited) —compare LITTLE³ (2) **3** **few and far between** rare; not happening often: *Sympathetic bosses like him are few and far between.* **4** **precious few** *infml* an extremely small number (of) **5** **quite a few** also **a good few**, *(fml)* **not a few**— a fairly large number (of): *Quite a few of us are getting worried.* | *You'll have to wait a good few weeks.*

▷ USAGE 1 Compare **(a) few** and **(a) little. (A) few** is used for plural nouns: *I have* **(a) few** *friends.* **(A) little** is used for uncountable nouns: *We drank* **(a) little** *coffee.* 2 Compare **few** and **a few**: *I have* **few** *friends* (=not many). | *I have* **a few** *friends.* (=some) Also **little** and **a little**: *There was* **little** *food left.* (=not much) | We ate **a little** *food* (=some). However it is more common to use **very few/very little** (=almost none) than **few/ little** alone: **very few** *friends/***very little** *food.* **Fewer** and **fewest** are the comparative and superlative of **few**; **less** and **least** are the comparative and superlative of **little**: *We have* **fewer** *students this year than last year.* | *I earn* **less** *money than my sister.* In informal English **less** and **least** are often used with plural nouns, but many people do not like this use. — see also LESS (USAGE), MORE (USAGE)◁

fey /feɪ/ *adj* **1** (of a person or their behaviour) strange, silly, and not thinking clearly **2** *ScotE* able to see into the future — ~ **ness** *n* [U]

Feyn·man /'faɪnmən/, **Richard Phillips** (1918–88) an American PHYSICIST who won a Nobel prize and wrote a best-selling book about his life shortly before he died

fez /fez/ *n* **fezzes** *or* **fezes** a round usu. red hat with a flat top and no BRIM, worn by some Muslim men —see picture at HAT

ff *written abbrev. for:* and the following (pages, VERSES, etc.): *See pages 17ff*

fi·an·cé /fi'ɒnseɪ‖ˌfiːɑːn'seɪ/ *fem.* **fiancée** (*same pronunciation*)— *n* the person one is going to marry; person to whom one is ENGAGED: *George is my fiancé.* | *Martha is my fiancée.*

Fi·an·na Fáil /ˌfiːənə 'fɔɪl/ an Irish political party organized in 1926 by people who were against the Anglo-Irish agreement of 1921 which established the Irish Free State. They have held power in the Republic of Ireland most of the time since then.

fi·as·co /fi'æskəʊ/ *n* **-cos** *BrE* ‖ **-coes** *AmE* [C;U] a complete failure of something planned: *The party was a total fiasco/ended in fiasco.*

fi·at /'faɪæt, 'fiːæt‖-ət/ *n fml, often derog* a command by someone in a position of power: *The matter was settled by presidential fiat.*

Fiat /'fiːət/ *tdmk* an Italian company which makes cars: *He works for Fiat.* | *I've just bought a new Fiat.*

fib /fɪb/ *v* **-bb-** [I] *infml* to tell a small unimportant lie —**fib** *n* : *to tell a fib* — ~ **ber** *n* : *What a fibber he is!*

Fib·ber Mc·Gee /ˌfɪbə mə'giː‖-bər-/ a character on an American radio programme in the 1940s which was called *Fibber McGee and Molly*. Every time Fibber McGee opened his CLOSET (=a large, built-in cupboard), everything fell out of it with a lot of noise. People often say of anything very untidy that it is like Fibber McGee's closet.

fi·ber·fill /'faɪbəfɪl‖-bər-/ *n* [U] man-made filling used in PILLOWS, DUVETS, etc.

fi·bre *BrE* ‖ **fiber** *AmE* /'faɪbər/ *n* **1** [C] any of the thin thread-like parts that together form many animal and plant growths such as wool, wood, or muscle; some plant fibres are spun (SPIN¹ (2)) and woven into cloth: *nerve fibres* **2** also **dietary fibre** – parts of plants that you eat. Although one cannot DIGEST fibre, it helps food move through your body and is thought to be good for you: *You need more fibre in your diet – eat more bran and apples.* **3** [U] a mass of threads used for making cloth, rope, etc.: *Cotton fibre is natural; nylon is a man-made fibre.* —see also FIBREGLASS **4** [U] a person's inner character: *He was shocked to* **the very fibre of his being.** (=extremely shocked) | *He lacks* **moral fibre.** (=has a weak character) —see also FIBROUS

fi·bre·board *BrE* ‖ **fiberboard** *AmE* /ˈfaɪbəbɔːd‖-bərbɔːrd/ *n* [U] board made of wood fibres pressed together

fi·bre·glass *BrE* ‖ **fiberglass** *AmE* /ˈfaɪbəglɑːs‖-bərglæs/ also **glass fibre**– *n* [U] material made from glass fibres that is used for making car bodies, small boats, and furnishing materials, and in buildings for keeping out the cold

fibre op·tics /ˌ·· ˈ··/ *n* [U] the use of very thin glass or plastic fibres to send light signals, esp. for carrying telephone signals

fi·bro·si·tis /ˌfaɪbrəˈsaɪt̬s/ *n* [U] a painful RHEUMATIC disorder of the muscles

fi·brous /ˈfaɪbrəs/ *adj* like or made of fibres: *The coconut has a fibrous outer covering.*

fib·u·la /ˈfɪbjʊlə/ *n* **-lae** /liː/ *or* **-las** *med* the outer of the two bones in the lower leg —see picture at SKELETON

FICA /ˈfaɪkə, ˌef aɪ siː ˈeɪ/ Federal Insurance Contributions Act; in the US, money which is taken out of one's pay to be used for SOCIAL SECURITY

fiche /fiːʃ/ *n* [C;U] *AmE for* MICROFICHE

fick·le /ˈfɪkəl/ *adj* likely to change suddenly and without reason, esp. in love or friendship; CAPRICIOUS: *a fickle lover* | (fig.) *The weather's so fickle – one moment it's raining, the next the sun's out.* — **~ness** *n* [U]

fic·tion /ˈfɪkʃən/ *n* **1** [U] stories or NOVELS about imaginary people and events, as compared to other sorts of literature like history or poetry: *a writer of popular fiction* | *I prefer light fiction to all those serious novels.* | *They say that truth is stranger than fiction.* —compare NONFICTION; see also SCIENCE FICTION **2** [S;U] an invention of the mind; an untrue story: *His account of the crime was (a) complete fiction.*

fic·tion·al /ˈfɪkʃənəl/ *adj* belonging to fiction; told as a story: *Jules Verne wrote a fictional account of a journey to the moon.* (=wrote about it as an imaginary event) —compare FICTITIOUS — **~ly** *adv*

fic·tion·al·ize also **-ise** *BrE* /ˈfɪkʃənəlaɪz/ *v* [T] to write about (a true event) as if it were a story, changing some details, introducing imaginary characters, etc. — **lzation** /ˌfɪkʃənəlaɪˈzeɪʃən‖-lə-/ *n* [S;U (of)]

fic·ti·tious /fɪkˈtɪʃəs/ *adj* untrue; invented; not real: *She invented a fictitious boyfriend to put him off.* | *His account of the incident was totally fictitious.* (=was completely different from the way it really happened) —compare FICTIONAL — **~ly** *adv*

fid·dle¹ /ˈfɪdl/ *n infml* **1** [C] *BrE* a dishonest practice: *It's a fiddle – they put different labels on the bottles and sell them at five times the proper price.* | *a tax fiddle* | *They suspected he was* **on the fiddle.** (=doing dishonest things) **2** [S] an activity that is difficult because it needs delicate use of the fingers: *It's a bit of a fiddle to get all these wires back in the box.* | *a VIOLIN*, esp. when used in JAZZ or popular music **4 as fit as a fiddle** *infml* very fit and healthy **5 play/be second fiddle (to)** to play/have a less important part (than): *She has never enjoyed playing second fiddle to the chairman.*

fiddle² *v infml* **1** [I(AROUND, **with**)] to move things aimlessly in one's fingers: *Put down that pen and stop fiddling!* | *Don't fiddle around with that gun – it might go off!* **2** [T] *BrE* to prepare (accounts) dishonestly to one's own advantage: *He was fined for trying to fiddle his income tax.* **3** [T] *BrE* to gain dishonestly: *He fiddled an extra ten pounds on his expenses claim.* **4** [T] *AmE* to repair or change slightly **5** [I] to play the VIOLIN **6 fiddle while Rome burns** to concern oneself with small matters while something important is happening (from the story of Nero who played the FIDDLE¹ (3) while the city of Rome was burning): *The government is fiddling*

while manufacturing industry is burning. —see also NERO —**fiddler** *n*

fiddle about/around *phr v* [I] to behave aimlessly or waste time on unimportant matters: *We can't fiddle about here all day; we've got to get going.*

fiddle with sthg. *phr v* [T] to touch or move (something that is not one's own): *I don't want you fiddling with my bicycle – leave it alone!*

fiddle-fad·dle /ˈfɪdlˌfædl/ *n* [U] *infml* nonsense: *Don't talk fiddle-faddle.*

fid·dle·sticks /ˈfɪdlˌstɪks/ *interj old-fash* Nonsense!

fid·dling /ˈfɪdlɪŋ/ *adj* [A] *infml* unimportant and silly PETTY; TRIVIAL

fid·dly /ˈfɪdli/ *adj BrE infml* **1** needing delicate use of the fingers: *It's a very fiddly job to get all these wires back into their holes.* **2** fiddling: *I can't be bothered with all these fiddly details.*

fi·del·i·ty /fɪˈdelɪti/ *n* [U (to)] **1** [(to)] faithfulness; loyalty: *fidelity to one's leader/ideals* **2** loyalty in marriage shown by having a sexual relationship only with one's husband or wife —compare INFIDELITY; see also FAITHFUL¹ (3) **3** (of something copied or reported) closeness in sound, facts, colour, etc., to the original; exactness: *the fidelity of a translation/of a sound recording* —see also HIGH FIDELITY

fid·get¹ /ˈfɪdʒɪt/ *v infml* **1** [I (**with**)] to move one's body around restlessly, so that one annoys people: *Stop fidgeting, children; just sit still and listen to the music.* | *I wish you'd stop fidgeting with that box of matches.* **2** [T] to make (someone) nervous and restless: *The dripping tap fidgeted me so much I had to get up and turn it off.*

fidget² *n infml* someone, esp. a child, who fidgets: *Sit still, you little fidget!*

fid·gets /ˈfɪdʒɪts/ *n* [the+P] *infml* an attack of fidgeting: *She's got the fidgets again.*

fid·get·y /ˈfɪdʒɪti/ *adj infml* restless; fidgeting or wanting to fidget

Fi·do /ˈfaɪdəʊ/ a name that is supposed to be a very common name given to dogs though dogs are in fact rarely named this: *They've called their mutt Fido as a joke.*

fie /faɪ/ *interj* [(**on**, **upon**)] *old use or humor* (expressing disapproval or shock) Shame!: *Fie upon you!*

Fied·ler /ˈfiːdlər/, **Arthur** (1894–1979) an American CONDUCTOR who conducted (CONDUCT) the BOSTON POPS ORCHESTRA for many years

field¹ /fiːld/ *n* **1** [C] an enclosed area of land, usu. part of a farm, used for animals or crops: *fields of corn* | *a field full of sheep* **2** [C] (*usu. in comb.*) an open area where **a** the stated game is played: *a football field* **b** the stated substance is mined (MINE⁴ (2)): *an oilfield* | *the Yorkshire coalfields* **c** the stated activity is practised: *an airfield* | *a battlefield/field of battle* **d** the surface is of the stated kind: *a snowfield/field of snow* **3** [C] a branch of knowledge or area of activity: *a lawyer famous in his own field* | *the field of politics/art/Greek history* | *That's* **outside my field.** (=not my special subject) | *exciting business opportunities in the electronics field* —see also **never in the field of human conflict...** (CONFLICT¹ (3)) **4** [*the*+S] the place where practical operations happen, as compared to places where they are planned or studied, such as offices, factories, and universities: *She's studying tribal languages* **in the field.** (=living with the people who speak them) | *Our class is doing a* **field trip** *to study animals and plants in the local countryside.* —see also FIELD-TEST, FIELDWORK **5** [C] (in PHYSICS) the area in which the stated force is felt: *the moon's gravitational field* **6** [C+*sing./pl. v*] all the horses in a race **a** except the FAVOURITE (=the one that is expected to win): *The betting is 9-4 the field.* **b** including the FAVOURITE: *The rest of the field is/are far behind Red Rum.* **7** [*the*+S+*sing./pl. v*] (in cricket or BASEBALL) the team that are fielding (=stopping) the ball rather than hitting it: *The captain brought the field in closer to stop the batsmen taking a quick run.* **8** [C] the part on the surface of a coin or flag that is not the pattern: *Their flag shows a red lion on a white field.* **9** [C] *tech* an area of fixed length within a DATA record set aside for a particular type of information: *The field for the user's name and surname is 25 characters.* **10 take the field: a** to go on to a sports field in order to begin play **b** to go to war **11 play the field** *AmE infml* to DATE (=go out with) many people of the

opposite sex rather than just one: *Don't expect a commitment from him, he likes to play the field.* —see also FIELD OF VISION

field² *v* **1** [T] (in cricket and BASEBALL) to stop (a ball that has been hit) **2** [I] to be (a member of) the team whose turn it is to do this because they are not batting (BAT² (2)): *We'll be fielding in the afternoon.* **3** [T] to produce or have (a team, army, etc.): *The school fields two football teams.* **4** [T] to answer (a difficult question) cleverly and skilfully: *The Minister had to field some tricky questions from the reporters.*

Field, The a British magazine which has articles on the countryside, field sports, and farming. "The Field" is connected in people's minds with wealthy people who live and own land in the country.

Field & Stream /ˌ· ˈ·/ an American magazine read mostly by men; that has articles about hunting, fishing, and outdoor life

field corn /ˈ· ·/ *n* [U] *AmE* MAIZE grown to be used as grain or to be fed to animals, rather than to be eaten as a vegetable —compare SWEET CORN

field day /ˈ· ·/ *n* **1** a day on which schoolchildren are taken outdoors for a planned activity such as sport or the study of nature **2 have a field day** *infml* to get great enjoyment or the greatest possible advantage, esp. when making full use of a chance to do what one likes doing: *If the newspapers get hold of this scandal they'll really have a field day!*

field·er /ˈfiːldər/ also **fields·man** *BrE— n* (in cricket or BASEBALL) a player in the team that is fielding (FIELD²) or one who fields regularly: *a first class fielder* —see pictures at BASEBALL and CRICKET

field e·vent /ˈ· ˌ·ˌ·/ *n* (in ATHLETICS) a sports event, such as weight-throwing or jumping, that is not a race but which is a competition —compare TRACK EVENT

field glass·es /ˈ· ˌ··/ *n* [P] BINOCULARS

field goal /ˈ· ·/ *n AmE* **1** (in FOOTBALL) the act of kicking the ball over the bar of the GOAL **2** also **basket—** (in BASKETBALL) putting the ball through a circle called a HOOP (=BASKET (3)) during play

field hock·ey /ˈ· ˌ··/ *n* [U] *esp. AmE for* HOCKEY —compare ICE HOCKEY

Fiel·ding /ˈfiːldɪŋ/, **Henry** (1707–54) an English writer most famous for his NOVEL *Tom Jones*

field mar·shal /ˈ· ˌ··/ *n* an officer of high rank in the British army —see TABLE 3

field of vi·sion /ˌ· · ˈ··/ *n* **fields of vision** the whole space within seeing distance; all that can be seen: *The tall building obstructed our field of vision.*

Fields /fiːldz/, **Dame Gra·cie** /ˈɡreɪsi/ (1898–1979) an English singer and entertainer from Lancashire, in NW England, who was known as "Our Gracie" at the height of her popularity in the 1930s. During the Second World War, her song "Wish Me Luck as You Wave Me Goodbye" was very popular.

Fields, W. C. (1880–1946) an American film actor and COMEDIAN who was famous esp. for not liking children

fields·man /ˈfiːldzmən/ *n* **-men** /mən/ a FIELDER

field sports /ˈ· ˌ·/ *n* [P] country sports, such as hunting, shooting, and fishing

field-test /ˈ· ·/ *v* [T] to try (something) out in the FIELD¹ (4): *The apparatus has all been field-tested in tropical conditions.* —**field test** *n*

field trip /ˈ· ·/ *n* a journey made (usu. by a group of students) for the purpose of study: *We're going to France on a geology field trip next year.*

field·work /ˈfiːldwɜːk‖-wɜːrk/ *n* [U] scientific or social study done in the FIELD¹ (4), such as measuring and examining things or asking people questions — **~ er** *n*

fiend /fiːnd/ *n* **1** a devil or evil spirit **2** *infml* someone very keen on the stated thing: *He's a fresh air fiend.* **3** *AmE infml* a person, esp. a child, who plays tricks and annoys people: *Her kids are little fiends.*

fiend·ish /ˈfiːndɪʃ/ *adj* **1** fierce and cruel: *She has a fiendish temper.* **2** *infml* unpleasantly clever or difficult; not plain or simple: *a fiendish plan/question* **3** (of difficulty or cleverness) very great: *He had worked out a plan of fiendish complexity.* | *fiendish cunning* — **~ ly** *adv* : *a fiendishly difficult question* — **~ ness** *n* [U]

fierce /fɪəs‖fɪərs/ *adj* **1** angry, violent, and likely to attack:*The house is guarded by a fierce dog.* | *He had a very fierce look on his face.* **2** marked by strong feeling: *They were having a fierce argument, and I thought they might end up hitting each other.* | *fierce loyalty* **3** very severe; INTENSE: *Because there is so much unemployment, the competition for jobs is fierce.* | *The plants wilted in the fierce heat of the tropical sun.* — **~ ly** *adv* : *fiercely loyal* | *the fiercely competitive job market* — **~ ness** *n* [U]

fi·er·y /ˈfaɪəri/ *adj* **1** (as if) on fire: *a fiery sunset* | *She has fiery red hair.* | *This curry is pretty fiery.* (=hot-tasting) **2** (likely to be) full of violent feeling: *He has a fiery temper.* | *His fiery speech roused his audience to anger.*

fi·es·ta /fiˈestə/ *n* (esp. in Spain and South America) a religious holiday with public dancing and other entertainments

Fiesta *n tdmk* a popular small car made by FORD

FIFA /ˈfiːfə/ Fédération Internationale de Football Association; the organization for international football and the World Cup

fife /faɪf/ *n* a small musical pipe with high notes that is played in military bands, often with drums

Fife a REGION in E Scotland between the FIRTHS of Tay and Forth and including Glenrothes, St Andrews, and Kirkaldy

fif·teen /ˌfɪfˈtiːn◄/ *determiner, n, pron* **1** (the number) 15 —see TABLE 1 **2 fifteen men on the dead man's chest — yo-ho-ho and a bottle of rum** *quote* lines from a song sung by PIRATES in the story *Treasure Island* by Robert Louis Stevenson —**-teenth** *determiner, n, pron, adv*

fifth /fɪfθ, fɪftθ/ *determiner, n, pron, adv* **1** 5th —see TABLE 1 **2** an amount equalling 1/5th of a GALLON (=just over a litre) of strong alcoholic drink: *a fifth of bourbon*

Fifth A·mend·ment /ˌ· ·ˈ··/ *[the] AmE law* **1** a part of the American CONSTITUTION which says that a person does not have to state facts against himself in a criminal trial and that no one can be put in prison or have their property taken away without a trial **2 plead/take the Fifth** to refuse to testify: (fig.) *"I plead the fifth," he said when his wife wanted to know where he'd been.*

Fifth Av·e·nue , 5th Avenue /ˌ· ˈ··/ *n* a street in New York, famous for its expensive shops —see colour map on page 1376

fifth col·umn /ˌ· ˈ··/ *n* a group of people who are secretly sympathetic to the enemies of the country they live in, and work to help them during a war — **~ ist** *n*

fifth-gen·er·a·tion com·put·er /ˌ· ···ˌ··· ·ˈ··/ *n* a type of computer that can develop knowledge and use it to make its own judgments and decisions, in a way that is similar to the processes of the human brain

fifth wheel /ˌ· ˈ·/ *n AmE infml* an unwanted person or thing: *She felt like a fifth wheel at the party since everyone else seemed to have paired off.*

fif·ties /ˈfɪftiz/ *n* [P] **1** *[the]* also **'50s—** the 1950s (=the years from 1950 to 1959): *There was a new era of material affluence in the fifties and living standards rose.* **2** in **his/her/their fifties** ages from 50 to 59: *He began to feel more financially secure in his early fifties.* **3** *[the]* the numbers from 50 to 59, esp. when used to measure temperature: *rather a cold day with the temperatures in the mid fifties*

fif·ty /ˈfɪfti/ *determiner, n, pron* (the number) 50 —see TABLE 1 —**-tieth** *determiner, n, pron, adv*

fifty-fif·ty /ˌ·· ˈ···◄/ *adj, adv* (of shares or chances) equal(ly): *We divided it up fifty-fifty/on a fifty-fifty basis.* | *Let's go* **fifty-fifty.** (=each be responsible for half) | *There's a fifty-fifty chance that he will succeed.*

fig /fɪɡ/ *n* **1** [C] (a broad-leaved tree that bears) a soft sweet fruit with many small seeds, growing chiefly in warm countries **2** [S *usu. in questions and negatives*] *infml* a worthless amount: *I don't* **care/give a fig (for)** *what you think.* (=I don't care at all) | *Her advice isn't worth a fig.* —see also FIG LEAF, and see picture at FRUIT

fig. *written abbrev. for:* **1** FIGURATIVE **2** FIGURE¹ (6)

fight¹ /faɪt/ *v* **fought** /fɔːt/ **1** [I;T] to use physical violence against (as if) in a battle: *Did your father fight in the last war?* | *Britain fought against/with the US in the War of*

Independence; the Americans were fighting for|fighting to gain their freedom. | *Stop fighting* (=each other), *you two!* | *The two dogs were fighting over* (=because of) *the scraps of food.* | *We vowed to* **fight on** (=continue fighting) *until all our demands were met.* | *I can fight any man here!* | *The two boxers* **fought to a finish.** (=until one was completely defeated) | (fig.) *He fought the other contenders for leadership of the party.* | (fig.) *Women have had to fight for equal rights.* | (fig.) *He fought his way through the crowd.* **2** [I(**over, about**)] to quarrel: *He and his wife are always fighting (about who will take the car).* **3** [T] to take part in (a war, battle, etc.): *They fought a duel.* | (fig.) *I'm afraid the rail unions are* **fighting a losing battle** (=one that they are certain to lose) *over driver-only trains.* **4** [T] to try to prevent; stand against: *The firemen fought the blaze very bravely.* | *The pressure group was formed to fight the closure of the hospital.* **5 fight shy of** to avoid getting mixed up in: *I rather fought shy of telling her the truth about her husband.* **6 fight the good fight** *saying from the Bible* to struggle to live one's life according to the rules and customs of one's religion: *He believed that all Christians should fight the good fight and spread the word.* **7 'Tis better to have fought and lost than never to have fought at all** *quote* a phrase from a poem by Arthur Hugh Clough **8 We shall fight on the beaches, we shall fight on the landing grounds, we shall fight in the fields and in the streets, we shall fight in the hills; we shall never surrender.** *quote* a phrase from a speech by Winston Churchill, made to the British Parliament in 1940. This speech is seen by British people as a sign of their determination to win the Second World War even if it meant suffering great hardship.

fight back *phr v* [I] to make a great effort to recover from a bad or losing position; defend oneself by fighting: *The government is agonizing about how to fight back at the terrorists without endangering the hostages.*

fight sbdy./sthg. ↔ **off** *phr v* [T] to keep away by violent action: *The pop star had to fight off all the screaming teenagers who were trying to touch him.* | (fig.) *She took various medicines to try to fight off her cold.*

fight sthg. **out** *phr v* [T] to settle (a disagreement) by fighting: *I'm not going to interfere in their quarrel; they'll have to fight it out between them.*

fight² *n* **1** [C] an act of fighting between two people, groups, countries, etc.; battle: *The police were called in to stop the fight (between the two gangs).* | *Are you going to the big fight* (=BOXING match) *tonight?* | (fig.) *The fight against drug abuse goes on.* | (fig.) *Our team* **put up a good fight** (=struggled well), *but were beaten in the end.* **2** [U] also **fighting spir·it** /ˌ·· ˈ···/ — the power or desire to fight: *There's not much fight left in him now.* | *The news of the defeat took all the fight out of us.*

fight·er /ˈfaɪtər/ *n* **1** someone who fights, esp. a professional soldier or BOXER: (fig.) *a tireless fighter against racism* **2** a small fast military aircraft that can destroy enemy aircraft in the air: *a fighter pilot* —compare BOMBER (1)

fighting chance /ˌ·· ˈ·/ *n* [S] *infml* a small but real chance if great effort is made: [+(*that*)] *There's just a fighting chance that we'll be able to escape.*

fight or flight syn·drome /ˌ· · ˈ· ˌ··/ also **fight or flight re·ac·tion** /ˌ·· ˈ· ·ˌ··/— *n* [the] the body's natural way of behaving in answer to danger, excitement, or STRESS. These include increases in heart rate, in the levels of HORMONES, and in the amount of blood sent to the muscles.

fig leaf /ˈ· ·/ *n* **1** the large leaf of the FIG tree. Fog leaves are often shown as covering people's sex organs in paintings, esp. paintings of Adam and Eve. **2** something that hides (something else), esp. unsuccessfully or dishonestly

fig·ment /ˈfɪgmənt/ *n* **a figment of someone's imagination** something believed but not real

Fig New·ton /ˌ· ˈ··/ *tdmk* a kind of BISCUIT filled with sweet FIGs and sold in the US

fig·u·ra·tive /ˈfɪgjʊrətɪv, -gə-/ *adj* (of a word, phrase, meaning, etc.) used in some way other than the main or usual meaning, to suggest a picture in the mind or make a comparison. Words or expressions used in a figurative way are marked (*fig.*) in this dictionary: *"A sweet temper" is a figurative expression, but "sweet coffee" is not.*

—compare LITERAL¹ (1) — **~ly** *adv* : *He's up to his eyes in paperwork — figuratively speaking, of course!*

fig·ure¹ /ˈfɪgər‖ˈfɪgjər/ *n* **1** (the shape of) a whole human body: *I could see a figure in the far distance, but I couldn't make out who it was.* | *There is a group of figures on the left of the painting.* **2** the human shape considered from the point of view of being attractive

▶ CULTURAL NOTE British and American people generally like to look SLIM. A man is usu. thought to have a good figure if he has broad shoulders, strong muscles, and slim, strong legs. A woman is thought to have a good figure if she has a narrow waist, long, slim legs, and quite large breasts: *She has a lovely figure.* | *He's doing exercises to improve his figure.* | *She's past forty now, but she's* **kept her figure.** (= still has a good shape) —see BODY (USAGE)◀

3 a person of a particular type: *He was one of the leading political figures of this century.* | *a central|key figure in the negotiations* **4** any of the number signs from 0 to 9: *Write the number in words and in figures.* | *I'm no good at figures|haven't* **got a head for figures!** (=sums) | *Her income is in six figures.* | *She has a six-figure income.* (=at least £100,000) **5** an amount, esp. of money: *They're asking a high figure for their house.* | *The crowd is very big, but I couldn't* **put a figure on it.** (=say exactly what the number of people is) **6** an often numbered drawing or DIAGRAM used in a book to explain something **7** a pattern performed in FIGURE SKATING

figure² *v* **1** [I (**as, in**)] to take an esp. important or noticeable part; appear: *His name did not figure in the list of those who had received awards.* | *The vice-president figured prominently in the peace negotiations.* **2** [T+(*that*); *obj*] *esp. AmE* to consider; believe: *I figured (that) you'd want to see me about it.* **3 That figures** *infml* That seems reasonable and is what I expected.

figure on sthg. *phr v* [T] *esp. AmE* to plan on; include in one's plans: [+*obj*|*v-ing*] *I'm figuring on (getting) a $600 pay increase.* [+*obj*+*v-ing*] *I figured on him leaving at 6 o'clock.*

figure sbdy./sthg. ↔ **out** *phr v* [T] to come to understand or discover by thinking: *I can't figure him out — he's a mystery!* [+*wh-*] *We still haven't figured out how to do it.*

fig·ured /ˈfɪgəd‖ˈfɪgjərd/ *adj* [A] decorated with a small pattern: *a dress of figured silk*

figured bass /ˌ·· ˈ·/ *n* CONTINUO

figurehead

figurehead

fig·ure·head /ˈfɪgəhed‖ˈfɪgjər-/ *n* **1** a representation in wood, usu. of the top half of a woman, that in former times was placed at the front of a ship **2** someone who is the head or chief in name only: *The President is just a figurehead; it's the party leader who has the real power.*

figure of eight /ˌ··· ˈ·/ also **figure eight** /ˌ·· ˈ·/ *AmE*— *n* something in the shape of the number 8, such as a knot, stitch, or dance pattern

figure of speech /ˌ··· ˈ·/ *n* an example of the FIGURATIVE use of words: *I didn't really mean that my boss is a rat; it was just a figure of speech.*

figure skat·ing /ˈ·· ˌ··/ *n* [U] SKATING in which one cuts patterns in the ice —**-er** *n*

fig·u·rine /ˌfɪgjʊˈriːn, ˈfɪgjʊriːn‖ˌfɪgjʊˈriːn/ *n* a small decorative human figure made of baked clay, cut stone, etc.

Fi·ji /ˈfiːdʒiː/ a country in the SW Pacific Ocean made up of many islands; capital Suva; population 732,000 (1989) —**Fijian** /fiːˈdʒiːən ‖ ˈfiːdʒiən/ *n, adj*

fil·a·ment /ˈfɪləmənt/ n a thin thread, such as the thin piece of metal inside an electric light BULB

fil·bert /ˈfɪlbət ‖ -bərt/ n AmE HAZEL¹ (3)

filch /fɪltʃ/ v [T] to steal (something of small value) secretly; PILFER

file¹ /faɪl/ n a steel tool with a rough face, used for rubbing down, making smooth, or cutting through hard surfaces —see also NAIL FILE, and see picture at TOOL

file² v [I+adv/prep;T] to rub or cut with a file: *The prisoner filed through his bars and escaped.* | *She was filing her nails.* | *File down this rough spot.* [+obj+adj] *He filed the wood smooth.*

file³ n 1 a box, FOLDER, etc. for storing papers in an ordered way, esp. in an office —see also FILING CABINET 2 [(on)] a collection of papers concerning one subject, stored in this way: *Here's our file on the Middle East.* | *I'll keep your report on file.* (=stored in a file) | *a confidential file* 3 a collection of information for a computer stored under one name on a DISK or CASSETTE: *a text file* | *a data file* | *a file name*

file⁴ v [T] 1 [(AWAY)] to put (papers or letters) in a FILE³: *Please file this letter (away), Mrs Jellaby.* 2 *law* to send in or record officially: *They filed an application to have their case heard early.* | *Charges have been filed against him.*
file for sthg. *phr* v [T] *law* to request officially: *They have filed for a divorce.*

file⁵ n [C+sing./pl. v] a line of people one behind the other —see also RANK AND FILE, SINGLE FILE

file⁶ v [I+adv/prep] to march in a FILE⁵: *They filed slowly past the grave of their leader.*

file foot·age /ˈ· ˌ··/ n [U] *AmE for* LIBRARY PICTURES

fil·et /ˈfɪlɪt ‖ ˈfɪlɪt, -leɪ, fɪˈleɪ/ n, v *AmE for* FILLET

fil·et mi·gnon /ˌfiːleɪ ˈmiːnjɒn ‖ fɪˌleɪ mɪnˈjɔːn/ n Fr a small, tender piece of BEEF STEAK. In the US filet mignon is considered to be something that rich people eat or that is served only in very expensive restaurants.

fi·li·al /ˈfɪliəl/ adj fml of or suitable to a son or daughter: *filial respect*

fil·i·bus·ter /ˈfɪlɪbʌstəʳ/ v [I] *esp. AmE* to try to delay or prevent action in a lawmaking body by making very slow long speeches —**filibuster** n

fil·i·gree /ˈfɪlɪɡriː/ n [U] delicate decorative wire work: *silver filigree jewellery*

filing cab·i·net /ˈ·· ˌ···/ n a piece of office furniture with drawers, shelves, etc. for storing FILES³

fil·ings /ˈfaɪlɪŋz/ n [P] very small sharp bits that have been rubbed off a metal surface with a FILE¹: *iron filings*

fill¹ /fɪl/ v 1 [I;T (with)] to make or become full: *The cinema was filling fast.* | *The apples filled the basket.* | *She filled the jug to the brim/fill it with water.* | *The wind filled* (=swelled out) *the sails.* [+obj+adj] *You've filled the bath too full.* | (fig.) *Laughter filled the room.* | (fig.) *The thought fills me with dread.* 2 [T] to be in or be put into (an office or position): *There is no one who can fill the office of president with as much credibility as our candidate.* | *John's the best person to fill this vacancy.* | *I'm afraid the post has already been filled.* (=the job has been given to someone else) 3 [T] to meet the needs or demands of; fulfil: *This should fill your requirements nicely.* 4 [T] to put a FILLING in (a tooth) 5 **fill the bill** *AmE for* **fit the bill** (FIT¹)
fill in *phr* v 1 [T] (**fill** sthg. ↔ **in**) to put in (whatever is needed to complete something): *You draw the people and the children can fill them in.* (=add colour to them) | *Fill in your name on this cheque.* | *Please fill in this application form.* 2 [T(on)] (**fill** sbdy. **in**) to supply the most recent information to: *Could you fill me in on what happened at the meeting?* 3 [I (for)] to take someone's place: *Can you fill in for Steve tonight as he's ill?* —see also FILL-IN 4 [T] (**fill** sthg. ↔ **in**) to use up (unwanted time): *What can we do to fill in the afternoon?*
fill out *phr* v 1 [I] to get fatter: *Her face is beginning to fill out as she puts on weight* 2 [T] (**fill** sthg. ↔ **out**) *esp. AmE for* **fill in** (1)
fill up *phr* v 1 [I;T (=fill sthg. ↔ **up**)] to make or become completely full: *The room soon filled up (with people).* | *Fill her up, please.* (said to someone putting petrol in one's car) 2 [T] (**fill** sthg. ↔ **up**) *esp. BrE* to complete

(a form) by answering the questions in the spaces provided

fill² n 1 [(of)] a full supply; the quantity needed to fill something: *Would you like a fill of my tobacco?* (=for your pipe) 2 **one's fill: a** as much as one can bear: *The children are getting on my nerves — I've had my fill of them for this evening!* **b** *lit* as much as one can eat or drink: *He drank his fill.*

filled gold /ˌ· ˈ·/ n [U] ROLLED GOLD

fill·er /ˈfɪləʳ/ n [S;U] 1 a substance that is added to another, to increase the size or weight 2 material used for filling cracks in wood, walls, etc. before painting 3 *AmE* written or drawn material, that is not very important and is only there to complete the page: *It seems like half the articles in this magazine are just filler.*

fil·let¹ also **filet** *AmE* /ˈfɪlɪt ‖ ˈfɪlɪt, -leɪ, fɪˈleɪ/ n a piece of meat or fish without bones, for eating: *a fillet steak* | *fillets of sole*

fil·let² also **filet** *AmE* v [T] to remove the bones from (fish): *Will you fillet it for me please?* | *filleted sole*

fill-in /ˈ· ·/ n *infml* someone or something that FILLs in (3): *I'm only here as a fill-in while Robert's away.*

fill·ing /ˈfɪlɪŋ/ n 1 (the material used for) the filling of a hole in a tooth to preserve it from decay: *The dentist gave me a temporary filling/a gold filling.* | *You've got a lot of fillings.* 2 a food mixture folded inside pastry to make a PIE, bread to make a SANDWICH, etc.

filling² adj (of food) that makes one's stomach feel full; satisfying

filling sta·tion /ˈ·· ˌ··/ also **petrol station** *BrE* ‖ also **gas station** *AmE*— n a place where petrol and oil are sold and repairs to motor vehicles may also be done — compare GARAGE¹ (2)

fil·lip /ˈfɪlɪp/ n [(to)] something that brings encouragement or increases attraction and interest: *A valuable order from Japan gave the new company a big fillip.*

Fill·more /ˈfɪlmɔːʳ/, **Mil·lard** /ˈmɪlɑːd ‖ -ərd/ (1800–74) the 13th US president

fil·ly /ˈfɪli/ n a young female horse —compare COLT

film¹ /fɪlm/ n 1 [C;U] (a roll of) material which is sensitive to light and which is used in a camera for taking photographs or moving pictures for the cinema: *I let some light in while I was loading the film into the camera.* | *The whole incident was recorded on film.* | *high-speed film* — see picture at ROLL 2 [C] *esp. BrE* ‖ usu. **movie** *esp. AmE*— a story, play, etc. recorded on film to be shown in the cinema, on television, etc.: *Have you seen any good films lately?* | *a film actor* | *a documentary/news film* — see also BLUE FILM, SILENT FILM 3 [S;U] a thin skin of any material: *A film of dust/oil formed on the surface of the water.* | *Cover the food with a piece of plastic film.*
film over *phr* v [I] to become dull, as if covered with a FILM¹ (3): *His eyes filmed over, and I thought he was going to cry.*

film² v 1 [I;T] to make a film for the cinema, television, etc.: *We'll be filming all day tomorrow.* | *We had to film the scene five times before we got it right.* 2 [I+adv] to be the subject of a cinema picture: *The duel scene filmed beautifully in the end.*

film prem·i·ère /ˈ· ˌ···‖ˈ· ·ˌ·/ n the first showing of a new cinema film

film star /ˈ· ·/ *esp. BrE* ‖ **movie star** *esp. AmE* — n a well-known actor or actress in cinema pictures

film stock /ˈ· ·/ n [U] cinema film that has not yet been used

film·strip /ˈfɪlmˌstrɪp/ n a length of photographic film used to PROJECT (=show) photographs, drawings, etc., separately one after the other as still pictures: *an educational filmstrip*

film·y /ˈfɪlmi/ adj (esp. of cloth) so fine and thin that one can see through it: *filmy mists* | *a filmy silk dress* —**iness** n [U]

Fi·lo·fax /ˈfaɪləʊfæks/ n tdmk a small book like a diary with LOOSE-LEAF pages for addresses and other information. It

Filofax

is thought of by many people as being used esp. by YUPPIES.

fi·lo pas·try /ˌfiːləʊ ˈpeɪstri/ n [U] a PASTRY made with extremely thin sheets of DOUGH

fil·ter[1] /ˈfɪltər/ n **1** an apparatus containing paper, sand, etc., through which a liquid or gas can be passed to make it clean or separate small pieces of solid matter: *the oil filter in a car | filter paper* —see picture at ENGINE **2** a (coloured) glass that reduces the quantity or changes the quality of the light admitted into a camera or TELESCOPE

filter[2] v **1** [T] to clean, change, etc., by passing through a filter: *You need to filter the drinking water.* **2** [I+adv|prep] (of a group) to move gradually: *Around 11 o'clock the crowds start filtering out of the theatres. | The students filtered into the exam room.* **3** [I] BrE (of traffic) to turn left or right while traffic going straight ahead must wait until a red light changes to green
  filter sthg. ↔ **out** phr v [T] to remove by means of a filter: *Filter out the sediment|the blue light.*
  filter through (sthg.) phr v [I (to);T] to pass through gradually or in a reduced form: *The news slowly filtered through to* (=became known to) *everyone in the office. | The sunlight filtered through the curtains.*

filter cof·fee /ˈ··· ˌ··/ n [C; U] (a cup of) a hot drink made by filtering water through coffee beans which have been ground (GRIND). It is thought by some people to have a better taste than INSTANT coffee: *We only ever drink filter coffee.*

filter tip /ˈ··· ·/ n (a cigarette with) a special end that filters the smoke before it enters the smoker's mouth —**filter-tipped** /ˌ·· ˈ·/ adj

filth /fɪlθ/ n [U] **1** very unpleasant dirt or waste matter: *Go and wash that filth off your hands.* **2** something very rude, immoral, or unpleasant: *I don't know how you can read such filth.*

filth·y /ˈfɪlθi/ adj **1** extremely dirty: covered with filth: *Take your filthy boots off before you come in.* **2** showing or containing something very rude or immoral: *She's always telling filthy jokes. | The film is disgusting – it's absolutely filthy!* —**ily** adv —**iness** n [U]

filthy lu·cre /ˌ·· ˈ··/ n [U] pomp or humor money

fil·tra·tion /fɪlˈtreɪʃən/ n [U] the process of passing through a filter

fin /fɪn/ n **1** any of the winglike parts that a fish uses in swimming: *a tail fin* **2** a part shaped like this on a car, aircraft, bomb, etc. —see picture at AIRCRAFT **3** AmE for FLIPPER (2) **4** AmE old fash sl a five-dollar bill

Fi·na /ˈfiːnə/ an oil company that operates petrol stations in Britain and other countries

fi·na·gle /fɪˈneɪgəl/ v AmE infml **1** [T (**out of**)] to cheat or trick (a person), usu. by talking them into something: *He finagled me out of ten bucks.* **2** [T] to obtain, sometimes by cheating: *How he finagled four front row seats to the game I'll never know.* —**gler** n : *an accomplished finagler*

fi·nal[1] /ˈfaɪnl/ adj **1** [A no comp.] last; coming at the end: *the final episode of the serial|The game is now in its final stages. | a final demand for payment of a bill* **2** (of a decision, offer, etc.) that cannot be changed: *I won't go, and that's final! | Is that your final offer?* **3** completely settled: *I'd love to marry you but my divorce won't be final until March.* —see also FINALLY

final[2] also **finals** pl.— **1** the last and most important in a set of matches: *I never expected to get through to the finals. | the World Cup Final* —see also SEMIFINAL **2** esp. BrE the last and most important examinations in a college course: *When do you take your finals?* **3** AmE the last and most important examination in a high school, college, or university class: *How did your finals go? | My final for Chem 1A is at 10 o'clock. | a biology final*

fi·na·le /fɪˈnɑːliǁfɪˈnæli/ n the last division of a piece of music or a musical show: (fig.) *That wonderful party made a fitting finale to their visit.*

fi·nal·ist /ˈfaɪnl-ɪst/ n one of the people or teams that reaches the FINAL[2] (1), after the others have been defeated

fi·nal·i·ty /faɪˈnælɪti/ n [U] the quality of being or seeming FINAL[1] (2): *"No!" he said with finality.*

fi·nal·ize also **-ise** BrE /ˈfaɪnəl-aɪz/ v [T] to bring (a plan, arrangement, etc.) into a finished and complete form: *The agreement between the two countries has now been*

finalized. —**ization** /ˌfaɪnəl-aɪˈzeɪʃənǁ-nələ-/ n [U]

fi·nal·ly /ˈfaɪnl-i/ adv **1** at last: *After several delays, the plane finally left at six o'clock.* **2** as the last of a number of things; lastly: *And finally, I'd just like to say this.* **3** so as not to allow further change: *It's not finally settled yet.* —see LASTLY (USAGE)

Final So·lu·tion /ˌ··· ·ˈ··/ [the] Adolf Hitler's plan to get rid of the Jewish people in Europe by killing them during the Second World War

fi·nance[1] /ˈfaɪnæns, fɪˈnænsǁfɪˈnæns, ˈfaɪnæns/ n [U] **1** the management of money, esp. of large amounts of money by governments, companies, or large organizations: *the Minister of Finance | the university's finance committee* **2** money, esp. provided by a bank or similar organization, to help run a business or buy something: *Unless we can get more finance, we'll have to close the hotel.* —see also FINANCES

fi·nance[2] /faɪˈnæns, fɪ-ǁˈfaɪnæns, fɪˈnæns/ v [T] rather fml to provide an esp. large amount of money for (a public activity or organization, business, etc.): *The repairs to the school will be financed by the education department.| The concert was financed by the Arts Council.*

finance com·pa·ny /ˈ·· ˌ···, ·ˈ· ˌ···/ n AmE a company whose business is lending money to people at very high rates of interest. They are often used by people who are refused loans by banks.

finance di·rect·or /ˈ·· ·ˌ··, ·ˈ· ·ˌ··/ n esp. BrE a person with a high position in a company whose job is to plan how money is to be earned and spent

finance house /ˈ·· ·, ·ˈ· ·/ n a company which can offer CREDIT, e.g. in the form of HIRE PURCHASE, to people or organizations

fi·nanc·es /ˈfaɪnænsɪz, fɪˈnænsɪzǁfɪˈnænsɪz, ˈfaɪnænsɪz/ n [P] the amount of money owned by a person, government, or business: *I'm afraid my finances won't run to* (=be enough for) *a holiday abroad this year.*

fi·nan·cial /fɪˈnænʃəl, faɪ-/ adj **1** connected with finance: *The City of London is a great financial centre. | Mr Briggs is our financial adviser. | The film was popular with the critics, but was not a financial success.* (=was not profitable) **2 financial aid** AmE money given or lent to students at college or university: *a financial aid package* —~**ly** adv : *The company is not financially sound.*

financial in·cen·tive /·ˌ··· ·ˈ··/ n a sum of money offered to someone to persuade them to take some action

financial in·sti·tu·tion /·ˌ··· ··ˈ··/ n an organization involved with the borrowing and lending of money, such as a bank, building society etc: *All the big financial institutions are cutting their interest rates.*

financial mar·kets /·ˌ·· ˈ··/ n [P] the areas of international finance, in which large TRANSACTIONS are made by financial institutions —see also MONEY MARKET

financial sweet·ener /·ˌ·· ˈ··/ also **sweetener**— n an amount of money offered, sometimes dishonestly, to persuade someone to make a business arrangement, e.g. to buy a company; BRIBE

Financial Times /·ˌ·· ˈ·/ also **FT**— [the] a serious British daily newspaper which contains a lot of business and financial news. It is printed on pink paper. —see also extra information on page 896

Financial Times In·dex /·ˌ·· ·ˈ··/ also **FT Index**— [the] a list of prices on the London STOCK EXCHANGE based on the daily average prices of 30 industrial SHARES[1] (2). It is thought to be useful in showing how the British STOCK MARKET in general is performing. Its full name is the **Financial Times Industrial Ordinary Share Index** —compare DOW JONES AVERAGE

financial year /·ˌ·· ·/ n the yearly period over which accounts are calculated, usu. from 6th April to 5th April in Britain: *Self-employed people pay their taxes at the end of the financial year.* —compare FISCAL YEAR

fi·nan·cier /fɪˈnænsɪər, faɪˈnæn-ǁˌfɪnənˈsɪər/ n someone who controls or lends large sums of money

finch /fɪntʃ/ n any of many kinds of small singing birds with strong beaks that eat seeds

find[1] /faɪnd/ v **found** /faʊnd/ [T] **1** to discover, esp. by searching; get (someone or something that was hidden, lost, or not known): *I can't find my boots! | We've found oil under the North Sea. | Where were the jewels found? |*

We looked everywhere for the keys, but they were **nowhere to be found.** (=we could not find them anywhere) | *They still have not found a replacement for the designer who left last month.* | *They found somewhere for him to live.* [+obj(i)+obj(d)] *They found him somewhere to live.* [+obj+v-ing] *They found the lost child hiding in the cave.* [+obj+adj] *He was found dead in the morning.* (=he was found by someone and he was already dead) *No one has yet found a solution to this difficult problem.* | *Do you think you can find your way home?* **2** to discover (someone or something) to be, by chance or experience: [+obj+adv/prep] *When we arrived, we found him* (=he was) *in bed.* | *I woke up to find myself* (=that I was) *in the hospital.* | *"I think she's mean." "I didn't find her so."* [+obj+adj] *I find it difficult to believe you.* [+obj+n] *I didn't find her an easy woman to work with.* (=in my experience it was not easy to work with her) [+(that)] *I find I have half an hour to spare, so we can have our talk now.* | *We're finding that fewer and fewer people are buying this brand.* **3** (of a thing) to reach; arrive at: *The bullet found its mark.* | *The water will soon find its own level.* **4** to obtain by effort: *How ever do you find the time to make cakes?* | *He's going to Mexico, and I'm going too if I can find the money.* | *At last she found the courage to tell him.* | *Once he'd* **found his tongue** (=gained the courage to speak) *he told them what he thought of them.* **5** [*not in progressive forms*] to know or see that (something) exists or happens: [+obj+adv/prep] *This type of snake is only found* (=lives, exists) *in South America.* [+obj+v-ing] *You won't find many students learning* (=not many students learn) *Latin now.* **6** [+obj+adj; *not in progressive forms*] *law* to decide (someone) to be: *The jury found the prisoner guilty/not guilty.* —compare FIND **against,** FIND **for 7** *BrE* to provide: *Do the men find their own tools, or is their employer responsible?* | *The cook gets paid £80 a week and* **all found.** (=and also has food, housing, etc., provided) **8 finders keepers, losers weepers** *saying* the person who finds something may keep it, the person who has lost it can do nothing **9 find it in one's heart/in oneself to** (*usu. in questions or negatives*) to be ready or willing: *Can't you find it in your heart to forgive her?* **10 find oneself** to discover one's own wishes, ability, and character: *Her year of voluntary work abroad helped her to find herself as an individual.* **11 find one's feet** to become used to new or strange surroundings; settle in: *He's only been at the school two weeks, and he hasn't really found his feet yet.* — ~ **er** *n : The finder of the lost articles will receive a reward.*

find against sbdy. *phr v* [T *no pass.*] *law* to give judgment against: *The jury found against the plaintiff.*

find for sbdy. *phr v* [T *no pass.*] *law* to give judgment in favour of: *The judge found for the plaintiff.*

find out *phr v* **1** [I; T (=**find** sthg. ↔ **out**)] to learn or discover (a fact that was hidden or not known): *I won't tell you – you'll have to find out for yourself!* | *I've been trying to find out her telephone number.* [+(that)] *I found out quite by chance that she intended to sell it.* [+wh-] *Nobody could find out how to operate it.* **2** [T] (**find** sbdy. **out**) to discover in a dishonest act: *After years of embezzling from his employers, he was finally found out.*

find² *n* something good or valuable that is found: *This little restaurant is quite a find/is a real find.*

fin de siè·cle /ˌfæn də ˈsjeklə/ *adj Fr* (typical) of the end of the 19th century, esp. when thought of as a time of DECADENT ideas in literature, art, etc.

find·ing /ˈfaɪndɪŋ/ also **findings** *pl.– n* **1** *law* a decision made by a judge or JURY **2** something learnt as the result of an official inquiry: *The findings of the committee on child care are due to be published soon.*

Fin·dus /ˈfɪndəs/ *n tdmk* a company which makes many different types of frozen (FREEZE (5)) food product

fine¹ /faɪn/ *adj* **1** beautiful and of high quality; better than most of its kind: *a fine house/musician/wine/view* | *It's a fine example of its kind.* | *I've never seen a finer animal.* | *This painting is really very fine.* | *He's an expert at getting the children ready for school; he's* **got it down to a fine art. 2** *a* very thin: *fine hair/thread/silk* | *a pencil with a fine point* | *This print's too fine* (=small) *for me to read.* | (fig.) *There's often a very fine line between truth and falsehood.* **b** in very small grains or bits: *fine sugar/dust* —opposite **coarse**; see also FINE PRINT; see THIN (USAGE) **3** (of weather) bright and sunny; not wet: *a fine summer morning* | *It's* **turned out fine** *again.* | (fig.)

I suppose I might be rich **one fine day.** (=at some uncertain time in the future) **4** [F *no comp.*] (of a person or situation) healthy and comfortable: *"How's your wife?" "She's fine, thank you."* | *How's the new job?" "It's fine, thank you."* | *This apartment's fine for two people, but not more.* **5** [A] delicate and difficult to understand or notice: *I missed some of the finer points in the argument.* | *That's a very fine distinction; I would have said a donkey and an ass were the same animal.* | **Not to put too fine a point on it** (=to express it plainly), *I think he's mad!* **6** (of statements) too grand and perhaps not true: *We've had enough of your fine speeches!* | *That's all very fine, but what about me and the children?* **7** [A] *infml* terrible: *That's a fine thing to say!* | *Your shoes will be in a fine state if you walk in the mud.* —see also FINELY – ~**ness** *n* [U]

fine² *adv* **1** so as to be very thin or in very small bits: *Cut up the vegetables very fine.* | *The cloth was woven of fine-spun silk.* **2** *infml* very well: *It suits me fine.* | *The machine works fine if you oil it.* | *"I'll leave the key on the table, OK?" "Fine."* (=yes, that is all right) **3 cut/run it fine** *infml* to allow only just enough time and no more: *You're cutting it a bit fine if you want to catch the 5.30 train!* —compare FINELY

fine³ *v* [I;T (DOWN)] **1** to make or become pure and clear: *Before the beer can be bottled it has to be fined.* **2** to improve by making or becoming thinner, less wasteful, or more exact: *Now that the original plans have been fined down, they are much more practical.*

fine⁴ *n* an amount of money paid as a punishment. Fines are usu. given to people for committing (COMMIT) small crimes, e.g. for parking in the wrong place, for driving too fast, or for dropping LITTER: *You'll have to pay a £50 fine/an* **on-the-spot fine.** (=a fine paid at once)

fine⁵ *v* [T (**for**)] to take money from as a punishment: *They fined him heavily (for breaking the speed limit).* [+obj(i)+obj(d)] *He was fined £200.*

fine art /ˌ· ˈ·/ *n* [U] paintings, drawings, music, SCULPTURE, etc., of high quality: *a lover of fine art*

fine arts /ˌ· ˈ·/ *n* [*the*] activities such as painting, music, and SCULPTURE, that are chiefly concerned with producing beautiful rather than useful things: *a student of the fine arts*

Fin·e Gael /ˌfɪnə ˈɡeɪl/ an Irish political party thought to be CONSERVATIVE and interested in reaching an agreement with the UK. Under leader Garrett Fitzgerald they joined in the Anglo-Irish agreement of 1985.

fine·ly /ˈfaɪnli/ *adv* **1** so as to be very thin or in very small bits: *finely cut vegetables* **2** closely and delicately: *These instruments are very finely set/tuned.* **3** *fml* very well, esp. in a moral sense: *I think he behaved finely.* —compare FINE²

fine print /ˌ· ˈ·/ *n* [(*the*) U] SMALL PRINT

fi·ne·ry /ˈfaɪnəri/ *n* [U] beautiful or showy clothes, jewellery, etc., esp. for a special occasion: *the guests in their wedding finery*

fines herbes /ˌfiːn ˈeəb‖-ˈeərb/ *n* [U] *Fr* a mixture of dried and cut plants such as PARSLEY, CHIVES, and TARRAGON, which is added to food during cooking to improve its taste

fi·nesse /fɪˈnes/ *n* [U] **1** delicate skill and self-confidence: *Paul played the sonata/handled the meeting with great finesse.* **2** (in card games) the holding back of one's highest card because one guesses that one will be able to win with a lower card

fine-tooth comb /ˌ· · ˈ·, ˌ· · ˈ·/ also **fine-toothed comb** /ˌ· · ˈ·/ *AmE— n* **with a fine-tooth comb** very carefully and in great detail: *They went through his statement with a fine-tooth comb, to see if they could find any inconsistencies.*

fine-tune /ˌ· ˈ·/ *v* [T] to make slight changes to (something) so as to make it work as well as possible —**fine-tuning** *n* [U]

Fin·gal's Cave /ˌfɪŋɡəlz ˈkeɪv/ a cave on Staffa Island in the INNER HEBRIDES in W Scotland famous for its PILLARS of rock

fin·ger¹ /ˈfɪŋɡəʳ/ *n* **1** any of the five movable parts with joints at the end of each hand: *He ran his fingers through his hair/drummed his fingers on the desk in frustration.* | *She let the sand fall through* (=between) *her fingers.*

—compare TOE and see picture at HAND   **2** any of four such parts, not including the thumb: *a beckoning finger* —see also INDEX FINGER, LITTLE FINGER, MIDDLE FINGER, RING FINGER   **3** the part of a GLOVE that covers a finger   **4** **be/feel all fingers and thumbs** *BrE infml* to use one's hands awkwardly or be unable to control them; be CLUMSY: *I'm sorry I dropped your cup – I'm all fingers and thumbs today.*   **5 give someone the finger** *AmE infml* to move the middle finger upwards in the direction of someone with whom one is angry, in an extremely offensive way   **6 (have) a finger in every pie** *infml* (to have) a part or interest in everything that is going on   **7 have/with one's fingers in the till** *infml* to steal/stealing money from the place where one works: *He was caught with his fingers in the till and dismissed.*   **8 keep one's 'fingers crossed** *infml* to hope: *We must just keep our fingers crossed that the weather will stay fine for our picnic tomorrow.*   **9 lay a finger on** (*usu. in negatives*) to harm; touch, even slightly: *It's not my fault – I never laid a finger on her!*   **10 lift/raise a finger** (*usu. in negatives*) to make any effort to help when necessary: *He was the only one who lifted a finger to help the victims.*   **11 pull/take/get one's finger out** *BrE infml* to start working hard; make an effort   **12 put one's finger on** *infml* to find or show exactly (the cause of trouble): *Something's wrong with this room, but I can't quite put my finger on what it is.*   **13 put two fingers up at** *BrE infml* to move the first two fingers of the hand upwards in the direction of someone with whom one is angry, in an extremely offensive way   **14 -fingered** /ˈfɪŋgəd‖-ərd/: **a** having the stated number or kind of fingers: *three-fingered long-fingered*   **b** using the stated number of fingers: *two-fingered typing* —see also BUTTERFINGERS, GREEN FINGERS, **burn one's fingers** (BURN[1]), **point the finger** (POINT[2]), **twist someone round one's little finger** (TWIST[1])

finger[2] *v* [T]   **1** to feel or handle with one's fingers: *She fingered the rich silk enviously.*   **2** [+obj+adv/prep] to perform (a piece of music) with the correct or stated fingers: *How do you finger this piece?*   **3** [(to)] *infml, esp. AmE* to point out, esp. as being a criminal: *He fingered the other members of the gang to the police.*

fin·ger·board /ˈfɪŋgəbɔːd‖-gərbɔːrd/ *n* the part of a stringed musical instrument against which the fingers press the strings in order to vary the note

finger bowl /ˈ··· ·/ *n* a small basin in which someone can wash their fingers before and after a meal. In Britain and the US, finger bowls are only used on formal occasions when people are eating food which is eaten with the fingers.

fin·ger·ing /ˈfɪŋgərɪŋ/ *n* [U] the use or position of the fingers when playing a musical instrument: *The fingering is difficult in this piece.*

fin·ger·lick·in' good /ˌfɪŋgəlɪkɪn ˈgʊd‖-gər-/ *adj a* phrase used in advertisements for Kentucky Fried Chicken

fin·ger·mark /ˈfɪŋgəmɑːk‖-gərmɑːrk/ *n* a mark made by dirty or sticky fingers on something clean: *Who's put greasy fingermarks all over my clean table?*

fin·ger·nail /ˈfɪŋgəneɪl‖-ər-/ *n* the hard flat piece that covers the top of the end of a finger: *long/painted fingernails | She bit her fingernails nervously.*

finger-paint /ˈ··· ˌ·/ *v* [I;T] to paint on paper using the fingers, usu. done by children: *Children love to finger-paint.* — ~ **ing** *n* [C;U] : *Finger-painting and drawing with crayons are often a child's first introduction to art. | a child's finger-painting*

fin·ger·plate /ˈfɪŋgəpleɪt‖-ər-/ *n* a metal or glass plate that is fastened to a door near the handle or keyhole, to keep off dirty fingermarks

fin·ger·print[1] /ˈfɪŋgəˌprɪnt‖-ər-/ *n*   **1** (a mark made by) the pattern of lines on the bottom of the end of a finger, as used in the discovery of crime: *Her fingerprints on the handle proved she'd been there. | The police* **took his fingerprints** *by pressing his fingertips onto an inked pad.*   **2** a mark or pattern that makes each one different or recognizable: *The graph of a patient with heart disease has its own particular fingerprint.* —see picture at PRINT

fingerprint[2] *v* [T] to take (someone's) fingerprints

fin·ger·stall /ˈfɪŋgəstɔːl‖-ər-/ *also* **stall** *BrE* ‖ **splint** *AmE— n* a cover for a hurt finger

fin·ger·tip[1] /ˈfɪŋgəˌtɪp‖-ər-/ *n*   **1** the end of a finger   **2 have something at one's fingertips** to have a complete and

ready knowledge of something: *You'd better ask David – he's got the whole subject at his fingertips.*   **3 to the/one's fingertips** *esp. BrE* completely; in all ways: *He's British to his fingertips.*

fingertip[2] *adj* [A *no comp.*] near and easy to reach: *fingertip information/controls*

fin·i·cky /ˈfɪnɪki/ *adj infml*   **1** too concerned about unimportant details, small likes and dislikes, etc.; FUSSY: *Eat up your spaghetti and don't be so finicky!*   **2** needing delicate attention to detail: *It's a very finicky job to get all these little bones out of the fish.*

fin·ish[1] /ˈfɪnɪʃ/ *v*   **1** [I;T] to come or bring to an end; reach the end of (an action or activity): *What time does the concert finish? | When do you finish your college course? | He interrupted her before she had finished what she was saying. | The building is still only half-finished.* [+v-ing] *Could I borrow that book when you've finished reading it?*   **2** [T] **a** [(OFF)] to put the last details to (something that one has made): *I must finish (off) this dress I'm making. I'm just giving it the last* **finishing touches**. **b** to provide with a final polish or coat of paint, etc.: *Wood which has not been finished is still rough.*   **3** [T (UP, OFF)] to eat or drink the rest of: *The cat will finish (up) the fish. | Let's finish (off) the wine.*   **4** [I+adv/prep] to arrive or end (in the stated place or way): *"Where did you finish in the 100 metres?" "I finished first."* (=I won) *| The party finished with a song.*   **5** [T (OFF)] *infml* to take all one's strength, hopes of success, patience, etc.: *Climbing all those stairs has really finished me (off).* (=tired me out) —see also FINISHED; see END (USAGE)

finish sthg./sbdy. ↔ **off** *phr v* [T] to kill or destroy (a person or animal, esp. one that is hurt or not strong): *That tiger is wounded – shall I finish him off?* —see also FINISH[1] (2,3,5)

finish up *phr v* [L] to be in the end (in the stated place, condition, etc.): *We toured Europe and finished up in Paris.* [+v-ing] *Everything went wrong, and I finished up wishing I'd never tried it.* —see also FINISH[1] (3)

finish with sthg./sbdy. *phr v* [T]   **1** to have no more use for: *I'll borrow the scissors if you've finished with them.*   **2** *infml* to (wish to) have no further relationship with (someone): *I've finished with Mary after the way she's treated me.*

finish[2] *n*   **1** [C] the end or last part, esp. of a race: *That was a close finish!* (=the competitors were almost level) *| The meeting was a fiasco* **from start to finish**. *| The two men* **fought to the finish**. (=until one was completely defeated)   **2** [S;U] the appearance or condition of having been properly finished, with paint, polish, etc.: *This antique French table has a beautiful finish. | (fig.) Her manners lack social finish.*

fin·ished /ˈfɪnɪʃt/ *adj*   **1** [A] properly made and complete: *the finished product | a very finished* (=of very high quality) *performance* —opposite **unfinished**   **2** [F] *infml* at the end of an activity, relationship, etc.: *The workmen were finished by 7.00.*   **3** [F] *infml* with no hope of continuing: *If the bank refuses to lend us the money, we're finished!*

finishing school /ˈ··· ·/ *n*   **1** a private school where rich young girls learn social skills   **2** *AmE derog* a college or university with very low standards, esp. one for women only

fi·nite /ˈfaɪnaɪt/ *adj*   **1** having an end or limit: *There is only a finite number of possibilities. | Light moves at a finite speed. | finite resources* —opposite **infinite**   **2** *tech* (of a verb form) marked to show a particular tense and subject: *"Am", "was", and "are" are finite forms of the verb "to be", but "being" and "been" are non-finite.* — ~ **ly** *adv*

fink /fɪŋk/ *v* [I] *AmE sl* to inform people, esp. the police, about the action of others, esp. criminals: *Who finked?*

fink *n AmE infml*   **1** a worthless or unpleasant person   **2** a person who tells the police or a parent when someone else has done something wrong

Fink, Mike (about 1770–1823) a popular and admired man in the US who was famous for taking boats up and down the Mississippi River, for being a good shot, and for his drinking and bragging (BRAG).

Fin·land /ˈfɪnlənd/ a country in Scandinavia in N Europe; capital Helsinki; population 4,962,000 (1989)

Finn /fɪn/ *n* a person who comes from, or whose parents come from, Finland

Finn, Huck·le·ber·ry /ˈhʌkəlbəri‖-beri/ also **Huck Finn**— a character in the NOVELS *Tom Sawyer* and *The Adventures of Huckleberry Finn* by Mark Twain. He is a very independent young boy who runs away from his father and has many adventures. —see colour picture on page 1145

Finnish /ˈfɪnɪʃ/ *adj* of Finland

fi·ord /ˈfiːɔːd, fjɔːd‖fiːˈɔːrd, fjɔːrd/ *n* a FJORD

fir /fɜːʳ/ also **firtree**— *n* any of many kinds of straight tree that mostly keep their thin sharp leaves (NEEDLES) in winter, form their seeds in CONES, and grow esp. in cold countries —see picture at TREE

fire[1] /faɪəʳ/ *n* **1** [U] the condition of burning; flames, light, and great heat: *Horses are afraid of fire.* | *Have you got fire insurance?* (=in case your house burns down) | *The pile of papers couldn't* **catch fire** (=start to burn) *by itself; someone must have* **set fire to** *it/***set** *it* **on fire** *deliberately.* | *The building had been seriously damaged by fire.*| *fire prevention measures* | (fig.) *Her performance was full of fire.* (=very excitingly and strongly expressed feeling) **2** [C] a mass of burning material, lit either on purpose for cooking, heat, etc., or by accident: *It's nice to have a real coal fire in the winter.* | *The hunters lit/made a fire to boil up some water.* | *Thousands of trees were lost in the* forest fire. | *It took them several hours to put out the fire.* **3** [C] *BrE* a gas or electrical apparatus for warming a room, with the flames or red-hot wires able to be seen: *to turn off the fire* —compare STOVE[1] **4** [U] shooting by guns; firing (FIRE[2] (1)): *We were* **under fire** (=being shot at) *from all sides.* | *We gave him* **covering fire** (=protected him by shooting) *as he dashed across the clearing.* | *If you stick your head up like that you'll* **draw the enemy's** *fire.* (=make them shoot at you) | *The captain ordered his guns to* **open/cease fire.** (=start/stop shooting) **5 Fire burn and cauldron bubble** *quote* part of a speech by the three witches (WITCH) in Shakespeare's play *Macbeth* —see also **Double, double, toil and trouble** (TOIL) **6 go through fire and water (for)** *old-fash* to face great hardship and danger (for) **7 keep the home fires burning** a phrase from a British song popular during the First World War, meaning that soldiers' families should remain cheerful and keep their homes ready to welcome the soldiers home at the end of the war **8 on fire** (of something not meant to burn) burning: *The house is on fire!* **9 play with fire** to take great risks **10 pull something out of the fire** to make something successful in spite of difficulties: *We just managed to pull the game out of the fire.* (=win it) **11 -fired** /faɪəd‖-ərd/ operated by the stated FUEL: *oil-fired central heating* | *a coal-fired power station* —see also **hang fire** (HANG[1])

▷ USAGE If you want something to burn you usually **light** it: *to* **light** *a cigarette/the kitchen fire/a candle.* You **set fire** (either by accident or on purpose) to things which usually you do not want to burn: *Who* **set fire** *to the house?* When something begins to burn, esp. by accident, it **catches fire**: *Her dress* **caught fire.**◁

fire[2] *v* **1** [I (at)] (of a person or gun) to shoot off bullets: *He's firing at us!* | *The captain ordered his men to start firing.* **2** [T (at)] (of a person) to shoot off bullets from (a gun): *He ran into the bank and fired his gun into the air.* **3** [T (at)] (of a person, gun, or BOW[3] (1)) to shoot off (bullets or ARROWS): *They fired poisoned arrows/antiaircraft missiles at us.* **4** [T] *infml* to dismiss from a job; SACK: *Get out! You're fired!* **5** [T (with)] to produce (strong feelings) in (someone); INSPIRE: *Her stories fired the little boy's imagination.* | *He was suddenly fired with the desire to visit China.* **6** [T] to bake (clay pots, dishes, etc.) in a KILN

fire away *phr v* [I *usu. imperative*] *infml* to begin to speak or do something: *If anyone has any questions, fire away!*

fire a·larm /ˈ· ·ˌ·/ *n* (an apparatus, e.g. a bell, that gives) a signal to warn people of fire, usu. in a building: *The fire alarm went off/sounded.*

fire and brim·stone /ˌ· · ˈ··/ *n* [U] a phrase used in the Bible to describe Hell. It is often used by religious people warning other people about what will happen to them if they lead wicked lives.

fire·arm /ˈfaɪərɑːm‖-ɑːrm/ *n* [*usu. pl.*] a gun, esp. a small one

fire·ball /ˈfaɪəbɔːl‖-ər-/ *n* a ball of fire, such as the very hot

cloud of burning dust and gases formed by an atomic explosion, a very bright METEOR, etc.

fire·boat /ˈfaɪəbəʊt‖-ər-/ *n* a boat which carries equipment for fighting fires

fire·bomb /ˈfaɪəbɒm‖-əbɑːm/ *n* a bomb which can cause a fire when it explodes

fire·box /ˈfaɪəbɒks‖-əbɑːks/ *n* the place for the fire in a steam engine or boiler

fire·brand /ˈfaɪəbrænd‖-ər-/ *n* **1** a flaming piece of wood **2** a person who regularly causes anger and unrest among others; AGITATOR

fire·break /ˈfaɪəbreɪk‖-ər-/ *n* a narrow piece of land cleared of trees to prevent forest fires from spreading

fire·brick /ˈfaɪəbrɪk‖-ər-/ *n* a brick made of a substance which is not damaged by heat, used in fireplaces, chimneys, etc.

fire bri·gade /ˈ· ·ˌ·/ *BrE* ‖ **fire de·part·ment** /ˈ· ·ˌ···/ *AmE*— *n* [C+*sing./pl. v*] an organization for preventing and putting out fires: *Quick! Call the fire brigade!*

fire·bug /ˈfaɪəbʌg‖-ər-/ *n* *infml* a person who purposely starts fires to destroy property; person who performs an act of ARSON

fire·crack·er /ˈfaɪəˌkrækəʳ‖-ər-/ also **cracker**— *n* a small FIREWORK that explodes loudly

fire·damp /ˈfaɪədæmp‖-ər-/ *n* [U] an explosive mixture of gases that forms in mines and becomes dangerous when mixed with air

fire·dog /ˈfaɪədɒg‖-ərdɔːg/ *n* an ANDIRON

fire door /ˈ· ˌ·/ *n* a door which is kept closed and helps to prevent the spread of a fire: *Hotels are required to fit fire doors.*

fire drill /ˈ· ·/ *n* [C;U] (the act of doing) the set of actions that must be performed to leave a burning building safely, practised regularly by pupils in a school, workers in a factory, etc.: *to hold/have a fire drill*

fire-eat·er /ˈ· ˌ··/ *n* **1** an entertainer who appears to put flaming material into his/her mouth **2** *infml* a person with violent opinions who likes to quarrel

fire en·gine /ˈ· ˌ··/ also **fire truck** *AmE*— *n* a special vehicle that carries firemen (FIREMAN) and special equipment to put out fires

fire es·cape /ˈ· ·ˌ·/ *n* a way by which people can escape from a burning building, esp. a set of metal stairs leading down outside of a building to the ground

fire ex·tin·guish·er /ˈ· ·ˌ···/ also **extinguisher**— *n* a smallish metal container with water or chemicals inside for putting out a fire

fire fight /ˈ· ˌ·/ *n* a short battle between people, usu. soldiers or the police, using guns

fire fight·er /ˈ· ˌ··/ *n* a person who puts out fires, either as a FIREMAN or as a special helper during forest fires or in wartime

fire fight·ing /ˈ· ˌ··/ *n* [U] **1** actions taken to put out large unwanted fires in buildings, etc. **2** actions taken to discover and remove causes of sudden trouble, in organizations, machines, etc.

fire·fly /ˈfaɪəflaɪ‖-ər-/ *n* an insect with a tail that shines in the dark

fire·guard /ˈfaɪəgɑːd‖-ərgɑːrd/ also **firescreen** *AmE*— *n* a protective metal framework put round a fireplace to stop children going too near

fire·house /ˈfaɪəhaʊs‖-ər-/ *n* -**houses** /ˌhaʊzɪz/ *AmE* a small FIRE STATION, esp. in a small town

fire hy·drant /ˈ· ˌ··/ also **hydrant** *BrE* ‖ **fireplug** *AmE*— *n* a water pipe in a street used as a water supply for fighting fires

fire i·rons /ˈ· ˌ·/ *n* [P] the metal tools used for looking after a coal fire in a home

fire·light /ˈfaɪəlaɪt‖-ər-/ *n* [U] the light produced from a fire in the fireplace, often considered warm, gentle, and ROMANTIC: *She looked beautiful in the firelight.*

fire·light·er /ˈfaɪəˌlaɪtəʳ‖-ər-/ *n* [C;U] *esp. BrE* (a piece of) a substance which burns easily and helps to light a coal fire

fire·man /ˈfaɪəmən‖-ər-/ *n* -**men** /mən/ **1** a person whose job is putting out fires —see picture at HELMET **2** a person who looks after the fire in a steam engine or FURNACE

Fire of Lon·don /ˌ· ·ˈ··/ also **Great Fire of London**– [the] a very bad fire that destroyed large parts of London in 1666

fireplace

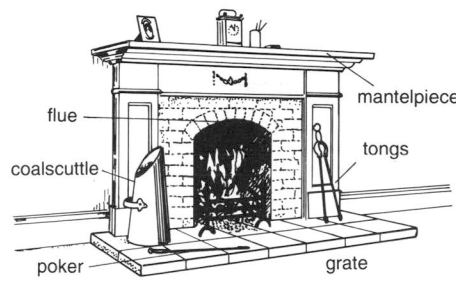

flue

mantelpiece

coalscuttle

tongs

poker

grate

fire·place /ˈfaɪəpleɪs‖-ər-/ n the opening for a coal or wood fire in the wall of a room, with a chimney above it and usu. a HEARTH and MANTELPIECE around it

fire-plug /ˈ· ·/ n AmE for FIRE HYDRANT

fire-pow·er /ˈfaɪəˌpaʊəʳ‖-ər-/ n [U] tech the ability to deliver gunfire or use other kinds of weapon effectively: the enemy's superior firepower

fire-proof /ˈfaɪəpruːf‖-ər-/ v [T] to make (a material, building, etc.) not able to be damaged by heat or flames – **fireproof** adj

fire-rais·ing /ˈ· ·ˌ··/ n [U] BrE the crime of starting fires on purpose; ARSON –-er n

fire sale /ˈ· ·/ n a sale of goods that have been slightly damaged by a fire, or of goods that must be sold because, as the result of a fire, there is nowhere to keep them

fire-screen /ˈfaɪəskriːn ‖ -ər-/ AmE for FIREGUARD

Fire Ser·vice /ˈ· ·ˌ··/ [the] the organization in Britain which manages the supply of firemen (FIREMAN) and FIRE ENGINES to put out fires

fire·side /ˈfaɪəsaɪd‖-ər-/ n [usu. sing.] the area around the fireplace, often thought of as representing the comfort and pleasures of home life: He sat by the fireside drinking his cocoa.

fireside chat /ˌ·· ·ˈ·/ n 1 a friendly conversation by a fireside 2 one of a group of speeches given on American radio by American President Franklin D. Roosevelt, which told people in an informal way what the government was doing. Roosevelt was the first president to tell people in a direct way what he was thinking and doing. All the presidents after him have used either radio or television in the same way though not always so regularly.

fire sta·tion /ˈ· ·ˌ··/ n a building for firemen (FIREMAN) and their vehicles and equipment

Fire-stone /ˈfaɪəstoʊn ‖ ˈfaɪər-/ an American company that makes tyres and other rubber products

fire-storm /ˈfaɪəstɔːm‖-ərstɔːrm/ n a very large fire, usu. started by bombs, that is kept burning by the high winds that are drawn into it

fire-trap /ˈfaɪətræp‖-ər-/ n a building which is dangerous because it may easily catch fire and/or be difficult to escape from in case of fire

fire truck /ˈ· ·/ n AmE a FIRE ENGINE

fire-watch·er /ˈfaɪəwɒtʃəʳ‖-ərwɑːtʃər, -wɔːtʃ-/ n one of the people who kept watch for fire bombs in British cities when they were being bombed by German aircraft during the Second World War. Firewatchers usu. waited on the tops of tall buildings and tried to put out fires as soon as they started.

fire-wat·er /ˈfaɪəˌwɔːtəʳ‖-ər-, -ərˌwɔː-, -ˌwɑː-/ n [U] humor strong alcoholic drink, such as WHISKY

fire-wood /ˈfaɪəwʊd‖-ər-/ n [U] wood cut for burning on fires: chopping firewood in the yard

fire-work /ˈfaɪəwɜːk‖-ərwɜːrk/ n [usu. pl.] a small container filled with an explosive chemical powder that burns or explodes to produce a show of light, noise, and smoke –see colour picture on page 1211

▶CULTURAL NOTE In Britain, people usu. have fireworks on GUY FAWKES NIGHT and sometimes also for other special

celebrations. Anyone over the age of 16 is allowed to buy fireworks. In the US, fireworks are used to celebrate the FOURTH OF JULY and also for other special celebrations. In some parts of the US people can buy fireworks for the Fourth of July, but in many places it is illegal to buy fireworks because they are considered to be too dangerous. Many people go to see firework displays in parks or other public places.◀

fire·works /ˈfaɪəwɜːks‖-ərwɜːrks/ n [P] infml a show of anger: I told you there'd be fireworks if you attempted to contradict her.

Fireworks Night /ˈ·· ·ˌ·/ GUY FAWKES NIGHT

firing line /ˈ·· ·/ [the] a position or situation in which one is the object of (often undeserved) attack, blame, etc.: It's the police who are always in the firing line when there are political demonstrations.

firing squad /ˈ·· ·ˌ·/ n [C+sing./pl. v] a group of soldiers with the duty of putting a person to death by shooting

firm¹ /fɜːm‖fɜːrm/ adj 1 solidly fixed in place: I don't think that chair's firm enough to stand on. (=it may slip or fall over) 2 not changing or likely to change: I'm a firm believer in always telling the truth. | The pound stayed firm (=did not change its value) against the dollar in London but fell a little in New York. | Our offer was met with a firm refusal. 3 strong and giving a feeling of trust: She has a good firm handshake. | He kept a firm hold on my arm as he helped me over the fence. 4 determined in purpose; RESOLUTE: Our army stood firm in the face of a terrible onslaught. | Always hold firm to your beliefs. | You'll have to be firm with class three; they're a noisy lot. – ~ly adv : I firmly believe that we are justified in taking this course of action. – ~ness n [U]

firm² v [I;T UP] to (cause to) become firm: Stock market prices have firmed. (=become steady) | We should be able to firm up the agreement (=put it into a fixed form) today.

firm³ n a business company: She works for an engineering firm|a firm of stockbrokers.

fir·ma·ment /ˈfɜːməmənt‖ˈfɜːr-/ n [the] lit or old use the sky

firm of·fer /ˌ· ·ˈ··/ n a price suggested for a service or for goods which becomes legally fixed if accepted

firm·ware /ˈfɜːmweəʳ‖ˈfɜːrm-/ n [U] tech instructions for controlling the operation of a computer, stored on a CHIP¹ (6), such as a ROM –compare HARDWARE, SOFTWARE

first¹ /fɜːst‖fɜːrst/ determiner, adv 1 before anything else; before the others: George arrived first|was the first person to arrive. | "Let's go." "I'll have to find my keys first." | First, let me deal with the most important difficulty. | It was the first time I had ever been in a plane. | We left at first light. (-very early in the morning) | First impressions are very important. 2 for the first time: Is this your first visit to New York? | I remember when I first met him. 3 at the beginning: When we first lived here there were no buses. | First I want to establish some basic points. | The first few days passed very quickly. | a first-year student at the university 4 more willingly: I'll never allow you to do that: I'll die first! 5 at first hand directly; FIRSTHAND: I got the news from her at first hand. 6 first among equals the person who leads a group of people but is not seen as being better or more important than the other members of the group 7 first and foremost most importantly; above all else: He's written many different kinds of books, but he's first and foremost a poet. 8 first of all as the first or most important thing: First of all let me say how glad I am to be here. | I'm interested in old coins but first of all I'm a stamp collector. 9 first off infml before other things: First off, let's see where we agree and disagree. 10 first thing at the earliest time in the morning: I'll come round to collect it first thing tomorrow. 11 first things first let us take things in the proper order of importance 12 in the first instance esp. BrE as the first act in a set of actions: Anyone wishing to purchase tickets should apply in the first instance to the secretary. 13 not the first infml not the slightest; no: I haven't got the first idea how to do it. 14 of the first water old-fash or pomp of the highest quality: a scientist of the first water –see also FIRSTLY 15 on the first day of Christmas the first line of a popular Christmas song:
On the first day of Christmas my true love sent to me
A partridge in a pear tree...

first² n, pron 1 [(the) S] the person, thing, or group before all others: "Are we the first?" he asked, as their host opened *the door.* | *The minister's television appearance – his first since taking office – was a great success.* [+to-v] *He was the first|one of the first to collect Picasso's paintings.* | *Whoever is (the) first to finish will get a prize.* | *the first of a series of programmes on life in Russia* –compare LAST² **2** [C (**in**)] the highest class of British university degree: *He got a first in history.* –see also DEGREE (CULTURAL NOTE) **3** [C] *infml* something never done before: *Roger Bannister scored a notable first when he ran the mile in under four minutes.* **4** [U] FIRST GEAR **5 at first** at the beginning: *At first I didn't like him but now I do.* –compare **at last** (LAST²); see FIRSTLY (USAGE) **6 first come, first served** the person who arrives first will be served first: *The number of tickets is limited, so it's a case of first come, first served.* (=people who come late may not get tickets) **7 from the (very) first** from the beginning: *I knew from the first it would never succeed.* **8 the first shall be last, and the last shall be first** *phrase from the Bible* the people who have power now will one day have no power, and the people with no power now will one day have power

first aid /ˌ· '·/ *n* [U] treatment to be given by an ordinary person (as opposed to a doctor, nurse, etc.) to a person who has been hurt in an accident or suddenly taken ill: *Do you know anything about first aid?* | *I'm going to do a first-aid course.*

first aid kit /ˌ· '· ˌ·/ also **first aid box**– *n* a collection of equipment such as BANDAGES, PLASTERS etc., which can be used to treat people who have been hurt in an accident or suddenly taken ill

First A·mend·ment /ˌ· ·'··/ [*the*] a part of the American CONSTITUTION which gives American citizens the rights of freedom of speech, freedom of the PRESS, freedom of religion, and freedom of ASSEMBLY (=the right to gather together as a group). Many cases concerning the rights included in the First Amendment have been taken to the SUPREME COURT. People in the US usually feel very strongly about the questions that these cases raise.

first base /ˌ· '·/ *n* also **first**– *AmE* **1** (in BASEBALL) the first of the four places which a player must touch before gaining a point (RUN): *He plays first base for the Red Sox.* **2** the first stage of success in an attempt to achieve something: *You've gotten to first base if you've landed an interview.*

first·born /'fɜːstbɔːn‖'fɜːrstbɔːrn/ *adj, n* **firstborn** [A;C] *lit or bibl* (the) eldest among the children in a family: *the firstborn child*

▶ CULTURAL NOTE The firstborn son (= the eldest son) used to be considered the most important child in a family because he was the one who would INHERIT most of the family's land and wealth. This idea is not so strong today but in some noble or royal families it is still the case that the first born son inherits the family's wealth. ◀

first class /ˌ· '·◀/ *n* **1** [U] **a** (in Britain) a class of mail in which letters and parcels are delivered as quickly as possible, and which is more expensive than second class mail **b** (in the US) the class of mail used for ordinary business and personal letters **2** [U] (on a train, ship, or aircraft) the best and most expensive travelling conditions: *There's a lot more space in first class.* | *a first-class ticket* –compare BUSINESS CLASS, CLUB CLASS, ECONOMY CLASS, SECOND CLASS **3** [C] *fml for* FIRST² (2) –**first class** *adv* : *You'd better send it first class.* | *I always travel first class.*

first-class *adj* of the highest or best quality: *Your work is first-class; I'm very pleased with it.*

First Com·mu·nion /ˌ· ·'··/ *n* (the act of) receiving Holy Communion for the first time: *Rachel's making her First Communion on Saturday.*

first cous·in /ˌ· '··/ *n* a COUSIN

first day cov·er /ˌ· · '··/ *n* (in Britain) a special envelope on which newly produced stamps are stuck and marked with a POSTMARK on their first day of use. Some people in Britain like to collect first day covers which sometimes later become very valuable.

first-de·gree /ˌ· ·'·◀/ *adj* [A] **1** (of a burn) of the lowest level of seriousness **2** *AmE* (of a crime) of the highest level of seriousness: *first-degree murder*

First Di·vi·sion /ˌ· ·'··◀/ [*the*] a group of English football teams that compete with each other. The First Division is below the PREMIER LEAGUE. –see also FOOTBALL (1)

first e·di·tion /ˌ· ·'··/ *n* one of the copies of a book that was produced the first time that book was printed. Some first editions of old books are now very valuable.

first-ev·er /ˌ· '···◀/ *adj* happening for the first time ever; that has never happened before: *The town had its first-ever snowfall last year.* | *my first-ever trip to New York*

first fam·i·ly /ˌ· '···/ *n* the family of the president of the US

first floor /ˌ· '·◀/ *n* [*the*] **1** *BrE* the first floor of a building above ground level **2** *AmE* the floor of a building at ground level –compare GROUND FLOOR; see FLOOR (USAGE)

first-footing /ˌ· '··/ *n* [U] *ScotE* the custom in Scotland of visiting people soon after the New Year has begun, at 12 o'clock at night on December 31st –**first-footer** *n*

▶ CULTURAL NOTE In Scotland people usu. celebrate HOGMANAY and the New Year as much as CHRISTMAS. There are usu. parties on Hogmanay followed by celebrations at 12 o'clock when the New Year starts. After 12 o'clock people **go first-footing**, hoping to find another party or just to wish friends a **Happy New Year**. It is supposed to be lucky if the first person to enter your house is a tall, dark man carrying a piece of coal. Therefore **first-footers** should take coal with them, although this is not often done now. ◀

first gear /ˌ· '·/ *n* the lowest GEAR in a car or other motor vehicle, used when the vehicle is started or when going up a very steep hill

first gen·e·ra·tion /ˌ· ··'···/ *n* [*the*] the children of parents who have moved to live in a new country, esp. the US. These children grow up speaking the language of their new country at school and the language of their parents at home. –**first-generation** *adj* : *first-generation children*

first half /ˌ· '·/ *n* the first of two equal periods into which a sports match is divided: *That was a tough first half for Wales.*

first·hand /ˌfɜːst'hænd◀‖-ɜːr-/ *adj, adv* (learnt) directly from the point of origin: *I heard her news firsthand.* (=from her) | *It's not firsthand information, so I don't know if you can completely believe it.* –compare SECONDHAND¹ (2); see also **at first hand** (FIRST¹)

first la·dy /ˌ· '··/ *n* (*sometimes cap.*) (in the US) the wife of the President, or of the GOVERNOR of a state

first lan·guage /ˌ· '··/ *n* the language that one knows best and speaks most naturally, usu. the language first learnt as a child: *His first language is Spanish, but he also speaks French and Italian.*

first lieu·ten·ant /ˌ· ·'··◀/ *n* an officer in the US army, air-force, or MARINES –see TABLE 3

first·ly /'fɜːstli‖-ɜːr-/ *adv* as the first of a set of things; FIRST¹: *Firstly, let me deal with the most urgent problem.*

▷ USAGE Compare **first(ly)** and **at first**. **Firstly** (and **first**²) are often used when separating the points you want to make and putting them in order: *First(ly) I'll mention the advantages, then I'll mention the disadvantages.* | *There are three reasons why I hate him:* **first(ly)** *he's a cheat,* **second(ly)** *he's a liar, and* **third(ly)|finally** *he owes me money.* **At first** cannot be used in this way. **At first** refers to a point of time and often marks a contrast with a later time: **At first** *I didn't understand, but afterwards it became very clear.* | *You'll find it difficult* **at first,** *but it'll soon get easier.*◁

first name /'· ·/ also **forename** *fml* ‖ **given name** *AmE*– *n* the name or names that stand before one's SURNAME (=family name); one's personal name(s): *Mr Smith's first name is Peter.* | *His first names are Peter Alexander.* | *She's* **on first-name terms** *with her teachers.* (=knows them well enough to call them by their first names) | He's **on a first name basis** (*AmE*) *with his boss.*

▷ USAGE In English-speaking countries, your **first name** usually means the first of the names given to you by your parents at birth, but it may also include *all* the names given to you by your parents. In Christian countries, **Christian name** is sometimes used in the same way. **Given name(s)** and (less commonly) **forename(s)** are also used in this way, especially on official forms. **Given name** or **given names** is the most suitable expression for people, such as Chinese, who usually say their SURNAMES first.◁

first night /ˌ· '·/ *n* the evening on which the first public performance of a show, play, etc., is given

first of·fend·er /₁· ·'··/ *n* a person found guilty of breaking the law for the first time

first past the post /₁· · ·'·/ *n* [U] a voting system used in British national and local elections, in which the person with more votes than any other wins the election. The winner does not need to have more votes than the losers have together. —compare PROPORTIONAL REPRESENTATION

first per·son /₁· '··◄/ *n* [*the*+S] **1** *tech* a form of verb or PRONOUN that is used to show the speaker: *"I", "me", "we", and "us" are first person pronouns.* | *"I am" is the first person present singular of "to be".* **2** a way of telling a story in which the teller uses the first person: *The story was written in the first person: it began "I was born in. . .".* —compare SECOND PERSON, THIRD PERSON

first-rate /₁· '·◄/ *adj* very good; of the highest quality: *This is first-rate beer!* —compare SECOND-RATE

First Read·ing /₁fɜːst 'riːdɪŋ‖₁fɜːrst-/ *n* **1** the first reading out of a suggested new law in parliament: *The new transport bill will get its first reading in the House of Commons tomorrow.* **2** (in the US) the introduction of a suggested new law into Congress —see BILL¹ (2) (CULTURAL NOTE)

first re·fus·al /₁· ·'··/ *n* [(*the*) U] *BrE* the right to decide whether to buy something before it is offered to other people: *If you sell your house, will you let me have first refusal on it?*

first school /'· ·/ *n* (in Britain) a school for children between the ages of five and eight

first strike /₁· '·◄/ *n* an attack made on your enemy before they (can) attack you: *a new weapon system that gives us a* **first-strike capability**

first-string /₁· '·◄/ *adj* [A] being a regular member of a team, group, etc., rather than one who sometimes comes in to take the place of another —compare SECOND-STRING

first-time buy·er /₁· · '··/ *n* someone who is buying a flat or house for the first time. In Britain, first-time buyers are often offered favourable financial deals by banks and building societies (BUILDING SOCIETY).

First World /₁· '·◄/ *n* [*the*+*sing.*/*pl.v*] the highly industrial countries of the world —**first world** *adj* [A] : *first world economies*

First World War /₁· · '·/ *BrE* ‖ usu. **World War I** *AmE*— [*the*] (1914–18) a war fought in Europe between France, Britain, Russia, and the US (the ALLIES) on one side and Germany, Austria–Hungary, and Turkey on the other, in which about 10 million people were killed

▶ CULTURAL NOTE Although the Allies won the First World War, British people do not usu. talk of the war or the victory with pride, because of the very large numbers of men, esp. young men, who were killed. People remember the names of the main battles of the war, esp. Passchendaele and the Somme, and these names have come to represent the sadness and wastefulness of war. ◄

firth /fɜːθ‖fɜːrθ/ *n* (*often cap. as part of a name*) (esp. in Scotland) a narrow arm of the sea, or place where a river flows out: *the Firth of Tay*

fir·tree /'fɜːtriː‖'fɜːr-/ *n* a FIR

fis·cal¹ /'fɪskəl/ *adj fml* of or related to public money, taxes, debts, etc.: *the government's fiscal policy* — ~ **ly** *adv*

fiscal² *n infml for* PROCURATOR FISCAL

fiscal year /₁·· '·/ also **FY** *AmE*— *n* the yearly period over which the amount of tax payable is calculated. In Britain, the fiscal year for companies starts on 1st April and for private persons it starts on 6th April. In the US the government fiscal year starts on October 1st; for INDIVIDUALs it is the same as the CALENDAR YEAR. Businesses may start their own fiscal years. —compare FINANCIAL YEAR

Fisch·er /'fɪʃər/, **Bobby** (1943–) an American CHESS player famous for reaching a professional level of play at the age of 15

fish¹ /fɪʃ/ *n* **fish** *or* **fishes** **1** [C] an animal which lives in water, is covered in SCALES² (1), and uses its FINs and tail to swim: *We caught three little fishes/several fish.* | *to gut/fillet a fish* **2** [U] the flesh of a fish when used as food: *We had fish/some fish/a piece of fish for dinner.* | *What kind of fish is this?* **3** [C] *infml* a person of the stated kind (used esp. in the phrases **a cold/odd/queer fish**) **4** have ¹**other fish to fry** *infml* to have other affairs to attend

to, esp. that are more important **5 like a fish out of water** uncomfortable because one is in a strange place or situation —also COLD FISH, **a pretty kettle of fish** (KETTLE) **6 neither fish nor fowl** neither one thing nor another **7 there are plenty more fish in the sea** (a phrase used to someone who has just suffered the ending of a relationship) there are plenty of other people to have a relationship with

fish² *v* **1** [I (**for**)] to try to catch fish: *Let's go fishing.* | *We're fishing for trout* —compare ANGLE³ **2** [T] to catch fish in (an area of water): *This river has been fished too much.* **3** [I+ABOUT, AROUND, **for**] *infml* to search: *She was fishing around in her handbag trying to find the key.* | *From the way he spoke I could tell he didn't know and was just fishing for information.* **4 fish for compliments** to try to make someone say something admiring about oneself, usu. by asking them a question: *"Did you like the play?" "Stop fishing for compliments. You know you acted brilliantly."* **5 fish in troubled waters** to try to gain advantage out of other people's troubles **6 fish or cut bait** *AmE infml* either do what you are saying you will do, or stop talking about it: *"I'll show these guys how the game is really played." "Fish or cut bait, buddy."*

fish *sthg./sbdy.* ↔ **out** *phr v* [T] *infml* **1** to pull from the water: *Jean fell into the river, and we had to fish her out.* **2** to bring out, esp. after searching: *He fished out a coin/a handkerchief from his pocket.*

fish *sthg.* ↔ **up** *phr v* [T] to pull up, as if catching a fish: *He fished up an old shoe out of the lake.*

Fish, Mi·chael /'maɪkəl/ (1944–) a weather reporter for BBC radio and television

fish and chips /₁· · '·/ *n* [U;P] a meal consisting of fish which is dipped into a mixture of flour and milk (BATTER²) and then cooked in oil, served with long, thin pieces of potato cooked in oil (CHIPS)

▶ CULTURAL NOTE Fish and chips is very popular in Britain, and is considered to be a typically British meal. It is usu. bought ready cooked at special shops (**fish and chip shops**) and taken away wrapped in paper, to be eaten at home or outside. It is quite cheap to buy and is usu. eaten as a quick meal or a SNACK. ◄

fish and chip shop

fish and chip shop /₁· · '· ·/ *n* a shop where fish and chips and some other foods are cooked and sold

fish·cake /'fɪʃkeɪk/ *n* a small round flat cake made of cooked fish mixed with cooked potato

fish·er /'fɪʃər/ *n* **I will make you fishers of men** a phrase used in the Bible by Christ, telling his followers, who were fishermen, that they should stop trying to catch fish and instead should try to attract more people to follow him

fish·er·man /'fɪʃəmən‖-ʃər-/ *n* **-men** /mən/ a man who catches fish, for sport or as a job —compare ANGLER

Fisherman's Friend /₁··· '·/ *n tdmk* a strong-tasting sweet which one sucks to help a cough get better

fish·e·ry /'fɪʃəri/ *n* a part of the sea used for the business of catching sea fish: *coastal fisheries*

fish-eye lens /₁· · '·/ *n* a type of very curved LENS for a camera that allows one to take pictures that cover a very wide angle

fish farm /'· ·/ *n* an area of water used for breeding fish for eating — ~ **ing** *n* [U]

fish fin·ger /₁· '··/ *esp. BrE* ‖ **fish stick** *esp. AmE*— *n* a small finger-shaped piece of fish covered with BREADCRUMBs, esp. popular with small children

fish·ing /'fɪʃɪŋ/ n [U] (the sport or job of) catching fish: *We're going to do some fishing in the holidays.* | *The sign says "No fishing".* (=you are not allowed to catch fish here) | *a fishing rod/net*

fishing ex·pe·di·tion /'·· ··,·,··/ n AmE an inquiry that tries to find secret information: *reporters on a fishing expedition at the mayor's residence*

fishing tack·le /'·· ,·/ n [U] all the things, e.g. fishing rod and net, needed for catching fish in a river or lake

fish ket·tle /'· ,·/ n a long, deep dish used for cooking whole fish

fish knife /'· ·/ n a kind of table knife without a sharp edge, used for eating fish —see picture at PLACE SETTINGS

fish mar·ket /'· ··/ n a market where fish is sold

fish meal /'· ·/ n [U] dried fish crushed into a powder and put onto the land to help food plants grow

fish·mon·ger /'fɪʃmʌŋgəʳ‖-maːŋ-, -mʌŋ-/ n esp. BrE a person who owns or works in a shop (**fishmonger's**) which sells fish: *I bought a nice piece of cod from the fishmonger|at the fishmonger's.*

fish 'n' chips /ˌfɪʃ ən 'tʃɪps/ n [P] infml FISH AND CHIPS; used esp. on signs and advertisements

fish·net stock·ings /ˌfɪʃnet 'stɒkɪŋz‖-'staː-/ n [P] STOCKINGS made of material with lots of small holes in it. Fishnet stockings are thought to make a woman look sexy and drawings of PROSTITUTEs often show them wearing fishnet stockings.

fish slice /'· ·/ BrE ‖ **slotted spatula** AmE— n a kitchen tool with a wide flat blade and a long handle, used esp. for lifting and turning food when cooking —see picture at KITCHEN

fish stick /'· ·/ n AmE for FISH FINGER

fish·tail /'fɪʃteɪl/ v [I] (of a car, or other motor vehicle, or plane) to slide from side to side: *The driver panicked as the car fishtailed on the icy road.*

fish·wife /'fɪʃwaɪf/ n -wives /waɪvz/ derog a woman who shouts in a loud, angry, rude way: *Stop shrieking like an old fishwife and listen to me!*

fish·y /'fɪʃi/ adj 1 (tasting or smelling) of fish 2 infml seeming false; making one doubtful; SUSPICIOUS: *His story sounds/smells very fishy to me.*

fis·sile /'fɪsaɪl‖-səl/ adj tech 1 able to split by atomic fission 2 tending to split along natural lines of weakness: *fissile wood*

fis·sion /'fɪʃən/ n [U] tech 1 the splitting into parts of certain atoms to free their powerful forces —compare FUSION 2 the act of splitting or dividing, esp. of one living cell into two or more

fis·sure /'fɪʃəʳ/ n a deep crack, esp. in rock or earth

fist /fɪst/ n 1 (the shape of) the hand with the fingers closed in tightly: *She shook her fist angrily.* | *I* **clenched my fists** (=closed my hands very tightly) *to try and stop the pain.* 2 **make a good/bad etc. fist of** BrE infml rare to make a successful/unsuccessful attempt at —see also HAM-FISTED, TIGHTFISTED, **hand over fist** (HAND¹ (23))

fist·ful /'fɪstfʊl/ n (**of**) an amount which is as much as can easily be held in a fist

Fistful of Dol·lars /ˌ·· · '··/, A a SPAGHETTI WESTERN made in 1964 with Clint Eastwood —see colour picture on page 685

fis·ti·cuffs /'fɪstɪkʌfs/ n [P] old use or humor fighting with the fists

fit¹ /fɪt/ v -tt- 1 [I;T not in progressive forms] to be the right size or shape (for): *The lid fits badly.* | *This jacket fits like a glove.* (=very well and closely) | *This dress doesn't fit me.* | *Will your key fit the lock?* | (fig.) *Your theory fits all the facts.* | (fig.) *They didn't give me the job because* **my face doesn't fit.** (=they do not regard me as a suitable person for that company) 2 [T (**for**) not in progressive forms] to be suitable (for): *to make the punishment fit the crime* [+obj+to-v] *Her experience and abilities fit her admirably for the job/to do the job.* —see also FITTING¹ 3 [T] to provide and put correctly into place: *We're fitting new locks/We're having new locks fitted on all the doors.* —see also FITTED (2) 4 **fit the bill** to do or be what is wanted or needed: *We needed a journalist with specialist knowledge, and he fitted the bill.*

▷ USAGE The usual past form of **fit** is **fitted,** but in the

first meaning **fit** can also be used in American English: *When he left the shop, the suit fit him perfectly.*◁

fit in phr v 1 [I;T (=**fit** sthg. ↔ **in**)] to (cause to) match or agree; HARMONIZE: *His ideas did not quite fit in with our aims.* | *Mary joined the local drama club but didn't seem to fit in, so she left.* | *I'll try to fit my holidays in with yours.* 2 [T] (**fit** sbdy./sthg. ↔ **in**) to find time to see (someone) or do (something), esp. when one is extremely busy: *Doctor Jones can fit you in on Thursday afternoon.* | *We must try and fit in a visit to Westminster Abbey while we're in London.*

fit sbdy./sthg. ↔ **out** phr v [T] to supply (a person or place) with necessary things; EQUIP or furnish: *The ship has been newly fitted out.*

fit sbdy./sthg. ↔ **up** phr v [T] 1 esp. BrE to furnish or arrange (esp. a place); EQUIP: *We had to fit up one of the bedrooms as an office.* 2 BrE sl to cause to seem guilty of a crime; FRAME² (3): *He was fitted up for the murder.*

fit² adj -tt- 1 [+**for**/to-v] right and suitable for a particular purpose, person, or situation: *I don't think she's really fit for the job.* | *a meal fit for a king* (=a very good meal) | *The health inspector said the food in the restaurant was not fit for human consumption.* | *She's not fit to be in charge of small children|not a fit person to be in charge of small children.* | *Go and wash! You're not fit to be seen.* 2 physically healthy and strong, esp. as a result of regular exercise: *He runs three miles every morning; that's why he's so fit.* | *She goes to keep-fit classes and does exercises every day.* —opposite **unfit** 3 (**as**) **fit as a fiddle/flea** infml perfectly healthy 4 **fit to be tied** AmE infml upset, anxious, or angry 5 **fit to burst** infml as if about to explode: *They were laughing fit to burst.* 6 **fit to drop** (as if) about to fall on the ground, esp. because of extreme tiredness: *We worked till we were fit to drop.* 7 **see/think fit (to do)** to decide; consider it right (to do): *It's your responsibility — you must do as you see fit.*

fit³ n [S] the particular way in which something fits: *This coat's a beautiful fit.* | *I'll try to climb through, but it's a tight fit.*

fit⁴ n 1 [(**of**)] a short attack of a slight illness or violent feeling: *a fit of coughing* | *I hit her in a fit of anger/of pique.* | (fig.) *She kept them in fits (of laughter) with her jokes.* 2 a period of loss of consciousness, with strange uncontrolled movements of the body: *She suffers from epileptic fits.* | (fig., infml) *The boss will have a fit/throw a fit* (=be very angry) *when he hears what you've done.* 3 **in/by fits and starts** continually starting and stopping; not regularly

fit·ful /'fɪtfəl/ adj irregular; happening for short periods of time: *fitful showers of rain* – ~ **ly** adv : *He slept fitfully.*

fit·ment /'fɪtmənt/ n [often pl.] BrE a piece of fitted furniture: *bathroom fitments*

fit·ness /'fɪtn̩s/ n [U] 1 the state of being physically fit: *They're doing exercises to improve their fitness.* 2 [+**for**/to-v] the quality of being suitable: *No one questions her fitness for the job/to do the job.*

fitness freak /'·· ,·/ n often derog a person who spends a lot of time doing exercises to keep their body strong and in good condition

fit·ted /'fɪtn̩d/ adj 1 [F+**with**] including (a part, piece of apparatus, etc.): *Is the car fitted with a radio?* 2 [A] fixed in place: *a fitted carpet* | *fitted cupboards*

fit·ter /'fɪtəʳ/ n 1 a person who puts together or repairs machines or electrical parts: *a gas fitter* 2 a person who cuts out clothes and/or makes them the correct size for other people

fit·ting¹ /'fɪtɪŋ/ adj fml right for the purpose or occasion; suitable: *It is fitting that we should honour their memory.* | *a fitting tribute to the dead soldiers*

fitting² n 1 [usu. pl.] something necessary that is fixed into a building but able to be moved: *electric light fittings* —compare FIXTURE 2 an occasion when one puts on clothes that are being made for one, to see if they fit: *I'm going for a fitting on Tuesday.*

Fitz·ger·ald /fɪts'dʒerəld/, **El·la** /'elə/ (1918–) an American JAZZ singer who became successful in the US in the 1940s and then internationally when she toured the world with the big bands of Duke Ellington and Count Basie

Fitzgerald, F Scott (1896–1940) an American writer known esp. for the books *Tender is the Night* and *The Great Gatsby*

Fitzgerald, Dr Gar·rett /ˈgærət/ (1926–) an Irish politician and PRIME MINISTER of the Republic of Ireland until 1987

five /faɪv/ *determiner, n, pron* **1** (the number) 5 —see TABLE 1 **2** *AmE* a five-dollar bill: *Have you got a five?*

five-and-ten /ˌ· · ˈ·/ also **dime store, five-and-dime, five-and-ten-cent store** /ˌ· · · ˈ· ˌ·/— *n AmE* a shop which sells many different types of inexpensive goods, esp. for the house: *Run down to the five-and-ten and get me a broom, please, honey.*

five-barred gate /ˌ· · ˈ·/ *n* a large gate made of wooden bars, usu. used at the entrance to a field

five o'clock shad·ow /ˌ· ·· ˈ··/ *n* [S] *infml* a darkness caused by hair growing on the face of a man who has not shaved (SHAVE) since the morning

501's /ˌfaɪv əʊ ˈwʌnz/ *n* [P] *tdmk* a type of JEANS made by Levi Strauss, Inc (LEVIS) which have buttons in the front instead of a ZIP. They are considered fashionable, esp. if they are old and faded (FADE).

fiv·er /ˈfaɪvəʳ/ *n BrE infml* £5 or a five-pound note: *It costs a fiver.* | *I've only got fivers.*

fives /faɪvz/ *n* [U] a British ball game in which the ball is hit with the hand against any of three walls —compare HANDBALL; see also **a bunch of fives** (BUNCH¹ (3))

five-spot /ˈ· ·/ *n AmE sl* a five-dollar bill

five-star /ˈ· ·/ *adj* [A] of the highest standard or quality: *a five-star hotel*

fix¹ /fɪks/ *v* [T] **1** [+obj+adv/prep] to fasten firmly in position: *I fixed it to the wall with a nail.* | *She fixed a new handle on the door.* | (fig.) *The address is fixed in my mind.* | (fig.) *He fixed his eyes on her.* | (fig.) *Don't try and* **fix the blame on** *me.* —see also FIXED **2** [(UP)] to arrange and establish (an exact time, place, price, etc.), esp. through agreement: *Let's fix (up) a time for the meeting.* | *The rent was fixed at £45.* | *Have you got anything fixed for the weekend?* (=Have you arranged to do anything?) | *If you want to meet them, I can fix it.* [+wh–] *We haven't fixed (up) where to stay yet.* [+to-v] *They've fixed to go to Borneo.* —compare FIX on, FIX up (1) **3** to repair: *I must get the radio fixed.* **4** *esp. AmE* to cook or prepare (esp. food or drink): *She's fixing breakfast.* [+obj(i)+obj(d)] *Let me fix you a drink.* **5 a** to arrange the result of (something) dishonestly: *The election was fixed.* | *She accused the chairman of fixing the vote.* **b** *infml* to influence dishonestly, esp. by BRIBERY: *Can they fix the judge?* **6** *infml* to deal with (someone who has harmed you); get even with (EVEN² (2)) **7** *AmE infml* to NEUTER² a pet, esp. a dog or cat: *We took the cat in to be fixed last week.* **8** [I (TO)] *AmE infml* to prepare or plan (to do sthg.): *I was just fixing to call you.* | *They're fixing to go camping this weekend.* **9** *tech* to protect (colours or photographic film) from the effects of light by chemical treatment

  fix on sthg./sbdy. *phr v* [T] to choose or decide after considering: *We've fixed on the 14th of April for the wedding.* —compare FIX¹ (2)

  fix sbdy./sthg. ↔ **up** *phr v* [T] **1** [(with)] *infml* to provide (someone) with something they need, usu. by making arrangements: *Can you fix me up with a bed for the night?* —compare FIX¹ (2) **2** to repair, change, or improve to make suitable for new needs: *My mother's getting too old to live on her own, so we're fixing up the spare room for her.*

  fix sbdy. **with** sthg. *phr v* [T] to look for a long time at (someone) with: *He fixed me with an intense stare and I couldn't move.*

fix² *n* **1** [C] *infml* an awkward or difficult position; PREDICAMENT: *We're in a real fix – there's nobody to look after the baby!* **2** [S] *infml* something that has been dishonestly arranged: *The election was a fix!* —see also FIX¹ (5) **3** [C (of)] *sl* (used by drug-takers) an INJECTION: *He didn't know where his next fix was coming from.* **4** [C (on)] the (calculation of) the position of a ship, spacecraft, etc., found by looking at the stars, taking measurements, etc.

fix·a·ted /fɪkˈseɪtɪd/ *adj* [F (on)] thinking, talking, etc. continuously about one particular thing, so as not to give enough attention to anything else: *The popular newspapers seem to be fixated on stories about sex and drugs.*

fix·a·tion /fɪkˈseɪʃən/ *n* **1** [(about, with)] a strong unhealthy feeling (about) or love (for); OBSESSION: *He has a fixation about cleanliness.* | *a mother fixation* **2** *tech* a stopping of the growth of the mind and character at a certain stage, so that the person remains childish

fix·a·tive /ˈfɪksətɪv/ *n* [C;U] a chemical used for sticking things together, holding things, esp. hair or false teeth, in position, or fixing colours

fixed /fɪkst/ *adj* **1** fastened; not movable or changeable: *The tables are firmly fixed to the floor.* | *The date is fixed now.* | (fig.) *He has very fixed ideas on this subject.* **2** [F (for)] *infml* supplied with something that one needs: *How are you fixed for money?* (=How much do you have?)

fixed as·sets /ˌ· ˈ··/ *n* [P] things which a business has or owns which are likely to be used over a long period of time, e.g. land, buildings, equipment, etc.

fixed cap·i·tal /ˌ· ˈ···/ *n* [U] buildings or machines which a business owns and which can be used for a long period of time in the production of other goods

fixed charge /ˌ· ˈ·/ *n* a cost which does not change for some time

fixed costs /ˌ· ˈ·/ *n* [P] costs of rent, rates, etc. which an organization has to pay even when no production is taking place

fix·ed·ly /ˈfɪksɪdli/ *adv* steadily; with great attention: *He stared fixedly at the woman in black.*

fixed star /ˌ· ˈ·/ *n* a star so distant that its movement can be measured only by very exact calculations over long periods, unlike that of the PLANETs

fix·er /ˈfɪksəʳ/ *n infml* a person who is good at arranging that a desired result or state of affairs happens, esp. by using influence or dishonesty

fix·ings /ˈfɪksɪŋz/ *n* [the+P] *AmE infml* foods that go with a main dish for a meal: *turkey with all the fixings*

Fix·it /ˈfɪksɪt/ *BrE infml* a name given to a person who manages to arrange or organize things for other people: *He's known in the hospital as Mr Fixit.* —see also Jimmy SAVILE

fix·i·ty /ˈfɪksɪti/ *n* [U] *fml* the quality of being fixed; firmness: *fixity of purpose*

fix·ture /ˈfɪkstʃəʳ/ *n* **1** something necessary, such as a bath, that is fixed into a building and sold with it: *The price includes all fixtures and fittings.* | *bathroom fixtures* —compare FITTING², FURNISHINGS **2** *BrE* a match or sports competition taking place on an agreed date: *to arrange this season's fixtures* **3** someone or something that is always present in a place or that is strongly connected with a place or activity: *I can't believe she's leaving the company – I thought she was a permanent fixture!*

fizz¹ /fɪz/ *v* [I] to make the sound of BUBBLES of gas bursting: *The firework fizzed.* | *She uncorked the champagne and it fizzed out.* (=came out fizzing)

fizz² *n* **1** [S] the sound of fizzing **2** [U] BUBBLES of gas in a liquid: *You didn't put the top back on the soda and now all the fizz has gone out of it.*

fiz·zle /ˈfɪzəl/
  fizzle out *phr v* [I] *infml* to fail or end disappointingly, esp. after a good start: *The game fizzled out into a tame draw.*

fiz·zy /ˈfɪzi/ *adj* (of a liquid) containing BUBBLES of gas

fizzy drink /ˌ·· ˈ·/ *n* a sweet, non-alcoholic drink, usu. drunk by children: *Try to reduce the number of sweets and fizzy drinks your child has.*

fjord , fiord /ˈfiːɔːd, fjɔːd‖fiːˈɔːrd, fjɔːrd/ *n* a narrow arm of the sea between cliffs or steep slopes, esp. in Norway

FL *written abbrev. for:* FLORIDA

flab /flæb/ *n* [U] *infml derog* soft loose flesh on a person's body: *She's gone on a diet and is trying to do more exercise in an effort to* **fight the flab** (=become thinner)

flab·ber·gast /ˈflæbəɡɑːst‖-ərɡæst/ *v* [T *usu. pass.*] *infml* to surprise very much; fill with shocked wonder, usu. so that one is unable to think clearly: *I was absolutely flabbergasted when she told me the price.*

flab·by /ˈflæbi/ *adj derog* **1** having soft loose flesh; (of muscles) soft and lacking firmness: *I became rather flabby after I stopped playing football regularly.* **2** lacking force or effectiveness: *a flabby, unconvincing argument* —**bily** *adv* —**biness** *n* [U]

flac·cid /ˈflæsɪd, ˈflæksɪd/ adj not firm enough; weak and soft: *flaccid plant stems* — ~ly adv — ~ity /flæˈsɪdɪti, flæk-/ n [U]

flack /flæk/ n [U] FLAK

flag¹ /flæg/ n **1** a square or OB-LONG piece of material, usu. with a pattern or picture on it, that is put up as a sign of a country, organization, etc., or to make signals. Flags are often flown at HALF-MAST when an important person has died: *The French flags were flapping/fluttering in the breeze.* | *The danger flag was flying.* (=being shown) | *The children waved their flags as the queen passed by.* | (fig.) *Most of the countries that once lived under the British flag* (=were ruled by Britain) *are now independent.*

▶CULTURAL NOTE In the US the American flag is a very important SYMBOL of the country and is supposed to be treated with respect. Children repeat the Pledge of Allegiance to the flag (= promise to be loyal to the country and its flag) at school and are usually taught how to fold it correctly. In the 1960s some American people burned the flag to protest against the Vietnam War, and many Americans felt very strongly that this was wrong.◀

2 keep the flag flying to continue to represent one's beliefs, or continue to represent one's own country in another country: *When the island became independent, only a few Dutch teachers and nurses remained to keep the flag flying.* **3 show the flag** to remind people of the political and military presence and power of one's country: *An American naval force is showing the flag in various Mediterranean ports.* —see also RED FLAG, WHITE FLAG and see picture at GOLF

flag² v -gg- [T] to put a special mark on (something) so it can be picked out from among others
 flag sthg./sbdy. ↔ **down** phr v [T] to cause (a vehicle or its driver) to stop by waving at the driver: *I tried to flag down a taxi.*

flag³ v -gg- [I] to be or become weak and less alive or active: *After walking for four hours we were beginning to flag.* | *I tried to revive his flagging interest in the subject.* —see also UNFLAGGING

flag⁴ n a FLAGSTONE

flag⁵ n a plant with long blade-like leaves that grows in wet places

flag day /ˈ· ·/ n BrE a day on which money is collected for a CHARITY by asking people in the street to give money. Those who give receive paper flags or small STICKERS

Flag Day June 14th, a day in the US when people fly the US flag, remembering the day in 1777 when the STARS AND STRIPES (=US flag) was officially accepted and first used

fla·gel·lant /ˈflædʒɪlənt, fləˈdʒelənt/ n tech someone who whips himself or herself as a religious punishment

fla·gel·late /ˈflædʒɪleɪt/ v [T] fml to whip, esp. as a religious punishment or for sexual pleasure —**lation** /ˌflædʒɪˈleɪʃən/ n [U]

flag foot·ball /ˈ· ˌ··/ n [U] a game of American football played mainly in schools in which tearing off one of the flags a player wears around his waist stops play

flag of con·ve·ni·ence /ˌ· · ·ˈ···/ n the flag of a country in which a ship owned by someone from another country is officially recorded, in order to avoid the rules and taxes of its home country

flag·on /ˈflægən/ n a large container for liquids such as wine, usu. with a lid, a handle, and a lip or SPOUT for pouring

flag·pole /ˈflægpəʊl/ n a long pole to raise a flag on, fixed in the ground or on a building

fla·grant /ˈfleɪgrənt/ adj (of a bad action or person) open and with no sign of guilt; OUTRAGEOUS: *a flagrant abuse of the*

flags

The Union Jack

The Stars and Stripes

taxpayers' money | *a flagrant liar* — ~ly adv —**grancy** n [U]

flag·ship /ˈflægʃɪp/ n **1** the chief ship among a group of naval warships, on which the ADMIRAL sails **2** the finest or most expensive product in a set of things made by a company: *The new car is the flagship of the Ford range.*

flag·staff /ˈflægstɑːf‖-stæf/ n a flagpole

flag·stone /ˈflægstəʊn/ also **flag**— n a hard, smooth, flat piece of stone for a floor or path

flag stop /ˈ· ·/ n AmE for REQUEST STOP

flag-wav·ing /ˈ· ˌ··/ n [U] derog the noisy expression of national military feeling; JINGOISM

flail¹ /fleɪl/ n a wooden tool consisting of a stick swinging from the end of a long handle, used esp. in former times for threshing (THRESH)

flail² v [I;T] **1** to beat (grain) with a flail **2** to (cause to) wave violently but aimlessly about: *He ran down the hill at full speed, his arms flailing wildly.*

flair /fleəʳ/ n **1** [S;U (for)] (a) natural ability to do some special thing well: *She has a flair for writing poetry.* **2** [U] a way of doing things which is different, interesting, and has style: *The new director certainly has got flair.*

flak , flack /flæk/ n [U] **1** firing from guns that shoot at enemy aircraft from the ground **2** infml severe disapproval or opposition: *Their proposal to increase the price of school dinners has* **run into/come in for a lot of flak.**

flake¹ /fleɪk/ n [(of)] **1** (often in comb.) a light leaf-like little bit (of something soft): *soap flakes* | *flakes of snow* **2** a thin flat broken-off piece (of something hard): *A flake of bone had lodged itself in his knee.* —see picture at PIECE

flake² v [I (OFF)] to fall off in flakes: *The paint's beginning to flake (off).*
 flake out phr v [I] infml **1** to fall asleep or become unconscious because of great tiredness **2** AmE to become slightly mad

flake³ n AmE sl a person whose behaviour is strange or slightly mad, or who behaves in a way one cannot trust: *I wouldn't depend on a ride from Kevin; he's a real flake.*

Flake n tdmk a type of milk chocolate bar made by Cadbury's

flak jack·et /ˈ· ˌ··/ n a JACKET of a heavy material with metal bands inside it to protect the wearer from FLAK. They are worn by esp. soldiers who are in danger of being hit by flak, or by people who think them fashionable.

flak·y /ˈfleɪki/ adj **1** made up of flakes or tending to break into flakes **2** AmE sl behaving irresponsibly and foolishly, and in a way one cannot trust: *My brother's getting so flaky! He locked himself out of the house yesterday.* —see FLAKE³ —**iness** n [U]

flaky pas·try /ˌ·· ˈ··/ n [U] a rich PASTRY made up of many very thin LAYERS

flam·bé /ˈflɒmbeɪ‖flɑːmˈbeɪ/ also **flam·béed** /ˈflɒmbeɪd‖flɑːmˈbeɪd/ adj Fr (of food) with alcohol such as BRANDY poured over it, and lit to give a flame

flam·boy·ant /flæmˈbɔɪənt/ adj **1** brightly coloured and noticeable: *a flamboyant orange shirt* **2** (of a person or their behaviour) showy and confident: *With a flamboyant gesture he threw off the covering to reveal the new statue.* — ~ly adv —**ance** n [U]

flame¹ /fleɪm/ n [C;U] (a area of) red or yellow burning gas seen when something is on fire: *The candle flame flickered and went out/died.* | *The dry sticks* **burst into flames.** | *The whole city was in flames.* (=burning) | *It's very dangerous to hold* **a naked flame** (=a flame which is not covered by glass, etc.) *anywhere near petrol.* —see also OLD FLAME

flame² v [I] **1** to be brightly filled with the colours of flame: *The evening sky flamed with red and orange.* | *Her cheeks flamed (red).* **2** to break out with sudden violence: *His anger flamed up.* | *He was flaming with anger.* | *I was in a* **flaming temper.** | *He had a* **flaming row** *with his wife.* —see also FLAMING

fla·men·co /fləˈmeŋkəʊ/ n [U] a form of very fast and exciting Spanish dance and music: *We went to see some flamenco dancing last night.*

flame proof /ˈ· ·/ also **flame re·sist·ant** /ˈ· ·ˌ··/ n made of a substance that does not burn easily

flame-throw·er /ˈ· ˌ··/ n a gun-like instrument that throws out flames or burning liquid under pressure, used as a weapon or in clearing wild land

flam·ing /ˈfleɪmɪŋ/ adj [A] infml (used for adding force to an expression): You flaming idiot!

fla·min·go /fləˈmɪŋɡəʊ/ n -gos or -goes a tall tropical water bird with long thin legs, pink and red feathers, and a broad beak that curves downwards −see picture at WATER BIRD

flam·ma·ble /ˈflæməbəl/ adj AmE or tech for INFLAMMABLE −opposite **nonflammable**

▷ USAGE **Flammable** and **inflammable** are not opposite in meaning. They have the same meaning, but **flammable** is used in the US and is also the British English technical word; both British English and American English use **inflammable** when it means "easily excited".◁

flan /flæn/ n a round open case of pastry or cake, with a filling of fruit, cheese, etc. −see PIE (USAGE)

Flan·ders /ˈflɑːndəz‖ˈflændərz/ a REGION of the Low Countries in what is now part of Belgium and Holland, which was an important battleground in the First World War

Flanders, Mi·chael /ˈmaɪkəl/ (1922−75) an English entertainer known esp. as one of the pair **Flanders and Swann**. He wrote the words for the many funny songs that he and Donald Swann performed together. −see also Donald SWANN

Flanders, Moll a main character in the book *The Fortunes and Misfortunes of the famous Moll Flanders* by Daniel Defoe. In the book, Moll tells the story of her many marriages, relationships, and life of crime in a way which is amusing and makes the reader sympathetic towards her.

flange /flændʒ/ n the flat edge that stands out from the main surface of an object such as a railway wheel, to keep it in position

flank¹ /flæŋk/ n **1** the side of a person or animal, between the RIBS and the HIP −see picture at HORSE **2** the side of an army at war: The enemy attacked us on the left flank.

flank² v [T often pass.] to be placed beside; BORDER: The road was flanked with/by tall trees.

flan·nel¹ /ˈflænl/ n **1** [U] a smooth loosely woven woollen or cotton cloth with a slightly furry surface: grey flannel trousers | flannel sheets −see also FLANNELS **2** [C] esp. BrE ‖ **washcloth** AmE− a piece of cloth used for washing oneself **3** [U] infml, esp. BrE meaningless though attractive words used to avoid giving a direct answer, to deceive, etc.: That's just a lot of flannel − tell me the truth!

flannel² v -ll- BrE ‖ -l- AmE [T] infml, esp. BrE to deceive, FLATTER, etc., by using FLANNEL¹ (3)

flan·nel·ette BrE ‖ also **flannelet** AmE /ˌflænəlˈet◂/ n [U] cotton cloth with a furry surface that looks like flannel: flannelette sheets

flan·nels /ˈflænlz/ n [P] esp. BrE men's flannel trousers, esp. as worn for summer games like cricket −see PAIR (USAGE)

flap¹ /flæp/ n **1** [C] a wide flat thin part of anything that hangs down, esp. so as to cover an opening: He wore a cap with flaps to cover his ears. | We crept under the flap of the tent. | Stick down the flap of the envelope. **2** [S] the sound of flapping: the slow flap of the sails **3** [S] infml a state of excited anxiety: Don't get in a flap − we'll soon find it! −see also UNFLAPPABLE

flap² v -pp- **1** [I;T] to wave (something large and soft) or move slowly up and down or backwards and forwards, usu. making a noise: The bird flapped its wings. | The sails flapped in the wind. **2** [I+adv/prep] (of a usu. large bird) to fly: The eagle flapped across the sky. **3** [I] BrE infml to be in a state of excited anxiety: There's no need to flap.

flap·jack /ˈflæpdʒæk/ n **1** a PANCAKE cooked in a pan on top of the fire **2** BrE‖**granola bar** AmE− a mixture of OATS and other things baked into a sweet cake

flap·per /ˈflæpər/ n a fashionable woman in the 1920s who wore short dresses and had modern ideas

flare¹ /fleər/ v **1** [I (UP)] to burn brightly, but with an unsteady flame or for a short time: A match flared (up) in the darkness. **2** [I;T] to (cause to) open outwards, esp. to widen gradually towards the bottom: Her nostrils flared with anger. | flared trousers

flare up phr v BrE ‖ also **flare out** AmE− [I] to show sudden increased anger, activity, or violence: Street fighting has flared up again in the big cities. | His anger flared out momentarily before he regained self-control. −**flare-up** /ˈ· ·/ n

flapper

flare² n **1** [S] a flaring light: There was a sudden flare as she lit the gas. **2** [C] (something that provides) a bright light out of doors, often used as a signal: After the ship sank the survivors fired off flares in the hope someone would see them. **3** [C] a widening towards one end: trousers with wide flares

flare path /ˈ· ·/ n a lit-up path for aircraft to land on

flares /fleəz‖fleərz/ n [P] trousers that become wider below the knee. Flares were fashionable esp. in the 1960s and '70s and are now connected in people's minds with this period.

flash¹ /flæʃ/ v **1** [I] (of a light) to appear as a sudden very bright flame or flare: The lightning flashed. | We watched the flashing lights of the cars. | (fig.) Her eyes flashed with anger. **2** [T (at)] to make a flash with; shine for a moment: Why is that driver flashing his lights (at me)? | Stop flashing that light in my face. | (fig.) She flashed a shy smile at him. [+obj(i)+obj(d)] She flashed him a shy smile. **3** [I+adv/prep] to move very fast: The days seem to flash by. | (fig.) An intriguing idea suddenly flashed across/into/through my mind. **4** [T+obj+adv/prep] to show for a moment: They flashed a message up on the cinema screen. | She flashed a £5 note at the man by the door and he let her in. | (fig.) George certainly flashes his money around! (=makes a show of having lots of money by spending it freely) **5** [T+obj+adv/prep] to send by radio, SATELLITE, etc: They flashed the news back to London. **6** [I] infml (of a man) to show the sexual organs in public, usu. in order to get sexual pleasure −compare STREAK

flash back phr v [I (to)] to return suddenly to an earlier time (as if) in a FLASHBACK: My mind flashed back to last Christmas.

flash forward phr v [I (to)] to go forward in time in a cinema film to show what happens later in the story

flash² n **1** [C (of)] a sudden quick bright light: Flashes of lightning illuminated the scene. | (fig.) a sudden flash of inspiration/wit **2** [C] a single movement of a light or flag in signalling **3** [C] infml a quick look: Go on, give me a quick flash! **4** [C] a short news report: They interrupted the programme with a **news flash** saying the President had died. **5** [C;U] (in photography) the method or apparatus for taking photographs in the dark: Did you use a flash? **6** [C] the sign of a military group, worn on the shoulder of a uniform **7 flash in the pan** a sudden success that is not repeated: His brilliant novel turned out to be a flash in the pan; he never wrote another one. **8 in a/like a/quick as a flash** infml very quickly, suddenly, or soon; (almost) at once: I'll be back in a flash.

flash³ adj **1** [A] **a** (of a flood, fire, etc.) sudden, violent, and short: Flash fires have broken out in several parts of the country. **b** (in comb.) done very quickly: flash-freezing −see also FLASH FLOOD **2** BrE infml, often derog modern, attractive, and expensive-looking; FLASHY: That's a very flash car − where did you get it?

Flash n [U] tdmk a cleaning substance made by Procter and Gamble Ltd, used to remove dirt from esp. floors; it is sold as a liquid or as a powder which can be mixed with water

flash·back /ˈflæʃbæk/ n **1** [C;U] a scene in a film, play, etc. that goes back in time to show what happened earlier in the story: The events of his childhood are shown in (a) flashback. −see also FLASH **back 2** [C] a burst of flame backwards up a tube, into a container, etc.

flash·bulb /ˈflæʃbʌlb/ n an electric lamp in which metal wire or FOIL burns brightly for a moment, used for taking a photograph

flash burn /ˈ· ·/ n a burn caused by a very sudden, very strong heat, e.g. when there is an explosion

flash·card /ˈflæʃkɑːd‖-kɑːrd/ n a card with a word, number, or picture on it used in teaching

flash·cube /ˈflæʃkjuːb/ n four flashbulbs packed together, for taking four photographs one after the other

flash·er /ˈflæʃəʳ/ n **1** something that flashes, such as a traffic signal or a light on a car **2** sl a man who habitually shows his sexual parts unexpectedly to strangers, esp. women, and is excited by the thought of shocking them —compare STREAKER; see also DIRTY MAC BRIGADE

flash flood /ˌ· ˈ·/ n a very sudden flood in a small area because of extremely heavy rain

flash freeze /ˌ· ˈ·/ v [T] AmE for QUICKFREEZE

Flash Gor·don /ˌ· ˈ··/ a character who appeared in American COMICS and films in the 1930s. In the stories, Flash Gordon travels through space and saves the Earth from many dangers.

flash·gun /ˈflæʃɡʌn/ n a piece of equipment which holds a FLASHBULB and makes it work at the moment when the photograph is taken

flash·light /ˈflæʃlaɪt/ n **1** also **flash**— esp. BrE a piece of equipment for taking flash photographs: Did you bring your flashlight|your flash? **2** esp. AmE a small electric light carried in the hand to give light; TORCH

Flash·man /ˈflæʃmən/ a character in the story Tom Brown's Schooldays who is cruel and bullies (BULLY) boys who are younger than he is —see also TOM BROWN'S SCHOOLDAYS

flash point /ˈ· ·/ n [C;U] **1** the lowest temperature at which the gas (VAPOUR) from oil will burn if a flame is put near it **2** a point or place at which violent action may be expected: I could tell from the look in his eyes that he was reaching (his) flash point. | Beirut is one of the flash points of the Middle East.

flash·y /ˈflæʃi/ adj derog unpleasantly big, bright, decorated, etc., and perhaps not of good quality: a large flashy car | cheap flashy clothes —compare FLASH³(2) —**ily** adv: flashily dressed —**iness** n [U]

flasks

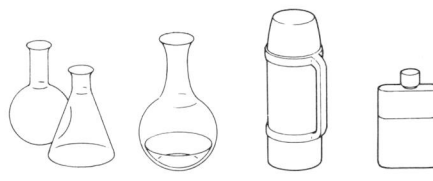

carafe　　thermos flask　　hip flask

flask /flɑːsk‖flæsk/ n **1** a narrow-necked bottle used in a LABORATORY **2** a flat bottle for carrying alcohol or other drinks in one's pocket, fastened to one's belt, etc. —see also HIP FLASK and see picture at LABORATORY **3** also **thermos flask, thermos**— a bottle with two thin glass walls between which there is a VACUUM, used to keep liquids either hot or cold **4** [(of)] the amount of liquid that a flask contains: We drank a whole flask of tea|whisky.

flat¹ /flæt/ n **1** [C] BrE ‖ **apartment** esp. AmE— a set of rooms in a building, esp. on one floor, including a kitchen and bathroom: They divided the house into flats. | Who lives in the top flat? | They're building a block of flats. —see HOUSE (USAGE) and see picture at HOUSE **2** [C] also **flats** pl.— a low level plain, esp. near water: mud flats **3** [the] (of) the flat part or side: I hit him with the flat of my hand|my sword. **4** [C] esp. AmE a flat tyre: Stop — I think we've got a flat! **5** [C] (in music) **a** a FLAT² (8) note **b** the sign (♭) for this — compare SHARP³, NATURAL² (2) **6** [C] a flat movable piece of stage scenery **7 on the flat** not on a slope; on level ground: I can walk at four miles an hour on the flat. —see also FLATS

flat² adj -tt- **1** smooth and level; not rounded or lumpy: I need something flat to write on. | Spread the map out flat on the floor. | a flat surface **2** not very thick or high: flat cakes | a flat hat **3** (of a tyre) without enough air in it **4** BrE (of a BATTERY) ‖ **dead** AmE— having lost some or all of its electrical power **5** (of beer and other gassy

drinks, or their taste) no longer fresh because the gas has been lost **6** [F] dull and lifeless: Everything seems so flat after the Christmas and New Year celebrations are over. **7** [F] (in music) lower than the correct note: You're flat. Sing it again. —compare SHARP¹ (10) **8** [after n] (of a note in music) lower than the stated note by a SEMITONE: a symphony in the key of E flat —compare SHARP¹ (11), NATURAL¹ (6) **9** [A no comp.] complete; firm; with no more argument: My request was met with a flat refusal. | The allegations provoked a flat denial. | I won't go, and that's flat! **10** [A] (of an amount of money, a charge, etc.) fixed; not variable: They charge a flat rate/flat fee. —see FLATLY, fall flat (FALL¹), lay someone/something flat (LAY² (10)) **11 flat as a pancake** very flat —~ness n [U]

flat³ adv **1** in or into a flat or level position: Spread the map out flat on the floor. **2** (in music) lower than the correct note: You're singing flat. —compare SHARP² (3) **3** infml (after an expression of time, showing surprise at its shortness) exactly; and not more: I got dressed in three minutes flat. **4 flat broke** completely without money **5 flat out** at full speed: He worked flat out to get it finished. | The car does 100 miles an hour flat out.

flat cap /ˌ· ˈ·/ n a CLOTH CAP

flat car /ˈ· ·/ n AmE a flat railway car used to carry goods

flat-chest·ed /ˌ· ˈ··◂/ adj usu. derog (of a woman) having small breasts

Flat Earth So·ci·e·ty /ˌ· ˈ· ·ˌ···/ [the] an American organization, a branch of which also exists in Britain, which believes that the Earth is flat and science cannot be trusted or believed

flat feet /ˌ· ˈ·/ n [P] a condition in which the curved bone structure in the foot is flattened, so that it rests flat on the ground. People with flat feet cannot walk for very long distances and so cannot join the army.

flat·fish /ˈflæt͵fɪʃ/ n -fish or -fishes a sea fish with a thin flat body, such as a SOLE or PLAICE

flat-foot·ed /ˌ· ˈ··◂/ adj **1** having FLAT FEET **2 catch someone flatfooted** AmE— to surprise someone, usu. unpleasantly: My mother-in-law dropped in and caught us flatfooted, with dirty dishes piled everywhere.

Flat I·ron Build·ing /ˈ· ·· ͵··/ [the] a large office building in Manhattan, New York, which is shaped like a very large iron

flat·let /ˈflætlət/ n BrE a very small FLAT¹ (1)

flat·ly /ˈflætli/ adv **1** in a dull level way: "It's hopeless," he said flatly. **2** (esp. in expressions of refusal, disagreement, etc.) completely; firmly: He flatly denied it. | She flatly refused to give us any information. — compare FLAT¹ (9)

flat·mate /ˈflætmeɪt/ n BrE someone who shares a FLAT¹ (1) with another —compare ROOMMATE

flat rac·ing /ˈ· ͵··/ n [U] the sport of horseracing on flat ground with no jumps —compare STEEPLECHASE (1)

flat rate /ˌ· ˈ·/ n a fixed rate of payment or fixed charge for a piece of work

flats /flæts/ n **1** [the+P] BrE a block of FLATS¹ (1): Do you live in the flats across the road? **2** [P] infml shoes with flat SOLES¹ (2) **3** [P] FLAT¹ (2) —compare HEELS

flat share /ˈ· ·/ n BrE an arrangement by which people, usu. young people, share a flat with each other

flat spin /ˌ· ˈ·/ n **1** (in flying) a fast and often uncontrollable drop while spinning round and round in a level position **2 go into/be in a flat spin** esp. BrE infml to go into/be in a state of excited confusion

flat·ten /ˈflætn/ v **1** [I;T (OUT)] to make or become flat: The rabbit was flattened by a passing car. | I flattened myself against the wall as the soldiers passed. | The hills flatten (out) as they near the coast. **2** [T] (in music) to play or sing (a note) flat
　flatten out phr v [I] (of an aircraft) to come to an upright position with the wings parallel to the ground: The plane did a steep dive and flattened out at 10,000 feet.

flat·ter /ˈflætəʳ/ v [T] **1** [(on)] to praise (someone) too much or insincerely, esp. in order to gain advantage: He flattered her (on her cooking). | flattering remarks —compare COMPLIMENT² **2** [often pass.] to give pleasure to: She was flattered at the invitation/flattered to be invited/flattered that they had invited her. **3** (of a picture or photograph) to make (the person shown there) look better or more beautiful: *a flattering photograph* | *The picture certainly doesn't flatter you.* **4 flatter oneself** to deceive oneself by imagining that one is more important than one really is: *"They're all watching me." "You flatter yourself!"* **5 flatter oneself (that)** to have the pleasant though perhaps mistaken opinion (that): *We flatter ourselves that we provide the best service in town.* — ~ er *n*

flat·ter·y /'flætəri/ *n* [U] **1** flattering remarks **2 flattery will get you nowhere** *saying* you will not gain what you want by saying flattering things to people

flat·top /'flæt-tɒp‖-tɑːp/ *n AmE infml* a man's haircut which is short and flat on top —**flattop** *adj* : *a flat-top haircut*

flattop

flat·u·lence /'flætjʊləns‖-tʃə-/ *n* [U] *fml* (the feeling of discomfort caused by) too much gas in the stomach —**lent** *adj*

flat·ware /'flæt,weəʳ/ *n* [U] *AmE* knives, forks, and spoons; CUTLERY

Flau·bert /'fləʊbeəʳ‖fləʊ'beər/, **Gus·tave** /'ɡʊstɑːv‖'ɡʌs-/ (1821–80) a French writer whose best known book is *Madame Bovary*

flaunt /flɔːnt‖flɔːnt, flɑːnt/ *v* [T] *derog* to show (oneself or something one is proud of) for public admiration; make (something) too plain: *She was flaunting her new fur coat.* | *I dislike the way he flaunts his success.*

flau·tist /'flɔːtɪst/ *BrE* ‖ **flutist** *AmE* — *n* someone who plays the FLUTE

fla·vour¹ *BrE* ‖ **flavor** *AmE* /'fleɪvəʳ/ *n* **1** [C] a taste; a quality that only the tongue can experience: *This dish has a strong flavour of cheese.* | *Choose from six popular flavours!* **2** [U] the quality of tasting good or pleasantly strong: *This bread hasn't much flavour/has plenty of flavour.* **3** [S] a particular quality or character: *This newspaper has a sporting flavour.* **4 flavour of the month** the idea, plan, person, etc., which is the most popular at present **5 -flavoured** /fleɪvəd‖-vərd/ having the stated flavour: *strawberry-flavoured ice cream* — ~ less *adj*

flavour² *BrE* ‖ **flavor** *AmE*— *v* [T (with)] to give flavour to: *She flavoured the cake with chocolate.*

fla·vour·ing *BrE* ‖ **flavoring** *AmE* /'fleɪvərɪŋ/ *n* [C;U] something added to food to give or improve the flavour: *All their products are free from artificial colourings and flavourings.*

flaw¹ /flɔː/ *n* [(in)] a fault or weakness that makes something not perfect: *The flaw in this stamp makes it less valuable.* | *Your argument has one fatal flaw.*

flaw² *v* [T] to make a flaw in: *The scar flawed her beauty.* | *a flawed masterpiece*

flaw·less /'flɔːləs/ *adj* perfect; with no flaw: *a flawless gem* | *a flawless performance* — ~ ly *adv*

flax /flæks/ *n* [U] **1** a plant with blue flowers, that is grown for its stem and oily seeds **2** the thread made from the stems of this plant, used for making LINEN

flax·en /'flæksən/ *adj esp. lit* (of hair) pale yellow

flay /fleɪ/ *v* [T] **1** to remove the skin from: *They flayed the dead horse.* **2** *lit* to whip violently **3** to attack severely in words: *The newspapers really flayed him.*

flea /fliː/ *n* **1** a small jumping insect without wings that feeds on the blood of humans and animals —see picture at INSECT **2 a 'flea in one's ear** *infml* a short severe scolding (SCOLD), esp. that makes one feel foolish: *He tried to kiss her, but she sent him off with a flea in his ear.*

flea·bag /'fliːbæɡ/ *n* **1** *esp. BrE* a dirty disliked person or animal: *She loves her cat, but nobody else can bear the old fleabag.* **2** *esp. AmE* a cheap dirty hotel

flea·bite /'fliːbaɪt/ *n* **1** the bite of a flea **2** *esp. BrE* a small problem or cost: *I lost £5 at the races, but that's only a fleabite.*

flea col·lar /'· ,··/ *n* a collar worn by a cat or a dog which

contains special chemicals to keep fleas away from the animal

flea mar·ket /'· ,··/ *n* a market usu. in the street, where old or used goods are sold

flea·pit /'fliː,pɪt/ *n BrE infml humor* a cheap dirty cinema or theatre

fleck¹ /flek/ *n* [(of)] a small mark or spot; a grain: *She wore a brown blouse with flecks of red.* | *flecks of dust*

fleck² *v* [T (with)] *often pass.*] to mark or cover with flecks: *The grass under the trees was flecked with sunlight.*

fledg·ling, **fledgeling** /'fledʒlɪŋ/ *n* a young bird that has developed wing feathers and is learning to fly: (fig.) *the fledgling* (=new or young) *republic*

flee /fliː/ *v* **fled** /fled/ [I;T] *esp. lit* to escape (from) by hurrying away, esp. because one is afraid: *The spectators fled in panic when the bull got loose.* | *We were forced to* **flee the country.** (=go abroad for safety)

fleece¹ /fliːs/ *n* a sheep's woolly coat —see also GOLDEN FLEECE

fleece² *v* [T] *infml* to rob by a trick; charge too much money: *They really fleeced us at that hotel!*

fleec·y /'fliːsi/ *adj* (seeming) woolly like a fleece: *a fleecy nightgown*

fleet¹ /fliːt/ *n* [C+sing./pl. v] **1** a number of ships under one command, such as warships in the navy **2** a group of buses, aircraft, etc., under one control

fleet² *adj lit* fast; quick: *a fleet-footed runner* — ~ ness *n* [U]

fleet ad·mi·ral /'· ,···/ *n* a rank in the US navy —see TABLE 3

fleet·ing /'fliːtɪŋ/ *adj* passing quickly; not lasting long: *The fans caught* **a fleeting glimpse** *of their idol as he ran into the waiting car.* — **ly** *adv*

Fleet Air Arm /,· '· ,·/ [*the*] the branch of the British navy that used to look after and fly naval aircraft

Fleet Street /'· ·/ **1** the area in London where most of the important newspaper offices used to be. Although most newspaper offices have now left Fleet Street, the name is still used to describe the newspaper industry: *Fleet Street was buzzing with excitement at the thought of a general election.* **2** (the influence of) British national newspapers/newspaper writing: *Fleet Street can make or break a politician.*

Fleet·wood Mac /,fliːtwʊd 'mæk/ a popular music group made up of British and American musicians, popular esp. in the 1960s and 1970s

Flem·ing /'flemɪŋ/, **Sir Al·ex·an·der** /,ælɪɡ'zɑːndəʳ‖-'zæn-/ (1881–1955) Scottish scientist who discovered PENICILLIN

Fleming, I·an /'iːən/ (1908–64) an English writer who wrote the many books about the SECRET AGENT James Bond

Flem·ish¹ /'flemɪʃ/ *n* [U] the Germanic language spoken in N Belgium

Flemish² *adj* of or from the part of Belgium where Flemish is spoken

flesh¹ /fleʃ/ *n* **1** [U] the soft part of the body of a person or animal that covers the bones and lies under the skin **2** [U] the soft part of a fruit or vegetable, which can be eaten —see picture at FRUIT **3** [*the*] the physical human body as opposed to the mind or soul: *His life was devoted to the* **pleasures of the flesh.** | *The spirit is willing but the flesh is weak.* **4 go the way of all flesh** *lit* to die **5 in the flesh** in real life; in physical form: *She's even more beautiful in the flesh than in photographs.* **6 make someone's 'flesh creep** to shock or frighten, esp. in a way that causes unpleasant physical feelings: *The latenight horror movie made my flesh creep.* **7 press the flesh** *infml* to shake hands with a large number of people; usu. done by members of the royal family or politicians: *The new Prime Minister was pressing the flesh and chatting to people in the crowd.* **8 (the spirit is willing but) the flesh is weak** I would like to do something but my body is not strong enough to do it

flesh² *v*

flesh sth. ↔ **out** *phr v* [T (with)] to add more substance to: *Try to flesh out your argument (with a few relevant facts).*

flesh and blood /,· · '· ·/ *n* [U] **1** relatives; family: *I must help them — they're my own flesh and blood.* **2** *esp. lit* human nature: *These sorrows are more than flesh and blood can bear.*

flesh-col·oured /ˈ· ˌ··/ *BrE* **flesh-tone** /ˈ· ·/ *AmE adj* of the colour of European people's skin: *a flower with flesh-coloured petals*

flesh·ly /ˈfleʃli/ *adj* [A] *lit* physical, esp. sexual: *fleshly desires*

flesh·pot /ˈfleʃpɒt‖-pɑːt/ *n* [*usu. pl.*] *usu. humor or derog* a place supplying good food, drink, singing and dancing, etc., esp. a place where people go for sexual pleasure

flesh wound /ˈfleʃ ˌwuːnd/ *n* a wound which does not damage the bones or the important organs of the body

flesh·y /ˈfleʃi/ *adj* **1** having much flesh; fat: *fleshy cheeks* **2** of or like flesh: *a fleshy texture* —**iness** *n* [U]

fleur-de-lis , **fleur-de-lys** /ˌflɜː də ˈliːs, -ˈliː‖ˌflɜːr dəˈliː/ *n* a pattern formed of three curved parts joined together that is used on COATS OF ARMS

flew /fluː/ *past tense of* FLY

flex¹ /fleks/ *v* [T] to bend and move (a limb, one's muscles, etc.) so as to stretch and loosen, esp. in preparation for physical exercise or work: *The runners flexed their muscles as they waited for the race to begin.*

flex² *n* [C;U] *esp. BrE* (a length of) electrical wire enclosed in a protective covering, used for connecting an electrical apparatus to a supply

flex·i·ble /ˈfleksɪbəl/ *n* **1** that can bend or be bent easily **2** that can change or be changed to be suitable for new needs, changed conditions, etc.: *We can visit you on Saturday or Sunday; our plans are fairly flexible.* — opposite **inflexible** —**bly** *adv* —**bility** /ˌfleksɪˈbɪləti/ *n* [U]

flexible friend /ˌ··· ˈ·/ *n BrE infml* a CREDIT CARD (from an advertisement for ACCESS® cards, in which the cards were given human characteristics and described as *Your flexible friend*)

flex·i·time /ˈfleksɪtaɪm/ *BrE* ‖ also **flex·time** /ˈflekstaɪm/ *AmE*— *n* [U] a system by which people work a certain number of hours each week or month, but can choose from a usu. limited range of daily starting and finishing times and are sometimes allowed to take time off work once they have completed a certain number of hours: *Do you work flexitime?*

flib·ber·ti·gib·bet /ˌflɪbətiˈdʒɪbɪt‖-bər-/ *n infml* a silly unsteady person, usu. a woman, who talks too much, etc.

flick¹ /flɪk/ *n* a short light sudden blow, or movement with a whip, finger, etc.: *He hit the ball with just a flick of the wrist.* —see also FLICKS, SKIN FLICK

flick² *v* **1** [I+*adv/prep*;T] to (cause to) move with a light quick sudden movement: *The snake's tongue flicked from side to side.* | *He flicked the switch.* | *The cow flicked the flies away with its tail.* **2** [T] to strike with a light quick sudden blow from a whip, finger, etc.: *The driver flicked the horse with his whip to make it go faster.*

flick·er¹ /ˈflɪkəʳ/ *v* **1** [I] to burn unsteadily; shine with an unsteady light: *a flickering candle* | (fig.) *The hope still flickered within her that her husband might be alive.* **2** [I;T] to (cause to) move backwards and forwards unsteadily: *Shadows flickered on the wall.* | *flickering eyelids*

flick·er² *n* [S] **1** a flickering movement or light: *We watched the flicker of the firelight on the wall.* **2** a feeling that lasts a very short time: *a flicker of interest/excitement*

flick knife /ˈ· ·/ *BrE* ‖ **switchblade** *AmE*— *n* a knife with a blade inside the handle that springs into position when a button is pressed. Flick knives are connected in people's minds with violent criminals, esp. young men who enjoy fighting.

flicks /flɪks/ *n* [*the*+P] *esp. BrE infml* the cinema

fli·er , **flyer** /ˈflaɪəʳ/ *n* **1** someone or something that flies, esp. a pilot **2** *infml for* FLYING START **3** a LEAFLET which is produced for advertising purposes and is given to people in the street or handed out door-to-door (DOOR)

flies /flaɪz/ *n* **1** [P] *BrE* the front opening of a pair of trousers; FLY⁴ (2) **2** [*the*+P] the large space above a stage from which people control and move the scenes used in a play

flight¹ /flaɪt/ *n* **1** [C;U] (an act of) flying: *She photographed the bird in flight.* | *It was the bird's first flight from the nest.* **2** [C] (the distance covered in) a journey through

air or space: *several flights a day from London to New York* | *I've booked you on a direct flight to Paris.* | *The airline provides good in-flight entertainment.* | *Flight BA 447 to Geneva* (=the plane making this journey) *is now boarding.* | *a charter flight* | *an internal flight* (=within one country) —see also CHARTER FLIGHT **3** [C] a set of stairs between one floor and the next: *She fell down a flight of stairs.* | *He lives two flights up.* **4** [C] a group of birds or aircraft flying together: *a flight of pigeons* **5** [C (**of**)] an unusually fine performance or effort of imagination: *His entertaining speech contained some amusing* **flights of fancy.** **6** [U] *esp. lit* fast movement or passage: *the flight of time* **7 in the first flight** *esp. BrE* excellent; in a leading place

flight² *n* [C;U] (an example of) the act of running away or escaping: *Our army will quickly* **put** *the enemy* **to flight.** (=make them run away) | *When the police arrived the thieves* **took** (**to**) **flight** (=ran away), *leaving the jewels behind.* | (fig.) *The crisis in the country led to a flight of capital abroad.* (=a movement of money out of the country)

flight at·ten·dant /ˈ· ·ˌ··/ *n AmE* a person who looks after the comfort of the passengers in an aircraft during the flight

flight da·ta re·cord·er /ˈ· ·· ·ˌ··/ *n* a FLIGHT RECORDER

flight deck /ˈ· ·/ *n* **1** the surface of a ship (AIRCRAFT CARRIER) used for the take-off or landing of military aircraft **2** the room in an aircraft which contains the controls and where the pilot sits

Flight into E·gypt /ˌ· ·· ˈ··/ [*the*] the story in the Bible, in which Joseph, Mary, and the baby Jesus run away to Egypt to escape from King Herod, who has ordered all male newborn children to be killed —see also HEROD, MASSACRE OF THE INNOCENTS

flight·less /ˈflaɪtləs/ *adj* unable to fly: *a flightless bird*

flight lieu·ten·ant /ˌ· ·ˈ··◂/ *n* a rank in the British airforce —see TABLE 3

flight path /ˈ· ·/ *n* the (planned) course which a plane, spacecraft, etc., takes

flight re·cord·er /ˈ· ·ˌ··/ also **flight data recorder** *fml*, **black box** *infml*— *n* a piece of equipment in an aircraft which records the speed at which the aircraft travels, the direction in which it travels, etc. This information is used to explain what has happened if an aircraft crashes.

flight ser·geant /ˈ· ˌ··/ *n* a rank in the British airforce — see TABLE 3

flight·y /ˈflaɪti/ *adj* (esp. of a woman or a woman's behaviour) unsteady; too influenced by sudden desires or ideas; often changing, esp. from one lover to another —**ily** *adv* —**iness** *n* [U]

flim·flam /ˈflɪmflæm/ *v* [T] to trick or deceive for personal gain: *He was going door-to-door flimflamming old ladies.* —**flimflam** *adj* : *a flimflam man*

flim·sy /ˈflɪmzi/ *adj* **1** (of material) light and thin: *She felt cold in her flimsy dress.* **2** (of an object) easily broken or destroyed; lacking strength: *a flimsy old wooden shed* **3** weak; that does not CONVINCE: *What a flimsy excuse!* —**sily** *adv* —**siness** *n* [U]

flinch /flɪntʃ/ *v* [I (**from**)] to move back when shocked by pain, or in fear of something unpleasant; WINCE: *She didn't flinch once when the doctor was cleaning the wound.*| (fig.) *I flinched from telling her the news.*

fling¹ /flɪŋ/ *v* **flung** /flʌŋ/ **1** [T+*obj*+*adv/prep*] to throw violently or with force, esp. with lack of care for the object that is thrown: *She flung her shoe at the cat.* | *Every morning he flings the windows open and breathes deeply.* | (fig.) *The military government flung its opponents into prison.* **2** [I+*adv/prep*;T+*obj*+*adv/prep*] to move (oneself or part of one's body) quickly or with force: *The two old friends flung their arms round one another in delight.* | *He flung out of the room in a violent rage.* **3 fling oneself into** to begin to do (something) with great eagerness: *He flung himself into the job with great enthusiasm.* **4 fling up one's hands in horror** to show signs of being very shocked

fling² *n* [S] **1** an occasion or period of enjoying oneself, often with no sense of responsibility: *Let's have a fling and eat at that expensive restaurant for a change.* | *a final fling before getting married* **2 have a fling (at)** to make an attempt (at) —see also HIGHLAND FLING

flint /flɪnt/ n **1** [C;U] (a piece of) very hard grey stone that makes small flashes of flame when struck against steel **2** [C] a small piece of iron or other metal that makes a small flash of flame when struck, used in cigarette LIGHTERS to light the gas or petrol —**flinty** adj

flint·lock /ˈflɪntlɒk‖-lɑːk/ n a type of gun used in former times

Flint·stones /ˈflɪntstəʊnz/, **The** a funny American television CARTOON about a family of cavemen (CAVEMAN) and their friends

The Flintstones

flip[1] /flɪp/ v **-pp- 1** [T] to send (something) spinning, often into the air, by striking with a light quick blow: *They flipped a coin to decide who would go first.* **2** [I] sl also **flip one's lid— a** to become mad or very angry: *My brother really flipped when I told him I'd smashed up his car.* **b** to become full of excitement and interest: *I knew you'd flip when you saw my new car.* **3 flip someone the bird** AmE infml to flip someone off

flip off phr v [T (=**flip** sbdy. ↔ **off**)] to move the middle finger upwards in the direction of someone with whom one is angry, in an extremely offensive way; **give someone the finger** (FINGER[1]): *The cabbie flipped off the driver who cut in front of him.*

flip out phr v [I] AmE infml **1** to become very angry: *He flipped out when I told him his car was totalled.* **2** to lose one's mind: *His mother flipped out and had to be institutionalized.*

flip over phr v [I;T (—**flip** sthg. ↔ **over**)] to turn over: *The pages of the magazine flipped over in the breeze.* | *He flipped the egg over in the pan.*

flip through sthg. phr v [T] to read or look at (a book, paper, etc.) rapidly or carelessly

flip[2] n **1** [C] a quick light blow, esp. one that sends something spinning into the air: *the flip of a coin* **2** [C] a SOMERSAULT, esp. when performed in the air

flip[3] adj **-pp-** infml flippant: *a flip remark*

flip-flop[1] /ˈ·-·/ BrE ‖ also **thongs** AmE— n [usu. pl.] **1** a type of open shoe (SANDAL), which is usu. made of rubber and is held on by the toes and loose at the back —see PAIR (USAGE), and see picture at SHOE **2** AmE infml a change of mind: *He has done so many flip-flops no one knows what he really thinks.*

flip-flop[2] v AmE infml [I] to change one's mind: *If he continues to flip flop on this issue, the decision will be made for him.*

flip·pant /ˈflɪpənt/ adj disrespectful about serious subjects, esp. when trying to be amusing: *A hospital is scarcely the place for such flippant remarks about death.* — ~**ly** adv —**pancy** n [U]

flip·per /ˈflɪpəʳ/ n **1** a limb of certain large sea animals, esp. SEALS, with a flat edge used for swimming **2** also **fin** AmE— a rubber shoe shaped like an animal's flipper, worn when swimming, esp. under water —see PAIR (USAGE)

Flipper an American television show of the early 1960s which was about a friendly DOLPHIN

flip·ping /ˈflɪpɪŋ/ adj, adv [A] BrE euph sl BLOODY[2]: *Don't be so flipping rude!*

flip side /ˈ·-·/ n [the] **1** the side of a record that has a song or piece of music on that is of less interest or less popular than that on the other side **2** the opposite, usually bad, side of a question or situation: *The flip side is that it may cause more pollution.*

flirt[1] /flɜːt‖flɜːrt/ v [I (**with**)] to behave with a member of the opposite sex in a way that attracts (sexual) interest and attention: *I don't like going to parties because my husband always flirts with every woman in the room.*

flirt with sthg. phr v [T no pass.] **1** to think about, but not very seriously: *I've been flirting with the idea of changing my job, but I probably won't.* **2** to risk, esp. needlessly or lightly: *Bullfighters regularly flirt with death.*

flirt[2] n usu. derog a person, esp. a woman, who regularly flirts with members of the opposite sex

flir·ta·tion /flɜːˈteɪʃən‖flɜːr-/ n **1** [U] the act of flirting **2** [C] a short love affair which is not serious **3** [C (**with**)] a passing interest in or connection with something: *After a brief flirtation with ancient languages, she finally settled on history as her subject of study.*

flir·ta·tious /flɜːˈteɪʃəs‖flɜːr-/ adj tending to flirt: *a flirtatious young girl* | *He had a flirtatious twinkle in his eye.* — ~**ly** adv — ~**ness** n [U]

flit /flɪt/ v **-tt-** [I+adv/prep] to fly or move lightly or quickly: *The birds flitted (about) from branch to branch.* —see also MOONLIGHT FLIT

float[1] /fləʊt/ v **1** [I;T] to (cause to) stay on the surface of a liquid without sinking: *Does this type of wood float?* | *We are trying to float the sunken ship.* **2** [I+adv/prep; T+obj+adv/prep] to (cause to) move easily and lightly as on moving liquid or air: *The logs floated down the river.* | *We floated the canoe out into the middle of the river.* **3** [I+adv/prep] to move aimlessly from place to place; DRIFT: *The old man floats from town to town with nowhere to go and nothing to do.* **4** [T] to suggest; offer for consideration: *The idea was first floated before the war.* **5** [T] to establish (a business, company, etc.) by selling shares —see also FLOTATION **6** [I;T] to (allow to) vary freely in value against other countries' money from day to day: *It was decided to float the pound because having a fixed value was damaging exports.* **7** [T] AmE to write (a cheque) which one does not have enough money in the bank to pay: *He personally floated cheques worth $56,000.* — ~**er** n

float[2] n **1** something that floats, esp. a piece of wood or other light object used on a fishing line or to support the edge of a fishing net —see also DEAD-MAN'S FLOAT **2** AmE (usu. in comb.) a drink with ICE CREAM floating in it: *I'll have a coke float please.* | *a root-beer float* **3** a large flat vehicle on which special shows, decorative scenes, etc., are drawn in processions —see also MILK FLOAT **4** a sum of money provided for giving change, etc.: *The sales reps in this company have floats for their travelling expenses.*

floa·ta·tion /fləʊˈteɪʃən/ n [C;U] FLOTATION

float·ing /ˈfləʊtɪŋ/ adj **1** not fixed or settled in a particular place: *London has a large floating population.* **2** tech (of a bodily part) not properly connected or not in the usual place: *a floating rib/kidney*

floating cap·i·tal /ˌ·· ·····/ also **circulating capital**— n [U] money available for carrying on a business, e.g. goods available for sale, the money the business has, and money owed to the business

floating vot·er /ˌ·· ·····/ n someone who does not necessarily vote for the same political party at each election

flock[1] /flɒk‖flɑːk/ n [C+sing./pl. v] **1** a group of sheep, goats, or birds —compare HERD[1] **2** [+of] infml a crowd; large number of people: *a flock of tourists* **3** the group of people who regularly attend a church: *The priest warned his flock against breaking God's law.*

flock[2] v [I+adv/prep] to gather or move in large numbers: *People are flocking to the cinema to see the new film.*

flock[3] n [U] **1** small pieces of wool, cotton, etc., used for filling CUSHIONS, etc. **2** soft material that forms decorative patterns on the surface of wallpaper, curtains, etc.

Flod·den /ˈflɒdn‖ˈflɑːdn/ a hillside in Northumberland, England, where a battle took place in 1513 between the Scots and the English. King James IV of Scotland and many men were killed.

floe /fləʊ/ n a large mass of ice floating on the surface of the sea

flog /flɒg‖flɑːg/ v **-gg-** [T] **1** to beat severely with a whip or stick, esp. as a punishment **2** BrE infml to sell: *He makes a living flogging encyclopedias.* **3 flog a dead horse** infml to waste time or effort by returning to a subject or argument which has already been settled: *You'll just be flogging a dead horse if you try to make her change her mind about it.* **4 flog to death** infml to spoil (a story, request, idea, etc.) by repeating too often

flog·ging /ˈflɒgɪŋ‖ˈflɑːgɪŋ/ n [C;U] (a) severe beating with a whip or stick, esp. as punishment

Flo-Jo /ˈfləʊ dʒəʊ/ (1959–   ) an American runner whose full name is **Florence Griffeth Joyner**. She won several

Olympic gold MEDALS, and was known esp. for her fashionable appearance and clothes and her long finger nails.

flood[1] /flʌd/ also **floods** pl.— n **1** the covering with water of a place that is usu. dry; a great overflow of water: *The town was destroyed by the floods after the storm.* | *The water rose to flood level.* | *The river was in flood.* (=overflowing) **2** a large quantity or flow: *There was a flood of complaints about the bad language after the show.* | *She was in floods of tears.*

flood[2] v **1** [I;T] to (cause to) be filled or covered with water: *Every spring the river floods the valley.* | *Our street floods whenever we have rain.* **2** [I] to overflow: *After such a storm I'm surprised the river hasn't flooded.* **3** [I+adv/prep;T] to go or arrive (at) in large numbers: *Requests for information flooded in after the advertisement.* | *Settlers flooded from Europe to America in the 19th century.* | *After the show, complaints flooded the television company's offices.* **4** [I+adv/prep;T] to cover or spread into completely; OVERFLOW: *The room was flooded with light.* | *Apples* **flooded the market** (=were for sale in large numbers), *so their price went down.*

flood sbdy. ↔ **out** phr v [T usu. pass.] to force to leave home because of floods: *Most of the people who were flooded out during the storm have now returned home.*

Flood [the] **1** the story told in the Bible of a great flood that covered the whole world. According to the story, God caused the Flood because he was angry at the wickedness of people on Earth and wanted to punish them. He made it rain for 40 days and 40 nights, and most of the people and animals on Earth were killed. Only one man, Noah, and his family were saved. God told them to build a large boat (ARK) and to save two of every kind of animal. When the Flood was going down Noah sent out a DOVE to look for land, and it returned carrying an OLIVE BRANCH to show that the land was reappearing. —see also ARK, OLIVE BRANCH **2 before the Flood** infml a very long time ago

flood·gate /'flʌdgeɪt/ also **floodgates** pl.— n **1** a gate used for controlling the flow from a large body of water **2 open the floodgates** to allow feelings to be suddenly expressed or action suddenly taken after being (forcibly) held back: *The new law opened the floodgates as many more people suddenly applied for government aid.*

flood·light[1] /'flʌdlaɪt/ n (a large electric light that produces) a very powerful and bright beam of light, used for lighting the outside of buildings, football grounds, etc., at night

floodlight[2] v **-lighted** or **-lit** /lɪt/ [T] to light by using floodlights: *Buckingham Palace is floodlit at night.*

flood plain /'· ·/ n the usu. flat areas of land on either side of a river which are (regularly) covered with water when the level of the river rises: *the flood plain of the Ganges*

flood tide /'· ·/ n the flow of the TIDE inwards; rising tide —opposite **ebb tide**

floor[1] /flɔːʳ/ n **1** [C] the surface on which one stands indoors; surface nearest the ground: *I must sweep the kitchen floor.* | *A* **dance floor** *is a level area specially prepared for dancing.* —see LAND (USAGE) **2** [C] a level of a building; STOREY: *Our office is on the sixth floor.* | *the third floor* (=the people who live or work there) *are having a Christmas party tomorrow.* —see USAGE **3** [the (of)] the bottom of the sea, a CAVE, etc.: *the ocean floor* **4** [the] the part of a parliament, council building, public meeting place, etc., where those attending sit: *The member for Brighton* **has the floor.** (=has the right to speak, so others must not interrupt) | *After the visiting speaker has finished, I shall ask for questions* **from the floor.** (=from those listening) **5 go through the floor** infml (of a price) to sink to a very low level **6 take the floor**

Flo-Jo

to start dancing at a party, in a dance hall, etc. —see also SHOP FLOOR, **wipe the floor with** (WIPE[1])

▷ USAGE In American English the bottom floor of a building (at ground level) is called the **first floor.** In British English this is called the **ground floor.** The next level up is called the **second floor** in American English and the **first floor** in British English.◁

floor[2] v [T] **1** to provide with a floor: *The room was floored with tiles.* **2** infml to knock down: *The soldier floored his attacker with one heavy blow.* | (fig.) *The news really floored me; I hadn't been expecting it at all.* **3** infml to beat; defeat: *I was floored by his argument and had to admit defeat.*

floor·board /'flɔːbɔːd‖'flɔːrbɔːrd/ n a board in a wooden floor

floor cloth /'· ·/ n esp. BrE a piece of cloth used for washing or cleaning floors

floor cov·er·ing /'· ,···/ n [C;U] something used to cover a floor, e.g. CARPET: *We'll need some sort of floor covering.*

floor·ing /'flɔːrɪŋ/ n [U] material used for making floors: *wooden flooring*

floor lamp /'· ·/ n AmE for STANDARD LAMP —see pictures at LIGHT and LIVING ROOM

floor lead·er /'· ,···/ n a leader in the House of Representatives or Senate who is elected by the members of his political party. Floor leaders help arrange the timetable and work to pass bills that are important to their party.

floor mod·el /'· ,··/ [I] also **floor sample** AmE— n an electrical APPLIANCE for the home such as a washing machine or piece of furniture which has been on show in a shop and is often sold at a cheaper price

floor show /'· ·/ n a number of acts (such as dancing, singing, etc.) performed in a restaurant, NIGHTCLUB, etc.

floor·walk·er /'flɔː,wɔːkəʳ‖'flɔːr-/ n esp. AmE for SHOPWALKER

floo·zy , **-zie**, **-sie** /'fluːzi/ n old-fash derog sl a girl or woman who is, or appears to be, sexually immoral

flop[1] /flɒp‖flɑːp/ v **-pp-** [I] **1** [+adv/prep] to move or fall in a loose, heavy, or awkward way: *She flopped down exhausted in an armchair.* **2** infml (of a plan, performance, etc.) to fail; be unsuccessful: *The new play flopped and was taken off Broadway after a week.*

flop[2] n **1** [S] the movement or noise of flopping: *He fell with a flop into the water.* **2** [C] infml a failure: *The party was a complete flop.* —see also BELLY FLOP

flop·house /'flɒphaʊs‖'flɑːp-/ n **-houses** /ˌhaʊzɪz/ AmE sl a cheap hotel

flop·py[1] /'flɒpi‖'flɑːpi/ adj soft and falling loosely: *a floppy hat* —**pily** adv —**piness** n [U]

floppy[2] n a floppy disk

floppy disk /ˌ··· '·/ n a piece of bendable plastic with a thin coat of a MAGNETIC substance on which information for a computer can be stored —compare HARD DISK, and see picture at COMPUTER

Flop·sy /'flɒpsi‖'flɑːp-/ a rabbit character in several stories for children by Beatrix Potter: *Flopsy, Mopsy, Cottontail and Peter*

flo·ra /'flɔːrə/ n [C;U] all the plants of a particular place, country, or period: *the flora of chalk areas* | *stone-age flora* —compare FAUNA

Flora n tdmk [U] a kind of MARGARINE available in Britain

flo·ral /'flɔːrəl/ adj of flowers: *He chose a nice material with a floral pattern for the curtains.*

Flor·ence /'flɒrəns‖'flɔː-/ a city in central Italy, famous for its art and ARCHITECTURE

flor·id /'flɒrɪd‖'flɔː-, 'flɑː-/ adj **1** often derog too much decoration; (too) showy: *He played the piece in a very florid style, with lots of extra ornamental flourishes.* **2** having a red face: *a florid complexion* —**~ly** adv

Flor·i·da /'flɒrɪdə‖'flɔː-/ written abbrev: **FL** a state in SE US. Florida is known in the US for its good weather all year round, and many older people RETIRE there (=go there to live when they have stopped working). In the spring, many college and university students go to cities near the beaches in Florida for a short holiday. —see colour map on pages 1374–5

Florida Keys /ˌ··· '·/ [the+P] a group of small islands and REEFs off the southern coast of Florida, where many

American people go on holiday —see colour map on pages 1374–5

flor·in /ˈflɒrɪ̱n‖ˈflɔː-, ˈflɑː-/ n (in Britain before 1971) a silver-coloured coin worth two SHILLINGs, ten of which made £1 (a pound)

flor·ist /ˈflɒrɪst‖ˈflɔː-/ n a person who owns or works in a shop (**florist's**) which sells flowers: *He had a dozen red roses sent to his wife from the florist's.*

Flor·sheim /ˈflɔːʃaɪm ‖ ˈflɔːr-/ tdmk an American company which makes good quality shoes, which are often called FLORSHEIMS

floss[1] /flɒs‖flɑːs, flɔːs/ n [U] fine silk, spun (SPIN) but not twisted, used for sewing, etc. —see also CANDYFLOSS, DENTAL FLOSS

floss[2] v [T] AmE to clean (one's teeth) with DENTAL FLOSS

flo·ta·tion , floa- /fləʊˈteɪʃən/ n [C;U] an act or the action of getting money or other support in order to start up a business company: *a share flotation*

flo·til·la /fləˈtɪlə‖fləʊ-/ n a group of small ships, esp. warships

flot·sam /ˈflɒtsəm‖ˈflɑː-/ n [U] broken pieces of wood, plastic, and other waste materials from a shipwreck floating about together in the sea, or washed up onto the shore —compare JETSAM

flotsam and jet·sam /ˌ···ˈ···/ n 1 [U] a collection of broken unwanted things lying about in an untidy way 2 [P] people without homes or work, who move helplessly through life: *the flotsam and jetsam of society*

flounce[1] /flaʊns/ v [I+adv/prep] to move violently, esp. to express anger or attract attention: *She slapped him on the face and flounced off in a huff.*

flounce[2] n a band of cloth gathered and sewn onto clothing as a decoration, esp. in fashions of former times — **flounced** adj: *a flounced skirt*

floun·der[1] /ˈflaʊndər/ v [I] 1 to move about helplessly or with great difficulty, esp. in water, mud, snow, etc.: *The little dog was floundering around in the snow, so I picked it up.* | *The fish floundered on the river bank, struggling to breathe.* 2 to struggle or lose control when speaking or doing something: *When one of his listeners laughed rudely, he lost the thread of his argument and started floundering.*

flounder[2] n **flounder** or **flounders** a small flat fish, used as food

flour[1] /flaʊər/ n [U] powder made by crushing grain, esp. wheat, and used for making bread, pastry, cakes, etc. — see also PLAIN FLOUR, SELF-RAISING FLOUR

flour[2] v [T] to cover with flour: *Flour the pastry board so that the dough doesn't stick to it.*

flour·ish[1] /ˈflʌrɪʃ‖ˈflɜːrɪʃ/ v 1 [I] to be alive and well; to grow healthily: *Very few plants will flourish without sunlight.* | *"How are the children?" "They're flourishing!"* 2 [I] to be active and successful: *The company has really flourished since we moved our factory to Scotland.* | *Jazz flourished in America in the early part of the century.* | *a flourishing black market* 3 [T] to wave in the hand and so draw attention to (something): *"I've passed my exam!" shouted the boy, flourishing a letter in his mother's face.* — **~ingly** adv

flourish[2] n 1 a showy movement or manner that draws people's attention to one: *He opened the door with a flourish.* 2 a decorative curve in writing 3 a loud showy part of a piece of music, esp. one to mark the entrance of an important person

flour·mill /ˈflaʊəˌmɪl‖-ər-/ n a place where flour is made from grain; MILL

flour·y /ˈflaʊəri/ adj 1 covered with flour: *She was making pastry and her hands were floury.* 2 soft and rather powdery: *floury potatoes*

flout /flaʊt/ v [T] to treat without respect; go against: *No one can flout the rules and get away with it.*

flow[1] /fləʊ/ v [I] 1 to move smoothly (as if) in a stream: *The river flowed along rapidly.* | *Blood was flowing from his wound.* | *The cars flowed in a steady stream along the main road.* | (fig.) *As they sat around the fire, the conversation began to flow freely.* 2 (of the TIDE) to rise; come in —see also FLOWING

flow[2] n 1 [S (of)] a smooth steady movement or supply: *He could not staunch the flow of blood.* | *The flow of oil*

had to be cut off because of the threat of fire. | *Her questions interrupted his flow of thought.* | *The flow of traffic is always slow at rush hours.* | *His method of treating the disease goes against the flow of* (=is in opposition to) *current medical opinion.* – see also CASH FLOW 2 *[the (of)]* the rise (of the TIDE) —compare EBB[1] (1)

flow·chart /ˈfləʊtʃɑːt‖-ɑːrt/ also **flow di·a·gram** /ˈ·· ˌ···/‖ **flow sheet** AmE – n a drawing in which particular shapes and connecting lines are used for showing how each particular action in a system is connected with or depends on the next or another: *The factory manager used a flowchart to explain the production process.* – **flowchart** v [T]

flowers

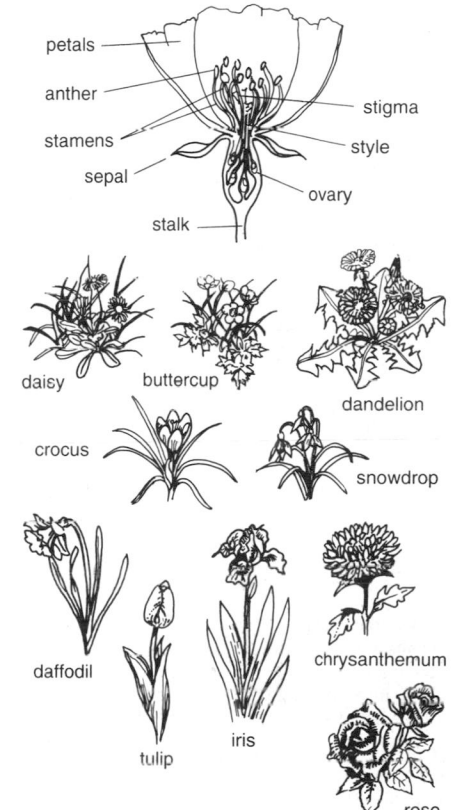

petals
anther
stamens
sepal
stalk
stigma
style
ovary

daisy
buttercup
dandelion
crocus
snowdrop
daffodil
chrysanthemum
tulip
iris
rose

flow·er[1] /ˈflaʊər/ n 1 [C] the part of a plant, often beautiful and coloured, that produces seeds or fruit: *There was a vase of flowers on the table.* | *The roses are **in flower*** (=the flowers are open) *now.* | *He used to send her huge bouquets of flowers.*

▶ CULTURAL NOTE Flowers are often given to someone as a sign of love, to say thank you to someone, or to say sorry. Flowers are also put on the grave of someone who has died, and are given to people in hospital to make them feel better. ◀

2 [C] a plant that is grown for the beauty of this part: *He grows flowers in the front garden, and vegetables in the back.* 3 *[the+of]* lit the best part; the most perfect (of a group): *The flower of the nation's youth was lost in the war.* 4 **say it with flowers** a phrase used by sellers of flowers to encourage people to give flowers to others to show their feelings 5 **the flowers that bloom in the spring, Tra la** quote a phrase from the OPERA *Mikado* by Gilbert and Sullivan – **~less** adj: *Ferns are flowerless plants.*

flower[2] v [I] 1 (of a plant) to produce flowers: *This bush flowers in the spring.* | *flowering plants* 2 fml to be fully developed; be in its best state: *His genius as a painter flowered very early.*

flower ar·rang·ing /ˈ··· ·ˌ··/ n [U] the art of arranging fresh or dried (DRY) flowers in an attractive way. It is usu. done by women, as a HOBBY, and is often taught at evening classes.

flow·er·bed /ˈflaʊəbed‖-ər-/ also **bed**— n a piece of prepared ground in which flowers are grown —see picture at HOUSE

flower child /ˈ·· ˌ·/ n —**children** AmE one of the FLOWER PEOPLE

flow·ered /ˈflaʊəd‖-ərd/ adj decorated with flower patterns: *flowered dress material*

flower girl /ˈ··· ·/ n **1** BrE a girl or woman who sells flowers in a street or market **2** AmE a little girl who carries flowers in a wedding procession —compare BRIDESMAID, BEST MAN, MATRON OF HONOUR, PAGE BOY

flow·er·ing /ˈflaʊərɪŋ/ n [S] a high point of development: *Many would say the Renaissance saw the finest flowering of European culture.*

flower peo·ple /ˈ·· ˌ··/ BrE ‖ **flower children** AmE— n [the+P] young people in the 1960s and 1970s who were in favour of peace, love, and beauty and often carried flowers to show their beliefs. They were known for their long hair, unusual clothes, and use of SOFT DRUGS. In the US, they joined the protests against the Vietnam War and used the phrase "Make Love not War" —see also HIPPIE

flow·er·pot /ˈflaʊəpɒt‖-ərpɑːt/ n a plastic or clay pot in which plants can be grown —see picture at POT

Flowerpot Men /ˈ··· ˌ·/, **The** two characters in a British television programme for young children popular in the 1960s. The Flowerpot Men were two small men made out of flowerpots who spoke in strange voices and whose names were Bill and Ben. They had a friend called Little Weed, who was a tall flower.

flower po·wer /ˈ·· ˌ··/ n [U] the beliefs and way of life of the flower people, thought of esp. in connection with certain events or occasions, e.g. the POP music FESTIVAL at Woodstock

flow·er·y /ˈflaʊəri/ adj **1** decorated with flowers: *a flowery pattern* **2** usu. derog (of speech or writing) full of fanciful words and expressions; not expressed simply and clearly

flow·ing /ˈflaʊɪŋ/ adj [A] moving, curving, or hanging gracefully: *The letter was written in flowing handwriting.* — ~ly adv

flown /fləʊn/ past participle of FLY

flow sheet /ˈ· ·/ n AmE for FLOW CHART

fl. oz. n written abbrev for: FLUID OUNCE

flu /fluː/ also **influenza** fml— n [U] an infectious disease which is like a bad cold but more serious: *She's in bed with flu.*

flub /flʌb/ v [I;T] AmE infml to make a mistake: *He flubbed his lines.* | *I really flubbed that test.*

fluc·tu·ate /ˈflʌktʃueɪt/ v [I] to change continually or frequently: *The price of vegetables fluctuates according to the weather.* | *His feelings fluctuated between excitement and fear.* —**-ation** /ˌflʌktʃuˈeɪʃən/ n [C;U (in)]

flue /fluː/ n a metal pipe or tube, esp. in a chimney, through which smoke or heat passes: *The fire won't burn because the flue's blocked up.* —see picture at FIREPLACE

flu·ent /ˈfluːənt/ adj **1** (in) (of a person) speaking, writing, or playing a musical instrument in an easy smooth manner: *He is fluent in five languages.* **2** (of speech, writing, etc.) expressed readily and without pause: *She speaks fluent English.* — ~ly adv —**ency** n [U (in)]

fluff¹ /flʌf/ n **1** [U] thin soft hair or feathers; DOWN⁶ **2** [U] esp. BrE soft light loose waste from woollen or other materials: *The room hasn't been properly cleaned; there's fluff and dust under the furniture.* **3** [C] infml an awkward unsuccessful attempt, esp. at acting or at playing a stroke in a game —see also BIT OF FLUFF

fluff² v [T] **1** [(OUT, UP)] to make (something soft) appear larger by shaking or by brushing or pushing upwards: *The bird fluffed (out) its feathers in the sun.* **2** infml to do (something) badly or unsuccessfully: *The actress fluffed her lines.* (=forgot what she had to say) | *The cricketer fluffed the catch.* (=dropped the ball he was trying to catch)

fluff·y /ˈflʌfi/ adj like or covered with fluff: *a fluffy little kitten* —**iness** n [U]

flu·id¹ /ˈfluːɪd/ adj **1** having the quality of flowing, like liquids, air, gas, etc.; not solid **2** unsettled; not fixed: *We've only just begun to plan the work, and our ideas on the subject are still fluid.* — ~ity /fluːˈɪdɪti/ n [U]

fluid² n [C;U] **1** a liquid: *The doctor removed some fluid from her injured knee.* | *He's still very weak, and must be fed fluids only.* **2** tech any fluid substance

fluid ounce /ˌ·· ˈ·/ n (a unit of liquid measurement equal to) 0.05 (1/20) of a PINT or 0·0284 of a litre in Britain, and to 0.0626 (1/16) of a pint in the US

fluke /fluːk/ n infml a piece of accidental good fortune: *He passed his examination by a fluke; he knew very little about his subject.* | *a fluke discovery* —**fluky, -ey** adj: *a fluky shot*

flume /fluːm/ n a sloped channel through which water flows: *The creek is diverted into a concrete flume just above the town.*

flum·mox /ˈflʌməks/ v [T] infml to confuse completely: *She was completely flummoxed by the second question.*

flung /flʌŋ/ past tense & participle of FLING

flunk /flʌŋk/ v infml, esp. AmE **1** [I;T] to fail (an examination or study course): *"Did you pass?" "No, I flunked."* | *He flunked chemistry.* **2** [T] to mark the examination answers of (someone) as unsatisfactory: *The teacher flunked her.*

flunk out phr v [I (of)] AmE infml to be dismissed from a school or college for failure: *He flunked out of college but went on to become a successful businessman.*

flun·key, -ky /ˈflʌŋki/ n **1** sometimes derog a male servant in ceremonial dress **2** derog a person who tries to win someone's favour by behaving with too much respect and obedience or by over-praising them: *The princess was always surrounded by flunkeys.*

flu·o·res·cent /fluəˈresənt‖fluə-, flɔː-/ adj **1** (of a substance) having the quality of giving out bright white light when electric or other waves are passed through **2** (of lighting) producing light by means of electricity passed through a tube covered with fluorescent material **3** (of colours) very bright and seeming to give out light: *She was wearing a fluorescent pink t-shirt.* —**cence** n [U]

flu·o·ri·date /ˈfluərɪdeɪt‖ˈfluə-, ˈflɔː-/ v [T] to add fluoride to (a water supply) in order to protect people's teeth —**dation** /ˌfluərɪˈdeɪʃən‖ˌfluə-, ˌflɔː-/ n [U]

flu·o·ride /ˈfluəraɪd/ n [U] a compound of fluorine, esp. one that helps protect teeth against decay, contained in many TOOTHPASTES

flu·o·rine /ˈfluəriːn/ n [U] a non-metallic substance, usu. in the form of a poisonous pale greenish-yellow gas

fluo·ro·car·bon /ˌfluərəʊˈkɑːbən‖-ˈkɑːr-/ n any chemical which contains the simple substances FLUORINE and CARBON in a particular atomic arrangement. Fluorocarbons are widely used in industry; and their presence in the air is thought to have damaged the OZONE LAYER. —see also CFC

flur·ry¹ /ˈflʌri‖ˈflɜːri/ n **1** [C] a sudden sharp rush of wind or rain or light fall of snow: *Snow flurries are expected this evening.* **2** [S (of)] sudden confusion or excitement: *A flurry of excitement went round the hall as the party leader came in.*

flurry² v [T often pass.] to confuse; make nervous and uncertain

flush¹ /flʌʃ/ n **1** [C] an act of cleaning with a sudden flow of liquid, esp. water: *The pipe is blocked; give it a good flush (out).* **2** [C] an apparatus for cleaning a TOILET with a flow of water **3** [S] a red appearance of the face: *The sick boy had an unhealthy flush and breathed with difficulty.* —see also HOT FLUSH **4** [S+of] a sudden feeling of anger, excitement, etc.: *a flush of anger/triumph* **5 in the first flush of** in the first part of something pleasant: *In the first flush of success he ordered drinks for everybody.* | (euph or humor) *She's no longer in the first flush of youth.* (=is no longer young)

flush² v **1** [T (OUT)] to clean or drive out by a sudden flow of water: *The waste pipe is blocked; try flushing it (out) with hot water.* **2** [I;T] to (cause to) become empty of waste matter by means of a flow of water: *The toilet won't flush; I've tried flushing it several times, but it won't work.* **3** [T+obj+adv/prep] to make (someone) leave a hiding place: *The police flushed the criminals out of their lair.* | *to flush birds from their hiding places* **4** [I;T *usu. pass.*] to (cause) to become red in the face: *The young man flushed with embarrassment when his stomach rumbled loudly in the middle of the meeting.* —see also FLUSHED

flush³ *adj* **1** [(with)] exactly on a level (with); even in surface: *These cupboards are flush with the wall.* (=they do not stick out) | *a flush door* **2** [F] *infml* having plenty of money: *He felt very flush on his first payday, and bought drinks for everyone.*

flush⁴ *adv* [+prep] **1** in a FLUSH³ (1) way: *The door fits flush into its frame.* **2** *infml* exactly; fully: *I hit him flush on the jaw.*

flush⁵ *n* (in card games) a set of cards dealt to a person, in which all the cards belong to only one of the four different types (SUITS (2)) —compare RUN² (12); see also ROYAL FLUSH

flushed /flʌʃt/ *adj* [F+with] excited and eager; filled with pleasure and pride: *The soldiers, flushed with their first success, went on to gain another victory.*

flus·ter¹ /ˈflʌstəʳ/ *v* [T] to cause (someone) to be nervous and confused: *The shouts of the crowd flustered the speaker and he forgot what he was going to say.* | *Take your time; don't get flustered.*

fluster² *n* [S] a state of being flustered: *I got in an awful fluster at the traffic lights, so I failed my driving test.*

flute¹ /fluːt/ *n* a musical instrument of the WOODWIND family, with no REED, played by holding it sideways, and blowing across it —see picture at WOODWIND

flute² *v* [T] to make long thin inward curves in (something) as a decoration, esp. parallel curves along the whole length of a pillar: *a fluted column* | *a pastry case with fluted edges*

flut·ing /ˈfluːtɪŋ/ also **flutings** *pl.*— *n* [U] a set of hollow curves cut on a surface as decoration: *The plates and dishes of this old dinner set are edged with fluting.*

flut·ist /ˈfluːtɪ̩st/ *n AmE for* FLAUTIST

flut·ter¹ /ˈflʌtəʳ/ *v* **1** [I;T] (of a bird, an insect with large wings, etc.) to move (the wings) quickly and lightly: *The bird fluttered her wings up and down, hoping to frighten the cat away from her eggs.* | *The butterfly fluttered from flower to flower.* **2** [I] (of a thin object) to move by waving quickly and lightly: *The flag fluttered in the wind.* | *The dead leaves fluttered to the ground.* **3** [I;T] to (cause to) move in a quick irregular way: *The boy's heart fluttered with excitement.* | *She fluttered her eyelashes at him.*

flutter² *n* **1** [S] a fluttering movement: *There was a flutter of wings among the trees.* **2** [S] *infml* an excited condition; state of excited interest: *The news of the Queen's visit to the factory put them in/into a flutter.* **3** [C *usu. sing.*] *infml, esp. BrE* the risking of a small amount of money; a small BET: *He likes to have a flutter on the horses.* **4** [C] *med* an irregular movement of the heart **5** [U] *tech* a shaking movement that causes a fault in the action of a machine, esp. in the wings of an aircraft or in a machine for playing recorded sound, causing faulty high sounds —compare WOW⁴

flu·vi·al /ˈfluːviəl/ *adj tech* of, found in, or produced by rivers

flux /flʌks/ *n* [U] **1** continual change; condition of not being settled: *Our future plans are very unsettled. Everything's in a state of flux.* **2** a substance added to a metal to help melting, or to help in soldering (SOLDER) two pieces of metal together

fly¹ /flaɪ/ *v* flew /fluː/, flown /fləʊn/ **1** [I] to move or be moved through the air by means of wings: *Most birds and some insects fly.* | *A bee flew in through the open window.* | *The damaged aircraft was flying on only one engine.* **2** [I;T] to control and guide (an aircraft or similar vehicle) in flight: *He was the first man ever to fly that type of aircraft.* | *She's learning to fly.* (=to be a pilot) **3** [I] to travel by aircraft: *Are you going by train or are you going to fly?* | *He's never flown before.* **4** [T *pass. rare*] to use (a particular AIRLINE) for travelling by: *I always fly British Airways.* **5** [T] to carry or send (someone or something) in an aircraft: *How many passengers does this airline fly weekly?* | *He's flying his car to Europe.* **6** [T] to cross (a broad stretch of water) by means of flying: *Louis Blériot was the first man to fly the English Channel.* **7** [I] to pass up into or through the air as a result of the wind or some directed force: *The player gave a great kick, and the foot-*

ball flew across the field. | Arrows were flying thick and fast from the fort. | (fig.) Angry words were flying as the crowd grew more and more threatening. **8** [I;T] to (cause to) wave or float in the air while being fixed at one end: *The national flag was flying from its pole.* | *The warship was flying the national flag.* **9** [I] to pass rapidly; hurry; move at speed: *The day has simply flown (by).* | *The train flew past.* | *I'm late; I must fly.* (=leave quickly) **10** [I+adv/prep] to move suddenly and with force: *The window flew open.* | *The head of the hammer was loose, and it flew off the handle.* | (fig.) *He flew into a temper/a rage when I mentioned her name.* **11** [I (from);T] to escape (from); FLEE: *He was forced to fly the country.* | *The thief was flying from justice.* **12** fly a kite *BrE* to say or do something in order to find out what the public opinion about a particular subject is **13** fly in the face of to intentionally act in opposition to (what is usual, reasonable, etc.); DEFY: *Such behaviour flies in the face of convention.* **14** fly off the handle *infml* to become suddenly and unexpectedly angry **15** Go fly a kite *AmE* Go away and stop being annoying! **16** knock/send someone/something flying: **a** to knock (someone) over or backwards **b** to cause (something) to move through the air, esp. by hitting it hard **17** let fly (at): **a** to attack with blows or words **b** to shoot —see also FLYING, FLYING COLOURS **as the crow flies** (CROW¹); see DRIVE (USAGE)

fly at sbdy./sthg. || also **fly into** sbdy./sthg. *AmE— phr v* [T *no pass.*] to attack suddenly and violently: *The fierce dog flew at the postman.*

fly² *v* flied [I] (in BASEBALL) to hit a FLY BALL, esp. one that is caught by a player from the other team: *He flies to right field and Smith catches the ball easily.*

fly out *phr v* [I] (in BASEBALL) to be put OUT¹ (16) by hitting a FLY BALL which a player from the other team catches: *He flied out to left field.*

fly³ *n* **1** (*often in comb.*) a small flying insect with two wings, esp. the HOUSEFLY —see picture at INSECT **2** a hook that is made to look like a fly, used for catching fish **3** a FLYSHEET **4** a FLY BALL **5** fly in the ointment *infml* something that spoils the perfection of something, makes something less valuable, pleasurable, etc.: *I've been offered a wonderful job — the only fly in the ointment is that the pay is not too good.* **6** like flies *infml* in very large numbers: *The plague raged through the city, and people were dying like flies.* **7** on the fly *AmE infml* quickly; without stopping: *She ate her sandwiches on the fly.* **8** there are no flies on someone *BrE infml* someone is not a fool and cannot be tricked

fly⁴ *n* **1** a band of strong cloth (CANVAS) over the entrance to a tent, forming a kind of door **2** also **flies** *pl. BrE*— the front opening of a pair of trousers, with a band of cloth on one side to cover the fastenings: *Your fly is undone.* | *He did up his fly buttons.*

fly⁵ *adj old-fash infml, esp. BrE* sharp and clever; not easily tricked

fly·a·way /ˈflaɪəweɪ/ *adj* [A] (esp. of hair) soft and loose and easily falling out of place

fly ball /ˈ· ·/ also **fly**— *n* (in BASEBALL) a ball which has been hit into the air: *It's a long fly ball to left field.*

fly-blown /ˈflaɪbləʊn/ *adj* **1** (of meat) containing flies' eggs and so unfit to eat **2** *esp. BrE* || **flyspecked** *esp. AmE*— covered with the small spots that are the waste matter of flies: *a dirty flyblown window* **3** *derog* **a** not pure or bright and new; in a bad condition: *a few flyblown old chairs* **b** worthless because used many times before: *He always brings out the same flyblown old stories when he makes an after-dinner speech.*

fly-boy /ˈ· ·/ *n AmE infml* an AIRFORCE pilot

fly-by /ˈflaɪbaɪ/ *n* -bys *AmE* **1** *for* FLYPAST **2** a flight of a SPACECRAFT close to the moon or a star, esp. to collect information **3** a spacecraft that makes a flyby

fly-by-night /ˈ· · ˌ·/ *adj* [A] *derog* not firmly established in business, but interested only in making quick profits, esp. by slightly dishonest methods

fly·catch·er /ˈflaɪˌkætʃəʳ/ *n* a small bird that catches flies in the air

fly drive /ˈ· ˌ·/ *adj* (of a holiday) by plane and then with a car available for one's use: *We're taking a fly drive holiday to Italy this year.*

fly·er /ˈflaɪəʳ/ *n* a FLIER

fly·fish·ing /'·ˌ··/ n [U] the practice of fishing in a river or lake with a FLY² (2)

fly half /ˌ·ˈ·/ also **standoff half**— n (in RUGBY) a fast-running player whose job is to pass the ball out to the line of players who will try to gain points with it

fly·ing¹ /'flaɪ-ɪŋ/ adj [A] **1** (of a jump) made after running: *The stream was several feet wide, but she took a flying leap and got safely across.* **2** lasting a very short time: *It's just a flying visit; we can't stay long.*

flying² n [U] travelling by aircraft, as a means of getting from one place to another or as a sport: *I don't like flying; it makes me feel sick.* | *a flying club*

flying boat /'·· ·/ n an aircraft with an underside shaped like the bottom of a boat, able to land on water

flying but·tress /ˌ·· ˈ··/ n a half arch joined at the top to the outside wall of a large building (such as a church, a castle, etc.), used for supporting the weight of the wall

flying col·ours /ˌ·· ˈ··/ n **with flying colours** very successfully; splendidly: *He passed his exams with flying colours.*

flying doc·tor /ˌ·· ˈ··/ n (often cap.) (esp. in Australia) a doctor who goes by aircraft to visit the sick in distant lonely places, in answer to radio messages

Flying Dutch·man /ˌ·· ˈ··/, **The** n a GHOST ship which, in stories, appears in stormy weather and warns of terrible events to come

flying fish /ˌ·· ˈ·/ n a tropical sea fish that can jump out of the water and move forward supported by long wing-like parts (FINS)

flying fox /ˌ·· ˈ·/ n a FRUIT BAT

flying of·fic·er /'·· ˌ···/ n a rank in the British airforce – see TABLE 3

flying pick·et /ˌ·· ˈ··/ n in Britain, someone who PICKETs a place of work other than their own, esp. as part of a group that travels from place to place. The Conservative government of Margaret Thatcher (1979–91) introduced laws in Britain, limiting the powers of TRADE UNIONs which included making the use of flying pickets ILLEGAL.

flying sau·cer /ˌ·· ˈ··/ n a usu. plate-shaped spaceship which is said to be piloted by creatures from another world. Not many people believe in flying saucers, but they often appear in children's stories and in SCIENCE FICTION. —see also UFO and see picture at SPACESHIP

Flying Scots·man /ˌ·· ˈ··/, **The** a fast train that runs between London and Edinburgh

flying squad /'·· ·/ n [C+sing./pl. v] (often cap.) in Britain, a group of special police who are always ready for quick action when a serious crime takes place

flying start /ˌ·· ˈ·/ n [S] **1 a** a start to a race in which the competitors are already moving when they cross the starting line or receive the starting signal **b** also **flier** infml— a start to a race in which one competitor begins to move before the others and so gains an unfair advantage over them **2** a very good beginning: *He's got off to a flying start in his new job.*

fly·leaf /'flaɪliːf/ n **-leaves** /liːvz/ a page on which there is usu. no printing, at the beginning or end of a book, fastened to the cover

Fly·mo /'flaɪməʊ/ tdmk a type of LAWN MOWER with a ROTARY blade which is held a little way above the ground by a current of air forced from beneath it

Flynn /flɪn/, **Er·rol** /'erəl/ (1909–59) an Australian-born American actor who often played the part of an active and physically strong man: *Siegfried runs down the aisle and Roy trapezes in overhead like Errol Flynn.*

Errol Flynn as Robin Hood

fly·o·ver /'flaɪ-əʊvəʳ/ n **1** BrE ‖**overpass** AmE — a place where two roads or railways cross each other at different levels **2** AmE a flypast

fly·pa·per /'flaɪˌpeɪpəʳ/ n [U] a length of paper covered with a sticky or poisonous substance to trap flies in a room

fly·past /'flaɪpɑːst ‖-pæst/ BrE ‖ **flyby, flyover** AmE — n the actions of a group of aircraft flying in a special formation on a ceremonial occasion, esp. at a low level in front of a crowd

fly·sheet /'flaɪʃiːt/ also **fly**— n an additional sheet that is put over a tent for protection from rain or sun

fly·specked /'flaɪspekt/ adj esp. AmE for FLYBLOWN (2)

fly·swat·ter /'flaɪˌswɒtəʳ‖-ˌswɑː-/ n an instrument for killing flies, usu. made of a flat square piece of plastic or wire net fixed to a handle

fly·weight /'flaɪweɪt/ n a BOXER (1) of the lightest class, weighing 112 POUNDs (51 kilos) or less —see also BANTAMWEIGHT

fly·wheel /'flaɪwiːl/ n a wheel which, because of its heavy weight, keeps a machine working at an even speed

fly·whisk /'flaɪˌwɪsk/ n BrE a bunch of long horse hairs fastened to a handle, used for keeping flies away from the face

FM /ˌef 'em◄/ n [U] frequency modulation; a system of broadcasting, usu. on VHF, in which the electric signal that carries the sound waves has a wave that is always of the same strength but comes at a varying number of times per second, and provides very clear words and music for the listener: *an FM radio* —compare AM

▶ CULTURAL NOTE In the US, FM radio stations are thought to have better quality programmes and fewer COMMERCIALS. ◀

Fo /fəʊ/, **Dar·i·o** /'dæriəʊ/ (1926–) an Italian actor and writer for the theatre, well-known for his plays which are very funny but deal with serious social and political events, e.g. *Accidental Death of an Anarchist* and *Can't Pay, Won't Pay*

foal¹ /fəʊl/ n a young animal of the horse family

foal² v [I] to give birth to a foal

foam¹ /fəʊm/ n [U] **1** a whitish mass of very small bubbles on the surface of a liquid, on skin, etc.: *foam-flecked waves* | *He complained to the barman about the amount of foam on his beer.* | *Many fire extinguishers are filled with chemical foam.* **2** infml foam rubber: *a foam mattress* —**foamy** adj

foam² v [I] to produce foam: *The dying animal was found foaming at the mouth.* | (fig.) *He could hardly speak; he was foaming with anger.* (=was very angry)

foam rub·ber /ˌ· ˈ··◄/ n [U] soft rubber full of air bubbles, used for making chair seats, the soft part of beds, etc.

fob¹ /fɒb‖fɑːb/ v **-bb-**
  fob sthg./sbdy. ↔ **off** phr v [T] to wave aside; take no notice of: *He took no notice of our suggestions; he fobbed them/us off and talked of something else.*
  fob sthg. ↔ **off on** sbdy. phr v [T] to pass or sell to, esp. by deceit: *He fobbed this painting off on me as a genuine Renoir, but I later found out it was a fake.* —compare PALM **off** (1)
  fob sbdy. **off with** sthg. phr v [T] to persuade into accepting (something worthless), esp. by deceit: *The salesman fobbed the old lady off with a faulty machine.* | *Don't try and fob me off with that feeble excuse again!* —compare PALM **off** (2)

fob² n **1** also **fob chain** /'· ·/— a short chain or band of cloth to which a FOB WATCH is fastened **2** a small decorative TAG¹(1) fixed to a key ring

FOB /ˌef əʊ 'biː/ adj free on board; with no charge for delivery at the stated place: *All the new car prices are quoted FOB Detroit.*

fob watch /'· ·/ n a watch that fits into a pocket, or is pinned to a woman's dress

fo·cal /'fəʊkəl/ adj [A] of a focus

focal length /ˌ·· ˈ·/ n [(the) (of)] the distance from the middle of a piece of glass (LENS) that collects light into one beam, to its focus

focal point /'·· ·/ n [(the) (of)] a central point; FOCUS: *The fireplace is the focal point of the room.*

fo'c'sle /'fəʊksəl/ BrE ‖ **forecastle** AmE— n the front part of a ship, where the sailors live

fo·cus¹ /'fəʊkəs/ n **-cuses** or **-ci** /kaɪ, saɪ/ **1** [C] the point at which beams of light or heat or waves of sound meet after their direction has been changed (e.g. by REFLECTION) **2** [(the) (of)] a centre of attention, activity, or interest: *She always wants to be the focus of attention.* | *The* new union will provide a focus for discontented teachers. **3 in(to)/out of focus** (not) having, giving, or being a clear picture: *This photo of John isn't in focus; I can't see his face clearly.*

focus² *v* **-s-** *or* **-ss-** **1** [I;T **(on)**] to come to or bring to a focus: *The beams of light moved across the sky and focused on the aircraft.* | *All eyes were focused on him.* (=Everyone was looking at him.) **2** [I;T **(on)**] to direct (one's attention) to something: *Focus your attention on your work.* | *Today we're going to focus on the question of homeless people.* | *He was very tired and couldn't focus* (=he couldn't give his full attention) *at all.* **3** [T **(on)**] to arrange the LENS in (an instrument) so as to obtain a clear picture (of): *The astronomer focused his telescope (on the moon).*

fod·der /ˈfɒdəʳ‖ˈfɑː-/ *n* [U] **1** food for horses and farm animals **2** *derog* things or people used for supplying a continuous demand of the stated kind: *"We are just factory fodder," complained the workers.* —see also CANNON FODDER

foe /fəʊ/ *n lit* an enemy

FoE /ˌef əʊ ˈiː/ *abbrev. for:* FRIENDS OF THE EARTH

foetal po·si·tion /ˈ·· ·ˌ··/ [*the*] the body position of an unborn child inside the mother, in which the legs are drawn up against the chest

foe·tus , fetus /ˈfiːtəs/ *n* a young human or other creature before birth, esp. at a later stage when all its parts have been developed —compare EMBRYO (1) **--tal** *adj*

fog¹ /fɒg‖fɑːg, fɔːg/ *n* [C;U] **1** (a state or time of) very thick mist: *There are patches of thick fog on the motorway.* | *We often have bad fogs on the south coast during winter.* **2** mistiness on a photographic plate or film, or on a print from such a film **3 in a fog** *infml* in a confused and uncertain state of mind: *My son's in a complete fog about his science lesson; he has no idea at all what it means.*

fog² *v* **-gg-** to (cause to) become covered with fog: *The steam has fogged my glasses.* | *My glasses have fogged up in this steamy room.* | *The light you let into the camera has fogged the film.* **2** [T] to confuse or hide: *irrelevant accusations which fogged the real issues*

fog·bound /ˈfɒgbaʊnd‖ˈfɑːg-, ˈfɔːg-/ *adj* prevented by fog from working or travelling as usual: *fogbound air traffic*

Fogg /fɒg‖fɑːg/**, Phil·e·as** /ˈfɪliəs/ the main character in the book *Around the World in Eighty Days* by Jules Verne. Phileas Fogg is an Englishman who travels around the world and has many adventures.

fog·gy /ˈfɒgi‖ˈfɑːgi, ˈfɔːgi/ *adj* **1** not clear because of fog; very misty: *It's unpleasant to be out on a foggy day.* **2** not exact; unclear: *I didn't hear all she said; I've only a foggy idea/notion what it was all about.* **3 not have the foggiest (idea)** *infml* not to know at all: *"What are you going to do this evening?" "I haven't the foggiest."* **--gily** *adv* **--giness** *n* [U]

Foggy Bot·tom /ˈ·· ˌ··/ the American Department of State (from the fog that often surrounds the offices of the State Department and the SWAMP (wet land) that the offices are built on)

fog·horn /ˈfɒghɔːn‖ˈfɑːghɔːrn, ˈfɔːg-/ *n* a loud horn used as a warning of fog by and to ships: *She's got a* **voice like a foghorn.** (=a very loud unpleasant voice)

fog lamp /ˈ·· ·/ *BrE* ‖ **fog light** *AmE*— *n* a lamp on the front of a car or other vehicle that gives a strong beam of light to help driving during fog

fo·gy , fogey /ˈfəʊgi/ *n derog* a slow usu. old person who dislikes changes and does not understand modern ideas: *The judge was an* **old fogy** *and was completely out of touch with modern life.* | *a young fogy* (=a young person who does not keep up with fashion or modern ideas)

▶CULTURAL NOTE In the US while Ronald Reagan was president (1980 – 88), young people who supported the REPUBLICAN party and CONSERVATIVE values were called **young fogies.**◀

foi·ble /ˈfɔɪbəl/ *n* a small rather strange and stupid personal habit or weakness of character: *My father was always buying new hats; it was just one of his foibles.*

foie gras /ˌfwɑː ˈgrɑː/ *n* [U] *infml for* PATE DE FOIE GRAS

foil¹ /fɔɪl/ *v* [T **(in)**] to prevent (someone) from succeeding in (some plan): *The thief was foiled in his attempt to enter the house.* | *We foiled his attempt to escape.*

foil² *n* **1** [U] (*often in comb.*) metal beaten or rolled into very thin paperlike sheets: *Milk bottle tops are made of tin foil.* | *Wrap the chicken in foil before you cook it.* **2** [U] paper covered with this: *Cigarettes are wrapped in foil to keep them fresh.* **3** [C (**for, to**)] a person or thing of a kind that makes the better or different quality of another more noticeable: *In the play, a wicked old uncle acts as a foil to the noble young prince.*

foil³ *n* a light narrow sword used in FENCING —compare EPEE, SABRE(2)

foist /fɔɪst/ *v*
foist sbdy./sthg. **on** sbdy. *phr v* [T] **1** to cause (someone or something unwanted) to be borne or suffered for a time by (someone): *They didn't invite him to go out with them, but he foisted himself/his company on them.* **2** [(OFF)] to pass or sell to, esp. by deceit: *Don't trust that shopkeeper; he'll try to foist damaged goods (off) on you.*

Fok·ker /ˈfɒkəʳ‖ˈfɑː-/**, Anthony** (1890–1939) a Dutch aircraft maker who supplied planes to Germany during the First World War. He moved to the US in 1925 and made planes for the American aircraft industry.

fold¹ /fəʊld/ *v* **1** [T (UP)] to turn or press back one part of (something, esp. paper or cloth) and lay it on the remaining part; bend into two or more parts: *She folded the handkerchief and put it in her pocket.* | *Fold up the tablecloth and put it away, please.* | *The paper must be folded in half|into quarters.* —opposite CREASE **2** [I] to be able to be bent back; close up: *Does this table fold?* | *These doors fold back against the wall.* | *a folding bed* **3** [T] to press (a pair of limbs) together: *He folded his arms.* (=crossed them over his chest) | *The insect folded its wings.* **4** [T+obj+adv/prep] to wrap; cover: *He found some seeds folded in a little piece of paper.* **5** [I (UP)] (esp. of a business) to fail and close: *Our New York operation has folded.* **6** [T;I] (in card games) to put down (one's cards) to show that one can no longer play in the game: *He was sure he had better hands so he folded.*
fold in *phr v* [T] **1** (**fold** sthg. ↔ **in**) to mix (something eatable) into a mixture that is to be cooked, by turning over gently with a spoon: *Fold in two eggs and then cook gently for thirty minutes.* **2** (**fold** sbdy. **in** sthg.) to wrap (one's arms) round (someone); EMBRACE in: *She folded the child in her arms.*
fold sthg. **into** sthg. *phr v* [T] to mix (something eatable) into (a mixture that is to be cooked), by turning over gently with a spoon
fold up *phr v* **1** [I] to break down, esp. emotionally: *She just folded up when we told her the bad news about her son.* **2** [T;I] (esp. of a business) to fail and close: *The shop folded up two weeks after it opened.*

fold² *n* **1** a line made in material, paper, etc., by folding: *Each fold in the skirt should be exactly the same width.* | *The curtain hung in heavy folds.* **2** a hollow part inside something folded: *She put her book in the fold of the newspaper to protect it from the rain.* **3** *esp. BrE* **a** a bend in a valley **b** a hollow in a hill **4** *tech* a bend in the bands of rock and other substances that lie one under the other beneath the surface of the earth

fold³ *n* **1** [C] a sheltered corner of a field where farm animals, esp. sheep, are kept for protection, surrounded by a fence or wall **2** [*the*] the place or situation where one belongs and/or is protected, such as one's home or religion: *The church is always willing to welcome repentant sinners back to the fold.*

fold·a·way /ˈfəʊldəweɪ/ *adj* [A] made in such a way that can be folded up out of the way or out of sight: *a foldaway bed*

fold·er /ˈfəʊldəʳ/ *n* a folded piece of cardboard used for holding loose papers

Fo·ley /ˈfəʊli/**, Thomas** (1929–) a long-serving US CONGRESSMAN who became Speaker of the House in 1989

fo·li·age /ˈfəʊli-ɪdʒ/ *n* [U] *fml or tech* the leaves of a plant or plants: *Most trees lose their foliage in winter.*

Fo·lies-Ber·gère /ˌfɒli beəˈʒeəʳ‖ˌfəʊˌliː beər-/ [*the*] a music hall in Paris, famous since the 19th century for its shows which have featured many different kinds of performers, including women wearing few clothes

fo·li·o /ˈfəʊliəʊ/ *n* **-lios** *tech* **1** [C] a single numbered sheet of paper in a book; both sides of a page: *The manuscript you sent me has a folio missing.* **2** [U] the (size of) paper produced by folding a large sheet of paper once so as to give two sheets or four pages in all —compare OCTAVO,

QUARTO **3** [C] a book of the largest size, made up of large sheets folded once: *She owns a Shakespeare* **first folio.** | *This book on art has been brought out* **in folio.**

folk[1] /fəʊk/ *n* **1** [P] *BrE* ‖ also **folks** *AmE*— people belonging to a particular race or nation, or sharing a particular kind of life: *They are just simple country folk.* —see also FOLKS **2** [P] *BrE* ‖ **folks** *AmE*— people: *Some folk are just so inconsiderate.* **3** [U] FOLK MUSIC: *Do you prefer folk or jazz?*

▷ USAGE Compare **people** and **folk. People** is the usual word for the mass of the population in a country, city, or area: *The* **people** *of Liverpool demand the right to work.* **Folk** is used especially of people who share a certain way of life, or who belong to a small COMMUNITY: *the old* **folk** *of the village.*◁

folk[2] *adj* [A *no comp.*] of music or any other art that has grown up among working and/or country people as an important part of their way of living and belongs to a particular area, trade, etc., or that has been made in modern times as a copy of this: *folk music* | *a folk concert* | *folk art*

folk dance /ˈ· ˌ·/ *n* (a piece of music for) an old country dance, usu. performed by a set of dancers –**folk dancer** *n*

folk he·ro /ˈ· ˌ··/ *n* a person who is well-known, popular, and respected by ordinary people; usu. for a brave action or way of life: *Casey Jones is a well-known American folk hero.*

folk·lore /ˈfəʊklɔːʳ/ *n* [U] (the scientific study of) all the knowledge, beliefs, habits, etc., of a racial or national group, still preserved by memory, or in use from earlier and simpler times

folk medi·cine /ˈ· ˌ··/ *n* medicines such as those made from HERBS which are not based on modern medical science

folk mu·sic /ˈ· ˌ··/ *n* [U] music of working or country people of a particular nation or area, developed over many years and of which the original songwriter or COMPOSER is not usu. known

folks /fəʊks/ *n* [P] *infml* **1** one's parents or relations: *I'd like you to meet my folks.* **2** (used esp. when addressing people in a friendly way) people: *Well, folks, shall we go out this afternoon?* **3** *AmE for* FOLK[1] (2)

folk sing·er /ˈ· ˌ··/ also **folksinger**— *n* a person who sings folk songs

folk song /ˈ· ·/ *n* a simple song (in the style) of working or country people often with repeating words and tune

folk·sy /ˈfəʊksi/ *adj infml, esp. AmE* **1** simple and friendly; not formal **2** *derog* pretending to be or trying to appear simple in ways, likes, etc.: *They're a pretty folksy couple next door, growing all their own vegetables, keeping hens in the backyard, making pottery and so on.*

folk·tale /ˈfəʊkteɪl/ *n* a popular story passed on by speech over a long period of time in a simple society

fol·li·cle /ˈfɒlɪkəl‖ˈfɑː-/ *n* any of the small holes in the skin of a person or animal from which hairs grow

fol·low /ˈfɒləʊ‖ˈfɑː-/ *v* **1** [I;T] to come, arrive, go, or leave after; move behind in the same direction: *The boy followed his father out of the room.* | *Don't keep following me about everywhere I go.* | *I'm sending the letter today; the packet will follow (later).* | *The film star walked to his car, followed by a crowd of journalists.* | (fig.) *He'll be a difficult man to follow.* (=it will be difficult for anyone to take his place because he is/was so good) **2** [I;T] to happen, take place, or come directly after (something): *May follows April.* | *The flash of lightning was followed by loud thunder.* | *The number 5 follows the number 4.* | *We expect even greater successes to follow.* | *The late-night movie follows the 10 o'clock news.* **3** [T] to go in the same direction as; continue along: *The railway line follows the river for several miles.* | *Follow the road until you come to the hotel.* **4** [T] to go after in order to catch: *I think we're being followed!* **5** [T] to keep in sight; watch: *The cat followed every movement of the mouse.* | *He followed her with his eyes.* (=watched her movements closely) **6** [T] to attend or listen to carefully: *He followed the speaker's words with the greatest attention.* **7** [I;T] to understand clearly: *I didn't quite follow (what you were saying; could you explain it again?* **8** [T] to take a keen interest in: *He follows all the baseball news.* | *I've been following her career since I first saw her acting in "The Tempest".* –see also FOLLOWER **9** [T] to (accept and) act according to: *Why didn't you follow my advice?* | *The vil-*

lagers still follow the customs of their grandfathers. **10** [I;T] to be or happen as a necessary effect or result (of): *When there is war, social unrest often follows.* | *Disease often follows war.* [+(*that*)] *"If the door was not opened by force, it follows that* (=it is reasonable to believe that) *the burglar had a key." "No that doesn't necessarily follow: there may be another explanation."* **11** [T] to carry on (a certain kind of work): *You will have to study hard if you intend to* **follow the law.** (=be a lawyer) **12 as follows** as now to be told; as given in the list below: *The results are as follows: Philip Carter 1st, Sam Cohen 2nd, Sandra Postlethwaite 3rd.* **13 follow in the footsteps of** to follow an example set by (someone) in the past: *The girl's following in her father's footsteps and studying to be a doctor.* **14 follow suit a** to do the same as someone else has: *Once one bank raised its interest rate, all the others followed suit.* **b** (in a card game) to play a card of the same suit[1](2) as one played earlier: *If you can't follow suit, you can trump it.* **15 follow that car** a phrase often used in old films when someone wants to follow or catch someone else: *They climb into a taxi and give the order "follow that car!"* **16 to follow** as the next dish; as the next thing to eat: *"What will you have to follow, sir?" asked the waiter.* | *...and to follow, some fresh fruit*

follow on/**upon** sthg. *phr v* [T *no pass.*] to result from: *Her illness followed on her mother's death.*

follow through *phr v* **1** [T] (**follow sthg. ↔ through**) also **follow out**— to complete; carry out exactly to the end: *The police have followed through several lines of inquiry, but are no nearer to finding the culprit.* | *Even though he followed out all the instructions carefully, he couldn't get the machine to work.* **2** [I] (in tennis, GOLF, etc.) to complete a stroke by continuing to move the arm after hitting the ball —see also FOLLOW-THROUGH

follow sthg. ↔ **up** *phr v* [T] **1** to take further action on (something): *I decided to follow up her suggestion.* **2** [(**with**)] to take further action after (something) (by means of something else): *I followed up my letter with a visit.* —see also FOLLOW-UP

fol·low·er /ˈfɒləʊəʳ‖ˈfɑː-/ *n* someone who follows or supports a particular person, belief, or cause, etc.: *He's a faithful follower of his home football team.* | *Many ancient Greeks were followers of Socrates.* | *a follower of fashion* —see also CAMP FOLLOWER

fol·low·ing[1] /ˈfɒləʊɪŋ‖ˈfɑː-/ *adj* **1** [*the*+A] next: *He was sick in the evening, but on the following day he seemed quite well again.* **2** [*the*+A] that is/are to be mentioned now: *Payment may be made in any of the following ways: by cash, by cheque, or by credit card.* [also *n, the*+C, *pl.* **following**] *The following* (=these people) *have been selected to play in tomorrow's match: Duncan Ferguson, Hugh Williams, ...* | *The following is a summary of the President's speech.* **3** [A] (of wind or sea) moving in the same direction as a ship; helping: *The sailing boat made good speed, thanks to a following wind.*

following[2] *n* [usu. *sing.*] a group of supporters or admirers: *This politician has quite a large following in the North.* —see also FOLLOWING[1] (2)

following[3] *prep* after: *Following the speech, there will be a few minutes for questions.*

follow-my-lead·er /ˌ··· · ˈ··/ *BrE* ‖ **follow-the-leader** *AmE*— *n* [U] a children's game in which one of the players does actions which all the other players must copy

follow-on /ˈ··· ·/ *n* a second INNINGS that must be played by a cricket team that has made a much smaller SCORE than the opposing team in its first innings

follow-through /ˈ··· ·/ *n* **1** (in sports) the part of a stroke made after hitting the ball **2** *AmE* the action taken to complete a plan: *Their idea was good but their follow-through was abysmal.* —see also FOLLOW **through**

follow-up /ˈ··· ·/ *adj, n* [A;C] (of or being) a thing done or action taken to continue or add to the effect of something done before: *follow-up visits* | *Our newspaper story on the sex trial was a great success; we must get someone to write a follow-up.* —see also FOLLOW **up**

fol·ly /ˈfɒli‖ˈfɑːli/ *n* **1** [C;U] *fml* (an act of) stupidity: *It would be sheer folly to reduce public spending on the health service.* | *The old man smiled sadly as he remembered the follies of his youth.* **2** [C] a building of strange or fanciful shape, that has no particular purpose, esp. as built only to be looked at

Fol·som /ˈfəʊlsəm/ a prison for criminals who have broken US FEDERAL (2) law

fo·ment /fəʊˈment/ v [T] *fml* to help (something evil or unpleasant) to develop, esp. over a long period of time: *He accused the government's enemies of deliberately seeking to foment rebellion.* — ~**ation** /ˌfəʊmenˈteɪʃən, -mən-/ n [U]

fond /fɒnd‖fɑːnd/ adj **1** [F+of] having a great liking or love (for someone or something, esp. as the result of a long relationship): *She has many faults, but we're all very fond of her.* | *My young nephews are fond of playing practical jokes on me.* **2** [A] loving in a kind, gentle, or tender way: *a fond farewell* **3** [A] foolishly loving; giving in weakly to loving feelings: *A fond mother may spoil her child.* **4** [A] foolishly trusting or hopeful: *She's waiting patiently in the fond belief he'll come back to her.* —see also FONDLY – ~**ness** n [S;U (for)]

Fon·da /ˈfɒndə‖ˈfɑː-/, **Henry** (1905–82) an American actor who made many films including *The Grapes of Wrath, Twelve Angry Men,* and *On Golden Pond*

Fonda, Jane (1937–) an American actress, daughter of Henry Fonda, known also for her left-wing views esp. her support for Vietnam and her opposition to the American government during the Vietnam War. Her films include *Klute, The China Syndrome,* and, with her father, *On Golden Pond.* She is also known for her interest in active physical exercise. —see colour picture on page 228

Fonda, Peter (1939–) an American actor and director best-known for his film *Easy Rider*; son of Henry Fonda

fon·dant /ˈfɒndənt‖ˈfɑːn-/ n [C;U] a sweet made of very small grains of sugar, that melts in the mouth

fon·dle /ˈfɒndl‖ˈfɑːndl/ v [T] to touch gently and lovingly; stroke softly: *The old lady fondled her cat.*

fond·ly /ˈfɒndli‖ˈfɑːndli/ adv **1** in a loving way: *She greeted her old friend fondly.* **2** in a foolishly hopeful manner: *She fondly imagined that she could pass her exam without working.*

fon·due , -du /ˈfɒndjuː‖fɑːnˈduː/ n [C;U] **1** a dish from Switzerland made with melted cheese, into which pieces of bread are dipped **2** (*often in comb.*) a dish consisting of small pieces of food, such as meat or fruit, that are cooked in or dipped into a hot liquid

font /fɒnt‖fɑːnt/ n **1** a large container in a church, usu. made of stone, that holds the water used for baptizing (BAPTIZE) people in the Christian religion —see picture at CHURCH **2** a FOUNT²

Fon·teyn /fɒnˈteɪn‖fɑːn-/, **Dame Mar·got** /ˈmɑːɡəʊ‖ˈmɑːr-/ (1919–91) an English BALLET dancer with the Royal Ballet (1935–59), known esp. for her dancing partnership with Rudolph Nureyev

Fonz /fɒnz‖fɑːnz/ also **the Fonz**— the central character in the American television SERIES called HAPPY DAYS. Fonz is a popular teenage boy who is known for wearing a black leather jacket and giving the THUMBS-UP sign. —see colour picture on page 686

food /fuːd/ n **1** [U] something that living creatures take into their bodies to provide them with strength to do things and to help them to develop and to live: *Milk is the natural food for young babies.* | *a serious food shortage* | *a new sort of liquid plant-food* **2** [C;U] something solid for eating: *We always get lots of food there, but they never give us much to drink.* | *Too many sweet foods, like cakes and pastry, may increase your weight.* **3** [U+for] subject matter (for an argument or careful thought); that which helps ideas to start working in the mind: *The teacher's advice gave me plenty of food for thought.* **4** **if music be the food of love, play on** *quote* a phrase from Shakespeare's play *Twelfth Night*

food ad·di·tive /ˈ· ˌ···/ n a substance added to food to preserve it or to give it taste or colour. Under EC rules only those considered safe can be used and they are given E numbers.

▶ CULTURAL NOTE Many people think that even additives with E numbers are not good for the health. In the US, E numbers are not used but the FDA gives advice on which additives are safe to use. Many Americans also think, however, that additives are not good for people's health. ◀

food aid /ˈ· ·/ n [U] food provided by richer countries to countries who are in difficulty and cannot produce or do not have enough food themselves: *The Foreign Minister asked for large-scale western financial help, technical assistance and extra food aid.*

Food and Ag·ri·cul·ture Or·gan·i·za·tion /ˌ· · ˈ···· ···ˌ··/ [the] see FAO

Food and Drug Ad·min·i·stra·tion /ˌ· · ˈ· ···ˌ··/ [the] see FDA

food bank /ˈ· ·/ n *AmE* a place which gives food to poor people

food chain /ˈ· ·/ n a group of animals (and sometimes plants) arranged in a SERIES in which each member eats the one below it and is eaten by the one above it

food cou·pon /ˈ· ˌ··/ n see FOOD STAMP

food·ie /ˈfuːdi/ n *infml* someone who is very interested in cooking and good food

food la·bel·ling /ˈ· ˌ··/ n [U] a way of describing the contents of ready-packed food now demanded by law in most Western countries. Under EC and FDA rules all contents and FOOD ADDITIVES must be put in a list and a date given when the food should be sold and eaten by.

food poi·son·ing /ˈ· ˌ··/ n [U] a painful stomach disorder caused by eating food that contains harmful bacteria or poisonous substances

food pro·ces·sor /ˈ· ˌ··/ n a piece of electrical equipment that performs a number of operations in preparing food, such as cutting and mixing

food stamp /ˈ· ·/ also **food coupon** n (in the US) an official paper which the government gives to people who are unemployed or on a low income. They can be used to buy food and some other necessary things: *This store accepts food stamps.* | *My daughter's on food stamps.* | *Are you eligible for food stamps?*

food·stuff /ˈfuːdstʌf/ n [*often pl.*] a substance used as food, esp. a simple food material that is to be cooked and/or mixed with other foods for eating

fool¹ /fuːl/ n **1** [C] a person who is lacking in judgment or good sense: *What fool has put that wet paintbrush in my chair?* | *What a fool I was to think that she really loved me.* | *Don't do it like that, you silly little fool!* | *That fool of a secretary* (=that secretary, who is a fool) *has forgotten to book the conference room!* **2** [C] (in former times) a manservant at the court of a king or noble, whose duty was to amuse his master; JESTER **3** [C;U] (*usu. in comb.*) esp. BrE a dish made of cooked soft fruit which is made into a liquid and beaten up with cream: *gooseberry fool* **4** **any fool** anyone at all: *Any fool could have told you it wasn't genuine!* **5** **fools rush in where angels fear to tread** *quote* a phrase from Alexander Pope's Essay on Criticism and used about acts stupidly or without thinking: *The emotional traumas of the past two years have taught me the wisdom of not rushing in where angels fear to tread.* **6** **make a fool of oneself** to behave unwisely or in a silly way and lose people's respect: *She was never keen on performing in public because she was afraid of making a fool of herself.* **7** **make a fool of someone** to trick someone; make someone seem stupid: *Are you trying to make a fool of me? Anyone can see it's a fake!* **8** **(the) more fool you/him, etc.** *esp. BrE* I think you were, he was, etc., a fool to do, accept, expect, etc., that: *"He picked up a strange cat and it bit him." "More fool him; he should have known better."* **9** **no/nobody's/no one's fool** a person who cannot be tricked: *He tried to sell me that old car, but I'm nobody's fool; I could see it hadn't got an engine.* **10** **play the fool** to act in a foolish manner: *Johnny's always playing the fool during lessons.* —see also APRIL FOOL

fool² v **1** [T] to deceive; trick: *She fooled the old man out of all his money.* | *He's fooled a lot of people into believing he's a rich man.* **2** [I] to speak without serious intention; joke: *Don't worry, he was only fooling.* **3** **You can fool all the people some of the time, and some of the people all the time, but you cannot fool all the people all the time.** *quote* a phrase used in a speech by Abraham Lincoln, saying that people will not always be deceived by politicians **4** **You could have fooled 'me!** *infml* I don't believe you or agree with you!

fool about/around *phr v* [I] *derog* **1** to spend time doing nothing useful: *He never does any work; he just fools about all day long.* **2** [(with)] to behave in a foolish or irresponsible way: *You shouldn't fool around with*

dangerous chemicals. **3** [(with)] to amuse oneself by having sexual relationships, esp. with people who are already married: *He's always fooling around with other men's wives.*

fool³ *adj* [A] *infml, esp. AmE* stupid; foolish: *That fool son of mine has smashed up his new car.*

fool·e·ry /ˈfuːləri/ *n* [C;U] (an example of) silly behaviour

fool·har·dy /ˈfuːlhɑːdi‖-ɑːr-/ *adj* foolishly daring; taking unwise risks; RECKLESS: *You were very foolhardy to jump off the bus while it was still moving.* **—diness** *n* [U]

fool·ish /ˈfuːlɪʃ/ *adj derog* **1** unwise; without good sense: *It would be foolish to spend money on something you can't afford.* | *a foolish remark* **2** like a fool; stupid: *I felt rather foolish when I couldn't answer the teacher's question.* | *with a foolish grin on his face* **— ~ly** *adv* **— ~ness** *n* [U]

fool·proof /ˈfuːlpruːf/ *adj* **1** that cannot go wrong: *I've found a foolproof way of doing it.* | *a foolproof plan* **2** *infml* very simple to understand, use, work, etc.: *a foolproof machine*

fools·cap /ˈfuːlskæp/ *n* [U] a large size of paper, esp. writing paper

fool's er·rand /ˌ· ˈ··/ *n* [S] a useless or unnecessary piece of work or effort: *I found I'd gone/been sent on a fool's errand; the man I'd been told to contact was out of the country.*

fool's gold /ˌ· ˈ·/ *n* [U] **1** any of various yellow metals which look like gold **2** something which seems attractive or exciting, but will cause disappointment: *He's off chasing fool's gold.*

fool's par·a·dise /ˌ· ˈ···/ *n* [S] a carelessly happy state for which there is no good reason: *You're* (**living**) *in a fool's paradise if you think your husband's never been unfaithful to you.*

foot¹ /fʊt/ *n* **feet** /fiːt/ **1** [C] the movable part of the body at the end of the leg, below the ankle, on which a person or animal stands: *I stepped on a nail, and my foot's very sore.* | *It's nice to sit down after being* **on your feet** (=standing or walking) *all day.* | *This medicine will soon have you back on your feet* (=well) *again.* | *He* **got to his feet** (=stood up) *when he heard the bell.* | *She found it difficult to* **keep (on) her feet** (=not to fall) *on the slippery surface.* | *The congregation* **rose to their feet** *when the priest walked down the aisle.* | *She said she wouldn't* **set foot in** (=enter) *the room until it had been properly cleaned.* —see also PAW **2** [C *usu. sing.*] the part of a sock or STOCKING that covers the foot: *There's a hole in the foot.* **3** [U] *esp. lit* particular manner of walking; step: *He's very* **fleet of foot.** (=He walks/runs very fast.) **4** [*the* (*of*)] the bottom part or lower end: *He stood at the foot of the stairs and shouted up at me.* | *There's something written at the foot of the page.* | *He sat on the foot of the bed.* | *She laid some flowers at the foot of her friend's grave.* **5** [C] (*pl. sometimes* **foot**) (*written abbrev.* **ft**) (a measure of length equal to) 12 inches (INCH) or about 0·305 metres: *Three feet make one yard.* | *He's six feet/foot tall, but she's only five foot one.* (=five feet and one INCH tall) **6** [C] a division of a line in poetry, in which there is usu. a strong beat and one or two weaker ones: *In the line "The way/was long/the wind/was cold", the words between each pair of upright lines make up a foot.* **7 feet first** dead: *You'll go out feet first if you keep driving so fast.* **8 a foot in both camps** connected or concerned with two groups of people who have different or opposing ideas, beliefs, etc. **9 a foot in the door** a favourable position from which to advance, gain influence, etc.: *Now she's got a foot in the door in show business, I think her talent will carry her a long way.* **10 get/start off on the right/wrong foot** to begin (sthg.) in a good or bad way: *He started off on the right foot when he complimented her mother on her cooking.* **11 have/keep both (one's) feet on the ground** to be sensible and REALISTIC: *Despite her rise to stardom she has kept both feet firmly on the ground.* **12 have/with one foot in the grave** *infml derog* (to be/who is) very old and near death **13 my foot!** *infml* I don't believe it: *"She says*

foot

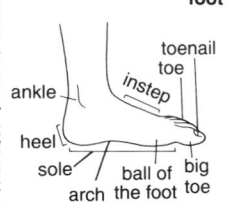

toenail
toe
ankle — instep
heel
sole
ball of
the foot
big toe
arch

she's too busy to speak to you." "Busy, my foot! She just doesn't want to." **14 on foot** (by) walking: *It's easier to get there on foot than by car.* —see TRANSPORT (USAGE) **15 put a foot wrong** also **not put a foot right**— *esp. BrE* to say or do the wrong things: *She answered all our questions perfectly; she never put a foot wrong.* **16 put one's best foot forward: a** to walk as fast as possible: *It's a long way to the village, but if you put your best foot forward you'll reach it before the evening.* **b** to do the best one can: *You've been so lazy in the past few months; you'll have to put your best foot forward if you want to pass that exam now.* **17 put one's feet up** *infml* to rest by lying down or sitting with one's feet supported on something: *It's nice to put your feet up after a long day's work.* **18 put one's foot down** *infml* **a** to speak and act firmly on a particular matter, esp. to forbid something: *The father didn't like his son staying out at night, so he put his foot down and forbade him to do it again.* **b** *BrE* to drive very fast: *As soon as they left the town he put his foot down and soon reached the next village.* **19 put one's foot in it** *esp. BrE* ‖ **put one's foot in one's mouth** *esp. AmE— infml* to say something wrong or unsuitable, usu. as a result of thoughtlessness, and so cause an awkward situation: *I really put my foot in it when I asked him how his wife was; she's left him for another man.* **20 -footed** /fʊtɪd/ having feet of the stated kind or number: *four-footed/flat-footed* | *Ducks are web-footed.* **21 -footer** /fʊtər/ a person or thing that is a stated number of feet long, tall, or high: *My brother is a six-footer.* —see also COLD FEET, FEET OF CLAY, UNDERFOOT, **drag one's feet** (DRAG¹), **fall on one's feet** (FALL¹), **tie/bind someone hand and foot** (HAND¹ (34)), **be rushed off one's feet** (RUSH¹), **stand on one's own (two) feet** (STAND¹ (28)), **sweep someone off their feet** (SWEEP¹)

foot² *v* **foot the bill** *infml* to pay the bill: *My parents footed the bill for the wedding.*

Foot, Mi·chael /ˈmaɪkəl/ (1913–) a British politician on the left-wing of the Labour Party who became party leader in 1980 but was replaced by Neil Kinnock after Labour's defeat in the general election in 1983. He is known also as a political thinker, writer, and member of CND.

foot·age /ˈfʊtɪdʒ/ *n* [U] (the length in feet of) cinema film used for a scene, subject, etc.: *They screened some interesting old footage of the first flight across the Atlas Mountains.*

foot-and-mouth dis·ease /ˌ·· ˈ· ·ˌ·/ *n* [U] a disease of cattle, sheep, and goats, in which spots appear in the mouth and on the feet, and which often causes death

foot·ball /ˈfʊtbɔːl/ *n* **1** [U] also **Association football** *fml— BrE* a game that is played between two teams of 11 players using a round ball that is kicked but not handled; SOCCER: *a football player* | *a football match* —see colour picture on page 884 **2** [U] *AmE* ‖ **American football** *BrE—* an American game, rather like RUGBY, played between two teams of 11 players using an OVAL (=egg-shaped) ball that can be handled or kicked —see colour picture on page 884 **3** [C] a large leather or plastic ball filled with air, used in these games **4** [C] something (e.g. an idea) which is used as the starting point for an argument, disagreement, etc., rather than being considered for its own qualities: *The issue has become* **a political football.** —see REFEREE (USAGE) and see also extra information on page 501 **— ~er** *n*: *a professional footballer*

Football As·so·ci·a·tion /ˈ··· ····ˌ···/ [*the*] see FA

football fan /ˈ·· ˌ·/ *n* a very keen supporter of football, esp. of a particular team: *Football fans paraded through the town centre after the match.*

football field /ˈ·· ˌ·/ *n* an area covered with grass, marked out for the game of football

football hoo·li·gan /ˈ·· ˌ···/ *n* in Britain, a noisy, rough usu. young man, who causes trouble at football matches or near football grounds by fighting and breaking things.

▶ CULTURAL NOTE Most football supporters blame hooligans for spoiling the game for others. In Britain, football clubs try to prevent hooliganism by forbidding alcohol in the ground, keeping the supporters of each team apart, building special fences, and providing more seats. ◀

Football League /ˌ·· ˈ·/ [*the*] the organization of professional football teams for competition in England, Wales, and Scotland. The team with the most points at the end

Football

Football (soccer *AmE*) is a very popular sport in Britain, played between August and May (the **football season**). Many people, esp. men, support a particular team and may go to watch the games that their team plays. Professional football is controlled by two organizations, the FOOTBALL LEAGUE and the Football Association (the FA). In England and Wales, there are 93 teams in the League, organized into four divisions:

Premier League
(22 teams)
↑
1st Division
(24 teams)
↑
2nd Division
(24 teams)
↑
3rd Division
(23 teams)

In Scotland, there are 38 teams in the League, organized into three divisions:

Premier Division
(12 teams)
↑
1st Division
(12 teams)
↑
2nd Division
(14 teams)

Teams play regularly against the other teams in their league or division according to a fixed programme. At the end of the season the team in the Premier League (or the Premier Division in Scotland) with the most points is the **League Champion**. This competition is called the **League Championship**.

The other important competition is the FA CUP, often just called the cup. This is open to all AMATEUR football teams that belong to the FA as well as the 93 professional teams. The teams play against each other in a KNOCKOUT competition which starts in August and ends in May. The two teams left in the competition play in the **FA Cup Final** at Wembley Stadium in London. This is a very important national sporting occasion, watched by millions of people on television.

Team names usu. include the name of the town or city where the team is based, e.g. Leeds United, Sheffield Wednesday, Wolverhampton Wanderers (Wolves), Dundee United, etc.

football (soccer *AmE*)

Football

Football (American football *BrE*) is a very popular sport in the US. Many people, esp. men, support a particular team and watch the games that their team plays.

Each team has a name, which usually includes the name of the town or city that the team is associated with. Some examples of names are: **New York Jets, Washington Redskins, New England Patriots**, and **Green Bay Packers.**

The season starts in early autumn and ends at the end of January with the SUPER BOWL, which is the NFL championship game. The two teams that play in the Super Bowl are determined by games within the divisions and conferences. The Super Bowl is only one game, and at the end of the game, they have a **sudden-death play-off**, in which the first team to gain points wins the game.

Professional football games are organised in the US in the following way:

National Football League

Conference (NFC)			Conference (AFC)		
(14 teams)			(14 teams)		
Eastern	Central	Western	Eastern	Central	Western
division	division	division	division	division	division

football (American football *BrE*)

of the playing season wins the League Championship. —see also FOOTBALL (1) and see extra information on page 501

football pools /ˈ·· ˌ·/ n [the+P] see POOLS

football shirt /ˈ·· ˌ·/ BrE ‖ **football jer·sey** /ˈ·· ˌ··/ AmE— n a shirt worn when playing football. Football shirts are usu. brightly coloured and help the players and people watching to tell the two teams apart. They show each player's number (and sometimes their name) on the back.

foot·bridge /ˈfʊtˌbrɪdʒ/ n a narrow bridge to be used only by people walking

foot·fall /ˈfʊtfɔːl/ n esp. lit the sound of a footstep

foot fault /ˈ·· ·/ n (in games like tennis) a mistake that happens when the feet of the player who is serving (SERVE¹ (7)) are not behind the BASELINE —see picture at TENNIS -**foot-fault** v [I]

foot·hill /ˈfʊtˌhɪl/ n [usu. pl.] a low hill at the bottom of a mountain or chain of mountains: the foothills of the Himalayas

foot·hold /ˈfʊthəʊld/ n somewhere where a foot can be firmly placed to help one to continue to climb up or down: The mountain climber couldn't find many footholds on the melting ice. | (fig.) It isn't easy to get/gain a foothold (=a first position from which to advance) in the film world.

foot·ing /ˈfʊtɪŋ/ n [S] 1 a firm placing of the feet; a surface for the feet to stand on: She lost her footing on the muddy road and fell. 2 a particular (stated) kind of position or base: Is this business on a firm footing? (=properly planned, with enough money to support it) | International tension was high, and the army was put on a war footing. | I like to keep my relationship with my colleagues on a business footing; it doesn't do to get too friendly. | They all started off on an equal footing.

foo·tle /ˈfuːtl/ v [I (ABOUT, AROUND)] old-fash infml to behave in a careless way, without giving serious attention to what one is doing: Get on with your work and stop footling about. —see also FOOTLING

foot·lights /ˈfʊtlaɪts/ n [P] a row of lights along the front edge of the floor of a stage at the theatre, to show up the actors —see picture at THEATRE

foot·ling /ˈfuːtlɪŋ/ adj old-fash derog worthless; unimportant: Don't waste my time with such footling questions. — see also FOOTLE

foot lock·er /ˈ·· ˌ··/ n AmE a strong, usu. metal box which can be locked; usu. used by soldiers and placed at the bottom end of the bed

foot·loose /ˈfʊtluːs/ adj free to go wherever one pleases and do what one likes; having no family or business duties to limit one's freedom: I wish I could be **footloose and fancy-free** like you.

foot·man /ˈfʊtmən/ n -men /mən/ a manservant who opens the front door, introduces visitors, waits at table, etc., and is often dressed in a uniform

foot·note /ˈfʊtnəʊt/ n a note at the bottom of a page in a book, to explain some word or sentence, add some special remark or information, etc.

foot·pad /ˈfʊtpæd/ n old use a thief who attacks travellers on the roads and takes their money —compare HIGHWAYMAN

foot·path /ˈfʊtpɑːθ‖-pæθ/ n -paths /pɑːðz‖pæðz/ esp. BrE a narrow path or track for people to walk on: A public footpath led across the fields.

foot·plate /ˈfʊtpleɪt/ n (esp. formerly) a metal plate covering the floor of a railway engine, where the people driving the train stand

foot·print /ˈfʊtˌprɪnt/ n a mark made by the foot of a person or animal: The hunter recognized the footprints of a bear near the river bank. | Who left these muddy footprints on the kitchen floor? —see picture at PRINT

foot·race /ˈfʊt-reɪs/ n a race for runners, usu. over level ground

foot·sie /ˈfʊtsi/ n infml **play footsie (with someone): a** to rub one's feet on someone else's in a sexually playful way: They were playing footsie under the table. **b** AmE to work together (with someone), esp. in a way that is not completely honest or fair: Senators and congressmen play footsie (with each other) while the situation gets steadily worse.

Footsie n see FT-SE INDEX

foot·slog /ˈfʊtslɒg‖-slɑːg/ v -gg- [I] BrE infml to march or walk a long way in tiring conditions — ~ging n [U]

foot·sore /ˈfʊtsɔːʳ/ adj having tender, painful, or swollen feet, esp. as a result of much walking: After a long day's walk in the country, they came home hungry and footsore.

foot·step /ˈfʊtstep/ n 1 (the sound of) a person's step: Her footsteps were clearly marked in the snow. | He heard soft footsteps coming up the stairs. 2 the distance covered by one step: The servant walked two or three footsteps behind his master. —see also **follow in the footsteps of** (FOLLOW)

foot·stool /ˈfʊtstuːl/ n a low support on which a seated person can rest their feet

foot·wear /ˈfʊtweəʳ/ n [U] shoes, boots, etc., worn on the feet: You can buy shoelaces in the footwear department.

foot·work /ˈfʊtwɜːk‖-wɜːrk/ n [U] the use of the feet, esp. skilfully in sports, dancing, etc.: Her footwork is very poor.

fop /fɒp‖fɑːp/ n derog a man who takes too much interest in his clothes and personal appearance — ~ **pish** adj — ~ **pishness** n [U]

for¹ /fəʳ; strong fɔːʳ/ prep **1** intended to belong to or be given to: I've got a present for you. | They've bought some new chairs for the office. | Save some of the cake for Arthur. —see USAGE 2 **2** (shows purpose): This knife is for cutting bread. | What's this handle for? (=What is its purpose?) | I've sent my coat away for cleaning. (=to be cleaned) **3** instead of; so as to help: Let me lift that heavy box for you. **4** as a help to; in order to improve the condition of: The doctor's given her some medicine for her cold. **5** because of: He was rewarded for his bravery. | There's a prize for finding the most mistakes. | We could hardly see for the thick mist. | He couldn't speak for laughing. | For several reasons, I'd rather not meet him. —see also **for fear of** (FEAR¹) **6** at the time of; on the occasion of: We've invited our guests for 9 o'clock. | I've got an appointment with the doctor for the 5th of March. | I'm warning you for the last time. | She's coming home for Christmas. | He bought his son a boat for his birthday. **7** (shows length of time): She didn't answer for several minutes. | I haven't seen her for years. | That's all for today. — compare SINCE²; see USAGE 1, DURING (USAGE) **8** (shows distance): They ran fast for a mile or two. **9** as regards or in regard to: France is famous for its wines. | I have no ear for music. | I've put my name down for four tickets. | Are you still all right for money? (=Have you enough?) | He has a great respect for his father. | It's difficult for someone in her position to think clearly. | He's a great one for details. (=He always wishes all details to be correct.) | **For all** (=as far as) I know, he may be dead. | Fortunately for him, he can swim. | The men are all ready for action. | She's the very person for the work. | You're too strong for me! (=much stronger than me) | It's not for the pupil (=it is not suitable for the pupil) to tell the teacher what to do. **10** in order to have, get, or obtain: They're waiting for the bus. | For details of this offer, write to Jones & Co. | The demand for coal is greatest in the winter. | He's gone for a swim. | Run for (=in order to save) your life! | The kids ran through the streets, pressing all the doorbells for a laugh/for fun. | **"Now for** (=now I will have/let's have) a nice cool drink," he said, opening the bottle. **11** (shows payment, price, or amount): I bought this book for £3. | I paid £3 for the book. | These cigarettes are £2 for twenty. | She wouldn't go up in an aircraft for anything. (=whatever she was offered or paid) | He wouldn't harm anybody **for (all) the world.** (=on any account) **12** as being or as part of: I took him for a fool. | We've got duck for dinner today. | He says so, and **I for one** believe him. (=I believe him even if no one else does) | I don't want to buy it; **for one thing** I don't like the colour, **and for another** the price is too high. —see also **for example** (EXAMPLE¹), **for instance** (INSTANCE¹) **13** representing; meaning; as a sign of: What's the word for "to travel" in French? | Red is for danger. **14** in favour of; in support of; in agreement with; in defence of: I'm **all for** the young enjoying themselves. | Are you for the government or against it? | He plays football for England. | Let's have three cheers for the captain! **15** towards; so as to reach: The children set off for school. | This train is for Brighton only. (=it doesn't stop anywhere else) | I bought a first-class ticket for Oxford. **16** (following a comparative) after; as the result of; because of: You look all the better for your holiday. | This table's the worse for wear. (=looks old and damaged as the result of long use) **17** considering; considered as; considering that (someone or something) is ... : It's cold for the time of year. | He's heavy for a small boy.   **18** (followed by **each, every,** or a number) in addition to; compared with: For every mistake you make, you'll lose half a mark. | For every three who do agree with you, there are two who don't.   **19** (followed by a noun or pronoun and an infinitive with **to**) (introduces a phrase that is used instead of a CLAUSE): **a** (as the subject of a sentence, often introduced by **it is**): For an old man to run fast (=that an old man should run fast) is dangerous. | It isn't convenient for him to visit us (=that he should visit us) next week. **b** (following a verb of type L): Our plan was for one of us to travel (=that one of us should travel) by train with all the bags. **c** (following an adjective or adverb, esp. with **too** or **enough**): It's plain for all to see. (=so that all may see it) | He speaks too softly for her to hear. (=so softly that she cannot hear) | My parents don't live near enough for me to visit them very often. **d** (following a noun): There's no need for us to argue (=that we should argue) about this. **e** (following a verb): I can't bear for her to be angry (=that she should be angry) with me. **f** (following than): There's nothing worse than for a person to ill-treat (=than that a person should ill-treat) a child. **g** (used instead of a CLAUSE with **if**): His father must have allowed him to stay up very late, for him to be so tired. (=if he is/was so tired) **h** (used instead of a CLAUSE of purpose, where the infinitive may sometimes be left out): I've sent my coat away for it to be cleaned. (=in order that it may be cleaned) | The bell rang for the lesson (to begin). (=in order that it should begin) | For the plants to do well (=in order that they should do well) they must be watered. —see also FOR¹ (3)   **20 be (in)** '**for it** infml, esp. BrE to be likely to be punished, get into trouble, etc.: You'll be (in) for it if father finds out you've not been to school for three days!   **21 for all: a** in spite of: For all his efforts, he didn't succeed. | He's mean and bad-tempered and snores, but she loves him **for all that.** (=in spite of everything he does) | For all that (=in spite of the fact that) she has a good sense of balance, she can't dance well. —compare DESPITE¹, NOTWITHSTANDING **b** considering how little: For all the improvement you've made in the last year, you might as well give up singing.   **22 if it weren't/if it hadn't been for** if something were not true or had not happened: If it hadn't been for your help (=if you had not helped), we'd never have finished it.   **23 that's** ... **for** you often derog that's typical of ... ; that's the trouble with ... : When I arrived late I couldn't get a hot bath or a good meal; still, that's country hotels for you. **24 there's** ... **for you** derog that's not what I would call ... ; that's the complete opposite of ... : I help her and she ignores me — there's gratitude for you. —see also WHAT FOR, **as for** (AS⁴), **except for** (EXCEPT²), **for good** (GOOD²)

▷ USAGE 1 Compare **for** and **in** with time. After first, only, and negative or superlative forms American English may use **in** where British English uses **for**: the first time **in** (for BrE) many years | the worst accident **in** (for BrE) months | He hadn't eaten a good meal **in** (for BrE) a long time. 2 When we talk about buying or making something for someone we omit **for** in sentences like She bought her friend a drink. (=She bought a drink **for** her friend.) However, you must use **for** in sentences like He bought a new chair **for** the office.◁

for² conj fml or lit (used after the main statement) and the reason is that; because: The old lady does not go out in the winter, for she feels the cold a great deal.

for·age¹ /ˈfɒrɪdʒ‖ˈfɑː-, ˈfɔː-/ n   **1** [U] food supplies for horses and cattle   **2** [S;U] (an act of) foraging

forage² v [I+adv/prep]   **1** to wander about looking for food or other supplies: The campers went foraging for wood to make a fire.   **2** infml to hunt about or search, turning many things over: She foraged about in her handbag, but she couldn't find her ticket.

for·as·much as /ˌfərəzˈmʌtʃ əz‖ˌfɔːrəzmʌtʃ əz/ conj esp. old use because; as it is a fact that

for·ay¹ /ˈfɒreɪ‖ˈfɔː-, ˈfɑː-/ n   **1** a sudden rush into enemy country, usu. by a small number of soldiers, in order to damage or seize arms, food, etc.: The officer sent a few of his men on a foray.   **2** a short attempt to become active in an activity that is quite different from one's usual activity: After his unsuccessful foray into politics, he went back to his law practice.

foray² v [I (**into**)] to go out and attack enemy country suddenly, esp. in order to carry off food or other supplies

for·bear¹ /fɔːˈbeəʳ, fə-‖fɔːr-, fər-/ v -**bore** /ˈbɔːʳ/, -**borne** /ˈbɔːn‖ˈbɔːrn/ [I (**from**);T obj] fml to hold oneself back from doing something, esp. with an effort of self-control or in a generous and forgiving way: He deserved to be punished several times, but I've forborne (from doing so). [+v-ing|to-v] The judge forbore sending|to send her to prison on condition that she behaved better in future. | I could scarcely forbear from laughing out loud.

for·bear² /ˈfɔːbeəʳ‖ˈfɔːr-/ n [usu. pl.] a FOREBEAR

for·bear·ance /fɔːˈbeərəns‖fɔːr-/ n [U] patience; forgiveness: The child doesn't understand that he's doing wrong; you must treat him with forbearance.

for·bear·ing /fɔːˈbeərɪŋ‖fɔːr-/ adj long-suffering; gentle and willing to forgive: He has a forbearing nature; he accepts all his troubles with a smile.

for·bid /fəˈbɪd‖fər-/ v -**bade** /ˈbeɪd‖ˈbæd/ or -**bad** /ˈbæd/, -**bidden** /ˈbɪdn/ or -**bid** ; present participle -**bidding** [T]   **1** to refuse to allow; command against, esp. officially or with the right to be obeyed: The law forbids the use of chemical fertilizers. | Smoking is forbidden during takeoff. [+obj+to-v] I forbid you to tell anyone.   **2** [+obj(i) +obj(d)] fml to refuse to allow (someone) to have (something): He forbade his children sweets because he didn't want their teeth to be ruined.   **3** to prevent: Lack of time forbids any further discussion at this point.

for·bid·den /fəˈbɪdn‖fər-/ adj not allowed, esp. by law or rule: It's a rule of this club that religion and politics may not be talked about; they're **forbidden ground/territory**.

Forbidden Cit·y /ˌ·ˈ··ˌ ˈ··/ [the] a range of buildings enclosed by a wall in Beijing which was once forbidden to everyone except the EMPEROR's family and servants, but which is now open to the public

forbidden fruit /ˌ·ˌ·· ˈ·/ n [U] a pleasure or enjoyment that is disapproved of or not allowed (and perhaps therefore more enjoyable), esp. a sexual act (from the story of Adam and Eve in the Bible, who ate the fruit of a tree in the Garden of Eden which God had told them not to eat. As a result, they were forced to leave the Garden of Eden.)

for·bid·ding /fəˈbɪdɪŋ‖fər-/ adj having a fierce, unfriendly, or dangerous appearance: She's very nice, but because she has a forbidding manner she's slow in making friends. | The travellers' way was blocked by a forbidding range of mountains. – – **ly** adv – – **ness** n [U]

force¹ /fɔːs‖fɔːrs/ n   **1** [U] natural or physical power; active strength: The force of the explosion broke all the windows in the building. | He had to use force to get the lid off the tin.   **2** [U] fierce or uncontrolled use of strength; violence: The thief took the money from the old man by force.   **3** [C;U] tech (measurement of) a power that changes or may produce change of movement in a body on which it acts or presses: The force of gravity makes things fall to earth. —see picture at DIAGRAM   **4** [C] a person, thing, belief, action, etc., that has a strong enough influence to cause widespread changes in a way of living, or that has uncontrollable power over living things: She was a powerful force in the women's movement. | Many forces have been at work in the last fifty years that have improved the standard of living. | Modern wars let loose terrible forces of destruction. | The forces of evil attack us on all sides. | Some countries are greatly at the mercy of the forces of nature; they suffer from floods, earthquakes, etc. | Force of circumstances prevented us from doing anything else. —see also MARKET FORCES   **5** [U] strong influence on the mind: The force of his argument was so great that many people changed their minds overnight. | I did it from force of habit. (=because it was my habit to do so)   **6** [C] a group of people brought together or trained for some kind of action, esp. military action: Both land and sea forces were employed in the attack on the island. | The British air fighting force is called the Royal Air Force. | She joined the police force. | A small force of doctors and nurses was rushed to the scene of the big fire.   **7 in force** in large numbers: Trouble was expected at the football match, so the police turned out in force.   **8 in(to) force** (of a rule, order, law, etc.) in(to) effect, use, or operation: Are the new charges for postage stamps in force yet? | What's the use of a government making new laws if they can't be put into force?   **9 join/combine forces (with)** to come together (with) for a common purpose: We're joining forces with some friends to hire a hall for a party. | The two countries joined forces to fight their common enemy. —see also FORCES

force² v [T] **1** to make (an unwilling person or animal) do something; drive: I didn't want to do it; he forced me. | The rider forced his horse on through the storm. [+obj+to-v] His arguments forced them to admit he was right. | She won't do it unless you force her (to). **2** to use physical force on: "I'm trying to get some more books into this box." "Don't force them; you'll break the box." [+obj+adv/prep] He tried to force the suitcase through the tiny hole in the fence. | We had to force our way through (the dense crowd).| We had to force the window open. | The thieves **forced an entry/forced their way** into the house. (=got in by force) | The lock had been forced. (=broken open by force)| (fig.) The government forced the bill through parliament against fierce opposition. **3** to produce with difficulty or by unwilling effort: Although he was in great pain, he forced a smile. —see also FORCED **4** to make (a plant) grow faster by the use of heat: forced rhubarb **5 force someone's hand** to make someone act as one wishes or before they are ready: He was delaying signing the contract for the house, but the man selling it forced his hand by threatening to accept another offer.

force sthg. **from/out of** sthg. phr v [T] to get from (an unwilling person): They forced a confession out of him.

force sbdy./sthg. **on/upon** sbdy. phr v [T] to cause to be accepted by (an unwilling person): He didn't want to be paid, but we forced the money on him because we knew he needed it. | I don't want to force myself/my company on you, but I'd be grateful for a lift if you've got some extra room in the car.

Force [the] (in the film Star Wars) a type of magic power which only a few acquire and learn to control and which can be used for good or evil. It can be seen in a beam of light which can be used like a sword and its protective qualities are called upon in the phrase "The Force be with you." —see also STAR WARS

forced /fɔːst‖fɔːrst/ adj **1** [A no comp.] done or made because of a sudden happening which makes it necessary to act without delay: The aircraft had to make a **forced landing** because two of its engines were on fire. **2** produced unwillingly and/or with difficulty: I thought their laughter was rather forced.

force-feed /ˈ· ·/ v -**fed** /fed/ [T] to feed (a person or animal) by forcing food or esp. liquid down the throat: One prisoner refused to eat, so he had to be force-fed. | (fig.) Schoolchildren shouldn't be force-fed with Shakespeare before they are old enough to really appreciate his plays.

force·ful /ˈfɔːsfəl‖ˈfɔːrs-/ adj apprec (of a person, words, ideas, etc.) strong; powerful: She made a forceful speech.| He isn't forceful enough to make a good leader. – ~ **ly** adv – ~ **ness** n [U]

force ma·jeure /ˌfɔːs mæˈʒɜːʳ‖ˌfɔːrs mɑː-/ n Fr an event beyond one's control, e.g. a STRIKE² (1), government rules, ACTS rmof GOD, or war

force·meat /ˈfɔːs-miːt‖ˈfɔːrs-/ n [U] esp. BrE a mixture containing bread, HERBS, and often meat, which is cut up very small and used esp. for putting inside a chicken, joint of meat, etc., that is to be cooked

for·ceps /ˈfɔːseps, -sᵻps‖ˈfɔːr-/ n forceps a medical instrument with two long thin blades joined at one end or in the middle, used for holding objects firmly: When a baby is delivered by having its head held and pulled by forceps, it is called a **forceps delivery.** —see PAIR (USAGE)

forc·es /ˈfɔːsᵻz‖ˈfɔːr-/ n [(the) P] (often cap.) the army, navy, and air force of a country: In wartime most young men are expected to join the forces. | the armed forces

for·ci·ble /ˈfɔːsᵻbəl‖ˈfɔːr-/ adj [A] **1** using physical force: The police had to make a forcible entry into the house where the thief was hiding. **2** (esp. of a manner of speaking) strong and effective; powerful: The burglary at her neighbour's house was a forcible reminder that she should lock up carefully every time she went out. --**bly** adv: Her ideas are always forcibly expressed.

ford¹ /fɔːd‖fɔːrd/ n a place in a river where the water is not very deep, and where it can be crossed on foot, in a car, etc., without using a bridge

ford² v [T] to cross (a river, stream, etc.) by means of a ford – ~ **able** adj

Ford tdmk a company which makes cars —see also Henry FORD

Ford, Ford Mad·dox /fɔːd ˈmædəks‖fɔːrd-/ (1873–1939) a British writer of many poems, articles and NOVELs including The Good Soldier and Parade's End about his experiences as an army officer in France in the First World War

Ford, Ger·ald /ˈdʒerəld/ R (1913–) an American Republican politician who became president of the US when Richard Nixon resigned (RESIGN) after the Watergate affair in 1974. He was defeated in the next presidential election in 1976 by Jimmy Carter. Ford once fell down the steps of an airplane and some jokes were made about his clumsiness (CLUMSY).

Ford, Glenn (1916–) a Canadian actor who made many films in the 1940s–1960s, often playing a HERO

Ford, Harrison (1942–) an American actor known esp. for his adventure films such as Star Wars and Raiders of the Lost Ark —see picture at Indiana JONES

Ford, Henry (1863–1947) an American industrialist and maker of the first motor cars. He set up the Ford Motor Company in 1903, designed (DESIGN) the famous Model T car in 1908 and by 1924 his company was producing two million cars a day. He is known as one of the richest, most successful American businessmen.

Ford, John (1586–1639) an English poet and writer for the theatre. His plays include 'Tis Pity She's a Whore and The Broken Heart

Ford, John (1895–1973) an American film director esp. known for his WESTERNs including Stagecoach and How the West was Won and The Grapes of Wrath

fore¹ /fɔːʳ/ n **to the fore** to a noticeable, active, or leading position: She passed her law examinations when she was very young, and soon **came to the fore** as a lawyer. | The crisis in the Middle East suddenly brought him to the fore as an expert negotiator.

fore² adj, adv [A] in or towards the front part of a boat or aircraft: Your seat's in the fore part of the aircraft. – opposite aft

fore³ interj (a warning shouted by a GOLF player who has just hit the ball)

fore- see WORD FORMATION

fore and aft /ˌ· · ˈ·/ adj (of a ship's sails) set in a line along the length of the ship rather than across —compare SQUARE-RIGGED

fore·arm¹ /ˈfɔːrɑːm‖-ɑːrm/ n the lower part of the arm between the hand and the elbow

fore·arm² /ˌfɔːrˈɑːm‖-ˈɑːrm/ v [T usu. pass.] to prepare for an attack before the time of need —compare FOREWARN

fore·bear , for- /ˈfɔːbeəʳ‖ˈfɔːr-/ n [usu. pl.] fml or lit a person from whom one is descended; ANCESTOR: My forebears lived in the west of Scotland.

fore·bode /fɔːˈbəʊd‖fɔːr-/ v [T] fml to be a warning of (something unpleasant)

fore·bod·ing /fɔːˈbəʊdɪŋ‖fɔːr-/ n [C;U] a feeling of coming evil; PREMONITION: She thought of a lonely future with foreboding. [+that] She had a strange foreboding that she'd never see him again.

fore·cast¹ /ˈfɔːkɑːst‖ˈfɔːrkæst/ v -**cast** or -**casted** [T] to say, esp. with the help of some kind of knowledge (what is going to happen at some future time); PREDICT: He confidently forecast a big increase in sales, and he turned out to be right. [+that] The teacher forecast that fifteen of his pupils would pass the exam. [+wh-] I wouldn't like to forecast whether he will resign. – – **er** n: a weather forecaster

forecast² n a statement of future events, based on some kind of knowledge or judgment: The weather forecast on the radio said there would be heavy rain. | the government's economic forecasts for the coming year [+that] The newspaper's forecast that the government would only last for six months turned out to be wrong.

fore·castle /ˈfəʊksəl ‖ ˈfəʊksəl, ˈfɔːrkæsəl/ n AmE for FO'C'SLE

fore·close /fɔːˈkləʊz‖fɔːr-/ v [I (on);T] to take back property because of someone's failure to repay (a MORTGAGE): The building society will be forced to foreclose (this mortgage) because regular repayments have not been made. --**closure** /ˈkləʊʒəʳ/ n [C;U]

fore·court /ˈfɔːkɔːt‖ˈfɔːrkɔːrt/ n **1** a large open area in front of a large building: He parked his car in the station *forecourt.* **2** the area of a GARAGE[1] (2) where petrol and oil are sold

fore·doomed /fɔːˈduːmd‖fɔːr-/ *adj* [(to)] *fml* intended (as if) by fate to reach a usu. bad state or condition: *The plan was foredoomed to failure.*

fore·fa·ther /ˈfɔːˌfɑːðəʳ‖ˈfɔːr-/ *n* [*usu. pl.*] a person from whom the stated person is descended; relative in the far past; (male) ANCESTOR: *One of his forefathers was an early settler in America.* —see also FAMILY TREE

fore·fin·ger /ˈfɔːˌfɪŋɡəʳ‖ˈfɔːr-/ *n* INDEX FINGER

fore·foot /ˈfɔːfʊt‖ˈfɔːr-/ *n* **-feet** /fiːt/ either of the two front feet of a four-legged animal

fore·front /ˈfɔːfrʌnt‖ˈfɔːr-/ *n* [*the* (of)] the most forward place; leading position: *She has been in/at the forefront of the struggle for women's rights.*

fore·go /fɔːˈɡəʊ‖fɔːr-/ *v* **-went** /ˈwent/, **-gone** /ˈɡɒn‖ˈɡɔːn/ [T *past tense rare*] to FORGO

fore·go·ing /ˈfɔːɡəʊɪŋ‖ˈfɔːr-/ *adj, n* [A;*the*+C] foregoing *fml* (the one) that has just been mentioned: *The foregoing (paragraph) is a brief summary of the situation; in what follows I shall go into more detail.*

foregone con·clu·sion /ˌ··· ·ˈ···/ *n* [S] a result that is or was certain: *"Do you think he'll win again?" "He won the last four matches so I think it's a foregone conclusion."*

fore·ground /ˈfɔːɡraʊnd‖ˈfɔːr-/ *n* the nearest part of a scene in a view, a picture, or a photograph: *a photograph of our town, with the church in the foreground* | (fig.) *She talks a great deal, because she likes to keep herself in the foreground.* (=as noticeable as possible) —compare BACKGROUND

fore·hand /ˈfɔːhænd‖ˈfɔːr-/ *n* (in games such as tennis) (the ability to make) a stroke with the front of the hand (the PALM) turned in the direction of movement: *She has a very strong forehand.* —compare BACKHAND –**forehand** *adj, adv*: *a forehand smash*

fore·head /ˈfɒrɪd, ˈfɔːhed‖ˈfɔːrɪd, ˈfɑːrɪd, ˈfɔːrhed/ *n* the part of the face between the eyes and above the hair: *a man with a high* (=wide) *forehead* —see picture at HEAD

for·eign /ˈfɒrɪn‖ˈfɔːr-, ˈfɑː-/ *adj* [*no comp.*] **1** to, from, of, in, being, or concerning a country or nation that is not one's own or not the one being talked about or considered: *foreign travel* | *These oranges are foreign produce.* | *I collect foreign stamps.* | *Have you had any foreign experience as a teacher?* (=Have you taught in other countries?) | *He's visited many foreign countries and has learnt several foreign languages.* | *I can't understand what he says; he must be foreign.* —compare DOMESTIC[1] (4), NATIVE[1]; see OVERSEAS (USAGE) **2** [F+to] *fml* having no place (in); having no relation (to): *He's a very good person; unkindness is foreign to his nature.* **3** [A] *fml* coming or brought in from outside; not belonging; harmful: *The swelling on her finger was caused by a foreign body in it.* (=a small piece of something that had entered it by accident)

foreign af·fairs /ˌ··· ·ˈ·/ *n* [P] matters concerning international relations and the interests of one's own country in foreign countries: *the Ministry of Foreign Affairs*

foreign aid /ˌ·· ˈ·/ *n* [U] money, goods, etc., given to poor countries; AID[2] (3)

soldiers of the Foreign Legion

Foreign and Com·mon·wealth Of·fice /ˌ·· · ˈ··· ˌ··/ [*the*] see FCO

for·eign·er /ˈfɒrɪnəʳ‖ˈfɔːr-, ˈfɑː-/ *n* a person belonging to a foreign race or country: *Could you help me, please? I'm a foreigner, and I can't read the signs.*

foreign ex·change /ˌ··· ·ˈ·/ *n* [U] (the practice of buying and selling) foreign money

Foreign Le·gion /ˌ·· ˈ··/ [*the*] the French army of VOLUN-TEERS which mainly consists of foreigners and was used in the French colonies (COLONY) during the First and Second World Wars. It is connected in people's minds with strong, rough men able to suffer difficult and severe conditions.

foreign min·is·ter /ˌ·· ˈ···/ *n* the head of the foreign office, the government department responsible for a country's relations with other countries. In Britain the head of the Foreign Office is called the Foreign Secretary: *The foreign ministers of the 12 EC countries meet in Brussels today.*

Foreign Of·fice /ˈ·· ˌ··/ [*the*] *infml* FOREIGN AND COMMON-WEALTH OFFICE

foreign pol·i·cy /ˌ·· ˈ···/ *n* [U] the general plan of one country concerning its relations with other countries: *It is not yet clear who will be in charge of foreign policy in the new government.*

Foreign Sec·re·ta·ry /ˌ·· ˈ····/ *n* (in Britain) the head of the Foreign Office —compare SECRETARY OF STATE, see FCO

Foreign Ser·vice /ˈ·· ˌ··/ [*the*] a part of the US STATE DEPARTMENT which sends DIPLOMATs to foreign countries to deal with business abroad

fore·knowl·edge /fɔːˈnɒlɪdʒ‖fɔːrˈnɑːl-/ *n* [U (of)] *fml* knowledge about something before it happens

fore·leg /ˈfɔːleɡ‖ˈfɔːr-/ *n* either of the two front legs of a four-legged animal

fore·lock /ˈfɔːlɒk‖ˈfɔːrlɑːk/ *n* **1** a piece of hair growing just above and falling over the forehead: *She brushed her horse's mane and forelock before the show jumping began.* —see picture at HORSE **2 tug at/touch one's forelock** *BrE* to be (too) respectful to someone in a position of power, someone of a higher social class, etc.

fore·man /ˈfɔːmən‖ˈfɔːr-/ **forewoman** *fem.*— *n* **-men** /mən/ **1** a skilled and experienced worker who is put in charge of other workers **2** (in a court of law) the leader of the 12 people (JURY) appointed to decide whether a person on trial is guilty or not

fore·most /ˈfɔːməʊst‖ˈfɔːr-/ *adj* [*the*+A] most important; leading: *He was the foremost conductor of his day.* —see also **first and foremost** (FIRST[1])

fore·name /ˈfɔːneɪm‖ˈfɔːr-/ *n fml for* FIRST NAME

fore·noon /ˈfɔːnuːn‖ˈfɔːr-/ *n fml* the time before midday; morning

fo·ren·sic /fəˈrensɪk, -zɪk/ *adj* [A] *tech* related to or used in the law and the tracking of criminals: *The use of scientific methods by the police is known as* **forensic science.** | *A specialist in* **forensic medicine** *was called as a witness in the murder trial.*

forensic ev·i·dence /·ˌ·· ˈ···/ *n* [U] something physical, e.g. blood, hair, fingerprints, or drugs, which proves something in law: *The rapist was convicted on the basis of forensic evidence.*

fore·or·dain /ˌfɔːrɔːˈdeɪn‖ˌfɔːrɔːr-/ *v* [T *often pass.*] *fml* to arrange or decide from the very beginning that, or how, something or someone shall happen, act, or be done: *He believed his success was foreordained.* [+obj+to-v] *His followers were convinced that he was foreordained to lead them to victory.* [+that] *God foreordained that she would one day be queen.*

fore·play /ˈfɔːpleɪ‖ˈfɔːr-/ *n* [U] sexual activity, such as touching the sexual organs and kissing, that is done before SEXUAL INTERCOURSE

fore·run·ner /ˈfɔːˌrʌnəʳ/ *n* [+of] **1** a sign or warning that something is going to happen: *A few isolated signs were the forerunner of a massive run on the Stock Exchange.* **2** a person or group who prepares the way for, or is a sign of the coming of, a more important person or group: *Mrs Pankhurst, who fought for votes for women, was a forerunner of the modern women's movement.*

fore·see /fɔːˈsiː‖fɔːr-/ *v* **-saw** /ˈsɔː/, **-seen** /ˈsiːn/ [T] to see or form an idea about (what is going to happen in the future) in advance; expect: *We should have foreseen this trouble months ago and made provisions for it.* [+(that)] *He foresaw that his journey would be delayed by bad weather.* [+wh-] *It's impossible to foresee whether she'll be well enough to come home from hospital next month.* — see also UNFORESEEN

fore·see·a·ble /fɔːˈsiːəbəl‖fɔːr-/ *adj* that can be foreseen: *It was a foreseeable accident.* | *The house certainly needs a new roof, but we can't afford one* **in the foreseeable future.** (=as far ahead in time as we can see)

fore·shad·ow /fɔːˈʃædəʊ‖fɔːr-/ *v* [T] *esp. lit* to be a sign of (what is coming); represent or be like (something that is going to happen)

fore·shore /ˈfɔːʃɔːʳ‖ˈfɔːr-/ *n* [*the*] the part of the seashore **a** between the highest point the sea reaches and the lowest point it goes back to **b** between the edge of the sea and the part of the land that has grass, buildings, etc.

fore·short·en /fɔːˈʃɔːtn‖fɔːrˈʃɔːrtn/ *v* [T] **1** to draw (an object or scene) with the lines and shapes in the distance smaller, shorter, and closer together, as they appear to the human eye **2** to make (objects or scenes) seem smaller, shorter, and/or closer together than is really the case: *Television cameras foreshorten the picture you see.*

fore·sight /ˈfɔːsaɪt‖ˈfɔːr-/ *n* [U] *usu. apprec* the ability to imagine what will probably happen, allowing one to act to help or prevent developments; care or wise planning for the future: *He had the foresight to invest his money carefully.* —compare HINDSIGHT

fore·skin /ˈfɔːˌskɪn‖ˈfɔːr-/ *n* a loose fold of skin covering the end of the PENIS (=the male sex organ)

for·est /ˈfɒrɟst‖ˈfɔː-, ˈfɑː-/ *n* [C;U] (a large area of land thickly covered with) trees and bushes: *A large part of Russia is made up of thick forest(s).* | *a pine forest* | *a clearing in the forest* | *a forest fire* | (fig.) *When the teacher asked the children an easy question, a forest of hands shot up.* —compare JUNGLE, WOOD; —see also RAIN FOREST

fore·stall /fɔːˈstɔːl‖fɔːr-/ *v* [T] to prevent, defeat, etc., (a person or their plans) by acting first: *We forestalled any attempt to steal the jewels by having them moved to a safer place.* | *I meant to meet my friend at the station, but she forestalled me/my plan by arriving on an earlier train and coming to the house.*

for·est·er /ˈfɒrɟstəʳ‖ˈfɔː-, ˈfɑː-/ *n* a person who works in or is in charge of a forest

Forester, C S (1899–1966) a British writer best-known for his stories about the Royal Navy in the days of sailing ships, esp. those about the character Captain Horatio Hornblower

Forest Hills /ˌ·· ˈ·/ *n* a town in New York state where tennis competitions are held

for·est·ry /ˈfɒrɟstri‖ˈfɔː-, ˈfɑː-/ *n* [U] the science of planting and caring for large areas of trees

Forestry Com·mis·sion /ˈ··· ·,·/ [*the*] an organization concerned with the care of trees in Britain, including the cutting down and replanting of trees, the control of DISEASEs, and the providing of walks and camping grounds in forests

fore·taste /ˈfɔːteɪst‖ˈfɔːr-/ *n* [S (of)] a small early experience (of something that will come later): *The unusually warm spring day seemed like a foretaste of summer.*

fore·tell /fɔːˈtel‖fɔːr-/ *v* **-told** /ˈtəʊld/ [T] to tell (what will happen in the future); PROPHESY: *The fortune-teller foretold the man's death.* [+that] *She foretold that the man would die.* [+wh-] *Who can foretell how the world will end?*

fore·thought /ˈfɔːθɔːt‖ˈfɔːr-/ *n* [U] wise planning for future needs; consideration of what is to come: *If you'd had the forethought to bring your raincoat, you wouldn't have got wet.*

for·ev·er /fərˈevəʳ/ *adv* **1** also **for ever** — for all future time: *When her son went to fight in the war, his mother felt she'd said goodbye to him forever.* | *I'll love you for ever and ever.* **2** (*used only with verbs in progressive forms*) continually and annoyingly: *The little boy is forever asking questions.* **3 take forever** to take an extremely long time: *Go by underground — it'll take you forever if you go by bus.* **4 forever and a day** an extremely long time: *It took me forever and a day to finish the assignment.* —see also **Diamonds are forever** (DIAMOND (1))

fore·warn /fɔːˈwɔːn‖fɔːrˈwɔːrn/ *v* [T (**of, against, about**)]

to warn (someone) of coming danger, unpleasantness, etc.; advise (that something will happen or be done): *We were forewarned of/about the sudden collapse in shares.* [+obj+that] *They forewarned us that our first year in business would not be easy.* | *As I always say,* **forewarned is forearmed.** (=if you know about something in advance, you can be properly prepared to deal with it)

fore·went /fɔːˈwent‖fɔːr-/ *past tense of* FOREGO

fore·wom·an /ˈfɔːˌwʊmən‖ˈfɔːr-/ *n* **-women** /ˌwɪmɪn/ a female FOREMAN

fore·word /ˈfɔːwɜːd‖ˈfɔːrwɜːrd/ *n* a short introduction at the beginning of a book, esp. in which someone who knows the writer and their work says something about them — see PREFACE (USAGE)

for·feit¹ /ˈfɔːfɟt‖ˈfɔːr-/ *v* [T] to have (something) taken away from one because some agreement or rule has been broken, or as a punishment, or as the result of some action: *If you don't return the article to the shop within a week, you forfeit your chance of getting your money back.* – **-able** *adj* – **-er** *n*

forfeit² *n* what must be lost or forfeited for something; price: *Some scientists who have studied dangerous substances have* **paid the forfeit** *of their lives in the cause of knowledge.*

forfeit³ *adj* [F (**to**)] *fml or old use* taken from one by law as a punishment: *If a man put his country in danger by helping the enemy, his life and possessions were forfeit to the crown.*

for·fei·ture /ˈfɔːfɟtʃəʳ‖ˈfɔːr-/ *n* [U (**of**)] *fml* forfeiting or being forfeited

for·gath·er /fɔːˈgæðəʳ‖fɔːr-/ *v* [I] *fml* to gather together; meet, esp. in a friendly way

for·gave /fəˈgeɪv‖fər-/ *past tense of* FORGIVE

forge¹ /fɔːdʒ‖fɔːrdʒ/ *v* [T] **1** to make a copy of (something) in order to deceive: *He got the money dishonestly, by forging his brother's signature on a cheque.* | *She tried to get into the country on a forged passport.* —see also FORGERY **2** to form by heating and hammering: *forging the links of a chain* | (fig.) *new efforts to forge unity in our political party* —compare WELD

forge² *n* **1** (a building or room containing) a large apparatus with a fire inside, used for heating and shaping metal objects: *Horseshoes are made in a blacksmith's forge.* **2** (a part of a factory containing) a large apparatus that produces great heat inside itself, used for melting metal, making iron, etc.

forge³ *v* [I+adv/prep] to move with a sudden increase of speed and power: *One of the runners forged into the lead as they came round the last bend.* | (fig.) *She didn't do very well when she first went to school, but she's* **forged ahead** *in the last two years.*

forg·er /ˈfɔːdʒəʳ‖ˈfɔːr-/ *n* a person who forges money, papers, etc.

for·ge·ry /ˈfɔːdʒəri‖ˈfɔːr-/ *n* [C;U] (something made by) forging (FORGE¹ (1)): *When he bought the picture he was told it was a Rubens, but he later found out that it was a forgery.* | *They were sent to prison for forgery.*

for·get /fəˈget‖fər-/ *v* **-got** /ˈgɒt‖ˈgɑːt/, **-gotten** /ˈgɒtn‖ˈgɑːtn/ [*not usu. in progressive forms*] **1** [I;T] to fail to remember or keep in the memory: *Be there at five o'clock — don't forget!* | *I'm sorry, I've forgotten your name.* [+to-v] *Don't forget to bring the cases.* [+(that)] *I'm sorry, I was forgetting (that) you don't like beans.* [+v-ing] *I'll never forget finding that rare old coin in my garden.* [+wh-] *I forget who said it.* | *"What's her name?" "I forget."* **2** [I (**about**); T] to fail to remember to do, bring, buy, etc. (something): *Don't forget the cases.* | *"Did you lock the door when you left the house?" "No, I'm afraid I forgot (all) about it."* **3** [I (**about**);T] to stop thinking about; put out of one's mind: *They agreed to forget their disagreements and be friends again.* | *"I'm sorry I broke your teapot."* **"Forget it."** (=It doesn't matter at all.) | *"Our former neighbours came to see us yesterday." "I'd forgotten (all) about them."* | *However hard he tried, he couldn't forget her.* | *Don't hold grudges against people who have hurt you; you should* **forgive and forget. 4** [T] to fail to give attention to; treat with inattention: *He forgot his old friends when he became rich.* | *"Don't forget me," said the little boy as his aunt was giving out jelly to the other children.* **5** [T] to stop regarding (something) as a possibility; give up (a plan): *If we can't get any financial backing, we might as well forget the whole thing.* **6 forget oneself** to lose one's temper or self-control, or act in a way that is unsuitable or makes one look foolish: *The little girl annoyed him so much that he forgot himself and hit her.* **7 lest we forget** *quote* a phrase from a work by Rudyard Kipling, used esp. on MEMORIALs to those people who died during the two World Wars

for·get·ful /fəˈgetfəl‖fər-/ *adj* [(of)] having the habit of forgetting: *My aunt has become rather forgetful in her old age.* – ~ly *adv* – ~ness *n* [U]

forget-me-not /ˈ·ˈ· ˌ·/ *n* a type of low-growing plant with small usu. pale blue flowers

forg·ing /ˈfɔːdʒɪŋ‖ˈfɔːr-/ *n* a piece of forged (FORGE¹ (2)) metal

for·giv·a·ble , **-give-** /fəˈgɪvəbəl‖fər-/ *adj* (of a thing) that can be forgiven: *It was a forgivable mistake.* –**bly** *adv*

for·give /fəˈgɪv‖fər-/ *v* **-gave** /ˈgeɪv/, **-given** /ˈgɪvən/ **1** [I; T (**for**) *not in progressive forms*] to say or feel that one is no longer angry with (someone) or about (something); to say or feel that one no longer blames (someone) for (something): *I'm afraid I've smashed up your car – can you ever forgive me?* | *I'll never forgive you for what you said to me last night.* | *It's best to* **forgive and forget.** [+*obj(i)+obj(d)*] *He forgave her the awful things she said about him.* | (used to express annoyance, disagreement, etc.) *"Forgive me, Minister," said the interviewer, "but you haven't answered my question yet."* **2 Father forgive them for they know not what they do** the words spoken by Christ in the Bible, asking God to forgive the people who were killing Him

for·give·ness /fəˈgɪvnɪs‖fər-/ *n* [U] **1** [(of)] the act of forgiving or state of being forgiven: *He asked God's forgiveness|for forgiveness of his wrong-doings.* **2** willingness to forgive

for·giv·ing /fəˈgɪvɪŋ‖fər-/ *adj* willing or able to forgive: *a gentle forgiving nature* – ~ly *adv*

for·go , **fore-** /fɔːˈgəʊ‖fɔːr-/ *v* **-went** /ˈwent/, **-gone** /ˈgɒn‖ˈgɔːn/ [T *past tense rare*] *fml* to give up; (be willing) not to have (esp. something pleasant): *You shouldn't forgo the opportunity of hearing a live concert.*

for·got /fəˈgɒt‖fərˈgɑːt/ *past tense of* FORGET

for·got·ten /fəˈgɒtn‖fərˈgɑːtn/ *past participle of* FORGET

fork¹ /fɔːk‖fɔːrk/ *n* **1** an instrument for holding food or carrying it to the mouth, having a handle at one end with two or more points at the other, and usu. made of metal or plastic: *He picked up his knife and fork.* –see KNIFE (USAGE) and see picture at PLACE SETTING **2** a farm or gardening tool for breaking up the soil, lifting dried grass, etc., having a handle with two or more metal points at one end –see picture at GARDENING EQUIPMENT **3** a place where something divides into branches, or one of the divided parts: *We came to a fork in the road, and we couldn't decide whether to take the left fork or the right.* **4** also **forks** *pl.* – a pair of parallel metal points between which the front wheel of a bicycle, motorcycle, etc., is fixed –see picture at BICYCLE

fork² *v* **1** [T+*obj+adv/prep*] to lift, carry, move, or turn (soil, grass, etc.) with a fork: *Fork over the garden before you plant the peas.* **2** [I] (of something long and narrow) to divide into two or more parts: *You'll see our house on the left, just before the road forks.* **3** [I+*adv/prep*] (of a person) to take one fork of a road, path, etc.: *Fork left at the pub.*

fork (sthg. ↔) **out** *phr v* [I;T (**for, on**)] *infml* to pay (money) unwillingly: *I had to fork out £200 for my last telephone bill.*

fork up *phr v* [I (**for**) *often imperative*] *infml* to FORK out: *Come on, fork up!*

forked /fɔːkt‖fɔːrkt/ *adj* [*no comp.*] **1** having one end divided into two or more points: *Snakes have forked tongues.* **2 White man speaks with forked tongue** a phrase used in old WESTERN films, said by Native Americans when they believe a white man is not telling the truth

forked light·ning /ˌ·ˈ··/ *n* [U] lightning in the form of a line in the sky, usu. dividing into two or more parts near the bottom –compare SHEET LIGHTNING

fork·lift truck /ˌfɔːklɪft ˈtrʌk‖ˌfɔːrk-/ *n* a small vehicle with a movable apparatus on the front used for lifting and lowering heavy goods –see picture at TRUCK

for·lorn /fəˈlɔːn‖fərˈlɔːrn/ *adj esp. lit. or fml* **1** (typical of one who is) left alone and unhappy: *She had a forlorn look (on her face).* –see ALONE (USAGE) **2** left empty and in poor condition: *a row of forlorn old buildings down by the port* – ~ly *adv* – ~ness *n* [U]

forlorn hope /·ˌ· ˈ·/ *n* [S] a plan or attempt that is very unlikely to succeed

form¹ /fɔːm‖fɔːrm/ *n* **1** [C;U] shape; outward appearance: *In the early morning light we could just make out|see the dark forms of the mountains.* | *The tall graceful form of a woman appeared at the top of the stairs.* | *Churches are often built* **in the form of** (=shaped like) *a cross.* **2** [C (**of**)] a general plan or arrangement; way something shows or expresses itself; kind or sort: *Different countries have different forms of government.* | *Name three forms of air travel.* | *This illness* **takes the form of** (=shows itself as) *high fever and sickness over a period of several days.* | *She dislikes any form of exercise.* | *There are two forms of the past of "to dream": "dreamed" and "dreamt".* | *I don't like sport* **in any shape or form.** (=of any kind) **3** [U] *tech* the way in which a work of art is put together: *Some writers are masters of form, but the content of their books isn't interesting.* **4** [U] (esp. in sport) degree of fitness, skill, etc., esp. as this influences performance or success: *"What kind of form is he in?"* (=How well is he playing?) *"He's been* **in bad form|out of form** *recently."* | *If it's really* **on form** (*esp. BrE*)/**in form** (*esp. AmE*), *this horse should win easily.* | *He was* **in great form|**(also *BrE*) **on great form** (=in good spirits) *at the party last night.* | *We were hoping to make a profit this year, but* **on present form** (=judging by our present performance) *that looks unlikely.* **5** [C] an official paper with spaces in which to answer questions and give other information: *If you wish to be considered for this job, you must* **fill in/fill up/fill out a form** *giving your age, name, experience, etc., and send it to the company.* | *Hand your completed form in at the desk.* | *I'm sorry, I don't understand (how to fill in) this form.* | *a badly-designed form* | *a visa application form* **6** [(*the*)U] the correct or usual custom or practice; PROCEDURE: *I'd like to join the library; what's the form?* (=what do I have to do?) | *I'll have to ask for your name and address, sir, but it's purely* **a matter of form.** **7** [U] *old-fash* behaviour as judged by accepted social standards; manners: *It is considered very* **bad form** *to arrive too early at a dinner party.* **8** [C] a class in a British school, and in some American schools: *Children who have just started school go into the first form; the oldest children are in the sixth form.* –compare GRADE¹ (2) **9** [C] *BrE* a long wooden seat, usu. without a back **10** [U] *BrE sl* a record of having been found guilty of crimes **11 -former** *BrE* a pupil of the stated FORM (8): *a sixth-former*

form² *v* **1** [I;T] to come or bring gradually into existence; develop. *A cloud of smoke formed over the burning city.* | *A plan began to form in his mind.* | *I formed the impression that she was not being completely honest.* | *School helps to form a child's character.* **2** [T] to make or produce, esp. by combining parts: *The past tense of "cook" is formed by adding "-ed ".* | *The leader of the winning party has been invited to form a government.* | *We used branches and leaves to form a rough shelter.* **3** [L+*n*] to take the shape of: *The school buildings formed a hollow square, with a playground in the middle.* **4** [L+*n*] to be; be the substance of; CONSTITUTE: *Flour, eggs, fat, and sugar form the main ingredients of a cake.* **5** [I+*adv/prep*; T] to (cause to) stand or move in (a certain order): *The men formed a chain to pass the goods from the carts to the boats.* | *The teacher formed her class into five groups.* | *The soldiers formed up into a line.*

form·al /ˈfɔːməl‖ˈfɔːr-/ *adj* **1 a** based on or done according to correct or accepted rules, e.g. of social behaviour or official business: *As it's a formal dinner party, we will have to wear formal dress.* | *They told me on the phone that I could have the job, but I haven't yet had a formal offer.* **b** *esp. tech* (of words or a style of writing or speaking) suitable for official occasions, serious writing, etc., but not for ordinary conversation. Formal words or phrases are marked *fml* in this dictionary: *"Purchase" means the same as "buy", but it is more formal.* | *Government reports are usually written in formal language.*

▶ CULTURAL NOTE **Formal dress** usu. means a black DINNER JACKET, trousers, and BOW TIE for men, and a stylish dress which need not be long for women. ◀

2 exact and correct in manner and behaviour: *He's very formal with everyone; he never joins in a laugh.* **3** having a set or regular shape: *a formal garden with straight paths and neat hedges* —opposite **informal** (for 1,2,3) **4** [*no comp.*] *fml* in outward appearance only: *There's only a formal resemblance between the two brothers – their characters are very different.* – ~ **ly** *adv* : *At the police station he was formally charged with murder.*

formal² *n AmE* a woman's formal dress: *The only time I ever wore that formal was to the junior prom.*

for·ma·lin /ˈfɔːməlɪn‖ˈfɔːr-/ *n* [U] a liquid made by mixing the colourless gas **formaldehyde** with water, used for killing bacteria and keeping things clean, preserving dead bodies for science, making plastic, etc.

form·al·is·m /ˈfɔːməlɪzəm‖ˈfɔːr-/ *n* [U] *often derog* (too great and exact an) obedience to rules and ceremonies, esp. in art and religion --**ist** *n, adj*

for·mal·i·ty /fɔːˈmælɪti‖fɔːr-/ *n* **1** [U] careful attention to rules and accepted forms of behaviour: *Even with close friends he observes a certain formality.* **2** [C] **a** an act in accordance with law or custom: *There are a few formalities to go through before you enter a foreign country, such as showing your passport.* **b** an act like this which has lost its real meaning: *The written part of the exam is just a formality; no one ever fails it.*

for·mal·ize also **-ise** *BrE* /ˈfɔːməlaɪz‖ˈfɔːr-/ *v* [T] *fml* **1** to put (an agreement, plan, etc.) into clear usu. written form: *The agreement must be formalized before it can have the force of law.* **2** to introduce formality into (an occasion, event, etc.) --**ization** /ˌfɔːməlaɪˈzeɪʃən‖ˌfɔːrmələ-/ *n* [U]

For·man /ˈfɔːmən‖ˈfɔːr-/, **Mi·los** /ˈmiːlɒs‖-ləʊʃ/ (1932–) a Czech film director who has worked in the US since 1968. He is best known for his film *One Flew Over the Cuckoo's Nest.*

for·mat¹ /ˈfɔːmæt‖ˈfɔːr-/ *n* **1** the size, shape, etc., in which something, esp. a book, is produced **2** the general plan or arrangement of something: *a new format for the six o'clock TV news* | *Official reports are usually written in a set format.*

format² *v* **-tt-** [T] to arrange (a book, computer information, etc.) in a particular format

for·ma·tion /fɔːˈmeɪʃən‖fɔːr-/ *n* **1** [U] the shaping or developing of something: *Damp conditions are needed for the formation of mould.* | *School life has a great influence on the formation of a child's character.* **2** [C;U] (an) arrangement of people, ships, aircraft, etc.; order: *The soldiers were drawn up in battle formation.* (=in the correct position to begin a battle) | *a team of aircraft that does formation flying* (=flying that makes patterns in the sky) **3** [C;U] a thing which is formed or the way in which it is formed: *several kinds of cloud formations* | *Geologists study rock formation.* —see also BACK FORMATION

for·ma·tive /ˈfɔːmətɪv‖ˈfɔːr-/ *adj* [A] having influence in forming or developing: *Parents have the greatest formative effect on their children's behaviour.* | *The child's in her formative years.* (=the time when her character is formed) – ~ **ly** *adv*

Form·by /ˈfɔːmbi‖ˈfɔːrm-/, **George** (1904–61) an English COMEDIAN of MUSIC HALL and films from the North of England. He often acted as a rather stupid common man and sang humorous songs while playing the UKELELE (=a type of musical instrument with strings).

for·mer¹ /ˈfɔːməʳ‖ˈfɔːr-/ *adj* [A *no comp.*] of an earlier period: *her former husband* | *In former times people were hanged for stealing in Britain.* | *He made us laugh all the evening; he seemed more like his former self.* (=as he was before he was changed by trouble, age, illness, etc.)

former² *adj, n* **former** [A *no comp.*;C] *rather fml* the first (of two people or things just mentioned): *Of Nigeria and Ghana, the former (country) has the larger population.* | *Of the two possibilities, the former seems more likely.* – opposite **latter**

for·mer·ly /ˈfɔːməli‖ˈfɔːrmərli/ *adv* in earlier times: *Peru was formerly ruled by the Spanish.* | *Formerly he worked in a factory, but now he's a teacher.*

For·mi·ca /fɔːˈmaɪkə‖fɔːr-/ *n* [U] *tdmk* (*often not cap.*) a strong plastic made in thin sheets, used for making the top surface of tables and other articles of furniture

for·mic ac·id /ˌfɔːmɪk ˈæsɪd‖ˌfɔːr-/ *n* [U] an acid obtained

from ants, and now also produced artificially, used esp. in colouring cloth and making leather

for·mi·da·ble /ˈfɔːmɪdəbəl, fəˈmɪd-‖ˈfɔːr-,fər-/ *adj* **1** very great and frightening; causing anxiety, fearful respect, etc.: *He has a formidable voice.* (=very loud) | *His mother is a most formidable lady.* **2** difficult to defeat or deal with; needing much effort to succeed against: *a formidable enemy* | *They climbed the last part of the mountain in formidable weather conditions.* | *The examination paper contained several formidable questions.* --**bly** *adv*

form·less /ˈfɔːmləs‖ˈfɔːrm-/ *adj* **1** without shape: *a strange formless creature* **2** *usu. derog* lacking order or arrangement: *The experimental music was rather formless.* – ~ **ly** *adv* – ~ **ness** *n* [U]

form let·ter /ˈ· ˌ··/ *n* a standard letter that is sent to a number of people, with details such as name and address added

form of ad·dress /ˌ· · ·ˈ·/ *n* **forms of address** the correct, polite title to be used when speaking or writing to someone: *"Your Majesty" is the form of address used with the queen.* | *What form of address is appropriate when speaking to a bishop?*

form room /ˈ· ·/ *BrE* ‖ **homeroom** *AmE*– *n* the classroom used by the pupils in the same form¹ (8) where the teacher takes the attendance and discusses various social or ADMINISTRATIVE matters

form teach·er /ˈ· ˌ··/ *BrE* ‖ **homeroom teacher** *AmE*– *n* the teacher responsible for the pupils of one form¹ (8), often dealing with personal and social matters as well as teaching them: *Talk to your form teacher if you have any problems.*

for·mu·la /ˈfɔːmjʊlə‖ˈfɔːrm-/ *n* **-las** or **-lae** /liː/ **1** [C (**for**)] *tech* a general law, rule, fact, etc., expressed in a short form by means of a group of letters, signs, numbers, etc.: *The chemical formula for water is* H_2O. | *There is a special formula for calculating distance, if speed and time are known.* **2** [C (**for**)] a list of the esp. chemical substances used in making a medicine, a FUEL, a drink, etc., sometimes also including a description of how they are to be mixed: *Someone has stolen the secret formula for the new drink.* –compare RECIPE **3** [C (**for**)] a method or set of principles used for gaining a particular result: *The two sides worked out an acceptable formula* (=combination of suggestions, plans, etc.) *for settling the strike.* | *A good education and hard work seems to be a formula for success.* (=they will almost certainly lead to success) **4** [C] (before a number) a particular type of racing car or car race: *Formula One cars are the most powerful.* | *a formula 5000 race* **5** [U] *AmE* liquid milk-like food for babies

for·mu·la·ic /ˌfɔːmjʊˈleɪ-ɪk‖ˌfɔːrm-/ *adj fml or tech* containing or made up of fixed expressions or set forms of words: *formulaic poetry* – ~ **ly** *adv*

Formula One /ˌ··· ˈ·◂/ *n* [U] a type of car racing which uses expensive, purpose-built cars and competes in GRAND PRIX events: *a Formula One racing car*

for·mu·late /ˈfɔːmjʊleɪt‖ˈfɔːrm-/ *v* [T] **1** to express in an exact way; FRAME: *He took care to formulate his reply very clearly.* **2** to invent and prepare (a plan, suggestion, etc.): *The government is trying to formulate a new policy on Northern Ireland.* --**lation** /ˌfɔːmjʊˈleɪʃən‖ˌfɔːrm-/ *n* [C;U]

for·ni·cate /ˈfɔːnɪkeɪt‖ˈfɔːr-/ *v* [I] *esp. law or bibl* to have sexual relations with someone to whom one is not married --**cation** /ˌfɔːnɪˈkeɪʃən‖ˌfɔːr-/ *n* [U]

for·sake /fəˈseɪk‖fər-/ *v* **-sook** /ˈsʊk/, **-saken** /ˈseɪkən/ [T] *lit or bibl* to desert; leave for ever; give up completely: *She forsook her worldly possessions to devote herself to the church.* | *In the mist and rain the little village had a forsaken look about it.*

for sale /· ˈ·/ *adj* (*often cap.*) offered to be sold, esp. by a private owner: *There's a "For Sale" sign outside their house.* –see also SALE

for·sooth /fəˈsuːθ‖fər-/ *adv old use* indeed; certainly; in truth

For·ster /ˈfɔːstəʳ‖ˈfɔːr-/, **E M** (1879–1970) an English writer of stories who is best known for his NOVELs *Howards End* and *A Passage to India*, and *Room With a View*. Several of his novels have been made into films.

for·swear /fɔːˈsweəʳ‖fɔːr-/ *v* **-swore** /ˈswɔːʳ/ **-sworn** /ˈswɔːn‖ˈswɔːrn/ [T] *fml* to make a solemn promise to give up or to stop doing (something): *The priests of some religions must forswear possessions and marriage.* [+*v-ing*] *He forswore drinking.*

For·syte Sa·ga /ˈfɔːsaɪt ˌsɑːgə‖ˈfɔːr-/, **The** a long story by John Galsworthy, told in three books, about the Forsyte family. It was made into a television SERIES (=set of programmes) in the 1960s.

For·syth /ˈfɔːsaɪθ‖ˈfɔːr-/, **Bruce** (1928–   ) an English COMEDIAN and presenter of game shows on television, esp. the "Generation Game". He is known esp. for saying "Nice to see you, to see you nice!"

For·syth /fɔːˈsaɪθ‖fɔːr-/, **Fred·e·rick** /ˈfredərɪk/ (1938–   ) an English writer of exciting stories of crimes and violence. His books include *The Day of the Jackal* and *The Dogs of War* which have been made into films.

for·sy·thi·a /fɔːˈsaɪθiə‖fərˈsɪ-/ *n* [U] a bush that produces bright yellow flowers before its leaves appear

fort /fɔːt‖fɔːrt/ *n* a strongly made building or set of buildings used for defence at some important place; castle – see also **hold the fort** (HOLD¹)

for·te¹ /ˈfɔːteɪ‖ˈfɔːrt/ *n* [*usu. sing.*] a strong point in a person's character or abilities: *Games are his forte; he plays cricket and football unusually well.*

for·te² /ˈfɔːteɪ‖ˈfɔːr-/ *n, adj, adv* (a piece of music) played loudly –compare PIANO²

forth /fɔːθ‖fɔːrθ/ *adv esp. bibl or lit* **1** (after a verb) out; forward: *He went forth into the desert to pray.* **2** on into the future: *From that day forth, the lovers were never parted.* –see also BRING **forth, and so forth** (AND)

Forth [*the*] a river in S central Scotland which flows into the Firth of Forth and the North Sea

Forth Bridge /ˌ· ˈ·/ [*the*] **1** a railway bridge built in the late 19th century over the Firth of Forth, considered to be a great ENGINEERING achievement of its day **2** a road bridge built in 1964 next to the railway bridge. It is one of the longest SUSPENSION BRIDGES in the world. **3 like painting the Forth Bridge** *BrE* having no end; having to start again at the beginning as soon as one finishes: *Feeding this family is like painting the Forth Bridge.*

the Forth railway bridge

forth·com·ing /ˌfɔːθˈkʌmɪŋ◂‖ˌfɔːrθ-/ *adj* **1** [*no comp.*] happening or appearing in the near future: *On the noticeboard there was a list of forthcoming events at school.* **2** [F *no comp., usu. in negatives*] ready; supplied; offered when needed: *When she was asked why she was late, no answer was forthcoming.* **3** [*usu. in negatives*] *infml* ready to be helpful and friendly: *I asked several villagers the way to the river, but none of them was very forthcoming.*

forth·right /ˈfɔːθraɪt‖ˈfɔːrθ-/ *adj* (too) direct in manner and speech; expressing one's thoughts and feelings plainly; FRANK: *She made the point in her usual forthright manner.* – ~ness *n* [U]

forth·with /fɔːθˈwɪð, -ˈwɪθ‖fɔːrθ-/ *adv fml* at once; without delay

for·ties /ˈfɔːtiz‖ˈfɔːr-/ *n* **1** [*the*] also **'40s**– the 1940s (=the years from 1940 to 1949): *The forties were dominated by the Second World War.* **2 in his/her/their forties** aged from 40 to 49: *She remarried in her early forties.* **3** [*the*] the numbers from 40 to 49, esp. when used to measure temperature

for·ti·eth /ˈfɔːtiəθ‖ˈfɔːr-/ *determiner, n, pron, adv* 40th –see TABLE 1

for·ti·fi·ca·tion /ˌfɔːtʲfʲˈkeɪʃən‖ˌfɔːr-/ *n* **1** [C *usu. pl.*] towers, walls, gun positions, etc., set up as a means of defence **2** [U] the act or science of fortifying

for·ti·fy /ˈfɔːtʲfaɪ‖ˈfɔːr-/ *v* [T] **1** to build forts on; strengthen against possible attack: *a fortified city* | *They fortified the coastal areas.* **2** to make stronger, more effective, etc.: *This breakfast cereal is fortified with vitamins.* | *Sherry is a fortified wine.* (=a wine with strong alcohol added) – **-fiable** *adj* – **-fier** *n*

for·ti·tude /ˈfɔːtʲtjuːd‖ˈfɔːrtʲtuːd/ *n* [U] firm and lasting

ourage in bearing trouble, pain, etc., without complaining: *She bore her illness with great fortitude.*

Fort Knox /ˌ· ˈ·/ a military FORT in Kentucky which holds the US's gold BULLION. It is known for being heavily guarded and impossible to break into: *His house is like Fort Knox.*

fort·night /ˈfɔːtnaɪt‖ˈfɔːrt-/ *n* [*usu. sing.*] *BrE* two weeks: *I'm going away for a fortnight's holiday.* | *I see them about once a fortnight.* (=once every two weeks) | *He's coming in a fortnight's time.* (=two weeks from today) | *Her birthday is Tuesday fortnight.* (=two weeks later than next Tuesday)

fort·night·ly /ˈfɔːtnaɪtli‖ˈfɔːrt-/ *adj, adv BrE* (happening, appearing, etc.) every fortnight or once a fortnight: *a fortnightly visit* | *She is paid fortnightly.*

Fort·num and Ma·son /ˌfɔːtnəm ənd ˈmeɪsən‖ˌfɔːrt-/ a famous department store in Piccadilly in London which sells quality goods and is thought of being a place where rich people go for afternoon tea

For·tran /ˈfɔːtræn‖ˈfɔːr-/ *n* [U] a high-level computer language, mainly for scientific use

for·tress /ˈfɔːtrʲs‖ˈfɔːr-/ *n* a large FORT; place strengthened for defence: *The army stormed the fortress and occupied it.* | *a fortress town*

for·tu·i·tous /fɔːˈtjuːʲtəs‖fɔːrˈtuː-/ *adj* **1** *fml* happening by chance; accidental: *Our meeting was quite fortuitous.* **2** *nonstandard* fortunate; lucky – ~**ly** *adv* – ~**ness** *n* [U]

for·tu·nate /ˈfɔːtʃənʲt‖ˈfɔːr-/ *adj* having or bringing a good condition or situation; lucky: *He's fortunate to have/in having a good job.* | *It was fortunate for her that her husband arrived at that moment.* | *He came at a very fortunate time.* | *She's fortunate enough to have very good health.* –opposite **unfortunate**

for·tu·nate·ly /ˈfɔːtʃənʲtli‖ˈfɔːr-/ *adv* by good chance; luckily: *I was late in getting to the station, but fortunately for me, the train was late too.* | *Fortunately, the fire was discovered soon after it had started.* –opposite **unfortunately**

for·tune /ˈfɔːtʃən‖ˈfɔːr-/ *n* **1** [C] a great amount of money, possessions, etc.: *He dreamed of making a/his fortune.* | *She won a fortune in a lottery.* | *This family made their fortune in/from computers.* | *That diamond necklace she was wearing must be* **worth a fortune.** | (*infml*) *I seem to have spent an absolute fortune on food this week!* –see also SMALL FORTUNE **2** [U] chance, esp. as an important influence on a person's life; fate: *She had the (great) good fortune to be free from illness all her life.* | (*fml*) **Fortune smiled on** *their enterprise.* (=everything went well for it) **3** [C *usu. pl.*] whatever happens by chance, good or bad: *Through all his* **changing fortunes,** *he never lost courage.* | *The* **fortunes of war** *bring death to many, while others escape unharmed.* –see also SOLDIER OF FORTUNE **4** [C] what will happen to a person in the future: *That old gipsy woman* **tells fortunes.** (=claims to tell people about their futures by examining their hands, studying a pack of cards, a glass ball, etc.) | *I had my fortune told last week.* –see also **seek one's fortune** (SEEK)

fortune cook·ie /ˈ·· ˌ·-/ *n AmE* a BISCUIT which contains a piece of paper telling what is going to happen in the future or a humorous statement. They are typically provided at the end of a meal in Chinese restaurants.

Fortune 500 /ˌfɔːtʃən faɪv ˈhʌndrʲd‖ˌfɔːr-/ *n, adj* [*the*] 500 largest CORPORATIONS in the US, as they appear in the yearly list in *Fortune* magazine. It is considered PRESTIGIOUS (=deserving respect and admiration) to be included in this group: *She's a VP at a Fortune 500 company.*

fortune hunt·er /ˈ·· ˌ·-/ *n usu. derog* a person who tries to marry someone for their money –see also GOLD DIGGER (1)

fortune teller

fortune-tell·er /ˈ·· ˌ·-/ *n* a person who claims to be able to tell people what will happen to them in the future. The STEREOTYPE of a fortune teller is of a woman wearing a colourful SCARF on her head and large EARRINGS. She looks into a CRYSTAL BALL to see what is going to happen in the future and she asks people for money by asking them to "cross my palm with silver". –compare PALMIST

Fort Worth /ˌ· ˈ·/ a city in N Texas, in the US, known as an industrial centre, esp. for oil and gas. Its airport, which it shares with nearby Dallas, is one of the largest in the world. –see colour map on pages 1374–5

for·ty /ˈfɔːti‖ˈfɔːrti/ *determiner, n, pron* **1** (the number) 40 –see TABLE 1 **2 life begins at forty** *saying* you can begin to enjoy life at the age of forty

forty-five /ˌ·· ˈ·/ *n infml* **1** also **·45, Colt 45** *tdmk* –a small gun held in the hand (PISTOL). The inside of its barrel is 0·45 of an INCH wide. **2** also **45**– a small record, usu. with only one song on each side, that is played by causing it to turn round 45 times every minute –compare SEVENTY-EIGHT

Forty-five [*the*] the REBELLION in Scotland in 1745 led by Prince Charles Edward Stuart to try to bring back the Stuarts as the ruling family in Britain. They had been forced to leave the country in 1688 after the Glorious Revolution .

forty-nin·er /ˌ·· ˈ··/ *n* a person who took part in the GOLD RUSH to California in 1849

Forty-Sec·ond Street, 42nd Street /ˌ·· ˈ·· ˌ·/ a street in New York City where there are many theatres. A very popular MUSICAL², also called **42nd Street**, is still performed from time to time and was made into a film. This helped to connect 42nd Street with the excitement of life in the theatre.

Forty Thieves /ˌ·· ˈ·/ [*the*] see ALI BABA

forty winks /ˌ·· ˈ·/ *n* [P] *infml* a short sleep in the daytime: *Mum always has forty winks after lunch.*

for·um /ˈfɔːrəm/ *n* **1** (in ancient Rome) an open place used for public business **2 a** [(**for**)] a place where public matters may be talked over and argued about: *The letters page of this newspaper is a forum for public argument.* **b** a meeting for such a purpose: *They're holding a forum on new ways of teaching history.*

for·ward¹ /ˈfɔːwəd‖ˈfɔːrwərd/ also **forwards**– *adv* **1** towards the front, the end, or the future: *The soldiers crept forward under cover of darkness.* | *to bend/step/edge/fall forward* | *They never met again* **from that day forward.** | *to put the clock forward* (=so that it shows a later time) | *Their plans are going forward satisfactorily.* –see LOOK **forward to** **2** towards an earlier time: *We'll bring the date of the meeting forward from the 20th to the 18th.* **3** into a noticeable position: *The lawyer brought forward some new evidence.* | *to push oneself forward* –compare BACKWARDS

forward² *adj* **1** [A *no comp.*] at or directed towards the front, the end, or the future: *a forward movement* | *the forward part of the train* | *forward planning* **2** [*often negative*] advanced or early in development: *We aren't very far forward with our plans yet.* **3** too confident; too sure of oneself: *That young lady is rather forward; she's introducing herself to all the guests.* –compare BACKWARD

forward³ *v* [T] **1** [(**to**)] to send forward or pass on (letters, parcels, etc.) to a new address: *When we moved, we asked the people who took our old house to forward all our mail to our new address.* | *The man who left yesterday didn't leave a* **forwarding address,** *so I don't know where to send this letter that's come for him.* **2** [(**to**)] *fml* to send: *We will forward the goods when we receive your cheque.* [+*obj(i)*+*obj(d)*] *We are forwarding you a copy of our latest catalogue under separate cover.* **3** *fml* to help advance the development of: *We are doing all we can to forward the progress of the talks.*

for·ward⁴ /ˈfɒrəd, ˈfɔːwəd‖ˈfɔːrərd, ˈfɔːrwərd/ *adv naut* in or towards the front part of a ship: *We moved the cargo forward of the mast.* –compare AFT

for·ward⁵ /ˈfɔːwəd‖ˈfɔːrwərd/ *n* **1** (in sports such as football) one of the attacking players in a team –compare BACK¹ (6), CENTRE¹ (5) **2** in BASKETBALL, one of two players on a team who usually play nearest the basket

forward-look·ing /ˈ·· ˌ··/ *adj apprec* planning for or concerned with the future; PROGRESSIVE: *a dynamic forward-looking little company*

for·ward·ly /ˈfɔːwədli‖ˈfɔːrwərdli/ *adv* in a FORWARD² (3) manner

forward mar·ket /ˈ·· ˌ··/ also **futures market**– *n* a market in which contracts are made to buy and sell products at a future date at an agreed price

for·ward·ness /ˈfɔːwədnəs‖ˈfɔːrwərd-/ *n* [U] the state or quality of being FORWARD¹ (2, 3)

for·wards /ˈfɔːwədz‖ˈfɔːrwərdz/ *adv* FORWARD¹

for·went , fore- /fɔːˈwent‖fɔːr-/ *past tense of* FORGO

Fos·bu·ry flop /ˌfɒzbəri ˈflɒp‖ˌfɑːzberi ˈflɑːp/ *n* (in sport) a TECHNIQUE of high jumping (HIGH JUMP) by bending the back and jumping over the bar backwards

Fosse Way /ˌfɒs ˈweɪ‖ˌfɑːs-/ [*the*] a famous road between Lincoln and Exeter built by the Romans

fos·sil¹ /ˈfɒsəl‖ˈfɑː-/ *n* **1** a hardened part or print of an animal or plant that died many thousands of years ago, that has been preserved in rock, ice, etc.: *to go fossil hunting* | *The ginkgo tree is a* **living fossil** (=a plant or animal that has remained unchanged for many thousands of years) **2** *humor or derog* an (old) person with unchanging ideas or habits (esp. in the phrase **old fossil**) –see also LIVING FOSSIL

fossil² *adj* [A] **1** being or in the condition of a fossil: *a fossil seashell* **2** made of substances that were living things many thousands of years ago: *Coal is a fossil fuel.*

fos·sil·ize also **-ise** *BrE* /ˈfɒsəlaɪz‖ˈfɑː-/ *v* [I;T] to (cause to) become a fossil: *animal remains fossilized in the rocks of the valley* | (fig.) *fossilized ideas* (=fixed ideas which do not change or develop) **–-ization** /ˌfɒsəlaɪˈzeɪʃən‖ˌfɑːsələ-/ *n* [U]

fos·ter /ˈfɒstəʳ‖ˈfɔː-, ˈfɑː-/ *v* [T] **1** to take (someone else's child) into one's family for a certain period only, and without taking on the full legal responsibilities of the parent: *We fostered the little girl for several months while her mother was in hospital.* –compare ADOPT **2** *fml* to help (feelings or ideas) to grow or develop: *We hope these meetings will help foster friendly relations between our two countries.* | *The captain did his best to foster a sense of unity among the new recruits.*

▶CULTURAL NOTE Children are often fostered when their parents cannot look after them because of illness, difficult behaviour, or because the children are not cared for properly or treated badly. Foster parents receive some money towards the care of the child but have no legal rights over the child who may return to the natural parents.◀

Foster, Norman (1935–) an English ARCHITECT

Foster, Ste·phen /ˈstiːvən/ (1826–64) American songwriter remembered for his many popular songs known to most Americans such as *Oh Susanna* and *Camptown Races*

foster- see WORD FORMATION

Fou·cault /ˈfuːkəʊ‖fuːˈkəʊ/, **Jean Ber·nard Lé·on** /ʒɒn ˈbeənɑːʳ ˈleɪɒn‖ʒɑːn beərˈnɑːr leɪˈɑːn/ (1819–68) a French PHYSICIST who studied the speed of light. He is known for **Foucault's Pendulum** which showed the earth's movement round a fixed point, and for his invention of the GYROSCOPE.

fought /fɔːt/ *past tense & participle of* FIGHT¹

foul¹ /faʊl/ *adj* **1** *often infml* very bad or unpleasant: *There's a foul smell in here!* | *She was in a foul temper.* | *foul language* (=full of curses) **2** very dirty; unclean; impure: *The air in this room is foul; open the window!* **3** (of weather) rough; stormy: *It's a foul night tonight.* **4** *lit* very bad; evil; cruel: *a foul deed* | *They are determined to win the election* **by fair means or foul.** (=in any way they can, using honest or dishonest methods) –see also **fall foul of** (FALL¹), **murder most foul** (MURDER) **–~ly** *adv* **–~ness** *n* [U]

foul² *n* [(**against, on**)] (in sports) an act that is against the rules: *The footballer was sent off the field for a foul against an opponent; he had kicked him.*

foul³ *v* **1** [I;T] (in sports, esp. football) to be guilty of a foul: *He was sent off for fouling the other team's goalkeeper.* **2** [T] *fml* to make dirty with waste or impure matter: *Anyone whose dog fouls the footpath will be fined.* **3** [I;T] *esp. naut* (of a rope, chain, etc.) to get mixed up or twisted with (something)

foul out *phr v* [I] in sports (such as BASKETBALL), to be made to stop playing because of making too many fouls: *He fouled out in the fourth quarter.*

foul sthg. ↔ **up** *phr v* [T] *infml* to spoil (an occasion, etc.): *He fouled things up, as usual!* | *The bad weather completely fouled up our plans for the weekend.* –see also FOUL-UP

foul ball /ˌ· ˈ·/ n in sports, such as BASEBALL, a ball that has landed outside the border of the playing area —see also OUT-OF-BOUNDS

foul-mouthed /ˌ· ˈ·◁/ adj derog (habitually) writing or esp. speaking, using language that is full of angry swearing, and that therefore offends people

foul play /ˌ· ˈ·/ n [U] **1** (in sports) unfair play; actions that are against the rules **2** tech criminal violence, esp. in association with a person's death; murder: The police aren't sure how the man died, but they suspect foul play.

foul-up /ˈ· ·/ n infml a state of confusion caused by carelessness or lack of skill —see also FOUL³ **up**

found¹ /faʊnd/ past tense & participle of FIND¹

found² v [T] **1** to start the building or development of; establish: The Romans founded a great city on the banks of this river. | The company was founded in 1955. **2** to start and support by supplying money: The rich man founded a hospital and a school in the town where he was born. **3** [(on, upon)] often pass.] to provide with a base: The castle is founded on solid rock. | (fig.) Is the story a complete invention, or is it founded on fact? —see also FOUNDATION

found³ v [T] **1** to melt (metal) and pour into a MOULD — see also FOUNDRY **2** to make (something) of metal in this way

foun·da·tion /faʊnˈdeɪʃən/ n **1** [U] the act of founding a city, hospital, organization, etc.: The university has been famous for medical studies ever since its foundation. **2** [U] the fact or principle on which something is based; BASIS: The rumour was completely without foundation/had no foundation in fact. (=was untrue) **3** [C] (often cap. as part of a name) an organization that gives out money for certain special purposes: The Gulbenkian Foundation gives money to help artists. **4** [C] a building and the organization connected with it, established and supported in some special way: This school is an ancient foundation. **5** [C;U] also **foundation cream** /·ˈ·· ·/ —a mixture of oils and other substances that is rubbed into the skin of the face before face powder is put on —see also FOUNDATIONS

foundation course /·ˈ·· ˌ·/ BrE n a course of study covering a usu. wide range of subjects, such as one that is taught in the first year in some universities

foundation gar·ment /·ˈ·· ˌ·/ n old fash an article of underclothing worn by women, shaped so as to press the body into shape and make it look thinner —see also FOUNDATIONS

foundations

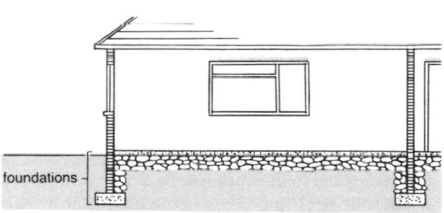

foundations

foun·da·tions /faʊnˈdeɪʃənz/ n [P] **1** the solid stonework, brickwork, etc., first set in holes dug deep in the earth, to support a building: The workmen are **laying the foundations** of the new hospital. | The explosion shook the building **to its foundations**. (=caused it to shake dangerously) | (fig.) He laid the foundations of his success by study and hard work. **2** AmE old use women's UNDERGARMENTS that press the body into shape and make it look thinner: Foundations are on the third floor, next to the cosmetics department.

foundation stone /·ˈ·· ·/ n a large block of stone, on which words are usually cut, which is laid in the foundations of a building, often with a public ceremony —compare CORNERSTONE

found·er¹ /ˈfaʊndəʳ/ n a person who establishes a school, hospital, organization, etc.: King Henry was the founder of Trinity College, Cambridge.

founder² v [I] lit or fml **1** (of a ship) to fill with water and sink: The ship foundered in the heavy seas. **2** to come to

othing; fail: The plan was a good one, but it foundered for lack of support.

founder mem·ber /ˌ·· ˈ··/ BrE ‖ **founding member** AmE— n one of the first members who helped to establish an organization, club, etc.

founding fa·ther /ˌ·· ˈ··/ n [often pl.] lit or fml a person who begins the development of something; FOUNDER: Louis Pasteur was one of the founding fathers of modern medicine.

Founding Fa·thers /ˌ·· ˈ··/ n [the +P] the group of men, including George Washington, Thomas Jefferson, and others, who wrote the US Constitution and Bill of Rights and thus started the US as a country: The Founding Fathers conceived of Congress acting to promote "the general welfare", not to advantage any one group and disadvantage another.

founding mem·ber /ˌ·· ˈ··/ n AmE for FOUNDER MEMBER

found·ling /ˈfaʊndlɪŋ/ n esp. lit an unknown young child left by its parents and found by others

foun·dry /ˈfaʊndri/ n a place where metals are melted down and poured into shapes to make separate articles or parts of machinery, such as bars, wheels, etc.: an iron foundry | foundry workers

fount¹ /faʊnt/ n [(of)] esp. lit the place where something begins or comes from; SOURCE: That old man is **a fount of wisdom**. (=is full of wise thoughts and words)

fount² /font, faʊnt‖fɑːnt, faʊnt/ also **font** — n tech a complete set of letters (TYPE) of one kind and size for printing books, newspapers, etc.

foun·tain /ˈfaʊntɪn/ n **1** a usu. decorative structure, often set in a lake or pool, which produces a stream of water that rises into the air: The parks of this city are famous for their spectacular/ornate fountains. **2** [(of)] a flow of liquid, esp. rising straight into the air: A fountain of water shot up from the burst pipe. — see also DRINKING FOUNTAIN, SODA FOUNTAIN

Fountain of Youth /ˌ·· · ˈ·/ [the] in old stories, a flow of water which was believed to make anyone who drank from it stay young forever

fountain pen /ˈ·· ·/ n a pen with a metal point (NIB) and a container giving a continuous supply of ink as one writes

Fountains Ab·bey /ˌ·· ˈ··/ a 12th-century Benedictine ABBEY in NE England, now a ruin

four /fɔːʳ/ determiner, n, pron **1** (the number) 4 —see TABLE 1 **2** something which has four units or members: Will you **make up a four** for a game of cards? (=complete the group of four people) | He drove up in **a coach and four**. (=a COACH pulled by four horses) **3** (in cricket) four RUNS (8a), usu. gained by hitting the ball to the edge of the field: He hit a four. **4** the four corners of the earth the most distant parts of the world **5 on all fours** down on one's hands and knees: He was crawling around on all fours. —see also **scatter to the four winds** (SCATTER¹)

four·eyes /ˈfɔːraɪz/ n infml (used as a humorous or rude way of addressing a person who wears glasses)

4-F /ˌfɔːr ˈef/ n AmE (of or being) a person considered unsuitable for military service because of poor health or HOMOSEXUALITY: He got a 4-F from the draft board. | He's 4-F.

Four Free·doms /ˌ· ˈ··/ [(the)] four things that president Franklin Roosevelt said were worth fighting for, in a speech he gave in 1941 before the US entered the Second World War. They are Freedom of Speech and Expression, Freedom of Worship, Freedom from Want, and Freedom from Fear.

4GL /ˌfɔː dʒiː ˈel‖ˌfɔːr-/ n FOURTH-GENERATION LANGUAGE

4H, 4-H /fɔːr ˈeɪtʃ/ a programme paid for by the government in RURAL (=outside cities) areas of the US that helps young people learn useful skills

Four Horse·men of the A·poc·a·lypse /ˌ· ˌ··· · · ·ˈ··/ [the+P] figures from the Bible representing war, FAMINE, death, and PESTILENCE, the four things which cause suffering to humans

four-leaved clo·ver /ˌ· · ˈ··/ also **four-leaf clover**— n [C;U] a CLOVER plant that has a set of four leaves instead of the usual three, and is believed to bring good luck to a person who finds it

four-let·ter word /ˌ· ·· ˈ·/ n any of various words, often made up of four letters, that are considered extremely impolite. Such words are marked *taboo* in this dictionary and are very offensive to most people: *The actor uttered a string of four-letter words during the interview.* — see also F-WORD

▶CULTURAL NOTE These words are very offensive to most people as they refer to sexual organs or bodily functions, such as CUNT, FUCK, or SHIT. People say 'a four-letter word' when referring to such a word, esp. in print or on television where they are not usu. allowed to say them.◀

four·post·er /ₗ· '··◀/ also **four-poster bed** /ₗ·· '·/— *n* a large bed with posts at the four corners to support a frame for curtains, used esp. in former times. They are thought of as very special and ROMANTIC, and are often put in HONEYMOON SUITEs in hotels.

four·some /'fɔːsəm‖'fɔːr-/ *n* a group of four people often two men and two women, esp. for playing games or sports: *Let's make up a foursome for tennis.* | *They went to the cinema in a foursome.*

four·square /ₗfɔː'skweəʳ◀‖ₗ'fɔːr-/ *adj* **1** *usu. apprec* showing confidence and determination; FORTHRIGHT: *a four-square decision* **2** (esp. of a building) shaped like a square; solid and firm

four-star /'· ·/ *adj* [A] of a high standard or quality: *a four-star restaurant*

four-star gen·er·al /ₗ·· '···/ *n AmE* the rank of general which is higher than **Brigadier General, Major General,** or **Lieutenant General**: *The order was given by a four-star general.*

four-stroke /'· ·/ *adj,n* (of, being, or driven by) an INTERNAL-COMBUSTION ENGINE in which all the events happening inside the engine are completed in two up-and-down movements of a PISTON: *a four-stroke cycle* — compare TWO-STROKE

four·teen /ₗfɔː'tiːn◀‖ₗfɔːr-/ *determiner, n, pron* (the number) 14 —see TABLE 1 – ~ **th** *determiner, n, pron, adv*

Fourteenth A·mend·ment, 14th Amendment /ₗ·· ·'··/ [*the*] an AMENDMENT (addition) to the US Constitution which gave former slaves the right to be citizens of the US. The amendment gives all citizens the right to be protected by the law.

fourth /fɔːθ‖fɔːrθ/ *determiner, n, pron, adv* 4th —see TABLE 1

fourth di·men·sion /ₗ·· ·'··/ *n* [(*the*)] (used esp. by scientists and writers of SCIENCE FICTION) time; something outside ordinary experience, as opposed to the other dimensions which are in space

fourth es·tate /ₗ·· ·'·/ [*the*] *BrE lit or pomp* (*often cap.*) newspapers and the people who write for them, esp. considered with regard to their political influence; the press, radio, and television together

fourth-gen·e·ra·tion lan·guage /ₗ·· ··ₗ·· '··/ also **4GL** *n* a computer language which contains programming SHORT CUTS (=a faster way to do something) not available in previous languages. It is also easier to use than earlier languages.

Fourth of Ju·ly /ₗ·· ·'·/ also **Independence Day** [*the*] the national Independence Day of the US, a holiday celebrating the signing of the DECLARATION OF INDEPENDENCE in 1776. The Fourth of July is celebrated all over the US with PARADES, PICNICS, and FIREWORKs at night. Many homes and businesses fly the American flag and decorate buildings in colours of red, white, and blue.

four-wheel drive /ₗ·· '·/ also **4WD**— *adj, n* [U] (of or being) a motor vehicle in which the power of the engine is given to all four wheels: *You'd better put it in four-wheel drive to get up this icy hill.* | *a four-wheel drive pickup* —see also GRANNY GEAR

fowl /faʊl/ *n* **fowls** or **fowl** **1** a farmyard bird, esp. a hen kept for its meat or eggs **2** *old use & poet* a bird: *God made all the fowls of the air.* —see also WATERFOWL, WILDFOWL

Fow·ler /'faʊləʳ/, **Henry Watson** (1858–1933) an English writer of dictionaries of the English language. He is known esp. for his *Dictionary of Modern English Usage.*

Fowles /faʊlz/, **John** (1926–) an English writer best known for *The French Lieutenant's Woman*

fowl pest /'· ·/ *n* [U] a quickly spreading disease of fowls

fox¹ /fɒks‖faːks/ *n* **1** [C] **vixen** *fem.*— a small doglike flesh-eating wild animal with a reddish coat and a wide furry tail. It is often hunted for sport in Britain and is said to have a clever and deceiving nature —see also FOX-HUNT **2** [U] the skin of this animal, used as fur on coats and other clothing **3** [C] *infml, usu. derog* a person who deceives others by means of clever tricks: *You can't trust him, he's a sly old fox.* **4** [C] *AmE apprec sl* a sexually attractive woman —see also FOXY

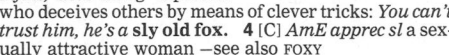
fox

fox² *v* [T] *infml* **1** *BrE* to confuse; to be too difficult for (someone) to understand: *The second question on the exam paper completely foxed me.* **2** to deceive cleverly; trick: *He managed to fox them by wearing a disguise.*

FOX /fɒks ‖ faːks/ the newest of the American television networks

Fox, Charles James (1749–1806) an English politician known for his wish to stop the slave trade and his opposition to the taxing of the American colonies (COLONY)

Fox, George (1624–91) an English religious leader who established the Society of Friends (Quakers)

Fox, Mi·chael /'maɪkəl/ **J** (1961–) a Canadian-born actor who has appeared in American films, esp. *Back to the Future* parts 1, 2, and 3. He is popular with young girls.

Fox, Sa·man·tha /sə'mænθə/ (1966–) an English singer who was famous as a PAGE THREE GIRL

Fox and the Grapes /ₗ·· ·'·/, **The** the title of a well-known story by Aesop in which a fox tries repeatedly to reach some GRAPEs above his head, but cannot, so he leaves them saying "They're probably sour ANYWAY." —see also SOUR GRAPES

fox·glove /'fɒksglʌv‖'faːks-/ *n* a tall straight poisonous plant that has pink or white bellshaped flowers all the way up its stem

fox·hole /'fɒkshəʊl‖'faːks-/ *n* a hole in the ground which soldiers use to fire at or hide from the enemy

fox·hound /'fɒkshaʊnd‖'faːks-/ *n* a dog with a sharp sense of smell, trained to track down and kill foxes (FOX¹(1))

fox·hunt·ing /'fɒkshʌntɪŋ‖'faːks-/ *n* the sport of hunting foxes (FOX¹ (1)) with foxhounds, by people riding on horses —see also HUNT SABOTEUR **foxhunt** *n* : *Foxhunts are colourful and lively occasions.*

▶CULTURAL NOTE Foxhunting started in the 13th century. It takes place in Britain every year between November and the spring. Riders often wear red coats and the hunt is controlled by the Master of Foxhounds. It is thought of as an occupation for the rich, esp. landed class who fiercely defend their right to hunt. Many people in Britain would like to see hunting stopped as they believe it is a cruel sport.◀

fox·hunt·er /'fɒkshʌntəʳ‖'faːks-/ *n* a horse used in foxhunting

fox ter·ri·er /ₗ· '···/ *n* a type of small dog often kept as a pet, formerly used to dig out foxes (FOX¹(1))

fox·trot /'fɒkstrɒt‖'faːkstraːt/ *n* (a piece of music for) a type of formal dance with short quick steps

fox·y /'fɒksi‖'faːksi/ *adj infml* **1** *derog* like a FOX¹(1) in nature; not to be trusted: *Watch out! He's a bit of a foxy character!* **2** like a FOX¹(1) in appearance: *She has rather foxy features.* **3** *AmE apprec sl* sexually attractive: *She's a real foxy lady!*

foy·er /'fɔɪeɪ‖'fɔɪər/ *n* **1** also **lobby** *AmE*— an entrance hall to a theatre, where people gather and talk: *They arranged to meet in the foyer ten minutes before the play started.* **2** *AmE* an entrance hall to a private house or flat —compare LOBBY

Foyles /fɔɪlz/ a large bookshop in the centre of London

FPA /ₗef piː 'eɪ/ *abbrev. for:* **1** Family Planning Association **2** Foreign Press Association

FPO /ₗef piː 'əʊ/ fleet post office; used in addresses to American soldiers who are at sea —compare APO

Fr *written abbrev. for:* **1** Father (as a religious title) **2** FRANC **3** France **4** French

frac·as /'frækaː‖'freɪkəs/ *n* **fracas** /'frækaːz‖'freɪkaːz/, *AmE* **-cases** /kəsⁱz/ *fml* a noisy quarrel in which a number of people take part, and which often ends in a fight: *The new wages policy caused a terrible fracas at the meeting yesterday.*

frac·tion /ˈfrækʃən/ n **1** (in MATHEMATICS) a division or part of a whole number: ⅓ *and* ⅚ *are fractions.* —see also COMMON FRACTION, IMPROPER FRACTION, PROPER FRACTION, VULGAR FRACTION **2** [(of)] a very small piece or amount: *When the factory closed, the machinery was sold off for only a fraction of its true value.* | *The car missed me by a fraction of an inch.*

frac·tion·al /ˈfrækʃənəl/ adj **1** so small as to be unimportant: *The difference between his wages and yours is only fractional.* **2** (in MATHEMATICS) of or being a fraction

frac·tion·al·ly /ˈfrækʃənəli/ adv to a very small degree: *If calculations in planning to send a spacecraft to the moon are even fractionally incorrect, the project will fail.*

frac·tious /ˈfrækʃəs/ adj fml (esp. of a child or an old or sick person) restless and complaining; bad-tempered about small things and ready to quarrel: *Babies tend to be fractious when their new teeth are growing.* – –**ly** adv – –**ness** n [U]

frac·ture¹ /ˈfræktʃər/ n [C;U (of)] med or fml (an example of) the cracking or breaking of something, esp. a bone: *a fracture of the hip* | *The flood was caused by a fracture in the water pipe.* —see also COMPOUND FRACTURE, SIMPLE FRACTURE

fracture² v [I;T] tech, esp. med, or fml to (cause to) break or crack: *He fell and fractured his upper arm.* (=the bone in his arm broke) | *The rock fractured under the tremendous pressure.*

fra·gile /ˈfrædʒaɪl‖-dʒəl/ adj **1** easily broken or damaged: *This old glass dish is very fragile.* | *The parcel was labelled: "Fragile, handle with care."* | (fig.) *a fragile relationship* (=not likely to last) **2 a** having a small thin body or weak in health: *The old lady was very fragile after her operation.* **b** usu. humor not in a good condition of health and spirits; weak: *"I'm feeling rather fragile this morning," he said. "I must have drunk too much last night."* —compare FRAIL ––**gility** /frəˈdʒɪlɪ̯ti/ n [U]

frag·ment¹ /ˈfrægmənt/ n [(of)] a small broken-off or incomplete piece or part: *She dropped the bowl and it broke into tiny fragments.* | *a fragment of poetry* | (fig.) *There's not even the smallest fragment of truth in what he says!*

frag·ment² /frægˈment‖ˈfrægment/ v **1** [I] to break into fragments **2** [T often pass.] to form from incomplete parts, esp. that are not easy to understand: *We received a rather fragmented account of the incident.* – –**ation** /ˌfrægmənˈteɪʃən, -men-/ n [U] : *A fragmentation bomb is one that explodes into small pieces.*

frag·ment·ary /ˈfrægməntəri‖-teri/ also **frag·ment·al** /frægˈmentl/— adj made up of pieces; not complete: *My knowledge of the subject is no more than fragmentary.*

fra·grance /ˈfreɪgrəns/ n [C;U] a (sweet or pleasant) smell: *the fragrance of spring flowers* | *This furniture polish comes in three new fragrances.* –**fragrance** v [T] : *a new air-freshener to fragrance your room*

fra·grant /ˈfreɪgrənt/ adj having a sweet or pleasant smell, esp. of flowers: *The air in the garden was warm and fragrant.* – –**ly** adv

frail /freɪl/ adj **1** weak in body or health: *She is now eighty, and becoming too frail to live alone.* | (fig.) *What a frail excuse!* **2** not strongly made or built: *a frail shelter of leaves* —compare FRAGILE

frail·ty /ˈfreɪlti/ n **1** [U] the quality of being frail **2** [C] a weakness of character or behaviour: *I suppose laziness is one of the frailties of human nature.* **3 frailty, thy name is woman** quote a phrase from Shakespeare's play *Hamlet*

frame¹ /freɪm/ n **1** a firm border or case into which something is fitted or set, or which holds something in place: *In a silver frame on the table there was a photograph of his son.* | *I can't close the door; it doesn't fit properly into its frame.* | *a window|picture frame* **2** the main supports of which something is built or over and around which something is stretched: *a bicycle frame* | *This old bed has an iron frame.* | *In some parts of the world small boats are made of skins stretched over a wooden frame.* **3** (the form or shape of) a human or animal body: *The athlete had a powerful frame.* **4** a large wooden box covered with transparent material in which young plants are grown outdoors: *a cucumber frame* **5** any of a number

of small photographs making up a cinema film **6** a complete stage of play in the games of SNOOKER and BOWLING —see also CLIMBING FRAME

frame² v [T] **1** to surround with a solid protecting edge; put a border round: *I'm having this picture framed, so that I can hang it on the wall.* | (fig.) *A large hat framed the girl's pretty face.* | (fig.) *He was standing there, framed in the light of the doorway.* **2** to give shape to (words, sentences, ideas, etc.); express; FORMULATE: *An examiner must frame his questions clearly.* | *The government is framing a new bill to control gambling.* **3** [(up)] infml to cause (someone) to seem guilty of a crime by means of carefully planned but untrue statements or proofs: *He's been framed! I know that he's innocent.* —see also FRAME-UP

frame of mind /ˌ· · ˈ·/ n **frames of mind** [usu. sing.] the state or condition of one's mind or feelings at a particular time: *I'm in the wrong frame of mind to make a decision now.*

frame of ref·er·ence /ˌ· · ˈ···/ n **frames of reference** a set or system of accepted facts, ideas, standards, etc., which help one to make clear the meaning of a statement, judgment, etc.

frames /freɪmz/ n [P] the metal or plastic part of GLASSES that hold the lenses (LENS): *I like your new frames.* | *These frames cost ten dollars more than my old ones.* —see picture at GLASSES

frame-up /ˈ· ·/ n infml a carefully prepared plan to make someone appear guilty of a crime: *As a result of a frame-up, he served a sentence for a crime he did not commit.* – see also FRAME² (3)

framework

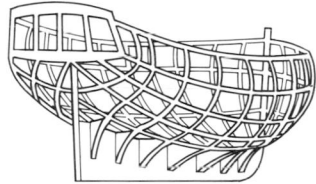

the framework of a ship

frame·work /ˈfreɪmwɜːk‖-wɜːrk/ n a supporting frame; structure: *The block of office buildings was built of concrete on a steel framework.* | (fig.) *These political strikes threaten to destroy the whole framework of our democracy.*

franc /fræŋk/ n the standard unit of money of France, Switzerland, Belgium, and many countries that were formerly ruled by France

France /frɑːns‖fræns/ a country in western Europe which has a DEMOCRATIC government and is a member of the European Community; capital Paris; population 56,160,000 (1989). In Britain, France is known esp. for its good food and drink, esp. its wines.

fran·chise¹ /ˈfræntʃaɪz/ n **1** [the] the right to vote in a public election, esp. one held to choose a parliament: *In England, women were given the franchise in 1918.* **2** [C] a special right given or sold by a company to one person or group of people that allows that person or group to sell the company's goods or services in a particular place: *That fast food business has expanded all over the world through the sale of franchises.*

franchise² v [T] to give or sell a FRANCHISE¹ (2) to

Fran·cis /ˈfrɑːnsɪs‖ˈfræn-/, **Dick** (1920–) an English writer who used to be a professional horse rider and racer. He is known for his mystery stories about the horse-racing world.

Fran·cis·can /frænˈsɪskən/ adj, n (a member) of a Christian religious group established by St Francis in 1209

Francis of As·si·si /ˌfrɑːnsɪs əv əˈsiːsi‖ˌfræn-/, **Saint** (1182–1226) an Italian religious man who formed the Franciscan ORDER¹ (9) of MONKS. He is known for his love of nature and is often shown surrounded by birds and animals.

Fran·co /ˈfræŋkəʊ/, **Fran·cis·co** /frænˈsɪskəʊ/ (1892–1975) a Spanish GENERAL and head of the Spanish state after the CIVIL WAR (1936–39). Many people saw him as a DIC-TATOR who kept control of the country by force.

Franco- see WORD FORMATION

frank¹ /fræŋk/ adj often apprec open and direct in speech or manner; plain and honest and not trying to hide the truth: *He's an extremely frank person.* | *If you want my frank opinion, I don't think the plan will succeed.* | *To be perfectly frank (with you), I think you have very little chance of getting the job.* —see also FRANKLY - ~ **ness** n [U] : *I appreciate your frankness.* | *with refreshing frankness*

frank² n AmE (short for) FRANKFURTER

frank³ v [T] BrE to print a sign on (a letter) to show that the charge for posting has been paid: *Companies that send out a lot of letters save time by using a* **franking machine.** | *franked envelopes* —see also POSTAGE METER

Frank, Anne (1929–45) a Jewish girl from the Netherlands who died in a Nazi CONCENTRATION CAMP. Her *Diary of a Young Girl* tells the story of her family while they lived in hiding.

Fran·ken·stein /'fræŋkₐnstaɪn/ a NOVEL by Mary Shelley, which tells the story of a scientist, called Frankenstein, who makes a creature by joining together bits of dead bodies and then brings it to life by passing an electric current through its body. The creature is gentle at first, but later becomes violent and attacks its maker. People often call the creature Frankenstein. The story is very popular and has been made into many films.

Frank·furt /'fræŋkfət‖-fərt/ an industrial city and port in W Germany —**Frankfurter** n

frank·fur·ter /'fræŋkfɜːtəʳ‖-ɜːr-/ also **frank, Wiener** AmE infml— n a small reddish smoked SAUSAGE, used esp. in HOT DOGS

frank·in·cense /'fræŋkₐnsens/ n [U] a sticky substance obtained from certain trees which is burnt to give a sweet smell, used esp. at religious ceremonies —see also **gold, frankincense, and myrrh** (GOLD)

Frank·lin /'fræŋklₐn/, **A·re·tha** /ə'riːθə/ (1942–) an American singer, also known as The Queen of Soul. Her hits include *Chain of Fools* and *Respect*.

Franklin, Ben·ja·min /'bendʒəmₐn/ (1706–90) an American politician, scientist and writer. He is known for his involvement in the Declaration of Independence in 1776 and for his writings, particularly his AUTOBIOGRAPHY and *Poor Richard's Almanack*, and for showing that lightning is a form of electricity by an experiment which involved flying a KITE during a storm.

Benjamin Franklin

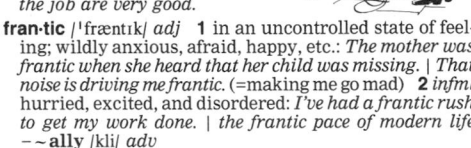

frank·ly /'fræŋkli/ adv **1** in an open and honest manner **2** speaking honestly and plainly: *Frankly, I don't think your chances of getting the job are very good.*

fran·tic /'fræntɪk/ adj **1** in an uncontrolled state of feeling; wildly anxious, afraid, happy, etc.: *The mother was frantic when she heard that her child was missing.* | *That noise is driving me frantic.* (=making me go mad) **2** infml hurried, excited, and disordered: *I've had a frantic rush to get my work done.* | *the frantic pace of modern life* - - ~ **ally** /kli/ adv

frap·pé /'fræpeɪ‖fræˈpeɪ/ also **frappe** /'fræpeɪ‖fræp/— n [C;U] **1** AmE a kind of thick MILK SHAKE **2** a strong alcoholic drink poured over very small pieces of ice **3** a partly frozen drink, e.g. fruit juice —**frappé** /'fræpeɪ‖fræˈpeɪ/ adj

frat /fræt/ n AmE infml a fraternity (2): *frat house* | *frat rat* (=student who lives in a fraternity house)

fra·ter·nal /frə'tɜːnl‖-ɜːr-/ adj **1** of, belonging to, or like brothers **2** friendly; brotherly: *The party sent its fraternal greetings to the trade union meeting.* - - ~ **ly** adv

fra·ter·ni·ty /frə'tɜːnₐti‖-ɜːr-/ n **1** [C+sing./pl. v] pomp an association of people having the stated work, interests, etc., in common: *He's a member of the medical fraternity.* (=is a doctor) **2** [C] also **frat** infml— (at some American

universities) a club of male students usu. living in the same house. Fraternities are named after Greek letters, and members are sometimes called **Greeks**. Most fraternities do work for CHARITY, and they are also known for their drinking parties. —see also RUSH² (6), compare SORORITY **3** [U] fml the state of being brothers; brotherly feeling

frat·er·nize also **-nise** BrE /'frætənaɪz‖-ər-/ v I (**with**)] **1** to meet and be friendly with someone as equals: *The teachers at the university tend not to fraternize with their students.* —compare SOCIALIZE (1) **2** derog to have friendly relations with members of an enemy nation —**nization** /ˌfrætənaɪˈzeɪʃən‖-ərnə-/ n [U (**with**)]

frat·ri·cide /'frætrₐsaɪd/ n **1** [U] fml the act of murdering one's brother or sister **2** [C] tech a person guilty of this crime —**-cidal** /ˌfrætrₐˈsaɪdl◄/ adj

Frau /frau/ n (used as a title for a German woman, esp. a married woman): *Frau Schmidt*

fraud /frɔːd/ n **1** [C;U] (an act of) deceitful behaviour for the purpose of making money, which may be punishable by law: *She got a five-year jail sentence for fraud.* | *He carried out a number of frauds on trusting people who lent him money.* **2** [C] derog someone or something that is not what they claim or are claimed to be: *He said he was an insurance salesman, but later she discovered he was a fraud.*

Fraud Squad /'· ˌ·/ [the] a special part of the police force in London who examine fraud in businesses

fraud·u·lent /'frɔːdjₐlənt‖-dʒə-/ adj deceitful; got or done by fraud: *They obtained the top-secret information by fraudulent means.* - - ~ **lence** n [U]

fraught /frɔːt/ adj **1** [F+**with**] full of something unpleasant: *The expedition through the jungle was fraught with difficulties and danger.* **2** infml troubled by anxieties; very TENSE

fräu·lein also **Fräulein** /'frɔɪlaɪn/ n a German unmarried woman

fray¹ /freɪ/ v [I;T] **1** to (cause to) have loose threads developing: *Constant rubbing had frayed his shirt cuffs.* | *This dress material frays very quickly when you cut it.* | *The electric cord is fraying and could be dangerous to handle.* **2** to cause (a person's temper, nerves, etc.) to become worn out: *After spending a day with screaming children, her nerves were completely frayed.* | *Tempers began to fray in the hot weather.*

fray² n [the] lit a fight; battle: *He rushed into the fray.* (=joined fearlessly in the fighting) | (fig.) *Are you ready for the fray?* (=ready for action, ready to begin)

Fra·zer /'freɪzəʳ/, **Sir James George** (1854–1941) a Scottish anthropologist (ANTHROPOLOGY), best known for *The Golden Bough*, a study of magic and religion

fraz·zle /'fræzəl/ n [S] infml **1** a condition of being completely tired in body and mind, owing to hard work or other difficulties: *I've been trailing round the shops all day, and I'm absolutely* **worn to a frazzle.** **2** a thoroughly burnt condition: *He forgot about the food he was frying, and it got* **burnt to a frazzle.** –**frazzled** adj

FRB /ˌef ɑː 'biː‖-ɑːr-/ abbrev. for FEDERAL RESERVE BANK

FRCM /ˌef ɑː siː 'em‖-ɑːr-/ abbrev. for: Fellow of the Royal College of Music

FRCP /ˌef ɑː siː 'piː‖-ɑːr-/ abbrev. for: Fellow of the Royal College of Physicians

FRCS /ˌef ɑː siː 'es‖-ɑːr-/ abbrev. for: Fellow of the Royal College of Surgeons

FRCVS /ˌef ɑː ˌsiː viː 'es‖-ɑːr-/ abbrev. for: Fellow of the Royal College of Veterinary Surgeons

freak¹ /friːk/ n **1** a living creature of unnatural form: *One of the new lambs is a freak; it was born with two tails.* | *This dwarf tree is a* **freak of nature. 2** a strange, unexpected happening: *By some strange freak, a little snow fell in the middle of the summer.* **3** infml a person with rather strange habits, ideas, or appearance: *He looks a real freak in his pink trousers and orange shirt.* **4** infml a person who takes a very strong interest in the stated thing; FAN: *a film freak* —see also CONTROL FREAK

freak² adj [A] very unusual and unexpected: *freak weather conditions, with snow falling in the middle of summer* | *a freak storm* | *a freak result*

freak³ v [I] *AmE infml* to become frightened or anxious very suddenly: *He freaked when he saw the police coming and took off down the alley.*

freak out *phr v* [I;T (=**freak** sbdy. ↔ **out**)] *old-fash infml* to (cause to) become greatly excited or anxious, esp. because of drugs

freak·ish /ˈfriːkɪʃ/ *adj* unusual; unreasonable; strange: *Her behaviour's becoming so freakish that I wonder if she's going mad.* | *a freakish hairstyle* – ~**ly** *adv* – ~**ness** *n* [U]

freck·le /ˈfrekəl/ *n [usu. pl.]* a small flat brown spot on the skin: *When she lies in the sun, her face gets covered in freckles.* —compare MOLE² –**led** *adj : a freckled nose*

Fred Per·ry /ˌfred ˈperi/ *adj* [A] *tdmk* a British make of sports clothes, esp. tennis clothes –see also PERRY, Fred

free¹ /friː/ *adj* **1** able to act as one wants; not in prison or under anyone's control: *This is a free country.* (=the state does not control everything) [F+to-v] *You are free to* (=you may) *go anywhere you wish.* | *Do feel free to ask questions.* | *They agreed to set all their prisoners free.* **2** not limited in any way, esp. by rule or custom: *He gave me free access to his valuable collection of scientific books.* (=let me use them whenever I wanted) | *It's a very free translation.* (=one in which the meaning is translated without giving an exact translation of every single word) | *The people won the right to free speech and a free press.* (=they could express ideas and judgments in public and in the newspapers) | *Their quarrel developed into a free fight.* (=everyone joined in) **3** [no comp.] without payment of any kind; costing nothing; given away: *He gave me two free tickets for the concert.* | *A free gift* | *"Are the drinks free?" "No, you have to pay for them."* [after *n*] *The goods will be sent to you postage free.* (=with no charge added on for posting) | *She lives there rent free.* **4** [no comp.] not busy; without work or duty; having time to give attention to someone or something: *He has very little free time during the week.* | *She gets a free afternoon once a week.* | *The doctor will be free in ten minutes' time; can you wait that long?* –see also FREE PERIOD **5** [no comp.] not being used; empty; not kept for or promised to anyone: *Is this seat free?* | *I was late because I couldn't find a free parking space.* | *She picked it up with her free hand.* | (fig.) *I'll try and phone you back when I've got my hands free.* (=when I am not busy) **6** (of a way or passage) open; not blocked: *The way is free; we can make our escape now.* | *Ice sometimes prevents the free passage of ships in the winter.* **7** [no comp.] not fixed onto anything; not set in position; loose: *The free end of the flag has been torn by the wind.* **8** [F+**from, of**] without (someone or something unwanted); safe from; untroubled or unspoilt by: *The old lady is never free from/of pain.* | *Keep the surface free from/of dirt by putting a cover over it.* | *Meals will be provided free of charge.* (–for no money) | *She's been nothing but a nuisance; I'll be glad to be free of her when she leaves next week.* | *All our food products are completely free of artificial flavourings and colourings.* | (*in comb.*) *trouble-free* | *duty-free* **9** (esp. of physical action) natural; graceful; not stiff or awkward: *Hit the ball with a long free swing of the arm.* | *The skirt hung in free folds from the waist.* **10** [F+**with**] ready to give; generous: *She's very free with her money.* | *He's too free with his advice.* (=gives advice when it isn't wanted) **11** *fml* too friendly; lacking in respect; not controlled by politeness: *Your son's manner is rather free in the presence of his teachers.* **12** [no comp.] *tech* (in chemistry) not combined with any type of matter (ELEMENT); pure: *free oxygen* **13 for free** *infml* without payment: *I got this ticket for free.* **14 free and easy** lacking in too great seriousness and ceremony; cheerful and unworried: *She leads a free and easy sort of life and never troubles much about anything.* **15** [+ (on)] **free ride** something obtained free that another must pay for: *welfare recipients getting a free ride on taxpayers' money* | *She's been taking a free ride on her boss's expense account.* **16 make free with** to use (something) without respect or as if it is one's own: *She's made free with my cigarettes during my absence.* (=has taken as many as she wanted without asking me) –see also FREEDOM, FREELY

free² *adv* **1** without payment: *Babies are allowed to travel free on buses.* **2** in an uncontrolled manner: *Don't let the dog run free on the main road.* **3** in a loose position; so as to be no longer joined: *Two screws in this old wooden door have worked themselves free.* (=loosened or fallen out

as a result of use) | *The window had stuck, but I pushed it hard and it swung free.*

▷ USAGE Compare **free** and **freely** in the following sentences: *You can travel free with this special ticket.* (=without payment) | *You can travel freely to all parts of the country.* (=without limitation)◁

free³ v **freed** /friːd/ [T] **1** [(**from**)] to allow to go free; RELEASE: *When will the prisoners be freed?* | *She freed the bird from its cage.* **2** [(**from**)] to move or loosen (a person or thing that is prevented from moving): *Part of the old wall fell on the workman, and it took half an hour to free him.* | *Her dress got caught on a rose bush, and she tore it when she tried to free it/herself from the thorns.* **3** [+obj+to-v] to take away conditions that stop someone doing something: *Giving up my job freed me to spend more time with the children.*

free sbdy./sthg. **from/of** sthg. *phr v* [T] to take away from (a person, animal, or place) anything uncomfortable, inconvenient, difficult, unwelcome, etc.: *We must free the world from hunger.* | *She can't free herself of the idea that someone's watching her all the time.* | *He opened the window to free the room of smoke.*

free up *phr v* [T (**free** sbdy./sthg. **up**)] to make available for use: *If I cancel this appointment it will free up two hours this afternoon.* | *Take this bag so I can free a hand up to open the door.*

-free see WORD FORMATION

free a·gent /ˌ· ˈ··/ *n* someone who can act as they choose: *No one can force you to do that – you're a free agent.*

free-and-ea·sy /ˌ· · ˈ··◂/ *adj* not controlled by or needing formal rules or instructions: *a free-and-easy lifestyle/manner of speaking*

free as·so·ci·a·tion /ˌ· ·ˌ···ˈ··/ *n* [U] *tech* (in PSYCHOLOGY) a way of studying someone's SUBCONSCIOUS mind by getting them to say the first word they think of when each of a number of words is spoken to them

free·base /ˈ· ·/ v [I] *sl* to smoke a specially prepared mixture of the drug COCAINE

free·bie , -bee /ˈfriːbiː/ *n infml, esp. AmE* something, such as a meal or a gift, that is given or received without payment

free·board /ˈfriːbɔːd‖-bɔːrd/ *n* [C;U] the distance between the level of the water and the upper edge of the side of a boat

free·boot·er /ˈfriːbuːtəʳ/ *n lit* a person who makes war in order to grow rich by seizing other people's money and goods; PIRATE

free-born /ˌfriːˈbɔːn‖-ˈɔːrn◂/ *adj* not born as a slave

Free Church /ˌ· ˈ·◂/ *n* a church in Britain which is not Anglican or Roman Catholic (the established churches), including the Baptist, the United Reformed, the Methodist, and the Church of Scotland. Many people think of these churches as having STRICT MORALS, esp. about alcohol and sex.

Free Church of Scot·land /ˌ· · · ˈ··/ *[the]* a small group of Protestant Christians mainly in the Highlands of Scotland, esp. known for being against any form of work on Sundays. Its members are often called **wee frees**. –see also FREE PRESBYTERIAN CHURCH OF SCOTLAND

free col·lec·tive bar·gain·ing /ˌ· ··· ˈ···/ *n* [U] *BrE* talks between TRADE UNIONS and employers about increases in pay, improvements in conditions, etc., that are not controlled by legal limits

free·dom /ˈfriːdəm/ *n* **1** [U (**from**)] the state of being free; not being under control: *During the school holidays the children enjoyed their freedom.* | *The people there are fighting to gain their freedom from foreign control.* | *He's enjoying his new-found freedom.* | *freedom from anxiety* **2** [C;U (**of**)] the power to do, say, think, or write whatever one wants to: *Two of the four freedoms spoken of by President Roosevelt in 1941 are* **freedom of speech** *and* **freedom of religion**. | *The journalists claimed that they were being denied* **freedom of expression**. | *You may have complete freedom of action in dealing with this matter; do what you think best.* | *Tight clothes don't allow enough freedom of movement.* [+to-v] *She's old enough to have the freedom to do as she likes.* **3** [*the*+**of**] certain rights, often given as an honour: *They gave her the freedom of their house.* (=gave her the right to use it as if it were her own) –compare LIBERTY

Freedom of In·for·ma·tion Act /ˌ·· ··'·· ˌ·/ n [the] an American law that makes any information held by the American government on any person or organization freely available to anyone with a reason to see the information —compare OFFICIAL SECRETS ACT

freedom fight·er /'·· ˌ··/ n a person who takes up arms against a government which is seen as ILLEGAL or REPRESSIVE —compare GUERRILLA, TERRORIST

freedom of the cit·y /ˌ·· · · '··/ n [U] the right to be a full member of a city, which may be given to someone by a city council in Britain. In modern times, the freedom of the city does not give a person any special rights or advantages, but is given as an honour.

free en·ter·prise /ˌ· '···/ n [U] an economic system in which supply and demand are very important, and in which private trade, business, etc., is carried on without much government control

free-fall /ˌ· '·◄/ n [U] **1** the condition of moving or falling freely through air or space without being held back by anything **2** the part of a jump or fall from an aircraft which is made before the jumper opens a PARACHUTE

free-float·ing /ˌ· '···◄/ adj not having firm feelings of support for a set of ideas, purpose, etc.; UNCOMMITTED

free·fone , -phone /'friːfəʊn/ n [U] BrE an arrangement by which a company pays the cost of telephone calls made to it, esp. in answer to an advertisement —compare FREEPOST, TOLL-FREE, 800 NUMBER

free-for-all /ˌ· · '·/ n infml an argument, quarrel, fight, etc., in which many people join, esp. in a noisy way

free-form /'·· ·/ adj without recognizable rules or patterns: free-form furniture/poetry/education

Free French /ˌ· '·/ [the] French people during the Second World War who opposed the rule of the German-led Vichy government of their country and worked, mostly outside France, to bring it down

free·hand /'friːhænd/ adj (of drawing or a drawing) done by natural movements of the hand, without the use of a ruler or other instrument: She drew me a freehand map so that I could find her house. –**freehand** adv : I can't draw very well freehand.

free hand /ˌ· '·/ n [S] unlimited freedom of action; complete rights: She's given me a completely free hand to manage the business during her absence. | You have a free hand to make all the changes you wish.

free·hold /'friːhəʊld/ adj, adv, n BrE (with) ownership of land or buildings for an unlimited time and without any conditions: All these houses are freehold properties. | They bought the land freehold. | They have bought the freeholds of their houses. —compare COMMONHOLD, LEASEHOLD

free·hold·er /'friːhəʊldər/ n BrE an owner of freehold land or property

free house /ˌ· '·, '· ·/ n (in Britain) a PUB not controlled by a particular beer-making firm, but getting and selling whatever kind of beer it chooses —compare TIED HOUSE

free kick /ˌ· '·/ n (in football) an unopposed kick given to one team when a rule of the game is broken by the other team

free-lance¹ /'friːlɑːns‖-læns/ also **free-lan·cer** /-lɑːnsər‖ -læn-/— n a writer or other trained worker who earns their money without being in the regular employment of any particular organization –**freelance** adj, adv : a freelance journalist | She does freelance translation work for several agencies. | He works freelance.

freelance² v [I] to work as a freelance

free·load /'friːləʊd/ v [I(on, off)] infml derog to live on money and goods given by other people, without giving anything in return; SPONGE² (3) – –**er** n

free love /ˌ· '·/ n [U] the practice of, or belief in having sexual relations outside marriage without any OBLIGATIONS. This is thought of esp. in connection with the HIPPY movement of the 1960s and 1970s.

free lunch /ˌ· '·/ phrase **There's no such thing as a free lunch** nothing is free, and things that appear to be free must be paid for in some way. A book about ECONOMICS in the 1970s by Milton Friedman used this phrase as its title.

free·ly /'friːli/ adv **1** willingly; readily: I freely admit that what I said was wrong. **2** openly; plainly; without hid-

ing anything: You can speak quite freely in front of me; I won't tell anyone what you say. **3** without any limitation on movement or action: Oil the wheel; then it will turn more freely. | freely available **4** generously: People have given very freely to the fund for victims of the floods. —see FREE² (USAGE)

free·man /'friːmən/ n -men /mən/ [(of)] BrE a person who, as an honour, has been given certain special rights in a city: The famous politician was made a freeman of the City of London. —see also FREEDOM (3)

free mar·ket /ˌ· '··/ n **1** on the STOCK EXCHANGE, a market in SHARES¹(2) which can be bought or sold without difficulty **2** a situation in which prices are not controlled or limited in any way

free mar·ket e·con·o·my /ˌ· ˌ·· ·'···/ n a system of trade in which there is free competition

Free·ma·son /'friːˌmeɪsən, ˌfriːˈmeɪsən/ BrE ‖ also **Mason**— n (sometimes not cap.) a man belonging to an ancient and widespread secret society, the members of which give help to each other and to other people and have certain signs and words by which they recognize each other, e.g. a special kind of HANDSHAKE. It is sometimes suggested that many important people in British organizations are Freemasons and that they will only give important jobs to other Freemasons. —see also SHRINER

free·ma·son·ry /'friːˌmeɪsənri, ˌfriːˈmeɪ-/ n [U] **1** also **masonry**— (often cap.) the system and practices of the Freemasons **2** the natural unspoken understanding and friendly feeling between people of the same kind, or having the same interests, beliefs, etc.: There's a sort of freemasonry among racing drivers.

free pa·per /ˌ· '··/ n a free local newspaper delivered to houses in an area, usu. containing mostly advertisements with some local news and details of events taking place

free par·don /ˌ· '··/ n law an official act of forgiving someone and allowing them to go free as though they had never done anything wrong: to grant someone a free pardon

free pass /ˌ· '·/ n an official paper giving a person the right to travel or go to the theatre, cinema, etc., without payment

free pe·ri·od /ˌ· '···/ n an amount of time during a school day when a pupil or teacher does not have a class. The time may be used for study or other work but it is usu. spent in the school, not at home.

free·phone /'friːfəʊn/ n [U] FREEFONE

free port /ˌ· '·/ n a port where goods of all countries may be brought in or taken out without paying tax

free·post /'friːpəʊst/ BrE ‖ **business reply mail** AmE— n [U] (in Britain) an arrangement by which a company pays the cost of letters sent to it by post: Send it freepost to this address. —compare FREEFONE, POST-FREE

Free Pres·by·te·ri·an Church of Scot·land /ˌ· ··ˌ··· ˌ· · '··/ [the] a small group of Protestant Christians mainly in the Highlands of Scotland. It has similar views to the Free Church of Scotland, esp. in connection with keeping Sunday for study of the Bible and worship of God. —see also FREE CHURCH OF SCOTLAND

free-range /ˌ· '·◄/ adj BrE being, concerning, or produced by farm animals, esp. hens, that are kept under natural conditions in a farmyard or field: free-range hens | I like free-range eggs. —compare BATTERY (3)

free·si·a /'friːziə‖-ʒə/ n a plant with sweet-smelling white, yellow, or red flowers

free·stand·ing /ˌfriːˈstændɪŋ◄/ adj standing alone without being fixed to a wall, frame, or other support

free·stone /'friːstəʊn/ n [U] building stone, such as SANDSTONE or LIMESTONE, that is easily cut in any direction

free·style /'friːstaɪl/ n [U] **1** a competition or method of swimming using the CRAWL stroke: Which swimmer won the 100 metres freestyle? **2** the use of wrestling (WRESTLE (2)) holds according to choice, not set rules –**freestyle** adj, adv

free·think·er /ˌfriːˈθɪŋkər/ n someone who forms their opinions using their own powers of reasoning, and does not just accept official teachings, esp. in religious matters –**-thinking** adj

free throw /ˌ· '·/ *n* a chance for a BASKETBALL player to shoot the ball after he has been fouled (FOUL)

Free·town /'friːtaʊn/ the capital city of Sierra Leone on the Atlantic coast which is a port and industrial centre

free trade /ˌ· '·◂/ *n* [U] the system by which foreign goods are allowed to enter a country in unlimited quantities and without payment of high charges

free verse /ˌ· '·/ *n* [U] poetry in a form that does not follow any regular or accepted pattern —compare BLANK VERSE

free·way /'friːweɪ/ *n AmE abbrev.* **fwy**— (in the US) a MOTORWAY that is free for drivers to travel on, esp. one near or between cities: *the Santa Monica Freeway* —see also EXPRESSWAY (USAGE)

free·wheel /ˌfriː'wiːl/ *BrE* ‖ **coast** *AmE*— *v* [I] to ride a bicycle or drive a vehicle, esp. downhill, without providing power from the legs or the engine —compare COAST[2]

free·wheel·ing /ˌfriː'wiːlɪŋ◂/ *adj infml* not greatly worrying about rules, formal behaviour, responsibilities, or the results of actions

free will /ˌ· '·/ *n* [U] **1** the ability of someone to decide freely what they will do: *She did it* **of her own free will.** (=it was completely her own decision) **2** the belief that human effort can influence events, and they are not fixed in advance by God —compare PREDESTINATION

free world /ˌ· '·/ *[the]* all the non-Communist countries of the world

freeze¹ /friːz/ *v* **froze** /frəʊz/, **frozen** /'frəʊzən/ **1** [I;T (UP)] to (cause to) harden, esp. into ice, as a result of extreme cold: *Water freezes at the temperature of 0 degrees Celsius.* | *The pond has frozen up.* | *The cold was severe enough to freeze the milk.* | *The cold has frozen the earth solid.* | *Many roads in northern Scotland are frozen.* (=covered with ice or snow) —compare MELT, THAW **2** [I;T (UP)] to (cause to) be unable to move or work properly as a result of ice or very low temperatures: *The engine has frozen up.* | *The cold has frozen the lock on the car door.* **3** [*it*+I] (of weather) to be at or below the temperature at which water becomes ice: *Do you think it will freeze tonight?* | *a freezing cold night* **4** [I;T] *infml* to (cause to) be, feel, or become extremely cold: *It's freezing in this room; put the fire on!* | *The mountain climbers were lost in the snow, and nearly* **froze to death.** (=died of cold) | *I'm getting* **frozen stiff** *here; please close the window!* | (fig.) *His terrible stories* **made our blood freeze.** (=made us cold with fear) **5** [I;T] **a** to preserve (food) by means of very low temperatures: *We'll eat some of the beans now, and freeze the rest.* | *frozen peas* **b** (of food) to be able to be preserved by freezing: *Some sorts of fruit don't freeze well.* **6** [I;T] to (cause to) stop suddenly or be unable to move (because of fear, etc.). *The burglar froze (to the spot) when he heard footsteps approaching.* | *The teacher froze the noisy class with a single look.* | *"Freeze!" he said, pointing the gun at me.* | *A wild animal will sometimes freeze in its tracks when it smells an enemy.* **7** [T] to fix (prices or wages) officially at a particular level for a certain length of time **8** [T] to prevent (business shares, bank accounts, etc.) from being used, esp. by government order: *frozen assets*
    freeze sbdy./sthg. **↔ out** *phr v* [T] *infml* to prevent from being included: *I tried to join in their conversation but they froze me out.*
    freeze over *phr v* [I;T (=**freeze** sthg. **↔ over**)] to (cause to) turn into ice on the surface: *The lake has frozen over.*

freeze² *n* [S] **1** a period of extremely cold icy weather: *He slipped and broke his leg during the big freeze last winter.* **2** a fixing of prices, wages, or the number of jobs at a certain level: *a wage freeze* | *a freeze on jobs* (=no new jobs will be made available) **3** a stopping of some activity, often because of the lack of money to continue it: *a hiring freeze* | *He put a freeze on that project till the end of the fiscal year.* —see also DEEP FREEZE

freeze-dry /ˌ· '·◂/ *v* [T] to preserve (esp. food) by drying in a frozen state: *freeze-dried vegetables/coffee*

freez·er /'friːzər/ *n* **1** also **deep freeze**— a large FRIDGE in which supplies of food can be stored at a very low temperature for a long time: *a chest freezer in a shop* | *an upright freezer* —compare FRIDGE and see picture at KITCHEN **2** also **freezing compartment** /'··· ·,··/— an enclosed part of a FRIDGE in which there is a specially low temperature for making ice CUBES, frozen foods, etc.

free·zer bag /'··· ·/ *n* a transparent plastic bag used to store food in, esp. in a freezer

freez·ing point /'··· ·/ *n* **1** [U] also **freezing** *infml*— the temperature (0 degrees Celsius) at which water becomes ice: *It's very cold today; the temperature has dropped to freezing point.* | *It must be five degrees below freezing today.* **2** [C (**of**)] the temperature at which any particular liquid freezes: *The freezing point of alcohol is much lower than that of water.* —compare BOILING POINT

freight¹ /freɪt/ *n* [U] goods carried by ship, train, plane, etc.: *This aircraft company carries freight only; it has no passenger service.* | *You can send this trunk by* **air freight** *or by* **sea freight.** | *What will be the cost of freight?* | *a freight train*

freight² *v* [T] to send (something) as freight

freight·er /'freɪtər/ *n* a ship or aircraft for carrying goods

freight·lin·er /'freɪtˌlaɪnər/ also **linertrain**— *n esp. BrE* a train that carries large amounts of goods in special containers

Fré·mont /'friːmɒnt‖-mɑːnt/, **John Charles** (1813–90) an American EXPLORER and politician. A PEAK in the Rocky Mountains is named after him.

french /frentʃ/ *v* [I] *AmE infml* to kiss with mouths open and tongues touching: *I caught them frenching behind the lockers.* —see also FRENCH KISS

French¹ *adj* of France, its people, etc.: *French wine* | *a French restaurant* (a restaurant outside France which serves food cooked in a French style)

French² *n* **1** *[the+P]* the people of France: *The French have voted for the proposal.* **2** [U] the language of France: *He speaks French.* | *a French lesson* **3** *humor* **pardon/excuse someone's French** to forgive someone for using offensive language: *I wish we'd never come to this bloody place, if you'll pardon my French.*

French, Dawn (1957–) a British actress and COMEDIENNE probably best-known for her appearances with another comedienne, Jennifer Saunders, esp. in the television show *French and Saunders*

French and In·di·an War /ˌ· · ·ˌ··· '·/ *[the]* the name for a number of battles that took place in North America between the French and the British before the American Revolution

French bean /ˌ· '·/ *n BrE for* GREEN BEAN

French bread /ˌ· '·/ *n* [U] bread in the form of French loaves (FRENCH LOAF)

French Ca·na·di·an /ˌ· ·'···◂/ *n* a French speaking Canadian, esp. a person whose family came originally from France

French chalk /ˌ· '·/ *n* [U] CHALK used for drawing lines on material in dress-making

French Con·nec·tion /'· ·,··/, **The** a film about drug smuggling (SMUGGLE) with Gene Hackman which won several OSCARS

French crick·et /ˌ· '··/ *n* [U] a game played with a ball and a BAT to hit it with, usu. by or with children, the aim being to hit the legs of the person with the ball

french dip /ˌ· '·/ *adj, n AmE* a SANDWICH served with clear BEEF soup into which the sandwich is dipped

French doors /ˌ· '·/ *n* [P] *esp. AmE for* FRENCH WINDOWS

French dress·ing /ˌ· '··/ *n* [U] **1** a liquid made of oil and VINEGAR, used for putting on dishes made with raw vegetables (SALADS) **2** *AmE* a thick liquid made of MAYONNAISE and KETCHUP

French fries /ˌ· '·/ *n* [P] *esp. AmE* long thin pieces of potato cooked in deep fat; CHIPS[1] (3) —see picture at CHIP

French Gui·a·na /ˌfrentʃ giˈɑːnə‖-ˈænə/ a country in NE South America, a French DEPARTMENT (2); capital Cayenne; population 93,540 (1989). It is known esp. for its large prison on Devil's Island.

French horn /ˌ· '·/ *n* a brass musical instrument made of thin pipe wound round and round into a circular form, having a wide bell-shaped mouth, and played by blowing —see picture at BRASS

French kiss /ˌ· '·/ *n* a kiss made with the mouth open, and usu. with the tongues touching

French leave /ˌ· '·/ *n* [U] *BrE old-fash or humor* absence from work or duty taken without permission: *The young*

soldier was punished for taking French leave to visit his girlfriend.

French let·ter /ˌ· ˈ··/ *n BrE infml* a CONDOM

French loaf /ˌ· ˈ·/ *n* a long thin round loaf

French·man /ˈfrentʃmən/ **French·wom·an** /-ˌwumən/ *fem.— n* **-men** /mən/ a French citizen born in France or of French parents

French pol·ish /ˌ· ˈ··/ *n* [U] a liquid mixture of SHELLAC and alcohol rubbed onto wooden furniture to give a hard and lasting shine **–French-polish** *v* [T]

French Pol·y·ne·si·a /ˌ· ··ˈ···/ a French possession consisting of many tropical islands in the E Pacific Ocean

French Quar·ter /ˈ· ˌ··/ *[the]* a part of the city of New Orleans, Louisiana, originally settled by French people and now famous as a tourist ATTRACTION

French Riv·i·e·ra /ˌ· ··ˈ··/ *n [the]* the Mediterranean coast of SE France. People think of the French Riviera as a fashionable place for the rich and famous to have a house or to spend a lot of time: *He spends most of the winter writing another novel somewhere on the French Riviera.*

French Rev·o·lu·tion /ˌ· ··ˈ··/ *[the]* the REVOLUTION which began in France in 1789 with the storming (STORM= attack) of the Bastille prison. The French king, Louis XVI, was killed and a republic was declared. During the revolution the people demanded "Liberty, Equality, and Fraternity".

French seam /ˌ· ˈ·/ *n* (in dress-making) a double SEAM to hide the edges that have been cut

French toast /ˌ· ˈ·/ *n* [U] *esp. AmE* pieces of bread dipped in beaten egg and cooked in hot oil

French West In·dies /ˌ· · ˈ··/ *[the]* a group of islands in the West Indies belonging to France

French win·dows /ˌ· ˈ··/ also **French doors** *esp. AmE— n* [P] a pair of light outer doors made of glass in a frame, usu. opening out onto the garden or a BALCONY of a house

fre·net·ic /frɪˈnetɪk/ *adj* showing frenzied activity; overexcited: *She worked at a frenetic pace to finish the work.* **– –ally** /kli/ *adv*

fren·zied /ˈfrenzid/ *adj* full of uncontrolled excitement and/or wild activity; mad; FRANTIC: *The house was full of frenzied activity on the morning of the wedding.* **– –ly** *adv*

fren·zy /ˈfrenzi/ *n* [S;U] a state of wild uncontrolled feeling, expressed with great force; a sudden, but not lasting, attack of madness: *In a frenzy of hate he killed his enemy.* | *The fans at the rock concert worked themselves up into a frenzy.*

fre·quen·cy /ˈfriːkwənsi/ *n* **1** [U] **(of)** the happening of something a large number of times: *The frequency of accidents on that road has forced the council to lower the speed limit.* | *Accidents are happening with increasing frequency.* **2** [C;U] *tech* a rate at which something happens or is repeated; the number of times that something happens in a given period: *This radio signal has a frequency of 200,000 cycles per second.* | *low frequency radiation* **3** [C] a particular number of radio waves per second at which a radio signal is broadcast: *This radio station broadcasts on three different frequencies.* –see also FM, VHF

fre·quent¹ /ˈfriːkwənt/ *adj* common; found or happening often; repeated many times; habitual: *Sudden rainstorms are frequent on this part of the coast.* | *She's a frequent visitor to our house.* –opposite **infrequent**; see NEVER (USAGE) **– –ly** *adv*

fre·quent² /frɪˈkwent‖frɪˈkwent, ˈfriːkwənt/ *v* [T] *fml* to be often in (a place, esp. a place of entertainment, people's company, etc.): *Police visited all the bars that the suspect frequented.* | *These woods are frequented by all kinds of birds.*

fres·co /ˈfreskəu/ *n* **-coes** or **-cos** [C;U] (a picture made by) painting in water colour on a surface, usu. of a wall, made of wet PLASTER: *This church is famous for its frescoes.*

fresh¹ /freʃ/ *adj* **1** (of meat, vegetables, flowers, etc.) in good natural condition, and not spoilt in taste, smell, or appearance by being kept too long; new: *You can buy fresh fruit and vegetables in the market.* | *This fish smells; I don't think it's quite fresh.* | *These flowers don't look very fresh.* **2** (of food) not preserved by freezing, putting in cans, or other means: *Canned fruit never tastes quite the same as fresh fruit.* | *Are those peas fresh or frozen?* **3** [A no comp.] (of water) not salty: *I prefer swimming in fresh water to sea water.* **4** [(from) no comp.] that has recently arrived, happened, grown, been found, or been supplied: *There's been no fresh news of the fighting since yesterday.* | *This bread's fresh from the oven.* (=is newly baked) | *This paint's fresh* (=just put on); *don't touch it!* | *The new teacher is fresh from university.* | *Can you throw any fresh light on this subject?* (=add anything that will help to explain it) **5** [A no comp.] another and different; new: *Let me make you a fresh pot of tea.* | *I've spoilt this drawing; I'll have to start again on a fresh piece of paper.* | *It's time to take a fresh look at this problem.* | *When she came out of prison, she decided to* **make a fresh start.** (=begin life again) **6** [F] not tired; young, healthy, and active: *She always seems fresh, however much work she's done.* | *The plants look fresh after the rain.* | (*infml*) *He woke up* **fresh as a daisy** (=very fresh) *after his long sleep.* **7** [A] (of skin) clear and healthy: *She has dark hair and a fresh complexion.* **8** [A] (of air) pure; cool: *Open the window and let in some fresh air.* | *I'm just going out for a* **breath of fresh air.** **9** *often tech* (of wind) rather strong; gaining in force: *The winds will be fresh or strong tonight, according to the weather report.* **10** [F] *infml* (of weather) cool and windy: *It's a bit fresh today.* **11** [F **(with)**] *infml* rudely confident with someone of the opposite sex: *He started* **getting fresh** *with me so I slapped his face.* –see also AFRESH, FRESHLY **– ~ness** *n* [U]

fresh² *adv* **1** (*in comb.*) just; newly: *I like fresh-ground coffee.* **2 fresh out of** *infml, esp. AmE* having just used up one's supplies of: *The store was* **fresh out of** *coffee.* (=had just sold its last jar of coffee)

fresh·en /ˈfreʃən/ *v* [I] (of wind) to gain in force; become stronger or colder

freshen up *phr v* [I;T] (=**freshen** sbdy./sthg. ↔ **up**)] to (cause to) feel less tired, look more attractive, etc.: *I must just go and freshen (myself) up before dinner.* | (fig.) *She's freshened up the house with a new coat of paint.* | *Can I freshen up your drink?* (=add more liquid, esp. alcohol, to it)

fresh·ly /ˈfreʃli/ *adv* (before a past participle) recently; just lately: *"This coffee smells good." "Yes, it's freshly made."* | *His shirts have been freshly washed and ironed.*

fresh·man /ˈfreʃmən/ *n* **-men** /mən/ **1** also **fresh·er** /-ʃər/– *BrE infml* a student in the first year at college or university **2** *AmE* a student in the first year at a HIGH SCHOOL, college, or university –compare SENIOR (3), JUNIOR (4), SOPHOMORE

fresh·wa·ter /ˈfreʃwɔːtər‖-wɔː-, -wɑː-/ *adj* [A] of, living in, or being a river or inland lake; not belonging to the sea: *freshwater fish* | *freshwater lakes* –opposite **saltwater**

fret¹ /fret/ *v* **-tt-** **1** [I;T] to (cause to) be continually worried or dissatisfied about small or unnecessary things: *Don't fret (yourself); everything will be all right.* | *The old lady is always fretting about/over something.* | *You mustn't fret your life away!* **2** [T] *rare* to make a wavy pattern on (water)

fret² *n* [S] *infml* an anxious complaining state of mind: *She gets in a fret whenever we're late.* –see also FRETFUL

fret³ *v* **-tt-** [T] to decorate with wood cut out in patterns

fret⁴ *n* any of the raised lines on the NECK (=the long thin part) of a GUITAR or similar musical instrument with strings

fret·ful /ˈfretfəl/ *adj* complaining and anxious, esp. because of dissatisfaction or discomfort: *The child was tired and fretful.* **– ~ly** *adv* **– ~ness** *n* [U]

fret·saw /ˈfretsɔː/ *n* a metal cutting tool that has a thin blade with fine teeth held in a deep frame, used for cutting out patterns in thin sheets of wood

fret·work /ˈfretwɜːk‖-wɜːrk/ *n* [U] (the making of) patterns cut in thin wood: *The cupboard was decorated with fretwork.* | (fig.) *The ground beneath the trees was a fretwork of sunlight and shadow.* (=formed a pattern of lines and spaces)

Freud /frɔid/, **Sig·mund** /ˈsɪgmənd/ (1856–1939) an Austrian doctor who developed the THEORY (=system of ideas) and practice of PSYCHOANALYSIS, based on FREE ASSOCIATION and the ANALYSIS (=examination) of dreams. His ideas have had a lot of influence on 20th century thinking. He was the AUTHOR of *The Interpretation of Dreams* and *The Ego and the Id.*

Freud·i·an /ˈfrɔɪdɪən/ adj **1** of or in accordance with the ideas and practices developed by Sigmund Freud concerning the way in which the mind works, and how it can be studied **2** infml (of a remark, action, etc.) concerned with or coming from ideas, esp. of sex, in the mind that are not openly expressed

Freudian slip /ˌ··· ˈ·/ n infml an act of accidentally saying something different from what was intended, by which one seems to show one's true thoughts

Fri. written abbrev. for: Friday

fri·a·ble /ˈfraɪəbəl/ adj tech easily broken into small bits or into powder: friable soil --**bility** /ˌfraɪəˈbɪlɪti/ n [U]

fri·ar /ˈfraɪəʳ/ n a man belonging to a Christian religious group who, esp. in former times, were very poor and travelled around the country teaching the Christian religion —compare MONK

Friar's bal·sam /ˌ·· ˈ··/ n [U] tdmk a medicine that is breathed in (INHALED) to help people who have colds

Fri·ar Tuck /ˌ·· ˈ·/ (in the stories of Robin Hood) one of Robin Hood's companions, usu. seen in pictures as a fat and cheerful MONK —see ROBIN HOOD and see colour picture on page 622

fri·ar·y /ˈfraɪəri/ n a building in which friars lived, when their rules of living were changed to allow them to stay in one place

fric·as·see /ˈfrɪkəseɪ‖ˌfrɪkəˈsiː/ n [C;U] a dish made of pieces of meat, cooked and served in a thick white SAUCE: chicken fricassee

fric·a·tive /ˈfrɪkətɪv/ adj, n tech (a consonant sound such as /f/ or /z/) made by forcing air out through a narrow opening between the tongue or lip and another part of the mouth

fric·tion /ˈfrɪkʃən/ n [U] **1** the force which tries to stop one surface sliding over another: He pushed the box very hard down the slope, but friction gradually caused it to slow down and stop. **2** the rubbing, often repeated, of one surface against another: Friction against the rock, combined with the weight of the climber, caused his rope to break. **3** unfriendliness and disagreement caused by two opposing wills or different sets of opinion, ideas, or natures: Mary's neat and Jane's untidy, so if they have to share a room there'll probably be friction.

friction tape /ˈ·· ˌ·/ AmE ‖ **insulating tape** BrE— n [U] sticky narrow material made from cloth or plastic that keeps water out and is used to wrap electrical wires

Fri·day /ˈfraɪdi/ (written abbrev. **Fri.**) n [C;U] **1** the fifth day of the week, between Thursday and Saturday: He'll arrive on Friday. | (BrE infml & AmE) He'll arrive Friday. | It happened on Friday morning. | She left last Friday. | I usually work late on Fridays. | My birthday is on a Friday this year. | He arrived on the Friday and left on the Sunday. (=arrived on the fifth day of the week being spoken of) **2** Friday the thirteenth the 13th day of a month, when it falls on a Friday. It is thought by many people to be an unlucky day: "I lost my cheque book on Friday." "Well, it was Friday the thirteenth!" **3** Thank God it's Friday! also TGIF— =I am very glad that it is the last day of the working week! —see DAY (CULTURAL NOTE); —see also GIRL FRIDAY, GOOD FRIDAY, MAN FRIDAY

fridge /frɪdʒ/ also **refrigerator** BrE fml or AmE, **icebox** old-fash AmE— n a large box or cupboard, used esp. in the home and operated by electricity, in which food and drink can be stored at a low temperature, but without being frozen —compare FREEZER (1) and see picture at KITCHEN

fridge-freez·er /ˌ·· ˈ··/ BrE ‖ also **refrigerator-freezer** AmE— n a large box or cupboard divided into two parts, one of which is a fridge and the other a FREEZER —see picture at KITCHEN

Frie·dan /ˈfriːdn/, **Bet·ty** /ˈbeti/ (1921–) American FEMINIST who questioned the idea that the ROLE of women was to be mothers and housewives. She is esp. known for her book The Feminine Mystique.

Fried·man /ˈfriːdmən/, **Milton** (1912–) an American ECONOMIST who supported the control by the government of the supply of money in a country's economic system (MONETARISM). He wrote Capitalism and Freedom and the Counter-Revolution in Monetary Theory.

Friel /friːl/, **Bri·an** /ˈbraɪən/ (1929–) an Irish writer of plays who writes mainly about Irish people and the sit-

uation in Ireland today. He is best known for Translations and Dancing at Lughnasa.

friend /frend/ n **1** a person who shares the same feelings of natural liking and understanding, the same interests, etc., but is not a member of the same family: Bill and Ben are friends. | "Bill is my friend," said Ben. | Bill is **friends with** (=has a friendship with) Ben. | The children are good friends. (=like each other very much) | Although Peter is a **close friend**, David is my **best** (=closest) friend. | Mary is a friend of mine. (=one of my friends) | She's an old friend (of mine) — we've known each other for sixteen years. | "There's your friend John." "He's **no friend of mine**; I don't like him at all." | I wish you children wouldn't quarrel all the time. Can't you be friends? —see also BOYFRIEND, GIRLFRIEND **2** [(of, to)] a helper; supporter; adviser; person showing kindness and understanding: That rich lady is a friend of the arts; she provides money for concerts in the town. | Our doctor's been a good friend to us; he's always helped us when we've needed him. | He says he's no friend of the government. | He didn't get the post on his own abilities; he had **friends in high places**. (=people in a position to influence others to help him) | (fig.) Bright light is the painter's best friend. **3** someone who is not an enemy; a person from whom there is nothing to fear: "Who goes there? Friend or foe?" was the question asked by the soldier on guard duty in former times. | They told the escaped prisoner: "Don't worry, you're among friends — we won't tell the police about you." **4** a person who is being addressed or spoken to politely in public: Friends, we have met here tonight to talk over a very serious matter. | In court, lawyers speak of each other as "My learned friend". **5** a stranger noticed for some reason, usu. with amusement or displeasure: Our friend with the loud voice is here again! **6** a **friend in need** a true friend, who comes to help you when you are in trouble **7 Friends, Romans, countrymen, lend me your ears; I come to bury Caesar, not to praise him.** quote a phrase from Shakespeare's play Julius Caesar, said by Mark Antony in a speech to the crowd at Caesar's funeral —see colour picture on page 1146 **8 How to win friends and influence people** the title of a book by Dale Carnegie aimed at helping people to be successful in business **9 just good friends** a phrase used to say that a new relationship with someone is not close or sexual: We're just good friends, nothing more than that. **10 make friends: a** (of one or more people) to form friendships: He has a pleasant manner, and finds it easy to make friends. **b** (of two or more people) to form a friendship: Sammy and Joey have only just met, but they've made friends already. | The little boys fought over a game, and then made friends again. (=forgave each other) **11 make friends with** to form a friendship with: Have you made friends with your new neighbours yet? **12 with friends like these who needs enemies?** infml, often humor a phrase used to or about friends who have said or done something unpleasant to you —see also BEFRIEND, **diamonds are a girl's best friend** (DIAMOND (1))

Friend n a member of the Christian group called the **Society of Friends**; QUAKER

friend·less /ˈfrendləs/ adj without friends or help – ~**ness** n [U]

friend·ly[1] /ˈfrendli/ adj **1** [(to, towards)] acting or ready to act as a friend: a friendly person | He's not very friendly to/towards newcomers. | You're always sure of a friendly welcome at this hotel. **2** [F (with)] having the relationship of friends (with): She gets free tickets to the theatre because she's friendly with the manager. **3** [F+to] favouring; ready to accept (ideas): This company has never been friendly to change. **4** not an enemy: a friendly nation **5** (of a game, argument, etc.) done for pleasure or practice and so not causing or containing unpleasant feelings: We've been having a friendly argument on politics/a friendly game of cards. —opposite **unfriendly** (for 1,3,4) —see also FRIENDLY FIRE, USER-FRIENDLY --**liness** n [U] : Do you think his friendliness is genuine?

friendly[2] n esp. BrE a game that is played for pleasure or practice and not as part of a serious competition: Manchester United beat Celtic in a friendly.

friendly fire /ˌ··· ˈ·/ n [U] euph in a war, bombs or bullets which accidentally kill people on the side which has fired the weapons: The soldiers were killed by friendly fire when the pilot thought they were the enemy.

friendly so·ci·e·ty /'·· ·,···/ n (often cap.) (in Britain) an association to which the members pay small regular sums, and which provides money when they are ill and/or in their old age

friend of the court /ˌ· · · '·/ also **amicus curiae**– n tech a person or group who has an interest in a legal case, although they are not a PARTY¹ (4) to the case. In the American legal system they can present their point of view to the court in the hope of influencing it.

friend·ship /'frendʃɪp/ n **1** [U] the condition of sharing a friendly relationship; the feeling and behaviour that exists between friends: *Real friendship is more valuable than money.* **2** [C] a particular example or period of this: *He finds it difficult to form lasting/close friendships.*

Friends of the Earth /ˌ· · · '·/ [(the)] an international group which tries to influence people and governments to care more for the environment: *Friends of the Earth want the government to spend more money on encouraging recycling.*

fri·er /'fraɪəʳ/ n see FRYER

fries /fraɪz/ n see FRENCH FRIES

Frie·si·an /'friːziən‖-ʒən/ esp. BrE ‖ **Holstein** esp. AmE– n a black-and-white cow of a breed that gives a large quantity of milk

frieze /friːz/ n a border along the top of the wall of a building or along the top of wallpaper in a room, usu. decorated with pictures, patterns, etc.: *There was an animal frieze in the little girl's bedroom.*

frig /frɪg/ v **-gg-** [I;T] taboo sl to have sex with
   frig about/around phr v esp. BrE taboo sl **1** [I] to act in a foolish, pointless, and probably annoying manner: *Would you stop frigging about and help me for a while?* **2** [T=**frig** sbdy/sthg **about**] to treat or use in an improper way

frig·ate /'frɪgɪt/ n a small fast-moving armed naval ship, used for travelling with and protecting other ships –see picture at SAIL

frig·ging /'frɪgɪŋ/ adj, adv [A] taboo (used for giving force to an expression, esp. showing annoyance)

fright /fraɪt/ n **1** [U] the feeling or experience of fear: *He was shaking with fright; I thought he must have seen a ghost.* | *The horse* **took fright** (=had an attack of fear) *at the sound of the explosion.* **2** [C] an experience that causes sudden fear; shock: *You* **gave me a fright** *by knocking so loudly on the door.* | *I* **got the fright of my life** (=the biggest fright I've ever had) *when the machine burst into flames.* **3** [S] infml a person or thing that looks silly or unattractive: *She looks a fright in that old black dress.*

fright·en /'fraɪtn/ v [T] **1** to fill with fear: *The little girl was frightened by the big dog.* | *a frightening dream* **2** [+obj+adv/prep] to influence or drive by fear: *The bird came to the window, but I moved suddenly and frightened it away.* | *The burglars were frightened off by the sound of our dog barking.* | *He frightened the old lady into signing the paper.* – ~**ingly** adv

fright·ened /'fraɪtnd/ adj **1** [(of)] full of fear: *a frightened animal* | *Don't be frightened (of the dog) – he won't bite.*| *He was frightened at the thought that he might drown.* [F+to-v] *I was frightened to look down from the top of the tall building.* [F+(that)] *The little girl was frightened (that) her mother wouldn't come back.* | (infml) *They were* **frightened to death/out of their wits** (=extremely frightened) *by the ghost.* **2** [F+of] habitually afraid: *We leave that light on because the children are frightened of the dark.*
   ▷ USAGE 1 Compare **frightened** and **afraid: a** You can be **frightened by** a particular object, animal, or person: *I was* **frightened by** *a large dog.* and **frightened at/by** a particular thought or event: **frightened at/by** *the idea of flying* | **frightened at/by** *the arrival of the police.* You can be **frightened of** or, more commonly, **afraid of** something which causes long-lasting fear: *I'm* **afraid of/frightened of** *snakes.* | *Ile's* **afraid of/frightened of** *flying.* **b** Frightened can come before or after the noun: *a* **frightened** *child* | *The child was* **frightened. Afraid** must come after the noun: *He's* **afraid** *of the dark.* 2 Compare **scared, frightened, terrified,** and **petrified. Scared** is the weakest in this group of words: *I felt a bit* **scared** *when the plane took off.* **Terrified** and **petrified** are the strongest: *I was*

terrified *when the tiger ran towards me.* | *We stood* **petrified** *as we felt the earthquake begin.*◁

fright·en·ers /'fraɪtnəz‖-nərz/ n [the] BrE sl **put the frighteners on** to make someone do what you want by threatening them, usu. to keep silent: *The witnesses refused to give evidence because the criminals had put the frighteners on them.*

fright·ful /'fraɪtfəl/ adj **1** terrible; shocking; causing fear: *The battlefield was a frightful scene.* **2** infml, rather old-fash very bad; unpleasant; difficult: *We're having frightful weather this week.* | *The exam questions were frightful!* – ~**ness** n [U]

fright·ful·ly /'fraɪtfəli/ adv infml, rather old-fash very; extremely: *I'm afraid I'm frightfully late.*

fri·gid /'frɪdʒɪd/ adj **1** (usu. of a woman) **a** tech unable to reach ORGASM during sexual activity **b** derog having an unnatural dislike for sexual activity **2** cold in manner; unfriendly; lacking in warmth and life: *She returned his smile with a frigid glance.* **3** [no comp.] tech very cold; having a continuously low temperature: *The parts of the world near the North and South Poles are called the* **frigid zones.** – ~**ly** adv – ~**ity** /frɪ'dʒɪdɪti/, ~**ness** /'frɪdʒɪdnəs/ n [U]

Fri·gi·daire /ˌfrɪdʒɪ'deəʳ/ n AmE tdmk a popular kind of FRIDGE in the US; often used for any kind of fridge

frill /frɪl/ n **1** a decorative edge to a piece of material made of a band of cloth gathered together on one side and sewn on: *She sewed a frill on the bottom of her skirt.* **2** [usu. pl.] infml, often derog something decorative or pleasant, but not necessary; EXTRA² : *I just want an ordinary car, without the frills.* | *We got a no-frills deal on our car rental.*

frill·y /'frɪli/ also **frilled** /frɪld/– adj having many FRILLs (1): *The little girl wore a frilly party dress.* –**iness** n [U]

fringe¹ /frɪndʒ/ n **1** a decorative edge of hanging threads on a curtain, tablecloth, GARMENT, etc. **2** BrE ‖ **bangs** pl. AmE– a short border of hair usu. cut in a straight line, hanging over a person's forehead: *The girl wore her hair in a fringe.* **3** [(of)] also **fringes** pl.– the part farthest from the centre; edge: *It was easier to move about on the fringe of the crowd.* | *The woodcutter had a little house on the fringes of the forest.* | (fig.) *A* **fringe group** *separated from the main political party.* –see also LUNATIC FRINGE

fringe² v [T] to act as a fringe or border to: *A line of trees fringed the pool.*

Fringe [the] the name of the theatre productions in the **Edinburgh Festival** which are not in the official programme: *a Fringe production* | *The comedian was a great success at the Fringe.*

fringe ben·e·fit /'· ·,···/ n [often pl.] an added favour or service given with a job, besides wages, such as the use of a car, free or cheap meals, or free insurance; PERK: *One of the fringe benefits of this job is free health insurance.* –compare EMOLUMENT

frip·pe·ry /'frɪpəri/ also **fripperies** pl.– n foolish, unnecessary, and useless decoration(s), esp. on an article of clothing

Fris·bee /'frɪzbi/ n tdmk (often not cap.) a plate-like piece of plastic that people throw to each other as a game: *The boys are playing (with a) frisbee in the park.*

frisk /frɪsk/ v **1** [I] (of an animal or child) to run and jump about playfully: *The new lambs are frisking in the fields.* **2** [T] to search (someone) for hidden weapons, goods, etc., by passing the hands over the body: *The passengers were frisked before they were allowed to board the plane.* –**frisk** n

frisk·y /'frɪski/ adj infml, often humor overflowing with life and activity; joyfully alive and playful: *The spring weather's making me feel quite frisky.* | *He may be over seventy, but he can still be quite frisky!* (=sexually playful) –**ily** adv –**iness** n [U]

fris·son /'friːsɒn‖friː'səʊn/ n a feeling of excitement and/or pleasure, esp. caused by something dangerous or forbidden of which one is slightly afraid

frit /frɪt/ adj BrE, dial frightened. The word became well known throughout Britain when Margaret Thatcher used it in the British Parliament.

Fri·tos /'friːtəʊz/ n [P] tdmk a popular kind of 'CORN CHIPS sold in the US

frit·ter[1] /ˈfrɪtəʳ/ n (often in comb.) a thin piece of fruit, meat, or vegetable, covered with a mixture of egg and flour (BATTER) and cooked in hot fat: *apple fritters*

fritter[2] v
fritter sthg. ↔ **away** phr v [T (on)] derog to waste (time, money, etc.) on small unimportant things: *She fritters away all her money on clothes and trips to the cinema.*

fri·vol·i·ty /frɪˈvɒlɪti‖-ˈvɑː-/ n **1** [U] derog the condition of being frivolous: *Your frivolity is out of place on such a solemn occasion.* **2** [C usu. pl.] **a** derog a frivolous act or remark: *One doesn't expect a serious political speech to be full of frivolities.* **b** any form of light pleasure or amusement: *Most people enjoy a few frivolities during their holidays.*

friv·o·lous /ˈfrɪvələs/ adj derog **1** not taking important matters seriously or sensibly; FLIPPANT: *When he tried to make a little joke, the judge warned him not to give frivolous replies to the lawyer's questions.* **2** liking to spend time in light useless pleasures: *He has a frivolous nature.* | *Are you playing cards again? What a frivolous way of spending your time!* – –**ly** adv – –**ness** n [U]

frizz /frɪz/ v [T (OUT, UP)] infml to cause (hair) to go into tight short curls –**frizz** n [S;U]

friz·zle /ˈfrɪzəl/ v [I (UP)] infml to become burnt by being cooked in hot fat: *I left the stew cooking for too long and it frizzled up and stuck to the pan.*

frizz·y /ˈfrɪzi/ adj infml (of hair) in lots of tight short curls: *Some people have naturally frizzy hair.*

fro[1] /frəʊ/ adv –see TO-AND-FRO

fro[2] n AmE infml for an AFRO: *He's got his hair in a fro now; I hardly recognized him.*

frock /frɒk‖frɑːk/ n **1** old-fash a woman's or girl's dress: *a party frock* **2** a long loose GARMENT worn by some Christian MONKs

frock coat /ˌ· ˈ·‖ˈ· ·/ n a knee-length coat for men, worn in the 19th century

Fro·do /ˈfrəʊdəʊ/ a HOBBIT character in the book *The Lord of the Rings* by JRR Tolkien

frog /frɒg‖frɑːg, frɔːg/ n **1** a small hairless tailless animal, usu. brownish-green, that lives in water and on land, has long back legs for swimming and jumping, and CROAKS (=makes a deep rough sound). People sometimes make jokes about kissing frogs to make them turn into an attractive prince, because this happens in some children's fairy stories. –see also FROG PRINCE **2** **a** **'frog in the/one's throat** infml a difficulty in speaking because of roughness in the throat

frog

Frog n infml, derog a French person (usu. considered offensive)

frog·man /ˈfrɒgmən‖ˈfrɑːg-, ˈfrɔːg-/ n -**men** /mən/ a skilled underwater swimmer who wears a special APPARATUS for breathing and FLIPPERS (=large flat shoes) to increase the strength of his leg movements: *Police frogmen were called in to search the lake for the missing child.* –compare SKIN-DIVE

frog·march /ˈfrɒgmɑːtʃ‖ˈfrɑːgmɑːrtʃ, ˈfrɔːg-/ v [T+obj +adv/prep] BrE to force (a person) to move forward with the arms held together firmly from behind: *They frogmarched him into the yard where the firing squad was waiting.*

Frog Prince /ˌ· ˈ·/, **The** a fairy story in which a prince has been turned into a frog by an evil WITCH. He becomes a prince again when a princess kisses the frog. The prince and princess then get married and live happily ever after.

frog·spawn /ˈfrɒgspɔːn‖ˈfrɑːg-, ˈfrɔːg-/ n [U] a nearly transparent mass of frog's eggs

frol·ic[1] /ˈfrɒlɪk‖ˈfrɑː-/ v -**ck**- [I (ABOUT)] to play and jump about happily; FRISK: *The young lambs were frolicking in the field.*

frolic[2] n an active and enjoyable game of amusement: *The children are having a frolic before bedtime.*

frol·ic·some /ˈfrɒlɪksəm‖ˈfrɑː-/ adj esp. lit playful; merry: *Kittens are naturally frolicsome.*

from /frəm; strong frɒm‖frəm; strong frʌm, frɑːm/ prep **1**

starting at (the stated place, position, or condition): *The train from London arrives here at nine o'clock.* | *He flew from London to New York.* | *A cool wind blew from the sea.* | *She went from shop to shop trying to find what she wanted.* | *He rose from office boy to managing director in fifteen years.* | *Translate this letter from French into English.* | *The situation seems to be going from bad to worse.* **2** starting at (the stated time): *From the moment he saw her, he loved her.* | *We've been working from morning to night.* (=without stopping) | *We hope to go on holiday a month from* (=after) *today.* | *The shop will be open from about half past eight until six o'clock.* | **From now on**, *I will only be working in the mornings.* **3** beginning at (the stated lower limit): *These coats are from £50.* (=the cheapest costs £50) | *There were from 60 to 80 people* (=between 60 and 80) *present.* **4** using (the stated thing) as a position: *From the top of the hill you can see the sea.* | *He was looking at me from over the top of his newspaper.* | (fig.) *From a child's point of view this book isn't very interesting.* **5** in a state of separation with regard to: *His absence from class was soon noticed.* | *It's hard for a child to be kept apart from its mother.* | *She took the matches away from the boys.* | *If you subtract 10 from 15, you are left with 5.* | *The wind blew his hat from his head.* | *Could you pass me that book down from the top shelf?* | *He ran away from home at the age of 14.* **6** out of: *He took a knife from his pocket.* **7** distant in regard to: *The village is five miles (away) from the coast.* | *She lives a few miles from here.* | (fig.) *Nothing could have been further from my mind.* (=my intentions or thoughts were quite opposite) **8** in a state of protection or prevention with regard to: *She saved the child from drowning.* | *A tree gave us shelter from the rain.* | *I think we ought to keep the bad news from her.* **9** compared with; as being unlike: *He's different from his brother in character.* | *I don't know anything about cars; I can't tell one make from another.* **10** sent or given by; originating in: *I had a letter from her yesterday.* | *You get eggs from hens.* | *Light comes from the sun.* | *He gets his good looks from his mother.* | *"Where are you from?" "I'm from Scotland."* (=I'm Scottish.) | *The man from* (=employed and sent by) *the gas company called today.* | *This music is from* (=is part of) *one of Mozart's operas.* | *Tell your brother from me* (=pass my message on to him) *that I want him to return my book.* **11** using: *Bread is made from flour.* | *She played the music from memory.* **12** because of; as a result of; through: *She suffered from heart disease.* | *She was exhausted from all the sleepless nights.* | *The explorers died from cold before they reached the North Pole.* **13** judging by; considering: *You can't tell how old he is from the way he looks.* | *From what John tells me, they're very rich.* **14 From Russia With Love** a film about James Bond based on the NOVEL by Ian Fleming. The title is often used in a changed form in newspapers: *From the government with love.* | *From India with an upset stomach.*

from·age frais /ˌfrɒmɑːʒ ˈfreɪ‖frɑˌmɑːʒ-/ n [U] Fr a soft food, usu. served in a small pot, made from soft cheese and cream, and sometimes sugar, and fruit

frond /frɒnd‖frɑːnd/ n a leaf of a FERN or of a PALM

front[1] /frʌnt/ n **1** [C (**of**) usu. sing.] the most forward position; the part in the direction that something moves or faces: *The restaurant car is at the front of the train.* | *The teacher called the boy to the front of the class.* | *We managed to get seats at the front of the hall.* | *The front of the postcard shows a picture of our hotel.* | *The front of the school faces south.* | *This dress fastens at the front.* | *I've spilt some soup down my front.* (=my chest) | *He's sitting in the front of the car, beside the driver.* | *Write your name at the front of the book* (=on the first page inside it)/*on the front of the book.* (=on the cover) | *Iron the fronts of the shirts and then the backs.* –opposite **back**; compare REAR[1] (1) **2** [C] a side of a large important building: *The west front of the church contains some fine old windows.* **3** [the] a road, often built up and having a protecting wall, by the edge of the sea, esp. in a town where people go for holidays: *The hotel is right on the sea front.* | *We walked along the front to enjoy the air.* –compare PROMENADE[1] (1) **4** [C] (sometimes cap.) a line along which fighting takes place in time of war, together with the part behind it concerned with supplies; FRONT LINE: *He lost his life at the front.* | *The Minister of Defence paid a visit to the Western Front.* | *There has been heavy fighting on several fronts.* | (fig.) *The fight against disease is making advances on all fronts.* –see also HOME FRONT **5** [C usu.

sing.] a combined effort or movement against opposing forces: *The opposition parties can only defeat the government if they* **present a united front.** | *During the war, she worked on the home front* (=in her own country), *helping to produce weapons for the army.* | *a political party called the Popular Front* **6** [*C usu. sing.*] a particular area of activity, esp. one in which difficulties are faced: *The government has reduced inflation, but has not made much progress on the employment front.* **7** [S] the outward manner and appearance of a person: *Whatever his problems, he always presents a smiling front to the world.*| *Although she was feeling very nervous she put on a brave front.* (=acted as if she wasn't afraid) **8** [C (**for**) *usu. sing.*] *infml* a person, group, or thing used for hiding the real nature of a secret or unlawful activity: *A travel company was used as a front for bringing illegal drugs into the country.* | *Her job at the embassy was just a front for her spying activities.* –see also FRONT² **for** **9** [C] *tech* a line of separation between two masses of air of different temperature: *A* **cold front** *will reach the south coast overnight, bringing icy weather to the southern region.* | *a* **warm front** **10 in front: a** ahead: *The old woman walked slowly, and the children ran on in front.* **b** in the most forward or important position: *The driver sits in front, and the passengers sit behind.* –compare BEHIND² (1) **11 in front of: a** in the position directly before: *She couldn't watch the television because he was standing in front of the screen.* | *A van was parked right in front of my car.* –opposite **behind b** in the presence of: *You shouldn't use such bad language in front of the children.* **c** in a more important position than; BEFORE ¹(5): *He won't consider our request in front of all the others.* **12 out front** *infml* **a** among the people watching a theatrical or other performance: *The author's family are out front this evening for the first performance of his new play.* **b** in front of the place where one is speaking: *Is that your car out front with the broken tail light?* | *A cop just pulled up out front.* **13 up front** *infml* as payment in advance, esp. as a sign of trust that other payments will follow: *He demanded £5,000 up front before agreeing to go ahead with the deal.* –see also FRONTAL, UPFRONT, **back to front** (BACK¹)

▷ **USAGE** Use **in front of** when one thing is separate from the other: *A child ran out* **in front of** *the bus* (=in the road outside the bus), *so the driver had to stop.* Use **at/in the front of** when one thing is inside or part of the other: *She got a seat* **at/in the front** *of the bus* (=in the front part of the bus), *so we had a good view.* | *I was sitting right* **at the front** *of the cinema* (=in the front part of the room) *but then someone sat* **in front of** *me, so I couldn't see a thing!*◁

front² *adj* [A] **1** at the front: *Write your name on the front cover of the exercise book.* | *One of his front teeth got knocked out.* | *We have tickets for the front row at the concert.* | *She sat in the front garden.* | *The incident made* (=was reported on) *the front page (of the newspaper).* **2** *infml* being a FRONT¹ (8): *a front man* | *The travel firm was just a front organization for the importing of heroin.* **3** *tech* (of a vowel sound) made by raising the tongue at the front of the mouth –opposite **back**

front³ *v* **1** [I+*prep,* esp. **onto**; T] (of a building) to have the front towards; face: *The hotel fronts onto the main road.*| *A large, well-kept lawn fronted the house.* **2** [T *usu. pass.*] to give a surface to the wall of (a building): *The house is fronted with brick.* **3** [T] to head in a way that attracts usu. favourable attention: *We want to get a well-known businessman to front our organization.*

front for sbdy./sthg. *phr v* [T] *infml* to act as a FRONT¹ (8) for: *The police suspected her of fronting for a gang of forgers.*

front·age /ˈfrʌntɪdʒ/ *n* a part of a building or of land that stretches along a road, river, etc.: *The shop has frontages on two busy streets.* | *The boat-building company is looking for a yard with a wide river frontage.*

frontage road /ˈ··· ˌ·/ *n AmE* a road, parallel to a larger road, from which it is possible to reach buildings that do not have a direct connection to the larger road: *Get off the freeway at exit 46 and follow the frontage road for half a mile till you see our turnoff.*

front·al /ˈfrʌntl/ *adj* [A] *fml* **1** of, at, or to the front: *The brain has two* **frontal lobes.** | *Are there any* **full frontal** *scenes* (=showing people with no clothes from the front) *in this film?* **2** (of an attack) direct; (as if) from

the front **3** of or being a weather FRONT¹ (9): *A new* **frontal system** *is moving towards Britain from the west.* – ~**ly** *adv*

front·bench /ˌfrʌntˈbentʃ◂/ *n* the front row of seats on each side of the British parliament; the PRIME MINISTER and ministers who speak officially for the government sit on one side, and leading opposition speakers sit on the other: *a front bench spokesman* –compare BACK-BENCH

front·bench·er /ˌfrʌntˈbentʃəʳ◂/ *n* a person who sits on the front bench –compare BACK-BENCHER

front door /ˌ· ˈ·/ *n* the main entrance door to a house, usu. at the front –see picture at HOUSE –compare BACK DOOR

front end /ˈ· ·/ *n AmE* the part of a computer system operated by people, as opposed to the part which is in the background: *We're hoping to get a new front end without updating our mainframe.*

front-end *adj AmE infml* happening or needed at the beginning: *She wants a front-end payment of $50,000 with the rest due in six months.*

fron·tier /ˈfrʌntɪəʳ‖frʌnˈtɪər/ *n* **1** [C (**between, with**)] the limit or edge of the land of one country, where it meets the land of another country; border: *They were shot trying to cross the frontier.* | *Sweden has frontiers with Norway and Finland.* **2** [*the*] the area between settled and wild country, esp. in the US in former times: *Areas near the frontier were rough and lawless in the old days.* **3** [C (**of**)] also **frontiers** *pl.* – a border between what is known and what is unknown: *They are pushing back the frontiers of medical knowledge.*

fron·tiers·man /ˈfrʌntɪəzmən‖frʌnˈtɪərz-/ *n* **-men** /mən/ a man living on the edge of a settled area (FRONTIER (2)); an early settler

fron·tis·piece /ˈfrʌntɪspiːs/ *n* a picture or photograph at the beginning of a book, usu. on the left-hand page opposite the title page

front line /ˌ· ˈ·◂/ *n* [*the*] **1** the most advanced or important position: *in the front line of the fight against disease* **2** the area where fighting takes place in a war; FRONT¹ (4): *soldiers in the front line* –**front-line** *adj* [A] : *front-line soldiers*

front-line states /ˌ· · ˈ·◂/ *n* [P] the name given to the countries nearest South Africa, such as Mozambique, Zimbabwe, and Botswana, which oppose the system of APARTHEID in South Africa

front man /ˈ· ·/ *n* someone who explains the views or future plans of esp. a large company or illegal organization to the public: *a front man for the Mafia/Bureau of Indian Affairs*

front-page /ˈ· ·/ *adj* [A] *infml* so interesting, important, or exciting that it is worthy of being printed on the front page of a newspaper: *front-page news* | *a front-page story*

front room /ˌ· ˈ·/ *n* a LIVING ROOM in a small house or flat, not usu. in a large house

front-run·ner /ˌ· ˈ··/ *n* a person (or sometimes a thing) that has the best chance of success in competing for something: *"Who do you think will get the job?" "Thomson, Murray, and Jenkinson are the three front-runners."* | *The government has several options for increasing its revenue, but the current front-runner is an increase in local taxes.*

frost¹ /frɒst‖frɔːst/ *n* **1** [U] a white powdery substance (frozen DEW) formed on outside surfaces when the temperature of the air is below freezing point: *The grass was covered with frost in the early morning.* **2** [C;U] (a period or state of) weather at a temperature below the freezing point of water: *There was a hard* (=severe) *frost last night.* | *The young shoots on the trees have been damaged by a late frost.* (=one towards the end of spring) | *Frost has killed several of our new young plants.* | (*tech*) *There was five* **degrees of frost** *last night.* (=the temperature was –5° Celsius) –see also FROSTY, JACK FROST

frost² *v* **1** [I;T (OVER, UP)] to (cause to) become covered with frost: *The cold has frosted the windows.* | *The fields have frosted over.* | *The car windscreen has frosted up.* **2** [T] to make (something, esp. glass) look as if it is covered with frost: *frosted glass* (=glass through which you cannot see clearly) | *Her cocktail glass was frosted with sugar.* **3** [T] *esp. AmE* to cover (a cake) with a mixture of fine powdery sugar and liquid; ICE² (2)

Frost, David (1939–) an English television CHATSHOW

host, who has had many successful television shows in Britain and the US

Frost, Rob·ert /ˈrɒbət‖ˈrɑːbərt/ (1874–1963) an American poet remembered for his many popular poems about ordinary people and nature such as *Mending Wall* and *Stopping by Woods on a Snowy Evening*

frost·bite /ˈfrɒstbaɪt‖ˈfrɔːst-/ *n* [U] harmful swelling and discoloration of a person's limbs, caused by great cold: *The rescued climbers were brought down from the mountain suffering from frostbite.* —**bitten** *adj* : *frostbitten toes*

frost·bound /ˈfrɒstbaʊnd‖ˈfrɔːst-/ *adj* (of the ground) hardened by FROST: *We can't plant the vegetables while the earth is still frostbound.*

frost·ing /ˈfrɒstɪŋ‖ˈfrɔːstɪŋ/ *n* [U] **1** a non-shiny surface on glass or metal **2** *esp. AmE* a covering on a cake made from fine sugar and liquid; ICING

frost·y /ˈfrɒsti‖ˈfrɔːsti/ *adj* **1 a** very cold: *It was a frosty morning.* **b** covered with FROST: *The fields look frosty this morning.* **2** unfriendly; cold: *She gave me a frosty greeting.* —**ily** *adv* —**iness** *n* [U]

froth¹ /frɒθ‖frɔːθ/ *n* **1** [S;U] a white mass of small bubbles formed on top of a liquid, or in the mouth; FOAM: *the froth on a glass of beer* **2** [U] *derog* a light empty show of talk or ideas: *The play was amusing, but it was little more than froth.* —see also FROTHY

froth² *v* [I] to make or produce froth: *The beer frothed as it was poured out.* | *The sick animal was* **frothing at the mouth.** | (*humor*) *"Is he annoyed about it?" "Yes, he's frothing at the mouth!"* (=showing signs of great excitement and anger)

troth·y /ˈtrɒθi‖ˈfrɔːθi/ *adj* **1** full of or covered with froth: *frothy beer* | *frothy coffee* **2** *sometimes derog* light and amusing; without serious content: *a frothy piece of entertainment* —**ily** *adv* —**iness** *n* [U]

frown¹ /fraʊn/ *v* [I] to bring the EYEBROWS together in anger or effort, causing lines to appear on the forehead: *He frowned with displeasure as he read his son's school report.* | *A fiddly task, like threading a needle, often makes you frown.* | (fig.) *frowning cliffs* (=having an unfriendly threatening appearance) – ~**ingly** *adv*

    frown on/upon sthg. *phr v* [T] to disapprove of: *Mary wanted to go to Europe by herself, but her parents frowned on the idea.* | *Smoking in the canteen is rather frowned on here.*

frown² *n* a serious or displeased look, causing lines on the forehead: *She looked at her exam paper with a worried frown.*

frowst·y /ˈfraʊsti/ *adj infml, esp. BrE* (of the conditions inside a room) hot and airless; STUFFY

frow·zy , -sy /ˈfraʊzi/ *adj* **1** (of a person, clothes, etc.) not neat or clean because not well cared for; SHABBY **2** (of a house or room) having a closed-in heavy smell

froze /frəʊz/ *past tense of* FREEZE¹

fro·zen /ˈfrəʊzən/ *past participle of* FREEZE¹. *I'm absolutely frozen.* (=extremely cold) | *frozen peas* | *The lake is frozen over.*

fruc·ti·fy /ˈfrʌktɪfaɪ/ *v* [I;T] *fml* **1** to (cause to) produce fruit **2** to (cause to) produce successful results —**fication** /ˌfrʌktɪfɪˈkeɪʃən/ *n* [U]

fru·gal /ˈfruːgəl/ *adj* **1** not wasteful; careful in the use of money, food, etc.: *Although he's become rich, he's still very frugal with his money.* | *frugal habits* **2** small in quantity and cost; MEAGRE: *a frugal supper of bread and cheese* – ~**ly** *adv* – ~**ity** /fruːˈgælɪti/ *n* [U]

fruit¹ /fruːt/ *n* **1** [C;U] (a particular variety of) the parts of a tree or bush that contain seeds and are often eaten for their usu. sweet flesh: *Apples, oranges, strawberries, and bananas are kinds of fruit*/*are all fruit.* | *Would you like fruit or cheese after your main course?* | *The potato is a vegetable, not a fruit.* | *This drink is made from four tropical fruits.* | *a fruit bowl* | *a fruit flan* | *dried fruit* —see also SOFT FRUIT **2** [C] *tech* a seed-containing part of any plant: *The tomato is technically a fruit, although it is eaten as a vegetable.* **3** [C] also **fruits** *pl.*— a result: *It was a tragedy that he died before he could enjoy the fruits* (=rewards) *of all his hard work.* | *Their plans haven't* **borne fruit.** (=had a successful result) —see also FRUITFUL **4** *BrE old-fash sl* (used for addressing a male friend): *Hello, old fruit!* **5** [C] *AmE derog sl* a male HOMOSEXUAL

flesh

stone *BrE*/
pit *AmE*   peach

skin

pear

plum

apple

cherries

segment

pip *BrE*/
seed *AmE*   oranges

peel

bananas

seeds *BrE*/
pips *AmE*

pineapple

melon

mango   papaya

figs

grapes

olives   lychees

fruit² *v* [I] *tech* (of a tree, bush, etc.) to produce fruit: *The apple trees are fruiting early this year.*

Fruit and Nut /ˌ· · ·ˈ·/ *n* a type of milk chocolate bar made by Cadbury's which contains RAISINS and nuts

fruit bat /ˈ· ·/ also **flying fox**— *n* a large type of flying animal (BAT³) that lives in hot countries and feeds on fruit

fruit·cake /ˈfruːtkeɪk/ *n* **1** [C;U] a cake containing small dried fruits, nuts, etc. **2** [C] *sl* a person who acts in an odd manner: *She's a strange person, in fact, she's a bit of a fruitcake.*

fruit·er·er /ˈfruːtərər/ *n tech* (a person who has) a shop in which fruit is sold

fruit fly /ˈ· ·/ *n* any of several types of small fly that feed on fruit or decaying vegetable matter

fruit·ful /ˈfruːtfəl/ *adj* **1** successful; useful; producing good results: *It was a very fruitful meeting; we made a lot of important decisions.* —opposite **fruitless 2** *old use* (of living things) producing many young or much fruit – ~**ly** *adv* – ~**ness** *n* [U]

fru·i·tion /fruˈɪʃən/ n [U] *fml* fulfilment (of plans, aims, desired results, etc.): *After much delay, the plan to build the new hospital finally* came to fruition/was brought to fruition.

fruit·less /ˈfruːtləs/ *adj* (of an effort) useless; unsuccessful; not bringing the desired result: *So far the search for the missing boy has been fruitless.* —opposite fruitful – ~ly *adv* – ~ness n [U]

fruit ma·chine /ˈ· ·ˌ·/ n *BrE for* ONE-ARMED BANDIT

Fruit of the Loom /ˌ· · · ˈ·/ an American maker of clothing, best known for UNDERWEAR and informal clothes

fruit sal·ad /ˌ· ˈ··/ n [C;U] a dish made of several types of fruit cut up and served in a bowl at the end of a meal

fruit·y /ˈfruːti/ *adj* 1 *usu. apprec* like fruit; tasting or smelling of fruit: *The medicine had a fruity taste.* | *This red wine is soft and fruity.* 2 *infml* (of a voice) too rich and deep: *a fruity laugh* 3 *BrE infml* (of talk, a remark, etc.) amusing in a slightly shocking or impolite way, esp. about matters of sex: *I was surprised to hear my mother-in-law telling such a fruity story.* 4 *derog* typical of male HOMOSEXUALS; EFFEMINATE: *He started acting really fruity when we were alone together.*

frump /frʌmp/ n *infml* a dull unattractive person, esp. a woman, who wears old-fashioned clothes – ~ish *adj* – ~y *adj*

frus·trate /frʌˈstreɪt‖ˈfrʌstreɪt/ v [T] 1 to cause (someone) to have feelings of annoyed disappointment or dissatisfaction: *After two hours' frustrating delay, our train at last arrived.* | *I'm feeling rather frustrated in my present job; I need a change.* 2 to prevent the fulfilment of; cause the failure of (someone or someone's effort); THWART: *The bad weather frustrated our hopes of going out.* | *The prisoner was frustrated in his attempt to escape by a watchful guard.* —**tration** /frʌˈstreɪʃən/ n [C;U] : *The players' frustration mounted as the rain continued to pour down outside.* | *Life is full of frustrations.*

fry /fraɪ/ v 1 [I; T] to cook or be cooked in hot fat or oil: *Shall I fry the fish for dinner?* | *The eggs were frying in the pan.* | *fried rice* 2 [I] *infml* to get SUNBURN: We'll fry if we stay too long in this hot sun. —see also DEEP FRY, SMALL FRY, STIR-FRY; see COOK (USAGE)

fry·er , frier /ˈfraɪəʳ/ n 1 (*often in comb.*) a deep pan for frying food: *a fish fryer* 2 *AmE* a chicken for frying

frying pan /ˈ·· ˌ·/ also **skillet** *AmE*– n 1 a flat pan with a long handle, used for frying food: *a non-stick frying pan* 2 **out of the frying pan into the fire** out of a bad position into an even worse one –see picture at PAN

fry-up /ˈ· ·/ n *BrE infml* (a dish cooked by) frying various foods, such as eggs, SAUSAGES, potatoes, etc., in order to make a quick meal: *I'm going to do/have a fry-up for supper.*

FS *written abbrev. for:* FOREIGN SERVICE

FSLIC /ˌef es ˌel aɪ ˈsiː/ [*the*] Federal Savings and Loan Insurance Corporation, which INSURES (=*protects*) the money people have in US SAVINGS AND LOAN ASSOCIATIONS

f-stop /ˈ· ·/ n the number which tells the size of the APERTURE of a camera; the f-stop can usu. be changed by the person using the camera, to let in more or less light

ft *written abbrev. for:* FOOT¹ (5): *He is 6ft (=feet) tall.*

FT /ˌef ˈtiː◄/ [*the*] *abbrev. for:* FINANCIAL TIMES

FTC /ˌef tiː ˈsiː/ [*the*] Federal Trade Commission; the department of the US government that is concerned with trade laws and practices

FT index /ˌef tiː ˈɪndeks/ *abbrev. for:* FINANCIAL TIMES INDEX

FT 100 Share Index /ˌef tiː wʌn ˌhʌndrəd ˈʃeər ˌɪndeks/ also **FT-SE-100, FT-SE, Footsie** *infml*– n [*the*] Financial Times Stock Exchange 100 Index; the main measure of the amount by which the leading 100 shares sold on the London STOCK EXCHANGE have gone up or down in value. It is brought up to date every minute of the working day.

FT-SE index /ˈfʊtsi ˌɪndeks/ n see FT 100 SHARE INDEX

fuch·sia /ˈfjuːʃə/ n a graceful garden bush with hanging bell-shaped flowers in two colours of red, pink, bluish-red, or white

fuck¹ /fʌk/ v [I;T] *taboo sl* to have sex (with)
fuck about/around *phr v* [I] *taboo sl, esp. BrE* to waste time; act in a useless or stupid way
fuck off *phr v* [I *usu. imperative*] *taboo sl* 1 to go away 2 to stop being troublesome or annoying

fuck sthg. ↔ **up** *phr v* [T] *taboo sl* to spoil; ruin –**fuck-up** /ˈ· ·/ n *taboo sl*: *He's been responsible for a series of major fuck-ups.*

fuck² n [*usu. sing.*] *taboo sl* 1 an act of having sex 2 **not care/give a fuck** not to care at all

fuck³ *interj taboo sl* (used as an expression of annoyance)

fuck all /ˈ· ·/ n [U] *taboo sl, esp. BrE* nothing at all: *It's got fuck all to do with you, so just mind your own business!*

fuck·er /ˈfʌkəʳ/ n *taboo sl* a stupid or greatly disliked person, esp. a man; fool

fuck·ing /ˈfʌkɪŋ/ *adj, adv* [A] *taboo* 1 (used to give force to an expression, esp. showing extreme annoyance): *You fucking idiot!* 2 (used as an almost meaningless addition to speech): *I got my fucking foot caught in the fucking chair!*

fud·dle¹ /ˈfʌdl/ v [T] *infml* to make (a person, the mind, etc.) slow and unable to work clearly, esp. as a result of drinking too much alcohol: *Too much strong drink will fuddle your brain.* | *a fuddled old man*

fuddle² n **in a fuddle** *infml* unable to think clearly; confused: *My grandad gets in a fuddle if he has too many things to do.*

fud·dy-dud·dy /ˈfʌdi ˌdʌdi/ n *derog* a person who does not understand or approve of modern ideas: *Uncle Ernest's a bit of an old fuddy-duddy; he still believes women shouldn't smoke.* | *fuddy-duddy ideas*

fudge¹ /fʌdʒ/ n [U] 1 a soft creamy light brown sweet made of sugar, milk, butter, etc. 2 an action which provides an answer to a problem but not in a satisfactory way

fudge² v *derog* 1 [T (UP)] to put together roughly or dishonestly: *There's nothing new in this book; the writer has fudged up a lot of old ideas.* | *The figures on the latest report have been fudged.* 2 [I (on);T] to avoid taking firm action on (something): *The government have fudged the issue of equal rights because they're afraid it would make them unpopular.* | *They have tended to fudge on matters of economic policy.*

fuel¹ /ˈfjuːəl/ n [C;U] (a) material that is used for producing heat or power by burning or by atomic means: *Petrol is no longer a cheap fuel.* | *Wood, coal, oil, gas, and plutonium are different kinds of fuel.* | *a fuel pump* | *fuel bills* | *high fuel consumption* | *a fuel-efficient engine* | (fig.) *The workers weren't satisfied with their wages, and when they were asked to work longer hours, it* added fuel to the flames. (=made them even more angry)

fuel² v -**ll-** *BrE* ‖ -**l-** *AmE* 1 [T] to provide with fuel: *The car is being fuelled in preparation for the race.* | (fig.) *His provocative words only fuelled the argument further.* 2 [I (UP)] to take in fuel: *Aircraft sometimes fuel (up) in midair.* —see also REFUEL

fuel in·jec·tion /ˈ·· ·ˌ··/ n [U] a method of putting liquid fuel directly into an INTERNAL-COMBUSTION ENGINE which allows a car to ACCELERATE more quickly. Cars with fuel injection engines are relatively expensive and have a modern, sporty image. —compare GTI –**fuel injected** *adj*

fug /fʌg/ n [S] *infml, esp. BrE* a heavy unpleasant airless condition of a room, etc., caused by heat, smoke, or the presence of many people: *There's a terrible fug in here; please open the window!* – ~**gy** *adj* : *a fuggy atmosphere*

fu·gi·tive /ˈfjuːdʒɪtɪv/ n [(**from**)] *fml* a person escaping from the law, the police, danger, etc.: *Three fugitives are still at large* (=haven't been caught) *following the prison escape.* | *a fugitive from justice*

fugue /fjuːg/ n a piece of music in which one or two tunes are repeated by different parts or voices

führ·er , fuehrer /ˈfjʊərəʳ/ n a leader with extreme authority, esp. Adolf Hitler, leader of the Nazis, before and during the Second World War

Fu·ji /ˈfuːdʒi/, **Mount** a VOLCANO, which is no longer active and is the highest point in Japan. It is a place of PILGRIMAGE and it is known for its perfectly formed snow-covered top.

Fujitsu a Japanese company making computers, FAX machines and other electronic products

Ful·bright Schol·ar·ship /ˈfʊlbraɪt ˌskɒləʃɪp‖-ˌskɑːlər-/ n any of a number of SCHOLARSHIPS (1) which provide for exchanges of university students and teachers between the US and other countries –**Scholar** n

ful·crum /ˈfʊlkrəm, ˈfʌl-/ n **-crums** or **-cra** /krə/ tech the point on which a bar (LEVER) turns, balances, or is supported in lifting or moving something

ful·fil BrE ‖ also **fulfill** AmE /fʊlˈfɪl/ v **-ll-** [T] **1** to carry out (an order, conditions, etc.); obey: *The conditions of the contract must be fulfilled exactly.* **2** fml to do or perform (a duty, etc.): *A nurse has many duties to fulfil in caring for the sick.* | *This chimney fulfils the function of taking away gas fumes.* **3** to supply or satisfy (a need, demand, or purpose): *The travelling library fulfils an important need for people who live in country areas.* | *This company should be able to fulfil our requirements.* | *He finds his work very fulfilling.* (=enjoys it very much) **4** to make or prove to be true; cause (something wished for or planned) to happen: *The old prophecy that the world would come to an end after a thousand years was not fulfilled.* | *If he's lazy, he'll never fulfil his ambition to be a doctor.* | *"I'll never learn to speak English!" "That's a self-fulfilling prophecy."* (=if you believe this, it will come true) **5** to develop and express the abilities, qualities, character, etc., of (oneself) fully: *She succeeded in fulfilling herself both as an actress and as a mother.*

ful·fil·ment BrE ‖ also **fulfillment** AmE /fʊlˈfɪlmənt/ n [U] **1** the act of fulfilling or state of being fulfilled: *After many years, our plans have come to fulfilment.* | *the fulfilment of a promise* **2** satisfaction after successful effort: *He gets a great sense of fulfilment from his work with the mentally handicapped.*

Ful·ham /ˈfʊləm/ an area of west London which has become a more fashionable place to live in recent years

Fulham Pal·ace /ˌ·· ˈ···◂/ the official home of the Bishop of London

full¹ /fʊl/ adj **1** [(of, UP)] (of a container or space) holding as much or as many as possible or reasonable; filled completely: *You can't put any more liquid into that bottle — it's full.* | *After the storm, the holes in the road were full of rainwater.* | *The train's full (up); there are no seats left at all.* | *The drawer was full up with old clothes.* | *It's rude to talk with your mouth full.* | *The wine glass was already full to the brim.* (=there was no room for even a single drop of wine) | *(infml) The little cinema was full to bursting.* (=could not hold any more people) | *(fig.) The doctor has a full day before him.* (=has work to do all the time) **2** [(of)] (of a container) holding liquid, powder, etc., as near to the top as is needed or convenient: *They brought us out a pot full of steaming coffee.* | *This bag of flour is only half full.* (=contains half the amount that it can hold) | *Don't fill my cup too full.* **3** [F+of] containing or having plenty (of): *The field was full of sheep.* | *This work's full of mistakes.* | *Her eyes were full of tears.* | *Every time they meet us, they're full of complaints about something.* | *The children were full of excitement at the thought of their coming holiday.* | *a soup full of flavour* **4** [(UP)] infml well fed, often to the point of discomfort; satisfied: *I can't eat any more; I'm full (up).* | *You shouldn't go swimming on a full stomach.* (=just after you have eaten a meal) **5** [A] complete; whole: *The full truth of the matter can never be told.* | *Please write down your full name and address.* | *You have my full support.* | *He's been away for a full year now.* | *For a full report on the prime minister's speech, turn to page seven.* | *It was only later that I realized the full implications of what she had said.* | *She rose to her full height.* (=stood up very straight and proudly) | *Only full members of the club* (=those with all the rights of membership) *are allowed to vote at meetings.* | *My foot caught in the step, and I fell full length.* (=flat on the ground) | *The incident took place in full view of the television cameras.* | *He has led a full life.* (=has had every kind of experience) | *I believe her, but I don't think she's telling us the full story.* (=everything she knows) **6** [A] the highest or greatest possible: *He drove the car at full speed through the town.* | *Only a very good student can obtain full marks in such a difficult exam.* | *Up on the hill, the full force of the wind can be felt.* | *The riders crossed the plain at full gallop.* (=as fast as they could) **7** [F+of] having the mind and attention fixed only (on); thinking and talking of nothing else (except): *Some people are too full of their own troubles to care about anyone else.* | *She's rather full of herself.* (=she thinks she's very important) | *He's full of his plans to visit America.* (=talks a lot about them) **8** (of clothing) containing a lot of material; fitting loosely: *The wedding dress had a tight bodice, full sleeves, and a full*

skirt. **9** (of a shape, a body, or its parts) **a** often apprec round; rounded; fleshy: *Her face was full/She was full in the face when she was younger; now it's much thinner.* | *full breasts* **b** euph fat: *This shop sells dresses for the fuller figure.* **10** apprec (of colour, smell, sound, taste, or substance) deep, rich, and powerful: *He likes a wine with a full body.* (=having strength or substance) | *This cheese should be served at room temperature to bring out its lovely full flavour.* —see also FULLNESS, FULLY, **full of beans** (BEAN), **(at) full blast** (BLAST¹ (7)), **come full circle** (CIRCLE¹), **in full cry** (CRY²), **(at) full pelt** (PELT²), **in full swing** (SWING²), **(at) full tilt** (TILT²)

full² adv [+adv/prep] **1** straight; directly: *The ball struck him full on the chest.* | *The sun shone full in her face.* **2** very; quite: *They knew full well that he wouldn't keep his promise.* **3** full out rare at full power; at top speed; **flat out** (FLAT³)

full³ n **1** in full completely: *The debt must be paid in full.* **2** to the full to the greatest degree: *To appreciate this opera to the full, you need to read the story first.*

full-back /ˈfʊlbæk/ n **1** (esp. in football) a defending player whose position is at the end of their own half of the field, farthest from the centre **2** in American football, an attacking player who usually works to block the defending team and keep them away from the QUARTERBACK —compare HALFBACK

full beam /ˌ· ˈ·/ n [S] BrE the full strength of a car's HEADLIGHTS

full-blood·ed /ˌ· ˈ···◂/ adj [A] **1** of unmixed race: *He's a full-blooded Indian.* **2** having all the typical qualities (of something) to a great degree: *a full-blooded Socialist* **3** forceful: *They were having a full-blooded argument.* — ~ness n [U]

full-blown /ˌ· ˈ·◂/ adj **1** [A] fully developed; possessing all the usual or necessary qualities: *We're afraid that the fighting on the border may develop into a full-blown war.* | *He has developed full-blown AIDS.* **2** often lit (of a flower) completely open

full board /ˌ· ˈ·/ n [U] (in hotels, etc.) the providing of all meals: *The room with full board will be £60 a week.* —compare HALF BOARD

full-bod·ied /ˌ· ˈ···◂/ adj apprec strong; heavy and rich in taste: *a fine full-bodied red wine*

full-court press /ˌ· · ˈ·/ n AmE infml (in BASKETBALL) a method of defence in which the team with the ball is followed all over the playing area, not only in the part where their basket is: *(fig.) The Justice Department and the DEA have launched a full-court press against Noriega, with dozens of people working on the case.*

full-cream /ˌ· ˈ·◂/ BrE ‖ **whole** AmE— adj made of milk which has not had any of the cream removed —compare SEMI-SKIMMED

full dress /ˌ· ˈ·/ n [U] special dress worn on special or ceremonial occasions —compare EVENING DRESS, HIGHLAND DRESS, MORNING DRESS

full em·ploy·ment /ˌ· ·ˈ··/ n [U] a situation existing in a country, society, etc. where everyone who wants a job is able to get one because there is enough work available —compare UNEMPLOYMENT

Ful·ler /ˈfʊləʳ/, **Rich·ard Buck·min·ster** /ˈrɪtʃəd ˈbʌkmɪnstəʳ‖-tʃərd-/ (1895–1983) an American ARCHITECT and engineer

fuller's earth /ˌ·· ˈ·/ n [U] dried clay sometimes made into a powder, used in former times for removing oil from cloth, but now used esp. in treating impure oils, to make them clearer and lighter

full-fash·ioned /ˌ· ˈ···◂/ adj AmE for FULLY-FASHIONED

full-fledged /ˌ· ˈ·◂/ adj esp. AmE for FULLY-FLEDGED

full-grown /ˌ· ˈ·◂/ also **fully-grown** BrE— adj (esp. of an animal, plant, or (tech) person) completely developed; that is not going to grow any larger: *A full-grown elephant can weigh over 6000 kilograms.*

full house /ˌ· ˈ·/ n **1** (at a cinema, sports ground, etc.) an occasion when every seat is taken: *We've had five full houses this week — it's a very popular film.* **2** (in the card game of POKER) three cards of one kind and a pair of another kind: *I've got a full house, fives over jacks.* (=three fives and two jacks)

full-length /ˌ· ˈ·◂/ adj **1** (of a photograph, painting, etc.)

showing all of a person, from their head to their feet: *a full-length portrait of the queen* **2** (of clothing) reaching to the ground: *a full-length evening dress* **3** (of a play, book, etc.) not short; not shorter than is usual: *a full-length feature film*

full moon /ˌ· ˈ·/ *n* the moon when seen as a complete circle: *A full moon shone brightly.* —compare HALF MOON, NEW MOON

▶ CULTURAL NOTE Some people believe that a full moon can cause people to behave in a strange or dangerous manner. In stories, people sometimes turn into werewolves (WEREWOLF) when there is a full moon. ◀

full·ness , fulness /ˈfʊlnᵻs/ *n* [U] **1** the condition of being full: *a contented feeling of fullness* **2 in the fullness of time** *esp. lit or fml* when the right time comes/came: *You may have to suffer hardships now, but in the fullness of time you will have your reward.*

full-page /ˌ· ˈ·◂/ *adj* [A] covering the whole of a page, esp. in a newspaper or magazine: *a full-page advertisement*

full pro·fes·sor /ˌ· ·ˈ··/ *n* a PROFESSOR (=teacher) at an American university who has the highest rank and possesses TENURE (=the right to keep a job) —compare ASSISTANT PROFESSOR, ASSOCIATE PROFESSOR

full-scale /ˌ· ˈ·◂/ *adj* **1** (of a model, drawing, copy, etc.) of the same size as the object represented: *There is a full-scale model of an elephant at the museum.* **2** [A] complete; total; with the use of all possible means: *The government has ordered a full-scale inquiry into the train crash.* | *The dispute between the countries nearly developed into a full-scale war.* | *a full-scale attack on the enemy position*

full-size /ˌ· ˈ·◂/ *adj* containing or being the usual amount or size of a thing: *Send in two proof-of-purchase seals from full-size packets of Crimples for your free recipe book.*

full stop /ˌ· ˈ·/ *n* **1** also **period** *AmE*— a point (.) marking the end of a sentence or a shortened form of a word: *Put in a full stop after "now".* —see picture at PUNCTUATION MARK **2** *esp. BrE for* PERIOD (5b): *I'm not going, full stop!* **3 come to a full stop** to stop completely, esp. because of a problem or difficulty

full-term /ˌ· ˈ·◂/ *adj* born after a PREGNANCY of the usual length: *a full-term baby* —compare PREMATURE (2)

full-time /ˌ· ˈ·◂/ *adj, adv* working or giving work during the whole of the usual working period: *After a lot of part-time jobs he's finally got a* **full-time job.** | *She's a* **full-time student** *at the university.* | *He used to work full-time, but now he only works four days a week.* | *He's in full-time employment.* | (fig.) *It's a full-time job* (=leaves one no free time) *looking after three young children.* —compare PART-TIME

▶ CULTURAL NOTE Jobs which require 35 or more hours a week are usually considered full-time. Wages and FRINGE BENEFITS offered with a job often vary according to whether the job is full-time or part-time. ◀

full time /ˌ· ˈ·/ *n* [U] *BrE* (in certain sports, esp. football) the end of the fixed period of time during which a match is played: *At full time neither team had scored, so they had to play another half hour to decide the match.* —compare HALF TIME

full toss /ˌ· ˈ·/ also **full pitch**— *n BrE* a ball which is bowled (BOWL²(16)), esp. in cricket, so that it does not touch the ground before reaching the BATSMAN

ful·ly /ˈfʊli/ *adv* **1** completely; altogether: *I don't fully understand his reasons for leaving.* | *Is she fully satisfied with the present arrangement?* | *a fully-trained nurse* **2** *fml* quite; at least: *It's fully an hour since he left.*

fully-fash·ioned /ˌ··· ˈ···◂/ *BrE* ‖ **full-fashioned** *AmE*— *adj* (of knitted (KNIT) clothing) made to fit the shape of the body exactly: *fully-fashioned tights*

fully-fledged /ˌ··· ˈ·◂/ *esp. BrE* ‖ **full-fledged** *esp. AmE*— *adj* **1** (of a young bird) having grown all its feathers, and now able to fly **2** completely trained: *After seven years of training she's now a fully-fledged doctor.*

fully-grown /ˌ··· ˈ·◂/ *adj esp. BrE for* FULL-GROWN

ful·mar /ˈfʊlməʳ, -maːʳ/ *n* a seabird that lives near the coasts of cold northern countries

ful·mi·nate /ˈfʊlmᵻneɪt, ˈfʌl-/ *v* [I (**against, at**)] *fml* to declare one's opposition very strongly and angrily: *The*

preacher fulminated against the use of alcohol. —**nation** /ˌfʊlmᵻˈneɪʃən, ˌfʌl-/ *n* [C;U]

ful·ness /ˈfʊlnᵻs/ *n* [U] FULLNESS

ful·some /ˈfʊlsəm/ *adj fml* giving an unnecessarily large amount of praise; EFFUSIVE: *I was embarrassed by their fulsome expressions of admiration.* | *Her speech of thanks was a little too fulsome.* – ~ **ly** *adv* – ~ **ness** *n* [U]

Ful·ton /ˈfʊltən/, **Rob·ert** /ˈrɒbət‖ˈraːbərt/ (1765–1815) an American engineer and inventor who produced several STEAMSHIPS

Fu Man·chu /ˌfuː mænˈtʃuː/ *n* an evil Oriental character in stories by Sax Rohmer. He is remembered for his heavy MOUSTACHE with ends that turn down and for having his hair in a PIGTAIL (tied together at the back): *wearing a Fu Manchu moustache and heavy sunglasses*

fum·ble /ˈfʌmbəl/ *v* **1** [I (**ABOUT, AROUND, FOR**)] to move the fingers or hands awkwardly in search of something, or in an attempt to do something: *She fumbled about in her handbag for a pen.* | *He fumbled for the light switch.* | (fig.) *He's not a very good public speaker; he often has to fumble for the right word.* **2** [T] to spoil or not succeed at by mishandling: *He fumbled the catch and dropped the ball.* **3** [I;T] (in American football) to drop (the ball) after having taken hold of it –**fumble** *n*

fume /fjuːm/ *v* [I] **1** to be angry and restless, but often without expressing one's feelings fully: *She was fuming with annoyance because the books hadn't arrived.* | *He fumed at the delay.* | *"Was he angry?" "Yes, he was really fuming."* **2** *rare* to give off fumes; smoke

fumes /fjuːmz/ *n* [P] heavy strong-smelling air given off from smoke, gas, fresh paint, etc., that causes an unpleasant sensation when breathed in: *She felt sick from breathing in paint fumes.* | *The air in the railway carriage was thick with tobacco fumes.* | *Petrol fumes from car engines poison the air.*

fu·mi·gate /ˈfjuːmᵻgeɪt/ *v* [T] to clear of disease, bacteria, or harmful insects by means of chemical smoke or gas: *The man was found to have an infectious disease, so all his clothes, his bed, and his room had to be fumigated.* –compare SMOKE out –**gation** /ˌfjuːmᵻˈgeɪʃən/ *n* [U]

fun¹ /fʌn/ *n* [U] **1** (a cause of) amusement, enjoyment, or pleasure: *Children get a lot of fun out of dressing in older people's clothes.* | *You're sure to have fun at the party tonight.* | *It's fun to try out new recipes.* | *There's no fun in spending the evening doing nothing.* | *Have fun!* (=Enjoy yourself!) | *Swimming in the sea is great/good fun.* (=is very enjoyable) | *He's learning French* **for fun/for the fun of it.** (=just for pleasure) | *It's not much fun being unemployed.* | *What fun!* (=How enjoyable!) **2** amusement caused by laughing at someone else: *He's become just a* **figure of fun** – *no one takes him seriously any more.* **3** playfulness: *The little dog's full of fun.* **4 in fun** in playfulness; without serious or harmful intention: *The children played a trick on the teacher but it was all in good fun.* **5 make fun of** to laugh, or cause others to laugh, rather unkindly at: *People make fun of her because she wears such strange hats.* —see also FUNNY, **poke fun at** (POKE¹)

fun² *adj* [A] *apprec, esp. AmE* providing pleasure, amusement, or enjoyment: *She's a fun person to be with.*

fun and games /ˌ· · ˈ·/ *n* [P] *infml* **1** playful tricks; high-spirited behaviour of a group: *The children were having some fun and games while the teacher was out of the room.* **2** exciting activity: *There'll be some fun and games if the newspapers get hold of this scandal!*

func·tion¹ /ˈfʌŋkʃən/ *n* **1** [C] a natural or usual duty (of a person) or purpose (of a thing): *The function of a chairman is to lead and control meetings.* | *The brain performs a very important function; it controls the nervous system of the body.* | *to fulfil a useful social function* **2** [U] the way in which something works: *a disease impairing the function of the brain* **3** [C] **a** a public ceremony: *The minister has to attend all kinds of official functions, such as dinners to welcome foreign guests of the government, and the openings of new schools and hospitals.* **b** *infml* a large or important gathering of people for pleasure or on some special occasion: *"You look as if you're dressed for some function or other." "Yes, I'm going to a friend's wedding."* **4 a** [(C **of**)] *tech* (in MATHEMATICS) a value which varies as another value varies: *In x=5y, x is a function of y.* **b** [+**of**] a quality or fact which depends on and varies with another: *The size of the crop is a function of the quality of the soil and the amount of rainfall.*

function² *v* [I] (esp. of a thing) to be in action; work; operate: *The machine will not function properly if it is not kept well-oiled.*

function as sthg. *phr v* [T] to fulfil the duty or purpose of; be: *This chair can also function as a bed.*

func·tion·al /ˈfʌŋkʃənəl/ *adj* **1** made for or concerned with practical use only, without decoration: *I don't like this functional modern furniture; it's so uncomfortable.* | *a rather functional piece of writing* **2** [no comp.] functioning; working properly: *"Is this machine functional?" "No; it needs repairing."* **3** [no comp.] having a function: *"Is this handle functional?" "No; it's only for decoration."* — opposite **nonfunctional** – ~**ly** *adv*

func·tion·al·is·m /ˈfʌŋkʃənəlɪzəm/ *n* [U] the idea and practice of making buildings and other objects for use and convenience without considering beauty or appearance —**ist** *n, adj*

func·tion·a·ry /ˈfʌŋkʃənəri‖-neri/ *n often derog* a person who has unimportant or unnecessary official duties

function key /ˈ··· ·/ *n* a key on the KEYBOARD of a machine such as a computer or a calculator which tells the machine which action to perform

fund¹ /fʌnd/ also **funds** *pl.*— *n* a supply or sum of money set apart for a special purpose: *Part of the school sports fund will be used to improve the football pitch.* | *We made a contribution to the famine relief fund.* | *The cost is being repaid out of government funds.* | *She's the manager of a pension fund for a large manufacturer.* | *(infml or humor) I'm a bit* **short of funds** *(=I haven't got much money) at the moment.* | *(fig.) She's got a fund of amusing jokes.*

fund² *v* [T] **1** to provide money for (an activity, organization, etc.): *The scientists' search for a cure for this disease is being funded by the government.* **2** *tech* to make (a debt) into a lasting debt on which a fixed yearly interest will be paid

fun·da·men·tal /ˌfʌndəˈmentl◄/ *adj* **1 a** (of a quality, idea, development, etc.) being at the base, from which all else develops; deep; BASIC: *There's a fundamental difference in attitude between these two politicians.* | *The changes will have to be fundamental if they are to have any effect.* **b** of the greatest importance; having a greater effect than all others: *The fundamental purpose of my plan is to encourage further development.* [+to] *A knowledge of economics is fundamental to any understanding of this problem.* **2** [A] (of a quality) belonging to a person's or thing's deep true character: *He has some rather strange ideas sometimes, but no one can doubt his fundamental good sense.* —see also FUNDAMENTALLY

fundamental² *n* [often pl.] a rule, law, etc., on which a system is based; necessary or important part: *If the boys are going to camp for ten days, they'll need to know the fundamentals of cooking.*

fundamental force /ˌ···· ·ˈ·/ *n tech* any of the four forces in the universe that are said to be properties of matter. They are GRAVITY, ELECTROMAGNETISM, the STRONG FORCE, and the WEAK FORCE.

fun·da·men·tal·is·m /ˌfʌndəˈmentəlɪzəm/ *n* [U] **1** the practice of following the rules of a religion, such as Christianity or Islam, very strictly and exactly **2** an American religious movement among some Protestant Christians, esp. in the south, which includes belief in the VIRGIN BIRTH, the SECOND COMING of Christ, and that the truth of the Bible must not be questioned. Fundamentalists do not believe in EVOLUTION and have sometimes tried to stop it being taught in schools.

fun·da·men·tal·ist /ˌfʌndəˈmentəl-ɪst/ *n* someone who follows the rules of a religion, such as Christianity or Islam, very strictly and exactly: *Islamic fundamentalists* –**fundamentalist** *adj*

fun·da·men·tal·ly /ˌfʌndəˈmentəli/ *adv* in every way that really matters or is important; ESSENTIALLY: *Although a few of your facts aren't right, your answer is fundamentally correct.* | *She is fundamentally unsuited to office work.*

fund·hold·er /ˈfʌndhəʊldəʳ/ *n BrE* a NHS doctor who controls his/her own BUDGET (=amount of money set aside for spending)

fund rais·er /ˈ· ˌ··/ *n* a person or an event which collects money for a specific cause, usu. in support of a CHARITY –**fund raising** *n* [U]

fu·ne·ral /ˈfjuːnərəl/ *n* **1** a ceremony, usu. religious, of burying or burning a dead person: *The old lady's funeral was held at the local church.* | *The bishop conducted her funeral service.* | *a funeral procession* | *a funeral pyre* — see also **ashes to ashes, dust to dust** (ASH), **in the midst of life we are in death** (LIFE) **2 be someone's funeral** *infml* to concern or be important for someone, and no one else: *If you miss the train, that's your funeral — don't expect the rest of us to wait for you.*

▶ CULTURAL NOTE Funerals usually take place in a church or CHAPEL. Anyone who wants to may go to a funeral, and it is usual for close friends and relatives of the dead person to attend. The COFFIN (= long box for the dead body) is carried to the church or chapel in a special black car (HEARSE), with close relatives following in other black cars. At some funerals in the US the coffin is open and people look at the dead person before the funeral service starts. The funeral service usually includes music and prayers, and sometimes there is a special speech about the life of the person who has died. After the funeral, the body is either buried in a churchyard or CEMETARY, or burned (CREMATEd) in a special building (CREMATORIUM). If the person is buried, there is usually a short ceremony beside the person's GRAVE (= hole where they are buried) and people throw earth into the grave. If the body is burnt the ASHES are usu. given to the family later, who then spread them around a pleasant place such as a garden. People usually wear black or dark-coloured clothes to funerals. Women in the family of the dead person sometimes wear VEILS (= pieces of cloth they can see through) over their faces. People usually send flowers in advance to a funeral, with a short message about the person who has died. ◀

funeral di·rec·tor /ˈ··· ·ˌ··/ also **mortician** *AmE— n fml* a person whose business is to arrange for dead people to be buried or burned; UNDERTAKER

funeral home /ˈ··· ˌ·/ also **funeral parlor** /ˈ··· ···/ *AmE— n* a funeral director's place of business

fu·ne·ra·ry /ˈfjuːnərəri‖-nəreri/ *adj* [A] *tech* suited or used for a funeral: *a funerary urn* (=a large container for the ashes of a person)

fu·ne·re·al /fjuːˈnɪəriəl/ *adj* heavy and sad; suitable for a funeral: *They went along at a funereal pace.* (=very slowly) | *funereal music* – ~**ly** *adv*

fun·fair /ˈfʌnfeəʳ/ *BrE* ‖ **carnival** *AmE— n* a noisy brightly-lit outdoor show at which one can ride on machines, play games of skill for small prizes, and enjoy other amusements, and that usu. moves from town to town

fun·gi·cide /ˈfʌndʒ₃̣saɪd, -gₗ-/ *n* [C;U] a chemical substance used for destroying or preventing fungus

fun·goid /ˈfʌŋgɔɪd/ *adj* like a fungus; of the nature of a fungus: *fungoid growths*

fun·gous /ˈfʌŋgəs/ *adj tech* **1** of, like, or related to fungus **2** caused by a fungus: *fungous plant diseases*

fungus

fun·gus /ˈfʌŋgəs/ *n* -**gi** /dʒaɪ, gaɪ/ *or* -**guses** **1** [C] a simple fast-growing plant without flowers, leaves, or green colouring, which may either be in a large form, with a fleshy stem supporting a broad rounded top (MUSHROOMS, TOADSTOOLS, etc.), or in a very small form, with a powderlike appearance (MILDEW, MOULD, etc.): *edible fungi* **2** [U] these plants in general, esp. considered as a disease: *My roses were suffering from fungus.* | *Fungus can cause wooden floorboards to decay.*

fu·nic·u·lar /fjuːˈnɪkjŭ̩ləʳ/ also **funicular rail·way** /·ˌ··· ˈ··/ — *n* a small railway up a slope or a mountain, worked by a thick metal rope, often with one carriage going up as another comes down

funk¹ /fʌŋk/ n **in a (blue) funk** old-fash in a state of great fear; unable to face a difficulty or an unpleasant duty

funk² v [T] old-fash to (try to) avoid (something or doing something) because of fear or lack of will: [+v-ing] We all funked telling her the truth.

funk³ n [U] a type of modern popular esp. dance music with a heavy regular beat

funk·hole /ˈfʌŋkhəʊl/ n AmE sl a place where one can hide for shelter or esp. to avoid military service

funk·y /ˈfʌŋki/ adj infml, esp. AmE **1** (of JAZZ or similar music) having a simple direct style and feeling **2** apprec (of clothes, cars, possessions) not new but still usable and sometimes unusual in appearance or purpose: He has a funky old Rambler but it starts every morning. | We just bought $10 worth of funky clothes at the Salvation Army.

funky chick·en /ˌ·· ˈ··/ n [the] a type of dance done to popular music that was fashionable in the 1970s

fun·nel¹ /ˈfʌnl/ n **1** a wide-mouthed tube used for pouring liquids or powders into a container with a narrow neck: He poured oil into the bottle through a funnel. —see picture at LABORATORY **2** also **smokestack** AmE— a metal chimney for letting out smoke from a steam engine or steamship

funnel² v -ll- BrE ‖ -l- AmE **1** [I+adv/prep] (esp. of something large or made up of many parts) to pass through a narrow space: The large crowd funnelled out of the gates after the football match. **2** [T+obj+adv/prep] to pass (as if) through a funnel: He funnelled the oil into the bottle.

fun·nies /ˈfʌniz/ also **funny papers**— n [the + P] AmE infml COMICS

fun·ni·ly /ˈfʌnl̩i/ adv **1** in a strange or unusual way: She's been acting rather funnily just recently. **2** in an amusing way **3** **funnily enough** BrE ‖ **funny enough** AmE— strangely or unexpectedly: Funnily enough, I was just about to phone you when you called me.

fun·ny /ˈfʌni/ adj **1** causing laughter; amusing: a funny joke/speech | He's a very funny man. (=can make people laugh with amusing stories, etc.) | I don't think that's at all funny. (=is a fit cause for laughter) | She was angry at first, but then she **saw the funny side** of the situation. **2** strange; unexpected; hard to explain: What can that funny noise be? | It's a funny thing, but I put the book on the table five minutes ago, and now I can't find it. | It's funny that she left so suddenly. | He's a funny sort of person. (=I don't understand him.) | (infml) This telephone's gone funny! (=it doesn't work properly) —see also FUN·NILY **3** infml not quite correct; marked by dishonesty or cheating: When I saw them whispering I knew there was something funny going on. | Don't try anything funny with me! (=Don't try to trick me!) **4** [F] infml a slightly ill: She always feels a bit funny if she looks down from a height. **b** euph slightly mad: He went a bit funny (in the head) after his wife died. **5** **funny peculiar or funny ha-ha** a phrase used to make it clear when you use the work "funny" whether you mean "strange" or "amusing": He had ever such a funny look on his face — I mean funny peculiar not funny ha-ha.

funny bone /ˈ·· ·/ also **crazy bone** AmE— n infml the tender part of the elbow, which hurts very much if it is knocked sharply

funny busi·ness /ˈ·· ˌ··/ n [U] infml **1** dishonest dealing: As soon as I examined the accounts I could see there'd been some funny business going on. **2** silly or careless behaviour: "Just keep your hands in the air," said the gunman. "I don't want any funny business."

funny farm /ˈ·· ·/ n humor or derog, esp. AmE a MENTAL HOSPITAL

funny mon·ey /ˈ·· ˌ··/ n [U] infml (a sum of) money that is so large as to seem unreal

funny pa·pers /ˈ·· ˌ··/ also **funnies**— n [the +P] AmE infml **1** COMICS **2** **see you in the funny papers** Good-bye

fun run /ˈ· ·/ n an event in which many people run over a long distance in order to collect money for people who are in need of help. Children may take part in a fun run as well as adults and, unlike a MARATHON, a fun run is not a serious competition but is purely for enjoyment and to raise money: a fun run to raise money for the earthquake victims

fur¹ /fɜː/ n **1** [U] the soft thin hair that grows thickly over the body of some types of animal, such as bears, rabbits, cats, etc.: The cat's fur was matted with blood. | coarse/silky fur —compare HAIR (1,2) **2** [C] (clothing made from) a hair-covered skin of certain types of animal, such as foxes, rabbits, MINK, etc.: She was wearing a silver fox fur across her shoulders. | The Canadian fur trader had a fine load of furs to sell after his hunting trip. | a fur coat —see also FURRIER, SKIN¹ (2)

▶ CULTURAL NOTE Furs are expensive and it was formerly considered PRESTIGIOUS to wear them, but many people now believe that animals should not be killed for their fur and think that wearing furs is wrong. ◀

3 [U] a hard covering on the inside of pots, hot-water pipes, etc., formed by CALCIUM in heated water —see also SCALE² (2) **4** [U] an unhealthy greyish covering on the tongue. It happens when people are ill or have a HANGOVER **5** **the fur begins/starts to fly** a very fierce argument starts: When she accused him of taking the money the fur really started to fly. —see also FURRY

fur² v -rr- [I;T (UP)] to (cause to) become covered with FUR¹ (3,4): The kettle was furred up. | a furred tongue

fur·bish /ˈfɜːbɪʃ/ ‖ ˈfɜːr-/ v [T (UP)] rare to improve the appearance of (something old and worn) —see also REFURBISH

Fu·ries /ˈfjʊəriz/, **The** [P] in CLASSICAL MYTHOLOGY, three terrible winged female goddesses who punished people who did wrong, esp. to their own family

fu·ri·ous /ˈfjʊəriəs/ adj **1** [F (with, at)] very angry in an uncontrolled way; in a FURY: He'll be furious with us if we're late. | I was furious at being kept waiting. | She was furious to find (=when she found) that they had gone without her. **2** [A] wild; uncontrolled: a furious temper | There was a furious knocking at the door. — ~ly adv — ~ness n [U]

furl /fɜːl/ ‖ fɜːrl/ v fml [T] to roll or fold up (a sail, flag, UMBRELLA, etc.) —see also UNFURL

fur·long /ˈfɜːlɒŋ ‖ ˈfɜːrlɔːŋ/ n (a measure of length equal to) 220 yards (201 metres), now used mainly in horse racing

fur·lough /ˈfɜːləʊ ‖ ˈfɜːr-/ n [C;U] absence from duty, usu. for a length of time, esp. as permitted to government officers, soldiers, and others serving outside their own country; holiday: He's home on furlough.

fur·nace /ˈfɜːnɪs ‖ ˈfɜːr-/ n **1** an apparatus in a factory, in which metals and other substances are heated to very high temperatures in an enclosed space —see also BLAST FURNACE **2** a large enclosed fire used for producing hot water or steam: This room's like a furnace. (=it's much too hot) **3** AmE an apparatus which produces heat for the home

fur·nish /ˈfɜːnɪʃ ‖ ˈfɜːr-/ v [T] **1** to put furniture in; supply with furniture: It's costing us a fortune to furnish our new flat. | They're renting a furnished flat. (=one with furniture already in it) | a well-furnished room | a room furnished with antiques **2** fml to supply (what is necessary for a special purpose): This shop furnishes everything that is needed for camping.

furnish sbdy./sthg. **with** sthg. phr v [T] fml to supply with (something necessary): He furnished himself with a pencil and paper, and began to draw. | Our company can furnish you with all the necessary details.

fur·nish·ings /ˈfɜːnɪʃɪŋz ‖ ˈfɜːr-/ n [P] articles of furniture or other articles fixed in a room, such as a bath, curtains, etc. —compare FIXTURE; see also SOFT FURNISHINGS

fur·ni·ture /ˈfɜːnɪtʃəʳ ‖ ˈfɜːr-/ n [U] large or quite large movable articles such as beds, chairs, and tables, that are placed in a house, room, or other area, in order to make it convenient, comfortable, and/or pleasant as a space for living in: This old French table is a very valuable piece of furniture. | garden furniture

fu·ro·re /fjʊˈrɔːri, ˈfjʊərɔːʳ ‖ ˈfjʊərɔːr/ BrE ‖ **fu·ror** /ˈfjʊərɔːʳ/ AmE— n [S] a sudden burst of angry or excited interest among a large group of people: The news that the football club was selling its best player caused quite a furore.

fur·ri·er /ˈfʌriəʳ ‖ ˈfɜːr-/ n a person who prepares furs for use as clothing, makes fur GARMENTS, and/or sells them

fur·row¹ /ˈfʌrəʊ ‖ ˈfɜːr-/ n **1** a long narrow track cut by a PLOUGH in farming land when the earth is being turned over in preparation for planting **2** any long deep cut or narrow hollow between raised edges, esp. in the earth **3** a deep line or fold in the skin of the face, esp. the forehead, often seen as a sign of worry or STRESS

furrow² *v* [T] to make furrows in: *The telescope showed the deeply furrowed surface of the planet.* | *She looked at the exam paper with a furrowed brow.* (=her forehead had lines in it because she was worried)

fur·ry /ˈfɜːri/ *adj* of, like, or covered with fur: *a furry little rabbit* | *furry material*

fur·ther¹ /ˈfɜːðər‖ˈfɜːr-/ *adv* **1** (*comparative of* FAR) at or to a greater distance or more distant point; FARTHER: *He's too tired to walk any further.* | *He can swim further than I can.* [+adv/prep] *Our house is a bit further along the road.* | *The records don't go any further back than 1960.* | *No, I'm not thinking of getting married — nothing could be further from my mind!* **2** more; to a greater degree: *Don't try my patience any further.* | *We'll enquire further into this question tomorrow.* | *I have nothing further to say.* **3** *fml* in addition; FURTHERMORE: *The house is not large enough for us, and further, it is too far from the town.* **4 further to** *fml* (used esp. in business letters) continuing the subject of: *Further to our letter of February 5th, we can now confirm that all the spare parts you requested are available.* **5 go further** to give, do, or say more: *We'll go further into this question tomorrow.* (=make more enquiries) | *He was a very fine man; indeed I'll go (even) further, he was the most courageous man I ever knew.* — see FARTHER (USAGE)

further² *adj* [A] (*comparative of* FAR) **1** later than the one spoken of: *There'll be a further performance of the play next week.* | *The office will be closed* **until further notice.** (=until we inform you that it is open again) **2** more; additional: *Have you any further questions (to ask)?* | *If you have no further use for this book, I'll give it to someone else.* | *There being no further business, the meeting was closed.*

further³ *v* [T] to help (something) advance or succeed: *This success should further your chances of promotion.* | *The society was dedicated to furthering the cause of world peace.*

fur·ther·ance /ˈfɜːðərəns‖ˈfɜːr-/ *n* [U] (**of**)] *fml* development; continuation: **In furtherance of** *their aim of improving the school, the Governors are building a new set of science classrooms.*

further ed·u·ca·tion /ˌ… ···‖···/ *n* [U] *BrE* education after leaving school, but not at a university. It is most commonly available in **further education colleges** and many of the courses are intended to prepare people for work: *further education classes at the local college* — compare ADULT EDUCATION, CONTINUING EDUCATION, HIGHER EDUCATION

fur·ther·more /ˌfɜːðəˈmɔːr‖ˈfɜːrðərmɔːr/ *adv fml* also; in addition to what has been said: *The house is too small for a family of four, and furthermore it is in a bad location.*

fur·ther·most /ˈfɜːðəməʊst‖ˈfɜːrðər-/ *adj esp. lit* most distant; farthest away: [A] *In the furthermost corner of the hall sat a tall thin man.* [F+from] *in the corner furthermost from the door*

fur·thest /ˈfɜːðəst‖ˈfɜːr-/ *adj, adv* (*superlative of* FAR) **1** at or to the greatest distance; FARTHEST: *Who can jump (the) furthest?* [+adv/prep] *He lives the furthest from us.* **2** greatest in degree, distance, or time: *She went (the) furthest in condemning their policies.* —see FARTHER (USAGE)

fur·tive /ˈfɜːtɪv‖ˈfɜːr-/ *adj* quiet and secret; trying to escape notice or hide one's intentions: *She cast a furtive glance down the hotel corridor before leaving her room.* – **~ly** *adv* – **~ness** *n* [U]

Furt·wäng·ler /ˈfʊətvɛŋɡlər‖ˈfʊərtvɛŋlər, **Wil·helm** /ˈvɪlhelm/ (1886–1954) a German CONDUCTOR and leader of the Berlin Philharmonic Orchestra for many years

fu·ry /ˈfjʊəri/ *n* **1** [C;U] (a state of) very great anger; (an occasion of) being FURIOUS: *It's no use trying to argue with you when you* **fly into a fury** (=get very angry) *for the slightest reason.* | (fig.) *At last the* **fury** (=wild force) *of the storm lessened.* **2** [S (**of**)] a wildly excited state (of feeling or activity); FEVER: *There was a fury of activity on the morning of their departure.* **3** [C] *old-fash infml* a fierce angry woman or girl **4 like fury** *infml* with great force or effort: *They worked like fury to get the car ready in time.* —see also **full of sound and fury** (SOUND¹ (5))

furze /fɜːz‖fɜːrz/ *n* [U] a wild bush with prickly leaves and bright yellow flowers; GORSE

fuse¹ /fjuːz/ *n* a (small container with a) short thin piece of wire, placed in an electric apparatus or system, which melts if too much electric power passes through it, and thus breaks the connection and prevents fires or other damage: *a five-amp fuse* | *You'll* **blow a fuse** (=make it melt) *if you try and plug the washing machine and the electric heater into the same socket.* | (fig.) *When her son broke the window, she blew a fuse.* (=lost her temper) — see also FUSED

fuse² *v* [I;T] **1** *BrE* to (cause to) stop working owing to the melting of a fuse: *If you plug in all these appliances at once, you'll fuse all the lights.* | *The lights have fused.* **2** to join or become joined by melting: *The aircraft came down in flames, and the heat fused most of the parts together into a solid mass.* —see also FUSION **3** to melt or cause (metal) to melt in great heat: *Lead will fuse at quite a low temperature.*

fuse³ *n* **1** a long string or narrow pipe used for carrying fire to an explosive article and so causing it to blow up: *He paid out the fuse, lit it, and ran behind the rock for safety.* | (fig.) *She has a rather* **short fuse.** (=gets angry quickly) **2** an apparatus in a bomb, SHELL¹ (2), or other weapon, which causes it to explode

fuse box /ˈ· ·/ *n* a box in which the electric fuses for a house are stored

fused /fjuːzd/ *adj* (of a piece of electrical apparatus) fitted with a FUSE¹

fu·se·lage /ˈfjuːzəlɑːʒ‖-sə-/ *n* the main body of an aircraft, in which travellers and goods are carried —see picture at AIRCRAFT

fu·sil·lade /ˌfjuːzɪˈleɪd‖-sɫ-/ *n* [(**of**)] a rapid continuous firing of shots: *As the soldiers marched forward, they were met by a fusillade of bullets from the fort.* | (fig.) *a fusillade of criticism*

fu·sion /ˈfjuːʒən/ *n* [U] *esp. tech* (a) joining together (as if) by melting: *This metal is formed by the fusion of two other types of metal.* | **Nuclear fusion** *works by the combining of atomic nuclei, which releases huge amounts of energy.* | *Her work is a fusion of several different styles of music.* —compare FISSION; see also COLD FUSION

fusion bomb /ˈ·· ˌ·/ *n* a HYDROGEN BOMB

fuss¹ /fʌs/ *n* **1** [S;U] unnecessary, useless, or unwelcome expression of excitement, anger, impatience, etc.: *What a fuss about nothing!* | *Don't make so much fuss over losing a pen.* **2** [S] an expression of annoyance, esp. for a good reason: *There's sure to be a fuss when my parents find the window's broken.* | *I'm going to have to make a fuss* (=complain) *about the service in this restaurant.* | (*infml*) *The local residents are* **kicking up a fuss** *about the plans for the new airport.* **3** [S] *an anxious nervous condition:* *There's no need to get into a fuss; calm down!* **4 make a fuss of** to pay a lot of attention to, in order to please or to show liking for: *Mary always makes a great fuss of her nieces.* —see also FUSSY

fuss² *v* **1** [I] to act or behave in a nervous, restless, and anxious way over small matters: *Don't fuss; we'll get there on time.* | *She fusses too much about her health.* **2** [T] to make nervous: *If you fuss him while he's adding up all those figures, he'll make a lot of mistakes.* **3 not be fussed (about)** *BrE infml* not to care greatly (about something): "*Do you want to eat at once or later?*" "*I'm not fussed.*" (=it doesn't matter to me)
  fuss over sthg./sbdy. *phr v* [T] to pay too much attention to: *The old lady fusses over her little dog as if it were a sick child.*

fuss·pot /ˈfʌs-pɒt‖-pɑːt/ also **fuss·bud·get** /ˈfʌsˌbʌdʒɪt/ — *n infml derog* someone who gets anxious about small matters or is too concerned about unimportant details: *Stop worrying, you old fusspot!*

fuss·y /ˈfʌsi/ *adj* **1** *usu. derog* (of a person) too concerned about details: *He's very fussy about his food; if it isn't cooked just right, he won't eat it.* | *a fussy eater* —compare FASTIDIOUS **2** *derog* (of dress, furniture, etc.) having too much detailed decoration: *a fussy hat* **3** *usu. derog* (esp. of a person's actions) nervous and excitable: *She patted her hair with small fussy movements of her hands.* **4** [F (**about**) *usu. in questions and negatives*] *infml* (of a person) concerned; caring: "*Would you like tea or coffee?*" "*I'm not fussy.*" (=I would like either.) [+wh-] *Are you*

fussy what time we have dinner? --**ily** *adv* --**iness** *n* [U]

fus·ti·an /ˈfʌstiən‖-tʃən/ *adj, n* [A;U] **1** (made from) a type of rough heavy cotton material **2** *rare* (consisting of) empty, important-sounding words

fus·ty /ˈfʌsti/ *adj derog* **1** (of a room, box, clothes, etc.) having an unpleasant smell as a result of having been shut up for a long time, esp. when not quite dry **2** *infml* not modern; old-fashioned: *We want to clear away all these fusty ideas about education and bring in some up-to-date methods.* --**tiness** *n* [U]

fu·tile /ˈfjuːtaɪl‖-tl/ *adj* **1** (of an action) having no effect; unsuccessful; useless: *All my attempts to unlock the door were futile, because I was using the wrong key.* | *Don't waste time by asking futile questions.* | *It's futile to complain.* **2** *rare* (of a person) lacking ability to succeed; IN-EFFECTUAL --**tility** /fjuːˈtɪlɨti/ *n* [U] : *the futility of war*

fu·ton /ˈfuːtɒn‖-tɑːn/ **1** a large bag filled with cotton, feathers, etc. for sleeping on, used in Japan, which can be rolled up and put away during the day —see picture at BED **2** a similar MATTRESS, on a wooden frame, used in other countries as a SOFA that can be used as a bed at night

fu·ture¹ /ˈfjuːtʃəʳ/ *n* **1** [*the*] the time after the present; time that has not yet come: *It's a good idea to save some money for the future.* | *The old lady claims to be able to tell what will happen in the future.* | *At some time in the future, we may all work fewer hours a day.* | **In the distant future** (=much later) *people may live on the moon.* | *We're hoping to move to Scotland* **in the near future** (=soon)/**in the not too distant future.** (=quite soon) **2** [C] that which will happen to someone or something in the future: *I wish you a very happy future.* | *The company's future is uncertain.* | *He has a great future ahead of him as an actor.* (=he is likely to become successful and famous)* | *These unemployed young people have not got much of a future.* (=much chance of becoming successful) **3** [U (**in**) *usu. in questions and negatives*] *infml* likelihood of success: *There's no future in trying to sell fur coats in a hot country.* **4** [*the*] *tech* (in grammar) the form of a verb that shows that the act or state described will happen or exist at a later time: *In the sentence "I will leave tomorrow", the verb 'will' indicates the future.* **5 in future** *BrE* ‖ **in the future** *AmE* (used esp. in giving warnings) from now on: *In future, make sure you get here on time.* —compare PAST **6 I have seen the future** *quote* a phrase used by Lincoln Steffens (1866–1936) and reused today in many ways: *"I have seen the future and it costs a packet."* | *"They have seen the future and it stinks."*

future² *adj* [A] **1** belonging to or happening in the time after the present: *I'd like you to meet my future wife.* (=the woman I am going to marry) | *This brilliant young player may be a future member of the England team.* | *You couldn't have known about it, but* **for future reference** (=remember this for the next time), *his parents must be consulted first.* **2** *tech* (in grammar) being the form of a verb used to show a future act or state: *the future tense*

future per·fect /ˌ·· ˈ··/ *n* [*the*] *tech* (in grammar) the form of a verb that shows that the action described by the verb will be complete before a particular time in the future, formed in English by **will have** or **shall have** and a past participle –**future perfect** *adj*

fu·tures /ˈfjuːtʃəz‖-ərz/ *n* [P] *tech* (agreements or contracts for) goods bought and sold in large quantities at the present price, but not produced or sent until a later time: *the futures market*

futures market /ˈ·· ˌ··/ see FORWARD MARKET

fu·tur·is·m /ˈfjuːtʃərɪzəm/ *n* [U] (*often cap.*) a new style of painting, music, and literature in the early 20th century which claimed to express the violent active quality of life in the modern age of machines --**ist** *n*

fu·tur·is·tic /ˌfjuːtʃəˈrɪstɪk◂/ *adj* **1** dealing with the future, esp. by imagining what may happen then: *She writes futuristic novels about voyages to distant galaxies.* **2** *infml, often derog* of strange modern appearance; having no connection with known forms of art: *futuristic furniture, made of steel tubes and plastic* --**tically** /kli/ *adv*

fuzz¹ /fʌz/ *n* **1** [U] *infml* a mass of soft thin hair, or hairlike substance: *Apricots are covered in fuzz.* **2** *AmE for* FLUFF¹ (2)

fuzz² *v* [T] to make (something) fuzzy

fuzz³ *n* [*the*+*sing.*|*pl. v*] *sl, becoming old-fash* the police

fuzz·y /ˈfʌzi/ *adj infml* **1** (of hair) standing up in a light short mass **2** (of something seen or heard) not clear in shape or sound: *The television picture|sound is rather fuzzy tonight.* **3** (of cloth, clothing, etc.) having a raised soft hairy surface --**ily** *adv* --**iness** *n* [U]

f-word /ˈef wɜːd‖-wɜːrd/ *n* [*the*] *euph for* FUCK (used only when talking about the word "fuck", and not used instead of the word): *That child has terrible language – he uses the f-word without even thinking about it!*

fwy *written abbrev. for:* FREEWAY

FX¹ /ˌef ˈeks/ *n* [U] FOREIGN EXCHANGE

FX² *n* [U] SPECIAL EFFECTS

FY /ˌef ˈwaɪ/ *n* [S] *AmE abbrev. for:* FISCAL YEAR: *We expect record profits in FY1993.*

FYI *abbrev. for:* for your information

G

G /dʒiː/ **G's, g's** or **Gs, gs** the seventh letter of the English alphabet

G¹ a note in Western music; the musical KEY¹ (4) based on this note

G² abbrev. for: **1** tech **a** GRAVITY **b** the amount of force caused by GRAVITY on an object that is lying on the Earth, used as a measure: *The people in a space vehicle have to suffer the effects of several G when it leaves the ground.* **2** AmE sl 1000 dollars; GRAND² (2): *The thieves got away with 100G from the local bank.* —see also G-STRING

G³ n, adj (in the US) (a film) that children of any age may be admitted to see in a cinema: *a G movie* —see also U³

G7 /ˌdʒiː ˈsevən/ adj abbrev. for GROUP OF SEVEN: *The first G7 summit was in the 1970s.* | *the G7 leaders*

GA written abbrev for: GEORGIA

gab /gæb/ v **-bb-** [I (ON, about)] infml derog to talk continuously and without thought; CHATTER: —see also **the gift of the gab** (GIFT)

gab·ar·dine , -erdine /ˈgæbədiːn, ˌgæbəˈdiːn‖ˈgæbərdiːn/ n **1** [U] a strong material which usu. does not allow water to go through and is often used for making coats **2** [C] an article of clothing made from gabardine, esp. **a** a raincoat **b** a long CLOAK worn by Jews in the Middle Ages

gab·ble¹ /ˈgæbəl/ v [I (AWAY, ON); T (OUT)] to say (words) in such a way, esp. so quickly, that they cannot be heard clearly: *The announcer gabbled (out) some incomprehensible message over the public address system.* | *What on earth are you gabbling about?* (=What are you trying to explain?)

gabble² n [(the) S] words or word-like sounds spoken so quickly that they cannot be heard clearly: *The gabble of excited children could be heard coming from the classroom.*

ga·ble /ˈgeɪbəl/ n the three-cornered upper end of a wall where it meets the sloping part of the roof

Gable, Clark (1901–60) an American film actor. He is best known for his ROLE as Rhett Butler in *Gone with the Wind* but also appeared in many other Hollywood films, including *Mutiny on the Bounty* and *The Misfits.* —see colour picture on page 685

ga·bled /ˈgeɪbəld/ adj having one or more gables

Ga·bon /gæˈbɒn‖-ˈbəʊn/, **Republic of** a country in W central Africa, which used to be part of French Equatorial Africa; capital Libreville; population 1,233,000 (1989) — **Gabonese** /ˌgæbəˈniːz◂/ adj,n

Ga·bri·el /ˈgeɪbriəl/ n (in the Bible) the ANGEL who brought news from God to people on Earth. Gabriel was sent by God to tell Mary she would be the mother of Jesus. He is often shown blowing a horn.

gad /gæd/ v **-dd-**
gad about (sthg.) phr v [I;T] infml, often derog to travel round (a place) to enjoy oneself, esp. when one should be doing something else: *She spent a few months gadding about (Europe) before her exams.*

gad·a·bout /ˈgædəbaʊt/ n infml, often derog a person who goes out or travels frequently and to many places for amusement: *She's become quite a gadabout since she left home.*

Gad·daf·i, Qaddafi /gəˈdæfi‖-ˈdɑː-/, **Colonel (Mo·a·mar al** /ˈməʊəmɑːˈ æl/ (1942–) an officer in the army of Libya and Libya's president since 1977. He was formerly Libyan chairman of the Revolutionary Command Council.

Gad·dis /ˈgædɪs/ **William** (1922–) an American writer of NOVELs including *Carpenter's Gothic*

gad·fly /ˈgædflaɪ/ n **1** a fly which bites cattle **2** rare someone who, usu. intentionally, annoys people, esp. by pointing out faults

gad·get /ˈgædʒɪt/ n infml a small machine or useful apparatus; DEVICE: *a clever little gadget for peeling potatoes* —see MACHINE (USAGE)

gad·get·ry /ˈgædʒɪtri/ n [U] infml, often derog gadgets: *Their kitchen is so full of gadgetry that you can hardly move.*

Gae·lic /ˈgeɪlɪk, ˈgælɪk/ adj, n [(the) U] (of or being) any of the Celtic languages, esp. that of Scotland, or those of Ireland and the Isle of Man. Gaelic is still spoken in some parts of Scotland and Ireland but by fewer and fewer people: *Does that family MacKenzie have the Gaelic?* (=speak Gaelic) —see also ERSE

Gaelic cof·fee /ˌ·· ˈ··/ n [C;U] IRISH COFFEE

Gaelic foot·ball /ˌ·· ˈ··/ n [U] a type of football that is played in Ireland and parts of the US, between teams of 15 players using a round ball and a low net between RUGBY posts

gaff /gæf/ n a stick with a hook at the end, used to pull big fish out of the water —see also **blow the gaff** (BLOW¹)

gaffe /gæf/ n an unintentional social mistake; FAUX PAS: *From the way she looked at me when I asked how much money she earned I realized I'd committed an awful gaffe.*

gaf·fer /ˈgæfəʳ/ n **1** someone in charge of the lighting in making a cinema film **2** BrE infml a man in charge, esp. in a factory; BOSS² **3** dial an old man

gag¹ /gæg/ n **1** something, such as a piece of cloth, put over or into someone's mouth to prevent them from talking or shouting **2** an official forbidding of speech or writing on a given subject: *The White House have issued a gag order on the latest developments.* **3** infml a joke or funny story: *That comedian always tells the same gags.*

gag² v **-gg-** **1** [T] to prevent (someone) from speaking by putting a gag into or over their mouth: *She was bound and gagged by the kidnappers.* | (fig.)*The newspapers have been gagged, so nobody knows what really happened.* **2** [I (on)] esp. AmE to be unable to swallow and seem about to bring up food from the stomach; CHOKE: *She gagged on a piece of hard bread.* **3 gag me with a spoon!** AmE humor interj (said to express a strong feeling of dislike, and usu. used by older children): *"You should see what's for lunch in the school cafeteria — gag me with a spoon!"*

ga·ga /ˈgɑːgɑː/ adj infml derog **1** having or showing a weak mind, esp. in old age; SENILE **2** [F(about, over)] having a strong but probably not long-lasting feeling of love; INFATUATED: *She's gaga over him.*

Ga·ga·rin /gəˈgɑːrɪn/, **Yu·ri** /ˈjʊəri/ (1934–68) a Soviet ASTRONAUT. On 12th April 1961 he became the first man in space when he travelled round the earth in Vostok I.

gage /geɪdʒ/ n, v AmE for GAUGE

gag·gle /ˈgægəl/ n [S (of)] **1** a number of geese (GOOSE) together **2** [+sing./pl. v] a group of noisy people who talk a lot: *A gaggle of schoolgirls followed the tennis star to his car.*

gai·e·ty /ˈgeɪəti/ n [U] **1** cheerfulness: *The gaiety of the music made everyone want to dance.* **2** also **gaieties** pl.— old-fash happy events and activities,esp. at a time of public holiday —compare GAYNESS; see also GAY¹

gai·ly /ˈgeɪli/ adv **1** in a cheerful manner: *gaily-coloured decorations* **2** in an insensitive, thoughtless way: *They gaily went on talking after the film had started.*

gain¹ /geɪn/ v **1** [I (by, from);T] rather fml to obtain (something useful, advantageous, wanted, profitable, etc.): *They stand to gain a fortune on the deal.* | *I hope you'll gain by the experience.* (=learn a useful lesson from it) | *We've got nothing to gain by delaying the meeting.* | *The revolutionaries are gaining thousands of supporters for their cause.* | *The thieves gained entry* (=got in) *through an upstairs window.* [+obj(i) +obj(d)] *He had gained himself a reputation for unfairness.* **2** [T] to have an increase in: *I think he's gaining weight.* | *The car gained speed as it went down the hill.* **3** [I (on, upon)] to reduce the distance between oneself and the person or thing one is chasing: *She was gaining on the leader throughout the final lap, and just overtook her before the finishing line.* | *"Drive faster! The police are gaining on us!"* **4** [I;T] (of a watch or clock) to work too fast by (an amount of time): *My watch is gaining five minutes a week.* —see CLOCK¹ (USAGE) **5** [T] fml or lit to reach (a place), esp. with effort or difficulty: *We cut a path through the forest and gained the river next day.* **6 gain ground: a** to GAIN (2) **b** to become stronger, more popular, etc.: *The People's Party is gaining ground in the country.* | *The idea that*

smoking is unhealthy has gained ground considerably in recent years. —opposite **lose** (for 1,2, 4) — **~ er** *n*

▷ USAGE Compare **gain, win,** and **earn.** You can **gain** something useful or necessary whether or not you deserve it: *to gain attention|knowledge|favour.* You can **gain** or **win** something as a result of great effort or ability: *People disliked him at first, but in the end his willingness to work hard gained/won their approval.* You can **earn: a** something which you deserve: *Take a rest now. You've earned it!* **b** money for work you do: *He's earning £300 a week at present.*◁

gain² *n* **1** [U] also **gains** *pl.—* (the act of making) a profit; (increase in) wealth: *He put a lot of money into the firm with the hope of gain in the future.* | *The thief escaped to Europe with his **ill-gotten gains.*** (=the money and property he had stolen) —see also CAPITAL GAINS **2** [C] an increase in amount: *Stocks this week have shown a significant gain over last week's prices.* —opposite **loss**

gain·ful /ˈgeɪnfəl/ *adj* [*no comp.*] *fml* which provides money; for which one is paid: *gainful employment* — **~ ly** *adv*

gain·say /ˌgeɪnˈseɪ/ *v* **-said** /ˈsed/ [T *usu. in negatives*] *fml* to say that something is not so; DENY: *There's no gainsaying her ability.*

Gains·bo·rough /ˈgeɪnzbərə‖-bɜːrəʊ/, **Thomas** (1727–88) an English artist best known for his PORTRAITS and LANDSCAPE paintings. He was involved in the establishment of the Royal Academy in London.

gait /geɪt/ *n* a way of walking: *He had a strange rolling gait, like a sailor on a ship.*

gai·ter /ˈgeɪtə³/ *n* either of a pair of cloth or leather coverings worn, esp. formerly, to cover either the ankle or the leg from knee to ankle —see PAIR (USAGE)

gal /gæl/ *n* **1** *AmE infml* a girl or woman: *What are you gals doing this weekend?* **2** *BrE* (used to suggest an old-fash,* UPPER-CLASS pronunciation) a girl

ga·la /ˈgɑːlə‖ˈgeɪlə, ˈgælə/ *n* **1** an occasion of planned enjoyment or special public entertainment: *This is a gala occasion; it calls for champagne.* | *It was a gala night at the opera; all the stars were going to perform, and the audience wore their finest clothes.* **2** *esp. BrE* a sports meeting, esp. a swimming competition: *She's competing in three races at the school's swimming gala.*

Gal·a·had /ˈgæləhæd/, **Sir** a man who behaves in a very polite way (from the story of the most VIRTUOUS of King Arthur's Knights of the Round Table who regained the Holy Grail): *I happened to be passing by and played a kind of Sir Galahad by helping to get her wheelchair out of the van.* —see also ARTHURIAN LEGEND

Ga·láp·a·gos Is·lands /gəˈlæpəgəs ˌaɪləndz‖gəˈlɑːpəgəʊs-/ [*the*] a group of islands in the Pacific Ocean, W of Ecuador. They were visited by Charles Darwin in 1835, who collected information which led him to his ideas about EVOLUTION. They are also famous for the GIANT TORTOISES living there.

gal·ax·y /ˈgæləksi/ *n* **1** any of the large groups of stars which make up the universe: *a spiral galaxy* **2** [(of)] a splendid gathering of people, esp. famous, beautiful, or clever people: *A galaxy of film stars attended the première.* **—-actic** /gəˈlæktɪk/ *adj* [A]

Galaxy¹ *n* [*the*] the large group of stars in which our own sun and its PLANETS lie

Galaxy² *n* [C;U] *tdmk* a type of milk chocolate made by Mars Confectionary

gale /geɪl/ *n* **1** a very strong wind: *The old tree was blown down in a gale.* | *The weathermen forecast a Force Nine gale.* **2** [+of] also **gales** *pl. —* a sudden burst, esp. of laughter: *As the door opened, gales of laughter came from inside.* —see WIND (USAGE)

Gal·i·lee /ˈgælɪliː/ an area in N Israel in which the main city is Nazareth. It is known as the area in which Jesus lived and worked.

Galilee, Sea of a lake in NE Israel through which the River Jordan flows and which is found in many New Testament Bible stories

Gal·i·le·o /ˌgælɪˈleɪəʊ/ (1564–1642) an Italian astronomer (ASTRONOMY), MATHEMATICIAN, and PHYSICIST who made several important scientific discoveries, and by building the first TELESCOPE discovered the four largest SATELLITEs of Jupiter. In 1633 he was brought before the INQUI-

SITION in Rome and forced to DENY his claim that the sun was the centre of the universe.

gall¹ /gɔːl/ *n* [U] **1** daring rudeness or bad manners: *I don't know how you can **have the gall** to turn up here again after the way you've behaved in the past.* **2** *old use for* BILE

gall² *n* **1** a painful place on an animal's skin, esp. on that of a horse, usu. caused by something rubbing against the skin **2** a swelling on a tree or plant caused by an insect laying its eggs, infection, or damage

gall³ *v* [T] to cause to feel annoyed disappointment or anger: *It galled him that his father left him no money when he died.* | *a galling experience*

gal·lant¹ /ˈgælənt/ *adj fml or lit* courageous: *a gallant soldier* | *It was a gallant deed to risk almost certain death to save his friend.* **— ~ly** *adv*

gal·lant² /gəˈlænt, ˈgælənt‖gəˈlænt, gəˈlɑːnt/ *adj fml or lit* (of a man) attentive and polite to women **— ~ly** *adv* : *He bowed gallantly and asked her for the next dance.*

gal·lant³ /ˈgælənt, gəˈlænt‖gəˈlænt, gəˈlɑːnt/ *n old use* a man, esp. a young man, who is particularly well dressed and/or politely attentive to women

gal·lan·try /ˈgæləntri/ *n* [C;U] *fml or lit* **1** (an act of) bravery, esp. in battle: *He was awarded a medal for gallantry.* **2** (an act of) polite unselfish attention paid by a man to a woman

gall blad·der /ˈ· ˌ···/ *n* an organ of the body, like a small bag, in which BILE is stored

gal·le·on /ˈgæliən/ *n* a large sailing ship used in former times, esp. by the Spaniards —see picture at SAIL

gal·le·ry /ˈgæləri/ *n* **1** a room, hall, or building where works of art are shown and sometimes offered for sale: *It's in Gallery 15.* | *an art gallery* **2** an upper floor built out from an inner wall of a hall, from which activities in the hall may be watched: *the public gallery in Congress* **b** the highest upper floor in a theatre —see picture at THEATRE **3** a long narrow room: *a shooting gallery* **4** a level underground passage in a mine or joining natural CAVES —see also **play to the gallery** (PLAY² (26))

gal·ley /ˈgæli/ *n* **1** (in former times) a long low ship with sails, which was rowed along by slaves, esp. an ancient Greek or Roman warship —see picture at SAIL **2** a ship's kitchen **3** also **galley proof** /ˈ·· ·/— any of the sheets of paper on which a printer prints a book so that mistakes can be put right before it is divided into pages

Gal·lic /ˈgælɪk/ *adj* typical of France or the French: *He kissed her hand with Gallic charm.*

Gal·lip·o·li /gəˈlɪpəli/ an area in Turkey where a battle by the Allies, including soldiers from Australia and New Zealand took place during the First World War. The battle ended unsuccessfully for the Allies: *the Gallipoli landings*

gal·li·vant /ˈgælɪvænt/ *v* [I (ABOUT)] *infml or humor, often derog* to go around amusing oneself; GAD **about:** *You can't spend the rest of your life gallivanting about; get yourself a steady job.*

gal·lon /ˈgælən/ *n* a measure for liquids —see TABLE 2

▶ CULTURAL NOTE In Britain the gallon was the measure commonly used for buying petrol until the late 1980s since when it has also been sold in litres. Gallons are still used in the US for petrol and some other liquids: *a gallon of milk | ten gallons of gas*◀

gal·lop¹ /ˈgæləp/ *n* **1** [S] the movement of a horse at its fastest speed, when all four feet come off the ground together: *The horse went off at a gallop across the field.* | *The horses broke into a gallop.* (=began to gallop) **2** [C] a ride at this speed: *She took her pony out to the countryside for a good gallop.* **3 at a gallop** *infml* in a rush or hurry: *She ate her lunch at a gallop.*

gallop² *v* [I;T] **1** (to cause to) move at the speed of a gallop: *The horse/The rider galloped down the hill.* | (fig.) *He galloped through his work so that he could leave the office early.* —compare CANTER², TROT² (1)

gal·lop·ing /ˈgæləpɪŋ/ *adj* [A] increasing or changing very quickly: *The country is suffering from galloping inflation; the value of its money has halved in the past six months.*

gal·lows /ˈgæləʊz/ *n* **gallows** the wooden frame on which criminals used to be killed by hanging from a rope: *The* *murderer was sent to the gallows for his crimes.*

gallows hu·mour /ˈ·· ˌ··/ *n* [U] *lit* humour which makes very unpleasant or dangerous things or people seem funny; BLACK HUMOUR

gall·stone /ˈgɔːlstəʊn/ *n* a hard stone or grain which forms in the GALL BLADDER and may have to be removed by an operation or other treatment

Gal·lup poll /ˈgæləp pəʊl/ *n tdmk* a special count of opinions in a country, done esp. in order to try to say what the result of a political election will be, by questioning a number of people chosen to represent the whole population. Gallup polls are named after the American STATISTICIAN, George Horace Gallup, who invented them, and are often printed in newspapers.

ga·lore /gəˈlɔːr/ *adj* [after *n*] in large amounts or numbers: *There are bargains galore in the sales this year.*

ga·losh /gəˈlɒʃ‖gəˈlɑːʃ/ also **overshoe**, also **rubber** *AmE— n* [*usu. pl.*] a rubber shoe worn over an ordinary shoe, esp. by older people, when it rains or snows —see PAIR (USAGE)

Gals·wor·thy /ˈgɔːlzwɜːði‖-wɜːr-/, **John** (1867–1933) an English writer of books and plays who won the Nobel Prize for literature in 1932. He is best known for his books *The Forsyte Saga* about a rich MIDDLE-CLASS English family called the Forsytes.

Gal·ti·e·ri /ˌgæltiˈeəri/, **General Le·o·pol·do** /leɪəˈpəʊldəʊ/ (1926–   ) an Argentinian leader who ordered the Falkland Islands (Malvinas) to be seized in 1982, leading to the war with Britain. He was sent to prison in 1986.

ga·lumph /gəˈlʌmf/ *v* [I+*adv/prep*] *infml* to move in a cheerful carefree way, but heavily and awkwardly: *The sea lion galumphed up to the zookeeper to take the fish.*

gal·van·ic /gælˈvænɪk/ *adj* 1 [*no comp.*] *tech* of or concerning the production of electricity by the action of an acid on a metal: *a galvanic cell* 2 *fml* (of actions and events) sudden, unnaturally strong, etc.: *The warning about the bomb had a galvanic effect, and people ran everywhere trying to find it.*

gal·va·nis·m /ˈgælvənɪzəm/ *n* [U] *tech* the production of electricity by chemical means, esp. as in a BATTERY

gal·va·nize also **-nise** *BrE* /ˈgælvənaɪz/ *v* [T] 1 to put a covering of metal, esp. ZINC, over (a sheet of another metal, esp. iron), by using electricity: *galvanized iron* 2 [(into)] to shock (someone) into sudden action: *The announcement of the general election galvanized the party members into activity.*

Gal·way¹ /ˈgɔːlweɪ/ a COUNTY in the W of the Republic of Ireland, which contains the town of Galway

Galway², **James** (1939–   ) a Northern Irish FLUTE player who has played with ORCHESTRAs as well as making popular records and appearing on television

Ga·ma /ˈɡɑːmə/, **Vas·co da** /ˈvæskəʊ də‖ˈvɑːs-/ (?1469–1524) a Portuguese NAVIGATOR who was the first European to travel to India by sea and who opened up the SPICE trade which began the Portuguese EMPIRE

Gam·bi·a /ˈgæmbiə/ [*the*] a country in West Africa which became independent from Britain in 1965 and a republic in 1970; capital Banjul; population 835,000 (1989) **—bian** *n, adj*

gam·bit /ˈgæmbɪt/ *n* an action made to produce a future advantage, esp. an opening move in a game, an argument, or a conversation: *That was a clever gambit, to move your bishop out so early in the chess game.* | *"Do you come here often?" is a hackneyed conversational gambit.* | *It was a poor* **opening gambit** *to accuse him of stealing – you should have introduced the subject more gently.* —compare PLOY

gam·ble¹ /ˈgæmbəl/ *v* 1 [I;T (on)] to risk (money, property, etc.) on the result of something uncertain, such as a card game, a horse race, a business arrangement, etc.: *to gamble at poker/on the stock exchange* | *He gambled away* (=risked and lost) *the fortune his grandmother left him.* | *The police regularly raid these* **gambling dens.** (=places where people go to play cards, etc., illegally) 2 [I (on, with);T+*that; obj*] to do something risky that depends for its success on certain things happening as one wishes: *They carried out the robbery on Christmas Day, gambling on no one being in the building.* | *He's gambling with his passengers' lives, driving as fast as that.* **—bler** *n*

gamble² *n* [S] a risky matter or act: *The operation may succeed, and it may not; it's a bit of a gamble.*

gam·bol /ˈgæmbəl/ *v* **-ll-** *BrE* ‖ **-l-** *AmE* [I (ABOUT)] to jump about in play: *The lambs are gambolling (about) in the fields.* —**gambol** *n*

game¹ /geɪm/ *n* 1 [C] a form of play or sport, or one example or type of this: *Football is a game which doesn't interest me.* | *Let's have a game of cards.* | *The children were in the garden, playing a game of hide-and-seek.* | *Chess and draughts are* **board games.** 2 [C] a single part of a set into which a match is divided, e.g. in tennis, BRIDGE³, etc. 3 [U] wild animals, birds, and fish which are hunted or fished for food, esp. as a sport: *Pheasants and partridges are* **game birds.** | *A strong red wine goes well with game.* —see also BIG GAME 4 [C] *infml* a profession or activity, esp. one in which people compete against each other: *the advertising game* | *Can you help me plan the meeting – I'm new to this game.* 5 [C] *infml* a trick or secret plan: *What's your little game, then?* | *Don't play games with me – just tell me what you want.* | *I'll tell you what we're planning for Jane's birthday, as long as you promise not to* **give the game away.** (=tell Jane about it) 6 **make game of** *old-fash* to laugh at or make fun of 7 **on the game** *sl, esp. BrE* in the business of being a PROSTITUTE 8 **the game's** '**up** your/our trick or plan has been found out and can succeed no further —see also GAMES, FAIR GAME, MUG'S GAME, WAR GAME, **the name of the game** (NAME¹), **play the game** (PLAY² (24)), **two can play at that game** (TWO); see RECREATION (USAGE)

game² *adj* 1 brave, determined, and ready for action: *The little boy was hurt by the fall, but he was game enough to get up and try again.* 2 [F (for)] willing: *"Who's game for a swim?" "I'm game!"* [+to-*v*] *I'm game to try.* **– ~ly** *adv*

game³ *v* [I] *fml* to GAMBLE at cards and other games of chance: *She spends every evening at the* **gaming tables.**

game⁴ *adj* [A] *old-fash for* GAMMY

game·cock /ˈgeɪmkɒk‖-kɑːk/ *n* a male chicken specially trained to fight others

game·keep·er /ˈgeɪmˌkiːpər/ *n* a man employed to raise and protect GAME¹ (3), esp. birds, on private land

game park /ˈ· ·/ also **game reserve** – *n* a large area of country which is set aside for wild animals to live in, esp. in Africa

game·plan /ˈgeɪmplæn/ *n* a plan for gaining success by a number of steps, used esp. in business or sports; TACTICS: *The businessman eventually forced the board to agree to his gameplan.*

game point /ˈ· ·/ *n* [C;U] the situation in games such as tennis in which one player will win the game if he or she wins the next point —compare MATCH POINT

game re·serve /ˈ· ·ˌ·/ *n* a GAME PARK

games /geɪmz/ *n* **games** 1 [P;U] *BrE* (the playing of) team games and other forms of physical exercise out of doors at school: *We have games on Wednesday afternoons.* 2 [*the*+C+*sing./pl. v*] (*often cap. in names*) a particular set of sports competitions: *The 1984 (Olympic) Games were/was held in Los Angeles.* | *the Commonwealth Games* —see also FUN AND GAMES

game show /ˈ· ·/ *n* a television programme in which competitors, esp. members of the public, play games for prizes. Game shows are usu. funny and noisy rather than serious or meaningful, and valuable prizes e.g. cars, or large amounts of money can be won.

games·man·ship /ˈgeɪmzmənʃɪp/ *n* [U] *often derog* the art of winning by using the rules to one's own advantage without actually cheating

gam·ey /ˈgeɪmi/ *adj* GAMY

gam·ma /ˈgæmə/ *n* the third letter (Γ, γ) of the Greek alphabet

gamma glob·u·lin /ˌgæmə ˈglɒbjʊlɪn‖-ˈglɑː-/ *n* [U] a natural substance found in the body, a form of ANTIBODY, which gives protection against certain diseases

gamma ray /ˈ·· ·/ *n* [*usu. pl.*] a beam of light of short wave length, which goes through solid objects

gam·mon /ˈgæmən/ *n* [U] *esp. BrE* the meat, preserved by salt or smoke, from the back part and leg of a pig: *gammon steaks* —compare BACON, HAM (1)

gam·my /ˈgæmi/ also **game** old-fash— adj infml, esp. BrE (esp. of a human leg) damaged or painful, esp. in such a way that one cannot walk properly or comfortably; usu. in older people

gam·ut /ˈgæmət/ n [(the) S (of)] the complete range of a subject, including the smallest details and the most general ideas: He's **run the whole gamut of** (=experienced all of) human experience.

gam·y , **gamey** /ˈgeɪmi/ adj (of meat) having the strong taste of GAME¹ (3) which has been hung up for some time before cooking —compare HIGH¹ (9) —**iness** n [U]

Gan·dalf /ˈgændælf‖ˈgɑːndɑːlf/ a WIZARD character in the book The Lord of the Rings by JRR Tolkien

gan·der /ˈgændəʳ/ n 1 [C] a male GOOSE 2 [S (at)] infml a look: "Come and take a gander at this!" he said, with his eye to the keyhole.

Gan·dhi¹ /ˈgændi/, **In·di·ra** /ɪndɪərə/ (1917–84) the PRIME MINISTER of India 1966–77 and 1980–84 and the daughter of India's first PRIME MINISTER, Nehru. She was murdered by one of her Sikh bodyguards.

Gandhi², **Mo·han·das Kar·am·chand** /məʊhənˈdæs kærəmˈtʃænd/ (1869–1948) an Indian lawyer, social worker, Hindu leader and nationalist known as **Mahatma Gandi** who believed in non-violent action in the nationalist movement for Indian independence. He was murdered soon after India gained independence.

Gandhi³, **Ra·jiv** /rəˈdʒiːv/ (1944–91) the son of Indira Gandhi who was elected PRIME MINISTER of India after his mother was killed in 1984 and remained in power until 1989. He was murdered in 1991 while campaigning (CAMPAIGN) in the Indian elections.

Gandhi

G & T /ˌdʒiː ənd ˈtiː/ n [C;U] see GIN AND TONIC

gang¹ /gæŋ/ n [C+sing./pl. v] **1 a** a group of criminals: The gang was/were planning a robbery. | the leader of the James Gang **b** a group of esp. young men who cause trouble and/or fill other people with fear: They were attacked by a gang of skinheads. | a gang fight **2** a group of friends, esp. TEENAGERS: Have you seen any of the/our gang lately? **3** a group of people working together, such as prisoners or building workers —see also CHAIN GANG

gang² v

gang up phr v [I (**on**, **against**)] derog to work together as a close group (against someone); CONSPIRE: She feels that everyone's ganging up on her.

gang-bang /ˈ· ˌ·/ n sl an occasion on which several different men have sex with the same woman, esp. against her wishes —**gang-bang** v [I;T]

gang·er /ˈgæŋəʳ/ n BrE the FOREMAN (=leader) of a group of workers, esp. building workers

Gan·ges /ˈgændʒiːz/ [the] a river in N India which provides water for the fields in India and Bangladesh. It is considered to be SACRED by Hindus.

gang·land /ˈgæŋlænd, -lənd/ n [U] the world of professional and esp. violent crime: A group of gangland bosses met to decide who would control which territory. | gangland killings

gang·ling /ˈgæŋglɪŋ/ adj (esp. of a boy) unusually tall and thin, so as to appear awkward in movement

gan·gli·on /ˈgæŋliən/ n med **1** a mass of nerve cells **2** a (painful) swelling containing liquid, often on the back of the wrist

Gang of Four /ˌ· · ˈ·/ [the] **1** a group of four strong supporters of Mao Tse-tung important in the Cultural Revolution in China, who were seized in 1976 and given long prison sentences **2** four former British ministers who left the Labour Party in 1981 to start the Social Democratic Party

gang·plank /ˈgæŋplæŋk/ n a wooden board which is used to make a bridge to get into or out of a ship or to pass from one ship to another

gan·grene /ˈgæŋgriːn/ n [U] the decay of the flesh of part of the body because blood has stopped flowing there, usu. after a wound —**grenous** /grɪnəs/ adj

gang·ster /ˈgæŋstəʳ/ n a member of a group (GANG) of usu. armed criminals. In Britain, the image many people have of a gangster is of a man in a very SMART suit who carries a big gun hidden in a case meant for holding a VIOLIN. Most people associate the word with Al Capone and the Chicago gangsters of the 1920s and 1930s.

gangster

gang·way /ˈgæŋweɪ/ n **1 a** usu. large GANGPLANK **2** a clear space between two rows of seats in a cinema, theatre, bus, or train; AISLE **3 Gangway!** (used to clear a passage through a crowd of people) Please get out of the way!

gan·net /ˈgænɪt/ n gannets or gannet **1** a large bird that lives near the sea and catches fish by diving (DIVE) into the sea **2** sl someone who eats a lot and who eats any type of food

gan·try /ˈgæntri/ n a metal frame which is used to support movable heavy machinery or railway signals

Gan·y·mede /ˈgænɪmiːd/ in old Greek stories, a beautiful young boy who was taken to Olympus by Zeus to be a servant to the gods

gaol /dʒeɪl/ n, v BrE for JAIL

gaol·bird /ˈdʒeɪlbɜːd‖-bɜːrd/ n BrE for JAILBIRD

gaol·er /ˈdʒeɪləʳ/ n BrE for JAILER

gap /gæp/ n [(**in**, **between**)] **1** an empty space between two objects or two parts of an object: The gate was locked but we went through a gap in the fence. | (fig.) There are wide gaps in my knowledge of history. | (fig.) a gap in the conversation | (fig.) bridging the gap between school and university —see also CREDIBILITY GAP, GENERATION GAP **2 gap in the market** an area, usu. in the buying and selling of goods and services, which is not fully developed, and therefore offers someone a chance to start a suitable business and make money out of it: She just saw the gap in the market, borrowed money from the bank and set up the business. Just like that!

gape /geɪp/ v [I] **1** [(**at**)] to look hard in surprise or wonder, esp. with the mouth open: "What are you gaping at?" "This letter says I've just won half a million pounds!" —compare GAWP **2** to come apart or open widely: Holes gaped in the road. | His shirt gaped open where the button had come off. | a gaping wound | (fig.) There were gaping holes in (=large parts left out of) his account of the incident, so we thought he must be trying to hide something. —see GAZE (USAGE)

gar·age /ˈgærɑːʒ, -ɪdʒ‖gəˈrɑːʒ/ n **1** a building in which motor vehicles can be kept: She put the car away in the garage. | a bus garage —compare CARPORT, see picture at HOUSE **2** also **service station**— a place where motor vehicles are repaired and petrol and oil may also be sold: The car's at the garage. —compare FILLING STATION

garage² v [T] to put or keep in a garage

garage sale /ˈ·· ˌ·‖ˈ· ˌ·/ n a sale of used articles from people's houses, often taking place in a garage

ga·ram ma·sa·la /ˌgɑːrəm məˈsɑːlə, mɑː-/ n [U] a mixture of SPICES which give a hot taste to food, used esp. in Indian cooking

garb¹ /gɑːb‖gɑːrb/ n [U] fml or lit clothing of a particular style, esp. clothing which shows one's type of work or is of unusual appearance: He was clothed in a judge's solemn garb.

garb² v [T (**in**) usu. pass.] fml or lit to dress: The priest was garbed in black.

gar·bage /ˈgɑːbɪdʒ‖ˈgɑːr-/ n [U] **1** esp. AmE ‖ **rubbish** esp. BrE— waste material, e.g. from a house or office, to be thrown away; REFUSE² **2** derog stupid and worthless ideas, words, etc.: Don't talk such **a load of garbage!** **3 garbage in, garbage out** (used esp. in computing (COMPUTE)) if you put RUBBISH, e.g. bad DATA, into a machine, you will get bad results

gardening equipment

rake   hoe   fork   spade

lawn mowers

shears

trowel

secateurs/
pruning shears

sprinkler

hose

watering
can

hover mower

gar·bage can /ˈ·· ·/ *n AmE for* DUSTBIN —see picture at HOUSE

gar·bage col·lec·tor /ˈ·· ·ˌ··/ also **garbage man** /ˈ·· ˌ·/—*n AmE for* DUSTMAN

gar·bage dis·pos·al /ˈ·· ·ˌ··/ also **disposal** *infml*— *n AmE* a small machine in the kitchen SINK which breaks vegetable rubbish into small pieces so that it can be allowed to go down the pipes that carry waste water away: *Can apple skins be put in the garbage disposal?* | *Will these go down the disposal?*

gar·bage truck /ˈ·· ·/ *n AmE for* DUSTCART

gar·ban·zo /ɡɑːˈbænzəʊ‖ɡɑːrˈbɑːn-/ *n Sp* CHICK PEA

gar·ble /ˈɡɑːbəl‖ˈɡɑːr-/ *v* [T] to repeat in a confused way which gives a false idea of the facts: *He was overexcited, and gave a garbled account of the meeting.*

Gar·bo /ˈɡɑːbəʊ‖ˈɡɑːr-/, **Gret·a** /ˈɡretə/ (1905–90) an American film actress, born in Sweden, whose films include *Queen Christina*, *Anna Karenina*, and *Camille*. Greta Garbo was known for her beauty, for saying "I want to be alone" and, towards the end of her life, for becoming a RECLUSE in her New York home. see picture on page 228

gar·bol·o·gy /ɡɑːˈbɒlədʒi‖ɡɑːrˈbɑː-/ *n* [U] *AmE* the study of waste or GARBAGE, e.g. for scientific purposes

Gar·cí·a Lor·ca /ɡɑːˌsiːə ˈlɔːkə‖ɡɑːrˌsiːə ˈlɔːr-/, **Fed·e·ri·co** /ˌfedəˈriːkəʊ/ (1898–1936) a Spanish poet and writer of plays, known for plays such as *Blood Wedding* and *The House of Bernarda Alba*. He was shot during the Spanish Civil War.

Gar·cí·a Már·quez /ɡɑːˌsiːə ˈmɑːkes‖ɡɑːrˌsiːə ˈmɑːr-/, **Gabriel** (1928–   ) a Colombian writer who won the Nobel Prize for literature in 1982 and whose books include *One Hundred Years of Solitude* and *Love in the Time of Cholera*

gar·çon /ˈɡɑːsɒn‖ɡɑːrˈsəʊn/ *n Fr* a waiter, esp. in a French restaurant

gar·den¹ /ˈɡɑːdn‖ˈɡɑːr-/ *n* **1** a piece of land, often around or at the side of a house, which may be covered with grass or planted with flowers, fruit, and vegetables: *She's out in the garden, mowing the lawn.* | *the back/front garden* | *a herb garden* | *a rose garden* | *a garden seat* —see picture at HOUSE; compare YARD² **2** (in the US) that part of a YARD which is planted with flowers or vegetables: *We have a little garden in our backyard.* | *We were thinking of planting a garden this year, but it's so much work digging up the yard.* **3** also **gardens** *pl.* – a public park with flowers, grass, paths, and seats —see also KITCHEN GARDEN, MARKET GARDEN, **lead someone up the garden path** (LEAD¹) **4 Come into the garden, Maud** the title and first line of a song popular in Britain at the beginning of this century

garden² *v* [I] to work in a garden, keeping it tidy, making

plants grow, etc. — ~ **er** *n* — ~ **ing** *n* [U] : *Many retired people take up gardening as a hobby.* | *gardening gloves* | *It was a sunny day so I decided to do some gardening.*

garden cen·tre /ˈ·· ˌ··/ *BrE* ‖ **nursery** *AmE*— *n* a place where equipment and tools for gardening, and plants and flowers are sold

garden cit·y /ˌ·· ˈ··/ *n esp. BrE* a town or part of a town (a **garden suburb**), planned and built to have grass, trees, and open spaces, rather than factories and signs of industry —compare NEW TOWN

garden flat /ˈ·· ˌ·/ *BrE* ‖ **garden a·part·ment** /ˈ·· ·ˌ··/ *AmE*— *n* a flat in a BASEMENT or on the ground floor which has a garden

gar·de·ni·a /ɡɑːˈdiːniə‖ɡɑːr-/ *n* a tropical bush with large white or yellow sweet-smelling flowers

Garden of E·den /ˌ·· · ˈ··/ [*the*] see EDEN

Garden of En·gland /ˌ·· · ˈ··/ [*the*] the popular name for the COUNTY of Kent, because of its AGRICULTURAL produce, esp. ORCHARDS

garden par·ty /ˈ·· ˌ··/ also **lawn party** *AmE*— *n* a formal party held out of doors on the grass, esp. in a large garden
▶ CULTURAL NOTE Every year, the Queen holds several garden parties, usu. at Buckingham Palace, to which guests are invited in recognition of their work or achievements, and it is considered a great honour to go to one. ◀

garden-va·ri·e·ty /ˈ·· ·ˌ··/ *adj AmE sometimes derog* ordinary; not unusual: *She's a stripper and her husband's a garden-variety criminal.* | *garden-variety complaints about public transportation*

garden wed·ding /ˈ·· ˌ··/ *n AmE* a wedding which takes place in a garden

Gard·ner /ˈɡɑːdnəʳ‖ˈɡɑːr-/, **Erle Stan·ley** /ɜːl ˈstænli‖ɜːrl-/ (1889–1970) an American writer of crime FICTION who invented the character of Perry Mason, the DETECTIVE (2)

Gar·field¹ /ˈɡɑːfiːld‖ˈɡɑːr-/ *n* a CARTOON cat character invented by Jim Davis which appears daily in hundreds of American newspapers, and in some British newspapers. Garfield is very popular in both the US and Britain and there are many Garfield books and toys on sale , esp. a toy cat which people stick on their car windows.

Garfield², **James** (1831–81) president of the US in 1881, who was killed while in office

Gar·fun·kel /ˈɡɑːfʌŋkəl‖ˈɡɑːr-/, **Art** (1941–   ) an American popular music singer and actor, best known as half of the very successful singing pair, Simon and Garfunkel —see also SIMON AND GARFUNKEL

gar·gan·tu·an /ɡɑːˈɡæntʃuən‖ɡɑːr-/ *adj* extremely large; GIGANTIC: *a gargantuan meal* | *He had a gargantuan appetite.*

gar·gle¹ /ˈɡɑːɡəl‖ˈɡɑːr-/ *v* [I (**with**)] to wash the throat or mouth by blowing air from the LUNGs through liquid held in the throat or mouth; people may do this with medicine if they have a sore throat, or with a preparation to make the breath smell fresh

gargle² n **1** [S] an act of gargling: *Have a good gargle.* **2** [C;U] (a) liquid with which one gargles

gar·goyle /ˈgɑːgɔɪl‖ˈgɑːr-/ n an often ugly stone figure of a person or animal on a roof or wall, esp. of a church, through whose mouth rainwater is carried away —see picture at CHURCH

Gar·i·bal·di /ˌgærᵻˈbɔːldi◂/, **Giu·sep·pe** /dʒuˈsepi/ (1807–82) an Italian nationalist (born in France) who led 1,000 soldiers to take over Sicily and Naples and reunite Italy in 1860. He was elected to the Italian parliament in 1874.

Garibaldi bis·cuit /ˌ···· ˈ··/ n BrE a type of flat square BIS-CUIT containing CURRANTs

gar·ish /ˈgeərᵻʃ/ adj unpleasantly bright: *garish colours* | *a garish jacket* – –**ly** adv – –**ness** n [U]

gar·land¹ /ˈgɑːlənd‖ˈgɑːr-/ n a circle of flowers, leaves, or both, esp. one that is worn round the neck for decoration or as a sign of victory —compare WREATH

garland² v [T (**with**)] to put one or more garlands on: *They garlanded him with flowers.*

Garland, Judy (1922–69) an American film actress and singer who was most famous as the character of Dorothy in the film of *The Wizard of Oz* —see colour picture on page 685

gar·lic /ˈgɑːlɪk‖ˈgɑːr-/ n [U] a plant rather like an onion, which is used in cooking to give a strong taste: *a clove of garlic* | *a garlic press* – –**ky** adj : *his garlicky breath*

gar·ment /ˈgɑːmənt‖ˈgɑːr-/ n fml or tech an article of clothing

gar·ner /ˈgɑːnəʳ‖ˈgɑːr-/ v [T] lit to collect or store

gar·net /ˈgɑːnᵻt‖ˈgɑːr-/ n **1** [C] a red jewel **2** [U] a deep red colour

Gar·nett /ˈgɑːnᵻt‖ˈgɑːr-/, **Alf** /ælf/ a character in the BBC television COMEDY programme *Till Death Us Do Part* played by the actor Warren Mitchell. Alf Garnett is a British WORKING-CLASS man with very RIGHT-WING political opinions. He is very PATRIOTIC and believes strongly in the British Queen and royal family. He also believes that foreign people, esp. black people, should not be allowed to live in Britain. His name is now often used when talking about people with similar opinions: *He's your average Sun reader – a real Alf Garnett type.* | *policies aimed at attracting the Alf Garnett vote*

gar·nish¹ /ˈgɑːnɪʃ‖ˈgɑːr-/ n anything that is used to improve the appearance or taste of food, such as small pieces of fruit or vegetable

garnish² v [T (**with**)] to add a garnish to (food): *The chicken was garnished with watercress and tiny new potatoes.* – see DECORATE (USAGE)

garnish³ also **gar·nish·ee** /ˌgɑːnᵻˈʃiː‖ˌgɑːr-/ v [T] AmE to take money from (a person's wages) by a court order because he has failed to pay a debt: *They're garnishing my wages to pay my wife alimony.*

gar·ret /ˈgærᵻt/ n esp. lit a small usu. unpleasant room at the top of a building. People often think of poor writers and artists living in garrets, as these rooms were often cheap to rent. —compare ATTIC

Gar·rick Club /ˈgærɪk ˌklʌb/ [the] (in Britain) a gentleman's CLUB¹ (3) in West London which has a strong association with the theatre

gar·ri·son¹ /ˈgærᵻsən/ n **1** [+sing./pl. v] a group of soldiers living in a town or fort and defending it: *The garrison was/were called out when news of the enemy's advance was received.* **2** a fort or camp where such soldiers live: *In the old days this used to be a garrison town.*

garrison² v [T] to (send a group of soldiers to) guard (a place): *The government will garrison the coastal towns.* | *Our regiment will garrison the town next month.*

gar·rotte /gəˈrɒt‖gəˈrɑːt/ v a metal collar or wire which may be tightened round the neck to prevent someone from breathing and so kill them —**garrotte** v [T]

gar·ru·lous /ˈgærᵊləs/ adj fml habitually talking too much – –**ly** adv – –**ness** n [U]

gar·ter /ˈgɑːtəʳ‖ˈgɑːr-/ n **1** a band of elastic material worn round the leg to keep a sock or STOCKING up. It is a cus-

tom in Britain for BRIDEs (=women getting married) to wear a garter on one leg. **2** AmE for SUSPENDER

Garter, Order of the [the] the highest order of British KNIGHTHOOD. The sign of the Order of the Garter is a blue VELVET garter.

garter snake /ˈ·· ˌ·/ n a small, non-poisonous North American snake with stripes down the length of its back

gas¹ /gæs/ n **gases** or **gasses 1** [C;U] (a type of) substance like air, which is not solid or liquid and usually cannot be seen: *Oxygen and nitrogen are gases.* | *a gas cylinder* **2** [U] a substance of this type, esp. NATURAL GAS, which is burnt in the home for heating and cooking and formerly also for light: *a gas cooker/fire* | *He turned on/lit the gas.* | *A gas main exploded.* **3** [U] a substance of this type which is used to poison or cause extreme discomfort: *The police used tear gas to control the riot.* **4** [U] AmE infml petrol: *We're out of gas.* | *a gas tank* **5** [U] AmE for WIND¹ (3) **6** [S] infml, esp. AmE something funny, entertaining, or enjoyable: *Woody Allen's latest film's a real gas!* **7** [U] infml derog, esp. BrE unimportant talk: *Don't pay any attention; it's all gas!* —see also LAUGHING GAS

gas² v -**ss**- **1** [T] to poison or kill (someone) with gas **2** [I] infml, esp BrE to talk for a long time about unimportant things; CHAT: *Well, I can't sit here gassing all day; I must get on with some work.*

gas·bag /ˈgæsbæg/ also **windbag**– n infml a person who talks too much

gas cham·ber /ˈ· ˌ··/ n a room in which people or animals are killed with poison gas. The Nazis used gas chambers to kill thousands of Jews in the Second World War. They are used today in some American states which allow CAPITAL PUNISHMENT.

Gas·coigne¹ /ˈgæskɔɪn/, **Bam·ber** /ˈbæmbəʳ/ (1935–) a British writer who introduces television programmes; known esp. as the question master in the television programme *University Challenge*

Gascoigne², Paul (1967–) a very popular English footballer, also known as **Gazza**. He is generally considered to be a very good player, and he also became very famous in Britain after crying while playing in England's SEMI-FINAL match in the 1990 World Cup.

gas·e·ous /ˈgæsiəs/ adj esp. tech of or like gas

gas-fired /ˌ· ˈ·◂/ adj esp. BrE using NATURAL GAS or PROPANE: *gas-fired central heating*

gas fit·ter /ˈ· ˌ··/ BrE ‖ **pipe fitter** AmE– n a person whose job is to supply or repair the pipes for gas in the home and the apparatuses worked by it, such as heaters, etc.

gas guz·zler /ˈ· ˌ··/ n AmE a large car or other motor vehicle that uses a lot of petrol —**ling** adj

gash /gæʃ/ v [T] to wound with a large deep cut: *He gashed his foot on a piece of broken glass.* —**gash** n : *a nasty gash in her arm*

gas·hold·er /ˈgæsˌhəʊldəʳ/ also **gasometer**– n a very large round metal container from which gas is carried in pipes to houses and buildings

gas·ket /ˈgæskᵻt/ n a flat piece of soft material which is placed between two surfaces so that steam, oil, gas, etc., cannot escape: *That car has* **blown a (head) gasket.** (=steam is escaping from the engine) | (fig.) *She really* **blew a gasket** (=became very angry) *when I asked for more money.*

gas·light /ˈgæs-laɪt/ n **1** [U] the light produced from burning gas **2** [C] also **gas·lamp** /-læmp/– a lamp in the house or on the street which gives light from burning gas

gas·man /ˈgæsmæn/ n -**men** /men/ a man who works in the gas industry, esp. an official who visits one's home to see how much gas one has used in order to calculate payment

gas mask /ˈ· ·/ n a breathing apparatus worn over the face to protect the wearer against poisonous gases

gas me·ter /ˈ· ˌ··/ n a piece of equipment that measures how much gas is used in a building, esp. in a house, in order to calculate how much money is owed: *I've come to read the (gas) meter.*

gas·o·hol /ˈgæsəhɒl‖-hɔːl/ n [U] esp. AmE petrol with a small amount of alcohol in it. It can be used in cars and is cheaper than petrol.

gas·o·line , -**lene** /ˈgæsəliːn/ also **gas** infml– n [U] AmE petrol

gas·om·e·ter /gæˈsɒmᵻtəʳ‖-ˈsɑː-/ n a GASHOLDER

gasp¹ /gɑːsp‖gæsp/ v **1** [I (**at, with, in**)] to take in one's breath suddenly and in a way that can be heard, esp. because of surprise, shock, etc.: *The circus audience gasped with/in amazement as she put her head in the lion's mouth.* **2** [I] to breathe quickly, esp. with difficulty, making a noise: *I came out of the water* **gasping for breath.** **3** [T (OUT)] to say while breathing in this way: *He gasped out the message.*

gasp² n **1** an act of gasping: *She gave a gasp of surprise.* **2** **at the last gasp** at the last possible moment

gas ped·al /ˈ· ˌ··/ n AmE for ACCELERATOR —see picture at CAR

gas per·me·a·ble lens /ˌ· ····· ˈ·/ n a kind of CONTACT LENS available from the 1980s that allows oxygen to reach the eye of the wearer

gasp·ing /ˈgɑːspɪŋ‖ˈgæ-/ adj [F] BrE infml very thirsty

gas ring /ˈ· ·/ BrE ‖ **burner** AmE— n a metal ring on the top of a cooker through which gas passes to feed a flame over which food can be cooked —see picture at RING

gas sta·tion /ˈ· ˌ··/ n AmE for FILLING STATION

gas·sy /ˈgæsi/ adj full of (a) gas: *I don't like this gassy beer.* **—siness** n [U]

gas·tric /ˈgæstrɪk/ adj [A] tech of the stomach: *The* **gastric juices** *are acids which break down food in the stomach.* | *a gastric ulcer* | *gastric flu*

gas·tri·tis /gæˈstraɪtɪs/ n [U] an illness in which the inside of the stomach is swollen, so that a burning pain is felt

gas·tro·en·te·ri·tis /ˌgæstrəʊ-entəˈraɪtɪs/ n [U] an illness in which the food passages, including the stomach and INTESTINES, are swollen

gas·tro·nome /ˈgæstrənəʊm/ n sometimes humor a person who is skilled in gastronomy or enjoys good food

gas·tron·o·my /gæˈstrɒnəmi‖gæˈstrɑː-/ n [U] the art and science of cooking and eating good food **—mic** /ˌgæstrəˈnɒmɪk◂‖-ˈnɑː-/ adj **—mically** /kli/ adv

gas tur·bine /ˈ· ˈ··/ n an INTERNAL-COMBUSTION ENGINE in which a wheel of special blades is driven round at high speed by hot gases

gas·works /ˈgæswɜːks‖-ɜːr-/ n gasworks [C+sing./pl. v] a place where gas for use in the home is made from coal

gate /geɪt/ n **1** a movable frame, often with bars across it, which closes an opening in a fence, wall, etc., and provides a way of entering or leaving a usu. outdoor place: *Someone left the gate open and the cows wandered out of their field.* | *park gates* —compare DOOR, and see picture at HOUSE **2** an entrance or way out, esp. in an airport: *Our flight is boarding at gate number 12.* —see also PEARLY GATES **3** BrE **a** the number of people who go in to see a sports event, esp. a football match: *Gates are down on last season.* (=fewer people are going to matches) **b** also **gate mon·ey** /ˈ· ˌ··/— the money paid by these people **4** (in comb.) a political SCANDAL in connection with the stated place (from the **Watergate** affair in 1972): *Irangate*

GATE /geɪt/ Guaranteed Accommodation and Training for Employment; a British organization set up in 1991 to help the homeless

gâ·teau /ˈgætəʊ‖gɑːˈtəʊ/ n **-teaux** /təʊz/ BrE [C;U] any of various kinds of large sweet cakes often filled and decorated with cream, fruit, nuts, etc.

gate·crash /ˈgeɪtkræʃ/ also **crash** infml— v [I;T] to go to (a party) without having been invited **— ~er** n

gate·house /ˈgeɪthaʊs/ n **-houses** /ˌhaʊzɪz/ a building that surrounds the gate of a castle or city wall, or that stands beside the gate to a park or the land surrounding a big house

gate·keep·er /ˈgeɪtˌkiːpəʳ/ n a person who is in charge of the opening and closing of a gate

gate-legged ta·ble /ˌ· · ˈ··/ also **gate-leg table** n a table which has a leg on a HINGE that can swing in to let down part of the table

gate·post /ˈgeɪtpəʊst/ n a post beside a gate, from which the gate is hung or to which it fastens —see also **between you, me, and the gatepost** (BETWEEN¹); see picture at HOUSE

gate·way /ˈgeɪt-weɪ/ n **1** [C] an opening in a fence, wall, etc., across which a gate may be put **2** [the (**to**)] a way

of reaching or gaining (esp. something desirable): *Hard work is the gateway to success.*

Gateway one of a group of British SUPERMARKETS selling mainly food, but also other things

gath·er¹ /ˈgæðəʳ/ v **1** [T (IN, UP)] esp. lit to collect (flowers, crops, several objects, etc.), esp. by moving from one place to another: *Gather your toys up.* | *The farmers are gathering in the corn.* **2** [T] to gain or obtain (information, qualities, etc.) by a process of gradual increase: *He travels about the world gathering facts about little-known diseases.* | *As we came onto the slope we* **gathered speed.** | *I hate to see such good equipment* **gathering dust.** (=not being used) **3** [T (**from**)] to understand from something said or done: *I didn't gather much from the confused story he told me.* [+(that)] *I gather she's been ill, so she may not be able to come.* **4** [I (ROUND)] to come together: *Gather round, and I'll tell you a story.* | *A crowd gathered to see what had happened.* **5** [T] to pull (a material or piece of clothing) **a** around or close to something: *He gathered his cloak around him.* **b** into small folds, usu. by making small stitches with a long thread, then pulling the thread so that the folds are pushed together: *a skirt gathered at the waist* **6** **gather ye rosebuds while ye may** quote a phrase from a poem by Robert Herrick, telling young girls to enjoy their beauty while it lasts because it will not last for ever

▷ USAGE Compare **gather, collect, accumulate,** and **amass.** You can **gather** things which are irregularly distributed, or not clearly separated from one another: *to* **gather** *flowers/crops/information.* **Collect** is like **gather,** but suggests that the things you are gathering are separate, or can be dealt with one at a time: *Collect the books and put them on the shelf.* | *I'm* **collecting** *signatures for a petition.* It is used esp. when you want to keep things together to form a collection: *She* **collects** *stamps/coins.* If you **accumulate** things you collect more and more of them over a period of time (often without having a strong intention to do this): *I've* **accumulated** *quite a lot of rare books over the years.* **Amass** is rather formal, and is used esp. of money, goods, or power collected gradually, but in very large amounts: *George Blake has* **amassed** *a fortune through his business dealings.*◁

gather² n a small fold produced by gathering (GATHER¹ (5))

gath·er·ing /ˈgæðərɪŋ/ n **1** a meeting: *a small social gathering* **2** a gather or group of gathers in material

Ga·to·rade /ˈgeɪtəreɪd/ n [U] tdmk a drink sold in the US which is supposed to replace chemicals in the body which are lost when one plays sports for a long time

Gatsby see GREAT GATSBY

GATT /gæt/ General Agreement on Tariffs and Trade; an agreement between 76 countries which aims to encourage trade between the members. *GATT talks*

Gat·wick Air·port /ˌgætwɪk ˈeəpɔːt‖-ˈeərpɔːrt/ one of the airports serving London, which is used for international flights and handles a large number of passengers. It is 25 miles south of London.

gauche /gəʊʃ/ adj awkward, esp. in social behaviour; doing and saying the wrong things

gau·cho /ˈgaʊtʃəʊ/ n **-chos** a S American COWBOY, esp. of the plains (PAMPAS) of Argentina

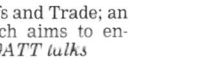

La Sagrada Familia by Antonio Gaudí

Gau·dí /ˈgaʊdi/, **An·to·ni·o** /ænˈtəʊniəʊ/ (1852–1926) a Spanish ARCHITECT known esp. for the *Templo Sagrada Familia* in Barcelona

gau·dy /ˈgɔːdi/ adj too bright in colour and/or with too much decoration: *a gaudy display of trinkets/of wealth* **—dily** adv **—diness** n [U]

gauge¹ ‖ also **gage** AmE— /geɪdʒ/ n **1** an instrument for measuring size, amount, etc., e.g. the width of wire or the amount of rain that has fallen: *a rain gauge* | *the fuel gauge in a car* —see picture

at CAR **2** the thickness of wire or certain metal objects, or the width of the barrel of a gun: *a 12 gauge shotgun* **3** the distance between the RAILs of a railway or between the wheels of a train: *standard gauge* (4' 8½") —see also BROAD GAUGE, NARROW GAUGE **4** a standard measure of weight, size, etc., to which objects can be compared

gauge² *v* [T] **1** to measure by means of a gauge: *A thermometer gauges the temperature.* | (fig.) *He gauged the height of the tunnel with his eye.* **2** to make a judgment about: *Can you gauge what her reaction is likely to be?*

Gau·guin /ˈɡəʊɡæn‖ɡəʊˈɡæn/, **Paul** (1848–1903) a French painter who went to live in Tahiti, where he painted scenes which showed his interest in the life of the people there, using pure, bright colours

Gaul·list /ˈɡəʊlₐst‖ˈɡɔːl-/ *n* **1** someone who supported the French political movement during the Second World War led by Charles de Gaulle in opposition to the Vichy Regime **2** a follower of de Gaulle's political principles and ideas —see also DE GAULLE —**Gaullist** *adj*

gaunt /ɡɔːnt/ *adj* thin, as if ill or hungry: *He had gaunt cheeks and hollow eyes after his long illness.* | (fig.) *The old house stood gaunt and empty, a complete ruin.* — ~ness *n* [U]

gaunt·let /ˈɡɔːntlₐt/ *n* **1** [C] a long GLOVE covering the wrist, worn to protect the hand in certain sports or industrial processes **2** [C] a GLOVE covered in metal, used as armour by soldiers in former times **3** [the] an invitation to fight, esp. when two people's beliefs are opposed (esp. in the phrases **throw down/pick up the gauntlet**) **4 run the gauntlet (of)** to suffer or experience (attack, blame, danger, etc.): *He ran the gauntlet of newspaper attacks.*

gauze /ɡɔːz/ *n* [U] **1** fine thin net-like material, used esp. as a curtain or in medicine to cover wounds: *cotton gauze* **2** *AmE for* BANDAGE¹ —**gauzy** *adj*

Gav·as·kar /ˈɡævəskɑːʳ/, **Sun·il** /ˈsʊnɪl/ (1949–) an Indian cricket player who scored (SCORE) a record number of runs in a record number of test matches between 1971 and 1987

gave /ɡeɪv/ *past tense of* GIVE

gav·el /ˈɡævəl/ *n* a small hammer used by a CHAIRPERSON, a US judge, or an AUCTIONEER selling things in public, for striking a table in order to get attention

ga·votte /ɡəˈvɒt‖ɡəˈvɑːt/ *n* (a piece of music for) a fast happy dance from France, danced esp. in former times

gawk /ɡɔːk/ *v* [I (at)] to look at something in a foolish way; gawp: *Don't just stand there gawking!* — ~er *n*

gaw·ky /ˈɡɔːki/ *adj* (of a person) awkward in movement, esp. because of long thin limbs —-kiness *n* [U]

gawp /ɡɔːp/ *v* [I (at)] *BrE* to look at something in a foolish way, esp. with the mouth open: *The little boys gawped at the princess as she stepped out of the taxi.* —compare GAPE, GOGGLE

gay¹ /ɡeɪ/ *adj* **1** *infml for* HOMOSEXUAL: *gay rights*

▶CULTURAL NOTE The word **gay** is used by gay people themselves and is not offensive.◀ **2** bright or attractive, so that one feels happy to see it, hear it, etc.: *gay colours* **3** cheerful; happy; full of fun —see also GAILY

gay² *n infml* a HOMOSEXUAL person, esp. a man

gay com·mu·ni·ty /ˌ· ·ˈ···/ [the] those members of the population who are gay, esp. those who are open about it, and are united by shared beliefs and views about political questions, rights, or other subjects which particularly concern them: *The book was strongly criticized by leading members of the gay community.*

Gaye /ɡeɪ/, **Marvin** (1939–84) an American soul singer and songwriter whose many successful songs were part of the Detroit MOTOWN sound, and included *I Heard It Through the Grapevine*

gay·ness /ˈɡeɪnₐs/ *n* [U] the quality of being gay (esp. of being HOMOSEXUAL) —compare GAIETY

gay rights /ˌ· ˈ·/ *n* [P] legal measures and protection for HOMOSEXUAL men and women that result in their being treated the same as all people in matters such as housing, jobs, insurance, etc. Many US cities and states have politically active gay groups that have influenced new laws to help them, though there is usu. some opposition to this from religious and CONSERVATIVE groups. In Britain there is less organization of political activity among gay people: *a gay rights activist/demonstration* | *Does the party platform say anything about gay rights?*

Ga·za Strip /ˌɡɑːzə ˈstrɪp/ [the] a coastal area in the Middle East, between Egypt and Israel, which has been held by Israel since 1967 and is inhabited mainly by Palestinians.

gaze¹ /ɡeɪz/ *v* [I+adv/prep] to look steadily, esp. for a long time and often without being conscious of what one is doing: *She sat gazing at the fire/gazing out of the window.*

▷ USAGE Compare **gaze**, **stare**, and **gape**. **Gaze** is used when a person looks steadily at something, often with admiration or pleasure: *We stood gazing at the beautiful scenery.* **Stare** is used when a person keeps their eyes open and fixed on something in wonder, fear, anger or deep thought: *He stared at me, trying to remember who I was.* **Gape** means "to look hard in surprise, esp. with the mouth open": *They gaped at me when I told them about the gold I had found.*◁

gaze² *n* [S] a steady fixed look: *She turned her worried gaze from one person to the other.* | *He turned his head away, feeling too ashamed to meet her gaze.*

ga·ze·bo /ɡəˈziːbəʊ‖-ˈzeɪ-, -ˈziː-/ *n* -bos a shelter or hut, usu. in a garden, where one can sit and look at the view

ga·zelle /ɡəˈzel/ *n* -zelles *or* -zelle an animal like a small deer, which jumps in graceful movements and has beautiful large eyes

ga·zette /ɡəˈzet/ *n* **1** an official newspaper, esp. one from the government giving lists of people who have been employed by them, important notices, etc. **2** *AmE* a newspaper

gaz·et·teer /ˌɡæzₐˈtɪəʳ/ *n* a list of names of places, printed as a dictionary or as a list at the end of a book of maps

gaz·pach·o /ɡæzˈpætʃəʊ‖ɡəˈspɑː-/ *n* [U] a Spanish cold soup made from TOMATO, green pepper, CUCUMBER, and onion

ga·zump /ɡəˈzʌmp/ *v* [T] *BrE infml* (of the owner of a house) to refuse to sell a house to (someone who thinks they have bought it) and sell it instead to someone who has offered more money

ga·zun·der /ɡəˈzʌndəʳ/ also **gaz·welch** /ɡəzˈweltʃ/— *v* [T] *BrE* to try to force (someone selling a house) to lower the price by threatening to pull out after an agreement on the sale has been reached. This is thought to be an unfriendly and unfair thing to do, but it is not against the law in England.

Gaz·za /ˈɡæzə/ see Paul GASCOIGNE

GB /ˌdʒiː ˈbiː/ *abbrev. for:* Great Britain

GBH /ˌdʒiː biː ˈeɪtʃ/ *abbrev. for:* GRIEVOUS BODILY HARM

GCE /ˌdʒiː siː ˈiː◂/ *n* General Certificate of Education; an examination in any of a range of subjects taken in British schools before 1988 by pupils aged 15 or over. The examinations were O LEVELS and A LEVELS, and GCSE examinations have now taken the place of O levels.

GCHQ /ˌdʒiː siː eɪtʃ ˈkjuː/ Government Communication Headquarters; a place near Cheltenham where the British government collects information about enemy countries, esp. by listening to their radio messages. It came into the news in 1984 when the British government announced that workers at GCHQ would no longer have the right to belong to a union and there was much protest.

GCSE /ˌdʒiː siː es ˈiː/ *n* General Certificate of Secondary Education; a school examination in any of a range of subjects which the took place of O LEVELS and CSEs in Britain in 1988, and involves not only final examinations but also work done on a two-year course. GCSEs are taken by pupils of all abilities: *She's taking seven GCSEs* —see also CONTINUOUS ASSESSMENT; compare O LEVEL and see also extra information on page 408

Gdansk /ɡəˈdænsk/ a city and port in Poland, known for its shipyards where RIOTS by the workers in 1970 led to government changes and the establishment of the trade union Solidarity in 1980; formerly known as Danzig

g'day /ɡəˈdeɪ/ *interj AustrE for* GOOD DAY (1)

GDP /ˌdʒiː diː ˈpiː/ [the] Gross Domestic Product; the total value of all the goods and services produced in a country, usu. in a single year, except for income received from abroad —compare GNP

gear¹ /ɡɪəʳ/ *n* **1** [C;U] an apparatus, esp. one consisting of a set of toothed wheels, that allows power to be passed from one part of a machine to another so as to control the power, speed, or direction of movement: *She changed gear to make the car go up the hill faster.* | *Most cars have four forward gears.* | *She put the van into bottom gear (BrE)/low gear (AmE) to climb the hill.* | *"The car isn't moving!" "That's because you're not in gear."* | *The truck screeched to a halt with* **a crashing of gears.**| *reverse gear* | (fig.) *The industry has been* **out of gear** (=not working well) *since before the dispute began.* **2** [U] **a** a set of equipment or tools, esp. used for a particular purpose: *climbing gear* (=boots, ropes, etc.) **b** (*often in comb.*) clothing or an article of clothing, esp. for a particular purpose: *football gear* | *headgear* **3** [U] an apparatus or part of a machine which has a special use in controlling a vehicle: *the landing gear of an aircraft* (=its wheels and wheel supports)

gear² *v*

　gear sthg. **to** sthg. *phr v* [T *often pass.*] to allow (an activity or course of action) to be dependent on or influenced by (a particular fact or condition): *We must gear the amount of products we make to the level of public demand.* | *Education should be geared to the children's needs and abilities.*
　gear sbdy. **up** *phr v* [T *usu. pass.*] *infml* to put (esp. oneself) into a state of excited or anxious expectation about an activity: *The party is all geared up for the forthcoming election campaign.* | *I was all geared up to have an argument about it and then she said it didn't matter.*

gear·box /ˈgɪəbɒks‖ˈgɪərbɑːks/ *n* a metal case containing the gears of a vehicle

gear le·ver /ˈ· ˌ··/ also **gear stick** /ˈ· ·/*BrE* ‖ **gear shift** *AmE*— *n* a movable metal rod with which one controls the gears of a vehicle —see picture at CAR and at BICYCLE

GEC /ˌdʒiː iː ˈsiː/ the General Electric Company plc; a British firm that specializes in ELECTRONICS, TELECOMMUNICATIONS, and other HIGH-TECHNOLOGY products, and operates in many countries around the world

geck·o /ˈgekəʊ/ *n* **-os** *or* **-oes** a small animal of the LIZARD family, esp. of tropical countries

GED /ˌdʒiː iː ˈdiː/ *n* general equivalency diploma; in the US, a degree, equivalent to a HIGH SCHOOL DIPLOMA which can be studied for at anytime by those who left high school without finishing

gee¹ /dʒiː/ *interj infml, esp. AmE* (an expression of surprise)

gee² *v*

　gee up *phr v BrE* **1** [T] (**gee** sbdy./sthg. ↔ **up**) *infml* to encourage forcefully into greater activity or effort: *This class has been very lazy lately; maybe the new teacher will gee them up a bit.* **2 gee up** (used as a command to a horse) Go faster!

gee-gee /ˈ· ·/ *n BrE sl* (used esp. by or to children or in horse racing) a horse

geek /giːk/ *n sl* **1** *AmE* someone who bites the heads off animals that are alive as part of a show **2** a stupid or annoying person —**geeky** *adj*

geese /giːs/ *pl. of* GOOSE

gee whiz /ˌdʒiː ˈwɪz/ *interj AmE infml* an expression of surprise

gee·zer /ˈgiːzəʳ/ *n sl* a man, often one who is thought to be a little strange: *I didn't realize that funny old geezer was your grandpa!*

Geh·rig /ˈgerɪg/, **Lou** /luː/ (1903–41) an American BASEBALL player who set a record for playing in the greatest number of games without missing any

Gei·ger count·er /ˈgaɪgə ˌkaʊntəʳ‖-gər-/ *n* an instrument for finding and measuring RADIOACTIVITY

gei·sha /ˈgeɪʃə/ also **geisha girl** /ˈ·· ·/— *n* a Japanese woman who is trained in the art of dancing, singing, and providing entertainment, esp. for men

gel¹ /dʒel/ *n* [C;U] a substance in a state between solid and liquid; JELLY: *hair gel*

gel² *v* **-ll-** [I] to JELL

gel·a·tine /ˈdʒelətiːn‖-tn/ also **gel·a·tin** /ˈdʒelətᵻn‖-tn/ *AmE* — *n* [U] a clear substance obtained from boiled animal bones, used for making jellies (JELLY)

ge·lat·i·nous /dʒᵻˈlætᵻnəs/ *adj esp. tech* like JELLY; in a state between solid and liquid

geld /geld/ *v* [T] to remove the TESTICLES (=sexual organs) of (certain male animals)

geld·ing /ˈgeldɪŋ/ *n* an animal, usu. a horse, that has been gelded

Gel·dof /ˈgeldɒf‖-ɔːf, -ɑːf/, **Bob** (1954–) an Irish singer who sang with his band **The Boomtown Rats**, before becoming involved in raising money for people dying from hunger in Ethiopia with the CHARITY **Band Aid** and the **Live Aid** concerts in the 1980s

gel·ig·nite /ˈdʒelɪgnaɪt/ *n* [U] a very powerful explosive

Gel·ler /ˈgeləʳ/, **U·ri** /ˈjʊəri/ (1946–) an Israeli PSYCHIC performer, who claimed that he could use his special powers to bend objects such as FORKS

gem /dʒem/ *n* **1** a precious stone, esp. when cut into a regular shape; jewel **2** a thing or person regarded as esp. good, clever, valuable, etc.: *My secretary is an absolute gem/a real gem.*

Gem·i·ni /ˈdʒemᵻnaɪ‖-ni/ *n* **1** [U] the third sign of the ZODIAC, represented by a set of TWINS (=two people born together) **2** [C] a person born between May 23 and June 21 —see ZODIAC (USAGE) and see picture at ZODIAC

Gemini pro·gram /ˈ··· ˌ··/ [*the*] an American space programme of the mid-1960s which prepared for the Apollo program

gen¹ /dʒen/ *n* [U (**on**)] *BrE old-fash infml* the correct or complete information: *She gave me all the gen on the new office arrangements that were made while I was away.*

gen² *v* [T] (of a computer system) to form from various parts (of SOFTWARE) so as to make a whole: *This system was genned in October 1990.*

　gen up *phr v* [I (**on**);T (=**gen** sbdy. **up**)(**on**, **about**)] *BrE infml* to (cause to) learn the facts thoroughly: *I must gen up on the route before we leave.* | *She's thoroughly genned up about all our procedures.*

gen·darme /ˈʒɒndɑːm‖ˈʒɑːndɑːrm/ *n* a French policeman

gen·der /ˈdʒendəʳ/ *n* [C;U] **1** *tech* (in grammar) **a** the system (in some languages) of marking words such as nouns, adjectives, and PRONOUNS as being MASCULINE, FEMININE, or NEUTER: *One of the ways of showing difference of gender in French is by changing the endings of adjectives.* **b** any of these three divisions: *German has three genders but French only has two.* **2** *tech or euph* the division into male or female; sex: *gender differentiation within a species*

gender-bend·er /ˈ·· ˌ··/ *n sl* **1** someone, often a popular singer or entertainer, who takes on some of the ways of behaving, dressing, etc., of someone of the opposite sex **2** something that fits onto a male PLUG to make it work as a female, or onto a female plug to make it work as a male

gene /dʒiːn/ *n* any of several small parts of the material at the NUCLEUS (=centre) of a cell, that control the development of all the qualities in a living thing which have been passed on from its parents

ge·ne·al·o·gy /ˌdʒiːniˈælədʒi/ *n* **1** [U] (the study of) the history of the members of a family from the past to the present **2** [C] an account of this for one particular family, esp. when shown in a drawing with lines and names spreading like the branches of a tree —see also FAMILY TREE —**gist** *n* —**gical** /ˌdʒiːniəˈlɒdʒɪkəl◄/ ‖ -ˈlɑː-/ *adj* —**gically** /kli/ *adv*

gene pool /ˈ· ˌ·/ *n* all of the genes available to a named (or the human) SPECIES

gen·e·ra /ˈdʒenərə/ *pl. of* GENUS

gen·e·ral¹ /ˈdʒenərəl/ *adj* **1** concerning or influencing the lives of all or most people: *There is a general feeling that this law isn't working properly.* | *It's not* **in the general interest** *to close railways.* (=it's not good for most people) | *The* **general public** (=ordinary people) *weren't allowed in to the secret trial.* | *Is the staff car park for general use or only for the senior staff?* | *Worry about high food prices has now become fairly general.* **2** not limited in range; concerning or including most cases, things, etc.: *The school gives a good general education.* (=in many subjects) | *She took a general degree at university.* | *a general store* (=a small shop that sells many different types of things) | *Rain will become general overnight.* | *I don't give interviews* **as a general rule** (=usually), *but in this case I'll make an exception.* **3** not detailed; describing the main things only: *Just give me a general idea of the work.* **4** [*after n*] (as the second part of an official title) chief: *the Postmaster-General* | *Attorney General* | *Surgeon General* **5 in general** usually; in most cases: *In general, people like her.* | *People in general like her.* —see also GENERALLY

general² n **1** a high rank in the army or airforce —see TABLE 3 **2** a person in command of an army or other fighting force: *Here is the report, General.*

General Ac·ci·dent /ₗ··· ·'··/ a British company that deals in LIFE ASSURANCE

General As·sem·bly /ₗ··· ·'··/ n [C+*sing./pl.v*] **1** the main DELIBERATIVE body of the United Nations in which each member country has one vote **2** the top governing body of some religious DENOMINATIONs, esp. the Church of Scotland and other Presbyterian churches **3** a law-making body, esp. in a US state

General Bel·gra·no /ₗdʒenərəl bel'grɑːnəʊ/ [*the*] an Argentinian ship sunk by the British in 1982 in the Falklands War —see BELGRANO AFFAIR

general coun·sel /ₗ··· '··/ n **1** the chief legal officer of an American company **2** a firm of US lawyers which gives general rather than specialist advice

general de·liv·er·y /ₗ··· ·'··/ n [U] *AmE for* POSTE RESTANTE

general e·lec·tion /ₗ··· ·'··/ n an election in which all the voters in a country take part at the same time to choose the members of a government —see also extra information on page 412

General E·lec·tric /ₗ··· ·'··/ an American company that makes electrical and electronic equipment

General Hos·pi·tal /ₗ··· '··/ a long-running daytime SOAP OPERA on American television. It is seen as typical of soap operas, esp. when people are talking in a humorous way: *Her personal life is right out of General Hospital.*

gen·e·ra·lis·si·mo /ₗdʒenərə'lɪsɪməʊ/ n **-mos** (in certain countries) a commander of the army, navy, and airforce, esp. one who has political as well as military power

gen·e·ral·i·ty /ₗdʒenə'rælɪti/ n **1** [C *often pl.*] a general statement; point for consideration which is not detailed: *We all know there's a lack of food in the world, but let's move on from generalities to the particular problems of feeding the people of this country.* **2** [*the*+P **(of)**] *fml* the greater part; most: *The generality of people are neither good nor bad, but somewhere in between.* **3** [U] *fml* the quality of being general

gen·e·ral·i·za·tion also **-isation** *BrE* /ₗdʒenərəlaɪ'zeɪʃən‖-lə-/ n **1** [U] the act of generalizing **2** [C] *sometimes derog* a general statement, principle, or opinion formed from (sometimes incomplete) consideration of particular facts: *The report's conclusion is full of* **sweeping generalizations,** *some of them based on very little evidence.*

gen·e·ral·ize also **-ise** *BrE* /'dʒenərəlaɪz/ v **1** [I **(about)**] to make a general statement: *Our history teacher is always generalizing; he never deals with anything in detail.* **2** [I **(from)**] to form a general principle, opinion, etc., after considering only a small number of the facts: *It is unfair to generalize from these two accidents and say that all young people are bad drivers.* **3** [T] to put (a principle, statement, rule, etc.) into a more general form that covers a larger number of particular cases: *to generalize a law*

general know·ledge /ₗ··· '··/ n [U] knowledge of facts from a number of different subjects, e.g. the capitals of countries, political events or people, historical events and dates, famous books and writers, people in sports and entertainment, etc.: *a general knowledge quiz*

gen·er·al·ly /'dʒenərəli/ adv **1** usually: *We generally go to France for our holidays.* **2** by most people: *It is generally agreed that smoking is bad for you.* | *The plan has been generally accepted.* **3** without considering particular cases or details, but only what is true in most cases: **Generally speaking,** *the more you pay for stereo equipment, the better the system.*

General Mo·tors /ₗ··· '··/ the largest maker of cars and TRUCKs in the US, including Chevrolet, Oldsmobile, Pontiac, and Buick

general prac·tice /ₗ··· '··/ n **1** [U] work in a profession, esp. law or medicine, that is of different kinds and not limited to a special kind: *He did five years of general practice before concentrating on criminal law.* **2** [C] (the office of) a group of lawyers or doctors who do all kinds of work in their profession: *She works in a general practice on 15th Street.*

general prac·ti·tion·er /ₗ··· ·'··/ *fml for* GP

general pub·lic /ₗ··· '··/ n [*the*+S+*sing./pl.v*] PUBLIC² (1)

general pur·pose /ₗ··· '··/ adj that is suitable for most uses of the stated thing: *a general purpose fire extinguisher* (=puts out all kinds of fires) | *general purpose tyres*

gen·er·al·ship /'dʒenərəlʃɪp/ n [U] an army commander's military skill

general staff /ₗ··· '·/ n [(*the*) S+*sing./pl. v*] the group of army officers who work for a commanding officer

general strike /ₗ··· '·/ n the stopping of work by most of the workers in a country at the same time. In Britain the only general strike has been the one in 1926, when many people stopped work in support of the men who worked in the COALMINES. The strike had a great effect but was not successful in its political aims.

General Syn·od /ₗ··· '··/ [*the*] the group of people who govern the Church of England, which includes BISHOPs and representatives from the church, both official and unofficial

gen·e·rate /'dʒenəreɪt/ v [T] **1** *fml* to cause (esp. feelings or ideas) to exist; produce: *The accident generated a lot of public interest in the nuclear power issue.* | *The personnel department seems to be generating a lot of paperwork these days.* | *to generate 15 million dollars' worth of business* | *This computer program will generate a list of random numbers.* **2** *tech* to produce (heat or electricity): *an electricity generating station*

gen·e·ra·tion /ₗdʒenə'reɪʃən/ n **1** [C] a period of time in which a human being can grow up and have a family, about 25 or 30 years: *Members of my family have lived in this house for generations.* **2** [C+*sing./pl. v*] **a** all the members of a family of about the same age: *This valuable heirloom has been passed down from generation to generation.* (=from parents to children) | *This family photo shows three generations: myself, my parents, and my grandparents.* **b** all people of about the same age: *The younger generation only seems/seem to be interested in pop music and clothes.* | *Most people of my father's generation have experienced war.* **3** [C] all the members of a developing class of things at a certain stage: *The latest generation of anti-tank missiles has several new refinements.* —see also FIFTH-GENERATION COMPUTER **4** [U] the act or process of generating: *the generation of electricity*

generation gap /·'·· ₗ·/ n [*the*] the difference in ideas, feelings, and interests between older and younger people, esp. considered as causing lack of understanding: *How can teachers help to bridge the generation gap between parents and their teenage children?*

gen·e·ra·tive /'dʒenərətɪv/ adj having the power to produce or generate

gen·e·ra·tor /'dʒenəreɪtəʳ/ n a machine which generates something, esp. electricity —compare DYNAMO, MAGNETO

ge·ner·ic /dʒɪ'nerɪk/ adj **1** *tech* of a GENUS: *The Latin term "Vulpes" is the generic name for the various types of fox.* **2** shared by or typical of a whole class of things **3** *esp. AmE* cheaper because of not having a TRADEMARK: *a generic drug* | *generic canned goods* — **~ally** /kli/ adv

gen·e·ros·i·ty /ₗdʒenə'rɒsɪti‖-'rɑː-/ n **1** [U] the quality of being generous **2** [C *usu. pl.*] a generous act

gen·e·rous /'dʒenərəs/ adj **1** showing readiness to give money, help, kindness, etc.; unselfish: *It was very generous of you to lend them your new car for their holiday.* | *She's not very generous with the food.* (=she gives small amounts) | *a generous and forgiving nature* —compare MEAN¹ **2** larger, kinder, etc., than usual: *a generous meal* | *generous gifts* | *These farmers receive generous subsidies from the government.* — **~ly** adv : *Please give generously to this deserving charity.*

gen·e·sis /'dʒenɪsɪs/ n [(*the*)+S **(of)**] *fml* the beginning or origin: *We cannot yet satisfactorily explain the genesis of the universe.*

Genesis the first part of the Bible, in which the Creation, Adam and Eve, the Flood, and many other events important in Christianity and Judaism are described. Most people know the first words of Genesis: "In the beginning God created the heaven and the earth."

ge·net·ic /dʒɪ'netɪk/ adj of GENEs or GENETICS: *genetic defects* — **~ally** /kli/ adv

genetic code /·'·· '·/ n [*the*] the arrangement of GENEs which controls the way a living thing develops

genetic en·gin·eer·ing /·ₗ··· ·'··/ n [U] the changing of the nature of a creature or of its organs, cells, etc., by the artificial changing of its GENES

genetic fin·ger·print /·ˌ·· ·ˈ···/ also **DNA fingerprint** // n the pattern of genetic information which is different for each person, used to show a person's IDENTITY and used esp. to show whether a person is guilty of a crime

genetic fin·ger·print·ing /·ˌ·· ·ˈ···/ n [U] the process of using genetic fingerprints to show who a person is and whether they are guilty of a crime: *The murderer was caught through genetic fingerprinting.*

ge·net·i·cist /dʒɪˈnetɪsɪst/ n a person who studies genetics

ge·net·ics /dʒɪˈnetɪks/ n [U] the study of how living things develop according to the effects of those substances passed on in the cells from the parents —see also GENE, HEREDITY

Ge·ne·va /dʒəˈniːvə/ a city in Switzerland, known for being the main base for organizations such as the Red Cross, and the World Health Organization

Geneva Con·ven·tion /·ˌ·· ·ˈ··/ [the] any of several agreements, accepted by most countries, about how to treat people hurt or taken prisoner in war: *He can't shoot those captured pilots — it's against the Geneva Convention.*

Gen·ghis Khan /ˌdʒeŋɡɪs ˈkɑːn, ˌɡen-/ (?1160–1227) ruler of the Mongol people in China who took over N India and sent his army as far as the Crimea. He was a law maker, but is known esp. for his cruelty in battle. People with very RIGHT-WING political opinions are sometimes described as being like Genghis Khan: *"What are her politics?" "Oh, she's somewhat to the right of Genghis Khan".*

ge·ni·al /ˈdʒiːniəl/ adj cheerful, friendly, and good-tempered: *he's a genial man* | *He greeted us with a genial smile.* — **ly** adv —**ity** /ˌdʒiːniˈælɪti/ n [U]

ge·nie /ˈdʒiːni/ also **djinn**— n **-nies** or **-nii** /niaɪ/ a magical spirit in Arab fairy stories, often contained in a bottle or oil lamp. He becomes the slave of the person who rubs the lamp and makes him appear: *Aladdin rubbed his lamp, and the genie appeared.*

gen·i·tal /ˈdʒenɪtl/ adj of or having an effect on the sex organs: *genital herpes* — **ly** adv : *genitally transmitted*

gen·i·tals /ˈdʒenɪtlz/ also **gen·i·ta·li·a** /ˌdʒenɪˈteɪliə/tech— n [P] the outer sex organs

gen·i·tive /ˈdʒenɪtɪv/ n tech a particular form of a noun in certain languages, such as Latin and Greek, which shows that the noun is a possessor or an origin —compare POSSESSIVE —**genitive** adj

ge·ni·us /ˈdʒiːniəs/ n **1** [U] great and rare powers of thought, skill, or imagination: *There's genius in the way this was painted.* | *Rembrandt's self-portraits are works of genius.* **2** [C] a person of very great ability or very high INTELLIGENCE: *Einstein was a genius.* **3** [S (for)] a special ability or skill; TALENT: *She has a genius for saying the wrong thing.* **4** [C] someone who has the stated influence, usu. a bad influence, over someone else: *He was her evil genius, leading her into a life of crime against her will.* —see also **I have nothing to declare but my genius** (DECLARE (3))

▷ USAGE **Genius** is a very strong word. It is only used of very rare ability or of the person who has it: *Einstein had genius/was a genius.* **Talent** is less strong. It is used of special ability: *a young actress with a lot of talent/She has a talent for music.* | *He's one of the bright young talents in music today.*◁

genius lo·ci /ˌdʒiːniəs ˈləʊsaɪ/ n [(the) S] Lat the typical character of a place, as shown by the feelings it produces in one

Gen·o·a /ˈdʒenəʊə/ a port on the Gulf of Genoa, in NW Italy

gen·o·cide /ˈdʒenəsaɪd/ n [U] the killing of a whole group of people, esp. a whole race

gen·re /ˈʒɒnrə//ˈʒɑːnrə/ n Fr **1** a class of works of art, literature, or music marked by a particular style, form, or subject: *Many of his finest works belong to the genre of nature poetry.* | *What genre of films do you like?* **2** fml a sort or kind

Gen·scher /ˈɡenʃəʳ/, **Hans-Die·trich** /hæns ˈdiːtrɪk, -ɪx/ (1927–) a West German politician, chairman of the Free Democratic Party from 1974–85

gent /dʒent/ n infml or humor a gentleman: *You're a real*

---

ent! | *What are you drinking tonight, gents?* —see also CITY GENT, GENTS

gen·teel /dʒenˈtiːl/ adj **1** showing unnaturally polite manners, esp. so as to appear socially important: *She always talks in such a genteel voice when she's on the phone.* | *They live in* **genteel poverty.** (=though poor, they try to appear of a higher social class) **2** old use of a high social class — **ly** /dʒenˈtiːl-li/ adv

gen·tian /ˈdʒenʃən/ n a plant with blue flowers which grows in some mountainous areas

gen·tile /ˈdʒentaɪl/ n, adj [A] (sometimes cap.) (a person who is) not Jewish; this word is used esp. by those Jewish people who think it is important to marry someone of their own race or religion: *Their daughter married a gentile.*

gen·til·i·ty /dʒenˈtɪlɪti/ n [U] the quality of being genteel

gen·tle /ˈdʒentl/ adj not rough, violent, or severe in movement, character, etc.; soft: *Be gentle when you brush the baby's hair.* | *A gentle breeze stirred the leaves.* | *a gentle rebuke* | *The slope is quite gentle.* (=not steep) —**tly** adv : *"Don't cry", he said gently.* | *Careful when you lift that desk —* **gently does it!** (=be gentle) — **ness** n [U]

gen·tle·folk /ˈdʒentlfəʊk/ also **gentlefolks** /-fəʊks/— n [P] old use people of high social class; GENTRY

gen·tle·man /ˈdʒentlmən/ n **-men** /mən/ **1** a man who behaves well towards others and who can be trusted to keep his promises and always act honourably: *He was a* **perfect gentleman** *and looked the other way while she took off her wet clothes.* | *I wouldn't do business with him —* he's **no gentleman. 2** polite a man: *Say thank you to the kind gentleman, Billy.* | *Good evening,* **ladies and gentlemen.**

▷ USAGE **Lady** and **gentleman** can be used as a respectful way of speaking about a woman or a man. The words are used esp. in the person's presence: *Mr Smith, there's a* **gentleman/lady** *here to see you. Shall I show him/her in,* or when speaking to a gathering of people: **Ladies** *and* **gentlemen,** *I'd like to introduce our speaker for this evening.* In other cases **woman** and **man** are the usual words: *Is the director a* **man** *or a* **woman?** | *the first* **woman** *prime minister* | *I met a very interesting* **man/woman** *on the train.* —see also FEMALE (USAGE)◁

gentleman-at-arms /ˌ···· ·ˈ·/ n **gentlemen-at-arms** a man who is one of a group who guard a king or queen on important occasions

gentleman farm·er /ˌ··· ·ˈ··/ n BrE a man of high social class who has a farm for pleasure rather than profit

gen·tle·man·ly /ˈdʒentlmənli/ adj fair, kind, and honourable in behaviour; typical of a gentleman

gentleman's a·gree·ment /ˌ··· ·ˈ··/ n an unwritten agreement made between people who trust each other

gentleman's club /ˈ··· ˌ·/ n a club which does not usu. allow women members. It is often old, well established, and in a pleasant part of a city. Gentlemen's clubs usu. have a library, a bar, and a restaurant. Gentlemen's clubs are associated esp. with upper-class men.

gentleman's gen·tle·man /ˌ··· ·ˈ··/ n a VALET

gentle sex /ˌ·· ·ˈ·/ also **fair sex**— n [the+sing./pl. v] the female sex; women

gen·tle·wom·an /ˈdʒentlˌwʊmən/ n **-women** /ˌwɪmɪn/ old use a woman of high social class; lady

gen·tri·fi·ca·tion /ˌdʒentrɪfɪˈkeɪʃən/ n [U] infml the process by which a street or area formerly lived in by poor people is changed by people with more money going to live there. This is considered a bad thing by some people because it means that poor people, who may have been born and grown up in the area, can no longer afford to live there. —**gentrify** /ˈdʒentrɪfaɪ/ v [T usu. pass.]

gen·try /ˈdʒentri/ n [(the) P] people of high social class: *The* **landed gentry** *are those who own land from which they obtain their income.*

gents /dʒents/ BrE || also **men's room** AmE— n (often cap.) a public TOILET for men —compare LADIES; see TOILET (USAGE)

gen·u·flect /ˈdʒenjʊflekt/ v [I (before)] fml to bend one's knee as a sign of respect: *They genuflected before the altar.* — **ion** /ˌdʒenjʊˈflekʃən/ n [C;U]

gen·u·ine /ˈdʒenjuɪn/ adj **1** actually being what he/she/it seems to be; real: *"Is this a genuine Ming vase?" "No, it's*

a fake." | "This service is only available to genuine tourists." **2** without dishonesty or pretending; sincere: *We all feel genuine concern for their plight.* | *She's a very genuine person.* | *a genuine attempt to settle their disagreements* – – **ly** *adv* – – **ness** *n* [U]

ge·nus /'dʒiːnəs/ *n* **genera** /'dʒenərə/ *tech* a division of animals or plants, below a FAMILY and above a SPECIES – see also GENERIC

geo- see WORD FORMATION

ge·o·cen·tric /ˌdʒiːəʊˈsentrɪk◂/ *adj* having, or measured from, the Earth as the central point: *In former times, people thought the universe was geocentric.*

ge·o·de·sic /ˌdʒiːəʊˈdiːsɪk◂‖-ˈdes-/ *n,adj tech* of or being the shortest distance between two points on a non-flat surface, such as a SPHERE (=ball-like object): *flying on the geodesic between New York and Tokyo*

geodesic dome /ˌ···· ˈ·/ *n tech* a large ball-shaped building made from small, straight pieces connected together to form POLYGONS

ge·og·ra·phy /dʒiˈɒgrəfi, 'dʒɒgrəfi‖dʒiˈɑːg-/ *n* **1** [U] the study of the countries of the world and of the seas, rivers, towns, etc., on the Earth's surface: *a geography lesson* – see also PHYSICAL GEOGRAPHY **2** [*the*+of] the arrangement or positions of the parts of (a particular place): *Until you know the geography of the building it's not easy to find your way out!* —**pher** *n* —**phical** /ˌdʒiːəˈgræfɪkəl◂/ *adj*: *geographical knowledge* —**phically** /kli/ *adv*

ge·ol·o·gy /dʒiˈɒlədʒi‖-ˈɑːlə-/ *n* [U] the study of the materials (rocks, soil, etc.) which make up the Earth, and of their changes during the history of the world —**gist** *n* —**gical** /ˌdʒiːəˈlɒdʒɪkəl‖-ˈlɑː-/ *adj* : *geological formations* —**gically** /kli/ *adv*

ge·o·met·ric /ˌdʒiːəˈmetrɪk◂/ also **geo·met·ri·cal** /-ɪkəl/— *adj* **1** concerning geometry **2** (esp. of straight lines and regular patterns) like the figures in geometry: *Muslim art is characterized by geometric patterns.* – – **ally** /kli/ *adv*

geometric pro·gres·sion /ˌ···· ·ˈ··/ also **geometrical progression** /·ˌ··· ·ˈ··/— *n* a set of numbers in order, in which each is multiplied by a fixed number to produce the next (as in *1, 2, 4, 8, 16, …*) —compare ARITHMETIC PROGRESSION

ge·om·e·try /dʒiˈɒmətri‖-ˈɑːm-/ *n* [U] the study in MATHEMATICS of the angles and shapes formed by the relationships of lines, surfaces, and solids in space

ge·o·phys·ics /ˌdʒiːəʊˈfɪzɪks/ *n* [U] the study of the movements and activities of parts of the Earth, including the sea bed —**ical** /ˌdʒiːəʊˈfɪzɪkəl◂/ *adj*

ge·o·pol·i·tics /ˌdʒiːəʊˈpɒlɪtɪks‖-ˈpɑː-/ *n* [U] the study of the effect of a country's position, population, etc., on its politics —**tical** /ˌdʒiːəʊpəˈlɪtɪkəl◂/ *adj*

Geor·die /'dʒɔːdi‖'dʒɔːr-/ *n BrE infml, sometimes derog* **1** [C] a name used for someone, esp. a man, from Tyneside in NE England: *He's a Geordie.* **2** [U] a way of speaking typical of people from Tyneside —**Geordie** *adj*

George I /ˌdʒɔːdʒ ðə ˈfɜːst‖ˌdʒɔːrdʒ ðə ˈfɜːrst/, **King** (1660–1727) King of Great Britain and Ireland from 1714 to 1727 but he could not speak English and was very unpopular, spending most of his time in Germany. His lack of interest in government led to Britain having its first PRIME MINISTER

George II /ˌdʒɔːdʒ ðə ˈsekənd‖ˌdʒɔːrdʒ-/, **King** (1683–1760) King of Great Britain and Ireland from 1727 to 1760. He was the last king to lead his men personally in battle.

George III /ˌdʒɔːdʒ ðə ˈθɜːd‖ˌdʒɔːrdʒ ðə ˈθɜːrd/, **King** (1738–1820) King of Great Britain and Ireland from 1760 to 1820. He is remembered for having been INSANE.

George IV /ˌdʒɔːdʒ ðə ˈfɔːθ‖ˌdʒɔːrdʒ ðə ˈfɔːrθ/, **King** (1762–1830) King of Great Britain and Ireland from 1820 to 1830. He acted against a STRICT education by marrying first a Catholic WIDOW (which is not thought acceptable by the royal family) and secondly a princess whom he later tried to DIVORCE. Before he became king, he ruled as Prince Regent because his father, George III, was INSANE.

George V /ˌdʒɔːdʒ ðə ˈfɪfθ‖ˌdʒɔːrdʒ-/, **King** (1865–1936) King of Great Britain and Ireland, and the British Commonwealth from 1910 to 1936. In 1917 he stopped using German titles for his family, and the name of the royal

house was changed from Saxe-Coburg-Gotha (known as Brunswick or Hanover) to Windsor.

George VI /ˌdʒɔːdʒ ðə ˈsɪksθ‖ˌdʒɔːrdʒ-/, **King** (1895–1952) King of Great Britain, Ireland, and the British Commonwealth from 1936 to 1952. He married Lady Elizabeth Bowes-Lyon (the Queen Mother) in 1923 and they had two children, Queen Elizabeth II and Princess Margaret.

George Cross /ˌ· ·ˈ/ [*the*] an honour given to British people not in the armed forces who do something extremely brave, e.g. saving someone else's life at great danger to themselves. It is given very rarely and thought to be a sign of great respect and admiration.

George Med·al /ˌ· ·ˈ·/ [*the*] an honour in the form of a red RIBBON with five blue STRIPES. It is given for similar acts of bravery as the George Cross but is not such a high honour.

George, Saint see SAINT GEORGE

George·town /'dʒɔːdʒtaʊn‖'dʒɔːr-/ **1** a wealthy shopping and living area of Washington DC, also known for its university **2** the capital city of Guyana, at the mouth of the Demerara river on the Atlantic ocean **3** town and capital of the Cayman Islands

Geor·gia /'dʒɔːdʒə‖'dʒɔːr-/ *written abbrev.:* **GA**— **1** a state in the SE of the US, named after King George II of Britain. It was one of the 13 original colonies (COLONY) –see colour map on pages 1374–5 **2** a country in SE Europe bordered on the W by the Black Sea, to the S by Turkey, Armenia, and Azerbaijan, and to the N by Russia; capital Tblisi; population 5,449,000 (1989)

Geor·gian /'dʒɔːdʒən, -dʒiən‖'dʒɔːrdʒən/ *adj* **1** of the country of Georgia, in the Caucasus **2** (in the style) of the period of rule of the British kings George the First, Second, and Third, esp. from 1714 to 1811. Georgian buildings are considered to be very attractive, and are often built in red brick with white stone decoration. –see colour picture on page 227 **3** of or being English poetry of the time of King George the Fifth, esp. from 1912 to 1922

Geor·gie Por·gie /ˌdʒɔːdʒi ˈpɔːdʒi‖ˌdʒɔːrdʒi ˈpɔːr-/ a little boy in a NURSERY RHYME (=an old song or poem for children):

> *Georgie Porgie pudding and pie,*
> *Kissed the girls and made them cry.*
> *When the boys came out to play,*
> *Georgie Porgie ran away.*

ge·o·sta·tion·ar·y /ˌdʒiːəʊˈsteɪʃənəri◂‖-eri◂/ also **ge·o·syn·chro·nous** /ˌdʒiːəʊˈsɪŋkrənəs◂/— *adj* of or being a spacecraft or SATELLITE that goes round the Earth at the same speed as the Earth moves, so that it always stays above the same place on the Earth

geo·ther·mal /ˌdʒiːʊˈθɜːməl◂‖-ˈɜːr-/ *adj* of the heat found deep inside the earth: *a geothermal spring*

Gep·hardt /'gəphɑːrt ‖ -hɑːrt/, **Richard** (1941-) a US CONGRESSMAN who became MAJORITY LEADER of the House of Representatives in 1989

ge·ra·ni·um /dʒəˈreɪniəm/ *n* any of many closely related plants with red, pink, or white flowers and round leaves that are often grown in gardens or in pots in houses

ger·bil /'dʒɜːbəl‖'dʒɜːr-/ *n* a small animal that lives in deserts and has long back legs on which it jumps. They are sometimes kept as pets, esp. by children.

Gere /gɪər/, **Richard** (1949–) an American actor known esp. for his part in the films *American Gigolo* and *Pretty Woman* —see colour picture on page 228

ger·i·at·ric /ˌdʒeriˈætrɪk◂/ *adj* **1** [*A no comp.*] of or for geriatrics: *a geriatric hospital* **2** *derog* very old and unable to work properly: *the country's geriatric leadership*

ger·i·a·tri·cian /ˌdʒeriəˈtrɪʃən/ *n* a doctor who specializes in geriatrics

ger·i·at·rics /ˌdʒeriˈætrɪks/ *n* [U] the medical treatment and care of old people —compare GERONTOLOGY

Ger·i·tol /'dʒerɪtɒl‖-tɑːl/ *n* [U] *tdmk* a PATENT MEDICINE sold in the US which contains a lot of iron; it is usually taken by older people: *the Geritol generation/set* (=old people)

germ /dʒɜːm‖dʒɜːrm/ *n* **1** [C] a disease-producing bacterium; MICROBE: *This disinfectant kills all known household germs.* **2** [*the*+of] something that may develop into something larger or more important: *It's just the germ of an idea, but I think we might make something of it.* —see also WHEAT GERM

Ger·man /'dʒɜːmən‖'dʒɜːr-/ n 1 [C] a person who comes from or whose parents come from Germany 2 [U] the language of Germany, Austria, and large parts of Switzerland —**German** adj

ger·mane /dʒɜː'meɪn‖dʒɜːr-/ adj [(to)] fml (of ideas, remarks, etc.) suitably connected with something; RELEVANT: *He makes some interesting points, but they are not really germane to the argument.*

Ger·man·ic /dʒɜː'mænɪk‖dʒɜːr-/ adj 1 (of style, appearance, etc.) of or typical of Germany or the Germans 2 of the language family that includes German, Dutch, Swedish, English, etc.

German mea·sles /ˌ·· '··/ also **rubella** med– n [U] an infectious disease in which red spots appear on the body for a short time. It may damage unborn children if caught by their mothers when PREGNANT.

German shep·herd /ˌ·· '··/ n esp. AmE for ALSATIAN —see picture at DOG

German U·ni·fi·ca·tion /ˌ·· ···\·\·/ the uniting of East and West Germany in 1990 after they had been separated since 1945. This followed the opening of the Berlin Wall in 1989 and then the COLLAPSE of the East German government.

Ger·man·y /'dʒɜːməni‖'dʒɜːr-/ a country in central Europe, divided from 1945 until 1990 into West Germany and East Germany; capital Berlin; population 78,620,000 (1990) — see also BERLIN WALL

germ cell /'· ·/ n a small part or cell of a living thing that can grow into a new plant, animal, etc.

ger·mi·cide /'dʒɜːmɪ̥saɪd‖'dʒɜːr-/ n [C;U] a substance in liquid or powder form which kills germs

ger·mi·nate /'dʒɜːmɪ̥neɪt‖'dʒɜːr-/ v [I;T] to start or cause (a seed) to start growing: *Heat and moisture will germinate the seeds.* | (fig.) *I don't know how the idea first germinated in my mind.* —**nation** /ˌdʒɜːmɪ̥'neɪʃən‖ˌdʒɜːr-/ n [U]

germ war·fare /'·· '··/ n [U] the use of germs to spread disease in war, not allowed by international agreement

Ge·ro·ni·mo /dʒɪ̥'rɒnɪ̥məʊ‖-'rɑː-/ 1 (1829–1909) an Apache Indian chief who fought Americans coming on to land belonging to his tribe in Arizona and New Mexico. When he was caught he was taken to Oklahoma, where he became a farmer and wrote the story of his life. 2 a cry used by American PARATROOPERs, and by children copying them in games, esp. when jumping off a high place

ger·on·tol·o·gy /ˌdʒɛrɒn'tɒlədʒi‖ˌdʒɜrən'tɑː-/ n [U] the scientific study of old age, its changes in the body, the effects of these, etc. —compare GERIATRICS

ger·ry·man·der /'dʒɛrimændəʳ, ˌdʒɛri'mændəʳ/ v [I;T] derog to divide (an area) for election purposes so as to give one group or party an unfair advantage over others

Ger·shwin /'gɜːʃwɪ̥n‖'gɜːr-/, **George** (1898–1937) an American COMPOSER known esp. for his OPERA *Porgy and Bess* and his JAZZ music such as *Rhapsody in Blue*. His brother **Ira Gershwin** (1896–1983) wrote the words for many of his popular songs.

ger·und /'dʒɛrənd/ n a VERBAL NOUN

ge·stalt /gə'ʃtɑːlt/ n tech a whole which is different from all its parts put together and has qualities that are not present in any of its parts: **Gestalt psychology** *is esp. concerned with patterns of experience as wholes.*

ge·sta·po /ge'stɑːpəʊ/ n -pos [C+sing./pl. v] (often cap.) a secret police force using cruel methods, esp. the secret police of the Nazi period in Germany in the 1930s and 1940s

ges·ta·tion /dʒe'steɪʃən/ n 1 [U] tech the carrying of a child or young animal inside the mother's body before birth 2 [S] also **gestation period** /·'·· ˌ···/– a tech the time during which this happens b the time of development of a thought or idea, before it is made known

ges·tic·u·late /dʒe'stɪkjʊ̥leɪt/ v [I] to make esp. rapid or excited movements of the hands and arms to express something, usu. while speaking —**lation** /dʒeˌstɪkjʊ̥'leɪʃən/ n [C;U]: *angry gesticulations*

ges·ture¹ /'dʒestʃəʳ/ n 1 [C;U] (an example of) the use of movement of the body, esp. of the hands, to express a certain meaning: *She shrugged her shoulders in a gesture of impatience.* | *He made an angry gesture.* | *English people do not use as much gesture as Italians.* 2 [C] an action which is done to show one's feelings or intentions: *We invited our new neighbours to dinner as a gesture of*

friendship. | *Their offer to renew the peace talks was a conciliatory gesture.*

gesture² v [I+adv/prep; T+obj+adv/prep] to call or direct with a movement of the body: *She gestured to the waiter to bring some more coffee.* | *He gestured me over with a movement of his head.*

ge·sund·heit /gə'zʊndhaɪt/ interj AmE used to wish good health to someone who has just sneezed (SNEEZE)

get /get/ v **got** /gɒt‖gɑːt/, **got** esp. BrE ‖ **gotten** /'gɒtn‖'gɑːtn/ AmE, present participle **getting** ■ to receive or obtain something 1 [T no pass.] to receive or experience: *I got a letter today.* | *I got a shock when I looked at the electricity bill.* | *Unless you improve your work, you'll* **get the sack.** (=be dismissed) | *This part of the country doesn't get much rain.* | *One of the advantages of teaching is that you get long holidays.* | *I get the impression that they weren't very interested.* | *You won't get much* (=much money) *for that old piano.* | *He got five years* (=in prison) *for smuggling diamonds.* 2 [T (for)] to obtain; begin to have: *You'll have to get her permission before you do that.* | *I didn't get a good look at it.* | *I'm afraid she's getting a reputation for careless work.* | *Where did you get* (=buy) *those new shoes?* [+obj(i)+obj(d)] *Will you get this book for me/get me this book from the library?* | *What did she get you for your birthday?* 3 [T no pass.] to catch (an illness): *I got flu twice last year.* | *I always get a headache if I drink too much.* ■ shows a change in position: to move or be moved 4 to catch (a bus, train, etc.): *We got the six o'clock (train) from London.* 5 [I+adv/prep; T+obj+adv/prep] to (cause to) come, go, or move: *"Get out of my house!" he shouted.* | *I got into the car.* | *He got off his bike.* | *They got onto the plane at Cairo.* | *Where has my pen got to?* (=I can't find it) | *It's late; I must be getting (back) home.* | *My feet are so swollen I can't get my boots on/off.* | *I've got so fat that I can't get into my jeans.* | *We finally got the box through the hole.* | *Get that cat out of the house before mother sees it!* | *I managed to get these watches through customs without being questioned.* | (fig.) *He gets into a terrible temper if you contradict him.* | (fig.) *I finally succeeded in* **getting (off) to sleep** *at midnight.* | (fig.) *If you tell the teacher about it you'll get me into dreadful trouble.* 6 [I+adv/prep] to arrive at or reach a place or point: *We got to Paris at 8 o'clock.* | *When did you get here?* | *We got home very late.* | *What time does the train get into Edinburgh?* | *"How far have you got with your book?" "I've got up to the last chapter."* | *We're* **getting nowhere** *with this plan; we'll have to try something else.* 7 [T] to bring from one place to another; FETCH or collect: *I'm just going to get the children from school.* ■ shows a change in state 8 [L] to become: [+adj] *The food's getting cold.* | *They must have got lost.* | *I want to plant the roses before it gets dark.* | *My cat's getting too old to catch any mice.* | *They're getting worried about her exams.* | *They've just got married.* | *He's getting better.* (=after an illness) | *"Where's David?" "He's upstairs getting ready to go out."* | *It gets really cold here in the wintertime.* | *You'll soon get used to your new job.* [+v-ing] *Let's get going.* | *Our report is late; we must* **get going/moving/weaving.** (=start work on it) 9 [L+v-ed] (used like the PASSIVE) to be: *His finger got trapped in the door.* | *If you go there alone after dark you might get attacked and robbed.* 10 [T] to bring into or cause to be in a certain state: [+obj+adj] *I'll get the children ready for school.* | *Let me get this clear: is she married or not?* | *He got all the answers wrong.* | *This cold weather is really* **getting me down.** (=making me unhappy) | *I'm so disorganized – I really must* **get myself together.** [+obj+v-ed] *I got the work finished just in time.* | *I must get this radio mended.* 11 [T] to cause (to do or be): [+obj+to-v] *I got him to help me when I moved the furniture.* | *I can't get the car to start.* [+obj+v-ing] *We'll get the party going with some music.* | *I got the radio working again by twiddling with some wires.* 12 [I+to-v] **a** to do something gradually or with the passing of time: *He's getting to be an old man now.* | *When you* **get to know** *him you'll find he's quite nice.* **b** to have it happen that one does something, by chance or permission: *If I get to see him I'll ask him about it.* | *She never gets to drive the car.* ■ other meanings 13 [T] to prepare (a meal): *I'm in the middle of getting (the) dinner.* [+obj(i)+obj(d)] *Will you get the children their supper tonight?* 14 [T] to hear: *I didn't quite get what you said; would you speak a little louder?* 15 [T] to understand: *I don't get it; why did he do that?* | *I try to make him understand that I'm not interested in him, but he never*

gets the message. | *Now don't get me wrong; I never meant to imply I didn't like him.* **16** [T] to succeed in making a telephone call to, or receive a telephone call or a radio or television signal from: *I wanted to speak to the managing director, but I got the office boy.* | *"The phone's ringing." "I'll get it."* | *Can you get Peking on your radio?* | *I've been ringing his office all day, but I can't* **get hold of** *him.* [+obj(i)+obj(d)] *Get me New York please, operator.* | *Sorry, you've got the wrong number.* **17** [T *no pass.*] *infml* to annoy: *It really gets me when he says those stupid things.* **18** [T] *infml* **a** [(for)] to punish or harm (someone) in return for harm they have done to you: *I'll get you for that, you swine!* **b** to catch or attack: *If they try to escape from the island, the crocodiles will get them.* **c** to hit or wound: *I got the minister on the ear with a potato.* | *Where did the bullet get you?* **19** [T *no pass.*] *infml* to defeat or confuse (someone): *"What's the square root of three?" "I don't know; you've got me there."* ■ fixed phrases **20 get you/him/her, etc.** *sl* (used as an expression of disapproval) look at or listen to you/him/her, etc.: *Get her! Who does she think she is, trying to give us orders like that?* **21 have got** to have: *I've got a dog called Fido.* | *Have you got the time, please?* **22 you get** *infml* there is/are: *In winter you get strong winds here.* —see also **get one's own back** (OWN¹) ■ phrasal verbs
get about/around *phr v* [I] **1** to move or travel from place to place: *He's getting old and he doesn't get about much any more.* | *She gets about quite a lot, working for an international company.* **2** also **get round** *BrE—* (of news, etc.) to spread; CIRCULATE: *The news of their secret wedding soon got about.*
get across *phr v* [I;T (=get sthg. ↔ across) (to)] to (cause) to be understood or accepted, esp. by a large group: *Our teacher is clever, but not very good at getting his ideas across (to us).* | *The message got across at last.*
get along *phr v* [I] **1** (of a person) to continue, often in spite of difficulties; manage: *He didn't even offer to help us, but I'm sure we can get along quite well without him.* **2** to advance; GET on: *How's the work getting along?* **3** [(with)] to form or have a friendly relationship; GET on: *Do you get along well with your aunt?* **4** (of a person) to leave: *I must be getting along now; it's late.* **5 Get along with you!** *infml* I don't believe you! **b** *BrE* **b** *AmE* leave now!
get around *phr v* **1** [I] to GET **about** **2** [T] (**get around** sthg.) also **get round—** to avoid or find a way to deal with (something) to one's advantage; CIRCUMVENT: *If you're clever, you can sometimes get around the tax laws.*
get around/round to sthg. *phr v* [T] to find time for; do at last: *I've been meaning to see that film for ages, and I finally got around to it last week.* [+v-ing] *After a long delay, he got around to writing the letter.*
get at sbdy./sthg. *phr v* [T] **1** to reach or find: *Put the food where the cat can't get at it.* | *Let's hope this public enquiry can get at the truth.* | *I'm dying to get at that fudge cake.* **2** [*no pass.*; *in progressive forms*] to suggest indirectly; IMPLY: *I'll soon get into the way of doing things. I get what I might be better suited to a different job?* | *I don't see what you're getting at.* (=I don't understand your meaning) **3** [*often pass.*] *infml, esp. BrE* to (try to) influence unfairly by offers of money: *Some of the jurors had been got at.* **4** *BrE* [*usu. in progressive forms*] *infml* to say unkind things to, esp. repeatedly: *Stop getting at me!*
get away *phr v* [I] **1** to succeed in leaving: *I'm sorry I'm late; I was in a meeting and couldn't get away.* **2** to escape, esp. from the scene of a crime or from being caught: *The thieves got away (with all our money).* | *I caught a really big fish but it got away.* —see also GETAWAY **3 one can't get away from** also **there's no getting away from—** one has to admit the truth of (something, esp. something unpleasant): *You can't get away from the fact that it would cost a lot of money.*
get away with sthg. *phr v* [T] **1** to do (something wrong) without being caught or punished: *Don't try to deceive the taxman; you'll never get away with it.* [+v-ing] *How did he get away with cheating?* **2 get away with murder** *infml* to escape punishment for something wrong that you have done: *His mother's much too soft; she lets him get away with murder.*
get back *phr v* **1** [I] to return, esp. to one's home: *It's late; we must be getting back.* | *I heard you were away. When did you get back?* | *I wish you would* **get back to basics** (=return to important matters) *and stop all this talk about winning the lottery.* **2** [I (IN)] to return to political power after having lost it: *Will the Labour Party*

get back in at the next election? **3** [I (FROM)] stand away from: *Get back! There's a train coming.* | *Please get back from the road.* **4** [T] (**get** sthg. ↔ **back**) to obtain again after loss or separation: *He got his old job back.*
get back at sbdy. *phr v* [T] *infml* to punish (someone) in return for a wrong done to oneself: *I'll get back at him one day!*
get back to sbdy. *phr v* [T] to speak or write to again later: *I can't give you a definite answer now, but I'll get back to you about it.*
get behind *phr v* [I (with)] to fail to produce something at the proper time: *They've got behind with their rent again.*
get by *phr v* [I] **1** to have enough money for one's needs or way of life: *We can't get by on my salary alone.* **2** to be good enough but not very good; be acceptable: *Your work will get by, but try to improve it.*
get down *phr v* **1** [I] *AmE infml* to enjoy oneself, esp. at a party or with others: *We're really going to get down on Saturday night.* **2** [T] (**get** sthg. ↔ **down**) to swallow, esp. with difficulty: *Try to get the medicine down.* **3** [T] (**get** sthg. ↔ **down**) to record in writing: *Get down every word she says.* **4** [T] (**get** sbdy. **down**) to cause to feel nervous, ill, or sad; DEPRESS: *This continual wet weather is getting me down.* **5** [I] (of a child) to leave the table after a meal: *Please may I get down?*
get down to sthg. *phr v* [T] to begin to give serious attention to: *It's hard to get down to work after a nice holiday.* [+v-ing] *I really must get down to filling in my tax form.* —see also **get down to brass tacks** (BRASS)
get in *phr v* **1** [I] to arrive: *The plane got in late.* | *We didn't get in* (=home) *until 3 o'clock in the morning.* **2** [I] to be elected to a position of political power: *She's running for Congress but I doubt if she'll get in.* **3** [T] (**get** sthg. ↔ **in**) to collect or buy a supply of: *The farmers are getting the crops in.* | *We'd better get in some more coal before the price goes up.* **4** [T] (**get** sbdy. ↔ **in**) to call to one's help, esp. in the house: *We'll have to get the plumber in.* **5** [T] (**get** sthg. ↔ **in**) to deliver to the proper place: *Can you get your essay in by next week?* **6** [I (**at**, **on**)] to take part in an activity: *It sounds like a very profitable enterprise; I'd like to get in on it.* **7** [I;T (=**get** sbdy. **in**)] to (cause) to be admitted to a place of education or a class, esp. after an examination or test: *He applied to do medicine at university but he didn't get in.* | *I couldn't get my best pupil in.* **8** [T] (**get** sthg. ↔ **in**) *BrE infml* to buy (a set of drinks for all the people one is with) in a bar
get into *phr v* [T *no pass.*] **1** (**get into** sbdy.) to influence or take control of (someone) so as to make them act strangely: *I don't know what's got into him; she's been behaving very oddly.* **2** (sbdy.) **into** sthg.) to put (oneself or someone else) into (a bad condition): *Don't get into a temper.* | *I'm sorry if I got you into trouble.* | *She got herself into a real state* (=became very anxious) *about her driving test.* **3** (**get into** sthg.) **a** to learn or become used to: *I'll soon get into the way of doing things.* **b** *I get into bad habits* **b** to develop a strong interest in: *I'm really getting into fitness since I joined the health club*
get off *phr v* **1** [I] to start a journey; leave: *I'd better be getting off now.* | *We have to get off early tomorrow.* **2** [I] *AmE infml* to have an ORGASM **3** [T] (**get** sthg. **off**) to send: *I'd like to get this letter off by the first post.* **4** [I;T (=**get** sbdy. ↔ **off** (sthg.)) to (cause to) escape punishment (for): *The man went to prison but the two boys got off (with a warning).* | *You'll need a good lawyer to get you off (that charge).* **5** [I;T (=**get** sbdy. **off**)] to (cause to) be able to fall asleep: *I'll come downstairs as soon as I've got the baby off (to sleep).* **6** [I;T (=**get off** sthg.) *no pass.*] to leave (work) with permission: *"What time do you get off work?" "I get off at 6 o'clock." | I got off early today.* **7 tell someone where they (can) get off/where to get off** *infml* to tell someone how to behave, or esp. tell someone not to misbehave: *They tried to stop me going in, but I soon told them where they could get off – I've been a member of that club for years, you know.*
get off on sthg. *phr v* [T] *sl* to be excited by; enjoy: *I really get off on that music.*
get off to sthg. *phr v* [T *no pass.*] to make or have (a start of the stated type): *His performance got off to a bad start when he couldn't remember his first words.*
get off with sbdy. *phr v* [T] *infml, esp. BrE* to start a (sexual) relationship with: *She got off with him soon after the party started.*
get on *phr v* **1** [I] *esp. BrE* ‖ **get along** *AmE* (of a

person or activity) to advance or develop, esp. in the stated way: *You'll have to pass your exams if you want to get on.| How is your work getting on? | Young Johnny isn't getting on very well at school.* **2** [I; *in progressive forms*] **a** (of time) to become late: *Time is getting on.* **b** (of a person) to become old: *Now grandfather's getting on a bit he doesn't go out so much.* **3** [I (**with**)] to continue, often after interruption: *I must be getting on. | Get on with your work!* **4** [I] to manage; GET **along**: *How will we get on without you?* **5** [I (**with**, TOGETHER)] *esp. BrE* ‖ **get along** *AmE* to form or have a friendly relationship: *Do you get on well with your boss? | My brother and I have never really got on (together).* **6 get it on** *AmE sl* to have sex: *"Let's get it on."* **7 get on with it** *infml* hurry up: *Get on with it! We've got a train to catch.* **8 Get on with you!** *BrE infml* I don't believe you!

get on for sthg. *phr v* [L+*n*; *in progressive forms*] *esp. BrE* to be almost reaching, in time, age, number, or distance; be nearly: *Grandfather is getting on for 80. | There were getting on for two thousand people there.*

get onto sbdy./sthg. *phr v* [T *no pass.*] **1** to speak or write to; CONTACT: *I'll see the director and see if he can help.* **2** to find out about deceit by (someone): *He was cheating his customers for years until the police got onto him.* **3** to be elected or appointed to: *My neighbour got onto the City Council.* **4** to begin to talk about or work at: *How did we get onto that subject?*

get out *phr v* **1** [I; T (=**get** sbdy. **out**)] to (cause to) escape: *One of the lions has got out (of the zoo). | The lawyer got his client out (=of police care) on bail.* **2** [I] (esp. of secret information) to become known; LEAK out: *I don't know how the news got out.* **3** [T] (**get** sthg. ↔ **out**) to produce or PUBLISH: *We hope to get the report out very soon.* **4** [T] (**get** sthg. ↔ **out**) to speak with difficulty: *He managed to get out a few words.*

get out of *phr v* [T] **1** (**get** (sbdy.) **out of** sthg.) to (cause to) avoid (a responsibility or duty): *I'll see if I can get you out of tonight's homework.* [+*v*-*ing*] *He tried to get out of helping me.* **2** (**get** sthg. **out of** sbdy.) to force or persuade (someone) to tell, give, pay, etc.: *The police finally got the truth out of her.* **3** (**get** sthg. **out of** sthg.) to gain from: *I can't understand why people smoke; what do they get out of it? | He seems to* **get a kick out of** (=to enjoy) *being nasty to her.*

get over *phr v* [T] **1** (**get over** sthg./sbdy.) to return to one's usual state of health, happiness, etc., after (a bad experience or a (sexual) relationship with a person): *He's just getting over an illness. | Sooner or later you'll get over the shock. | Her affair with Dick ended months ago, but she hasn't really got over him yet.* **2** [(WITH)] (**get** sthg. **over**) to do and reach the end of (usu. something necessary but unpleasant): *You'll be glad to get your operation over (with).* **3** [(to)] (**get** sthg. ↔ **over**) to make clear; cause to be understood; GET **across**: *I don't think you got it over to them that they can't miss any meetings.* **4** (**get over** sthg.) to find a way to deal with: *How shall we get over this difficulty?* **5 I can't/couldn't get over** *infml* I am/was very surprised, amused, etc., by: *I couldn't get over his beard/him growing a beard!*

get round *BrE* ‖ **get around** *AmE phr v* **1** [I] (of news, etc.) to spread; GET **about**: *The story soon got round.* **2** [T] (**get round** sthg.) to avoid: *They got round the immediate problem by borrowing a lot of money.* **3** [T] (**get round** sbdy.) to persuade (someone) to accept one's own way of thinking: *Father doesn't want to let us go, but I know I can get round him.*

get round to sthg. *phr v* [T] to GET **around to**

get through *phr v* **1** [I; T (=**get** sbdy./sthg. **through** (sthg.))] to (cause or help to) pass, pass through, or come successfully to the end of: *We were all delighted when we heard you'd got through (your exam). | Her mother's support got her through her depression. | The government managed to get the new law through (parliament) despite strong opposition.* **2** [T] (**get through** sthg.) to complete or use up the whole of; finish: *We got through a whole chicken at one sitting! | They won a million dollars, but they got through the whole lot in less than five years.* **3** [I (**with**)] *esp. AmE* to finish: *When you get through (with your work), let's go out.* **4** [I (**to**)] to reach someone, esp. by telephone: *I tried to telephone you but I couldn't get through. | I can't get through to Paris.* **5** [I; T (=**get** sthg. **through**) (**to**)] to (cause to) be understood by someone: *When he's in this strange mood I just can't get through to him.* [+*that*] *Her father has been trying to get it through*

to her that she must work harder if she wants to pass the exam.

get together *phr v* **1** [I (**with**)] to have a meeting or party: *When can we get together for a drink?* —see also GET-TOGETHER **2 get it together** *AmE infml* to be in control of (a particular job, situation, or one's life) and be doing everything reasonably well: *"Come on, Mark, get it together—we leave in half an hour". | I don't know what's wrong with me these days; I just can't seem to get it together.*

get up *phr v* **1** [I;T (=**get** sbdy. **up**)] to (cause to) rise from bed in the morning: *What time do you normally get up? | I'm sorry to phone so early; did I get you up? | I woke up at six, but I didn't get up till an hour later.* **2** [I] to rise to one's feet; stand up: *Everyone got up when the judge came in.* **3** [I] *BrE* (of a wind, fire, etc.) to start and increase **4** [T] (**get** sthg. ↔ **up**) to arrange or bring together; ORGANIZE: *I'm getting up a little group to visit the theatre; would you like to come along?* **5** [T (**as**)] (**get** sbdy. **up**) *BrE* ‖ (**do** sbdy. **up**) *AmE* to decorate or change the appearance of in the stated way: *She got herself up as a Roman soldier for the school play.* —see also GETUP **6** [T] (**get** sthg. ↔ **up**) *BrE old-fash* to study or gain knowledge of **7 get up speed/steam** to increase the amount of speed or steam (in an engine) **8 get it up** *AmE sl taboo* to have an ERECTION (3)

get up to sthg. *phr v* [T *no pass.*] *infml* to do (esp. something bad): *The children are very quiet; I wonder what they're getting up to.*

get·a·way /ˈgetəweɪ/ *n* [S] *infml* an escape made after a crime: *The burglar made his getaway across the roof. | As the thieves ran out of the bank the* **getaway car** *was waiting with its engine running.* —compare DRIVEAWAY CAR —see also GET **away** (2)

Geth·sem·a·ne /geθˈseməni/ a garden where Jesus went with his followers, and where he was betrayed (BETRAY) by one of them, Judas, and taken prisoner by the Romans

get-to·geth·er /ˈ· ·ˌ···/ *n* a friendly informal meeting for enjoyment: *When you're next in town we must have a little get-together.* —see also GET **together**

Get·ty /ˈgeti/, **J. Paul** (1892–1976) an American businessman and owner of an oil company who became very rich and set up the Getty Museum in California where he kept his very valuable art collection

Get·tys·burg Ad·dress /ˌgetɪzbɜːg əˈdres‖-bɜːrg-/ [*the*] a famous speech made by Abraham Lincoln in 1863 in the town of Gettysburg, Pennsylvania. He expressed his grief for the soldiers killed in the American Civil War, and talked about the principles that they died for, in words that are often remembered by Americans: *Four score and seven years ago, our fathers brought forth on this continent a new nation, conceived in liberty and dedicated to the proposition that all men are created equal...... We here highly resolve that these dead shall not have died in vain; that this nation, under God, shall have a new birth of freedom; and that government of the people, by the people, and for the people shall not perish from the earth.*

get·up /ˈgetʌp/ *n infml* a set of clothes, esp. unusual clothes: *She looks ridiculous in that getup.* —see also GET **up** (5)

get-up-and-go /ˌ·· · · ˈ·/ *n* [U] *infml apprec* a forceful active quality of mind; determined desire to get things done

gey·ser /ˈgiːzəʳ‖ˈgaɪ-/ *n* **1** a natural spring of hot water which from time to time rises suddenly into the air from the earth **2** *BrE* an apparatus which is used in kitchens, bathrooms, etc., for heating water by gas

Gha·na /ˈgɑːnə/ a country in W Africa, formerly British and known as the **Gold Coast** and now part of the British Commonwealth; capital Accra; population 14,566,000 (1989) **Ghanaian** /gɑːˈneɪən/ *adj, n*

ghast·ly /ˈgɑːstli‖ˈgæstli/ *adj* **1** *infml* extremely bad or unpleasant; terrible: *We had a ghastly holiday; it rained all the time. | a ghastly mistake* **2** causing very great fear or dislike: *a ghastly crime* **3** [F] (of a person) very pale and ill-looking: *You look ghastly; what's wrong with you?* —**liness** *n* [U]

ghat , ghaut /gɔːt/ *n IndE & PakE* **1** a narrow way between mountains; PASS **2** [*usu. pl.*] a mountain **3** a set of steps, as from a house or temple, leading down to a river or lake **4** a place where dead bodies are ceremonially burnt

ghee , ghi /giː/ n [U] *IndE & PakE* melted butter made from cow's or BUFFALO's milk, used in Indian cooking

gher·kin /ˈɡɜːkɪn‖ˈɡɜːr-/ n a small green vegetable (a type of CUCUMBER) which is usually eaten after being kept in VINEGAR

ghet·to /ˈɡetəʊ/ n -tos or -toes 1 a part of a city in which a group of people live who are poor and/or are not accepted as full citizens —compare SLUM 2 a part of a city where people mostly of one race, class or group live: *a gay/Hispanic ghetto*

ghetto blaster

ghetto blast·er /ˈ·· ˌ··/ also **boom box** AmE— n sl, often derog a large TAPE RECORDER that can be carried around, and is often played very loudly in public places

ghost

ghost¹ /ɡəʊst/ n 1 (the spirit of) a dead person who appears again: *Do you believe in ghosts?* | *He looked so terrified I thought he'd seen a ghost.*

▶CULTURAL NOTE There are two main STEREOTYPES of ghosts. The first is of a faint, shapeless figure with empty, round eyes which frightens people by making a strange wailing (WAIL) sound. It floats through the air and can go through walls and closed doors. Children often wear a white sheet over their head to dress up as this kind of ghost. The second STEREOTYPE is of a young man or woman in Elizabethan clothes. They have had their head cut off and carry it around under their arm. They may have chains round their arms or legs, which make a clanking (CLANK) sound as they walk.◀

2 also **ghost·writ·er** /ˈɡəʊstˌraɪtəʳ/— someone who writes a book, article, etc., for someone else, who then often pretends it is their own work 3 a second, fainter image, esp. on a television picture 4 **give up the ghost** infml to die: (fig.) *My old car's finally given up the ghost.* 5 **the ghost of a** infml the slightest: *You haven't got the ghost of a chance of getting the job.* 6 **the ghost of Christmas past** quote a character in Charles Dickens' *A Christmas Carol* who comes to show Scrooge scenes from his past. The phrase is sometimes changed and used in other writing now: *the ghost of companies past*

ghost² v [T] also **ghost·write** /ˈɡəʊst-raɪt/— to write (something) as a GHOST¹ (2): *A journalist ghosted the general's memoirs.*

Ghost·bust·ers /ˈɡəʊstbʌstəz‖-ərz/ either of two popular films of the 1980s about an imaginary firm in New York which tries to rid buildings of ghosts

ghost·ly /ˈɡəʊstli/ adj like a ghost, esp. in having a faint or uncertain colour and shape: *I saw a ghostly light ahead of me in the darkness.* —**liness** n [U]

ghost town /ˈ· ·/ n an empty town, esp. one that was once

busy because people came to find gold or other precious substances, and left when there was no more to be found

ghoul /ɡuːl/ n 1 a spirit which, in the stories told in some Eastern countries, takes bodies from graves to eat them 2 a person who delights in (thoughts of) dead bodies and other unpleasant things — ~ **ish** adj : *Some people take a ghoulish delight in visiting the scenes of road accidents.* — ~ **ishness** n [U]

GHQ /ˌdʒiː eɪtʃ ˈkjuː/ abbrev. for: General Headquarters; the place from which a large esp. military operation is controlled

ghyll /ɡɪl/ n NW EngE for GORGE (1)

GI /ˌdʒiː ˈaɪ◀/ n GI's or GIs a soldier in the American army, esp. during the Second World War

▶CULTURAL NOTE In Britain in the Second World War GIs were seen as attractive and exciting by people, esp. women, partly because they could provide things which were not easily available in Britain at that time, such as certain types of clothes and food, and many men did not like their presence for that reason. Some women married American soldiers and went to live in the US, becoming known as **GI brides**. —see also GI BILL, GI JOE◀

gi·ant¹ /ˈdʒaɪənt/ n 1 **gi·ant·ess** /-tes/fem.— (in children's stories) a creature in the form of an extremely tall strong man, esp. one who is cruel to humans 2 a man who is much bigger than is usual 3 a person of great ability: *Shakespeare is a giant among writers.* | *sporting giants of the past* —see also RED GIANT 4 a very large company: *Honda is a giant in the international market.*

giant² adj [A] extremely large: *The giant (size) packet gives you more for less money!* | *a giant US electronics corporation*

giant kil·ler /ˈ·· ˌ··/ n esp. BrE a person, sports team, etc., that defeats a much stronger opponent —see also JACK AND THE BEANSTALK

giant pan·da /ˌ·· ˈ··/ also **panda**— n a large bear-like animal from China that has black and white fur

Giant's Cause·way /ˌ·· ˈ··/ [the] a number of unusually shaped rocks on the coast of Northern Ireland, formed by a flow of LAVA into the sea. A story says that it was once used as a bridge for giants crossing between Ireland and Scotland.

gib·ber /ˈdʒɪbəʳ/ BrE ‖ **jabber** AmE— v [I] to talk very fast, esp. because of fear or shock, in a way that is meaningless for the hearer: *What on earth are you gibbering about? Pull yourself together and speak calmly!* | *a gibbering idiot*

gib·ber·ish /ˈdʒɪbərɪʃ/ n [U] sounds, talk, or writing that is meaningless or hard to understand: *This essay is pure gibberish; you'll get no marks for it at all.*

gib·bet /ˈdʒɪbɪt/ n a wooden post with another piece at right angles at the top, from which in former times criminals were hanged by the neck until dead

gib·bon /ˈɡɪbən/ n an animal like a monkey with no tail and long arms, which lives in trees in Asia and is the smallest APE

gib·bous /ˈɡɪbəs/ adj tech (of the moon) having the bright part filling more than half a circle

gibe , jibe /dʒaɪb/ n [(about, at)] a remark which makes someone look foolish, or points out someone's faults: *She finished her speech with a gibe at the prime minister.* — **gibe at** phr v [T]

GI Bill /ˌdʒiː ˈaɪ ˌbɪl/ [the] a law passed in the US in 1944 which is still effective. It provides for education and other BENEFITS for people who have served in the armed forces: *go to college on the GI Bill*

gib·lets /ˈdʒɪblɪts/ n [P] the parts of a bird, such as the heart and LIVER, which are taken out before the bird is cooked, but may themselves be cooked and eaten

Gi·bral·tar /dʒɪˈbrɔːltəʳ/ a town and port on the **Rock of Gibraltar** on the S coast of Spain. It is a British possession which formerly belonged to Spain, and is the subject of disagreement between Britain and Spain because both countries think that it should belong to them.

▶CULTURAL NOTE Many tourists visit Gibraltar, and one attraction is the group of monkeys which live there, known as Barbary APES. A famous story says that when they leave the Rock, the British will also leave.◀

—**tarian** /ˌdʒɪbrɔːlˈteəriən/ n, adj

Gib·son /'gɪbsən/, **Mel** /mel/ (1956–) an Australian actor whose films include *The Year of Living Dangerously* and *Hamlet*

gid·dy /'gɪdi/ *adj* **1** feeling unsteady, usu. in an unpleasant way, as though everything is moving round oneself and/or as though one is falling; DIZZY: *The children enjoyed twirling round and round, but I felt giddy just watching them.* **2** [A] causing a feeling of unsteady movement and/or falling: *We looked down from a giddy height.* **3** *infml, BrE old-fash or AmE* not serious; too interested in amusement; FRIVOLOUS —**dily** *adv* : *He reeled giddily across the room.* —**diness** *n* [U] : *a sudden attack of giddiness*
    giddy up /ˌ·· ·/ (used as a command to a horse) Go faster!

Gid·e·on Bi·ble /ˌgɪdiən 'baɪbəl/ *n* a (copy of a) Bible placed in a hotel room or somewhere similar, by a member of the **Gideons**, a Christian organization, in the hope that people will read it

Giel·gud /'giːlgʊd/, **Sir John** (1904–) an English actor and director who has played many parts from Shakespeare's plays, as well as making film appearances, e.g. in *Arthur* in 1981 when he won an Oscar

gift /gɪft/ *n* **1** something which is given willingly; a present: *Christmas gifts | My grandmother made me a gift of her silver cutlery. | With each packet of soap powder you get a free gift of a plastic flower. | a gift shop* (=that sells things suitable to be given as presents) | *That legacy of £5000 was a gift from the Gods.* (=something very desirable got by lucky chance) | (fig.) *The last question in my exam paper was a gift.* (=very easy) —see also GOD'S GIFT **2** [(for)] a natural ability to do something; TALENT: *She has a gift for music|for learning languages. | Her tactfulness is a remarkable gift.* —see also GIFTED **3** [*usu. sing.*] *BrE infml* something obtained easily or cheaply: *At £2 it's a gift!* **4 gift of the gab** *infml* the ability to speak well continuously, and esp. to persuade people **5 in someone's gift** *BrE fml* in someone's power to give, to whoever they want: *The chairmanship of this committee is in the gift of the minister|in the minister's gift.*

gift cer·tif·i·cate /ˌ· ·,···/ *n AmE for* GIFT TOKEN

gift·ed /'gɪftᵻd/ *adj* having one or more special abilities; TALENTED: *a very gifted musician*

gifted child /ˌ·· '·/ *n* a child that is generally very clever or clever in one particular subject: *a school for gifted children*

gift horse /'· ·/ *n* **Don't/Never look a gift horse in the mouth** *infml* Be grateful for something that is given to you, without asking questions about it or finding fault with it

gift to·ken /'· ˌ··/ also **gift voucher** *BrE* ‖ **gift certificate** *AmE* — *n* a gift card for a certain value that can be exchanged for an article in a shop: *My aunt gave me a £10 gift token for Christmas.*

gift-wrap /'· ·/ *v* **-pp-** [T] to wrap (esp. something intended as a present) to make it look attractive: *Some shops provide a gift-wrapping service.*

gig[1] /gɪg/ *n infml* **1** a performance by a musician or group of musicians playing modern popular music or JAZZ, e.g. at a concert or club: *The band played a final gig in Amsterdam before splitting up. | a fantastic gig* **2** an arrangement for such a performance; BOOKING —**gig** *v* **-gg-** [I]

gig[2] /gɪg/ *n* a small two-wheeled carriage pulled by one horse and used esp. in former times

gig·a·byte /'gɪgəbaɪt/ *n tech* one BILLION BYTES: *new machines with 3 gigabytes of memory*

gi·gan·tic /dʒaɪ'gæntɪk/ *adj* extremely large in amount or size: *a gigantic building | The company has made gigantic losses this year, and will probably go out of business.* —**~ally** /kli/ *adv*

gig·gle[1] /'gɪgəl/ *v* [I] to laugh quietly in a silly childish uncontrolled way; often in a way which suggests that one is laughing about someone or something secret, which one finds amusing: *Stop giggling, girls; this is a serious matter. | a fit of hysterical giggling* —see LAUGH (USAGE)

giggle[2] *n* **1** [C] an act of giggling: *George has got the giggles again.* (=has a fit of giggling) **2** [S] *infml, esp. BrE* something that amuses; PRANK: *Wouldn't it be a giggle*

to tie his shoelaces together while he isn't looking! | They only did it for a giggle.

gig·o·lo /'ʒɪgələʊ, 'dʒɪ-/ *n* **-los** a man who is paid to be a woman's lover and companion

GI Joe /ˌdʒiː aɪ 'dʒəʊ/ *n* **1** *infml* an American soldier, esp. one in the Second World War **2** a DOLL (=child's toy in the shape of a person) that looks like a soldier, popular with American children

Gil·bert and Sul·li·van /ˌgɪlbət ənd 'sʌlᵻvən‖-bərt-/ two men, Sir William Gilbert and Sir Arthur Sullivan, who worked together during the second half of the 19th century on many OPERETTAS such as *HMS Pinafore, The Pirates of Penzance,* and *The Mikado*

gild /gɪld/ *v* [T] **1** to cover with a thin coat of gold or gold paint (GILT): *a gilded statue | (fig.) Sunshine gilded the rooftops.* **2** to give an attractive appearance to, often in a way intended to deceive **3 gild the lily** to try to improve something that is already good enough, so spoiling the effect

gill[1] /gɪl/ *n* **1** an organ through which a fish breathes **2 green/white about the gills** *infml or humor* having a pale sick-looking face as a result of fear, illness, etc.

gill[2] /dʒɪl/ *n* a measure of liquid

Gil·les·pie /gᵻ'lespi/, **Dizzy** (1917–93) an American JAZZ TRUMPET player who invented and played the style of BEBOP with Charlie Parker

Gil·lette /dʒɪ'let/ *n tdmk* a company which makes several different types of RAZOR and other equipment for shaving (SHAVE (1)) such as SHAVING FOAM

gil·lie, **gilly** /'gɪli/ *n* (in Scotland) a man who acts as a guide and helper to someone who is shooting or fishing for sport

Gil·more /'gɪlmɔːr/, **Gar·y** /'gæri/ (1940–1977) an American criminal remembered for demanding that his death sentence be carried out. He was shot by a FIRING SQUAD.

gilt[1] /gɪlt/ *n* **1** [U] shiny material, esp. gold, used as a thin covering: *silver gilt | The plates have a gilt edge.* **2** [C] *tech* a GILT-EDGED SHARE[1] (2) **3 take the gilt off the gingerbread** *BrE infml* to take away the part that makes the whole attractive

gilt[2] *n esp. AmE* a young female pig

gilt-edged /ˌ· '·◂/ *adj* (of STOCKS[1] (3) and SHARES[1] (2), esp. those sold by the government) paying a small rate of interest but unlikely to fail, and therefore considered safe

gim·let /'gɪmlᵻt/ *n* a tool which is used to make holes in wood so that screws may enter easily: (fig.) *He has eyes like gimlets.* (=which look very hard and searchingly)

gim·me /'gɪmi/ *nonstandard* give me: *Gimme some bread, mister!*

gim·mick /'gɪmɪk/ *n infml, often derog* a trick or object which is used only to attract people's attention, esp. in an attempt to sell something: *The pretty girl on the cover of the book is just a sales gimmick.* —**~y** *adj* : *Having bingo games in newspapers is just a gimmicky idea that won't last long.*

gin[1] /dʒɪn/ *n* [C;U] (a glass of) a colourless strong alcoholic drink made from grain and certain berries —see also PINK GIN, GIN AND TONIC

gin[2] also **gin trap** /'· ·/— *n* a trap for catching small animals or birds —see also COTTON GIN

gin[3] *n infml for* GIN RUMMY

gin and ton·ic /ˌ· · '··/ also G & T— *n* [C;U] a popular alcoholic drink served with ice and a SLICE of LEMON, thought of as a typical middle-class drink

gin·ger[1] /'dʒɪndʒər/ *n* [U] **1** (a plant with) a root with a very hot strong taste, which is used in cooking or covered with sugar and eaten as a sweet, etc.: *ground ginger | preserved ginger | crystallized ginger* **2** an orange-brown colour: *She has bright ginger hair.* **3** *infml* an active cheerful quality

ginger[2] *v*
    ginger sthg. ↔ **up** *phr v* [T] to make more effective, exciting, or active: *We need some new young recruits to ginger up the company.*

ginger ale /ˌ··· '·‖'··· ·/ *n* [C;U] (a glass of) a gassy non-alcoholic drink made with ginger and often mixed with other drinks

ginger beer /ˌ··· '·‖'··· ·/ *n* [C;U] (a glass of) a gassy non-alcoholic drink with a strong taste, made with ginger

gin·ger·bread /ˈdʒɪndʒəbred‖ -dʒər-/ n [U] a cake or BISCUIT with ginger in it: *She baked some gingerbread men.* (=biscuits in the shape of people)

gingerbread man

Gingerbread a British organization which provides support and practical help for single parents and their children

ginger group /ˈ·· ·/ n [C+*sing.|pl. v*] *BrE* a group of people, usu. within a political party, who try to urge the leaders of the party to take stronger action on a particular matter

gin·ger·ly /ˈdʒɪndʒəli‖-ər-/ *adv, adj* (in a way that is) careful and controlled in movement so as not to cause harm: *I reached out gingerly to touch the snake.* | *She sat down in a rather gingerly fashion on the rickety old chair.*

ginger nut /ˈ·· ·/ *esp. BrE*‖**gin·ger·snap** /ˈdʒɪndʒəsnæp‖ -ər-/ *esp. AmE*— n a hard BISCUIT with ginger in it

ging·ham /ˈgɪŋəm/ n [U] cotton which is usu. woven with a pattern of squares and used for making clothes, tablecloths, etc. In Britain it is often used for making summer dresses for girls to wear to school.

gin·gi·vi·tis /ˌdʒɪndʒ‍ᵻˈvaɪt‍‍ᵻs/ n [U] a medical condition in which the GUMS (=flesh out of which the teeth grow) are red, swollen, and painful

gi·nor·mous /dʒaɪˈnɔːməs‖-ɔːr-/ *adj BrE infml* very large

gin rum·my /ˌ·ˈ·‍·/ also **gin** *infml, esp. AmE*— n a simple card game for two people; form of RUMMY

Gins·berg /ˈgɪnzbɜːg‖-bɜːrg/, **Allen** (1926–   ) an American poet, leader of the BEAT GENERATION, who criticized American society for its MATERIALISM in the 1950s and 1960s. He travelled in Asia and was influenced by Buddhism.

gin·seng /ˈdʒɪnseŋ‖-sæŋ, -seŋ/ n [U] (a medicine made from the root of) a Chinese plant used originally in China and Korea, and now very popular in the West, being taken by people who believe that it keeps them young and healthy —compare ROYAL JELLY

gin sling /ˌ·ˈ·‍·/ n a drink made from GIN[1] mixed with water, sugar, and sometimes other things e.g. LEMON juice

gin trap /ˈ· ·/ n a GIN[2]

Giot·to /ˈdʒɒtəʊ‖ˈdʒɑː-/ (1266–1337) an Italian painter (**Giotto di Bandone**) and ARCHITECT. He was one of the most important 13th and 14th century painters, esp. of religious subjects.

gip·py tum·my /ˌdʒɪpi ˈtʌmi/ n [S;U] *infml, esp. BrE* a condition in which one has stomach pains and often needs to pass waste matter from the body, caused esp. by eating food that is bad or which one is not used to

gip·sy , gypsy /ˈdʒɪpsi/ n (*often cap.*) a member of a dark-haired race which may be of Indian origin. They often live and travel about in covered carts (CARAVANS), earning money as horse traders, musicians, basket makers, FORTUNE-TELLERS, etc. —compare NEW AGE TRAVELLER

► CULTURAL NOTE Gipsies are often treated with disapproval, lack of trust, and lack of understanding because their way of life is so different to the way most other British people live. Gipsies live in most European countries. There are very few gipsies in the US, and there the word refers to anyone who has a wandering way of life. ◄

Gipsy Moth IV /ˌdʒɪpsi ˌmɒθ ðə ˈfɔːθ ‖ -ˌmɔːθ ðə ˈfɔːrθ-/ the YACHT (=boat) in which Sir Francis Chichester sailed alone round the world in 1966–67

gi·raffe /dʒ‍ᵻˈrɑːf‖-ˈræf/ n -**raffes** or -**raffe** an extremely tall African animal with a very long neck and legs and pale brown fur with dark spots, which eats the leaves from the branches of trees

gird /gɜːd‖gɜːrd/ v **girded** or **girt** /gɜːt‖gɜːrt/ [T] **1** *lit* to fasten (something) round or to (something or someone): *The knight girded on his sword.* **2 gird (up) one's loins** *bibl, pomp, or humor* to get ready for action

gir·der /ˈgɜːdə‍ʳ‖ˈgɜːrr/ n a strong beam, usu. of iron or steel, which supports a floor, roof, or bridge

gir·dle[1] /ˈgɜːdl‖ˈgɜːr-/ n **1** a firm article of underwear for

women, worn round the waist and HIPS, that supports and shapes the stomach, hips, and bottom **2** *esp. lit* something which surrounds something else: *A girdle of islands enclosed the lagoon.*

girdle[2] v [T] *esp. lit* to go all the way round: *Our airline's routes girdle the world.*

girl /gɜːl‖gɜːrl/ n **1** a young female person: *There are more girls than boys in this school.* | *a girl acrobat* —see CHILD (USAGE) **2** a daughter, esp. young: *My little girl is ill.* | *Their eldest girl is getting married on Saturday.* **3** *infml* a woman: *The men have invited the girls to play football against them.* **4 a** (*often in comb.*) a woman worker: *the office girls* | *shop girls* **b** (esp. formerly) a female servant: *a girl who looks after the children* **5** *infml old-fash* a girlfriend: *John's girl* **6 a girl in every port** a phrase used about sailors, who are often mentioned in jokes as having a different girl waiting for them at each of the ports they visit **7 there was a little girl and she had a little curl** the first line of a NURSERY RHYME (=an old song or poem for children):

> *There was a little girl, and she had a little curl*
> *Right in the middle of her forehead;*
> *And when she was good she was very, very good,*
> *And when she was bad she was horrid!*

8 what are little girls made of? a line from a NURSERY RHYME (=an old song or poem for children). The answer is "sugar and spice and all things nice". —see also **what are little boys made of?** (BOY[1] (8)) **9 What's a nice girl like you doing in a place like this?** a phrase which people believe is often used by a man as a way of introducing himself to a woman whom he is interested in her sexually, now often used humorously

▷ USAGE Some people, esp. women, feel that it is offensive to call a woman a **girl** after she has become an adult, particularly in a situation where men are not called boys, e.g. at (3) above◁

girl Fri·day /ˌ·ˈ·‍·/ n a female secretary or general helper in an office —compare MAN FRIDAY

girl·friend /ˈgɜːlfrend‖ˈgɜːrl-/ n **1** the regular female friend of a boy or man. The word is used esp. when talking about the relationships of young people. Older people prefer to use the word "partner" or "friend". **2** a female lover **3** *esp. AmE* a woman's female friend with whom she spends time and shares amusements: *She's always on the phone to her girlfriends.* —see WOMAN (USAGE); see also BOYFRIEND

girl guide /ˌ·ˈ·‍·/ n a member of the **Girl Guides Association** set up in 1910 to teach girls practical skills and develop their character

girl guides

a British   an American
girl guide   girl scout

girl·hood /ˈgɜːlhʊd‖ˈgɜːrl-/ n [C *usu. sing.*; U] the state or time of being a young girl — see also BOYHOOD, CHILDHOOD

girl·ie, girly /ˈgɜːli‖ˈgɜːrli/ *adj* [A] *infml* (esp. of a magazine or picture) showing young women with (almost) bare bodies, photographed in positions which are intended to be sexually exciting. As long as they are not considered to be PORNOGRAPHIC, girlie magazines can be sold openly in shops. Some people would like to change this, to make them less easily available. —compare PAGE THREE GIRL

girl·ish /ˈgɜːlɪʃ‖ˈgɜːr-/ *adj* of or like a girl: *sounds of girlish laughter* | *his girlish shyness* —~**ly** *adv* —~**ness** n [U]

girl scout /ˌ·ˈ·‍·/ n a member of the **Girl Scouts** organization set up in the US in 1912. It is similar to the Girl Guides Association.

gi·ro /ˈdʒaɪərəʊ/ n **1** [U] a system of banking used in Britain, run by a bank or post office, in which a central computer handles the accounts which are held at different branches, so that payments can be made directly from one person's account to that of another **2** [C] (in Britain) a cheque from the state to a person who is unemployed: *I haven't got any money, my giro hasn't come yet.*

Gi·ro·bank /ˈdʒaɪərəʊbæŋk/ a bank which one deals with by post, or by telephone, or through the POST OFFICE

girt /gɜːt‖gɜːrt/ *past tense & participle of* GIRD

girth /gɜːθ‖gɜːrθ/ *n* **1** [C;U] *esp. tech* the measure of thickness round something: *the girth of a tree* | *(humor) his rather ample girth* (said of a fat person) **2** [C] a band which is passed tightly round the middle of a horse, DONKEY, etc., to keep the load or SADDLE (=rider's seat) firmly on its back —see picture at HORSE

Gis·card d'Es·taing /ˌʒiːskɑː desˈtæŋ‖-kɑːr-/, **Val·é·ry** /ˈvæləri/ (1926–) a French politician who was president from 1974–81

Gish /gɪʃ/, **Lil·li·an** /ˈlɪliən/ (1893–1993) an American actress known for her roles in silent films

gis·mo , **gizmo** /ˈgɪzməʊ/ *n esp. AmE infml* a small piece of equipment intended for a particular purpose; GADGET

gist /dʒɪst/ *n* [*the* (**of**)] the main points or general meaning: *I haven't time to read this report; can you give me the gist of it?*

gite /ʒiːt/ *n Fr* a furnished house in a country area of France that people can book for a holiday. They are quite popular with British people because they are cheaper than hotels and more comfortable than camping. Gites are popular esp. with MIDDLE-CLASS people in Britain.

give¹ /gɪv/ *v* **gave** /geɪv/, **given** /ˈgɪvən/ ■ to cause or allow someone to have something **1** [T+*obj*(*i*)+*obj*(*d*)] to cause someone to have, hold, receive, or own: *Give me the tickets.* [+*obj*(*d*)+**to**] *Give the tickets to me.* | *Their teacher gave them a lot of homework.* | *My mother gave us chicken for lunch.* | *A 30-year-old man has been given an artificial heart in a special operation.* | *I'll give you our plants to look after while we're away.* | *He gave me his coat to mend.* | *(fig.) He gave the old lady his arm* (=allowed her to lean on it) *as she crossed the road.* **2 a** [T+*obj*(*i*) +*obj*(*d*)] to hand (something) over as a present: *I gave my father some socks for Christmas.* [+*obj*(*d*)+**to**] *I gave those socks to my father.* | *We've just been given a piano by some friends of ours.* | *This piano was given to us by some friends of ours.* **b** [I+*obj*/*prep*] to supply (money); CONTRIBUTE: *It's a very deserving charity; please give generously.* —see also GIVE OF **3** [T+*obj*(*i*)+*obj*(*d*)] to allow to have: *Give him enough time to get home before you telephone.* | *I'll give you 24 hours to make a decision.*| *Were you given a choice, or did you have to do it?* | *(infml) I'd give their marriage a year at most.* (=I think it will only last a year) | **Given the chance** (=if someone gave me the chance), *I'd love to try again.* —see also GIVEN² **4** [T (**to**)] to provide or supply; cause someone, or people in general, to have (esp. something non-material): *The shop gives a generous discount on large orders.* | *The apple tree doesn't give much fruit.* | *to give evidence in a murder trial* [+*obj*(*i*)+*obj*(*d*)] *Whatever gave you that idea?* | *Can you give me more information?* | *Who gave you permission to do that?* | *I'd like you to give me your honest opinion of my work* | *Please give your parents my regards.* | *Digging the garden gave me a pain in the back.* | *The drop in prices should give sales a boost.* | *Has official approval been given to the scheme?* **5** [T (**for**)] to pay in order to buy; pay in exchange (for something): *I can't believe you gave £3000 for that broken-down old car!* [+*obj*(*i*)+*obj*(*d*)] *How much will you give me for this silver teapot?* ■ to perform an action; make something happen or exist **6** [T] **a** to perform or carry out (an action): *Give the signal to fire!* | *He gave a deep sigh.* | *The prisoner gave a shrug of indifference.* **b** [+*obj*(*i*)+*obj*(*d*)] to cause (an action) to be performed on or to (something or someone): *Give me a kiss.* | *She gave the tin a good polish.* | *He gave her hand a reassuring squeeze.* | *I gave the ball a kick* **7** [T (**to**)] to produce (an effect, appearance, etc.): *She gives the impression of being very well organized.* | *His books give pleasure to millions.* [+*obj*(*i*)+*obj*(*d*)] *The news gave us a shock.* | *I hope my son didn't give you any trouble.* **8** [T] to cause (a performance, amusement, or public event) to take place: *He gave a reading of his poetry.* | *Another performance will be given next week.* | *The President is giving a press conference tomorrow.* [+*obj*(*i*) +*obj*(*d*)] *Give us a song!* | *We are giving John a party for his birthday.* ■ other meanings **9** [T] to set aside (time, thought, strength, etc.) for a purpose: *They have given their lives in the cause of preserving democracy.* [+*obj*(*i*) +*obj*(*d*)] *You must give more attention to your work*|*give your work more attention.* | *The unemployment problem must now be given top priority.* **10** [T+*obj*(*i*)+*obj*(*d*)] to punish in the stated way, esp. to send to prison for the stated time: *The judge gave her two years.*| *He was given*

a life sentence for murder. | *The boy was given a beating for stealing the money.* **11** [T+*obj*(*i*)+*obj*(*d*)] *infml* to admit the truth of: *It's too late to go to the party, I give you that. But we could go somewhere else.* **12** [T+*obj* +*to-v*; *often pass.*] *fml* to cause to believe, esp. wrongly, because of information given: *They gave me to understand they would wait for me, but they left without me.* | *I was given to understand that he was ill.* **13** [T+*obj*(*i*) +*obj*(*d*)] to offer as an excuse or explanation: *Don't give me that nonsense about your bad leg!* **14** [T+*obj*(*i*) +*obj*(*d*)] *esp. BrE* to call on (people present) to drink to the health of; ask (people) to drink a TOAST¹ to: *Gentlemen, I give you the President!* **15** [T+*obj*+*adv*; *often pass.*] *BrE* (in certain games) to declare (a player or ball) to be in the stated condition: *The centre forward was given offside.* | *The linesman gave the ball out.* **16** [I] to bend or stretch under pressure: *The branch he was sitting on began to give.* | *(fig.) There's a lot of tension in the international situation at present; something has got to give soon.* —see also GIVE² ■ fixed phrases **17 give as good as one gets** to answer or fight with force equal to that of one's opponent in an argument or fight **18 give it to someone (straight)** *infml* to tell someone something unpleasant (in a direct way) **19 give me (something)** I like (something) best: *Give me a nice old house any day|every time.* (=I like old houses much better than new ones.) **20 give or take (a certain amount)** (a certain amount) more or less: *It will take an hour, give or take a few minutes (either way).* **21 I/he/they/etc. don't/ couldn't give a damn/hoot/etc.** I/he/they/etc. don't care at all: *He couldn't give a damn about her.* [+*wh*-] *I don't give a damn how you do it, so long as it gets done.* **22 I/he/they/etc. would give a lot/anything/the world, etc.** I/he/they/etc. would very much like (to do or have something): *The boys would give anything to meet that football player.* | *I'd give my right arm to be able to sing like that!* **23 it is better to give than to receive** *quote* a slightly changed phrase from the Bible **24 What gives?** *infml* (used for showing surprise) What's happening? —see also **give way** (WAY¹ (17)) —**giver** *n* ■ phrasal verbs

give sbdy./sthg. ↔ **away** *phr v* [T] **1** to get rid of by giving: *She gave away all her money to the poor.* | *No one wants to buy last year's fashions; you can't even give them away.* | *(fig.) He gave away* (=lost carelessly) *his last chance of winning the election when he said the wrong thing on TV.* **2** to give ceremonially; PRESENT: *The local MP will give away the prizes at the school speech day.* **3** [(**to**)] to give information about; tell (a secret): *Someone in the gang gave him away to the police.* [+*wh*-] *She made me promise not to give away where it was hidden.* | *I'll tell you our plan to surprise David if you promise not to* **give the game away.** **4** to show the truth about; REVEAL: *She tried to appear indifferent, but her eyes gave her away.* **5** to officially hand over (a woman) to her husband at a wedding: *Mary was given away by her father.* —see also GIVEAWAY

give sthg. ↔ **back** *phr v* [T (**to**)] to return (something) to its owner or original possessor: *Give it back (to me).* [+*obj*(*i*)+*obj*(*d*)] *Give me back my pen.* | *The operation gave her back the use of her legs.*

give in *phr v* [(**to**)] **1** [I] to give way; allow oneself to be beaten; SURRENDER: *The boys fought until one gave in.*| *Don't give in to their demands.* | *I gave in to temptation and had a cigarette.* **2** [T] (=**give** sthg. ↔ **in**) to deliver; hand in: *Give your exam papers in (to the teacher) when you've finished.*

give of sthg. *phr v* [T] *fml* to give (time, effort, etc.) without expecting anything in return: *They have given unstintingly of their time and money to help the poor.*

give off sthg. *phr v* [T] to send out (esp. a liquid, gas, or smell); EMIT: *The eggs were giving off a bad smell.*

give on/onto sthg. *phr v* [T *no pass.*] *BrE* to have a view of, or lead straight to: *That door gives onto the garden.*

give out *phr v* **1** [T (**to**)] (=**give** sthg. ↔ **out**) to give to each of several people; DISTRIBUTE: *Give out the exam papers.* | *Give the money out to the children.* **2** [T] (**give** sthg. ↔ **out**) *esp. BrE* to make known publicly; ANNOUNCE: *The date of the election will be given out soon.* [+*that*] *They gave out on the radio that the president had died.* **3** [T] (**give out** sthg.) to send out (esp. a noise): *The radio is giving out a strange signal.* | *She gave out a yell.* **4** [I] to come to an end; be completely used up: *Our supply of sugar has given out.* | *My strength gave out.* **5** [I] *infml* to stop working; break down: *The engine gave out.*

give over (sthg.) *phr v* [I;T+*v-ing; often imperative*] *BrE infml* to stop (doing something): *Do give over! I'm sick of your complaints!* | *Give over hitting your little brother!*

give over to *phr v* [T] **1** (**give** sthg. **over to** sthg.) to set (a time or place) apart for a particular purpose or use: *The building was given over to the youth club.* | *The evening was given over to singing and dancing.* **2** (**give** sbdy./sthg. **over to** sthg.) to give (oneself or something) completely to: *After her husband's death she gave herself over to her work.* | *He gave his life over to helping people.*

give up *phr v* **1** [I;T (=**give** sthg. ↔ **up**)] to stop having or doing: *"Do you smoke?" "No, I gave up last year."* | *The doctor told him to give up alcohol.* | *He had to give up his studies through lack of money.* [+*v-ing*] *I've given up eating meat.* **2** [I] to stop attempting something; admit defeat: *I give up* (=I can't guess); *tell me the end of the story.* | *All the girls swam the lake except two, who gave up halfway.* **3** [T] (**give** sbdy. **up**) to stop believing that (someone) can be saved, esp. from death: *The doctors had almost given her up when she made a dramatic recovery.* | *The boy was* **given up for dead. 4** [T] (**give** sbdy. ↔ **up**) to stop having a relationship with: *She gave up a lot of her friends when she got married.* **5** [T (to)] (**give** sbdy. **up**) to offer (someone or oneself) as a prisoner: *The murderer gave himself up (to the police).* **6** [T (to)] (**give** sthg. ↔ **up**) to deliver or allow to pass (to someone else): *We had to give up the town (to the enemy).* | *Give your seat up to the old lady, Jimmy.* —see also **give up the ghost** (GHOST¹)

give up on sbdy. *phr v* [T *no pass.*] *infml* to have no further hope for: *I give up on you: you'll never get anywhere with that attitude.*

give sbdy. **up to** sthg. *phr v* [T] to allow (oneself) to feel completely the effects of: *She had given herself up to despair.*

give² *n* [U] the quality of bending, stretching, or loosening under pressure: *Shoes get slightly larger after wearing because of the give in the leather.* | *There was too much give in the rope, and it slipped off the box it was holding.* —see also GIVE¹ (16)

give-and-take /ˌ· · ·ˈ·/ *n* [U] willingness of each person to give way to (some of) the other's wishes; willingness to COMPROMISE: *There has to be a lot of give-and-take in any successful marriage.*

give·a·way¹ /ˈgɪvəweɪ/ *n* **1** [S] *infml* something unintentional that makes a secret known: *She tried to hide her feelings, but the tears in her eyes were a* **dead giveaway. 2** [C] something given in a shop with a certain product to encourage people to buy that product —see also GIVE away

giveaway² *adj* [A] *infml* (of a price) very low

giv·en¹ /ˈgɪvən/ *adj* **1** [A] fixed for a purpose and stated as such: *The work must be done at/within the given time.* | *In a circle, the distance from the centre to the edge is the same at any given point.* **2 be given to** to be in the habit of or to have a tendency to: *He's given to drinking rather heavily.* | *She's given to depression.*

given² *prep* if one takes into account: *Given their inexperience, they've done a good job.* [+*that*] *Given that they're inexperienced, they've done a good job.* —see also GIVE¹ (3)

given name /ˈ·· ·/ *n esp. AmE for* FIRST NAME

Gi·za /ˈgiːzə/ a city in Egypt near Cairo where the Pyramids and the Sphinx attract many tourists

giz·mo /ˈgɪzməʊ/ GISMO

giz·zard /ˈgɪzəd‖-ərd/ *n* the second stomach of a bird, where food is broken up with the help of small stones the bird has swallowed

gla·cé /ˈglæseɪ‖glæˈseɪ/ *adj* [A] (of a fruit) covered with sugar: *glacé cherries*

glacé ic·ing /ˌ·· ·‖·ˌ·· ·/ *n* [U] a type of ICING often used on birthday cakes, made from icing sugar and water, often with colouring added

gla·cial /ˈgleɪʃəl/ *adj* **1** of ice or glaciers **2** [A] of an ICE AGE: *Two thirds of the continent was covered in ice during glacial periods.* **3** *infml* very cold: *a glacial wind* | (fig.) *He gave me a glacial smile.* (=without friendliness)

gla·ci·er /ˈglæsiə‖ˈgleɪʃər/ *n* a mass of ice which moves very slowly down a mountain valley —see picture at MOUNTAIN

glad /glæd/ *adj* -**dd- 1** [F (**about**)] pleased and happy about

something: *I'm glad about his new job.* [+(*that*)] *I'm glad he's got the job.* [+*to-v*] *You'll be glad to hear he's got the job.* **2** [F+*of*] grateful for: *I'd be glad of some help with carrying these boxes.* **3** [F+*to-v*] polite very willing: *I'll be only too glad* (=extremely willing) *to help you repair the car.* | *"Would you give me a hand?" "Yes, I'll be glad to."* **4** [A] causing happiness: *I'm pleased to be the first to bring you the* **glad tidings.** (=good news) —see also GLADLY — ~ **ness** *n* [U]

glad·den /ˈglædn/ *v* [T] to make glad or happy: *The sight of the child running about after his long illness* **gladdened** *his father's* **heart.**

glade /gleɪd/ *n lit* an open space without trees in a wood or forest; CLEARING

glad eye /ˌ· ·ˈ·, ·ˈ· ·/ *[the] BrE old-fash sl* a look of sexual invitation: *The boys were all giving her the glad eye.*

glad hand /ˌ· ·ˈ·, ·ˈ· ·/ *n [the] old-fash infml* a warm welcome or greeting, esp. one made in order to gain personal advantage

glad·i·a·tor /ˈglædieɪtər/ *n* (in ancient Rome) an armed man who fought against men or wild animals in a public place as a form of entertainment — ~ **ial** /ˌglædiəˈtɔːriəl◄/ *adj*

glad·i·o·lus /ˌglædiˈəʊləs/ *n* -**li** /laɪ/ *or* -**luses** ‖ also -**lus** *AmE* a garden plant with long sword-shaped leaves and brightly-coloured flowers

glad·ly /ˈglædli/ *adv polite* very willingly; eagerly: *I'll gladly come and help you; why didn't you ask me before?*

glad rags /ˈ· ·/ *n* [P] *BrE infml* (one's) finest or best clothes: *They're putting their glad rags on for the party.*

Glad·stone /ˈglædstən‖-stəʊn/, **Wil·liam Ew·art** /ˈwɪljəm ˈjuːət‖-ərt/ (1809–98) a British Liberal politician, who was PRIME MINISTER from 1868 to 1874, from 1880 to 1885, in 1886, and from 1892 to 1894. He established national education, introduced the secret BALLOT, and supported free trade and home rule for Ireland.

Glamorgan see MID GLAMORGAN, SOUTH GLAMORGAN, WEST GLAMORGAN

glam·o·rize also -**our-** *BrE* also -**rise** *BrE* /ˈglæməraɪz/ *v* [T] to make (something) appear better, more attractive, more exciting, etc. than it really is — ~ **rization** /ˌglæməraɪˈzeɪʃən‖-mərə-/ *n* [U]

glam·or·ous , also -**ourous** *BrE* /ˈglæmərəs/ *adj* having glamour: *a glamorous woman* | *Being in publishing/in the theatre isn't as glamorous as some people think.* — ~ **ly** *adv*

glam·our *BrE* ‖ -**or** *AmE* /ˈglæmər/ *n* [U] **1** the exciting and charming quality of something unusual or special, with a magical power of attraction: *Foreign travel has never lost its glamour for me.* | *the glamour of a job in the pop music business* **2** strong personal attraction which excites admiration, esp. sexually exciting beauty: *They know they'll get bigger audiences if they give the parts to* **glamour girls** *rather than talented actresses.*

glance¹ /glɑːns‖glæns/ *v* [I] **1** [+*adv/prep*] to give a quick short look: *He glanced at his watch.* | *I glanced round the room before I left.* | *She glanced down the list of names.* **2** *esp. lit* (of a bright surface) to flash with light: *The glasses glanced and twinkled in the firelight.*

glance off (sthg.) *phr v* [I;T] to touch (something) with a light blow and move quickly off at an angle: *The bullet just glanced off the top of the car.* | *The sword glanced off the shield.* —see also GLANCING

glance² *n* **1** [(**at**)] a quick short look: *He gave her an admiring glance.* | *One glance at his face told me he was ill.* | *She* **cast/took a** (**quick**) **glance** *at the notepad to see if there were any messages for her.* | **At first glance,** *the figures don't look good, but on closer examination you'll find they're not bad at all.* **2 at a glance** with one look; at once: *I could tell at a glance that she'd been crying.*

▷ USAGE Compare **glance** and **glimpse. Glance** means "to look at something quickly": *As I was making the speech, I glanced at the clock.* (=looked quickly at it) **Glimpse** (or more commonly **catch a glimpse of**) means "to see by chance, just for a moment": *I glimpsed/caught a glimpse of the Town Hall clock as we drove quickly past.*◁

glanc·ing /ˈglɑːnsɪŋ‖ˈglæn-/ *adj* [A] (of a blow) which slips to one side; not having the (intended) full force: *He caught me* (=hit me) *with a glancing blow on the chin.* —see also GLANCE off — ~ **ly** *adv*

gland /glænd/ n an organ of the body which produces a liquid substance, either to be poured out of the body or into the bloodstream: *Mumps makes the glands in your neck swell up.* | *the pituitary gland*

glan·du·lar /ˈglændjᵿləʳ‖-dʒə-/ adj concerning one or more glands, or produced from a gland

glandular fe·ver /ˌ··· ˈ··/ *BrE* ‖ **mononucleosis, mono** *AmE*— n [U] an infectious disease in which one has a fever and the LYMPH glands swell up, and which makes one feel weak for some time afterwards

glare¹ /gleəʳ/ v [I] **1** [(at)] to look in an angry way: *They didn't fight, but stood there glaring at one another.* **2** [+adv/prep] to shine with a strong light and/or in a way that hurts the eyes: *She put on dark glasses because the sun was glaring in her eyes.* | (fig.) *The mistakes in this report really glare at you.*

glare² n **1** [C] an angry look or STARE: *I was going to offer help, but the fierce glare on his face stopped me.* **2** [(the) S] a hard unpleasant effect given by a strong light: *She was almost blinded by the glare of headlights from the approaching car.* | (fig.) *I feel sorry for famous people who live their lives* **in the (full) glare of publicity.**

glar·ing /ˈgleərɪŋ/ adj **1 a** (of light) hard and too bright: *This glaring light hurts my eyes.* **b** (of a colour) too bright: *a glaring red* **2** (of something bad) very noticeable: *The report is full of glaring errors.* | *an example of glaring injustice* — ~**ly** adv : *The mistakes were glaringly obvious.*

Glas·gow /ˈglɑːzgəʊ‖ˈglæs-/ a city and port in W Scotland on the River Clyde. It is the main city in the Strathclyde area and has a university and CATHEDRAL. —see colour map on page 818

Glasgow Her·ald /ˌ··· ˈ··/ n one of Scotland's main newspapers, read esp. in the West of Scotland —see also extra information on page 896

glas·nost /ˈglæsnɒst‖ˈglɑːsnəʊst/ n [U] the willingness of an organization, esp. the government of the former USSR, to act openly and discuss its behaviour and actions publicly: *the spirit of glasnost* | *policy of glasnost* —compare PERESTROIKA

glasses

wine glass

sherry glass

brandy glass *BrE*/ snifter *AmE*

beer glass/ beer mug

glass¹ /glɑːs‖glæs/ n **1** [U] a transparent solid easily-broken material made from sand melted under great heat and used esp. to make windows and containers for liquids: *a glass bottle* | *The glazier fitted a new pane of glass in the window.* | *I cut my hand on some broken glass.* | *I grew these cucumbers* **under glass.** (=in a FRAME¹ (4)) | *a shop window made of strengthened glass* **2** [U] also **glassware**— objects, esp. dishes, drinking glasses, etc., made of this: *the museum's valuable collection of medieval Italian glass* **3** [C] (the contents of) a small usu. glass container for drinking from: *a wine glass* | *a broken/cracked glass* | *I drink several glasses of water a day.* | *a plastic glass* —see picture at PLACE SETTING **4** [C] *infml, BrE for* LOOKING GLASS **5** [*the*] *BrE* the measurement shown on an apparatus with a pointer which moves downwards when bad weather is coming (BAROMETER): *The glass is falling; it's going to rain.* **6 people in glass houses shouldn't throw stones** *saying* people who have faults of their own should not criticize other people, because they might be criticized in return **7 through a glass darkly** *phrase from the Bible* we do not see clearly now: *As for the outlook for next year—through a glass darkly indeed.* —see also GLASSES, CUT GLASS, GROUND GLASS, MAGNIFYING GLASS, PLATE GLASS, STAINED GLASS

glass² v

glass sthg. ↔ **in** *phr v* [T] to cover with or enclose in glass

Glass, Philip (1937–) an American COMPOSER who was influenced by Far Eastern music. His works include *Einstein on the Beach.*

glass-blow·er /ˈglɑːsˌbləʊəʳ‖ˈglæs-/ n a person who shapes glass into bottles, glass animals, etc., by blowing air through a tube into a ball of hot liquid glass

glass cei·ling /ˌ· ˈ··/ n an imaginary limit that allows people to see their aims but prevents them from achieving them, usu. because of RACISM or SEXISM

glass·cut·ter /ˈglɑːsˌkʌtəʳ‖ˈglæs-/ n **1** a person who cuts glass into pieces or cuts patterns on glass objects **2** a tool for cutting glass

glasses

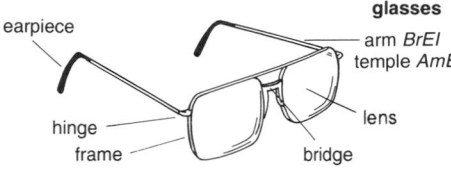

earpiece

arm *BrE*/ temple *AmE*

hinge

lens

frame

bridge

glass·es /ˈglɑːsɪz‖ˈglæ-/ n [P] **1** two pieces of specially-cut glass in a frame, worn in front of the eyes for improving a person's ability to see; SPECTACLES (*BrE*): *He wears glasses for reading.* | *I need some new glasses/a new pair of glasses.* | *The film star was wearing dark glasses.* **2 men never make passes at girls who wear glasses** *saying* men do not find women who wear glasses attractive —see also OPERA GLASSES, SUNGLASSES

glass fi·bre /ˌ· ˈ··◂/ n [U] FIBREGLASS

glass·house /ˈglɑːshaʊs‖ˈglæs-/ n *BrE* **-houses** /ˌhaʊzɪz/ **1** [C] a building used for growing plants; GREENHOUSE **2** [*the*] *sl* military prison

glass slip·per /ˌ· ˈ··/ n a special glass shoe worn by Cinderella —see CINDERELLA, and see colour picture on page 357

glass·ware /ˈglɑːsweəʳ‖ˈglæs-/ n [U] glass objects generally, esp. dishes, drinking glasses, etc.

glass·works /ˈglɑːswɜːks‖ˈglæswɜːrks/ n **glassworks** a factory where glass is made

glass·y /ˈglɑːsi‖ˈglæsi/ adj **1** like glass, esp. smooth and shining: *a glassy pond* **2** (of eyes) having a fixed expression, as if without sight or life: *glassy eyes* | *a glassy stare*

Glas·ton·bur·y /ˈglæstənbəri‖-beri/ a town in SW England where many things from the Iron Age have been found. It has associations with King Arthur's Isle of Avalon and with the story of St Joseph of Arimathea. It is popular with HIPPIES and NEW AGE TRAVELLERS

Glas·we·gian /glæzˈwiːdʒən‖glæs-/ n *BrE infml* **1** [C] a name used for someone, esp. a man, from Glasgow: *I'm a Glaswegian born and bred.* **2** [U] a way of speaking typical of people from Glasgow —**Glaswegian** adj

glau·co·ma /glɔːˈkəʊmə/ n [U] a disease of the eye in which there is increased pressure within the eyeball, which gradually causes loss of sight

glau·cous /ˈglɔːkəs/ adj *tech* (of a leaf, fruit, etc.) covered with a fine whitish powdery surface

Glax·o /ˈglæksəʊ/ a British company, operating in many countries, which makes drugs and medicines

glaze¹ /gleɪz/ v **1** [T] to put a shiny surface on (pots and bricks) **2** [T] to cover (food) with a substance giving a shiny surface: *glazed fruit* **3** [T] to provide or fit with glass: *a glazed door* —see also DOUBLE-GLAZING **4** [I (OVER)] (of eyes) to become dull and lifeless: *His eyes glazed over and he fell back unconscious.* | *a glazed expression*

glaze² n **1** a shiny surface, esp. one fixed on pots by heat **2** a transparent covering of oil paint spread over solid paint, esp. to change the effect of the colours in a painting **3** a liquid substance which may be spread over cold cooked meats or fruit, and which produces a shiny surface when it sets

gla·zi·er /ˈgleɪziəʳ‖-ʒər/ n a person whose job is to fit glass, esp. into window frames

G

glaz·ing /ˈgleɪzɪŋ/ n [U] **1** the action or job of a glazier **2** glass used to fill a window —see also DOUBLE-GLAZING

GLC /ˌdʒiː el ˈsiː/ [the] Greater London Council; formed in 1964, this body had members from all the London BOROUGH COUNCILS, and was the local authority for Greater London. It was the subject of much fierce political argument and opposed many of the policies of the Conservative government of Margaret Thatcher. In 1985 it was removed and its responsibilities were given back to the local borough councils.

gleam¹ /gliːm/ n **1** [(of)] a gentle light, esp. one that is small and/or shines for a short time: *the red gleam of the firelight* | *Gleams of sunshine came through the breaks in the cloud.* **2** [+of] a sudden showing of a feeling or quality for a short time: *A gleam of interest came into his eye.* | *a gleam of hope* —compare GLIMMER, GLOW

gleam² v [I] **1** to give out a gentle light; shine softly: *We saw the lights of the little town gleaming in the distance.* | *a gleaming new Cadillac* **2** [+adv/prep] (of a feeling) to be expressed with a sudden light (in the eyes): *Amusement gleamed in his eyes.*

glean /gliːn/ v **1** [T] to gather (facts or information) in small amounts and often with difficulty: *From what I was able to glean, it appears they don't intend to take any action yet.* **2** [I;T] to collect (grain that has been left behind) after crops have been cut

glean·ings /ˈgliːnɪŋz/ n [P] **1** small amounts of information or news, perhaps gathered with difficulty **2** the grain gathered in the fields after the crops have been cut

Glea·son /ˈgliːsən/, **Jackie** (1916–87) an American actor and COMEDIAN, best remembered for his part in the long-running television programme *The Honeymooners*

glebe /gliːb/ n **1** [the] poet the earth or soil **2** [C] tech the land held by a priest to provide part of his income

glee /gliː/ n **1** [U] a feeling of joyful satisfaction at something which pleases one: *The little girl jumped about in glee when she saw the new toys.* **2** [C] a song for three or four voices together, often sung by the members of a **glee club** (=AmE a particular type of CHOIR)

glee·ful /ˈgliːfəl/ adj showing joy and delight – ~ ly adv

glen /glen/ n a narrow mountain valley, esp. in Scotland or Ireland

Glen Coe /ˌ· ˈ·/ a valley in the W Highland Region of Scotland. It is important in Scottish history as the place where a famous battle took place in 1692.

Glen·ea·gles /glenˈiːgəlz/ two popular Scottish hotel GOLF courses. In 1977 heads of Commonwealth governments met here to agree the **Gleneagles Principle** which said that all sporting links with South Africa should be cut because of APARTHEID.

Glen·fid·dich /glenˈfɪdɪk, -ɪx/ n [U] tdmk a type of MALT WHISKY

Glenn /glen/, **John** (1921–) the first American ASTRONAUT to ORBIT (=travel in a large circle) around the earth. In 1974 he became a US SENATOR representing Ohio.

glib /glɪb/ adj **-bb-** often derog **1** good at speaking quickly, cleverly, and in a way that is likely to persuade people, whether speaking the truth or not: *a glib salesman/politician* | *He's got a glib tongue.* **2** spoken too easily to be true: *She's always ready with a glib excuse/reply.* – ~ ly adv – ~ ness n [U]

glide¹ /glaɪd/ v [I] **1** [+adv/prep] to move (noiselessly) in a smooth continuous manner, which seems easy and without effort: *The boat glided over the lake.* | *The dancers glided across the floor.* —compare SLIDE **2 a** (of a bird) to fly smoothly through the air without moving the wings **b** (of a person) to fly in a glider: *He goes gliding at weekends.* —see also HANG GLIDING

glide² n **1** a gliding movement **2** (in music) the act of passing from one note to another without a break in sound **3** tech (in PHONETICS) a sound made while passing from one position of the speech organs to another, e.g. when pronouncing a DIPHTHONG

glid·er /ˈglaɪdər/ n a light plane without an engine that can only fly after being pulled into the air by another plane

glim·mer¹ /ˈglɪmər/ v [I] to give a very faint unsteady light: *A light glimmered at the end of the passage.*

glimmer² n **1** a faint unsteady light **2** [+of] also **glim·mer·ing** /ˈglɪmərɪŋ/– a small uncertain sign:

There's still a glimmer of hope left for the lost climbers. | *She spoke enthusiastically, but her audience didn't show a glimmer of interest.* —compare GLEAM, GLOW

glimpse¹ /glɪmps/ v [T] to have a quick incomplete view of: *I glimpsed her among the crowd just before she disappeared from sight.*

glimpse² n a quick look at or incomplete view of: *I only caught a glimpse of the thief, so I can't really describe him.* —see GLANCE² (USAGE)

glint¹ /glɪnt/ v [I] to give out small flashes of light: *The gold glinted in the sunlight.* | (fig.) *Their eyes glinted when they saw the money.*

glint² n a flash of light, as from a shiny metal surface: *brown hair with golden glints* | *I could tell he was angry by the glint in his eye.*

glis·ten /ˈglɪsən/ v [I (with)] to shine (as if) from wetness: *His brow/forehead glistened with sweat.* – ~ ingly adv

glis·ter /ˈglɪstər/ v [I] **all that glisters is not gold** quote a phrase from Shakespeare's play *The Merchant of Venice* meaning that not everything that appears attractive and good actually is: *For the man at the head of Britain's biggest jewellery chain, all that glisters is not gold.*

glitch /glɪtʃ/ n AmE infml **1** a small fault in the operation of something **2** a false ELECTRONIC signal caused by a sudden increase in electrical power

glit·ter¹ /ˈglɪtər/ v [I] **1** to shine brightly with flashing points of light: *The diamond ring glittered on her finger.* | (fig.) *The film première was a glittering occasion, with royalty and many famous stars in attendance.* **2 all that glitters is not gold** quote a slightly changed phrase from Shakespeare's play *The Merchant of Venice*, meaning that not everything that appears attractive actually is

glitter² n **1** [S] a brightness, as of flashing points of light: *the glitter of the sun on the waves* | *The torturer had a cruel glitter in his eyes.* **2** [U] attractiveness; GLAMOUR: *Beneath its surface glitter, the fashion industry is a tough place to work in.* **3** [U] very small glittering objects used for decoration: *She sprinkled silver glitter in her hair.* | *a tube of glitter* – ~ y adj

Glitter, Gar·y /ˈgæri/ (1940–) a British popular music singer, successful in the 1970s, known esp. for his tight, shiny clothes and his large boots with thick, high heels

glit·te·ra·ti /ˌglɪtəˈrɑːti/ n [(the)P] sl fashionable and usu. rich and famous people whose social activities are widely reported (from a humorous combination of glitter and LITERATI): *Hollywood's glitterati*

glitz /glɪts/ n [U] sl an exciting fashionable quality (without seriousness or deep meaning) – ~ y adj : *one of the year's glitziest parties, reported in all the newspaper gossip columns*

gloam·ing /ˈgləʊmɪŋ/ [the] poet (the time of) half darkness in the early evening; DUSK

gloat /gləʊt/ v [I (over)] to look at or think about something with unpleasant satisfaction: *The thief gloated over the stolen jewels.* | *Don't gloat; the same misfortune may happen to you one day.* –**gloat** n : *I'm sure he'll have a good gloat over this.* – ~ ingly adv

glo·bal /ˈgləʊbəl/ adj **1** of or concerning the whole world: *events of global importance* | *Global climatic changes may have been responsible for the extinction of the dinosaurs.* **2** taking account of or including (almost) all possible considerations: *The report takes a global view of the company's problems.* – ~ ly adv

glo·bal·is·m /ˈgləʊbəlɪzəm/ n [U] the quality of being concerned with causes and effects over the whole world, not just single parts of it –**ist** adj, n : *globalist economic policies*

global warm·ing /ˌ· ˈ··/ n [U] a general increase in world temperatures caused by CARBON DIOXIDE collecting in space immediately around the Earth —see also GREEN-HOUSE EFFECT

globe /gləʊb/ n **1** [C] an object in the shape of a round ball; SPHERE **2** [C] an object like this on which a map of the Earth or sky is painted, and which may be turned round and round on its base **3** [the] lit the Earth: *She has travelled all round the globe.*

globe ar·ti·choke /ˌ· ˈ···/ n an ARTICHOKE (1)

Globe Thea·tre /ˌ· ˈ··/ [the] the theatre in London where Shakespeare's plays were first performed. It was

A scene from one of the Carry On films

Laurel and Hardy

Charlie Chaplin

Eddie Murphy

Dame Edna

The Blues Brothers

Robin Williams

enny Hill

Woody Allen

Buddy Holly

The Beatles

David Bowie

Luciano Pavarotti

Tina Turner

Michael Jackson

Madonna

Elvis Presley

Frank Sinatra

Elton John

The Rolling Stones

destroyed in the 17th century and is now being rebuilt exactly as it was.

globe·trot·ter /ˈgləʊbtrɒtəʳ‖-traː-/ *n infml* a person who travels a lot —**ting** *adj, n*

glob·u·lar /ˈglɒbjᵿləʳ‖ˈglaː-/ *adj* in the form of a globule or globe

glob·ule /ˈglɒbjuːl‖ˈglaː-/ *n* a small drop of a liquid or melted solid; BLOB: *Globules of wax fell from the candle.*

glock·en·spiel /ˈglɒkənspiːl‖ˈglɑː-/ *n* a musical instrument made up of a set of flat metal bars of different lengths each of which gives out a different musical note, played by striking with two small hammers

gloom /gluːm/ *n* **1** [S;U] a feeling of deep sadness or hopelessness: *The news of defeat filled them all with gloom.* | *A deep gloom settled on them when they heard the company was going to close down.* | *to spread gloom and despondency/gloom and doom* **2** [U] *esp. lit* darkness: *We inched forwards in the gathering gloom.*

gloom·y /ˈgluːmi/ *adj* **1** almost dark, esp. in an unpleasant way: *a gloomy day* **2** having or giving little hope or cheerfulness: *He's such a gloomy chap; you can never get him to smile.* | *Our future seems gloomy.* —**ily** *adv* —**iness** *n* [U]

glop /glɒp‖glaːp/ *n* [U] *AmE sl derog* a thick liquid mass, usu. of unwanted food: *What is this glop?*

glo·ri·fy /ˈglɔːrᵻfaɪ/ *v* [T] **1** to give (sometimes undeserved) glory or fame to: *Her brave deeds were glorified in song and story.* | *Many modern films glorify war and violence.* **2** to give praise and thanks to (God); worship (God) **3** [(with)] *infml* to cause to appear more important than in reality; give sthg. a name which it does not deserve: *I wouldn't glorify it with the name of a dictionary; it's more of a phrase book.* | *She calls it a country house, but I call it a glorified bungalow!* —**fication** /ˌglɔːrᵻfᵻˈkeɪʃən/ *n*

glo·ri·ous /ˈglɔːriəs/ *adj* **1** having or deserving great fame, honour, and admiration: *a glorious victory* | *the glorious dead* **2** beautiful and splendid: *glorious colours* | *a glorious day* **3** *infml* very enjoyable: *We had a glorious time at the seaside.* — –**ly** *adv* : *a gloriously sunny day*

Glorious Rev·o·lu·tion /ˌ··· ··ˈ··/ [*the*] the time in British history (1688–89) when King James II was removed from power, and his daughter Mary and her husband William of Orange became joint rulers. It was also called the **Bloodless Revolution**.

Glorious Twelfth /ˌ··· ·ˈ·/ [*the*] August 12th, the date when the season for the sport of shooting GROUSE begins. There is a race to see who can eat the first GROUSE in expensive restaurants in London.

glo·ry¹ /ˈglɔːri/ *n* **1** [U] great fame, honour, and admiration. *Those who died bravely in battle earned everlasting glory.* | *He can hardly be said to have emerged from that episode* **covered in/with glory.** (=regarded favourably by everyone) | *Her son has been honoured by the President, so she's basking in* **reflected glory.** (=the glory of another, usu. closely related, person) **2** [U] beautiful and splendid appearance: *The bright moonlight showed the Taj Mahal* **in all its glory.** | *After years of decay, this fine old house has now been restored to its former glory.* **3** [(*the*) C+**of**] something that is esp. beautiful or gives cause for pride: *When that bush comes into flower it is the glory of the whole garden.* | *Being knighted by the Queen was the* **crowning glory** *of his long and successful career.* | *the cultural glories of China* **4** [U] praise, honour, and thanks: *Glory be to God!* —see also MORNING GLORY

glo·ry² *v*

glory in sthg. *phr v* [T] **1** to be very happy about; get great pleasure from: *They gloried in their new freedom.* **2** *derog* to enjoy in an unpleasant or selfish way: *She gloried in the fact that she had beaten everyone else.* | *He accused the government of glorying in slaughter.*

glory hole /ˈ·· ·/ *n BrE old-fash infml* a room, cupboard, or drawer where unwanted articles are left; esp. a room which is very untidy, causing embarrassment

gloss¹ /glɒs‖glɔːs, glaːs/ *n* [S;U] **1** shiny brightness on a surface: *the gloss on a polished table/on her hair* —compare MAT², MATT **2** a pleasant but deceiving outer appearance: *They hide their dislike for each other under a surface gloss of good manners.* **3** an explanation of a

piece of writing, esp. in the form of a note at the end of a page or book: *Some of Shakespeare's language is so different from today's that I could never understand it without the gloss.* —compare GLOSSARY

gloss² *v* [T] to provide a GLOSS¹ (3) for: *In this dictionary we often gloss difficult expressions with an explanation in brackets.*

gloss over sthg. *phr v* [T] to speak well of (something bad), usu. with the intention of deceiving or hiding faults: *The company's annual report tried to gloss over recent heavy losses, but angry shareholders forced the chairman to explain them.*

glos·sa·ry /ˈglɒsəri‖ˈglɔː-, ˈglaː-/ *n* a list of explanations of words, esp. unusual ones, at the end of a book —compare GLOSS¹

gloss paint /ˈ· ·/ *n* [U] paint which is shiny when it dries, used esp. on wood inside and outside buildings —compare EMULSION PAINT

gloss·y /ˈglɒsi‖ˈglɔːsi, ˈglaːsi/ *adj* shiny and smooth: *Our cat has glossy black fur.* —**iness** *n* [U]

glossy mag·a·zine /ˌ··· ··ˈ·‖ˌ·· ˈ···/ also **glossy** *infml* — *n esp. BrE* a magazine printed on good quality paper with a shiny surface, usu. having lots of colour pictures

glot·tal stop /ˌ·· ·ˈ·/ *n tech* a speech sound made by completely closing and then opening the glottis, which in English may take the place of /t/ between vowel sounds or may be used before a vowel sound

glot·tis /ˈglɒtᵻs‖ˈglaː-/ *n* the space between the VOCAL CORDS (=the fleshy parts of the air passage inside the throat), which produce the sound of the voice by movements in which this space is repeatedly opened and closed —see picture at RESPIRATORY —**tal** *adj*

Glouces·ter /ˈglɒstəʳ‖ˈglaː-/ **1** a CATHEDRAL town on the river Severn in SW England, where the local government for Gloucestershire is based **2** also **double Gloucester**— a kind of hard cheese originally from the area around Gloucester

Glouces·ter·shire /ˈglɒstəʃəʳ‖ˈglaːstər-/ a COUNTY in SW England

gloves

  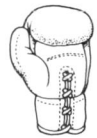 

glove   mitten   boxing gloves   baseball glove/ baseball mitt

glove /glʌv/ *n* **1** a GARMENT which covers the hand, esp. one with separate parts for the thumb and each finger: *woollen/leather gloves* —compare MITTEN **2** a large leather glove used in BOXING **3** a large leather glove used in BASEBALL —see PAIR (USAGE); see also KID GLOVES, **hand in glove** (HAND¹), **the iron hand/fist in the velvet glove** (IRON¹)

glove com·part·ment /ˈ· ·,··/ also **glove box** /ˈ· ·/— *n* a small space or shelf in a car in front of the passenger seat, where small articles may be kept —see picture at CAR

gloved /glʌvd/ *adj* [A] (of a hand) wearing a glove

glove pup·pet /ˈ· ,··/ *n* a PUPPET (2)

Glov·er /ˈglʌvəʳ/, **Jane** (1949–) a musical CONDUCTOR, known for her television programmes on music

glow¹ /gləʊ/ *v* [I (**with**)] **1** to give out heat and/or soft light without flames or smoke: *The iron bar was heated until it glowed.* | *The cat's eyes glowed in the darkness.* | (fig.) *It was painted in glowing colours.* **2** to show redness and heat, esp. in the face, e.g. after hard work or because of strong feelings: *She was glowing with health and happiness.* | *His cheeks glowed with embarrassment.* | (fig.) *She glowed with pride at her son's achievements.* —see also GLOWING; compare GLEAM, GLIMMER

glow² *n* [S] **1** a soft light from something burning without flames or smoke: *There was a dull red glow in the night sky above the steelworks.* **2** brightness of colour: *the warm glow of copper pans in the kitchen* **3** [(**of**)] the feeling and/or signs of heat and colour in the body and face, e.g. after exercise or because of good health: *the glow of*

health   **4** [+**of**] a strong feeling: *She felt a glow of pride|of satisfaction at her son's achievements.*

glow·er /ˈglaʊəʳ/ *v* [I (**at**)] to look with an angry expression; GLARE: *Instead of answering he just glowered (at me)|gave me a glowering look.* | (fig.) *The glowering clouds promised rain.* – ~**ingly** *adv*

glow·ing /ˈgləʊɪŋ/ *adj* showing strong approval; very favourable: *She gave a glowing description of the film, which made me want to see it for myself.* | *The director referred to your work in glowing terms.* – ~**ly** *adv*

glow-worm /ˈ· ·/ *n* an insect whose female has no wings and gives out a greenish light from the end of its tail

glu·cose /ˈgluːkəʊs/ *n* [U] a natural form of sugar found in fruit and used in the body

glue[1] /gluː/ *n* [U] a sticky substance which is made chemically or obtained from animal or fish bones and is used for joining things together: *Put a dab of glue on each corner.* | *a tube of glue*

glue[2] *v present participle* **gluing** *or* **glueing** [T] **1** to join or stick with glue: *It's no use tying it; you'll have to glue it.* | *She glued down the corner of the paper.* | *I glued the broken pieces together.* **2 glued to** *infml* continually close to, looking at, or directed towards: *I stayed glued to his side because I was so afraid of getting lost.* | *The children have been glued to the television all day.* | *She stood there as if* **glued to the spot.** (=unable to move)

glue ear /ˈ· ˌ·/ *n* [U] an illness of the ear which can prevent people from hearing properly

glue-snif·fing /ˈ· ˌ··/ *also* **solvent abuse** *fml* – *n* [U] the harmful breathing in of FUMES of glue or similar substances through the nose or mouth to produce a state of excitement or changed consciousness. It is illegal to sell certain kinds of glue to children in case it is used for glue-sniffing, which can sometimes cause death. –**fer** *n*

glue·y /ˈgluːi/ *adj* **1** sticky like glue **2** covered with glue

glum /glʌm/ *adj* -mm- sad; in low spirits; GLOOMY: *"You look very glum." "I've just lost all my money."* – ~**ly** *adv* – ~**ness** *n* [U]

glut[1] /glʌt/ *n* [(**of**) *usu. sing.*] a larger supply than is necessary: *There was a glut of oil (on the market) a few months ago.* | (fig. *derog*) *a glut of old films on television*

glut[2] *v* -tt- [T *often pass.*] to supply with too much; overfill: *The shops are glutted with apples because of this year's record crop.*

glu·ten /ˈgluːtn/ *n* [U] a sticky PROTEIN substance that is found in flour made from wheat

glu·ti·nous /ˈgluːtₐnəs/ *adj fml* sticky: *a bowl of glutinous rice*

glut·ton /ˈglʌtn/ *n* **1** *derog* a person who eats too much **2** [+**for**] *infml* a person who is always ready to do or accept something hard or unpleasant: *She kept coming to work even when she was ill: she's a real* **glutton for punishment!**

glut·ton·ous /ˈglʌtənəs/ *adj derog* like a glutton; GREEDY, esp. for food – ~**ly** *adv*

glut·ton·y /ˈglʌtəni/ *n* [U] *fml derog* the habit of eating (and drinking) too much. Gluttony is one of the Seven Deadly Sins. –see also SEVEN DEADLY SINS

gly·ce·rine , **-rin** /ˈglɪsərɪn/ *n* [U] a sweet sticky colourless liquid made from fats, which is used in making soap, medicines, and explosives, and in some foods to help them to set

Glynde·bourne /ˈglaɪndbɔːn‖-bɔːrn/ *a* 16th-century country house in a village in the south of England, now famous as a place where there is an annual OPERA FESTIVAL. The operas are attended esp. by rich, UPPER-CLASS people.

gm *written abbrev. for:* GRAM

GM /ˌdʒiː ˈem/ *abbrev. for:* GENERAL MOTORS

GMC /ˌdʒiː em ˈsiː/ [*the*] General Medical Council; the professional organization to which British doctors have to belong

G-Men /ˈdʒiː men/ *n* [P] *old fash AmE* government men; a name used in the 1930s for men working for the FBI

GMT /ˌ· · ˈ·/ *abbrev. for:* GREENWICH MEAN TIME

gnarled /nɑːld‖nɑːrld/ *adj* **1** (of a tree or its trunk or branches) rough and twisted, with hard lumps, esp. as a result of age **2** (of hands and fingers) twisted, with swollen joints and rough skin, esp. as a result of hard

work or old age **3** (of a person) rough in appearance, as if from many years in rough wind and weather: *a gnarled old fisherman*

gnash /næʃ/ *v* [T] to strike (one's teeth) together: *gnashing his teeth in fury* –see also **wailing and gnashing of teeth** (WAIL) –**gnash** *n*

gnat /næt/ *n* a small flying insect that stings: *a gnat bite* | *a cloud of gnats*

gnaw /nɔː/ *v* [I (AWAY, **at**); T] to keep biting steadily on (something hard), esp. so as to make a hole or until it is destroyed: *The dog gnawed (away at) the bone.* | *Rats can gnaw holes in wood.* | *She gnawed anxiously at her fingernails.* | (fig.) *The problem's been gnawing at me* (=worrying me) *for some time.*

gnaw·ing /ˈnɔːɪŋ/ *adj* [A] painful or worrying, esp. in a small but continuous way: *gnawing hunger|anxiety*

gneiss /naɪs/ *n* [U] a hard rock with light and dark bands formed from earlier rocks which were pressed together under heat

gnome /nəʊm/ *n* **1** (in children's stories) a little (old) man who lives under the ground and guards stores of gold, silver, jewels, etc. **2** a (stone or plastic) figure representing this: *a garden gnome* **3 the gnomes of Zurich** *infml* certain powerful bankers, esp. Swiss ones, who are said to control supplies of money to foreign governments

garden gnomes

Gnos·tic Gos·pels /ˌnɒstɪk ˈgɒspəlz‖ˌnɑːstɪk ˈgɑːs-/ *n* [*the*+P] ancient writings which are believed by some people to have once been part of the BIBLE, and to have been taken out by early priests who disagreed with their messages

GNP /ˌdʒiː en ˈpiː/ [*the*] Gross National Product; the total value of all the goods and services produced in a country, usu. in a single year –compare GDP

gnu /nuː/ *also* **wildebeest**– *n* **gnu** *or* **gnus** a large southern African animal with a tail and curved horns

go[1] /gəʊ/ *v* **went** /went/, **gone** /gɒn‖gɔːn/*3rd person sing. present* **goes** ■ to move or travel **1** [I] to leave a place (so as to reach another); DEPART: *I wanted to go, but she wanted to stay.* | *It's late; I must go|I must be going.* | *When does the train go?* | *He went early.* | *I left my pen on the desk and now it's gone; who's taken it?* | (fig.) *The summer is going fast.* –see USAGE; see also **be going to** (GO[1]); compare COME[1] **2** [I+*adv/prep*] to travel or move in a particular way or in a particular direction: *We went by bus.* | *It can go by post.* | *He went away and left me.* | *The car's going too fast.* | *Where are you going?* | *We went to France for our holidays.* | *We're going* (=are intending to go) *to my parents' for Christmas.* | *His hand went to his pocket.* | (fig.) *Your suggestion will go* (=be sent) *before the committee.* | (fig.) *I don't know where all my money goes (to)!* **3** [I+*v-ing*] to travel somewhere in order to do the stated activity: *He's gone shopping.* | *We're going swimming this afternoon.* | *She went house-hunting at the weekend.* **b** *infml* to perform the stated undesirable action: *Don't go blaming yourself!* | *It's a secret, so don't go telling everyone about it!* ■ to be in or pass into a particular state **4** [L+*adj*] to pass into a different, often less favourable state, either by a natural change or by changing on purpose; become: *Her hair's/She's going grey.* | *The milk went sour.* | *He's gone mad.* | *This used to be a state school, but it's gone independent.* | *The company has gone bankrupt.* | *He went white with anger.* –see BECOME (USAGE) **5** [L+*adv/adj*] to be or remain in a particular usu. undesirable state: *After his enemy's threats he went in fear of his life.* | *Her complaints went unnoticed.* | *Should a murderer go free|go unpunished?* | *When the crops fail, the people go hungry.* **6** [I] to become weak, damaged, or worn out: *My voice has gone because of my cold.* | *These old shoes are beginning to go.* ■ to start an activity or perform an action **7** [I] to start an action or activity: *All the preparations for the project have been completed, so we're ready to go.* | *The signal to begin a race is "One, two, three, go!" or "Ready, steady, go!"* | *If we don't* **get going** *on this work soon it'll never be ready in time.* **8** [I] (of a machine) to work (properly): *This clock* *doesn't go.* | *I can't get the car to go.*   **9** [T] **a** to make the stated sound: *Ducks go "quack".* | *The guns went "boom".* **b** *nonstandard* to say: *So then she goes "Don't you ever do that again!", and he laughs.*   **10** [I+*adv*|*prep*] to make a particular movement: *When he was explaining it, he went like this with his hands.*   ■ **other meanings** **11** [I+*adv*|*prep*; *not in progressive forms*] to reach (as far as stated): *Which road goes to the station?* | *The valley goes from east to west.* | *The roots of the plant go deep.* | *The belt's too short — it won't go round my waist.* | (fig.) *She's very talented; I'm sure she'll* **go far.** (=be very successful) | (fig.) *A pound doesn't* **go far** (=buy much) *these days.* **12** [I *not in progressive forms*] **a** to fit: *Your foot's too big — it won't go (into the shoe).* **b** [(**into**)] to divide a certain number, esp. so as to give an exact figure: *Three into two won't go.* | *Two goes into ten five times.*   **13** [I+*adv*|*prep*; *not in progressive forms*] to be placed, esp. usually placed: *The chairs can go against that wall.* | *Which cupboard do these plates go in?*   **14** [I (**for, to**)] to be sold: *The house went for £30,000.* | *The oranges were going cheap, so I bought ten.* | *Each lot will go to the highest bidder.* | *"Any more bids for this lot, the silver tray?" said the auctioneer;* *"going ... going ... gone!"* (=I have sold it)   **15** [I] (with **must, can, have to**) to be got rid of: *The car must go — we can't afford it any more.* | *It's no use; that secretary will have to go. She can't even spell!*   **16** [I+*adv*|*prep*; *not in progressive forms*] to be stated, said, or sung in a particular way: *I can't remember how this poem goes.* | *The tune goes something like this.* [+*that*] *The story goes that he was murdered by his wife.*   **17** [I; *not in progressive forms*] to (have to) be accepted or acceptable: *As far as my boss is concerned,* **anything goes.** (=we can do what we like) | *You may not like it, but he's in charge and what he says goes.*   **18** [I+*adv*|*prep*] to happen or develop in the stated way: *The party went well.* | **How are things going**|*infml* **How's it going**|(*old-fash*) **How goes it?** (=Is everything happening satisfactorily?) | *Everything's going fine*|*nicely*|*swimmingly at the moment.* | (*BrE fml*) *It will* **go hard with** *any boy caught cheating.* (=he will be in serious trouble)   **19** [I] *euph* to die: *Now her husband's gone*|**dead and gone,** *she's all on her own.*   ■ **fixed phrases** **20 as**|**so far as something goes** up to but not beyond the limits of something's quality; in itself: *A bike's quite good as far as it goes, but you need a car to be really mobile.*   **21 as someone**|**something goes** compared with the average person or thing of that type: *She's not a bad cook, as cooks go, but she's no expert.* | *It's cheap, as these things go.*   **22 be going** *infml* to be present for use or enjoyment: *Is there any food going?*   **23 be going to (do or happen)** (showing the future; not usu. in sentences containing a condition) **a** (of a person) to intend to: *He's going to buy her some shoes.* (compare *He'll buy her some shoes if she asks him to.*) | *They're going (to go) to Cairo next year.* | *She's going to ring us from the station.* **b** (of a thing or event that cannot be controlled) to be certain to, or expected to, at some time in the future: *Is it going to rain?* | *I'm going to be sick!* | *She's going to have a baby.* —see GONNA (USAGE)   **24 go and: a** to go in order to: *I'll just go and get my pen.* | *It's time you went and saw your mother.* —compare **try and** (TRY[1]) **b** *infml* (often used for expressing surprise) to do the stated thing: *He's gone and ordered a brand new car!* | *You've really* **gone and done it** *now!* (=done something terrible)

▷ USAGE In *AmE* "and" is sometimes left out after "go", but never after "went" or "gone": *Someone's at the door—go see who it is.* | *I'm just about to go do my homework.*◁

25 go as far as ‖ also **so far as** *BrE* to make such a strong statement or take such strong action as: *I wouldn't go so far as to say he's handsome, but he's certainly quite nice-looking.*   **26 go it** *BrE old-fash* to go at a very fast speed: *To get from London to Glasgow in six hours by car is certainly going it!*   **27 go it alone** to act independently: *She's decided to go it alone and start her own business.* **28 go one better** to do better; go beyond: *Very impressive; but I can go one better (than you): I actually spoke to the Queen.*   **29 go steady** *old-fash* (of a boy and girl) to go out together regularly: *They've been going steady for years.*   **30 go too far** to go beyond the limits of what is considered reasonable: *I know he was rude to you, but I think you went too far, insulting his wife like that.*   **31 to go: a** still remaining before something happens: *Only three days to go before*|*to Christmas!* **b** *AmE* (of cooked food sold in a shop) to be taken away and not eaten in the

shop: *Two chicken dinners with corn to go!* —compare TAKEAWAY   **32 that's the way it goes** (an expression used when trying not to feel unhappy about something that has failed, or about bad news) good things and bad things happen, according to chance, and there is nothing you can do about it: *Your sister can't come to visit? Oh well, that's the way it goes.*   **33 -goer** /gəʊəʳ/a person who goes regularly to the stated place or activity: *church-goers* | *filmgoers* —see also GOER   **34 -going** /gəʊɪŋ/(*in* [A] *adjectives and* [U] *nouns*) (the activity of) going regularly to the stated place or activity: *the theatregoing public* | *churchgoing* —see also GOING[1,2], GONE

▷ USAGE The usual past participle of **go** is **gone,** but if we mean "visit" or "go to a place then leave it" it is **been.** Compare: *George has* **gone** *to Paris.* (=he's there now) | *George has* **been** *to Paris.* (=he's visited Paris in the past) | *The doctor hasn't* **gone** *yet.* (=he's still in the house) | *The doctor hasn't* **been** *yet.* (=he has not yet visited the house)◁

■ **phrasal verbs**
go about *phr v* **1** [T] (**go about** sthg.) to perform or do: *It was a typical Monday morning and people were going about their work*|*their business in the usual way.* **2** [T] (**go about** sthg.) also **set about**— to begin working at; TACKLE: *That's not the best way to go about it.* [+*v-ing*] *I wouldn't have the first idea how to go about mending a clock.*   **3** [I] (of a ship) to turn round to face in the opposite direction   **4** [I+**with**/TOGETHER] to GO **around** (2)
go after sthg.|sbdy. *phr v* [T *pass. rare*] to try to obtain or win; chase: *to go after a job*|*a girl*|*a prize*
go against sbdy.|sthg. *phr v* [T *no pass.*] **1** to act in opposition to: *She went against her mother's wishes.*   **2** to be unfavourable to (someone): *Opinion is going against us.* | *The case may go against you.* (=you may lose it)   **3** to be opposite to; not be in agreement with (something): *It would go against my principles to work for a company that manufactured weapons.*
go ahead *phr v* [I]   **1** to go in advance of others: *You go (on) ahead; we'll catch up with you later.*   **2** [(**with**)] to begin: *Go ahead, we're all listening.* | *The council gave us permission to go ahead with our building plans.* | *"Do you mind if I smoke?" "Go ahead."* (=No, I do not mind.) **3** to continue; advance: *Work is going ahead.* —see also GO-AHEAD
go along *phr v* [I] to continue with an activity, movement, plan, etc.; PROCEED: *I like to add up my bank account as I go along.* | *You'll get more used to the job as you go along.*
go along with sbdy.|sthg. *phr v* [T]   **1** to agree with; support: *They were quite happy to go along with our suggestion.* | *I'd go along with you there.*   **2 Go along with you!** *BrE infml* I don't believe you!
go around *phr v* [I]   **1** [*usu. in progressive forms*] also **go round**— (of an illness) to spread: *There are a lot of very bad colds going around at the moment.*   **2** [+**with**/TOGETHER] also **go about**— to be often out in public (with someone): *Why do you go around with such strange people?*   **3** to be enough for everyone; GO **round 4 go at** sthg. *phr v* [T *no pass.*] *infml* to deal with or begin to do with great force or effort; TACKLE: *He went at his breakfast as if he hadn't eaten for days.*
go back *phr v* [I]   **1** to return to a former place, state, method, etc.: *Let's go back home now.* | *If the new arrangement doesn't work out, we'll go back to the old one.* | *Let's go back to what the chairman said earlier.*   **2** [+*adv*|*prep*] to have one's origins in (an earlier time): *Some of the university buildings go back as far as medieval times.* **3** to have been friends with for (a long time): *He and I go back years and years.*
go back on sbdy.|sthg. *phr v* [T *pass. rare*] to break or not keep (a promise, agreement, etc.): *He went back on his word and refused to lend us the money.*
go by *phr v*   **1** [I] to pass (in place or time): *A car went by.* | *Two years went by.* | *She let the chance go by.* (=lost it)   **2** [T *no pass.*] (**go by** sthg.) to act according to; be guided by: *He always goes by the rules.* | *Don't go by that old map; it might be out of date.*   **3** [T *no pass.*] (**go by** sthg.) to judge by: *Going by her clothes, she must be very rich.*
go down *phr v* [I]   **1** to become lower in price, value, level, quantity, etc.: *The standard of work has gone down.* | *The (value of the) dollar has gone down again.* | *Eggs are going down (in price).* | *He's gone down in my opinion since I discovered his political views.* | *This*

neighbourhood has gone down (=to a lower social level) *in the last few years.* **2** to sink; disappear from sight or below a surface: *Three ships went down in the storm.* | *The sun is going down.* **3** to become less swollen: *My ankle has gone down, so I should be able to walk again soon.* | *This tyre's going down; I'll pump it up.* **4** (of a computer or machine) to stop working suddenly: *The central computer went down this morning, so we can't check whether that's been paid or not.* **5** [+*adv/prep*] to be accepted: *Her speech went down well (with the crowd).* **6** (of food and drink) to pass down the throat: *The pills wouldn't go down so I dissolved them in some water.* **7** *AmE* to happen: *"What's going down, bro?"* | *"We're going out to see what's going down."* **8** [+*adv/prep*, esp. **in**] to be recorded: *This day will go down in history.* **9** [+*adv/prep*, esp. **to**] to reach as far as: *The mountains go right down to the sea.* **10** [(**from, to**)] *BrE* to leave a university after a period of study, or a city for a less important place: *He went down without taking a degree.* | *We're going down to the country for the weekend.* **11** [(**for**)] *sl* to be sent to prison: *He went down for five years.* **12 go down the tubes/drain** *infml, derog* to become poorer in quality: *This place has really gone down the tubes.*

go down with sthg. *phr v* [T *no pass.*] *infml* to catch (an infectious illness): *They all went down with scarlet fever.*

go for sbdy./sthg. *phr v* [T *no pass.*] **1** to attack, physically or with words: *Our dog went for the postman this morning!* | *She really went for me when I came in late.* **2** to try to obtain or win: *I hear you're going to go for that job in the accounts department.* | *Smith is going for gold* (=will try to win the GOLD MEDAL) *in the 200 metres.* **3** to choose or take: *When you offer him sweets he always goes for the biggest one.* **4** to like or be attracted by: *Do you go for modern music?* | *I don't go for men of his type.* **5** to concern or be true for (someone or something): *I think this report is badly done, and that goes for all the other work done in this office.* | *He thought the lunch was terrible, and the same goes for all the rest of us too.* (=we also thought it was terrible) **6 Go for it!** *infml* do it; try it; get it (said about something exciting): *I think the team's got the ball – go for it!* **7 go for nothing** to be wasted; have no result: *All my hard work went for nothing.*

go in *phr v* [I] **1** (of the sun, moon, etc.) to become covered by cloud **2** [(**with**)] to join: *They invited me to go in with them to form a new company.*

go in for sthg. *phr v* [T] **1** to take part in (a test of skill or knowledge); enter: *to go in for a competition* | *Several people went in for the race.* **2** to make a habit of (doing), esp. for enjoyment: *I don't go in for sports.* [+*v-ing*] *I've never gone in (much) for dancing.*

go into sthg. *phr v* [T] **1** [*no pass.*] to enter (a profession, state of life, etc.): *She plans to go into politics when she leaves university.* | *He went into business as an undertaker.* **2** [*no pass.*] to be put into: *Three years' work has gone into this scheme.* **3** to explain in depth: *He didn't go into details, but I gather from what he said that she was seriously injured.* | *This new textbook goes into all the complexities of grammatical theory.* **4** to examine thoroughly: *There's something mysterious about his death; it'll have to be gone into by the police.*

go off *phr v* **1** [I] **a** to explode: *Don't touch that unexploded bomb; it might go off!* **b** to ring or sound loudly: *The alarm went off when the thieves got in.* **2** [I] to stop operating: *The heating goes off at night.* | *The lights went off.* **3** [I+*adv/prep*] to happen in the stated way; COME **off** (2): *The conference went off very well* (= was a success). **4** [I] (of food) to go bad: *This milk has gone off.* **5** [I] *BrE* to stop being felt: *The pain went off after three treatments.* **6** [T] (**go off** sthg./sbdy.) **a** *BrE infml* to lose interest in or liking for: *I've gone off coffee recently.* [+*v-ing*] *Mary and I have gone off cooking, so we live on salads these days.* **b** *AmE* to stop using, eating, or drinking something: *The doctor said to go off coffee and chocolate.* **7** [I] *BrE infml* to go down from a higher level of skill, quality, interest, etc.: *The lessons have gone off since we had a new teacher.* | *The book goes off after the first 50 pages.*

go off with sthg./sbdy. *phr v* [T] **1** *infml* to take away without permission: *Someone's gone off with my pen!* **2** to leave one's marriage partner and start living with (someone else): *He went off with his secretary.*

go on *phr v* **1** [I] to take place or happen: *There's a children's party going on next door.* | *What's going on here?* | *Their secretive behaviour made me suspect there was some-*

thing illegal going on. –see also GOINGS-ON **2** [I] to begin to operate: *I've set the heating to go on at six o'clock.* | *The lights went on.* **3** [T *no pass.*] (**go on** sthg.) **a** to use as a reason, proof, or base for further action: *We were just going on what Aunt Jess told us of the situation.* | *A bloody handkerchief and the name "Margaret" were all the police had to go on to catch the killer.* **b** to start using (a drug): *I'm going on the birth control pill next week.* | *to go on tranquillizers* **4** [I] to go in advance of others; GO **ahead**: *You go on; we'll catch up with you later.* **5** [I] (of time) to pass: *As time went on, things began to change.* | *As the day went on, it became hotter.* **6** [I (**with**)] **a** to continue without stopping or without change: *Go on with your work.* | *We can't go on like this – I want a divorce!* [+*v-ing*] *She didn't want to go on being a secretary all her life, so she went back to college.* **b** to continue talking, esp. after stopping or in order to pass to a new subject: *Go on, I'm listening.* | *He paused for a sip of coffee, then went on with his story.* [+*to-v*] *After describing the planned improvements, she went on to explain how much they would cost.* –see also ONGOING **7** [I+*adv/prep*] to behave continually in a certain way: *If he goes on like this he'll lose his job.* | *To judge by the way she's going on, she's very nervous about something.* **8** [I (**at**)] to keep complaining or criticizing: *She's always going on at her husband.* **9** [I] *infml* to keep talking to the point of being annoying: *He does go on so!* | *She goes on and on.* **10** [I] *infml* to advance or develop; GET **on**: *How's the work going on?* **11 Go on (with you)!** *infml* I don't believe you! **12 to go/be going on with** *infml, esp. BrE* (to use) for the present time: *Here's £30 to be going on with; I'll give you some more tomorrow.*

go out *phr v* [I] **1** to leave the house, esp. for amusement: *She's gone out for a walk.* | *He goes out drinking two or three times a week.* **2** [(TOGETHER, **with**)] to spend time, esp. regularly (with someone of the opposite sex): *They've been going out (together) for two years.* **3** [(**to**)] to travel to a usu. distant place, esp. in order to live there: *My friends went out to Australia.* **4** to be made public, be sent: *Have the notices all gone out?* **5** (of a fire, light, etc.) to stop burning or shining: *Without more coal, the fire will soon go out.* | (fig.) *As soon as he got into bed, he went out like a light.* (=went to sleep very quickly) **6** (of the sea) to go back to its low level: *The tide's going out.* –opposite **come in 7** to stop being fashionable: *Short skirts went out some time ago.* –opposite **come in 8** [+*adv/prep*, esp. **to**] *fml* (of feelings) to be in sympathy (with): *Our thoughts go out to our friends abroad.* **9** [+*adv/prep*] *esp. lit* (of time) to end: *March went out with high winds and rain.*

go over *phr v* **1** [T] (**go over** sthg.) **a** to visit and examine: *We went over several houses before we found the one we wanted.* **b** to look at and examine for a purpose; CHECK: *We went over the accounts very thoroughly but couldn't find any mistakes.* –see also GOING-OVER **2** [T] (**go over** sthg.) to repeat: *If they don't understand it the first time, go over it (again) until they do.* **3** [I+*adv/prep*] (of a performance) to be received in the stated way: *His speech went over well.* **4** [I+**from/to**] to change (one's political party, religion, etc.): *He went over from the Democrats to the Republicans.* | *I've gone over to (eating) vegetarian food.* **5** [I (**to**)] (in television or radio) to cause the broadcast to be made from another place: *We're now going over to the House of Commons for an important announcement.*

go round *phr v* [I] **1** also **go around**– to be enough for everyone: *If there aren't enough chairs to go round, some people will have to stand.* **2** (of an illness) to spread; GO **around 3** (of words, ideas, etc.) to be continuously present: *There's a tune going round in my head.*

go slow *phr v* [I] *BrE* to refuse to put more than the least amount of effort into one's work, as a form of STRIKE –see also GO-SLOW

go through *phr v* **1** [T] (**go through** sthg.) to suffer or experience; ENDURE: *The country has gone/been through too many wars.* | *I admire the way she's still so cheerful after all she's been through.* **2** [T] (**go through** sthg.) to use up; to finish; GET **through** (2): *Have you gone through all your money already?* **3** [I;T (=**go through** sthg.)] (of a law, etc.) to pass through or be accepted (by): *The bill has gone through (Parliament) without a vote.* | *The plan must go through several stages.* **4** [T] (**go through** sthg.) to practise (a ceremony or performance): *Let's go through it again, this time with the music.* **5** [T] (**go through** sthg.) to look at or examine carefully: *I'm* sure it's there — I'll go through the file again. | She went through his jacket pockets and eventually found the keys.

go through with sthg. *phr v* [T] to complete (something which has been agreed or planned), often with difficulty: *He promised to marry her, but now he doesn't want to go through with it.*

go to sthg. *phr v* [T *no pass.*] **1** to cause oneself to experience: *He went to a lot of trouble for me.* | *They went to great expense to educate their children.* | *They went to great lengths* (=took a lot of trouble) *to ensure that no one would find out the truth.* **2** to start experiencing or causing (a state or action): *Be quiet; I'm trying to go to sleep.* | *Britain and Germany went to war in 1939.* —see also **go to pieces** (PIECE¹)

go together *phr v* [I] **1** (of two or more things) to match or suit each other **2** *AmE, infml* (usu. said by older children) to **go steady** (STEADY³): *We're going together.* | *Do you want to go together?*

go under *phr v* [I] **1** (of a ship or floating object) to sink below the surface **2** to fail, be defeated, or get into difficulties: *Unless the company's sales improve soon, it will go under.*

go up *phr v* [I] **1** to rise; increase: *Prices have gone up again.* **2** to be built: *There are new houses going up everywhere round here.* **3** to explode or be destroyed in fire: *The whole house went up in flames.* —see also **go up in smoke** (SMOKE¹) **4** (of the curtain on stage) to open and start the performance: *What time does the curtain go up?* **5** [(to)] *BrE* to go to a university, esp. to begin a course of study, or to a more important place: *to go up to London* **6** [+*adv/prep*, esp. **to**] to reach as far as: *The trees go right up to the riverbank.*

go with *phr v* [T *no pass.*] **1** to match or suit: *Mary's blue dress goes with her eyes.* | *Mint sauce goes well with roast lamb.* **2** to be gained with or included with, esp. as a result: *Happiness doesn't necessarily go with money.* [+*v-ing*] *Responsibility goes with becoming a father.* **3** *infml* to spend time socially, or (*euph*) sexually, with (someone of the opposite sex): *He goes with a different girl every week.* **4** *AmE, infml* to choose: *f I were you I'd go with the red one, Pete.* **5** **go with the crowd/the times/the stream/the flow** to behave or think in the same way as most people **6** **go with that/it** *AmE, infml* to continue to do or to develop something, such as a course of action or an idea: *I know university has been difficult, but go with it for just a while longer.*

go without (sthg.) *phr v* [I;T+*obj/v-ing*] **1** to succeed in living without (something), do without. *She went without sleep/without sleeping for five days.* | *We can't afford it, so we'll just have to go without.* **2 it goes without saying** it is clear without needing to be stated: *If you take a job as a journalist, it goes without saying that sometimes you'll have to work at weekends.*

go² *n goes infml* **1** [C] *esp. BrE* one's turn, esp. in a game: *It's my go now.* **2** [C (**at**)] *esp. BrE* an attempt to do something: *"I can't open this jar." "Let me* **have a go.**" | *He had several goes at the exam before he passed.* **3** [U] an active lively quality; VITALITY: *The children are full of go. They run and play all day.* | *She's got plenty of go, and is sure to do well in her job.* —see also GET UP AND GO **4** [C *usu. sing.*] *BrE old-fash* an (awkward or strange) state of affairs: *This is a bit of a rum go!* **5 (all) the go** *BrE infml* very fashionable **6 have a go** *infml, BrE* a to complain: *My boyfriend is sure to have a go at me for spending so much money.* **b** to attempt to catch or stop a wrongdoer by force: *This criminal may be armed, so the police advise the public against having a go.* **7 it's all go** *BrE infml* it is very busy: *It's all go in the postal service at Christmas time!* **8 (it's) no go** *infml* it has not happened or it will not happen: *I tried to persuade her to accept your plan, but (it was) no go, I'm afraid.* —see also NO-GO AREA **9 make a go of** *infml* **a** *BrE* to make a success of: *Do you think they'll ever make a go of their marriage?* **b** *AmE* to try (to do something): *I think we can reach the top — do you want to make a go of it?* **10 on the go** *infml* working all the time or very busy: *I've been on the go all day and I'm worn out.*

goad¹ /gəʊd/ *v* [T] **1** [(**into**, ON)] to cause (someone) to do something by strong or continued annoyance: *If you keep goading her with those insults she may turn nasty.* | *They goaded him into doing it by saying he was a coward.* | *He was tired of working but the need for money goaded him on.* **2** to drive (esp. cattle) with a goad

goad² *n* a sharp-pointed stick for driving cattle or other

animals forward: (fig.) *They needed the goad of threatened fines to make them take action.*

go-a·head¹ /ˈ·· ·ˌ·/ *n* [S] permission to take action: *We're ready to start the new building as soon as we get/we are given the go-ahead from the council.* —see also GO **ahead**

go-ahead² *adj BrE* active in using new methods; PROGRESSIVE: *It's a very go-ahead company; they were among the first to introduce profit-sharing.*

goal /gəʊl/ *n* **1** (in games such as football and HOCKEY) the area, usu. between two goalposts, where the ball, PUCK, etc., must go for a point to be gained: *He kicked the ball into the goal.* | (*BrE*) *He has kept goal* (=been goalkeeper) *for England.* —see picture at SOCCER **2** the point gained when the ball is caused to do this: *He scored a goal.* | *Brazil beat France by two goals to one.* **3** one's aim or purpose; a position or object one wishes to reach or obtain: *Her goal is a place at university.* | *The company has achieved all its goals this year.* | *Before starting on a project like this, you have to set yourself some clearly defined goals.* —see also OWN GOAL

goal·keep·er /ˈgəʊlˌkiːpə^r/ also **goal·ie** /ˈgəʊli/ *infml*— *n* the player in a football or other sports team who is responsible for preventing the ball from getting into his or her team's goal: *The goalkeeper made a marvellous save.*

goal kick /ˈ· ·/ *n* (in football) a FREE KICK taken by the defending team when the ball is sent over the goal line by the opposing team

goal line /ˈ· ·/ *n* a line at either end and usu. running the width of a playing area, on which a GOAL (1) is placed

goal·mouth /ˈgəʊlmaʊθ/ *n* the area directly in front of the GOAL (1)

goal·post /ˈgəʊlpəʊst/ *n* [*usu. pl.*] one of the two posts, with a bar along the top or across the middle, and usu. with a net at the back, that form the GOAL (1) in games like football and HOCKEY —see also **move the goalposts** (MOVE¹)

goat /gəʊt/ *n* **1** a horned animal related to the sheep, which also gives milk and wool, and which can climb steep hills and rocks and eat almost anything **2** *esp. BrE infml, esp. derog or humor* a man who is very active sexually; esp. one who is old or not sexually attractive **3 get someone's goat** *infml* to make someone extremely annoyed —see also BILLY GOAT, KID¹ (3), NANNY GOAT

goat

goa·tee /gəʊˈtiː/ *n* a little pointed beard on the bottom of the chin, like the hair on a male goat's chin

goat·herd /ˈgəʊthɜːd‖-hɜːrd/ *n* a person who looks after a FLOCK (=a group) of goats

goat·skin /ˈgəʊtˌskɪn/ *n* [C;U] (leather made from) the skin of a goat

gob¹ /gɒb‖gɑːb/ *n BrE sl, impolite* the mouth: *Shut your gob!*

gob² *n* [(**of**)] *sl* **1** a mass of something wet and sticky: *gobs of spit* **2** also **gobs** *AmE infml* a large amount of: *gobs of money* | *He gave me a whole gob of extra work to do just as he was leaving.*

gob·bet /ˈgɒbᵻt‖ˈgɑː-/ *n* [(**of**)] *infml* a lump or piece of something, esp. food

gob·ble¹ /ˈgɒbəl‖ˈgɑː-/ *v* [I;T (UP)] *infml* to eat very quickly, and sometimes noisily: *Don't gobble your breakfast.* | (fig.) *Inflation soon gobbled up our pay increase.*

gobble² *v* [I] to make the sound a TURKEY makes —**gobble** *n*

gob·ble·dy·gook , **-degook** /ˈgɒbəldiguːk‖ˈgɑːbəldɪguk, -guːk/ *n* [U] *infml derog* meaningless t ut important-sounding official language; often very difficult to understand: *bureaucratic gobbledygook*

go-be·tween /ˈ· ·ˌ·/ *n* a person who takes messages from one person or side to another, because the two sides cannot meet or do not wish to meet: *She acted as a go-between in the delicate negotiations.*

Go·bi /ˈgəʊbi/ also **Gobi Des·ert** /ˌ·· ˈ···/— [the] one of the world's largest deserts, covering half a million square miles, in central Asia

gob·let /ˈgɒblɪt‖ˈgɑːb-/ *n esp. old use* a container for drinking, usu. of glass or metal, with a base and stem but no handles, and used esp. for wine

goblin

gob·lin /ˈgɒblɪ̯n‖ˈgɑːb-/ *n* a small, often ugly, FAIRY that is usu. unkind or evil and plays tricks on people —see also HOBGOBLIN

gob·smacked /ˈgɒbsmækt‖ˈgɑːb-/ also **gob·struck** /ˈgɒbstrʌk‖ˈgɑːb-/— *adj BrE infml* suffering from great surprise, disappointment, pleasure, or other strong emotion; flabbergasted (FLABBERGAST)

gob·stop·per /ˈgɒbstɒpəʳ‖ˈgɑːbstɑː-/ *BrE*‖**jawbreaker** *AmE*— *n* a large, round, hard sweet

god /gɒd‖gɑːd/ *n* a being who is worshipped, esp. for having made or for ruling over the world or a part of the world: *They made a sacrifice to the god of rain.* | *The ancient Greeks had many gods.* | (fig.) *He* **makes a god of** *his work* (=gives too much importance to it), *and forgets his family.* —see also GODS, TIN GOD, **in the lap of the gods** (LAP¹)

God **1** the being who in the Christian, Jewish, and Muslim religions is worshipped as maker and ruler of the world: *to pray to God* | *a mosque built to the glory of God* —see also ACT OF GOD, GOD'S GIFT

▶CULTURAL NOTE British and American people often imagine God as a very old man with a white beard.◀

2 **God (alone) knows** *infml* it's impossible to say: *God knows where he went!* | *It'll cost God knows how much.* **3** **God forbid (that)** I very much hope it will not happen (that): *God forbid that I should ever have to work with him again.* **4** **God moves in mysterious ways** *quote* a phrase from a religious song, often used humorously when saying that an unexpected event may bring advantages **5** **God's in his heaven, all's right with the world** *quote* a phrase from a poem by Robert Browning **6** **God willing** if all goes well **7** **Man proposes, God disposes** an old saying, meaning that people can make plans, but whether or not they are successful depends on the will of God **8** **My God, My God, why hast thou forsaken me?** *quote from the Bible* the phrase used in the Bible by Christ just before he died on the cross **9** **Nearer my God to Thee** the title of a religious song, believed to have been sung by the people on the ship "Titanic" as it sank **10** **Oh God/My God/Good God!** (strong expressions of surprise, fear, annoyance, etc.) **11** **thank God** (an expression of happiness that trouble has passed): *Thank God you're safe!* —see also ACT OF GOD **12** **you cannot serve both God and Mammon** *quote from the Bible* you cannot serve two gods, i.e. spend all your time trying to get rich and be a Christian

▷USAGE 1 **God grant (that)** is usually used in a religious way. **God forbid (that)** is often used in a non-religious way to express strong dislike of a possibility: *"I expect Smithson will be the next Prime Minister." "Smithson? God forbid!"* **Oh God/My God/Good God/For God's sake** are used in a non-religious way, though some people may find them offensive. —see also JESUS (USAGE), SAKE (USAGE) 2 **God** is written with a capital letter. The pronouns which refer to **God** are **He, Him,** and **His,** and they too are written with a capital letter: *We prayed to God, and He answered our prayers.*◁

God·ard /ˈgɒdɑː‖ˈgɑːdɑːrd/, **Jean-Luc** /ʒɒn luːk‖ʒɑin-/ (1930–) a French film DIRECTOR remembered esp. for the film *Breathless*

god·aw·ful /ˌ·ˈ··◀/ *adj sl* very bad or unpleasant

god·child /ˈgɒdtʃaɪld‖ˈgɑːd-/ *n* **-children** /ˌtʃɪldrən/ (in the

Christian religion) the child (**godson** or **goddaughter**) for whom a GODPARENT takes responsibility by making promises at a ceremony (BAPTISM) e.g. to look after them if anything happens to their parents and to bring them up in the Christian faith

god·damn , **goddam** /ˈgɒdæm‖ˈgɑː-/also **god·damned** /-ˈdæmd/ *adj, adv, interj* [A] DAMN¹, ²

god·dess /ˈgɒdɪs‖ˈgɑː-/ *n* a female being who is worshipped, esp. for having made or for ruling over the world or part of the world: *the goddess of the moon*

god·fa·ther /ˈgɒdˌfɑːðəʳ‖ˈgɑːd-/ *n* **1** a male GODPARENT **2** *sl (often cap.)* the head of a criminal organization or Mafia family

the actor Marlon Brando as The Godfather

Godfather, The a film based on a book by Mario Puzo about an Italian godfather (2) who was a powerful member of the Mafia, and arranged crime using his family and friends. The Godfather was played by the actor Marlon Brando. Later two more films were made as part of the same story.

god·fear·ing /ˈ·ˌ··/ *adj old-fash* morally good and closely following the rules of the Christian religion; GODLY

god·for·sak·en /ˈgɒdfəseɪkən‖ˈgɑːdfər-/ *adj derog* (of a place) far from cities and towns and containing nothing useful, interesting, attractive, or cheerful, and often in very bad condition, in very wild country, etc.: *He was sent to work in some godforsaken remote village.*

god·head /ˈgɒdhed‖ˈgɑːd-/ *n [the] fml* God

Lady Godiva

Go·di·va /gəˈdaɪvə/, **Lady** an 11th-century British woman of high rank who is believed to have ridden a horse through Coventry with no clothes on as a PROTEST, to persuade her husband to lower the local taxes

god·less /ˈgɒdləs‖ˈgɑːd-/ *adj fml* wicked; not showing respect for God or belief in God — ~ **ly** *adv* — ~ **ness** *n* [U]

god·like /ˈgɒdlaɪk‖ˈgɑːd-/ *adj* like or suitable to God or a god: *godlike beauty/calm*

god·ly /ˈgɒdli‖ˈgɑːd-/ *adj fml* showing obedience to God by leading a good life —**·liness** *n* [U]

god·moth·er /ˈgɒdˌmʌðəʳ‖ˈgɑːd-/ *n* a female godparent — see also FAIRY GODMOTHER

god·pa·rent /ˈgɒdˌpeərənt‖ˈgɑːd-/ *n* the person (**godfather** or **godmother**) who makes promises to help a Christian newly received into the church at a special ceremony (BAPTISM) —see also GODCHILD

God Rest You Mer·ry Gen·tle·men /ˌ·ˌ··ˌ··ˈ···/ a religious song (CAROL) sung at Christmas

gods /gɒdz‖gɑːdz/ *n [the+P] infml* the seats high up at the back of a theatre

God Save the Queen /ˌ·ˈ··ˌˈ·/ the name of the British NATIONAL ANTHEM. "Queen" changes to "King" when a king rules.

god·send /ˈgɒdsend‖ˈgɑːd-/ *n infml* an unexpected lucky chance or event, often badly needed: *That legacy from my* *uncle's will was a godsend, because I was very short of money.*

God's gift /ˌ· '·/ *infml* **God's gift to men/women/ mankind** *often derog* a man or woman who thinks that he/she is perfect, esp. by being very attractive: *He seems to think he's God's gift to women!*

God Slot /'· ·/ *n BrE infml* a regular religious broadcast on radio or television

god·speed /ˌgɒd'spiːd‖'gɑːdspiːd, ˌgɑːd'spiːd/ *n* [U] *old use* good luck, esp. in a journey or activity: *We wished/bade him godspeed as he set off on his quest.*

God squad /'· ·/ *[the] infml derog* a word used to describe Christians who go about trying to persuade people to join their religion

Godt·haab /'gɒdhɔːb ‖ 'gɑːd-/ a former name for NUUK

God·win-Aus·ten /ˌgɒdwɪn 'ɒstɪn‖ˌgɑːdwɪn 'ɔːs-/, Mount see K2

Goeb·bels /'gɜːbəlz/, **Paul Joseph** (1897–1945) a German Nazi politician who controlled German PROPAGANDA during the Second World War

go·er /'gəʊəʳ/ *n infml, esp. BrE* **1** a person or thing that moves or does things fast: *My new car's a real goer.* **2** a person who is always ready for new activity, esp. sexual activity: *She's a bit of a goer.* —see also **-goer** (GO¹ (3))

Goe·ring /'gɜːrɪŋ/, **Her·mann Wil·helm** /'hɜːmən 'wɪlhelm‖'hɜːr-/ (1893–1946) a German Nazi military commander who was head of the German airforce in the Second World War

Goe·the /'gɜːtə/, **Jo·hann Wolf·gang von** /'jəʊhæn 'wʊlfgæŋ vɒn‖-hɑːn-, -vɑːn/ (1749–1832) a German poet and scientist, and one of the best known writers of plays and books of all time, known esp. for his play *Faust*

go·fer /'gəʊfəʳ/ *n esp. AmE* a person whose job is to get or take things for other people —compare GOPHER

Gog and Ma·gog /ˌgɒg ənd 'meɪgɒg‖ˌgɑːg ənd 'meɪgɑːg/ in old stories, the last two of a race of GIANTS living in Britain in Roman times. In the Apocalypse in the Bible they represent the future enemies of the kingdom of God.

go-get·ter /ˌ· '··, '· ˌ··‖'· ˌ··/ *n* someone who is forceful and determined and likely to succeed in getting what they want. This kind of person is usu. admired: *She's a real go-getter.*

gog·gle /'gɒgəl‖'gɑː-/ *v* [I (**at**)] to look hard with the eyes wide open or moving around, usu. in great surprise: *The children goggled in amazement at the peculiar old man.* —compare GAWP

goggle box /'·· ·/ ‖ **boob tube** *AmE n* [*the*+S] *humor, esp. BrE* television

goggle-eyed /ˌ··· '·◄/ *adj infml* with the eyes standing out as if surprised

goggles

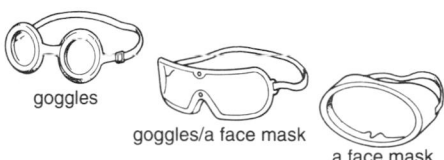

goggles

goggles/a face mask

a face mask

gog·gles /'gɒgəlz‖'gɑː-/ *n* [P] (a pair of) large round pieces of glass or plastic with an edge which fits against the skin so that dust and wind or water cannot get near the eyes: *motorcycle goggles | ski goggles* —see PAIR (USAGE)

go-go /'· ·/ *adj* [A] **1** of or being a form of fast dancing with sexy movements, usu. performed by one or more girls in a nightclub, bar, etc.: *go-go dancing* **2** *infml* up-to-date and eager: *a go-go style of management*

go·ing¹ /'gəʊɪŋ/ *n* [U] **1** the act of someone's leaving: *Her going will be a great loss to the company.* **2** the rate of travel or advance towards an aim: *We climbed the mountain in three hours, which was very good going. | The going was slow on the project because of a shortage of skilled workers.* **3** the condition or possibility of movement or travel: *The mud made it rough/hard going for the car. | Let's leave* **while the going's good.** (=while we can) | (fig.) *I found the book very* **heavy going.** (=dull and

difficult to read) —see also **comings and goings** (COMING¹)

going² *adj* **1** [F] able to be obtained: *Are there any jobs going in your factory?* **2** [A] as charged at present: *The* **going rate** *for the job is £6 an hour.* **3** [after *superlative adj* + *n*] in existence: *He's the biggest fool going. | That's the best car going.* **4** **have a lot/plenty/nothing going for one** *infml* to have many/no advantages or good qualities: *I think this new system has a lot going for it.*

going con·cern /ˌ·· '·/ *n* a business which is operating in the usual way, making a profit, and expected to continue to do so

going-o·ver /ˌ·· '··/ *n* **goings-over** *infml* **1** a (thorough) examination and/or treatment: *The car needs a proper going-over before we use it again.* —see also GO **over** (1) **2** *BrE* a severe beating or an angry complaint: *If he refuses to pay, I'll get the boys to* **give** *him* **a going-over.** | *She got a real going-over (from her parents) for coming home late.*

goings-on /ˌ·· '·/ *n* [P] *infml* activities or events, usu. of an undesirable kind: *Stories of scandalous goings-on at the palace began to leak out to the papers.* —see also GO **on** (1)

goi·tre *BrE* ‖ **-ter** *AmE* /'gɔɪtəʳ/ *n* [U] a medical condition in which an organ (the THYROID) in the front of the neck gets larger, sometimes because the body lacks certain chemical substances

go-kart ‖also **go-cart** *AmE* /'gəʊ kɑːt‖-kɑːrt/ *n* a small racing vehicle made of an open frame on four wheels, with an engine

Go·lan Heights /ˌgəʊlæn 'haɪts‖-lɑːn-/ *[the*+P] a range of hills and mountains E of the Jordan River, occupied by Israel since 1967.

gold¹ /gəʊld/ *n* **1** [U] a valuable soft yellow metal that is a substance (ELEMENT) and is used for making coins, jewellery, etc.: *a rich vein of gold in the rock | The men were panning for gold in the river. One of them suddenly* **struck gold.** (=found gold) | *a gold mine* **2** [U] coins, jewellery, or other objects made of this metal: *People used to pay in gold. | She wore so much jewellery that she seemed to be covered in gold.* **3** [U] the colour of this metal: *the gold of her hair* **4** [C] a GOLD MEDAL —see also **as good as gold** (GOOD¹) **5** **gold, frankincense, and myrrh** (in the Bible) the gifts brought by the Three Wise Men to the baby Jesus **6** **there's gold in them thar hills** *humor* (a phrase used to suggest that something is likely to be profitable. The phrase is supposed to represent the speech of an old American gold-miner.

gold² *adj* **1** made of gold: *a gold bar/ingot | a gold watch* **2** of the colour of gold: *a gold car | gold paint* —compare GOLDEN

Gold·berg /'gəʊldbɜːg‖-bɜːrg/, **Whoop·i** /'wʊpi/ (1949–) an American film actress who appeared in *The Color Purple* and *Ghost*

Whoopi Goldberg

Gold Blend /ˌ· '·/ *n tdmk* a type of INSTANT coffee made by Nescafé

gold·brick¹ /'gəʊldbrɪk/ *n AmE infml derog* a worthless thing that appears to be valuable: *This new all-in-one personal organizer is a goldbrick if I ever saw one.*

goldbrick² *v* [I] *AmE infml* to stay away from one's work or responsibilities, esp. with the false excuse that one is ill: *George called in sick but I think he's goldbricking; he's got tickets for the baseball game.*

gold card /'· ˌ·/ *n tdmk* a CREDIT CARD available to people with a lot of money or property

Gold Coast /'· ˌ·/ *n* **1** the former name of **Ghana** before 1957 **2** [C] *AmE* an expensive area of nice homes, esp. one near water: *Chicago's Gold Coast along Lake Shore Drive*

Gold Cup /ˌ· '·/ *[the]* a horse race held every March in Cheltenham, England

gold dig·ger /'· ˌ··/ *n* **1** *old-fash derog sl* a woman who tries to attract rich men so that she can get money and presents **2** a person who tries to find gold by digging in the earth

gold dust /ˈ·ˌ·/ n [U] gold in the form of a fine powder: (fig.) *Good computer personnel are like gold dust.* (=very valuable and hard to find)

gold·en /ˈɡəʊldən/ adj **1** esp. lit made of gold: *a golden crown* **2** esp. lit of the colour of gold: *golden hair* **3** [A] very favourable or advantageous: *I missed a golden chance/opportunity to make a lot of money.* **4** [A] very successful or having qualities that promise future success: *He's one of the company's golden boys; sales have doubled since he took over as marketing director. | the golden girl of US tennis* —compare GOLD²

golden age /ˈ·· ·/ n [(of)] a period of time, either real or imaginary, when everyone was happy, the best work was done, etc.: *The 17th century was the golden age of Dutch painting. | People are always harking back to an imaginary golden age.*

golden an·ni·ver·sa·ry /ˌ··· ··ˈ···/ n AmE for GOLDEN WEDDING

golden calf /ˌ·· ˈ·/ n a CALF (=young cow) made from gold which, in a Bible story, was worshipped by the Jews. It is now used to represent the false worship of material things, rather than God.

golden ea·gle /ˌ·· ˈ··/ n a large golden-brown meat-eating bird that lives in northern parts of the world

golden egg /ˌ·· ˈ·/ n an egg made of gold laid by the GOLDEN GOOSE

golden fleece /ˌ·· ˈ·/ [the] in CLASSICAL MYTHOLOGY, the gold FLEECE of a magical flying RAM which Jason and the Argonauts obtained after many adventures

Golden Gate /ˌ·· ˈ·/ [the] the stretch of water, crossed by the **Golden Gate Bridge**, which joins San Francisco Bay in California, US, to the Pacific Ocean —see colour map on pages 1374–5

the Golden Gate Bridge

Golden Globe A·ward /ˌ·· ˈ· ·ˌ·/ n a prize given by a group of newspaper writers for excellent work in films or television. Many of the people, films, or television programmes that win these prizes go on to win an Academy Award or an Emmy Award.

Golden Gloves /ˌ·· ˈ·/ n [the] an American competition for AMATEUR (=unpaid) BOXERs

golden goose /ˌ·· ˈ·/ n a magical GOOSE in an old story, which laid one golden egg each day. The owners of the goose tried to open the goose up, to get out all the eggs that were inside, but in doing so they killed the goose. —see also GOOSE (3)

golden hand·cuffs /ˌ·· ˈ··/ n [P] a large amount of money given to someone by their employer to persuade them to stay in their present job and not leave for another job

golden hand·shake /ˌ·· ˈ··/ n BrE a large amount of money given to someone when they leave a job, esp. when the company has asked them to leave

golden hel·lo /ˌ·· ·ˈ·/ n a payment offered to someone to persuade them to join a company

golden ju·bi·lee /ˌ·· ˈ··/ n the date that is exactly 50 years after the date of some important personal event, esp. of becoming a king or queen —compare DIAMOND JUBILEE, SILVER JUBILEE

golden mean /ˌ·· ˈ·/ n [(the) S] a balance between two extreme positions, ideas, etc.

golden old·ie , golden oldy /ˌɡəʊldən ˈəʊldi/ n a popular song that may be many years old, but that people still enjoy listening to: *This radio station only plays golden oldies.*

golden par·a·chute /ˌ·· ˈ···/ n infml part of an EXECUTIVE's contract according to which she/he will be paid a large sum of money when the contract ends, even if she/he did not work well

golden rule /ˌ·· ˈ·/ n [S] a very important fact, principle, way of behaving, etc. that must be remembered

Golden Rule, The an idea from the Bible that people should treat others in the way that they want to be treated themselves: *I've always tried to live by the Golden Rule.*

golden syr·up /ˌ·· ˈ··/ n [U] BrE a sweet thick liquid made from sugar, that is spread on bread and used in cooking

Golden Tem·ple /ˌ·· ˈ··/ [the] the centre of the Sikh religion in Amritsar, India, a temple which stands in the middle of a holy lake and contains the holy book of the Sikhs. In 1984 a group of Sikhs took over the temple and there was a battle between the Sikhs and Indian soldiers. Many people were killed.

Golden Tri·an·gle /ˌ·· ˈ···/ [the] part of SE Asia where OPIUM poppies (POPPY) are grown. Most of the world's raw opium comes from this area.

golden wed·ding /ˌ·· ˈ··/ n also **golden wedding an·ni·ver·sa·ry** /ˌ·· ·ˈ···ˌ···/ ‖ also **golden anniversary** AmE— the date that is exactly 50 years after the date of a wedding —compare DIAMOND WEDDING, SILVER WEDDING

Golden Won·der /ˌ·· ·ˈ··/ n tdmk a type of potato CRISP (1); there are many different FLAVOURs of Golden Wonder crisps. Golden Wonder is a division of Dalgety Spillers Foods Limited

gold·field /ˈɡəʊldfiːld/ also **goldfields** pl.— n an area of land where gold can be found

gold·finch /ˈɡəʊldˌfɪntʃ/ n a small singing bird with some yellow feathers

gold·fish /ˈɡəʊldˌfɪʃ/ n goldfish a small shiny esp. orange fish which is kept as a pet in glass bowls in houses, and in ORNAMENTAL pools in gardens

goldfish bowl /ˈ·· ˌ·/ also **fishbowl** AmE— n **1** a glass bowl, usu. very rounded in shape, in which fish are kept as pets **2 in a goldfish bowl** open to public view: *Film-stars live in a goldfish bowl.*

Gold·i·locks /ˈɡəʊldilɒks‖-lɑːks/ n **1** a children's story (full title, *Goldilocks and the Three Bears*) in which a little girl with golden-coloured hair (Goldilocks) visits the Three Bears' house while they are out. She tries their chairs, their PORRIDGE, and their beds, until she finds what she wants and falls asleep. The Bears return and know that someone has been there, saying "Who's been sitting on my chair?" etc. until they find her in bed and she runs away. **2** a name sometimes used in a joking way for a little girl with golden hair (from *Goldilocks and the Three Bears*)

Gol·ding /ˈɡəʊldɪŋ/, **William** (1911–93) an English writer who was given the 1983 Nobel Prize for literature and is famous esp. for his NOVEL *Lord of the Flies*

gold leaf /ˌ·· ˈ·/ n [U] gold which has been beaten into extremely thin sheets for use in picture frames, decorative writing, etc.

gold med·al /ˌ·· ˈ··/ also **gold—** n a usu. round flat piece of gold given to the winner of a race or competition, or by a society, etc. as a sign of special achievement —see also BRONZE MEDAL, SILVER MEDAL

gold·mine /ˈɡəʊldmaɪn/ n **1** a place where gold is mined (MINE⁴) from the rock **2** infml a successful business or activity which makes large profits: *That little restaurant is a real goldmine. | He doesn't realize it, but with that new invention he's sitting on a goldmine.* (=he possesses something very valuable)

gold plate /ˌ·· ˈ·/ n [U] **1** old use articles, such as dishes, made of gold **2** a covering of gold on top of another metal **—plated** /ˌ·· ˈ··◂/ adj : *Is it solid gold or gold-plated?*

gold rush /ˈ·· ·/ n **1** a rush to a place where gold has just been discovered, by people hoping to collect large amounts of it easily **2** (with caps.) the famous gold rush in California in 1849

gold·smith /ˈɡəʊldˌsmɪθ/ n a person who makes things out of gold

Goldsmith, Ol·i·ver /ˈɒlɪvəʳ‖ˈɑː-/ (1728–74) an Irish poet and writer of books and plays. His works include the book *The Vicar of Wakefield* and the play *She Stoops to Conquer.*

gold stan·dard /ˈ· ˌ··/ [the] the practice of using the value of gold as a fixed standard on which to base the value of money, usu. with the purpose of preventing the value of the money from changing

gold star /ˌ·· ˈ·/ n a small piece of gold paper shaped like

a golf course

a star given to young school children as a reward for good behaviour or good work

gold watch /₁· ˈ·/ n a watch made of gold, or coloured like gold, often given as a mark of respect to people who have worked for a company for a long time and have come to the end of their working life

Gold·wyn /ˈgəʊldwɪn/, **Sam·u·el** /ˈsæmjuəl/ (1882–1974) American film producer, head of one of the companies which later became MGM. Goldwyn is famous for saying odd things like "Include me out!"

go·lem /ˈgəʊlem/ n (in old Jewish stories) an artificial person made by magic; now often used to mean a stupid person, or a person easily controlled

golf /gɒlf‖gɑːlf, gɔːlf/ n [U] a game in which people hit small hard white balls into holes in the ground with a set of special sticks (GOLF CLUBS), trying to do so with as few strokes as possible: *They played a round of golf.*

golf ball /ˈ· ·/ n 1 a small hard white ball used in the game of golf 2 (an electric TYPEWRITER that has) a small ball on which the letters of the alphabet are raised, which moves to press them onto the paper —compare DAISY WHEEL PRINTER

golf club /ˈ· ·/ n 1 a club for golfers, with the land and buildings it uses 2 a long-handled wooden or metal stick used for hitting the ball in golf —see also IRON¹ (3), WOOD (3)

golf course /ˈ· ·/ n an area of land with small hills, ditches, etc., across which the ball must be hit from hole to hole in golf —see picture at GOLF

gol·fer /ˈgɒlfər ‖ ˈgɑː-, ˈgɔː-/ n a person who plays GOLF

golf·ing /ˈgɒlfɪŋ‖ˈgɑː-, ˈgɔː-/ n [U] playing golf: *He goes golfing on Sundays.* | *a golfing holiday*

golf links /ˈ· ·/ n golf links a golf course, esp. by the sea

Gol·goth·a /ˈgɒlgəθə ‖ ˈgɑːl-/ according to the Bible, the place where Jesus was crucified (CRUCIFY)

Go·li·ath /gəˈlaɪəθ/ a very strong GIANT killed by the boy David in the Bible: (fig.) *How can a small computer company compete with the goliaths of the industry?* —see also DAVID; and see colour picture on page 424

gol·li·wog , golly- /ˈgɒliwɒg‖ˈgɑːliwɑːg/ also **golly-** n (in Britain) an old-fashioned child's toy (DOLL) made of soft material, dressed like a little man, and with a black face with big white eyes and black hair standing out round its head. Many people who are against RACISM find golliwogs offensive because they show an old-fashioned STEREOTYPE of black people, but many other people think that golliwogs are just toys and that their appearance is not important.

gol·ly /ˈgɒli‖ˈgɑːli/ interj old-fash infml (an expression of surprise)

Go·mor·rah /gəˈmɒrə‖-ˈmɔː-/ see SODOM AND GOMORRAH

go·nad /ˈgəʊnæd/ n tech a male or female organ in which the cells from which young may be formed are produced

gon·do·la /ˈgɒndələ‖ˈgɑːn-, gɑːnˈdəʊlə/ n 1 a long narrow flat-bottomed boat with high points at each end, used only on the waterways (CANALS) in Venice in Italy 2 a vehicle or arrangement of seats that hangs down underneath an AIRSHIP or large BALLOON 3 the enclosed part of a CABLE CAR (1) which carries the passengers

gon·do·lier /₁gɒndəˈlɪər‖₁gɑːn-/ n a man who guides and drives a GONDOLA (1)

Gon·dwa·na·land /gɒnˈdwɑːnəlænd‖gɑːn-/ the large mass of land that existed before it broke up to form Antarctica, Australia, Africa, South America, and India —see also LAURASIA, PANGAEA

gone¹ /gɒn‖gɔːn/ past participle of GO —see GO (USAGE)

gone² adj infml 1 [F] suffering from illness, the effects of alcohol or drugs, etc.: *We tried to make him understand, but he was too far gone to take in what we were saying.* 2 BrE [after n] having been PREGNANT (=with an unborn child growing inside one) for the stated period of time: *She's six months gone.* 3 [F (on)] having a very great liking or fondness (for): *She's really gone on that boy next door.*

gone³ prep BrE later or older than; past: *We didn't get home until gone midnight.* | *Considering that she's gone eighty she's very vigorous.*

gon·er /ˈgɒnər‖ˈgɔː-/ n infml someone or something that will soon die or be in a hopeless position: *When she catches him, he's a goner!*

Gone With The Wind /₁gɒn wɪð ðə ˈwɪnd‖₁gɔːn-/ a NOVEL by Margaret Mitchell, set in Georgia, US, during the American Civil War. The novel and the film of it (1939) are extremely popular. *Gone With The Wind* has many associations: the HEROINE, Scarlett O'Hara, is a beautiful woman with wild, strong feelings; the HERO, Rhett Butler, is attractive but dangerous; and the book and esp. the film have many very sad moments, such as when Scarlett's house is burnt down because of the war. —see colour picture on page 685

gong /gɒŋ‖gɑːŋ, gɔːŋ/ n 1 a round piece of metal hanging in a frame, which when hit with a stick gives a deep ringing sound 2 BrE sl for MEDAL

Gong Show /ˈ· ·/, **The** a former American television programme, in which non-professional and often very bad performers would sing, dance, tell jokes, etc. until someone struck a gong to show that they had seen enough

gon·na /ˈgɒnə, gənə‖ˈgɑːnə, gənə/ going to: *I'm gonna get you for that!*

▷ USAGE **Gonna** is used to suggest an American English or nonstandard British English pronunciation of

going to. It is pronounced and written like this only when it comes before a verb to show the future: "I'm **gonna** *find her," he said.* **Gonna** would not be written or said in this sentence: *"I'm* **going to** *Canada", he said.*◁

gon·or·rhe·a , **-rhoea** /ˌɡɒnəˈriːə‖ˌɡɑː-/ *n* [U] a disease of the sex organs, passed on during sexual activity and causing a burning feeling when urinating (URINATE) — compare SYPHILIS

gon·zo jour·nal·is·m /ˈɡɒnzəʊ ˌdʒɜːnəl-ɪzəm‖ˈɡɑːnzəʊ ˌdʒɜːr-/ *n* [U] *AmE infml* reporting, esp. in newspapers, which is considered unprofessional because it is untrue, too emotional, or too sensational —**ist** *n*

goo /ɡuː/ *n* [U] *infml* **1** unpleasantly sticky material: *"What's all that goo at the bottom of this bag?" "The chocolate must have melted."* **2** *derog* (words which seem to express) unnaturally sweet feelings; SENTIMENTALISM —see also GOOEY **3 goo-goo ga-ga** *AmE* (used to describe or copy the sounds a baby makes when learning to talk)

Gooch /ɡuːtʃ/, **Gra·ham** /ˈɡreɪəm/ (1953–) an English cricket player who was made captain of the England team in 1990, and made a SCORE of 333 in one INNINGS against India. Gooch began to play cricket for England in 1975, but was not allowed to play for three years after he went to South Africa with a cricket team in 1982.

good[1] /ɡʊd/ *adj* **better** /ˈbetəʳ/, **best** /best/ **1** having qualities that are very satisfactory, favourable, or worthy of praise; of the right or desirable kind: *"Hamlet" is a very good play.* | *He is a good husband/a good father/a good person to work for.* | *Her exam results were very good.* | *She put forward quite a good case for appointing him.* | *She received the best medical treatment.* | *The weather remains good.* | *This watch keeps good* (=correct) *time.* | *good news* | *a school with a good reputation* | *Come on, give them a few hours of your time – it's all in a* **good cause!** (=for a good purpose) | *It's good that we didn't go to the park because it's started to rain.* **2** useful or suitable (for a particular purpose): *It's a good day for a trip to the beach.* | *a good knife for cutting vegetables* | *good advice* | *Just because his wife doesn't like cooking, he thinks she's good for nothing.* (=completely useless) — see also GOOD-FOR-NOTHING **3** enjoyable; pleasant: *Did you* **have a good time** *at the party?* | *Oh no! It's raining: I knew this weather was* **too good to last!** | *It's good to see you again.* **4** [(for)] in a satisfactory condition; not broken, damaged, decayed, or ineffective: *You need good shoes for walking on the hills.* | *To test eggs, put them in a bowl of water: if they float they're bad, if they sink they're good.* | *They've fixed the car and it's* **as good as new.** (=in perfect condition) | *This ticket is good* (=can be used) *for one month.* **5** of pleasing appearance; attractive: *She was jealous of her sister's good looks.* | *You're looking very good – living in the country must suit you.* **6** [(for)] useful to the health or character; BENEFICIAL: *The water isn't good; we have to boil it before we drink it.* | *Milk is good for you.* | *It isn't good for children to give them everything they want.* —see also GOOD[2] (1) **7** [(at)] clever or skilful; having the ability to do something: *She's a good skier.* | *He's good at languages/good with his hands.* | *a good liar* **8** morally right; in accordance with religious standards: *People who do good deeds and lead a good life will go to heaven.* —see also GOOD[2] (2,3) **9** [(to, about)] (of a person) kind; helpful: *She's always been very good to me.* | *I had some time off work when my mother was ill, but the boss was very good about it.* | *It's good of you to help.* | (in formal requests) *Would you be good enough to close the door?* **10** (esp. of a child) well-behaved: *Be good when we visit your aunt.* | *a prize for good conduct* **11** [A] complete; thorough: *Take a good look at it.* | *Their team gave us a good beating.* | *She had a good cry.* **12** safe from loss of money: *a good risk* | *a good debt* **13** [A] (used with **a**): a large or fairly large in quantity, size, or degree: *I waited a good while.* (=quite a long time) | *We travelled a good distance.* | *I've had* **a good deal of** (=a lot of) *trouble with it.* | *She feels* **a good deal** (=much) *better today.* | *I've been there* **a good few/a good many** (=quite a large number of) *times.* | *There's a good chance he'll be at the meeting.* (=it is quite likely) **b** at least or more than: *It's a good mile away.* | *We wasted a good three hours.* **14** (in greetings): *Good morning/afternoon/evening.* **15 all in good time** (it will happen) at a suitable later time; be patient **16 as good as** almost (the same thing as): *He as good as refused.* | *We're as good as ruined.* | *She's as*

good as dead. | *(BrE) He really shouts at her, but she* **gives as good as she gets!** (=she shouts back at him) **17 as good as gold** *infml* (esp. of a child) very well-behaved **18 be as good as one's word** to keep one's promise **19 Good!** I'm pleased, satisfied, etc.: *"I'll be back tomorrow." "Good!"* **20 good and** ... *infml* very or completely: *Don't rush me; I'll do it when I'm good and ready.* **21 good for** likely to produce (an effect or money): *It's not a good film, but it's good for a laugh.* | *He'll be good for* (=will be willing to lend) *a few dollars.* **22 good God/gracious/grief/heavens/Lord!** (used as an expression of surprise or other strong feeling) **23 Good show** *BrE old-fash infml* I am glad **24 in good time** early (enough): *We must make sure we get to the station in good time, because we've still got to buy our tickets.* **25 in one's own good time** *infml* when one is ready, and not before **26 it's a good thing/job** it is fortunate: *It's a good thing you didn't tell me that bad news last night, because I would have been too worried to sleep.* | *(BrE) He's gone, and a good job, too.* (=I am glad) **27 make (it) good** to become successful, and esp. wealthy: *a boy from a small town who made good in New York* **28 make good (something): a** to pay for (something lost or missing): *The loss to the company was made good by contributions from its subsidiaries.* **b** to put (something) into effect: *The prisoners slipped over the wall and made good their escape.* (=succeeded in escaping) | *He made good his promise and returned the money.* **c** esp. *BrE* to repair (something that one has damaged): *The builders agreed to make good the whole area under the windows.* **29 no good/not much good/not any good** useless or bad: *It's no good talking to him, because he never listens.* | *A car's not much good to me; I can't drive.* | *The film wasn't any good.* | *Is your new doctor any good?* **30 too much of a good thing** something which is usually pleasant but has become unpleasant because it has gone on too long or become too big **31 very good** *BrE old-fash* polite of course; certainly: *"Please tell the cook to come up." "Very good, sir."* —see also BEST, BETTER, **so far so good** (FAR[1]), **hold good** (HOLD[1] (19)), **for good measure** (MEASURE[1]), **well and good** (WELL[1])

good[2] *n* **1** [U] something that brings gain, advantage, or improvement: *I go swimming for the good of my health.* (=not for fun) | *You should drink the medicine, not because I want you to, but* **for your own good.** | *It'll* **do you good** *to have a holiday.* | *His ex-wife's presence at the wedding will* **do more harm than good.** | *A long holiday would do him* **a power of good/the world of good.** (=a great deal of good) **2** [U] action or behaviour that is morally right, worthy of praise, or in accordance with religious beliefs and principles: *By behaving well you can be an influence for good.* | *The company claims it has done a lot of good for the town by providing employment.* | *There's good in her, in spite of her bad behaviour.* —see also DO-GOODER **3** [*the*+P] good people generally; those who do what is right: *Christians believe the good go to heaven when they die.* **4 for good (and all)** for ever: *We thought she'd come for a visit, but it seems she's staying for good.* **5 good for you** ‖ also **good on you** *AustrE & dial BrE*— (used to express approval and pleasure at someone's success, good luck, etc.) **6 to the good** with a profit of (an amount): *I sold it for more than I paid for it, so I'm £5 to the good.* **7 up to no good** doing or intending to do something wrong or bad: *When I saw him climbing through the window behind the shop I knew he was up to no good.* **8 What's the good of** ... ? also **What good is** ... ?— What is the use or purpose of (something or doing something)?: *What's the good of buying a boat when you don't have enough spare time to use it?* | *What good is money when you haven't any friends?* —see also GOODS **9 the good, the bad, and the ugly** *humor* (a phrase used to mean "all sorts of people or things", originally the title of a film)

good af·ter·noon /ˌ· ˌ·ˈ·/ *interj, n* (an expression used when meeting, or being met by, someone in the afternoon)

good book /ˌ· ˈ·/ [*the*] *old-fash, sometimes humor* the Bible

good·bye /ɡʊdˈbaɪ/ also **bye** *infml*— *interj, n* (an expression used when leaving, or being left by, someone): *We said our goodbyes and left.* | *"I'm off now. Bye!" "Goodbye, John. See you tomorrow."*

good day /ˌ· ˈ·/ *interj, n* **1** esp. *AustrE & AmE* (an expression used when meeting, or being met by, someone, esp. in the morning or afternoon) **2** *old-fash, esp. BrE* HELLO or goodbye

good deed /ˌ· ˈ·/ *n* an action which helps others, esp. done by Scouts and Guides, who were supposed to do a good deed every day: *Have you done your good deed for the day?*

good eve·ning /ˌ· ˈ··/ *interj, n* (an expression used when meeting, or being met by, someone in the evening) — compare GOOD NIGHT

good faith /ˌ· ˈ·/ *n* **in good faith** (of a deal, etc.) made with honesty and no intention to deceive: *The contract was drawn up in good faith.*

good-for-noth·ing /ˌ· · ˈ··, ˈ· · ··/ *n* a person who is worthless, useless, etc.: *Get out of bed, you lazy good-for-nothing!* —**good-for-nothing** /ˈ· · ··/ *adj* [A]

Good Fri·day /ˌ· ˈ··/ *n* [C;U] (in the Christian religion) the Friday before EASTER

Good House·keep·ing /ˌ· ˈ···/ a British monthly magazine read esp. by women who are interested in decorating their homes. It has articles about food and fashions and pictures of the insides of people's houses. There is also an American magazine with the same name.

Good Hu·mor /ˌ· ˈ··/ *tdmk* a kind of ICE CREAM sold in the US, esp. in summer by a person (**Good Humor Man**) who drives around in a TRUCK that plays music (**Good Humor Truck**)

good-hu·moured /ˌ· ˈ···◂/ *adj* having or showing a cheerful friendly state of mind: *a good-humoured smile* | *He was very good-humoured about the mess my children made of his kitchen.* —see also HUMOUR¹ (3) — ~**ly** *adv*

good·ie , goody /ˈgʊdi/ *n* someone who is good or an opponent of bad people, esp. in books, films, etc.

good·ish /ˈgʊdɪʃ/ *adj* [A] *BrE* **1** quite good (but not very good) in quality **2** [A] (with **a**) rather; to quite a high degree: *You can walk from here to the park but it's a good-ish distance.* (=quite a long way)

good life /ˌ· ˈ·/ [the] a simple way of living in which people are close to nature, e.g. by growing their own food: *Many people have moved to remote parts of Britain in search of the good life.*

good look·er /ˌ· ˈ··/ *n infml* an unusually good-looking person, esp. a woman

good-look·ing /ˌ· ˈ···◂/ *adj* **better-looking, best-looking** (esp. of a person) having an attractive appearance —see BEAUTIFUL (USAGE)

good looks /ˌ· ˈ·/ *n* [P] a person's attractive appearance: *She's kept her good looks in old age.*

good·ly /ˈgʊdli/ *adj* [A] *old use or pomp* **1** large (in amount): *There were a goodly number of people present.* **2** pleasant or satisfying in appearance: *The table spread with food made a goodly sight.*

Good·man /ˈgʊdmən/, **Benny** (1909–86) an American JAZZ musician and bandleader who played the CLARINET and helped make big band jazz popular in the 1930s. He was known as the "King of Swing".

good mor·ning /ˌ· ˈ··/ *interj, n* (an expression used when meeting, or being met by, someone in the morning)

good-na·tured /ˌ· ˈ···◂/ *adj* naturally kind; ready to help, to forgive, not to be angry, etc. — ~**ly** *adv* — ~**ness** *n*

good·ness /ˈgʊdnɪs/ *n* [U] **1** the quality of being good **2** the best part, esp. the part of food which is good for the health: *If you boil the vegetables too long they'll lose all their goodness.* **3** (used in expressions of surprise and annoyance): **My goodness!** | **Goodness (gracious) me!** | **For goodness' sake,** *stop talking!* | *I wish to goodness he'd be quiet.* —see SAKE (USAGE)

Good News Bi·ble /ˌ· ˈ· ˈ··/, **The** a modern translation of the Bible which first came out in 1976 and is written in simple English

good night /ˌ· ˈ·/ *interj, n* (an expression used when leaving, or being left by, someone at night, esp. before going to bed or to sleep): *Good night, sleep tight.* —compare GOOD EVENING

good of·fic·es /ˌ· ˈ···/ *n* [P] *fml* services provided, esp. by someone in a position of power or influence, that help someone out of a difficulty: *Through the good offices of the ambassador we were able to get special permission to travel.*

goods /gʊdz/ *n* **1** [P] articles for sale: *There's a large variety of consumer goods in the shops.* | *frozen goods* **2** [P] *BrE* ‖ **freight** *esp. AmE* — heavy articles which can be carried by road, train, etc.: *a goods train/waggon* **3** [P] possessions which can be moved, as opposed to houses,

land, etc.; personal property: *He bequeathed her all his worldly goods.* **4** [the+P] *BrE infml* a desirable thing or person: *She thinks he's the goods.* | *He's full of promises but in fact he rarely* **comes up with/delivers the goods.** (=produces what is needed or expected) —see also DRY GOODS, GOODS AND CHATTELS

good Sa·mar·i·tan /ˌ· · ·ˈ···/ *n* someone who gives help to people in trouble or need, without thinking of themselves (from the Bible story of the **Good Samaritan**, who made a special effort to help someone who other people had taken no notice of)

goods and chat·tels /ˌ· · ˈ···/ *n* [P] *law* personal possessions

Good Shep·herd /ˌ· ˈ··/ [the] a name used in the Bible for Jesus

good·will /ˌgʊdˈwɪl/ *n* [U] **1** kind feelings towards or between people and/or willingness to take action that will bring advantage to the others: *Given sufficient goodwill on both sides, there's no reason why this dispute shouldn't be resolved.* **2** the value of the popularity, the regular customers, etc., of a business calculated as part of its worth when being sold: *We paid £30,000 for the shop, plus £5000 for the goodwill.*

Good·win Sands /ˌgʊdwɪn ˈsændz/ [the+P] a dangerous area of sand just under the sea off the S coast of England, near Dover, where many ships have been wrecked

Good·wood /ˈgʊdwʊd/ (the race held on) a horse-racing course near Chichester, S England. Races are held at Goodwood every year in July and August: *the Goodwood winner* (=the horse that wins the races held there)

good word /ˌ· ˈ·/ *n* **1** [S] a favourable statement: *They hadn't* **a good word (to say) for** *her.* (=everything they said about her was unfavourable) | *When you're talking to the director,* **put in a good word for** *me.* (=mention me favourably) **2** [the] *AmE* good news: *What's the good word?*

good·y¹ /ˈgʊdi/ *n* [usu. pl.] *infml* **1** a pleasant thing to eat: *She had got us all sorts of delicious goodies for tea.* **2** something particularly attractive, pleasant, or desirable: *They had all the goodies — new cars, a big house, holidays abroad — that a higher income brings.* **3** *a* GOODIE

goody² *interj* (an expression of pleasure, used esp. by children)

Good·year /ˈgʊdjɪəʳ, -jɜːʳ‖-jɪər/ a company known around the world for its tyres and other rubber products

goody-good·y /ˈ·· ˌ·◂/ ‖ also **goody-two-shoes** *AmE— n* **goody-goodies** *infml derog* (used esp. by children about other children) a person who likes to appear faultless in behaviour so as to please others, not because he or she is really good: *Who's a little goody-goody then, helping the teacher?*

goody-two-shoes /ˌ··· ˈ· ˌ·/ *n* **goody-two-shoes** *AmE for* goody-goody

goo·ey /ˈguːi/ *adj infml* **1** sticky and usu. sweet: *gooey cakes* **2** *derog* over-sweet; SENTIMENTAL: *She gets very gooey about babies and young animals.* —see also GOO

goof¹ /guːf/ *n infml* **1** a foolish person: *The poor goof still hasn't twigged* (=realized) *that they're pulling his leg* (=that they are joking). **2** *esp. AmE* a silly mistake

goof² *v* [I] *infml, esp. AmE* to make a silly mistake **goof off** *phr v* [I] *AmE infml* to waste time or avoid work

goof·y /ˈguːfi/ *adj infml* appearing stupid or silly —**iness** *n* [U]

goo·gly /ˈguːgli/ *n* (in cricket) a ball bowled (BOWL²(1)) as if to go in one direction after bouncing (BOUNCE) which in fact goes in the other direction

goo-goo eyes /ˈ·· ˌ·/ *n* [P] *AmE infml humor* a look at another person that suggests love or sexual desire: *Don't look at me with your goo-goo eyes!* | *I think that man in the suit is* **making goo-goo eyes** *at you.*

goo·ly, goolie /ˈguːli/ *n BrE, sl, not polite* a TESTICLE

goon /guːn/ *n infml* **1** a silly or stupid person **2** *esp. AmE* a violent criminal hired to frighten or attack people

Goon Show /ˈ· ˌ·/ [the] a British radio COMEDY show of the 1950s, whose four performers (Spike Milligan, Peter Sellers, Michael Bentine, and Sir Harry Secombe) called themselves **the Goons**. It was different from anything which had gone before and influenced a lot of later British humour.

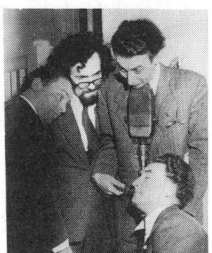

The Goons

goose /guːs/ *n* **geese** /giːs/ **1 gander** *masc.* – a bird that is similar to a duck but larger and makes a hissing (HISS) or honking (HONK) noise **2** (*pl.* **gooses**) *old-fash infml* a silly person **3** (**kill**) **the goose that lays/laid the golden egg(s)** (to spoil or destroy) the thing that is or will be the main cause of one's profit or success (from the story of the GOLDEN GOOSE) –see also HONK[1], MOTHER GOOSE, WILD-GOOSE CHASE, **can't/couldn't say boo to a goose** (BOO[1]), **cook someone's goose** (COOK[1])

goose·ber·ry /ˈguzbəri, ˈguːz-, ˈguːs-‖ˈguːsberi/ *n* **1** a small round green sharp-tasting fruit that grows on a bush – see picture at BERRY **2** *infml, esp. BrE* a third person who stays in the company of two lovers although they want to be alone: *When her boyfriend came over I went out because I didn't want to* **play gooseberry.**

gooseberry bush /ˈ··· ˌ·/ *n* the small bush on which gooseberries grow. In the past British children were sometimes told that new babies are found under gooseberry bushes. –see picture at BERRY

goose·flesh /ˈguːsfleʃ/ *BrE*, also **goose pim·ples** /ˈ· ˌ··/ ‖ *usu.* **goose·bumps** /ˈguːsbʌmps/ *AmE– n* [U] a condition in which the skin is raised up in small points because a person is cold or frightened

Goose Green /ˌ· ˈ·/ a settlement in the Falkland Islands where British soldiers fought with Argentinians in May 1982. Many people were killed.

goose-step /ˈguːs-step/ *n* [(*the*) S] a way of marching, used by soldiers in some countries, in which each step is taken without bending the knee. This word is connected by many people with the marching style of the German soldiers in the Second World War. –**goosestep** *v* -**pp-** [I]

GOP /ˌdʒiː əʊ ˈpiː/ [*the*] *esp. AmE* Grand Old Party; the Republican Party in US politics

go·pher /ˈgəʊfər/ *n* a ratlike animal of North and Central America which makes and lives in holes in the ground –compare GOFER

Gor·ba·chev /ˈgɔːbətʃɒf‖ˈgɔːrbətʃɔːf/, **Mi·khail** /miˈkaɪl, -ˈxaɪl/ also **Gor·by** /ˈgɔːbi‖ˈgɔːr-/ *infml–* (1931–) a political leader of the USSR who started the processes of economic and political change (PERESTROIKA) and freedom of expression (GLASNOST) which greatly improved relations with the West (1985–92)

Gorbachev

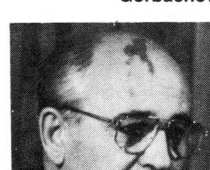

Gor·bals /ˈgɔːbəlz‖ˈgɔːr-/ [*the*] an area of the city of Glasgow. For many years this area was one of Britain's worst SLUMS, and its name still makes people think of low quality houses, people with no jobs or low wages, crime, and violence.

Gor·di·an knot /ˌgɔːdiən ˈnɒt‖ˌgɔːrdiən ˈnɑːt/ *n* **cut the Gordian knot** to settle a difficulty or remove a problem by direct action, without thinking too much of the results (from the ancient story which said that whoever undid the complicated knot used by King Gordius would rule all Asia. Alexander the Great is supposed to have cut through it with his sword.)

Gor·di·mer /ˈgɔːdʒmər‖ˈgɔːr-/, **Na·dine** /nəˈdiːn/ (1923–) a South African novelist who won the Nobel Prize for literature in 1992

Gor·don /ˈgɔːdn‖ˈgɔːr-/, **Charles** (1833–85) a British GENERAL who fought in the Crimean War and then in China. He was killed at Khartoum, when British soldiers were trapped there.

Gor·don /ˈgɔːdn‖ˈgɔːr-/, **No·ele** /ˈnəʊəl/ (1923–85) an English actress and singer best remembered for playing the

character Meg Richardson in the old television programme *Crossroads*

Gordon High·land·ers /ˌ·· ˈ···/ *n* [*the*+P] a Scottish REGIMENT (=large division of men) in the British army

Gor·don's /ˈgɔːdnz ‖ ˈgɔːr-/ *n tdmk* a company which makes different types of GIN; it is best known for its London Special Dry Gin

Gor·don·stoun /ˈgɔːdnztən‖ˈgɔːr-/ a well-known PUBLIC SCHOOL in the north of Scotland, where some members of the royal family were educated

gore[1] /gɔːr/ *v* [T] (of an animal) to wound with the horns or TUSKs: *The bullfighter was badly gored.*

gore[2] *n* [U] *lit* blood, esp. blood that has flowed from a wound and thickened. This word is often used when speaking of films which show a lot of people being killed, etc.: *too much blood and gore* –see also GORY

gore[3] *n* a piece of material which widens towards the bottom and is used in making a garment, usu. a skirt – **gored** *adj* : *a gored skirt*

Gore, Albert (1948–) a senator from Tenessee who became Vice President of the US in 1993. His wife's name is **Tipper** (1948–)

gorge[1] /gɔːdʒ‖gɔːrdʒ/ *n* **1** a deep narrow valley with steep sides usu. made by a stream which runs or has run through it –see VALLEY (USAGE) **2 make someone's ˈgorge rise** to make someone feel sickened or feel strong dislike: *When I saw the torturers and their victims it made my gorge rise.*

gorge[2] *v* **gorge oneself on/with** *usu. derog* to fill oneself completely with (food); eat in a GREEDY way: *He gorged himself on cream cakes.*

gor·geous /ˈgɔːdʒəs‖ˈgɔːr-/ *adj infml* **1** wonderful; delightful: *What a gorgeous day!* (=warm and sunny) | *This cake is gorgeous.* **2** very beautiful: *Our show features fifty gorgeous dancing girls.* – –**ly** *adv* – –**ness** *n* [U]

gor·gon /ˈgɔːgən‖ˈgɔːr-/ *n* **1** *infml* an ugly angry-looking woman whose appearance causes fear **2** (*usu. cap.*) any of three imaginary sisters in ancient Greek stories who had snakes on their heads instead of hair, and turned anyone who looked at them to stone

Gor·gon·zo·la /ˌgɔːgənˈzəʊlə‖ˌgɔːr-/ *n* [U] an Italian cheese which is white with blue marks and has a strong taste

go·ril·la /gəˈrɪlə/ *n* **1** a very large African monkey that is the largest of the manlike monkeys (APEs) –see picture at APE **2** *sl* an ugly or rough man: *The gang boss had brought his gorillas in case there was any trouble.*

Gor·ky /ˈgɔːki ‖ ˈgɔːr-/, **Maxim** (1868–1936) a Russian writer of NOVELs remembered esp. for his book about his own life

gor·mand·ize also **-ise** *BrE* /ˈgɔːməndaɪz‖ˈgɔːr-/ *v* [I] *fml* to eat a lot for pleasure rather than from hunger –see also GOURMAND

gorm·less /ˈgɔːmləs‖ˈgɔːrm-/ *adj BrE infml* stupid and thoughtless; slow in understanding: *a gormless-looking young man* – –**ly** *adv*

gorse /gɔːs‖gɔːrs/ also **furze–** *n* [U] a prickly bush with bright yellow flowers, which grows wild in country areas

gor·y /ˈgɔːri/ *adj* **1** *infml* full of extreme violence and unpleasantness: *a gory film* | *The newspaper account of the accident gave all* **the gory details. 2** *lit* covered in blood –see also GORE[2]

gosh /gɒʃ‖gɑːʃ/ *interj infml* (an expression of surprise)

gos·ling /ˈgɒzlɪŋ‖ˈgɑːz-, ˈgɔːz-/ *n* a young GOOSE

go-slow /ˌ· ˈ·◂/ *n BrE* ‖ **slowdown** *AmE– a period of working as slowly and with as little effort as possible, as a form of STRIKE[2] (1) –compare WORK-TO-RULE; see also **go slow** (GO[1])

gos·pel /ˈgɒspəl‖ˈgɑːs-/ *n* [U] **1** also **gospel truth** /ˌ·· ˈ·/ – something that is completely true: *What I'm telling you is gospel/the gospel truth.* **2** also **gospel mu·sic** /ˈ·· ˌ··/ – a style of popular music usu. performed by black American singers in which religious songs are sung strongly and loudly: *a gospel singer* –see also HOT-GOSPELLER

Gospel *n* any of the four accounts of Christ's life in the Bible: *the Gospel according to St Matthew/St Mark/St Luke/St John*

gos·sa·mer /ˈgɒsəmər‖ˈgɑː-/ *n* [U] **1** light silky thread which SPIDERs leave on grass and bushes and between trees **2** a very light thin material

gos·sip¹ /ˈgɒsᵻp‖ˈgɑː-/ n **1** [C;U] (a) conversation or report about the details of other people's behaviour and private lives, often including information that is not actually true: *All this talk about his love affairs is just idle gossip.* | *I haven't had a good gossip since you left.* | *Many newspapers have a gossip column, where the private lives of famous people are reported.* —compare RUMOUR **2** [C] a person who likes talking about other people's private lives

gossip² v [I] to spend time in gossip: *She was gossiping with her friend about the boss's love life.*

gos·sip·y /ˈgɒsᵻpi‖ˈgɑː-/ adj infml full of gossip or liking gossip: *I got a long gossipy letter from my sister.* | *a gossipy person*

got /gɒt‖gɑːt/ past tense & participle of GET —see GOTTEN (USAGE), HAVE² (USAGE)

got·cha /ˈgɒtʃə‖ˈgɑː-/ interj I've got you! (said to surprise or frighten someone, or to show that one has gained a sudden advantage). During the Falklands War, the Sun newspaper used **Gotcha!** in its HEADLINE when the British sank an Argentine ship. Many people found this insensitive and offensive.

Goth /gɒθ‖gɑːθ/ a member of a group of people (the **Goths**) from the area of Germany who invaded (INVADE) the Roman Empire several times between the 3rd and 5th centuries AD

Goth·am /ˈgɒθəm‖ˈgɑː-/ AmE infml the name for New York City used in the Batman stories

Goth·ic /ˈgɒθɪk‖ˈgɑː-/ adj **1** of or in a style of building common in Western Europe between the 12th and 16th centuries, with pointed arches, tall PILLARS, and tall thin pointed windows often with coloured glass in them: *Notre Dame in Paris is a Gothic cathedral.* **2** of or like a style of writing popular in the late 18th century which produced stories set in lonely frightening places: *Gothic novels* | *Gothic horror films, with ruined castles, haunted graveyards, and eerie noises* **3** being a type of printing with thick pointed letters

𝕲𝖔𝖙𝖍𝖎𝖈 𝕷𝖊𝖙𝖙𝖊𝖗𝖎𝖓𝖌

got·ta /ˈgɒtə‖ˈgɑːtə/ nonstandard **1** have/has got to **2** have/has a

▷ USAGE **have got to** and **have got a** are often pronounced like this in ordinary speech, but **gotta** is used in writing only to suggest a very informal or nonstandard pronunciation: *I gotta go.* (=I must go) | **Gotta** *match?* (=Have you got a match?)◁

got·ten /ˈgɒtn‖ˈgɑːtn/ AmE past participle of GET —see also ILL-GOTTEN

▷ USAGE In American English **gotten** is more common than **got** as the past participle of **get**, except where it means **a** "possess", compare: *I've got a new car* (=I possess one) and *I've gotten a new car* (=I've bought one) or **b** "must", compare: *I've got to go* (=I must go) and *I've gotten to go* (=I've succeeded in going).◁

got·tle o'geer /ˌgɒtl ə ˈgɪəʳ/ interj infml humor (a phrase used by someone pretending to be a bad VENTRILOQUIST who is actually trying to say "bottle of beer")

gou·ache /ɡʊˈɑːʃ, ɡwɑːʃ/ n [C;U] (a picture produced by) a method of painting using colours that are mixed with water and thickened with a sort of GUM² (1)

Gou·da /ˈɡaʊdə, ˈɡuːdə/ n [U] a flat Dutch cheese which is yellowish in colour and not very strong in taste

gouge¹ /ɡaʊdʒ/ n a tool for cutting out hollow areas in wood

gouge² v
gouge sthg. ↔ **out** phr v [T] to press or dig out with force: *They tortured him and then gouged his eyes out.*

gou·lash /ˈɡuːlæʃ‖-lɑːʃ, -læʃ/ n [U] a dish originally from Hungary consisting of meat cooked in liquid with PAPRIKA, a hot-tasting pepper

Gould /ɡuːld/, **Glenn** (1932–82) a Canadian piano player remembered esp. for his excellent recordings of the music of J.S. Bach

gourd /ɡʊəd‖ɡɔːrd, ɡʊərd/ n **1** a round fruit which has a hard outer shell and cannot usually be eaten **2** the shell

of this fruit that can be used for drinking from or keeping things in

gour·mand /ˈɡʊəmənd‖ˈɡʊər-/ n a person who is too interested in eating and drinking —see also GORMANDIZE

gour·met¹ /ˈɡʊəmeɪ‖ˈɡʊər-, ɡʊərˈmeɪ/ n a person who knows a lot about food and drink and is good at choosing combinations of dishes, good wines, etc.

gourmet² adj (of food) suitable for a gourmet, of excellent quality: *This restaurant serves gourmet French dishes.*

gout /ɡaʊt/ n [U] a disease which makes esp. the toes, fingers, and knees swell and give pain. In the past, gout was often thought to be caused by drinking too much of certain kinds of alcohol, e.g. PORT³. — **~y** adj : *an irritable old lord with a gouty leg*

gov·ern /ˈɡʌvən‖-ərn/ v **1** [I;T] to control and direct the affairs of (a country, city, etc. and its people), using political power: *The country was governed by a small élite of military officers.* | *In Britain the Queen is the formal head of state, but it is the prime minister and cabinet who govern.* **2** [T] to control, fix, or guide; DETERMINE: *The price of coffee is governed by the quantity that has been produced.* | *a change in the rules governing the use of seat belts* **3** [T] (in grammar) (of a word) to cause another word to be in (the stated form): *In German, prepositions usually govern the accusative or dative cases.*

gov·ern·ess /ˈɡʌvənᵻs‖-ər-/ n (esp. in former times) a female teacher who lives with a rich family and educates their children at home

gov·ern·ing /ˈɡʌvənɪŋ‖-ər-/ adj [A] having the power of ruling or controlling: *The governing party doesn't want an election yet.* | *The university's governing body (=the group of people in control) has decided to expand the Computer Centre.*

gov·ern·ment /ˈɡʌvəmənt, ˈɡʌvənmənt‖ˈɡʌvərn-/ n **1** [C+sing./pl. v] (often cap.) the group of people who govern (esp. a nation or state): *The Government is/are planning new tax increases.* | *the Swiss government* | *changes in education policy under the last Labour government* (=during the period of their rule) | *a military/civilian government* **2** [U] the form or method of governing: *a return to democratic government* | *She is in charge of a government department.* **3** [U] the act or process of governing; rule: *the art of government* | *Government has been entrusted to the elected politicians.* —see also CENTRAL GOVERNMENT, LOCAL GOVERNMENT, NATIONAL GOVERNMENT and see extra information on page 565 — **~al** /ˌɡʌvən ˈmentl‖ˌɡʌvərn-/ adj

government bond /ˌ··· ˈ·/ n a SECURITY (5) produced by a government on which the holder receives a fixed rate of interest until the repayment date

government health warn·ing /ˌ··· ˈ· ˌ··/ n a notice that, by law, must be put on certain products to warn people that they are considered harmful: *All cigarette packets now carry a government health warning.*

government stock /ˌ··· ˈ·/ n [U] savings BONDs¹ (3) or other forms of GILT-EDGED SECURITY

gov·er·nor /ˈɡʌvənəʳ/ n **1** a person who controls any of certain types of organization or place. The office of governor is the highest in American state government: *After the mass riot the prison governor resigned.* | *He was elected governor of the state of California.* | *British colonies were ruled by governors.* —see also extra information on page 565 **2** a member of a group or committee that broadly directs or controls a school, hospital, or similar organization: *The head teacher is appointed by the school governors.* | *She was invited to join the board of governors of the opera house.* **3** a part of a machine that controls how the machine works, esp. by limiting it in some way **4** esp. BrE GUVNOR —see also GUBERNATORIAL — **~ship** n [U]

governor-gen·e·ral /ˌ··· ˈ···/ n **governors-general** or **governor-generals** (usu. cap.) a person who represents the King or Queen of Britain in other Commonwealth countries which are not REPUBLICs: *the Governor-General of Australia*

Governor of the Bank of En·gland /ˌ··· ··· ˌ·· ˈ··/ the head of the Bank of England, one of the most important people in the City of London

Government in Britain

National government

The centre of government in Britain is PARLIAMENT, which makes all the important laws for the country about crimes and punishment, taxation, etc. Parliament is made up of the House of Commons, the House of Lords, and the monarch. The HOUSES OF PARLIAMENT are in Westminster in London and sometimes "Westminster" itself is used to mean Parliament.

The HOUSE OF COMMONS (or the COMMONS) is the lower but more powerful of the two Houses. It has 650 elected members, called MEMBERS OF PARLIAMENT or MPS, each representing people in a particular area or CONSTITUENCY. The HOUSE OF LORDS (or the Lords) is the higher but less powerful of the two Houses. It has over 1,000 members, none of whom is elected. These members include: people who have titles like Lord or Viscount which have been passed down to them on the death of their father (**hereditary peers**); people who are given titles as a reward for their long service in public life, but whose children do not INHERIT their title (**life peers**); and some important leaders of the Church of England (ARCHBISHOPS and BISHOPS).

The government brings BILLS (=suggested laws) to the House of Commons, which are discussed by MPs. The bills then go to the House of Lords to be discussed. The House of Lords can suggest changes to a bill, but does not have the power to REJECT it (=refuse permission for it to be passed). When bills come back to the Commons, MPs vote on them and if they are passed they are signed by the monarch and become **Acts of Parliament**.

At present England, Scotland, Wales, and N Ireland are all governed by Parliament in Westminster. In N Ireland the political parties are different but their MPs still go to the House of Commons. In Scotland there is a lot of discussion about whether Scotland should have some separate or partly separate form of government. The same is true in Wales.

Local government

Local government in Britain, also known as COUNCILS, can make small laws (BYLAWS) which only apply in their area, but these are usually about small, local matters. For instance, they may be about fines that will be made to people who park in certain streets.

Councils are paid for by local taxes and also by an amount of money given to them each year by the national government. Their main job is the organizing and providing of local services, e.g. hospitals, schools, libraries, public transport, street-cleaning, etc. They are also responsible for setting the amount of local tax that people must pay and for collecting this tax.

Local councils are elected by people within each town, city, or country area. The people who are elected, known as COUNCILLORS, usually represent one of the national political parties, but are often elected because of their policies on local issues rather than the national policies of their party.

Government in the US

All levels of government in the US (FEDERAL, STATE, AND LOCAL) are elected by the people of the country.

Federal government

The Constitution of the US specifically limits the power of the federal (=national) government mainly to defence, foreign affairs, printing money, controlling trade and relations between the states, and protecting human rights. The federal government is made up of the CONGRESS, the PRESIDENT, and the SUPREME COURT.

Congress

Congress, the central law-making body in the US, is made up of the House of Representatives and the Senate. The HOUSE OF REPRESENTATIVES is the lower but more important of the two houses of Congress. It has 435 members, called REPRESENTATIVES or CONGRESSMEN/CONGRESSWOMEN elected by their state. The number of Representatives for each state depends on the size of the population of the state, with each state having at least one Representative. The SENATE is the higher but less powerful of the two houses of Congress. It has 100 members, called SENATORS, elected by their state. Each state has two Senators.

Congress decides whether a BILL (=suggested law) becomes law. If the Senate and the House of Representatives both agree to a bill, the President is asked to agree. The President can veto (=say no to) the bill, but Congress can still make it a law if 2/3 of the members of each house agree to it.

State government

State government has the greatest influence in people's daily lives. Each state has its own written CONSTITUTION (=set of fixed laws), and among the states there are sometimes great differences in law on matters such as property, crime, health, and education. The highest elected official of each state is the GOVERNOR. Each state also has one or two elected law-making bodies (state LEGISLATURE) whose members represent the various parts of the state.

Local government

Local government concerns laws made at the town, city or COUNTY level. These laws are usually limited to a small area and concern such things as traffic, where and when alcoholic drinks can be sold, or keeping animals. The highest elected official of a town or city is usually the MAYOR; a small law-making body is usually called the town or city COUNCIL.

Every law at every level of government must be in agreement with the United States constitution. Any citizen who thinks he or she has not been given their rights under the law may argue their case through all the courts up to the Supreme Court (the final COURT OF APPEAL in the US) if necessary, and any law which is found not in agreement with the constitution (unconstitutional) cannot be kept in force. —see also pages 412 and 949

Gow·er /ˈgaʊəʳ/, **David** (1957–) an English cricket player who was captain of the England cricket team in 1984–85, and again for a short time in 1989

gown /gaʊn/ n **1** a woman's dress, esp. a long one worn on formal occasions: *She wore a blue silk evening gown.* **2** a long loose usu. black outer garment worn for special ceremonies by judges, teachers, lawyers, and members of universities **3** (*often in comb.*) a long loose garment worn for some special purpose: *The gown a surgeon wears during an operation is usually green.* —see also DRESSING GOWN

Go·ya /ˈgɔɪə/, **Fran·cis·co de** /frænˈsɪskəʊ də/ (1746–1828) a Spanish artist, considered to be the greatest of his time, many of whose works are paintings of people, esp. the royal families of Spain

GP /ˌdʒiː ˈpiː/ also **general practitioner** *fml, esp. BrE—* n a doctor who is trained in general medicine and whose work (**general practice** /ˌ··· ˈ··/) is to treat people in a certain local area: *My GP sent me to a specialist.* —see also extra information on page 825

GPA /ˌdʒiː piː ˈeɪ/ GRADE POINT AVERAGE

GPO /ˌ·· ˈ·◄/ *abbrev. for:* **1** *BrE tdmk* General Post Office; the former name of the organization that controls the mail in Britain (now the Post Office) **2** *AmE* Government Printing Office, a government department which prints and gives away or sells US government documents —compare HMSO

grab¹ /græb/ v *-bb-* [T] **1** to take hold of (a person or thing) with a sudden rough movement, esp. for a bad or selfish purpose: *He grabbed the money and ran off.* | *They grabbed her by the arm and forced her into their car.* | (fig.) *Don't miss this chance to travel – grab it before the boss changes her mind.* **2** *infml* to get quickly and perhaps unfairly: *She grabbed the seat near the fire before I could.* | *I missed breakfast but I managed to grab a sandwich on the way here.* **3** *infml* to have an effect on; find favour with: *How does the idea of a holiday in Spain grab you?* (=Would you like one?)
grab at sthg./sbdy. *phr v* [T] to make a sudden attempt to grab: *She grabbed at the fish, but the cat was too fast for her.*

grab² n **1** a sudden attempt to take hold of something: *The thief made a grab at my bag but I pushed him away.* **2 up for grabs** *infml* ready for anyone to take or win: *They've decided to change their advertising company, so there's a big contract up for grabs.*

grab bag /ˈ· ·/ n *AmE for* LUCKY DIP (1)

grace¹ /greɪs/ n **1** [U] a fine and attractive quality in movement or form, esp. when this seems effortless and natural: *She danced with marvellous natural grace.* **2** [S; U] willingness to behave in a fair and honourable way: *She had the grace to admit that I was right.* | *He agreed to the proposed changes with (a) good/bad grace.* (=willingly/unwillingly) **3** [U] a delay allowed as a favour, usu. for the stated period: *I'll give you a week's grace, but if the work is not finished then, I'll write to my lawyers.* **4** [U] a prayer before or after meals, giving thanks to God: *Who'll say grace today?* **5** [U] the favour or MERCY (of God): **By the grace of God** *the ship came safely home through the storm.* **6** [U] (in the Christian religion) the state of the soul when freed from evil: *to die in a state of grace* **7 fall from grace: a** to fall/a fall from a position of favour **b** to fall/a fall back into bad old ways of behaving **8 in someone's good graces** in someone's favour —see also GRACES, SAVING GRACE **9 there but for the grace of God go** ¹I (a phrase used when you see someone else in a difficult or unfortunate situation, and feel lucky that you are not in that situation)

grace² v [T] *fml or humor* **1** [(**with, by**) *usu. pass.*] to give honour or favour to: *We're flattered that you were able to grace us with/by your presence.* (=said formally to an important guest, or humorously to someone arriving late) **2** to decorate or make beautiful; ADORN: *The photo of him meeting the Queen graces his mantelpiece.*

Grace n (used as a title for addressing or speaking of a DUKE, DUCHESS, or ARCHBISHOP): *Good morning, Your Grace.* | *Their Graces the Duke and Duchess of Bedford.*

Grace, Princess see Grace KELLY

Grace, W G (1848–1915) an English cricketer, generally thought of as the best ever. He was a very large man with a long, thick beard.

grace·ful /ˈgreɪsfəl/ adj **1** attractively and usu. effortlessly fine and smooth; full of grace: *a graceful dancer* | *her graceful movements* **2** showing a willingness to behave fairly and honourably: *a graceful apology* —see GRACIOUS (USAGE) – ~ly adv – ~ness n [U]

Grace·land /ˈgreɪslənd/ the former home of singer Elvis Presley in Memphis, Tennessee, now a tourist attraction

grace·less /ˈgreɪsləs/ adj **1** awkward in movement or form **2** lacking in good manners – ~ly adv – ~ness n [U]

Grac·es /ˈgreɪsɪz/, **The** also **The Three Graces** Greek and Roman goddesses of grace and beauty who often appear in art

gra·cious /ˈgreɪʃəs/ adj **1** polite, kind, and pleasant, esp. in a generous way: *Busy as she was, she was gracious enough to show us round her home.* **2** [A] having those qualities which are made possible by wealth, such as comfort, beauty, and freedom from hard work: *All this gracious living isn't for me; I prefer the simple life.* **3** [A] *fml* (used in speaking of a royal person): *Her Gracious Majesty Queen Elizabeth* **4** (of God) forgiving; MERCIFUL **5 Gracious!** also **Good gracious!** – *rather old-fash* (used to show surprise) – ~ly adv – ~ness n [U]

▷ USAGE Compare **gracious** and **graceful**. **Graceful** means attractive or pleasant and is used especially to describe bodily movements or form: *a graceful dancer* | *a deer running gracefully through the forest.* **Graceful** can also be used of people's manners, especially when they are saying they are sorry for something, or accepting defeat: *He admitted gracefully that he was wrong.* | *The losing candidate accepted the result of the election gracefully.* **Gracious** is usually used of people's manners and suggests an important person being polite to someone less important: *The Queen thanked them graciously.*◁

grad /græd/ n *infml* a GRADUATE¹'². *a reunion of old grads*

gra·da·tion /grəˈdeɪʃən/ n [(**in, of**)] *fml* a stage in a set of changes or degrees of development: *There are many gradations in/of colour between light blue and dark blue.* – compare GRADUATION

grade¹ /greɪd/ n **1** a particular level of rank or quality: *He's not in the first grade as a musician.* | *low-grade apples* | *weapons-grade plutonium* (=of a quality suitable for using in weapons) | *This grade of wool can be sold at a lower price.* **2** (in the American school system) a particular year of one school course: *She's in the second/eighth grade.* | *He had a fifth-grade education.* (=left school after completing the fifth grade) —compare FORM¹ (8)

▶ CULTURAL NOTE There are twelve years of education in the US, and these are called "first grade", "second grade", etc., up to "twelfth grade". The last four grades are spent in HIGH SCHOOL. Most Americans go to college or university after the twelfth grade. **First graders** are usu. six years old; **twelfth graders** are usu. seventeen years old.◄

3 *esp. AmE* a mark for the standard of a piece of schoolwork or of the schoolwork for all or part of the year: *She got good grades last semester.* **4** *esp. AmE* a degree of slope, esp. in a road or railway **5 make the grade** to succeed; reach the necessary standard: *I don't think she'll make the grade as a fashion model.*

grade² v [T] to separate into levels of rank or quality: *These potatoes have been graded according to size and quality.* —**gradable** adj : *"Rich" is a gradable adjective but "nuclear" is not.*

grade cross·ing /ˈ· ·ˌ··/ n *AmE for* LEVEL CROSSING

grade point av·er·age /ˌ· · ˈ·ˌ···/ also **GPA** *abbrev.—* n (in the US) the average of a student's marks (GRADES¹ (3)) over a period of time. Each grade is given a number (A = 4, B = 3, C = 2, D = 1, F = 0) and an average is calculated. A 4·0 (pronounced "four-point-O") is the highest possible grade point average. Often these numbers are used to decide whether a HIGH SCHOOL student will be accepted into a particular college or university.

grade school /ˈ· ·/ n *AmE old-fash for* ELEMENTARY SCHOOL

gra·di·ent /ˈgreɪdiənt/ also **grade** *AmE—* n a degree of slope, esp. in a road or railway: *A gradient of 1 in 4 is a rise or fall of one metre for every four metres forward.* | *a steep gradient*

grad school /ˈ· ·/ n a GRADUATE SCHOOL

grad·u·al /ˈgrædʒuəl/ adj happening or developing slowly and by degrees; not sudden: *There has been a gradual increase in the birth rate.* | *a gradual slope* | *a gradual phasing-out of the old equipment* − ~ **ly** *adv* − ~ **ness** *n* [U]

grad·u·ate[1] /ˈgrædʒuɪt/ *n* **1** a person who has completed a university degree course, esp. for a first degree − compare UNDERGRADUATE **2** *AmE* a person who has completed a course at a college, school, etc.: *a high school graduate*

graduate[2] *n, adj AmE for* POSTGRADUATE: *graduate school* | *a graduate student*

graduates

grad·u·ate[3] /ˈgrædʒueɪt/ *v* **1** [I (**from**)] to obtain a degree, esp. a first degree, at a university: *She graduated from Oxford with a first-class degree in physics.* **2** [I (**from**)] *AmE* to complete an educational course: *He graduated from high school last year.* **3** [T] to divide into levels or GRADES: *The salary scale is graduated, so I will get an annual increase.* **4** [T] *tech* to make marks showing degrees of measurement on: *a graduated ruler*

graduated pen·sion scheme /ˌ·····ˈ···ˌ·/ *n* a British government PENSION SCHEME in addition to the OLD AGE PENSION. Employed people make payments according to their earnings and employers pay a similar sum.

graduate school /ˈ···ˌ·/ also **grad school** *n AmE* a college or university where one can study for a MASTER'S or DOCTORATE DEGREE, having already obtained a BACHELOR'S DEGREE −see also extra information on page 408

grad·u·a·tion /ˌgrædʒuˈeɪʃən/ *n* **1** [U] (a ceremony for) the receiving of a first university degree or an American school DIPLOMA −see also extra information on page 408 **2** [C] a mark showing a measure of degree, esp. on a SCALE[1] (2) −compare GRADATION

Graeco- see WORD FORMATION

Graf /græf/, **Stef·fi** /ˈstefi/ (1969−) a German tennis player who has won many prizes and won the women's competition at Wimbledon in 1990 and 1992

graf·fi·ti /græˈfiːti, grə-/ *n* [U] drawings or writing on a wall, etc., esp. of a rude, humorous, or political nature: *The men's toilet is full of the usual graffiti.*

graffiti

graffiti art /·ˌ·· ˈ·/ *n* [U] graffiti, esp. names of people, painted on walls etc. in a decorative way, usu. with an AEROSOL, and considered by some people to be a kind of art

graft[1] /grɑːft‖græft/ *n* **1** [C] a piece cut from one plant and tied to or placed inside a cut in another, so that it grows there **2** [C] a piece of healthy living skin or bone taken from a person's body and placed instead of such a substance in another part of the body which has been damaged: *Her severe burns were treated with skin grafts.* **3** [U] *esp. AmE* the practice of obtaining money or advantage by the dishonest use of esp. political influence: *He rose to power through graft and corruption.*

graft[2] *v* [T (ON, onto)] to put onto a plant or body as a graft: *They grafted a piece of skin from his thigh onto his badly*

burnt face. | (fig.) *You could see that the last part of the report had just been grafted on as an afterthought.*

graft[3] *n* [U] *infml, esp. BrE* work: *It's* **hard graft** *peeling potatoes for a hundred people.*

graft[4] *v* [I] *infml, esp. BrE* to work hard − ~ **er** *n* : *She may be slow, but she's a real grafter.*

Gra·ham /ˈgreɪəm/, **Billy** (1918−) an American EVANGELIST who has visited many countries of the world to give public speeches attempting to spread belief in Christ and the Christian religion

Graham, Mar·tha /ˈmɑːθə ‖ ˈmɑːr-/ (1894−1991) an American dancer and CHOREOGRAPHER remembered esp. for her work in developing modern dance

graham crack·er /ˈ·· ˌ··/ *n (often cap.)* a flat, plain, slightly sweet American BISCUIT: *S'more's are made with chocolate and toasted marshmallows between graham crackers.*

Gra·hame /ˈgreɪəm/, **Ken·neth** /ˈkenɪθ/ (1859−1932) a Scottish writer famous esp. for his children's story *The Wind in the Willows*

Grail /greɪl/ *n* [*the*] the HOLY GRAIL

grain /greɪn/ *n* **1** [C] a single seed of rice, wheat, or other similar food plants: *a grain of rice* **2** [U] crops from plants which produce these seeds, esp. wheat: *a cargo of grain* | *the grain harvest* **3** [C (of)] a single very small piece of a hard substance: *a grain of sand/salt* | (fig.) *The story sounded most improbable, but there may be a* **grain of truth** (=some but not much truth) *in it.* −see picture at PIECE **4** [(*the*) U] the natural arrangement of the threads or FIBRES in wood, flesh, rock, and cloth, or the pattern of lines one sees as a result of this: *It's easiest to cut wood in the direction of the grain.* **5** [C] the smallest measure of weight, as used for medicines (1/7000 of a pound or ·0648 gram) **6 go against the grain** to be something that one does not like doing: *It goes against the grain for me to borrow money.* −see also **with a grain of salt** (SALT)

gram also **gramme** *BrE* /græm/ (*written abbrev.* **gm**) *n* (a measure of weight equal to) 1/1000 of a kilogram −see TABLE 2 and picture at POUND

-gram see WORD FORMATION

gram·mar /ˈgræməʳ/ *n* **1** [U] (the study or use of) the rules by which words change their forms and are combined into sentences: *I find German grammar very difficult.* | *His pronunciation is good, but his grammar is terrible.* | *"It's 'they were', not 'they was'," he said, correcting my grammar.* **2** [C] a book which describes or teaches these rules: *an Italian grammar/a grammar of Italian*

gram·mar·i·an /grəˈmeəriən/ *n* a person who studies and knows about grammar, esp. a writer of grammar books

grammar school /ˈ··· ·/ *n* **1** (in Britain, esp. formerly) a school for children over the age of 11, who are specially chosen to study for examinations which may lead to higher education −compare COMPREHENSIVE, SECONDARY MODERN; see also ELEVEN-PLUS **2** (in the US) *becoming rare* an ELEMENTARY SCHOOL

gram·mat·i·cal /grəˈmætɪkəl/ *adj* **1** [A *no comp.*] concerning grammar: *grammatical rules* **2** correct according to the rules of grammar: *"What means this word?" is not a grammatical question in modern speech.* − ~ **ly** /kli/ *adv* − ~ **ity** /grəˌmætɪˈkælɪti/ *n* [U]

gramme /græm/ *n* GRAM

Gram·my /ˈgræmi/ *n* an AWARD given by the US National Academy of Recording Arts and Sciences for special achievement in the record industry

gram·o·phone /ˈgræməfəʊn/ *n old-fash for* RECORD PLAYER

gramophone rec·ord /ˈ··· ·ˌ··/ *n old-fash for* RECORD[2] (4)

Gram·pi·an /ˈgræmpiən/ **1** a REGION (=area) in NE Scotland **2** one of the British television companies controlled by the ITC, transmitting programmes to NE Scotland

Gram·pi·ans /ˈgræmpiənz/ also **Grampian Moun·tains** /ˌ··· ˈ··/ [*the*+P] a mountain range in Scotland which includes Ben Nevis and the Cairngorms

gram·pus /ˈgræmpəs/ *n* **1** a type of sea creature which blows out air and water; kind of WHALE **2 breathe/puff/wheeze like a grampus** *infml, now rare* to breathe noisily

gran /græn/ *n esp. BrE infml* a grandmother

Gra·na·da /grəˈnɑːdə/ **1** a city in S Spain famous for its historical Moorish buildings, esp. the Alhambra palace **2** also **Granada Television** one of the British television companies controlled by the ITC, transmitting programmes to the NW of England **3** *tdmk* a kind of large comfortable car made by the Ford Motor Company

gra·na·ry[1] /ˈgrænəri‖ˈgreɪ-, ˈgræ-/ *n* a storehouse for grain, esp. wheat: (fig.) *The Midwest is often called the granary of the US.* (=because a lot of wheat is grown there)

granary[2] *adj BrE* (of bread) containing a mixture of white and WHOLEMEAL flours, and some whole grains of wheat: *a granary loaf‖granary bread*

grand[1] /grænd/ *adj* **1** splendid in appearance or style; IMPRESSIVE: *How grand the mountains look in the early light.* | *a millionaire who entertained his guests on a grand scale* **2** (of a person) important but perhaps too proud: *The king's court was full of nobles and grand ladies.* **3** *old-fash infml* or *dial* very pleasant; delightful: *That was a grand party.* – ~**ly** *adv* – ~**ness** *n* [U]

grand[2] *n* **1** (*pl* **grands**) *infml for* GRAND PIANO: *a concert grand* | *a* **baby grand** (=a small one) **2** (*pl.* **grand**) *sl* a thousand pounds or dollars: *That fur coat cost me five grand!*

gran·dad , granddad /ˈgrændæd/ *n infml* **1** a grandfather **2** (an impolite way of speaking to an old man): *Come on, grandad!*

gran·dad·dy , grand·dad·dy /ˈgrændædi/ *n infml* **1** [*the*+S+**of**] the first, greatest, or most powerful example: *Louis Armstrong was the grandaddy of jazz trumpeters.* | *Last night we had the grandaddy of all thunderstorms.* **2** [C] a grandfather

Grand Ca·nal /ˌ· ·ˈ·/ [*the*] **1** a CANAL in Venice, Italy, which is the main way through the town and has many famous buildings on its banks **2** a canal in E China. Part of it, connecting the Yangtze and Yellow Rivers, was built in the 5th century BC.

Grand Ca·na·ry /ˌ· ·ˈ·/ an island in the Atlantic Ocean, part of the Canary Islands

Grand Can·yon /ˌ· ˈ··/ [*the*] an extremely large GORGE cut over millions of years through the rocks of Arizona, US. It is up to 1·6 km (1 mile) deep, 6–29 km (4–18 miles) wide, and over 320 km (200 miles) long, and is one of America's main tourist spots. –see colour map on pages 1374–5

the Grand Canyon

Grand Cen·tral Sta·tion /ˌ· ··ˈ··/ the main railway station in New York City. Grand Central Station is a very busy place, and in the US people often mention it humorously to say how busy another place is: *Our house was like Grand Central Station last night!* –see colour map on page 1376

grand·child /ˈgræntʃaɪld/ *n* **grandchildren** /ˈgrænˌtʃɪldrən/ (more *fml* in the singular than **granddaughter** or **grandson**) the child of someone's son or daughter

grand·daugh·ter /ˈgrænˌdɔːtər/ *n* the daughter of someone's son or daughter

gran·dee /grænˈdiː/ *n* a Spanish or Portuguese nobleman of the highest rank

gran·deur /ˈgrændʒər/ *n* [U] **1** great beauty or power, often combined with great size: *You can't help being impressed by the grandeur of the scenery in the Alps.* **2** personal importance: *He suffers from* **delusions of grandeur.** (=thinks he is more important than he really is)

grand·fa·ther /ˈgrændˌfɑːðər/ *n* the father of someone's father or mother

grandfather clock /ˈ··· ˌ·/ *n* a tall clock which stands on the floor, with a long wooden outer case and the face at the top –see picture at CLOCK

grand fi·na·le /ˌ· ·ˈ··/ *n* the last and most impressive or exciting part of a show etc.: *As a grand finale, the orchestra played a rousing march.*

Grand Ho·tel /ˌ· ·ˈ·/ an American film of 1932 with Joan

Crawford and Greta Garbo, about the problems of wealthy and GLAMOROUS people

gran·dil·o·quent /grænˈdɪləkwənt/ *adj fml, often derog* (of a person or speech) using long important-sounding words; POMPOUS – **quence** *n* [U]

gran·di·ose /ˈgrændiəʊs/ *adj usu. derog* intended to have the effect of seeming important, splendid, etc.: *He always has grandiose ideas but where's the money for them?* | *grandiose schemes*

grand ju·ry /ˌ· ˈ··/ *n* (in the US) a group of usu. 23 people chosen to consider the facts about someone who is charged with a crime, and to then decide whether a TRIAL (=a formal hearing and judging of a person) is necessary. At a trial, a smaller JURY of between 6 and 12 people decide whether a person is guilty or not. –compare COURT OF INQUIRY and see also extra information on page 742

Grand La·ma /ˌ· ˈ··/ [*the*] the DALAI LAMA

grand lar·ce·ny /ˌ· ˈ··/ *n* [U] *AmE law* the stealing of very valuable goods

grand·ma /ˈgrænmɑː/ *n infml* a grandmother –compare GRANDPA

grand mal /ˌgrɒn ˈmæl‖ˌgrɑːn-/ *n* [U] *Fr* a serious form of the disease EPILEPSY –compare PETIT MAL

Grandma Mo·ses /ˌ·· ˈ··/ (1860–1961) an American US artist who painted colourful pictures in a PRIMITIVE[2] (2) style, and who did not begin painting until she was 75 years old

Grand Mar·ni·er /ˌgrɒn ˈmɑːnieɪ‖ˌgrɑːn mɑːrnˈjeɪ/ *n* [C;U] *tdmk* a strong alcoholic drink usu. drunk from a small glass after a meal

grand mas·ter /ˌ· ˈ··/ *n* a CHESS player of a very high level of skill

Grand Met·ro·pol·i·tan /ˌ· ··ˈ···/ also **Grand Met** /ˌ· ˈ·/ *infml*– a British company dealing in milk products, hotels, and breweries (BREWERY)

grand·moth·er /ˈgrænˌmʌðər/ *n* the mother of someone's father or mother –see also LITTLE RED RIDING HOOD

Grand Na·tion·al /ˌ· ˈ···/ [*the*] a famous horse race held each year at the AINTREE course near Liverpool. Many people who never usu. show interest in racing risk their money on the horse they think will win the Grand National.

Grand Old Duke of York /ˌ· · ·, · ·ˈ·/, **The** a character in a British NURSERY RHYME (=an old song or poem for children), often mentioned when someone seems to keep doing something and then doing the opposite:
> *Oh the Grand Old Duke of York*
> *He had ten thousand men,*
> *He marched them up to the top of the hill*
> *And he marched them down again.*

Grand Old Man /ˌ· · ·ˈ·/ *n* a name given to a person who has been involved in a subject or an activity for a long time and is highly respected: *the Grand Old Man of the cinema*

Grand Ole Op·ry /ˌgrænd əʊl ˈɒpri ‖ -ˈɑːpri/ [*the*] a country music entertainment centre in Nashville, Tennessee, from which radio and television broadcasts of performers were made for many years. In 1974 it moved to **Opryland USA**, near Nashville, and is still an important centre for country music.

grand op·e·ra /ˌ· ˈ···/ *n* [C;U] (an) OPERA in which all the words are sung, usu. on a serious subject

grand·pa /ˈgrænpɑː/ *n infml* a grandfather –compare GRANDMA

grand·par·ent /ˈgrænˌpeərənt/ *n* [*usu. pl.*] the parent of someone's father or mother

grand pi·an·o /ˌ· ·ˈ··/ also **grand** *infml*– *n* a large piano with strings set parallel to the ground, not up and down –compare UPRIGHT PIANO

grand prix /ˌgrɒn ˈpriː‖ˌgrɑːn-/ *n* **grands prix** *(same pronunciation) Fr (often caps.)* any of a set of important races, esp. car races, held under international rules

grand slam /ˌ· ˈ·/ *n* **1** the winning of all of a set of important sports competitions **2** the winning of all the card TRICKS[1] (5) possible at one time, esp. in the game of BRIDGE[3] **3** (in BASEBALL) a hit which is a HOME RUN made with players on the bases, so that four players can run to HOME BASE, gaining four runs

grand·son /ˈɡrænsʌn/ n the son of someone's son or daughter

grand·stand /ˈɡrændstænd/ n a set of seats, arranged in rising rows and sometimes covered by a roof, from which people watch sports matches, races, etc.

Grandstand a British television sports programme on Saturday afternoons which shows matches and competitions from several different sports

grand tour /ˌ· ˈ·/ n 1 [the] (formerly) a tour of Europe taken by upper-class young English people as part of their education: *Has she made the grand tour yet?* 2 *humor* any thorough tour of an esp. large building or place: *They took us on a grand tour of their new home.*

Grand U·nion Ca·nal /ˌ· ˌ·· ·ˈ·/ [the] a CANAL opened in 1801 connecting London with the English Midlands

grand wiz·ard /ˌ· ˈ···/ n (*often cap.*) the leader of the Ku Klux Klan

grange /ɡreɪndʒ/ n (*often cap. as part of a name*) a large country house with farm buildings: *They want to buy the old grange and turn it into a hotel.* | *Askham Grange*

gran·ite /ˈɡrænɪt/ n [U] a very hard usu. grey rock, used for building and making roads

gran·ny¹, **grannie** /ˈɡræni/ n *infml* a grandmother

granny², **grannie** adj [A] *infml, esp. BrE* of a style used by old women: *granny shoes*

granny flat /ˈ··· ·/ n a separate place to live, within or next to a person's house, intended for an old relative, esp. a parent

granny gear /ˈ··· ˌ·/ n [C;U] *infml* 1 *AmE for* FOUR-WHEEL DRIVE 2 *BrE* a very low GEAR on esp. a touring bicycle

granny knot /ˈ··· ˌ·/ n a REEF KNOT that is crossed the wrong way and therefore comes undone easily

Granny Smith /ˌ·· ˈ·/ n a kind of eating apple with a green skin and hard, white, sweet flesh

gra·no·la /ɡrəˈnəʊlə/ n [U] *AmE* breakfast food made from mixed, toasted (TOAST (2)) grains, seeds, and nuts, usu. sweetened

granola bar /·ˈ·· ˌ·/ n *AmE for* FLAPJACK (2)

grant¹ /ɡrɑːnt‖ɡrænt/ v [T] 1 *fml* to agree to fulfil or allow to be fulfilled: *They granted her request.* | *At last my wish was granted.* (=what I wished for happened) 2 *fml* to give, esp. as a favour: *In response to the lawyer's appeals, the Home Secretary granted a free pardon.* [+obj(i)+obj(d)] *The country was granted its independence in 1961.* | *They have been granted permission to pull down the old theatre.* 3 to admit the truth of (something) to (someone): *I had to grant the logic of his argument.* [+obj+(that)] *I grant you (that) the government isn't very popular at the moment, but I still think it will win the next election.* 4 **granted** yes (but): *"We were very successful last year." "Granted. But can we do it again this year?"* 5 **granted that** (in an argument) even though; even supposing that: *Granted that he should send money to help with the bills, it doesn't mean he will.* 6 **take something/someone for granted: a** to accept a fact or situation without questioning its rightness: *I took it for granted that you'd want to come with us, so I bought you a ticket.* **b** to treat someone or something with too little attention or concern; not recognize the true value of: *He's so busy with his job that he takes his family for granted.*

grant² n money given esp. by the state for a particular purpose, such as to a university or to a student during a period of study: *She finds it difficult to live on her grant.* | *We got a home improvement grant* (=money to spend on improving our house) *from the local council.*

Grant, Car·y /ˈkæri‖ˈkeɪ-/ (1904–86) a British-born American actor who is remembered esp. for his COMIC films, including *The Philadelphia Story* and *Bringing Up Baby*

Grant, Russell (1952–) an English radio and television ASTROLOGER who also writes about his subject

Grant, Ulysses S. (1822–85) an American army general and commander of the UNION (=the North's) army during the American Civil War. Grant is considered most responsible for the Union winning the war. He later became the 18th president of the US (1869–77) —compare Robert E LEE

Gran·ta /ˈɡrɑːntə‖ˈɡræn-/ a magazine which publishes (PUBLISH) new writing, esp. NOVELs, poetry, etc.

grant-aided school /ˌ· ·· ˈ·/ n AIDED SCHOOL

grant-in-aid /ˌ· · ˈ·/ n grants-in-aid *AmE* 1 an amount of money from taxes given by the national government to state or city governments for a specific purpose 2 an amount of money given to support a student, artist, or organization by a government or a CHARITY

grant-main·tained school /ˌ· ·· ˌ·/ n a British state school controlled by its governors and headteacher and not by the local education authority

Grant Thorn·ton /ˌɡrɑːnt ˈθɔːntən‖ˌɡrænt ˈθɔːrn-/ a British ACCOUNTANCY firm

gran·u·lar /ˈɡrænjʊlər/ adj made of, full of, or covered with granules

gran·u·lat·ed /ˈɡrænjʊleɪtɪd/ adj (of white sugar) in the form of not very fine powder —compare CASTER SUGAR

gran·ule /ˈɡrænjuːl/ n a small bit like a fine grain: *a granule of sugar* | *instant coffee granules*

grape /ɡreɪp/ n a small round juicy fruit usu. either green (called "white") or dark purple (called "black"), which grows on a VINE and is used for making wine: *a bunch of grapes* —see also SOUR GRAPES, and see picture at FRUIT

grape·fruit /ˈɡreɪpfruːt/ n grapefruit or grapefruits a round yellow fruit with a thick skin, like a very large orange but with a more acid taste

Grape Nuts /ˈ· ·/ [U] *tdmk* a type of breakfast CEREAL, made from wheat, which is hard and CRUNCHY

grape·shot /ˈɡreɪpʃɒt‖-ʃɑːt/ n [U] small iron balls fired together in a mass from large guns in former times

Grapes of Wrath /ˌ· · ˈ·/, **The** a book by John Steinbeck which describes the hard conditions faced by farmers who had to move away from their land in the central US during the Depression of the 1930s. It was made into a successful film. —see colour picture on page 1145

grape·vine /ˈɡreɪpvaɪn/ n 1 [the+S] an unofficial way of spreading news: *I heard about your success on/through the office grapevine.* 2 [C] *rare* a climbing plant that bears grapes; VINE

graph /ɡræf, ɡrɑːf‖ɡræf/ n a planned drawing, such as a curved line, which shows how (usu. two) different values are related to each other: *This graph shows how the number of road accidents has increased over the last ten years.* —see picture at CHART

graph·ic¹ /ˈɡræfɪk/ adj 1 giving a clear and detailed description or lifelike picture, esp. in words, sometimes more detailed than necessary or than one would like; VIVID: *The newspaper article gave a graphic description of the earthquake.* | *Spare me* (= don't tell me) *all the graphic details!* 2 [A *no comp.*] concerned with or including drawing, printing, LETTERING, etc.: *The graphic arts include calligraphy and lithography.*

graphic² n [usu. pl.] a drawing or similar representation of an object: *The graphics on the package suggest a high-tech product* —see also COMPUTER GRAPHICS

graph·i·cally /ˈɡræfɪkli/ adv 1 in a graphic manner: *She described the events so graphically that I could almost see them.* 2 *fml* by means of a graph: *It is easier to represent these statistics graphically than to describe them in words.*

graphic de·sign /ˌ··· ·ˈ·/ n [U] the art of combining pictures, words, and decoration in the making of books, magazines, advertisements, etc. – ~**er** n

graph·ite /ˈɡræfaɪt/ n [U] a black substance which is a kind of CARBON and is used for the writing material in the middle of pencils (when it is usu. called "lead") and also in paints, oil for machines, and electrical equipment

gra·phol·o·gy /ɡræˈfɒlədʒi‖-ˈfɑː-/ n [U] the study of handwriting as a guide to character —**gist** n

graph pa·per /ˈ· ˌ··/ n [U] paper with squares marked on it, on which GRAPHs can be easily measured out and drawn

grap·nel /ˈɡræpnəl/ n a grappling iron

Grap·pel·li /ɡrəˈpeli/, **Stéph·ane** /ˈstefən‖steˈfɑːn/ (1908–) a French JAZZ musician who plays the VIOLIN

grap·ple /ˈɡræpəl/ v **grapple with** sbdy./sthg. *phr v* [T] 1 to take hold of and struggle with: *She grappled with the bank robber, but was thrown to the ground.* 2 to work hard to deal with something difficult: *Don't interrupt John; he's grappling with the accounts.*

grappling i·ron /ˈ··· ··/ also **grappling hook** /ˈ··· ·/— n an iron instrument with several hooks, which when tied to a rope can be used for holding a boat still, for searching for an object on the bottom of a river or lake, or (formerly) for pulling an enemy's boat close to one's own

Gras·mere /ˈɡrɑːsmɪəʳ‖ˈɡræs-/ a village in the Lake District, NW England, near a lake which is also called Grasmere. The village is famous as the home of the poet William Wordsworth, whose house, Dove Cottage, is popular with tourists.

grasp¹ /ɡrɑːsp‖ɡræsp/ v [T] **1** to take or keep a firm hold of, esp. with the hands: *Grasp the rope with both hands.* **2** to succeed in understanding: *I think I grasped the main points of the speech.* | *They failed to grasp the full significance of these events.* **3** to try or be eager to take: *to grasp an opportunity* **4 grasp the nettle** to deal firmly with an unpleasant job or subject —see CLASP² (USAGE) **grasp at** sthg. *phr v* [T] to reach for; try to take or hold: (fig.) *He grasped at the first flimsy excuse that came to his mind.*

grasp² *n* [S] **1** a firm hold with the hands or arms: *I kept her hand in my grasp.* | *The kitten wriggled out of my grasp.* **2** one's power or ability to reach or gain something: *Success is within our grasp.* **3** one's power or ability to understand something: *This work is beyond my grasp.* | *She seems to have a good grasp of the subject.* **4** *esp. lit* control or power: *in the grasp of wicked men*

grasp·ing /ˈɡrɑːspɪŋ‖ˈɡræs-/ *adj derog* eager for more, esp. more money, and often ready to use unfair or dishonest methods: *Don't let those grasping taxidrivers overcharge you.*

grass¹ /ɡrɑːs‖ɡræs/ n **1** [U] various kinds of common lowgrowing green plants whose blades and stems are eaten by sheep, cows, etc., on hills and in fields **2** [U] land covered by grass: *Don't walk on the grass.* | *I'm just going to cut the grass.* (=LAWN) **3** [C *usu. pl.*;U] any of various green plants with tall straight stems and flat blades: *He hid behind some tall grasses.* | *There was an attractive arrangement of dried grasses in the vase.* **4** [C] *BrE derog sl* someone, often a criminal, who informs the police about the (other) people concerned in a crime; INFORMER —see also SUPERGRASS **5** [U] *sl for* MARIJUANA **6 let the grass grow under one's feet** [*usu. in negatives*] to delay action; waste time in inactivity: *As soon as you approve it I'll get started — I'm not one to let the grass grow under my feet!* **7 out to grass** *BrE*, **out to pasture** *infml* no longer working: *Some of these old judges are nearly 80, you know; it's time they were put out to grass!* **8 the grass is always greener on the other side of the fence** *saying* something that you have not got always seems more attractive or exciting than the thing that you have got

grass² *v* **1** [T (OVER)] to cover (land) with grass **2** [I (on)] *BrE sl* (esp. of a criminal) to inform the police about the action of (other) criminals

Grass /ɡræs/, **Gün·ter** /ˈɡjʊntəʳ, ˈɡʊn-/ (1927) a German poet and writer of books and plays known esp. for his book *The Tin Drum*

grass·hop·per /ˈɡrɑːsˌhɒpəʳ‖ˈɡræsˌhɑː-/ n an insect which can jump high and makes a sharp noise by rubbing its legs against its body —see also **knee-high to a grasshopper** (KNEE-HIGH)

grass·land /ˈɡrɑːslænd‖ˈɡræs-/ also **grasslands** *pl.*— n [U] a stretch of land covered mainly with grass, esp. wild open land used for cattle to feed on

grass roots /ˌ· ˈ·/ n [P] the ordinary people or ordinary members of a group, rather than the ones with power or special knowledge: *Opinion at (the) grass roots (level) is sympathetic to the strikers.* | *Grass roots opinion is in favour of a strike.*

grass snake /ˈ· ·/ n a non-poisonous snake found in many parts of Europe

grass wid·ow /ˌ· ˈ··/ **grass wid·ow·er** /ˌ· ˈ···/*masc.*— n *sometimes humor* a woman whose husband is away for a period of time

gras·sy /ˈɡrɑːsi‖ˈɡræsi/ *adj* covered with growing grass

grate¹ /ɡreɪt/ n the bars and frame which hold the coal, wood, etc., in an old-fashioned fireplace —see picture at FIREPLACE

grate² v **1** [T] to rub (esp. food) against a rough or sharp surface so as to break it into small pieces: *grated cheese*

2 [I (on)] to make a sharp sound, unpleasant to the hearer: *The teacher's chalk grated on the blackboard.* | *His monotonous whistling grated on her nerves.* —see also GRATING²

grate·ful /ˈɡreɪtfəl/ *adj* [(for, to)] feeling or showing thanks to another person: *I was most grateful to John for bringing the books/for his kindness.* | *The rescuers deserve our grateful thanks.* [F+(that)] *I'm grateful that you didn't tell my husband about this.* [F+ to-v] *We were grateful to get back on dry land after our rough boat trip.* —opposite **ungrateful** — ~**ly** *adv* — ~**ness** n [U]

grat·er /ˈɡreɪtəʳ/ n an instrument for grating things into small pieces, often one having or consisting of a metal surface full of sharp-edged holes: *a cheese grater*

grat·i·fy /ˈɡræt̮əfaɪ/ v [T] *fml* **1** [*often pass.*] to give pleasure and satisfaction to: *I was gratified/It gratified me to see how much my wedding present was appreciated.* **2** to satisfy (a desire): *Now she has a job in France she can gratify her desire to see Europe.* — ~**·fication** /ˌɡræt̮əfəˈkeɪʃən/ n [C;U] : *His family's success was a great gratification to him in his old age.*

grat·i·fy·ing /ˈɡrætʃfaɪ-ɪŋ/ *adj* giving pleasure and satisfaction: *It is gratifying to see the widespread response to our charity appeal.* — ~**ly** *adv*

grat·ing¹ /ˈɡreɪtɪŋ/ n a frame or network of bars, usu. metal, to protect a hole or window: *The rainwater ran along the gutter into a grating at the side of the road.* (=one which covers a hole connecting with a water system)

grating² *adj* (of a noise or sound) sharp, hard, and unpleasant —see also GRATE² (2) — ~**ly** *adv*

grat·is /ˈɡrætʃs, ˈɡreɪtʃs/ *adv, adj* [F] free; (given) without payment

grat·i·tude /ˈɡrætʃtjuːd‖-tuːd/ n [U (to, for)] the state or feeling of being grateful; kind feelings towards someone who has been kind: *She showed me her gratitude by inviting me to dinner.* | *We all owe* **a debt of gratitude** *to the local council, without whose help this event could not have been staged.* —opposite **ingratitude**

gra·tu·i·tous /ɡrəˈtjuːɪtəs‖-ˈtuː-/ *adj fml* **1** *derog* not deserved or necessary: *a gratuitous insult* | *an unpleasant film with a lot of gratuitous violence in it* **2** *rare* done freely, without reward or payment being expected — ~**ly** *adv* — ~**ness** n [U]

gra·tu·i·ty /ɡrəˈtjuːɪti‖-ˈtuː-/ n **1** *fml* a gift of money for a service done; TIP⁵ **2** *esp. BrE* a gift of money to a worker or member of the armed forces when they leave their employment

grave¹ /ɡreɪv/ n **1** [C] the place in the ground where a dead person is buried —compare TOMB **2** [*the*+S] *esp. lit* death: *Is there life beyond the grave?* | *The state takes care of its people* **from the cradle to the grave.** (=from birth to death) **3 turn in one's grave** (of someone who is dead) to be very annoyed or worried if they were still alive: *The way young people behave nowadays would make my grandfather turn in his grave.* —see also **dig one's own grave** (DIG¹), **have one foot in the grave** (FOOT¹), **silent as the grave** (SILENT¹)

grave² *adj* **1** giving cause for worry and/or needing urgent attention; very serious: *grave news* | *The situation poses a grave threat to peace.* | *a matter of grave concern* **2** serious or solemn in manner: *His face was grave as he told them about the accident.* —see also GRAVITY (2) — ~**ly** *adv*

grave³ /ɡrɑːv/ *adj* [A] (of an ACCENT¹ (3) put above a letter to show pronunciation) being the mark over è —compare ACUTE (6), CIRCUMFLEX

grav·el¹ /ˈɡrævəl/ n [U] small stones usu. mixed with sand and used to make a surface for paths, roads, etc.: *a gravel pit* (=place where gravel is dug out of the ground)

gravel² v *BrE* -ll- ‖ -l- *AmE* [T *often pass.*] to cover (a path or road) with gravel: *a gravelled path*

grav·el·ly /ˈɡrævəli/ *adj* **1** of, containing, or covered with gravel **2** having a low rough hard sound; GRATING²: *a gravelly voice*

Graves /ɡreɪvz/, **Rob·ert** /ˈrɒbət‖ˈrɑːbərt/ (1895–1985) an English poet and writer, known to many people for his HISTORICAL NOVELS *I, Claudius* and *Claudius the God*, which were made into a very successful SERIES of television programmes

grave·stone /ˈɡreɪvstəʊn/ also **tombstone**— n a stone put up over a grave bearing the name, dates of birth and death, etc., of the dead person

grave·yard /ˈgreɪvjɑːd‖-jɑːrd/ n a piece of ground, sometimes around a church, where people are buried; a CEMETERY or CHURCHYARD: (fig.) *The area had become a graveyard for old cars.* (=a place where people left them) —compare CEMETERY, CHURCHYARD

graveyard shift /ˈ·· ˌ·/ n AmE infml for NIGHT SHIFT

grav·i·tas /ˈgrævɪtæs/ n [U] fml seriousness of manner which causes respect or trust

grav·i·tate /ˈgrævɪteɪt/ v
gravitate to/towards sthg. *phr v* [T] **1** to be attracted by and move gradually towards: *In the 19th century, industry gravitated towards the north of England.* | *From amateur tennis he eventually gravitated to the professional circuit.* **2** to fall or be drawn towards something, under the influence of gravity: *However often you mix it up in the water, the mud will gravitate towards the bottom again.*

grav·i·ta·tion /ˌgrævɪˈteɪʃən/ n [U] **1** [+ **to, towards**] the process of gravitating towards something **2** GRAVITY (1) **– ~al** adj : *gravitational forces* | *They had entered the planet's* **gravitational field.**

grav·i·ty /ˈgrævɪti/ n [U] **1** the natural force by which objects are attracted to each other, esp. that by which a large mass pulls a smaller one to it. It is one of the four FUNDAMENTAL FORCES of nature: *Anything that is dropped falls towards the ground because of the force of gravity.* —see also Isaac NEWTON **2** fml a worrying importance: *He doesn't seem to understand the gravity of the situation.* **b** seriousness of manner —see also GRAVE², CENTRE OF GRAVITY

gra·vure /grəˈvjʊəʳ/ n [U] the method of printing from copper or wooden plates on which a picture has been marked

gra·vy /ˈgreɪvi/ n [U] **1** the juice which comes out of meat as it cooks, thickened with flour, etc., to serve with meat and vegetables **2** sl, esp. AmE something pleasing or valuable that happens or is gained easily

gravy boat /ˈ·· ˌ·/ n a small deep long-shaped container with a handle, from which gravy can be poured at a meal — see picture at JUG

gravy train /ˈ·· ˌ·/ n [the+S] infml, esp. AmE something from which many people can make money or profit without much effort, and which one would therefore like to join in: *There's so much money invested in this political campaign that everyone's trying to climb on the gravy train.*

gray¹ /greɪ/ adj, v AmE for GREY¹, ³: *gray hair* | *Her hair is graying.*

gray² n AmE **1** [C;U] GREY² **2** [C] (usu. cap.) (a member of) the Confederate (CONFEDERATE² (3)) army

Gray¹, Dorian see PICTURE OF DORIAN GRAY

Gray², Thomas (1716–71) an English poet whose best-known work, *Elegy written in a Country Churchyard*, is usually called **Gray's Elegy**

Gray's Inn /ˌ·ˈ·/ one of the four Inns of Court in London —see INNS OF COURT

graze¹ /greɪz/ v **1** [I;T] (of an animal) to feed on growing grass (in): *The cattle are grazing (in the field).* **2** [T] to cause (an animal) to feed on grass: *We can't graze the cattle till summer.* | *The bottom field is being kept for grazing.*

graze² v [T] **1** to break the surface of (esp. the skin) by rubbing against something: *She fell down and grazed her knee.* **2** to touch (something) lightly while passing: *The wing seemed to graze the treetops as the plane climbed away.* | *The car just grazed the gate as it drove through.*

graze³ n [usu. sing.] a surface wound: *She has a nasty graze on her elbow.*

GRE /ˌdʒiː ɑːr ˈiː/ n (in the US) Graduate Record Exam; an examination which any graduate can take. The resulting mark is then sent to graduate schools that the student would like to attend, and the graduate schools generally choose those students with the highest marks. The GRE is managed by a private company, and students can take it again to improve their results. —compare SAT

grease¹ /griːs/ n [U] **1** animal fat when soft after being melted: *You'll never get the bacon grease off the plates if you don't use detergent.* **2** any thick oily substance, esp. one used to help the moving parts of machines to run

smoothly: *Put some grease on the door hinges to stop them squeaking.* | *He puts grease on his hair to make it shiny.*

grease² /griːs, griːz/ v [T] **1** to put grease on: *Grease the dish with butter before pouring in the egg mixture.* | *Ask the mechanic to grease the axle.* **2 grease someone's palm** infml to give money to someone in a secret or dishonest way in order to persuade them to do something —see also OIL THE WHEELS (OIL²)

greased light·ning /ˌ· ˈ··/ n [U] infml something extremely fast: *You should see Carl Smith run the 100 metres; he's like greased lightning!*

grease gun /ˈ· ˌ·/ n a hand instrument for forcing GREASE¹ (2) into machinery

grease·paint /ˈgriːs-peɪnt/ n [U] a thick soft substance that comes in many colours and is used by actors and actresses on their faces, hands, etc., to change their appearance when acting

grease·proof pa·per /ˌgriːs-pruːf ˈpeɪpəʳ/ n [U] a type of paper which grease or oil cannot pass through, used in Britain esp. for wrapping food or in cooking

greas·er /ˈgriːsəʳ, -zəʳ/ n **1** a person who puts grease on machinery to make it run smoothly **2** AmE taboo derog a person from Latin America, esp. Mexico

greas·y /ˈgriːsi, -zi/ adj **1** covered with or containing grease: *greasy food/skin/hair* **2** slippery: *The roads are greasy after the rain.* **3** derog insincerely polite; SMARMY: *I detest his greasy smile.* **—iness** n [U]

greasy spoon /ˌ·· ˈ·/ n sl a cheap often dirty restaurant that mainly serves fried food (FRY)

great¹ /greɪt/ adj **1** very large in degree or amount: *Take great care.* | *The show was a great success.* | *I lost* **a great deal** *of money.* | *There were* **a great many** *people there.* | *She lived to* **a great age.** (=to be very old) | *The sense of loss we felt at his death was very great.* | *It gives me great pleasure to introduce our special guest for this evening.* | *The plan as supported by* **the great majority of** (=nearly all) *the members* **2** of excellent quality or ability: *a great war leader* | *a great achievement* | *In my view she's one of the greatest modern novelists.* | *Muhammad Ali, the boxing champion, called himself "the Greatest".* **3** [A] of special importance and seriousness: *Most great state occasions, like coronations, are televised nowadays.* | *one of the great political issues of our times* **4** [(at)] infml splendid; very good: *What a great idea!* | *This new singer is really great!* | *I think this new singer has a great future.* (=will be very successful) | *"I've got the use of a car."* *"Great! We can go to the seaside."* | *He's really great at playing the guitar.* | *It's great to see you again!* **5** [A] (of a person) unusually active in the stated way: *He's a great talker.* (=talks a lot) | *We're great* (=very close) *friends.* **6** [A] infml (usu. with another adjective of size) big: *That great (big) tree takes away all the light.* | *There's a huge great spider in the bath!* **7** [A] (used in names to mark something important of its type): *King Alfred the Great* —see also GREATER **8 go great guns** infml to get on with great speed and success **9 great with child** bibl for PREGNANT **10 no great shakes** infml not very good, skilful, effective, etc.: *I'm no great shakes as a pianist, but I can play a few simple tunes.* **11 he/she/it has gone to the great… in the sky** infml humor he/she/it has died: *Old Fred the cat has gone to the great mouse-hunting ground in the sky.* **12 some men are born great, some achieve greatness, and some have greatness thrust upon them** quote a phrase from Shakespeare's play *Twelfth Night* **13 great- : a** being the parent of a grandfather or grandmother: *great-grandfather* **b** being the child of a child of a son or daughter: *great-granddaughter* **c** being the brother or sister of a grandfather or grandmother: *great-aunt* **d** being the child of a NEPHEW or NIECE: *great-nephew* —see BIG (USAGE), see also GREATLY **– ~ness** n [U]

great² n **greats** or **great** an important or leading person: *Charlie Chaplin is one of the* **all-time greats** *of the cinema.* | *He's always talking about his connections with the great.*

Great Bar·ri·er Reef /ˌ· ˌ··· ˈ·/ [the] the largest CORAL REEF¹ in the world, off the NE coast of Australia. It is around 2000 km (1250 miles) long.

Great Bear /ˌ· ˈ·/ [the] a group of stars

Great Brit·ain /ˌ· ˈ··/ see UK (USAGE)

great cir·cle /ˌ· ˈ··/ n a circle on the Earth's surface, with the centre of the Earth as its centre: *The great circle route is the quickest way to fly from London to Beijing.*

great·coat /ˈgreɪtkəʊt/ *n* a heavy usu. military OVERCOAT

Great Crash /ˌ· ˈ·/ *[the]* the CRASH² (5)

Great Dane /ˌ· ˈ·/ *n* a very large tall dog with smooth hair

Great De·pres·sion /ˌ· ·ˈ·ˑ/ *[the]* a very severe economic DEPRESSION (=period of reduced business activity and high unemployment) in the 1930s which followed a CRASH (=business failure) on WALL STREET (=the US STOCK MARKET) in October 1929. The US was esp. involved, with 16 million people unemployed in 1933. The effects of the Great Depression were also felt in Europe.

Great Di·vide /ˌ· ·ˈ·/ *n [the]* CONTINENTAL DIVIDE

Great·er /ˈgreɪtəʳ/ *adj* [A] (in names) including the outer areas of a city: *Greater Manchester | the Greater Buffalo area*

Greater Lon·don /ˌ·· ˈ·ˑ/ a local government area including the whole of London and parts of other areas surrounding London

Greater Man·ches·ter /ˌ·· ˈ·ˑˑ/ a former COUNTY in NW England including the whole of Manchester and parts of other counties

Great Ex·hi·bi·tion /ˌ· ··ˈ·ˑ/ *[the]* an EXHIBITION in the Crystal Palace in London in 1851. It was intended to show human progress, esp. in science and TECHNOLOGY.

Great Ex·pec·ta·tions /ˌ· ··ˈ·ˑ/ a NOVEL by Charles Dickens about a young man who believes that he will become rich by inheriting (INHERIT) money

Great Fire of Lon·don /ˌ· ˌ· · ˈ·ˑ/ *[the]* a fire in 1666 which started in a baker's shop in Pudding Lane, London. Thousands of buildings were destroyed but only four people were killed.

Robert Redford and Mia Farrow in *The Great Gatsby*

Great Gats·by /ˌgreɪt ˈgætsbi/, **The** a book by F. Scott Fitzgerald about rich, GLAMOROUS people in the US in the Jazz Age (the 1920s)

Great Lakes /ˌ· ˈ·/ *[the]* a group of five lakes along the US–Canadian border. They form part of an important shipping and are popular with tourists many of whom go esp. to see Niagara Falls. —see colour map on pages 1374–5

Great Leap For·ward /ˌ· · ˈ·ˑ/ *[the]* a programme of bringing more people into industry in China (1959–60) in an attempt to improve the country's economic situation. The Great Leap Forward did not work, because the country was producing less food than the government had thought, and many people died of hunger.

great·ly /ˈgreɪtli/ *adv* (with verb forms, esp. past participles) to a large degree; very: *Her reading has improved greatly since she changed schools. | The effects of this policy have been greatly exaggerated by its opponents.*

Great Or·mond Street Hos·pi·tal /ˌgreɪt ˌɔːmənd striːt ˈhɒspɪtl‖-ˌɔːr-, -ˈhɑː-/ a children's hospital in London

Great Plains /ˌ· ˈ·/ *[the]* a large area of flat, high land in the western central US

Great Rift Val·ley /ˌ· ˌ· ˈ·ˑ/ *[the]* a very deep, wide valley which is 3000 miles long and runs across most of E Africa and into SW Asia

Great Salt Lake /ˌ· · ˈ·/ *[the]* a lake in the US state of Utah which is about 70 miles long and has strong salt water —see colour map on pages 1374–5

Great Seal of the U·nit·ed States /ˌ· ˌ· · ·ˑ·· ˈ·/ *[the]* an official mark which represents the authority of the US government. It shows an EAGLE (=kind of large bird) on one side and a PYRAMID on the other. Both sides can be seen on the back of a $1 bill.

Great Smok·y Moun·tains /ˌ· ˌ··· ˈ·ˑ/ also **Great Smokies** /ˌ· ˈ··/, **Smokies** *[the+P]* a range of mountains along the border between the US states of North Carolina and Tennessee

Great Train Rob·be·ry /ˌ· ˈ· ˌ·ˑ/ *[the]* the name given to an event in 1963 when several men robbed a mail train in Britain and escaped with over £2,000,000. It is still remembered because of the large amount of money involved and because not all the men were caught. —see also Ronald BIGGS

Great U·ni·ver·sal Stores /ˌ· ˌ···· ˈ·/ a British MAIL ORDER company

Great Wall of Chi·na /ˌ· ˌ· · ˈ·ˑ/ *[the]* an ancient wall built across N China for defence purposes

Great War /ˌ· ˈ·/ *[the]* *BrE* the FIRST WORLD WAR

Great West·ern /ˌ· ˈ··◄/ *[the]* a PADDLE STEAMER built in 1838 by I. K. Brunel. The Great Western was the first steam ship made specially for carrying passengers across the Atlantic Ocean.

Great Western Rail·way /ˌ· ·· ˈ·ˑ/ *[the]* a British railway built by I. K. Brunel and opened in 1841 to connect London and Bristol

Greaves /ˈgriːvz/, **Jimmy** (1940–) a former England footballer now introducing sports programmes on British television and well-known for his direct opinions. He is often called **Greavsie**.

grebe /griːb/ *n* a bird rather like a duck but with separate toes, which can swim under water in lakes and rivers

Gre·cian /ˈgriːʃən/ *adj lit* (of style or appearance) Greek, esp. of ancient Greece

Greco, El see EL GRECO

Greco- see WORD FORMATION

Greece /griːs/ a country in SE Europe; capital Athens; population 10,031,000 (1989). It is considered by many people to be the birthplace of many of the arts and sciences, and it is also a popular place for holidays.

greed /griːd/ *n* [U (**for**)] *usu. derog* a strong desire to have a lot of something, esp. food, money, or power, often in a way that is selfish or unfair to other people: *It was pure greed that made me finish all those chocolates! | The speculators' greed (for profit) has left several small investors penniless.*

greed·y /ˈgriːdi/ *adj* **1** *usu. derog* full of greed for food: *Don't be so greedy — leave some of the food for the rest of us. | You greedy pig!* **2** [F+**for**] full of a strong desire (for): *greedy for power/fame* —**ily** *adv* —**iness** *n* [U]

greedy-guts /ˈ··· ·/ *n infml, esp. BrE* (used esp. by children) a person who likes to eat too much; GLUTTON

Greek¹ /griːk/ *n* **1** [U] the language of ancient or modern Greece **2** [C] a person who comes from Greece or whose parents come from Greece **3** [C] *AmE* a member of a FRATERNITY or a SORORITY at a college or university **4 beware of Greeks bearing gifts** a warning not to trust someone who seems to be being kind to you because they may wish to harm you (from the story of the Trojan Horse)

Greek² *adj* **1** of the people, language, art, etc. of Greece **2 be all Greek to someone** *infml* (esp. of speech or writing) to be beyond someone's understanding: *She tried to explain her theories about modern poetry but it was all Greek to me.* **3** *AmE* of a FRATERNITY or a SORORITY

Greek god /ˌ· ˈ·/ *n* a very good-looking man: *He's not exactly a Greek god, but he's very nice.*

Greek Or·tho·dox /ˌ· ˈ···◄/ *adj* of or belonging to the Greek Orthodox Church: *a Greek Orthodox priest*

Greek Orthodox Church /ˌ· ··· ˈ·/ *[the]* a branch of the Christian Church in E Europe and SW Asia, which split away from the Western (now Catholic) Church in 1054 AD

green¹ /griːn/ adj **1** of a colour between yellow and blue, which is the colour of leaves and grass: *The countryside is very green* (=covered in fresh grass and leaves) *in spring.* | *A* **green salad** *has only green vegetables, such as lettuce and cucumber.* | *When the traffic lights turn green you can go.* | *I painted the door green.* —see also BOTTLE GREEN **2** (of a plant) of this colour when young or unripe: *Green apples are sour.* | *Wood which is green is not dry enough to burn.* **3** concerned with, or not causing harm to, the environment; ENVIRONMENT FRIENDLY: *He's very green-minded/very green.* | *Our local government is very green – they won't allow chemicals to be dumped in the river.* **4** *infml* unhealthily pale in the face because of sickness, fear, etc.: *She turned green when she smoked her first cigarette.* —see also **green about the gills** (GILL¹) **5** *infml* young and/or inexperienced and therefore easily deceived and ready to believe anything **6** [F] *infml* very jealous: *He was absolutely* **green (with envy)** *when he saw my new Jaguar car.* **7** *lit* (esp. of a memory) fresh, strong, and full of life, in spite of the passing of time – – **ness** /ˈgriːn-nɪs/ n [U]

green² n **1** [C;U] the colour which is green: *She was dressed in green.* | *The room was decorated in bright greens and blues.* **2** [C] a smooth stretch of grass for a special purpose, such as for playing a game or for the general use of the people of a town: *They are dancing on the green.* | *The golfer got to the green in one stroke.* —see also GREENS, BOWLING GREEN, VILLAGE GREEN and see picture at GOLF

green³ v [T] to fill with growing plants, esp. so as to lessen the ugliness caused by human activity on the Earth: *the greening of our cities*

Green¹ adj of the Green Party: *Green issues* | *a Green spokeswoman*

Green² n (a member or supporter of) the Green Party: *There are a lot of Greens in Devon.* | *I'm voting Green* (=for the Green Party) *this year.*

Green·a·way /ˈgriːnəweɪ/, **Kate** /keɪt/ (1846–1901) an English painter known for her pictures for children's books

green·back /ˈgriːnbæk/ n old-fash AmE infml an American banknote, esp. a one-dollar bill

green bean /ˌ· ˈ·/ also **French bean** BrE– n a bean having a narrow green case (POD) used as a vegetable. Both the contents and the case are eaten.

green belt /ˈ· ·/ n [C;U] esp. BrE a stretch of land, round a town or city, where building is not allowed, so that fields, woods, etc., remain

green ber·et /ˌ· ˈ··‖ˌ· ˈ·/ n a member of a special force of soldiers in the US Army who wear special green hats and are thought to be esp. brave

green card /ˌ· ˈ·/ n **1** Br E a document of motor insurance protecting vehicles driven abroad: *Have you got your green card?* **2** Am E a document necessary in order to work legally in the US: *I'm getting my green card in another six months.*

green cross code /ˌ· · ˈ·/ [the] Br E a set of rules for children on how to cross roads safely

Greene /griːn/, **Graham** (1904–91) an English writer of NOVELS and plays, famous esp. for the novel *Brighton Rock* and for the film *The Third Man*, for which he wrote the story

green·e·ry /ˈgriːnəri/ n [U] green leaves and plants (FOLIAGE), esp. when used for decoration —compare GREENS (2)

green-eyed mon·ster /ˌ· · ˈ··/ n [the] lit or humor jealousy

green fin·gers /ˌ· ˈ··/ n [P] esp. BrE ‖ **green thumb** esp. AmE– natural skill in making plants grow well –**green-fingered** adj

green·fly /ˈgriːnflaɪ/ n **greenfly** or **greenflies** a very small green insect which feeds on the juice from young plants: *The roses have got greenfly again.*

green·gage /ˈgriːngeɪdʒ/ n a soft juicy greenish-yellow fruit; kind of PLUM

Green Gi·ant /ˌ· ˈ··/ n tdmk a company which produces tinned and frozen (FREEZE (5)) vegetables; it is best known for its SWEETCORN

green·gro·cer /ˈgriːnˌgrəʊsər/ n esp. BrE a person who owns or works in a shop (**greengrocer's**) which sells vegetables and fruit: *I bought some onions at the greengrocer's.* —compare GROCER

Green·ham Com·mon /ˌgriːnəm ˈkɒmən‖-ˈkɑː-/ an airforce base at the village of Greenham Common in S England for British and American soldiers. Since 1981 groups of women have been camping around the base, originally protesting against the NUCLEAR weapons, esp. the CRUISE MISSILES, which were kept there. —compare MOLESWORTH

green·horn /ˈgriːnhɔːn‖-hɔːrn/ n infml an inexperienced person, usu. male, esp. one who is easily cheated

green·house /ˈgriːnhaʊs/ n **-houses** /ˌhaʊzɪz/ a building with a glass roof and glass sides and often some form of heating, used for growing plants which need heat, light, and freedom from winds. Many people have them in their gardens to protect young plants from the cold before planting them outside, or to store plants for the winter.

greenhouse ef·fect /ˈ·· ·ˌ·/ [the] the gradual slight warming of the air surrounding the Earth because heat cannot escape through its upper levels, said to be caused by POLLUTION (2) in the air. Some people do not believe that the greenhouse effect exists, while others blame every change in the weather on it —see also GLOBAL WARMING

greenhouse gas /ˈ·· ˌ·/ n a gas, esp. CARBON DIOXIDE or METHANE, which is thought to trap heat above the Earth and cause the greenhouse effect

green·ish /ˈgriːnɪʃ/ adj slightly green

Green Jackets n [P] see ROYAL GREEN JACKETS

Green·land /ˈgriːnlənd, -lænd/ an island in the N Atlantic near NE Canada; capital Godthaab (Nuuk); population 56,000 (1989). Greenland belongs to Denmark but has a great deal of independence.

green light /ˌ· ˈ·/ [the] permission, esp. official permission, to begin an action: *We're ready to rebuild our house; we're just waiting for the green light from the Council.* –compare RED LIGHT

green·light /ˈgriːnlaɪt/ v **greenlighted** [T] AmE sl to give the authority to happen, esp. for something that needs a lot of money: *Will Congress greenlight the new aid program?* | *Only the studio heads can greenlight new movies.*

green·mail /ˈgriːnmeɪl/ n [U] AmE money that a company uses to buy back shares from someone who has attempted a TAKEOVER –**greenmail** v [T] : *Acme Appliances is greenmailing the Harris Group to regain control of the company.*

green on·ion /ˌ· ˈ··/ n AmE for SPRING ONION

green pa·per /ˌ· ˈ··/ n a small book put out by the British government containing suggestions to be talked about which may later be used in making new laws –compare WHITE PAPER, BILL¹ (2)

Green Par·ty /ˌ· ˈ··/ n **1** [the] a British political party started in 1973 which wants a NUCLEAR-free society and whose ideas centre around caring for the environment. Originally it was called the Ecology Party, changing its name in 1985 in order to get closer to similar European parties. **2** [C] any of a number of European political parties whose ideas are concerned with care of the environment: *Are they a green party?*

Green·peace /ˈgriːnpiːs/ an international organization which actively works to protect the environment from harm. It is known esp. for its direct non-violent actions and wants to stop damage to the environment caused by NUCLEAR testing, the pouring of poisonous waste into the sea, and the killing of WHALES.

green pep·per /ˌ· ˈ··/ also **sweet pepper** ‖ also **bell pepper** AmE– n a vegetable with firm shiny green flesh and white seeds used raw or cooked to give a particular taste to food

green pound /ˌ· ˈ·/ [the] the unit of CURRENCY used in the European Community's Common Agricultural Policy as a value of the pound STERLING. The use of **green money** is to protect farm prices from changes in the EXCHANGE RATE

green rev·o·lu·tion /ˌ· · ˈ··/ [the] a large increase in crop production, esp. the one that happened around the world in the 1960s and 1970s as a result of using better varieties of plants and more chemicals

green·room /ˈgriːnruːm, -rʊm/ n a room behind the stage

(BACKSTAGE) in a theatre or television studio, where performers may relax

greens /griːnz/ n [P]　**1** green leafy vegetables that are cooked and eaten　**2** *AmE* leaves and branches used for decoration, esp. at Christmas —compare GREENERY　**3** |*the*| (*cap*) (supporters of) the Green Party

Green Shield Stamp /ˌ· · ˈ·/ n [C *usu.* P] *tdmk* a type of TRADING STAMP, also called a **Green Stamp**. Green Shield stamps are probably the best-known trading stamps in Britain, introduced in the 1950s and after a break reintroduced in 1988. The name comes from their green colour. In the US, Green Stamps were widely used in the 1950s and 60s, but are less common now.

Green·sleeves /ˈgriːnsliːvz/ a favourite English song of the Elizabethan period well known in Britain and the US

green stuff /ˈ· ·/ n [U] *AmE sl* money

green·sward /ˈgriːnswɔːd‖-ɔːrd/ n *old use or lit* a stretch of grassy land

green tea /ˌ· ˈ·/ n [U] light-coloured tea which is made from leaves which have been heated with steam, not dried in the ordinary way

green thumb /ˌ· ˈ·/ n [S] *esp. AmE* for GREEN FINGERS

Green Wel·lie Bri·gade /ˌ· ˈ·· ·ˌ·/ |*the*| *usu. derog* a name given to the richer classes of British society who enjoy country life esp. hunting, horseriding, etc. The name comes from the green WELLINGTONS (=rubber boots) which they often wear.

green wel·lies /ˌ· ˈ··/ n [P] *BrE* green WELLINGTONS (=rubber boots). They are associated esp. with rich, UPPER-CLASS people who enjoy life in the country.

Green·wich /ˈgrenɪtʃ, ˈgrɪnɪdʒ/ a BOROUGH in SE London, on the River Thames. The original British Royal Observatory (=a place from which scientists watched the stars) is there, and the 0° MERIDIAN (=an imaginary line dividing east from west) passes through the grounds of the Observatory.

Green·wich Mean Time /ˌ··· ˈ· ·/ (*abbrev.* **G.M.T.**) n [U] the time at Greenwich in London. Times in the rest of the world are compared to this and said to be a number of hours earlier or later: *European time is usually one hour later than Greenwich Mean Time.*

Greenwich Vil·lage /ˌ··· ˈ··/ an area of New York City, known for being the home of many artists, esp. those who are young and who do not want to live according to the accepted standards of society. It is also known as a fashionable place where many HOMOSEXUALs live. —see colour map on page 1376

Greer /grɪəʳ/, **Ger·maine** /dʒɜː·ˈmeɪn‖dʒɜr-/ (1939–　) an Australian writer who had a big influence on the WOMEN'S MOVEMENT esp. through her book *The Female Eunuch*

greet /griːt/ v [T]　**1** to welcome with words or actions: *He greeted us by shouting a friendly "Hello!"* | *She greeted him with a loving kiss.*　**2** [+*obj*+*adv*/*prep*] to receive with an expression of feeling: *The speech was greeted by loud cheers/in stony silence.*　**3** to be suddenly seen or heard by: *As we entered the room complete disorder greeted us.* | *I woke up and was greeted by bird song.*

greet·ing /ˈgriːtɪŋ/ n　**1** a form of words or an action used when meeting someone: *"Good morning," I said, but she didn't return the/my greeting.*　**2** [*usu. pl.*] a good wish: *We sent her a card with birthday/Christmas greetings.* | *a greetings telegram*

gre·gar·i·ous /grɪˈgeərɪəs/ adj　**1** (of a person) liking the companionship of others; not enjoying being alone; SOCIABLE　**2** *tech* (of an animal or person) tending to live in a group — ~**ly** adv — ~**ness** n [U]

Gre·go·ri·an cal·en·dar /grɪˌgɔːrɪən ˈkælɪndəʳ/ n |*the*| the system of arranging the 365 days of the SOLAR YEAR in days and months and numbering the years from the birth of Christ, which has been generally used in the West since 1582, when Pope Gregory XIII introduced it — compare HEGIRA CALENDAR

Gregorian chant /·ˌ··· ˈ·/ n [C;U] a kind of church music for voices alone

grem·lin /ˈgremlɪn/ n *infml* an imaginary wicked spirit that is believed to cause damage to engines and other machines or equipment: *There seems to be a gremlin in the computer.* (=it isn't working properly)

Gre·na·da /grəˈneɪdə/ an island nation in the West Indies, made up of the main island of Grenada, the southern part of the Windward Islands, and various small islands called the **Grenadines**. In 1983, American soldiers attacked Grenada in order to return to power a former government that had been removed by force by some members of the army of Grenada. Many people around the world were opposed to this action by the US. —**dian** *adj,n*

gre·nade /grɪˈneɪd/ n a small bomb which can be thrown by hand or fired from a gun: *The hijackers managed to smuggle guns and hand grenades aboard the plane.*

gren·a·dier /ˌgrenəˈdɪəʳ◂/ n a member of a famous REGIMENT (=large division of men) in the British army, the **Grenadiers** or **Grenadier Guards** (/ˌ··· ˈ·/)

gren·a·dine /ˈgrenədiːn, ˌgrenəˈdiːn/ n [U] a sweet liquid made from POMEGRANATEs and used in drinks

Gren·fell /ˈgrenfəl/, **Joyce** (1910–75) a British entertainer who wrote and performed humorous songs and speeches in which she represented many different women, esp. English women. One of her most famous characters was a teacher of small children.

Gret·na Green /ˌgretnə ˈgriːn/ a village in S Scotland on the border with England. Until 1940 people could get married there without following the usual English rules, and in the past young English people sometimes ran away to Gretna Green to get married, esp. if they wanted to get married without their parents' agreement.

Gretz·ky /ˈgretski/, **Wayne** (1961–　) a Canadian ICE HOCKEY player

grew /gruː/ *past tense of* GROW

grey[1] ‖ *usu.* **gray** *AmE* /greɪ/ adj　**1** of the colour like black mixed with white; the colour of lead, ashes, and rain clouds: *grey clouds* | *an old lady with grey hair* | *a grey coat*　**2** [F] having grey hair: *She's gone quite grey in the last few years.*　**3** (of a person's face) of a pale colour because of sudden fear or illness: *His face turned grey as he heard the bad news.*　**4** dull and without light; GLOOMY: (fig.) *Life seems grey and joyless.* — ~**ness** n [U]

grey[2] *usu.* **gray** *AmE*– n [C;U] (a) grey colour: *She was dressed in grey.* | *dull greys and browns*

grey[3] *usu.* **gray** *AmE*– v [I] (esp. of hair) to become grey: *greying hair* | *He's greying at the temples.*

Grey, Lady Jane (1537–54) a woman who was queen of England for 9 days in 1553, before she was put in prison by Mary I, and later killed

grey ar·e·a /ˌ· ˈ···/ n an area of knowledge that is not clear or certain or not fully understood: *The legal status of the unborn child is still a grey area.*

Grey Cup /ˈ· ˌ·/ n |*the*| a prize given to the best Canadian FOOTBALL (2) team each year

grey·hound /ˈgreɪhaʊnd/ n a type of thin dog with long thin legs that can run very fast in hunting and esp. racing — see picture at DOG

Greyhound Bus /ˌ··· ˈ·/ n *tdmk* (in the US) one of the buses which travel usu. long distances, owned by a private national company. Greyhound buses travel all over the US, and many tourists use them because they are cheaper than hiring a car or flying. However, they often make very many stops in small towns along the way, so journeys can take a long time. —see picture at BUS

greyhound rac·ing /ˈ··· ˌ··/ n [U] a popular sport in Britain in which greyhounds run around a track chasing a model HARE, driven by an electric motor. People risk their money on which dog will win the race. This sport is also found in the US, but is not as popular there as in Britain.

grey·ish *usu.* **grayish** *AmE* /ˈgreɪ-ɪʃ/ adj slightly grey

grey mat·ter /ˈ· ˌ··/ n [U]　**1** the substance of the brain and nervous system which contains cell bodies, esp. the central part of the brain　**2** *infml* brain power; the power of thought

grid /grɪd/ n　**1** a set of bars set across each other in a frame; GRATING[1]: *a grid over a drain* —see also CATTLE GRID　**2** *BrE* a network of electricity supply wires connecting power stations: *the national grid*　**3** a system of numbered squares printed on a map so that the exact position of any place on it may be stated or found　**4** a set of starting positions for all the cars in a motor race

grid·dle /'grɪdl/ n **1** an iron plate which was used esp. formerly for cooking things, such as flat cakes (**griddle cakes** /'··· ·/), over a fire **2** AmE a flat, usu. round, plate used for cooking things, e.g. PANCAKES, on top of a COOKER

grid·i·ron /'grɪdaɪən‖-ərn/ n **1** an open frame of metal bars for cooking meat or fish over a very hot fire **2** AmE a field marked in white lines for American football

grief /griːf/ n [U] **1** great sorrow or feelings of suffering, esp. at the death of a loved person: *She went nearly mad with grief after the child died.* | *the* **grief-stricken** *relatives of the murdered man* **2 come to grief** to fall or fail, causing harm or loss to oneself: *She cycled fast down the hill but came to grief when she went over a stone.* | *Their plans came to grief when the bank refused to lend them more money.* —see also **good grief** (GOOD¹ (22))

Grieg /griːg/, **Ed·vard** /'edvɑːd‖-vɑːrd/ (1843–1907) a Norwegian writer of music (COMPOSER) who is best known for the SUITE (3) *Peer Gynt*

griev·ance /'griːvəns/ n a complaint or cause for complaint, esp. when one feels one has been unfairly treated: *She has a very real grievance against the hospital, since the operation which ruined her health.* | *A committee was set up to look into the workers' grievances.* | **Nursing a grievance** (=thinking about it continuously) *makes you bitter; it's better to try and remedy it.*

grieve /griːv/ v **1** [I (for)] to suffer from grief or great sadness: *She is still grieving (for her dead husband).* **2** [T] fml to cause grief to; make very unhappy; DISTRESS: *It grieves me to see him wasting his youth.*

griev·ous /'griːvəs/ adj [A] fml **1** very seriously harmful: *You have made a grievous mistake, which could affect the rest of your life.* **2** (of a wound, pain, etc.) severe: *a grievous wound* **– –ly** adv **– –ness** n [U]

grievous bod·i·ly harm /ˌ··· ···· '·/ n [U] BrE law physical harm done to a person in an attack, for which the attacker may be charged in a court of law. These words are often shortened to GBH, the first letters only, in conversation: *He was in prison for three years for GBH.*

grif·fin , **griffon, gryphon** /'grɪfən/ n an imaginary animal in stories with a lion's body and the wings and head of an EAGLE (=a large bird)

griffin

Grif·fith /'grɪfɪθ/, **D W** (1875–1948) an American film maker known esp. for his use of new photographic methods, and for his film *Birth of a Nation*

grift /grɪft/ v [T] AmE sl to obtain (money, etc.) by deceiving someone **grifter** n

grill¹ /grɪl/ v **1** [I;T] BrE‖**broil** AmE— to cook (something) under or over direct heat: *grilled sausages* | (fig.) *He's grilling (himself) out there in the midday sun.* —see COOK (USAGE) **2** [T] infml (esp. of the police) to question severely and continuously: *When the woman identified him as the criminal, he was grilled for two hours before the police accepted his alibi.*

grill² n **1** BrE ‖ **broiler** AmE— an arrangement of a metal shelf under a gas flame or electric heat, used to cook food quickly: *Put the bread under the grill to make toast.* | *a* **grill pan** (=a part of the metal shelf, a container to catch fat etc.) —see COOK (USAGE) **2** a set of bars which can be put over a hot open fire, so that food can be cooked quickly: *Put the steaks on the grill.* —see also MIXED GRILL, and see picture at KITCHEN, and see picture at PAN

grille /grɪl/ n a frame of usu. upright metal bars filling a space in a door or window, such as one in a bank or post office separating a clerk from the customers, or one at the front of a car, where it protects the RADIATOR

grilled cheese /ˌ· '·/ n AmE a SANDWICH of melted cheese between slices of bread that have been lightly fried

grim /grɪm/ adj **-mm-** **1** causing great fear or anxiety: *The judge's expression was grim as he told them they were to be hanged.* | *There's more grim news from the war zone; over a thousand of our men were killed today.* | *The staff now face the grim prospect of redundancy.* **2** determined in spite of fear or great difficulty: *a grim smile* **3** infml unpleasant; not cheerful: *I've had a grim day.* | *I had to spend the whole evening listening to Mr Watson's fishing*

stories; it was pretty grim, I can tell you! **4 like grim death** infml with great determination, in spite of difficulty: *She hung on like grim death till the firemen arrived with their ladders.* **– –ly** adv **– –ness** n [U]

gri·mace¹ /grɪ'meɪs, 'grɪməs‖'grɪməs, grɪ'meɪs/ v [I (**at, with**)] to make an expression of pain, annoyance, etc., which makes the face look unnaturally twisted: *She grimaced with pain.* | *The teacher grimaced as he looked at my work.*

grimace² n an unnatural twisting of the face, as in pain or annoyance: *a grimace of pain*

grime /graɪm/ n [U] a surface of thick black dirt: *His face and hands were covered with grime from the coal dust.*

Grimm /grɪm/, **Jacob** (1785–1863) a German who studied language and FOLKLORE. He is best known for the book he wrote with his brother Wilhelm, *Grimm's Fairy Tales*, a collection of nearly 200 stories, which are still popular with children in Britain and the US —see also FAIRY TALE

Grim Reap·er /ˌ· '··/ [the] esp. lit (a name for death, considered as a person). The Grim Reaper is often thought of as a SKELETON in a CLOAK with a HOOD, carrying a SCYTHE to REAP (=gather) his crop (=the dead).

the Grim Reaper

grim·y /'graɪmi/ adj covered with dark-coloured dirt or grime **– –iness** n [U]

grin¹ /grɪn/ v **-nn-** [I (**with, at**)] **1** to make a wide smile: *They grinned with pleasure when I gave them the sweets.* —see picture at SMILE **2 grin and bear it** infml to suffer something unpleasant without complaint: *I hate having my wife's parents to stay, but I suppose I'll just have to grin and bear it.* —see also **grin like a Cheshire cat** (CHESHIRE CAT)

grin² n a wide smile which usu. shows the teeth: *She gave a cheeky grin.* | *He stood there with an embarrassed grin on his face.* | **Take/Wipe that grin off your face;** *this is a serious matter!* —see SMILE (USAGE)

Grinch /grɪntʃ/ AmE **How the Grinch Stole Christmas**, a children's story by Dr Seuss about a nasty, unkind, green creature called the Grinch who almost spoiled Christmas. Someone who is very bad-tempered may be called a Grinch.

grind¹ /graɪnd/ v **ground** /graʊnd/ **1** [T (UP)] to crush into small pieces or into powder by pressing between hard surfaces: *We grind (up) the wheat to make flour.* | *freshly-ground coffee* **2** [T] to rub (esp. the teeth) together so as to make a crushing noise: *Some people grind their teeth while they're asleep.* **3** [T] to make smooth or sharp by rubbing on a hard surface: *A man came to grind the knives and scissors.* | *The lenses for giant telescopes are very expensive to grind.* **4** [T+obj+adv/prep] to press down hard on (something) with a strong, twisting movement: *In anger, he ground his knee into the man's stomach, and hit him in the face.* | *The dirt was deeply ground into the carpet.* **5** [I+adv/prep] infml, esp. AmE, now rare to study hard, esp. for an examination; SWOT²: *They're grinding away for their exam/grinding across at their French.* **6 grind the faces of the poor** to make poor people work very hard and give them almost nothing in return **7 grind to a halt** to come slowly and/or noisily to a stop —see also **have an axe to grind** (AXE¹)

grind sbdy. **↔ down** phr v [T] to keep in a state of suffering and hopelessness; OPPRESS: *Most of the people were ground down by hunger and poverty.*

grind sthg. **↔ out** phr v [T] derog to produce (esp. writing or music) continuously, but like a machine: *She grinds out romantic stories for the women's magazines.* | *The juke box ground out its monotonous tunes.*

grind² n infml **1** [S] hard uninteresting work: *I find any kind of study a real grind.* | *the* **daily grind** *of the housework* **2** [S] a long steady tiring effort of movement, such as a difficult race: *It was a terrible grind getting up that long hill.* **3** [C] AmE, often derog a student who is always working; SWOT¹

grind·er /'graɪndər/ n a machine or person that grinds: *a coffee grinder* | *a knife grinder* —see also ORGAN GRINDER

grind·stone /ˈgraɪndstəʊn/ n **1** a round stone which is turned and rubs against tools, knives, etc. to sharpen them. Formerly people had their knives sharpened by a man with a grindstone who would visit their area regularly. **2 one's nose to the grindstone** *infml* in a state of continuous hard work: *He's got to keep his nose to the grindstone to feed his six children.*

grin·go /ˈgrɪŋgəʊ/ n -s *usu. derog* a N American or English-speaking foreigner in Latin America, esp. in Mexico

grip¹ /grɪp/ v -pp- **1** [I;T] to take a very tight hold (of): *She gripped my hand in fear.* | *car tyres that grip the road well* **2** [T] to take hold of the attention or feelings of: *The pictures gripped my imagination.* | *The whole country was gripped by panic.* —see CLASP (USAGE); see also GRIPPING

grip² n **1** [C *usu. sing.*] a very tight forceful hold: *The thief would not let go his grip on my handbag.* | (fig.) *The president keeps a firm grip on his country's foreign policy.* (=keeps it under his control) | (fig.) *The country is in the grip of severe winter storms.* **2** [S] understanding, control, or skill in a subject or activity: *I played badly today; I seem to be* **losing my grip.** **3** [C] a special way of holding: *To improve your golf/tennis strokes you try using a different grip.* **4** [C] **a** a (part of a) handle suitable to be gripped: *She has a leather grip on her tennis racket.* **b** a part of an apparatus which grips —see also HAIRGRIP **5** [C] a bag or case for a traveller's personal belongings **6** [C] a person whose job is to move the cameras around in the making of a film or television show **7 come/get to grips with** to deal seriously with (something difficult): *The speaker talked a lot, but never really got to grips with the subject.* **8 get/keep a grip on oneself** to (start to) act in a (more) sensible, calm, and controlled manner

gripe¹ /graɪp/ v [I (**at, about**)] *infml* to complain continually and annoyingly: *He's griping about his income tax again.* —**griper** n

gripe² n *infml* a complaint: *My main gripe is, there's no hot water.*

gripe³ v [I] to cause or feel sharp pain, esp. in the stomach: *a griping pain*

gripes /graɪps/ n [*the*+P] *old-fash infml* sudden and severe stomach pains: *He's got the gripes.*

gripe water /ˈ· ˌ··/ n a liquid given to babies when they have stomach pains

grip·ping /ˈgrɪpɪŋ/ adj holding the attention; very interesting and exciting: *a gripping film* —see also GRIP¹ (2) —~**ly** adv

gris·ly /ˈgrɪzli/ adj extremely unpleasant because of death, decay, or destruction which is shown or described: *the grisly remains of the bodies* | *a grisly story about people who ate human flesh* —compare GRUESOME

grist /grɪst/ n (**all**) **grist to one's/the mill** something that can be used for one's advantage or profit: *As a writer, even life's problems are all grist to his mill.*

gris·tle /ˈgrɪsəl/ n [U] the part of meat which is not soft enough to eat, found near the bones; CARTILAGE in cooked meat —~**tly** adj

grit¹ /grɪt/ n [U] **1** small pieces of a hard substance, usu. stone: *Grit is spread on roads to make them less slippery in icy weather.* | *I've got a piece of grit in my eye.* **2** *infml* determination; strength and courage during difficulty: *It takes a lot of grit to overcome a physical handicap.* —**gritty** adj : *a gritty surface* | *gritty determination*

grit² v -tt- [T] **1** to put grit on (esp. a road) **2 grit one's teeth** to become determined when in a position of difficulty: *The snow was blowing in his face, but he gritted his teeth and went on.*

grit·ter /ˈgrɪtə/ also **gritting lor·ry** /ˈ·· ˌ··/ **salt truck** *AmE*— n *BrE* a LORRY with equipment for spreading grit and usu. salt on roads which are icy or likely to become icy: *I bet there'll be lots of ice on the minor roads where the gritters haven't been.*

grits /grɪts/ n [U+*sing./pl. v*] *AmE* HOMINY grain which is roughly crushed, or uncrushed but with the outer skin removed, often eaten for breakfast in the southern states of the US —compare HOMINY

griz·zle /ˈgrɪzəl/ v [I] *BrE infml derog* **1** (esp. of a young child) to cry quietly and continually as though tired or worried **2** to complain in a self-pitying way

griz·zled /ˈgrɪzəld/ adj [A] *esp. lit* having grey or greyish hair

griz·zly bear /ˌ··· ˈ·ǁˈ·· ·/ also **grizzly**— n a very large brownish-grey bear of the Rocky Mountains of N America —see picture at BEAR

groan¹ /grəʊn/ v [I] to make a groan: *The old man who had been in the accident lay groaning beside the road.* | (fig.) *The table groaned with food.* (=there was lots of food on it) | *He's always* **moaning and groaning** (=complaining) *about something.*

groan² n a sound of suffering, worry, complaint, or disapproval, which is made in a deep voice: *There were loud groans from the boys when the girls started to win.* | *groans of disappointment/despair/pain* | (fig.) *The old chair gave a groan when the fat woman sat down on it.*

groat /grəʊt/ n a former British coin of low value

groats /grəʊts/ n [P] grain, esp. OATS, from which the outer shell has been removed, and which may also have been broken into pieces

gro·bag , growbag /ˈgrəʊbæg/ n a large plastic bag containing specially prepared earth for growing vegetables, e.g. tomatoes

gro·cer /ˈgrəʊsə/ n a person who owns or works in a shop (**grocer's**) which sells dry and preserved foods, like flour, coffee, sugar, rice, and other things for the home, such as matches and soap: *I bought some flour at the grocer's (shop).* —compare GREENGROCER

gro·cer·ies /ˈgrəʊsəriz/ n [P] the goods sold by a grocer or a SUPERMARKET: *She put the box of groceries in the car.*

gro·cer·y /ˈgrəʊsəri/ n **1** [C] also **grocery store** /ˈ··· ˌ·/ *AmE* —the shop of a grocer: *The nearest grocery is in Smith St.* **2** [U] the trade of a grocer: *a grocery business*

gro·dy /ˈgrəʊdi/ adj *AmE sl* very unpleasant or offensive

grog /grɒgǁgrɑːg/ n [U] **1** a mixture of strong drink (esp. RUM) and water, esp. as drunk by sailors **2** *infml, esp. AustrE* any alcoholic drink

grog·gy /ˈgrɒgiǁˈgrɑːgi/ adj *infml* weak because of illness, shock, tiredness, etc., and often unable to walk steadily: *I felt a bit groggy after 15 hours on the plane.* —**gily** adv

groin /grɔɪn/ n **1 a** the hollow place where the tops of the legs meet the front of the body **b** *euph* the male sex organs: *a kick in the groin* **2** a GROYNE

Gro·my·ko /grəˈmiːkəʊ/, **An·drei** /ˈɑːndreɪ/ (1908–89) a Soviet politician and head of state (1985–88), best remembered as foreign minister, a position he held for 28 years from 1957

groom¹ /gruːm, grʊm/ n **1** someone who is in charge of feeding, cleaning, and taking care of horses **2** a BRIDEGROOM

groom² v **1** [T] to take care of (horses), esp. by rubbing, brushing, and cleaning them **2** [T] to take care of the appearance of (oneself), by dressing neatly, keeping the hair tidy, etc.: *He always looks very well-groomed.* **3** [I;T] (of an animal) to clean the fur and skin of (itself or another animal): *Monkeys groom each other.* **4** [T (**for**)] to prepare (someone) for a special position or occasion: *They were grooming her for stardom.* (=to play big parts in plays or films) [+*to-v*] *She's being groomed to take over the chairman's job when he retires.*

groove /gruːv/ n **1** a long narrow usu. regular path or track made in a surface, esp. to guide the movement of something: *The needle is stuck in the groove of the record, so it keeps repeating the same bit of music.* | *The door fits into this metal groove and slides shut.* **2** a track made by repeated movement; RUT: (fig.) *My parents don't like change; they're happy to stay in the same old groove.*

grooved /gruːvd/ adj having grooves

groov·y /ˈgruːvi/ adj *old-fash sl* attractive or interesting; fashionably modern. This word is connected esp. with the 1960s, when it was a very popular, fashionable word.

grope¹ /grəʊp/ v **1** [I+*adv/prep*, esp. **for**] to try to find something by feeling with the hands in a place one cannot see (properly): *He groped (about) in his pocket for his ticket.* | (fig.) *She groped for the right word.* | (fig.) *The two sides are groping towards an agreement.* **2** [T+*obj*+*adv/prep*] to make (one's way) by feeling with outstretched hands (as if) in the dark: *I groped my way to a seat in the dark cinema.* **3** [T] *derog sl* to (try to) feel over the body of (a person, usu. a woman) so as to get sexual pleasure

grope² *n* an act of groping

gross¹ /grəʊs/ *adj* **1** [A *no comp.*] total: *my gross income, before taxes are deducted* | *The gross weight of the box of chocolates is more than the weight of the chocolates alone.* —compare NET³ **2** [A] *fml* clearly wrong; inexcusable: *The court found the doctor guilty of gross negligence.* | *It was an act of the grossest insolence.* | *gross inequalities* **3** (esp. of people's speech and habits) rough, impolite, and offensive; COARSE: *She was shocked by his gross behaviour at the party.* **4** unpleasantly fat: *He's become really gross in old age.* **5** *infml, esp. AmE* very unpleasant or offensive – – **ly** *adv* – – **ness** *n* [U]

gross² *v* [T] to gain as total profit or earn as a total amount: *The film grossed over $15 million.*

gross³ *determiner, n* **gross** or **grosses** a group of 144; 12 DOZEN: *The shopkeeper ordered ten gross of candles.*

gross do·mes·tic prod·uct /ˌ· ·ˌ·· ˈ··/ *n* the total value of all the goods and services produced in a country, usu. in a single year, except for income received from abroad. It is also known as GDP.

gross mar·gin /ˌ· ˈ··/ also **gross profit**– *n* the difference between what something costs to be produced and what it is sold for

gross na·tion·al prod·uct /ˌ· ˌ··· ˈ··/ *n* the total value of all the goods and services produced in a country, usu. in a single year. Also known as GNP, it is seen as a measure of a country's economic performance.

gross prof·it /ˌ· ˈ··/ *n* see GROSS MARGIN

gross re·ceipts /ˌ· ·ˈ·/ *n* [P] the total amount of money received before any costs are taken off

gro·tesque¹ /grəʊˈtesk/ *adj* strange and unnatural so as to cause fear, disbelief, or amusement; OUTLANDISH: *grotesque paintings of two-headed animals with fangs and staring eyes* | *The fat old man looked grotesque in his tight trousers.* | *Her account of the incident was a grotesque distortion of the truth.* – – **ly** *adv* – – **ness** *n* [U]

gro·tesque² *n* [C; *the*+S] (a picture or object showing) grotesque qualities: *Hieronymus Bosch was a master of the grotesque in painting.*

grot·to /ˈgrɒtəʊǁˈgrɑː-/ *n* **-toes** or **-tos** **1** a natural CAVE, esp. of LIMESTONE, or a man-made one set in a garden and often decorated with shells **2** a small place for religious worship in the shape of a CAVE

grot·ty /ˈgrɒtiǁˈgrɑːti/ *adj BrE infml* bad, nasty, unpleasant, etc.: *She lives in a grotty little room with nowhere to cook.* —**tiness** *n* [U]

grouch¹ /graʊtʃ/ *n infml* **1** [*usu. sing.*] a bad-tempered complaint: *She's always got a grouch about something; if it's not the weather, it's the cost of living.* **2** a person who keeps complaining: *Quit being a grouch!* —**grouchy** *adj* – – **iness** *n* [U]

grouch² *v* [I] *infml* to complain in a bad-tempered way; GRUMBLE

ground¹ /graʊnd/ *n* **1** [(*the*) U] the surface of the earth: *The branch broke and fell to the ground.* | *The injured man was lying on the ground.* | *high ground* | *They built a bomb shelter* **below ground.** | *Moles seldom come* **above ground.** —compare FLOOR¹ (1); see also UNDERGROUND **2** [U] soil; earth: *The ground is dry/frozen.* —see LAND (USAGE) **3** [C] (*usu. in comb.*) a piece of land used for a particular purpose: *soldiers marching on a parade ground* | *a football ground* —see also PLAYGROUND **4** [U] the bottom of the sea or the shore: *Our ship touched ground.* **5** [C] **a** the colour on which a pattern is placed; background: *The curtains have white flowers on a blue ground.* **b** the first covering of paint on a painting **6** [U] **a** an area of knowledge, study, or experience: *It was absurd to try to cover so much ground* (=talk about so much) *in such a short lecture.* | *The book says nothing new — it just goes over the same old ground.* | *I'm on fairly familiar ground here because I've had a lot of experience with computers.* **b** a base for argument: *You'll be* **on safe ground** *as long as you avoid the subject of politics.* | *You're* **on dangerous ground** *if you mention pop music to him —he hates it!* | *Just when I thought I had won the argument she* **shifted her ground** *and put forward a whole new set of objections.* **7** [U] a position of advantage to be won or defended: *The army lost ground/was forced to give ground*

when the enemy started its new offensive. | *This big contract will help us to* **gain ground on** (=get closer to in success) *our competitors.* | *The president has lost a lot of ground in the popularity polls.* | *The idea of equal pay for women is* **gaining ground.** (=gradually becoming accepted) **8** [C] *esp. AmE for* EARTH¹ (4) **9 into the ground** beyond what is sensible or necessary, esp. so as to be very tired: *Don't work so hard; you're driving yourself into the ground.* **10 off the ground** successfully started: *Lack of money meant we couldn't even get the plan off the ground/the plan didn't even get off the ground.* **11 on the ground** at the actual place where something, esp. a war, is happening, rather than in another place where the situation is being watched or discussed: *While the politicians discussed possible peace plans, the situation on the ground was tense.* | *We turn now to our reporter on the ground for an up-to-the-minute run-down of events.* **12 to ground** *BrE* into hiding to escape: *The criminals went* **to ground** *in a deserted old farm house.* —see also GROUNDS, **break new ground** (BREAK¹), **cut the ground from under someone's feet** (CUT¹ (32)), **have/keep one's ear to the ground** (EAR¹), **have/keep both one's feet on the ground** (FOOT¹ (11)), **stand one's ground** (STAND¹ (25)), **suit someone down to the ground** (SUIT²)

ground² *v* **1** [I;T] to strike or cause (a boat) to strike against the bottom of the sea, a river, etc.: *The ship grounded on a hidden sandbank.* | *He grounded his ship in two metres of water.* **2** [T] **a** to prevent (a plane or pilot) from flying: *All aircraft have been grounded because of thick fog.* | *He's been grounded for dangerous flying.* **b** *AmE infml* to prevent (a child) from going out as a punishment: *My father grounded me for coming in late.* **3** [T+*obj*+*adv/prep*, esp. **on, in**] to base: *Our development plans are grounded on the results of our market research.* | *Our fears proved to be well grounded.* **4** [T] *esp. AmE for* EARTH²

ground sbdy. **in** sthg. *phr v* [T *usu. pass.*] to teach the main points or rules of (a subject) as a base for further study: *Our English teacher made sure that we were well grounded in basic grammar.* —see also GROUNDING

ground³ *past tense & participle of* GRIND: *freshly ground coffee*

ground bait /ˈ· ·/ *n* [U] food which is thrown onto a river, lake, etc., to attract fish to the place where one is fishing

ground ball /ˈ· ·/ also **ground·er** /ˈgraʊndər/– *n* (in BASEBALL) a ball which travels along the ground after being hit —compare FLY BALL

ground beef /ˌ· ˈ·/ *n* [U] *AmE* BEEF that has been cut very finely, often used to make HAMBURGERS

ground cloth /ˈ· ·/ *n AmE for* GROUNDSHEET

ground cover /ˈ· ˌ··/ *n* [U] plants that cover the ground, in a forest or in a place where they have been planted specifically for that purpose: *We need some ground cover for that corner of the garden.*

ground crew /ˈ· ·/ also **ground staff** *BrE*– *n* [C+*sing./pl. v*] the team of people at an airport who do not fly aircraft but take care of them between flights

ground floor /ˌ· ˈ·◂/ *n* **1** the part of a building at or near ground level: *My office is on the ground floor.* —compare FIRST FLOOR (2); see FLOOR (USAGE) **2 get/be in on the ground floor** to be part of an activity, business operation, etc. from the time it starts

ground forc·es /ˈ· ˌ··/ *n* [P] the part of the armed forces that fights on the ground, not in the air or at sea

ground glass /ˌ· ˈ·◂/ *n* [U] **1** glass which has had the surface partly rubbed away so that it can spread the light which passes through it **2** glass in powder form

ground·hog /ˈgraʊndhɒgǁ-hɑːg, -hɔːg/ also **woodchuck, marmot**– *n* a small N American animal of the MARMOT family, that has thick, brown fur and lives in holes in the ground

Groundhog Day /ˈ··· ˌ·/ *n* (in the US) 2nd February. On this day, according to popular stories, the groundhog comes out of its hole for the first time since winter began. If it sees its shadow, it is frightened back into its hole and there will be six more weeks of winter, but if it is cloudy and the groundhog cannot see its shadow, there will be an early spring.

ground·ing /ˈgraʊndɪŋ/ *n* [S (**in**)] a complete training in the main points of a subject: *All our students receive a good grounding in English grammar.*

ground·less /'graʊndləs/ adj (of feelings, ideas, etc.) without base or good reason: *Fortunately my fears/suspicions proved groundless.* — ~**ly** adv — ~**ness** n [U]

ground·ling /'graʊndlɪŋ/ n a person of low position in relation to others, esp. in former times one watching a performance from the cheapest part of the theatre

ground·nut /'graʊndnʌt/ n esp.tech a PEANUT or peanut plant

Groundnut Scheme /'·· ˌ·/ n BrE an expensive plan which fails because of lack of thought

ground plan /'· ·/ n **1** a drawn plan of a building at ground level **2** a general plan of arrangements for a particular piece of work

ground rent /'· ·/ n [C;U] rent paid during a certain time (in England usu. 99 years) to the owner of land (FREEHOLDER) by a person whose house is built on this land

ground rule /'· ·/ n [often pl.] a rule used as a base for deciding how to deal with something: *One of the ground rules of/for social behaviour is to avoid offending people.*

grounds /graʊndz/ n [P] **1** [(for)] a reason; the facts or conditions that provide a base for an action or feeling: *We have good grounds for thinking that he stole the money.* | *He left on (the) grounds of ill-health/on the grounds that he was ill.* | *She refused on moral grounds.* **2** land surrounding a large building, such as a country house or hospital, usu. made into gardens and enclosed by a wall or fence **3** a large area used for the stated purpose: *fishing grounds* | *hunting grounds* **4** small bits of solid matter which sink to the bottom of a liquid, esp. coffee: *coffee grounds*

ground·sheet /'graʊndʃiːt/ BrE ‖ **groundcloth** AmE— n a sheet of WATERPROOF material (=through which water cannot pass), used by someone sleeping outdoors or put under a tent

grounds·man /'graʊndzmən/ n -men /mən/ esp. BrE a man employed to take care of a sports field or large gardens

ground squir·rel /'· ˌ··/ n one of several types of N American RODENT that often damage crops

ground staff /'· ·/ n [C+sing./pl. v] BrE **1** a team of people employed at a sports ground to look after the grass, the sports equipment, etc. **2** GROUND CREW

ground stroke /'· ˌ·/ n a stroke made in tennis and similar games by hitting the ball after it has hit the ground

ground·swell /'graʊndswel/ n **1** [S (of)] a sudden and quickly-developing growth of a feeling among large numbers of people: *There is a groundswell of public opinion in favour of letting these refugees enter the country.* **2** [S;U] the strong movement of the sea which continues after a storm or strong winds

ground·wa·ter /'graʊndwɔːtəʳ‖-wɔː-, -wɑː-/ n [U] water that can be found under the earth by digging wells

ground·work /'graʊndwɜːk‖-wɜːrk/ n [U] the work which forms the base for some kind of study, skill, or activity: *These preliminary talks laid the groundwork for the meeting between the two leaders.*

group¹ /gruːp/ n [C+sing./pl. v] **1** [(of)] a number of people, things, or organizations placed together or connected in a particular way: *A group of tall trees stands on top of the hill.* | *A group of us are going up to London for the day.* | *a photo of a family group* | *"Which blood group do you belong to?" "Group A."* | *a small group of congressmen campaigning for tougher anti-pollution laws* | *English belongs to the Germanic group of languages.* | *the Longman Group of companies* —see also AGE GROUP **2** a small number of players of popular music, sometimes with a singer: *The Beatles were the best-known pop group of the 1960s.*

group² v [I+adv/prep; T] to form into one or more groups: *The children grouped round the piano.* | *We can group animals into several types.* | *Let's group all the history books together.*

group cap·tain /ˌ· '··◂/ n an officer in the British airforce —see TABLE 3

group·ie /'gruːpi/ n infml, sometimes derog a person, esp. a young girl, who follows pop groups (POP) to their concerts, hoping to meet and perhaps have sex with the players: (fig.) *a tennis groupie*

group·ing /'gruːpɪŋ/ n an arrangement of people or things into a group: *The new grouping of classes means that there are larger numbers in each class.*

Group of Sev·en /ˌ· · '··/ also **G7**— [the] the seven most important industrial nations in the world: Canada, France, Germany, Great Britain, Italy, Japan, and the US

group prac·tice /ˌ· '··/ n [C;U] a working partnership among a number of doctors

Group Thea·tre /ˌ· '··/ [the] a group of actors and DIRECTORs in the US who wanted to produce plays with political meaning. It began in 1931 and stopped producing plays in 1940, but many of the people in the group were very important in the American theatre. —see also Elia KAZAN, Lee STRASBERG

group ther·a·py /ˌ· '···/ n [U] a way of treating disorders of the mind by bringing sufferers together to talk about their difficulties, usu. with a doctor or specially trained leader

grouse¹ /graʊs/ n grouse a smallish fat bird which is shot for food and sport. In Britain, grouse shooting begins every year on August 12th (known as the "Glorious Twelfth") and ends on December 10th. It is popular esp. with the ARISTOCRACY and richer classes of British society.

grouse² v [I (about)] infml to complain; GRUMBLE

grouse³ n infml a complaint; GRUMBLE —compare GROUCH

grove /grəʊv/ n **1** esp. lit a small group of trees **2** an area planted with certain types of trees, esp. CITRUS fruit trees: *an orange grove* | *olive groves on the hillside* —compare ORCHARD **3** (usu. cap. as part of a name) a road with trees along the sides: *Lisson Grove*

grov·el /'grɒvəl‖'grɑː-, 'grʌ-/ v -ll- BrE ‖ -l- AmE [I (to)] derog **1** to show extreme respect and willingness to obey someone in a position of power, in the hope of gaining their favour: *I had to grovel to my boss before she would agree to let me go on holiday.* **2** to lie or move flat on the ground, esp. in fear of or obedience to someone powerful: *When he shouted at the dog it grovelled at his feet.* — ~**ler** n

grow /grəʊ/ v grew /gruː/, grown /grəʊn/ **1** [I] (of a living thing) to increase in size by natural development: *Grass grows after rain.* | *He's grown six inches (taller).* | *A lamb grows into a sheep.* | *She doesn't like her hair short, so she's letting it grow.* | *Growing children need lots of food.* **2** [I+adv/prep] (of a plant) to exist and be able to develop, esp. after planting: *Cotton grows wild here.* | *Oranges grow in Spain.* **3** [T] to cause or allow (esp. plants and crops) to grow: *We grow vegetables in our garden.* | *Plants grow roots.* | *Snakes can grow a new skin.* | *Cattle often grow horns.* | *He's grown a beard.* | *She's grown her hair long.* **4** [I] to increase in amount, size, or degree: *The company has grown rapidly in the last five years.* | *Fears are growing for the climbers' safety.* | *A growing number of people are taking part-time jobs.* | *the world's fastest-growing hotel company* **5** [L+adj] esp. fml or lit to become (gradually).*She's growing fat.* | *The noise grew louder.* | *It's growing dark.* | *The sound of the music grew faint as the band marched away.* **6** to begin gradually: [I to-v] *In time you will grow to like him.* (=as you learn to know him you will like him) **7 grow on trees** [usu. in negatives] infml to be very common or easy to get: *Money doesn't grow on trees, you know.*

grow away from sbdy. phr v [T no pass.] to begin gradually to have a less close relationship with (esp. one's parents, husband, or wife)

grow into sbdy./sthg. phr v [T no pass.] **1** to become as a result of growing: *He's grown into a fine young man.* **2** to become big enough for (clothes, shoes, etc.) by growing: *The coat is too long now, but she'll grow into it.* —compare GROW out of (1) **3** to become used to (work and activities): *You need time to grow into the job.*

grow on sbdy. phr v [T no pass.] to become gradually more pleasing or more of a habit to: *His music is difficult to listen to, but after a while it starts to grow on you.*

grow out of sthg. phr v [T] **1** to become too big for (clothes, shoes, etc.) by growing: *My daughter has grown out of all her old clothes.* —compare GROW **into** (2) **2** to lose (a childish or youthful weakness) as one becomes older: *to grow out of a bad habit* [+v-ing] *He'll soon grow out of wetting the bed.*

grow up phr v [I] **1** (of a person) to develop from being a child to being a man or woman: *What do you want to be when you grow up/are grown up?* | *I wish you'd grow up!* (=stop behaving childishly) **2** to become established; develop: *The custom grew up of dividing the* *father's land between the sons.* —see also GROWN-UP

grow·bag /ˈgrəʊbæg/ *n* GROBAG

grow·er /ˈgrəʊəʳ/ *n* **1** a person who grows something for sale: *apple growers* | *wine growers* (=who grow GRAPES to make wine) **2** a plant which grows in the stated way: *This rose is a slow grower.*

growing pains /ˈ··ˌ/ *n* [P] **1** aches and pains in the limbs of children who are growing up, commonly believed to be the result of growing too fast **2** difficulties that are experienced at the beginning of a new activity but will probably not last: *I hear Clive's business is having a few growing pains.*

growl /graʊl/ *v* [I (**at**)] (esp. of animals) to make a deep rough sound in the throat to show anger or give warning: *Our dog always growls at strangers.* | *Dad's in a bad mood and he's growling at everyone today.* —**growl** *n* : *He answered with a growl of anger.* —**growler** *n*

Grow·more /ˈgrəʊmɔːʳ/ *n* [U] *tdmk* a substance that is put on the garden to make crops grow better

grown /grəʊn/ *adj* [A] (of a person) of full size or development; adult: *A grown man like you shouldn't behave like that.* —see also FULL-GROWN, INGROWING

grown-up¹ /ˌ·ˈ·◂/ *adj* fully developed; no longer being or like a child: *She has a grown-up daughter who lives abroad.* | *I'd expect more grown-up behaviour of you.*

grown-up² /ˈ·ˌ·/ *n infml* a fully grown person; adult. Most adults use the word "adult" except when talking to children, who usu. talk about "grown-ups": *Go to bed now and let the grown-ups have a little time to themselves.* —see also GROW UP

growth /grəʊθ/ *n* **1** [U] the process or rate of growing and developing: *Trees take many years to reach their full growth.* | *The report condemns the slowness of the growth of world literacy.* | *vitamins that are essential for healthy growth* **2** [S;U (**in**)] increase in size, amount, or degree: *There has been a sudden growth|a 50% growth in the market for home computers.* | *a high rate of population growth* | *a period of rapid economic growth* **3** [C] something which has grown: *Nails are thin horny growths at the ends of the fingers.* **4** [C] a lump produced by an unnatural and often unhealthy increase in the number of cells in a part of the body: *The surgeons removed a growth from the patient's neck.* —compare TUMOUR

growth in·dus·try /ˈ· ˌ···/ *n* an industry which grows faster than other industries under the same conditions

groyne , groin /grɔɪn/ *n* a low wall built out from the shore into the sea, to prevent the sea from washing away (parts of) the shore

grub¹ /grʌb/ *n* **1** [C] an insect in the soft thick wormlike form it has after coming out of its egg **2** [U] *infml* food: *Grub's up!* (=the meal is ready)

grub² *v* -**bb**- **1** [I+*adv*/*prep*] to turn over the soil, esp. by digging with the hands or PAWs: *The dog was grubbing (about) under the bush, looking for a bone.* **2** [T+*obj*+*adv*, esp. UP, OUT] to dig up by the roots

grub·by /ˈgrʌbi/ *adj infml* rather dirty: *grubby hands* | *That white shirt's looking rather grubby.*

grub·stake /ˈgrʌbsteɪk/ *n infml, esp. AmE* money provided to develop a new business in return for a share of the profits

grudge¹ /grʌdʒ/ *v* [T] to give or allow (something) unwillingly; BEGRUDGE: [+*v-ing*] *He grudged paying so much for such bad food.* [+*obj*(i)+*obj*(d)] *I don't grudge you your success.*

grudge² *n* [(**against**)] (something that causes) a deep feeling of dislike for another person, esp. based on a belief that they have harmed one in some way: *I always feel she has a grudge against me, although I don't know what wrong I've done her.* | *I'm not one to* **bear a grudge/grudges.** (=continue to feel angry about someone's past actions) | *This big boxing match is billed as a* **grudge fight.** (=because the fighters dislike each other)

grudg·ing /ˈgrʌdʒɪŋ/ *adj* unwilling or showing unwillingness: *She was very grudging in her thanks/praise.* | *his grudging acceptance of our decision* — ~**ly** *adv* : *He gave his permission grudgingly.*

gru·el /ˈgruːəl/ *n* [U] a thin liquid food given in the past to a person who was ill, made by boiling crushed OATS (=a

type of grain) in milk or water. Formerly it was often the only food a poor person could afford or would be given if they lived in the WORKHOUSE (=former state building for the homeless and unemployed)

gru·el·ling *BrE* ‖ **grueling** *AmE* /ˈgruːəlɪŋ/ *adj* very hard and tiring; demanding great effort and determination: *All the runners were exhausted after the gruelling race.* — ~**ly** *adv*

grue·some /ˈgruːsəm/ *adj* (esp. of something connected with death or suffering) very shocking and sickening: *a gruesome report about torture in a prison camp* — compare GRISLY, MACABRE — ~**ly** *adv* — ~**ness** *n* [U]

gruff /grʌf/ *adj* **1** (of a person's voice) deep and rough, sometimes because bad-tempered **2** (of a person's behaviour) unfriendly or impatient, esp. in one's manner of speaking: *a gruff manner/reply* — ~**ly** *adv* — ~**ness** *n* [U]

grum·ble¹ /ˈgrʌmbəl/ *v* [I] **1** to express discontent or dissatisfaction; complain in a quiet but bad-tempered way: *They were all grumbling about the company's refusal to increase their pay.* | (*BrE infml*) *"How are you today?" "Mustn't grumble."* (=I'm fairly well) **2** to make a low dull sound; RUMBLE: *Thunder grumbled in the distance.* —**bler** *n*

grumble² *n* **1** [C] a complaint or expression of dissatisfaction: *Take your grumbles to the boss, not to me.* **2** [(*the*) S] a low, esp. continuing, noise; RUMBLE: *the distant grumble of the guns*

grum·bling /ˈgrʌmblɪŋ/ *adj not tech* (of the human APPENDIX) causing pain or discomfort from time to time

grump·y /ˈgrʌmpi/ *adj infml* bad-tempered and tending to complain: *She's very grumpy when her tooth aches.* —**ily** *adv* —**iness** *n* [U]

grun·gy /ˈgrʌndʒi/ *adj AmE s;* dirty and perhaps badsmelling, in a way that offends: *grungy blue jeans*

grunt¹ /grʌnt/ *v* **1** [I] (esp. of a pig) to make short deep rough sounds in the throat, as if the nose were closed **2** [I;T] (of a human being) to make a sound like this or express with such a sound, esp. when dissatisfied or unwilling to talk: *When I asked her if she wanted some tea, she just grunted.* | *He grunted his agreement without looking up from his newspaper.*

grunt² *n* a short deep rough sound (like that) of a pig: *He gave a grunt of approval.*

Gru·yère /ˈgruːjeəʳ‖gruːˈjeər/ *n* [U] a sort of hard cheese with holes in it, from Switzerland

gryph·on /ˈgrɪfən/ *n* a GRIFFIN

g-spot /ˈdʒiː spɒt ‖ -spɑːt/ *n taboo, sl* a centre of sexual sensation inside a woman's VAGINA

Gstaad /gəˈʃtɑːd/ a town in Switzerland, famous as a place where esp. rich people go skiing (SKI²)

G-string /ˈdʒiː ˌstrɪŋ/ *n* a very small piece of cloth, leather, etc., worn on the lower part of the body esp. by STRIP-TEASE dancers

GTI /ˌdʒiː tiː ˈaɪ/ *adj* (of motor cars) grand tourer injection; having a special FUEL system which means the car can go at high speeds —compare FUEL INJECTION

gua·ca·mo·le /ˌgwɑːkəˈməʊli/ *n* [U] *Sp* a dish made of crushed AVOCADO flesh

Guang·zhou /ˌgwɑːŋˈdʒəʊ/ the modern name for Canton, China

gua·no /ˈgwɑːnəʊ/ *n* [U] the waste matter passed from the stomachs of seabirds, which is used to feed soil where plants are grown

guar·an·tee¹ /ˌgærənˈtiː/ *n* [(**of**)] **1** a formal declaration that something will be done, esp. a written agreement by the maker of an article to repair or replace it if it is found to be imperfect within a certain period of time. Not all goods have a guarantee but they must still do the job for which they were made and last a reasonable amount of time according to the rules of the Consumer Council in Britain, and the Consumer Protection Agency in the US: *The radio has a two-year guarantee.* | *The car is less than a year old, and therefore still* **under guarantee.** [+*that*] *Can you give me your guarantee* (=firm promise) *that the goods will be delivered before Friday?* | (fig.) *Clear skies are no guarantee of continued fine weather/that the weather will stay fine.* —compare WARRANTY **2** an agreement to be responsible for the fulfilment of someone else's promise, esp. for paying a debt **3** something of value given to someone to keep until the owner has fulfilled a promise, esp. to pay what is owing —compare SECURITY (4)

guarantee² *v* [T] **1** to give a guarantee: *The manufacturers guarantee the watch for three years.* [+(*that*)] *They have guaranteed that any faulty parts will be replaced free of charge.* [+*to-v*] *Our products are guaranteed to last for years.* [+*obj+adj*] *All our food is guaranteed free of artificial preservatives* **2** to promise (that something will certainly be so): *They have guaranteed delivery within three days.* [+(*that*)] *Go and see that play – I guarantee (that) you'll enjoy it.* —see also WARRANTY

guar·an·tor /ˌgærənˈtɔːʳ/ *n law* a person who agrees to be responsible for another person's fulfilling a promise, esp. paying a debt

guar·an·ty /ˈgærənti/ *n law* a guarantee, esp. of payment – see also WARRANTY

guard¹ /gɑːd‖gɑːrd/ *n* **1** [C] a person, esp. a soldier, policeman, or prison officer, who watches over a person or place to prevent escape, danger, attack, etc.: *The camp guards are changed every night.* | *security guards at the airport* **2** [(*the*) S+*sing.*|*pl. v*] a group of people, esp. soldiers, whose duty it is to guard someone or something: *The prisoner was brought in* **under armed guard.** | *Lots of tourists go to Buckingham Palace to see the* **changing of the guard.** —see also OLD GUARD **3** [U] a state of watchful readiness to protect or defend: *There are soldiers* **on guard** *at the gate, to prevent anyone getting in or out.* | *The police are* **keeping guard** *over the house.* | *The soldiers* **stood/mounted guard** *over* (=guarded) *the palace.* | *The Rock of Gibraltar* **stands guard over** *the entrance to the Mediterranean.* **4** [C] (*often in comb.*) an apparatus which covers and protects: *Football players often wear* **shin guards.** (=to protect the lower part of their legs) – see also FIREGUARD, MUDGUARD **5** [C] *BrE* ‖ **conductor** *AmE* – a railway official in charge of a train **6** [U] a position of being ready to defend oneself or protect oneself from danger, esp. in a fight: *I got in under my opponent's guard.* (=hit him although he was defending himself) | *Be* **on your guard** *against pickpockets.* | *The question caught her* **off (her) guard,** *and she couldn't think of an answer.*

guard² *v* [T] **1** [(**against, from**)] to watch over in order to protect from harm or danger or to prevent from escaping; keep safe: *The dog guarded the house (against intruders).* | *the heavily-guarded presidential palace* | (fig.) *Guard the secret with your life: tell it to no one!* **2** to keep under control: *You must guard your tongue carefully.* (=be careful what you say)

guard against sthg. *phr v* [T] to (try to) prevent by special care: *Brush your teeth regularly to guard against tooth decay.* [+*v-ing*] *You should wash your hands when preparing food, to guard against spreading infection.*

guard·ed /ˈgɑːdɪd‖ˈgɑːr-/ *adj* (of a person or what they say) careful; not saying too much; NONCOMMITTAL: *He gave a guarded reply.* – – **ly** *adv*

guard·house /ˈgɑːdhaʊs‖ˈgɑːr-/ *n* **-houses** /ˌhaʊzɪz/ [*usu. sing.*] a building for military guards, esp. at the entrance to a camp, sometimes also used for imprisonment of soldiers

guard·i·an /ˈgɑːdiən‖ˈgɑːr-/ *n* **1** [(**of**)] *esp. fml or lit* someone who guards or protects: *It is not this newspaper's job to be guardian of the nation's morals.* **2** *law* someone who has the responsibility of looking after a child that is not their own, esp. after the parents' death. The guardian is usu. a member or close friend of the child's family. —compare WARD¹ (3)

Guardian [*the*] a national daily newspaper in Britain —see also extra information on page 896

guardian an·gel /ˌ… ˈ…/ *n* **1** a good spirit which protects a person or place. It is esp. children who believe in guardian angels. **2** a person who helps and protects another person

Guardian An·gels /ˌ… ˈ…/ [*the*] people who, unpaid, travel on the New York SUBWAYs or the London Underground and protect the other passengers from criminals

Guardian read·er /ˈ… ˌ…/ *n BrE* a person who is well educated and has liberal or left-wing political opinions, thought to be the sort of person who reads the Guardian newspaper

guard·i·an·ship /ˈgɑːdiənʃɪp‖ˈgɑːr-/ *n* [U] the position of, responsibility of, or period of time as a (legal) guardian

guard·rail /ˈgɑːd-reɪl‖ˈgɑːrd-/ *n* **1** a protective bar or RAIL intended **a** to prevent people from falling from a bridge or stairs or **b** *esp. AmE* to prevent drivers from going off the road **2** an additional railway line, fitted on curves to prevent the train running off the lines

guard·room /ˈgɑːd-rʊm, -ruːm‖ˈgɑːrd-/ *n* a (room of a) GUARDHOUSE

Guards /gɑːdz‖gɑːrdz/ also **Guards Di·vi·sion** /ˈ… ˌ…/– [*the* + P] a group of REGIMENTs (=large divisions of men) in the British Army, originally those who guarded the King or Queen. The Guards are considered to be some of the finest soldiers in the British Army, and becoming an officer in the Guards is thought to be a good CAREER for esp. upper-class young men. —see also COLDSTREAM GUARDS, GRENADIER, IRISH GUARDS, SCOTS GUARDS, WELSH GUARDS

guards·man /ˈgɑːdzmən‖ˈgɑːr-/ *n* **-men** /mən/ (esp. in Britain) a soldier in the Guards

guard's van /ˈ… ·/ *BrE* ‖ **caboose** *AmE*– *n* the part of a train, usu. at the back, where the GUARD¹ (5) travels. Bicycles, pets, and large boxes, cases, etc. can also travel here.

Gua·te·ma·la /ˌgwɑːtəˈmɑːlə/ an independent republic in Central America, the home of the Mayan civilization for 1000 years; capital Guatemala; population 8,935,000 (1989) —**malan** *n, adj*

gua·va /ˈgwɑːvə/ *n* (a small tropical tree bearing) a round fruit with pink or white flesh and seeds in the centre. Guavas are not often on sale in Britain and are fairly expensive as they come from abroad. In the US **guava nectar** can be found in areas that have a large Hispanic population.

gu·ber·na·to·ri·al /ˌguːbənəˈtɔːriəl‖-bər-/ *adj fml or tech* of a governor: *the gubernatorial elections in the US*

Guc·ci /ˈguːtʃi/ *tdmk* an Italian maker of fashion clothes, esp. leather products: *a Gucci handbag*

Guer·ni·ca /ˈgɜːnɪkə‖ˈgweər-/ a town in the Basque area of N Spain bombed by German aircraft in the Spanish Civil War (1937). The event is strikingly recorded in Pablo Picasso's painting *Guernica*.

guern·sey /ˈgɜːnzi‖ˈgɜːr-/ *n* **-seys** a woollen SWEATER with a special pattern of raised stitches across the shoulder

Guernsey an island in the English Channel near NW France. Guernsey is one of the Channel Islands. It is popular for holidays and famous as a place where people pay very little tax.

guer·ril·la , guerilla /gəˈrɪlə/ *n* a member of an unofficial military group, esp. one fighting to remove a government, which attacks its enemy in small groups unexpectedly: *guerrilla warfare|guerilla tactics* –compare FREEDOM FIGHTER, TERRORIST

guess¹ /ges/ *v* **1** [I (**at**); T] to form a judgment (about) or risk giving an opinion (on) without knowing or considering all the facts: *"I don't know the answer." "Well just guess!"* | *Can you guess (at) the price?* [+(*that*)] *I guessed I'd find you in here!* [+*wh-*] *You'll never guess how much|what it cost.* [+*obj+to-v*] *I'd guess it to be about £300.* **2** [T] to get to know by guessing: *She guessed my thoughts.* | *"I suppose he's late again." "You've guessed it!"* **3** [T+(*that*); *obj*; *not in progressive forms*] *infml, esp. AmE* to suppose; consider likely: *I guess you don't have time to go out now that you have young children.* | *"Will you be coming tomorrow?" "I guess so."* **4** **keep someone guessing** to keep someone uninformed and uncertain what will happen next —see also EDUCATED GUESS, SECOND-GUESS

guess² *n* **1** [(**at**)] an attempt to guess: *Have (BrE)|Take (AmE) a guess at the answer.* | *She made a wild guess, but it was completely wrong.* | *I'd say that,* **at a guess** (=without being certain or exact)*, there were about 500 people there.* **2** an opinion formed by guessing: *My guess is that he didn't come because his parents wouldn't let him.* | *It's* **anybody's guess** (=no one knows) *when they'll arrive.* | *"Where do you think she's gone?" "I don't know –* **your guess is as good as mine."**

guess·ti·mate /ˈgestɪmət/ *n infml* an inexact judgment, esp. of quantity, made by guessing; a guessed ESTIMATE

Guess Who's Com·ing to Din·ner? /ˌ… ·ˌ… ·ˈ…/ a 1967

American film in which a white girl invites her black boyfriend home to meet her parents

guess·work /ˈgeswɜːk‖-wɜːrk/ n [U] the act of guessing, or the judgment which results: *She arrived at the right answer by pure guesswork.*

guest¹ /gest/ n **1** a person who is in someone's home by invitation, either for a short time or to stay: *a dinner guest | I have to give up my bedroom when we have guests.* —compare HOST¹ **2** a person who is invited out and paid for at a theatre, restaurant, etc.: *They are coming to the concert as my guests.* **3** a person who is lodging in a hotel or in someone's home: *Guests are requested not to remove the coathangers. | She takes in* **paying guests** *during the summer.* **4** a person, esp. an entertainer, who is invited to take part in a show, concert, etc., often in addition to those who usually take part: *Ladies and gentlemen, please welcome tonight's special guest. | She made a guest appearance on his TV show.* **5 be my guest!** *infml* I would not mind if you did so; please feel free to do so: *"Can I borrow your pen?" "Be my guest!"* —compare HOST¹ (1); see CUSTOMER (USAGE), VISITOR (USAGE)

guest² v [I(on)] *esp. AmE* to take part as a guest performer: *She's guesting on the Bob Hope Show.*

guest·house /ˈgesthaʊs/ n **-houses** /ˌhaʊzɪz/ a private house where visitors can stay and have meals for payment; a small hotel. Guesthouses are often used when people are on holiday or working away from home and are usu. cheaper than hotels.

guest·room /ˈgest-rʊm, -ruːm/ n a bedroom in a private house which is kept for visitors to sleep in

guest work·er /ˈ· ˌ··/ n a foreign worker working in another country for a limited time. Guest workers usu. come from poorer countries, are employed in unskilled jobs, and are not always treated fairly or well.

Guevara, Ché see CHE GUEVARA

guff /gʌf/ n [U] *infml* nonsense: *That's all* **a load of guff!**

guf·faw /gəˈfɔː/ v [I] to laugh loudly, and perhaps rudely – **guffaw** n : *He gave a loud guffaw.* —see LAUGH (USAGE)

Gug·gen·heim Mu·se·um /ˈgʊgənhaɪm mjuːˌziːəm/ [*the*] an important collection of modern art in New York. Its full name is the **Solomon R. Guggenheim Museum**, after a famous American industrialist of that name (1861–1949). It is famous for its large circular building designed by Frank Lloyd Wright.–see picture at WRIGHT (Frank Lloyd) and see colour map on page 1376

the Guggenheim Museum designed by Frank Lloyd Wright

guid·ance /ˈgaɪdəns/ n [U] **1** help and advice, esp. on problems connected with one's work, education, or personal life: *The agency offers practical guidance to people starting their own businesses. | a marriage guidance counsellor* **2** the process of directing the course of a MISSILE in flight: *a sophisticated electronic guidance system*

guidance coun·sel·or /ˈ·· ˌ···/ n *AmE* someone employed by a HIGH SCHOOL to give advice to students about what subjects to study and to help students with personal or emotional problems

guide¹ /gaɪd/ n **1** something or someone that shows the way, esp. a person whose job is to show a place to tourists: *You need a guide to show you the city.* **2** [(to)] something that provides a model on which behaviour, opinions, etc. can be based: *These opinion polls are not a very reliable guide to the way people are likely to vote.* **3** [(to)] also **guide book** /ˈ· ·/– a book which gives a description of a place, for the use of visitors **4** [(to)] a book which teaches the way to do something or provides information about something: *a parents' guide to children's diseases* **5** also **girl guide** *BrE* ‖ **girl scout** *AmE*– (*often cap.*) a member of an association (the **Girl Guides Association**) for training girls in character and self-help. Originally established by Agnes, sister of Lord Baden-Powell and including a junior section (the Brownie Guides), the Guides is an international movement recognizable by its uniform and known for its aim of developing good citizenship among its members —compare SCOUT¹ (1)

guide² v [T] **1** [+obj+adv/prep] to show (someone) the way by leading: *He guided us through the narrow streets to the railway station. | The light guided them back to harbour.| (fig.) An experienced lawyer guided them through the complex application procedure.* —see LEAD (USAGE) **2** [+obj+adv/prep] to control (the movements of): *The pilot guided the plane onto the runway. | (fig.) The government will guide the country through the difficulties ahead.* **3** [*usu. pass.*] to influence strongly: *Be guided by your feelings, and tell her the truth before it's too late.*

guided mis·sile /ˌ·· ·ˈ··/ n a MISSILE that is guided by electrical means to the thing it is aimed at

guide dog /ˈ· ·/ *BrE* ‖ **seeing eye dog** *AmE*– n a dog (usu. a Labrador) trained to guide a blind person

guided tour /ˌ·· ·ˈ·/ n a tour on which people are shown places and told things about them by a guide¹ (1): *a guided tour of Blenheim Palace|of the Speedwell Caverns*

guide·lines /ˈgaɪdlaɪnz/ n [P] informal rules or instructions on how something should be done: *The new pay settlement goes outside the government's guidelines. | Before you start on this project, let me give you a few guidelines.*

guild /gɪld/ n **1** an association for businessmen or skilled workers who joined together in former times to help one another and to make rules for training new members **2** an association of people with similar interests: *the Townswomen's Guild*

guil·der /ˈgɪldəʳ/ also **gulden**– n the standard money unit of the Netherlands

Guild·ford /ˈgɪldfəd‖-fərd/ a town in Surrey, SW of London

Guildford Four /ˌ·· ·ˈ·/ n [*the*+P] four people who were sent to prison for life in 1975 for IRA bombings in the English town of Guildford. They were freed in 1989, and it was suggested that the police had acted wrongly to make them seem guilty. Along with other cases, this case has raised questions in Britain about police questioning of people they have caught for a crime, and about the way mistakes in justice are put right. —compare BIRMINGHAM SIX, MAGUIRE SEVEN, TOTTENHAM THREE

guild·hall /ˌgɪldˈhɔːl, ˈgɪldhɔːl‖ˈgɪldhɔːl/ n a building in which members of a guild used to meet

Guildhall [*the*] the meeting hall of the Corporation of the City of London, used officially for important occasions, esp. large formal meals

guile /gaɪl/ n [U] *fml* deceit, esp. of a clever indirect kind; CUNNING: *He persuaded her to sign the document by guile.* – –~**ful** *adj* – –~**fully** *adv*

guile·less /ˈgaɪl-ləs/ *adj* (appearing to be) lacking in any deceit; INGENUOUS – –~**ly** *adv* – –~**ness** n [U]

guil·le·mot /ˈgɪlɨmɒt‖-maːt/ n any of several kinds of seabirds with narrow BEAKs that live in northern parts of the world

guil·lo·tine¹ /ˈgɪlətiːn/ n **1** a piece of equipment used esp. in France for cutting off the heads of criminals, which works by means of a heavy blade sliding down between two posts. It was used esp. during the FRENCH REVOLUTION to kill members of the ARISTOCRACY. **2** a piece of equipment used for cutting paper **3** an act of fixing a time to vote on a law in a law-making body, so that argument about it will not go on too long. Some people think that governments will do this in order to get the result they want: *to apply a guillotine*

guillotine² v [T] **1** to cut off the head of (a person) with a guillotine **2** to limit (argument) in a law-making body: *Discussion of the bill was guillotined.*

guilt /gɪlt/ n [U] **1** the fact of having broken a moral rule or official law: *The jury acquitted him* (=let him go free) *because his guilt could not be proved. | an admission of guilt* –opposite **innocence** **2** responsibility for something wrong; blame: *When children behave badly the guilt sometimes lies with the parents for not caring sufficiently.* **3** the feelings produced by knowledge or belief that one has done wrong; REMORSE: *She was tortured by guilt. | feelings of guilt* – –~**less** *adj* – –~**lessly** *adv* – –~**lessness** n [U]

guilt·y /ˈgɪlti/ *adj* **1** [(of)] having broken a law or disobeyed a rule: *The jury found her guilty of murder. | "Prisoner at the bar, how do you plead: guilty or not guilty?"* (=a formal question in a British court of law) *| The police suspect that the secretary may be the* **guilty party.** (=person) –opposite **innocent** **2** [(of)] responsible for behaviour that is morally wrong or socially unacceptable: *Politicians of all parties are guilty of ignoring this serious problem.* | *Whoever wrote this is guilty of appalling bad taste.* **3** [(about)] having or showing a feeling of guilt or shame: *She had a guilty look on her face.* | *a guilty conscience* | *I feel very guilty about forgetting to post your letter.* —**ily** *adv* —**iness** *n* [U]

guin·ea /ˈgɪni/ *n* (the value of) a former British gold coin, worth £1.05

Guinea a country in W Africa; capital Conakry; population 6,706,000 (1989) —**Guinean** *n, adj*

Guinea-Bis·sau /ˌgɪni bɪˈsaʊ/ a country in W Africa; capital Bissau; population 966,000 (1989)

guinea fowl /ˈ··· ·/ *n* **guinea fowl** a grey African bird with white spots which may be kept for its eggs and for food

guinea pig /ˈ··· ·/ *n* **1** a small roundish furry animal rather like a rabbit but with short ears and no tail, which is often kept by children as a pet, and is sometimes used in scientific tests **2** a person who is the subject of some kind of test: *I must try this new recipe out on someone. Will you be my guinea pig?* | *They're using us as guinea pigs for their experiment.*

Guin·e·vere /ˈgwɪnɪˌvɪəʳ/ the wife of King Arthur —see ARTHURIAN LEGEND

Guin·ness /ˈgɪnɪs/ *n tdmk* **1** [C;U] a strong dark beer (a STOUT) with a creamy white FROTH on top of it. Guinness is generally considered to be the national drink of the Irish and has a well-known advertising phrase, "Guinness is good for you", which many people believe to be true. **2** a British company which produces this beer

Guinness, Sir Al·ec /ˈælɪk/ (1914–) an English theatre and film actor well-known for playing many different parts. His best known films are *Lawrence of Arabia*, *The Bridge on the River Kwai*, and *Kind Hearts and Coronets*, in which he played eight parts

Guinness Af·fair /ˈ·· ·ˌ·/ [*the*] a 1990 criminal case in which four men connected with the Guinness company were fined (FINE) and/or put in prison for FRAUD

Guinness Book of Rec·ords /ˌ··· · · ˈ··/ *n* [*the*] a book brought out every year containing details of things that have happened more, faster, better, etc. than ever before. People often talk about getting into (=having their name entered in) the Guinness Book of Records because not all the records are serious and many are a result of amusing activities done to collect money for good causes.

guise /gaɪz/ *n fml* an outer appearance, esp. one that is intended to deceive: *There is nothing new here; just the same old ideas in a different/new guise.* | *In his new film he appears in various guises: as a lawyer, a soldier, a window cleaner, etc.*

gui·tar /gɪˈtɑːʳ/ *n* a musical instrument that has usu. six strings, with a long neck, played by striking or plucking (PLUCK) the strings with the fingers or a small piece of hard material (a PLECTRUM *BrE* ‖ PICK *AmE*). It can have either a hollow wooden body (**acoustic guitar**) or, when played using electricity, a solid plastic body (**electric guitar**). —**~ist** *n*

Guj·a·ra·ti , Gujerati /ˌgʊdʒəˈrɑːti◂/ *n* **Gujarati 1** the language of an area of India (**Gujarat**) and neighbouring areas **2** a member of a people mainly from Gujarat speaking Gujarati. A number of people living in Britain are either from or descended from people from this area and continue speaking the language.

gu·lag /ˈguːlæg‖-lɑːg/ *n* any of various prison camps in the former USSR, established in 1930. The bad conditions in gulags were described by Alexander Solzhenitsyn in his book *The Gulag Archipelago*.

gulch /gʌltʃ/ *n AmE* (esp. in the western US) a narrow stony valley with steep sides formed by a rushing stream

gul·den /ˈgʊldən‖ˈguːl-/ *n* **guldens** *or* **gulden** a GUILDER

gulf /gʌlf/ *n* **1** (*often cap. as part of a name*) a large deep stretch of sea partly enclosed by land: *the Persian Gulf* **2** [(**between**)] an area of serious difference or separation, esp. between opinions: *There seems no hope of a reconciliation; if anything the gulf between the two families is widening.* **3** *lit* a deep hollow place in the Earth's surface; CHASM

Gulf also **Arabian Gulf, Persian Gulf** [*the*] a part of the Indian Ocean between the Iranian and the Arabian Peninsula.

It is strategically very important in the Middle East.

Gulf an American company producing oil and petrol: *There is a Gulf garage on the corner.*

Gulf of Mex·i·co /ˌ·· ·ˈ···/ [*the*] an area of the Atlantic Ocean, bordered by Cuba, Mexico, and the US —see colour map on pages 1374–5

Gulf States /ˈ· ·ˌ·/ [*the*] **1** the small Arab states on the Gulf: Bahrain, Kuwait, Qatar, and the United Arab Emirates. These countries are very rich in oil. **2** *AmE* the US states that border on the Gulf of Mexico

Gulf Stream /ˈ· ·/ [*the*] a current of warm water which flows north eastward in the Atlantic Ocean from the Gulf of Mexico towards Europe. It is thought that the Gulf Stream keeps Britain much warmer that it would be otherwise.

Gulf War /ˌ· ˈ·/ [*the*] a war which began in 1991 after the Iraqi army occupied Kuwait declaring it the 19th PROVINCE of Iraq. Forces, mainly from the US, under the flag of the United Nations intervened and they were successful in driving the Iraqis out of Kuwait.

gull¹ /gʌl/ also **seagull**— *n* any of several kinds of common fairly large black and white or grey and white flying seabirds —see picture at WATER BIRD

gull² *v* [T] *esp. lit or old-fash* to cheat or deceive

gul·let /ˈgʌlɪt/ *n infml* the (inner) throat; foodpipe from the mouth to the stomach: *A piece of food got stuck in his gullet.* | (fig.)*This kind of dishonesty sticks in my gullet.* (=is unacceptable to me)

gul·li·ble /ˈgʌlɪbəl/ *adj* easily tricked or persuaded to believe something: *He's so gullible you could sell him any thing.* —**bly** *adv* —**bility** /ˌgʌlɪˈbɪlɪti/ *n* [U]

Gul·li·ver's Trav·els /ˌgʌlɪvəz ˌtrævəlz ‖ -vərz-/ the title of a book by Jonathan Swift about the adventures of a character named Gulliver. Gulliver travels to many imaginary places, the best remembered being **Lilliput**, where he meets a race of tiny people (**Lilliputians**). The most moral and highly developed creatures that he meets on his travels are a race of talking horses called the **Houyhnhnms**, while the worst creatures he meets are called **Yahoos**, who look very much like humans.

gul·ly , -ley /ˈgʌli/ *n* **1** a small narrow valley cut esp. into a hillside by heavy rain —see VALLEY (USAGE), and see picture at MOUNTAIN **2** a deep ditch or other small waterway

gulp¹ /gʌlp/ *v* **1** [T (DOWN)] to swallow hastily: *She gulped (down) her coffee and rushed out.* **2** [I] to make a sudden swallowing movement as if surprised or nervous: *He gulped when he saw the bill.*
gulp sthg. ↔ **back** *phr v* [T] to prevent the expression of feeling (as if) by swallowing: *She gulped back her tears.*

gulp² *n* **1** [(**of**)] a large mouthful: *She took a few gulps of coffee and rushed out of the house.* **2** an act of gulping: *He gave a nervous gulp.*

gum¹ /gʌm/ *n* [*usu. pl.*] either of the two areas of firm pink flesh in which the teeth are fixed, at the top and bottom of the mouth: *Massage your gums after cleaning your teeth.* —see picture at TEETH

gum² *n* **1** [U] any of several sticky substances obtained from the stems of some trees and bushes **2** [U] a sticky substance used for sticking things together: *These labels have gum on the back.* **3** [U] CHEWING GUM or BUBBLE GUM **4** [C] also **gumdrop**— a hard transparent jelly-like sweet: *a fruit gum* **5** [C] a GUM TREE

gum³ *v* **-mm-** [T+obj+adv/prep] to stick (something) in position with GUM² (2): *She gummed the labels to her suitcase.*
gum sthg. ↔ **up** *phr v* [T] *infml* to prevent from working properly: *All this dirt that has got into my watch has gummed up the works.*

gum⁴ *n* **by gum** *BrE dial, AmE dial, or humor* (used as an expression of surprise)

gum·bo /ˈgʌmbəʊ/ *n* **-bos** [U] **1** a soup with meat or seafood, vegetables, and OKRA to thicken it, made popular by CAJUN cooking from the southern US **2** *AmE dial* for OKRA

gum·boil /ˈgʌmbɔɪl/ *n infml* a painful swelling on the GUM¹, usu. near a tooth which is decayed; ABSCESS

gum·boot /ˈgʌmbuːt/ *n esp. BrE* a WELLINGTON

gum·drop /ˈɡʌmdrɒp‖-drɑːp/ *n* a hard jelly-like sweet; GUM² (4)

gum·my /ˈɡʌmi/ *adj* sticky; covered with sticky GUM² (2) —**miness** *n* [U]

gump·tion /ˈɡʌmpʃən/ *n* [U] *infml* **1** the ability to think and act in a practical way; good sense: *When the pan of chips caught fire he had the gumption to cover it with a damp cloth.* **2** the ability to take action needing courage and determination: *It takes a lot of gumption to start up your own business single-handed.*

gum·shoe /ˈɡʌmˌʃuː/ *n AmE sl for* DETECTIVE

gum tree /ˈ· ·/ *n* **1** any of various trees that produce gum **2** the American sweet gum tree **3** also **gum**— *esp. AustrE* the EUCALYPTUS tree **4 up a gum tree** *BrE infml* in a difficult situation with no means of escape

gun¹ /ɡʌn/ *n* **1** a weapon from which bullets or SHELLS¹ (2) are fired through a metal tube (BARREL). Gun ownership is strictly controlled in Britain, and most of the police force do not carry guns. In the US, the police carry guns and the public often own them. —see GUN CONTROL **2** a tool which forces out and spreads a substance by pressure: *a grease gun* **3** *infml, esp. AmE for* GUNMAN: *a hired gun* —see also SON-OF-A-GUN, **go great guns** (GREAT¹), **jump the gun** (JUMP¹), **spike someone's guns** (SPIKE²), **stick to one's guns** (STICK to)

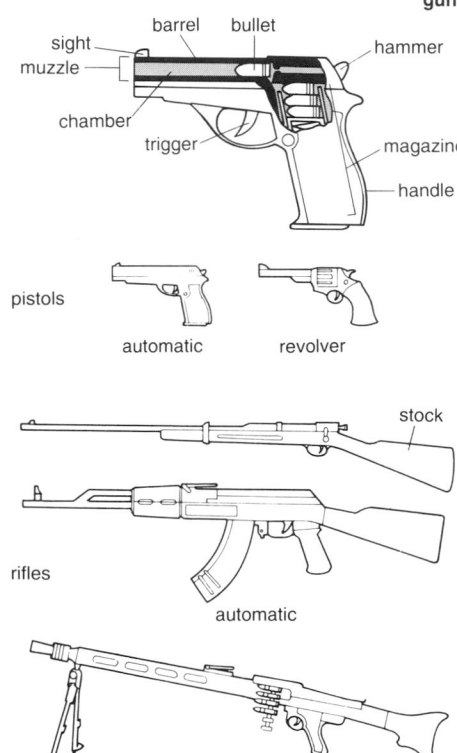

guns

sight
barrel bullet
muzzle
hammer
chamber
trigger
magazine
handle

pistols
automatic   revolver

stock
rifles
automatic

machine gun

cannon

gun² *v*

gun sbdy. ↔ **down** *phr v* [T] *infml* to shoot and kill or wound with a gun, esp. without pity: *Innocent villagers were gunned down by the terrorists.*

gun for sbdy. *phr v* [T] *infml, esp. BrE* to try to find rea-

sons for attacking or harming (someone): *Ever since I proved he'd made a mistake in the accounts he's been gunning for me, trying to get me dismissed.*

gun·boat /ˈɡʌnbəʊt/ *n* a small but heavily armed naval warship for use in waters near the coast

gunboat di·plo·ma·cy /ˈ·· ·ˌ···/ *n* [U] *derog* the use of a threat of armed force by a country to support a claim, demand, complaint, etc., against another

gun car·riage /ˈ· ˌ··/ *n* a frame with wheels on which a heavy gun is moved from place to place

gun con·trol /ˈ· ·ˌ/ *n* [U] laws which forbid or greatly restrict the possessing or using of guns. In the US, gun control is a subject about which everyone has a strong opinion. Guns kill so many people every year that many people would like them to be forbidden by law. However, the American Constitution states that every American has the right to have arms, and many people fear that gun control would stop them from being able to defend themselves, and being able to hunt. The National Rifle Association works to stop the American government forbidding guns.

gun cot·ton /ˈ· ˌ··/ *n* [U] a powerful explosive

gun·dog /ˈɡʌndɒg‖-dɔːg/ also **bird dog** *AmE*— *n* a dog trained to help in the sport of shooting birds, esp. by finding and bringing back the dead bird

gun·fight /ˈɡʌnfaɪt/ *n esp. AmE* a fight between two or more people, using esp. hand-held guns: *a fierce gunfight between police and criminals | rival gangs in a street gunfight* —see colour picture on page 358

► CULTURAL NOTE Gunfights are often thought of in connection with the American WILD WEST. ◄

gun·fight·er /ˈɡʌnfaɪtəʳ/ *n* a person who fights others, using a gun, esp. formerly in the American Wild West —see colour picture on page 358

gun·fire /ˈɡʌnfaɪəʳ/ *n* [U] the sound or act of firing one or more guns

gunge /ɡʌndʒ/ *BrE* ‖ **gunk** /ɡʌŋk/*AmE*— *n* [U] *infml* an unpleasant, dirty, and/or sticky substance: *What's this horrible gunge in the bottom of the bucket?*

gung-ho /ˌɡʌŋ ˈhəʊ/ *adj infml* showing extreme, often foolish eagerness, esp. to attack an enemy: *a gung-ho attitude to international relations*

gun lob·by /ˈ· ˌ··/ *[the]* (in the US) any group or groups who try to influence the Congress to defeat laws that will limit people's rights to buy and keep guns —see also NATIONAL RIFLE ASSOCIATION

gun·man /ˈɡʌnmən/ *n* -**men** /mən/ a man armed with a gun, esp. a criminal or TERRORIST

gun·met·al /ˈɡʌnˌmetl/ *n* [U] **1** a metal which is a mixture of copper, tin, lead, and ZINC from which chains, belt fasteners, etc., are made **2** a dark blue grey colour

gun·nel /ˈɡʌnl/ *n* GUNWALE

gun·ner /ˈɡʌnəʳ/ *n* **1** any member of the armed forces whose job is to aim or fire a gun **2** a soldier in a part of the British army which uses heavy guns (ARTILLERY): *Gunner Smith*

gun·ner·y /ˈɡʌnəri/ *n* [U] the science and practice of shooting with heavy guns: *a gunnery officer*

gun·ny·sack /ˈɡʌnisæk/ *n AmE* a sack, usu. measuring about 1 m deep, made from HESSIAN, in which potatoes, coal, etc. are stored

gun·point /ˈɡʌnpɔɪnt/ *n* **at gunpoint** under a threat of death by shooting: *They were forced at gunpoint to hand over the money.*

gun·pow·der /ˈɡʌnˌpaʊdəʳ/ *n* [U] an explosive substance in the form of a powder

Gunpowder Plot /ˈ··· ˌ·/ *[the]* a plan by English Catholics led by Guy Fawkes to kill King James I and destroy Parliament by means of explosives on November 5th 1605. The plan failed when one of the Catholics warned a relative not to attend Parliament that day and all the people in the Plot were caught and killed. The event is remembered every November 5th on Guy Fawkes Night. —see also Guy FAWKES, GUY FAWKES NIGHT

gun·run·ner /ˈɡʌnˌrʌnəʳ/ *n* a person who secretly and illegally brings guns into a country, esp. for the use of those who wish to fight against their own government. —**running** *n* [U]

gun·shot /ˈgʌnʃɒt‖-ʃɑːt/ n **1** [C] the act or sound of firing a gun: *gunshot wounds* **2** [U] the distance reached by a shot from a gun: *The animal was out of gunshot.*

gun·shy /ˈgʌnʃaɪ/ adj (esp. of a GUNDOG) easily frightened by the noise of a gun being fired

gun·smith /ˈgʌnˌsmɪθ/ n a person who makes and repairs small guns

Gun·smoke /ˈgʌnsməʊk/ a long-running American television programme, set in Dodge City, a town in the Wild West. Though the programme has ended, its characters are still remembered, including Matt Dillon, the MAR-SHAL (=policeman) of the town, and Miss Kitty, who owned a SALOON (=bar).

gun·wale, gunnel /ˈgʌnl/ n tech the upper edge of the side of a small ship or a boat —see picture at YACHT

gur·gle¹ /ˈgɜːgəl‖ˈgɜːr-/ v [I] **1** [(with)] (esp. of a baby) to make a sound like water flowing unevenly, e.g. out of a bottle or over stones: *The baby gurgled with pleasure.* **2** [+adv/prep] to flow with such a sound: *The water gurgled down the plughole.*

gurgle² n [(the) S] the sound of gurgling: *the gurgle of the brook* (=small stream) *over the little pebbles*

Gur·khas /ˈgɜːkəz‖ˈgɜːr-/ [the] a REGIMENT (=large division of men) in the British army. Originally from Nepal, the Gurkhas are best known for their bravery in battle and fierce fighting qualities.

gu·ru /ˈguruː/ n **1** an Indian religious leader or teacher of religious practices, esp. those that produce peace of mind **2** infml a greatly respected person whose ideas are followed: *J M Keynes was the great guru of economics.* | *one of the president's foreign policy gurus*

gush¹ /gʌʃ/ v **1** [I+adv/prep] (of liquid) to flow or pour out in large quantities (as if) from a hole or cut: *Oil gushed out from the broken pipe.* | *Blood gushed from the wound.|a gushing fountain* **2** [T] to send out (liquid) in large quantities: *The wound gushed blood.* **3** [I (over)] derog to express admiration, pleasure, etc., too strongly and perhaps without true feeling: *Look at them all gushing over the new baby.*

gush² n [S (of)] a (sudden) flow of liquid in large quantities: *When he removed the bandage there was a gush of blood.* | (fig.) *a gush of congratulations*

gush·er /ˈgʌʃəʳ/ n an OIL WELL from which oil rushes out strongly without pumping being necessary

gush·ing /ˈgʌʃɪŋ/ also **gush·y** /ˈgʌʃi/infml— adj expressing admiration, pleasure, etc. too strongly and perhaps without true feeling: *a gushing account of the two presidents' meeting* | *She's rather gushing.*

gus·set /ˈgʌsɪt/ n a three or four-sided piece of cloth sewn into a larger garment to strengthen or widen it at a particular place such as under the arm

gust¹ /gʌst/ n [(of)] a sudden strong rush of air, or of rain, smoke, etc., carried by wind: *A gust of wind blew the door shut.* | (fig.) *a gust of anger*   see WIND (USAGE)

gust² v [I] (of wind) to blow in gusts: *The wind will gust up to 45 miles an hour.*

gus·ta·to·ry /ˈgʌstətəri‖-tɔːri/ adj tech or pomp connected with tasting

gus·to /ˈgʌstəʊ/ n [U] eager enjoyment (in doing or having something); ZEST: *He started eating with great gusto.*

gust·y /ˈgʌsti/ adj (with wind) blowing in gusts: *a gusty day* | *a gusty wind*

gut¹ /gʌt/ n **1** [C] med the foodpipe which passes through the body, esp. the part below the stomach **2** [U] a strong thread made from this part of animals: *a fishing line made of gut* —see also GUTS, CATGUT

gut² v **-tt-** [T] **1** to take out the inner organs, esp. GUTS of (a dead animal): *Gut the rabbit before you cook it.* **2** [often pass.] to destroy the inside of (a building) completely, esp. by fire: *The factory was gutted by flames.*

gut³ adj [A] infml coming from or concerning one's natural feelings, rather than from careful thought: *I had a gut feeling that something would go wrong.* | *My gut reaction is to refuse, but I can't explain why.*

gut course /ˈ· ·/ n AmE sl a course of study in a college or university in which a passing mark can be got without much work

Gu·ten·berg Bi·ble /ˌguːtənbɜːg ˈbaɪbəl‖-bɜːrg-/ [the] a Bible which was the first book to be printed using movable TYPE¹ (2) (named after the printer Johann Gutenberg (1397–1468))

Guth·rie /ˈgʌθri/, **Woody** (1912–67) an American FOLK² singer, songwriter, and GUITAR player, esp. remembered for his songs against war

gut·less /ˈgʌtlɒs/ adj infml cowardly — ~ness n [U]

gut·rot /ˈgʌtrɒt‖-rɑːt/ n [U] BrE infml a pain in the stomach

guts /gʌts/ n [P] infml **1** the bowels or INTESTINES: *I've got a terrible pain in my guts|in the guts.* **2** bravery and determination: *We all agreed the boss was making a terrible mistake, but no one had the guts to tell him.* | *It takes a lot of guts to do something like that.* **3** the inner working parts of something, esp. of machinery **4 hate someone's guts** infml to hate someone very strongly

guts·y /ˈgʌtsi/ adj infml apprec brave and determined: *That young boxer is a gutsy fighter.*

gut·ter¹ /ˈgʌtəʳ/ n **1** [C] a small ditch or CHANNEL beside a road, between it and the path, to collect and carry away rainwater —see picture at HOUSE **2** [C] an open pipe fixed at the lower edge of a roof to collect and carry away rainwater **3** [C] the long narrow BOWLING place where the bowls are rolled in **4** [the] the lowest poorest level of society: *He picked her up out of the gutter and made her rich and famous.*

gutter² v [I] lit (of a candle) to burn with an uneven flame; FLICKER

gutter press /ˈ·· ˌ·/ n [the+sing.|pl. v] derog newspapers which tend to be full of shocking stories about people's personal lives. These papers are not generally considered to contain much serious news but are quite easy to read and very popular with many people. —see also extra information on page 896

gut·ter·snipe /ˈgʌtəsnaɪp‖-ər-/ n infml derog a child of the poorest parts of a town, living in the worst conditions, and usu. dressed in torn dirty clothes

gut·tur·al /ˈgʌtərəl/ adj (of speech or a speech sound) which seems to be produced deep in the throat: *a guttural accent/voice/sound*

guv /gʌv/ n BrE sl GUVNOR (2)

guv·nor , **guv'nor** /ˈgʌvnəʳ/ n BrE sl **1** a man who is in a position of control over one, such as an employer or father: *I'm only the office boy here, you'd better ask the guvnor.* **2** also **guv**— old use (used for addressing a man, esp. of higher position or social class): *Have you got the time guvnor?*

guy¹ /gaɪ/ n **1** infml **a** a man: *He's quite a nice guy when you get to know him.* **b** esp. AmE any person, male or female: *Come on, you guys!* —see also WISE GUY **2** a figure of a man, burnt in Britain on Guy Fawkes Night. Shortly before Guy Fawkes Night, children make guys and ask people for money, saying "a penny for the guy!". They then spend the money on FIREWORKS.

guy² also **guy rope** /ˈ· ·/ n a rope stretched from the top or side of a pole or from the side of a tent to the ground, to hold it in place

guy³ v [T] rare to copy or show (esp. a person) in a funny way so as to make people laugh

Guy·an·a /gaɪˈænə/ a country in NE South America, formerly British Guiana; capital Georgetown; population 1,024,000 (1989) **Guyanese** /ˌgaɪəˈniːz◂/ n, adj

Guy Fawkes' Night /ˌgaɪ ˈfɔːks naɪt/ also **Bonfire Night, Fireworks Night**— n [C;U] November 5th, when in Britain people light FIREWORKS and burn a GUY on a BONFIRE. This is in memory of the time when Guy Fawkes tried to destroy Parliament in London in 1605. The historical meaning of the occasion is no longer important —see also Guy FAWKES, GUNPOWDER PLOT and colour picture on page 1211

Guy's /gaɪz/ Guy's Hospital, an important teaching hospital in London

guz·zle /ˈgʌzəl/ v [I;T] often derog to eat or drink eagerly, quickly, and often continuously: *He's been guzzling beer all evening.* —**guzzler** n : (fig.) *These big cars are real gas guzzlers.* (=use a lot of petrol)

Gwent /gwent/ a COUNTY in S Wales

Gwyn /gwɪn/, **Nell** /nel/ (1650?–87) an English actress and lover of Charles II. She also sold oranges on the streets of London, and is often shown carrying a basket of oranges.

Nell Gwyn

Gwyn·edd /ˈgwɪnɪð/ a COUNTY in NW Wales

gym /dʒɪm/ n infml **1** [C] a gymnasium, esp. one where people go to do fitness training, e.g. lifting weights **2** [U] indoor exercises for the development of the body, esp. as a school subject: *gym shoes* | *a gym lesson* — compare PT

gym·kha·na /dʒɪmˈkɑːnə/ n esp. BrE a local sports meeting for horse racing, horse jumping, and competitions for horse and carriage

gym·na·si·um /dʒɪmˈneɪziəm/ n a hall with wall bars, ropes, and other equipment for climbing, jumping, and similar forms of exercise

gym·nast /ˈdʒɪmnæst, -nəst/ n a person who is skilled in doing certain physical exercises, esp. one who enters competitions

gym·nas·tics /dʒɪmˈnæstɪks/ n [U] the art or practice of training the body by means of certain exercises, such as swinging on bars or jumping over things, often performed in competition with others: (fig.) *verbal gymnastics* (=using words very skilfully) | *Working out that puzzle really took some mental gymnastics!* (=some clever thinking) —**tic** adj [A]

gym shoe /ˈ· ·/ n BrE for PLIMSOLL —see picture at SHOE

gym·slip /ˈdʒɪmˌslɪp/ n BrE a sort of dress without SLEEVEs, formerly worn by schoolgirls as part of a uniform

gymslip moth·er /ˌ·· ˈ··/ n BrE a girl who has a baby while she is still at school and esp. under the AGE OF CONSENT

gy·nae·col·o·gy gynecology AmE /ˌgaɪnɪˈkɒlədʒi‖-ˈkɑː-/ n [U] the branch of medicine dealing with the workings and diseases of women's bodies, esp. of the female sex organs —**ogist** n —**ogical** /-kəˈlɒdʒɪkəl◂‖-ˈlɑː-/ adj

gyp[1] /dʒɪp/ n [U] sl, esp. BrE sharp pain or punishment: *My bad tooth is really giving me gyp this morning.*

gyp[2] v -**pp**- [T] sl to cheat

gyp·sum /ˈdʒɪpsəm/ n [U] a soft white chalklike substance, from which PLASTER OF PARIS is made

gyp·sy /ˈdʒɪpsi/ n a GIPSY

gy·rate /dʒaɪˈreɪt‖ˈdʒaɪəreɪt/ v [I] fml to swing round and round on a fixed point, either in one direction or with changes of direction: *The dancers gyrated wildly to the strong beat of the music.* —**ration** /dʒaɪəˈreɪʃən/ n [C;U]

gy·ro·scope /ˈdʒaɪərəskəup/ also **gy·ro** /ˈdʒaɪərəu/ infml n a heavy wheel which spins inside a frame, used for keeping ships and aircraft steady, and also as a children's toy —**scopic** /ˌdʒaɪərəˈskɒpɪk◂‖-ˈskɑː-/ adj

H

H /eɪtʃ/ **H's, h's** or **Hs, hs** the eighth letter of the English alphabet –see also H-BOMB

H adj (of a pencil) having a hard centre and producing a light black mark. 2H is harder than H. –compare B, HB

H₂O /ˌeɪtʃ tuː ˈəʊ/ n [U] tech water, as expressed in chemistry (sometimes used humorously in ordinary speech)

ha /hɑː/ interj (used as a shout of surprise, interest, etc.) –see also AHA, HA-HA

ha·be·as cor·pus /ˌheɪbiəs ˈkɔːpəs‖-ˈkɔːr-/ n [U] law Lat (protection against unlimited imprisonment without charges, given by) the right of someone in prison to appear in a court of law so that the court can decide whether they should stay in prison: She applied for a **writ of habeas corpus.** (=a written order for someone to appear in court for this purpose)

hab·er·dash·er /ˈhæbədæʃəʳ‖-bər-/ n old-fash or tech **1** BrE a shopkeeper who sells pins, sewing thread, and other small things used in dressmaking **2** AmE a shopkeeper who sells men's clothing, esp. hats, GLOVES, etc.

hab·er·dash·er·y /ˈhæbədæʃəri‖-bər-/ n [C;U] old-fash or tech (the goods sold in) a haberdasher's shop or a haberdasher's department in a department store

hab·it /ˈhæbɪt/ n **1** [C; U] a tendency to behave in a particular way or do particular things, esp. regularly and repeatedly over a long period: She has an annoying habit of biting her fingernails. | I smoke only **out of/from habit;** I wish I could **break the habit.** | Cigarettes are **habit-forming.** (=make you want to keep smoking them) | I'm not **in the habit of** lending money, (=I don't usually do it) but I'll make an exception in this case. | You can borrow some money this time, but don't **make a habit of it.** | bad habits | eating habits **2** [C] a special set of clothes, esp. that worn by MONKS and NUNS

▷ USAGE Compare **habit, custom, practice,** and **convention.** A **habit** usually means something which is done regularly by a single person: He has an annoying **habit** of biting his nails. A **custom** usually means something which has been done for a long time by a whole society: the **custom** of giving presents at Christmas. **Practice** can mean **custom,** but often with a derogatory meaning: the **practice** of eating one's enemies. It can also mean the usual way of doing things in business, law, etc.: The normal **practice** in this company is to send the bill as soon as the job is done. The **conventions** of a society are its generally accepted standards of behaviour: As a matter of **convention,** people attending funerals wear dark clothes.◁

hab·i·ta·ble /ˈhæbɪtəbəl/ adj fml good enough to be lived in: Their damp draughty house was scarcely habitable. –opposite **uninhabitable**

hab·i·tat /ˈhæbɪtæt/ n the natural home of a plant or animal: The polar bear's habitat is the icy wastes of the Arctic. | I prefer to see animals in their **natural habitat,** rather than in zoos.

Habitat (a shop owned by) a British company which manufactures and sells a range of furniture and furnishings for houses. Habitat products are known for being practical, attractive, and reasonably priced, and are often made from natural materials, e.g. wood. They are popular esp. with MIDDLE-CLASS people.

hab·i·ta·tion /ˌhæbɪˈteɪʃən/ n fml **1** [U] the act of living in a place: This dilapidated old house is **unfit for human habitation. 2** [C] a house or place to live in

ha·bit·u·al /həˈbɪtʃuəl/ adj fml **1** [A] usual; customary: her habitual rudeness/greeting **2** done as a habit or doing something from habit: He's a **habitual** coffee drinker – he gets through about ten cups a day. | habitual cigarette smoking – **~ly** adv : habitually late

ha·bit·u·ate /həˈbɪtʃueɪt/ v **habituate** sbdy. **to** sthg. phr v [T often pass.] fml to allow (oneself) to get used to: to become habituated to a drug [+v-ing] Over the centuries, these animals have become habituated to living in such a dry environment.

ha·bit·u·é /həˈbɪtʃueɪ/ n [(**of**)] a regular attender: a habitué of the nightclub

Habs·burg /ˈhæpsbɜːg‖-bɜːrg/ adj HAPSBURG

ha·ci·en·da /ˌhæsiˈendə/ n Sp (the main house of) a large farm in Spanish speaking countries

hack¹ /hæk/ v **1** [I+adv/prep; T+obj+adv/prep] to cut (up), esp. roughly, violently, or in uneven pieces: She hacked away at the frozen ice, trying to make a hole. | They hacked their way through the jungle. | One of the police officers was hacked to death by the mob. **2** [T] sl to bear: I've been doing this job for years but I just can't hack it anymore. **–hack** n [(**at**)] : He made a hack at the log.

hack² n **1** derog a writer who does a lot of poor quality work, esp. writing stories or newspaper articles: Fleet Street hacks | hack journalism –see also HACKWORK **2** derog, esp. BrE an unimportant politician who is concerned mainly with party matters: The meeting was attended by the usual old party hacks. **3** an old tired horse **4** a light horse for riding **5** BrE a ride on horseback **6** AmE infml a taxi

hack³ v [I;T+obj+adv/prep] BrE to ride (a horse) at an ordinary speed along roads or through the country

hack·er /ˈhækəʳ/ n infml someone who is able to use or change the information in other people's computer systems without their knowledge or permission **–hacking** n [U]

hacking cough /ˌ·· ·ˈ/ n a repeated, often painful, cough with a rough unpleasant sound

hacking jack·et /ˈ·· ˌ·/ n BrE a special JACKET worn when riding a horse

hack·les /ˈhækəlz/ n [P] **1** the long feathers or hairs on the back of the neck of certain birds and animals, which stand up straight in times of danger **2 make someone's ¹hackles rise** to make someone feel very angry: His insensitive remarks about foreigners made her hackles rise. | I could feel my hackles rising as I watched the President being interviewed on TV.

hack·ney /ˈhækni/ n a horse of a breed which lifts its feet very high as it steps

Hackney a BOROUGH of N London

hackney car·riage /ˈ·· ˌ··/ n **1** a horse-drawn carriage used for hire, esp. formerly **2** also **hackney cab** /ˈ·· ˌ·/– fml or tech a taxi

hack·neyed /ˈhæknid/ adj derog (of a phrase, statement, etc.) meaningless because used and repeated too often; TRITE: hackneyed phrases/remarks

hack·saw /ˈhæksɔː/ n a tool (SAW) that has a fine-toothed blade and is used esp. for cutting metal –see picture at TOOL

hack·work /ˈhækwɜːk‖-wɜːrk/ n [U] derog uninteresting work, esp. writing, done to earn money and not because one likes it

had /d, əd, həd; strong hæd/ **1** past tense & participle of HAVE –see NOT (USAGE) **2 be had** /hæd/ infml to be tricked or made a fool of: I've been had! Those eggs I bought are all bad!

had·dock /ˈhædək/ n **haddock** a common fish found in northern seas, used as food

Ha·des /ˈheɪdiːz/ (in CLASSICAL MYTHOLOGY) the land of the dead; HELL

hadj /hædʒ/ n a HAJ

had·ji /ˈhædʒi/ n a HAJJI

had·n't /ˈhædnt/ short for: had not: If I hadn't seen it myself, I'd never have believed it.

Ha·dri·an's Wall /ˌheɪdriənz ˈwɔːl/ a stone wall built across the N of England by order of the Roman ruler Hadrian between 122 AD and 128 AD to defend the N border of Roman Britain. Part of the wall and some of the forts built along its course can still be seen.

hae·mo·glo·bin BrE‖**hemoglobin** AmE /ˌhiːməˈgləʊbɪn‖ ˈhiːməgləʊbɪn/ n [U] a red colouring matter in the blood which contains iron and carries oxygen

hae·mo·phil·i·a BrE‖**hemophilia** AmE /ˌhiːməˈfɪliə/ n [U] med a serious disease in which the blood is unable to CLOT². The disease affects only males, but is carried by females. It is treatable in some cases.

hae·mo·phil·i·ac BrE‖**hemophiliac** AmE /ˌhiːməˈfɪliæk◂/ n a person suffering from haemophilia

haem·or·rhage[1] *BrE*||**hemorrhage** *AmE* /ˈhemərɪdʒ/ *n* [C;U] a flow of blood, esp. a long or large and unexpected one

haemorrhage[2] *BrE*||**hemorrhage** *AmE v* [I] to have a haemorrhage

hae·mor·rhoids *BrE*||**hemorrhoids** *AmE* /ˈhemərɔɪdz/ *n* [P] *med or fml* swollen BLOOD VESSELS (=blood-carrying tubes) at the ANUS (=the opening at the lower end of the bowel) —see also PILES

haft /hɑːft||hæft/ *n tech* the handle of an AXE or of some long-handled weapons

hag /hæg/ *n derog* an ugly or unpleasant woman, esp. one who is old and is thought to be evil

hag·gard /ˈhægəd||-ərd/ *adj* having lines on the face and hollow places around the eyes and in the cheeks (as if) through tiredness, lack of sleep, or anxiety: *The haggard faces of the rescued miners showed what they had suffered.*

Haggard, Sir H Rider (1856–1925) an English writer remembered esp. for his adventure story *King Solomon's Mines*

hag·gis /ˈhægɪs/ *n* [C;U] a food eaten in Scotland, made from the heart and other organs of a sheep cut up and boiled inside a skin made from the sheep's stomach. Haggis is typically eaten with boiled TURNIPS and potatoes, known in Scotland as "neeps and tatties". It is considered to be typical Scottish food.

hag·gle /ˈhægəl/ *v* [I (**over, about**)] to argue, esp. in an attempt to fix a price: *He haggled over the price of the horse.* | *It's not the custom to haggle in British and American shops.*

hag·i·og·ra·phy /ˌhægiˈɒgrəfi||-ˈɑːg-/ *n* [C;U] **1** (a book giving) information about the lives of SAINTS or other holy people **2** (a) BIOGRAPHY which is too admiring or favourable towards its subject

Hag·man /ˈhægmən/, **Lar·ry** /ˈlæri/ (1930–) an American film actor, known esp. for acting the part of J R Ewing in the SOAP OPERA *Dallas*

hag·rid·den /ˈ·ˌ··/ *adj lit* continually worried by something as if by a bad dream

Hague /heɪg/, **The** a city in the Netherlands where that country's government is based

ha-ha[1] /ˌ·ˈ·ˈ·/ *interj* (a shout of laughter) —see also AHA, HA

ha-ha[2] /ˈ·· ·/ *n* **ha-has** (a wall or fence set in) a ditch used to divide property without interrupting the view

Haight-Ash·bu·ry /ˌheɪt ˈæʃbəri/ a part of San Francisco, California, where the HIPPIE movement began in the 1960s

hai·ku /ˈhaɪkuː/ *n* haiku a type of Japanese poem with three lines consisting of 5, 7 and 5 SYLLABLES

hail[1] /heɪl/ *n* **1** [U] frozen rain drops which fall as little hard balls of ice —see RAIN (USAGE) **2** [S+of] a number of things which strike suddenly with violence, causing pain or damage: *a hail of bullets* | *a hail of abuse*

hail[2] *v* [*it*+I] (of hail) to fall: *It's hailing outside.*

hail[3] *v* [T] to call out to or try to attract the attention of: *An old friend hailed me from the other side of the street.* | *We waited until they were within hailing distance, and then shouted to attract their attention.* | *The hotel doorman will hail a cab for you.*

    hail sthg./sbdy **as** sthg. *phr v* [T *often pass.*] to recognize and describe as (something good): *Her latest book is being hailed as a masterpiece.*

    hail from sthg. *phr v* [T *no pass.*] *esp. pomp or humor* to come from; have as one's home: *She hails from Liverpool.*

Hai·le Se·las·sie /ˌhaɪli sɪˈlæsi/ (1892–1975) the EMPEROR of Ethiopia from 1930 to 1974, who is remembered esp. for having modernized his country. He was removed from power by his army in 1974 but is still important to his followers, called RASTAFARIANS, who regard him as a god. He is also sometimes called **Ras Tafari**, the **Lion of Judah**.

hail-fel·low-well-met /ˌ· ··· ˈ·/ *adj* [F] *old-fash, sometimes derog* (of a person or their behaviour) very cheerful and friendly from the moment of greeting; HEARTY

Hail Ma·ry /ˌ· ˈ··/ a special Roman Catholic prayer to Mary, the mother of Jesus, to ask for her help

hail·stone /ˈheɪlstəʊn/ *n* a small ball of hail

hail·storm /ˈheɪlstɔːm||-ɔːrm/ *n* a storm when hail falls heavily

hair /heəʳ/ *n* **1** [C] a fine threadlike growth from the skin of a person or animal: *The cat has left white hairs all over my black sweater.* | *I found a woman's hair on my husband's jacket.* —see picture at HEAD **2** [U] a mass of these growths, esp. on the head of human beings: *She brushed her hair.* | *a woman with curly blonde hair* | *I'm going to the hairdresser to have/get my hair cut.* —compare FUR[1]; see also HEAD OF HAIR and see picture at HEAD **3 get in someone's hair** *infml* to annoy someone, esp. by being continually present: *I find the children get in my hair during the school holidays.* **4 I'm washing my hair** *humor* a phrase supposedly used by women as an excuse to stay at home when they do not want to go out with someone **5 keep one's hair on** [*usu. imperative*] *infml* to remain calm; not get annoyed **6 let one's hair down** *infml* to behave freely and perhaps wildly, esp. after a period of controlled behaviour: *You should have seen the teachers letting their hair down at the school dance.* **7 make someone's** ˈ**hair stand on end** to make someone very afraid; TERRIFY someone **8 not turn a hair** to show no fear, worry, or surprise; remain calm: *When we told him there were 500 plates to be washed, he didn't turn a hair, but just got on and did them.* **9 the/a hair of the dog (that bit you)** *humor* an alcoholic drink taken in the morning because it is said to cure illness caused by drinking too much alcohol the night before **10 -haired** /heəd||heərd/ having hair of the stated length, colour, type, etc.: *long-haired* | *fair-haired* —see also **split hairs** (SPLIT[1]), **tear one's hair (out)** (TEAR[2])

Hair a very successful MUSICAL of the 1960s. It included scenes which showed naked people, and was very shocking to a lot of people at that time.

hair·breadth /ˈheəbredθ, -bretθ||ˈheər-/ *n* HAIR'S BREADTH

hair·brush /ˈheəbrʌʃ||ˈheər-/ *n* a brush used for the hair to make it smooth and to get out dirt —see picture at BRUSH

hair·cut /ˈheəkʌt||ˈheər-/ *n* **1** an occasion of having the hair cut: *I'm going for a haircut.* **2** the style the hair is cut in: *Do you like my new haircut?*

hair·do /ˈheəduː||ˈheər-/ *n* **-dos** *infml old-fash in BrE* **1** a woman's HAIRSTYLE **2** an occasion of a woman having her hair shaped into a style: *A hairdo costs such a lot nowadays.*

hair·dress·er /ˈheəˌdresəʳ||ˈheər-/ *n* a person who shapes people's hair into a style by cutting, setting (SET[1] (10)), etc., and who usu. works in a shop (**hairdresser's**): *I've got an appointment at the hairdresser's.* —compare BARBER —**-ing** *n* [U]

hair-dry·er, **-drier** /ˈheəˌdraɪəʳ||ˈheər-/ *n* a machine that blows out hot air for drying hair

hair·grip /ˈheəgrɪp||ˈheər-/ *BrE* || **bobby pin** *AmE* — *n* a flat HAIRPIN with ends pressed close together —see picture at PIN

hair·less /ˈheələs||ˈheər-/ *adj* with no hair; BALD

hair·line /ˈheəlaɪn||ˈheər-/ *n* **1** the line around the head, esp. above the forehead, where the hair starts growing **2** a very thin line or crack: *She had a* **hairline fracture** (=a very slight one) *of her forearm.*

hair·net /ˈheənet||ˈheər-/ *n* a net, worn esp. by women, which stretches over the hair to keep it in place

hair·piece /ˈheəpiːs||ˈheər-/ *n often euph* a piece of false hair used to make one's own hair seem thicker

hair·pin /ˈheəˌpɪn||ˈheər-/ *n* a pin made of wire bent into a U-shape to hold long hair in position on the head —see picture at PIN

hairpin bend /ˌ·· ˈ·/ *n* a very sharp U-shaped curve in a road, as when going up a steep hill: *The truck nearly came off the road on a hairpin bend in the mountains.*

hair-rais·ing /ˈ· ˌ··/ *adj* causing a mixture of fear and surprise: *a hair-raising experience* | *He told us some hair-raising stories about his exploits as a mountaineer.*

hair-re·stor·er /ˈ·· ·ˌ··/ *n* [C;U] (a) substance or liquid that is supposed to make hair grow again

hair's breadth /ˈ·· ·/ *also* **hairbreadth**— *n* [S] a very short distance: *The car came careering round the bend and missed us* **by a hair's breadth**; *it came* **within a hair's breadth** *of hitting us.*

hair shirt /ˌ· ˈ·/ *n* a shirt made of rough uncomfortable cloth containing hair, worn formerly by religious people, esp. MONKs, to punish themselves

hair slide /'· ·/ also **slide** BrE ‖ **barrette** AmE— n a small often decorative fastener to keep a girl's or woman's hair in place

hair-split·ting /'· ˌ··/ n [U] derog the act or habit of paying too much attention to small unnecessary differences and unimportant points of detail, esp. in argument —see also **split hairs** (SPLIT¹)

hair·spray /'heəspreɪ‖'heər-/ n [U] a transparent or coloured substance used by women to keep their hairstyle in place, usu. sprayed (SPRAY¹) from an AEROSOL

hair·spring /'heəˌsprɪŋ‖'heər-/ n a delicate spring inside a watch that helps to make the watch run evenly

hair·style /'heəstaɪl‖'heər-/ n the style in which someone's hair has been cut or shaped

hair trig·ger /ˌ· '··◂/ n a TRIGGER on a gun that needs only a very gentle pressure to fire the gun: (fig.) He's got a hair-trigger temper. (=very quickly and easily gets angry)

hair·y /'heəri/ adj 1 having a lot of body hair: a hairy man | hairy legs | a hairy chest 2 infml frighteningly or excitingly dangerous: It was rather hairy driving down that narrow road in the dark. —-iness n [U]

Hai·ti /'heɪti/ a country in the Caribbean, on the western third of the island of Hispaniola; capital Port au Prince; population 5,609,000 (1989) —Haitian /'heɪʃən/ n, adj

haj, hadj /hædʒ/ n a PILGRIMAGE (=religious journey) to Mecca, which all Muslims aim to make at least once in their lifetime

haj·ji, hadji /'hædʒi/ n (used as a title for) a Muslim who has made a haj

hake /heɪk/ n hake or hakes a sea fish used as food

ha·kim /hɑː'kiːm/ n a Muslim doctor

ha·lal /hə'lɑːl/ n [U] meat from an animal that has been killed in the manner approved of by Muslim law

hal·berd /'hælbəd‖-bərd/ n a weapon with a blade on a long handle, used in former times

hal·cy·on days /ˌhælsiən 'deɪz/ n [P] esp. lit a time of peace and happiness: She recalled with a wistful smile the halcyon days of her youth. | the halcyon days of full employment

hale /heɪl/ adj **hale and heart·y** /ˌ· · '··/ (esp. of an old person) very healthy and active

Hale, Na·than /'neɪθən/ (1755–76) an American nationalist who was hanged by the British as a SPY during the American War of Independence. He is famous for saying "I regret (=am sorry) that I have but one life to give for my country."

Ha·ley /'heɪli/, **Bill** (1927–81) an American popular music singer whose record Rock Around the Clock first made ROCK 'N' ROLL music popular in the 1950s

half¹ /hɑːf‖hæf/ n, pron **halves** /hɑːvz‖hævz/ **1** either of the two equal parts into which something is or could be divided; ½; 50%: Half of 50 is 25. | (One) half of the children study chemistry, (the other) half study Spanish. | Almost half of all road accidents are caused by drunkenness. | The company has 60 microcomputers but only half are used regularly. | She bought a kilo and a half (=1½kilos) of rice. | He cut the cake **in half**. (=into two equal parts) | You haven't heard/don't **know (the) half of it** yet ! (=the most surprising or shocking part has still to be told) **2** either of two parts into which something is divided: He's in the bottom half of the class. | He broke the chocolate in two and took the bigger half for himself. | in the latter half of the 20th century **3** either of two equal periods into which a sports match is divided: England scored in the second half. **4** the number ½: Three halves makes 1½. **5** (pl. also **halfs**) BrE half a PINT, esp. of beer: a half of lager | A pint and two halfs, please. **6** (pl. also **halfs**) BrE a child's ticket: One and two halves to Waterloo, please. **7** (pl. also **halfs**) a HALFBACK **8 and a half** infml of very good quality: That was a meal and a half! **9 by halves** in part; incompletely; in a HALF-HEARTED way: I recommended that wine to him, and he bought ten cases of it; he never does anything by halves. **10 go halves** infml to share something equally: Since it was so expensive, we agreed to go halves in/on it. (=share the cost equally) | I'll go halves with you. **11 half past** half an

hour later than the stated hour: He went out at half past nine. (=9:30) —see also OTHER HALF

half² predeterminer, adj [A] **1** being ½ in amount: Half the boys are already here. | I've lived there half my life. | I waited half an hour|a (full) half hour. | She bought half a kilo of rice. | She ran in the half-mile race. | They stood in a half circle. | He bought **half a dozen** (=six) apples. | She gave a sort of half smile. (=not quite a smile) | The buses come every hour **on the half hour.** (=at 1:30, 2:30, 3:30, etc.) **2** BrE infml half past (the stated time): He went out at half nine. (=9:30) —see also HALF¹ (11) **3 half a loaf is better than no bread** saying a small amount of something is better than none at all **4 half the battle** the biggest part of the difficulty (finished): Persuading her it's a good idea is half the battle; once she's convinced, she'll do a good job.

▷ USAGE 1 When 1½ is said as one and a half it is plural: One and a **half** months have passed since I saw him. But when it is said as a … and a half it is usually singular: A month and a **half** has passed since I saw him. 2 In American English some people think it is better to say a **half** mile than half a mile.◁

half³ adv **1** partly; not completely: These potatoes are only half cooked. | She looked half starved. (=very hungry) | He was half under the bed, with his legs sticking out. | a half empty bottle **2** to an equal degree: She was half laughing, half crying. **3 half and half** ½ one and ½ the other; two equal parts of two things: "Is it made with milk or water?" "Half and half". —see also HALF-AND-HALF **4 half as much again** one-and-a-half times as much **5 not half** BrE infml **a** very (much); to a great degree: It wasn't half good! (=it was very good) | It isn't half windy today! (=it's very windy) | He didn't half complain! | "Was she annoyed?" "Not half!" **b** (to be) not at all: The food's **not half bad.** (=it's quite good) **6 not half as** not nearly as: I didn't feel half as cold once they'd put the heating on.

half a crown /ˌ· · '·/ also **half crown**— n half crowns (in Britain before 1971) a large silver-coloured coin, eight of which made £1 (a pound)

half-and-half /ˌ· · '·/ n **1** [C;U] BrE a drink made of equal amounts of bitter beer and MILD (=not strong in taste) beer: They were drinking half-and-half. | A half-and-half, please. **2** [U] AmE a mixture of cream and milk, used for tea and coffee

half-arsed /ˌhɑːf 'ɑːst◂/ BrE ‖ **-assed** AmE adj sl, not polite **1** not good enough and not producing a good result: he made a half-arsed attempt to clean up the mess he had made **2** stupid

half-back /'hɑːfbæk‖'hæf-/ also **half**— n **1** (in British football) a player who plays in the middle of the field, sometimes attacking and sometimes defending **2** (in American football) a player who at the start of play is behind the front line of players at the right or left of the FULLBACK

half-baked /ˌ· '·◂/ adj infml (esp. of an idea, suggestion, etc.) stupid because not properly planned or thought about: Another of her half-baked schemes!

half board /ˌ· '·/ n [U] esp. BrE (in lodgings, hotels, etc.) the providing of a bed and either the midday meal or the evening meal as well as breakfast —compare FULL BOARD

half-breed /'· ·/ n, adj taboo (a person) with parents of different races, esp. with one white parent and one Native American parent

half-broth·er /'· ˌ··/ n a brother related through one parent only

half-caste /'· ·/ n, adj usu. taboo (a person) with parents of different races

half cock /ˌ· '·/ n **go off (at) half cock** (esp. of a planned event) to fail to satisfy expected standards because of poor preparation, bad luck, etc.

half crown /ˌ· '·◂/ n HALF A CROWN

half-heart·ed /ˌ· '··◂‖'· ˌ··/ adj (of a person or action) showing little effort and no real interest: The children made a half-hearted attempt to tidy their room. —~ly adv —~ness n [U]

half-hol·i·day /ˌ· '···/ ‖ **half-day** /'· ·/AmE— n half a day which is free from school, studies, etc.

half-length /ˌ· '·◂‖'· ·/ adj for or of the upper half of a person: a half-length portrait|coat

half-life /ˈ··/ n the time it takes for half the atoms in a RADI-OACTIVE substance to decay

half-light /ˈ··/ n [(the) U] a dull greyish light like the light at sunset or in a badly-lit room

half-mast /ˌ·ˈ·/ n [U] **1** a point near the middle of a flag-pole where the flag flies as a sign of sorrow, esp. when an important political leader has died: *All the flags were at half-mast when the king died.* **2 (at) half-mast** *humor. esp. BrE* (of full-length trousers) too short, so that the ankles can be seen

half mea·sures /ˈ·ˌ··/ n [P] actions or methods that are not firm or effective enough to deal with a difficult situation: *If we want to stop drug addiction it's no use trying half measures.*

half moon /ˌ·ˈ·/ n **1** the shape of the moon seen when half the side facing the Earth is showing **2** something of this shape —compare FULL MOON, NEW MOON

half note /ˈ··/ n *AmE for* MINIM —see picture at NOTATION

Hal·fords /ˈhælfədz‖-fərdz/ one of a group of British shops which sell articles connected with cars and bicycles

half·pence /ˈheɪpəns/ n [P] **1** pl. of HALFPENNY[1,2] **2** a small amount of money: *It only costs* **a few halfpence.** —see also THREE-HALFPENCE

half·penny /ˈheɪpni/ n **halfpennies** or **halfpence 1** (in Britain in the past) a very small BRONZE coin, two of which made a PENNY; ½p **2 not have two halfpennies to rub together** *BrE infml* to be very poor

half·penny·worth /ˈheɪpniwəθ, ˌhɑːfˈpenəθ‖ˈheɪpəniwɔrθ/ also **hap'orth**– n **halfpennyworth** [(of)] *old-fash BrE* **1** [C] an amount of something bought for a HALFPENNY[2]: *three halfpennyworth of sweets* **2** [S] a small amount: *If he had a halfpennyworth of sense, he'd accept their offer.*

half-pint /ˈ··/ n **1** a measure for liquids that is half of a PINT: *The recipe requires a half-pint of milk.* **2** *infml* a short or small person, esp. one who is considered unimportant: *A half-pint like your little brother won't be of any use in our team.*

half-sis·ter /ˈ·ˌ··/ n a sister related through one parent only

half term /ˌ·ˈ··/ n [U] (in Britain) a short holiday, usu. two or three days, in the middle of a school TERM

half-tim·bered /ˌ·ˈ··◂/ adj of an old style of house building with the wood of the frame showing in the walls, esp. the outer walls

half time /ˌ·ˈ·◂‖ˈ··/ n [U] the short period of rest between two parts of a game, such as a football match: *The referee blew his whistle for half time.* | *They were leading by two goals at half time.* —see also FULL TIME

half·tone /ˌhɑːfˈtəʊn◂‖ˈhæftəʊn/ n **1** [U] the method of printing) a picture made from a black-and-white photograph, with varying shades shown by dots **2** [C] also **half step**– *AmE for* SEMITONE

half-truth /ˈ··/ n *derog* or *euph* a statement that is only partly true or is nearly a lie: *His replies were full of evasions and half-truths.*

half vol·ley /ˌ·ˈ··/ n **1** (esp. in tennis) a stroke in which the ball is hit as it BOUNCES **2** (in cricket) a ball that can easily be hit by the BATSMAN as it bounces

half·way /ˌhɑːfˈweɪ◂‖ˌhæf-/ adj, adv **1** at the middle point between two things: *The runners reached the halfway mark in the race after 49 seconds.* [+adv/prep] *Oxford is halfway between London and Stratford-on-Avon.* | *I was halfway to the office when I realized I'd forgotten my briefcase.* | *She'd got halfway through the book by lunchtime.* **2** by a small or incomplete amount: *These government measures only go halfway towards solving the problem.* —see also **meet someone halfway** (MEET[1])

halfway house /ˌ··ˈ·◂/ n **1** [S (**between**)] something that is halfway between two other things, and loses some of the qualities of both: *It's not really a history and it's not really a guidebook – it's a sort of halfway house.* **2** [C] a home for former prisoners, MENTAL PATIENTS, etc. who can stay for a limited time to get used to life outside prison, hospital, etc.

half-wit /ˈ··/ n *derog* a weak-minded or stupid person – **~ted** /ˌ·ˈ··◂/ – **tedly** /ˌ·ˈ··/ *adv*

hal·i·but /ˈhæliꞵət/ n **-but** or **-buts** a very large flat sea fish used as food

Hal·i·fax /ˈhæliꞵæks/ **1** a town in W Yorkshire, N England, known, esp. in the past, for its wool industry **2** a port

in Nova Scotia, SE Canada, on the Atlantic coast

Halifax [*the*] a British BUILDING SOCIETY, branches of which are found in many towns and cities in Britain

hal·i·to·sis /ˌhæliꞵˈtəʊsɪs/ n [U] a condition in which the breath from the mouth smells bad; a more formal word for bad breath

hall /hɔːl/ n **1** also **hallway** *esp. AmE*– the passage just inside the entrance of a house, from which the other rooms and usu. the stairs are reached: *Hang your coat up in the hall.* **2** also **hallway** *AmE* a CORRIDOR in a house or other building **3** a large room in which meetings, dances, etc., can be held –see also CITY HALL, TOWN HALL **4** (in a college or university) **a** *esp. BrE* the room where all the members eat together: *to dine in hall* **b** a HALL OF RESIDENCE: *Do you live* **in hall** *or in lodgings?* – see also MUSIC HALL

Hal·lé /ˈhæleɪ/, **Sir Charles** (1819–95) a German PIANIST and CONDUCTOR who came to live in Britain and set up the **Hallé Orchestra** in Manchester (1857)

hal·le·lu·ja /ˌhæliˈluːjə◂/ also **alleluia**– *interj, n* (a song, shout, etc., that is an expression of) praise, joy, and thanks to God

Hallelujah Cho·rus /ˌ··ˈ·ˌ··/ [*the*] a joyful part of the *Messiah*, a long piece of religious music with singing, written in the 18th century by Handel

Hal·ley's com·et /ˌhæliz ˈkɒmꞵt, ˌheɪl-‖-ˈkɑː-/ a bright COMET that moves around the sun in a period of about 76 years (named after Edmund Halley (1656–1742), an English ASTRONOMER (=person who studies the stars))

hal·liard /ˈhæljəd‖-jərd/ n a HALYARD

hall·mark[1] /ˈhɔːlmɑːk‖-mɑːrk/ n **1** a mark made on objects of precious metal to prove that they are silver or gold **2** [(of)] a particular quality, way of behaving, etc. that is very typical of a certain person or thing: *Clear expression is the hallmark of good writing.* | *This fascination with small details is one of the hallmarks of her painting.*

hallmark[2] v [T] to mark with a hallmark: *hallmarked silver*

hal·lo /həˈləʊ, he-, hæ-/ *interj, n* **-los** *BrE for* HELLO

Hall of Fame /ˌ··ˈ·/ n **Halls of Fame** *AmE* **1** a group of people considered to have achieved greatness in a particular sport or activity: *He's in the baseball Hall of Fame.* **2** a building where the lives and achievements of such a group of people are recorded: *Be sure to visit the Country Music Hall of Fame.*

hall of res·i·dence /ˌ··ˈ···/ also **hall** *BrE* ‖ **dormitory** *AmE*– n a building belonging to a college or university where many students live and sleep

hal·low /ˈhæləʊ/ v [T *often pass.*] **1** *fml* to set apart as holy: *Murderers were not buried in* **hallowed ground. 2 Hallowed be thy name** a phrase from the LORD'S PRAYER

Hal·low·een‖ **Hallowe'en** *AmE* /ˌhæləʊˈiːn◂/ the night of October 31, when it was formerly believed that the spirits of the dead appeared

▶ CULTURAL NOTE Hallowe'en is celebrated by children in both Britain and the US. They dress up as WITCHes, GHOSTs, etc. and sometimes make lamps from hollowed-out PUMPKINs. Esp. in the US, children go out in groups and knock on people's doors, where they are expected by most people. The children call out "trick or treat!" and the person at the door gives each child a treat, usu. a sweet. Children and older people often have Hallowe'en parties, where they play games, e.g. trying to catch floating apples with their teeth. ◀

hal·lu·ci·nate /həˈluːsɪneɪt/ v [I] to see things or experience things which are not real: *As soon as the drug took effect, she started hallucinating.*

hal·lu·ci·na·tion /həˌluːsɪˈneɪʃən/ n [C;U] (the experience of seeing or feeling) something that is imagined although it is not really there, often as the result of a drug or an illness of the mind

hal·lu·ci·na·to·ry /həˈluːsɪnətəri‖-tɔːri/ adj *fml* causing or like a hallucination: *a hallucinatory image/experience*

hal·lu·ci·no·gen·ic /həˌluːsɪnəˈdʒenɪk◂/ adj causing hallucination: *hallucinogenic drugs*

hall·way /ˈhɔːlweɪ/ n esp. AmE for HALL (1)

ha·lo /ˈheɪləʊ/ n **-loes** or **-los 1** a golden circle representing light around the heads of holy people (SAINTs) in religious paintings **2** a bright circle of light, such as that seen around the sun or moon in misty weather

Hals /hæls ‖ hɑːls/, **Frans** /fræns ‖ frɑːns/ (?1580–1666) a Dutch painter known for his PORTRAITS, esp. the *Laughing Cavalier* —see colour picture on page 1016

halt¹ /hɔːlt/ v [I;T] *rather fml* to (cause to) stop: *"Halt! Who goes there?" shouted the sentry.* | *The train was halted by work on the line.* | *government measures designed to halt the decline in our car industry.*

halt² n **1** [S] a stop or pause: *The car came to a halt just in time to prevent an accident.* | *Production was* **brought to a halt** *by an unofficial strike.* | *It's about time we* **called a halt** (=stopped) *all this senseless arguing.* **2** [C] BrE a small country railway station without proper buildings: *country halts*

halt³ n [the+P] *old use* people who cannot walk properly; those who are LAME

hal·ter /ˈhɔːltəʳ/ n **1** a rope or leather band fastened round a horse's head, esp. to lead it **2** an upper garment for women that is tied behind the neck and across the back, leaving the arms and back uncovered **3** *old use or lit* a piece of rope for hanging criminals

hal·ter·neck /ˈhɔːltənek‖-tər-/ adj, n [A;C] (a garment, esp. a dress) that leaves the wearer's back and arms uncovered and is held in place by a narrow band of material that is tied behind the neck

halt·ing /ˈhɔːltɪŋ/ adj stopping and starting as if uncertain: *a halting voice* | *halting steps* —~ly adv

halve /hɑːv‖hæv/ v [T] **1** to reduce by half: *By introducing robots we've managed to halve the time it takes to assemble a car.* **2** to divide into halves: *to halve an apple*

halves /hɑːvz‖hævz/ pl. of HALF

hal·yard, **halliard** /ˈhæljəd‖-jərd/ n tech a rope used to raise or lower a flag or sail

ham¹ /hæm/ n **1** [C;U] (meat from) the upper part of a pig's leg preserved with salt or smoke for use as food: *two slices of ham* | *ham and eggs for breakfast* | *a ham sandwich* | *two whole hams* —compare BACON, GAMMON; see MEAT (USAGE) **2** [C] the upper part of the leg **3** [C] an actor whose acting is unnatural, esp. with too much movement and expression: *a ham actor* **4** [C] someone who receives and sends radio messages using their own apparatus: *a radio ham*

ham² v **-mm-** [I;T (UP)] to perform or tell unnaturally or wildly, like a ham actor: *It was a good script but they spoiled it by* **hamming it up.**

ham·burg·er /ˈhæmbɜːgəʳ‖-ɜːr-/ also **burger**— n **1** [C] a flat round cake of finely cut BEEF, cooked and eaten in a round bread ROLL¹ (2) **2** [U] AmE for MINCE² (1)

ham-fist·ed /ˌ· ˈ··◂/ also **ham-hand·ed**— adj infml derog awkward in using the hands; CLUMSY: (fig.) *the government's ham-fisted approach to dealing with the strike*

Ham·il·ton /ˈhæmʒltən/, **Al·ex·an·der** /ˌælɪgˈzɑːndəʳ‖ˈzæn ɪ/ (1755?–1804) one of the first politicians of the US, whose ideas influenced the Constitution. His picture is on the American 10-dollar BILL¹ (3).

ham·let /ˈhæmlʒt/ n a small village

Hamlet one of the most famous plays written by William Shakespeare. The chief character, Prince Hamlet of Denmark, is often taken as an example of a thoughtful, sad, self-questioning person. He is often pictured holding a SKULL. There are many well-known phrases from the play, but the most famous are "To be or not to be, that is the question" and "Alas, poor Yorick". —see also OPHELIA, YORICK; see picture at Laurence OLIVIER and see colour picture on page 1146

ham·mer¹ /ˈhæməʳ/ n **1** a tool with a heavy metal head for forcing nails into wood, or for striking things to break them or move them **2** a part of a machine or instrument made to hit another part, e.g. in a piano or gun —see picture at GUN **3** tech one of the bones in the ear **4** be/go at it hammer and tongs BrE infml **a** with great force **b** (of two or more people) to fight or argue very hard **5** come under the hammer to be offered for sale at an AUCTION: *Her art collection came under the hammer yesterday.* **6** throwing the hammer a sport in which competitors throw a metal ball fixed to a handle as far as possible

hammer² v **1** [I;T+obj+adv/prep] to use a hammer on (something), esp. so as to force it into a desired position: *I wish they'd stop hammering.* | *Hammer the nails in.* | *Hammer the nail into the wall.* | *The back of the car got*

dented *and I'm trying to hammer it back into shape.* **2** [I (AWAY, at);T] to hit repeatedly: *The police hammered at the door.* **3** [T] infml to defeat beyond any doubt, by fighting or in a game: *We really hammered the other team/gave them a real hammering.* **4** [I (AWAY, at)] to keep working at something: *I hammered away at the problem all afternoon.*

hammer sthg. ↔ **in** phr v [T] to force understanding of (something) by repeating: *The teacher has been trying to hammer in the facts.* | *I've been trying to hammer into them the importance of writing clearly.*

hammer out phr v [T] **1** (**hammer out** sthg.) to talk about in detail and come to a decision about: *We've got to get together and try to hammer out a solution.* **2** (**hammer** sthg. ↔ **out**) to remove by hammering: *Can you hammer out the dent in the side of my car?*

Hammer, Ar·mand /ˈɑːmənd‖ˈɑːr-/ (1899–1990) an American businessman who had strong trade connections with the former Soviet Union

hammer and sick·le /ˌ··· · ˈ··/ [the] the sign of a hammer crossing a SICKLE, used as a representation of COMMUNISM: *For how much longer will the hammer and sickle* (=the flag of the former USSR) *fly over the republics?*

Hammer House of Hor·ror /ˌ··· · · ˈ··/ [the] a name for the set of HORROR FILMS produced by a film company called Hammer Film Productions during the 1950s and 60s

Ham·mer·smith and Ful·ham /ˌhæməsmɪθ ənd ˈfʊləm‖ˌhæmər-/ a BOROUGH in W London

Ham·mer·stein /ˈhæməstaɪn‖-mər-/, **Oscar** (1895–1960) an American songwriter who is famous for his work with Richard Rogers on MUSICALS such as *South Pacific* and *The Sound of Music*

ham·mock /ˈhæmək/ n a long piece of strong cloth or net which can be hung up by the ends to sleep in

Hamp·den Park /ˌhæmdən ˈpɑːk‖-ˈpɑːrk/ a football STADIUM in Glasgow where the Scottish Cup Final is played

ham·per¹ /ˈhæmpəʳ/ v [T] to cause difficulty in movement or activity: *The search was hampered by appalling weather conditions.*

hamper² n **1** esp BrE a large basket with a lid, often used for carrying food: *a picnic hamper* **2** AmE for LAUNDRY BASKET

Hamp·shire /ˈhæmpʃəʳ/ a COUNTY of S England, bordering on the English Channel

Hamp·stead /ˈhæmpstʒd, -sted/ an area of N London, about five miles NW of the City. Hampstead is an expensive place to live and is considered a desirable area.

Hamp·ton /ˈhæmptən/, **Li·o·nel** /ˈlaɪənəl/ (1913–) an American JAZZ musician, singer, and bandleader who played the piano, drums, and VIBRAPHONE and was known for his exciting, lively performances

Hamp·ton Court /ˌ·· ˈ·/ a large house in SW London, begun by Cardinal Wolsey in 1514 but taken over by King Henry VIII and used as a royal palace until the 18th century

ham·ster /ˈhæmstəʳ/ n a small animal with pockets (POUCHes) in its cheeks for storing food, kept as a pet

ham·string¹ /ˈhæmˌstrɪŋ/ v **-strung** /ˌstrʌŋ/ [T] to make (a person or group) ineffective or powerless; CRIPPLE² (2): *a government hamstrung by lack of funds*

hamstring² n a cordlike TENDON at the back of the leg, joining a muscle to a bone

Han·cock /ˈhænkɒk‖-kɑːk/, **John** (1737–93) an American leader in the American Revolutionary War, remembered most for being the first to sign the Declaration of Independence. He was later the first governor of the state of Massachusetts. —see also JOHN HANCOCK

Hancock, Tony (1924–1968) a British COMEDIAN, famous esp. for his show called *Hancock's Half Hour* on radio and television

hand¹ /hænd/ n **1** [C] either of the movable parts at the end of a person's arm, including the fingers: *She had a gun in her hand.* (=she was holding a gun) | *I've got a nasty cut in/on my left hand.* | *I held it in the palm of my hand.* | *The two lovers were holding hands (with each other).* | *He led the child by the hand.* | *She's very* **good with her hands.** (=good at making things, mending things, etc.) | *Wait until I* **get my hands on** *him!* (=catch him) | (fig.) *I can't do it today — I've* **got my hands full.**

hand

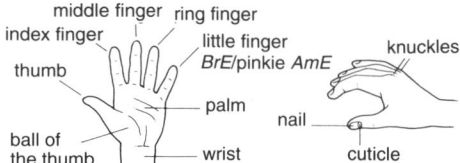

middle finger   ring finger
index finger   little finger
thumb   BrE/pinkie AmE   knuckles
palm
nail
ball of   wrist   cuticle
the thumb

(=I'm very busy) | (fig.) *He asked for her hand in marriage.* (=asked to marry her) | (fig.) *That child needs a firm hand!* (=should be firmly controlled) **2** [C] a pointer or needle on a clock, machine, or measuring instrument: *the second/minute/hour hand* | *the big/little hand* (=children's phrases for the hour/minute hand of a clock) **3** [S] handwriting: *He wrote in a neat hand.* **4** [C] **a** a set of playing cards held by one person in a game: *a good hand* | *a winning hand* **b** a game of cards: *a couple of hands of poker* **5** [C] a unit equal to 0.1 metres, used in measuring a horse's height at the shoulder **6** [C] a sailor on a ship: *All hands on deck!* (=a call for all sailors to come up to deal with some trouble) **7** [C] (*usu. in comb.*) a worker: *a factory hand* | *a farmhand* | (*AmE*) *a hired hand on a farm* **8** [C] someone with skill, knowledge, or experience of the stated kind: *BrE I'm* **a dab hand** (=very skilled) *at making pastry.* | *You don't need to tell her how to do it – she's* **an old hand** at *this sort of work.* | *an old China hand who'd lived there and knew it well* **9** [S] encouragement given by clapping (CLAP¹) the hands; a burst of APPLAUSE: *Let's give the singer a big hand!* **10** [S] help (esp. in the phrase **give/lend a hand to**): *Could you give me a hand with this heavy table, please?* **11** [S (**in**)] an influence or share in some action or event: *I suspect John had a hand in this.* | *Some observers detected the hand of the Americans in the coup.* (=believed that they influenced or took part in it) **12** [C *usu. pl.;*U] control, power, or responsibility: *The meeting is* **getting out of hand** – *will everybody stop talking at once!* | *The whole affair is now in the hands of the police.* (=they are responsible for dealing with it) | *I've got a lot more free time now that the children are* **off my hands.** (=I'm no longer responsible for them) | *Several of the border villages have* **fallen into enemy hands.** (=been taken by the enemy). – compare **out of hand** (HAND¹ (32)) **13 at first hand** by direct personal experience, or that of another person: *I heard about it at first hand from my neighbour.* | *He's one of the few Westerners who has experienced conditions there at first hand.* –see also FIRSTHAND **14 at hand** *rather fml* near in time or place: *The great day is at hand.* **15 at second/third/fourth hand** when passed on through one, two, or three people: *I heard it (at) second hand, when his father, who saw the fire, told my mother, who told me.* – see also SECOND-HAND **16 at someone's hands** from or because of someone: *They suffered terribly at the hands of the invaders.* **17 bite the hand that feeds you** *infml* to do something to upset or hurt a person you depend on for money, e.g. your employer **18 by hand: a** by a person, not a machine: *written by hand, not typed or printed* **b** delivered directly from one person to another, not sent through the post **19 (from) hand to mouth** with only just enough money to live on and nothing for the future: *living from hand to mouth* | *a hand-to-mouth existence* **20 give someone a free hand** to allow someone to do things in their own way: *The new director has been given a free hand to reorganize the company.* **21 hand in glove (with)** closely connected or working together (with someone), esp. in something bad **22 hand in hand: a** holding each other's hand (usu. with the left hand of one in the right hand of the other), esp. to show love **b** happening together and closely connected: *Dirt and disease go hand in hand.* | *Dirt goes hand in hand with disease.* **23 hand over fist** *infml* very quickly and in large amounts: *making money hand over fist* **24 in hand** ready or able to be used or done:*money in hand* | *Don't worry: we've still got three days in hand before the work is due.* –compare **take/have in** (HAND¹ (33)) **25 in good, safe, etc. hands** under someone's good, safe etc. protection or responsibility: *Don't worry about the children – they're in good hands.* | *We left the project in the capable hands of our deputy manager.* **26 keep one's hand in** to keep one's skill in something by continuing

to practise it **27 many hands make light work** *saying* if many people work together, they can do a job quickly **28 not do a hand's turn** *BrE infml derog* to do no work **29 on every hand** *lit* in all directions; all around **30 on hand** ready for use or ready when needed: *The nurse will be on hand if you need her.* **31 on the one/other hand** (used for comparing different things or ideas) as one point in the argument/as an opposite point: *I know this job of mine isn't well paid, but on the other hand I don't have to work long hours.* –see CONTRARY (USAGE) **32 out of hand** (esp. of decisions not to do something) at once and without any further thought: *I refused their offer out of hand.* –compare **getting out of hand** (HAND¹ (12)) **33 take/have in hand** to bring/have under control: *We have the matter (well) in hand.* | *These young offenders must be taken in hand.* – compare **in hand** (HAND¹ (24)) **34 (tie/bind someone) hand and foot** (to tie) both the hands and feet of: *The prisoners were tied hand and foot.* | (fig.) *We're bound hand and foot by all the safety regulations.* (=we are unable to act freely) **35 to hand** within reach **36 turn one's hand to** to (have the ability to) practise (a skill): *He can turn his hand to any kind of manual work.* **37 -handed** /hændɪd/ **a** having a hand or hands of the stated kind or number **b** using the stated hand or number of hands: *right-handed* | *serving left-handed* | *Is left-handedness inherited?* | *a one-handed catch* –see also RED-HANDED, SINGLE HANDED **38 -hander** /hændəʳ/someone using the stated hand: *The players are both left-handers.* –see also FREE HAND, HANDS OFF, HANDS-ON, OLD HAND, SECOND-HAND, **force someone's hand** (FORCE²), **overplay one's hand** (OVERPLAY (2)), **wash one's hands of** (WASH¹), **win hands down** (WIN¹)

hand² *v* [T] **1** to give from one's own hand into someone else's: [+*obj*+*adv/prep*] *Will you hand it back when you've finished with it?* | *I handed round the box of chocolates.* (=offered them to everyone) | *She handed her ticket to the ticket-collector.* [+*obj(i)*+*obj(d)*] *Hand me that book, please.* | *Will you hand me down that box from the shelf, please?* **2 (have to) hand it to someone** to (have to) admit someone's success, esp. in the stated activity: *You've got to hand it to him, he's a good talker.*

hand down *phr v* [T (**to**)] **1** [*often pass.*] (**hand** sthg. ↔ **down**) to give or leave to people who are younger or live after: *This ring has been handed down in my family for generations.* –see also HAND-ME-DOWN **2** (**hand down** sthg.) (of a person or group in a position of power) to declare publicly and officially: *The board of directors will hand down its decision on Monday.* | *The judge handed down heavy sentences to the rioters.* –compare INHERIT

hand sthg. ↔ **in** *phr v* [T] to deliver; give by hand: *Please hand in your papers at the end of the exam.*

hand sthg. ↔ **on** *phr v* [T (**to**)] **1** to give from one person to another (esp. something that can be used by many people one after the other): *Please read this leaflet and hand it on.* **2** to HAND **down** (1)

hand sthg. ↔ **out** *phr v* [T (**to**)] to give to each member of a group of people; DISTRIBUTE: *Hand out the pencils (to everyone in the class).* | (fig.) *He's very good at handing out advice!* (=he gives it too freely) –see also HANDOUT

hand over *phr v* **1** [T (**to**)] (**hand** sbdy./sthg. ↔ **over**) to give into someone else's care or control: *The thief was handed over to the police.* | *I know you've got it – now hand it over!* **2** [I;T (=**hand** sthg. ↔ **over**)] to give (power, responsibility, or control of something) to someone else: *The captain was unwilling to hand over the command of his ship (to a younger man).* | *The old government will hand over (power) to its successors next week.* –see also HANDOVER

hand·bag¹ /ˈhændbæg/ also **purse, pocketbook** *AmE– n* a small bag, esp. one used by a woman to carry her money and personal things. People sometimes make jokes about women hitting people with their handbags if they are angry. –see picture at PURSE

handbag² *v* to attack, usu. used to describe a woman, esp. a politician, who makes a verbal attack on somebody

hand·ball /ˈhændbɔːl/ also **racketball**– *n* [U] **1** a game played in the US usu. by two or four players, where a ball (a **handball**) is hit against a wall by the hand –compare FIVES **2** (in football) the offence of touching the ball with one's hand

hand·bill /ˈhændˌbɪl/ n a small printed notice or advertisement to be given out by hand

hand·book /ˈhændbʊk/ n a short book giving all the most important information about a subject: *a handbook of roadsigns* | *a tourist handbook* —compare MANUAL[2]

hand·brake /ˈhændbreɪk/ n an apparatus (BRAKE) that stops a vehicle, worked by the driver's hand, not by the foot —see picture at CAR

handbrake turn /ˈ·· ˌ·/ n BrE the action of making a car turn to one side suddenly by putting on the handbrake when the car is moving quickly, making the back wheels SKID. Handbrake turns are dangerous and are typically done by HOTTERS (=young people who steal cars and drive them fast).

hand·car /ˈhændkɑːʳ/ n AmE a railway vehicle operated by large handles pushed up and down which cause the wheels to turn

hand·cart /ˈhændkɑːt‖-kɑːrt/ n a small cart which can be pushed or pulled by hand

hand·clap /ˈhændklæp/ n a clapping (CLAP[1]) action of the hands —see also SLOW HANDCLAP

hand cream /ˈ· ·/ n [U] a substance which is rubbed into the hands to keep them soft and to prevent the skin from cracking

hand·cuff /ˈhændkʌf/ v [T] to put handcuffs on (someone)

hand·cuffs /ˈhændkʌfs/ n [P] a pair of metal rings joined together by a short chain and fastened with a key, for holding together the wrists of a prisoner

Han·del /ˈhændl/, **George Fred·e·rick** /dʒɔːdʒ ˈfredərɪk‖ dʒɔːrdʒ-/ (1685–1759) a British COMPOSER, born in Germany, noted for his ORATORIOs, such as the *Messiah*, and his ORCHESTRAL music, particularly his *Water Music* and *Music for the Royal Fireworks*

hand·ful /ˈhændfʊl/ n 1 [C (**of**)] an amount which is as much as can easily be held in the hand: *a handful of nuts/of small change* 2 [C (**of**)] a small number (of people): *We invited 30 people, but only a handful (of them) came.* 3 [S] infml a person or thing that is so active that it is difficult to control: *That child is quite a handful/Those children are quite a handful.*

hand·gun /ˈhændgʌn/ n esp. AmE a small gun held in one hand while firing, not raised against the shoulder; a PISTOL —compare RIFLE

hand·i·cap[1] /ˈhændɪkæp/ n 1 **a** a disability of the body or mind that causes a person serious difficulty: *Blindness is a great handicap.* **b** any condition or situation likely to cause disadvantage or difficulty: *Not being able to drive is quite a handicap if you live in the country.* 2 (in a race or other sport or game) a disadvantage given to the stronger competitors, such as carrying more weight or starting from a worse position: *He has a handicap of 100 metres.* (=He starts 100 metres behind slower runners.) | *a three-stroke handicap in golf*

handicap[2] v **-pp-** [T] 1 (of a quality or situation) to cause (someone) to have a disadvantage: *We were handicapped by lack of money.* 2 [usu. pass.] (of a physical or MENTAL disability) to prevent (someone) from acting and living as most people do

hand·i·capped /ˈhændɪkæpt/ adj having a disability of the body or mind: *physically handicapped* [also n, the+P] *a special school for the mentally handicapped* (=for people who are mentally handicapped)

hand·i·craft /ˈhændɪkrɑːft‖-kræft/ also **craft** n [usu. pl.] a skill needing careful use of the hands, such as sewing, weaving, making baskets, etc.

hand·i·work /ˈhændɪwɜːk‖-wɜːrk/ n [U] 1 work demanding the skilful use of the hands: *an exhibition of handiwork by the schoolchildren* 2 the result, esp. the undesirable result, of someone's action or efforts: *This explosion looks like the handiwork of terrorists.*

hand job /ˈ· ·/ n taboo sl an act of MASTURBATION, esp. when performed on another person

hand·ker·chief /ˈhæŋkətʃʃf‖-kər-/ **-chiefs** or **chieves** /tʃiːvz/ n a piece of cloth or thin soft paper for drying the nose, eyes, etc.: *a paper handkerchief*

▶ CULTURAL NOTE There is a well-known STEREOTYPE of an older British man wearing a handkerchief, knotted at each corner, to protect his head from the sun when he is on holiday. ◀

han·dle[1] /ˈhændl/ n 1 a part of an object which is specially made for holding it or for opening it: *a door handle* | *Pick up the typewriter case by the handle.* —see pictures at CAR, GUN, and TOOL 2 old-fash infml a title or a name, esp. one that sounds important 3 infml the call-sign of a CB user —see also **fly off the handle** (FLY[1])

handle[2] v 1 [T] **a** to pick up, touch, or feel with the hands: *Customers are asked not to handle the goods in the shop.* **b** to move by hand: *Glass — handle with care!* (a notice on a box) 2 [T] to deal with; control: *It was a difficult situation and he handled it very well.* | *She really knows how to handle a fast car!* 3 [T] to have responsibility for; be in charge of: *Ms Brown handles the company's accounts.* 4 [T] to treat; behave towards: *He's not a very good teacher — he doesn't know how to handle children.* 5 [T] to buy, sell, or deal with (goods or services) in business or trade: *We don't handle that sort of book.* | *The dockers refused to handle South African imports.* | *a handling charge* (=money charged for selling or dealing with goods) 6 [I+adv/prep] (of a car, boat, etc.) to obey controlling movements in the stated way: *The boat handles well, even in rough weather.*

handlebar mous·tache /ˌ·· ·ˈ·‖ˌ··· ˈ··/ n a long heavy MOUSTACHE which curves upwards at both ends. This kind of moustache was esp. popular with men in the British airforce in the Second World War.

handlebar moustache

han·dle·bars /ˈhændlbɑːz‖-bɑːrz/ n [P] the usu. curved bar above the front wheel of a bicycle or motorcycle, which controls the direction it goes in —see picture at BICYCLE

han·dler /ˈhændləʳ/ n a person who controls an animal: *a dog handler*

hand·loom /ˈhændluːm/ n a small machine (a LOOM) for weaving by hand

hand lug·gage /ˈ· ˌ··/ n [U] a traveller's light or small bags, cases, etc., which can be carried by hand: *You can take your hand luggage with you on the plane.*

hand·made /ˌhændˈmeɪd◂/ adj made by hand, not machine: *These shoes were expensive, but they're handmade.*

hand·maid·en /ˈhændˌmeɪdn/ also **hand·maid** /ˈhændmeɪd/— n old use a female servant

hand-me-down /ˈ· · ˌ·/ also **reach-me-down** BrE— n [usu. pl.] a garment used by one person after belonging to another usu. older person: *wearing my big brother's hand-me-downs* | *hand-me-down clothes*

hand·out /ˈhændaʊt/ n 1 something given free, such as food, clothes, etc., esp. to someone poor 2 information given out, e.g. to students attending a talk esp. in the form of a printed sheet: *Please read the handout carefully.* see also HAND **out**

hand·o·ver /ˈhændəʊvəʳ/ n an act of passing something, esp. power or responsibility, from one person or group to another; TRANSFER: *the handover of power to the new government* —see also HAND **over**

hand·picked /ˌhændˈpɪkt◂/ adj (esp. of a person or people) chosen with great care, usu. for a special purpose: *a handpicked audience* | *a squad of handpicked commandos*

hand·rail /ˈhændreɪl/ n a bar of wood or metal that is fixed beside a place where people walk for holding onto, esp. near stairs —compare BANISTER, RAILING

hands down /ˌ· ˈ·/ adv AmE easily; without effort: *The Bulls beat the Lakers hands down last night.*

hand·shake /ˈhændʃeɪk/ n 1 an act of taking each other's right hand when two people meet or leave each other. FREEMASONS are said to have a special kind of handshake, and this is sometimes mentioned in stories and jokes. — see also GOLDEN HANDSHAKE 2 the way a person does this: *I like a man with a firm handshake.*

hand·shak·ing /ˈhændʃeɪkɪŋ/ n [U] tech an exchange of signals between two pieces of electronic equipment, such as MODEMs, to see if they have a workable way of exchanging information

hands off /ˌ· ˈ·◂/ interj Don't touch: (fig.) *"Hands off the unions!" the strikers shouted.*

hands-off /ˈ· ·/ adj [A] letting other people act and make decisions, without trying to tell them what to do: *a hands-off management policy*

hand·some /ˈhænsəm/ adj **1 a** (esp. of men) good-looking; of attractive appearance **b** (esp. of women) strong-looking; attractive with a firm, large appearance rather than a delicate one —see BEAUTIFUL (USAGE); see also **tall, dark, and handsome** (TALL (3)) **2** large in quantity; PLENTIFUL: *a handsome reward* **3** generous: *a handsome gesture/contribution* — ~ly adv

handsome prince /ˌ·· ˈ·/ often caps. a character in fairy stories who sometimes changes from a FROG (=small green water animal) into a prince or breaks a SPELL, then marries the princess so that the story ends happily: *women who are tired of waiting for their handsome prince* —see also FROG PRINCE

hands-on /ˈ· ·/ adj [A] providing or being practical experience of something, esp. of using computers, rather than just information about it: *The computer course includes plenty of hands-on training.*

hand·stand /ˈhændstænd/ n a movement in which the legs are kicked into the air so that the body is upside down and supported on the hands

hands up /ˌ· ˈ·/ interj (used by gunmen) Put your arms above your head!

hand-to-hand /ˌ·· ˈ·◂/ adj,adv involving physical touching: *The soldiers were engaged in* **hand-to-hand** *combat* (=fighting without weapons).

hand tow·el /ˈ· ˌ··/ n a small TOWEL for drying one's hands

hand·writ·ing /ˈhændˌraɪtɪŋ/ n [U] **1** writing done by hand **2** the style or appearance of handwriting done by a particular person: *very clear handwriting*

hand·writ·ten /ˌhændˈrɪtn◂/ adj written by hand, not printed

hand·y /ˈhændi/ adj **1** useful and simple to use: *a handy little gadget for peeling potatoes* **2** [(with)] clever in using the hands: *handy with her needle* (=good at sewing) **3** [(for)] infml near; easily reached: *The shops are quite handy.* | *The house is quite handy for the shops.* | *Keep a pencil and paper handy.* **4 come in handy** to be useful: *A few more traveller's cheques may come in handy on holiday.* —ily adv —iness n [U]

Handy, W C (1873–1958) an American JAZZ musician thought to be the first to write BLUES music, known esp. for his song *St Louis Blues*

hand·y·man /ˈhændimæn/ n -men /men/ a person who does repairs and practical jobs well, esp. in the house

hang¹ /hæŋ/ v **hung** /hʌŋ/ **1** [T] to fix (something) at the top so that the lower part is free: *to hang curtains* | *Hang your coat (up) on the hook.* **2** [I+adv/prep] to be in such a position: *Her coat was hanging on the door.* | *They climbed up a rope that hung down from the roof.* **3** [I;T] (past tense & participle usu. **hanged**) to (cause to) die, esp. in punishment for a crime, by dropping with a rope around the neck: *The murderer was condemned to be hanged.* | *He hanged himself in a fit of remorse.* | *You'll hang for this!* **4** [T usu. pass.] to show (a painting) publicly: *His pictures were hung in the Museum of Modern Art.* **5** [T] **a** to fix (wallpaper) on a wall **b** to fix (a door) in position on HINGES **6** [I;T] **a** (of certain kinds of meat) to hang until ready to be eaten: *Let the pheasant hang for a few days.* **b** to cause (certain kinds of meat) to hang until ready to be eaten: *The flavour improves if you hang it for a few days.* **7** [I;T] old-fash infml (used to express annoyance or a wish that someone will suffer misfortune, esp. in the phrases **I'll be hanged, Hang it (all)!, Go hang!**): *I'll be hanged if I'll let you insult my wife!* | *He can go hang for all I care!* **8 hang by a thread** to be in great danger: *The sick man's life hung by a thread.* **9 hang fire** to be delayed in development; stop happening or continuing: *We're working very hard on the new house, so our plans for a holiday will have to hang fire for a time.* **10 hang in the balance** to be in an uncertain position in which things may end well or badly: *The government's future now hangs in the balance.* **11 hang in there** infml to remain brave or firm in spite of difficulties **12 hang one's head** to appear ashamed **13 hang up one's hat** infml to stop doing a habitual activity, esp. one's work: *At the age of 60, he hung up his hat and retired.* **14 One**

may as well be hanged for a sheep as a lamb infml One may as well do something very wrong if the punishment for something less serious is just as severe

hang about ‖ **hang around** AmE— phr v BrE infml **1** [I;T (=**hang about** sthg.)] also **hang around**— to wait or stay near (a place) without doing anything or with no clear purpose: *I hung about (the station) for an hour but he didn't come.* **2** [I] to delay or move slowly; DAWDLE: *Don't hang about, we have a train to catch!* | *Hang about* (=wait a minute) — *I'm nearly ready.*

hang back phr v [I] to be unwilling to speak, act, or move, esp. because of fear or lack of confidence: *The bridge looked so unsafe that we all hung back.* | *Don't hang back — go and introduce yourself to her.*

hang on phr v **1** [I (**to**)] to keep hold of something: *Hang on (to the strap): the bus is about to start.* **2** [I] to continue waiting: *I finish work at five but I'll hang on until half past to meet you.* | *(esp. BrE) I'm afraid the (telephone) line is engaged, would you like to hang on?* **3** [T] to continue in spite of difficulties; PERSEVERE: *I know you're tired, but try to hang on a bit longer.* **4** [T] (**hang on/upon** sthg.) to pay close attention to: *The boy admires his teacher and* **hangs on his every word. 5** [T no pass.] (**hang on** sthg.) to depend on: *The future of the company hangs on the outcome of this meeting.* [+wh] *Everything hangs on where they went next.*

hang onto sthg./sbdy. phr v [T] infml to try to keep: *We should hang onto the house and sell it later when prices are higher.*

hang out phr v [I+adv/prep] **1** infml to live or spend a lot of time in a particular place: *He hangs out in Green Street.* | *They normally hang out in the pub.* **2 let it all hang out** old-fash sl to behave exactly as you want to —see also HANGOUT

hang over sthg./sbdy. phr v (esp. of an unpleasant event) to be about to happen or seem likely to happen soon: *The prospect of defeat is now hanging over them.* | *The threat of war hung over Europe for 21 years.* | *With the exams* **hanging over her head**, *she can't sleep at nights.* —see also HANGOVER

hang together phr v [I] **1** to remain united: *"We must indeed all hang together, or ... we shall all hang* (=be hanged) *separately."* (Benjamin Franklin) **2** to form a whole in which the separate parts agree with each other; be CONSISTENT (2): *The witness's story just doesn't hang together, and I don't see how it can be true.*

hang up phr v [I] **1** [(**on**)] to finish a telephone conversation by putting the RECEIVER back: *It's a bad line; hang up and I'll call you back.* | *I was so angry I hung up on her.* (=while she was still talking) —see TELEPHONE (USAGE) **2** to hang (clothes) on a HANGER: *Would you please hang up your clothes?* **3 be hung up on/about** infml to be anxious or have a fixed idea about: *She's very hung up about being alone.* —see also HANG-UP

hang² n [the+S] **1** the shape or way something hangs: *I don't like the hang of this coat at the back.* **2 get/have the hang of something** infml to learn how to do something or use something, esp. when this needs skill: *Press this button when the light goes on — you'll soon get the hang of it.*

han·gar /ˈhæŋər/ n a big building where aircraft are kept between flights or when being built or repaired

hang·dog /ˈhæŋdɒg‖-dɔːg/ adj [A] (of an expression on the face) unhappy esp. because ashamed or sorry

hang·er /ˈhæŋər/ also **coat hanger**— n a frame with a hook and crosspiece which is put inside the shoulders of a dress, coat, etc., so that it can be hung up and will keep its shape

hanger-on /ˌ·· ˈ·/ n **hangers-on** usu. derog a person who tries to be friendly with another person or group, esp. for his or her own advantage: *The rock group arrived with all their hangers-on.*

hang glid·ing /ˈ· ˌ··/ n [U] the sport of gliding (GLIDE (2b)) using a large KITE (2) (a **hang glider**) instead of a plane

hang·ing¹ /ˈhæŋɪŋ/ n **1** [U] the punishment in which death is caused by hanging a person from a rope round the neck: *When was hanging abolished here?* **2** [C] a death of this type: *There have been no hangings in Britain for many years.*

hanging² adj [A] **1** connected with the punishment of people by hanging: *a hanging offence* (= crime punishable by death) | *a hanging judge* (= a severe judge in times past who often ordered people to be hanged) **2**

it's/that's no hanging matter *infml* the problem, or your mistake, is not as bad as you think it is

hang gliding

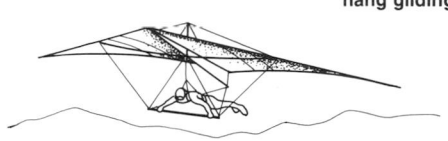

hang·ings /ˈhæŋɪŋz/ *n* [P] curtains and any other materials hanging over the walls, windows, doors, etc., of a house: *wall hangings*

hang·man /ˈhæŋmən/ *n* -**men** /mən/ the person whose work is hanging criminals

hang·nail /ˈhæŋneɪl/ *n* a piece of skin that has come loose near the bottom of the fingernail where it grows out from the skin

hang·out /ˈhæŋaʊt/ *n sl* a place that a person lives in or often visits: *one of my favourite hangouts* —see also HANG out

hang·o·ver /ˈhæŋəʊvəʳ/ *n* **1** the feeling of headache, sickness, etc., the day after drinking too much alcohol **2** [(**from**)] a condition or effect resulting from an earlier event or situation: *The licensing laws are a hangover from wartime.*

hang-up /ˈ· ·/ *n infml* something that a person gets unusually worried about, perhaps without good reason: *She's got a real hang-up about her appearance.* —see also HANG up (2)

han·ker /ˈhæŋkəʳ/ *v*
    hanker after/for sthg. *phr v* [T] *infml* to have a strong wish for (usu. something one cannot have); YEARN for: *He's lonely and hankers after friendship.*

han·ker·ing /ˈhæŋkərɪŋ/ *n* [(**for, after**)] *infml* a strong wish; LONGING: *a hankering after fame and wealth*

han·kie , -ky /ˈhæŋki/ *n infml* a handkerchief

hank·y-pank·y /ˌhæŋki ˈpæŋki/ *n* [U] *infml, often humor* cheating or deceit or sexually improper behaviour of a not very serious kind: *a bit of hanky-panky at the office party*

Han·ni·bal /ˈhænɪbəl/ (247–183 BC) a general who led the army of Carthage against the Romans between 218 and 201 BC. Hannibal is famous esp. for having crossed the Alps into Italy with around 35,000 men and 37 ELEPHANTS.

Ha·noi /hæˈnɔɪ/ the capital city of Vietnam, on the Red River

Han·o·ver /ˈhænəʊvəʳ/ a city in NW Germany, the capital city of Lower Saxony; German name **Hannover**

Han·o·ve·ri·an /ˌhænəʊˈvɪəriən/ *adj* of or supporting the line of English kings and queens which originally came from Hanover and ruled from 1714 to 1901: *George III was a Hanoverian king.*

Han·sard /ˈhænsɑːd‖-sərd/ the printed report of what is said and done in the British parliament: *Read about the debate in Hansard.* —compare CONGRESSIONAL RECORD

Han·se·at·ic League /ˌhænsiætɪk ˈliːg/ [*the*] a trade organization of German towns which existed from the 13th to the 17th centuries to protect each other against competition from abroad. Bremen, Hamburg, and Lübeck are still known as Hanseatic cities.

Han·sel and Gret·el /ˌhænsəl ənd ˈgretl/ the chief characters in the fairy story of that name by the Grimm Brothers. Hansel, a boy, and Gretel, a girl, are left alone in a forest. They discover a house made of GINGERBREAD and belonging to a wicked WITCH. The witch wants to eat the children, but Gretel pushes her into an OVEN and the children go home with her riches.

han·som /ˈhænsəm/ also **hansom cab** /ˈ·· ·, ˌ·· ˈ·/— *n* a two-wheeled horse-drawn carriage whose driver sits on a high outside seat at the back, used until early in the 20th century, usu. as a kind of taxi

Han·son Group /ˈhænsən ˌgruːp/ a British company dealing in industrial services, food products, etc. It was begun by Lord Hanson.

Ha·nuk·kah, Chanukah /ˈhɑːnʊkə‖ˈkɑːnəkə, ˈhɑː-/ an eight-day Jewish holiday marking an ancient victory in Israel, when Jewish children get presents

hap·haz·ard /ˌhæpˈhæzəd◂‖-ərd◂/ *adj* happening in an unplanned disorderly manner: *The town grew in a haphazard way.* —~**ly** *adv*

hap·less /ˈhæpləs/ *adj* [A] *poet* unlucky: *a hapless lover*

hap·ly /ˈhæpli/ *adv lit or old use* perhaps: *"Haply I may remember,/And haply may forget."* (Christina Rossetti)

hap·orth /ˈheɪpəθ‖-ərθ/ *n* **hap'orth** [(*of*)] *old-fash BrE* a HALFPENNYWORTH

hap·pen¹ /ˈhæpən/ *v* [I] **1** (of an event or situation) to come into existence, esp. without being planned; OCCUR: *What time did the accident happen?* | *No one knew who had fired the gun — it all happened so quickly.* | *I can't understand how this happened.* | *They keep saying inflation will fall soon, but it hasn't happened yet.* —see also HAPPEN to **2** to be the result of an event or course of action: *She pressed hard on the brake but nothing happened.* | *What would happen if your parents found out?* **3** to be or do as if by chance: [+*to-v*] *I happened to see her on my way to work.* | *If you happen to find it, please let me know.* [*it*+I+(*that*)] *It happened that they were out when we called.* | *They were out,* **as it happened.** | (used to show annoyance or to give force to a statement) *I happen to like her, so don't be so rude about her.* | *That happens to be my car you're leaning on.* | **It just so happens** *that you're wrong.*

▷ USAGE Compare **happen, occur,** and **take place.** Events usually **happen** or (more formal) **occur** by accident: *When did the explosion* **happen/occur?** Events usually **take place** by arrangement: *When will the wedding* **take place?**◁
    happen on/upon sbdy./sthg. *phr v* [T *no pass.*] to find or meet by chance: *I happened on an old country inn, and stopped to have a meal.*
    happen to sbdy./sthg. *phr v* [T *no pass.*] (of an event) to take place and have an effect on: *I wonder what's happened to Jane — she's two hours late.* | *Whatever happened to that singer you used to like so much?*

hap·pen² *adv NEngE* perhaps

hap·pen·ing /ˈhæpənɪŋ/ *n* **1** something that happens; an event **2** (esp. in the 1960s and early 1970s) an unprepared performance or other event that catches attention

hap·pi·ly /ˈhæpɪli/ *adv* **1** in a happy manner: *laughing happily* **2** fortunately: *Happily, the accident was not serious.*

hap·pi·ness /ˈhæpɪnəs/ *n* [U] the state of being happy

hap·py /ˈhæpi/ *adj* **1 a** feeling or showing pleasure and contentment: *a happy child/smile* | *The news made us all very happy.* [F+(*that*)/*to-v*] *I'm so happy that you could come!* | *You'll be happy to know that she's just had a baby girl.* **b** causing pleasure and contentment: *a happy marriage* | *one of the happiest days of my life* —opposite **unhappy** **2** [F (**about, with**)] feeling that something is right or good; satisfied: *The government won't be very happy about the latest unemployment statistics.* | *Are you happy with his work?* **3** [A] (of events) fortunate: *By a happy coincidence we were all booked in to the same hotel.* **4** *fml or lit* (of behaviour, thoughts, etc.) suitable; FELICITOUS: *His choice of words was not a happy one.* **5** [F+*to-v; no comp.*] willing; glad; not finding it difficult (to): *I'll be happy to meet him when I have some free time.* **6** [A *no comp.*] (used in wishes about events or occasions) full of pleasure and success (esp. in phrases like **Happy New Year, Happy Birthday**): *Happy Anniversary!* | *Happy Christmas!* —see also SLAPHAPPY, TRIGGER-HAPPY

Happy Days /ˌ·· ˈ·/ an American television SERIES for teenagers set in the 1950s. The central character is called Fonz —see also FONZ and see colour picture on page 686

Happy Days are Here A·gain /ˌ··· ˌ· ˌ· ˌ· ˈ·/ the title of a popular song of the 1930s, now used to say that a general situation is improving

Happy Eat·er /ˌ·· ˈ···/ *n* one of a group of restaurants placed beside roads and MOTORWAYS everywhere in Britain – compare LITTLE CHEF

happy e·vent /ˌ·· ·ˈ·/ *n BrE* the birth of a child

happy-go-luck·y /ˌ··· ··ˈ··◂/ *adj usu. not derog* (of people or their behaviour) showing a lack of careful thought or planning; tending not to worry; CAREFREE

happy hour /ˈ·· ˌ·/ *n infml* a limited period in a day when alcoholic drinks are sold at lower than the usual prices in a bar, PUB, etc.

happy me·di·um /ˌ·· ˈ···/ n [usu. sing.] a way of doing something that is halfway between two opposite ways that are possible: COMPROMISE: We try to **strike a happy medium** between working too hard and not working at all.

Haps·burg /ˈhæpsbɜːg‖-bɜːrg/ adj of or supporting a family of German princes that ruled in Austria from 1278 to 1918 and in Spain from 1516 to 1700; German name **Habsburg**

har·a·ki·r·i /ˌhærə ˈkɪri/ n [U] a way of ceremonially killing oneself by cutting open the stomach, formerly used in Japan by male members of the Samurai class

ha·rangue[1] /həˈræŋ/ n a loud or long speech, esp. one which blames those listening to it or tries to persuade them: The minister of propaganda delivered his usual harangue.

harangue[2] v [T] to attack or try to persuade with a long often loud and attacking speech: The teacher harangued us all about our untidy work. | I didn't come here to be harangued!

Ha·ra·re /həˈrɑːri/ the capital city of Zimbabwe, formerly called Salisbury

har·ass /ˈhærəs, həˈræs‖həˈræs, ˈhærəs/ v [T] **1** to make (someone) worried and unhappy by causing trouble, esp. on repeated occasions: a busy, harassed housewife | I feel rather harassed by all the pressures at the office. **2** to cause problems for by making repeated attacks against: Our soldiers harassed the enemy. ~ **ment** n [U] : a campaign against harassment of immigrants by the police — see also SEXUAL HARASSMENT

har·bin·ger /ˈhɑːbɪndʒəʳ‖ˈhɑːr-/ n [(of)] lit a person or thing showing that something is going to happen or is on its way: Daffodils are a harbinger of spring. —compare HERALD

har·bour[1] BrE ‖ **harbor** AmE /ˈhɑːbəʳ‖ˈhɑːr-/ n [C;U] an area of water by a coast which is sheltered from rougher waters so that ships are safe inside it

harbour[2] BrE ‖ **harbor** AmE v [T] **1** to give protection, esp. by giving food and shelter, to (something or someone bad) either on purpose or without knowing: Harbouring criminals is an offence in law. **2** to keep in the mind (thoughts or feelings, esp. when bad): He harbours a secret grudge against his father.

hard[1] /hɑːd‖hɑːrd/ adj **1** firm and stiff; difficult or impossible to break, press down, or bend: The snow has frozen hard. | The plate smashed as it fell on the hard floor. | This ice cream is as hard as rock. —opposite **soft** **2** difficult to do or understand: There were some hard questions on the exam paper. [+to-v] It's hard to know what he's really thinking. | He is a hard person to understand. —opposite **easy** **3 a** using force: I gave it a hard push/a hard kick. **b** needing force or effort of body or mind: hard work | (fig.) We must take a **long hard look** at this plan. (=examine it very carefully) **4** [A] putting great effort into the stated activity; DILIGENT: She's a hard worker. (=She works hard.) | John's **a hard drinker.** (=drinks a lot of alcohol) **5** full of difficulty and trouble; not pleasant: a hard life | The police gave me **a hard time.** (=hurt, annoyed, or threatened me) **6** [(on)] (of people, punishments, etc.) not gentle; showing no kindness; severe: You're a hard woman. | Don't be too hard on them. | I'm afraid I said some very hard things to her. | She drives a hard bargain. (=makes agreements to her own advantage but not necessarily to anyone else's) **7** (of seasons and weather) very cold; severe: a hard winter | a hard frost —opposite **mild** **8** not tech (in English pronunciation): **a** (of the letter c) pronounced as /k/ rather than /s/ **b** (of the letter g) pronounced as /g/ rather than /dʒ/: The letter "g" is hard in "get" and soft in "gentle". **9** (of water) containing minerals that prevent soap from mixing properly with the water —opposite **soft** **10** [A] (of a drug) considered dangerous and/or ADDICTIVE to users —opposite **soft** **11** [A] based on what is clearly true or can be proved: The police have several theories about the case, but no hard evidence. | Can linguistics ever be **a hard science** like physics? **12 be hard on** to wear (something) out easily or quickly: Children are very hard on their shoes. **13 do something the ˈhard way** to learn by difficult experience, not by being taught **14 take (some/a few) hard knocks** to have painful experiences, bad luck, difficulties, etc. —see also HARDLY; see HARDEN (USAGE) —**hardness** n [U]

hard[2] adv **1** using great and steady effort; in a STRENUOUS way: I tried so hard to please her. | You've been working much too hard. | I thought long and hard about the problem. | Listen hard and you might just hear it. | a hard-fought election campaign **2** strongly; heavily; in large amounts over a period of time: It's raining harder than ever. **3 be hard done by** to be unfairly treated: I felt hard done by when I got less money than anybody else, after I had worked twice as hard. **4 be hard hit (by)** to suffer loss because of (some event): The farmers were hard hit by the bad weather. **5 be hard put (to it) to** to have great difficulty (in doing something): We were hard put to find a replacement for our assistant. **6 (it) go(es) hard with someone** to be (an experience that is) difficult for someone to accept: It goes hard with him to be alone so often. **7 hard ˈat it** working with all one's force in some activity; working as hard as one can: I'm glad to see you're still hard at it! **8 hard on the heels of** close behind; very soon after: War came hard on the heels of the economic depression. **9 take (it) hard** to suffer deeply: Don't take it so hard: you'll feel better tomorrow. | She's taking her father's death very hard. —see also HARD BY, HARD UP, HARD UPON, **die hard** (DIE[1] (5)); see TRY (USAGE)

hard-and-fast /ˌ· · ˈ·◂/ adj (of rules) fixed and unchangeable

hard·back /ˈhɑːdbæk‖ˈhɑːrd-/ n a book with a strong stiff cover. Hardbacks are usu. more expensive than paperbacks (=books with thin cardboard covers): Is it available **in hardback**? —compare PAPERBACK

hard·ball /ˈhɑːdbɔːl‖ˈhɑːrd-/ n [U] AmE **1** BASEBALL rather than SOFTBALL **2 play hardball** infml to use methods that are not gentle and may even be unfair: He played political hardball to get a government job.

hard-bit·ten /ˌ· ˈ···◂/ adj (appearing) firm and strong, esp. when made like this by long and hard experience: a hard-bitten old soldier

hard·board /ˈhɑːdbɔːd‖ˈhɑːrdbɔːrd/ n [U] strong material made out of fine pieces of wood pressed into sheets and used in making things instead of e.g. a light wood

hard-boiled /ˌ· ˈ·◂/ adj **1** (of an egg) boiled until the yellow part is hard —compare SOFT-BOILED **2** infml (of a person) not showing feelings or influenced by feelings, esp. because of bitter experience

hard·bound /ˈhɑːdbaʊnd‖ˈhɑːrd-/ adj HARDCOVER

hard by /ˌ· ˈ·/ adv, prep esp. lit very near: The house stood hard by (the river).

hard can·dy /ˌ· ˈ···/ n [C;U] AmE a BOILED SWEET, or boiled sweets in general: They sell hard candy. | a dish of hard candies

hard cash /ˌ· ˈ·/ n [U] money in coins and notes; CASH: I offered to give him a cheque, but he demanded hard cash.

hard ci·der /ˌ· ˈ···/ n [C;U] AmE for alcoholic CIDER. Alcoholic cider cannot usu. be bought in the US, but freshly pressed apple juice which has naturally turned alcoholic, accidentally or otherwise, is called hard cider.

hard cop·y /ˈ· ˌ··/ n [U] tech readable information from a computer, esp. when printed on paper —compare SOFT COPY

hard core[1] /ˌ· ˈ·/ n **1** [S+sing./pl. v] (ˌ·ˈ·/) often derog the small central group that takes the most active part within a larger group or organization: The hard core of party activists make/makes all the decisions. **2** [U] (/ˈ·◂/) BrE the broken brick, stone, etc., used as a base when a road is built

hard-core[2] /ˌ· ˈ·◂/ adj [A] **1** often derog very strongly following a particular belief or activity, and unlikely to change: hard-core opposition to the government | a hard-core criminal type **2** showing or describing sexual activity in a very open and detailed way: hard-core pornography

hard·cov·er /ˈhɑːdˌkʌvəʳ‖ˈhɑːrd-/ also **hardbound**— adj (of a book) having a firm stiff cover (BINDING); being a HARDBACK

hard cur·ren·cy /ˌ· ˈ···/ n [C;U] money which is used in international trade, usu. because the country has a favourable BALANCE OF PAYMENTS and a steady EXCHANGE RATE

hard disk /ˌ· ˈ·/ n a piece of firm plastic with a coat of a MAGNETIC substance on which information for a computer can be stored. It can store much more information than a FLOPPY DISK —compare FLOPPY DISK

hard drink /ˌ· '·/ also **hard liquor**— *n* [U] strong drink which contains a lot of alcohol, such as WHISKY

Hard Ec·u /ˌ· '··/ [*the*] a standard unit of money which, it was planned, would be used in Europe in the future together with existing national money systems, until all Europe changed to using just one standard unit (the **ecu**)

hard·en /ˈhɑːdn‖ˈhɑːrdn/ *v* [I;T] **1** to make or become firm or stiff: *The snow hardened until ice was formed.* | *He hardened his hold on the door.* (=held it more tightly) **2** to make or become severe, unkind, or lacking in human feelings: *I hardened my heart against him.* | *Police described the man as a hardened criminal.* **3** to make or become stronger and more able to deal with difficulty, pain, etc: *Life in the mountains hardened me.* | *Opposition to the military government hardened after the massacre.*

▷ USAGE **Harden** means "to make or become hard", but should only be used when **hard** means "firm and stiff" or "unkind and severe": *Leave the wet cement to* **harden.** | *She* **hardened** *her heart.* In other cases use **get hard(er):** *The exercises in this book gradually get* **harder** (=become more difficult). | *Life is* **getting hard** *for people on low incomes.*◁

    harden sbdy. **to** sthg. *phr v* [T *usu. pass.*] to make (someone) more used to and less sensitive to (something unpleasant): *Dennis is becoming hardened to failure/to failing.*

hard feel·ings /ˌ· '··/ *n* **no hard feelings** (used to tell someone with whom you have quarrelled that you do not dislike them or feel anger towards them)

hard hat /ˈ· ·/ *n* **1** a protective hat made of hard material, esp. worn by workers who do building work —compare HELMET **2** *infml* a CONSTRUCTION worker

hard·head·ed /ˌhɑːdˈhedȷd‖ˌhɑːrd-/ *adj* **1** practical, firm, and thorough, esp. in business: *a hardheaded businesswoman/decision* **2** *esp. AmE* stupid or difficult to persuade

hard·heart·ed /ˌ· '··◁/ *adj* having no kind or sympathetic feelings; HARD¹ (6) —opposite **soft-hearted** — ~ **ly** *adv* — ~ **ness** *n* [U]

hard·hit·ting /ˌ· '··◁/ *adj* forceful and effective: *The magazine published a hard-hitting exposé of organized crime.*

har·di·ness /ˈhɑːdinȷs‖ˈhɑːr-/ *n* [U] the quality of being HARDY

Hard·ing /ˈhɑːdɪŋ‖ˈhɑːr-/, **Warren G** (1865–1923) the 29th president of the US (1921–23)

hard la·bour /ˌ· '··/ *n* [U] (a punishment which consists of) hard physical work such as digging or building. Hard labour has not been used in Britain since 1948: *He was sentenced to three years' hard labour.*

hard land·ing /ˌ· '··/ *n* a sudden fall after a period of economic increase

hard left /ˌ· '·◁/ *n* **1** [*the*] *BrE* people, esp. within a political party, whose views are considered to be very left-wing and who are seen as being very active and extreme in their ideas **2** [C] *esp. AmE* a sharp left-hand turn when travelling by car: *Go down this road and take a hard left at the traffic light.*

hard line /ˌ· '·◁/ *n* [S (**on**)] a firm unchanging opinion or plan of action, esp. one that is not influenced by points of view: *They're taking a hard line in the pay negotiation, and have refused to improve on their original offer.* — **hard-line** *adj* —**hard-liner** /ˌ· '··, ·· '··/ *n*

hard liq·uors /ˈ· ˌ··/ *n* [U] HARD DRINK

hard luck /ˌ· '·◁/ also **tough luck**, also **hard lines** *BrE*— *interj, n* [U] *infml* (sorry about your) bad luck: *You failed your exam? Hard luck!*

hard luck sto·ry /ˌ· '· ˌ··, ˌ·· '··/ *n infml, usu. derog* a story about one's misfortunes, typically told to a friend to get pity, help, or money: *Don't give me any of your hard luck stories.*

hard·ly /ˈhɑːdli‖ˈhɑːrdli/ *adv* **1** almost not; only with difficulty (often with **can** or **could**): *I can hardly wait to hear the news.* | *I could hardly speak for tears.* **2** almost not: *I hardly ever go out these days.* (=almost never) | *You've hardly eaten anything.* | *You've eaten hardly anything.* (=almost nothing) | *Hardly anyone* (=almost no

one) *likes him, because he's so bad-tempered.* —see NEVER (USAGE) **3** only just; not really: *I hardly know the people I work with.* | *We had hardly started/Hardly had we started* (=we had only just started) *when the car got a flat tyre.* —see USAGE **4** not at all; not reasonably: *This is hardly the time for buying new clothes — I've only got just enough money for food.* | *You can hardly blame me if you didn't like the place, as you were the one who begged me to take you there.*

▷ USAGE Compare **hardly, scarcely, barely,** and **no sooner. 1 Hardly, scarcely,** and **barely** are followed by *when*, but **no sooner** is followed by *than* in sentences like these: *The game had* **hardly/scarcely/barely** *begun when it started raining.* | *The game had* **no sooner** *begun than it started raining.* **2** When the sentence begins with any of these words the word order is changed like this: **Hardly/scarcely/barely** *had the game begun when it started raining.* | **No sooner** *had the game begun than it started raining.* **3 Hardly, scarcely,** and (less commonly) **barely** can be followed by *any* and *ever* to mean "almost no", and "almost never": *We've* **hardly/scarcely/barely** *any money left.* | *He's* **hardly/scarcely/barely** *ever late for work.* Sentences with **hardly, scarcely,** and **barely** can also contain *at all* to mean "almost not". *We* **hardly/scarcely/barely** *got wet at all.*◁

hard-nosed /ˌ· '·◁/ *adj infml* extremely determined, firm, and practical in behaviour, esp. in getting what one wants: *a hard-nosed, no-nonsense approach to business*

hard nut /ˌ· '·/ *n infml* a difficult thing/person to deal with (esp. in the phrase **a hard nut to crack**)

hard of hear·ing /ˌ· · '··/ *adj* [F] *euph* unable to hear properly; (rather) *infml* DEAF: *Could you speak up a bit, as my mother's rather hard of hearing?*

hard-on /ˈ· ·/ *n taboo sl for* ERECTION (3)

hard pal·ate /ˌ· '··/ *n* the bony front part of the top of the mouth —compare SOFT PALATE

hard porn /ˈ· ·/ *n* [U] *infml* books, films, etc. that are considered to be extremely PORNOGRAPHIC —compare SOFT PORN

hard-pressed /ˌ· '·◁/ *adj* [(**for**)] experiencing severe or continual difficulties: *a hard-pressed housewife* | *hard-pressed for cash* [F+to-v] *We'll be hard-pressed to finish on time.* (=It will be difficult for us to do so)

hard right /ˌ· '·◁/ *n* **1** [*the*] *BrE* people, esp. within a political party, whose views are considered to be very right-wing and who are seen as being very active and extreme in their ideas **2** [C] *esp. AmE* a sharp right-hand turn when travelling by car: *Go down this road and take a hard right.*

hard rock /ˌ· '·◁/ *n* a type of ROCK³ music, which has a strong beat, and fast, loud ELECTRIC GUITAR playing

Hard Rock Ca·fe /ˌ· · ' '·/ any of an international group of restaurants in big cities which are fashionable, esp. with young people, and where people often wait outside for a long time in order to get in

hard sauce /ˌ· '·/ *n AmE* a liquid mixture of butter and sugar, and sometimes cream and FLAVOURING, served on top of cakes, etc.

hard sell /ˌ· '·◁/ *n* [(**the**) S] the method of trying to sell something by putting repeated forceful pressure on buyers: *She gave me the hard sell and I ended up buying it.* | *hard-sell methods* —opposite **soft sell**

hard·ship /ˈhɑːdʃɪp‖ˈhɑːrd-/ *n* [C;U] (an example of) difficult conditions of life, such as lack of money, unemployment, etc.

hard shoul·der /ˌ· '··/ ‖ usu. **shoulder** *AmE*— *n esp. BrE* an area of ground beside a road, esp. a MOTORWAY, that has been given a hard surface where cars can stop if in difficulty, because stopping is not allowed on the road itself

hard tack /ˈ· ·/ *n* [U] SHIP BISCUIT

Hard Times /ˌ· '·/ a NOVEL by Charles Dickens about a very practical man, Thomas Gradgrind, who lives in an industrial city and spoils his children's lives because he only thinks about profits

hard·top /ˈhɑːdtɒp‖ˈhɑːrdtɑːp/ *n* a type of car with a metal roof which cannot be moved

hard up /ˌ· '·◁/ *adj* [F (**for**)] *infml* in need (of); not having enough (esp. money): *We were very hard up when I lost my job.* | *We're a bit hard up for new ideas.*

hard up·on /ˈ·· ·ˌ·/ also **hard on** /ˈ·· ·/— *prep esp. lit* **1** soon after **2** close behind: *He left, and I followed hard on his heels.* (=close behind him)

hard·ware /ˈhɑːdweəʳ‖ˈhɑːrd-/ *n* [U] **1** equipment and tools for the home and garden, such as pans, garden tools, etc. **2** *tech* the machinery which makes up a computer, as opposed to the systems that make it perform particular jobs —compare FIRMWARE, SOFTWARE **3** the physical equipment needed for the operation of any system: *military hardware such as tanks* | *tape recorders and other educational hardware*

hardware store /ˈ·· ·ˌ·/ also **ironmonger's** *BrE*— a shop that sells hardware (1)

hard·wear·ing /ˌhɑːdˈweərɪŋ◄‖ˌhɑːrd-/ *BrE* ‖ also **longwearing** *AmE*— *adj apprec* (esp. of a material or clothes, shoes, etc.) that lasts for a long time, even when used a lot

hard-wired /ˌ·· ˈ·/ *adj* [(for)] (of computer operations) controlled by HARDWARE rather than SOFTWARE and thus not readily changed by the user: *The printing out of crash dumps is hard-wired on this system.* | (fig.) *My boss is hard-wired to ignore any requests for time off.*

hard·wood /ˈhɑːdwʊd‖ˈhɑːrd-/ *n* **1** [U] strong heavy wood from trees like the OAK, used to make good furniture **2** [C] a tree that has wood of this type —compare SOFTWOOD

har·dy /ˈhɑːdi‖ˈhɑːrdi/ *adj* **1** (of people or animals) strong; able to bear cold, hard work, etc.; ROBUST —see also HARDINESS **2** *tech* (of plants) able to live through the winter above ground: *This bush is a* **hardy perennial.**

Hardy, Ol·i·ver /ˈɒlɪvəʳ‖ˈɑːl-/ see LAUREL AND HARDY

Hardy, Thomas (1840–1928) an English writer and poet, most of whose books are set in Dorset, where he was born, and often describe the unhappy side of life. His best known books include *Far From the Madding Crowd, Tess of the D'Urbervilles,* and *Jude the Obscure.*

Hardy Boys /ˈ·· ·ˌ·/ brothers who are characters in a number of American books for boys and young men (**Hardy Boys mysteries**). The boys always have unusual adventures and narrowly escape great dangers.

hardy-har-har /ˌhɑːdi hɑː ˈhɑːʳ‖ˌhɑːrdi hɑːr-/ *interj AmE infml, humor* (a phrase supposed to sound like a laugh, but usually used in a SARCASTIC way to mean that something is not very funny)

hare¹ /heəʳ/ *n* **hares** or **hare** **1** an animal like a rabbit, but usu. larger, with long ears, a short tail, and long back legs which make it able to run fast —see also MARCH HARE and see picture at RABBIT **2** **run with the hare and hunt with the hounds** to try to support both sides in an argument or not disagree with either of two opposed groups

hare² *v* [I+*adv/prep*] *BrE infml* to run very fast: *He hared off down the road.*

Hare and the Tor·toise /ˌ· · · ˈ·ˌ·/, **The** *n* see TORTOISE AND THE HARE

hare·bell /ˈheəbel‖ˈhear-/ *n* a wild plant with bell-shaped blue flowers on top of a thin stem

hare·brained /ˈheəbreɪnd‖ˈhear-/ *adj* (of people or plans) very impractical and foolish: *another one of his harebrained schemes*

hare cours·ing /ˈ·· ˌ·/ *n* [U] the sport of coursing (COURSE² (2))

Ha·re Krish·na /ˌhæri ˈkrɪʃnə‖ˌhɑːr-/ *n* **1** a branch of the HINDU religion worshipping the god Krishna. Hare Krishna is noted for the way its members gather to repeat a pattern of holy words, including "Hare Krishna", in public. **2** [C] a member of Hare Krishna

hare·lip /ˌheəˈlɪp‖ˌhear-/ *n* [S;U] (the condition of having) the top lip divided into two parts, because it did not develop properly before birth: *He has a harelip.* —**lipped** /ˌheəˈlɪpt◄‖ˌhear-/ *adj*

har·em /ˈheərəm, hɑːˈriːm‖ˈhærəm/ *n* **1** a separated place in a Muslim house where only women live **2** [+*sing./pl. v*] the women who live in a harem **3** [+*sing./pl. v*] a group of females living with, or under the protection of, one male

harem trou·sers /ˈ·· ·ˌ·, ·ˈ· ·ˌ·‖ˈ·· ·ˌ·/ *n* [P] a fashionable type of women's trousers which have a great width of material gathered into folds at the waist

Har·greaves /ˈhɑːɡriːvz‖ˈhɑːr-/, **James** (died 1778) an English inventor known for inventing machines such as the SPINNING JENNY, which allowed one person to spin several threads at the same time

har·i·cot /ˈhærɪkəʊ/ also **haricot bean** /ˌ··· ˈ·/— *n* a small white bean

Har·in·gey /ˈhærɪŋɡeɪ/ a BOROUGH in N London

hark /hɑːk‖hɑːrk/ *v* [I *usu. imperative*] *lit* to listen; HEARKEN **hark at** sbdy. *phr v* [T *imperative*] *BrE infml* to listen to (someone who is saying something very stupid, unreasonable, etc.): *Hark at him criticizing us! I bet he couldn't do any better!*
hark back *phr v* [I (to)] *infml, sometimes derog* to mention or return to events, subjects, etc. of an earlier time: *You're always harking back to how things were when you were young.* | *This book harks back to the author's earlier works on philosophy.*

har·ken /ˈhɑːkən‖ˈhɑːr-/ *v* [I (to)] to HEARKEN

Hark! The Her·ald An·gels Sing /ˌ·· ·ˌ·· ·ˌ· ˈ·/ the title and first line of a religious song (CAROL) sung at Christmas

Har·lem /ˈhɑːləm‖ˈhɑːr-/ an area in NE Manhattan in New York City, known esp. for being a poor and dangerous neighbourhood of mostly black people and HISPANICS

Harlem Globe·trot·ters /ˌhɑːləm ˈɡləʊbtrɒtəz‖ˌhɑːrləm ˈɡləʊbtrɑːtərz/ [*the*+P] a BASKETBALL team with black players who travel around the world to play games in which they entertain people with excellent basketball skills and funny acts

har·le·quin /ˈhɑːlɪkwɪn‖ˈhɑːr-/ *n* (*often cap.*) a character on the stage who wears a special type of bright clothes and plays tricks. He does not speak, and is the lover of Columbine in various old plays.

Harlequin Ro·mance /ˌ··· ·ˈ·/ *n* one of a series of books published (PUBLISH) in the US containing stories about women and men who fall in love. The stories are often simple, and they usu. have a happy ending.

Harley Davidson

Har·ley-Da·vid·son /ˌhɑːli ˈdeɪvɪdsən‖ˌhɑːr-/ *n tdmk* a large, heavy, expensive American MOTORCYCLE

Har·ley Street /ˈhɑːli striːt‖ˈhɑːr-/ (a street in the centre of) an area of London where important doctors (esp. SPECIALISTS) work, who charge money for treatment. Harley Street is a famous and expensive place to get treatment: *a well-known Harley Street doctor*

har·lot /ˈhɑːlət‖ˈhɑːr-/ *n old use or lit* a PROSTITUTE

harm¹ /hɑːm‖hɑːrm/ *n* [U (to)] **1** damage or wrong: *His film was a complete failure, and this did his reputation a lot of harm.* | *He* **means no harm** (=does not intend to offend anyone) *by saying what he thinks, but people tend to be upset by it.* | *What harm is there in staying up a little later?* | *It wouldn't do her any harm to work a bit harder.* (=it would be good for her) | *I don't think you should punish them for this — it would probably* **do more harm than good.** (=have a damaging rather than helpful effect) —see also GRIEVOUS BODILY HARM **2** **come to harm** [*usu. in negatives*] to be hurt: *My brother's ship was caught in a storm but he came to no harm.* **3** **out of harm's way** in a position in which one is **a** safe from harm or **b** unable to cause harm

harm² *v* [T] **1** to cause harm to; hurt (esp. a person): *There was a fire in our street, but no one was harmed.* | *Getting up early won't harm you!* **2** **he/she, etc., wouldn't harm a fly** *infml* he/she, etc., is very gentle by nature

harm·ful /ˈhɑːmfəl‖ˈhɑːrm-/ adj [(to)] causing or likely to cause harm: *Smoking is harmful to health.* — ~**fully** adv — ~**fulness** n [U]

harm·less /ˈhɑːmləs‖ˈhɑːrm-/ adj unable or unlikely to cause harm: *The dog seems fierce, but he's harmless.* — ~**ly** adv — ~**ness** n [U]

har·mon·ic /hɑːˈmɒnɪk‖hɑːrˈmɑː-/ adj 1 of or relating to (the laws of) music: *harmonic scales | harmonic intervals* 2 AmE characterized by HARMONY; harmonious: *a harmonic relationship/meeting* —**ically** adv

har·mon·i·ca /hɑːˈmɒnɪkə‖hɑːrˈmɑː-/ also **mouthorgan** infml — n a small musical instrument played by being held to the mouth, moved from side to side, and blown into or sucked through

har·mo·ni·um /hɑːˈməʊniəm‖hɑːr-/ n a musical instrument played like a piano but working by pumped air (as in an ORGAN (4))

har·mo·nize also **-nise** BrE /ˈhɑːmənaɪz‖ˈhɑːr-/ v [I;T] 1 [(with)] to (cause to) be in agreement with each other or something else, e.g. in purpose, method, style, or colour: *The colours don't seem to harmonize (with each other) at all.* 2 to sing or play (music) in HARMONY (1): *The singing teacher taught them to harmonize (the new song).*

har·mo·ny /ˈhɑːməni‖ˈhɑːr-/ n 1 [C;U] notes of music combined together in a pleasant sounding way 2 [U (with)] a state of complete agreement (in feelings, ideas, etc.): *Her ideas were no longer in harmony with ours. | My cat and dog never fight — they live together in perfect harmony.* 3 [U] the pleasant effect made by parts being combined into a whole: *The harmony of sea and sky makes a beautiful picture.* —compare DISCORD —**nious** /hɑːˈməʊniəs‖hɑːr-/ adj : *a harmonious combination of sounds | Relations with our neighbours are not harmonious at the moment.* —**niously** adv —**niousness** n [U]

har·ness[1] /ˈhɑːnɪs‖ˈhɑːr-/ n [C;U] 1 an apparatus for controlling a horse consisting of leather bands held together by metal 2 a similar apparatus used to control, fasten, or support a person or animal: *a baby's harness | a safety harness* 3 **in harness:** a infml in one's usual work: *back in harness after a long holiday* b living or working closely with another person, esp. one's husband or wife, or one's business partner

harness[2] v [T] 1 [(to)] a to put a harness on (esp. a horse) b to fasten together or fasten to a vehicle: *I harnessed the horse to the cart/the oxen to the plough.* 2 to use (a natural force) to produce useful power: *a new scheme to generate electricity by harnessing the power of the wind*

Har·old II /ˌhærəld ðə ˈsekənd/ (1022?–1066) the last ANGLO-SAXON king, who died in battle against William the Conqueror at Hastings

harp[1] /hɑːp‖hɑːrp/ n a large musical instrument with strings that are stretched from top to bottom of an open three-cornered frame, played by moving the hands across the strings —see also JEW'S HARP — ~**ist** n

harp[2] v
  harp on (sthg.) phr v [I (about);T] infml, usu. derog to talk about (something) repeatedly or continually: *My grandfather still harps on (about) his pre-war illness. | Don't keep harping on like that.*

Har·per's and Queen /ˌhɑːpəz ənd ˈkwiːn‖ˌhɑːrpərz-/ tdmk a British magazine written for wealthy, fashionable people

Har·pic /ˈhɑːpɪk ‖ ˈhɑːr-/ n [U] tdmk a liquid made by Reckitt & Colman Limited, used to clean and remove GERMS from TOILETS

har·poon /hɑːˈpuːn‖hɑːr-/ n a spear with a long rope, used for hunting large sea animals, esp. WHALES —**harpoon** v [T]

harp·si·chord /ˈhɑːpsɪkɔːd‖ˈhɑːrpsɪkɔːrd/ n a musical instrument, used esp. formerly, which is played like a piano but produces a different sound

har·py /ˈhɑːpi‖ˈhɑːrpi/ n 1 an evil creature in old stories with the head of a woman and the body of a bird 2 infml a cruel or nasty woman

har·ri·dan /ˈhærɪdən/ n old-fash a bad-tempered, unpleasant woman; HAG

har·ri·er /ˈhæriər/ n 1 a kind of dog used for hunting HARES 2 (used esp. in the names of running clubs) a CROSS-COUNTRY runner 3 a kind of meat-eating bird with broad wings and long legs

Harrier jump jet /ˌ··· ˈ· ·/ n tdmk a plane used by the Royal Air Force because of its short take-off and landing ability. The Royal Navy use the **Sea Harrier** which is very similar.

Har·ris /ˈhærɪs/, **Em·my·lou** /ˈemiluː/ (1949–) an American popular music singer

Harris, Rolf /rɒlf‖rɑːlf/ (1930–) an Australian singer, writer, and painter who moved to Britain in the 1950s and became a well-known television star. He is remembered by British people esp. for his way of painting pictures very quickly, and also for playing unusual musical instruments, esp. the DIDGERIDOO.

Har·ri·son /ˈhærɪsən/, **Ben·ja·min** /ˈbendʒəmɪn/ (1833–1901) the 23rd president of the US (1889–93)

Harrison, George (1943–) an English popular musician and song writer who played with **The Beatles**. His songs include *My Sweet Lord.*

Harrison, Rex (1908–90) a British actor known esp. for his part in the film *My Fair Lady*

Harris poll /ˈ·· ˌ·/ n a study of public opinion made by Louis Harris Associates of New York, or one of their connected companies in Britain or France

Harris Tweed /ˌ·· ˈ·◄/ n [U] tdmk a type of woollen cloth woven by hand on Harris, an island off the W coast of Scotland

Har·rods /ˈhærədz/ a famous and expensive DEPARTMENT STORE in Knightsbridge, W London —see colour map on page 817

Harrods

Har·ro·gate /ˈhærəgət‖-geɪt/ a SPA town in North Yorkshire, England, which is a popular holiday and RETIREMENT place

har·row /ˈhærəʊ/ n a farming machine with sharp metal teeth used to break up the earth and make it smooth — **harrow** v [I;T]

Harrow also **Harrow School** /ˈ··· ˈ·/ a British PUBLIC SCHOOL for boys, at Harrow-on-the-Hill, NW London. It is one of the most expensive and PRESTIGIOUS public schools in Britain. Men who have been educated at Harrow are known as Old Harrovians. —see also ETON

har·rowed /ˈhærəʊd/ adj feeling or showing anxiety and suffering; FRAUGHT: *You're looking rather harrowed. | a harrowed expression*

har·row·ing /ˈhærəʊɪŋ/ adj causing great suffering and anxiety in the mind; DISTRESSING: *To see someone killed is very harrowing/is a very harrowing experience.*

har·ry /ˈhæri/ v [T] fml or lit 1 [(for)] to worry or annoy continually: *The tax authorities have been harrying her (for repayment).* 2 to attack repeatedly and with great effect, esp. in war: *The army harried the enemy's borders.*

Harry, Deb·bie /ˈdebi/ (1945–) an American popular music singer, who led the group **Blondie**

Harry, Prince see Prince HENRY

harsh /hɑːʃ‖hɑːrʃ/ adj 1 unpleasant or painful to the senses, e.g. because very loud or very bright: *harsh colours | a harsh voice | a harsh light* (=too strong for the eyes) 2 (of people, punishments, etc.) showing cruelty and a lack of sympathy, esp. in dealing with bad behaviour or mistakes; severe: *harsh discipline/punishments* — ~**ly** adv — ~**ness** n [U]

hart /hɑːt‖hɑːrt/ n harts or hart esp. BrE a male deer, esp. of the RED DEER family, over five years old; STAG — compare HIND

Hart, Lor·enz Mil·ton /ˈlɒrənz ˈmɪltən‖ˈlɔː-/ (1895–1943) an American song writer who worked with Richard Rodgers on MUSICALS

Hart, Gar·y /ˈgæri/ (1936–) an American Democrat politician who was unsuccessful in the 1988 presidential CAMPAIGN, after stories in the newspapers about his private life

har·te·beest /ˈhɑːtˌbiːst‖ˈhɑːr-/ n hartebeests or hartebeest a large ANTELOPE of southern Africa

Hart·nell /ˈhɑːtnəl‖ˈhɑːrt-/, **Sir Norman** (1901–79) a British fashion DESIGNER who became the official dressmaker for Queen Elizabeth II

har·um-scar·um /ˌheərəm ˈskeərəm/ *adj, adv old-fash infml* (behaving) wildly and thoughtlessly: *children dashing harum-scarum around the playground*

Har·vard /ˈhɑːvəd‖ˈhɑːrvərd/ Harvard University in Cambridge, Massachusetts, the oldest and probably most famous American university, opened in 1636: *a Harvard law student*

har·vest¹ /ˈhɑːvɪst‖ˈhɑːr-/ *n* **1** [C;U] the act or time of gathering the crops: *We all helped with the harvest.* | *It's harvest time.* **2** [C] the (size or quality of) the crops that have been gathered: *a large harvest* | *this year's excellent grape harvest* **3** [S] the results of past work or action: *The government is now* **reaping the harvest** *of its past mistakes.*

harvest² *v* **1** [I;T] to gather (a crop) —compare REAP **2** [T] *rare* to receive or suffer (the results of past work or action)

har·vest·er /ˈhɑːvɪstəʳ‖ˈhɑːr-/ *n* **1** a person who gathers the crops **2** a machine which cuts grain and gathers it in, esp. a COMBINE³ (2)

harvest fes·ti·val /ˌ··ˈ···/ *n (often cap.) esp. BrE* a religious occasion when thanks are given for the crops which have been gathered, marked by services in churches, schools, etc. For the harvest festival, churches are decorated inside with fruit, vegetables and corn. —compare THANKSGIVING

harvest home /ˌ··ˈ·/ *n now rare* a ceremonial meal given to the workers after all the crops have been gathered

harvest moon /ˌ··ˈ·/ *n* the full moon in autumn at the time when day and night are of equal length (EQUINOX)

Har·vey /ˈhɑːvi‖ˈhɑːr-/, **Paul** (1918–   ) an American radio personality whose **News and Comment** is heard on many different radio stations around the country

Har·vey's /ˈhɑːviz ‖ ˈhɑːr-/ *n tdmk* a company which makes different types of SHERRY; Harvey's is based in Bristol and its best-known sherry is Harvey's BRISTOL CREAM

Har·well /ˈhɑːwəl‖ˈhɑːr-/ a government centre for atomic RESEARCH near a village in Oxfordshire, S England with the same name

Har·wich /ˈhærɪtʃ, -ɪdʒ/ a port in Essex, E England which has connections by sea with Denmark, Belgium, and the Netherlands

has /z, əz, həz; *strong* hæz/ *3rd person sing. present tense of* HAVE —see NOT (USAGE)

has-been /ˈ· ·/ *n infml, derog* a person or thing that no longer has its former importance, popularity, or effectiveness: *Many pop stars are has-beens after only a few years.*

hash¹ /hæʃ/ *n* **1** [C;U] a meal containing meat cut up in small pieces, esp. when re-cooked **2** [S] something done badly or unsuccessfully; MESS: *I made a complete hash of my driving test.* —see also HASH up **3** [C] *sometimes derog* old material, ideas, etc., in a new form; REHASH **4** [U] *sl* hashish

hash² *v*
  hash sthg. ↔ **up** *phr v* [T] *infml* to do or perform (something) badly; spoil; MESS **up**: *He was so nervous at the interview that he completely hashed it up.* —see also HASH¹ (2)

hash browns /ˈ· ·/ *n* [P] potatoes which are cut into very small pieces, cooked in oil, pressed together, and eaten hot

hash·ish /ˈhæʃiːʃ, -ɪʃ/ *also* **hash** *sl—* *n* [U] the strongest form of the drug CANNABIS. It is the RESIN (=the hardened juice) of the Indian HEMP plant. —compare BHANG, MARIJUANA

has·n't /ˈhæzənt/ *short for:* has not: *She hasn't enough time to see you.* | *Hasn't he finished yet?*

hasp /hɑːsp‖hæsp/ *n* a metal fastener for a box, door, etc., which usu. fits over a hook and is kept in place by a PADLOCK

Has·sam /ˈhæsəm/, **Childe** /tʃaɪld/ (1859–1935) an American painter and printmaker whose work was influenced by Impressionism

Has·san II /hə₁sɑːn ðə ˈsekənd/, **King** (1929–   ) the king of Morocco since 1961

has·sle¹ /ˈhæsəl/ *n infml* **1** [S] a situation causing difficulty or annoyance; struggle: *It's a real hassle to get the children to eat/getting the children to eat.* | *I came by bus because I couldn't be bothered with the hassle of parking.* **2** [C] *esp. AmE* an argument or fight

hassle² *v infml* **1** [T] to annoy, esp. continuously; HARASS: *I wish you would stop hassling me (about stopping smoking).* **2** [I (**with**)] to argue: *hassling with the umpire over a disputed point*

has·sock /ˈhæsək/ *n* **1** a small CUSHION for kneeling on in church **2** *AmE for* POUF (1)

hast /hæst/ **thou hast** *old use or bibl* (when talking to one person) you have

haste /heɪst/ *n* [U] **1** quick movement or action, esp. when one has very little time to do something; speed: *He packed his bags* **in haste** *when he heard the police were looking for him.* | *(old use)* Make haste! *(=hurry)* **2** too much speed, often with bad or unwanted results: *"More haste, less speed!"* (old saying) | *In his haste, he forgot to take his umbrella.*

has·ten /ˈheɪsən/ *v* **1** [I+adv/prep;T] *fml* to (cause to) move or happen fast or faster: *She hastened home.* | *The strike hastened the downfall of the government.* **2** [I+to-v] to be quick (to say something), in case the hearer imagines something else: *Some of the staff are to be dismissed, but I hasten to add you won't be among them.*

Has·tings /ˈheɪstɪŋz/ a town on the SE coast of England. The **Battle of Hastings** took place near Hastings. King Harold of England was defeated and killed by William the Conqueror's army in 1066.

has·ty /ˈheɪsti/ *adj* **1** done in a hurry: *a hasty meal* (=made or eaten in a hurry) **2** too quick in acting or deciding, often with bad or unwanted results; RASH: *He soon regretted his hasty decision to get married.* —**ily** *adv* —**iness** *n* [U]

hats

stetson

Tam o' shanter

bowler hat

peaked cap

top hat

panama hat

baseball cap

sombrero

fez

straw boater

woolly hat *(BrE)*
stocking cap *(AmE)*

hat /hæt/ *n* **1** a covering for the head, typically having a wide flat bottom part and a higher central part **2** **keep something under one's hat** *infml* to keep (something) secret **3** **my hat!** *old-fash* I don't believe (that) **4** **I'll eat my hat** I'll be very surprised: *If the train arrives on time I'll eat my hat.* **5** **pass the hat round** to collect money, esp. to give to someone who deserves it **6** **take one's hat off to** *infml* to express admiration for (someone): *I take my hat off to him for the superb way he organized the party.* —see also OLD HAT, **bad hat** (BAD¹ (9)), **at the drop of a hat** (DROP²), **hang up one's hat** (HANG¹), **to talk through one's hat** (TALK¹)

hat·band /ˈhætbænd/ *n* a band of cloth, leather, etc., running round a hat above the BRIM²

hatch¹ /hætʃ/ *v* **1** [I;T (OUT)] **a** (of an egg) to break, letting the young bird out: *Three eggs have already hatched (out).* **b** to cause (an egg) to hatch: *We hatch the eggs by keeping them in a warm place.* **2** [I;T (OUT)] **a** (of a young bird) to break out through an egg: *Three chicks have hatched (out).* **b** to cause (a young bird) to hatch: *She has hatched all her chickens.* **3** [T] to form (a plan) secretly, esp. to do something bad: *They hatched a plot to murder the king.*

hatch² *n* **1** also **hatchway**– (the covering for) an opening in a wall, floor, etc., through which people or things can pass: *She went through the hatch to the upper deck to look at the sea.* | *There's a serving hatch between the kitchen and the dining room.* —see picture at AIRCRAFT **2 Down the hatch!** *infml* (a phrase used before swallowing a drink)

hatch·back /'hætʃbæk/ *n* a car with a door at the back which opens upwards —compare ESTATE CAR, SALOON, SPORTS CAR

hatch·er·y /'hætʃəri/ *n* a place for hatching eggs, esp. fish eggs

hatch·et /'hætʃ↓t/ *n* a small AXE with a short handle —see also **bury the hatchet** (BURY), and see picture at AXE

hatchet-faced /'·· ,·/ *adj* having an unpleasantly thin sharp face

hatchet job /'·· ,·/ *n infml* a cruel attack in speech or writing: *The reviewers did a hatchet job on her latest novel.*

hatchet man /'·· ·/ *n infml* a person who is paid by someone to attack or kill an enemy, or destroy his/her REPUTATION

hatch·ing /'hætʃɪŋ/ *n* [U] fine lines drawn on or cut into a surface —see CROSS-HATCHING

hatch·way /'hætʃweɪ/ *n* a HATCH² (1)

hate¹ /heɪt/ *v* [T *not in progressive forms*] **1** to have a very strong dislike of; DETEST: *I hate violence.* | *They really hate each other.* | (*infml*) *I hate his guts.* (=hate him very much) **2** *infml* to dislike: *I hate cabbage.* | *I hate it when people ask me for money.* [+to-v] *She hates to be late for work.* [+v-ing] *She hates being late for work.* [+obj+to-v] *I'd hate you to think we were late on purpose.* [+obj+v-ing] *He hates people asking him for money.* —opposite **love 3** [+to-v/v-ing; obj] *infml* to be sorry; REGRET: *I hate (having) to tell you this, but I've just damaged your car.*

hate² *n* [C;U] a strong dislike: *She looked at me with hate in her eyes.* | *Rock'n'roll is her pet hate.* (=something she greatly dislikes) —opposite **love**; see also HATRED

hate·ful /'heɪtfəl/ *adj* [(to)] very bad, unpleasant, or unkind: *Ironing shirts is a hateful job.* – ~ ly *adv* – ~ ness *n* [U]

hate mail /'· ·/ *n* [U] letters which contain threats, rude language, or offensive words, sent to a person in order to frighten them or make them change their behaviour: *After the rapist was caught, he received a lot of hate mail from the local community.*

hath /hæθ/ *old use or bibl* has

Hath·a·way /'hæθəweɪ/, **Anne** (1557?–1623) the wife of William Shakespeare. Her house in Stratford-upon-Avon (**Anne Hathaway's Cottage**) is a famous tourist attraction

hat·pin /'hæt,pɪn/ *n* a long, strong pin, often decorative, used to keep a woman's hat in place. Hatpins were popular in the late 19th and early 20th centuries: *She jabbed her attacker with a hatpin.*

ha·tred /'heɪtr↓d/ *n* [S;U (of, for)] extreme dislike; hate: *She is full of hatred for the men who killed her husband.* | *They have a hatred of bad workmanship.*

hat·ter /'hætər/ *n* a maker and/or seller of hats —see also **as mad as a hatter** (MAD (7)), MAD HATTER

Hat·ters·ley /'hætəzli||-tər-/, **Roy** /rɔɪ/ (1932–) a British Labour politician who was DEPUTY leader of the Labour Party from 1983 to 1992

hat trick /'· ·/ *n BrE* three successes of the same type in one period of activity, esp. in sports, e.g. (in cricket) when three players have been dismissed by the same person or (in football) when the same player has made three GOALs in one game: *He scored a brilliant hat trick.* | (fig.) *a hat trick of election victories*

Hau·ghey /'hɔːhiː/, **Charles** (1925–) the PRIME MINISTER of the Republic of Ireland from 1987–1992

haugh·ty /'hɔːti/ *adj* (of people or their behaviour) seeming to consider oneself better or more important than others; ARROGANT: *a haughty look/manner/young lady* —**tily** *adv* —**tiness** *n* [U]

haul¹ /hɔːl/ *v* **1** [+adv/prep; T] to pull with effort or difficulty: *to haul logs* | *They hauled away on the ropes.* |

to haul up the fishing nets | *The protesters were hauled off to jail.* | (fig.) *They hauled down the enemy's flag when they captured the city.* **2** [T] to carry (goods) in a vehicle, esp. a TRUCK **3** [T+obj+adv/prep] *infml* to force to appear before an official body, esp. a court of law; SUMMONS²: *He's been hauled (up) before the court/in front of the magistrate on a charge of dangerous driving.* —see also HAVE **up 4 haul someone over the coals** to speak to someone angrily and severely for something they have done wrong; REPRIMAND

haul off *phr v* [I] *AmE sl* to raise one's arm (before hitting someone): *He hauled off and hit Pete on the jaw.*

haul² *n* **1** [C (of) *usu. sing.*] **a** the amount of fish caught when fishing with a net **b** *infml* the amount of something gained, esp. stolen or forbidden goods: *The smugglers got through customs with a huge haul of cannabis.* **2** [S] the act of hauling **3** [S] the distance over which a load is hauled: (fig.) *It was a long haul home and we arrived exhausted.* —see also LONG-HAUL

haul·age /'hɔːlɪdʒ/ *n* [U] **1** the business of carrying goods by road: *road haulage* **2** the charge for this

haul·i·er /'hɔːliər/ *BrE* ‖ **haul·er** /'hɔːlər/*AmE*– *n* a person who runs a haulage business

haunch /hɔːntʃ/ *n* **1** [*usu. pl.*] the fleshy part of the human body between the waist and legs; HIP: *The men were squatting on their haunches.* **2** either of the back legs of a four-legged animal —compare HINDQUARTERS

haunt¹ /hɔːnt/ *v* [T *not in progressive forms*] **1** [*often pass.*] (of a spirit, esp. of a dead person) to visit (a place), appearing in a strange form: *The ghost of a headless man haunts the castle.* | *a haunted house* **2** [*usu. pass.*] (esp. of something strange or sad) to be always in the thoughts of (someone): *I was haunted by his last words to me.* | *She had a haunted look, as if she were constantly anxious or afraid.* **3** *infml* to visit (a place) regularly; FREQUENT

haunt² *n* a place which a particular person visits frequently: *This pub is one of my favourite haunts.* | *The area was a haunt of criminals.*

haunt·ing /'hɔːntɪŋ/ *adj* strange in a pleasant or sad way and remaining in one's thoughts: *the haunting memory of her beautiful face* | *a haunting melody* – ~ ly *adv*

haut·bois , **-boy** /'əubɔɪ, 'həubɔɪ/ *n* **-bois** /-bɔɪz/ *or* **-boys** *old use* an OBOE

haute cou·ture /,əut kuː'tjuər‖-'tuər/ *n* [U] COUTURE

haute cui·sine /,əut kwɪ'ziːn/ *n* [U] cooking, esp. French cooking, of a very high standard: *a restaurant renowned for its haute cuisine*

hau·teur /əu'tɜːr‖hɔː'tɜːr/ *n* [U] *fml* haughtiness (HAUGHTY)

Ha·van·a¹ /hə'vænə/ the capital of Cuba. Havana is connected in the minds of some British people with Graham Greene's book *Our Man in Havana* and the famous film made of it.

Havana² *n* a CIGAR made in Cuba

have¹ /v, əv, həv; *strong* hæv/ *v* **had** /d, əd, həd; *strong* hæd/; *3rd person sing.* present tense **has** /z, əz, həz; *strong* hæz/, *negative short forms* **haven't** /'hævənt/, **hasn't** /'hæzənt/, hadn't /'hædnt/ [*auxiliary verb*] **1 a** (used with the past participle to form perfect tenses of verbs): *I've been reading.* | *I've written six letters today.* | *He had already been to New York earlier in the week.* | *He'll have finished by tomorrow.* | *I would have gone by car if I had known the train would be late.* | *It's silly not to have gone after having accepted the invitation.* | *He said he'd been there before.* | *"Have you finished?" "No, I haven't."* | *We've met before, haven't we?* **b Had (I, he, etc.)** *rather fml* if (I, he, etc.) had: *Had they searched more closely, they would have found what they wanted.* | *Had I known you were going to be late, I would have taken the next train.* —see NOT (USAGE) **2 had better/best (do/not do)** ought (not) to; should (not): *I'd better tell him before he goes home.* | *We'd better not go until your sister arrives, or else she'll be angry.* | (used in giving orders or warnings) *You'd better not tell anyone about this!* **3 have had it** *infml* **a** to be ruined, useless, dead, or dying: *This old TV's had it – it's time we bought a new one.* | *That plant of yours has had it, I'm afraid.* **b** to have experienced, worked, or suffered enough, or more than enough: *That's it, I've had it! I'm going home.* | *I've had it with all your complaining!*

have² also **have got**– *v* [T *not in progressive forms*] **1 a** to possess, own, or be able to use or give: *He has a new*

car. | *"Have you got a pencil?" "Yes, I have."* | *She's got plenty of money.* | *Have you got a minute (to spare)?* | *I'll have time to see you on Monday.* | *Have you got* (=can you tell me) *the time, please?* **b** to show as part of one's character: *He has a good memory|a bad temper.* | *She's got no imagination.* **c** to contain or include as a part: *He's got a big nose.* | *This coat has no pockets.* (=There are no pockets in this coat.) | *Spiders have eight legs.* **2 a** to experience or be experiencing: *I have bad colds every year.* | *I've got a bad cold now.* | *Have you ever had malaria?* **b** [+*obj*+*v-ing*] to experience as happening in the stated way: *We have reports coming into the office from all over the world.* **c** [+*obj*+*to-v*] to experience the need to deal with in the stated way: *I have things to do.* | *We've got a schedule to keep.* **3** to keep or feel in the mind: *Have you any doubt about his guilt?* | *I've got no idea what to do. Have you?* | *Have you got any hope of finding it?* | *I had a feeling we were being followed.* | *I'm not sure who did it, but I have my suspicions.* | *It's her own fault — I have no sympathy with her!* **4 have coming** also **have got coming**— to deserve (esp. something bad): *We weren't surprised when he lost his job — he'd had it coming (to him) for a long time.* **5 I have it!** also **I've got it!**— (an expression when one suddenly sees the right way to deal with something) **6 You 'have me there** also **You've 'got me there**— *infml* **a** That's a good point against me. I will have to think again about my argument, plan, etc., because of what you said **b** I don't know: *"Who won the election in 1928?" "I'm sorry: you have me there."* **7 to have and to hold from this day forward** *quote* a phrase from the Christian marriage service, in which the people getting married promise to care for each other from the day they are married until they die —see also MARRIAGE

▷ USAGE 1 The opposite of *He has a beard* is: *He hasn't got a beard.* | *He doesn't have a beard.* | *He has no beard.* Use **hasn't/haven't** only when another word comes between **have** and the noun: *I haven't (got) any money.* | *He hasn't (got) a very good temper.* 2 Both **have got** and **have** are acceptable in English, especially in cases of **a** permanent possession, compare: *She's got blue eyes* and *She has blue eyes* **b** questions, short answers, and negatives, compare: **"Have you got a car?" "Yes I have."** and **"Do you have a car?" "Yes, I do."** 3 **Got** is not usual in past tense forms: *She had blue eyes.* | **Did** you have *a car when you were a student?* 4 Do not use **got** when talking about habits or repeated experiences: **"Do** you ever **have** colds?" "Yes, I nearly always **have** a cold at this time of year."◁

have³ *v* [T *rarely pass.*] **1** [*not in progressive forms*] to receive or obtain: *I had some good news today.* | *We must have your answer by Friday.* | *I had a shock when I saw the size of the bill.* | *I had a win in a competition.* | *Let me have it back when you've finished with it.* | *We tried to get a copy of her book, but* **there was none to be had. 2** [*not in progressive forms*] to show (a quality): *He had the impudence to ask me for more money.* | *She had the grace to apologize immediately.* | (*pomp*) *Have the goodness to answer when I ask you a question!* (shows great displeasure) **3** *infml, esp. BrE ‖ usu.* **take** *AmE* (used esp. before a noun that has the same form as a verb) to perform the actions connected with; do (something): *Have a look at this.* | *to have a read* (=read for a while) | *BrE to have a swim|a walk|a run|a wash|a chat* | *AmE to take a swim|a walk; or go for a swim|a walk|a run; to wash; to have a chat* | *She had another sip of her tea.* —see USAGE **4** to eat, drink, or smoke: *We were having breakfast.* | *He always has a cigarette with his coffee.* | *Have another drink, Mary* **5** [+*obj*+*adv|prep*] to have invited as a guest in the home: *We're having some people over tonight.* | *We're having guests for|to dinner.* | *When did we last have her round?* **6** [*usu. in negatives*] to (be willing to) permit; allow: *I won't have all this noise.* | *I'm not having any more of your nonsense!* [+*obj*+*v-ing*] *We can't have you going everywhere by taxi.* **7** to give birth to: *His wife has just had a baby.* | *She's having a baby in March.* **8** [+*obj*+*to-v|v-ing*] to cause (someone) to (do something): *I had John find me a house.* | *I had them all laughing at my jokes.* **9** [+*obj*+*v-ed*] to cause or arrange for (something) to be done by someone: *to have the roof fixed* | *to have one's hair cut* | *Will you have my cases sent up, please?* **10** to cause to be in the stated place or condition: [+*obj*+*adv|prep*] *Can we have our ball back, please, sir?* | *I'll have your cat down from the tree in a minute,*

Mrs Jones [+*obj*+*adj*] *Make sure you have the car ready by tomorrow.* | *It had me worried when I heard about your accident.* **11** [+*obj*+*v-ed*] to experience (something) as having been treated in the stated way: *I had my watch stolen last night.* | *She had her camera confiscated by the police.* **12** to enjoy or suffer; experience, often as part of a group: *We're having a party|a meeting.* | *We all had a good time.* (note the fixed phrase: **a good time was had by all**) | *We're having a bit of trouble with the car.* **13** [*usu. pass.*] *infml* to cheat; trick: *I'm afraid you've been had.* **14** [*not in progressive forms*] *old-fash* to know: *She has a little French, but not much Latin.* **15** [+*obj*+*to-v*] *old use or fml* (with **will** or **would**) to wish for: *Would you have me go home alone?* | *I would have you know that I am a person of some importance in this company!* | *What would you have me say?* **16** *sl* to perform the act of sex with (esp. someone desired but not loved) **17 have done with** to finish (something) and not do it or deal with it again: *Let's have done with all this quarrelling.* **18 have it: a** to say; MAINTAIN: *Rumour has it that they're getting divorced.* | *He will have it* (=he keeps saying very firmly, even if wrongly) *that it was my fault.* **b** to get to know something: *I had it from John.* | *I* **have it on good authority** (=from someone who should know) *that the election will be in June.* **19 have it 'in for** to want to be unkind to or hurt (someone) on purpose: *One of the teachers really has it in for Charlie — she shouts at him all the time.* **20 have it 'in one** *infml* to have a (hidden or unexpected) quality or ability: *We were all surprised when he won — we never knew he had it in him.* **21 have on/about one** to be carrying, esp. in a pocket or on HANDBAG: *Have you got any money on you?* **22 have something against someone** to dislike someone because of a particular quality or a particular thing they have done: *I have nothing against her — I just don't think she's the right person for the job.* **23 not having any** *sl* not accepting; not willing to listen, take an interest in, etc.: *I tried to get her to help me with the cooking, but she wasn't having any* (*BrE*)*|wouldn't have any of that* (*AmE*).

▷ USAGE Nouns like *a look, a swim,* which are formed from verbs (*to look, to swim*) are used with **have** or **take:** *to take a look* | *to have a swim.* These phrases are more informal than *to look, to swim.*◁

have sbdy./sthg. ↔ **in** *phr v* [T *no pass.*] **1** [*not in progressive forms*] also **have got in**— *esp. BrE* to have or keep a supply of (something): *Have we got enough sugar in?* **2** to call (someone) to the house to do some work: *We're having the builders in next week to improve the kitchen.*

have sthg. **off** *phr v* [T *no pass.*] *esp. BrE* **1** [*not in progressive forms*] *old-fash* to have learnt, ready to speak from memory: *I have the whole poem off already.* **2 have it off (with)** *sl* to have sex (with)

have on *phr v* [T *no pass.*] **1** [*not in progressive forms*] (**have** sthg. ↔ **on**) also **have got on**— to be wearing (something): *He had nothing on except a hat.* **2** (**have** sbdy. **on**) also **put on** *AmE*— to trick (someone), usu. by pretending something that is not true; TEASE: *You didn't believe her, did you? She was just having you on.* **3** [*not in progressive forms*] (**have** sthg. **on**) also **have got on**— *infml* to have (something) to do; have promised or arranged to do (something): *I haven't got anything on tonight.* | *We've got a lot of work on at the moment.* **4** [*not in progressive forms*] (**have** sthg. **on** sbdy.) also **have got** sthg. **on** sbdy.— *infml* to have information recorded against (someone): *You can't take me to the police station, you've got nothing on me.* **5 have nothing on** *infml* to be not nearly so good as: *Sam may have money, but for brains he has nothing on Janet.*

have sthg. **out** *phr v* [T *no pass.*] **1** to get (something) taken out, usu. a tooth or an organ of the body: *He had to go to the dentist and have the tooth out.* | *Have you had your tonsils out?* **2** [(**with**)] to settle (a difficulty) by talking freely and openly, or sometimes angrily: *Let's have the whole thing out.* | *I must have it out with him, and stop all this uncertainty.*

have sbdy. **up** *phr v* [T (**for**) *usu. pass.*] *BrE infml* to take to court: *He was had up for dangerous driving.*

have⁴ *v* [+*to-v*] **1** also **have got**— to be forced to; must: *Do you have to go now?* | *Have you got to go now?* | *I've got to go to a meeting.* | *I hate having to get up so early.* | *It has to be done|It's got to be done by tomorrow.* | *I'll have to phone you later.* | *You don't have to go|haven't got to go if you don't want to.* | (*infml*) *That has to be* (=I am sure it is) *the stupidest idea I've ever heard!* —see MUST (USAGE) **2 have to do with** —see DO **with** (5)

Hav·el /ˈhævel, -vəl/, **Vác·lav** /ˈvɑːtslæf/ (1936–) the president of Czechoslovakia since 1989 and a writer for the theatre. Havel was put in prison by Czechoslovakia's COMMUNIST rulers, but led a successful peaceful movement against them.

ha·ven /ˈheɪvən/ n **1** a place of calm and safety: *The school library is a little haven of peace and quiet.* | *safe in the haven of his mother's arms* **2** rare a HARBOUR —see also TAX HAVEN, SAFE HAVEN

have-nots /ˌ· ˈ·/ n [(*the*) P] the poor people in a country or society: *This government gives to the haves and ignores the have-nots.* —opposite **haves**

have·n't /ˈhævənt/ *short for:* have not: *They haven't replied to my letter.* | *Haven't I met you before?*

hav·er·sack /ˈhævəsæk‖-ər-/ n a bag carried usu. over one shoulder when walking, esp. to hold food and clothing —compare BACKPACK, RUCKSACK

haves /hævz/ n [(*the*) P] the rich people in a country or society —opposite **have-nots**

hav·oc /ˈhævək/ n [U] widespread damage or serious disorder: *The earthquake* **wreaked havoc** *(on the city).* | *The transport strike* **played havoc with** *everyone's holiday plans.*

Ha·vre /ˈɑːvrə/ see LE HAVRE

haw¹ /hɔː/ v see hum and haw (HUM²)

haw² *interj* (the sound made in a loud laugh)

Ha·wai·i /həˈwaɪ-i/ *written abbrev.* **HI**— a state of the US consisting of eight main islands in the Pacific (the **Hawaiian Islands**); capital Honolulu, on the island of Oahu. It is a popular place for Americans to go on holiday. British people have a mental picture of Hawaii as a wonderfully warm place where friendly pretty girls wearing grass skirts greet visitors by placing GARLANDS of flowers, called **leis**, round their necks. —see colour map on pages 1374–5 — ~**an** /həˈwaɪən/ n, adj

Haw-Haw /ˈhɔːhɔː/, **Lord** (1906–46) the name given to William Joyce, an Englishman who broadcast against Britain from Germany during the Second World War. He was called Lord Haw-Haw because he tried to speak in a very upper-class way. After the war he was executed (EXECUTE).

Haw·ick /ˈhɔːɪk/ a town in Scotland where woollen clothes are made and sold

hawk

dove   hawk

hawk¹ /hɔːk/ n **1** a type of bird which catches other birds and small animals with its feet (CLAWs) for food, is active during the day, and is believed to have very good eyesight —compare EAGLE **2** a person who believes in strong action or the use of force, esp. one who supports warlike political ideas —opposite **dove** — ~**ish** adj : *a hawkish foreign policy* — ~**ishness** n [U] : *the hawkishness of their political views*

hawk² v [T] **1** to sell (goods) on the street or at the doors of houses, esp. while moving from place to place **2** to spread (information, ideas, etc.) around, esp. by speech: *hawking one's ideas around* — ~**er** n

Hawke /hɔːk/, **Rob·ert** /ˈrɒbət‖ˈrɑːbərt/ (**Bob**) (1929–) an Australian political leader and former Prime Minister

Haw·ker Sidde·ley /ˌhɔːkə ˈsɪdli/ a British company formerly producing aircraft. One of the most famous Hawker Siddeley aircraft was the Hurricane which, with the Supermarine Spitfire, played an important part in the Battle of Britain.

hawk-eyed /ˈ· ·/ adj lit **1** having very good eyesight **2**

watching everything and everyone closely; very OBSERVANT: *hawk-eyed customs officers*

Haw·king /ˈhɔːkɪŋ/, **Ste·phen** /ˈstiːvən/ (1942–) an English PHYSICIST who wrote *A Brief History of Time* (1988)

haw·ser /ˈhɔːzər/ n a thick rope or steel CABLE as used on a ship

Hawks·moor /ˈhɔːksmʊər/, **Nicholas** (1661–1736) an English ARCHITECT who worked with Sir Christopher Wren on St Paul's Cathedral, and built many churches in London

Hawn /hɔːn/, **Gol·die** /ˈɡəʊldi/ (1945–) an American actress known esp. for appearing in COMEDY films

Ha·worth /ˈhaʊwəθ‖ˈhɔːwərθ/ a small village in Yorkshire in the N of England which tourists visit because the English writers the Brontë sisters lived there. The area is described in Emily Brontë's famous book *Wuthering Heights.*

haw·thorn /ˈhɔːθɔːn‖-ɔːrn/ also **may**– n a type of tree with white or red flowers (BLOSSOMS) which often grows beside country roads, and has red berries in autumn

Haw·thorne /ˈhɔːθɔːn‖-ɔːrn/, **Na·than·i·el** /nəˈθæniəl/ (1804–64) an American writer of NOVELs and short stories whose most famous novel is *The Scarlet Letter*

hay /heɪ/ n [U] **1** grass which has been cut and dried, esp. for using as cattle food **2 make hay** to dry grass in the sun **3 make hay while the 'sun shines** *infml* to make good use of chances —see also **hit the hay** (HIT¹) – ~**making** n [U]

hay·cock /ˈheɪkɒk‖-kɑːk/ n now rare a small, usu. round pile of hay, ready to be taken out of the field

Hay·dn /ˈhaɪdn/, **Joseph** (1732–1809) an Austrian writer of music (COMPOSER) whose works are very popular and frequently performed. His *Creation* is sung very often by choral societies (CHORAL SOCIETY).

Hayes /heɪz/, **Ruth·er·ford Bir·chard** /ˈrʌðəfəd ˈbɜːtʃəd‖ -ðərfərd ˈbɜːrtʃərd/ (1822–93) the 19th president of the US (1877–81)

hay fe·ver /ˈ· ˌ·-/ n [U] an illness rather like a bad cold, but caused by POLLEN (=dust from plants) which is breathed in from the air

hay·fork /ˈheɪfɔːk‖-fɔːrk/ n a long-handled fork with two points (PRONGS), used for turning over hay in the field or for gathering it

Hay·mar·ket /ˈheɪmɑːkɪt‖-mɑːr-/ [*the*] a street in the West End of London where there is a theatre also called **The Haymarket**

hay·ride /ˈheɪraɪd/ n AmE **1** a night-time ride in an open CART filled with HAY, in which young men and women get to know each other better **2 no hayride** infml humor not easy or enjoyable: *"How was your weekend with the in-laws?" "It was no hayride."*

hay·stack /ˈheɪstæk/ also **hay·rick** /-rɪk/– n a large pile of hay gathered, usu. outdoors, for storing —see also **needle in a haystack** (NEEDLE¹)

Hay·wain /ˈheɪweɪn/ [*the*] a famous painting by John Constable which is in the National Gallery in London —see colour picture on page 1016

Hay·ward Gal·le·ry /ˈheɪwəd ˌɡæləri‖-wərd-/ [*the*] an art GALLERY on London's South Bank

hay·wire /ˈheɪwaɪər/ adj [F] infml in a state of disorder and confusion: *The computer's* **gone haywire** – *it's printing numbers at random.* | *Our plans have (all) gone haywire since the rail strike.*

haz·ard¹ /ˈhæzəd‖-ərd/ n **1** [(**to**)] something likely to cause damage or loss; a danger or risk: *a hazard to health* | *There are many serious health hazards associated with smoking.That big box of papers is a* **fire hazard.** (=something that increases the risk of fire) **2** a difficult move or place in certain games or sports **3 in/at hazard** at risk; in danger

hazard² v [T] fml **1** to offer (a suggestion, a guess, etc.) when there is a risk of being wrong or saying something unwelcome; VENTURE: *Would you care to hazard a guess as to how many people will come?* **2** fml to risk; put in danger: *He hazarded all his money in the attempt to save the business.*

haz·ard·ous /ˈhæzədəs‖-zər-/ adj (esp. of an activity) which contains risks or danger: *a hazardous occupation/ journey/route* — ~**ly** adv

hazardous waste /ˌ··· ˈ·/ n [U] waste which contains harmful chemicals or RADIOACTIVE materials

hazard warn·ing lights /ˌ··· ˈ··· ˌ·/ n [P] special lights on a car or other road vehicle which can be made to flash to warn other drivers if there has been an accident or if the vehicle is parked in a dangerous place

Haz·chem /ˈhæzkem/ BrE a written sign placed as a warning on the outside of buildings and containers which have dangerous chemicals inside

haze¹ /heɪz/ n **1** [S;U] a light mist or smoke: *I could hardly see her through the haze of cigarette smoke.* | *a heat haze in the distance* **2** [S] a feeling of confusion or uncertainty in the mind —see also HAZY

haze² v [I (OVER)] to become hazy: *The sky hazed over at the end of the day.*

haze³ v [T] AmE **1** to make (someone) worried or uncomfortable by forcing them to do unpleasant work or by saying unpleasant things about them; HARASS **2** to play tricks on (a young college student) as part of the ceremony of joining a club or FRATERNITY (4). Hazing used to be common in military schools, but now is rare and forbidden by the schools.

ha·zel¹ /ˈheɪzəl/ n **1** [C] a small tree or bush that bears nuts which can be eaten **2** [U] the wood of this tree **3** also **hazelnut** the nut of this tree, which is good to eat —see picture at NUT

hazel² adj having a light brown or greenish brown colour: *She has hazel eyes.* —**hazel** n [U]

ha·zel·nut /ˈheɪzəlnʌt/ also **filbert** AmE— n HAZEL¹(3)

Haz·litt /ˈhæzlɪt/, **William** (1778–1830) an English writer and CRITIC whose works include the collection of ESSAYS called *Table Talk*

haz·y /ˈheɪzi/ adj **1** misty; rather cloudy: *The mountains were hazy in the distance.* **2** unclear; uncertain: *I'm rather hazy about the details of the arrangement.* —**ily** adv —**iness** n [U]

HB /ˌeɪtʃ ˈbiː/ adj (on a British pencil) having a centre between hard and soft. The letters stand for hard-black.

H-Block /ˈeɪtʃ blɒk‖-blɑːk/ a large building, shaped like a letter H, which is part of the Maze Prison in Northern Ireland where members of the IRA and other violent political organizations are kept. In 1980, a group of IRA prisoners went on HUNGER STRIKE because they were not treated as political prisoners, and some of them died in 1981.

HBO /ˌeɪtʃ biː ˈəʊ/ n see HOME BOX OFFICE

H-bomb /ˈeɪtʃ bɒm‖-bɑːm/ n a HYDROGEN BOMB

HCF /ˌeɪtʃ siː ˈef/ abbrev. for: highest common factor —see FACTOR (2)

HDTV /ˌeɪtʃ ˌdiː tiː ˈviː/ abbrev. for HIGH-DEFINITION TELEVISION

he¹ /i, hi; strong hiː/ pron (used as the subject of a sentence) **1** that male person or animal already mentioned: *"Where's John?" "He's gone to the cinema."* | *Be careful of that dog — he sometimes bites.* **2** (with general meaning): *Everyone should do what he considers best.* —compare THEY (4) **3** **he who** fml or lit the person who: *"He who laughs last laughs longest."* (saying)

▷ USAGE Some people, especially women, do not like the use of **he** with a general meaning. Instead they use **he or she**, **she or he** or **they**: *Everyone should do what he or she thinks best.* | *Everyone should do what they think best.* In writing, **he/she** is commonly used, or **s/he** (especially in American English).◁

he² /hiː/ n a male: *Is your dog a he or a she?*

he- see WORD FORMATION

H.E. n abbrev. for His Excellency or Her Excellency (used before the name of an important official such as an AMBASSADOR to show their rank) .

head¹ /hed/ n **1** [C] **a** the part of the body which contains the eyes, ears, nose, and mouth, and the brain: *She nodded her head in agreement.* | *They looked him over from head to foot.* | *The children were standing on their heads.* | *His crimes cost him his head.* (=it was cut off) **b** (in humans) the part of the head above and behind the eyes: *My head aches.* | *I hit my head on the low ceiling.* **2** [(the) S (of)] the end where the head rests: *at the head of the bed/the grave* **3** [C] the mind or brain: *Can't you get it into your head* (=understand) *that the adjective*

head

comes before the noun, not after it. | *His heart rules his head.*(=He is influenced more by feeling than by reason.)| *He just stood there watching; it never entered his head to help me.* | *He suddenly took it into his head* (=decided, esp. foolishly) *to buy a big new car.* | *What was it that put the idea into your head?* | *Two heads are better than one.* (= A problem or job is easier to deal with if it is shared with someone else.) **4** [C usu. sing.] infml, esp. BrE a headache: *I've got a bad head.* **5** [S (for)] a ability of the stated kind; APTITUDE: *She has a good business head.* | *I haven't got much of a head for figures.* **b** the power to be in control of oneself; COMPOSURE: *to keep one's head in a crisis* | *She managed to* **keep a cool head/a clear head** *in a difficult situation.* | *I haven't got much of a* **head for heights.** (=an ability to be in a high place without being frightened) **6** [S] a measure of height or distance equal to a head: *He is half a head taller than his brother.* | *The horse won the race by a short head.* (=by only a small amount) **7 a** [S] a person (esp. in the phrase ... **a/per head**): *It costs about £10 a head to eat there.* | *I did a quick* **head count** *and discovered that member of the class was missing.* **b** (pl. **head**) [C usu. pl.] (used in counting animals, esp. cattle) an animal: *three thousand head (of cattle)* **8** [C (**of**)] someone who is in control of a place, organization, etc.; a ruler or leader: *the head of the English department/the family* | *heads of state/of government* | *the head waiter* **9** BrE a head teacher in a school: *The head's busy at the moment.* **10** [(the) S (**of**)] a part at the top of an object (esp. of a tool) which is different or separate from the body: *the head of a hammer* | *the head of the nail* —see picture at TOOL **11** [(the) S (**of**)] **a** the top of a page: *I put my address at the head of the letter.* **b** the top or front; the highest or furthest point: *I waited at the head of the queue.* | *officers marching at the head of a column of soldiers* **12** [C] the title at the top of a piece of writing; HEADING **13** [C] the top part of some plants, esp. when several leaves or flowers grow together there:*The heads of the flowers were blown off in the storm.*| *heads of lettuce* **14** [C] the white FROTH on the top of drinks such as beer: *a beer with a good head on it* **15** [(the) S (**of**)] the upper part or end: *the head of the lake* | *at the head of the stairs* **16** [C] (esp. in names) a HEADLAND: *Beachy Head* **17** [the (**of**)] the most important place: *sitting at the head of the table* **18** [C] the white or black centre of a swollen spot on the skin (a BOIL or PIMPLE) when it is about to burst **19** [S (**of**)] the pressure or force produced by a body of water or by a quantity of steam **20** taboo sl ORGASM or sexual pleasure **21** [C] tech (in grammar) the word in a group of words that is its central part and that is used in the same way as the whole group: *The word "man" is the head of the noun phrases "an old man" and "the man in the street".* **22** [C] also **magnetic head**— **a** the part of a TAPE RECORDER which records sound **b** the part of a computer that reads and writes DATA **23 above someone's head** beyond someone's ability to understand; too difficult **24 an old head on young shoulders** (a young person who has) the sensible behaviour of an experienced person **25 bang/bash/beat/hit/knock one's head against a brick wall** to waste one's effort or hurt oneself by trying to do something impossible: *Trying to get that class to learn anything is just banging your head against a brick wall!* **26 bring/come to a head** to bring to a point where something must be done or decided: *The assassination of the president brought matters to a head.* **27 eat/talk/shout, etc., one's head off** infml to eat/talk/shout, etc. repeatedly, for a long time, loudly, etc.: *She laughed her head* *off when I told her what had happened.* **28 give someone their head** *BrE* to allow someone freedom to do as they like **29 go to someone's head: a** to make someone drunk; INTOXICATE **b** to over-excite someone: *The thrill of watching the race had gone to his head — he was jumping up and down and screaming.* **c** to make someone too proud or CONCEITED: *I hope her new important job won't go to her head.* **30 have one's ˈhead in the clouds** to be extremely impractical; not act according to the realities of life **31 have/bury one's head in the sand** to refuse to think about an unpleasant situation **32 have one's ˈhead screwed on** *infml apprec* to be sensible and practical **33 head and shoulders above** very much better than: *This book is/stands head and shoulders above all the others on the subject.* **34 head over heels: a** turning over in the air *headfirst* **b** completely; uncontrollably: *head over heels in love* **35 Heads will roll** certain people will be punished (said when a serious mistake has been made) **36 keep one's head** to remain calm in a difficult situation or an EMERGENCY: *She kept her head and put a damp blanket over the flames.* **37 keep one's head above water** to be only just able to live on one's income **b** to be only just able to keep going, working, etc. **38 lose one's head** to suddenly lose one's calmness and self-control **39 not be able to make head or tail of** to be unable to understand; be completely confused by **40 off one's head** *infml* mad; CRAZY: *He must be off his head to go jogging in this weather!* **41 out of one's head** *sl* behaving as if mad, esp. when under the influence of a drug or alcohol **42 over someone's head: a** beyond someone's ability to understand: *The lecture was a bit over their heads.* **b** without first talking to or getting the permission of someone of lower rank: *He went over the captain's head to complain to the general.* —compare OVERHEAD **43 put our/your/their heads together** to think out a plan with other people **44 take it into one's head to…** to suddenly get a silly but firm idea to… **45 talk one's head off** to talk a great deal **46 turn someone's head: a** to make someone too proud or CONCEITED: *Success had not turned his head.* **b** to make someone fall in love: *Her beauty had quite turned his head.* **47 two heads are better than one** *saying* two people thinking together can find an answer to a problem more easily than one person thinking alone **48 -headed** /hedʒd/a having a head or heads of the stated type or number: *a three-headed monster | red-headed* (=having red hair) **b** having a mind or brain of the stated type: *empty-headed* (=stupid) *| level-headed* (=calm and not easily upset) *| clear-headed* (=able to think clearly) – see also HEADS, SWOLLEN HEAD, **bite someone's head off** (BITE¹), **knock something on the head** (KNOCK¹), **standing on one's head** (STAND¹)

head² *v* **1** [T (UP)] **a** to lead; be at the front of: *The president's car headed the procession.* **b** to be in charge of: *a commission of inquiry headed by Lord Scarman | The sales director heads a team of 20 representatives.* **2** [I+adv|prep] to move in a certain direction: *After the battle, the army headed back towards Rome. | We're heading home.* **3** [T] to strike (a ball) with the head, esp. in football: *He headed it into the goal.* **4** [T] to be at the top of; provide a HEADING for: *[+obj+adj|n] The memorandum was headed "Confidential".*

head for sthg. *phr v* [T] to move towards; go to: *"Where are you heading for/headed for?" "Manchester." | After the play we all headed for the bar. | (fig.) You're heading for trouble/heading for an accident if you drive after drinking. | (fig.) The company seems to be heading for bankruptcy.* —compare ASK **for**

head sbdy./sthg. ↔ **off** *phr v* [T] **1** to cause to change direction by moving in front of: *They were running towards the house, but we headed them off at the gate.* **2** to prevent (something unwanted); FORESTALL: *The company changed its plans in order to head off a rebellion by shareholders.*

head·ache /ˈhedeɪk/ *n* **1** a pain in the head: *I always get headaches after reading. | I've got a bad headache.*

▶ CULTURAL NOTE Saying that one has a headache is a well-known excuse for not having sex, and is often mentioned in jokes. —see ACHE (USAGE)◀

2 *infml* a difficult or worrying problem: *Trying to make the children eat is one big headache!* —**achy** *adj infml* : *a headachy feeling | feeling headachy* —see also SICK HEADACHE

Head and Shoul·ders /ˌ· · ˈ··/ *n* [P;U] *tdmk* a type of SHAMPOO which is made by Procter & Gamble Ltd and which is used to remove DANDRUFF as well as to clean the hair

head·band /ˈhedbænd/ *n* a band worn around the head, usu. to keep the hair back from the face, typically worn by tennis players

head·bang /ˈhedbæŋ/ *v* [I] to move one's head violently backwards and forwards to the beat of HEAVY METAL music

head·bang·er /ˈhedˌbæŋəʳ/ *n BrE sl* **1** a person who headbangs **2** a person who behaves in a stupid or mad way: *headbangers who drive at 90 miles an hour in the fog*

head·board /ˈhedbɔːd‖-bɔːrd/ *n* an upright board forming the HEAD (=the top end) of a bed

head boy /ˌ· ˈ·/ *n* the most important boy in a school, chosen to lead a team of older boys (PREFECTS) in controlling the younger ones, and to represent the school on public occasions

head·cheese /ˈhedtʃiːz/ *n* [U] *AmE for* BRAWN (2)

head·dress /ˈhed-dres/ *n* a covering that decorates the head: *The Indian chief wore a feathered headdress.*

head·ed /ˈhedʒd/ *adj* having a LETTERHEAD: *She wrote on headed notepaper.*

head·er /ˈhedəʳ/ *n BrE* **1** a fall or a jump into water (DIVE), with the head going down before the feet **2** (in football) an act of striking the ball with the head **3** also **header tank** a TANK in a car's engine into which water is put to keep up the correct water pressure in the car's RADIATOR —see picture at ENGINE

head·first /ˌhedˈfɜːst‖-ˈɜːrst/ *adj, adv* **1** (moving) with the rest of the body following the head: *I fell headfirst down the stairs/into the water* **2** (done) with unthinking speed: *He's gone headfirst into trouble again.*

head·gear /ˈhedɡɪəʳ/ *n* [U] (a) covering for the head: *They issued caps, berets, helmets, and other types of headgear to the rescue party.*

head girl /ˌ· ˈ·/ *n* the most important girl in a British school, chosen to lead a team of older girls (PREFECTS) in controlling the younger ones, and to represent the school on public occasions

head·hunt·er /ˈhedˌhʌntəʳ/ *n* **1** a person who cuts off his enemies' heads and keeps them **2** *infml* a person who tries to attract specially able people to jobs, esp. by offering them better pay and more responsibility —**headhunt** *v* [T]

head·ing /ˈhedɪŋ/ *n* the words written as a title at the top of a piece of writing, or at the top of each part of it

head·lamp /ˈhedlæmp/ *n old-fash* HEADLIGHT

head·land /ˈhedlənd/ *n* an area of land running out from the coast into the sea; PROMONTORY

head·less /ˈhedləs/ *adj* without a head: *The headless body of a man was found in the woods.*

Headless Horse·man /ˌ··· ˈ··/ *[the]* (in ghost stories) a headless man who rides a horse, esp. in the story *The Legend of Sleepy Hollow* by Washington Irving —see colour picture on page 620

head·light /ˈhedlaɪt/ also **head·lamp** /-læmp/ *old-fash— n* [*often pl.*] a powerful light, usu. one of a pair fixed at the front of a vehicle —compare SIDELIGHT, and see picture at CAR

head·line¹ /ˈhedlaɪn/ *n* **1** the heading printed in large letters above a story in a newspaper: *The new road plan is in the headlines again.* **2** [*usu. pl.*] a main point of the news, as read on radio or television: *The time is 12 o'clock: here are the news headlines.* —see also **hit the headlines** (HIT¹)

headline² *v* [T] **1** to give a headline to: *The newspaper headlined the changes in the government.* **2** to direct attention to; bring to notice **3** *AmE* to be the leading performer in: *Frank Sinatra headlines tonight's show.*

head·long /ˈhedlɒŋ‖-lɔːŋ/ *adv, adj* **1** (done) with foolish or unthinking speed: *They rushed headlong into marriage.* **2** (happening) quickly, suddenly, and without control: *a headlong descent into anarchy and disorder* **3** HEADFIRST (1)

head·man /ˈhedmən/ *n* **-men** /mən/ a chief, esp. of a tribal village

head·mas·ter /ˌhedˈmɑːstəʳ‖ˈhedˌmæstər/ *BrE* ‖ **principal** *AmE*— *n* the male teacher in charge of a school

head·mis·tress /ˌhedˈmɪstr‰s‖ˈhedˌmɪstr‰s/ *BrE* ‖ **principal** *AmE*— *n* the female teacher in charge of a school

head of hair /ˌ‚ · ˈ‚/ *n* [S] *apprec* a thick mass of hair on a person's head: *She has a beautiful/fine/thick head of hair.*

head of state /ˌ‚ · · ˈ‚/ *n* (*often caps.*) the formal leader of a state, e.g. the Queen in Britain, as opposed to the head of government, e.g. the Prime Minister in Britain

head-on /ˌ‚ ˈ‚◂/ *adv, adj* with the head or front parts meeting, usu. violently: *The cars collided head-on.* | *a head-on collision* | (fig.) *The government and the unions are set for a head-on confrontation.*

head·phones /ˈhedfəʊnz/ *n* [P] a piece of equipment made to fit over the ears so that a person can receive radio messages, listen to recordings, etc.: *listening to the music on (a pair of) headphones*

head·piece /ˈhedpiːs/ *n* **1** something which fits closely over the head, such as the HELMET of a suit of armour **2** (in printing) a decorative heading at the top of a page or piece of writing

head·quar·ters /ˈhedˌkwɔːtəz, ˌhedˈkwɔːtəz‖-ɔːrtərz/ (*abbrev.* **HQ**) *n* **-ters** [C+*sing.*/*pl. v.*] the central office or place where the people work who control a large organization, such as the police or army or a private company: *Our headquarters is/are in Geneva.*

head·rest /ˈhed-rest/ *n* **1** something which supports the head, usu. a suitably shaped part of the back of a chair or of a front seat in a car **2** *AmE for* HEAD RESTRAINT

head re·straint /ˈ‚ · ·ˌ‚/ *BrE* ‖ **headrest** *AmE*— *n* a piece fitted on to the top of a front seat in a car to prevent a person's neck being injured in an accident

head·room /ˈhed-rʊm, -ruːm/ *n* [U] **1** the amount of space above a vehicle passing under a bridge, through a TUNNEL, etc.: *not enough headroom* **2** the amount of space above the heads of the passengers in a vehicle: *The new car has very generous headroom.*

heads /hedz/ *n* [U] **1** the front side of a coin, which often has the head of a king, queen, president, etc. on it **2 Heads or tails?** (a question someone asks when they TOSS a coin to decide something) **3 Heads I win, tails you lose** *humor* (used to describe a situation in which the person being spoken to cannot win)

head·scarf /ˈhedskɑːf‖-ɑːrf/ also **scarf**, **headsquare** *n* **-scarfs** *or* **-scarves** /-skɑːvz‖-skɑːrvz/ a square piece of cloth folded from one corner to the opposite one, worn on the head and tied under the chin. In Britain and the US headscarves are no longer fashionable, and are worn esp. by older upper-class women.

head·set /ˈhedset/ *n* HEADPHONES, often with a connected MICROPHONE

head·ship /ˈhedʃɪp/ *n* [C;U] **1** *BrE* the position or period in office of a HEADMASTER or HEADMISTRESS: *She's applied for a headship at a big London school.* **2** the position or period in office of a person in charge of an organization

head·shrink·er /ˈhedˌʃrɪŋkəʳ/ *n humor* a PSYCHOANALYST

head·stand /ˈhedstænd/ *n* an act of supporting the body upside down, with the head on the floor or ground and the feet in the air, using the hands for balance: *Can you do a headstand?*

head start /ˌ‚ · ˈ‚/ *n* [S] (**over, on**) an advantage, esp. in a race or competition: *She's got a head start over her friends who are learning French, because she has already lived in France for a year.*

head·stone /ˈhedstəʊn/ *n* a stone which marks the top end of a grave, usu. having the buried person's name on it; GRAVESTONE

head·strong /ˈhedstrɒŋ‖-strɔːŋ/ *adj* determined to do what one wants in spite of all advice

heads up /ˌ‚ · ˈ‚/ *interj infml* (used as a warning of danger coming from above) put your heads up and see what is coming: *Heads up — here comes the ball!*

head ta·ble /ˌ‚ · ˈ‚·/ *n AmE for* TOP TABLE

head teach·er /ˌ‚ · ˈ‚·/ ‖ **principal** *AmE*— *n* the teacher who is in charge of a school; a HEADMASTER or HEADMISTRESS: *J. Beilby Smith, leader of the Head Teachers' Association*

head wait·er /ˌ‚ · ˈ‚·/ *n* the person in charge of WAITERS

(=people who bring food to the tables in a restaurant)

head·way /ˈhedweɪ/ *n* **make headway** to advance or gain good results in dealing with a difficulty: *They're trying to reduce expenditure by 10% but they're not making much headway.*

head·wind /ˈhedˌwɪnd/ *n* a wind coming from in front and blowing directly against one

head·word /ˈhedwɜːd‖-wɜːrd/ *n* the word which is written at the beginning of a description of its meaning, esp. in dictionaries: *The next headword is "heady".*

head·y /ˈhedi/ *adj* **1** (of alcohol and its effects) tending to make people drunk, GIDDY, etc. **2** giving or having a feeling of lightness and excitement: *heady with success* | *On the last day of term there was a heady atmosphere of excitement and relief.*

heal /hiːl/ *v* **1** [I (OVER, UP)] (of a wounded part of the body) to become healthy again, esp. to grow new skin: *The cut will soon heal up/heal over.* **2** [T (**of**)] *fml or old use* to make (a person or part of the body) healthy again; CURE: *This ointment will help to heal the wound.* | *He was healed of his sickness.* | *The leader tried to heal the divisions within his party.* —see also FAITH HEALING

heal·er /ˈhiːləʳ/ *n* a person who has, or is thought to have, the power to heal others

Hea·ley /ˈhiːli/, **Den·is** /ˈden‰s/ (1917–) a British politician who was the Labour Minister of Defence in the 1960s and Chancellor of the Exchequer (=finance minister) in the 1970s

healing touch /ˌ‚·· ˈ‚/ [*the*] the power to heal people by touching them: *The King was formerly thought to have the healing touch.* | (fig.) *She put my car right in next to no time—she's definitely got the healing touch!*

Heal's /hiːlz/ a large shop in London which sells good quality modern furniture

health /helθ/ *n* **1** [U] the state of being well in the body and mind, and free from disease: *Health is more important to me than money.* | *physical/mental health* **2** [U] the condition of the body with regard to disease: *in poor health* | *I've always enjoyed* (=had) *good health.* | *Cigarette smoking damages your health.* **3** [C;U] (before drinking) (a wish for) someone's success and continued freedom from illness (esp. in the phrases **drink someone's health**, **Your (good) health!**) —see also BILL OF HEALTH, DRINK¹ (3), NATIONAL HEALTH SERVICE

health and safe·ty /ˌ‚ · · ˈ‚·/ *n* an area of British government and law concerned with people's health and safety, esp. at work. **Health and safety inspectors** visit factories, offices, restaurants, etc. to check that the law is being obeyed, and many institutions have their own **health and safety officer**.

Health and Safe·ty at Work Act /ˌ‚ · · ˌ‚··· · ˈ‚ ˌ‚/ [*the*] a set of laws made in Britain in 1974 in order to protect people at work and make sure that they do not have to work in dangerous conditions or without proper clothing, etc.

Health and Safe·ty Com·mis·sion /ˌ‚ · · ˈ‚·· ·ˌ‚·/ [*the*] a British organization which, since 1974, has been responsible for making sure that people do not have to work in dangerous conditions, esp. in industry

Health and Safe·ty Ex·ec·u·tive /ˌ‚ · · ˈ‚· ··ˌ‚···/ also **HSE** *abbrev.*— [*the*] a British government organization with powers to advise on and control standards of health and safety at work

health care /ˈ‚ ·/ *n* [U] the process of looking after people's health, including medical treatment and advice on how to stay healthy. In Britain, health care is provided partly by the National Health Service and partly by PRIVATE MEDICINE.

health cen·tre /ˈ‚ ˌ‚·/ *n* in Britain, a building where several doctors work and a person can go to see their doctor or to have treatment from a nurse

health club /ˈ‚ ·/ *n* a privately owned place with special equipment where people can go to take exercise. In the 1980s exercising to be healthy became fashionable in Britain, and many health clubs were established. It is usu. quite expensive to be a member. In the US, the fashion of health clubs goes back to the 1970s.

health farm /ˈ‚ ·/ *n* an establishment, usu. in the country, where rich or fashionable people go when they want to lose weight

health food /ˈ· ·/ n [C;U] (a kind of) food that is believed to be good for health, esp. food that is in the natural state, without added chemicals: *Is there a health food shop in town?*

▶ CULTURAL NOTE For some people health food is very important and a very good thing. Other people laugh at people who eat it and say that they are CRANKS (= people who hold silly ideas very strongly). —compare JUNK FOOD ◄

health·ful /ˈhelθfəl/ adj old-fash or lit likely to produce good health: *the healthful mountain air*

health in·su·rance /ˈ· ·ˌ··/ n [U] a contract with an insurance company which promises that if a person pays a regular amount of money usu. each month, the insurance company will pay all or most of any medical bills if that person becomes ill or is hurt in an accident. Because there is no national health service in the US, medical care is extremely expensive. Most people have some kind of health insurance, which is partly paid by their employer or by a family member's employer —compare HEALTH MAINTENANCE ORGANIZATION, LIFE INSURANCE

health main·te·nance or·gan·i·za·tion also **HMO** abbrev. /ˈ· ,··· ···,··/ n (in the US) a hospital or group of hospitals run by one organization in order to treat paying members of that organization. People who are members may go to any of those hospitals for treatment when they are ill. —compare HEALTH INSURANCE

Health Min·is·ter /ˈ· ,···/ n the member of the British government who is the head of the Department of Health

Health Ser·vice /ˈ· ,··/ [the] the British NATIONAL HEALTH SERVICE

health vis·it·or /ˈ· ,···/ n (in Britain) a nurse whose job is to visit people in their homes and give them advice. Health visitors work mainly with women who have just had a baby, old people, and people who have a physical disability.

health·y /ˈhelθi/ adj **1** physically strong and not often ill; usually in good health: *healthy children* | (fig.) *The country's economy is not very healthy.*

▶ CULTURAL NOTE In Britain and the US, it has become fashionable to take plenty of exercise, to eat WHOLEFOODS, to avoid food containing E NUMBER chemicals, and to lose weight. People who are very careful about their health are popularly called **health freaks**, and jokes sometimes suggest that health freaks do not have much fun, esp. because the food they eat is simple and does not contain fat, sugar, or other unhealthy but enjoyable things. ◄

2 a likely to produce good health: *healthy seaside air* **b** good for the mind or character: *That book is not healthy reading for a child.* **3** showing good health: *a clear healthy skin* | *a healthy appetite* —opposite **unhealthy**: **b** showing a good or favourable condition: *healthy profits from our overseas operations* **c** showing a strong or sensible character; natural: *The children have a healthy dislike of school|a healthy disrespect for these silly rules.* —**-ily** adv —**-iness** n [U]

Hea·ney /ˈhiːni/, **Sea·mus** /ˈʃeɪməs/ (1939–) an Irish poet. His collections of poems include *Death of a Naturalist* and *Seeing Things.*

heap¹ /hiːp/ n [(of)] **1** a disorderly pile or mass of things one on top of the other: *The books lay in a heap on the floor.* | *a heap of dirty clothes waiting to be washed* | *a heap of sand|leaves* **2** [often pl.] infml a lot: *We have heaps of time.* | *a whole heap of trouble* **3 be struck/knocked all of a heap** old-fash infml to be very surprised or confused —see PILE (USAGE), and see picture at PILE

heap² v **1** [T+obj+adv|prep] to pile up in large amounts: *Some old furniture had been heaped up in the corner.* [+obj+with] *He heaped the plate with food.* [+obj+on] *He heaped food on the plate.* | *a heaped tablespoonful of flour* **2 heap** praises **on/upon** to give a lot of praise to

hear /hɪəʳ/ v **heard** /hɜːd‖hɜːrd/ **1** [I;T not in progressive forms] to receive (sounds) with the ears: *I heard a funny noise in the middle of the night.* | *I can't hear very well.* [+obj+to-v-v] *I heard her say so.* | (fml) *He was heard to observe that he did not agree with the verdict.* [+obj+v-ing] *I can hear someone knocking.* —compare LISTEN; see CAN¹ (USAGE), SEE (USAGE) **2** [T not usu. in progressive forms] to be told or informed: *Have you heard the latest news?* [+(that)] *I hear there's going to be an election in March.* | *I've* **heard it said** *that she's a tough business-*

woman. | *"I passed my driving test." "Yes, so I've heard."* | *We've been hearing quite a lot about that young tennis player recently.* | *Have you heard anything of Bob lately?* (=received any news about him) —see also HEAR **about**, HEAR **of 3** [T] (esp. of a person in an official position) to listen with attention: *The Judge heard the case in court.* | *The priest heard my confession.* **4 Hear! Hear!** (an expression of agreement). This is the usual expression of Members of Parliament when they support what is being said in parliament. **5 hear tell (of)** infml to get to know by being told: *I've often heard tell of the wonderful parties she gives, but I've never been invited.* **6 'hear things** infml to imagine that one hears something that has not been said: *I must be hearing things* (=I can't believe what I have heard) — *they can't really have given the job to that idiot!* —see also **see things** (SEE¹) **7 won't/wouldn't hear of** refuse(s) to allow: *I won't hear of you walking to the station — let me give you a lift!* **8 have you heard the one about...** infml (a common beginning for a joke) — ~ **er** n

▷ USAGE Compare **hear** and **listen (to).** 1 You **hear** something, but you **listen to** something. 2 To **hear** is to take in sound with the ears, whether one wants to or not: *I'm a little bit deaf so I didn't* **hear** *him knocking.* To **listen** is to pay attention in order to hear: *We always* **listen to** *the six o'clock news on the radio.* | *If you* **listen** *hard, you can hear what the neighbours are saying.*◁

hear about sbdy./sthg. phr v [T] to get to know: *Did you hear about the party? — It was a complete failure.* [+obj+v-ing] *Have you heard about Gatsby jumping into the pool with all his clothes on?*

hear from sbdy. phr v [T] to receive news from (someone), usu. by letter: *I heard from him last week.* | *I look forward to hearing from you in the near future.* (=written at the end of a letter) —compare HEAR **of**

hear of sbdy./sthg. phr v [T usu. in questions and negatives] to have knowledge of or receive information about (a fact, the existence of a person or thing, etc.): *Who's he? — I've never heard of him.* [+obj+v-ing] *I've never heard of anyone doing a thing like that.* | *He disappeared in the Amazon region and hasn't been heard of since|and that's the last we heard of him.* —compare HEAR **from**; see also UNHEARD-OF

hear sbdy./sthg. **out** phr v [T pass. rare] to listen to (a person or their words) until they have finished speaking: *Don't interrupt, just hear me out.*

hear·ing /ˈhɪərɪŋ/ n **1** [U] the sense by which one hears sound: *Her hearing is getting worse.* —see also HARD OF HEARING **2** [U] the distance at which one can hear; EARSHOT: *Don't talk about it in her hearing.* (=so that she can hear) **3** [C] an act or occasion of listening: *At first hearing I didn't like the music.* **4** [C] a chance to be heard explaining one's position: *She felt that her proposal hadn't been given a fair hearing.* **5** [C] a trial of a case before a judge or any official inquiry at which witnesses are heard

hearing aid /ˈ··· ·/ also **deaf-aid** BrE infml— n a small electric machine fitted near the ear, which makes sounds louder for people with weak hearing —compare LISTENING DEVICE

hear·ken, harken /ˈhɑːkən‖ˈhɑːr-/ v [I (to)] lit to listen

hear·say /ˈhɪəseɪ‖ˈhɪər-/ n [U] things which are said rather than proved: *I'm told he didn't resign; he was fired — but it's only hearsay.* | *Hearsay evidence is not acceptable to the court.*

hearse /hɜːs‖hɜːrs/ n a vehicle which is used to carry a body in its COFFIN to the funeral before being put in the grave

Hearst /hɜːst‖hɜːrst/, **Wil·liam Ran·dolph** /ˈwɪljəm ˈrændɒlf‖-dɑːlf/ (1863–1951) an American businessman who owned many popular newspapers. It is thought that Orson Welles' film *Citizen Kane* was based on Hearst.

heart /hɑːt‖hɑːrt/ n **1** [C] the organ inside the chest which controls the flow of blood by pushing it round the body: *a weak heart* | *The patient's heart is beating strongly.* | (fig.) *My heart stood still when I saw her.* (=I was unable to move or think clearly) —see picture at RESPIRATORY **2** [C] the heart when thought of as the centre of a person's feelings, esp. of kind or sincere feelings: *Don't let your heart rule your head.* (=Don't let your feelings influence your ideas, decisions, etc.) | *My* **heart bled** (=I was very sorry) *for the starving children.* | *I felt* **sick at heart.** (=sad and without hope) | *He has a kind|warm|cold*

heart. | *Have a heart!* (=be sympathetic/forgiving) | *You can't expect me to do all that work in one day!* | *She died of a* **broken heart.** | *I thanked her with all my heart|from the bottom of my heart.* (=very sincerely) | *The nuclear issue is a subject* **close to her heart.** (=something she is deeply concerned about) | *She originally said she wouldn't help us, but she seems to have had a* **change of heart.** (=her feelings have changed) | *The political party campaigned to win the* **hearts and minds** *of the young people* (=to gain their complete and eager support) **3** [C] something in a shape supposed to be like the shape of a heart. A heart is used to represent the love between a man and a woman. It frequently appears on VALENTINE cards which people, esp. young unmarried people, send to the man or woman they love on VALENTINE'S DAY. **4** [C] **a** a heart-shaped figure printed in red on a playing card **b** a card belonging to the SUIT (=set) of cards that have one or more of these figures printed on them: *the five|queen of hearts* | *I have only two hearts in my hand.* —see CARDS (USAGE) and see picture at CARDS **5 a** [(*the*) S (**of**)] the central or most important part: *in the heart of New York's financial district* | *Let's get to the heart of the matter|the subject.* | *new reforms that* **strike at the heart of** *the capitalist system* **b** [C] the firm middle part of some leafy vegetables: *artichoke hearts* **6** [U] determination or strength of purpose: *I did the job for a few weeks but* **my heart wasn't in it.** | *I used to dig the garden every week, but I* **lost heart** *when the rain washed all the plants away.* | *I didn't* **have the heart** *to tell her the bad news.* **7 after one's own heart** similar to oneself or of the type one likes: *He's a man after my own heart.* **8 at heart: a** really; in fact: *He seems friendly, but he's just a ruthless businessman at heart.* **b** in one's care or thoughts: *Believe me, I have your best interests at heart.* **9 by heart** by memory: *to learn a poem by heart* **10 have one's heart in the right place** *infml* to be a kind or generous person, perhaps in spite of one's outward manner **11 heart and soul** with all one's attention and strength; completely **12 in one's heart of hearts** in one's most secret feelings; in reality: *I told her I loved her, but in my heart of hearts I knew it wasn't true.* **13 my heart sank** I suddenly lost hope: *My heart sank when I saw the length of the queue.* **14 my heart was in my mouth** *infml* I was full of fear for a short time: *My heart was in my mouth as she made her last jump.* **15 take heart** to be encouraged **16 set one's heart on something** to want something very much and to expect to have or do it: *The children have set their hearts on going to the zoo, so we can't disappoint them.* **17 take something to heart** to feel the effect of something deeply (and take suitable action): *She took your criticisms very much to heart and she's working harder now.* | *Don't take what she says so much to heart.* **18 the way to a man's heart is through his stomach** *saying* the way to make a man love you is to cook good food for him **19 to one's heart's content** as much as one wants: *It's the weekend, so you can sleep to your heart's content.* **20 -hearted** /ˈhɑːtɪd‖ˈhɑːr-/ having a heart or character of the stated kind: *kind-hearted* | *cold-hearted* (=without kind feelings) | *stout-hearted* (=full of determination) —see also BROKEN-HEARTED, LONELY HEARTS, PURPLE HEART, **eat one's heart out** (EAT), **lose one's heart to** (LOSE), **wear one's heart on one's sleeve** (WEAR¹)

heart·ache /ˈhɑːteɪk‖ˈhɑːrt-/ *n* [U] *esp. lit* deep feelings of sorrow

heart at·tack /ˈ· ·ˌ·/ *n* a sudden serious medical condition in which the heart stops working properly, usu. because of a CORONARY² —compare HEART DISEASE

heart·beat /ˈhɑːtbiːt‖ˈhɑːrt-/ *n* **1** [U] the action or sound of the heart as it pushes the blood round the body **2** [C] one pushing movement of the heart: *We thought he was dead, but then we detected a heartbeat.*

heart·break /ˈhɑːtbreɪk‖ˈhɑːrt-/ *n* [U] deep sorrow or terrible disappointment

heart·break·ing /ˈhɑːtˌbreɪkɪŋ‖ˈhɑːrt-/ *n* causing deep sorrow or terrible disappointment: *a heartbreaking news report about starving children* – –**ly** *adv*

heart·brok·en /ˈhɑːtˌbrəʊkən‖ˈhɑːrt-/ also **broken-hearted**– *adj* (of a person) deeply hurt in the feelings; full of sorrow: *absolutely heartbroken over the death of her pet cat*

heart·burn /ˈhɑːtbɜːn‖ˈhɑːrtbɜːrn/ *n* [U] *not tech* a condition in which one feels an unpleasant burning in the chest,

caused by acid acting on food in the stomach; it is a sign of INDIGESTION

heart dis·ease /ˈ· ·ˌ·/ *n* [C;U] (an) illness which prevents the heart from working properly. Britain has one of the highest rates of heart disease in the world. —compare HEART ATTACK

heart·en /ˈhɑːtn‖ˈhɑːr-/ *v* [T *often pass.*] to cause to feel happier or more hopeful; encourage: *We were heartened by the fall in the unemployment figures.* | *heartening news* –opposite **dishearten** – –**ingly** *adv*

heart fail·ure /ˈ· ˌ·/ *n* [U] the stopping of the movement of the heart, esp. resulting in death

heart·felt /ˈhɑːtfelt‖ˈhɑːrt-/ *adj* deeply felt; sincere: *a heartfelt apology* | *my heartfelt thanks*

hearth /hɑːθ‖hɑːrθ/ *n* **1** the area around the fire in a house, esp. the floor of the fireplace. The hearth is often thought of as the centre of a family's life. —see picture at FIREPLACE **2 hearth and home** home as a centre of family life

hearth·rug /ˈhɑːθrʌg‖ˈhɑːrθ-/ *n* a RUG (=type of floor covering) in front of the fireplace

heart·i·ly /ˈhɑːtɪli‖ˈhɑːr-/ *adv* **1 a** with strength, force, etc.: *He laughed heartily.* **b** in large amounts: *They ate heartily.* **2** thoroughly: *I'm heartily sick of your constant complaining.*

heart·land /ˈhɑːtlænd‖ˈhɑːrt-/ *n* the central or most important part of a country or area: *the Russian heartland*

heart·less /ˈhɑːtləs‖ˈhɑːrt-/ *adj* cruel; unkind; pitiless: *a heartless refusal|attitude* | *How can you be so heartless?* – –**ly** *adv* – –**ness** *n* [U]

heart-lung ma·chine /ˌ· ˈ· ·ˌ·/ *n* a machine which can do the work of a person's heart while a doctor is operating on the heart

Heart of En·gland /ˌ· · ˈ·‖/ [*the*] the central area of England. This expression is used esp. to tourists to make the area sound attractive.

Heart of Mid·lo·thi·an /ˌ· · ·ˈ·‖·/ also **Hearts** *infml* a football team based in Edinburgh, Scotland (from the name of an old Edinburgh prison)

heart·rend·ing /ˈhɑːtˌrendɪŋ‖ˈhɑːrt-/ *adj* causing deep sorrow or pity; PITIFUL: *the heartrending cries of the starving children* – –**ly** *adv*

heart·search·ing /ˈ· ˌ·/ *n* [U] painful thinking about one's attitude or behaviour in a difficult situation: *After much heart-searching, they decided to have the baby adopted.*

heart·sick /ˈhɑːtˌsɪk‖ˈhɑːrt-/ *adj* *esp. lit* feeling very unhappy or disappointed

Hearts of Oak /ˌ· · ˈ·/ an 18th-century British song and march which celebrate Britain's skill in naval matters

heart·strings /ˈhɑːtˌstrɪŋz‖ˈhɑːrt-/ *n* [P] someone's deep feelings of love and sympathy: *The sight of the little boy crying* **tugged at my heartstrings.**

heart·throb /ˈhɑːtθrɒb‖ˈhɑːrtθrɑːb/ *n sl* a man who is very attractive and with whom girls fall in love

heart-to-heart /ˌ· · ˈ·◂/ *n, adj* [A] (a talk) that is open and sincere, esp. between two people, mentioning personal details, without hiding anything: *It's time we had a heart-to-heart (chat) about your work.*

heart·warm·ing /ˈhɑːtˌwɔːmɪŋ‖ˈhɑːrtˌwɔːr-/ *adj* giving a feeling of pleasure, esp. when someone has been very kind: *a heartwarming response to our appeal for help* – ~**ly** *adv*

heart·wood /ˈhɑːtwʊd‖ˈhɑːrt-/ *n* [U] the older harder wood at the centre of a tree —compare SAPWOOD

heart·y /ˈhɑːti‖ˈhɑːrti/ *adj* **1** friendly and sincere; WARM-HEARTED: *a hearty welcome* **2** (of a person) strong and healthy; full of VIGOUR: *He's very* **hale and hearty** *for a man of 75.* **3** (of meals) large; SUBSTANTIAL **4** *infml, esp. BrE* (too) cheerful, esp. when noisy and trying to appear friendly **5 my hearties** *old use* (a friendly form of address used by and to men, esp. sailors): *Pull away, my hearties!* —see also HEARTILY –**iness** *n* [U]

heat¹ /hiːt/ *v* [I;T (UP)] to make or become warm or hot: *We'll heat (up) some milk for the coffee.* | *a pan of water heating on the stove* | *a heated swimming pool*

heat² *n* **1** [U] the degree of hotness; temperature: *Use the circular switch to adjust the heat of the oven.* **2** [U] a condition of being hot; high temperature: *The heat from* *the fire dried their clothes.* | *a chemical reaction that produces tremendous heat* | *The spacecraft is made of heat-resistant metal.* **b** hot weather: *I can't walk about in this heat.* | *We liked living in a tropical country but we couldn't stand the heat.* **3** [U] a state or time of great excitement or activity, or strong feeling: *In the heat of the moment|argument I lost my self-control.* | *The heat is on.* (=activity, excitement, and pressure have started) | *take the heat off* (=reduce the pressure) | *He tried to take the heat out of the debate.* (=tried to calm the feelings of those taking part) —see also HEATED **4** [U] a state of sexual excitement happening regularly to certain female animals, such as female dogs (esp. in the phrases **on heat** (*BrE*)/**in heat** (*AmE*)) **5** [C] a part of a race or competition whose winners then compete against other winners to decide the end result: *She was knocked out in the qualifying heats.* **6** [U] *tech* the force produced by the movement of groups of atoms —see also DEAD HEAT, PRICKLY HEAT, WHITE HEAT **7 the heat is on** someone is under a lot of pressure, usu. to work harder: *The heat is on for him now — he either improves his work or he loses his job.* **8 If you can't stand the heat, get out of the kitchen** *saying* if you cannot accept the problems and pressure that come with a job or situation, you should leave the situation

heat·ed /ˈhiːt̬ᵻd/ *adj* with strong, excited, and often angry feelings; IMPASSIONED: *a heated debate* | *She got very heated about it.* —compare HOT¹ (3) — **~ly** *adv*

heat·er /ˈhiːtəʳ/ *n* a machine for heating air or water: *Did you remember to turn the heater off?* | *a fan heater* — compare STOVE¹, and see picture at CAR

heat ex·chang·er /ˈ· ·ˌ··/ *n* a piece of equipment in a car heater or POWER STATION (=place where electricity is produced) which makes heat go from one liquid or gas to another

heat ex·haust·ion /ˈ· ·ˌ·/ *n* [U] weakness and sickness caused by doing too much when it is very hot: *Many of the refugees are suffering from heat exhaustion.*

heath /hiːθ/ *n* **1** [C] an open piece of wild unfarmed land where grass and other plants grow; MOOR¹ or COMMON² **2** [U] a kind of bush with small flowers; HEATHER or LING

Heath, Sir Edward (Ted /tɛd/) (1916–) a British Conservative politician who was PRIME MINISTER from 1970 to 1974 and led Britain into the European Community

Heath·cliff /ˈhiːθklɪf/ the central character in the book *Wuthering Heights* by Emily Brontë. Attractive to Catherine Earnshaw (Cathy) because of his wildness, he is prevented from marrying her and later punishes those who have ruined his life.

hea·then¹ /ˈhiːðən/ *n old-fash* **1** [*the* +P] people, esp. in a distant or wild place, who are not Christians. This word was used esp. in the 19th century when Britain was building its EMPIRE (=possession of other countries by force). As companies went to these countries to get cheap goods, missionaries (MISSIONARY) went to teach Christianity to the heathen, people they thought of as either wicked or not knowing about the right ways to behave: *They went out to Africa to convert the heathen.* —compare PAGAN **2** a person, esp. in a distant or wild place, who does not belong to one of the large established religions **3** *infml, often derog* a person who is regarded as wild and uncivilized: *He's nothing but a heathen.*

heathen² *adj* not Christian and usu. living in a distant or wild place

heath·er /ˈhɛðəʳ/ *n* [U] a small bush which grows on open windy land and has small purple, pink or white flowers. People connect heather with Scotland where the mountainsides are purple with heather in the autumn. White heather is said to be lucky and gypsies (GYPSY) sometimes try to sell it.

Heath Rob·in·son /ˌ· ˈ···/ *adj BrE, usu. humor* (of a machine or system) very clever and COMPLICATED, but in an impractical and amusing way (after W Heath

Pit Head **by Heath Robinson**

Robinson (1872–1944), an English artist who drew complicated imaginary machines to do simple jobs): *He had rigged up an extraordinary Heath Robinson contraption for watering the plants in his sitting room.*

Heath·row Air·port /ˌhiːθrəʊ ˈeəpɔːt‖-ˈeərpɔːrt/ also **Heathrow** /ˌhiːθˈrəʊ◂, ˈhiːθrəʊ‖ˈhiːθrəʊ/ an important international airport to the W of London, the largest airport in Britain

heat·ing /ˈhiːtɪŋ/ ‖ also **heat** *AmE*— *n* [U] a system for keeping rooms and buildings warm: *Turn the heating down.* | *a big heating bill* —see also CENTRAL HEATING

heat light·ning /ˈ· ˌ··/ *n* [U] *esp. AmE* LIGHTNING without thunder or rain, and which is a flash of light over a large area, seen esp. in warm countries —compare SHEET LIGHTNING

heat·proof /ˈhiːtpruːf/ *adj* not damaged by heat: *a heatproof work surface*

heat pump /ˈ· ·/ *n* an apparatus which collects heat from one place and moves it to another, usu. into a building, by means of warm air or water, usu. sent through pipes

heat rash /ˈ· ·/ also **prickly heat**— *n* [C;U] painful red spots close together on the skin caused by heat and SWEAT (=liquid which comes out of the body through the skin)

heat-re·sis·tant /ˈ· ·ˌ··/ *adj* (of dishes, surfaces, etc.) not easily damaged by heat: *a tray with a heat-resistant surface*

heat-seek·ing /ˈ· ··/ *adj* having a guiding apparatus that looks for and then tries to get to a hot place, esp. the hot gases coming from an aircraft, ROCKET, etc.: *heat-seeking missiles*

heat shield /ˈ· ·/ *n* the part of a spacecraft which prevents the front from getting too hot as it comes back to the Earth

heat·stroke /ˈhiːtstrəʊk/ *n* [U] a sometimes severe condition of fever and weakness caused by too much heat — compare SUNSTROKE

heat wave /ˈ· ·/ *n* a period of unusually hot weather

heave¹ /hiːv/ *v* **1** [I;T+obj+adv|prep] to lift and pull or push with great effort: *We heaved him to his feet.* | *We heaved the piano up the steps.* | *They heaved away at the heavy crate, but it didn't move an inch.* **2** [T+obj+adv|prep] *infml* to throw (esp. something heavy): *The children have just heaved a brick through my window.* **3** [I] to rise and fall regularly: *Her chest heaved as she breathed deeply after the race.* **4** [T] (of a person) to give out (a sound, esp. a sad sound): *We all heaved a sigh of relief.* | *to heave a groan* **5** [I] to try to bring up food from the stomach, esp. because of illness; RETCH **6** *BrE* **be heaving** *infml* be extremely busy: *"How was the supermarket?" "Oh, it was absolutely heaving. I'd forgotten there was a holiday tomorrow."* **7** [I+adv|prep] (*past tense usu.* **hove**) *tech* (of a ship) to move in the stated direction or manner: *As we came into harbour another ship hove alongside.* | (fig., humor) *We were just about to go when my old friend Pete hove into view.*

heave to *phr v* **hove** /həʊv/ [I] *tech* (of a ship) to stop moving; come to rest: *When the ship received the signal, she hove to.*

heave² *n* **1** [C] an act of heaving something: *One more heave, boys, and the stone will be in place.* **2** [U (of)] a regular rising and falling movement: *the heave of the sea*

heave-ho /ˌ· ˈ·/ *n sl* **give (someone) the (old) heave-ho** to dismiss (someone) from a job

heav·en /ˈhɛvən/ also **heavens** *pl.*— *n esp. lit* the sky: *a grey heaven* | *Suddenly, the heavens opened.* (=it began to rain very hard)

Heaven, heaven *n* **1** the place where God or the gods are supposed to live; a place of complete happiness where the souls of good people go after death

▶CULTURAL NOTE In the Christian religion, Heaven is thought of as a place full of light and the home of ANGELs, servants of God with wings, who play musical instruments (HARPS). People are said to go **up** to Heaven and **down** to Hell, and Heaven is often thought of as high in the sky. The gates of Heaven are guarded by Saint Peter, who holds the keys to Heaven. When people arrive at the gates of Heaven, Saint Peter asks them questions to find out whether they have been good enough to be let in. — compare HELL◀

2 [U] *infml* a state of great happiness: *I was in heaven*

Heaven

when I heard the good news. The beach was heaven. | It was **sheer heaven** being able to stay in bed all day. —see also SEVENTH HEAVEN, **move heaven and earth** (MOVE¹) **3** (often in expressions of surprise or annoyance) God: Heaven help us if the newspapers ever find out about this. | Heaven knows (=I can't imagine) what would have happened if the police hadn't arrived. | For Heaven's sake shut up! **4 Heavens! Good Heavens! Heavens alive!** (expressions of surprise or annoyance)

heav·en·ly /ˈhevənli/ adj **1** infml wonderful; giving great pleasure: What heavenly weather! **2** [A] existing or belonging to heaven, the sky, or space: The sun, moon, and stars are **heavenly bodies**. | a heavenly choir of angels

Heavenly Twins /ˌ··· ˈ·/ [the+P] see CASTOR AND POLLUX

heaven-sent /ˌ··· ˈ·◄‖ˈ·· ·/ adj happening at just the right moment: a heaven-sent opportunity

heav·en·wards /ˈhevənwədz‖-wərdz/ also **heav·en·ward** /-wəd‖-wərd/ AmE— adv towards Heaven or the sky

heav·ies /ˈheviz/ [the+P] BrE, infml serious newspapers; QUALITY PAPERS —compare TABLOID

heav·y¹ /ˈhevi/ adj **1** of a relatively great weight, esp. of a weight that makes lifting or moving difficult: a heavy rock | This bag is too heavy for me to lift. | a heavy winter coat **2** of unusually great force, amount, or degree: heavy rain | Reports are coming in of heavy fighting in Beirut. | The judge imposed a heavy fine. | heavy traffic | The army suffered heavy casualties/a heavy defeat. | She's a heavy smoker/drinker. (=she smokes/drinks a lot) | She's a heavy sleeper. (=she sleeps deeply) **3 a** demanding great effort of the mind or great physical effort: The report makes pretty heavy reading. | Moving that piano was heavy work. **b** (esp. of periods of time) full of hard work: I've had a heavy day. **4** feeling or causing sadness or disappointment: a heavy heart | heavy news **5 a** feeling or showing difficulty or slowness in moving: My head is heavy. | heavy movements | a heavy breathing **b** difficult to dig or move in: heavy soil **6** (of food) rather solid and difficult for the stomach to DIGEST: a heavy fruitcake **7 a** (of the sky) full of dark clouds; OVERCAST **b** (of the sea) rough and stormy, with big waves **8** [F+on] infml a severe or unsympathetic (in dealing with): Don't be too heavy on her. **b** using in large quantities: This car is heavy on oil. **9** old-fash sl troublesome or threatening. When people hear this word they often think of HIPPIEs and the popular way of life of the 1960s: It's too heavy here, man. We'd better leave. **10 find something heavy going** to find that something is very difficult, esp. something that needs great effort of the mind: I tried to read the report but I found it heavy going. **11 make heavy weather of something** to make a job or problem seem more difficult than it really is —opposite **light** (esp. for 1,2,3,4) —**ily** adv: moving/breathing/drinking heavily | They are heavily dependent on imported oil. | heavily-armed guards —**iness** n [U]

heavy² adv in a dull unsatisfying way (in the phrases **lie heavy on/hang heavy on**): Time hung heavy on his hands. (=seemed to pass slowly)

heavy³ n **1** infml a rough and violent person; THUG: a gang of heavies **2** a serious usu. male part in a play, esp. a bad character

heavy breath·er /ˌ··· ˈ··/ n **1** a person who breathes loudly when asleep **2** a man who telephones a woman, usu. a woman he does not know, and breathes noisily to frighten her or to suggest sexual pleasure **heavy breathing** n [U]

heavy cream /ˌ··· ˈ·/ n [U] AmE thick cream

heavy-du·ty /ˌ··· ˈ···◄/ adj **1** (of clothes, TYRES, machines, etc.) made to be used a lot, or strong enough for rough treatment **2** infml (of people and social occasions) causing worry, pressure, STRAIN² (2), etc.

heavy goods ve·hi·cle /ˌ··· ˈ· ˌ···/ also **HGV** n BrE a large vehicle used for carrying goods from one place to another, for example from the WAREHOUSE to the SUPERMARKET

heavy-hand·ed /ˌ··· ˈ···◄/ adj **1** unkind, unfair, or severe in the way one treats other people: a heavy-handed style of management **2** not careful in speech and action; TACTLESS: a heavy-handed compliment **3** awkward in movements of the hands; CLUMSY —~ly —~ness n [U]

heav·y-heart·ed /ˌheviˈhɑːtɪd◄‖-ˈhɑːr-/ adj esp. lit sad; DEPRESSED

heavy hit·ter /ˌ··· ˈ··/ n AmE **1** a BASEBALL player who hits the ball hard and often gains points for his/her team **2** a person who has a lot of power, esp. in business or politics, and so can get things done to his/her advantage: The Russians are bringing on their heavy hitters in this latest round of arms talks.

heavy hy·dro·gen /ˌ··· ˈ···/ n [U] tech a type of HYDROGEN heavier than the more common ISOTOPE

heavy in·dus·try /ˌ··· ˈ···/ n [U] the branch of industry that produces large goods, such as cars or aircraft, or materials (such as coal, steel, or chemicals) which are used in the production of other goods —compare LIGHT INDUSTRY

heavy-lad·en /ˌ··· ˈ···◄/ adj **1** carrying a heavy load **2** lit having too many worries and troubles

heavy met·al /ˌ··· ˈ···/ n [U] loud ROCK MUSIC with a strong beat and with the GUITAR sound increased by electric instruments.

▶CULTURAL NOTE Heavy metal attracts men more than women. Some people who are keen on heavy metal HEADBANG, that is, they shake their heads violently in time with the beat. They often have long hair and wear black clothes, esp. black leather JACKETS, and clothes with chains on them. Some are interested in the association of heavy metal with evil. —compare HARD ROCK, CLASSIC ROCK◄

heavy pet·ting /ˌ··· ˈ··/ n [U] sexual activity up to but not including SEXUAL INTERCOURSE

heavy-set /ˌ··· ˈ·◄/ adj (of people) rather broad and stronglooking, sometimes rather fat

heavy wa·ter /ˌ··· ˈ··/ n [U] tech water containing HEAVY HYDROGEN

heav·y·weight /ˈheviweɪt/ n **1** a person or thing that is a of more than average weight **b** of great importance or influence: one of the heavyweights of the film industry **2** a BOXER of the heaviest class, weighing 175 pounds (79 kilos) or more —see also LIGHT HEAVYWEIGHT

heb·dom·a·dal /hebˈdɒmədl‖-ˈdɑː-/ adj fml rare weekly —~ly adv

He·bra·ic /hɪˈbreɪ-ɪk/ adj of or concerning the Hebrew people, language, or civilization

He·brew /ˈhiːbruː/ n **1** [C] a member of the Jewish people, esp. in ancient times **2** [U] the language used by the Jews, in ancient times and at present —**Hebrew** adj

Heb·ri·des /ˈhebrɪdiz/ [the + P] a group of islands W of the Scottish mainland, made up of the **Inner Hebrides** (the largest islands of which are Skye, Raasay, Rhum, Eigg, Coll, Tiree, Mull, Jura, Colonsay, and Islay), and the **Outer Hebrides** (Lewis and Harris, North Uist, Benbecula, South Uist, and Barra) —see colour map on page 818 —**bridean** /ˌhebrɪˈdiːən◄/ n, adj

heck /hek/ interj, n sl (used to show annoyance, give force to an expression, etc.): Oh heck! I've lost my keys again! | a heck of a lot of money | It's rather expensive, but what **the heck!** (=it doesn't matter)

heck·le /ˈhekəl/ v [I;T] to interrupt (a speaker or speech) with disapproving or unfriendly remarks, esp. at a political meeting —**ler** n

heck·u·va /ˈhekəvə/ also **helluva**— adj AmE infml heck of a; very good, ADMIRABLE: I think I'd make a heckuva farm wife.

hec·tare /ˈhektɑːʳ, -teəʳ‖-teər/ n a unit for measuring area —see TABLE 2

hec·tic /ˈhektɪk/ adj full of excitement or hurried activity: a hectic day at the office —~ally /kli/ adv

hec·tor /ˈhektəʳ/ v [I;T] to behave in a noisy threatening way towards (someone), esp. in order to get them to do what one wants

Hector the leader of the Trojans in the Trojan War, whose body was dragged around the walls of Troy by Achilles, who killed him

he'd /id, hid; *strong* hiːd/ *short for:* **1** he would: *He'd go if he could.* **2** he had: *By the time I got there, he'd gone.*

hedge¹ /hedʒ/ n **1** a row of bushes or small trees planted close together, usu. cut level at the top, which divides one garden or field from another —see picture at HOUSE **2** [(against)] something that gives protection, esp. against possible loss: *Buying a house will be a hedge against inflation.*

hedge² v **1** [T] to make a hedge round (a field) **2** [I] to refuse to answer directly: *You're hedging again − have you got the money or haven't you?* **3** [I] *tech* (of the STOCK MARKET) to buy or sell a COMMODITY (1) to establish a definite price for future use **4 be hedged about with/around with** *fml* to be full of or surrounded by, esp. in a way that causes difficulty or limits one's actions: *We're trying to build an extension to the house, but the whole procedure seems to be hedged about with problems.* **5 hedge one's bets** to protect oneself against possible loss, e.g. by supporting more than one side in a competition or argument
hedge sbdy./sthg. ↔ **in** *phr* v [T] to surround or enclose, esp. so that escape is impossible

hedge·hog /ˈhedʒhɒg‖-hɔːg/ n a type of small insect-eating animal which is active at night. It has SPINES (=stiff, sharp-pointed parts) which stand out from its back to protect it when it rolls itself into a ball after being attacked. People have a friendly attitude to hedgehogs, and some people leave bread and milk for them in their gardens at night. —compare PORCUPINE

hedgehog

prickle/spine

snout

hedge·row /ˈhedʒrəʊ/ n a row of bushes or low trees growing on a bank of earth, esp. along a country road or separating fields

hedge spar·row /ˈ·ˌ··/ n a common small bird of Europe and America

he·don·is·m /ˈhiːdən-ɪzəm/ n [U] the practice of living one's life purely for pleasure, esp. physical pleasure —compare EPICUREAN **—ist** n **—istic** /ˌhiːdəˈnɪstɪk◂/ adj

hee·bie-jee·bies /ˌhiːbi ˈdʒiːbiz/ n [the+P] *infml* nervous anxiety caused by fear

heed¹ /hiːd/ v [T] *fml* to give attention to; consider seriously: *She didn't heed my warning/advice.*

heed² n [U] *fml* careful attention, esp. to advice or requests; notice (esp. in the phrases **pay heed to**, **take heed of**): *Pay heed to/Take heed of her advice.* **− ~ful** adj **− ~less** adj : *Heedless of our advice, he went for a swim and was attacked by a shark.*

Hee Haw /ˈhiː hɔː/ an American television programme which featured simple humour about country people and country music

hee-haw n [S] the sound made by a DONKEY

heel¹ /hiːl/ n **1** the rounded back part of the foot —see picture at FOOT **2 a** the part of a shoe, sock, etc., which covers the heel **b** the raised part of a shoe underneath the back of the foot —see also HEELS, and see picture at SHOE **3** *old-fash sl* a man with no sense of honour; CAD **4 bring to heel** to bring under control; force to obey **5 come to heel: a** (of a dog) to follow close to its master **b** (of a person) to begin to obey or stop disobeying **6 kick one's heels** not to have anything particular to do: *I'm just kicking my heels until the meeting.* **7 lay someone by the heels** *BrE old use* to catch someone and put them in prison **8 on/at one's heels** (following) very closely behind: *The police were (hot) on our heels.* | *Heavy rain followed (hard) on the heels of the thunder.* **9 take to one's heels** to run away at once **10 turn on one's heel** to turn away suddenly, esp. angrily or rudely **11 under the heel of** completely in the power of: *The whole country was under the heel of a foreign army.* —see also ACHILLES' HEEL, DOWN-AT-HEEL, WELL-HEELED, **cool one's**

heels (COOL²), **dig one's heels in** (DIG¹), **show a clean pair of heels** (SHOW¹)

heel² v **1** [T] to put a heel on (a shoe) **2** [I *usu. imperative*] (of a dog) to move along at the heels of someone **3** [T] (in RUGBY) to send (the ball) backwards with the heel
heel over *phr* v [I] to lean over at an angle, ready to fall: *The ship heeled over in the storm.*

heels /hiːlz/ n [P] HIGH HEELS —compare FLATS

Heep /hiːp/, **U·ri·ah** /juːˈraɪə/ a wicked character in Dickens's story *David Copperfield* who pretends to be very willing to do everything his master wishes, but in reality controls him and cheats him. He is known esp. for saying repeatedly that he is **so very 'umble** (=HUMBLE).

Hef·ner /ˈhefnəʳ/, **Hugh** /hjuː/ (1926−   ) an American who started Playboy magazine and is connected with Playboy Clubs

hef·ty /ˈhefti/ adj **1** big and powerful: *a hefty man* | *a hefty punch on the jaw* **2** large in amount: *The judge imposed a hefty fine.* **3** (of objects) big and difficult to move; BULKY **—tily** adv

He·gel /ˈheɪgəl/, **Ge·org Wil·helm Fried·rich** /ˈɡeɪɔːɡ ˈvɪlhelm ˈfriːdrɪk, -ɪx‖ˈɔːrg-/ (1770−1831) a German thinker (PHILOSOPHER)

he·gem·o·ny /hɪˈɡeməni, ˈhedʒ₁məni‖hɪˈdʒeməni, ˈhedʒ₁məʊni/ n [U] *fml* leadership and control of one state over other states; DOMINANCE

He·gi·ra, Hejira /ˈhedʒ₁rə, hɪˈdʒaɪərə/ [the] the escape of Muhammad from Mecca to Medina in the year AD 622

Hegira cal·en·dar /ˌ··· ˈ···, ·ˌ·· ˈ···/ [the] the Muslim system of dividing a year of 354 days into 12 months and numbering the years from the Hegira —compare GREGORIAN CALENDAR

Hei·del·berg /ˈhaɪdəlbɜːɡ‖-bɜːrɡ/ a university town in SW Germany

Hei·di /ˈhaɪdi/ a little girl who is the chief character in the children's book *Heidi* by Johanna Spyri (1827−1901)

heif·er /ˈhefəʳ/ n a young cow which has not yet given birth to a CALF —compare BULLOCK, OX, STEER

heigh-ho /ˈheɪ ˌhəʊ/ *interj* (used humorously to express tired acceptance of something unpleasant, e.g. that it is time to start work again): *Heigh-ho, I suppose we'd better get back to work.*

height /haɪt/ n **1** [C;U] the quality or degree of being tall or high: *His height makes him easy to see in the crowd.* | *What's the height of the Empire State Building?* (=How high is it?) **2** [C] (a point at) a fixed or measured distance above another given point: *a window at a height of 5 metres above the ground* | *During the floods the river rose to the height of the main road beside it.* **3** [C] *also* **heights** *pl.* − a high position or place: *We looked down from a great height to see the whole town below us.* | *the Golan Heights* | *I'm afraid of heights.* **4** [(the)] S (**of**) **a** the highest degree: *It's the height of stupidity to go sailing when you can't swim.* | *She always dresses in the height of fashion.* **b** the main or most active point: *at the height of the storm/the tourist season* | *when the crisis/the famine was at its height*

height·en /ˈhaɪtn/ v [I;T] to make or become higher or greater: *to heighten a wall* | *As she waited, her excitement heightened.* | *The dramatic lighting heightened the effect of the exhibition.* | *a heightened awareness of the problem*

Heim·lich ma·noeu·vre /ˈhaɪmlɪk məˌnuːvəʳ, -lɪx-/ *also* **abdominal thrust** *esp. BrE* − n a method of saving someone who is CHOKING (=dying because something stuck in the throat prevents breathing). A person standing behind the person in trouble puts his/her arms around the person and pushes into the person's chest quickly and suddenly to force the object out of the person's throat. The Heimlich manoeuvre can be learned in a FIRST AID course —see also FIRST AID

Hei·ne /ˈhaɪnə/, **Hein·rich** /ˈhaɪnrɪk, -ɪx/ (1797−1856) a German poet noted for his political SATIRE

Hei·ne·ken /ˈhaɪnₐkən/ n [U] *tdmk* beer made by the Dutch company Heineken. Many people remember their advertisements, which had amusing pictures and the words "Heineken. Refreshes the parts other beers cannot reach." People sometimes use these words humorously when they are talking about other subjects.

hei·nous /ˈheɪnəs/ adj *lit or fml* (of morally bad people or

acts) extremely wicked or shameful: *a heinous crime* −
~ly *adj* − ~ness *n* [U]

Heinz /haɪnz/ *tdmk* a well-known company that makes
tinned food, esp. BAKED BEANS. On their tins it says
"Heinz 57 varieties", and people sometimes mention this
when they want to say that there are many different
kinds of something: *Heinz baby food* | (fig., humor) *Our
dog's a bit of a Heinz.* (i.e. it is a MONGREL, with many
different varieties of dog in its family)

heir /eər/ *n* [(**to**)] the person who has the legal right to
receive the property or title of another person, usu. an
older member of the same family, when that person dies:
The king's eldest son is the heir to the throne | *the birth
of a son and heir* (=first son)

heir ap·par·ent /ˌ · ·ˈ··/ *n* **heirs apparent** [(**to**)] the heir
whose right to receive the family property or title can-
not be taken away until he dies: *the heir apparent to the
throne* | (fig.) *the heir apparent to the party leadership* −
compare HEIR PRESUMPTIVE

heir·ess /ˈeərɪs, ˈeəres/ *n* a female heir, esp. to great
wealth. People sometimes make jokes about men dreaming of marrying wealthy heiresses, and popular
newspapers often have stories about unmarried wealthy
heiresses and the men they are seen with: *He hopes to
marry a rich heiress and stop working.*

heir·loom /ˈeəluːm‖ˈeər-/ *n* a valuable object that has been
passed on by older members of a family to younger ones
over many years or even several centuries: *I wouldn't sell
that vase. It's an heirloom.*

heir pre·sump·tive /ˌ · ·ˈ··/ *n* **heirs presumptive** [(**to**)] an
heir whose right to a title or property can be taken away
if someone else with a stronger right is born −compare
HEIR APPARENT

Hei·sen·berg /ˈheɪzənbɜːg‖-bɜːrg/, **Wer·ner Karl** /ˈveənə
kɑːl‖ˈveərnər kɑːrl/ (1901−76) a German PHYSICIST noted
for his work on the behaviour of atoms, who won the 1932
Nobel Prize for PHYSICS

Heis·man Tro·phy /ˈhaɪsmən ˌtrəʊfi/ also **Heisman
Me·mo·ri·al Tro·phy** /ˌ · ·ˈ··· ˌ··/ *fml− n* a prize given
each year to the best college FOOTBALL (2) player in the
US

heist /haɪst/ *n AmE infml* an act of stealing something, usu.
of great value; a ROBBERY or BURGLARY **heist** *v* [T] : *Somebody heisted $50,000 from the safe over the weekend.*

He·ji·ra /ˈhedʒɪrə, hɪˈdʒaɪərə/ [*the*] the HEGIRA

held /held/ *past tense & participle of* HOLD

Hel·en of Troy /ˌhelən əv ˈtrɔɪ/ also **Helen**− in CLASSICAL
MYTHOLOGY, the wife of Menelaus and the most beautiful of women

▶ CULTURAL NOTE In the West, Helen of Troy is still one
of the most famous beautiful women. She was the wife of
a Greek, Menelaus, but followed her lover Paris to Troy.
The Greeks went to war against Troy (the TROJAN WAR) and,
by hiding their men inside a wooden horse (the TROJAN
HORSE) which they gave as a gift to the men of Troy, succeeded in getting her back. Troy was destroyed. This story
was told by Homer in the *Iliad*, and has been retold many
times in European literature. In the later story of Faust, in
which a man sells his soul to the Devil for the pleasures
of this world, Faust chooses Helen. The phrase "Is this the
face that launched a thousand ships?", speaking of the
beauty of Helen, comes from Christopher Marlowe's play
about Faust (1588). ◀

hel·i·cop·ter /ˈhelɪkɒptər‖-kɑːp-/ also **whirlybird** *AmE
infml− n* a type of aircraft which is made to fly by a set
of large fast-turning metal blades fixed on its top, and
which can land in a small space and take off without running over the ground

he·li·o·graph /ˈhiːliəɡrɑːf‖-ɡræf/ *n* an instrument which
sends messages by directing flashes of sunlight with a
mirror

he·li·o·trope /ˈhiːliətrəʊp, ˈhe-‖ˈhiː-/ *n* **1** [C] a type of
garden plant with purplish flowers which turn towards
the sun **2** [U] the colour of this flower

hel·i·port /ˈhelɪpɔːt‖-pɔːrt/ *n* a usu. small airport for
helicopters

he·li·um /ˈhiːliəm/ *n* [U] a gas that is a simple substance
(ELEMENT) that is lighter than air, will not burn, and is
used in AIRSHIPs and some kinds of lights

he·lix /ˈhiːlɪks/ *n tech* something with the form of a SPIRAL[1]
(2)

hell

hell /hel/ *n* **1** [U] (*often cap.*) (esp. in the Christian and Muslim religions) a place where the souls of the DAMNED (bad
people) are said to be punished after death.

▶ CULTURAL NOTE In the Christian religion, Hell is thought
of as a place full of darkness and fire, where people burn
for ever. People are said to go **up** to heaven and **down** to
Hell, and Hell is often thought of as deep below the ground.
Satan, the devil, has control of the people in Hell. −
compare HEAVEN ◀

2 [S;U] a state or experience of great suffering: *The troops
at the front went through hell.* | *The new airport has made
our lives hell because of the continual noise.* | *Central Lon-
don was* **sheer** *hell on the Saturday before Christmas.* **3**
[(*the*)S;U] *sl* (a swear word, used in anger or to give force
to an expression) −see also HELLUVA: *What the hell's that
thing on your head?* | *That's a hell of a price to pay for
a shirt.* | *a hell of a lot of money* | *He's got* **a hell of a cheek**
coming in here and expecting us to do his work. | *"Are you
going to do his work?" "The hell I am!"* (=No, certainly
not.) | *If you don't like it, you can go to hell!* | *Oh hell −
I've missed the last train!* **4** All **'hell broke loose** a sudden noisy disorder broke out **5 come hell or high
water** in spite of whatever difficulties may happen: *They
were determined to finish the job, come hell or high water.*
6 for the hell of it *infml* just for fun and for no other reason: *We decided to go swimming at midnight just for the
hell of it.* **7 give someone hell** *infml* to treat or speak
to someone very angrily or severely: *My father was in bed
when I came in late, but he gave me hell next morning.* **8
hell for leather** *infml, esp. BrE* very fast; used of movement by people: *I was half an hour late for work, and I
cycled hell for leather down the hill.* **9 Hell hath no fury
like a woman scorned** *quote* a slightly changed phrase
from a poem by William Congreve, used when saying
how cruel women can be when they have been hurt or
upset by a man **10 hell's bells** *infml* (an expression of
surprise) **11 Hell on earth** a very unpleasant situation
or way of life **12 hell to pay** *sl* serious trouble or
punishment: *There'll be hell to pay if the boss finds out
about this.* **13 like a bat out of hell** *infml* extremely
quickly: *I ran out of there like a bat out of hell!* **14 like
hell** *infml* **a** (used after the phrase) very much: *We
worked like hell to finish the job.* **b** (used before the
phrase) not at all so: *"Did he pay for the meal?" "Like hell
he did! I had to pay for it myself!"* **15 play hell with**
infml to cause disorder or confusion to: *The sudden cold
weather played hell with the weekend sports programme.*
16 when hell freezes over *infml* never (because hell is
believed to be hot with fire, and will never freeze)

he'll /iːl, hiːl; *strong* hiːl/ *short for:* **1** he will **2** he shall

hell-bent /ˌ · ˈ·◀/ *adj* [F+on] *infml* completely determined
to do something, without considering possible dangers:
She's hell-bent on climbing that mountain.

hell-cat /ˈhelkæt/ *n* a fierce hot-tempered woman

Hel·lene /ˈheliːn/ *n fml* a Greek, esp. an ancient Greek

Hel·len·ic /heˈlenɪk/ *adj* of or concerning the history, civilization, or art of the Greeks, esp. during the ancient period
before the death of Alexander the Great (323 BC)

Hel·le·nis·tic /ˌheliˈnɪstɪk◀/ *adj* of or concerning the history, civilization, or art of ancient Greece and other countries of the Eastern Mediterranean during the period
after the death of Alexander the Great (323 BC)

Hel·les·pont /ˈheliˌspɒnt‖-pɑːnt/ [*the*] a former name for the
Dardanelles

hell·hole /ˈhelhəʊl/ *n* a place in which conditions for a human are extremely bad

hell·ish /ˈhelɪʃ/ *adj* **1** *infml* very bad or unpleasant; *hellish weather* | *I've had a hellish day at work.* **2** of or like HELL (1) – ~**ly** *adv* : *a hellishly difficult exam*

Hell·man /ˈhelmən/, **Lil·li·an** /ˈlɪliən/ (1905–84) an American writer of plays known especially for *The Children's Hour* and *The Little Foxes.* She is also remembered for refusing to name anyone as a Communist in front of HUAC.

hel·lo /həˈləʊ, he-/ also **hallo, hullo** BrE– *interj, n* **-los 1 a** (the usual word used when greeting someone): *Hello, John! How are you?* | *I don't know her name but she always says hello to me in the street.* **b** (the word used for starting a telephone conversation): *Hello, is Mrs Brown there?* | *Hello, who's speaking, please?* **2** *esp. BrE* (an expression of surprise): *Hello! Where's he gone?* **3** (a call for attention to a distant person): *Hello! Is anybody there?* **4 Hello, hello, hello, what's all this here?** *BrE* a phrase used by policemen in humorous stories and jokes

hell's angels

hell's an·gel /ˌ· ˈ··/ *n* (*often caps.*) a member of a group (CHAPTER) of badly behaved and sometimes violent young people who wear black clothes and ride MOTORBIKES. Hell's Angels were common in the 1960s.

hell·uv·a /ˈheləvə/ *adj infml* a hell of a; a great deal of: *It makes a helluva difference.*

helm /helm/ *n* **1 a** the TILLER or wheel which guides a ship (esp. in the phrase **at the helm**) **b** the position from which things are controlled: *How long has the present director been at the helm?* **2** *old use* a helmet

helmets

astronaut's helmet   crash helmet   fireman's helmet

see also picture at **hat**

hel·met /ˈhelmɪt/ *n* a strong covering to protect the head, as formerly worn by soldiers in armour, and now worn by people who might hurt their heads in accidents or at work, such as CYCLISTs, MOTORCYCLISTs, policemen, firemen, or miners –compare HARD HAT; see also CRASH HELMET

hel·met·ed /ˈhelmɪtɪd/ *adj* wearing a helmet

Helms /helmz/, **Jes·se** /ˈdʒesi/ (1921–) a Republican senator from North Carolina who is known for being REACTIONARY (=strongly opposed to social change)

Helms·ley /ˈhelmzli/, **Le·o·na** /liˈəʊnə/ (1921–) an American owner of expensive New York hotels, who often appeared in advertisements before them. In 1989 she was found guilty of tax EVASION (=not paying taxes she owed) and she began serving a prison sentence in 1992.

helms·man /ˈhelmzmən/ *n* **-men** /mən/ *esp. lit* a person who guides and controls, esp. when at the HELM of a boat

Hél·o·ïse /ˈeləʊiːz‖ˈhe-/ the lover and wife of Peter Abelard –see Peter ABELARD

help¹ /help/ *v* **1** [I;T (**with**)] to make it possible for (someone) to do something, by doing part of the work oneself;

be of use to (someone in doing something); ASSIST: *Is there anything I can do to help?* | *Thank you for helping us.* | *Can you help me with my homework?* [+obj+to-v] *The neighbours helped us to move the piano.* [+obj+to-v] *They helped us move it.* [+obj+adv/prep] *Let me help you in with those bags.* (=Let me help you bring them in.) | *I helped her into her coat.* | *"Can I help you?"* (=May I show you anything?) *said the shop assistant.* **2** [T] to encourage, improve, or produce favourable conditions for (something): *The fall in the oil price will help our economic development.* | *Helped by favourable weather, the country produced a record harvest.* [+obj+to-v/to-v] *All this arguing isn't going to help us (to) win the election.* **3** [I;T] to make (a person or situation) better or less painful; RELIEVE: *Crying won't help (you).* | *What have you got that will help a cold?* **4** [T] to avoid, prevent, or have control over (only with **can/can't/couldn't**): *He can't help his rather loud voice.* | *She can't help herself, she doesn't mean to be so rude.* | *I can't help it* (=It's not my fault) *if all the trains are cancelled.* | *He never does any more work than he can help.* (=He does as little as possible.) [+v-ing] *I couldn't help laughing when I saw his haircut.* | *I can't help thinking that we've made a big mistake.* **5** [T (**to**)] to give something to (someone) or take something for (oneself): *"Can I have a drink?" "Help yourself!"* | *Let me help you to some more potatoes.* | *The money was on the table and no one was there, so he helped himself (to it).* (=he stole it) **6 be helping the police with their inquiries** *BrE* to be being questioned by the police because they think that you have committed (COMMIT) a crime **7 It can't be helped** these things happen, we must accept it: *It's a pity the weather's so bad for our holiday, but it can't be helped.* **8 so help me/so help me God** on my solemn promise: *I swear to tell the truth, so help me God.* | *I'll pay you back, so help me (I will)!* – ~**er** *n*

▷ USAGE Compare **help, assist,** and **aid. 1 Help** and **assist** often have the same meaning but **assist** is more formal and always suggests that the person being assisted is doing part of the work: *I can't push the car on my own – will someone* **help/assist** *(fml) me?* If someone is in difficulties you **help** (not **assist**) them: *They* **helped** (=saved) *the drowning man.* | *His job consists of* **helping** *old people who live alone.* **Aid** *fml* is like **help** but is not so commonly used. **2 Help** can be followed by a verb in the infinitive form: *He* **helped** *me (to) pass my exam* (=I passed). **Assist** and **aid** are not used in this way.◁

help (sbdy.) **out** *phr v* [I;T] to give help (to someone) at a time of need: *My mother helped me out (with some money) when I lost my job.* | *The children help out in their father's shop when things are busy.*

help² *n* **1** [U] the act of helping; AID; ASSISTANCE: *Can I give you any help?* | *Can I be of any help?* | *We got it open with the help of a knife.* | *I couldn't have done it without your help.* | *I'm afraid the patient is* **beyond help.** (=can no longer be helped) **2** [C (**to**)] something or someone that helps: *You've been a great help.* | *I find this new machine quite a help.* **3** [C] *BrE* ‖ **helper** AmE– a person, esp. female, who is employed to do some of someone else's housework: *a home help provided by the local authority* | *She has a help in twice a week.* **4** [U] *esp. AmE* workers, esp. house servants: *Good help is hard to find.* **5 Help!** Please bring help, I'm in danger! **6 There's no help for it** The damage has been done, and nothing can now be done to improve the situation

help·ful /ˈhelpfəl/ *adj* [(**to, in**)] providing help or willing to help; useful: *a helpful boy/map/suggestion* | *It was very helpful of you to do that typing for me.* – ~**ly** *adv* – ~**ness** *n* [U]

help·ing /ˈhelpɪŋ/ *n* [(**of**)] a serving of food; PORTION: *I'd like a second helping, I'm still hungry!* | *large helpings*

helping hand /ˌ·· ˈ·/ *n* **give/lend someone a helping hand** to give help and support to someone who needs it

help·less /ˈhelpləs/ *adj* unable to look after oneself or take action to help oneself: *a helpless child* | *Without proper defences, we'd be helpless against an enemy attack/helpless to prevent an enemy attack.* – ~**ly** *adv* – ~**ness** *n* [U]

help·line /ˈhelplaɪn/ *n* a telephone number you can ring if you need the special advice or information offered, e.g. on personal problems or financial matters –compare CRISIS LINE

help·mate /ˈhelpmeɪt/ also **help·meet** /-miːt/– *n esp. bibl* a helpful partner, usu. a wife

Help the Ag·ed /ˌ· · ˈ··/ a British organization (CHARITY) which collects money and helps old people

Hel·sin·ki /helˈsɪŋki/ the capital of Finland

Helsinki Ac·cords /·ˌ·· ·ˈ·/ also **Helsinki A·gree·ment** /·ˌ·· ·ˈ··/ *[the]* a written agreement which encourages peace in Europe. It was signed in August 1975 by 35 European countries, including Britain, and by the US, Canada, and the USSR.

hel·ter-skel·ter[1] /ˌheltə ˈskeltəʳ‖ˌheltər-/ *n esp. BrE* an amusement in a FAIRGROUND where one sits down and slides from the top of a tower to the bottom, moving round and round it

helter-skelter[2] *adv, adj* (done) in a great and disorderly hurry: *She ran helter-skelter down the stairs.*

helve /helv/ *n* the handle of an AXE or a similar tool

Hel·vel·lyn /helˈveləˌn/ a mountain in the Lake District in NW England

hem[1] /hem/ *n* the edge of a piece of cloth that is turned under and sewn down, esp. the lower edge of a skirt or dress: *The dress was too long, so I took the hem up.* (=made it shorter)

hem[2] *v* **-mm-** [T] **1** to put a hem on **2** *AmE* to take the hem up in order to shorten: *Could you hem my trousers?*
hem sbdy. ↔ **in** *phr v* [T] to surround tightly so that movement is impossible; CONFINE: *The army was hemmed in by the enemy with no hope of escape.* | (fig.) *hemmed in by planning restrictions*

he-man /ˈ· ·/ ‖ also **macho-man** *AmE*– *n infml, often humor* a man who wants people to see that he is a strong man with powerful muscles

He·ming·way /ˈhemɪŋweɪ/, **Er·nest** /ˈɜːnəˌst‖ˈɜːr-/ (1898–1961) one of the great 20th-century American writers. He wrote many NOVELS and short stories in a very direct style, celebrating men who are strong.

hem·i·sphere /ˈheməˌsfɪəʳ/ *n* **1** half a SPHERE (an object which is round like a ball) **2** a half of the Earth, esp. the northern or southern halves above and below the EQUATOR, or the eastern or western half: *What is the largest city in the southern hemisphere?* –see picture at GLOBE **3** either of the two halves of the brain: *the right hemisphere of the brain*

hem·line /ˈhemlaɪn/ *n* the length of a dress, skirt, etc., as shown by the position of the hem. At most times in the history of fashion the height of women's hemlines has been very important.

hem·lock /ˈhemlɒk‖-lɑːk/ *n* [C;U] (poison made from) a poisonous plant with white flowers and finely divided leaves. When they hear this word some people think of the ancient Greek thinker Socrates, who was killed by being made to drink hemlock.

Hemlock So·ci·e·ty /ˈ·· ·ˌ···/ *n* an American organization which supports the belief that SUICIDE (=killing oneself) is a reasonable choice, esp. for the old and sick, and should be made legal and discussed –compare EXIT and see also EUTHANASIA

he·mo·glo·bin /ˌhiːməˈgləʊbəˌn‖ˈhiːməˌgləʊbəˌn/ *n* [U] HAEMOGLOBIN

he·mo·phil·i·a /ˌhiːməˈfɪliə/ *n* [U] HAEMOPHILIA

he·mo·phil·i·ac /ˌhiːməˈfɪliæk◂/ *n* HAEMOPHILIAC

hem·or·rhage /ˈheməʳrɪdʒ/ *n* [C;U] HAEMORRHAGE

hem·or·rhoids /ˈheməroɪdz/ *n* [*usu. pl.*] HAEMORRHOIDS

hemp /hemp/ *n* [U] any of a family of plants which are used for making strong rope and a rough cloth, and some of which produce the drug CANNABIS

hen /hen/ *n* **1** a female bird often kept for its eggs on farms; female chicken –see also CHICK, CLUCK[1] A woman who worries about her children and wants to know where they are is sometimes compared to a mother hen. **2** any female bird of which the male is the COCK: *The cock has brighter coloured feathers than the hen.* | *a hen pheasant* **3** (used informally as a friendly form of address in Scotland): *What's the matter, hen?*

hen·bane /ˈhenbeɪn/ *n* [C;U] (poison made from) a poisonous wild plant with yellow flowers

hence /hens/ *adv fml* **1** (often in a phrase without a verb) for this reason or from this origin; therefore: *The town was built near a bridge on the River Cam: hence the name Cambridge.* **2** from here or from now: *2 miles hence* | *3 days hence*

hence·forth /ˌhensˈfɔːθ, ˈhensfɔːθ‖-ɔːrθ/ also **hence·for·ward** /ˌhensˈfɔːwəd‖-ˈfɔːrwərd/– *adv fml* from this time on; from now: *Following our merger with Brown Brothers, the company will henceforth be known as Johnson and Brown Inc.* –compare HEREAFTER

hench·man /ˈhentʃmən/ *n* **-men** /mən/ *usu. derog* a faithful supporter, esp. of a political leader or criminal, who obeys without question and may use violent or dishonest methods

Hen·drix /ˈhendrɪks/, **Jim·i** /ˈdʒɪmi/ (1942–70) an American popular music singer and GUITAR player who was one of the most influential ROCK[3] musicians and known for his exciting performances. His early death was caused by drink and drugs.

Jimi Hendrix

hen house /ˈ· ·/ *n* a usu. wooden hut in which hens are kept. In Britain now some people still have hens which they put in a henhouse at night, but most eggs and chickens are produced in BATTERY farms.

Hen·ley Re·gat·ta /ˌhenli rɪˈgætə/ also **Henley**– a meeting for races between rowing boats at **Henley**, a town on the Thames. Henley Regatta is an important social event for upper-class and fashionable people, and also at this event businesses entertain people who might buy goods from them.

hen·na /ˈhenə/ *n* [U] a reddish-brown DYE made from a type of bush and used to colour the hair, fingernails, etc.

hen par·ty /ˈ· ˌ··/ *n infml* a party for women only, esp. one just before a woman's wedding –compare STAG PARTY

hen·pecked /ˈhenpekt/ *adj* (of a man) continually nagged (NAG) by one's wife and completely obedient to her: *a henpecked husband*

Hen·ry I /ˌhenri ðə ˈfɜːst‖-ˈfɜːrst/ (1068–1135) an English king (1100–35), the youngest son of William the Conqueror

Henry II /ˌhenri ðə ˈsekənd/ an English king (1154–89). Henry II tried to gain more power for the state and to weaken the power of the Church. He got his men to murder the Archbishop of Canterbury (head of the Church in England), Thomas à Becket.

Henry III /ˌhenri ðə ˈθɜːd‖-ˈθɜːrd/ (1207–72) an English king (1216–72). He fought many wars which made him unpopular with the BARONS (=noblemen). Led by Simon de Montfort they fought him, but lost.

Henry IV /ˌhenri ðə ˈfɔːθ‖-ˈfɔːrθ/ **1** (1366–1413) an English king (1399–1413) who seized power from Richard II, and spent his time as king fighting the Welsh, the Scots, and others opposed to his rule **2** a play by William Shakespeare about the life of King Henry IV

Henry V /ˌhenri ðə ˈfɪfθ/ **1** (1387–1422) an English king (1413–22) who is remembered esp. for defeating the French at the Battle of Agincourt **2** a play by William Shakespeare about the life of King Henry V –see colour picture on page 1146

Henry VI /ˌhenri ðə ˈsɪksθ/ (1421–71) an English king (1422–61, 1470–71). During Henry's rule there was great dissatisfaction with the government. This led to the Wars of the Roses, in which Henry was finally murdered.

Henry VII /ˌhenri ðə ˈsevənθ/ also **Henry Tudor**– (1457–1509) an English king (1485–1509). He defeated Richard III at the battle of Bosworth Field, and married to unite the families of York and Lancaster and so ended the Wars of the Roses between the two families.

Henry VIII /ˌhenri ðə ˈeɪtθ/ (1491–1547) the most famous English king (1509–47). The most well-known fact about Henry VIII is that he had six wives. His first wife, Catherine of Aragon, failed to bear him a son, but the Pope would not allow him to DIVORCE her. As a result, the Church of England broke away from the Roman Catholic church, and Henry married Anne Boleyn. She was later found guilty of ADULTERY (=making love with another man) and Henry had her head cut off. His other wives were Jane Seymour, who died while giving birth to a child, Anne of Cleves, who Henry divorced, Catherine Howard, who was executed (EXECUTE), and Catherine Parr, who lived on after Henry's death. Henry encouraged learning and allowed the Bible to be printed in English. Under Henry England became richer and more powerful.

King Henry VIII

Henry, John a character in American stories and FOLK songs who worked on railways and was very strong

Henry, Len·ny /ˈleni/ (1958–) a popular British entertainer and COMEDIAN, often seen on television

Henry, O. (1862–1910) an American writer of short stories

Henry, Pat·rick /ˈpætrɪk/ (1736–99) an American leader during the American Revolution, famous for his phrase "Give me liberty, or give me death!"

Henry, Prince (1984–) the second son of the Prince and Princess of Wales. He is known as **Prince Harry**.

Henry Tudor /ˈ·· ˈ··/ see HENRY VII

Henry Wood Prom·e·nade Con·cert /ˌ·· · ˌ·/ n fml a PROMENADE CONCERT: *Tonight we come to the fifth in our season of Henry Wood Promenade Concerts.*

Hen·son /ˈhensən/, **Jim** /dʒɪm/ (1936–90) the man who thought of, made, and operated the Muppets, a popular set of PUPPETS (=toy people and animals made to move by a person who is hidden from the viewer) including Kermit the frog, Miss Piggy, Oscar, and the Cookie Monster, who appeared on the television shows *Sesame Street* and *The Muppet Show*

hep·a·ti·tis /ˌhepəˈtaɪtəs◂/ n [U] a disease of the LIVER that causes physical weakness and JAUNDICE (=yellowness of the skin)

hepatitis A /ˌ···· ˈ·/ n [U] a usu. less severe form of hepatitis, carried by infected food or water

hepatitis B /ˌ···· ˈ·/ n [U] a form of hepatitis carried in infected blood or HYPODERMIC needles

Hep·burn /ˈhepbɜːn‖-bɜːrn/, **Au·drey** /ˈɔːdri/ (1929–93) an actress of great beauty who appeared in British and American films of the 1950s and 1960s, and was later known for her work with children in the Third World

Katharine Hepburn and Spencer Tracey

Hepburn, Kath·a·rine /ˈkæθərɪn/ (1909–) an American film actress remembered esp. for her role in the films *Guess Who's Coming to Dinner* and *On Golden Pond*

He·phaes·tus /hɪˈfiːstəs‖-ˈfes-/ in CLASSICAL MYTHOLOGY the Greek god of fire and metalwork (Roman name Vulcan)

hep·ta·gon /ˈheptəgən‖-gɑːn/ n a shape with seven sides — ~**al** /hepˈtægənəl/ adj

Hep·worth /ˈhepwɜːθ‖-wərθ/, **Bar·ba·ra** /ˈbɑːbərə ‖ ˈbɑːr-/ (1903–75) an English SCULPTOR known for the ABSTRACT style of her work

her¹ /ər, hər; strong hɜːr/ determiner (possessive form of SHE) **1** of or belonging to her: *Mary sat down in her chair.* |

You should ask her opinion. | *It was her first attempt.* **2** (used of vehicles, countries, etc., that are thought of as female): *the ship with all her passengers*

her² pron (object form of SHE): *Where is she? Can you see her?* | *Give her the keys/Give the keys to her.* | | *Which is the girl you know? Is that her?* | *God bless this ship and all who sail in her!* —see ME (USAGE)

He·ra /ˈhɪərə/ in CLASSICAL MYTHOLOGY, the wife of Zeus and the Greek goddess who protected women and marriage. She was well-known for her jealousy. (Roman name Juno)

her·ald¹ /ˈherəld/ n **1** (in former times) a person who carried messages from a ruler and gave important news to the people **2** (esp. in Britain) an official person who keeps records of the COATS OF ARMS of noble families **3** [(of)] lit something that is a sign of something about to come, happen, etc.: *a herald of spring* —compare HARBINGER

herald² v [T (IN)] fml or lit to be a sign of (something coming or about to happen): *Their new offer may herald a breakthrough in the peace talks.* | *The singing of the birds heralded (in) the day.*

he·ral·dic /heˈrældɪk/ adj of or concerning heraldry

Herald of Free En·ter·prise /ˌ··· ··· ˈ···/ also **Herald**– [the] a cross-Channel FERRY which turned over in the port of Zeebrugge in Belgium in 1987, drowning many people. The accident happened because the doors at the front of the ship (the BOW (5) doors) had been left open.

her·ald·ry /ˈherəldri/ n [U] the study and use of COATS OF ARMS

Herald Trib·une /ˌ·· ˈ··/ also **International Herald Tribune** [the] a daily international English-language newspaper which gets some of its articles from American newspapers, and is esp. popular with Americans abroad

herb /hɜːb‖ɜːrb, hɜːrb/ n any of several kinds of small plant which are used to improve the taste of food or to make medicine: *The sauce is flavoured with herbs, including marjoram and basil.*

her·ba·ceous /həˈbeɪʃəs ‖ hɜːrˈbeɪ-, ɜːrˈbeɪ-/ adj fml or tech (of a plant) soft-stemmed, not woody

herbaceous bor·der /·ˌ·· ˈ··/ n a long flower bed of herbaceous plants that do not die in the winter. Herbaceous borders are a typical feature of English gardens and are usu. very colourful in the summer.

herb·al¹ /ˈhɜːbəl‖ˈɜːr-, ˈhɜːr-/ adj made of herbs: *herbal medicine* | *herbal tobacco*

herbal² n a book, usu. an old one, about herbs, esp. about their use as medicine

herb·al·ist /ˈhɜːbəlɪst‖ˈɜːr-, ˈhɜːr-/ n a person who grows, sells, or uses herbs, esp. one who uses herbs to treat disease. In Britain, herbalists do not usu. work within the National Health Service, and herbal medicine is considered to be an ALTERNATIVE MEDICINE.

herbal medi·cine /ˌ··· ˈ·· ‖ ˌ·· ˈ···/ n [U,C] the prevention or treatment of ill health with the use of particular plants known for their medicinal properties —see also ALTERNATIVE MEDICINE

Her·bert /ˈhɜːbət‖ˈhɜːrbərt/, **George** (1593–1633) an English METAPHYSICAL poet

herb gar·den /ˈ· ˌ··/ n a garden in which only herbs are grown. Very often different herbs are grown in different parts to make a pattern.

herb·i·cide /ˈhɜːbɪsaɪd‖ˈhɜːrb-, ˈɜːrb-/ n [C;U] tech a substance used to kill WEEDS (=unwanted wild plants); WEEDKILLER

her·bi·vore /ˈhɜːbɪvɔːʳ ‖ ˈhɜːr-, ˈɜːr-/ n a plant-eating animal: *Rabbits are herbivores; lions are not.* —compare CARNIVORE, OMNIVORE —**·vorous** /hɜːˈbɪvərəs ‖ hɜːr-, ɜːr-/ adj

Her·ce·go·vi·na /ˌhɜːtsəɡəˈviːnə‖ ˌheɑːrts-/ see BOSNIA-HERZEGOVINA

Her·cu·le·an, herculean /ˌhɜːkjʊˈliːən, hɜːˈkjuːliən‖-ɜːr-/ adj fml needing or using very great strength or determination: *a Herculean task* | *a Herculean effort*

Her·cu·les /ˈhɜːkjʊliːz‖ˈhɜːr-/ in CLASSICAL MYTHOLOGY, a man admired for performing the 12 **Labours of Hercules**, actions which were extremely difficult and needed great strength. The name is now often used to describe someone who completes difficult jobs or has great strength: *a difficult job even for Hercules*

herd¹ /hɜːd‖hɜːrd/ n 1 [C+sing./pl. v] a group of animals of one kind which live and feed together: *a herd of cattle|elephants* —compare FLOCK¹ (1) 2 [C] (*in comb.*) someone who looks after a herd: *a shepherd | a goatherd* 3 [*the*+S+sing./pl. v] derog people generally, thought of as easily led or influenced, without having their own thoughts or opinions: *to follow the herd* (=do just what everyone else does) | *the* **herd instinct** (=a feeling which makes a group act alike, esp. in being unfriendly towards strangers)

herd² v 1 [T] to look after or drive (animals) in a herd: *to herd cattle* 2 [I+adv/prep; T+obj+adv/prep] to come or bring together in a large group, esp. roughly: *They herded together|herded into the corner. | They herded the prisoners into the courtyard. | The tourists were herded into their bus.*

herds·man /ˈhɜːdzmən‖-ɜːr-/ n -men /mən/ a man who looks after a herd of animals

here¹ /hɪəʳ/ adv 1 at, in, or to this place or point: *How long have you lived here? | It's about two miles from here. | Come here! | It hurts just here. | Here in London, the temperature is 20 degrees. | Here is where I want to stay. | Come over* (=across to) *here. | They're here!* (=They have arrived.) | *At last the holidays are here.* (=the time for them has come) | (fig.) *You may not like computers, but they're* **here to stay.** (=they have become, and will remain, a part of life) 2 at this point: *Here we agree. | We've found the cause of the problem, so* **where do we go from here?** (=what should we do next?) 3 a (used for drawing attention to something or someone): *Here comes John. | Here he comes! | Here it is!* (=I've found it.) | *It is ten o'clock and here is the news.* b (used when giving something to someone): *Here's the pound I owe you. | Here you are, John.* 4 [after n] being present; in this place: *The sergeant here will take a statement from you. | It's this one here that I want.* 5 **here and there** scattered about: *There were clothes lying here and there on the floor.* 6 **Here goes!** Now I'm going to have a try (to do something, esp. something difficult): *I've never been on a horse before — well, here goes!* 7 **Here's to** (said when drinking a TOAST¹ (2)): *Here's to Sarah in her new job!* 8 **here, there, and everywhere** infml in every place 9 **here today and gone tomorrow** infml remaining a very short time 10 **neither here nor there** not connected with the matter being talked about; IRRELEVANT: *I know a lot of people like the idea, but that's neither here nor there: we just can't afford it.*

here² interj 1 (used to call someone's attention or express annoyance): *Here! What do you think you are doing?* 2 **Look here** also **See here—** Pay attention or my warning: *Look here, I can't allow this kind of behaviour in my house.*

here·a·bouts /ˌhɪərəˈbaʊts, ˈhɪərəbaʊts/ also **here·a·bout** /-aʊt/AmE— adv somewhere near here: *I think I saw a post office somewhere hereabouts.*

here·af·ter¹ /ˌhɪərˈɑːftəʳ‖-ˈæf-/ adv fml after this time; in the future —compare HENCEFORTH, THEREAFTER

hereafter² n [(*the*)S] the life after death: *Her religion promises happiness in the hereafter. | Do you believe in a hereafter?* —compare AFTERLIFE

here·by /ˌhɪəˈbaɪ, ˈhɪəbaɪ‖-ər-/ adv fml or law by means of this statement, law, etc.; by doing or saying this: *I hereby declare her elected.* —compare THEREBY

Here Comes the Bride /ˌ· ˌ· · ˈ·/ a piece of music which is often played at the beginning of a marriage ceremony, when the BRIDE begins to walk up the AISLE of the church —compare WEDDING MARCH

her·e·dit·a·ment /ˌherɪˈdɪtəmənt/ n law land and property which can be passed on after the death of the owner to his/her relatives

he·red·i·ta·ry /hɪˈredɪtəri‖-teri/ adj 1 a (of a position, title, etc.) which can be passed down from an older to a younger person, esp. in the same family: *a hereditary peer|peerage* b (of a person) having the legal right to receive such a position, title, etc.: *a hereditary peer* 2 (of a quality or condition of the mind or body) which can be passed down from parent to child in the cells of the body: *a hereditary disease | a hereditary ability* —see also INHERIT —**·rily** adv

he·red·i·ty /hɪˈredɪti/ n [U] 1 the fact that living things have the ability to pass on their own qualities from parent to child in the cells of the body: *Some diseases are present by heredity.* 2 the passing of possessions as well as qualities of mind and body from parents to children, esp. from father to oldest son: *Heredity is very important to the upper classes. They like the continuity suggested by the passing down of property from one generation to another.*

Here·ford /ˈherɪfəd‖-fərd/ a small city with a cathedral in the W of England

Hereford and Worces·ter /ˌ··· · ˈ··/ a COUNTY in the W of central England

He·re·ford·shire /ˈherɪfədʃəʳ‖-fər-/ one of the old counties (COUNTY) of England, which is now part of Hereford and Worcester

here·in /ˌhɪərˈɪn/ adv fml or law in this piece of writing, esp. in this: *... and everything herein contained | The law does not recognize this type of evidence, and herein lies the problem.* —compare THEREIN

here·in·af·ter /ˌhɪərɪnˈɑːftəʳ‖-ˈæf-/ adv law later in this official paper, statement, etc.: *Messrs Wilson and Cartwright, hereinafter referred to as "the insurers", ...*

here·of /ˌhɪərˈɒv‖-ˈʌv, -ˈɑːv/ adv fml or law of or belonging to this: *... every part hereof* —compare THEREOF

her·e·sy /ˈherəsi/ n [C;U] (the fact of holding) a belief that is against the official or accepted beliefs of a religion or other group: *She was burned at the stake for heresy in the 14th century. | The minister's speech will be regarded as heresy by most members of her party.*

her·e·tic /ˈherətɪk/ n a person who is guilty of heresy — ~ **al** /həˈretɪkəl/ adj

here·to /ˌhɪəˈtuː‖ˌhɪərˈtuː/ adv fml or law to this (agreement or piece of writing)

here·to·fore /ˌhɪətuˈfɔːʳ‖ˈhɪərtʊfɔːr/ adv fml or law until now; before this time; HITHERTO: *Meetings will continue to be held on Thursdays, as heretofore.*

here·up·on /ˌhɪərəˈpɒn‖-ˈpɑːn/ adv fml at or after this point in time —compare THEREUPON

Here We Go /ˌ· · ˈ·/ a song sung in Britain by large groups of young men, esp. football supporters, to encourage each other and frighten other people

here·with /ˌhɪəˈwɪð‖ˌhɪər-/ adv fml (esp. in business) with this (letter or written material): *I enclose herewith two copies of the contract.*

Her·gé /ˈeəʒeɪ‖eərˈʒeɪ/ (1907–83) a Belgian writer, famous esp. for the *Tintin* stories

Her·i·ot-Watt U·ni·ver·si·ty /ˌheriət ˌwɒt juːnɪˈvɜːsɪti‖-ˌwɑːt juːnɪˈvɜːr-/ a university in Edinburgh which specializes in scientific and technical subjects

her·i·ta·ble /ˈherɪtəbəl/ adj fml or law 1 (of property, qualities, etc.) which can be passed on to one's descendants; HEREDITARY 2 having the right to INHERIT

her·i·tage /ˈherɪtɪdʒ/ n [S;U] an object, custom, or quality which is passed down over many years within a nation, social group, or family, and is thought of as something valuable and important which belongs to all its members: *These beautiful old churches are part of our national heritage. | preserving our cultural heritage* —compare INHERITANCE; see also NATIONAL HERITAGE

her·maph·ro·dite /hɜːˈmæfrədaɪt‖hɜːr-/ n, adj (a living thing) with the organs or appearance of both male and female —**·ditic** /hɜːˌmæfrəˈdɪtɪk◂‖hɜːr-/ adj

Her·mes /ˈhɜːmiːz‖ˈhɜːr-/ the Greek name for the Roman messenger of the Gods, Mercury —see MERCURY

her·met·ic /hɜːˈmetɪk‖hɜːr-/ adj 1 tech very tightly closed; AIRTIGHT: *A hermetic seal prevents the escape of radioactive material.* 2 old use concerning magic or ALCHEMY: *hermetic writings* — ~ **ally** /kli/ adv : *The container is hermetically sealed.*

her·mit /ˈhɜːmɪt‖ˈhɜːr-/ n a person who lives alone, esp. for religious reasons

her·mit·age /ˈhɜːmɪtɪdʒ‖ˈhɜːr-/ n a place where a hermit lives or has lived

Hermitage [*the*] one of the world's great MUSEUMs, in St Petersburg in the former USSR, esp. famous for its IMPRESSIONIST paintings

the
March Hare

Alice

the Mad Hatter

dormouse

The Mad Hatter's Tea Party from the book
***Alice's Adventures in Wonderland* by Lewis Carroll**

There is a famous scene in this book where Alice has tea with the
Mad Hatter, the March Hare and the dormouse

Wendy

Tinkerbell

Peter Pan

Tick Tock

Captain Hook

***Peter Pan* by J. M. Barrie**
The picture shows Peter Pan, Tinkerbell and Wendy and her brothers flying
above Captain Hook and the pirates.

Robin Hood and his followers who were known as the Merry Men

The Merry Men

The Sheriff of Nottingham

Maid Marion

Robin Hood

Friar Tuck

Little John

They all lived in Sherwood Forest and took money from the rich to give to the poor. Their enemy was the Sheriff of Nottingham.

Headless Horseman

Ichabod Crane

The Legend of Sleepy Hollow by Washington Irving
In this story Ichabod Crane is chased by the Headless Horseman (a rider with no head).

hermit crab /ˈ‥ ˌ·/ n a kind of CRAB that lives in the empty, used shells of other sea creatures

her·ni·a /ˈhɜːniə‖ˈhɜːr-/ also **rupture**— n [C;U] the medical condition in which an organ pushes through its covering wall, usu. when the bowel is pushed through the stomach wall

he·ro /ˈhɪərəʊ/ n -roes 1 heroine fem.— a someone who is admired for their bravery, goodness, or great ability, esp. someone who has performed an act of great courage under very dangerous conditions: a war hero | The real hero of the match was the Tottenham goalkeeper. b the most important character in a play, poem, story, etc. — compare ANTIHERO 2 AmE a SANDWICH made of a long loaf of bread filled with meat, cheese, SALAD, etc. —see also SUBMARINE SANDWICH

Her·od /ˈherəd/ n a wicked king in Israel when Jesus Christ was born. He had all the young Jewish boys killed to try and make sure that Jesus did not become king, but Jesus' mother Mary and her husband Joseph took the young Jesus to safety in Egypt —see also FLIGHT INTO EGYPT, OUT-HEROD

he·ro·ic /hɪˈrəʊɪk/ adj 1 showing the qualities of a hero; extremely courageous: heroic deeds | heroic resistance to the evil dictator 2 tech of or concerning heroes: heroic poems — ~ **ally** /kli/ adv

heroic coup·let /·ˌ·‥ ˈ‥·/ n a pair of lines of a type once common in English poetry, which RHYME (=end with the same sound) and have five beats each —compare IAMBIC PENTAMETER

he·ro·ics /hɪˈrəʊɪks/ n [P] usu. derog speech or behaviour which is intended to appear grand or brave but means nothing

her·o·in /ˈherəʊɪn/ n [U] a powerful drug made from MORPHINE, which the user can quickly become ADDICTED to (=dependent on). It is used medically for lessening pain but is also used illegally for pleasure: the heroin traffic|a heroin addict

▶ CULTURAL NOTE Misuse of heroin is growing in Britain, and has been a problem in American cities for many years. Many ADDICTs (= people who keep taking it) die. Addicts now have a new danger, the disease AIDS which they can get by sharing the needle they use to INJECT (= put in) heroin. ◀

her·o·ine /ˈherəʊɪn/ n see HERO (1)

her·o·is·m /ˈherəʊɪzəm/ n [U] very great courage: an act of great heroism

her·on /ˈherən/ n -ons or -on a type of long-legged bird which lives near water —see picture at WATER BIRD

hero wor·ship /ˈ‥ ˌ·/ n [U] great and often secret admiration for someone who is thought to be brave, good, or have great ability. People sometimes use this word in a way that suggests that hero-worship is a rather childish emotion. It is thought to be usual in growing up that TEENAGERs go through a period of hero-worship. —**hero-worship** v [T]

her·pes /ˈhɜːpiːz‖ˈhɜːr-/ n [U] a very infectious skin disease which causes painful sores on the skin, esp. of the face or GENITALS

Herr /heəʳ/ n (used as a title for a German man): Herr Brandt

her·ring /ˈherɪŋ/ n -rings or -ring a type of fish which swims in large groups in the sea and is used for food — see also RED HERRING

her·ring·bone /ˈherɪŋbəʊn/ n a pattern in which two sides slope in opposite directions, forming a continuous line of V's, e.g. in a material or in a decorative arrangement of bricks: herringbone tweed —see picture at PATTERN

Her·ri·ot /ˈheriət/, **James** (1916–) a British writer of stories about the life of a country VET (=animal doctor). Many of his stories have been made into popular television plays.

hers /hɜːz‖hɜːrz/ pron (possessive form of SHE) of that female person or animal already mentioned: This is my coat and hers (=her coat) is over there. | My shoes are brown and hers are red. | She's a friend of hers.

her·self /əˈself, hə-; strong hɜː-‖ər-, hər-; strong hɜːr-/ pron 1 (reflexive form of SHE): She hurt herself. | She bought herself a car. 2 (strong form of **she**): She told me so herself. | She herself said so. 3 infml (in) her usual state of

mind or body: She was ill yesterday, but she's more herself today. 4 (all) by herself alone; without help: The little girl wrote the letter all by herself. | She lives by herself in the country. 5 to herself for her private use; not shared: a bedroom to herself —see YOURSELF (USAGE)

Her·shey bar /ˈhɜːʃi bɑːʳ‖ˈhɜːr-/ n tdmk a bar of chocolate made by the Hershey company and sold in the US. The Hershey company also makes a small chocolate wrapped in silver-coloured paper called a **Hershey's Kiss**

Hert·ford /ˈhɑːfəd‖ˈhɑːrtfərd/ a town N of London, where the local government for Hertfordshire is based

Hert·ford·shire /ˈhɑːtfədʃəʳ‖ˈhɑːrtfərd-/ a COUNTY in SE England, N of London

hertz /hɜːts‖hɜːrts/ n **hertz** (a measure meaning) one time each second: These radio waves are transmitted at a frequency of 15,000 cycles per second: that's 15 kilohertz or 15,000 hertz.

Hertz n tdmk an international company which hires out cars to people

he's /iz, hiz; strong hiːz/ short for: 1 he is: He's a writer.| He's reading. 2 (in compound tenses) he has: He's got two cars. | He's had a cold.

Hes·el·tine /ˈhesəltaɪn/, **Mi·chael** /ˈmaɪkəl/ (1933–) an important Conservative minister in the British government in the 1980s, who left the government over the Westland Affair. In 1990 he competed with Mrs Thatcher and John Major for the leadership of the Conservative Party, and became a minister in John Major's government. He is sometimes called Tarzan in the popular newspapers because of his hairstyle.

hes·i·tan·cy /ˈhezɪtənsi/ n [U] the quality of being hesitant; INDECISION

hes·i·tant /ˈhezɪtənt/ adj showing uncertainty or slowness about deciding to act; tending to hesitate: She's hesitant about making new friends. | his hesitant attempts to speak English — ~ **ly** adv

hes·i·tate /ˈhezɪteɪt/ v 1 [I] to pause before taking an action or making a decision: Don't hesitate when you're crossing the road. | She hesitated for a moment, and then gave her agreement. 2 [T+to-v; obj] to be unwilling to do something, esp. because it is unpleasant or because one is uncertain whether it is right: If you need any help, don't hesitate to ask. | The government will not hesitate to take the severest measures against these terrorists. 3 **he who hesitates is lost** saying if you do not do something immediately, you may never again get the chance to do it — ~ **tatingly** adv

hes·i·ta·tion /ˌhezɪˈteɪʃən/ n [C;U] (an example of) the act of hesitating: Without a moment's hesitation, she jumped into the river after the child. | I have no hesitation in recommending him for the job.

Hess /hes/, **Ru·dolf** /ˈruːdɒlf‖-ɑːlf/ (1894–1987) a German Nazi politician, second to Hitler. After the Second World War he was put in Spandau Prison in Berlin until he died.

Hes·se /ˈhesə/, **Her·mann** /ˈhɜːmən‖ˈhɜːr-/ (1877–1962) a German writer and poet

hes·si·an /ˈhesiən‖ˈheʃən/ BrE ‖ **burlap** AmE— n [U] a type of thick rough cloth made from HEMP; SACKS used to be made of it: hessian floor|wall coverings

Hes·ton /ˈhestən/, **Charlton** (1923–) an American film actor who played the leading male part in some big films full of brave action and excitement

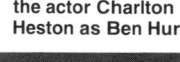

the actor Charlton Heston as Ben Hur

het /het/ adj see HET UP

het·e·ro·dox /ˈhetərədɒks‖-dɑːks/ adj fml (of beliefs, practices, etc.) against accepted opinion, esp. in religion; not ORTHODOX — compare UNORTHODOX

het·e·ro·ge·ne·ous /ˌhetərəʊ-ˈdʒiːniəs/ also **het·e·ro·ge·nous** /hetəˈrɒdʒənəs‖-ˈrɑː-/ AmE— adj fml consisting of parts or members that are very different from one another; not HOMOGENEOUS: a

heterogeneous mix of nationalities — ~ly *adv* —-ity /ˌhetərəʊdʒʒˈniːʒti/ *n* [U]

het·e·ro·sex·u·al /ˌhetərəˈsekʃuəl◂/ *adj, n* (of or being) a person who is sexually attracted to people of the other sex —compare BISEXUAL, HOMOSEXUAL, LESBIAN — ~ly *adv* — ~ity /ˌhetərəsekʃuˈælʒti/ *n* [U]

het up /ˌhet ˈʌp/ *adj* [F (**about**)] *infml, usu. derog, esp. BrE* nervous, excited, and confused: *There's no need to get so het up about it, it's only an examination.*

heu·ris·tic /hjʊəˈrɪstɪk/ *adj fml* **1** (of education) based on learning by one's own personal discoveries and experiences **2** helping one in the process of learning or discovery — ~ally /kli/ *adv*

heu·ris·tics /hjʊəˈrɪstɪks/ *n* [P;U] (the study of) the use of experience and practical efforts to find answers to questions or to improve performance

hew /hjuː/ *v* **hewed, hewed** or **hewn** /hjuːn/ *fml or lit* **1** [I; T] to cut or cut down using an AXE or other cutting tool; CHOP: *to hew down a tree/hew off a branch* **2** [T+*obj*+*adv*/*prep*] to cut and shape out from a larger mass: *to hew a canoe out of a tree trunk* | *to hew one's way through the forest* — ~er *n*

hew·er /ˈhjuːəʳ/ *n* **hewers of wood and drawers of water** *BrE fml* or *humor* a class of people used to do the heaviest physical work

Hew·lett Pack·ard /ˌhjuːlʒt ˈpækɑːd‖-ɑːrd/ a maker of computers and electronic equipment that operates in many countries

hex¹ /heks/ *n* [(**on**)] *esp. AmE* an evil curse which brings trouble: *There seems to be a hex on this car – it's always breaking down.*

hex² *v* [T] *esp. AmE* to put an evil curse on, esp. to cause harm or bad luck

hex³ *adj infml* hexadecimal: *What's the hex code for 128?*

hex·a·dec·i·mal /ˌheksəˈdesʒməl◂/ also **hex** *infml— adj tech* based on the number 16, and using 0-9 as in decimal numbers and A-F to represent 10-15. Hexadecimal numbers have many uses in computers.

hex·a·gon /ˈheksəgən‖-gɑːn/ *n* a shape with six sides — ~al /hekˈsægənəl/ *adj*

hex·a·gram /ˈheksəgræm/ *n* a six-pointed star made up from two three-sided shapes (TRIANGLEs)

hex·am·e·ter /hekˈsæmʒtəʳ/ *n* a line of poetry with six main beats

hey /heɪ/ *interj infml* (a shout used to call attention or to express surprise, interest, etc.): *Hey! Where are you going?*

hey·day /ˈheɪdeɪ/ *n* [(the) S] the time of greatest power, influence, success, or popularity: *The 1930s were the heyday of the big Hollywood musical.* | *In her heyday she was one of the highest-paid actresses in the country.*

Hey·er /ˈheɪəʳ/, **Geor·gette** /ˌdʒɔːˈʒet‖ˌdʒɔːr-/ (1902–72) a writer of popular historical love stories

hey pres·to /ˌheɪ ˈprestəʊ/ *interj infml, esp BrE* (used by someone performing a magic trick) Here is the result of my trick!

Hey·sel /ˈhaɪsəl, ˈheɪ-/ also **Heysel Sta·di·um Di·sas·ter** /ˌ··ˈ···· ·ˌ···/— *n* the death of 39 people at a Belgian football ground in 1985, caused by a wall which fell down when English supporters of Liverpool attacked other people. After this, English teams were not allowed to play in European competitions, and action was taken to stop football violence.

Hez·bo·llah /ˌhezbʊˈlɑː/ also **Hizbollah**— a Shi'ite MILITIA group supported by Iran, who were fighting the Amal group supported by Syria, in Lebanon in the 1980s

HGV /ˌeɪtʃ dʒiː ˈviː/ *n BrE* a HEAVY GOODS VEHICLE, esp. a LORRY

HGV li·cence /ˌ··ˈ·· ˌ··/ *n BrE* official written permission to drive a large vehicle, given after passing a special test

hi /haɪ/ *interj infml* (used as a greeting): *Hi, Barbara, how are you?*

HI *written abbrev. for* HAWAII

hi·a·tus /haɪˈeɪtəs/ *n* [*usu. sing.*] **1** *fml* a break or interruption: *Talks between the two countries have resumed after a six-year hiatus.* **b** a space where something is missing, esp. in a piece of writing **2** *tech* a pause between (or lack of a sound which joins) two vowel sounds

Hi·a·wath·a /ˌhaɪəˈwɒθə‖-ˈwɔː-/ a Native American chief who helped to end tribal wars in the 1400s. He is the subject of a long poem by LONGFELLOW called *The Song of Hiawatha*. American children often learn parts of this poem, so many people are familiar with the lines:

> *...By the shore of Gitche Gumee,*
> *By the shining Big-Sea-Water,*
> *Stood the wigwam of Nokomis,*
> *Daughter of the Moon, Nokomis...*

hi·ber·nate /ˈhaɪbəneɪt‖-ər-/ *v* [I] (of some animals) to be or go into a state like a long sleep during the winter: *Squirrels and hedgehogs hibernate.* —-nation /ˌhaɪbəˈneɪʃən‖ -bər-/ *n* [U] : *They've gone into hibernation.*

Hi·ber·ni·an /hɪˈbɜːniən‖-ˈbɜːr-/ also **Hibs** /hɪbz/ *infml* a football team based in Edinburgh

hi·bis·cus /haɪˈbɪskəs/ *n* [C;U] a tropical plant with large bright flowers

hic·cup¹, **hic·cough** /ˈhɪkʌp, -kəp/ *n* [*often pl.*] **1** (a sudden sharp sound caused by) a movement in the chest which stops the breath: *In the middle of the church service there was a loud hiccup from my husband.* | *an attack of hiccups* **2** [(in)] a small delay or interruption: *There's been a slight hiccup in the schedule due to a computer failure.*

hiccup² *v* [I] to have hiccups: *I couldn't stop hiccuping.*

hick /hɪk/ *n esp. AmE infml, often derog* an uneducated person from the country; YOKEL —compare REDNECK

hic·key /ˈhɪki/ *n* **hickeys** *AmE* a red mark on the neck or elsewhere on the body caused by sucking the skin. They are usu. seen on young people (TEENAGERs) who get them from a boyfriend or girlfriend: *Where did Janet get that gigantic hickey?*

Hick·ok /ˈhɪkɒk‖-ɑːk/, **Wild Bill** (1837–76) an American FRONTIERSMAN whose real name was James Butler Hickok

hick·o·ry /ˈhɪkəri/ *n* [C;U] (the hard wood of) a North American tree which bears nuts

Hicks /hɪks/, **Edward** (1780–1849) an American painter and PREACHER

hidden a·gen·da /ˌ··· ··ˈ··/ *n* a secret intention to carry out actions that would be criticized or found unacceptable if they were spoken of openly: *She came to the meeting with a hidden agenda to gain control of the budget.* | *What is the hidden agenda of the Democrats?*

hide¹ /haɪd/ *v* **hid** /hɪd/, **hidden** /ˈhɪdn/ [(**from**)] **1** [T] to put or keep out of sight; prevent from being seen or found; CONCEAL: *I hid the broken plate in the drawer.* | *The house was hidden from view by a row of tall trees.* | *Their conversation was recorded by a hidden microphone.* **2** [I] to place oneself or be placed so as to be unseen: *I'll hide behind the door.* | *(humor) Where's that book hiding?* **3** [T] to keep (facts, feelings, etc.) from being known: *I couldn't hide my disappointment.* | *I think she's hiding some important information.* | *There's a hidden meaning in this poem.* **4** **hide one's light under a bushel** *phrase from the Bible* to hide, or be MODEST about, one's ability or skill: *Come on, Bill, I know you're a good piano player – don't hide your light under a bushel!*

hide² *BrE* ‖ **blind** *AmE— n* a place from which a person can watch animals or birds, without being seen by them, esp. in order to take photographs or shoot them

hide³ *n* **1** an animal's skin, esp. when removed to be used for leather **2 not hide or/nor hair of** *infml* no sign of: *I haven't seen hide or hair of them for 20 years at least!*

hide-and-seek /ˌ·· ·ˈ·/ ‖ also **hide-and-go-seek** /ˌ··· ·ˈ·/ *AmE— n* [U] a children's game in which some hide and others search for them

hide·a·way /ˈhaɪdəweɪ/ *n infml* a place, such as a house, where one can go to avoid people

hide·bound /ˈhaɪdbaʊnd/ *adj derog* (of people) having fixed, unchangeable opinions; not willing to consider new ideas; NARROW-MINDED

Hi-de-hi /ˌhaɪ diː ˈhaɪ/ the title of a British television COMEDY programme about life in a holiday camp. In the programme, the people who work in the holiday camp use the words "hi-de-hi" as a cheerful greeting to the guests.

hid·e·ous /ˈhɪdiəs/ *adj* extremely ugly and/or shocking to the senses; REPUGNANT: *a hideous face* | *a hideous scream* | *hideous wounds* — ~ly *adv* — ~ness *n* [U]

hid·ing[1] /ˈhaɪdɪŋ/ n infml **1 a** a beating: *I'll give you a good hiding when we get home!* **b** a defeat: *The English team got quite a hiding in Paris.* **2 be on a hiding to nothing** BrE infml to completely waste one's time with no chance of success: *You're on a hiding to nothing if you think you can get her to change her mind.*

hid·ing[2] n [U] the state of being hidden (in phrases like **go into hiding, be in hiding**)

hie /haɪ/ v **hied, hying** or **hieing** [I;T] old use or humor to cause (one or oneself) to hurry or go quickly: *I will hie (me/myself) to the market.*

hi·er·ar·chy /ˈhaɪərɑːki‖-ɑːr-/ n **1** [C;U] a system by which the members of an organization are grouped and arranged according to higher and lower ranks, esp official ranks: *There's a very rigid hierarchy in the Civil Service.| the principle of hierarchy* **2** [C+sing./pl. v] **a** the group of people in an organization who have power or control: *The party hierarchy has/have the final say on matters of policy.* **b** tech a group of ruling priests —**·chical** /haɪəˈrɑːkɪkəl‖-ɑːr-/ adj —**·chically** /kli/ adv

hi·e·ro·glyph /ˈhaɪərəglɪf/ n a picture-like sign which represents a word, esp. in the writing system of ancient Egypt — ~ **ic** /ˌhaɪərəˈglɪfɪk◂/ adj

hieroglyphics

hi·e·ro·glyph·ics /ˌhaɪərəˈglɪfɪks/ n [P] a system of writing which uses hiero- glyphs

hi-fi /ˈhaɪ faɪ, ˌhaɪ ˈfaɪ/ n **hi-fis** becoming old-fash **1** [C] a piece of high-quality ELECTRONIC equipment for playing recorded sound, usu. including a record player: *Have you seen our new hi-fi? | a hi-fi shop | a* **hi-fi system** (=radio, TAPE DECK, record player, and often CD player in one unit, with suitable LOUDSPEAKERS **2** [U] HIGH FIDELITY

Hig·gins /ˈhɪgɪnz/, **Professor Henry** a character in George Bernard Shaw's play *Pygmalion*, who teaches Eliza Doolittle, a COCKNEY woman, to speak in an upper class manner

hig·gle·dy-pig·gle·dy /ˌhɪgəldi ˈpɪgəldi/ adj, adv infml in disorder; mixed together without system

high[1] /haɪ/ adj **1** (not usu. of living things) having a top that is some distance, esp. a large distance, above the ground: *How high is the wall/the mountain? | It's a very high building. | The water was waist-high.* (=as high as one's waist) **2** [after n] measuring in height: *four metres high | a building twenty storeys high* **3** at a point well above the ground or above what is usual: *That shelf is too high for me – I can't reach it. | The plane is high in the sky.* **4** near the top of the set of sounds which the ear can hear: *She sang a high note. | She has a very high voice.* **5** above the usual level, amount, rate, or degree: *I have a high opinion of her work. | the high cost of food | high blood pressure | a high salary | an area of high unemployment | a high-risk investment | high speed | high winds* **6** of great rank, importance, or influence: *She held high office in the last government. | He claims to have* **friends in high places.** (=people in very important positions) | *high society | I have it on the highest authority that he intends to resign.* **7** [A] (of time) the mid-point or most important point of: *high summer | It's* **high time** *we were going.* (=We should go at once.) | *(lit) high noon* **8** showing goodness in morals and character; worthy of admiration: *high principles | high moral standards* **9** (of certain foods) not fresh; spoilt by age: *The venison is high.* —compare GAMY **10** [F] infml a drunk **b** [(on)] under the effects of drugs: *high on marijuana* —opposite **low** (for 1,3,4,5,6,8); see also HIGHER, HIGHLY

▷ USAGE We use **high** (opposite **low**) for measurements of most things (not people), especially when we are thinking only of distance above the ground: *a* **high** *shelf | a* **high** *mountain | You can see the city from the top of that* **high** *building.* We use **tall** (opposite **short**) for people: *a* **tall** *man* and for ships: *a* **tall** *ship.* We can also use **tall** for things which are high and narrow, especially when we are thinking of the complete distance

from top to bottom: *a* **tall/high** *building | a* **tall/high** *tree*◁

high[2] adv **1** to or at a high level in position, movements or sound: *She threw the ball high into the air. | The bird sang high and clearly. | The dollar stayed high after a busy day on the foreign exchanges.* **2** to or at a high or important level in society, in an organization, etc.: *He's risen high in the world. | You've got to aim high if you want to succeed.* **3 high and dry** in a helpless situation: *They took all the money and left us high and dry.* **4 high and low** everywhere: *We searched high and low but we couldn't find it anywhere.* **5 high on the hog** AmE sl well and richly: *They've been living high on the hog since they struck oil.*

high[3] n **1** [C] a high point; the highest level: *The price of oil reached a new high/an* **all-time high** *this week.* **2** [U] esp. bibl or lit a high place, esp. heaven (in the phrase **on high**): *The Lord looked down from on high. | (humor) These decisions are handed down to the workforce from on high.* **3** [C] infml a state of great excitement and often happiness produced by or as if by a drug: *She's on a high today.* **4** [C] a weather condition with a high-pressure area; ANTICYCLONE **5 the high and mighty** derog very rich and important people, esp. the rulers of a country: *The high and mighty just don't know what it's like to have to struggle to make a living.*

-high see WORD FORMATION

high a·chiev·er /ˌ· ·ˈ···/ n someone whose work is usu. excellent or who usu. succeeds, esp. in school

high-and-might·y /ˌ· · ˈ··◂/ adj infml too proud and certain of one's own importance; ARROGANT

high·ball /ˈhaɪbɔːl/ n esp. AmE an alcoholic drink, esp. WHISKY or BRANDY mixed with water or SODA and served with ice

high·born /ˈhaɪbɔːn‖-bɔːrn/ adj fml or lit born into the highest social class; of noble birth

high·boy /ˈhaɪbɔɪ/ n AmE for TALLBOY

high·brow /ˈhaɪbraʊ/ n sometimes derog a person who is thought to have more than average knowledge of, or interest in, artistic and INTELLECTUAL matters —compare LOWBROW, MIDDLEBROW —**highbrow** adj

high chair /ˌ· ˈ·‖ˈ· ·/ n a chair with long legs at which a baby or small child can sit, esp. when eating from a table or from a special TRAY joined to the chair —see picture at CHAIR

High Church /ˌ· ˈ·◂/ adj of the part of the Church of England which places great importance on ceremony, and is closest in its beliefs to the Roman Catholic Church. High Church services include the burning of CANDLES and sweet-smelling INCENSE. —compare LOW CHURCH — ~ **man** n

high-class /ˌ· ˈ·◂/ adj **1** of good quality; SUPERIOR **2** of high social position

high com·mand /ˌ· ·ˈ·/ n [U;C] (the offices of) the top leaders and officers of a military force

high com·mis·sion /ˌ· ·ˈ··/ n [C+sing./pl. v] (often caps.) (the group of people who work in) the office (like an EMBASSY) of a high commissioner

high com·mis·sion·er /ˌ· ·ˈ···/ n (often caps.) a person who is the chief official representative of one Commonwealth country in another: *the British High Commissioner in New Delhi* —compare AMBASSADOR, CONSUL (1)

high court /ˌ· ˈ·◂/ n **1** [C] a court which is at a higher level than ordinary courts and which can be asked to change the decision of a lower court: *a high court judge* **2** [the] (caps) also **High Court of Jus·tice** /ˌ· ˌ· ·ˈ··/— the lower branch of the Supreme Court of England and Wales consisting of the Queen's Bench Division, the Chancery Division, and the Family Division —see also extra information on page 737

High Court of Jus·ti·cia·ry /ˌhaɪ ˌkɔːt əv dʒʌˈstɪʃəri ‖ -ˌkɔːrt-/ [the] the high criminal court of Scotland, dealing with murder, RAPE, and all cases involving heavy punishment —see also extra information on page 737

high-def·i·ni·tion tel·e·vi·sion /ˌ· ··ˌ·· ·····, ˌ· ··ˌ·· ··ˈ··/ also **HDTV** abbrev.— n [U;C] (a television set which uses) a modern system of broadcasting television pictures which gives a much sharper image than previous systems

high·er¹ /ˈhaɪəʳ/ *adj* **1** *comparative of* HIGH **2** [A] more advanced, esp. in development, organization, or knowledge needed: *higher animals | higher nerve centres| higher mathematics*

higher² *n* the higher level of the Scottish Certificate of Education —see also SCE —compare O GRADE —see also extra information on page 408

higher ed·u·ca·tion /ˌ··· ··ˈ··/ *n* [U] education at a university or college —compare ADULT EDUCATION, FURTHER EDUCATION

higher-up /ˌ··· ˈ·◂/ *n* [*usu. pl.*] *infml* an important person of high rank in an organization

high ex·plo·sive /ˌ··· ·ˈ···◂/ *n* [C;U] a powerful explosive

high·fa·lu·tin /ˌhaɪfəˈluːtɪ̣n◂‖-tn◂/ *adj infml derog* foolishly trying to appear serious or important; PRETENTIOUS: *a highfalutin manner*

high fi·del·i·ty /ˌ··· ·ˈ···◂/ also **hi-fi—** *n* [U] the ability (of TAPE RECORDERS, RECORD PLAYERS, etc.) to give out sound which represents very closely the details of the original sound before recording: *high fidelity equipment* —see also HI-FI

high-fli·er /ˌ··· ˈ··/ *n* an unusually clever person who has a strong desire to succeed and is regarded by others as likely to gain a high position

high-flown /ˌ··· ˈ·◂/ *adj usu. derog* (of language) important-sounding, though lacking in deep meaning: *high-flown rhetoric*

high-fly·ing /ˌ··· ˈ···◂/ *adj* **1** which flies high: *high-flying aircraft* **2** like a high-flier; AMBITIOUS

High·gate /ˈhaɪgeɪt/ an area of N London which has a large burial ground (**Highgate Cemetery**) where many famous people, including Karl Marx, are buried

high-grade /ˌ··· ˈ·◂/ *adj* of high quality: *high-grade cloth for suits | high-grade oil*

High·grove House /ˌhaɪgrəʊv ˈhaʊs/ a house in Gloucestershire, England, which is owned by the Prince and Princess of Wales

high-hand·ed /ˌ··· ˈ···◂/ *adj* using one's power too forcefully and without considering the wishes or feelings of other people; ARBITRARY: *high-handed treatment|attitudes | It was rather high-handed of him to take that decision without consulting you first.* — ~ly *adv* — ~ness *n* [U]

high heels /ˌ··· ˈ·/ also **heels—** *n* [P] women's shoes with high heels

high horse /ˈ·· ·, ·ˈ·/ *n* **on one's high horse** *infml derog* behaving, esp. talking, as if one knows best, or more than others

high in·terest ac·count /ˌ··· ˈ·· ·ˌ·/ *n* a bank account in which money saved earns a higher rate of interest than in other savings accounts, if you keep at least a certain sum in the account

high jinks /ˈ·· ··, ·ˈ·/ *n* [P] *infml old-fash* wild fun of a harmless type

high jump /ˈ· ·/ *n* [*the*+S;C] **1** (a sport in which someone makes) a jump over a bar which is gradually raised higher and higher —see colour picture on page 883 **2 be for the high jump** *BrE infml* to be about to be in trouble or get a serious punishment: *You'll be for the high jump when they find out you've crashed the firm's car.* — ~er *n*

high·land¹ /ˈhaɪlənd/ *n* a mountainous area

highland² *adj* [A] **1** of a mountainous area: *highland vegetation* **2** (*often cap.*) of the Scottish Highlands: *a Highland clan*

Highland a REGION of Scotland, covering a large area in the N and NW of the country and many of the inner islands

Highland dress /ˌ··· ˈ·/ a special kind of clothing worn by some Scottish men on special occasions. Highland dress includes a formal JACKET, a BOW TIE, a KILT with a SPORRAN, long socks, and a small knife kept under the fold at the top of the sock.

high·land·er /ˈhaɪləndəʳ/ *n* (*often cap.*) a person from a mountainous area, esp. in Scotland

Highland fling /ˌ··· ˈ·/ *n* a Scottish country dance that is fast and full of movement, done by one person. The Highland fling is one of several Scottish dances, and is not often performed except at special EXHIBITIONS of dancing.

Highland Games /ˌ··· ˈ·/ also **Highland Gath·er·ing** /ˌ···

ˈ···/— a FESTIVAL with competitions in Scottish sports, dancing, and music, held every year in the Highlands. The best-known Highland Games is the one held at Braemar, though similar festivals take place in other Scottish towns, some of which are outside the Highlands. Typical sports include tossing (TOSS) the CABER.

High·lands /ˈhaɪləndz/ [*the*+P] mountainous areas, esp. those in the north of Scotland —compare LOWLANDS

Highlands and Is·lands /ˌ··· ˈ··/ [*the* +P] a general name for the N, NW, and island areas of Scotland, whose business interests are helped by the **Highlands and Islands Development Board**

high-lev·el /ˌ··· ˈ···◂/ *adj* [A] **1** at a high level **2** done by or including people of high rank or importance: *high-level discussions about the future of the company* **3** *tech* (of a language for computer PROGRAMS) similar to human language, rather than to machine language: *BASIC is a high-level programming language.*

high life /ˈ· ·/ *n* [U] **1** [(*the*)] the enjoyable life of rich and fashionable people, which includes lots of amusement, good food, etc. **2** a type of music and dance popular in W Africa

high·light¹ /ˈhaɪlaɪt/ *n* [*often pl.*] **1** [(of)] an important, noticeable, or special part of something bigger, e.g. of a performance or sports event: *Recorded highlights of today's big football game will be shown after the news.* **2** a lighter area in the hair, often made lighter by artificial means. Highlights are often used as a way of hiding grey hairs. **3** *tech* the area on a picture or photograph where most light appears to fall

highlight² *v* [T] to pick out (something) as an important part; throw attention onto: *facts that highlight the need for change*

high·light·er /ˈhaɪlaɪtəʳ/ *n* a kind of pen which writes with a very bright colour which does not cover up the words underneath it, and is used to highlight words on a page

high·ly /ˈhaɪli/ *adv* **1** (often before adjectives made from verbs) to a great degree; very: *highly amused | highly skilled | highly enjoyable | highly unlikely* **2 a** very well: *highly paid | She speaks|thinks very highly of your work.* (=praises it/thinks it is very good) **b** in a high or important position: *highly placed government officials*

highly-strung /ˌ··· ˈ··◂/ also **high-strung—** *adj* easily upset or excited; nervous. This word is often used to excuse a person who has strong emotional feelings about problems.

high mass /ˌ··· ˈ·/ *n* [C;U] (esp. in the Roman Catholic Church) a very formal MASS (=type of church service) with singing and music

high-mind·ed /ˌ··· ˈ···◂/ *adj* having or showing very high esp. moral standards, perhaps too high — ~ly *adv* — ~ness *n* [U]

High·ness /ˈhaɪnɪ̣s/ *n* (used as a title for speaking to or about certain royal persons): *His (Royal) Highness Prince Leopold | Thank you, Your Highness. | Their Highnesses the Prince and Princess of Wales will visit the university in March.*

high-oc·tane /ˌ··· ˈ···◂/ *adj* (of petrol) of good quality

high-pitched /ˌ··· ˈ·◂/ *adj* **1** (of a sound or voice) at a level close to the highest that can be heard; not low or deep: *She let out a high-pitched scream.* **2** (of a roof) sloping steeply

high point /ˈ· ·, ·ˌ·/ also **high spot—** *n* [(of)] the best or most important moment or event of a period or activity, esp. one that is remembered with great pleasure: *One of the high points of our holiday was the visit to the Grand Canyon.*

high-pow·ered /ˌ··· ˈ···◂/ *adj* showing great force, ability, etc.: *high-powered selling methods | a high-powered car | The new professor is very high-powered.*

high-pres·sure¹ /ˌ··· ˈ···◂/ *adj* [A] **1** of, at, or using high pressure, esp. air pressure that is higher than usual **2** (esp. of a salesperson or method of selling) using strong and continuous argument and talk: *I was talked into buying it by a high-pressure salesman.*

high-pressure² /ˈ·· ·ˌ·/ *v* [T (into)] *esp. AmE* to persuade (someone) to do or buy something by high-pressure methods

high priest /ˌ··· ˈ·/ **high priest·ess** /ˌ··· ˈ···|*fem.*— *n* the chief

high-prin·ci·pled /ˌ·ˈ···◂/ adj honourable; HIGH-MINDED

high pro·file /ˌ·ˈ··◂/ n [usu. sing.] the state or quality of attracting a lot of attention to oneself or one's actions: *The company has a high profile in the area of personal computers.* —**high-profile** adj :*a high-profile job as the President's personal spokesman*

high-rank·ing /ˌ·ˈ··◂/ adj [A] of high rank: *high-ranking government officials* | *one of the highest-ranking members of the government*

high re·lief /ˌ·ˈ·ˈ·/ n [U] a form of art in which figures are cut out of the stone or wooden surface of a wall so that they stand well out from the background, which has been cut away —compare BAS-RELIEF

high-rise /ˈ·ˈ·/ adj [A] describing a very tall building, esp. a block of flats with more than a few floors (STOREYs). In Britain, high-rise buildings are usu. in inner city areas and are lived in by people who are not very rich, but in the US, some high-rise flats are very attractive and very expensive. —compare LOW-RISE —**high rise** n : *We live on the twentieth floor of a high rise.* —see picture at HOUSE

high road /ˈ·ˈ·/ n 1 [(the)S] esp. BrE (often cap. as part of a name) a main road; HIGH STREET: *We got it at a shop in Kilburn High Road.* 2 [the+S+to] the easiest, best, or most direct way: *the high road to health*

high school /ˈ·ˈ·/ n [C;U] 1 (in Britain) a SECONDARY SCHOOL for children, often for girls, aged between 11 and 18; used esp. in names: *Manchester High School* 2 (in the US) a school for children aged between 15 and 18 — see also extra information on page 400

high school di·plo·ma /ˌ·ˈ·ˈ···/ n AmE a document given to those who complete the twelve years of education required in the American School system. It is necessary for all but the most unskilled jobs

high seas /ˌ·ˈ·/ n [the+P] the oceans of the world which do not belong to any particular country

high sea·son /ˌ·ˈ··/ n [(the)U] the time of year when business is most active and prices are highest: *Your ticket will cost more if you fly during (the) high season.* —compare LOW SEASON

high se·cu·ri·ty pris·on /ˌ·ˈ···· ˈ···/ n a prison for dangerous criminals, from which it is very difficult to escape

High Sher·iff /ˌ·ˈ···/ also **Sheriff**— n (in England and Wales) the chief officer of the King or Queen in a COUNTY with various mostly ceremonial duties

high-sid·ed ve·hi·cle /ˌ·ˈ·· ˈ···/ n BrE a vehicle such as a large VAN or a bus which has high sides. Some bridges in windy places are closed to high-sided vehicles in very windy weather, because these vehicles might be in danger of being blown over.

high-sound·ing /ˌ·ˈ··◂/ adj often derog (of words, ideas, etc.) seeming important or very good but often having no meaning

high-speed /ˌ·ˈ·◂/ adj [A] which travels, works, etc., very fast: *a high-speed train*

high-spir·it·ed /ˌ·ˈ···◂/ adj 1 (of a person or their behaviour) full of fun; adventure-loving; LIVELY 2 (of an animal, esp. a horse, or of animal behaviour) active, esp. nervously active, and hard to control

high spot /ˈ·ˈ·/ n [(of)] the best or most important part; HIGH POINT

high street /ˈ·ˈ·/ BrE ‖ **main street** AmE— n [(the)S] (often cap. as part of a name) the most important shopping and business street of a town: *Camden High Street* | *There are several banks in the high street.* —**high-street** adj [A] : *one of the big high-street shoe shops*

high street bank /ˌ·ˈ·· ˈ·/ n BrE a bank which provides services to ordinary people and small companies. Branches of high street banks, e.g. NatWest, Midlands, Barclays, can be found in most towns and cities in Britain.

high-strung /ˌ·ˈ·◂/ adj HIGHLY-STRUNG

high ta·ble /ˌ·ˈ··/ n [U] (in Britain) the table at which the teachers at a college eat, which is at a level raised above that of the area where the students eat. This expression is used esp. at the universities of Oxford and Cambridge.

high·tail /ˈhaɪteɪl/ v **hightail it** infml, esp. AmE to go or leave in a great hurry: *We'd better hightail it out of here before the law shows up.*

high tea /ˌ·ˈ·/ n [U] BrE an early-evening meal taken in some parts of Britain instead of afternoon tea or a later dinner, esp. by children whose parents eat separately after the children are in bed

high tech, hi-tech /ˌhaɪ ˈtek/ n [U] 1 a style of decorating houses, offices, etc., using modern industrial building materials 2 high technology —**high tech, hi-tech** adj

high tech·nol·o·gy /ˌ·· ·ˈ···/ n [U] the use of the most modern and advanced machines, processes, and methods, e.g. in business or industry

high-ten·sion /ˌ·ˈ··◂/ adj [A] carrying a powerful electrical current: *high-tension cables*

high tide /ˌ·ˈ·/ n 1 [C;U] the moment when the water is highest up the sea shore because the TIDE has come in —opposite **low tide** 2 [C usu. sing.] the highest point of success

high time /ˌ·ˈ·/ n [U] the proper time (for something that has been delayed too long): [+(that)] *It's high time you had your hair cut; it's getting much too long.*

high-toned /ˌ·ˈ·◂/ adj (seeming to be) concerned with great aims, high principles, or noble ideas

high trea·son /ˌ·ˈ··/ n [U] the crime of putting one's country or its ruler in great danger, e.g. by planning to kill the king, giving military secrets to foreign enemies, etc.; TREASON of the very worst kind

high wa·ter /ˌ·ˈ··/ n [U] the moment when the water in a river is at its highest point because of the TIDE —opposite **low water** —see also **come hell or high water** (HELL)

high water mark /ˌ·ˈ·· ·/ n 1 a mark showing the highest point reached by a body of water, such as a river 2 the highest point of success —opposite **low water mark**

high·way /ˈhaɪweɪ/ n 1 [C] esp. AmE or law a broad main road used esp. by traffic going in both directions, and often leading from one town to another 2 [the+S+to] BrE the best or most direct way; HIGH ROAD (2)

Highway Code /ˌ·· ·ˈ·/ n [the] the official list of rules for drivers on the road in Britain. People are tested on their knowledge of the Highway Code as part of their driving test

high·way·man /ˈhaɪweɪmən/ n -men /mən/ (in former times) a man who used to stop horsemen and carriages on the roads and rob them of their money, jewels, etc. Dick Turpin was probably the most famous highwayman in Britain. Highwaymen are thought of as holding a PISTOL and saying "stand and deliver!" —compare FOOTPAD

highwayman

high wire /ˈ· ˌ·/ n TIGHTROPE

hi·jack¹ /ˈhaɪdʒæk/ v [T] 1 to take control of (esp. an aircraft) using the threat of force, usu. in order to make political demands: *They hijacked a British Airways flight and threatened to blow the plane up if their government did not release its political prisoners.* | (fig.) *Some people think the party has been hijacked by political extremists.* 2 to stop (a moving vehicle, such as a train) in order to rob it —~er n —~ing n [C;U]

hijack² n a case of hijacking

hike¹ /haɪk/ n 1 a long walk in the country, esp. over rough ground, usu. taken for pleasure: *to go on a hike* 2 infml a rise in prices, etc: *recent hikes in the cost of petrol*

hike² v 1 [I] to go on a hike —compare TREK 2 [T (UP)] infml, esp. AmE to increase suddenly and steeply: *trying to hike rents* —compare HITCHHIKE —**hiker** n

hike sthg./sbdy. ↔ **up** phr v infml, esp. AmE [T] to raise or pull with a sudden movement: *He hiked his son up on his shoulders to see the marching soldiers.* | *She hiked up her skirt, and got on the horse.*

hi·lar·i·ous /hɪˈleəriəs/ adj full of or causing wild laughter: *The party got quite hilarious after they brought more wine.* | *a hilarious joke* —~**ly** adv —~**ness** n [U]

hi·lar·i·ty /hɪˈlærɪti/ n [U] cheerfulness, expressed in laughter; MIRTH

hill /hɪl/ n 1 a raised area of land, not as high as a mountain, and not usu. as bare or rocky: *Sheep were grazing on the side of the hill.* | *The castle stands on a hill.* | *a hill* farmer **2 the Hill** *AmE* CAPITOL HILL **3 over the hill** *infml* no longer young

Hill¹, Benny (1925–92) a British COMEDIAN best known for his very successful television programmes made in the 1950s and 60s which were very much liked, and also often criticized, for the large number of jokes about sex or involving young women wearing very little clothing —see colour picture on page 553

Hill², Joe /dʒeʊ/ (1879–1915) an American TRADE UNION leader

Hil·la·ry /ˈhɪləri/, **Sir Ed·mund** /ˈedmənd/ (1919–) a New Zealand mountain climber known for being the first to reach the top of Mount Everest in 1953. He also went to the South Pole overland, in 1958.

hill·bil·ly /ˈhɪlbɪli/ *n AmE, often derog or humor* an uneducated person from a mountain area, esp. from the Appalachian Mountains, living far from a town

hill·ock /ˈhɪlək/ *n* a little hill

Hills·bo·rough /ˈhɪlzbərə/ also **Hillsborough Di·sas·ter** /ˈ··· ·ˌ··/— the death of 96 people and the INJURY of 170 which happened because of overcrowding at the Sheffield Wednesday football ground in 1989

hill·side /ˈhɪlsaɪd/ *n* the sloping side of a hill, as opposed to the top (**hilltop**)

Hill Street Blues /ˌ·· · ˈ·/ an American television programme in the 1980s about a police station and the policemen who worked there

hill·y /ˈhɪli/ *adj* full of hills

hilt /hɪlt/ *n* **1** the handle of a sword, or of a knife which is used as a weapon —see picture at SWORD **2 (up) to the hilt** (usu. of something undesirable) completely: *She's up to the hilt in debts.* | *We're mortgaged up to the hilt.* | *I'll support you to the hilt.*

Hil·ton /ˈhɪltən/ *[the] tdmk* also **Hilton ho·tel** /ˌ··· ·ˈ·/— a particular one of many hotels belonging to the same group and named after the original owner. Hilton hotels are known to be very expensive and extremely comfortable: *We're staying at the Hilton.*

Hilton Head /ˌ·· ˈ·/ an island off the coast of South Carolina, US, which is popular, esp. with wealthy tourists

him /ɪm; *strong* hɪm/ *pron* (object form of **he**): *The dog never comes in when I call him.* | *Which is the boy you were talking about? Is that him?* | *Have you given him the book?* | *I carried his case for him.* | *She wants to marry him, and him at least 75 years old!* —see ME (USAGE)

Him·a·lay·as /ˌhɪməˈleɪəz/ a long mountain range in S Asia which includes the world's highest mountain, Mount Everest, and others which only very experienced climbers try to climb

Him·mler /ˈhɪmləʳ/, **Hein·rich** /ˈhaɪnrɪk, -rɪx/ (1900–45) a German Nazi leader who controlled the SS and the Gestapo during the Second World War

him·self /ɪmˈself; *strong* hɪm-/ *pron* **1 a** (reflexive form of **he**): *Did he hurt himself when he fell?* | *The old man was talking to himself.* **b** (with general meaning): *Everyone should be able to defend himself.* **2** (strong form of **he**): *I want to speak to the director himself, not his secretary.* | *The President himself did it.* | *He did it himself.* | *The Minister of Sport, himself a keen football supporter, has been very critical of the behaviour of football crowds.* **3** *infml* (in) his usual state of mind or body: *I don't think he's very well — he doesn't* **seem himself** *today/he hasn't* **been himself** *lately.* **4 (all) by himself** alone, without help: *The baby can walk by himself now.* | *He lives all by himself in the country.* **5 to himself** for his own private use: *a bedroom to himself* —see YOURSELF (USAGE)

hind¹ /haɪnd/ *n* **hinds** *or* **hind** a female deer, esp. of the RED DEER family —compare HART

hind² *adj* [A] (usu. of animals' legs) at the back or forming the back part: *The dog stood up on its hind legs.*

Hin·de·mith /ˈhɪndəmɪt/, **Paul** (1895–1963) a German COMPOSER and writer on music

hin·der /ˈhɪndəʳ/ *v* [T (**from**)] to stop or delay the advance or development of (a person or activity); prevent or get in the way of; OBSTRUCT: *This unfortunate incident may hinder the progress of the peace talks.*

Hin·di /ˈhɪndi/ a language spoken in N central India. Hindi is one of the two official languages of India and is closely related to Urdu.

Hind·ley /ˈhɪndli/, **My·ra** /ˈmaɪrə/ a child murderer who has been in prison in Britain for many years. Her name is usu. connected with that of Ian Brady, another child murderer.

hind·most /ˈhaɪndməʊst/ *adj old use* furthest behind

hind·quar·ters /ˈhaɪndˌkwɔːtəz‖-ˌkwɔːrtərz/ *n* [P] the back part of an animal, including the legs —compare HAUNCH and see picture at HORSE

hin·drance /ˈhɪndrəns/ *n* [(**to**)] **1** [U] the act of hindering: *This delay has caused some hindrance to my plans.* **2** [C] someone or something that hinders: *He offered to help me with the cleaning, but he was* **more of a hindrance than a help.** | *Lack of adequate funding is a serious hindrance to the progress of our research.*

hind·sight /ˈhaɪndsaɪt/ *n* [U] understanding the nature of or reasons for an event after it has actually happened: *It's easy to say now what we should have done then —* **with the wisdom/benefit of hindsight!** (=with the advantage of knowing what has now actually happened) —compare FORESIGHT

Hin·du /ˈhɪnduː, hɪnˈduː/ *n* **Hindus** a person whose religion is Hinduism —**Hindu** *adj*

Hin·du·is·m /ˈhɪndu-ɪzəm/ *n* [U] the chief religion of India which includes belief in DESTINY and REINCARNATION

Hines /haɪnz/, **Earl** (1903–83) an American JAZZ musician, piano player, and bandleader

hinge¹ /hɪndʒ/ *n* a metal part which joins two objects together and allows the first to swing around the second, such as one joining a door or gate to a post, or a lid to a box: *The gate is creaking — I think the hinges need oiling.* —see picture at GLASSES

hinge

hinge² *v* [T *often pass.*] to fix (something) on hinges: *The cupboard door is hinged on the right, so it opens on the left.*

hinge on/upon sthg./sbdy. *phr v* [T *not in progressive forms*] to depend on; have as a necessary condition: *The success of the operation hinges on the support we get from our allies.* [+*wh*-] *Everything hinges on where we go next.*

hint¹ /hɪnt/ *n* **1** a statement or action that gives a small or indirect suggestion: *She* **dropped** (=made) *a few* **hints** *about her birthday, to make sure that no one would forget it.* | *I kept looking at my watch, but she* **can't take a hint** (=understand what is meant by it), *and it was after midnight before she left.* | *a* **broad hint** (=a very clear one) **2** [(**of**)] a small sign or small amount: *There's a hint of summer in the air, although it's only May.* | *a spaghetti sauce with a hint of garlic* [+*that*)] *He gave no hint* (=did not show) *that he was in pain.* **3** [*often pl.*] useful advice: *helpful hints for people travelling to China*

hint² *v* [I (**at**);T+(*that*); *obj*] to suggest or mention indirectly; INTIMATE: *The prime minister has hinted at the possibility of an early election.* | *I hinted (to him) that I was dissatisfied with his work.*

hin·ter·land /ˈhɪntəlænd‖-ər-/ *n* [*the*+S] the inner part of a country, beyond the coast or the banks of an important river

hip¹ /hɪp/ *n* the fleshy part of either side of the human body above the legs: *Women have rounder hips than men.* | *He stood with his hands on his hips.*

hip² also **rose hip**— *n* [*usu. pl.*] the red fruit of some kinds of rose bush

hip³ *interj* **hip, hip, hooray!** (a shout or cheer of approval)

hip⁴ *adj* **-pp-** [(**to**)] *sl* of, knowing about, or interested in the latest fashions in behaviour, music, amusements, etc.: *hip to everything that's happening*

hip-bath /ˈhɪpbɑːθ‖-bæθ/ *n* a bath in which one can sit but not lie. Hipbaths are not common in Britain or the US

hip flask /ˈ· ·/ *n* a small often curved FLASK made to fit into a hip pocket, and used esp. for carrying strong alcoholic drinks —see picture at FLASK

hip hop /ˈ· ·/ *n* [U] a kind of popular music with a regular heavy beat and special musical effects as a background to spoken words. Hip hop is part of a youth CULTURE which comes from the US and includes GRAFFITI ART and BREAKDANCE.

hip-hug·gers /ˈhɪphʌgəz‖-ərz/ *n* [P] *AmE for* HIPSTERS

hip·pie, hippy /ˈhɪpi/ n (esp. in the 1960s and 1970s) a person who opposes, or is thought to oppose, the accepted standards of ordinary society, esp. when showing this by dressing in unusual clothes, having long hair (both men and women), living in groups together, and (sometimes) taking drugs for pleasure. Hippies believed in peace, and one of their sayings was "make love, not war". —see also FLOWER PEOPLE

hippies

hip pock·et /ˌ· ˈ··/ n a pocket on the HIP¹, or at the back, of a pair of trousers or of a skirt

Hip·poc·ra·tes /hɪˈpɒkrətiːz‖-ˈpɑː-/ (460?–?377 BC) a Greek doctor who is considered to be the man who began the study of medicine

Hip·po·crat·ic oath /ˌhɪpəkrætɪk ˈəʊθ/ [the] the promise made by doctors to try to save life and to follow the standards set for the medical profession (named after Hippocrates)

Hip·po·drome /ˈhɪpədrəʊm/ [the] a typical name given to a theatre: the Birmingham Hippodrome

hippopotamus

hip·po·pot·a·mus /ˌhɪpəˈpɒtəməs‖-ˈpɑː-/ also **hip·po** /ˈhɪpəʊ/ infml— n -muses or -mi /maɪ/ a large African animal with a large head and wide mouth, large body, and thick hairless dark grey skin, which lives near and in water

hip·py /ˈhɪpi/ n a HIPPIE

hip·sters /ˈhɪpstəz‖-ərz/ BrE ‖ **hiphuggers** AmE— n [P] trousers that fit up to the HIPs, not the waist. Hipsters were popular esp. in the 1960s.

hire¹ /haɪəʳ/ v [T] **1** BrE ‖ **rent** AmE to get the use of (something) for a special occasion or a limited time on payment of a sum of money: We hired a car for a week when we were in Italy. **2 a** to employ (someone) for a short time or for a particular purpose: Let's hire a plumber. | a hired killer **b** esp. AmE to employ or appoint to a job

▷ USAGE 1 In BrE you **hire** things for just a short time and the owner **hires** them **out**. Let's hire a car for the weekend. | I'll have to **hire** a suit for the wedding. You **rent** things for a longer period: Is that your own television or do you **rent** it? You **rent** a house or a flat and the owner **lets** it (**out**). But in AmE you **rent** all of these things, and the owner **rents** them **out**. 2 In AmE you **hire** people (=employ them), but in BrE you only **hire** people for a particular purpose, not for a long period; otherwise they are **appointed**: We hired an advertising company to help sell our new product. | We're going to **appoint** a new history teacher. 3 In BrE and AmE things like buses, ships, and planes are **chartered** for special use by a group or organization.◁

hire sthg./sbdy. ↔ **out** ‖ **rent out** AmE phr v [T (to)] **1** to give the use of (something) for payment: Why don't you hire out your car to your neighbours while you're away, and make some money? **2** to give the use of (oneself or one's services) for payment: farm labourers who hire themselves out for the harvest

hire² n [U] **1** BrE the act of hiring or state of being hired: Boats for hire. | to pay for the hire of a room | a car hire company **2** payment for this: to work for hire

hire·ling /ˈhaɪəlɪŋ‖ˈhaɪər-/ n derog a person whose services may be hired by anyone willing to pay: hireling politicians

hire pur·chase /ˌ· ˈ··/ BrE ‖ **installment plan** AmE— n

[U] a system of payment for goods by which one pays small sums of money regularly after receiving the goods (usually paying more than the original price in total): to get a new fridge on hire purchase

Hi·ro·hi·to /ˌhɪərəʊˈhiːtəʊ/ (1901–89) the EMPEROR of Japan from 1926 to 1989

Hi·rosh·i·ma /hɪˈrɒʃɪmə‖ˌhɪrəʊˈʃiːmə/ a city in Japan. It was destroyed in 1945 when an American ATOMIC bomb was dropped on it. A large number of people were killed in the attack. It is now a large industrialized city again.

Hirs·horn /ˈhɜːʃ-hɔːn‖ˈhɜːrʃ-hɔːrn/ the Hirshorn MUSEUM and Sculpture Garden; a museum of MODERN ART in Washington, DC, part of the SMITHSONIAN INSTITUTION, given by J H Hirshorn in 1966

hir·sute /ˈhɜːsjuːt, hɜːˈsjuːt‖ˈhɜːrsuːt, hɜːrˈsuːt/ adj **1** fml or tech hairy **2** fml or humor with untidy hair on the face; with the beard and hair of the head uncut

his¹ /ɪz; strong hɪz/ determiner (possessive form of HE) **1** of or belonging to him: He lost his keys. | John's away on his honeymoon. | It was his first visit to England. **2** (with general meaning): Everyone must do his best. —compare THEIR (2)

his² /hɪz/ pron (possessive form of HE) **1** that/those belonging to him: Which coat is John's? Is this one his? | His is/are on the table. | That fool of a brother of his! **2** (with general meaning): Everyone wants only what is his by right. —compare THEIRS (2)

his 'n' hers also **his and hers** /ˌ·· ˈ··/ adj [A] (of a pair of things) matching, but one intended for use by the man, and one by the woman, of a (usu. married) COUPLE¹ (2): They've even got his 'n' hers monogrammed towels in the bathroom.

Hi·span·ic /hɪˈspænɪk/ adj of Spanish-speaking or Portuguese-speaking countries. In the US, Hispanic is usu. used to talk about people from Latin America (=all countries south of the US). —**Hispanic** n

His·pan·i·o·la /ˌhɪspæniˈəʊlə‖-pənˈjəʊlə/ an island in the Caribbean, formerly called **Santo Domingo** and now divided into the countries of Haiti and the Dominican Republic

hiss /hɪs/ v **1** [I] to make a sound like a continuous "s": The cat hissed at the dog. | The hot iron hissed as it pressed the wet cloth. | Gas escaped with a hissing noise from the broken pipe. **2** [T] to say in a sharp whisper: The boy hissed a warning to be quiet. **3** [T] to hiss at in order to show disapproval and dislike: The crowd hissed the speaker when he said taxes should be increased. | She was hissed off the stage. (=made to leave by people hissing at her) —**hiss** n : The snake gave an angry hiss.

Hiss, Al·ger /ˈældʒəʳ/ (1904–) an American government official sent to prison for five years for spying (SPY² (1)) for the Communists. Many people in the US believe he was not guilty.

hist /hɪst/ interj old use (a sound used for getting attention or asking for silence)

his·ta·mine /ˈhɪstəmiːn/ n [U] a chemical compound which can increase the flow of blood, either when used as a drug or when produced as a natural substance in the body — see also ANTIHISTAMINE

his·to·gram /ˈhɪstəgræm/ n a BAR CHART

his·tol·o·gy /hɪˈstɒlədʒi‖-ˈstɑː-/ n [U] the study of the cells of the body

his·to·ri·an /hɪˈstɔːriən/ n a person who studies history and/or writes about it

his·tor·ic /hɪˈstɒrɪk‖-ˈstɔː-, -ˈstɑː-/ adj **1** important in history; having or likely to have an influence on history: a historic battle | a historic meeting between two great leaders | historic buildings —see HISTORY (USAGE) **2** of the times whose history has been recorded —compare PREHISTORIC

his·tor·i·cal /hɪˈstɒrɪkəl‖-ˈstɔː-, -ˈstɑː-/ adj **1** connected with history as a study: historical research | a historical society **2** based on or representing events in the past: a historical play/novel —see HISTORY (USAGE) — ~ **ly** /kli/ adv

historical nov·el /·ˌ··· ˈ··/ n a book which tells a story that is not true (NOVEL) but which happens in a definite time in the past and which mentions real people or events from that time

historic pres·ent /·ˌ·· ˈ··/ also **historical pres·ent** /·ˌ·ᐟ ˈ··ᐟ·/ n [the+S] the present tense as used in many languages to describe events which happened in the past, when the teller wants to make them sound more real

his·to·ry /ˈhɪstəri/ n   **1** [U] (the study of) events in the past, such as those of a nation, arranged in order from earlier to later times, esp. events concerning the rulers and government of a country, social and trade conditions, etc.: *a history lesson at school | She has a degree in European history.*   **2** [S;U] (**of**) (the study of) the development of something during the period in which it has existed: *the history of the English language | The English language has an interesting history. | The worst disaster in the history of space travel.*   **3** [C] (**of**) a (written) account of past events, and developments, esp. in a particular subject, period, or place: *a short history of the last war*   **4** [C] (**of**)] a record of what has happened to or been done by someone in their life, esp. with regard to illness, social difficulties, criminal activity, etc.: *She has a history of back trouble.* (=she has often suffered from it in the past) | *The defendant had a history of violent assaults against women.* —see also CASE HISTORY   **5** [U] a story or course of events that is already well known: *He met her at a dance, they fell in love — and* **the rest is history.**   **6** [C] a long story including details of many events: *She told me her whole life history.*   **7 make history** to do or be concerned in something important which will be recorded and remembered: *Neil Armstrong made history when he stepped on the moon. | He made legal history when he won the case.*   **8 past/ancient history** what may have been true in the past, but is no longer important: *She loved me once, but that's all ancient history now.*   **9 history is bunk** =history is nonsense; a phrase used by Henry Ford, the American industrialist —see also NATURAL HISTORY

▷ USAGE 1 Compare **story** and **history**. A **story** [C] tells of a number of connected events which may or may not really have happened: *She told the children a* **story**. **History** [U] is the real events of the past: *We studied* **history** *at school.* 2 Compare **historic** and **historical**. **Historical** characters and events are those which really existed or happened in the past. **Historic** places or events are those which are thought to be very important in history. Thus the Battle of Hastings (1066) was a **historical** event (it really happened) and also a **historic** event (it had an important influence on English history).◁

his·tri·on·ic /ˌhɪstriˈɒnɪk◂‖-ˈɑːnɪk◂/ adj   **1** derog behaving or done in a too theatrical way, esp. in showing feelings that are insincere or pretended   **2** rare concerning the theatre or acting — ~**ally** /kli/ adv

his·tri·on·ics /ˌhɪstriˈɒnɪks ‖ -ˈɑːn-/ n [P] behaviour which is like a theatrical performance, showing strong but insincere feelings

hit¹ /hɪt/ v **hit, hitting** [T]   **1** to bring the hand, or something held in the hand, forcefully against (a person or thing); strike: *He hit me in the stomach. | She hit the tennis ball over the net.* —compare KICK¹ (1); see STRIKE (USAGE)   **2 a** to come against with force: *The ball hit the window. | The car hit the wall. | The bullet hit him in the chest.* **b** to cause (esp. a part of the body) to do this by accident or on purpose: *She fell down and hit her head. | I hit my knee on/against the chair.*   **3** infml to arrive at; reach: *We hit the main road two miles further on. | (esp. AmE) We'll look for work as soon as we* **hit town**. *| I hit a difficult point in my work, and decided it was time for a cup of tea. | The singer hit a high note at the end of the song. | The dollar* **hit an all-time low** (=reached its lowest point ever) *on the money markets today. | A cool drink really* **hits the spot** (=is just what is needed) *on a summer's day.*   **4** to have a bad effect on: *The increase in food prices hits everyone's pocket.* (=means they have less money) *| The company has been badly hit/hard hit by the rise in interest rates.*   **5** to get or make by hitting, in a ball game: *The batsman hit three runs. | The batter hit a home run.*   **6** sl, esp. AmE to attack or kill   **7 hit it off (with)** to have a good relationship (with); become good friends   **8 hit someone where it hurts (most)** to attack someone through their weaknesses or the things they feel most strongly about   **9 hit the bottle** infml to (start to) drink too much alcohol   **10 hit the deck** infml to lie down suddenly: *"It's a bomb!" he shouted, and everyone hit the deck.*   **11 hit the hay** also **hit the sack**— sl to go to bed   **12 hit**

the headlines to get into the news, esp. by being important enough to appear in the HEADLINES on the front page of a newspaper or on radio or television news   **13 hit the jackpot** infml to have a big success   **14 hit the nail on the head** to be exactly right in words or action   **15 hit the road** infml to start on a journey; leave   **16 hit the roof** also **go through the roof, hit the ceiling**— infml to become very angry

hit back phr v [I (**at**)] to reply forcefully to an attack on oneself: *The prime minister has hit back angrily at these criticisms.*

hit on/upon sthg. phr v [T] to find by lucky chance or have a good idea about: *I hope that someone will hit on a solution to our problem.*

hit out at sbdy./sthg. phr v [T]   **1** also **hit out against**— express strong, esp. public, disapproval of; CONDEMN: *The bishop has hit out at what he describes as an "immoral" defence policy.*   **2** to (try to) hit: *He hit out at me without thinking.*

hit sbdy. **up for** sthg. phr v [T] AmE, sl to ask (someone) for (something): *Can I hit you up for some cigarettes?*

hit² n   **1** a blow, esp. with the hand or something held in the hand: *an unfair hit, below the belt*   **2** a shot, movement, etc. that brings one thing against another with force: *I scored a direct hit with my first shot.*   **3** something, such as a musical or theatrical performance, which is successful: *The record was a big hit and sold a million copies. | a Broadway hit*   **4** [(**at**)] a remark which causes the desired effect, esp. if unpleasant: *That joke was a nasty hit at me.*   **5** sl, AmE an act of breathing in the smoke of CANNABIS   **6** sl, esp. AmE a murder   **7 make a hit (with)** to be successful (with): *You've really made a hit with her.*

hit-and-miss /ˌ··ˈ·ᐟ/ adj HIT-OR-MISS

hit-and-run /ˌ··ˈ·◂/ adj [A]   **1 a** (of a road accident) of a type in which the guilty driver does not stop to help **b** (of a military attack) of a type in which the attackers arrive suddenly and unexpectedly, and leave as soon as possible   **2** (of a person) who causes a hit-and-run accident: *a hit-and-run driver*

hitch¹ /hɪtʃ/ v   **1** [T+obj+adv/prep] to fasten by hooking a rope or metal part over another object: *He hitched the horse's rope over the pole. | Another railway carriage has been hitched on.*   **2** [I;T] infml to (try to) get (a ride in someone else's car) as a way of travelling; hitchhike: *They hitched across Europe. | We hitched a ride/a lift in a truck.* —compare THUMB²   **3 get hitched** infml to get married

hitch sthg. ↔ **up** phr v [T]   **1** to pull upwards into the proper position: *John hitched up his trousers.*   **2** to fasten to something by hitching: *We hitched up the horses (to the cart).*

hitch² n   **1** a difficulty which delays something for a while: *a slight hitch | A technical hitch prevented the book from coming out on time. | The royal visit went off without a hitch.* (=was a complete success)   **2** a short sudden push or pull (up); TUG: *He gave his sock a hitch (up) when he felt it slipping down.*   **3** a knot used by sailors

Hitch·cock /ˈhɪtʃkɒk‖-kɑːk/, **Sir Al·fred** /ˈælfrədᴢ/ (1899–1980) a British filmmaker whose films are known for the terror experienced by people watching them. Two famous Hitchcock films are *The Thirty-nine Steps* and *Psycho.* —see picture on page 685. Hitchcock's face was familiar to film-goers, because he made small, quick appearances in his own films.

Alfred Hitchcock

hitch·hike /ˈhɪtʃhaɪk/ v [I] to travel by getting rides in other people's cars, usu. by standing at the side of the road and signalling to drivers. —**hiker** n

▶CULTURAL NOTE Hitchhiking is less common in Britain and the US than it used to be because there have been several cases in which either hitchhikers or drivers have been attacked, so many people feel that it is unsafe to hitchhike or to give a ride to a hitchhiker. —compare HIKE² ◀

hi-tech /ˌhaɪ ˈtek◂/ adj, n [U] HIGH TECH

hith·er /ˈhɪðəʳ/ adv **1** old use to this place; here **2 hither and thither** in all directions

hith·er·to /ˌhɪðəˈtuː◂‖-ər-/ adv fml until this/that time; up until now

Hit·ler /ˈhɪtləʳ/, **Ad·olf** /ˈædɒlf‖ˈeɪdɑːlf/ (1889–1945) the leader of the German Nazi party, born in Austria. He became CHANCELLOR of Germany in 1933. Under his control, Germany invaded (INVADE) several other European countries, which led to the start of the Second World War in 1939. He wanted to create a pure Germanic race, and many people esp. Jews and Communists who did not fit in with this idea were put in prison or killed. Hitler killed himself in 1945, just before Germany's DEFEAT in the war. His name is now often used when talking about someone who is a RACIST, or someone who allows no opposition to their power: *an opposition figure who was forced to flee Hitler's Germany* | *He is a ruthless leader, and has been described as a new Hitler.*

Hitler Youth /ˌ·· ˈ·/ an organization set up by Adolf Hitler in 1933 to train German boys in the principles of Nazism

hit list /ˈ· ·/ n infml a list of people or organizations against whom some (bad) action is planned: *The unions claimed that the company had a hit list of factories which it intended to close.*

hit man /ˈ· ·/ n infml, esp. AmE a criminal who is employed to kill someone

hit-or-miss /ˌ· · ˈ·/ adj depending on chance; not planned carefully

hit pa·rade /ˈ· ·ˌ·/ n old-fash a list of popular records (of songs) showing which ones have sold most. The ten most popular records are now called "the top ten".

HIV /ˌeɪtʃ aɪ ˈviː◂/ n [U] a type of VIRUS that enters the body through the bloodstream and can cause AIDS: *She has been diagnosed HIV positive* (=having the virus present in the body). —see also AIDS

hive¹ /haɪv/ n **1 a** also **beehive**– a place where bees are kept, like a small hut or box **b** [+sing./pl. v] the group of bees who live there together **2** a crowded busy place (esp. in the phrases **a hive of industry/activity**): *The newspaper office was a real hive of industry.*

hive

hive² v

hive off phr v **1** [T] (**hive** sthg. ↔ **off**) (esp. in business) to separate from a larger group or organization: *The government is planning to hive off the more profitable sections of the national car company by selling them on the open market.* **2** [I] infml, esp. BrE to disappear or go away without warning: *Where's Jim? I suppose he's hived off again.*

hives /haɪvz/ n [P;U] a skin disease in which the skin is red and painful, usu. a reaction to something physical or emotional: *I break out in hives whenever I eat seafood.*

Hiz·bol·lah /ˌhɪzbʊˈlɑː/ see HEZBOLLAH

h'm also **hmm** /m, hm/ interj (a sound made with the lips closed to express doubt, pausing, disagreement, or dissatisfaction)

HM /ˌeɪtʃ ˈem◂/ BrE His/Her Majesty; the official way to talk about the Queen is to call her **Her Majesty** or **Her Majesty the Queen**. The Queen Mother is called **Her Majesty the Queen Mother.**

HMI /ˌeɪtʃ em ˈaɪ/ n Her/His Majesty's Inspector; a British government official who examines the working of schools

HMO /ˌeɪtʃ em ˈəʊ/ n abbrev. for: HEALTH MAINTENANCE ORGANIZATION

HMS /ˈeɪtʃ em es/ n His/Her Majesty's Ship; a title for a ship in the British Navy and for some land-based stations: *HMS Belfast*

HMSO /ˌeɪtʃ em es ˈəʊ/ His/Her Majesty's Stationery Office; a government organization which prints and publishes (PUBLISH) government papers, documents, and books – compare GPO

the dog symbol used by HMV records

HMV /ˌeɪtʃ em ˈviː/ the trademark, originally of a British company which produces recordings of music etc. The letters "HMV" stand for "His Master's Voice", and the companys advertisement shows a small dog listening to a record.

ho /həʊ/ interj usu. lit (used to express surprise or draw attention): *Land ho!*

hoar /hɔːʳ/ adj HOARY

hoard¹ /hɔːd‖hɔːrd/ n [(of)] a (secret) store, esp. of something valuable to the owner: *He kept a little hoard of chocolates in his top drawer.*

hoard² v **1** [I;T] to store secretly, esp. more than is needed or allowed: *After the war, they were shot for hoarding (food).* **2** [T (UP)] to save in large amounts for future use: *The squirrel hoards up nuts for the winter.* – –er

hoard·ing /ˈhɔːdɪŋ‖ˈhɔːr-/ n BrE **1** a high fence round a piece of land, esp. when building work is going on **2** also **billboard** AmE– a high fence or board on which large advertisements are stuck

hoar·frost /ˈhɔːfrɒst‖ˈhɔːrfrɔːst/ ‖ usu. frost AmE– n [U] white frozen drops of water, esp. those seen on grass and plants after a cold night

hoarse /hɔːs‖hɔːrs/ adj **1** (of a voice) rough-sounding, as though the surface of the throat is rougher than usual, e.g. when the speaker has a sore throat –compare HUSKY¹ **2** (of a person) having a hoarse voice: *We shouted ourselves hoarse* (=shouted until we were hoarse) *at the football match.* – –ly adv – –ness n [U]

hoar·y /ˈhɔːri/ also **hoar** lit– adj **1** (of hair) grey or white with age: (fig.) *a hoary old joke that we'd all heard many times before* **2** (of people) having grey or white hair in old age —-iness n [U]

hoax¹ /həʊks/ n a trick, esp. one which makes someone believe something that is not true, and take action based on that belief. *The telephone caller said there was a bomb in the hotel, but it later turned out to be a hoax.* | *a bomb hoax*

hoax² v [T] to play a trick on (someone) – ~er n

hoax call /ˈ· ˌ·/ n a telephone call to give false information, esp. to say that a bomb is in a particular place when it is not – ~er n

hob /hɒb‖hɑːb/ n BrE **1** the flat top of a gas or electric cooker, on which pans are placed **2** (esp. in former times) a metal shelf beside an open fire where food and water could be cooked or warmed

Hobbes /hɒbz‖hɑːbz/, **Thomas** (1588–1679) an English PHILOSOPHER best known for his book *Leviathan*, in which he argues that man is selfish and best governed by a single powerful authority

hob·bit, Hobbit /ˈhɒbɪt‖ˈhɑː-/ n one of many similar creatures which appear in books by J R R Tolkien. Hobbits are said to look like humans but are much smaller and live in holes in the ground. —see also LORD OF THE RINGS

hob·ble /ˈhɒbəl‖ˈhɑː-/ v **1** [I] to walk in an awkward way and with difficulty, esp. as a result of damage to the legs or feet: *I hurt my foot, and had to hobble home.* **2** [T] to fasten together two legs of (esp. a horse): *The horse has been hobbled so that he can't run away.*

hob·ble·de·hoy /ˈhɒbəldihɔɪ‖ˈhɑː-/ n old use an awkward or rude young person, esp. a young man

hob·by /ˈhɒbi‖ˈhɑː-/ n an activity which one enjoys doing in one's free time: *One of her hobbies is collecting stamps.* —see RECREATION (USAGE)

hob·by·horse /'hɒbihɔːs‖'haːbihɔːrs/ n **1** a child's toy like a horse's head on a stick, which the child pretends to ride on **2** a fixed idea to which a person keeps returning, esp. in conversation: *Of course, as soon as we mentioned the strike, he* **got on his hobbyhorse** *and started criticizing the unions.*

hob·gob·lin /hɒb'ɡɒblən, 'hɒbɡɒb-‖'haːbɡaːb-/ n a GOBLIN that plays tricks on people

hob·nail /'hɒbneɪl‖'haːb-/ n a large nail with a big head used to make heavy shoes and boots stronger underneath (esp. in the phrase **hobnail boots**) — ~ **ed** adj

hob·nob /'hɒbnɒb‖'haːbnaːb/ v **-bb-** [I (**with**)] *sometimes derog* to have a (pleasant) social relationship, often with someone in a higher social position: *I've been hobnobbing with the directors at the office party.*

ho·bo /'həʊbəʊ/ n **hoboes** *or* **hobos** *AmE infml* a person who has no regular work or home; TRAMP² (1)

Hob·son's choice /ˌhɒbsənz 'tʃɔɪs‖ˌhaːb-/ n [U] lack of choice; a situation in which there is only one thing that one can choose, only one course of action that one can take, etc. (from a hirer of horses called Hobson who did not give customers any choice)

Ho Chi Minh Cit·y /ˌhəʊ tʃiː mɪn 'sɪti/ a city in Vietnam, formerly known as **Saigon** and capital of South Vietnam

hock¹ /hɒk‖haːk/ n **1** esp. AmE a piece of meat from above the foot of an animal, esp. a pig: *ham hocks* **2** the middle joint of an animal's back leg —see picture at HORSE

hock² n [U] esp. BrE a German white wine

hock³ n **in hock** sl **a** pawned (PAWN¹) **b** in debt: *The country is completely in hock to the international banks.*

hock⁴ v [T] sl for PAWN¹

hock·ey /'hɒki‖'haːki/ n [U] **1** esp. BrE ‖ **field hockey** esp. AmE— a game played by two teams of 11 players each, with sticks and a ball. Hockey is usu. played in winter. **2** esp. AmE for ICE HOCKEY —see REFEREE (USAGE), and see picture at STICK

Hock·ney /'hɒkni‖'haːk-/, **David** (1937–) an English artist known esp. for his paintings of people and water

ho·cus-po·cus /ˌhəʊkəs 'pəʊkəs/ n [U] **1** the use of tricks to deceive; TRICKERY **2** pointless activity or words, esp. when they draw people's attention away from the real facts or situation

hod /hɒd‖haːd/ n a container shaped like a box with a long handle, used by builders' workmen for carrying bricks

hodge·podge /'hɒdʒpɒdʒ‖'haːdʒpaːdʒ/ n [S] esp. AmE for HOTCHPOTCH

hoe¹ /həʊ/ n a long-handled garden tool used for breaking up the soil and removing wild plants (WEEDS) —see picture at GARDEN

hoe² v **hoed, hoeing** [I;T] to use a hoe (on)

Hof·fa /'hɒfə ‖ 'hɔːfə, 'haː-/, **Jimmy** (1913–75?) an American TRADE UNION leader, president of the Teamsters, who was believed to be associated with the Mafia and who was sent to prison for FRAUD (deception) and several other crimes. He is thought to have been murdered in 1975, but his body has not been found.

Hoff·man /'hɒfmən‖'haːf-/, **Dus·tin** /'dʌstən/ (1937–) an American film actor best known for his roles in the films *The Graduate, Kramer vs. Kramer,* and *Midnight Cowboy* —see colour picture on page 228

hog¹ /hɒɡ‖haːɡ, hɔːɡ/ n **1** AmE a pig, esp. a fat one for eating **2** a male pig that cannot produce young and is kept for meat —compare BOAR (1), SOW² **3** a person who eats too much: *You greedy hog!* **4** go the whole hog infml to do something thoroughly; go to the limits of what is possible: *Instead of ordering a glass of wine each, we went the whole hog and ordered a bottle.* —see also ROAD HOG

hog² v **-gg-** [T] infml **1** to keep or use (all of something) for oneself, esp. unfairly: *He's been hogging the bathroom and no one else can get in.* **2 hog the road** to drive so that other cars cannot get past

Ho·gan /'həʊɡən/, **Paul** (1939–) an Australian actor, famous esp. for his film *Crocodile Dundee* in which he plays a hunter, living in the OUTBACK, who is invited to visit New York

Ho·garth /'həʊɡaːθ‖-aːrθ/, **William** (1697–1764) an English

artist whose most famous work shows the weaknesses and wicked pleasures of his times

hog·gish /'hɒɡɪʃ‖'haː-, 'hɔː-/ adj (of people or habits) piglike, dirty, selfish, etc.

Hog·ma·nay /'hɒɡmənei‖ˌhaːɡmə'nei/ n [U] (in Scotland) New Year's Eve and the parties, drinking, etc., which take place then

▶ CULTURAL NOTE In Scotland, Hogmanay is a very important celebration. Many people go to parties and drink a lot of alcohol. At midnight, when the old year ends and the new year begins, people kiss each other, sing *Auld Lang Syne,* and often go to visit friends to have a drink with them. This visiting is called **First Footing.**◀

hogs·head /'hɒɡzhed‖'haːɡz-, 'hɔːɡz-/ n **1** a barrel, esp. one which holds 52½ GALLONS (=238·5 litres) in Britain, or 63 GALLONS in the US **2** the amount of liquid which can be held in a hogshead

hog·wash /'hɒɡwɒʃ‖'haːɡwaːʃ, 'hɒːɡ-, -wɔːʃ/ n [U] esp. AmE stupid talk; nonsense: *That's a load of hogwash!*

ho-hum /ˌ· '·/ adj infml derog uninteresting, ordinary, or boring: *It was a ho-hum sort of day.* | *I thought the show was pretty ho-hum, which was disappointing.*

hoi pol·loi /ˌhɔɪ pə'lɔɪ/ n [the+P] derog the ordinary people; the MASSES. This expression is used by someone who considers such people to be uneducated and of little worth.

hoist¹ /hɔɪst/ v [T (UP)] **1** to raise, lift, or pull up (a flag or something heavy), esp. using ropes: *The sailors hoisted the flag|hoisted the cargo onto the deck.* | *He hoisted the sack over his shoulder.* **2 hoist with one's own petard** pomp or humor made to suffer by some evil plan by which one had intended to harm others

hoist² n **1** an upward push **2** an apparatus for lifting heavy goods

hoi·ty-toi·ty /ˌhɔɪti 'tɔɪti/ adj old-fash derog behaving in a proud way, as if thinking one is more important than other people; HAUGHTY

Hok·kai·do /hɒ'kaɪdəʊ‖həʊ-/ the second largest island of Japan, in the N

ho·kum /'həʊkəm/ n [U] sl, esp. AmE foolish talk, esp. when intended to deceive or cause admiration; nonsense

Hol·born /'həʊbən‖-bərn/ an area in central London, to the W of the City, with many famous buildings

hold¹ /həʊld/ v **held** /held/, **holding** to keep or support something **1** [T] to keep or support using the hands or arms (or another part of the body): *He was holding a knife in one hand and a fork in the other.* | *She held her daughter's hand as they crossed the road.* | *I held the baby in my arms.* | *Hold it by the handle at the side.* | *The dog held a newspaper between its teeth.* **2** [T] to bear the weight of; support: *Will this branch hold me?* **3** [T+obj+adv| prep] to put or keep (oneself or a part of the body) in a particular position: *They held their heads up.* | *The dog held its tail between its legs.* | (fig.) *We held ourselves in readiness for the attack.* to stay in or keep something in a particular place, position, or state **4** [T+obj+adv|prep] to cause to remain in the stated condition or position: *The picture is held in place by a hook.* | *She held the lid down while I locked the suitcase.* | *The roof is held up by pillars.*| *Hold it over the fire until it's dry.* | *The children held out their hands and I gave them some sweets.* —see also HOLD **back** (1) **5** [I] **a** to remain unchanged; last: *How long will this good weather hold?* | *If our luck holds* (=if we continue to be lucky) *we'll win the competition.* **b** to remain in position, esp. in spite of pressure, weight, etc.: *Can our line hold, or will the enemy push us back?* | *I don't think the shelf will hold if we put anything else on it.* **c** to remain true; continue to have effect: *What I said yesterday still holds.* **6** [T] to keep and not allow to leave; CONFINE (2): *Police are holding two men in connection with the jewel robbery.* | *The terrorists* **held them prisoner/held them hostage.** **7** [T] **a** (of a ship or aircraft) to continue to follow (a direction): *The plane held a northwesterly course.* **b** (of a singer) to continue to sing (a musical note): *to hold a high note* to have or keep control over something **8** [T] to keep control over; not use: *The general ordered his men to* **hold their fire.** (=not shoot) | *We held our breath in fear.* | *Hold your tongue!* (=Be quiet!) **9** [T] (esp. of an army) to keep or defend against attack: *The French army held the town for three days.* | *At the election, the Republicans held this seat, but with a reduced majority.* **10** [T] to keep (the interest or attention) of (someone): *His speech held everyone's attention.* **11** [T *not in progressive forms*] to possess (money, land, or position): *He holds a half share in the business.* | *She holds the office of chairman.* —see also HOLDER (1) other meanings **12** [T *not in progressive forms*] to (be able to) contain; have space for: *How much water does the pan hold?* | *The cinema holds about 500.* | (fig.) *Life holds many surprises.* **13** [T *not in progressive forms*] to have or express (a belief, opinion, etc.): *She holds strong left-wing views.* [+*that*] *I hold that this policy is mistaken.* [+*obj*+*to*-*v*] *The court held him to have* (=believed he had) *told the truth.* [+*obj*+*adj*] *I hold you responsible for this fiasco.* **14** [T] to cause to take place; make happen: *The meeting will be held at the Town Hall.* | *to hold an election* **15** [I] also **hold the line**— to wait until the person one has telephoned is ready to answer: *Ms Smith's line is engaged — will you hold?* fixed phrases **16 be left holding the baby** (*BrE*)/**the bag** (*AmE*) to find oneself responsible for doing something which someone else has started and left unfinished **17 hold all the cards** to have a very strong advantage **18 hold court** *often humor* to receive admirers in a group **19 hold good** to be or remain true: *This rule holds good at all times and places.* **20 hold hands (with)** to hold the hand (of someone else) or the hands (of each other), esp. as a sign of love. Holding hands is often thought to be typical of young and inexperienced lovers: *He wanted to do a bit more than just holding hands!* **21 Hold it!** *infml* **a** Stay like that; don't move! **b** (used when interrupting someone talking) Stop for a moment! **22 hold one's head high** to show pride or confidence in oneself, esp. in a difficult situation **23 hold one's own: a** to keep one's (strong) position, even when attacked **b** not to get worse or weaker: *"How is she, doctor?" "She's holding her own."* **24 hold the fort** to look after everything while someone is away: *When she had to go to America, her daughter held the fort at home.* **25 hold the road** (of a car) to stay in position on the road while moving, esp. in spite of speed, wet weather, etc. **26 hold water** (*usu. in questions or negatives*) to be or seem true, reasonable, or believable: *His explanation of where he got the money from just doesn't hold water.* **27 Hold your horses!** *infml* Don't rush too quickly into an action or decision! **28 not hold a candle to** *infml* to be unable to match someone or something else in quality, skill, etc.: *In terms of value for money this car can't hold a candle to the French one.* **29 speak now, or forever hold your peace** state your opposition now, or it will be too late and you will have to remain silent (a phrase based on part of the Christian marriage service) **phrasal verbs**

hold sthg. **against** sbdy. *phr v* [T] to allow (something bad done by someone) to influence one's feelings about (that person): *It's not fair to hold the boy's past bad behaviour against him.* | *Don't hold it against him that he's been in prison.*

hold back *phr v* **1** [T] (**hold** sthg. ↔ **back**) to make (something) stay in place; prevent from moving, esp. in spite of pressure: *They built banks of earth to hold back the rising flood waters.* —see also HOLD¹ (4) **2** [T] (**hold** sthg. ↔ **back**) to prevent the expression of (feelings, tears, etc.); control: *Jim was able to hold back his anger and avoid a fight.* **3** [T] (**hold** sbdy. ↔ **back**) to prevent the development of: *You could become a good musician, but your lack of practice is holding you back.* **4** [I] to be slow or unwilling to act, esp. through nervousness or carefulness —compare HOLD **off** (1) **5** [I;T (=**hold** sthg. ↔ **back**)] to keep (something) secret; WITHHOLD: *You must tell us the whole story: don't hold (anything) back.*

hold sthg./sbdy. ↔ **down** *phr v* [T] **1** to keep at a low level: *We must try to hold down the rate of interest.* **2** to control or limit the freedom of; OPPRESS: *The people were held down by a ruthless secret police.* **3 hold down a job** to manage to stay in a job for a fairly long period; keep a job: *She hasn't managed to hold down a job for more than a few weeks.*

hold forth *phr v* [I (**about, on**)] *usu. derog* to speak or express one's opinions at length

hold off *phr v* **1** [T] (**hold** sbdy./sthg. ↔ **off**) to cause to remain at a distance; prevent the advance of: *We somehow managed to hold off the enemy's attack.* —compare HOLD **back** (4) **2** [T] (**hold** sthg. ↔ **off**) to delay: [+*obj*/*v*-*ing*] *The committee will hold off their decision/hold off making their decision until Monday.* **3** [I] to be delayed;

stay away: *Do you think the rain will hold off until after the game?*

hold on *phr v* [I] **1** to wait (often on the telephone); HANG **on** (2): *Hold on a minute — I'll just get a pen.* **2** to continue in spite of difficulties: *Try and hold on until help arrives.*

hold onto sbdy./sthg. *phr v* [T] to keep possession of, esp. in spite of difficulties: *She managed to hold onto her job when several of her colleagues lost theirs*

hold out *phr v* **1** [T] (**hold out** sthg.) to offer: *These plans hold out the prospect of new jobs for the area.* | *I don't hold out much hope that the weather will improve.* **2** [I] to continue to exist; last: *How much longer can our supplies hold out?* **3** [I] to continue in spite of difficulties; ENDURE: *The town was surrounded but the people held out until help came.*

hold out for sthg. also **stick out for** sthg.— *phr v* [T] to demand firmly and wait in order to get: *The men are still holding out for more pay.*

hold out on sbdy. *phr v* [T] *infml* to refuse to give support, information, etc. to; keep something back from: *Why didn't you tell me at once, instead of holding out on me?*

hold sthg. **over** *phr v* [T *often pass.*] to move to a later date; DEFER: *The concert was held over until the following week because of the singer's illness.* —see also HOLDOVER

hold to *phr v* [T] **1** (**hold** sthg.) to (cause to) follow exactly or remain loyal to: *Whatever your argument, I shall hold to my decision.* | *We held him to his promise.* (=made him keep it) **2** (**hold** sbdy. to sthg.) to not allow to do better than or get more than: *We managed to hold the other team to a draw.*

hold together *phr v* [I;T (=**hold** sbdy./sthg. ↔ **together**)] to (cause to) remain united: *The needs of the children held their marriage together.* | *The party has held together in spite of differences of opinion.*

hold sthg./sbdy. ↔ **up** *phr v* [T] **1** [*often pass.*] delay: *The building of the new road has been held up by bad weather.* | *An unofficial strike has held up production.* **2** to (try to) rob by using the threat of violence: *The criminals held up the train/the bank and took all the money.* **3** [(**as, to**)] to show as an example: *The old man always held up his youngest son as a model of hard work.* —see also HOLDUP

hold with sthg. *phr v* [T *usu. in negatives*] to approve of; agree with: *She doesn't hold with these modern ideas.* [+*v*-*ing*] *I don't hold with letting people smoke in public.*

hold² *n* **1** [U] the act of holding (esp. in the phrases **take/get/lose/lay hold of**): *I got hold of it in both hands and lifted it onto the table.* | *He lost hold of the rope and fell.* **2** [C] something which can be held, esp. in climbing: *Can you find a hold for your hands?* —see also FOOTHOLD **3** [S] **a** the forceful closing of the hand: *He's got a strong hold.* **b** [(**of, on**)] influence; control: *She's got a good hold of her subject.* | *trying to keep a hold on* (=not lose) *his sanity* **4 get hold of: a** to find and make use of: *I must get hold of some more writing paper.* **b** to find someone for a reason: *I'll try to get hold of her and ask her where the books are.* **5 have a hold over** to know something which gives one an influence over (someone) **6 no holds barred** not keeping to any rules or limits: *a no holds barred contest* **7 on hold: a** waiting to speak or be spoken to on the telephone: *The caller is on hold.* | *Put him on hold.* (=make him wait) **b** delayed; in a state in which no action is taken for a time: *We've put the project on hold for a month.*

hold³ *n* the part of a ship (below DECK) where goods are stored

hold-all /ˈhəʊld-ɔːl/ ‖ also **carryall** *AmE*— *n* a large bag or small case for carrying clothes and articles necessary for travelling

hold-er /ˈhəʊldəʳ/ *n* (*often in comb.*) **1** a person who possesses or has control of a place, land, money, or titles: *The holder of the office of chairman is responsible for arranging meetings.* —see also HOLD¹ (11) **2** something which holds or contains the stated thing: *a candle holder* —see also CIGARETTE HOLDER

hold-ing /ˈhəʊldɪŋ/ *n* something which one possesses, esp. land or SHARES¹ (2) in a company —see also SMALLHOLDING

holding com-pa-ny /ˈ··· ˌ···/ *n* a company that holds a controlling number of the SHARES¹ (2) of other companies — compare INVESTMENT COMPANY

hold-o-ver /ˈhəʊldˌəʊvəʳ/ *n* [(**from**)] *esp. AmE* something

a Californian beach

people may go walking or camping in the mountains. Many people have CAMPERs or small TRAILERs in which to travel, or if they are in a car, they may stay at MOTELs on the journey. Disneyland and Disneyworld are also popular and people can go skiing (SKI) in the Rocky Mountains of Colorado, Wyoming and Montana.

It is also very common to use vacations to visit relatives who may live in states a long distance away. Some children go to SUMMER CAMP for a holiday during the summer vacation from school, where they do special activities such as sports or CRAFTs (eg, making things from wood or cloth).

When Americans want a holiday for sun and rest, they usually go to Florida, Hawaii, Mexico or the Caribbean. They may go

Paid holidays

People in the US get 2 weeks a year paid vacation (=holiday) from their job. Most British people have four or five weeks paid holiday a year. Americans often complain that two weeks is not enough holiday, especially when they hear about the longer holidays that EUROPEANs get. In addition, there are 8 days in each country which are public holidays (BrE =BANK HOLIDAY) and many of these fall on a Monday giving people a LONG WEEKEND (also called THREE-DAY WEEKEND in AmE or Bank Holiday weekend in BrE). In Britain, so many people drive to another part of the country, especially the coast, on Bank Holiday weekends that there are serious TRAFFIC JAMs (=lines of cars not able to move) which may stretch for many miles.

Popular holiday places

Within the US, outdoor vacations are popular, for example at the Grand Canyon or Yosemite or Yellowstone or other national parks or forests. Young

a British seaside holiday

to Europe for CULTURE (2) (for example to see art, plays, and places of historic interest).

In Britain, many people like to go to the SEASIDE (=place by the sea) for holidays. There are places near the sea, such as Blackpool, Scarborough and Bournemouth, where there is plenty to do even if it rains. In a traditional British seaside holiday, the children can watch a PUNCH AND JUDY show, eat CANDY FLOSS and ROCK (2,4) (=sweets) and make SANDCASTLEs, while older people can hire a DECKCHAIR to sit on the BEACH. People also like to go to the country, especially to walk, in places like Scotland, Wales and the Lake District.

When the British go abroad they usually want to go somewhere warm. Spain and the Spanish islands of Majorca and Ibiza are popular as are other places in southern Europe. For skiing, people often go to the Alps.

Where people stay on holiday

The less expensive ways of going on holidays are to take a camper or CARAVAN in which you can stay or to go camping. It is also cheaper when travelling abroad to go on a PACKAGE TOUR in which your hotel and flight are arranged for you. You can stay in a BED AND BREAKFAST (also called a B AND B) which is usually a private house which takes paying guests and provides them with a room for the night and breakfast for the following morning. In Britain this is usually cheaper than a hotel though in the US it is more expensive. Some people buy TIMESHAREs, that is they become part owners of a holiday home and it is theirs to use a certain time every year. Companies which sell timeshares are famous for trying very hard to persuade people to buy their houses, often offering prizes as a reward for buying them. Some British people go on SELF-CATERING holidays where they buy and cook their own food.

Bank Holiday traffic

that has continued to exist longer than expected —see also HOLD **over**

hold·up /ˈhəʊld-ʌp/ n **1** a delay, e.g. of traffic **2** also **stickup** infml— an attempt at robbery by threatening people with a gun —see also HOLD **up**

hole¹ /həʊl/ n **1** [(in)] **a** an empty space inside something solid; CAVITY: *The men have dug a hole in the road.* **b** a space or opening through something; GAP: *There's a hole in my sock.* | *We squeezed through a hole in the fence.* **2 a** (often in comb.) the home of a small animal: *a rabbit hole* **b** infml a small unpleasant living-place: *What are you doing living in this hole?* **3** infml a position of difficulty; PREDICAMENT: *John's resignation puts us in a bit of a hole.* **4** [(in)] infml a fault in reasoning: *trying to* **pick holes in** *the other side's arguments* (=to find the weak points) | *Her theory is full of holes.* **5** ‖ also **cup** AmE— (in GOLF) **a** a hollow place in the ground into which the ball must be hit **b** an area of play with such a hole at the far end: *an 18-hole golf course* | *The next hole is 450 yards long.* —see picture at GOLF **6 make a hole in** infml to use up a large part of: *The cost of the repairs had made a big hole in our savings.* **7 need something like a hole in the head** infml to see something as unwelcome and adding to other problems: *I needed another bill like I needed a hole in the head.* —see also BLACK HOLE, WATERING HOLE

hole² **1** [T] to make a hole in: *Our ship was holed and began to sink.* **2** [I (OUT);T] to hit (the ball) into a HOLE¹ (5) in GOLF
    hole up phr v [I+adv/prep] sl to hide as a means of escape: *After the bank robbery, the criminals holed up in a disused factory.*

hole-and-cor·ner /ˌ· · ˈ· ·◁/ adj [A] (of actions) secret or hidden, esp. because dishonest; FURTIVE: *"I'm sick of this hole-and-corner relationship!" she shouted.*

hole in one /ˌ· · ˈ·/ n (in GOLF) an act of hitting the ball from the starting place into the hole with only one stroke

hole in the heart /ˌ· · ˈ·/ n [S] infml a medical condition sometimes found at birth where the two sides of the heart are not properly separated: *She has had an operation for* (=to cure) *a hole in the heart.* —**hole-in-the-heart** adj : *a hole-in-the-heart baby*

hole-in-the-wall /ˌ· · · ˈ·/ n **1** BrE for CASH DISPENSER **2** AmE a small business, esp. a restaurant, that may not be easy to find

hol·i·day¹ /ˈhɒlɪdi‖ˈhɑːlɪˌdeɪ/ ‖ usu. **vacation** AmE— n **1** a time of rest from work, esp. **a** also **public holiday**— a day on which there is a general stopping of work: *Next Friday is a holiday.* | *The Fourth of July is a national holiday of the US.* **b** esp. BrE a day or period in which one does not go to work, school, etc.: *According to your contract, you get 25 days' paid holiday a year.* | *The school holidays start on Wednesday.* **c** also **holidays** pl.— esp. BrE a period of free time in which one travels to another place for enjoyment: *We're going to Spain for our holiday(s).* | *a skiing holiday* | *They have a holiday retreat* (=a house etc. in a peaceful place, where they spend their holidays) *in the mountains.* **2 on holiday/on one's holidays** having a holiday, esp. over a period of time: *away on holiday* —see also BANK HOLIDAY, BUSMAN'S HOLIDAY —see also extra information on page 632

▷ USAGE Compare **holiday(s)**, **vacation**, and **leave**. **Holiday** is the general word in British English for a period of rest from work, although it is not usually used for a single **day off** from work (unless the day is given to everyone), and it is not usually used of the **weekend**. The plural **holidays** can be used of any of the longer periods of rest from work in a year (but not of a single day or weekend). The general word in American English is **vacation**: *In this job you get four weeks* **holiday** (BrE)/**vacation** (AmE) *a year.* | *We're going to France during the summer* **holiday(s)** (BrE)/**vacation** (AmE). In British English **vacation** is used for the period when universities are closed: *The library is closed during the college* **vacation**. Soldiers and people employed by the government go on **leave** and this word is also used in expressions like *sick* **leave** and **leave** *of absence.*◁

holiday² also **vacation** AmE— v [I+adv/prep] to spend one's holiday: *holidaying in Majorca*

Holiday, Bil·lie /ˈbɪli/ (1915–59) an American JAZZ singer, often considered the greatest jazz singer ever, with an easily recognizable style. She came from a poor background and her early death was caused by drugs.

holiday bro·chure /ˈ··· ˌ·· ‖ ˈ··· ·ˌ·/ n a small thin book with a paper cover advertising holidays arranged by a travel company, usu. with brightly coloured pictures of places where one can spend holidays: *We spent the evening looking at holiday brochures, planning where to go in summer.*

holiday camp /ˈ··· ·/ n BrE a place, often by the sea, where people can go for their holidays. Holiday camps have buildings where people can sleep, restaurants, bars, and often a FUNFAIR, all in the same area. Holidays in holiday camps were very popular in the 1950s and 1960s when many people could not afford to go abroad for their holidays.

holiday home /ˈ··· ·/ n a house, flat, etc. where people, esp. a family, go during the holidays: *Dozens of Welsh cottages have been bought by English people as holiday homes.*

Holiday Inn /ˌ··· ˈ·/ n tdmk one of a group of American hotels, found in the US and many other countries

hol·i·day·mak·er /ˈhɒlɪdiˌmeɪkəʳ‖ˈhɑːlɪˌdeɪ-/ also **vacationer** AmE— n a person who has travelled to another place for a holiday —**-ing** n [U]

hol·i·er-than-thou /ˌ··· · ˈ·◁/ adj derog thinking oneself to be morally better than other people; SANCTIMONIOUS

hol·i·ness /ˈhəʊlɪnəs/ n [U] the state or quality of being holy

Holiness n (a title of the Pope): *Your Holiness* | *His Holiness Pope John Paul* | *His Holiness the Pope*

ho·lis·tic /həʊˈlɪstɪk/ adj based on the principle that a whole thing or being is more than just a collection of parts added together: *holistic medicine* (=which treats the whole person, not just the diseased part) | *a holistic approach to education* — **~ally** /kli/ adv

Hol·land /ˈhɒlənd‖ˈhɑː-/ see NETHERLANDS

hol·ler /ˈhɒləʳ‖ˈhɑː-/ v [I (at);T] infml, esp. AmE to shout out, e.g. to attract attention or because of pain: *"Let go," he hollered.* | *Just holler if you need me!* —**holler** n : *She let out a holler when she saw me.*

hol·low¹ /ˈhɒləʊ‖ˈhɑː-/ adj **1** having an empty space inside: *The pillars look solid, but in fact they're hollow.* **2** (of parts of the body) lacking flesh so that the skin sinks inwards: *hollow cheeks* **3** (of sounds) having a ringing sound like the note when an empty container is struck: *the hollow sound of a large bell* **4** (of feelings, words, events, etc.) without real meaning or value: *the hollow promises of insincere politicians* | *a hollow victory* —see also **beat someone hollow** (BEAT¹) — **~ly** adv — **~ness** n [U]

hollow² n a space made in the surface of something, esp. in the ground

hollow³ v
    hollow sthg. ↔ **out** phr v [T] **1** to make a hollow place in: *to hollow out a log* **2** to make by doing this: *to hollow out a canoe from a log*

Hol·lo·way /ˈhɒləweɪ‖ˈhɑːl-/ a prison for women in London

hol·ly /ˈhɒli‖ˈhɑːli/ n [U] (a small tree) with dark green shiny prickly leaves and red berries. At Christmas, British and American people decorate their houses with holly.

holly

Holly, Buddy (1936–59) an American popular music singer, GUITAR player, and songwriter who was very influential and had an easily recognizable style. He was killed in a plane crash. —see colour picture on page 554

Holly and the I·vy /ˌ··· · ˈ··/, The the title and first line of a religious song (CAROL) sung at Christmas

hol·ly·hock /ˈhɒlihɒk‖ˈhɑːlihɑːk/ n a garden flower which grows very tall

Hol·ly·wood /ˈhɒliwʊd‖ˈhɑːl-/ an area of Los Angeles which is known as the centre of the American film industry. It is generally thought that everyone living in Hollywood is extremely rich, famous, and concerned with appearances but in fact many parts of Hollywood today are poor, dirty, and badly cared for. —see colour map on page 1374–5

Hollywood Bowl /ˌ··· ˈ·/ [the] a theatre in Hollywood,

California, with a covered stage for performers and outdoor seats for people to watch and listen. It is usu. used for musical entertainment.

Holmes /həʊmz/, **Sher·lock** /ˈʃɜːlɒk‖ˈʃɜːrlɑːk/ a DETECTIVE in stories by Sir Arthur Conan Doyle. Holmes smokes a pipe, plays the VIOLIN, and uses his impressive brain to understand mysterious deaths and other problems. He often says "Elementary, my dear Watson" to his friend Dr Watson, to show how easy to understand something is.

Hollywood

Sherlock Holmes

hol·o·caust /ˈhɒləkɔːst‖ˈhɑː-/ n great destruction and the loss of many lives, esp. by burning: *Millions of lives would be lost in a* **nuclear holocaust.**

Holocaust [*the*] the period of killing and cruel treatment of Jews by Hitler and the Nazi Party in the 1930s and 1940s

hol·o·gram /ˈhɒləgræm‖ˈhəʊl-, ˈhɑːl-/ n a photograph-like picture of something made with LASER light, which, when this light is shone on it again, makes the thing appear to be solid rather than flat —compare HOLOGRAPH

hol·o·graph /ˈhɒləgrɑːf‖ˈhəʊləgræf, ˈhɑːl-/ n a book etc. written by hand by the author —compare HOLOGRAM

hol·o·graph·y /hɒˈlɒgrəfi‖həʊˈlɑː-/ n [U] the science of producing holograms

hols /hɒlz‖hɑːlz/ n [P + *sing./pl.v*] *BrE infml* HOLIDAY[1] (2) **b** and **c**

Holst /həʊlst/, **Gus·tav** /ˈɡʊstɑːv‖ˈɡʌs-/ (1874–1934) a British COMPOSER whose most famous musical work is called *The Planets*

Hol·stein /ˈhɒlstən, ˈhɒlstiːn‖ˈhɑː-/ n *esp. AmE for* FRIESIAN

hol·ster /ˈhəʊlstəʳ/ n a leather holder for a PISTOL (=small gun), esp. one that hangs on a belt round the waist

ho·ly /ˈhəʊli/ *adj* 1 [*no comp.*] connected with God and religion; SACRED: *the Holy Bible* | *the holy city of Mecca/Benares* 2 giving oneself to the service of God and religion; pure and good: *a holy man* | *to lead a holy life* 3 [A] *sl euph* very bad (esp. in the phrase **a holy terror** (=a person who causes a lot of usu. not very serious trouble)) —see also UNHOLY

Holy Bi·ble /ˌ·· ˈ··/ [*the*] the BIBLE

holy cit·y /ˈ·· ˌ··/ n 1 a city which is a centre of religious activity and has been such a centre for some time 2 **the Holy City** JERUSALEM

Holy Com·mu·nion /ˌ·· ·ˈ··/ n [U] COMMUNION

Holy Fam·i·ly /ˌ·· ˈ··/ [*the*] Jesus, his mother Mary, and her husband Joseph

Holy Fa·ther /ˌ·· ˈ··/ [(*the*)] God

Holy Ghost /ˌ·· ˈ·/ [*the*] the HOLY SPIRIT

Holy Grail /ˌ·· ˈ·/ also **Grail**— [*the*] the cup believed to have been used by Christ before his death, and in which, it is said, some of his blood was collected. It was searched for by King Arthur's KNIGHTS but never found: (fig.) *economic growth without inflation – the politicians' Holy Grail* (=they try to get it but never can)

Hol·y·head /ˈhɒlihed‖ˈhɑː-/ 1 an island off the NW coast

of Anglesey 2 the main town on Holyhead, a port from which ferries (FERRY[1]) sail to Ireland

Holy Is·land /ˌ·· ˌ·/ an island off the NE coast of Northumberland, also known as **Lindisfarne**

Holy Land /ˌ·· ˌ·/ [*the*] a general name for those parts of the Middle East connected with the first Christians, Jews, and Muslims, also known as Palestine, in which most of the events mentioned in the Bible took place

Holy Loch /ˌ·· ˈ·/ an INLET of the Atlantic Ocean, on the W coast of Scotland NW of Glasgow, where the US navy used to have a base for NUCLEAR SUBMARINES

holy of ho·lies /ˌ·· ˈ··/ [*the*] 1 the most holy inner part of a Jewish temple 2 *sometimes humor* a place where people are not usu. allowed to go: *The headmaster invited us into that holy of holies, his study.*

Holy Rol·ler /ˌ·· ˈ··/ n *AmE infml derog* a member of a (Christian) church which has rather loud and emotional services

Holy Ro·man Em·pire /ˌ·· ˌ·· ˈ··/ [*the*] a large collection of lands ruled by one man, mainly in what is now Germany and Italy, which lasted from the ninth century until 1806

Hol·y·rood Pal·ace /ˌhɒliruːd ˈpælɪs‖ˌhɑː-/ a large house in Edinburgh owned by the British royal family

Holy See /ˌ·· ˈ·/ [*the*] *fml* the office of the Pope (=the most important priest in the Roman Catholic church)

Holy Spir·it /ˌ·· ˈ··/ also **Holy Ghost**— [*the*] (according to many Christian churches) God in the form of a spirit

holy war /ˌ·· ˈ·/ n a war fought in the name of a religion, for example to defend its beliefs

Holy Week /ˈ·· ·/ (in the Christian church) the week between Palm Sunday and Easter. In Britain people work as usual during Holy Week except that GOOD FRIDAY is a public holiday.

Holy Writ /ˌ·· ˈ·/ n [U] 1 the Bible 2 any writing or statement that is regarded as completely true and unquestionable

hom·age /ˈhɒmɪdʒ‖ˈhɑː-/ n [S;U (to)] *fml* signs of great respect, shown esp. to a ruler (esp. in the phrases **pay/do homage to someone**)

hom·burg /ˈhɒmbɜːg‖ˈhɑːmbɜːrg/ n a soft FELT[2] hat for men, with a wide piece (BRIM) standing out round the edge

home[1] /həʊm/ n 1 [C;U] **a** the house, flat, etc. where one lives. One's home is considered to be a safe and comfortable place which others only enter by invitation: *I left my briefcase at home.* | *They have a charming home in London.* | *Now that we have more furniture, the flat is beginning to feel like home.* | (fig.) *Has this pan got a home?* (=a place where it is usually kept) **b** a house, flat, etc. considered as property: *home buyers* | *"Attractive modern homes for sale"* (advertisement) | *home owners* | *There has been an increase in home ownership.* (=in the number of people who are buying or have bought their own homes) **c** the place where one was born or habitually lives and to which one usu. has emotional ties: *Nigeria is my home, but I'm living in London just now.* | *She was born in Denver, but she's made Los Angeles her home.* — see HOUSE (USAGE) 2 [C;U] the house and family one belongs to: *She came from a poor home.* | *a happy home life* | *He didn't leave home until he was 21.* 3 [*the*+S+of] **a** a place where a plant or animal can be found living or growing wild, esp. in large numbers: *India is the home of elephants and tigers.* **b** the place where something was originally discovered, made, or developed: *America is the home of baseball.* 4 [C] a place for the care of a group of people or animals of the same type, who do not live with a family, and who usu. have special needs or problems: *a children's home* | *an old people's home* | *If he gets worse we'll have to put him in a home.* —see also REST HOME 5 [U] (in some games and sports) a place which a player must try to reach, such as the GOAL or the finishing line of a race —see also HOME RUN, HOME STRETCH 6 **at home** *old-fash* ready to receive visitors: *If he telephones, say I'm not at home to visitors until ten.* 7 **be/feel at home** to be comfortable; not feel worried, esp. because one has the right skills or experience: *She's completely at home with computers.* 8 **Home, James, and don't spare the horses!** a phrase used humorously when telling someone to drive you home quickly 9 **make oneself at home** (*often imperative*) to behave freely, sit where one likes, etc., as if one were in one's own home **10 home sweet home** a phrase used when saying how pleasant it is to be in your own home **11 there's no place like home** a phrase from an old popular song, meaning that your own home is the nicest place to be — see also HOME FROM HOME

home² *adv* **1** to or at one's home: *Is he home from work yet?* | *I'm going home.* | *I really must be getting home in a moment.* (said by a guest who is about to go home) **2** as far as possible and/or to the right place: *He struck the nail home.* | (fig.) *He drove his point home with plenty of facts.* **3 come home to someone/bring something home to someone** to be clearly understood by someone/to make someone clearly understand something: *At last it's come home to us that they've been tricking us all the time.* **4 home and dry** *infml, esp. BrE* having safely or successfully completed something —see also **till the cows come home** (COW¹ (6)), **nothing to write home about** (WRITE)

▷ USAGE When speaking of movement towards **home**, use the adverb form without **to**: *I'm coming* **home**. | *Let's send the children* **home**. | *Henry'll be* (=come) **home** *before seven.* When there is no movement the usual form in British English is **at home**: *Let's stay at* **home** *this evening.* | *Is Henry* **at home**? In American English **home** is often used without the preposition: *Let's stay* **home** *this evening.* | *I've been* **home** *all day.*◁

home³ *adj* [A] **1** of or being a home, place of origin, or base of operations: *the home office of an international firm* | *What's your home address?* **2** not foreign; DOMESTIC¹ (4): *the home country* | *Are these cars made for the home market or for export?* —see also HOME OFFICE **3** prepared, done, or intended for use in a home: *home cooking* | *home-baked bread* | *a home computer* **4** played or playing at one's own sports field, rather than that of an opponent: *the home team* | *home games* —opposite **away** **5 homebase** *esp. AmE* **a** also HOME PLATE **b** a place or situation which is like one's home: *Eventually I'll return to Scotland, which is homebase.*

home⁴ *v*

home in on sthg. *phr v* [T] to aim exactly towards: (fig.) *Now that we've got all the facts, we're homing in on the right answer.*

home bak·ing /ˌ·ˈ··/ *n* [U] (cakes etc. made by) baking things at home rather than in a factory: *Granny's home baking always tastes so much better than the cakes you buy in the shops.*

Home·base /ˈhəʊmbeɪs/ one of a group of DO-IT-YOURSELF stores in Britain owned by J Sainsbury plc

home·bod·y /ˈhəʊmˌbɒdi‖-ˌbɑːdi/ *n infml* a person who enjoys being at home. This word is usu. used to describe a woman who chooses to stay at home rather than go out to work.

Home Box Of·fice /ˌ· '· '·/ also **HBO**— *n tdmk* an American CABLE TELEVISION company which usu. shows films

home·boy /ˈhəʊmbɔɪ/ *n AmE infml* **1** a person who comes from the same town as you **2** a friend, used esp. by black men **3** a member of a GANG¹ (1b), used esp. by other members of the gang: *"You, home boy! Come here!"*

home brew /ˌ· ˈ·/ *n* [U] beer made at home — ~ **ed** /ˌ· ˈ·◁/ *adj*

home·com·ing /ˈhəʊmˌkʌmɪŋ/ *n* **1** an arrival home, esp. after long absence **2** *AmE* an occasion when former students return to a high school or college for a REUNION (=reuniting) and usu. a football game

▶ CULTURAL NOTE Homecoming is usu. every autumn. It is celebrated by the students as well as by the returning GRADUATEs, and includes dances and parties, and esp. in high schools, the choosing of a **homecoming queen**. She is a student, usu. chosen because she is popular and attractive.◀

Home Coun·ties /ˌ· ˈ··/ [the+P] the counties (COUNTY) around London, in SE England. People living in the Home Counties are often considered to be relatively wealthy and to share a comfortable way of life.

home e·co·nom·ics /ˌ· ··ˈ··/ *n* [U] DOMESTIC SCIENCE

home from home /ˌ· · ˈ·/ *BrE* ‖ **home a·way from home** /ˌ· ··· ˈ·/ *AmE*— *n* a place as pleasant, comfortable, welcoming, etc., as one's own house

home front /ˌ· ˈ·/ *n* [the] (the activities of) the people working in their own country, while others are away at war

home fry /ˈ· ·/ *n* ~ **fries** *AmE* a CHIP¹ (3) (=long thin piece of potato) fried with its skin still on: *steak and home fries*

home-grown /ˌhəʊmˈɡrəʊn◁/ *adj* **1** (of plants for food) **a** grown in the home country, not abroad **b** grown in one's own garden, not bought in a shop **2** *infml* made or produced in one's own country: *homegrown TV programmes*

Home Guard /ˌ· ˈ·/ *n* [the+sing./pl. v] (in the Second World War) the citizen army formed at home to help to defend Britain in case of attack from abroad —compare TERRITORIAL ARMY

home help /ˌ· ˈ·/ *n* a person who is sent in by the medical and social services in Britain or is employed to do cleaning and cooking esp. for someone who is ill or very old

home im·prove·ments /ˌ· ·ˈ··/ *n* [P] work, e.g. building new rooms, fitting better windows, insulating (INSULATE (1)) the walls, etc., which is done to a house to improve its standard of comfort

home·land /ˈhəʊmlænd, -lənd/ *n* **1** the country where a person was born **2** any of several large areas of land set aside for the black population by the government of South Africa, according to the system of APARTHEID

home·less /ˈhəʊmləs/ *adj* without a home and therefore often forced to sleep without shelter in streets or parks: *Londoners are concerned about the growing numbers of homeless people living in the city.* | (also *n, the*+P) *help for the homeless* — ~ **ness** *n* [U]

home loan /ˌ· ˈ·/ *n infml for* MORTGAGE

home·ly /ˈhəʊmli/ *adj* **1** *esp. BrE* simple; not trying to seem important or special: *a homely meal of bread and cheese* **2** *AmE* (of people, faces, etc.) not good-looking; unattractive —compare HOMEY —**liness** *n* [U]

home·made /ˌhəʊmˈmeɪd◁/ *adj* (of clothes, food, etc.) made at home, not bought from a shop

home·mak·er /ˈhəʊmˌmeɪkəʳ/ *n euph, esp. AmE* a housewife

home mov·ie /ˌ· ˈ··/ *n* a film made privately and intended to be shown at home, not in a cinema

Home Of·fice /ˈ· ˌ··/ *n* [the] the British government department under the control of the Home Secretary, responsible for justice and controls on people entering Britain. A similar department in a foreign government is usu. known as the Ministry of the Interior. —compare FCO

Home on the Range /ˌ· · · ˈ·/ an American FOLK song whose words are often used and repeated:
O give me a home where the buffalo roam,
Where the deer and the antelope play;
Where seldom is heard a discouraging word,
And the skies are not cloudy all day.

ho·me·o·path, homoeo- /ˈhəʊmiəˌpæθ/ *n* a person who practises homeopathy

ho·me·op·a·thy, homoeop- /ˌhəʊmiˈɒpəθi‖-ˈɑːp-/ *n* [U] a system of medicine in which disease is treated by giving very small amounts of a substance which, in larger amounts, would usu. produce an illness similar to the disease. Homeopathy is a form of ALTERNATIVE MEDICINE and is not usu. practised by GPs in Britain. It is not usu. available under the National Health Service, so people must pay for treatment. —**thic** /ˌhəʊmiəˈpæθɪk◁/ *adj* —**thically** /kli/ *adv*

home·own·er /ˈhəʊmˌəʊnəʳ/ *n* a person who owns their house or flat

home plate /ˌ· ˈ·/ also **home, homebase**— *n* (in BASEBALL) the point over which a PITCHER must throw the ball for the hitter and the last point a runner must touch in order to make a RUN² (10) —see picture at BASEBALL

ho·mer¹ /ˈhəʊməʳ/ *n AmE infml* a HOME RUN

homer² *v* [I] *AmE infml* to hit a HOME RUN: *Rodriguez homered in the bottom of the sixth to bring the score to 5-all.*

Ho·mer a Greek poet who lived about 800 to 900 years before Christ, whose EPIC poems the *Iliad* and the *Odyssey* have had a great influence on Western literature

Homer, Wins·low /ˈwɪnzləʊ/ (1836–1910) an American artist, remembered for his WATERCOLOURs

home room /ˈ· ·/ *n AmE* a classroom where students have to go at the beginning of every school day

home rule /ˌ· ˈ·/ *n* [U] **1** self-government by an area that was once politically dependent. This expression is sometimes used by Scots people instead of "DEVOLUTION" when speaking of independence for Scotland. **2 Home Rule** (in British use) self-government for Ireland, the aim of

Irish nationalists from around 1870 until 1921, when the Irish Free State was established

home run /ˌ· ˈ·/ also **homer** *infml*— *n* (in BASEBALL) a long hit which allows the hitter to run round the complete course and gain a point: *Until Hank Aaron came along, Babe Ruth had hit more home runs than any other player.*

Home Sec·re·tar·y /ˌ· ˈ····/ *n* the British government minister who is head of the Home Office. A similar minister in a foreign government is usu. called the Minister of the Interior.

home·sick /ˈhəʊmˌsɪk/ *adj* feeling a great wish to be at home, when one is away from it. People feel homesick because they miss their family and friends or places and customs that are familiar to them. — ~ **ness** *n* [U]

home·spun /ˈhəʊmspʌn/ *adj* **1** (of cloth) woven or spun (SPIN¹ (2)) at home, esp. in former times **2** simple and ordinary in a way that is admired: *homespun philosophy*

home·stead¹ /ˈhəʊmsted, -stʌd/ *n* **1** a house and its surrounding land, esp. a farm with its buildings **2** *esp. AmE* a piece of land given by the state (esp. in former times) on condition that the owner farms it

homestead² *v* [I;T] *AmE* to settle on (land) for a fixed period of time as a way of getting ownership of it: *My parents homesteaded some land in Alaska.* —**er** *n* : *homesteaders of the American West*

home stretch /ˌ· ˈ·/ *n* [*the*] **1** also **home straight** *BrE*— the last part of a race **2** the last part of an activity or journey

home·town /ˌhəʊmˈtaʊn/ *n* the town where one was born and/or spent one's childhood

home truth /ˌ· ˈ·/ *n* [*often pl.*] a fact about someone which is unpleasant for them to know, but true: *She told him a few home truths about his selfishness.*

home·ward /ˈhəʊmwəd‖-wərd/ *adj* [A] going towards home: *the homeward journey* —opposite **outward**

home·wards /ˈhəʊmwədz‖-wərdz/ ‖ usu. **homeward** *AmE*— *adv* towards home

home·work /ˈhəʊmwɜːk‖-wɜːrk/ *n* [U] **1** studies which must be done at home by students to help them to learn and prepare for what is studied at school **2** preparation done before taking part in an important activity: *The MP's speech showed she'd done her homework well.* —compare HOUSEWORK

home·work·ing /ˈhəʊmˌwɜːkɪŋ‖-ˌwɜːr-/ *n* [U] working for a company from one's home instead of travelling to the company's offices every day

hom·ey, homy /ˈhəʊmi/ *adj AmE infml* pleasant, like home —compare HOMELY

hom·i·cid·al /ˌhɒmɪˈsaɪdl◂‖ˌhɑː-/ *adj* (of a person or character) likely to murder: *a homicidal maniac*

hom·i·cide /ˈhɒmɪsaɪd‖ˈhɑː-/ *n fml or law* **1** [C;U] (an act of) murder **2** [C] a murderer

hom·i·ly /ˈhɒmɪli‖ˈhɑː-/ *n* **1** *usu. derog* a long talk, which gives advice on how to behave **2** a SERMON (1)

hom·ing /ˈhəʊmɪŋ/ *adj* [A] **1** of or having the ability, which is found in certain birds and animals, to find one's way home: *a homing pigeon | the homing instinct* **2** (of certain machines, esp. weapons) having the ability to guide themselves onto the place they are aimed at: *a missile equipped with a homing device*

homing pi·geon /ˈ·· ˌ··/ *n* a CARRIER PIGEON

hom·i·ny /ˈhɒmɪni‖ˈhɑː-/ *n* [U] a sort of American corn, esp. when boiled —compare GRITS

ho·mo /ˈhəʊməʊ/ *n* a Latin word used with other Latin words to describe different kinds of human or human-like animals: *Our species is called Homo Sapiens.*

ho·moe·o·path /ˈhəʊmiəˌpæθ/ *n* a HOMEOPATH

ho·moe·op·athy /ˌhəʊmiˈɒpəθi‖-ˈɑːp-/ *n* [U] HOMEOPATHY

ho·mo·ge·ne·ous /ˌhəʊməˈdʒiːniəs/ also **ho·mog·e·nous** /həˈmɒdʒɪnəs‖-ˈmɑː-/— *adj* formed of parts of the same kind; the same all through —compare HETEROGENEOUS — ~ **ly** *adv* —**ity** /ˌhəʊməˌdʒɪˈniːˌti/ *n* [U]

ho·mo·ge·nize also **-nise** *BrE* /həˈmɒdʒənaɪz‖-ˈmɑː-/ *v* [T] to make (the parts of a whole, esp. a mixture) become evenly spread through the whole: *homogenized milk* (=in which there is no cream, because the fat is broken up all through the liquid)

hom·o·graph /ˈhɒməɡrɑːf, ˈhəʊ-‖ˈhɑːməɡræf, ˈhəʊ-/ *n* a word that has the same spelling as another, but is different in meaning, origin, grammar, or pronunciation: *The noun "record" and the verb "record" are homographs (of each other).*

hom·o·nym /ˈhɒmənɪm, ˈhəʊ-‖ˈhɑː-, ˈhəʊ-/ *n* a word that has both the same sound and spelling as another, but is different in meaning or origin: *The noun "bear" and the verb "bear" are homonyms (of each other).*

ho·mo·pho·bi·a /ˌhəʊməˈfəʊbiə, ˌhɒ-‖ˌhəʊ-/ *n* [U] fear or hatred of homosexuality, expressed as violence against or unfairness in dealing with homosexuals and matters that concern them: *homophobia in the media* —**bic** *adj* : *a homophobic attack*

hom·o·phone /ˈhɒməfəʊn, ˈhəʊ-‖ˈhɑː-, ˈhəʊ-/ *n* a word that sounds the same as another but is different in spelling, meaning, and origin: *"Knew" and "new" are homophones (of each other).*

Ho·mo sa·pi·ens /ˌhəʊməʊ ˈsæpienz‖-ˈseɪpiənz/ *Lat* the human race; the type of human being now alive on the Earth (as opposed to earlier types)

ho·mo·sex·u·al /ˌhəʊməˈsekʃuəl◂, ˌhɒ-‖ˌhəʊ-/ also **gay**— *adj, n* (of or being) a person who is sexually attracted to people of the same sex —compare BISEXUAL, HETEROSEXUAL, LESBIAN; see also COME **out** (7) — ~ **ity** /ˌhəʊmə ˌsekʃuˈælˌti, ˌhɒ-‖ˌhəʊ-/ *n* [U]

▶ CULTURAL NOTE In Britain, it was illegal in the past for men to have sex with each other. It is now legal in Britain between men aged over 21, but it is still illegal in the Isle of Man and in the Republic of Ireland. In the US, some states still have laws against homosexual actions, but in most states it is unlikely that these laws would be enforced (ENFORCE). While many homosexuals are more open about their sexuality, many people still do not find homosexuality acceptable. ◀

hom·y /ˈhəʊmi/ *adj AmE infml* HOMEY

hon 1 /ɒn‖ɑːn/ *abbrev. for:* HONORARY²: *the hon chairman* **2** /hʌn/ *AmE infml for* HONEY²: *"Hi, hon, I'm home."*

Hon *written abbrev. for:* HONOURABLE: *the Hon member for Liverpool West*

hon·cho /ˈhɒntʃəʊ‖ˈhɑːn-/ *n AmE infml* the person in charge; the BOSS: *"Who's the head honcho here?"*

Hon·da /ˈhɒndə‖ˈhɑːn-/ *tdmk* a MOTORCYCLE or car made by the Japanese company Honda

Hon·du·ras /hɒnˈdjʊərəs‖hɑːnˈdjʊərəs, -ˈdʊə-/ a country in Central America; capital Tegucigalpa; population 4,951,000 (1989). Honduras is important to the US because it is a friendly nation in an area in which many countries are against the US. —**ran** *n, adj*

hone /həʊn/ *v* [T] to sharpen (knives, swords, etc.)

Hon·e·cker /ˈhɒnəkəʳ‖ˈhɑː-/, **Er·ich** /ˈerɪk, -ɪx/ (1912–) a former East German politician, and head of state of East Germany (1971–89)

hon·est /ˈɒnəst‖ˈɑːn-/ *adj* **1** (of a person) trustworthy; not likely to lie, cheat, or steal: *an honest politician/employee* —opposite **dishonest 2** (of actions, appearance, etc.) typical of an honest person: *an honest face | honest dealings* **3** open and direct; not hiding facts; FRANK: *To be quite honest with you, I don't think you will pass. | Give me your honest opinion.* **4 make an honest living** to earn one's pay fairly, without cheating, breaking the law, etc. **5 make an honest woman of** now usu. humor to marry (a woman) after having a sexual relationship with her

hon·est·ly /ˈɒnəstli‖ˈɑːn-/ *adv* **1** in an honest way **2 a** really; speaking truthfully: *I can't honestly say it matters to me. | I didn't tell anyone, honestly I didn't. | Quite honestly, I don't think his work is very good.* **b** (used for expressing strong feeling, usu. mixed with disapproval): *Honestly! What a stupid thing to do!*

honest-to-good·ness /ˌ··· ˈ··◂/ *adj* [A] *infml apprec* pure and simple; in a natural state; STRAIGHTFORWARD

hon·es·ty /ˈɒnəsti‖ˈɑːn-/ *n* [U] **1** the quality of being honest: *We've never doubted her honesty. | I must tell you,* **in all honesty** (=being completely open and truthful), *that your chances of passing the test are not very high.* —opposite **dishonesty 2 honesty is the best policy** *saying* it is better to be honest and tell people the truth

hon·ey /ˈhʌni/ *n* **1** [U] the sweet sticky usu. golden-brown substance produced by bees, which can be eaten on bread and used in cooking **2** also **hon·ey·bunch** /ˈhʌnibʌntʃ/ ‖ *esp. AmE* **a** (used when speaking to someone you love): *Gee, honey, that's a swell dress you've got on!* **b** (used informally as a friendly form of address, esp. by or to a woman) **3** [C] *infml, esp. AmE* something excellent: *That's a honey of a car!*

hon·ey·bee /ˈhʌnibiː/ *n* a bee which makes honey

hon·ey·comb /ˈhʌnikəʊm/ *n* **1** a container made by bees out of WAX and consisting of six-sided cells in which honey is stored —see picture at CELL **2** something like this in shape or pattern, such as an arrangement of bricks

hon·ey·combed /ˈhʌnikəʊmd/ *adj* [F (**with**)] filled with holes, hollow passages, etc.

hon·ey·dew mel·on /ˌhʌnidjuː ˈmelən‖-duː-/ *n* a common type of MELON with a pale skin and flesh and a very sweet taste

hon·eyed /ˈhʌnid/ *adj lit* (of words) sweet and pleasing and often insincere

hon·ey·moon¹ /ˈhʌnimuːn/ *n* **1** the holiday taken by a man and woman who have just got married. They usu. leave for their honeymoon immediately after the RECEPTION which follows the wedding ceremony, and often do not tell anyone where they are going: *a honeymoon couple* | *the hotel's honeymoon suite* (=a specially comfortable set of rooms used by people on their honeymoon) **2** a short period of agreement, good relations, etc. at the beginning of a new piece of work, period of office, etc.: *The honeymoon is over – people are starting to criticize the new government.*

honeymoon² *v* [I+*adv/prep*] to have or spend one's honeymoon: *honeymooning in the Bahamas* – **~er** *n*

hon·ey·pot /ˈhʌnipɒt‖-paːt/ *n infml* something, esp. the possibility of financial reward, which attracts a lot of people: *The North Sea oil industry has* | *Spring sales in London have always been a honeypot.*

hon·ey·suck·le /ˈhʌniˌsʌkəl/ *n* [C;U] a climbing plant with sweet-smelling yellow flowers

Hong Kong /ˌhɒŋ ˈkɒŋ◂‖ˈhɑːŋ ˌkaːŋ/ **1** a COLONY of Britain in SE China which is an important financial and trade centre. Hong Kong will be given back to the People's Republic of China in 1997. **2** one of a number of islands in this COLONY

Hon·i soit qui mal y pense /ˌɒni swɑː kiː ˌmæl iː ˈpɒns‖ ˌɔːn-, -ˈpɑːns/ *Fr* the MOTTO of the Order of the Garter. It means "let bad things happen to the person who thinks bad thoughts about others".

honk¹ /hɒŋk‖haːŋk, hɔːŋk/ *n* **1** the sound a GOOSE makes **2** the sound made by a car horn

honk² *v* [I;T (**at**)] to (cause to) make a honk: *He honked his horn as he went past.*

hon·ky, honkie /ˈhɒŋki‖ˈhɔːŋ-, ˈhaːŋ-/ *n AmE derog sl* a white person

honky-tonk¹ /ˈhɒŋki tɒŋk‖ˈhaːŋki taːŋk, ˈhɔːŋki tɔːŋk/ *n AmE* a kind of bar esp. popular in the 1950s which featured country music, dancing, and drinking. Many COUNTRY AND WESTERN songs from this period are about honky-tonks.

hon·ky-tonk² *adj* [A] **1** of or used in a merry form of piano-playing: *a honky-tonk piano/pianist* **2** cheap and brightly coloured; lacking good taste: *a honky-tonk restaurant.* **3** of a honky-tonk: *a honky-tonk singer/man*

Hon·o·lu·lu /ˌhɒnəˈluːluː‖ˌhaːn-/ the capital of Hawaii, a port and trade centre on the island of Oahu which also attracts many tourists —see colour map on pages 1374–5

hon·or *AmE for* HONOUR

hon·or·a·ble *AmE for* HONOURABLE

hon·o·rar·i·um /ˌɒnəˈreəriəm‖ˌaːnə-/ *n* **-iums** *or* **-ia** /iə/ a sum of money offered for professional services, for which by custom the person does not ask to be paid

hon·or·a·ry /ˈɒnərəri‖ˈaːnəreri/ *adj* **1** (of a rank, a university degree, etc.) given as an honour, not according to the usual rules **2** holding an office or position without payment for one's services: *She's the honorary chairman.* – compare HONOURABLE

hon·or·if·ic /ˌɒnəˈrɪfɪk◂‖ˌaːnə-/ *adj, n* (a title or expression) which shows respect, esp. as used in Far Eastern languages – **~ally** /kli/ *adv*

honor roll /ˈ··· ·/ *n AmE* a list of students who have achieved the highest marks (GRADES) in a school or college: *Are you on the honor roll this year?*

hon·ors *AmE for* HONOURS

honor so·ci·e·ty /ˈ··· ·,···/ *n AmE* an organization for the recognition of high ACADEMIC standards in students, either within a particular school or on a local or national level: *The honor society will meet after school on Thursday.*

honor sys·tem /ˈ··· ,··/ *n AmE* a way of operating some activity in which people are trusted to be honest and obey rules, and no checks are made on them: *We run the coffee shop on an honor system: take what you want and leave the money in the box.*

hon·our¹ *BrE*‖**honor** *AmE* /ˈɒnəʳ‖ˈaːnər/ *n* **1** [U] the great respect and admiration which people have for a person, country, etc., often publicly expressed: *to win honour on the field of battle* | *fighting for the honour of one's country* | *a party* **in honour of** (=to show respect to) *the visiting president* | *The queen was welcomed at the airport by* **a guard of honour.** (=special group of soldiers) **2** [U] high principles and standards of behaviour; nobleness of character: *a man of honour* | *It's* **a point of honour** *with me to repay all my debts promptly.* | *I give you* **my word of honour** (=I promise) *that I did not take the money.* **3** [S (**to**)] a person or thing that brings great pride and pleasure: *He's an honour to the school.* | *It's a great honour to have the Queen here today.* | (*polite or fml*) *Will you* **do me the honour of** *dancing with me?* **4** [U] *now usu. humor* the CHASTITY of a woman (esp. in the phrase **lose one's honour**) **5 (in) honour bound** forced by one's standards of good behaviour: *I feel* **(in)** *honour bound to repay the money I borrowed.* **6 on one's honour** on trust; being trusted to behave rightly: *He was on his honour not to tell the secret.* —see also HONOURS, MAID OF HONOUR

hon·our² *BrE* ‖ **honor** *AmE* – *v* [T] **1** *esp. fml or pomp* to show or bring honour to: *We're deeply honoured that you should agree to join us.* | *Today the Queen honoured us with/by her presence.* **2** to keep (an agreement), often by making a payment: *The bank has refused to honour his cheque.* | *Please honour your agreement/contract by working until the project is finished.*

Honour *BrE* ‖ **Honor** *AmE*– *n* (used as a title for a judge): *His Honour Judge Sachs* | *Good morning, Your Honour.*

hon·our·a·ble *BrE*‖**honorable** *AmE* /ˈɒnərəbəl‖ˈaːn-/ *adj* **1** bringing or deserving honour: *honourable deeds* | *an honourable settlement of the dispute* **2** showing high principles and good character —compare HONORARY —**bly** *adv*

Honourable (*written abbrev.* **Hon.**) *adj* [A] (a title given to the children of certain British nobles and to certain high officials, including Members of Parliament when talking to one another in the House of Commons): *Will the Honourable member please answer the question?* | *the Honourable Glencora Smith-Fortescue*

honourable men·tion /ˌ····· ˈ··/ *n* [C;U] a special mark of honour in a competition or show, given for work of high quality that has not actually won a prize

hon·ours *BrE*‖**honors** *AmE* /ˈɒnəz‖ˈaːnərz/ *n* [P] **1** marks of respect: *buried with* **(full) military honours** (=a special ceremony which soldiers attend in their best uniforms) **2** a level gained in an honours degree: *She graduated with first-class honours.* | *with high honours* —compare CUM LAUDE **3** *BrE* the highest playing cards in a game **4 do the honours** *infml* to act as the host or hostess, e.g. by offering drinks, introducing people, etc.

honours de·gree /ˈ··· ·,·/ *n* a specialized British university UNDERGRADUATE degree: *What class of honours degree did she graduate with?*

honours list /ˈ··· ,·/ *n* [*the*] (in Britain) a list of important people to whom titles are to be given as a sign of respect. The honours list is produced each year by the Prime Minister but the titles are actually given by the Queen in a special ceremony: *He got a peerage* (=became a Lord) *in the New Year's honours list.*

Hon·shu /ˈhɒnʃuː‖ˈhaːn-/ the largest of the four main islands of Japan. Most of Japan's largest cities are on Honshu.

hooch, hootch /huːtʃ/ *n* [U] *AmE sl* strong alcoholic drink, esp. WHISKY, esp. that which is made illegally

hood /hʊd/ n **1** a covering for the whole of the head and neck **a** except the face, usu. fastened on at the back to a coat, etc., so that it can be pushed back when not needed **b** including the face, worn by criminals to avoid recognition **2** something that covers or fits over the top of something else, such as **a** a covering over a cooker to draw cooking smells out of the room **b** a folding cover over a car, PRAM, etc. —see picture at PRAM **3** AmE the BONNET (2) covering the engine of a car —see picture at CAR and at ENGINE **4** sl a hoodlum

Hood, Robin see ROBIN HOOD

hood·ed /'hʊdɪd/ adj covered with or wearing a hood

hood·lum /'huːdləm/ n sl a violent and/or criminal person

hoo·doo /'huːduː/ n -doos [(on)] infml, esp. AmE a person or thing that brings bad luck

hood·wink /'hʊdˌwɪŋk/ v [T (into)] to trick or deceive

hoo·ey /'huːi/ n [U] AmE sl stupid talk; NONSENSE

hoof /huːf‖hʊf/ n hoofs or hooves /huːvz‖hʊfs/ **1** the hard foot of certain animals, e.g. the horse —see picture at HORSE **2 on the hoof** (of an animal kept for its meat) before being killed for meat; still alive

hoof·er /'huːfər/ n AmE sl a dancer, esp. one who TAP DANCEs

hoo-ha /'huː haː/ n [U] esp. BrE infml noisy talk about something unimportant; FUSS

hooks

picture hook   fish hook   coat hook

hook¹ /hʊk/ n **1** a curved piece of metal or plastic used **a** for hanging things on: Hang your coat on the hook. **b** for catching fish: a fish hook **c** with an EYE¹ (6) for fastening clothing —see picture at FASTENER **2 a** (in cricket, GOLF, etc.) a stroke which sends the ball away from a straight course towards the side of the player's weaker hand **b** (in BOXING) a blow given with the elbow bent: a left/right hook **3** the part on which a telephone RECEIVER rests or is hung: They took/left the phone **off the hook** so no calls would disturb them. **4 by hook or by crook** infml by any means possible, perhaps including dishonest or illegal means **5 hook, line, and sinker** infml (with expressions of belief) completely: She swallowed the whole unlikely story hook, line, and sinker. **6 off the hook** infml no longer in a position of difficulty: The barman has told the police that Jane was in the bar at the time of the bank robbery, so that **lets her off the hook.** —see also BILLHOOK, BOAT HOOK, **sling one's hook** (SLING)

hook² v [T] **1** to catch with a hook: to hook a fish **2** [+obj+adv/prep] to hang on or fasten (as if) with a hook: Hook the rope over that nail. **3** to hit (a ball) with a hook stroke

     hook sthg. ↔ **up** phr v [T (to) often pass.] to connect to a power supply or central system: The BBC is hooked up by satellite to the American network in order to broadcast the President's speech.

Hook, Captain see CAPTAIN HOOK

hook·ah /'hʊkə/ also **water pipe**— n a tobacco pipe whose smoke is drawn through water by a long tube before reaching the mouth

hook and lad·der /ˌ· · '··/ n AmE a FIRE ENGINE with long ladders fixed to it

hooked /hʊkt/ adj **1** shaped like a hook: a hooked nose **2** having one or more hooks **3** [F (on)] infml **a** dependent (on drugs); ADDICTED **b** having a great liking for and very frequently using, doing, eating, etc.: hooked on jogging

hook·er /'hʊkər/ n sl, esp. AmE for PROSTITUTE

hook-nosed /ˌ· '·◁/ adj having a nose that curves outwards and downwards to a point

Hook of Hol·land /ˌ· · '··/ [the] a port on the SW coast of the Netherlands. The Dutch name is **Hoek van Holland**.

hook-up /'· ·/ n a temporary connection between things, usu. for the purpose of moving power, FUEL, or information from one to the other: a satellite hook-up to televise the Barcelona Olympics | We need a campground with a gas hook-up for our camper.

hook·worm /'hʊkwɜːm‖-wɜːrm/ n **1** [C] a worm which lives in the INTESTINEs of humans or animals **2** [U] the disease caused by this worm

hook·y, hookey /'hʊki/ n **play hooky** to stay away from school without permission; play TRUANT

hoo·li·gan /'huːlɪɡən/ n a noisy rough person who causes trouble by fighting, breaking things, etc. In Britain, people who are noisy and violent at football matches are called football hooligans. — ~ **ism** n [U]

hoop /huːp‖hʊp, huːp/ n **1** a circular band of wood or metal round a barrel **2** a similar circular band, such as one used **a** as a child's toy **b** (formerly) to hold women's skirts out **c** for animals to jump through at the CIRCUS **3** a metal arch through which the ball is driven in CROQUET **4 put/go through the hoop(s)** to (cause someone to) go through a difficult test

hoop·la /'huːp laː‖'huːp-, 'hʊp-/ n [U] **1** BrE a game in which prizes are won when a ring is thrown right over them **2** esp. AmE noise and excitement intended to attract attention, and also perhaps deceive, and sometimes used as an advertisement for whatever is happening; BALLYHOO: the hoop-la of a circus coming to town.

hoop·ster /'huːpstər/ n AmE sl a BASKETBALL player: One of the best hoopsters of all time.

hoo·ray /hʊ'reɪ, huː'reɪ◁/ interj, n HURRAY

Hooray Hen·ry /ˌ·ˌ· '··, ˌ·· '··/ n BrE usu. humor an upper-class man who makes a noisy show of enjoying himself and is considered to be a fool by most other people

hoose·gow /'huːsɡaʊ/ n AmE sl a prison: He'll be up in the hoosegow for years.

hoot¹ /huːt/ n **1** [C] the sound an OWL makes **2** [C] the sound made by a car's or ship's horn **3** [C] a shout of disapproval, unpleasant laughter, etc.: a speech that was greeted with loud hoots/with hoots of derision **4** [S] infml something very amusing: That play was an absolute hoot. **5 not care/give a hoot/two hoots** infml not to care at all: He doesn't care two hoots what people think.

hoot² v [I;T (at)] **1** to (cause to) make a hoot: I could hear an owl hooting. | She hooted at me with her horn/hooted her horn at me. **2** infml to laugh loudly (at), esp. to show disrespect or disapproval: The audience hooted with derision. | They hooted him off the stage. (=made him leave by hooting)

hoot·en·an·ny /'huːtn-æni/ n AmE an informal concert usu. of FOLK MUSIC at which anyone can sing or play an instrument: The Glacier Hotel has a hootenanny every Tuesday night.

hoot·er /'huːtər/ n **1** esp. BrE something that makes a hooting sound, such as a car horn or a horn or whistle that signals the beginning or end of work **2** BrE sl the nose. This word is used esp. to talk about a large nose with amusement or disrespect.

hoo·ver¹ /'huːvər/ n tdmk (often cap.) (a type of) VACUUM CLEANER

hoover² v [I;T] BrE to clean with a VACUUM CLEANER

Hoover, Herbert Clark (1874–1964) the president of the US (1929–33). Hoover was president during the first years of the Great DEPRESSION.

Hoover, J. Ed·gar /ˌdʒeɪ 'edɡər/ (1895–1972) the most important director of the FBI who held that position from 1924 until his death. Hoover was respected for his improvement of the FBI, but after his death it was learned that the FBI kept information about many people and groups that it should not have had, and many people felt that Hoover had had too much power.

Hoover Dam /ˌ·· '·/ also **Boulder Dam** [the] a DAM on the COLORADO RIVER in the SW US which supplies electricity and water to several states. It is one of the highest dams in the world. —see colour map on pages 1374–5

hooves /huːvz‖hʊfs/ pl. of HOOF

hop¹ /hɒp‖haːp/ v -pp- **1** [I] **a** (of people) to jump on one leg **b** [+adv/prep] (of small animals, birds, etc.) to jump: The bird hopped onto my finger. **2** [T] to cross by hopping **3** [I+adv/prep] infml to get onto/into or off/out of a vehicle: Hop in and I'll drive you to the station. | We hopped onto the bus while it was still moving. **4** [T] esp.

AmE infml to make a trip, esp. a short one or on a plane: *They hopped a plane for Los Angeles.* | *He's hopped up to New York for the day.* **5 Hop it!** *BrE sl* Go away! **6 hopping mad** *infml* very angry

hop² *n* **1** an act of hopping; a jump **2** *old-fash infml* a dance at which popular music is played **3** *infml* a distance travelled by a plane before landing: *It's only a short hop from London to Paris.* **4 on the hop** *infml* unprepared; without warning: *I'm afraid your order has caught us on the hop — the goods aren't available yet.*

hop³ *n* **1** a tall climbing plant with flowers **2** [*usu. pl.*] the seed-cases of this plant, esp. when dried and used for giving taste to beer

hope¹ /həʊp/ *v* [I (**for**); T *obj*] **1** to wish and expect; want (something) to happen and have some confidence that it will happen: *We're hoping for a big order from the Middle East.* [+to-v] *She hopes to go to university next year.* [+(that)] *I hope you'll come and see us when you're in London.* | *We* **hope and pray** *that she will recover.* | *"Will he come back?" "I sincerely hope so|not."* | *The* **hoped-for** *improvement in trade has still not happened.* **2 hope against hope** to continue to hope when there is little chance of success **3 hope for the best** to trust that things will go well, esp. when a rather risky or unsatisfactory arrangement has been made: *You don't need to make the soup carefully; just mix everything together and hope for the best.*

▷ USAGE Compare **hope** and **wish**. You **hope** for things that are possible, but **wish** for things that you think are impossible or unlikely: *I* **hope** *you pass your exam.* (=I think it is possible) | *I* **hope** *you will help me.* (=I want you to, and I think you can) | *I* **wish** *I were 20 years younger.* (=but that is impossible) | *I* **wish** *you would help me.* (=I want you to, but it seems unlikely judging by your behaviour so far) —see also EXPECT (USAGE)◁

hope² *n* **1** [C;U (**of**)] the expectation that something will happen as one wishes: *The situation looks bad, but don't give up hope.* | *Hopes of (reaching) a peace settlement are now fading.* [+that] *Is there any hope that she'll recover?* | *We've postponed the game until Monday in the hope that* (=hoping that) *the weather will improve.* | *The doctors don't* **hold out much hope** *for her.* | *We're* **pinning all our hopes on** *the new manager.* (=all our hopes depend on him/her) | *Things look bad but we* **live in hope**. (=we haven't given up hoping yet) | *The one* **glimmer/ray of hope** *is the possibility that the government will provide emergency assistance.* | *Her* **hopes** *were* **dashed** (=destroyed) *when she failed the exam.* **2** [C] a person or thing that seems likely to bring success: *You're my last hope.* | *They're our only hope.* **3 beyond/past hope** beyond the possibility of a good result —see also WHITE HOPE **4 hope springs eternal in the human breast** *quote* a phrase from a work by Alexander Pope, meaning that people will by nature always feel hopeful about things

▷ USAGE Compare *I have no* **wish** *to go* (=I don't want to go) and *I have no* **hope** *of going* (=I want to go but I know I can't).◁

Hope, Anthony (1863–1933) an English writer, known esp. for his NOVEL *The Prisoner of Zenda*

Hope, Bob (1903–) an American actor and COMEDIAN born in England, who was a star of many amusing films. In the US, Bob Hope is also known for the kind of humour he uses, the ONE-LINER (a very short joke), and for entertaining soldiers during wartime.

hope chest /'· ·/ *n AmE for* BOTTOM DRAWER

hope-ful¹ /'həʊpfəl/ *adj* **1** [(**of**)] (of people) feeling hope: *hopeful of success* [+that] *I'm hopeful that he'll arrive early.* **2** giving cause for hope of success: *hopeful signs of economic recovery* – – **ness** *n* [U]

hopeful² *n* a person who wants to succeed or seems likely to succeed, esp. in the performing arts: *The audition was attended by scores of young hopefuls.*

hope-ful-ly /'həʊpfəli/ *adv* **1** in a hopeful way: *The little boy looked at her hopefully as she handed out the sweets.* **2** if our hopes succeed: *Hopefully we'll be there by dinnertime.*

▷ USAGE This second meaning of **hopefully** is now very common, especially in speech, but it is thought by some people to be incorrect.◁

hope-less /'həʊpləs/ *adj* **1** showing lack of hope: *hopeless*

tears **2** giving no cause for hope: *Our position is hopeless; we'll never get out alive.* | *a hopeless case* **3** *infml* very bad or unskilled: *I'm hopeless at maths.* – –**ly** *adv* – –**ness** *n* [U]

Ho·pi /'həʊpi/ [C; *the* +P] (a member of) a Native American people from Arizona, US –see NATIVE AMERICAN (CULTURAL NOTE)

Hop·kins /'hɒpkɪnz ‖ 'hɑːp-/, **Anthony** (1937–) a Welsh actor known for his many roles on the stage and in films

Hopkins, Ger·ard Man·ley /'dʒerɑːd 'mænli‖dʒə'rɑːrd-/ (1844–89) an English poet who was also a priest. Many of his poems deal with SPIRITUAL or religious ideas.

Hop o' My Thumb /ˌ· · · '·/ also **Little Thumb**– the title of a French FAIRY STORY in which Hop o' my Thumb, the youngest of seven children, protects his brothers and sisters after their parents leave them in the forest because they have no more money. He steals an OGRE's magic boots and uses them to make money which he gives to his parents.

hop·per /'hɒpəʳ‖'hɑː-/ *n* a large FUNNEL through which grain or coal is passed

Hopper, Edward (1882–1967) an American painter

hop·scotch /'hɒpskɒtʃ‖'hɑːp-skɑːtʃ/ *n* [U] a children's game in which a stone is thrown onto numbered squares and each child HOPs and jumps from one to another. The game is usu. played in the school yard or street, where squares are drawn with CHALK.

hopscotch

hop, step, and jump /ˌ· ˌ· · '·/ *n* [*the*] *infml for* TRIPLE JUMP

Hor·ace /'hɒrɪs‖'hɔː-/ (65–8 BC) a Roman poet and writer of SATIRE, whose Latin name was Quintus Horatius Flaccus

horde /hɔːd‖hɔːrd/ *n* also **hordes** *pl.*– [(**of**)] a large moving crowd, esp. one that is noisy or disorderly: *a horde of children* | *Hordes of children were running round the building.*

ho·ri·zon /hə'raɪzən/ *n* **1** [*the*] the limit of one's view across the surface of the earth, where the sky seems to meet the earth or sea: *We could see a ship on the horizon.* | *The setting sun disappeared below the horizon.* | (fig.) *Business is good at the moment, but there are one or two problems on the horizon.* (=that can be expected in the future) **2** [C] also **horizons** *pl.*– the limit of one's ideas, knowledge, or experience: *This series of talks is intended to broaden our horizons.*

hor·i·zon·tal /ˌhɒrɪ'zɒntl‖ˌhɑːrɪ'zɑːntl◀/ *adj* in a flat position, along or parallel to level ground; level with the horizon: *a horizontal line/surface* –compare VERTICAL – –**ly** *adv*

horizontal² *n esp. tech* [C;(*the*) U] a horizontal line, surface, or position

Hor·licks /'hɔːlɪks ‖ 'hɔːr-/ *n* [P] *tdmk* a type of hot milky drink produced by SmithKline Beecham; it is prepared by mixing powder with hot milk or water and it is usu. drunk in the evening before going to bed

hor·mone /'hɔːməʊn‖'hɔːr-/ *n* any of several substances directed from organs of the body into the blood so as to influence growth, development, etc.

hormone re·place·ment ther·a·py /ˌ· ··· '·· ˌ···/ also *abbrev.* **HRT**– *n* [U] treatment given to some middle-aged women to help control certain unwanted effects of the MENOPAUSE. These women are given small quantities of female sex hormones

horn¹ /hɔːn‖hɔːrn/ *n* **1** [C] a hard pointed part that grows, usu. as one of a pair, on the heads of cattle, sheep, goats, and some wild animals **2** [C] something which stands out from an animal's head like a horn, e.g. on a SNAIL – see picture at DEER **3** [U] the substance that horns are made of: *The knife has a horn handle.* **4** [C] (*often in comb.*) something, esp. a container, originally made from a horn: *a drinking horn* (=a container for drinking from) **5** [C] **a** any of a number of musical instruments consisting of a long metal tube, usu. bent several times and played by blowing: *a hunting horn* –see also ENGLISH

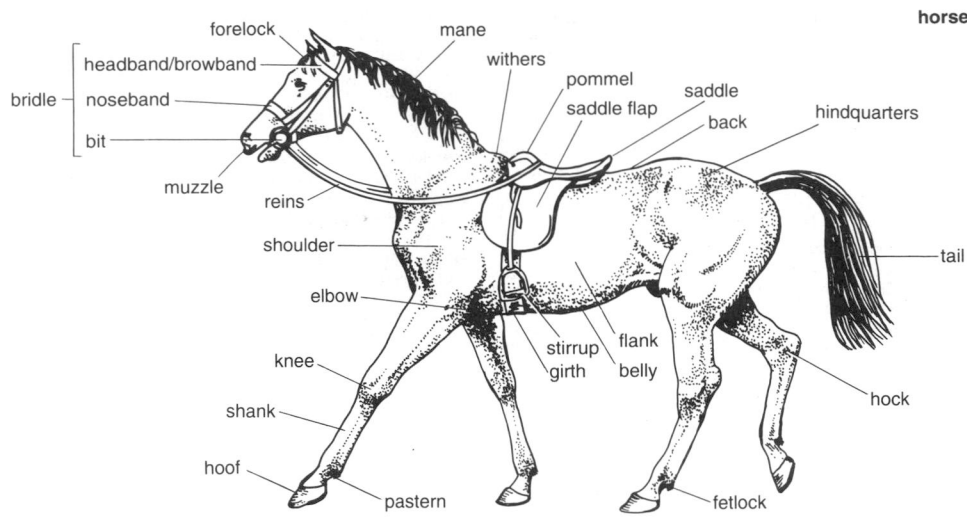

HORN, FRENCH HORN, POST HORN **b** *infml* any of the larger WIND INSTRUMENTS, esp. a TRUMPET **6** [C] an apparatus, e.g. in a car, which makes a loud usu. short warning sound: *The driver blew/sounded her horn when the child stepped in front of the car.* | *a ship's foghorn* —compare SIREN, and see picture at CAR **7 draw in/pull in one's horns** to reduce the amount of one's activities, spending, etc. **8 on the horns of a dilemma** having to choose between two unpleasant things or courses of action —see also ENGLISH HORN, FRENCH HORN, **blow one's own trumpet/horn** (BLOW¹), **take the bull by the horns** (BULL¹), **lock horns** (LOCK²) —**horned** /hɔːnd‖hɔːrnd/ *adj* : *horned cattle*

horn²
   horn in *phr v* [(**on**)] to interrupt or come in where one is not wanted: *He horned in on our conversation.* | *She's always horning in though it's none of her business.*

Horn [*the*] see CAPE HORN

horn·bill /ˈhɔːnˌbɪl‖ˈhɔːrn-/ *n* a bird with a horn-like growth on its beak

Horn·blow·er /ˈhɔːnbləuəʳ‖ˈhɔːrn-/, **Ho·ra·ti·o** /həˈreɪʃiəu/ an officer in the British navy, the chief character in the *Hornblower* stories by C S Forester

horn·book /ˈhɔːnbʊk‖ˈhɔːrn-/ *n AmE* **1** a piece of paper with the alphabet or numbers on it and covered with a thin sheet of horn, used formerly to teach children **2** *rare* any first schoolbook teaching a child letters or numbers

hor·net /ˈhɔːnɪt‖ˈhɔːr-/ *n* a large insect which can sting, related to the WASP —see picture at WASP

hornet's nest /ˈ·· ˌ·/ *n* [*usu. sing.*] a lot of trouble and anger between people (esp. in the phrase **stir up a hornet's nest**)

Horn of Af·ri·ca /ˌ· · ˈ···/ [*the*] the part of E Africa that includes Somalia and some of Ethiopia

horn of plen·ty /ˌ· · ˈ···/ *n* a CORNUCOPIA

horn·pipe /ˈhɔːnpaɪp‖ˈhɔːrn-/ *n* **1** a dance performed esp. by sailors **2** the music for this dance

horn-rimmed /ˌ· ˈ·◂/ *adj* (of glasses for the eyes) surrounded by an edge made of horn or a similar material

horn·y /ˈhɔːni‖ˈhɔːrni/ *adj* **1** hard and rough: *The old gardener had horny hands.* **2** *taboo sl* sexually excited

hor·o·scope /ˈhɒrəskəup‖ˈhɑː-, ˈhɔː-/ *n* a written or spoken description of someone's character, life, and future, which is gained by knowing the positions of the stars or PLANETS at the time of his/her birth and the effects these are said to have. Many people in Britain and the US read their horoscope each day in the paper, but few really believe it is true —see also ZODIAC

Hor·o·witz /ˈhɒrəvɪts, -wɪts‖ˈhɔːrəwɪts/, **Vlad·i·mir** /ˈvlæd‚-

miəʳ/ (1904–89) an American piano player born in Russia who played CLASSICAL music

hor·ren·dous /hɒˈrendəs, hə-‖hɑː-, hɔː-/ *adj* **1** really terrible; causing great fear **2** *infml* extremely unpleasant: *What horrendous weather!* — — **ly** *adv* — —**ness** *n* [U]

hor·ri·ble /ˈhɒr‚bəl‖ˈhɔː-, ˈhɑː-/ *adj* **1** terrible: *a horrible accident* **2** *infml* very unkind or unpleasant; AWFUL: *What a horrible dress!* | *a horrible man* | *I have a horrible feeling we're going to miss the plane.* —**bly** *adv*

hor·rid /ˈhɒr‚d‖ˈhɔː-, ˈhɑː-/ *adj* [(to)] *esp. BrE* very unkind or unpleasant; nasty: *Don't be horrid (to me)!* — —**ly** *adv* — —**ness** *n* [U]

hor·rif·ic /hɒˈrɪfɪk, hə-‖hɔː-, hɑː-/ *adj* causing or intended to cause horror; horrifying: *The film showed the most horrific murder scenes.* — —**ally** /kli/ *adv*

hor·ri·fy /ˈhɒr‚faɪ‖ˈhɔː-, ˈhɑː-/ *v* [T] to shock greatly; fill with horror: *We were horrified to hear that she had been murdered.* | *horrifying news* — —**ingly** *adv*

hor·ror /ˈhɒrəʳ‖ˈhɔː-, ˈhɑː-/ *n* **1** [U] a feeling of great shock, anxiety, and dislike: *The news of the plane crash filled us with horror.* | *I cried out in horror as I saw him fall in front of the car.* **2** [C *usu. pl.*; U] (an event, activity, etc. that has) the quality of causing this feeling: *It's hard to describe the horror of their lives.* | *the horrors of modern warfare* **3** [C] *esp. BrE* an unpleasant person, usu. a child: *The little horror never stops playing tricks on his parents.* **4 have a horror of** to hate; dislike very much: *I have a horror of snakes.* **5 the horrors** *infml* a state of extreme fear, worry, or sadness —compare TERROR

horror film /ˈ·· ˌ·/ *n* a cinema film in which frightening and often unnatural things happen, such as dead people coming to life, people turning into animals, etc.

horror-strick·en /ˈ·· ˌ··/ also **horror-struck** /ˈ·· ·/— *adj* filled with horror; deeply shocked: *We were horror-stricken to hear of her murder.*

hors de com·bat /ˌɔː də ˈkɒmbɑː‖ˌɔːr də ˈkɑːmbɑː/ *adj, adv* [F] *Fr* unable to fight, because wounded: (fig.) *Their best player is hors de combat with a knee injury.*

hors d'oeu·vre /ˌɔː ˈdɜːv‖ˌɔːr ˈdɜːrv/ *n* -**d'oeuvres** /ˈdɜːv‖ ˈdɜːrvz/ SAVOURY food served in small amounts at the beginning of a meal instead of soup or another starter

horse¹ /hɔːs‖hɔːrs/ *n* **1** [C] a large strong four-legged animal with hard feet (HOOVES), which people ride on and use for pulling heavy things: *learning to ride a horse* | *A male horse is called a stallion, and a female horse a mare.* | *We went to see the horse races.* —see BICYCLE (USAGE); see also FOAL, NEIGH **2** [C] an exercise apparatus for jumping over; VAULTING HORSE **3** [P] *old use, esp. BrE* soldiers riding on horses; CAVALRY: *a regiment of horse* **4** [U] *sl for* HEROIN **5 a horse! a horse! my kingdom for a horse!** *quote* a phrase from Shakespeare's play *Richard III*, said by the King when he needs a horse very badly and now often used humorously when someone needs something badly   **6 a horse of another/a different colour** a completely different thing or situation   **7 (straight) from the horse's mouth** *infml* (of information) from the actual person concerned, not told indirectly —see also CLOTHESHORSE, DARK HORSE, GIFT HORSE, HIGH HORSE, TROJAN HORSE, WHITE HORSE, **put the cart before the horse** (CART¹), **flog a dead horse** (FLOG), **Hold your horses!** (HOLD¹ (28))

horse² *v*
  horse around/about *phr v* [I] *infml* to play roughly or waste time in rough play

horse·back¹ /'hɔːsbæk‖'hɔːrs-/ *n* **on horseback** (riding) on a horse: *Police on horseback broke up the demonstration.*

horseback² *adj, adv* [A] *esp. AmE* on the back of a horse: *horseback riding*

horse·box /'hɔːsbɒks‖'hɔːrsbɑːks/ ‖ usu. **horse car, horse trailer** *AmE— n* a large enclosed container that is fixed to or pulled by a motor vehicle, used for carrying horses from one place to another

horse chest·nut /ˌ·ˈ··‖ˌ·ˈ·/ also **chestnut—** *n* **1** a large tree with white or pink flowers   **2** a shiny brown nut from this tree —see also CONKER, and see picture at TREE

horse·flesh /'hɔːsfleʃ‖'hɔːrs-/ *n* [U] *sl* horses generally, esp. with regard to their fitness for racing. This word is usu. used by people with a professional interest in racing: *a good judge of horseflesh*

horse·fly /'hɔːsflaɪ‖'hɔːrs-/ *n* a large fly that stings horses and cattle

Horse Guards /'· ˌ·/ [*the* +P] the ROYAL HORSE GUARDS

Horse Guards Pa·rade /ˌ· · · ·ˈ·/ a wide square in central London used for public shows by the Horse Guards and other British army units

horse·hair /'hɔːsheəʳ‖'hɔːrs-/ *n* [U] the long hair from a horse, esp. from the MANE and tail, esp. when used to fill the inside of furniture

horse·laugh /'hɔːslɑːf‖'hɔːrs-læf/ *n* a loud (impolite) laugh

horse·man /'hɔːsmən‖'hɔːrs-/ **horsewoman** *fem.— n* **-men** /mən/ a person who rides a horse, esp. skilfully

horse·man·ship /'hɔːsmənʃɪp‖'hɔːrs-/ *n* [U] the practice or skill of horse-riding

Horse of the Year Show /ˌ· · · · '· ˌ·/ [*the*] a SHOW JUMPING competition held every year in London

horse op·e·ra /'· ˌ···/ *n humor, esp. AmE for* WESTERN² — compare SOAP OPERA

horse·play /'hɔːspleɪ‖'hɔːrs-/ *n* [U] rough noisy behaviour, usu. in fun

horse·pow·er /'hɔːsˌpaʊəʳ‖'hɔːrs-/ (*abbrev.* **HP**)— *n* **horsepower** [C;U] (a measure of) the power of an engine: *This car has a 40 horsepower engine.*

horse rac·ing /'· ˌ··/ *n* [U] the running of races between horses ridden by JOCKEYS. Horse racing is a popular sport in Britain and the US, and while very few people own racehorses, many people are interested in the races and risk money on the horse which they think will win a race.

horse·rad·ish /'hɔːsˌrædɪʃ‖'hɔːrs-/ *n* [U] a plant whose root is used to make a strong-tasting SAUCE (**horseradish sauce**) which is eaten with meat, esp. with ROAST BEEF

horse sense /'· ·/ *n* [U] *infml for* COMMON SENSE

horse·shit /'hɔːsˌʃɪt‖'hɔːrs-/ *n* [U] *taboo sl, esp. AmE* nonsense; BULLSHIT

horse·shoe /'hɔːʃ-ʃuː, 'hɔːs-‖'hɔːr-/ *n* **1** also **shoe—** a curved piece of iron nailed on under a horse's foot   **2** something in the shape of a horseshoe, such as a decorative card given at weddings to bring good luck

horse·shoes /'hɔːʃ-ʃuːz, 'hɔːs-‖ 'hɔːr-/ *n* [U] an American outdoor game in which one throws horseshoes at a fixed marker

horse·trad·ing /'· ˌ··/ *n* [U] the process by which two sides try to reach agreement with each other, e.g. about prices, the details of a contract, etc.: *Each side got what it wanted by clever political horse-trading.*

horse trail·er /'· ˌ··/ *n AmE for* HORSEBOX

horse·whip /'hɔːsˌwɪp‖'hɔːrs-/ *v* **-pp-** [T] to beat (someone) hard, esp. with a whip for a horse

horse·wom·an /'hɔːsˌwʊmən‖'hɔːrs-/ *n* **-women** /ˌwɪmɪn/

a woman who rides a horse, esp. skilfully

hors·y, **horsey** /'hɔːsi‖'hɔːrsi/ *adj* **1** *BrE* (esp. of a woman, often one of high social class) interested in horses, fond of riding, etc.   **2** *usu. derog* of an appearance which reminds one of horses —**-iness** *n* [U]

hor·ti·cul·ture /'hɔːtɪˌkʌltʃəʳ‖'hɔːr-/ *n* [U] the practice or science of growing fruit, flowers, and vegetables — compare AGRICULTURE —**-tural** /ˌhɔːtɪˈkʌltʃərəl‖ˌhɔːr-/ *adj* —**-turalist** *n*

ho·san·na /həʊˈzænə/ *n, interj bibl* a shout of praise to God

hose¹ /həʊz/ ‖ also **hose·pipe** /'həʊzpaɪp/ *BrE— n* [C;U] (a piece of) rubber or plastic tube which can be moved and bent to direct water onto fires, gardens, etc.
  ▶ CULTURAL NOTE In many parts of Britain, during long periods without rain, there is a **hosepipe ban** i.e. people are not allowed to use their hoses because the water is needed for other purposes. In the US, people are asked to save water during periods of DROUGHT in many different ways but are not prevented from using their hoses. —see picture at GARDEN◀

hose² *v* [T (DOWN)] to use a hose on, esp. for washing: *hosing the car down* | *to hose the garden*

hose³ *n* [U] **1** (used esp. in shops) TIGHTS, STOCKINGS, or socks   **2** tight-fitting leg coverings worn by men in former times

ho·sier /'həʊzɪəʳ‖'həʊʒər/ *n old-fash or tech* a shopkeeper who sells socks and men's underclothes

ho·sier·y /'həʊʒəri‖'həʊʒəri/ *n* [U] *old-fash or tech* TIGHTS, STOCKINGS, and socks in general

hos·pice /'hɒspɪs‖'hɑː-/ *n* **1** a house for travellers to stay and rest in, esp. when kept by a religious group   **2** a hospital for people with incurable illnesses

hos·pi·ta·ble /'hɒspɪtəbəl, hɒ'spɪ-‖hɑː'spɪ-, 'hɑːspɪ-/ *adj* [(**to, towards**)] (of people or their behaviour) friendly and welcoming towards guests or visitors, esp. by feeding them, inviting them into one's home, etc.: *Americans have the reputation of being very hospitable people.* — opposite **inhospitable** —**-bly** *adv*

hos·pi·tal /'hɒspɪtl‖'hɑː-/ *n* [C; (*esp. BrE*) U] a place where people who are ill or hurt have medical treatment. In Britain hospital treatment is free for anyone who does not choose to pay for private medical insurance: *After the accident, Jane was rushed to the hospital/(BrE) to hospital.* | *The sick man has been admitted to a hospital/(BrE) to hospital.*

hos·pi·tal·i·ty /ˌhɒspɪˈtælɪti‖ˌhɑː-/ *n* [U] **1** the quality of being hospitable; welcoming behaviour towards guests   **2** food, a place to sleep, etc., when given to a guest

hos·pi·tal·ize also **-ise** *BrE* /'hɒspɪtl-aɪz‖'hɑː-/ *v* [T *usu. pass.*] to put (a person) into hospital: *He broke a leg and was hospitalized for a month.* —**-ization** /ˌhɒspɪtl-aɪˈzeɪʃən‖ˌhɑːspɪtələˈzeɪ-/ *n* [U]

host¹ /həʊst/ *n* **1 a** a person who receives guests and provides food, drink, and amusement for them: *At the end of the party we thanked our host and went home.* **b** a person, place, or organization that provides the necessary space, equipment, etc. for a special event: *The Grand Hotel is* **playing host to** *this year's sales conference.* (=it is being held in the hotel) | *the host country for the next Olympic Games* —compare GUEST¹   **2** a person who introduces other performers, such as those on a TV show; COMPERE   **3** *tech* an animal or plant on which some lower form of life is living as a PARASITE

host² *v* [T] *infml* to act as host of (a party, friendly meeting, TV show, etc.): *Moscow and Los Angeles have hosted the Olympic Games.*

host³ *n* [C+*sing./pl. v*] **1** [+**of**] a large number: *The machine comes with a whole host of useful accessories.*   **2** *old use or bibl* an army

host⁴ *n* [*the*] (*often cap.*) the holy bread eaten in the Christian service of COMMUNION

hos·tage /'hɒstɪdʒ‖'hɑː-/ *n* **1** a person who is kept as a prisoner by an enemy so that the other side will do what the enemy demands: *The terrorists kidnapped the children and are keeping them as hostages.* | *They are* **holding** *the children* **hostage.**   **2 give hostages to fortune** to accept responsibilities, esp. having a family, that may limit one's freedom of action in the future

hos·tel /'hɒstl‖'hɑː-/ *n* **1** a building in which certain types

of people can live and eat, such as students, young people working away from home, etc. Hostels are less expensive than hotels, and guests stay there for longer. — compare HOTEL   **2** a YOUTH HOSTEL

hos·tel·ler *esp. BrE* ‖ usu. **hos·tel·er** *AmE* /ˈhɒstələʳ‖ˈhɑː-/ *n* a person travelling from one YOUTH HOSTEL to another

hos·tel·ry /ˈhɒstəlri‖ˈhɑː-/ *n old use or humor* a PUB

host·ess /ˈhəʊstↃs/ *n* **1** a female host   **2** an AIRHOSTESS   **3** *AmE* a woman who shows one to a seat in a restaurant   **4** a young woman who acts as a companion, dancing partner, etc., and sometimes as a PROSTITUTE, in a social club

hos·tile /ˈhɒstaɪl‖ˈhɑːstl, ˈhɑːstaɪl/ *adj* **1** [(to)] showing extreme dislike or disapproval; unfriendly: *The prime minister was greeted by a hostile crowd/was given a hostile reception.* **2** belonging to an enemy: *hostile territory*

hos·til·i·ties /hɒˈstɪlↃtiz‖hɑː-/ *n* [P] acts of fighting in war: *Their meeting led to a cessation of hostilities between the two countries.*

hos·til·i·ty /hɒˈstɪlↃti‖hɑː-/ *n* [U (**to**)] a state of extreme unfriendliness; ENMITY: *There is now open hostility between the two leaders.*

hos·tler /ˈhɒsləʳ‖ˈhɑːs-/ *n esp. AmE for* OSTLER

hot¹ /hɒt‖hɑːt/ *adj* **-tt-** **1** having a certain degree of heat, esp. a high degree: *How hot is the water?* | *The water isn't hot yet.* | *Bake the pie in a hot oven for half an hour.* | *I feel hot after all that running.* | *It's very hot in here — can I open the window?* | *The soup was* **piping hot**. (=very hot) —see COLD¹ (USAGE)   **2** causing a burning taste in the mouth: *Pepper makes food hot.* | *a hot curry* —opposite **mild**   **3** (esp. of people) expressing strong feelings; excitable: *a hot temper* —compare HEATED   **4 a** *esp. lit* (of people) (tending to be) sexually excited; ARDENT: *hot with passion* **b** sexually exciting: *one of the hottest books ever written*   **5** (of news) very recent; fresh: *a hot news item* | *a story* **hot off the press** (=only just printed)   **6** [F (**on**)] *infml* (of people) well-informed and very interested (in the stated thing): *She's hot on jazz.*   **7** likely to cause strong feelings and argument, and therefore difficult to deal with; CONTROVERSIAL: *a hot political issue* | *The Watergate scandal eventually proved* **too hot to handle**, *and the president resigned.*   **8** *AmE* popular at a particular point in time: *Michael Jackson was really hot a few years ago.*   **9** *sl* (of stolen goods) difficult to sell because still known to the police, esp. soon after the crime has taken place   **10** (of JAZZ) with a strong exciting beat   **11** [F] (esp. in children's games) very near to finding a hidden object, the answer, etc. —compare COLD¹ (4), WARM¹ (6)   **12 blow hot and cold** *infml* to seem very keen on something or someone at times, and at other times to seem not keen at all   **13 hot and bothered a** worried and confused by a feeling that things are going wrong **b** *AmE* sexually excited   **14 hot on someone's trail/track** chasing someone and almost on the point of catching them   **15 hot on the heels of** following or happening just after   **16 hot under the collar: a** angry or excited and ready to argue **b** confused and embarrassed (EMBARRASS)   **17 in hot pursuit of** following (someone) very closely and eagerly: *The thieves got away in a stolen car, but the police were soon in hot pursuit.*   **18 make it (too) hot for someone** to put someone in a difficult or uncomfortable position, esp. causing them to leave   **19 not so hot** *infml* not very good; not as good as expected —see also HOTLY, HOTS, RED-HOT

hot² *v* **-tt-**
hot up *phr v* [I] *infml, esp. BrE* to increase in activity which is often exciting or dangerous; INTENSIFY: *The election campaign is hotting up.* | *"Air raids began to hot up about the beginning of February."* (George Orwell)

hot air /ˌ· ˈ·/ *n* [U] *infml derog* meaningless talk or ideas

hot-air bal·loon /· ˈ· ·ₐ·/ *n* a BALLOON¹ (1) large enough to lift several people, filled with hot air which causes it to rise

hot·bed /ˈhɒtbed‖ˈhɑːt-/ *n* [+**of**] a place or condition where the stated undesirable thing can exist and develop: *The city is a hotbed of crime.* | *a hotbed of intrigue*

hot-blood·ed /ˌ· ˈ··◂/ *adj* having strong excitable feelings; PASSIONATE

hot cake /ˌ· ˈ·/ *n AmE* a PANCAKE (2) —see also **go/sell like hot cakes** (CAKE¹ (4))

hotch·potch /ˈhɒtʃpɒtʃ‖ˈhɑːtʃpɑːtʃ/ *esp. BrE* ‖ usu. **hodge-**

podge *AmE*— *n* [S] a number of things mixed up without any sensible order or arrangement

hot-cross bun /ˌ· · ˈ·/ *n* a small sweet cake made of bread with a cross-shaped mark on top, which is eaten on Good Friday, just before Easter

hot dish /ˈ· ·/ *n AmE* a CASSEROLE (2): *Sitting together on folded chairs eating hot dish off paper plates* | *Will you all please sign up to bring a hot dish or a dessert.*

hot dog /ˌ· ˈ·‖ˈ· ·/ *n* a cooked FRANKFURTER or other SAUSAGE in a long bread ROLL. In the US hot dogs and HAMBURGERs are considered to be very American foods and are very popular.

hot-dog /ˈhɒtdɒg ‖ ˈhɑːtdɔːg/ *v* [I] *AmE infml* to behave in a showy, attention-getting way, esp. by performing actions requiring physical skills, strength, or daring: *skiers hotdogging down the slopes*

ho·tel /həʊˈtel/ *n* a building that provides rooms for people to stay in (usu. for a short time) and usu. also meals, in return for payment. Hotels are usu. more expensive to stay in than GUESTHOUSEs or BED AND BREAKFAST but offer a higher standard of comfort. —compare HOSTEL; see INN (USAGE)

ho·tel·i·er /həʊˈtelieɪ, -liəʳ/ *n* a person who owns and/or runs a hotel

hot flush /ˌ· ˈ·/ *esp. BrE* ‖ usu. **hot flash** *AmE*— *n* a sudden feeling of heat in the skin, esp. as experienced by women at the MENOPAUSE (=the time when they stop being able to bear children)

hot·foot¹ /ˌhɒtˈfʊt◂‖ˈhɑːtfʊt/ *adv infml* moving quickly and eagerly: *We ran hotfoot to find out the news.*

hotfoot² *v* **hotfoot it** *infml* to move fast: *We hotfooted it down the street.*

hot-gos·pel·ler /ˌ· ˈ···/ *n BrE infml, often derog* a religious speaker who tries to fill his hearers with excitement and strong feelings —**-ling** *n* [U]

hot·head /ˈhɒthed‖ˈhɑːt-/ *n* **1** a person who does things too quickly, without thinking   **2** a person who gets angry easily — **~ed** /ˌhɒtˈhedↃd◂‖ˌhɑːt-/ *adj* — **~edly** *adv*

hot·house /ˈhɒthaʊs‖ˈhɑːt-/ *n* **-houses** /ˌhaʊzↃz/ **1** a warm building where flowers and delicate plants can grow; a GREENHOUSE, esp. a large one   **2** a place or situation in which people are interested in and discuss many ideas and activities, and which encourages other people to do the same: *Vienna was a hothouse of artistic activity.*

hot line /ˈ· ·/ *n* **1** a direct telephone line between heads of government, to be used at times of great difficulty, esp. when war is threatened   **2** a telephone line that can be used for a particular purpose, esp. for making inquiries: *The police have set up a hot line for relatives to contact about the plane crash.*

hot·ly /ˈhɒtli‖ˈhɑːtli/ *adv* **1** with anger or other strong feelings: *The rumour was hotly denied.* | *a hotly-debated issue*   **2** closely and eagerly (often in the phrase **hotly pursued**)

hot pad /ˈ· ·/ *n AmE* a POT HOLDER

hot·plate /ˈhɒtpleɪt‖ˈhɑːt-/ *n* a metal surface, usu. on an electric cooker, which can be heated and on which food can be cooked in a pan —see COOK¹ (USAGE)

Hot·point /ˈhɒtpɔɪnt‖ˈhɑːt-/ *tdmk* an American company which makes electrical equipment for use in people's houses

hot·pot /ˈhɒtpɒt‖ˈhɑːtpɑːt/ *n* [C;U] a mixture of MUTTON (=sheep meat), potatoes, and onions, cooked slowly in a pot, which is eaten esp. in the north of England: *Lancashire hotpot*

hot po·ta·to /ˌ· ·ˈ···/ *n infml* something difficult or dangerous to deal with: *a political hot potato*

hot rod /ˈ· ·/ *n sl, esp. AmE* an old car rebuilt for high speed rather than appearance —compare STOCKCAR

hots /hɒts‖hɑːts/ *n sl* **have/get the hots for** to have a strong sexual interest in: *She could tell he had the hots for her.*

hot seat /ˈ· ·/ *n* [*the*] **1** *infml* a position of difficulty from which one must make important decisions, answer difficult questions, etc.: *As chief accountant for the firm, she's* **in the hot seat**.   **2** *AmE sl* an ELECTRIC CHAIR used in prisons to kill prisoners who have been given a death sentence

hot-shot /ˈhɒtʃɒt‖ˈhɑːtʃɑːt/ *adj AmE infml* very successful, confident, and showy: *a hotshot young lawyer* —**hot shot** *n* : *He thinks he's such a hot shot.*

hot spot /'· ·/ *n* a place where there is likely to be much trouble and perhaps war or unsettled government

hot stuff /ˌ· '·/ *n* [U] *infml* **1** someone or something of great ability or very good quality **2** someone or something exciting or dangerous, esp. sexually

hot-tem·pered /ˌ· '··· / *adj* having a readiness to become angry quickly and easily; quick-tempered

hot·ter /'hɒtər‖'hɑː-/ *n BrE sl* a JOYRIDER, usu. a young man, who performs dangerous tricks e.g. HANDBRAKE TURNs with a stolen car —**hotting** *n* [U]

hot tick·et /ˌ· '··/ *n AmE infml* a fashionable or very popular person whom everyone wants to see: *Julia Roberts seems to be this year's hot ticket.*

hot tub /'· ˌ·/ *n* a small, heated bath in which several people can sit and which is often fitted with equipment to send JETs of water into the bath, below the level of the bath water. Many people think of hot tubs as only for people who love pleasure.

hot wa·ter /ˌ· '··/ *n* **get into/be in hot water** *infml* to get into/be in a difficult situation: *His gambling activities eventually got him into hot water.*

hot-water bot·tle /ˌ· '·· ˌ··/ *n* a rubber container into which hot water is put, and which is placed inside a bed to warm it —see picture at BOTTLE

hot-wire /'· ·/ *v* [T] *sl* to start the engine of (a car or other vehicle) without the key by using the wires of the IGNITION system. This method is usu. used by car thieves: *Police said that thieves had hot-wired the car.*

Hou·di·ni /huːˈdiːni/, **Harry** (1874–1926) an American escape artist famous for escaping from chains and locked containers

hou·mous, houmus, humus /'humʊs, 'huː-/ *n* HUMMUS

hound¹ /haʊnd/ *n* **1** (*often in comb.*) a hunting dog, esp. one that uses smell in hunting: *to ride to hounds* (=hunt foxes) —see also FOXHOUND, NEWSHOUND **2** *old-fash* a person who is disliked and considered unpleasant

hound² *v* [T] to chase or worry continually; HARASS: *I must finish the work so my boss will stop hounding me.* | *He was hounded out of public life by the persistent attacks of the popular newspapers.*

Hound of the Bas·ker·villes /ˌhaʊnd əv ðə 'bæskəvɪlz‖ -kər-/, **The** a story by Sir Arthur Conan Doyle in which the DETECTIVE Sherlock Holmes tries to find out who is responsible for killings that appear to have been done by a large, fierce dog

hour /aʊər/ *n* **1** a period of 60 minutes: *There are 24 hours in a day.* | *The journey takes about three hours.* | *a three-hour journey* | *I'll be back* **in an hour/in an hour's time.** | *the hours of darkness* (=night time) | *They are paid* **by the hour.** | *We spent many happy hours together.* | *I've been waiting here* **for hours.** (=for a long time) **2** a time of day when a new hour starts: *The clock struck the hour.* | *The trains leave at five minutes past the hour.* | *The attack began at sixteen hundred hours/1600 hours.* (=4 o'clock in the afternoon) **3** the distance travelled or work done in an hour: *It's only an hour away by car.* **4** [*often pl.*] a fixed point or period of time, esp. one that is set aside for a particular purpose or activity: *I'll see you in my lunch hour.* | *During office hours I can be contacted at this number.* | *the hospital's visiting hours* **5** an important moment or period: *In my hour of need* (=when I needed help) *no one helped me.* | *It was our country's* **finest hour.** (=a time giving cause for great pride, etc.) | *one of the burning* (=important) *questions of the hour* (=of the present time) **6** **after hours** later than the usual times of work or business **7** **at all hours** (at any time) during the whole day and night **8** **(every hour) on the hour** at 1.00, 2.00, 3.00, etc. **9** **hour after hour** continuously for many hours: *I waited at the airport hour after hour.* **10** **keep late/regular, etc. hours** to go to bed late/at regular times, etc. **11** **out of hours** before or after the usual times **12** **this was their finest hour** *quote* a phrase from a speech by Winston Churchill describing the actions of the British PILOTs who fought in the Battle of Britain —see also ELEVENTH HOUR, HAPPY HOUR, RUSH HOUR, SMALL HOURS, ZERO HOUR

hour·glass /'aʊəglɑːs‖'aʊərglæs/ *n* a glass container for measuring time, which is narrow in the middle like a

figure 8 so that the sand inside can run slowly from the top half to the bottom, taking exactly one hour: (fig.) *She has an* **hourglass figure.** (=with a very narrow waist)

hou·ri /'hʊəri/ *n* -s (according to the Koran) a beautiful young woman in the Muslim heaven

hour·ly /'aʊəli‖'aʊərli/ *adj, adv* **1** (happening, appearing, etc.) every hour or once an hour: *an hourly inspection* | *hourly-paid workers* **2** at any time soon (esp. in the phrase **expect someone hourly**)

house¹ /haʊs/ *n* **houses** /'haʊzɪz/ **1 a** a building for people to live in, often one that has more than one level (STOREY) and is intended for use by a single family: *Do you live in a house or a flat?* | (*esp. BrE*) *We're going to* **move house** (=move to another house) *next month.* | *a big rise in house prices* **b** the people in such a building: *The whole house was woken up by the noise.* **2** (*usu. in comb.*) a building for animals or goods: *the monkey house at the zoo* | *a hen house* —see also WAREHOUSE **3** (*often cap. as part of a name*) an important family, esp. noble or royal: *The House of Windsor is the British royal family.* **4** *BrE* **a** a building in which children live at some private BOARDING SCHOOLs, with its own name **b** a division of a school, esp. for sports competitions **5 a** a business firm, formerly often one controlled by a single family: *These shops belong to the House of Fraser.* | *a publishing house* | *a software house* (=producing computer SOFTWARE) **b** (*often in comb.*) a usu. large building used for a particular purpose or by a company or other organization: *The union's headquarters is in Transport House.* | *a courthouse* | *a picture house* **6 a** (*often cap.*) (the members of) a law-making body, esp. when one of two: *The President addressed both houses of Congress.* | *Will the Prime Minister please inform the House what she intends to do?* —see also LOWER HOUSE, UPPER HOUSE **b** (*cap.*) the US House of Representatives: *The Senate approved the bill, but the House voted against it.* **7** [*usu. sing.*] the people voting after a DEBATE: *The motion in the debate was "This house does not support capital punishment."* **8** [*usu. sing.*] the people watching a performance in a theatre, concert hall, etc.; AUDIENCE: *a full house* | *The play was taken off after playing to almost empty houses for two weeks.* **9** (*cap. in names in* ASTROLOGY) a group of stars, with its usual name: *the House of the Lion* **10** (in certain phrases) a place where people meet for a particular purpose: *a house of prostitution* —see also COFFEE HOUSE, FREE HOUSE, PUBLIC HOUSE **11** HOUSE MUSIC **12 bring the house down** (of a performance or play) to cause great admiration, usu. expressed loudly **13 get on like a** **house on fire** to have a very friendly relationship, or start one very easily **14 keep house** to manage a house, doing or controlling the cleaning, cooking, and similar jobs —see also HOUSEKEEPER **15 on the house** (usu. of drinks) paid for by the people in charge, e.g. by the owner of a PUB, by a company, etc. **16 put/set one's house in order** to arrange one's affairs so that they are in better order, either in business or by improving one's private behaviour **17 round the houses** *BrE* from one person or place to another (esp. when trying to get information): *He was sent round the houses when he tried to find out about his insurance claim.* —see also HALFWAY HOUSE, SAFE HOUSE, TOWN HOUSE, **eat someone out of house and home** (EAT (11)), **keep open house** (OPEN HOUSE)

▷ USAGE 1 A **house** is a building for people to live in and often has more than one level (storey). A **cottage** is a small, usu. old house, especially in the country and in the US is usu. used as a holiday home. A **bungalow** is a fairly modern house built on only one level. A set of rooms (including a kitchen and bathroom) within a larger building is called a **flat** in British English or an **apartment** or **condominium** in American English. An **apartment** is usu. rented (RENT² (1)), and a **condominium** is usu. owned, by the person who lives there. A small one-room flat is a **bedsitter** in British English. A large, grand house is called a **mansion** or (if it belongs to a king or queen) a **palace.** 2 Compare **house** and **home.** The place where you live is your **home**, whatever type of **house** it is: *After the party we went home to our flat.* British speakers often consider that your **home** is the place where you belong and feel comfortable and is more than just a **house**: *Our new house is beginning to look more like a real home.* In American English **home** can also be used for the actual building: *She has a beautiful home.* | *"New Homes for Sale."*◁

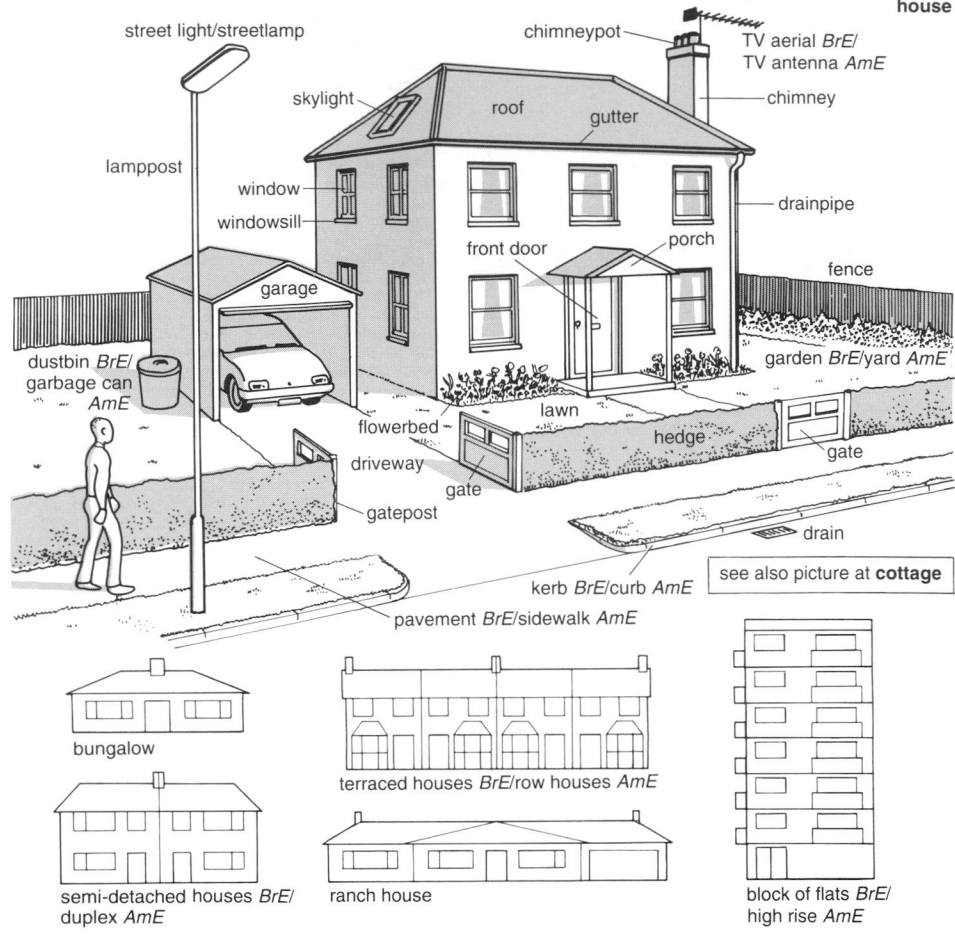

house

street light/streetlamp
chimneypot
TV aerial *BrE*/
TV antenna *AmE*
chimney
skylight
roof
gutter
lamppost
window
windowsill
front door
porch
drainpipe
garage
fence
dustbin *BrE*/
garbage can
AmE
garden *BrE*/yard *AmE*
flowerbed
lawn
hedge
gate
driveway
gate
gatepost
drain
kerb *BrE*/curb *AmE*
see also picture at **cottage**
pavement *BrE*/sidewalk *AmE*

bungalow

terraced houses *BrE*/row houses *AmE*

semi-detached houses *BrE*/
duplex *AmE*

ranch house

block of flats *BrE*/
high rise *AmE*

house² *adj* [A] **1** used by or intended for people working in a particular firm or industry: *a house magazine* | *Our* **house style** *is to use the spelling "-ization" rather than "-isation".* **2** (of wine) provided by a restaurant, esp. to be drunk with meals: *The house wine is usually cheaper.*

house³ /haʊz/ *v* [T] **1** to provide with a place to live **2** to provide space for: *This new building will house the Department of Chemistry.*

house ar·rest /ˈ· ·ˌ·/ *n* **under house arrest** forbidden to leave one's house because the government believes one is dangerous

house·boat /ˈhaʊsbəʊt/ *n* a boat with a covered place where one can sleep, cook, and wash. Houseboats are used for living in all the time or can be hired for short trips.

house·bound /ˈhaʊsbaʊnd/ *adj* unable to move out of the house, or to spend much time outside it, usu. because of illness

house·boy /ˈhaʊsbɔɪ/ *n* now usu. *considered derog* a boy or man who does general work in a house or hotel. Houseboys were employed by British people in Africa in COLONIAL times.

house·break·er /ˈhaʊsˌbreɪkəʳ/ *n* a thief who enters a house by force, esp. during the day —compare BURGLAR

house·bro·ken /ˈhaʊsˌbrəʊkən/ *adj AmE for* HOUSE-TRAINED

house·coat /ˈhaʊskəʊt/ *n* a garment worn by women at home, esp. when partly undressed just before or after their night's sleep

house·craft /ˈhaʊs·krɑːft‖-kræft/ *n* [U] *esp. BrE for* DOMESTIC SCIENCE

house·fa·ther /ˈhaʊsˌfɑːðəʳ/ *n* a male HOUSEPARENT

house·fly /ˈhaʊsflaɪ/ *n* the most common type of fly, which comes into the house esp. in hot weather

house·ful /ˈhaʊsfʊl/ *n* [S+of] an amount or number which is as much as a house can hold: *a houseful of guests*

house·hold¹ /ˈhaʊshəʊld/ *n* [C+*sing.*/*pl. v*] all the people living together in a house: *The whole household was/were up early.*

house·hold² *adj* [A] concerned with the management of a house; DOMESTIC: *household expenses* | *household chores*

Household Cav·al·ry /ˌ·· ·ˈ···/ [*the*] a body of horse soldiers who have the special responsibility of guarding the British king or queen, or the royal palace. The Household Cavalry consists of two British REGIMENTS (=divisions of the army), the Life Guards and the Blues and Royals.

household clean·er /ˌ·· ·ˈ··/ *n* [C;U] a chemical mixture suitable for cleaning various kinds of surface in a house

house·hold·er /ˈhaʊsˌhəʊldəʳ/ *n* a person who owns or is in charge of a house

household name /ˌ·· ·ˈ·/ also **household word**— *n* a person or thing that is very well known or talked about by almost everyone: *After the tremendous success of her third novel, she became a household name.*

house hus·band /ˈ· ˌ··/ *n* a husband who stays at home and cleans the house, cooks meals, etc. while his wife goes out to work; a male HOUSEWIFE

house jour·nal /ˈ· ˌ··/ ‖also **house organ** *AmE*— *n* a magazine produced regularly by a company for its workers to inform them about the company's activities

house·keep·er /ˈhaʊsˌkiːpəʳ/ *n* a person who is responsible for housekeeping, esp. one who is employed to do this —see also HOUSE¹ (13)

house·keep·ing /ˈhaʊsˌkiːpɪŋ/ n [U] **1** the management of a house, esp. with regard to cleaning, cooking, buying food, etc. **2** also **housekeeping mon·ey** /ˈ··· ˌ··/— an amount of money set aside to pay for food and other things needed in the home **3** jobs that need to be done to keep a computer system working properly, such as making copies of FILES

house lights /ˈ· ·/ n [P] the lights used in the part of a cinema or theatre where people sit

house·maid /ˈhaʊsmeɪd/ n (esp. in former times) a female servant who cleans the house

housemaid's knee /ˌ·· ˈ·/ n [U] a swelling of the knee, caused esp. by too much kneeling on floors while cleaning them

house·man /ˈhaʊsmən/ BrE‖**intern** AmE— n -men /mən/ a doctor of low rank (man or woman) completing hospital training, and often (esp. in Britain) living in the hospital. Housemen often work very long hours because they must be available day and night. —compare INTERN[1]

house mar·tin /ˈ· ˌ··/ n a European bird of the SWALLOW family

house·mas·ter /ˈhaʊsˌmɑːstəʳ‖-ˌmæ-/ **house·mis·tress** /-ˌmɪstrɪs/ fem. — n esp. BrE a teacher who is in charge of one of the houses (HOUSE[1] (4)) in a school

house·moth·er /ˈhaʊsˌmʌðəʳ/ n a female HOUSEPARENT

house mu·sic /ˈ· ˌ··/ also **house**— n [U] a kind of popular music involving complicated mixtures of sounds made by SYNTHESIZERs, a fast, repeated beat, and few words. House music was intended for dancing to, and was popular at the Acid House parties of the late 80s.

house of cards /ˌ·· ˈ·/ n [usu. sing.] **1** an arrangement of playing cards built up carefully but easily knocked over **2** a plan or situation which is too badly arranged to succeed

House of Com·mons /ˌ·· ˈ··/ also **House, Commons**— n [the] the larger and more powerful of the two parts of the British or Canadian parliament, the members of which are elected by citizens over 18 years of age. Each member represents people in a particular area and is their MP. The British House of Commons has 650 members. MPs serve for five years, except when a General Election is held before the end of that period. When a new law is introduced, it is passed first in the House of Commons, then sent to the House of Lords to be discussed and approved. Finally it must be approved by the queen and given the ROYAL ASSENT. —compare HOUSE OF LORDS; see extra information on page 565 and colour picture on page 949

house of God /ˌ·· ˈ·/ [the] lit or pomp a church

house of ill re·pute /ˌ·· · ·· ·ˈ·/ n a BROTHEL

House of Lords /ˌ·· ˈ·/ also **House, Lords**— n [the] **1** the smaller and less powerful of the two parts of the British parliament, the members of which are not elected but have positions because of their rank or titles of honour. Members of the House of Lords include Lords, BISHOPS (=leaders of the Church of England), and LIFE PEERs (=people who have been given a title as a reward for important public service). —compare HOUSE OF COMMONS; see extra information on page 565 and colour picture on page 949 **2** the group of LAW LORDS of the House of Lords who make up the highest Court of Appeal in Britain

House of Rep·re·sen·ta·tives /ˌ·· · ··ˈ··/ also **House**— n [the] the larger and more powerful of the two parts of the central law-making organization in such countries as New Zealand, Australia, and the US. In the US, the House has 435 members, called **Representatives** or **Congress·men/women**, elected by their state. The number of Representatives per state depends on the size of its population. A Representative serves for two years. —compare CONGRESS, SENATE (1); see extra information on page 565 and colour picture on page 949

house or·gan /ˈ· ˌ··/ n AmE for HOUSE JOURNAL

house·par·ent /ˈhaʊsˌpeərənt/ n a person who acts as a parent to children who have no families or need special care, and who live together in a special home

house par·ty /ˈ· ˌ··/ n a party lasting for several days in a private house, esp. a large house in the country

house·phone, house phone /ˈhaʊsfəʊn/ n a telephone which can only make calls within a building, esp. a hotel: Use the housephone to reach the concierge.

house·plant /ˈhaʊsplɑːnt‖-plænt/ n a usu. decorative plant that is grown indoors —see picture at LIVING ROOM

house point /ˈ· ˌ·/ n BrE a mark given to pupils in some schools as a reward for good behaviour or for doing well at sport, studies, etc.

house-proud /ˈ· ·/ adj liking to have everything in perfect order in the house and spending a lot of time on keeping it clean and tidy, perhaps too much so

house·room /ˈhaʊsruːm, -rʊm/ n [U] esp. BrE **1** space in a house for a person or thing **2 give sbdy./sthg. houseroom** usu. negative be willing to find a place in one's home for: I think it's ugly—I wouldn't give it houseroom!

Houses of Par·lia·ment /ˌ·· · ˈ··/ [the+P] the buildings in which the British parliament sits, or the parliament itself: We bring you a report on today's debate in the Houses of Parliament. —see colour map on page 817

house spar·row /ˈ· ˌ··/ n the most common bird of the SPARROW family

House that Jack Built /ˌ·· · ˈ· ˌ·/, **The** the title of a well-known NURSERY RHYME (=an old song or poem for children) which begins "This is the house that Jack built"

house-to-house /ˌ·· ˈ·◂/ also **door-to-door**— adj [A] (done by) visiting each house in turn: a house to house collection

house·tops /ˈhaʊs-tɒps‖-tɑːps/ n **from the housetops** publicly, so that everyone will hear or know: shouting their demands from the housetops

house trail·er /ˈ· ˌ··/ n AmE a MOBILE HOME

house-trained /ˈ· ·/ BrE ‖ **housebroken** AmE— adj **1** (of house pets) trained to go out of the house to empty the bowels or BLADDER **2** humor (of people) taught to be tidy and useful at home

House Un-A·mer·i·can Ac·tiv·i·ties Com·mit·tee /ˌ·· ·ˌ·· · ···· ·ˈ··· ·ˌ··/ n [the] see HUAC

house·wares /ˈhaʊsweəz‖-weərz/ n [P+sing./pl.v] AmE (the department of a large shop which sells) small articles used in the home, such as cooking equipment, lamps, small furniture, etc.

house·warm·ing /ˈhaʊsˌwɔːmɪŋ‖-ˌwɔːr-/ n a party given when one has moved into a new house, and to which guests sometimes bring presents for the home

house·wife /ˈhaʊs-waɪf/ n -wives /waɪvz/ [C] a woman who works at home for her family, cleaning, cooking, etc., esp. one who does not work outside the home — ~ly adj

house·work /ˈhaʊswɜːk‖-wɜːrk/ n [U] work done in taking care of a house, esp. cleaning: to do the housework — compare HOMEWORK

hous·ing /ˈhaʊzɪŋ/ n **1** [U] (the act of providing) places for people to live in: government housing policy | Too many people are living in bad housing (conditions). **2** [C] a protective covering, esp. for a piece of machinery: the engine housing

Housing and Ur·ban De·vel·op·ment /ˌ·· · ˌ·· ·ˈ···/ n see HUD

housing as·so·ci·a·tion /ˈ·· ···ˌ··/ n in Britain, a society formed by a group of people so that they can build houses or flats for themselves or buy the houses or flats in which they live

housing ben·e·fit /ˈ·· ˌ··/ n [U] in Britain, money given by local councils to people who cannot afford to pay the rent for their room, house, or flat

housing es·tate /ˈ·· ·ˌ·/ BrE ‖ **housing de·vel·op·ment** /ˈ·· ·ˌ··/ AmE— n a piece of land on which houses have been built, usu. close together, in a planned way —see colour picture on page 162

housing list /ˈ·· ·/ n BrE a list of people waiting to be given a house or flat by the local council

housing pro·ject /ˈ·· ˌ··/ n esp. AmE a group of houses or flats usu. built with government money for families who have little money: drug-dealing in the housing projects

Hous·ton /ˈhjuːstən/ a city in the American state of Texas where the American government space centre (NASA) is based —see colour map on pages 1374–5

Houston, Sam·u·el /ˈsæmjuəl/ (1793–1863) an American soldier, FRONTIERSMAN, and politician. Sam Houston fought against Mexico to gain independence for Texas. While he was president of Texas he persuaded the American government to make Texas a state (1845).

Hous·ton /'huːstən/, **Whit·ney** /'wɪtni/ (1963–) an American popular music singer who became one of the most successful singers in the late 1980s, selling millions of records in Britain and the US

hove /həʊv/ *tech or humor past tense & participle of* HEAVE²

hov·el /'hɒvəl‖'hʌ-, 'hɑː-/ *n often derog or humor* a small dirty place where people live

hov·er /'hɒvəʳ‖'hʌ-, 'hɑː-/ *v* [I] **1** (of birds, certain aircraft, etc.) to stay in the air in one place **2** (of people) to stay around one place, esp. in a way that annoys other people: *I wish you'd stop hovering (round) and let me get on with some work!* **3** [(**between**)] to be in an uncertain state: *He's hovering between life and death.* – ~**er** *n*

hov·er·craft /'hɒvəkrɑːft‖'hʌvərkræft, 'hɑː-/ *n* -**craft** *or* -**crafts** a vehicle, esp. a large one for carrying passengers, that flies over land or water keeping very close to the surface, and is kept in flight by a strong current of air forced out beneath it –compare HYDROFOIL

hover mow·er /'·· ‚··/ *n* a LAWN MOWER that is supported just above the ground on a cushion of air and has a blade that spins round and round very fast

Hov·han·ess /həʊv'hænʲs/, **Al·an** /'ælən/ (1911–) an American COMPOSER

Ho·vis /'həʊvɪs/ *n tdmk* a company which makes different types of BREAD; it is best known for its brown bread which is considered to be good for you

HOV lane /‚eɪtʃ əʊ 'viː leɪn/ *also* **diamond lane**– *n AmE* High Occupancy Vehicle Lane; a LANE (2) on a FREEWAY which only cars with two or more people in them can drive in

how¹ /haʊ/ *adv* **1** (in questions) **a** in what way or by what means: *How can I get to Cambridge?* | *Will you tell me how I can get to Cambridge?* | *How is this word spelt?* | *Can you remember how to get there?* | (shows surprise or anger) *How could you do such a stupid thing?* **b** in what condition, of health or mind: *How is your mother?* | *How are you (feeling)?* | *I want to know how he feels about having to work at weekends.* **c** by what amount; to what degree: *How much does this cost?* | *How old are you?* | *I don't know how long this will take.* | *I wonder how soon he'll come.* | *It depends on how large a salary you earn.*| *I forget how many there are.* **2** (in expressions of strong feeling): *How pleased they were to see us!* | *How nice of you to come.* | *How we laughed!* –compare WHAT²; see USAGE **3 And how!** *infml, esp. AmE* Very much so: *"Did they enjoy themselves?" "And how!"* **4 How are you?** /‚· '·· ·/ **a** (a question about someone's health) **b** (a phrase used when meeting someone you already know. The reply is often *"Fine (thanks). (And) how are you* /‚· · '·/?*"*) **5 How come?** *infml* (expressing surprise) Why is it? How can it be that … ?: *How come he got the job when she was the best-qualified person?* **6 How do you do?** (a phrase used to someone you have just met for the first time; this person replies with the same phrase. They usually shake hands at the same time.) –see also HOW DO YOU DO **7 How so?** Why? In what way?: *"I think she's stuck-up." "How so?" "She never says hello when she passes me in the street."* **8 How's that?** Please repeat; What did you say? –see also **how about** (ABOUT²)

▷ USAGE Both **how** and **what** are used in exclamations. **How** usually comes before an adjective or adverb: **How** *nice she is!* | **How** *kind of you to invite me!* | **How** *slowly he walks!* **What** comes before a noun or noun phrase: **What** *a nice person she is!* | **What** *an idiot I was!*◁

how² *conj* **1** the fact that: *Do you remember how she used to smoke fifty cigarettes a day?* **2** *infml* HOWEVER¹: *In your own home you can act how you like.*

how³ *n* the how and the why the way something can be done and the reason for it

How·ard /'haʊəd ‖ -ərd/, **Trev·or** /'trevəʳ/ (1916–88) an English actor remembered esp. for his roles in films, esp. *Brief Encounter*

Howard Johnson's one of a group of American restaurants which are usu. found close to large roads, in order to be convenient to travellers

Howard League for Pe·nal Re·form /‚·· ‚· ·‚· ·'·/ [*the*] a British organization which is against physical punishment and the death sentence, and wants change in international attitudes to punishment and imprisonment

how·dah /'haʊdə/ *n* a usu. decorative seat for a person to sit on an elephant's back

how do you do /‚haʊ djə 'duː, ‚haʊ də jʊ 'duː/ *also* **how d'ye do** /‚haʊ djə 'duː/– *n* a **fine how do you do** *infml* an unpleasantly surprising situation –see also HOW¹ (6)

how·dy /'haʊdi/ *interj AmE infml* (used when meeting someone) HELLO

How·dy Doo·dy /‚haʊdi 'duːdi/ an American television programme for children in which the main character, called Howdy Doody, was a PUPPET with FRECKLES and red hair who dressed like a COWBOY. The programme was on from the 1940s until 1960 and many people know that it began with the words "It's Howdy Doody time" and that the children who were present while it was being filmed were called "the peanut gallery".

Howe /haʊ/, **Geof·frey** /'dʒefri/ (1926–) a British Conservative politician who was Chancellor of the Exchequer in Margaret Thatcher's government from 1979–83

Howe, Gor·die /'gɔːdi‖'gɔːr-/ (1928–) an American ICE HOCKEY player who played for twenty-six years in the NHL (National Hockey League)

How·erd /'haʊəd‖-ərd/, **Frank·ie** /'fræŋki/ (1921–92) a British COMEDIAN who appeared in films, on television, and in the theatre. He is remembered esp. for playing the part of a Roman slave in the British television SERIES *Up Pompeii* and also for appearing in many "Carry On" films.

how·ev·er¹ /haʊ'evəʳ/ *conj* in whatever way: *I'm going by car but you can go however you like.*

however² *adv* **1** to whatever degree: *However cold it is, she always goes swimming.* | *I won't accept their offer, however favourable the conditions.* | *We'll have to finish it, however long it takes.* **2** *rather fml* in spite of this; NEVERTHELESS: *The company's profits have fallen slightly. However, this is not a serious problem.* | *There is, however, another side to this problem.* | *My room is small. It's very comfortable, however.* **3** (showing surprise) how: *However did you find it?* –see EVER (3)

How Green was My Val·ley /‚· ‚· · '··/ a NOVEL by Richard Llewellyn, which came out in 1939 and which tells the story of a MINER's family in Wales

how·it·zer /'haʊɪtsəʳ/ *n* a heavy gun which fires SHELLS¹ (4) high over a short distance

howl¹ /haʊl/ *n* a long loud sound, e.g. of pain, anger, etc., esp. that made by certain animals, such as wolves (WOLF) and dogs

howl² *v* **1** [I (**with**)] to make a howl: *The dogs howled all night.* | (fig.) *The wind howled in the trees.* | *We all howled with laughter.* **2** [T (**OUT**)] to say or express with a howl **3** [I (**with**)] to cry loudly, in pain, sorrow, or anger: *howling with pain*
   howl sbdy./sthg. ↔ **down** *phr v* [T] to make a loud disapproving noise so as to prevent (someone) from being heard

howl·er /'haʊləʳ/ *n infml* a very silly mistake which makes people laugh, esp. one in which the wrong word is used in a piece of writing so that the meaning is completely changed

howl·ing /'haʊlɪŋ/ *adj* [A] *infml* very great; extreme: *a howling success*

how·so·ev·er /‚haʊsəʊ'evəʳ/ *adv lit* to whatever degree; HOWEVER² (1)

how·zat /haʊ'zæt/ *also* **how's that**– *interj* (a call used in CRICKET to say that someone is OUT¹ (16))

Ho·xha /'hɒdʒə‖'hɑː-/, **En·ver** /'envəʳ/ (1908–85) the Communist leader of Albania from 1944 to 1982, regarded by many as an evil TYRANT

hoy·den /'hɔɪdn/ *n lit* a girl who is wild and rough rather than gentle and polite – ~**ish** *adj*

HP /‚eɪtʃ 'piː/ *abbrev. for:* **1** HORSEPOWER **2** (*BrE*) HIRE PURCHASE: *We got it on (the) HP.*

HP sauce /‚eɪtʃ piː 'sɔːs/ *n* [U] *BrE tdmk* a thick dark brown liquid made of vegetables, fruit, and SPICES, which is sold in bottles and eaten esp. with meat

HQ /‚eɪtʃ 'kjuː/ *n* [C;U] HEADQUARTERS: *See you back at HQ in half an hour.*

hr, hrs *written abbrev. for:* hour

HRH *abbrev. for:* His/Her Royal Highness: *HRH the Prince of Wales*

HRT /ˌeɪtʃ ɑː ˈtiː ‖ -ɑːr-/ *abbrev. for* HORMONE REPLACEMENT THERAPY

HSE /ˌeɪtʃ es ˈiː/ [*the*] *abbrev.* for HEALTH AND SAFETY EXECUTIVE

ht *written abbrev. for:* height

HTV /ˌeɪtʃ tiː ˈviː/ Harlech Television; one of the British television companies controlled by the ITC, transmitting programmes to Wales and the West Country

HUAC /ˈhjuːæk, ˌeɪtʃ juː eɪ ˈsiː/ *n* [U] House Un-American Activities Committee; the group in the American House of Representatives which examined possible cases of SUB-VERSIVE actions (=actions dangerous to the American government). HUAC was formed in 1938 but is most known for its actions during the 1950s when Senator Joseph McCarthy began looking at possible cases of Communism within the government, in the army, and among other important people. In 1969 HUAC took a new name but it stopped operating in 1975. –see also COMMUNIST, Joseph MCCARTHY, MCCARTHYISM

hua·ra·che /wəˈrɑːtʃi, hə-/ *n Sp* a SANDAL often made in Mexico whose top is of leather bands woven together

hub /hʌb/ *n* **1** the central part of a wheel, round which it turns and into which the AXLE fits –see picture at BICY-CLE **2** [(of)] the centre of activity or importance: *For him, his department is the hub of the universe.* (derog)

Hub·bard /ˈhʌbəd‖-ərd/, **L Ron** /rɒn‖rɑːn/ (1911–86) an American writer of SCIENCE FICTION, and the man who began the Church of SCIENTOLOGY

Hub·ble Tel·e·scope /ˈhʌbəl ˌtelɪskəʊp/ *n* [*the*] a TELESCOPE on a SATELLITE which can see further into space than telescopes on Earth

hub·bub /ˈhʌbʌb/ *n* [S;U] a mixture of loud noises; DIN

hub·by /ˈhʌbi/ *n infml* a husband

hub·cap /ˈhʌbkæp/ *n* a metal covering over the centre of the wheel of a motor vehicle –see picture at CAR

hu·bris /ˈhjuːbrɪs/ *n* [U] *fml* great and unreasonable pride, often bringing great misfortune to the person who shows it

huck·le·ber·ry /ˈhʌkəlbəri‖-beri/ *n* a dark blue fruit which grows in North America

Huckleberry Finn /ˌ···· ˈ·/ see Huckleberry FINN

huck·ster /ˈhʌkstə/ *n* **1** a person who sells small things in the street or at the doors of houses **2** *AmE, often derog* a person who writes advertisements, esp. for radio and television

HUD /hʌd/ *n* Housing and Urban Development; a part of the US government which deals with housing and the development of cities

hud·dle¹ /ˈhʌdl/ *v* [I;T (TOGETHER, UP) *usu. pass.*] **1** to (cause to) crowd together, in a group or in a pile: *The boys huddled together under the rock to keep warm.* | *They were huddled together for warmth.* | (*esp. BrE*) *Your clothes are all huddled up inside that bag getting spoilt.* **2 huddled masses** *quote* a phrase taken from the words written on the Statue of Liberty in New York Harbour, used to talk about groups of poor people huddled together –see also STATUE OF LIBERTY

huddle² *n* **1** a crowd of people or things, close together and not in any ordered arrangement **2** (in American football) a group made by a team before they separate to make the next play **3 go into a huddle** to get into a small group, away from other people, in order to talk privately or secretly

Hud·son /ˈhʌdsən/, **Rock** (1925–85) an American film actor known for his attractive appearance

Hudson Bay /ˌ·· ˈ·/ a large area of sea in northern Canada which is frozen for most of the year

Hudson Riv·er /ˌ·· ˈ··/ [*the*] a river in New York State in the US, which meets the Atlantic Ocean in New York City. The Hudson is named after the EXPLORER, Henry Hudson. –see colour map on page 1376

Hudson River School /ˌ··· ˈ·· ˌ·/ *n* a group of American painters of the 1800s who painted LANDSCAPEs (views of nature) in a ROMANTIC style

Hudson's Bay Com·pa·ny /ˌ··· ˈ· ˌ···/ *n tdmk* a company which did business for fur with the Native Americans and which once owned much land in what is now Canada

hue /hjuː/ *n* **1** *esp. lit or tech* (the degree of brightness in)

a colour: *The diamond shone with every hue under the sun.* **2** *fml* a type or sort: *Political opinions of every hue were represented at the conference.*

hue and cry /ˌ·· ˈ·/ *n* [S] a noisy expression of anger, disapproval, etc., esp. when showing opposition to something: *There was a great hue and cry against the new rule.*

huff¹ /hʌf/ *v* **1** [I] to breathe with a noisy movement of air, e.g. when climbing: *They went huffing and puffing up the stairs.* **2** [T] (in the game of DRAUGHTS) to take a piece belonging to (an opponent who has failed to take a piece)

huff² *n* [S] a state of bad temper when one is offended or displeased: *He went off in a huff when she criticized his work.*

huff·y /ˈhʌfi/ also **huff·ish** /ˈhʌfɪʃ/– *adj derog* **1** in a huff; SULKY **2** easily offended; TOUCHY –**ily** *adv*

hug¹ /hʌɡ/ *v* **-gg-** [T] **1 a** to hold (someone) tightly in the arms, esp. as a sign of love **b** (of a bear) to hold (a person) tightly with the front PAWs (=legs) **2** to hold (something) in one's arms, close to one's chest: *hugging a pile of books* **3** to go along while staying near: *The boat hugged the coast.* **4** to hold on to (an idea) with a feeling of pleasure or safety **5 hug oneself** to feel very pleased with oneself

hug² *n* an act of hugging: *He gave his little boy a (great big) hug at bedtime.* –see also BEAR HUG

huge /hjuːdʒ/ *adj* **1** extremely large: *a huge house* | *a huge amount of money* **2** very great in degree: *a huge success* –**~ly** *adv* : *hugely successful* –**~ness** *n* [U]

hug·ger-mug·ger /ˈhʌɡə ˌmʌɡə‖ ˈhʌɡər-/ *n* [U] *esp. old use* **1** secrecy **2** disorder –**hugger-mugger** *adj, adv*

Hughes /hjuːz/, **Howard** (1905–76) a very wealthy American who was important in the aircraft and film industries and who avoided all but a few people for the last 26 years of his life

Hughes, Lang·ston /ˈlæŋstən/ (1902–67) a black American poet and writer famous for using African-American speech and RHYTHMs in his work

Hughes, Ted /ted/ (1930–   ) a British poet, appointed POET LAUREATE in 1984, who is well known for his use of animal imagery

Hu·go /ˈhjuːɡəʊ/, **Victor** (1802–85) a French writer of poems, plays, and NOVELs. Hugo's two most famous novels are *The Hunchback of Notre Dame* and *Les Misérables.*

Hu·gue·not /ˈhjuːɡənəʊ‖-nɑːt/ *n, adj* [C *usu. pl.*] (of) a member of a group of French Protestants of the 16th and 17th centuries –see also RICHELIEU

huh /hʌh/ *interj infml* (used for asking a question or for expressing surprise or disapproval): *It's pretty big, huh?*

hu·la /ˈhuːlə/ also **hula hula** /ˌ·· ˈ··/– *n* a Polynesian dance, involving gentle rocking movements of the hips performed by women

hula hoop /ˈ·· ·/ *n AmE tdmk* a toy in the shape of a circular band which children move by putting it around their waists and moving their HIPs

hulk /hʌlk/ *n* **1** the body of an old ship, no longer used at sea and left in a bad state **2** a heavy awkward person or thing

hulk·ing /ˈhʌlkɪŋ/ *adj* [A] big, heavy, and awkward: *We can't move that hulking great table on our own.*

hull¹ /hʌl/ *n* the main body of a ship –see picture at YACHT

hull² *v* [T] to take the outer covering off (a vegetable, grain, etc.): *Rice is gathered, cleaned, and hulled before being sold.* | *hulled peas*

Hull also **Kingston upon Hull**– an industrial city and fishing port in NE England

hul·la·ba·loo /ˌhʌləbəluː, ˌhʌləbəˈluː/ *n* -**loos** [*usu. sing.*] a lot of noise, esp. of voices; UPROAR

hul·lo /hʌˈləʊ/ *interj, n* -**los** *esp. BrE* HELLO

hum¹ /hʌm/ *v* -**mm-** **1** [I] (of bees and certain animals) to make a continuous low sound; BUZZ **2** [I;T] (of people) to make a sound like a continuous **m**, esp. as a way of singing (a tune) with closed lips: *to hum a song* **3** [(**with**)] to be full of life or activity: *The office was really humming (with activity).* –**hum** *n* [S]

hum² *v BrE* ‖ **hem** *AmE*– -**mm-** *usu. derog* **hum and haw** /ˌ·· ˈ·/ *BrE* ‖ **hem and haw** *AmE* to express uncertainty, esp. annoyingly

hu·man¹ /ˈhjuːmən/ *adj* **1** of or concerning people, esp. as opposed to animals, plants, or machines: *the human voice* | *The archaeologists have found several human skeletons.* | *Some ancient societies used to practise human sacrifice.* | *The broken-down old house was not fit for human habitation.* (=not suitable for people to live in) | *The accident was caused by* **human error**, *not by a fault in the machine.* **2** concerning or typical of ordinary people: *Everyone makes mistakes sometimes – we're only human.* | *It's only* **human nature** *to want a comfortable life.* | *a newspaper story with plenty of* **human interest**, *about a little boy and his dog* **3** showing the feelings, esp. those of KINDNESS, which people are supposed to have: *He's quite human when you get to know him.* – opposite **inhuman**; compare HUMANE; see also HUMANLY

human² also **human be·ing** /ˌ·· ˈ··/ – *n* a man, woman, or child, not an animal –see MAN (USAGE) –see picture at SKELETON

hu·mane /hjuːˈmeɪn/ *adj* **1** showing human kindness, thoughtfulness, and sympathy for the suffering and misfortune of others, etc.: *a humane method of killing animals* (=one that causes the least possible pain) – opposite **inhumane**; compare HUMAN **2** [A] *fml, now rare* (of studies) concerned with the ARTS, such as literature and history – ~**ly** *adv*

Humane So·ci·e·ty /·ˈ· ˌ···/ [*the*] an American organization which is mainly concerned about the humane treatment of animals

human immuno deficiency virus /ˌhjuːmən ˌɪmjʊnəʊ dɪˈfɪʃənsi ˌvaɪərəs/ see HIV

hu·man·is·m /ˈhjuːmənɪzəm/ *n* [U] (*often cap.*) **1** a system of beliefs and standards concerned with the needs of people, and not with religious ideas **2** the study in the Renaissance of the ideas of the ancient Greeks and Romans –**ist** *n, adj* –**istic** /ˌhjuːməˈnɪstɪk·/ *adj*

hu·man·i·tar·i·an /hjuːˌmænɪˈteəriən/ *n, adj* (a person) concerned with trying to improve people's lives, e.g. by providing better conditions to live in and by opposing injustice – ~**ism** *n* [U]

hu·man·i·ties /hjuːˈmænɪtiz/ *n* [*the*+P] studies such as ancient and modern literature, history, etc.; the ARTS (1)

hu·man·i·ty /hjuːˈmænɪti/ *n* [U] **1** the quality of being humane or human **2** human beings generally

hu·man·ize also **-ise** *BrE* /ˈhjuːmənaɪz/ *v* [T] to cause to be or seem human or humane

hu·man·kind /ˌhjuːmənˈkaɪnd/ *n* [U] human beings generally; MANKIND

hu·man·ly /ˈhjuːmənli/ *adv* according to human powers: *It's not* **humanly possible** *to finish that work in a week.* (=it's completely impossible)

hu·man·oid /ˈhjuːmənɔɪd/ *adj* (esp. of a machine) having human shape or qualities: *a humanoid robot* – **humanoid** *n*

human race /ˌ·· ˈ·/ [*the*] human beings thought of as a group; MANKIND –see MAN (USAGE)

human re·sourc·es /ˌ··· ·ˈ··/ *n* [P] (the abilities, skills, etc. of) people: *Closing down this factory is a waste of the industry's human resources.*

human rights /ˌ·· ·ˈ·/ *n* [P] the non-political rights of freedom, equality, etc., which belong to any person without regard to race, religion, colour, sex, etc.: *an international agreement on human rights* | *a human rights campaigner* | *human rights violations/abuses*

human shield /ˌ·· ·ˈ·/ *n* [C *usu. sing.*] non-military people, esp. of the same nationality as an attacking force, brought into a military area by the defenders to discourage attack (by increasing the risk that the attacker may kill or INJURE his own people). This phrase was used a lot during the Gulf War.

Hum·ber·side /ˈhʌmbəsaɪd‖-bər-/ a COUNTY in NE England including the ESTUARY of the River **Humber**, which is crossed by the **Humber Bridge**

hum·ble¹ /ˈhʌmbəl/ *adj* **1** of low rank or position (in society, in an organization, etc.): *just a humble clerk* | *He rose from humble origins to become prime minister.* **2** having a low opinion of oneself and a high opinion of others; UNASSUMING –opposite **proud** **3 eat humble pie** to have to admit that one was wrong or that one has failed **4 your humble servant** (a very polite and formal way

of ending a letter before signing it, used esp. formerly) –**bly** *adv*

humble² *v* [T] *fml* to cause (someone or oneself) to lose pride or position: *to humble one's enemy* | *a humbling experience*

hum·bug¹ /ˈhʌmbʌg/ *n* **1** [U] *old-fash* an insincere expression of shock, disapproval, etc: *This newspaper is always talking about the decline of moral standards, but that's sheer humbug because it's full of pornographic pictures.* **2** [U] *old-fash* nonsense **3** [C] *old-fash* a deceitful person who pretends to be something he/she is not; IMPOSTOR **4** [C] *BrE* a sweet made of hard boiled sugar and usu. tasting of MINT³

humbug² *interj* nonsense!

hum·ding·er /hʌmˈdɪŋəʳ/ *n infml* a wonderful person or thing

hum·drum /ˈhʌmdrʌm/ *adj* too ordinary; without variety or change; MONOTONOUS: *our humdrum lives*

Hume /hjuːm/, **Cardinal Basil** (1923–) the ARCHBISHOP OF Westminster (=the head of the Roman Catholic church in Britain) from 1976

Hume, David (1711–76) an influential Scottish writer on PHILOSOPHY (1) and history, whose best known works are *A Treatise of Human Nature* and his *History of England*

hu·mer·us /ˈhjuːmərəs/ *n tech* the long bone in the top half of the arm –see picture at SKELETON

hu·mid /ˈhjuːmɪd/ *adj* (of air and weather) containing a lot of water VAPOUR; DAMP: *a humid day/climate* –compare DRY¹ (2); see DAMP (USAGE)

hu·mid·i·fy /hjuːˈmɪdɪfaɪ/ *v* [T] to make humid –**fier** *n*

hu·mid·i·ty /hjuːˈmɪdɪti/ *n* [U] the (amount of) water VAPOUR contained in the air: *It's not the heat but the humidity that makes it so uncomfortable today.*

hu·mil·i·ate /hjuːˈmɪlieɪt/ *v* [T] to cause to feel ashamed or to lose the respect of others: *It was so humiliating to be corrected by the head teacher in front of the whole school.* –**ation** /hjuːˌmɪliˈeɪʃən/ *n* [C;U]

hu·mil·i·ty /hjuːˈmɪlɪti/ *n* [U] the quality of being HUMBLE (2); lack of pride

hum·ming·bird /ˈhʌmɪŋbɜːd‖-bɜːrd/ *n* a very small bird whose wings beat very fast and make a humming noise (HUM)

hum·mock /ˈhʌmək/ *n* a very small hill; HILLOCK

hummus /ˈhʊmʊs, ˈhuː-/ , also **houmous, houmus, humus**– *n* [U] a thick mixture made mainly from CHICKPEAS (=a kind of vegetable), eaten as food esp. in Greece and the Middle East

hu·mor·ist /ˈhjuːmərˌst‖ˈhjuː-, ˈjuː-/ *n* a person who makes jokes, esp. in writing

hu·mor·ous /ˈhjuːmərəs‖ˈhjuː-, ˈjuː-/ *adj* funny; that makes people laugh: *a humorous play/remark/character in a play* – ~**ly** *adv*

hu·mour¹ *BrE* ‖ **humor** *AmE* /ˈhjuːməʳ‖ˈhjuː-, ˈjuː-/ *n* **1** [U] (the ability to understand and enjoy) what is funny and makes people laugh: *He hasn't got much of a sense of humour.* **2** [U] the quality of causing amusement: *a story full of humour* | *She couldn't see the humour in the situation.* **3** [C *usu. sing.*] *old-fash fml* a state of mind; MOOD¹: *in a good humour* **4** [C] any of four liquids which were formerly thought to be present in the body in varying degrees, and to influence the character **5 out of humour** *old-fash fml* in a bad temper; MOODY **6** **-humoured** *BrE* ‖ **-humored** *AmE* /hjuːməd‖hjuːmərd, juː-/ having the stated condition of mind: *good-humoured* | *ill-humoured* –see also BLACK HUMOUR

humour² *BrE* ‖ **humor** *AmE*– *v* [T] to accept the wishes, esp. foolish or unreasonable wishes, of (someone) esp. in order to keep them happy or prevent them from complaining

hump¹ /hʌmp/ *n* **1** [C] a large lump or round part which stands out noticeably: *There's a hump in the road to slow down the traffic.* **2** [C] a lump on the back, esp. **a** of a CAMEL **b** of a HUNCHBACK **3** [*the*] *BrE infml* a feeling of bad temper or dislike of life in general: *It's giving me the hump, all this bad weather!* **4 over the hump** past the worst part

hump² *v* **1** [T+*obj*+*adv*/*prep*] *BrE infml* to carry (something heavy), esp. with difficulty: *We humped the* *cupboard upstairs.* | *I'm tired of humping all this luggage around.* **2** [I;T] *taboo sl* to have sex (with)

hump·back /'hʌmpbæk/ n a back with a hump; HUNCHBACK —**backed** adj

humpbacked bridge /ˌ··· '·/ n esp. BrE a short sharp rise and fall in the surface of a road as it goes over a bridge

Hum·per·dinck /'hʌmpədɪŋk‖-pər-/, **En·gel·bert** /'eŋgəl-bɜːt‖-bɜːrt/ (1854–1921) a German COMPOSER best known for his OPERA *Hansel und Gretel*

Humperdinck, Engelbert (1936–) a British popular music singer who was successful in the 1960s with slow love songs which were popular with people of all ages

humph, h'm /hʌmf, hmh, hm/ interj (a sound made with the lips closed to express a feeling of doubt or dissatisfaction with something said or done)

Hum·phries /'hʌmfriz/, **Bar·ry** /'bæri/ (1931–) an Australian entertainer who appears dressed as characters he has invented, esp. Dame Edna Everage and Sir Les Patterson —see also DAME EDNA

Hump·ty Dump·ty /ˌhʌmpti 'dʌmpti/ a character shaped like an egg in a NURSERY RHYME (=an old song or poem for children):

> *Humpty Dumpty sat on a wall,*
> *Humpty Dumpty had a great fall.*
> *All the King's horses and all the King's men*
> *Couldn't put Humpty together again.*

Humpty Dumpty

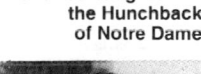
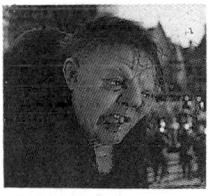

hu·mus[1] /'hjuːməs/ n [U] rich soil made of decayed plants, leaves, etc.

humus[2] /'hʊmʊs, 'huː-/ n HUMMUS

Hun /hʌn/ n derog a name for Germans esp. used in the First and Second World Wars

hunch[1] /hʌntʃ/ n an idea based on feeling rather than on reason or facts: *"How did you know that horse was going to win?" "It was just a hunch."* [+(that)] *I have a hunch that she didn't really want to go.*

hunch[2] v [T (UP)] to pull (all or part of) the body) into a rounded shape: *She hunched (up) her shoulders over her book.* | *sitting hunched up in a corner*

hunch·back /'hʌntʃbæk/ n (a person who has) a back that sticks out in a large rounded lump —**backed** adj

Hunch·back of Not·re Dame /ˌ··· · ˌ·· '·/, **The** a book by the French writer Victor Hugo which tells a story of love and death in 15th century Paris and is remembered for the character **Quasimodo**, a hunchback

Charles Laughton as the Hunchback of Notre Dame

hun·dred /'hʌndrəd/ determiner, n, pron -**dred** or -**dreds** (the number) 100: *a hundred years* | *two hundred miles* | (infml) *I've been there hundreds of times.* (=very often) —see TABLE 1

hundreds and thou·sands /ˌ··· · '··/ BrE ‖ **nonpareil** AmE— n [P] small, thin pieces of coloured sugar used to decorate cakes and other food which is to be eaten by children

hun·dredth /'hʌndrədθ/ determiner, n, pron, adv 100th —see TABLE 1

hun·dred·weight /'hʌndrədweɪt/ (written abbrev. **cwt**)— n -**weight** a measure of weight —see TABLE 2

Hundred Years' War /ˌ··· ˌ· '·/ [the] a war (1337–1453) between England and France resulting from royal quarrels, particularly over land, and ending in the defeat of the English as they were pushed back out of France

hung /hʌŋ/ **1** past tense & participle of HANG[1] **2** adj [A] (of a parliament, council, or JURY) evenly divided between opposing parties or opinions, so that decisions cannot be made

Hun·ga·ri·an /hʌŋ'geəriən/ n **1** [C] a person who comes

from or whose parents come from Hungary **2** [U] the official language of Hungary

Hun·ga·ry /'hʌŋgəri/ a country in central Europe, formerly under COMMUNIST rule; capital Budapest; population 10,576,000 (1989)

hun·ger[1] /'hʌŋgər/ n **1** [U] the wish or need for food **2** [U] lack of food, esp. for a long period: *people dying of hunger* **3** [S (for)] a strong wish: *a hunger for change/adventure*

hunger[2] v [I] old use to feel hunger
hunger for/after sthg. phr v [T] esp. lit to want very much

hunger march /'··· ·/ n a procession made esp. by unemployed and poor people, to make known the difficulties of those who cannot afford to eat —**hunger marcher** n

hunger strike /'··· ·/ n a refusal to eat, esp. by people in prison, as a sign of strong dissatisfaction —**hunger striker** n

hung·o·ver /hʌŋ'əʊvər/ adj suffering the effects of drinking too much the night before; having a HANGOVER (1): *Jerry's hungover from his all-night stag party.*

hung par·lia·ment /ˌ· '···/ n BrE a parliament in which no political party has more elected representatives than the others

hun·gry /'hʌŋgri/ adj **1** feeling or showing hunger: *hungry children* | *If you can't be bothered to go to the shops you'll just have to go hungry.* (=remain without food) **2** causing hunger: *hungry work* **3** [(for)] having a strong eager wish: *We're hungry for news of our brother in Australia.* —**grily** adv

hunk /hʌŋk/ n **1** [(of)] a thick piece, esp. of food, broken or cut off: *a hunk of bread* —see CHUNK (USAGE), and see picture at PIECE **2** often humor a strong-looking man with big muscles

hun·ker /'hʌŋkər/ v [I] to sit on one's heels; SQUAT: *They hunkered by the fire, warming themselves.* | *The soldiers hunkered down in the trench.*

hun·kers /'hʌŋkəz‖-ərz/ n [P] esp. BrE infml the part of the body between the waist and legs; HAUNCHes: *they all sat down on their hunkers*

hun·ky-dor·y /ˌhʌŋki 'dɔːri/ adj [F] infml (esp. of a situation) very satisfactory

hunt[1] /hʌnt/ v **1** [I;T] to chase in order to catch and kill (animals and birds), either for food or for sport **2** [I;T] **a** to chase (foxes) on horseback with HOUNDs (=hunting dogs) **b** to do this in (an area): *to hunt the county* **3** [I (for);T] to search (for); try to find: *I've hunted high and low* (=everywhere) *for my socks.* | *We spent the weekend house-hunting.* (=looking for a new house) **4** [T] to follow in order to catch: *hunting an escaped prisoner*

▷ USAGE In Britain, *to go* **hunting** normally means to use dogs (HOUNDs) to chase the animal (usually a fox) while riding a horse. The sport of killing animals or birds with a gun is called **shooting**. But in the US the word **hunting** is used for both these sports.◁

▶ CULTURAL NOTE In the US, hunting is a popular sport among some people, while others think of hunting as INHUMANE. In Britain, there is particularly strong opposition to the hunting of foxes. —see also HUNT SABOTEUR ◀
hunt sbdy./sthg. ↔ **down/out/up** phr v [T] to succeed in finding after much effort

hunt[2] n **1** (often in comb.) an act of hunting: *the long hunt through the fields and woods* | *a bear-hunt* | *an elephant-hunt* **2** BrE **a** an occasion of hunting foxes; a FOXHUNT **b** [+sing./pl. v] the people who regularly hunt foxes together **c** the area in which they hunt **3** [(for)] a search, esp. one that is long and difficult: *The hunt for these terrorists still continues.* | *He's left his job so* **the hunt is on** (=has begun) *for a new director.*

Hunt, Wil·liam Hol·man /ˌwɪljəm 'həʊlmən/ (1827–1910) an English painter who, with Millais and Rossetti, began the Pre-Raphaelite Brotherhood —see also PRE-RAPHAELITE

hunt·er /'hʌntər/ n **1** a person or animal that hunts something, usu. wild animals **2** a strong horse used in fox-hunting (FOXHUNT) **3** BrE a watch with a metal cover over its FACE (=the front) —see also FORTUNE HUNTER

hunter-gath·er·er /ˌ··· '···/ n a member of a very early society that lived by hunting animals and gathering wild crops for food, moving around as needed to find enough to eat

hunting ground /ˈ··· ·/ n **1** a place where animals are hunted **2** a place where one may hope to find what one is searching for: (fig., *humor*) *They've gone to* **the happy hunting ground.** (=heaven)

hunt·in', shoot·in', and fish·in' /ˌhʌntɪn ˌʃuːtɪn ənd ˈfɪʃɪn/ n, adj (interested in) outdoor activities, esp. hunting, shooting GROUSE, and fishing, which are considered to be typically done by British upper-class people. The manner of speaking of these people is meant to be shown by the missing letters.

hunting pink /ˌ·· ˈ·/ n [U] (the colour of) the bright red coats worn by people in Britain who ride horses and hunt foxes

hunt·ress /ˈhʌntrʌs/ n esp. lit a female hunter

hunt sab·o·teur /ˈ· ··,·/ n a person, usu. one of a group, who tries to stop a hunt because he/she believes that wild animals such as FOXes should not be killed in this way

hunts·man /ˈhʌntsmən/ n -men /mən/ **1** a person, usu. a man, who hunts; hunter **2** the person in charge of the HOUNDs (=dogs) during a FOXHUNT

hunt the thim·ble /ˌ·· ˈ··/ n [U] a popular children's game in Britain, in which a THIMBLE is hidden in a room and the children have to find it

Hurd /hɜːd‖hɜːrd/, **Douglas** (1930–) a Conservative minister in the British parliament from 1979 and foreign minister from 1990

hur·dle¹ /ˈhɜːdl‖ˈhɜːr-/ n **1** a frame for jumping over in a race **2** a difficulty which must be dealt with: *He overcame many hurdles to become a lawyer.*

hurdle² v [I] to run a hurdle race —**hurdler** n

hur·dy-gur·dy /ˈhɜːdi ˌgɜːdi‖ˌhɜːrdi ˈgɜːrdi/ n a small BARREL ORGAN

hurl /hɜːl‖hɜːrl/ v [T] **1** to throw (esp. something big and heavy) with force: *He hurled a brick through the window.* **2** to shout out violently: *He hurled abuse at the driver who almost crashed into him.*

hurl·ing /ˈhɜːlɪŋ‖ˈhɜːr-/ n [U] an Irish ball game played between two teams of 15 players

hur·ly-bur·ly /ˈhɜːli ˌbɜːli‖ˌhɜːrli ˈbɜːrli/ n [S;U] noisy activity: *the hurly-burly of city life*

Hu·ron /ˈhjʊərən/, **Lake** the second largest of the Great Lakes, on the border between the US and Canada —see colour map on pages 1374–5

hur·ray, hooray /hʊˈreɪ/ also **hur·rah** /hʊˈrɑː/old-fash-interj, n (a shout of joy or approval) (note the phrase **hip, hip, hurray**): *Three cheers for the winner: Hip, hip, hurray!* —see CHEER (CULTURAL NOTE)

hur·ri·cane /ˈhʌrɪkən‖ˈhɜːrɪkeɪn/ n a violent storm with a strong fast circular wind in the western Atlantic ocean —compare CYCLONE, TYPHOON; see STORM (USAGE)

Hurricane n a type of British fighter aircraft which became famous in the Second World War for its success against enemy bombers and fighters —see also SPITFIRE

hurricane lamp /ˈ···· ·/ n a lamp which has a strong cover to protect the flame inside from wind —see picture at LIGHT

hur·ried /ˈhʌrid‖ˈhɜːrid/ adj done very quickly, perhaps too quickly: *hurried work* —**~ly** adv

hur·ry¹ /ˈhʌri‖ˈhɜːri/ v **1** [I;T] to (cause to) be quick in action or movement, sometimes too quick: *There's no need to hurry; we're not late.* | *She hurried across the road to catch the bus.* | *Don't hurry me; I'm working as fast as I can!* **2** [T+obj+adv/prep] to send or bring quickly: *Doctors and nurses were hurried to the scene of the accident.*
   hurry up phr v **1** [I;T (=**hurry** sbdy. **up**)] to (cause to) act or move more quickly: *I tried to hurry him up, but he wouldn't walk any faster.* | *If you don't hurry up we'll miss the plane.* **2** [T] (**hurry** sthg. **up**) to do faster: *We have to hurry this job up if we want to finish by Thursday.*

hur·ry² n [U] **1** movement or activity that is quicker than is usual or necessary: *We've got plenty of time — what's all the hurry for?* **2** need for quickness: *Don't drive so fast: there's no hurry.* **3 in a hurry: a** (too) quickly: *You make mistakes if you do things in a hurry.* **b** anxiously eager: *She seemed to be in a hurry to leave.* | *I'm in no hurry to go.* **c** [usu. in negatives] infml easily or quickly: *I won't forget her kindness in a hurry.* **d** [usu. in negatives] infml willingly: *I won't help her again in a hurry — she's*

been so ungrateful. | *I'm in no hurry to help her again.*

hurt¹ /hɜːt‖hɜːrt/ v **hurt** **1** [T] to cause physical pain and/or damage to (esp. a part of the body); INJURE: *She hurt her leg when she fell.* | *The two cars collided, but luckily no one was seriously hurt.* **2** [I;T] to produce a feeling of pain (in): *My leg hurts.* | *Is that tight shoe hurting you/your foot?* | *"Where does it hurt, Mr Jones?" "Just here, doctor."* **3** [T] to cause (a person) to suffer pain of the mind, esp. by unkindness; upset: *I was deeply hurt by the way she just ignored me.* | *I'm sorry if I hurt your feelings.* **4** [I;T] to cause harm or difficulty (to): *A lot of companies will be hurt by these new tax laws.* | *This will hurt his reputation/his chances of being elected.* | (infml) *It won't hurt you to get up early for once.* | *Have another drink — one more won't hurt.* **5** (**he**) **wouldn't hurt a fly** (he) is a kind and gentle person

▷ USAGE When **hurt** is used in the sense of bodily damage, you may be *slightly*/*badly*/*seriously* **hurt**, but do not use these adverbs when speaking of unhappiness caused by someone's behaviour. Compare *She was badly*/*slightly* **hurt** *when she fell off the ladder* and *She was very*/*rather*/*deeply* **hurt** *by his unkind words.* —see also WOUND³ (USAGE)◁

hurt² n [(**to**)] fml **1** [U] harm; damage, esp. to feelings **2** [C often pl.] damage; INJURY to the body

hurt·ful /ˈhɜːtfəl‖ˈhɜːrt-/ adj [(**to**)] painful to the feelings; unkind: *There's no need to make such hurtful remarks.* —**~ly** adv —**~ness** n [U]

hur·tle /ˈhɜːtl‖ˈhɜːr-/ v [I+adv/prep] to move or rush with great speed: *Rocks hurtled down the cliffs*/*through the air.*

hus·band¹ /ˈhʌzbənd/ n **1** the man to whom a woman is married: *Have you met her husband?* | *John would make an ideal husband for her.* | *her ex-husband* (=to whom she was formerly married) **2 husband and wife** a married pair **3 my husband and I** pomp or humor a phrase used by the British Queen and, esp. humorously, by other women instead of "we" when talking about themselves and their husbands —see also HOUSE HUSBAND

husband² v [T] fml to save carefully and/or make the best use of: *to husband one's strength*/*resources*

hus·band·man /ˈhʌzbəndmən/ n -men /mən/ old use or bibl a farmer

hus·band·ry /ˈhʌzbəndri/ n [U] fml or tech farming: *animal husbandry*

hush¹ /hʌʃ/ v [often imperative; T] to (cause to) be silent and/or calm —compare SHUSH
   hush sthg. **↔ up** phr v [T] to keep (something that should be publicly known) secret: *The President tried to hush up the fact that his adviser had lied.* —**hush-up** /ˈ· ·/ n [S]

hush² n [S;U] (a) silence, esp. a peaceful one: *A hush fell over*/*on the room.* | *Can we have a bit of hush, please!*

hush-a-bye ba·by /ˌ·· · · ˈ··/ (the first words of) an old British song sung by adults to put babies to sleep

hush-hush /ˌ·· ˈ·‖ˈ·· ·/ adj infml (of plans, arrangements, etc.) hidden, or to be hidden, from other people's knowledge; secret

hush mon·ey /ˈ· ˌ··/ n [U] infml money paid secretly to prevent some shameful fact from being known publicly — compare BLACKMAIL

Hush Pup·pies /ˈ· ˌ··/ n [P] tdmk a kind of shoe made from soft leather (SUEDE) and said to be very comfortable

hush pup·py /ˈ· ˌ··/ n AmE a small fried cake of MAIZE flour which is typical of the Southern US

husk /hʌsk/ n **1** the dry outer covering of some fruits and seeds: *Brown bread contains the husk of wheat.* **2** the useless outside part of something

hus·ky¹ /ˈhʌski/ adj **1** (of a person or voice) difficult to hear and breathy, as if the throat were dry —compare HOARSE **2** infml (of a man) big and strong —**kily** adv —**kiness** n [U]

husky² n a rather large working dog with thick hair that lives in northern Canada, Alaska, and eastern Siberia, and is used by ESKIMOs to pull SLEDGEs over the snow

hus·sar /hʊˈzɑːʳ/ n a soldier in that part of the British CAVALRY (=horse soldiers) which carries light weapons

Hus·sein /hʊˌseɪn/, **King** (1935–) the king of Jordan from 1952. He is often seen as a calming force in Middle Eastern politics.

Hus·sein, Sad·dam /sæˈdæm/ (1937–) the president of Iraq and leader of the socialist Ba'ath party. Under his rule, Iraq was involved in a long war with Iran and attempted to take over Kuwait. In the war that followed (the Gulf War), United Nations forces from a number of countries, including Britain and the US, forced Iraq to leave Kuwait.

hus·sy /ˈhʌsi, ˈhʌzi/ n old-fash a girl or woman who is impolite or sexually improper: *You* **brazen/shameless hussy!**

hus·tings /ˈhʌstɪŋz/ n [the+P] BrE the process of making speeches, attempting to win votes, etc., which goes on before an election: *All politicians are out* **on the hustings** *in the run-up to the election.*

hus·tle¹ /ˈhʌsəl/ v **1** [I;T] to (cause to) move fast: *She hustled the children off to school and started working.* **2** [T (into)] infml, esp. AmE to persuade by forceful, esp. deceitful activity: *We didn't want them, but he hustled us into buying them.* **3** [I] infml, esp. AmE to work as a PROSTITUTE

hustle² n [U] hurried activity (esp. in the phrase **hustle and bustle**)

hus·tler /ˈhʌslər/ n **1** infml an active busy person, esp. one who tries to persuade people to buy things, etc. **2** sl, esp. AmE a male PROSTITUTE **3** AmE sl a swindler (SWINDLE)

Hus·ton /ˈhjuːstən/, **John** (1906–87) an American filmmaker who is known for *The Treasure of the Sierra Madre, The African Queen*, and many others

hut /hʌt/ n a small simply-made building, usu. for living or working in: *They lived in a mud hut.* | *a wooden hut* —compare SHED¹

hutch /hʌtʃ/ n **1** a small box or cage with one side made of wire, esp. one for keeping rabbits in **2** AmE for WELSH DRESSER

Hux·ley /ˈhʌksli/, **Al·dous** /ˈɔːldəs/ (1894–1963) a British writer whose most famous book, *Brave New World*, is about a society of the future which appears to be controlled by kindly means but which offers people little freedom

hy·a·cinth /ˈhaɪəsɪnθ/ n a plant with a head of bell-shaped flowers and a sweet smell, which grows from a BULB below the ground and opens in spring

hy·ae·na /haɪˈiːnə/ n a HYENA

hy·brid /ˈhaɪbrɪd/ n **1** a living thing produced from parents of different breeds: *The hybrid from a donkey and a horse is called a mule.* **2** a machine that contains parts of different machines

Hyde /haɪd/, **Mr** see JEKYLL AND HYDE

Hyde Park /ˌ· ˈ·◂/ **1** a large London park where people go to walk or to relax –see also SPEAKER'S CORNER and see colour map on page 817 **2** a large neighbourhood on the S side of Chicago, where the University of Chicago is based

Hyde Park Cor·ner /ˌ· · ˈ··/ a busy meeting place of several roads at the SE corner of Hyde Park, London

hy·dra /ˈhaɪdrə/ n **1** (in ancient Greek stories) a snake with many heads which grew again when they were cut off **2** an evil thing which is difficult to destroy

hy·dran·gea /haɪˈdreɪndʒə/ n a plant which grows as a bush with its brightly-coloured flowers growing in large round groups

hy·drant /ˈhaɪdrənt/ n a water pipe in the street from which one may take water from the public supply, esp. for putting out a fire

hy·drate /ˈhaɪdreɪt/ n [C;U] tech (often in comb.) a combination of a chemical substance with water

hy·draul·ic /haɪˈdrɒlɪk, -ˈdrɔː-‖-ˈdrɔː-/ adj concerning or moved by the pressure of water or other liquids: *a hydraulic pump* | *hydraulic brakes* – ~ **ally** /kli/ adv

hy·draul·ics /haɪˈdrɒlɪks, -ˈdrɔː-‖-ˈdrɔː-/ n [U] the science which studies the use of water to produce power

hydro- see WORD FORMATION

hy·dro·car·bon /ˌhaɪdrəˈkɑːbən‖-ˈkɑːr-/ n a chemical compound of HYDROGEN and CARBON, such as petrol

hy·dro·chlor·ic ac·id /ˌhaɪdrəklɒrɪk ˈæsɪd‖-klɔː-/ n [U] an acid containing HYDROGEN and CHLORINE

hy·dro·e·lec·tric /ˌhaɪdrəʊ-ɪˈlektrɪk/ adj concerning or producing electricity by the power of falling water: *a*

hydroelectric power station | *a country with good hydroelectric resources* – ~ **ally** /kli/ adv

hy·dro·foil /ˈhaɪdrəfɔɪl/ n a large motorboat fitted with an apparatus which raises it out of the water when it moves at high speed —compare HOVERCRAFT

hy·dro·gen /ˈhaɪdrədʒən/ n [U] a gas that is a simple substance (ELEMENT), without colour or smell, is lighter than air, and burns very easily: *Water contains hydrogen and oxygen.* –see also HEAVY HYDROGEN

hy·dro·ge·nat·ed oil /ˌhaɪdrədʒəneɪtɪd ˈɔɪl ‖ haɪˌdrɑːdʒ-/ n [C;U] oil which has been chemically changed from a liquid to a solid, usu. for use in prepared foods. This changes it from an UNSATURATED FAT to a SATURATED FAT, which is considered much less healthy.

hydrogen bomb /ˈ··· ·/ also **H-bomb, fusion bomb**– n a very powerful NUCLEAR bomb using HEAVY HYDROGEN which explodes when the central parts of the atoms join together

hydrogen per·ox·ide /ˌ··· ·ˈ··/ n [U] tech for PEROXIDE

hy·dro·pho·bi·a /ˌhaɪdrəˈfəʊbiə/ n [U] **1** tech for RABIES **2** fear of water

hy·dro·plane /ˈhaɪdrəpleɪn/ v [I] AmE AQUAPLANE

hy·dro·pon·ics /ˌhaɪdrəˈpɒnɪks‖-ˈpɑː-/ n [U] the science of growing plants in water with chemical substances added, rather than in soil – **ic** adj

hy·dro·ther·a·py /ˌhaɪdrəʊˈθerəpi/ n [U] the treatment of illnesses by the use of water, esp. by bathing and exercising parts of the body in water containing special chemical substances. Hydrotherapy is a form of COMPLEMENTARY MEDICINE and is not used on its own to treat serious diseases.

hy·e·na , hyaena /haɪˈiːnə/ n an African and Asian animal, rather like a dog, which eats meat, often from animals already dead, and has a wild cry like a laugh

hy·giene /ˈhaɪdʒiːn/ n [U] **1** the study and practice of how to keep good health and prevent the spreading of disease, esp. by paying attention to cleanness: *public hygiene* (=keeping public places, esp. restaurants etc., clean) **2** habitual cleanness generally

hy·gien·ic /haɪˈdʒiːnɪk‖-ˈdʒe-, -ˈdʒiː-/ adj showing careful attention to cleanness, esp. so that disease will not be spread: *The food is processed in an up-to-date factory in very hygienic conditions.* –opposite **unhygienic** – ~ **ally** /kli/ adv

hy·gien·ist /ˈhaɪdʒiːnɪst, haɪˈdʒiːnɪst/ ‖ **dental hygienist** AmE– n a person who helps a DENTIST by looking after the cleanness and health of teeth

hy·men /ˈhaɪmən/ n a fold of skin partly closing the entrance (VAGINA) to the sex organs of a VIRGIN (=a woman who has never had sex)

hy·me·ne·al /ˌhaɪməˈniːəl◂/ adj poet of marriage

hymn¹ /hɪm/ n a song of praise, esp. to God, usu. one of the religious songs of the Christian church which all the people sing together during a service

hymn² v [T] poet to sing (praise)

hym·nal /ˈhɪmnəl/ also **hymn book** /ˈ· ·/– n a book containing written hymns

Hymns An·cient and Mod·ern /ˌ· ˌ··· ˈ··/ a standard book of hymns much used in the Church of England

hype¹ /haɪp/ v [T] infml, often derog to try to get a lot of public attention for, especially more than is deserved: *hyping their latest record with a lot of interviews*

hype² n [U] infml, often derog attempts to get a lot of public attention for things or people by saying loudly and often that they are very good, or better than they really are: *media hype*

hyped up /ˌ· ˈ·/ adj [F] infml very excited and anxious: *getting all hyped up about the exams*

hy·per /ˈhaɪpər/ adj infml, esp. AmE very excitable; MANIC

hyper- see WORD FORMATION

hy·per·ac·tive /ˌhaɪpərˈæktɪv/ adj too active; unable to rest or be quiet: *hyperactive children*

hy·per·bo·la /haɪˈpɜːbələ‖-ɜːr-/ n a curve whose two ends are always going away from each other and are never parallel

hy·per·bo·le /haɪˈpɜːbəli‖-ɜːr-/ n [C;U] (an example of) a way of describing something in order to make it sound bigger, smaller, better, worse, etc. than it really is: *To say "This chair weighs a ton" is an example of hyperbole.*

hy·per·bol·ic /ˌhaɪpə'bɒlɪk◂‖-pər'bɑː-/ *adj* **1** of or tending to use hyperbole **2** of or like a hyperbola — ~**ally** /kli/ *adj*

hy·per·crit·i·cal /ˌhaɪpə'krɪtɪkəl◂‖-pər-/ *adj* [(of)] too eager to see faults or things which are wrong, rather than noticing the good qualities; too CRITICAL — ~**ly** /kli/ *adv*

hy·per·in·fla·tion /ˌhaɪpərɪn'fleɪʃən/ *n* [U] economic INFLA-TION (=continuous rise in prices) at such a fast rate that people lose confidence in their economic system and find ways to avoid using it. Hyperinflation is usu. seen in poor countries, and often after wars.

hy·per·mar·ket /'haɪpəˌmɑːkɪt‖-pərˌmɑːr-/ *n BrE* a very large SUPERMARKET which is often built outside a town

hy·per·sen·si·tive /ˌhaɪpə'sensɪtɪv‖-pər-/ *adj* [(to, about)] unusually sensitive; having feelings which are too easily hurt: *hypersensitive to cold* | *hypersensitive about her appearance* —**tivity** /ˌhaɪpəsensɪ'tɪvɪti‖-pər-/ [U (to, about)]

hy·per·ten·sion /ˌhaɪpə'tenʃən‖-pər-/ *n med* an illness caused by having high blood pressure

hy·phen /'haɪfən/ *n* a short written or printed line (-) which can join words or SYLLABLES: *"Co-operate" can be written with a hyphen.* —compare DASH² (4)

hy·phen·ate /'haɪfəneɪt/ *v* [T] to join with a hyphen —**-ation** /ˌhaɪfə'neɪʃən/ *n* [U]

hyp·no·sis /hɪp'nəʊsɪs/ *n* [U] (the production of) a sleep-like state in which a person's mind and actions can be influenced by the person who produced the state: *Under hypnosis* (=while in a state of hypnosis) *the patient described her early childhood in great detail.* —**tic** /hɪp'nɒtɪk‖-'nɑː-/ *adj* —**tically** /kli/ *adv*

hyp·no·ther·a·pist /ˌhɪpnəʊ'θerəpɪst/ *n* a person who practises hypnotherapy. It is not necessary to be a doctor to be a hypnotherapist.

hyp·no·ther·a·py /ˌhɪpnəʊ'θerəpi/ *n* [U] the use of hypnosis to treat people who are mentally or physically ill or who have problems of behaviour. Hypnotherapy is a form of ALTERNATIVE MEDICINE and is not used on its own to treat serious diseases.

hyp·no·tis·m /'hɪpnətɪzəm/ *n* [U] the practice of hypnosis

hyp·no·tist /'hɪpnətɪst/ *n* a person who practises hypnotism, esp. in public for entertainment, and can produce HYPNOSIS

hyp·no·tize also **-tise** *BrE* /'hɪpnətaɪz/ *v* [T] to produce HYP-NOSIS in: (fig.) *hypnotized by her lovely singing*

hy·po /'haɪpəʊ/ *n* **hypos** *infml* a HYPODERMIC

hypo·al·ler·gen·ic /ˌhaɪpəʊælə'dʒenɪk‖-lər-/ *adj* (of COS-METICS or jewellery) not causing infection or allergies (ALLERGY)

hy·po·chon·dri·a /ˌhaɪpə'kɒndriə‖-'kɑːn-/ *n* [U] a state of unnecessary anxiety and worry about one's health

hy·po·chon·dri·ac /ˌhaɪpə'kɒndriæk‖-'kɑːn-/ *n* a person suffering from hypochondria —**hypochondriac** *adj*

hy·poc·ri·sy /hɪ'pɒkrɪsi‖-'pɑː-/ *n* [U] the act of pretending to believe, feel, or be something very different from, and usu. better than, what one actually believes, feels, or is; extreme insincerity: *The government's claim to be concerned about unemployment is sheer hypocrisy.*

hyp·o·crite /'hɪpəkrɪt/ *n* a person who says one thing and does another, usu. something worse; someone who practises hypocrisy: *He's such a hypocrite: he claims to be a socialist but he sends his children to an expensive private school.* —**critical** /ˌhɪpə'krɪtɪkəl◂/ *adj* —**critically** /kli/ *adv*

hy·po·der·mic¹ /ˌhaɪpə'dɜːmɪk◂‖-ɜːr-/ *n* an instrument with a hollow needle for putting drugs directly into the body through the skin; small SYRINGE for medical use

hypodermic² *adj* (of an instrument or substance put into the body) which is made to enter or injected (INJECT) beneath the skin: *a hypodermic needle/injection* — ~**ally** /kli/ *adv*

hy·pot·e·nuse /haɪ'pɒtɪnjuːz‖-'pɑːtənuːs, -nuːz/ *n* the longest side of a RIGHT-ANGLED TRIANGLE (=three-sided figure), which is opposite the RIGHT ANGLE (=angle of 90 degrees) —see picture at TRIANGLE

hy·po·ther·mi·a /ˌhaɪpəʊ'θɜːmiə‖-ɜːr-/ *n* [U] a serious medical condition in which the body temperature falls below the usual level, esp. as happens to old people during cold weather: *They died of hypothermia.*

hy·poth·e·sis /haɪ'pɒθɪsɪs‖-'pɑː-/ *n* **-ses** /siːz/ an idea which is suggested as a possible way of explaining facts, proving an argument, etc.: *If we accept this hypothesis, it may provide an explanation for the recent changes in the weather.* [+that] *He put forward the hypothesis that the bones belonged to an extinct type of reptile.*

hy·po·thet·i·cal /ˌhaɪpə'θetɪkəl◂/ *adj* based only on a suggestion that has not been proved or shown to be real; imaginary: *She asked me how I would deal with the problem if I were the president, but that is a purely hypothetical situation.* (=because I am not and never will be the president) — ~**ly** /kli/ *adv*

hys·ter·ec·to·my /ˌhɪstə'rektəmi/ *n* [C;U] the medical operation for removing the WOMB (=the female organ in which a baby develops before birth)

hys·te·ri·a /hɪ'stɪəriə‖-'stɪriə/ *n* [U] **1** a condition of nervous excitement in which the sufferer laughs and cries uncontrollably and/or shows strange changes in behaviour or physical state **2** wild uncontrolled excitement, esp. of a crowd of people: *News of the victory produced mass hysteria in the streets of the capital.* —**ric** /hɪ'sterɪk/ *n*

hys·ter·i·cal /hɪ'sterɪkəl/ *adj* **1** (of people) in a state of hysteria: *They became hysterical after the accident.* **2** (of feelings, words, etc.) expressed wildly, in an uncontrolled manner: *hysterical crying/laughter* | *a hysterical statement* (=made as a result of hysteria) **3** *infml* extremely funny: *You should go and see the film — it's absolutely hysterical.* — ~**ly** /kli/ *adv*

hys·ter·ics /hɪ'sterɪks/ *n* [P] an attack of hysteria: *He always has hysterics at the sight of blood.* | *The clown had the children* **in hysterics.** (=made them laugh uncontrollably)

Hz *written abbrev. for:* HERTZ

I

Icarus

I¹ /aɪ/ **I's, i's** or **Is, is** **1** the ninth letter of the English alphabet **2** the ROMAN NUMERAL representing the number one

I² *pron* (used as the subject of a sentence) the person speaking: *I hurt my hand.* | *I'm not late, am I?* | *I'm next, aren't I|(fml) am I not?* —see ME (USAGE)

I³ *AmE abbrev. for* INTERSTATE: *driving on the I70*

IA *written abbrev. for* IOWA

I·a·coc·ca /ˌaɪəˈkəʊkə/, **Lee** (1924–) an American businessman who greatly increased the profits made by the car company Chrysler at a time when the company had not been very successful. Iacocca also wrote a best-selling AUTOBIOGRAPHY in the early 1980s while he was still famous for his work with Chrysler.

I·a·go /iˈɑːgəʊ/ a character in William Shakespeare's play *Othello.* Iago ruins the life of his friend Othello by telling lies about Othello's wife. Someone who is **Iagoesque** deceives people who should be able to trust him.

i·amb /ˈaɪæm‖ˈaɪæm, ˈaɪæmb/ also **i·am·bus** /aɪˈæmbəs/— *n* **-s** /ˈaɪæmz/ *tech* a measure of poetry consisting of one weak (or short) beat followed by one strong (or long) beat, as in "alive" —compare TROCHEE – **~ ic** /aɪˈæmbɪk/ *adj, n* : *written in iambic lines|iambics*

iambic pen·tam·e·ter /ˌ·ˌ·· ·¹··/ *n* [U;C] a common measure in English poetry, each line consisting of five iambic FEET (=divisions of the line) —compare HEROIC COUPLET

IATA /aɪˈɑːtə/ *abbrev. for* INTERNATIONAL AIR TRANSPORT ASSOCIATION

IBA /ˌaɪ biː ˈeɪ/ *n* [*the*] Independent Broadcasting Authority; the organization representing those British television broadcasting companies which are paid for by advertisers. It will be replaced by the ITC in 1993.

I-beam /ˈaɪ biːm/ *n AmE* a kind of steel beam used in large buildings which, when looked at from an end, looks like a capital I

I·be·ri·a /aɪˈbɪəriə/ Spain and Portugal considered together – **-rian** *adj* : *the Iberian peninsula*

i·bex /ˈaɪbeks/ *n* **ibexes** *or* **ibex** a wild goat of the Alps and Pyrenees

ib·id /ˈɪbɪd/ also **ib·i·dem** /ˈɪbɪdem, ɪˈbaɪdem/— *adv Lat* in the same place, usu. in a (part of a) book already mentioned

i·bis /ˈaɪbɪs/ *n* **ibises** *or* **ibis** a large bird with a long curved beak, living in warm wet areas, which was considered SACRED in ancient Egypt

I·bi·za /ɪˈbiːθə, aɪ-/ a Spanish island SW of Majorca, where many European people go on holiday

IBM /ˌaɪ biː ˈem/ International Business Machines; a very large American-based international business computer company

IBM-com·pat·i·ble¹ /ˌ·····¹···/ *n* a computer which is very similar to the PERSONAL COMPUTERS made by IBM, and can be connected with these machines and can use the same DISKs and equipment as these machines

IBM-compatible² *adj* (of a computer, a piece of computer equipment, etc.) that can be used with a PERSONAL COMPUTER made by IBM: *Is your printer IBM-compatible?*

Ib·sen /ˈɪbsən/, **Hen·rik** /ˈhenrɪk/ (1826–1906) a Norwegian writer of plays known esp. for writing about social problems and criticizing social CONVENTIONs

IC /ˌaɪ ˈsiː/ *n,adj* INTEGRATED CIRCUIT: *IC technology*

ICA /ˌaɪ siː ˈeɪ/ [*the*] Institute of Contemporary Arts; a building in London where modern paintings, films, etc. are shown. The ICA is generally considered to be politically LEFT-WING and some of its EXHIBITIONs cause a lot of argument and discussion.

Ic·a·rus /ˈɪkərəs/ in CLASSICAL MYTHOLOGY, a Greek man who tried to fly using wings held together with WAX. The wax melted when he got too near the sun and he fell and died. —see also DAEDALUS

ICBM /ˌaɪ siː biː ˈem/ *n* intercontinental ballistic missile; a MISSILE that can be fired a very great distance

ICC /ˌaɪ siː ˈsiː/ *abbrev. for* INTERSTATE COMMERCE COMMISSION

ice¹ /aɪs/ *n* **1** [U] water which has frozen to a solid as a result of reaching a very low temperature: *ice on the lake in winter* | *Her hands were like ice|were as cold as ice.* | *The ice has melted.* **2** [C] *old-fash, esp. BrE* a serving of ice cream: *Two ices, please.* **3** [C] *also* **water ice** *BrE* ‖ **sherbet** *AmE*– a type or a serving of a cold sweet food like ice cream, but made with fruit juice instead of milk or cream **4** [U] *AmE old fash sl* jewellery, esp. diamonds **5 keep/put something on ice** take no immediate action about something: *Let's keep that suggestion on ice for now.* —see also ICY, BLACK ICE, DRY ICE, **break the ice** (BREAK¹ (25)), **cut no ice** (CUT¹ (25)), **skating on thin ice** (SKATE²)

ice

icc cream   ice-cream soda

ice cube

ice² *v* [T] **1** to make very cold by using ice: *iced drinks* **2** *also* **frost** *AmE* to cover (a cake) with ICING (=a mixture of fine powdery sugar and liquid) **ice over/up** *phr v* [I;T (=**ice** sthg. ↔ **over/up**) *usu. pass.*] to (cause to) become covered with ice: *The lake iced over during the night.* | *It's too dangerous to drive – the roads are all iced up.*

ice age /ˈ· ·/ *n* (*often cap.*) any of several periods when ice covered many northern countries

ice axe /ˈ· ·/ *n* an ICE PICK

ice-ball /ˈaɪsbɔːl/ *n* [U] a team game played on ice in which the ball is passed by throwing with the aim of getting GOALs

ice·berg /ˈaɪsbɜːg‖-bɜːrg/ *n* a very large piece of ice floating in the sea, most of which is below the surface: *The ship struck an iceberg and sank.* —see also **the tip of the iceberg** (TIP¹ (4))

iceberg

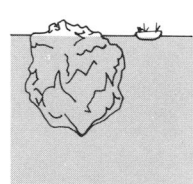

iceberg let·tuce /ˌ·· ¹··/ *n* [C;U] a round LETTUCE whose leaves are fairly firm when fresh

ice-box /ˈaɪsbɒks‖-bɑːks/ *n* **1** a box where food is kept cool with blocks of ice **2** *AmE for* FRIDGE

ice-break·er /ˈaɪsˌbreɪkəʳ/ *n* **1** a ship which cuts a passage through floating ice **2** *AmE* something which makes a situation easier or less tense: *"We've got to have a good icebreaker to help everyone get to know each other."*

ice buck·et /ˈ· ˌ··/ *n* **1** a container with pieces of ice in it, used for keeping wine cool, as in a restaurant: *The girl was very impressed when the waiter appeared with a bottle of champagne and an ice bucket.* **2** a container with pieces of ice in it for adding to drinks such as WHISKY or GIN, in a BAR¹ (3)

ice cap /ˈ· ·/ also **ice sheet**— *n* a lasting covering of ice, such as that on the North and South Poles

ice-cold /ˌ· ˈ·◂/ *adj* extremely cold; as cold as ice: *ice-cold drinks|hands*

ice cream /ˌ· ˈ·◂‖ˈ· ·/ *n* [C;U] (a type or a serving of) a soft sweet mixture which is frozen and eaten cold, typically containing milk products and often eggs: *Two ice creams, please.* | *chocolate ice cream* | *an ice-cream cone* —see picture at ICE

ice-cream so·da /ˌ· · ˈ··/ also **soda**— *n* a dish made from ice cream, sweet SYRUP, and SODA WATER, usu. served in a tall glass —see picture at ICE

ice cube /ˈ· ·/ *n* a cube of ice, often used to cool alcoholic or soft drinks —see picture at ICE

iced cof·fee /ˌ· ˈ··/ *n* [C;U] (a glass of) cold coffee with ice and usu. milk, popular in the US as a summer drink

iced tea /ˌ· ˈ·/ *n* [C;U] (a glass of) cold tea, often served with LEMON or sugar in the US and Canada, and drunk esp. in the summer

ice floe /ˈ· ·/ *n* a sheet of ice floating on the sea

ice hock·ey /ˈ· ˌ··/ also **hockey** esp. AmE — *n* [U] a team game like HOCKEY played on ice. Ice hockey is very popular in Canada and is the national sport. —compare FIELD HOCKEY

Ice·land /ˈaɪslənd/ an island country in the Atlantic ocean just south of the Arctic Circle; capital Reykjavik; population 252,000 (1989) — ~**er** *n*

Ice·lan·dic /aɪsˈlændɪk/ *adj* of Iceland, its people, or their language

ice lol·ly /ˈ· ˌ··/ BrE ‖ **Popsicle** AmE tdmk— *n* a piece of sweet-tasting ice on a stick. Ice lollies often taste of fruit

ice·man /ˈaɪs-mæn/ *n* **-men** /men/ AmE (esp. in former times) a man who delivers ice to the home for use in an ICEBOX

I·ce·ni /aɪˈsiːnaɪ, -ni/ [the+P] an ancient British tribe of E England who fought against the Romans under the command of their queen, Boudicca

ice pack /ˈ· ·/ *n* a bag containing ice, used to make parts of the body cool esp. where there is a pain or INJURY — see also PACK ICE

ice pick /ˈ· ·/ also **ice axe**— *n* a tool for breaking ice —see picture at AXE

ice rink /ˈ· ·/ *n* a specially prepared surface of ice for skating (SKATE)

ice sheet /ˈ· ·/ *n* an ICE CAP

ice-skating

ice-skate /ˈ· ·/ *v* [I] to SKATE on ice —see colour picture on page 1212 —**ice-skater** *n* —**ice-skating** *n* [U] : *Ice-skating is my favourite winter sport.*

ice skate /ˈ· ·/ *n* a SKATE that is worn on the feet for moving over ice —compare ROLLER SKATE; see PAIR¹ (USAGE)

ice wa·ter /ˈ· ˌ··/ *n* [U] water made very cold and used esp. for drinking

Ich·a·bod Crane /ˌɪkəbɒd ˈkreɪn ‖ -bɑːd-/ the main character in the story *The Legend of Sleepy Hollow* by Washington Irving. In the story, he is frightened by what he thinks is a headless man riding a horse. —see colour picture on page 620

I Ching /ˌaɪ ˈtʃɪŋ, ˌiː ˈdʒɪŋ/ [the] an ancient Chinese book, also called the Book of Changes, which some people believe helps you to understand things which are happening in your daily life and tells you what is going to happen in the future

ich·neu·mon fly /ɪkˈnjuːmən flaɪ‖-ˈnuː-/ *n* an insect which lays eggs inside the LARVA (=the young) of another insect

ICI /ˌaɪ aɪ ˈsiː/ Imperial Chemical Industries; a large international company which makes and sells drugs, paints, FERTILIZERS etc. all over the world and does a lot of RESEARCH. People often mention ICI when they want to give an example of a very large company.

i·ci·cle /ˈaɪsɪkəl/ *n* a pointed stick of ice formed when water freezes as it runs down or falls in small drops: *icicles hanging from the roof*

ic·ing /ˈaɪsɪŋ/ esp. BrE ‖ also **frosting** AmE— *n* [U] a mixture of fine powdery sugar with liquid, used to cover cakes: *chocolate|lemon icing* | (fig.) *All those nice extras they're offering are just* **the icing on the cake***: is the plan itself any good?*

icing sug·ar /ˈ·· ˌ··/ also **powdered sugar** AmE— *n* [U] the very fine powdery sugar used to make icing

ick·y /ˈɪki/ *adj infml* very unpleasant, but in a usu. harmless way: *What icky weather for a picnic!* | *These dumplings look really icky, I hope they taste good.* —**ickiness** *n* [U]

i·con, ikon /ˈaɪkɒn‖-kɑːn/ *n* **1** a picture or figure of a holy person, used in worship by the Eastern branches of Christianity **2** a famous person, admired by many people, who is believed to represent something important: *Marilyn Monroe is an icon of popular culture.* **3** a small sign shown on a computer SCREEN which, when you point to it with a MOUSE (3), makes the computer perform a particular operation

i·con·o·clast /aɪˈkɒnəklæst‖-ˈkɑː-/ *n* a person who attacks established beliefs or customs — ~**ic** /aɪˌkɒnəˈklæstɪk◂‖ -ˌkɑː-/ *adj*

ICU /ˌaɪ aɪ ˈsiː ˈjuː/ *n* AmE med intensive care unit; a place in a hospital for people who are very sick: *After his brain surgery he was in an ICU for two days.*

ic·y /ˈaɪsi/ *adj* **1** extremely cold: *My hands are icy.* | *an icy wind from the north* | (fig.) *She gave me an icy look.* **2** covered with ice: *Icy roads are dangerous.* —**icily** *adv* — **iciness** *n* [U]

I'd /aɪd/ *short for:* **1** I had: *I'd gone.* | (esp. BrE) *I'd no time left.* **2** I would: *I decided I'd go.*

id /ɪd/ *n* (in Freudian PSYCHOLOGY) the one of the three parts of the mind that is completely unconscious, but has needs and desires —compare EGO (2), SUPEREGO

I·da·ho /ˈaɪdəhəʊ/ *written abbrev.* **ID**— a STATE in the NW of the US, known for its farming, esp. of potatoes —see colour map on pages 1374–5

ID card /ˌaɪ ˈdiː kɑːd‖-kɑːrd/ *n* an IDENTITY CARD

i·dea /aɪˈdɪə/ *n* **1** [C] a plan, thought, or suggestion for a possible course of action: *What a good idea!* | *Somebody had the bright idea of recording the meeting.* | *a meeting to discuss new ideas* | *What gave you the idea for the book?* [+to-v|that] *It was Mary's idea to hold|that we should hold the party outside.* **2** [C;U] (of) a picture in the mind; CONCEPTION: *I've got a fairly good idea of what they want.* | *Have you any idea of what I'm trying to explain?* | The **very idea** of *going sailing* (=just thinking about it) *makes me feel seasick.* | *His idea of a good night out is getting drunk and fighting with his friends.* **3** [C;U] (of) knowledge or understanding: *The report will give you an idea|give you some idea of the problems involved.* [+wh-] *I haven't the slightest idea who she is.* (=I don't know at all) | **You have no idea** *how worried I was!* (=I was extremely worried) | *It was so hot — you've no idea!* **4** [C] a guess; feeling that something is probable: *I don't know where she is, but I've got a pretty good idea.* [+(that)] *I've an idea that she likes him better than anyone else.* | *You thought I was the boss? Whatever gave you that idea?* **5** [C] an opinion or belief: *She's got some pretty strange political ideas.* [+that] *This discovery disproved the idea that the world was flat.* **6** [the (of)] a plan or intention: *She went shopping with the idea of buying some shoes, and bought some boots instead.* | *I thought the idea was to go for a drink after work.* | *What was the idea of telling him that?* (usu. used to suggest that something was a bad idea) **7 get the idea (that)** to come to believe (often mistakenly): *Don't get the wrong idea: I really like her.* **8 put ideas in someone's head** to make someone hope for things they cannot have **9 The idea!/What an idea!** (an expression of surprise at a strange thought or suggestion, or of disagreement with a silly thought or suggestion)

i·deal¹ /ˌaɪˈdɪəl◂/ *adj* **1** perfect in every way: *an ideal marriage* | *It's an ideal place for a holiday.* **2** [(for)] very suitable: *This picture book is ideal for young children.* **3** expressing possible perfection which is unlikely to exist in the real world: *the ideal system of government* —see also IDEALLY

ideal² *n* **1** [*often pl.*] (a belief in) high principles or perfect standards: *a woman with/of high ideals* | *They share our democratic ideals.* **2** [(of)] a perfect example: *That's my ideal of what a house should be like.*

Ideal Home /ˌ·· ˈ·/ a British magazine containing photographs of, and articles about, beautiful homes, with ideas on how to make one's own home more attractive

Ideal Home Ex·hi·bi·tion /ˌ·· ˈ· ··ˌ··/ [*the*] an EXHIBITION of furniture and objects for the house, held every year in London

i·deal·is·m /aɪˈdɪəlɪzəm/ *n* [U] **1** the quality or habit of living according to one's ideals, or the belief that such a way of life is possible: *youthful idealism* —compare MATERIALISM **2** (in art) the principle of showing the world in a perfect form, although such perfection may not exist —compare REALISM (2), NATURALISM (1)

i·deal·ist /aɪˈdɪəlɪ̖st/ *n sometimes derog* a person who tries to live according to high principles or perfect standards, often in a way that is impractical or shows a lack of understanding of the real world: *a youthful idealist* — ~**ic** /ˌaɪdɪəˈlɪstɪk◂/ *adj* — ~**ically** /kli/ *adv*

i·deal·ize also **-ise** *BrE* /aɪˈdɪəlaɪz/ *v* [T] to imagine or represent as perfect or as better than reality: *He tends to idealize the time he spent in the army.* | *Her books give a rather idealized picture of life in 19th-century England.* | *The theory works only when applied to an idealized model of language.* —**ization** /aɪˌdɪəlaɪˈzeɪʃən‖-lə-/ *n* [C;U]

i·deal·ly /aɪˈdɪəli/ *adv* **1** in an ideal way: *ideally beautiful* | *ideally suited* **2** in an ideal situation; if conditions were perfect: *Ideally, we should have twice as much office space as we have now.*

id·em /ˈɪdem, ˈaɪdem/ *pron Lat* (of a book, writer, etc., already mentioned) the same

i·den·ti·cal /aɪˈdentɪkəl/ *adj* **1** [(to, with)] exactly alike: *two sisters with identical voices* | *Your voice is identical to hers.* **2** the same: *This is the identical hotel we stayed at last year.* —**cally** /kli/ *adv*

identical twin /·ˌ··· ˈ·/ *n* [*usu. pl.*] either of a pair of children or animals born from one egg of the mother and usu. looking extremely alike

i·den·ti·fi·ca·tion /aɪˌdentɪ̖fɪ̖ˈkeɪʃən/ *n* [U] **1** the act of identifying or fact of being identified: *The body had been badly burned so identification was difficult.* **2** something (such as an official paper) which is proof or a sign of identity: *Let me see your identification.* | *His only means of identification was his passport.* | *baggage identification tags* | *vehicle identification numbers* **3** [(with)] the feeling that one shares the ideas, feelings, problems, etc. of another person, esp. a character in a story: *his identification with the hero of the book*

identification pa·rade /·ˌ···ˈ·· ·ˌ·/ *BrE* ‖ **line-up** *AmE* — *n* a process by which a person who saw a crime take place is asked by the police to look at a group of people and say which one took part in the crime

i·den·ti·fy /aɪˈdentɪ̖faɪ/ *v* [T] **1** [(as)] to prove or show the identity of: *She was asked to identify the criminal.* | *She identified herself to the police as the driver of the vehicle.* | *The dead man has been identified as Mr James Gould.* **2** to discover or recognize: *They have now identified the main cause of the problem.*

identify with *phr v* [T] **1** (**identify with** sbdy./sthg.) to feel one shares the (ideas, feelings, problems, etc.) of (someone, esp. a person in a story): *Reading this book, we can identify with the main character/with the main character's struggle.* **2** (**identify** sbdy. **with** sthg.) to cause or consider (someone) to be connected with: *He is too closely identified with the previous administration to be given a job in this one.*

i·den·ti·kit /aɪˈdentɪkɪt/ *BrE* ‖ **composite** *AmE* — *n* a collection of photographs or DRAWINGs of parts of faces which can be fitted together to produce pictures of different faces, so that witnesses to a crime may choose the face that looks most like that of the criminal: *Police have issued an identikit picture of the killer.* | (fig.) *identikit pop*

stars who all look and sound alike —compare CLONE (2), PHOTOFIT

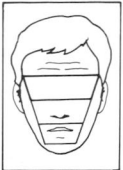

identikit

i·den·ti·ty /aɪˈdentɪ̖ti/ *n* **1** [C;U] who or what a particular person or thing is: *The identity of the murdered woman has not yet been established.* | *She experienced a loss of identity/an identity crisis after giving up her career to get married.* (=felt as if she lacked self-confidence and had no particular purpose in life) **2** [U] sameness; exact likeness

identity card /·ˈ··· ·/ also **ID card**— *n* a card with one's name, photograph, signature, etc., which proves one's identity

id·e·o·gram /ˈɪdiəgræm/ also **id·e·o·graph** /-grɑːf‖-græf/— *n* a written sign (as in Chinese writing) which represents an idea or thing rather than the sound of a word

i·de·o·logue /ˈaɪdiəˌlɒg‖-ˌlɔːg, -ˌlɑːg/ *n usu. derog* a person who is strongly influenced by a particular ideology and tries to follow it very closely

i·de·ol·o·gy /ˌaɪdiˈɒlədʒi‖-ˈɑːlə-/ *n* [C;U] *sometimes derog* a set of ideas, esp. one on which a political or economic system is based: *Marxist ideology* | *the free market ideology of the extreme right* —**ogical** /ˌaɪdiəˈlɒdʒɪkəl◂‖-ˈlɑː-/ *adj* —**ogically** /kli/ *adv* : *Ideologically, they have many differences.* | *As a socialist, I don't feel that buying shares in companies sold off by the government is ideologically sound.*

ides /aɪdz/ *n* [P] *lit* (in the ancient Roman CALENDAR) a date or period of time around the middle of the month

Ides of March /ˌ· · ˈ·/ [*the*+P] March 15th, famous for being the day on which Julius Caesar was killed by a group of his former friends because they thought he had too much power. Caesar is supposed to have been warned by a FORTUNE-TELLER to "Beware the Ides of March."

id·i·o·cy /ˈɪdiəsi/ *n* **1** [U] the state of being an idiot **2** [C] a stupid action

id·i·o·lect /ˈɪdiəlekt/ *n tech* a particular person's use of language

id·i·om /ˈɪdiəm/ *n* **1** a phrase which means something different from the meanings of the separate words from which it is formed: *To "kick the bucket" is an English idiom meaning "to die"* **2** the way of expression typical of a person or a group in their use of language: *the idiom of the young* | (fig.) *the new and exciting idiom of modern popular music*

id·i·o·mat·ic /ˌɪdiəˈmætɪk◂/ *adj* **1** of or containing an idiom: *To "kick the bucket" is an idiomatic expression.* **2** (of a word, way of speaking, etc.) typical of the natural speech of a person speaking in their first language: *a Frenchman who speaks idiomatic English* — ~**ally** /kli/ *adv*

id·i·o·syn·cra·sy /ˌɪdiəˈsɪŋkrəsi/ *n* a strange or unusual habit or way of behaving that a particular person has: *Keeping pet snakes is an idiosyncrasy of his.* —**cratic** /ˌɪdiəsɪnˈkrætɪk◂/ *adj*

id·i·ot /ˈɪdiət/ *n* **1** a foolish person: *What did you do that for, you idiot!* **2** *old use or tech* a person of very weak mind, usu. from birth —compare IMBECILE (2) — ~**ic** /ˌɪdiˈɒtɪk◂‖-ˈɑːt-/ *adj* — ~**ically** /kli/ *adv*

idiot light /ˈ··· ·/ *n AmE* a light on the DASHBOARD of a car which goes on when something is wrong with the car: *The idiot light flashed on to show that the engine was about to overheat.*

i·dle¹ /ˈaɪdl/ *adj* **1** not working or operating productively: *Owing to the electricity strike, a lot of factory workers were left idle.* | *We can't afford to have all this expensive machinery lying idle.* | *the idle rich* (=rich people who do not work for a living) **2** lazy; wasting time —see also BONE-IDLE **3** not based on fact or good reason: *idle*

rumour/gossip/talk | *His words were just idle threats: he can't hurt us.* **4** [A] having no particular purpose: *I don't know why I asked – just idle curiosity.* **–idly** adv **– ~ness** n [U]

idle² v [I] **1** to waste time doing nothing **2** (of an engine) to run slowly while disconnected from the TRANSMISSION: *Put the car out of gear and let the engine idle.* **–idler** n **idle away** phr v [T] to waste (time) doing nothing: *We idled away the hours.*

i·dol /ˈaɪdl/ n **1** an image worshipped as a god **2** someone or something admired or loved too much: *The football player was the idol of the younger boys.*

i·dol·a·ter /aɪˈdɒlətəʳ‖-ˈdɑː-/ **i·dol·a·tress** /-trɪs/ fem. **–** n a worshipper of idols

i·dol·a·trous /aɪˈdɒlətrəs‖-ˈdɑː-/ adj **1** worshipping idols **2** like IDOLATRY (2): *idolatrous love of money* **– ~ly** adv

i·dol·a·try /aɪˈdɒlətri‖-ˈdɑː-/ n [U] **1** the worship of idols **2** too great admiration of someone or something

i·dol·ize also **-ise** BrE /ˈaɪdəl-aɪz/ v [T] to treat as an idol: *He idolizes his father.* (=he loves or admires him too much and thinks he is perfect)

id·yll, idyl /ˈɪdɪl‖ˈaɪdl/ n a simple happy period of life, often in the country, or a scene (as if) from such a time: *an idyll of two young lovers* **– ~ic** /ɪˈdɪlɪk‖aɪ-/ adj : *an idyllic scene* **– ~ically** /kli/ adv : *idyllically happy*

i.e. /ˌaɪ ˈiː/ abbrev. id est; that is; by which is meant: *The cinema is only open to adults, i.e. people over 18.* **–see** NAMELY (USAGE)

if¹ /ɪf/ conj **1** (not usu. followed by the future tense) **a** on condition that: *We'll go if the weather stays fine, but if it rains we'll stay at home.* | *If you promise not to tell anyone else, I'll tell you how much I paid for it.* **b** supposing that: *If she phones/(fml) If she should phone, tell her I'm out.* | *Just ask John if you need any help/(fml) should you need any help.* | *If he told you that, he was lying.* | *Get out of here at once. If not, I'll phone the police.* | *If John was/were here, he would know what to do.* | *If you'd listened to me/(fml) Had you listened to me, you wouldn't be in such trouble now.* **c** in any situation in which; whenever: *If you pour oil on water, it floats.* | *If I go to bed late, I find it hard to get up in the morning.* **–see** UNLESS (USAGE) **2** accepting that; although: **a** (often with **even**) *We'll go even if it rains.* (=We'll go, whether it rains or not.) | *If she's poor, at least she's honest.* **b** (joining nouns, adjectives, or adverbs): *a pleasant if noisy child* | *It was a nice meal, if a little expensive.* | *Too sweet? – I thought it was a little dry, if anything.* **3** (in reported questions, or after verbs like **know, remember,** or **wonder**) whether: *Do you know if/whether she's coming?* | *I wonder if she isn't mistaken?* (=I think she is.) | *I'll see if he wants to talk to you.* | *Could you ask her if she'll be coming to the meeting?* | *I couldn't remember if you took sugar in your coffee or not.* **4** (used like **that** after words expressing surprise, sorrow, or pleasure): *I'm sorry if she's annoyed.* | *I don't care if she is ten years older than me – I love her.* | *Do you mind if I smoke?* (=May I smoke?) **5 if I were you** (used when giving advice): *If I were you I'd leave at once.* **6 it isn't/it's not as if** (often expressing annoyance) it is not true that: *I don't know why he's so mean – it isn't as if he hasn't got any money!* (=he has plenty of money) **–see also if you like** (LIKE¹ (9))

▷ USAGE You can use **if** with *will/won't* when the meaning is "be willing": **If** *you will just sign here please* (=a polite request) *I'll give you the money.* | **If** *you won't help me* (=if you refuse) *I'll shoot myself.* Compare **If** *he signs the cheque I'll be really happy.* **–see also** WHETHER (USAGE), **even if** (AS²), **if only** (EVEN²), **if only** (ONLY²)◁

if² n **ifs and buts** BrE ‖ **ifs, ands, or buts** AmE reasons given for delay: *I don't want any ifs and buts – just make sure the goods are delivered tomorrow!*

if·fy /ˈɪfi/ adj infml full of uncertainty: *Until the contract is signed, we're in a rather iffy situation.*

ig·loo /ˈɪgluː/ n **-loos** a house made of hard icy blocks of snow, esp. as built by the Inuit **–see picture at** ESKIMO

ig·ne·ous /ˈɪgniəs/ adj tech (of rocks) formed from LAVA

ig·nis fat·u·us /ˌɪgnɪs ˈfætʃuəs/ ‖ also **will-o'-the wisp** n **ignes fatui** /ˌɪgniːz ˈfætʃuiː/ [usu. sing.] Lat a moving light seen over wet ground because of the burning of waste gases

ig·nite /ɪgˈnaɪt/ v [I;T] fml to (cause) to start to burn

ig·ni·tion /ɪgˈnɪʃən/ n [U] **1** the act or action of igniting **2** the means or apparatus for starting an engine (such as a car engine) by using electricity **–see picture at** CAR

ig·no·ble /ɪgˈnəʊbəl/ adj esp. lit dishonourable; which one should be ashamed of **––bly** adv

ig·no·min·i·ous /ˌɪgnəˈmɪniəs◂/ adj bringing or deserving strong (esp. public) disapproval; damaging to one's pride: *an ignominious defeat* | *ignominious behaviour* **– ~ly** adv

ig·no·mi·ny /ˈɪgnəmɪni/ n **1** [U] a state of shame or dishonour **2** [C] an act of shameful behaviour

ig·no·ra·mus /ˌɪgnəˈreɪməs/ n an ignorant person

ig·no·rance /ˈɪgnərəns/ n [U (**of**)] **1** lack of knowledge, information, or consciousness, esp. of something one ought to know about: *Ignorance of the law is no excuse.* | *The workers were kept in complete ignorance of the company's financial situation.* | *It shows appalling ignorance not to know who the present prime minister is.* **2 ignorance is bliss** saying if one does not know something, one cannot worry about it: *"Have you seen the new plans yet?" "No, ignorance is bliss!"*

ig·no·rant /ˈɪgnərənt/ adj **1** [(**of**)] lacking knowledge, education, or consciousness, esp. of something one ought to know about: *ignorant of even the simplest facts* | *I'm afraid I'm rather ignorant about computers.* **–see** IGNORE (USAGE) **2** infml rude or impolite, esp. because of lack of social training **3** caused by or showing ignorance: *ignorant ideas*

ig·nore /ɪgˈnɔːʳ/ v [T] to take no notice of; refuse to pay attention to: *My advice was completely ignored.* | *The government would be unwise to ignore the growing dissatisfaction with its economic policies.*

▷ USAGE Compare **ignore** and **be ignorant of:** *He was driving very fast because he* **was ignorant of** *the fact that* (=didn't know) *there was a speed limit.* | *He* **ignored** *the speed limit* (=he knew about it, but paid no attention to it) *and drove very fast.*◁

i·gua·na /ɪˈgwɑːnə/ n **-nas** or **-na** a large LIZARD of tropical America

IKBS /ˌaɪ keɪ biː ˈes/ n intelligent knowledge-based system; a type of computer system that uses ARTIFICIAL INTELLIGENCE

i·kon /ˈaɪkɒn‖-kɑːn/ n an ICON

il- see WORD FORMATION

IL written abbrev. for ILLINOIS

ILEA /ˈɪliə, ˌaɪ el iː ˈeɪ◂/ [the] Inner London Education Authority; an organization which used to be responsible for schools and colleges in London and which was closed down in 1990

i·lex /ˈaɪleks/ n **1** an OAK tree with EVERGREEN leaves **2** tech any of a family of trees and bushes including HOLLY

Il·i·ad /ˈɪliæd, -əd/, **The** an ancient Greek poem by Homer about the Trojan War **–compare** ODYSSEY

Il·i·um /ˈɪliəm/ see TROY

ilk /ɪlk/ n [S] kind, type, etc. (usu. in the phrase **of that ilk**)

ill¹ /ɪl/ adj **worse** /wɜːs‖wɜːrs/, **worst** /wɜːst‖wɜːrst/ **1** [F] not in good health; not well: *She's ill, so she can't come.* | *ill with worry* | *She suddenly* **fell ill**/*was suddenly* **taken ill.** (=became ill) | *mentally ill*

▷ USAGE In the US, **ill** and **sick** are used in almost the same way: *He is very sick.* | *He is very ill.* In Britain, the phrase *I feel sick* means that one's stomach is upset and one feels like vomiting (VOMIT¹), but in the US it may mean that one is not well, has a sore throat, etc. In the US, **ill** is somewhat more formal than **sick.** **–see also** SICK (USAGE)◁

2 [F] BrE hurt; suffering in the stated way from the effects of INJURY: *A week after the riots, two policemen were still seriously/critically ill in hospital with gunshot wounds.* **3** [A] bad; harmful: *ill luck* | *an ill omen* | *There's a lot of* **ill feeling** (=jealousy, anger, etc.) *about her being promoted.*

ill² adv (often in comb.) **1** badly, cruelly, or unpleasantly: *The child was* **ill-treated.** **2** not well; not enough; hardly: *ill-suited to the job* | *ill-informed* (=not having the right information or enough information) | *I* **can ill afford** *the time to speak to you.* | *"I see one-third of a nation ill-housed, ill-clad, ill-nourished."* (F. D. Roosevelt) **3**

unfavourably: *to think/speak ill of someone* | (*fml*) *It* ill becomes you *to say such unkind things.*

ill³ *n* [*often pl.*] a bad thing, esp. a problem or cause of worry: *the social ills of unemployment and poverty*

I'll /aɪl/ *short for:* I will or I shall

ill-ad·vised /ˌ· ·'··◂/ *adj* unwise: *They were ill-advised to buy that old house.*

ill-as·sort·ed /ˌ· ·'··◂/ *adj* that do not go well together; not well matched: *an ill-assorted pair*

ill at ease /ˌ· · '·/ *adj* [F] nervous and uncomfortable, esp. because of lack of social skill: *He's always ill at ease at parties.*

ill-bred /ˌ· '·◂/ *adj* badly behaved or rude, probably as the result of being badly brought up as a child: *an ill-bred remark* | *ill-bred children* —opposite well-bred

ill-dis·posed /ˌ· ·'··◂/ *adj* unfriendly; unsympathetic: *She was ill-disposed towards the idea of their marriage.*

il·le·gal /ɪˈliːɡəl/ *adj* against the law: *It's illegal to park your car here.* | *an illegal immigrant* (=someone who has entered a country illegally) | *It's illegal for people under 17 to drive a car in Britain.* —opposite legal; compare ILLEGITIMATE — ~ ly *adv*

illegal a·li·en /·ˌ·· '··◂/ *n AmE* an illegal immigrant

illegal im·mi·grant /·ˌ·· '··◂/ *n* someone who comes into a country from abroad to make their home there without official permission. In many countries it is a crime to be an illegal immigrant and many governments refuse to let illegal immigrants stay in the country.

il·le·gal·i·ty /ˌɪlɪˈɡælətɪ/ *n* 1 [U] the state of being illegal 2 [C] an illegal act

il·leg·i·ble /ɪˈledʒəbəl/ *adj* difficult or impossible to read, esp. because of extreme untidiness: *Can you see what this note says — his writing is almost illegible!* —compare UN-READABLE —bly *adv* —bility /ɪˌledʒəˈbɪlətɪ/ *n* [U]

il·le·git·i·mate /ˌɪlɪˈdʒɪtəmət/ *adj* 1 born to parents who are not married.

► CULTURAL NOTE So many children in Britain and the US have parents who are not married that this is now considered acceptable by most of society, especially if the parents are living together, although in the past it was seen as something to be very ashamed of. The word illegitimate is now used esp. in official situations, e.g. in court. ◄

2 not allowed by the rules —compare ILLEGAL — ~ ly *adv* —macy *n* [U]

ill e·quipped /ˌ· ·'·/ *adj* not fitted for; unable to provide what is necessary for doing something: *He was ill-equipped for the journey.* | *Because of her upbringing, she was ill-equipped to deal with rejection.* —opposite well-equipped

ill-fat·ed /ˌ· '··◂/ *adj* unlucky; bringing misfortune: *an ill-fated attempt that ended in death*

ill-fa·voured /ˌ· '··◂/ *adj lit* (of a person) not good-looking, esp. in the face; ugly

ill-got·ten /ˌ· '··◂/ *adj* obtained by dishonest means (usu. in the phrase ill-gotten gains)

il·lib·e·ral /ɪˈlɪbərəl/ *adj* 1 not supporting freedom of expression or of personal behaviour, both of which are considered to be good things in western society: *illiberal opinions* 2 ungenerous — ~ ly *adv* — ~ ity /ɪˌlɪbəˈrælətɪ/ *n* [U]

il·lic·it /ɪˈlɪsət/ *adj* (done) against a law or a rule: *an illicit act* | *illicit trade in drugs* — ~ ly *adv*

Il·li·nois /ˌɪlɪˈnɔɪ/ *written abbrev.* IL a state in the Midwest of the US. Chicago is its largest city, and its economic life is based on farming and industry —see colour map on pages 1374–5

il·lit·e·rate /ɪˈlɪtərət/ *adj* 1 (of a person, esp. an adult) who has not learnt to read or write: (fig.) *an illiterate note* (=badly written) 2 *infml* having little knowledge of art, literature, etc.; badly educated —compare PRELITERATE — ~ ly *adv* —racy *n* [U]

ill-man·nered /ˌ· '··◂/ *adj* rude; impolite —opposite well-mannered

ill-na·tured /ˌ· '··◂/ *adj* of a bad-tempered character; DISAGREEABLE: *an ill-natured remark* —opposite good-natured; see ANGRY (USAGE)

ill·ness /ˈɪlnəs/ *n* [C;U] (a) disease; unhealthy state of the body or mind: *There seems to be a lot of illness in that*

family. | *physical and mental illness* | *Tuberculosis is a very serious illness.* —see DISEASE (USAGE)

il·lo·gi·cal /ɪˈlɒdʒɪkəl‖ɪˈlɑː-/ *adj* 1 going against what is sensible and reasonable 2 *infml* (of people, behaviour, or ideas) going against the principles of LOGIC — ~ ly /klɪ/ *adv*

ill-o·mened /ˌ· '···◂/ *adj* not likely to bring success; ILL-FATED

ill-starred /ˌ· '·◂/ *adj lit* unlucky; ILL-FATED

ill-tem·pered /ˌ· '···◂/ *adj* habitually bad-tempered; IRRITABLE —see ANGRY (USAGE)

ill-timed /ˌ· '·◂/ *adj* (done) at the wrong time; UNTIMELY: *an ill-timed comment that hurt her feelings*

ill-treat /ˌ· '·/ *v* [T] to be cruel to; MALTREAT: *an unhappy, ill-treated child* — ~ ment *n* [U]

il·lu·mi·nate /ɪˈluːmɪneɪt, ɪˈljuː-‖ɪˈluː-/ *v* [T] 1 a to give light to; fill (esp. a room) with light: *illuminated by candles* | (fig.) *a sudden smile illuminated her face* b to decorate (buildings, streets, etc.) with lights for a special occasion 2 to cause to understand; explain; make clear 3 (esp. in former times) to decorate (a piece of writing) with gold paint and other bright colours: *an illuminated manuscript*

il·lu·mi·nat·ing /ɪˈluːmɪneɪtɪŋ, ɪˈljuː-‖ɪˈluː-/ *adj* that helps to explain: *an illuminating remark, which showed her real character/made everything clear*

il·lu·mi·na·tion /ɪˌluːmɪˈneɪʃən, ɪˌljuː-‖ɪˌluː-/ *n* 1 [U] the act of illuminating or state of being illuminated 2 [C *usu. pl.*] (esp. in former times) a picture or decoration painted on a page of a book 3 [U] the strength of light: *The illumination is too weak to show the detail of the painting.*

il·lu·mi·na·tions /ɪˌluːmɪˈneɪʃənz, ɪˌljuː-‖ɪˌluː-/ *n* [P] *esp. BrE* a show of (coloured) lights used to make a town bright and colourful: *the famous Blackpool illuminations* —compare SON ET LUMIERE

il·lu·sion /ɪˈluːʒən/ *n* 1 a false idea, esp. about oneself: [*+that*] *He cherished the illusion that she loved him, but he was wrong.* 2 something seen wrongly, not as it really is: *The mirrors all round the walls give an illusion of greater space.* | *The mirrors produce an optical illusion.* 3 be under an illusion to believe wrongly: *They were under the illusion that the company was doing well, but in fact it was in serious trouble.* 4 have no illusions about to be fully conscious of the true nature of something, esp. something bad, difficult, etc.: *I have no illusions about his ability — he's just no good.*

illusion

an optical illusion

Is this a vase or two faces?

▷ USAGE Compare illusion and delusion. An illusion is something which people might reasonably believe to be true, but is in fact false: *The sun appears to go round the Earth, but this is an* illusion. A delusion is something that is believed to be true (perhaps by only one person) but is obviously false: *The patient suffers from the* delusion *that he is Napoleon.*◁

il·lu·sion·ist /ɪˈluːʒənəst/ *n* an entertainer (a MAGICIAN) who plays tricks on the eyes in a stage performance

il·lu·so·ry /ɪˈluːsərɪ/ also il·lu·sive /ɪˈluːsɪv/— *adj fml* deceiving and unreal; based on an illusion: *an illusory belief/victory*

il·lus·trate /ˈɪləstreɪt/ *v* [T] 1 to add pictures to (something written): *a beautifully illustrated book* 2 to make the meaning of (something) clearer by giving related examples: *His story about her illustrates her true generosity very clearly.*

il·lus·tra·tion /ˌɪləˈstreɪʃən/ *n* 1 [C] a picture to go with the words of a book, speaker, etc.: *The illustrations are better than the text.* 2 [C (of)] an example which explains, shows, or helps to prove something: *a typical illustration of his meanness* 3 [U] the act of illustrating 4 by way of illustration as an example

il·lus·tra·tive /ˈɪləstreɪtɪv, -strət-‖ɪˈlʌstrətɪv/ *adj* used for explaining the meaning of something: *an illustrative example* —see also ILLUSTRATE (2) — ~ ly *adv*

il·lus·tra·tor /ˈɪləstreɪtəʳ/ n a person who draws pictures, esp. for a book

il·lus·tri·ous /ɪˈlʌstriəs/ adj famous; widely known and admired for one's great works: *the illustrious name of Shakespeare* – –ly adv

ill will /ˌ· ˈ·/ n [U] hatred or strong dislike; HOSTILITY: *Despite the way they treated her, she* **bears them no ill will**. (=does not feel ill will towards them)

I Love Lu·cy /ˌaɪ lʌv ˈluːsi/ an American television programme of the 1950s and 1960s which has Lucille Ball as its star. *I Love Lucy* is still popular in the US and old programmes are still shown on television. The character Lucy often gets involved in funny, complicated situations which she often tries to hide from her husband Ricky with the help of her neighbours Fred and Ethel Mertz.

I'm /aɪm/ short for: I am: *I'm a doctor.* | *I'm going now.*

im- see WORD FORMATION

im·age /ˈɪmɪdʒ/ n **1** [C (of)] a picture formed in the mind: *She had a clear image of how she would look in twenty years' time.* **2** [C] a picture formed of an object in front of a mirror or LENS, such as the picture formed on the film inside a camera or one's REFLECTION in a mirror **3** [C] the general opinion about a person, organization, etc., esp. one that has been intentionally formed in people's minds: *The government will have to improve its image if it wants to win the next election.* | *The company tries to project an image of being innovative and progressive.* **4** [(the) (of)] a copy: *He's the (very) image of his father.* **5** [the+of] a phrase giving an idea of something in a poetical form, esp. a METAPHOR or SIMILE **6** old use likeness; form: *According to the Bible, man was made in the image of God.* –see also MIRROR IMAGE, SPITTING IMAGE

im·ag·e·ry /ˈɪmɪdʒəri/ n [U] images (IMAGE (5)) generally, esp. as used in literature

i·ma·gi·na·ble /ɪˈmædʒɪnəbəl/ adj that can be imagined: *We tried every imaginable means|every means imaginable, but we couldn't wake her up.* –opposite **unimaginable**

i·ma·gi·na·ry /ɪˈmædʒɪnəri‖-dʒəneri/ adj not real, but produced from pictures or ideas in someone's mind; existing only in imagination: *All the characters in this book are imaginary.* | *My little daughter has an imaginary friend.* –compare IMAGINATIVE

i·ma·gi·na·tion /ɪˌmædʒɪˈneɪʃən/ n **1** [C;U] the ability to imagine: *The story shows plenty of imagination.* | *a vivid|fertile imagination* | *I'll leave the gory details to your imagination.* (=I will not describe them) | *His story about sailing around the world single-handed* **stretches the imagination** *somewhat.* (=is very hard/impossible to believe) | *The pantomime really captured the children's* **imagination** *and they talked about it for weeks.* **2** [C] the mind: *The difficulties are all in your imagination.* (=they are not real) **3** [U] *infml* something only imagined and not real: *Her pains are mostly pure imagination.*

i·ma·gi·na·tive /ɪˈmædʒɪnətɪv/ adj **1** that shows use of the imagination: *imaginative writing* | *an imaginative design* –compare IMAGINARY **2** good at inventing imaginary things or artistic forms, or at producing new ideas: *an imaginative child* – –ly adv

i·ma·gine /ɪˈmædʒɪn/ v [T] **1** [not usu. in progressive forms] to form (a picture or idea) in the mind: *I can imagine the scene quite clearly.* | *You can imagine my surprise when they told me the news.* [+wh-] *You can imagine how surprised I was.* [+(that)] *Try to imagine that you're all alone on a desert island.* [+v-ing] *It's hard to imagine living in a place where there are no cars.* [+obj+v-ing] *Can you imagine George cooking the dinner?* **2** to believe or have an idea about (something that is false or does not exist): *There's nobody following us – you're just imagining it!* [+(that)] *He imagines that people don't like him, but they do.* **3** [+(that); obj; not in progressive forms] to suppose; think: *I imagine she was pretty annoyed when she found out.* **4 (just) imagine (it/that)!** (an expression of surprise or disapproval): *"She's dyed her hair purple." "Imagine that!"*

im·am /ˈɪmɑːm, ˈɪmæm/ n a Muslim priest and/or prince, or someone who studies Muslim law

im·bal·ance /ɪmˈbæləns/ n a lack of balance or proper relationship; a noticeable and usu. undesirable difference, esp. between two qualities or between two examples of one thing: *a population imbalance, in which more males* are born than females | *a serious trade imbalance between the two countries*

im·be·cile /ˈɪmbəsiːl‖-səl/ n **1** a fool or stupid person **2** old use or tech a person of weak mind, but less weak than an IDIOT

im·be·cil·i·ty /ˌɪmbəˈsɪlɪti/ n **1** [U] the state of being an imbecile **2** [C] an act of great foolishness

im·bed /ɪmˈbed/ v -dd- [T (in)] to EMBED

im·bibe /ɪmˈbaɪb/ v [I;T] fml or humor to drink or take in (esp. alcohol): (fig.) *imbibing knowledge at his mother's knee* (=as a small child)

im·bro·gli·o /ɪmˈbrəʊliəʊ/ n -glios **1** an occasion filled with confused action **2** a misunderstanding or difficult and confusing situation, esp. in a play

im·bue /ɪmˈbjuː/ v
imbue sbdy. **with** sthg. phr v [T usu. pass.] to fill with (something, esp. a strong feeling or opinion): *A president should be imbued with a sense of responsibility for the nation.*

IMF /ˌaɪ em ˈef/ abbrev. for INTERNATIONAL MONETARY FUND

im·i·tate /ˈɪmɪteɪt/ v [T] **1** to copy (the behaviour, appearance, speech, etc.) typical of (a person); MIMIC: *James can imitate his father|his father's speech perfectly.* –compare IMPERSONATE **2** to take as an example or model: *You should imitate her way of doing things.* –**tator** n

im·i·ta·tion /ˌɪmɪˈteɪʃən/ n **1** [C;U] the act or an action of imitating: *She did a brilliant imitation of the Queen.* **2** [C] a copy of the real thing: *It's not real leather: it's only an imitation.* | *imitation jewellery* **3 imitation is the sincerest form of flattery** saying if you copy what another person does, you are showing that you admire that person

im·i·ta·tive /ˈɪmɪtətɪv‖-teɪtɪv/ adj [(of)] sometimes derog following the example of someone or something else, esp. in a way that shows a lack of original ideas – –ly adv – –ness n [U]

im·mac·u·late /ɪˈmækjʊlət/ adj **1** clean and unspoilt: *immaculate white shoes* **2** pure; without fault: *immaculate behaviour* – –ly adv : *immaculately dressed*

Immaculate Con·cep·tion /·,··· ·ˈ··/ [the] the Roman Catholic belief that Christ's mother Mary did not have the fault (ORIGINAL SIN) that Christians believe all ordinary people have when they are born

im·ma·nent /ˈɪmənənt/ adj fml or tech **1** (of qualities) spreading through something: *hope, which seems immanent in human nature* –compare EMINENT, IMMINENT **2** (of God) present in all parts of the universe –**-nence, -nency** n [U]

im·ma·te·ri·al /ˌɪməˈtɪəriəl/ adj **1** unimportant; IRRELEVANT: *When it happened is immaterial: I want to know why it happened.* **2** not having material form; without substance: *The body is material but the soul is immaterial.*

im·ma·ture /ˌɪməˈtʃʊəʳ‖-ˈtjʊər/ adj **1** not fully formed or developed **2** not MATURE; showing a lack of good sense and control over one's feelings which is expected of people who are old enough to have learned this: *rather immature for a man of 30* – –ly adv –**-turity** n [U]

im·mea·su·ra·ble /ɪˈmeʒərəbəl/ adj too big or great to be measured: *This scandal has done immeasurable damage to the company's reputation.* –**-bly** adv

im·me·di·a·cy /ɪˈmiːdiəsi/ also **im·me·di·ate·ness** /-diət-nəs/– n [U] the nearness or urgent presence of something, which causes it to be noticed or dealt with without delay: *the immediacy of the danger* | *Television brings a new immediacy to world problems.*

im·me·di·ate /ɪˈmiːdiət/ adj **1 a** done or needed at once and without delay: *an immediate reply* | *taking immediate action to avert catastrophe* **b** [A] of or related to the present time: *We have no immediate plans for expansion.* | *Our immediate concern was to prevent the fire from spreading to other buildings.* **2** [A] nearest in time, space, or degree; next: *in the immediate future* | *My immediate family consists of my son and my wife.* | *Guards were posted in the immediate neighbourhood of the palace.* **3** [A] with nothing in between; direct: *He's been unwell for some time, but the immediate cause of his death was heart failure.*

im·me·di·ate·ly /ɪˈmiːdiətli/ adv **1** without delay; at once:

Stop that immediately![+adv/prep] *I came immediately after I'd eaten.* **2** with nothing in between; directly: *All those who are immediately involved will be informed of the decision.* [+adv/prep] *I'd parked immediately in front of the theatre.*

immediately² *conj BrE* as soon as; DIRECTLY²: *"Immediately your application is accepted you will be covered by the ... Plan."* (insurance advertisement)

im·me·mo·ri·al /ˌɪmɪˈmɔːriəl◂/ *adj* going back to ancient times (esp. in the phrase **from/since time immemorial**)

im·mense /ɪˈmens/ *adj usu. apprec* extremely large in size or degree: *an immense palace/improvement*

im·mense·ly /ɪˈmensli/ *adv* very much; to a great degree: *I enjoyed it immensely.* | *immensely rich/popular*

im·men·si·ty /ɪˈmensɨti/ also **immensities** *pl.* — *n* [U] very great size: *the immensity/immensities of space*

im·merse /ɪˈmɜːs‖-ɜːrs/ *v* [T (**in**)] **1** to put deep into a body of liquid: *He lay immersed in a hot bath.* | *Immerse the cloth in the dye.* **2** to cause (oneself) to enter deeply into an activity; ABSORB: *I immersed myself in work so as to stop thinking about her.*

im·mer·sion /ɪˈmɜːʃən, -ʒən‖ɪˈmɜːrʒən/ *n* [U] **1** the action of immersing or state of being immersed **2** BAPTISM by going under water **3** the language teaching method in which people are put in situations where they have to use the new language most of the time so that they learn faster

immersion heat·er /·ˈ·· ˌ··/ also **immersion** *infml*— *n BrE* an electric water heater placed in a TANK that provides hot water for use in the home

im·mi·grant /ˈɪmɨɡrənt/ *n* someone coming into a country from abroad to make their home there.

▶ CULTURAL NOTE Many immigrants have come to live in Britain. Some were REFUGEES, esp. before and during the Second World War. In the 1950s and 1960s many people came to Britain from the COMMONWEALTH (1), and more recently a number of BOAT PEOPLE arrived from Vietnam. The US has received large numbers of immigrants from all over the world since the country was established. —compare EMIGRANT; see EMIGRATE (USAGE); see also ILLEGAL IMMIGRANT ◀

im·mi·grate /ˈɪmɨɡreɪt/ *v* [I] *rare* to come into a country to make one's life and home there —see EMIGRATE (USAGE)

im·mi·gra·tion /ˌɪmɨˈɡreɪʃən/ *n* [U] the process of entering another country to make one's life and home there: *the immigration office at the airport* —see EMIGRATE (USAGE)

Immigration and Nat·u·ral·i·za·tion Ser·vice /···ˌ·· · ˌ···· ˈ· ˌ··/ also **INS** *abbrev.*— [the] an American government organization which makes sure that people obey laws about who is allowed to enter the US legally and who may become a citizen

immigration con·trols /···ˈ·· ·ˌ·/ *n* [P] the rules used to limit the number of immigrants who come to live in a country, esp. by making it difficult for them to get official permission to immigrate: *There are strict immigration controls in this country.* —see also ILLEGAL IMMIGRANT

im·mi·nence /ˈɪmɨnəns/ also **im·mi·nen·cy** /-nənsi/— *n* [U] *fml* the nearness of something which is going to happen, esp. something unpleasant: *The imminence of the exams made them work harder.*

im·mi·nent /ˈɪmɨnənt/ *adj* which is going to happen very soon: *There's a storm imminent.* | *in imminent danger of death* —compare EMINENT, IMPENDING, IMMANENT — ~ly *adv*

im·mo·bile /ɪˈməʊbaɪl‖-bəl/ *adj* unmoving; unable to move: *to keep a broken leg immobile* —**bility** /ˌɪməʊˈbɪlɨti/ *n* [U]

im·mo·bi·lize also **-lise** *BrE* /ɪˈməʊbɨlaɪz/ *v* [T] to make unable to move or travel: *immobilized by bad weather* | (fig.) *The company was immobilized by lack of finance.* —**lization** /ɪˌməʊbɨlaɪˈzeɪʃən‖-bələ-/ *n* [U]

im·mod·e·rate /ɪˈmɒdərɨt‖ɪˈmɑː-/ *adj fml* not kept within sensible and reasonable limits; EXCESSIVE: *immoderate eating* | *immoderate wage demands* — ~ly *adv* —**racy** *n* [U]

im·mod·est /ɪˈmɒdɨst‖ɪˈmɑː-/ *adj fml* **1** showing or tending to express a high opinion of oneself and one's abilities, perhaps higher than is really deserved; not MODEST **2** (usu. concerning women) not following the standards of sexual behaviour that are regarded as socially accept-

able: *an immodest dress* | *immodest behaviour* —compare INDECENT — ~ly *adv* — ~y *n* [U]

im·mo·late /ˈɪməleɪt/ *v* [T] to kill (esp. oneself) for religious or political reasons, esp. by burning —**lation** /ˌɪmə-ˈleɪʃən/ *n* [U]

im·mor·al /ɪˈmɒrəl‖ɪˈmɔː-/ *adj* **1** not good or right; not following accepted moral principles: *Using other people for one's own profit is immoral.* **2** going against accepted standards of sexual behaviour: *A pimp lives off the immoral earnings of a prostitute.* | *an immoral book that some people called obscene* —compare AMORAL — ~ly *adv*

im·mo·ral·i·ty /ˌɪməˈrælɨti/ *n* **1** [U] immoral behaviour **2** [C *usu. pl.*] an act which goes against accepted standards

im·mor·tal /ɪˈmɔːtl‖-ɔːr-/ *adj* **1** that will never die; that will live for ever: *the immortal gods* **2** that will continue or be remembered for ever: *Shakespeare's immortal plays* —**immortal** *n* : *Shakespeare is one of the immortals.*

im·mor·tal·i·ty /ˌɪmɔːˈtælɨti‖-ɔːr-/ *n* [U] the state of being immortal; never-ending life or endless fame

im·mor·tal·ize also **-ise** *BrE* /ɪˈmɔːtəl-aɪz‖-ɔːr-/ *v* [T] to give endless life or fame to: *Dickens's father was immortalized as Mr Micawber in "David Copperfield".*

Immortal Mem·o·ry /·ˌ·· ˈ···/, **The** (esp. in Scotland) the title of a TOAST¹ (2) (=expression of good wishes) to Robert Burns, usu. made at parties on BURNS NIGHT

im·mo·va·ble /ɪˈmuːvəbəl/ *adj* **1** impossible to move **2** impossible to change: *The government is immovable on that issue.* (=will not change its mind) —**bly** *adv*

im·mune /ɪˈmjuːn/ *adj* **1** [(**to**)] unable to be harmed because of special qualities in oneself: *immune to disease* | *The president seems to be immune to criticism.* **2** [(**from**)] specially protected: *The criminal was told he would be immune from prosecution if he helped the police.* —**munity** *n* [U] : *diplomatic immunity*

immune sys·tem /·ˈ· ˌ··/ [the] the bodily system by which special substances called antibodies (ANTIBODY) are produced to fight against disease-causing substances (ANTIGENS) that have entered the body

im·mu·nize also **-nise** *BrE* /ˈɪmjʊnaɪz/ *v* [T (**against**)] to protect from disease by putting certain substances into the body, usu. by means of an INJECTION —compare INOCULATE, VACCINATE —**nization** /ˌɪmjʊnaɪˈzeɪʃən‖-nə-/ *n* [C;U]

im·mu·no·de·fi·cien·cy /ˌɪmjʊnəʊdɪˈfɪʃənsi, ˌɪmjuːnəʊ-/ *n* [C,U] an inability of the body to fight infection (e.g. when a person has AIDS) —**immunodeficient** *adj*

im·mure /ɪˈmjʊəʳ/ *v* [T] *fml or lit* to imprison; shut (someone) away alone

im·mu·ta·ble /ɪˈmjuːtəbəl/ *adj fml* unchangeable: *the immutable laws of nature* —**bly** *adv* —**bility** /ɪˌmjuːtəˈbɪlɨti/ *n* [U]

imp /ɪmp/ *n* **1** a little devil **2** a child who misbehaves in a not very serious way —see also IMPISH

im·pact¹ /ˈɪmpækt/ *n* **1** the force of one object hitting another **2** [(**on**)] an esp. strong or powerful influence or effect caused or produced by an idea, invention, event, etc.: *The computer has had/made a great impact on modern life.* | *The full impact of these changes has not yet been felt.* **3 on impact** at the moment of hitting: *The cup hit the wall and broke on impact.*

im·pact² /ɪmˈpækt/ *v* [I+**on**;T] *esp. AmE* to have an impact (on): *These costs will impact on our profitability.*

im·pact·ed /ɪmˈpæktɨd/ *adj* (usu. of a WISDOM TOOTH) growing under another tooth instead of upwards into the mouth

im·pair /ɪmˈpeəʳ/ *v* [T] to weaken or make worse: *His illness has impaired his efficiency.* | *impaired hearing* — ~ment *n* [U]

im·pa·la /ɪmˈpɑːlə/ *n* **impalas** or **impala** a large brownish graceful African deerlike animal (ANTELOPE)

im·pale /ɪmˈpeɪl/ *v* [T (**on**)] to run a sharp stick or weapon through (someone's body): *He fell out of the window and was impaled on the iron railings.* —compare TRANSFIX — ~ment *n* [U]

im·pal·pa·ble /ɪmˈpælpəbəl/ *adj fml* **1** which cannot be felt by touch; not PALPABLE **2** not easily understood: *impalpable ideas floating through his mind*

im·pan·el /ɪmˈpænl/ *v* [T] to EMPANEL

im·part /ɪmˈpɑːt‖-ɑːrt/ v [T (**to**)] fml **1** to give or pass (qualities, feelings, etc.): *The music imparts a feeling of excitement to the film.* | *The herbs imparted a delicious flavour to the stew.* **2** to make known (information, etc.): *He had no news to impart.*

im·par·tial /ɪmˈpɑːʃəl‖-ɑːr-/ adj fair; not giving special favour or support to any one side: *an impartial judge* | *an impartial news report* – –ly adv – –ity /ˌɪmˌpɑːʃiˈælɨti‖-ɑːr-/ n [U]

im·pass·a·ble /ɪmˈpɑːsəbəl‖ɪmˈpæ-/ adj which cannot be travelled over: *The snow has made the road impassable.*

im·passe /æmˈpɑːs‖ˈɪmpæs/ n [usu. sing.] a point at which further movement or development is blocked: *The negotiations have reached an impasse.* (=neither side will agree)

im·pas·sioned /ɪmˈpæʃənd/ adj (usu. of speech) filled with deep feelings: *an impassioned plea for justice*

im·pas·sive /ɪmˈpæsɪv/ adj sometimes derog showing or seeming to have no feelings; without EMOTION: *The defendant remained impassive as the judge sentenced him to death.* –compare IMPERTURBABLE – –ly adv –sivity /ˌɪmpæˈsɪvɨti/ n [U]

im·pa·tience /ɪmˈpeɪʃəns/ n [U] **1** inability or unwillingness to accept delays, other people's weaknesses, etc.: *There is growing impatience at the government's inability to solve the problem.* **2** [+for/to-v] great eagerness: *She arrived too early in her impatience to see him.*

im·pa·tient /ɪmˈpeɪʃənt/ adj **1** showing impatience: *too impatient with slow learners* | *an impatient reply* **2** [F+for/to-v] very eager: *impatient for his dinner* | *impatient to leave* – –ly adv

im·peach /ɪmˈpiːtʃ/ v [T] **1** fml to raise doubts about: *to impeach someone's motives/character* **2** law **a** to say that (someone) is guilty of a serious crime, esp. against the state **b** (esp. in the US) to charge (a public official) with serious misbehaviour in office – –ment n [U]

im·pec·ca·ble /ɪmˈpekəbəl/ adj free from fault or blame; FLAWLESS: *impeccable character/credentials* –bly adv : *impeccably dressed*

im·pe·cu·ni·ous /ˌɪmpɪˈkjuːniəs◀/ adj fml, sometimes humor having little or no money, esp. continually – –ly adv – –ness n [U]

im·ped·ance /ɪmˈpiːdəns/ n [S;U] tech (a measure of) the power of a piece of electrical apparatus to stop the flow of an ALTERNATING CURRENT

im·pede /ɪmˈpiːd/ v [T] to get in the way of or slow down the movement or development of; HINDER: *The rescue attempt was impeded by bad weather.*

im·ped·i·ment /ɪmˈpedɨmənt/ n **1** [(**to**)] a fact or event which makes action difficult or impossible: *The main impediment to development is the country's huge foreign debt.* **2** a physical or nervous difficulty which prevents a person from speaking clearly: *a speech impediment*

im·ped·i·men·ta /ɪmˌpedɨˈmentə/ n [P] bags and possessions in the form of LUGGAGE, esp. supplies carried by an army: (fig., humor) *They brought their children, the cat, the dog, and the rest of their impedimenta.*

im·pel /ɪmˈpel/ v -ll- [T (**to**)] (esp. of an idea, feeling, etc.) to drive (someone) to take action: *impelled to greater effort* [+obj+to-v] *I was so annoyed that I felt impelled to write a letter to the paper.* –compare COMPEL; see also IMPULSE

im·pend·ing /ɪmˈpendɪŋ/ adj (usu. of something unpleasant) about to happen: *impending doom* | *the impending exams* –compare IMMINENT

im·pen·e·tra·ble /ɪmˈpenɨtrəbəl/ adj **1** impossible to go into or through: *the impenetrable forest* | (fig.) *impenetrable darkness* (=in which the eye can see nothing) **2** extremely difficult or impossible to understand: *an impenetrable mystery*

im·pen·i·tent /ɪmˈpenɨtənt/ adj fml not sorry (for wrongdoing): *an impenitent criminal* – –ly adv –tence n [U]

im·per·a·tive¹ /ɪmˈperətɪv/ adj **1** urgent; which must be done: *Prompt action is imperative. It's imperative that you (should) tell him immediately.* **2** showing proud power: *an imperative manner* **3** tech (in grammar) expressing a command or having the form of a command –compare DECLARATIVE, INTERROGATIVE – –ly adv

imperative² n **1** tech (in grammar) a verb form, or a set of verb forms (MOOD²), that expresses a command: *In*

"Come here!" the verb "come" is an imperative/is in the imperative. –compare INDICATIVE², SUBJUNCTIVE **2** fml something that must be done: *Job creation has become an imperative for the government.* | *a moral imperative*

im·per·cep·ti·ble /ˌɪmpəˈseptɨbəl‖-pər-/ adj not noticed because very small or slight; not PERCEPTIBLE: *an almost imperceptible movement of her eyelid* –bly adv –bility /ˌɪmpəseptɨˈbɪlɨti‖-pər-/ n [U]

im·per·fect¹ /ɪmˈpɜːfɪkt‖-ɜːr-/ adj **1** not perfect; faulty: *an imperfect knowledge of French* **2** [A] tech being the form of a verb used to show incomplete action in the past – –ly adv – –ion /ˌɪmpəˈfekʃən‖-pər-/ n [C;U]

imperfect² [the] tech (in grammar) the form of a verb that shows incomplete action in the past: *"I was walking along the road" is in the imperfect.*

im·pe·ri·al /ɪmˈpɪəriəl/ adj (often cap.) **1** of an EMPIRE or its ruler: *Britain's imperial expansion in the 19th century* | *an imperial power* (=a country that rules a lot of other countries) –compare IMPERIOUS **2** (of weights and measures) of the British standard: *The imperial gallon is not the same size as the US one.* –compare METRIC; see TABLE 2; see also METRIC (CULTURAL NOTE) – –ly adv

Imperial Can·cer Re·search /·ˌ·· ˌ··· ·'·, ·ˌ··· '··/ a British organization that does work to find what causes CANCER and how it can be cured

Imperial Col·lege /·ˌ··· '··/ (abbrev. **IC**) a college that is part of the University of London, and does RESEARCH in science, MINING, ENGINEERING, and COMPUTING

im·pe·ri·al·is·m /ɪmˈpɪəriəlɪzəm/ n [U] **1** (the practice of) forming a large group of countries all under the direct political control of a single state or ruler **2** derog the gaining of political and trade advantages over poorer nations by a powerful country which rules them or controls them indirectly –compare COLONIALISM –ist n, adj –istic /ɪmˌpɪəriəˈlɪstɪk◀/ adj –istically /kli/ adv

Imperial War Mu·se·um /·ˌ··· '· ·ˌ··/ [the] a military MUSEUM in London, which contains information about the wars which Britain has fought

im·per·il /ɪmˈperɨl/ v -ll- BrE ‖ -l- AmE [T] rather fml to put in danger: *The whole project is imperilled by lack of funds.*

im·pe·ri·ous /ɪmˈpɪəriəs/ adj (too) commanding; expecting obedience: *an imperious voice/manner* –compare IMPERIAL – –ly adv – –ness n [U]

im·per·ish·a·ble /ɪmˈperɨʃəbəl/ adj fml or tech which will always exist or cannot wear out; that cannot PERISH: *The manufacturers claim that the material is imperishable.* | *imperishable memories*

im·per·ma·nent /ɪmˈpɜːmənənt‖-ɜːr-/ adj which will change or be lost; not PERMANENT: *an impermanent arrangement* –nence n [U]

im·per·me·a·ble /ɪmˈpɜːmiəbəl‖-ɜːr-/ adj which substances (esp. liquids) cannot pass through –compare IMPERVIOUS

im·per·mis·si·ble /ˌɪmpɜːˈmɪsɨbəl‖-ɜːr-/ adj fml which cannot be allowed

im·per·son·al /ɪmˈpɜːsənəl‖-ɜːr-/ adj **1** not showing or including personal feelings: *an impersonal letter* | *a large impersonal organization* **2** tech (in grammar) having no subject, or a subject represented by a meaningless or empty word like "it": *"Rain" is an impersonal verb in a sentence like "It rained".* – –ly adv

im·per·so·nate /ɪmˈpɜːsəneɪt‖-ɜːr-/ v [T] to pretend to be (another person) by copying their appearance, behaviour, etc.: *He impersonates all the well-known politicians.* | *He was arrested for impersonating an army officer.* –compare IMITATE –nation /ɪmˌpɜːsəˈneɪʃən‖-ɜːr-/ n [C;U] : *She does a marvellous impersonation of the principal.* –nator /ɪmˈpɜːsəneɪtəʳ‖-ɜːr-/ n

im·per·ti·nent /ɪmˈpɜːtɨnənt‖-ɜːr-/ adj rude or not respectful, esp. to an older or more important person –see IMPOLITE (USAGE) – –ly adv –nence n [U]

im·per·tur·ba·ble /ˌɪmpəˈtɜːbəbəl‖-pərˈtɜːr-/ adj that cannot be worried; remaining calm and steady in spite of difficulties or confusion –compare IMPASSIVE –bly adv –bility /ˌɪmpətɜːbəˈbɪlɨti‖-pərtɜːr-/ n [U]

im·per·vi·ous /ɪmˈpɜːviəs‖-ɜːr-/ adj [(**to**)] **1** not allowing anything to pass through: *impervious to gases and liquids* **2** not easily influenced or changed, esp. in one's opinions: *impervious to reason/criticism* | *impervious to her charms* –compare IMPERMEABLE

im·pe·ti·go /ˌɪmpɪˈtaɪgəʊ/ n [U] an infectious skin disease

im·pet·u·ous /ɪmˈpetʃuəs/ adj tending to take quick action but without careful thought; IMPULSIVE: *an impetuous decision which she soon regretted* – **~ly** adv **–osity** /ɪmˌpetʃuˈɒsˌti‖-ˈɑːs-/, **~ness** /ɪmˈpetʃuəsnˌs/ n [U]

im·pe·tus /ˈɪmpɪtəs/ n **1** [U] the force of something moving; MOMENTUM: *The car ran down the hill under its own impetus.* | (fig.) *The campaign is gaining impetus.* **2** [S;U] something that encourages action; STIMULUS: *The government's encouragement gave fresh impetus to these reforms.*

im·pi·e·ty /ɪmˈpaɪˌti/ n **1** [U] lack of respect, esp. for religion; lack of PIETY –see also IMPIOUS **2** [C *often pl.*] an act of impiety

im·pinge /ɪmˈpɪndʒ/ v
impinge on/upon sthg./sbdy phr v [T *pass. rare*] to have an effect on; influence: *The effects of the recession are impinging on every aspect of our lives.*

im·pi·ous /ˈɪmpiəs/ adj lacking respect, esp. for religion; showing IMPIETY – **~ly** adv – **~ness** n [U]

imp·ish /ˈɪmpɪʃ/ adj not usu. derog like an IMP (=a little devil); MISCHIEVOUS: *an impish grin* | *a charmingly impish child* – **~ly** adv – **~ness** n [U]

im·plac·a·ble /ɪmˈplækəbəl/ adj impossible to satisfy, change, or make less angry: *an implacable enemy* | *implacable demands*

im·plant /ɪmˈplɑːnt‖ɪmˈplænt/ v [T (**in, into**)] to fix in deeply, usu. into the body or mind: *deeply implanted fears/insecurity* –compare TRANSPLANT –**implant** /ˈɪmplɑːnt ‖ -plænt/ n : *an artificial heart implant*

im·plau·si·ble /ɪmˈplɔːzˌbəl/ adj seeming to be untrue, unreasonable, or unlikely: *an implausible excuse/explanation* –**bly** adv –**bility** /ɪmˌplɔːzˌˈbɪlˌti/ n [U]

im·ple·ment¹ /ˈɪmplˌmənt/ n a tool or instrument: *farming/gardening implements* –see MACHINE (USAGE)

im·ple·ment² /ˈɪmplˌment/ v [T] to carry out or put into practice: *The committee's suggestions will be implemented immediately.*

im·pli·cate /ˈɪmplˌkeɪt/ v [T (**in**)] to show that (someone else) is also concerned (in an esp. criminal activity): *a letter implicating him in the robbery* –compare INVOLVE

im·pli·ca·tion /ˌɪmplˌˈkeɪʃən/ n **1** [C;U] (an example of) the act of implying: *She said very little directly, but a great deal* **by implication.** **2** [C] a possible later effect of an action, decision, etc.: *What are the implications (of the government's announcement) for the future of our project?* | *an article assessing the wider implications of the nuclear accident* **3** [U] the act of implicating –compare INFERENCE

im·pli·cit /ɪmˈplɪsˌt/ adj **1** [(**in**)] implied or understood though not directly expressed: *Their request for information seems to contain an implicit threat.* | *She didn't openly attack the plan, but her opposition was implicit in her failure to say anything in support of it.* –compare EXPLICIT **2** unquestioning and complete: *implicit trust (in you)* – **~ly** adv : *She trusted the doctor implicitly.*

im·plode /ɪmˈpləʊd/ v [I] to explode inwards –**plosion** /ɪmˈpləʊʒən/ n [C;U]

im·plore /ɪmˈplɔːr/ v [T] *fml* to ask (for) in a begging manner; ENTREAT: *an imploring look* | *She implored his forgiveness.* [+obj+to-v] *I implore you to go now.*

im·ply /ɪmˈplaɪ/ v [T] **1** to express, show, or mean indirectly; suggest: *Their failure to reply to our letter seems to imply a lack of interest.* [+(that)] *She didn't actually say she had been there, but she certainly implied that she had.* | *Are you implying that we are not telling the truth?* | *an implied threat/criticism* –see INFER (USAGE) **2** to cause to be necessary; ENTAIL: *Rights imply duties.*

im·po·lite /ˌɪmpəˈlaɪt◂/ adj not polite: *It was impolite of her not to say goodbye.* – **~ly** adv – **~ness** n [C;U]

▷ USAGE **Rude** can have a similar meaning to **impolite,** but it is stronger, and suggests a real wish to be unpleasant. Compare *It was rather* **impolite** *of you not to write and thank the hosts* and *He's never forgiven her since she was* **rude** *about his cooking.* **Impertinent, impudent, cheeky** BrE, and **sassy** AmE *infml* mean rude, esp. to an older or more important person: *I can hardly believe the* **impudent** *things he says to the boss.*| *a* **cheeky** *child.*◁

im·pol·i·tic /ɪmˈpɒlˌtɪk‖-ˈpaː-/ adj *fml* (of an action or decision) not well-judged for one's purpose; not wise; not POLITIC

im·pon·de·ra·ble¹ /ɪmˈpɒndərəbəl‖-ˈpaːn-/ adj of which the importance cannot be calculated or measured exactly

imponderable² n [*usu. pl.*] something whose effects are imponderable

im·port¹ /ɪmˈpɔːt‖-ɔːrt/ v [T (**from**)] to bring in (something, esp. goods) from another place or esp. another country: *a rise in the number of imported cars/of cars imported from France* –compare EXPORT¹

im·port² /ˈɪmpɔːt‖-ɔːrt/ n **1** [C *often pl.*] something brought into a country from abroad: *(The volume of) imports rose last month.* **2** [U] the act or business of importing: *the import of food from abroad* –compare EXPORT² **3** [(*the*) S] *fml* the meaning: *The import of his speech was that we should all work harder.* **4** [U] *fml* importance: *a matter of no great import*

im·por·tance /ɪmˈpɔːtəns‖-ɔːr-/ n [U] **1** the quality or state of being important: *a matter of little importance/of the utmost importance/of national importance* | *How much* **importance** *do you* **attach** *to the latest events?* **2** the reason why something or someone is important: *The real importance of this new law is the protection it gives to female workers.*

Importance of Be·ing Ear·nest /·ˌ·· ·· ˈ··/, **The** a play by Oscar Wilde in which a man pretends that his name is Ernest because he thinks this will give him an advantage with a woman he admires

im·por·tant /ɪmˈpɔːtənt‖-ɔːr-/ adj **1** which matters a lot; having or likely to have great effect, value, or influence: *an important meeting/decision* | *He had to cancel his holiday owing to important developments which required his attention.* | *an important new book about American history* | *It's important (for people) to learn to read.* | *It's important that he (should) learn to read.* | *Privacy is important to her.* (–has a high value for her) **2** (of people) having influence or power: *one of the most important people in the company* | *an important new writer* – opposite **unimportant** – **~ly** adv : *You must finish, and, more importantly, you must finish on time.*

im·por·ta·tion /ˌɪmpɔːˈteɪʃən‖-ɔːr-/ n **1** [U] the act or business of importing –compare EXPORTATION **2** [C] something brought in from another place or country, esp. an object or way of behaviour typical of another place

import con·trols /ˈ·· ·ˌ·/ n [P] limits on the number of imports allowed into a country, set by a government in order to protect the country's own industries

import du·ty /ˈ·· ˌ··/ n [C;U] (a) tax on goods which enter one country from another, according to their value, quantity, etc.: *You'll have to pay import duty on that machinery.*

im·por·ter /ɪmˈpɔːtər ‖ ·ɔːr / n a person or country that imports: *The US is a big importer of goods.* –compare EXPORTER

import li·cence /ˈ·· ˌ··/ n a document giving permission to bring certain goods into a country

im·por·tu·nate /ɪmˈpɔːtʃˌnˌt‖-ɔːr-/ adj *fml* always demanding things: *importunate people/requests* – **~ly** adv **–nity** /ˌɪmpəˈtjuːnˌti‖ˌɪmpərˈtuː-/ n [U]

im·por·tune /ˌɪmpəˈtjuːn‖ˌɪmpərˈtuːn/ v [T] *fml* to make repeated requests to, often in an annoying or troubling way: *We were importuned with requests for assistance.*

im·pose /ɪmˈpəʊz/ v [(**on, upon**)] **1** [T] to establish (an additional payment) officially: *A new tax has been imposed on wine.* **2** [T] to force the acceptance of (usu. something difficult or unwanted): *The bank has imposed very strict conditions for the repayment of the loan.* | *The magistrate imposed a fine of £500.* | *Economic sanctions were imposed on the nation.* **3** [I] to take unfair advantage, in a way that causes additional work and trouble: *Thanks for the offer but I won't stay the night – I don't want to impose on you.* –**imposition** /ˌɪmpəˈzɪʃən/ n [C;U] : *It's quite an imposition to ask us to stay late at work.* | *protesting against the imposition of a sales tax on books*

im·pos·ing /ɪmˈpəʊzɪŋ/ adj grand in appearance or large in size; IMPRESSIVE: *an imposing view across the valley* | *an imposing building* – **~ly** adv

im·pos·si·ble /ɪmˈpɒsˌbəl‖ɪmˈpaː-/ adj **1** that cannot happen or exist, or be done or fulfilled: *Lack of money made*

further progress impossible. | *an impossible request* | *It's impossible (for us) to come.* | *You're asking me to* **do the impossible.** (=do something that is impossible) [F+*to-v*] *demands that were impossible to accept* [F+(*that*)] *It's impossible that he forgot our meeting: he must have stayed away on purpose.* **2** difficult or awkward to accept or deal with: *His bad temper makes life impossible for the whole family.* | *You're the most impossible person I've ever met!* | *Her refusal has put me in an impossible position.* —**bly** *adv* : *impossibly difficult* —**bility** /ɪmˌpɒsə-ˈbɪlɪti‖ɪmˌpɑː-/ *n* [U]

im·pos·tor ‖ also **-ter** *AmE* /ɪmˈpɒstər‖ɪmˈpɑːs-/ *n* someone who deceives by pretending to be someone else

im·pos·ture /ɪmˈpɒstʃər‖ɪmˈpɑːs-/ *n* [C;U] *fml* (an example of) being an impostor

im·po·tent /ˈɪmpətənt/ *adj* **1** unable to take effective action, esp. because lacking power: *a government that seems impotent in its dealings with the trade unions* [F+*to-v*] *We felt quite impotent to resist the will of the dictator.* **2** (of a man) unable to perform the sex act — ~**ly** *adv* —**tence** *n* [U]

im·pound /ɪmˈpaʊnd/ *v* [T] *fml or law* to take and keep officially until claimed (esp. something lost or not taken care of): *The police will impound your car if you leave it there.*

im·pov·e·rish /ɪmˈpɒvərɪʃ‖ɪmˈpɑː-/ *v* [T *usu. pass.*] **1** to make poor: *an impoverished student* | (fig.) *spiritually impoverished* **2** to make worse or incomplete by the removal of something important: *Our lives have been impoverished by the death of that great artist.*

im·prac·ti·ca·ble /ɪmˈpræktɪkəbəl/ *adj* that cannot be used or done in practice; not PRACTICABLE: *The idea sounds good, but I'm afraid it's impracticable.* —**bly** *adv* —**bility** /ɪmˌpræktɪkəˈbɪlɪti/ *n* [U]

im·prac·ti·cal /ɪmˈpræktɪkəl/ *adj* not sensible or clever in dealing with practical matters: *an impractical person who can't even boil an egg* | *an ingenious but impractical suggestion* — ~**ly** /kli/ *adv* — ~**ity** /ɪmˌpræktɪˈkælɪti/ *n* [U]

im·pre·ca·tion /ˌɪmprɪˈkeɪʃən/ *n fml* **1** [C] a curse; a SWEARWORD **2** [U] the act of cursing

im·preg·na·ble /ɪmˈpregnəbəl/ *adj* which cannot be entered or taken by force: *an impregnable fortress* | (fig.) *an impregnable argument* —**bly** *adv* —**bility** /ɪmˌpregnəˈbɪlɪti/ *n* [U]

im·preg·nate /ˈɪmpregneɪt‖ɪmˈpreg-/ *v* [T] **1** *fml* to make PREGNANT **2** [(**with**)] to cause a substance to enter and spread completely through (another substance): *a cleaning cloth impregnated with polish* **3** (of a substance) to enter and spread completely through (another substance)

im·pre·sa·ri·o /ˌɪmprɪˈsɑːriəʊ/ *n* **-os** a person who arranges for performances in theatres, concert halls, etc.

im·press¹ /ɪmˈpres/ *v* [T] **1** [*often pass.*; *not in progressive forms*] to influence deeply, esp. with a feeling of admiration: *The teachers were most impressed/very impressed by your performance in the exam.* | *The thing that impresses me most about her books is the way she draws her characters.* | *We've tried the new product and we're favourably impressed with it.* (=we think it is good) **2** to make the importance of (something) clear to (someone): [+**on/upon**+*obj*] *My father impressed on me the value of hard work.* [+*obj*+**with**] *My father impressed me with the value of hard work.* **3** [(**into, on**)] to press (something) into something else, or to make (a mark) as a result of this pressure: *a pattern impressed on the clay pots before baking*

im·press² /ˈɪmpres/ *n fml or lit* a mark or pattern made by impressing (IMPRESS (3))

im·pres·sion /ɪmˈpreʃən/ *n* **1** [C (**on**)] an image or effect that is produced in the mind by a person, event, experience, etc.: *The house was very untidy — it didn't create a very good impression, I'm afraid.* | *Her speech made quite an impression on the audience.* (=had an effect on them, esp. by being good) | *First impressions are often wrong.* | *What's your impression of him as a worker?* (=do you think he is good or bad?) **2** [C *often sing.*] a not very clear feeling or idea about something: *On waking, I had a vague impression of shapes and bright colours, but I didn't know where I was.* [+(*that*)] I **got** the **distinct impression** (*that*) *they'd just had an argument.* | *I asked him for a job* **under the impression that** *he was the*

manager — but he wasn't. **3** [C] a mark left by pressure: *He took an impression of the key.* | *the impression of a heel in the mud* **4** [C (**of**)] an attempt to copy in a funny way the most noticeable parts of a person's appearance or behaviour: *He did a brilliant impression of the president.* **5** [C *often sing.*] all the copies of something (such as a book) made at one printing —compare EDITION, REPRINT² **6** [U] the act of impressing or state of being impressed

im·pres·sio·na·ble /ɪmˈpreʃənəbəl/ *adj* (of a person) easy to influence, often with the result that one's feelings and ideas change easily and one is too ready to admire other people: *The child is at an impressionable age.* —**bly** *adv* —**bility** /ɪmˌpreʃənəˈbɪlɪti/ *n* [U]

im·pres·sion·is·m /ɪmˈpreʃənɪzəm/ *n* [U] (*often cap.*) **1** a style of painting (used esp. in France between 1870 and 1900 by painters such as Monet, Cézanne, and Pissarro) which produces effects (esp. of light) by use of colour rather than by details of form. The French impressionists often painted directly from nature. **2** a style of music (in France 1870–1914, and in England later) that produces feelings and images by the quality of sounds rather than by a pattern of notes —compare EXPRESSIONISM

im·pres·sion·ist¹ /ɪmˈpreʃənɪst/ *n* **1** (*often cap.*) a person who practises impressionism in painting or music **2** a person who does IMPRESSIONS (4), esp. as a theatrical performance

impressionist² *adj* (*often cap.*) of or about impressionism: *an impressionist painter/painting*

im·pres·sion·is·tic /ɪmˌpreʃəˈnɪstɪk◂/ *adj* based on impressions rather than on knowledge, fact, or detailed study: *an impressionistic account of what happened* — ~**ally** /kli/ *adv*

im·pres·sive /ɪmˈpresɪv/ *adj* causing admiration, esp. by giving one a feeling of size, importance, or great skill; making a strong or good impression: *an impressive speech/speaker* | *the great cathedral with its impressive spire* — ~**ly** *adv* — ~**ness** *n* [U]

im·pri·ma·tur /ˌɪmprɪˈmeɪtər, -ˈmɑː-/ *n* [*usu. sing.*] **1** official permission to print a book, esp. as given by the Roman Catholic Church **2** *sometimes humor* approval, esp. from an important person

im·print¹ /ɪmˈprɪnt/ *v* [T (**on**)] **1** to print or press (a mark) on something: *The shape of the coin was imprinted on his tightly clenched hand.* | (fig.) *Every detail is imprinted on my mind.* **2** (*usu. pass*) to give (a bird or animal) an image of the family it belongs to, usu. by being the first thing it sees after birth: *Christine reared the duck from birth, and it thinks she's its mother — it's been imprinted by her.*

im·print² /ˈɪmprɪnt/ *n* **1** a mark left on or in something: *the imprint of her foot in the moist sand* **2** the name of the PUBLISHER as it appears on a book: *This dictionary is published under the Longman imprint.*

im·pris·on /ɪmˈprɪzən/ *v* [T] to put in prison or keep in a place or state which one is not free to leave: *The crew were imprisoned in the plane by the hijackers.* — ~**ment** *n* [U]: *He was sentenced to* **life imprisonment.** (=for life or a very long time)

im·prob·a·ble /ɪmˈprɒbəbəl‖-ˈprɑː-/ *adj* not likely to happen or be true: *They may win, but it's improbable.* | *rather improbable explanation* | *It is improbable that he drove home in less than an hour.* —**bly** *adv* —**bility** /ɪmˌprɒbəˈbɪlɪti‖-ˌprɑː-/ *n* [C;U]

im·promp·tu /ɪmˈprɒmptjuː‖ɪmˈprɑːmptuː/ *adj, adv* (said or done) at once without preparation: *an impromptu speech*

im·prop·er /ɪmˈprɒpər‖-ˈprɑː-/ *adj* **1** not suitable; INAPPROPRIATE: *improper behaviour for such a serious occasion* **2** not in accordance with fact, truth, or rules; not correct: *The director of the charity was accused of improper use of funds.* | *the improper use of a singular verb with a plural subject* **3** showing thoughts which are socially unacceptable, esp. about sex: *What an improper suggestion!* —see also PROPER — ~**ly** *adv* : *improperly dressed for the occasion*

improper frac·tion /·,·· ˈ··/ *n* a FRACTION, such as $^{107}/_8$, in which the number above the line is greater than the one below it —compare PROPER FRACTION

im·pro·pri·e·ty /ˌɪmprəˈpraɪɪti/ *n fml* **1** [U] the quality or state of being improper **2** [C] an improper act —see also PROPRIETY

im·prove /ɪmˈpruːv/ v **1** [T] to make better; bring to a better or more acceptable state: *I want to improve my English.* | *If the company refuses to improve its pay offer, we shall go on strike.* **2** [I] to get better: *Let's hope the weather improves before Saturday.* | *Business prospects have improved enormously.* | *The wine improves with age.* **3** [T] to increase the value of (land or property) by farming, building, etc.
　improve on/upon sthg. *phr v* [T] to produce or be something better than: *The leading contestant has scored 165 points, and I don't think anyone will improve on that.*

im·prove·ment /ɪmˈpruːvmənt/ n [C;U (**in, on**)] (a sign or result of) the act of improving or the state of being improved: *Your work shows considerable improvement.* | *There has been a slight improvement/a significant improvement in the company's trading position.* | *to carry out home improvements* | *Your English is getting better, but there is still* **room for improvement**. (=it is still possible for it to improve even more)
　▷ USAGE You can speak of an **improvement** *in* something if it has got better: *There has been an* **improvement** *in the weather.* You can speak of an **improvement** *on* something if you compare two things, the second of which is better than the first: *Today's weather is an* **improvement** *on* (=is better than) *yesterday's.*◁

im·prov·i·dent /ɪmˈprɒvɪ̥dənt‖-ˈprɑː-/ adj *fml* (esp. of someone who wastes money) not preparing for the future — ~**ly** *adv* —**dence** *n* [U]

im·pro·vise /ˈɪmprəvaɪz/ v [I;T] **1** to do or make (something one has not prepared for) owing to an unexpected situation, sudden need, etc.: *I forgot to bring the words of my speech, so I just had to improvise.* | *We slept by the road in an improvised shelter.* **2** to make up (music) as one is playing —**visation** /ˌɪmprəvaɪˈzeɪʃən‖ɪmˌprɑːvə-/ *n* [C;U]

im·pru·dent /ɪmˈpruːdənt/ adj unwise and thoughtless; not PRUDENT — ~**ly** *adv* —**dence** *n* [U]

im·pu·dent /ˈɪmpjʊ̥dənt/ adj rude and disrespectful, esp. to an older or more important person: *an impudent child/remark* — ~**ly** *adv* —**dence** *n* [U]

im·pugn /ɪmˈpjuːn/ v [T] *fml* to raise doubts about (someone's behaviour, qualities, etc.)

im·pulse /ˈɪmpʌls/ n **1** [C;U] a sudden wish to do something; sudden urge: *He bought the car* **on (an) impulse**. (=without planning or deciding in advance) [+*to-v*] *an irresistible impulse to start dancing* | **impulse buying** *of goods one does not really want* —*compare* IMPULSIVE **2** [C] *fml* a reason or aim which is the cause of activity; STIMULUS: *The prime impulse of capitalism is the making of money.* **3** [C] *tech* a single push, or a force acting for a short time in one direction along a wire, nerve, etc.: *an electrical impulse* | *a nerve impulse*

im·pul·sion /ɪmˈpʌlʃən/ n **1** [U] the act of impelling or state of being impelled (IMPEL) **2** [C] an urge or impulse

im·pul·sive /ɪmˈpʌlsɪv/ adj having or showing a tendency to act suddenly without thinking about the suitability or possible results of what one is doing —*compare* IMPULSE (1) — ~**ly** *adv* — ~**ness** *n* [U]

im·pu·ni·ty /ɪmˈpjuːnɪ̥ti/ n **with impunity** without any danger of being punished

im·pure /ɪmˈpjʊəʳ/ adj **1** not pure, but mixed with something else: *impure drugs* **2** morally bad, esp. with regard to sexual behaviour: *impure thoughts*

im·pu·ri·ty /ɪmˈpjʊərɪ̥ti/ n **1** [U] the state of being impure **2** [C] something that is impure or that makes something else impure: *Refined sugar has had all the impurities removed.*

im·pu·ta·tion /ˌɪmpjʊˈteɪʃən/ n [(**of, to**)] *fml* **1** [U] the act of imputing something to someone **2** [C] a criminal charge or suggestion of something bad: *an imputation of guilt*

im·pute /ɪmˈpjuːt/ v
　impute sthg. **to** sbdy./sthg. *phr v* [T] *fml* to claim that (someone or something) possesses or has done, esp. unjustly: *How can they impute such dishonourable motives to me?*

in¹ /ɪn/ *prep* **1** (shows a position) **a** contained by (something with depth, length, and height); within (an enclosed space); inside: *We keep the money in a box.* | *Put*

the plate in the cupboard. | *She's in the bathroom.* | *to sit in a car* (compare *on a bicycle*) | *to go swimming in the sea* (compare *sailing on the sea*) | *lying in bed* (compare *lying on the bed, outside the covers*) | (*infml*) *He came in* (=into) *the room.* | *Get in* (=into) *the car!* | (fig.) *I wonder what's in his mind.* (=what he is thinking about or planning) (compare *I wonder what's on his mind* = what he is worrying about) **b** surrounded by (an area); within and not beyond (an open space): *cows in a field* | *The children are playing in the garden/in the street.* | *I saw a face in* (=within the frame of) *the window.* | *She had a cigarette in her mouth.* | *in the corner of the room* (compare *at the corner of Broadway and 42nd Street*) | *wounded in the leg* **2** (with the names of countries, seas, towns, and villages) not outside: *They live in London/in France.* | *an island in the Atlantic* **3** (with the name of a place connected with an activity) attending for the usual purpose: *in prison for stealing* | *in church praying* | *George is in hospital (BrE)/in the hospital (AmE) with a broken leg.* (compare *George works at the hospital.*) | (*esp. AmE*) *George is in school studying.* (=George is at school studying.) **4** being included as part of: *a character in a story* | *Can you see the mistake in this sentence?* | *an interesting article in today's paper* | *the people in this photograph* **5** (showing an area of employment or activity): *She's in business/in politics/in insurance.* | *a university degree in history* | *He was in conversation with a priest.* **6** wearing: *dressed in silk* | *a girl in red/in a fur coat* | *a man in armour/in uniform* **7** (showing direction of movement): *They drove off in the direction of London/in the wrong direction.* | *The wind is in the east.* (=coming from the east) | *The sun is in my eyes.* (=shining directly towards them) **8** using to express oneself; with or by means of: *Write it in pencil/in ink/in French.* | *printed in red* | *She called out in a loud voice.* **9** (with certain periods of time) at some time during; at the time of: *in January* | *in Spring* | *in 1986* | *in the 18th century* | *in the (early) afternoon* (compare *on Monday afternoon*) | *in the night* (compare *at night*) | *in his youth* | *in the 1930s* | *He was killed in the First World War.* | *in the past* **10** (with lengths of time) **a** during not more than (the space of): *He learnt English in three weeks.* (=and then he knew it) (compare *He learnt English for three weeks.*) **b** after; at the end of: *It'll be finished in five minutes.* | *It's two o'clock; I'll come in an hour.* (=at three o'clock) (compare *for an hour*=from two to three) —compare **in time** (TIME¹ (34)) **c** (*often with negatives*) during; for: *He hasn't had a good meal in weeks.* | *the first time I've seen her in two years* —compare WITHIN¹; see FOR (USAGE) **11** (showing the way something is done or happens): *She looked at me in horror.* | *I don't like speaking in public.* (=publicly) | *in secret* (=secretly) | *speaking in anger/in fun* | *In all seriousness* (=I am speaking seriously) *I think you ought to give up your job.* **12** (showing the condition of a person or thing): *They were living in terrible poverty.* | *in difficulties* | *in danger* | *in good health* | *in ruins* | *in a hurry* | *in doubt* | *in tears* | *to be/fall in love* | *in a bad mood* **13** (showing division and arrangement) so as to be: *Pack them in tens.* (=ten in each parcel) | *in rows* | *in groups* | *We stood in a circle.* | *Cut it in two.* (=into two halves) **14** (showing a relation or PROPORTION) per: *to pay a tax of 40p in the pound* | *One child in twenty suffers from this disease.* **15** (showing quantity or number): *in large numbers* | *They arrived in (their) thousands.* | *in part* (=partly) **16** with regard to: *weak in judgment* | *lacking in courage* | *blind in one eye* | *better in every way* | *They're equal in distance.* | *10 feet in length/in depth* **17** as a/an; by way of: *What did you give him in return?* | *She said nothing in reply.* **18** (naming or describing who or what you mean): *In her I see a future leader.* | *You have a good friend in me.* | *unusual ability in such a young child* **19** [+*v-ing*] when; while: *In studying other cultures, you can learn more about your own.* —compare ON¹ (6) **20 in all** together; as the total: *The cost of the repairs came to $800 in all.* **21 in that** because: *I'm in a slightly awkward position, in that my secretary is on holiday at the moment.* —see also INASMUCH

in² *adv* **1** (so as to be) contained or surrounded; away from the open air, the outside, etc.: *Open the box and put the money in.* | *The water looked warm so I jumped in.* | *strong walls to keep the prisoners in* | *Let's go in there where it's warm.* | (BrE) *a cup of tea with sugar in* (=with sugar in it) | *The door burst open and in they came.* (note word order) **2** (so as to be) present (esp. at home or under the roof of a building): *I'm afraid Mr Jones is out, but he'll be in again soon.* | *Let's spend the evening in* (=at home) *watching television.* | *Some thieves broke in* (=entered the house) *while we were out.* | *"Come in!"* (said when someone knocks at a door) | *The train isn't in yet.* | *It will be in in five minutes.* **3 a** inwards; towards the middle: *There was a loud explosion and the walls fell in.* | *It curves in at the edges.* **b** from a number of people, or from all directions to a central point: *Letters of support have been coming|pouring in from all over the country.* | *Entries to the competition must be in by Monday.* | *to bring the harvest in* **4** so as to be added or included where not formerly present: *The picture is almost finished — I can paint in the sky|paint the sky in later.* | *Fill in your name and address on the form.* **5 a** (of one side in a game such as cricket) having a turn to BAT: *Our side were in|went in to bat first.* **b** (of the ball in a game such as tennis) inside the line **6 a** so as to have a position of power: *Do you think the Nationalist Party will get in again* (=be elected) *at the election?* **b** (so as to be) fashionable: *Long hair for men went out in the 1970s, but it's in again|it's come in again now.* **7** back towards the shore or coast: *The ship went out to sea, then sailed back in.* | *When does the tide come in?* (=When does the sea reach a high point close to the coast?) **8 be in at** to be present at (an event): *I want to be in at the finish.* **9 be in for** to be about to have (trouble, bad weather, etc.): *We're in for some trouble|in for it if we don't finish quickly.* **10 be|get in on** *infml* to take part in; have|get a share in: *I want to be in on the discussion too.* **11 be in with** *infml* to be friendly with: *He's (well) in with the Board of Directors.* **12 go|be in for** to enter|be entered on the list for (a competition) **13 have (got) it in for someone** *infml* to dislike someone and intend to harm them **14 in and out (of)** sometimes inside and sometimes outside: *He's been in and out of prison for years.*

in³ *adj* **1** [A] directed inwards; used for sending or going in: *the in door* **2** [A] *infml* fashionable: *That new restaurant is the in place to go now.* | *the in crowd* (=people) **3** [A] shared by only a few favoured people; private: *an in joke* **4** [F] (of a fire) lit; burning: *Is the fire still in?* —see also INS AND OUTS —compare ON² (5)

in- see WORD FORMATION

IN *written abbrev. for* INDIANA

in·a·bil·i·ty /ˌɪnəˈbɪlɪti/ *n* [S;U+*to-v*] lack of power, skill, or ability: *(an) inability to work alone|to stop smoking*

in·ac·ces·si·ble /ˌɪnəkˈsesɪbəl◂/ *adj* [(to)] difficult or impossible to reach —**bly** *adv* —**bility** /ˌɪnəksesɪˈbɪlɪti/ *n* [U]

in·ac·cu·rate /ɪnˈækjʊrɪt/ *adj* not correct; not ACCURATE — **~ ly** *adv* —**racy** *n* [C *usu. pl.*; U]

in·ac·tion /ɪnˈækʃən/ *n* [U] lack of action or activity; quality or state of doing nothing

in·ac·tive /ɪnˈæktɪv/ *adj* not active — **~ ly** *adv* —**tivity** /ˌɪnækˈtɪvɪti/ *n* [U]

in·ad·e·qua·cy /ɪnˈædɪkwəsi/ *n* **1** [U] the quality of being inadequate: *a feeling of personal inadequacy* **2** [C *often pl.*] an example of incompleteness or poor quality; SHORTCOMING: *several inadequacies in your report*

in·ad·e·quate /ɪnˈædɪkwɪt/ *adj* [(to, for)] not good enough in quality, ability, size, etc. (for a particular purpose or activity); not ADEQUATE: *The food was inadequate for 14 people.* | *inadequate parking facilities|safety measures* | *She's so clever she makes me feel inadequate.* — **~ ly** *adv*

in·ad·mis·si·ble /ˌɪnədˈmɪsɪbəl◂/ *adj* which cannot be allowed; not ADMISSIBLE: *This evidence is inadmissible in a court of law.* —**bly** *adv* —**bility** /ˌɪnədmɪsɪˈbɪlɪti/ *n* [U]

in·ad·ver·tent /ˌɪnədˈvɜːtənt◂ ‖ -ɜːr-/ *adj* (done) without paying attention or by accident — **~ ly** *adv*: *He inadvertently knocked over the bowl of flowers.* —**tence** *n* [U]

in·a·lien·a·ble /ɪnˈeɪliənəbəl/ *adj fml* which cannot be taken away (often in the phrase **inalienable rights**)

i·nam·o·ra·ta /ɪˌnæməˈrɑːtə/ *n* **-tas** /-təz/ *lit or old use* the woman a man loves —compare PARAMOUR

i·nane /ɪˈneɪn/ *adj* meaningless or extremely stupid: *an inane remark* — **~ ly** *adv* —**inanity** /ɪˈnænɪti/ *n* [C *often pl.*;U]

in·an·i·mate /ɪnˈænɪmɪt/ *adj* not living; not ANIMATE: *A stone is an inanimate object.* —compare DEAD, INORGANIC

in·ap·pli·ca·ble /ˌɪnəˈplɪkəbəl, ɪnˈæplɪkəbəl/ *adj* [(to)] not directly related to or not having an effect on; not APPLICABLE: *Most of the questions on the form were inapplicable to me.* —**bly** *adv* —**bility** /ˌɪnəplɪkəˈbɪlɪti, ɪnˌæplɪkəˈbɪlɪti/ *n* [U]

in·ap·pro·pri·ate /ˌɪnəˈprəʊpri-ɪt/ *adj* [(for, to)] not suitable; not APPROPRIATE: *Your short dress is inappropriate for a formal party.* [+*to-v*] *It was a rather inappropriate moment (for us) to visit them.* — **~ ly** *adv* : *inappropriately dressed* — **~ ness** *n* [U]

in·apt /ɪnˈæpt/ *adj fml* (of statements, ideas, etc.) unsuitable: *an inapt comment* —compare INEPT — **~ ly** *adv* — **~ ness** *n* [U]

in·ar·tic·u·late /ˌɪnɑːˈtɪkjʊlɪt◂ ‖ -ɑːr-/ *adj* **1** (of speech) not well-formed; not clearly expressed **2** not speaking or expressing oneself clearly, so that the intended meaning is not expressed or is hard to understand; not ARTICULATE — **~ ly** *adv* — **~ ness** *n* [U]

in·as·much /ˌɪnəzˈmʌtʃ/ *adv fml* **inasmuch as** owing to the fact that; to the degree that: *Their father is also guilty, inasmuch as he knew what they were planning to do.*

in·at·ten·tion /ˌɪnəˈtenʃən/ *n* [U (to)] lack of attention: *inattention to detail*

in·at·ten·tive /ˌɪnəˈtentɪv◂/ *adj* [(to)] not giving attention: *an inattentive student* — **~ ly** *adv* — **~ ness** *n* [U]

in·au·di·ble /ɪnˈɔːdɪbəl/ *adj* too quiet to be heard —compare INVISIBLE —**bly** *adv* —**bility** /ɪnˌɔːdɪˈbɪlɪti/ *n* [U]

in·au·gu·rate /ɪˈnɔːgjʊreɪt/ *v* [T] **1** to open (a new building or service) or start (a public event) with a ceremony **2** [*usu. pass.*] to introduce (someone important) into a new place or job by holding a special ceremony **3** to be the beginning of (something, esp. an important period of time): *The introduction of free milk in British schools inaugurated a period of better health for children.* —**ral** *adj* [A] : *an inaugural ceremony to open the new hospital* —**ration** /ɪˌnɔːgjʊˈreɪʃən/ *n* [C;U] : *the president's inauguration* | *the inauguration ceremony*

Inauguration Day /·ˌ··ˈ··· ·/ the day an American president is inaugurated, which is always held on January 20. There is usually a PARADE and the new president makes a speech about what he plans for the US. —see picture on page 950

in·aus·pi·cious /ˌɪnɔːˈspɪʃəs◂/ *adj fml* seeming to show that bad luck will come; not giving good hopes for the future; not AUSPICIOUS — **~ ly** *adv* — **~ ness** *n* [U]

in·board /ˈɪnbɔːd ‖ -bɔːrd/ *adj* inside a boat: *an inboard motor* —compare OUTBOARD MOTOR

in·born /ˌɪnˈbɔːn◂ ‖ -ɔːrn◂/ *adj* present from birth; part of one's nature; INNATE: *Birds have an inborn ability to fly.*

in·bound /ˈɪnbaʊnd/ *adj AmE* moving towards the speaker or the starting place; INCOMING —opposite **outbound**

in·bred /ˌɪnˈbred◂/ *adj* **1** having become part of one's nature as a result of early training: *inbred courtesy* **2** resulting from inbreeding

in·breed·ing /ˈɪnbriːdɪŋ/ *n* [U] breeding from (closely) related members of a family: *Inbreeding is sometimes used to produce pure white animals or plants.* —compare INTERBREED

Inc /ɪŋk; *fml* ɪnˈkɔːpəreɪtɪd ‖ -ɔːr-/ *adj* [after *n*] incorporated; (in the US) formed into a CORPORATION (1). An incorporated company may sell shares (SHARE¹ (2)) to raise money: *General Motors, Inc* —compare LTD, PLC

In·ca /ˈɪŋkə/ *n* **Incas** *or* **Inca** [C;*the*+P] (a member of) a South American people of Peru who ruled a large area of the Andes from Ecuador to Chile in the 15th century until the Spanish destroyed their rule in the 16th century. The Incas are known especially for their achievements in building roads and cities.

in·cal·cu·la·ble /ɪnˈkælkjʊləbəl/ *adj* **1** which cannot be counted or measured, esp. because too great or too many: *a policy that has done incalculable damage to our education service* **2** (esp. of people's feelings, character, etc.) changeable; UNPREDICTABLE —**bly** *adv* : *incalculably great|damaging*

in·can·des·cent /ˌɪnkænˈdesənt ‖ -kən-/ *adj* giving a bright light when heated — **~ ly** *adv* —**cence** *n* [U]

in·can·ta·tion /ˌɪnkænˈteɪʃən/ *n* [C;U] (the saying of) words used in magic

in·ca·pa·ble /ɪnˈkeɪpəbəl/ *adj* [F] **1** [+*of*] not having the power or ability to do something or show a quality: *He* seems to be incapable of understanding simple instructions. | incapable of kindness|hard work | I'm incapable of deceiving you. **2** unable to behave in an ordinary sensible way: He was arrested for being **drunk and incapable.** —**bly** adv —**bility** /ɪnˌkeɪpə'bɪlᵻti/ n [U]

in·ca·pac·i·tate /ˌɪnkə'pæsᵻteɪt/ v [T (**for**)] to make (someone) unable to do something: incapacitated (for work) after the accident

in·ca·pac·i·ty /ˌɪnkə'pæsᵻti/ n [S;U (**for**)] lack of power or ability (to do something): his incapacity for kindness|hard work

in·car·ce·rate /ɪn'kɑːsəreɪt‖-ɑːr-/ v [T] fml to keep or shut (as if) in a prison —**ration** /ɪnˌkɑːsə'reɪʃən‖-ɑːr-/ n [U]

in·car·nate¹ /ɪn'kɑːnᵻt‖-ɑːr-/ adj in physical form rather than in the form of a spirit or idea: [after n] the devil incarnate

in·car·nate² /ɪn'kɑːneɪt‖-ɑːr-/ v [T (**in, as**)] **1** [usu. pass.] to put (an idea, quality, etc.) into bodily form **2** [often pass.] to EMBODY (2)

in·car·na·tion /ˌɪnkɑː'neɪʃən‖-ɑːr-/ n **1** [U] the act of incarnating or state of being incarnate **2** [C] time passed in a particular bodily form or state: She believed that in a previous incarnation she had been an Egyptian queen. —see also REINCARNATION **3** [the+of] a person or thing that is the perfect example of a quality —compare PERSONIFICATION: She's the incarnation of goodness.

Incarnation [the] (in Christianity) the coming of God to Earth in the body of Jesus Christ. The Christian belief is that there was a union of God and Man in Jesus Christ.

in·cau·tious /ɪn'kɔːʃəs/ adj not showing careful thought; (doing things) which will lead to trouble: His incautious remark was seized upon by the newspapers. — ~**ly** adv — ~**ness** n [U]

in·cen·di·a·rism /ɪn'sendiərɪzəm/ n [U] incendiary action or behaviour

in·cen·di·a·ry /ɪn'sendiəri‖-dieri/ adj [A] **1** causing fires: an incendiary bomb|device **2** (of a person or behaviour) causing or intended to cause trouble or anger; INFLAMMATORY

in·cense¹ /'ɪnsens/ n [U] any of several substances that give off a sweet smell when burnt, esp. as used in religious services

in·cense² /ɪn'sens/ v [T often pass.] to make (someone) extremely angry; OUTRAGE: We were incensed by|at their bad behaviour. —see ANNOY (USAGE)

in·cen·tive /ɪn'sentɪv/ n [C;U (**to**)] something which encourages one to greater activity: His interest gave me an incentive and I worked twice as hard. | incentive payments to increase productivity | The promise of a bonus acted as an incentive to greater effort. [+to-v] Our research has not shown us anything so far, so there is little incentive to continue with it. —opposite **disincentive**

in·cep·tion /ɪn'sepʃən/ n [usu. sing.] fml the beginning: The programme has been successful since its inception.

in·cer·ti·tude /ɪn'sɜːtᵻtjuːd‖ɪn'sɜːrtᵻtuːd/ n [U] pomp uncertainty

in·ces·sant /ɪn'sesənt/ adj (esp. of something bad) continuous over a long period of time; never stopping: tired of his incessant complaining — ~**ly** adv

in·cest /'ɪnsest/ n [U] a forbidden sexual relationship between close relatives in a family, e.g. between brother and sister or parent and child, usu. considered unnatural and in most countries against the law

in·ces·tu·ous /ɪn'sestʃuəs/ adj **1** of or performing acts of incest: an incestuous relationship **2** esp. derog (of relationships) unusually close, esp. in a way that does not include people from outside or that is thought to be unhealthy: Publishing can be rather incestuous, with senior staff always moving around from firm to firm. — ~**ly** adv — ~**ness** n [U]

inch¹ /ɪntʃ/ n **1** a unit for measuring length —see TABLE 2 **2** a very small amount or distance: The car got through the gate with hardly an inch to spare. | They have sworn to defend every inch of their territory. | The bus missed our car by inches. (=almost hit it) **3 inch by inch** by small degrees or stages **4 every inch** completely; in all ways: every inch a gentleman **5 Give him an inch and he'll take a yard/a mile** If you allow him a little freedom or power he'll try to get a lot more **6 within an inch of**

very near: We came within an inch of death. **7 not give/budge an inch** not to change one's opinions when other people try to make you agree to theirs: I tried every argument, but she didn't budge an inch.

inch² v [I+adv|prep;T+obj+adv|prep] to (cause to) move slowly and with difficulty: I inched (my way) through the narrow space between the cars. | We inched the heavy box along the corridor.

in·cho·ate /ɪn'kəʊᵻt/ adj fml (of desires, wishes, plans, etc.) at the beginning of development; not fully formed

in·ci·dence /'ɪnsᵻdəns/ n [S (**of**)] the rate at which something, esp. something undesirable, happens or exists: There's a high incidence of disease|burglary there.

in·ci·dent /'ɪnsᵻdənt/ n **1** an event; a happening, esp. one that is unusual: one of the strangest incidents in my life | We completed the journey **without further incident.** (=with nothing unusual happening) **2** an event that includes or leads to violence, danger, or serious disagreement: The attack was the latest in a series of incidents in the area. | The spy scandal caused a diplomatic incident.

in·ci·den·tal¹ /ˌɪnsᵻ'dentl◂/ adj [(to)] happening or existing in connection with something else that is more important: an event incidental to the main action | minor, incidental details | You are allowed to claim for the **incidental expenses** of a business trip, such as taxi fares and food.

incidental² n [usu. pl.] something incidental, esp. something that is needed after the main things have been done, bought, etc.: We'd better leave some money to pay for incidentals.

in·ci·den·tal·ly /ˌɪnsᵻ'dentəli/ adv (used for adding something to what was said before, either on the same or another subject) by the way: I must go now. Incidentally, if you want that book I'll bring it next time.

▷ USAGE **Incidentally** like **by the way** can be used to introduce an important subject while making it seem as if it is not really very important to you: **Incidentally,** I think you still owe me some money. —see also WAY (USAGE)◁

incidental mu·sic /ˌ··· '··/ n [U] descriptive music played during a play, film, etc. to give the right feeling or to go with the action

in·cin·e·rate /ɪn'sɪnəreɪt/ v [T often pass.] to destroy (unwanted things) by burning —**ration** /ɪnˌsɪnə'reɪʃən/ n [U]

in·cin·e·ra·tor /ɪn'sɪnəreɪtəʳ/ n a machine or container for burning unwanted things

in·cip·i·ent /ɪn'sɪpiənt/ adj fml or med at an early stage: incipient disease — ~**ly** adv —**ence, -ency** n [U]

in·cise /ɪn'saɪz/ v [T (**in, into**) often pass.] tech to make (a cut) into (something)

in·ci·sion /ɪn'sɪʒən/ n [C;U (**in, into**)] tech, esp. med (the act of making) a cut into something, done with a special tool: An incision was made into the diseased organ.

in·ci·sive /ɪn'saɪsɪv/ adj apprec going directly to the main point of the matter that is being considered: incisive comments|questions — ~**ly** adv — ~**ness** n [U]

in·ci·sor /ɪn'saɪzəʳ/ n any of the teeth at the front of the mouth, which have one cutting edge. In humans there are four in each jaw. —compare CANINE TOOTH, MOLAR, and see picture at TEETH

in·cite /ɪn'saɪt/ v [T (**to**)] to cause or encourage (someone) to (a strong feeling or action); PROVOKE: He was charged with inciting a riot|inciting the crowd to rebellion. [+obj+to-v] He incited them to rise up against their officers. — ~**ment** n [U (**to**)] : Incitement to violence is sometimes a crime.

in·ci·vil·i·ty /ˌɪnsᵻ'vɪlᵻti/ n [C;U] fml (an act of) impoliteness

in·clem·ent /ɪn'klemənt/ adj fml (of weather) bad, esp. cold or stormy —**ency** n [U]

in·cli·na·tion /ˌɪnklᵻ'neɪʃən/ n **1** [C often pl.;U (**for, to, towards**)] what one likes or wants to do; liking; PREFERENCE: You always follow your own inclinations instead of thinking of our feelings. [+to-v] I've no inclination to change my job. **2** [C+to-v] fml a tendency: an inclination to see everything in political terms **3** [C (of) usu. sing.] a movement from a higher to a lower level: a slight inclination of her head **4** [S] a slope; a sloping surface

in·cline¹ /ɪn'klaɪn/ v [not usu. in progressive forms] **1** [T] to influence or encourage (someone) to have a particular feeling, belief etc.: [+*obj*+*to-v*] *Her arguments incline me to change my mind.* [+*obj*+*adv/prep*] *Her arguments incline me towards a different view of the matter.* **2** [I] **a** to tend (to); feel drawn (esp. to a particular belief or idea):[+*to-v*] *I incline to take the opposite point of view.* [+*adv/prep*, esp. **to, towards**] *I think she inclines towards our point of view.* **b** to be likely to show a particular state or quality: [+*to-v*] *I incline to get tired easily.* [+*adv/prep*, esp.**to, towards**] (*fml*) *I incline to/towards tiredness in winter.*—compare INCLINED (2) **3** [T] to cause to move downwards: *to incline one's head (in greeting)* **4** [I;T] to (cause to) slope

in·cline² /ˈɪnklaɪn/ *n* a slope: *a steep incline*

in·clined /ɪnˈklaɪnd/ *adj* [F+*to-v*] **1** encouraged; feeling a wish (to): *The news makes me inclined to change my mind.* **2** likely; tending (to): *I'm inclined to get tired easily.*

in·close /ɪnˈkləʊz/ *v* [T] to ENCLOSE

in·clos·ure /ɪnˈkləʊʒər/ *n* [C;U] (an) ENCLOSURE

in·clude /ɪnˈkluːd/ *v* [T(**in**)] **1** [*not in progressive forms*] to have as a part; contain in addition to other parts: *The price includes postage charges.* | *Is service included in the bill?* [+*v-ing*] *My job doesn't include making coffee for the boss!* —see COMPRISE (USAGE) **2** to put in with something or someone else; take in or consider as part of a group, set, etc.: *Please include me in the list.* | (*humor*) *Include me out!* (=I don't want to be included.) | *There are six of us in the family, or seven if you include the dog.* —opposite **exclude**

in·clud·ed /ɪnˈkluːdd/ *adj* [after *n*] including: *all of us, me included*

in·clud·ing /ɪnˈkluːdɪŋ/ *prep* having as a part; which includes: *six people, including three women* | *all of us, including me* | *I'm ordering some extra office equipment, including some new desks and a word processor.* —opposite **excluding**

in·clu·sion /ɪnˈkluːʒən/ *n* **1** [U (**in**)] the act of including or the state of being included: *The editor was against the inclusion of a gossip column in the newspaper.* —opposite **exclusion 2** [C] something that is included

in·clu·sive /ɪnˈkluːsɪv/ *adj* **1** also **all-inclusive**— containing or including everything (or many things): *an inclusive charge* | *It's an all-inclusive price; there's nothing extra to pay.* **2** [(**of**) after *n*] (of a price or charge) including other costs that are often paid separately: *The rent is £80 inclusive (of heating charges).* **3** [after *n*] *esp. BrE* including all the numbers or dates: *from the 5th to the 18th inclusive* —see USAGE — ~**ly** *adv*

▷ USAGE American speakers often use **through** in expressions where British speakers use **inclusive**: *Monday to Friday* **inclusive** (*BrE*) | *Monday* **through** *Friday* (*AmE*).◁

in·cog·ni·to /ˌɪnkɒɡˈniːtəʊ◂ || ˌɪnkɑːɡˈ-/ *adj, adv* [F] hiding one's IDENTITY (=who one is), esp. by taking another name when one's own is well-known: *travelling incognito*

in·co·her·ent /ˌɪnkəʊˈhɪərənt◂/ *adj* showing an inability to express oneself clearly, with suitable connections between ideas or words: *the incoherent ravings of a madman* | *She became quite incoherent as the disease got worse.* — ~**ly** *adv* —**ence** *n* [U]

in·come /ˈɪŋkʌm, ˈɪn-/ *n* [C;U] money which one receives regularly, usu. as payment for one's work or interest from INVESTMENTs: *Half of our income goes on rent.* | *government help for low-income families* | *People on fixed incomes are hurt by inflation.* | *to live within one's income* | *unearned income* (=income from savings, industrial shares, etc., rather than from work) | *a private income* (=an income provided by one's family rather than earned by working) —compare EXPENDITURE, OUTGOINGS; see PAY¹ (USAGE)

incomes pol·i·cy /ˈ·· ˌ···/ *n* a government policy to slow down the continuing rise in prices by setting limits on wage increases

income sup·port /ˈ·· ·ˌ·/ *n* [U] *BrE* (in Britain) a payment made by the government to people who do not have enough money to live on, e.g. the old or unemployed, introduced in 1988 to replace SUPPLEMENTARY BENEFIT — compare UNEMPLOYMENT BENEFIT, WELFARE, and see also SOCIAL SECURITY

income tax /ˈ·· ·/ *n* [C;U] (a) direct tax on one's income. In Britain and the US, people with higher incomes pay

a higher rate of tax than people with lower incomes. Governments often make changes to the system for economic or political reasons. Many people try to find legal ways to avoid paying income tax, and most people complain about paying it, but the Inland Revenue (in the US, the Internal Revenue Service) checks to see that people are paying what they should, and can take people to court if they do not.

income tax re·turn /ˈ·· ·· ·ˌ·/ *n* a form which is filled in each year by income tax payers who state how much they have earned and what money they do not have to pay tax on, and is used to calculate how much tax they must pay

in·com·ing /ˈɪnkʌmɪŋ/ *adj* [A] arriving, coming in, starting a period in office: *the incoming tide* | *the incoming president* | *incoming radio signals* —compare OUTGOING

in·com·mode /ˌɪnkəˈməʊd/ also **discommode**— *v* [T] *fml or pomp* to cause (someone) inconvenience

in·com·mo·di·ous /ˌɪnkəˈməʊdiəs◂/ *adj usu. lit or fml* not convenient, satisfactory, or large enough — ~**ly** *adv*

in·com·mu·ni·ca·do /ˌɪnkəmjuːnɪˈkɑːdəʊ/ *adv* (of people) kept away from people outside, and not able to give or receive messages: *The prisoner was held incommunicado.*

in·com·pa·ra·ble /ɪnˈkɒmpərəbəl||-ˈkɑːm-/ *adj* too great in degree or amount to be compared; without equal; not COMPARABLE: *incomparable wealth/beauty* —**bly** *adv* : *This model is incomparably the best/incomparably better than the others.* —**bility** /ɪnˌkɒmpərəˈbɪlˌti||-ˌkɑːm-/ *n* [U]

in·com·pat·i·ble /ˌɪnkəmˈpætˌbəl/ *adj* [(**with**)] not suitable to be together with (another thing or person/each other): *Those two are basically incompatible; I'm sure they'll soon get divorced.* | *An expensive project like this is incompatible with the government's aim of reducing public spending.* | *The two ideas are mutually incompatible.* (=each prevents the other) | *The two computer systems are incompatible with each other.* (=cannot be used together) —**bly** *adv* —**bility** /ˌɪnkəmpætˌˈbɪlˌti/ *n* [U]

in·com·pe·tence /ɪnˈkɒmpˌtəns||-ˈkɑːm-/ *n* [U] lack of ability and skill, resulting in bad work

in·com·pe·tent /ɪnˈkɒmpˌtənt||-ˈkɑːm-/ *adj* completely lacking skill or ability: *an incompetent teacher* [F+*to-v*] *quite incompetent to be the leader* —**incompetent** *n* : *a hopeless incompetent* — ~**ly** *adv*

in·com·plete /ˌɪnkəmˈpliːt◂/ *adj* not complete — ~**ly** *adv* — ~**ness** *n* [U]

in·com·pre·hen·si·ble /ɪnˌkɒmprɪˈhensˌbəl||-ˌkɑːm-/ *adj* [(**to**)] difficult or impossible to understand: *incomprehensible behaviour* | *His signature was an incomprehensible scrawl.* —**bly** *adv* —**bility** /ɪnˌkɒmprɪhensˌˈbɪlˌti||-ˌkɑːm-/ *n* [U]

in·com·pre·hen·sion /ɪnˌkɒmprɪˈhenʃən||-ˌkɑːm-/ *n* [U] the state of not understanding

in·con·cei·va·ble /ˌɪnkənˈsiːvəbəl/ *adj* too strange to be thought real or possible; impossible to imagine: *It once seemed inconceivable that people should travel to the moon.* —**bly** *adv* —**bility** /ˌɪnkənsiːvəˈbɪlˌti/ *n* [U]

in·con·clu·sive /ˌɪnkənˈkluːsɪv◂/ *adj* not leading to a clear decision or result: *inconclusive evidence* | *an inconclusive meeting between the unions and the management* — ~**ly** *adv* — ~**ness** *n* [U]

in·con·gru·i·ty /ˌɪnkənˈɡruːˌti/ *n* **1** [U] also **in·con·gru·ous·ness** /ɪnˈkɒŋɡruəsˌs||-ˈkɑːŋ-/— the state of being incongruous **2** [C] an act or event which seems strange and out of place because of its difference from what is happening around it

in·con·gru·ous /ɪnˈkɒŋɡruəs||-ˈkɑːŋ-/ *adj* strange or surprising in relation to the surroundings; out of place: *a modern building that looks incongruous in that quaint old village* — ~**ly** *adv*

in·con·se·quen·tial /ɪnˌkɒnsˌˈkwenʃəl||-ˌkɑːn-/ *adj* unimportant; INSIGNIFICANT: *an inconsequential event* — ~**ly** *adv* —**tiality** /ɪnˌkɒnsˌkwenʃiˈælˌti||-ˌkɑːn-/ *n* [U]

in·con·sid·e·ra·ble /ˌɪnkənˈsɪdərəbəl/ *adj* rather small; not worth considering: *a* **not inconsiderable** (=quite large) *sum of money* —compare CONSIDERABLE

in·con·sid·er·ate /ˌɪnkənˈsɪdərˌt◂/ *adj derog* not thinking of other people's feelings; thoughtless: *It was rather inconsiderate of her to keep us waiting like that.* — ~**ly** *adv* — ~**ness** *n* [U]

in·con·sis·tent /ˌɪnkən'sɪstənt◂/ *adj* **1** [(with)] (of ideas, opinions, etc.) not in agreement with each other or with something else: *What the government is saying now is inconsistent with its earlier statement on this subject.* | *The two statements are inconsistent.* | *He felt that his job in the bank was inconsistent with his socialist principles.* **2** tending to change; ERRATIC: *Her work is rather inconsistent — sometimes it's very good and sometimes it's awful.* —opposite **consistent** — ~ly *adv* —**tency** *n* [C;U]

in·con·so·la·ble /ˌɪnkən'səʊləbəl/ *adj* too sad to be comforted: *She was inconsolable (at the loss of her friend).* | *inconsolable grief.* —**bly** *adv*

in·con·spic·u·ous /ˌɪnkən'spɪkjuəs◂/ *adj* not easily seen or noticed; not attracting attention — ~ly *adv* — ~ness *n* [U]

in·con·stant /ɪn'kɒnstənt‖-'kɑːn-/ *adj fml* (of people or behaviour) tending to change; unfaithful in feeling: *an inconstant lover* —**stancy** *n* [C *usu. pl.*;U]

in·con·tes·ta·ble /ˌɪnkən'testəbəl◂/ *adj* clearly true; INDISPUTABLE: *incontestable proof* —**bly** *adv* —**bility** /ˌɪnkəntestə'bɪlɪti/ *n* [U]

in·con·ti·nent /ɪn'kɒntɪnənt‖-'kɑːn-/ *adj* **1** unable to control the passing of URINE and FAECES from the body **2** *lit or old use* unable to control oneself sexually —opposite **continent** —**nence** *n* [U]

in·con·tro·ver·ti·ble /ˌɪnˌkɒntrə'vɜːtɪbəl‖ˌɪnˌkɑːntrə'vɜːr-/ *adj fml* impossible to disprove; INDISPUTABLE —**bly** *adv*

in·con·ve·ni·ence[1] /ˌɪnkən'viːniəns/ *n* **1** [U] a state of difficulty, discomfort, or annoyance: *The station authorities apologized for any inconvenience caused by the late arrival of the train.* **2** [C] something that causes inconvenience: *It's no inconvenience to drive you to the station.* —see also CONVENIENCE

inconvenience[2] *v* [T] to cause inconvenience to: *I hope it won't inconvenience you to drive me to the station.*

in·con·ve·ni·ent /ˌɪnkən'viːniənt◂/ *adj* causing difficulty, discomfort, or annoyance; not CONVENIENT: *The meeting is at an inconvenient time (for me): I'm afraid I can't come.* — ~ly *adv*

in·cor·po·rate /ɪn'kɔːpəreɪt‖-ɔːr-/ *v* [T (**in, into, with**)] to make (something) a part of a group or of something larger; include: *They incorporated her suggestions into their plans.* | *The new plan incorporates the old one.* | *a new desktop computer incorporating an electronic mail facility* —**ration** /ɪnˌkɔːpə'reɪʃən‖-ɔːr-/ *n* [U]

in·cor·po·rat·ed /ɪn'kɔːpəreɪtɪd‖-ɔːr-/ *adj* see INC

in·cor·po·re·al /ˌɪnkɔː'pɔːriəl‖-kɔːr-/ *adj fml* without a body; not made of any material substance — ~ly *adv*

in·cor·rect /ˌɪnkə'rekt◂/ *adj* not correct — ~ly *adv* — ~ness *n* [U]

in·cor·ri·gi·ble /ɪn'kɒrɪdʒɪbəl‖-'kɔː-/ *adj often not derog* (of people or behaviour) very bad and unable to be changed or improved: *He's an incorrigible liar!* —**bly** *adv* : *incorrigibly naughty* —**bility** /ɪnˌkɒrɪdʒɪ'bɪlɪti‖-ˌkɔː-/ *n* [U]

in·cor·rup·ti·ble /ˌɪnkə'rʌptɪbəl/ *adj* **1** too honest to be improperly influenced or bribed (BRIBE) **2** which cannot decay or be destroyed —see also CORRUPT —**bly** *adv* : *incorruptibly honest* —**bility** /ˌɪnkərʌptɪ'bɪlɪti/ *n* [U]

in·crease[1] /ɪn'kriːs/ *v* [I;T] to make or become larger in amount, number, or degree: *The population of this town has increased.* | *They have increased the price of petrol by almost 20%.* | *This method should lead to increased efficiency.* | *increasing difficulty* | *Her remarks have increased speculation about a possible fall in interest rates.* —opposite **decrease**; compare REDUCE

in·crease[2] /'ɪnkriːs/ *n* **1** [(**in**)] a rise in amount, numbers, or degree: *an increase in crime* —opposite **decrease**; compare REDUCTION **2 on the increase** increasing: *Crime is on the increase.*

in·creas·ing·ly /ɪn'kriːsɪŋli/ *adv* more and more all the time: *I find it increasingly difficult to live within my income.*

in·cred·i·ble /ɪn'kredɪbəl/ *adj* **1** too strange to be believed; unbelievable or very hard to believe: *an incredible idea/excuse* | *That's the most incredible coincidence I've ever heard of!* —see also CREDIBLE **2** *infml* wonderful; unbelievably good: *She has an incredible house!* —**bility** /ɪnˌkredɪ'bɪlɪti/ *n* [U]

Incredible Hulk /·ˌ··· '·/ [*the*] a character in COMICS[2] (1), films and television, a man who sometimes changed into a very large green person with great strength but kept his ordinary human feelings

in·cred·i·bly /ɪn'kredɪbli/ *adv* **1** very; extremely: *an incredibly nice/stupid man* **2** in a way that is hard to believe: *Incredibly, the smallest horse won the race!*

in·cre·du·li·ty /ˌɪnkrɪ'djuːlɪti‖-'duː-/ *n* [U] disbelief: *She gave me a look of complete incredulity.*

in·cred·u·lous /ɪn'kredjʊləs‖-dʒə-/ *adj* showing disbelief: *an incredulous look* —see also CREDULOUS — ~ly *adv* — ~ness *n* [U]

in·cre·ment /'ɪŋkrɪmənt/ *n* an increase in money or value: *an annual increment in one's salary* — ~**al** /ˌɪŋkrɪ'mentl◂/ *adj* — ~**ally** *adv*

in·crim·i·nate /ɪn'krɪmɪneɪt/ *v* [T] to cause (someone) to seem guilty of a crime or fault: *incriminating evidence* —**nation** /ɪnˌkrɪmɪ'neɪʃən/ *n* [U]

in·crus·ta·tion /ˌɪnkrʌ'steɪʃən/ *n* [(**of**)] dirt or other material that is laid down on top of something else and forms a LAYER: *incrustations of salt*

in·cu·bate /'ɪŋkjʊbeɪt/ *v* [I;T] **1 a** (of eggs) to be kept warm until the young birds come out **b** to sit on and keep (eggs) warm until the young birds come out **2** *med* **a** to be holding in one's body (an infection which is going to develop into a disease) **b** (of such an infection) to be incubated in the body —**bation** /ˌɪŋkjʊ'beɪʃən/ *n* [U] : *the incubation period (of a disease)*

in·cu·ba·tor /'ɪŋkjʊbeɪtər/ *n* a heated container for **a** keeping eggs warm until the young birds come out **b** keeping alive PREMATURE babies (=babies that are still too small to live and breathe in ordinary air)

in·cu·bus /'ɪŋkjʊbəs/ *n* **-buses** *or* **-bi** /baɪ/ **1** a male devil supposed to have sex with a sleeping woman —compare SUCCUBUS **2 a** a very worrying problem **b** *lit* a bad dream; NIGHTMARE

in·cul·cate /'ɪŋkʌlkeɪt‖ɪn'kʌl-/ *v* [T] *fml* to fix (ideas, principles, etc.) in the mind of (someone): [+*obj*+**in/into**] *They inculcated the will to succeed in all their children.* [+*obj*+**with**] *They inculcated all their children with the will to succeed.* —**cation** /ˌɪŋkʌl'keɪʃən/ *n* [U]

in·cul·pate /'ɪŋkʌlpeɪt‖ɪn'kʌl-/ *v* [T] *fml* to show that (someone) is guilty of crime; INCRIMINATE

in·cum·ben·cy /ɪn'kʌmbənsi/ *n* the period in office of an incumbent: *during his incumbency as president*

in·cum·bent[1] /ɪn'kʌmbənt/ *n* **1** a priest in the Church of England who is in charge of a church and its PARISH **2** the holder of an official position, esp. a political one

incumbent[2] *adj* **1** [F+**on/upon**] *fml* being the duty or responsibility (of someone): *It's incumbent on the purchaser to/check the contract before signing.* **2** [A] holding the stated office: *the incumbent priest* | *the incumbent president*

in·cur /ɪn'kɜːr/ *v* **-rr-** [T] to receive (esp. something unpleasant) as a result of one's actions; bring upon oneself: *I incurred her displeasure somehow; was it something I said?* | *Invoice the company for any expenses that you incur in the course of your work.* | *The company incurred heavy losses in its first year.*

in·cur·a·ble /ɪn'kjʊərəbəl/ *adj* that cannot be cured: *an incurable disease* | (fig.) *an incurable optimist* —**bly** *adv* —**bility** /ɪnˌkjʊərə'bɪlɪti/ *n* [U]

in·cu·ri·ous /ɪn'kjʊəriəs/ *adj* lacking natural interest in things; not CURIOUS to know more: *incurious about the outside world*

in·cur·sion /ɪn'kɜːʃən, -ʒən‖ɪn'kɜːrʒən/ *n* [*often pl.*] *fml* a sudden attack on or entrance into a place which belongs to other people: *Enemy forces have made incursions into our territory.* —compare INROADS

in·debt·ed /ɪn'detɪd/ *adj* [+**to**] very grateful to (someone) for help given: *I'm indebted to all the people who worked so hard to make the party a success.* — ~ness *n* [U(**to**)]

in·de·cent /ɪn'diːsənt/ *adj* **1** morally offensive, esp. sexually improper: *an indecent remark/joke* —compare IMMODEST (2) **2** *infml* not reasonable; not suitable (in amount or quality): *You've given us an indecent amount of work to do.* (=too much) | *He left with indecent haste.* (=too fast) — ~ly *adv* : *indecently dressed* —**cency** *n* [U]

indecent as·sault /·ˌ·· ·'·/ *n* [C;U] *law* an attack on a person which includes some form of sexual violence

indecent ex·po·sure /·ˌ··· ·'··/ *n* [U] the intentional showing of part of one's body (esp. the male sex organ) in a place where this is likely to offend people; EXHIBITIONISM —see also FLASHER (2), (2)

in·de·ci·pher·a·ble /ˌɪndɪˈsaɪfərəbəl/ *adj* which cannot be deciphered (DECIPHER) or understood —**bly** *adv* —**bility** /ˌɪndɪsaɪfərəˈbɪlᵻti/ *n* [U]

in·de·ci·sion /ˌɪndɪˈsɪʒən/ also **in·de·ci·sive·ness** /ˌɪndɪˈsaɪsɪvnᵻs/— *n* [U] a state of being unable to decide between two things, possible courses of action, etc.

in·de·ci·sive /ˌɪndɪˈsaɪsɪv◂/ *adj* **1** having or showing inability to make decisions: *a weak and indecisive leader* **2** giving an uncertain result; INCONCLUSIVE: *an indecisive answer/battle* – ~**ly** *adv*

in·dec·o·rous /ɪnˈdekərəs/ *adj fml or euph* showing bad manners – ~**ly** *adv* – ~**ness** *n* [U]

in·deed /ɪnˈdiːd/ *adv* **1** *rather fml* (used for making an answer more forceful) certainly; really: *Yes, it is indeed beautiful weather.* | *"Did you hear the explosion?" "Indeed I did."* **2** it is even true (that): *I didn't mind. Indeed, I was pleased.* | *They'll be surprised when they get here, if indeed they get here at all.* **3** (used after **very** + adjective or adverb for making the meaning even stronger): *The crowds were very large indeed.* | *We enjoyed it very much indeed.* **4** (showing surprise and often disbelief, unfavourable interest, or annoyance): *"He left without finishing his work." "Did he, indeed?"* | *"I earn $1,000 a minute." "Indeed!"* | *"Why would he say such a strange thing?" "Why indeed?"*

in·de·fat·i·ga·ble /ˌɪndɪˈfætɪɡəbəl/ *adj* showing no sign of ever getting tired —**bly** *adv*

in·de·fen·si·ble /ˌɪndɪˈfensᵻbəl/ *adj* **1** too bad to be excused or defended: *indefensible behaviour* **2** which cannot be defended: *The enemy's position is indefensible.* —**bly** *adv*

in·de·fi·na·ble /ˌɪndɪˈfaɪnəbəl/ *adj* difficult or impossible to DEFINE or describe: *an indefinable air of tension in the town* —**bly** *adv*

in·def·i·nite /ɪnˈdefᵻnᵻt/ *adj* **1** not clear; not PRECISE: *indefinite opinions* | *indefinite responsibilities* **2** not fixed, esp. as to time: *absent for an indefinite period* | *an indefinite ban on imports of gold* —see also DEFINITE, INDEFINITELY – ~**ness** *n* [U]

indefinite ar·ti·cle /ˌ·ˈ···· ˈ···/ *n* **1** (in English) the words "a" or "an" **2** (in other languages) a word used like "a" and "an" —compare DEFINITE ARTICLE; see also ARTICLE¹ (4)

in·def·i·nite·ly /ɪnˈdefᵻnᵻtli/ *adv* **1** for a period of time without a fixed end: *You can keep the book indefinitely.* | *postponed indefinitely* **2** in an indefinite way – see also DEFINITELY

in·del·i·ble /ɪnˈdeləbəl/ *adj* which makes marks that cannot be rubbed out: *indelible ink* | *an indelible pencil* | (fig.) *an indelible stain on his character* —**bly** *adv* : *an experience indelibly printed on my memory*

in·del·i·cate /ɪnˈdelᵻkᵻt/ *adj* not careful enough to avoid offending people's feelings; improper: *It was rather indelicate of her to mention her urinary problems at dinner.* – ~**ly** *adv* —**cacy** *n* [U]

in·dem·ni·fi·ca·tion /ɪnˌdemnᵻfᵻˈkeɪʃən/ *n* [(**against, for**)] **1** [U] the act of indemnifying or state of being indemnified **2** [C;U] money or something else received to repair the effect of loss or damage; INDEMNITY (2)

in·dem·ni·fy /ɪnˈdemnᵻfaɪ/ *v* [T] **1** [(**against, for**)] to promise to pay (someone) in case of loss or damage **2** [(**for**)] to pay (someone) for loss, hurt, or damage

in·dem·ni·ty /ɪnˈdemnᵻti/ *n* **1** [U] protection against loss, esp. in the form of a promise to pay —see also DOUBLE INDEMNITY **2** [C] payment for loss of money, goods, etc.: *When a country has been defeated in war, it sometimes has to pay an indemnity to the victors*

in·dent¹ /ɪnˈdent/ *v* **1** [T] to make a usu. toothlike or V-shaped mark on the surface or edge of; NOTCH: *an indented surface/coastline* **2** [T] to start (a line of writing) further into the page than the others: *In English, the first line of a new paragraph is often indented.* **3** [I (**for**)] *esp. BrE* to order goods by indent

in·dent² /ˈɪndent/ *n* [(**for**)] *esp. BrE* **1** an order for goods to be sent abroad, or for stores in the army **2** an official, usu. written, order for goods

in·den·ta·tion /ˌɪndenˈteɪʃən/ *n* **1** [U] the act of indenting or state of being indented **2** [C] a space made as if by cutting into something: *the indentations in a coastline* **3** [C] a space at the beginning of a line of writing, esp. at the beginning of a new PARAGRAPH

in·den·ture¹ /ɪnˈdentʃəʳ/ also **indentures** *pl.*— *n* a formal contract, esp. one in former times between an APPRENTICE and his master

indenture² *v* [T(**to, as**)] to cause to enter employment on conditions stated in indentures: *an indentured bricklayer*

▶CULTURAL NOTE Some **indentured servants** in the 1600s to 1800s would agree to work in America for their employers for five to seven years in return for their employers paying for them to travel to America. ◀

in·de·pen·dence /ˌɪndᵻˈpendəns/ *n* [U] **1** [(**from**)] the quality or state of being independent; freedom: *This money gives me independence from my family.* | *Nigeria gained independence from Britain in 1960.* | *political and economic independence* —compare LIBERTY **2** the time when a country becomes politically independent: *The country has made great progress since independence.*

Independence Day /ˌ···ˈ·· ˌ·/ see FOURTH OF JULY

Independence Hall /ˌ····· ˈ·/ the building in Philadelphia, Pennsylvania, where the Declaration of Independence was signed, which today is visited by many tourists

in·de·pen·dent /ˌɪndᵻˈpendənt◂/ *adj* [(**of**)] **1** [*no comp.*] not governed by another country; self-governing: *India became independent (of Britain) in 1947.* **2** usu. apprec not depending on the help, advice, or opinions of others; habitually taking actions or decisions alone. This is usu. considered admirable in most Western countries: *She went on holiday alone – she's very independent.* **3** [*no comp.*] earning or providing enough money to live on, so that one does not have to depend on others. This is usu. considered admirable in most Western countries: *She is financially independent (of her family).* | *a woman of independent means* (=with her own income) **4** [*no comp.*] not connected with, controlled by, or influenced by others: *They are demanding an independent inquiry into the behaviour of the police at the demonstration.* | *Three independent studies in three different countries all arrived at the same conclusions.* – ~**ly** *adv* : *Charles Darwin and Alfred Russel Wallace discovered evolution independently (of each other).*

In·de·pen·dent *n* (*sometimes not cap.*) a person who does not always support the same political party

Independent, The a national daily newspaper in Britain. It is a QUALITY PAPER. —see also extra information on page 896

independent clause /ˌ····· ˈ·/ also **main clause**— *n tech* (in grammar) a CLAUSE which can make a sentence by itself. It may have one or more DEPENDENT CLAUSES as parts of it or joined to it: *In the sentence "She decided to leave because the film was bad", "She decided to leave" is an independent clause.*

Independent on Sun·day /ˌ··ˌ·· · ˈ··/ [*the*] a serious British newspaper which is printed and sold every Sunday —see also extra information on page 896

independent school /ˌ····· ˈ·/ *n BrE* (in Britain) a private school which does not receive money from the government. Only a MINORITY of children go to independent schools but some of these, esp. the PUBLIC SCHOOLS, are considered very important and influential.

in-depth /ˈ· ·/ *adj* [A] thorough and giving careful attention to detail: *an in-depth study*

in·de·scri·ba·ble /ˌɪndɪˈskraɪbəbəl/ *adj* impossible to describe, either because extremely good or extremely bad, or because description is too difficult to attempt —**bly** *adv* : *indescribably delicious/awful*

in·de·struc·ti·ble /ˌɪndɪˈstrʌktᵻbəl/ *adj* too strong to be destroyed —**bly** *adv* —**bility** /ˌɪndɪstrʌktᵻˈbɪlᵻti/ *n* [U]

in·de·ter·mi·na·ble /ˌɪndɪˈtɜːmᵻnəbəl‖-ɜːr-/ *adj* impossible to decide or fix: *The exact position of those particles is indeterminable by any method now available.* —**bly** *adv*

in·de·ter·mi·nate /ˌɪndɪˈtɜːmᵻnᵻt‖-ɜːr-/ *adj* not clearly seen as, or not fixed as, one thing or another: *Our holiday plans are still at an indeterminate stage.* —**nacy** *n* [U]

in·dex¹ /ˈɪndeks/ *n* **1** (*pl.* **indexes**) **a** an alphabetical list at the back of a book, of names, subjects, etc., mentioned in it and the pages where they can be found **b** also **card index** *BrE* ‖ **card catalog** *AmE*— a similar alphabetical list, e.g. of books and writers that can be found in a library, written on separate cards (**index cards**) **2** (*pl.* **indices** *or* **indexes**) *fml* a sign by which something can be judged or measured: *This local election will provide* *a useful index of the national political mood.* —compare INDICATION **3** (*pl.* **indices** *or* **indexes**) the system of numbers by which prices, costs, etc., can be compared to a former level, usu. fixed at 100: *An index-linked pension goes up when the cost of living does.* —see also DOW JONES, FT INDEX

index² *v* [I;T] to prepare an index (for) — ~**er** *n*

in·dex·a·tion /ˌɪndekˈseɪʃən/ *n* [U] the putting of something on an INDEX (3), esp. an arrangement by which if one thing, such as the cost of living, rises or falls, then so does another, such as wages, by a similar amount

index fin·ger /ˈ·· ˌ··/ also **forefinger**— *n* the finger next to the thumb —see picture at HAND

index fund /ˈ·· ˌ·/ *n* a fund in which money is invested (IN-VEST) and the value of the SHARES rises and falls according to the rise and fall in the STOCK MARKET

index-linked gilts /ˌ·· · ˈ·/ *n* [P] (in Britain) a type of government STOCK¹(3) where the value and interest change as RETAIL prices change

In·di·a /ˈɪndiə/ a large country in S Asia; capital New Delhi; population 811,817,000 (1989). The official languages are Hindi and English and most people are Hindu by religion.

In·di·an /ˈɪndiən/ *n* **1** a person who comes from or whose parents come from India **2** NATIVE AMERICAN —see colour picture on page 358 —**Indian** *adj*

In·di·an·a /ˌɪndiˈænə/ *written abbrev.* **IN**— a state in the US, in the Midwest, where farming is important —see colour map on pages 1374–5

In·di·a·nap·o·lis /ˌɪndiəˈnæpəlɨs/ the capital city of the state of Indiana in the US. An important car race called the **Indianapolis 500** is held there each year. —see colour map on pages 1374–5

Indian corn /ˌ·· ·/ *n* [U] *old-fash esp. AmE for* MAIZE

Indian file /ˈ·· ·/ *adv, n infml* SINGLE FILE; used mainly to children

Indian giv·er /ˌ·· ˈ··/ *n AmE infml derog* a person who gives a gift and then takes it back. The expression came out of a misunderstanding of Native American customs and is not used much any more as it is considered offensive to Native Americans.

Indian Guide /ˌ·· ˈ·/ also **Y-Indian Guide** *fml*— *n* a member of a club for young boys and their fathers run by the YMCA in the US. The YWCA runs a similar programme for young girls and their mothers called **Indian Maidens**.

Indian ink /ˌ·· ·/ *BrE* ‖ **India ink** /ˈ·· ˌ·/ *AmE*— *n* [U] dark black ink made from natural substances, such as that used for Chinese and Japanese writing with a brush

Indian Mu·ti·ny /ˌ·· ˈ···/ [*the*] the REVOLT of Indian soldiers in 1857 which led to a general protest and refusal to accept British rule. The British established their control again in 1858.

Indian O·cean /ˌ·· ˈ··/ [*the*] the third largest ocean in the world, E of Africa, S of Asia, W of Australia, and N of Antarctica

Indian sum·mer /ˌ·· ˈ··/ *n* **1** a period of warm weather in the late autumn **2** a pleasant or successful time happening near the end of a certain period, esp. towards the end of a person's life

Indian Ter·ri·to·ry /ˈ·· ˌ·····/ *n* [U] an area west of the Mississippi River in the US, now mainly in Oklahoma, to which many Native Americans were forced to move in the mid-1800s. The land was later taken back by the government. —see also TRAIL OF TEARS

Indian Wars /ˌ·· ˈ·/ [*the*+P] the wars in the US between the white settlers and the Native Americans in the 18th and 19th centuries. These increased particularly after 1815 when the American government began moving Native Americans onto RESERVATIONS —see also WOUNDED KNEE

india rub·ber /ˌ·· ˈ···◂/ *n* [U] *tech or old-fash* (*sometimes cap.*) rubber, esp. as used for making toys or rubbing out pencil marks: *an india-rubber ball*

In·dic /ˈɪndɪk/ *adj* of the Sanskrit language group and the modern languages related to it

in·di·cate /ˈɪndɨkeɪt/ *v* **1** [T] to point to; draw attention to: *I asked him where my sister was and he indicated the shop opposite.* **2** [T] to show or make clear, esp. by means of

a sign: *He indicated his willingness with a nod of his head.* [+(*that*)] *The government has indicated that it intends to cut taxes.* | *Research indicates that men find it easier to give up smoking than women.* [+wh-] *She indicated where I should go.* **3** [I;T] *esp. BrE* ‖ **signal** *AmE*— to show (the direction in which one is turning in a vehicle) with hand signals, lights, etc.: *He's indicating left.* | *Don't forget to indicate before turning.* **4** [T *often pass.*] *esp. med* to show a need for; suggest: *The change in his illness indicates the use of stronger drugs.* | *Stern measures may be indicated in a crisis.*

in·di·ca·tion /ˌɪndɨˈkeɪʃən/ *n* [C;U (of)] a sign or suggestion that indicates something: *There is every indication* (=a very strong probability) *of a change in the weather.* | *Can you give me any indication of how I did in the test?* [+*that*] *There are some indications that interest rates will soon fall.* —compare INDEX¹ (2)

in·dic·a·tive¹ /ɪnˈdɪkətɪv/ *adj* **1** [F+of] showing or suggesting: *His presence is indicative of his willingness to help.* **2** of or being the indicative: *an indicative verb (form)* — ~**ly** *adv*

indicative² *n tech* (in grammar) a verb form, or a set of verb forms (a MOOD²), that describes an action or states a fact: *In the sentences "He comes here often" and "She passed the test" the verbs "comes" and "passed" are indicatives/are in the indicative.* —compare IMPERATIVE² (1), SUBJUNCTIVE

in·di·ca·tor /ˈɪndɨkeɪtəʳ/ *n* **1** a needle or pointer on a machine showing a measurement, e.g. of temperature, pressure, amount of petrol, etc. **2** *esp. BrE* ‖ **turn signal, signal** *AmE*— any of the lights on a car which flash to show which way it is turning —see picture at CAR **3** a fact, quality, or situation that indicates something: *All the main economic indicators suggest that trade is improving.*

in·di·ces /ˈɪndɨsiːz/ *pl. of* INDEX¹ (2,3)

in·dict /ɪnˈdaɪt/ *v* [T (for)] to charge (someone) officially with an offence in law — ~**ment** *n* [C;U]

in·dict·a·ble /ɪnˈdaɪtəbəl/ *adj law* for which one can be indicted: *an indictable offence*

in·die /ˈɪndi/ *n* a small, independent company, esp. one which produces popular music recordings or television programmes

indie mu·sic /ˈ·· ˌ··/ *n* [U] popular music recordings produced by a small, independent company

in·dif·fer·ent /ɪnˈdɪfərənt/ *adj* **1** [F (to, towards)] not interested in; not caring about or noticing: *I was so excited to see snow that I was indifferent to the cold.* | *His manner was cold and indifferent.* **2** not very good; MEDIOCRE: *Was it good, bad, or indifferent?* | *I'm an indifferent cook.* — ~**ly** *adv* —**ence** *n* [U (to, towards)] : *He treats her with complete indifference.*

in·di·ge·nous /ɪnˈdɪdʒənəs/ *adj* [(to)] *fml or tech* originating, growing, or living naturally (in a particular place): *a plant indigenous to New Zealand* — ~**ly** *adv*

in·di·gent /ˈɪndɪdʒənt/ *adj fml* poor, lacking money and goods —**gence** *n* [U]

in·di·ges·ti·ble /ˌɪndɪˈdʒestɨbəl/ *adj* **1** (of food) which cannot be easily broken down in the stomach into substances to be used by the body **2** (of facts) which cannot easily be taken into the mind —**bly** *adv* —**bility** /ˌɪndɪdʒestɨˈbɪlɨti/ *n* [U]

in·di·ges·tion /ˌɪndɪˈdʒestʃən/ *n* [U] illness or pain caused by the stomach being unable to deal with the food which has been eaten —compare DIGESTION

in·dig·nant /ɪnˈdɪgnənt/ *adj* [(at)] expressing or feeling surprised anger (because of something wrong or unjust) — ~**ly** *adv*

in·dig·na·tion /ˌɪndɪgˈneɪʃən/ *n* [U (at)] feelings of surprised anger (because of something wrong or unjust): *I expressed my indignation at being unfairly dismissed.* | *righteous indignation*

in·dig·ni·ty /ɪnˈdɪgnɨti/ *n* [C;U] a state or situation that makes one feel ashamed or feel loss of respect (DIGNITY): *I suffered the indignity of having to say I was sorry in front of all those people.*

in·di·go /ˈɪndɪgəʊ/ *adj* dark blue-purple —**indigo** *n* [U]

in·di·rect /ˌɪndɨˈrekt◂/ *adj* **1** not straight; not directly connected (to or with): *an indirect route to avoid the town centre* **2 a** meaning something which is not directly mentioned: *an indirect remark/answer* | *an indirect way of telling me to leave* **b** happening in addition to, or instead of, what is directly intended: *The accident was the indirect result of the bus being late* **3** (of a tax) not paid directly but through an additional price added to the cost of goods or services − − **ly** *adv* − − **ness** *n* [U]

indirect free kick /ₗ⋯ ᵗ·/ *n* (in football) a FREE KICK given to one team, from which a direct shot at GOAL cannot be made −compare DIRECT FREE KICK, PENALTY KICK

indirect ob·ject /ₗ⋯ ˡ·/ *n tech* the noun, noun phrase, or PRONOUN that is concerned in the result of an action shown by a TRANSITIVE verb; person or thing that the DIRECT OBJECT is given to, made for, done to, etc.: *"Him" is the indirect object in "I asked him a question", and "door" is the indirect object in "I gave the door a kick".* −compare DIRECT OBJECT

indirect speech /ₗ⋯ ˡ·/ also **reported speech** ‖ usu. **indirect discourse** *AmE*− *n* [U] *tech* the style used in writing to report what someone said without repeating their actual words. This is done by changing the grammar and usu. using the form [+(*that*)], e.g. in a sentence like *Julia said (that) she didn't want to go* (her actual words were "I don't want to go"). −compare DIRECT SPEECH

indirect tax·a·tion /ₗ⋯ ·ˡ·/ *n* [U] tax not collected directly from the taxpayer, e.g. VAT which is paid by the producer of the goods, the cost being passed on to the customer in the form of a higher selling price

in·dis·cer·ni·ble /ₗɪndɪˈsɜːnᵻbᵊl‖-ɜːr-/ *adj* (often of something small or hidden by darkness) very difficult to see or notice: *a path almost indiscernible in the mist*

in·dis·ci·pline /ɪnˈdɪsᵻplᵻn/ *n* [U] a state of disorder because of lack of control; lack of DISCIPLINE

in·dis·creet /ₗɪndɪˈskriːt◂/ *adj* not acting carefully and politely, esp. in the choice of what one says and does not say; not DISCREET − − **ly** *adv*

in·dis·cre·tion /ₗɪndɪˈskreʃᵊn/ *n* **1** [U] the quality of being indiscreet; lack of DISCRETION **2** [C] **a** a careless impolite act **b** *euph* a piece of bad behaviour, such as small crimes and sexual experiences which are socially undesirable: *his youthful indiscretions*

in·dis·crim·i·nate /ₗɪndɪˈskrɪmᵻnᵻt◂/ *adj* not showing the ability to make judgments (esp. moral judgments) or to see a difference in value between two people, groups, things, etc.: *the terrorists' indiscriminate violence against ordinary people* − − **ly** *adv*

in·di·spen·sa·ble /ₗɪndɪˈspensᵊbᵊl/ *adj* [(to)] too important or too useful to be without; not DISPENSABLE: *She has become quite indispensable to the company.* | *A telephone is an indispensable piece of equipment for any office.* −**bly** *adv* −**bility** /ₗɪndɪspensᵊˈbɪlᵻti/ *n* [U]

in·dis·posed /ₗɪndɪˈspəʊzd◂/ *adj* [F] *fml* **1** *often euph* not very well (in health): *temporarily indisposed* **2** [+to-v] not very willing; not DISPOSED: *indisposed to do it/to help*

in·dis·po·si·tion /ɪnₗdɪspəˈzɪʃᵊn/ *n fml* **1** [C;U] a slight illness **2** [U+to-v] a certain degree of unwillingness: *Their indisposition to help makes everything more difficult.*

in·dis·pu·ta·ble /ₗɪndɪˈspjuːtᵊbᵊl/ *adj* too certain to be questioned; beyond doubt: *an indisputable fact* −**bly** *adv* : *indisputably first-rate*

in·dis·so·lu·ble /ₗɪndɪˈsɒljᵊbᵊl‖-ˈsɑː-/ *adj fml* impossible to separate or break up; lasting −compare DISSOLVE (esp. 4), INSOLUBLE −**bly** *adv* : *indissolubly united* −**bility** /ₗɪndɪsɒljᵊˈbɪlᵻti‖-sɑː-/ *n* [U]

in·dis·tinct /ₗɪndɪˈstɪŋkt◂/ *adj* not clear to the eye or ear or mind: *Those events are just an indistinct memory now.* | *an indistinct area in a photograph* −see also DISTINCT − − **ly** *adv* − − **ness** *n* [U]

in·dis·tin·guish·a·ble /ₗɪndɪˈstɪŋgwɪʃᵊbᵊl/ *adj* [(from)] which cannot be seen or known to be different from something else or each other: *The twin sisters are almost indistinguishable.* | *The material is indistinguishable from real silk, but much cheaper.* −**bly** *adv*

in·di·vid·u·al¹ /ₗɪndᵻˈvɪdʒuᵊl◂/ *adj* **1** [A] separate or particular; existing as an individual: *Each individual leaf on the tree is different.* | *The education department decides on general teaching policies, but the exact details are left to the individual schools.* | *individual portions* (=enough for one person) *of cheese* **2** [A] suitable for each person or thing, but not necessarily for any others: *Individual attention must be given to every fault in the material.* **3**

(of a manner, style, or way of doing things) particular to the person, thing, etc., concerned (and different from others); DISTINCTIVE: *She wears very individual clothes.* − see also INDIVIDUALLY

individual² *n* **1 a** a single person or thing, considered separately from the class or group to which he, she, or it belongs: *The rights of the individual are perhaps the most important rights in a free society.* **b** a person whose ideas, behaviour, etc. may not be the same as other people's: *Do social pressures make it hard for us to become individuals?* **2** *infml* a person of a particular kind: *a bad-tempered individual*

in·di·vid·u·al·is·m /ₗɪndᵻˈvɪdʒuᵊlɪzᵊm/ *n* [U] the idea that the rights and freedom of the individual are the most important rights in a society, a central belief in most western countries, esp. the US

in·di·vid·u·al·ist /ₗɪndᵻˈvɪdʒuᵊlᵻst/ *n, adj* (a person who is) noticeably independent and individual in opinions and/or style − − **ic** /ₗɪndᵻₗvɪdʒuᵊˈlɪstɪk/ *adj* − − **ically** /kli/ *adv*

in·di·vid·u·al·i·ty /ₗɪndᵻₗvɪdʒuˈælᵻti/ *n* [U] the character and qualities that make someone or something different from all others: *a dull woman, who lacks individuality*

in·di·vid·u·al·ize also **-ise** *BrE* /ₗɪndᵻˈvɪdʒuᵊlaɪz/ *v* [T] to cause to change according to the special needs or character of a person or thing; give individuality to −**ization** /ₗɪndᵻₗvɪdʒuᵊlaɪˈzeɪʃᵊn‖-lᵻ-/ *n* [U]

in·di·vid·u·al·ly /ₗɪndᵻˈvɪdʒuᵊli/ *adv* **1** one by one; separately: *Individually, they're nice children but when they're in a group they can be quite troublesome.* **2** in an INDIVIDUAL¹ (3) way: *dressing very individually*

Individual Re·tire·ment Ac·count /ₗ⋯ ·ˡ·· ·ₗ·/ *n* see IRA²

in·di·vis·i·ble /ₗɪndᵻˈvɪzᵊbᵊl◂/ *adj* which cannot be divided or separated into parts −**bly** *adv* −**bility** /ₗɪndᵻₗvɪzᵊˈbɪlᵻti/ *n* [U]

Indo- see WORD FORMATION

In·do·chi·na /ₗɪndəʊˈtʃaɪnə◂/ the name given to SE Asia by Europeans during the 19th century. Indochina included Vietnam, Kampuchea, Burma, Thailand, Malaysia, and Laos.

in·doc·tri·nate /ɪnˈdɒktrᵻneɪt‖ɪnˈdɑːk-/ *v* [T (**with**)] *usu. derog* to train (someone) to accept a set of (esp. political) ideas without questioning them: *indoctrinated with mindless anti-communism* −**nation** /ɪnₗdɒktrᵻˈneɪʃᵊn‖ɪnₗdɑːk-/ *n* [U]

In·do-Eu·ro·pe·an /ₗ⋯ ·ˡ·⋯◂/ *adj* **1** of or being a group of languages that includes most of those spoken in Europe (and now spread to America and parts of Africa), Iran, and India: *English is an Indo-European language.* **2** of or being a member of a group which speaks any of these languages

in·do·lent /ˈɪndᵊlᵊnt/ *adj fml* lazy; disliking effort or activity − − **ly** *adv* −**lence** *n* [U]

in·dom·i·ta·ble /ɪnˈdɒmᵻtᵊbᵊl‖ɪnˈdɑː-/ *adj* too strong and brave to be discouraged: *an indomitable spirit in the face of adversity* −**bly** *adv*

In·do·ne·si·a /ₗɪndəʊˈniːziə, -ˈniːʒə‖-ˈniːʒə, -ˈniːʃə/ a country in SE Asia consisting of more than 3000 islands including Java, Sumatra, Borneo and Bali; capital Jakarta; population 179,136,000 (1989)

In·do·ne·sian /ₗɪndəˈniːʒᵊn◂, -ˈniːziᵊn◂‖-ʒᵊn◂, -ʃᵊn◂/ *adj* of Indonesia, its peoples, or their official national language

in·door /ˈɪndɔːʳ/ *adj* [A] existing, happening, done, or used inside a building: *indoor sports* | *indoor clothes* | *an indoor swimming pool* −opposite **outdoor**

in·doors /ₗɪnˈdɔːz‖-ɔːrz/ *adv* **1** into or inside a building: *We went indoors.* | *We stayed indoors.* −opposite **outdoors 2 'er indoors** *BrE infml humor* one's wife: *I wanted to spend Sunday fishing, but 'er indoors wouldn't wear it!* (=did not allow me to)

in·dorse /ɪnˈdɔːs‖-ɔːrs/ *v* [T] to ENDORSE

in·du·bi·ta·ble /ɪnˈdjuːbᵻtᵊbᵊl‖ɪnˈduː-/ *adj fml* which cannot be doubted; unquestionable −**bly** *adv*

in·duce /ɪnˈdjuːs‖ɪnˈduːs/ *v* [T] **1** [+*obj*+to-v] *fml* to lead (someone) to do something, often by persuading: *Nothing could induce her to be disloyal to him.* **2** [*often pass.*] **a** to cause (LABOUR¹ (3)) to begin by medical means **b** to cause (a baby) to be born, or (a mother) to give birth, by medical means: *She had to be induced because the baby was four weeks late.* **3** *fml* to cause or produce: *The medicine may induce drowsiness.*

in·duce·ment /ɪnˈdjuːsmənt‖ɪnˈduːs-/ *n* [C;U] (something which provides) encouragement to do something: [+*to-v*] *They offered her a share in the business as an inducement to stay.*

in·duct /ɪnˈdʌkt/ *v* [T (**into**) often pass.] **1** to introduce (someone, esp. a priest) into an official position in a special ceremony **2** *esp. AmE* to introduce (someone) officially into a group or organization, esp. into the army

in·duct·ee /ˌɪndʌkˈtiː/ *n AmE for* CONSCRIPT²

in·duc·tion /ɪnˈdʌkʃən/ *n* **1** [U (**into**)] the act of inducting **2** [U] the act of inducing: *the induction of labour after a long pregnancy* **3** [C;U] a ceremony in which a person is inducted into a position or organization **4** [C;U] (an) introduction into a new job, company, etc.: *an induction course* **5** [U] *tech* the production of electricity in one object by another which already has electrical (or MAGNETIC) power **6** [C;U] (an example or result of) a process of reasoning using known facts to produce general rules or principles —compare DEDUCTION

in·duc·tive /ɪnˈdʌktɪv/ *adj* using INDUCTION (6); reasoning from known facts to produce general principles: *inductive reasoning* —compare DEDUCTIVE — ~**ly** *adv*

in·due /ɪnˈdjuː‖ɪnˈduː/ *v*
indue sbdy. **with** sthg. *phr v* [T] *AmE for* ENDUE with

in·dulge /ɪnˈdʌldʒ/ *v* **1** [T] to allow (oneself or someone else) to have or do what they want, esp. habitually: *They may spoil their grandchildren by indulging them too much.* **2** [T] to let oneself or someone else have (their wish to do or have something, etc.): *They indulge my every whim.* | *to indulge a love of expensive wines* **3** [I (**in**)] *infml* to allow oneself to have or do something that one enjoys, esp. something that is considered rather bad or harmful: *I wouldn't say he's a heavy drinker but he tends to indulge* (=drink too much) *at parties.* | *I occasionally indulge in a big fat cigar.*

in·dul·gence /ɪnˈdʌldʒəns/ *n* **1** [U (**to, towards**)] the habit of allowing someone to do or have what they want —see also SELF-INDULGENCE **2** [U] *infml* the habit or activity of indulging in something, esp. too much food or alcohol **3** [C] something in which one indulges: *Sweets are/smoking is my only indulgence.* **4** [C;U] (in the Roman Catholic Church) freedom from punishment by God for wrong-doing, given by a priest —**gent** *adj* : *indulgent grandparents* | *indulgent to their grandchildren* —**gently** *adv*

in·dus·tri·al /ɪnˈdʌstriəl/ *adj* **1** of industry and the people who work in it: *industrial unrest/democracy/output* | **Industrial relations** *concerns the relationship between the management and the workers in an industry.* **2** having highly developed industries: *an industrial nation* —compare INDUSTRIOUS — ~**ly** *adv* : *an industrially developed country*

industrial ac·tion /·ˌ···ˈ··/ *n* [U] *esp. BrE* action by workers (such as a STRIKE or a WORK-TO-RULE) intended to put pressure on employers to agree to the workers' demands

industrial ar·chae·ol·o·gy /·ˌ····ˈ···/ *n* [U] the study of the factories, machinery, and products of earlier stages of the INDUSTRIAL REVOLUTION

industrial art /·ˌ··· ˈ·/ also **shop class, shop** *n* [U] *AmE* a subject taught in school on how to use tools and machinery: *Industrial Arts classes offered this semester are Automotive Repair, Printing, Woodworking, and Electronics.*

industrial dis·pute /·ˌ··· ·ˈ·, ·ˌ··· ˈ··/ *n* a disagreement between an employer or the management of a business or industry and the people working there, who are usu. represented by a TRADE UNION. If agreement cannot be reached, a trade union may instruct its members to WORK TO RULE, refuse OVERTIME or go on STRIKE. In Britain, if an industrial dispute continues for a long time and agreement cannot be reached, the two sides may go to ACAS, an independent body which tries to find agreement in industrial disputes. In the US, such a dispute may go to an arbitrator (ARBITRATE) who has been agreed upon by both sides.

industrial es·pi·o·nage /·ˌ··· ˈ·····/ *n* [U] the action of a business or industry in trying to find out the secrets of another, usu. in order to gain an advantage

industrial es·tate /·ˌ··· ·ˈ·/ *BrE* ‖**industrial park** /·ˌ··· ˈ·/, **science park, business park** *AmE*— *n* a piece of land, often on the edge of a city, with buildings on it, planned as a place for small factories and businesses

in·dus·tri·al·is·m /ɪnˈdʌstriəlɪzəm/ *n* [U] the system by which a society gains its wealth through industries and machinery

in·dus·tri·al·ist /ɪnˈdʌstriəlɪst/ *n* the owner or manager of a factory, industrial company, etc.

in·dus·tri·al·ize also **-ise** *BrE* /ɪnˈdʌstriəlaɪz/ *v* [I;T] to (cause to) become industrially developed: *a meeting of finance ministers from the major industrialized countries* —**ization** /ɪnˌdʌstriəlaɪˈzeɪʃən/-lə-/ *n* [U]

industrial re·la·tions /·ˌ··· ·ˈ··/ *n* [P] the (good or bad) relationship between an employer or the management of a business or industry and the people working there who are usu. represented by a TRADE UNION

industrial rev·o·lu·tion /·ˌ··· ··ˈ··/ *n* (*often caps.*) a period of time when machines are invented and factories set up, and the changes which take place during this time (as in Britain around 1750–1850): *Will computers and automation bring about a new Industrial Revolution?*

industrial tri·bu·nal /·ˌ··· ·ˈ··/ *n* in Britain, an official organization which makes decisions in INDUSTRIAL DISPUTEs, usu. those involving an individual

in·dus·tri·ous /ɪnˈdʌstriəs/ *adj* hard-working; DILIGENT —compare INDUSTRIAL — ~**ly** *adv* — ~**ness** *n* [U]

in·dus·try /ˈɪndəstri/ *n* **1** [U] the production of goods for sale, esp. in factories, or of materials that can be used in the production of goods: *a decline in manufacturing industry* **2** [U] the people and organizations that work in the production of goods: *Are the government's policies helpful to industry?* | *an agreement that will be welcomed by both sides of industry* (=by employers and workers) **3** [C] a particular branch of industry or trade, usu. employing large numbers of people and using machinery and/or modern methods: *the steel/food/aerospace/clothing industry* | *The tourist trade has become a real industry.* | (*fig. derog*) *yet another book from the Shakespeare industry* **4** [U] continual hard work; industriousness: *Success comes with industry.* —see also HEAVY INDUSTRY, SUNRISE INDUSTRY

i·ne·bri·ate /ɪˈniːbrieɪt/ *v* [T *usu. pass.*] *fml or pomp* to make drunk: *They were totally inebriated by the end of the party.* —**inebriate** /-bri-ɪt, -brieɪt/ *n* —**ation** /ɪˌniːbriˈeɪʃən/ *n* [U]

in·ed·i·ble /ɪnˈedɪbəl/ *adj* not suitable for eating —**bly** *adv* —**bility** /ɪnˌediˈbɪlɪti/ *n* [U]

in·ed·u·ca·ble /ɪnˈedjʊkəbəl‖-dʒə-/ *adj* impossible to educate esp. because of weakness of mind —**bly** *adv* —**bility** /ɪnˌedjʊkəˈbɪlɪti‖-dʒə-/ *n* [U]

in·ef·fa·ble /ɪnˈefəbəl/ *adj fml* **1** too wonderful to be described: *ineffable joy* **2** (esp. of the name of God in some religions) not to be spoken aloud: *the ineffable name* —**bly** *adv* —**bility** /ɪnˌefəˈbɪlɪti/ *n* [U]

in·ef·fec·tive /ˌɪnɪˈfektɪv◂/ *adj* not resulting in or able to produce good or intended effects: *In terms of improving the economic situation, this policy has been largely ineffective.* | *an ineffective manager* — ~**ly** *adv* — ~**ness** *n* [U]

in·ef·fec·tu·al /ˌɪnɪˈfektʃuəl◂/ *adj* not producing satisfactory or intended results or not able to get things done: *an ineffectual plan* | *He won't be able to deal with the situation; he's too ineffectual.* — ~**ly** *adv*

in·ef·fi·cient /ˌɪnɪˈfɪʃənt◂/ *adj* not working or performing in a satisfactory way, esp. because of wastefulness or lack of ability and organization; not EFFICIENT: *an inefficient heating system* | *an inefficient secretary* — ~**ly** *adv* —**ciency** /ɪnɪˈfɪʃənsi/ *n* [U] : *Due to the inefficiency of the postal system, her letters took two weeks to arrive.*

in·el·e·gant /ɪnˈelɪgənt/ *adj* lacking in grace or good taste; not ELEGANT: *an inelegant gesture* — ~**ly** *adv* —**gance** *n* [U]

in·el·i·gi·ble /ɪnˈelɪdʒɪbəl/ *adj* [(**for**)] not suitable to be chosen or included; not ELIGIBLE: *ineligible for election because too young* [F+*to-v*] *He was ineligible to vote, because he didn't belong to the club.* —**bility** /ɪnˌelɪdʒɪˈbɪlɪti/ *n* [U]

in·e·luc·ta·ble /ˌɪnɪˈlʌktəbəl/ *adj lit* impossible to escape from; unavoidable —**bly** *adv*

in·ept /ɪˈnept/ *adj* **1** [(**at**)] not effective; CLUMSY: *I made a rather inept attempt to remedy the situation.* **2** foolishly unsuitable: *What an inept remark to make on such a*

formal occasion. —compare INAPT – ~ **ly** *adv* – ~ **itude,** ~ **ness** *n* [U]

in·e·qual·i·ty /ˌɪnɪˈkwɒlˌti‖-ˈkwɑː-/ *n* [C *usu. pl*;U] (a) lack of fairness or equality: *There are many inequalities in the law.* | *social inequality*

in·eq·ui·ta·ble /ɪnˈekwˌtəbəl/ *adj fml* not equally fair to everyone; unjust: *an inequitable distribution of the money* —**bly** *adv*

in·eq·ui·ty /ɪnˈekwˌti/ *n* [C;U] *fml* (an example of) injustice or unfairness

in·e·rad·i·ca·ble /ˌɪnɪˈrædɪkəbəl/ *adj fml* which cannot be completely removed, esp. from a person's character: *an ineradicable flaw* —**bly** *adv*

in·ert /ɪˈnɜːt‖-ɜːrt/ *adj* **1** without the strength or power to move: *He lay completely inert on the floor and we feared he was dead.* **2** *tech* not acting chemically when combined with other substances: *inert gases* – ~ **ly** *adv* – ~ **ness** *n* [U]

in·er·tia /ɪˈnɜːʃə‖-ɜːr-/ *n* [U] **1** the force which keeps a thing in the position or state it is in until it is moved or stopped by another force: *A ball will keep rolling* **under its own inertia** *until friction stops it.* | (fig.) *The inertia of the parliamentary system ensures that such inequalities are never put right.* **2** the state of being powerless to move or too lazy to move: *a feeling of inertia on a hot summer day*

inertia reel /·ˈ··· ˌ·/ *n* a wound length, esp. of a SEAT BELT in a car, that will unwind if it is pulled steadily but sticks if it is pulled suddenly

inertia sel·ling /·ˌ·· ˈ··/ *n* [U] *esp. BrE* the selling of goods by sending them to people who have not asked for them and demanding payment if they are not returned

in·es·ca·pa·ble /ˌɪnɪˈskeɪpəbl◂/ *adj* impossible to avoid: *Your son was the only person there, so the inescapable inference is that he stole the money.* —**bly** *adv*

in·es·sen·tial[1] /ˌɪnˌˈsenʃəl◂/ *adj* [(to)] not needed; unnecessary

inessential[2] *n* [*often pl.*] something that is not needed: *This report does not concern itself with inessentials; it gets directly to the main point.*

in·es·ti·ma·ble /ɪnˈestˌməbəl/ *adj fml apprec* too great or excellent to be calculated: *Your advice has been of inestimable value to us.* —**bly** *adv*

in·ev·i·ta·ble /ɪˈnevˌtəbəl/ *adj* **1** which cannot be avoided or prevented from happening; certain to happen: *A confrontation was inevitable because they disliked each other so much.* | *They reached the inevitable conclusion that the money must have been stolen.* | *the inevitable consequences of his actions* | *Given the current financial situation, it was inevitable that the pound would be devalued.* **2** [A] *infml* which always happens or is always present: *The head teacher made his inevitable joke about the school food.* —**bly** *adv* : *He was, inevitably, upset by her departure, but he soon got over it.* —**bility** /ɪˌnevˌtəˈbɪlˌti/ *n* [U]

in·ex·act /ˌɪnɪgˈzækt◂/ *adj* not exact: *Sociology is an inexact science.* – ~ **itude,** ~ **ness** *n* [U]

in·ex·cu·sa·ble /ˌɪnɪkˈskjuːzəbəl/ *adj* too bad to be excused: *inexcusable behaviour/lateness/rudeness* —**bly** *adv*

in·ex·haus·ti·ble /ˌɪnɪgˈzɔːstˌbəl/ *adj* existing in such large amounts that it can never be finished or used up: *inexhaustible patience* | *an inexhaustible supply of funny stories* —**bly** *adv*

in·ex·o·ra·ble /ɪnˈeksərəbəl/ *adj* **1** whose actions or effects cannot be changed or prevented by one's efforts: *the slow but inexorable workings of British justice* | *inexorable price rises* **2** *fml* not able to be persuaded to act differently: *an inexorable opponent* —**bly** *adv* : *The runaway train bore down inexorably on the trapped rabbit.* —**bility** /ɪnˌeksərəˈbɪlˌti/ *n* [U]

in·ex·pe·di·ent /ˌɪnɪkˈspiːdiənt/ *adj fml* not useful, advisable, or convenient; not EXPEDIENT —**ency, -ence** *n* [U]

in·ex·pen·sive /ˌɪnɪkˈspensɪv◂/ *adj often euph* reasonable in price; not expensive – ~ **ly** *adv* – ~ **ness** *n* [U]

in·ex·pe·ri·ence /ˌɪnɪkˈspɪəriəns/ *n* [U] lack of experience

in·ex·pe·ri·enced /ˌɪnɪkˈspɪəriənst◂/ *adj* (of a person) lacking the knowledge which one gains by experiencing some activity or life generally: *a rather inexperienced young salesman*

in·ex·pert /ɪnˈekspɜːt‖-ɜːrt/ *adj* [(at, in)] not good at doing something; unskilled: *his inexpert attempts to cook/to speak French* – ~ **ly** *adv* – ~ **ness** *n* [U]

in·ex·plic·a·ble /ˌɪnɪkˈsplɪkəbəl‖ɪnˈeksplɪkəbəl, ˌɪnɪkˈsplɪk-/ *adj* too strange to be explained or understood: *the inexplicable disappearance of the woman, who was never seen again* —**bility** /ˌɪnɪkˌsplɪkəˈbɪlˌti/ *n* [U]

in·ex·plic·a·bly /ˌɪnɪkˈsplɪkəbli/ *adv* **1** in an inexplicable way **2** it is an inexplicable fact (that): *Inexplicably, journalists failed to report the affair, and the scandal was hidden from the public for several weeks.*

in·ex·pres·si·ble /ˌɪnɪkˈspresˌbəl/ *adj fml* (of a feeling) too great or too strong to be expressed in words: *inexpressible joy/sorrow/relief* —**bly** *adv* —**bility** /ˌɪnɪkspresˌˈbɪlˌti/ *n* [U]

in·ex·press·ive /ˌɪnɪkˈspresɪv◂/ *adj* lacking expression or meaning: *an inexpressive face*

in·ex·tin·guish·a·ble /ˌɪnɪkˈstɪŋgwɪʃəbəl/ *adj fml* (of fire and feelings) which cannot be destroyed or put out: *inextinguishable hope* | (fig.) *the inextinguishable flame of liberty*

in ex·tre·mis /ˌɪn ɪkˈstriːmɪs/ *adv Lat fml* (as if) at the moment of death: *The government's incomes plan was saved in extremis* (=when it was about to fail) *by some last-minute concessions to the unions.*

in·ex·tri·ca·ble /ɪnˈekstrɪkəbəl, ˌɪnɪkˈstrɪ-/ *adj fml* **1** from which it is impossible to get free: *inextricable financial troubles* **2** which cannot be untied or separated: *The history of scientific advance and the history of warfare are inextricable.* —**bly** *adv* : *The country's high birthrate and low life expectancy are inextricably linked.*

in·fal·li·ble /ɪnˈfælˌbəl/ *adj* **1** never making mistakes or doing anything bad: *So what if I did get the answer wrong? I'm not infallible, you know!* | *an infallible memory* **2** (of a thing) always having the right effect: *an infallible remedy/cure* —**bly** *adv* —**bility** /ɪnˌfælˌˈbɪlˌti/ *n* [U] : *Catholics are required to believe in the infallibility of the Pope.*

in·fa·mous /ˈɪnfəməs/ *adj* **1** well known for being bad, esp. morally wicked: *an infamous criminal/traitor* | (fig.) *Steve's infamous for his practical jokes.* **2** *fml* evil; wicked: *infamous behaviour* —see FAMOUS (USAGE)

in·fa·my /ˈɪnfəmi/ *n fml* **1** [U] the quality of being infamous **2** [C *often pl.*] an infamous act

in·fan·cy /ˈɪnfənsi/ *n* [S;U] **1** the period of being an infant; early childhood **2** a beginning or early period of existence: *The company is still only* **in its infancy.**

in·fant /ˈɪnfənt/ *n* **1** a very young child, esp. one who has not learnt to speak or walk: *a high rate of infant mortality* —see CHILD (USAGE) **2** *BrE* a very young schoolchild, esp. below the age of eight: *Our little boy is in the infants' class.* | *an infant teacher*

in·fan·ta /ɪnˈfæntə/ *n* (*often cap.*) the daughter of a Spanish or Portuguese king

in·fan·ti·cide /ɪnˈfæntˌsaɪd/ *n* **1** [C;U] *fml* the crime of killing a child, esp. an infant. Infanticide is still practised in some societies where girl children are killed in countries where male children are considered more valuable. **2** [C] *tech* a person guilty of this crime

in·fan·tile /ˈɪnfəntaɪl/ *adj usu. derog* like or typical of a small child; PUERILE: *infantile humour* | *His behaviour is appallingly infantile!* (=foolishly childlike)

infantile pa·ral·y·sis /ˌ···· ·ˈ····/ *n* [U] *old-fash for* POLIO

infant mor·tal·i·ty rate /ˌ··· ·ˈ···· ·/ *n* (*abbrev.* **IMR**) the number of deaths of babies under one year old, expressed per 1000 babies born alive in a year. This figure is regarded as a measure of a country's wealth and social development.

infant prod·i·gy /ˌ··· ˈ···/ *also* **child prodigy**— *n* a (young) child with unusually great ability and understanding: *Mozart was an infant prodigy: he composed a symphony at the age of seven.*

in·fan·try /ˈɪnfəntri/ *n* [(the) U+*sing./pl. v*] soldiers who fight on foot: *Our infantry was/were fighting bravely.* | *My son's in the infantry.* —compare CAVALRY

in·fan·try·man /ˈɪnfəntrimən/ *n* -**men** /mən/ a soldier who fights on foot

infant school /ˈ··· ·/ *n* (in Britain) a school for children aged 5 to 7 or 8 —compare ELEMENTARY SCHOOL; —see also PRIMARY SCHOOL and see extra information on page 408

in·fat·u·at·ed /ɪnˈfætʃueɪtɪd/ adj [(with)] usu. derog (of a person) filled with a strong, unreasonable, but usu. not long-lasting, feeling of love. Many people think of being infatuated as something experienced by young people, esp. TEENAGERS at school, sometimes with someone of the same sex: *She's really infatuated with that boy next door.* | (fig.) *He's infatuated with his own importance.*

in·fat·u·a·tion /ɪnˌfætʃuˈeɪʃən/ n [C;U (with)] a state or period of being infatuated: *It's only an infatuation; she'll get over it soon enough.*

in·fect /ɪnˈfekt/ v [T (with)] **1** (of disease) to get into the body of (someone), often through the air: *The open wound soon became infected.* | *Don't come near me if you've got a cold – I don't want to be infected.* **2** to make (air, food, etc.) impure by spreading disease into it; CONTAMINATE: *infected food* **3** to make (someone else) have feelings of the same type: *She infected the whole class with her enthusiasm.*

in·fec·tion /ɪnˈfekʃən/ n [C;U] the act or result of infecting, or a disease spread by infecting: *a lung/chest infection* | *Sterilize the needle to prevent infection* —compare CONTAGION

in·fec·tious /ɪnˈfekʃəs/ adj (of a disease) that can be passed from one person to another by infection, esp. in the air: *Colds are infectious.* | (fig.) *infectious laughter* —compare CONTAGIOUS – – **ly** adv – – **ness** n [U]

in·fer /ɪnˈfɜːr/ v **-rr-** [T (from)] to form an opinion from or make a judgment based on (something); DEDUCE: *What can we infer from his refusal to see us?* [+that] *I infer from your letter that you have not yet made a decision.*
▷ USAGE Compare **infer** and **imply**. The speaker or writer **implies** something, and the listener or reader **infers** it. *His remarks* **implied** (=suggested indirectly) *that he hadn't enjoyed his holiday.* | *I* **inferred** (=understood) *from his remarks that he hadn't enjoyed his holiday.*◁

in·fer·ence /ˈɪnfərəns/ n **1** [U] the act of inferring: *Our conclusions were arrived at by inference, not by direct evidence.* **2** [C] the judgment that one forms about the meaning of something done, said, etc.: *He never arrives on time; the inference is that he feels the meetings are useless.* —compare IMPLICATION

in·fer·en·tial /ˌɪnfəˈrenʃəl/ adj which can be or has been inferred; not direct: *inferential proof* – – **ly** adv

in·fe·ri·or¹ /ɪnˈfɪəriər/ adj [(to)] **1** not good or less good in quality or value: *His work is inferior to mine.* | *She's so clever, she makes me feel inferior.* | *an inferior mind* | *goods of inferior quality* **2** fml or tech lower in position: *an inferior court of law* —compare SUPERIOR; see MAJOR (USAGE) – – **ity** /ɪnˌfɪəriˈɒrɪti/-ˈɔːr-/ n [U]

inferior² n often derog a person of lower rank, esp. in a job; SUBORDINATE —compare SUPERIOR² (1)

inferiority com·plex /ˌ · · · · · · / n [(about)] a condition of the mind in which someone believes himself or herself to be much less important, clever, etc. than other people, sometimes resulting in avoiding other people or trying to attract attention —compare SUPERIORITY COMPLEX

in·fer·nal /ɪnˈfɜːnl‖-ɜːr-/ adj **1** [A] old-fash infml (used esp. to express anger or annoyance) extremely unpleasant; terrible: *What an infernal racket/din!* | *an infernal nuisance* **2** [no comp.] lit of HELL: *the infernal powers* – – **ly** adv : *infernally noisy* | *an infernally long time*

in·fer·no /ɪnˈfɜːnəʊ‖-ɜːr-/ n **-nos** a place of very great heat and large uncontrollable flames: *The oilrig caught fire and quickly became a raging inferno.* —see also DANTE'S INFERNO

in·fer·tile /ɪnˈfɜːtaɪl‖-ɜːrtl/ adj **1** [no comp.] not able to produce young: *infertile eggs* **2** (of land) not able to grow plants

in·fer·til·i·ty /ˌɪnfɜːˈtɪlɪti‖-ɜːr-/ n [U] the state of being infertile: *the infertility of the soil*

in·fest /ɪnˈfest/ v [T (with)] (of something harmful, dangerous, or unwanted) to be present (in a place) in large numbers or to a great degree: *Mice infested the old house.* | *It would be crazy to swim in these shark-infested waters.* – – **ation** /ˌɪnfeˈsteɪʃən/ n [C;U] : *an infestation of lice/dry rot*

in·fi·del /ˈɪnfɪdəl/ n old use derog (used esp. in former times by Christians and Muslims of each other) someone who does not follow one's own religion; an unbeliever: *war against the infidels*

in·fi·del·i·ty /ˌɪnfɪˈdelɪti/ n [C;U (to)] **1** (an example or act of) not being faithful **2** (an act of) sex with someone other than one's marriage partner —compare FIDELITY

in·field /ˈɪnfiːld/ n **1** the part of a cricket field nearest to the player who hits the ball **2** the part of a BASEBALL field inside the four bases —see picture at BASEBALL **3** [+sing./pl. v] the players in this part of the field —compare OUTFIELD – – **er** n

in·fight·ing /ˈɪnfaɪtɪŋ/ n [U] competition and disagreement, often bitter, which goes on between close members of a group, e.g. partners in a company or members of a political party: *political infighting*

in·fil·trate /ˈɪnfɪltreɪt‖ɪnˈfɪltreɪt, ˈɪnfɪl-/ v [T (into)] to (cause to) go into (a place) or become part of (an organization), secretly or without being noticed, and usu. with an unfriendly purpose: *She claimed that Communist sympathizers had infiltrated our organization.* | *We infiltrated some of our troops into enemy territory.* —**tration** /ˌɪnfɪlˈtreɪʃən/ n [C;U] —**trator** /ˈɪnfɪltreɪtər‖ɪnˈfɪltreɪtər, ˈɪnfɪl-/ n

in·fi·nite¹ /ˈɪnfɪnɪt/ adj **1** without limits or end; not FINITE: *The universe is infinite.* | *an infinite number of possibilities* **2** very great: *with infinite care/patience* | *This is an infinite improvement on your previous work.* | *My father has decreed,* **in his infinite wisdom** (=I completely disagree), *that all motorbikes are killers, so I can't buy one.* – – **ly** adv : *infinitely large/better*

infinite² [the] (often cap.) the highest power of the spirit; God

in·fin·i·tes·i·mal /ˌɪnfɪnɪˈtesɪməl/ adj extremely small: *an infinitesimal amount* – – **ly** adv

in·fin·i·tive /ɪnˈfɪnɪtɪv/ n the form of a verb that is usually used with **to** and can follow a noun, adjective, or other verb (for example, **go** in *a desire to go, It is important to go,* and *I want to go*) and can sometimes be used without **to** when following certain verbs (for example, **go** in *You may go* and *I saw her go*) —see TO³ (USAGE); see also SPLIT INFINITIVE – **infinitive** adj : *an infinitive construction*

in·fin·i·tude /ɪnˈfɪnɪtjuːd‖-tuːd/ n [S;U] fml largeness; wideness; lack of limits: *the vast infinitude of space*

in·fin·i·ty /ɪnˈfɪnɪti/ n [U] **1** a point at an infinite distance away: *The universe stretches out to infinity.* | *Parallel lines meet at infinity.* **2** a number too large to be calculated

in·firm /ɪnˈfɜːm‖-ɜːrm/ adj weak in body or mind, esp. from age: *old and infirm*

in·fir·ma·ry /ɪnˈfɜːməri‖-ɜːr-/ n **1** a hospital **2** a room or other place where people who are ill are given care and treatment: *the school infirmary*

in·fir·mi·ty /ɪnˈfɜːmɪti‖-ɜːr-/ n fml **1** [C usu. pl.;U] (a) weakness of body or mind: *the infirmities of old age* | *suffering from age and infirmity* **2** **infirmity of purpose** lit inability to decide

in fla·gran·te de·lic·to /ɪn fləˌɡrænti dɪˈlɪktəʊ/ adv Lat, often humor in an act of SEXUAL INTERCOURSE, esp. one with someone else's husband/wife

in·flame /ɪnˈfleɪm/ v [T (with)] to make (more) violent or angry: *His indiscreet comments only served to inflame the dispute.* | *inflamed with desire*

in·flamed /ɪnˈfleɪmd/ adj (of a part of the body) red and swollen because hurt or diseased: *an inflamed eye*

in·flam·ma·ble /ɪnˈflæməbəl/ adj **1** also **flammable** esp. AmE or tech— which can easily be set on fire and which burns quickly: *Clothes shouldn't be made of inflammable material.* | *Petrol is highly inflammable.* | (fig.) *The situation is highly inflammable.* —opposite **nonflammable, flameproof 2** easily excited or made angry — compare INFLAMMATORY; see FLAMMABLE (USAGE)

in·flam·ma·tion /ˌɪnfləˈmeɪʃən/ n [C;U] (a) swelling and soreness on or in the body, which is often red and hot to the touch: *an inflammation of the lungs* —see also INFLAMED

in·flam·ma·to·ry /ɪnˈflæmətəri‖-tɔːri/ adj likely to cause strong feelings or violence: *inflammatory remarks* — compare INFLAMMABLE; see also INFLAME

in·fla·ta·ble /ɪnˈfleɪtəbəl/ adj which must be inflated for use: *an inflatable raft/life jacket*

in·fla·ta·bles /ɪnˈfleɪtəbəlz/ n [P] BrE inflatable objects which children use in a swimming pool to help them float

in·flate /ɪnˈfleɪt/ v fml **1** [I;T] to (cause to) fill until swelled with air or gas; blow up: *She inflated the balloon.* | *Pull this cord to inflate the life jacket.* **2** [T] to raise (a price) by INFLATION (2)

in·flat·ed /ɪnˈfleɪtɪd/ adj **1** (of prices) risen or put up to a high level: *charging ridiculously inflated prices for their goods* **2** derog increased to a level (e.g. of importance or value) that is falsely high: *an inflated opinion of himself* | *artificially inflated statistics* **3** blown up (e.g. with air): *an inflated lung|balloon—* opposite **deflated**

in·fla·tion /ɪnˈfleɪʃən/ n [U] **1** (the rate of) a continuing rise in prices: *The government is determined to bring down inflation (to below 5%).* | *The annual rate of inflation was 10%.* | *an* **inflation-proof** *pension* (=which rises in value at the rate of inflation) —compare DEFLATION, REFLATION **2** the act of inflating or state of being inflated

in·fla·tion·a·ry /ɪnˈfleɪʃənəri‖-ʃəneri/ adj of or likely to cause inflation: *inflationary pressures in the economy* | *inflationary wage increases*

inflationary spi·ral /·,····ˈ··/ n the continuing rise in wages and prices which happens because an increase in wages tends to produce an increase in prices, so that wages have to be increased again: *The economy is caught in an inflationary spiral.*

in·fla·tion·is·m /ɪnˈfleɪʃənɪzəm/ n [U] the idea of causing economic inflation by increasing the supply of money in a country (=CURRENCY)

in·flect /ɪnˈflekt/ v [I;T] esp. tech **1** to change or cause (a word) to change in form according to its meaning or use: *The word "child" inflects|is inflected in the plural by adding "-ren" to it.* | *German is a highly inflected language.* —compare CONJUGATE (1,2), DECLINE¹ (4) **2** to change or cause (the voice) to change, esp. in level, according to the needs of expression

in·flec·tion also **inflexion** BrE /ɪnˈflekʃən/ n esp. tech **1** [U] the process or result of inflecting; the change in the form of a word to show difference in its meaning or use **2** [C] a word part which is added to another word when inflecting it: *In "largest", "-est" is the inflection meaning "most".* **3** [C] a movement up or down of the voice: *A sentence that asks a question usually ends on a rising inflection.* —compare INTONATION — ~ **al** adj : *an inflectional suffix*

in·flex·i·ble /ɪnˈfleksəbəl/ adj **1** difficult or impossible to bend; stiff and firm: *The new plastic is completely inflexible.* **2** usu. derog (of a person) refusing to be turned away from one's purpose, esp. in an unreasonable way; UNBENDING: *You'll never get him to change his mind; he's so inflexible.* **3** (of an idea, decision, etc.) which cannot be changed, even when change is desirable: *His attitude has become even more rigid and inflexible than it was before.* —**bly** adv —**bility** /ɪnˌfleksəˈbɪləti/ n [U] : *The inflexibility of the country's labour market seriously impedes its economic recovery.*

in·flict /ɪnˈflɪkt/ v [T (on, upon)] to force (something or someone unpleasant or unwanted) on someone: *The judge inflicted the severest possible penalty.* | *Don't inflict your ridiculous ideas on me!* | *Mary has inflicted the children on her mother for the weekend.* —**infliction** /-ˈflɪkʃən/ n [C;U (on, upon)] : *He seems to delight in the infliction of pain.* (=causing pain to people)

in·flight /ˈ··ˈ·/ adj [A] happening or provided during a trip by plane: *in-flight meals|entertainment*

in·flow /ˈɪnfləʊ/ also **influx—** n [C;U] the action or process of flowing in or something which does: *the inflow of money to the banks* | *a big inflow of refugees*

in·flu·ence¹ /ˈɪnfluəns/ n [C;U] **1** [(over, on, upon, with)] (the power to have) an effect on someone or something without the use of direct force or command: *He promised to use his influence with the chairman to get me the job.* | *The stars' influence on people's lives has not been proved.* | *She's a woman of some influence in government circles.* | *They had come* **under the influence of** *a strange religious sect.* | *Listening to the music had a calming influence on her.* **2** [(for, on)] a person or thing that has this power: *I wish she wouldn't go around with that boy; he's such a* **bad influence** *(on her).* | *Gospel music and blues are the main influences on his music.* **3** **under the influence (of alcohol)** infml drunk: *He was fined for driving under the influence.*

influence² v [T] to have an effect on (a person or their

behaviour), esp. in causing or persuading someone to act in a particular way but without the use of direct force or command; AFFECT²: *Don't let me influence your decision.* | *Her writing has obviously been influenced by Virginia Woolf.* [+obj+to-v] *What were the factors that influenced you to take the job?*

in·flu·en·tial /ˌɪnfluˈenʃəl◂/ adj having great influence: *an influential writer|newspaper|speech* — — **ly** adv

in·flu·en·za /ˌɪnfluˈenzə/ n [U] fml for FLU

in·flux /ˈɪnflʌks/ n **1** [C (of)] usu. sing.] the esp. sudden arrival of large numbers or quantities: *a sudden influx of imported electronic goods onto the market* | *a great influx of tourists into the town in the summer months* **2** [C;U] an INFLOW

in·fo /ˈɪnfəʊ/ n [U] infml information

in·form /ɪnˈfɔːm‖-ɔːrm/ v [T (of, about)] usu. fml to give information or knowledge to; tell: *I wasn't informed of the decision until too late.* | *Why wasn't I informed?* [+obj+(that)] *I informed him that I would not be able to attend.* [+obj+wh-] *Could you please inform me how to go about contacting a lawyer?* —see SAY¹ (USAGE)

inform against/on sbdy. phr v [T] sometimes derog to give the police, or someone in a position of power, information about the guilt of (someone): *I'm amazed to hear that she was the one who informed on her husband.*

in·for·mal /ɪnˈfɔːməl‖-ɔːr-/ adj **1** not formal; not following official or established rules, methods, etc.: *an informal agreement|meeting* | *We have made preliminary, informal approaches to the committee.* | *informal talks between the two leaders* **2 a** (of clothes, behaviour, etc.) suitable for ordinary everyday situations but not for official occasions **b** esp. tech (of words or a style of writing or speaking) suitable for ordinary conversation, e.g. with friends or people one works with, but not for serious writing or official occasions. Informal words or phrases are marked *infml* in this dictionary: *"Info" is an informal word for "information".* — ~ **ly** adv : *I told him informally that he'd got the job, but that official confirmation wouldn't come for a few days.* — ~ **ity** /ˌɪnfɔːˈmælɪti‖ -ɔːr-/ n [U]

in·for·mant /ɪnˈfɔːmənt‖-ɔːr-/ n fml **1** someone who gives information, esp. to the police, a government, etc.: *The FBI were warned about the spy ring by a confidential informant.* **2** someone who gives information, esp. someone who gives details of their language, social customs, etc., to a person who is studying them —compare INFORMER

in·for·ma·tion /ˌɪnfəˈmeɪʃən‖-fər-/ n [U (about, on)] **1** (something which gives) knowledge in the form of facts, news, etc.: *Could you give me some information about flights to Cairo, please?* | *an interesting piece of information* | *This book gives all sorts of useful information on how to repair cars.* | *Acting on information received, the police have arrested two suspects.* [+that] *We have received information that they may have left the country.* | *(fml) According to my information* (=I have been told), *he is no longer here.* | *classified information* (=officially secret information) **2** AmE (often cap.) the telephone service which provides telephone numbers to people who ask for them: *Her number's not in the book yet but you can get it from information.* | *How do you get information for Los Angeles?* DIRECTORY ENQUIRIES — -**tional** adj

information cen·tre /·ˈ··ˌ·ˈ·/ n a place, often in somewhere such as a big EXHIBITION, a hospital, a place which tourists visit, or a NATURE RESERVE, where people can get information: *I wonder if there's an information centre anywhere?* | *For further information, write to the National Building Information Centre, 138 Birchanger Street...*

information re·triev·al /·ˈ··· ·ˌ··/ n [U] tech the finding of stored information when it is needed, esp. from a computer

information sci·ence /ˌ·····ˈ··/ n [U] the science of collecting, arranging, storing, retrieving (RETRIEVE), and sending out information

information tech·nol·o·gy /·ˈ··· ·ˌ····/ also **IT** abbrev.— n [U] the science or practice of collecting, storing, using, and sending out information by means of computer systems and TELECOMMUNICATIONS

information theo·ry /·ˈ··· ·ˌ··/ n [U] the mathematical principles that deal with information and the sending of information between humans and machines

in·for·ma·tive /ɪnˈfɔːmətɪv‖-ɔːr-/ adj providing useful facts or ideas: *an informative television documentary* — opposite **uninformative** – – ly adv

in·formed /ɪnˈfɔːmd‖-ɔːr-/ adj 1 [(**about, on**)] having or showing knowledge; having information: *well-informed | badly informed | Please keep me informed of any developments in the situation. | Informed sources/observers predict serious repercussions on the government.* 2 using one's knowledge of a situation: *I don't know exactly how many votes he will get, but I can make an informed guess.*

informed o·pin·ion /·,· · ·ˈ··/ n [U] esp. BrE those people who are in a position to know: *Informed opinion has it that/says she's coming today.*

in·form·er /ɪnˈfɔːməʳ‖-ɔːr-/ n sometimes derog a person who informs against someone else, esp. to the police in return for money —compare INFORMANT

in·frac·tion /ɪnˈfrækʃən/ n [C;U (**of**)] fml (an example of) the breaking of a rule or law: *Any infraction of the regulations will be punished.*

in·fra dig /ˌɪnfrə ˈdɪg/ adj [F] infml, esp. BrE below one's standard of social or moral behaviour: *It's a bit infra dig for him to wear brown shoes on such a formal occasion.*

in·fra·red /ˌɪnfrəˈred◂/ adj of or being RAYS of light of long WAVELENGTH that cannot be seen but give heat: *an infrared grill/lamp | infrared radiation* —compare ULTRAVIOLET

in·fra·struc·ture /ˈɪnfrəˌstrʌktʃəʳ/ n the system or structures which are necessary for the operation of a country or an organization: *Vast sums are needed to maintain the infrastructure* (=water/power/road systems) *| a country's economic infrastructure* (=its banks and other organizations which handle and control its money)

in·fre·quent /ɪnˈfriːkwənt/ adj fml not (happening) often; rare: *infrequent visits | an infrequent visitor* – – ly adv —**quency** n [U]

in·fringe /ɪnˈfrɪndʒ/ v 1 [I (**upon, on**); T] fml to go against (a law, etc.) or take over (the right of another person): *to infringe a copyright/a patent | He considers that the school is infringing (upon) his rights as a parent by punishing his son in that way. | to infringe upon a nation's fishing rights* – – ment n [C;U] : *an infringement of the law*

in·fu·ri·ate /ɪnˈfjʊərieɪt/ v [T] to make (someone) extremely angry: *His casual attitude infuriates me! | infuriating delays* —see ANNOY (USAGE) —**atingly** adv

in·fuse /ɪnˈfjuːz/ v 1 [T] to fill (someone) with (a quality): [+obj+**with**] *His speech infused the men with a desire to win.* [+obj+**into**] *His speech infused a desire to win into the men.* 2 [I;T] to stay or cause (a substance such as tea) to stay in hot water so as to give the liquid the taste of the substance: *Let the tea infuse for a few minutes.*

in·fu·sion /ɪnˈfjuːʒən/ n 1 [U] the act of infusing 2 [C] a liquid made by infusing, often for medical use: *The old woman recommended an infusion of special herbs for my cold.* 3 [C;U (**into**)] (an example of) the act of mixing or filling with something new: *an infusion of new ideas into the department*

Inge /ɪŋ/, **Wil·liam Ralph** /ˈwɪljəm rælf/ (1860–1954) an English writer and Dean of St Paul's Cathedral, known as the "Gloomy Dean" because of the unhappy and hopeless nature of his SERMONS (=talks in church)

in·ge·ni·ous /ɪnˈdʒiːniəs/ adj usu. apprec showing cleverness at making or inventing things: *What an ingenious gadget! | an ingenious person/idea/excuse* —compare INGENUOUS; see also GENIUS – – ly adv

in·ge·nue, **-gé-** /ˈænʒeɪnjuː‖ˈændʒənuː/ n Fr a young inexperienced girl, esp. in plays and films: *With her innocent looks, she always gets the ingenue roles.*

in·ge·nu·i·ty /ˌɪndʒɪˈnjuːɪti‖-ˈnuː-/ n [U] skill and cleverness in making, inventing, or arranging things: *It took some ingenuity to squeeze all the furniture into the little room.*

in·gen·u·ous /ɪnˈdʒenjuəs/ adj often derog (of a person or their behaviour) simple, direct, and inexperienced; NAIVE: *Only the most ingenuous person would believe such a feeble excuse. | an ingenuous smile* —compare INGENIOUS; see also DISINGENUOUS – – ly adv – – ness n [U]

in·gest /ɪnˈdʒest/ v [T] tech to take (food) into the stomach —compare DIGEST – – **ion** /ɪnˈdʒestʃən/ n [U]

in·gle·nook /ˈɪŋgəlnʊk/ n (a seat in) a partly enclosed space near a large open fireplace; CHIMNEY CORNER

in·glo·ri·ous /ɪnˈglɔːriəs/ adj lit 1 shameful; bringing dishonour: *an inglorious defeat* 2 old use not famous; unknown: *"Some mute inglorious Milton may here rest."* (Gray's *Elegy*) – – ly adv

in·got /ˈɪŋgət/ n a lump of metal in a regular shape, often brick-shaped: *gold ingots*

in·grained /ɪnˈgreɪnd/ adj fixed firmly and deeply into the surface or inside, so that it is difficult to remove or destroy: *ingrained dirt |* (fig.) *ingrained habits/prejudices |* (fig.) *a deeply ingrained dislike of small children*

In·grams /ˈɪŋgrəmz/, **Richard** (1937–　) a British writer who was the EDITOR of the British SATIRICAL magazine *Private Eye* and later of a magazine started in 1992, *The Oldie*. He also appears on radio and television programmes.

in·grate /ɪnˈgreɪt, ˈɪŋgreɪt‖ˈɪŋgreɪt/ n fml or lit derog an ungrateful person

in·gra·ti·ate /ɪnˈgreɪʃieɪt/ v [T (**with**)] derog to gain approval or favour for (oneself) by making oneself pleasant, showing admiration, etc: *He is obviously trying to ingratiate himself with the boss.* —compare INSINUATE **into**

in·gra·ti·at·ing /ɪnˈgreɪʃieɪtɪŋ/ adj derog (of a person or their behaviour) showing that one wishes to gain favour: *an ingratiating smile/manner* – – ly adv

in·grat·i·tude /ɪnˈgrætɪtjuːd‖-tuːd/ n [U] ungratefulness

in·gre·di·ent /ɪnˈgriːdiənt/ n [(**of**)] any of the things that are formed into a mixture when making something, esp. in cooking: *Flour and fat are the most important ingredients. |* (fig.) *Imagination and hard work are the ingredients of success.*

In·gres /ˈæŋgrə/, **Jean Au·guste Dom·i·nique** /ʒɒn ˈəʊgjuːst ˈdɒminiːk‖ʒɑːn əʊˈgjuːst duːmɪˈniːk/ (1780–1867) a French painter, leader of the NEOCLASSICAL school, known for his pictures of people (PORTRAITS) and historical works

in·gress /ˈɪŋgres/ n [U] fml or lit the act of entering or the right to enter —opposite egress

in-group /ˈ· ·/ n [C+sing./pl. v] often derog a social group that shows favour to those who belong to it and tries to keep out non-members; CLIQUE: *There's a little in-group in that department that seems to keep all the good jobs for itself.*

in·grow·ing /ˌɪnˈgrəʊɪŋ◂/ esp. BrE ‖ **in·grown** AmE /ˌɪnˈgrəʊn◂/ adj [A no comp.] growing inwards, esp. into the flesh: *an ingrowing toenail*

in·hab·it /ɪnˈhæbɪt/ v [T] fml or tech (esp. of animals or large groups of people) to live in (a place or area): *Woodpeckers inhabit hollow trees. | tribes who inhabit the tropical forests |* (fig.) *Who knows what dark fears inhabit the mind of a madman?* —see LIVE (USAGE) – – **able** adj : *an inhabitable area*

in·hab·i·tant /ɪnˈhæbɪtənt/ n [(**of**)] a person, or sometimes an animal, that lives in a particular place regularly, usually, or for a long period of time: *a city of 6 million inhabitants*

in·ha·lant /ɪnˈheɪlənt/ n [C;U] something, esp. a medicine, that is inhaled

in·hale /ɪnˈheɪl/ v [I;T] 1 to breathe (something) in: *He inhaled deeply. | These days we can't help inhaling car exhaust fumes.* —opposite exhale 2 to take (cigarette smoke) into the lungs – **halation** /ˌɪnhəˈleɪʃən/ n [C;U]

in·hal·er /ɪnˈheɪləʳ/ n an apparatus which is used for inhaling medicine in the form of VAPOUR, usu. to make breathing easier

in·har·mo·ni·ous /ˌɪnhɑːˈməʊniəs‖-ɑːr-/ adj fml not going well with something else/each other: *an inharmonious set of colours | inharmonious sounds* – – ly adv – – ness n [U]

in·here /ɪnˈhɪəʳ/ v
　　inhere in sthg. phr v [T] fml or tech to be a natural part of

in·her·ent /ɪnˈhɪərənt, -ˈher-/ adj [(**in**)] present naturally as a part of; not able to be thought of as separate: *I'm afraid the problems you mention are inherent in the system; to get rid of them we'd have to change the whole system. | the inherent contradictions in his arguments*

in·her·ent·ly /ɪnˈhɪərəntli, -ˈher-/ adv by its or one's nature; intrinsically (INTRINSIC): *inherently different*

in·her·it /ɪnˈherɪt/ v 1 [I;T (**from**)] to receive (property, a title, etc.) left by someone who has died: *If he dies without making a will, his closest relative will inherit.* | *She inherited the land from her grandfather.* | (fig.) *The government claims it has inherited all its difficulties from the previous administration.* **2** [T (**from**)] to receive (qualities of mind or body) from one's parents, grandmother or grandfather, etc.: *He's inherited his father's nose|bad temper.* | *an inherited characteristic|trait* —compare HAND **down**; see also DISINHERIT

in·her·i·tance /ɪnˈherɪtəns/ *n* **1** [C *usu. sing.*] something that has been inherited, esp. property, money, or a title: *He spent all his inheritance in less than a year.* | *to come into|take possession of one's inheritance* **2** [U] the act of inheriting —compare HERITAGE, LEGACY

inheritance tax /·ˈ··· ·/ *n* [U] a tax on money given or inherited from one person to another **2** a tax on property or money that is left to a person when someone dies. This tax is known to be very complicated because of the rules about who pays and who does not pay. —see also DEATH DUTIES, ESTATE TAX, PROBATE

in·hib·it /ɪnˈhɪbɪt/ *v* [T] **1** to prevent or hold back; RESTRICT (something): *Loosen any tight clothing, which may inhibit breathing.* | *The mild weather has inhibited the sales of winter clothing.* | *regulations that have inhibited the growth of new businesses.* **2** to make (someone) inhibited: *His presence inhibits me.* | *an inhibiting influence* **inhibit** sbdy. **from** sthg. *phr v* [T+*v-ing*] to prevent from (doing something), esp. by some controlling influence: *Fear inhibited him from talking.*

in·hib·it·ed /ɪnˈhɪbɪtɪd/ *adj* (of a person or their character) unable to express what one really feels or do what one really wants: *I feel very inhibited when people are watching me.* | *too inhibited to laugh freely|to talk about sex* — opposite **uninhibited** – ~ly *adv*

in·hi·bi·tion /ˌɪnhɪˈbɪʃən/ *n* [C;U] the state of, or a feeling of, being inhibited: *She soon loses her inhibitions when she's drunk two or three glasses of wine.* | *sexual inhibitions* | *He has no inhibitions about performing in public.*

in·hos·pi·ta·ble /ˌɪnhɒˈspɪtəbəl‖-hɑː-/ *adj* [(**to, towards**)] *derog* **1** (of a person or action) not showing kindness, esp. not giving food and shelter in one's own home: *It was very inhospitable of them not even to offer us a cup of coffee.* **2** (of a place) not suitable to stay in or live in, esp. because of severe weather, lack of shelter, etc.: *inhospitable desert areas* —**bly** *adv*

in·house, in-house /ˌɪnˈhaʊs◂/ *adj* carried on within a group or organization: *Is she an inhouse worker or a freelance?* —**inhouse** *adv* : *Do you work inhouse?*

in·hu·man /ɪnˈhjuːmən/ *adj* **1** very cruel: *an inhuman tyrant* **2** lacking warm human feelings; IMPERSONAL **3** not human: *A sinister inhuman scream rang out across the moors.* —compare SUBHUMAN, SUPERHUMAN

in·hu·mane /ˌɪnhjuːˈmeɪn◂/ *adj* not showing ordinary human kindness or sympathy, esp. when it should be shown: *inhumane treatment of animals* – ~ly *adv*

in·hu·man·i·ty /ˌɪnhjuːˈmænɪti/ *n* [C *often pl.*; U] (an act showing) the quality of being cruel and harming others: *an example of man's inhumanity to man*

in·im·i·cal /ɪˈnɪmɪkəl/ *adj* [(**to**)] *fml* very unfavourable; HOSTILE: *conditions inimical to economic development*

in·im·i·ta·ble /ɪˈnɪmɪtəbəl/ *adj apprec* too good for anyone else to copy with the same high quality: *He delivered the speech in his own inimitable style.* —see also IMITATE —**bly** *adv*

in·iq·ui·tous /ɪˈnɪkwɪtəs/ *adj fml* extremely unjust or wicked: *an iniquitous suggestion* | *iniquitous tax increases* – ~ly *adv*

in·iq·ui·ty /ɪˈnɪkwɪti/ *n* [C;U] (an act or case of) injustice or wickedness: *The bar in the old harbour was a* **den of iniquity**. (=place of great wickedness)

i·ni·tial¹ /ɪˈnɪʃəl/ *adj* [A *no comp.*] which is (at) the beginning: *The initial talks formed the basis of the later agreement.* | *After she'd got over|overcome her initial shyness, she became very friendly.* | *the initial investment|outlay*

initial² *n* [*usu. pl.*] a CAPITAL (=large) letter at the beginning of a name, esp. when used alone to represent a person's first name(s) and last name: *His initials are PHJ: they stand for Peter Henry Johnson.*

initial³ *v* **-ll-** *BrE* ‖ **-l-** *AmE* [T] to write one's initials on (a piece of writing), usu. to show approval or agreement: *Please would you initial these memos, sir?*

i·ni·tial·ly /ɪˈnɪʃəli/ *adv* at the beginning; at first: *Initially, she opposed the plan, but later she changed her mind.*

initial teach·ing al·pha·bet /·ˌ·· ˈ·· ˌ···/ [*the*] a 44-character PHONETIC alphabet used to teach children to read English

i·ni·ti·ate¹ /ɪˈnɪʃieɪt/ *v* [T] **1** to be responsible for starting: *The government has initiated a massive new housebuilding programme.* **2** [(**into**)] to give (someone) some secret or mysterious knowledge: *to initiate someone into the mysteries of a secret religion* **3** [(**into**)] *often pass.*] to introduce (someone) into a club, group, etc., esp. with a special ceremony —see also UNINITIATED —**ation** /ɪˌnɪʃiˈeɪʃən/ *n* [C;U (**into**)] : *Many tribes have* **initiation ceremonies** *for young men and women when they become adults.*

i·ni·ti·ate² /ɪˈnɪʃiɪt/ *n* a person who is instructed or skilled in some special field, esp. one who knows its secrets or mysteries: *rituals known only to initiates*

i·ni·tia·tive /ɪˈnɪʃətɪv/ *n* **1** [U] *apprec* the ability to make decisions and take action without asking for the help or advice of others: *I wish my son would show a bit more initiative.* | *Don't keep asking me for advice;* **use your (own) initiative.** **2** [C] the first movement or action which starts something happening: *He* **took the initiative** *in organizing a party after his brother's wedding.* | *The government is making some fresh initiatives to try to resolve the dispute.* **3** [*the*] the position of being able to take action or influence events: *Because of a stupid mistake, we lost the initiative in the negotiations; the other side* **has the initiative** *now.* **4** the process which allows voters to suggest a law by signing a PETITION which is then voted on in an election or approved by the LEGISLATURE (=people who make laws) —compare REFERENDUM **5 on one's own initiative** (done) according to one's own plan and without help; not suggested by someone else

in·ject /ɪnˈdʒekt/ *v* [T (**with, into**)] to put (liquid) into (someone) with a special needle (SYRINGE): *This drug can't be swallowed; it has to be injected.* | *The lab assistant injected the rat with the new drug.* | (fig.) *The arrival of our friends with several crates of beer injected new life into the flagging party.*

in·jec·tion /ɪnˈdʒekʃən/ *n* [C;U (**into**)] an act of injecting: *The drug is taken by injection.* | (fig.) *The organization will need a massive injection of government money.*

in·joke /ˈ·· ˌ·/ *n* a joke which is understood only by a particular group of people: *taxi-drivers' in-jokes about tourists*

in·ju·di·cious /ˌɪndʒuːˈdɪʃəs/ *adj fml* (of an action or statement) not wise or sensible; showing bad judgment: *an injudicious remark* – ~ly *adv* – ~ness *n* [U]

In·jun /ˈɪndʒən/ *n infml* (*offensive to Native Americans*) **1** a Native American **2** honest Injun *esp. AmE* truthfully; really: *He told me everything, honest Injun.*

in·junc·tion /ɪnˈdʒʌŋkʃən/ *n* [(**against**)] *law* a command or official order to do or not to do something: *The court has issued an injunction forbidding them to strike for a week.* | *The financier* **took out an injunction** *against the magazine to prevent them from publishing the story.*

in·jure /ˈɪndʒər/ *v* [T] **1** to cause physical harm to (a person or animal), esp. in an accident; hurt seriously: *Two people were killed and seven were injured, some of them seriously, when the car hit the bus.* | *He can't play today because he's injured his knee.* | *She was badly injured in the accident.* | (fig.) *I hope I didn't injure* (=offend) *her feelings.* **2** to damage: *His reputation will be badly injured by these vicious rumours.* —see WOUND³ (USAGE)

in·jured /ˈɪndʒəd‖-ərd/ *adj* hurt: *an injured knee* | *injured pride* [also *n, the*+P] | *Among the dead and injured were six children.* —see WOUND³ (USAGE)

in·ju·ri·ous /ɪnˈdʒʊəriəs/ *adj* [(**to**)] *fml* causing injury; damaging: *Smoking is injurious to health.* – ~ly *adv*

in·ju·ry /ˈɪndʒəri/ *n* [(**to**)] **1** [U] harm; damage to a living thing: *insurance against injury at work* | (fig.) *injury to one's pride* **2** [C] a physical hurt or wound, esp. when caused accidentally: *The driver of the car received|sustained serious injuries to the legs and arms.* | *Be careful lifting that heavy box – you'll* **do yourself an injury!** — see also **add insult to injury** (ADD)

injury time /ˈ··· ˌ·/ *n* [U] *BrE* additional playing time at the end of a match, esp. in football, played to make up for time lost through injuries to players

in·jus·tice /ɪnˈdʒʌstɪs/ n **1** [U] the fact of not being just; unfairness **2** [C] an act or situation showing this: *one of life's little injustices* **3 do someone an injustice** to judge someone in an unfair way and/or believe something bad about them which is untrue: *You do him an injustice to say he's lazy; he's just a slow worker.*

ink¹ /ɪŋk/ n [C;U] coloured liquid used for writing, printing, or drawing: *written in ink* | *a bottle of ink* | *a selection of different-coloured inks* —see also INDIAN INK

ink² v [T] to put ink on: *He inked the printing plate.*
ink sthg. ↔ **in** *phr* v [T] to complete (something drawn in pencil or left unfilled) using ink: *to ink in a pencil sketch*

ink·blot test /ˈɪŋkblɒt ˌtest‖-blɑːt-/ n a PSYCHOLOGICAL test based on a person's reactions to marks (BLOTs) made by ink

In·ka·tha Free·dom Par·ty /ɪnˌkɑːtə ˈfriːdəm ˌpɑːti- ‖ -ˌpɑːr-/ [*the*] a black South African nationalist movement representing the Zulu people and led by Chief Buthelezi

ink·jet print·er /ˈɪŋkdʒet ˌprɪntəʳ/ n an electronic printer, often connected to a small computer, which gets ink on the paper by shooting it through very small holes in a moving part

ink·ling /ˈɪŋklɪŋ/ n [S (**of, as to**) *usu. in questions or negatives*] a slight idea or suggestion: *Could you give me an/some/any inkling of what the committee's findings are likely to be?* [+(*that*)] *I didn't have the slightest inkling* (=didn't know at all) *that she was so ill.* [+*wh*-] *He hasn't got an inkling how to do it.*

ink·pad /ˈɪŋkpæd/ n a small box containing ink on a thick piece of cloth or other material, used for putting ink onto a marker (STAMP²(3)) that is to be pressed onto paper

ink·stand /ˈɪŋkstænd/ n a container for pens, pots of ink, etc., usu. kept on a desk

ink·well /ˈɪŋk-wel/ n an ink container which fits into a hole in a desk

ink·y /ˈɪŋki/ adj **1** marked with ink: *inky fingers* **2** very dark: *I stared out into the inky blackness of the night.*
—**-iness** n [U]

INLA /ˌaɪ en el ˈeɪ/ *abbrev. for* IRISH NATIONAL LIBERATION ARMY

in·laid /ˌɪnˈleɪd◂/ adj [*no comp.*] **1** [(**in, into**)] set attractively into another substance: *gold inlaid in(to) wood* | *inlaid gold* **2** [(**with**)] having another substance set in it: *wood inlaid with gold and precious stones* | *inlaid wood*

in·land¹ /ˈɪnlənd/ adj [A *no comp.*] done or placed inside a country, not near the coast or near other countries: *an inland sea* | *inland waterways* | *inland trade*

in·land² /ɪnˈlænd/ adv towards or in the middle of the country: *We drove/headed further inland.* | *There are mountains inland.*

Inland Rev·e·nue /ˌɪˌ ˈ···/ also **the Revenue**— [*the*] the government department which collects national taxes in Britain. The Inland Revenue collects taxes directly from income and capital. —compare INTERNAL REVENUE SERVICE

in-laws /ˈ·· ·/ n [P] *infml* one's relatives by marriage, esp. the father and mother of one's husband/wife

In·lay /ˈɪnleɪ/ n **1** [C;U] an inlaid pattern, surface, or substance: *wood with an inlay of gold* **2** [C] a filling of a metal or another substance used in the inside of a decayed or damaged tooth

in·let /ˈɪnlet, ˈɪnlɪt/ n **1** a narrow stretch of water reaching from a sea, lake, etc., into the land or between islands **2** a way in, esp. for water or other liquid: *a fuel inlet* — compare OUTLET

in lo·co pa·ren·tis /ɪn ˌləʊkəʊ pəˈrentɪs/ adv *Lat fml* having the responsibilities of a parent towards someone else's children: *Teachers at a boarding school are in loco parentis.*

in·mate /ˈɪnmeɪt/ n someone who lives in or esp. is kept in a place, typically with many other people, such as a prisoner in a prison, a patient in a MENTAL HOSPITAL, etc.: *One of the inmates has escaped.*

in me·mo·ri·am /ɪn mɪˈmɔːriəm/ prep *Lat* (used before the name marked on a stone above a grave, or in a newspaper advertisement) in memory of: *In Memoriam John Jones 1871–1956*

in·most /ˈɪnməʊst/ also **innermost**— adj [A *no comp.*] farthest inside: *the inmost depths of the cave* | (fig.) *one's inmost feelings* —opposite **outermost**

inn /ɪn/ n **1** esp. *BrE* a small PUB or hotel, esp. one built (in the style of) many centuries ago: *an old country inn* —see also INNS OF COURT **2 no room at the inn** *quote* a slightly changed phrase from the story in the Bible telling of the birth of Jesus. Jesus was born in a STABLE because there was no room for his mother, Mary, in an inn. —see also NATIVITY

▷ USAGE British people use the word **inn** only when talking about a particular, old-style pub or hotel: *I know a very nice little inn quite close to here.* The usual word is **pub** or **hotel**: *Let's find a pub and have a drink.* | *Where's the nearest hotel?* In American English, **inn** does not have any special meaning apart from **hotel** or **restaurant** and is sometimes used instead of them in the names of businesses wanting to appear old-fashioned.◁

in·nards /ˈɪnədz‖-ər-/ n [P] *infml* the inner parts, usu. of the stomach: *a pain in her innards* | *He'd spread the innards of the engine all over the kitchen floor.*

in·nate /ɪˌɪˈneɪt◂/ adj (of a quality) which someone was born with: *innate kindness/laziness* | *an innate sense of fun* | (fig.) *the innate flaws in the plan* – **~ly** adv : *innately kind*

in·ner /ˈɪnəʳ/ adj [A *no comp.*] **1** on the inside or close to the middle: *the inner ear* | *an inner room* | *inner London* **2** close to the centre of control: *an inner circle* (=group) *of ministers* | *the inner workings of government* **3** not expressed; secret, esp. of the spirit: *She suspected his comments had an inner meaning.* | *an inner certainty* | *He knows nothing about my inner self.* **4** of the mind or spirit: *the inner life* —compare OUTER

inner ci·ty /ˌɪˌ ···◂/ n the central part of a city, esp. an area with a high (usu. poor) population, old buildings in bad condition, etc.: *The government plans an extensive building programme to revitalize the inner cities/the inner city areas.* | *inner city decay*

Inner Heb·ri·des /ˌɪˌ ˈ···/ [*the* +P] a large group of islands close to the NW coast of Scotland

inner light /ˌɪˌ ˈ·/ n [S] (*often caps.*) a heavenly presence, esp. in the Quaker religion, to help and guide the soul

Inner Lon·don /ˌɪˌ ˈ···◂/ the parts of London including the City, Westminster, and the BOROUGHs that border them. Most of these boroughs have councils controlled by the Labour Party.

inner man /ˌɪˌ ˈ·/ **inner wom·an** /ˌɪˌ ˈ··|fem.— n [*the*] **1** the soul; the mind **2** *humor* desire for food; APPETITE: *A juicy steak and kidney pudding should satisfy the inner man!*

Inner Mon·go·li·a /ˌɪˌ ·ˈ···/ an area in N China known for its large grasslands

in·ner·most /ˈɪnəməʊst‖-nər-/ adj [A *no comp.*] INMOST

inner plan·et /ˌɪˌ ˈ··/ n any of the planets Mercury, Venus, Earth, or Mars, whose ORBITs are nearer the sun than those of the other PLANETs

inner space /ˌɪˌ ˈ·/ n [U] **1** space at or near the Earth's surface, esp. under the sea **2** the unconscious human mind

Inner Tem·ple /ˌɪˌ ˈ··/ [*the*] the oldest of the four Inns of Court in London —see INNS OF COURT

inner tube /ˈ··· ·/ n the circular air-filled tube inside a TYRE

inner-tube /ˌɪˌ ·ˈ·/ v [I] *AmE* to ride on an inner tube either in water or down a snow-covered hill: *Let's go inner-tubing after school!*

in·ning /ˈɪnɪŋ/ n any of the usu. nine playing periods into which a game of BASEBALL or SOFTBALL is divided

in·nings /ˈɪnɪŋz/ n innings **1** the period of time during which a cricket team or player BATs: *England made 302 in their first innings.* | *He played a brilliant innings.* **2** *BrE infml* a time when one is active, esp. in a public position, or alive: *I've had a good innings, but it's time for me to retire.*

inn·keep·er /ˈɪnˌkiːpəʳ/ n *old use* a person who owns or runs an inn —compare PUBLICAN (1)

in·no·cent /ˈɪnəsənt/ adj **1** [(**of**)] (of a person) not guilty of a crime or SIN; blameless: *He was innocent of the crime.* | *They hanged an innocent man.* | *acts of terrorism against innocent people* | *In the British and American legal systems, an accused person is* **innocent till proven guilty.** **2** (of a thing) harmless in effect or intention: *innocent enjoyment/pleasures* | *He was startled by their*

angry response to his innocent remark. **3** *often derog* (of a person) having little experience of the world and not able to recognize evil; NAIVE: *an innocent young child* — ~ **ly** *adv* —**cence** *n* [U] : *He protested his innocence loudly as they dragged him off to prison.*

Innocents' Day /ˈ··· ͵·/ 28 December, a day on which people in the Roman, Greek, and Anglican churches remember the killing of the children of Bethlehem by Herod — see also MASSACRE OF THE INNOCENTS

in·noc·u·ous /ɪˈnɒkjuəs‖ɪˈnɑːk-/ *adj* **1** (esp. of an action or statement) not likely to or intended to harm or offend: *I made what I thought was a perfectly innocuous remark and he got most upset.* **2** not having harmful effects: *Would you like to try some of the local wine? It's quite innocuous!* — ~ **ly** *adv* — ~ **ness** *n* [U]

in·no·vate /ˈɪnəveɪt/ *v* [I] to make changes, introduce new ideas, inventions, etc. —**vator** *n*

in·no·va·tion /͵ɪnəˈveɪʃən/ *n* **1** [C] a new idea, method, or invention: *recent innovations in printing techniques* **2** [U] the introduction of new things: *If our industries shy away from innovation, we will never compete successfully with other countries.*

in·nov·at·ive /ˈɪnə͵veɪtɪv/ also **in·nov·a·tor·y** /-təri/ *BrE— adj apprec* **1** newly invented or introduced; different from, and esp. better or cleverer than, previous ones: *innovative printing techniques* | *innovative ideas* **2** tending or liking to introduce new ideas or methods: *a very innovative manager|firm*

Inns·bruck /ˈɪnzbrʊk/ a city in SW Austria known as an industrial centre and a summer and winter tourist RESORT

Inns of Court /͵· · ˈ·/ [*the*+P] the four law societies and their buildings in London, for students and practising BARRISTERS, which an English barrister must belong to. The four societies are Lincoln's Inn, the Inner Temple, the Middle Temple, and Gray's Inn.

in·nu·en·do /͵ɪnjuˈendəʊ/ *n* -**does** or -**dos** **1** [C] a remark that suggests something unpleasant or disapproving without saying it directly **2** [U] (the making of) such unpleasant remarks: *scurrilous newspapers that print rumour and innuendo* —see also INSINUATION

In·nu·it /ˈɪnjuɪt, ˈɪnuɪt/ *n, adj see* INUIT

in·nu·me·ra·ble /ɪˈnjuːmərəbəl‖ɪˈnjuː-, ɪˈnuː-/ *adj* too many to be counted

in·nu·mer·ate /ɪˈnjuːmərɪt‖ɪˈnjuː-, ɪˈnuː-/ *adj BrE* not understanding calculation with numbers; not NUMERATE — compare ILLITERATE — **acy** *n* [U]

i·noc·u·late /ɪˈnɒkjʊleɪt‖ɪˈnɑː-/ *v* [T (**with, against**)] to introduce a weak form of a disease into (someone), esp. by INJECTION, as a protection against the disease: *The doctor inoculated her with the serum.* | *Have you been inoculated against hepatitis?* —compare IMMUNIZE, VACCINATE —**lation** /ɪ͵nɒkjʊˈleɪʃən‖ɪ͵nɑː-/ *n* [C;U] : *a certificate of inoculation*

in·of·fen·sive /͵ɪnəˈfensɪv◄/ *adj* (of a person or their behaviour) not causing any harm or offence: *an inoffensive manner* | *a quiet inoffensive little man* — ~ **ly** *adv* — ~ **ness** *n* [U]

in·op·e·ra·ble /ɪnˈɒpərəbəl‖ɪnˈɑː-/ *adj* **1** (of an illness or a growth) that cannot be treated or removed by an operation so as to cure the person: *I'm afraid her condition is inoperable.* | *an inoperable tumour* **2** *fml* which cannot be put into practice; not practical

in·op·e·ra·tive /ɪnˈɒpərətɪv‖ɪnˈɑː-/ *adj* **1** (esp. of a machine) not working or able to work as usual **2** (of a law, rule, etc.) not in effect or not able to be put into effect

in·op·por·tune /ɪnˈɒpətjuːn‖͵ɪnɑːpərˈtuːn/ *adj fml* unsuitable, esp. because happening at an inconvenient time: *They called at an inopportune moment, when we were about to go out.* | *an inopportune visit|remark* — ~ **ly** *adv* — ~ **ness** *n* [U]

in·or·di·nate /ɪˈnɔːdənɪt‖-ɔːr-/ *adj fml* beyond reasonable limits: *inordinate demands for higher wages* | *It has taken an inordinate length of time.* (=too long) — ~ **ly** *adv*

in·or·gan·ic /͵ɪnɔːˈgænɪk◄‖-ɔːr-/ *adj* **1** not of living material; not ORGANIC **2** not showing the pattern or organization typical of natural growth —compare INANIMATE — ~ **ally** /kli/ *adv*

inorganic chem·is·try /͵···· ˈ···/ *n* [U] the scientific study of inorganic material

in·pa·tient /ˈɪ· ͵··/ *n* someone staying in a hospital for treatment —compare OUTPATIENT

in per·so·nam /͵ɪn pəˈsəʊnæm‖pər-/ *adj, adv Lat* (of a legal action) against a person, to make the person accept a RESPONSIBILITY or duty — compare IN REM

in pro·pri·a per·so·na /ɪn ͵prəʊpriə pəˈsəʊnə‖-pər-/ *adv Lat* in person, without the help of a lawyer

in·put¹ /ˈɪnpʊt/ *n* [S;U] **1** something that is put in for use, esp. by a machine, such as electrical current or information for a computer: *As the input of energy is increased, the volume gets louder.* **2** something, such as advice, information, or effort, that is provided in order to help something succeed or develop: *We mustn't forget the sales department's input.* (=the help, information, etc. they gave)

input² *v* -**tt**-; *past tense & participle* **inputted** *or* **input** [T (**into**)] to put (information) into a computer: *Have you inputted the new data yet?*

input/out·put /͵·· ˈ··/ *n, adj see* I/O

in·quest /ˈɪŋkwest/ *n* [(**on, into**)] an official inquiry, usu. to find out the cause of a sudden or unexpected death, esp. when there is a possibility of crime: *The inquest on his death will be held next Thursday.* | (fig.) *There's bound to be an inquest into the England team's terrible performance.*

in·qui·e·tude /ɪnˈkwaɪɪtjuːd‖-tuːd/ *n* [U] *fml* anxiety; lack of peace of mind

in·quire, en- /ɪnˈkwaɪəʳ/ *v* [I (**about, into**); T] **1** to ask for information: *I'll inquire about the trains.* | *I inquired the way to the station.* [+*wh*-] *I inquired whether the 6:00 train would leave on time.* **2 inquire within** (a sign or notice saying that information can be found inside) —see ASK (USAGE) — ~ **quirer** *n*
   inquire after sbdy./sthg. *phr v* [T] to ask about the health or well-being of: *She inquired after her mother's health|after his mother.*
   inquire into sthg. *phr v* [T] to make a search or inquiry into, in order to discover information; INVESTIGATE: *The court ordered the council to inquire into the conduct of the two officers.*
   inquire sthg. **of** sbdy. *phr v* [T] *fml* to ask (someone) about (something): [+*wh*-] *I must inquire of you where you obtained this money, sir.*

in·quir·ing, en- /ɪnˈkwaɪərɪŋ/ *adj* **1** [A] as if asking a question: *an inquiring look* **2** *apprec* showing an interest in knowing about things: *She has a very inquiring mind.* — ~ **ly** *adv* : *He looked at me inquiringly.*

in·quir·y, en- /ɪnˈkwaɪəri‖ˈɪŋkwəri, ɪnˈkwaɪəri/ *n* **1** [C;U (**into, about**)] (an act of) inquiring: *We made some inquiries into her movements|into what she had done on that day.* | *After months of fruitless inquiry we finally discovered the truth.* **2** [C (**into**)] an attempt to find out the reason for something or how something happened, usu. in the form of official meetings and other actions: *a government inquiry into the air crash* | *to conduct a public inquiry* **3 helping the police with their inquiries** *BrE* being held and questioned by the police about a crime, but not yet officially charged with the crime. This phrase is used esp. by the police: *Two people were shot dead by a gunman in central Birmingham today. A man is helping the police with their inquiries.*

▷ USAGE **Enquiry** and **inquiry** are almost exactly the same. **Inquiry** is more often used for a long serious study: *an inquiry into the diseases caused by smoking.*◁

inquiry a·gent /·ˈ·· ͵··‖ˈ··· ͵··, ·ˈ·· ͵··/ *n BrE* a PRIVATE DETECTIVE

in·qui·si·tion /͵ɪŋkwɪˈzɪʃən/ *n usu. derog* an inquiry, esp. one that is carried out with little regard for the rights of the people being questioned: *I was subjected to a lengthy inquisition by the tax inspector.*

Inquisition [*the*] (in former times) the official Roman Catholic organization for discovering and punishing HERESY (=unacceptable religious beliefs). People connect the Inquisition with the use of TORTURE, and almost certain death: *the Spanish Inquisition*

in·quis·i·tive /ɪnˈkwɪzɪtɪv/ *adj often derog* (of a person or their behaviour) trying to find out (too many) details about things and people: *Don't be so inquisitive!* — ~ **ly** *adv* : *He peeped inquisitively into the drawer.* — ~ **ness** *n* [U]

in·quis·i·tor /ɪnˈkwɪz₄tər/ n 1 usu. derog a person making an inquisition: *My inquisitor considered my answer for a moment.* 2 (*often cap.*) (in former times) an officer of the Inquisition, esp. one who is very cruel when making an inquiry —see also TORQUEMADA

in·quis·i·to·ri·al /ɪnˌkwɪz₄ˈtɔːriəl/ adj fml, usu. derog like or typical of an inquisitor — ~ly adv

in·quo·rate /ɪnˈkwɔːr₄t/ adj tech (of a meeting) not having enough people present, so that it cannot officially be held

in re /ɪn ˈriː/ prep regarding; concerning; RE²; (used mostly in business letters but sometimes in speech)

in rem /ɪn ˈrem/ adj or adv Lat (of a legal action) against a thing, such as a right or piece of property, in order to get the use of it —compare IN PERSONAM

in·res·i·dence /ˌ· ˈ···/ adj [after n] being officially connected with an organization in the stated position: *She was made poet-in-residence at the university, and worked with the students for a year.*

in·roads /ˈɪnrəʊdz/ also **inroad** sing.— n [(on, upon, in, into)] 1 an attack upon or advance into a new area, esp. one held by an enemy or competitor: *The company is starting to make inroads into the lucrative soft-drinks market.* —compare INCURSION 2 an effort or activity that lessens the quantity or difficulty of something: *The long illness made (serious) inroads on his savings.* | *We're beginning to make some inroads into changing people's attitude towards unemployment* (=people are beginning to change their way of thinking)

INS /ˌaɪ en ˈes/ abbrev. for IMMIGRATION AND NATURALIZATION SERVICE

in·sa·lu·bri·ous /ˌɪnsəˈluːbriəs◄/ adj fml unhealthy: *an insalubrious climate*

ins and outs /ˌ· · ˈ·/ n [the+P (of)] infml the details (of a difficult situation, problem, etc.): *Bill explained all the ins and outs of the case to me.*

in·sane /ɪnˈseɪn/ adj seriously ill in the mind; mad: *He went insane.* | (fig.) *You must be insane to go out in this weather!* | *insane jealousy* [also n, the+P] *a hospital for the insane* — ~ly adv : *insanely jealous*

in·san·i·ta·ry /ɪnˈsæn₄təri‖-teri/ adj likely to harm the health by causing disease: *insanitary conditions*

in·san·i·ty /ɪnˈsæn₄ti/ n [U] madness.
► CULTURAL NOTE In criminal law if a person **pleads insanity** (= claims he or she was insane) they are not considered responsible for their actions and would be put into a hospital rather than a prison. Judgments on insanity are often CONTROVERSIAL as it is difficult to prove: *The defence entered a plea of insanity.* —see also DIMINISHED RESPONSIBILITY◄

in·sa·tia·ble /ɪnˈseɪʃəbəl/ adj [(for)] that cannot be satisfied: *an insatiable desire/appetite* | *They were insatiable for news of the royal family.* —**bly** adv : *insatiably thirsty*

in·scribe /ɪnˈskraɪb/ v [T] fml to write, print, or ENGRAVE (something), esp. as a lasting record; mark (a surface) with (something written, printed, etc.): [+obj+**in, on, upon**] *He inscribed his name in the book* | *The Queen was presented with a specially inscribed copy of the book.* | (fig.) *They have inscribed their names upon the pages of history.* [+obj+**with**] *He inscribed the book with his name.*

in·scrip·tion /ɪnˈskrɪpʃən/ n something inscribed, such as a a piece of writing marked into the surface of stone b a piece of handwriting at the beginning of a book saying who gave the book to whom and giving the date, year, etc.

in·scru·ta·ble /ɪnˈskruːtəbəl/ adj very difficult to understand; whose meaning or way of thinking is not at all clear; mysterious. British and American people sometimes say that people from Asia are inscrutable because they cannot tell what Asian people are thinking from the expression on their faces: *an inscrutable smile* —**bly** adv —**bility** /ɪnˌskruːtəˈbɪl₄ti/ n [U]

in·sect /ˈɪnsekt/ n 1 a small creature with no bones, six legs, a body divided into three parts (the head, THORAX, and ABDOMEN), and usu. two pairs of wings, such as an ant or fly 2 not tech any small creature that creeps along the ground, such as a SPIDER or worm 3 infml derog a person of no worth or importance

in·sec·ti·cide /ɪnˈsekt₄saɪd/ n [C;U] (a) chemical substance made to kill insects: *to spray insecticide on crops* — compare PESTICIDE —**cidal** /ˌɪnˌsekt₄ˈsaɪdl◄/ adj

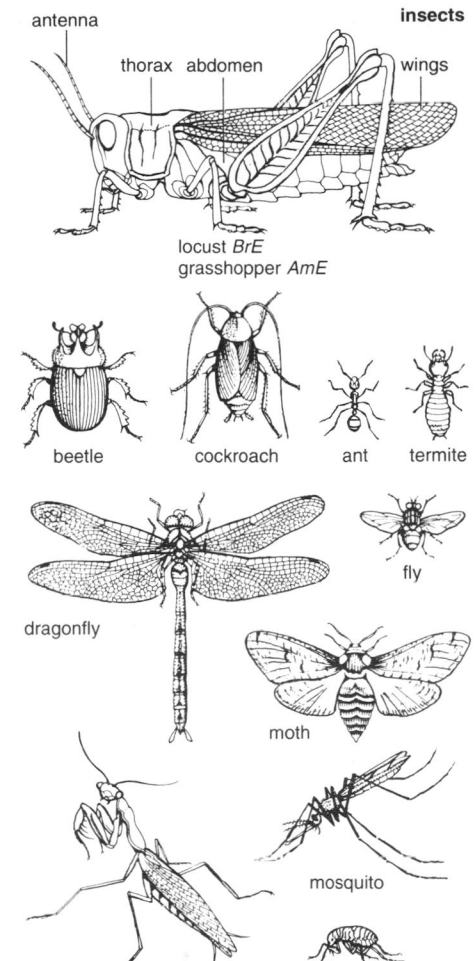

insects

antenna
thorax abdomen wings

locust *BrE*
grasshopper *AmE*

beetle   cockroach   ant   termite

dragonfly

fly

moth

mosquito

praying mantis   flea

in·sec·ti·vore /ɪnˈsekt₄vɔːr/ n an insectivorous creature

in·sec·tiv·o·rous /ˌɪnsekˈtɪvərəs/ adj eating insects as food: *Many birds are insectivorous.* —see also CARNIVORE, HERBIVORE, OMNIVOROUS

in·se·cure /ˌɪnsɪˈkjʊər◄/ adj 1 not safe; which cannot give support or is not properly supported; likely to fall: *an insecure wall* | *I feel very insecure up this ladder.* 2 not giving one a feeling of safety; likely to be lost: *an insecure job/investment* 3 anxious and unsure of oneself; not confident: *He's very insecure − that's why he is always bad-tempered.* — ~ly adv —**curity** n [U] : *His confident manner is really just a way of hiding his (feelings of) insecurity.*

in·sem·i·nate /ɪnˈsem₄neɪt/ v [T] to put male seed into (a female), by the sexual act or by an artificial process: *Cows are usually inseminated artificially nowadays.* —see also ARTIFICIAL INSEMINATION —**nation** /ɪnˌsem₄ˈneɪʃən/ n [U]

in·sen·sate /ɪnˈsenseɪt/ adj fml 1 without the power to have feelings; INANIMATE 2 unreasoning; wild: *insensate rage*

in·sen·si·bil·i·ty /ɪnˌsens₄ˈbɪl₄ti/ n fml 1 [U] unconsciousness 2 [S;U (to)] old use inability to have deep feelings, such as love, sympathy, anger, etc.

in·sen·si·ble /ɪnˈsens₄bəl/ adj fml 1 unconscious − compare SENSELESS (2) 2 [F (of)] lacking knowledge; UNAWARE: *insensible of his danger* 3 [F (to)] unable to have feelings, esp. to feel pain: *insensible to pain/to the cold* —see also INSENSITIVE 4 too small to be noticed: *an insensible change* —**bly** adv

▷ USAGE **Insensible** is not the opposite of **sensible**.◁

in·sen·si·tive /ɪnˈsensɪtɪv/ *adj* [(to)] **1** (of a person or their behaviour) not kind to others because one does not think about how they feel; lacking thoughtfulness and sympathy: *How can you be so insensitive as to laugh at someone in pain?* | *an insensitive remark* | *It was very insensitive of you to tell her about your promotion when she's been unemployed since last year.* **2** not listening to or acting upon (a request, demand, etc.): *Why is the union leadership so insensitive to the feelings of its members?* **3** not showing or feeling the effect of (a force or the presence of something): *This paper is insensitive to light.* | *insensitive to pain* − ~**ly** *adv* − **-tivity** /ˌɪnsensɪˈtɪvɪti/ *n* [S;U]

in·sep·a·ra·ble /ɪnˈsepərəbəl/ *adj* [(from)] impossible to separate from something else or from one another; always together: *The three boys are inseparable.* | *The issue of human rights is inseparable from our struggle for democracy.* −**-bly** *adv* −**-bility** /ɪnˌsepərəˈbɪlɪti/ *n* [U]

in·sert¹ /ɪnˈsɜːt‖-ɜːrt/ *v* [T (in, into)] to put or place something in (something else): *to insert a key in a lock* | *to insert an amendment into the contract*

in·sert² /ˈɪnsɜːt‖-ɜːrt/ *n* something that is or can be inserted, esp. written or printed material put in between the pages of a book

in·ser·tion /ɪnˈsɜːʃən‖-ɜːr-/ *n* **1** [U] the act of inserting: *The insertion of the needle under the skin made him wince.* **2** [C] something inserted, esp. an advertisement or AN-NOUNCEMENT in a newspaper

in·ser·vice /ˌɪˈ‖ˈ‖ˌ‖◂/ *adj* [A no comp.] (taking place) during one's working time: *In this job you receive* **in-service training**.

in·set¹ /ˈɪnset/ *n* something put as an addition into something else, esp. a small picture or map set in one corner of a larger one

in·set² /ɪnˈset/ *v* **-tt-**; *past tense & participle* inset *or* insetted [T (in, into)] to put (something) in as an inset

INSET /ˈɪnset/ *n* in-service training; (in Britain) training for teachers in STATE SCHOOLs during the school year: *an INSET day*

in·shore /ˌɪnˈʃɔːʳ◂/ *adv* near, towards, or to the shore: *He rowed further inshore.* −compare OFFSHORE −**inshore** *adj* [A no comp.] : *inshore fishing*

in·side¹ /ɪnˈsaɪd, ˈɪnsaɪd/ *n* **1** [(*the*) S] the inner part of a solid object; the part that is nearest to the centre, or that faces away from the open air: *We examined the inside of the house.* | *The inside of an orange is full of juice.* | *This lock can only be opened from the inside.* −opposite **outside 2** [*the*] the side of a road or path nearest to the edge or to the buildings along it: *That car tried to pass me on the* **inside**. −opposite **outside 3** [*the*] *infml* a position in which one is able to know special or secret information: *He could only have been told about it by someone* **on the inside**. **4** [C] also **insides** *pl.*− *infml* one's stomach: *a pain in my insides* **5 inside out: a** with the usual inside parts on the outside: *He put his socks on inside out.* | *She turned her drawers* **inside out** (=searched them very thoroughly, probably throwing things onto the floor) *looking for her passport.* **b** *infml* with complete knowledge; very thoroughly: *She knows the subject inside out.*

in·side² /ˈɪnsaɪd/ *adj* [A] **1** facing or at the inside: *the inside pages of a newspaper* | *driving slowly in the inside lane* −opposite **outside 2** from or about those most directly or secretly concerned: *an inside joke* | *As I had some* **inside information** *I was able to buy at exactly the right time.* | *The papers are trying to get the* **inside story** (=what really but secretly happened) *on the royal divorce.* −see also INSIDE JOB

in·side³ /ɪnˈsaɪd/ *adv* **1** to or in the inside: *The children are playing inside* (=indoors) *because it's raining.* | *I opened the box and looked inside.* | (fig.) *I tried to appear calm, but I felt pretty scared inside.* (=in my mind) − opposite **outside 2** *BrE* downstairs in a bus with two floors **3** *sl, esp. BrE* in prison: *inside for murder* **4 inside of: a** INSIDE⁴ (2) **b** *AmE for* INSIDE⁴ (1)

inside⁴ *prep* **1** to or on the inside of; within: *inside the car/the house/my mouth* −opposite **outside 2** *infml* in less time than: *I'll be back inside an hour.*

▷ USAGE Compare **inside** and **within**. 1 Both words can express the idea of being surrounded by something, but **inside** is more usual in this sense. **Within** is more

formal and mostly used of large areas: **inside** *the box* | **within** *the castle.* 2 Both words can mean "in no greater time/distance than" but **within** is more usual in this sense: **within** *a mile* | **within** *three weeks.*◁

inside job /ˈ‖ ˌ‖/ *n infml* a robbery done by someone connected with the place, organization, etc. which has been robbed

in·sid·er /ɪnˈsaɪdəʳ/ *n* someone who is recognized or accepted as a member of a group, esp. someone who has special information or influence −compare OUTSIDER

insider trad·ing /ˌ‖ˌ‖/ also **insider dealing**− *n* [U] the illegal practice of buying and selling business shares by people (such as company directors) who take advantage of their special knowledge of the plans and business affairs of the companies for which they work

inside track /ˌ‖ˌ‖/ *n* [*the*] **1** (in racing) the track nearest the inside, which is shorter **2** *AmE* an advantageous position in a competition: *the inside track to success in business*

in·sid·i·ous /ɪnˈsɪdiəs/ *adj* acting gradually and without being noticed, but causing serious harm; secretly harmful: *the insidious spreading of dry rot* | *the insidious trend towards a police state* − ~**ly** *adv* − ~**ness** *n* [U]

in·sight /ˈɪnsaɪt/ *n* [(into)] **1** [U] *apprec* the power of using one's mind to see or understand the true nature of a situation: *a woman of great insight* **2** [C] a sudden, clear, but not always complete understanding: *Her autobiography gave me an insight into the way government actually works.*

in·sig·ni·a /ɪnˈsɪɡniə/ *n* [P] BADGES or objects which represent the power of an official or important person: *the royal insignia of crown and sceptre* | *Naval officers have stripes on their sleeves as insignia of their rank.*

in·sig·nif·i·cant /ˌɪnsɪɡˈnɪfɪkənt/ *adj* of no value and/or importance: *It was a mere detail which seemed insignificant at the time but later proved to be crucial.* | *an insignificant little man* − ~**ly** *adv* −**-cance** *n* [U]

in·sin·cere /ˌɪnsɪnˈsɪəʳ◂/ *adj* not sincere; pretended or false: *insincere flattery* | *an insincere smile* − ~**ly** *adv* −**-cerity** /ˌɪnsɪnˈserɪti/ *n* [U]

in·sin·u·ate /ɪnˈsɪnjueɪt/ *v* [T] to suggest (something unpleasant) indirectly by one's behaviour or remarks: *What are you insinuating?* [+(*that*)] *Are you insinuating that I'm not telling the truth?* | *I think he's insinuating that the witness has been bribed, Your Honour.*

insinuate sbdy. **into** sthg. *phr v* [T] *fml or humor* to cause (esp. oneself) to become part of (something), esp. by unpleasantly indirect methods; gain acceptance (for oneself) into (something): *He tried to insinuate himself into the boss's favour.* −compare INGRATIATE

in·sin·u·a·tion /ɪnˌsɪnjuˈeɪʃən/ *n* [C;U] (an act of) insinuating; (an) indirect suggestion: *She blamed him, not directly but by insinuation.* [+*that*] *They made unpleasant insinuations that he might not be quite honest.* −see also INNUENDO

in·sip·id /ɪnˈsɪpɪd/ *adj derog* lacking a strong character, taste, or effect: *insipid food* | *an insipid character* − ~**ly** *adv* − ~**ness**, ~**ity** /ˌɪnsɪˈpɪdɪti/ *n* [U]

in·sist /ɪnˈsɪst/ *v* [I (on, upon); T+(*that*); *obj*] **1** to declare firmly, esp. in the face of doubt or opposition: *He insisted on his innocence/on the truth of his story, even though the police refused to believe him.* | *He still insists he wasn't there at the time.* **2** to order or demand (that something must happen or be done): *They are insisting on immediate repayment.* | *I insisted that he (should) go.* | *You must come with us − I insist!* | *All right, I'll do it,* **if you insist**. (=I don't really want to)

insist on/upon sthg. *phr v* [T] to consider very important; place great importance on: *He insists on discipline in the classroom.* [+*v-ing*] *I insist on having a holiday abroad every year.*

in·sis·tence /ɪnˈsɪstəns/ *n* [U] **1** the act of insisting: *At the director's insistence* (=because the director insisted) *the new product was kept secret.* | *the government's insistence on a price freeze* **2** also **insistency** /ɪnˈsɪstənsi/− the quality or state of being insistent −compare PERSISTENT

in·sis·tent /ɪnˈsɪstənt/ *adj* [(on, upon)] repeatedly insisting: *The company is insistent on immediate payment.* [F+(*that*)] *He's very insistent that he'll finish in time.* **2** needing to be done, answered, or dealt with; urgent: *insistent demands* | *the baby's insistent screams* − ~**ly** *adv*

in·si·tu /ˌɪn ˈsɪtjuː‖ˌɪn ˈsaɪtuː/ *adv Lat* in its original place

in·so·far /ˌɪnsəˈfɑːʳ/ *adv* see **in so far as** (FAR¹ (9))

in·sole /ˈɪnsəʊl/ *n* a piece of material inside a shoe or boot, shaped to fit the bottom of the foot

in·so·lent /ˈɪnsələnt/ *adj* showing disrespectful rudeness: *insolent children* | *insolent behaviour* — ~**ly** *adv* —**lence** *n* [U]

in·sol·u·ble /ɪnˈsɒljŭbəl‖ɪnˈsɑːl-/ *adj* **1** to which no answer or explanation is/seems possible: *an insoluble problem* **2** which cannot be dissolved (DISSOLVE (1,2)): *insoluble in water* —compare INDISSOLUBLE

in·sol·va·ble /ɪnˈsɒlvəbəl‖ɪnˈsɑːl-, ɪnˈsɔːl-/ *adj esp. AmE for* INSOLUBLE (1)

in·sol·vent /ɪnˈsɒlvənt‖ɪnˈsɑːl-/ *n, adj tech* (a person) not having enough money to pay debts: *an insolvent estate* | *The bank was declared insolvent.* —compare BANKRUPT¹ —**vency** *n* [U]

in·som·ni·a /ɪnˈsɒmniə‖-ˈsɑːm-/ *n* [U] habitual inability to sleep

in·som·ni·ac /ɪnˈsɒmniæk‖ɪnˈsɑːm-/ *adj, n* (of or being) a person who habitually cannot sleep, or can sleep only for a short period of the night

in·so·much /ˌɪnsəʊˈmʌtʃ/ *adv* **insomuch as** to the degree that; inasmuch as (INASMUCH)

in·sou·ci·ance /ɪnˈsuːsiəns/ *n* [U] *fml* a cheerful lack of care or worry —**ant** *adj*

in·spect /ɪnˈspekt/ *v* [T] **1** to examine (something) closely or in detail, esp. in order to judge quality or correctness: *After they had finished building the wall the foreman inspected it to make sure they'd done it properly.* | *Let's go and inspect the damage.* | *Nobody inspected my ticket before I got on the train.* **2** to make an official visit to judge the quality of (an organization, machine, etc.): *The sergeant-major inspects the barracks every day.*

in·spec·tion /ɪnˈspekʃən/ *n* [C;U] (an act of) inspecting: *I gave the car a thorough inspection before buying it.* | *He thought it was a moth, but on closer inspection it turned out to be a butterfly.* | *an official inspection* | *a tour of inspection*

in·spec·tor /ɪnˈspektəʳ/ *n* **1** an official who inspects something: *A ticket inspector got on the train.* | *a tax inspector* **2** a police officer of middle rank: *Can I have a word with you, Inspector?* **3** an official who visits schools to advise on and judge the quality of the teaching; an HMI — ~**ate** *n*

Inspector Morse /ɪnˌspektə ˈmɔːs‖-tər ˈmɔːrs/ *a* police DETECTIVE in a British television programme. The stories take place in Oxford, and Morse is a clever, highly educated man who finds it difficult to talk to ordinary people. He is helped by Sergeant Lewis, who is younger and understands ordinary people better.

in·spi·ra·tion /ˌɪnspɪˈreɪʃən/ *n* **1** [U] the act of inspiring or state of being inspired: *by divine inspiration* **2** [C;U (for)] something or someone which gives a person the urge or the ability to do something, esp. to produce works of the imagination: *These events provided the inspiration for her first novel.* | *She was an inspiration to all who knew her.* | *His journey to South America was a source of fresh ideas and inspiration.* **3** [C] a sudden good idea: *to have an inspiration* — ~**al** *adj*

in·spire /ɪnˈspaɪəʳ/ *v* [T] **1** [(to)] to encourage in (someone) the desire and ability to take effective action, by filling with eagerness, confidence, etc.: *He tried to inspire them to greater efforts.* [+obj+to-v] *I was inspired to work harder by her example.* **2** to be the force which produces (usu. a good result): *The memory of his mother inspired his best music.* **3** to fill (someone) with (a feeling) by means of one's behaviour or example: [+obj+in] *His driving hardly inspires confidence (in his passengers).* [+obj+with] *His driving hardly inspires his passengers with confidence.* — see also AWE-INSPIRING

in·spired /ɪnˈspaɪəd‖-ərd/ *adj* so clever or good as to seem to show inspiration, esp. from God: *an inspired guess/performance*

in·spir·ing /ɪnˈspaɪ ərɪŋ/ *adj* that gives one the urge or ability to do great things; providing inspiration: *inspiring music/leadership*

inst /ɪnst/ *BrE fml, becoming rare* (used after a date in business letters) of this month: *The meeting will be held on the 24th inst.*

in·sta·bil·i·ty /ˌɪnstəˈbɪlŧti/ *n* [U] lack of STABILITY; unsteadiness, e.g. in a situation or a person's character, producing a tendency to change suddenly: *He's showing signs of instability — he could be heading for a nervous breakdown.* | *political instability in this region*

in·stall /ɪnˈstɔːl/ *v* [T (in)] **1** to set (an apparatus) up, ready for use: *We're having central heating installed.* **2** [+obj +adv/prep] *infml* to settle firmly: *Once she's installed herself in front of the fire for the evening you won't get her to move.* **3** to settle (someone) in an official position, esp. with ceremony: *The new bishop has been installed.*

in·stal·la·tion /ˌɪnstəˈleɪʃən/ *n* **1** [U] the act of installing or state of being installed: *The installation of the shower only took a few minutes.* | *the installation of a computer in the accounts department* **2** [C] an apparatus in a fixed state ready for use: *new central-heating installations* **3** [C] a military or naval base or fort: *American nuclear installations in Europe*

installment plan /·ˈ···· / /ˈ···/ *n* [(the) U] *AmE for* HIRE PURCHASE

in·stal·ment *BrE* ‖ **installment** *AmE* /ɪnˈstɔːlmənt/ *n* **1** [C] a single part of a book, play, or television show which appears in regular parts until the story is completed: *a play in six instalments* **2** [C] a single payment of a set which, in time, will complete full payment of a debt: *to pay the last instalment of a loan* **3** [U] INSTALLATION (1)

in·stance¹ /ˈɪnstəns/ *n* [(of)] **1** a single fact, event, etc., expressing a general idea; example; case: *There have been several instances of terrorists planting bombs in the city.* | *I usually support people who take such actions, but in this instance I have to condemn them.* **2 at someone's instance** *fml* because of someone's wish **3 for instance** for example: *You can't rely on her: for instance, she arrived an hour late for an important meeting yesterday.* — see also **in the first instance** (FIRST)

in·stance² *v* [T] *fml* to give as an example: *As one example of what I mean about youth today, let me instance the growing rate of vandalism.*

in·stant¹ /ˈɪnstənt/ *n* **1** [usu. sing.] a moment of time: *I'll be back in an instant.* | **Not for an instant** (=not at all) *did I believe he had lied.* **2 (at) the instant** as soon as: *(At) the instant I saw him I knew he was the man the police were looking for.*

in·stant² *adj* **1** happening or produced at once: *I took an instant dislike to him.* | *At the turn of a tap you get instant hot water.* | *an instant success* **2** (of food) which can be very quickly prepared for use: *instant coffee/mashed potato* (=coffee/potato in powder form that needs only the addition of boiling water)

► CULTURAL NOTE Many people consider instant food and drinks to be of poor quality and often make excuses when offering them: *Would you like a coffee? I'm afraid I've only got instant.* —see also INSTANTLY◄

in·stan·ta·ne·ous /ˌɪnstənˈteɪniəs/ *adj* happening at once: *She accidentally swallowed the poison and death was instantaneous.* | *an instantaneous reaction* — ~**ly** *adv* — ~**ness** *n* [U]

in·stant·ly /ˈɪnstəntli/ *adv* at once: *The police came to my help instantly.*

instant re·play /ˌ·· ˈ··/ *n AmE for* ACTION REPLAY

in·stead /ɪnˈsted/ *adv* **1** in place of that: *It's too wet to go for a walk; let's go swimming instead.* | *If you don't want to go, I'll go instead.* **2 instead of** in place of: *You should be working instead of lying there in bed.* | *Will you go to the meeting instead of me?*

in·step /ˈɪnstep/ *n* **1** the upper surface of the foot between the toes and the ankle —see picture at FOOT **2** the part of a shoe, sock, etc., which covers the instep —see picture at SHOE

in·sti·gate /ˈɪnstŧɡeɪt/ *v* [T] *fml* **1** to start (something happening) by one's action; be responsible for starting: *The police have instigated a search for the missing boy.* | *to instigate criminal proceedings* **2** [+obj+to-v] to cause (someone else) to act usu. wrongly, esp. by forceful speech; INCITE —**gator** *n usu. derog*: *the instigators of all this unrest* —**gation** /ˌɪnstŧˈɡeɪʃən/ *n* [U]: *He did it at my instigation.* (=I told him to or suggested that he should)

in·stil *BrE* ‖ **instill** *AmE* /ɪnˈstɪl/ *v* -**ll**- [T (in, into)] to put (ideas, feelings, etc.) gradually but firmly into someone's mind by a continuous effort: *We instilled the need for discipline and obedience into the new recruits.* —**stillation** /ˌɪnstŧˈleɪʃən/ *n* [U]

in·stinct /ˈɪnstɪŋkt/ n [C;U] (a) natural ability or tendency to act in a certain way, without having to learn or think about it: *the nest-building instinct in birds* | *Don't ask me; follow/trust your instincts and do what you think is right.* | *an instinct for survival* [+*to-v*] *Lions have an instinct to hunt.* —compare INTUITION

in·stinc·tive /ɪnˈstɪŋktɪv/ adj resulting from instinct: *instinctive behaviour* | *an instinctive dislike of extreme political opinions* | *an instinctive mistrust of strangers* — ~ly adv : *Instinctively, I knew she was ill.* | *He ducked instinctively as the bullet whistled past his head.*

in·sti·tute¹ /ˈɪnstɪtjuːt‖-tuːt/ n a society or organization formed to do special work or for a special purpose: *a research institute*

institute² v [T] *fml* to set up (a society, rules, actions in law, etc.) for the first time: *The police have instituted legal proceedings against her.*

Institute of Di·rec·tors /ˌ··· · ·ˈ··/ [the] a British organization for businessmen

institute of ed·u·ca·tion /ˌ··· ··ˈ··/ n (often caps.) a teacher training institution in England and Wales

in·sti·tu·tion /ˌɪnstɪˈtjuːʃən‖-ˈtuː-/ n **1** [C] **a** a habit, custom, etc., which has been in existence for a long time: *the institution of marriage* **b** *infml, often humor* a person who has been seen in the same place and/or doing the same thing for a long time: *That old man in the park is a regular institution.* **2** [C] (a large building for) an organization, usu. a long-established or well-respected one: *the big City institutions* (=the banks and other companies in the City of London that deal with money) | *The Royal Institution is a British organization for scientists.* **3** [C] *euph for* MENTAL HOSPITAL: *He went rather strange and had to be put into an institution.* **4** [C] *derog* a place where a lot of people live, usu. in the care of an official organization, such as a children's or old people's HOME (4): *I could never put my mother into an institution — she'd hate it.* **5** [U] the act of instituting: *the institution of a new law* — ~al adj : *institutional food*

in·sti·tu·tion·al·ize also **-ise** *BrE* /ˌɪnstɪˈtjuːʃənəlaɪz‖-ˈtuː-/ v [T] **1** to cause to become an INSTITUTION (1a): *inefficient practices that have been allowed to become institutionalized* | *They described corporal punishment in schools as "institutionalized violence".* **2** *euph* to put into an INSTITUTION (3,4) **3** [*usu. pass.*] to cause or allow (a person) to gradually begin to behave in the way that people behave when they are kept in a prison, hospital, etc., for a long time: *After 20 years in prison, he had become so institutionalized that he was completely unable to adapt to life outside.*

in·store /ˌɪnˈstɔːʳ◂/ adj operating, or in use, within a large DEPARTMENT STORE: *an instore detective*

in·struct /ɪnˈstrʌkt/ v [T] **1** [+*obj*+*to-v*] to give orders or directions to, esp. with the right or expectation of being obeyed: *I've been instructed to wait here until the teacher arrives.* | *I am instructed* (=I have been told) *to inform you that the minister is not willing to make a statement.* | *The union issued an order instructing its members not to work overtime.* **2** [(**in**)] to give knowledge or information (usu. of something practical) to: *The sergeant was instructing the soldiers (in how to do the drill).* —see TEACH (USAGE) **3** [+*obj*+*that*; *usu. pass.*] *law* to advise or inform officially: *I have been instructed that the defendant is unwell, and I therefore adjourn the case.* **4** *law* to employ (a lawyer) to handle a case in court —see ORDER (USAGE)

in·struc·tion /ɪnˈstrʌkʃən/ n **1** [C *often pl.*] an order: *You must obey my instruction.* | *to give someone instructions* [+*to-v*] *I have instructions not to let anyone in.* [+(*that*)] *My instructions are that I must not let anyone in.* —see also INSTRUCTIONS **2** [U] the act of instructing; teaching: *He's not trained yet; he's still* **under instruction**. (=being instructed) | *an instruction manual* — ~al adj

in·struc·tions /ɪnˈstrʌkʃənz/ n [P] advice on how to do something: *I didn't follow the instructions printed on the box, and broke the machine.*

instruction set /·ˈ··· ·/ n the complete set of instructions that a computer understands, each instruction controlling one operation in the MICROPROCESSOR

in·struc·tive /ɪnˈstrʌktɪv/ adj (not of a person) giving useful information that increases knowledge or understanding: *a most instructive lecture/visit* — ~ly adv

in·struc·tor /ɪnˈstrʌktəʳ/ n **1** a person who teaches, esp. a physical, practical, or scientific activity: *a swimming/driving instructor* —see also SKI INSTRUCTOR **2** *AmE* a person who teaches a subject, esp. in a college or university: *a social studies instructor*

in·stru·ment /ˈɪnstrʊmənt/ n **1** an object used to help in work, esp. in work where exact detail and measurements are necessary, such as medicine and science: *The pilot studied his instruments* (=ALTIMETER, FUEL GAUGE, etc.) *anxiously.* | *surgical instruments* | *an instrument of torture* **2** also **musical instrument**— an object, such as a piano, horn, drum, etc., played to give musical sounds —see also STRINGED INSTRUMENT, WIND INSTRUMENT **3** [(**of**)] *esp. lit* someone or something which seems to be used by an outside force to cause something to happen: *an instrument of fate*

▷ USAGE An **instrument** is a man-made tool, usually without power, used in science or art. A microscope, a compass, and a thermometer are examples of **instruments**. A piano, an organ, and a violin are examples of (**musical**) **instruments**. —see also MACHINE (USAGE)◁

in·stru·men·tal /ˌɪnstrʊˈmentl◂/ adj **1** [*no comp.*] (of music) for instruments, not voices: *an instrumental work* **2** [F+(**in**)] *fml* helpful (in); being (part of) the cause of: *He/His information was instrumental in catching the criminal.*

in·stru·men·tal·ist /ˌɪnstrʊˈmentəlɪst/ n a person who plays a musical instrument, esp. with a group of singers —compare VOCALIST

in·stru·men·ta·tion /ˌɪnstrʊmenˈteɪʃən/ n [U] **1** the way in which a piece of music is arranged for the different instruments of a band —compare ORCHESTRATE **2** a set of instruments, esp. to help in controlling a machine: *the complex instrumentation in an aircraft's cockpit*

instrument fly·ing /ˈ··· ˌ··/ n [U] flying an aircraft on a course using instruments only, e.g. at night or in thick cloud when the pilot cannot see ahead

instrument land·ing /ˈ··· ˌ··/ n a landing in an aircraft, using instruments and RADAR only, e.g. in bad weather

instrument pan·el /ˈ··· ˌ··/ n a board on which instruments are set, esp. in an aircraft; DASHBOARD

in·sub·or·di·nate /ˌɪnsəˈbɔːdənət‖-ɔːr-/ adj *derog* (of a person of lower rank or their behaviour) intentionally disobedient; not showing willingness to take orders — ~ly adv —**nation** /ˌɪnsəbɔːdəˈneɪʃən‖-ɔːr-/ n [U] : *The captain will not tolerate any insubordination.*

in·sub·stan·tial /ˌɪnsəbˈstænʃəl◂/ adj **1** *derog* lacking firmness or solidity; weak or unsatisfying: *an insubstantial meal* **2** lacking substance or material nature; without material reality

in·suf·fe·ra·ble /ɪnˈsʌfərəbəl/ adj unbearable (in behaviour) esp. because too proud in manner; INTOLERABLE: *your insufferable little brother* | *insufferable rudeness* | *He's absolutely insufferable!* —**bly** adv

in·suf·fi·cient /ˌɪnsəˈfɪʃənt◂/ adj [(**for**)] (esp. of power, money, or RESOURCES) not enough: *The food was insufficient for our needs.* | *cancelled due to insufficient interest/funds* [+*to-v*] *There was insufficient food to feed everyone.* — ~ly adv —**ciency** n [S;U (**of**)] *fml* : *an insufficiency of money*

in·su·lar /ˈɪnsjʊləʳ‖ˈɪnsələr, ˈɪnʃə-/ adj **1** *derog* narrow (in mind); interested only or mainly in one's own group, country, etc.: *an insular outlook* | *Don't be so insular!* —compare PAROCHIAL (2) **2** [*no comp.*] of or like an island — ~ity /ˌɪnsjʊˈlærɪti‖-sə-, -ʃə-/ n [U] : *the insularity of the British*

in·su·late /ˈɪnsjʊleɪt‖ˈɪnsə-/ v [T (**from, against**)] **1** to cover (something) so as to prevent electricity, heat, sound, etc., from getting out or in: *Many houses could be warmer if they were insulated against heat loss.* | *She covered the bare wires with* **insulating tape** *to make them safe.* **2** to protect (a person) from ordinary experiences: *The royal family is insulated from many of the difficulties faced by ordinary people.* —compare ISOLATE

in·su·la·tion /ˌɪnsjʊˈleɪʃən‖ˌɪnsə-/ n [U] **1** (esp. in relation to a house) the action of insulating or the state of being insulated: *Insulation can save on heating bills.* | *a house with good insulation* **2** material which insulates: *Glass fibre is sometimes used as insulation for water tanks.*

in·su·la·tor /ˈɪnsjʊleɪtəʳ‖ˈɪnsə-/ n an object or material which insulates, esp. one which does not allow electricity to pass through it

in·su·lin /ˈɪnsjʊ̈lən‖ˈɪnsə-/ n [U] a substance produced naturally in the body which allows sugar to be used for ENERGY. People with DIABETES often need to take extra insulin into their bodies because their bodies do not produce enough.

in·sult¹ /ɪnˈsʌlt/ v [T] to be rude to or treat with lack of respect; offend: *You will insult her if you don't go to her party.* | *This book insults the reader's intelligence.* (=treats them as if they were stupid) | *an insulting remark* | *insulting behaviour*

in·sult² /ˈɪnsʌlt/ n [(to)] a rude or offensive remark or action: *He shouted/hurled insults at the boy who had kicked him.* | *His refusal to attend the memorial service is an insult to the memory of our brave soldiers.* —see also **add insult to injury** (ADD)

in·su·pe·ra·ble /ɪnˈsjuːpərəbəl‖ɪnˈsuː-/ adj (of something in one's way) which is too difficult to be defeated or passed: *insuperable difficulties* —compare INSURMOUNTABLE —**bly** adv

in·sup·por·ta·ble /ˌɪnsəˈpɔːtəbəl‖-ˈpɔːr-/ adj fml unbearable (because bad): *insupportable behaviour/pain*

in·sur·ance /ɪnˈʃʊərəns/ n **1** [U (**against**)] agreement by contract to pay money to someone if something, esp. a misfortune, such as illness, death, or an accident, happens to them: *All drivers in Britain must have third-party insurance.* | *Does your insurance cover damage by flooding?* | *a well-known insurance company* | *to* **take out (life) insurance 2** [U (**on**)] money paid to an insurance company in order to make or keep such a contract: *The insurance on my house is very high.* | *a crippling insurance premium* **3** [U] the business of making this type of contract and providing such payments: *She works in insurance.* **4** [S;U (**against**)] protection: *I bought some new locks as an additional insurance against burglary.* —see also ASSURANCE, NATIONAL INSURANCE —**able** adj : *an insurable risk*

insurance bro·ker /ˈ·ˈ·· ˌ·ˈ·/ also **insurance agent** n a person who arranges different kinds of insurance for other people and who receives payment for doing it

insurance pol·i·cy /ˈ·ˈ·· ˌ·ˈ·/ n a POLICY² : (fig.) *Are nuclear weapons a credible insurance policy against attack?*

in·sure /ɪnˈʃʊər/ v [T] **1** [(**against**)] to protect (someone or something) by insurance, esp. against loss of money, life, goods, etc.: *My house is insured against fire.* | *Are you insured for all risks?* **2** esp. AmE for ENSURE

▷ USAGE Compare **insure**, **ensure**, **assure**, and **reassure**. 1 You usually **insure** against future misfortune by paying money to an **insurance** company: *fire insurance.* But it is possible to **insure/assure** (BrE, tech) against death: *life insurance AmE/assurance BrE.* 2 **Ensure** means "to make sure that something happens": *Please ensure that the lights are switched off before leaving the building.* 3 If you **assure** a person of something you promise them or tell them that something will happen: *The doctor assured me that I would get better.* But when followed by an abstract noun, **assure** is like **ensure**: *Weeks of practice assured/ensured success in the match.* 4 **Reassure** means "to comfort someone who is anxious": *I was feeling worried about the exam, but the teacher reassured me.*◁

in·sured /ɪnˈʃʊəd ‖ ɪnˈʃʊərd/ n **insured** [the+C] an insured person: *If the camera is stolen the insured receives a sum of money.*

in·sur·er /ɪnˈʃʊərər/ n a person or company that provides insurance: *If the camera is stolen the insurer will pay a sum of money.*

in·sur·gent /ɪnˈsɜːdʒənt‖-ɜːr-/ n [often pl.] a person who is not an official soldier but is fighting against those in power, usu. in his or her own country: *The insurgents are gaining strength/gathering in the north of the country.* —compare GUERRILLA; see also COUNTERINSURGENCY — **insurgent** adj : *insurgent forces* —**gency** n [C;U]

in·sur·moun·ta·ble /ˌɪnsəˈmaʊntəbəl‖-sər-/ adj too large, difficult, etc., to be dealt with: *insurmountable problems/obstacles* —compare INSUPERABLE

in·sur·rec·tion /ˌɪnsəˈrekʃən/ n [C;U] (an act of) opposing by force and trying to defeat the people who have power, such as the government — ~ **ist** n

in·tact /ɪnˈtækt/ adj whole because no part has been touched, spoilt, or broken: *The fragile parcel arrived intact.* | (fig.) *Somehow his reputation survived the scandal intact.*

in·ta·gli·o /ɪnˈtɑːliəʊ/ n -**glios** [C;U] (the result of) the art of making a picture, decoration, etc., by cutting a pattern deeply into the surface of a hard substance, esp. a jewel

in·take /ˈɪnteɪk/ n **1** [S (**of**)] the amount or number allowed to enter or taken in: *If you want to lose weight, you should reduce your intake of fat and alcohol.* | *this year's intake of students* **2** [C] an opening in a tube, pipe, etc., where air, gas, or liquid is taken in: *the air intakes of a jet engine*

in·tan·gi·ble /ɪnˈtændʒɨbəl/ adj **1** which by its nature cannot be known by the senses or described, though it can be felt: *an intangible quality* | *As soon as we entered the house, we felt an intangible sense of gloom and hopelessness.* **2** which is hidden or not material, but known to be real: *intangible assets* (=things belonging to a business which are not material, such as the loyalty of its customers) —**bly** adv /ɪnˌtændʒɨˈbɪlɨti/ n [U]

in·te·ger /ˈɪntɨdʒər/ n a whole number: *6 is an integer, but 6⅔ is not.* —compare DECIMAL²

in·te·gral /ˈɪntɨɡrəl/ adj [(**to**)] necessary (to complete something); which cannot be left out: *an integral part of the argument/of our defence strategy* | *She is our best player, and is integral to our team.*

integral cal·cu·lus /ˌ··· ˈ···/ n [U] (in MATHEMATICS) a way of measuring the distance which a moving object has covered at a particular moment; one of the two ways of making calculations about quantities which are continually changing —compare DIFFERENTIAL CALCULUS

in·te·grate /ˈɪntɨɡreɪt/ v [(**with**, **into**)] **1** [I;T] to join or cause (a member of a social group) to join in society as a whole; (cause to) spend time with members of other groups and develop habits like theirs: *Not all foreign immigrants want to integrate (with us/into our society).* | *It is difficult to integrate released prisoners back into society.* **2** [T] *rather fml* to join to something else so as to form a whole: *Many schools are now integrating computer programs into the curriculum.* —**gration** /ˌɪntɨˈɡreɪʃən/ n [U] : *racial integration*

in·te·grat·ed /ˈɪntɨɡreɪtɨd/ adj (*often in comb.*) showing a usu. pleasing mixture of qualities, groups, etc.: *an integrated school with children of different races and social classes* | *(well-)integrated characters* | *a poorly-/badly-integrated person* (=who is not calm or happy and gets on badly with other people)

integrated cir·cuit /ˌ···· ˈ··/ n a very small set of electrical connections printed on a single piece of SEMICONDUCTOR material, such as a CHIP¹ (6). Integrated circuits are important for electrical equipment because they are small, easily made, and unlikely to develop faults.

in·teg·ri·ty /ɪnˈteɡrɨti/ n [U] **1** *apprec* strength and firmness of character or principle; honesty; trustworthiness: *a man of complete integrity* **2** *fml* a state of being whole and undivided; completeness: *Our integrity as a nation is threatened by these separatist forces.*

in·teg·u·ment /ɪnˈteɡjʊ̈mənt/ n tech an outer covering, such as a shell, the skin of a fruit, etc.

in·tel·lect /ˈɪntɨlekt/ n **1** [C;U] the ability to use the power of reason (rather than to feel or take action); ability to think intelligently and understand: *a woman of superior intellect* **2** [C] someone with a great intellect —see INTELLIGENT (USAGE)

in·tel·lec·tual¹ /ˌɪntɨˈlektʃuəl◂/ adj **1** of, using, or needing the use of the intellect: *intellectual topics* | *The argument was too intellectual for me; I couldn't follow a word of it.* | *an intellectual film* | *an intellectual giant* (=an extremely clever person) **2** having a high intellect: *an intellectual family* —see INTELLIGENT (USAGE) — ~ **ly** adv : *intellectually unsatisfactory* | *Intellectually speaking, it's a very weak piece of work.* — ~ **ize** v [I;T]

intellectual² n someone who has the ability to reason well, and (often) who uses this ability in their work —see INTELLIGENT (USAGE)

intellectual prop·er·ty /ˌ····· ˈ···/ n [U] anything which a person has invented or has the only right to make or sell, e.g. something protected by COPYRIGHT or by a TRADEMARK

in·tel·li·gence /ɪnˈtelɨdʒəns/ n [U] **1** (good) ability to learn, reason, and understand: *a boy of low intelligence* (=not very clever) | *Use your intelligence!* (=don't be so foolish) | *an intelligence test* —see also ARTIFICIAL INTELLIGENCE **2** [+*sing.*|*pl. v*] (*sometimes cap.*) (a group of people who gather) information, esp. about an enemy country: *He works in intelligence.* | *Our intelligence reports indicate that rebel groups are planning an attack.* | *military intelligence* | *Our intelligence is that the spies plan to leave the country soon.* —see also CIA, MI5, MI6

intelligence gath·er·ing /·ˈ··· ˌ···/ *n* [U] the finding out of military, political, or industrial information about another country or organization. Modern methods include the use of SATELLITES, LISTENING DEVICES, and COMPUTER ANALYSIS.

intelligence quo·tient /·ˈ··· ˌ··/ *n* see IQ

intelligence test /·ˈ··· ˌ·/ also **IQ test**— *n* a test which is supposed to show how clever a person is, formerly given to all school children —see also IQ

in·tel·li·gent /ɪnˈtelɪdʒənt/ *adj* having or showing powers of learning, reasoning, or understanding, esp. to a high degree: *Human beings are much more intelligent than animals.* | *an intelligent suggestion* | *The collie is an intelligent dog, easily trained to control sheep.* — —**ly** *adv*

▷ USAGE 1 Compare **intelligent** *adj*, **intellectual** *n*|*adj*, and **intellect** *n*. An **intelligent** person is someone with a quick and clever mind, but an **intellectual** (person) is someone who is well-educated and interested in subjects which need long periods of study. A small child, or even a dog, can be **intelligent** but cannot be called an **intellectual**. In British English, **intellectual** may suggest a person who looks down on others less clever than themselves. In American English, **intellectual** does not generally have this negative association. 2 When used to mean a person, **intellect** suggests someone who has a very good brain, but perhaps not much practical ability: *I'm sure he's a real intellect, but he'd be nowhere without his wife.* —see also CLEVER (USAGE)◁

in·tel·li·gent·si·a /ɪnˌtelɪˈdʒentsiə/ *n* [(*the*) S+*sing.*|*pl. v*] the people in society who are highly educated and often concern themselves with ideas and new developments, esp. in art or politics: *leading members of the intelligentsia*

in·tel·li·gi·ble /ɪnˈtelɪdʒɪbəl/ *adj* [(to)] (esp. of speech or writing) which can be understood: *His argument was so confused that it was barely intelligible.* | *This report would be intelligible only to an expert in computing.* — opposite **unintelligible**; compare ARTICULATE¹ —**bly** *adv* —**bility** /ɪnˌtelɪdʒɪˈbɪlɪti/ *n* [U]

in·tem·per·ate /ɪnˈtempərɪt/ *adj fml* (of a person or their behaviour) not keeping within the usual limits, esp. of drinking alcohol: *intemperate habit* | *The decision was made with intemperate haste.* — —**ly** *adv* —**ance** *n* [U]

in·tend /ɪnˈtend/ *v* [T] **1** to have in one's mind as a plan or purpose; mean (to do): *He took it as an insult, which wasn't at all what I had intended.* [+*to-v*] *She intended to catch the early train, but she didn't get up in time.* | *I intend to report you to the police.* [+*obj+to-v*] *It was meant to be a surprise; I didn't intend you to see it so soon.* [+(*that*)] (*fml*) *We do not intend that they should know at this stage.* **2** [*obj*; *usu. pass.*] to have a plan for (something) in one's mind: [+*obj+for, as*] *The chair was intended for you, but she took it away.* | *That remark was intended as a joke.* | *The book is intended for young adults in their first year of learning English.* [+*obj+to-v*] *It was intended to be cooked slowly.*

in·tend·ed /ɪnˈtendɪd/ *n* [*usu. sing.*] *old use or humor* someone's future husband or wife: *Let me introduce my intended.*

in·tense /ɪnˈtens/ *adj* **1** strong or great, esp. in quality or feeling; extreme: *There was intense competition between the rival companies to get the contract.* | *intense heat*|*pain* | *intense hatred* **2** having feelings or opinions which are (too) strong, serious, etc.: *I find her exhausting to be with — she's too intense.* | *an intense young man who takes life too seriously.* — —**ly** *adv* —**tensity** *n* [U] : *The poem showed great intensity of feeling.* | *the intensity of the light*

in·ten·si·fi·er /ɪnˈtensɪfaɪər/ *n tech* a word, usu. an adverb, that is used to add stronger feeling to the meaning of an adjective, verb, or adverb (for example, **absolutely** in *That's absolutely wonderful* and *I absolutely disagree*)

in·ten·si·fy /ɪnˈtensɪfaɪ/ *v* [I;T] to (cause to) become more intense: *The strong wind seemed to intensify the cold.* |

Efforts to reach the injured men have been intensified because of a sudden deterioration in weather conditions. —**fication** /ɪnˌtensɪfɪˈkeɪʃən/ *n* [U] : *The intensification of the industrial dispute has caused alarm in government circles.*

in·ten·sive /ɪnˈtensɪv/ *adj* **1** giving a lot of attention or action to a small amount of something or in a small amount of time; CONCENTRATED: *intensive study* | *Intensive efforts are being made to resolve the dispute.* | *an intensive course in English* **2** -**intensive** using or needing a lot of the stated thing: *disk-intensive computer operations* —see also CAPITAL-INTENSIVE, LABOUR-INTENSIVE — ~**ly** *adv*

intensive care /·ˌ··· ˈ·/ *n* [U] a department in a hospital which gives special attention and treatment to people who are very seriously ill or hurt: *He's in*|*out of intensive care.* | *the intensive care unit*

in·tent¹ /ɪnˈtent/ *n* [(with) U] **1** (the stated) purpose or intention: *She behaved foolishly but with good intent.* **2** *law* intending to do something bad: *The policemen arrested him for loitering with intent.* [+*to-v*] *The court has to decide if he entered the building with intent to steal.* **3** to|**for all intents (and purposes)** in almost every way; very nearly: *The work is, to all intents and purposes, finished.*

intent² *adj* **1** [(on, upon)] showing fixed or eager attention (in doing or wishing to do): *an intent stare* | *intent on her work* **2** [F+on] having a determined intention: *He's intent on going to France to continue his studies.* — ~**ly** *adv* — ~**ness** *n* [U]

in·ten·tion /ɪnˈtenʃən/ *n* [C;U] **1** a plan which one has; purpose: *She felt offended at my remarks, but it wasn't my intention to hurt her.* | *I had no intention of changing* (=did not intend to change) *my mind.* | *He's full of good intentions, but can't really do anything to help.* | (*old-fash*) *I hope your intentions are honourable, young man.* (=that you intend to marry the woman you have expressed your love to) **2** -**intentioned** /ɪnˈtenʃənd/ having or showing intentions of the stated type: *a well-intentioned effort*

in·ten·tion·al /ɪnˈtenʃənəl/ *adj* (esp. of something bad) done on purpose; DELIBERATE: *an intentional insult* | *His exclusion from the meeting was quite intentional.* —opposite **unintentional** — ~**ly** *adv*

in·ter /ɪnˈtɜːr/ *v* -**rr**- [T] *fml* to bury (a dead person) — opposite **disinter**; see also INTERMENT

inter- see WORD FORMATION

in·ter·act /ˌɪntərˈækt/ *v* [I (with)] **1** to have an effect on each other or something else by being or working close together: *The two ideas interact.* **2** talk to people easily in a social situation: *Our son has difficulty interacting with other children.* | *She interacts very well with older people.* — ~**ion** /ˈækʃən/ *n* [C;U (between, with)] : *There should be a lot more interaction between the social services and local doctors.*

in·ter·act·ive /ˌɪntərˈæktɪv◂/ *adj* **1** that interacts **2** of or for the exchange of information between a computer and a user while a PROGRAM is in operation: *interactive educational software* —compare BATCH PROCESSING — ~**ly** *adv*

in·ter a·li·a /ˌɪntər ˈeɪliə, -ˈɑːliə/ *adv Lat fml* among other things: *Our success depends, inter alia, on the number of trained people we can employ.*

in·ter·breed /ˌɪntəˈbriːd‖-ər-/ *v* -**bred** /ˈbred/ [I (with);T] to (cause to) produce young from parents of different breeds, groups, etc.: *Can lions and tigers interbreed?* —compare CROSSBREED², INBREEDING

in·ter·cede /ˌɪntəˈsiːd‖-ər-/ *v* [I (with, for)] to speak in favour of someone, esp. in order to save them from punishment: *I was saved because he interceded with the governor for me*|*on my behalf.* —see also INTERCESSION

in·ter·cept /ˌɪntəˈsept‖-ər-/ *v* [T] to stop and usu. catch or destroy (someone or something moving from one place to another): *We intercepted and decoded a secret message from their embassy.* | *See if you can intercept her before she gets here.* — ~**ion** /ˈsepʃən/ *n* [C;U]

in·ter·cep·tor /ˌɪntəˈseptər‖-tər-/ *n* a light fast military aircraft

in·ter·ces·sion /ˌɪntəˈseʃən‖-tər-/ *n* **1** [U (with)] the act of interceding: *intercession with the governor on her behalf* **2** [C;U] a prayer which asks for other people to be helped, cured, etc.

The characters Darth Vader and
Luke Skywalker from *Star Wars III*

Clint Eastwood in
A Fistful of Dollars

Julie Andrews in
The Sound of Music

Jaws

Humphrey Bogart and Ingrid
Bergman in *Casablanca*

Gene Kelly in
Singin' in the Rain

Sylvester Stallone
as *Rocky*

Judy Garland in
The Wizard of Oz

ET

Vivien Leigh and
Clark Gable in
Gone With The Wind

John Travolta in
Saturday Night Fever

Arnold Schwarzenegger in
Terminator II

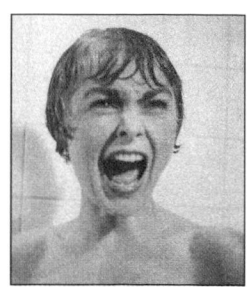

Janet Leigh in
Psycho

Coronation Street

Happy Days

Thunderbirds

Dr Who

Cheers

Fawlty Towers

The Cosby Show

in·ter·change¹ /ˌɪntəˈtʃeɪndʒ‖-ər-/ v [I;T (**with**)] to put each of (two things) in the place of the other; exchange: *The thief interchanged the diamonds with some pieces of glass.*

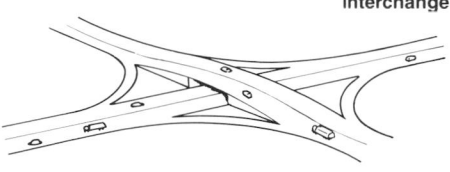

interchange

a motorway interchange

in·ter·change² /ˈɪntətʃeɪndʒ‖-ər-/ n **1** [C;U] (an act of) interchanging; exchange: *a useful interchange of ideas* **2** [C] a system of smaller roads by which two or more main roads are connected: *We should leave the motorway at the next interchange.*

in·ter·chan·gea·ble /ˌɪntəˈtʃeɪndʒəbəl‖-tər-/ adj [(**with**)] which can be used in place of each other or something else —**bly** adv : *The two words are used interchangeably.* —**bility** /ˌɪntəˌtʃeɪndʒəˈbɪlɨti‖-tər-/ n [U]

in·ter·cit·y /ˌɪntəˈsɪti◄‖-tər-/ adj [A] travelling fast between cities or leading from one city to another: *intercity roads*

InterCity n, adj tdmk **1** (of) a type of British Rail train which carries passengers quickly from one city or large town in Britain to another. InterCity trains travel faster and make fewer stops than other trains, and the service is considered to be better: *I'm catching an InterCity at four o'clock.* | *The InterCity network* **2** (of) the division of British Rail which runs these trains: *InterCity has made a profit this year.* | *InterCity management*

in·ter·col·le·giate /ˌɪntəkəˈliːdʒɨt◄‖-tər-/ adj (done) among members of different colleges: *intercollegiate sports*

in·ter·com /ˈɪntəkɒm‖ˈɪntəkɑːm/ n a system by which one can talk through a machine to someone in a near place. Intercoms can be either one-way or two-way: *The airport manager spoke to the waiting passengers on/over the intercom.*

in·ter·com·mu·ni·cate /ˌɪntəkəˈmjuːnɨkeɪt‖-tər-/ v [I] **1** to make feelings, news, etc., known to each other **2** to have a door or doors opening into each other: *All three rooms intercommunicate.* —**cation** /ˌɪntəkəˌmjuːnɨˈkeɪʃən‖-tər-/ n [U]

in·ter·con·ti·nen·tal /ˌɪntəkɒntɨˈnentl◄‖-tərkɑːn-/ adj between CONTINENTS (=different land masses): *intercontinental trade/flights*

intercontinental bal·lis·tic mis·sile /ˌ········ ·ˌ·· ˈ··/ n see ICBM

in·ter·course /ˈɪntəkɔːs‖ˈɪntəkɔːrs/ n [U] **1** fml an exchange of feelings, actions, etc., which make people know each other more closely: *social intercourse* **2** SEXUAL INTERCOURSE

in·ter·de·nom·i·na·tio·nal /ˌɪntədɨˈnɒmɨˌneɪʃənəl‖ˌɪntərdɨˌnɑː-/ adj between or among different branches of the Christian religion

in·ter·de·part·men·tal /ˌɪntəˌdiːpɑːtˈmentl‖ˌɪntərdɪˌpɑːrt-ˈmentl/ adj between different departments (of a firm, school, etc.): *intense interdepartmental rivalry* | *an interdepartmental conference*

in·ter·de·pen·dent /ˌɪntədɪˈpendənt◄‖-tər-/ adj depending on each other; necessary to each other: *Central government and local government are interdependent.* — ~**ly** adv — **-dence** n [U]

in·ter·dict /ˈɪntədɪkt‖-ər-/ n fml an order not to do something, esp. a punishment in the Roman Catholic Church preventing one from taking part in the important services: *a papal interdict*

in·ter·dis·ci·plin·ary /ˌɪntəˌdɪsɨˈplɪnəri‖ˌɪntərˈdɪsəplənəri/ adj of two or more branches of learning studied at a university: *an interdisciplinary course*

in·terest¹ /ˈɪntrɨst/ n **1** [C; U (**in**)] (a) readiness or desire to give attention to, be concerned with, or learn about something: *I have no interest in politics.* | *My son is already showing an interest in music.* | *I wish you'd take a bit more interest in your work.* **2** [U (**to**)] the quality in a thing that causes attention to be given: *Sport doesn't* hold much interest for my family.* | *That's of no interest to me.* (=I am not interested in it.) **3** [C] an activity, subject, etc., which one gives time and attention to: *Job application forms often ask you to list your leisure-time interests.* | *Eating seems to be his only interest in life!* **4** [C] also **interests** pl.— advantage, advancement, or favour: *You may not like these suggestions, but it would be in your interest/in your (best) interests to follow them.* | *He gave up his share in the interests of fairness.* (=in order to be fair) **5** [U] a charge made for the borrowing of money: *They lent me the money at 6% interest.* | (fig.) *She returned the insults with interest.* (=with additional force) —see also COMPOUND INTEREST, SIMPLE INTEREST **6** [C (**in**)] a share in a company, business, property, etc.: *She sold her interest in the company.* | *His business interests are very extensive.* **7** [C (**in**)] the fact of being connected with something, esp. so that one makes a profit from it: *If an MP wants to speak in parliament about something he's financially connected with, he has to declare his interest.* —see also VESTED INTEREST, CONFLICT OF INTEREST

interest² v [T] **1** to cause (someone) to have a feeling of interest: *Politics doesn't interest me.* **2** [(**in**)] to make (someone) want to buy, eat, or do something: *Can I interest you in this book?*

in·terest·ed /ˈɪntrɨstɨd/ adj **1** [(**in**)] having or showing interest: *an interested look on his face.* | *Are you interested in football?* [F+to-v] *I'd be interested to hear your opinion about this.* [F+(that)] *I'm interested that you (should) agree with him.* **2** [A] personally concerned, esp. so as to be unable to make a fair judgment from the outside: *Interested parties* (=people) *are excluded from the discussion.* —see also DISINTERESTED, UNINTERESTED — ~**ly** adv

interest group /ˈ·· ·ˌ·/ also **special interest group**— n [C+sing./pl. v] a group of people that share an INTEREST, esp. an organization that attempts to influence government action —compare PRESSURE GROUP

in·terest·ing /ˈɪntrɨstɪŋ/ adj that takes (and keeps) one's interest; giving ENTERTAINMENT: *an interesting book/person/idea* | *How interesting!* — ~**ly** adv : *Interestingly enough* (=this fact is interesting) *the Prime Minister made no attempt to deny the rumour.*

interest rates /ˈ·· ·ˌ/ n [P] the PERCENTAGE amounts charged for borrowing money by the big banks and building societies (BUILDING SOCIETY), according to the BASE RATE set in Britain by the Bank of England, or the PRIME RATE set by banks in the US. Both governments use changes in interest rates as a method of controlling the ECONOMY: *Bank interest rates are going to rise this month.* | *High interest rates will help to keep inflation down.* —see also FEDERAL RESERVE SYSTEM

in·ter·face¹ /ˈɪntəfeɪs‖ ər / n [(**between**)] a place or area where different things meet and have an effect on each other: *the man-machine interface* —see also USER INTERFACE

interface² v [I;T (**with**)] to connect or be connected by means of a computer: *to interface two computer systems*

in·ter·fac·ing /ˈɪntəfeɪsɪŋ‖-ər-/ n [U] material which can be sewn into articles of clothing to stiffen parts such as the collar or the LAPELS

in·ter·fere /ˌɪntəˈfɪər‖-tər-/ v [I (**in, between**)] derog to enter into or take part in a matter which does not concern one, and in which one is not wanted: *I never interfere between husband and wife/in his affairs.* | *He's just an interfering old busybody.*
  interfere with sbdy./sthg. phr v [T] **1** to get in the way of; prevent from working or happening: *The sound of the radio upstairs interferes with my work.* **2** to touch or move (something) in a way that is annoying or not allowed: *Who's been interfering with my books?* **3** euph to touch or annoy (someone) sexually: *He got put in prison for interfering with little girls.*

in·ter·fer·ence /ˌɪntəˈfɪərəns‖-tər-/ n [U] **1** [(**in, with, between**)] the act of interfering: *I resented his interference in my affairs.* **2** the noises and shapes which spoil the working of electrical equipment, esp. when a radio or television station is difficult to listen to or look at because of the effect of another one near to its WAVELENGTH: *We apologize for the interference, which is due to bad weather conditions.*

in·ter·fer·on /ˌɪntəˈfɪərɒn‖ˌɪntərˈfɪərɑːn/ n [U] a chemical substance produced by the body to fight against certain disease-producing substances, esp. VIRUSes

in·ter·ga·lac·tic /ˌɪntəgəˈlæktɪk◂‖-tər-/ adj [A] (happening or done) between the galaxies (GALAXY). The idea of intergalactic war is often the subject of SCIENCE FICTION: *intergalactic space*

in·ter·im¹ /ˈɪntərɪm/ adj [A no comp.] (done) as a less complete part of something to be given in full later: *The government is taking interim measures to help those in immediate need.* | *an interim report*

interim² n **in the interim** MEANWHILE: *A room has been booked from September onwards. In the interim meetings will be held at my house.*

in·te·ri·or¹ /ɪnˈtɪərɪər/ n **1** [C (**of**) usu. sing.] the part which is inside, indoors, or farthest from the edge or outside: *the interior of the cave* | *The outside of the house needs to be decorated, but the interior is in excellent condition.* – opposite **exterior 2** [*the*] the inside of a country or the part of a country which is away from the coast: *She led an expedition into the interior.*

interior² adj inside, indoors, or furthest from the edge or outside: *an interior room* –opposite **exterior**

interior dec·o·ra·tor /·ˌ··· ˈ·····/ also **interior de·sign·er** /·ˌ··· ·ˈ··/, **decorator**– n someone who plans and chooses the colours, furnishings, etc., for the inside of someone else's room or house (but usu. does not do the actual work of putting them in)

Interior, Department of the [*the*] see DEPARTMENT OF THE INTERIOR

interior min·is·ter /·ˌ··· ˈ··/ n the head of a British government department, the **interior ministry**/MINISTRY OF THE INTERIOR, which is responsible for public order inside a country and controls organizations such as the police and the fire service, as well as the movement of people into the country. In Britain this minister is known as the Home Secretary and the department is called the Home Office.

interior mon·o·logue /·ˌ··· ˈ···/ n a speech in a play in which a character tells his/her thoughts to the AUDIENCE (=the people watching)

interior sprung mat·tress /·ˌ··· · ˈ··/ n a MATTRESS which contains many springs. Interior sprung mattresses are thought to be more comfortable and less harmful to one's back than filled mattresses.

in·ter·ject /ˌɪntəˈdʒekt‖-ər-/ v [I;T] fml to make (a sudden remark) between other remarks: *"I don't agree at all!" he interjected.* | *If I may interject a few comments at this point …*

in·ter·jec·tion /ˌɪntəˈdʒekʃən‖-tər-/ n **1** [C] a phrase, word, or set of sounds used as a sudden remark, usu. expressing a strong feeling such as shock, disapproval, or pleasure; EXCLAMATION: *"Good Heavens!" and "Ouch!" are interjections.* **2** [U] the act of interjecting

in·ter·lace /ˌɪntəˈleɪs‖-ər-/ v [T (**with**)] to join together or to something else by twisting over and under the other: *interlaced branches*

in·ter·lard /ˌɪntəˈlɑːd‖ˌɪntərˈlɑːrd/ v [T (**with**)] to mix (speech or writing) with foreign phrases, photographs, etc.

In·ter·lin·gua /ˌɪntəˈlɪŋgwə‖-tər-/ an INTERNATIONAL LANGUAGE developed in 1951 which has been used as the common language at medical and scientific meetings –compare ESPERANTO; see also INTERNATIONAL LANGUAGE

in·ter·link /ˌɪntəˈlɪŋk‖-ər-/ v [T (**with**)] to join (things) together, or (one thing) with something else: *interlinked fates*

in·ter·lock /ˌɪntəˈlɒk‖ˌɪntərˈlɑːk/ v [I;T] to fasten or be fastened together, esp. in a certain order or so that movement of one part causes movement in others: *The two gear wheels have interlocked.*

in·ter·loc·u·tor /ˌɪntəˈlɒkjʊtər‖ˌɪntərˈlɑːk-/ n fml the person who is talking to one: *my interlocutor*

in·ter·lop·er /ˈɪntələʊpər‖-tər-/ n derog a person who enters a place or group with no right to be there: *They threw the interloper out.* –compare INTRUDER

in·ter·lude /ˈɪntəluːd‖-ər-/ n **1** a period of time or an event, esp. of a different kind, which comes in between two other events, activities, etc.: *a brief interlude of*

democracy before a return to military rule **2 a** the time (INTERVAL) between parts of a play, film, concert, etc. **b** a short piece of music, talk, etc., used for filling this time

in·ter·mar·riage /ˌɪntəˈmærɪdʒ‖-ər-/ n [U] **1** marriage between members of different groups (families, races, etc.) **2** marriage within one's own group or family

in·ter·mar·ry /ˌɪntəˈmæri‖-ər-/ v [I (**with**)] **1** to become connected by marriage with each other or someone else of another group, family, etc.: *The two tribes have been intermarrying for hundreds of years.* **2** to marry each other or someone within the same group, family, etc.: *Members of some ancient races intermarried with their own sisters.*

in·ter·me·di·a·ry /ˌɪntəˈmiːdiəri‖ˌɪntərˈmiːdieri/ n a person who comes between two people or groups of people, esp. in order to bring them into agreement: *He acted as an intermediary in the dispute.* –compare ARBITRATE

in·ter·me·di·ate /ˌɪntəˈmiːdiət◂‖-tər-/ adj [(**between**) no comp.] (done or happening) between two others; halfway: *at an intermediate stage of development* | *intermediate schools*

intermediate school /·· ˈ··· ·ˌ·/ n AmE a JUNIOR SCHOOL or MIDDLE SCHOOL

intermediate tech·nol·o·gy /ˌ····· ·ˈ··/ n [U;C] (a) practical science which is uncomplicated, easy to learn, and cheap, and therefore suitable for use in developing countries (DEVELOPING COUNTRY)

in·ter·ment /ɪnˈtɜːmənt‖-ɜːr-/ n [C;U] fml burial –see also INTER

in·ter·mez·zo /ˌɪntəˈmetsəʊ‖-tər-/ n -zos or -zi /tsi/ a short piece of music played alone, or one which connects longer pieces

in·ter·mi·na·ble /ɪnˈtɜːmɪnəbəl‖-ɜːr-/ adj derog (seeming) endless, esp. when very uninteresting: *interminable delays* | *an interminable speech* –**bly** adv

in·ter·min·gle /ˌɪntəˈmɪŋgəl‖-tər-/ also **in·ter·mix** /-ˈmɪks/– v [I (**with**)] (usu. of groups or masses) to mix together or with something else: *The waters of the streams met and intermingled.* | *They intermingled with the crowd in the hope that their pursuers would lose sight of them.*

in·ter·mis·sion /ˌɪntəˈmɪʃən‖-tər-/ n esp. AmE for INTERVAL (2)

in·ter·mit·tent /ˌɪntəˈmɪtənt◂ ‖ -tər-/ adj happening, then stopping, then happening again, with pauses in between; not continuous: *Today will be mostly fine and sunny, with intermittent showers.* –**ly** adv

in·tern¹ /ɪnˈtɜːn‖-ɜːrn/ v [T] to put in prison or limit the freedom of movement of (someone considered dangerous), esp. in wartime or for political reasons: *to intern enemy aliens*

in·tern² /ˈɪntɜːn‖-ɜːrn/ n esp. AmE a person who has nearly or recently finished professional training, esp. in medicine or teaching, and is gaining controlled practical experience, esp. in a hospital or classroom –compare HOUSEMAN – ~**ship** n

in·ter·nal /ɪnˈtɜːnl‖-ɜːr-/ adj **1** [(**to**)] of or in the inside, esp. of the body: *The doctor x-rayed her to see if there were any internal injuries.* | *the internal organs* **2** of one's own country; not foreign: *internal trade* | *the Minister of Internal Affairs* **3** from the place, organization, etc., which is under consideration rather than from outside it: *an internal audit* | *There is internal evidence that the poem was not written by Chaucer.* –opposite **external** – ~**ly** adv : *The matter will be settled internally; we needn't involve outsiders.* | *"Not to be taken internally."* (instruction on a medicine bottle, tube, etc.)

internal-com·bus·tion en·gine /·ˌ··· ·ˈ·· ·ˌ·/ n an engine, such as a car engine, which produces power by the burning of a substance, such as petrol, inside itself

internal ex·am·in·er /·ˌ··· ·ˈ···/ n BrE an examiner who is a teacher at the institution where students are doing an examination –compare EXTERNAL EXAMINER

in·ter·nal·ize also **-ise** BrE /ɪnˈtɜːnəlaɪz‖-ɜːr-/ v [T] to make (esp. a principle or a pattern of behaviour) a conscious or unconscious part of the self as the result of learning or repeated experience ––**ization** /ɪnˌtɜːnəlaɪˈzeɪʃən‖ ɪnˌtɜːrnələ-/ n [U]

internal medi·cine /ɪˌ··ˈ··ǁ·ˌ··ˈ···/ *n* [U] *AmE med* a type of medical knowledge in which doctors DIAGNOSE (=say what is wrong with a person) and treat illnesses but do not perform SURGERY

Internal Rev·e·nue Ser·vice /ɪˌ··ˈ···ˌ··/ also **Internal Revenue**, *abbrev.* **IRS**— [*the+sing|pl. v*] the office which collects national taxes in the US —compare INLAND REVENUE

in·ter·na·tion·al[1] /ˌɪntəˈnæʃənəlǁ-tər-/ *adj* concerning, taking place between, or recognized by more than one nation: *international trade agreements | international arms-limitation talks | an international football match | international terrorism | an international star* (=famous in more than one country) — ~ **ly** *adv* : *internationally famous*

international[2] *n* **1** an international sports match **2** someone who plays for their country's team in such a match: *an England|English international*

International *n* any of four international LEFT-WING political associations

International Air Trans·port As·so·ci·a·tion /ˌ······ ·ˈ··ˌ··,··/ also **IATA** *abbrev.*— [*the*] an international association of AIRLINE operators that aims to encourage safe, regular, reasonably-priced airline services

International Bank for Re·con·struc·tion and De·vel·op·ment /ˌ······ ·ˌ··ˌ···ˌ···/ [*the*] see WORLD BANK

International Court of Jus·tice /ˌ······ ·ˌ· ˈ··/ [*the*] a court in the Hague, also known as the World Court, which judges legal questions brought there by countries in the United Nations

International Crim·i·nal Po·lice Or·ga·ni·za·tion /ˌ······ ˌ··· ·ˈ· ···ˌ··/ [*the*] see INTERPOL

international date line /ˌ······ ˈ· ·/ [*the*] (*often caps*) an imaginary line that goes from the NORTH POLE to the SOUTH POLE through the middle of the Pacific, to the east of which the date is one day later than it is to the west. It is necessary because it makes sure that in all countries of the world, the time is related to day and night. —see also GREENWICH MEAN TIME

In·ter·na·tio·nale /ˌɪntænæʃəˈnælǁ-tər-/ *n* [*the*] the international SOCIALIST song

International House /ˌ····· ˈ·/ an organization which has English Language schools in many countries

in·ter·na·tion·al·is·m /ˌɪntəˈnæʃənəlɪzəmǁ-tər-/ *n* [U] the principle that nations should work together, because their differences are less important than the needs they have in common —**ist** *n*

in·ter·na·tion·al·ize also **-ise** *BrE* /ˌɪntəˈnæʃənəlaɪz‖-tər-/ *v* [T] to make international or bring under international control —**ization** /ˌɪntənæʃənəlaɪˈzeɪʃən‖ˌɪntər-næʃnəl-/ *n* [U]

international lan·guage /ˌ····· ˈ··/ *n* a language which can be used as a common means of COMMUNICATION by people of different nationalities. Some artificial languages have been specially invented for this purpose, though many people today consider English to be an international language, esp. in the business world. —see also ESPERANTO, INTERLINGUA

international law /ˌ····· ˈ·/ *n* [U] a collection of laws which is recognized by different countries and used in their relations with each other. The United Nations has the right to force its member countries to obey international law.

International Mon·e·ta·ry Fund /ˌ····· ˈ···· ˌ·/ also **IMF** *abbrev.*— [*the*] an international organization whose aims are to encourage the growth of trade and the strength of nations' money systems, as well as helping poor countries to pay their debts. It is part of the United Nations and has been based in Washington, DC since it was established in 1944.

international re·la·tions /ˌ······ ·ˈ··/ *n* [U] the area of politics which is concerned with the relations between different countries

international re·lief a·gen·cy /ˌ······ ·ˈ· ˌ···/ *n* any organization, such as Oxfam, the Red Cross, etc., which works in countries all over the world to lessen the suffering of the poor, hungry, and sick

in·ter·ne·cine /ˌɪntəˈniːsaɪn◂‖ˌɪntərˈniːsən◂, -ˈnesiːn◂/ *adj fml* (of fighting, etc.) between members of the same group, nation, etc.: *internecine strife*

in·tern·ee /ˌɪntɜːˈniːǁ-ɜːr-/ *n* someone who is interned (INTERN[1])

in·tern·ist /ˈɪntɜːnɪst‖ -ɜːr-/ *n AmE med* a doctor who has a general knowledge about all illnesses and medical conditions and who does not perform SURGERY —see also extra information on page 829

in·tern·ment /ɪnˈtɜːnmənt ‖ -ɜːr-/ *n* [C;U] the imprisonment of people, usu. without their being taken to court and found guilty of any crime, because they are considered dangerous, esp. in wartime and for political reasons.

▶CULTURAL NOTE In 1942, the US government ordered the internment of Japanese Americans after Japanese forces had bombed Pearl Harbor. This policy was greatly criticized.◀

In the 1970s the British government introduced internment for certain people thought to be members of the IRA, but this method of dealing with violence in Northern Ireland was ended after much criticism.

in·ter·per·son·al /ˌɪntəˈpɜːsənəl◂‖-tərˈpɜːr-/ *adj* being, related to, or concerning relations between people —compare INTRAPERSONAL

in·ter·plan·e·ta·ry /ˌɪntəˈplænɪtəri◂‖ˌɪntərˈplænɪteri/ *adj* [A] (happening or done) between the PLANETs: *interplanetary travel|space*

in·ter·play /ˈɪntəpleɪ‖-ər-/ *n* [U (of, between)] the action or effect of two or more things on each other: *the interplay of the sparkling light on the water*

In·ter·pol /ˈɪntəpɒl‖ˈɪntərpoʊl/ the International Criminal Police Organization; an international police organization for helping national police forces to catch criminals. More than 100 countries are members of Interpol, which provides them with information about international criminals and helps to catch them, esp. criminals involved in counterfeiting (COUNTERFEIT[1]), FORGERY, smuggling (SMUGGLE), and the drugs trade.

in·ter·po·late /ɪnˈtɜːpəleɪt‖-ɜːr-/ *v* [T] *fml* **1** ((into)) to put in (additional words): *He interpolated a phrase about the growth of profits into the report.* **2** to interrupt by saying: *"But that's not true!" she interpolated.* —**lation** /ɪnˌtɜːpəˈleɪʃən‖-ˌtɜːr-/ *n* [C;U]

in·ter·pose /ˌɪntəˈpəʊz‖-tər-/ *v* [T (between)] *fml* **1** to put between two other things: *He interposed himself* (=his body) *between them to stop them fighting*. **2** to introduce or say between the parts of a conversation or argument: *If I may interpose a few comments at this stage …* —**position** /ˌɪntəpəˈzɪʃən‖-tər-/ *n* [C;U]

in·ter·pret /ɪnˈtɜːprɪt‖-ɜːr-/ *v* **1** [T (as)) to understand the likely meaning of (a statement, action, etc.); place a particular meaning on: *I interpreted his silence as a refusal.| to interpret a dream* —see also MISINTERPRET **2** [T] to show one's own ideas of the meaning of (a work of art) in one's performance: *Not everyone agreed with the way she interpreted the piano sonata, but it was a technically perfect performance.* **3** [I;T] to put (something spoken) in one language into the words of another language: *I don't speak Russian; will you interpret (what she says) for me?* —compare TRANSLATE (1)

in·ter·pre·ta·tion /ɪnˌtɜːprɪˈteɪʃən‖-ɜːr-/ *n* [C;U] **1** (an act of) interpreting; explanation: *So that's your interpretation of the current political situation? I would* put a different interpretation on *it myself.* (=explain it differently) | *a judge's interpretation of the law* **2** (a) performance giving the performer's ideas of how something should be performed and what it means: *a wonderful interpretation of the symphony|the role of Macbeth*

in·ter·pre·ta·tive /ɪnˈtɜːprɪtətɪv‖ɪnˈtɜːrprəteɪtɪv/ also **in·ter·pre·tive** /ɪnˈtɜːprɪtɪv‖-ɜːr-/— *adj* of or for interpretation: *the conductor's interpretative skill*

in·ter·pret·er /ɪnˈtɜːprɪtər‖-ɜːr-/ *n* **1** a person who INTERPRETs (3), esp. as a job —compare TRANSLATOR **2** a computer PROGRAM that changes an instruction into a form that can be used directly by the computer, so that the instruction can be carried out at once

in·ter·ra·cial /ˌɪntəˈreɪʃəl◂/ *adj* (done, happening, etc.) between different races of human beings: *interracial harmony* — ~ **ly** *adv*

Inter-Rail /ˈɪntə reɪl‖-tər-/ *v* [I] to travel by train using an Inter-Rail pass: *We spent three weeks Inter-Railing around Europe.*

Inter-Rail pass /ˈ··· ˌ·/ *n* a British railway ticket sold for a fixed price that allows the holder unlimited travel on railways in many European countries for a fixed time. Inter-Rail passes are very popular with people esp. students who want to see a lot of foreign countries cheaply.

in·ter·reg·num /ˌɪntəˈregnəm/ n **-nums** or **-na** /nə/ **1** a period of time when a country has no king or queen, because the new ruler has not yet taken up his or her position **2** a period of time between events, esp. when waiting for someone to take up an important position

in·ter·re·late /ˌɪntərɪˈleɪt/ [I;T (**with**)] to connect or be connected to each other or with something else in a way that makes one depend on the other: *Wages and prices interrelate|are interrelated.*

in·ter·re·la·tion /ˌɪntərɪˈleɪʃən/ also **in·ter·re·la·tion·ship** /ˌɪntərɪˈleɪʃənʃɪp/— n [C;U (**between**)] a (close) connection; relation of dependence: *the interrelation between wages and prices*

in·ter·ro·gate /ɪnˈterəgeɪt/ v [T] **1** to question formally for a special purpose, esp. for a long time and perhaps with the use of threats or violence: *The police interrogated the suspect for several hours.* —see ASK (USAGE) **2** to (try to) get direct information from: *to interrogate a computer* —**gator** n : *He refused to tell his interrogators anything.* —**gation** /ɪnˌterəˈgeɪʃən/ n [C;U]

interrogation mark /····ˈ·· ˌ·/ n a QUESTION MARK

in·ter·rog·a·tive[1] /ˌɪntəˈrɒgətɪv/|-ˈrɑː-/ adj fml or tech (esp. in grammar) asking a question or having the form of a question: *the interrogative mood of a verb | "Who" and "what" are interrogative pronouns.* —compare DECLARATIVE, IMPERATIVE — ~ **ly** adv

interrogative[2] n tech **1** [the] (in grammar) the form used for asking questions: *Put this statement into the interrogative.* **2** [C] a word (such as **who, what, which**) used in asking a question

in·ter·rupt /ˌɪntəˈrʌpt/ v **1** [I;T] to break the flow of speech or action of (someone) by saying or doing something: *Don't interrupt (me), children; it's rude. | She's studying for an exam tomorrow, so you'd better not interrupt her.* **2** [T] to break the flow of (something continuous): *The calm of the afternoon was interrupted by a loud bang.* **3** **as I was saying before I was so rudely interrupted** humor (a phrase used when continuing to say something after someone has interrupted you) — ~ **ion** /ˈrʌpʃən/ n [C;U] : *several infuriating interruptions*

in·ter·sect /ˌɪntəˈsekt‖-ər-/ v [I;T] to cut across (each other or something else): *intersecting paths|lines*

in·ter·sec·tion /ˌɪntəˈsekʃən, ˈɪntəsekʃən‖-tər-/ n **1** [U] the act of intersecting **2** [C] a point where roads, lines, etc., intersect, esp. where two roads cross; CROSSROADS: *an accident at the intersection of North Road and Lemsford Road*

in·ter·sperse /ˌɪntəˈspɜːs‖ˌɪntərˈspɜːrs/ v [T] to set (something) here and there among other things: [+obj+**in**, **among, throughout**] *There were small dots interspersed in the pattern.* [+obj+**with**] *The pattern was interspersed with small dots. | Sunny periods will be interspersed with occasional showers.*

in·ter·state[1] /ˌɪntəˈsteɪt◄‖-ər-/ adj [A] done between, happening, or connecting states, such as the states of the US: *interstate highways*

interstate[2] adv AustrE from the state one is in to another: *I'm heading interstate tonight.*

Interstate n any of the MOTORWAYs of four or more LANES in the US, marked by red and blue signs and numbered: *There was an accident out on the Interstate this morning.| west on Interstate 80* —see EXPRESSWAY (USAGE)

Interstate Com·merce Com·mis·sion /ˌ··· ˈ·· ·, ·ˌ·/ also **ICC** abbrev.— [the] the branch of the US government that is concerned with trade within the 50 states

in·ter·stel·lar /ˌɪntəˈstelər◄‖-tər-/ adj [A] (happening or done) between the stars: *interstellar gases|space*

in·ter·stice /ɪnˈtɜːstɪs‖-ɜːr-/ n [(of, in, between**) usu. pl.] fml a small space or crack between things placed close together

in·ter·twine /ˌɪntəˈtwaɪn‖-ər-/ v [I;T (**with**)] to (cause to) twist together or with something else: *intertwining branches | (fig.) Their fates were **inextricably intertwined.** (=firmly joined together)

in·ter·val /ˈɪntəvəl‖-tər-/ n **1** [(between)] a period of time between events, activities, etc.: *After a long interval he replied. | the interval between receiving bills and paying them | Tomorrow it will be mostly cloudy, with a few sunny intervals. | During the six-month interval between his arrest and the trial, new evidence came to light.* **2** BrE‖ **intermission** AmE— such a period of time between the parts of a play, concert, etc.: *I like to eat ice cream in the interval.* **3** the difference in PITCH between two musical notes **4 at intervals (of)** happening regularly after equal periods of time or appearing at equal distances (of): *The bell rang at 20-minute intervals. | These seeds are planted at intervals of three inches.* (=three inches apart) | *at regular intervals*

in·ter·vene /ˌɪntəˈviːn‖-ər-/ v [I] **1** [(**in**)] (of a person) to interrupt, esp. in order to prevent a bad result: *They were about to start fighting when their father intervened. | The government intervened to stabilize the pound.* **2** (of an event) to happen so as to prevent or cause something: *He was going to go to university, but the war intervened.* **3** [(**between**)] (of time) to come between events: *I hadn't seen him since 1980, and he had aged a lot in the intervening years.*

in·ter·ven·tion /ˌɪntəˈvenʃən‖-tər-/ n [C;U (**in**)] (an act of) intervening: *The government's intervention in this dispute will not help.*

in·ter·ven·tion·is·m /ˌɪntəˈvenʃənɪzəm‖-tər-/ n [U] the practice of intervening, esp. by a government which intervenes in economic affairs in its own country or in the political affairs of another country

in·ter·view[1] /ˈɪntəvjuː‖-ər-/ n an occasion when a person is asked questions by one or more other people, either **a** to decide whether he or she is a suitable person to be given a job, a place at a college, etc. or **b** to find out about his or her opinions, ideas, etc., so that they can be printed in a newspaper, magazine, etc., or broadcast: *When she was still at school, she had her first interview, for a job in a shoeshop. | The film star agreed to give an interview immediately after his wedding.*

interview[2] v [T] to ask questions of (someone) in an interview: *She's being interviewed for the job. | A reporter from the "Washington Post" interviewed the President.* — ~ **er** n

in·ter·view·ee /ˌɪntəvjuːˈiː‖-ər-/ n someone who is being or is to be interviewed, esp. for a job

in·ter·war /ˌɪntəˈwɔːr◄‖-ər-/ adj happening between the First World War and the Second World War: *the interwar years|period*

in·ter·weave /ˌɪntəˈwiːv‖-ər-/ v **-wove** /ˈwəʊv/, **-woven** /ˈwəʊvən/ [T (**with**)] to weave together or with something else: *They interwove the red and gold threads. | (fig.) Our lives are interwoven.* (=seem joined together)

in·tes·tate /ɪnˈtesteɪt, -stət/ adj law not having made a WILL[2] (5) which leaves one's property to named people: *The old man **died intestate.***

intestinal for·ti·tude /·ˌ··· ˈ···/ n [U] AmE infml courage or the ability to bear something very difficult

in·tes·tine /ɪnˈtestən/ also **intestines** pl.— n the long tube that carries waste matter from the stomach out of the body; bowels —see also LARGE INTESTINE, SMALL INTESTINE —**tinal** adj

In the Bleak Mid-Win·ter /ˌ·· ·ˌ· ˈ··/ the title and first line of a religious song (CAROL) sung in Britain at Christmas

in·ti·fa·da /ˌɪntɪˈfɑːdə/ [the] (often cap.) a movement started by Palestinian Arabs in the late 1980s in protest at the Israeli holding of the West Bank and the Gaza Strip

in·ti·ma·cy /ˈɪntəməsi/ n **1** [S;U (**with**)] the state of being intimate: *His claims to (an) intimacy with|to be on terms of intimacy with the President are somewhat exaggerated.* **2** [C often pl.] a remark or action of a kind that happens only between people who know each other very well: *exchanging intimacies with one's close friends* **3** also **intimacies** pl.— [U (**with**)] euph the act of sex: *"He went up to her room and intimacy took place," said the policeman.*

in·ti·mate[1] /ˈɪntəmət/ adj **1** [(**with**)] having an extremely close relationship: *intimate friends | He is intimate with the President. | They are on intimate terms.* **2** providing or suggesting warm or private surroundings for making close (esp. sexual) relationships: *an intimate candlelit dinner for two* **3** fml detailed; resulting from close study or association: *She has an intimate knowledge of the law.* **4** [A] personal; private: *She confided her most intimate thoughts to her diary.* **5** [F (**with**)] euph having sex:

"They were intimate three times," reported the policeman. − ~**ly** *adv*

intimate² *n* someone who is a close friend of, and shares secrets with, another person: *an intimate of the President's*

in·ti·mate³ /ˈɪntɪˌmeɪt/ *v* [T] *fml* to make known indirectly; suggest; IMPLY: *He intimated a wish to go by saying that it was late.* [+*that*] *He intimated that he wanted to go|that we should leave.* −**mation** /ˌɪntɪˈmeɪʃən/ *n* [C;U]

in·tim·i·date /ɪnˈtɪmɪˌdeɪt/ *v* [T (**into**)] to frighten, esp. by making threats: *They tried to intimidate him into doing what they wanted.* | (fig.) *an intimidating pile of dirty dishes to do* −**dation** /ɪnˌtɪmɪˈdeɪʃən/ *n* [U] : *After bribes had proved useless, they tried threats and intimidation.| the intimidation of defence witnesses*

intnl *written abbrev. for* INTERNATIONAL

in·to /ˈɪntə; *before vowels* ˈɪntʊ; *strong* ˈɪntuː/ *prep* **1** so as to be in: *It started to rain so they went into the house.* | *She jumped into the water.* | *He changed into his uniform.* | *He went into* (=got a job in) *the clothing trade.* | *They worked far into the night.* | *You'll get into trouble if you do that.* | *He scared them into silence.* **2** so as to be: *She translated it into French.* | *She developed into a beautiful woman.* | *The frog turned into a prince.* | *Roll the clay into a ball.* **3** against; so as to hit: *He bumped into me and knocked me over.* **4** (used when dividing one number by another): *Seven into eleven won't go.* **5** *infml* keen on; interested in: *He's given up photography and now he's into computers.* | *She's really into modern dance.*

in·tol·e·ra·ble /ɪnˈtɒlərəbəl‖-ˈtɑː-/ *adj* which is too difficult, painful, unfair, bad, etc., to be borne; unbearable: *intolerable pain|rudeness* | *an intolerable situation* −**bly** *adv*

in·tol·e·rant /ɪnˈtɒlərənt‖-ˈtɑː-/ *adj* [(**of**)] not able or willing to accept ways of thinking and behaving which are different from one's own: *intolerant of any opposition* | *intolerant bigots* − ~**ly** *adv* −**rance** *n* [U] : *racial intolerance*

in·to·na·tion /ˌɪntəˈneɪʃən/ *n* [C;U] *esp. tech* (a pattern of) rise and fall in the level (PITCH³) of the voice, which often adds meaning to what is being said (e.g. to show that a question is being asked, that the speaker is angry, etc.): *Questions are spoken with a rising intonation.* −compare INFLECTION, STRESS¹ (4)

in·tone /ɪnˈtəʊn/ *v* [I;T] to say (a poem, prayer, etc.) in an almost level voice; CHANT: *The priest intoned the blessing.*

in to·to /ˌɪn ˈtəʊtəʊ/ *adv Lat* totally; as a whole: *They accepted the plan in toto.*

in·tox·i·cant /ɪnˈtɒksɪkənt‖ɪnˈtɑːk-/ *n tech* something which intoxicates, esp. an alcoholic drink

in·tox·i·cate /ɪnˈtɒksɪˌkeɪt‖ɪnˈtɑːk-/ *v* [T] **1** *tech* (of alcohol) to make drunk: *He was fined for driving while intoxicated.* | *intoxicating liquor* **2** [*often pass.*] *fml* to bring out strong feelings of wild excitement in: *Intoxicated by his success|by the thought of all the money he might win* −**cation** /ɪnˌtɒksɪˈkeɪʃən‖ɪnˌtɑːk-/ *n* [U]

in·trac·ta·ble /ɪnˈtræktəbəl/ *adj fml* **1** very difficult to deal with or find an answer to: *intractable problems* **2** having such a strong will as to be difficult to control: *an intractable child* −**bly** *adv* −**bility** /ɪnˌtræktəˈbɪlɪti/ *n* [U]

in·tra·mu·ral /ˌɪntrəˈmjʊərəl◂/ *adj* (happening) within a place or organization: *intramural courses at college* | *intramural sports* (=between teams from the same school or college) −opposite **extramural**

in·tran·si·gent /ɪnˈtrænsɪdʒənt/ *adj fml derog* (of a person or their behaviour) showing extreme ideas, esp. in politics, which cannot be changed by other people's wishes or arguments: *The government were urged on all sides to change their proposals, but they remained completely intransigent.* − ~**ly** *adv* −**gence** *n* [U]

in·tran·si·tive /ɪnˈtrænsɪtɪv/ *adj tech* (of a verb) having a subject but no object. Intransitive verbs are marked [I] in this dictionary: *"Break" is intransitive in the sentence "My cup fell and broke" but transitive in "I broke the cup".* −compare DITRANSITIVE, TRANSITIVE −**intransitive** *n* − ~**ly** *adv*

in·tra·per·son·al /ˌɪntrəˈpɜːsənəl◂ ‖ -ˈpɜːr-/ *adj* happening in the mind rather than between two people −compare INTERPERSONAL

in·tra·u·te·rine de·vice /ˌɪntrəˈjuːtəraɪn dɪˈvaɪs ‖ -tərən-/ *n* see IUD

in·tra·ve·nous /ˌɪntrəˈviːnəs◂/ *adj* (done) into or by way of a VEIN (=tube in the body taking blood back to the heart): *The drug was administered by* **intravenous injection.** − ~**ly** *adv*

in tray /ˈ· ·/ *n* a box used for storing work, letters, etc. which need to be dealt with: *When I came back from my holiday, my in tray was overflowing.* −compare OUT TRAY −see picture at TRAY

in·trench /ɪnˈtrentʃ/ *v* [T] to ENTRENCH

in·trep·id /ɪnˈtrepɪd/ *adj apprec, esp. lit* showing no fear; brave: *the intrepid mountaineers* − ~**ly** *adv* − ~**ity** /ˌɪntrəˈpɪdɪti/ *n* [U] *fml*

in·tri·ca·cy /ˈɪntrɪkəsi/ *n* **1** [U] the quality or state of being intricate: *the intricacy of the lace|the problem* **2** [C *often pl.*] something intricate: *the intricacies of political manoeuvring*

in·tri·cate /ˈɪntrɪkɪt/ *adj* containing many detailed parts, and thus sometimes difficult to understand: *an intricate pattern|story* − ~**ly** *adv*

in·trigue¹ /ɪnˈtriːg/ *v* **1** [T] to interest greatly, esp. because strange, mysterious, or unexpected; FASCINATE: *He's always been intrigued by machinery.* | *You intrigue me; tell me more!* **2** [I (**against**)] to make secret plans; PLOT

in·trigue² /ˈɪntriːg, ɪnˈtriːg/ *n* **1** [U] the act or practice of planning something secretly: *She got to her present high position by plotting and intrigue.* **2** [C (**against**)] a secret plan or activity between two or more people

in·tri·guing /ɪnˈtriːgɪŋ/ *adj* very interesting, esp. because of some strange quality; FASCINATING: *an intriguing idea|story|woman* − ~**ly** *adv*

in·trin·sic /ɪnˈtrɪnsɪk, -zɪk/ *adj* [(**to**)] being part of the nature or character of someone or something; INHERENT: *her intrinsic goodness* | *He admitted the intrinsic merits of my idea, but said it would need a lot of refinement before it could be put into practice.* | *difficulties that are intrinsic to such a situation* − ~**ally** /kli/ *adv* : *He's intrinsically honest, although he is tempted to cheat sometimes.*

int·ro /ˈɪntrəʊ/ *n* -**s** [(**to**)] *infml* an introduction: *Can you arrange an intro to the chairman for me?*

in·tro·duce /ˌɪntrəˈdjuːs‖-ˈduːs/ *v* [T] **1** [(**to**)] to make known for the first time to each other or someone else, esp. by telling two people each other's names: *I introduced John to|and Mary last year, and now they're married.* | *Have you two been introduced?* | *Let me introduce myself: my name is (John) Simpson.* | (fig.) *Let me introduce you to the pleasures of wine-tasting.* **2** [(**into, to**)] to bring in, esp. for the first time: *Potatoes were introduced into Europe from South America.* | *His unfortunate remarks introduced a note of bitterness into the conversation.* **3** to bring (new laws, PROCEDURES, etc.) into practice or use; INSTITUTE: *The government has introduced a ban on the advertising of cigarettes.* **4** to be a sign that (something) is about to happen; signal the start of: *An enormous orchestral crescendo introduces the climax of the opera.*

   introduce sthg. **into** sthg. *phr v* [T] *fml* to put (something) into (something): *He introduced the pipe into the hole.*

in·tro·duc·tion /ˌɪntrəˈdʌkʃən/ *n* **1** [U (**to, into**)] the act of introducing or the fact of being introduced: *the introduction of a new brand of soap* | *The union opposed the introduction of the new technology because of the loss of jobs it would cause.* **2** [C (**to**) *often pl.*] an occasion of telling people each others' names: *Shall I make the introductions? Robert, this is Julia.* | (fig.) *This little book is a very good introduction to* (=provides the most important facts or principles of) *geometry.* **3** [C (**to**)] a written or spoken explanation at the beginning of a book or speech: *The introduction tells you how to use the book.* | *In the chairman's brief introduction she told us a little about the speaker's work.* −see PREFACE (USAGE) **4** [C] a type of plant or animal that was originally brought from another part of the world: *The potato is an introduction; it didn't use to grow here.*

in·tro·duc·to·ry /ˌɪntrəˈdʌktəri◂/ *adj* which happens or is said at the beginning to explain or advertise what is to follow: *The chairman made a few introductory remarks.* | *introductory courses in computer programming*

introductory of·fer /ˌ····· ˈ··/ *n* a special deal, such as a reduced price or an increased amount, which is offered for a short time on a new product, to encourage people to buy it

in·tro·spec·tion /ˌɪntrəˈspekʃən/ n [U] the habit of looking into one's own thoughts and feelings to find out their real meaning, the reasons for them, etc. Introspection has been considered an important method in PSYCHOLOGY and LINGUISTICS.

in·tro·spec·tive /ˌɪntrəˈspektɪv◂/ adj tending to think (too) deeply about oneself – – **ly** adv

in·tro·vert /ˈɪntrəvɜːt‖-ɜːrt/ n a person of an introverted type —compare EXTROVERT

in·tro·vert·ed /ˈɪntrəvɜːtɪd‖-ɜːr-/ adj concerning oneself with one's own thoughts, acts, personal life, etc., rather than spending much time sharing activities with others: *I like Bill, but he's rather introverted.* —**version** /ˌɪntrə-ˈvɜːʃən‖-ˈvɜːrʒən/ n [U]

in·trude /ɪnˈtruːd/ v [(**into, on, upon**)] **1** [I] to enter unwanted or unasked: *I don't want to intrude (on you) if you're busy.* | *It would be very insensitive to intrude upon their private grief.* **2** [T] fml to bring in, esp. without good reason or permission: *A translator shouldn't intrude his own opinions into what he's translating.* —compare OBTRUDE

in·trud·er /ɪnˈtruːdə^r/ n a person who has come in unasked and usu. secretly, esp. one intending to steal —compare INTERLOPER

in·tru·sion /ɪnˈtruːʒən/ n [(**on, upon**)] **1** [U] the act of intruding **2** [C] something that intrudes on or interrupts something: *I have so many intrusions on my time that it's difficult to get my work done.* | *These questions are an intrusion upon people's privacy.*

in·tru·sive /ɪnˈtruːsɪv/ adj derog or tech tending to intrude: *intrusive neighbours* | *Some people pronounce an intrusive "r" at the end of "law" in "law and order".*

in·trust /ɪnˈtrʌst/ v [T] to ENTRUST

in·tu·it /ɪnˈtjuːɪt‖-ˈtuː-, -ˈtjuː-/ v [I;T] to get knowledge (of) by intuition

in·tu·i·tion /ˌɪntjuˈɪʃən‖-tu-, -tju-/ n **1** [U] the power of understanding or knowing something without reasoning or learned skill: *My intuition told me he wasn't to be trusted.* | *"How did you know that, Jane?" "Woman's intuition!"* **2** [C] an example of this, or a piece of knowledge that results: [+(*that*)] *She had an intuition that her friend was ill.* —compare INSTINCT

in·tu·i·tive /ɪnˈtjuːɪtɪv‖-ˈtuː-, -ˈtjuː-/ adj usu. apprec showing or formed by intuition: *She's a very intuitive person.* | *He seemed to have an intuitive knowledge of how I was feeling.* – – **ly** adv – – **ness** n [U]

In·u·it, Innuit /ˈɪnjuɪt, ˈɪnuɪt/ n Inuit or Inuits [C] **1** (a member) of a race of people living in the icy northern part of N America. This is thought to be a better word for Eskimo. —see picture at ESKIMO **2** [U] the language of these people

in·un·date /ˈɪnəndeɪt/ v [T (**with**) often pass.] to flood over in large amounts, esp. so as to cover: *The river overflowed and inundated the village.* | (fig.) *After winning the competition, I was inundated with requests for money.* —**dation** /ˌɪnənˈdeɪʃən/ n [C;U]

in·ure /ɪˈnjʊə^r/ v
inure sbdy. **to** sthg. phr v [T] to get used to (something unpleasant) by long experience: *Nurses gradually become inured to the sight of people in pain/to people suffering.*

in·vade /ɪnˈveɪd/ v **1** [I;T] to go or come into and attack, so as to take control of (a country, city, etc.): *Hitler invaded Poland in 1939.* | (fig.) *These microorganisms can easily invade diseased tissue.* | (fig.) *Holidaymakers invade the seaside towns* (=enter them in large numbers) *in summer.* | (fig.) *Doubts invaded his mind.* **2** [T] derog to enter into and spoil: *The motorbikes invaded the calm of the summer afternoon.* —see also INVASION —**vader** n

in·val·id¹ /ɪnˈvælɪd/ adj not correct or correctly expressed, esp. in law; not (any longer) suitable for use: *Your arguments are invalid.* | *Your ticket has passed its expiry date, so it is now invalid.* – – **ly** adv

in·va·lid² /ˈɪnvəliːd, -lɪd‖-lɪd/ n a person who is disabled or suffers from habitual ill-health: *He never fully recovered, and spent the rest of his life as an invalid.* —**invalid** adj : *my invalid mother*

invalid³ v
invalid sbdy. ↔ **out** phr v BrE [T (**of**) usu. pass.] to allow (someone) to leave esp. a military force because of ill-health: *He was invalided out of the army when he lost the sight of one eye.*

in·val·i·date /ɪnˈvælɪdeɪt/ v [T] to make (something) invalid; show that (something) is not correct: *The fact that there is almost no critical discussion of his paintings invalidates this book's claims to be the standard work on Blake.* —**dation** /ɪnˌvælɪˈdeɪʃən/ n [U]

invalid chair /·ˈ··· ˌ·/ n BrE a WHEELCHAIR

in·va·lid·i·ty /ˌɪnvəˈlɪdɪti/ n [U] **1** the state of being INVALID¹: *the invalidity of her arguments* **2** the state of being an INVALID²: *an invalidity pension*

invalidity ben·e·fit /·ˈ···· ˌ···/ n [C;U] (in Britain) a payment made by the government to someone who has been unable to work because of illness for more than a certain length of time

in·val·ua·ble /ɪnˈvæljʊbəl/ adj [(**for, to**)] apprec too valuable for the worth to be measured; extremely useful: *An electric drill would have been invaluable for this job.* | *your invaluable help* | *His advice has been invaluable to the success of the project.* —see VALUABLE (USAGE)

in·var·i·a·ble /ɪnˈveəriəbəl/ adj which cannot or does not vary or change: *an invariable quantity* | *She came to see me with the invariable request* (=the request she always makes) *for a loan.* —**bility** /ɪnˌveəriəˈbɪlɪti/ n [U]

in·var·i·a·bly /ɪnˈveəriəbli/ adv **1** in an invariable way **2** always: *It invariably rains when I go there.*

in·va·sion /ɪnˈveɪʒən/ n an act of invading (INVADE), esp. an attack in war when the enemy spreads into and tries to control a country, city, etc.: *the invasion of Normandy* —**sive** /ˈveɪsɪv/ adj : *invasive cancer cells*

invasion of priv·a·cy /·ˌ··· ˈ···/ n an INTRUSION into the personal affairs of another person: *Opening my letter was an inexcusable invasion of privacy.*

in·vec·tive /ɪnˈvektɪv/ n [S;U] fml (a) forceful attacking speech used for blaming someone for something and often including swearing: *They cringed under the force of his withering invective.*

in·veigh /ɪnˈveɪ/ v
inveigh against sthg./sbdy. phr v [T] fml to attack strongly with words: *The speaker was inveighing against the evils of drink.*

in·vei·gle /ɪnˈveɪgəl, ɪnˈviː-‖ɪnˈveɪ-/ v [T] to obtain by deceit or tricks: *I inveigled fifty bucks from her with my hard luck story.*
inveigle sbdy. **into** sthg. phr v [T+obj+v-ing] to trick (someone) into (doing something) by persuading (them) cleverly

in·vent /ɪnˈvent/ v [T] **1** to make or produce (esp. a new or useful thing or idea) for the first time: *Alexander Graham Bell invented the telephone in 1876.* **2** to think of (a story, lie, etc.) esp. in order to deceive; produce (something untrue or unreal): *They invented a very convincing alibi.* | *He invented a hundred reasons why he couldn't go.*
▷ USAGE You **discover** something that existed before but was not known, such as a place or a fact. You **invent** something that did not exist before, such as a machine or a method: *They* **discovered** *oil in the North Sea.* | *Who* **invented** *the computer?*◁

in·ven·tion /ɪnˈvenʃən/ n **1** [U] the act of inventing: *the invention of the telephone* **2** [C] something invented: *The telephone is a wonderful invention.* | *The whole story is a complete invention; I don't believe a word of it!*

in·ven·tive /ɪnˈventɪv/ adj apprec having or showing the ability to invent or think in new and different ways: *an inventive person/mind* – – **ly** adv – – **ness** n [U]

in·ven·tor /ɪnˈventə^r/ n a person who invents something new, esp. one whose job is inventing things

in·ven·to·ry /ˈɪnvəntri‖-tɔːri/ n **1** [(**of**)] a list, esp. one of all the goods in a place: *An inventory of all the stock has to be made before the shop can be sold.* **2** AmE all the goods in one place; STOCK

In·ver·ness /ˌɪnvəˈnes◂‖-vər-/ a town in N Scotland which is known as the capital of the Highlands

Inverness-shire /ˌɪnvəˈnes-ʃə‖-vər-/ a former COUNTY in N Scotland, now part of Highland REGION

in·verse /ˌɪnˈvɜːs◂‖-ɜːrs◂/ n, adj [A; the (**of**)] (something which is) opposite, esp. in order or position: *The inverse of 4* (=⁴/₁) *is ¹/₄.* | *Amazingly, his enthusiasm for a job seems to be in* **inverse relation/proportion** *to the amount he gets paid for it!* (=the less he gets paid, the more he likes it) – – **ly** adv

in·ver·sion /ɪnˈvɜːʃən‖-ˈvɜːrʒən/ n 1 [U] the act of inverting 2 [C] a weather condition in which the air nearest the ground is cooler than the air above it. In cities this is connected with POLLUTION.

in·vert /ɪnˈvɜːt‖-ɜːrt/ v [T] fml or tech to put in the opposite position or order, esp. to turn upside down: She caught the insect by inverting her cup over it.

in·ver·te·brate /ɪnˈvɜːtɨbrɨt, -breɪt‖-ɜːr-/ n tech a living creature which has no BACKBONE: Worms and insects are invertebrates. —compare VERTEBRATE —**invertebrate** adj

inverted com·ma /·ˌ·· ˈ·ˌ/ n BrE 1 QUOTATION MARK 2 **in inverted commas** BrE ‖ **in quotes** AmE— (used, esp. in speech, for suggesting the opposite of what has just been said): "Her friends, in inverted commas, all disappeared when she was in trouble." (=so they were not really her friends; compare, in writing: Her "friends" all disappeared…) —compare SO-CALLED

inverted snob /·ˌ·· ˈ·/ BrE ‖ **reverse snob** AmE— n someone who makes a show of disliking grand things and admiring things typical of low social class — ~ **bery** n [U]

in·vest /ɪnˈvest/ v 1 [I;T(in)] to put (money) in a particular use, e.g. by buying SHARES in a business, in order to make a profit: Your bank manager will advise you how/where to invest your money. | He invested £1000 in an oil company. | You can make a lot of money by investing in antique furniture. (=buying it so as to make a profit when the price goes up) | (fig.) I've invested a lot of time and effort in this plan, and I don't want it to fail. 2 [T] old use to surround with soldiers or ships so as to prevent escape or entrance
  invest in sthg. phr v [T] infml to buy: I've decided to invest in a new car.
  invest sbdy. **with** sthg. phr v [T often pass.] fml or lit to give officially to (a person) (the outward signs of rank or power, or the power itself): She was invested with full authority. | (fig.) Don't invest his words with too much importance! (=take them too seriously)

in·vest·ed /ɪnˈvestɨd/ adj [(in)] AmE strongly connected or interested, often in an emotional way: I'm too invested in this situation to be objective about it. | She's really invested in her boyfriend at the moment.

in·ves·ti·gate /ɪnˈvestɨɡeɪt/ v [I;T] to try to find out more information about; examine the reasons for (something), the character of (someone), etc.: The police are investigating the crime. | He has been investigated and found blameless. | to investigate the causes of cancer —**gator** n —**gation** /ɪnˌvestɨˈɡeɪʃən/ n [C;U (into)] —**gative** /ɪnˈvestɨɡətɪv‖-ɡeɪtɪv/ adj : investigative journalism (=where newspapers try to find out things of public importance, uncover secrets, etc.)

in·ves·ti·ture /ɪnˈvestɨtʃəʳ‖-tʃʊəʳ/ n a ceremony to accept someone into office, to give them certain powers, etc.: the investiture of the Prince of Wales

in·vest·ment /ɪnˈvestmənt/ n [(in)] 1 [U] the act of investing (INVEST (1)) 2 [C] something invested or in which one INVESTS: She made an investment of £1000 in the new firm. | He sold off all his investments in South America. | The government is trying to attract more investment into the shipbuilding industry. | Antique furniture is a very safe/good investment.

investment com·pa·ny /·ˈ·· ˌ··/ n a company whose main business is to buy the SHARES or securities (SECURITY (5)) of other companies purely for investment purposes — compare HOLDING COMPANY

investment trust /·ˈ·· ˌ·/ n an investment company that buys securities (SECURITY (5)) for its investors. Investment trusts are free to choose which securities they buy for their investors as their aim is to give investors the best possible income from their money.

in·ves·tor /ɪnˈvestəʳ/ n a person who puts money to a particular use, e.g. by buying SHARES¹ (2) in a business, in order to make a profit: We have to protect the interests of our investors. | a major investor in the new company

in·vet·e·rate /ɪnˈvetərɨt/ adj [A] 1 firmly settled in a usu. bad habit; HABITUAL: an inveterate liar | (humor) I'm afraid I'm an inveterate reader of trashy romances! (=I know most people do not approve of them) 2 (of a habit) firmly established

in·vid·i·ous /ɪnˈvɪdiəs/ adj tending to cause ill-will or make people unnecessarily offended or jealous: It would be invidious (of me) to single out (=choose) any one member

of the team for praise. | invidious comparisons — ~ **ly** adv — ~ **ness** n [U]

in·vi·gi·late /ɪnˈvɪdʒɨleɪt/ BrE‖**proctor** AmE— v [I;T] to watch over (an examination or the people taking it) in order to prevent dishonesty —**lator** n —**lation** /ɪnˌvɪdʒɨˈleɪʃən/ n [U]

in·vig·o·rate /ɪnˈvɪɡəreɪt/ v [T] to give a feeling of freshness and healthy strength to: an invigorating swim before breakfast

in·vin·ci·ble /ɪnˈvɪnsɨbəl/ adj apprec too strong to be defeated: an invincible army —**bly** adv —**bility** /ɪnˌvɪnsɨˈbɪlɨti/ n [U]

in·vi·o·la·ble /ɪnˈvaɪələbəl/ adj fml which is too highly respected to be attacked, changed, etc.; which cannot be violated (VIOLATE): inviolable rights —**bility** /ɪnˌvaɪələˈbɪlɨti/ n [U]

in·vi·o·late /ɪnˈvaɪələt/ adj lit not violated (VIOLATE): The sanctity of the temple remains inviolate.

in·vis·i·ble /ɪnˈvɪzɨbəl/ adj 1 [(to)] that cannot be seen; hidden from sight: Germs are invisible to the naked eye. | The magician drank the mixture to make himself invisible. | He felt that he was powerless; some invisible force seemed to be directing his life. | a secret message written in invisible ink (=which can be read only when heated or treated with a chemical) | The house is invisible from the road, being surrounded by trees. —compare INAUDIBLE 2 that is not usually recorded, esp. in statements of profit and loss: Insurance is one of Britain's most profitable invisible exports. (=sale of services, rather than goods, abroad) —**bly** adv: "Where's the torn place?" "It's been invisibly mended." —**bility** /ɪnˌvɪzɨˈbɪlɨti/ n [U]

invisible earn·ings /·ˌ··· ˈ··/ n [P] income from e.g. the tourist trade, which is difficult to IDENTIFY separately from other earnings, as it is unclear when and by what people the money involved is spent

invisible ink /·ˌ··· ˈ·/ n [U] a type of ink used for writing secret messages which is invisible until it is developed, usu. by heating. It is rarely used in real life but it is often written about in DETECTIVE stories.

Invisible Man /·ˌ··· ˈ·/, **The** 1 (the main character in) a book by H. G. Wells which was later made into a film and a set of television programmes 2 a book by the American writer Ralph Ellison about the difficult life of a young black man in New York

in·vi·ta·tion /ˌɪnvɨˈteɪʃən/ n 1 [C (to)] a written or spoken request made to someone, asking them to come to a place, take part in an activity, etc.: "Did you get an invitation to the party?" "Yes, I replied to it this morning." | They sent out 200 invitations to their wedding. [+to-v] Their ambassador has accepted/declined (=not accepted) an invitation to meet with the president and discuss this issue. | I've got a **standing/an open invitation** to visit my friend in China (=I can go at any time) 2 [U] the act of inviting: Entrance is by written invitation only. 3 [S+to] an encouragement to an action, usu. a bad action; INDUCEMENT: These enticing displays of goods in shops are an invitation to theft. —see REFUSE (USAGE)

in·vite¹ /ɪnˈvaɪt/ v [T] 1 [(to)] to ask (someone) to come esp. to a social occasion: We invited all our relatives (to the wedding). | Let's invite some people over/round (=to our house) for a drink. [+obj+to-v] They've invited us to stay for the weekend. | She was polite but she didn't invite me in. | The film was shown to a specially invited audience. 2 to ask for or request, esp. politely or formally: Questions were invited after the meeting. | to invite offers on a house/bids for a contract [+obj+to-v] The television interviewer invited the minister to comment on the recent events. 3 to (seem to) encourage (something bad): You're just inviting trouble if you do that. [+obj+to-v] Some shops invite people to steal by making it too easy to take things.

invite² /ˈɪnvaɪt/ n infml an invitation (1): Did you get an invite to the mayor's reception?

in·vit·ing /ɪnˈvaɪtɪŋ/ adj attractive; encouraging one to take a suitable action: an inviting prospect | an inviting-looking cake/armchair — ~ **ly** adv

in vi·tro /ɪn ˈviːtrəʊ/ adj, adv Lat (done) outside a living body, in a piece of scientific equipment —compare IN VIVO

in vitro fer·ti·li·za·tion /·ˌ· ···ˌ···/ n [U] a process in which a human OVUM is taken from a woman's body and FERTILIZED by a man's SPERM in a LABORATORY before being returned to the woman's body for the usual development. This has been used since 1978 as a way of helping people to have children if they have had difficulty in doing so. —see also TEST-TUBE BABY

in vi·vo /ɪn ˈviːvəʊ/ *adj, adv Lat* (done) inside a living body —compare IN VITRO

in·vo·ca·tion /ˌɪnvəˈkeɪʃən/ *n fml* **1** [U] the act of invoking: *their invocation of diplomatic immunity in order to escape arrest* **2** [C (**to**)] a form of words calling for help, esp. from God or the gods; prayer

in·voice¹ /ˈɪnvɔɪs/ *n* a list of goods supplied or work done, stating quantity and price: *to make out/submit/process/ pay an invoice*

invoice² *v* [T] **1** to prepare an invoice for (goods supplied or work done): *several orders waiting to be invoiced* **2** to send an invoice to (someone): *We will be invoicing you separately for these items.*

in·voke /ɪnˈvəʊk/ *v* [T] *fml* **1** to call or bring into use (esp. a right or law)/or operation: *The government invoked "reasons of national security" in order to justify arresting its opponents.* **2** to make an urgent request to (a power, esp. God) for help **3** to request or beg for: *She invoked their help/their forgiveness.* **4** to call on and cause (spirits) to appear —see also INVOCATION

in·vol·un·ta·ry /ɪnˈvɒləntəri‖ɪnˈvɑːlənteri/ *adj* made or done without conscious effort or intention: *involuntary muscular movements* | *He gave an involuntary smile/gasp/shudder.* —**tarily** *adv*

in·volve /ɪnˈvɒlv‖ɪnˈvɑːlv/ *v* [T *not usu. in progressive forms*] **1** [(**in, with**)] to cause (someone or oneself) to become connected or concerned: *Don't involve other people in your mad schemes!* | *If I were you I wouldn't get involved in their problems.* —compare IMPLICATE **2** [(**in**)] to have as a necessary part or result; ENTAIL: *I didn't realize putting on a play involved so much work/that so much work was involved in putting on a play.* [+*v-ing*] *The job involves travelling abroad for three months each year.* **3** (of a situation or action) to have as the people or things taking part: *The accident involved a bus and a truck.* | *a big police operation involving over a hundred officers.* —**ment** *n* [U (**in, with**)] : *The police are investigating his possible involvement in the crime.*

in·volved /ɪnˈvɒlvd‖ɪnˈvɑːlvd/ *adj* **1** having related parts which are difficult to understand; COMPLICATED: *a long and involved explanation* **2** [F (**with**)] (of a person) closely connected in relationships and activities with others, esp. in a personal or sexual way: *He's deeply involved with a married woman.*

in·vul·ne·ra·ble /ɪnˈvʌlnərəbəl/ *adj* [(**to**)] impossible to harm by attack: *an invulnerable castle* | (fig.) *She seems invulnerable to criticism.* —**bly** *adv* —**bility** /ɪnˌvʌlnərəˈbɪlʒti/ *n* [U]

in·ward /ˈɪnwəd‖-wərd/ *adj* [A] **1** (placed) on the inside **2** moving towards the inside **3** in or towards the mind or spirit: *a very inward-looking philosophy* | *a feeling of inward satisfaction* —compare OUTWARD —**ly** *adv* : *She smiled, but she was fuming* (=very angry) *inwardly.*

in·wards /ˈɪnwədz‖-wərdz/ also **inward** *AmE*— *adv* towards the inside: *They screamed as the walls fell inwards.* —opposite **outwards**

I/O /ˌaɪ ˈəʊ/ *n, adj* [U;C] *tech* input/output; (of) the part of a computer that both receives information and after processing, sends the resulting information back or to another computer: *We're getting faster disk I/Os with this new software.* | *terminal I/O* | *an I/O fault*

IOC /ˌaɪ əʊ ˈsiː/ [*the*] International Olympic Committee; the governing body of the Olympic Games: *The IOC meets today to discuss the venue for the 1996 Olympics.*

i·o·dine /ˈaɪədiːn‖-daɪn/ *n* [U] a simple substance (ELEMENT) that is used on wounds to prevent infection and in photography

IOM *written abbrev. for* ISLE OF MAN

i·on /ˈaɪən‖ˈaɪən, ˈaɪɑːn/ *n* an atom which has been given (+) POSITIVE or (−) NEGATIVE force by the taking away or addition of an ELECTRON

I·o·na /aɪˈəʊnə/ an island off W Scotland, one of the Inner Hebrides, famous as the starting place in the 6th century of Scots Christianity, and the home of the **Iona Community**, an ECUMENICAL Christian group

I·o·nes·co /ˌiːəˈneskəʊ/, **Eu·gène** /juːˈʒiːn/ (1912–) a

modern French writer of plays born in Romania, who writes about the ABSURDITY of human life. His plays include *The Bald Prima Donna* (1956), *Rhinoceros* (1960), and *Exit the King* (1963)

I·on·ic /aɪˈɒnɪk‖aɪˈɑː-/ *adj* of, like, or typical of a style of ancient Greek building that is not very highly decorated: *an Ionic column* —compare CORINTHIAN, DORIC

i·on·ize also **-ise** *BrE* /ˈaɪənaɪz/ *v* [I;T] to (cause to) form ions —**ization** /ˌaɪənaɪˈzeɪʃən‖-nə-/ *n* [U]

i·on·i·zer also **-iser** *BrE* /ˈaɪənaɪzəʳ/ *n* a machine that produces negative IONS, which is believed to make the air inside a room or building more healthy. Ionizers are often used by people who suffer from ASTHMA.

i·on·o·sphere /aɪˈɒnəsfɪəʳ‖aɪˈɑː-/ [*the*] the part of the AT-MOSPHERE which is between about 40 and 400 kilometres above the Earth. It is used in helping to send radio waves around the Earth, because radio waves will BOUNCE off the ionosphere (=hit it and return to Earth). —**spheric** /aɪˌɒnəˈsferɪk‖-ˌɑːn-/ *adj*

i·o·ta /aɪˈəʊtə/ *n* [S (**of**) *usu. in negatives*] a very small amount; any at all: *There's not an iota of truth in what she said!*

IOU /ˌaɪ əʊ ˈjuː/ *n* "I owe you"; a piece of paper saying that one owes a certain amount of money to someone, with one's signature at the bottom: *I haven't any cash on me; can I give you an IOU for the £5?*

IOW *written abbrev. for* ISLE OF WIGHT

I·o·wa /ˈaɪəwə ‖ ˈaɪəʊə/ *written abbrev.* **IA** a state in the Midwest of the US. Iowa's economic life is based on farming and it is a leading producer of corn and SOYA BEANS —see colour map on pages 1374–5

IPA /ˌaɪ piː ˈeɪ‖ [*the*]U] International Phonetic Alphabet; a system of special signs, each one of which represents a sound made in speech: *A form of (the) IPA is used for showing the pronunciations in this dictionary.*

ipse, IPSE /ɪps/ integrated project support environment; a set of system development tools used in the planning, development, and testing of some large computer systems

ip·so fac·to /ˌɪpsəʊ ˈfæktəʊ/ *adv Lat fml* (used for showing that something else is known from or proved by the known facts) by the fact itself: *If she admits it is her signature on the cheque, she is ipso facto guilty.* —compare DE FACTO

Ip·swich /ˈɪpswɪtʃ/ the main town of Suffolk, E England, a port and industrial centre where the local government for Suffolk is based

IQ /ˌaɪ ˈkjuː/ *n* intelligence quotient; a measure of human INTELLIGENCE, with 100 representing the average. A person's IQ is often determined using an **IQ test** consisting of problems related to letters, numbers, and shapes. These tests are quite CONTROVERSIAL because many people think they are biased (BIAS) against people of certain races: *She has an IQ of 127.*

ir- see WORD FORMATION

IRA¹ /ˌaɪ ɑːr ˈeɪ/ [*the*] Irish Republican Army; an illegal organization whose aim is to unite Northern Ireland and the Republic of Ireland as one republic. Part of the IRA, the PROVISIONAL IRA, is known for its use of TERRORIST methods. —see also SINN FEIN

IRA² /ˈaɪrə/ Individual Retirement Account; a personal PENSION plan available to American citizens and other people who live in the US

I·ran /ɪˈrɑːn, -æn/ a country in SW Asia, officially known as the Islamic Republic of Iran and called Persia until 1935; capital Tehran; population 54,203,000 (1989). Iran is one of the leading producers of oil in the world. Iran was at war with Iraq from 1980 to 1988.

I·ran·gate /ɪˈrɑːŋgeɪt, ɪˈræn-/ also **the Iran-Con·tra Af·fair** /ˌ·ˌ ˈ··· ·ˌ/ a political SCANDAL in the US, uncovered in 1986 and 1987, in which members of the Reagan ADMINIS-TRATION were found to have sold weapons to Iran in exchange for the return of American HOSTAGEs, and to have sent the profits to support the Contra REBELs in Nicaragua

I·ra·ni·an /ɪˈreɪniən/ *n* a person who comes from or whose parents come from Iran —**Iranian** *adj*

I·raq /ɪˈrɑːk, -æk/ a country in SW Asia, officially called the Republic of Iraq, which is one of the leading producers of oil in the Middle East; capital Baghdad; population 17,610,000 (1989). Iraq was at war with Iran from 1980 to 1988. In 1990, under Saddam Hussein, Iraq invaded (INVADE) Kuwait, which led to the GULF WAR. Iraq was forced to leave Kuwait in 1991.

I·raq·i /ɪˈrɑːki, -æki/ n a person who comes from or whose parents come from Iraq —**Iraqi** adj

i·ras·ci·ble /ɪˈræsɪbəl/ adj fml (of a person) tending to get angry easily: an irascible old man —**bly** adv —**bility** /ɪˌræsɪˈbɪlɪti/ n [U]

i·rate /ˌaɪˈreɪt◂/ adj very angry, esp. because one's moral feelings have been offended: The television station got lots of complaints from irate viewers. | an irate letter − ~**ly** adv

ire /aɪəʳ/ n [U] esp. lit anger − ~**ful** /fʊl/ adj

Ire·land /ˈaɪələnd ‖ ˈaɪər-/ the second largest island in the British Isles, which lies W of Scotland, England, and Wales, and is separated from them by the Irish Sea. It is divided politically into Northern Ireland and the Republic of Ireland (Eire). Northern Ireland is part of the British Isles and the majority of the people there are PROTESTANTs. The Republic of Ireland has been an independent state since 1921 and the majority of the people there are Roman Catholics. Ireland, esp. the Republic of Ireland, is known for its beautiful, green countryside. It is sometimes called the **Emerald Isle**. —see also NORTHERN IRELAND, REPUBLIC OF IRELAND; see colour map on page 818

ir·i·des·cent /ˌɪrɪˈdesənt◂/ adj showing changing colours as light falls on it: the butterfly's iridescent wings −**cence** n [U]

ir·i·dol·o·gy /ˌɪrɪˈdɒlədʒi ‖ -ˈdɑː-/ n [U] a method of discovering an illness by looking carefully at the round coloured part of a person's eye

i·ris /ˈaɪərɪs/ n **1** a tall wild or garden flower with long thin leaves —see picture at FLOWER **2** the round coloured part of the eye which surrounds the black PUPIL² —see picture at EYE

I·rish¹ /ˈaɪərɪʃ/ adj of Ireland, its people, or their language

Irish² n **1** [the +P] the people of Ireland **2** [U] also **Irish Gae·lic** /ˌ··ˈ··/ the Celtic language of Ireland

Irish cof·fee /ˌ·· ˈ··/ n [C;U] coffee with cream and WHISKY added

Irish Guards /ˌ·· ˈ·/ [the+P] a REGIMENT (=large division of men) in the British army that is part of the GUARDS

Irish joke /ˈ·· ˌ·/ n a joke about an Irish person or people in which they appear to be quite stupid. Such jokes are usu. told by English people and are considered offensive, esp. by Irish people themselves.

I·rish·man /ˈaɪərɪʃmən/ **I·rish·wom·an** /-ˌwʊmən/fem. n -**men** /mən/ a person who comes from or whose parents come from Ireland

Irish Na·tion·al Lib·er·a·tion Ar·my /ˌ·· ˌ··· ··ˈ·· ˌ·/ also **INLA** abbrev.− [the] an illegal organization which wants the two parts of Ireland to be united in one state, and which uses violence to achieve this

Irish Re·pub·lic /ˌ·· ·ˈ··/ [the] the REPUBLIC OF IRELAND

Irish Re·pub·li·can Ar·my /ˌ·· ·ˌ··· ˈ··/ [the] the IRA

Irish Sea /ˌ·· ˈ·/ [the] part of the Atlantic Ocean between Great Britain and Ireland —see colour map on page 818

Irish stew /ˌ·· ˈ·/ n [C;U] a dish consisting of meat, potatoes, and onions which have been boiled together

Irish whis·key /ˌ·· ˈ··/ n a strong alcoholic drink made in Ireland, usu. from MALT or BARLEY, by a process of DISTILLATION. Irish whiskey is considered to taste different from Scotch whisky, and is always spelt differently.

irk /ɜːk ‖ ɜːrk/ v [T] infml to annoy; trouble: It irks me to have to admit it, but he was quite right.

irk·some /ˈɜːksəm ‖ ˈɜːrk-/ adj troublesome or annoying: irksome duties

i·ron¹ /ˈaɪən ‖ ˈaɪərn/ n **1** [U] a very common and useful metal that is a simple substance (ELEMENT), is MAGNETIC, is used in the making of steel, and is found in very small quantities in certain foods and in the blood: iron gates | an iron foundry | iron ore | a diet low in iron | iron pills —see also CAST IRON, WROUGHT IRON **2** [C] a heavy object with a flat bottom and a handle on top, shaped in a point at the front, which is heated, usu. electrically, and used for making cloth and clothes smooth —see picture at SYMBOL **3** [C] any of the set of nine GOLF CLUBs (numbered

from one to nine) which have metal heads with sloping faces: a six iron (=the one with the number six) | an iron shot (=made using an iron) —compare WOOD (3) **4 have several irons in the fire** to have various different interests, activities, or plans at the same time **5 the iron hand/fist in the velvet glove** a very firm intention hidden under a gentle appearance —see also IRONS, CLIMBING IRON, **rule with a rod of iron** (RULE²), **strike while the iron's hot** (STRIKE¹ (20))

iron² v [T] to make (clothes) smooth with an IRON: She ironed her blouse. —see also IRONING
iron sthg. ↔ out phr v [T] **1** to remove by ironing: She ironed out the wrinkles in her skirt. **2** infml to remove or find an answer to: It didn't take long to iron out the difficulties.

iron³ adj [A] usu. apprec very strong and firm: a man of iron will/resolve

Iron Age /ˈ·· ·/ [the] the time about 3000 years ago when iron was used for making tools, weapons, etc., which was a more advanced period than the Bronze Age before it —compare BRONZE AGE, STONE AGE

I·ron·bridge /ˈaɪənbrɪdʒ ‖ -ərn-/ a town in Shropshire, W England, where iron was first produced in 1709, and which became a centre of the INDUSTRIAL REVOLUTION

iron·clad /ˌ·· ˈ·◂/ adj very strong; unbreakable: an iron-clad alibi

Iron Cur·tain /ˌ·· ˈ··/ [the] the name formerly given to the western border between the Communist countries of Eastern Europe and the rest of the world: Many Western pop groups were popular **behind the Iron Curtain**. —compare BAMBOO CURTAIN

iron-grey /ˌ·· ˈ·◂/ adj dark grey

i·ron·ic /aɪˈrɒnɪk ‖ aɪˈrɑː-/ also **i·ron·i·cal** /-kəl/− adj expressing IRONY: How ironic that he should have been invited to play for the England team on the very day that he broke his leg.

i·ron·i·cal·ly /aɪˈrɒnɪkli ‖ aɪˈrɑː-/ adv **1** in an ironic way: She smiled ironically. **2** it is ironic (that): Ironically, his cold got better on the last day of his holiday. —compare PARADOXICALLY

i·ron·ing /ˈaɪənɪŋ ‖ -ər-/ n [U] **1** the work of making cloth or clothes smooth with an iron: He hates doing the ironing. **2** cloth or clothes that need to be ironed or have been ironed: a basket of ironing

ironing board /ˈ···· ·/ n a long narrow usu. folding table on which clothes are spread to be ironed

Iron La·dy /ˌ·· ˈ··/ [the] a NICKNAME given to Margaret Thatcher while she was Prime Minister of Britain, because of her forceful style of government

iron lung /ˌ·· ˈ·/ n a machine for helping some ill people to breathe by forcing air into and out of their lungs

i·ron·mon·ger /ˈaɪənˌmʌŋgəʳ ‖ ˈaɪərnˌmʌŋ-, -ˌmɑːŋ-/ n BrE a person who owns or works in a shop (**ironmonger's**) which sells HARDWARE (1), esp. if made of metal: I bought a spade at the ironmonger's.

iron-on /ˈ·· ·/ adj that can be placed on material using a hot iron: iron-on stickers of cartoon characters for children's clothes

iron ra·tions /ˌ·· ˈ··/ n [P] small amounts of substances with high food value, such as chocolate, carried by soldiers, climbers, etc., for use in an EMERGENCY

i·rons /ˈaɪənz ‖ ˈaɪərnz/ n [P] esp. lit chains or chains to keep a prisoner from moving: The captain ordered the mutinous sailors to be **clapped in irons**. (=put in chains)

i·ron·work /ˈaɪənwɜːk ‖ ˈaɪərnwɜːrk/ n articles made of iron

i·ron·works /ˈaɪənwɜːks ‖ ˈaɪərnwɜːrks/ n **ironworks** [C+sing./pl. v] a factory for preparing iron or steel and making it into heavy objects

i·ron·y /ˈaɪərəni/ n **1** [U] use of words which are clearly opposite to one's meaning, usu. either in order to be amusing or to show annoyance (e.g. by saying "What charming behaviour" when someone has been rude) —compare SARCASM **2** [C;U] a course of events or a condition which has the opposite result from what is expected, usu. a bad result: We went on holiday to Greece because we thought the weather was certain to be good, and it rained almost every day; the irony of it is, that at the same time there was a heat-wave back at home! —compare PARADOX; see also DRAMATIC IRONY

Ir·o·quois /ˈɪrəkwɔɪ/ n [C;the+P] (a member of) a Native American people formerly living in New York state —see NATIVE AMERICAN (CULTURAL NOTE)

ir·ra·di·ate /ɪˈreɪdieɪt/ v [T] **1** *esp. lit* to make bright by throwing light on: (fig.) *His little face was irradiated by happiness.* **2** *tech* to treat with X-RAYS or similar beams of force: *The surgeons irradiated the tumour.* —see also RADIATION —**ation** /ɪˌreɪdiˈeɪʃən/ n

irradiation treat·ment /····· ˌ··/ n [U] the treatment of food with X-RAYS to kill bacteria and make it last longer

ir·ra·tion·al /ɪˈræʃənəl/ adj not (done) by using reason; against reasonable behaviour: *After taking the drug she became quite irrational.* | *a completely irrational decision* — —**ly** adv —**ity** /ɪˌræʃəˈnæləti/ n [U]

ir·rec·on·ci·la·ble /ɪˌrekənˈsaɪləbəl/ adj [(with)] which cannot be settled or brought into agreement together or with something else: *irreconcilable differences of opinion* | *irreconcilable enemies* | *Holding a government post was irreconcilable with his outside commercial activities, so he had to resign.* —**bly** adv

ir·re·cov·e·ra·ble /ˌɪrɪˈkʌvərəbəl/ adj which cannot be got back or recovered (RECOVER): *irrecoverable debts* —**bly** adv

irredeemable /ˌɪrɪˈdiːməbəl/ adj **1** *fml* which nothing can take the place of: *an irredeemable loss* **2** *fml derog* too bad to be put right; hopeless: *the irredeemable awfulness of the performance* **3** (of STOCK (3)) which cannot be exchanged for the original sum paid, but only for the regular interest payments —**bly** adv

ir·re·du·ci·ble /ˌɪrɪˈdjuːsɪbəl‖-ˈduː-/ adj fml which cannot be made smaller or simpler: *the irreducible minimum* —**bly** adv

ir·re·fu·ta·ble /ˌɪrɪˈfjuːtəbəl, ɪˈrefjŭtəbəl/ adj fml too strong to be disproved: *an irrefutable argument* —**bly** adv

ir·reg·u·lar¹ /ɪˈregjŭlər/ adj **1** (of shape) having different-sized parts; uneven; not level: *an irregular polygon* | *an irregular coastline* | *She has irregular features.* (her face is not the same on both sides) **2** (of time) at unevenly separated points; not equal: *He visits us at irregular intervals.* | *She dislikes working such irregular hours.* **3** fml not according to the usual or accepted rules, habits, etc.: *But there's no official stamp on your permit; this is most irregular!* | *His behaviour is rather irregular.* (=immoral or unacceptable) **4** not continuous: *Her work as an actress is so irregular that she supplements her income by working in a bar.* **5** (in grammar) not following the usual pattern: *an irregular verb* **6** AmE euph suffering from CONSTIPATION — —**ly** adv

irregular² n a soldier in an army which is not the official army of a country but has been brought together for a special purpose

ir·reg·u·lar·i·ty /ɪˌregjŭˈlærəti/ n **1** [U] the state of being irregular: *the irregularity of the coastline* **2** [C] something irregular: *You'll need to flatten out the irregularities in the lawn with a roller.* **3** [C;U] fml euph something that goes against the rules, esp. (an act of) wrongdoing: *He couldn't explain the irregularities in the balance sheet, and I suspect him of taking the money.* **4** [U] AmE euph CONSTIPATION

ir·rel·e·vance /ɪˈreləvəns/ also **ir·rel·e·van·cy** /-vənsi/— n **1** [U] the state of being irrelevant **2** [C] an irrelevant remark or fact

ir·rel·e·vant /ɪˈreləvənt/ adj [(to)] not having any real connection with or relation to something else: *If he can do the job well, his age is irrelevant.* (=does not matter) — —**ly** adv

ir·re·li·gious /ˌɪrɪˈlɪdʒəs◂/ adj fml derog against religion or showing a lack of religious feeling

ir·re·me·di·a·ble /ˌɪrɪˈmiːdiəbəl/ adj fml which cannot be put right: *irremediable damage* —**bly** adv

ir·rep·a·ra·ble /ɪˈrepərəbəl/ adj which cannot be repaired or put right: *The storm caused irreparable damage to the house.* | *Her death is an irreparable loss to the firm.* —**bly** adv

ir·re·place·a·ble /ˌɪrɪˈpleɪsəbəl/ adj too special, unusual, or valuable for anything else to take its place: *Don't break my Ming vase — it's irreplaceable!* | *We'll miss him when he leaves the company, but no one's irreplaceable.* (=someone else will be able to do his job)

ir·re·pres·si·ble /ˌɪrɪˈpresˌbəl/ adj too full of force, excitement, etc. to be stopped or held back: *irrepressible cheerfulness|good humour|high spirits* | *an irrepressible talker* —**bly** adv

ir·re·proa·cha·ble /ˌɪrɪˈprəʊtʃəbəl/ adj fml so good that no blame at all could be given; faultless: *His conduct was irreproachable.* —**bly** adv

ir·re·sis·ti·ble /ˌɪrɪˈzɪstˌbəl/ adj **1** too nice, charming, attractive, etc. to refuse; impossible to dislike or RESIST: *What irresistible chocolates!* | *an irresistible little baby* **2** so strong or powerful that one cannot help being influenced by it: *the irresistible force of his logic* —**bly** adv

ir·res·o·lute /ɪˈrezəluːt/ adj fml derog (typical of a person who is) unable to make decisions and take action; weak in character — —**ly** adv: *He hesitated, then moved irresolutely towards the door.* —**lution** /ɪˌrezəˈluːʃən/ n [U]

ir·re·spec·tive /ˌɪrɪˈspektɪv/ adv **irrespective of** without regard to: *a film that can be enjoyed by anyone, irrespective of age* (=however old they are) —compare REGARDLESS (2)

ir·re·spon·si·ble /ˌɪrɪˈspɒnsˌbəl‖-ˈspaːn-/ adj derog having or showing lack of ability to behave carefully, think of the effect of one's actions on others, etc.: *It was irresponsible of her to leave the children by themselves in the swimming pool.* | *irresponsible driving* —**bly** adv —**bility** /ˌɪrɪspɒnsˌˈbɪlˌti‖-spaːn-/ n [U]

ir·re·trie·va·ble /ˌɪrɪˈtriːvəbəl/ adj that cannot be got back or put back into the original better state: *an irretrievable loss* | *We were four-nil down with five minutes to go, so the game looked completely irretrievable.* (=we would certainly lose it) | *They gave the* **irretrievable breakdown** *of their marriage as grounds for divorce.* —**bly** adv

ir·rev·e·rent /ɪˈrevərənt/ adj showing lack of respect for important people or organizations: *It would be considered very irreverent for a man not to take his hat off in church.* | *the irreverent humour of the students' magazine* — —**ly** adv —**rence** n [U]

ir·re·ver·si·ble /ˌɪrɪˈvɜːsˌbəl ‖ -ɜːr-/ adj which cannot be changed to bring things back to the way they were before: *an irreversible judgment* —**bly** adv

ir·rev·o·ca·ble /ɪˈrevəkəbəl/ adj that cannot be changed once it has been started or made: *an irrevocable decision* —**bly** adv

ir·ri·gate /ˈɪrɪgeɪt/ v [T] **1** to supply water to (dry land): *They have built canals to irrigate the desert.* **2** med to wash (a wound) with a flow of liquid —**gable** /ˈɪrɪgəbəl/ adj —**gation** /ˌɪrɪˈgeɪʃən/ n [U]

ir·ri·ta·ble /ˈɪrˌtəbəl/ adj tending to get angry at small things; easily annoyed: *He gets irritable when he's got toothache.* —see ANGRY (USAGE) —**bly** adv —**bility** /ˌɪrˌtəˈbɪlˌti/ n [U]

irritable bow·el syn·drome /ˌ···· ˈ·· ˌ··/ n [U] a medical problem of the INTESTINE which causes pain and discomfort and sometimes DIARRHOEA

ir·ri·tant /ˈɪrˌtənt/ n, adj (something) which irritates

ir·ri·tate /ˈɪrˌteɪt/ v [T] **1** to make angry or impatient: *Her habit of biting her nails irritates me.* | *irritating delays* **2** to make painful and sore: *Wool irritates my skin.* —see AGGRAVATE (USAGE), ANNOY (USAGE)

ir·ri·ta·tion /ˌɪrˌteɪʃən/ n **1** [C;U] (an example of) the act of irritating or the state of being irritated: *the irritations of driving in busy towns* | *"Don't be so silly!" he said with some irritation.* **2** [C] a sore place or feeling: *a skin irritation*

ir·rup·tion /ɪˈrʌpʃən/ n [(into)] fml a sudden violent rush (of people or force) into a place

IRS /aɪ ɑːr ˈes/ n [the] see INTERNAL REVENUE SERVICE

Ir·ving /ˈɜːvɪŋ‖ˈɜːr-/, **Washington** (1783–1859) an American writer remembered mostly for his stories set in New England, including *Rip Van Winkle* and *The Legend of Sleepy Hollow*

is /s, z, əz; strong ɪz/ 3rd person sing. present tense of BE: *She is living here now.* | *Here he is!* | *Is it 6:00 yet?* —see NOT (USAGE)

I·saac /ˈaɪzək/ the son of Abraham and the subject of many stories in the Bible

I·sai·ah /aɪˈzaɪə/ **1** a Hebrew PROPHET of the 8th century BC, who said that God would send a ruler to save the Jews **2** a book in the Old Testament

ISBN /ˌaɪ es biː 'en/ n International Standard Book Number; the number which is printed on a book, usu. on the back cover, or (on a HARDBACK) inside, to avoid confusion with other books

Is·car·i·ot /ɪˈskæriət, **Judas** see JUDAS

ISDN /ˌaɪ es diː 'en/ n [U] Integrated Services Digital Network; a system of international telephone lines to be used for all types of TELECOMMUNICATIONS, including voice, DATA, FAX, and others —compare PSTN

I·seult /ɪˈsuːlt/ see TRISTRAM AND ISOLDE

I·sis¹ /ˈaɪsɪs/ [the] the river Thames, at and UPSTREAM of Oxford

Isis² the most important Egyptian nature-goddess, the sister and wife of Osiris

Is·lam /ˈɪslɑːm, ˈɪz-, ɪsˈlɑːm/ n [U] **1** the Muslim religion, started by Muhammad **2** the people and countries that practise this religion — ~ **ic** /ɪzˈlæmɪk, ɪs-/ adj

Is·lam·a·bad /ɪzˈlɑːməbæd, ɪs-/ the capital city of Pakistan

Is·lam·ic Ji·had /ɪzˌlæmɪk dʒɪˈhæd, ɪs-‖-/ an Islamic organization extremely opposed to what it sees as Western IMPERIALISM, responsible for the kidnapping (KIDNAP¹) of several Westerners who were kept HOSTAGE for a number of years and finally RELEASEd in 1991 —see also JIHAD

is·land /ˈaɪlənd/ n **1** a piece of land surrounded by water: *Britain is an island.* | *a small island in the middle of the lake* | *the Maldive Islands* | *the island of Madagascar* | (fig.) *a little island of peace in the noisy city* **2** also **traffic island,** also **safety island** AmE– a raised place in the middle of the road where people crossing can wait for traffic to pass **3 no man is an island** quote a phrase from a poem by John Donne, used when saying that everyone needs friends and the support of other people

is·land·er /ˈaɪləndər/ n a person who lives on an island: *The islanders live by fishing.*

Is·lay /ˈaɪlə, -leɪ/ an island off W Scotland, in the Inner Hebrides, much visited by tourists and famous for its WHISKY

isle /aɪl/ n poet or used in names an island: *the Scilly Isles*

Isle of Dogs /ˌ· · ˈ·/ [the] an area of E London just N of, and surrounded on three sides by, the river Thames. The Isle of Dogs is part of the area generally known as Docklands.

Isle of Man /ˌ· · ˈ·/ also **Man**– [the] (abbrev. **IOM**) an island in the Irish Sea which is under British control but which has its own government and laws. Many rich British people live or keep their money on the Isle of Man because taxes are lower there than in the rest of Britain. —see also TYNWALD and colour map on page 818

Isle of Wight /ˌ· · ˈ·/ [the] (abbrev. **IOW**) an island off the coast of S England, and an English COUNTY. The Isle of Wight is a popular place for family holidays and for sailing. —see also COWES and see colour map on page 818

is·let /ˈaɪlɪt/ n esp. tech or old use a small island

Is·ling·ton /ˈɪzlɪŋtən/ a BOROUGH in NE central London

is·m /ˈɪzəm/ n infml, sometimes derog a set of usu. political or religious ideas or principles, with a name ending in -ism: *socialism, communism, and all the other isms of the modern world*

-ism see WORD FORMATION

is·n't /ˈɪzənt/ short for: is not: *The tea isn't ready.* | *It's Monday, isn't it?* | *"He's 40." "He isn't, is he?"*

ISO¹ /ˌaɪ es ˈəʊ/ [the] International Standards Organization; a group with members from about 70 countries which sets standards of size, shape, performance, etc. of a wide range of industrial and CONSUMER goods. At present it is very active in computer and TELECOMMUNICATIONS products. —compare BSI, ANSI

ISO² AmE abbev. for: in search of (in personal advertisements): *Single Pisces man ISO female 20-30.*

i·so·bar /ˈaɪsəbɑːr/ n a line on a map joining places where the air pressure is the same

i·so·late /ˈaɪsəleɪt/ v [T (**from**)] **1** to keep apart; separate from others: *Several villages have been isolated by the floods.* | *to isolate a child with an infectious disease* | *The radical group in the ruling party is becoming increasingly isolated.* (=is losing support) **2** esp. tech to separate (one substance) from others so that it can be used or examined on its own: *They have isolated the bacterium in its pure form.* —compare INSULATE —**lation** /ˌaɪsəˈleɪʃən/ n [U] :

living in complete isolation in the country | *an isolation ward in a hospital* (=for infectious patients) | *a feeling of total isolation*

i·so·lat·ed /ˈaɪsəleɪtd/ adj not near any others: *a very isolated farmhouse* (–far out in the country, away from other buildings or people) | *Apart from a few isolated cases,* (=rare ones, not happening in groups) *we have managed to avoid delays.*

i·so·la·tion·is·m /ˌaɪsəˈleɪʃənɪzəm/ n [U] often derog the political principle that a country should not concern itself with the affairs of other countries or join international political organizations —**ist** n

isolation pe·ri·od /···ˈ·· ˌ···/ n the length of time for which a person with an infectious illness should be kept apart from other people: *The isolation period for German measles is seven days.* —compare QUARANTINE

I·sol·de /ɪˈzɒldə‖ɪˈzəʊl-/ see TRISTRAM AND ISOLDE

i·sos·ce·les /aɪˈsɒsəliːz‖-ˈsɑː-/ adj [A] tech (of a TRIANGLE) having two equal sides —compare EQUILATERAL, SCALENE, and see picture at TRIANGLE

i·so·therm /ˈaɪsəθɜːm‖-θɜːrm/ n a line on a map joining places where the temperature is the same

i·so·tope /ˈaɪsətəʊp/ n any of two or more kinds of atom of a simple substance (ELEMENT) which are of the same chemical type but a different ATOMIC weight

I·spy /ˌ· ˈ·/ n [U] a game, usu. played by children, in which an object which can be seen by the players is guessed from the first letter of its name. The person who chooses the object says "I spy, with my little eye, something beginning with [e.g.] 's'."

Is·rael /ˈɪzreɪl/ a country in the Middle East, bordered by Lebanon, Syria, Jordan, and Egypt; population 4,509,000 (1989). Israel was established as the home of the Jewish people in 1947. Before that it was part of Palestine. Many of the Arab states are opposed to the State of Israel and would not regard Jerusalem as the capital, although the Israelis do. There has been great trouble and often fighting and war in the region.

Is·rae·li /ɪzˈreɪli/ n a person who comes or whose parents come from the state of Israel —**Israeli** adj

Is·rael·ite /ˈɪzrəlaɪt‖ˈɪzriə-/ n, adj (in the Bible) (a person) of the ancient kingdom of Israel

is·sue¹ /ˈɪʃuː, ˈɪsjuː‖ˈɪʃuː/ n **1** [C] a subject to be talked about, argued about, or decided: *Parliament will debate the nationalization issue next week.* | *one of the key issues in the election campaign* | *I don't want to* **make an issue of it.** (=quarrel about it) **2** [C] something which is produced so as to be publicly sold or given out: *The Christmas issue of the magazine had a picture of carol singers on its cover.* | *There's a new issue of stamps to commemorate the Royal Wedding.* **3** [U] the act of coming out or being produced: *I bought the new stamp the day of its issue.* | *(fml) the issue of blood from a wound* **4** a company's SHARES? (2) **5** [U+sing./pl. v] old use and law children (esp. in the phrase **die without issue**) **6** [C] fml what happens in the end; the result: *to await the issue* **7 at issue** under consideration, esp. because of some doubt: *Her ability is not at issue; it's her character I'm worried about.* **8 take issue** with fml to disagree with (a person) —see also RIGHTS ISSUE, SIDE ISSUE

issue² v [T] **1** to produce (esp. something printed and/or official): *Banknotes of this design were first issued 20 years ago.* | *The government is expected to issue a statement about the crisis.* **2** to give out or provide officially: *Our new uniforms haven't been issued yet.* [+obj+**with**] *They issued the firemen with breathing equipment.* [+obj+**to**] *They issued breathing equipment to the firemen.*

  issue forth phr v [I] lit to go or come out

  issue sth. phr v [T no pass.] fml to come to or result from: *smoke issuing from the chimneys* | *Our economic problems issue from a lack of investment.*

Is·tan·bul /ˌɪstænˈbʊl/ a city in NW Turkey, formerly called Constantinople and in ancient times known as Byzantium

isth·mus /ˈɪsməs/ n a narrow piece of land with water on each side, that joins two larger pieces of land: *the Isthmus of Panama*

I·su·zu /iːˈsuːzuː/ tdmk a Japanese company that makes motor vehicles esp. ones that are suitable for use on rough ground

it¹ /ɪt/ pron (used as subject or object) **1 a** that thing, group, idea, etc., already mentioned: I picked up the plate and put it on the table. | "Whose coat is this?" "It's mine." | "Where's my dinner?" "The cat ate it." | The government has become very unpopular since it was elected. | They were all shouting; it (=the situation) was terrible. | "I've broken a plate." "It (=the breaking of the plate) doesn't matter." **b** that person or animal whose sex is unknown or not thought to be important: What a beautiful baby — is it a boy? **2** that person: "Who's that?" "It's me!"/"It's Harry!"/"It's the postman!" —see THERE (USAGE²) **3 a** (used in the pattern **it**+**be**+a noun or adjective, for making a statement about esp. weather, time, or distance): It's raining. | It's hot. | It's a beautiful day. | It's Thursday. | It'll soon be breakfast time. | It's not far to Paris.| It's 112 miles from London to Birmingham. | It's my turn next. **b** that thing or situation not mentioned but understood by the speaker and the hearer: I can't stand it (=this situation) any longer! | How's it (=your life, work, etc.) going? | The worst of it is that we'll have to get the repairs done again. **4** (used as a subject or object in various verb patterns where the real subject or object comes later): It makes me sick the way she's always complaining. [+v-ing] It's fun being a singer. (=Being a singer is fun.) | What's it like being married? | It's no use worrying. | It felt funny watching myself on television. [+to-v] It cost £800 to mend the roof. (=The mending of the roof cost £800.) | It proved difficult to reach an agreement. | It's easy for you to criticize, but could you do any better? | It surprised me to hear she was leaving. | It's important to continue with the experiment. | Would it be possible to borrow your car? [+(that)] It's true that he stole the jewels. (=he did steal them) | It's a pity (that) you forgot. | It says in the paper that the game has been cancelled. | I take it that you don't agree with me. (=I liked her kissing me.) | I hate it when I have to speak in French on the phone. | It is said that she opposes this plan. | They kept it quiet that the President was dead. [+wh-/if] Is it known where they went? | I liked it when she kissed me. | Does it matter if I don't wear a tie? | I can't help it if she's always late. [it +**be**+adj+**of**] It is very kind of you to help us. (=In helping us, you are being very kind) | It was silly of him to say that. **5** (used as the subject of **seem, appear, happen,** or **look**): It seems (that) she lost her way. | "She's drunk." "So it appears!" | As it happens, I know the person you mean. | Since it happened to be a nice day, we decided to go to the beach. | It looks as if we're going to be late. **6** (used to make one part of the sentence more important) **a** (with the subject): It was Jane who bought dinner yesterday. (=I didn't buy it) **b** (with the object): It was dinner that Jane bought yesterday. (=she didn't buy LUNCH) **c** (with an adverb or PREPOSITIONAL PHRASE): It was yesterday that Jane bought dinner. (=not today) | It was in London that I last saw her. **7** usu. infml (used as a meaningless object of certain verbs): They ran for it. (=tried to escape) | He lorded it over his friends. (=behaved like a more important person) | She's decided to leave her job and go it alone as a businesswoman. **8 if it weren't for/hadn't been for** without the help or existence of: If it weren't for Tom, I wouldn't be alive today. | If it hadn't been for the snow, we could have got there much earlier. **9 That's it:** **a** That's complete; there's nothing more to come: You can have one more sweet and that's it. | Is that it? (=Is that all/everything?) **b** That's right: Move the ladder for me — that's it! —see also **catch it** (CATCH¹ (16)), **have had it** (HAVE¹ (3)), **have what it takes** (TAKE¹ (29))

it² n [U] **1** the most important person in a children's game, esp. the one who finds the others who are hiding **2** old-fash Italian VERMOUTH (only in the phrase **gin and it**) **3** sl the important moment: This is it — I'll have to make my mind up now. **4** sl **a** SEXUAL INTERCOURSE **b** old-fash SEX APPEAL —see also **with it** (WITH)

IT /ˌaɪ ˈtiː/ n [U] INFORMATION TECHNOLOGY

I·tal·i·an /ɪˈtæliən/ n **1** [C] a person who comes from or whose parents come from Italy **2** [U] the language of Italy —**Italian** adj

Italian dres·sing /·ˌ··· ˈ··/ n [U] a liquid poured on SALAD, usu. made from oil, VINEGAR, and HERBs which are typically used in Italian cookery

i·tal·i·cize also **-cise** BrE /ɪˈtælɪˌsaɪz/ v [T] to put or print (something) in italics

i·tal·ics /ɪˈtælɪks/ n [P;U] (the style of writing or printing with) sloping letters: This example is printed in italics.

—compare ROMAN —**italic** adj : italic script | handwriting

Italo- see WORD FORMATION

It·a·ly /ˈɪtəli/ a country of Europe lying between the Adriatic and Mediterranean seas, with borders in the N with France, Switzerland, Austria, Slovenia, and Croatia; capital Rome; population 57,517,000 (1989). Italy is known as the place where the Renaissance began, and where many great painters lived and worked. It is now very popular with tourists.

ITC /ˌaɪ tiː ˈsiː/ [the] Independent Television Commission; the organization which controls private television companies in Britain, which will replace the IBA in 1993

itch /ɪtʃ/ v [I] **1** to cause or feel a slight uncomfortable soreness which makes one want to SCRATCH the skin: The wound itches all the time. | I'm itching all over. **2** be **itching to/for** infml to want very much to do something soon: I'm itching to go. | I'm itching for them to leave so I can open my presents.

itch² n [usu. sing.] **1** a feeling of itching **2** infml a strong desire: [+ to-v] an itch to travel —see also SEVEN-YEAR ITCH

itch·y /ˈɪtʃi/ adj feeling or causing an itch: I felt itchy all over. | rough itchy woollen socks —**-iness** n [U]

itchy feet /ˌ·· ˈ·/ n [P] infml the desire to travel or habit of wandering, esp. to other countries

itchy palm /ˌ·· ˈ·/ also **itching palm**— n infml a great desire for money, esp. as (secret) payment for doing unfair favours

it'd /ˈɪtəd/ short for: **1** it would: It'd be better if I had more money. **2** it had: It'd been raining earlier that morning.

ITDG /ˌaɪ tiː diː ˈdʒiː/ Intermediate Technology Development Group; a British CHARITY organization that helps people esp. in poor countries to develop small industries using INTERMEDIATE TECHNOLOGY

i·tem¹ /ˈaɪtəm/ n [(of)] **1** a single thing on a list or among a set: The police examined several items of clothing. (=several clothes) | an interesting news item|item of news in today's paper **2** infml a subject of GOSSIP, esp. two people who are thought to have a (secret) emotional or sexual relationship: Have you noticed that Jill and Matt are absent on the same days? I wonder if they're an item.

item² adv fml, esp. old use (used in a list for introducing each article except the first) and in addition; also

i·tem·ize also **-ise** BrE /ˈaɪtəmaɪz/ v [T] to set out all the details of (each thing on a list): an itemized restaurant bill | itemized tax deductions

Ith·a·ca /ˈɪθəkə/ in CLASSICAL MYTHOLOGY, the home of Odysseus

i·tin·e·rant /aɪˈtɪnərənt/ adj [A] fml habitually travelling from place to place, esp. to practise one's trade or profession: an itinerant labourer|preacher

i·tin·e·ra·ry /aɪˈtɪnərəri‖-nəreri/ n a plan of a journey

it'll /ˈɪtl/ short for: it will: It'll rain tomorrow.

ITN /ˌaɪ tiː ˈen·/ Independent Television News; a British news service which provides news reports for ITV

its /ɪts/ determiner (possessive form of IT¹ (1)) of or belonging to it: The cat drank its milk and washed its ears. | It's a nice jug, but its handle is broken. | The plan has its merits.

it's short for: **1** it is: It's raining. | It's too small, and its handle is broken. **2** it has: It's been raining.

it·self /ɪtˈself/ pron (reflexive form of IT¹ (1)): The cat's washing itself. | The government made itself unpopular. **2** (strong form of IT): We won't buy new tyres when the car itself is so old. **3 (all) by itself** alone; without help: The door opened all by itself. **4 in itself** without considering the rest: The problem is unimportant in itself, but its long-term effects could be very serious. **5 to itself** for its private use; not shared —see YOURSELF (USAGE)

it·sy-bit·sy /ˌɪtsi ˈbɪtsi·/ also **it·ty-bit·ty** /ˌɪti ˈbɪti·/— adj [A] humor very small: an itsy-bitsy piece of cake

ITV /ˌaɪ tiː ˈviː/ n Independent Television; a system of British television companies supported by advertising: She watched a programme on ITV. —compare BBC, CHANNEL 4

IUD /ˌaɪ juː ˈdiː/ n intrauterine device; a plastic or metal object fitted inside a woman's childbearing organ (WOMB) as a form of CONTRACEPTION (=to prevent her from having children)

I·van·hoe /ˈaɪvənhəʊ/ a book by Sir Walter Scott about the imaginary brave KNIGHT Sir Wilfred of Ivanhoe

I·van the Ter·ri·ble /ˌaɪvən ðə ˈterɪbəl/ (1530–84) the first Russian ruler to take the title TSAR, remembered for his cruel and unfair leadership

I've /aɪv/ short for: I have: *I've been here before.* | *I've got lots of time.* | *I've a feeling you're right.*

IVF /ˌaɪ viː ˈef◂/ n abbrev. for IN VITRO FERTILIZATION

i·vied /ˈaɪvid/ adj esp. lit covered with ivy: *the ancient ivied walls*

i·vo·ry /ˈaɪvəri/ n **1** [U] the hard white substance of which an elephant's TUSKs are made. Ivory can be used to make valuable things, such as jewellery, and in many places the sale of it has been forbidden to prevent people from illegally killing elephants to obtain the ivory from their tusks. **2** [U] the colour of this substance; creamy white **3** [C often pl.] something made of this substance, esp. a small figure of a person or thing: *my collection of Chinese ivories* —see also **tickle the ivories** (TICKLE¹ (5))

ivory tow·er /ˌ··· ˈ··/ n often derog an imaginary place where very clever people (INTELLECTUALs) are supposed to avoid the difficult realities of ordinary life: *university professors in their ivory towers*

i·vy /ˈaɪvi/ n [U] a climbing plant with shiny three- or five-pointed leaves —see also POISON IVY

ivy

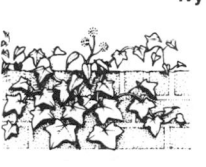

Ivy League /ˌ·· ˈ·◂/ adj [A] *AmE* belonging to or typical of a group of old and respected universities of the eastern US. These are Brown, Columbia, Cornell, Harvard, Princeton, and Yale Universities, Dartmouth College, and the University of Pennsylvania. The phrase Ivy League is also used more broadly to include other very highly-respected universities and colleges: *an Ivy League college* | *Ivy League clothes/manners/football*

I·wo Ji·ma /ˌiːwəʊ ˈdʒiːmə/ a Pacific island where Americans won a very difficult battle in the Second World War. There is a statue in Washington, DC of US Marines raising the flag on Iwo Jima.

J

J /dʒeɪ/ **J's, j's** or **Js, js** the tenth letter of the English alphabet

jab¹ /dʒæb/ v **-bb-** [I+adv/prep; T+obj+adv/prep] to push (something pointed) hard; strike quickly from a short distance: *He jabbed his fork into the meat.* | *Careful! You might jab my eye out with that stick!* | *She jabbed me in the ribs with her umbrella.* | *He jabbed angrily at the page with his finger.*

jab² n **1** a sudden forceful push with something pointed **2** *infml, esp. BrE for* INJECTION: *Have you had your jabs for Africa yet?* | *a cholera jab*

jab·ber /ˈdʒæbəʳ/ v [I (AWAY); T (OUT)] to talk or say quickly and not clearly: *I can't understand you if you keep jabbering (away) like that.* | *He jabbered (out) a confused apology.* —**jabber** n [S;U] : *a jabber of excited voices* — ~ **er** n

jab·ber·wock·y /ˈdʒæbəwɒki‖-bərwɑː-/ n [U] a piece of non-sense, written as a poem, or spoken (from the nonsense poem *Jabberwocky* by Lewis Carroll in *Through the Looking-Glass*)

jack¹ /dʒæk/ n **1** a piece of equipment for lifting a heavy weight, such as a car, off the ground —see also JACK up **2** also **knave** *BrE*— [(of)] a playing card with a picture of a man on it and a rank between the ten and the queen: *the jack of hearts* —see CARDS (USAGE) **3** the small white ball at which the players aim in the games of BOWLS and BOULES —see also MAN JACK, UNION JACK **4** an electronic connection for a telephone or other electric device

jack² v
jack sthg. ↔ **in** phr v [T] BrE sl to stop; give up: *As soon as I've got enough money I'm going to jack this boring job in.*
jack off phr v [I;T] AmE taboo sl for MASTURBATE
jack sthg. ↔ **up** phr v [T] to lift with a jack: *Jack up the car.* | (fig.) *They've jacked up the price.* (=increased it a lot)

jack·al /ˈdʒækɔːl, -kəl‖-kəl/ n an African and Asian wild animal of the dog family, which often eats what other animals have killed

jack·a·napes /ˈdʒækəneɪps/ n **-napes** [usu. sing.] old-fash a child who plays annoying tricks

Jack and Jill /ˌdʒæk ənd ˈdʒɪl/ two children in a NURSERY RHYME (=an old song or poem for children):
Jack and Jill went up the hill
To fetch a pail of water;
Jack fell down and broke his crown,
And Jill came tumbling after.

Jack and the Bean·stalk /ˌdʒæk ənd ðə ˈbiːnstɔːk/ also **Jack the Gi·ant-kil·ler** /ˌ· · ˈ·· ˌ·· /— a children's story in which a boy, Jack, sells his mother's cow for some magic beans. The mother, in anger, throws the beans out of the window. The next day a very tall bean plant (the **Bean-stalk**) has grown up into the clouds. Jack climbs it and finds himself in a strange country outside a GIANT's house. He enters and has to hide from the giant, who sings, "Fee fi fo fum, I smell the blood of an Englishman." Jack robs the giant of a hen that lays golden eggs and a HARP that plays by itself, and escapes down the beanstalk with the giant following. Arriving at the ground first, Jack takes an AXE and cuts down the beanstalk, and the giant falls and is killed.

Jack·a·no·ry /ˌdʒækəˈnɔːri/ a popular British television show in which well-known actors read favourite chil-dren's stories

jack·ass /ˈdʒæk-æs/ n **1** infml taboo in AmE a person who behaves foolishly: *Don't be a jackass — come down off the roof!* **2** now rare a male ASS —see also LAUGHING JACKASS

jack·boot /ˈdʒækbuːt/ n **1** [C] a military boot which covers the leg up to the knee **2** [the] the cruel rule of military men, often used in association with the Nazis in Ger-many: *living under the jackboot*

jack·daw /ˈdʒækdɔː/ n a bird of the CROW family, believed to steal small bright objects

jack·et /ˈdʒækɪt/ n **1** a short coat with SLEEVES: *a tweed jacket* | *a man's three-piece suit includes a jacket, trousers,* and a waistcoat. | *It's in my jacket pocket.* —see also LIFE JACKET, NORFOLK JACKET **2** BrE the skin of a cooked potato: *potatoes baked in their jackets* | *a jacket potato* **3** an outer cover for certain machines or containers that get very hot **4** a DUST JACKET **5** AmE a SLEEVE (2) for a record: *He wrote the jacket notes* (=information on the sleeve) *for her new album.*

Jack Frost /ˌ· ˈ·/ a name for FROST, considered as a person. Children are told that Jack Frost comes at night and leaves frost on the windows.

jack·ham·mer /ˈdʒækˌhæməʳ/ n esp. AmE for PNEUMATIC DRILL

Jack·ie /ˈdʒæki/ a British magazine for girls around the age of PUBERTY, containing ROMANTIC stories, articles on popular music, and advice on various areas of life

jack-in-the-box /ˈ· · · · ˌ·/ n a children's toy which is a box from which an amusing figure on a spring jumps when the top is opened: *He jumps up like a jack-in-the-box whenever the phone rings.*

Jack in the Box n a FAST-FOOD restaurant in the US which serves HAMBURGERS and Mexican-style food

jack knife /ˈ· ·/ n **jack knives** /-naɪvz/ **1** a knife with a blade that folds into the handle **2** a DIVE in which the body is bent and then straightened before entering the water

jack-knife v [I] (esp. of a two-part vehicle) to bend suddenly in the middle and go out of control: *The articulated lorry skidded and jack-knifed.*

jack-of-all-trades /ˌ· · ˈ· ·/ n (sometimes cap.) a person who can do many different kinds of work (but who may not be very good at any of them)

jack-o'-lan·tern /ˌdʒæk ə ˈlæntən‖-ərn/ n (sometimes cap.) a lamp made by putting a candle inside a hollow PUMP-KIN which has had holes cut into it in the shape of eyes and a mouth. Jack-o'-lanterns are often made at Hal-lowe'en. —see colour picture on page 1211

jack·pot /ˈdʒækpɒt‖-pɑːt/ n the biggest amount of money to be won in a game of cards or in any competition decided by chance —see also **hit the jackpot** (HIT¹)

jack·rab·bit /ˈdʒækˌræbɪt/ n a large N American HARE with long ears

Jack Rob·in·son /ˌ· ˈ··· / n before one could/can say Jack Robinson *infml* very quickly or suddenly

Jack Rus·sell /ˌ· ˈ··/ n a breed of dog which is a kind of TERRIER, with a smooth white coat with black and/or brown markings, short legs, and a small body —see pic-ture at DOG

jacks /dʒæks/ n [P] a children's game in which the player tries to pick up small metal objects (**jacks**) at the same time she or he is bouncing (BOUNCE) a rubber ball, using only one hand

Jack·son /ˈdʒæksən/ the capital of the state of Mississippi, US, named after President Andrew Jackson

Jackson, Andrew (1767–1845) an American Democrat politician, the seventh president of the US (1829–37), who was a very successful lawyer, judge, and military commander

Jackson, Bo /bəʊ/ (1962–) an American FOOTBALL and BASEBALL player

Jackson, Glen·da /ˈglendə/ (1936–) a British actress who has made many appearances on stage, and in television and films, including *Women in Love* in 1971, and as Queen Elizabeth I in *Elizabeth R*. She became involved in Labour Party politics and entered Parliament as an MP in 1992.

Jackson, the Reverend Jes·se /ˈdʒesi/ (1941–) an Ameri-can Democratic politician and supporter of issues con-cerning black people, known for his public speaking. He tried unsuccessfully to be chosen to represent the Democrats in the elections for president in 1984 and 1988.

Jackson, Mi·chael /ˈmaɪkəl/ (1958–) an American popular music singer and songwriter, the youngest brother of the group The Jackson Five who had many hit records in the 1970s. Michael on his own had great success in the 1980s, with the ALBUMS *Thriller* and *Bad*, and his performances in concert. People often talk about the fact that he has had his face greatly changed by PLAS-TIC SURGERY. —see colour picture on page 554

Jackson, Stonewall the name given to Thomas Jackson

(1824–63), an American Confederate GENERAL. He fought at the battle of Bull Run in the American Civil War and helped to defeat the Union army.

Jack Sprat /ˌ·ˈ·/ a character in a NURSERY RHYME (=an old song or poem for children):
Jack Sprat would eat no fat,
His wife would eat no lean,
And so between them both, you see,
They licked the platter clean.

jack tar /ˌ·ˈ·/ also **tar**— *n infml, now rare (sometimes cap.)* a British sailor

Jack the Lad /ˌ·ˈ·/ *n BrE sl* a showily confident and successful young WORKING-CLASS man

Jack the Rip·per /ˌ·ˈ··/ a name given by the public to the man who killed and cut up the bodies of five women who were PROSTITUTES, in the Whitechapel area of London in 1888. The case was very famous and caught the interest of the public, and seeing it in films or hearing it mentioned still makes people think of these particularly nasty crimes. Similar, more recent criminals are sometimes called after him. —see also YORKSHIRE RIPPER

Ja·cob /ˈdʒeɪkəb/ a character in the Old Testament, whose 12 sons were the ANCESTORS of the 12 tribes of Israel

Jac·o·be·an /ˌdʒækəˈbiːən◂/ *adj* of the period 1603 to 1625, when James I was the king of England: *Jacobean poetry/furniture*

Jac·o·bite /ˈdʒækəbaɪt/ *adj, n* (esp. in the 17th and 18th centuries) (of or being) a person who wanted a descendant of King James II to be the king of England

Jac·o·bite Ris·ing /ˌ···ˈ··/ also **Jacobite Re·bel·li·on** /ˌ··· ·ˈ···/ [*the*] **1** the failed attempt in 1715–16 to make James Edward Stuart (the Old Pretender) King of England **2** the attempt in 1745–46 led by Charles Edward Stuart (the Young Pretender) which ended all hope of making the Stuarts kings of England again

Ja·cob's /ˈdʒeɪkəbz/, **The Jacob's Bakery Limited** *n tdmk* a company which makes many different types of BISCUIT

Jacques /dʒeɪks/, **Hat·tie** /ˈhæti/ (1924–80) an English actress known esp. for her humorous parts in many Carry On films, and television work with Eric Sykes

ja·cuz·zi /dʒəˈkuːzi/ *n tdmk* a bath or pool fitted with a system of fast currents of hot water, used as a way to relax, or to cure or improve certain medical conditions such as backache. Jacuzzis are thought of as being part of an expensive way of life.

jade[1] /dʒeɪd/ *n* [U] **1** a precious usu. green stone from which jewellery, small decorative figures, etc. are made **2** the colour of this stone; milky green

jade[2] *n old use* **1** *derog or humor* a woman, esp. a rude or immoral woman **2** a worn-out old horse

ja·ded /ˈdʒeɪdɪd/ *adj* [(with)] tired or uninterested because of having had too much experience of something: *After all these years of travelling I'm feeling rather jaded (with it all).*

Jae·ger /ˈjeɪgər/ a British company which sells expensive and SOPHISTICATED clothes

Jaf·fa cake /ˈdʒæfə keɪk/ *n* a type of cake made by McVitie's, which consists of a SPONGE CAKE covered with orange JELLY and chocolate; Jaffa cakes are small and look like BISCUITS

Jaf·fa or·ange /ˌ··ˈ··/, also **Jaffa**— *n* a variety of large orange with a thick skin, grown in Israel

jag /dʒæg/ *n* **1** *BrE infml* a short period of uncontrolled activity, esp. of drinking alcohol: *on a crying jag* — compare SPREE, BINGE **2** (*usu. cap*) *infml* a Jaguar car

jag·ged /ˈdʒægɪd/ also **jag·gy** /ˈdʒægi/— *adj* having a rough uneven edge, often with sharp points: *jagged rocks* | *a jagged tear in her sleeve* — ~**ly** *adv*

jagged

a jagged line

Jag·ger /ˈdʒægər/, **Mick** /mɪk/ (1943–) an English popular music singer and songwriter, part of the group The Rolling Stones. He is known especially for the sexual nature of his singing style and performance on stage.

jag·u·ar /ˈdʒægjuər‖ˈdʒægwɑːr/ *n* a large spotted wild cat of Central and South America —see picture at BIG CATS

Jaguar *n tdmk* also **Jag** *infml* a type of large British car, known for being expensive, fast, and of good quality, often driven by company DIRECTORS, politicians, etc.

jai a·lai /ˌhaɪ əˈlaɪ‖ˈhaɪ laɪ/ *n* [U] a game played by two, four, or six people in which they use a basket-like RACQUET to throw a ball against one of the three walls in the playing area

jail[1] also **gaol** *BrE* /dʒeɪl/ *n* [C;U] a place where criminals are kept as part of their punishment; prison

jail[2] also **gaol** *BrE*— *v* [T] to put in jail: *He was jailed for life for murder.*

jail·bird also **gaolbird** *BrE* /ˈdʒeɪlbɜːd‖-bɜːrd/ *n infml* a person who has spent a lot of time in prison

jail·break also **gaolbreak** *BrE* /ˈdʒeɪlbreɪk/ *n* an escape from prison, esp. by more than one person

jail·er also **gaoler** *BrE* /ˈdʒeɪlər/ *n esp. old use* a person who is in charge of a prison or prisoners

Jain /dʒaɪn/ *n* a person who believes in and follows the religion of Jainism

Jain·is·m /ˈdʒaɪnɪzəm/ *n* [U] a religion practised in India, which teaches that the soul does not die but is reborn until it reaches perfection and is then freed. The gods of Jainism are such perfect souls which have become free.

Ja·kar·ta /dʒəˈkɑːtə‖-ˈkɑːr-/ the capital city of Indonesia, NW Java

jal·a·pe·ño /ˌhæləˈpeɪnjəʊ◂‖ˌhɑːl-/ *n* a small very hot green pepper used in cooking Mexican food: *stuffed jalapeños* | *jalapeño relish*

ja·lop·y /dʒəˈlɒpi‖-ˈlɑːpi/ *n humor* a worn-out old car

jam[1] /dʒæm/ *n* [U] **1** very thick sweet liquid made from fruit boiled and preserved in sugar, used esp. for spreading on bread: *strawberry jam* —see also MARMALADE, **money for jam** (MONEY) **2 jam tomorrow** (the promise of) good things to come, for those who are patient

jam[2] *v* -**mm**- **1** [I+*adv/prep*;T+*obj*+*adv/prep*] to pack, crush, or gather tightly into a small space: *One of the lifts was out of order, so we all had to jam into the other one.* | *I can't jam another thing into this bag.* | *The bus was so full that I was jammed in and couldn't move.* **2** [T] to fill with people, cars, etc., so that movement is difficult or impossible: *The crowds jammed the streets, and no cars could pass.* **3** [T *usu. pass.*] to make so many telephone calls to a place at the same time that (its telephone system) cannot work properly: *The company's switchboard was jammed with complaints.* **4** [T+*obj*+*adv/prep*] to press hard and suddenly: *She jammed the top of the box down on my hand.* | *I jammed on the brakes/jammed the brakes on.* **5** [I (UP)] (esp. of moving parts, e.g. of machines) to get stuck: *The door has jammed and I can't open it.* **6** [T] to broadcast noise on a radio signal so that (the radio shows that should be on that signal) cannot be heard: *The Russians have been jamming broadcasts to Eastern Europe.* **7** [I] *infml* to play in a JAM SESSION

jam[3] *n* **1** a mass of people or things pressed so close together that movement is difficult or impossible: *Their car was stuck in a traffic jam for hours.* **2 be in/get into a jam** *infml* be in/to get into a difficult situation

JAMA /ˌdʒeɪ eɪ em ˈeɪ/ *tdmk Journal of the American Medical Association*; a highly-respected American magazine which reports the latest medical research —see also LANCET, NEW ENGLAND JOURNAL OF MEDICINE

Ja·mai·ca /dʒəˈmeɪkə/ an island in the Caribbean Sea, now an independent state in the COMMONWEALTH (1); capital Kingston; population 2,375,000 (1989). Jamaica was an important centre of the slave trade in former times, but is now known for its trade in sugar and bananas, and its attractions for tourists. — ~**can** *n, adj*

jamb /dʒæm/ *n tech* a side post of a door or window

jam·ba·la·ya /ˌdʒæmbəˈlaɪə/ *n* [U] a Cajun rice dish from the S of the US, containing OKRA, chicken, and seafood

jam·bo·ree /ˌdʒæmbəˈriː/ *n* **1** *infml* a big noisy happy party **2** a large gathering of SCOUTS or GUIDES

James I /ˌdʒeɪmz ðə ˈfɜːst‖-ˈfɜːrst/, **King** (1566–1625) the King of England from 1603, who was James VI of Scotland (from 1567). He was the son of Mary, Queen of Scots

James II /ˌdʒeɪmz ðə ˈsekənd/, **King** (1633–1701) the King of England from 1685 and Scotland (as James VII). He became a Catholic and was forced to run away to France, and was later defeated at the battle of the Boyne in 1690.

James /dʒeɪmz/, **Henry** (1843–1916) an American writer who wrote about the effect of Europe on Americans who travelled there. His books include *Washington Square*, *The Bostonians*, and the SUPERNATURAL story *The Turn of the Screw*. —**sian** *adj* : *a Jamesian plot*

James, Jes·se /ˈdʒesi/ (1847–82) an American bank and train robber who, with his brother Frank, led a GANG of robbers, one of whom killed him. His name became famous even in Britain, as an exciting character who is still both written and sung about.

James, P D (1920–) a British writer of DETECTIVE stories who invented the character Adam Dalgliesh. Many of her books have now been filmed for television, such as *Death of an Expert Witness* and *A Taste for Death*.

James, Sid /sɪd/ (1913–76) an actor known esp. for his humorous parts in many Carry On films, as well as television programmes such as *Bless This House*

James·town /ˈdʒeɪmztaʊn/ the first permanent settlement of English people in N America (1607). It is in Virginia, and is now a popular place for tourists to visit.

jam jar /ˈ·· ·/ *n* a small glass container (=JAR¹ (1)) for JAM¹, sometimes used to store other things instead: *The children went fishing with a net and a jam jar* —see picture at CONTAINER

jam·mies /ˈdʒæmiz/ *n* [U] *infml* PYJAMAS

jam·my /ˈdʒæmi/ *adj BrE sl* **1** easy: *That was a really jammy examination.* **2** (used esp. with *taboo* words) lucky, esp. in a way that makes other people annoyed: *The jammy bugger passed the exam without doing any work!*

jam-packed /ˌ· ˈ·◂/ *adj* [(with)] *infml* full with many people or things very close together; very CROWDED: *The theatre was jam-packed for the first night of the play.*

jam ses·sion /ˈ· ˌ··/ *n* a JAZZ or ROCK³ performance in which the musicians play together without practising together first

Jane /dʒeɪn/ the female companion of Tarzan in the Tarzan books and films —see TARZAN

Jane Doe /ˌ· ˈ·/ *AmE* an UNIDENTIFIED woman, esp. one in a law case who does not want her name to be known: *The case of Jane Doe vs Acme Electronics* —compare JOHN DOE

Jane Eyre /ˌdʒeɪn ˈeəʳ/ the title of a book by Charlotte Brontë written in 1847, about a woman who becomes a GOVERNESS and falls in love with her employer, Mr Rochester. The book describes Jane's situation and her relationship with the HERO in a powerful and clever style and is one of the most widely read English NOVELs even today.

jan·gle /ˈdʒæŋɡəl/ *v* **1** [I;T] to (cause to) make a sharp sound, like metal striking against metal: *The brass bells jangled on the horse's collar.* **2** [T] to excite unpleasantly; upset: *his jangled nerves*

jan·is·sa·ry /ˈdʒænɪˌsəri|-seri/ also **jan·i·za·ry** /-zəri‖-zeri/— *n* a member of a special group of soldiers in Turkey in former times

jan·i·tor /ˈdʒænɪtəʳ/ *n* **1** *AmE & ScotE for* CARETAKER (1) **2** *old-fash* a person who guards the main door of a large building —compare PORTER¹ (3)

Jan·u·a·ry /ˈdʒænjuəri, -njuri‖-jueri/ (*written abbrev.* **Jan.**) *n* [C;U] the first month of the year, between December and February. When people think of January, they think of the New Year and also of cold weather, snow, and ice: *It happened on January the fifth|on the fifth of January|on January fifth (AmE).* | *This office opened in January 1991.* | *I started work here last January|the January before last.*

Ja·nus /ˈdʒeɪnəs/ in CLASSICAL MYTHOLOGY, the Roman god of beginnings, gates and doorways, who was thought of as having one old face pointing into the old year and one young face pointing into the new year, and therefore gave his name to the month of January

Jap /dʒæp/ *n infml* a Japanese person (usu. considered offensive)

ja·pan /dʒəˈpæn/ *v* **-nn-** [T] to cover (wood or metal) with a special paint giving a black shiny surface: *a japanned box*

Japan a country in E Asia consisting of four large islands (Hokkaido, Kyushu, Honshu and Shikoku) and many smaller islands. Capital Tokyo; population 122,380,000 (1987); language Japanese. The main religions are Shinto and Buddhism. Japan is a very rich, industralized country, with great success in car production and electronic goods such as televisions, VIDEOS, and AUDIO equipment.

Jap·a·nese /ˌdʒæpəˈniːz◂/ *n* Japanese **1** [*the* +P] people from Japan **2** [U] the language of Japan —**Japanese** *adj*

Japanese lan·tern /ˌ···ˈ···/ *n* a paper LANTERN that folds up, usu. used for decorative purposes

jape /dʒeɪp/ *n old-fash* a playful trick

ja·pon·i·ca /dʒəˈpɒnɪkə‖-ˈpɑː-/ *n* [C;U] a decorative bush with red or white flowers

jar¹ /dʒɑːʳ/ *n* **1** a short-necked wide-mouthed pot or bottle made of glass, stone, clay, etc.: *a jam jar* **2** also **jar·ful** /-fʊl/— the amount a jar will hold: *For this recipe you need a whole jar of marmalade.*

jar² *v* **-rr-** **1** [I (**on**)] to upset by making an unpleasant sound: *This experimental music jars (on my nerves) somewhat.* **2** [T] to shake unpleasantly: *The fall jarred every bone in my body.* **3** [I (**with**)] to be in noticeable opposition; not match; CLASH: *jarring opinions|colours*

jar³ *n* (something that causes) an unpleasant shaking sensation: *We felt a jar as the wheels hit a bump.*

jar·gon /ˈdʒɑːɡən‖ˈdʒɑːrɡən, -ɡɑːn/ *n* [C;U] *often derog* difficult or strange language which uses words known only to the members of a certain group: *computer jargon* | *the jargon of the advertising business*

Jarls·berg /ˈjɑːlzbɜːɡ‖ˈjɑːrlzbɜːrɡ/ *n* [U] a kind of cheese made in Norway, with a pale yellow colour and a MILD (=not strong) taste

Jar·row /ˈdʒærəʊ/ an industrial town in NE England on the river Tyne, which had important shipyards and steelworks until 1930, when the economic problems of the Great Depression led to many people becoming unemployed. In 1936 many unemployed people walked from Jarrow to London as a protest, which became known as **the Jarrow March**.

Jar·u·zel·ski /ˌjæruːˈzelski/, **Woj·ciech** /ˈvɔɪtʃek/ (1923–) a Polish general and leader who was president of Poland from 1985 until 1989. He did not allow any opposition or TRADE UNION activity but was forced to accept changes after the elections in 1989.

jas·mine /ˈdʒæzmɪn/ *n* [C;U] a climbing plant with sweet-smelling white or yellow flowers

Ja·son /ˈdʒeɪsən/ in CLASSICAL MYTHOLOGY, a man who sailed with his companions, the **Argonauts**, passing through many dangerous adventures in order to regain the Golden Fleece and whose story was made into a highly successful film called *Jason and the Argonauts*

Jason, David (1940–) a British character actor, mostly seen on television and known best for *Open All Hours*, *Only Fools and Horses*, and *The Darling Buds of May*

jas·per /ˈdʒæspəʳ/ *n* [U] a decorative red, yellow or brown stone, not of great value

jaun·dice /ˈdʒɔːndɪs‖ˈdʒɔːn-, ˈdʒɑːn-/ *n* [U] a medical condition in which the skin, the white part of the eyes, etc. turn yellow

jaun·diced /ˈdʒɔːndɪst‖ˈdʒɔːn-, ˈdʒɑːn-/ *adj* **1** *often derog* tending to judge people and things unfavourably, esp. (as if) from long and disappointing experience of human affairs: *jaundiced opinions* | *a jaundiced view of life* | *He looks on these modern ideas with a rather jaundiced eye.* **2** *rare* suffering from jaundice

jaunt /dʒɔːnt‖dʒɔːnt, dʒɑːnt/ *n* a short journey for pleasure: *We're going on|for a little jaunt to the seaside this afternoon.* —**jaunt** *v* [I]

jaun·ty /ˈdʒɔːnti‖ˈdʒɔːnti, ˈdʒɑːnti/ *adj* (showing that one feels) cheerful, confident, and pleased with life: *a jaunty hat|person|wave of the hand* —**tily** *adv* —**tiness** *n* [U]

Ja·va /ˈdʒɑːvə/ an island which is part of Indonesia, in the Indian Ocean — ~**nese** /ˌdʒɑːvəˈniːz◂/ *n, adj*

jav·e·lin /ˈdʒævəlɪn/ *n* a light spear for throwing, now used mostly in sport —see colour picture on page 883

jaw¹ /dʒɔː/ *n* **1** [C] either of the two bony parts of the face in which the teeth are set: *the upper|lower jaw* —see pictures at SKELETON and at HEAD **2** [C] the appearance of the lower jaw: *A strong square jaw is supposed to be a sign of firm character.* **3** [C;U] *infml, sometimes derog* (a) talk: *We hadn't seen each other for months, and we sat down for a good jaw.* —see also JAWS

jaw² *v* [I (AWAY)] *infml, sometimes derog* **1** to talk: *They've been jawing away for hours.* **2 to jaw-jaw is better than to war-war** *quote* a phrase originally spoken by Winston Churchill during the COLD WAR, and often used by somebody who thinks that discussion e.g. of political problems is better than fighting or other violent action

jaw·bone /'dʒɔːbəʊn/ *n* either of the big bones of the jaws, esp. the lower jaw

jaw·break·er /'dʒɔːˌbreɪkəʳ/ *n infml* **1** a word that is hard to pronounce **2** *AmE infml* a hard round piece of CANDY

jaws /dʒɔːz/ *n* [P] **1** the mouth of a (fierce) animal: *The crocodile opened its jaws|clamped its jaws shut.* | (fig.) *to escape from the jaws of death* (=from a situation in which one might have been killed) **2** the two parts of a machine or tool, esp. a VICE², between which something can be held tightly or crushed

Jaws a film, based on a book by Peter Benchley, about a SHARK (=dangerous biting fish) which kills swimmers – see colour picture on page 685

jay /dʒeɪ/ *n* a noisy brightly-coloured bird of the CROW family –see also BLUE JAY

Jay·cee /ˌdʒeɪˈsiː/ *n* a member of the **Jaycees**, an organization with branches in many American towns and cities which encourages useful and interesting activities for local people

jay·walk /'dʒeɪwɔːk/ *v* [I] to cross streets in a careless and dangerous way, esp. in the wrong place or without paying attention to the traffic lights. Jaywalking is against the law in some countries and most states of America but the police usu. do not stop people for it. If someone is **picked up for jaywalking**, it is usu. because the police want them for some other reason. – **~er** *n*

jazz¹ /dʒæz/ *n* [U] **1** music with a strong beat and some free playing by each musician, originated by black Americans **2** *AmE sl* empty meaningless talk, esp. if used to confuse or deceive **3 and all that jazz** *sl, usu. derog* and other things like that: *I'm fed up with being told about rules, responsibilities, duties, and all that jazz.*

jazz² *v*

  jazz sthg. ↔ **up** *phr v* [T] *infml* to make more active, interesting, or enjoyable, often with cheap bright decoration: *to jazz up the room with some bright red curtains*

Jazz Age /'· ˌ·/ [*the*] the period of great popularity of jazz music during the ten years or so after the First World War

jazz·y /'dʒæzi/ *adj infml* **1** attracting attention, as with (too) bright colours: *a very jazzy dress* **2** like jazz music **—ily** *adv*

JCB /ˌdʒeɪ siː ˈbiː/ *n tdmk* a large machine for moving earth

J C Pen·ney /ˌdʒeɪ siː ˈpeni/ also **Penney's** a group of shops, and a MAIL ORDER company, in the US. Penney's is known for quality goods at reasonable prices.

J.D., JD /ˌdʒeɪ ˈdiː/ *n* Doctor of Jurisprudence; the degree given by American law schools to students who have successfully completed their courses: *She got her JD in 1987.* | *Robert Pole, J.D.*

jeal·ous /'dʒeləs/ *adj* [(of)] *often derog* **1** unhappy and angry because (you think that) **a** someone who should like you, likes someone else better: *When she kisses the baby, it makes the older child jealous.* **b** someone who you feel belongs to you is being admired too much by someone else: *If other men spoke to his wife, he got terribly jealous.* **2** wanting to have what someone else has; ENVIOUS: *He is jealous of their success.* **3** wanting to keep what one has; POSSESSIVE: *He is jealous of his possessions|of his rights.* – **~ly** *adv* : *The dog guarded its bone jealously.* | *She jealously defended the honour of her family.*

▷ USAGE 1 **Jealousy** is usually considered to be a more unpleasant feeling than **envy**. Compare *Ann has got a very nice job – I'm envious|full of envy|I envy her* (=I wish I had a job like that) and *Tom is jealous of Ann* (=feels strong dislike for Ann) *because he thinks that he should have got the job.* 2 **Jealous** is often used about someone who is afraid of letting a person (especially a husband or wife) be liked or admired by others: *If other men spoke to his wife he was immediately jealous.*◁

jeal·ous·y /'dʒeləsi/ *n* [C;U] (a) jealous feeling

jeans /dʒiːnz/ also **blue jeans** *AmE– n* [P] trousers made

of DENIM (=a strong, usu. blue, cotton cloth), worn informally by men, women, and children, and thought very fashionable among young people –see PAIR (USAGE), SLACKS, and see picture at OVERALL

Jed·da /'dʒedə/ also **Jid·dah** /'dʒɪdə/ the largest port of Saudi Arabia, on the Red Sea

jeep, Jeep *tdmk* /dʒiːp/ *n* a type of small car made for travelling over rough ground: *to cross the desert by jeep*

jeer /dʒɪəʳ/ *v* [I (at); T] to laugh or shout disrespectfully (at): *The team was playing dreadfully, and the crowd jeered (at) them* | *jeering laughter* –**jeer** *n* : *abusive jeers* – **~ingly** *adv*

Jeeves /dʒiːvz/ *n* a very good male personal servant, who looks after his employer's clothes, food, etc., and is useful and trusted in personal matters (from the VALET named **Jeeves** in the many humorous books by P G Wodehouse)

Jef·fer·son /'dʒefəsən‖-fər-/, **Thomas** (1743–1826) the third president of the US (1801–09). Jefferson wrote a large part of the Declaration of Independence. He is also considered to be the FOUNDER of the Democratic Party.

Je·ho·vah /dʒɪˈhəʊvə/ (a name given to God in the Old Testament (=first part of the Bible))

Jehovah's Wit·ness /·ˌ·· '··/ *n* a member of a religious organization that believes in every word of the Bible and sends its members to people's houses to discuss religious matters. Jehovah's Witnesses believe that war is wrong, and are also opposed to the authority of organized government in matters of conscience.

je·june /dʒɪˈdʒuːn/ *adj fml derog* **1** childish; NAIVE: *jejune political opinions* **2** (esp. of written material) dull; uninteresting: *jejune lectures*

Jek·yll and Hyde /ˌdʒekɪl ənd ˈhaɪd/ *n* a person who has two different natures and can change from one to the other: *He's a bit of a Jekyll and Hyde.* (from the story "The Strange Case of Dr Jekyll and Mr Hyde" by R L Stevenson, in which the main character has one good nature (Dr Jekyll) and one evil nature (Mr Hyde)) **—Jekyll-and-Hyde** *adj* :a *Jekyll-and-Hyde character*

jell, gel /dʒel/ *v* [I] **1** (of a liquid) to become firmer, like jelly **2** (of ideas, thoughts, etc.) to take a clear shape: *I found the film confusing – a lot of different ideas that didn't really jell.*

jel·lied /'dʒelid/ *adj* cooked and served in jelly: **Jellied eels** *are thought of as a favourite food of working-class Londoners.*

jel·lo /'dʒeləʊ/ also **jell-o**– *n* [U] *tdmk, AmE* **1** *for* JELLY (1b) **2 jello salad** a dish made from jello mixed with fruit, nuts, or sometimes vegetables, served with whipped cream

jel·ly /'dʒeli/ *n* **1 a** [S;U] *esp. BrE* a soft quite solid substance which shakes when it is moved: *The juices from the cooked meat solidify into a jelly.* | (fig.) *He had beaten his victim's head to a jelly with a hammer.* **b** [C;U] also **jello** *AmE* (a dish of) such a substance made with sweetened fruit juice and GELATINE, often eaten with ice cream at children's parties: *an orange jelly* | *I was so nervous I was shaking like a jelly.* **2** [U] clear, quite solid JAM¹ containing no pieces of fruit, seeds, etc.: *apple jelly*

jelly ba·by /'·· ·/ *n BrE* a small soft jelly-like sweet made in the shape of a baby, in a variety of colours, often eaten by children

jelly bean /'·· ·/ *n* a small soft sweet that comes in many different tastes and colours, is shaped like a bean, and which one has to chew a lot. Jelly beans are popular in the US, esp. at Easter, when they are put in EASTER BASKETS.

jel·ly·fish /'dʒelifɪʃ/ *n* **-fish** *or* **-fishes** a sea creature that has a soft nearly transparent body and sometimes stings

jelly roll /'·· ·/ *n AmE for* SWISS ROLL

jem·my /'dʒemi/ *BrE* ‖ **jimmy** *AmE* – *n* a metal bar used esp. by thieves to break open locked doors, windows, etc. **—jemmy** *v* [T]

Je·na /'jeɪnə/ a town in the E of Germany, famous for its glass industry –see also ZEISS

je ne sais quoi /ˌʒə nə seɪ ˈkwɑː/ *n* [S;U] *Fr, often pomp or humor* a desirable quality that cannot be described or expressed: *Her reading of the poem lacked a certain je ne sais quoi.*

Jen·kins /ˈdʒeŋkɪnz/, **Roy** /rɔɪ/ (1920–) a British politician who held several important positions in Labour governments in the 1960s and 70s. In 1981 he was one of the "Gang of Four" who established the Social Democratic Party, and in 1987 became **Baron Jenkins of Hillhead**.

Jen·ner /ˈdʒenər/, **Edward** (1749–1823) an English doctor who discovered the principle of VACCINATION, and tested his ideas by giving small amounts of COWPOX (a disease of cows) to humans, which protected them from SMALL-POX (a disease which killed many people until then)

jenny n see SPINNING JENNY

jeop·ar·dize also **-dise** BrE /ˈdʒepədaɪz‖-ər-/ v [T] to put at risk or in danger: If you're rude to him it may jeopardize your chances of promotion.

jeop·ar·dy /ˈdʒepədi‖-ər-/ n [U] risk of loss, defeat, harm, etc.; danger: His foolish behaviour may put his whole future in jeopardy. —see also DOUBLE JEOPARDY

jer·e·mi·ad /ˌdʒerɪˈmaɪəd/ n lit, often derog a long sad-sounding complaint

Jer·e·mi·ah /ˌdʒerɪˈmaɪə/ (6th century BC) a Hebrew PROPHET who said that terrible things would happen because God would become angry with the Jews. His thoughts are given in the Old Testament of the Bible. A person who says that terrible things are going to happen is sometimes called a **Jeremiah**.

Jer·i·cho /ˈdʒerɪkəʊ/ an ancient city N of the Dead Sea in Israel, thought to be the oldest known settlement in the world. It was taken by Joshua in about 1300 BC, and destroyed and then rebuilt by Herod the Great in about 30 BC.

jerk¹ /dʒɜːk‖dʒɜːrk/ v **1** [T] to pull suddenly: He jerked the string and the puppet jumped. **2** [I] to move with jerks: The bus jerked to a stop.

jerk off phr v [I;T] taboo sl, esp. AmE for MASTURBATE

jerk² n **1** a short quick pull or (backward) movement: The knife was stuck but she pulled it out with a jerk. | The train stopped with a jerk. —see also PHYSICAL JERKS **2** derog sl, esp. AmE a stupid person, esp. a man who is insensitive to women: Stop dancing on my feet, you jerk!

jer·kin /ˈdʒɜːkɪn‖-ɜːr-/ n a short coat, usu. without SLEEVES, worn esp. by men in former times

jerk·y /ˈdʒɜːki‖-ɜːr-/ adj not smooth in movement; with sudden starts and stops: We had a very jerky ride in the back of the old truck. —ily adv —iness n [U]

jer·o·bo·am /ˌdʒerəˈbəʊəm/ n a very large wine bottle that holds four times the amount of an ordinary wine bottle

Je·rome /dʒɪˈrəʊm/, **Jerome K** (1859–1927) an English writer who wrote humorous books, such as Idle Thoughts of an Idle Fellow and Three Men in a Boat

Jer·ry¹ /ˈdʒeri/ see TOM AND JERRY

Jerry² n BrE old-fash derog a German (used esp. during the Second World War)

jer·ry-built /ˈ··· ·/ adj derog built quickly, cheaply, and badly: a jerry-built house

jer·sey /ˈdʒɜːzi‖-ɜːr-/ n **1** [C] a woollen garment for the upper part of the body; SWEATER **2** [U] fine usu. woollen cloth used esp. for women's dresses **3** [C] AmE a soft shirt worn by players of some sports: His name and number are on the back of his jersey.

Jersey n **1** the largest of the Channel Islands, between England and France, with influences from both countries. Jersey is known for DAIRY products such as cream, as well as potatoes and TOMATOes **2** a light brown cow that produces creamy milk **3** AmE infml NEW JERSEY

Je·ru·sa·lem /dʒɪˈruːsələm/ **1** the city between the Mediterranean and the Dead Sea, which is of great religious and historical importance to Christians, Jews and Muslims. It has many important places for all these religions, such as the Dome of the Rock, the Mount of Olives and the Wailing Wall. Although the Israelis regard Jerusalem as their capital, this is not agreed with by many people, particularly Arabs. **2** a well-known religious song based on a poem written by William Blake

Je·ru·sa·lem ar·ti·choke /·ˌ··· ˈ···/ n an ARTICHOKE (2)

Jerusalem Bi·ble /·ˌ··· ˈ··/ n a translation of the Bible which was published (PUBLISH) in English in 1966, based on work done in Jerusalem

jest /dʒest/ v [I (**with, about**)] fml to speak without serious

intention; joke: Don't jest with me, young man! | a jesting remark —**jest** n [C;U] : He said it as a jest/said it in jest. — ~**ingly** adv

jest·er /ˈdʒestər/ n a man kept by a ruler in former times to amuse him, tell jokes, etc.; FOOL¹ (2)

Je·su·it /ˈdʒezjuː‖ɪt‖ˈdʒeʒuː‖ɪt, ˈdʒezuː‖ɪt/ n a Roman Catholic man who is a member of the Society of Jesus and lives a religious life. People sometimes think of Jesuits in connection with the words "Give us a child until it is seven, and it is ours for life", originally said by a Jesuit teacher. — ~**ical** /ˌdʒezjuːˈɪtɪkəl‖ˌdʒeʒuː-, ˌdʒezuː-/ adj — ~**ically** /kli/ adv

Je·sus¹ /ˈdʒiːzəs/ also **Jesus Christ** /·ˌ·· ˈ·/, Christ— the FOUNDER of the Christian religion. As told in the New Testament, Jesus was born in Bethlehem, the son of God and the Virgin Mary, and lived as a CARPENTER in Nazareth with Mary and her husband Joseph. Jesus gathered 12 followers, called DISCIPLEs, and travelled around Palestine teaching and healing (HEAL) people who were sick. He also performed MIRACLEs e.g. walking on water and turning water into wine. However, there was much opposition to his message and the Roman authorities caught him and crucified (CRUCIFY) him by nailing him to a cross. Christians believe that he rose from the dead after three days and went up to heaven. This is known as the Resurrection. —see also CHRIS-TIANITY, NATIVITY; and see colour picture on page 424

Jesus² interj sl (a strong word used to express surprise, anger, etc.)

▷ USAGE Some people, especially those who believe in the Christian religion, are offended by the use of **Jesus** and **Christ** as interjections. **God** is more commonly used and is not felt to be so strong, but some people do not like this use either.◁

Jesus Christ Su·per·star /·ˌ·· ·ˌ· ˈ···/ a musical show about the life of Jesus, made into a film in 1973

Jesus freak /ˈ··· ·/ n becoming old-fash a person who combines the practice of some form of Christianity with a HIPPIE way of life. The STEREOTYPE of a Jesus freak is of a young man with long hair and a beard, who wears loose clothes and SANDALS.

Jesus move·ment /ˈ·· ˌ···/ [the] a Christian movement which began in the 1970s and consisted of esp. young people who reject the practice of most of the established Christian churches and believe in spreading the teachings of Jesus by talking about them a lot

jet¹ /dʒet/ n **1** an aircraft with a JET ENGINE: Enemy jets attacked our positions. | travelling by jet | a jet aircraft — see picture at AIRCRAFT **2** [(**of**)] a fast narrow stream of liquid, gas, etc., coming out of a small hole: The firemen directed jets of water at the burning building. **3** a narrow opening from which this is forced out: Put a match to the gas jet to light the gas.

jet² v -tt- **1** [I+adv/prep; T (OUT)] to come or send out of a small opening in a fast narrow stream: Water jetted from the pipe/jetted out. | The flamethrower jetted (out) flames. **2** [I+adv/prep] infml to travel by jet aircraft: jetting around the world

jet³ n [U] a hard black material used, when polished, for making small decorative objects and jewellery

Jet tdmk a company which deals in oil: Turn right just after the Jet garage.

jet-black /ˌ· ˈ·◄/ adj deep black

jet en·gine /ˌ· ˈ··/ n an engine that pushes out a stream of hot air and gases behind it, used for aircraft —see picture at AIRCRAFT

jet foil /ˈdʒetfɔɪl/ n a boat that rises out of the water on leglike structures when travelling fast; HYDROFOIL

jet-lag /ˈ· ·/ n [U] the tired and confused feeling that people may get after flying to a part of the world where the time is different, e.g. morning when it ought to be bed-time: suffering from jet lag —**jet-lagged** adj : Thomas was jet-lagged after his ten-hour flight

jet-pro·pelled /ˌ·· ·ˈ·◄/ adj driven by a JET ENGINE

jet pro·pul·sion /ˌ·· ·ˈ··/ n [U] the use of JET ENGINEs

jet·sam /ˈdʒetsəm/ n [U] things thrown from a ship (and floating towards the shore) —compare FLOTSAM

jet set /ˈ· ·/ n [the+sing./pl. v] infml the international social group of rich, successful, and fashionable people who travel a lot: *By marrying a Greek shipping millionaire she gained immediate entry into the jet set.* | *a jet-set party* — **jet-setter** *n* : *My son's a real jet-setter these days.*

jet-ski /'··/ *n* a very small boat in the form of a platform with HANDLEBARS, ridden over water as a form of sport —**jet-ski** *v* [I]

jet stream /'··/ *n* [*the*] a current of very strong winds high up above the Earth's surface

jet·ti·son /'dʒetɪsən, -zən/ *v* [T] **1** to throw away, esp. from a moving vehicle: *We had to jettison the cargo to make the plane lighter.* **2** to get rid of: *If this company is ever to return to profitability, it's got to jettison its outmoded management practices.*

jet·ty /'dʒeti/ *n* a wall or PLATFORM built out into water, used either for getting on and off ships or as a protection against the force of the waves, and usu. smaller than a PIER

Jeux Sans Fron·ti·ères /ˌ33: sɑːn fronti'eəʳ‖-frɑːn-/ *an* international television game show involving teams who play humorous games and run races against each other for entertainment. Its English name is *It's a Knockout.*

Jew /dʒuː/ **Jew·ess** /'dʒuːɪs/*fem., not polite— n* a member of a people whose religion is JUDAISM and whose language was Hebrew, who lived in ancient times in the land of Israel, some of whom now live in the modern state of Israel and others in various countries all over the world. *— ~ish adj: My husband is Jewish.* | *the Jewish religion*

jew·el /'dʒuːəl/ *n* **1** a small piece of decorative and valuable stone, e.g. a diamond or EMERALD; GEM **2** [*usu. pl.*] a decoration that contains one or more of these and is worn on clothes or on the body: *She locked her jewels in the safe.* —see also CROWN JEWELS **3** a very small real or artificial stone fitted in the machinery of a watch, to make it run smoothly **4** a person or thing of great value: *This painting is the jewel of my collection.* (=is my finest painting)

jewel in the crown /ˌ·· ·· '·/ *n* [*the*] the best thing, etc. among many good ones. It was said in the past that India was the jewel in the crown of the British Empire: *His shares in ICI are the jewel in the crown of his portfolio.*

jew·elled *BrE* ‖ **jeweled** *AmE* /'dʒuːəld/ *adj* decorated or fitted with jewels: *a jewelled bracelet*

jew·el·ler *BrE* ‖ **jeweler** *AmE* /'dʒuːələʳ/ *n* **1** a person who owns or works in a shop (**jeweller's** *BrE*, **jeweler's** *AmE*) which sells jewellery, watches, etc. **2** a maker of jewellery

jew·el·lery *BrE* ‖ **-elry** *AmE* /'dʒuːəlri/ *n* [U] body decorations such as rings, NECKLACEs, etc.: *This diamond brooch is my most valuable piece of jewellery.* | *a jewellery box* —see also COSTUME JEWELLERY

Jew·ish /'dʒuːɪʃ/ *adj* of or connected with Jews and their way of life. *a Jewish ceremony/delicatessen*

Jew's harp /ˌ· '·‖'· ·/ *n* a small musical instrument held between the teeth and played by striking a piece of metal with one finger

Jez·e·bel /'dʒezəbəl, -bel/ *n derog, usu. lit or humor* an immoral woman who tries to attract men sexually

JFK /ˌdʒeɪ ef 'keɪ/ *n* **1** also **Kennedy** New York's main international airport: *I'm flying into JFK but out of Newark.* **2** *abbrev. for* John Fitzgerald KENNEDY

Jiang Qing /ˌdʒiæŋ 'tʃɪŋ/ (1913–) a Chinese politician and former actress who became the third wife of Mao Zedong —see also GANG OF FOUR

jib¹ /dʒɪb/ *n* a long beam which stands out from a CRANE, and from which the hook hangs down

jib² *n* a small sail —see picture at YACHT; see also **the cut of someone's jib** (CUT²)

jib³ *v* **-bb-** [I (*at*)] *BrE* to become suddenly unwilling to go further; HESITATE: *He jibbed a bit when I told him the price, but eventually he agreed* | *She jibbed at signing the contract without legal advice.*

jibe /dʒaɪb/ *n, v* GIBE

jif·fy /'dʒɪfi/ *n* [S] *infml* a moment: *I'll be ready in a jiffy.* (=I'll be ready very soon)

jif·fy bag, **Jiffy bag** /'·· '·/ *n tdmk* a (make of) padded (PAD² (1)) bag in which breakable things are often sent through the post

jig¹ /dʒɪg/ *n* (music for) a quick merry dance

jig² *v* **-gg-** **1** [I] to dance a jig **2** [I+*adv/prep*; T+*obj+adv/prep*] to (cause to) move up and down with quick short movements : *They were jigging up and down in time to the music.*

jig·ger /'dʒɪgəʳ/ *n* **1** a small usu. metal cup used in measuring alcoholic drinks **2** *rare esp. AmE* any small piece of apparatus: *Have you seen that jigger I fix the radio with?*

jig·gered /'dʒɪgəd‖-ərd/ *adj* [F] *infml* **1** very surprised: *Well, I'll be jiggered!* (=I am very surprised) **2** *old-fash* very tired: *I'm completely jiggered after that game of football.*

jig·ger·y-po·ker·y /ˌdʒɪgəri 'pəʊkəri/ *n* [U] *infml, esp. BrE* secret dishonest behaviour: *By the look of these election results, there's been some jiggery-pokery.*

jig·gle /'dʒɪgəl/ *v* [I;T] *infml* to (cause to) move from side to side with short quick light movements: *Jiggle the key in the lock and see if it will open the door.* —**jiggle** *n*

jig·saw /'dʒɪgsɔː/ *n* **1** also **jigsaw puz·zle** /'·· ˌ··/—a picture cut up into many small pieces to be fitted together: *to do a jigsaw* | (fig.) *The police have found a vital clue to the murder, and hope that the other pieces of the jigsaw will now fall into place.* (=so that the rest of the mystery will be explained) **2** a SAW for cutting out shapes in thin pieces of wood

jigsaw

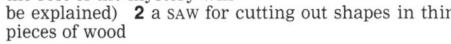

ji·had /dʒɪ'hɑːd, dʒɪ'hæd/ *n* a holy war fought by Muslims as a religious duty

jilt /dʒɪlt/ *v* [T] *derog* to suddenly refuse to see (a lover) any more; unexpectedly refuse to marry (someone) after having promised to do so

jim crow /ˌdʒɪm 'krəʊ/ *adj* [A] *AmE* (*often caps.*) **1** *derog* unfairly disadvantageous to blacks: *Jim Crow laws* **2** for blacks only, and usu. of poor quality: *Jim Crow schools* —see also CIVIL RIGHTS MOVEMENT

jim·jams /'dʒɪmdʒæmz/ *n* [*the*+P] *BrE humor sl* the JITTERS

jim·my /'dʒɪmi/ *n AmE for* JEMMY

Jimmy (used informally by Scottish men, esp. men from Glasgow, as a form of address to another man): *I'm talking to you, Jimmy.*

jin·gle¹ /'dʒɪŋgəl/ *v* [I;T] to (cause to) sound with a jingle: *The coins in his pocket jingled as he walked.*

jingle² *n* **1** a repeated sound like small bells ringing or light metal objects striking against each other **2** a very short simple song, usu. of poor quality, esp. as part of a radio or TV advertisement: *I can't stop humming that awful soap powder jingle.*

Jingle Bells /ˌ·· ˌ·/ the title and first words of a popular Christmas song

jin·go·is·m /'dʒɪŋgəʊɪzəm/ *n* [U] *derog* a belief that one's country is better than others, esp. expressed threateningly —**ist**, *n* —**istic** /ˌdʒɪŋgəʊ'ɪstɪk◄/ *adj*

jinks /dʒɪŋks/ *n* see HIGH JINKS

jinn /dʒɪn/ also **jin·ni** /'dʒɪni/— *n* a GENIE

Jin·nah /'dʒɪnə/, **Mo·ham·med Al·i** /məʊ'hæmɪd 'æli‖-'ɑːli/ (1876–1948) a Muslim lawyer who was the FOUNDER of Pakistan when he persuaded the British to separate it from India when India was made independent in 1947

jinx¹ /dʒɪŋks/ *n* [(*on*)] something that brings bad luck: *There seems to be a jinx on our team when we play there, because we always lose.*

jinx² *v* [T] *infml* to bring bad luck to: *That family is jinxed.* (=has continuing bad luck)

jit·ter·bug /'dʒɪtəbʌg‖-ər-/ *n* a fast active popular dance of the 1940s

jit·ters /'dʒɪtəz‖-ərz/ *n* [*the*+P] *infml* anxiety, esp. before an important or difficult event: *I've got the jitters about my driving test.* | *That mad look in his eyes gives me the jitters.* —**tery** /'dʒɪtəri/ *adj*

jiu·jit·su /ˌdʒuː'dʒɪtsuː/ *n* [U] JUJITSU

jive¹ /dʒaɪv/ *n* [U] **1** (a style of very fast dancing performed to) a kind of popular music with a strong regular beat; SWING² (5) or ROCK 'N' ROLL **2** *AmE sl* deceiving or foolish talk **3** *AmE sl* also **jivetalk, jivetalking** the variety of

English spoken by esp. URBAN (=living in cities) black people

jive² *v* [I] to dance to jive music

Jnr *BrE written abbrev. for* JUNIOR¹

Joan see DARBY AND JOAN

Joan of Arc /ˌdʒəʊn əv ˈɑːk ‖ -ˈɑːrk/ see SAINT JOAN OF ARC

job /dʒɒb‖dʒɑːb/ *n* **1** [C] regular paid employment: *"What does she do?" "She has a good job in a bank."* | *The factory closed down and she lost* (=was dismissed from) *her job.* | *He's got a safe job in the Civil Service.* (=he is unlikely to lose his job) | *a part-time job* | *He's been out of a job* (=unemployed) *for months.* | *I'm looking for a new job, one where I get a bit more* **job satisfaction.** | *I love being a soldier; I could never do an ordinary* **nine-to-five job.** (=with regular hours of work every day) | *No, I can't let you look at the confidential files — it'd be* **more than my job's worth.** (=I would lose my job) | *to fill in a job application* | *a government job-creation scheme* —see also JOBSWORTH

▶ CULTURAL NOTE If a person is looking for a job they will often look in a newspaper or at a JOBCENTRE and when they find something they are interested in, they send a written APPLICATION and their CV. If they are successful they are invited to an INTERVIEW¹ and asked questions about themselves, and may be asked to give the names of former employers who can talk about their work. In most companies there is an official process for giving someone a job and it is not usual to get a job just because you have a friend or relative who can help you. ◀

2 [C] a piece of work: *I've got a job for you: wash these dishes, please.* | *The plumber's done a good job*|*a good* **job of work.** | *I think Peter's just* **the man for the job.** (=exactly the right person to do this piece of work) —see also ODD JOB MAN **3** [S] something hard to do: *It was a (real) job to talk with all that noise.* | *I had a job finishing that piece of work on time.* **4** [S] one's affair; duty: *It's not my job to interfere.* **5** *infml* [C *usu. sing.*] an example of a certain type: *That new car of yours is a beautiful job.* (=a beautiful car) **6** [C] *infml* a PLASTIC SURGERY operation: *She's had a nose job.* **7** [C] *sl* a crime, esp. a robbery: *He's in prison for* **pulling a job** (=doing a crime) *up north.* | *a bank job* —see also INSIDE JOB **8 give something up as a bad job** to decide that something is impossible, and stop trying to do it **9 gi'z a job** (=give me a job) a phrase used in the British television SERIES *Boys from the Blackstuff.* The phrase was used by a young man looking for a job in Liverpool at a time when there was high unemployment. **10 jobs for the boys** *usu. derog* good employment for one's friends or supporters **11 just the job** exactly the thing wanted or needed: *That spanner you lent me was just the job.* **12 make the best of a bad job** *BrE* to do as well as possible in unfavourable conditions: *They wouldn't let us use the house, so making the best of a bad job we held our party in the garden.* **13 on the job: a** while working; at work: *We're not allowed to smoke on the job.* | *on-the-job training* **b** (*BrE infml, humor*) while having sex: *He died on the job.* —see also PUT-UP JOB, **a good job** (GOOD¹)

▷ USAGE What you do to earn your living is your **job** [C], your **work** [U], or (more formal) your **occupation:** *Please state your* **occupation** *on the form.* **Post** and **position** are more formal words for a particular job: *He was appointed to the* **post/position** *of lecturer in English at Newcastle University.* A **trade** is a skilled job in which you use your hands: *She's an electrician by* **trade.** A **profession** is a job such as that of a doctor or lawyer, for which you need special training and a good education. Some **professions,** such as teaching and nursing, are also called **vocations,** which suggests that people do them in order to help others. A **career** is a job that you hope to do all your life, with more and more success: *Her political* **career** *began 20 years ago.*◁

Job /dʒəʊb/ a man in the Bible who was patient in spite of many misfortunes: *You need the patience of Job to work in the complaints department.*

job·ber /ˈdʒɒbəʳ‖ˈdʒɑː-/ *n* see MARKET MAKER

job·bing /ˈdʒɒbɪŋ‖ˈdʒɑː-/ *adj* [A] *BrE* doing separate small jobs for various people: *a jobbing gardener*

job cen·tre /ˈ· ˌ··/ also **employment exchange** *n* a British government office which helps people to find work or workers. Most large towns have a job centre.

Job·club /ˈdʒɒbklʌb‖ˈdʒɑːb-/ *n* a government organization in Britain which helps unemployed people find work

job de·scrip·tion /ˈ· ·ˌ··/ *n* the description of the duties involved in a particular job, and the things for which the job holder is responsible, often in the form of an official document: *My job description includes liaising with our marketing department.*

job-hunt·ing /ˈdʒɒbhʌntɪŋ‖ˈdʒɑːb-/ *n* [U] the activity of looking for a job, e.g. by looking in the special part of a newspaper where jobs are advertised: *advice to help you with your jobhunting* | *How's the jobhunting going?*

job·less /ˈdʒɒbləs‖ˈdʒɑːb-/ *adj* without a job; unemployed: [(also *n, (the)* P)] *There are over 1000 jobless in our town.*

job los·ses /ˈ· ˌ··/ *n* [P] figures representing the number of jobs lost in a particular place, usu. given in a news statement about a factory closing, or in a total of such losses of jobs for a certain area, or over a period of time: *The town suffered heavy job losses when the steelworks shut down.*

job lot /ˈ· ·, ˌ· ˈ·/ *n* [(of)] (*often derog*) a group of things of different kinds, all bought or sold together

Job's com·fort·er /ˌdʒəʊbz ˈkʌmfətəʳ‖-fər-/ *n rare* a person whose attempts to make others feel better actually make them feel worse

job-shar·ing /ˈdʒɒbʃeərɪŋ‖ˈdʒɑːb-/ *n BrE* [U] the practice of dividing a full-time job between two people so that each works for half the time. This practice is becoming more popular, esp. as a way of helping women with children return to work.

jobs·worth /ˈdʒɒbzwɜːθ‖ˈdʒɑːbzwɜːrθ/ *n BrE infml, often humor* a usu. uniformed male attendant, esp. in an unimportant post, who sticks closely to rules rather than using common sense. His favourite saying when refusing to meet a request is "It's more than my job's worth" (e.g. to let someone do something) (=he would lose his job if he let them do it).

jock /dʒɒk‖dʒɑːk/ *n AmE infml often derog* a sportsman, esp. a college student who is very keen on sport and not very clever

Jock *n BrE infml, often derog* a name used for a man from Scotland. This word is usu. used by English people, and can be annoying to Scotsmen.

jock·ey¹ /ˈdʒɒki‖ˈdʒɑːki/ *n* a person who rides in horse races, esp. professionally —see also DISC JOCKEY

jockey² *v* [T+*obj*+*adv/prep*, esp. **into**] to persuade gradually and skilfully: *They were reluctant at first, but we managed to jockey them into signing the agreement.* —see also **jockey for position** (POSITION¹ (8))

Jockey Club /ˈ·· ·/ [*the*] the organization in charge of horseracing in Britain

Jockey shorts /ˈ·· ˌ·/ *n* [P] *tdmk* a type of men's UNDERPANTS.

jock·strap /ˈdʒɒkstræp ‖ ˈdʒɑːk-/ also **athletic supporter** *AmE— n infml* a tight-fitting undergarment for supporting the male sex organs, worn while doing sports

jo·cose /dʒəˈkəʊs, dʒəʊ-/ *adj lit or fml* joking; meant to or meaning to cause amusement — ~**ly** *adv* — ~**ness, jocosity** /dʒəˈkɒsˌti, dʒəʊ-‖-ˈkɑː-/ *n* [U]

joc·u·lar /ˈdʒɒkjʊləʳ‖ˈdʒɑː-/ *adj fml* meant to or meaning to cause amusement, perhaps in reply to a serious question: *a jocular reply*|*person* — ~**ly** *adv* — ~**ity** /ˌdʒɒkjʊˈlærˌti‖ˌdʒɑː-/ *n* [U]

joc·und /ˈdʒɒkənd‖ˈdʒɑː-/ *adj lit & poet* merry; cheerful — ~**ity** /dʒəʊˈkʌndˌti, dʒə-/ *n* [U]

jodh·purs /ˈdʒɒdpəz‖ˈdʒɑːdpərz/ *n* [P] trousers for horse riding that are tight from the ankle to the knee and loose above the knee —see PAIR (USAGE)

Jod·rell Bank /ˌdʒɒdrəl ˈbæŋk‖ˌdʒɑː-/ an OBSERVATORY (=place from which scientists study the stars, etc.) in Cheshire, NW England

Joe Bloggs /ˌdʒəʊ ˈblɒgz‖-ˈblɑːgz/ also **Joe Pub·lic** /ˌ· ˈ··/, **Joe Soap** *BrE infml*‖**Joe Blow, John Q. Public** /ˌ· · ˈ··/ *AmE, AustrE infml*— an average man or male member of the public: *What would Joe Bloggs think?* | *It was a brilliant design of motorbike, but expensive–and Joe Public refused to pay up.* —see also **man in the street** (MAN)

jog¹ /dʒɒg‖dʒɑːg/ *v* **-gg-** **1** [T] to push or knock slightly with the arm, hand, etc.: *She jogged my elbow and made* *me spill my coffee.* **2** [I+*adv/prep*] to move slowly, shaking up and down or from side to side: *The carriage jogged along the rough road.* **3** [I] to run slowly and steadily, esp. for exercise: *I go jogging in the park before breakfast.* | (fig.) *Our lives just jog along* (=move uneventfully) *from day to day.* —see RUN (USAGE)   **4 jog someone's memory** to make someone remember

jog² *n* **1** a slight shake, push, or knock: *I gave him a jog to wake him up.* **2** a slow steady run, esp. for exercise, a fashionable thing to do, esp. in the 1980s: *I go for a jog in the park every morning.*

jog·ger /ˈdʒɒɡəʳ‖ˈdʒɑː-/ *n* a person who runs slowly and steadily for exercise, but who is not fit or fast enough to be called a runner. —**jogging** *n*

jog·gle /ˈdʒɒɡəl‖ˈdʒɑː-/ *v* [I;T] *infml* to (cause to) shake often, but slightly —**joggle** *n*

jog trot /ˈ· ·/ *n* [S] a slow steady run (of a person) or TROT (of a horse)

Jo·han·nes·burg /dʒəʊˈhænəsbɜːɡ‖-bɜːrɡ/ the largest city in South Africa, a centre for business and TRANSPORT¹ (2)

john /dʒɒn‖dʒɑːn/ *n AmE sl* **1** *for* TOILET **2** a word used by American PROSTITUTEs for one of their customers

John see SAINT JOHN

John, El·ton /ˈeltən/ (1947–   ) an English popular music singer, piano player, and songwriter known for his unusual, brightly decorated clothes and glasses and his financial support for Watford Football Club in London. His many successful songs include *Crocodile Rock* and *Candle In The Wind.* —see colour picture on page 554

John, King (1167–1216) King of England from 1199. He is remembered esp. for signing the Magna Carta in 1215. —see also MAGNA CARTA

John Bar·ley·corn /ˌdʒɒn ˈbɑːlɪkɔːn‖ˌdʒɑːrn ˈbɑːrlikɔːn/ *AmE old fash* alcoholic drink, represented as a man

John Brown's Bod·y /ˌ· · ˈ··/ an American song, written by Charles Hall, about a famous fighter against slavery: *John Brown's body lies a-mouldering in the grave, But his soul goes marching on...* —see also John BROWN

John Bull /ˌ· ˈ·/ *n lit* **1** England; the English people **2** [C] *usu. derog* a typical Englishman, esp. one considered to dislike foreigners. John Bull is shown in pictures as a large, rather fat man wearing leather boots and a WAISTCOAT with the pattern of the UNION JACK on it. There is often a BULLDOG beside him. —compare BRITANNIA

John Deere /ˌdʒɒn ˈdɪəʳ‖ˌdʒɑːn-/ an American company that makes industrial and farm vehicles and machines

John Doe /ˌ· ˈ·/ *n* **1** an UNIDENTIFIED man, esp. one in a law case who does not want his identity to be known —compare JANE DOE **2** [C] *esp. AmE* an average man

John Han·cock /ˌ· ˈ··/ *n* [S] *AmE infml* a SIGNATURE (1) (after the American STATESMAN of that name who was the first to sign Declaration of Independence. He is said to have made his signature very large, so that the king of England could read it without his glasses: *Put your John Hancock on the dotted line.*

John Lew·is /ˌ· ˈ··/ (in Britain) one of a group of shops found in large towns, selling things for the home, clothing, toys, etc.

John·nie Walk·er /ˌdʒɒni ˈwɔːkəʳ ‖ ˌdʒɑː-/ *n* [U] *tdmk* a type of blended (BLEND (2)) WHISKY

john·ny /ˈdʒɒni‖ˈdʒɑːni/ *n* **1** *old-fash infml* (*often cap.*) a man **2** *BrE sl for* CONDOM **3** *AmE sl* PENIS

johnny-come-late·ly /ˌ·· · ˈ··/ *n AmE* a NEWCOMER to a job or an activity, esp. one who is successful and receives a lot of attention

John of Gaunt /ˌ· · ˈ·/ (1340–99) an English politician, son of Edward III, who acted as head of government until Richard II was old enough to rule

John O'Groats /ˌdʒɒn ə ˈɡrəʊts‖ˌdʒɑːn-/ a place in NE Scotland, thought of as being (though not actually) the most northern part of the mainland of Britain, esp. in the phrase "from Land's End to John O'Groats" —compare LAND'S END

John Paul I /ˌdʒɒn pɔːl ðə ˈfɜːrst‖ˌdʒɑːn-, -ˈfɜːrst/, **Pope** (1912–78) a POPE who ruled for only 34 days before he died, but encouraged a simpler style of leading the Catholic Church

John Paul II /ˌdʒɒn pɔːl ðə ˈsekənd‖ˌdʒɑːn-/, **Pope** (1920–   ) the first Polish POPE, elected in 1978 and known for his

support of Roman Catholic teachings on issues such as BIRTH CONTROL and marriage, and opposition to ideas such as women becoming priests and modern dress for MONKS and NUNS

johns /dʒɒnz‖dʒɑːnz/ *n* [P] see LONG JOHNS

John·son /ˈdʒɒnsən‖ˈdʒɑːn-/, **A·my** /ˈeɪmi/ (1904–41) a British pilot who flew alone from London to Australia in 1930, and England to Cape Town in 1932. Her plane disappeared over the English Channel during the Second World War.

Johnson, Andrew (1808–75) an American Democrat politician, the 17th president of the US 1865–69

Johnson, Ben (1961–   ) a Canadian runner who broke the world record for the 100 metres race in 1987, and again at the 1988 Olympic Games but was later disqualified (DISQUALIFY) for using drugs to help his performance

Johnson, Dame Ce·li·a /ˈsiːliə/ (1908–82) an English actress remembered esp. for her role in the film *Brief Encounter*

Johnson, Lyn·don Baines /ˈlɪndən beɪnz/ also **LBJ** (1908–73) the 36th president of the USA (1963–69), a DEMOCRAT. As John F. Kennedy's vice-president, Johnson became president when Kennedy was killed. He was re-elected in 1964 and helped start many social programmes in his plans for a **Great Society**, but he became unpopular after increasing US involvement in Vietnam. Johnson was from Texas; his wife's name was **Lady Bird**.

Johnson, Magic (1959–   ) an American BASKETBALL player famous for his excellent play and teamwork and for his happy attitude. In 1991 doctors told Johnson that he was HIV-positive (that he has the VIRUS which causes AIDS) and he began working to inform people about the illness.

Magic Johnson

Johnson, Sam·u·el /ˈsæmjuəl/ (1709–84), known as **Dr Johnson**, an English CRITIC and dictionary writer, and a well-known figure in London society in the 18th century. He is considered to be a very well educated person and is often thought of in association with James Boswell, who wrote his life story (BIOGRAPHY).

John the Bap·tist /ˌ· · ˈ··/ see SAINT JOHN THE BAPTIST

joie de viv·re /ˌʒwɑː də ˈviːvrə/ *n* [U] *Fr* great enjoyment of life: *She's full of/has lots of joie de vivre.*

join¹ /dʒɔɪn/ *v* **1** [T (**to**, TOGETHER, UP)] to fasten or bring together; connect; unite: *Join the pieces of cloth with a loose stitch before finally sewing them together.* | *The hip bone is joined to the thigh bone.* | *The two towns are joined by a railway.* | (*fml*) *to join two people in marriage* **2** [T] to come together with; become united with; meet: *You go home and I'll join you later.* | *Will you join me for a drink?* (=come and sit, etc. with me and have a drink)*Will you join me in a drink?* (=have a drink with me) | *I'm sure you'll all join me in congratulating the bride and groom.* | *Where does this stream join the river?* **4** [I;T] to become united: *Where do the two streams join?* **4** [I;T] to become a member (of): *to join the army* | *to join the Labour party* **5** [T] to take part in (an activity) as a member of a group: *Come on in and join the fun/the party!* **6 join battle** *fml* to begin fighting **7 join hands (with)** to hold (each other's) hands: *They all joined hands and danced round in a circle.* —see also **join forces** (FORCE¹ (9))

join in *phr v* [I;T (=**join in** sthg.)] to take part in (an activity) as a member of a group: *She started singing and we all joined in.* | *We all joined in the singing.*

join up *phr v* [I] to become a member of an army, navy, etc.

join with sbdy. *phr v* [T (**in**) *no pass.*] to act together with; do the same thing as: *Will you now all join with me in drinking a toast to the bride and groom!*

join² *n* a place where two things are joined together: *It's so well made that you can't see the join.*

join·er /ˈdʒɔɪnəʳ/ *n* **1** a maker of wooden doors, door-frames, windowframes, etc. —compare CARPENTER **2** *infml* a person who likes to join organizations: *He's never been much of a joiner.*

join·er·y /ˈdʒɔɪnəri/ *n* [U] the trade or work of a JOINER — compare CARPENTRY

joint¹ /dʒɔɪnt/ *n* **1** a connection between two bones, esp. one that can be bent: *The finger joints are called "knuckles".* | *The old lady had an artificial hip joint fitted.* **2** a place where things are joined together: *the joints in a pipe* —see also UNIVERSAL JOINT **3** *BrE* ‖ **roast** *AmE*— a large piece of meat for cooking, esp. containing a bone, often eaten as part of a Sunday dinner with potatoes and other vegetables: *a joint of pork* **4** *derog sl* a public place, esp. one where people go for entertainment and usu. cheap or having a bad character or REPUTATION —see also CLIP JOINT **5** *sl* a cigarette containing the drug CANNABIS —see also **put someone's nose out of joint** (NOSE¹)

joint² *adj* [A] shared by two or more people: *We did it together; it was a joint effort.* | *our joint bank account* | *to take joint action* | *joint owners* — ~ **ly** *adv*

joint³ *v* [T] to cut (meat) into JOINTS (2)

Joint Chiefs of Staff /ˌ· ˌ· · ˈ·/ *n* [the] the group of leaders of the four main divisions of the American army

joint cus·to·dy /ˌ· ˈ···/ *n* [U] the act or right of caring for someone, shared by two people, esp. when given in a court of law: *After the divorce, the parents were awarded* **joint custody** *of their children.*

joint·ed /ˈdʒɔɪntɪd/ *adj* having joints, esp. movable ones: *a jointed doll*

joint hon·ours /ˌ· ˈ···/ *n BrE* [U] a university degree course in which more than one main subject is studied and included in the name of the degree —compare SINGLE HONOURS

joint res·o·lu·tion /ˌ· ··ˈ···/ *n* a decision or law approved by both houses of the US Congress and signed by the president

joint-stock com·pa·ny /ˌ· ˈ· ˌ···/ ‖ also **stock company** *AmE*— *n* a business company owned by all the people who have bought shares in it

joint ven·ture /ˌ· ˈ···/ *n* a business activity begun by two or more companies acting together, sharing the costs, risks, and profits

joist /dʒɔɪst/ *n* any of the beams onto which a floor is fixed

joke¹ /dʒəʊk/ *n* [C] **1** something said or done to amuse people and cause laughter, esp. a funny story or amusing trick: *She told/made/cracked some very funny jokes.* | *He played a joke on me by pretending he'd lost the tickets.* | *I was having* (=sharing) *a joke with her.* | *Can't you take a joke?* (=be amused by a joke against yourself) | *I don't see the joke.* (=understand what is funny) | *a dirty joke.* (=a joke about sex) —compare TRICK¹ (1,3) **2** something foolish; a person, thing, or event that is not taken seriously: *The exam was so easy it was a joke.* | *Your behaviour is/has gone beyond a joke.* (=is too serious to laugh at) | *It was no joke carrying those heavy bags.* (=it was very difficult, annoying, etc.) **3 the joke's on him/her** he/she looks foolish, instead of the person he/she tried to play a joke on —see also PRACTICAL JOKE

joke² *v* [I (about, with)] to speak unseriously, or not seriously enough: *You mustn't joke with him about religion.* | *We often joke about the crazy things we used to do.* | *joking remarks* | *"Have you finished that job yet?" "You must be joking!* *I've hardly even started it."* | *Yes, that's very funny. But, joking apart/aside* (=we should now speak seriously), *what did he really say?* —**jokingly** *adv*: *I'm sure his remarks were meant jokingly.*

jok·er /ˈdʒəʊkəʳ/ *n* **1** a person who likes to make jokes **2** *infml* a person who is not serious or who should not be taken seriously **3** an additional CARD¹ (1) with no fixed value, used in certain games **4 joker in the pack** something or someone whose possible effect on future events cannot be known or guessed

Jol·i·et /ˈʒɒliei ‖ ʒəʊlˈjei/, **Lou·is** /ˈluːi/ (1645–1700) a French-Canadian EXPLORER who, with Jacques Marquette, discovered the upper Mississippi River in 1673

jol·li·fi·ca·tion /ˌdʒɒlɪfɪˈkeɪʃən‖ˌdʒɑː-/ also **jollifications** *pl.*— *n* [C;U] *infml* harmless fun and enjoyment

jol·ly¹ /ˈdʒɒli‖ˈdʒɑːli/ *adj* cheerful; happy; pleasant: *a jolly person/laugh* —**jollily** *adv* —**jollity, jolliness** *n* [U]

jolly² *adv BrE infml* **1** very: *We all had a jolly good time.* | *The questions were jolly difficult.* **2 jolly well** (used for giving force to an expression) certainly; really. This use of **jolly** is often thought to be typical of upper-class people: *I jolly well told him what I thought of him.*

jolly³ *v* [T +*obj*+**into, out of**] *infml, esp. BrE* to persuade; urge gently: *They jollied her into going with them.*

jolly sbdy. **along** *phr v* [T] to encourage in a joking or friendly way: *He wasn't very keen to finish the job, but I jollied him along.*

jolly sthg. ↔ **up** *phr v* [T] *infml* to make (esp. a place) bright and cheerful: *to jolly up the room with some red cushions*

Jolly Ro·ger /ˌ· ˈ··/ *n* [(the) C] the flag of a PIRATE of former times, showing a SKULL and bones crossed under it

Jol·son /ˈdʒəʊlsən/, **Al** /æl/ (1886–1950) a white American singer, born in Lithuania, who, like other performers at the beginning of the century, used to paint his face to look like a black man. He is known for his very emotional and exciting performances, and for being the star of the first film with sound, *The Jazz Singer*, in 1927. His many famous songs include *Swanee* and *My Mammy*.

Al Jolson

jolt¹ /dʒəʊlt/ *v* [I;T] to (cause to) shake forcefully: *The cart jolted (along) over the rough road.* | *The fall jolted every bone in his body.* | (fig.) *Her angry words jolted* (=shocked) *him (out of his dream).*

jolt² *n* a sudden forceful shake: *We felt a series of jolts as the plane touched down.*

jo·nah /ˈdʒəʊnə/ *n* (*often cap.*) a person who seems to bring bad luck

Jonah a character in the Old Testament whose duty was to warn of the destruction of the city of Nineveh. He tried to escape this by getting on a ship but was thrown into the sea by the CREW as a bringer of bad luck, and spent three days and nights inside a WHALE before coming to land.

Jones¹ /dʒəʊnz/, **Ca·sey** /ˈkeɪsi/ (1863–1900) an American train driver and FOLK HERO who saved the lives of passengers in a train crash, but was killed himself

Jones², **Indiana** a character played by the actor Harrison Ford in three films directed by Steven Spielberg including *Raiders of the Lost Ark*. The films were very popular and full of action and excitement: *"The dashing archaeological adventurer Indiana Jones is back on a new quest — and in a deadly race against evil..."*

Harrison Ford as Indiana Jones

Jones³, **In·i·go** /ˈɪnɪgəʊ/ (1573–1652) an English AR-CHITECT and theatre DESIGNER who was responsible for many important houses and buildings, esp. in London

Jones⁴, **Tom** (1940–) a British popular music singer from S Wales, who was successful in Britain in the 1960s and later in the US. He is known for wearing tight trousers and dancing in a way that is thought to be sexually exciting.

Jones·es /ˈdʒəʊnzɪz/ *n* see **keep up with the Joneses** (KEEP **up**)

Jones·town /ˈdʒəʊnztaʊn/ a settlement in Guyana of the followers of **Jim Jones**, a religious CULT leader. In a religious ceremony, the people living there all killed themselves by drinking poison together, in what became known as the **Jonestown massacre**.

Jon·son /ˈdʒɒnsən‖ˈdʒɑːn-/, **Ben** (1572–1637) an English writer of plays, poetry and criticism, known for plays such as *Volpone*, *The Alchemist*, and *Bartholomew Fair*

Jop·lin /ˈdʒɒplɪn‖ˈdʒɑːp-/, **Jan·is** /ˈdʒænɪs/ (1943–70) an American popular music singer, known for her wild, very active performances in the 1960s and for her wild private life. Her early death was thought to have been caused by drugs, and for many people she represents the PSYCHEDELIC, ACID ROCK, HIPPIE period.

Joplin, Scott (1868–1917) an American piano player and COMPOSER known esp. for his RAGTIME music, such as *The Entertainer*, which was used in the film *The Sting* in 1973, making Joplin famous again

Jor·dan¹ /ˈdʒɔːdən‖ˈdʒɔːr-/ an Arab state in the Middle East, bordering on Israel, Syria, and Saudi Arabia; capital Amman. The country is divided by the River Jordan, which runs from the N to the S of the country, separating it into the West Bank (occupied by Israel since 1967) and the East Bank; East Bank population 3,100,000 (1989); West Bank population 1,000,000 (1989). —**ian** /dʒɔːˈdeɪnɪən‖dʒɔːr-/ *n, adj*

Jordan² [*the*] a river in Israel and Jordan which flows to the Dead Sea. It is mentioned in the Bible.

Jordan, Mi·chael /ˈmaɪkəl/ (1963–) a BASKETBALL player for the Chicago Bulls team, who is a very popular personality in the US, esp. with young people

Jor·dans /ˈdʒɔːdənz‖ˈdɔːr-/ *n* [P] *tdmk* a make of sports shoes

Jo·seph /ˈdʒəʊzɪf/ in the Bible, one of the sons of Jacob. Jacob gave Joseph a COAT OF MANY COLOURS but his brothers, jealous of him, sold him as a slave to some Egyptians. Joseph became an adviser to Pharaoh, king of Egypt, and in the end brought his people to settle in Egypt.

Joseph in the Bible, the husband of the Virgin Mary. Joseph was a CARPENTER in Nazareth

Joseph, Sir Keith /kiːθ/ (1918–) a politician in the British Conservative Party who was secretary of state for education and science (1981–86) in Margaret Thatcher's government

Joseph, Chief (1840?–1904) a leader of a TRIBE of Native Americans who fought against the US army when the army tried to force them to move from their lands to a RESERVATION. When Chief Joseph gave up the fight, he said "I am tired of fighting. My heart is sick and sad. From where the sun now stands I will fight no more forever." —see also NATIVE AMERICAN (CULTURAL NOTE)

Joseph and the A·maz·ing Tech·ni·col·or Dream·coat /ˌdʒəʊzɪf ənd ði əˌmeɪzɪŋ ˌteknɪkʌlə ˈdriːmkəʊt‖-lər-/ a musical play based on the life of Joseph, the son of Jacob in the Bible

Jo·se·phine /ˈdʒəʊsəfiːn/ (1763–1814) the EMPRESS of France from 1796 to 1809, the wife of Napoleon, who divorced (DIVORCE) her in 1809 because she had not produced any children. She is known esp. in connection with the phrase "Not tonight, Josephine", said to have been spoken by Napoleon, refusing his wife's desire for sex, and used in a humorous way today. —see colour picture on page 1015

Joseph of Ar·i·ma·the·a /ˌdʒəʊzɪf əv ˌærɪməˈθɪːə/ in the Bible, a follower of Jesus who asked for the body of Jesus after the CRUCIFIXION. He buried it in a TOMB of rock.

josh /dʒɒʃ‖dʒɑːʃ/ *v infml, esp. AmE* **1** [I] to joke **2** [T] to make fun of, without wanting to hurt: *He's always been keen on collecting unusual hats, although all his friends josh him about it.* —**josh** *n*

Josh·u·a /ˈdʒɒʃjuːə‖ˈdʒɑːʃuːə/ a character in the Old Testament who led the Jews to the land of Canaan. People know of him in connection with Jericho, where he is said to have blown his TRUMPETs and caused the walls to fall down.

joss stick /ˈdʒɒs ˌstɪk‖ˈdʒɑːs-/ *n* a stick of INCENSE¹

jos·tle /ˈdʒɒsəl‖ˈdʒɑː-/ *v* [I;T] (of a person) to knock or push against (someone) rather roughly: *The players were jostled by an angry crowd as they left the field.*

jot¹ /dʒɒt‖dʒɑːt/ *n* [S (**of**) *usu. in negatives*] a very small amount; IOTA: *There isn't a jot of truth in it.*

jot² *v* -**tt**- [T (**DOWN**)] to write quickly, esp. without preparation: *I'll jot down some notes while he's speaking.* | *He jotted her address down on his newspaper.*

jot·ter /ˈdʒɒtəʳ‖ˈdʒɑː-/ *n BrE* a number of pieces of paper joined together, used for writing notes on

jot·ting /ˈdʒɒtɪŋ‖ˈdʒɑː-/ *n* [*usu. pl.*] a short note, usu. written quickly: *It's not really an article, just a few preparatory jottings.*

joule /dʒuːl‖dʒuːl, dʒaʊl/ *n tech* a measure of ENERGY or work

jour·nal /ˈdʒɜːnl‖-ɜːr-/ *n* **1** a serious magazine, usu. produced by a specialist society: *the British Medical Journal* | *the Journal of the Cricket Society* **2** *lit* a usu. daily record of events; DIARY: *I kept a journal during my visit to China.*

▷ USAGE Both **journal** *lit* and **diary** can mean "(a book containing) a record of the events in a person's life" but **diary** is the more usual word for a record of ordinary, daily life. **Diary** *esp. BrE*/**calendar** *AmE* (not **journal**) is the word for the book in which you write down appointments and things to be done in the future.◁

jour·nal·ese /ˌdʒɜːnəlˈiːz‖-ɜːr-/ *n* [U] *derog* language considered to be typical of newspapers, esp. in being full of too-often-used expressions

jour·nal·is·m /ˈdʒɜːnəl-ɪzəm‖-ɜːr-/ *n* [U] the profession of writing for newspapers and magazines —**istic** /ˌdʒɜːnəlˈɪstɪk◂‖-ɜːr-/ *adj*

jour·nal·ist /ˈdʒɜːnəl-ɪst‖-ɜːr-/ *n* a person whose profession is journalism —compare REPORTER

jour·ney¹ /ˈdʒɜːni‖-ɜːr-/ *esp. BrE* ‖ usu. **trip** *AmE n* a trip from one place to another, esp. by land over quite a long distance: *a long train journey across Europe* | *It was years since I'd made the journey to* (=gone to) *Scotland.* | *If you're going on a long car journey, make sure the vehicle's in good condition.* | *It's three days' journey/a three-day journey from here to Berlin.* | *Have a safe journey!* | *They* **broke** (=interrupted) **their journey** *and stayed the night at a hotel.* | *some books to read on your journey* | (*lit*) *to reach one's journey's end* (=the end of one's journey) —see TRAVEL (USAGE)

journey² *v* [I+*adv/prep*] *lit* to travel; go on a journey: *journeying across Africa on horseback*

jour·ney·man /ˈdʒɜːniːmən‖-ɜːr-/ *n* -**men** /mən/ (*usu. in comb.*) **1** a trained workman who works for another person and is often paid by the day: *a journeyman printer* **2** an experienced person whose work is fairly (but not very) good: *an example of the journeyman work this painter produced in his later years*

jour·no /ˈdʒɜːnəʊ‖-ɜːr-/ *n* -**nos** *sl for* JOURNALIST

joust /dʒaʊst/ *v* [I (**with**)] (in former times) to fight on horseback with LANCEs (=long spears), esp. as a sport; this was often done in the form of a TOURNAMENT to entertain a king

Jove /dʒəʊv/ **1** the god Jupiter **2** (*poet*) the PLANET Jupiter **3 By Jove!** *old-fash infml* (an expression of surprise, also used for adding force to other expressions): *By Jove, you're right!*

jo·vi·al /ˈdʒəʊviəl/ *adj* cheerful; friendly: *a jovial greeting/old man* —**ly** *adv* —**ity** /ˌdʒəʊviˈælɪti/ *n* [U]

jowl /dʒaʊl/ *also* **jowls** *pl.*— *n* **1** the lower part of the side of the face, esp. loose skin and flesh near the lower jaw **2 -jowled** /dʒaʊld/ having jowls of the stated kind: *a heavy-jowled dog* —see also **cheek by jowl** (CHEEK¹)

joy /dʒɔɪ/ *n* **1** [U] great happiness: *She was filled with joy at the thought of seeing her daughter again.* | *They* **jumped for joy** (=were very happy) *when they heard the good news.* | *To his mother's joy, he won first prize.* **2** [C] a person or thing that causes joy: (*fml*) *She had remained a staunch friend throughout all the joys and sorrows of life.* | (*fml*) *My children are a great joy to me.* | (*infml*) *This car is a joy to drive.* (=is easy, and therefore pleasing, to drive) | *This rose bush is my husband's* **pride and joy**. **3** [U *usu. in questions and negatives*] *BrE infml* success: *I tried to get her on the telephone, but I didn't have any joy.* (=I wasn't able to)

Joyce /dʒɔɪs/, **James** (1882–1941) an Irish writer who greatly influenced (INFLUENCE) the way English NOVELs were written, with his use of unusual and invented words and different style of writing. His novels include *Ulysses* and *Finnegans Wake*.

joy·ful /ˈdʒɔɪfəl/ *adj fml* full of or causing joy: *Imagine the joyful scene when they were reunited with their lost daughter.* —**ly** *adv*: *The bells rang out joyfully.* —**ness** *n* [U]

joy·less /ˈdʒɔɪləs/ *adj* without joy; unhappy: *The funeral supper was a joyless affair.* —**ly** *adv* —**ness** *n* [U]

Joy of Cook·ing /ˌ· · '··/, **The** the name of a very popular American cookbook which has instructions on how to cook many standard American and foreign dishes

joy·ous /'dʒɔɪəs/ *adj lit* full of or causing joy: *a joyous heart/song/occasion* — ~ **ly** *adv* — ~ **ness** *n* [U]

joy·ride /'dʒɔɪraɪd/ *n infml* a ride for pleasure in a vehicle, esp. a stolen car, often with careless driving —**joyride** *v* [I] —**rider** *n* : *Your car was taken by joyriders, sir, and dumped a few miles away.*

joy·stick /'dʒɔɪˌstɪk/ *n* an upright handle moved to control the operation of something, esp. the movement of an aircraft: *the joystick of a video game* | *a computer joystick*

JP /ˌdʒeɪ 'piː/ *n* a Justice of the Peace; MAGISTRATE

Jr *written abbrev. for:* JUNIOR¹

JR /ˌdʒeɪ 'ɑːʳ/ J R Ewing, a character in the American television SERIES *Dallas* which was very popular in the US and Britain. JR was the oldest brother of the Ewing family and head of their oil company. Although he was RUTHLESS and deceitful, he was a very popular character. His fame spread even to people who did not watch the programmes, esp. when someone tried to kill him, and "Who shot JR?" became a popular phrase. —see also DALLAS

Juan Car·los /ˌhwɑːn 'kɑːlɒs‖-'kɑːrlɒus/, **King** (1938–) the King of Spain since 1975, responsible for introducing DEMOCRACY to Spain after the DICTATORSHIP of Franco

jub·i·lant /'dʒuːbɨlənt/ *adj* filled with or expressing great joy, esp. at a success: *The team were jubilant after their victory in the Cup.* | *jubilant shouts* — ~ **ly** *adv*

ju·bi·la·tion /ˌdʒuːbɨ'leɪʃən/ *n* [U] great joy; REJOICING: *There was jubilation in the winning team's home town.*

ju·bi·lee /'dʒuːbɨliː, ˌdʒuːbɨ'liː/ *n* (a special occasion marking) the return of the date of some important event —see also DIAMOND JUBILEE, GOLDEN JUBILEE, SILVER JUBILEE

Ju·dah /'dʒuːdə/ in the Bible, a son of Jacob

Ju·da·is·m /'dʒuːdeɪ-ɪzəm, 'dʒuːdə-‖'dʒuːdə-, 'dʒuːdi-/ *n* [U] the religion of the Jews; the religion based on the Old Testament of the Bible, the Talmud, and the later teachings of the RABBIS. Judaism is the oldest religion with one God, and both Christianity and Islam are descended from it. Jews believe that God made an agreement with them to protect them if they served Him faithfully, obeyed his law, and recognized no other gods. The law is believed to have been given to Moses in the form of the Ten Commandments. The Jews came to believe in a Messiah after they had spent many years without a country of their own, but they do not agree with Christians that Jesus Christ was the true Messiah. Features of the religion today include keeping the Sabbath, celebrating Passover and other holy days, and eating KOSHER food, all of which have helped in the preservation of Judaism — see also ZIONISM /dʒuː'deɪ-ɪk/ *adj*

Ju·das /'dʒuːdəs/ **1** also **Judas Iscariot** in the Bible, the follower of Jesus who betrayed (BETRAY) him, leading to his ARREST and death. Judas received "thirty pieces of silver" for betraying Jesus —see colour picture on page 424 **2** *derog* a disloyal person who secretly helps the enemies of his friends; TRAITOR: *You Judas!*

jud·der /'dʒʌdəʳ/ also **jutter** *AmE*— *v* [I] *BrE* (esp. of a vehicle) to shake violently: *The driver pulled the emergency brake and the train juddered to a halt.*

Jude the Ob·scure /ˌdʒuːd ðɪ əb'skjuəʳ/ a book by Thomas Hardy, written in 1895. It is a very sad story, set in Wessex, about a young man's life.

judge¹ /dʒʌdʒ/ *v* **1** [T] to act as a judge in (a law case); TRY¹ (5): *Who will judge the next case?* **2** [I;T] to decide the result of (a competition) or give an official decision about (people or things taking part in a competition): *to judge a talent contest* | *to judge the exhibits at a flower show* **3** [I;T] to form or give an opinion about (someone or something), esp. after carefully considering all the information: *It seems like a good proposal, but without all the facts I can't really judge.* | *Try to judge the distance from here to that car.* | *Schools tend to be judged by the performance of their students in exams.* | **Judging by** *what everyone says about him, I'd say he has a good chance of winning.* [+*wh*-] *It's difficult to judge where the responsibility for the accident really lies.* | [+*that*] *The committee judged that the scheme was unlikely to produce an acceptable profit.* | [+*obj*+*adj/n*] *The scheme was judged (to be) unprofitable.*

judge² *n* **1** (*often cap.*) a public official who has the power to decide questions brought before a court of law: *a high-court judge* | *The judge sentenced her to 12 months' imprisonment.* | *Judge Jeffreys* —see colour picture on page 751 and see also extra information on page 742

▶ CULTURAL NOTE In Britain judges of the High Court are chosen by the Lord Chancellor from BARRISTERS. SOLICITORS who have more than 13 years' experience can be appointed as judges in the Crown Court and County Court. In the US, Supreme Court judges are chosen by the president and must be approved by the Senate. Many judges in the lower courts are elected by the people.◀

2 a person who has been appointed to decide the result of a competition: *The panel of judges included several well-known writers.* **3** [(of)] a person who has the knowledge and experience to give valuable opinions: *I'm no judge of music, but I know what I like.* | *She's a good judge of character.* | *I don't like this wine — not that I'm any judge.*

judg·ment, judgement /'dʒʌdʒmənt/ *n* **1** [U] the ability to make decisions that are based on careful consideration of facts, principles, etc.: *a man of sound/weak judgment* | *Her decision seems to show a lack of political judgment.* | *an error of judgment* | *I can't decide for you; you'll have to use your own judgment.* | *He did the right thing, but more by luck than judgment.* **2** [C] an opinion: *to form a judgment* | *In my judgment, we should accept the employer's offer.* | *I let him go, against my better judgment.* (=although I knew it was probably a mistake) **3** [C;U (on)] an official decision given by a judge or a court of law: *He passed* (=gave) *judgment on the guilty man.* | *an impartial judgment* **4 sit in judgment on** to take the responsibility of judging (a person or their behaviour), esp. in order to find fault: *You have no right to sit in judgment on her; you'd probably have done exactly the same thing if you'd been in her position.* —see also VALUE JUDGMENT

judg·men·tal, judgemental /dʒʌdʒ'mentl/ *adj often derog* too quick to form (usu. moral) judgments; moralistic: *His parents tend to be quite judgmental about his friends.*

judgment day /'·· ·/ also **day of judgment, last judgment**— (*often cap.*) (according to various religions, esp. Christianity) the day when, after the world has come to an end, God will judge everyone for the things they have done in life, and the dead will also rise up and be judged on their lives' actions

ju·di·ca·ture /'dʒuːdɨkətʃəʳ/ *n* **1** [*the*+S+*sing./pl. v*] the judiciary **2** [U] *fml* the power of giving justice in a court of law

ju·di·cial /dʒuː'dɪʃəl/ *adj* of or related to a court of law, judges, or their judgments: *a judicial decision/ruling* | *to bring/take judicial proceedings* —compare JUDICIOUS, LEGISLATIVE — ~ **ly** *adv*

ju·di·ci·a·ry /dʒuː'dɪʃəri‖-ʃieri, -ʃəri/ *n* [*the*+*sing./pl. v*] all the judges in the courts of law, considered as one group, and forming one of the branches of government: *The judiciary has/have been consulted.* —compare EXECUTIVE² (2), LEGISLATURE

ju·di·cious /dʒuː'dɪʃəs/ *adj fml* having or showing the ability to form sensible opinions, make sensible decisions, etc.; PRUDENT: *a judicious choice/move* —compare JUDICIAL — ~ **ly** *adv* — ~ **ness** *n* [U]

ju·do /'dʒuːdəʊ/ *n* [U] a type of self-defence from the Far East, based on holding and throwing one's opponent, often practised as sport: *a black belt at judo* | *judo lessons*

Judy see PUNCH AND JUDY SHOW

jug¹ /dʒʌg/ *n* **1** [C] *BrE* | **pitcher** *AmE*— **a** a container for holding liquids that has a handle and a lip for pouring: *a glass/earthenware jug* **b** also **jugful** /-fʊl/— the amount a jug will hold: *two jugs/jugfuls of water* —see picture on page 711 **2** [C] *AmE* **a** a pot for holding liquids that has a narrow opening at the top that can usu. be closed with a CORK **b** also **jugful**— the amount this will hold **3** [(*the*)] U] *old-fash BrE sl* prison: *He's back in (the) jug again.*

jug² *v* **-gg-** [T] *BrE* to cook (meat, esp. HARE) in liquid in a closed pot: *jugged hare*

jug·ger·naut /'dʒʌgənɔːt‖-ər-/ *n* **1** *BrE infml, usu. derog* a very large heavy TRUCK that carries loads over long distances **2** a great force or object that destroys everything it meets

jug·gle /'dʒʌgəl/ *v* [I (**with**);T] **1** to keep (several objects) in the air at the same time by throwing them up quickly and catching them again: *His favourite party trick is juggling with plates.* **2** to arrange or deal with (something) cleverly, esp. in order to deceive: *By juggling (with) the figures, they gave the impression that the company had made a profit.* —**gler** *n*

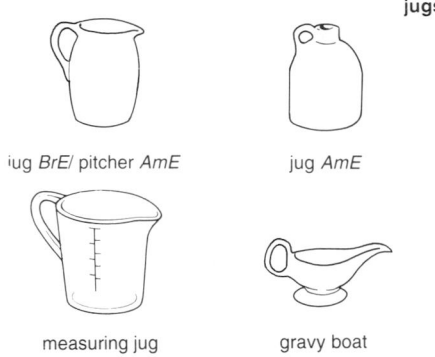

jugs

iug *BrE*/ pitcher *AmE*   jug *AmE*

measuring jug   gravy boat

jug·u·lar /ˈdʒʌɡjʊ̈ləʳ/ *n* **1** a jugular vein **2 go for the jugular** *infml* to attack very fiercely so as to cause as much hurt or damage as possible: *When threatened with the sack he really went for the jugular, accusing his boss of lying and corruption.*

jugular vein /ˌ··· ˈ·/ *n* [*usu. sing.*] either of two large tubes in the body, one on each side of the neck, that take blood from the head back to the heart

juice¹ /dʒuːs/ *n* **1** [C;U] the liquid from fruit, vegetables, or meat: *Is this orange juice sweetened or unsweetened?* | *a carton of tomato juice* **2** [C *usu. pl.*;U] the liquid in certain parts of the body, esp. the stomach, that helps people and animals to use (DIGEST) food: *digestive/gastric juices* **3** [U] *sl* something that produces power, such as electricity, gas, or petrol: *Our car uses a lot of juice.*

juice² *v*
  juice sthg. ↔ **up** *phr v* [T] *AmE infml* to give more life, excitement, fun, etc., to

juic·y /ˈdʒuːsi/ *adj* **1** containing a lot of juice: *a juicy orange* | *a juicy steak* **2** *infml* interesting, esp. because providing information about bad behaviour: *I want to hear all the juicy details of the scandal!* **3** *infml* desirable, esp. because likely to produce a lot of money: *a fat juicy contract that will make us all rich* —**iness** *n* [U]

ju·jit·su, jiujitsu /ˌdʒuːˈdʒɪtsuː/ *n* [U] a type of fighting and self-defence from the Far East in which one holds, throws, and often hits one's opponent

ju·ju /ˈdʒuːdʒuː/ *n* [C;U] (the power of) a magic charm in West Africa

ju·jube /ˈdʒuːdʒuːb/ *n* a small jelly-like sweet, often with throat medicine added

juke·box /ˈdʒuːkbɒks‖-baːks/ *n* a music machine, found in places of entertainment, PUBS, etc., which plays records when a coin is put into it

ju·lep /ˈdʒuːlɪp/ also **mint julep**— *n* an American drink in which alcohol and sugar are mixed and poured over ice, and MINT³ is added. Americans connect this drink with summertime and the South, where it is popular. It is a custom to drink it while watching the Kentucky Derby.

Ju·li·et /ˈdʒuːliət/ **1** the female lover in Shakespeare's play *Romeo and Juliet* —see also ROMEO AND JULIET and see colour picture on page 1146 **2** the female half of any COUPLE in love: *She was his Juliet.*

Ju·li·us Cae·sar /ˌdʒuːliəs ˈsiːzəʳ/ a play by William Shakespeare, in which the Roman leader Julius Caesar is murdered. One of the murderers is his friend, Brutus, who thinks Caesar is taking too much power. After his death, his friend Mark Antony makes a famous speech to the crowd beginning with the words "Friends, Romans, countrymen, lend me your ears". —see also Mark ANTONY, BRUTUS, Julius CAESAR, and see colour picture on page 1146

Ju·ly /dʒʊˈlaɪ/ (*written abbrev.* **Jul.**) *n* [C;U] the seventh month of the year, between June and August: This office

opened in July 1991. | She started work here last July/the July before last.

▶CULTURAL NOTE People connect July with summer, warm weather, and the start of the long school holidays. In the US, 4th July is Independence Day.◀

jum·ble¹ /ˈdʒʌmbəl/ *v* [T (UP, TOGETHER) *often pass.*] to mix in disorder: *Various books and papers were jumbled up/jumbled together on her desk.*

jumble² *n* **1** [S (of)] a disorderly mixture (of things or ideas): *a jumble of confused ideas* **2** [U] *BrE* unwanted things suitable for a jumble sale

jumble sale /ˈ·· ·/ *BrE* ‖ **rummage sale** *AmE*— *n* a sale of used articles as a way of collecting money for a good purpose, e.g. to help a hospital or a school: *We're holding a jumble sale to raise money for the famine victims.*

jumble sale

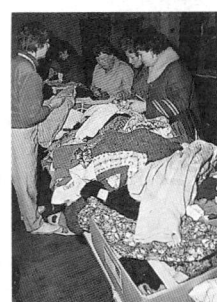

jum·bo /ˈdʒʌmbəʊ/ also **jumbosized** /ˈ·· ·/— *adj* [A] *infml* larger than others of the same kind: *a jumbo-sized plate of ice cream*

Jumbo a name for an ELEPHANT, as used by children, and in stories and songs

jumbo jet /ˌ·· ·/ also **jumbo** *infml*, **747**— *n* a very large passenger aircraft built by the Boeing Corporation

jump¹ /dʒʌmp/ *v* **1** [I] to push oneself into the air or away from a surface by the force of one's legs; spring: *The children jumped up and down.* | *I jumped over the wall/out of the window/into the river.* | *She jumped to her feet and ran out of the room.* | *We managed to jump clear of the car before it hit the wall.* **2** [T] to cross or go over by jumping: *He jumped the stream.* | *The horse jumped the fence.* **3** [I] to make a quick sudden movement as a result of strong feeling: *His heart jumped when he heard the news.* | *I nearly jumped out of my skin when I saw the snake under my bed.* **4** [I+adv/prep] to move suddenly from one point to another, often missing out what comes in between: *Her lecture was hard to follow because she kept jumping from one subject to another.* | *I jumped (ahead) to the last section of the report to see what the committee had recommended.* **5** [I] (esp. of money or quantity) to rise suddenly and by a large amount: *The price of oil jumped sharply in 1973.* | *Their profits jumped from £3.5 million to £22 million in a single year.* **6** [T] *infml* to leave, pass, or escape from (something) illegally or without permission: *One of the sailors* **jumped ship** *at Gibraltar.* | *to jump the (traffic) lights* | *to jump bail* **7** [T] *infml, esp. AmE* to travel on (a train) without paying: *He jumped a freight (train) in Texas.* **8** [T] *infml* to attack suddenly: *A gang of youths jumped me in the park.* **9** [T] JUMP-START **10 jump a claim** *esp. AmE* to try to claim valuable land which someone else already owns **11 jump down someone's throat** *infml* to attack someone in words, strongly and unexpectedly, esp. before they have finished talking **12 jump rope** *AmE for* SKIP¹ (5) **13 jump the gun** *infml* to take action too soon or before the proper time: *I know he's a suspect, but isn't it jumping the gun a bit to arrest him immediately?* **14 jump the queue** *BrE* ‖ **cut in line** *AmE* to obtain an unfair advantage over others who have been waiting longer **15 jump to it** *infml* to hurry: *You'll have to jump to it if you want to catch the train.*
  jump at sthg. *phr v* [T] to accept eagerly: *She jumped at the chance to go abroad.*
  jump on sbdy. *phr v* [T] *infml* to speak to sharply, showing disapproval, esp. unfairly: *She jumps on me every time I make the slightest mistake.*

jump² *n* **1** an act of jumping: *a good jump* **2** a thing to be jumped over: *The horse cleared all the jumps.* **3 be/stay one jump ahead** *infml* to do the right thing because one knows or guesses what one's competitors are going to do —see also HIGH JUMP, LONG JUMP, RUNNING JUMP

jump ball /ˈ· ·/ *n* (in BASKETBALL) an action at the beginning of a game and at some times during it in which the ball is thrown into the air by the REFEREE (judge) and one player from each team jumps to gain control of it

jumped-up /ˌ·ˈ·◂/ *adj* [A] *infml derog, esp. BrE* having too great an idea of one's own importance, esp. because of having just risen to a higher position or higher social class

jump·er /ˈdʒʌmpəʳ/ *n* **1** a person or animal that jumps **2** *BrE* ‖ **sweater** *AmE* a woollen garment for the top half of the body **3** *AmE* a dress without SLEEVEs, usu. worn over a BLOUSE

jumper ca·bles /ˈ·· ˌ··/ *n* [P] *AmE for* JUMP-LEADS

jumping-off place /ˌ··· ˈ· ˌ·/ also **jumping-off point**— *n* a point to start from, esp. at the beginning of a journey or plan

jump-jet /ˈ· ·/ *n esp. BrE* a JET aircraft which can take off and land straight from or onto the ground, without needing a long RUNWAY —see also HARRIER JUMP JET

jump-lead /ˈdʒʌmp liːd/ *n* [P] *BrE* ‖ **jumper cables** *AmE* thick wires used to connect the batteries (BATTERY (1)) of two cars in order to jump-start one of them

jump shot /ˈ· ·/ *n* (in BASKETBALL) a throw of the ball towards the basket in which the player jumps before throwing the ball

jump-start /ˌ· ˈ·/ *v* [T] to start (a car) using the power of the BATTERY from another car

jump-suit /ˈdʒʌmpsuːt, -sjuːt‖-suːt/ *n* a one-piece garment combining top and trousers

jump·y /ˈdʒʌmpi/ *adj* nervously excited, esp. because of guilt or because one is expecting something bad to happen —**·ily** *adv* —**·iness** *n* [U]

junc·tion /ˈdʒʌŋkʃən/ *n* a place where things join or come together: *a busy railway junction where lines from all over the country meet* | *at the junction of Vine Street and Gordon Road*

junc·ture /ˈdʒʌŋktʃəʳ/ *n fml* a particular point in time or in a course of events: *At this critical juncture in the negotiations we must be careful not to upset the other side.*

June /dʒuːn/ (*written abbrev.* **Jun.**) *n* [C;U] the sixth month of the year, between May and July: *It happened on June the second|on the second of June|(AmE) on June second.* | *This office opened in June 1991.* | *She started work here last June|the June before last.*

▶CULTURAL NOTE People connect June with the beginning of summer, warm weather, and events in Britain such as Wimbledon, Ascot, etc.◀

Ju·neau /ˈdʒuːnəʊ/ the capital city of Alaska, US

Jung /jʊŋ/, **Carl Gus·tav** /kɑːl ˈɡʊstɑːv‖kɑːrl ˈɡʌs-/ (1875–1961) a Swiss PSYCHIATRIST who worked with Sigmund Freud, and studied the importance of dreams and religion in problems of the mind —**ian** *adj* : *Jungian analysis*

Jung·frau /ˈjʊŋfraʊ/ [*the*] a mountain in the Swiss Alps, in SW central Switzerland

jun·gle /ˈdʒʌŋɡəl/ *n* **1** [C;U] a tropical forest too thick to walk through easily: *the jungles of South America* | *jungle animals* | *jungle warfare* | (fig.) *Your garden's a bit of a jungle.* **2** [C] a disorderly mass of things that is hard to understand: *the jungle of tax laws* —compare FOREST; see also CONCRETE JUNGLE, LAW OF THE JUNGLE

Jungle Book /ˈ·· ˌ·/, **The** a book of stories by Rudyard Kipling, about a young boy called Mowgli who is brought up in the jungle by animals, such as Baloo the bear and Bagheera the PANTHER. It was made into a successful CARTOON film by Walt Disney.

jungle gym /ˈ·· ˌ·/ *n AmE for* CLIMBING FRAME

ju·ni·or /ˈdʒuːniəʳ/ *n, adj* [(to)] **1** (someone) who is younger: *He is my junior (by several years).* —compare SENIOR (1) **2** (someone) of low or lower rank: *a very junior officer|minister* | *He is junior to me, though he's older.* | *a junior partner in a law firm* —compare SENIOR (2) **3** *BrE* a pupil at a JUNIOR SCHOOL **4** *AmE* (a student) of the third year in a four-year course at HIGH SCHOOL or university —compare FRESHMAN, SENIOR, SOPHOMORE and see MAJOR (USAGE)

Junior¹ (*written abbrev.* **Jr** or **Jnr**) *adj* [after *n*] *esp. AmE* the younger, esp. of two men in the same family who have exactly the same name: *Martin Luther King Junior* —compare SENIOR

Junior² *n* (a name for) one's son: *Bring Junior to the party.* | *Come here, Junior.*

junior col·lege /ˌ··· ˈ··/ *n* [C;U] a college in the US or Canada where the students study for two years for an ASSOCIATE DEGREE —see also DEGREE (3)

junior high school /ˌ··· ˈ· ·/ also **junior high, intermediate school** *n* (in the US) a school for children aged 12 and 13, GRADES 7 and 8, attended after ELEMENTARY SCHOOL and before HIGH SCHOOL —see also HIGH SCHOOL; compare MIDDLE SCHOOL; see also extra information on page 408

junior school /ˈ··· ˌ·/ *n* [C;U] (in Britain) a school for children aged between 7 and 11 —see also extra information on page 408

ju·ni·per /ˈdʒuːnɪpəʳ/ *n* [C;U] a low bush with berries, whose prickly leaves remain green all year

junk¹ /dʒʌŋk/ *n* [U] **1** *infml* old or unwanted things, usu. of low quality or little use or value: *The attic was full of junk.* | *I bought this old table in* **a junk shop.** **2** *sl* a dangerous drug, esp. HEROIN —see also JUNKIE

junk² *v* [T] *infml* to get rid of as worthless: *We're going to have to junk these computers; they're obsolete.*

junk³ *n* a flat-bottomed Chinese sailing ship with square sails

junk bond /ˈ· ˌ·/ *n* an official document giving the owner the right to certain property, which may or may not be profitable and has a high risk. Junk bonds are bought and sold on the STOCK EXCHANGE, esp. to pay for an intended TAKEOVER.

Jun·kers /ˈjʊŋkəz‖-kərz/, **Hugo** (1859–1935) a German aircraft builder. His planes were used by the Germans in the Second World War.

jun·ket /ˈdʒʌŋkɪt/ *n* **1** [C] *infml, esp. AmE, often derog* a trip or journey, esp. one made by a government official and paid for with government money: *off on a junket* **2** [U] milk thickened by adding an acid, sweetened, and often given a particular taste

jun·ket·ing /ˈdʒʌŋkɪtɪŋ/ *n BrE infml* **1** [C;U] (a) happy social gathering with lots of eating and drinking **2** [U] going on a trip or journey, esp. paid for with government money

junk food /ˈ· ·/ *n* [U] *infml* bad quality unhealthy food, esp. chemically treated food containing a lot of sugar, fat, and CARBOHYDRATEs —compare HEALTH FOOD

junk·ie, junky /ˈdʒʌŋki/ *n sl* a person who habitually takes a drug such as HEROIN and is dependent on it: (fig.) *I'm a real sugar junkie.*

junk mail /ˈ· ·/ *n* [U] *derog* mail, usu. for advertising, that is sent to people who have not asked for it, which some people find very annoying

junk·yard /ˈdʒʌŋkjɑːd‖-jɑːrd/ *n AmE* **1** TIP⁴ (1) **2** a place where old or unwanted items can be left, bought and sold

Ju·no /ˈdʒuːnəʊ/ in CLASSICAL MYTHOLOGY, the Roman goddess of women and marriage, wife of Jupiter (Greek name Hera)

Ju·no·esque /ˌdʒuːnəʊˈesk◂/ *adj sometimes humor* (of a tall woman) graceful and attractive

jun·ta /ˈdʒʌntə, ˈhʊntə ‖ ˈhʊntə/ *n* [C+*sing./pl. v*] *often derog* a government, esp. a military one, that has come to power by force rather than through elections

Ju·pi·ter /ˈdʒuːpɪtəʳ/ **1** the largest PLANET, fifth in order from the sun —see picture at SOLAR SYSTEM **2** in CLASSICAL MYTHOLOGY, the king and ruler of the Roman gods. He was god of the sky and the weather, and threw THUNDERBOLTs (imaginary weapons that cause thunder and lightning when they are thrown) when he was angry; Greek name Zeus

Ju·ra /ˈdʒʊərə/ [*the*+P] a range of low mountains along the border between France and Switzerland

ju·rid·i·cal /dʒʊəˈrɪdɪkəl/ *adj fml* of or related to the law or judges

jur·is·dic·tion /ˌdʒʊərɪsˈdɪkʃən/ *n* [U] the right to use the power of an official body, esp. in order to make decisions on questions of law: *The prisoner refused to accept the jurisdiction of the court.* | *That area does not fall within the jurisdiction of the city health authority.* | *The UN court has no jurisdiction over non-members.*

ju·ris·pru·dence /ˌdʒʊərɪsˈpruːdəns/ *n* [U] *fml* the science or study of law

ju·rist /ˈdʒʊərɪst/ *n fml* a person with a thorough knowledge of law; a legal EXPERT —compare JUROR

ju·ror /ˈdʒʊərəʳ/ also **ju·ry·man** /ˈdʒʊərimən/ masc, **ju·ry·wom·an** /-ˌwʊmən/fem.— n a member of a jury — compare JURIST

ju·ry /ˈdʒʊəri/ n [C+sing.|pl. v] **1** a group of usu. 12 people chosen to hear all the details of a case in a court of law and give their decision on it: The jury has|have returned (=given) a verdict of guilty. | There were eight women on the jury. | the jury's still out (=is still deciding) —see also extra information on page 742 **2** a group of people chosen to judge a competition: Now let's ask the jury to pick the winners of the song contest. —see also GRAND JURY

jury box /ˈ·· ·/ n the place where the jury sit in a court — see colour picture on page 751

jury ser·vice /ˈ·· ˌ··/ BrE ‖ **jury duty** esp. AmE— n [U] service as a member of a jury, a duty which every adult is supposed to do if called, except when there are reasons why they cannot (by itself, work is not a good enough reason): I've been called up to do jury service.

▶ CULTURAL NOTE In MAINLAND Britain anyone between the ages of 18 and 65 who has lived in Britain for five years since the age of 13 can be called on for jury service, except people such as judges and priests, and anyone from Northern Ireland. In the US, anyone who is able to vote can be called upon to serve on a jury or grand jury. ◀

just¹ /dʒəst; strong dʒʌst/ adv **1** exactly: She was sitting just here. | He arrived just as I was leaving. | That's just what I wanted. (compare That's not quite what I wanted.) | She looks just like her mother. | He makes just as much money as you do. | Just what do you mean by that remark? (shows annoyance) | The accident was serious, but we can't yet tell just how serious. | That's **just my luck!** (=exactly the sort of bad luck I always have) | That ladder is **just the thing** (=exactly what is needed) for picking apples. **2** only; no more than: Just a little more, please. | She's just a child. | Just a moment! (=Wait a moment!) | I don't want any dinner, just coffee. | Answer me, don't just stand there laughing! | Just listen to this! (used to make a command stronger) **3 a** only a short time ago; only now and no sooner: You're too late; the train's just left. | I've just been reading a very interesting book. | I'd just got into bed when the phone rang. | (BrE) It's just gone 8 o'clock. | (AmE) It just turned 8 o'clock. —see USAGE **b** starting to; on the point of: I'm just coming. | He's just about to leave. **c** (with words about time) only a little: They left just before|just after Christmas. | It lasted just over two hours. **4** (often with **only**) almost not; hardly: The line is just over|just under three centimetres long. | The skirt comes just below my knees. | I can only just lift it. (=it's almost too heavy) | We got there just in time to save him. | He arrived on time, just. **5** in a way that offers no other choice or possibility; simply: If you can't come tomorrow, we'll just have to postpone the meeting till next week. | I don't know where that book is — it seems to have just disappeared. **6** infml completely; very: That's just perfect. | Isn't that just beautiful! **7 just about** almost; very nearly: "Have you finished?" "Just about." | We were just about ready to leave when it started snowing. **8 just as soon** rather, prefer (to): I'd just as soon do it tomorrow. | I'd just as soon have the yellow one. **9 just as well: a** lucky or suitable: It's just as well I brought my coat — it's freezing in here! **b** (with **may**, **might**, etc.) with good reason, considering the situation: Since there's no more work to do, we might just as well go home. **10 just now: a** a moment ago: Paul telephoned just now. **b** at this moment: We're having dinner just now — can you come back later? **11** BrE just on nearly; almost exactly: just on 90 years ago | it's just on ten past six **12 just so** also **quite so**— BrE fml yes; I agree **13 just so** tidy; with everything in its proper place: I like my house to be just so. **14 just yet** [only in negatives] quite yet: I can't leave just yet. —see also **just the same** (SAME¹)

▷ USAGE **Just**, **already**, and **yet** were at one time not used with the simple past tense when speaking of time. But expressions like: The bell just rang. | I already saw him. | Did you eat yet? are common in informal American English. It is still considered more correct in British English to say The bell has just rung. | I've already seen him. | Have you eaten yet?◁

just² /dʒʌst/ adj **1** morally right and proper; fair: a just man|decision | I don't think you were being just in punishing him but not her. | It's only just that we should get some compensation. **2 get one's just deserts** to be treated as one deserves, esp. by being punished: Don't worry, he'll get his just deserts one of these days! — **~ly** adv : justly deserved criticism — **~ness** n [U]

jus·tice /ˈdʒʌstɪs/ n **1** [U] the quality of being just; fairness: They have at last received compensation, so justice has been done. (=they have been treated fairly) | He claimed — with justice — that he had not received his fair share. (=his claim was right) | I wouldn't dispute the justice of his remarks. —opposite **injustice**; see also POETIC JUSTICE **2** [U] the action or power of the law: The police do all they can to bring criminals to justice. (=catch them and bring them to be tried in court) | a court of justice

▶ CULTURAL NOTE Justice is often represented as a woman with her eyes covered, holding a sword in one hand and a pair of scales in the other. There is a very famous STATUE of this figure on the Old Bailey, the main court for criminal cases in London. ◀

3 [C] (often cap.) a judge in a law court: Mr Justice Smith (=a judge's official name) —see also CHIEF JUSTICE **4 do justice to someone/something** also **do someone/something justice**— to treat in a fair or proper way; get the best results from: She cooked a delicious dinner, but we couldn't really do it justice (=eat enough of it) because we'd eaten too much already. | She didn't do herself justice in the exam. (=did not answer the questions as well as she could have)

Justice of the Peace /ˌ··· ·ˈ·/, abbrev. **JP** n a person who judges less serious cases in small courts of law and, in the US, has the power to perform the marriage ceremony —see also MAGISTRATE

jus·ti·fi·a·ble /ˈdʒʌstɪˌfaɪəbəl/ adj that can be justified: justifiable pride —opposite **unjustifiable** —**bly** adv : justifiably angry

justifiable hom·i·cide /ˌ····· ·ˈ···/ n [U] an act of killing someone which is not against the law, e.g. when done by a policeman or person carrying out an official punishment

jus·ti·fi·ca·tion /ˌdʒʌstɪfɪˈkeɪʃən/ n [U] a good or proper reason for doing something: I know he's upset, but that is no justification for his rude behaviour. | What can be said **in justification of** their actions?

jus·ti·fied /ˈdʒʌstɪfaɪd/ adj **1** [(in)] having a good or proper reason: Is he justified in his criticisms? | I think I'm completely justified in asking for his resignation. **2** (of written or printed matter) having a straight edge where all the words line up: The right margin on this page isn't justified.

jus·ti·fy /ˈdʒʌstɪfaɪ/ v [T+obj|v-ing] **1** to give a good reason for; explain satisfactorily: How can you justify such an expense|justify spending so much money? | The government will find it difficult to justify this decision (to the public). **2** to be a good reason for: Nothing can justify such rudeness.

Just Sev·en·teen /ˌ· ··ˈ·/ a British magazine for teenage girls, containing photographic stories, articles on popular music, beauty, and other nonfiction matters, and a problem page

Just Wil·liam /ˌ· ˈ··/ a SERIES of story books for children by the English writer Richmal Crompton about William Brown, an 11-year-old schoolboy who has many adventures

jut /dʒʌt/ v -tt- [I+adv|prep, esp. OUT] to stick up or out further than the things around it; PROJECT: The balcony juts out over the sea. | mountains jutting into the sky

jute /dʒuːt/ n [U] a plant substance used for making rope and rough cloth

Jut·land /ˈdʒʌtlənd/ a piece of land in northern Europe belonging partly to Denmark and partly to Germany. There was a large naval battle there in the First World War.

ju·ve·nile¹ /ˈdʒuːvənaɪl‖-nəl, -naɪl/ adj **1** [A no comp.] esp. law of or for young people, no longer babies but not yet fully grown: a juvenile court **2** childish and foolish: his juvenile sense of humour

juvenile² n fml or tech **1** a young person, no longer a baby but not yet fully grown **2** an actor or actress who plays such a person: She was getting a bit too old to be the juvenile lead.

juvenile de·lin·quent /ˌ···· ·ˈ··/ n a child or young person who shows no concern for other people or behaves in a criminal way. Young people (below the age of 18) who misbehave or are criminals are not put in prison but may be sent to a special school to be educated or trained, to try to prevent them offending again. In court they are usu. tried **as a juvenile** rather than as an adult and the court uses different rules for them. —**juvenile delinquency** *n* : *an increase in juvenile delinquency*

Ju·ven·tus /juːˈventəs/ an Italian football team, based in Turin

jux·ta·pose /ˌdʒʌkstəˈpəʊz‖ˈdʒʌkstəpəʊz/ *v* [T] *fml* to place side by side or close together: *We tried to juxtapose the sculptures to give the best effect.* —-**position** /ˌdʒʌkstəpəˈzɪʃən/ *n* [U]

JVC /ˌdʒeɪ viː ˈsiː/ a Japanese company making electronic products, such as VIDEOS, CD players, etc.

K

K¹ /keɪ/ **K's, k's** or **Ks, ks** the 11th letter of the English alphabet

K² written abbrev. for: **1** 1024 BYTEs of computer DATA: *a computer with a 128 K memory* —see also KILOBYTE **2** infml one thousand: *a £20K salary*

K2 /ˌkeɪ ˈtuː/ also **Mount Godwin Austen**— the second highest mountain in the world after Mount Everest, on the border between Kashmir and China

K-12 /ˌkeɪ ˈtwelv/ adj AmE connected with KINDERGARTEN and/or GRADES¹ (2) 1–12 of the American education system, which includes all education paid for by the government: *a K-12 teacher* (=able to teach any level from kindergarten to 12th grade): *the K-12 curriculum*

kaa·ba /ˈkɑːbə/ a small stone building in the court of the Great Mosque at Mecca. It contains a special black stone which Muslims believe to be holy, and which they turn to when they pray.

Ka·ba·la /kæˈbɑːlə/ n [U] the CABALA

ka·bob /kəˈbɑːb/ n AmE for KEBAB

Ka·bul /ˈkɑːbul/ the capital city of Afghanistan

kad·dish /ˈkædɪʃ‖ˈkɑː-/ n **-shim** /-dɪʃɪm/ [C;U] (often cap.) a prayer in praise of God, said in Jewish religious services and also by Jewish people when a member of the family has died: *saying Kaddish for their father*

kaf·fir /ˈkæfəʳ/ n SAfrE a black African. This word is used only by white people and is considered offensive to black people.

Kaf·ka /ˈkæfkə‖ˈkɑːf-/, **Franz** /frænts‖frɑːnts/ (1883–1924) a Czech writer who wrote in German, known for NOVELs such as *The Trial*, and short stories including *The Metamorphosis*, in which a man turns into a BEETLE (=a kind of insect). His stories are often SURREAL, and many deal with the struggle of people on their own against the state, large organizations, etc. — ~**esque** /ˌkæfkəˈesk‿/ adj

kaf·tan /ˈkæftæn‖kæfˈtæn/ n a CAFTAN

kail /keɪl/ n KALE

Kai·ser /ˈkaɪzəʳ/ n [(the)] (the title of) the king of Germany (between 1871 and 1918): *Kaiser Wilhelm was nicknamed "Kaiser Bill" by the Allied troops.*

Kal·a·ha·ri Des·ert /ˌkæləhɑːri ˈdezət‖-zərt/, **Kalahari** /ˌkælɔˈhɑːri‿/ [the] a large desert in southern Africa

ka·lam /kəˈlɑːm/ n [U] a school of Islamic religious belief

Ka·lash·ni·kov /kəˈlæʃnɪkɒf‖-kɔːf/ n a type of RIFLE¹ which can fire very rapidly, made in the former USSR. It has been sold to many countries in the Third World, and is often used by GUERRILLAS.

kale, kail /keɪl/ n [C;U] a dark green CABBAGE (=type of vegetable) with curled leaves

ka·lei·do·scope /kəˈlaɪdəskəup/ n **1** a tube with mirrors and pieces of coloured glass fitted inside at one end which shows many-coloured patterns when turned **2** a pattern or scene that has many different bright colours or details, often changing: *the fairground was a kaleidoscope of colour* | (fig.) *the kaleidoscope of European history*

ka·lei·do·scop·ic /kəˌlaɪdəˈskɒpɪk‿‖-ˈskɑː-/ adj (esp. of scenes and bright colours) changing quickly and often — ~**ally** /kli/ adv

kal·ends /ˈkælendz/ n [the+P] the first day of ancient Roman months

Ka·li /ˈkɑːli/ in Hindu MYTHOLOGY, a goddess of death and destruction

Ka·ma·su·tra, Kama Sutra /ˌkɑːmə ˈsuːtrə/ [the] an ancient Hindu book about love and marriage, known in the West esp. for its many suggested positions for sexual acts

kam·i·ka·ze¹ /ˌkæmɪˈkɑːzi‿/ n **1** one of a group of Japanese pilots (in the Second World War) who deliberately crashed on a military or naval TARGET, killing themselves as well as damaging the building, ship, etc. attacked. Kamikaze pilots were regarded as dying a hero's death in the service of their country. **2** an aircraft carrying explosives, used in such an attack

kamikaze² adj [A, no comp] **1** of or being a kamikaze: *a kamikaze pilot.* **2** seeming to take no care to protect one's own life: *a kamikaze driver*

kam·ma /ˈkɑːmə/ KARMA

Kam·pa·la /kæmˈpɑːlə‖kɑːm-/ the capital city of Uganda, on Lake Victoria

Kam·pu·che·a /ˌkæmpuˈtʃiːə/ a republic in SE Asia, formerly **Cambodia**; capital Phnom Penh. It was bombed by the US during the Vietnam War, and is known esp. in association with the leader Pol Pot (1975–79), during whose time in power 3 million people are believed to have died of hunger or been killed by the communist Khmer Rouge government. —see also KHMER REPUBLIC, VIETNAM WAR —**Kampuchean** n, adj

Kan·chen·jun·ga /ˌkæntʃənˈdʒʊŋgə‖ˌkɑːn-/ one of the world's highest mountains, on the border between India and Nepal

kan·ga /ˈkæŋgə/ n a woman's dress of African origin, consisting of a length of cloth wound round the body

kan·ga·roo /ˌkæŋgəˈruː‿/ n **-roos** or **-roo** an Australian animal which jumps along on its large back legs and which carries its young in a POUCH (=a special pocket of flesh)

kangaroo

pouch

kangaroo court /ˌ··· ˈ·/ n derog an unofficial court established by some members of a group to examine and usu. to punish other members of the same group: *The factory workers had set up/held a kangaroo court to try the men who'd refused to support the strike.*

Kan·sas /ˈkænzəs/ written abbrev. **KS** an American state in the Great Plains area of central US which produces large amounts of wheat —see colour map on pages 1374–5

Kansas Cit·y /ˌ·· ˈ··/ written abbrev. **KC 1** a city and port in W Missouri, USA **2** a city and port in NE Kansas, USA —see colour map on pages 1374–5

▶ CULTURAL NOTE When people in the US refer to Kansas City, they usu. mean Kansas City, Missouri. ◀

Kap·i·tal /kæpɪˈtɑːl/, **Das** /dæs/ a book written by Karl Marx, in which he described his theories of economics —see Karl MARX

Kant /kænt ‖ kɑːnt/, **Im·man·u·el** /ɪˈmænjuəl/ (1724–1804) a German PHILOSOPHER who believed that moral decisions must be based on reason, and wrote books arguing about the existence of God and about how we understand the world. His most important book is the *Critique of Pure Reason.* — ~**ian** adj

ka·o·lin /ˈkeɪəlɪn/ n [U] a fine white clay used for making cups, plates, etc., and also in medicine

ka·pok /ˈkeɪpɒk‖-pɑːk/ n [U] a very light cotton-like material used for filling soft things such as CUSHIONs

Ka·po·si's sar·com·a /kəˌpəuziz sɑːˈkəumə‖-ˌpəusiz sɑːr-/ n [U] a type of CANCER which people with AIDS often suffer from

ka·put /kəˈpʊt/ adj [F] sl broken; no longer able to be used: *The TV's kaput.*

Ka·ra·chi /kəˈrɑːtʃi/ a city in S Pakistan, formerly the capital and still the main port and industrial centre

Kar·a·jan /ˈkærəjɑːn‖ˈkɑː-/, **Herbert von** (1908–89) an Austrian CONDUCTOR and director of the Berlin Philharmonic Orchestra who made many musical recordings

kar·a·o·ke /ˌkæriˈəuki‖ˌkɑːrə-/ n **1** [C] a machine which plays recorded music that a person can sing to **2** [U] the practice of singing to recorded BACKING (3) music as a form of relaxation, usu. in a bar. Karaoke became very popular in British PUBs and American bars in the 1990s, having been introduced from Japan.

kar·at /ˈkærət/ n AmE a CARAT

ka·ra·te /kəˈrɑːti/ n [U] a style of fighting and self-defence from the Far East, including hitting with the hands and kicking

Ka·ri·ba Dam /kəˌriːbə ˈdæm/ [*the*] a DAM (=wall to keep back the water) across the Zambezi river in S central Africa, one of the world's largest dams

Kar·loff /ˈkɑːlɒf‖ˈkɑːrlɔːf, **Bor·is** /ˈbɒrɪs‖ˈbɔː-/ (1887–1969) a British actor known for his work in American HORROR FILMS, esp. as the MONSTER in *Frankenstein* in 1931

kar·ma /ˈkɑːmə‖-ɑːr-/ also **kamma–** *n* [U] **1** (in Hinduism and Buddhism) the force produced by a person's actions in life which will influence them later or in future lives. Bad actions in this life lead to being born again as a poor or unfortunate person or as an animal, but good ones lead to rebirth as a better or more fortunate person. **2** *infml* luck resulting from one's actions; fate: *bad karma* **–mic** *adj*

Kar·nak /ˈkɑːnæk‖ˈkɑːr-/ a village in Egypt where many TEMPLEs of the PHARAOHs have been found, esp. the Great Temple of Amon

Kash·mir /ˌkæʃˈmɪər/ a state on the NW border of India, which was divided in 1949 when India became independent. Part of Kashmir now lies in India and part in Pakistan, and there is often fighting between Hindus and Muslims who live there. **–Kashmiri** *n, adj*

Kath·e·rine of Ar·a·gon /ˌkæθərɪn əv ˈærəgən‖-gɑːn/ see CATHERINE OF ARAGON

Kath·man·du, Katmandu /ˌkætmænˈduː◂/ the capital city of Nepal, in the Himalayas

Ka·un·da /kɑːˈʊndə/, **Ken·neth** /ˈkenɪθ/ (1924–) a Zambian politician who became the first president of Zambia when it became an independent country in 1964

Ka·wa·sa·ki /kɑʊwəˈsɑːki/ *tdmk* a motorcycle made by the Japanese company Kawasaki

kay·ak /ˈkaɪæk/ *n* a light narrow covered boat, esp. as used by the Inuit or in sport **–aker** *n*

Kaye /keɪ/, **Dan·ny** /ˈdæni/ (1913–87) an American singer, actor, and COMEDIAN who appeared in many films, such as *The Secret Life of Walter Mitty* and *Hans Christian Andersen*

Ka·zakh·stan /ˌkæzækˈstɑːn/ a country in S central Asia, stretching from the Caspian Sea to China; capital Alma Ata; population 16,538,000 (1989)

Ka·zan /kəˈzɑːn/, **E·lia** /ˈiːljə/ (1909–) an American theatre and film director known for his work with the Group Theatre and for directing important plays such as *The Skin of Our Teeth*, *A Streetcar Named Desire*, and *Death of a Salesman*

ka·zoo /kəˈzuː/ *n* a simple musical instrument played by holding it in the lips and making sounds through it

KC /ˌkeɪ ˈsiː/ *abbrev. for* **1** KANSAS CITY **2** KENNEL CLUB **3** KING'S COUNSEL; (the title given, while a king is ruling, to) a British BARRISTER (=lawyer of high rank): *Sir Peter is a leading KC* | *Sir Peter Jones, KC* **–compare** QC **4** KNIGHTS OF COLUMBUS

Kea·ting /ˈkiːtɪŋ/, **Paul** (1944–) an Australian political leader, who became PRIME MINISTER in 1991

Kea·ton /ˈkiːtn/, **Buster** (1896–1966) an American actor and COMEDIAN known for his many silent films made in the 1920s

Keats /kiːts/, **John** (1795–1821) an English poet, a leading figure in the Romantic movement, known for poems such as *To Autumn* and *Ode to a Nightingale*, which are often studied in schools in Britain

ke·bab /kᵻˈbæb‖kᵻˈbɑːb/ *BrE* | **kabob** *AmE* – *n* a dish of small pieces of meat and usu. vegetables cooked on a stick, eaten as part of a Greek meal, or cooked on a BARBECUE

kedg·e·ree /ˈkedʒəriː/ *n* [U] a dish of rice, fish, and eggs mixed together

Kee·gan /ˈkiːgən/, **Kev·in** /ˈkevᵻn/ (1951–) an English footballer who played for Liverpool and other teams, as well as being captain of the England team

keel¹ /kiːl/ *n* **1** a bar along the bottom of a boat from which the whole frame of the boat is built up –see picture at YACHT **2 on an even keel** steady; without sudden changes: *We must try and get the company back on an even keel.*

keel² *v*

  keel over *phr v* [I] to fall over sideways: *The ship keeled over in the storm.* | *My drink must have been drugged; when I tried to stand up, I keeled over.*

Kee·ler /ˈkiːləʳ/, **Chris·tine** /ˈkrɪstiːn/ (1942–) an English model known for her part in the Profumo SCANDAL in 1963 –see PROFUMO SCANDAL

keen¹ /kiːn/ *adj esp. BrE* **1** [(on)] (of a person) having a strong, active interest in something; eager to do something: *a keen golfer/student of politics* | *She's keen on* (=likes) *football/growing roses.* | *He's very keen on the girl next door.* [F +*to-v*] *She's very keen to go.* | *Her father is keen for her to go to university.* **2** (of a competition or struggle) done with eagerness and activity on both sides; INTENSE: *There's been keen competition for the job.* **3** (of the mind, the feelings, the senses, etc.) good, strong, quick at understanding, etc.: *a keen mind* | *keen eyesight* **4** *lit* sharp: *a keen-edged sword* | (fig.) *a keen wind blowing from the east* **5 as keen as mustard** *infml, esp. BrE* a extremely eager **b** very quick to understand; clever – **~ly** *adv* **–~ness** *n* [U]

keen² *n* (in Ireland) a loud sad song or cry of grief for the dead **–keen** *v* [I]

keep¹ /kiːp/ *v* **kept** /kept/ **1** [T] to have without needing to give back: *You can keep it; I don't need it.* | *"The price is £4.50, sir." "Here's £5; keep the change."* **2** [T] to continue to have for some time or for more time; avoid losing: *Will you keep my place in the queue for me* (=prevent anyone else from taking it) *while I go and make a phone call?* | *These old clothes are not worth keeping.* | *I won't smoke the cigar now; I'll keep it for later.* | *I'll keep his address in case I need it.* | *He kept the chairmanship of the committee, despite strong opposition.* | *I think we should keep an open mind* (=not make a firm decision) *on this until we know all the facts.* | *She just managed to keep her temper.* (=not become angry) | *The police struggled to keep order.* **3** [T] to cause to remain or continue in a particular state or situation: [+*obj*+*adj/adv/prep*] *This coat will keep you warm.* | *This will keep the children amused.* | *The illness kept her in hospital/kept her away from work for six weeks.* | *I keep* (=store) *the plates in this cupboard.* [+*obj*+*v-ing*] *I'm sorry to keep you waiting.* (=to make you wait for a long time) | *They use computers to keep the traffic running smoothly.* **4** [I;L] **a** to continue to be in a particular place or condition; remain; stay: [+*adv/prep*] *Try to keep out of trouble.* | *Keep back! It may explode.* | *Keep off the grass.* | *Keep left when you get to the end of the street.* [+*adj*] *It's difficult to keep warm here.* | *Try to keep calm – there's nothing to worry about.* **b** [+ *v-ing*] to continue in an activity: *I wish you wouldn't keep (on) interrupting.* (=wouldn't make continuous interruptions) | *The children keep pestering me to take them to the zoo.* | *Keep going* (=do not stop) *till you reach the traffic lights.* **5** [T] to fulfil: *She kept her promise/word.* (=did what she promised she would do) | *My train was badly delayed, so I was unable to keep my appointment.* **6** [T (from)] to hold back; delay or prevent: *You're late; what kept you?* | *I know you're busy; I won't keep you (from your work).* | *Can't you keep your dog from coming into my garden?* – see also **keep the wolf from one's door** (WOLF) **7** [T] to know (a secret) without telling it: *She kept his secret for 15 years.* **8** [T] to make regular written records of or in: *Keep an account of what you spend.* | *Do you keep a diary?* **9** [T] to take care of and provide with food, money, etc.; support: *She kept her brother's children when he died.* **10** [T] to own and/or have the use of: *They keep chickens in their back garden.* | *She keeps* (=owns and runs) *a small shop.* | *You need to be very rich now to keep* (=employ) *servants.* **11** [I] (of food) to remain fresh and fit to eat: *This fish won't keep; we must eat it now.* | (fig.) *"I've got something to tell you!" "Won't it keep until* (=can't you tell me about it) *later?"* **12** [I+*adv*, esp. **well**] *old-fash infml* to be in the stated condition of health: *"How are you keeping?" "I'm keeping quite well, thank you."* **13** [T (from)] *fml* to guard; protect: *May God keep you (from harm)!* **14** [T] *old-fash* to behave suitably in relation to (an esp. religious day), meaning to perform all the usual customs, eat the usual foods etc., which have always been done/eaten on that day: *The Victorians certainly knew how to keep Christmas.* **15 keep (oneself) to oneself** not to mix with or talk to other people very much **16 keep one's shirt on** also **keep one's hair on** *BrE– infml* to remain calm; not to become upset or angry: *It was only a joke – keep your shirt on!* –see also **keep someone company** (COMPANY), **keep time** (TIME)

  keep around *phr v* [I] *infml* to keep something which may seem to have no value because it may be useful later : *I think I'll keep those old boots around in case we* go climbing. | *She wanted to sell the car but I told her to keep it around.*

keep (sbdy.) **at** sthg. *phr v* [T *no pass.*] *infml* to (force to) continue working at: *The work is tiring, but he'll keep at it until he's finished.* | *The teacher kept us at it all afternoon.*

keep sthg. ↔ **back** *phr v* [T] **1** not to tell; keep silent about; WITHHOLD: *She told them most of the story, but kept back the bit about her uncle.* **2** to keep (usu. some of something) in one's possession; RETAIN: *His employers kept back some of his wages to pay for the damage he'd done.*

keep sbdy./sthg. ↔ **down** *phr v* [T] **1** to control; prevent from increasing: *Chemicals are used for keeping insects down.* | *The government is trying to keep down inflation.* | *Would you keep it down* (=not make noise) *in there. I'm on the telephone.* **2** to keep in a state like slavery; OPPRESS **3** to prevent (food or drink) from passing back from the stomach through the mouth: *I can't keep this horrible medicine down.*

keep from *phr v* [T+*v-ing*] **1** (**keep** sthg. **from** sbdy.) not to tell (someone) about (something); prevent from hearing about: *We thought it best to keep the bad news from him.* **2** [+*v-ing*] (**keep from** sthg.) to prevent oneself from (doing something): *I could hardly keep from laughing.* —see also KEEP[1] (6)

keep sbdy./sthg. ↔ **in** *phr v* [T] to force (a person or animal) to stay inside, esp. a child in school as a punishment: *The whole class was kept in for being so noisy.*

keep in with sbdy. *phr v* [T] to (try to) remain friendly with, esp. for one's own advantage

keep off *phr v* [I;T (=**keep** sthg. ↔ **off**)] to (cause to) not come or happen: *Take a beach umbrella to keep the sun off.* (=to stop it shining on you) | *If the rain keeps off,* (=if it doesn't rain) *we'll go out.*

keep on *phr v* **1** [L+*v-ing*] to continue doing something: *Prices keep on increasing.* —see also KEEP[1] (4b) **2** [T] (**keep** sbdy./sthg. ↔ **on**) to continue to have or employ: *I'll keep the flat on through the summer.* | *Will you be able to keep your secretary on?* **3** [I (**about, at**)] *esp. BrE infml derog* to talk continuously: *He keeps on about his operation.* [+*to-v*] *His wife kept on at him* (=continually tried to persuade him) *to change his job.*

keep out *phr v* [I;T (=**keep** sbdy./sthg. ↔ **out**)] to (cause to) stay away or not enter: *Can't you boys read? The notice says "Keep out!"* | *Warm clothing will keep out the cold.* | *I try to keep out of* (=not become concerned with) *their family quarrels.*

keep to *phr v* [T] **1** (**keep to** sthg.) to follow closely or limit oneself to: *Don't raise irrelevant matters, we must try and keep to the subject.* | *Let's keep to the original plan.* **2** (**keep to** sthg.) to remain in the stated position or place: *Traffic in Britain keeps to the left.* | *He kept to his room for the first few days of term.* **3** (**keep** sthg. **to** sbdy.) to cause (something) to remain known only to (oneself): *I'm resigning — but keep it to yourself!*

keep up *phr v* **1** [T] (**keep** sthg. ↔ **up**) to prevent from falling or dropping: *a belt to keep my trousers up* | (fig.) *She kept up her spirits* (=remained cheerful) *by singing.* **2** [I;T (=**keep** sthg. ↔ **up**)] to (cause to) continue: *Keep up the good work!* | *Keep it up; don't stop now!* | *Will the fine weather keep up?* **3** [I (**with**)] to remain level: *I had to run to keep up (with the girls).* | (fig.) *I can't keep up with these changes in fashion.* (=they change too quickly for me to know about each one) **4** [T] (**keep** sbdy. **up**) *infml* to prevent from going to bed: *I hope I'm not keeping you up.* **5** [T] (**keep** sthg. ↔ **up**) to look after and keep in good condition: *How do you keep up this large house?* —see also UPKEEP **6 keep up appearances** to behave in an ordinary way when one is in difficulties, esp. when one has become poor, so as to persuade others that nothing is wrong **7 keep up with the Joneses** *derog* to compete with one's neighbours socially, esp. by buying the same expensive new things that they buy: *"Oh, she only bought those new curtains to keep up with the Joneses."*

keep with *phr v* [T] *AmE infml, old fash* to agree with (a practice or set of values): *I've kept with the Catholic faith all my life.* | *I don't keep with drinking.*

keep[2] *n* **1** [U] (the cost of providing) necessary goods and services, esp. food and lodgings: *She made her do odd jobs around the house to* **earn her keep**. **2** [C] a large strong tower, usu. in the centre of a castle —see also KEEPS

Keep A·mer·i·ca Beau·ti·ful /ˌ· ·ˌ··· ˈ···/ (the SLOGAN of) a

CAMPAIGN[1] (2) to encourage American people not to drop LITTER in the streets

keep-a·way /ˈ· ·ˌ·/ *n* [U] a game played by children in the US in which the object is to throw a ball between two people without letting a third person in the middle catch it

Keep Brit·ain Ti·dy /ˌ· ˌ·· ˈ··/ (the SLOGAN of) a CAMPAIGN[1] (2) to encourage British people not to drop LITTER in the streets

keep·er /ˈkiːpəʳ/ *n* (*often in comb.*) a person who guards, protects, or looks after: *The (zoo) keeper is feeding the animals.* | *a shopkeeper* | *a goalkeeper* —see also **Am I my brother's keeper?** (BROTHER)

keep fit /ˌ· ˈ·/ *n* [U] activities intended to keep one in good physical condition: *I go to keep fit on Thursdays.* | *She's really into keep fit.* —**keep-fit** *adj* [A] : *keep-fit classes*

keep·ing /ˈkiːpɪŋ/ *n* [(**in**) U] **1** the state of being looked after or guarded: *She left her jewellery in her sister's keeping.* | *Don't worry: your jewels are* **in safe keeping** (=being guarded carefully) —see also SAFEKEEPING **2 out of/in keeping (with something)** unsuitable/suitable (for something): *His silly jokes weren't really in keeping with the solemn occasion.*

keeps /kiːps/ *n* **for keeps** *infml* for ever: *He came home for keeps.*

keep·sake /ˈkiːpseɪk/ *n* something, usu. small, given (esp. in former times) to be kept in memory of the giver: *She gave him a lock of her hair as a keepsake.*

keg /keg/ *n* a small barrel, esp. for beer —see also POWDER KEG

keg·ger /ˈkegəʳ/ *n AmE* a big usu. outdoor party where beer is served from kegs

Keil·lor /ˈkiːlɔ̯ʳ/, **Garrison** (1942–) an American humorous writer, known esp. for *Lake Wobegon Days* and *Leaving Home*

Kei·tel /ˈkeɪtl/, **Wil·helm** /ˈvɪlhelm/ (1882–1946) a German army commander in the Second World War who signed Germany's SURRENDER in Berlin in 1945. He was hanged for war crimes.

Kel·ler /ˈkeləʳ/, **Hel·en** /ˈhelən/ (1880–1968) an American writer and social REFORMER, known esp. for the way she was taught to speak after becoming blind and DEAF as a baby

Kel·logg Pact /ˈkelɒg pækt‖-lɔːg/ [the] an international agreement, also called the **Kellogg-Briand Pact**, to settle arguments peacefully, without war or weapons. It was suggested by Aristide Briand, the French Foreign Minister, to Frank B. Kellogg, the US Secretary of State, and signed in 1928.

Kel·logg's /ˈkelɒgz‖-lɔːgz/ *tdmk* an American company, the best-known maker of breakfast CEREALs (2), esp. CORN-FLAKES, in the US and Britain

Kells /kelz/, **The Book of** an illuminated (ILLUMINATE (3)) Gospel written in the eighth century, at a MONASTERY in the town of Kells in the Republic of Ireland

Kel·ly[1] /ˈkeli/, **Gene** /dʒiːn/ (1912–) an American film actor, dancer, and director who appeared in many musicals of the 1940s and 50s, including *Singin' in the Rain*, in which he sang and danced to a song with the same name —see picture on page 685

Kelly[2], **Grace** (1928–82) an American film actress, star of *High Noon* and *High Society* in the 1950s, who became **Princess Grace of Monaco** when she married Prince Rainier

Grace Kelly

Kelly, Ned /ned/ (1854–80) an Australian armed robber who robbed banks and stole horses with his brother Daniel. In 1880 he was caught and hanged.

kelp /kelp/ *n* [U] a kind of large brown SEAWEED

kel·pie also **kelpy** /ˈkelpi/ *n ScotE* a water-spirit or devil often in the form of a horse, said to stay near water and enjoy drowning (DROWN) people

kel·vin /ˈkelvɪn/ n a unit of temperature —see TABLE 2

Kem·pis /ˈkempɪs/, **Thom·as à** /ˈtɒməs ə || ˈtɑː-/ (1380–1471) a German Augustinian MONK and religious writer

ken[1] /ken/ v -nn- [I;T+obj (that)] ScotE to know

ken[2] n **beyond one's ken** sometimes humor outside the limits of one's knowledge

ken·do /ˈkendəʊ/ n [U] an ancient Japanese fighting art, in which two people fight with long BAMBOO sticks, which they use like swords

Ken·nedy[1] /ˈkenɪdi/ also **JFK**— the main international airport serving New York

Kennedy[2], **Edward Moore** also called **Ted** /ted/ or **Teddy**— (1932–) a US SENATOR of the Democratic party, brother of John, who wanted to represent his party in the 1980 elections but failed, mainly because of his association with a car crash at Chappaquiddick in 1969 when his female passenger was drowned. He is known today esp. for his LIBERAL political opinions. —see also CHAPPAQUIDDICK

Kennedy[3], **Jackie** the wife of John Fitzgerald Kennedy — see picture on page 752

President John F. Kennedy and Jackie Kennedy

Kennedy[4], **John Fitzgerald** also called **Jack Kennedy**, **JFK**— (1917–63) the 35th president of the US (1961–63), a Democrat and the first Roman Catholic to be elected, who was shot and killed in Dallas, Texas by Lee Harvey Oswald. He was one of the four sons of Joseph Patrick Kennedy, all of whom entered politics. John F Kennedy is remembered for the Bay of Pigs INVASION of Cuba in 1961, and his programme of social change which was carried out by Lyndon Johnson after Kennedy's death. Kennedy was very popular and people were very sad when he was killed, although since that time many facts have appeared showing that his character and behaviour were not as good as they seemed. Many people can still remember what they were doing when they heard the news of his death, and many theories (THEORY) have been suggested which say that Oswald was not his killer. —see picture on page 752

Kennedy[5], **Ni·gel** /ˈnaɪdʒəl/ (1956–) a British musician who plays the VIOLIN. He is known for playing CLASSICAL and JAZZ music, and for his often informal way of dressing.

Kennedy[6], **Rob·ert Fran·cis** /ˈrɒbət ˈfrɑːnsɪs || ˈrɑːbərt ˈfræn-/ also **Bobby Kennedy** (1925–68) the brother of John F. Kennedy and also a political leader. He was killed in 1968 while trying to become president.

Kennedy Cen·ter /ˈ··· ˌ··/ [the] John F. Kennedy Center for the Performing Arts, the National Cultural Center of the US and the official MEMORIAL to President John F. Kennedy

ken·nel[1] /ˈkenl/ n **1** a small hut for a dog **2** AmE for KENNELS

kennel[2] v -ll- BrE || -l- AmE [T] to keep or put in a kennel or a kennels

Kennel Club /ˈ·· ·/ [the] written abbrev **KC** an organization of dog breeders which keeps records of the PEDIGREEs of all British pure-bred dogs, and decides what physical features each breed must have

ken·nels /ˈkenlz/ n kennels BrE a place where dogs **a** are looked after while their owners are away: They left their dog in a kennels when they went on holiday. **b** are bred (BREED[1] (2))

Ken·sing·ton and Chel·sea /ˌkenzɪŋtən ənd ˈtʃelsi/ a BOROUGH in W London just N of the river Thames. People think of Kensington and Chelsea as a place where rich and fashionable people live, but it also contains poorer areas, esp. in the northern part.

Kensington Gar·dens /ˌ··· ˈ··/ a park in London which was formerly the grounds of Kensington Palace. There is a STATUE of Peter Pan there.

Kensington Pal·ace /ˌ··· ˈ··/ an official royal RESIDENCE in London, rebuilt by Christopher Wren for William III, where Queen Victoria was born. Parts of it are open to the public.

Kent /kent/ a COUNTY in SE England, known as the "Garden of England" because of its fruit and vegetable crops

Kent, Bruce (1929–) an Englishman who was a Catholic priest, and then worked for the Campaign for Nuclear Disarmament. He has written about peace, Christianity, and giving up NUCLEAR weapons.

Kent, Clark an imaginary character from COMIC STRIPs and films. Clark Kent is a very ordinary, uninteresting man who works for a small newspaper as a REPORTER, but secretly he is also Superman. —see also SUPERMAN

Kent State /ˌ· ˈ·/ an event in 1970 when soldiers from the National Guard killed four students who were part of a large PROTEST MARCH against the Vietnam War at **Kent State University** in Ohio

Ken·tuck·y /kenˈtʌki || kən-/ written abbrev: **KY** a state in the American South, known as the Bluegrass State. It is known for country music and is an important producer of WHISKEY. —see colour map on pages 1374–5

Kentucky Der·by /ˌ·ˌ·· ˈ··/ [the] a famous race for three-year-old horses held each year on the first Saturday in May in Louisville, Kentucky

Kentucky Fried Chick·en /ˌ·ˌ·· · ˈ··/ tdmk (one of a group of shops selling) fried chicken sold as FAST FOOD. The company is originally American, but is now also very widespread in Britain. The chicken is described by the company's advertisements as being "finger-lickin' good".

Ken·wood /ˈkenwʊd/ a British firm which makes esp. food mixers and FOOD PROCESSORs

Ken·ya /ˈkenjə, ˈkiː-/ a country in E Africa, on the EQUATOR, which became independent in 1963 and which is known for production of coffee and tea; capital Nairobi; population 24,872,000 (1989) —**Kenyan** n, adj

Ken·yat·ta /kenˈjætə || -ˈjɑː-/, **Jo·mo** /ˈdʒəʊməʊ/ (about 1893–1978) a Kenyan politician, Prime Minister from 1963 and president from 1964 until his death. He was imprisoned for his association with the Mau Mau organization, and active in making Kenya independent from British rule.

Ke·ogh Plan /ˈkiːəʊ plæn/ in the US, a personal PENSION plan for self-employed people

Kep·ler /ˈkeplər/, **Jo·hann** /ˈjəʊhæn || -hɑːn/ (1571–1630) a German ASTRONOMER (=person who studies the stars) on whose ideas Isaac Newton's work was based

kept /kept/ past tense and past participle of KEEP

kept wom·an /ˌ· ˈ··/ n old use or humor a woman who is supplied with (money and) a place to live by a man who visits her regularly for sex

kerb BrE || **curb** AmE /kɜːb || kɜːrb/ n a line of raised stones (**kerbstones** /ˈkɜːbstəʊnz || ˈkɜːrb-/) or CONCRETE along the edge of a PAVEMENT, separating the pavement from the road —see picture at HOUSE

kerb craw·ler /ˈ· ˌ··/ BrE n a man looking for PROSTITUTEs, who follows women slowly in a car when they are walking along a street, usu. asking them to have sex with him —**kerb crawling** n [U]

ker·chief /ˈkɜːtʃɪf || ˈkɜːr-/ n old use a square piece of cloth worn to cover the head, neck, etc.

Kermit and Miss Piggy

ker·fuf·fle /kəˈfʌfəl || kər-/ n [C;U (**about**)] BrE infml (unnecessary and) noisy excitement; FUSS: There's been a tremendous kerfuffle about the plan to move the bus stop.

Ker·mit /ˈkɜːmɪt || ˈkɜːr-/ a PUPPET in the form of a FROG, who appears on British and American television in The Muppet Show and also in Sesame Street

Kern /kɜːn‖kɜːrn/, **Je·rome** /dʒəˈrəʊm/ (1885–1945) an American popular music COMPOSER and songwriter who wrote many songs and musical shows, e.g. *Showboat*, which included the famous song *Ol' Man River*

ker·nel /ˈkɜːnl‖ˈkɜːr-/ *n* **1** [C] the part of a nut, large grain, fruit stone, or seed, inside its hard covering –see picture at NUT **2** [S+of] *lit or fml* the important part of something, often surrounded by unimportant or untrue matter: *I think there's a kernel of truth in these otherwise frivolous comments.*

ker·o·sene, -sine /ˈkerəsiːn/ *n* [U] *AmE, AustrE, & NZE for* PARAFFIN

Ker·ou·ac /ˈkeruæk/, **Jack** (1923–69) an American writer who was a leading figure of the 1950s BEAT GENERATION. His books include *On the Road* and *Big Sur*.

Ker·ry /ˈkeri/ a COUNTY on the SW coast of the Republic of Ireland, popular with tourists because of its beautiful mountains and lakes

Kes·sel·ring /ˈkesəlrɪŋ/, **Albert** (1885–1960) a German military commander in the Second World War. He was found guilty of war crimes but later set free.

kes·trel /ˈkestrəl/ *n* a type of small FALCON

ketch /ketʃ/ *n* a small sailing ship with two MASTs

ketch·up /ˈketʃəp/ also **catsup** *esp. AmE* – *n* [U] a thick red liquid made from tomatoes (TOMATO), used for giving a pleasant taste to food. People sometimes make jokes about ketchup being used as artificial blood in plays, films, etc.

ket·tle /ˈketl/ *n* **1** a metal or plastic container with a lid, a handle, and a SPOUT (=a narrow curved mouth for pouring), used mainly for heating water: *Please* **put the kettle on** (=start heating it) | *an electric kettle* –see picture at KITCHEN **2** **a pretty/fine/different kettle of fish** *infml* a situation that is difficult or awkward, or different from what is expected: *She's not nervous about speaking to a lot of people, but speaking to a TV camera is a different kettle of fish.*

ket·tle·drum /ˈketldrʌm/ *n* a large metal musical drum with a round bottom, used in an ORCHESTRA –see TIMPANI

Kev·in /ˈkevɪn/ *BrE infml* a CHRISTIAN NAME for a man, used in Britain and the US. In Britain, it is often given as an example of a typical name of a young, WORKING-CLASS man with rough manners. –compare SHARON AND TRACEY

Kew Gar·dens /ˌkjuː ˈɡɑːdnz‖-ˈɡɑːr-/ a large park in the W of London, open to the public, where scientific study of plants is carried out and which contains plants from all over the world

key¹ /kiː/ *n* **1** a specially shaped piece of metal for locking or unlocking a door, winding a clock, starting and stopping a car engine, etc.: *I've lost the ignition key/the car keys* | *She put the key in the lock and turned it.* **2** [(to)] something that explains or helps one to understand: *There's a key underneath the diagram that explains the symbols.* | (fig.) *The discovery of the murder weapon provided the key to the mystery.* | (fig.) *The weather holds the key to our success or failure.* (=they depend on the weather) **3** any of the parts in a writing or printing machine or musical instrument that are pressed down to make it work: *the keys of a piano/a typewriter* –see picture at TYPEWRITER **4** a set of musical notes with a certain starting or base note: *a tune played in the key of C* | *I can't sing this – it's in too high a key for me.* | (fig.) *The police want to keep the operation in a fairly low key.* (=make it not very noticeable) –see also LOW-KEY

key² *v* [T (IN, into)] to put (information) into a machine such as a computer by using the KEYBOARD¹: *She keyed in all the new data.* –see also KEYED UP

 key *sthg.* to *sthg.* *phr v* [T *often pass.*] to make suitable to: *The course is keyed to the needs of school leavers.*

key³ *adj* very important; on which others depend: *a key position in the firm* | *key men/industries* | *a key issue in the forthcoming election* | *a key witness*

key⁴ *n* a small island, esp. one near the coast of Florida: *Key West* | *Key Largo* | *the Florida Keys*

Key, Francis Scott (1779–1843) the American writer of the song *The Star-Spangled Banner*, the national song of the US

key·board¹ /ˈkiːbɔːd‖-bɔːrd/ *n* **1** a row or several rows of keys on a musical instrument or a machine: *the keyboard*

of a piano/a typewriter/a computer –see picture at COMPUTER **2** *also* **keyboards** *pl* a musical instrument with a keyboard: *Sally plays keyboards in a rock group.*

keyboard² *v* [I;T] **1** to work the keyboard of (esp. a computer) **2** *also* **key–** to provide a machine with (information) by working a keyboard – ~ **er** *n*

keyed up /ˌ· ˈ·/ *adj* [F (about)] anxiously excited or nervous: *He's very keyed up about the exam.*

key·hole /ˈkiːhəʊl/ *n* a hole for a key, esp. in a door lock. People sometimes look through or listen at the keyhole to find out about something private that is taking place on the other side of a closed door.

key mon·ey /ˈ· ˌ··/ *BrE‖security deposit AmE–* *n* [U] money, additional to the rent and usual charges, sometimes demanded before a person is allowed to begin living in a flat or house

Keynes /keɪnz/, **John May·nard** /dʒɒn ˈmeɪnɑːd‖dʒɑːn ˈmeɪnɑːrd/ (1883–1946) a British ECONOMIST whose ideas on financial matters influenced much of the thought on ECONOMICS during the 20th century. His **Keynesian** ideas advised government action to increase demand and therefore employment.

key·note /ˈkiːnəʊt/ *n* **1** [(of)] the main point, which establishes a general situation: *The keynote of the discussion was concern for the jobless.* | *We'd invited a world-famous expert to give the keynote speech at the conference.* **2** the particular note on which a musical key is based

key·pad /ˈkiːpæd/ *n* **1** a small KEYBOARD which can be held in the hand, such as the ones used for REMOTE CONTROL of a television **2** part of the KEYBOARD of a computer, usu. on the right-hand side, that has keys (usu. of numbers) arranged separately from the letter keys

key·punch /ˈkiːpʌntʃ/ *n AmE for* CARDPUNCH – ~ **er** *n*

key ring /ˈ· ·/ *n* a ring or ring-shaped object on which keys are kept and carried, often with a FOB²

key sig·na·ture /ˈ· ˌ···/ *n tech* a mark in a system of musical writing that shows the key of a piece of music

key·stone /ˈkiːstəʊn/ *n* [*usu. sing.*] **1** the middle stone in the top of an arch, which keeps the other stones in position **2** [(of)] an idea, belief, etc., on which everything else depends: *Social justice is the keystone of their political programme.*

Keystone Kops /ˌ· ˈ·/ [*the* + P] a group of silly policemen in a set of British COMEDY films made in about 1920

key·stroke /ˈkiːstrəʊk/ *n* the action of pressing down and letting up a key on a TYPEWRITER or computer KEYBOARD¹: *I'll show you a way to perform that function using fewer keystrokes.*

Key West /ˌ· ˈ·/ an island off the coast of Florida, one of the Florida Keys, which is the point furthest south in the US. It is popular with tourists because of its fine weather, interesting buildings, and the unusual people who live there.

kg *written abbrev. for:* KILOGRAM(s)

KGB /ˌkeɪ dʒiː ˈbiː/ *n* [*the+sing./pl.v*] the secret police of the former USSR, responsible for state SECURITY in the Soviet Union and ESPIONAGE abroad

kha·ki /ˈkɑːki‖ˈkæki, ˈkɑːki/ *n* [U] **1** a yellow-brown colour **2** cloth of this colour, esp. as worn by soldiers –**khaki** *adj*

kha·kis /ˈkɑːkiz‖ˈkækiz, ˈkɑː-/ *n* [P] *AmE* trousers made of khaki –see USAGE NOTE at PAIR

kha·lif /ˈkeɪlɪf/ *n* a CALIPH

kha·li·fate /ˈkeɪlɪfeɪt/ *n* a CALIPHATE

khan /kɑːn/ *n* (*often cap.*) (a title of) a ruler or official in Asia

Khar·toum /kɑːˈtuːm‖kɑːr-/ the capital city of Sudan, known to many British people as the place where General Gordon was killed during a long battle in the 1880s

Khmer Re·pub·lic /ˌkmeə rɪ ˈpʌblɪk, kə ˌmeə- ‖ kə ˌmeər-/ [*the*] a former name (1970–75) of Kampuchea

Khmer Rouge /ˌkmeə ˈruːʒ, kə ˌmeə-‖kə ˌmeər-/ *n* [*the+sing./pl.v*] a military body which took over the government of Kampuchea in 1975 under the leader Pol Pot. Around 3 million Kampucheans are believed to have been killed under this government's rule. –see also KILLING FIELDS, POL POT

Kho·mei·ni /kɒˈmeɪni‖kəʊ-/, **Ayatollah** (1900–89) a political and religious leader of Iran from 1919 until his death who demanded the exact following of Islamic laws.

Ayatollah Khomeini

Khrush·chev /ˈkrʊstʃɒf‖ˈkrʌstʃef, -tʃɔːf/, **Ni·ki·ta** /nɪˈkiːtə/ (1894–1971) a political leader of the former USSR whose ideas replaced those of Stalin and led to the REVOLTs in Poland and Hungary in 1956 —see also BAY OF PIGS

Khy·ber Pass /ˌkaɪbə ˈpɑːs‖ -bər ˈpæs/ [the] a steep mountain pass joining Pakistan and Afghanistan, for centuries the main road to India from the west

kHz written abbrev. for: KILOHERTZ

kib·butz /kɪˈbʊts/ n -zim /sɪm/ or -zes a farm or settlement in Israel where many people live and work together. At one time, many young foreign people, esp. students, worked on kibbutzim for short periods.

ki·bosh /ˈkaɪbɒʃ‖-bɑːʃ/ n BrE **put the kibosh on** old-fash sl to put an end to (esp. a hope, plan, etc.); ruin

kick¹ /kɪk/ v **1** [T] to strike with the foot: The boy kicked the ball. | The horse kicked me. | (fig.) I could **kick myself** for making such a stupid mistake. | He kicked the chair over. | He kicked open the gate. | She kicked sand in my face. | She kicked a hole in the door. —compare HIT¹ (1) **2** [T] to SCORE by kicking: He kicked two penalty goals in the rugby match. **3** [I] to move the legs violently as if kicking something: Babies kick to exercise their legs. **4** [I] (of a gun) to move backwards violently when fired **5** [T] sl to stop or give up (a harmful activity): I'm trying to kick the habit. **6 kick against the pricks** BrE lit or fml to complain uselessly about something that cannot be changed **7 kick ass** AmE taboo sl to move very quickly: That new car he's got really kicks ass. **8 kick over the traces** BrE to free oneself from control; unexpectedly start to act wildly **9 kick someone in the teeth** infml to discourage or disappoint someone very much, esp. when they need support or hope **10 kick someone upstairs** infml to move someone to a job which appears more important than their present one, but which really has less power **11 kick the bucket** humor sl to die —see also **kick one's heels** (HEEL¹) – ~**er** n

kick about/around phr v infml **1** [=**kick about** sthg.)] to lie unnoticed or unused in (a place): That old typewriter has been kicking about the house for years. | "Where's my cap?" "Oh, it's kicking around somewhere." **2** [T] (**kick** sbdy./sthg. **about/around**) infml to treat roughly or give unnecessary orders to: " ... You won't have me to kick around any more." (Richard Nixon) **3** [T] (**kick** sthg. ↔ **about/around**) to talk about and compare informally: Let's kick around a few ideas and see if we can come up with a solution. **4** [T] (**kick about** sthg.) to travel in (a place) with no fixed plan: He's been kicking about Africa for years.

kick against/at sthg. phr v [T] to be strongly unwilling to obey or act in accordance with: At school he always kicked against authority.

kick in phr v AmE **1** [I;T **kick in** sthg.) CONTRIBUTE: We're going to buy Bob a present – do you want to kick in (something)? **2** [I] (to begin) to have an influence: I took a painkiller an hour ago, I wish it would kick in.

kick off phr v [I] to start a game of football: What time do we kick off? | (fig.) The lecturer kicked off (=began his talk) with a few jokes. —see also KICKOFF

kick sbdy. ↔ **out** phr v [T (of)] infml to remove or dismiss, esp. violently: He was kicked out of college for cheating in exams.

kick up sthg. phr v [T] infml to cause or make (trouble): He **kicked up a fuss/a row** about the broken furniture. (=complained forcefully about it)

kick² n **1** [C] an act of kicking: Give the door a good kick to open it. | I knocked him down and gave him a smart kick in the ribs for good measure. | He's so lazy; he could do with a good kick up the rear. **2** [C] sl a strong feeling

of excitement, pleasure, etc.: He **gets** some kind of **a kick out of** making her suffer. | She drives fast (just) **for kicks**. **3** [S;U] infml strength; power to produce an effect: This home-made whisky has a real kick to it. **4** [C] an extremely strong new interest: She's **on a health food kick** at the moment.

kick·back /ˈkɪkbæk/ n [C;U] sl money paid, usu. secretly or dishonestly, to someone in return for doing something: For arranging the contract he got a kickback of $20,000.

kick·ball /ˈkɪkbɔːl/ n [U] an American game with rules like BASEBALL, except that the ball is kicked rather than hit, and it may be thrown at a player to get him out

kick·box·ing /ˈkɪkbɒksɪŋ‖-bɑːk-/ n [U] an Oriental sport which allows punching (PUNCH¹ (1)), and kicking with bare feet —**kickboxer** n

kick·off /ˈkɪk-ɒf‖-ɔːf/ n the first kick of a game of football: The kickoff is at three o'clock today. —see also KICK off

kick·stand /ˈkɪkstænd/ n a metal rod fixed to a bicycle or MOTORCYCLE that can be folded down to make it able to stand by itself

kick-start /ˈ· ·/ also **kick-start·er** /ˈ· ˌ··/ – n a LEVER which is kicked down to start the engine of a motorcycle —**kick-start** v [T] : (fig.) The scheme to encourage more women into the workforce was kick-started last autumn with the launch of Opportunity 2000.

kid¹ /kɪd/ n **1** [C] infml a child: I'm taking the kids (=my children) to the zoo this afternoon. **2** [C] infml a young person: college kids | They're just kids; it's immoral to put them in uniform and send them out to be killed. —see CHILD (USAGE 2) **3** [C;U] (leather made from the skin of) a young goat

kid² v -dd- infml **1** [I; T] to deceive (someone), esp. playfully; joke: He's not really hurt: he's only kidding. | You're kidding!|You must be kidding (me)! (=I don't believe you!) | (humor) I kid you not. (=I'm telling you the truth) | Yes, it's true; no kidding! **2** [T] to make (oneself) believe something untrue or unlikely: [+obj+ (that)] He's been trying to kid himself that he's got a chance of winning. – ~**der** n

kid³ adj [A] infml, esp. AmE (of a brother or sister) younger: his kid sister

kid·die, -dy /ˈkɪdi/ n,adj infml (for) a small child: I carry my little boy in a kiddy seat on the back of my bike.

kid·dush /ˈkɪdəʃ/ n [U] a ceremonial blessing used in a Jewish home or SYNAGOGUE before eating bread or drinking wine on a holy day: to say kiddush

kid gloves /ˌ· ˈ·/ n [P] gentle methods of dealing with people (as if with gloves made of very soft leather): He's pretty angry; you'll have to handle him with kid gloves. —**kid-glove** /ˈ· ·/ adj [A] : kid-glove treatment

kid·nap¹ /ˈkɪdnæp/ v -pp- BrE ‖ -p- or -pp- AmE [T] to take (someone) away illegally and usu. by force, in order to demand esp. money for their safe return – ~**per** n : The boy's kidnappers demanded an enormous ransom.

kidnap² n an act of kidnapping: took part in a kidnap (attempt)

Kid·napped /ˈkɪdnæpt/ an adventure story for children by Robert Louis Stevenson about the kidnapping of a boy, David, who has seen a man being killed. He has to travel across the Highlands of Scotland to escape.

kid·ney /ˈkɪdni/ n **1** [C] either of the pair of bodily organs in the lower back area, which separate waste liquid from the blood **2** [C;U] such an organ or organs from an animal, used as food: steak and kidney pie

kidney bean /ˈ·· ·/ n a dark red bean that is shaped like a kidney and eaten as a vegetable

kidney ma·chine /ˈ·· ·ˌ·/ n a large machine, esp. in a hospital, that can do the work of human kidneys, for people whose own kidneys do not work or have been removed

kid's stuff /ˈ· ·/ BrE ‖ **kid stuff** AmE – n [U] infml something that is suitable only for children because it is too simple, UNSOPHISTICATED, or boring: The exam was kid stuff compared to the one we had last year.

Kiel /kiːl/ an industrial centre, port, and naval base in Germany, on an arm of the Baltic Sea

Kier·ke·gaard /ˈkɪəkəɡɑːd‖ˈkɪərkəɡɑːrd/, **Sö·ren Aa·bye** /ˈsɜːrən ˈɑːbi/ (1813–55) a Danish thinker and writer, the FOUNDER of EXISTENTIALISM

Ki·ev /ˈkiːef, -ev/ the capital city of the Ukraine, an industrial centre and important port —see also CHICKEN KIEV

kike /kaɪk/ n AmE taboo sl an offensive word for a Jewish person

Ki·ku·yu /kɪˈkuːjuː/ n [C;U] (a member of) one of the peoples of N Kenya —see also MAU MAU

Kil·dare /kɪlˈdeəʳ/ a COUNTY in the E of the Republic of Ireland

Kil·i·man·ja·ro /ˌkɪlɪmənˈdʒɑːrəʊ/ also **Mount Kilimanjaro**— a mountain in Tanzania. It has two PEAKs; the taller is the highest mountain in Africa.

Kil·ken·ny /kɪlˈkeni/ a COUNTY in the SE of the Republic of Ireland

kill¹ /kɪl/ v **1** [I;T] to cause death or cause to die: *Handle these toxic substances carefully; they can kill.* | *He was killed in the war|in a car crash.* | *The cold weather killed all the plants.* | (fig.) *My feet are killing me!* (=hurting very much) | (fig.) *The boss will kill me* (=be very angry at me) *if she finds out about this!* | *This guy really kills me!* (= makes me laugh a lot) **2** [T] to cause to stop, finish, or fail: *That mistake has killed his chances.* | *His tactless remark killed the conversation.* | *The newspaper editor killed the story (before it was printed).* | *He drinks to kill the pain.* | *Kill the lights.* (=turn them off) **3** [T] to destroy, weaken, or spoil the effect of (something) by comparison with it or closeness to it: *That red sofa kills (the effect of) the grey wall.* **4 kill someone with kindness** to treat someone too kindly, so that they feel uncomfortable **5 kill the fatted calf** esp. humor or pomp to welcome joyfully and with generous entertainment someone who has returned after a long absence (from the welcoming party given on the return of the PRODIGAL SON in the Bible) **6 kill time** to make time pass quickly by finding something to do: *We killed time by playing cards.* **7 kill two birds with one stone** to get two good results from one action: *Since Wendy lives near my mother, I'll call in on her as well and kill two birds with one stone.* —see also **dressed to kill** (DRESS¹ (9))

▷ USAGE **Kill** is a general word meaning to cause (anything) to die: *My uncle was killed in a plane crash.* | *The cold weather killed our tomato plants.* **Murder** means to kill a person on purpose: *She was sent to prison for murdering her husband.* **Slaughter** and **butcher** mean to kill animals for food, but both words are also used to describe cruel or unnecessary killing of humans: *Our army was butchered by the enemy's much larger forces.* | *Thousands of people are needlessly slaughtered in road accidents.* To **assassinate** means to kill an important political figure: *an attempt to assassinate the president.* To **massacre** means to kill large numbers of (defenceless) people: *The army entered the city and massacred all the women and children.*◁

kill sthg. **off** phr v [T] to kill (a lot of living things), usu. one at a time: *The trees were killed off by the severe winter.*

kill² n **1** [S] an animal killed in hunting: *The lion was eating his kill.* —see also ROAD KILL **2** [the] the act or moment of killing esp. hunted birds or animals: (fig.) *All his business rivals came to the bankruptcy proceedings to be* **in at|on the kill.**

kill·er /ˈkɪləʳ/ n a person, animal, or thing that kills: *This disease is a killer.* | *killer sharks* | *There's a killer at large.*

killer in·stinct /ˈ·· ˌ··/ n the natural ability or tendency to try to harm or kill another animal: (fig.) *Jim's really showing his killer instinct now that his company is in trouble.*

killer whale /ˈ·· ·/ n a small fierce meat-eating WHALE

kill·ing¹ /ˈkɪlɪŋ/ n **1** a murder: *a series of gangland killings* **2 make a killing** to make a lot of money suddenly, esp. in business

killing² adj infml extremely tiring: *This work is really killing.* — ~ly adv

Killing Fields /ˈ·· ˌ·/, **The** a film made in 1984 about the killing of Cambodians by the Khmer Rouge during the Pol Pot rule (1975–79)

kill·joy /ˈkɪldʒɔɪ/ n derog a person who intentionally spoils the pleasure of other people

kiln /kɪln/ n a box-shaped heating apparatus for baking pots or bricks, or for drying wood: *a brick kiln* | *kiln-dried oak*

Kil·ner jar /ˈkɪlnə dʒɑːʳ‖-nər-/ n BrE tdmk a glass bottle with a lid that can be sealed (SEAL³ (3)), used for preserving fruit or vegetables —compare MASON JAR

ki·lo /ˈkiːləʊ/ n kilos infml a KILOGRAM: *I weigh 52 kilos.* | *A kilo of apples, please.*

kilo- see WORD FORMATION

kil·o·byte /ˈkɪləbaɪt/ n also **K** 1000 or 1024 BYTES of computer information

kil·o·cal·o·rie /ˈkɪləkæləri/ n a CALORIE (1)

kil·o·gram , -gramme /ˈkɪləgræm/ (written abbrev. **kg**) n a unit of weight equal to 2.20 pounds: *The sack weighed 30 kilograms.* —see TABLE 2

kil·o·hertz /ˈkɪləhɜːts‖-ɜːr-/ also **kil·o·cy·cle** /ˈkɪləˌsaɪkəl/— n -hertz 1000 HERTZ

kil·o·joule /ˈkɪlədʒuːl‖-dʒuːl, -dʒəʊl/ n a unit of work or ENERGY equal to 1000 JOULES

kil·o·li·tre BrE ‖ **-ter** AmE /ˈkɪləˌliːtəʳ/ n a unit of amount —see TABLE 2

kil·o·me·tre BrE ‖ **-ter** AmE /ˈkɪləˌmiːtəʳ, kɪˈlɒmɪtəʳ‖ kɪˈlɑːmɪtəʳ/ (written abbrev. **km**) n a unit for measuring length: *The bridge is almost 2 kilometres long.* —see TABLE 2

kil·o·watt /ˈkɪləwɒt‖-wɑːt/ n 1000 WATTS

kilowatt hour /ˌ··· ˈ·/ written abbrev. **kwh** n the amount of ENERGY produced by a kilowatt over a period of an hour. It is the unit usu. used by electricity companies for setting their prices.

Kil·roy /ˈkɪlrɔɪ/ an unknown man, the subject of the sentence "Kilroy was here", which from the Second World War on has been found written on walls as GRAFFITI; its origin is unknown

kilt /kɪlt/ n a skirt with many pressed folds at the back and sides, and usu. of a TARTAN pattern, worn esp. by Scotsmen. People often make jokes about the fact that men are believed to wear nothing under their kilt. — ~ **ed** adj [A]: *kilted Highlanders*

kil·ter /ˈkɪltəʳ/ n **out of kilter|off kilter** not working properly or in good condition

ki·mo·no /kɪˈməʊnəʊ/ n -nos **1** a long traditional Japanese garment made of thin silk or other material **2** esp. AmE a loose DRESSING GOWN, worn esp. by women

kin /kɪn/ n [P] BrE old use or fml; AmE infml **1** also **kinfolk** the members of one's family; one's relatives **2 next of kin** a person's closest relative or relatives: *His next of kin were told of his death.* —compare KINDRED; see also KITH AND KIN

Kin·car·dine·shire /kɪnˈkɑːdɪnʃəʳ‖-ɑːr-/ a former COUNTY in E Scotland, now part of Grampian REGION

kind¹ /kaɪnd/ n **1** [C (of)+sing.|pl. v] a group whose members share certain qualities; type; sort: *all kinds of people* | *the only one of its kind* | *It's a kind of reddish-brown colour.* (=is rather reddish brown) | *There's red wine or white; which kind would you prefer?* | *The film was OK, if you like that kind of thing.* | *Haven't you got any other kind?* | *Those kind of watches are stronger than the others.* —see USAGE 1 **2** [U] the qualities that make something what it is, and different from others; nature: *You can't compare them — there is a fundamental difference in kind.* | *"You said he was old." "I never said anything of the kind!"* (=I said nothing at all like that) **3 a kind of** an unclear or unusual sort of: *He had a kind of feeling (AmE)|a kind of a feeling (BrE) that she would phone him.* **4 in kind: a** (of payment) using goods or natural products rather than money **b** with the same treatment: *I paid him back in kind for cheating me.* (=I cheated him) **5 kind of** infml in a certain way; rather: *I'm feeling kind of tired.* | *She kind of hoped to be invited.* —see USAGE 2 **6 of a kind: a** of the same kind: *Father and son are two of a kind; they're both very generous.* **b** of a not very good kind: *It was advice of a kind, but it wasn't very helpful.*

▷ USAGE 1 Sentences like: *Those* **kind/sort** *of questions are very difficult* are common in speech but are thought by teachers to be incorrect. In writing it is better to use this form: *That* **kind/sort** *of question is very difficult*, or: *Questions of that* **kind/sort** *are very difficult.* 2 **Kind of** and **sort of**. In informal conversation these expressions can be used to show that you are not sure or have doubts about something: *"Do you like red wine?" "Yes,* **kind of/sort of.**" | *"Did he help you?" "Well,* **kind of.**" (=not as much as I hoped). In very informal speech **kind of** and **sort of** are sometimes used without any particular meaning: *He* **sort of** *came up to me and pushed me. So I* **kind of** *hit him in the face.* This is not considered to be good English.◁

kind² *adj* [(**to**)] (that shows one is) caring about the happiness or feelings of others: *a kind person/action/thought* | *She's very kind to animals.* | *It was very kind of you to visit me when I was ill.* | *They've been very kind about letting our children play in their garden.* | *(fml) Would you be kind enough to do it for me?* | *(fml) Would you be so kind as to do it?* —opposite **unkind**; see also KINDLY¹, KINDNESS

kin·der·gar·ten /ˈkɪndəgɑːtn‖-dərgɑːrtn/ *n* [C;U] a school or class for young children, usu. age five. In the US kindergarten is usu. the beginning of formal, state-controlled education. Most GRADE SCHOOLS have kindergarten classes, where children attend for half a day. —compare NURSERY SCHOOL; see also extra information on page 408

kind-heart·ed /ˌ·ˈ···◁‖ˈ·ˌ··/ *adj* having or showing a kind nature: *a kind-hearted person/action* — ~**ly** *adv* — ~**ness** *n* [U]

Kind Hearts and Cor·o·nets /ˌ·ˌ·ˌ·ˈ···/ a British COMEDY film made in 1949, with Alec Guiness playing eight members of an UPPER CLASS family who are all killed by someone who wants to become a DUKE

kin·dle /ˈkɪndl/ *v* [I;T] to (cause to) start burning: *to kindle a fire* | *(fig.) I'm afraid our publicity campaign failed to kindle much interest among the public.*

kin·dling /ˈkɪndlɪŋ/ *n* [U] materials for lighting a fire, esp. dry wood, leaves, grass, etc.

kind·ly¹ /ˈkaɪndli/ *adv* **1** in a kind way: *She spoke kindly to the old man.* —opposite **unkindly 2** (esp. used to show annoyance) please: *Will you kindly put that book back?* | *Kindly put it back.* **3 not take kindly to** not to accept willingly: *He didn't take kindly to being told how to behave.*

kindly² *adj fml* pleasantly; friendly or generous, esp. to those who are younger, weaker, or less important than oneself: *a kindly uncle/smile* —**-liness** *n* [U]

kind·ness /ˈkaɪndnɪs/ *n* [(**to**)] **1** [U] the quality of being kind: *to show kindness to animals* **2** [C] a kind action: *I think it would be a kindness to tell him the bad news straight away.* —opposite **unkindness**; see also **kill with kindness** (KILL¹ (4))

kin·dred¹ /ˈkɪndrɪd/ *n old use or fml* **1** [P] one's relatives —compare KIN **2** [U (**with**)] family relationship; KINSHIP: *He claims kindred with royalty.*

kindred² *adj* [A] belonging to the same group; related: *Italian and Spanish and other kindred languages* | *He and I are* **kindred spirits***: we have the same tastes and the same opinions.*

kine /kaɪn/ *n* [P] *old use* cattle

ki·net·ic /kɪˈnetɪk, kaɪ-/ *adj fml or tech* of or about movement: **Kinetic art** *involves the use of moving objects.* — ~**ally** /kli/ *adv*

kinetic en·er·gy /·ˌ·· ˈ···/ *n* [U] *tech* the power of something moving, such as running water

ki·net·ics /kɪˈnetɪks, kaɪ-/ *n* [U] the science that studies the action of force in producing or changing movement — compare DYNAMICS¹

kin·folk /ˈkɪnfəʊk/ also **kinfolks**— *n* [P] *AmE for* KINSFOLK

king /kɪŋ/ *n* **1** [(**of**)] (*sometimes cap.*) (the title of) the male ruler of a country, usu. the son of a former ruler: *He became king on the death of his father.* | *The King of Spain* | *King Edward IV* (=the fourth) **2** [(**of**)] the most important man or male animal in a group, esp. a chief among competitors: *a cotton king* (=a powerful businessman in the cotton industry) | *The lion is king of the jungle/of beasts.* **3 a** the most important piece in CHESS **b** [(**of**)] any of the four playing cards with a picture of a king: *the king of diamonds* —see CARDS (USAGE), and see picture at CHESS; see also QUEEN, UNCROWNED KING

King¹, The a name sometimes used for the American singer Elvis Presley

King², Bil·lie Jean /ˈbɪli dʒiːn/ (1943–) an American tennis player, winner of four US Open titles and twenty titles at Wimbledon, where she was CHAMPION six times

King³, Don (1931–) an arranger and advertiser of BOXING (fighting) matches known for being associated with important BOXERs and for his unusual hair style and behaviour

King⁴, Martin Luther (1929–68) a Black American minister and CIVIL RIGHTS leader, who received the 1964 Nobel Peace Prize, advised non-violence in fighting RACISM and was shot and killed in Memphis, Tennessee. He is remembered esp. for his famous speech which began with the words "I have a dream..." and expressed big hopes for the future of black people. —see picture on page 752

Don King

King⁵, Rod·ney /ˈrɒdni ‖ ˈrɑːd/ a black American who, in 1991, was badly beaten by a group of white policemen in Los Angeles. A citizen filmed the beating, and it was later shown on television. In 1992 the policemen involved in the event were found not guilty of using too much force by a JURY in Los Angeles, and this led to the Los Angeles RIOTs.

King⁶, Ste·phen /ˈstiːvən/ (1947–) a popular American writer of frightening stories such as *Carrie* and *The Shining*

King and Coun·try debate /ˌ·· · ˈ··· ·ˌ·/ [*the*] a famous DEBATE¹ (1) at Oxford University in 1933, in which students noted that they would not fight for their king and country. People at the time found this very shocking.

king·dom /ˈkɪŋdəm/ *n* **1** a country governed by a king or queen, or of which a king or queen is the head of state: *He ruled his kingdom wisely.* | *the* **United Kingdom** *of Great Britain and Northern Ireland* | *(fig.) the kingdom of God* —compare EMPIRE **2** an area in which the stated thing has the greatest influence; REALM: *the kingdom of the mind* **3** any of the three great divisions of natural objects: *the animal/plant/mineral kingdom* **4 kingdom come** *infml, often humor* **a** the state after death: *The bomb blew him to kingdom come.* (=killed him) **b** an extremely long time: *You'll have to wait until kingdom come for him to buy you a drink!* **5 Thy Kingdom come** a phrase from the LORD'S PRAYER

▷ USAGE A **kingdom** may be ruled over by a **queen**, like Britain is at present.◁

Kingdom Hall /ˌ·· ˈ·/ *n* a place of worship for Jehovah's Witnesses

King Ed·ward /· ˈ··/ *n* a common British variety of potato

king·fish·er /ˈkɪŋˌfɪʃərʳ/ *n* a small brightly-coloured bird that feeds on fish in rivers, lakes, etc. —see picture at BIRD

King James Ver·sion /· ˌ· ˈ··/ also **King James Bible** — [*the*] the AUTHORIZED VERSION of the Bible, produced in 1611 when James I was king of Britain. It is still the most popular VERSION of the Bible.

King Kong /ˌkɪŋ ˈkɒŋ‖-ˈkɑːŋ/ an extremely large GORILLA in the 1933 film of the same name, which terrorized (TERRORIZE) the people of New York, taking a young woman prisoner and climbing the Empire State Building holding her under his arm

King Lear /ˌkɪŋ ˈlɪərʳ/ a play by William Shakespeare about an old king who divides his KINGDOM among his three daughters according to how much each says she loves him. Deceived by their words, he gives all the kingdom to the two who do not love him at all, leading to sad and terrible events.

king·ly /ˈkɪŋli/ *adj fml* belonging to or suitable to a king: *a kingly manner/feast*

king·mak·er /ˈkɪŋˌmeɪkərʳ/ *n BrE* a person who can influence appointments to very high political office: *The party chairman is trying to play the role of kingmaker.*

king of the cas·tle /ˌ·· · ˈ··/ [*the*] the person in the most commanding, successful, etc., position (from the words of a RHYME¹ (1) in a children's game in which one child stands on something and the others try to pull him/her off it and take his/her place)

King of the Jews /ˌ·· · ˈ·/ another name for Jesus which is used in the Bible

king·pin /ˈkɪŋˌpɪn/ *n* [(**of**)] the most important person in a group, upon whom the success of the group depends;

LINCHPIN: *Sir George was the kingpin of the steel industry.*

King's Bench /ˌ· ˈ·/ also **King's Bench Di·vi·sion** /ˌ· ˈ· ·ˌ··/— *n* [*the*] (the name given, while a king is ruling, to) a division of the High Court of Justice in England — compare QUEEN'S BENCH

King's Col·lege Chap·el /ˌ· ˌ·· ˈ··/ the church at King's College in Cambridge, England, where every Christmas Eve a CAROL service is held, led by a CHOIR of boys

King's Coun·sel /ˌ· ˈ··/ *n* see KC

Kings Cross /ˌ· ˈ·◄/ an area of London where there are two main line railway stations and an Underground station. A very bad fire there in 1987 killed many travellers on the Underground. The area is also known as a place where many PROSTITUTEs work. —see colour map on page 817

King's Eng·lish /ˌ· ˈ··/ [*the*] (the expression sometimes used, when a king is ruling, to describe) good correct English as spoken in Britain —compare QUEEN'S ENGLISH

king's ev·i·dence /ˌ· ˈ···/ *n* [U] *BrE* see QUEEN'S EVIDENCE

king's e·vil /ˌ· ˈ··/ *n* [*the*] *old use for* SCROFULA

king·ship /ˈkɪŋʃɪp/ *n* [U] the condition or official position of a king: *the responsibilities of kingship*

king-size /ˈ· ·/ also **king-sized**— *adj* larger than the standard size: *a king-size bottle|packet|*(fig.) *hangover* | *a king-size bed*

Kings·ley /ˈkɪŋzli/, **Charles** (1819–75) an English writer of historical NOVELs such as *Westward Ho!*, as well as the children's story *The Water Babies*

King Sol·o·mon's Mines /kɪŋ ˌsɒləmənz ˈmaɪnz‖-ˌsɑː-/ a book written by Henry Rider Haggard in 1885, an adventure story set in Africa

Kings Road /ˌ· ˈ·/ [(*the*)] (an area of London including) a road which used to be a centre of fashionable life in the 1960s, esp. among young people. It is still fashionable, but has become much more expensive.

Kings·ton /ˈkɪŋstən/ the capital city of Jamaica and the island's business centre, main port, and largest town

Kingston-u·pon-Thames /ˌ··· ·· ˈ·/ a town in Surrey, England, where the local government for that COUNTY is based

King Tut /kɪŋ ˈtʊt, -ˈtʌt/ —see TUTANKHAMEN

kink /kɪŋk/ *n* **1** [(**in**)] an (unwanted) sharp turn or twist in hair, a rope, a chain, a pipe, etc.: *The water isn't coming out because there's a kink in the hosepipe.* **2** *infml* a strangeness of the mind or character, esp. with regard to sexual behaviour —**kinky** *adj* : *kinky ideas* | *a shop specializing in kinky black leather and rubber clothes*

Kinks /kɪŋks/, **The** a British popular music group successful in the 1960s and 1970s

Kin·nock /ˈkɪnək/, **Neil** /niːl/ (1942   ) a British politician, leader of the Labour Party from 1983 to 1992, born in Wales. He was leader of the Labour Party when it was very unpopular, and did much to improve its image, although some people think the party is now too rightwing. He resigned in 1992 following the party's defeat in the general election.

Kin·ross-shire /kɪnˈrɒsʃəʳ‖-ˈrɔːs-/ a former COUNTY in central Scotland, now part of Tayside REGION

Kin·sey /ˈkɪnzi/, **Al·fred Charles** /ˈælfrəd tʃɑːlz‖-tʃɑːrlz/ (1894–1956) an American scientist who studied human sexual behaviour. His works, usu. called the **Kinsey Reports**, surprised everyone when they were published (PUBLISH) because they showed that people's sexual practices were very different from what most people thought.

kins·folk /ˈkɪnzfəʊk/ also **kinfolk** *AmE*— *n* [P] *old-fash* the members of one's family

kin·ship /ˈkɪnʃɪp/ *n* **1** [U (**with**)] family relationship: *The kinship system in that tribe is very complicated.* **2** [S;U (**with, between**)] likeness in character, understanding, etc.: *I feel a certain kinship with him.* | *a strong feeling of kinship between us*

Kin·ski /ˈkɪnski/, **Klaus** /klaʊs/ (1926–92) a German actor who was in many Werner Herzog films such as *Nosferatu* and *Venom*

kins·man /ˈkɪnzmən/ **kins·wom·an** /-ˌwʊmən/ *fem.*— *n* **-men** /mən/ *old use* a relative

ki·osk /ˈkiːɒsk‖-ɑːsk/ *n* **1** a small open hut, such as one used for selling newspapers **2** *BrE fml* a public telephone box, indoors or outdoors

kip¹ /kɪp/ *n* [S;U] *BrE sl* (a period of) sleep: *to have a kip* | *I didn't get much kip last night.*

kip² *v* **-pp-** [I] *BrE sl* **1** to sleep **2** [+*adv/prep*] to go to bed: *Let's kip (down) here for the night.*

Kip·ling /ˈkɪplɪŋ/, **Rud·yard** /ˈrʌdjəd‖-jərd/ (1865–1936) an English writer born in India, where his stories and poems are set. He is best known for his *Jungle Book*, the poem *If*, and stories for children. He received the Nobel Prize for literature in 1907.

kip·per /ˈkɪpəʳ/ *n* a salted HERRING (=kind of fish) to which salt has been added and that is preserved by being treated with smoke

Kir·ghiz·i·a /kɜːˈgɪziə‖kɪr-/ a country in S central Asia, bordering on China in the E; capital Bishkek; population 4,291,000 (1989)

Kir·i·bat·i /ˌkɪrɪˈbɑːti/ a country in the Pacific, near the Equator, consisting of 33 islands; capital Tarawa; population 72,298 (1987). It was formerly a British COLONY called the **Gilbert Islands** but has been independent since 1979.

kirk /kɜːk‖kɜːrk/ *n ScotE* a church

Kirk [*the*] *ScotE* the Church of Scotland

Kirk, Captain James T the captain of the SPACESHIP *Starship Enterprise* in the television programme *Star Trek* —see also STARTREK

Kirk·cud·bright·shire /kəˈkuːbrɪʃəʳ‖kər-/ a former COUNTY in SW Scotland, now part of Dumfries and Galloway REGION

Kirk·wall /ˈkɜːkwɔːl ‖ ˈkɜːrk-/ a town on the largest island of the Orkneys, where the local government for the islands is based

kirsch /kɪəʃ‖kɪərʃ/ *n* [U] a strong alcoholic drink made from CHERRY juice

kis·met /ˈkɪzmet, ˈkɪs-/ *n* [U] *lit* fate; DESTINY

kiss¹ /kɪs/ *v* **1** [I; T] to touch with the lips as a sign of love or as a greeting: *In the final scene of the film, they kiss.* (=kiss each other on the lips) | *Kiss me!* | *He kissed her on the forehead.* | (fig., *lit*) *The wind kissed the trees.* (=touched and moved them gently)

► CULTURAL NOTE To kiss on the mouth is a sign of (usu. sexual) love; a kiss on the cheek, forehead, etc. is more a sign of friendship or family love. In most Western countries it is unusual for men to kiss each other, unless they are members of the same family or HOMOSEXUAL. ◄

2 [T] to express (something) to someone by kissing: [+*obj*(*i*)+*obj*(*d*)] *He kissed his wife goodbye|kissed his children goodnight.* [+*obj*+**to**] (fig.) *If you fail that exam you can kiss goodbye to* (=you will have lost) *your chance of going to university.* **3** **kiss hands** (in Britain) to ceremoniously kiss the king's or queen's hand as an official sign of being appointed to a high position in the government — ~ **able** *adj*

kiss² *n* an act of kissing: *I gave her a kiss.* | *a passionate kiss* —see also FRENCH KISS, KISS OF DEATH, KISS OF LIFE, **blow someone a kiss** (BLOW¹ (15))

kiss·a·gram, kiss-a-gram /ˈkɪsəgræm/ —see KISSOGRAM

kiss-and-tell /ˌ· · ˈ·/ *adj* [usu. A] (of sexual affairs, or newspaper etc. accounts of them) retold in public, and often in great detail, by one of the lovers after the affair is over. Often famous people are involved: *Kiss-and-tell stories in the tabloids* | *a kiss-and-tell lover*

kiss·er /ˈkɪsəʳ/ *n* **1** a person who kisses **2** *old-fash sl* the mouth

kissing cous·in /ˌ·· ˈ··/ *n AmE old-fash* a COUSIN or other relative family member who one knows well enough to greet with a kiss

Kis·sin·ger /ˈkɪsɪndʒəʳ/, **Henry** (1923–   ) an American politician and adviser who played an important part in American foreign POLICY in the 1970s. He received the 1973 Nobel Peace Prize for helping to stop the fighting in North Vietnam.

kiss-me-quick hat /ˌ·· ˈ· ·/ *n BrE* a cheap, usu. black, hat, with "kiss me quick" or some other SLOGAN on it, worn for fun usu. by young women at a FAIRGROUND or the SEASIDE

kiss of death /ˌ· · ˈ·/ [*the*] *infml* something that makes failure certain: *The withdrawal of government funding gave our plan the kiss of death.*

kitchen

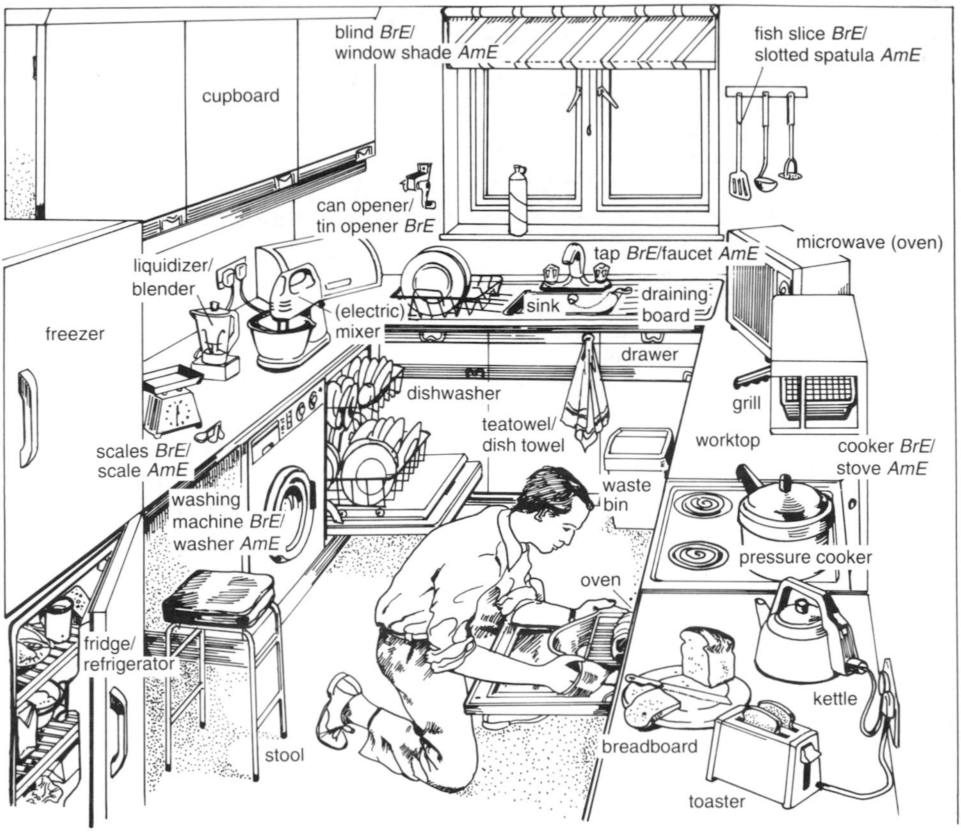

Illustration labels:
- cupboard
- blind *BrE*/ window shade *AmE*
- fish slice *BrE*/ slotted spatula *AmE*
- can opener/ tin opener *BrE*
- liquidizer/ blender
- tap *BrE*/faucet *AmE*
- microwave (oven)
- freezer
- (electric) mixer
- sink
- draining board
- drawer
- dishwasher
- grill
- teatowel/ dish towel
- worktop
- cooker *BrE*/ stove *AmE*
- scales *BrE*/ scale *AmE*
- waste bin
- washing machine *BrE*/ washer *AmE*
- pressure cooker
- oven
- fridge/ refrigerator
- kettle
- stool
- breadboard
- toaster

---

kiss of life /ˌ· · ˈ·/ [*the*] *esp. BrE* MOUTH-TO-MOUTH RESUS-CITATION

kis·so·gram, kissagram, kiss-a-gram /ˈkɪsəɡræm/ *n* **1** a message, often a humorous greeting, sent by way of a person dressed in COSTUME, who may either sing or speak it, and usu. gives the person receiving it a kiss **2** the person in such a costume who delivers the message

kit¹ /kɪt/ *n* **1** [C] a set of articles or tools needed for a particular purpose or job: *a shaving/repair kit* | *a survival kit* (=containing necessary food, tools, etc. to keep one alive for a time) | *first aid kit* (=containing supplies for medical EMERGENCY) **2** [U] *BrE* a set of clothes and other articles needed for daily life, esp. by soldiers, sailors, etc., or for playing a particular sport: *The captain wants to inspect your kit.* | *my football kit* **3** [C] a set of parts sold ready to be put together: *a model aircraft kit* | *This furniture comes as a kit/in kit form.* **4 kit and caboodle** *AmE infml* everything: *She threw all my stuff out. Everything. The whole kit and caboodle.*

kit² *v* **-tt-**
   kit sbdy. ↔ **out/up** *phr v* [T (**with**) *often pass.*] *esp. BrE* to supply with necessary things, esp. clothes: *They were all kitted out (with boots and trousers) for skiing.*

kit bag /ˈ· ·/ *n esp. BrE* a long narrow bag used by soldiers, sailors, etc., for carrying kit —compare DUFFEL BAG

kit car /ˈ· ·/ *n* a car whose engine, body parts, and CHASSIS are bought separately and put together by the buyer

kitch·en /ˈkɪtʃən/ *n* **1** a room where food is prepared and cooked: *We usually eat breakfast in the kitchen.* | *kitchen appliances, such as food mixers* **2 everything but the kitchen sink** *humor* a larger amount than seems necessary: *He's only staying three days, but he arrived with everything but the kitchen sink.* (=lots of bags, cases, etc.)

Kitch·en·er /ˈkɪtʃənər/, **Ho·ra·ti·o** /həˈreɪʃiəʊ/, **First Earl** (1850–1916) a British soldier, also known as **Lord**

Kitchener or **Field Marshal Earl Kitchener**, who fought in the Sudan, won victory over the Boers, and greatly increased the size of the British army in the First World War. He appeared on a POSTER in the First World War with the SLOGAN **Your country needs you**, urging men to join the British Army.

kitch·en·ette /ˌkɪtʃəˈnet/ *n* a very small kitchen, or a part of a room used for cooking

kitchen gar·den /ˌ· · ˈ·/ *n esp. BrE* a garden where fruit and vegetables are grown, usu. for eating at home rather than for sale

kitchen roll /ˈ· ·/ also **kitchen pa·per** /ˈ· ·ˌ·/, **towel** *BrE* ‖ **paper towel** *AmE*– *n* [C;U] thick, ABSORBENT paper used mainly in the kitchen for cleaning up small amounts of food, liquid, dirt, etc.: *Pass me a piece of kitchen roll/paper towel*

kitchen-sink dra·ma /ˌ· · ˈ· ˌ·/ *n* [C;U] a serious play or plays about working-class home life, esp. as written in Britain in the late 1950s and the 1960s

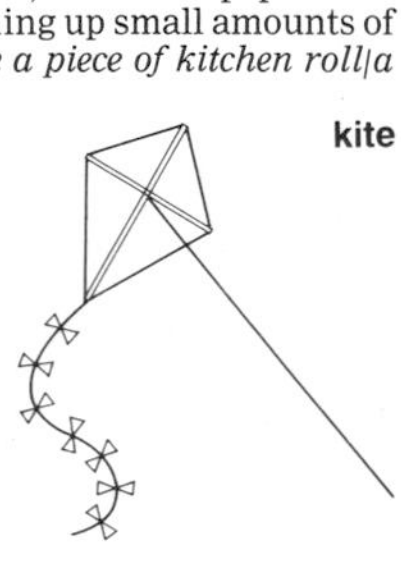

kite¹ /kaɪt/ *n* **1** a paper-covered or cloth-covered frame flown in the air at the end of a long string using the power of the wind, esp. for amusement: *The children are*

Lord Kitchener

kite

on the hillside *flying their kites*. —see also **fly a kite** (FLY¹ (12)), **go fly a kite** (FLY¹ (15)) **2** a large bird (HAWK) that kills and eats small birds and animals

kite² *v* [I;T] *AmE* to obtain money or goods by writing a cheque or using a CREDIT CARD when one does not have the money in the bank to cover the payment: *One member kited 996 checks totaling $251,000.*

Kit-E-Kat /ˈkɪtikæt/ *n tdmk* a company which makes tinned and dried food for cats

kite·mark /ˈkaɪtmɑːk‖-mɑːrk/ *n* a special mark put on many kinds of goods in Britain to show that they meet the safety standards of the British Standards Institution

kitemark

kith and kin /ˌkɪθ ən ˈkɪn/ *n* [P] people of one's own family, country, etc.: *You can't refuse to help them; they're your own kith and kin.*

Kit·Kat /ˈkɪtkæt/ *tdmk n* a sweet made of (two or four) fingers of BISCUIT joined together by, and covered with, chocolate

kitsch /kɪtʃ/ *n* [U] *derog* popular decorative objects, writing, etc., that pretend to be art but are silly and worthless: *She's decorated her flat with all kinds of plastic kitsch.* | *His new film is pure kitsch.* —~**y** *adj*

kit·ten /ˈkɪtn/ *n* **1** a young cat **2 have a kitten/kittens** *infml* to be very nervous and anxious: *I thought she was going to have kittens when I told her the job would be late.*

kit·ten·ish /ˈkɪtn-ɪʃ/ *adj often derog* (esp. of a woman) playful like a kitten, esp. so as to attract sexual attention — ~**ly** *adv*

kit·ti·wake /ˈkɪtiweɪk/ *n* a kind of GULL (=a seabird) with long wings

kit·ty¹ /ˈkɪti/ *n* **1** (in some card games) an amount of money collected from all the players at the beginning and taken by the winner **2** *infml* a sum of money collected by a group of people, and used for an agreed purpose: *All the prize money won by individual players goes into the team's kitty.*

kitty² *n* (used, esp. by children, for calling or talking to) a cat or KITTEN: *"Here, kitty kitty," called the little girl.*

kitty-cor·ner /ˈ·· ˌ·-/ also **catty-corner**— *adv AmE infml* diagonally (DIAGONAL) across the street from the stated place (usu. a corner): *There's a drugstore kitty-corner from the bank.* | *I live kitty-corner from/to the school.*

Kitty Hawk /ˈ·· ˌ·/ the place in North Carolina where the Wright Brothers first flew an aeroplane successfully in 1903

Ki·wa·nis /kɪˈwɑːnɪz/ *[the]* a SERVICE CLUB which has branches across the US, esp. in small towns. A member of the club is called a **Kiwani**.

ki·wi /ˈkiːwiː/ *n* **1** a New Zealand bird with very short wings that cannot fly **2** *sl* (*usu. cap.*) a New Zealander

kiwi fruit /ˈ·· ·/ *n* a small fruit with a brown skin and green flesh, popular in fruit SALADS and DESSERTS

KKK /ˌkeɪ keɪ ˈkeɪ/ *[the]* *abbrev. for* KU KLUX KLAN

Klam·mer /ˈklæməʳ/, **Franz** /fræns ‖ frɑːnts/ (1953–) an Austrian SKIER, one of the best of all time, winner of one Olympic and five world titles

klatch *n* see COFFEE KLATCH

klax·on /ˈklæksən/ *n* a very loud usu. electric horn, used, esp. formerly, on motor vehicles

Kleen·ex /ˈkliːneks/ *n* [C;U] *tdmk* (a sheet of) thin soft paper, used as a handkerchief. The word is sometimes used, esp. in *AmE*, for any kind of paper handkerchief: *Do you have a/any Kleenex?* —see TISSUE (3)

Klein /klaɪn/, **Calvin** (1942–) an American clothes DESIGNER, known esp. for his informal (CASUAL) clothes

klep·to·ma·ni·a /ˌkleptəˈmeɪniə/ *n* [U] a disease of the mind causing an uncontrollable desire to steal

klep·to·ma·ni·ac /ˌkleptəˈmeɪniæk/ *infml* **klep·to** /ˈkleptəʊ/ *n* a person suffering from kleptomania

Klon·dike /ˈklɒndaɪk‖ˈklɑːn-/ *[the]* an area in NW Canada, in the Yukon. Gold was discovered there in the 1890s, leading to the **Klondike Gold Rush** when many people

went to the area to look for gold. —see also GOLD RUSH (1)

klutz /klʌts/ also **clutz**— *n AmE* a person who is awkward and ungraceful in their movements or actions

km *written abbrev. for:* kilometre(s)

K Mart /ˈkeɪ mɑːt‖-mɑːrt/ a large chain of popular department stores in the US that sells everything cheaper than the usual price —**K-Mart** *adj* : *K-Mart shoppers*

knack /næk/ *n* [(*the*) S] *infml* a special skill or ability, usu. the result of practice: *He has a/the knack of making friends wherever he goes.* | *It's not so difficult to thread these wires through the holes once you've got the knack of it.*

knack·ered /ˈnækəd‖-ərd/ *adj* [F] *BrE sl* extremely tired; exhausted (EXHAUST 1). The word is not usu. used in polite company.

knack·er's yard /ˈnækəz ˌjɑːd‖-ərz ˌjɑːrd/ *n BrE* a place where old horses are killed, esp. so that their flesh can be sold as animal food: (fig.) *That old car of yours is only fit for the knacker's yard.* (=you should get rid of it)

knap·sack /ˈnæpsæk/ *n* RUCKSACK

knave /neɪv/ *n* **1** *BrE* the CARD¹ (1) with a value between the ten and the queen; the JACK —see CARDS (USAGE) **2** *old use* a dishonest man or boy —**knavish** *adj* — **knavishly** *adv*

knav·e·ry /ˈneɪvəri/ *n* [C;U] *esp. old use* (a piece of) dishonest behaviour

knead /niːd/ *v* [T] **1** to press (esp. a flour-and-water mixture for making bread) firmly and repeatedly with the hands: *The cook kneaded the dough.* **2** to press or make other movements on (a muscle or other part of the body) to cure pain, stiffness, etc.: *The masseur kneaded my back.*

knee¹ /niː/ *n* **1** the middle joint of the leg, where it bends: *He got down on his hands and knees to crawl under the table.* | *a baby sitting on its father's knee* | *She went down on her knees to pray/to beg for mercy.* | *pain in the knees* —see picture at HORSE **2** the part of a pair of trousers, TIGHTS, etc., that covers the knee: *big holes in the knees of his old trousers* **3 bend the knee to** (someone) *lit* to admit that (someone) has control over one **4 bring someone to their knees** to force someone to admit defeat —see also **the bee's knees** (BEE), **at one's mother's knee** (MOTHER¹), **weak at the knees** (WEAK)

knee² *v* -**d** [T (**in**)] to hit with the knee: *The wrestler kneed his opponent in the stomach.*

knee breech·es /ˈ· ˌ·-/ *n* [P] old-fashioned short tight trousers reaching to just below the knee, esp. as worn on ceremonial occasions —see PAIR¹ (USAGE)

knee·cap¹ /ˈniːkæp/ *n* the bone at the front of the knee — see picture at SKELETON

kneecap² *v* -**pp-** [T] to shoot the kneecaps of (someone), usu. as an unofficial punishment. This form of punishment has often been used by TERRORISTS in Northern Ireland.

knee-deep /ˌ· ˈ·◂/ *adj* [(**in**)] deep enough to reach the knees: *The water is knee-deep.* | *He was knee-deep in mud.* | (fig.) *knee-deep in work* (=having a lot of work to do)

knee-high /ˌ· ˈ·◂/ *adj* **1** tall enough to reach the knees: *The grass was knee-high.* **2 knee-high to a grasshopper** *infml humor* (esp. of a child) very small or young

knee-jerk /ˈ· ·/ *adj* [A] *derog* (of opinions) held or produced without thought, as the result of long habit: *his knee-jerk reaction to feminism* | *a knee-jerk Liberal*

kneel /niːl/ *v* **knelt** /nelt/ ‖ also **kneeled** *AmE*— [I (DOWN, on)] to go down onto or remain on one's knee(s): *She knelt (down) on the mat and began to pray.*

knee-length /ˈ· ·/ *adj* long enough to reach the knees: *a knee-length skirt* | *knee-length boots*

knee sock /ˈ· ·/ *n* a sock which comes up to the knee. Knee socks are worn esp. by young girls.

knees-up /ˈ· ·/ *n esp. BrE infml* a party or other celebration, usu. involving dancing: *The office Christmas party was a real knees-up.*

knell /nel/ *n lit* the sound of a bell rung slowly, esp. for a death or funeral: (fig.) *His decision sounds* **the death knell** *for all our hopes.* (=means that our hopes will not be fulfilled)

Knes·set /ˈkneset/ *[the]* the Israeli parliament

K

knew /njuː‖nuː/ *past tense of* KNOW[1]

knick·er·bock·er glo·ry /ˌnɪkəbɒkə ˈɡlɔːri ‖ -kərbɑːkər-/ *n* a sweet dish made from fruit, ice cream, JELLY, and cream, served in a tall glass; a SUNDAE

knick·er·bock·ers /ˈnɪkəˌbɒkəz‖ˈnɪkərˌbɑːkərz/ *n* [P] short loose trousers made to fit tightly just below the knees, worn esp. in former times —see PAIR[1] (USAGE)

knick·ers[1] /ˈnɪkəz‖-ərz/ *n* [P]   **1** *BrE infml* a short undergarment worn by women and girls, covering the area between the waist and the top of the legs; PANTIES: *a pair of frilly knickers* —compare UNDERPANTS   **2** *AmE* knickerbockers   **3 get one's knickers in a twist** *BrE humor sl* to become angry or confused —see PAIR[1] (USAGE)

knickers[2] *interj BrE humor sl* (used as an expression of fearless disrespect)

knick-knack, nicknack /ˈnɪk næk/ *n infml* a small cheap decorative object, esp. for the house: *various knick-knacks on the mantelpiece*

knife[1] /naɪf/ *n* **knives** /naɪvz/   **1** a blade fixed in a handle, used for cutting as a tool or weapon; in Britain, it is illegal to carry a knife around with you, as it is considered to be a dangerous weapon: *He picked up the knife and stabbed her.* | *a table knife* (=for cutting up one's food) | *hunting knives* | *to sharpen a blunt knife* —see also FORK[1]   **2** *BrE* **have/get one's knife in/into someone** *infml* to continue to treat someone as an enemy: *I don't know why, but she's really got her knife in him at the moment.* —see picture at PLACE SETTING, and see also PAPER KNIFE

▷ USAGE Note the fixed phrase **knife and fork**: *Put your* **knife and fork** *down on the plate if you've finished eating.*◁

knife[2] *v* [T (**in**)] to stick a knife into (someone); STAB: *He was knifed in the stomach during a street-fight.*

knife-edge /ˈ·ˌ·/ *n* **1** something narrow and sharp: *a knife-edge of rocks just below the surface of the sea* | *knife-edge pleats in a skirt*   **2 on a knife-edge: a** (of a person) very anxious about the future result of something: *on a knife-edge about the exams* **b** delicately balanced; with the result extremely uncertain: *The success or failure of the plan was balanced on a knife-edge.*

knight

knight[1] /naɪt/ *n*   **1** (in former times) a man of noble rank trained to fight, esp. on horseback: *knights in armour* — see also ROUND TABLE, WHITE KNIGHT   **2** a man who has the title SIR, given to him by the king or queen —compare DAME; see also DUB   **3** (in CHESS) a piece, usu. with a horse's head, that moves two squares forward or backward and one or two squares sideways, moving three squares altogether —see picture at CHESS   **4 knight in shining armour** a brave or admirable person, esp. one who saves a person from a dangerous or difficult situation. In old stories, a **knight in shining armour** (=a noble man wearing a suit of ARMOUR) often rescued (RESCUE) a young noble woman called a **damsel in distress**. —see also DAMSEL

knight[2] *v* [T] to make (someone) a knight: *He has been knighted by the Queen for services to British industry.*

knight-er·rant /ˌ·ˈ·ˌ·/ *n* **knights-errant** a knight in former times who wandered in search of adventures, esp. ones which included helping people in trouble

knight·hood /ˈnaɪthʊd/ *n* [C;U] the rank, title, or state of a knight: *He received a knighthood for his services to British industry.*

knight·ly /ˈnaɪtli/ *adj lit* of or suitable to a knight, esp. in being brave and noble: *knightly conduct*

Knights·bridge /ˈnaɪtsbrɪdʒ/ an area of W central London which has a number of expensive, fashionable shops, and where it is generally very expensive to live

Knights of the Round Ta·ble /ˌ·····ˌ· ˈ··/ [*the* +P] according to old stories, the KNIGHTS (KNIGHT[1] (1)) of the court of King Arthur, who all sat at a round table so that none appeared to be more important than any others —see also ARTHURIAN LEGEND

Knights Tem·plars /ˌnaɪts ˈtempləz‖-ərz/ [*the*+P] members of the military religious order of the Poor Knights of Christ, also called **Knights of the Temple of Solomon**. They protected people travelling in the Holy Land during the Crusades.

knit[1] /nɪt/ *v* **knitted** *or* **knit** [I;T]   **1** to make (things to wear) by joining woollen threads into a close network with long needles (**knitting needles**). Knitting is usu. done by women: *to knit a sweater* | *I can knit while I watch TV.* [+obj(i)+obj(d)] *She's knitting the baby a pair of bootees.* —compare CROCHET[2]   **2** *tech* to use a PLAIN[4] stitch in making (something) in this way: *Knit one, purl one.* | *Knit to the last ten stitches.* —compare PURL   **3** [(TOGETHER)] to join (people or things) closely: *It's not a serious break; the bone should knit (together) in a couple of weeks.*   **4 knit one's brows** *lit* to show displeasure, worry, or deep thought by frowning (FROWN[1]) —see also CLOSE-KNIT —~ **ter** *n* : *She's a fast knitter.*

knit[2] *n* PLAIN[4]

knit·ting /ˈnɪtɪŋ/ *n* [U] something which is being knitted: *She keeps her knitting in a bag.*

knitting ma·chine /ˈ·· ·ˌ·/ *n* a machine used for knitting

knit·wear /ˈnɪt-weər/ *n* [U] knitted clothing: *This shop sells knitwear.*

knives /naɪvz/ *pl. of* KNIFE[1]

knob /nɒb‖nɑːb/ *n*   **1** a round lump, esp. on the surface or at the end of something: *a stick with a knob on the end* | *a knob of butter*   **2** a round handle or control button: *the knobs on a TV*   **3** *Br taboo sl* a PENIS   **4 with knobs on** *BrE old-fash sl* (used to make esp. an angry remark stronger): *"You're an idiot!" "And the same to you, with knobs on!"*

knob·bly /ˈnɒbli‖ˈnɑːbli/ *BrE* ‖ **knob·by** /ˈnɒbi‖ˈnɑːbi/ *AmE— adj* having round knob-like lumps: *knobbly knees*

knock[1] /nɒk‖nɑːk/ *v*   **1** [I] **a** [(**against**)] to come into forceful connection with, usu. making a noise when doing so: *a branch knocking against the window* **b** [(**on, at**)] to hit a door firmly with esp. one's hand or a KNOCKER (1), esp. in order to inform the people inside of one's presence: *Please knock (on/at the door) before entering.* —compare TAP[3]   **2** [T] **a** to hit hard: *Don't knock those glasses, they're fragile!* [+obj+adv/prep] *He knocked the fish on the head to kill it quickly.* | *She knocked a cup off the table.* | *She knocked some nails into the wall.* | *He knocked their heads together to make them see sense.* [+obj+adj] *A falling branch knocked him unconscious.* **b** [+obj+adv/prep] to make (something) by hitting hard: *He knocked a hole in the wall.*   **3** [T] *infml* to express unfavourable opinions about; CRITICIZE: *Stop knocking him; he's doing his best.*   **4** [I] (of a car engine) to make a noise because something is wrong: *If the engine starts knocking, it could be a worn big-end bearing.* —see also ANTIKNOCK   **5 knock someone cold: a** to KNOCK out (1a) **b** also **knock someone sideways/for six** to surprise someone and usu. make them unable to act in reply: *The news of her sudden death really knocked me for six.*   **6 knock something on the head** *infml* to prevent a hope, plan, suggestion, etc. from being put into action   **7 knock someone's block off** (esp. in threats) to hit someone very severely: *If you insult my wife again I'll knock your block off!*   **8 knock spots off** *BrE infml* to defeat easily; be much better than: *He can knock spots off me at tennis.*   **9 knock the bottom out of** *infml* to take away the necessary support on which something rests: *The bad news knocked the bottom out of market prices.* | *That knocks the bottom out of my argument.*   **10 take a knock** to suffer a physical blow: (fig.) *Her hopes of becoming an MP have taken quite a knock.*   **11 you could have knocked me**

down/over with a feather *infml, often humor* I was extremely surprised −see also **knock one's head against a brick wall** (HEAD¹ (25)) **12 knock on wood** *AmE* ‖ **touch wood** *BrE* (used to keep away bad luck, so that something good will continue): *My house has never been burgled, knock on wood.*

knock about/around *phr v infml* **1** [I;T (=**knock about** sthg.) *no pass.*] to remain unnoticed in (a place): *That old typewriter has been knocking about (the house) for years.* **2** [I+*adv/prep*] to be active, and esp. to travel continuously: *He's knocked about in Africa for years.* **3** [I (**with**, TOGETHER)] to be seen in public (with someone); have a relationship, often sexual: *Sally's been knocking about with Jim for years.* **4** [T] (**knock** sbdy. **about**) to treat roughly, esp. by hitting: *They say he knocks his wife about.* | *The prisoner seemed to have been knocked about a bit.* −see also KICK¹ **about/around**

knock back *phr v* [T] *infml* **1** (**knock** sthg. ↔ **back**) to drink quickly or in large quantities: *I've seen him knock back ten whiskies in an evening.* **2** (**knock** sbdy. **back** sthg.) *BrE* to cost (a large amount): *That car must have knocked you back a few pounds!* **3** (**knock** sbdy. **back**) to surprise; shock: *The news really knocked him back.*

knock sbdy./sthg. ↔ **down** *phr v* [T *often pass.*] **1** to destroy and remove the structure of (a building, bridge, etc.); DEMOLISH: *Our house is being knocked down to make way for a new road.* **2** *BrE* also **knock** sbdy. ↔ **over**− to hit (someone) with the vehicle one is driving, so that they fall to the ground: *Alec was knocked down by a bus yesterday.* **3** [(**to**)] to (cause to) reduce (a price): *The price was knocked down to £3. | I knocked him down to £3.* **4** [(**to**)] (at an AUCTION) to sell, usu. at a low price: *The wine was knocked down at £30/was knocked down to Mr Johnson for £30.* −see also KNOCKDOWN

knock sbdy. **into** *phr v* [T] to teach to (someone) by force (not usu. physical force): *Try to knock some sense into him/into his head.* −see also **knock something into shape** (SHAPE¹ (5))

knock off *phr v* **1** [T] (**knock** sthg. ↔ **off**) (of a seller) to lower a price by (the stated amount): *As it's slightly damaged, I'll knock $2 off.* **2** [I;T (=**knock off** sthg.) *no pass.*] *infml* to stop doing (something, esp. work): *Let's knock off (work) early today. | Here,* **knock it off!** (=stop being annoying) *Can't you see I'm trying to concentrate?* **3** [T] (**knock** sthg. ↔ **off**) *infml* to produce quickly or (too) easily: *He can knock off a fake Renoir in an afternoon.* −see also KNOCKOFF **4** [T] (**knock** sthg. ↔ **off**) *BrE sl* to steal: *He's knocked off a lorry-load of TV sets.* **5** [T] (**knock off** sthg.) also **knock over** *AmE*− *sl* to rob: *They knocked off the Post Office and got away with £4000.* **6** [T] (**knock** sbdy. ↔ **off**) *sl* to murder

knock sbdy./sthg. ↔ **out** *phr v* [T] **1 a** to knock unconscious **b** (in BOXING) to make (one's opponent) lose consciousness or be unable to rise before a count of ten seconds; see also KNOCKOUT¹ **2** *infml* (of a drug) to make (someone) go to sleep: *A few drops of morphia will knock him out.* −see also KNOCKOUT² **3** [(**of**) *often pass.*] to defeat and so dismiss from a competition; ELIMINATE: *Our team was knocked out in the first round of the competition.* **4** to cause to suddenly fail to work; make useless: *Telephone communications were knocked out by the storm.* **5** *sl* to fill with great admiration: *The way that group plays really knocks me out.*

knock over *phr v* [T] **1** (**knock** sbdy. **over**) to KNOCK **down** (2) **2** (**knock over** sthg.) *AmE for* KNOCK **off** (5)

knock sthg. ↔ **together** *phr v* [T] to make quickly and without great care: *She knocked together a meal out of leftovers.*

knock up *phr v* **1** [T] (**knock** sthg. ↔ **up**) *BrE infml* to make in a hurry: *I can probably knock up a meal if you wait a few minutes.* **2** [T] (**knock** sbdy. **up**) *BrE infml* to wake by knocking: *Knock me up at 7.30.* **3** [I] *BrE* (esp. in tennis) to practise before beginning a real game **4** [T] (**knock** sbdy. ↔ **up**) *AmE taboo sl* to cause (a woman, esp. one who is not married) to become PREGNANT

knock² *n* **1** (the sound of) a striking action: *a knock at the door* **2** *infml* a piece of bad luck or trouble: *He's taken/had quite a few hard knocks lately.* **3** a (single) sound made by an engine knocking (KNOCK¹ (4))

knock·a·bout /ˈnɒkəbaʊt‖ˈnɑː-/ *adj* [A] (of a theatre performance, a film, or a performer) causing laughter by wild silly behaviour; SLAPSTICK: *a knockabout comedy*

knock·down /ˈnɒkdaʊn‖ˈnɑːk-/ *adj* [A] (of a price) the lowest possible: *He couldn't sell them even at the knock-down price of £5.* −see also KNOCK **down**

knock-down-drag-out /ˌ·· ·ˈ·· ·/ *adj AmE* showing very violent behaviour and unwillingness to stop from fighting: *a knock-down-drag-out boxing match/divorce*

knock·er /ˈnɒkəʳ‖ˈnɑː-/ *n* **1** also **doorknocker**− a metal instrument fixed to a door and used by visitors for knocking at the door **2** *derog* a person who is always expressing unfavourable opinions

knock·ers /ˈnɒkəz‖ˈnɑːkərz/ *n* [P] *sl* a woman's breasts

knock-kneed /ˌ·ˈ·◄‖ˈ·ˌ·/ *adj* having knees that bend inwards and so often touch each other when walking

knock-knock joke /ˌ· ·ˈ· ˌ·/ *n* a joke which begins by the teller saying "Knock-knock"; the listener replies by saying "Who's there?" and the joke usu. is funny because of a clever way of using words (=PUN): *"Knock-knock." "Who's there?" "Ivan" "Ivan who?" "Ivan (=I've an) idea you don't want to let me in."*

knock·off /ˈnɒkɒf ‖ ˈnɑːkɔːf/ *n AmE infml* a cheap copy of something expensive: *knockoffs of fashionable sports shoes*

knock-on /ˈ·· ·/ *adj* [A] *esp. BrE* marked by a set of events, actions, etc., each of which is caused by the one before: *These price rises will have a* **knock-on effect** *throughout the economy.* −compare DOMINO EFFECT

knock·out¹ /ˈnɒk-aʊt‖ˈnɑːk-/ *n* **1** also **KO**− (in BOXING) an act of knocking one's opponent down so that he cannot get up again: *He won the fight by a knockout.* | (fig.) *The new regulations dealt a knockout blow to (=ruined) our chances of starting up a business.* −see also KNOCK **out 2** a competition from which one is dismissed if one loses a match: *Our team got to the final of the knockout competition.* **3** *infml* someone or something causing great admiration: *Their latest record's a real knockout.*

knockout² *adj infml* **1** causing great admiration: *a knockout dress/song* **2** causing unconsciousness: *knockout drops*

knock-up /ˈ·· ·/ *n* **1** [C] *BrE* (esp. in tennis) an act or period of knocking up (KNOCK **up**) **2** [U] *AmE taboo sl for* SEXUAL INTERCOURSE

knoll /nəʊl/ *n* a small round hill

knot¹ /nɒt‖nɑːt/ *n* **1** a fastening formed by tying together the ends of a piece or pieces of string, rope, wire, etc.: *She tied her belt with a knot.* | (fig., *pomp*) *Now that divorce is easier, untying the* **marriage knot** *is no longer such a problem.* −see also GRANNY KNOT, REEF KNOT **2** a hard mass formed in wood at the place where a branch joins a tree **3** [(**of**)] a small group of people close together: *Little knots of people had formed, excitedly whispering about the rumours.* **4** a hard swelling or mass: *The muscles of his arms stood out in knots as he lifted the heavy box.* **5** a measure of the speed of a ship, about 1853 metres (= 6080 feet) per hour −see also GORDIAN KNOT, **at a rate of knots** (RATE¹), **tie the knot, tie (up) in knots** (TIE²)

knot² *v* **-tt-** [T (TOGETHER)] **1** to join together (pieces of string, rope, wire, etc.) with a knot: *Knot the ends of the rope together.* | *She had a scarf knotted round her neck.* **2 Get knotted!** *BrE sl* (expresses great, sometimes pretended, annoyance at a person)

knot·ty /ˈnɒti‖ˈnɑːti/ *adj* **1** (of wood) containing knots: *knotty pine furniture* **2** full of difficulties: *a knotty problem*

Knotty Ash /ˌ··ˈ·/ a part of Liverpool famous for being the home of the Diddymen, characters invented by the British COMEDIAN Ken Dodd −see also DIDDYMEN, Ken DODD

know¹ /nəʊ/ *v* **knew** /njuː‖nuː/, **known** /nəʊn/ [*not in progressive forms*] **1** [I;T (**about**)] to have knowledge of (something), esp. as a result of personal experience; have (information) in the mind: *I asked her where you were, but she said she didn't know.* | *"He's very ill." "Yes, I know." | I think so, but I don't know for certain. | "Where's the library?" "I wouldn't know."* (=I don't know.) | *As far as/So far as I know, he's abroad.* (=I believe that he is) | *I think he knows about it, but he won't admit it.* | *Do you know the answer to this question? | What do you know about the disappearance of all this money? | He's missed the last three meetings — I* **might have known** *he'd miss this one. | He thinks he* **knows all the answers.** (=behaves as if he knows everything) | *When it comes to politics, she really* **knows what she's talking about.**

(=knows a lot about politics) | *"Be careful with that dynamite!" "Don't worry; I know what I'm doing."* (=I have enough skill and experience to deal with it properly) | *I want to know* (= to be told) *what you intend to do about this.* | *She knows LA* **like the back of her hand** (=very well indeed) [+*(that)*] *I know (that) she doesn't like it.* | *How was I to know it would explode?* (=I could not possibly have known it) [+*wh-*] *Do you know where they are?* | *The door opened and you-know-who came in.* (=you can guess who it was) | (*fml*) *I know him to be* (=know that he is) *a liar/dishonest.* **2** [T] to have learnt (and be able to do): *She really knows her job.* (= is very good at it) | *He knows all of Keats's poetry* **by heart.** | *Do you know* (=can you speak and read) *German?* [+*wh-*] *I don't know how to swim.* −see also KNOW-HOW **3** [T] to be familiar with (a person, place, etc.): *I've known Martin for years.* | *Do you know New York well?* | *He's a strange man, but quite pleasant when you* **get to know** *him.* | *He'll be late as usual, knowing him.* **4** [T **(by)**] to be able to recognize: *I'd know him again if I saw him.* | *She knows a good wine when she tastes it.* | *You'll know him by the colour of his hair.* −see also KNOW **apart,** KNOW **from 5** [T] **a** *fml* to experience (something) fully and deeply: *He has known both grief and happiness.* **b** [+ *obj+ to-v/to-v*; *only in past and perfect tenses*] to see, hear, etc.: *I've known him to run/(esp. BrE) known him run ten miles before breakfast.* (=this is what he sometimes does, surprisingly). | *She's never been known to be late.* (= She is never late.) **6 I don't know** (used for expressing slight disagreement): *"I reckon she's mad." "Oh, I don't know; I think she's just a bit strange."* **7 I know** (used when one suddenly has an idea, finds an answer to a problem, etc.): *What can we get her for her birthday? Oh, I know − let's give her some flowers.* **8 know a thing or two** *infml* to have practical useful information gained from experience **9 know better: a** to be wise or well-trained enough (not to): *She's old enough to know better than to take sweets from a strange man.* **b** to know or think that one knows more (than someone or anyone else): *He says he was there at the time, but I know better.* (=I know he was not) | *I suppose you think you know better than your parents!* **10 know one's business** to be good at doing one's work, arranging one's life, etc. **11 know one's own mind** to have firm ideas about what one wants, likes, etc. **12 know one's stuff/one's onions** *infml* to be good at or know all one should know about one's work, a subject, etc. **13 know which side one's 'bread is buttered** *infml* to know how to make oneself liked by people in power or how to gain their approval; know what is to one's advantage **14 let someone know** to tell or inform someone: *Let me know when you'll be coming.* | *Thank you for your application; we'll let you know.* (=tell you soon whether you have been successful in getting the job or not) **15 not know someone from Adam** *infml* not to know who someone, esp. a man, is or what they look like: *I've met her several times, but she says she doesn't know me from Adam.* **16 not that I know of** not so far as I know; not to my knowledge: *"Is there anything else to discuss?" "Not that I know of."* **17 there's no knowing** it is impossible to know: *There's no knowing what the eventual cost will be.* **18 (Well,) what do you know!** *infml, esp. AmE* (used as an expression of usu. pleased surprise): *"I'm getting married tomorrow." "Well, what do you know!"* **19 you know** *infml* **a** (used for adding force to a statement) −see USAGE **b** [ˈ·ˌ·/] (used when one is reminding someone of something): *"Who's Chris?" "Oh, you know, that boy she's been seeing."* **20 you never know** (often used to avoid giving a direct answer to a question) possibly; perhaps: *"Will you be coming next week?" "You never know."*

▷ USAGE 1 Compare **know** and **learn.** To **know** is to be conscious of (a fact), to have skill in (a subject), or to have met (a person) before: *I knew I had passed my exam before the teacher told me.* | *She knows about computers.* | *Do you know how to drive?* | *I don't know your brother* (=I haven't met him). To **learn** is to gain knowledge of (a fact or subject, but not a person): *I learnt that I had passed the test.* | *She's learning about computers.* | *I'm learning how to drive.* (=I can't drive yet) 2 In informal conversation **you know** is often used (sometimes too much) without very much meaning to attract or keep the attention of the listener, or just to fill pauses in the person's speech: *You know, I've been thinking about what you said yesterday ...* | *It's strange,*

you know, *that he hasn't phoned.* | *I'm very fond of you,* **you know.**◁

know things/people **apart** *phr v* [T] to be able to see the difference between: *The two sisters are so alike you'd hardly know them apart.*

know sthg./sbdy. **backwards** *phr v* [T] *infml* to know or understand perfectly: *We've been through this contract so many times that I know it backwards!*

know sthg./sbdy. **from** sthg./sbdy. *phr v* [T] to understand the difference between (one person or thing) and (another): *He doesn't know his left from his right/know good writing from bad.*

know of sbdy./sthg. *phr v* [T] to have heard of or about something: *Do you know of any way to get wine stains out of cloth?*

know² *n* **in the know** *infml* having more information (about something) than most people: *People in the know say the economy's in trouble.*

know-all /ˈ· ·/ also **know-it-all** *esp. AmE− n infml derog* someone who behaves as if they know everything: *OK Mr. Know-it-all, what's the capital of Namibia?*

know-how /ˈ· ·/ *n* [U] *infml* practical ability or skill; experience in a particular area of activity: *I haven't the technical know-how to attempt this repair job.* | *The Chinese are buying products, equipment, and know-how from abroad.*

know·ing /ˈnəʊɪŋ/ *adj* showing or suggesting that one knows all about something: *He said nothing but gave us a knowing look.*

know·ing·ly /ˈnəʊɪŋli/ *adv* **1** in a knowing manner **2** intentionally; with knowledge of the probable effect: *She would never knowingly hurt anyone.*

know-it-all /ˈ· · ˌ·/ *n esp. AmE* a KNOW-ALL

knowl·edge /ˈnɒlɪdʒ‖ˈnɑː-/ *n* **1** [S;U (**of**)] what a person knows; the facts, information, skills, and understanding that one has gained, esp. through learning or experience: *a man of considerable knowledge* (=who knows a lot) | *discoveries that have increased the sum of human knowledge* (= the amount that people know) | *She has a detailed knowledge of this period.* | *My knowledge of French is rather poor.* | *It's* **common knowledge** (=everyone knows) *that he's a compulsive gambler.* −compare LEARNING; see also WORKING KNOWLEDGE **2** [U] the state of being informed about something; awareness (AWARE): *The matter never came/was never brought to the knowledge of the minister.* (=He never found out or was never told about it.) | *They did it without my knowledge.* (=I didn't know about it) | *I reminded her about our agreement, but she* **denied all knowledge of it.** (= said she knew nothing about it) [+*that*] *We went to bed happy in the knowledge that our daughter was safe.* **3 to (the best of) one's knowledge** so far as one knows: *I am not quite sure, but to the best of my knowledge his story is true.* | *He has been there several times, to my (certain) knowledge.* | *"Has she arrived?" "Not to my knowledge."* **4** [*the*] *BrE* the practical information that a London taxi driver must learn before he is licensed (LICENSE²): *He quit his job at the cafe and now he's doing the knowledge.*

knowl·edge·a·ble /ˈnɒlɪdʒəbəl‖ˈnɑː-/ *adj* [(**about**)] (of a person) knowing a lot: *He's very knowledgeable about wines.* −−**bly** *adv* : *He speaks very knowledgeably about wines.*

known¹ /nəʊn/ *past participle of* KNOW¹: *a disease with no known cure*

known² *adj* **1** [A] generally recognized as being the stated thing: *a known criminal* **2 known as: a** generally recognized as: *She's known as a great singer.* **b** also publicly called; named: *Samuel Clemens, known as Mark Twain, became a famous American writer.* −see also AKA **3 known to** known by; familiar to: *He's known to the police.* (=as a criminal) **4 make oneself known to** *fml* to introduce oneself to **5 make something known** *fml* to tell people about something openly or publicly: *He made it known to his friends that he did not want to enter politics.*

Knox /nɒks‖nɑːks/, **John** (?1514−72) a Scottish religious reformer (REFORM) who established the Church of Scotland and Presbyterianism

knuck·le¹ /ˈnʌkəl/ *n* **1** a finger joint, esp. the one joining the finger to the hand: *I bruised my knuckles.* −see picture at HAND **2** a piece of meat including the lowest joint of the leg: *a knuckle of pork* **3 near the knuckle** *BrE* *infml* almost offensive because of being sexually improper: *That joke of his was a bit near the knuckle, don't you think?*

knuckle² *v*
    knuckle down *phr v* [I (**to**)] to start working hard: *You'll have to knuckle down if you want to pass the exam.*
    knuckle under *phr v* [I (**to**)] to be forced to accept the orders of someone more powerful: *He refused to knuckle under (to any dictatorship).*

knuckle·ball /ˈnʌkəlbɔːl/ *n* (in BASEBALL) a way of throwing a ball which makes the ball move slowly but in unexpected ways

knuckle-dust·er /ˈ·· ˌ··/ ‖ usu. **brass knuckles** *AmE*— *n* a metal covering for the knuckles, used as a weapon for hitting people

KO¹ /ˌkeɪ ˈəʊ/ *n infml for* KNOCKOUT

KO² *v* [T] *infml for* KNOCK out: *The boxer KO'd his opponent right in the first round.*

ko·a·la /kəʊˈɑːlə/ also **koala bear** /·ˌ·· ˈ·/— *n* an Australian tree-climbing animal like a small bear with no tail — see picture at BEAR

Ko·dak /ˈkəʊdæk/ *tdmk* one of the world's largest makers of photographic film, paper, and other related products

koh·i·noor /ˈkəʊinɔːʳ/ the name of a large DIAMOND that is part of the British CROWN JEWELS

kohl /kəʊl/ *n* [U] a powder used esp. in the East by women to darken the skin above and below the eyes

Kohl, Hel·mut /ˈhelmuːt/ (1930–) a German politician, CHANCELLOR of West Germany from 1982 and of united Germany from 1990

kohl·ra·bi /ˌkəʊlˈrɑːbi/ *n* [U] a vegetable of the CABBAGE family whose swollen stem is used for food

Ko·jak /ˈkəʊdʒæk/ an American television DETECTIVE SERIES about a policeman called Kojak, played by the actor Telly Savalas. He was well known for being BALD (=having no hair) and sucking LOLLIPOPS.

Kon-Ti·ki ex·pe·di·tion /kɒn ˈtiːki ekspəˌdɪʃən‖kɑːn-/ [*the*] the journey made in 1947 by the Norwegian EXPLORER Thor Heyerdahl and five others. They sailed a RAFT, the **Kon-Tiki**, from Callao in Peru to Tuamoto Island in the South Pacific, to show that the Polynesian people had done this in earlier times and were therefore descended from the Incas.

kook /kuːk/ *n AmE infml* a person whose ideas or behaviour are unusual or silly

kook·a·bur·ra /ˈkʊkəbʌrə/ also **laughing jackass**— *n* an Australian bird with a call like laughter

kook·y /ˈkuːki/ *adj AmE infml* (esp. of a person) odd; behaving in a silly unusual manner —**iness** *n*

Kool-Aide /ˈkuːleɪd/ *n* [U] *tdmk* a powder which when mixed with water and sugar makes a drink. Kool-Aide is usu. drunk by children: *grape Kool-Aide*

Kop /kɒp‖kɑːp/ [*the*] part of the Anfield football STADIUM in Liverpool where the Liverpool supporters stand

ko·peck , -pek /ˈkəʊpek/ *n* 100th of a ROUBLE, the money used in the former USSR

Ko·ran, Qur'an /kɔːˈrɑːn, kə-‖kəˈræn, -ˈrɑːn/ [*the*] the holy book of the Muslims, containing the writings of Muhammad. These are accepted by Muslims as coming from Allah, being told to Muhammad by Gabriel. — ~ **ic** *adj*

Kor·but /ˈkɔːbət‖ˈkɔːr-, **Ol·ga** /ˈɒlgə‖ˈəʊl-/ (1955–) a Soviet GYMNAST who became famous when she won three gold MEDALS at the 1972 Olympics

Ko·re·a /kəˈriːə/ a country in E Asia, which in 1948 was separated into COMMUNIST North Korea (the Democratic People's Republic; capital Pyonguang; population 22,419,000 (1989)) and South Korea (the Republic of Korea; capital Seoul; population 42,380,000 (1989)) — ~ **an** *n, adj*

Ko·re·an War /kəˌriːən ˈwɔːʳ/ [*the*] a war between Chinese and North Korean forces on the one hand and UN and South Korean forces on the other. The war began in 1950 and ended in 1953, with neither side having won.

ko·sher /ˈkəʊʃəʳ/ *adj* **1** of, providing, or being food, esp. meat, prepared according to Jewish law: *kosher meat* | *a kosher restaurant* — see also JUDAISM **2** *infml* honest and trustworthy; customary or proper: *I don't think he or his business are quite kosher.*

Ko·sin·ski /kəˈzɪnski/, **Jer·zy** /ˈdʒɜːzi‖ˈdʒɜːr-/ (1933–91) an American writer, born in Poland

kow·tow /ˌkaʊˈtaʊ/ *v* [I (**to**)] **1** to obey without question; show too much respect or regard (for the wishes or opinions of): *Be polite, but don't kowtow (to him).* **2** (esp. formerly in SE Asia) to kneel and lower one's head to show respect

KP /ˌkeɪ ˈpiː/ *n AmE often humor* work to be done by soldiers in a kitchen: *He's assigned to KP today.*

kph *written abbrev. for:* kilometres per hour

kraal /krɑːl/ *n* **1** a village in South Africa with a fence around it **2** *SAfrE* an enclosed piece of ground in which cows, sheep, etc., are kept at night

Kraft /krɑːft‖kræft/ *n* [U] *tdmk* a company which produces different types of cheese, often in convenient packets

Kra·ken /ˈkrɑːkən/ *n* in Norse MYTHOLOGY a very large frightening sea-animal

Kray twins /ˈkreɪ ˌtwɪnz/ [*the*+P] (1933–) two brothers, **Ronnie Kray** and **Reggie Kray**, who were responsible for a great deal of violent crime in the East End of London in the 1960s. They were put in prison in 1969 for the murders of two men, the judge saying that they should serve at least 30 years.

Krem·lin /ˈkremlɪn/ [*the*] **1** the group of buildings in Moscow which was the centre of the government of the Soviet Union **2** [+*sing./pl. v*] the government of the Soviet Union: *How will the Kremlin answer the latest message from Washington?*

kris /kriːs/ *n* (in Malaysia or Indonesia) a knife with a wavy blade, used as a weapon

Krish·na /ˈkrɪʃnə/ in Hindu MYTHOLOGY, a god who represents Vishnu, in the form of a COWHERD

Kriss Krin·gle /ˌkrɪs ˈkrɪŋgəl/ *AmE* SANTA CLAUS

kro·na /ˈkrəʊnə/ *n* **-nor** /nɔːʳ/ the standard coin in the money system of Sweden and Iceland

kro·ne /ˈkrəʊnə/ *n* **-ner** /nəʳ/ the standard coin in the money system of Denmark and Norway

Kru·ger·rand /ˈkruːgəˌrænd/ *n* a South African gold coin. They are not used as money, but are bought esp. by foreigners as a way of investing (INVEST (1)) in gold.

kryp·ton /ˈkrɪptɒn‖-tɑːn/ *n* [U] a gas, found in the air, which is a simple substance (= ELEMENT)

Krypton the imaginary PLANET (=other world) where the character Superman was born — see also SUPERMAN

Kryp·ton·ite /ˈkrɪptənaɪt/ *n* [U] a type of imaginary rock that comes from the PLANET Krypton in the Superman stories. It is harmful to Superman. — see also SUPERMAN

KS¹ /ˌkeɪ ˈes/ *n* KAPOSI'S SARCOMA

KS² *written abbrev. for* KANSAS

Kt *written abbrev. for:* KNIGHT

Kua·la Lum·pur /ˌkwɑːlə ˈlʊmpʊəʳ‖-lʊmˈpʊəɪ/ the largest city and capital of the Federation of Malaysia, SE Asia

Kub·lai Khan /ˌkuːblə ˈkɑːn ‖ -ˈkɑːn, -blaɪ/ (1216–94) a Mongol EMPEROR of China, the GRANDSON of Genghis Khan. He moved the capital of China to Peking.

Ku·brick /ˈkuːbrɪk/, **Stanley** (1928–) an American film director and producer. His films include *Dr Strangelove, 2001: A Space Odyssey, A Clockwork Orange,* and *The Shining.*

ku·dos /ˈkjuːdɒs‖ˈkuːdɑːs/ *n* [U] *esp. BrE* public admiration and glory (for something done); PRESTIGE: *He gained a lot of kudos by winning the literary competition.*

Ku Klux Klan /ˌkuː klʌks ˈklæn/ [*the*] also **KKK**— a secret US political organization of Protestant white men who oppose people of other races or religions. It was particularly violent towards black people during the CIVIL RIGHTS protests of the 1960s, showing little or no regard for the law. Members meet in secret and wear long white clothes and long pointed hats which hide their faces. — see picture on page 730

kuk·ri /ˈkʊkri/ *n* a curved knife used as a weapon by the fighting men of Nepal

küm·mel /ˈkʊməl‖ˈkɪməl/ *n* [U] a strong alcoholic drink which tastes of CARAWAY

kum·quat, cumquat /ˈkʌmkwɒt‖-kwɑːt/ *n* a very small sort of orange

kung fu /ˌkʌŋ ˈfuː/ *n* [U] a Chinese style of fighting without weapons that includes hitting with the hands and feet

Kurd /kɜːd‖kɜːrd/ *n* a member of an Islamic people living in various countries, esp. Iran and Iraq. The Kurds have attempted without success to gain independence and have been attacked several times by the Iraqi government. After the Gulf War of 1990–91, a place of safety, a **safe haven**, was set up inside Iraq by the UN, but they remain under threat of attack.

Ku Klux Klan

Kurd·ish /ˈkɜːdɪʃ‖ˈkɜːrd-/ adj of the Kurds or their language

Kurd·is·tan /ˌkɜːdɪˈstɑːn, -stæn‖ˌkɜːrd-/ the HOMELAND of the Kurds which lies in parts of Turkey, Iran, Iraq, Syria, and the Soviet Union

Ku·ro·sa·wa /ˌkʊərəˈsɑːwə/, **A·ki·ra** /əˈkɪərə/ (1929–) a Japanese film director, probably the best known and

with the greatest influence outside Japan, whose films include *Seven Samurai* and *Kagemusha*

Ku·wait /kʊˈweɪt/ a country in the Middle East, at the NW corner of the Gulf, which has borders with Saudi Arabia and Iraq; capital Kuwait City; population 2,048,000 (1984). It was invaded (INVADE) by Iraq in 1990, and after the resulting Gulf War was returned to the Kuwaitis in 1991. — ~ i n, adj

kw *written abbrev. for:* KILOWATT(s)

kwash·i·or·kor /ˌkwɒʃiˈɔːkəʳ‖ˌkwɑːʃiˈɔːr-/ n [U] a tropical disease of children caused by not eating enough food containing PROTEIN

kwe·la /ˈkweɪlə/ n [U] a kind of dance music popular among black South Africans, that includes a type of whistle among its instruments

kwh *written abbrev. for:* KILOWATT HOUR

Kwik-fit /ˈkwɪk fɪt/ one of a group of GARAGES[1] (2) in Britain where tyres, EXHAUSTS[2] (1), and other spare parts for cars and other vehicles are sold and fitted

Kwik-save /ˈkwɪkseɪv/ one of a group of shops which sell food and other goods cheaply, found in many towns and cities in Britain

KY *written abbrev. for:* KENTUCKY

KY jel·ly /ˌkeɪ waɪ ˈdʒeli/ n [U] *tdmk* a type of JELLY used medically to LUBRICATE certain parts of the body such as the VAGINA. People often make jokes about it because it is connected with sex.

Ky·u·shu /kiˈuːʃuː/ the furthest S and third largest island of Japan

L

L , l /el/ **L's**, **l's** or **Ls**, **ls** **1** the 12th letter of the English alphabet **2** the ROMAN NUMERAL (number) for 50 **3** *AmE infml* ELEVATED RAILWAY

l *written abbrev. for:* **1** (*often cap.*) (on a map) lake **2** line **3** litre

la /lɑː/ *n* [S;U] the sixth note in the SOL-FA musical scale

LA[1] /ˌel ˈeɪ◂/ LOS ANGELES

LA[2] *written abbrev. for:* LOUISIANA

laa·ger /ˈlɑːgəʳ/ *n* [S] (esp. in connection with politics in South Africa) a position of opposing all change and uniting to defend the existing social and political conditions: *Demands for major reforms may simply drive the whites back into their laager.* | *a laager mentality*

lab /læb/ *n infml* **1** *for* LABORATORY **2** LABRADOR

Lab *written abbrev. for:* LABOUR PARTY

la·bel[1] /ˈleɪbəl/ *n* a piece of paper or other material, fixed to something, which gives information about what it is, where it is to go, who owns it, etc.: *luggage labels* | *The label on the bottle says "Poison".* | *The group's latest hit record is on the Ace Sounds label.* (=is produced by the Ace Sounds record company)

label *v* **-ll-** *BrE*‖**-l-** *AmE* [T] **1** to fix or tie a label on: *Make sure your luggage is properly labelled.* [+*obj*+*n*/*adj*] *The doctor labelled the bottle poison/poisonous.* **2** [+*obj*+*n*/*adj*] to describe as belonging to a particular kind or class: *The newspapers had unjustly labelled him (as) a coward.*

la·bi·al /ˈleɪbɪəl/ *n, adj tech* (a speech sound) made using one or both lips —compare BILABIAL

La Bo·hème /lɑː bəʊˈem/ an OPERA written in 1896 by the Italian COMPOSER Giacomo Puccini. It tells the story of a young woman who falls in love with a painter and later dies.

la·bor·a·tory /ləˈbɒrətri‖ˈlæbrətɔːri/ *n* a special building or room in which a scientist works to examine, test, or prepare materials: *This is our new research laboratory.* | *a*

laboratory experiment | *laboratory animals* (=animals used for scientific tests) —see also LANGUAGE LABORATORY

Labor Day /ˈ·· ·/ in the US and Canada, the first Monday in September, taken as a public holiday. Labor Day was originally meant to honour workers, but now many people celebrate it as marking the end of summer. Many people have PICNICs or BARBECUEs over **Labor Day Weekend** and enjoy having the extra day off work.

la·bo·ri·ous /ləˈbɔːrɪəs/ *adj* **1** needing great effort: *Breaking up the stones was a laborious task.* **2** *derog* showing signs of being done with difficulty: *This essay of his is a laborious piece of work.* **~ ly** *adv* : *They made their way laboriously up the mountainside.* **~ ness** *n* [U]

labor u·nion /ˈ·· ˌ··/ *n AmE for* TRADE UNION —see also AFL-CIO, TEAMSTERS

la·bour[1] *BrE* ‖ **labor** *AmE* /ˈleɪbəʳ/ *n* **1** [U] effort or work, esp. tiring physical work: *Building roads still involves* **manual labour**. (= work with hand-held tools) | *The garage charged us for parts and labour.* —see WORK[1] (USAGE) **2** [U+*sing.*/*pl. v*] workers, esp. those who use their hands, considered as a group or class: *It is up to organized labour to band together to fight the government's anti-union laws.* | *plans to cut the company's* **labour force** (=the number of workers) | *Labour relations* (=between the workers and employers) *have improved recently.* **3** [S;U] the act of giving birth: *She was in labour for several hours.* | *labour pains* **4** [C] *fml* (the doing of) a piece of work: *Sit down and rest after your labours!* —see also HARD LABOUR

labour[2] *BrE* ‖ **labor** *AmE v* **1** [I] to work, esp. hard: *They laboured for years to build this monument.* | *I laboured over the report, trying to get it exactly right.* **2** [I+*adv*/*prep*] to move slowly and with difficulty: *She laboured up the hill with her heavy bags.* **3** [T] *also* **belabour**— to describe or deal with (something) in too great detail or by repeating too much: *There's no need to* **labour the point;** *we're all well aware what you mean.* **4** [I] (of an engine) to be working with difficulty at too low a speed

labour under sthg. *phr v* [T] *fml* to have or be influenced by (a mistaken idea): *If you think you're going to be promoted soon I'm afraid you're* **labouring under a delusion.**

Labour[1] /ˈleɪbəʳ/ *n* [U+*sing.*/*pl.v*] the British LABOUR PARTY

laboratory

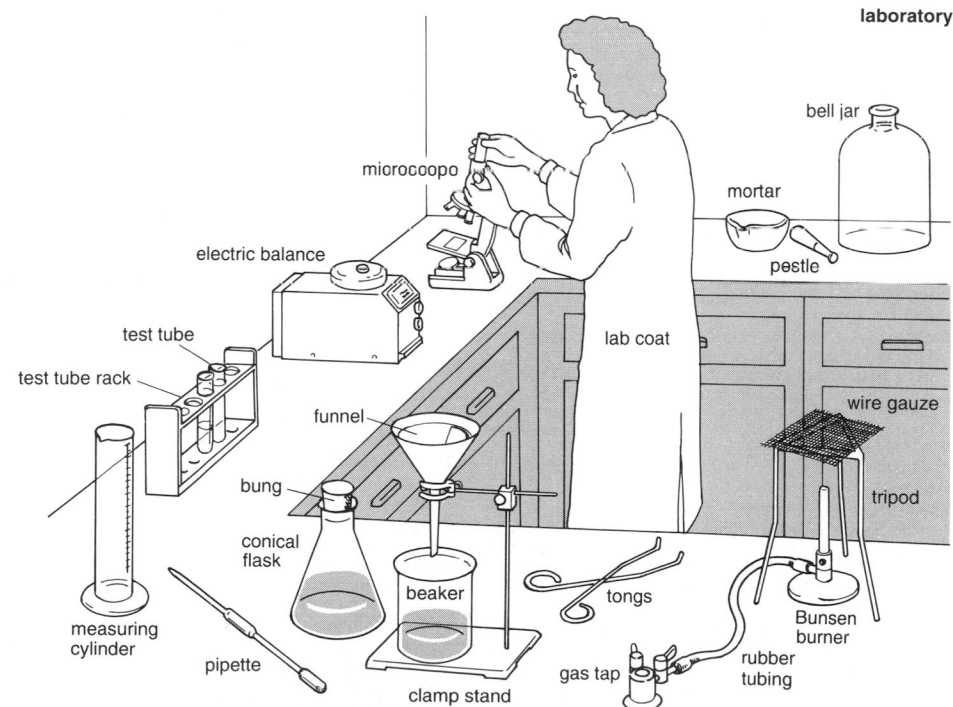

microscope
bell jar
mortar
pestle
electric balance
test tube
lab coat
test tube rack
wire gauze
funnel
tripod
bung
conical flask
beaker
tongs
Bunsen burner
measuring cylinder
pipette
gas tap
rubber tubing
clamp stand

Labour² *adj* supporting or having a connection with the Labour Party: *Do you think Labour will win?* | *We're all Labour in our family.* —see also LABOUR PARTY

la·boured *BrE* ‖ **labored** *AmE* /ˈleɪbəd‖-bərd/ *adj* showing signs of effort and difficulty: *You could tell from the laboured way he read out his speech that he didn't know much English.* | *laboured breathing*

la·bour·er *BrE* ‖ **laborer** *AmE* /ˈleɪbərəʳ/ *n* a worker whose job needs strength rather than skill, esp. one who works outdoors

labour ex·change /ˈ·· ·ˌ·/ *n* *BrE* *old-fash* for JOB CENTRE

labour-in·ten·sive /ˌ··· ·ˈ···◂/ *adj* (of an industry) needing a lot of workers compared to its other needs, such as money —compare CAPITAL-INTENSIVE

labour mar·ket /ˈ·· ˌ··/ *[the]* the supply of workers in a particular country, area, etc., who are ready or suitable for work

labour of love /ˌ··· ·ˈ·/ *n* **labours of love** a piece of work done for one's own pleasure, or to please someone else, and not for money or other gain

Labour Par·ty /ˈ·· ˌ··/ *[the]* a political party trying to obtain social improvement, esp. for workers and less wealthy people —see SOCIALIST (USAGE)

► CULTURAL NOTE The British Labour Party, sometimes called the SOCIALISTs, is one of the two main political parties and has a close association with the TRADE UNIONS (2), although it is not now as left-wing as it used to be. It has not been in power since 1979 but still has many supporters esp. among WORKING-CLASS and MIDDLE-CLASS people. Americans, who are generally more CONSERVATIVE politically than Europeans, associate labour parties with powerful TRADE UNIONS, and take a somewhat negative view of them.◄

la·bour·sav·ing /ˈleɪbəˌseɪvɪŋ‖-bər-/ *adj* that reduces or takes away the need to do work, esp. with one's hands: *laboursaving electrical appliances such as food mixers* | *a laboursaving device*

Lab·ra·dor /ˈlæbrədɔːʳ/ also **Labrador re·triev·er** /ˌ··· ·ˈ··/— *n* a large dog with usu. black or yellow hair —see picture at DOG

la·bur·num /ləˈbɜːnəm‖-ɜːr-/ *n* [C;U] a small decorative tree with long hanging stems of yellow flowers and poisonous seeds

lab·y·rinth /ˈlæbərɪnθ/ *n* [(of)] **1** a network of passages or paths that meet and cross each other, through which it is difficult to find one's way; MAZE: *We made our way through a labyrinth of narrow, twisting alleyways.* | (fig.) *You need an expert to guide you through the labyrinth of rules and regulations on this subject.* **2** *usu. cap* [in] CLASSICAL MYTHOLOGY, a very complicated labyrinth from which few people ever escaped. It was built by Daedalus on the island of Crete and the Minotaur was kept there. —see also THESEUS, MINOTAUR — ~ **ine** /ˌlæbəˈrɪnθaɪn◂, -θ‿n/ *adj*

lace¹ /leɪs/ *n* **1** [U] a netlike decorative cloth made of fine thread: *lace curtains* —see also LACY **2** [C] a string or cord that is pulled through holes in the edges of an opening, esp. in shoes (SHOELACE) or clothing, to pull the edges together and fasten them —see PAIR (USAGE), and see picture at SHOE

lace² *v* [T] **1** [(UP)] to pull together or fasten by tying a lace: *If you don't lace up your shoes, you'll trip over.* **2** [(UP)] to pass a string, thread, lace, etc., through holes in (something): *I always have trouble lacing these football boots.* **3** [(with)] to add a small amount of something strong to (a drink): *coffee laced with brandy* | *She laced her husband's bedtime drink with poison.*
    lace into sbdy. *phr v* [T] *infml rare* to attack physically or with words

la·ce·rate /ˈlæsəreɪt/ *v* [T] to tear or roughly cut (skin, part of the body, etc.) as with fingernails or broken glass: (fig.) *Nothing could soothe her lacerated (=hurt) feelings.* —**ration** /ˌlæsəˈreɪʃən/ *n* [C;U] : *He was thrown through the window, and received severe lacerations of/to the face and chest.*

lace-up /ˈ· ·/ *n* [usu. P] *esp. BrE* a shoe or boot that is fastened with laces. They are usu. thought of as sensible and unexciting: *My mother would only let me wear lace-ups to school.*

lach·ry·mal /ˈlækrɨməl/ *adj* *tech* of tears or the part of the

body (**lachrymal gland**) that produces them

lach·ry·mose /ˈlækrɨməʊs/ *adj* *fml* **1** often crying; TEARFUL **2** *often derog* tending to cause tears; sad: *lachrymose poetry*

lack¹ /læk/ *v* [T] **1** to be without; not have, or not have enough of (esp. something needed or wanted): *The female bird lacks the male's bright coloration.* | *He's good at his job but he seems to lack confidence.* | *What the company lacks is sufficient money to invest in new products.* —see also LACKING **2 lack for nothing** to have everything one needs

▷ USAGE Compare **lack** and **be short of.** Both can mean "not to have enough of something" but **lack** (or commonly **be lacking in**) is used especially with abstract nouns: *The teacher said that the child* **lacked/was lacking in** *confidence.* **Be short of** is more common than **lack** when talking about objects and materials: *We're* **short of** *sugar/apples.* (**Lack** would be very formal in sentences like these.)◁

lack² *n* [S;U] **(of)** the state of not having (enough of) something: *The plants died through/for lack of water.* | *There's a certain lack of enthusiasm for these changes among the membership.*

lack·a·dai·si·cal /ˌlækəˈdeɪzɪkəl◂/ *adj* *derog* not showing (enough) interest or effort; lazy: *She has a rather lackadaisical approach to her work.* — ~ **ly** /kli/ *adv*

lack·ey /ˈlæki/ *n* *derog* a person who behaves like a servant by always obeying

lack·ing /ˈlækɪŋ/ *adj* [F] **1** not present; missing: *We can't confirm these rumours because accurate information is lacking.* | *I was happy as a child, but there was something lacking (in my life).* **2** [+ **in**] without the usual or needed amount of (a quality, skill, etc.): *I'm afraid he's somewhat lacking in intelligence/tact/initiative.*

lack·lus·tre *BrE* ‖ **-ter** *AmE* /ˈlækˌlʌstəʳ/ *adj* *derog* unexciting; dull: *a lacklustre speech/performance*

la·con·ic /ləˈkɒnɪk‖-ˈkɑː-/ *adj* *fml* using few words: *a laconic way of speaking* — ~ **ally** /kli/ *adv* : *"Wait and see!" he replied laconically.*

lac·quer¹ /ˈlækəʳ/ *n* [U] a transparent or coloured substance used for forming a hard shiny surface on metal or wood, or for making hair stay in place

lacquer² *v* [T] to cover with lacquer

lacrosse

la·crosse /ləˈkrɒs‖ləˈkrɔːs/ *n* [U] a game played on a field by two teams, each player having a long stick with a net at the end to throw, catch, and carry the small hard ball. In Britain many people think of lacrosse as being played only by girls at private schools. —see picture at STICK

lac·ta·tion /lækˈteɪʃən/ *n* [U] *tech* **1** the production of milk for babies by a human or animal mother **2** the time that this lasts

lac·tic /ˈlæktɪk/ *adj* *tech* of or obtained from milk

lactic a·cid /ˌ·· ·ˈ··/ *n* [U] an acid found in sour milk

lac·tose /ˈlæktəʊs/ *n* [U] a sugary substance found in milk, sometimes used as a food for babies and sick people

la·cu·na /ləˈkjuːnə‖-ˈkuː-/ *n* **-nae** /niː/ *or* **-nas** *fml* an empty space where something is missing, esp. in a piece of writing

lac·y /ˈleɪsi/ *adj* of or like LACE¹

lad /læd/ *n* **1** *esp. BrE infml* a boy or young man: *He's just a lad.* | *It's my eldest lad's* (=son's) *birthday today.* **2** *BrE infml* a playfully rude man: *Ron's* **a (bit of a) lad,** *isn't he? He flirts with all the girls.* **3** a STABLE BOY: *the head lad* —compare LASS; see also LADS, JACK THE LAD

La·da /ˈlɑːdə/ *n* *tdmk* a type of car made in the former Soviet Union and sold in Britain at a very low price compared to most cars

Lad·brokes /ˈlædbrʊks/ one of Britain's largest betting

(BET¹) companies, which has shops in many towns and cities

lad·der¹ /ˈlædəʳ/ n **1** a structure consisting of two bars or ropes joined to each other by steps (RUNGs), and used for climbing, e.g. up the side of a building or ship: *He was standing on a ladder picking apples.* | (fig.) *She's working hard to try to get up the promotion ladder.*

▶ CULTURAL NOTE There is an old SUPERSTITION which says that it is unlucky to walk under a ladder. ◀

2 *BrE* ‖ **run** *AmE*– a long thin upright fault in STOCKINGs, etc., caused by stitches coming undone **3** (in sports such as SQUASH and TABLE TENNIS) a list of players who play each other regularly in order to decide who is best. A winner goes up the list; a loser goes down.

ladder² v [I;T] *BrE* to develop or cause (TIGHTS, etc.) to develop a ladder: *My tights laddered/I laddered my tights on a nail.*

lad·die , -dy /ˈlædi/ n *infml, esp. ScotE* a boy; lad

la·den /ˈleɪdn/ adj [(**with**)] (heavily) loaded: *the heavily laden ship* | *The lorry was* **fully laden.** | *The bushes were laden with fruit.* | (fig., lit) *He was laden* (=deeply troubled) *with sorrow.*

la·di·da, lah·di·dah /ˌlɑː di ˈdɑː/ adj infml derog pretending to be in a higher social position than one actually is in, by using unnaturally delicate manners, ways of speaking, etc.: *She/her voice/her manner is a bit too la-di-da for my liking.*

la·dies /ˈleɪdiz/ *BrE* ‖ **ladies room** /ˈ·· ·/ *AmE*– n ladies a women's TOILET –compare GENTS; see TOILET (USAGE)

Ladies' Day /ˈ·· ˌ·/ **1** the second day of RACING at Ascot, when ladies wear unusual hats and fashionable clothes –see also ASCOT **2** *AmE* a day when women may attend an event at a reduced cost: *It's Ladies' Day at the ballpark today so women can get in for half price.*

Ladies' Home Jour·nal /ˌ·· ˌ· ˈ··/ an UPPER-CLASS and rather old-fashioned British magazine for women

ladies' man /ˈ·· ·/ n a man who likes to spend his time with women, and is (sexually) attractive to them

Ladies' night /ˈ·· ·/ **1** (in the UK) a special evening when women are allowed into a men's club as guests of a member **2** *AmE* a night when women may attend an event at a reduced cost: *On Tuesday they're having a Ladies' night with half-price drinks.*

la·dies·wear /ˈleɪdizweəʳ/ n [U] women's clothing; a word used on signs or in departments in shops

la·ding /ˈleɪdɪŋ/ n [C;U] see BILL OF LADING

la·dle¹ /ˈleɪdl/ n a large deep spoon with a long handle, used esp. for lifting liquids out of a container: *a soup ladle* – see picture at SPOON

ladle² v [T (OUT, **into**)] to serve (food, soup, etc.), esp. with a ladle

ladle sthg. ↔ **out** phr v [T] *infml, usu. derog* to give out in large amounts and usu. without careful judgment: *He ladles out compliments to everyone, but he's not really sincere.*

lads /lædz/ n [the+P] *BrE infml* a group of men that one knows and likes

▶ CULTURAL NOTE The word is usually used by or about young WORKING-CLASS men, who typically have a large group of male friends with whom they may play sport, esp. football, or go out drinking in PUBs: *He spends every evening at the pub with the lads.* | *The lads* (= my/our team) *played brilliantly this afternoon.* | *Jeff's one of the lads.* (= a loyal member of the group) ◀

la·dy /ˈleɪdi/ n **1** a *polite* woman: *Good morning, ladies!* | *the lady of the house* (=the wife and mother in the family) | *a lady doctor* **b** a woman of good manners and behaviour or of high social position: *They could tell as soon as they saw her that she was a lady.* **c** apprec a woman of the stated type: *The new boss is a very businesslike lady.* **2** old use and poet a man's wife or female friend: *the captain and his lady* **3** sl, esp. AmE (used for addressing a woman): *You dropped your handkerchief, lady!* **4** **and all because the lady loves Milk Tray** a phrase used in advertisements for Milk Tray chocolates –see MILK TRAY **5** **the lady's not for turning** a phrase, slightly changed from the title of a play *The Lady's not for Burning* by Christopher Fry, used by Margaret THATCHER when refusing to change her policies (POLICY) and afterwards often used about her; see also BAG LADY,

FIRST LADY, LEADING LADY, OLD LADY; see GENTLEMAN (USAGE)

Lady n **a** a woman of noble rank: *Good morning, my lady.* **b** the wife or daughter of a nobleman or the wife of a KNIGHT: *Sir Harold and Lady Wilson* **c** a woman with a high position: *Lady President* –see also LADYSHIP, OUR LADY

Lady, The a small, rather old-fashioned British magazine in which UPPER-CLASS women often advertise for servants

Lady and the Tramp /ˌ·· · · ˈ·/ a CARTOON film made in 1955 by Walt Disney, about two dogs that fall in love with each other. One of the dogs (**the Lady**) is of a special breed and very well cared for, while the other (the **Tramp**) is a mixture of breeds and has to take care of himself.

la·dy·bird /ˈleɪdibɜːd‖-bɜːrd/ *BrE* ‖ **la·dy·bug** /ˈleɪdibʌg/ *AmE*– n a small round BEETLE (type of insect) that is usu. red with black spots

Ladybird 1 *tdmk* a make of children's clothing **2** the name of a set of books with hard covers for children, now produced by Ladybird Books Ltd in England: *the Ladybird reading scheme*

Lady Boun·ti·ful /ˌ·· ˈ···/ derog a rich woman who makes a show of giving to the poor: *She likes to think she's Lady Bountiful.*

Lady Chap·el /ˈ·· ˌ··/ a CHAPEL in a Christian, esp. a ROMAN CATHOLIC, church where people go to pray to Mary, the mother of Christ. It usu. contains a picture or STATUE of her.

Lady Chat·ter·ley /ˌleɪdi ˈtʃætəli‖-tər-/ a character in *Lady Chatterley's Lover*, a book by D H Lawrence which was banned (BAN¹) for years after it was written in 1928 because of its use of TABOO language and the fact that Lady Chatterley, an UPPER-CLASS woman, had a sexual affair with her GAMEKEEPER. It was finally published (PUBLISH) in Britain in 1960, after a court ruled that it was not OBSCENE.

Lady Day /ˈ·· ·/ 25 March, the day on which, according to the Bible, the news was given to the Virgin Mary by the Angel Gabriel that she would become the mother of the son of God. Until 1752 it was the official beginning of the year in law.

Lady Di /ˌ·· ˈ·/ a name by which the Princess of Wales was informally known before she was married. Her full name was Lady Diana Spencer.

lady fin·ger /ˈ·· ˌ··/ n AmE a small, finger-shaped cake that is used to make DESSERTs

lady friend /ˈ·· ˌ·/ n usu. humor. a man's female friend; a girlfriend: *I saw you in the pub last night with your lady friend.* –compare YOUNG LADY

lady-in-wait·ing /ˌ·· · ˈ··/ n ladies-in-waiting a lady who looks after and serves a queen or princess

lady-kill·er /ˈ·· ˌ··/ n infml, sometimes derog a man who charms and attracts all the women he meets: *He thinks he's a real lady-killer, but the girls all laugh at him.*

la·dy·like /ˈleɪdilaɪk/ adj old fash apprec (of a woman or her behaviour) looking like, behaving like, or suitable to a lady; having good manners: *scratching herself in a way that was certainly not ladylike*

Lady Macbeth see Lady MACBETH

lady of the eve·ning /ˌ·· · · ˈ··/ n ladies of the evening euph a PROSTITUTE¹

Lady of the Lake /ˌ·· · · ˈ·/, **The** a rather unreal, shadowy figure with magic powers who appears in stories about King Arthur, most famously as a hand rising from a lake to catch Arthur's sword when he is dying and as one of the three queens who take him by boat to Avalon to die –see ARTHURIAN LEGEND

Lady of the Lamp /ˌ·· · · ˈ·/ see Florence NIGHTINGALE

la·dy's fin·gers /ˈ·· ˌ··/ n [P] OKRA

la·dy·ship /ˈleɪdiʃɪp/ n (often cap.) (used as a title for addressing or speaking of) a woman with the title of Lady: *Good morning, your ladyship.* | *Her ladyship will not be pleased when she hears about this.*

La Fon·taine /ˌlæ fɒnˈteɪn‖ˌlɑː fɑːn-/, **Jean De** /ˈʒɒn də‖ʒɑːn-/ (1621–95) a French poet most famous for his *Fables*, a collection of moral stories in which the characters are animals

lag¹ /læg/ v **-gg-** [I (BEHIND, **behind**)] to move or develop more slowly (than others); considered to be a fault: *He*

lagged behind the rest of the children because he kept stopping to look in shop windows. | *Why is this country lagging behind in the development of space technology?*

lag² *n* a TIME LAG

lag³ *v* **-gg-** [T (**with**)] *BrE* to cover (water pipes and containers) with a special material to prevent loss of heat: *We've lagged the hotwater tank with felt.*

lag⁴ *n* see OLD LAG

la·ger /ˈlɑːɡəʳ/ *n* [C;U] *BrE* (a glass of) a light kind of beer; lager is popular with younger people

lager lout /ˈ·· ˌ·/ *n BrE* a young man who drinks too much lager (or other alcohol) and then misbehaves by making anything from unpleasant remarks to violent attacks on people and property, usu. in the company of others

lag·gard /ˈlæɡəd‖-ərd/ *n old use* a person or thing that is very slow or late

lag·ging /ˈlæɡɪŋ/ *n* [U] *BrE* material used to LAG³ a water pipe or container

la·goon /ləˈɡuːn/ *n* a lake of sea water partly or completely separated from the sea by banks of sand, rock, CORAL, etc.: *a tropical lagoon*

La·gos /ˈleɪɡɒs‖-ɡɑːs/ the largest city and former capital of Nigeria

La Guar·di·a /lə ˈɡwɑːdiə‖-ɑːr-/ one of New York's main airports, used mostly for flights within the US

lah-di-dah /ˌlɑː di ˈdɑː/ *adj* LA-DI-DA

laid /leɪd/ *past tense and participle of* LAY¹

laid-back /ˌ· ˈ·◂/ *adj infml* (of a person or behaviour) cheerfully informal and/or unworried; RELAXED

lain /leɪn/ *past participle of* LIE¹

lair /leəʳ/ *n* the place where a wild animal hides, rests, and sleeps: (fig.) *The police tracked the thieves to their lair.*

laird /leəd‖leərd/ *n* a Scottish landowner —compare SQUIRE (1)

lais·sez-faire , **laisser-faire** /ˌleseɪ ˈfeəʳ, ˌleɪ-/ *n, adj* [U] *Fr* (the principle of) allowing people's activities, esp. business activities, to develop without control: *a laissez-faire attitude/policy*

la·i·ty /ˈleɪ³ti/ *n* [*the*+P] members of a religious group without the special training of priests; laymen (LAYMAN (2))

lake¹ /leɪk/ *n* **1** a large area of water, esp. non-salty water, surrounded by land: *sailing on the lake* | *Lake Michigan* —compare POND **2** a very large amount of the stated usu. liquid product that is additional to what is needed or used: *European economic policies have created a wine lake.* —compare MOUNTAIN (3)

lake² *n* [U] a deep bluish-red colour, esp. of paint

Lake Dis·trict /ˈ· ˌ··/ [*the*] an area in NW England where there are a number of lakes in beautiful mountain scenery which attract many tourists. It includes England's highest mountain, Scafell Pike.

Lake District

Lake Okeechobee see OKEECHOBEE

Lake Wo·be·gon /leɪk ˈwəʊbɪɡɒn‖-ɡɔːn/ *n* a town in the stories of Garrison Keillor which is supposed to be typical of a small town in Minnesota

lakh /læk/ *determiner, n IndE & PakE* a hundred thousand

La-la Land /ˈ·· ˌ·/ see LOS ANGELES

LA Law /ˌel eɪ ˈlɔː/ an American television SERIES set in a law firm

La·lique /læˈliːk/, **Re·né** /ˈreneɪ ‖ rəˈneɪ/ (1860–1945) a French designer of jewellery remembered esp. for his Art Nouveau style

lam¹ /læm/ **-mm-** *v*
　　lam into sbdy./sthg. *phr v* [T] *BrE sl* to beat or attack physically or with words

lam² *n AmE infml* **on the lam** escaping, esp. from the police: *he broke out of jail and now he's on the lam.*

la·ma /ˈlɑːmə/ *n* a Buddhist priest of Tibet, Mongolia, etc. —see also DALAI LAMA

La·ma·is·m /ˈlɑːmə-ɪzəm/ *n* [U] a type of Buddhism practised in Tibet, Mongolia, etc.

La Manche /læ ˈmɒnʃ‖lɑː ˈmɑːnʃ/ the French name for the English Channel

la·ma·se·ry /ˈlɑːməsəri‖-seri/ *n* a building or group of buildings where lamas live

La·maze meth·od /ləˈmɑːz ˌmeθəd/ *n* [*the*] a method developed by a French doctor, **Fernand Lamaze**, for women to learn before giving birth to control their muscles and their breathing while giving birth: *Lamaze classes*

lamb¹ /læm/ *n* **1** [C] a young sheep —see also BAA **2** [U] the meat of a young sheep —see MEAT (USAGE) **3** [C] *infml* a harmless gentle person **4** as/**like a lamb to the slaughter** said of blameless people who are about to experience something bad which they don't deserve or know about: *He walked into the press conference as a lamb to the slaughter.*

lamb² *v* [I] to give birth to lambs: *The sheep are lambing this week.*

Lamb, Charles (1775–1834) an English writer of ESSAYS and criticism, who worked with his sister **Mary Lamb** (1764–1847) on *Tales from Shakespeare*, a book telling the stories of Shakespeare's plays

lam·ba·da /læmˈbɑːdə/ [*the*] (a piece of music for) a sexually suggestive dance originally from Brazil, which became fashionable in Britain in the early 1990s —**lambada** *v* [I]

lam·baste /ˈlæmbeɪst/ also **lam·bast** /-bæst/— *v* [T] *infml* to beat or attack fiercely, either physically or with words: *Her new play was really lambasted by the critics.*

lam·bent /ˈlæmbənt/ *adj lit* **1** (of a flame) having a soft light and moving over a surface without burning it **2** (of light) softly shining **3** gently or playfully clever: *lambent wit*

Lam·beth /ˈlæmbəθ/ an inner London BOROUGH on the S side of the river Thames, a mainly WORKING-CLASS area

Lambeth Con·fer·ence /ˌ·· ˈ···/ [*the*] any of the formal meetings of the world's Church of England BISHOPS (1) held every ten years; the first one was held at Lambeth Palace in 1867

Lambeth Pal·ace /ˌ·· ˈ··/ **1** the official home in London of the ARCHBISHOP OF CANTERBURY, the head of the CHURCH OF ENGLAND **2** (+ *sing./pl.v*) the CHURCH OF ENGLAND speaking officially: *Lambeth Palace has condemned Government policies on the inner city.*

Lambeth walk /ˌ·· ˈ·/ [*the*] a dance which was popular in the past, in which dancers form a long line, usu. in the street. It was danced to a popular song with the same name.

Lamb of God /ˌ·· · ˈ·/ [*the*] another name for Jesus

lamb·skin /ˈlæmˌskɪn/ *n* [C;U] (leather made from) the skin of a lamb, esp. with the wool on it

lame¹ /leɪm/ *adj* **1** not able to walk properly because one's leg or foot is hurt or has some sort of weakness: *The horse went lame.* **2** *infml* not easily believed; weak: *a lame excuse* — ~**ly** *adv* — ~**ness** *n* [U]

lame² *v* [T] to cause to become lame

la·mé /ˈlɑːmeɪ‖lɑːˈmeɪ/ *n* [U] cloth containing gold or silver threads: *a gold lamé skirt*

lame-brain /ˈleɪmbreɪn/ *n AmE sl* a stupid person: *Don't do it that way, lamebrain! you'll break it.*

lame duck /ˌ· ˈ·/ *n* **1** a person or business that is helpless or ineffective **2** *AmE* a political official whose period in office will soon end: *a lame duck president/presidency*

la·ment /ləˈment/ *v* [I (**over**);T] **1** to feel or express deep sorrow (for or because of): *The nation lamented the passing* (=death) *of its great war leader.* | (*fml or pomp*) *The decline in good manners is to be lamented.* **2** **the late lamented** *fml or humor* the recently dead (person)

lament² *n* [(**for**)] a strong expression of deep sorrow, esp. in the form of a song or piece of music; a common form of bagpipe music (BAGPIPES)

lam·en·ta·ble /ˈlæməntəbəl, ləˈmentəbəl/ *adj fml* very unsatisfactory: *This government's performance/attitude is absolutely lamentable.* —**bly** *adv*

lam·en·ta·tion /ˌlæmən'teɪʃən/ n [C;U] *fml or bibl* (an expression of) deep sorrow: *There was lamentation throughout the land at the news of the defeat.*

lam·i·nar flow /ˌlæmɪnə 'fləʊ‖-nər-/ n [U] a smooth flow of a gas or liquid over a solid surface, such as an aircraft's wing

lam·i·nate¹ /'læmɪneɪt/ v [T] **1** to make (a strong material) by joining many thin sheets of the material on top of each other: *laminated steel* **2** to cover with thin metal or plastic sheets: *The work surface is made of wood laminated with plastic.*

lam·i·nate² /'læmɪnɪt, -neɪt/ n [C;U] material made by laminating sheets of plastic, metal, etc.

La·mont /lə'mɒnt‖-'mɑːnt/, **Norman** (1942–) a British Conservative politician, Chancellor of the Exchequer in John Major's government

lamp /læmp/ n **1** an apparatus, esp. a movable one, for giving light, using oil, gas, or electricity: *to light an oil lamp* | *A miner's lamp is fixed onto his helmet.* | *a table lamp* | *a streetlamp* —see pictures at BICYCLE and at LIGHT **2** an electrical apparatus used for producing healthgiving forms of heat: *an infrared lamp* —see also BLOWLAMP, HURRICANE LAMP, SAFETY LAMP, SUNLAMP **3** **new lamps for old** see ALADDIN

lamp-black /'· ·/ n [U] a fine black colouring material made from the SOOT (=black powder) produced by the smoke of a burning oil or gas lamp

lam·poon¹ /læm'puːn/ n a piece of writing fiercely attacking a person, government, etc., by making them seem foolish

lampoon² v [T] to attack in a lampoon: *In his essays he lampooned all the major political figures of the time*

lamp·post /'læmp-pəʊst/ n a tall thin support for a lamp which lights a street or other public area —see picture at HOUSE

lam·prey /'læmpri/ n a snakelike fish with a sucking mouth

lamp·shade /'læmpʃeɪd/ n a usu. decorative cover placed over a lamp, esp. to reduce or direct its light

LAN /læn/ n local area network; a system connecting computer TERMINALS in a building

Lan·ark·shire /'lænəkʃər‖-nər-/ a former COUNTY in central Scotland, now part of Strathclyde REGION

Lan·ca·shire /'læŋkəʃər/ *written abbrev* **Lancs.** a COUNTY in NW England, known esp. in the past for its TEXTILE and coal industries

Lan·cas·ter /læŋkəstər‖-kæs-/, **Burt** /bɜːt‖bɜːrt/ (1913–) an American actor who made many important films between the 1940s and 1980s. He won an Oscar in 1960 for *Elmer Gantry.*

lance¹ /lɑːns‖læns/ n a long spearlike weapon used by soldiers on horseback in former times

lance² v [T] to cut (flesh) open with a medical instrument, esp. to let infected material out: *That boil will have to be lanced.*

lance cor·po·ral /'· ˌ···◂/ n a military rank —see TABLE 3

Lan·ce·lot /'lɑːnsəlɒt‖'lænsəlɑːt/, **Sir** the most famous of the KNIGHTS of King Arthur, lover of Arthur's wife Guinevere, and father of Sir Galahad —see also ARTHURIAN LEGEND

lanc·er /'lɑːnsər‖'læn-/ n a soldier in a REGIMENT (=a military group) (formerly) armed with lances

lan·cet /'lɑːnsɪt‖'læn-/ n a small very sharp pointed knife with two cutting edges, used by a doctor to cut flesh

Lancet, The a British magazine for medical workers, produced by the British Medical Association, which reports on recent discoveries in medicine, drugs, etc. Its technical language is generally suitable only for doctors and other medical professionals. —see also NEW ENGLAND JOURNAL OF MEDICINE

Lan·ci·a /'lɑːnsiə/ *tdmk* (a company which makes) a sporty type of Italian car

Lancs. *written abbrev for*: LANCASHIRE

land¹ /lænd/ n **1** [U] the solid dry part of the Earth's surface: *After working at sea for several years, I got a job on land.* | *We finally sighted land/made land* (=reached the shore) *after a voyage of two weeks.* | *land-based nuclear weapons* —see also DRY LAND **2** [U] also **lands** pl. — (*usu. in comb.*) a part of the Earth's surface all of the same

(stated) natural type: *the heathlands of Northern Germany* —see also HIGHLAND, LOWLAND, WOODLAND **3** [C] *esp. lit* a country; nation: *People came from many lands to take part.* | *England is my native land.* (=I was born there) | (fig.) *the land of the dead* —see also CLOUD-CUCKOO-LAND, DREAMLAND; see also **land of milk and honey** (MILK¹ (3)) **4** [U] also **lands** pl. — ground owned as property: *You are on my land.* | *Land prices have risen quickly.* | *The duke's lands stretch for many miles in all directions.* **5** [U] ground used for farming: *This is excellent land for wheat.* | *He works (on) the land.* (=is a farmer) **6** [the] life in the country as opposed to life in towns and cities: *People who live in towns often dream of getting* **back to the land. 7 see/find out how the land lies** to try to discover the present state of affairs before taking action **8 land of the living** *humor* a state of being awake, esp. after being asleep or ill: *Is John back in the land of the living yet?*

▷ USAGE 1 The surface of the world, when compared with the sea, is called the **land**, but when compared with the sky or space it is called **earth** or the **Earth:** *After a week at sea, the sailors saw* **land.** | *After a week in space, the spacecraft returned to* **earth.** 2 An area considered as property is a piece of **land:** *the high price of* **land** *in London.* The substance in which plants grow is the **soil** or **earth:** *a tub filled with* **soil/earth,** or (when we think of it as having an area) **ground:** *a small piece of* **ground** *where I could plant a few potatoes.* But when we are talking about large areas used for farming, we say **land:** *There is good* **land** *here for growing corn.* The surface we walk on is called the **ground,** but when this is inside a building it is the **floor:** *The horse fell to the* **ground.** | *The plate fell to the* **floor.**◁

land² v **1** [I;T] to come or bring down from the air onto a surface, esp. of the Earth or water: *The plane landed only five minutes late.* | *We landed at Dubai for refuelling.* | *A drop of rain landed on my head.* | *The pilot landed the plane very skilfully in difficult conditions.* **2** [T] to bring to or put on land from water or from the air: *The ship landed the goods at Dover.* | *The troops were landed by helicopter.* **3** [T] to catch (a fish): (fig.) *She landed* (=succeeded in getting) *the top job in the record company.* **4** [T+obj(i)+obj(d)] *infml* to hit: *I landed him a punch on the nose.* —see also **land on one's feet** (FOOT)

land sbdy. **in** sthg. *phr v* [T] (of an event or course of action) to bring (someone) into (an undesirable state or position): *That sort of behaviour could land you in prison.* | *Her sudden resignation landed us in a real mess.*

land up *phr v* [I+adv/prep] to reach the stated (often undesirable) state or position at the end of a course of action or events: *After years of bad management the company landed up in serious debt.* [+v-ing] *We landed up wandering around with nowhere to stay.* —see also END UP

land sbdy. **with** sthg. *phr v* [T] *infml* to give (someone) (something unwanted): *I've been landed with the job of organizing the Christmas party.*

Land, Ed·win Her·bert /'edwɪn 'hɜːbət‖-'hɜːrbərt/ (1909–91) the American inventor of Polaroid glass, film and cameras (sometimes known as Polaroid Land cameras)

land a·gent /'· ˌ··/ n *esp. BrE* someone who looks after the land, cattle, farms, etc., belonging to someone else

lan·dau /'lændɔː‖-daʊ/ n a four-wheeled horsedrawn carriage with two seats and a top that folds back in two parts, used esp. in former times

land·ed /'lændɪd/ *adj* [A] **1** owning large amounts of land: *the* **landed gentry 2** *tech* made up of land: *landed property*

Lan·ders /'lændəz‖-ərz/, **Ann** /æn/ (1918–) a well-known American AGONY AUNT whose writings appear daily in hundreds of American newspapers

land·fall /'lændfɔːl/ n the first sight of land or arrival on land after a journey by sea or air; used esp. when the journey has taken a long time or is over a long distance: *We made landfall on the 84th day.*

land·fill /'lændfɪl/ n **1** [C;U] (an example of) the act of burying waste under the soil **2** [U] waste buried in this way: *a* **landfill site** (=place where this waste is buried)

land·girl /'lændgɜːl ‖ -gɜːrl/ n a member of the Women's Land Army in Britain during the Second World War. Landgirls worked on farms to replace men who were away fighting in the war.

land·ing /ˈlændɪŋ/ n **1** the level space at the top of a set of stairs or between two sets of stairs **2** an act of arriving or bringing something to land: *an emergency landing|crash landing*

landing craft /ˈ·· ·/ n a flat-bottomed boat that opens at one end, used for landing soldiers and army vehicles directly on the shore

landing field /ˈ·· ·/ n a LANDING STRIP

landing gear /ˈ·· ·/ n [U] an aircraft's wheels and wheel supports —see picture at AIRCRAFT

landing net /ˈ·· ·/ n a net on a long handle used for lifting a caught fish out of the water

landing stage /ˈ·· ·/ n a level surface, floating in or supported over the water, onto which passengers and goods are landed

landing strip /ˈ·· ·/ also **landing field**— n a stretch of prepared ground for aircraft to take off from and land on; a landing strip is used in country areas where there is no proper airport, and is sometimes just a flat field.

land·la·dy /ˈlændˌleɪdi/ n **1** a woman who owns and runs a BOARDING HOUSE (=a small hotel): *Seaside landladies are often thought of as fearsome or eccentric.* **2** a woman from whom someone rents a room, a building, land, etc.: *My landlady keeps complaining about the noise.* —compare LANDLORD

land·locked /ˈlændlɒkt‖-lɑːkt/ adj enclosed or almost enclosed by land: *Switzerland is a landlocked country, with no port for sea trade.*

land·lord /ˈlændlɔːd‖-lɔːrd/ n **1** a man from whom someone rents a room, a building, land, etc. **2** a man who owns or is in charge of a hotel, PUB, etc.: *There's a new landlord at the King's Head.* —compare LANDLADY

land·lub·ber /ˈlændˌlʌbəʳ/ n infml, often derog a person who is not used to the sea and ships; used mainly by people who are used to the sea and ships — ~ly adj

land·mark /ˈlændmɑːk‖-mɑːrk/ n **1** an easily recognizable object, such as a tall tree or building, by which one can tell one's position **2** an important point in a person's life, in the development of knowledge, etc.: *The discovery of penicillin was a landmark in the history of medicine.*

land·mass /ˈlændmæs/ n fml or tech a large area of land: *the European landmass*

land·mine /ˈlændmaɪn/ n an explosive apparatus hidden in or on the ground, which blows up when a person or vehicle passes over it

Land of Hope and Glo·ry /ˌ· · ·ˌ· · ˈ··/ the title and first words of a song, with music by Elgar, used on PATRIOTIC occasions to describe Britain. It is often now thought of as JINGOISTIC, but still sung esp. on the LAST NIGHT OF THE PROMS

Land of My Fa·thers /ˌ· · · ˈ··/ the English title of the NATIONAL ANTHEM (=national song) of Wales

Land of Nod /ˌ· · ˈ·/ [the] in children's stories, the place where one goes when one sleeps: *The children are all safely in the Land of Nod.*

land·own·er /ˈlændˌəʊnəʳ/ n a person who owns land: *a large landowner* — ~ship n [U] —**landowning** adj, n : *the landowning classes*

land re·form /ˈ· ·ˌ·/ n [U] the sharing out of farm land, esp. by government, to make a fairer system

Land Re·gis·try /ˈ· ˌ···/ [the] the central record of who owns what land in Britain

Land Rov·er /ˈ· ˌ··/ n tdmk a type of strong car, made by the Rover Group in Britain, suitable for travelling over rough ground —compare JEEP

Lan·dry /ˈlændri/, **Tom** (1924–) an American FOOTBALL COACH (teacher)

land·scape¹ /ˈlændskeɪp/ n **1** [C] a wide view of country scenery: *the gently rolling landscape of Devon* —see picture at MOUNTAIN **2** [C] a picture of such a scene: *a Cézanne landscape* —compare SEASCAPE **3** [U] the art of representing scenery in paintings, etc. —see SCENERY (USAGE); see also **blot on the landscape** (BLOT¹) **4** LANDSCAPE MODE

landscape² v [T] to make (the land around new houses, factories, etc.) more like interesting natural scenery: *We're having the hotel grounds landscaped.*

landscape ar·chi·tect /ˈ·· ˌ···/ n someone whose profession is to arrange land, including roads, buildings, and planted areas, for human use —**landscape architecture** n [U]

landscape gar·den·ing /ˌ·· ˈ···/ n [U] the art of arranging trees, paths, etc., in gardens and in parks to give a pleasing effect —**landscape gardener** n

landscape mode /ˈ·· ˌ·/ also **landscape**— [U] tech in landscape mode (of paper, or a picture on a page) with the longer edge from left to right (=HORIZONTAL) and the shorter edge from top to bottom (=VERTICAL): *I can't get my file to print out in landscape (mode).* —compare PORTRAIT MODE

Land's End /ˌ· ˈ·/ **1** the point of the English coast that is furthest west, in the extreme SW of the country **2** **from Land's End to John O'Groats** from the extreme south to the extreme north of Britain. Most people think of Land's End as being the furthest southern point of MAINLAND Britain, although in fact the lizard is further south —compare JOHN O'GROATS

land·slide /ˈlændslaɪd/ n **1** a sudden fall of earth or rocks down a hill, cliff, etc. **2** a very large, often unexpected, success in an election: *The Republicans won in a landslide|had a* **landslide victory.**

land·slip /ˈlændslɪp/ n a small LANDSLIDE (1)

land·ward /ˈlændwəd/ adj towards the land, esp. from the sea —compare EARTHWARD

land·wards /ˈlændwədz‖-wərdz/ esp. BrE ‖ usu. **landward** AmE— adv towards the land, esp. from the sea —compare EARTHWARDS

lane /leɪn/ n **1** a narrow often winding road or way between fields, houses, etc.: *country lanes* | *picturesque lanes in the Old Town* | *Her house is in Ivy Lane.* **2** any of the parallel parts into which wide roads are divided to keep fast and slow cars apart: *The outside lane is the fast lane.* | *Get in lane for* (=the right part of the road to get to) *Los Angeles.* | *lane closures on the M1* **3** a path marked for each competitor in a running or swimming race: *The champion is running in lane five.* **4** a fixed path across the sea or through the air used regularly by ships or aircraft: *the busy shipping lanes of the English Channel* —see also **in the fast lane** (FAST¹)

lane clo·sure /ˈ· ˌ··/ n an act of closing a LANE (2) e.g. for a road to be repaired or built or to prevent accidents: *Watch out for lane closures on the M6.* | *lane closures due to fog*

Lang /læŋ/, **Fritz** /frɪts/ (1890–1976) an American film director, born in Austria, who went to the US in 1936. His films include *Fury* and *The Big Heat.*

Lang·try /ˈlæŋtri/, **Lil·lie** /ˈlɪli/ (1853–1929) an English actress known as the **Jersey Lily** and considered to be very beautiful. She was the MISTRESS (2) of the future Edward VII.

lan·guage /ˈlæŋgwɪdʒ/ n **1** [U] the system of human expression by means of words: *Experts disagree about the origins of language.* **2** [C] a particular system of words, as used by a people or nation: *"How many languages can you speak?"* *"Two: English and French."* | *English is my first|native language.* | *the English language* | *a language course* (=to learn a foreign language) **3** [C;U] a system of signs, movements, etc., used to express meanings or feelings: *The language this computer uses is BASIC.* | *Whales have a language of squeaks and clicks.* —see also BODY LANGUAGE, SIGN LANGUAGE **4** [U] a particular style or manner of expression: *poetic language* | (fig.) *I like him; he talks my (kind of) language.* (=has the same opinions as me and expresses them similarly) **5** [U] often euph rude or shocking words and phrases, esp. FOUR-LETTER WORDS: *The teacher threw him out for using* **bad language.** | *He expressed his disagreement in rather* **strong language.**

language la·bor·a·tory /ˈ·· ·ˌ···‖ˈ·· ˌ····/ n a room in which people can learn foreign languages by means of special teaching machines, esp. TAPE RECORDERS

language school /ˈ·· ˌ·/ n a school that teaches one or more languages to students from other countries

lan·guid /ˈlæŋgwɪd/ adj without strength or any show of effort; slow, esp. in a graceful way: *She stretched out a languid arm to brush the cigar ash off the couch.* — ~ly adv

lan·guish /ˈlæŋgwɪʃ/ v [I] sometimes lit **1** [(in)] to experience long suffering: *She languished in prison for* *fifteen years.* **2** to be or become weaker: *The plants are languishing because of lack of water.* **3** [(**for**)] to become weak or unhappy through desire

lan·guor /ˈlæŋgəᵊ/ *n esp. lit* **1** [U] usu. pleasant tiredness of mind or body; lack of strength or will **2** [U] pleasant or heavy stillness: *the languor of a hot summer's afternoon* **3** [C *often pl.*] a feeling or state of mind of tender sadness and desire: *the languors of a lovesick poet* — ~ **ous** *adj* — ~ **ously** *adv* : *She lowered her eyelids languorously and stretched out in front of the fire.*

lank /læŋk/ *adj derog* (of hair) straight and lifeless — ~ **ly** *adv* — ~ **ness** *n* [U]

lank·y /ˈlæŋki/ *adj* (esp. of a person) ungracefully tall and thin — **iness** *n* [U]

lan·o·lin /ˈlænəl-ᵻn/ *n* [U] a fatty substance obtained from sheep's wool, used in skin creams

lan·tern /ˈlæntən‖-ərn/ *n* **1** a container, usu. of glass and metal, that encloses and protects the flame of a light; more often used outside than inside — see picture at LIGHT **2** *tech* the top of a building or tower, such as a LIGHTHOUSE, with windows on all sides — see also CHINESE LANTERN, MAGIC LANTERN

lantern-jawed /ˌ·· ˈ·◂/ *adj* (of a person) having long narrow jaws and cheeks that sink inwards

lan·tern·slide /ˈlæntənslaɪd‖-ər-/ *n* an early type of SLIDE² (4), made of glass, as used in a MAGIC LANTERN

lan·yard /ˈlænjəd‖-jərd/ *n* **1** a short piece of rope, used on ships for tying things **2** a thick string on which a knife or whistle is hung round the neck, esp. by sailors

Laos /laʊs‖ˈlɑːʊs/ a country in SE Asia, bordered by China, Vietnam, Kampuchea, Thailand, and Myanmar; capital Vientiane; population 3,972,000 (1989)

lap¹ /læp/ *n* **1** the front part of a seated person between the waist and the knees: *The child sat on its mother's lap.* **2 in the lap of luxury** *infml* in very great comfort: *He wants to marry a millionairess and live in the lap of luxury.* **3 in the lap of the gods** dependent on chance or fate; uncertain

lap² *v* **-pp-** **1** [T (UP)] (of animals) to drink by taking up with quick movements of the tongue: *The cat lapped the milk.* | (fig.) *She lapped up the compliments.* (=accepted them eagerly or without thought) **2** [I (**against**);T] (of water) to move or hit with little waves and soft sounds: *waves gently lapping (against) the shore*

lap³ *n* **1** [C] an act of lapping a liquid with the tongue **2** [*the*] the sound of lapping, e.g. of waves

lap⁴ *n* (in racing, swimming, etc.) a single journey round or along the track: *a three-lap race* | (fig.) *The last lap* (=the last stage) *of our journey is from Frankfurt to London.*

lap⁵ *v* **-pp-** **1** [I+*adv/prep*] (in racing) to race completely round the track: *Niki Lauda lapped in under two minutes.* **2** [T] (in racing, swimming, etc.) to pass (a competitor) having covered a complete lap more than them **3** [T+*obj+adv/prep*] *esp. lit* to fold over or round; wrap round; surround

lap·a·ros·cop·y /ˌlæpəˈrɒskəpi‖-ˈrɑː-/ *n* [C;U] (an) examination of the inside of the body using an instrument (**laparoscope**) with a lighted tube that the doctor can look down

lap·dog /ˈlæpdɒg‖-dɔːg/ *n* **1** *often derog* a small pet dog **2** *derog* a person completely under the control of another (usu. important) person

la·pel /ləˈpel/ *n* the part of the front of a coat or JACKET that is joined to the collar and folded back on each side towards the shoulders: *narrow lapels* — compare REVERS

lap·i·da·ry¹ /ˈlæpᵻdəri‖-deri/ *adj* [A] **1** *tech* (of words) cut in stone: *lapidary inscriptions* **2** *BrE pomp apprec* (of something said or written) very clever, amusing, etc., and deserving to be remembered

lapidary² *n* a person skilled in cutting precious stones, making them shine, etc.

lap·is laz·u·li /ˌlæpᵻs ˈlæzjʊli‖-ˈlæzəli/ *n* [C;U] (the colour of) a bright blue SEMIPRECIOUS stone

Lap·land /ˈlæplænd/ a cold area of N Europe consisting of parts of Norway, Sweden, Finland, and the former USSR. It is thought of by British children as the home of Father Christmas. — **er** *n*

lap of honour /ˌ·· ˈ··/ *n* **laps of honour** a LAP⁴ of a track,

completed after a race by the winner while people cheer

Lapp /læp/ *n, adj* (a native) of Lapland

lapse¹ /læps/ *n* **1** [C (**of**)] a small fault or mistake, esp. one that is quickly put right: *a memory lapse/lapse of memory* **2** [C] a failure in correct behaviour, belief, duty, etc.: *I started to eat the peas with my knife, but I don't think anyone noticed my little lapse.* **3** [S (**of**)] a passing away, esp. of time: *After a lapse of several years he came back to see us.*

lapse² *v* [I] **1** to pass gradually into a less active or less desirable state: *Standards have lapsed recently.* | *No one could think of anything more to say, and the meeting lapsed into silence.* | *After a year of fame the singer lapsed back into obscurity.* **2** (of a business agreement, official title, legal right, etc.) to come to an end, esp. because of lack of use, death, or failure to claim: *Her membership of the club lapsed because she failed to pay her subscription.*

lapsed /læpst/ *adj* [A] **1** no longer following the practices of esp. one's religion: *a lapsed Catholic* **2** *law* no longer in use: *a lapsed title*

lap·top , laptop /ˈ· ·/ *adj, n* [A] (of) a computer small enough to be held on one's knees for use: *I'll take the laptop and do some work on the train.*

lap·wing /ˈlæpˌwɪŋ/ also **peewit**— *n* a small bird with raised feathers on its head; its cry sounds like the name peewit

lar·ce·ny /ˈlɑːsᵊni‖ˈlɑːr-/ *n* [C;U] *law* (an act of) stealing — see also PETTY LARCENY

larch /lɑːtʃ‖lɑːrtʃ/ *n* a tall upright tree with bright green needle-like leaves and hard-skinned fruit (CONES)

lard¹ /lɑːd‖lɑːrd/ *n* [U] pig fat made pure by melting, used in cookery

lard² *v* [T] **1** to put small pieces of BACON into or on (other meat) before cooking **2** [(**with**)] to use lots of noticeable phrases, esp. of a particular kind, in one's (speech or writing): *His conversation was liberally larded with obscenities.*

lar·der /ˈlɑːdəʳ‖ˈlɑːr-/ *n* a storeroom or cupboard for food in a house — compare PANTRY

la·res and pe·na·tes /ˈlɑːreɪz ənd peˈnɑːteɪz‖ˌlæriːz ənd pəˈneɪ-/ *n* [P] in classical MYTHOLOGY, the Roman gods of the house, the lares being protectors of people and the penates protectors of possessions

large /lɑːdʒ‖lɑːrdʒ/ *adj* **1** more than usual in size, number, or amount; big: *a large house/sum of money/number of people* | *large employers* (=firms who employ lots of people) | *The company is too small to manufacture clothes on a large scale.* — opposite **small** **2 (as) large as life** *infml* (of a person) unexpectedly present: *We thought he'd gone to Australia, but there he was, (as) large as life!* **3 at large: a** (esp. of a dangerous person or animal) free; uncontrolled: *Two of the escaped prisoners are still at large.* **b** as a whole; altogether: *The country at large is hoping for great changes.* — see BIG (USAGE); see also LARGELY, **by and large** (BY²) — ~ **ness** *n* [U]

Large, Ed·die /ˈedi/ (1942–) a British COMEDIAN best known for his partnership with Syd Little esp. in the British television show *Little and Large*. Large is a big man and Little is small.

large in·tes·tine /ˌ· ··/ *n* the lower bowel, including the COLON and RECTUM, where food is changed into solid waste matter — compare SMALL INTESTINE

large·ly /ˈlɑːdʒli‖ˈlɑːr-/ *adv* to a great degree; mostly; mainly: *This country is largely desert.* | *His success is largely due to his own hard work.*

lar·gesse also **-gess** *AmE* /lɑːˈʒes‖lɑːrˈdʒes/ *n* [U] (something given in) generosity to people who do not have enough.

lar·go /ˈlɑːgəʊ‖ˈlɑːr-/ *n, adj, adv* **-os** (a piece of music) played slowly and solemnly

lar·i·at /ˈlæriət/ *n esp. AmE for* LASSO

lark¹ /lɑːk‖lɑːrk/ *n* a small light brown singing bird with long pointed wings, esp. the SKYLARK

lark² *n esp. BrE infml; rather old-fash* something done as a joke or for amusement; bit of fun: *We hid the teacher's books for a lark.*

lark³ *v*

    lark about/around *phr v* [I] *esp. BrE infml; rather*

old-fash to play rather wildly: *I'm sorry we broke the chair — we were only larking about.*

Lar·kin /ˈlɑːkɪn‖ˈlɑːr-/, **Philip** (1922–85) an English poet. He often wrote about death and loneliness and his poems are sometimes very sad, but people like them because they are written in plain and simple language. His most famous poems are *Aubade, High Windows,* and *Whitsun Weddings.*

Lark Rise to Can·dle·ford /ˌlɑːk ˌraɪz tə ˈkændlfəd‖ˌlɑːrk, -fərd/ a set of three books written by Flora Thompson between 1939 and 1945, about her life in the country in England in the early 20th century and the customs of that way of life, which no longer exists in England

lark·spur /ˈlɑːkspɜːr‖ˈlɑːr-/ *n* a DELPHINIUM

La Rue /lə ˈruː/, **Dan·ny** /ˈdæni/ (1927–) an Irish actor and entertainer well known through his own television show and for dressing up as a woman for part of his act

lar·va /ˈlɑːvə‖ˈlɑːrvə/ *n* **-vae** /viː/ the wormlike young of an insect between leaving the egg and changing into a winged form —**-val** *adj*

lar·yn·gi·tis /ˌlærənˈdʒaɪtɪs/ *n* [U] a painful swollen condition of the larynx which makes it difficult to speak: *suffering from (acute) laryngitis*

lar·ynx /ˈlærɪŋks/ also **voice box** *infml* — *n* **-ynges** /ləˈrɪndʒiːz/(*med*) *or* **-ynxes** the hollow boxlike part at the upper end of the throat in which the sounds of the voice are produced by the VOCAL CORDS —see picture at RESPIRATORY

la·sa·gna , **-gne** /ləˈsænjə, -ˈzæn-‖-ˈzɑːn-/ *n* [U] (an Italian dish made with) broad flat pieces of PASTA, meat or vegetables, and usu. cheese

La Salle /lə ˈsæl/, **Ren·é Ro·bert** /reneɪ ˈrɒbeər ‖ rəˈneɪ rɑːˈbeər/, **Sieur de** /ˈsjɜːr də/ (1643–87) a French EXPLORER who travelled through N America, down the Mississippi river, and established Louisiana. He was killed by his companions after getting lost.

La Sca·la /læ ˈskɑːlə‖ˈlɑː-/ a famous theatre in Milan where OPERAS are performed. Most of the very best singers have sung there.

las·civ·i·ous /ləˈsɪviəs/ *adj derog* feeling or showing uncontrolled sexual desire: *a lascivious look* – *~* **ly** *adv* – *~* **ness** *n* [U]

la·ser /ˈleɪzər/ *n* (an apparatus for producing) a very hot narrow beam of light, used for cutting metals and other hard substances and in medical operations, etc.; also sometimes used in light shows for entertainment: *laser beams* | *laser surgery* —compare MASER

laser print·er /ˈ·· ˌ··/ *n* a machine, esp. one connected to a computer system, that produces printed material by means of laser light

lash¹ /læʃ/ *v* **1** [T] to hit hard (as if) with a whip: *He lashed the horse cruelly.* | (fig.) *The newspaper headline is "Judge lashes drug dealers".* (=attacks them violently with words) **2** [I+adv/prep;T] to hit or move violently or suddenly: *The waves lashed (against) the rocks.* | *The rain lashed down.* **3** [T+prep, esp. **into**] to cause to have sudden strong violent feelings: *The speaker lashed the crowd into a fury of hatred.* **4** [T+obj+adv/prep] to tie firmly, esp. with rope: *We had to lash the cargo to the ship's deck during the storm.*

    lash out *phr v* **1** [I (**at, against**)] to make a sudden violent attacking movement: (fig.) *In his speech he lashed out at his critics.* **2** [I;T (=**lash out** sthg.) (**on**)] *BrE infml* to spend (a lot of money), esp. wastefully: *He lashed out (£12,000) on a new car.*

lash² *n* **1** a hit with a whip: *His punishment was thirty lashes.* **2** the thin bendable part of a whip **3** a sudden or violent movement: *With a lash of its tail the tiger leaped at her.* **4** an EYELASH

lash·ings /ˈlæʃɪŋz/ *n* [P (**of**)] *infml, esp. BrE* a large amount, esp. of food and drink; lots: *apple pie with lashings of cream*

lash-up /ˈ· ·/ *n BrE infml; often derog* an arrangement of e.g. electrical apparatus put together quickly to be used for only a limited period

Las Pal·mas /læs ˈpælməs‖lɑːs ˈpɑːl-/ a popular tourist town on Gran Canaria in the Canary Islands, much visited by the British on holiday

lass /læs/ also **lassie** – *n esp. ScotE & N EngE* **1** a girl or young woman **2** a GIRLFRIEND —compare LAD

Las·sie /ˈlæsi/ a dog who was the main character in seven films made between 1943 and 1951 and later television programmes and CARTOONS. In the films, etc. Lassie often bravely and cleverly saved her human family and others from danger.

las·si·tude /ˈlæsˌtjuːd‖ˈlæsətjuːd, -tuːd/ *n* [U] *fml* **1** tiredness **2** laziness: *He accused the official of moral lassitude.* (=failure to keep up good moral standards)

las·so¹ /ləˈsuː, ˈlæsəʊ/ also **lariat** *esp. AmE*— *n* **-sos** a rope with one end that can be tightened in a circle (NOOSE), used esp. in the US for catching horses and cattle

lasso² *v* [T] to catch with a lasso: *The cowboy lassoed the wild horse.*

last¹ /lɑːst‖læst/ *determiner, adv* **1** after anything else; after the others: *George arrived last/was the last person to arrive.* **2** being the only remaining; FINAL: *This is my last £5.* | *We've almost finished packing – this is the last suitcase.* | *That is the last time I invite him to dinner.* (=I will not invite him again.) **3** on the occasion nearest in the past; most recent(ly): *last night* | *last January* | *When did you last see him?* | *I arrived in France last week.* (=in the week before this) | *I've been here for the last week.* (=for the last seven days) | *This week's class was shorter than last week's.* —compare NEXT¹ (2) **4** the least suitable or likely: *He's the last person I'd have expected to see here.* **5** LASTLY **6 last but not least** important(ly), although coming at the end: *Last but not least, our thanks are due to the technicians working behind the scenes.* **7 on one's/its last legs** *infml* **a** very tired **b** nearly worn out or failed: *This car's on its last legs.* **c** close to death

▷ USAGE **1** When our point of view is in the present, looking back to the past, we say **last** *night*, **last** *week*, etc.: *I'm sure I saw George at the club* **last** *week*. But when our point of view is in the past, looking even further back into the past, we use expressions like *the night* **before that,** *the* **previous** *week*, etc.: *I was sure I had seen George at the club the* **previous** *week.* **2** Compare **latest** and **last**. **Latest** means "new and most recent": *Have you heard the* **latest** *news?* **Last** before a noun means "coming at the end" or "before the **latest** one": *"The Magic Flute" was Mozart's* **last** *opera.* | *Have you read Steinway's* **latest** *novel? It's much better than his* **last** *one.*◁

last² *n, pron* [(*the*) S] **1** the person, thing, or group after all others: *"I hope I'm not the last," he said, as he arrived at the party.* [+*to-v*] *I was the last to arrive.* | *The last I heard she was in Spain.* (=that is the most recent information I have heard about her) —compare FIRST² (1) **2** the only remaining; the end: *They drank up the last of the wine.* | *I'm sure you haven't heard the last of the matter.* (=The matter is not yet finished.) **3** the one or ones before the present one: *He was here the week* **before last.** (=two weeks ago) **4 at (long) last** in the end; after a long time: *At last we found out what had really happened.* | *He's here, at last!* —compare **at first** (FIRST²); see LASTLY (USAGE) **5 to the last** until the latest moment; until the end: *The condemned man continued to the last* (=until he was officially killed) *to insist that he was innocent.* — see also **breathe one's last** (BREATHE), **the first shall be last and the last shall be first** (FIRST² (8))

last³ *v* **1** [L+*n*; I+*adv/prep*] to continue for the stated length of time; go on: *The lessons last less than an hour.* | *The hot weather lasted until September/for several weeks.* **2** [I (OUT)] to remain in good condition, in existence, or alive: *Her bad mood won't last.* | *This cheap watch won't last (for) very long.* | *I don't know how much longer we can last out without water.* **3** [T (OUT)] to continue in good condition or alive beyond the end of: *He's very ill, and isn't expected to last (out) the night.* **4** [L (+*obj*)+*n*] to be enough for: *This food will only last (them) three days.*

last⁴ *n* a piece of wood or metal shaped like a human foot, used by shoemakers and shoe repairers

last call /ˌ· ˈ·/ *n AmE* LAST ORDERS

last-ditch /ˌ· ˈ·◄/ *adj* [A] done as one last effort before accepting defeat: *In a last-ditch attempt to save the company from collapsing, they asked the government to lend them money.*

last·ing /ˈlɑːstɪŋ‖ˈlæs-/ *adj* continuing for a long time; unending: *searching for a lasting peace after so many terrible wars* | *His policies had a lasting effect on our country's economy.*

last judg·ment /ˌ· ˈ··/ [*the*] (*often cap.*) JUDGMENT DAY

last·ly /ˈlɑːstli‖ˈlæst-/ adv after everything else: ... and lastly, let me mention the great support I've had from my assistant.
▷ USAGE Compare **lastly, finally, at last,** and **in the end. Lastly** and **finally** are often used when you are separating the points you want to make and are putting them in order: There are three reasons why I hate him: first(ly) he's a cheat, second(ly) he's a liar, and **lastly/finally** he owes me money. **At last** and **in the end** cannot be used in this way. These words mean "after a long time; after a lot of waiting": I tried over and over again and **at last/in the end** I succeeded. **Finally** (but not **lastly**) can also be used with this meaning: I waited for hours and **finally/at last/in the end** he arrived.◁

last min·ute /ˌ· ˈ·◂/ n [the] the moment just before an event, decision, etc.: At the last minute she changed her mind and turned down the job. | last-minute preparations

last name /ˈ· ·/ n esp. AmE SURNAME

Last Night of the Proms /ˌ· ˌ· · · ˈ·/ [the] the last of London's PROMENADE CONCERTS held each summer, when the second half of the programme always consists of the same well-loved tunes and songs which the standing crowds in the Albert Hall sing along with. The programme ends with the song Land of Hope and Glory, a PATRIOTIC song, and people sing it while waving Union Jacks (=British national flags).

last num·ber re·call /ˌ· ˌ·· ˈ··/ also **-redial**— n [U] a feature on a telephone which has the ability to DIAL² again the last number called without the caller having to dial it by hand

Last of the Mo·hi·cans /ˌ· · · · ·ˈ··/, **The** a NOVEL by James Fenimore Cooper written in 1826 about the lives of Native Americans and early settlers

last or·ders /ˌ· ˈ··/ BrE ‖ **last call** AmE— (the words called out at) the time when a PUBLIC HOUSE or bar is about to close and there is just time for one more set of drink orders to be taken

last post /ˌ· ˈ·/ [the] a tune played on a BUGLE at military funerals, or to call soldiers back to camp for the night —see also TAPS

last rites /ˌ· ˈ·/ n [P] see RITE

last straw /ˌ· ˈ·/ [the] the difficulty, trouble, etc., that makes the total unbearable when it is added to one's present difficulties or troubles: After losing my credit cards and having my camera stolen, breaking my leg really was the last straw. —see also **the straw that breaks the camel's back** (STRAW (6))

Last Sup·per /ˌ· ˈ··/ [the] **1** in the Bible, the meal taken by Jesus and his followers on the evening before he was crucified (CRUCIFY). Jesus shared bread and wine among his followers, beginning the Christian ceremony of the EUCHARIST —see also EUCHARIST **2** a painting of this gathering esp. the one by Leonardo da Vinci (1498)

last word /ˌ· ˈ·/ [the] **1** [(on)] the word or phrase that ends an argument, usu. giving advantage to the speaker: She always has to have the last word. | That's my last word on the subject. **2** the deciding judgment: The last word must rest with the boss. **3** [+in] infml the most modern example: This computer is the last word in high technology.

Las Ve·gas /læs ˈveɪɡəs‖ˈlɑːs-/ a city in the desert of Nevada, USA, famous for its very large CASINOS and its entertainment. It grew where it did because gambling (GAMBLE¹ (1)) was not legal in California, and Las Vegas is just over the border in Nevada, where it is legal. —see colour map on pages 1374–5

lat written abbrev. for: LATITUDE

latch¹ /lætʃ/ n **1** a simple fastening for a door, gate, window, etc., worked by dropping a bar into a U-shaped space: To open the gate, lift up the latch. **2** a fastening for a house door that can be opened from the inside with a handle but from the outside only with a key: I'll leave the door **on the latch.** (=fastened only with the latch, not locked)

latch² v [I;T] to fasten or be able to be fastened with a latch: Remember to latch the gate behind you.
latch on phr v [I] infml to understand; CATCH **on:** He's not very clever, so it took him some time to latch on.
latch onto sbdy./sthg. phr v [T] infml **1** to gain an

understanding of: He soon latched onto how to do it. **2** to start trying to talk to (someone), be friendly with them, etc., and refuse to go away: He latched onto me at the party and bored me for hours with silly gossip. **3** to take hold of with the mind; develop an interest in or recognition of: It has taken the company a long time to latch onto all the new technology now available.

latch·key /ˈlætʃkiː/ n a key for opening a lock on an outside door of a house or flat

latchkey child /ˈ·· ˌ·/ n a child whose parents are often not at home and who therefore often returns esp. from school to an empty house. The word is used esp. by people who think that women who have young children should not go out to work.

late¹ /leɪt/ adj **1** [(for)] arriving, happening, etc., after the usual, arranged, necessary, or expected time: The train was late. | We were late for the train. (=it left before we arrived) | I was late for the meeting. (=it should have) started before I arrived) | She was a late **developer.** | Spring is late this year. | The doctors were too late to save him. (=his illness had developed too far) [after n] The train was ten minutes late. —compare EARLY¹ (1) **2** happening or being towards the end of the day, life, a period, etc.: She returned in the late afternoon. | It's getting late; we must go home. | late September | the late eighteenth century | She's in her late forties, I think —compare EARLY¹ (2) **3** [A no comp.] euph who has died recently: her late husband | the late president **4** [A no comp.] existing or operating in the recent past but not now; former: the late government/chairman **5** [A] happening a short time ago; recent: the late changes in the government **6** [A no comp.] just arrived; new; fresh: Some late news of the war has just come in. **7** **better late than never** an old saying — see also LATELY, LATEST — ~**ness** n [U]

late² adv **1** after the usual, arranged, necessary, or expected time: They stayed up late to watch the election results on the television. [after n] The bus arrived five minutes late. **2** towards the end of a period: late in the evening/at night | The bush was planted late in the season. **3** until or at a late time of the night: We went to bed late. | working late **4** [of] fml until recently; LATELY: Dr Smith, late of the Maudsley Hospital, has now taken up private practice. **5** of late recently; LATELY: He's been behaving very strangely of late. —compare EARLY²

late book·ing /ˌ· ˈ··/ n [C;U] (esp. in Britain) holiday arrangements made, or the practice of making such arrangements, a very short time before one goes. This is often very much cheaper than the same arrangement made a long time before: Late bookings! Leave tomorrow for only £50!

late·com·er /ˈleɪtˌkʌmər/ n someone who arrives late

late·ly /ˈleɪtli/ adv **1** in the recent past and up until now: I've not been feeling very well (just) lately. **2** fml until recently (but no longer): Professor Brown, lately of Edinburgh, is now head of department at Manchester.

late-night /ˈ· ·/ adj [A] of or happening late at night: The late-night news

late-night shop·ping /ˌ· · ˈ··/ also **late shopping**— n [U] BrE shopping until 8 o'clock at night or later. In Britain, shops usu. close at 5.30 or 6 o'clock, but they often stay open for late-night shopping on one evening a week and during very busy periods, e.g. just before Christmas: We're going into town for the late-night shopping. | We close at six, except for late shopping on Thursdays till eight.

la·tent /ˈleɪtənt/ adj usu. fml present but not yet noticeable, active, or fully developed: a latent infection | latent aggression | These aggressive tendencies remained latent. —**tency** n [U]

latent heat /ˌ· ˈ·/ n [U] tech the additional heat necessary to change a solid (at its MELTING POINT) into a liquid, or a liquid (at its BOILING POINT) into a gas

lat·er /ˈleɪtər/ adv **1** at a later time; afterwards: At first he denied all guilt, but he later made a partial confession. | I'll tell/see you later. (=after some time has passed) **2** later on afterwards: It wasn't until later on that we realized she'd gone.

lat·e·ral¹ /ˈlætərəl/ adj fml of, at, from, or towards the side: lateral movement — ~**ly** adv

lateral² n tech something, such as a branch, which is at or comes from the side

lateral think·ing /ˌ··· ˈ··/ n [U] a CREATIVE way of thinking which tries to use imagination and humour to find new and clever answers to problems. It was invented by Edward de Bono.

late shop·ping /ˌ· ˈ··/ n LATE-NIGHT SHOPPING

lat·est[1] /ˈleɪtɟst/ adj [A] most recent: *Her latest book is selling very well.* —see LAST[1] (USAGE)

latest[2] n [the] **1** [(in)] the most recent example, news, or fashion: *This case is the latest in a series of British spy scandals.* | *Have you heard the latest about the war?* | *The salesman showed us the latest in computer software packages.* **2 at the latest** not later than the stated time: *Please be here by 9 o'clock at the latest.* —opposite **at the earliest**

Late Sum·mer Hol·i·day /ˌ· ˌ·· ˈ···/ [the] see AUGUST BANK HOLIDAY

la·tex /ˈleɪteks/ n [U] **1** a thick whitish liquid produced by certain plants, esp. the rubber tree **2** a material produced from this: *latex goods*

lath /lɑːθ‖læθ/ n laths /lɑːðz, lɑːθs‖læðz, læθs/ a long flat narrow piece of wood used in building to support PLASTER (=wall-covering material) or TILES or SLATES (=roof-covering materials)

lathe /leɪð/ n a machine for shaping that turns a piece of wood or metal round and round against a sharp tool

la·ther[1] /ˈlɑːðəʳ‖ˈlæ-/ n [S;U] **1 a** a white mass produced by shaking a mixture of soap and water: *Brush the shaving cream until a lather forms.* **b** a mass like this which is the result of heavy sweating (SWEAT), esp. by a horse **2 in a lather** BrE hot and anxious, esp. because of lack of time — ~ y adj

lather[2] v **1** [I] (esp. of soap) to produce a lather: *This detergent lathers easily.* **2** [T (UP)] to cover with lather: *He stood in the shower lathering his back.* **3** [T] infml rare to hit violently

Lat·i·mer /ˈlætɟməʳ/, **Hugh** /hjuː/ (1485–1555) an English BISHOP who was burned as a HERETIC in Oxford

Lat·in[1] /ˈlætɟn‖ˈlætn/ n **1** [U] the language of the ancient Romans **2** [C] a Latin person

Latin[2] adj **1** (written) in Latin: *a Latin inscription* **2** of a nation that speaks a language developed from Latin, such as Italian, Spanish, or Portuguese

Latin A·mer·i·can /ˌ··· ·ˈ····◂/ adj of the Spanish- or Portuguese-speaking countries of South and Central America (known as **Latin America**)

Latin lov·er /ˌ·· ˈ··/ n a man from southern Europe who is PASSIONATE and skilled at LOVEMAKING. It is often thought in Britain that the French, Italians, Greeks, etc. make better lovers than the British.

La·ti·no /læˈtiːnəʊ/ n AmE a person living in the US who is from or whose family was from a Central or South American culture: *The school is 65% latino, 30% black, and 5% white.* —**Latino** adj : *Latino culture*

Latin Quar·ter /ˈ·· ˌ·/ [the] a part of Paris on the left bank of the river Seine, where many students and artists live

lat·i·tude /ˈlætɟtjuːd‖-tuːd/ n **1** [C;U] the distance north or south of the EQUATOR measured in degrees: *The latitude of the island is 20 degrees south.* —compare LONGITUDE and see picture at GLOBE **2** [S] also **latitudes** pl.— an area at a particular latitude: *At this latitude/these latitudes you often get strong winds.* **3** [U] fml freedom to do, say, etc., what one likes: *The new law allows firms a lot less latitude than before in fixing the price of their goods.* —**tudinal** /ˌlætɟˈtjuːdɟnəl◂‖-ˈtuː-/ adj

lat·ke /ˈlɑːtkə/ n a Jewish potato PANCAKE

la·trine /ləˈtriːn/ n a TOILET, esp. an outdoor one in a camp, military area, etc.

lat·ter[1] /ˈlætəʳ/ adj [A no comp.] fml near to the end; later: *In the latter years of his life he lived alone and never welcomed visitors.*

latter[2] adj, n latter [A;C] rather fml the second (of two people or things just mentioned): *If offered red or white, I'd choose the latter (wine).* (=white wine) —opposite **former**

latter-day /ˈ··· ·/ adj [A no comp.] modern; recent: *a latter-day hero*

Latter-Day Saints /ˌ··· · ˈ·/ [the+P] the MORMONS

lat·ter·ly /ˈlætəli‖-ər-/ adv fml (more) recently —compare FORMERLY

lat·tice /ˈlætɟs/ also **lat·tice·work** /ˈlætɟswɜːk‖-wɜːrk/— n **1** a frame of flat pieces of wood or metal crossed over each other with open spaces between, used as a fence, a support for climbing plants, etc. —compare TRELLIS **2** also **lattice win·dow** /ˌ·· ˈ··/— an old type of window with many small pieces of glass held together by narrow pieces of lead

Lat·vi·a /ˈlætviə/ a country in NE Europe next to the Baltic sea, bordered by Russia, Estonia, and Lithuania; Capital Riga; population 2,681,000 (1989) —**Latvian** n, adj : *the Latvian ambassador*

laud /lɔːd/ v [T] old use or pomp to praise: *It's annoying to see a rival's work lauded to the skies.* (=praised very greatly)

Laud, William (1573–1645) an English priest who was Archbishop of Canterbury from 1633

Lau·da /ˈlaʊdə/, **Nik·i** /ˈnɪki/ (1949–) an Austrian motor-racing driver who was the Formula 1 world CHAMPION in 1975 and 1977. He was very badly burned in an accident in 1976 but was able to continue racing.

lau·da·ble /ˈlɔːdəbəl/ adj (esp. of behaviour, actions, etc.) good and deserving praise, even though perhaps not completely successful: *Despite his laudable attempts to bring the two sides together, the dispute continued to drag on.* —compare LAUDATORY —**bly** adv —**bility** /ˌlɔːdəˈbɪlɟti/ n [U]

lau·da·num /ˈlɔːdənəm/ n [U] a substance containing the drug OPIUM in alcohol, used, esp. formerly, as a medicine to lessen pain and for its pleasant effects

lau·da·to·ry /ˈlɔːdətəri‖-tɔːri/ adj fml expressing praise or admiration: *laudatory comments* —compare LAUDABLE

Lau·der /ˈlɔːdəʳ/, **Es·tée** /esˈteɪ/ (1908–), an American woman who began the cosmetics (COSMETIC[1]) business which bears her name and is now known internationally

laugh[1] /lɑːf‖læf/ v **1** [I (at)] to express amusement, happiness, careless disrespect, etc., by breathing out forcefully so that one makes sounds with the voice, usu. while smiling: *It was so funny, we couldn't help laughing.* | *Don't laugh – this is a serious matter.* | *I told him not to be so rude, but he just laughed.* | *No one laughs at my jokes.* | (fig.) *her laughing eyes* (=bright happy-looking eyes) **2** [T+obj+adv/prep] to bring, put, etc., with laughing: *The pathetic performance was laughed off the stage.* **3** [T+obj+adj] to cause (oneself) to become by laughing: *It was such a ridiculous suggestion that we all laughed ourselves silly.* (=laughed very much) | *He laughed himself hoarse.* **4 laugh all the way to the bank** to show pleasure because one has gained financially (often at someone else's EXPENSE (2)) **5 laugh and the world laughs with you; weep, and you weep alone** quote a phrase from a poem by Ella Wheeler Wilcox **6 laugh in someone's face** to show clear disrespect or disobedience towards someone: *I suggested that he should work late and he laughed in my face.* **7 laugh like a drain** BrE infml to laugh loudly, openly, and perhaps rudely **8 laugh on the 'other side of one's face** (usu. said unkindly) to experience disappointment, sorrow, failure, etc., after expecting success or joy: *Wait until you see the exam results; you'll be laughing on the other side of your face!* **9 laugh something out of court** to refuse to consider (something) because it is too silly: *The idea was laughed out of court.* **10 no 'laughing matter** serious; not a suitable subject for jokes: *Losing your job is no laughing matter, I can tell you.* **11 laugh up one's sleeve** to laugh secretly and often unkindly

▷ USAGE When you **laugh** you produce sounds with the voice while smiling. To **guffaw** (rare) means "to laugh loudly" and to **chuckle** means "to laugh quietly, with pleasure or satisfaction". To **giggle** (in Britain used especially about young girls) is to laugh repeatedly in an uncontrolled way. To **titter** is to **giggle** quietly in a nervous or silly way. If you laugh quietly in an unpleasant and rude way, you **snigger** (AmE **snicker**). All these words can be used both as verbs and as nouns. —see also SMILE (USAGE)◁

laugh at sthg./sbdy. phr v [T] **1** to treat as foolish or as not worth serious consideration: *They'll just laugh at you if you can't think of a better excuse than that.* | *Soccer hooligans just laugh at the sort of sentences courts give them.* **2** to take no notice of; not care: *She laughs at (the idea of) danger.*

laugh sthg. ↔ **off** phr v [T] to pretend, by laughing or joking, that (something) is less serious or important than it really is: *Publicly, they're trying to laugh off this latest failure, but in private they're very worried.*

laugh² *n* **1** [C] an act or sound of laughing: *She gave a (happy) laugh.* **2** [S] *infml* something done for a joke or amusement: *Wouldn't it be a laugh to tie his shoelaces together!* **3 have the last laugh** to win an argument, competition, etc., esp. after earlier defeats; have one's opinions, actions, etc., proved to be correct in the end **4 have the laugh on** to make a fool of someone who was trying to make others look foolish

laugh·a·ble /ˈlɑːfəbəl‖ˈlæ-/ *adj* **1** *derog* so bad or foolish that it cannot be taken seriously: *a laughable attempt to deceive the public* **2** *rare* amusing; funny **–bly** *adv* : *The proposals were almost laughably inadequate.*

Laugh-In /ˈ· ·/ an American television programme of the 1960s in which many now famous performers first appeared

Laughing Cav·a·lier /ˌ··· ··ˈ·/ [the] the name of a painting of an unknown man by Frans Hals –see colour picture on page 1016

laugh·ing gas /ˈ·· ·/ *n* [U] NITROUS OXIDE

laughing hy·e·na /ˌ·· ··ˈ·/ *n* a HYENA

laughing jack·ass /ˌ·· ˈ··/ *n* a KOOKABURRA

laugh·ing·ly /ˈlɑːfɪŋli‖ˈlæ-/ *adv* **1** with a laugh **2** not seriously; as a joke: *He's often laughingly referred to as the forgotten man of British politics.*

laugh·ing·stock /ˈlɑːfɪŋstɒk‖ˈlæfɪŋstɑːk/ *n* someone or something that is regarded as foolish and causes unkind laughter: *His silly behaviour made him a laughing-stock/made him the laughing-stock of the office.* (=everyone in the office laughed at him)

laugh·ter /ˈlɑːftəʳ‖ˈlæf-/ *n* [U] the act or sound of laughing

Laugh·ton /ˈlɔːtn/, **Charles** (1899–1962) an American character actor born in Britain, regarded as one of the great film actors of the first half of the 20th century – see picture at HUNCHBACK OF NOTRE DAME

launch¹ /lɔːntʃ/ *v* [T] **1** to send (a boat, esp. one that has just been built) into the water: *The new aircraft carrier was officially launched by the queen.* **2** to send (a modern weapon or instrument) into the sky or space, esp. with a ROCKET: *Our nuclear missiles can be launched at a moment's notice.* **3** to begin (an activity, plan, way of life, etc.): *He launched a fierce attack on his political opponents.* | *She's planning to launch a company to make electronic toys.* | *They held a special party to launch the new book.* (=to bring it to public attention when it came out) **4** [(at)] to throw very hard: (fig.) *He launched himself at the thief and brought him to the ground.* –see also the **face that launched a thousand ships** (FACE) – **cr** *n* : *a rocket launcher*

launch into sthg. *phr v* [T] to begin eagerly, forcefully, etc.: *He launched into a violent attack on my handling of the affair.*

launch out *phr v* [I+adv/prep] to make an important new beginning, esp. at something rather risky: *He left his father's shop and launched out into business for himself.*

launch² *n* an act of launching: *Were you at the launch of the new ship/book?*

launch³ *n* a usu. large motor-driven boat used for carrying people on rivers, lakes, HARBOURS, etc.

launch pad /ˈ· ·/ also **launching pad** /ˈ·· ·/– *n* a base from which a MISSILE or space vehicle is sent off into the sky: (fig) *The marketing campaign will be the launch pad for a whole range of new products.*

laun·der /ˈlɔːndəʳ/ *v* [T] **1** to wash, or wash and iron (clothes, sheets, etc.): *We must have these bedclothes laundered.* **2** *infml* to give (something, esp. money obtained illegally) the appearance of being legal

laun·derette, **laundrette** /lɔːnˈdret/ *esp. BrE* ‖ also **laun·dro·mat** /ˈlɔːndrəmæt/ *tdmk esp. AmE–* *n* a shop where the public can wash their clothes in machines that work when coins are put in them

laun·dry /ˈlɔːndri/ *n* **1** [C] a place or business where clothes, etc., are washed and ironed **2** [U] clothes, sheets, etc., that need to be washed or have just been laundered: *There's a lot of laundry in the basket.*

laundry bas·ket /ˈ·· ˌ··/ also **linen basket**, also **hamper** *AmE– n* a large basket in which dirty clothing, sheets, etc., are carried or put ready for washing

laundry list /ˈ·· ˌ·/ *n AmE infml* a list of things one needs: *The Pentagon presented Congress with a laundry list of new weapons.*

Lau·ra Ash·ley /ˌlɔːrə ˈæʃli/ (one of) a group of shops which, like the things sold in them, carry the name of their DESIGNER¹, Laura Ashley. People think of Laura Ashley shops esp. as selling women's clothes made of cotton with flowery patterns, but the shops also sell furniture, curtains and WALLPAPER. –see also Laura ASHLEY

Lau·ra·sia /lɔːˈreɪʃə‖-ˈreɪʒə/ the large land mass that existed before it split apart to form North America, Europe, Asia, and Greenland –see also GONDWANALAND, PANGAEA

laur·e·ate /ˈlɔːriᵻt/ *n* someone who has won a particular high honour: *a Nobel laureate in physics* –see also POET LAUREATE

laur·el /ˈlɒrəl‖ˈlɔː-, ˈlɑː-/ *n* **1** [C;U] a small tree with smooth shiny dark green leaves that do not fall in winter **2** [C] also **laurels** *pl.–* honour gained for something done: *The minister has been given the credit for achieving the settlement, but the laurels rightfully belong to the civil servants.* –see also **look to one's laurels** (LOOK to), **rest on one's laurels** (REST on)

Laurel and Har·dy /ˌ··· ··ˈ·/ an American film partnership, **Stan Laurel** (1890–1965) and **Oliver Hardy** (1892–1957), who made many humorous popular films in the 1930s with the same two central characters, Laurel being the smaller, thin one and Hardy the taller, fat one: *That thin little man and his huge wife look like Laurel and Hardy!* –see picture on page 553

Lau·ren /ˈlɔːrən/, **Ralph** /rælf/ (1939–   ) an American clothes DESIGNER known esp. for his informal clothes

la·va /ˈlɑːvə/ *n* [U] **1** rock in a very hot liquid state flowing from a VOLCANO **2** this material when it has become cool and turned into a grey solid with many small holes

lav·a·to·ri·al /ˌlævəˈtɔːriəl/ *adj derog, often humor* showing an unhealthily strong interest in the bodily processes connected with lavatories, and/or in sex

lav·a·tory /ˈlævətri‖-tɔːri/ also **lav** /læv/*infml– BrE n* a TOILET (1,2): *to go to the lavatory* | *a public lavatory* –see TOILET (USAGE)

lavatory pa·per /ˈ··· ˌ··‖ˈ···· ˌ··/ *n* [U] TOILET PAPER

lav·en·der /ˈlævᵻndəʳ/ *n* [U] **1** a plant with stems of small strongly smelling pale purple flowers **2** the dried flowers and stems of this plant used for giving stored clothes, sheets, etc., a pleasant smell **3** a pale purple colour: *lavender(-coloured) writing paper*

lavender wa·ter /ˈ··· ˌ··/ *n* [U] a PERFUME made from lavender oils and alcohol. Lavender water is rather old-fashioned and is connected esp. with old UPPER-CLASS ladies.

la·ver /ˈlɑːvəʳ/ *n* [U] a type of SEAWEED (=sea plant) which can be eaten and which is collected esp. on Scottish and Japanese coasts. Laver bread is a favourite Welsh dish usu. eaten at breakfast. The laver is cut up and boiled then fried (FRY) in butter. Although it is called "bread", it is more liquid than solid and feels slippery.

lav·ish¹ /ˈlævɪʃ/ *adj* **1** [(with, (*fml*) of)] very generous or wasteful in giving or using: *a lavish spender* (=who spends a lot, or perhaps too much) | *She'd been a bit too lavish with the salt, so the soup didn't taste very nice.* **2** given, spent, or produced in great (or perhaps too great) quantity: *lavish praise* | *expenditure on a lavish scale* – **~ly** *adv* **– ~ness** *n* [U]

lavish² *v*

lavish sthg. **on/upon** sbdy./sthg. *phr v* [T] to give to or spend on generously or wastefully: *He'd lavished most of his fortune on impractical business ventures.* | *She lavishes a lot of attention on her friends.*

law /lɔː/ *n* **1** [C (**against**)] a rule that is supported by the power of government and that controls the behaviour of members of a society: *Parliament makes/passes laws.* | *There ought to be a law against that sort of antisocial behaviour.* | *With the president's signature the bill becomes a law.* **2** [*the*+S] the whole set of such rules: *Once they are approved by Parliament, the new traffic regulations will become law.* (=people will have to obey them) | *There is nothing in law that requires it.* | *In court, the jury decides on matters of fact, but the judge advises them on matters of law.* | *The law forbids stealing.* | *If you break the law, you must expect to be punished.* | *Driving when you've*

In both Britain and the US, when a person is accused (ACCUSE) of a crime it must be shown that they are guilty 'beyond reasonable doubt'. A person is always innocent in the eyes of the law until they have been proved to be guilty. If the person is found guilty by a court they can sometimes ask for permission to APPEAL to a higher court in the hope that it will change this decision (see diagram below).

The Appeals System

The diagram shows the courts in order of importance, with arrows representing the appeals system

Criminal Courts in England & Wales
↑
House of Lords
↑
Court of Appeal (Criminal Division)
↑
Crown Court
↑
Magistrates' Court

Criminal law in England Wales

The diagram shows the possible events following an arrest

arrested by the police
↓
magistrate decides whether
there will be a trial
↙　　　　　↘
(serious offences)　　　(less serious offences)
trial in a Crown Court　　trial in a Magistrates'
with a judge and jury　　　Court
↘　　　　　↙
If found guilty it may
be possible to appeal to
a higher court

Criminal law in England and Wales

When someone is arrested (ARREST) by the police, a MAGISTRATE (=an official who judges cases in some types of courts) decides whether there is enough EVIDENCE against the person for the case to go to court. If there is enough evidence and the case is a serious one, the person accused of the crime (called 'the accused') is sent to a CROWN COURT for a TRIAL with a JUDGE and JURY (=12 members of the public who have to decide if the accused is innocent or guilty. If the VERDICT (=decision) of the jury is that the accused is guilty, then the judge decides the SENTENCE(2) (=punishment). If there is enough evidence against the accused but the crime is <u>not</u> a serious one (for example a traffic offence) then the case is heard in a MAGISTRATES COURT.

If found guilty in the Crown Court the accused may apply to the COURT OF APPEAL (Criminal Division) where he or she will be heard by a judge. Sometimes a HIGH COURT judge from the Queen's Bench Division assists in dealing with criminal matters in the Court of Appeal or Crown Court.

Criminal law in Northern Ireland

In Northern Ireland, as in England and Wales, someone accused of a crime may be tried in a Magistrates' Court or a Crown Court depending on how serious the crime is. Appeals from the Crown Court are heard in the Northern Ireland Court of Appeal.

Criminal law in Scotland

Scotland has a separate court system. After a person is arrested by the police, an official called the PROCURATOR FISCAL is in charge of deciding whether there is enough evidence against the accused for a trial. If there is enough evidence and the crime is a very serious one, the accused is sent to the HIGH COURT OF JUSTICIARY where there is a judge and jury (in Scotland there are 15 people on a jury). If there is enough evidence but the crime is a less serious one, the case is heard in a SHERIFF COURT (the SHERIFF is a trained lawyer who acts as a judge). Appeals from the Sheriff Court go to the High Court of Justiciary.

Criminal law in the US

The US has two separate court systems. In general terms STATE COURTS are used when someone has done something against the laws or CONSTITUTION of a particular state. FEDERAL COURTs deal with cases to do with the laws and constitution of the United States as a whole. Federal courts also hear cases where the US government is one of the sides involved. Cases for crimes which are not serious are likely to be heard in state courts. Serious crimes may be tried in either state courts or federal courts depending on the situation, for example, cases where a crime has taken place in another state are often heard in federal courts.

After a person has been arrested a magistrate, or in some cases a GRAND JURY made up of between 16 and 23 citizens, decides whether they should go to trial. If there is enough evidence for a trial the accused goes to state and has to state whether he/she is **guilty or not guilty** of the crime. If they say they are not guilty they are sent to trial with a judge and jury (of 6 or 12 citizens) in either a State or COUNTY COURT or, in federal cases, a DISTRICT COURT. If the accused is found guilty they may have the right to appeal to a higher court, as shown below.

The final court of appeal in the US federal system and for some cases in the state courts is the US SUPREME COURT. It is made up of a CHIEF JUSTICE and eight ASSOCIATEs. The accused does not have the right to be heard by the Supreme Court, but the Supreme Court decides which cases it will hear. — see also page 751.

The Appeals System

The diagram shows the courts in order of importance with arrows representing the appeals system.

Federal Courts	*State Courts*
Supreme Court	State Supreme Court
↑	↑
Court of Appeals	Appellate Court
↑	↑
District Court	State/County Court

had too much to drink is **against the law**. (=is illegal) | She's been studying law for five years. (=learning these rules and studying how they operate) | business law (=the set of laws concerned with business) | a leading London law firm (=a firm of lawyers) **3** [C] a rule of action in a sport, art, business, etc.: the laws of cricket/commerce **4** [C] a statement expressing what has been seen always to happen in certain conditions: Boyle's law is a scientific principle. | the law of gravity | the laws of nature **5** [the+sing./pl. v] infml the police or a policeman: The law was/were there in force. (=many policemen were there) **6** [the] cap. the instructions in the first five books of the BIBLE on how to live one's life, believed to have been written by Moses **7 be a law unto oneself** to take no notice of the law and other rules of behaviour, and do what one wishes **8 go to law** (of a private person, not the police or the state) to bring a matter to a court of law for a decision **9 law and order** respect and obedience for the law in society: to establish/keep law and order | a breakdown in law and order **10 law of averages** the rule that if the chances of anything happening or not happening are equal, it will happen exactly half the time (if attempted often enough) **11** pomp, humor **the long arm of the law** justice, esp. in the form of the police, considered as something that criminals cannot escape from **12 take the law into one's own hands** to take no notice of society's rules and act alone, usu. by force: He took the law into his own hands and shot the burglar. —see also CIVIL LAW, COMMON LAW, POOR LAW, ROMAN LAW, SOD'S LAW, UNWRITTEN LAW, **lay down the law** (LAY down) and see also extra information on page 742

law·a·bid·ing /ˈ· ·ˌ··/ adj habitually obeying the law: an honest, law-abiding citizen

law·break·er /ˈ· ˌ··/ n a person who breaks the law; a criminal —**law-breaking** n [U]: law-breaking is on the increase

law en·force·ment /ˈ· ·ˌ··/ n [U] the act of causing (a rule or law) to be obeyed or carried out effectively: a law enforcement officer | The police are responsible for law enforcement.

law en·force·ment a·gent /ˈ· ··· ˌ··/ n a policeman or officer of the law

law firm /ˈ· ˌ·/ n AmE a business company specializing in legal services and employing usu. many LAWYERS

law·ful /ˈlɔːfəl/ adj fml **1** allowed by law: I was going about my lawful business. **2** admitted by law to be the stated thing: a lawful marriage —see LEGAL (USAGE) — ~ly adv — ~ness n [U]

law·less /ˈlɔːləs/ adj **1** (of a country or place) not governed by laws: lawless frontier towns **2** uncontrolled; wild: lawless frontiersmen — ~ly adv — ~ness n [U]

Law Lords /ˈ· ˌ·/ [the+P] those members of the House of Lords who hold, or have held, high positions in the legal profession; members of the highest court in the English system

law·mak·er /ˈlɔːmeɪkər/ n [often pl.] AmE any elected official who is responsible for making laws: lawmakers in Washington | county lawmakers

law·man /ˈlɔːmæn/ n -men /men/ AmE any professional officer whose job is to make sure that the law is obeyed, esp. a SHERIFF: He's one of the finest lawmen I've ever met.

lawn /lɔːn/ n a stretch of usu. flat ground, esp. next to a house, covered with closely cut grass: Let's have tea on the lawn. | The grass is getting too long, we must mow the lawn. —see picture at HOUSE

lawn bowl·ing /ˈ· ˌ··/ n [U] AmE for BOWLS

lawn·mow·er /ˈlɔːnməʊər/ n a machine which can be pushed or driven along the ground to cut grass, esp. in gardens —see picture at GARDEN

lawn par·ty /ˈ· ˌ··/ n AmE for GARDEN PARTY

lawn ten·nis /ˌ· ˈ··/ n [U] fml or tech for TENNIS

law of the jun·gle /ˌ· · · ˈ··/ [the] the principle that only the strongest will succeed in life and that people should help themselves rather than others

Law·rence /ˈlɒrəns‖ˈlɔː-, ˈlɑː-/, **D. H.** (1885–1930) an English writer known esp. for his stories of life in industrial society in which his characters show great strength of emotion, particularly love, and strong sexual desires. His best known books are Sons and Lovers and Lady Chatterley's Lover. Several of his books were considered OBSCENE when they were written, esp. Lady Chatterley's

Lover which was banned (BAN) and not available until 1960.

Lawrence, T. E.S (1888–1935) a British soldier and writer, also known as **Lawrence of Arabia**, who helped the Arabs in their fight against the Turks (1914–18) and was strongly in favour of Arab independence. He wrote Seven Pillars of Wisdom about his desert adventures.

law school /ˈ· ·/ n [C;U] AmE a school of higher education where one studies to become a lawyer, having already earned a BACHELOR'S DEGREE

Law So·ci·e·ty /ˈ· ·ˌ···/ [the] the professional body in England and Wales dealing with the behaviour, education, and interests of SOLICITORS

Law·son /ˈlɔːsən/, **Ni·gel** /ˈnaɪdʒəl/ (1932–) a British politician who was Conservative Chancellor of the Exchequer (=British finance minister) from 1983 to 1989

law·suit /ˈlɔːsuːt, -sjuːt‖-suːt/ also **suit**— n a matter brought to a court of law for decision by a private person or company, not by the police or the state: The victims have started a lawsuit to get compensation for their injuries.

law·yer /ˈlɔːjər/ n a person whose business is to advise people about laws, write formal agreements, or to represent people in court: I suggest you consult a lawyer. —see also ADVOCATE, ATTORNEY, BARRISTER, SOLICITOR

▶ CULTURAL NOTE **Lawyer** is the general word for someone whose business is the law. In England and Wales there are two kinds of lawyer who have different training and perform different jobs. A **solicitor** advises people on legal matters such as contracts, wills, and the buying and selling of property. Solicitors may represent a person in a MAGISTRATE'S COURT, but have only been able to do so in a higher court since 1992. A **barrister** may represent a person in any court, but usu. only does so in the higher courts. A person's solicitor advises the barrister about the facts of the case, but does not tell the barrister what to say. In the US, a lawyer may also be called an **attorney**, and there are no differences between the two. A lawyer who represents someone during a trial is sometimes called a **counselor**. ◀

lax /læks/ adj **1** not paying enough attention to what is needed or lacking in control, esp. of oneself or others: That teacher's too lax with his class; no wonder they're so undisciplined. | lax morals | Lax security allowed the thieves to enter. **2** med (of bowels) emptying too easily — ~ly adv — ~ity, ~ness n [U]

LAX /ˌel eɪ ˈeks/ Los Angeles International Airport; the main airport serving the area around Los Angeles, California

lax·a·tive /ˈlæksətɪv/ n, adj (a medicine or something eaten for) causing the bowels to empty easily

lay¹ /leɪ/ v past tense of LIE¹

lay² v **laid** /leɪd/ **1** [T+obj+adv/prep] to put, esp. carefully, in a flat position; place: They laid the injured woman (down) on the grass. | He laid his coat over a chair. **2** [T] to set in proper order or position: He planned to build his own house, and was learning to lay bricks. | We're having a new carpet laid in the bedroom. **3** [T] to prepare; make ready: to lay plans | to lay a trap | (BrE) She laid the table. (=covered it with a cloth, knives, forks, etc., ready for a meal) **4** [T] to cause to settle, disappear, or no longer be active: The rain quickly laid the dust. | to lay a ghost **5** [I;T] (of a bird, insect, etc.) to produce (an egg or eggs): Last week they laid 30 eggs, but this week the hens aren't laying. **6** [T (on)] to risk (money) on the result of some happening, such as a race; BET²: She laid £5 on the favourite. **7** [T+obj+adv/prep] to put into a particular condition, esp. of weakness, helplessness, obedience, etc.: The country was laid in ruins. **8** [T+obj+adv/prep] to make (a statement, claim, charge, etc.) in a serious, official, or public way: Your employer has laid a serious charge against you. | The proposal was laid before the committee. | He laid the blame squarely on the police. **9** [T] taboo sl to have sex with: He's been trying to lay her for ages. | He only goes to parties to **get laid**. —see also LAY⁴ (1) **10 lay someone/something flat** to knock down to the ground **11 lay someone low: a** to make someone unable to perform their usual activities because of illness: I've been laid low with flu for a week. **b** esp. fml or lit to knock or bring someone down, esp. so as to wound them or make them helpless **12 lay something on the line: a** to state (a fact, one's intentions, etc.) forcefully; make clear **b** to risk: He laid his life on the line for his country. **13 lay waste** to make (a place) bare, esp.

by violence; destroy, as in war   **14 lay someone/oneself open to** to put someone/oneself into the position of receiving (blame, attack, etc.): *If you don't get the facts right, you'll lay yourself open to criticism/to ridicule* —see also **lay one's cards on the table** (CARDS), **lay a finger on** (FINGER¹)

▷ USAGE Do not confuse **lay** [T] (**laid, laid**) with **lie** [I] (**lay, lain**): *He laid his trousers on the bed.* | *He lay on the bed.* A third verb **lie** [I] (**lied, lied**) means "to tell a lie".◁

lay about sbdy. *phr v* [T] *BrE*   **1** to attack wildly: *He laid about his attackers with a club.*   **2 lay about one** *old use* to hit wildly in all directions: *She laid about her until her assailants ran off.*

lay sthg. ↔ **aside** *phr v* [T]   **1** to store for future use: *She'd managed to lay aside a few pounds out of her wages each week.*   **2** to stop using, doing, or preparing for a time: *We've had to lay aside our plans for expansion.*

lay sthg. ↔ **away** *phr v* [T] *AmE* to buy something, with the seller agreeing to hold it for a small amount of money and deliver it when the full amount is paid: *Only $10 will lay away a new electric blanket for those cold winter nights!* —see also LAYAWAY

lay sthg. ↔ **down** *phr v* [T]   **1** to put down (tools, weapons, etc.) as a sign that one will not use them: *Lay down your guns and come out with your hands up!*   **2** [(**for**)] to lose or stop having willingly in order to help others: *Greater love hath no man than this, that a man lay down his life for his friend.* (the Bible)   **3** to start the building or making of: *The foundations of the building were laid down in 1959.*   **4** [*often pass.*] to declare or state firmly or officially: [+*that*] *It's laid down in the regulations/The regulations lay down that members must always sign guests in.*   **5** to store (esp. wine) for future use   **6 lay down the law** to give an opinion or order in an unpleasant commanding manner

lay sthg. ↔ **in** *phr v* [T] to obtain and store (a supply of): *We laid in (a good supply of) candles in case there was a power cut.*

lay into sbdy. *phr v* [T] to attack physically or with words: *The boxer really laid into his opponent.* | (fig.) *You should have seen her laying into that cake!*

lay off *phr v*   **1** [T] (**lay** sbdy. ↔ **off**) to stop employing (a worker), esp. for a period in which there is little work: *During the recession they laid us off for three months.* —see also LAY-OFF   **2** [I;T (=**lay off** sthg.)] *infml* to stop (doing, having, using, etc.): *You'd better lay off (alcohol) for a while.* [+*v-ing*] *Lay off hitting me!*

lay on *phr v* [T]   **1** *esp. BrE* (**lay** sthg. ↔ **on**) to supply or provide, esp. generously: *The organizers laid on a huge meal for us.* | *They've laid on a car to meet us at the airport.*   **2** (**lay** sthg. **on** sbdy.) to cause to have (a serious responsibility) on: *That's rather a lot to lay on one person.*   **3 lay it on (a bit thick/with a trowel)** *infml* **a** to tell something in a way that goes beyond the truth **b** to praise or admire something too greatly, esp. in order to please

lay sthg. ↔ **open** *phr v*   **1** to uncover or make known   **2** to cut; wound: *The blow laid his head open.*

lay sbdy./sthg. **out** *phr v* [T]   **1** to spread out: *She laid out the map on the table.*   **2** to arrange or plan (a building, town, garden, etc.): *The garden is laid out in a formal pattern.* —see also LAYOUT   **3** to arrange (a dead body) in preparation for burial   **4** to knock (a person) down, esp. making them unconscious: *I laid him out with a blow to the head.*   **5** [(**on, for**)] *infml* to spend (money, esp. a large amount): *She laid out £600 on a new carpet.* —see also OUTLAY

lay over *phr v* [I] *AmE for* STOP **over**

lay to *phr v* [I;T (=**lay** sthg. **to**)] to stop or cause (a ship) to stop moving —compare LAY **up** (3), LIE **to**

lay sbdy./sthg. ↔ **up** *phr v* [T]   **1** to collect and store for future use: *to lay up food for the winter* | (fig.) *to lay up problems for the future*   **2** to keep indoors or in bed with an illness: *I've been laid up for a week with my bad back.*   **3** to stop using (a boat) for a time, esp. so that it can be repaired —compare LAY **to**

lay³ *adj* [A]   **1 a** of, done by, or being people who are not in official positions within a religion: *a lay preacher* **b** not holding an official position in an organization: *lay members of the union*   **2** not trained in or having knowledge of a particular profession or subject, such as law or medicine: *To the lay mind, these technical terms are incomprehensible.* —see also LAITY, LAYMAN

lay⁴ *n*   **1** *taboo sl* (someone, esp. a woman, considered for their part in) the sexual act: *She's a great lay!*   **2 lay of the land** *esp. AmE for* **lie of the land** (LIE²)

lay⁵ *n*   **1** a short poem that tells a story and is meant to be sung, esp. one written in former times   **2** *poet* a song

lay·a·bout /ˈleɪəbaʊt/ *n BrE infml* a lazy person who avoids work, responsibility, etc.

lay·a·way /ˈleɪəweɪ/ *n, adj* [U] *AmE* a method of buying in which goods are held by the seller for a small amount of money until the full price is paid: *a layaway plan* | *stove bought on layaway*

lay bro·ther /ˌ· ˈ··/ **lay sis·ter** *fem.*— *n* someone who belongs to but is not a full priestly member of a religious group, and who is employed mostly in general work in the kitchen or garden of a religious house

lay-by /ˈ· ·/ *n* **-bys** *BrE* a space next to a road where vehicles can park out of the way of traffic

lay·er¹ /ˈleɪəʳ/ *n*   **1** [(**of**)] a thickness of some substance, often one of many: *These seeds must be covered with a layer of earth.* | *There's a thin layer of coal between the two layers of rock.* | *She's wearing several layers of clothing to keep out the cold.* | (fig.) *trying to penetrate the layers of bureaucracy*   **2** (*usu. in comb.*) a person or thing that lays something: *a carpet layer* —see also BRICKLAYER, PLATELAYER   **3** a bird, esp. a hen, that lays eggs: *a good layer*   **4** *tech* a plant stem that has been fastened partly under the ground, in order to grow roots and so become a separate plant   **5 -layered** /leɪəd‖-ərd/ having the stated number of thicknesses: *many-layered*

layer² *v*   **1** [T] to make a layer of; put down in layers: *This dish is made of potatoes layered with cheese.*   **2** [T] to cut (hair) in layers rather than all to the same length   **3** [T] *tech* to fasten (a plant stem) down and cover it with earth   **4** *tech* [I] (of a plant) to form roots where a stem meets the soil

lay·ette /leɪˈet/ *n* a complete set of clothes and other things needed for a newborn baby

lay fig·ure /ˌ· ˈ··/ *n* a figure of the human body, usu. wooden, with movable limbs, used as a model when painting or drawing

laying on of hands /ˌ··· · ˈ·/ *n* [(*the*)] the act of putting hands on a person's (or animal's) body to cure illness, esp. with help from God. It is practised mostly by EVANGELICAL and FUNDAMENTALIST CHRISTIANS. —see also **speak in tongues** (SPEAK)

lay·man /ˈleɪmən/ *also* **layperson, laywoman** *fem.*— **-men** /mən/   **1** a person who is not trained in a particular subject or type of work, esp. as compared with those who are: *These technical terms are difficult for the layman to understand.* | *the gross domestic product, or, in layman's language/terms, the amount of goods produced by a country*   **2** a person who is not a priest in a religion

lay-off /ˈ· ·/ *n* the stopping of a worker's employment at a time when there is little work: *There have been a lot of lay-offs in the shipbuilding industry recently.* —see also LAY **off**

lay·out /ˈleɪaʊt/ *n*   **1** the way in which something large with many parts is arranged, such as a town, garden, building, etc., as shown in a drawing: *In the new layout for the conference hall, the platform is to be placed at the western end.* | *The robbers studied the layout of the bank.*   **2** the way in which printed matter is set out on paper: *The book designer will have to re-do the page layouts.* —see also LAY **out**

lay·o·ver /ˈleɪəʊvəʳ/ *n AmE* STOPOVER: *I've got a two-hour layover in Pittsburgh before flying on to Chicago.* —see also LAY **over**

lay·per·son /ˈleɪˌpɜːsən‖-ɜːr-/ *n* a LAYMAN or LAYWOMAN

lay read·er /ˈ· ˌ··/ *n* in certain Christian churches, a person who is not a priest but who may lead religious services and PREACH (=give the message of God)

lay sis·ter /ˌ· ˈ··/ *n* see LAY BROTHER

lay-up /ˈ· ·/ *n* (in BASKETBALL) a throw at the basket which takes place near the basket: *Bird drops a lay-up into the net.*

lay·wom·an /ˈleɪˌwʊmən/ *n* **-women** /ˌwɪmɪn/ see LAYMAN

Laz·a·rus /ˈlæzərəs/ a friend of Jesus' whose story is told in the Bible. When he died, Jesus brought him back to life.

laze¹ /leɪz/ v [I+adv/prep] to rest lazily: *He spent the after-noon lazing in a hammock.*
  laze about/around phr v [I] to waste time enjoyably, with little effort: *That's enough lazing around — it's time to start work.*
  laze sthg. ↔ **away** phr v [T] to spend (time) lazily: *She lazed away the afternoon in a deckchair by the pond.*

laze² n [S] a short period of restful and lazy inactivity

la·zy /'leɪzi/ adj **1** derog disliking and avoiding activity or work: *He won't work; he's just too lazy!* **2** (esp. of a period of time) suitable for doing nothing, or spent in doing nothing: *a lazy afternoon* **3** moving slowly: *a lazy river* —**zily** adv —**ziness** n [U]

la·zy·bones /'leɪzibəʊnz/ n **lazybones** infml a lazy person: *Come on, lazybones; it's time to get up!*

lazy Su·san /ˌleɪzi 'suːzən/ n a flat piece of plastic or wood which can be turned round and made to hold several dishes etc. on a dinner table so that everyone can reach what they want

lb written abbrev. for: pound (weight)

lbw /ˌel biː 'dʌbəljuː/ abbrev. for: **leg before wicket** (LEG¹)

LBJ /ˌel biː 'dʒeɪ/ see Lyndon Baines JOHNSON

LCD /ˌel siː 'diː/ n liquid crystal display; part of an APPARA-TUS on which numbers, letters, etc. are shown by pass-ing an electric current through a special liquid, so that they light up: *The time on my digital watch is shown on an LCD.* —compare LED

LCM /ˌel siː 'em/ written abbrev. for: LOWEST COMMON MULTIPLE

L-driv·er /'el ˌ.../ n BrE a person who is learning to drive

LDS written abbrev. for: Latter-Day Saints —see MORMON

lea /liː/ n poet an open piece of grassy land

LEA /ˌel iː 'eɪ/ abbrev. for: LOCAL EDUCATION AUTHORITY

Lea and Per·rins /ˌliː ənd 'perᵻnz/ n [U] tdmk a company in Britain which makes Worcestershire SAUCE. The sauce is made to a secret RECIPE which includes VINEGAR, SPICES, and anchovies (ANCHOVY) and is used to add FLAVOUR to food.

leach /liːtʃ/ v [OUT, AWAY, from] tech **1** [T] to separate (a substance) from a material, such as soil, by passing water through the material: *Alkali is leached out from ashes.* **2** [I] (of certain substances in a material) to be removed by water passing through the material: *All the minerals essential for plant growth gradually leached away.*

lead¹ /liːd/ v **led** /led/ **1** [T+obj+adv/prep, esp. to] to go with or in front of (a person or animal) so as to take them to a place or show them the way: *She led the blind man down the stairs.* | *The horses were led into the yard.* | (fig.) *The distant lights led me to the village.* | (fig.) *A single vital clue led the police to the murderer.* | (fig.) *The girl's father blamed her boyfriend for leading her astray.* (=causing her to behave wrongly) **2** [I (ON);T] to go in front (of), esp. so as to show the way: *You lead (on) and we'll fol-low.* | *The royal car led the procession.* **3** [I+adv/prep] to be the means of reaching a place, going through an area, etc.: *A path led through the wood.* | *This road leads to the village.* | (fig.) *Her careless spending led her into debt.* **4** [T+obj+to-v] to cause, esp. wrongly: *She led me to believe that she had a lot of influence.* (=but in fact she did not have such influence) **5** [I;T] to be in charge of (esp. a group): *Has she got the qualities necessary to lead?* | *A general leads an army.* | *He's been chosen to lead the cricket team.* **6** [I;T] to be ahead (of) in sports or games: *The English team was leading (France) 1-0 at half time.* | (fig.) *Japan leads the field* (=is ahead of all other coun-tries) *in electronics production.* **7** [T] to live (a particu-lar kind of life): *He led an exciting life.* **8** [I (with)] to make one's main attacking hits in BOXING: *He led with his left.* (=left hand) **9** [I;T (with)] to start or open a game of cards (with): *She led (with) her highest card.* **10 lead someone a (merry) dance** BrE infml to cause someone a lot of unnecessary trouble, such as making them fol-low you about from place to place without any advantage to themselves **11 lead someone by the nose** infml to have complete control over someone **12 lead someone up the garden path** infml to cause someone to believe something that is not true; deceive someone **13 lead the life of Riley** BrE sl to live in complete comfort, enjoy-ment, etc.
  ▷ USAGE To **lead** is to show the way by going first: *You*

lead *and we'll follow.* | *She* **led** *them down the moun-tain.* To **guide** is to go with someone (who needs help) in order to show the way and explain things: *He* **guided** *the blind woman across the road.* | *He* **guided** *the tourists round the castle.* To **direct** is to explain to some-one how to get to a place: *Could you* **direct** *me to the station, please?*◁

lead (sthg. ↔) **off** phr v [I;T (with)] **1** to make a start (to); begin: *She led off (the show) with a song.* **2** AmE to BAT² first in an INNING in BASEBALL: *Sandberg will lead off for the Cubs.*

lead sbdy. **on** phr v [T] **1** to cause to believe something that is not true: *She has no sense of humour, so she couldn't see he was leading her on.* | *He thought it was love but she was only leading him on.* **2** to influence (some-one) into doing something they should not do: *My little Tommy would never have got into trouble with the police if those friends of his hadn't led him on.*

lead to sthg. phr v [T no pass.] to result in: *This will lead to trouble in the future.* [+obj+v-ing] *The scandal led to him resigning.*

lead up to sthg. phr v [T] to come before and result in or be a preparation for: *His flattering words led up to a request for money.* | *the events leading up to his arrest*

lead² /liːd/ n **1** [C] a guiding suggestion or example: *We're waiting for the conductor to give us a lead.* | *I'll follow your lead.* **2** [the] the position ahead of all others: *The English team was in the lead* (=winning the game) *at half time.* | *He's playing the lead* (=the most important acting part) *in the new play.* | *Japan has taken the lead in car production.* (=is now producing more than any other country) | *It's up to someone to take the lead in con-demning these injustices.* (=to do so first, and set a good example to others) **3** [S (over)] the distance, number of points, etc., by which one competitor is ahead of another: *England had a lead of ten points to three at half time.* | *Japan will soon have/take an unassailable lead over other car-producing countries.* **4** [C] BrE ‖ **leash** AmE or BrE fml— a length of rope, leather, chain, etc., fastened to an animal, usu. a dog, to control it: *a dog on a lead* **5** [C] an electric wire for taking the power from the supply point to an instrument or apparatus **6** [C] a piece of in-formation that may lead to a discovery or to something being settled; CLUE: *The police have several useful leads.* **7** [(the) S] the right to play the first card in a game: *It's your lead, partner.*

lead³ /liːd/ adj [A] being most important or a leader: *a lead part in a play* | *a lead singer in a pop group*

lead⁴ /led/ n **1** [U] a soft heavy easily melted greyish-blue metal, used for waterpipes, to cover roofs, etc.: *lead pip-ing* **2** [C;U] (a thin stick of) GRAPHITE (=a black sub-stance) used in pencils: *I need a pencil with a soft lead.* **3 go down like a lead balloon** (of a joke, remark, etc.) to be received very badly: *His comment on her hairstyle really went down like a lead balloon* **4** [U] AmE sl bullets: *They filled him full of lead* (=they shot him many times). —see also LEADS, BLACK LEAD, WHITE LEAD, **swing the lead** (SWING¹)

lead·ed lights /ˌledᵻd 'laɪts/ also **leaded win·dows** /ˌ... '.../— n [P] esp. BrE windows with thin narrow pieces of LEAD⁴ (1) separating small PANES of glass. The glass is often in a diamond pattern and is thought to look old-fashioned and attractive.

leaded pet·rol /ˌledᵻd 'petrəl/ BrE ‖ **leaded gas·o·line** /ˌ... '.../, **leaded gas** /ˌ... '.../ AmE— n [U] petrol contain-ing lead, generally considered to be harmful to the environment —opposite **lead-free** or **unleaded petrol**

lead·en /'ledn/ adj **1** of the colour of lead; dull grey: *a leaden sky* **2** without cheerfulness or excitement: *With a leaden heart she opened the income-tax envelope.* | *a rather leaden performance*

lead·er /'liːdər/ n **1** [(of)] a person who guides or directs a group, team, organization, etc.: *the leader of the miners' union* | *He's always been a follower rather than a leader.* | *a born leader* **2** [(of, in)] a person or thing that is ahead of others: *Liverpool are the current leaders in the football championship.* | *The leader (of) in the race) is just coming into view.* **3** BrE ‖ **concertmaster** AmE— the chief VIO-LIN player of an ORCHESTRA **4** AmE for CONDUCTOR (1) **5** BrE for EDITORIAL²: *the "Times" leader writers* **6** tech the strongest stem or branch of a tree —see also LOSS LEADER

Leader of the House /ˌ.... · · '·/ also **Leader—** **1** the member of the government who arranges the business in the HOUSE OF COMMONS **2** the member of the government who arranges the business in the HOUSE OF LORDS

Leader of the Op·po·si·tion /ˌ· · · · ··ˈ··/ [the] the leader of the main party opposing the government in the British parliament

lead·er·ship /ˈliːdəʃɪp‖-ər-/ n **1** [U (of)] the position of leader: *He was elected to the leadership of the Labour party.* | *Britain has lost her leadership in the shipbuilding industry.* **2** [U] the qualities necessary in a leader: *She lacks leadership.* **3** [C+sing./pl. v] a group of people who lead: *The leadership of the movement is/are in agreement on this issue.*

lead-free pet·rol /ˌled friː ˈpetrəl/ BrE‖**lead-free gas·o·line** /ˌ· · ˈ··/, **lead-free gas** /ˌ· · ˈ·/ AmE— n [U] PETROL containing no lead

lead-in /ˈliːd ɪn/ n remarks made by someone to introduce a radio or television show

lead·ing[1] /ˈliːdɪŋ/ adj [A] most important; chief; main: *He was one of the leading composers of his time.* | *a leading role in the film*

lead·ing[2] /ˈledɪŋ/ n [U] **1** lead used for covering roofs, for window frames, etc. **2** the space left between lines of printed matter: *9 point type on a 10 point leading*

leading ar·ti·cle /ˌliːdɪŋ ˈɑːtɪkəl‖-ˈɑːr-/ n BrE for EDITORIAL[2]

leading edge /ˌliːdɪŋ ˈedʒ/ n **1** the front edge of an aircraft PROPELLER blade or wing **2** the edge of a sail that faces the wind

leading la·dy /ˌliːdɪŋ ˈleɪdi/ **leading man** /ˌ·· ˈ·/masc.— n the person who acts the leading female or male part in a film, play, etc.

leading light /ˌliːdɪŋ ˈlaɪt/ n [(in, of)] infml a person of importance or influence: *Bill is one of the leading lights of the local dramatic society.*

leading ques·tion /ˌliːdɪŋ ˈkwestʃən/ n a question formed in such a way that it suggests the expected answer. In a court of law, LAWYERS are not allowed to ask leading questions.

lead-off /ˈliːd ɒf‖-ɔːf/ adj AmE coming or going first, before others: *the lead-off pitcher for The Twins* | *The lead-off title in a new series of How-To books* —see also LEAD **off**

leads /ledz/ n [P] **1** sheets of lead used for covering a roof **2** narrow pieces of lead used for holding small pieces of glass together to form a LATTICE window

lead time /ˈliːd taɪm/ n the time taken in planning and producing a new product, before it is actually ready for sale

leaf[1] /liːf/ n **leaves** /liːvz/ **1** [C] any of the usu. flat green parts of a plant that are joined to its stems or branches: *autumn leaves* | *The trees are in/are coming into leaf.* **2** [C] a thin sheet of paper, esp. a page in a book —see also LOOSE-LEAF, OVERLEAF **3** [U] metal, esp. gold or silver, in a very thin sheet: *gold leaf* **4** [C] part of a tabletop, door, etc., that can be slid, folded, or taken into or out of use: *Pull out both leaves of the table.* **5 take a leaf out of someone's book** to follow someone's example **6 turn over a new leaf** to begin a new course of improved behaviour, habits, etc.: *I've decided to turn over a new leaf and do lots of exercise from now on.* **7 -leaved** /liːvd/also **-leafed** /liːft/— having leaves of the stated type or number: *a narrow-leaved plant*

leaf[2] v

leaf through sthg. phr v [T] to turn the pages of (a book, magazine, etc.) quickly without reading much: *I was leafing through an old school magazine when I came across your photo.*

leaf·let[1] /ˈliːflɪt/ n a small, often folded piece of printed paper, often advertising something, usu. given free to the public

leaflet[2] v -t BrE‖-tt esp. AmE— [I;T] esp. BrE to give out or post leaflets in (a certain area), esp. as part of political activity: *He's been out leafleting (the housing estate).*

leaf mould /ˈ· ·/ n [U] dead decaying leaves which form a rich top surface to soil

leaf·y /ˈliːfi/ adj **1** having many leaves: *a very leafy bush* **2** esp. lit having many trees: *the leafy suburbs of London*

league[1] /liːg/ n **1** a group of sports clubs or players that play matches among themselves: *the Football League* |

a darts league | *a league match* | *league football* —compare CONFERENCE (2); see also FOOTBALL LEAGUE **2** a group of people, countries, etc., who have joined together to protect or improve their position, or to bring about a particular result **3** infml a level of quality; class: *They're not in the same league as the French at making wine.* | *You'll find you're out of your league if you challenge him to a game — he's the chess club champion.* **4 in league (with)** working together (with), often secretly or for a bad purpose: *The police suspected that the bank clerk was in league with the robbers.*

league[2] v [I;T (TOGETHER)] rare to unite in or join a LEAGUE[1] (2)

league[3] n old use a measure of distance of about three miles or five kilometres

League a·gainst Cru·el Sports /ˌ· ··ˌ·· ˈ·/ [the] (in Britain) an organization established in 1924 which wants to make BLOOD SPORTS (= hunting, shooting, etc. of animals for sport) illegal —see also HUNT SABOTEUR

League of Na·tions /ˌ· ·· ˈ··/ [the] (1920–46) an international organization established to work for international peace and safety after the First World War. It served as a model for the existing United Nations.

League of Wom·en Vot·ers /ˌ· ·· ˌ·· ˈ··/ [the] an American organization that encourages women to vote and calls attention to political matters that might have an affect on their lives

league ta·ble /ˈ· ˌ··/ n (in Britain) a list of people or teams in a competition, showing their relative positions: *Liverpool have now reached top of the league table.*

leak[1] /liːk/ v **1** [I;T] to let (a liquid, gas, etc.) in or out of a hole or crack: *The tank is leaking (petrol).* **2** [I (OUT, IN)] (of a liquid, gas, etc.) to get out through a hole or crack: *Oil was leaking out of a hole in the tank.* | *water leaking in through a hole in the roof* **3** [T (OUT, to)] to make known (news, facts, etc., that ought to be secret): *Someone in the ministry had leaked the story to the press.*

▶CULTURAL NOTE As there is no Freedom of Information Act (= allowing the public knowledge of government business) in Britain, important information is often leaked by officials who think the public ought to know but do not want or are not allowed to tell them officially.◀

leak out phr v [I] (of news, facts, etc., that ought to be secret) to become known: *It has leaked out that they intend to increase the arms budget.*

leak[2] n **1** [C] a small accidental hole or crack through which something flows in or out: *You'd better repair that leak in the fuel pipe.* **2** [C] an escape of liquid, gas, etc., through such a hole: *a gas leak* | *a leak of nuclear waste* **3** [C] an accidental or intentional spreading of news, facts, etc., that ought to be secret: *a security leak* **4** [S] sl an act of passing water from the body: *I'm just going to take/have a leak.* (=to URINATE)

leak·age /ˈliːkɪdʒ/ n **1** [C;U] an example of something leaking: *The short circuit was due to (a) leakage of water.* **2** [C] something which has leaked in or out: *He wiped up the leakage.*

Lea·key /ˈliːki/, **Lou·is** /ˈluːi/ (1903–72) a British archaeologist (ARCHAEOLOGY) who discovered human FOSSILS (hardened bones) in Tanzania which he believed were important in discovering the development of man through EVOLUTION. His wife **Mary Leakey** (1913–) and his son **Richard Leakey** (1944–) are also archaeologists.

leak·y /ˈliːki/ adj letting things leak in or out: *a leaky bucket* | *a leaky committee, whose supposedly secret meetings were accurately reported in the press* —**iness** n [U]

lean[1] /liːn/ v **leant** /lent/ or **leaned** **1** [I] to slope or bend from an upright position: *The trees leant in the wind.* | *the leaning tower of Pisa* | *He leant forward/down/over to hear what she said.* **2** [I+adv/prep] to support or rest oneself in a bent or sloping position: *She leant against his shoulder.* | *He leant on the back of the chair.* **3** [T+obj+adv/prep] to place so as to be supported from the side in a sloping position: *Lean it (up) against the wall.* —see also **lean over backwards** (BACKWARDS) —**lean** n [S (of)] : *a lean of 20°*

▷ USAGE **Leaned** and **leant** are both used in British English, but **leaned** is the main form in American English.◁

lean on sbdy./sthg. phr v [T] **1** also **lean upon**— to

need the help of; depend on: *The minister leans on his advisers (for support).* **2** *infml* to influence forcefully, often by threats: *I'm being leant on to pay up straightaway.*
    lean towards sthg. *phr v* [T] to favour (an opinion, idea, etc.): *My wife intends to vote for the Democrats, but I find myself leaning towards the Republicans.*

lean² *adj* **1** (of meat) not having much fat. It is generally considered to be healthier to eat lean meat than fatty meat and it is often eaten by people trying to lose weight or people interested in eating healthy foods. **2** (of a person, esp. a man, or an animal) not having much flesh; healthily thin: *He had the lean fit look of a trained athlete.* | (fig.) *With our cuts in staff our company is leaner and more profitable.* **3** producing or having little value: *It's been a lean year for business.* –see THIN (USAGE) **4 a lean and hungry look** *quote* a phrase from Shakespeare's play *Julius Caesar.* Cassius, one of the men planning to kill Caesar, is described as having "a lean and hungry look" because he looks as if he is planning to do harm to someone. – ~ **ness** *n* [U]

lean³ *n* [*the* U] the part of meat that is not fat

Lean, David (1908–91) an English film director known for films such as *Brief Encounter, Bridge on the River Kwai, Dr Zhivago,* and *A Passage to India*

Lean Cui·sine /ˌ· ··ˈ·/ *n* [U] *tdmk* a range of prepared foods which contain very little fat, often eaten by people looking after their health or trying to lose weight

lean·ing /ˈliːnɪŋ/ *n* [(**towards**)] a slight tendency to favour one thing rather than another: *At an early age his leaning towards Socialism had become apparent.* | *She has artistic leanings.* (=thinks she may like to become an ARTIST)

Leaning Tow·er of Pi·sa /ˌliːnɪŋ ˌtaʊər əv ˈpiːzə/ [*the*] a round bell tower in Pisa, Italy which leans to one side. It is a popular tourist attraction but is now in danger of falling down completely.

lean-to /ˈ· ·/ *n* a small often roughly made building that rests against the side of a larger building or structure

leap¹ /liːp/ *v* **leapt** /lept/ *or* **leaped** /lept‖liːpt/ **1** [I+*adv/prep*] to jump, usu. so as to land in a different place: *The horse leapt across the chasm.* | *She leapt into the boat and grabbed the oars.* **2** [T] *esp. lit* to jump over: *He leapt the wall and ran away.* **3** [I+*adv/prep*] to act, move, rise, etc., quickly, as if with a jump: *He leapt up* (=suddenly stood up) *to complain.* | *She leapt to his assistance.* | *He leapt to their defence.* (–was quick to defend them)
    ▷ USAGE **Leapt** is more common in British English than **leaped** but **leaped** is more common in American English.◁
    leap at sthg. *phr v* [T] to accept (a chance, offer, etc.) eagerly: *She leapt at the chance of a trip to Europe.*
    leap out *phr v* [I (**at**)] to be very clearly noticeable: *His name leapt out at me from the newspaper.*

leap² *n* **1** a sudden jump: *She got over the stream with a single leap.* | (fig.) *It takes a considerable leap of the imagination to picture him as prime minister.* **2** [(**in**)] a sudden increase in number, amount, quantity, etc.: *There has been a leap in the number of births in Britain.* **3 by leaps and bounds** very quickly and successfully: *Her French is improving by leaps and bounds.* **4 leap in the dark** an action or risk taken without knowing what will happen as a result

leap·frog¹ /ˈliːpfrɒg‖-frɔːg, -frɑːg/ *n* [U] a game in which one person bends down and another jumps over them from behind

leapfrog² *v* **-gg-** [I (**over**);T] to advance well by missing out (something) on the way: *He leapfrogged two ranks and was promoted directly to colonel.*

leap year /ˈ· ·/ *n* [C;U] a year, every fourth year, in which February has 29 days instead of 28 days. Usually it is the custom in Britain for a man to ask a woman to marry him, but in a leap year, and esp. on February 29th, it is the custom that a woman can ask a man to marry her.

Lear, King see KING LEAR

Lear, Edward (1812–88) an English artist, traveller, and nonsense poet best known for his *Book of Nonsense*

Lear, Norman (1928–) an American maker of television programmes who began many popular programmes, esp. in the 1970s, including *All the Family* and *Maude.* Lear

is also known for running a political organization concerned with CIVIL RIGHTS

learn /lɜːn‖lɜːrn/ *v* **learned** *or* **learnt** /lɜːnt‖lɜːrnt/ **1** [I;T (**about**)] to gain knowledge of (a subject) or skill in (an activity), esp. through experience or through being taught: *The child is learning quickly.* | *I'm trying to learn French.* [+*to-v*] *She is learning to be a dancer.* [+*wh-*] *He is learning how to play the drums.* | *We hope he'll learn from his mistakes.* (=become wiser as a result of them) –compare TEACH (1) **2** [T+(*that*);*obj*] to come to understand; REALIZE: *You must learn that you can't treat people like servants.* **3** [T] to fix in the memory; MEMORIZE: *The teacher told us to learn the poem (by heart).* | *An actor learning his lines* **4** [I (**of, about**);T] *fml* to become informed (of): *She only learnt of* (=found out about) *her son's marriage long after the event.* | *Where did you learn this news?* [+(*that*)] *We were pleased to learn that he had arrived safely.* [+*wh-*] *We have yet to learn whether he arrived safely.* **5** [T] *BrE sl humor* to punish (someone) by shouting at them, hitting them, etc.: *That'll learn you to be cheeky!* **6 learn one's lesson** to suffer so much from doing something bad that one will not do it again –see also **live and learn** (LIVE¹)
    ▷ USAGE For the simple past form and past participle, **learned** and **learnt** are both common in British English, but the usual American English form is **learned**. –see also KNOW (USAGE)◁

learn·ed /ˈlɜːnɪd‖ˈlɜːr-/ *adj fml or pomp* **1** having much knowledge as the result of study and reading: *We consulted the most learned professors.* **2** [A] of or for advanced study: *a publisher of learned works* – ~ **ly** *adv*

learned so·ci·e·ty /ˌ··· ·ˈ···/ *n* a society where educated people discuss certain subjects involving study or reading

learn·er /ˈlɜːnər‖ˈlɜːr-/ *n* a person who is learning, esp. a person (**learner driver** /ˌ·· ˈ··/ (*BrE*)) who is learning to drive a car: *She's a rather slow learner.* (=is slow at learning)

learner's per·mit /ˈ··· ˌ··/ *AmE for* PROVISIONAL LICENCE

learn·ing /ˈlɜːnɪŋ‖ˈlɜːr-/ *n* [U] **1** deep and wide knowledge gained through reading and study: *a man of great learning* –compare KNOWLEDGE (1) **2 a little learning is a dangerous thing** *quote* a phrase from a work by Alexander Pope, often used when saying that it is not helpful to know a small amount about a subject

learning curve /ˈ··· ·/ *n* the rate at which someone learns something, e.g. a job, over a period of time

lease¹ /liːs/ *n* **1** a written legal agreement by which the use of a building or piece of land is given by its owner to someone for a certain time in return for rent: *She bought the house on a 99-year lease.* | *We've taken a lease on an office building.* | *The lease expires next month.*
    ▶CULTURAL NOTE A lease can be made for a very long time, perhaps for hundreds of years. The person who has the right to live in or use the property can sell that right for the remaining years of the lease to someone else. When the lease ends it may be RENEWED (= a new agreement may be made). –see also COMMONHOLD, FREEHOLD, GROUND RENT, LEASEHOLD◀
    2 a new lease of life (*BrE*)/**on life** (*AmE*) the ability to be happy, active, and successful again, esp. after being weak or tired: *That long holiday has given me a new lease of life.*

lease² *v* [T (**OUT**)] **1** to give or take the use of (land or buildings) on a lease: *This company leases out property.* [+*obj(i)+obj(d)*] *We will lease you the house for a year.* | *"Do you own the freehold of your house?" "No, I lease it."* **2** *tech* to rent or hire (expensive machinery or equipment): *Leasing (these cars) is tax-deductible.* | *We lease all our computers these days.*

lease·back /ˈliːsbæk/ *n* [C;U] an arrangement by which one sells or gives something to someone, but then continues to have the use of it in return for rent

lease·hold /ˈliːshəʊld/ *adj, adv esp. BrE* (of land or buildings) owned only for as long as is stated in a lease: *"Is your flat leasehold?" "Yes, we bought it leasehold."* –compare COMMONHOLD, FREEHOLD; see also LEASE¹ (1)
    ▶CULTURAL NOTE In England, Ireland, and Wales most flats are leasehold. Most houses and shops used to be leasehold, but many people have now bought their FREEHOLDs. In Scotland almost all property is freehold. ◀

lease·hold·er /ˈliːʃəʊldəʳ/ n someone who lives in a lease-hold house, flat, etc.

leash /liːʃ/ n AmE or BrE fml for LEAD² (4): Dogs must be kept on a leash. | (fig.) Let off the leash of government restrictions, the council increased its spending rapidly.

least¹ /liːst/ adv (superlative of LITTLE) **1** less than anything else or than any others: It happened just when we least expected it. | one of the least known of the modern poets –opposite most **2** least of all especially not: No one listened, least of all the children! **3** not least fml partly; quite importantly: Trade has been bad, not least because of the increased cost of imported raw materials.

least² determiner, pron (superlative of LITTLE) **1** the smallest number, amount, etc.: Buy the one that costs (the) least. | Finding enough money is the least of our problems! | "Thank you very much." "Not at all; it was the least I could do." (=a polite reply to thanks) –opposite most; see FEW (USAGE) **2** [usu. in negatives] slightest: I haven't the least idea where she is. (=I don't know at all) **3** at least: a (used for mentioning some small advantage in something, that makes its disadvantages seem not so bad): The food wasn't good, but at least it was cheap. **b** (used for lessening the force or certainty of something said): He left last Tuesday – at least, I think he did. **4** at (the) least not less than: It costs at least £5. | At the (very) least, it's going to cost £5. –opposite at (the) most (MOST²) **5** in the least [usu. in negatives] at all: He's not in the least worried. | "You must find such long hours very tiring." "Not in the least – I enjoy it." **6** to say the least (of it) (used for describing something bad without using strong words, but showing that one really disapproves of it a lot): It was rather thoughtless of him, to say the least.

least com·mon mul·ti·ple /ˌ· ·ˌ· ˈ···/ see LOWEST COMMON MULTIPLE

least·wise /ˈliːstwaɪz/ also **least·ways** /-weɪz/– adv AmE infml at least: He was there a minute ago, leastwise that's what Sue said.

leath·er /ˈleðəʳ/ n [U] **1** animal skin that has been treated to preserve it, used for making shoes, bags, etc.: a leather coat **2** the crack of leather on willow BrE the sound made by a CRICKET ball (made of leather) hitting a BAT (made of wood from the WILLOW tree), often used as a way of referring to the game of cricket

leath·er·ette /ˌleðəˈret/ n [U] tdmk a cheap material made to look like leather: a hideous leatherette sofa

leath·er·neck /ˈleðənek ‖ -əʳ-/ n AmE sl a member of the US Marine Corps

leath·er·y /ˈleðəri/ adj often derog like leather; hard and stiff: leathery meat/skin

leave¹ /liːv/ v left /left/ **1** [I (for);T] to go away (from): We must leave (the party) early. | When shall we leave for (=in order to go to) the party? | We're leaving from the main station at six o'clock. (=that is when our train journey starts) | He wanted to go to the toilet, and asked if he could leave the room. **2** [I;T] to stop being in or with (a place, organization, person, etc.): I'm leaving England and going to live in Spain. | He left his wife three months ago. | We're giving him a party when he leaves. (=stops working for our company, etc.) | a leaving present **3** [T (BE-HIND)] to go without taking: I must go back; I've left (=forgotten to bring) my car keys (behind). | We left the paperwork at the office. **4** [T] to cause to be or remain in a particular state or position: Let's leave the washing up (until tomorrow). (=not do it until tomorrow) | How were things left after the meeting? (=what arrangements were settled) | He left his car in the middle of the road. | Paying for the car repairs has left us without a penny. [+obj+adj] Will you leave the door open when you go out? | The president's sudden death has left the country leaderless. [+obj+v-ing] She left me waiting in the rain. | Her narrow escape left her feeling shaken. **5** [T] to cause to remain afterwards as an effect: The injury left a scar (on his face). **6** [T] to allow (something) to be the responsibility of (someone) or to be decided by (something): [+obj+with] He left the children with me while he went to get a paper. [+obj+to] "Which film shall we go and see?" "I'll leave it to you." (=you can choose) [+v-ing] I'll leave buying the tickets to you. [+obj+to-v] I'll leave you to buy the tickets. | I'll leave it to you to buy the tickets. **7** [T (OVER)] to allow to remain untaken, unused, unchanged, uneaten, etc.: Don't leave your cabbage. | There were some

chairs left over when everyone had sat down. **8** [T] to place or deliver (a letter, parcel, message, etc.): The postman has left a letter for you. [+obj(i)+obj(d)] The postman has left you a letter. | If I'm out, leave a message with my secretary. **9** [T] to have remaining after death: He leaves a wife and two children. | He left his family well provided for. **10** [T (to)] to give through a WILL² (5) after one's death: She left £250,000. | She left all her property to her husband. [+obj(i)+obj(d)] She left her husband all her property. **11** [L (+obj)+n] to give the stated result after taking one number away from another: Two from eight leaves (you) six. **12** leave go/hold of BrE infml to stop holding: Leave go of my hair! **13** leave it at that to do or say no more; not argue any further **14** leave someone/something alone to stop behaving annoyingly in someone's presence or touching something: Go away and leave me alone! | Leave that ornament alone; you might break it. **15** leave someone/something be to allow someone/something to remain untouched, unused, in proper position or order, etc.: "The baby's crying!" "Leave him be; he'll soon stop." –compare let someone/something be (LET¹) **16** leave someone cold to fail to excite or interest someone: Frankly, opera leaves me cold. **17** leave someone/something standing BrE infml to be much better than someone/something: This director's films leave the others standing. **18** leave someone to themself/to their own devices to allow or force someone to act on their own, without offering them any help, telling them what to do, etc. **19** leave well (enough) alone to make no change to something that is satisfactory, in case one makes things worse rather than better –leaver n : school leavers

leave off (sthg.) phr v [I;T] infml, rare in AmE to stop (doing something); give up: I wish the rain would leave off. | She was so ill she had to leave off work. [+v-ing] Leave off making that noise! Can't you see I'm trying to work?

leave sbdy./sthg. ↔ **out** phr v [T (of)] **1** to fail to include: You've left out the most important word in this sentence. | England has left Smith out (of their cricket team). | Don't leave me out when you're giving out the invitations! **2** to fail to accept or make welcome in a social group: No one speaks to him; he's always left out/he always feels left out. **3** Leave it out! BrE sl Stop lying, pretending, or being annoying!

leave² n **1** [C;U] time spent away from work or duty, esp. in government or army service: I'm in command of the regiment while the colonel's on leave. **2** [U] fml permission: It was done without leave from me/without my leave, I can assure you. [+to-v] Who gave you leave to do that? **3** take leave (of) to say goodbye (to); go away (from): (fig.) She must have taken leave of her senses (=gone mad) to do such a stupid thing. –see HOLIDAY¹ (USAGE); see also FRENCH LEAVE, SICK LEAVE

leav·en¹ /ˈlevən/ n **1** [U] a substance, esp. YEAST, that is added to a flour-and-water mixture to make it swell so that it can be baked into bread **2** [C;U] fml rare an influence that causes a gradual change in character

leaven² v [T] **1** to add leaven to (a cooking mixture, esp. flour and water) –see also UNLEAVENED **2** fml rare to influence; change

leav·en·ing /ˈlevənɪŋ/ n **1** [U] LEAVEN(1) **2** [S (of)] a small part which makes something different, esp. more cheerful: a leavening of humour in an otherwise serious book

Leav·en·worth /ˈlevənwɜːθ‖-wɜːrθ/ a town in the American state of Kansas, known for its prison: He's serving time at Leavenworth.

leave of ab·sence /ˌ· · ˈ··/ n [U] LEAVE² (1)

leaves /liːvz/ pl. of LEAF

Leaves of Grass /ˌ· · ˈ·/ a collection of poems written in FREE VERSE by Walt Whitman, which are thought to include some of his best work. They are also considered important in the historical development of American poetry.

leave tak·ing /ˈ· ˌ··/ n fml the act of saying goodbye and going away: tearful leave takings

leav·ings /ˈliːvɪŋz/ n [(the) P] BrE things that are left or unwanted, esp. food after a meal –compare LEFTOVERS

Leb·a·non /ˈlebənən, -nɒn‖-nən, -nɑːn/ a country in the Middle East, bordering on the Mediterranean; capital Beirut; population 2,897,000 (1989). Once a rich country, important for business, tourism and finance in the Middle East, there was a CIVIL WAR in the 1970s and 80's between different political and religious groups, some of which were supported by neighbouring states. − **Lebanese** /ˌlebəˈniːz◂/ *n, adj*

Le Car·ré /lə ˈkæreɪ/, **John** (1931–) an English writer of THRILLERs and SPY stories such as *The Spy Who Came in from the Cold*; *Tinker, Tailor, Soldier, Spy*, and *Smiley's People*

lech·er /ˈletʃəʳ/ *n derog* a man who continually looks for sexual pleasure: *a disgusting old lecher*

lech·er·ous /ˈletʃərəs/ *adj derog* (esp. of a man) having or showing a desire for continual sexual pleasure: *a lecherous old man* | *a lecherous look* − ~ **ly** *adv* − ~ **ness** *n* [U]

lech·er·y /ˈletʃəri/ *n* [U] *derog* continual searching for sexual pleasure, esp. when expressed in an unpleasant way. Lechery is one of the Seven Deadly Sins according to the Bible. −see also SEVEN DEADLY SINS

Le Cor·bu·si·er /lə kɔːˈbjuːzieɪ, -ˈbuː- ‖ -ˌkɔːrbuːzˈjeɪ/ (1887–1965) the name used by Charles Edouard Jeanneret, French ARCHITECT and writer (born in Switzerland). He was a great planner of modern cities and towns, most famously the city of Chandigarh in India.

lec·tern /ˈlektən‖-ərn/ *n* a sloping table for holding a book, esp. the Bible in a church

lec·ture[1] /ˈlektʃəʳ/ *n* [(**on, about**)] **1** a long talk given to a group of people on a particular subject, esp. as a method of teaching at universities: *He gave a series of lectures on medieval art.* | *Students have to attend ten lectures a week.* | *a French lecture* (=about French language, literature, etc.) **2** a long solemn talk expressing disapproval or warning: *He gave|(old-fash) read the child a lecture on the importance of punctuality.*

lecture[2] *v* [(**on, about**)] **1** [I] to give a LECTURE (1) **2** [T] to give a LECTURE (2) to: *I wish you'd stop lecturing me.*

lec·tur·er /ˈlektʃərəʳ/ *n* **1** a person who gives lectures, esp. at a university or college **2** [(**in**)] a person who holds the lowest teaching rank at a British or American university or college

lec·ture·ship /ˈlektʃəʃɪp‖-ər-/ *n* [(**in**)] the position of a LECTURER (2): *a lectureship in mathematics*

led /led/ *past tense & participle of* LEAD[1]

LED /ˌel iː ˈdiː/ *n* light-emitting diode; part of an apparatus on which numbers, letters, etc., are shown by using an electric current to produce usu. red or green light. LEDs are used in watches, clocks, and computers.

-led see WORD FORMATION

Le·da /ˈliːdə/ in CLASSICAL MYTHOLOGY, the wife of a king of Sparta, loved by Zeus who came to her as a SWAN

ledge /ledʒ/ *n* **1** a narrow flat shelf or surface, esp. one on the edge of an upright object: *a window ledge* (=below a window) **2** a flat surface of rock, esp. one that stretches a long way below the sea

led·ger /ˈledʒəʳ/ *n* **1** an account book recording the money taken in and given out by a business, bank, etc. **2** also **ledger line** /ˈ·· ·/, **leger, leger line**− a short line added above or below a STAVE on which music is written, for notes that are too high or too low to be recorded on the stave −see also ST LEDGER

Led Zep·pe·lin /ˌ·ˈ····/ a British HEAVY METAL rock music group, very successful in the 1970s

lee /liː/ *n* [*the*] *fml* **1** [(**of**)] shelter, esp. from rough weather or wind: *We took refuge in the lee of the wall.* **2** the side of esp. a ship that is away from the wind −see also LEE SHORE, LEE TIDE

Lee, Chris·to·pher /ˈkrɪstəfəʳ/ (1922–) a British film actor best known for playing the part of Dracula

Lee, General Rob·ert E /ˈrɒbət iː‖ˈrɑːbərt-/ (1807–70) an American army general and commander of the Confederate army during the American Civil War, often considered to be the best general of the war −compare Ulysses S. GRANT

Lee, Laur·ie /ˈlɒri‖ˈlɔː-/ (1914–) an English writer and poet, known esp. for his book *Cider with Rosie*, which describes country life at the time of his childhood

leech /liːtʃ/ *n* **1** a small wormlike creature living in wet places that fixes itself to the skin of animals and drinks their blood, formerly used for drinking sick people's blood to lower their blood pressure: *My shy little sister clung to me like a leech* (= stayed very close to me) *all through the party.* **2** *derog* a person who over a long

period takes advantage of another person's weakness by getting money, help, etc., from them **3** *old use or humor* a doctor

Leeds[1] /liːdz/ a city in W Yorkshire, central N England, which is an important industrial and business centre − see colour map on page 818

Leeds[2] [*the*] the **Leeds Permanent Building Society**, a British BUILDING SOCIETY, branches of which are found in many towns and cities in Britain

Leeds U·ni·ted /ˌ·ˈ·ˈ··/ an English football team based in Leeds, N England

Lee-En·field /liː ˈenfiːld/ *n tdmk* a type of RIFLE (=gun with a long barrel) used by the British army in the First and Second World Wars

leek /liːk/ *n* a vegetable that has a long white fleshy stem and broad flat green leaves and tastes slightly of onions. The leek is one of the national SYMBOLS of Wales. −see picture at VEGETABLE

leek

leer[1] /lɪəʳ/ *n derog* an unpleasant smile or sideways look expressing cruel enjoyment, rudeness, or thoughts of sex −see SMILE (USAGE)

leer[2] *v* [I (**at**)] *derog* to look with a leer: *Stop leering at those young girls!* − ~ **ingly** *adv*

leer·y /ˈlɪəri/ *adj* [F (**of**)] *infml* watchful and not trusting; WARY: *I'm a bit leery of him.*

lees /liːz/ *n* [*the*] P] the bitter undrinkable thick substance (SEDIMENT) found in the bottom of a wine bottle, barrel, etc. −compare DREGS

lee shore /ˌ· ˈ·/ *n tech* a shore onto which the wind blows from the sea

lee tide /ˌ· ˈ·/ *n tech* a TIDE (=a rise of the sea) moving in the same direction as the wind, and therefore greater than the usual rise

lee·ward[1] /ˈliːwəd, *tech* ˈluːəd‖-ərd/ *adj, adv naut* **1** (going) in the same direction as the wind: *We steered a leeward course|steered leeward.* **2** opposite to or away from the wind: *the leeward side of the ship* −opposite **windward**

leeward[2] *n* [U] *naut* the side or direction towards which the wind blows: *We steered a course to leeward.*

Lee·ward Is·lands /ˈliːwəd ˌaɪləndz‖-wərd-/ [*the* +P] a group of islands in the West Indies, between Puerto Rico and Martinique

lee·way /ˈliːweɪ/ *n* [S;U] **1** the chance to act freely, rather than being forced to act in a particular way: *The new law allows landlords much less leeway in fixing the amount of rent they can charge tenants.* **2** *BrE* loss of time or advance: *She's got a lot of leeway to make up in her studies after her illness.* **3** a sideways movement of a ship caused by strong wind

left[1] /left/ *adj* **1** [A] on the side of the body that contains the heart: *one's left arm|eye* **2** [A] on, by, or in the direction of one's left side: *the left bank of the stream* | *Take a left turn at the crossroads.* **3** of or supporting the LEFT[2] (2) in politics: *He's very left.* | *left-of-centre political views* −see also LEFT WING **4 the left hand doesn't know what the right hand is doing** one part of a group or an organization does not know what other parts are doing, with the result that things do not work smoothly − opposite **right**

left[2] *n* **1** [(*the*) U] the left side or direction: *Keep to the left.* | *He doesn't know his left from his right.* | *Take the next turning on|to your left.* (=the next one you come to on your left side) | *The Labour party is* **to the left of** *the Liberals.* **2** [*the*+*sing.|pl. v*] (*often cap.*) political parties or groups, such as Socialists and Communists, that favour the equal division of wealth and property and generally support the workers rather than the employers: *The left oppose(s) the new taxes.* **3** [C] a hit with the left hand: *I caught him on the chin with a straight left.* −opposite **right**

left[3] *adv* towards or in favour of the left: *Turn left at the crossroads.* −opposite **right**; see also **right and left** (RIGHT[5])

left[4] *past tense & participle of* LEAVE[1]

Left Bank /ₐ· '·◂/ *[the]* an area of Paris on the left river bank of the Seine, popular with students, artistic people, and free thinkers

left-brain /'··/ *adj* concerned with or resulting from the left side of the brain, which controls the right side of the body and also LOGICAL and ANALYTIC thinking

left field /'··/ *n* **1** a position in BASEBALL in the left side of the OUTFIELD as seen from home base –see picture at BASEBALL **2 (way) out in left field** (of opinions or ideas) strange; very different from what most people think –**der** *n* : *a left fielder for the Baltimore Orioles*

left-hand /ₐ· '·◂/ *adj* [A] **1** on or to the left side: *the left-hand page* | *on the left-hand side (of the street)* **2** turning or going to the left: *They drove too fast round the left-hand bend.* –opposite **right-hand 3** LEFT-HANDED (2)

left-hand·ed /ₐ· '··◂/ *adj* **1** using the left hand for most actions rather than the right: *I'm left-handed.* | *a left-handed golfer* **2** done with the left hand: *a left-handed shot* **3** made for a left-handed person to use: *left-handed scissors* –opposite **right-handed 4** AmE **left-handed compliment** something said to a person which both praises and offends them – ~ **ness** *n* [U]

left-hand·er /ₐ· '··/ *n* **1** also **lefty** AmE *infml*– someone who usu. uses their left hand for most actions rather than their right **2** a hit with the left hand –opposite **right-hander**

left-hand drive /ₐ·· '·/ *adj* (of a vehicle) having the STEERING WHEEL and driver's controls on the left-hand side – **left-hand drive** *n* [S] : *a car with left-hand drive*

left·ist /'left‿st/ *n, adj (often cap.) sometimes derog* (a supporter) of the LEFT[2] (2) in politics: *a leftist government* | *leftist guerillas* –opposite **rightist** –**ism** *n* [U]

left lug·gage of·fice /ₐ· '·· ‚··/ *BrE* || **baggage room, checkroom** AmE– *n* a place, esp. in a station, where one can leave one's bags for a certain period, to be collected later

left-of-cen·tre /ₐ·· '···◂/ *adj* (of a party or political party) having views that are left-wing to some degree: *She's definitely left-of-centre.*

left·o·ver /'leftəʊvəʳ/ *adj* [A] remaining; unused: *After cutting out the curtains, she made some cushion covers from the leftover material.*

left·o·vers /'left‿əʊvəz‖-ərz/ *n* [P] food remaining uneaten after a meal, esp. when served at a later meal: *She made a stew out of leftovers.* –compare LEAVINGS

left·ward /'leftwəd‖-wərd/ *adj* on or towards the left – opposite **rightward**

left·wards /'leftwədz‖-wərdz/ *esp. BrE* || **leftward** AmE– *adv* on or towards the left –opposite **rightwards**

left wing /ₐ· '·◂/ *n, adj [the]* **1** [+ *sing./pl. v*] (the members) of a group that favour greater political changes than others in the party: *The left wing of the Labour party wants/want reforms in the party's organization.* **2** [+*sing./pl. v*] (of) the LEFT[2] (2): *left-wing ideas* | *She's very left-wing.* **3** (on) the left-hand side of the field in such games as football: *He centred the ball from the left wing.* –opposite **right wing** –**left-winger** /ₐ· '··/ *n*

left·y , left·ie /'lefti/ *n infml* **1** *esp. BrE, usu. derog* a supporter of the LEFT[2] (2) in politics, esp. a COMMUNIST **2** *esp. AmE* a left-handed person

leg[1] /leg/ *n* **1** [C] a limb of a person or animal which includes the foot and is used to support the body and for walking: *Humans and birds have two legs; dogs have four.* | *The leg bends at the knee.* –see picture at CROSS-LEGGED **2** [C] the part of this limb above the foot: *She injured her leg.* **3** [C;U] the leg of an animal as food: *roast leg of lamb* **4** [C] the part of a garment that covers the leg: *There's a hole in your trouser leg.* **5** [C] any of the long thin upright supports on which a piece of furniture stands: *a table/chair leg* **6** [C] a single part or stage, esp. of a journey or competition: *The final leg of the race is from Newcastle to Edinburgh.* **7** [U] also **leg side** /'· ·/– the part of a cricket field behind and to the left of the (right-handed) BATSMAN as he/she faces the BOWLER: *He hit the ball to leg.* –opposite **off 8 break a leg** a phrase used to wish someone luck before a performance, esp. among actors, because it is considered unlucky to actually say "good luck" **9 give someone a leg up** BrE *infml* **a** to help someone to climb or get on something by

supporting the lower part of their leg **b** to help someone to improve their situation **10 leg before wicket** a way in which a cricketer's INNINGS can be ended when their leg is hit by a ball which would otherwise have hit the three posts of their WICKET **11 not have a leg to stand on** to have no support for one's position: *He had confirmed what I said, but then he changed his mind and denied it, and I was left without a leg to stand on.* **12 on its/his/her last legs** *infml* in very poor condition and about to die or stop working: *I think this car is really on its last legs now.* **13 pull someone's leg** *infml* to make playful fun of someone, e.g. by encouraging them to believe something untrue **14 short, fat, hairy legs** a phrase often used by the British COMEDIANs Eric Morecambe and Ernie Wise describing Ernie Wise's legs **15 -legged** /legd, leg‿d/having the stated number or kind of legs: *four-legged animals* | *He sat cross-legged on the floor.* –see also BOW-LEGGED, SEA LEGS, **on one's last legs** (LAST[1]), **shake a leg** (SHAKE[1]), **show a leg** (SHOW[1]), **stretch one's legs** (STRETCH[1])

leg[2] *v* **-gg- leg it** *old-fash infml, esp. BrE* to walk or run fast, esp. so as to escape

leg·a·cy /'legəsi/ *n* **1** money or other property that one receives from someone who has died, in accordance with their wishes officially recorded while they were alive: *I got a nice little legacy from my aunt.* **2** [(**of**)] something passed on or left behind by someone or something: *These buildings are a legacy of the last government.* (=it had them built) | *Disease and famine are often legacies of war.* (=are caused by and remain after wars) –compare INHERITANCE

le·gal /'liːgəl/ *adj* **1** allowed or made by law: *Don't worry, it's quite legal!* | *Schooling is a legal requirement for children over five years old in Britain and the US.* –opposite **illegal 2** [A] of or using the law: *a legal matter* | *The company intends to take legal action* (= SUE or PROSECUTE) *over this matter.* | *The case made legal history.* | *the* **legal profession** (=lawyers) – ~ **ly** *adv* : *The contract is not legally binding until it has been signed by both people.*

▷ USAGE Compare **legal, lawful,** and **legitimate.** Any action which is allowed by law is **legal:** *It is legal for people over 18 to buy alcohol.* **Legal** also means "connected with the law": *the* **legal** *profession.* **Lawful** means "existing according to law" and suggests that the law has moral or religious force: *a* **lawful** *marriage* | *your* **lawful** *king.* **Legitimate** means "accepted by law, custom, or common belief": *the* **legitimate** *government* | *He claimed that bombing the town was a* **legitimate** *act in war.* | *Her illness was a* **legitimate** *reason for being absent from work.*◁

legal age /ₐ· '·◂/ *n* [U] the age at which one is legally allowed to do certain things e.g. leave school, vote, etc.: *The legal age for drinking varies from state to state.* –see ADULT (CULTURAL NOTE)

legal aid /ₐ· '·/ *n* [U] the services of a lawyer in a court case provided free to people too poor to pay for them: *The defendant applied for/was granted legal aid.*

legal ex·ec·u·tive /ₐ·· '····/ *n* someone with legal knowledge but without QUALIFICATIONs who helps a professional SOLICITOR –compare PARALEGAL

le·gal·ist·ic /ₐliːgə'lIstIk◂/ *adj derog* placing great importance on keeping exactly to what the law says, rather than trying to understand and act in accordance with its true meaning and intention – ~ **ally** /kli/ *adv*

le·gal·i·ty /lI'gæl‿ti/ *n* [U] the condition of being allowed by law: *I would question the legality of the government's decision.*

le·gal·ize also **-ise** BrE /'liːgəlaIz/ *v* [T] to make legal: *Will the government legalize cannabis?* | *legalized abortion* –**ization** /ₐliːgəlaI'zeIʃən‖-gələ-/ *n* [U]

legal o·pin·ion /ₐ·· '··/ *n* [C;U] a formal opinion given by a lawyer stating that certain points of a document are true and correct

legal pad /'·· ·/ *n* yellow, lined writing paper sold in the US in PADs (2), and popular with lawyers, students, and many others: *taking notes on a legal pad*

legal pro·fes·sion /ₐ·· '···/ *[the]* all the people who are professionally trained to help people with legal problems –see also ATTORNEY, BARRISTER, LAWYER, LEGAL EXECUTIVE, PARALEGAL, SOLICITOR

witness stand (AmE)

jury box

a US courtroom

At the trial, the accused stands in the dock while lawyers question people who know about the crime (witnesses) to try to discover the truth. The witnesses stand in a witness box (witness stand AmE) where they are asked to make a serious promise (=swear an oath) to tell 'the truth, the whole truth, and nothing but the truth,' usually by putting their hand on the Bible.

a US judge

a British judge

statue of Justice

A jury, made up of members of the public, decides whether the person is innocent or guilty (the decision is called the verdict). The judge decides the punishment (=the sentence).

jury box

witness box (BrE)

a British courtroom

dock

In 1969 the American astronaut Neil Armstrong became the first man to walk on the moon

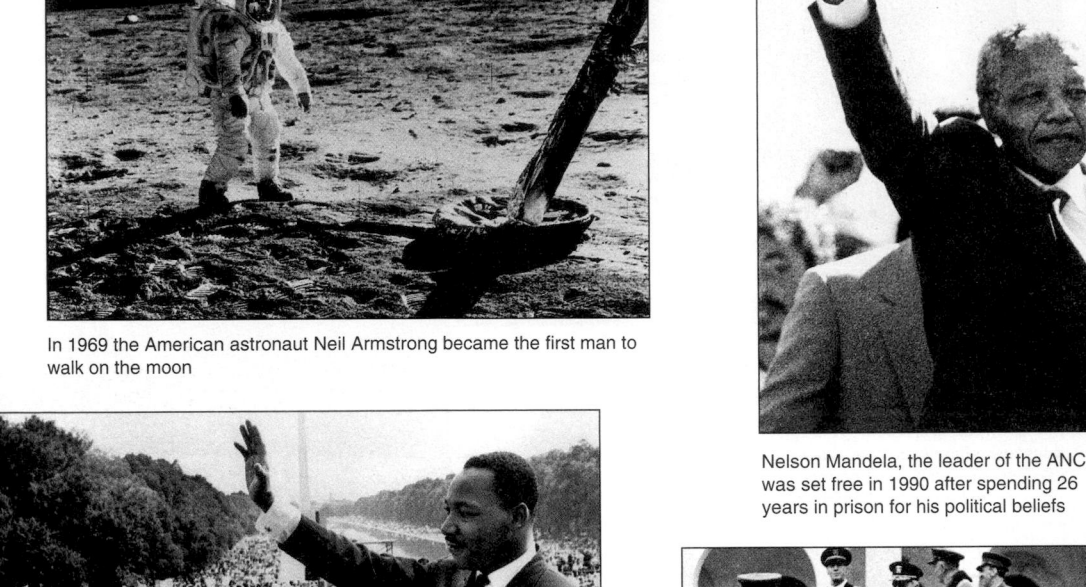

Nelson Mandela, the leader of the ANC, was set free in 1990 after spending 26 years in prison for his political beliefs

The American civil rights leader Martin Luther King, who was assassinated in 1968

Crowds destroying the Berlin Wall in 1989

The British Prime Minister Winston Churchill, the US President Franklin D. Roosevelt and the Soviet leader Joseph Stalin at the Yalta Conference in 1945

The coronation of Queen Elizabeth II in London in 1953

The American President John F. Kennedy was assassinated by Lee Harvey Oswald in 1963

legal-size /ˈ·· ·/ also **legal-** adj AmE (of paper) having a size of 8 × 13 inches: *The photocopier is out of legal-size paper.* —compare LETTER-SIZE

legal ten·der /ˌ·· ˈ··/ n [U] fml any form of money which by law must be accepted when offered in payment

leg·ate /ˈlegɪt/ n a high-ranking representative, esp. a priest appointed by the Pope as his representative

leg·a·tee /ˌlegəˈtiː/ n tech a person who receives a LEGACY (1)

le·ga·tion /lɪˈgeɪʃən/ n (the building or offices of) a group of officials who represent their government in a foreign country. It is lower in rank and importance than an EMBASSY: *the Cuban legation | a member of a legation* —compare EMBASSY

le·ga·to /lɪˈgɑːtəʊ/ adj, adv (of music) played smoothly, with the notes sliding smoothly into each other —compare STACCATO

leg-break /ˈ· ·/ n (in cricket) a slow ball that turns from the leg (LEG (7)) side to the off (OFF⁴) side when it bounces (BOUNCE)

leg·end /ˈledʒənd/ n **1** [C] an old story about great events and people in ancient times, which may not be true: *In the legend of ancient Troy, the Greeks got into the city by hiding in a wooden horse.* **2** [U] such stories collectively: *a character in Irish legend* **3** [C] a famous person or act, esp. in a particular area of activity: *He is a legend in his own lifetime for his scientific discoveries.* **4** [C] old-fash the words that explain a picture, map, table, etc., in a book —compare MYTH

le·gen·da·ry /ˈledʒəndəri‖-deri/ adj **1** of, like, or told in a legend: *legendary characters* **2** [(for)] very famous: *the legendary Elvis Presley | This restaurant is legendary for its fish.* (=it serves famously good fish)

Legend of Sleep·y Hol·low /ˌ·· · ˌ·· ˈ··/, **The** a story by Washington Irving in which the main character, Ichabod Crane, is frightened by what he thinks is a headless man riding a horse —see also HEADLESS HORSEMAN and see colour picture on page 620

le·ger /ˈledʒəʳ/ also **leger line** /ˈ·· ·/— n a LEDGER (2)

le·ger·de·main /ˌledʒədəˈmeɪn‖-dʒər-/ n [U] old-fash **1** quick skilful use of the hands in performing tricks: *the conjurer's legerdemain* **2** fml clever but rather deceitful use of argument: *The lawyer confused the jury with his legal legerdemain.*

leg·gings /ˈlegɪŋz/ n [P] coverings, usu. made of wool or of strong cloth, leather, etc., worn to keep the lower legs warm, or to protect them

leg·gy /ˈlegi/ adj (esp. of a child, a young animal, or a woman) having long rather thin legs, esp. in comparison with the rest of the body: *a leggy blonde* —**giness** n [U]

le·gi·ble /ˈledʒəbəl/ adj (of handwriting or print) that can be read, esp. easily: *His handwriting is barely legible.* (=is very difficult to read) —opposite **illegible** —**bly** adv: *Please write legibly when you fill in the form.* —**bility** /ˌledʒəˈbɪləti/ n [U]

le·gion¹ /ˈliːdʒən/ n [C+sing./pl. v] **1** a division of an army, esp. the army of ancient Rome: *Each legion contained between 3000 and 6000 soldiers.* **2** [(of)] also **legions** pl.— fml a large group of people: *She has a legion (=lots) of admirers.*

legion² adj [F no comp.] fml or pomp very many: *Her admirers are legion.*

le·gion·a·ry /ˌliːdʒənəri‖-neri/ n a member of a LEGION¹ (1)

le·gion·naire /ˌliːdʒəˈneəʳ/ n a member of a LEGION (1), esp. of the army of ancient Rome or of the French FOREIGN LEGION

legionnaire's dis·ease /ˌ··ˈ· ·ˌ·/ n [U] a serious infectious disease of the lungs, caught esp. by groups of people gathered together in a building such as a hospital or hotel. It first appeared in people attending a meeting of the American Legion in 1976.

le·gis·late /ˈledʒɪsleɪt/ v [I (for, against)] to make a law or laws: *The Senate has legislated against the importation of dangerous drugs.*

le·gis·la·tion /ˌledʒɪsˈleɪʃən/ n [U] **1** a law or set of laws: *The government will introduce legislation to restrict the sale of firearms.* **2** the act of making laws

le·gis·la·tive /ˈledʒɪslətɪv‖-leɪtɪv/ adj [A] having the power

and duty to make laws: *a legislative assembly* —compare EXECUTIVE (2), JUDICIAL

le·gis·la·tor /ˈledʒɪsleɪtəʳ/ n a maker of laws or a member of a lawmaking body

le·gis·la·ture /ˈledʒɪsleɪtʃəʳ, -lətʃəʳ/ n [C+sing./pl. v] a body of people who have the power to make and change laws —compare EXECUTIVE² (2), JUDICIARY and see also extra information on page 568

le·git /lɪˈdʒɪt/ adj sl for LEGITIMATE (1a): *I promise you, the deal's strictly legit.*

le·git·i·mate¹ /lɪˈdʒɪtəmət/ adj **1** correct or allowable **a** according to the law: *The Crown Prince has a legitimate claim to the throne. | Far from being a legitimate business, it was a front for a drugs racket.* **b** according to generally accepted standards of behaviour: *It's perfectly legitimate to question his instructions if you think they're wrong.* —opposite **illegitimate 2** born of parents who are legally married to each other —opposite **illegitimate 3** reasonable; sensible: *From her failure to reply we reached the quite legitimate conclusion that she wasn't interested.* —see LEGAL (USAGE) — —**ly** adv —**macy** n [U]

legitimate² v [T] AmE for LEGITIMIZE

le·git·i·mize also **-mise** BrE /lɪˈdʒɪtəmaɪz/ also **le·git·i·ma·tize, -tise** BrE /lɪˈdʒɪtəmətaɪz/‖also **legitimate** AmE— v [T] **1 a** to make legal **b** to make (esp. something bad) seem right or acceptable **2** to make (a child) legitimate, esp. by the marriage of the parents

leg·less /ˈlegləs/ adj infml, esp. BrE very drunk

Leg·o /ˈlegəʊ/ n [U] tdmk a set of small coloured plastic building blocks of various shapes and sizes which can be fitted together to make many different things; an educational toy esp. for young children. Many fine examples of its use are on show at **Legoland** in Denmark.

Lego

leg-pull /ˈ· ·/ n infml a playful attempt to make a fool of someone by telling them something that is not true — compare **pull someone's leg** (LEG¹)

leg·room /ˈlegruːm, -rʊm/ n [U] room enough to position one's legs comfortably when seated: *There's not much legroom in the back of this car.*

leg side /ˈ· ·/ n LEG¹ (7)

leg·ume /ˈlegjuːm, lɪˈgjuːm/ n **1** (the seed case of) a plant of the bean family that has its seeds in a POD (=a thin case) which breaks in two along its length **2** esp. AmE PULSE³ —**uminous** /lɪˈgjuːmɪnəs/ adj

leg-up /ˈ· ·/ n BrE infml **1** a help in getting up onto something by using somebody's joined hands as a step: *Give me a leg-up onto this wall, will you?* **2** (help in) advancing oneself: *It's a bit of a leg-up from barmaid to banker, isn't it?*

leg-warm·er /ˈ· ˌ··/ n a woollen covering for the leg from the ankle to the knee

leg·work /ˈlegwɜːk‖-wɜːrk/ n [U] infml work that needs much walking about or tiring effort: *He leaves someone else to do all the legwork of gathering information while he sits in the office and collates it.*

Le Ha·vre /lə ˈɑːvrə/ a city and port in N France on the river Seine and English Channel, receiving many ships from England

lei /leɪ/ n a circular bunch of flowers placed round one's neck as a greeting, esp. in Hawaii

Leib·niz, Leibnitz /ˈlaɪbnɪts/, **Gott·fried Wil·helm** /ˈgɒtfriːd ˈvɪlhelm◂‖ˈgɑː-/, **Baron von** (1646–1716) a German thinker and MATHEMATICIAN who invented the CALCULUS at the same time as, but independently of, Newton

Lei·ca /ˈlaɪkə/ a German company making high-quality cameras

Leices·ter /ˈlestəʳ/ a city in Leicestershire where the local government for that COUNTY is based

Leices·ter·shire /ˈlestəʃəʳ‖-tər-/ written abbrev. **Leics** a COUNTY in central England

Leicester Square /ˌ.. ˈ./ a square in central London with several cinemas, restaurants, and theatres. It is a popular place with tourists and young people. —see colour map on page 817

Leigh /liː/, **Jan·et** /ˈdʒænₐt/ (1927–   ) an American actress remembered esp. for her role in the film *Psycho* —see picture on page 685

Leigh, Viv·i·en /ˈvɪvɪən/ (1913–67) an English actress best remembered for playing the part of Scarlett O'Hara in the film *Gone with the Wind* —see colour picture on page 685

Leigh-Pem·ber·ton /ˌliː ˈpembətən‖-bər-/, **Robin** (1927–   ) an English banker who became Governor of the Bank of England in 1983

Lein·ster /ˈlenstəʳ/ a PROVINCE in the Republic of Ireland which includes 12 counties (COUNTY) and the city of Dublin

Leip·zig /ˈlaɪpsɪg/ an important business and CULTURAL centre in E central Germany, with a large university.

lei·sure /ˈleʒəʳ‖ˈliː-/ n [U] 1 time when one is free from work or duties of any kind; free time: *She's very busy; she doesn't get much leisure (time).* | *Fishing is a popular leisure pursuit/activity.* | *leisure shoes* | *a leisure suit* 2 **at one's leisure** at a convenient time: *Do it at your leisure; it's not urgent.*

leisure cen·tre /ˈ.. ˌ../ n BrE a place providing some of a range of leisure activities e.g. various sports, swimming, cinema, restaurant, etc.

lei·sured /ˈleʒəd‖ˈliːʒərd/ adj having no regular work and plenty of free time: *the leisured classes*

lei·sure·ly¹ /ˈleʒəli‖ˈliːʒərli/ adj moving, acting, or done without hurrying: *a leisurely stroll* | *I had a leisurely glass of beer.* (=I drank it without hurrying) —**liness** n [U]

leisurely² adv rare in a leisurely way

leisure suit /ˈ.. ˌ./ n AmE a suit of matching shirt and trousers, typically made of POLYESTER and worn by middle-aged and older men. Leisure suits are considered very unfashionable by young people and are often the subject of jokes: *When we saw all the leisure suits waiting in line we decided we'd better pick another movie.*

lei·sure·wear /ˈleʒəweəʳ ‖ ˈliːʒər-/ n [U] informal clothes suitable for sport or for relaxation

leit·mo·tiv , -tif /ˈlaɪtməʊˌtiːf/ n 1 a musical phrase that is played at various times during an OPERA or similar musical work to suggest or go along with a particular character or idea —compare MOTIF (3) 2 something in a work of art, a person's behaviour, etc., that appears repeatedly and is seen to be a controlling influence or important interest

Lei·trim /ˈliːtrₐm/ a COUNTY in the N of the Republic of Ireland

Le Mans /lə ˈmɒn ‖ -ˈmɑːn/ (a city in NW France known internationally for) a yearly 24-hour car race

lem·ming /ˈlemɪŋ/ n a ratlike animal living in cold northern parts of the world, which sometimes travels in large groups. Many of them drown in the sea on these journeys and it is popularly thought that they deliberately kill themselves in large numbers: *The soldiers continued their advance, possessed by some **lemming-like instinct** for self-destruction* —see picture at RODENT

lem·on /ˈlemən/ n 1 [C;U] a fruit with a hard yellow skin and sour juice: *fish served with slices of lemon* 2 [U] a drink made from this fruit 3 [U] pale yellow: *walls painted in lemon* 4 [C] BrE sl a foolish person: *Don't do it like that, you lemon!* 5 [C] sl something unsatisfactory or worthless; a failure: *That car he sold me turned out to be a real lemon; it hasn't got an engine!*

lem·on·ade /ˌleməˈneɪd◂/ n [U] 1 BrE a CARBONATED drink tasting of lemon 2 a drink made from fresh lemons with sugar and water added

lemon curd /ˌ.. ˈ./ n [U] BrE a cooked mixture of eggs, butter, and lemon juice, eaten on bread

lemon sole /ˌ.. ˈ./ n a flat fish used as food

lemon squash /ˌ.. ˈ./ n [U] esp. BrE a drink made from lemon juice and sugar, to which water is added before it is drunk

Lem·sip /ˈlemsɪp/ n '5[C;U] tdmk a type of medicine made by Reckitt & Colman for curing colds; Lemsip is a powder which is mixed with hot water to make a drink

le·mur /ˈliːməʳ/ n any of several mostly small monkey-like forest animals that are active at night, found esp. in Madagascar

lend /lend/ v **lent** /lent/ 1 [T (to)] to give (someone) the possession or use of (something, such as money or a car) on the condition that it or something like it will be returned later: *I never lend money.* | *Reluctantly I agreed to lend it to her.* [+obj(i)+obj(d)] *Can you lend me £10 until tomorrow?* 2 [I;T] to give out (money that must be repaid) so as to earn profit from interest, esp. as a business: *The bank currently lends (money) at 10 per cent interest.* 3 [T+obj(i)+obj(d)] to give as an additional quality: *The presence of the bishop lent the occasion a certain dignity.* [+obj+to] *The many flags lent colour to the streets.* 4 **lend an ear** to listen, esp. sympathetically: *She was talking about her operation to anyone willing to lend an ear.* 5 **lend itself to** rather fml (of a thing) to be suitable for: *This book lends itself admirably to film adaptation.* [+v-ing] *This play lends itself to being performed in an open-air theatre.* 6 **lend one's name to** to agree to be publicly connected with: *I'm surprised he lent his name to a cheap publicity stunt.* —compare BORROW (1); see also **lend a hand (with)** (HAND¹) — **-er** n

lending li·bra·ry /ˈ.. ˌ.../ n a library which lends books, music, etc.

lending rate /ˈ.. ˌ./ n the RATE¹ (2) charged by a bank or BUILDING SOCIETY for lending money —see also MINIMUM LENDING RATE

Len·dl /ˈlendl/, **I·van** /iːˈvɑːn/ (1960–   ) an American professional tennis player, born in Czechoslovakia. He was the World Singles Champion in 1982, and won the European Tennis Championship in 1985.

lend-lease /ˈ. ˈ./ n an arrangement during the Second World War by which the US sent necessary supplies to countries friendly to the US. These were either returned at the end of the war or a similar exchange was made.

length /leŋθ/ n 1 [C;U] the measurement of something from one end to the other or of its longest side: *The length of the room is ten metres; it is ten metres in length.* (compare *It is ten metres long.*) | *Take two pieces of string of different lengths.* —compare BREADTH, WIDTH 2 [U] the quality or condition of being long: *The students complained about the length of the exam paper.* (=complained that it was too long) 3 [the(of)] the distance from one end to the other: *We walked the length of* (=all along) *the street.* 4 [C] the measure from one end to the other of a horse, boat, etc., used in stating distances in races: *The horse won by three lengths.* 5 [C (of)] a piece of something, esp. of a certain length or for a particular purpose: *He tied it with a length of string.* 6 **at length** fml a using many words; in great detail: *She spoke at (great) length about the plight of the refugees.* b lit after a long time; at last: *At length he returned.* 7 **go to any length(s)/great/some/considerable/unprecedented lengths** to be willing to do anything, however difficult, dangerous, unpleasant, or morally wrong: *He'll go to any lengths to get his child back from his ex-wife.* | *They went to unprecedented lengths to limit press coverage of the trial.* 8 **the length and breadth of** in or through every part of: *He travelled the length and breadth of the country raising funds for the party.* —see also **at arm's length** (ARM¹), **measure one's length** (MEASURE¹)

length·en /ˈleŋθən/ v [I;T] to make or become longer: *to lengthen a skirt* | *The days lengthened as summer approached.* —opposite **shorten**

length·ways /ˈleŋθweɪz/ also **length·wise** /-waɪz/— adv in the direction of the longest side: *He laid the bricks lengthways.*

length·y /ˈleŋθi/ adj sometimes derog very long: *a lengthy meeting/speech/discussion* —**-ily** adv —**-iness** n [U]

le·ni·ent /ˈliːniənt/ adj not severe in judgment or punishment; gentle: *a lenient judge who passes lenient sentences* — **-ly** adv —**-ence, -ency** n [U]

Len·in /ˈlenₐn/, **Vlad·i·mir Il·yich** /ˈvlædₐmɪəʳ ˈɪlɪtʃ/ (1870–1924) a Russian Marxist REVOLUTIONARY and writer who was leader of the Bolshevik party and first leader of the Soviet Union (1918–24) —see picture on page 755

Len·in·grad /ˈlenₐngræd/ see ST PETERSBURG

Len·in·is·m /ˈlenₐnɪzəm/ n [U] the teachings of Lenin, based on those of Karl Marx, regarding political, economic, and social matters; MARXISM-LENINISM —**Leninist** n, adj **Leninite** n, adj

len·i·ty /ˈlenˌtiˈ/ n [U] *fml rare* gentleness; MERCY

Len·non /ˈlenən/, **John** (1940–80) an English singer, GUITAR player, and songwriter who was a member of the Beatles and joint writer of many songs with Paul McCartney. In 1969 the Beatles separated and John Lennon continued alone, producing songs of peace and love. He was murdered in the US. He was married to Yoko Ono. —see also BEATLES

Lenin

Len·o /ˈlenəʊ/, **Jay** (1950–) an American COMEDIAN who became host of the TONIGHT SHOW in 1992

lens /lenz/ n **1** a piece of glass, plastic, or other transparent material, curved on one or both sides, which makes a beam of light passing through it bend, spread out, become narrower, change direction, etc. It is used in glasses for the eyes, in cameras, in microscopes, etc.: *He has very thick lenses in his glasses.* —see pictures at CAMERA and GLASSES **2** a piece of round transparent flesh behind the PUPIL (=black opening in front of the eye), which acts like a glass lens in focusing (FOCUS) light —see picture at EYE **3** *infml for* CONTACT LENS

lent /lent/ *past tense and participle of* LEND

Lent n [U] the 40 days before Easter, during which Christians customarily do not allow themselves all their usual pleasures: *What are you giving up for Lent?*

len·til /ˈlentl/ n the small round seed of a beanlike plant, dried and used for food. Lentils are popular with people who like to eat healthily, esp. those who do not eat meat, and often made fun of by non-VEGETARIANS.

len·to /ˈlentəʊ/ adj, adv (of music) played slowly

Le·o /ˈliːəʊ/ n **1** the third sign of the ZODIAC, represented by a lion —see picture at ZODIAC **2** [C] a person born between July 23 and August 22: *He's (a) Leo, is he? I thought all Leos were lively.* —see ZODIAC (USAGE)

Leon·ard /ˈlenəd‖-ərd/, **Sugar Ray** (1956–) an American BOXER

Leonardo see Leonardo DA VINCI

le·o·nine /ˈliːənaɪn/ adj fml of or like a lion: *a noble leonine head*

leop·ard /ˈlepəd‖-ərd/ **leop·ard·ess** /ˈlepədes‖-ər-/ fem.— n **1** a large fierce meat-eating catlike animal, yellowish with black spots, that lives in Africa and southern Asia —see picture at BIG CATS **2 the leopard doesn't change his spots** saying people cannot change their basic nature or character

le·o·tard /ˈliːətɑːd‖-ɑːrd/ n a tight-fitting garment that covers the whole upper body from the neck to the legs, worn esp. by dancers

Le Pen /lə ˈpen/, **Jean-Ma·rie** /ʒɒn məˈriː‖ʒɑːrn-/ (1928–) a French extreme RIGHT-WING politician, leader of the French National Front, which supports capital punishment and sending people of other nationalities home to their countries of origin

lep·er /ˈlepəʳ/ n **1** *now usu. taboo* a person who has the disease leprosy. Formerly lepers were forced to live away from towns. They had to wear a bell and shout "unclean, unclean" to warn people not to come near them for fear of passing on the disease: *a leper hospital* **2** a person who is avoided by other people for social or moral reasons.

lep·re·chaun /ˈleprↄkↄːn‖-kɑːn, -kↄːn/ n (in old Irish stories) a kind of fairy in the form of a little man or ELF who usu. wears green, makes shoes for the fairies, and knows where gold is hidden

lep·ro·sy /ˈleprəsi/ n [U] a long-lasting infectious disease in which the skin becomes rough and thick with small round hard whitish marks, and the flesh and nerves are slowly destroyed —**-rous** adj

Ler·ner and Loewe /ˌlɜːnər ənd ˈləʊ‖ˌlɜːr-/ two American songwriters, Alan Jay Lerner (1918–86) who wrote the words and Frederick Loewe (1904–88) who wrote the music. Together they wrote many successful musical plays including *My Fair Lady* and *Gigi*.

Ler·wick /ˈlɜːwɪk‖ˈlɜːr-/ a town and port which is the capital of the Shetland Islands. Lerwick is on Mainland island and is a centre of the fishing industry.

les·bi·an /ˈlezbiən/ adj, n (of or being) a woman who is sexually attracted to women rather than to men —compare BISEXUAL (2), HETEROSEXUAL, HOMOSEXUAL — ~ **ism** n [U]

lese-ma·jes·ty also **lèse-ma·jes·té** /ˌliːz ˈmædʒↄsti, ˌleɪz ˈmædʒↄsteɪ/ — n [U] **1** *law* criminal action against a ruling king or government **2** *often humor* behaviour that makes an important person feel offended; lack of respect

Le·so·tho /ləˈsuːtuː‖-ˈsəʊtəʊ/ a mountainous country in S Africa surrounded by the republic of South Africa, and a member of the COMMONWEALTH (1); capital Maseru; population 1,700,000 (1989)

le·sion /ˈliːʒən/ n med **1** a wound: *multiple lesions on the back* **2** a dangerous change in the form or working of a part of the body, esp. after an operation or accident: *a brain lesion*

less[1] /les/ adv [(than)] **1** (*with adjectives and adverbs*) not so; not as; to a smaller degree (than): *I hope the next train will be less crowded than this one.* | *Try and speak less indistinctly.* | (*euph*) *I think she was being less than truthful.* (=was not at all truthful) —opposite **more 2** (*with verbs*) not so much: *Try to shout less.* | *He works less than he used to.* —opposite **more 3 less and less** increasingly rarely: *He comes here less and less.* **4 much/still less** and certainly not: *The baby can't even walk, much less run.*

less[2] *determiner, pron* (*comparative of* LITTLE) [(**of, than**)] **1** (*with* [U] *nouns and sing.* [C] *nouns*) a smaller amount; not so much: *Statistics show that people now drink less beer than they used to, and smoke fewer cigarettes.* | *I can't eat all that cake — could you give me a little less?* | *To get the balance right you need a bit less of the almond flavouring and a bit more of the cinnamon.* | *Why have I got less than you?* | *Fourteen is less than seventeen.* | *Nothing in this shop is less than* (=costs below) *£10.* | *Can we have a bit less noise/less of that noise?* (=Be quiet!) | *Increased taxes mean that people have less to spend on luxuries.* | *She's less of a fool than* (=not so foolish as) *I thought.* | *He's ggoing* (*even*) *less than usual.* | *I'll be back in less than no time.* (=very soon) | *No less than a thousand people came.* (=it was surprising that there were so many) | *There were not less than* (=at least) *a thousand people there.* | *Good heavens! It's the President himself, no less/It's no less a person than the President!* (=it is surprising to see such an important person) | *It's nothing* (**more or**) **less than** (=just the same as; no better than) *murder to send such a small group of soldiers out to attack those heavily defended enemy positions.* —opposite **more 2** (*with pl.* [C] *nouns*) a smaller number; not so many; fewer: *Now that our system's computerized, we hope there will be less problems than before.* —opposite **more;** see USAGE **3 less and less** (an amount) that continues to become smaller: *Margaret eats less and less/does less and less work/is less and less able to get out of bed.* —opposite **more and more 4 the less: a** to a smaller or lower amount, degree, etc.: *In spite of his misdeeds, I don't love him* **any the less.** | *They will think* (**all**) **the less** (=have a lower opinion) of *you for what you have done.* **b** (used for showing that two things get smaller, or change, together): *The less he eats the thinner he gets.* — see also NEVERTHELESS, NONETHELESS, **more or less** (MORE[2]); see MORE[2] (USAGE)

▷ USAGE In informal English many people now use **less** and **least** with plural nouns: *There are* **less** *cars on the road at night,* but this is still considered to be incorrect. **Fewer** and **fewest** are the accepted forms: *There are* **fewer** *cars on the road at night.* —see also FEW (USAGE)◁

less[3] *prep* not counting; but we subtract; MINUS[1]: *She gave me £100, less £5 for her own costs.* (=She gave me £95.)

-less see WORD FORMATION

less a·ble /ˌ· ˈ··/ adj, n [the+P] *euph* an expression used in education for those children who find learning more difficult

les·see /leˈsiː/ n a person who by a LEASE (=a written agreement) is given the use of a house, building, or land for a certain time in return for payment to the LESSOR (=the owner)

less·en /ˈlesən/ v [I;T] to make or become smaller in size, worth, importance, appearance, etc.: *This defeat lessens our chances of winning the championship.* | *His behaviour*

had lessened him in her eyes. (=given her a lower opinion of him) | *The noise lessened as the plane got further away.*

less·er /'lesə^r/ *adj, adv* [A] *rather fml* (*not used with* than) not so great or so much as the other (of two) in worth, degree, size, etc.: *the lesser of two evils* | *one of the lesser-known modern poets*

Les·sing /'lesɪŋ/, **Dor·is** /'dɒrɪs‖'dɔː-/ (1919–) a British writer brought up in Rhodesia (Zimbabwe). She wrote *The Golden Notebook* and a set of NOVELs, *The Children of Violence*, concerning politics and FEMINISM.

les·son /'lesən/ *n* **1** [(in, on)] (a period of time for) the teaching of something to someone, esp. to a pupil or class in school: *Each history lesson lasts 40 minutes.* | *She gives drawing lessons|lessons in drawing.* (=She teaches people to draw.) | *Today's French lesson will be on irregular verbs.* | *a driving lesson* **2** (good sense learnt from) a warning example or experience: *That accident taught me a lesson; I won't drive too fast again.* | *His car accident has been a lesson to him to stop driving too fast.* | *"There," I said,* **"let that be a lesson to you"** *when he fell off his bike after trying to ride it without holding on to the handlebars.* —see also **learn one's lesson** (LEARN) **3** a short piece read from the Bible during religious services

les·sor /le'sɔː^r/ *n* a person who gives the use of a house, building, or land by a LEASE (=a written agreement) to someone else (the LESSEE) for a certain time, in return for payment

lest /lest/ *conj fml or old-fash* **1** in order that the stated thing should not happen; in case: *Lest anyone (should) worry that this will lead to price increases, let me reassure them that it will not.* **2** (with words expressing fear) that: *I was afraid lest she (should) be offended.* **3 lest we forget** a phrase which is often written on British MONUMENTS to people killed in the First and Second World Wars, or on WREATHs put on such monuments, e.g. on Remembrance Day

let¹ /let/ *v let; pres. participle* **letting** [T] **1** [*not usu. pass.*] to allow (to do or happen): *I wanted to go out but my mum wouldn't let me.* [+*obj+to-v*] *She lets her children play in the street.* | *He's letting his beard grow.* | *He let a week go by before answering the letter.* | *Please let me buy you a drink.* (=a polite offer) | *She took off the dog's lead and let it loose.* | *They tied the prisoner to the fence and let the dogs at him.* (=allowed the dogs to attack) —see CAUSE (USAGE) **2** [+*obj+to-v*] (the named person) must, should, or can: *Let each man decide for himself.* | *Let him do what he likes; I don't care.* | *Let there be no mistake about it.* | *Don't let me have to speak to you again.* | *"Who shall I invite in place of Mary?"* **"Let me see** (=I must think carefully about this) – *what about Diana?"* | (when suggesting a plan) *"Let's* (=Let us) *have a party, shall we?" "No, let's not."* | *Let's not quarrel|(BrE) Don't let's quarrel about it.* | **Let's face it** (= we have to admit), *we're going to be late.* | (*fml*) *When a priest invites the congregation to pray, he says "Let us pray".* —see USAGE **3** [(**to, OUT**)] *esp. BrE* ‖ **rent** *esp. AmE*– to give the use of (a room, a building, land, etc.) in return for rent: *We're hoping to let our spare room to a student.* | *The top floor of the house is let (out) to a young couple.* | *There's a "To Let" sign on the house next door.* —compare LET **out** (5); see HIRE¹ (USAGE) **4** [+*obj+to-v*] *fml* (in plans or calculations) to suppose for the purpose of argument: *Let the line AB be equal in length to the line XY.* **5 let alone** (used for showing that the thing mentioned next is even less likely or believable than the one mentioned before): *The baby can't even walk, let alone run.* **6 let drop/fall** to make (a remark, suggestion, etc.) known, as if by accident but really on purpose: *She let drop the fact that she was expecting a baby.* **7 let go (of)** to stop holding: *Don't let go (of) the handle. Hold it tight and don't let go.* | *Let go! You're hurting my arm.* **8 let it go at that** to take no further action **9 let oneself go: a** to behave more freely and naturally than usual: *You should have seen the way he let himself go at the party, dancing on the table and singing!* **b** to take less care of one's appearance than usual: *Buy some new clothes and get your hair cut, my dear – you're letting yourself go these days.* **10 let someone go: a** to set someone free; allow someone to escape **b** *euph* to dismiss someone from a job **11 let someone/something alone** to leave someone/something alone (LEAVE¹) **12 let someone/something be** to leave

someone/something unworried; not INTERFERE with: *Let him be, he's doing no harm.* | *I told him I'd tried to fix the typewriter but he said let it be till he got home.* —compare **leave someone/something be** (LEAVE¹) **13 let well (enough) alone** to make no change to something that is satisfactory; end, so that the people attending can leave in case it is made worse rather than better —see also **let fly** (FLY¹), **let it all hang out** (HANG OUT), **let one's hair down** (HAIR), **let someone know** (KNOW¹), **let something pass** (PASS¹), **let something ride** (RIDE¹), **let something rip** (RIP¹), **let slip** (SLIP¹)

▷ USAGE **1 Let us** is usually shortened to **let's** in conversation when making a suggestion which includes the person you are speaking to: *Come on, Jim,* **let's** *dance!* Otherwise it must be **let us**: *Please sir,* **let us** *go now.* **2** The negative of **let's** is **let's** *not.* In British English *don't* **let's** is also possible: **Let's** *not waste time on this|(BrE) Don't* **let's** *waste time on this.*◁

let down *phr v* [T] **1** (let sthg./sbdy. ↔ **down**) to cause or allow to go down; lower: *Let down a rope so that I can climb up.* **2** (let sthg. ↔ **down**) also **lengthen** *AmE* to make (clothes) longer: *I'm going to let down this old dress for my daughter.* **3** (let sbdy. **down**) to fail to do for (someone) what they could reasonably expect one to do because one is supposed to be loyal to them, has made a promise to them, etc.: *I'm counting on you to support me; don't let me down.* | *The singer we had engaged let us down at the last moment, so we had to find a quick replacement.* —see also LETDOWN **4 let someone down lightly** to disappoint or give bad news to someone in a way that will not hurt their feelings too much

let sbdy./sthg. ↔ **in** *phr v* [T] **1** to allow or make it possible for (someone or something) to enter: *She opened the door and let me in.* | *This tent lets in the rain.* **2** to allow; admit: *This new evidence lets in the possibility of doubt.*

let sbdy. ↔ **in for** sthg. *phr v* [T] *infml* to cause to have or experience (something difficult or unpleasant): *When I agreed to help you, I didn't know what I was letting myself in for.*

let sbdy. ↔ **in on** sthg. *phr v* [T] *infml* to allow to share (a secret or something secret)

let sbdy./sthg. **into** sthg. *phr v* [T] **1** to allow or make it possible for (someone or something) to enter: *I let myself into the flat with a spare key.* **2** to allow to join: *They won't let women into their club.* **3** to place into (another material) so as to be level with and form a pattern on its surface: *The iron decoration has been let into the brickwork.* **4** to allow (someone) to know; LET **in on**: *I'll let you into a little secret: I've never even been there.*

let sbdy./sthg. **off** *phr v* [T] **1** to excuse from (punishment, duty, etc.): *If you promise not to do it again, I'll let you off.* | *She let the boy off (doing) his music practice.* | *He was expected to go to prison, but the judge let him off with a fine.* | *In my opinion he was* **let off lightly.** (=given less severe treatment than he deserved) **2** to allow to leave (a vehicle): *The conductor wouldn't let me off (the bus) until I'd paid the fare.* **3** to fire or cause to explode: *Don't let that gun|those fireworks off indoors.*

let on *phr v* **1** [T] (let sbdy./sthg. **on** (sthg.)) to allow to get on (a vehicle): *The conductor wouldn't let me on (the bus) with this big parcel.* **2** [I;T *obj*] *infml* to tell a secret: *I think he knows more about it than he's prepared to let on.* | *Don't let on about the meeting.* [+ *that|wh-*] *Don't let on that I told you|let on who told you.*

let out *phr v* **1** [T (**of**)] (let sbdy./sthg. ↔ **out**) to allow or make it possible for (someone or something) to leave: *They were let out of* (=freed from) *prison last week.* | *Someone's let the air out of this tyre.* **2** [T] (let out sthg.) to express loudly and violently: *He let out a cry of pain|a roar.* **3** [T] (let sthg. ↔ **out**) to make (clothes) wider: *Jack's put on so much weight that I've had to let out all his trousers.* —compare TAKE **in** (3) **4** [T] (let sthg. ↔ **out**) to allow (something) to become known: *News of the takeover bid was let out this morning.* [+*that*] *He accidentally let out that he hadn't been home for three weeks.* **5** [T] (let sthg. ↔ **out**) *esp. BrE* to give the use of (esp. vehicles or equipment) in return for payment —see HIRE¹ (USAGE) **6** [I] *AmE* to end, so that the people attending can leave: *When does school let out?* | *The movie lets out at 10 o'clock.* —see also **let the cat out of the bag** (CAT)

let up *phr v* [I] (esp. of something bad) to lessen or stop: *When will this rain let up?* —see also LETUP

let up on sbdy./sthg. *phr v* [T *no pass.*] *infml* to treat less severely: *You're always pressing her to work harder and do better; why don't you let up on her for a while?*

let² *n BrE* **1** an act of renting a house or flat to, or from, someone: *a long let* **2** a house or flat that is (to be) rented —compare MORTAL (3) — ~**ly** *adv*

let³ *n* **1** [C] (in tennis and similar games) a stroke that does not count and must be played again, esp. one in which a ball that has been served hits the top of the net on its way over **2** [U] *law* the act of preventing something from being done (esp. in the phrase **without let or hindrance**)

let·down /'letdaʊn/ *n infml* a disappointment: *We were going out today, but now it's raining so we can't; what a letdown!* —see also LET **down** (3)

le·thal /'liːθəl/ *adj* (having the power of) causing death: *A hammer can be a lethal weapon.* | *a lethal dose of a drug* | (fig.) *That cocktail looks fairly lethal!* (=very strong in alcohol) —compare MORTAL (3) — ~**ly** *adv*

leth·ar·gy /'leθədʒi‖-ər-/ *n* [U] *fml, often derog* the state of being sleepy, unnaturally tired, or (too) inactive; lazy state of mind: *The heat of the afternoon and the heavymeal combined to create a feeling of lethargy.* | *The government was accused of lethargy.* —**gic** /lɪˈθɑːdʒɪk‖-ɑːr-/ *adj* —**gically** /kli/ *adv*

Le·the /'liːθi/ [*the*] in GREEK MYTHOLOGY, a river in Hades which, if one drinks its water, produces forgetfulness

Let·ra·set /'letrəset/ *n* [U] *tdmk* letters printed on a special sheet in such a way that they can be put onto paper or other surfaces by the use of pressure

let·ter /'letəʳ/ *n* **1** [C] a written or printed message sent usu. in an envelope: *Could you post this letter for me when you go out?* | *I've had a letter from the tax inspector saying I owe him money.* | *I wrote her a letter last week, but I haven't received a reply yet.* | *the "letters to the Editor" column of the newspaper* | *Would you give me a letter of recommendation for my new employer?* **2** [C] any of the signs in writing or printing that represent a speech sound: *"B" is a capital letter; "b" is a small letter.* **3** [(*the* S] the words of an agreement, law, rule, etc., rather than its real, intended, or general meaning: *Going by the (strict)* **letter of the law**, *you could be charged with obstruction, but the police have agreed to overlook it.* —opposite **spirit** **4 to the letter: a** with close attention to the written details of an agreement, law, etc. **b** to the fullest degree; exactly: *You must follow my instructions to the letter.* —sec also LETTERS, CHAIN LETTER, DEAD LETTER, OPEN LETTER, DEAR JOHN LETTER

letter bomb /'·· ,·/ *n* a small bomb hidden in an envelope and sent by post to the person it is supposed to kill or harm. They are usually sent by TERRORIST or similar organizations to important people.

let·ter·box /'letəbɒks‖'letərbɑːks/ *esp. BrE* ‖ usu. **mailbox** *AmE— n* **1** a narrow opening in a front door, or at the entrance to a building; a box for receiving things delivered, esp. letters brought by the postman: *Another bill dropped through the letterbox.*

▶CULTURAL NOTE **Letter boxes** are much more common in Britain than in the US, where it is more usual to have a **mailbox** somewhere near your front door which is an actual box with a closing lid. In Britain anyone may put anything through a **letterbox**; in the US it is illegal for anyone except the Postal Service to use your **mailbox** and only mail that carries your name and address may be delivered there. —compare PILLAR BOX, POST BOX◀

2 a box in a post office, street, etc., in which letters can be posted or delivered; POSTBOX

letter car·ri·er /'·· ,···/ *n AmE for* POSTMAN

let·tered /'letəd‖-ərd/ *adj old-fash fml* (well) educated —opposite **unlettered**

let·ter·head /'letəhed‖-ər-/ *also* **let·ter·head·ing** /-,hedɪŋ/— *n* the name and address of a person or business printed at the top of a sheet of writing paper

let·ter·ing /'letərɪŋ/ *n* [U] **1** the art of writing or drawing letters or words: *Lettering is this designer's speciality.* **2** written or drawn letters, esp. of the stated style: *ornate old-fashioned lettering*

Let·ter·man /'letəmən‖-tər-/, **David** (1947–) the host of an American television talk show shown late at night. He is known for having unusual guests and for funny parts of the show, such as "stupid pet tricks".

letter of cred·it /,·· · '··/ *n* an official letter from a bank allowing a named person to take money from another bank, esp. in a foreign country

letter o·pen·er /'·· ,···/ *n AmE for* PAPER KNIFE

letter-per·fect /,·· '···◂/ *adj AmE for* WORD-PERFECT

let·ter·press /'letəpres‖-ər-/ *n* [U] a method of printing in which the words, pictures, etc., to be printed form a raised area on the printing machine

letter-qual·i·ty /'·· ,···/ *adj* (of a printer, producing characters of a quality) good enough to be used in sending business letters

let·ters /'letəz‖-ərz/ *n* [P] *fml or pomp* literature in general: *He was one of the foremost figures of|in English letters at the turn of the century.* —see also MAN OF LETTERS

letter-size /'·· ·/ *also* **letter—** *adj AmE* (of paper) having a size of 8 by 11 inches: *Have this printed on letter-size sheets.*

let·ting /'letɪŋ/ *n esp. BrE* a house or flat that is (to be) rented: *unfurnished lettings*

let·tuce /'letɪs/ *n* [C;U] a usu. round vegetable with thin pale green leaves, used raw in SALADS —compare CABBAGE, and see picture at VEGETABLE

let·up /'letʌp/ *n* [C;U] (a) stopping or lessening of activity: *It rained for twelve hours without (a) letup.* —see also LET **up**

leu·co·cyte , leuko- /'luːkəsaɪt/ *n med for* WHITE BLOOD CELL (=disease-fighting cell in the blood)

leu·cot·o·my /luːˈkɒtəmi‖-ˈkɑː-/ *n BrE for* LOBOTOMY

leu·ke·mia *also* **-kae-** *BrE* /luːˈkiːmiə/ *n* [U] a serious disease (a kind of CANCER) in which the blood contains too many white cells, causing weakness and sometimes death

Le·vant /ləˈvænt/ [*the*] the former name for the land to the east of the Mediterranean Sea, including Syria, Lebanon, and Israel —**ine** /'levəntaɪn/ *adj, n* : *Levantine customs*

lev·ee¹ /'levi/ *n esp. AmE* a bank built to stop a river overflowing

levee² /'levi, ləˈveɪ/ *n old use* a meeting in which a ruler receives visits from important people

lev·el¹ /'levəl/ *adj* **1** having a surface which is flat and smooth; not sloping; HORIZONTAL: *A football field needs to be level.* | *a level spoonful of sugar* **2** [F (**with**)] equal in height or standard: *The child's head is level with his father's knee.* | *The two teams finished level at ten points each.* **3** steady and unvarying: *He gave me a level look.* | *a calm level voice* **4 one's level best** *infml* one's best effort: *I did my level best* (=tried as hard as possible) *to help him.*

level² *n* **1** [C;U] a line or surface parallel to the ground; a position of height in relation to a flat surface: *The garden is arranged on two levels.* (–it has two parts, one higher than the other) | *an accident on level three of the mine* | *The top of this mountain is six kilometres above sea level.* | *an eye-level grill* (=equal with the height of a person's eyes) | (fig.) *The matter is being considered at ministerial level.* (=by important politicians) | (fig.) *high level|top-level discussions* —see also WATER LEVEL **2** [C] a general standard of quality or quantity: *a high level of achievement* | *The level of your work is not satisfactory.* | *We must increase production levels.* | *High levels of radiation were found in the sea nearby.* **3** [C] *also* **levels** *pl.—* a smooth flat surface, esp. a wide area of flat ground: *You should build on the level, not on the slope.* | *the Somerset Levels* **4** [C] *esp. AmE for* SPIRIT LEVEL **5 on the level** *infml* honest; truthful: *Is what you're telling me on the level?* | *Are you on the level?* —see also LEVEL **with**; A LEVEL; O LEVEL

level³ *v* **-ll-** *BrE* ‖ **-l-** *AmE* [T] **1** [(OUT, OFF)] to make flat and even: *She levelled off the wet concrete with a piece of wood.* **2** to knock or pull down to the ground: *The bombing raid practically levelled the town.*

level sthg. **at** sbdy./sthg. *phr v* [T] **1** to aim (a weapon) at **2** [*often pass.*] *also* **level** sthg. **against** sbdy./sthg.— to bring (a charge) against: *Serious accusations have been levelled against the minister.*

level off/out *phr v* [I] to stop climbing higher or falling lower, and continue at a fixed height: *The plane levelled off at 30,000 feet.* | (fig.) *Inflation has begun to level off.* | (fig.) *We expect the differences in their educational attainment to gradually level out.*

level with sbdy. *phr v* [T] *infml* to speak freely and truthfully to; not hide facts from —see also **on the level** (LEVEL²)

level⁴ *adv* [(**with**)] so as to be level: *a missile that flies level with* (=close to) *the ground*

level cross·ing /ˌ·· ¹··/ *BrE* ‖ **grade crossing** *AmE—* *n* a place where a road and a railway cross each other, usu. protected by gates that shut off the road while a train passes

level-head·ed /ˌ·· ¹··◄/ *adj apprec* calm and sensible in making judgments

lev·el·ler *BrE* ‖ **-eler** *AmE* /ˈlevələʳ/ *n esp. old use* a member of a political group that wishes to get rid of all social differences

Lev·el·lers /ˈlevələz‖-lərz/ [*the* +P] a religious and political group which began during the English Civil War and demanded equal legal rights and freedom of worship for all people

level peg·ging /ˌ·· ¹··/ *adv BrE* equal, neither ahead of nor behind a competitor: *It's level pegging between the two candidates, either of them could win.*

level play·ing-field /ˌ·· ¹·· ·/ *n* [*usu.* S] a situation in which no one has any unfair advantage: *If we know their secrets and they know ours, at least we're competing on a level playing-field.*

le·ver¹ /ˈliːvəʳ‖ˈle-, ˈliː-/ *n* **1** a bar or other strong tool used for lifting or moving something heavy or stiff. One end is placed under or against the object, the middle rests on a FULCRUM, and the other end is pushed down strongly: (fig.) *They used the threat of strike action as a lever* (=a strong influence) *to get the employers to agree to their demands.* **2** a bar or rod that is fixed to a machine at one end and is moved to work the machine; a handle: *Push the lever and the machine will start.* —see also GEAR LEVER and see picture at TYPEWRITER

lever² *v* [T+obj+adv/prep] to move (something) with a lever: *They levered it into position.* | (fig.) *They're trying to lever him out of his job as head of the firm.*

le·ver·age /ˈliːvərɪdʒ‖ˈle-, ˈliː-/ *n* [U] **1** the action, power, or use of a lever: *We'll have to use leverage to move this huge rock.* **2** influence over someone else, esp. of an unofficial or irregular kind: *She used political leverage to get that top job.*

le·ver·aged buy·out /ˌliːvərɪdʒd ˈbaɪaʊt‖ˌle-, ˌliː-/ *n* the TAKEOVER of a company, esp. by its management, using borrowed money, in the hope or expectation that the interest on the borrowings can be paid out of the profit on the company bought

lev·e·ret /ˈlevərɪt/ *n* a young HARE

le·vi·a·than /lɪˈvaɪəθən/ *n* **1** (in the Bible) a very large and frightening sea animal **2** *lit or pomp* something very large and strong, esp. a large ship or a WHALE (=a large sea animal)

Le·vis /ˈliːvaɪz/ *n* [P] *tdmk* a popular and fashionable kind of JEANS: *a pair of Levis* | *Do you stock Levis?*

lev·i·tate /ˈlevɪteɪt/ *v* [I;T] to (cause to) rise and float in the air as if by magic. Some MAGICIANS make people appear to levitate as a trick. Some MYSTICS claim that they can really levitate themselves or others, although many people do not believe them. —**-tation** /ˌlevɪˈteɪʃən/ *n* [U]

lev·i·ty /ˈlevɪti/ *n* [U] *fml or pomp* lack of respect for serious matters; lack of seriousness: *This is no time for levity — we have important matters to discuss.*

lev·y¹ /ˈlevi/ *v* [T (**on, upon**)] to demand and collect officially: *to levy a tax on tobacco*

levy² *n* an official demand and collection, esp. of a tax: *import levies*

lewd /luːd/ *adj derog* **1** wanting, thinking about, or suggesting thoughts of sex, esp. in a way that is not socially acceptable: *He gave her a lewd wink.* **2** rude; OBSCENE: *lewd songs* — **~ly** *adv* — **~ness** *n* [U]

Lew·es /ˈluːɪs/ a town in E Sussex, England, where the local government for that COUNTY is based

Lew·is¹ /ˈluːɪs/, **Carl** /kɑː‖ˈkɑːr‖/ (1961–) an American ATHLETE who won GOLD MEDALS for the LONG JUMP in the 1984 and 1992 Olympic Games, and also for the 4 x 100m relay in the 1992 Olympic Games.

Lewis², **C S** (1898–1963) an English writer, known for his children's, religious and adult LITERARY works, esp. *The*

Allegory of Love and the *Chronicles of Narnia* —see also NARNIA

Carl Lewis

Lewis³, **Jerry** (1926–) an American COMEDIAN on television and in films. He made many films with Dean MARTIN. He is known for seeming to be very stupid and silly. Lewis has also done a lot of work raising money for an organization that helps children who are ill.

Lewis⁴, **Sinclair** (1885–1951) an American writer of FICTION, whose books, including *Main Street* and *Elmer Gantry*, examined social problems of his time

Lewis and Clark /ˌ·· ·‖·/ *n* [P] the EXPLORERS **Meriwether Lewis** (1774–1809) and **William Clark** who travelled all over the recently bought LOUISIANA PURCHASE from 1804 to 1806, going up the Missouri River and over the Rocky Mountains to the Pacific coast of America. They recorded what they found and saw.

Lew·i·sham /ˈluːɪʃəm/ an inner London BOROUGH S of the river Thames. It is a mainly WORKING-CLASS area.

lex·i·cal /ˈleksɪkəl/ *adj tech* of or about words — **~ly** /kli/ *adv*

lex·i·cog·ra·phy /ˌleksɪˈkɒɡrəfi‖-ˈkɑː-/ *n* [U] the writing and making of dictionaries —**-pher** *n*

lex·i·col·o·gy /ˌleksɪˈkɒlədʒi‖-ˈkɑː-/ *n* [U] *tech* the study of the meaning and uses of words

lex·i·con /ˈleksɪkən‖-kɑːn, -kən/ *n* **1 a** a dictionary **b** a list of words with their meanings **2** *tech* all the words and phrases used in a particular language

Lex·ing·ton /ˈleksɪŋtən/ a city in N central Kentucky, US known for producing THOROUGHBRED horses and for its university

lex·is /ˈleksɪs/ *n* [U] *tech* all the words that belong to a particular subject or language, or that a particular person knows —compare VOCABULARY

Ley·land /ˈleɪlənd/ a British company that makes lorries (LORRY) and buses

ley line /ˈleɪ laɪn, ˈliː-/ *n BrE* a set of easily recognizable objects e.g. churches, wells, etc. following a line thought to be the line of an ancient track. Some people believe ley lines also follow lines of ENERGY.

li·a·bil·i·ty /ˌlaɪəˈbɪlɪti/ *n* **1** [U (**for, to**)] the condition of being liable: *The new law exempts them from all liability in these matters.* | *Taking extra vitamins may reduce your liability to colds.* **2** [C] something for which one is responsible, esp. by law: *A child is its parents' liability.* **3** [C] also **liabilities** *pl.— tech* the amount of debt that must be paid: *If your liabilities exceed your assets, you may go bankrupt.* —compare ASSET (1); see also CURRENT LIABILITIES, LIMITED LIABILITY **4** [C] *infml* someone or something that limits one's activities or freedom: *This old car's a real liability; I can't use it but I have to pay for somewhere to keep it.* —compare ASSET (2)

li·a·ble /ˈlaɪəbəl/ *adj* **1** [F+*to-v*] likely, esp. from habit or tendency: *He's liable to shout when he gets angry.* | *Be careful, the car is liable to overheat.* **2** [F+**to**] often suffering (from): *This part of town is liable to flooding.* **3** [F (**for**)] (legally) responsible for paying (for something): *He declared that he was not liable (for his wife's debts).* **4** [F+**to**] likely to be legally punished (with): *People who walk on the grass are liable to a fine of £5.*

▷ USAGE Compare **liable** and **likely**. **Liable** is used when talking about general characteristics: *The river is liable to flood in the winter.* | *This kind of cloth is liable to tear very easily.* **Likely** is used when you think there is a possibility on a particular occasion that something will happen: *The bus is likely to be late today because of the bad weather.*◁

li·aise /liˈeɪz/ *v* [I (**with**)] *BrE* (esp. in the army or in business) to make, have, or keep a connection, esp. so that information can be passed: *My job is to liaise with foreign clients.*

li·ai·son /liˈeɪzən‖ˈliːəzɑːn, liˈeɪ-/ *n* [(**with, between**)] **1**

[S;U] a working association or connection, esp. so that each side is well informed about what the other is doing: *close liaison between the army and the police* | *a liaison officer* **2** [C] *euph* a sexual relationship between a man and a woman not married to each other

li·a·na /li'ɑːnə, li'ænə/ *n* (a long climbing stem of) a woody tropical plant that climbs round trees, up walls, etc.

li·ar /'laɪəʳ/ *n* a person who tells lies

lib /lɪb/ *n* [U] *infml, becoming old-fash* (a movement for) social equality and the removal of disadvantages suffered by particular social groups (esp. in the phrases **women's lib, gay lib**) – – **ber** *n usu derog* : *The women's libbers are trying to get into this men's club.*

Lib *n, adj BrE* LIBERAL (PARTY)

li·ba·tion /laɪ'beɪʃən/ *n* **1** an offering of wine to a god, esp. in ancient Greece and Rome **2** *pomp or humor* a drink of wine or other alcohol

Lib Dem /ˌlɪb 'dem/ *BrE infml for* LIBERAL DEMOCRAT: *a Lib Dem candidate*

Lib Dems /ˌ· '·/ *n* [P] *infml* LIBERAL DEMOCRATS

li·bel¹ /'laɪbəl/ *n* **1** [C (**on**)] *law* a printed or written statement that says unfairly bad things about a person and may make others have a low opinion of him or her. Libel usually concerns famous people who may then go to court to clear their name. **2** [U] the making of such a libel: *The politician is suing the magazine for libel.* | *a libel action* —compare SLANDER¹ **3** [C (**on**)] *infml* an unfair or untrue remark, description of someone, etc.: *a libel on my character*

libel² *v* **-ll-** *BrE* ‖ **-l-** *AmE* [T] to make a libel against; DEFAME: *He claims he has been libelled in the press.*

li·bel·lous *BrE* ‖ **-belous** *AmE* /'laɪbələs/ *adj* being or containing a libel: *a libellous allegation* – **~ly** *adv*

Lib·e·ra·ce /ˌlɪbə'rɑːtʃi/ (1919–87) an American musician who played popular piano tunes in his own television SERIES, in which the decorations and his dress were both highly exaggerated (EXAGGERATE) in their richness. He always played with a CANDELABRUM (=a branched candle holder) on his piano.

Liberace

lib·e·ral¹ /'lɪbərəl/ *adj* **1** willing to understand and respect the ideas and feelings of others: *a liberal mind/thinker* | *a liberal-minded person* **2** supporting or allowing some change, e.g. in political or religious affairs: *The church has become more liberal in this century.* | *a liberal foreign policy* —compare REACTIONARY **3** encouraging or leading to a wide general knowledge, wide possibilities for self-expression, and respect for other people's opinions: *a liberal education* **4** giving freely and generously: *a liberal supporter of the hospital* **5** given freely; large: *a liberal supply of drinks* **6** neither close nor very exact: *a liberal interpretation of a rule* – **~ly** *adv*

liberal² *n* a person with liberal opinions or principles

Liberal *n, adj* in Britain, (a person) supporting or belonging to the former Liberal Party or the Liberal Democrats.

liberal arts /ˌ··· '·/ *n* [P] *esp. AmE* the areas of learning which develop the ability to think and reason, as well as general knowledge, rather than technical skills which prepare one for a particular job. The liberal arts include PHILOSOPHY, languages, literature, history, MATHEMATICS, and science. —compare LIBERAL STUDIES and see also HUMANITIES

Liberal Dem·o·crat /ˌ··· '····/ also **Lib Dem** *infml*– *n* a member of the Liberal Democrats

Liberal Dem·o·crats /ˌ··· '····/ also **Lib Dems** *infml*– Social and Liberal Democrats *fml n [the* +P] a British political party of the centre formed in 1988 from the LIBERAL PARTY and the SOCIAL DEMOCRATS. It is the third largest party, but it is quite small.

lib·e·ral·is·m /'lɪbərəlɪzəm/ *n* [U] (*sometimes cap.*) liberal opinions or principles, esp. with regard to social and political matters

lib·e·ral·i·ty /ˌlɪbə'rælɪti/ *n* **1** [U] also **lib·e·ral·ness** /'lɪbərəlnɪs/ – *fml* **a** generosity **b** respect for other people's opinions **2** [C] *old use* a gift given generously

lib·e·ral·ize also **-ise** *BrE* /'lɪbərəlaɪz/ *v* [T] to make liberal or more liberal, esp. by the removal of limits on freedom: *The divorce laws have been liberalized in recent years.* – **-ization** /ˌlɪbərəlaɪ'zeɪʃən‖-rələ-/ *n* [U]

Liberal Par·ty /'··· ·/ [*the*] **1** a political party that favours liberalism **2** a British political party which held power for many years in the 19th and early 20th centuries. With the rise of the Labour Party it lost much of its support —see also LIBERAL DEMOCRATS

liberal stud·ies /'··· ·/ *n* [P] *esp. BrE* subjects that are taught in order to increase general knowledge and the ability to write, speak, and study more effectively, esp. when taught to older students in addition to their main subjects —compare LIBERAL ARTS

lib·e·rate /'lɪbəreɪt/ *v* **1** [T (**from**)] *fml* to set free (from control, prison, duty, etc.): *The new government has liberated all political prisoners.* **2** *sl, esp. AmE* to steal –**-rator** *n* –**-ration** /ˌlɪbə'reɪʃən/ *n* [U]

lib·e·rat·ed /'lɪbəreɪtd/ *adj* **1** having or showing freedom of action in social and sexual matters: *a liberated woman* | *liberated attitudes* **2** (of an area or country) freed from OCCUPATION of a foreign army or government: *liberated Kuwait*

liberation the·ol·o·gy /ˌ··· ·,···/ *n* [U] religious teaching, esp. in Roman Catholic countries in South America, which places special importance on the need to improve people's social conditions and give them political freedom

Li·be·ri·a /laɪ'bɪəriə/ a country in W Africa on the Atlantic Ocean, bordered by Guinea; capital Monrovia; population 2,508,000 (1989) –**-rian** *adj,n*

lib·er·tar·i·an /ˌlɪbə'teəriən‖-bər-/ *n* a person who believes that people should be free to express their opinions, to have whatever religion they wish, etc. –**libertarian** *adj*

lib·er·tine /'lɪbətiːn‖-ər-/ *n* a person who leads an unusual or immoral life, esp. one who continually looks for pleasure

lib·er·ty /'lɪbəti‖-ər-/ *n* **1** [U] *esp. lit* the state of being free from conditions that limit one's actions, so that one can do what one likes without the permission of others; freedom: *The tyrant's oppressed subjects cry out for their liberty.* | *prisoners dreaming of liberty* (=of being set free from prison) —compare FREEDOM **2** [C;U] *fml* the right or permission to do or use something **3** [S] too much freedom in speech or behaviour, taken without permission and sometimes regarded as rude: (*fml*) (used to say sorry or as an excuse) *I took the liberty of reading this letter, even though it was addressed to you.* | (*BrE infml*) *"Whenever he needs a car he just takes mine, without asking whether I mind." "What a liberty!"* **4 at liberty: a** free from prison, control, etc. **b** *fml* having permission or the right (to do something): *I'm afraid I am not at liberty to discuss this matter.* **5 liberty, equality, fraternity** a phrase used during the French Revolution **6 take liberties (with): a** to behave in a rude, too friendly way (towards someone, esp. a woman) **b** to make unreasonable changes in (a piece of writing, history, etc.): *He may not tell lies, but he does often take liberties with the truth.* (=say things that are not completely true) —see also CIVIL LIBERTY, STATUE OF LIBERTY

Liberty the National Council for Civil Liberties; an independent British organization which aims to defend and increase the rights of INDIVIDUAL citizens

Liberty Bell /'··· ·/ [*the*] a historic bell kept in Philadelphia, US. It was rung in 1776 to tell people of the Declaration of Independence from Great Britain and the founding (FOUND² (1)) of the United States. –see also AMERICAN REVOLUTION

Liberty Is·land /ˌ··· '··/ the small island in New York Harbor where the Statue of Liberty stands –see colour map on page 1376

Lib·er·ty's /'lɪbətiz‖-ər-/ also **Liberty**– a department store established in 1875 to sell goods from the Far and Near East. It has branches in many cities in Britain. It is known esp. for its beautiful materials: *a Liberty fabric/ pattern/design*

liberty ship /'··· ·/ one of a large number of PREFABRICATED ships for carrying goods built in the US during the Second World War

li·bid·i·nous /lɪˈbɪdɪnəs/ *adj fml or tech* having or showing strong sexual desires — ~**ly** *adv* — ~**ness** *n* [U]

li·bi·do /lɪˈbiːdəʊ/ *n* **-dos** *tech* (esp. in FREUDIAN PSYCHOLOGY) **1** the sexual urge **2** the strong force of life in a person

Lib-Lab pact /ˌ· ˈ· ˌ·/ [*the*] an arrangement made in 1977 in Britain, by David Steel of the Liberal Party and James Callaghan's Labour government, in which the Liberals gave support to the government in exchange for certain rights

Li·bra /ˈliːbrə/ *n* **1** [U] the seventh sign of the ZODIAC, represented by a pair of scales **2** [C] a person born between September 23 and October 22 —see ZODIAC (USAGE) and see picture at ZODIAC

li·brar·i·an /laɪˈbreəriən/ *n* a person who is in charge of or helps to run a library — ~**ship** *n* [U]

li·bra·ry /ˈlaɪbrəri, -bri‖-breri/ *n* **1** a room or building containing books that can be looked at or borrowed by members of the public or by members of the group or organization that owns the library: *a public library* | *a college library* | *a reference library* | *Is that a library book or is it your own copy?* —compare BOOKSHOP **2** a collection of books, records, etc. **3** a set of books, records, etc., that are produced by the same company and have the same general appearance: *a library of modern classics issued by a well-known publisher* —see also RECORD LIBRARY, LENDING LIBRARY

Library of Con·gress /ˌ··· · ˈ··/ [*the*] the largest LIBRARY in the US, in Washington DC. It is supported by the government and is open to the public. It keeps a copy of all written material that is copyrighted (COPYRIGHT) in the US.

library pic·tures /ˈ··· ˌ··/ *BrE*‖**file footage** *AmE*— *n* [P] pictures shown esp. during a television news programme, which were made at a previous time and do not show the actual events mentioned in the programme. When such pictures are shown on television, the words "library pictures" are shown at the bottom of the SCREEN¹ (4)

li·bret·tist /lɪˈbretɪst/ *n* the writer of a libretto

li·bret·to /lɪˈbretəʊ/ *n* **-tos** the words of a musical play, such as an OPERA or ORATORIO: *the libretto of Mozart's "Marriage of Figaro"* —compare BOOK¹ (5)

Lib·y·a /ˈlɪbiə/ an oil producing country in N Africa on the Mediterranean Sea; capital Tripoli; population 4,385,000 (1989). —**Libyan** *n*, *adj*

lice /laɪs/ *pl. of* LOUSE

li·cence usu. **-cense** *AmE* /ˈlaɪsəns/ *n* **1** [C] an official paper, card, etc., showing that permission has been given to do something, usu. in return for a fixed payment and sometimes after a test: *a dog licence* | *a driving licence* | *a licence fee* [+*to-v*] *a licence to sell alcohol* | (fig.) *This government seems to think it has a licence to print money!* —see also SPECIAL LICENCE **2** [U] official permission to do something: *We manufacture these goods* **under licence** *from* (=with the permission of) *the original makers.* **3** [U] *fml* **a** freedom of action, speech, thought, etc.: *demands that they should be allowed greater licence in the exercise of their power* **b** *derog* uncontrolled freedom that causes harm or damage: *I'm in favour of liberty, of course — but against licence.* **4** [U] the freedom claimed by a painter, writer, etc., to change the facts of the real world in producing a work of art —see also POETIC LICENCE

li·cense ² also **-cence** *AmE* /ˈlaɪsəns/ *v* [T] to give official permission to or for: *licensing the sale of alcohol* [+*obj*+*to-v*] *He is licensed to sell alcohol.*

li·censed , **-cenced** /ˈlaɪsənst/ *adj BrE* having a licence, esp. to sell alcoholic drinks: *a licensed restaurant*

licensed prac·ti·cal nurse /ˌ··· ˌ··· ˈ·/ *n* also **licensed vo·cation·al nurse** /ˌ··· ·ˌ··· ˈ·/, **LPN, LVN**— (in the US) a trained person officially allowed to practise most of the duties of a nurse

licensed vict·ual·ler /ˌ··· ˈ···/ *n BrE tech* a keeper of a shop or pub who is allowed to sell alcoholic drink

li·cen·see /ˌlaɪsənˈsiː/ *n* a person to whom official permission is given, esp. to sell alcoholic drinks or tobacco

license plate /ˈ··· ·/ *n AmE for* NUMBERPLATE

▶ CULTURAL NOTE **License plates** in the US show where a car is from because each state makes its own. In Britain, **number plates** are associated with a particular car and stay with the car; in some states of the US, **license plates** are associated with a car owner. When the owner sells the car he/she can keep the plates and can later put them on another car. —see also VANITY PLATES and see picture at CAR◀

licensing hours /ˈ··· ˌ·/ *n* [P] the hours during which it is legal to sell alcohol in Britain

licensing laws /ˈ··· ˌ·/ *n* [P] *BrE* the laws that limit the sale of alcoholic drinks to certain times and places

li·cen·ti·ate /laɪˈsenʃiət/ *n tech* **1** [(of)] a person given official permission, esp. by a university, to practise a particular art or profession: *a licentiate of the Royal College of Music* **2** a (written) declaration that this permission has been given

li·cen·tious /laɪˈsenʃəs/ *adj fml derog* behaving in a sexually uncontrolled way — ~**ly** *adv* — ~**ness** *n* [U]

li·chen /ˈlaɪkən, ˈlɪtʃən/ *n* [U] a dry-looking greyish, greenish, or yellowish flat spreading plant that covers the surfaces of stones and trees —compare MOSS

lick¹ /lɪk/ *v* **1** [T] to move the tongue across the surface of (something) in order to make it wet, eat it, clean it, etc.: *to lick a postage stamp* | *to lick an ice cream* | *The dog licked the dish clean.* **2** [T (UP)] to drink by taking up with quick movements of the tongue: *The cat licked (up) the milk from its bowl.* **3** [I (**against**);T] (esp. of flames or waves) to pass lightly or with quick movements over or against the surface of (something): *The flames licked (against) the building.* **4** [T] *infml* to defeat in a game, race, fight, etc.: (fig.) *I think we've finally got the problem licked.* **5 lick one's lips** to experience pleasure at the thought of something good that is going to happen to one **6 lick one's wounds** to go away after a defeat feeling sorry for oneself but perhaps preparing to come back to make a new effort **7 lick someone's boots** to obey someone like a slave, through fear, admiration, or desire for favour —see also **lick into shape** (SHAPE¹)

lick² *n* **1** [C *usu. sing.*] an act of licking **2** [C (**of**)] *infml* a small amount (of a cleaning material, paint, etc.): *This door needs a lick of paint.* **3** [S] *infml, esp. BrE* (fast) speed: *running down the hill at quite a lick* (=fast) **4 a lick and a promise a** *BrE old-fash infml* a quick careless wash or clean **b** *AmE* (of a job or duty) an incomplete or hurried performance, usu. with the intention of doing it better later: *I gave the piano a lick and a promise this morning but I'm really going to practise this weekend.* —see also SALTLICK

lick·e·ty-split /ˌlɪkɪti ˈsplɪt/ *adv AmE* very fast; at high speed: *He was running lickety-split down the road.*

lick·ing /ˈlɪkɪŋ/ *n old-fash infml* **1** a severe beating **2** a defeat: *The other team gave us quite a licking.*

lic·o·rice /ˈlɪkərɪs, -rɪʃ/ *n* [U] LIQUORICE

lid /lɪd/ *n* **1** a cover for the open top of a pot, box, or other container that can be lifted up or removed **2** an EYELID **3 put the (tin) lid on** *infml* to ruin or put an end to (an activity, a person's hopes, etc.), esp. by being the last in a set of misfortunes **4 take the lid off** to make known the unpleasant truth about (something); EXPOSE: *a film that takes the lid off the world of organized crime*

li·do /ˈliːdəʊ, ˈlaɪ-‖ˈliːdəʊ/ *n* **-dos** *esp. BrE* an outdoor public swimming bath, a special part of a BEACH, or the edge of a lake used for swimming and lying in the sun, with changing rooms and places to get food and drink. Many lidos were built in Britain in the 1930s, but now people prefer heated pools indoors.

lie¹ /laɪ/ *v* **lay** /leɪ/, **lain** /leɪn/, *present participle* **lying** /ˈlaɪ-ɪŋ/ **1** [I+*adj/adv/prep*] to be or remain in a flat position on a surface: *They just lie on the beach all day.* | *Don't move: just lie still.* | *There was a book lying on the table.* | *He lay on the floor reading a book.* | *Father is lying down* (=resting on a bed) *for a while.* **2** [I+*adv/prep*, esp. DOWN] to put one's body into such a position: *The doctor told me to go and lie (down) on the bed.* **3** [I+*adv/prep*; L+*adj*] to be, remain, or be kept in the stated condition: *The criminals were lying in wait for* (=hiding in order to attack) *their victim.* | *The village lay in ruins after the war.* | *The machinery lay idle* (=not being used) *because of the strike.* | *Where do your best interests lie?* | *The final decision lies with the minister.* (=The minister must make the final decision.) | *We're trying to establish where the responsibility lies.* (=find out who is responsible) **4** [I+*adv/prep*] to be in the stated place, position, or direction: *The town lies about two miles to the east of us.* | *Liverpool are lying third* (=are in third position) *in the football* championship. | (fig.) *The truth lies somewhere between these two statements.* | (fig.) *The future lies before us.* **5** [I+*adv/prep*] *old use* to stay, e.g. with friends or at a hotel **6 lie heavy/heavily on** to have an uncomfortable effect on: *guilt lying heavy on one's conscience* **7 lie in state** (of the dead body of an important person) to be placed in a public place so that people may honour it **8 lie low** to hide so as to avoid being discovered —see LAY² (USAGE)

lie about/around *phr v* [I] *derog* to spend one's time lazily, doing nothing —see also LAYABOUT

lie behind sthg. *phr v* [T *no pass.*] to be the (hidden) reason or explanation for: *What lies behind her reluctance to speak?*

lie down *phr v* [I] **1 lie down on the job** to do work that is not good enough in quantity or quality **2 take something lying down** to suffer something bad without complaining or trying to stop it: *You mustn't take his rudeness lying down.* —see also LIE¹ (2), LIE-DOWN

lie in *phr v* [I] *esp. BrE* to stay in bed late in the morning —see also LIE-IN, LYING-IN

lie off (sthg.) *phr v* [I;T *no pass.*] *tech* (of a ship) to keep a short way from (the shore or another ship): *The fleet lay off (the coast).*

lie to *phr v* [I] *tech* (of a ship) to be still or almost still while facing the wind —compare LAY to

lie up *phr v* [I] **1** to stay in bed, esp. for a long period **2** *esp. BrE* to stay in hiding or avoid being noticed

lie with sbdy. *phr v* [T] *old use or bibl* to have sex with

lie² *n* [*usu. sing.*] **1** the way or position in which something lies, esp., in GOLF, the position in which the ball lies on the grass: *I had a terrible lie, amongst some long grass.* **2 the lie of the land** *BrE* ‖ **the lay of the land** *AmE*— **a** the appearance, slope, etc., of an area of land **b** the state of affairs at a particular time

lie³ *v* **lied**; *present participle* **lying** **1** [I] to make an untrue statement in order to deceive; tell a lie: *He said he'd never been there, but he was lying.* | *She lied (to them) about her age in order to get the job.* **2** [T+*obj*+*adv/prep*] to put into a particular condition by telling lies: *He lied himself out of trouble.* **3** [I] to have a misleading appearance: *Figures can lie when statistics are misused.* **4 lie in/through one's teeth** *infml* to tell a bad lie shamelessly —see also LIAR, **lies, damned lies and statistics** (STATISTICS)

lie⁴ *n* **1** an untrue statement purposely made to deceive: *to tell lies* | *a barefaced lie* | *an outright lie* | *She said she loved me, but it was all lies/all a lie.* (=it was untrue) | *Their explanation sounded convincing, but it was just a pack of lies/a tissue of lies.* (=it was completely untrue) **2 father, I cannot tell a lie** a phrase which is believed to have been used by George Washington when admitting to his father that he had cut down a CHERRY tree —see also George WASHINGTON **3** *BrE* **give the lie to** to show that (something) is untrue: *These figures give the lie to the government's claims!* —see also WHITE LIE

lieb·frau·milch /ˈliːbfraʊmɪlʃ, ˈliːp-, -mɪlk/ *n* [U;C] (*often cap.*) (a variety of) a popular German white wine

Liech·ten·stein /ˈlɪktənstaɪn/ a very small country between Austria and Switzerland; capital Vaduz; population 28,000 (1989). Many foreign companies have their head offices there because taxes are low and the banks keep companies' affairs secret. — ~ **er** *n*

lie·der /ˈliːdəʳ/ *n* [U;P] German songs for one voice and piano, esp. 19th-century settings of poems to music

lie de·tec·tor /ˈ· ·ˌ··/ also **polygraph** *tech— n* an instrument that is supposed to show when a person is telling lies: *Some civil servants were forced to take lie detector tests.*

lie-down /ˈ· ·, ˌ· ˈ·/ *n BrE infml* a short rest, usu. on a bed: *I'm just going upstairs for a lie-down.* —see also LIE¹ (2)

lief /liːf/ *adv old use or lit* willingly; gladly: *I would as lief go as stay.*

liege /liːdʒ/ *n old use* **1** also **liege lord** /ˌ· ˈ·/— a lord or ruler to whom others must give loyalty and service **2** also **liege man** /ˈ· ·/— a man or servant who must give loyalty and service to his lord

lie-in /ˈ· ·, ˌ· ˈ·/ *n infml, esp. BrE* a stay in bed later than usual in the morning —see also LIE in

lien /lɪən/ *n* [(on)] *law* the legal right to keep possession of something belonging to someone who owes money, until the debt has been paid: *The court granted me a lien on my debtor's property.*

lieu /ljuː, luː/‖/luː/ *n* **in lieu (of)** instead (of): *The company offered us time off in lieu (of extra payment).*

lieu·ten·ant /lefˈtenənt‖luːˈten-/ *n written abbrev.* **Lt.** **1** an officer of low rank —see TABLE 3 **2** (*in comb.*) an officer or official with the rank next below the one stated: *a lieutenant colonel* | *the Lieutenant Governor of the State of New York* **3** a person who acts for, or in place of, someone in a higher position; DEPUTY —see also FLIGHT LIEUTENANT and see picture at RANK

life /laɪf/ *n* **lives** /laɪvz/ **1** [U] the active force in animals and plants that makes them different from all other forms of matter, such as stones or machines or dead bodies: *The plant may recover; it's very dry and withered, but there's still life in it.* | a **life-sciences** *course at university* (=studying BIOLOGY, ZOOLOGY, etc.) | *Life began on Earth millions of years ago.* **2** [U] matter in which this force is present and which can grow, produce new forms, etc.: *There is no life on the moon.* | *There is little plant life in the desert.* **3** [C;U] the state or condition of being alive: *Once someone has died, they cannot be brought back to life.* | *Hurry, doctor! It's* **a matter of life and death.** | *Hundreds of* **lives** *were* **lost**/*Hundreds of people* **lost their lives** (=died) *in the floods.* | **Run for your lives!** (=Run away fast) *He's got a gun!* —compare DEATH (2) **4** [U] (the typical qualities of) human existence: *Life isn't all fun.* | *Life is full of surprises.* | *The story is very* **true to life.** (=represents life as it really is) —see also FACTS OF LIFE **5** [C;U] the period between birth and death, between birth and the present time, or between the present time and death: *to devote one's life to science* | *She's had a hard life.* | *I have lived all my life in England, but I'm going to spend the rest of my life abroad.* | *Since an early age he'd led a life of crime.* (=been a criminal) | *She got married quite late in life.* **6** [C] the period for which a machine, organization, etc., will work or last: *during the life of the present parliament* **7** [C;U] **a** a stated manner or type of existence: *country life* | *How are you enjoying married life?* **b** a stated part of one's existence: *her working life* | *my private life* | *the sex life of the frog* | *What do you think will happen in* **the life to come?** (=the supposed existence after life on earth) **8** [U] existence as a collection of widely different experiences: *You won't see much of life if you stay at home all the time.* **9** [U] activity; movement: *There was no* **sign(s) of life** *in the empty house.* **10** [U] active; cheerfulness; VIGOUR: *The children are* **full of life** *this morning.* **11** [U] the cause of interest, pleasure, or happiness in living: *His work is his (whole) life.* **12** [*the*+*of*] a person or thing that is the cause of enjoyment or activity in a group: *He was* **the life (and soul)** *of the party.* **13** [U] also **life imprisonment** /ˌ· ·ˈ···/ — the punishment of being put in prison for a (long) period of time which is not fixed: *sentenced to life for armed robbery* —see also LIFE SENTENCE **14** [C] a written or filmed account of a person's life; a BIOGRAPHY: *Boswell's Life of Johnson* **15** [U] reality as the subject of painting, drawing, etc.: *painted from life, not from photographs or memory* —see also STILL LIFE **16** all human **life is there** a phrase meaning that many different types of people and a wide variety of human experience are found in a particular place, situation, or type of work **17 (as) large as life** not able to be mistaken; real: *I'd thought he was in America, but when I turned round, there he was, large as life.* **18 come/bring to life: a** to (cause to) become conscious again after fainting **b** to (cause to) show or develop interest, excitement, etc. **19 for dear life** with the greatest possible effort, esp. in order to avoid harm: *I clung onto the branch for dear life.* **20 for the life of one** in spite of all one's efforts: *He couldn't for the life of him remember her name.* **21 In the midst of life we are in death** *quote* a phrase taken from the Christian prayer said when someone is buried or cremated (CREMATE) **22 life begins at forty** *saying* you can start to enjoy life once you are 40 years old **23 life, liberty, and the pursuit of happiness** *quote* a phrase from the American Declaration of Independence which states that these are things which no government has a right to take away from people **24 Not on your life!** Certainly not! **25 take one's (own) life** *fml* to kill oneself **26 take one's life in one's (own) hands: a** *infml* to put oneself in (continual) danger of death **b** to get into control of one's own life **27 take someone's life** *fml* to kill someone **28 to the life** copying or copied exactly: *What an accurate portrait — it's him to the life!* —see also CHANGE OF LIFE, HIGH LIFE, LOW LIFE, PRO-LIFE, TRUE-LIFE, AFTERLIFE

Life¹ a British organization of people who are against ABORTION

Life² a US magazine known for having many interesting photographs of different places around the world

life-and-death /ˌ·· '·◄/ also **life-or-death**— adj [A] **1** ending in life or death: a life-and-death struggle with a creature from outer space **2** having great importance: It's a life-and-death matter as far as the children are concerned.

life as·sur·ance /'·· ·ˌ··/ n [U] LIFE INSURANCE

life belt /'· ·/ n a belt or ring made of a material that will float, held or worn in order to prevent a person from sinking after falling into water

life·blood /'laɪfblʌd/ n [U] **1** something that gives continuing strength and force: Trade is the lifeblood of most modern states. **2** lit blood regarded as the thing that keeps one alive

life·boat /'laɪfbəʊt/ n **1** a strong boat kept on shore and used for saving people in danger at sea

▶ CULTURAL NOTE In Britain the lifeboat service is not provided by the Government, but by an organization called the Royal National Lifeboat Institution (RNLI), which uses people who give their services freely. The organization collects money from the public to pay for its equipment, etc. The sea is important to British people, and lifeboats, and the people who work in them, are popular. ◀

2 a small boat carried by a ship for escape in case of wreck, fire, etc.

life buoy /'· ·/ ǁ'· ˌ·, '· ·/ n a large ring made of material that will float; LIFE BELT

life class /'· ·/ n an art class in which students draw or paint a person who acts as a model

life cy·cle /'· ·ˌ··/ n the regular development or changes in the form of a living thing in the course of its life, such as that of insects from egg to worm-like form and then to winged form

life ex·pec·tan·cy /ˌ· ·'···/ also **expectation of life**— n [C;U] **1** the average number of years that a person is expected to live: Life expectancy for men is about 78 years in Japan. **2** the length of time that an object, an idea, or an arrangement will be in use

life form /'· ·/ n a class of plant or animal: Distinctive life forms have evolved to suit this harsh climate.

lifeguard

life·guard /'laɪfɡɑːd‖-ɡɑːrd/ n a swimmer employed, e.g. on a BEACH or at a swimming pool, to help swimmers in danger

Life Guards /'· ˌ·/ n [the +P] a REGIMENT (=a large division of men) of horse soldiers in the British army who provide a ceremonial guard at Horse Guards, a building in Whitehall in London, and to the MONARCH (=the king or queen) on special occasions. The guards, who wear colourful uniforms, perform a ceremony, the Changing of the Guard, which is very popular with tourists —see also CHANGING OF THE GUARD

life his·to·ry /ˌ· '···/ n all the events in the course of the life of one living thing

life im·pris·on·ment /ˌ· ·'···/ n LIFE (13) —see also LIFE SENTENCE

life in·sur·ance /'·· ·ˌ··/ n [U] a kind of insurance in which a person makes regular payments so that if they die, their wife or husband and children will receive a large sum

of money. Sometimes the insured person receives a large sum of money when they reach a certain age. —compare HEALTH INSURANCE

life jack·et /'· ˌ··/ n an air-filled garment worn round the upper body to support a person in water

life·less /'laɪfləs/ adj **1** esp. lit dead: a lifeless corpse **2** derog lacking force, interest, or activity: a lifeless performance —compare LISTLESS — ~ **ly** adv — ~ **ness** n [U]

life·like /'laɪflaɪk/ adj being a very close or exact representation: a lifelike photograph

life·line /'laɪflaɪn/ n **1** a rope used for saving people in danger, esp. at sea **2** a rope fastened to a swimmer who goes down to great depths, by which signals can be sent up **3** something on which one's life depends, such as one's only way of being connected with other people: He's severely disabled, so the telephone is his lifeline to the world.

life·long /'laɪflɒŋ‖-lɔːŋ/ adj [A] lasting all one's life: my lifelong friend

life mem·ber /ˌ· '··/ n a person who will belong to a club etc. until he/she dies and who usu. will have made a single large payment for membership

life mem·ber·ship /ˌ· '···/ n [U] the state of being a life member of a club etc.: She has life membership of the Youth Hostels Association.

Life of Bri·an /ˌlaɪf əv 'braɪən/, **The** an English film, featuring the actors from the Monty Python programmes, which is a humorous PARODY of the life of Jesus. Because of this subject matter, some people found the film offensive, while others who were used to the BLACK HUMOUR of Monty Python found it very funny.

life of Ri·ley /ˌlaɪf əv 'raɪli/ see lead the life of Riley (LEAD¹ (13))

life-or-death /ˌ· ·· '·◄/ adj [A] LIFE-AND-DEATH

life peer /ˌ· '·/ **life peer·ess** /ˌ· '··ǁfem— n a Briton who has the rank of PEER¹ but is not allowed to pass it on to a son or daughter after death

▶ CULTURAL NOTE Until 1958 all members of the House of Lords were the sons or daughters of lords. Life peers were introduced in an attempt to improve the House of Lords. They are chosen by the Government, with suggestions from the opposition parties, for their legal, political, or social experience. ◀

life pre·serv·er /'· ·ˌ··/ n esp. AmE a life-saving apparatus, such as a LIFE BELT or LIFE JACKET

lif·er /'laɪfəʳ/ n sl a person who has been sent to prison for life —see also LIFE (13)

life raft /'· ·/ also **raft**— n RAFT¹ (2)

life·sav·er /'laɪfseɪvəʳ/ n **1** someone or something that saves life or prevents difficulty **2** something that comes just in time to save one from a difficult or unpleasant situation: A cup of strong black coffee can be a real lifesaver at times.

Life Sav·er /'· ˌ··/ n tdmk (in the US) a small hard round sweet with a hole in the middle that comes in many different FLAVOURS

life·sav·ing /'laɪfseɪvɪŋ/ n [U] the set of skills necessary to protect or save someone from drowning, such as excellent swimming, carrying a drowning person through the water, and MOUTH-TO-MOUTH RESUSCITATION: You have to know lifesaving to apply for this job as a lifeguard. — compare FIRST AID

life sav·ings /ˌ· '···/ n [P] all the money which a person who is not very rich has managed to save during their life: Thieves broke in and stole her life savings.

life sci·en·ces /ˌ· '···/ n [P] also **life science** n [C;U]— a group of subjects studied at university, and concerned with plants, animals, and the human race

life sen·tence /ˌ· '···/ n a prison SENTENCE¹ (2) for a long period of time which is not fixed. In Britain, people are not punished by death, so a life sentence is given for murder or other violent crimes.

life-size /'· ·/ also **life-sized**— /'· ·/ adj (of a work of art) of the same size as what it represents: a life-sized statue of the president

life·span /'laɪfspæn/ n the average length of life of a sort of animal or plant or the time for which a material object will last: Men have a shorter lifespan than women. | These nuclear reactors have a pretty short lifespan. — compare LIFETIME

life sto·ry /ˈ⋅ ˌ⋅⋅/ *n* the story of someone's whole life: *I don't know why she needed to tell me her whole life story.*

life·style /ˈlaɪfstaɪl/ *n* a way of living, including the kind of home one lives in, the things one owns, the kind of job one does, and the LEISURE activities one enjoys; *the luxurious lifestyle of a Hollywood star*

life sup·port sys·tem /ˌ⋅ ⋅ˈ⋅ ˌ⋅⋅/ *n* 1 a piece of equipment which keeps a person alive when they are seriously ill

▶CULTURAL NOTE In the US esp. there are many people kept alive with this equipment who will never become conscious, and there are new moral and legal problems about deciding whether and when to switch off the equipment and let a person die. —see also LIVING WILL◀

2 a piece of equipment which keeps a person alive when they are in a place where people cannot live in the usual way, e.g. in space   3 a natural system which is necessary for life to continue, for example the process that produces OXYGEN for people to breathe

life's work /ˌ⋅ ˈ⋅/ also **life work**– *n* [U] an achievement for which someone has worked very hard for most of their life because they think it is very important: *The freeing of the slaves was his life's work.*

life·time /ˈlaɪftaɪm/ *n* the time during which a person is alive or a machine, organization, etc., continues to exist: *I doubt if there will be a female Pope in my lifetime.* | *the* **opportunity/chance of a lifetime** –compare LIFESPAN

Lif·fey /ˈlɪfi/ [*the*] a river in the Republic of Ireland which flows through Dublin

lift¹ /lɪft/ *v* 1 [T (UP)] to bring from a lower to a higher level; raise: *I can't lift this bag – it's too heavy.* | *If you lift up the chair I'll clean the carpet underneath it.* | *He was too weak even to lift his hand.* | (fig.) *She lifted her eyes* (=looked up) *from the book.* | (fig.) *The good news lifted my spirits.*   2 [I] (of movable parts) to be able to be lifted: *The top of this box won't lift (off).*   3 [T+obj+adv/prep] to take hold of and move to a higher or lower place or position: *I lifted the child down from the tree.* | *She lifted the baby out of the cot.*   4 [I] (esp. of low clouds, mist, etc.) to move upwards or disappear; DISPERSE: *The plane will take off once the fog has lifted.*   5 [T+obj+adv/prep] to carry by air; AIRLIFT   6 [T] to bring to an end; remove; RESCIND: *to lift an embargo/a ban*   7 [T] *infml, usu. derog* to take and use (other people's ideas, writings, etc.) as one's own without stating that one has done so; PLAGIARIZE: *All his main ideas in this article are lifted from other works.*   8 [T] *infml* to steal (esp. something small) —see also SHOPLIFT   9 [T] *tech* to dig up (vegetables that grow under the ground, or plants): *lifting potatoes*   10 [T (UP)] *lit* to make (the voice) loud, e.g. in singing —see also **lift a finger** (FINGER¹)

lift off *phr v* [I] (of an aircraft or spacecraft) to leave the ground; TAKE **off** —see also LIFT-OFF

lift² *n* 1 [C] an act of lifting. *One more lift and it's up!*   2 [C] *BrE* ‖ **elevator** *AmE*– an apparatus in a building for taking people and goods from one floor to another: *He pressed the button to call the lift.* | *He took the lift to the 14th floor.* | *the hotel lift*   3 [C] a free ride in a private vehicle: *Can I give you a lift home?*   4 [C;U] a lifting force, such as an upward pressure of air on the wings of an aircraft   5 [S] *infml* a feeling of increased strength, cheerfulness, etc.: *Passing the exam gave me a real lift.*   6 [C] any of various types of equipment for lifting

lift-off /ˈ⋅ ⋅/ *n* [C;U] the start of the flight of a spacecraft; TAKEOFF —see also **lift off** (LIFT¹)

lig·a·ment /ˈlɪgəmənt/ *n* any of the strong bands in the body that join bones or hold some part of the body in position: *He tore a ligament playing football.*

lig·a·ture /ˈlɪgətʃəʳ/ *n fml or tech* something used for tying, esp. a thread used for tying a BLOOD VESSEL to prevent loss of blood

light¹ /laɪt/ *n* 1 [U] the natural force that takes away darkness, so that objects can be seen: *sunlight* | *gaslight* | *firelight* | *She worked by the light of a candle/the moon.* | *Have you got enough light to read (by)?* | *The light isn't good/strong enough to take a photograph.* | *The lake was bathed in the soft* (=not very bright or strong) *light of the moon.* | *I must finish this painting while the light lasts.* (=before the darkness of evening starts to come) | *Come over into the light* (=an area that is not dark) *where I can see you.*

▶CULTURAL NOTE Light is often connected with goodness and knowledge, but **darkness** is connected with evil and ignorance. ◀

2 [C] **a** something that produces light and allows other things to be seen, such as a lamp or TORCH: *Turn off/Switch off the lights when you go to bed.* | *Shine your light over here, please.* | *The lights went down* (=gradually became less bright) *and the performance began.* | *the neon lights of the city* **b** a TRAFFIC LIGHT: *The lights are changing (to red); you'd better stop.* –see picture at LIVING ROOM   3 [U] the path by which a supply of light reaches a person: *I can't read while you're standing in my light.*   4 [S;U] (something that will cause) burning: *Have you got/Can you give me a light, please?* (=please provide me with a match, cigarette lighter, etc. to make my cigarette, etc., burn) | *The candle fell over and* **set light to** *the warehouse.*   5 [C] *tech* a window or other opening in a roof or wall that allows light into a room   6 [S;U] brightness, esp. in the eyes, showing happiness or excitement   7 [C *usu. sing.*;U] the bright part of a painting or photograph: *light and shade*   8 [U] the condition of being or becoming known: *Some new information has* **come to light** *about the accident.*   9 [S] *fml* the way in which something or someone appears or is regarded: *The workers and the employers see the situation in quite a different light.* | *This incident seems to show the company* **in a bad light.** (=in an unfavourable way)   10 [U] *lit or fml* (something that provides) knowledge, understanding, or explanation: *the light of truth* | *Does this information* **throw/shed any light** *on the problem?*   11 **according to one's own lights** *fml or lit* with regard to one's own personal opinions or ideas of right and wrong   12 **in the light of** *BrE* ‖ **in light of** *AmE*– taking into account; considering: *I wanted to hold the meeting today, but in the light of the changed circumstances it had better be postponed.*   13 **(to go) out like a light** *infml* (to fall) deeply asleep or unconscious   14 **let there be light (and there was light)** a phrase from the Bible used by God when creating light in the world, now used humorously to ask for light or when a light is put on   15 **light at the end of the tunnel** signs of the end of something which has been difficult or unpleasant: *The project has been going on for months but at last we can see the light at the end of the tunnel.*   16 **the light's on, but nobody's home** *infml* a person is awake but not involved in their surroundings —see also GREEN LIGHT, LEADING LIGHT, LIGHTS, NORTHERN LIGHTS, RED LIGHT

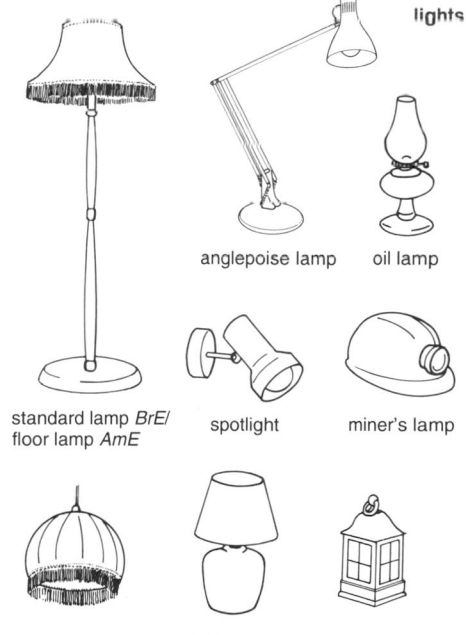

lights

anglepoise lamp   oil lamp

standard lamp *BrE*/
floor lamp *AmE*   spotlight   miner's lamp

table lamp   lantern

light² *v* **lit** /lɪt/ *or* **lighted**   1 [I;T (UP)] to (cause to) start to burn; IGNITE: *He lit (up) a cigarette.* | *The fire won't light.* —see FIRE (USAGE) **2** [T] to give light to: *The stage is lit by several powerful spotlights.* **3** [I;T (UP)] to (cause to) become bright with pleasure or excitement: *Suddenly a smile lit (up) her face.* | *Her face lit up (with joy) when she saw him coming.* **4** [T+obj+adv/prep] *old-fash* to show the way with a light: *I lighted him up the stairs to bed with a candle.*

▷ USAGE **Lit** is more common than **lighted** as the past and past participle of **light**, except in sense 4 or when it stands as an adjective before the noun: *He's* **lit** *a match.* | *The match is* **lit.** | *a* **lighted** *match*◁

light up *phr v* [I;T (=**light** sthg. **up**)] **1** to make or become bright with light or colour: *The candles on the Christmas tree lit up the room.* | (fig.) *The room lights up when she walks in!* **2** to cause (lamps) to begin giving out light: (BrE) *Lighting-up time is 6.50 tonight.* **3** *infml* to begin to smoke (a cigarette, CIGAR, or pipe)

light³ *adj* **1** having light; not dark; bright: *It's getting light: morning is coming.* **2** not deep or dark in colour; pale: *a light-coloured dress* | *light green curtains* —compare DEEP¹ (5) **3** (also **lite**) of food, not containing very much of a substance, e.g. fat, that is considered harmful: *New light cheese spread with only half the fat.* — ~**ness** *n* [U]

light⁴ *adj* **1** of little weight; not heavy: *It's so light a child could lift it.* **2** of little weight as compared with size or the usual weight: *a light summer suit* | *a light metal* | *This case is surprisingly light.* **3** of less than the correct weight: [after *n*] *The crate is a pound (too) light.* **4** small in amount; less than average or expected: *a light crop of wheat* | *light traffic* **5** easy to bear or do; not severe, difficult, or tiring: *light punishment* | *light duties* **6** intended only for entertainment; not serious or deep in meaning: *light reading* | *light comedy* **7** soft; gentle; having little force: *a light wind* | *Give it a light tap with a hammer.* **8** quick and graceful in movement: *She's* **light on her feet.** **9 a** (of sleep) from which one wakes easily; not deep **b** [A] easily woken: *a light sleeper* **10 a** (of meals) small in amount **b** (of food) easy to DIGEST **11** [A] (of a person) habitually eating, drinking, smoking, etc., in small amounts: *She's a light smoker.* **12** (of wine and other alcoholic drinks) not very strong **13** *lit* happy, cheerful, or free of worries: *light of heart* —see also LIGHT-HEARTED **14** (of the head) having an unsteady feeling, as when in a feverish condition or after drinking alcohol; DIZZY —see also LIGHT-HEADED **15** (of soil) easily broken up; sandy **16 make light of** to treat as of little importance, and even to joke about: *We shouldn't make light of the difficulties this will cause.* —see also LIGHTLY — ~**ness** *n* [U]

light⁵ *adv* without many cases or possessions (LUGGAGE) (esp. in the phrase **travel light**)

light⁶ *v* **lit** *or* **lighted** [I+adv/prep, esp. **on, upon**] *old use or lit* to come down from flight and settle; ALIGHT
  light out *phr v* [I (**for**)] *AmE infml* to run away (towards): *The fox lit out for the forest.*
  light upon/on sthg./sbdy. *phr v* [T] *old use or lit* to discover or find (esp. something or someone pleasant) by chance

light air·craft /ˌ· '···/ *n* a small aircraft typically driven by a PROPELLER

light ale /ˌ· '·/ also **pale ale** *BrE*— *n* [U] a type of rather weak pale beer, usu. kept in bottles

light beer /ˌ· '·/ *n* [C;U] (a glass of) a kind of beer which does not contain much alcohol

Light Brigade [*the*] see CHARGE OF THE LIGHT BRIGADE

light bulb /'·· ·/ also **bulb**— *n* a usu. round hollow container of thin glass with a wire inside, which lights up when electricity is passed through it: *The light bulb's gone* (=stopped working)*; can you put a new 100-watt bulb in?*

light-e·mit·ting di·ode /ˌlaɪt ɪˌmɪtɪŋ 'daɪəʊd/ *n* LED

light·en¹ /'laɪtn/ *v* [I;T] to (cause to) become brighter or less dark: *The sky began to lighten after the storm.* | *Paint the ceiling white to lighten the room.* —compare DARKEN

light·en² *v* [I;T] **1** to make or become less heavy, forceful, etc.: *The taking on of a new secretary lightened her workload considerably.* **2** to make or become more cheerful or less troubled: *Her mood lightened.* **3 Lighten up!** *AmE infml* Be calm!; Don't worry!

light·er¹ /'laɪtər/ also **cigarette lighter**— *n* a small instrument that produces a flame for lighting cigarettes, pipes,

or CIGARS: *a gas lighter* (=that produces a flame by burning gas)

lighter² *n* a large open flat-bottomed boat used for loading and unloading ships —compare PINNACE

light-fin·gered /ˌ· '···/ *adj* **1** *infml* having the habit of stealing small things **2** having fingers that move easily and quickly, as in playing an instrument

light-head·ed /ˌ· '···/ *adj* **1** unable to think clearly or move steadily, e.g. during fever or after drinking alcohol; DELIRIOUS **2** not sensible or serious; FRIVOLOUS — ~**ly** *adv* — ~**ness** *n* [U]

light-heart·ed /ˌ· '···/ *adj* **1** cheerful; happy **2** not serious: *a television comedy that takes a light-hearted look at life in prison*

light heav·y·weight /ˌ· '···/ *n, adj* (a BOXER) heavier than a MIDDLEWEIGHT but lighter than a HEAVYWEIGHT

light·house /'laɪthaʊs/ *n* -**houses** /ˌhaʊzɪz/ a tower or other building with a powerful flashing light that guides ships or warns them of dangerous rocks

light in·dus·try /ˌ· '···/ *n* [U] the branch of industry which produces small goods, e.g. things used in the house

light·ing /'laɪtɪŋ/ *n* [U] the system, arrangement, or equipment that lights a room, building, street, theatre, etc., or the quality of the light produced: *You can completely change the atmosphere of a room if you change the lighting.*

lighting up time /ˌ··· '· ·/ *n* [U] *BrE* the time at which vehicles must by law put their lights on in the evening, when it begins to get dark

light·ly /'laɪtli/ *adv* **1** with little weight or force; gently: *He tapped her lightly on the shoulder.* **2** to a slight or little degree: *lightly cooked* | (fig.) *Only six months in prison for murder — I call that* **getting off lightly!** (=with little punishment) **3** without careful thought or consideration: *I'm not making these accusations lightly, you know!* **4** without appearing to be concerned: *"Don't worry about it at all," he said lightly.*

light me·ter /'· ˌ··/ *n* a piece of equipment used by a photographer to measure how much light there is: *a camera with a built-in light meter*

light·ning /'laɪtnɪŋ/ *n* [U] **1** a powerful flash of light in the sky caused by electricity passing from one cloud to another or to the earth, usu. followed by thunder: *The tower has been struck by lightning.* —see also FORKED LIGHTNING, GREASED LIGHTNING, HEAT LIGHTNING, SHEET LIGHTNING **2 lightning never strikes twice in the same place** *saying* the same piece of bad luck does not happen to a person twice

lightning bug /'··· ·/ *n AmE for* FIREFLY

lightning con·duc·tor /'··· ·ˌ··/ *BrE* ∥ **lightning rod** /'·· ˌ·/*AmE*— *n* a metal wire or bar leading from the highest point of a building to the ground to protect the building from damage by lightning

lightning strike /ˌ··· '· ·/ *n* a sudden STRIKE (=stopping of work) by dissatisfied workers without the usual warning of intention

light pen /'· ˌ·/ *n* **1** an object like a pen used in shops to tell the prices of goods from the BAR CODEs on them **2** a piece of equipment like a pen used to draw lines on a computer SCREEN

Light Rail Ve·hi·cle /ˌ· '· ˌ···/ *n* LRV

light rail·way /ˌ· '·/ *n* a railway that uses light trains and usu. carries only passengers, not goods. Light railways usu. run in cities, sometimes along streets.

lights /laɪts/ *n* [P] *old-fash* the lungs of sheep, pigs, etc., used as food

light·ship /'laɪtˌʃɪp/ *n* a small ship that is fixed near a dangerous place at sea and warns and guides other ships by means of a powerful flashing light

lights-out /ˌ· '·, '·ˌ·/ *n* [U] the time when a group of people in beds (in a school, the army, etc.) must put the lights out and go to sleep: *No talking after lights-out!*

light·weight /'laɪtˌweɪt/ *n* **1** a person or thing of less than average weight **2** a BOXER heavier than a FEATHERWEIGHT but lighter than a WELTERWEIGHT **3** *derog* someone who is of little importance or does not have the ability to think deeply: *He's an intellectual lightweight.* —**lightweight** *adj* : *I find his articles rather lightweight.*

light year /'· ·/ *n* **1** (a measure of length equal to) the distance that light travels in one year (about 9,500,000,000,000 kilometres or 6,000,000,000,000 miles), used for measuring distances between stars **2** also **light years** *pl.— infml* a very long time: *light years ago*

lig·ne·ous /ˈlɪgnɪəs/ *adj tech* like wood

lig·nite /ˈlɪgnaɪt/ *n* [U] a soft material like coal, used for burning

li·ka·ble , likeable /ˈlaɪkəbəl/ *adj* (esp. of people) pleasant; easy to like

like¹ /laɪk/ *v* [T *not usu. in progressive forms*] **1** to regard with pleasure or fondness; have good feelings about; enjoy: *I like your new dress.* | *She's very friendly — everyone likes her.* | *She is very well-liked.* | *"Do you like Chinese food?" "Yes I love it!"* | *I don't like it when she tells me how to do things.* [+*v-ing*] *The children like watching television.* [+*to-v*] *I like to visit her as often as possible.* | (*infml* used to mean the opposite, esp. so as to show annoyance) *I like the way he just comes in here and tells everyone what to do!* | *I like your cheek!* (=I don't like your rudeness!) **2** [+*to-v/v-ing; only in negatives*] to be willing (to): *I know she could help, but I don't like to ask her when she's so busy.* | *I don't like interrupting her when she has visitors.* **3** (with **should**, **would**) **a** to wish: [+*to-v*] *I'd like to see you again soon.* [+*obj+to-v*] *I wouldn't like you to think I was being unfair.* | *We'd like him to come.* [+*obj+v-ed*] *I'd like this work finished by Friday, please.* **b** (used for adding politeness to what you are saying): [+*to-v*] *I'd like to thank everyone who helped me.* (=I thank everyone …) | *We'd like to wish you good luck.* **4 a** (with **should, would**) to choose to have; want: *I'd like the red one, please.* (=Please give me the red one.) | (used in making an offer) *Would you like a cigarette/a cup of tea?* [+*obj+adj*] *I'd like my steak well-done.* (=Please cook it thoroughly) [+*obj+v-ed*] *I'd like to see this work finished by Friday, please.* **b** to have habitually: *When do you like your breakfast?* | *What do you like for tea?* | *"How do you like your coffee?" "I like it black."* **5 How do you like …?** (used when asking for an opinion or judgment): *How do you like this dress?* (=does it seem good to you?) | (shows annoyance or surprise) *"My boyfriend has just told me to go on a diet." "Well how do you like that!"* **6 How would you/he/they like** … ? How would you/he/they feel about (something)?; What would your/his/their reaction to (something) be?: *How would you like to be treated like that?* (=in such a bad way) | (used in making a threat) *How would you like a punch on the nose?* **7 I'd like to** (used in disbelief or angrily) I would be surprised/interested to: *I'd like to see him do better, even if he does think he's so clever.* (=I don't think he could do better) | *I'd like to know what you mean by that.* **8 I like that!** *infml* That is very annoying!: *"He said you were fat." "Well, I like that!"* **9 if you like: a** if it would please you; if that is what you want: *We can go out if you like.* **b** if I may express it in this way: *It wasn't actually a holiday, more a working break, if you like.*

▷ USAGE 1 **Like** used on its own means "to be fond of or enjoy": *I like coffee.* (=I'm fond of it) | *I like watching* (also *to watch AmE*) *television.* 2 When asking for something, or to be allowed to do something, *I'd like* is more common and more polite than *I want*: *I'd like a cup of coffee.* | *I'd like to watch television tonight.* 3 When offering something to someone say **Would** *you* **like** … ?: **Would** *you* **like** *a cup of tea?* | Would *you* like *me to help you with your homework?* —see also WANT (USAGE)◁

like² *prep* **1** in the same way as: *Do it like this.* | *He cried like a baby when they told him the news.* **2** with the same qualities as; similar to: *He was like a son to me.* | *She's very like her mother.* | *When the car's painted it will look like new.* | *There's nothing like* (=nothing as nice as) *a nice hot bath.* | *What's your new job like?* (=is it interesting, enjoyable, etc.?) **3** typical of: *It was (just) like him to think of helping her.* | *It's not like her to be so late.* (=She's not usually so late.) **4** (esp. with **look, sound**) in a way that shows the likelihood of (being): *It looks like rain.* | *From what you say, she sounds like the right person for the job.* (=it seems that she might be the right person) **5** *infml* (used in forming phrases that add force): *We ran like mad.* | *It hurts like hell/like anything.* (=hurts very much) **6** for example; such as: *There are several people interested, like Mrs Jones and Dr Simpson.* **7 like father, like son** a phrase used about a son who looks/acts etc. very similar to his father: *Michael always* forgets my birthday—*like father, like son, I suppose!* **8 something like** about; more or less: *It'll cost something like £100.* —see also **feel like** (FEEL¹)

▷ USAGE Note the difference between these uses of **like** and as: *He has been playing tennis* **as** *a professional for two years.* (=he is a professional) | *He plays tennis* **like** *a professional.* (=he is not a professional but he plays as well as a professional)◁

like³ *n* **1** [*the*+(*of*)] someone or something which is like another, esp. in having equally high value; equal: *Will we ever see the like of Mozart again?* | *I've never seen its like/the like of it.* **2 and the like** and something of the same kind: *running, swimming, and the like* —see also LIKES

like⁴ *adj* **1** *fml* with the same or similar qualities: *We have like attitudes/are* **of like mind** (=are in agreement) *in this matter.* **2** [A] *fml* of the same type; SUCHLIKE: *running, swimming, and like sports* **3** [F+*to-v*] *old use or dial* likely **4 as like as two peas (in a pod)** *infml* the same in all ways

like⁵ *conj* **1** *infml* as; in the same way as: *Do you make bread like you make cakes?* | *Like I said, I can't get there on Saturday.* (=I have said this before) **2** *nonstandard* as if: *He acts like he's the boss.*

like⁶ *adv* **1** *nonstandard* (used in speech, either after an inexact, unusual, or unclear expression or as a meaningless addition): *He went up to her all innocent, like, as if he'd done nothing.* **2** *old use* in the same way (in the phrases **like as, like to, like unto**) **3 as like as not** *infml* probably **4 like enough** *infml* probably

-like see WORD FORMATION

like·a·ble /ˈlaɪkəbəl/ *adj* LIKABLE

like·li·hood /ˈlaɪklihʊd/ *n* [U (**of**)] **1** the fact or degree of being likely; probability: *There's no likelihood/little likelihood of rain.* [+(*that*)] *There's not much likelihood he'll succeed.* **2 in all likelihood** probably

like·ly¹ /ˈlaɪkli/ *adj* **1** that can reasonably be expected; probable: *The likely winner of the election.* | *Rain is likely in all parts of the country today.* | *A new pay settlement is the most likely outcome of these discussions.* | *If, as seems likely, we fail — what then?* [F+*to-v*] *He's likely to arrive a bit late.* | *It's likely that they will lose the election.* — opposite **unlikely**; see APT (USAGE), PROBABLE (USAGE) **2** [A] suitable to give (good) results: *That's the likeliest suggestion we've heard yet.* | (*BrE infml*) *a likely lad, who's bound to succeed* **3 (That's) a 'likely story!** *infml* (said to show that one disbelieves what someone has said)

likely² *adv* **1** probably (esp. with **most** or **very**): *They'll very likely come by car.* **2 as likely as not** *infml* probably **3 Not likely!** *infml* (used esp. for refusing) Certainly not!

Likely Lads /ˈ·· ˌ·/, **The** a British television SERIES popular esp. in the 1960s, about two young, unmarried men from the NE of England who spent a lot of time drinking in PUBs and enjoying themselves and were full of hope and plans for their future lives

like-mind·ed /ˌ· ˈ···◁/ *adj* having the same ideas, interests, etc.: *He got together with a group of like-minded people to organize a protest against the plan.* — **~ness** *n* [U]

lik·en /ˈlaɪkən/ *v* **liken** sthg./sbdy. **to** sthg./sbdy. *phr v* [T *often pass.*] *fml* to compare to: *Life can be likened to a journey with an unknown destination.*

like·ness /ˈlaɪknɪs/ *n* **1** [C;U (**to**)] sameness, esp. in appearance; RESEMBLANCE: *a family likeness* | *His mannerisms bear a strong likeness to those of his father.* **2** [C] a photograph or painting of a person esp. a good one that is really like the person; PORTRAIT: *That's a good likeness of Julie.*

likes /laɪks/ *n* [P] **1** things that one likes (usu. in the phrase **likes and dislikes**) —see also LIKING **2 the likes of** *infml* people of the stated type: *High-class restaurants aren't for the likes of us.* (=people like us) —see also LIKE³

like·wise /ˈlaɪk-waɪz/ *adv fml* **1** in the same way; similarly: *The stockbroker bought shares in the company and advised his clients to do likewise.* (=to do the same) | *"I'm very pleased to meet you." "Likewise."* (="I am similarly glad to meet you.") **2** also; in addition: *You must pack plenty of food. Likewise, you'll need warm clothes, so pack them too.*

lik·ing /ˈlaɪkɪŋ/ n 1 [S+for] fondness: *to have a liking for sweets* 2 **to one's liking** *sometimes pomp* suiting one's needs, wishes, or expectations: *Was the meal to your liking, madam?* (=did you like it?)

Li·kud /lɪˈkʊd‖-ˈkuːd/ [*the*] a RIGHT-WING political party in Israel

li·lac /ˈlaɪlək/ n 1 [C] a tree with pinkish purple or white flowers giving a sweet smell 2 [U] a colour like the pale purple colour of these flowers

Lil·ith /ˈlɪlɪθ/ in Jewish FOLKLORE, a female devil, the first wife of Adam, who is said to be a VAMPIRE

Lille /liːl/ a large industrial city in the N of France

Lil·lee /ˈlɪli/, **Den·nis** /ˈdenɪs/ (1949–) an Australian cricket player who has played for the English Northamptonshire team since 1988

Lil·li·bur·le·ro /ˌlɪlɪbəˈleərəʊ‖-bər-/ the name of a popular old song based on Irish words "Lero, lero, lilliburlero" in which the words are repeated after every VERSE

Lil·li·put /ˈlɪlɪpʌt, -pʊt/ a country in the book *Gulliver's Travels* by Jonathan Swift where all the people and things are very small. The people are called **Lilliputians**

Lil·li·pu·tian /ˌlɪlɪˈpjuːʃən∢/ adj fml extremely small; MINIATURE: *a doll's house with Lilliputian furniture*

Lil·ly·white's /ˈlɪliwaɪts/ one of a group of shops selling sports equipment and clothing, with branches in central London and other cities

Li·lo /ˈlaɪləʊ/ n **-los** BrE tdmk (often without cap.) an AIRBED, used as a bed esp. when camping, or for lying on when by the sea or to float on water

lilt /lɪlt/ n [S] a regular usu. pleasant pattern of rising and falling sound, esp. in speaking or singing: *He speaks with a Welsh lilt.*

lil·ting /ˈlɪltɪŋ/ adj having a lilt: *a lilting voice* | *a lilting tune*

lil·y /ˈlɪli/ n 1 any of several plants with large flowers of various colours, esp. one with clear white flowers. A white lily is often used as a SYMBOL of purity and beauty. —see also **gild the lily** (GILD), WATER LILY 2 **consider the lilies of the field; they toil not neither do they spin** *quote* a slightly changed phrase from the Bible, used when saying that things are important even if they do not serve any very useful purpose

lily-liv·ered /ˌ··ˈ··∢/ adj infml cowardly

lily of the val·ley /ˌ··· · ˈ··/ n **lilies of the valley** a plant with several small white bell-shaped flowers with a sweet smell

lily pad /ˈ·· ·/ n the leaf of the WATER LILY, which floats on the surface of the water

lily-white /ˌ·· ˈ·∢/ adj esp. lit or humor pure white: *a lily-white complexion* | (fig.) *a person of lily-white character* (=of very pure and honest character)

Li·ma /ˈliːmə/ an important industrial and university city; the capital of Peru

li·ma bean /ˈliːmə biːn‖ˈlaɪ-/ n a bean of tropical American origin with flat seeds which are often dried for later eating

limb /lɪm/ n fml or tech 1 a leg or arm of a person or animal, or the wing of a bird 2 a (large) branch of a tree 3 **out on a limb** alone without support, esp. in opinions or argument 4 **-limbed** /lɪmd/ having the stated type or number of limbs: *strong-limbed* —see also **in wind and limb** (WIND¹) − ∼**less** adj

lim·ber¹ /ˈlɪmbəʳ/ v
limber up phr v [I] to make the muscles stretch and move easily by exercise, esp. when preparing for a race, game, etc.

limber² adj apprec, fml or lit loose (in muscle); moving and bending easily; SUPPLE

lim·bo¹ /ˈlɪmbəʊ/ n [U] 1 (often cap.) (in the Roman Catholic religion) a place which is neither heaven nor HELL where the souls of those who have not done evil may go after death, even though they were not Christians during their life —compare PURGATORY 2 a state of uncertainty: *I'm in limbo, waiting to know whether or not I've got the job.*

limbo² n **-bos** a West Indian dance in which a dancer leans backwards and passes under a rope or bar which is lowered closer and closer to the floor

lime¹ /laɪm/ n [U] 1 also **quicklime**− a white substance obtained by burning LIMESTONE 2 a white powder made by adding water to this, used in making cement, for liming fields, etc.

lime² v [T] tech to add lime to (fields, land, etc.) in order to control acid substances

lime³ also **lime tree** /ˈ· ·/ ‖ also **linden** esp AmE− n a tree sometimes planted along streets because of its attractive appearance and sweet-smelling yellow flowers

lime⁴ n 1 a tree which bears a small juicy green fruit with a sour taste 2 the fruit of this tree: *a glass of lime juice*

lime·ade /ˌlaɪmˈeɪd/ n [U] a green drink made of the juice of limes, with sugar added, and sometimes gas

lime green /ˌ· ˈ·∢/ adj, n (of) a light yellow green colour

lime·light /ˈlaɪmlaɪt/ n 1 [*the*] the centre of public attention: *a hospital that has been in the limelight because of the new techniques of heart surgery being pioneered there* | *when a famous author's husband steals the limelight and writes a best-seller* 2 [U] a bright white light produced by heating lime in a strong flame, which was formerly used in theatres to light the stage

lim·e·rick /ˈlɪmərɪk/ n a usu. humorous short poem with five lines, three long and two short ones. An example of a limerick is:
There was a young man from Bengal,
Who went to a fancy-dress ball,
He decided, for fun,
To dress as a bun,
But a dog ate him up in the hall.

Limerick 1 a COUNTY in the SW of the Republic of Ireland 2 the main town of this county

lime·stone /ˈlaɪmstəʊn/ n [U] a type of rock containing CALCIUM and other substances −see also LIME¹

li·mey /ˈlaɪmi/ n **-meys** sl, esp. AmE, usu. humor or derog an Englishman

lim·it¹ /ˈlɪmɪt/ n 1 [C] also **limits**− the farthest point or edge, which cannot or must not be passed: *Other countries' vessels are not allowed to fish within a 12-mile limit of our coast.* | *to reach the limit of one's patience* | *I'll help as much as I can, but there's a limit to what I can do* (=I can't do everything). | *I can't walk 10 miles; I know my limits.* | (fig.) *Her ambition knows no limit(s).* (=is extremely great) 2 [C] the greatest or smallest amount or number which is fixed as being legal, correct, necessary, etc.: *The government has imposed an 8% limit on pay awards.* | *The bank has written to say I've gone over my credit limit.* (=I have borrowed more than I am allowed) | *safety limits* | *time limit* | *The motorist was found by police to be below/over the limit.* (=having less/more than the highest level of alcohol in the blood at which one may legally drive a vehicle) 3 [*the*] infml someone or something that is too annoying, difficult, painful, etc. to bear: *This is the third time in a week that the electricity supply has been cut off − it really is the limit.* 4 **off limits (to)** esp. AmE where one is not allowed to go; out of BOUNDS (to): *The town is off limits to military personnel.* 5 **within limits** not beyond a certain point, amount, time, etc.: *to keep our spending within (reasonable) limits* | *You can do what you like − within limits.*

limit² v [T (to)] to keep within a certain size, number, area, or place; RESTRICT: *We must limit our spending.* | *We must limit ourselves to an hour/to one cake each.*

lim·i·ta·tion /ˌlɪmɪˈteɪʃən/ n 1 [U] the fact or condition of limiting or being limited 2 [C usu. pl.] something that limits; the limit beyond which no more can be done: *I won't even try to fix the car myself; I know my limitations as a mechanic.* | *It's a good little car, but it has its limitations.* (=cannot do so much as a bigger or more powerful one)

lim·it·ed /ˈlɪmɪtɪd/ adj 1 [(to)] not very great in amount, power, etc., and not able to increase or improve; having limits or limitations: *a student of rather limited ability/intelligence* | *Seating is limited to 500.* | *limited resources/funds* | *a limited edition of a book* (=with only a certain number printed) −opposites **unlimited**, **limitless** 2 (abbrev. **Ltd**) [A; after n] BrE (of a company) having limited liability: *J. Marsh and Sons Limited* − compare INC, PLC

limited com·pa·ny /ˌ··· ˈ···/ also **limited-li·a·bil·i·ty com·pa·ny** /ˌ··· ··ˈ··· ˌ···/ n a company whose owners only have to pay a limited amount if the company gets into debt

limited e·di·tion /ˌ··· ·ˈ··/ *n* copies of a book, picture, etc. made at one time and limited to a certain number so that the quality will be good and the value may increase

limited li·a·bil·i·ty /ˌ··· ··ˈ···/ *n* [C;U] *tech* the legal duty to pay back debts only up to the limit of the money owned (by a company): *a limited-liability company* —see also LIMITED COMPANY

limited-o·vers crick·et /ˌ···· ·· ˈ··/ *n* ONE-DAY CRICKET

lim·it·ing /ˈlɪmɨtɪŋ/ *adj* which prevents improvement, increase, etc.: *A limiting factor in health care is lack of doctors.*

lim·it·less /ˈlɪmɨtləs/ *adj* without limit or end: *limitless possibilities* – ~ly *adv* – ~ness *n* [U]

limn /lɪm/ *v* [T] *old use* **1** to describe **2** to paint or draw

Li·moges /lɪˈməʊʒ/ a city in W central France where fine cups, plates, etc. are made

lim·ou·sine /ˈlɪməziːn, ˌlɪməˈziːn/ *n* also **lim·o** /ˈlɪməʊ/ *infml* – a big expensive comfortable car –see also STRETCH LIMO

limp¹ /lɪmp/ *v* [I] **1** to walk with an uneven step, one foot or leg moving less well than the other **2** *derog* (of speech, music, poetry, etc.) to have an uneven pattern

limp² *n* [S] a limping way of walking: *to walk with/have a limp*

limp³ *adj derog* lacking strength or stiffness: *I like lettuce to be crisp, not limp and soggy.* | *a limp handshake* – ~ly *adv* – ~ness *n* [U]

lim·pet /ˈlɪmpɨt/ *n* a small sea animal with a shell (SHELLFISH), which holds on tightly to the rock where it lives: *She clung to his side like a limpet.* –see picture at SEA

lim·pid /ˈlɪmpɨd/ *adj esp. lit* (esp. of liquid) clear; transparent: *eyes like limpid pools* – ~ly *adv* – ~ity /lɪmˈpɪdɨti/ *n* [U]

Lim·po·po /lɪmˈpəʊpəʊ/ *[the]* a river in South Africa which flows across Mozambique to the Indian Ocean

limp-wrist·ed /ˌ· ˈ··◂/ *adj derog* (of a man) lacking manly forcefulness

lim·y /ˈlaɪmi/ *adj* covered in or containing LIME¹: *limy soil*

linch·pin /ˈlɪntʃˌpɪn/ *n* [(of)] an important part or member which keeps the whole thing or group together

Lin·coln¹ /ˈlɪŋkən/ a city in Lincolnshire where the local government for that COUNTY is based. It is famous esp. for its CATHEDRAL.

Lincoln² *tdmk* an American LUXURY car made by Ford: *She drove up in a Lincoln Continental.*

Lincoln³, Abraham (1809–65) a self-educated lawyer, Republican President of the US (1861–65). Lincoln was against an increase in slavery, and when he came to power the Southern states, which depended on the work of slaves, wanted to leave the US. This led to the American Civil War in which he fought the South. In 1863 he said that the slaves would be freed. He also made the Gettysburg Address in favour of DEMOCRACY. After the war he was shot by an actor called John Wilkes Booth. He is remembered as one of the greatest American presidents and his picture can be seen on the five-dollar bill.

Abraham Lincoln

Lincoln Cen·ter /ˈ·· ˌ··/ *[the]* The Lincoln Center for the Performing Arts; a large group of theatres and concert halls in New York City where plays, concerts, and OPERAS are performed: *The concert will be broadcast live from Lincoln Center.*

Lincoln green /ˌ·· ˈ·/ *n* [U] (cloth of) a bright green colour originally made at Lincoln. Robin Hood and his men are said to have worn this colour. –see ROBIN HOOD

Lincoln Me·mo·rial /ˌ··· ·ˈ···/ *[the]* a building in Washington, DC, with a large stone figure of Abraham Lincoln inside it. It was built to preserve his memory.

Lincoln's Birth·day /ˌ·· ˈ··/ *n* [U] the birthday of Abraham Lincoln, February 12th, which is a legal holiday in many American states —see also PRESIDENT'S DAY

Lin·coln·shire /ˈlɪŋkənʃər/ *written abbrev.* **Lincs** a COUNTY in E England, bordering on the North Sea

Lincoln's Inn /ˌ··· ˈ·/ one of the four INNS OF COURT in London —see INNS OF COURT

Lincoln Tun·nel /ˌ··· ˈ··/ *[the]* a traffic tunnel under the Hudson River that connects Manhattan with New Jersey —see colour map on page 1376

Lincs *written abbrev. for:* Lincolnshire

linc·tus /ˈlɪŋktəs/ *n* [U] *BrE* liquid medicine to cure coughing

Lind /lɪnd/, **Jen·ny** /ˈdʒeni/ (1820–87) a Swedish singer known for her sweet voice and called the "Swedish NIGHTINGALE"

lin·dane /ˈlɪndeɪn/ *n* [U] a chemical for killing insects, now thought dangerous to humans

Lind·bergh /ˈlɪndbɜːg‖-bɜːrg/, **Charles** (1902–74) an American AVIATOR; in 1927 he became the first person to fly non-stop and alone across the Atlantic, flying from New York to Paris in his plane the **Spirit of St Louis**. Later his baby son was kidnapped (KIDNAP¹) and murdered.

lin·den /ˈlɪndən/ *n poet and AmE* a LIME³ tree

Lin·dis·farne /ˈlɪndɨsfaːn‖-faːrn/ another name for HOLY ISLAND

Lin·dis·farne Gos·pels /ˌ··· ˈ··/ *[the +P]* a handwritten, decorated book containing the Christian Gospels, written at Lindisfarne (**Holy Island**) before AD 700 and now preserved in the British Museum

line¹ /laɪn/ *n* **1** [C] a long narrow mark (drawn) on a surface: *Do not write below this line.* | *She drew a wavy line under the word.* | *With his finger he traced the curving line of the road on the map.* **2** [C] a long mark used as a limit or border: *The British runner was first to cross the finishing line, but was later disqualified.* | *If the ball goes over the line, it's out of play.* | *a white line in the middle of the road* | *a line judge in tennis* **b** a border or edge: *the line between North and South Korea* | (fig.) *There's a very fine (dividing) line between genius and madness.* —see also MASON-DIXON LINE, PLIMSOLL LINE **3** [S (of)] a direction of movement: *He's had so much to drink that he could hardly walk in a straight line.* | *a ball's line of flight* **4** [C] a row: *A line of coats hung on the wall.* **5 a** [C;U] a number of people side by side or one behind the other: *The recruits were standing in line to be examined.* | *Children, get into (a) line/form a line.* | *If we don't get in line now we'll never get a seat.* —compare QUEUE¹ **b** [C] a set of people following one another in time, esp. a family: *He comes from a long line of actors.* | *a line of kings* **6** [C] also **lines** *pl.* – a railway track: *Passengers are not allowed to cross the lines.* | *the main line from London to Leeds* **7** [C] a row of words **a** on a printed page: *There are 12 words to a line.* (=on each line) **b** in a poem: *Each line has five beats.* **8** [C] a long thin mark in the skin; WRINKLE: *The old man's face is covered with lines.* **9** [C] an OUTLINE: *the sleek elegant lines of a racing yacht* **10** [C; U] (a piece of) string or cord: *clothes drying on the washing line* | *a fishing line* | *50 metres of line* **11** [C] a telephone wire or connection: *The lines went down in the storm.* | **Hold the line**, please (=do not put your telephone down) – *I'm trying to connect you.* | *I'm afraid this is rather a bad line – could you speak a bit more clearly?* | *I'm sorry, sir, the line is busy/engaged – would you like to call back later?* –see also HOT LINE, PARTY LINE **12** [S] *infml* a short letter: *Drop me a line* (=write me a letter) *when you know your exam results.* **13** [C] (*usu. in comb.*) (a company that provides) a system for travelling by or moving goods by road, railway, sea, or air; a TRANSPORT system or company: *an airline* | *a shipping line* **14** [C *often pl.*] a course or method of action: *This failed to persuade her, so we tried a new line of argument.* | *The police are following various lines of inquiry.* | *You haven't got the right answer, but you're* **on the right lines**. (=following the right method, and likely to succeed) | *What line shall we take at the meeting?* | *The judges have been urged to* **take a tough line** *with violent criminals.* –see also HARD LINE **15 a** [C] (esp. in politics) an officially stated set of ideas, methods, etc.: *to follow the party line* **b** [U] (in certain phrases) the state of being in agreement with this: *This pay settlement will* **bring us into line** *with the government's guidelines.* | *The party leadership managed to* **keep** *the members* **in line**/*to prevent them from* **stepping out of line**. | *They disagreed at first but in the end they* **fell into line**. **16** [C] *infml* an area of interest, activity, or work: *Her line is insurance.* | *That's not really in my line of business.* | *Fishing isn't really my line.* **17** [C] a type of goods: *This dress is one of our latest lines.* | *a new line in shoes* | (fig.) *She does/has a good line in funny stories.* **18** [C] *infml* a way of talking that seems to be intended to deceive or persuade: *Don't give me that line about not having any money!* **19** [*the*] *tech* the EQUATOR: *crossing the line* **20** [C] a row of military defences, esp. that nearest the enemy: *He was parachuted behind enemy lines.* | *the Maginot line* | (fig.) *the body's first line of defence against disease* —see also FRONT LINE **21** [*the*] **a** (in the British army) the regular foot soldiers of the army: *a line regiment* **b** (in the US army) all the regular fighting forces **22** [C] also **line of battle** /ˌ· · ˈ··/– the arrangement of soldiers, ships, etc., side by side: (*old-fash*) *a ship of the line* (=a large warship) **23** [S (**on**)] *infml* a piece of useful information: *Can you give me a line on the new head of department? I can't seem to get a line on her.* **24 all along the line** in every part and/or from the beginning: *He's been opposing me all along the line.* **25 down the line** *infml, esp. AmE* completely or fully, e.g. in support or encouragement: *I'll support him down the line on that issue.* **26 Hard lines!** *BrE infml* (an expression of sympathy) What bad luck you had! **27 in line for** about to or likely to get: *in line for the job/for promotion* **28 in line with** straight or level compared with: *The wheel at the back isn't in line with the one at the front.* | (fig.) *That isn't in line with my ideas at all.* **29 on the line** at serious risk; in danger: *Work hard: your job is on the line.* (=you may lose it) | *to put one's reputation on the line* **30** (**reach**) **the end of the line** (to reach) the last stages, esp. the point of failure —see also LINES, BOTTOM LINE, STORY LINE, **draw the line at** (DRAW¹), **lay something on the line** (LAY²), OFFLINE, ONLINE, **read between the lines** (READ¹)

line² *v* [T] **1** to draw lines on: *lined paper* **2** to mark with lines or WRINKLES: *Signs of worry lined his face.* **3** to form rows along: *The crowds lined the streets.* | *tree-lined avenues*

    line up *phr v* **1** [I;T (=**line** sbdy./sthg. ↔ **up**)] to (cause to) form into a row, side by side or one behind the other: *He lined up behind the others to wait his turn.* | *Line up the glasses and I'll fill them.* | *Everybody line up, facing the front.* **2** [T (**for**)] (**line** sthg./sbdy. ↔ **up**) to arrange for (an event) to take place or (a person) to take part in an event: *We've lined up a great race to celebrate the centenary, with some of the best runners in the world taking part.* | *We've lined up Pavarotti for the main role in the opera.* [+obj+to-v] *We've lined him up to sing the main role.* —see also LINEUP

line³ *v* [T (**with**) *often pass.*] **1** to cover the inside of (something) with material: *I lined the box with paper before I put the clothes in.* | *a coat lined with silk* | *Are these curtains lined?* —see also LINING **2** to be an inner covering for: *the soft slippery substance that lines the stomach* **3 line one's pocket(s)/purse** to make money for oneself in a way that is disapproved of

lin·e·age¹ /ˈlɪni-ɪdʒ/ *n* [C;U] *fml* the way in which members of a family are descended from other members: *a family of ancient/royal lineage*

line·age² /ˈlaɪnɪdʒ/ *n* [U] the number of lines in something written or printed

lin·e·al /ˈlɪniəl/ *adj fml* in a set of people following each other directly in time, esp. from parent to child — ~**ly** *adv*

lin·e·a·ment /ˈlɪniəmənt/ *n* [*usu. pl.*] *fml or lit* **1** a FEATURE of the face **2** a typical quality

lin·e·ar /ˈlɪniər/ *adj* **1** of or in lines: *a linear diagram* **2** [A] of length: *linear measurements*

linear ac·cel·e·ra·tor /ˌ··· ·ˈ····/ *n* a piece of equipment used by scientists to find out about the nature of matter; it makes small pieces of atoms called PARTICLES travel in a straight line at increasingly high speed —compare CYCLOTRON

linear per·spec·tive /ˌ··· ·ˈ··/ *n* [U] a way of drawing and painting in which lines which are really PARALLEL meet. It is used to give the idea of depth and distance.

line·back·er /ˈlaɪnbækər/ *n* a player in American football who tries to spoil attacking plays by tackling (TACKLE¹) members of the other team

line draw·ing /ˈ· ˌ··/ *n* a drawing done with a pen or pencil and made up only of lines

line drive /ˈ· ·/ *n* a BASEBALL hit with great force in a straight line fairly near the ground

Lin·e·ker /ˈlɪnɪkər/, **Gar·y** /ˈgæri/ (1960–) an English football player, originally in the Leicester City team, who played for England in 1984 and again in the World Cup in 1986 and 1990. He is known for being a nice person and for not using offensive language.

line·man /ˈlaɪnmən/ also **linesman**— *n* -**men** /mən/ a man whose job is to take care of railway lines or telephone wires

line man·age·ment /ˈ· ˌ···/ *n* [U] the method of passing information and instructions along lines of people up and down an organization, each person telling the one immediately above or below them —**line manager** *n*

lin·en /ˈlɪnən/ *n* [U] **1** cloth made from the plant FLAX and used to make good-quality tablecloths, furnishing cloth, and clothes; it wears well but is very expensive; before the introduction of cotton, it was used for sheets **2** sheets, tablecloths, etc.: *to buy bed linen* | *a linen cupboard* **3** *old use* underclothes, esp. white: *to change one's linen* —see also **wash one's dirty linen** (WASH¹)

linen bas·ket /ˈ·· ˌ··/ *n* a LAUNDRY BASKET

linen cup·board /ˈ·· ˌ··/ *n* a special cupboard where sheets, tablecloths, TOWELS, etc. are kept. In Britain, if this cupboard is heated, it can be called an AIRING CUPBOARD.

line of coun·try /ˌ· · ˈ··/ *n* [S] *BrE infml* kind of job: *What line of country are you in?*

line of du·ty /ˌ· · ˈ··/ **It's all in the line of duty.** It's part of the responsibility that goes with the position that someone holds. People say this when you thank or praise them for doing something and they want to say that they are only doing their job.

line of scrim·mage /ˌ· · ˈ··/ *n* in American football, a line running parallel to the width of the field where the ball is placed at the beginning of each play

line of sight /ˌ· · ˈ·/ also **line of vision** /ˌ· · ˈ··/— *n* **lines of sight** the imaginary straight line along which one looks towards an object

line-out /ˈ· ·/ *n* the method in RUGBY UNION by which the ball is returned to play by being thrown in between two lines of players from each team

line print·er /ˈ· ˌ··/ *n* a machine which prints out information from a computer at a very high speed —see picture at COMPUTER —**-ing** *n* [U]

lin·er /ˈlaɪnər/ *n* **1** [C] a large passenger ship esp. one of several owned by a company: *an ocean liner* —see also AIRLINER, CRUISE LINER **2** [C;U] an EYELINER **3** [C] a piece of material used inside another to protect it: *a nappy liner* | *a bin liner* | *A semi-rigid polythene liner was used for the pool.*

liner notes /ˈ·· ·/ *n* [P] *AmE for* SLEEVE NOTES

lin·er·train /ˈlaɪnətreɪn‖-ər-/ *n* a FREIGHTLINER

lines /laɪnz/ *n* [P] **1** the words learnt by an actor to be said in a play: *Have you learnt your lines yet?* **2** *BrE* a usu. stated number of written lines to be copied by a pupil as a punishment: *The teacher gave me 100 lines.* **3** *lit* a poem: *"Lines on the Death of Nelson"* —see also MARRIAGE LINES

lines·man /ˈlaɪnzmən/ *n* -**men** /mən/ **1** (in sport) an official who stays near the lines marking the side of the playing area and helps the UMPIRE or REFEREE, esp. by deciding when a ball has gone outside the limits —see picture at TENNIS **2** a LINEMAN

line·up /ˈlaɪn-ʌp/ *n* [*usu. sing.*] **1 a** an arrangement of people, esp. side by side in a line looking forward **b** *AmE* a line of this sort arranged by the police, containing a person thought to be guilty of a crime and looked at by a witness who tries to recognize the criminal **2** the (arrangement of) players or competitors at the beginning of a race or game: *There are seven horses in the lineup.* **3** a set of events, following one after the other: *What's next on the lineup?* —see also LINE **up**

ling /lɪŋ/ *n* [U] a plant very like HEATHER, with bell-shaped pink flowers

lin·ger /ˈlɪŋgər/ *v* [I (**ON**)] **1** to remain for a time instead of going, esp. because one does not wish to leave; delay going: *She lingered outside the school after everyone else had gone home.* | *They lingered over coffee and missed the train.* **2** to be slow to disappear: *The pain lingered on* *for weeks.* | *The event is over, but the memory lingers on.* —see also LINGERING **3** to be close to dying for a long time, esp. when suffering from a disease — ~ **er** *n*

lin·ge·rie /ˈlænʒəriː||ˌlɑːnʒəˈreɪ, ˈlænʒəriː/ *n* [U] underclothes for women, esp. for sale in shops: *Underwear and nightdresses are in the lingerie department.*

lin·ger·ing /ˈlɪŋgərɪŋ/ *adj* [A] slow to reach an end or disappear: *a lingering death/illness* | *The official announcement finally extinguished any lingering hopes we might have had.* — ~ **ly** *adv*

lin·go /ˈlɪŋgəʊ/ *n* -**goes** *sl* a language, usu. foreign: *I'd like to go to France but I don't speak the lingo.*

lin·gua fran·ca /ˌlɪŋgwə ˈfræŋkə/ *n* a language used between peoples whose main languages are different. It may originally be made up of parts of several languages: *English serves as a lingua franca in some parts of the world.* —compare PIDGIN

lin·gual /ˈlɪŋgwəl/ *adj tech* **1** of the tongue **2** (of a sound) made by the movement of the tongue —see also BILINGUAL

lin·gui·ni /lɪŋˈgwiːni/ *n* [U] *AmE* a flat, thin PASTA in the shape of long narrow pieces

lin·guist /ˈlɪŋgwɪst/ *n* **1** a person who studies and is good at foreign languages **2** also **lin·guis·ti·cian** /ˌlɪŋgwɪˈstɪʃən/— a person who studies linguistics

lin·guis·tic /lɪŋˈgwɪstɪk/ *adj* of languages, words, or linguistics: *linguistic development/change* — ~ **ally** /kli/ *adv*

lin·guis·tics /lɪŋˈgwɪstɪks/ *n* [U] the study of language in general and of particular languages, their structure, grammar, history, etc. —compare PHILOLOGY

lin·i·ment /ˈlɪnɪmənt/ *n* [U] a liquid substance containing oil, to be rubbed on the skin to cure soreness and stiffness of the joints —compare EMBROCATION

lin·ing /ˈlaɪnɪŋ/ *n* [C;U] (a piece of) material covering the inner surface of an article of clothing, a box, etc.: *a coat with a silk lining* | *brake linings* —see picture at SHOE; see also SILVER LINING

link¹ /lɪŋk/ *n* **1** a single ring of a chain **2** [(**between, with**)] something which connects two or other parts: *Research has established a link between smoking and lung cancer.* | *a new rail link between two towns* (=a train service between them) | *The country has now severed* (=broken) *all links with its former ally.* —see also LINKS, CUFF LINK, MISSING LINK

link² *v* **1** [T (UP)] to join or connect: *The road links all the new towns.* | *The police suspect that the two crimes may be linked.* | *They walked with linked arms/with their arms linked.* | *The road will link Manchester and Birmingham with/to London.* **2** [I (TOGETHER, UP, **with**)] to be joined or connected: *In the second part of the programme, we'll be linking up with American radio for an interview with the President.* | *My own work links up with the research you are doing.* —see also LINKUP

Link *n* [S] (in Britain) a system which allows people to get money from their bank accounts using a special plastic card (a **Link card**) in a machine

link·age /ˈlɪŋkɪdʒ/ *n* **1** [C] a system of links or connections **2** [S;U (**between, with**)] a connecting relationship (between things or ideas) **3** [S;U (**between, with**)] the idea of connecting two or more different questions in the hope of getting an agreement on both: *A union spokesman rejected linkage between a wage increase and changes in working practices.*

link·man /ˈlɪŋkmæn/, **link·wom·an** /-ˌwʊmən/*fem.*— -**men** /men/ *n* a person whose job is to introduce all the separate parts of a television or radio broadcast

links /lɪŋks/ *n* **links** [C+*sing./pl. v*] a piece of ground on which GOLF is played, esp. near the sea; GOLF LINKS

link-up /ˈlɪŋk-ʌp/ *n* an arrangement by which different things are connected: *a live TV linkup between studios throughout Europe*

Lin·nae·us /lɪˈniːəs, -ˈneɪ-/, **Ca·ro·lus** /ˈkærˈrəʊləs/ (1707–78) a Swedish scientist who studied animals and plants and invented a system (the **Linnaean System**) for putting them into classes

lin·net /ˈlɪnɪt/ *n* a small brown singing bird

li·no·cut /ˈlaɪnəʊkʌt/ *n* **1** the art of cutting a pattern on a block of linoleum **2** [C] a picture printed from such a block

li·no·le·um /lɪˈnəʊliəm/ also **li·no** /ˈlaɪnəʊ/*BrE*— *n* [U]

smooth shiny material in flat sheets used as a floor-covering, made up of strong cloth combined with a hard material. It is used esp. in kitchens because it is easy to clean.

Li·no·type /ˈlaɪnəʊtaɪp/ *n tdmk* [U] a system for setting (SET¹ (6)) type in the form of solid metal lines: *a Linotype operator*

lin·seed /ˈlɪnsiːd/ *n* [U] the seed of FLAX

linseed oil /ˌ· ˈ·/ *n* [U] the oil from linseed, used in linoleum, and in some paints, inks, etc.

lint /lɪnt/ *n* [U] **1** soft material used for protecting wounds **2** esp. *AmE for* FLUFF¹ (2)

lin·tel /ˈlɪntl/ *n* a piece of stone or wood across the top of a window or door, forming part of the frame

Li·nus /ˈlaɪnəs/ a character in the **Peanuts** CARTOONs, a very young child who always takes his BLANKET everywhere because he would not feel happy without it. People may call something a **Linus blanket** if they feel safe or comfortable because it is there: *For many people the church is a kind of Linus blanket, even though they never go there.*

li·on /ˈlaɪən/, **li·on·ess** /ˈlaɪənes, -n̩s/*fem*— **1** a large yellowish-brown animal of the cat family which hunts and eats meat, and lives mainly in Africa, the male having a thick growth of hair (a MANE) over its head and shoulders: *as brave as a lion* | *the lion's roar* —see picture at BIG CATS

▶CULTURAL NOTE The lion is thought of as brave and frightening, and as the king of the JUNGLE (= tropical forest). A lion is sometimes used to represent Britain. People sometimes also mention the idea from the Bible that one day the lion will lie down with the lamb, that is there will be peace and happiness. ◀

2 a famous and important person: *a literary lion* **3 in the lion's den** (from the story of Daniel in the Bible) in a difficult situation, esp. because one is surrounded by people who are not friendly: *A job interview can feel like being in the lion's den.* —see also DANIEL **4 the 'lion's share (of)** the greatest part (of); most (of) **5 thrown/ tossed to the lions** (from the custom in ancient Rome of throwing Christians to lions in an ARENA) left to an unpleasant fate, esp. by people who were thought to be friendly: *The workers felt they'd been thrown to the lions to save other people's jobs.*

Lion *n* (used as a title for a member of the Lions Club): *Contact Lion Jim Cole for details of the forthcoming Lions Club Summer Gala.*

Lion, the Witch and the War·drobe /ˌ··· · ˈ··· ˈ··/, **The** a children's book by C S Lewis, the best known of his seven *Narnia* books, describing the imaginary country of Narnia and the adventures that a group of children have there —see also NARNIA

lion-heart·ed /ˌ··· ˈ··•/ *adj esp. lit* very brave

li·on·ize also **-ise** *BrE*— /ˈlaɪənaɪz/ *v* [T] to treat (a person) as important or famous —**-ization** /ˌlaɪənaɪˈzeɪʃən||-nə-/ *n* [U]

Lions /laɪənz/ [*the*+P] see BRITISH LIONS

Lions Club /ˈ·· ·/ *n* an international organization of business and PROFESSIONAL¹ (1) people who perform services for their communities, such as CHARITY work

lions' den /ˌ·· ˈ·/ *n* a place where there is someone that one is frightened of —see also DANIEL

lip /lɪp/ *n* **1** [C] **a** either of the two edges of the mouth where the skin is delicate and usu. redder than the surrounding skin: *He kissed her on the lips.* | *I cut my lip on the cracked glass.* | *pursed lips* **b** the ordinary skin around these, esp. above the mouth: *A small moustache adorned his upper lip.* —see picture at HEAD **2** [C *usu. sing.*] the edge (of a hollow container or opening): *the lip of the cup* **3** [U] *sl* rude or arguing talk: *I'll have none of your lip, my lad!* **4 -lipped** /lɪpt/having lips of the stated type: *thick-lipped* —see also STIFF UPPER LIP, TIGHT-LIPPED **5 my lips are sealed** I will keep it secret **6 read my lips** *infml* listen very carefully to what I am saying. The phrase was used by George Bush when promising that he would introduce "no new taxes"

Li Peng /ˌliː ˈpʌŋ/ (1928–) the PRIME MINISTER of China from 1988

lip gloss /ˈ· ·/ *n* [C; U] a substance in a small pot used to make the lips look very shiny

lip·id /ˈlɪpɪd/ n tech any of a class of FATTY substances in living things, such as fat, oil, or WAX

Lip·man /ˈlɪpmən/, **Mau·reen** /ˈmɔːriːn/ (1946–) an English theatre and film actress famous for her part in television advertisements for British Telecommunications

lip·o·suc·tion /ˈlɪpəʊsʌkʃən/ n [U] a way of removing unneeded fat from a person's body by cutting the skin and drawing the fat out by means of SUCTION

lip-read /ˈlɪp riːd/ v [I;T] (usu. of people who cannot hear) to watch people's lip movements so as to understand (what they are saying) — ~ing n [U]

lip ser·vice /ˈ· ˌ··/ n pay lip service to to support in words, but not in fact; give loyalty, interest, etc., in speech, while really thinking the opposite: *The government are only paying lip service to the idea of equality for women.*

lip·stick /ˈlɪpˌstɪk/ n [C;U] (a stick-shaped piece of) a substance for brightening the colour of the lips

lip synch /ˈlɪp sɪŋk/ n [U] the activity of moving the lips at the same time that a recording is being played, to give the appearance that one is talking or singing —**lip-synch** v [I] : *They said it was live but I think she was lip-synching from her record.*

liq·ue·fac·tion /ˌlɪkwɪˈfækʃən/ n [U] esp. tech the act of making or becoming liquid

liq·ue·fy /ˈlɪkwɪfaɪ/ v [I;T] fml to (cause to) become liquid: *Butter liquefies in heat.*

li·ques·cent /lɪˈkwesənt/ adj tech becoming or tending to become liquid

li·queur /lɪˈkjʊəʳ‖lɪˈkɜːr/ n any of several types of very strong alcoholic drink, each of which has a special, often sweet or fruity taste, usu. drunk in small quantities after a meal —compare LIQUOR

liq·uid¹ /ˈlɪkwɪd/ n 1 [C;U] a substance which is not a solid or a gas, which flows, is wet, and has no fixed shape: *Water is a liquid.* 2 [C] tech either of the consonant sounds /l/ and /r/

liquid² adj 1 (esp. of something which is usu. solid or gas) in the form of a liquid: *liquid soap | liquid oxygen* 2 apprec, esp. fml or lit clear, as if covered in clean water: *liquid colours/eyes* 3 apprec, esp. fml or lit (of sounds) clear and flowing, with a pure quality 4 that can easily be exchanged or sold for money (esp. in the phrase **liquid assets**) 5 **liquid refreshment** pomp or humor drink, esp. alcoholic

liquid as·sets /ˌ·· ˈ··/ n [P] CASH and other ASSETS that a business has, that can easily be exchanged for money

liq·ui·date /ˈlɪkwɪdeɪt/ v 1 [T] to get rid of; destroy or kill: *The opposition leaders were liquidated on the orders of the dictator.* 2 [I;T] a to close down (a business company), esp. when it has too many debts b (of a company) to close down in this way, esp. by going BANKRUPT 3 [T] tech to pay (a debt)

liq·ui·da·tion /ˌlɪkwɪˈdeɪʃən/ n [U] 1 the closing down of a company which can no longer pay its debts. A liquidator sells off all the company's ASSETS, and the money is used to pay CREDITORS. 2 the paying of a debt

liq·ui·da·tor /ˈlɪkwɪdeɪtəʳ/ n an official who ends the trade of a particular business, esp. so that its debts can be paid

liquid crys·tal di·splay /ˌ··· ˌ·· ·ˈ·/ n LCD

liq·uid·i·ty /lɪˈkwɪdɪti/ n [U] tech 1 the state of having money in one's possession, or goods that can easily be sold for money 2 the state of being liquid

liq·uid·ize also **-ise** BrE /ˈlɪkwɪdaɪz/ v [T] to crush (esp. fruit or vegetables) into a liquid-like form

liq·uid·iz·er /ˈlɪkwɪdaɪzəʳ/ n BrE for BLENDER —see picture at KITCHEN

liquid lunch /ˌ·· ˈ·/ n humor a visit to a PUB or bar to have an alcoholic drink instead of eating food at LUNCH time

liq·uor /ˈlɪkəʳ/ n [U] 1 AmE strong alcoholic drink, such as WHISKY —compare LIQUEUR 2 lit or tech alcoholic drink 3 rare, esp. BrE the liquid produced from cooked food, such as the juice from meat

liq·uo·rice , licorice /ˈlɪkərɪs, -rɪʃ/ n 1 [U] a black substance produced from the root of a plant, used in medicine and sweets 2 [C;U] a sweet or sweets made from this

liquorice all·sorts /ˌlɪkərɪs ˈɔːlsɔːts, -rɪʃ-‖-sɔːrts/ n [P] a mixture of different shaped brightly coloured sweets containing liquorice

lir·a /ˈlɪərə/ n lire /ˈlɪəreɪ/ or liras 1 the unit of money in Italy 2 the unit of money in Turkey or Syria; the Turkish or Syrian POUND¹ (2)

Lis·bon /ˈlɪzbən/ n the capital and main port of Portugal, with a large university and CATHEDRAL

lisle /laɪl/ n [U] cotton material, used in the past for GLOVEs and STOCKINGS

lisp¹ /lɪsp/ v [I;T] to speak or say unclearly, pronouncing s-sounds as /θ/ — ~ingly adv

lisp² n [S] the habit of lisping: *She speaks with a lisp.*

lis·som , lissome /ˈlɪsəm/ adj lit apprec (esp. of a woman or her body) thin and graceful in shape and movement — ~ly adv — ~ness n [U]

list¹ /lɪst/ n [(of)] a set of words, names, numbers, etc., usu. written one below the other, so that one can remember them or keep them in order so that they can be found: *a list of things to buy | a shopping list | an alphabetical list | How many people are there on the council's housing list?* —see also LISTS, CIVIL LIST, DANGER LIST, HIT LIST, SHORT LIST, WAITING LIST

list² v [T] 1 to put into or include in a list: *She listed all the things she had to do.* 2 to put on a government list of buildings of historical interest which must be protected

list³ v [I] (esp. of a ship) to lean or slope to one side: *listing to port* —**list** n

list⁴ v [I] old use to wish; desire

list⁵ v [I] old use to listen

listed build·ing /ˌ·· ˈ··/ n (in Britain) a building on a government list of buildings which are of historical interest and must be protected. Listed buildings must not be changed in any important way or pulled down.

lis·ten¹ /ˈlɪsən/ v [I (to)] 1 to give attention in hearing: *We sat listening to music/listening to a play on the radio. | If you listen carefully you can hear a funny sound in the engine.* 2 to take notice; hear or consider with thoughtful attention: *I warned him not to go but he just wouldn't listen. | She never listens to me/to my advice. | Listen, I think we may be able to solve your problem.* —see HEAR (USAGE)

listen for sthg./sbdy. phr v [T] to pay attention so as to be sure of hearing: *Listen for the moment when the music changes.*

listen in phr v [I] 1 [(to)] to listen to a broadcast on the radio: *to listen in to the news* —see also TUNE **in** 2 [(on, to)] to listen to the conversation of other people, esp. secretly and without permission: *I think the police have been listening in on my phone calls.*

listen out phr v [I (for)] BrE infml to listen carefully, esp. for an expected sound: *Listen out for the baby in case she wakes up.*

listen² n [S] infml an act of listening: *Have a listen to this new album!*

lis·ten·a·ble /ˈlɪsənəbəl/ adj [(to)] infml pleasant to hear: *The music is quite listenable (to).*

lis·ten·er /ˈlɪsənəʳ/ n a person who listens or is listening, esp. to the radio: *Good morning, listeners! | Regular listeners will remember that a few weeks ago … | If you've got any problems, she's a good listener.* (=listens patiently and sympathetically to what you want to say) —compare VIEWER

Listener, The a former British weekly magazine produced by the BBC and the IBA, with articles about television and radio programmes

listening bank /ˈ··· ˌ·/ [the] a description of itself used in an advertisement for the Midland Bank. The idea was that the bank would listen to its customers and try to help them.

listening de·vice /ˈ··· ·ˌ·/ n something which allows one to hear other people's conversations usu. secretly; a BUG¹ (4) —compare HEARING AID

Lis·ter /ˈlɪstəʳ/, **Joseph** (1827–1912) an English doctor who introduced the idea of ANTISEPTIC medicine, esp. using STERILE instruments during operations to prevent infection

lis·te·ri·a /lɪˈstɪəriə/ n [U] any of various kinds of bacteria which cause an illness called listeriosis, a kind of FOOD POISONING

Lis·te·rine /ˈlɪstəriːn/ n [U] tdmk a type of MOUTHWASH made by Warner Lambert Healthcare

listing par·tic·u·lars /ˈ·· ·ˌ·ˌˈ·ˈ/ n [P] BrE tech a document which an existing company must have printed when it is offering shares for sale which number 10 per cent or more of shares already owned —compare PROSPECTUS

list·ings /ˈlɪstɪŋz/ n [P] lists of films, plays, and other events which will take place soon, with the time and place of each. The listings appear in some newspapers and in some special magazines.

list·less /ˈlɪstləs/ adj lacking movement, activity, and interest, as if tired; LANGUID: Heat makes some people listless. —compare LIFELESS − −**ly** adv − −**ness** n [U]

list price /ˈ·· ·/ n a price which is suggested for an article by the people who make it, but which a shopkeeper does not necessarily have to charge

lists /lɪsts/ n BrE **enter the lists** to (start to) take part in a competition, argument, etc.

Liszt /lɪst/, **Franz** /frænts‖frɑːnts/ (1811–86) a Hungarian COMPOSER and piano player who wrote poetic music full of feeling

lit¹ /lɪt/ past tense & participle of LIGHT²,⁶

lit² abbrev. for: **1** literature or LITERARY: lit crit (=literary CRITICISM) **2** litre

lit·a·ny /ˈlɪtəni/ n a form of long prayer in the Christian church in which the priest calls out and the people reply, always in the same words: (fig.) They continued with a long litany of complaints.

li·tchi /ˈlaɪtʃiː/ -s n a LYCHEE

lite /laɪt/ adj see LIGHT³ (3)

lite beer /ˌ· ·/ also **light beer**− n [U] AmE a beer which has fewer CALORIES than other beer

li·ter /ˈliːtəʳ/ n AmE for LITRE see picture at LITRE

lit·e·ra·cy /ˈlɪtərəsi/ n [U] fml the state or condition of being LITERATE (=able to read and write): an adult-literacy campaign | (fig.) computer-literacy (=a simple understanding of how computers work)

lit·e·ral¹ /ˈlɪtərəl/ adj **1** being or following the exact or original meaning of a word, phrase, etc. without any additional meanings (e.g. without METAPHOR or ALLEGORY): The literal meaning of "blue" is a colour, but it can also mean "unhappy". | a literal interpretation −compare FIGURATIVE **2** giving a single word in place of each original word: A literal translation is not always the closest to the original meaning. **3** derog not showing much imagination; PROSAIC: a boring literal-minded person − −**ness** n [U]

literal² BrE ‖ **typo, typographical error** AmE− n tech a printing mistake, esp. in the spelling of a word

lit·e·ral·ly /ˈlɪtərəli/ adv **1 a** in a literal sense; really: The Olympic Games were watched by literally billions of people around the world. **b** (used for giving force to an already strong and esp. METAPHORICAL expression): She was literally blue with cold. | He was literally blazing with anger. **2** so as to give a single word in place of each original word: to translate literally **3** according to the words and not the intention: I took what he said literally, but afterwards it became clear that he really meant something else.

▷ USAGE **Literally** should really be used to mean "exactly as stated": Their house is literally 10 metres from the sea. (=I am telling the exact truth.) It is often used more generally to give force to an expression, but many teachers feel this is incorrect: He literally exploded with anger. (=his anger was very like an explosion)◁

lit·e·ra·ry /ˈlɪtərəri‖ˈlɪtəreri/ adj **1** (typical) of literature. Literary words or phrases are marked lit in this dictionary: a literary style | one of the most coveted literary prizes **2** [A] fond of, studying, or producing literature: a literary man | a literary society

lit·e·rate /ˈlɪtərət/ adj **1** able to read and write −compare NUMERATE **2** having studied or read a great deal **3** -**literate** having enough knowledge to use the stated thing: computer-literate −opposite **illiterate**; see also LITERACY − −**ly** adv − −**ness** n [U]

lit·e·ra·ti /ˌlɪtəˈrɑːti/ n [the + P] fml, sometimes derog people with great knowledge of literature, esp. forming a fairly small group in society

lit·e·ra·ture /ˈlɪtərətʃəʳ‖-tʃʊər/ n **1** [U] **a** written works which are of artistic value: one of the great works of English literature **b** such works as a subject for study:

studying language and literature | a course in modern African literature **2** [S;U] all the books, articles, etc. on a particular subject: She is trying to keep abreast of the literature (in her field). | There is now a vast literature on the subject. **3** [U] infml printed material, esp. giving information: Have you got any literature on the new car? | sales literature | promotional literature

lithe /laɪð/ adj (esp. of people or animals) able to bend and move easily and gracefully: the lithe bodies of the dancers − −**ly** adv

lith·i·um /ˈlɪθiəm/ n [U] a soft silver-white simple substance (ELEMENT) that is the lightest known metal. A **lithium battery** does not lose quality quickly, so is used when a small BATTERY is needed to supply a little electricity over a long period, e.g. in a camera, watch, or calculator.

lith·o·graph¹ /ˈlɪθəgrɑːf‖-græf/ n a picture, print, etc., made by lithography

lithograph² v [I;T] to print by lithography

li·thog·ra·phy /lɪˈθɒɡrəfi‖lɪˈθɑː-/ n [U] a process for printing patterns, pictures, etc., from a piece of stone or metal −−**phic** /ˌlɪθəˈɡræfɪk◂/ adj −−**phically** /kli/ adv

Lith·u·a·ni·a /ˌlɪθjuˈeɪniə‖ˌlɪθu-/ a country on the E coast of the Baltic Sea; capital Vilnius; population 3,690,000 (1989)

Lith·u·a·ni·an /ˌlɪθjuˈeɪniən‖ˌlɪθu-/ n **1** [C] a person who comes from or whose parents come from Lithuania **2** [U] the main language spoken in Lithuania − **Lithuanian** adj

lit·i·gant /ˈlɪtɪɡənt/ n tech a person on one side or the other in a noncriminal case being decided by a law court

lit·i·gate /ˈlɪtɪɡeɪt/ v [I] tech to take a noncriminal matter to a court of law for a decision

lit·i·ga·tion /ˌlɪtɪˈɡeɪʃ ən/ n [U] tech the process of making and defending claims in a court of law, in noncriminal matters

li·ti·gious /lɪˈtɪdʒəs/ adj fml, often derog habitually liking to take matters of disagreement to a court of law; fond of litigation − −**ness** n [U]

lit·mus /ˈlɪtməs/ n [U] a substance which turns red when touched by an acid substance and blue when touched by an ALKALI

litmus pa·per /ˈ·· ˌ··/ n [U] (a piece of) paper treated with litmus used to test whether a liquid is acidic or ALKALINE

litmus test /ˈ·· ˌ·/ n [S] **1** something which makes it clear what someone's opinions, feelings, or abilities are: His views on the siting of the new town are a litmus test of the Government's policy on the environment. **2** a test using litmus paper

li·to·tes /ˈlaɪtətiːz, laɪˈtəʊtiːz/ n [U] tech a way of expressing a thought by its opposite, esp. with "not" (as in **not bad** = "good"); UNDERSTATEMENT

litre

1 litre BrE/   1 pint (in UK)   1 pint (in USA)
liter AmE

li·tre BrE ‖ -**ter** AmE /ˈliːtəʳ/ n a metric measure of liquid: a litre of oil −see TABLE 2

lit·ter¹ /ˈlɪtəʳ/ n **1** [U] waste material thrown away, esp. bits of paper scattered untidily in a public place: The streets were full of litter. **2** [C+sing./pl. v] a group of young animals, such as KITTENS or PIGLETS born at the same time to one mother **3** [U] **a** a pile of STRAW used as an animal's bed **b** a special substance in the form of small grains kept on a **litter tray** to be used by house animals, esp. cats, to empty their bowels on when indoors: cat litter **4** [C] a bed or seat with handles, used esp. in former times for carrying people who were wounded or ill, or rich people

litter² v [T (**with**)] to cover untidily with scattered litter or something similar: The streets were littered with old cans and other rubbish. | Piles of books and papers *littered her desk.* | (fig.) *The book is littered with* (=full of) *mistakes.*

lit·te·ra·teur /ˌlɪtərəˈtɜːʳ/ *n often derog* a person who is interested in or works with literature, esp. a writer whose work is not considered very serious

lit·ter bin /ˈlɪtəˌbɪn‖-ər-/ *also* **litter bas·ket** /ˈ·· ˌ·-/— *n BrE* a container for objects to be thrown away, esp. in a public place —compare WASTEPAPER BASKET

lit·ter lout /ˈlɪtəlaʊt‖-ər/ *BrE* ‖ **lit·ter·bug** /-bʌg/*esp. AmE*— *n derog* a person who leaves litter in public places

lit·tle[1] /ˈlɪtl/ *adj* **1** small, esp. in a way that is attractive or produces sympathy: *They live in a little cottage in Scotland.* | *What a nice little garden!* | *There were two little birds on the windowsill.* **2** [A] short: *She sat with him for a little while.* **3** young: *a little boy* | *my little girl* (=my daughter) | *my little* (=younger) *brother* | *She's too little to ride a bicycle.* —see CHILD (USAGE) **4** [A] not important; TRIVIAL: *the little things of life* | *one or two little problems to sort out* **5 little things please little minds** *derog* a phrase used to criticize someone who is too concerned with small, or unimportant things

▷ USAGE Compare **little** and **small**. **Little** often suggests that you are talking about something which is pleasantly small: *I used to go there when I was a little girl.* | *I'd like to have a little house of my own.* **Small** does not have this suggestion: *Some small boys tried to steal a tape-recorder from my car.* | *I wouldn't like to live in such a small house.*◁

little[2] *adv* **less, least** **1** to only a small degree: *a little-known fact* | *The book is little more than* (=not much more than) *a rehash of old ideas.* **2** *fml or pomp* (with verbs of feeling and knowing) not at all: *They little thought that the truth would be discovered.* | *Little did they know that we were watching them.* **3** rarely: *I go there very little/as little as possible.*

little[3] *determiner, pron, n* **less, least** **1** [U] (with [U] nouns; used without **a** or **only,** to show the smallness of the amount) not much; not enough: *I have very little (money) left.* | *I understood little of what she said.* | *I have so little time to enjoy myself.* (compare *I have so few chances …*) | *There is little hope of an agreement being reached.* | *It would take less* (=not so much) *time if you went by train.* | *no less than a mile* | *the one that costs the least (money)* (=the smallest amount) | *We did what little we could to help the refugees.* (=we did what we could, but this was not very much) | *We see very little of our children* (=we do not see them often) *now that they are grown up.* —compare FEW (1), PLENTY[1] **2** [S](with [U] nouns; used with **a** or **the**) a small amount, but at least some: *a few eggs and a little milk* | *There's only a (very) little left.* | *Give me a little more of that wine.* | *It tastes nice if you add a little salt.* | *"Would you like some more tea?" "Just a little."* | *We had a little trouble finding the house.* | *She speaks a little French.* —compare FEW (2) **3** [S] a short time or distance: *He came back after a little.* | *Can't you stay a little longer?* | *a little over 60 years ago* | *We walked a little further along the road.* **4 a little** *also* **a little bit** *infml*— to some degree; rather: *I was a little annoyed.* | *(fml) I was not a little annoyed.* (=I was really rather annoyed.) | *He thinks it's all a little bit stupid* **5 little by little** gradually: *Little by little things returned to normal.* **6 make little of** *fml* **a** to treat as unimportant: *She made little of her worries.* **b** to not understand much of: *I could make very little of his explanation.* —compare **make much of** (MUCH[1]); see FEW (USAGE), MORE[2] (USAGE) **7 too little too late** not enough of something, esp. money, and given too late: *He described the government's rescue package as "too little too late"*

Little Bear /ˌ·· ˈ·/ [the] a group of stars, URSA MINOR

Little Big·horn /ˌlɪtl ˈbɪɡhɔːn‖-hɔːrn/ [the] the river in Montana where General George CUSTER fought and was killed by Native Americans led by SITTING BULL and CRAZY HORSE This is sometimes called the **Battle of the Little Bighorn**.

little black book /ˌ·· · ˈ·/ *n infml, humor* a small book in which someone esp. a man keeps the names and telephone numbers of his girlfriends: *"Have you got Sandra's number?" "I'll just look in my little black book."*

little black dress /ˌ·· · ˈ·/ *also* **little black num·ber** /ˌ·· · ˈ··/— *n infml humor* a woman's dress with thin SHOULDER STRAPS, made of a black usu. silky material and worn to COCKTAIL parties. This kind of dress was originally

designed (DESIGN[1] (1)) by the French fashion designer Coco Chanel.

Little Bo-peep /ˌlɪtl bəʊ ˈpiːp/ a little girl in a NURSERY RHYME (=an old song or poem for children), who lost the sheep she was looking after:
> *Little Bo Peep has lost her sheep*
> *And doesn't know where to find them;*
> *Leave them alone, and they'll come home,*
> *Bringing their tails behind them.*

Little Boy Blue /ˌ·· · ˈ·/ a boy in a NURSERY RHYME (=old song or poem for children) who was dressed in blue and went to sleep under a HAYSTACK instead of looking after the cows and sheep

Little Chef /ˌ·· · ˈ·/ *n* one of a group of modern roadside restaurants in Britain which provide FAST FOOD for people who are travelling: *We stopped at a Little Chef for lunch.* —compare HAPPY EATER

Little Dip·per /ˌ·· ˈ··/ *esp. AmE* [the] a group of stars, URSA MINOR

Little Dor·rit /ˌlɪtl ˈdɒrɪt‖-ˈdɔːr-/ a NOVEL by Charles Dickens, written in 1857. It is a rather SENTIMENTAL story about a young woman, Amy, (Little Dorrit) and her love for her father and then for her future husband.

little fin·ger /ˌ·· ˈ··/ *also* **pinkie** *ScotE & AmE*— *n* the smallest finger on the hand, which is farthest from the thumb. It used to be considered polite to keep the little finger straight when holding something like a cup, but people now think this is AFFECTED and amusing. —see picture at HAND

little green men /ˌ·· · ˈ·/ *n infml* [P] living beings thought to come from another PLANET, esp. Martians (=imaginary creatures from the planet Mars): *little green men in a flying saucer* | *What causes the crop circles? Little green men or human hoaxers—or neither?*

Little Jack Hor·ner /ˌlɪtl dʒæk ˈhɔːnəʳ‖-ˈhɔːr-/ a character from a NURSERY RHYME (=old song or poem for children):
> *Little Jack Horner sat in a corner,*
> *Eating his Christmas pie;*
> *He put in his thumb, and pulled out a plum,*
> *And said "What a good boy am I".*

Little John /ˌ·· ˈ·/ (in the stories about Robin Hood) one of Robin Hood's men. He was very big and strong, and was called Little John for a joke. —see colour picture on page 620

Little League /ˈ·· ˌ·/ a BASEBALL LEAGUE for children in the US, arranged in the summer in many different towns and cities using money from local businesses: *Are your kids playing in Little League this year?*

▶CULTURAL NOTE Some parents whose children play in Little League become very concerned that their children play well and win games. Parents who put too much pressure on their children to win are sometimes called **Little League parents**, even if the sport their child is involved in is not baseball. —compare BIG LEAGUE◀

Little Lord Faunt·le·roy /ˌlɪtl lɔːd ˈfɔːntlərɔɪ‖-lɔːrd-/ a character in a children's book by Frances Hodgson Burnett. He is a young boy of noble birth, known for his long golden curls, his neat clothes, and his very polite behaviour.

Little Mer·maid /ˌ·· ˈ··/, **The** a story by Hans Christian Andersen in which a MERMAID (=creature that is half-woman, half-fish) falls in love with a human prince and changes her mermaid's body for legs, even though it is very painful. The prince marries a human princess, and the little mermaid dies. The story has been made into a popular CARTOON film.

Little Miss Muf·fet /ˌlɪtl mɪs ˈmʌfɨt/ a character from a NURSERY RHYME (=old song or poem for children) who was frightened away by a SPIDER

Little Nell /ˌlɪtl ˈnel/ a character in the book *The Old Curiosity Shop* by Charles Dickens. People think of the death of Little Nell as one of the saddest things in English literature, although some people consider the story to be too SENTIMENTAL (2).

Little Or·phan An·nie /ˌlɪtl ˌɔːfən ˈæni ‖ -ˌɔːr-/ an American COMIC STRIP character. She is an ORPHAN who gets into a lot of trouble, esp. when the man who takes care of her, Daddy Wabucks, is away.

little peo·ple /ˈ·· ˌ··/ [the +P] *infml* **1** fairies (FAIRY), esp. the Irish LEPRECHAUNS: *He thinks he's talking to the* *little people.* **2** the people in a country or organization who have no power: *It's the little people who get hurt by these policies, not the wealthy.*

Little Red Book /ˌ··· ˈ·/, **The** a book written by Mao Tse Tung and also known as the *Thoughts of Chairman Mao*

Little Red Hen /ˌ··· ˈ·/, **The** a children's story, in which the Little Red Hen cannot persuade her friends to help her in her work. Each time they refuse, the little red hen says "I'll do it myself."

Little Red Riding Hood and the Big Bad Wolf

Little Red Rid·ing·hood /ˌlɪtl red ˈraɪdɪŋhʊd/ also **Red Riding Hood**— a character in a children's story of the same name. In the story a WOLF eats Little Red Ridinghood's grandmother and puts on her clothes. When Little Red Ridinghood goes to visit her grandmother she is surprised by her appearance and says, "Oh, Grandma, what big teeth you've got!" "All the better to eat you with", says the wolf. A wood-cutter kills the wolf, cuts open its stomach, and saves Little Red Ridinghood and her grandmother.

Little Rock /ˈ··· ·/ the capital of the US state of Arkansas. It is famous as the place where in 1957 the US army supported an order that black and white children should mix in the same school.

little toe /ˌ··· ˈ·/ n the smallest toe on the outside of the foot

little wom·an /ˌ··· ˈ··/ [*the*] (an expression for mentioning) one's wife; often considered offensive, esp. by women

Little Wo·men /ˌ··· ˈ··/ the title of a famous children's book by Louisa M. Alcott, an American writer, about a family of four sisters

Lit·tle·wood /ˈlɪtlwʊd/, **Joan** /dʒəʊn/ (1914–) an English left-wing theatre director who tried new ways of expressing (esp. political) ideas in the theatre

Lit·tle·woods /ˈlɪtlwʊdz/ one of a group of British shops selling clothes, food, and electrical goods

Littlewoods Pools /ˌ··· ˈ·/ n [P] POOLS arranged in Britain by a company called Littlewoods. People risk small amounts of money on the results of certain football matches, and those who guess the results correctly win large shares of the money that everyone has put in.

lit·to·ral /ˈlɪtərəl/ n, adj tech (an area of land) near the coast

li·tur·gi·cal /lɪˈtɜːdʒɪkəl‖-ɜːr-/ adj fml like or used in a liturgy – – **ly** /kli/ adv

lit·ur·gy /ˈlɪtədʒi‖-ər-/ n **1** [C] a form of worship in the Christian church, using prayers, songs, etc., according to fixed patterns in religious services **2** [*the*] (*sometimes cap.*) the written form of these services

Lit·vi·nov /lɪtˈviːnɒf‖-nɔːf/, **Maxim** (1876–1951) a Soviet politician who obtained US recognition of the USSR

liv·a·ble , liveable /ˈlɪvəbəl/ adj **1** [(IN)] suitable to live in; HABITABLE: *The house is not livable (in).* **2** [(WITH)] bearable; endurable (ENDURE): *The pain is bad, but it's livable (with).*

live¹ /lɪv/ v **1** [I] to be alive; have life: *Humans and animals have an equal right to live.* **2** [I] to continue to be alive: *His illness is so serious, he is unlikely to live.* | *She lived to a great age.* | *She won't live much longer if she keeps taking drugs.* | (fig.) A *writer's words can live beyond his death.* | (written on a wall) *'Elvis lives!'* (=We feel that Elvis Presley is still alive.) | (fml) *Long live the King!* (an expression of loyal support) **3** [I+adv/prep] to have one's home: *Where do you live?* | *I live in Maple Road/in Liverpool.* | *Fish live in water.* | (fig., infml) *Where does this hammer live?* (=where is it usually kept?) **4** [I (by, on)]

to keep oneself alive (with food, money, work, etc.): *They barely earn enough to live.* | *Sheep live on* (=live by eating) *grass.* | *The islanders live by fishing.* | *Their little bit of land doesn't provide enough food to live on.* **5** [I +adv/prep;T] to pass or spend (one's life): *to live one's life alone* | *to live a life of luxury* | *She lived in fear of her life/of being attacked.* | *He lived ten years as a monk.* | *I don't know how she lives like that, never leaving the house.* **6** [I] to lead an interesting varied life: *My job's OK, but I want to live, not just to exist!* | *Now we're really living!* **7 and they all lived happily ever after** a phrase used at the end of old stories for children, now often used humorously **8 live a lie** to continually behave in a way that hides what one is really like or how one feels: *My marriage was never really happy—I was living a lie all those years.* **9 live and learn** to have learnt something surprising: *Do Americans really have a higher body temperature than Europeans? Well, you live and learn!* **10 live and let live** to accept the behaviour of other people; be TOLERANT **11 live by/on one's wits** to get money by clever tricks rather than by an ordinary job, esp. dishonestly **12 live on borrowed time** to continue to be alive or exist after the time when one could have been expected to die **13 live in sin** old-fash, euph or humor (of two unmarried people) to live together as if married **14 live it up** infml to have a wild good time; enjoy oneself with eating and drinking, parties, spending, etc.

▷ USAGE 1 When talking about the place where people live, **dwell** (*lit*) and **reside** (*fml* or *pomp*) are used like **live**: *I live in London.* | *We visited the wise man who dwelt in the mountains.* | *People residing abroad are not subject to tax.* **Inhabit** means "to live in" and is usually used in formal descriptions of animal or human populations: *These monkeys inhabit the tropical forests.* | *Nomadic tribes inhabit the Northern deserts.* 2 When talking about a short period of time use **stay** and not **live**: *Which hotel are you staying at?* | *I'm staying with friends.*◁

live by sthg. *phr v* [T *no pass.*] to behave according to the rules of: *He lives by a strict moral code.* —see also LIVE¹ (4)

live sthg. ↔ **down** *phr v* [T] to make people forget about (something bad or shameful one has done), esp. by later good behaviour: *Do you remember when I was sick all over the mayoress's shoes? I don't think I'll ever live it down!*

live for sthg./sbdy. *phr v* [T *no pass.*] to give most attention to; seem to have as one's main reason for living: *She lives for her work/her children.*

live in *phr v* [I] (esp. formerly of a servant) to live in the place where one is employed —compare LIVE **out**(3); see also LIVE-IN

live off sthg./sbdy. *phr v* [T] *sometimes derog* to get one's food or income from: *I live off my investments.* | *He's nearly 30 and he still lives off his parents.* | *We were in enemy territory and had to live off the land.* (=get food from fields and trees, by killing animals, etc.)

live on *phr v* [I] to continue in life or use; SURVIVE: *She is dead but her memory lives on.* (=people still remember her) —see also LIVE¹ (4)

live out *phr v* **1** [T] (**live out** sthg.) to live till the end of: *Will the old man live out the month?* | *I don't want to live out my life in this hole.* **2** [T] (**live out** sthg.) to experience in reality: *Her success enabled her to live out her wildest fantasies.* **3** [I] (esp. formerly of a servant) to live in a place away from one's place of work —compare LIVE **in**

live through sthg. *phr v* [T] to remain alive during and in spite of (a difficult or dangerous period): *He lived through two world wars.* | *to live through a famine*

live together *phr v* [I] (of two people) to live with each other, having a sexual relationship, but without being married

live up to sthg. *phr v* [T] to keep to the high standards of: *Did the film live up to your expectations?* (=was it as good as you expected?)

live with sbdy./sthg. *phr v* [T] **1** to live in the same house as (someone else) in a sexual relationship, but without being married **2** to accept (a difficult or unpleasant situation, esp. one that continues for a long period): *I don't enjoy the situation, but I can live with it.*

live² /laɪv/ adj **1** [A] alive; living: *The cat was playing with a live mouse.* —opposite **dead 2** (of lighted coal, wood, etc.) still burning: *a live match* **3** still able to explode:

live ammunition —compare DEAD[1] (3) **4** carrying electricity which can give a shock to anyone who touches it: *live wires* —compare DEAD[1] (3) **5 a** (of broadcasting) seen and/or heard as it happens: *It wasn't a recorded show; it was live.* **b** (of popular entertainers) actually appearing in person: *Liza Minelli live in concert* **6** still able to attract interest: *a live issue/concern* **7 a real live** ... *infml* (used, esp. by or to children, for giving force to a noun, esp. when something unexpected is seen): *Look! A real live elephant!*

live³ /laɪv/ *adv* with a performance, event, etc., being shown as it actually happens: *The President's speech was broadcast live.*

Live Aid /ˈlaɪv eɪd/ the name of two popular music concerts held in London and Philadelphia on the same day in 1985, arranged by Bob Geldof to raise money for people dying of hunger in Ethiopia. Many famous popular musicians took part without being paid. Seen on television by many people around the world, the concerts raised millions of pounds and led to other events such as Sport Aid and Comic Relief to help people in THIRD WORLD countries. — see also BAND AID, COMIC RELIEF

live birth /ˌlaɪv ˈbɜːθ‖-ˈbɜːrθ/ *n* a birth in which the baby is born alive; an expression used in official figures: *the number of live births per thousand of population*

-lived see WORD FORMATION

lived-in /ˈ·ˌ·/ *adj* (of a room or a house) used by people for real everyday activities and not kept unnaturally beautiful, clean, and tidy just for show: *The sitting-room had a lived-in look.*

live-in /ˈlɪv ɪn/ *adj* [A] **1** *infml* ‖also **sleep-in** *AmE* being someone who sleeps and eats in a house where they are employed: *a live-in housekeeper* **2** *often derog.* being someone who lives with their sexual partner without being married: *a live-in boyfriend/lover*

live·li·hood /ˈlaɪvlihʊd/ *n* the way one earns money to live on: *I don't just do it for fun — it's my livelihood.*

live·long /ˈlɪvlɒŋ‖-lɔːŋ/ *adj* [A] *poet* (of the day or night) whole: *all the livelong day*

live·ly /ˈlaɪvli/ *adj* **1** full of quick and often cheerful movement, thought, activity, etc.: *a lively song | a lively mind | The subject produced a lively debate in Parliament.* **2** bright; VIVID: *lively colours* **3** (in sport) which has or causes quick movement (of the ball): *bowling the ball at a lively pace* **4** in BASEBALL, likely to travel far once hit: *It's a lively ball — there've been three doubles this inning alone.* **5** *infml or humor* troublesome; difficult: *We'll make it lively for him/give him a lively time!* —**liness** *n* [U]

Lively, Pe·nel·o·pe /pɪ̩ˈneləpi/ (1933–) an English writer who has written several NOVELS and children's stories, and won the Booker Prize in 1987

liv·en /ˈlaɪvən/ *v*
liven up *phr v* [I;T (=liven sthg. ↔ up)] to (cause to) become lively: *Let's liven up the party with a little dancing.*

liv·er¹ /ˈlɪvəʳ/ *n* **1** [C] a large organ in the body which produces BILE and cleans the blood **2** [U] this organ from an animal's body, used as food: *liver and onions*

liver² *n* a person who lives in the stated way: *a clean liver* (=someone who leads a healthy or morally correct life)

live rail /ˌlaɪv ˈreɪl/ *n* a thick metal bar which runs alongside the track of an electric railway and supplies electricity to the trains' motors: *"Danger — live rail"* (notice near a railway track)

Li·ver Buil·ding /ˈlaɪvə ˌbɪldɪŋ‖-vər-/ [the] a well-known building in Liverpool, on the side of the river Mersey. On it are two figures of the **Liver Bird**, an imaginary bird which is the SYMBOL of Liverpool.

liv·e·ried /ˈlɪvərid/ *adj* wearing LIVERY: *a liveried servant/chauffeur*

liv·er·ish /ˈlɪvərɪʃ/ *adj esp. BrE infml* feeling slightly ill, esp. after eating and/or drinking too much

Liv·er·pool /ˈlɪvəpuːl‖-vər-/ the third largest city in Britain, on the river Mersey in the NW of England —see colour map on page 818

▶CULTURAL NOTE Liverpool was formerly a great port. Many people left England from Liverpool for a new life in America, and many Irish people came to Liverpool to look for work. Work in the port and in industry has decreased sharply and Liverpool has a serious unemployment

problem, as well as problems with housing and local government. Liverpool has been important in the popular music world, esp. in the 1960s when the **Beatles** started there. A person who comes from Liverpool is called a **Liverpudlian** or (*infml*) a **Scouser**. The kind of English spoken in Liverpool is known informally as **Scouse.◀**

Liverpool Street /ˈ··· ·/ one of the mainline railway stations in London —see colour map on page 817

Liv·er·pud·li·an /ˌlɪvəˈpʌdliən◀‖-vər-/ *n, adj* (a person) of or from Liverpool

liver saus·age /ˈ··· ˌ··/ *esp. BrE* ‖ **liv·er·wurst** /ˈlɪvəwɜːst ‖ ˈlɪvərwɜːrst/*AmE*— *n* [U] a type of cooked soft SAUSAGE made mainly of LIVER, and eaten (often spread) on bread

liv·er·wort /ˈlɪvəwɜːt‖-vərwɜːrt/ *n* a small flat green flowerless plant growing in wet places which is like MOSS except that it has leaves

liv·e·ry /ˈlɪvəri/ *n* **1** [C;U] uniform of a special type for servants employed by a particular person: *The door was opened by a servant in livery.* **2** [U] *poet* clothing or covering: *the trees with their green livery of spring*

livery com·pa·ny /ˈ··· ˌ···/ *n* any of several ancient trade associations (GUILDS) in London

liv·e·ry·man /ˈlɪvərimən/ *n* -**men** /mən/ a member of a livery company

livery sta·ble /ˈ··· ˌ··/ also **livery stables** *pl.*— *n* a place where people can pay to have their horses kept, fed, etc., or where horses can be hired for use

lives /laɪvz/ *pl. of* LIFE

live·stock /ˈlaɪvstɒk‖-stɑːk/ *n* [P] animals kept on a farm, such as cattle or sheep

live wire /ˌlaɪv ˈwaɪəʳ/ *n* **1** a wire charged with electricity **2** a very active person

liv·id /ˈlɪvɪd/ *adj* **1** *infml* very angry; FURIOUS: *She'll be livid if she finds out.* **2** blue-grey, as of marks on the skin after being hit: *livid bruises* **3** *lit* (of the face) very pale — ~**ly** *adv*

liv·ing¹ /ˈlɪvɪŋ/ *adj* **1** alive now: *She has no living relatives.| the greatest living English writer | She is* **living proof** *of the effectiveness of this operation.* (=the fact that she is alive proves it is effective) [also *n, the* +P] *the living and the dead* **2** existing in use: *a living language* —compare DEAD[1] (2) **3** exact in likeness: **the living image of** *his father*

living² *n* **1** [C] a means of providing oneself with what is necessary for life: *She earns a living as a writer.* | *What do you do for a living?* (=What is your job?) | *He makes a good living* (=earns a lot of money) *by selling insurance.* **2** [U] (*often in comb.*) a standard or way of arranging one's life: *plain living | a decline in living standards* —see also COST OF LIVING, STANDARD OF LIVING **3** [C] a BENEFICE

living death /ˌ·· ˈ·/ *n* [*usu. sing.*] a life so bad that it would be better to be dead

living fos·sil /ˌ·· ˈ··/ *n* an animal or plant of a very ancient type, which lives now although it was thought no longer to exist

living le·gend /ˌ·· ˈ··/ *n* a person who is very famous like a person in an old story that everyone knows, but who is still alive: *Bannister's four-minute mile made him a living legend.*

living mem·o·ry /ˌ·· ˈ···/ *n* **within/in living memory** (of an event or time) which is not very long ago because there are people still alive who can remember it: *the worst storm in living memory*

living quar·ters /ˈ·· ˌ··/ *n* [P] a place where people live, esp. on a ship or in an army or industrial camp: *the cramped living quarters on a submarine | The quarrymen's living quarters were close to their place of work.*

living room /ˈ·· ·/ also **sitting room** *BrE*— *n* the main room in a house where people usu. sit and do things together, usu. apart from eating —compare DRAWING ROOM, FRONT ROOM, LOUNGE, PARLOUR (2)

living stan·dard /ˈ·· ˌ··/ also **living standards**— *n* [P] STANDARD OF LIVING

Liv·ing·ston /ˈlɪvɪŋstən/ a town in central SE Scotland, redeveloped as a NEW TOWN in 1962

Liv·ing·stone¹ /ˈlɪvɪŋstən, -stəʊn/, **Doctor David** (1813–73) a Scottish MISSIONARY and EXPLORER of Africa; the first European to see the Zambezi River and the Victoria Falls. A JOURNALIST, Henry Stanley, who did not know

living room

- light
- bookcase
- picture
- pelmet *BrE*/valance *AmE*
- houseplant
- standard lamp *BrE*/floor lamp *AmE*
- curtain
- stereo
- armchair
- television
- cushion
- radiator
- speaker
- video
- table lamp
- coffee table
- radio
- pouffe
- sofa/settee/couch *AmE*
- rug
- skirting board *BrE*/baseboard *AmE*
- carpet

Livingstone, went to look for him. When they met he said, just as if they were meeting in London, "Dr Livingstone, I presume." People sometimes say this as a joke.

Livingstone², **Ken** (1945–) the Labour leader of the Greater London Council, the local government of London until 1986 when it was broken up by the Conservative government of Mrs Thatcher. He is now an MP. He is sometimes called **Red Ken** because of his LEFT-WING views.

living things /ˌ‥ ˈ‥/ n [P] plants and animals, including humans, that are alive

living wage /ˌ‥ ˈ‥/ n [S] a wage which is enough to buy the necessary things for daily life

living will /ˌ‥ ˈ‥/ n AmE a written instruction on what medical and legal decisions should be made if one becomes very ill and unable to express one's wishes. Living wills are not legal documents so doctors, lawyers, and the person's family can decide not to do what the person has said, but they can help make it clear what decisions the person would have made

Liv·y /ˈlɪvi/ (59BC–AD17) a Roman HISTORIAN who wrote a history of Rome and the Roman Empire

liz·ard /ˈlɪzəd‖-ərd/ n a usu. small creature which is a REPTILE, with a rough skin, four legs, and a long tail

Lizard [the] a piece of land in the SW of England that sticks out into the sea. It is the place furthest to the south in the British MAINLAND.

Ljub·lja·na /luːbˈljɑːnə‖liːˌuː-/ the capital of Slovenia in NW Yugoslavia

ll written abbrev. for: lines: see ll 104–201

lla·ma /ˈlɑːmə/ n -mas or -ma a South American animal with thick woolly hair, rather like a CAMEL but without a HUMP, sometimes used for carrying goods

Llan·dud·no /lænˈdɪdnəʊ/ a holiday town in N Wales

Llan·fair·pwll·gwyn·gyll·go·ger·y·chwyrn·dro·bwll·llan ·ty·si·lio·go·go·goch /hlænˌvaɪrpʊhlˌgwɪŋɪhlgɒˌgerə xwɪrnˌdrɒbʊhlˌhlæntɪˌsɪljɒˌgɒgɒˈgɒx ‖ -əʊ- for -ɒ-/ also **Llanfair PG** /ˌlænfeə piː ˈdʒiː ‖ -ˈfeər-/ a small village in Wales, famous for having the longest place-name in Britain

LLB n abbrev. for: Bachelor of Laws; a title for someone who has a first university degree in law

LLD n abbrev. for: Doctor of Laws; a title for someone who has a DOCTORATE in law

Lloyd /lɔɪd/, **Ma·rie** /ˈmɑːri/ (1870–1922) a famous MUSIC HALL performer who used to sing humorous songs full of

sexual suggestion. Some of her songs are still popular, e.g. A Little of What you Fancy Does you Good.

Lloyd George /ˌ‥ ˈ‥/, **David** (1863–1945) a Liberal politician whose parents were Welsh and who was British PRIME MINISTER from 1916 to 1922. He was against increasing the British Empire and in favour of political change. He introduced PENSIONS and National Insurance. There is an old popular song called Lloyd George knew my father and most people know this phrase.

Lloyd's /lɔɪdz/ **1** also **Lloyd's of London**– an association of people who offer insurance, esp. for high-risk activities such as shipping **2** Lloyd's Bank

Lloyd's Bank /ˌ‥ ˈ‥/ also **Lloyd's**– one of the main British banks, branches of which can be found in many towns and cities in Britain

Lloyd's Re·gis·ter of Ships /ˌ‥ ‥‥ ‥ ˈ‥/ a list of ships, boats etc. produced every year, containing information about the condition and size of the VESSELS (=ship, boat, etc.)

Lloyd Web·ber /ˌlɔɪd ˈwebər/, **Sir Andrew** (1948–) an English writer of very successful MUSICALS including Cats and The Phantom of the Opera. He also directs performances in the theatre.

LMS /ˌel em ˈes/ n [U] local management of schools; (in Britain) a system by which the school rather than the local education authority is responsible for the financial and ADMINISTRATIVE management of STATE SCHOOLS

lo /ləʊ/ interj old use look —see also LO AND BEHOLD

load¹ /ləʊd/ n **1** something that is being or is to be carried, esp. something heavy that is carried by a vehicle, ship, person, animal, etc.: a cargo ship carrying a load of grain | a woman with a load of shopping | A truck has **shed its load** (=its load has accidentally fallen off) on the motorway. | (fig.) Her grief is a heavy load to bear. **2** (in comb.) the amount which the stated vehicle can carry: a bus-load of schoolchildren | I've ordered two lorry-loads of sand. **3** the amount of work that must be done by a member of a group, a machine, etc.: I have a fairly light teaching load this term. (=I do not have many lessons to teach) | The machine can't cope with such a heavy work load. **4** the (amount of) weight borne by the frame of a building or structure: a load-bearing wall | What is the maximum load that the bridge will take? **5** the power of an electricity supply **6 a load off someone's mind** the removing of a worry: When I heard they'd arrived safely it was a great load off my mind. **7 get a load of** sl (usu. in commands) to look at or pay attention to (something surprising, exciting, shocking, etc.) **8 loads of** also **a load of**– infml a large amount of; a lot of: She's got loads of money. | Thanks loads. | That book is **a load of** (old) rubbish.

load² v **1** [I;T (UP)] to put (a load) on or in (a vehicle, structure, etc.): Have you finished loading (up)? | Load up the van. | Load the furniture into the van. | Load the van (up) with furniture. | (fig.) They loaded me with presents. —see also LADEN   **2** [T] to put bullets, etc. into (a gun) or film into (a camera): Don't move! This gun is loaded.   **3** [T] to put a PROGRAM into (a computer): You'll have to load the program before you can play the game.

load sbdy./sthg. ↔ **down** phr v [T (**with**)] to cause or force to carry heavy things: I was loaded down with books|(fig.) with all my worries. —compare WEIGH **down**

load·ed /ˈləʊdɪd/ adj   **1** unfairly favouring one side: a loaded statement | The argument was loaded in his favour.   **2** usu. derog (of a question) put in such a way as to suggest a particular answer   **3** [F] sl having lots of money: Let him pay: he's loaded!   **4** [F] sl drunk   **5** (of DICE) weighted so that they fall in only a certain way: a pair of loaded dice meant to roll double sevens

load·ing /ˈləʊdɪŋ/ n an additional amount added to the cost of insurance because of a special risk

loading gauge /ˈ·· ˌ·/ n the limit on the amount that can be loaded on to a railway WAGON

Loads·a·mon·ey /ˈləʊdzəmʌni/ an amusing British television character invented by Harry Enfield who talks proudly about always having lots of money

load·star /ˈləʊdstɑːʳ/ n a LODESTAR

load·stone /ˈləʊdstəʊn/ n a LODESTONE

loaf¹ /ləʊf/ n **loaves** /ləʊvz/   **1** [C] a single mass of bread shaped and baked in one piece, which is usu. fairly large and can be cut into SLICES: a loaf of bread —compare ROLL² (4) —see also FRENCH LOAF

▶CULTURAL NOTE Most people know the Bible story in which Jesus was able to feed 5000 people with only five loaves and two fishes.◀

2 [C;U] (usu. in comb.) food (e.g. a sweet or SAVOURY mixture) prepared in a solid piece: (a) meat loaf | a slice of walnut loaf   **3 half a loaf is better than none/no bread** it is better to have half of something than nothing at all   **4** BrE old-fash sl **use one's loaf** to behave (more) sensibly

loaf² v [I (ABOUT, AROUND)] infml to waste time, esp. by not working when one should

loaf·er /ˈləʊfəʳ/ n   **1** someone who loafs   **2** a light shoe with a flat bottom and leather top that you slip your foot into

loam /ləʊm/ n [U] good quality soil made of sand, clay, and decayed plant material —**loamy** adj

loan¹ /ləʊn/ n   **1** something which is lent, esp. money: a £1000 loan | We took out a loan (=borrowed some money) to expand the business. | How much interest do they charge on loans?   **2** the act of lending; permission to borrow: She offered me the loan of her car.   **3 on loan** being borrowed, as a book is from a library: This picture is on loan from the Louvre to the National Gallery.

loan² v [T (**to**)]   **1** esp. AmE to give (someone) the use of (something); lend: [+obj(i)+obj(d)] Can you loan me your tennis racket?   **2** to lend (esp. something valuable) for a long period: She loaned her collection of paintings to the gallery. —compare BORROW

loan cap·i·tal /ˈ· ˌ···/ n [U] the money a company has borrowed, either on a MORTGAGE or by the ISSUE of DEBENTURES

lo and be·hold /ˌ· · ·ˈ·/ interj infml (an expression of surprise at something unexpected): She had looked everywhere for her key when lo and behold there it was in her bag!

loan shark /ˈ· ˌ·/ n derog someone who lends money at unreasonably high INTEREST rates

loan·word /ˈləʊnwɜːd/ n a word taken into one language from another: In English there are loanwords from many other languages.

loath, loth /ləʊθ/ adj   **1** [F+to-v] unwilling; RELUCTANT: I've had this old car a long time; I'm loath to part with it.   **2 nothing loath** lit quite willing

loathe /ləʊð/ v [T not in progressive forms] to feel hatred or great dislike for: He is loathed by most of his staff because of his unfairness and ruthlessness. [+v-ing] I loathe having to get up so early in the morning!

loath·ing /ˈləʊðɪŋ/ n [S;U] hatred; a feeling of DISGUST

loath·some /ˈləʊðsəm/ adj which causes loathing; extremely unpleasant: the loathsome smell of rotting flesh — —**ly** adv — —**ness** n [U]

loaves /ləʊvz/ pl. of LOAF¹

lob¹ /lɒb||lɑːb/ n [C] (in sports, esp. TENNIS) a ball hit or thrown in a slow high curve

lob² v **-bb-** [T] to send (a ball) in a lob: She lobbed the ball high over her opponent's head.

lob·by¹ /ˈlɒbi||ˈlɑːbi/ n   **1** a wide hall or passage which leads from the entrance to the rooms inside a public building: the hotel lobby —compare FOYER   **2** (in the British Parliament) **a** a hall where members of parliament and the public meet **b** either of two passages where members go to vote for or against something   **3** [+sing./pl. v] a group of people who try to persuade a Member of Parliament, a member of Congress, or public official to support or oppose certain actions: The minister was met by a lobby of industrialists. —see also LOBBY²   **4** [+sing./pl. v] a group of people who unite for or against a planned action in an attempt to persuade those in power to change their minds: The clean-air lobby is/are against the plans for the new factory. | a powerful anti-smoking lobby

lobby² v [I (**for, against**);T] to meet or attempt to influence (someone with political power) in order to persuade them to support one's actions, needs, or beliefs. In Britain PRESSURE GROUPS (=groups who want a particular change in the law) lobby members of parliament to try to achieve what they want. In the US, **lobbyists** lobby Congress to try to achieve their aims: They are lobbying for a reduction in defence spending. [+obj+to-v] We are lobbying our MP to support the new law.

Lobby cor·re·spon·dent /ˈ·· ··ˌ·ˌ·/ also **Lobby jour·nal·ist** /ˈ·· ˌ···/— n a newspaper writer or broadcaster who is allowed to work in the British parliament

lobe /ləʊb/ n   **1** also **earlobe**— the round fleshy piece at the bottom of the ear —see picture at HEAD   **2** tech a rounded division of an organ, esp. of the brain or lungs —see picture at HEAD —**lobed** /ləʊbd/ adj

lo·bot·o·my /ləʊˈbɒtəmi, lə-||-ˈbɑː-/ also **leucotomy** BrE— n (an operation for) the cutting away of part of the brain in order to make violent or uncontrolled PATIENTS calm. The operation is performed less often now than formerly because it has an effect on the person's ability to think and make decisions. —**mize, -mise** v [T]

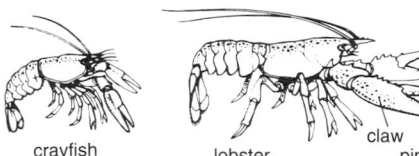

lobster

crayfish   lobster   claw   pincer

lob·ster /ˈlɒbstəʳ||ˈlɑːb-/ n   **1** [C] a large eight-legged sea animal with a shell and two large CLAWS. Its meat is quite expensive, and can be eaten after boiling, when the shell turns bright red.   **2** [U] lobster meat as food

lob·ster·pot /ˈlɒbstəpɒt||ˈlɑːbstərpɑːt/ n a trap shaped like a basket, in which lobsters are caught

lo·cal¹ /ˈləʊkəl/ adj   **1** of, in, or serving the needs of, a certain place or area, esp. the place one lives in: the/our local doctor | local news | a local radio station   **2** tech limited to one part, esp. of the body: a local infection | a local anaesthetic —see also LOCALLY; see TOPICAL (USAGE)

local² n infml   **1** [often pl.] someone who lives in the area where one finds them: I asked one of the locals which way to go.   **2** BrE a PUB near where one lives, esp. a pub which one often drinks at: having a pint in/at his local —see also PUB   **3** esp. AmE a bus, train, etc., that stops at all regular stopping places —compare EXPRESS² (1)   **4** AmE a branch of a trade union

lo·cal /ˌləʊ ˈkæl◄/ adj LOW-CAL

local ar·e·a net·work /ˌ·· ·ˌ·· ˈ··/ n see LAN

local au·thor·i·ty /ˌ·· ·ˈ···/ n [C + sing./pl.v] in Britain, the government for the city, town, or area, responsible for services such as schools and street-cleaning: cuts in local authority spending

local col·our /ˌ·· ˈ··/ n [U] additional details in a story or picture which are true to the place being represented, making it seem real

local coun·cil /ˌ·· ˈ··/ n a small division of British local government, responsible for providing services e.g.

housing and RECREATION in a particular area, usu. a town

local der·by /ˌ·· ˈ··/ n BrE a football match between two teams from the same area

lo·cale /ləʊˈkɑːl/ n fml a place where something particular happens or is done: We must choose a suitable locale for the outdoor scenes in the film.

Local Ed·u·ca·tion Au·thor·i·ty /ˌ·· ··ˈ·· ·ˌ···/ also **LEA**— n [C+sing.|pl.v] the organisation which in Britain is responsible for schools and colleges in a particular area and pays the wages of the teachers in that area —compare SCHOOL DISTRICT

local e·lec·tions /ˌ·· ·ˈ··/ n [P] (in Britain) elections in which COUNCILLORs are chosen for a local government area

local gov·ern·ment /ˌ·· ˈ···/ n [C;U] the government of cities, towns, etc. —see also extra information on page 568

local health au·thor·i·ty /ˌ·· ·ˈ·ˌ···/ n (in Britain) an organization which controls hospitals and medical services in a particular area, e.g. a COUNTY[1]

local his·tor·i·an /ˌ·· ·ˈ···/ n a person who studies the history of a particular area, usu. the one where she/he lives

local his·to·ry /ˌ·· ˈ···/ n [U] the history of a particular area: She knows a lot about local history—she'll be able to tell you when these houses were built.

lo·cal·i·ty /ləʊˈkælɪti/ n rather fml a particular area; DISTRICT: There are several cinemas in the locality. (=near the place being spoken of)

lo·cal·ized also **-ised** BrE /ˈləʊkəlaɪzd/ adj esp. fml or tech (esp. of something undesirable) within a small area: a localized infection | localized outbreaks of fighting

lo·cal·ly /ˈləʊkəli/ adv **1** in a local area: Most of the country will be dry, but there may be some rain locally. (=in particular areas) **2** near the place one is talking about: We have no shops locally. | I live locally, so it's easy to get to this office.

local op·tion /ˌ·· ˈ··/ n BrE the right which a part of a country may have to decide whether alcohol should be sold in that area

local pa·per /ˌ·· ˈ··/ also **local rag** /ˌ·· ˈ·/ BrE infml— n a newspaper which gives the news and carries advertisements from people and businesses in the area where it is published (PUBLISH): Where's the local paper? I want to see what's on at the pictures. | My daughter's wedding was in the local paper.

local ra·di·o /ˌ·· ˈ···/ n [U] the group of radio stations operated by the BBC or the IBA which broadcast programmes esp. intended for a particular small area, e.g. local news and programmes of interest to local people: The village fete was advertised on local radio.

local time /ˈ·· ·/ n [U] the time system in a particular part of the world: We will arrive in New York at ten o'clock local time.

lo·cate /ləʊˈkeɪt‖ˈləʊkeɪt/ v fml **1** [T] to find the position of: We've located the source of the signals, sir. **2** [T+obj+adv|prep; usu. pass.] to fix or set in a certain place; SITUATE: The house is located by the river. | The offices are conveniently located in the centre of town. **3** [I+adv|prep] AmE to come and establish oneself or itself: The firm finally located in Dallas.

lo·ca·tion /ləʊˈkeɪʃən/ n **1** [C] rather fml a particular place or position: a suitable location for a camp —see POSITION (USAGE) **2** [C;U] a place outside or away from a film STUDIO, where one or more scenes are made for a film: It was difficult to find a suitable location. | Most of the film was shot **on location** in Africa. **3** [U] the act of locating or state of being located: the location of the plane by radar

loch /lɒx, lɒk‖lɑːk, lɑːx/ n ScotE **1** a lake **2** a part of the sea partly enclosed by land

Loch Lo·mond /ˌlɒx ˈləʊmənd, ˌlɑːk-‖ˌlɑːk-, ˌlɑːx-/ a lake in W Scotland near Glasgow, popular with tourists. There is a well-known old song about Loch Lomond which contains the words:
    For me and my true love will never meet again
    On the bonnie bonnie banks o' Loch Lomond.

Loch Ness Mon·ster /ˌlɒx nes ˈmɒnstəʳ, ˌlɒk- ‖ ˌlɑːk nes ˈmɑːn-, ˌlɑːx-/ also **Nessie**— [the] the name given to a very large animal, supposed to live in **Loch Ness** (a large, very deep lake in N Scotland), which people say does not look like any other animal alive today. Although some people

the Loch Ness Monster

believe the Loch Ness Monster really exists and say they have seen it, there is no scientific proof, and for most people it is just a story. It is often shown in pictures etc. as a creature like a large black or green DINOSAUR.

lo·ci /ˈləʊsaɪ/ pl. of LOCUS

lock[1] /lɒk‖lɑːk/ n **1** [C] an apparatus for closing and fastening something, usu. by means of a key: Turn the key in the lock to open the door. | After the burglary she had all the locks changed. | a childproof lock on the car doors —see also COMBINATION LOCK and see picture at CAR **2** [C] a stretch of water closed off by gates, esp. on a CANAL, so that the water level can be raised or lowered to move boats up or down a slope: The lock keeper closed the lock gates. **3** [C] a hold which some fighters can use, esp. wrestlers (WRESTLE), to prevent their opponent from moving: an arm lock **4** [U] (in a machine) the state of being stopped in such a way that operation is not possible: in the lock position **5** [C;U] esp. BrE the degree to which a STEERING WHEEL can be turned to change the direction of travel: full lock **6 lock, stock, and barrel** (of an act that has an effect on several things) completely: We had to sell all our possessions|the whole company, lock, stock, and barrel. **7 under lock and key: a** safely hidden and fastened in **b** imprisoned

lock[2] v **1** [I;T] to fasten with a lock: Lock the door. | The door won't lock. **2** [T+obj+adv|prep] to put in a safe place and lock the entrance or opening: She locked her jewels in the safe. **3** [T +obj+adv|prep; usu. pass.] to hold or fasten firmly: The two fighters were locked together. | The lovers were locked in a deep embrace. | (fig.) We found ourselves locked into a senseless dispute with the management. **4** [I] to become fixed or blocked: I can't control the car: the wheels have locked. (=cannot be turned or moved) —**able** adj **5** infml **lock horns** to fight or argue with someone: She locked horns with him over the subject of equal pay for women.

    lock sbdy./sthg. ↔ **away** phr v [T] to LOCK up (2, 4): We looked all our valuables away before we went on holiday.

    lock sbdy./sthg. ↔ **in** phr v [T] to put or keep (esp. a person or animal) in an enclosed place and prevent them from leaving, esp. by locking a door: Help me, somebody — I'm locked in!

    lock onto sthg. phr v [T] (esp. of a MISSILE) to find and follow closely (the object to be attacked)

    lock sbdy. ↔ **out** phr v [T] **1** [(of)] to keep out of a place by locking the entrance: I forgot my key and found myself locked out of my flat. **2** usu. derog to prevent (workers) from entering a place of work until a disagreement is settled as the employers want it —see also LOCKOUT

    lock up phr v **1** [I;T (=lock sthg. ↔ up)] to make (a building) safe by locking the doors, esp. for the night: Lock (the house) up when you leave. **2** [T] (**lock** sthg. ↔ up) also **lock away**— to put in a safe place and fasten the lock: Lock it up in a drawer. **3** [T] (**lock** sthg. ↔ up) to put (money) where it cannot easily be moved or changed into CASH: All our money is locked up in foreign companies. **4** [T] (**lock** sbdy. ↔ up) also **lock away**— infml **a** to put in prison —see also LOCKUP **b** to put (someone) in a special hospital for mad people: She's crazy; she ought to be locked up!

lock[3] n a small piece of hair: She keeps a lock of his hair. —see also LOCKS

Locke /lɒk‖lɑːk/, **John** (1632–1704) an English PHILOSOPHER whose ideas on religious and political freedom were influential, esp. in France and the US, where they influenced the DECLARATION OF INDEPENDENCE

lock·er /ˈlɒkəʳ‖ˈlɑː-/ n **1** a small cupboard for keeping

things in, esp. in a school, factory, or sports building where people can leave their outdoor clothes and personal belongings while they are working or playing —see also DAVY JONES'S LOCKER **2** *AmE* a very cold room used for storing food, as in a restaurant or factory: *a meat locker*

Lock·er·bie /ˈlɒkəbi ‖ ˈlɑːkər-/ a town in SW Scotland. Lockerbie became famous when an American plane crashed onto the town in December 1988 killing 270 people. The plane was carrying a bomb thought to have been put there by TERRORISTS although nobody claimed responsibility. In 1992 the police gave out photographs and names of two Libyan men they believe put the bomb in the aeroplane, but they have not yet been able to arrest the men.

locker room /ˈ··· ·/ *n* a place where lots of lockers are kept, esp. in a sports building, for leaving clothes in

lock·et /ˈlɒkɪt‖ˈlɑː-/ *n* a small piece of jewellery for the neck, consisting of a metal case usu. on a chain in which small pictures or locks of hair can be kept

Lock·heed Cor·po·ra·tion /ˈlɒkhiːd kɔːpəˌreɪʃən ‖ ˈlɑːkhiːd kɔːr-/ an American company that makes aircraft and AEROSPACE products

lock·jaw /ˈlɒkdʒɔː‖ˈlɑːk-/ *n* [U] *infml for* TETANUS

lock keep·er /ˈ· ˌ··/ *n* a person whose job is to open and close the gates of a LOCK[1] (2) on a river or CANAL

lock·out /ˈlɒk-aʊt‖ˈlɑːk-/ *n* the action by an employer of not allowing workers to go back to work, esp. in a factory, until they accept an agreement —see also LOCK **out** (2); compare STRIKE[2] (1)

locks /lɒks‖lɑːks/ *n* [P] *poet* the hair of the head: *"Her locks were yellow as gold … "* (Coleridge, *The Ancient Mariner*) | *flowing locks* —see also LOCK[3]

lock·smith /ˈlɒkˌsmɪθ‖ˈlɑːk-/ *n* a person who makes and repairs locks

lock·stitch /ˈlɒkˌstɪtʃ‖ˈlɑːk-/ *n* the usual type of stitch of a sewing machine in which a thread from above the material and one from below fasten together at small distances apart

lock·up /ˈlɒk-ʌp‖ˈlɑːk-/ *n* a prison, esp. a small one where a criminal can be kept for a short time, as in a village or small town —see also LOCK **up** (4a)

lock-up gar·age /ˌ·· ˈ···‖ˌ·· ·ˈ·/ *n* a garage (=a place to keep cars etc.) which is separate from the user's house, is usu. one of a set of such garages built together, and can be locked up. People whose house does not have its own garage often rent a lock-up garage: *a block of council flats with a row of lock-up garages behind it*

lo·co /ˈləʊkəʊ/ *adj* [F] *sl, esp. AmE* mad; CRAZY

lo·co·mo·tion /ˌləʊkəˈməʊʃən/ *n* [U] *tech* movement; ability to move

lo·co·mo·tive[1] /ˌləʊkəˈməʊtɪv/ *n fml or AmE* a railway engine

locomotive[2] *adj tech* concerning or causing movement: *locomotive power*

lo·co·weed /ˈləʊkəʊwiːd/ *n* an American plant which causes disease in animals if eaten

lo·cum /ˈləʊkəm/ *n esp. BrE* someone, esp. a person in healthcare work, who does another person's job for a limited time: *While our doctor was on holiday his locum treated us.*

lo·cus /ˈləʊkəs/ *n* **-ci** /ˈləʊsaɪ/ *tech or fml* a position or point, esp. where something happens or can be found

locus clas·si·cus /ˌləʊkəs ˈklæsɪkəs/ *n loci classici* /ˌləʊsaɪ ˈklæsɪˌsaɪ/ *Lat, fml* a passage from a written work which has become well known in connection with a particular subject and is often mentioned

lo·cust /ˈləʊkəst/ *n* an Asian and African insect which flies from place to place in large groups, eating and destroying crops over large areas: *a swarm of locusts* —see picture at INSECT

▶ CULTURAL NOTE A Bible story tells how God punished the Egyptians by sending a PLAGUE of locusts. ◀

lo·cu·tion /ləʊˈkjuːʃən/ *n fml or tech* **1** a way of speaking **2** a phrase, esp. one used locally or within a special group of people

lode /ləʊd/ *n tech* an amount of metal in its natural form (ORE)

lode·star, **load-** /ˈləʊdstɑːr/ *n esp. lit* **1** the POLE STAR, used as a guide by sailors **2** a guide or example to follow

lode·stone, **load-** /ˈləʊdstəʊn/ *n* [C;U] (a piece of) iron which acts as a MAGNET

lodge[1] /lɒdʒ‖lɑːdʒ/ *v* **1** [I+*adv/prep*] *fml* to stay, usu. for a short time in return for paying rent: *to lodge at a friend's house|with friends* **2** [T] *esp. BrE* to give or find (someone) a home for a time, usu. for payment: *We lodge students during term time.* **3** [I+*adv/prep*; T+*obj+adv/prep*] to (cause to) settle or become fixed firmly in a position: *A small chicken bone lodged in his throat, and had to be removed by a doctor.* | *The bullet became lodged in her spine.* —see also DISLODGE **4** [T (**with**)] to make (a statement or report) officially to an official person or body: *to lodge a complaint|a protest|an appeal* **5** [T+*obj+adv/prep*] to put into a safe or proper place: *The surveyor's report was lodged with the building society.*

lodge[2] *n* **1** a room for a person who is responsible for seeing who enters a building, as in a block of flats or a college: *the porter's lodge* **2 a** [+*sing./pl. v*] a local branch of some types of social club: *a Masonic lodge* **b** the building where this branch meets **3** a small house for hunters, skiers (SKI[2]), etc., to stay in while crossing wild country or mountains —compare CHALET (2) **4** a small house on the land of a larger house **5** a BEAVER's home **6** *AmE* a WIGWAM **7** *AmE* a hotel building at a RESORT or in the mountains

Lodge[1], David (1935–) an English NOVELIST known for his humorous books such as *Changing Places* and *Small World*

Lodge[2], David (1921–) an English theatre and television actor

lodg·er /ˈlɒdʒər‖ˈlɑː-/ *also* **roomer** *AmE*— *n* a person who pays rent to stay in someone's house

lodg·ing /ˈlɒdʒɪŋ‖ˈlɑː-/ *n* [S;U] a place to stay: *a night's lodging* | *to find lodging* —compare BOARD[1] (3); see also LODGINGS

lodging house /ˈ··· ·/ *also* **rooming house** *AmE*— *n* a building where rooms may be rented for days or weeks

lodg·ings /ˈlɒdʒɪŋz‖ˈlɑː-/ *also* **digs** *BrE infml*— *n* [P] one or more rented furnished rooms: *to stay in lodgings* —compare BOARD[1]

lo·ess /ˈləʊes, -ɪs‖les, lɜːrs, ˈləʊɪs/ *n* [U] a type of soil like a yellowish powder, common in China and parts of Europe and N America

Loewe /ləʊ/, **Fred·e·rick** /ˈfredərɪk/ see LERNER AND LOEWE

loft[1] /lɒft‖lɔːft/ *n* **1 a** a room or space under the roof of a building; an ATTIC **b** *esp. AmE* an upper floor of a business building, esp. one that was originally a single large room used for storing things: *He's living in a converted loft in lower Manhattan.* **2** a room over a STABLE, where HAY is kept: *a hayloft* **3** *tech* a GALLERY (2) in a church: *an organ loft* **4** *tech* a quality of wool, DOWN, or SYNTHETIC materials which allows it to provide warmth: *Sleeping bags filled with synthetic fibres retain their loft when wet and so are more practical in damp conditions.*

loft[2] *v* [T] (esp. in cricket and GOLF) to hit (a ball) high

loft con·ver·sion /ˈ· ·ˌ··/ *n* rooms or a room made out of a house's LOFT (=the space under the roof), some time after the house was built: *We couldn't afford to move to a larger house, so we had a loft conversion done instead.*

Loft·ing /ˈlɒftɪŋ‖ˈlɔːf-/, **Hugh** /hjuː/ (1886–1947) an English writer of children's books, best known for the *Doctor Dolittle* stories about a man who could talk to animals

loft·y /ˈlɒfti‖ˈlɔːfti/ *adj* **1** (of ideas, feelings, writing, etc.) of unusually high moral quality: *lofty aims|ideals* **2** showing that one thinks one is better than other people; HAUGHTY: *a lofty smile* | *lofty disdain* **3** *esp. lit* high: *the lofty walls of the city* —**ily** *adv* : *When I asked for help, he just smiled loftily and turned away.* —**iness** *n* [U]

log[1] /lɒg‖lɔːg, lɑːg/ *n* **1** a thick unshaped piece of wood from a tree, either the whole trunk that has been cut down, or smaller pieces cut off: *chopping logs for the fire* | *a log fire* **2** an official written record of a journey, esp. in a ship or plane: *The captain described the accident in the ship's log.* —see also **sleep like a log** (SLEEP[2])

log[2] *v* **-gg-** **1** [T] to record (in a LOG[1] (2) **2** [T(UP)] (esp. of a ship or plane) to travel (a distance or length of time): *The old plane had logged (up) hundreds of hours of flying time.* **3** [T;I] *AmE* to cut down trees: *This part of the forest was logged three years ago.*

log in/on *phr v* [I] *tech* to begin a period of using a computer system by performing a fixed set of operations: *In order to log in (to the system) you have to type in a special password.*

log off/out *phr v* [I] *tech* to finish a period of using a computer system by performing a fixed set of operations

Lo·gan /ˈləʊgən/, **Mount** a mountain in SW Yukon territory, the highest mountain in Canada

lo·gan·ber·ry /ˈləʊgənbəri‖-beri/ *n* a soft dark-red fruit similar to a RASPBERRY

log·a·rith·m /ˈlɒgərɪðəm‖ˈlɔː-, ˈlɑː-/ also **log** *infml*— *n* a number which represents a value (a POWER¹ (9)) of another number, and which can be used for additions instead of multiplying the original number; the number of times a fixed number (usu. 10) must be multiplied by itself to equal a stated number: *The logarithm of 100 is 2 because 10² =100.* —compare ANTILOGARITHM —**rithmic** /ˌlɒgəˈrɪðmɪk◂‖ˈlɔː-, ˌlɑː-/ *adj* —**rithmically** /kli/ *adv*

log·book /ˈlɒgbʊk‖ˈlɔːg-, ˈlɑːg-/ *n* **1** *BrE for* REGISTRATION DOCUMENT **2** *AmE for* LOG¹ (2)

log cab·in /ˌ·ˈ··/ *n* a house, usu. a small one, made of logs of wood

log cabin

► CULTURAL NOTE In the US until the mid-1900s, politicians would sometimes say they had been born in a log cabin. This was supposed to tell people that they understood people's everyday problems and to suggest that they were like Abraham Lincoln, one of America's great presidents who really was born in a log cabin. ◄

loge /ləʊʒ/ *n* in a theatre or concert hall, the front part of the BALCONY: *We had seats in the loge.*

log·ger /ˈlɒgəʳ‖ˈlɔː-, ˈlɑː-/ *n* a person whose job is to cut down trees

log·ger·heads /ˈlɒgəhedz‖ˈlɔːgər-, ˈlɑː-/ *n* **at loggerheads (with)** always disagreeing (with); holding completely opposing views (to)

log·gi·a /ˈlɒdʒiə‖ˈləʊdʒə/ *n* a sort of open-sided room at the side of a house or other building

lo·gic /ˈlɒdʒɪk‖ˈlɑː-/ *n* [U] **1** the science or study of careful reasoning by formal methods **2** a particular way of reasoning: *I didn't follow her logic.* | *business logic* **3** *infml* reasonable thinking; good sense: *There's no logic in spending money on things you don't need.*

lo·gic·al /ˈlɒdʒɪkəl‖ˈlɑː-/ *adj* **1** according to the rules of logic: *a logical argument* **2** having or showing good clear reasoning; sensible: *the logical thing to do* | *It's logical that people who earn more money should pay higher taxes.* —opposite **illogical**

▷ USAGE When they mean "sensible", **logical** and **reasonable** can often be used in the same way: *It's a logical/reasonable thing to do.* **Logical** (but not **reasonable**) is used of careful thinking which follows the exact rules of logic: *Mathematics requires logical thinking.* | *She has a logical mind.* Compare a **reasonable** *person* (=sensible, willing to listen to others) and *a logical person/thinker* (=someone whose thinking follows a clear method).◁

lo·gic·al·ly /ˈlɒdʒɪkli/ *adv* **1** in a logical way: *Think logically.* **2** according to what is reasonable or logical: *Logically, one should become wiser with experience, but some people never do!*

lo·gi·cian /ləˈdʒɪʃən‖-ləʊ-/ *n* a person who studies or is skilled in logic

lo·gis·tics /ləˈdʒɪstɪks‖ləʊ-/ *n* **1** [P (**of**)] the planning and organization that is needed to carry out any large and difficult operation: *The logistics of supplying food to all the famine areas were very complex.* **2** [U] the study or skill of moving soldiers, supplying them with food, etc. —**tic** *adj* —**tically** /kli/ *adv*

log·jam /ˈlɒgdʒæm‖ˈlɔːg-, ˈlɑːg-/ *n* **1** a tightly-packed mass of floating logs on a river **2** *esp. AmE* a difficulty that prevents one from continuing; IMPASSE

lo·go /ˈləʊgəʊ/ *n* **-gos** a small pattern or picture that is the sign of a particular organization: *The Longman logo, a small sailing ship, is on the cover of this book.*

LO·GO /ˈləʊgəʊ/ *n* [U] an easy-to-use computer language often used in schools

log·roll·ing /ˈlɒgˌrəʊlɪŋ‖ˈlɔːg-, ˈlɑːg-/ *n* [U] *AmE infml* **1** the practice of giving praise or help to someone's work in return for receiving the same **2** the practice in the US Congress of helping one member pass a bill in return for receiving the same help at a later time **3** the sport in which two people stand on and roll a log floating on water, each trying to make the other fall off

lo·gy /ˈləʊgi‖ˈlɔː-, ˈlɑː-/ *adj* [F] *AmE infml* of or being a dull heavy feeling that produces a lack of activity: *I'm feeling rather logy after all that eating and drinking last night.*

loin /lɔɪn/ *n* [C;U] (a piece of) meat from the lower part of an animal's back —see also LOINS, SIRLOIN

loin·cloth /ˈlɔɪnkləʊθ‖-klɔːθ/ *n* **-cloths** /klɒθs‖klɔːðz, klɔːθs/ a loose covering for the loins, usu. for men, worn in hot countries esp. by poor people

loins /lɔɪnz/ *n* [P] **1 a** the lower part of the body below the waist and above the legs on both sides **b** *euph* the area of the body around the sexual organs **2 the fruit of his loins** *bibl* his children —see also **gird up one's loins** (GIRD)

Loire /lwɑːʳ/ [*the*] a river in central France which is famous for the many beautiful castles called châteaux (CHATEAU) along its banks and for the wine which is made in the area

loi·ter /ˈlɔɪtəʳ/ *v* [I] **1** to stand or wait somewhere, esp. in a public place, without any clear reason: *The men were loitering near the bank suspiciously.* | (*esp. AmE*) *The sign said "No loitering."*

► CULTURAL NOTE **Loitering with intent** is a crime which you can be sent to prison for because it means standing and waiting for the best time to do something bad, e.g. rob a bank: *He was arrested and charged with loitering with intent.* ◄

2 to move slowly or keep stopping when one should be going forward: *Stop loitering or the other people will get there first.* —**~er** *n*

Lo·ki /ˈləʊki/ in Norse MYTHOLOGY, the god of evil and destruction

Lo·li·ta /ləˈliːtə/ a character in a book of that name by Vladimir Nabokov. Lolita was a young girl who was the subject of a middle-aged man's PASSION. The name is sometimes used for a girl who is too young to have SEXUAL INTERCOURSE but who does, or wishes to —see also NYMPHET

loll /lɒl‖lɑːl/ *v* **1** [I+*adv/prep*] to be in a lazy loose position: *She was lolling in a chair, with her arms hanging over the sides.* **2** [I;T] to (allow to) hang down loosely; DROOP: *The dog's tongue lolled out.*

lol·li·pop ‖also **lollypop** *AmE* /ˈlɒlipɒp‖ˈlɑːlipɑːp/ *n* **1** also **sucker** *AmE*— a hard sweet made of boiled sugar and fixed on a stick, which is eaten by licking (LICK¹) **2** *esp. BrE* frozen juice, ice cream, etc., on a stick

lollipop man /ˈ··· ·/ **lollipop wom·an** /ˈ··· ··/, **lollipop lady** *fem.*— *n BrE* a person whose job is to stop traffic (so that school children can cross) by turning towards the cars a stick with a sign on top showing that they should stop

lollipop lady

Lol·lo·bri·gi·da /ˌlɒləˈbrɪdʒ⁀də‖ˌlɑːl-/, **Gi·na** /ˈdʒiːnə/ (1927–) an Italian film actress well known for playing GLAMOROUS parts

lol·lop /ˈlɒləp‖ˈlɑː-/ *v* [I+*adv/prep*] *infml* to move with long ungraceful steps: *He fired a warning shot and the elephant lolloped off.*

lol·ly /ˈlɒli‖ˈlɑːli/ *n BrE* **1** [C] *infml* a lollipop: *an ice lolly* **2** [U] *sl* money

Lom·bar·di /lɒmˈbɑːdi‖lɑːmˈbɑːr-/, **Vince** /vɪns/ (1913–70) an American football COACH whose team won the first two SUPERBOWLS

Lom·bard Street /ˈlɒmbəd striːt‖ˈlɑːmbərd-/ a street in the city of London known for financial and banking activity

Lon·don /ˈlʌndən/ the capital city of Great Britain. It is in south-east England on the river Thames and is an important port and a centre for business, industry, and TOURISM —see also CHANGING OF THE GUARD, CITY, INNER LONDON, UNIVERSITY OF LONDON, see picture at ESTUARY and colour maps on pages 817 and 818

London, Jack (1876–1916) an American writer whose books include *The Call of the Wild* and *White Fang*

London Bank·ers' Clear·ing House /ˌ··· ˌ·· ˈ··· ·/ an organization owned by the large banks, which processes daily all the cheque TRANSACTIONS of the member banks to find out how much is owed by and to each bank

London Blitz /ˌ·· ˈ·/ [*the*] the period of heavy German bombing of London during the Second World War, esp. in 1940 —see BLITZ (CULTURAL NOTE)

London Bridge /ˌ·· ˈ·/ **1** a bridge over the river Thames in London, connecting Southwark and the City. London Bridge is famous because of a NURSERY RHYME (=an old song or poem for children) called *London Bridge is Falling Down*. A new bridge was built in 1968 and the old one was sold and sent to a city in the US state of Arizona, where TOURISTS go to see it. **2** one of the mainline railway stations in London

London Col·i·se·um /ˌlʌndən kɒlɪˈsiːəm‖-kɑː-/ [*the*] a large theatre in London, where the English National Opera is based

Lon·don·der·ry /ˈlʌndənderi/ also **Derry**— **1** the second largest city in Northern Ireland —see colour map on page 818

▶CULTURAL NOTE Like Belfast, Londonderry is often in the news because of violence between Protestants and Catholics. The city is called Londonderry because of its historical associations with the City of London. —see also IRA, TROUBLES◀

2 a former COUNTY of Northern Ireland

Lon·don·er /ˈlʌndənəʳ/ *n* a person who lives in or was born in London —compare COCKNEY

London Li·bra·ry /ˌ··· ˈ···/ [*the*] a library in central London, well-known for its reading room and thousands of books

London Mar·a·thon /ˌ··· ˈ···/ [*the*] a long foot race run every year in London in which both professionals and non-professionals take part, many earn money for CHARITY —compare FUN RUN

London Marathon

London Pal·la·di·um /ˌlʌndən pəˈleɪdiəm/ [*the*] a theatre in London, noted for MUSICALs and VARIETY (4) shows

London Phil·har·mon·ic Or·ches·tra /ˌ··· ··ˈ·· ˌ···/ *abbrev* **LPO** [*the*] a top British SYMPHONY ORCHESTRA (=large group of musicians)

London Re·gion·al Trans·port /ˌ··· ˈ··· ˈ··/ also **London Transport**–, *abbrev* **LRT** a public company responsible for public TRANSPORT in and around London. It runs the UNDERGROUND, most of the buses, and the Docklands Light Railway.

London School of E·co·nom·ics /ˌ··· ˈ· ···· ˈ···/ *abbrev* **LSE** [*the*] a college, part of London University, where people can study ECONOMICS and politics.

London Sea·son /ˌ·· ˈ··/ [*the*] a programme of social events taking place every year in or near London and attended esp. formerly by UPPER-CLASS people, including parties for DEBUTANTES, the horse races at Ascot, Henley Regatta, and other events —see also ASCOT, HENLEY REGATTA

London Sym·pho·ny Or·ches·tra /ˌ··· ˈ··· ˌ···/ *abbrev* **LSO** [*the*] a top ORCHESTRA (=group of musicians) based at the Barbican in London

London Trans·port /ˌ··· ˈ··/ see LONDON REGIONAL TRANSPORT

London U·ni·ver·si·ty /ˌ··· ··ˈ···/ also **The University of**

London the third oldest university in England. It is a combination of many different colleges and offers an examination system which allows students overseas to take its DEGREES.

London weight·ing /ˌ·· ˈ··/ *n* [U] an additional payment added to the SALARY of a person who works in London, because of the higher cost of housing, TRANSPORT, etc. in the capital: *The salary includes London weighting.*

London Zoo /ˌ·· ˈ·/ a large old ZOO in London's Regent's Park and Britain's best-known zoo. As well as keeping and breeding many different animals and birds it studies wild animals and the things that have an effect on the way they live. In the 1990s it began to have severe financial problems.

lone /ləʊn/ *adj* [A] *lit or fml* **1** without other people or things; on one's own or on its own: *a lone rider* | *lone mothers on income support* —see ALONE (USAGE) **2**

Loneliness of the Long Dis·tance Run·ner /ˌ···· ·· ˌ·· ˈ··/, **The** a short story by Alan Sillitoe (1959) describing the REBELLION of a boy living in a BORSTAL, who is a very good runner but who deliberately loses an important race as a protest. It was made into a successful film.

lone·ly /ˈləʊnli/ *adj* **1** unhappy because of being alone or without friends: *He has been very/desperately lonely since his wife left him.* **2 a** (of a building or other object) with no others of the same type near: *a lonely house in the country* **b** *esp. lit* (of a place) without people; unvisited: *the lonely hillsides* —see ALONE (USAGE) —**-liness** *n* [U]

lonely hearts /ˌ·· ˈ·/ *adj, n* [A] (for) people who wish to find a friend or lover: *a lonely hearts club/column*

lone pa·rent /ˌ·· ˈ··/ *n* see SINGLE PARENT

lon·er /ˈləʊnəʳ/ *n* a person who spends a lot of time alone, esp. by choice; LONE WOLF

the Lone Ranger

Lone Rang·er /ˌ·· ˈ··/ [*the*] a character on an American television programme (a WESTERN²) of that name who wore a MASK to cover his face, rode a horse called Silver, and went with his NATIVE AMERICAN friend Tonto to protect people and prevent crimes. Several sentences from this programme are known to most British and American people: at the end of the show, someone the Lone Ranger had either helped or put in JAIL often said, "Who was that masked man?"; Tonto called the Lone Ranger "Kemo sabe"; and the Lone Ranger always said to his horse, "Hi ho Silver away!"

lone·some /ˈləʊnsəm/ *adj infml, esp. AmE* **1** lonely: *She is lonesome without the children.* **2** which makes one feel lonely: *a long lonesome road* —see ALONE (USAGE) **3 on/by one's lonesome** alone: *She's all by her lonesome as her husband's away.*

lone wolf /ˌ·· ˈ·/ *n* someone who likes to live, work, etc., alone

long¹ /lɒŋ‖lɔːŋ/ *adj* **1 a** measuring a large, or larger than average, amount from one end to the other: *long hair* | *a long road* | *She wore a long dress, reaching down to her feet.* **b** covering or lasting a great, or greater than average, distance or time: *a long illness/journey* | *We're a long way from home.* | *She's taking a long time to get here.* | (fig.) *Medical research has come a long way* (=made a lot of PROGRESS) *towards finding a cure for the disease.* —opposite **short** **2** covering a certain distance from one end to the other or a certain time: *How long is the film?* [after *n*] *It's an hour long.* | *The garden is 20 metres long and 15 metres wide.* **3** seeming to last more than usual or more than is wished: *I've had a long day;* (=with a lot of tiring work to do) *I need a drink!* **4** (of memory) able to remember things far back in time —opposite **short** **5**

(of a probability or BET) with a high risk of failing or not happening: *The odds against him winning are rather long.* (=he will probably lose) —see also LONG SHOT **6** [A] (of a drink) cool, containing little or no alcohol, and served in a tall glass: *I'm really thirsty — I'd like a nice long drink.* **7** (of a vowel) lasting longer than a short vowel in the same position **8 how long is a piece of string?** *humor* a phrase said as a reply to a question, the answer to which seems completely uncertain: *"How many people are likely to turn up?" "How long is a piece of string?"* **9 long in the tooth** *infml* old **10 long on** *infml, rather old-fash* with a lot of (a quality): *He's long on (good) looks, but short on brains.* **11 long time no see** *infml* an informal greeting used when you have not seen someone for a long time **12 not by a 'long chalk/shot** *infml* not at all; not nearly: *"Is it ready yet?" "No, not by a long chalk."* —see also **in the long run** (RUN[2]), **in the long term** (TERM[1]), **take the long view** (VIEW[1])

long² *adv* **1** (for) a long time: *How long will he be?* (=When will he come, finish what he is doing, etc.?) *I can't wait much longer.* | *Stay as long as you like.* | *He hasn't been back long.* | *Don't be long about (doing) it.* | *It was not long before we realized our mistake.* | *It won't take long to finish the job.* **2** [+adv/prep] at a long time: *long ago and far away* | *not long after that* (=a short time after) **3 as/so long as** if; on condition that; PROVIDED: *You can go out, as long as you promise to be back before 11 o'clock.* | *Our profits will be good so long as the dollar remains strong.* **4 no longer/(not) any longer** (not) any more; (formerly but not) now: *He no longer lives here.* | *He doesn't live here any longer.* | *I used to smoke 20 cigarettes a day, but not any longer!* **5 so long** *infml, esp. AmE* goodbye

long³ *n* **1 before long** also **ere long** *lit*— after a short period of time; soon: *They came back before long.* **2 for long** (*in questions or negatives*) for a long time: *Were you there for long?* | *I can't stay for long.* **3 the long and (the) short of it** *infml* the general result, expressed in a few words; UPSHOT: *I won't go into details, but the long and the short of it was that we missed the train.*

long⁴ *v* [T+*to-v; obj*] to want something very much: *I'm longing to see her again.* —see also LONGING[1,2]
long for sthg./sbdy. *phr v* [T] to want very much: *to long for freedom* [+*obj+to-v*] *I'm longing for him to arrive.* | *The longed-for day at last arrived.*

long⁵ *written abbrev. for:* LONGITUDE

Long, Hu·ey Pierce /ˈhjuːi pɪəs‖-pɪərs/ (1893–1935) an American politician, governor of Louisiana (1928–31) who was murdered

Long. *written abbrev. for:* Longford

long-awaited /ˌ·ˈ··◂/ *adj* that has been waited for a long time: *We finally got our long-awaited pay rise.*

long-boat /ˈlɒŋbəʊt‖ˈlɔːŋ-/ *n* the largest type of ROWING BOAT carried by a sailing ship —compare LONGSHIP

long·bow /ˈlɒŋbəʊ‖ˈlɔːŋ-/ *n* a large powerful BOW³ for shooting ARROWS, esp. as made in former times from a single long thin curved piece of wood (like the one used by the English HERO Robin Hood) —compare CROSSBOW

long-dis·tance¹ /ˌ·ˈ··◂/ *adj* [A] covering a long distance: *a long-distance runner/race*

long-distance² *adv* to or from a distant point: *to phone long-distance*

long-distance call /ˌ·ˈ·· ˈ·/ also **trunk call** *BrE old-fash*— *n* a telephone call made over a long distance

long dis·tance foot·path /ˌ·ˈ·· ˈ·◂/ *n* a public path in Britain going for many miles, such as the Pennine Way, used esp. by tourists and walkers

long di·vi·sion /ˌ·ˈ· ·ˈ··/ *n* [U] a method of dividing large numbers by others in which each stage is written out below the one before

long-drawn-out /ˌ·ˈ· ˈ·◂/ *adj* lasting (too) long; PROLONGED: *The official enquiry was a long-drawn-out affair.*

lon·gev·i·ty /lɒnˈdʒevⁱti‖lɑːn-, lɔːn-/ *n* [U] **1** *fml* long life **2** *tech* length of life: *the longevity of the rabbit*

long face /ˌ·ˈ·/ *n* an unhappy or complaining expression on the face: *She made/pulled a long face when I told her she would have to take the exam again.*

Long·fel·low /ˈlɒŋfeləʊ‖ˈlɔːŋ-/, **Hen·ry Wads·worth** /ˈhenri ˈwɒdzwəθ‖-ˈwɑːdzwərθ/ (1807–82) an American

poet who told the stories of American LEGENDS in long poems such as *The Song of Hiawatha, Paul Revere's Ride,* and *The Courtship of Miles Standish* —see also HIAWATHA

Long·ford /ˈlɒŋfəd‖ˈlɔːŋfərd/ *written abbrev.* **Long.** a COUNTY in Northern Ireland

Longford, Frank (1905–) an English politician, known as **Lord Longford**, who is a leading Catholic and worker for prison reform

long-haired /ˌlɒŋˈheəd◂‖ˌlɔːŋˈheərd◂/ *adj* **1** having long hair: *a longhaired dog* **2** [A] *old-fash derog* too concerned with art, literature, ideas, or spiritual matters: *longhaired intellectuals*

long·hand /ˈlɒŋhænd‖ˈlɔːŋ-/ *n* [U] ordinary writing by hand, not in any shortened or machine-produced form: *She wrote it out in longhand before typing it.* —compare SHORTHAND

long-haul /ˈ·ˈ·/ *adj* [A] (esp. of an aircraft flight) covering a long distance round the world: *Fog has delayed the departure of some long-haul flights.* | *Long-haul holidays are becoming more popular.* —compare SHORT-HAUL

long haul /ˌ·ˈ·/ *n* [S] a long and usu. difficult journey, job, or activity

long·horn /ˈlɒŋhɔːn‖ˈlɔːŋhɔːrn/ also **longhorn cattle, Texas longhorn**— *n AmE* a kind of cow, kept for their meat and now nearly EXTINCT, which has long horns and which was very popular in the West in the 1800s: *driving a herd of longhorns to Montana*

long·house /ˈlɒŋhaʊs‖ˈlɔːŋ-/ *n* **-houses** /ˌhaʊzɪz/ a kind of house used by some NATIVE AMERICAN tribes which was around one hundred feet long and was used by everyone in the tribe

long·ing¹ /ˈlɒŋɪŋ‖ˈlɔːŋɪŋ/ *n* [C;U (**for**)] a strong feeling of wanting something; strong wish; YEARNING: *a longing for fame* | *secret longings* | *The little boy looked with longing at the toys in the shop window.* —see also LONG⁴

longing² *adj* [A] showing a strong wish: *a longing look —* **~ly** *adv* : *She was looking longingly at him.*

long·ish /ˈlɒŋɪʃ‖ˈlɔːŋɪʃ/ *adj infml* quite long

Long Is·land /ˌ·ˈ··/ an island that contains the New York City BOROUGHs of Queens and Brooklyn. Further E it has many other towns and cities, and some seaside places that are popular in summer. —see colour map on pages 1374–5

lon·gi·tude /ˈlɒndʒⁱtjuːd‖ˈlɑːndʒⁱtuːd/ *n* [C;U] the position on the Earth east or west of a MERIDIAN usu. measured, in degrees, from Greenwich in England: *The town is at longitude 21° east.* —compare LATITUDE and see picture at GLOBE

lon·gi·tu·di·nal /ˌlɒndʒⁱˈtjuːdⁱnəl‖ˌlɑːndʒⁱˈtuː-/ *adj fml or tech* **1** of or measured according to longitude **2 a** in length; going from end to end, not across **b** in time: *a longitudinal study of educational development over five years* **— ~ly** *adv*

long johns /ˈ· ·/ *n* [P] *old-fash infml* men's underclothes with long legs, esp. worn for warmth

Long John Sil·ver /ˌ·· ˈ··/ a famous character from a children's adventure story called *Treasure Island* by Robert Louis Stevenson. Long John Silver is a cruel and frightening PIRATE who has part of one leg missing and a PARROT on his shoulder. —see also PIRATE

Long John Silver

long jump /ˈ· ·/ also **broad jump** *AmE*— [*the*] a sport in which someone jumps from a point and tries to land as far away as possible —see colour picture on page 883 —
~er *n*

long-lasting /ˌ·ˈ··◂/ *adj* **longer-lasting** lasting a long time: *Try the new long-lasting pack.*

Long·leat /ˈlɒŋliːt‖ˈlɔːŋ-/ a historic house in Wiltshire which is owned by the Marquess of Bath. It is known for its SAFARI PARK (=park which one can drive through where wild animals can be seen).

long-life /ˈ· ·/ adj [A] esp. BrE (of milk, fruit juice, etc.) treated so that it can be kept for a long time without going bad

long-lived /ˌlɒŋ ˈlɪvd◂‖ˌlɔːŋ ˈlaɪvd/ adj living or lasting a long time: a long-lived family | a long-lived friendship — compare SHORT-LIVED

long-lost /ˈ· ·/ adj [A] that has been lost or unknown for a long time: They greeted each other like long-lost brothers.

Long March /ˌ· ˈ·/ [the] the dangerous journey across China taken by an army of Communist Chinese soldiers and officials in 1934–35. Only one third of the people were alive at the end —see also MAO TSE-TUNG

long-play·ing rec·ord /ˌ· ·· ˈ···/ also **long-player** n an LP

long-range /ˌ· ˈ·◂/ adj [A] about or covering a long distance or time: long-range missiles | long-range weather forecasts predicting rain next month

long·ship /ˈlɒŋ ˌʃɪp‖ˈlɔːŋ-/ n a long narrow open warship once used by the Vikings, with OARs and a small square sail —compare LONGBOAT and see picture at VIKING

longship

long·shore·man /ˈlɒŋʃɔːmən‖ˈlɔːŋʃɔːr-/ n -men /mən/ esp. AmE for DOCKER

long shot /ˈ· ·/ n an attempt which is unlikely to succeed, but which one risks making —see also **not by a long shot** (LONG¹)

long-sight·ed /ˌlɒŋ ˈsaɪtɪd◂‖ˌlɔːŋ-/ esp. BrE ‖ **farsighted** esp. AmE— adj able to see objects or read things clearly only when they are far from the eyes —opposite **shortsighted**

long-stand·ing /ˌlɒŋ ˈstændɪŋ◂‖ˌlɔːŋ-/ adj having existed in the same form for a long time: a long-standing trade agreement between the countries | the long-standing rivalry between these two football clubs

long-suf·fer·ing /ˌlɒŋ ˈsʌfərɪŋ◂‖ˌlɔːŋ-/ adj patient in spite of continued difficulty, esp. bad or annoying treatment from another person: Although he keeps leaving her, his longsuffering girlfriend always takes him back.

long suit /ˌ· ˈ·/ n [S] rare infml someone's best quality or the thing they do best: Being tactful is not exactly his long suit. (=he has little TACT)

long-term , long term /ˌ· ˈ·◂/ adj, n [the] (concerning) a long period of time: (for or in) the distant future: a long-term plan | No one knows what the long-term effects of the new drugs will be. | In the long term we aim to train hundreds of medical workers. | training programmes for the long-term unemployed —opposite **short-term**

long-time /ˈ· ·/ adj [A] long-standing: a long-time love affair

long ton /ˌ· ˈ·/ n tech (a unit of weight equal to) 2240 pounds

lon·gueur /lɒŋ ˈgɜːr‖ˈlɔːŋ-/ n [usu. pl.] lit a very dull part or period

long va·ca·tion /ˌ· ·ˈ··/ also **long vac** /ˌ· ˈ·/infml— n BrE the period of three months in the summer when university students have holidays

long wave /ˌ· ˈ·◂/ written abbrev. **LW** n [U] radio broadcasting or receiving on waves of 1000 metres or more in length —compare MEDIUM WAVE, SHORT WAVE

long·ways /ˈlɒŋweɪz‖ˈlɔːŋ-/ esp. BrE ‖ usu. **longwise** AmE— adv along the length; LENGTHWAYS

long·wear·ing /ˌlɒŋ ˈweərɪŋ◂‖ˌlɔːŋ-/ adj AmE for HARDWEARING

long week·end /ˌ· ·ˈ·, ˌ· ˈ··‖ˌ· ˈ··/ n a short holiday or period of not working which includes the WEEKEND but lasts for longer than two days, usu. including Friday afternoon and Monday: We spent a long weekend in our country cottage.

long-wind·ed /ˌlɒŋ ˈwɪndɪd◂‖ˌlɔːŋ-/ adj (of a person, speech, piece of writing, etc.) going on too long and using too many words: That was the most longwinded speech I've ever had to sit through! — ~ly adv — ~ness n [U]

long·wise /ˈlɒŋwaɪz‖ˈlɔːŋ-/ adv esp AmE LONGWAYS

Lons·dale Belt /ˌlɒnzdeɪl ˈbelt‖ˌlɑːn-/ [the] the most important prize in British professional BOXING, a richly decorated belt which is given to a CHAMPION and is kept by

him if he wins it three times one after another

loo /luː/ n loos BrE infml for TOILET —see TOILET (USAGE)

Loo·by Loo /ˌluːbi ˈluː/ a PUPPET in the shape of a young girl with long, fair hair, who appeared with Andy Pandy in a British children's television SERIES of the 1950s

loo·fah , loofa /ˈluːfə/ n the long thin dried inner part of the fruit of a tropical plant, used as a SPONGE in washing the body

look¹ /lʊk/ v **1** [I+adv/prep, esp. at] to turn the eyes so as to see something or see in the stated direction: What are you looking at? | He looked angrily at the mess. | Look over there — I think something is burning. | to look round the corner/over the wall/out of the window | They looked away from the unpleasant sight. | Look at him jumping! | (esp. AmE) Look at him jump! **2** [I] to use the eyes in order to find something; search: You could see it if you'd only look. | We looked everywhere but we couldn't find it. | Try looking under the bed. —see also LOOK for **3** [L] to seem by expression or appearance: You look tired/well/happy. | The two children look alike. | She looks just like her sister. | Your room looks a mess. | "How does this hat look on me?" "It looks good." | The plan looks good on paper, but will it work? [+to-v] Judging by her letter, she looks to be the best person for the job. | It **looks like/looks as if** it's going to rain. (=It seems likely that it will rain.) **4** [T+wh-; usu. imperative] to look at; notice: Look how big it is! | Look (=be careful) where you're putting your feet! **5** [I+adv/prep] (esp. of a building) to face in the stated direction: Our house looks east/looks out on the river. | The offices look onto a park. **6** [T] to have an appearance that matches: He's beginning to look his age. | You have to look your best if you want the job. **7** [T+to-v; obj] infml to plan or expect to do something: If you're looking to buy a new car, I suggest you borrow some money from the bank. **8** [T] to express with the eyes: She said nothing but looked all interest. **9 here's looking at you, kid** quote a slightly changed phrase from the film Casablanca. The phrase was originally said by Humphrey Bogart. **10 Look alive/lively!** infml Act fast! Work fast! **11 look before you leap** think about possible dangers or difficulties before you do something **12 look daggers at** to look at (someone) extremely angrily **13 look down one's nose at** often derog to regard (someone or something) as unimportant or having a low social position —see also LOOK **down** on **14 look good** give a favourable effect: She looks good in that dress. **15 look on the ˈbright side (of things)** to be cheerful and hopeful in spite of difficulties **16 look sharp** infml, esp. BrE **a** to hurry up: You'll have to look sharp if you want to get there on time. **b** to watch out; be careful **17 look small** (of a person) to (be made to) appear unimportant or silly **18 look someone in the eye/face** to look directly and without fear at someone who is near: Can you look me in the eye and say you didn't steal it? **19 look someone up and down** to look at someone as if examining them carefully, esp. seeming ready to make a severe judgment: She looked me up and down, and then said, "Well, I suppose you look tidy enough." **20 look well** rather fml look good: The hat looks well on you.

look after sbdy./sthg. phr v [T] to take care of; be responsible for: Who will look after the baby while they're out? | I can look after myself. (=be independent and not let other people take advantage of me) | Are you being well looked after? | Look after yourself while you're away. (=take good care of yourself)

look ahead phr v [I] to plan for the future

look around/round phr v [I (for)] to search: looking around for a nice place to eat/for a new job

look at sbdy./sthg. phr v [T] **1** [+obj+adv/prep] to regard; judge: She looks at work in a different way now she's in charge. **2** to examine (something) to see if it is good or correct, if action needs to be taken, etc.: We're looking at a new idea for marketing our shampoos. | You ought to have that bad tooth looked at. | He looked carefully at the figures. —see SEE (USAGE) **3** [usu. in negatives] to consider: I wouldn't look at such a small offer! **4** [usu. imperative] to notice or remember and learn from: Look at Mrs Jones: drink killed her! **5 not much to look at** infml not attractive in appearance: He's not much to look at, but he has a kind heart.

look back phr v [I (to, on)] **1** to remember: I look back on those days as the happiest time of my life. **2 never look back** to continue to succeed: After he won the first game he never looked back. (=he kept on winning)

look down on sbdy./sthg. *phr v* [T] to have or show a low opinion of (esp. someone one considers socially IN-FERIOR or unimportant); DESPISE −opposite **look up to**

look for sbdy./sthg. *phr v* [T] **1** to try to find: *looking for a lost book/a new job* **2** *infml* to behave in a way that is likely to cause (something bad): *You're looking for trouble if you say things like that to me!* **3** *esp. old use* wish to have: *We look for improvement in your work, Smith.* −see also UNLOOKED-FOR

look forward to *phr v* [T] to expect with pleasure: *I'm really looking forward to your party.* [+*v-ing*] *I'm looking forward to going to your party.* | (in a business letter) *I look forward to receiving your reply as soon as possible.* −see EXPECT (USAGE)

look in *phr v* [I (**on**)] *infml* to make a short visit: *to look in on the party* −see also LOOK-IN

look into sthg. *phr v* [T] to examine the meaning or causes of; INVESTIGATE: *The police have received the complaint, and they're looking into it.* | *a report looking into the causes of unemployment*

look on *phr v* **1** [I] to watch while others take part −see also LOOKER-ON, ONLOOKER **2** [T+*obj+adv/prep*] (**look on** sbdy./sthg.) also **look upon**− to consider; regard: *I look on him as a friend.* | *Most people look on the government's promises with complete disbelief.*

look out *phr v* **1** [I *usu. imperative*] to take care: *Look out! There's a car coming!* **2** [I (**for**)] to keep watching (in order to see): *Look out for your aunt at the station.* −see also LOOKOUT **3** [T] (**look** sthg. ↔ **out**) *esp. BrE* to search for and choose from one's possessions: *to look out a dress for a party* **4 look out for number one** *usu. derog* to make sure that one's own needs and interests are treated as most important

look sthg./sbdy. ↔ **over** *phr v* [T] to examine, esp. quickly: *I've looked over the plans, but I haven't studied them in detail.* −see also OVERLOOK

look round *phr v BrE* ‖ **look around** *AmE*− **1** [I;T (=**look round** sthg.)] to look at and examine (a place), esp. while walking: *I don't want to buy anything; I'm just looking round.* | *Do we have to pay to look round the castle?* | *Let's look round the shops.* **2** [I (**for**)] to LOOK **around**

look through sthg./sbdy. *phr v* [T] **1** to examine, esp. for points to be noted: *Look through this proposal for me, and tell me what you think of it.* **2** to look at (someone) without seeming to notice them, on purpose or because of deep thought: *I tried to tell him about it, but he just looked (straight) through me.*

look to sbdy./sthg. *phr v* [T] **1** [(**for**)] to depend on for help, advice, etc.: *We look to you for support.* [+*obj+to-v*] *They're looking to the new manager to bring the company back to profitability.* **2** *fml* to pay attention to, esp. in order to improve: *We must each look to our own work.* **3** **look to one's laurels** to guard against competition; make sure one keeps one's good position

look up *phr v* **1** [I] *infml* (of a situation, business, etc.) to get better, esp. after being bad; improve: *Trade should look up later in the year.* | *Things are looking up!* **2** [T] (**look** sthg. ↔ **up**) to find (information) in a book: *Look up the word in the dictionary.* | *I'll look up the times of the trains.* **3** [T] (**look** sbdy. ↔ **up**) to find and visit (someone) when in the same area: *I must look up an old friend who lives nearby.*

look up to sbdy. *phr v* [T] to respect; admire −opposite **look down on**

look[2] *n* **1** [C (**at**) *usu. sing.*] an act of looking: *Have a look at that!* (=Look at that!) | *I took one look at the coat and decided I would have to buy it.* | *The country must have a long hard look at the tragedy of unemployment.* **2** [C] a (short) period of giving attention with the eyes; GLANCE: *She gave me an angry look.* **3** [C *usu. sing.*] an expression in the eyes or on the face: *I knew she didn't like it by the look on her face.* **4** [S] an appearance: *He has the look of a winner.* | *The deserted village had a sad look.* | *a new look in skirts* (=a new fashion in their appearance) | *I don't like the look of that hole in the roof.* (=its appearance suggests trouble) **5 by the look(s) of it, him, etc.** probably; judging from the way it, he, etc., appears or seems: *By the looks of it we shan't have much rain this month.* −see also LOOKS

look[3] *interj* also **look here**− (an expression used for drawing attention before saying something, esp. when one is angry or impatient): *Look, I don't mind you borrowing my car, but you ought to ask me first.* | *Now look here, you can't say things like that to me!*

look-a-like /ˈ···, ·/ *n infml* someone or something that looks very similar to someone or something else; a DOUBLE: *Let's hire that Humphrey Bogart look-alike for the TV commercial.* −compare CLONE

Look Back in An·ger /ˌ··ˈ··/ a play by the English writer John Osborne, which gave its name to the Angry Young Men, a group of British writers of plays in the 1950s −see also ANGRY YOUNG MAN

look·er /ˈlʊkəʳ/ also **good looker**− *n infml* a person, usu. a woman, with an attractive appearance: *She's a real looker.* −see also LOOKS

looker-on /ˌ··ˈ·/ *n* **lookers-on** an ONLOOKER

look-in /ˈ··/ *n* [S] *infml* **1** a chance to take part or succeed: *Their team was so much better than ours that we didn't even get a look-in.* (=we were completely beaten) **2** a short visit −see also LOOK **in**

look·ing glass /ˈ··· ·/ also **glass**− *n old-fash* a mirror

look·out /ˈlʊk-aʊt/ *n* **1** [S] the act of keeping watch: *keeping a lookout for the enemy* **2** [C] a person who keeps watch: *The general posted a lookout on top of the hill.* **3** [C] a place to watch from **4** [S (**for**)] *infml* a likely future course of events; OUTLOOK: *It's a bad lookout for the company if interest rates don't come down.* **5 one's own lookout** *BrE infml* an unpleasant situation one must take care of for oneself, without others' help: *If the teacher finds out you've been cheating, it's your own lookout.* **6 on the lookout for** searching for: *We're on the lookout for new computer programmers.* −see also LOOK **out**

looks /lʊks/ *n* [P] a person's appearance, esp. when attractive: *She kept her looks even in old age.* −see also LOOKER

look-see /ˌ··ˈ·/ *n AmE infml* LOOK[2](1): *Let's just have a look-see at the back of your throat; maybe your tonsils are swollen.*

loom[1] /luːm/ *n* a frame or machine on which thread is woven into cloth

loom[2] *v* **1** [I (UP)] to come into sight without a clear form, esp. so as to seem very large and threatening, causing fear: *A figure loomed (up) out of the mist.* | (fig.) *The threat of war loomed (over the country).* **2 loom large** to seem great and cause worry or other strong feeling: *Fear of failure loomed large in his mind.* | *The coming examination looms larger with every passing day.*

loon /luːn/ *n esp. lit* a foolish or mad person

loon·y /ˈluːni/ *n, adj sl* (a person who is) mad or foolish; LUNATIC

loony bin /ˈ··· ·/ *n sl, often humor for* MENTAL HOSPITAL; considered offensive by many people

loony left /ˌ··ˈ·/ [*the*] the name given in the 1980s to the extreme left of the British Labour party whose activities were thought to be damaging to the party −**loony leftie, lefty** *n* : *the loony lefties on the fringe of the party*

loop[1] /luːp/ *n* **1** the shape made by a piece of string, wire, rope, etc., when curved back on itself to produce a closed or slightly open curve: *To make a knot in a piece of rope, you first make a loop and then pass one end of the rope through it.* **2** something with this shape, esp. one used as a handle or fastening: *Carry the parcel by this loop of string.* **3** a type of IUD **4** also **loop line** /ˈ· ·/− a railway line that leaves the main track and then joins it again further on **5** a circle made by an aircraft while flying along, up, back, down, and then along again **6** a set of commands in a computer PROGRAM that are to be performed repeatedly

loop[2] *v* **1** [I;T] to make a loop or make into a loop **2** [T+*obj+adv/prep*] to fasten by using or forming a loop: *Loop the rope round the gate.* | *Loop that end of the rope through this and make a knot with it.* **3** [I;T] (of an aircraft) to fly a LOOP[1] (5) (often in the phrase **loop the loop**)

Loop [*the*] the central business area of Chicago. The name comes from an ELEVATED RAILWAY that forms a large circle around several blocks where different railways meet.

loop·hole /ˈluːphəʊl/ *n* a way of escaping or avoiding something, esp. one provided by a rule or agreement written without enough care: *a loophole in the tax laws*

loose[1] /luːs/ *adj* **1** not firmly or tightly fixed; movable when it should be firm: *a loose tooth* | *a loose button* | *This pole is coming/working loose; it'll soon fall over.* | *The*

radio wasn't working because of a loose connection in the wires. | (fig.) loose-limbed and graceful **2** [F] not fastened, tied up, shut up, etc.; free from control: The animals **broke loose** and ran away. | I **turned/let** the other animals **loose**. (=I freed them) **3** not tied or packed together, e.g. with string or in a box; not packaged (PACK-AGE): I bought these sweets loose, not in a box. **4** (of clothes) not fitting tightly **5** made of parts that are not tight together; not COMPACT: a loose weave/soil **6** not exact or controlled: a loose translation | loose accounting practices that have cost the firm a lot of money over the years **7** careless or irresponsible, esp. in what one says: Never tell him a secret; he's got a loose tongue. (=he will tell it to everyone else) | loose talk **8** old-fash derog having low sexual morals: a loose woman | loose living **9** (of the bowels) allowing waste matter to flow more than is natural **10 cut loose a** to break away from a group or situation **b** AmE infml to stop carefully controlling one's actions: Soon the music took hold of him and he cut loose, dancing uninhibitedly. **11 keep/stay loose** AmE infml to keep or stay in a calm unworried state **12 let someone loose on** to allow someone to deal with in their own way: Don't let him loose on the garden; he'll pull up all the flowers. – ~**ly** adv : Loosely translated, the word means "important". – ~**ness** n [U]

loose² v [T] fml or lit **1** to untie **2** to fire (an ARROW, a shot from a gun, etc.) **3** to free from control: The wine loosed his tongue. –compare LOOSEN

loose³ adv in a loose manner; loosely –see also **fast and loose** (FAST²)

loose⁴ n **on the loose** free, esp. having escaped from prison: a dangerous criminal on the loose

loose change /ˌ· ˈ·/ n [U] coins in one's pocket, PURSE, etc.

loose cov·ers /ˌ· ˈ··/ n [P] covers, made of cloth, used to protect and decorate pieces of furniture, esp. ARMCHAIRS and SOFAS

loose end /ˌ· ˈ·/ n [usu. pl.] **1** a part not properly completed: The committee's report was very good, but there are still just a few loose ends (to be tied up). **2 at a loose end** BrE || **at loose ends** AmE– having nothing to do: Can I come over? I'm at a loose end this morning.

loose-leaf /ˌ· ˈ·◄/ adj [A] (of a book) able to have pages put in and taken out: a loose-leaf binder (=a RING BINDER)

loos·en /ˈluːsən/ v [I;T] **1** to make or become less firm, fixed, tight, etc.: He loosened his grip on the handle. | I loosened my tie but I didn't take it off. | The government's control over the newspapers has loosened in recent years. **2** to make or become less controlled or more free in movement: a medicine that loosens the bowels | A few drinks loosened his tongue. (=made him talk more, and probably carelessly) –compare LOOSE²
    loosen up phr v **1** [I;T (=**loosen** sthg. ↔ **up**)] to (cause to) become ready for action by exercising the muscles: The runners are just loosening up before the race. | exercises to loosen up the muscles **2** [I] to become more free and relaxed (RELAX): After a few drinks we loosened up and began to enjoy ourselves.

loot¹ /luːt/ n [U] **1** goods, esp. valuable objects, taken away illegally, esp. by soldiers after defeating an enemy or by thieves

▶CULTURAL NOTE In CARTOONS, thieves are often seen carrying a large bag with the word "loot" written on it – compare SWAG (1)◄

2 AmE sl humor gifts, money, etc. considered as a group: The kids rushed downstairs to gape at their Christmas loot. | She came home from shopping with piles of loot.

loot² v [I;T] to steal, esp. in large quantities, and often causing widespread damage: Anyone found looting (the bombed houses and shops) will be shot. | There was an outbreak of looting. –compare PLUNDER² – –**er** n

lop /lɒp||lɑːp/ v -**pp**- [T (AWAY, OFF)] to cut (branches) off a tree: to lop the biggest branches off (a tree) | (fig.) They've lopped a few pounds off the price.

lope /ləʊp/ v [I+adv/prep] (esp. of an animal) to move easily and quite fast with springing steps: The noise alarmed the giraffe, and it loped off. –**lope** n [S] : going off at a lope

lop-eared /ˌ· ˈ·◄/ adj (of an animal) having ears that hang down loosely: a lop-eared rabbit/spaniel

lop-sid·ed /ˌ· ˈ··◄/ adj having one side heavier or lower than the other; not properly balanced: a lop-sided way of

walking | (fig.) The papers have been giving a rather lop-sided account of the strike.

loq·ua·cious /ləʊˈkweɪʃəs/ adj fml, often derog liking to talk a lot – ~**ly** adv –-**city** /-ˈkwæsɨti/ n [U]

loq·uat /ˈləʊkwɒt||-kwɑːt/ n the small yellowish fruit of a tree that grows mostly in China and Japan

Lorca see GARCÍA LORCA

lord¹ /lɔːd||lɔːrd/ n **1** a man of noble rank, esp. in Britain: The feudal lords forced the king to sign the treaty. | Dukes, earls, and barons are all lords. | Lord Hailsham addressed the meeting. | Will you step this way, my lord? –compare LADY; see also HOUSE OF LORDS **2** a powerful man in the stated industry: media lords –compare BARON (2) **3 one's lord and master** old use or humor a man who must be obeyed: Our lords and masters have changed the schedule yet again!

lord² v **lord it (over someone)** infml, usu. derog to behave (towards someone) as if one had the power to control them, e.g. by giving orders impolitely

Lord¹ n **1** [the] God: Praise the Lord! | (the) Lord God – see also OUR LORD **2** certain official people, originally only men: the first woman to become Lord Mayor of London **3 Lord (only) knows** infml no one knows: Lord knows where I left my bag! –see also LORDS

Lord² interj (an expression of surprise, fear, worry, etc., in such phrases as Oh Lord!, Good Lord!): Good Lord, how amazing! (=showing surprise) | Oh Lord, I forgot it! (=showing annoyance and worry)

Lord Ad·vo·cate /ˌ· ˈ···/ [the] the head of the Scottish legal system, which is different to the English legal system

Lord Cham·ber·lain /ˌ· ˈ···/ [the] the King or Queen of England's chief officer responsible for the ceremonial parts of royal activities

Lord Chan·cel·lor /ˌ· ˈ···/ [the] **Lords Chancellor** a political official who is the head of the legal system in England and Wales, the Speaker of the House of Lords and also usu. a member of the Cabinet. The responsibilities of the Lord Chancellor include appointing new judges and deciding if laws need to be changed. –see also SPEAKER

Lord Chief Jus·tice /ˌ· · ˈ··/ [the] **Lords Chief Justice** a judge who is second in importance after the Lord Chancellor

Lord Haw Haw see Lord HAW HAW

Lord is my Shep·herd /ˌ· · · ˈ··/, **The** the title and first words of a PSALM and HYMN, also known as the 23rd Psalm. It is the best-known of all the Psalms.

Lord Jim /ˌlɔːd ˈdʒɪm||ˌlɔːrd-/ a NOVEL by Joseph Conrad (1900) about a ship's officer who leaves his ship, thinking that it is about to sink, and spends the rest of his life trying to make up for this dishonourable action

Lord Lieu·ten·ant /ˌ· ·ˈ···/ [the] **Lords Lieutenant** an official who represents the King or Queen of England in a British COUNTY and performs ceremonial duties

lord·ly /ˈlɔːdli||-ɔːr-/ adj **1** often derog behaving like a lord, esp. in giving orders: a lordly manner **2** apprec, esp. lit suitable for a lord; grand: a lordly feast –-**liness** n [U]

Lord Mayor /ˌ· ˈ·||ˌ· ˈ··/ [the] the official title of the person elected each year by a council to be head of a city, the most important example being the Lord Mayor of London

Lord Mayor

Lord Mayor's Ban·quet /ˌ· · ˈ··||ˌ· · ˈ··/ [the] a BANQUET (=a formal dinner) held in the Guildhall, London every year after the new Lord Mayor of London has been elected. Many important people are invited to this banquet, including the Prime Minister, who makes a speech to mark the occasion.

Lord Mayor's Show /ˌ· ˈ· ·||ˌ· ˈ· ·/ [the] a street PARADE in which the new Lord Mayor of London travels in a golden carriage through the streets of London

Lord of the Flies /ˌ· ··· ˈ·/ the title of a NOVEL by William Golding about a group of boys who are stuck on a small island and behave in a cruel way towards one another

Lord of the Rings /ˌ· ··· ˈ·/, **The** a book by J R R Tolkien, following on from *The Hobbit* and originally intended as a children's story. It has many strange, magical characters in it, e.g. HOBBITs and the magician Gandalf.

Lord Priv·y Seal /ˌ·ˌ·· ˈ·/ [the] **Lords Privy Seal** an important member of the British Cabinet who is not responsible for a particular government department

lord pro·tect·or /ˌ·ˈ··-/ n [often caps.] the title taken by both Oliver and Richard Cromwell after the English Civil War as leaders of the country

Lords /lɔːdz‖lɔːrdz/ n **1** [the+P] the members of the House of Lords as a group **2** [the+sing.|pl.v] the House of Lords —compare HOUSE OF COMMONS

Lord's n the most important cricket ground in Britain. It is in London and is the HEADQUARTERS of the MCC

Lord's Day /ˈ·· ·/ [the] Sunday; the Christian SABBATH

Lord's Day Ob·ser·vance So·ci·e·ty /ˌ·· ·ˈ·· ·ˌ···/ [the] a British Christian society whose aim is to keep Sunday as a religious day. They object to activities involving buying and selling or sport on Sundays.

lord·ship /ˈlɔːdʃɪp‖-ɔːr-/ n **1** (often cap.) (used as a title for addressing certain noblemen or, in Britain, a BISHOP or high-ranking judge): *Good morning, your Lordship.* | *Their Lordships will give a decision tomorrow.* —compare LADYSHIP **2** [U (**over**)] the power or rule of a lord

Lord's Prayer /ˌ· ˈ·/ also **Our Father**— n [the] one of the most important prayers in the Christian church, taken from the Bible. Many phrases from it are very well known and often used: *Our Father, which art in heaven, Hallowed be thy Name. Thy kingdom come. Thy will be done, in earth as it is in heaven. Give us this day our daily bread. And forgive us our trespasses, As we forgive them that trespass against us. And lead us not into temptation; But deliver us from evil. For thine is the kingdom, the power and the glory, for ever and ever. Amen.*

Lords Spir·i·tu·al /ˌ· ˈ····/ n [the +P] the set of BISHOPs (=high-ranking priests) in the Church of England who are members of the House of Lords —compare LORDS TEMPORAL

Lord's Sup·per /ˌ· ˈ··/ [the] COMMUNION

Lords Tem·po·ral /ˌ· ˈ···/ n [the +P] the members of the House of Lords who are not Lords Spiritual

lore /lɔːʳ/ n [U] knowledge or old beliefs, not written down, about a particular subject: *old sea lore* —see also FOLKLORE

Lo·ren /ˈlɔːrən, ləˈren ‖ ˈlɔːrən/, **So·phi·a** /səˈfiːə/ (1934–) a beautiful Italian actress who is an international film star and has won two Academy Awards. She was most popular in the 1950s and 1960s.

lor·gnette /lɔːˈnjet‖-ɔːr-/ n a pair of glasses (of a type rarely used now) which are held in front of the eyes by a long handle

lorn /lɔːn‖lɔːrn/ adj poet sad and lonely; FORLORN —see also LOVELORN

Lor·na Doone /ˌlɔːnə ˈduːn‖ˌlɔːr-/ a NOVEL by R D Blackmore (1869), set on Exmoor in Devon

lor·ry /ˈlɒri‖ˈlɔːri, ˈlɑːri/ n BrE a large motor vehicle for carrying heavy goods; TRUCK —see DRIVE (USAGE), STEER (USAGE), TRANSPORT (USAGE), and see picture at TRUCK **2 it fell off the back of a lorry** infml it is stolen: *Where did you get that radio? Don't tell me, it fell off the back of a lorry!*

lorry driv·er /ˈ·· ˌ··/ n a person whose job is to drive a lorry. Most lorry drivers are men.
▶CULTURAL NOTE The STEREOTYPE of a lorry driver is a big, strong, sometimes rather fat man who drinks large MUGs of tea and eats large meals of fried (FRY) food in TRANSPORT CAFEs.◀

lorry park /ˈ·· ˌ·/ n BrE an open place where lorries can be parked

Los Al·a·mos /lɒs ˈæləmɒs‖lɔːs ˈæləməʊs/ a town in New Mexico, USA, which contains the LABORATORY in which the first ATOM BOMB and HYDROGEN BOMB were developed —see also MANHATTAN PROJECT

Los An·ge·les /lɒs ˈændʒəliːz‖lɔːs ˈændʒələs, -liːz/ also **LA** infml— the second largest city in the USA, which is in California on the Pacific coast —see colour maps on pages 1374-5
▶CULTURAL NOTE Los Angeles is famous for being the centre of the American film industry (in **Hollywood**) and for having lots of rich and beautiful people. Many people come to live in Los Angeles because of the good weather, but people who do not like Los Angeles think that only CRAZY or strange people live there and sometimes call Los Angeles La-La Land. There are many FREEWAYs in Los Angeles and it is difficult to go anywhere without using a car so Los Angeles is also a place with very bad air POLLUTION or SMOG because of the cars and industry. In 1992, there were serious race RIOTs in Los Angeles following a decision by a court to free four white policemen who had beaten a black man, Rodney King. A number of people were killed, and many buildings, esp. in the poor areas of the cities, were burned. —see also HOLLYWOOD◀

Los Angeles Times /ˌ· ˌ··· ˈ·/ [the] an important American newspaper sold in many parts of the US —see also extra information on page 892

lose /luːz/ v lost /lɒst‖lɔːst/ **1** [T] to no longer have (something) as a result of carelessness or accident, esp. by putting it somewhere and then being unable to find it: *I've lost my keys — have you seen them anywhere?* | *Here are the tickets: don't lose them.* | *The company stands to lose* (=will probably lose) *thousands of pounds if the contract falls through.* —opposite **find 2** [T] to no longer have as a result of death or destruction; stop possessing: *She lost her parents when she was very young.* (=they died) | *He lost an eye in the accident.* | *Many farm crops were lost as a result of the floods.* **3** [T+obj(i)+obj(d)] to cause the loss of; cost: *It was his nervousness in the interview that probably lost him the job.* | *The delays in production lost us several months' sales.* **4** [T] to fail to keep; not continue to have: *She used to be keen on photography, but she lost interest after a while.* | *I lost my balance and fell off the wall.* | *He was going to ask the boss for more money but he* **lost his nerve** (=his courage) *at the last minute.* | *She* **lost her temper** *and started shouting at them.* | *She probably won't lend you her car, but you've got* **nothing to lose** *by asking.* (=if she refuses, you won't be in a worse position than if you hadn't asked) —opposite **keep 5** [I (**by, to**);T] to fail to win; be unsuccessful in (a game, competition, etc.): *England lost the match against Brazil.* | *They lost to Brazil by two goals.* | *to lose an argument* —opposite **win 6** [T] to have less of: *The aircraft began to lose height.* | *He's lost a lot of weight.* | *She's losing a lot of blood; we must get her to hospital straightaway.* —opposite **gain 7** [I;T (**on**)] to have less (money) than when one started: *We lost (a lot of money) on that job.* —opposite **make 8** [T] to wander unintentionally away from; fail to find (one's way): *We lost our way and had to ask a policeman.* **9** [T] to (cause to) fail to hear, see, or understand: *Most of what she said was lost in the din.* | *He sped off, and became lost to view behind some trees.* | (infml) *I'm sorry, you've lost me: could you explain that again?* **10** [T] to fail to use; waste: *The doctor lost no time in getting the sick man to a hospital.* **11** [T (**in**)] to give all (one's) attention to something so as not to notice anything else; IMMERSE: *He lost himself in the book/in his work.* **12** [T] to confuse (oneself), esp. so as not to remember what one was going to do or say next: *I lost myself in the middle of trying to explain, so I had to start again.* **13** [I;T] (of a watch or clock) to work too slowly by (an amount of time): *This watch loses (50 minutes a day).* —opposite **gain;** see CLOCK (USAGE) **14 lose one's heart (to)** to fall in love (with) **15 lose one's shirt** AmE infml to lose everything one owns: *He lost his shirt in a bad business deal.* **16 lose sight of** to fail to consider; forget: *In the heat of the argument we mustn't lose sight of our main objective.* —see also LOST

lose out phr v [I] **1** [(**on**)] to make a loss, often large (from something): *The firm lost out (on the deal).* **2** [(**to**)] to be defeated or receive less favourable treatment: *The tax cuts are good news for the rich, but the poor lose out again.* | *The small companies are losing out to the big multinationals because of fierce competition.*

los·er /ˈluːzəʳ/ n **1** a person who loses: *There was a silver cup for the winner, and medals for the losers.* | *A good loser is somebody who doesn't get upset if he or she loses.* **2** derog a person who is unsuccessful in life, esp. because of lack of personal qualities; a failure: *I'm a born loser.*

loss /lɒs‖lɔːs/ *n* **1** [C;U] the act or an example of losing or failing to keep something: *Did you report the loss of your jewellery to the police?* | *The vehicle developed a loss of power.* | *We all expressed our condolences on his great loss.* (=the death of someone close to him) | *She's moved to another job; it's a great loss to our firm.* | *The British forces suffered heavy losses* (=many soldiers were killed) *on the first day of the battle.* **2** [C] the amount by which the cost of an article or business operation is greater than the income it produces: *a (net) loss of over £2 million* | *The company has made big losses this year.* (=has spent a lot more money than it has made) **3 at a loss: a** at a price lower than the original cost **b** uncertain what to do, think, or say; confused: *I was at a loss for words when she told me the news.* —see also DEAD LOSS

loss ad·just·er /ˈ· ·,··/ *n* a person employed by an insurance company to value losses and settle claims

loss lead·er /ˈ· ,··/ *n* an article sold at a low price in order to attract people into a shop

lost /lɒst‖lɔːst/ *adj* **1** that cannot be found by the owner: *a lost dog* | *lost keys* **2** [F] unable to find the way: *I got lost in the snow.* **3** no longer possessed or existing: *one's lost youth* | *a lost art* **4** not used, obtained, or won: *a lost chance/opportunity* **5** [F] destroyed, ruined, killed, drowned, etc.: *The boat and all its men were lost at sea.* **6** [F+to] not noticing: *He was reading his book, completely lost to the world.* **7** [F+on, upon] having no influence or effect on: *Good advice is lost on him.* **8 get lost** *sl* (used for telling people forcefully to go away): *He tried to introduce himself, but she told him to get lost.*

lost cause /ˌ· ˈ·/ *n* something which has no chance of success: *Give up that idea — it's a lost cause.*

Lost Gen·e·ra·tion /ˌ· ··ˈ··/ [the] **1** the group of people who became adults during or just after the First World War, and are seen as being socially or emotionally disadvantaged as a result **2** the young men who were killed in the First World War, seen as people who could have been influential in art, science, etc. **3** a group of American writers who grew up during the First World War, such as Ernest Hemingway and F. Scott Fitzgerald

lost prop·er·ty /ˌ· ˈ···/ *n* [U] articles found in public places because people have forgotten them, which are collected and kept in a special place (**lost property office** *BrE* ‖ **lost-and-found (office)** *AmE*) to which people who have lost something can go in the hope of getting it back

Lost Week·end /ˌ· ·ˈ·, ˌ· ˈ··‖ˌ· ˈ··/, **The** a 1945 American film in which a writer spends two days drinking a lot of alcohol and losing control of his life

lot[1] /lɒt‖lɑːt/ *n* **1** [C (**of**)] also **lots** *pl.*— a great quantity, number, or amount: *A lot of people/Lots of people came to the party.* | *She's got lots (and lots) of money.* | *I've got a lot (of work) to do.* | *They gave us lots to eat.* | *What a lot of food there is!* —compare PLENTY; see MANY (USAGE), MORE[2] (USAGE) **2** [*the*+*sing./pl. v*] the whole quantity, number, or amount: *Give me the lot.* (=all of it or all of them) | *The whole lot of you are mad!* **3** [C+*sing./pl. v*] a group or set of people or things of the same type; an amount of a substance or material: *Another lot of students is/are arriving soon.* | *This wine's no good but the next lot may be better.* **4 a** '**fat lot** *infml* none at all: *A fat lot you care!* (=You don't care at all.) | *We tried to make him change his mind, but a fat lot of good it did us!* **5 a lot/(infml) lots** (esp. in comparisons) much; a great deal: *This is a lot better.* | *This is lots more interesting.* **6 Thanks a lot!** Thank you very much!: *"I posted your letters." "Thanks a lot."* | (used to mean the opposite) *"I forgot to bring your money." "Oh, thanks a lot!"*

lot[2] *n* **1** [C] an article or a number of articles sold together, esp. at an AUCTION sale: *Lot 49, a fine old silver cigarette case.* —see also JOB LOT **2** [C] *esp. AmE* an area of land, esp. one for a particular purpose such as for building or parking cars on: *playing on an empty lot* —see also PARKING LOT **3** [C] a film STUDIO (=a building in which films are made) and the ground surrounding it **4** [C] any of a set of objects of different sizes or with different markings used for making a choice or decision by chance: *The children* **drew lots** (=chose such objects one by one) *to see who would go first.* **5** [U] the use of such objects to make a choice or decision: *The winner was chosen by lot.* —see also LOTTERY **6** [S] *fml or lit* the quality or manner of a person's life, regarded as something that cannot be

changed or avoided; fortune; fate: *Learn to be content with your lot (in life).*

Lot's wife /ˌ· ˈ·/ (in the Bible) a woman who was turned into a PILLAR of salt because she disobeyed God's command not to look back when she and her family were running from Sodom, which God was about to destroy

loth /ləʊθ/ *adj* [F+*to-v*] LOATH

Lo·tha·ri·o /ləˈθɑːriəʊ‖ləʊˈθeːr-/ *n lit or derog* a man whose main interest is having as many female lovers as possible without having a serious relationship with any of them: *a known Lothario*

Lo·thi·an /ˈləʊðiən/ a REGION in SE Scotland, which contains the city of Edinburgh

lo·tion /ˈləʊʃ*ə*n/ *n* [C;U] a liquid mixture, used on the skin or hair, e.g. to make it clean and healthy or less painful: *Put some lotion on your sunburn.* | *baby lotion* | *sun-tan lotion*

lot·te·ry /ˈlɒtəri‖ˈlɑː-/ *n* **1** [C] a system in which many numbered tickets are sold, some of which are later chosen by chance and prizes given to those who bought them —compare DRAW[2] (2), RAFFLE **2** [S] something whose result or worth is uncertain or risky: *Life is a lottery.*

lo·tus /ˈləʊtəs/ *n* **1** a white or pink flower that grows, esp. in Asia, on the surface of lakes **2** the shape of this flower used formally in decorative patterns, esp. in ancient Egyptian art **3** (in ancient Greek stories) a fruit which, when eaten, caused the eater to feel pleasantly dreamy, forgetful, and lazy

lotus-eat·er /ˈ·· ,··/ *n* a person who leads a lazy dreamy life and is not concerned with the business of the world (from the people in the *Odyssey* who behaved in this way after eating a fruit called a lotus)

lotus po·si·tion /ˈ·· ·,··/ [*the*] a position in YOGA in which you sit on the floor with your legs crossed and your hands on your knees, esp. when you want to MEDITATE

lotus position

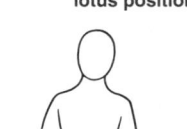

loud[1] /laʊd/ *adj* **1** having or producing great strength of sound: *The radio isn't loud enough; could you turn it up?* | *loud music* | *loud protests* **2** attracting attention by being unpleasantly noisy or colourful: *a loud young man who stood at the desk demanding to see the manager* | *He was wearing a rather loud shirt.* — ~**ly** *adv* — ~**ness** *n* [U]

loud[2] *adv* loudly; in a loud way: *Could you speak a little louder?* | *He read the news article* **out loud.** (=so people could hear it) —see also **for crying out loud** (CRY[1])

loud·hail·er /ˌlaʊdˈheɪlə*r*/ *n esp. BrE for* MEGAPHONE

loud·mouth /ˈlaʊdmaʊθ/ *n* -**mouths** /maʊðz/ *infml derog* a person who talks too much and in an offensive way — ~**ed** *adj*

loud·speak·er /ˌlaʊdˈspiːkə*r*, ˈlaʊdˌspiːkə*r*/ *n* **1** a SPEAKER (4) **2** an apparatus for making sounds louder: *The police addressed the crowd through a loudspeaker on their car.*

lough /lɒx, lɒk ‖ lɑːk, lɑːx/ *n* (in Ireland) a lake or a part of the sea almost surrounded by land

Lough Neagh /ˌlɒx ˈneɪ, lɒk-‖ˌlɑːk-, ˌlɑːx-/ a lake in Northern Ireland west of Belfast, the largest in the British Isles, popular with walkers and for sailing YACHTS

Lou·is XIV /ˌluːi ðə fɔːˈtiːnθ‖-fɔːr-/ (1638–1715) a King of France, who is also called the **Sun King** because of the beauty and RICHES of his court at Versailles —see also LOUIS QUATORZE

Louis XV /ˌluːi ðə fɪfˈtiːnθ/ (1710–74) the King of France from 1715 to 1774

Louis XVI /ˌluːi ðə sɪksˈtiːnθ/ (1754–93) the King of France at the time of the French Revolution, who was killed on the GUILLOTINE

Lou·is /ˈluːɪs/, **Joe** (1914–81) an American BOXER, the world HEAVYWEIGHT CHAMPION from 1937 to 1948

Lou·i·si·a·na /luːˌiːziˈænə/ *written abbrev:* **LA** a state in the southern US whose largest city is New Orleans —see colour map on pages 1374–5

Louisiana Pur·chase /·,····· '··/ also **Louisiana Ter·ri·to·ry** /·,····· '····/ [the] the area of land which the US bought from France in 1803. It covered the land between the Mississippi River and the Rocky Mountains and between Canada and the Gulf of Mexico. The Louisiana Purchase more than doubled the size of the US as it was then.

Louis Qua·torze /ˌluːi kæˈtɔːz‖-ˈtɔːrz/ adj typical of the ARCHITECTURE or furniture from the time of Louis XIV of France

Louis Quinze /ˌluːi ˈkænz/ adj typical of the ARCHITECTURE or furniture from the time of Louis XV of France

lounge¹ /laʊndʒ/ n **1** [C] a comfortable room for sitting in, such as: **a** esp. BrE a LIVING ROOM in a private house **b** a small public room in a hotel **c** AmE a large public room esp. in a hotel or theatre **d** LOUNGE BAR —see also COCK-TAIL LOUNGE **2** [S] BrE infml an act or period of lounging

lounge² v [I+adv/prep] **1** to stand or sit in a leaning lazy way: *lounging near the bar* **2** derog to spend time in a lazy way, doing nothing: *Don't lounge around/about all day: do something!*

lounge bar /'· ·/ n BrE for SALOON BAR

lounge liz·ard /'· ˌ··/ n AmE sl a man who goes to bars, NIGHTCLUBS, etc., in hopes of finding women who will buy him drinks or food or who will even support him with money

loung·er /ˈlaʊndʒəʳ/ n **1** derog a lazy person who does no work **2** a type of folding bed used in the garden for lying in the sun; a SUNBED

lounge suit /'· ·/ BrE ‖ **business suit** AmE— n a man's suit, for wearing during the day, e.g. in an office. In Britain and the US most men who work in a bank, office, etc. have to wear a lounge suit when they go to work, even when the weather is very hot or very cold. It is usu. in a dark colour such as grey or black, made of wool or similar material, and is always worn with a shirt and tie.

lour /ˈlaʊəʳ/ v [I] esp. BrE for LOWER³

Lourdes /lʊəd, lʊədz‖lʊərd/ a small town in SW France where Catholics believe that Saint Bernadette saw the Virgin Mary appear. For Catholics Lourdes is a holy place where MIRACLES can happen. Many sick people go there because they believe that the water there can heal them.

louse¹ /laʊs/ n **1** (pl. **lice** /laɪs/) any of several types of small wingless insect that live on the skin and in the hair of people and animals —see also DELOUSE **2** (pl. **louses** /ˈlaʊsɪz/) sl a worthless person

louse² v
louse sthg./sbdy. ↔ **up** phr v [T] AmE sl to make worse rather than better; MESS up: *The rain has loused up my plans.*

lou·sy /ˈlaʊzi/ adj **1** infml very bad, unpleasant, useless, etc.: *What lousy weather!* **2** [F+with] sl a derog filled (with): *The town was lousy with tourists.* **b** having plenty (of esp. money) **3** covered with lice (LOUSE)

lout /laʊt/ n derog a rough rude (young) man — ~ish adj ~ishness n [U]

Louth /laʊð, laʊθ/ the smallest COUNTY in the Republic of Ireland, on the NE coast

lou·vre also **lou·ver** AmE /ˈluːvəʳ/ n an arrangement of narrow sloping bands of wood, plastic, metal, etc., fixed in a frame that swings across a window, doorway, etc., esp. to allow some light in but keep rain or strong sun out — see picture at BLIND

Louvre /ˈluːvrə, luːv/ [the] the most famous French MUSEUM of art which is in Paris and has many important paintings, including the Mona Lisa

lov·a·ble , **loveable** /ˈlʌvəbəl/ adj easy to love or like; pleasant: *His vicious temper didn't make him the most lovable of men.* | *a lovable kitten*

love¹ /lʌv/ n **1** [U (for)] a strong feeling of fondness for another person, esp. between members of a family or close friends: *a mother's love for her child* —opposite **hate**, **hatred** **2** [U (for)] fondness combined with sexual attraction: *The young pair are* **in love** *(with each other).* | *They* **fell in love** *at once: it was* **love at first sight.** | *a love story*

▶ CULTURAL NOTE Some people, esp. women, think of love as being something perfect and better than reality. They

read love stories and believe in **love at first sight** (i.e. that two people can fall in love the moment they first see each other). They imagine love as leading to a beautiful white wedding and continuing happiness. Love is often represented by a red heart or by CUPID. ◀

3 [S;U (**of, for**)] warm interest and enjoyment (in) and attraction (to): *(a) love of music/sport* **4** [C] the object of such interest and attraction: *Music was one of the great loves of his life.* **5** [C] a person who is loved: *She was the great love of his life.* | *Yes, (my) love.* —compare LOVER (1) **6** also **luv** nonstandard or humor— BrE infml (a friendly form of address, esp. to or by a woman): *Would you like a cup of tea, love?* **7** [U] (in tennis) no points; NIL: *Becker leads 15-love.* | *a love game* (=where the opponent won no points) **8 the course of true love never runs smooth** an old saying **9 give/send someone one's love** to send friendly greetings to **10 love's young dream** a phrase used when talking about young people who are in love and believe that their love will last for ever and they will always be happy **11 make love (to): a** to have sex (with), but usu. suggesting greater fondness and tenderness than the phrase "have sex": *They made love.* | *He made love to her.* **b** esp. old use to show that one is in love (with) by always being with, kissing, etc. **12 make love not war** a phrase used by hippies (HIPPY) in the 1960s, encouraging people to make love (=have sex) rather than to fight **13 no love lost between** infml no friendship between: *There's no love lost between those two.* (=they dislike each other) **14 not for love or/nor money** infml not by any means: *You can't get that book for love or money: it's completely sold out.* **15 the ... you love to hate** saying of someone who is generally unpopular: *The taxman; the man you love to hate.*

love² v [not in progressive forms] **1** [I;T] to feel love, desire, or strong friendship (for): *I love my mother/husband.* **2** [T] to have a strong liking for; take pleasure in: *She loves this warm weather.* | *I'd love a cup of coffee.* [+v-ing] *I love sitting in the garden.* [+to-v] *We love to hear her sing.* [+obj+to-v] *I'd love you to come and see our new house.* — opposite **hate 3 Love thy neighbour as thyself** saying from the Bible people should be kind and understanding towards others **4 'Tis better to have loved and lost than never to have loved at all** quote a phrase from a poem by Tennyson

▷ USAGE **Beloved**, which is often formal or literary, is used about a person or thing you **love**; *My beloved husband*, but **dear** is more common: *My dear wife.* The person or thing that you like or love the best is your **favourite**: *My favourite song* | *John's a great favourite with his grandmother.*◁

love af·fair /'· ·ˌ·/ n a sexual relationship, esp. between a man and a woman who are not married or who are married to other people; an AFFAIR (3)

love·bird /ˈlʌvbɜːd‖-bɜːrd/ n any of various types of PARROT that stand in pairs

love·birds /ˈlʌvbɜːdz‖-bɜːrdz/ n [P] infml two people clearly in love with each other: *When are those two lovebirds going to get married?*

love-child /ˈlʌvtʃaɪld/ n old use or euph for BASTARD (1)

love-hate re·la·tion·ship /ˌ· '· ·ˌ···/ n a relationship in which the partners often argue or feel angry with each other, but do not wish to end the relationship: *It's more of a love-hate relationship than a happy marriage — but I'd be lost without him.* | (fig.) *a love-hate relationship with the computer*

love·less /ˈlʌvləs/ adj **1** without love: *a loveless marriage* **2** not giving or receiving love

love letter /'· ˌ··/ n a letter written by a person to someone with whom they are in love. A love letter is usu. meant to be private, and may contain secret hopes or thoughts: *My grandfather always kept the love letters my grandmother had written to him.*

love life /'· ·/ n [C;U] the part of a person's life that involves girlfriends, boyfriends, sex, marriage, etc.: *"How's your love life these days — got a boyfriend?"* | *gossiping about other people's love lives*

love·lorn /ˈlʌvlɔːn‖-lɔːrn/ adj esp. lit sad because one's love is not returned

love·ly¹ /ˈlʌvli/ adj **1** beautiful, attractive, etc., esp. to both the heart and the eye: *a lovely girl* | *a lovely view* **2** infml **a** very pleasant or enjoyable: *a lovely meal* | *lovely*

weather **b** *esp. BrE* (used for expressing thanks): *"The typing's done." "(That's) lovely, Sally."* —**liness** *n* [U]

▷ USAGE **Lovely** is not usually used to describe the physical appearance of men. Instead, **handsome** or **good-looking** is used. —see also BEAUTIFUL (USAGE)◁

lovely² *n infml, becoming rare* a beautiful woman

love-mak-ing /ˈlʌvˌmeɪkɪŋ/ *n* [U] *euph* sexual activity, esp. the act of having sex —see also **make love** (LOVE¹)

love nest /ˈ· ·/ (used esp. in newspapers) a small flat, room, or house used by two people having a sexual relationship, esp. one which is secret because they are not supposed to be together: *Pop star shared love nest with banker's wife.*

love po-tion /ˈ· ˌ··/ *n* a liquid mixture intended to make the person who drinks it fall in love with someone in particular. Most people in the West do not believe in this sort of magic, although love potions are found in old stories.

lov-er /ˈlʌvəʳ/ *n* **1** a person (usu. a man) who has a sexual relationship with another person outside marriage, esp. over a long period: *She has had many lovers.* | *He is her lover.* —compare LOVE¹ (5), MISTRESS (2) **2** a sexual partner: *Women today are expected to be wage-earner, wife, mother and lover.* **3** a person who is very fond of or interested in the stated thing: *a lover of good food* | *art/ music lovers*

lov-ers /ˈlʌvəz‖-ərz/ *n* [P] two people in love with and/or having a sexual relationship with each other: *They met in June and became lovers soon after.*

love-seat /ˈlʌvsiːt/ *n AmE* an S-shaped SOFA designed so that two people can sit side-by-side while facing each other: *A couch will be too big for this room but a loveseat will fit just fine.*

love-sick /ˈlʌvˌsɪk/ *adj* sad or ill because of unreturned love: *a lovesick poet*

Love's La-bour's Lost /ˌ· ·· ˈ·/ a humorous play by William Shakespeare in which a king and some of his noblemen (NOBLEMAN) swear to live away from the king's court, to study, and to have no dealings with women. However, they meet a princess and her ladies and find they cannot keep their promises.

Love Sto-ry /ˈ· ··/ the title of a popular book by Erich Segal and of a film with Ali McGraw and Ryan O'Neal in which two young people fall in love and get married, but the woman dies young of CANCER

lov-ey also **luvvie** /ˈlʌvi/ *n BrE infml* a word used to address a person, esp. a woman (though it is usu. considered offensive by them) or child: *Come here, lovey!*

lov-ey-dov-ey /ˌ··· ˈ··◂/ *adj infml derog* too loving in a ROMANTIC way; SENTIMENTAL: *I'm getting a bit sick of their lovey-dovey behaviour.*

lov-ing /ˈlʌvɪŋ/ *adj* showing or expressing love; fond: *a loving look* | *a loving father* — ~ **ly** *adv* : *They were looking at each other lovingly.* | *He polished his new sports car lovingly.*

loving cup /ˈ·· ·/ *n* a very large cup, usu. with two handles that used to be passed round at ceremonial meals in former times, to be drunk out of by everyone

loving kind-ness /ˌ·· ˈ··/ *n* [U] *esp. lit* gentle and tender care, friendship, or love

low¹ /ləʊ/ *adj* **1** not measuring much from the base to the top; not high: *He jumped over the low wall.* | *a long low building* **2** not far above the ground, floor, base, or bottom: *a low shelf* | *low clouds* | *The mirror is too low — I can't see the top of my head in it.* | *(fig.) That comes/is low on the list of jobs to be done.* (=It is not one of the most important jobs.) | *(fig., old use) a man of low* (=not noble) *birth* **3** being or lying below the usual level or height: *a low bridge* | *low ground* | *The river is getting low and will soon dry up.* **4** small in size, degree, amount, or value: *a low temperature* | *That figure seems very low; can it be right?* | *The price of oil is at its lowest level for ten years.* | *families on low incomes* | *a child of low intelligence* | *a low-budget film* **5** [F (on)] near or at the end of a supply or measure: *The coal's getting low/We're getting low on coal; we must order some more.* **6** [(in)] having only a small amount of a particular substance, quality, etc.: *This milk is low in fat* | *low-tar cigarettes* | *low-alcohol wine* **7** not loud; soft: *She heard a low moaning noise.* | *Keep your voices low — I don't want her to hear us.* **8** (of a musical note) deep: *This song is too low for*

a tenor. **9** unhappy; DEPRESSED: *She's still feeling a bit low about failing that exam.* | *in rather low spirits* **10** regarding something as of little worth; unfavourable: *I have a low opinion of that book.* **11** for a slow speed: *Use a low gear when driving slowly.* **12** not fair, generous, or honest; DISHONOURABLE: *That was a low trick.* — opposite **high** (for 1,2,3,4,6,8,10,11); see also **lay someone low** (LAY²), **lie low** (LIE¹); see HIGH¹ (USAGE) — ~ **ness** *n* [U]

low² *adv* **1** in or to a low position, degree, manner, or level: *He was bent low over a book.* | *We turned the heating down low.* | *low-paid workers* | *The price of coffee sank lower today due to rumours of a big harvest.* **2** near the ground, floor, base, etc.; not high: *The sun sank low in the sky.* | *Watch out for low-flying aircraft.* **3** (in music) in or with deep notes —opposite **high** **4** quietly; softly —see also LOWLY, **high and low** (HIGH²)

low³ *n* **1** [C] a low point, price, degree, or level: *Profits have reached an all-time low this month.* —opposite **high** **2** [C] an area of low pressure in the air —opposite **high** **3** [U] the GEAR that is used to make a vehicle move slowly

low⁴ *v* [I] *esp. lit* to make the sound of a cow; MOO

low-born /ˌləʊˈbɔːn◂‖-ɔːrn◂/ *adj lit* born to parents of low social class

low-brow /ˈləʊbraʊ/ *n usu. derog* a person who has no interest in literature, the ARTS, etc. —compare HIGHBROW, MIDDLEBROW —**lowbrow** *adj*

low-cal, lo-cal /ˈləʊ kæl/ *adj AmE infml* having few CALORIES: *a low-cal ice cream*

Low Church /ˌ· ˈ·◂/ *adj* (in the Christian religion, esp. the Church of England) believing in the importance of faith and studying the Bible, rather than in religious ceremonies —compare HIGH CHURCH

low com-e-dy /ˌ· ˈ···/ *n* [C;U] (a type of) funny play similar to FARCE

Low Coun-tries /ˌ· ˈ···/ [the+P] a REGION in NW Europe which includes Belgium, Luxembourg, the Netherlands, and the area which used to be called Flanders; also known as **Benelux**

low-cut /ˌ· ˈ·◂/ *adj* (of a dress or article of clothing worn on the upper half of the body, usu. by a female) cut in a way that shows the wearer's neck and top of the chest, or CLEAVAGE (2): *a low-cut evening dress* —compare LOW-NECKED

low-down /ˈləʊdaʊn/ *n* [the (on)] *sl* the true and often secret information about a person, event, etc.: *He says he has the lowdown on what happened at the negotiations.*

low-down /ˈ· ·/ *adj* [A] *infml* dishonest and dishonourable; CONTEMPTIBLE: *a dirty low-down trick*

Lowe /ləʊ/, **Arthur** (1914–82) an English theatre and film actor, famous esp. as Captain Mainwaring in the BBC television series *Dad's Army*

Low-ell /ˈləʊəl/, **Rob-ert** /ˈrɒbət ‖ ˈrɑːbərt/ (1917–77) an American poet and writer of plays. His opposition to the Vietnam War and support of Senator McCarthy are recorded in his *Notebook 1967–1968.*

low-er¹ /ˈləʊəʳ/ *adj* [A] in or being the bottom part: *He was wounded in the lower leg.* (=the bottom part of the leg) | *on the lower deck of the ship* —opposite **upper**

lower² *v* **1** [I;T] to make or become smaller in amount, degree, strength, etc.: *They've lowered the price from £15 to £10.* | *Please lower your voice.* **2** [T] to move or let down in height: *They lowered the coffin into the grave.* | *Flags were lowered to half-mast.* **3** [T *usu. in negatives*] to bring (someone, esp. oneself) down in worth or opinion by behaving in an immoral or dishonourable way: *I wouldn't lower myself to take part in such a dishonest business.*

low-er³ , **lour** /ˈlaʊəʳ/ *v* [I] **1** (of the sky or weather) to be dark and threatening: *a lowering sky before the storm* **2** [(at, on, upon)] to look in a dissatisfied bad-tempered manner; FROWN

lower case /ˌ·· ˈ·◂/ *n* [U] letters written or printed in the usual small form (such as *a, b, c*) rather than in the large (CAPITAL or UPPER CASE) form (such as *A, B, C*) —compare CAPITAL —**lower case** *adj*

lower class /ˌ·· ˈ·◂/ also **lower classes** *pl.*— *n* [the+sing./pl. v] often derog a social class of the lowest rank; WORKING CLASS: *a member of the lower class/lower classes* —compare MIDDLE CLASS, UPPER CLASS; see WORKING CLASS (USAGE) and see also extra information on page 1258

—lower-class *adj* : *a lower-class background*

Lower East Side /ˌ·· '· ˌ·/ also **East Side** *[the]* the southeastern part of Manhattan in New York, lived in mostly by people who have come to the US from other countries. This is one of the poorer parts of the city.

Lower House /ˌ·· '·/ also **Lower Cham·ber** /ˌ·· '··/— *[the]* either of the two branches of a law-making body, esp. the one that is larger, more representative, and more powerful, such as the British House of Commons or the American House of Representatives

lower mid·dle-class /ˌ·· ˌ·· '·/ *[the]* (in Britain) the part of society which sees itself and is seen by others as being between WORKING CLASS and MIDDLE CLASS. Typically, lower middle-class people work in offices and shops. They may enjoy some of the activities which middle-class people enjoy, but have not usu. had the good education which is typical of middle-class people. **—lower middle-class** *adj* : *My family are lower middle-class.*

low·er·most /ˈləʊəməʊst‖ˈləʊər-/ *adj fml* lowest

lower or·ders /ˌ·· ˌ··/ *[the+P] derog* people from the lower ranks of a society. This word is used by people who consider themselves to be more important than people of lower social rank: *unseemly outbursts of discontent among the lower orders*

lower sixth /ˌ·· '·/ *n [C+sing./pl.v]* the first year of the SIXTH FORM in British schools —compare UPPER SIXTH

lowest com·mon de·nom·i·na·tor /ˌ·· ˌ·· ·'····/ *n [U]* **1** *math* the smallest number that can be the DENOMINATOR in a group of FRACTIONS **2** the largest group of people who will watch or listen to something, esp. television, even if it is not very good: *The president's speech is designed to appeal to the lowest common denominator and doesn't actually say very much of importance.* | *TV shows often seem aimed at the lowest common denominator.*

lowest com·mon mul·ti·ple /ˌ·· ˌ·· '···/ also **LCM, least common multiple** the smallest number that two other numbers divide into exactly: *12 is the lowest common multiple of 4 and 6*

low-fat /ˌ·· '·◂/ *adj* (of food, cookery) containing or using only a small amount of fat: *low-fat skimmed milk* | *a low-fat way of cooking*

low-key /ˌ·· '·◂/ *adj* controlled in style or quality; not loud, bright, or forceful: *The prime minister made a low-key speech, hoping to calm the situation.*

low·land /ˈləʊlənd/ also **lowlands** *pl.* — *adj, n [A;U]* (of) an area of land that is lower than the land surrounding it: *These cattle thrive best in lowland areas.*

low·land·er /ˈləʊləndər/ *n* a person who lives in a lowland area

Low·lands /ˈləʊləndz/ *[the+P]* the central and eastern part of Scotland which is lower than the land surrounding it —compare HIGHLANDS

low-la·ther /ˌ·· '··◂/ *adj* (of washing powder etc.) producing less LATHER¹ than other products do

low life /'· ·/ *n [U]* **1** the life and behaviour of people of low social class, esp. those who live in big cities and take part in criminal activities: *a well-known novel about low life in Chicago during the 1930s* **2** *AmE sl* a person who takes part in criminal activities or who is bad: *John's turned out to be a real lowlife.*

low·ly¹ /ˈləʊli/ *adv [+v-ed]* in a low level or degree: *lowly paid workers* —see also LOW²

lowly² *adj* low in rank, position, or social class; HUMBLE: *a lowly bank clerk* **—liness** *n [U]*

low-ly·ing /ˌ·· '···◂/ *adj* **1** (of land) not much above the level of the sea; not high: *low-lying fields* **2** below the usual level: *low-lying clouds*

low-necked /ˌ·· '·◂/ *adj* (of an article of women's clothing) cut so as to leave the neck and shoulders uncovered —compare LOW-CUT

low-pitched /ˌ·· '·◂/ *adj* **1** (of a musical note) deep **2** (of a roof) not steep

low pro·file /ˌ·· '···◂/ *n [usu. sing.]* the state of not drawing attention to oneself or one's actions: *We'd better keep a low profile until the public outcry has died down.* —opposite **high profile** **—low-profile** *adj*

low·rid·er /ˈləʊraɪdər/ *n AmE* **1** a car whose bottom is very low to the ground, esp. one that is decorated inside and out with lights and other things that draw attention to

it **2** a person, usu. a TEENAGE boy, who drives such a car, often thought of as likely to cause trouble

low-rise /'· ·/ *adj* [A] (of a building) having only one or two floors (STOREYS) —compare HIGH-RISE

Low·ry /ˈlaʊri/, **L S** (1887–1976) an English artist whose paintings of the industrial North of England showing factories and crowds of people are all drawn in a very simple style as if done by a child

low sea·son /'· ˌ··/ *n [(the)* U] the time of year when business activity and prices are at their lowest: *Winter is (the) low season at seaside hotels.* —compare HIGH SEASON

low-so·di·um /ˌ·· '····◂/ *adj* (of food) containing only a small amount of SODIUM, usu. in the form of salt: *a low-sodium diet*

low-spir·it·ed /ˌ·· '····◂/ *adj* unhappy; LOW¹ (9)

Low Sun·day /ˌ·· '··/ the Sunday following Easter

low-tech /ˌ·· '·◂/ *adj* not using advanced machines, processes, or methods, e.g. in business or industry

low tide /ˌ·· '·/ *n [C;U]* the moment when the water is at its lowest point on the sea shore because the TIDE has gone out —opposite **high tide**

low wa·ter /ˌ·· '··/ *n [U]* the moment when the water in a river is at its lowest point because of the TIDE —opposite **high water**

low water mark /ˌ·· '·· ˌ·/ *n* **1** a mark showing the lowest point reached by a body of water, such as a river **2** the lowest point of success: *Our fortunes had reached their low water mark.* —opposite **high water mark**

lox /lɒks‖lɑːks/ *n [U] AmE* SALMON (a fish) preserved with smoke. Lox is often eaten with BAGELS.

loy·al /ˈlɔɪəl/ *adj [(to)]* faithful to one's friends, principles, country, etc.; always giving support: *He has remained loyal to the team even though they lose every game.* | *a loyal supporter of the government* — ~**ly** *adv*

loy·al·ist /ˈlɔɪəlɪst/ *n* a person who remains loyal to an existing government when opposed by those who want to change it **—loyalist** *adj*

Loyalist *n* **1** a Protestant in Northern Ireland who believes that it should remain part of the UK **2** someone who was loyal to the royal family during the English Civil War **3** someone who supported the elected government during the Spanish Civil War **4** someone who fought with the British during the War of American Independence **5** someone who supported the cause of the Union during the American Civil War **—Loyalist** *adj* : *the Loyalist flag/anthem*

loy·al·ty /ˈlɔɪəlti/ *n* **1** [U (to)] the quality of being loyal: *No one could ever doubt her loyalty.* **2** [C *usu. pl.*] a feeling of being loyal to someone or something: *She felt a strong loyalty to the old ideals.* | *He had divided loyalties; he wanted to be loyal to the company, but he also wanted to do what was best for his family.*

loz·enge /ˈlɒzɪndʒ‖ˈlɑː-/ *n* **1** a small flat sweet, esp. one that contains medicine and melts slowly in the mouth: *a cough lozenge* **2** *tech* a shape that has four straight and equal sides, with two sharp angles opposite each other and two wide angles

LP /ˌel ˈpiː/ also **long-player, long-playing record, album—** *n* a record that turns 33 times a minute, and usu. plays for between 20 and 25 minutes per side

LPG /ˌel piː ˈdʒiː/ *n [U]* liquefied petroleum gas; gas such as PROPANE, obtained from oil, kept in liquid form under pressure, and used as a FUEL for motor vehicles: *All the fork-lift trucks in this factory run on LPG.*   **L-plate**

L-plate /ˈel pleɪt/ *n BrE* either of two flat squares marked with a red letter L, that must be fixed to the front and back of a vehicle which is being driven by a learner

LPN /ˌel piː ˈen/ *n* LICENSED PRACTICAL NURSE

LPO /ˌel piː ˈəʊ/ *[the]* LONDON PHILHARMONIC ORCHESTRA

LRT /ˌel ɑː ˈtiː‖-ɑːr-/ LONDON REGIONAL TRANSPORT

LRV /ˌel ɑː ˈviː‖-ɑːr-/ also **Light Rail Vehicle—** *n* a kind of train whose tracks run in or between streets, used in many cities esp. in the US

LSAT /ˌel es eɪ ˈtiː/ n abbrev for Law School Admissions Test; a national examination necessary to enter an American law school

Lsd, £sd /ˌel es ˈdiː/ n [U] BrE infml (used esp. before decimal money was introduced in Britain) money

LSD /ˌel es ˈdiː/ also **acid** sl— n [U] an ILLEGAL drug that causes the user to see life and the world as much more beautiful, strange, frightening, etc., than usual, and sometimes to see things that do not exist. It was used esp. in the 1960s: He was on an LSD trip. (=experienced the effects of LSD)

LSE /ˌel es ˈiː/ abbrev. for: LONDON SCHOOL OF ECONOMICS

LSO /ˌel es ˈəʊ/ [the] LONDON SYMPHONY ORCHESTRA

Lt. n written abbrev. for: LIEUTENANT

Ltd written abbrev. for: LIMITED (2): M.Y. Dixon and Son, Ltd, Booksellers —compare INC, PLC

lu·au /ˈluːaʊ/ n AmE a party held outside which usu. has Hawaiian food or entertainment

lu·bri·cant /ˈluːbrɪkənt/ n [C;U] a substance, esp. a type of oil, used for making parts in a machine, etc., move easily and smoothly without rubbing or sticking

lu·bri·cate /ˈluːbrɪkeɪt/ v [T] to cause to move or work easily and smoothly without rubbing or sticking, esp. by means of a lubricant: This oil lubricates the machine. | (fig.) A few whiskies will lubricate his tongue. (=make him speak freely) —**cator** n : Oil is a good lubricator. —**cation** /ˌluːbrɪˈkeɪʃən/ n [U]

lu·bri·cious /luːˈbrɪʃəs/ adj fml showing too great an interest in sex, esp. in a way that is unpleasant or socially unacceptable

Luc·ca /ˈlʊkə‖ˈluː-/ a city in N Italy

lu·cerne /luːˈsɜːn‖-ɜːrn/ BrE ALFALFA

Lucerne a city in central Switzerland on **Lake Lucerne**

lu·cid /ˈluːsɪd/ adj **1** well expressed and easy to understand; clear: a lucid explanation **2** able to understand clearly, but perhaps only for a short time: The old man is confused most of the time but he does have lucid moments. — **~ly** adv — **~ity** /luːˈsɪdɪti/ n [U]

Lu·ci·fer /ˈluːsɪfər/ the ARCHANGEL in the Bible who led the ANGELS in a REVOLT and was forced to leave Heaven and live in Hell; Satan; the Devil

luck¹ /lʌk/ n [U] **1** the good or bad things that happen to a person in the course of events (as if) by chance; fate; fortune: Luck was with us/was on our side and we won easily. | I've had bad luck all week. | The hotel was full, so we decided to try our luck elsewhere. | **As luck would have it** (=by chance) a policeman was passing by. | (infml) He reached the food before I did, **worse luck!** (=unfortunately) | When I got to the theatre they had just sold the last ticket — that's **just my luck!** (=typical of my luck) **2** success or something good that happens as a result of chance; good fortune: Good luck! | I wish you luck/the best of luck. | She won £500 in the lottery; some people have all the luck! | This charm will bring you luck. | What a **stroke of luck** I met you in time to stop you! | Give it three drops of oil — and one more **for luck!** | I'm sorry you didn't pass your driving test — **better luck next time!** **3** **be down on one's luck** to have bad luck, esp. to be without money **4** **be in/out of luck** to have/not have good fortune: We're in luck; the train hasn't left yet. —see also HARD LUCK, **push one's luck** (PUSH¹)

luck² v

luck out phr v [I] AmE infml to be lucky: We really lucked out finding this nice apartment for such a low rent.

luck·i·ly /ˈlʌkɪli/ adv as a result of good luck: Luckily (for me), she was in when I called.

luck·less /ˈlʌkləs/ adj esp. lit without good fortune; unlucky: a luckless man

luck·y /ˈlʌki/ adj having, resulting from, or bringing good luck: a lucky man | a lucky escape | to wear a lucky charm [+to-v] We were lucky to escape injury. [+(that)] You should count yourself lucky (that) he didn't hear what you said. | Try once more — **third time lucky**. (=you should succeed the third time you try) | "I'm going to ask if I can take a month's holiday." "**You'll be lucky!**" (=you are very unlikely to get what you ask for, because you are asking for too much) —**iness** n [U]

► CULTURAL NOTE Some things which are considered lucky are: finding a FOUR-LEAVED CLOVER, seeing two MAGPIES together, and a black cat crossing one's path. Few people really believe that these things bring good luck, but lucky things are still mentioned in conversation. —see also SUPERSTITION, UNLUCKY◄

lucky dip /ˌ·· ˈ·/ n BrE **1** [C] **grab bag** AmE— a container filled with wrapped objects of various values, into which a person puts their hand and picks one out; it is often a way of giving small presents to children at a party **2** [S] infml something whose result depends on chance; LOTTERY

Lucky Jim /ˌlʌki ˈdʒɪm/ a NOVEL by Kingsley Amis (1954) about a college teacher who has RADICAL political ideas

Lu·co·zade /ˈluːkəzeɪd/ n [U] tdmk a soft drink which contains GLUCOSE. Advertisements for Lucozade claim that "Lucozade aids recovery" (=helps people to get better after they have been ill).

lu·cra·tive /ˈluːkrətɪv/ adj (esp. of a business, trade, or job) bringing in plenty of money; profitable — **~ly** adv

lu·cre /ˈluːkər/ n [U] derog or humor money or profit (esp. in the phrase **filthy lucre**)

Lu·cre·tius /luːˈkriːʃəs/ (99?–55 BC) a Roman thinker and poet whose best-known work is De rerum natura (on the nature of things)

lud·dite /ˈlʌdaɪt/ n derog (often cap.) someone who is opposed to change, esp. the introduction of new work methods and machinery (from the **Luddites**, groups of English industrial workers in the early 19th century who tried to destroy new labour-saving machinery as a protest against unemployment and low pay)

lu·di·crous /ˈluːdɪkrəs/ adj so foolish as to cause or deserve disrespectful laughter; RIDICULOUS: What a ludicrous suggestion! | Grandad looks absolutely ludicrous in Mum's old sunhat. — **~ly** adv — **~ness** n [U]

lu·do /ˈluːdəʊ/ BrE ‖ **Parcheesi** AmE tdmk— n [U] a children's game played with small flat objects (COUNTERS²(2)) on a board

luff /lʌf/ v [I (UP)] naut to bring the front of a sailing boat closer to or directly facing the wind

Luft·waf·fe /ˈlʊftwæfə‖-vɑːfə/ [the] the German Air Force just before and during the Second World War —see also BLITZ

lug¹ /lʌg/ v -gg- [T+obj+adv/prep] infml to pull or carry with great effort and difficulty: She lugged the heavy case up the stairs.

lug² n **1** a little piece, such as a small handle, that sticks out from something **2** a LUGHOLE **3** a LUGSAIL **4** a LUGWORM **5** AmE sl a rough, awkward, and stupid person

luge /luːʒ/ n [U;C] a sport in which a person slides down a track made of ice on a special vehicle with long metal blades instead of wheels (a **luge**)

Lu·ger /ˈluːgər/ n tdmk a German hand gun developed in 1902 by **George Luger** and used by German soldiers and sailors until 1938

lug·gage /ˈlʌgɪdʒ/ esp. BrE ‖ also **baggage** esp. AmE— n [U] the cases, bags, boxes, etc., of a traveller: I've put your luggage on the train. —see also HAND LUGGAGE

luggage rack /ˈ·· ·/ n esp. BrE a shelf in a train, bus, etc., for putting one's bags and cases on

lugg·age tro·lley /ˈ·· ˌ··/ n BrE **1** a metal frame with two wheels at the bottom, on which a heavy bag or SUITCASE can be fastened and pulled along **2** ‖ **baggage cart** AmE— a small cart which is often provided at an airport or station to help people move their luggage

luggage van /ˈ·· ·/ BrE ‖ **baggage car** AmE— n the part of a train in which only boxes, cases, etc., are carried

lug·ger /ˈlʌgər/ n a small boat with one or more lugsails

lug·hole /ˈlʌghəʊl, ˈlʌgəʊl/ also **lug**— n BrE humor an ear

lug·sail /ˈlʌgseɪl, -səl/ also **lug**— n a four-sided sail supported on a bar that hangs sloping from the main MAST of a boat

lu·gu·bri·ous /luːˈguːbriəs/ adj sorrowful; MOURNFUL: a lugubrious expression — **~ly** adv — **~ness** n [U]

lug·worm /ˈlʌgwɜːm‖-wɜːrm/ also **lug**— n a small worm that lives in the sand by the sea and is used by fishermen to catch fish

Lu Hsün /ˌluː ˈʃʊn/ see LU XUN

Luke, Saint see SAINT LUKE

luke·warm /ˌluːkˈwɔːm◄‖-ɔːrm◄/ adj usu. derog **1** (esp. of liquid) slightly warm; TEPID **2** showing hardly any interest; not eager: *His plan got a lukewarm reception from the committee.*

lull¹ /lʌl/ *v* [T] to cause to sleep, rest, or become less active: *The movement of the train lulled me to sleep.* | *Their plan was to* **lull** *their opponents* **into a false sense of security,** *and then strike.*

lull² *n* [S (**in**)] a (short) period of reduced activity: *a lull in the fighting*

lul·la·by /ˈlʌləbaɪ/ *n* a pleasant song used for causing children to sleep

lu·lu /ˈluːluː/ *n AmE infml* something very good or exciting: *The roller coaster at Magic Mountain is a real lulu.*

Lulu (1948–) the professional name of a Scottish female popular music singer who made several successful records in the 1960s, including *Shout*

lum·ba·go /lʌmˈbeɪgəʊ/ *n* [U] *not tech* pain in the lower back

lum·bar /ˈlʌmbəʳ/ *adj med* of the lower part of the back

lum·ber¹ /ˈlʌmbəʳ/ *v* [I+*adv/prep*] to move in a heavy awkward manner: *The old truck lumbered up the hill.*

lumber² *n* [U] **1** *esp. BrE* useless or unwanted articles, such as furniture, stored away somewhere **2** *esp. AmE for* TIMBER

lumber³ *v* **1** [T (**with**) *often pass.*] *BrE infml* to cause difficulty to (someone), esp. by giving them an unwanted object or responsibility: *The suppliers have lumbered me with 60 cases of wine I can't sell.* | *As usual, I got lumbered with (having to pay) the bill.* **2** [I] *AmE* to cut trees for wood into TIMBER

lumberjack

lum·ber·jack /ˈlʌmbədʒæk‖-ər-/ *n* (esp. in the US and Canada) a person who cuts down trees for wood

lum·ber·man /ˈlʌmbəmən‖-bər-/ *n* **-men** /mən/ *AmE* a man whose business is the cutting down of trees and the selling of wood

lum·ber·mill /ˈlʌmbəmɪl‖-ər-/ *n AmE for* SAWMILL

lumber-room /ˈ·· ·/ *n esp. BrE* a room in which useless or unwanted furniture, broken machines, etc., are stored

lum·ber·yard /ˈlʌmbəjɑːd‖-bərjɑːrd/ *n* a yard where building wood, boards, etc., are kept for sale

Lu·mi·ère Broth·ers /ˈluːmieə ˌbrʌðəz‖ˌluːmiˈeər ˌbrʌðərz/ [*the* + P] two French brothers, Auguste (1861–1954) and Louis (1864–1948), who operated a photographic company and in 1895 produced the first cinema film

lu·mi·na·ry /ˈluːmɪnəri‖-neri/ *n fml* someone who is famous and highly respected for their excellence in a particular art or activity: *the luminaries of the stage* (=famous actors)

lu·mi·nous /ˈluːmɪnəs/ *adj* able to shine, esp. in the dark: *luminous paint/safety clothing/road signs* – **~ly** *adv* **–nosity** /ˌluːmɪˈnɒsɪti‖-ˈnɑː-/ *n* [U]

Lum·ley /ˈlʌmli/, **Jo·an·na** /dʒəʊˈænə/ (1946–) an English theatre and film actress

lum·me , lummy /ˈlʌmi/ *interj old-fash infml BrE* (an expression of surprise)

lump¹ /lʌmp/ *n* **1** [C (**of**)] a mass of something solid without a special size or shape: *a lump of mud/lead/coal* | *There are lumps in the sauce.* | (fig.) *The scene where the lovers say goodbye really* **brought a lump to my throat.** (=made me feel very sad) —see CHUNK (USAGE), and see picture at PIECE **2** [C] a hard swelling on the body

▶ CULTURAL NOTE People sometimes feel worried or frightened if they feel a lump on their body because it may be a sign of CANCER, even though many lumps are often harmless. In most Western countries, women are encouraged to check their breasts regularly for lumps.◀

3 [C (**of**)] a small square-sided block (of sugar), esp. for use in tea or coffee: *Do you take one lump or two?* **4** [C] *infml* a stupid awkward ungraceful person: *You'll break it if you do it like that, you great lump!* **5** [*the+sing./pl. v*] *BrE infml* the group of workers in the building industry who are not employed on a continuous contract, but only as and when they are needed **6 take one's lumps** *AmE infml* to suffer the bad results of one's actions

lump² *v* **lump it** *infml* to accept without complaint a bad situation that cannot be changed: *I'm not going to turn my radio off; you'll just have to* (**like it or**) **lump it!**

lump sthg. ↔ **together** *phr v* [T] to consider as a single unit or type: *The cost of these two trips can be lumped together for tax purposes.* | *The media tend to lump all these groups together.*

lump·ec·to·my /lʌmpˈektəmi/ *n* a medical operation in which a TUMOUR is removed from a person's body, esp. from a woman's breast in order to stop the spread of CANCER

lump·ish /ˈlʌmpɪʃ/ *adj infml* awkward or stupid

lump sum /ˌ· ˈ·/ *n* an amount of money given or received as a single unit rather than in separate parts at different times

lump·y /ˈlʌmpi/ *adj* filled or covered with lumps: *This sauce is rather lumpy.* | *a lumpy mattress*

lu·na·cy /ˈluːnəsi/ *n* [U] **1** the condition of being sick in the mind; madness **2** foolish or wild behaviour: *It would be sheer lunacy to try to sail across the Pacific alone without a radio.* —see also LUNATIC

lu·nar /ˈluːnəʳ/ *adj* of, for, or to the moon: *a lunar eclipse* | *a lunar module* (=spacecraft that lands on the moon)

lunar month /ˌ·· ˈ·/ *n* a period of 28 or 29 days counted from one new moon to the next —compare CALENDAR MONTH

lu·nate /ˈluːneɪt/ *adj tech* shaped like a CRESCENT moon (=when only the curved edge of it can be seen)

lu·na·tic¹ /ˈluːnətɪk/ *n* **1** *derog* an extremely foolish person: *You lunatic – you nearly drove straight into me!* **2** *now taboo* a person who is suffering from an illness of the mind: *a lunatic asylum* (=a hospital for lunatics) – see also LUNACY

lunatic² *adj derog* wildly foolish: *lunatic behaviour*

lunatic fringe /ˌ··· ˈ·/ *n* [S+*sing./pl. v*] the people with the strangest or most unreasonable ideas or beliefs in a political or social group, esp. those whose ideas are the most RADICAL or the least acceptable to the people in power – see also LOONY LEFT

lunch¹ /lʌntʃ/ *also* **lunch·eon** /ˈlʌntʃən/ *fml* *n* [C;U] a usu. light meal eaten in the middle of the day: *We have lunch at one o'clock.* | *It happened at/during lunch.* | *a business lunch* (=at which business is talked about) | *What would you like for lunch?* | *He takes a* **packed lunch/bag lunch** *AmE* (=SANDWICHes, etc.) *to work.* | *We had a working lunch/a late lunch.* | *It's* **lunchtime!** –see also SUNDAY LUNCH, see DINNER (USAGE)

lunch² *v* [I] *fml* to eat lunch: *We're lunching with the Forsyths today.*

lunch·box /ˈlʌntʃbɒks‖-bɑːks/ *n* a light box with a closing lid in which food is carried, usu. used by schoolchildren and working men

lun·cheon·ette /ˌlʌntʃəˈnet/ *n AmE* a small restaurant that serves simple meals

luncheon meat /ˈ·· ·/ *n* [U] meat, usu. PORK, which has been pressed into a square shape, usu. bought in a tin and eaten with a SALAD or in a SANDWICH. Luncheon meat was popular in Britain after the Second World War, but it is no longer considered to be a fashionable food. –see also SPAM

luncheon vou·cher /ˈ·· ˌ··/ *also* **LV** *abbrev.– n* a kind of ticket sometimes given to people in Britain by their employers, in addition to their pay, which can be used to buy food at some restaurants or shops. Luncheon vouchers are often given to people such as office workers and although useful are not considered as desirable as PERKs which might be given to higher-paid employees, e.g. a company car or private medical insurance.

lunch hour /'· ·/ also **lunch break**— n the period of time in the middle of the day (about an hour), when most employers allow their workers to stop work and have something to eat. People usu. stop work for half an hour or an hour, beginning some time between 12 o'clock and one o'clock. Many people eat lunch in a CANTEEN at the place where they work.

Lun·dy /'lʌndi/ an island in the Bristol Channel, off Devon, SW England, kept as a safe place for wild flowers, SEALS, and birds, esp. PUFFINS

lung /lʌŋ/ n either of the two breathing organs in the chest of humans or certain other animals: *Smoking can cause lung cancer.* | (*humor*) *The baby has a good pair of lungs.* (=can cry loudly) | *She was screaming* **at the top of her lungs.** (=very loudly) —see picture at RESPIRATORY

lunge /lʌndʒ/ v [I (**at, towards**)] to make a sudden forceful forward movement, esp. with the arm and often in order to make an attack: *He lunged at me with a knife.* —**lunge** n : *He made a lunge at me.*

lunk·head /'lʌŋkhed/ n AmE infml a stupid person: *That's not the way to do it, you lunkhead!*

lu·pin BrE || **lupine** AmE /'luːpɪn/ n a garden plant with a tall stem covered in many flowers

lurch[1] /lɜːtʃ||lɜːrtʃ/ v [I] to move with irregular swinging or rolling movements: *The drunken man lurched across the street.* | *The truck lurched over the bumpy road.*

lurch[2] n **1** a lurching movement: *The boat gave a lurch and I fell overboard.* **2 leave someone in the lurch** infml to leave someone alone and without help in a place or time of difficulty; desert someone

lure[1] /lʊər, ljʊər||lʊər/ n **1** [*the* (**of**)] the power to attract, esp. by seeming to promise pleasure, profit, etc., which may not in fact exist: *The prospectors of 1849 were drawn to California by the lure of gold.* | *the lure of fame* **2** [C] a piece of equipment, such as a plastic bird or fish, to attract animals into a place where they can be caught; DECOY

lure[2] v [T+obj+adv/prep] usu. derog to attract or TEMPT by seeming to promise pleasure, profit, etc.; ENTICE: *She lured him into the shop doorway and her accomplice hit him over the head.* | *He's been lured to the Middle East by the promise of high wages.*

Lu·rex /'ljʊəreks||'lʊər-/ n [U] tdmk a type of thread which has an appearance like metal, usu. gold or silver, used in material for clothing, esp. evening wear: *a gold Lurex dress*

lur·gy /'lɜːgi||-ɜːr-/ n BrE humor an illness or disease

lu·rid /'lʊərɪd, 'ljʊərɪd||'lʊərɪd/ adj derog **1** unnaturally bright or strongly coloured: *a lurid sunset/carpet* **2** shocking, esp. because violent; unpleasant: *The papers gave all the lurid details of the murder.* — **~ly** adv — **~ness** n [U]

lurk /lɜːk||lɜːrk/ v [I+adv/prep] derog **1** to move or wait quietly and secretly, as if intending to do something wrong and not wanting to be seen: *The photographer lurked behind a tree, waiting for her to come past.* | *There's someone lurking about outside.* **2** to exist unseen: *Danger lurks in that quiet river.* | *doubts that lurk in my mind*

Lu·sa·ka /luː'sɑːkə/ the capital city of Zambia

lus·cious /'lʌʃəs/ adj apprec **1** having a very pleasant sweet taste or smell: *luscious fruit/wine* **2** infml (usu. considered offensive to women) very sexually attractive: *a luscious waitress* — **~ly** adv — **~ness** n [U]

lush[1] /lʌʃ/ adj **1** (of a plant, esp. grass) growing very well, thickly, and healthily: *the lush meadows* | *lush tropical vegetation* **2** infml providing great comfort, esp. as a result of wealth: *I felt out of place in such lush surroundings.*

lush[2] n sl, esp. AmE a person who habitually drinks too much alcohol; ALCOHOLIC

Lu·si·ta·ni·a /ˌluːsɪ'teɪniə/ [the] a British passenger ship sunk off the Irish coast in 1915 by the German navy during the First World War. 128 people, of the total 1195 killed, were Americans and the event added to anti-German feelings in America in favour of the US entering the war on the side of the Allies.

lust[1] /lʌst/ n derog **1** [U] very strong sexual desire, esp. when uncontrolled and not related to liking or love. Lust is one of the Seven Deadly Sins: *He attacked women to satisfy his lust.* —see also SEVEN DEADLY SINS **2** [C;U (**for**)] strong desire; eagerness to possess something: *his unbridled lust for power* —see DESIRE (USAGE)

lust[2] v

lust after/for sbdy./sthg. phr v [T] derog to desire very strongly, esp. sexually

lust·ful /'lʌstfəl/ adj derog full of strong esp. sexual desire — **~ly** adv — **~ness** n [U]

lus·tre BrE || **-ter** AmE /'lʌstər/ n [S;U] the brightness of a shiny polished surface: *the lustre of gold* | (fig.) *The company hope that this prestigious publication will add (a) new lustre* (=glory, fame) *to their image.*

lus·trous /'lʌstrəs/ adj esp. lit shining; BRILLIANT: *lustrous black hair* — **~ly** adv

lust·y /'lʌsti/ adj apprec full of strength, power, or health: *lusty singing* | *The baby gave a lusty cry.* —**ily** adv —**iness** n [U]

lu·ta·nist , **-tenist** /'luːtənɪst/ n a person who plays a lute

lute /luːt/ n a musical instrument with strings, having a long neck and a body shaped like a PEAR, played with the fingers and used esp. in former times

Lu·ther /'luːθər/, **Martin** (1483–1546) a German religious leader of the Reformation in Europe, which led to the establishment of the Protestant Church and its separation from the Catholic Church in the 16th century. He attacked the powers of the Pope and in 1517 he wrote 95 points criticizing the established church, which he nailed to the door of his church. He also translated the Bible into German. His ideas had great influence on German society and in other countries.

Lu·ther·an /'luːθərən/ n a member of a Church which is based on the work and ideas of Martin Luther. There are more than 70 million Lutherans around the world esp. in Scandinavian countries, Germany and North America. —**Lutheran** adj

Lu·ther·an·is·m /'luːθərənɪzəm/ n [U] the beliefs or practice of that branch of the Protestant church which is based on the teachings of Martin Luther, esp. the belief that SALVATION can be gained by faith alone

Lu·ton /'luːtn/ a town in Bedfordshire, England, with a busy international airport

Lu·ton Air·port /ˌ·· '··/ an airport near Luton, S central England

luv /lʌv/ n BrE, nonstandard or humor for LOVE[1] (6)

luv·vie /'lʌvi/ n LOVEY

Lux·em·bourg , **Luxemburg** /'lʌksəmbɜːg||-bɜːrg/, **the Grand Duchy of** a very small country in Western Europe bordered by Belgium, Germany, and France; capital Luxembourg; population 368,000 (1989) —**-er** n

Lux·em·burg /'lʌksəmbɜːg||-bɜːrg/, **Ro·sa** /'rəʊzə/ (1871–1919) a German political writer and ACTIVIST, born in Russian Poland, who helped establish the Socialist Party in Poland and a Marxist party in Germany. She was killed by soldiers in 1919.

Lux·or /'lʌksɔːr/ a city in central Egypt on the east bank of the River Nile, famous for its ancient temples and burial grounds

Lu Xun /ˌluː 'ʃʊn/ (1881–1936) a Chinese writer of great influence, whose real name was **Zhou Shuren**. He criticized Chinese government thinking and encouraged people in China to become interested in Western ideas and science. He is famous for his short stories, esp. *The True Story of Ah Q.*

lux·u·ri·ant /lʌg'zjʊəriənt, ləg'ʒʊəriənt||ləg'ʒʊəriənt/ adj **1** growing healthily and in large amounts: *Luxuriant forests covered the hills.* | *a luxuriant beard* **2** sometimes derog very highly decorated: *luxuriant prose* — **~ly** adv —**-ance** n [U]

lux·u·ri·ate /lʌg'zjʊərieɪt, ləg'ʒʊəri-||ləg'ʒʊəri-/ v

luxuriate in sthg. phr v [T] to consciously enjoy oneself in; take great pleasure in (esp. a situation of great comfort): *luxuriating in a hot bath with a good book*

lux·u·ri·ous /lʌg'zjʊəriəs, ləg'ʒʊəriəs||ləg'ʒʊəriəs/ adj **1** very fine and expensive: *a luxurious fur coat* **2** providing the greatest comfort: *She took a long luxurious hot bath.* — **~ly** adv

lux·u·ry /'lʌkʃəri/ n **1** [U] a condition of great comfort provided without any consideration of the cost: *They led a life of luxury.* | *a luxury hotel* **2** [C] something that is very pleasant and enjoyable, but not necessary and not often had or done: *Cream cakes are a luxury in our house.* | *We can't afford to spend money on luxuries.* | *Luxury items are heavily taxed.* | *It's a real luxury to be able to stay in bed instead of getting up for school.*

LV /ˌel ˈviː/ *abbrev. for:* LUNCHEON VOUCHER

LVN /ˌel viː ˈen/ *n AmE abbrev. for:* Licensed Vocational Nurse; a person who does almost the same work as a NURSE but only has two years of nursing education and is not allowed to give drugs, etc. —see also LICENSED PRACTICAL NURSE

LW *written abbrev. for:* LONG WAVE

-ly see WORD FORMATION

ly·can·thro·py /laɪˈkænθrəpi/ *n* [U] in stories, the condition of changing from a person into a WOLF (=wild dog) esp. at the time of the full moon —see also WEREWOLF

ly·cée /ˈliːseɪ‖liːˈseɪ/ *n* a French school for older pupils, either in France or for French children abroad

ly·ce·um /laɪˈsiːəm/ *n AmE old-fash.* a building used for public speeches, concerts, meetings, etc.

Lyceum [*the*] a BALLROOM (=large room for dancing) near the Strand, central London

ly·chee , litchi /ˈlaɪtʃiː/ *n* an Asian fruit with a hard rough nutlike shell and sweet white flesh that contains a single seed —see picture at FRUIT

lych-gate /ˈlɪtʃɡeɪt/ *n* a gate with a roof leading into the grounds of a church

Ly·cra /ˈlaɪkrə/ *n tdmk* [U] a man-made elastic material used esp. in sports clothing, e.g. for runners and cyclists. It became fashionable with young people in Britain and the US in the early 1990s: *black Lycra leggings*

ly·ing[1] /ˈlaɪ-ɪŋ/ *present participle of* LIE[1]

lying[2] *present participle of* LIE[3]

lying-in /ˌ··ˈ·/ *n* [*usu. sing.*] *old use* the period during which a woman remains in bed before the birth of a child; CONFINEMENT

lying in state /ˌ··· ·ˈ·/ *n* [S] the period of showing of the dead body, or the COFFIN containing it, of a famous and important person so that people may come and show their respect. In Western countries only very important people lie in state.

Lyle /laɪl/, **Sandy** (1958–) a British GOLF player who won the Open Championship in 1985 and the US Masters in 1988

Lyme dis·ease /ˈlaɪm dɪˌziːz/ *n* [U] a serious illness which is caused by the bite of a TICK[3] and which is dangerous and very difficult to cure if it is not noticed early

Lyme Re·gis /ˌlaɪm ˈriːdʒɪs/ a town in Dorset on the S coast of England, a popular place for holidays

Lymes·wold /ˈlaɪmzwəʊld/ *n* [U] *tdmk* a soft English blue cheese which does not have a very strong taste. It was first produced in 1983 and some people who prefer TRADITIONAL English cheeses dislike and disapprove of it.

lymph /lɪmf/ *n* [U] a clear watery liquid formed in the body which passes into the blood system

lym·phat·ic /lɪmˈfætɪk/ *adj* connected with, producing, or containing lymph

lymph gland /ˈ· ˌ·/ also **lymph node**— *n* a fleshy area in the body through which lymph passes to be made pure before entering the blood system

Ly·nam /ˈlaɪnəm/, **Des·mond** /ˈdezmənd/ (1942–) a reporter and presenter of esp. sports programmes on British radio and television probably best known for presenting the television programme *Grandstand*

lynch /lɪntʃ/ *v* [T] (esp. of a crowd of people) to take hold of (a person thought to be guilty of a crime) and kill them, esp. by hanging, without a legal trial. Many people think of lynching in the context of the American Wild West and with the illegal killing of blacks in the South by the Ku Klux Klan or a MOB.

Lynch, Bet a character in *Coronation Street* (a popular British television SERIES) who is what many people think is a typical BARMAID. She has blonde hair and large breasts and wears a lot of MAKE-UP and jewellery. The character has married, and is now called Bet Gilroy, although most people still think of her as Bet Lynch.

Bet Lynch

lynch law /ˈ· ·/ *n* [U] the punishment of someone who is thought to be guilty of a crime, usu. by death, without a legal trial

Lynn /lɪn/, **Lo·ret·ta** /ləˈretə/ (1935–) an American popular music singer. A film based on her life was called *Coal Miner's Daughter*, which was also the title of one of her songs.

Lynn, Dame Ve·ra /ˈvɪərə/ (1917–) an English singer who was very popular during the Second World War. She was known as the "Forces' Sweetheart", and entertained soldiers with songs such as *We'll Meet Again* and *White Cliffs of Dover.*

lynx /lɪŋks/ *n* **lynxes** *or* **lynx** a strong wild animal of the cat family with long legs and a short tail —see picture at BIG CATS

Ly·ons /ˈliːɒn‖liːˈɑːn/ the capital city of the Rhône department in the E of central France; French name **Lyon**

Ly·ons /ˈlaɪənz/ *tdmk* a British company selling tea, coffee, and a variety of food products

Lyons, Joseph (1848–1917) a British businessman who began the **J Lyons** company in 1894, and helped to make tea-shops and **Corner Houses** (types of restaurant) popular

lyre /laɪəʳ/ *n* an ancient Greek musical instrument with strings stretched on a U-shaped frame

lyre·bird /ˈlaɪəbɜːd‖ˈlaɪərbɜːrd/ *n* an Australian bird, the male having a long tail shaped like a lyre

lyr·ic[1] /ˈlɪrɪk/ *adj* expressing strong personal feelings, usu. in songlike form: *lyric poetry* | *a lyric poet*

lyric[2] *n* a usu. short lyric poem —see also LYRICS

lyr·i·cal /ˈlɪrɪkəl/ *adj* full of joy, admiration, eagerness, etc.; expressing direct and usu. very strong personal feeling: *There's a wonderfully lyrical flute solo in the middle of this symphony.* | *She* **waxed** (=became) **lyrical** *about the beauties of the scenery.* — ~ **ly** /kli/ *adv*

lyr·i·cis·m /ˈlɪrɪˌsɪzəm/ *n* [U] lyric or lyrical style or quality, esp. in poetry

lyr·i·cist /ˈlɪrɪs̩st/ *n* a writer of words for songs

lyr·ics /ˈlɪrɪks/ *n* [P] the words of a song, esp. a modern popular song

Lyt·tel·ton /ˈlɪtl-tən/, **Hum·phrey** /ˈhʌmfri/ (1921–) a British JAZZ musician, known as a TRUMPET player and band leader, who helped make New Orleans jazz popular in Britain in the 1950s

M

M /em/ **M's, m's** or **Ms, ms** 1 the 13th letter of the English alphabet 2 the ROMAN NUMERAL (number) for 1000

m written abbrev. for: 1 METRE 2 MARRIED 3 MILE

M abbrev. for: (BrE) MOTORWAY: driving up the M1

-'m /m/ short for: am: I'm ready. | "Are you French?" "Yes, I am|No, I'm not."

M1 /ˌem ˈwʌn◂/ [the] a British MOTORWAY connecting London and Leeds

M25 /ˌem twentiˈfaɪv◂/ [the] a British MOTORWAY which runs all round London. The M25 was intended to lessen crowding on roads around London, but has attracted so much traffic that traffic often travels very slowly on it.

ma /mɑː/ n infml (usu. cap.) 1 a mother: my old ma | Give me some milk, Ma! 2 sometimes not polite, esp. AmE (a name for an (old) woman): You've dropped your bag, Ma! | Old Ma Harris was taken to the hospital yesterday.

MA¹ /ˌem ˈeɪ/ n Master of Arts; (a title for someone who has) a university degree in an arts subject at the first level above the BA. At some Scottish universities an MA is a first degree, at the same level as a BA: Address it to Mary Jones, MA. | He has an MA in linguistics. —compare MSC, and see DEGREE (3) (CULTURAL NOTE)

MA² written abbrev. for: MASSACHUSSETTS

maa /mɑː/ v [I] to make the sound that a goat makes —maa n

ma'am /mæm, mɑːm, məm‖mæm/ n polite 1 (a short form for MADAM, used for addressing the Queen and, esp. formerly, women of high social class 2 AmE (a respectful word used for addressing a woman): Yes, ma'am, I will

Maas·tricht /ˈmɑːstrɪkt, -ɪxt/ a city in the Netherlands. In 1991, members of the EC met at Maastricht to discuss ways in which their countries could become closer in their political, economic, and monetary policies. The countries reached agreement and the Maastricht Treaty was signed in 1992.

Mab·i·nog·i·on /ˌmæbˌɪˈnɒgiɒn‖-ˈnəʊgiɑːn/, **The** a collection of old Welsh stories about magical and imaginary people and places

mac , mack /mæk/ n BrE infml for MACKINTOSH

Mac n AmE sl (used for speaking to a man whose name is not known)

ma·ca·bre /məˈkɑːbrə, -bəᵊ/ adj causing fear, dislike, and shock, esp. because connected with death and the dead: a macabre tale about grave robbers | a rather macabre sense of humour —compare GRUESOME

ma·cad·am /məˈkædəm/ AmE for TARMAC

mac·a·da·mia nut /ˌmækəˈdeɪmiə ˌnʌt/ n a nut from an Australian tree (macadamia tree) widely grown in Hawaii which can be eaten

Ma·cao , Macau /məˈkaʊ/ a Portuguese PROVINCE in SE China which will be handed to China in 1999. It is a centre for TOURISM and gambling (GAMBLE¹ (1)); main city Macao; population 448,000 (1989)

mac·a·ro·ni /ˌmækəˈrəʊni◂/ n [U] Italian PASTA (=food made from flour and water) in the shape of small pieces of thin pipe, cooked in boiling water —compare SPAGHETTI, TAGLIATELLE, VERMICELLI

macaroni cheese /ˌ···· ˈ·‖ BrE ‖ macaroni and cheese /···,··· ˈ·/ AmE— n [U] a dish made from cooked macaroni with a cheese SAUCE

mac·a·roon /ˌmækəˈruːn/ n a small flat cake made mainly of sugar, eggs, and crushed ALMONDS or COCONUT

Mac·Ar·thur /məˈkɑːθəᵊ‖-ɑːr-/, **Douglas** (1880–1964) an American GENERAL (=military leader) during the Second World War who was in charge of the Allied forces in the PACIFIC area and who organized the US forces in Japan after the war ended. He was the leader of the United Nations forces in Korea in 1950.

ma·caw /məˈkɔː/ n a large long-tailed Central and South American bird of the brightly-coloured PARROT family

Mac·beth /məkˈbeθ, mæk-/ 1 a king of Scotland (1040–57), who killed the previous king Duncan I in battle and was

himself later killed by Duncan's son, Malcolm 2 a play by William Shakespeare which gives an account of Macbeth's life. Macbeth is told by three witches (WITCH) that he will become king. To do so, he murders the present king Duncan, who is his guest. Although he feels very guilty about this, he kills several other people to keep his power. He is finally killed by Macduff. Actors believe it is unlucky to say the name Macbeth, so they often call it The Scottish Play. —see colour picture on page 1146

Macbeth, Lady the character of the wife of Macbeth in the play by William Shakespeare. She encourages her husband to kill Duncan and is a stronger, more evil person than Macbeth himself. After the murder, she feels as if she will never be able to clean the blood off her hands, and she walks in her sleep, rubbing her hands together as if washing them.

Mc·Calls /məˈkɔːlz/ a US magazine with articles of interest mostly to married women

Mc·Car·thy /məˈkɑːθi‖-ɑːr-/, **John** (1957–) an English JOURNALIST who was kidnapped (KIDNAP) in 1986 and held as a HOSTAGE in the Middle East until he was released in 1991

McCarthy, Joseph (1909–57) an American SENATOR (=politician of high rank) who achieved importance and power in the 1950s by claiming that important public figures were Communists

Mc·Car·thy·is·m /məˈkɑːθi-ɪzəm‖-ɑːr-/ n [U] (in the US in the 1950s) the hunting down and removal from public employment of all those believed to be Communists, which was carried out under Senator Joseph McCarthy. Many of the people accused were BLACKLISTED (=not allowed to work) or imprisoned. People were encouraged to give the names of their friends and people they worked with to help themselves. Today most Americans are embarrassed about this period in their history, and people who refused to give information about themselves or others are admired. McCarthyism is sometimes used to mean any accusation of disloyalty to the country that is made without proof. —see also BLACKLIST, COMMUNIST, HUAC

Mc·Cart·ney /məˈkɑːtni‖-ɑːr-/, **Paul** (1942–) an English popular music singer and GUITAR player, and one of the members of the Beatles. He wrote most of their songs with John Lennon. He later formed a new group, Wings, and continues to write songs and perform. —see also BEATLES

Mc·Clel·lan /məˈklelən/, **George** (1826–85) a GENERAL (=military leader) in the American Civil War

Mc·Coy /məˈkɔɪ/ infml **the real McCoy** the real or original article or thing, esp. something of high quality: This whisky is the real McCoy.

Mc·Crae /məˈkreɪ/, **John** (1872–1918) a Canadian poet who wrote the famous war poem In Flanders Fields

Mc·Cul·lers /məˈkʌləz‖-lərz/, **Carson** (1917–67) an American writer whose best known works include the NOVEL The Heart is a Lonely Hunter and a collection of short stories called The Ballad of the Sad Cafe. She often wrote about loneliness and many of her characters are people who do not fit into ordinary society.

Mac·don·ald /mək'dɒnəld‖-ˈdɑː-/, **Flora** (1722–90) a Scottish woman who helped Prince Charles Edward Stuart to escape from Scotland after the Battle of Culloden (1746)

Macdonald, Ram·say /ˈræmzi/ (1866–1937) a British political leader who became the first Labour PRIME MINISTER in 1924. He later led a COALITION (=a government formed from members of different political parties) during the Depression (DEPRESSION (2)) of the 1930s.

Macdonald, Ross (1915–) an American writer of DETECTIVE stories, whose real name is Kenneth Millar. The main character in his books is Lew Archer, a strong but sympathetic private detective.

Mc·Don·alds /mək'dɒnəldz‖-ˈdɑː-/ (one of) a large group of American-owned restaurants in the USA, Europe, and many other countries, which sell HAMBURGERS and other FAST FOOD. In Britain and the US, these restaurants are esp. popular with young people and children. McDonalds is thought to be a typical part of the American way of life.

McDou·gall's /mək'duːgəlz/ n tdmk a range of different types of flour made by RHM Foods Ltd

Mac·duff /mək'dʌf/ 1 a character in Shakespeare's play Macbeth, who kills Macbeth at the end of the play 2 **lead on, Macduff** a slightly changed phrase from Macbeth, now often used humorously when asking someone to lead you to a place

nace¹ /meɪs/ n **1** a decorative rod, often made of or covered with precious metals, which is carried or placed in front of an official in certain ceremonies as a sign of power

▶ CULTURAL NOTE There is a mace in the House of Commons which sits in front of the Speaker while Parliament is open and which is handed to an official of the Crown when it closes. ◀

2 a short heavy stick (CLUB) used as a weapon in former times, usu. of metal with sharp points sticking out around the head: *to swing a mace*

nace² n [U] **1** a powder made from the dried shell of a NUTMEG and used as a SPICE (=to give food a special taste) in cooking **2** AmE tdmk (usu. cap.) a chemical which causes painful stinging in the eyes and on skin. It is sometimes used as a weapon for defence, esp. by women: *a Mace spray*

Ma·ce·do·ni·a /ˌmæsɪˈdəʊniə/ a province of northern Greece, capital Thessaloniki, the birthplace of Alexander the Great

Mc·En·roe /ˈmækɪnrəʊ/, **John** (1959–) an American TENNIS player, one of the best in the world, who is known for becoming angry while playing tennis matches. British people remember him esp. as saying "You cannot be serious" when he disagreed with the UMPIRE's decision.

ma·cer·ate /ˈmæsəreɪt/ v [I;T] tech to (cause to) become soft by putting or being left in water: *Paper can be made from powdered wood which has been macerated.* **—-ation** /ˌmæsəˈreɪʃən/ n [U]

Mc·Ew·an's Ex·port /məˌkjuːənz ˈekspɔːt‖-ɔːrt/ n [U] tdmk a type of ALE that is made in Scotland

Mc·Gill U·ni·ver·si·ty /məˌgɪl juːnɪˈvɜːsɪti‖-ɜːr-/ n a university in Quebec, Canada

Mc·Gov·ern /məˈgʌvən‖-vərn/, **George Stanley** (1922–) one of the first leading American politicians to oppose the Vietnam War. He was defeated for the Presidency by Richard Nixon in 1972.

Mc·Guig·an /məˈgwɪgən/, **Bar·ry** /ˈbæri/ (1961–) an Irish BOXER who became a professional in 1981, fought 28 fights, winning all but one, and became the world FEATHERWEIGHT champion

Mach /mæk‖mɑːk/ n [U] the speed of an aircraft in relation to the speed of sound: *If a plane is flying at Mach 2, it is flying at twice the speed of sound.*

Mac·heath /məkˈhiːθ/, **Captain** a HIGHWAYMAN (=man who in the past stole money from travellers) who is the leading character of John Gay's *The Beggar's Opera* —see also BEGGAR'S OPERA

ma·chet·e /məˈʃeti, məˈtʃeti/ n a knife with a broad heavy blade, which is used as a cutting tool and weapon in South America and elsewhere

Mach·i·a·vel·li /ˌmækiəˈveli/, **Nic·co·lo** /ˈnɪkələʊ/ (1469–1527) an Italian political thinker who is best known for his book *The Prince*, which describes how a leader with no moral values may gain and keep power. He is often thought of as being cruel and interested only in power.

Mach·i·a·vel·li·an /ˌmækiəˈveliən◀/ adj usu. derog (of a person or action) showing skill in using cleverly indirect or immoral means to gain advantage or power, esp. in politics: *his Machiavellian cunning*

mach·i·na·tion /ˌmækɪˈneɪʃən, ˌmæʃɪ-/ n [usu. pl.] derog a clever plan for doing harm

ma·chine¹ /məˈʃiːn/ n **1** an instrument or apparatus which uses power, such as electricity, to perform work: *a sewing machine | a washing machine | a machine for producing car body parts | You can get tea or coffee from that drinks machine.* | (fig.) *The people in the accounts office behave more like machines than people.* (=without feelings or independent thoughts) | *The office runs like a well-oiled machine.* (=very smoothly and effectively) **2** esp. tech a computer: *machine translation | the man-machine interface* **3** infml a wheeled vehicle or aircraft: *He thundered down the street on his new machine.* (=motorcycle) **4** a group of people that controls and plans the activities of something, esp. a political party: *the government's propaganda machine | the party machine*

▷ USAGE Compare **device, gadget, machine,**

appliance, instrument, tool, and **implement. Device** is a general word for any man-made object used for doing work, and is usually used when there is no suitable particular word: *a device for catching mice | I had no idea how this device worked.* A **gadget** (infml) is a small and perhaps unusual device for doing a particular job: *a clever little gadget for opening bottles.* A **machine** usually uses power, and is not worked directly by hand: *the machines in the factory.* Electrical machines used in the home (such as washing machines) can also be called **appliances.** An **instrument** is an object used to help in exact or difficult work, usually without power: *medical instruments | A thermometer is a measuring instrument.* A **tool** is an object held in the hand, without power, and used for making things from wood, metal or other materials: *A hammer is one of a carpenter's tools.* An **implement** is usually larger than a tool, and is used for other jobs: *A plough is an implement used in farming.* —see also INSTRUMENT (USAGE)◁

machine² v [T] esp. tech **1** to make or produce by machine, esp. in sewing and printing **2** [(DOWN)] to produce according to exact measurements: *The edge must be machined down to 0·03 millimetres.*

machine code /·'· ·/ n [C;U] tech instructions in the form of numbers which are understood directly by the MICROPROCESSOR in a computer —compare SOURCE CODE

ma·chine-gun /məˈʃiːngʌn/ n a quick-firing gun, often supported on legs, which fires continuously as long as the TRIGGER is pressed —see picture at GUN **—machinegun** v **-nn-** [T]

machine lan·guage /·'· ˌ··/ n [C;U] **1** information that is recorded for a machine such as a computer to use **2** numbers or other instructions in a form that can be used by a computer

machine-read·a·ble /·ˌ· '···◀/ adj in a form that can be understood and used by a computer: *machine-readable text*

ma·chin·e·ry /məˈʃiːnəri/ n [U] **1** machines in general: *New machinery is being installed in the factory. | farm machinery* **2** the working parts of an apparatus: *He was tinkering about with the machinery, trying to get the motor to go.* **3** a system or process by which a result is obtained or a job is performed: *The machinery of the law works slowly. | the country's electoral machinery*

machine tool /·'· ˌ·/ n a power-driven tool for cutting and shaping metal, wood, etc.

ma·chin·ist /məˈʃiːnɪst/ n a person whose work is using a machine, esp. for sewing, or a machine tool

ma·chis·mo /məˈtʃɪzməʊ, -ˈkɪz-‖mɑː-, mə-/ n [U] usu. derog. the quality of being macho

mach·o /ˈmætʃəʊ‖ˈmɑː-/ adj usu. derog being or wishing to appear very typical of a man, esp. in being strong, brave, and without gentle feelings

▶ CULTURAL NOTE In many Western countries, attitudes to the way men and women should behave have changed. Many people now do not approve of men who want to appear strong and powerful but without gentle feelings. Although people may now criticize this kind of behaviour or find it amusing, many young men in Britain still want to be or appear macho. ◀

macho-man /'··· ·/ n usu. derog a man who is or likes to seem very macho

Ma·chu Pic·chu /ˌmɑːtʃuː ˈpiːktʃuː/ n the remains of an ancient city of the INCAS in the ANDES in Peru

mack , mac /mæk/ n BrE informal for MACKINTOSH

Mc·Kel·len /məˈkelən/, **Sir I·an** /ˈiːən/ (1939–) a British actor, one of the leading Shakespearian actors. He is also well-known for his work raising money for people with AIDS, and his work to gain equal rights for HOMOSEXUALS.

Mac·ken·zie /məˈkenzi/ **1** a river in NW Canada flowing from the Great Slave Lake into the Beaufort Sea **2** a mountain range in the Canadian Rockies

mack·e·rel /ˈmækərəl/ n mackerel or mackerels a sea fish which has bands of blue-green colour across the top of its body and has oily strong-tasting flesh

Mach·e·son /ˈmækɪsən/ n tdmk a type of STOUT² made by Whitbread Plc

McKinley, Mount see MOUNT McKINLEY

Mc·Kin·ley /məˈkɪnli/, **William** (1843–1901) the 25th

president of the US (1897–1901) who raised IMPORT and EXPORT taxes to the highest levels ever in the US and was shot and killed in Buffalo, New York State

mack·in·tosh /ˈmækɹ̩ntoʃ‖-tɑːʃ/ also **mac, mack** infml— n esp. BrE a coat made to keep out the rain

Mackintosh, Charles Ren·nie /tʃɑːlz ˈreni‖tʃɑːrlz-/ (1868–1928) a Scottish ARCHITECT, artist, and furniture DESIGNER. His work is considered to be among the best examples of the ART NOUVEAU style.

Ma·claine /məˈkleɪn/, **Shir·ley** /ˈʃɜːli‖ˈʃɜːr-/ (1934–   ) an American actress who wrote a book called *Dancing in the Light*

Mac·Laine /məˈkleɪn/, **Shir·ley** /ˈʃɜːli‖ˈʃɜːr-/ (1934–   ) an American film actress who has also written books telling of her unusual SPIRITUAL experiences and memories of former lives

Shirley MacLaine

Mc·Lar·en /məˈklærən/ a company which makes racing cars

Mac·lean /məˈkleɪn/, **Al·is·tair** /ˈælɹ̩steəʳ/ (1922–87) a Scottish writer of adventure stories many of which have been made into films, e.g. *The Guns of Navarone* and *Where Eagles Dare*

Maclean, Don·ald /ˈdɒnəld‖ˈdɑː-/ (1913–83) a British Foreign Office official who worked for the USSR as a SPY and escaped to the Soviet Union in 1951 with another British spy, Guy Burgess. Their names, "Burgess and Maclean", are usually remembered together. —see also Anthony BLUNT, Guy BURGESS, Kim PHILBY

Mc·Lu·han /məˈkluːən/, **Marshall** (1911–80) a Canadian with great knowledge of the MEDIA (=newspapers, radio, television, etc.) who said "the medium is the message", meaning that the way in which people receive information has more influence on what they think than the information itself

Mc·Mahon /məkˈmɑːn/, **Ed** (1923–   ) the assistant to Johnny Carson on *The Tonight Show*, an American television programme

Mac·mil·lan /məkˈmɪlən/, **Harold** (1894–1986) a British PRIME MINISTER and leader of the Conservative Party who worked to improve East-West relations and tried unsuccessfully to gain Britain's entry into the European Community. His government was damaged by the Profumo Scandal in 1963 and he gave up work in the same year because of ill health. In 1984, he became the Earl of Stockton. He made two expressions popular in Britain, when he told the British people "You've never had it so good" and when he talked about "the winds of change" blowing through Africa. In the newspapers, he was often called **Supermac**.

Mc·Na·ma·ra /ˌmæknəˈnɑːrə‖ˈmæknəˌmærə/, **Rob·ert Strange** /ˈrɒbət streɪndʒ‖ˈrɑːbərt-/ (1916–   ) an American Secretary of Defence, who resigned (RESIGN) because of doubts about the Vietnam War

Mc·Naugh·ten Rules, McNaghten Rules /məkˈnɔːtn ˌruːlz/ n [the+P] rules in English law which say that a person can PLEAD INSANITY (=use madness as a legal defence) after committing (COMMIT) a crime if it can be proved they did not know what they were doing or did not know that it was a crime (from the case against McNaughten in 1843)

Mac·Neil/Leh·rer Re·port /məkˌniːl ˈleərə rɪˌpɔːt‖ -rər rɪˌpɔːrt/ [the] a high quality American television news programme shown on PUBLIC TELEVISION

Mc·Pher·son /məkˈfɜːsən‖-ɜːr-/, **Ai·mee Sem·ple** /ˈeɪmi ˈsempəl/ (1890–1944) an American religious leader, very popular in the 1920s. She went to court for deceiving people into giving her money. She was found not guilty but there followed more legal problems with other business affairs. She may have died from accidentally taking too many sleeping PILLS.

Mc·Queen /məˈkwiːn/, **Steve** /stiːv/ (1930–80) an American actor and film star who was esp. popular in the 1960s and 1970s and was known for doing his own STUNTS. His films include *The Great Escape*, *Papillon*, and *The Hunter*.

ma·cra·mé /məˈkrɑːmi‖ˌmækrəˈmeɪ/ n [U] the art or practice of knotting string together in decorative patterns

mac·ro·bi·ot·ic /ˌmækrəʊbaɪˈɒtɪk◂‖-ˈɑːtɪk◂/ adj of a way of thinking which puts value on living according to nature, esp. by eating chiefly whole grains and vegetables: *a macrobiotic cookbook* —see also HEALTH FOOD

mac·ro·cos·m /ˈmækrəʊkɒzəm‖-kɑː-/ n **1** [the] the world as a whole; universe **2** [C] any large system containing smaller systems —compare MICROCOSM

mac·ro·ec·o·nom·ics /ˌmækrəʊekəˈnɒmɪks, -iːkə-‖-ˈnɑː-/ n [S] the study of large economic systems such as those of a country —compare MICROECONOMICS **macroeconomic** adj

Mac the Knife /ˌ· · ˈ·/ a character in Bertolt Brecht's *Threepenny Opera*

Mc·Vit·ie's /məkˈvɪtiz/ n tdmk a company which makes many different types of BISCUITS

Ma·cy's /ˈmeɪsiz/ one of a chain of large American shops that sell many different goods. The biggest Macy's is in New York City and most of the rest of the stores are in the eastern states. Each year Macy's holds a public procession on Thanksgiving Day.

mad /mæd/ adj -dd- **1** [(with)] esp. BrE ill in the mind; INSANE: *He went mad and had to be put into a mental hospital.* | *She was almost mad with grief/jealousy.* | (fig.) *Stop that noise; it's driving me mad!* (=annoying me very much) —opposite **sane** **2** esp. BrE very foolish: *You're mad to drive so fast.* | *What a mad idea!* | *You paid £50 for that hat? You must be* **stark raving mad! 3** [F+about, on] infml filled with strong feeling, interest, or admiration: *They're mad about football.* **4** [F (with, at)] infml, esp. AmE angry: *The director got mad at me because I forgot my lines.* | *It made me* **hopping mad.** (=very angry) **5** [A] wild; uncontrolled: *Everyone made a* **mad dash/rush** *for the door.* **6 like mad** infml very hard, fast, loud, etc.: *They ran like mad to catch the moving bus.* **7 (as) mad as a hatter/as a March hare** infml completely mad —see also MAD HATTER, MARCH HARE **8 mad dogs and Englishmen go out in the midday sun** quote a phrase from a song by Noël Coward which made fun of the way British people refused to take notice of local customs in COLONIAL times **9 mad keen** BrE infml extremely keen: *The children are mad keen to go to the zoo.* —see also MADLY; see also **mad dogs and Englishmen...**(ENGLISHMAN)

Mad·a·gas·car /ˌmædəˈgæskəʳ/ an island country in the Indian Ocean off the SE coast of Africa; capital Antananarivo; population 11,603,000 (1989) —**-can** n, adj

mad·am /ˈmædəm/ n **1** (often cap.) (a respectful way of addressing a woman, esp. a customer in a shop): *Are you being served, Madam?* —compare MISS[1], SIR **2** derog, esp. BrE a (young) female who likes to give orders: *She's a little madam – don't let her order you around.* **3** a woman who is in charge of a house of PROSTITUTES (=women who earn money by having sex), taking from them some of their payment

Madam n **Mesdames** /ˈmeɪdæm‖meɪˈdɑːm/ **1** (a word of address used at the beginning of a business letter to a woman, after the word **Dear**): *Dear Madam, ... –* compare SIR **2** (a word for addressing a woman official, followed by the name of her official position): *Madam President, may I ask a question?*

Ma·dame /ˈmædɑːm, məˈdɑːm‖məˈdæm/ n **Mesdames** (used as a title for a French-speaking woman, esp. a married woman) Mrs: *Madame Mitterrand*

Mad·ame But·ter·fly /ˌmædəm ˈbʌtəflaɪ‖-tər-/ **1** an OPERA by Giacomo Puccini (1904), set in Japan **2** the Japanese woman that the opera is about, who is left by her husband, a US naval officer

Madame Tus·saud's /ˌmædəm tʊˈsɔːdz‖ˌmædəm tʊˈsəʊz, məˌdæm-/ a MUSEUM in London which contains WAX figures of famous people, both living and dead. New models are made regularly as people become famous and old models are melted down. —see colour map on page 817

mad·cap /ˈmædkæp/ adj [A] infml wild and thoughtless; RECKLESS: *a madcap scheme to go mountain climbing in the middle of winter*

mad cow dis·ease /ˌ· · ·ˌ/ n [U] a deadly illness of the brain found esp. in cows. It is believed to be caused by eating food made from the bones and organs of other diseased animals, esp. sheep. The scientific name is **bovine spongiform encephalitis** or **BSE**. When the disease was found in cows in Britain in the late 1980s, many people were afraid to eat BEEF because it is not known whether the disease can be passed to humans.

MADD /mæd/ *abbrev. for:* Mothers Against Drunk Driving; an American organization, started by a woman whose daughter was killed by a drunk driver, that has done much to bring people's attention to the problem and encourage state and FEDERAL governments to make stronger laws against it

mad·den /ˈmædn/ *v* [T *often pass.*] to make extremely angry or annoyed; drive mad

mad·den·ing /ˈmædənɪŋ/ *adj* **1** causing much pain or worry: *maddening pain* **2** *infml* extremely annoying: *maddening delays* – ~ly *adv*

mad·der /ˈmædəʳ/ *n* [U] **1** a plant from whose roots a red colouring matter (DYE) is obtained **2** the red colouring matter obtained from this plant

made¹ /meɪd/ *past tense & participle of* MAKE: *Paper is made from wood.* | *made in England*

made² *adj* [F] **1** [+**from, of,** UP **of**] formed: *Clouds are made of water|made up of little drops of water.* **2** [+**for**] completely suited to: *Nick and Alison are made for each other.* **3** *infml* sure of success: *If you get that job you'll be* **made for life.** | *Now he's married a rich wife he's really* **got it made.**

▷ USAGE **Made of** and **made from** have very similar meanings, but often we use **made from** when the original material has been completely changed: *Paper is* **made from** *wood.* | *some jam* **made from** *the fruit in our garden.* | *Bread is* **made from** *flour and water.* We use **made of** when the original materials can still be recognized: *The table is* **made of** *wood.* | *a bag* **made of** *leather.*◁

Ma·dei·ra¹ /məˈdɪərə/ (the largest of) a group of Portuguese islands in the Atlantic Ocean, off the coast of Morocco; capital Funchal. It attracts many tourists and is famous for its wine.

Madeira² *n* [U] a strong sweet wine originally produced in the island of Madeira

Madeira cake /·ˈ··· ·/ *n* [U] BrE a plain rather solid yellow SPONGE CAKE

Mad·e·moi·selle /ˌmædəmwəˈzel/ *n* **Mesdemoiselles** /ˌmeɪdəmwəˈzel/ (used as a title for an unmarried French-speaking woman, esp. a young woman) MISS: *Mademoiselle Dubois*

made-to-mea·sure /ˌ··· ·ˈ··· ·/ *adj* (esp. of clothes) specially made to someone's measurements

made-up /·· ·/ *adj* **1** wearing MAKE-UP on the face: *She was heavily made-up.* **2** not true; invented: *a made-up story* –see also MAKE **up** (1) **3** BrE (of a road) covered with TARMAC

Mad Hat·ter /ˌ· ˈ··/ [*the*] a character in Lewis Carroll's book *Alice's Adventures in Wonderland.* Alice goes to the Mad Hatter's tea party where nobody eats or drinks anything, the Mad Hatter and the MARCH HARE talk nonsense and the DORMOUSE keeps falling asleep. –see also ALICE IN WONDERLAND and see colour picture on page 619

mad·house /ˈmædhaʊs/ *n* -**houses** /ˌhaʊzʒz/ **1** [*usu. sing.*] *infml* a place where there is a noisy and/or disorderly crowd of people: *The store is an absolute madhouse during the pre-Christmas period.* **2** *old use* a MENTAL HOSPITAL

Mad·i·son /ˈmædɨsən/, James (1751–1836) the fourth president of the US (1809–17), famous for helping to write the Constitution.

Madison Av·en·ue /ˌ··· ˈ···/ a street in New York City in the US famous as the centre of the advertising industry –see colour map on page 1376

▶ CULTURAL NOTE Madison Avenue can be used to mean advertising. People often accuse Madison Avenue of attitudes and practices such as treating people, things, and ideas in a very light way, when they mean that advertising does this.◀

Madison Square Gar·den /ˌ··· · ˈ··/ a place in New York City, USA, where concerts or sports events, esp. BOXING matches, are held which very large crowds of people attend –see colour map on page 1376

Madison Square Park /ˌ··· · ˈ·/ a small park in New York City, bordered by Madison Avenue, Broadway, and 23rd Street –see colour map on page 1376

mad·ly /ˈmædli/ *adv* **1** in a wild way as if mad: *People were rushing madly in all directions.* **2** *infml* very (much): *He's madly in love with her.*

Mad Mag·a·zine /ˌ· ···ˌ·/ a monthly humorous magazine, read mostly by young people, which specializes in SATIRE, and parodies (PARODY¹ (1)), of current affairs, films, personalities, etc.

mad·man /ˈmædmən/ **mad·wom·an** /-ˌwʊmən/ *fem.*– *n* -**men** /mən/ a person who is mad: *He drives like a madman: I'm sure he'll have an accident one day.*

mad mon·ey /ˈ· ˌ··/ *n* [U] AmE *infml* money kept aside for something unexpected or special: *I keep a little mad money in the zippered pocket of my purse.*

mad·ness /ˈmædnɨs/ *n* [U] **1** the state of being mad **2** very foolish behaviour: *It would be sheer madness to attempt to cross the desert on your own.* **3 that way madness lies** *quote* a phrase from Shakespeare's play *King Lear,* used when saying that a course of action would lead to a lot of difficulties or problems –see also **method in one's madness** (METHOD)

Ma·don·na¹ /məˈdɒnə‖məˈdɑː-/ *n* **1** [*the*] (in the Christian religion) Mary, the mother of Jesus Christ **2** [C] a picture or figure of Mary

Madonna² (1958–) a very successful American popular music singer known for her unusual, often extreme, styles in clothes and appearance and the sometimes sexual nature of her performances and behaviour. Her well known songs include *Like a Virgin.* –see colour picture on page 554

Ma·dras /məˈdrɑːs, -dræs/ a city and port in SE India, the capital of Tamil Nadu state

Ma·drid /məˈdrɪd/ the capital city of Spain, in the centre of the country

mad·ri·gal /ˈmædrɪgəl/ *n* a song for several singers without instruments

mael·strom /ˈmeɪlstrəm/ *n esp. lit* **1** a stretch of water moving with a strong circular movement, which can suck objects down; violent WHIRLPOOL **2** [*usu. sing.*] a situation in which the course of events seems uncontrollable and may lead to destruction: *She got* **sucked into the maelstrom of** *political controversy.*

mae·nad /ˈmiːnæd/ *n* **1** a female follower or priestess of the god of wine in ancient Greece or Rome **2** *lit* an unnaturally excited or upset woman

maes·tro /ˈmaɪstrəʊ/ *n* -**tros** *or* -**tri** /triː/ (*often cap.*) a great or famous musician, esp. a CONDUCTOR (=one who directs the playing of music)

Maestro *n tdmk* a type of car made by the Rover company

Mae West /ˌmeɪ ˈwest/ *n* a garment worn to support a person in water used esp. by British airforce pilots in the Second World War (named after the film star Mae West, because the shape of the life jacket reminded people of her breasts, which were famous)

Maf·e·king /ˈmæfɨkɪŋ/ a town in South Africa, now called **Mafikeng,** which British soldiers defended successfully for 217 days while under attack by the Boers in the Boer War

MAFF /mæf/ *abbrev. for:* MINISTRY OF AGRICULTURE, FISHERIES AND FOOD

maf·i·a /ˈmæːfiə‖ˈmɑːfiə/ *n* [S+*sing.|pl. v*] **1** [*the*] (*often cap.*) also **the Mob** an organization of criminals who control many ILLEGAL activities by threats of violence, esp. the one existing for many years in Sicily and more recently in the US. The Mafia has been the subject of many books and films e.g. *The Godfather.* **2** *derog* an influential group who support each other without any concern for people outside the group: *She claimed that the medical mafia had protected the doctor against complaints of negligence.*

maf·i·o·so /ˌmæfiˈəʊsəʊ‖ˌmɑː-/ *n* (*often cap.*) a member of the mafia

mag /mæg/ *n infml* a magazine

mag·a·zine /ˌmæɡəˈziːn‖ˈmæɡəziːn/ *n* **1** a sort of book with a paper cover and usu. large pages, which contains written articles, photographs, and advertisements, usu. on a special subject or for a certain group of people, and which is printed and sold every week or month: *a glossy fashion magazine*| *a photography/news/cricket magazine* | *a popular women's magazine* —compare JOURNAL **2** the part of a gun in which bullets are placed before firing — see picture at GUN **3** the place where the roll of film is kept away from the light in a camera or PROJECTOR (=an apparatus for showing pictures) **4** a storehouse or room for arms, explosives, bullets, etc.

Ma·gel·lan /mə'gelən, -'dʒe-‖-'dʒe-/, **Fer·di·nand** /'fɜ:dɪnænd‖'fɜ:r-/ (about 1480–1521) a Portuguese sailor who was the first person to go round the world. His journey proved that the Earth was round.

ma·gen·ta /mə'dʒentə/ *adj* having a dark purplish red colour —**magenta** *n* [U]

mag·got /'mægət/ *n* a small wormlike creature which is the young of a fly or certain other insects, found on flesh and food where flies have laid their eggs

Mag·gie /'mægi/ *abbrev. for* the name "Margaret", often used when speaking or writing about Margaret Thatcher: *Maggie quits! Margaret Thatcher has announced her resignation as leader of the Conservative Party.*

Ma·ghreb /'mɑ:greb/ [*the*] the area of NW Africa which includes the countries of Morocco, Algeria, Tunisia, and Libya where the people are Arab and Berber

Ma·gi /'meɪdʒaɪ/ also **Three Wise Men, Three Kings**— [*the* + P] according to the Bible, the three wise men who came from the East guided by a star and brought gifts of gold, FRANKINCENSE and MYRRH for the baby Jesus —see also NATIVITY and see picture on page 223

ma·gic¹ /'mædʒɪk/ *n* [U] **1** the use of secret forces to control events and people, usu. by calling on spirits, saying special words, performing special ceremonies, etc.: *to practise/work magic* —see also BLACK MAGIC, WHITE MAGIC

▶CULTURAL NOTE Very few people in Western countries believe in magic now. It is generally considered to be a form of SUPERSTITION. However, many people enjoy watching performers who perform magic tricks for entertainment, e.g. making things appear or disappear.◀

2 the art employed by an entertainer (CONJURER) who produces unexpected objects and results by tricks **3** a strange or wonderful influence, power, or quality: *And now, by the magic of satellite technology, we can take you live to Sydney, Australia.* | *the magic of the theatre* **4** like **magic/as if by magic** so well or suddenly as seems unreasonable or impossible to explain —see also MAGICIAN

magic² *adj* **1** [A] caused by or used in magic: *a magic trick* | (fig.) *She has a magic touch with the baby; he never cries when she's holding him.* **2** [F] *BrE sl* very good; wonderful: *Their latest record is really magic.*

ma·gic·al /'mædʒɪkəl/ *adj apprec* of strange power, mystery, or charm: *a magical evening beneath the bright stars* — ~ **ly** /kli/ *adv*

magic car·pet /ˌ·· '··/ *n* a flying CARPET which can carry people through the air from place to place (from a story in the Arabian Nights)

Magic Cir·cle /ˌ·· '··/ [*the*] the British association which people who practise magic as entertainment can join if they are very skilful. The secrets known by magicians must not be told to people who are not members. In 1991 women were allowed to join for the first time.

magic eye /ˌ·· '·/ *n infml for* PHOTOELECTRIC CELL

ma·gi·cian /mə'dʒɪʃən/ *n* **1** (in stories) a person who can make strange things happen by magic **2** an entertainer who performs magic tricks, e.g. making things appear or disappear; a CONJUROR.

▶CULTURAL NOTE The STEREOTYPE of a magician is a man wearing evening clothes and a black CLOAK. He waves a magic WAND and says magic words; e.g. **abracadabra**, and performs tricks such as sawing (SAW) a woman in half and producing a white rabbit out of a TOP HAT.◀

Magic King·dom /ˌ·· '··/ also **Magic Kingdom park** /ˌ·· ˌ· '·/— [*the*] *tdmk* a name sometimes used instead of DISNEYLAND or DISNEY WORLD: *"Welcome to the Magic Kingdom!" said a voice on the loudspeaker.*

magic lan·tern /ˌ·· '··/ *n* an apparatus for throwing images of pictures from glass plates onto a white sheet; early type of PROJECTOR

magic mush·room /ˌ·· '··/ *n* a type of MUSHROOM which causes HALLUCINATIONS when eaten. Some people look for

and eat these deliberately, because of their drug-like effects

magic wand /ˌ·· '·/ *n* a small stick used by a magician in doing magic tricks: (fig.) *The government can't just* **wave a magic wand** *and make this problem go away.*

Ma·gi·not Line /'mæʒɪnəʊ ˌlaɪn/ [*the*] a line of FORTS built before the Second World War to defend the E border of France. It was not successful in preventing the advance of the German army, which avoided it by going through part of Belgium to the N of the Line.

ma·gis·te·ri·al /ˌmædʒɪ'stɪəriəl◀/ *adj fml* **1** typical of someone who has complete control over a situation, great knowledge of a subject, etc.; AUTHORITATIVE: *His magisterial study of Roman law is likely to be the standard book on the subject for many years.* | *a magisterial manner* **2** [A] of or done by a magistrate — ~ **ly** *adv*

ma·gis·tra·cy /'mædʒɪstrəsi/ *n* **1** [(*the*) U] the office of magistrate **2** [*the*+*sing./pl. v*] magistrates considered as a group

ma·gis·trate /'mædʒɪstreɪt, -strɪt/ *n* an official who judges cases in the lowest courts of law: *The boy came up/appeared before the magistrate on a charge of theft.* —*see also extra information on page 738*

▶CULTURAL NOTE In England and Wales, a magistrate is also called a JUSTICE OF THE PEACE or JP. Magistrates do not have a special education or training in law and are not paid for their work which is part-time and VOLUNTARY. They are advised by a clerk on matters of law, but decide the cases themselves. It is considered a very responsible position in society.◀

Magistrates' Court /ˈ··· ˌ·/ *n* the lowest court in England and Wales where magistrates hear and decide on less serious criminal cases e.g. stealing, or decide if there is enough EVIDENCE for a more serious criminal case to go to a higher court. Over 90% of all criminal cases are heard in Magistrates' Courts, which are open to members of the public. —see also extra information on page 738

mag·lev /'mæglev/ *n* a train in Birmingham, England which takes passengers from the international airport to National Exhibition Centre. The name comes from the technical phrase "magnetic levitation".

mag·ma /'mægmə/ *n* [U] hot melted rock found below the solid surface of the earth

Mag·na Car·ta /ˌmægnə 'kɑ:tə‖-'kɑ:r-/ [*the*] a famous document in British history agreed in 1215 by King John of England at Runnymede, which set limits on royal powers. Later, esp. in the 17th century, it was seen as a statement of basic CIVIL RIGHTS. Four copies of the original still exist.

magna cum lau·de /ˌmægnə kʌm 'lɔ:di, -kʊm 'laʊdeɪ‖ -kʊm 'laʊdi/ *n Lat* the second of the three levels of high HONOURS (2) given to American university or college students when they finish their studies: *He graduated magna cum laude.* —see also CUM LAUDE, SUMMA CUM LAUDE, see DEGREE³ (CULTURAL NOTE 2)

mag·nan·i·mous /mæg'nænɪməs/ *adj fml apprec* showing very generous qualities towards others, beyond what is usual or necessary: *It was very magnanimous of you to overlook his rude behaviour.* — ~ **ly** *adv* —**mity** /ˌmægnə-'nɪmɪti/ *n* [U]

mag·nate /'mægneɪt, -nɪt/ *n sometimes derog* a wealthy and powerful man, esp. in business or industry: *an oil/shipping/media magnate*

mag·ne·sia /mæg'ni:ʃə, -ʒə/ *n* [U] a light white powder used as a stomach medicine

mag·ne·si·um /mæg'ni:ziəm/ *n* [U] a common silver-white metal that is a simple substance (ELEMENT), burns with a bright white light, and is used in making FIREWORKS and mixtures of metals

mag·net /'mægnɪt/ *n* **1** a piece of iron or steel which can make other metal objects come towards it either naturally or because of an electric current being passed through it **2** [(**for, to**)] a person or thing that attracts people: *Buckingham Palace is a great magnet for tourists.*

mag·net·ic /mæg'netɪk/ *adj* **1** having the qualities of a magnet: *The iron has lost its magnetic force.* | (fig.) *her magnetic personality* **2** of or using MAGNETISM, esp. for the purpose of recording and storing information for use in a computer system: *a magnetic disk* | *magnetic storage media* —compare OPTICAL (2) — ~ **ally** /kli/ *adv*

magnet

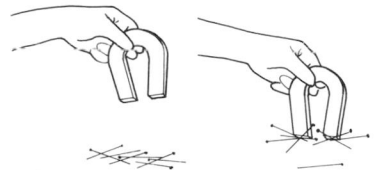

magnify

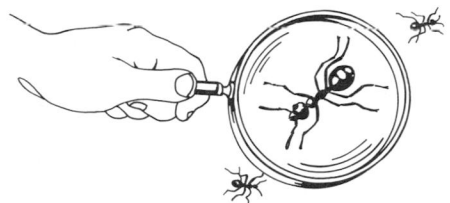

magnetic field /ˌ·ˌ·· ˈ·/ *n* the space in which a magnetic force is effective round an object which has magnetic power: *the Earth's magnetic field*

magnetic head /ˌ·ˌ·· ˈ·/ *n* a HEAD¹ (20)

magnetic me·di·a /ˌ·ˌ·· ˈ····/ [U] any of the magnetically co-vered plastics such as DISKS or MAGNETIC TAPE used for storing computer information: *The document was sent on magnetic media.*

magnetic north /ˌ·ˌ·· ˈ·/ *n* [U] the direction towards the north in the Earth's magnetic field as shown by the nee-dle of a COMPASS

magnetic pole /ˌ·ˌ·· ˈ·/ *n* either of two points, not firmly fixed but near the North Pole and the South Pole of the Earth, towards which the COMPASS needle points from any direction

magnetic storm /ˌ·ˌ·· ˈ·/ *n* a sudden change in the earth's magnetic field, caused by the sun, which can change radio waves and make it difficult to receive broadcasts

magnetic tape /ˌ·ˌ·· ˈ·/ also **mag tape** *infml*– *n* a TAPE on which sound or other information can be recorded

mag·net·is·m /ˈmægnˌtɪzəm/ *n* [U] **1** (the science dealing with) the qualities of MAGNETS **2** strong personal charm; the ability to attract: *He persuaded them to join him by the sheer magnetism of his personality.*

mag·net·ize also **-ise** *BrE* /ˈmægnˌtaɪz/ *v* [T] **1** to make into a magnet: *The iron was magnetized by passing elec-tricity through wire wound round it.* **2** to have a power-ful attraction or influence on: *Her speech magnetized the crowd.*

mag·ne·to /mægˈniːtəʊ/ *n* **-tos** a piece of equipment contain-ing one or more magnets used for producing electricity, esp. for igniting (IGNITE) the petrol in the engine of a car, motorcycle, etc. –compare DYNAMO, GENERATOR

mag·ne·to·sphere /mægˈniːtəʊsfɪəʳ/ *n* the part of the AT-MOSPHERE of the earth or other PLANET in which PARTICLES are influenced by the planet's MAGNETIC FIELD

magnet school /ˈ·· ˌ·/ *n* AmE a SECONDARY school which specializes in a particular subject, such as science or the arts, and draws its students from a wide area

Mag·nif·i·cat /mægˈnɪfˌkæt/ *n* a song praising God which is part of some Christian church services. It was origi-nally spoken by the Virgin Mary, according to the Bible.

mag·ni·fi·ca·tion /ˌmægnˌfˌˈkeɪʃən/ *n* **1** [U] the act of mag-nifying **2** [C] the power of magnifying to a stated num-ber of times bigger than in reality: *This microscope has a magnification of eight.* (=it makes things look eight times larger)

mag·nif·i·cent /mægˈnɪfˌsənt/ *adj* wonderfully fine, grand, generous, etc.: *The royal wedding was a magnificent oc-casion.* | *What a magnificent day!* (=a day of very fine weather) | *a magnificent gift* – ~ **ly** *adv* –**cence** *n* [U]

Magnificent Men in their Fly·ing Ma·chines /ˌ·ˌ···· ˌ··· · ˈ·· ·ˌ·/, **Those** the title of an old popular song, now often used when talking about the pilots of early aircraft

mag·ni·fy /ˈmægnˌfaɪ/ *v* [T] **1** to make (something) appear larger than it really is: *A microscope will magnify these germs, so that you can actually see them.* | (fig.) *The im-portance of his remark has been magnified out of all proportion.* **2** *old use or bibl* to praise (God) highly –**fier** *n*

magnifying glass /ˈ····· ·/ *n* a piece of glass (LENS), usu. curved on one or both sides, with a frame and handle, which magnifies things that are seen through it

mag·ni·tude /ˈmægnˌtjuːd‖-tuːd/ *n* **1** [U] *fml* greatness of size or importance: *I hadn't realized the magnitude of the problem.* **2** [C] *tech* the degree of brightness of a star: *a star of the second magnitude*

mag·no·li·a /mægˈnəʊliə/ *n* **1** [C] a tree with large sweet-smelling flowers **2** [U] a very pale pinkish-white colour

Mag·nox re·ac·tor /ˈmægnɒks riˌæktəʳ‖-naːks-/ *n tdmk* an old type of British NUCLEAR REACTOR

mag·num /ˈmægnəm/ *n* (a large bottle containing) a meas-ure of about 1·5 litres, esp. for wine

magnum o·pus /ˌ·· ˈ···/ also **opus magnum**– *n fml* a great book or work of art considered the most important piece of work of the person who produced it; MASTERPIECE

Mag·nus·son /ˈmægnəsən/, **Mag·nus** /ˈmægnəs/ (1929–) an Icelandic television presenter who asks the questions on the well-known British television QUIZ programme MASTERMIND. He is known esp. for saying "I've started so I'll finish."

mag·pie /ˈmægpaɪ/ *n* a noisy bird with black and white feathers, which often picks up and takes to its nest small bright objects

Ma·gritte /mæˈɡriːt/, **Re·né** /ˈrəneɪ‖rəˈneɪ/ (1898–1967) a Bel-gian SURREALIST painter known for the paradoxes (PARA-DOX) in his pictures, which often involved apples, hats, and windows

mag tape /ˌ·ˌ· ˈ·/ *n infml* MAGNETIC TAPE

Ma·guire Sev·en /məˌɡwaɪə ˈsevən‖-ˌɡwaɪər-/ [*the* + P] seven people, four of whom were from the Irish Maguire family, who were sent to prison in Britain in 1976 for set-ting up an IRA bomb factory. They were freed in 1991 after it was shown that scientific tests used to prove them guilty did not do so. Along with other cases, this case has raised questions in Britain about police questioning of people they have caught for a crime, and about the way mistakes in justice are put right –compare BIRMINGHAM SIX, GUILDFORD FOUR, TOTTENHAM THREE

Mag·yar /ˈmægjɑːʳ/ *n* **1** [C] a member of the largest group of people in Hungary **2** [U] the language of the Magyars –**Magyar** *adj*

ma·ha·ra·ja , **-jah** /ˌmɑːhəˈrɑːdʒə/ *n* (*often cap.*) a Hindu king or prince in India

ma·ha·ra·ni , **-nee** /ˌmɑːhəˈrɑːniː/ *n* (*often cap.*) the wife of a maharaja

Ma·ha·rish·i Ma·hesh Yo·gi /ˌmɑːhəˌriːʃi ˌmɑːheʃ ˈjəʊgi/ [*the*] an Indian religious leader who began the Spiritual Regeneration movement, which practises TRANSCENDENTAL MEDITATION. People remember him esp. in connection with The Beatles, who went to study under him.

ma·hat·ma /məˈhætmə‖məˈhɑːt-/ *n* (*often cap.*) a wise and holy man in India: *Mahatma Gandhi*

Ma·ha·ya·na /ˌmɑːhəˈjɑːnə/ *adj* of the form of Buddhism practised in Tibet and China, based on developments of the original teachings of the Buddha starting in the first century –compare THERAVADA

Mah·di /ˈmɑːdi/ *n* (a religious leader who claims to be) the MESSIAH whose arrival is expected by Muslims, and who will make all people in the world follow Islam

Mah·fouz /mɑːˈfuːz/, **Na·guib** /nɑːˈɡiːb/ (1911–) an impor-tant modern Egyptian writer who won the Nobel prize for literature in 1988

mah-jong , **-jongg** /ˌmɑː ˈdʒɒŋ‖-ˈʒɑːŋ/ *n* [U] a Chinese game for four players, played with small painted pieces of wood or bone. It is thought of as a game played by old, esp. UPPER-CLASS, women.

Mah·ler /ˈmɑːləʳ/, **Gus·tav** /ˈɡʊstɑːv‖ˈɡʌs-/ (1860–1911) an Austrian CONDUCTOR and writer of classical music, in-cluding nine symphonies (SYMPHONY) and the collections of songs *Das Lied von der Erde* (the song of the earth) and

Kindertotenlieder (songs of the deaths of children)

ma·hog·a·ny /məˈhɒgəni‖məˈhɑː-/ *n* [U] (the colour of) a dark reddish wood used for making fine furniture: *a mahogany table*

Ma·hon /məˈhɒn‖-ˈhəʊn/ a port and popular tourist centre on the Balearic island of Menorca

ma·hout /maːˈhuːt, məˈhaʊt‖məˈhaʊt/ *n* (in India) a person who drives an elephant, and keeps and trains elephants

maid /meɪd/ *n* **1** (*often in comb.*) a female servant, esp. in a large house in former times: *Her maid helped her to dress for the ball.* —see also HOUSEMAID, MILKMAID, NURSE-MAID **2** *lit or old use* a girl or (young) woman who is not married —see also OLD MAID

maid·en¹ /ˈmeɪdn/ *n* **1** *lit* a girl who is not married **2** *tech* a horse which has not won a race **3** also **maiden o·ver** /ˌ·· ˈ··/— (in cricket) an OVER in which no runs are made

maiden² *adj* [A] **1** first of its kind; earliest: *The aircraft makes its maiden flight tomorrow. | The new MP is making her maiden speech in Parliament tomorrow.* **2** (of a woman, esp. an older woman) unmarried: *a maiden aunt*

mai·den·hair /ˈmeɪdnheəʳ/ *n* [U] a kind of FERN

maid·en·head /ˈmeɪdnhed/ *n old use or lit* **1** [U] the state of being a female VIRGIN; fact of not having had sexual experience **2** [C] a HYMEN

Maidenhead a town in SE England, in Berkshire, on the river Thames

maid·en·hood /ˈmeɪdnhʊd/ *n* [U] *esp. lit* the condition or time of being a young unmarried girl

maid·en·ly /ˈmeɪdnli/ *adj esp. lit* like or suitable to a young unmarried girl: *maidenly modesty*

maiden name /ˈ·· ·/ *n* the family name a woman had before marriage

▶CULTURAL NOTE In Britain and the US it is usual for a woman to take her husband's family name after marriage, although some professional married women sometimes use their maiden names. In the US some women keep their maiden name and add their husband's family name to it using a HYPHEN: *Jane Smith-Robinson*◀

Maid Mar·i·an /ˌmeɪd ˈmæriən/ **1** (in the stories of Robin Hood) the woman who lived with Robin Hood —see ROBIN HOOD and see colour picture on page 620 **2** the May Queen in MORRIS DANCES and May Day games

maid of hon·our /ˌ·· ˈ··/ *n* **1** an unmarried lady who serves a queen or princess **2** the chief BRIDESMAID at a wedding **3** *BrE* a type of small cake

Maid of Or·le·ans /ˌmeɪd əv ɔːˈliːnz‖-ˈɔːrliənz/ [*the*] see SAINT JOAN OF ARC

maid·ser·vant /ˈmeɪdˌsɜːvənt‖-ɜːr-/ *n esp. old use* a female servant —compare MANSERVANT

Maid·stone /ˈmeɪdstən/ a town in Kent, England, where the local government for that COUNTY is based

Mai·gret /ˈmeɪgreɪ‖meɪˈgreɪ/ the main character in the very popular books by Georges Simenon, the Belgian writer. Maigret is a CHIEF INSPECTOR of police in Paris.

mail¹ /meɪl/ *n* **1** [(*the*);U] the postal system: *Airmail is quicker than sea mail. | I'll send it (by) first-/second-class mail. | (esp. AmE) It came in the mail.* **2** [U] letters and anything else sent or received by post, esp. those travelling or arriving together: *She was opening her mail.* **3** [C] also **mail train** /ˈ· ·/— (esp. in names) a train which carries mail **4** [U] a computer feature that enables users to send messages to each other which can be read, redirected, saved, copied, etc.: *Did you get my mail message about taking next Friday off?*

▷ USAGE 1 **Post** is the more usual word in British English except in certain combinations such as **airmail**. **Mail** is the usual word in American English. 2 **Mail**

is sometimes used in the names of newspapers, e.g. *the Daily* **Mail** and in the names of train or boat services, e.g. *the Irish* **Mail**.◁

mail² *v* [T (**to**)] *esp. AmE* to post (a letter, parcel, etc.)

mail³ *n* [U] armour made of metal plates or rings, worn by soldiers in former times: *a coat of mail* —see also CHAIN MAIL

Mail [*the*] the DAILY MAIL

mail·bag /ˈmeɪlbæg/ *n* **1** a large bag made of strong cloth for carrying mail in trains, ships, etc. **2** *AmE* a postman's bag for carrying mail to be delivered; POSTBAG

mail·box /ˈmeɪlbɒks‖-bɑːks/ *n AmE* **1** a place for posting letters, etc.; POSTBOX **2** a place where one's mail is left near one's house; a LETTERBOX separate from the door — see LETTERBOX and see picture at POST BOX

mail drop /ˈ· ·/ *n AmE* **1** a mailbox (2) **2** an address used in the sending of secret messages **3** an address which exists only for the purpose of receiving mail: *The police discovered that the address found on the murdered man was a mail drop.*

Mai·ler /ˈmeɪləʳ/, **Norman** (1923–) an American writer famous for his treatment of social and political subjects. His books include *The Naked and the Dead, The Armies of the Night*, and *The Executioner's Song*.

mailing list /ˈ·· ·/ *n* a list of names and addresses kept by an organization, to which it sends information by mail: *I'll put you on our mailing list, sir.*

mail·man /ˈmeɪlmæn/ *n* **-men** /men/ *AmE for* POSTMAN

Mail on Sun·day /ˌ· · ˈ··/ [*the*] a popular British newspaper which comes out on Sundays, produced by the same company and for the same readers as the DAILY MAIL. It is a TABLOID newspaper and known for its generally right-wing political news.

mail or·der /ˌ· ˈ··◂/ *n* [U] a method of selling goods in which the buyer chooses them at home, often from a book (CATALOGUE) which lists them, and the goods that have been ordered are sent by post

mail·shot /ˈmeɪlʃɒt‖-ʃɑːt/ *n* a sending of advertisements or other sorts of information to large numbers of people by post

maim /meɪm/ *v* [T] to wound very severely and usu. lastingly: *She survived the accident but she was* **maimed for life** *and will never walk again.*

main¹ /meɪn/ *adj* [A *no comp.*] of greater size, importance, or influence than all others; chief: *a busy main road | We have our main meal in the evening. | Note down the main points of the speech. | Soldiers guarded the main gates.* —see also MAINLY

main² *n* **1** also **mains** *pl.*— the chief pipe supplying water or gas, or a chief wire carrying electricity, into a building from outside: *The workman accidentally drilled a hole in the gas main. | She turned the water off* **at the mains.** (=so that the complete supply to the house was cut off) —see also MAINS **2** **in the main** on the whole; usually; mostly —see also **by/with might and main** (MIGHT²)

main chance /ˌ· ˈ·/ [*the*] *infml, esp. BrE* the possibility of making money or of other personal gain: *He always* **had an eye to** (=had as his purpose) **the main chance.**

main clause /ˌ· ˈ·/ *n* an INDEPENDENT CLAUSE

main course /ˈ· ·/ *n* the most important dish in a meal: *They served chicken as the main course.*

main drag /ˌ· ˈ·/ *n* [(*the*)] *esp. AmE* a chief street in a town or city where shops and businesses are found: *Let's take a cruise down the main drag and see what's going on. | It's a really small town. The main drag is only a block long.*

Maine /meɪn/ (*written abbrev.* **ME.**)– a state in the NE of the US, on the Atlantic coast and bordering on Canada —see colour map on pages 1374–5

main·frame /ˈmeɪnfreɪm/ *n* the largest and most powerful type of computer —compare MICROCOMPUTER, MINICOMPUTER, PERSONAL COMPUTER

main·land /ˈmeɪnlənd, -lænd/ *n* [*the*] a land mass, considered without its islands: *Ferry services operate between the islands and the mainland.* —**mainland** *adj* [A] : *the good road network in mainland Britain*

main·line /ˈmeɪnlaɪn/ *v* [I;T] *sl* to put (INJECT) a drug into one of the chief VEINS of the body, either for pleasure or because one is dependent on it, not for medical reasons

main line /ˌ·ˈ·◁/ *n* a chief railway line

main·ly /ˈmeɪnli/ *adv* [*no comp.*] in most cases or to a large degree; chiefly: *I don't know what her interests are, because we talk mainly about work when we meet.* | *His money comes mainly from business investments.*

main·mast /ˈmeɪnmɑːst, -məst‖-mæst, -məst/ *n* the largest or most important of the MASTs which hold up the sails on a ship

mains /meɪnz/ *n* [*the+sing./pl. v*] *esp. BrE* a supply of electricity produced centrally and brought to houses, etc., by wires: *Does your radio work off the mains or from a battery?* | *a mains radio*

main·sail /ˈmeɪnsəl, *not tech* -seɪl/ *n* the chief sail on a ship, usu. the one on the mainmast —see picture at YACHT

main·spring /ˈmeɪnsprɪŋ/ *n* **1** the chief spring in a watch **2** [(of) *usu. sing.*] the chief force or reason that makes something happen: *His belief in liberty was the mainspring of his fight against slavery.*

main·stay /ˈmeɪnsteɪ/ *n* [(of) *usu. sing.*] someone or something which provides the chief means of support: *Agriculture is still the mainstay of the country's economy.*

main·stream¹ /ˈmeɪnstriːm/ *n* [*the*] the main or most widely accepted way of thinking or acting in relation to a subject: *Their views lie outside the mainstream of current medical opinion.* —**mainstream** *adj* [A] : *mainstream philosophical thinking*

mainstream² *v* [T;I] *AmE* to include (a child with learning problems or physical disability) in a class with children developing in the expected way —**ing** *n* [U]

Main Street /ˈ·ˌ·/ *n AmE* **1** [C] (the name of) the most important business street in many small towns in the US. **2** [U] small towns in general, esp. in relation to their political and social values: *The president's speech wasn't received very well on Main Street.*

► CULTURAL NOTE A novel by Sinclair Lewis called *Main Street*, about life in a small Midwestern town, gave an image of CONSERVATISM and NARROW-MINDEDNESS in small towns. ◄

main·tain /meɪnˈteɪn, mən-/ *v* **1** [T] to continue to have, do, etc., as before; KEEP **up**: *He took the lead, and maintained it until the end of the race.* | *I hope you will maintain your recent improvement.* | *Part of her job is to maintain good relations with our suppliers.* **2** [T] to keep (something) in good condition by making repairs to it and taking care of it: *The railway lines have to be constantly maintained.* | *a well-maintained house* **3** [T] to (continue to) argue in favour of or declare to be true; ASSERT: *Throughout the trial he maintained his innocence.* [+(*that*)] *Some people still maintain that the Earth is flat.* **4** [T] **a** to support with money: *He is too poor to maintain his family.* **b** to keep in existence: *The supplies of food were scarcely enough to maintain life.* **5** [I] *AmE infml* to continue in one's present state or course of action — **~able** *adj*

main·te·nance /ˈmeɪntənəns/ *n* [U] **1** the act of maintaining, esp. of keeping something in good condition: *lessons in car maintenance* **2** *BrE* = money paid regularly by a DIVORCED person to his or her former partner, to help financially or support their children. The man and woman may agree the amount between themselves, but usually a court decides the amount and orders that it must be paid. Usually the man has to pay the woman, but if she earns more than he does she may have to pay, especially if the children live with their father. If the money is not paid regularly, the court may order the person's employers to take it out of their pay —compare ALIMONY, CHILD SUPPORT and see also DIVORCE¹

maintenance or·der /ˈ···ˌ·ˌ·/ *n BrE* an order made by a law court that a person shall pay for the support of others, esp. a man for his (former) wife and their children

mai·son·ette /ˌmeɪzəˈnet/ *n esp. BrE* a flat, usu. on two floors, that is part of a larger house but which has its own door to the outside

mai·tre d' /ˌmetrə ˈdiː‖ˌmeɪ-/ also **maître d'hô·tel** /ˌmetrə dəʊˈtel‖ˌmeɪ-/— *n* a person in charge of a restaurant, who tells guests where to sit and waiters what to do, etc.

maize /meɪz/ *esp. BrE* ‖ **Indian corn** *esp. AmE*, **corn** *esp. AmE & AustrE*— *n* [U] (the seed of) a type of tall plant grown, esp. in America and Australia, for its ears of yellow seeds, food for people and animals —see also SWEET CORN, and see picture at CEREAL

Maj. *written abbrev. for:* Major (MAJOR² (1))

ma·jes·tic /məˈdʒestɪk/ *adj apprec* having or showing majesty; STATELY — **~ally** /kli/ *adv* : *The great ship sailed slowly and majestically into harbour.*

ma·jes·ty /ˈmædʒəsti/ *n* [U] *apprec* a powerful quality that causes great admiration; GRANDEUR: *the snow-covered mountains in all their majesty*

Majesty *n* (used as a title for addressing or speaking of a king or queen): *Good morning, Your Majesty.* | *Her Majesty Queen Elizabeth the Second* | *Their Majesties will open the new bridge today.*

ma·jor¹ /ˈmeɪdʒəʳ/ *adj* **1** greater when compared with others in size, number, importance, or seriousness: *The car needs major repairs.* | *Shipbuilding used to be one of our major industries.* | *a major modern writer* | *He's going in for major surgery today.* | *The company's problems are fairly major.* —opposite **minor** **2** being or based on a musical SCALE on which there are SEMITONEs between the third and fourth and the seventh and eighth notes: *in a major key* [after *n*] *a symphony in D major* **3** [after *n*] *BrE old use* being the older of two boys of the same name at the same school: *Smith major* —opposite **minor**

▷ USAGE Neither **major** nor **minor** is used in comparisons with *than*. **Superior, inferior, senior,** and **junior** can be used in comparisons, but they are followed by *to* not *than*: *This restaurant is superior to the one we usually go to.* | *She is senior to everyone else in the company.*◁

ma·jor² *n* **1** an officer of middle rank in the British or US army or MARINEs or the US airforce —see also DRUM MAJOR —see TABLE 3 **2** *esp. AmE* (a student studying) a chief or special subject at a university: *She's a history major.* | *Her major is history.* —see also MAJOR **in** **3** *law* a person who has reached the age (now 18 in Britain and the US) at which they are fully responsible in law for their actions —compare MINOR²

ma·jor³ *v*

major in sthg. *phr v* [T] *esp. AmE* to study as the chief subject(s) when doing a university degree: *He's majoring in French.* —see also MAJOR² (2)

Major, John (1943–) a British politician in the Conservative Party who entered parliament in 1979 and became PRIME MINISTER in November 1990 when Margaret Thatcher resigned (RESIGN). He immediately faced the problems of the Gulf War and Britain's economic difficulties. When he first became prime minister, he was not well-known by the British public. He seemed to many people to be a pleasant man but rather dull and boring, esp. when compared with Mrs Thatcher. He was described as "Mr Nice" or "a grey man in a grey suit". He was re-elected as Prime Minister in the 1992 General Election. —see colour picture on page 950

Ma·jor·ca /məˈjɔːkə, -ˈdʒɔː-‖-ɔːr-/ a Spanish island in the W Mediterranean which is very popular with British tourists; the Spanish name is **Mallorca**. In Britain, it is often considered to be a place where large numbers of people go on cheap holidays. Some British people think that parts of the island, esp. on the coast, have been spoiled because there are too many new buildings and places of entertainment for tourists.

ma·jor·do·mo /ˌmeɪdʒəˈdəʊməʊ‖-dʒər-/ *n* **-mos** (esp. in former times) a person in charge of the servants in a large house, esp. in Spain or Italy

ma·jor·ette /ˌmeɪdʒəˈret/ also **drum majorette**— *n* one of a group of girls who wear brightly coloured uniforms including a short skirt and march in public PROCESSIONs with musical bands. They have sticks in their hands which they move in time to the music. Sometimes one girl marches alone in front of the band.

major gen·e·ral /ˌ··ˈ····◁/ *n* an officer of high rank in the British or US army or the US airforce —see TABLE 3

ma·jor·i·ty /məˈdʒɒrɪti‖məˈdʒɔː-, məˈdʒɑː-/ *n* **1** [S (of)+*sing./pl. v*] the larger number or amount, esp. of people; most: *The majority of doctors agree that smoking is extremely harmful to health.* | *A majority voted in favour of the proposal.* | *In the vast majority of cases, this is a very successful operation.* | *It was **a majority decision.*** (=more people agreed with it than disagreed) | *The majority party in parliament forms the government.* | *At the meeting, young people were **in the majority.*** **2** [C *usu. sing.*] the difference in number between a large and a smaller group: *He won by an overwhelming* (=very large) *majority/by a narrow* (=very small) *majority/by a majority of 900 votes.* **3** [U] *law* the age when one becomes a legally responsible adult —opposite **minority**

majority lead·er /·ˈ··· ˌ··/ *n* in the US, the person who is in charge of the organization of the members of the political party which has the most people elected in either the HOUSE OF REPRESENTATIVES or the SENATE: *Both Howard Baker and Bob Dole were effective Senate majority leaders, able to assert leadership over the diverse forces in Congress.* —compare MINORITY LEADER (2)

Major Leagues /ˌ··ˈ·/ also **majors**— *n* [*the* + P] the group of teams that make up American professional BASEBALL: *That catcher will be ready for the major leagues soon.* | (fig.) *You'll be playing in the major leagues if you get that job with Shearson Lehman Hutton.* (=you will have an important job working with professional people) — **major-league** *adj* : *major-league baseball* | *These articles are major-league stuff.* (=are very good) —see also BASEBALL

major suit /ˌ··ˈ·/ *n* (in the card game BRIDGE³) either HEARTS (4) or SPADES² (1), which have a higher value than the MINOR SUITS

Ma·kar·i·os III /məˌkɑːriəs ðə ˈθɜːd‖-əʊs ðə ˈθɜːrd/, **Archbishop** (1913–77) a religious leader, politician, and the first president of Cyprus. He led the movement which brought the island's independence from Britain in 1960.

make¹ /meɪk/ *v* **made** /meɪd/ to produce something **1** [T (**from, of, out of**)] to produce by work or action; cause to exist: *She made a cake.* | *Did you make this dress or buy it?* | *The children are making a lot of noise.* | *He's always making trouble.* | *Parliament makes laws.* | *"I haven't got time to do it." "Well, you must* **make time.**" | *He made a shelter from some branches and leaves.* | *The table is made of wood.* | *I'm going to make a skirt out of this material.* | *This car was made in Japan.* [obj(i)+obj(d)] *Will you make me a cup of coffee?* [+obj(d)+**for**] *Will you make a cup of coffee for me?* | (fig.) *This is his first real challenge; now we'll see* **what he's (really) made of.** (=see if he is brave, has a strong character, etc.) | (fig.) *No, I won't buy you a new coat — I'm not* **made of money** *you know!* —see USAGE to perform an action **2** [T] (used with nouns, often instead of a related verb, to show the doing of an action) to perform the actions connected with: *to make a decision* (=to decide) | *We made an important discovery.* (=We discovered something important.) | *to make an effort/a request* | *I think you've made a mistake here.* | *She made an offer of £10 for it.* | *The president is determined not to make any concessions to the terrorists* to cause to be or cause to do something **3** [T] to put into a certain state, position, etc.; cause to be: [+obj+adj] *Eating the unripe apples made him ill.* | *The decision made her very unpopular with the staff.* | *We made the house more secure by putting locks on the windows.* [+obj+v-ed] *He shouted to make himself heard across the room.* [+obj+n] *They have made her (a) director.* | *She has been made (a) director.* | *The Navy has* **made a man of him.** —see also **make a fool of oneself** (FOOL¹) **4** [T+obj+*to*-v] to force or cause (a person to do something or a thing to happen): *The pain made him cry out.* | *If you won't do it willingly, I'll make you do it!* | *Don't make me laugh!* | *Can't you make that dog stand still?* | *They made her wait.* | *She was made to wait for hours.* | *The extra cargo made the ship sink.* —see CAUSE (USAGE) **5** [T+obj+*to*-v] to represent as being, doing, happening, etc.; cause to appear as: *This photograph makes her look very young.* | *The shiny new office block makes our offices look rather drab.* | *In the film, the battle is made to take place in the winter.* to reach or gain something **6** [T] *infml* to arrive at or reach: *We made the station in time to catch the train.* | *The story made* (=was printed in) *all the papers.* | *I'm afraid I won't be able to make your party/to make it to your party.* | *If I don't make it* (=arrive) *by half past ten, assume I'm not coming.* **7** [T] to earn, gain, or get: *She makes a lot of money/£100 a week.* | *He makes a living by repairing cars.* | *The company has made a loss this year.* | *I see you've made a new friend.* [+obj(i)+obj(d)] *His ruthless behaviour made him many enemies.* **8** [T] to calculate (and get as a result): *He added up the figures and made a different answer from the one I got.* [+obj+n] *I make that £13.15 altogether.* | *What time do you make it?* to be or amount to **9** [L+n] to be when added together:

Two and two make four. **10** [L+n] to be counted as (first, second, etc.): *This makes our third party this month.* | *That makes four who want to go.* **11** [L (+obj)+n] to have the qualities of (esp. something good): *This story makes good reading.* | *The hall would make a good theatre.* | *"They say it will be sunny tomorrow." "That will* **make a change.**" | *She would make him a good wife.* other meanings **12** [T] *infml* to give the particular qualities of; complete: *It's the bright paint which really makes the room.* | *The good news really made my day!* (=meant I had a good day) **13** [T] to tidy (a bed that has just been slept in) by straightening the sheets, pulling over the cover, etc. **14** [T] *esp. old use* to travel (a distance): *He made a few more yards before he fell to the ground.* **15** [T+*to*-v; *obj*] *lit or old use* to be about (to): *He made to speak, but I stopped him.* **16** **make a go of sthg** to succeed; do something well: *They're really making a go of their marriage/business.* **17** **make as if/to** to be about to: *He made as if to speak, but I stopped him.* **18** **make a play for** *AmE infml* to try to get: *He made a play for the keys, but I held them out of his reach.* **19** **make believe** to pretend: *They made believe they were princes and princesses.* —see also MAKE-BELIEVE **20** **make do (with/without something)** *infml* to use (something) even though it may not be exactly what is wanted or needed: *We haven't got meat, so we'll have to make do with bread/make do without.* **21** **make good** a *AmE* [+ **on**] to keep a promise or repay a debt: *He made good on all his debts.* b to succeed: *You'll make good if you keep trying.* **22** **make it:** a to arrive in time: *I think we'll just make it!* b *infml* to succeed: *It's hard to make it to the top in show business.* **23** **make like** *AmE infml, sometimes derog* to act as if one were; pretend to be: *He makes like he's the biggest TV star around.* **24** **make my day** a threat or warning not to do sthg. because the speaker is ready for trouble: *Go on, hit me. Make my day.* **25** **make or break** (which will) cause success or complete failure: *What the critics say can make or break a new young performer.* | *a make-or-break decision* —see also MADE²

▷ USAGE 1 Compare **do** and **make**. These are used in many fixed expressions like **do** *a favour*, **make** *war*, where there is no rule about which one to use. But generally you **do** an action and **make** something which was not there before: *to* **do** *the shopping/the ironing/your exercises* | *to* **make** *a fire/a noise* | *"What are you* **doing**?" "Cooking." | *"What are you* **making**?" "A cake."* 2 When **make** means "to force" or "to cause", do not use *to* before a following verb unless the sentence is passive: *She* **made** *me cry.* | *I was* **made** *to walk home.*◁

make away with sbdy./sthg. *phr v* [T] *old-fash infml* **1** to kill (esp. oneself) **2** to steal

make for sthg. *phr v* [T *no pass.*] **1** to move in the direction of, usu. quickly or purposefully: *It started raining, so she made for the nearest shelter.* **2** to result in; make possible or likely: *The large print makes for easier reading.*

make (sthg./sbdy.) **into** sthg. *phr v* [T] to use or be usable in making; turn into: *I'm going to make this material into a skirt.*

make sthg. **of** sthg./sbdy. *phr v* [T] **1** to understand (partly or at all) by: *I don't know what to make of him/of his odd behaviour.* **2** to give (the usu. stated amount of importance) to: *She tends to make too much of her problems.* | *Well, do you want to make something of it?* (=a threatening reply to someone who is arguing)

make off *phr v* [I] to leave or escape in a hurry

make off with sthg. *phr v* [T] *infml* to steal

make out *phr v* **1** [T] (**make** sthg. ↔ **out**) to write in complete form: *to make out a cheque/a bill/a list* **2** [T] (**make** sthg./sbdy. ↔ **out**) *infml* to see, hear, or understand with difficulty: *I can just make out the writing.* | *He's an odd character; I can't quite make him out.* [+wh-] *I can't make out how to put the top back on.* **3** [T] *infml* to claim or pretend (that someone or something is so), usu. falsely: [+(*that*)] *He makes out he's the only person here who does any work.* [+obj+adj] *He makes himself out to be very important.* | *She's not as bad as she is made out (to be).* **4** [T] (**make** sthg. ↔ **out**) to prove by giving good reasons: *I'm sure we can* **make out a case** *for allowing you a longer holiday this year.* **5** [I] *infml* to succeed or advance, in business or life generally: *The firm isn't making out as well as was hoped.* | *How did she make out at the interview?* **6** [I;T (**with**)] *AmE sl* to kiss and touch another person in a sexual way: *They were making out in the back of a car.*

make sthg. ↔ **over** *phr v* [T] **1** [(to)] to pass over to someone else, esp. legally: *He made over his estate to his son before he died.* **2** *esp. AmE* to remake, ALTER: *They're going to make the whole thing over.* | *make over a dress* —see also MAKEOVER

make towards sthg. *phr v* [T *no pass.*] *fml* to move in the direction of; MAKE **for**: *traffic making towards the city in the morning*

make up *phr v* **1** [T] (**make** sthg. ↔ **up**) to invent (a story, a poem, an excuse, etc.), often in order to deceive —see also MADE-UP (2) **2** [I;T (=**make** sbdy./sthg. ↔ **up**)] to use special paint and powder on (someone or a part of someone's body, esp. the face) so as to change or improve the appearance: *She never goes out without making herself up first.* | *They made him up as an old man for the last act of the play.* —see also MADE-UP (1), MAKE-UP (1) **3** [T] (**make** sthg. ↔ **up**) to prepare, arrange, or put together ready for use: *The chemist made up the doctor's prescription/a bottle of medicine.* | *I can make up a bed for you on the floor.* | *I'm making up a parcel of old clothes for the jumble sale.* **4** [T] (**make** sthg. ↔ **up**) to form as a whole; CONSTITUTE: *Farming and mining make up most of the country's industry.* | *The committee is made up of representatives from all the universities.* —see also MAKE-UP (2) **5** [T (**into**)] (**make** sthg. ↔ **up**) to produce (something) from (material) by cutting and sewing: *I've made up the curtains.* | *She made the material up into a dress.* **6** [T (**to**)] (**make** sthg. ↔ **up**) to make (an amount or number) complete: *They made up a four at tennis.* | *I'll make up the money (to the amount you need).* **7** [T] (**make** sthg. ↔ **up**) to repay or give (an amount) in return: *You must make up what you owe before the end of the month.* **8** [I;T (=**make** sthg. ↔ **up**) (**with**)] to become friends again after (a quarrel): *to kiss and make up after an argument* | *It's time you made it up with your sister.* —see also **make up one's mind** (MIND¹) **9** [T] (**make** sthg. **up**) to do something after the time it was supposed to have been done: *I have to make up all the work I missed while I was ill.* | *Will you be able to make up the test?*

make up for sthg. *phr v* [T] to repay or COMPENSATE for (what was bad before) with something good: *This beautiful autumn makes up for the wet summer.* | *We're working fast to try and* **make up for lost time.** [+v-ing] *Nothing can make up for missing such a wonderful opportunity.*

make up to *phr v* [T] **1** (**make up to** sbdy.) *usu. derog* to try to gain the favour of by appearing friendly, pleasant, and full of praise: *People only make up to him because of his wealth.* **2 make it up to someone (for something)** to repay someone with good things in return for something good they have done or to make up for something bad experienced by them: *You've been so kind – I'll make it all up to you one day.* | *I do apologize for all the inconvenience this has caused – I'll make it up to you somehow.*

make with sthg. *phr v* [T] *sl, esp. AmE* to produce; bring: *I'm hungry; make with the dinner!*

make² *n* **1** [(of)] a type of product, esp. as produced by a particular maker: *This watch keeps going wrong; I wish I'd bought a better make.* | *What make (of car) is this?* **2 on the make** *derog* **a** actively trying to gain personal profit or advantage **b** trying to obtain a sexual experience with someone

▷ USAGE **Brand** and **make** can have similar meanings, but **brand** is usually used only with small or inexpensive things. Compare *What* **brand** *of toothpaste/soap powder do you use?* and *What* **make** *of computer did you buy?*◁

make-be·lieve /¹· ··ˌ·/ *n* [U] a state of pretending; believing things that have no connection with reality, esp. things that one would like to be true: *She lives in a world of make-believe if she thinks she can get to college without working hard.* —see also **make believe** (MAKE¹ (19))

make·o·ver /ˈmeɪkəʊvəʳ/ *n* a new haircut and usu. new MAKE-UP and clothes so that one looks different and usu. better than before: *This fashion magazine often has photographs of makeovers in it.*

mak·er /ˈmeɪkəʳ/ *n* **1 a** (*often in comb.*) a person who makes something: *a mapmaker* | *a filmmaker* | *a troublemaker* **b** also **makers** *pl.*— a firm that makes something: *My watch has gone wrong; I'm sending it back to the*

makers. **2** (*often cap.*) God: (*euph*) *He's gone to* **meet his maker.** (=has died)

make-shift /ˈmeɪkʃɪft/ *adj, n* (being) something made or used in the case of a sudden or urgent need, because there is nothing better: *a makeshift shelter*

make-up /¹· ·/ *n* **1** [C *usu. sing.*; U] powder, paint, etc., worn on the face, either by actors or (esp. by women) for improving one's appearance: *eye make-up* | *stage make-up* —see also MAKE **up** (2) **2** [C *usu. sing.*] a combination of members or qualities, esp. in a person's character: *The make-up of the crew is five Englishmen, two Americans, and an Australian.* | *You won't get him to change his behaviour at his age; it's in his make-up.* —see also MAKE **up** (4) **3** [C *usu. sing.*] the way in which the print, pictures, etc., in a newspaper or on a page are arranged **4** [C] *AmE* an examination taken to replace one that was missed: *I've got a make-up in Algebra for the test I missed when I was sick.*

make-weight /¹· ·/ *n* a person or thing added, invited, etc. only in order to make up a total value, number, etc., not for any value of its or their own

make-work /¹· ·/ *n* [U] *AmE* work which is not important but which keeps people busy: *The substitute teacher gave the students a lot of make-work in order to keep them quiet.*

mak·ing /ˈmeɪkɪŋ/ *n* **1** [U] (*usu. in comb.*) the process or business of producing something by work or activity, esp. with the hands: *shoemaking* | *dressmaking* | *film-making equipment* | *a lawmaking body* **2** [*the*+of] a means of gaining great improvement or success: *Hard work will be the making of him.* —compare UNDOING **3 in the making: a** in the process of being made: *The film is still in the making.* **b** ready to be produced: *There's a fortune in the making for anyone willing to work hard.*

mak·ings /ˈmeɪkɪŋz/ *n* [*the*+P+of] everything that is necessary for developing (into): *She has the makings of a good doctor.* | *The story has all the makings of a great movie.*

mal- see WORD FORMATION

Mal·a·bar Coast /ˌmæləbɑː ˈkəʊst‖-bɑːr-/ [*the*] the SW coast of India, which produces COCONUTS, rice, and SPICES

mal·a·chite /ˈmæləkaɪt/ *n* [U] a decorative green stone

mal·ad·just·ed /ˌmæləˈdʒʌstᵻd◂/ *adj* not having a good relationship with or attitude to other people or to one's surroundings, so that one is unhappy, dissatisfied with life, etc.; not WELL-ADJUSTED: *a home for maladjusted children* **—ment** *n* [U]

mal·ad·min·i·stra·tion /ˌmælədˌmɪnᵻˈstreɪʃən/ *n* [U] lack of proper care (and perhaps honesty) in carrying out duties, usu. by someone in an official position

mal·a·droit /ˌmæləˈdrɔɪt/ *n fml* not skilful in action or behaviour; awkward: *The chairman was criticized for his maladroit handling of the press conference.* **– ~ ly** *adv* **– ~ ness** *n* [U]

mal·a·dy /ˈmælədi/ *n fml or lit* **1** something that is wrong with a system or organization **2** *esp. old use* an illness

Mal·a·ga /ˈmæləgə/ a city and port in the S of Spain on the Mediterranean coast

ma·laise /mæˈleɪz/ *n* **1** [U] a feeling of illness without any particular pain or appearance of disease **2** [C *usu. sing.*; U] a general but not clearly expressed feeling of worry, dissatisfaction, and lack of confidence, esp. shown in lack of activity: *The underlying social malaise in this country is causing a steady decline in production and trade.*

Mal·a·mud /ˈmæləmʊd/, **Ber·nard** /ˈbɜːnəd‖bərˈnɑːrd/ (1914–86) an American writer who often wrote about Jewish life and customs. His books include *The Fixer* and *The Magic Barrel.*

Mal·a·prop /ˈmæləprɒp‖-prɑːp/, **Mrs** a character in Richard Sheridan's play *The Rivals*, known for her funny misuse of words (MALAPROPISMS)

mal·a·prop·is·m /ˈmæləprɒpɪzəm‖-prɑː-/ *n* an often amusing misuse of a word, such that the word incorrectly used sounds similar to the intended word but means something quite different

ma·lar·i·a /məˈleəriə/ *n* [U] a common disease of hot countries, spread by the bite of certain mosquitoes (MOSQUITO), which causes attacks of fever and coldness in turn which may be repeated periodically for many years **—larial** *adj*

ma·lar·key /mə'lɑːki‖-ɑːr-/ *n* [U] *infml* a speech or piece of writing which tries to deceive or be impressive to people but actually says little: *Everything he said was just a load of malarkey.*

Ma·la·wi /mə'lɑːwi/, **the Republic of** a country in the E of central Africa which has borders with Zambia, Tanzania, and Mozambique; capital Lilongwe; population 8,022,000 (1989) — **an** *adj, n*

Ma·lay /mə'leɪ‖mə'leɪ, 'meɪleɪ/ also **Ma·lay·an** /-ən/— *adj* of the people or language of Malaysia

Ma·lay·a /mə'leɪə/ *n* the former name of Peninsula or West Malaysia, now a part of Malaysia

Ma·lay·si·a /mə'leɪziə‖-ʒə, -ʃə/ a country in SE Asia consisting of the PENINSULA of Malaya which borders Thailand and, across the South China Sea, East Malaysia (the states of Sabah and Sarawak in N Borneo) which borders Indonesia; capital Kuala Lumpur; population 16,958,000 (1989) —**sian** /mɔːl'dɪviən/

Mal·colm X /ˌmælkəm 'eks/ (1925–65) a black American leader who became a Muslim while in prison. When he came out of prison in 1952 he spoke in favour of black SEPARATISM. Later he split away from the Black Muslims and formed the Organization of Afro-American Unity in 1964. He was murdered while making a speech in Harlem, New York City. In 1992 a film was made about his life.

mal·con·tent /'mælkəntent‖ˌmælkən'tent/ *n fml* a dissatisfied person who is likely to make trouble

Mal·dives /'mɔːldiːvz, -dɪvz, -daɪvz/ [*the*+P] a group of small islands forming an independent country in the Indian Ocean SW of Sri Lanka; capital Malé; population 206,000 (1989) —**divian** /mɔːl'dɪviən/

Ma·lé /'mɑːleɪ/ the capital of the Maldives

male¹ /meɪl/ *adj* **1** (typical) of the sex that does not give birth to young: *a male monkey* | *a male-voice choir* | *male characteristics* | *a magazine with a predominantly male readership* **2** (of a flower or plant) not producing fruit **3** *tech* made to fit into a hollow part: *a male plug* —see FEMALE (USAGE), FEMININE (USAGE) —**ness** *n* [U]

male² *n* a male person or animal: *In most birds the male is bigger and more brightly coloured than the female.*

male chau·vin·ist /ˌ· '····◂/ *n derog* a man who holds strongly to unreasoned opinions about the way men and women should behave and the parts they should play in life, esp. believing that men are better than women: *My boss is a male chauvinist who thinks no woman could do his job.* | **a male chauvinist pig** *whose wife stays at home doing housework while he goes out and has fun*

mal·e·dic·tion /ˌmælɪ'dɪkʃən/ *n esp. fml or lit* a curse

mal·e·fac·tor /'mælɪfæktər/ *n esp. fml or lit* a person who does evil things, esp. a criminal —compare BENEFACTOR

ma·lef·i·cent /mə'lefɪsənt/ *adj fml or lit* doing or able to do evil —**cence** *n* [U]

male men·o·pause /ˌ· '···/ *n* [S] a time in a man's life, when he is in his 40s or early 50s, when he wonders how much he has achieved. He may have emotional problems at this time similar to those faced by some women when they become too old to have children. The phrase is often used humorously to describe the behaviour of a middle-aged man who is not satisfied with his life at home or at work and may suddenly want to change his job or start showing an interest in much younger women: *He must be going through the male menopause.* —compare MENOPAUSE, MIDDLE AGE, MID-LIFE CRISIS

male-voice choir /ˌ· · '·/ *n* a group of singers, all men, who usu. perform in public with an ORCHESTRA. The Welsh are famous for their male-voice choirs.

ma·lev·o·lent /mə'levələnt/ *adj esp. lit* having or expressing a wish to harm others —compare BENEVOLENT — ~ **ly** *adv* —**lence** *n* [U]

mal·feas·ance /mæl'fiːzəns/ *n law* **1** [U] wrongdoing **2** [C] an unlawful act, esp. by an official in government

mal·for·ma·tion /ˌmælfɔː'meɪʃən‖-ɔːr-/ *n* **1** [U] the condition of being formed or shaped wrongly **2** [C] a shape, structure, or part (esp. a part of the body) that is formed badly or wrongly

mal·formed /ˌmæl'fɔːmd◂‖-ɔːr-/ *adj* made or shaped badly —compare DEFORM

mal·func·tion /mæl'fʌŋkʃən/ *n fml* a fault in operation:

Results have been delayed owing to a malfunction in the computer. —**malfunction** *v* [I]

Ma·li /'mɑːli/, **the Republic of** *n* in area one of the largest countries in W Africa, including part of the south Sahara; capital Bamako; population 7,960,000 (1989) — **Malian** *n, adj*

Mal·i·bu /'mælɪbuː/ a BEACH in California, in the US, famous for surfing (SURF²). Many rich and famous people, esp. film stars, live there.

mal·ice /'mælɪs/ *n* [U] **1** the wish, desire, or intention to hurt or harm someone: *He got no advantage out of it; he did it from pure malice.* | *I bear you no malice.* (=do not wish to harm you) **2 with malice aforethought** *law* (of a criminal act) planned before it was done; done on purpose

ma·li·cious /mə'lɪʃəs/ *adj* resulting from or expressing malice: *a malicious attack on his reputation* | *a malicious smile* — ~ **ly** *adv*

ma·lign¹ /mə'laɪn/ *v* [T] to say or write bad or unkind things about, esp. falsely: *She was maligned by the newspapers.* | *This much-maligned novel is in fact remarkable in many ways.*

malign² *adj derog, esp. lit* (of a thing) harmful; causing evil: *a malign influence* — ~ **ly** *adv* — ~ **ity** /mə'lɪɡnəti/ *n* [U]

ma·lig·nan·cy /mə'lɪɡnənsi/ *n* **1** [U] the state of being malignant **2** [C] *med* a dangerous growth of cells; a TUMOUR of a malignant kind

ma·lig·nant /mə'lɪɡnənt/ *adj* **1** full of hate and a strong wish to do harm: *a malignant nature|look* **2** *med* (of a disease) serious enough to cause death if not prevented: *a malignant tumour* —compare BENIGN — ~ **ly** *adv*

ma·lin·ger /mə'lɪŋɡər/ *v* [I] to avoid work by pretending to be (still) sick: *He says he's got flu, but I think he's malingering.* — ~ **er** *n*

Mal·i·now·ski /ˌmælɪ'nɒfski‖-'nɑːf-/, **Bron·i·slaw** /'brɒnɪslæf‖'brɑːn-/ (1884–1942) a British anthropologist (ANTHROPOLOGY), born in Poland, who established the first university department of anthropology in Britain and wrote several important books on the subject

mall /mɔːl, mæl‖mɔːl/ *n AmE* a large shopping centre, usu. enclosed, where cars are not permitted but there is plenty of space to park them outside —see also STRIP MALL

Mall, The **1** a straight road in Central London which connects Buckingham Palace and Trafalgar Square. Royal PROCESSIONS always go along The Mall, which is then decorated with flags. **2** a kind of park in Washington, D.C., surrounded by the Washington Monument and several famous MUSEUMS, esp. the Smithsonian Institution. The Mall is a very large grassy area which people use for PICNICS, games, concerts, etc.

mal·lard /'mæləd‖-ərd/ *n* mallard *or* mallards a wild duck, the male of which has a green head and a reddish-brown breast

mal·le·a·ble /'mæliəbəl/ *adj* **1** (of a metal) that can be beaten, pressed, rolled, etc., into a new shape **2** (of people or their character) easily influenced, changed, or trained; TRACTABLE —**bility** /ˌmæliə'bɪləti/ *n* [U]

mal·let /'mælɪt/ *n* **1** a wooden hammer with a large head —see picture at TOOL **2** a wooden hammer with a long handle used in the games of CROQUET and POLO

mal·low /'mæləʊ/ *n* a plant with pink or purple flowers and fine hairs on its stem and leaves —see also MARSHMALLOW

Mal·mö /'mælməʊ/ the city in SW Sweden, an important port and naval base

malm·sey /'mɑːmzi/ *n* [U] a dark type of MADEIRA (=a strong sweet wine)

mal·nour·ished /ˌmæl'nʌrɪʃt◂ ‖ -'nɜː-/ *adj* suffering from malnutrition

mal·nu·tri·tion /ˌmælnjʊ'trɪʃən‖-nʊ-/ *n* [U] (a poor condition of health resulting from) bad feeding, with food that is the wrong sort and/or too small in amount

mal·o·dor·ous /ˌmæl'əʊdərəs/ *adj fml or pomp* having a bad smell

Mal·o·ry /'mæləri/, **Sir Thomas** (1400?–71) an English writer famous for his book *Morte d'Arthur*, which tells the story of King Arthur and his KNIGHTS —see ARTHURIAN LEGEND

mal·prac·tice /ˌmæl'præktɪs/ *n* [C;U] (a) failure to carry out one's professional duty properly or honestly, often resulting in hurt, loss, or damage to someone: *She sued her doctor/solicitor for malpractice.*

Mal·raux /mælˈrəʊ/, **An·dré** /ˈɒndreɪ‖ˈɑːn-/ (1901–76) a French writer and thinker, very active in politics, whose many books include *La condition humaine* and *L'espoir*

malt¹ /mɔːlt/ *n* [U] grain, usu. BARLEY, which has been kept in water for a while until it grows a little and then dried for use in making drinks such as beer and WHISKY

malt² *v* [T] to make (grain) into malt

Mal·ta /ˈmɔːltə/ (the largest of) a group of islands in the Mediterranean Sea which became an independent republic and member of the COMMONWEALTH (1) in 1964 and is now popular with British tourists. It consists of three main islands; Malta, Gozo and Comino; capital Valletta; population 350,000 (1989)

malted milk /ˌ·· ˈ·/ *n* [C;U] **1** (a drink made from) milk treated with malt **2** *AmE* also **malted** (a drink made from) milk treated with malt, ICE CREAM, and a FLAVOUR-ING: *a chocolate malted milk | I'll have a strawberry malted.*

Mal·tese /ˌmɔːlˈtiːz◂/ *adj* of the people or language of Malta

Maltese cross /ˌ·· ˈ·/ *n* a cross with four equal arms that become wider as they go out from the centre

Mal·te·sers /mɔːlˈtiːzəz ‖ -zərz-/ *n* [P] *tdmk* chocolate sweets with a light, crisp centre

Mal·thus /ˈmælθəs/, **Thomas** (1766–1834) an English ECONOMIST famous for his work on population study. He is remembered esp. for stating that if the world's population is not controlled, either by disease and wars or by planning, it will grow faster than the world's food supply. —**Malthusian** /mælˈθjuːziən ‖ -ˈθuːʒən/ *adj*

malt liq·uor /ˌ·ˈ·ˌ/ *n* *AmE* a kind of BEER

mal·treat /mælˈtriːt/ *v* [T] to treat roughly and/or cruelly — ~ment *n* [U]

malt·ster /ˈmɔːltstər/ *n* a person whose job is to malt grain (MALT²)

Mal·vern /ˈmɔːlvən ‖ -vərn/ a town in W central England, in the Malvern Hills. It is known for the theatre and music FESTIVAL held every year.

Mal·vern Hills /ˌ·· ˈ·/ also **Malverns**— [*the*] a range of hills in the English Midlands. They are known esp. for their MINERAL WATER called **Malvern Water**, which is sold all over the country.

ma·ma¹, **mamma** /ˈmɑːmə/ also **momma**— *n* *AmE infml* (used only by or to very small children) mother

ma·ma² /məˈmɑː/ *n* *BrE old use* a mother: *Good morning, mama.*

mama's boy /ˈmɑːməz ˌbɔɪ/ *n* *AmE for* MOTHER'S BOY

mam·ba /ˈmæmbə‖ˈmɑːmbə, ˈmæmbə/ *n* a type of large very poisonous black or green African tree snake

Mam·et /ˈmæmət/, **David** (1947–) an American writer of plays and films, known esp. for *American Buffalo* and *Sexual Perversity in Chicago*

mam·mal /ˈmæməl/ *n* an animal of the type which is fed when young on milk from the mother's body: *Humans and dogs are mammals; birds and fish are not.* — ~**ian** /mæˈmeɪliən/ *adj* : *mammalian cells*

mam·ma·ry /ˈmæməri/ *adj* [A] *tech* of or being the breasts: *In female mammals the* **mammary glands** *produce milk.*

mam·mo·gram /ˈmæməgræm/ *n* an X-RAY photograph of the breasts done esp. to check for possible signs of CANCER

mam·mog·ra·phy /mæˈmɒgrəfi‖-ˈmɑː-/ *n* [U] examination of the breasts using X-RAY photographs, esp. to check for possible signs of CANCER

mam·mon /ˈmæmən/ *n* (often *cap.*) money or wealth, regarded as something that people think too much of. In the Bible, mammon was a word meaning wealth, but many people thought it meant a god of money: *You cannot worship God and Mammon. | New York was built to the glory of mammon — money, gain, the new god.*

mam·moth¹ /ˈmæməθ/ *n* a large hairy elephant which lived on Earth during the early stages of human development

mammoth² *adj* [A] extremely large; HUGE: *The problem is beginning to assume mammoth proportions. | a mammoth task*

mam·my /ˈmæmi/ *n* **1** *esp. IrE & AmE dial* (used esp. by or to children) a mother **2** *AmE old-fash, often derog* a black woman who looks after white children. She is often

mammoth

shown in CARTOONs as large and fat, with a loud voice.

man¹ /mæn/ *n* *men* /men/ **1** [C] an adult human male: *He's a nice man/a tall man/a hard-working man. | men, women, and children | If you want a good administrator he's* **your man.** (=the right man to choose) *| The army will* **make a man of** *him.* (=make him brave, strong, etc.) *| The boy tried to* **be a man** *and not cry, but the pain brought tears to his eyes.* **2** [C] a human being: *All men must die.* **3** [U] the human race: *Man must change in a changing world.* **4** [U] any of the sorts of human-like creatures that lived in former times: *prehistoric man* — see also NEANDERTHAL MAN **5** [C] an adult male in employment: *The men weren't happy with the employers' pay offer. | We'll send a man to look at your phone tomorrow.| a report from our man* (=representative) *in Italy* **6** a male of low rank in the armed forces: *the officers and men of the regiment* **7** a male member of a team: *The captain led his men onto the field.* **8** [C] *infml* a husband, lover, or other adult male with whom a woman lives: *waiting for her man to come out of prison* **9** *infml* a (used for addressing an adult male, esp. when the speaker is excited, angry, etc.): *Wake up, man, you can't sleep all day!* b *esp. AmE & CarE* (used for addressing someone, esp. an adult male): *This party's really great, man!* —see also MAN³ **10** [C] any of the objects moved by each player in a board game: *chess men* **11** **a man of few words** a man who does not talk very much and does not use many words to express himself **12** **a man of his word** someone who keeps their promises: *He's a man of his word, so if he said he'd help, he will.* **13** **a man of the people** a man who understands and represents the wishes and feelings of the general population **14** **a man of the world** a man with a lot of experience of life: *He's a man of the world. He won't be shocked.* **15** **a man's gotta do what a man's gotta do** a phrase supposed to be used in old COWBOY films when a man is bravely saying that he will do his duty even if it is difficult or dangerous. It is now used humorously. **16** **a man's home is his castle** *AmE saying* a person's home is very important to them, and they can do what they like there **17** **as one man** everyone together: *The audience stood as one man and applauded.* **18** **man alive** *AmE* (used to express great surprise: *Man alive, will you look at the size of that tomato!* **19** **man and boy** *old-fash* for the whole of his life: *He was born in the village and worked on the farm man and boy.* **20** **man and wife** *fml* married: *I'm afraid you can't share the same bedroom if you're not man and wife.* **21** **man's best friend** dogs: *It is ironical that man's best friend is so often ill-treated by humans.* **22** **man's inhumanity to man** a phrase used when talking about the cruelty of one group of people to another group **23** **no man is an island** *quote* a phrase from a poem by John Donne, used when saying that all people need other people **24** **one small step for a man, one giant leap for mankind** *quote* the phrase used by Neil Armstrong when he first stepped onto the surface of the moon in 1969 **25** **one's own man** independent in one's opinions and actions: *I shouldn't try telling him what to do; he's very much his own man.* **26** **the man in the moon** the face or shape of a man, seen in the moon's surface from Earth (often mentioned in children's poems and songs) **27** **the man in the street** (the idea of) the average person, who represents general opinion: *This kind of music doesn't appeal to the man in the street. | People who market goods need to find out what the man in the street wants.* **28** **(the) man of the match** the best or most notable player in a particular sports match: *Man of the match must be John Doe, with that brilliant hat trick.* **29** **the man on the Clapham omnibus** *infml* the average person who represents general opinion **30** **to a man** *becoming rare* every person: *They agreed, to a man.* **31** **to the last man**

until none was left **32 -man** /mən, mæn/ **a** a man who lives in or is from the stated place: *a Frenchman | a countryman* **b** a person, usu. a man, who has the stated job, skill, etc.: *a businessman | a postman* –see also BEST MAN, DIRTY OLD MAN, NEW MAN, OLD MAN; see GENTLEMAN (USAGE), PEOPLE (USAGE) – ~**like** *adj*

▷ USAGE Many people, especially women, do not like the use of **man** to mean human beings (men and women) in general. They prefer to use words like: **humans, human beings, the human race, people.** –see also PERSON (USAGE)◁

man² *v* **-nn-** [T] to provide with people for operation: *Man the lifeboats! | the first manned spacecraft to reach the moon* –see also OVERMANNED, UNDERMANNED, UNMANNED

man³ *interj AmE infml* (used for expressing strong feelings of excitement, surprise, etc.) –see also MAN¹ (9)

Man, Isle of *n* see ISLE OF MAN

man-a-bout-town /ˌ· ·· ˈ·/ *n* a (rich) man who spends a great deal of time at fashionable social events in clubs, theatres, etc., and often does not work

man·a·cle /ˈmænəkəl/ *n* [*usu. pl.*] either of a pair of iron rings joined by a chain, used for fastening the hands or feet of a prisoner –**manacle** *v* [T]

man·age /ˈmænɪdʒ/ *v* **1** [T] to be in control or charge of the affairs of, esp. the business affairs of; be or act as the manager of: *He managed the company while his father was away ill. | He manages the world tennis champion. | My wife manages our money very well. | a well-managed company* **2** [I;T] (often used with **can, could**) to succeed in dealing with (something or someone difficult): *"Do you need any help with those heavy bags?" "No, thanks, I can manage." | She knows how to manage him when he's angry.* [+*to-v*] *I finally managed to find what I was looking for* **3** [T] *infml* (often used with **can, could**) to succeed in taking, using, or doing: *I can't manage another mouthful. | I couldn't manage two weeks' holiday this year, only one. | Could you manage Friday for our meeting? | She could barely manage a smile.* [+*to-v*] *The little boy had somehow managed to tie his shoelaces together.* –see COULD (USAGE) **4** [I (**on**)] to succeed in living, esp. on a small amount of money: *They managed quite well on very little money.*

man·age·a·ble /ˈmænɪdʒəbəl/ *adj* easy or possible to control or deal with: *My hair is much more manageable since I had it cut short. | The rate of inflation has been brought down to a more manageable level.* –opposite **unmanageable** –**-bility** /ˌmænɪdʒəˈbɪlɨti/ *n* [U]

man·age·ment /ˈmænɪdʒmənt/ *n* **1** [U] the art or practice of managing, esp. of managing a business or money: *The company's failure was mainly due to bad management. | a management course | man management* (=controlling and dealing with people) **2** [C;U+*sing.*/*pl. v*] the people in charge of a company, industry, etc.: *The management is/are having talks with the workers. | The union has agreed to talks with senior management. | a management decision* **3** [U] skill in dealing with people or situations; judgment

management buy·out /ˌ··· ˈ··/ *n* the buying of SHARES in a business by the management so that they control the company

management con·sult·ant /ˈ··· ·ˌ··/ *n* a person who is paid to go to a company to give the management (2) advice on how to organize and run it

man·ag·er /ˈmænɪdʒəʳ/ *n* **1** a person who manages a business or other activity: *She's a bank manager/a hotel manager. | He's the party's campaign manager. | That was a terrible meal; I'm going to complain to the manager.* **2** a person who manages the business affairs of an entertainer: *the manager of a pop group* **3** a person who manages the training and other activities of a sportsman or team: *the England soccer manager* **4** someone who is skilled at managing their money, personal affairs, etc.: *She must be a very good manager to feed her children so well on so little money.*

man·ag·er·ess /ˌmænɪdʒəˈres‖ˈmænɪdʒərɨs/ *n* a woman who controls a business, esp. a shop or restaurant; female MANAGER (1)

man·a·ge·ri·al /ˌmænɨˈdʒɪəriəl◂/ *adj* of or concerning a manager or management: *a managerial position | managerial responsibilities*

managing di·rec·tor /ˌ··· ·ˈ··/ also **MD**– *n BrE* a person who is in charge of an organization, being responsible for its day-to-day running according to the decisions of the board of directors

Ma·nag·ua /məˈnægwə‖-ˈnɑː-/ the capital city of Nicaragua, in the W of the country. Managua was badly damaged by an EARTHQUAKE in 1972.

Ma·na·ma /məˈnɑːmə/ a city and port which is the capital of Bahrain

ma·ña·na /mænˈjɑːnə‖mən-/ *n Sp* not now, some other time (a Spanish word which means **tomorrow**): People use this word to describe the attitude of those who delay doing things because they are very relaxed or lazy: *Mexico is sometimes said to have a mañana culture.*

Man and Su·per·man /ˌ· · ˈ···/ a play by George Bernard Shaw, written in 1903

man-at-arms /ˌ· · ˈ·/ *n* **men-at-arms** a soldier of former times, esp. one with a horse and heavy armour and weapons

Man·ches·ter /ˈmæntʃɨstəʳ, -tʃes-/ a city in the NW of England. Manchester was formerly known for its wool and cotton industries and is now the CULTURAL and financial centre for the area. –see also GREATER MANCHESTER and see colour map on page 818

Manchester Cit·y /ˌ··· ˈ··◂/ also **Man Cit·y** /ˌ· ˈ··/ *infml*– an English football team from Manchester

Manchester Ship Ca·nal /ˌ··· ˈ· ·ˌ·/ a man-made stretch of water in NW England which runs from Manchester to the sea. It was built to help the cotton factories in the 19th century.

Manchester U·ni·ted /ˌ··· ··ˈ··/ also **Man United** *infml*– an English football team from Manchester with a long history of success. In 1958 an aeroplane carrying members of the team crashed in Munich, and several team members were killed. Many people still remember this event.

Man·cu·ni·an /mænˈkjuːniən/ *adj, n BrE* (a person) from Manchester

man·da·la /ˈmændələ, mænˈdɑːlə/ *n* (in Oriental art and religion) a usu. circular pattern which is believed to represent the universe

Man·da·lay /ˌmændəˈleɪ◂/ a city in Myanmar, known in Britain esp. because of the old popular song *The Road to Mandalay*

man·da·rin /ˈmændərɪn/ *n* **1** [C] also **mandarin or·ange** /ˌ··· ˈ··/– a small kind of orange with a special taste and a skin which comes off easily **2** [U] (*usu. cap.*) the official form of the Chinese language; the language of Beijing and northern China and of educated Chinese people generally –compare CANTONESE **3** [C] a government official of high rank in the former Chinese EMPIRE **4** [C] *BrE sometimes derog* a person who holds an important official position, and may be regarded as having too much influence: *British government policy is often influenced by Whitehall mandarins.* (=top British government servants)

mandarin duck /ˌ··· ˈ·/ *n* an attractive small duck with clearly marked areas of coloured feathers, and wing-feathers that stick up above its back

man·date¹ /ˈmændeɪt/ *n* [*usu. sing.*] **1** the right and power given to a government, or any body of people chosen to represent others, to act according to the wishes of those who voted for it: *to seek a mandate from the electorate* [+*to-v*] *I say the government does not have a mandate to introduce this new law!* **2** a formal command to act in a certain way, given by a higher to a lower official: *carrying out her mandate* **3** the power given to a country by the League of Nations after the First World War to govern (part of) another country

mandate² *v* [T *often pass.*] **1** to give a MANDATE¹ (1) to (someone) to do something **2** to put (a place) under a MANDATE¹ (3): *a mandated territory*

man·da·to·ry /ˈmændətəri‖-tɔːri/ *adj fml* which must be done; COMPULSORY: *It's mandatory to pay the debt within six months. | a mandatory election | Voting is not mandatory.*

Man·del·a /mænˈdelə/, **Nelson** (1918–) a South African black nationalist leader of the ANC. He was sentenced to life in prison for political offences by the South African government in 1964. He was freed in 1990 after international pressure and then continued to lead the ANC. He separated from his wife, Winnie Mandela, in 1992. –see colour picture on page 752

Mandela, Win·nie /ˈwɪni/ (1934–) the wife of Nelson Mandela and member of the ANC who helped lead the movement working to free her husband from prison. Her own activities were often limited by the South African government. In 1991, she appeared in court because it was said she had been involved in the murder of a young man, **Stompie Motchetsi**. She was found guilty of helping to KIDNAP him but appealed (APPEAL) against this decision. She and Nelson Mandela separated in 1992.

man·di·ble /ˈmændʒbəl/ n tech **1** a jaw which moves, esp. the lower jaw of an animal or fish, or a jawbone **2** the upper or lower part of a bird's beak **3** either of the two biting or holding parts in insects and CRABS

M & M's /ˌem ənd ˈemz/ n [P] AmE tdmk (a packet of) small round chocolate sweets with a hard coloured sugar covering. M & M's are advertised with the phrase "They melt in your mouth, not in your hand."

man·do·lin /ˌmændəˈlɪn/ n a round-backed musical instrument with eight metal strings, rather like a LUTE

man·drake /ˈmændreɪk/ n a plant from which drugs may be made, esp. those causing sleep, the root of which is in two parts, and which is said to have magic properties

man·drill /ˈmændrɪl/ n a large monkey like a BABOON with a brightly coloured face

M & S /ˌem ənd ˈes/ see MARKS AND SPENCER

Man·dy /ˈmændi/ n a British COMIC (=picture-story magazine) for young girls

mane /meɪn/ n **1** the long hair on the back of a horse's neck, or around the face and neck of a lion –see picture at BIG CATS and at HORSE **2** esp. humor the long thick hair on a person's head

man·eat·er /ˈ··ˌ···/ n **1** an animal or person that eats human flesh **2** derog humor **a** a woman who has many lovers **b** a woman with a powerful character who makes men feel afraid or foolish –**man-eating** adj : a man-eating lion

Man·et /ˈmæneɪ‖mæˈneɪ/, **Ed·ouard** /ˈedwəd‖-wərd/ (1832–83) a French painter who greatly influenced the Impressionists. Two of his most well-known works are The Balcony and The Fife Player.

ma·neu·ver /məˈnuːvəʳ/ n, v AmE for MANOEUVRE

ma·neu·ve·ra·ble /məˈnuːvərəbəl/ adj AmE for MANOEUVRABLE

Man for All Sea·sons /ˌ· ·· ˈ··/, A a play by Robert Bolt about the life and death of Thomas More

Man Fri·day /ˌ· ˈ··/ **1** a character in the book Robinson Crusoe by Daniel Defoe. He becomes Crusoe's servant and companion after Crusoe saves him from being killed by CANNIBALS. **2** also **man Friday** a loyal and trusted male servant –compare GIRL FRIDAY

man·ful /ˈmænfəl/ adj brave; determined: He made manful efforts to move the heavy furniture, but failed. – ~ly adv

man·ga·nese /ˈmæŋgəniːz/ n [U] a greyish-white metal that is a simple substance (ELEMENT) used in making glass, steel, etc.

mange /meɪndʒ/ n [U] a skin disease of animals, esp. dogs and cats, that results in the loss of areas of hair or fur –see also MANGY

man·gel-wur·zel /ˈmæŋgəl ˌwɜːzəl‖-ˈɜːr-/ also **mangel** AmE– n a vegetable with a large round root which can be eaten, often grown on farms as cattle food

man·ger /ˈmeɪndʒəʳ/ n a long container, open at the top, in which food is placed for horses and cattle –see also **dog in the manger** (DOG¹)

▶CULTURAL NOTE According to the Bible, Jesus was born in a STABLE and laid in a manger as a bed because there were no empty rooms in the town.◀

mange·tout /ˌmɒnʒˈtuː‖ˌmɑː-/ also **mangetout pea** /ˌ·· ˈ·/ BrE ‖ **snow pea** /ˈ· ·/ AmE– n a sort of PEA whose covering is eaten as well as its seeds

man·gle¹ /ˈmæŋgəl/ v [T] **1** [often pass.] to tear or cut to pieces; crush: After the accident they tried to identify the victims, but the bodies were too badly mangled to be recognized. | (fig.) The newspaper gave a very mangled version (=full of mistakes) of what happened. **2** to pass (clothes, etc.) through a mangle

mangle² n a machine with rollers turned by a handle between which water is pressed from clothes, sheets, etc.,

that are passed through, esp. of a kind used before modern electric washing machines were invented – compare WRINGER

man·go /ˈmæŋgəʊ/ n -goes or -gos a tropical fruit with a thin skin and sweet yellow-coloured flesh around a long hard seed –see picture at FRUIT

man·grove /ˈmæŋgrəʊv/ n a tropical tree which grows on muddy land and near water and puts down new roots from its branches: a mangrove swamp

Mangrove Club /ˈ·· ˌ·/ [the] a social club and CAFE in Notting Hill, W London which was a popular meeting place in the 1970s and 1980s esp. for young black people

mang·y /ˈmeɪndʒi/ adj **1** suffering from the disease of MANGE **2** infml of bad appearance because of loss of hair, as in MANGE: a mangy carpet (=old and with bare areas) –**ily** adv

man·han·dle /ˈmænhændl/ v [T] **1** to move by using the force of the body: We manhandled the piano up the stairs. **2** derog to handle (a person) roughly, using force: He complained that the guard manhandled him unnecessarily.

Man·hat·tan /mænˈhætn/ an island in New York Bay at the mouth of the Hudson River –see colour map on page 1376

▶CULTURAL NOTE Manhattan is the business and CULTURAL centre of New York City. The business area is centred on Wall Street on the southern end, where the STOCK EXCHANGE and the World Trade Centre are. Fifth Avenue has many expensive shops and department stores. There are many theatres near or on Broadway, and Manhattan has several important MUSEUMS, including the Metropolitan Museum of Art, which is on the edge of Central Park, a very large green area in the middle of Manhattan island. Harlem, at the north end of Central Park, has cheap housing, but other places in Manhattan are very expensive to live in. Often when people say they have been to New York they mean that they have been to Manhattan. The SKYLINE (the way the buildings look from a distance) of Manhattan is famous. –see also MADISON AVENUE, GREENWICH VILLAGE, TIMES SQUARE◀

Manhattan Pro·ject /·ˈ·· ˌ··/ [the] the secret American scientific plan established in 1942 to develop an ATOM BOMB –see LOS ALAMOS

man·hole /ˈmænhəʊl/ n an opening, usu. with a cover, on or near a road, through which someone can go down to a place where underground pipes and wires can be examined, repaired, etc.

man·hood /ˈmænhʊd/ n [U] **1** the condition or period of time of being a man, as opposed to being a boy or female **2** fml or lit all the men of a nation: America lost the flower (=best part) of its young manhood in the war. **3** euph when sexual powers of a man –compare WOMANHOOD

man·hour /ˈmæn-aʊəʳ/ n (a measure of) the amount of work done by one person in one hour

man·hunt /ˈmænhʌnt/ n a search for a wanted person, esp. a criminal: The police are conducting an extensive manhunt for the murderer.

ma·ni·a /ˈmeɪniə/ n [C (for);U] **1** tech a (dangerous) disorder of the mind: Kleptomania is a mania for stealing things. **2** infml (often in comb.) a desire or interest so strong that it seems mad: She has a mania for (driving) fast cars. | He's got motorcycle mania. | discomania

ma·ni·ac /ˈmeɪniæk/ n **1** a person (thought to be) suffering from (a) mania **2** infml a wild thoughtless person: Don't drive so fast, you maniac; you'll kill us all!

ma·ni·a·cal /məˈnaɪəkəl/ adj of or like a maniac: maniacal laughter – ~ly /kli/ adv

man·ic /ˈmænɪk/ adj **1** tech of or suffering from mania: manic depression/tidiness **2** very excited; wild in behaviour

manic-de·pres·sive /ˌ·· ·ˈ··/ n, adj (a person) suffering from an illness in which they have continual changes of feeling, states of great joyful excitement being followed by sad hopelessness

man·i·cure¹ /ˈmænɪkjʊəʳ/ n [C;U] (a) treatment for the hands and esp. the fingernails, including cleaning, cutting, etc. –compare PEDICURE

manicure² v [T] to give a manicure to (the hands): (fig.) a manicured garden (=very tidy, with neat edges, etc.)

manicure set /ˈ··· ˌ·/ n a set of small tools for cleaning, cutting, and shaping a person's nails

man·i·cur·ist /ˈmænᵻkjʊərᵻst/ n a person whose job is to manicure hands

man·i·fest¹ /ˈmænᵻfest/ adj fml very plain to see or clear to the mind: *Fear was manifest on his face.* | *their manifest failure to modernize the country's industries* — ~**ly** adv: *manifestly untrue*

manifest² v [T (in)] fml to show (something) plainly: *The disease typically manifests itself in a high fever and chest pains.* | *Her actions manifested a complete disregard for personal safety.* | *Their concern is manifested mainly in fine speeches, rather than in practical solutions.*

manifest³ n tech a list of goods carried, esp. on a ship

man·i·fes·ta·tion /ˌmænᵻfesˈteɪʃən‖-fə-/ n 1 [U] fml the act of showing or making clear and plain 2 [C] fml anything said or done which clearly shows or is proof of a fact, situation, feeling, belief, etc.: *This latest outbreak of violence is a clear manifestation of the growing discontent in the area.* 3 [C] an appearance, or other sign of presence, of a spirit

Manifest Des·ti·ny /ˌ··· ˈ···/ n [U] the idea in the 19th century that the US could move into and settle most of North America because God had planned that it would do so

man·i·fes·to /ˌmænᵻˈfestəʊ/ n -tos or -toes a usu. written statement making public the beliefs and intentions of a ruler or group of people, esp. a political party

▶ CULTURAL NOTE In Britain, the main political parties produce a manifesto before each general election, saying what they will do if they are elected: *The Labour Party manifesto for the next general election pledges to reduce unemployment.* —compare PLATFORM◀

man·i·fold¹ /ˈmænᵻfəʊld/ adj fml many in number and/or kind: *The problems facing the government are manifold.* | *her manifold talents*

manifold² n tech an arrangement of several pipes, esp. one that allows gases to enter or escape from a car engine: *an exhaust manifold* —see picture at ENGINE

man·i·kin , manni· /ˈmænᵻkᵻn/ n 1 a little man; DWARF 2 a figure of the human body used for art or teaching medical students

ma·nil·a, -nil·la /məˈnɪlə/ n [U] (*sometimes cap.*) 1 strong brown paper: *a manila envelope* 2 also **manila hemp** /ˌ·ᵻˈ·ᵻ/ a plant material used in making rope

Manila a city and port, the capital of the Philippines

Man·i·low /ˈmænᵻləʊ, -nəl-/, **Bar·ry** /ˈbæri/ (1946–) an American popular music singer and songwriter, known for his love songs and esp. popular with women

Man in the I·ron Mask /ˌ· · · ˌ·· ˈ·/ [the] a prisoner in the Bastille, Paris, who died in 1703. His face was always kept hidden by a MASK, and it was thought that he might be a brother of Louis XIV, but this is now considered unlikely.

man·i·oc /ˈmænɪɒk‖-ɑːk/ [C;U] CASSAVA

ma·nip·u·late /məˈnɪpjᵿleɪt/ v [T] 1 usu. derog to control or influence for one's own purposes: *He adores his sister and she manipulates him shamelessly.* | *He accused the government of manipulating public opinion.* 2 to work with skilful use of the hands: *Her dislocated shoulder was carefully manipulated back into place.* —**lation** n /məˌnɪpjᵿˈleɪʃən/ [C;U] : *skilful manipulation of the figures/the statistics* —**lative** /məˈnɪpjᵿlətɪv‖-leɪ-/ adj

Man·i·to·ba /ˌmænᵻˈtəʊbə/ a PROVINCE in central Canada

man·i·tou /ˈmænᵻtuː/ n [U] a SUPERNATURAL force thought by the Algonquian Indians of North America to exist throughout the natural world

Man·i·tou·lin /ˌmænᵻˈtuːlᵻn/ a large island in Lake Huron, Canada, the largest island surrounded by fresh (=not sea) water in the world

man jack /ˌ·ᵻ ˈ·/ n infml, esp. pomp or humor **every man jack** everyone; each person in a group: *We'll only succeed if every man jack of us works his hardest.*

man·kind /ˌmænˈkaɪnd/ n [U+sing./pl. v] the human race, both men and women: *for the good of all mankind* — compare HUMANKIND, WOMANKIND; see MAN (USAGE)

man·ky /ˈmæŋki/ adj BrE dial or infml nasty and dirty

Man·ley /ˈmænli/, **Mi·chael** /ˈmaɪkəl/ (1924–) a Jamaican politician, Prime Minister, and leader of the People's National Party

man·ly /ˈmænli/ adj apprec having qualities (believed to be)

typical of or suitable to a man: *a deep manly voice* | *The boy walked with a confident manly stride.* —compare MANNISH, WOMANLY —**liness** n [U]

man-made /ˌ·ˈ·◂/ adj 1 produced by people; not existing in nature: *The lake is man-made; there used to be a valley here until they dammed the river.* 2 (of a material) not made from natural substances, like wool or cotton, but from combinations of chemicals; SYNTHETIC: *Nylon is a man-made fibre.* —opposite **natural**

Mann /mæn/, **Thomas** (1875–1955) a German writer who won the Nobel prize for literature in 1929. His books include *Death in Venice* and *Doctor Faustus*.

man·na /ˈmænə/ n [U] the food which according to the Bible was provided by God for the Israelites in the desert after their escape from Egypt: (fig.) *That gift of money was* **manna from heaven.** (=provided great and unexpected help)

man·ne·quin /ˈmænᵻkᵻn/ n 1 a figure of the human body used for showing clothes in shop windows; DUMMY (2) 2 old-fash a person, usu. a woman, who is employed to wear new clothes and show them to possible buyers; MODEL

man·ner /ˈmænər/ n 1 [C usu. sing.] rather fml the way or method in which something is done or happens: *I agree it had to be done, but not in such an offensive manner.* | *a meal prepared in the Japanese manner* | *a painting in the manner of the early Impressionists* (=as they would have painted it) 2 [S] a personal way of acting or behaving towards other people: *He has a pleasant manner* | *her brisk, businesslike manner* 3 [S+of] old use kind or sort (of person or thing): *What manner of son can treat his mother so badly?* 4 **all manner of** every kind of: *The guests were served with* **all manner of** *food and drink.* 5 **(as) to the manner born** in a natural way, as if one is used to (something, esp. social position) from birth: *She played the queen as to the manner born.* 6 **in a manner of speaking** (used for making something seem less forceful than the words appear) if one may express it this way 7 **not by any manner of means** not at all; not to any degree 8 **-mannered** /mænəd‖-ərd/having MANNERS of the stated kind: *good-mannered* | *bad-mannered* —see also MANNERS

man·nered /ˈmænəd‖-ərd/ adj fml having an unnatural way of behaving; AFFECTED: *a mannered way of speaking*

man·ner·is·m /ˈmænərɪzəm/ n 1 [C] sometimes derog a particular and esp. odd way of behaving, speaking, etc., that has become a habit: *She has this strange mannerism of pinching her ear when she talks.* 2 [U] the use of unnatural ways of representing things in art, according to a set of styles

man·ners /ˈmænəz‖-ərz/ n [P] 1 (polite or generally accepted) social habits or ways of behaving: *His parents obviously didn't teach him (good) manners.* | *It's bad manners to eat like that.* —compare CHIVALRY, COURTESY, ETIQUETTE, TABLE MANNERS 2 fml social behaviour or ways of living, esp. of a nation or group of people

man·nish /ˈmænᵻʃ/ adj derog (of a woman) like a man in character, behaviour, or appearance —compare MANLY — ~**ly** adv — ~**ness** n [U]

ma·noeu·vra·ble BrE ‖ **maneuverable** AmE /məˈnuːvərəbl/ adj easy to move, direct, or esp. turn: *a very light and manoeuvrable car* —**bility** /məˌnuːvərəˈbɪlᵻti/ n [U]

ma·noeu·vre¹ BrE ‖ **maneuver** AmE /məˈnuːvər/ n 1 [often pl.] a large military movement or operation, esp. done for training purposes: *military/naval manoeuvres* | *The regiment is abroad* **on manoeuvres.** 2 a skilful or carefully planned process intended to deceive, to gain an advantage, to get out of a difficult position, etc.: *There were secret manoeuvres to get him removed from the job.* | *We're well below budget on this project so there's plenty of* **room for manoeuvre.** (=to spend more time, try new methods, etc.)

manoeuvre² BrE ‖ **maneuver** AmE— v [I+adv/prep; T+obj+adv/prep] to move or turn, esp. skilfully: *The car manoeuvres very well in wet weather.* (=it is easy to control its direction) | *It was difficult to manoeuvre the piano through the door.* | (fig.) *By secretly buying company shares he manoeuvred himself into a controlling position.* —see also OUTMANOEUVRE

man of let·ters /ˌ·ᵻ ˈ·ᵻ/ n fml or pomp a writer whose work is highly respected

man of straw /ˌ· · '·/ n **1** esp. BrE a person of weak character, esp. one who is unable to make decisions **2** also **straw man** esp. AmE an imaginary opponent whose arguments can easily be defeated

man-of-war /ˌ· · '·/ also **man-o'-war**— n old use a warship in the navy —see also PORTUGUESE MAN-OF-WAR

ma·nom·e·ter /məˈnɒmɪtəʳ‖-ˈnɑː-/ n an instrument for measuring the pressure of gases —**tric** /ˌmænəˈmetrɪk◂/ —**trically** /kli/ adv

man·or /ˈmænəʳ/ n **1** the land belonging to a nobleman (the **lord of the manor**) under the FEUDAL system, some of which he kept for his own use, the rest being rented to farmers who paid by giving services, esp. labour, and part of the crops they grew **2** a large house with land **3** BrE sl **a** a police area **b** an area that one lives or works in or knows well — ~ **ial** /məˈnɔːriəl/ adj : manorial lands

manor house /'·· ·/ n the house in which the owner of manorial land lives

man·pow·er /ˈmænˌpaʊəʳ/ n [U] the number of workers needed for a certain type of work: The police are seriously short of manpower.

man·qué /ˈmɒŋkeɪ‖mɑːˈŋkeɪ/ adj [after n] who could have been but failed to be or did not become (something): Our doctor paints beautiful pictures; I think he's really an artist manqué.

man·sard /ˈmænsɑːd‖-ɑːrd/ also **mansard roof** /'·· ·/— n a roof with a lower and upper part, the lower having a steeper slope

manse /mæns/ n a house belonging to **a** a Church of Scotland CLERGYMAN **b** a Methodist or Nonconformist CLERGYMAN

Man·sell /ˈmænsəl/, **Ni·gel** /ˈnaɪdʒəl/ (1954–) an English motor-racing driver, very successful in the 1980s and 1990s

man·ser·vant /ˈmænˌsɜːvənt‖-ɜːr-/ n esp. old use a male servant, esp. one who attends personally on a man; VALET —compare MAIDSERVANT

Mans·field /ˈmænsfiːld/, **Jayne** /dʒeɪn/ (1933–67) an American actress famous for her long BLONDE hair and large breasts. Her best-known film was The Girl Can't Help It.

Mansfield, Kath·e·rine /ˈkæθərɪn/ (1888–1923) a writer born in New Zealand who lived in England. She is well-known esp. for her short stories.

man·sion /ˈmænʃən/ n a large house, usu. belonging to a wealthy person —see HOUSE (USAGE)

Mansion House /ˌ·· '·/ [the] a large house in London, the official home of the Lord Mayor of London, where official dinners are held

man·sions /ˈmænʃənz/ n [P] BrE (usu. cap.) (in names of buildings) a building containing flats: Flat 14, Stirling Mansions

man-sized /'· ·/ also **man-size**— adj [A] infml (esp. used in advertising) large enough for a man: man-sized paper handkerchiefs | a man-sized helping of food

man·slaugh·ter /ˈmænˌslɔːtəʳ/ n [U] law the crime of killing a person illegally (ILLEGAL) but not intentionally: The driver was arrested on a charge of manslaughter. —compare MURDER[1] (1)

Man·son /ˈmænsən/, **Charles** (1956–) an American who with three others was found guilty of the murders of Sharon Tate and six other people in Los Angeles in 1969. Manson had a group of followers he called his "family" who took drugs with him and who thought that he was a kind of religious leader.

man·tel·piece /ˈmæntlpiːs/ also **man·tel** /ˈmæntl/— n a frame surrounding a fireplace, esp. the part on top which can be used as a shelf: photographs on the mantelpiece —see picture at FIREPLACE

man·tel·shelf /ˈmæntlʃelf/ n -**shelves** /ʃelvz/ the top part of a mantelpiece, forming a shelf

man·til·la /mænˈtɪlə/ n a decorative piece of thin material worn as a SHAWL by Spanish women, covering the head and falling onto the shoulders

man·tis /ˈmæntɪs/ n see PRAYING MANTIS and see picture at INSECT

man·tle[1] /ˈmæntl/ n [usu. sing.] **1** a loose article of outer clothing without SLEEVES, worn in former times, like a CLOAK: (fig.) a mantle of snow on the trees **2** general or official recognition, esp. of a person's importance or influence: Now that he is dead, she has taken over his mantle as the leading scholar in this field. **3** a small cover with holes in it put over the flame of a gas or oil lamp to make it give more light

mantle[2] v [T] lit to cover: Snow mantled the trees.

Mantle, Mickey (1931–) a famous BASEBALL player, remembered for his batting (BAT[2] (2)) ability

man-to-man /ˌ· · '·◂/ adj [A] infml open and honest; without unnecessary formality: man-to-man discussions —**man-to-man** adv : I think I should talk to him about it, man-to-man.

man·tra /ˈmæntrə/ n **1** a piece of holy writing in the Hindu religion esp. from the Vedas **2** in Hinduism and Buddhism a word or sound repeated again and again as a prayer or to help MEDITATION (=deep religious thought)

man·u·al[1] /ˈmænjuəl/ adj of or using the hands: manual dexterity | manual work — ~ **ly** adv : You have to change gear manually in this car; it's not automatic.

manual[2] n a (small) book giving information about how to do something, esp. how to use a machine: a car manual —compare HANDBOOK

manual la·bour /ˌ··· '··/ n work done with the hands and not needing much thought or skill, e.g. factory work. It is generally thought of as the lowest kind of work.

manual work·er /'··· ˌ··/ n a person whose job involves manual labour —see also BLUE-COLLAR

Man·uel /mænˈwel/ an amusing character in the popular British television programme Fawlty Towers. Manuel is a Spanish waiter who does not speak or understand much English so he is always asking ¿Qué? (= (Spanish for) What?) People in Britain sometimes copy this when they do not understand something and want to be funny. —see also FAWLTY TOWERS

man·u·fac·ture[1] /ˌmænjʊˈfæktʃəʳ/ v [T] **1** to make or produce esp. by machinery or other industrial processes and usu. in large quantities: This firm manufactures cars. | manufactured goods | the decline in jobs in the manufacturing sector (=in the branch of business that manufactures goods) **2** to invent (an untrue story, reason, etc.): You'll have to manufacture a good excuse if you don't go to your sister's wedding!

manufacture[2] n [U] manufacturing: The manufacture of these very small components is expensive.

man·u·fac·tur·er /ˌmænjʊˈfæktʃərəʳ/ also **manufacturers** pl.— n a firm that manufactures goods: The washing machine didn't work, so we sent it back to the manufacturers.

Man U·nit·ed /ˌ· ·'··/ see MANCHESTER UNITED

ma·nure[1] /məˈnjʊəʳ‖məˈnʊər/ n [U] waste matter from animals which is put on the land to make it produce better crops: a heap of manure —compare FERTILIZER

manure[2] v [T] to put manure on: manuring the roses

man·u·script /ˈmænjʊskrɪpt/ n **1** the first copy of a book or piece of writing, written by hand or typed before being printed: I read his novel in manuscript. **2** a handwritten book, from the time before printing was invented: a valuable medieval manuscript

Manx /mæŋks/ adj of the Isle of Man, its people, or the Celtic language originally spoken there

Manx cat /ˌ· '·/ n a type of cat from the Isle of Man which has no tail

man·y /ˈmeni/ determiner, pron **1** a large number (of); more than several but less than most: Many people find this kind of film unpleasant. | The apples had been stored so badly that many (of them) had rotted. | There are so many (nice things) that I find it hard to choose. | I haven't got as many as you. | You have (far) too many books on that shelf. | Not many of the children will pass the exam. | He bought four tickets, which was one too many. (=he only needed three) | They visited five countries **in as many days.** (=in five days) | He ate three and said he could eat **as many again.** (=three more) | This school has twice as many students as my last one. | There are many, many reasons against it. | How many letters are there in the alphabet? | He invited all his many friends to the party. | (fml) Many a good climber (=many good climbers) has met his death on this mountain. **2 a good many** quite a large number (of): We received a good many offers of support. **3 a great many** a very large number (of): There are a great many reasons why you shouldn't do it. **4**

'many's the time/day, etc., **(that)** there have been many times/days, etc., (that): *Many's the time I've wondered what happened to her.* **5 one too many** *infml* too much (alcohol) to drink: *Don't pay any attention to him — he's had one too many.* **6 one too many for** *old-fash infml* clever enough to beat (someone) —opposite **few**; compare MORE, MOST; see also MUCH, **in so many words** (WORD¹)

▷ USAGE Although **many** can be used alone in simple statements in the same way as **a lot of**, it is more formal and not usual in conversation: *He has* **many** *volumes in his library.* | *He has* **a lot of** *books.* | **Many** *people have expressed this opinion.* | **A lot of** *people think this.*◁

many-sid·ed /ˌ·· '··◄/ *adj* **1** with many sides **2** with many different qualities or interests — **~ ness** *n* [U]

man·za·nil·la /ˌmænzə'nɪlə/ *n* [U] a type of pale, dry SHERRY (=strong wine) from Spain, usu. drunk before a meal

Mao·is·m /'maʊɪzəm/ *n* [U] belief in and practice of the principles of Mao Tse-tung, the first leader of the People's Republic of China. Mao believed that SOCIALIST REVOLUTIONs would develop first in underdeveloped countries by workers on the land, not by industrial workers. He thought it was important to give encouragement and moral education to people to help them face their problems and build a new society. His ideas influenced many people outside China esp. in Third World countries. A number of small Maoist groups were established in western countries during the 1960s and early 1970s. **—ist** *adj, n*

Mao·ri /'maʊri/ *n* [C;*the*+P] (a member of) the original peoples of New Zealand, now only a small part of the population. In the 19th century, after wars with the European settlers and the building of towns, their numbers were greatly reduced and their old way of life was largely destroyed. **Maori** *adj*

Mao Tse-tung /ˌmaʊ ˌtseɪ 'tʊŋ/ also **Mao Ze-dong** /ˌmaʊ ˌdʒə 'dʊŋ/, **Mao, chairman Mao—** (1893–1976) a Chinese Communist leader. During the LONG MARCH (1934–35) to escape nationalist forces, he became leader of the Chinese Communist Party and in 1949, the first chairman of the People's Republic of China. He introduced the GREAT LEAP FORWARD in 1958 and the CULTURAL REVOLUTION (1966–69). When he became ill in the 1970s, he was influenced by his wife, Jiang Qing and the GANG OF FOUR. At the height of his power and success, he was greatly respected by the Chinese people who, at public meetings, waved copies of his little red book *The Thoughts of Chairman Mao*. His ideas influenced many people around the world.

map¹ /mæp/ *n* **1** [(of)] a representation of (part of) the Earth's surface as if seen from above, showing the shape of countries, the position of towns, the height of land, the rivers, etc.: *a map of the world/of Europe/of central London* | *a road map* | *If you don't know where it is, look it up on the map.* | *They got lost because they couldn't read* (=understand) *the map.* **2 off the map: a** (of a place) far away and unreachable **b** *infml* not in existence: *The bomb wiped their village off the map.* **3 (put something) on the map** *infml* (to cause someone or something to be) considered important: *Getting the part in the TV serial put me on the map, and a lead role in a film soon followed.* —see also RELIEF MAP

map² *v* **-pp-** [T] **1** to make a map of: *to map the surface of the moon* **2** [(onto)] *tech* to represent the pattern of (something) on something else
  map sthg. ↔ **out** *phr v* [T] to plan in detail in advance: *The girl's talent was spotted early, and a busy future was soon mapped out for her.* [+*wh-*] *We're mapping out where to go for our holidays.*

ma·ple /'meɪpəl/ *n* a tree with many-pointed leaves which grows in the northern half of the world —see picture at TREE. A red maple leaf is used to represent Canada, and appears on the Canadian flag.

maple syr·up /ˌ·· '··/ *n* [U] a sweet sticky liquid, obtained from some kinds of maple tree, which is eaten with WAFFLEs or PANCAKEs, esp. in the US and Canada

map·ping /'mæpɪŋ/ *n tech* (in MATHEMATICS) an act of fitting one member of a SET³ (10) exactly onto a member of another set

Ma·pu·to /mə'puːtəʊ/ a port on the Indian ocean, the capital city of Mozambique

mar /maːʳ/ *v* **-rr-** [T] *esp. lit* to make less perfect or complete; spoil: *The new power station mars the beauty of the countryside.*

Mar. *written abbrev. for:* March

mar·a·bou , **-bout** /'mærəbuː/ *n* a large African STORK (=a long-legged bird)

ma·ra·ca /mə'rækə‖-'rɑː-, -'ræ-/ *n* [*usu pl.*] either of a pair of hollow shells with small objects, such as stones, inside them that are shaken to provide a strong beat in Latin American music

Mar·a·don·a /ˌmærə'dɒnə‖-'dɑː-/, **Di·e·go** /di'eɪgəʊ/ (1960–) an Argentinian football player who helped his country win the World Cup in 1986. He is considered to be one of the best players in the world. In Britain, he is often remembered for the match between Argentina and England in the World Cup in 1986 when he scored (SCORE) a GOAL which many people thought should not have been allowed because he appeared to use his hand. After the match, when he was asked about it, Maradona said that it was "the hand of God". England lost the match.

mar·a·schi·no /ˌmærə'skiːnəʊ, -'ʃiː-/ *n* **-nos** (*sometimes cap.*) **1** [U] a sweet alcoholic drink (LIQUEUR) made from a kind of black CHERRY (=a small fruit) **2** [C] a sugar-covered CHERRY which has been kept in this or a similar drink, used for decorating drinks and sweet cakes and dishes

mar·a·thon¹ /'mærəθən‖-θɑːn/ *n* **1** (*often cap.*) a running race of about 26 miles or 42 kilometres (from the place-name of a Greek victory in 490 BC. A messenger ran this distance to Athens to report it.)

▶ CULTURAL NOTE Many big cities, e.g. London and Boston, have their own marathon every year which thousands of runners enter, both famous and ordinary people. The marathon is also an Olympic event: *a marathon runner*◀

2 an activity that tests one's power over a long time: *The meeting was a bit of a marathon.* | *a dance marathon*

marathon² *adj* [A] very long or needing much effort for a long time: *a marathon speech of six hours* | *It was a marathon job addressing all those envelopes.*

ma·raud·ing /mə'rɔːdɪŋ/ *adj* moving around in search of something to steal, burn, or destroy: *They were attacked by marauding tribesmen.* **—er** *n*

Mar·bel·la /mɑː'beɪə‖mɑːr-/ *n* a port and popular holiday place on the E coast of Spain

mar·ble /'mɑːbəl‖'mɑːr-/ *n* **1** [U] a sort of white or irregularly coloured LIMESTONE that is hard, cold to touch, smooth when polished, and used for buildings, STATUEs, gravestones, etc. **2** [C] a small hard ball of usu. coloured glass used in the game of MARBLES

Marble Arch /ˌ·· '·/ a large white stone arch in central London, where a number of big roads meet: *Turn left at Marble Arch and go up Edgware Road.*

mar·bled /'mɑːbəld‖'mɑːr-/ *adj* marked with irregular colours and lines like some kinds of MARBLE (1)

mar·bles /'mɑːbəlz‖'mɑːr-/ *n* **1** [U] a game in which small hard glass balls are rolled along the ground towards each other; it is usu. played by small children, esp. boys **2** [P] *humor* one's reason or good sense: *He hasn't got all his marbles/has lost his marbles.* (=is mad) —see also ELGIN MARBLES

mar·ca·site /'mɑːkəsaɪt‖'mɑːr-/ *n* [U] a metal that can be cut and polished to look rather like diamonds and is used for making a shiny sort of cheap jewellery

Mar·ceau /mɑː'səʊ‖mɑːr-/, **Mar·cel** /mɑː'sel‖mɑːr-/ (1923–) a French MIME artist, famous for his white-faced character, Bip. He has also produced plays using mime and dance.

march¹ /mɑːtʃ‖mɑːrtʃ/ *v* **1** [I] to walk with firm regular steps like a soldier: *The soldiers marched along the road.* | *"Squad, quick march!"* (=start marching) *shouted the sergeant-major.* | *She was very angry and marched out (of the shop).* | (fig.) *Time marches on.* (=advances regularly and quickly and cannot be turned back) **2** [T] to cover (a distance) by marching: *We'd marched 20 miles by sunset.* **3** [T+*obj*+*adv/prep*] to force to go, esp. on foot: *The police marched him off to prison.* —see also FROG-MARCH **— ~ er** *n* : *thousands of marchers on a demonstration*

march² *n* **1** [C;U] (an act of) marching: *The soldiers had* *a long march in front of them to reach the camp before nightfall.* | *They had to make a* **forced march** (=hurried and tiring march) *of three days to reach the safety of the city.* | *They paraded past at a march.* (=marching) | *Our armies are* **on the march.** (-have started marching) | (fig.) *Science is on the march.* (=is advancing and improving)* | (fig.) *We cannot resist the march* (=regular forward movement) *of time.* **2** [C] a piece of music played with a regular beat (as if) in time with marching feet —see also WEDDING MARCH **3** [C] the distance covered while marching in a certain (stated) period of time: *Our destination is a day's march away.* **4** [C] an act of walking by a large number of people from one place to another to show their opinions or dissatisfactions: *a peace march* —see also MARCHES, **steal a march on** (STEAL[1])

March (*written abbrev.* **Mar.**) *n* [C;U] the third month of the year, between February and April: *It happened on March the third|on the third of March|(AmE) on March third.* | *This office opened in March 1991.* | *She started work here last March|the March before last.*

▶ CULTURAL NOTE March is the first month of Spring. It is often cold and wet, with strong winds, but is also associated with Spring flowers, esp. DAFFODILS. People sometimes say that "March comes in like a lion and goes out like a lamb", meaning that it begins with cold, windy weather and ends with warmer weather.◀

mar·ches /ˈmɑːtʃɨz‖ˈmɑːr-/ *n* [P] (*often cap. as part of a name*) a border area, esp. between Scotland or Wales and England: *the Welsh Marches*

March Hare /ˌ· ˈ·/ [*the*] a character in Lewis Carroll's book *Alice's Adventures in Wonderland.* He is a mad HARE who talks nonsense —see also ALICE IN WONDERLAND, MAD HATTER, and see colour picture on page 619

marching band /ˈ·· ˌ·/ *n* a group of people playing musical instruments while they walk, all moving their legs at the same time with the beat of the music: *a parade with a marching band* | *She plays the tuba in a marching band.*

marching or·ders /ˈ·· ˌ·/ *BrE* ‖ **walking papers** *AmE*— *n* [P] *infml* official notice that one must leave: *He will get|The boss will give him his marching orders if he keeps being late like this.*

mar·chio·ness /ˈmɑːʃənɨs‖ˈmɑːr-/ *n* **1** the wife of a MARQUIS **2** a noblewoman with the rank of a MARQUIS

Marchioness [*the*] a pleasure boat which hit another boat and sank in the river Thames in London in 1989, killing 51 passengers. It had been hired for a private birthday party and most of the people killed were aged 20–30.

March of Dimes /ˌ· · ˈ·/ [*the*] an American CHARITY organization which raises money, esp. for DISABLED children

march-past /ˈ· ·/ *n* a ceremonial march of soldiers past a person or place of importance

Mar·ci·a·no /ˌmɑːsiˈɑːnəʊ‖ˌmɑːrsiˈænəʊ/, **Rocky** (1923–69) a famous American BOXER who became the world CHAMPION in 1952. He was never defeated and RETIRED in 1956.

Mar·co·ni /mɑːˈkəʊni‖mɑːr-/, **Gu·gliel·mo** /ɡʊlˈjɛlməʊ/ (1874–1937) an Italian inventor who formed the world's first radio company in 1897 and shared the Nobel prize for PHYSICS in 1909

Marco Polo see Marco POLO

Mar·cos /ˈmɑːkɒs‖ˈmɑːrkəʊs/, **Fer·di·nand** /ˈfɜːdɨnænd‖ˈfɜːr-/ (1917–89) the president of the Philippines from 1965 until he was forced to leave the country in 1986. He and his wife **Imelda** were very wealthy and known for their expensive way of life.

Marcos, I·mel·da /ɪˈmeldə/ (1930–) the wife of President Marcos of the Philippines, who left the country with him in 1986 and was the subject of legal action for EMBEZZLEMENT (=stealing money placed in one's care) in 1988. She is known for the expensive way of life she had while in the Philippines, and esp. for the very large number of shoes which she bought. In 1991 Imelda returned to the Philippines to try to become president, but she was accused (ACCUSE) of stealing from the people while her husband was in power.

Mar·cu·se /mɑːˈkuːzə‖mɑːr-/, **Herbert** (1898–1979) an American thinker and writer on politics, born in Germany, who attracted many followers in America in the 1960s. He wrote about the bad effects on people of modern economics, industry, and science.

Mar·di Gras /ˌmɑːdi ˈɡrɑː‖ˈmɑːrdi ɡrɑː/ (a CARNIVAL period held in some countries on or around the time of) the day before the first day of Lent; SHROVE TUESDAY. In the US, the city of New Orleans, Louisiana, holds a famous Mardi Gras celebration which many people travel to see.

mare /meəʳ/ *n* a female horse or DONKEY —compare STALLION

mare's nest /ˈ· ·/ *n* **1** a discovery which proves to be untrue or valueless; a HOAX **2** *AmE* a situation or place which is very confused or untidy

Mar·garet /ˈmɑːɡrət‖ˈmɑːr-/, **Princess** (1930–) a British princess, the younger sister of Queen Elizabeth II. She married a photographer, Anthony Armstrong-Jones (later Lord Snowdon) in 1960 and had two children, David (Viscount Linley) and Sarah. She was divorced (DIVORCE) in 1978.

mar·ga·rine /ˌmɑːdʒəˈriːn, ˌmɑːɡə-‖ˈmɑːrdʒərɨn/ also **marge** /mɑːdʒ‖mɑːrdʒ/*BrE infml*‖also *AmE*— *n* [U] a food similar to butter, which is made mainly from vegetable fats. Many people now eat margarine instead of butter because they believe that it is healthier, but most people think that butter tastes better. —see also SOFT MARGARINE

mar·ga·ri·ta /ˌmɑːɡəˈriːtə‖ˌmɑːr-/ *n AmE* an alcoholic drink consisting of TEQUILA and LEMON or LIME juice. It is usu. served in a glass with salt around the top

Mar·gate /ˈmɑːɡeɪt‖ˈmɑːr-/ a town on the E coast of England near London, which is a popular place for people from London, esp. WORKING-CLASS people, to go for the day or for their holidays

mar·gin /ˈmɑːdʒɨn‖ˈmɑːr-/ *n*   **margin**
1 an area down the side of a page near the edge, where there is no writing or printing: *Someone had scribbled some notes in the margin of the book.* | *a wide|narrow margin* —see picture at TYPEWRITER **2** an amount by which one thing is greater than another: *In the end we*   **margin**
won by a decisive margin. | *We must leave no* **margin for error.** (=we must make sure there is no chance at all of making a mistake) | *Our* **profit margin** (-the difference between the buying and selling price of our goods) *is very low.* **3** *lit* an area on the outside edge of a larger area: *on the margin of the forest*

mar·gin·al /ˈmɑːdʒɨnəl‖ˈmɑːr-/ *adj* **1** [A *no comp.*] (printed or written) on or in the margin of a page: *marginal illustrations|comments* **2** small in importance or amount: *The new law will have only a marginal effect on the lives of most people.* **3** (of land) too poor to produce many crops, and farmed only when there is a special need for additional crops – ~ **ly** *adv* : *This year's profits were marginally higher than last year's.*

marginal seat /ˌ··· ˈ·/ also **marginal con·sti·tu·en·cy** /ˌ··· ·ˈ····/, **marginal**— *n BrE* a SEAT[1] (3) in the British parliament which may be won or lost by a small number of votes, and so is quite likely to pass from the control of one political party to another —compare SAFE SEAT: *MPs in marginal seats were worried by the government's handling of the health service.*

mar·gin·al·ize also **-ise** *BrE*— /ˈmɑːdʒɨnəl-aɪz‖ˈmɑːr-/ *v* [T] to cause (a group of people) to become unimportant and powerless in society: *The decline in manufacturing industry has marginalized the Trade Unions involved in it, who now have far less influence.*

ma·ri·a·chi /mɑːriˈɑːtʃi/ *n Sp* a kind of dance music played esp. in Mexico — *adj* : *a mariachi band*

Mar·ie An·toi·nette /ˌmæri æntwəˈnet‖mæˌriː, mɑːriː-/ (1755–93) the queen of France, wife of Louis XVI, who tried to escape the REVOLUTION in 1791 but was caught and imprisoned. In 1793 she was killed by having her head cut off. When she was told that poor people did not have enough bread to eat, she is believed to have said, "Let them eat cake."

Marie Ce·leste /ˌmæri sɨˈlest, ˌmɑːri-‖məˌriː-/ [*the*] a sailing ship that was found in the Atlantic Ocean in 1872, with no one on it. The ship was undamaged, and a table was prepared for a meal. No one knows why the sailors left the ship, or what happened to them.

mar·i·gold /ˈmærɪɡəʊld/ n a plant with golden-yellow flowers

mar·i·jua·na, -huana /ˌmærɪˈwɑːnə, -ˈhwɑːnə/ also **grass, pot** infml— n [U] a form of the drug CANNABIS consisting of the dried flowers, stems, and leaves of the Indian HEMP plant, smoked to give pleasure —compare BHANG, HASHISH
► CULTURAL NOTE In Britain and in most of the US, the possession or use of marijuana is ILLEGAL but some people think that it should be made legal because it is not considered very harmful, compared with stronger drugs such as HEROIN or COCAINE. It became popular esp. in the 1960s. ◄

ma·rim·ba /məˈrɪmbə/ n a musical instrument like a XYLOPHONE

ma·ri·na /məˈriːnə/ n a small port for pleasure boats

mar·i·nade /ˌmærɪˈneɪd/ n [C;U] a mixture of oil, wine, and/or VINEGAR, SPICEs, etc., in which meat or fish can be kept before cooking to make it tender and give it a special taste

mar·i·nate /ˈmærɪneɪt/ also **mar·i·nade** /ˈmærɪneɪd/— v [T] to keep (meat or fish) in a marinade before cooking

Ma·rin Coun·ty /məˌrɪn ˈkaʊnti/ an area just N of San Francisco, California, where many wealthy people live.

ma·rine¹ /məˈriːn/ adj [A] **1** of, near, living in, or obtained from the sea: marine mammals such as whales and seals **2** of or for ships and their goods and trade at sea: marine insurance | marine law

marine² n (sometimes cap.) a soldier who serves on a naval ship, esp. a member of the Royal Marines or the Marine Corps —see also MERCHANT MARINE

Marine Corps /·ˈ· ·/ n also **Marines**— [the] a US armed force consisting of soldiers who serve on naval ships and on land. The Marine Corps are often considered to be the toughest and most skilled soldiers in the armed forces. They are often sent into battle first.

mar·i·ner /ˈmærɪnəʳ/ n tech or poet a sailor or seaman —see also ANCIENT MARINER

Ma·rines /məˈriːnz/ n [the+P] **1** the Marine Corps **2** the ROYAL MARINES **3 tell that to the Marines** saying I don't believe what you have just told me

mar·i·o·nette /ˌmæriəˈnet/ n a PUPPET (1)

mar·i·tal /ˈmærɪtl/ adj of marriage – ~ly adv

marital bliss /ˌ··· ˈ·/ n [U] a state of being completely happy which is thought to come with marriage. The phrase is often used humorously to describe young, newly-married people who have not yet experienced any difficulties or had any serious arguments.

marital sta·tus /ˌ··· ˈ··/ n [U] an official expression often used on forms to ask whether a person is married or not, or has ever been married: Marital status: single/married/divorced/separated (Delete as appropriate)

marital vows /ˌ··· ˈ·/ also **marriage vows**— n [P] the solemn promises made by a man and woman when they get married. —see also MARRIAGE

mar·i·time /ˈmærɪtaɪm/ adj **1** concerning ships or the sea: maritime law | That country was a great maritime power. (=had a strong navy) **2** near the sea: the country's maritime provinces

mar·jo·ram /ˈmɑːdʒərəm‖ˈmɑːr-/ n [U] a HERB with sweet-smelling leaves used in cooking

mark¹ /mɑːk‖mɑːrk/ n **1** [C] something, such as a spot or cut, on a surface that would otherwise be plain or clean: Do you think these marks in the sand are some kind of message? | This mark on your jacket won't come off. | His feet left dirty marks all over the floor. | The car had left tyremarks in the muddy ground. | There wasn't a mark (=no cuts or signs of blows) on the dead girl's body. | (fig.) The years in prison have left their mark (=had a lasting effect) on him/on his character. —see also BIRTHMARK **2** [C] a figure or printed or written sign which shows something: Every garment in the shop has a price mark sewn on it. —see also PUNCTUATION MARK, QUESTION MARK **3** [C usu. sing.] a fact or action that is a sign or proof of a quality, feeling, or condition: As a mark of respect they all stood up when he entered the room. | It is a mark of the company's strength that it has recovered so quickly from such a major setback. **4** [C] esp. BrE ‖ usu. **grade** AmE— a figure, letter, or sign which represents a judgment of the quality of someone's work, behaviour, performance in a competition, etc.: The highest mark in the test was

nine out of ten. | (fig.) I'll give him **full marks** for trying. (=I think he tried very hard.) **5** [C] the object or place one aims at: The bullet was aimed at his head, but luckily it missed its mark. | (fig.) Our estimate of the price was rather **wide of the mark**. (=not correct or close to the true figure) **6** [the] esp. BrE an acceptable level of quality: Your latest piece of work is not **up to/is below the mark**. | (fig.) I'm not feeling quite **up to the mark** (=not very well) today. **7** [C] (often cap. written abbrev. **Mk.**) (used esp. with numbers) a particular type of a machine: The Mark 4 gun is more powerful than the old Mark 3. **8** [C] (often cap., written abbrev. **Mk.**) (used esp. with numbers) a particular SETTING (2) for a machine, esp. a gas cooker: Cook for 40 minutes at gas mark 4. **9** [C] a sign, usu. in the form of a cross, made by someone who cannot write their name **10 make one's mark (on)** to become successful and influential (in a place or activity): He certainly made his mark (on the company) while he was here. **11 On your marks, get set, go!** (used for starting a running race) **12 quick/slow off the mark** infml quick/slow in understanding —see also BOOKMARK, LANDMARK

mark² v **1** [T] to make a mark or marks on, esp. one that spoils the appearance: The hot cups have marked the table badly. | The disease marked her face for life. **2** [I] to receive unwanted marks, causing a spoiled appearance: This table marks very easily; don't put that hot cup on it. **3** [T] to show the position of: The cross marks his grave. | She was careful to mark her place (=where she stopped reading) before she shut the book. **4** [T] to be typical of; CHARACTERIZE: She has all the qualities that mark a good nurse. | This writer's plays are marked by (=typically have) a gentle humour. **5** [T] esp. BrE ‖ **grade** AmE— to give MARKs¹ (4) to: I've got a pile of exam papers to mark. **6** [T] to be a sign of: Today's ceremony marks 100 years of trade between our two countries. | The opening of the new factory marked an important stage in the company's development. **7** [T] BrE to stay close to (an opposing player), esp. in football, so as to prevent them from getting the ball or gaining points **8** [T+obj/wh-] old use to watch or listen to carefully: Mark what your father is saying, young lady! **9 mark time: a** to make the movements of marching while remaining in the same place **b** to spend time on work, business, etc., without advancing **10 (you) mark my words!** you will see later that I am right: He'll get into trouble for doing that, you mark my words!

mark sbdy./sthg. ↔ **down** phr v [T] **1** [(as)] to note in writing: The teacher marked him down as absent. | (fig.) I marked him down as (=I thought he probably was) an American, but he turned out to be a Canadian. **2** to reduce the price of (goods): These winter coats have been marked down from £45 to £35. —see also MARKDOWN **3** to give a lower MARK¹ (4) to: He/His work was marked down for untidy writing.

mark sthg. ↔ **off** phr v [T] **1** to make into a separate area by drawing lines **2** to note (a piece of work, for example) as being done, esp. on a list

mark sbdy./sthg. ↔ **out** phr v [T] **1** to draw (an area) with lines: They marked out the tennis court with white paint. **2** [(as, for, from)] to show or choose as being likely to become (a successful person) or to gain (success): His qualities mark him out as a born leader. | She seemed marked out for political success from an early age.

mark sthg. ↔ **up** phr v [T] **1** to increase the price of (goods) —see also MARKUP **2** AmE write notes or instructions on: Someone had already marked up the alto part of the piece. | The manuscript is all marked up for printing.

mark³ n a German unit of money; DEUTSCHMARK

Mark, Saint see SAINT MARK

Mark Antony see ANTONY

mark·down /ˈmɑːkdaʊn‖ˈmɑːrk-/ n the amount by which a price is made lower: a markdown of £10 | The markdown price is on the back of the ticket. —compare MARKUP; see also MARK **down** (2)

marked /mɑːkt‖mɑːrkt/ adj **1** very noticeable: He showed a marked lack of interest. | a marked increase/improvement | This year's results, in **marked contrast to** last year's, were very encouraging. **2** a **marked man** a man who is in danger from a watching enemy – ~ly /ˈmɑːkɪdli‖ˈmɑːr-/ adv : They have markedly different approaches to the problem.

mark·er /ˈmɑːkəʳ‖ˈmɑːr-/ n **1** a tool or pen (**marker pen**) for making marks **2** an object which marks a place: *a book marker* **3** someone who gives MARKS¹ (4) in an exam, competition, etc. **4** an action or statement that makes one's intentions clear: *In refusing the request this time, he has put down a marker for future applicants.*

mar·ket¹ /ˈmɑːkɨt‖ˈmɑːr-/ n **1** [C] a building, square, or open place where people meet to buy and sell goods, esp. food and animals: *a fish market | a cattle market | the market square | an antiques market* **2** [C] a gathering of people to buy and sell on certain days at such a place: *There's no market this week. | Monday is market day.* **3** [C] an area or country where there is a demand for goods: *They sell mainly to the overseas market|the home market.| The sales director wants to open up new markets in the Far East.* **4** [S;U (**for**)] desire to buy; public demand (for a product, service, skill, etc.): *There's not much of a market for that kind of car.* (=not many people want to buy them)| *The potential market for this product is enormous.| He can't find a market for his skills.* (=anyone willing to employ him for them) | (fig.) *Are you* in the market for (=do you want to buy) *a used washing machine?* **5** [C] (the state of) trade in particular goods, or goods in general: *There's great activity in the tea market. | The market is rather depressed at the moment.* (=there is not much activity, prices are low, etc.) | *It's* a buyer's market (=prices are favourable for those wishing to buy) *so you ought to keep your shares until it's* a seller's market. | *They are aiming to increase their share of the market.* (=to sell more goods in comparison with others who sell the same goods) **6** on the market for sale; able to be bought: *the best small car on the market | They've put their house on the market.* —see also BLACK MARKET, EC, FLEA MARKET, the bottom has fallen out of the market (BOTTOM¹)

market² v [T] to offer for sale, esp. by using the skills of advertising and supplying: *The firm markets many types of goods.* | *If the deal is properly marketed, it should sell very well.* – – **able** *adj : marketable skills|products* – – **er** n – – **ability** /ˌmɑːkɨtəˈbɪlɨti‖ˌmɑːr-/ n [U]

market day /ˈ·· ·/ n [C;U] a day in the week when a town has a market, usu. once a week: *I usually go into town on market day. | Market days in Southall are Wednesday and Saturday.*

market e·con·o·my /ˌ··· ·ˈ···/ n a system of producing wealth based on the free operation of business and trade without government controls

mar·ket·eer /ˌmɑːkɨˈtɪəʳ‖ˌmɑːr-/ n **1** a person who supports a certain sort of system for buying and selling: *a free marketeer* **2** (in Britain) (*cap.*) a person who has a particular view on Britain's membership of the EEC: *anti-Marketeer|pro-Marketeer*

market forc·es /ˌ·· ˈ··/ n [P] the free operation of business and trade without any controls by government, so that prices and wage levels depend on the level of demand. Capitalist systems are based on the belief that this is the best way to operate.

market gar·den /ˌ·· ˈ··/ *BrE* ‖ **truck farm** *AmE*– n an area for growing vegetables and fruit for sale – – **er** n – – **ing** n [U]

mar·ket·ing /ˈmɑːkɨtɪŋ‖ˈmɑːr-/ n [U] **1** the branch of business concerned with advertising, PUBLICITY (2), etc.: *a job in marketing | marketing strategies | the marketing director* **2** *AmE* the act of doing one's shopping, esp. for food: *I have to go marketing in the morning. | When will you do the marketing?*

market lead·er /ˌ·· ˈ··/ n a service or product which sells better than any other of its kind

market mak·er /ˈ·· ˌ··/ n *tech* a dealer buying and selling securities (SECURITY (5)); usu. buying in large numbers and selling in smaller amounts

market niche /ˌ·· ˈ·/ n a space for a product or service to fill in the area of buying and selling: *Body Shop found a market niche for cosmetics not tested on animals.*

mar·ket·place /ˈmɑːkɨtpleɪs‖ˈmɑːr-/ n **1** [C] an open area, esp. a square, where a market is held **2** [the] the area of business activity which involves buying and selling: *We don't know if this new product will be successful until we test it out in the marketplace.*

market price /ˌ·· ˈ·/ n the price which buyers will actually pay for something

market re·search /ˌ··· ·ˈ·, ˌ·· ˈ··/ n [U] the process of collecting information about what people buy and why, usu. done by companies so that they can find ways of increasing sales: *We know the product will sell well because we've done a lot of market research on it.*

market share /ˌ·· ˈ·/ n the amount of a particular type of goods or services sold by a company when compared with the total amount of such goods etc. sold: *We are aiming to increase our market share in home computers.*

market town /ˈ··· ·/ n a town where a market is held, esp. one for buying and selling sheep, cattle, etc.

market val·ue /ˌ·· ˈ··/ n the value of a product, esp. a house; based on the price that people are willing to pay for it rather than the cost of making or building it

mark·ing /ˈmɑːkɪŋ‖ˈmɑːr-/ n [C *usu. pl.*;U] (any of a set of) coloured marks on an animal's skin, fur, or on a bird's feathers: *The leopard has beautiful markings.*

Mar·kov /ˈmɑːkɒv, -ɒf‖ˈmɑːrkɑːf, -ɔːf/, **Geor·gi** /ˈgjɔːgi‖ˈgjɔːr-/ (1929–78) a Bulgarian who disagreed with the government of Bulgaria and came to live in Britain. He worked for the BBC radio World Service and was killed when poison was put into his leg from the end of an UMBRELLA. It is said that the Bulgarian Secret Service was responsible for his murder.

Mar·ko·va /mɑːˈkəʊvə‖mɑːr-/, **Dame A·li·ci·a** /əˈlɪsiə/ (1910–) an English BALLET dancer, famous for the grace and beauty of her dancing, esp. in the ballet *Giselle*

Marks and Spen·cer /ˌmɑːks ənd ˈspensəʳ‖ˌmɑːrks-/ *tdmk* one of a group of very well-known department stores found in most large towns in Britain selling clothes, food, and other goods for the home under the name **St Michael**; it is sometimes just called **Marks** or **Marks and Sparks**, or abbreviated to **M & S**. Their clothes are generally considered to be of good quality and at reasonable prices, but not to include the most modern and most extreme fashions. Many people buy underwear from there. Their food products, esp. prepared meals, are thought to be very good quality and are popular esp. with MIDDLE-CLASS people who do not have time to cook.

marks·man /ˈmɑːksmən‖ˈmɑːrks-/ **marks·wom·an** /-ˌwʊmən/*fem.*– n -**men** /mən/ a person who can shoot well with a gun: *an expert marksman*

marks·man·ship /ˈmɑːksmənʃɪp‖ˈmɑːrks-/ n [U] the quality or ability of a marksman; skill in shooting

mark·up /ˈmɑːkʌp‖ˈmɑːrk-/ n the amount by which a price is raised by a seller to pay for costs and allow for profit: *a markup of 20% on cigarettes in the hotel shop* —compare MARKDOWN; see also MARK up

marl /mɑːl‖mɑːrl/ n [U] a soil formed of clay and LIME

Marl·bo·ro /ˈmɔːlbərə‖ˈmɑːrlbɜːrəʊ/ *tdmk* the name of a kind of American cigarettes. Marlboro advertisements typically show impressive outdoor scenes from the US, and adventurous-looking men like COWBOYS.

Marl·bo·rough /ˈmɑːlbərə‖ˈmɑːrlbɜːrəʊ/ a town in Wiltshire, SW England known for the famous PUBLIC SCHOOL, **Marlborough College**, established in 1843

Mar·ley /ˈmɑːli‖ˈmɑːr-/, **Bob** (1945–81) a Jamaican singer and songwriter who, with his group **The Wailers**, made Reggae music popular in many countries of the world. He was an exciting performer and his music often carried a social and political message. Like other RASTAFARIANS, he wore his hair in DREADLOCKS. His most famous songs include *No Woman, No Cry* and *Buffalo Soldier*.

Bob Marley

Mar·ley tiles /ˈ·· ˌ·/ n [P] *tdmk* TILES made of clay etc. (for roofs) or of a plastic material (for floors), made by a British company called Marley

mar·lin /ˈmɑːlɨn‖ˈmɑːr-/ n **marlin** *or* **marlins** a very large sea fish with a long sharp nose, which is hunted for sport

Mar·lowe /ˈmɑːləʊ‖ˈmɑːr-/, **Chris·to·pher** /ˈkrɪstəfəʳ/

(1564–93) an English writer of plays and poetry, best-known for his plays *Dr Faustus* and *Edward II*

Mar·lowe, Philip the main character in the DETECTIVE stories written by Raymond Chandler. Marlowe is very determined and tough, but he is honest and likes to see justice done. He is noted for his dry (=funny, without appearing to be so) humour and short, IRONIC statements.

mar·ma·lade¹ /ˈmɑːməleɪd‖ˈmɑːr-/ n [U] a JAM made from CITRUS fruits, esp. oranges; in Britain it is eaten at breakfast with TOAST and butter

marmalade² adj esp. BrE (esp. of a cat) dark orange in colour

Marmara, Sea of see SEA OF MARMARA

Mar·mite /ˈmɑːmaɪt‖ˈmɑːr-/ n [U] tdmk a soft, black, salty food eaten on bread or added to soups to give a savoury taste. Because it has been eaten in Britain for so many years, it is often connected with the past and considered typically British. It is often given to small children on long pieces of TOAST called **Marmite soldiers.**

mar·mo·set /ˈmɑːməzet‖ˈmɑːrməset, -zet/ n any of several types of very small hairy monkey from Central and South America, with large eyes

mar·mot /ˈmɑːmət‖ˈmɑːr-/ n a small European or American plant-eating animal that lives in holes in the ground — compare GROUNDHOG

Marne /mɑːn‖mɑːrn/, **Battle of the** n an important battle of the First World War when the Allies stopped the Germans from reaching Paris in September 1914. A second battle in 1918 saw the Allies stop the last German attack of the war.

Mar·on·ite /ˈmærənaɪt/ n a member of a group of Christians living esp. in Lebanon and connected to the Roman Catholic church

ma·roon¹ /məˈruːn/ v [T] to leave (someone) alone in a place where no one lives, with no means of getting away: *Our boat sank and we were marooned on a small island.*

maroon² adj having a very dark red-brown colour — **maroon** n [U]

maroon³ n a small ROCKET that explodes high in the air, used as a signal, esp. at sea

Mar·plan /ˈmɑːplæn‖ˈmɑːr-/ n a British organization that asks the public for its opinion on different subjects and prints the results in the newspapers esp. the *Financial Times* and the *Guardian*

Mar·ple /ˈmɑːpəl‖ˈmɑːr-/, **Miss Jane** a character in many of the stories written by Agatha Christie. Miss Marple is a very respectable, polite old lady who is also very clever at explaining mysteries and discovering criminals, esp. murderers.

mar·quee /mɑːˈkiː‖mɑːr-/ n **1** a large tent for outdoor public events, such as competitions or shows, or for eating and drinking in **2** AmE a sign above a theatre or cinema which gives the name of the play or film and sometimes its actors

mar·quet·ry /ˈmɑːkᵻtri‖ˈmɑːr-/ n [U] (the art of making) a type of pattern in wood, in which different coloured pieces are fitted together, esp. on the surface of furniture

Mar·quette /mɑːˈket | mɑːr-/, **Jacques** /ʒæk‖ʒɑːk/ (1637–75) a French Jesuit MISSIONARY and EXPLORER in N America; he and Louis JOLIET were the first Europeans to discover the Mississippi river

mar·quis , marquess /ˈmɑːkwᵻs‖ˈmɑːr-/ **marchioness** fem.— n a nobleman of high rank: *the Marquis of Bath*

Mar·ra·kesh, Marrakech /ˌmærəˈkeʃ/ a city in W central Morocco, with many fine buildings. It is popular with tourists and also famous for producing CARPETS and leather goods.

mar·ram grass /ˈmærəm grɑːs‖-græs/ n [U] a tall grass that grows by the sea

mar·riage /ˈmærɪdʒ/ n [C;U] **1** the union of a man and woman by a legal ceremony: *The marriage took place in church.* | *to take one's marriage vows* —see also WEDDING **2** the state of being married: *Her first marriage* (=her life with her first husband) *was not very happy.* —see also COMMON LAW MARRIAGE

▶ CULTURAL NOTE In Britain and the US it is now common, esp. among young people, for a man and a woman to live together without being married. Some couples decide to get married when they have children. About one in three

marriages ends in divorce, (in the US, almost one in two) so there are many parents bringing up children alone. These things are no longer considered as shocking as they were in the past. However, many people still consider to be happily married one of their main aims in life. Britain is a country of many different social groups and religions, so there are many different customs and attitudes to marriage, e.g. some British families of Asian origin may arrange marriages for their sons and daughters. —see DIVORCE, ONE-PARENT FAMILY, SINGLE PARENT, WEDDING ◀

mar·riage·a·ble /ˈmærɪdʒəbəl/ adj fml (esp. of a girl) suitable, esp. in age, character, appearance, etc., for marriage: *She has three very marriageable daughters.* | *of marriageable age* —compare ELIGIBLE —**-bility** /ˌmærɪdʒəˈbɪlᵻti/ n [U]

marriage bu·reau /ˈ⋯ ˌ⋯/ n an organization which brings together people who are looking for a husband or wife. A marriage bureau usu. asks its customers to answer a set of questions about themselves, e.g. their interests and things they like, so that they can be introduced to similar people.

marriage guid·ance /ˈ⋯ ˈ⋯/ n [U] advice given to people who are married, or are thinking of getting married, esp. to help them deal with relationship problems. Marriage guidance my be given by VOLUNTARY advisers from an organization such as Relate, or by a professional adviser (COUNSELLOR).

Marriage Guidance Coun·cil /ˌ⋯ ˈ⋯ ˌ⋯/ [the] see RELATE

marriage guid·ance coun·sel·lor /ˌ⋯ ˈ⋯ ˌ⋯/ n a person who tries to help people who are unhappy in their marriage by asking them both to talk to him or her about the problems and helping them to deal with the problems and to talk about their problems with each other

marriage li·cence /ˈ⋯ ˌ⋯/ n an official document which people must get before they are allowed to marry

marriage lines /ˈ⋯ ·/ n [P] BrE old-fash infml the CERTIFICATE (=official paper) which proves that a marriage has taken place

marriage of con·ve·ni·ence /ˌ⋯ ⋯ˈ⋯/ n **marriages of convenience** a marriage contract agreed for social, political, or economic advantage rather than for love, e.g. when a foreigner marries a citizen of a country in order to be allowed to stay in that country

Marriage of Fig·a·ro /ˌmærɪdʒ əv ˈfɪɡərəʊ/, **The** an OPERA by Mozart, based on a play of the same name by the French writer Beaumarchais

marriage vows /ˈ⋯ ˌ·/ see MARITAL VOWS

mar·ried /ˈmærɪd/ adj **1** having a husband or wife: *Is she married?* | *a married man* —compare SINGLE¹ (4), UNMARRIED **2** [F+to] having as a husband/wife; joined in marriage (to): *She's married to my brother.* | (fig.) *He's married to his work.* (=gives it all his attention) **3** [A] of the state of marriage: *married life* —see also MARRY

mar·rieds /ˈmærɪdz/ also **young marrieds** infml— n young married people, esp. recently married ones: *new homes for young marrieds*

Mar·ri·ner /ˈmærᵻnəʳ/, **Sir Nev·ille** /ˈnevəl/ (1924–) an English CONDUCTOR (=a person who directs the playing of a group of musicians)

mar·row /ˈmærəʊ/ n **1** [U] also **bone marrow**— the soft fatty substance in the hollow centre of bones: *It was so cold that he felt frozen to the marrow.* (=as if the cold had entered his bones) **2** [C] esp. BrE also **vegetable marrow**, also **squash** AmE— a large long round dark green vegetable that grows along the ground —see picture at VEGETABLE

mar·row·bone /ˈmærəʊbəʊn/ n a bone containing (a lot of) MARROW which can be used in cooking

mar·row·fat /ˈmærəʊfæt/ also **marrowfat pea** /ˌ⋯ ˈ·/— n a large PEA

mar·ry /ˈmæri/ v **1** [I;T] to take (a person) in marriage: *He married late in life.* | *They got married last April.* *They've been married for a year.* | *Will you marry me?* | *I don't think he'll ever marry. He's not the marrying kind.* (=the sort of person who marries) | (fig.) *She married money.* (=a rich man) **2** [T] (of a priest or official) to perform the ceremony of marriage for (two people): *The bishop married them.* **3** [T (to)] to cause to take in marriage: *She wants to marry her daughter to a rich man.* —see also MARRIED, MARRIAGE

▷ USAGE 1 **Get married** is less formal and more usual than **marry**, [I]: *My son's getting married next week.* | *They're saving up to get married.* 2 When both partners in the marriage are mentioned you can say *Ben and Jill are getting married.* You can also say *Ben is marrying (fml)/getting married to (infml) Jill or Jill is marrying (fml)/getting married to (infml) Ben —* see also DIVORCE (USAGE)◁

marry into sthg. *phr v* [T] to become a member of (a particular group or family) by marriage: *He married into a wealthy family.* | *(infml) married into money*

marry sbdy. ↔ **off** *phr v* [T (**to**)] to find a husband or wife for: *She married off her daughter to a diplomat.*

Mars /maːz‖maːrz/ 1 the PLANET fourth in order from the sun, and nearest to the Earth. It shines with a red colour —see picture at SOLAR SYSTEM

▶ CULTURAL NOTE People sometimes imagine that there are creatures who live on Mars, and usu. think of them as little green men.◀

2 in CLASSICAL MYTHOLOGY, the Roman god of war

Mars Bar /'·· ·/ *BrE* also **Mars‖Milky Way** *AmE tdmk— n tdmk* a chocolate bar with a soft filling which has been popular in Britain for many years. In advertisements for Mars Bars it is claimed that "A Mars a day helps you work, rest, and play."

Mar·sa·la /maːˈsɑːlə‖maːr-/ *n* [U] a sweet strong wine from Marsala in the island of Sicily

Mar·seil·laise /ˌmaːsəˈleɪz, -seɪˈez‖ˌmaːr-/ *n* [*the*] the NATIONAL ANTHEM of France

Mar·seilles /maːˈseɪ, -ˈseɪlz‖maːr-/ a city in S France which is an important sea port and industrial centre

marsh /maːʃ‖maːrʃ/ also **marshes** *pl.*, **marshland**— *n* [C;U] (a piece of) low land that is soft and wet —compare SWAMP¹ — ~ **y** *adj* : *marshy ground* | *a marshy area*

Marsh¹, Ngai·o /'naɪəʊ/ (1899–1982) a New Zealand writer of DETECTIVE stories, whose books include *A Man Lay Dead* and *Photo Finish*

Marsh², Pete /piːt/ a humorous name for **Lindow Man**, the body of a man from the Iron Age (about 3000 years ago) found in a PEAT BOG in Cheshire in 1984

mar·shal¹ /'maːʃəl‖'maːr-/ *n* 1 an officer of the highest rank in certain armies and airforces —see also AIR CHIEF MARSHAL, AIR VICE-MARSHAL, FIELD MARSHAL 2 *esp. BrE* an official in charge of making arrangements for an important public or royal ceremony or event 3 an official in charge of making arrangements for a race: *The marshals waved flags to warn the drivers of the danger ahead.* 4 (in the US) **a** an official who carries out the judgments given in a court of law; one who has the duties of a SHERIFF **b** a chief officer of a police or fire-fighting force

marshal² *v* -ll- *BrE* ‖ -l- *AmE* [T] 1 to arrange (esp. facts) in good or effective order. *To make a good speech you need to marshal your arguments very clearly.* 2 to lead or show (a person) ceremonially or carefully to the correct place: *Extra stewards had to be employed to marshal the crowds.* | *She marshalled the children into the museum.*

Mar·shall /'maːʃəl‖'maːr-/, **Thur·good** /'θɜːɡʊd‖'θɜːr-/ (1908–) the first black person to become a US Supreme Court justice. He served on the court from 1967 to 1991.

marshalling yard /'···· ·/ *n esp. BrE* a railway yard in which the parts of a train, esp. a goods train, are put together in preparation for a journey

Marshall Plan /'·· ˌ·/ [*the*] a programme which gave economic help to Europe after the Second World War, named after **George Marshall**, chief of the US army during the war, who organized and directed it

Marshal of the Roy·al Air Force /ˌ··· · ·ˌ· ·ˌ·/ *n* a high rank in the British airforce —see TABLE 3

marsh gas /'· ·/ *n* [U] gas formed by decayed vegetable matter under the surface of water in a marsh; METHANE

marsh·land /'maːʃlænd‖'maːr-/ *n* see MARSH

marsh·mal·low /ˌmaːʃˈmæləʊ‖'maːrʃmeləʊ/ *n* 1 a light soft round pink or white sweet often toasted (TOAST) on BONFIREs so that they melt 2 a plant with pink flowers that grows on marshes

Mar·ston Moor /ˌmaːstən ˈmʊəʳ‖ˌmaːr-/, **Battle of** an important battle near York in 1644 during the English Civil War, which gave Cromwell control of the north of England

mar·su·pi·al /maːˈsjuːpiəl‖maːrˈsuː-/ *n* any of various mainly Australian animals in which the female gives birth to partly developed young and then carries them in a POUCH (=pocket of skin) on her body for a time: *Kangaroos and koala bears are marsupials.*

Mar·tel·lo tow·er /maːˌteləʊ ˈtaʊəʳ‖maːr-/ *n* a circular tower formerly used in Britain for coastal defence. Some can still be seen on the south coast of Britain and in Jersey.

mar·ten /'maːtɪn, -tn‖'maːrtn/ *n* any of several small fierce flesh-eating animals that live mainly in trees

Mar·tha /'maːθə‖'maːr-/ a woman in the Bible who attended to the needs of Jesus and His DISCIPLEs, rather than listening to His teaching

Martha and Mary see SAINT MARTHA AND SAINT MARY

Mar·tha's Vine·yard /ˌ·· '··/ *n* an island off the NE coast of the US South of Cape Cod popular with writers and artists, and with tourists in the summer

mar·tial /'maːʃəl‖'maːr-/ *adj* of or suitable to war, soldiers, etc.: *martial music*

martial art /ˌ·· '·/ *n* any of various sports concerned with fighting skills, developed in Eastern countries: *Judo and karate are martial arts.*

martial law /ˌ·· '·/ *n* [U] law that provides for the government of a place by the army, esp. when there has been fighting against the established government: *After the rebellion, the whole country was put under martial law.*

Mar·tian /'maːʃən‖'maːr-/ *n, adj* (an imaginary creature) of or from the PLANET Mars —see also MARS

mar·tin /'maːtɪn‖'maːrtn/ *n* any of several sorts of bird (esp. the **house martin** and **sand martin**) of the SWALLOW family

Martin, Dean (1917–) an American actor and singer

Martin Chuz·zle·wit /ˌmaːtɪn 'tʃʌzəlwɪt‖ˌmaːrtn-/ a NOVEL by Charles Dickens published in 1843

mar·ti·net /ˌmaːtɪˈnet‖ˌmaːr-/ *n derog* a person who demands total, often unreasoning, obedience to rules and orders

mar·ti·ni /maːˈtiːni‖maːr-/ *n* [C;U] (a glass of) an alcoholic drink (COCKTAIL) made by mixing a spirit, usu. GIN and VERMOUTH: *a dry martini* (=one with a lot more gin than vermouth) | *a vodka martini*

Martini *n* [C;U] *BrE tdmk* (a glass of) an alcoholic drink made from wine with the addition of bitter or strong-tasting substances from roots and HERBs. It is usu. drunk before a meal, sometimes mixed with GIN.

Mar·ti·nique /ˌmaːtɪˈniːk‖ˌmaːrtnˈiːk/ a mountainous island in the Caribbean which is an overseas part of France. The main town is Fort-de-France; population 331,000 (1989)

mar·tyr¹ /'maːtəʳ‖'maːr-/ *n* 1 someone who is put to death or suffers for their beliefs, esp. for religious beliefs: *the early Christian martyrs* 2 *often derog* someone who gives up their own wishes or suffers something unpleasant in order to help other people or in the hope of receiving sympathy: *She only cleans all our shoes every evening because she enjoys being a martyr/enjoys making a martyr of herself.* 3 [(**to**)] *infml* someone who suffers something they cannot avoid, esp. a long-lasting illness: *She's a martyr to her rheumatism.*

martyr² *v* [T] to kill (someone) or cause (someone) to suffer greatly for a belief

mar·tyr·dom /'maːtədəm‖'maːrtər-/ *n* [U] the death or suffering of a martyr

mar·vel¹ /'maːvəl‖'maːr-/ *n* something (or someone) that causes wonder and admiration; wonderful thing or example: *What marvels met our eyes when we opened the treasure chest!* | *How they train those lions is a marvel to me.* | *This new furniture polish can do/work marvels.* (=produce wonderfully good results) | *He's a marvel; he still goes running every day even though he's over 80.*

marvel² *v* -ll- *BrE* ‖ -l- *AmE* [I (**at**);T] *fml* to be filled with great wonder, surprise, admiration, etc.: *We marvelled at their skill.* [+*that*] *The onlookers marvelled that he was unharmed after such a long fall.*

Mar·vell /'maːvəl‖'maːr-/, **Andrew** (1621–78) an English METAPHYSICAL poet and MP, known for his amusing love-poems. He also wrote SATIREs and political poems.

mar·vel·lous *BrE* ‖ **-velous** *AmE* /'maːvələs‖'maːr-/ *adj* causing great wonder, admiration, or pleasure, esp.

because extremely good, unusually clever, etc.: *What marvellous weather! | a marvellous idea − ~ly adv*

Mar·vin /ˈmɑːvɪ̯n‖ˈmɑːr-, **Lee** (1924–87) an American film actor known esp. for playing strong, violent characters in films such as *The Dirty Dozen* and *Point Blank*. He is also remembered for singing the song *I was Born under a Wandering Star* in a very deep voice.

Marx /mɑːks‖mɑːrks/, **Karl** /kɑːl‖kɑːrl/ (1818–83) a German political thinker and writer who, with Friedrich Engels, wrote the *Communist Manifesto* (1848) and established the basis for modern SOCIALISM and COMMUNISM. He was forced to leave Europe after the REVOLUTIONS of 1848, and lived in London where he wrote his most important work *Das Kapital*. Many people visit his grave in Highgate Cemetery, London. −see also COMMUNIST MANIFESTO

The Marx Brothers

Marx Broth·ers /ˈ· ˌ··/, **The** an American family of actors known for their special kind of humour and jokes. The most important members were **Groucho** (1895–1977), **Harpo** (1893–1964), who never spoke, and **Chico** (1891–1961). Their films include *Horse Feathers* and *Duck Soup*. Groucho is probably the best-known. He had large glasses, a MOUSTACHE, and a strange way of walking, and he always had a thick CIGAR. In the US he was also the host of a GAME SHOW called *You Bet Your Life* for many years.

Marx·is·m /ˈmɑːksɪzəm‖ˈmɑːr-/ n [U] the teachings of Karl Marx on which COMMUNISM and SOCIALISM are based, which explain the changes in history according to the struggle between social classes and say that this will in time lead to the fall of CAPITALISM and the victory of the working classes −−ist *n, adj*

Marxism-Len·in·is·m /ˌ··· ˈ····/ n [U] Marxism as explained, added to, and practised by Lenin, which says that society must be controlled by the workers until the establishment of a classless society −**Marxist-Leninist** *n, adj*

Ma·ry /ˈmeəri/, **the Virgin** according to the Bible, the mother of Jesus Christ and the most important SAINT, also called **Our Lady**. From earliest times, Christians (esp. CATHOLICS) have prayed to her when asking for help or cures.

Mary had a Lit·tle Lamb /ˌ··· ˌ· ˌ·· ˈ·/ a NURSERY RHYME (=an old song or poem for children):
Mary had a little lamb,
Its fleece was white as snow;
And everywhere that Mary went
The lamb was sure to go.

Mary I /ˌmeəri ðə ˈfɜːst‖-ˈfɜːrst/ also **Mary Tudor**− (1516–58) the daughter of Henry VIII of England and Katharine of Aragon. She became queen of England in 1553, and married Phillip II of Spain. She tried to make England return to the Catholic faith, and many Protestants who refused to do so were killed by being burnt. Because of this she was often called **Bloody Mary**.

Mary II /ˌmeəri ðə ˈsekənd/ see WILLIAM AND MARY

Ma·ry·land /ˈmeərɪlənd/ *written abbrev.* **MD**− a state on the E coast of the US, one of the 13 original colonies (COLONY). It has a very busy port at Baltimore. −see colour map on pages 1374–5

Mar·y·le·bone /ˈmærɪ̯ləbən‖ˈmerələbəʊn/ an area in W London, also the name of a railway station

Mary, Mary, Quite Con·tra·ry /ˌ··· ˌ··· ˌ· ·ˈ··/ the title and first line of a NURSERY RHYME (=an old song or poem for children):
Mary, Mary, quite contrary,
How does your garden grow?
With silver bells, and cockle shells,
And pretty maids all in a row.

Mary Mag·da·le·ne /ˌmeəri mægdəˈliːni, -ˈmægdəliːn/ see SAINT MARY MAGDALENE

Mary Pop·pins /ˌmeəri ˈpɒpɪ̯nz‖-ˈpɑː-/ (a character in) a children's book by P L Travers. Mary Poppins was a NANNY (=employed to take care of the children in a family) who had magical powers, e.g. being able to fly. The film *Mary Poppins* was very successful.

Mary Quant /ˌmeəri ˈkwɒnt‖-ˈkwɑːnt/ a British company, named after the woman who began it, that makes fashionable clothes for women, jewellery, and COSMETICS

Mary Queen of Scots /ˌ··· ˌ· · ˈ·/ also **Mary Stuart** /ˌ·· ˈ··/− (1542–87) the daughter of James V of Scotland and COUSIN of Elizabeth I of England. She became queen of Scotland as a baby. In 1567 she had to ABDICATE and ran away to England, where she spent the rest of her life as a prisoner. Many Catholics thought she should have been queen of England instead of Elizabeth I. She was thought to have been involved in a plan to kill Elizabeth, and Elizabeth ordered her to be killed. She was killed by having her head cut off. When Elizabeth died Mary's son, James VI of Scotland, also became king (James I) of England. In her life Mary had three husbands and many adventures. She is often thought of as a brave and beautiful woman and many stories and books have been written about her.

Mary Rose /ˌ·· ˈ·/, **The** a British warship which sank in the sea off the S coast of England on its first journey in 1545. The wreck was brought to the surface in 1982.

mar·zi·pan /ˈmɑːzɪ̯pæn‖ˈmɑːrtsɪ̯-, ˈmɑːrzɪ̯-/ n [U] a very sweet substance made from sugar, eggs, and finely crushed ALMONDS used for making sweets and for covering cakes, esp. wedding cakes

Ma·sai /ˈmɑːsaɪ/ n **1** [C] (a member of) a people of Kenya and Tanzania **2** [U] the language of the Masai −**Masai** *adj*

masc. *written abbrev. for:* MASCULINE (2)

mas·ca·ra /mæˈskɑːrə‖mæˈskærə/ n [U] a dark substance used by women to colour and thicken their eyelashes .
(EYELASH)

mas·cot /ˈmæskət‖ˈmæskɑːt/ n an object, animal, or person that is chosen as a SYMBOL and thought to bring good luck: *The football team's mascot is a goat.*

mas·cu·line /ˈmæskjʊlɪ̯n/ *adj* **1** of or having qualities that are considered typical of or suitable for a man, such as strength, authority, and a deep voice: *He looks very masculine in his new uniform. | She has a rather masculine voice.* **2** (in grammar) for or belonging to the class of words that usu. includes most of the words for males: *"Drake" is the masculine word for "duck". | The word for "book" is masculine in French. | a masculine ending −* compare FEMININE, NEUTER; see FEMININE (USAGE)

mas·cu·lin·i·ty /ˌmæskjʊˈlɪnɪti/ n [U] the quality of being MASCULINE (1)

Mase·field /ˈmeɪsfiːld/, **John** (1878–1967) an English writer and seaman, best known for his poems about the sea

ma·ser /ˈmeɪzəʳ/ n an apparatus for producing a very powerful electric force −compare LASER

Mas·e·ra·ti /ˌmæzəˈrɑːti‖ˌmɑːs-/ *tdmk* an expensive Italian car made by the Maserati company known for its speed and style

mash[1] /mæʃ/ v [T (UP)] to crush into a soft substance, often after cooking: *Mash (up) the potatoes with a fork.*

mash[2] n **1** [U] *BrE infml* mashed potatoes, esp. when eaten with SAUSAGES: *I love sausage and mash.* **2** [C;U] a mixture of grain, BRAN, etc., with water, forming a soft mass used as food for animals **3** [U] a mixture of MALT with hot water, used in making beer

M·A·S·H /mæʃ/ an American television programme made in the 1970s and 1980s and popular in the US and Britain, about an American army medical camp during the KOREAN WAR. Although a COMEDY, it also showed the effects that war has on people.

mashed po·ta·toes /ˌ·· ·ˈ··/ n [P] potatoes which have been boiled then crushed to make them soft

mask[1] /mɑːsk‖mæsk/ n a covering for the face or for part of the face (e.g. for the eyes or the nose or mouth) which hides or protects it, esp. so as to avoid being recognized, to protect the wearer from dangerous substances, or to protect others from infection: *Many of the dancers at the fancy dress ball wore colourful masks. | Surgeons wear*

Central London

N

Liverpool St. station

River Thames

1 km.

The City

Barbican Centre

Tower Bridge

Tower of London

St. Paul's Cathedral

The Old Bailey

Covent Garden

Embankment

National Theatre and Southbank

Waterloo station

Kings Cross station

British Museum

Leicester Square

National Gallery

Charing Cross station

Euston station

No 10.

St James Park

Houses of Parliament

Westminster Abbey

Regent's Park

Telecom Tower

West End

Trafalgar Square

Victoria station

Madame Tussauds

Oxford Street

Piccadilly Circus

Buckingham Palace

Baker Street

Paddington station

Hyde Park

Albert Hall

Harrods

The British Isles

The British Isles are made up of The United Kingdom (England, Scotland, Wales and Northern Ireland) and The Republic of Ireland.

The United Kingdom
capital city: London
money: pounds sterling

Northern Ireland
capital city: Belfast
patron saint: Saint Patrick
languages: English, Irish Gaelic

Republic of Ireland
capital city: Dublin
patron saint: Saint Patrick
languages: English, Irish Gaelic

Scotland
capital city: Edinburgh
patron saint: Saint Andrew
languages: English, Scottish Gaelic

England
capital city: London
patron saint: Saint George
language: English

Wales
capital city: Cardiff
patron saint: Saint David
languages: English, Welsh

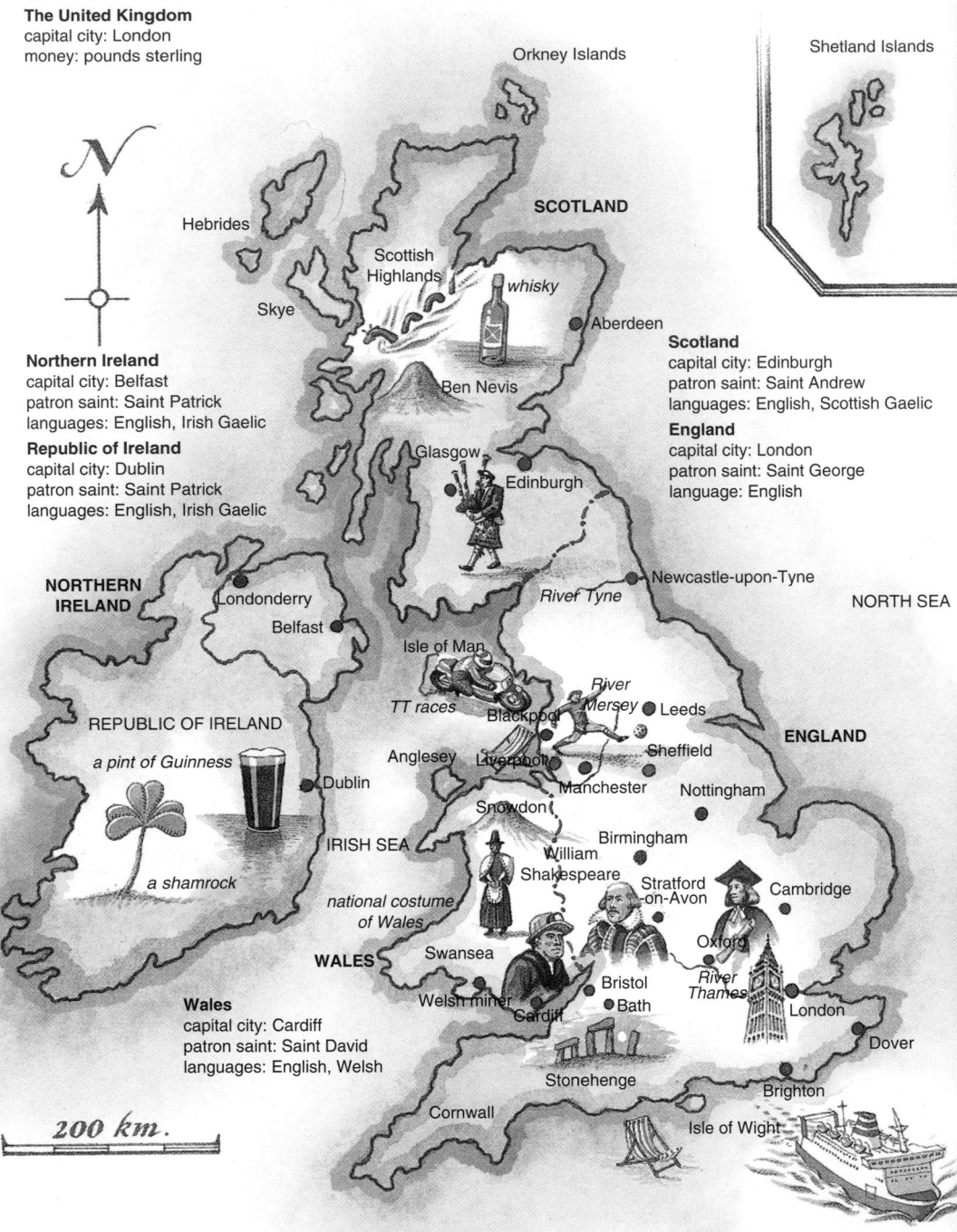

N

Orkney Islands

Shetland Islands

Hebrides

SCOTLAND

Scottish Highlands

whisky

Skye

Aberdeen

Ben Nevis

Glasgow

Edinburgh

Newcastle-upon-Tyne

River Tyne

NORTH SEA

NORTHERN IRELAND

Londonderry

Belfast

Isle of Man

TT races

River Mersey

Leeds

Blackpool

REPUBLIC OF IRELAND

Sheffield

ENGLAND

a pint of Guinness

Anglesey

Liverpool

Manchester

Nottingham

Dublin

Snowdon

Birmingham

a shamrock

IRISH SEA

William Shakespeare

Stratford-on-Avon

Cambridge

national costume of Wales

Oxford

WALES

Swansea

River Thames

Welsh miner

Bristol

London

Cardiff

Bath

Dover

200 km.

Stonehenge

Brighton

Cornwall

Isle of Wight

ENGLISH CHANNEL

cross-channel ferry

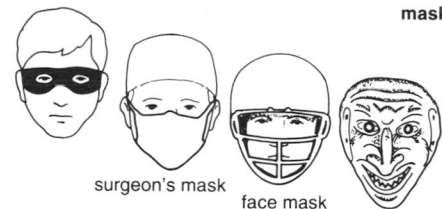

masks

surgeon's mask

face mask

masks to prevent the spread of infection. | a fencing mask | (fig.) *He hid his hatred under a mask of loyalty.* —see also DEATH MASK, GAS MASK and see picture at GOGGLES

mask² *v* [T] to hide (as if) with a mask; keep from being seen or noticed: *If you put in too much pepper you'll mask the delicate flavour of the sauce.* | *His smile masked his anger.* —see also UNMASK

masked /mɑːskt‖mæskt/ *adj* **1** wearing a mask: *The robbery was carried out by a gang of masked men.* **2** by or for people wearing masks: *a masked ball* **3 masked man** a way of referring to the Lone Ranger —see LONE RANGER

Mas·kell /'mæskəl/, **Dan** (1908–92) an English television and radio sports COMMENTATOR remembered esp. for his descriptions of tennis matches at Wimbledon

masking tape /'··· ·/ *n* [U] sticky material in a long narrow band used when painting a surface to cover the edge of any area which one wishes to leave unpainted

mas·o·chis·m /'mæsəkɪzəm/ *n* [U] **1** the gaining of pleasure from suffering pain or unpleasantness **2** the wish to be hurt so as to gain sexual pleasure —compare SADISM —**chist** *n* —**chistic** /ˌmæsəˈkɪstɪk◂/ *adj* : *masochistic tendencies*

ma·son /'meɪsən/ *n* **1** a STONEMASON **2** (*usu. cap.*) a FREEMASON

Mason, James (1909–84) a British actor who played ROMANTIC bad characters in British films in the 1940s and later worked in the US

Mason, Perry the main character in the books of Erle Stanley Gardner and in an American television programme of the 1960s about a lawyer who SOLVES crimes

Mason-Dix·on line /ˌmeɪsən ˈdɪksən laɪn/ [*the*] the border between the states of Maryland and Pennsylvania in the US. It is known for dividing the slave-owning states of the South from the free states of the North until the end of the American Civil War. Some people still consider it a dividing line between North and South.

ma·son·ic /məˈsɒnɪk‖məˈsɑː-/ *adj* (*often cap.*) of or connected with Freemasons or their beliefs, practices, etc.: *masonic rituals* | *a masonic lodge*

mason jar /'··· ·/ *n AmE* a glass pot with a tight lid used for preserving fruit and vegetables —compare KILNER JAR

ma·son·ry /'meɪsənri/ *n* [U] **1** stones from which a building, wall, etc., is made: *She was hurt by a piece of falling masonry.* **2** (*often cap.*) FREEMASONRY (1)

Ma·so·ra, Masorah /məˈsɔːrə/ [*the*] a set of notes about the Hebrew Old Testament, written in the thousand years up to 1000 AD

masque /mɑːsk‖mæsk/ *n* a theatrical play often performed in the 16th and 17th centuries for kings, queens, or noblemen, written in poetry and including music, dancing, and songs

mas·que·rade¹ /ˌmæskəˈreɪd/ *n* **1** something, esp. an action or way of behaving, that is intended to hide the truth; SHAM: *The neighbours know you've lost your job, so why keep up this masquerade of going out to work every day?* **2** a dance where people wear MASKS **3** *AmE for* FANCY DRESS: *We're going to have a masquerade party on Hallowe'en.*

masquerade² *v* [I (as)] to pretend (to be): *The robbers got into the bank by masquerading as security men.* —**rader** *n*

mass¹ /mæs/ *n* **1** [C (of)] a large solid lump or pile, usu. without a clear shape: *A great mass of rock had fallen from the cliff and now blocked the road.* **2** [C (of)] also

masses *pl.*— *infml* a large number; lots: *Her garden is a mass of flowers.* (=there are very many flowers in it) | *There are masses of people in here.* | *The mass of* (=most) *voters are in favour of these proposals.* **3** [U] *tech* (in science) the amount of matter in a body: *A litre of gas has less mass than a litre of water.* —see also MASSES

mass² *v* [I] to gather together in large numbers: *Crowds massed along the road where the queen would pass.* | *Dark clouds massed, and we expected rain.*

mass³ *adj* [A *no comp.*] of or for a large number, esp. of people: *a mass murderer* (=one who has killed many people) | *a mass walkout at the factory* | *mass unemployment*

mass⁴ *n* a piece of music written specially for all the main parts of the Mass

Mass *n* [C;(*the*) U] the main service in some Christian churches, esp. the Roman Catholic church. In it people eat bread and drink wine to represent the body and blood of Jesus Christ, which they believe he gave in order to save them: *to go to Mass* | *The priest* **celebrated (the) Mass.** —compare COMMUNION; see also HIGH MASS

Mas·sa·chu·setts /ˌmæsəˈtʃuːsɪts/ *written abbrev:* **MA, Mass.** a state in the NE of the US whose capital city is Boston. Massachusetts was where the PILGRIM FATHERS landed and was an important British COLONY before it became one of the 13 original states. —see colour map on pages 1374–5

mas·sa·cre¹ /'mæsəkər/ *n* **1** the cruel killing of large numbers of people, esp. those who cannot defend themselves: *the brutal massacre of thousands of innocent civilians* **2** *infml* a severe defeat: *It was a complete massacre; we lost 11-0!*

massacre² *v* [T] **1** to kill (a number of people) without pity: *They set fire to the city and massacred all its inhabitants.* —see KILL (USAGE) **2** *infml* to defeat severely

Massacre of the In·no·cents /ˌ····· · ·····/ [*the*] the killing of Jewish male children ordered by King Herod, as described in the Bible —see also HEROD

mas·sage¹ /'mæsɑːʒ‖məˈsɑːʒ/ *n* [C;U] (an act of) pressing and rubbing someone's body with one's hands, esp. in order to take away pain or stiffness from the muscles and joints: *to give/have a massage*

▶ CULTURAL NOTE When women advertise that they will give a massage in return for money, it is often understood that they are PROSTITUTES, but in some parts of the US massages are becoming very fashionable and some businesses even hire people to give their employees massages of the neck and shoulders. ◀

massage² *v* [T] **1** to give a massage to (someone or a part of the body) **2** to change (facts, figures, etc.), usu. in a dishonest way so that they appear better than they really are: *We suspected that the unemployment figures had been massaged.*

massage par·lour /'··· ˌ··‖·'·· ˌ··/ *n* **1** a place where one can pay to have a massage **2** *euph for* BROTHEL

▶ CULTURAL NOTE Because running a brothel is ILLEGAL in Britain and the US, houses where PROSTITUTES work are often advertised as massage parlours. ◀

mass·es /'mæsɪz/ *n* [*the*+P] *sometimes derog* the largest class of people in. society, esp. the WORKING CLASS: *He spent his life trying to improve the living conditions of the masses.*

mas·seur /mæˈsɜːʳ, mə-/ **mas·seuse** /mæˈsɜːz, mə-/ *fem.*— *n* someone who gives massages

Mas·sey Fer·gu·son /ˌmæsi ˈfɜːɡəsən‖-ˈfɜːr-/ a Canadian-owned company that makes and sells TRACTORs and farm machinery in many countries

mas·sif /'mæsiːf‖mæˈsiːf/ *n tech* a group of mountains forming one mass

mas·sive /'mæsɪv/ *adj* **1** of great size, esp. strong, solid, and heavy: *the castle's massive walls* | *the elephant's massive head* **2** great or greater than usual in degree, amount, power, severity, etc.: *He suffered a massive haemorrhage and died soon after.* | *massive efforts to improve productivity* | *massive doses of antibiotics to fight the infection* — ~ly *adv* — ~ness *n* [U]

mass me·di·a /ˌ· '····/ *n* [*the*+*sing.*/*pl. v*] the MEDIA

mass-pro·duce /ˌ· ·'·/ *v* [T] to produce (goods) in large numbers to the same pattern by machinery: *Mass-produced furniture is cheaper than furniture made by hand.*

mass pro·duc·tion /ˌ·· ·ˈ··/ n [U] the making of large numbers of the same article by a fixed method

mast /mɑːst‖mæst/ n **1** a long upright pole of wood or metal for carrying sails or flags on a ship —compare SPAR¹ (1), and see picture at YACHT **2** an upright metal framework for radio and television AERIALS **3** a flagpole —see also HALF-MAST **4 before the mast** *lit* on a sailing ship as an ordinary seaman, not as an officer

mas·tec·to·my /mæˈstektəmi/ n *med* an operation for the removal of a breast, usu. when BREAST CANCER has been discovered —compare LUMPECTOMY

mas·ter¹ /ˈmɑːstəʳ‖ˈmæ-/ n **1** a man in control of people, animals, or things: *The slaves rebelled against their masters.* | *His wife and children are always being rude to him and ordering him about. He's not even master in his own house.* | (fig.) *He prefers freelance work because he enjoys being* **his own master.** (=being independent) **2** *BrE* **mistress** *fem.*— a male teacher: *the maths master* — compare MISTRESS; see also HEADMASTER **3** a man who commands a ship carrying goods or passengers, or a large fishing boat **4** a man who has great skill in art or in working with his hands: *a master craftsman* | *The painting is the work of a master‖done by a master hand.* —see also GRAND MASTER, OLD MASTER, PAST MASTER **5** something from which copies are made: *a master tape* | *You've left your master (copy) in the photocopier.* **6** (*usu. cap., esp. BrE*) the head of certain university colleges: *the Master of King's College, Cambridge*

master² *adj* [A *no comp.*] **1** *tech or apprec* having a lot of skill as a result of long experience: *a master carpenter* | *a master chef* **2** chief; most important: *the master bedroom*

master³ *v* [T] **1** to learn thoroughly or gain a lot of skill in: *It takes years to master a new language.* | *He has never mastered the art of public speaking.* **2** to fight against (a bad feeling) so as not to be controlled by it: *He tried hard to master his fear of heights.*

Master *n old-fash* (used for addressing a young boy, esp. on a letter): *Master John Smith, 4 New Road*

master-at-arms /ˌ·· ·ˈ·/ n **masters-at-arms** an officer with police duties on a ship

master card /ˈ·· ·/ n a specially good reason, piece of knowledge, etc., which will have more effect than anything else: *At the climax of the meeting the chairman played his master card and announced that he had bought the company.*

Mas·ter·Card /ˈmɑːstəkɑːd‖ˈmæstərkɑːrd/ a large international CREDIT CARD system set up by a group of banks. Access is a member of the MasterCard system.

the symbol for **MasterCard**

mas·ter·ful /ˈmɑːstəfəl‖ˈmæstər-/ *adj apprec, esp. lit* (of people or behaviour) showing full control, understanding, etc. of people and situations: *The heroes of romantic fiction are supposed to be strong and masterful.* —compare MASTERLY — ~ **ly** *adv*

master key /ˈ·· ·/ n a key that will open several different locks

mas·ter·ly /ˈmɑːstəli‖ˈmæstərli/ *adj apprec* done or acting with very great skill: *a masterly summing-up of the situation* —compare MASTERFUL — **liness** n [U]

mas·ter·mind¹ /ˈmɑːstəmaɪnd‖ˈmæstər-/ n a very clever person, esp. one who is responsible for a plan: *the mastermind behind the robbery*

mastermind² *v* [T] *infml* to plan (an important or difficult course of action) cleverly: *to mastermind a crime*

Mastermind a British television programme in which members of the public compete to answer questions on general knowledge and on their own special subject. The programme is known for the large black chair that each person sits in to answer the questions and for the question master, Magnus MAGNUSSON. If a person does not know the answer to a question, they say "pass", and the next question is then asked. If the time for a person's questions finishes when Magnus Magnusson is in the middle of a question, he says "I've started so I'll finish" and he finishes asking the question.

Master of Arts /ˌ·· ·ˈ·/ n an MA

Master of Busi·ness Ad·min·is·tra·tion /ˌ·· ·ˈ·· ···ˌ·ˈ·/ n an MBA

master of ce·re·mo·nies /ˌ·· · ˈ····/ (*abbrev.* **MC**) ‖ also **emcee** *AmE*— n masters of ceremonies (*often caps.*) a person whose duty is to see that formal social occasions are carried out properly, to introduce speakers, etc.

Master of Sci·ence /ˌ·· · ˈ··/ n an MSC

Master of Fox·hounds /ˌ·· · ˈ··/ n Masters of Foxhounds the person, usu. a man, who arranges and controls the hunt in the sport of FOXHUNTING

Master of the Rolls /ˌ·· · · ˈ·/ n Masters of the Rolls a high-ranking judge in England and Wales who sits as head of the Court of Appeal

mas·ter·piece /ˈmɑːstəpiːs‖ˈmæstər-/ n a piece of work, esp. art, done with extreme skill, which is the best of its type or one of the best that a particular person has done: *The "Mona Lisa" was Leonardo's masterpiece.*

master plan /ˈ·· ·/ n a plan for controlling everything which happens in a complicated situation

mas·ter's /ˈmɑːstəz‖ˈmæstərs/ n *infml* (*often cap.*) **master's** a degree of MA, MSC, etc.: *He's planning on doing a master's in English literature.*

Masters and John·son /ˌ·· · ˈ··/ William Howell Masters (1915–) and Virginia Eshelman Johnson (1925–); an American team of scientists who have studied human sexual behaviour. Their best known work is *Human Sexual Response.*

Masters Tour·na·ment /ˈ·· ·ˌ··/ also **US Masters Tournament; US Masters**— [*the*] a GOLF competition held once each year in the US

mas·ter·stroke /ˈmɑːstəstrəʊk‖ˈmæstər-/ n a very skilful action or plan which results in complete success

master switch /ˈ·· ·ˌ·/ n a switch (SWITCH (1)) that controls all the other switches in an electrical CIRCUIT (3): *He threw the master switch and every light in the building went out.*

master·work /ˈmɑːstəwɜːk‖ˈmæstərwɜːrk/ n a MASTERPIECE, esp. one completed after long effort

mas·ter·y /ˈmɑːstəri‖ˈmæ-/ n [U] (**over, of**) **1** full power to control or defeat something: *mastery over‖of his fear* **2** great skill or knowledge in a particular subject or activity: *He shows complete mastery of his chosen subject.*

mast·head /ˈmɑːsthed‖ˈmæst-/ n **1** the top of a ship's MAST **2** the name of a newspaper, magazine, etc. often with the names of its owner, writers, etc. when printed at the top of the first page

mas·ti·cate /ˈmæstɪˌkeɪt/ v [I;T] *fml* to crush (food) thoroughly with the teeth; CHEW — **cation** /ˌmæstɪˈkeɪʃən/ n [U]

mas·tiff /ˈmæstɪf/ n a large powerful dog, often used to guard houses

mas·ti·tis /mæsˈtaɪtɪs/ n [U] *med* INFLAMMATION (swelling) of the breast

mas·to·don /ˈmæstədɒn‖-dɑːn/ n a large animal like an elephant, which no longer exists

mas·toid /ˈmæstɔɪd/ n *tech* a small bone behind the ear

Mas·troi·an·ni /ˌmæstrɔɪˈjɑːni/, **Mar·cel·lo** /mɑːˈtʃeləʊ‖mɑːr-/ (1923–) an Italian film actor, famous esp. for the film *La Dolce Vita*

mas·tur·bate /ˈmæstəbeɪt‖-ər-/ v [I] to excite one's own sex organs by handling, rubbing, etc. — **bation** /ˌmæstəˈbeɪʃən‖-ər-/ n [U]

▶ CULTURAL NOTE In the past, it was considered unhealthy to masturbate, and young men were told that if they did it they might become blind or go mad. ◀

mat¹ /mæt/ n **1** a piece of rough strong material for covering part of a floor; small RUG —SEE ALSO DOORMAT **2** a small piece of material for putting under objects on a table; TABLEMAT: *Put the hot dish down on the mat, so you don't burn the table.*

mat² *adj* not shiny; MATT —compare GLOSS¹

mat·a·dor /ˈmætədɔːʳ/ n the man who kills the BULL in a BULLFIGHT —compare PICADOR

Ma·ta Ha·ri /ˌmɑːtə ˈhɑːri/ (1876–1917) a Dutch dancer and member of the German secret service in Paris during the First World War, who obtained military secrets from Allied army officers of high rank. She was tried in court and shot by the French. She is often considered to be a good example of an attractive woman that men cannot refuse to please.

match[1] /mætʃ/ n **1** [C] esp. BrE a game or sports event where teams or people compete: *a football match* —see RECREATION (USAGE), TENNIS (USAGE) **2** [S (for)] a person who is equal to or better than another in strength, ability, etc.: *I'm no match for her when it comes to arithmetic.* | *He was very good at tennis, but he* met his match (=was beaten) *when he played the champion.* **3** [S (for)] a thing that is like another or is suitable to be put together with another, esp. by having a similar colour or pattern: *We can't find a match for this ornament.* | *The hat and shoes are a perfect match.* **4** [C *usu. sing.*] esp. old use **a** a possible husband or wife: *My son would be a good match for your daughter.* **b** a marriage of the stated kind: *Both her daughters made good matches.*

match[2] v **1 a** [I (UP);T] to be like or suitable for use with (another or each other), esp. in colour or pattern: *The curtains don't match the paint.* | *The curtains and the paint don't quite match.* | *a matching skirt and sweater* **b** [T (UP)] to find something like or suitable for use with: *I'm trying to match this yellow wool.* **2** [T] **a** [(in, for)] to be equal to or find an equal for: *His latest film doesn't match his previous ones.* | *This hotel can't be matched for* (=provides excellent) *service and food.* **b** [(to)] to make equal or suitable: *to match one's spending to one's income* **3** well-/ill-matched (of a pair) suitable/not suitable to be with, or to compete with, each other: *a well-matched husband and wife* | *The two boxers aren't very well-matched.* (=one is much better than the other)

match sbdy./sthg. **against** sbdy./sthg. *phr v* [T] to cause to compete against: *Ann will be matched against Jane in the semifinal.*

match up to/with sthg. *phr v* [T] to be as good as (something expected): *It wasn't a bad holiday, but the weather didn't match up to our hopes.*

match[3] n a short thin stick, usu. of wood, with a special substance covering one end which burns when the end is struck against a rough surface: *She lit her cigarette with a match.* | *to strike a match* | *a box/book of matches* —see SAFETY MATCH

match·book /'mætʃbʊk/ n a small, folded piece of heavy paper which contains paper matches. In the US, matchbooks often contain advertising and are given away free by businesses.

match·box /'mætʃbɒks‖-bɑːks/ n a small box in which matches are sold, with rough material along one or both sides on which to strike them

match·less /'mætʃləs/ adj fml or lit which has no equal in quality: *her matchless beauty* — ~ **ly** adv

match·mak·er /'mætʃˌmeɪkəʳ/ n a person who tries to arrange marriages or relationships, e.g. by introducing people to each other at social events —**-making** n [U]

Match of the Day /ˌ·· '·/ a television sports programme broadcast by the BBC which shows usu. the most important football match played on that day

match point /ˌ· '·‖'·· ·/ n [C;U] the situation in a game, esp. tennis, when one player will win the match if he/she gains the next point

match·stick /'mætʃˌstɪk/ n a single MATCH[3], esp. one that has been used

match·wood /'mætʃwʊd/ n [U] small thin pieces of wood: *The impact splintered the thin walls to matchwood.*

mate[1] /meɪt/ n **1** (*often in comb.*) a friend, or person one works with: *Her mates/workmates/schoolmates waited for her by the gate.* | *He's a mate of mine.* —see also RUNNING MATE, SOUL MATE **2** one of a male–female pair, usu. of animals: *The male hunts for food while his mate guards the nest.* **3** (not in the navy) a ship's officer next in rank below the captain: *the first mate* **4** BrE & AustrE infml (a friendly way of addressing a man, used esp. by working men): *"What time is it, mate?"* —see also MATEY **5** someone who works with and helps the stated kind of skilled workman: *a builder's/plumber's mate*

mate[2] v [I;T (with)] to become or make into a pair, esp. of animals, for the production of young: *Birds mate in the spring, the* mating season. | *They mated a horse with a donkey.*

mate[3] n, v CHECKMATE[1,2]

ma·té /'mɑːteɪ/ n [U] a kind of tea made from the leaves and stems of a South American plant

ma·ter /'meɪtəʳ, 'mɑː-‖'meɪ-/ n BrE (*sometimes cap.*) mother: *I'll have to ask Mater.* The word was formerly used by young UPPER-CLASS people, esp. boys at PUBLIC SCHOOL; now rarely used except humorously —compare PATER

ma·te·ri·al[1] /mə'tɪəriəl/ n **1** [C;U] anything from which something is or can be made; natural or man-made substance: *What kind of material is the bridge made of?* | *Rubber is a hard-wearing material.* | *Building materials are expensive.* | *writing materials, such as paper and pens* | (fig.) *He's excellent officer material.* (=a good enough soldier to become an officer) **2** [C;U] cloth: *a few metres of dress material* —see CLOTHES (USAGE) **3** [U (for)] information from which a (written) work is to be produced: *She's collecting material for a book.*

material[2] adj **1 a** of or having an effect on real or solid matter or substance, not spirit: *The storm did a great deal of material damage.* (=damaged buildings, property, etc.) **b** of the body, rather than the mind or soul; physical: *Food is a material need.* **2** [A] important and having a wide effect; SIGNIFICANT: *a material change in our plans* **3** [(to)] having an important connection; RELEVANT: *facts material to the investigation* —opposite **immaterial** — ~ **ly** adv

ma·te·ri·al·is·m /mə'tɪəriəlɪzəm/ n [U] **1** esp. derog (too) great interest in and desire for possessions, money, etc., rather than spiritual matters, art, etc. **2** tech the belief that only matter exists, and that there is no world of the spirit —compare IDEALISM —**-istic** /mə,tɪəriə'lɪstɪk◂/ adj: *our materialistic society* —**-istically** /kli/ adv

ma·te·ri·al·ist /mə'tɪəriəlʌst/ n **1** a person who believes that human actions are governed by the wish to gain things for oneself **2** a person who believes in MATERIALISM (2) —**materialist, materialistic** adj

ma·te·ri·al·ize also **-ise** BrE— /mə'tɪəriəlaɪz/ v **1** [I;T] to (cause to) begin to have physical form; appear: *The shape of a man materialized out of the shadows.* | *The magician appeared to materialize the rabbit from thin air!* | (fig.) *I'd arranged to meet him at seven, but he never materialized.* (=he did not come to meet me) **2** [I] (of something planned or expected) to become real or actual: *He always wanted a large family, but his hopes never materialized.* —**-ization** /mə,tɪəriəlaɪ'zeɪʃən‖-lə-/ n [U]

ma·ter·nal /mə'tɜːnl‖-ɜːr-/ adj **1** of, like, or natural to a mother: *her maternal feelings/instincts* | *maternal love* — compare MOTHERLY **2** [A] related to a person through the mother's side of the family: *my maternal grandfather* (=my mother's father) —compare PATERNAL — ~ **ly** adv

ma·ter·ni·ty[1] /mə'tɜːn‿ti‖-ɜːr-/ n [U] **1** fml the state of being a mother: *Maternity suits you!* —compare PATERNITY **2** a hospital department for the care of women before and after giving birth and for the care of newly born babies: *Trainee nurses have to work for some weeks in maternity.*

maternity[2] adj [A] for PREGNANCY and giving birth: *a maternity dress* | *the hospital's maternity ward*

maternity al·low·ance /·'···· ·,··/ also **maternity benefit**— n [U] (in Britain) money provided by the government to a woman before and after the birth of her child if she does not receive MATERNITY PAY —compare MATERNITY PAY

maternity ben·e·fit /·'···· ,····/ n see MATERNITY ALLOWANCE

maternity leave /·'···· ·,·/ n time that a mother spends away from work immediately before or after the birth of her baby. Maternity leave is taken with permission from the employer and usu. with part or full pay. In Britain, the law says that women who have worked for an employer for more than six months must be given maternity leave with some pay by the employer. In the US, maternity leave is decided by the employer, but many employers do not allow very much. —compare PATERNITY LEAVE

maternity pay /·'···· ·,·/ also **Statutory Maternity Pay** (SMP)— n (in Britain) money paid to a woman by her employer before and after the birth of her child if she has worked for that employer for more than six months — compare MATERNITY ALLOWANCE

Mates /meɪts/ tdmk a type of CONDOM sold in Britain

mat·ey /'meɪti/ adj infml, esp. BrE friendly

math·e·mat·i·cal /ˌmæθ‿'mætɪkəl◂/ adj **1** of or using mathematics: *a mathematical formula* | *a mathematical genius* **2** (of numbers, reasoning, etc.) exact; PRECISE: *It's a mathematical certainty.* (=is completely certain) | *a mathematical mind* —see picture at NOTATION — ~ **ly** /kli/ adv

math·e·ma·ti·cian /ˌmæθ‿məˈtɪʃən/ n a person who studies and understands mathematics

mathematical instruments

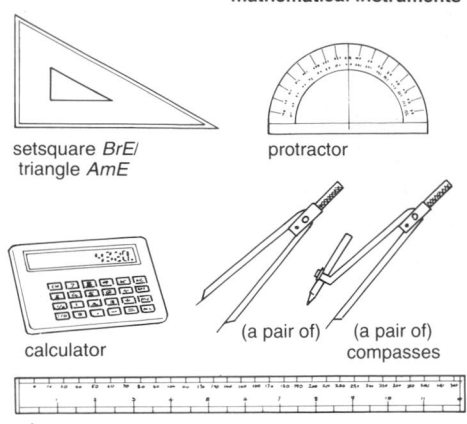

setsquare *BrE*/
triangle *AmE*

protractor

calculator

(a pair of) (a pair of)
compasses

ruler

math·e·mat·ics /ˌmæθˈmætɪks/ also **maths** /mæθs/*BrE* *infml* ‖ **math** /mæθ/*AmE*— n [U] the science of numbers and of the structure and measurement of shapes, including ALGEBRA and GEOMETRY as well as ARITHMETIC

Math·er /ˈmæðəʳ/, **Cotton** (1663–1728) an American PURITAN religious leader whose preaching (PREACH) helped make the fear of WITCHCRAFT worse —see also SALEM

mat·i·née /ˈmæt‿neɪ‖ˌmætənˈeɪ/ n a performance of a play or film given in the daytime, usu. in the afternoon

matinée i·dol /ˈ··· ˌ·‖·ˈ·ˌ·ˈ·/ n (esp. in the 1930s and 1940s) an actor who is very popular, esp. with women

matinée jack·et /ˈ··· ˌ··‖·ˈ·ˌ··/ n a short woollen coat for a baby

mat·ins , mat·tins /ˈmæt‿nz‖ˈmætnz/ n [U+*sing./pl. v*] (*often cap.*) MORNING PRAYER

Ma·tisse /mæˈtiːs/, **Hen·ri** /ˈɒnri‖ˈɑːn-/ (1869–1954) a French painter and SCULPTOR who was one of the leaders of Fauvism, a movement in French painting which used strong, pure colours

Mat·lock /ˈmætlɒk‖-lɑːk/ a town in Derbyshire, England, where the local government of that COUNTY is based

ma·tri·arch /ˈmeɪtriɑːk‖-ɑːrk/ n a woman, esp. a mother or grandmother, who rules a family or a group of people — compare PATRIARCH

ma·tri·ar·chal /ˌmeɪtriˈɑːkəl◂‖-ˈɑːr-/ adj **1** ruled or controlled by women: *a matriarchal society* **2** of or like a matriarch

ma·tri·ar·chy /ˈmeɪtriɑːki‖-ɑːr-/ n [C;U] (an example of) a social system in which the oldest woman is head of the family, and passes power and possessions on to her daughters —compare PATRIARCHY

mat·ri·cide /ˈmætr‿saɪd/ n **1** [U] *fml* the murder of one's mother **2** [C] *tech* a person guilty of this crime — compare PARRICIDE, PATRICIDE

ma·tric·u·late /məˈtrɪkjɣleɪt/ v [I] to become a member of a university, esp. after an examination or test —**lation** /məˌtrɪkjɣˈleɪʃən/ n [U]

mat·ri·mo·ny /ˈmætr‿məni‖-məʊni/ n [U] *fml* the state of being married —compare PATRIMONY —**nial** /ˌmætr‿ˈməʊniəl◂/ adj

ma·trix /ˈmeɪtrɪks/ n matrices /-tr‿siːz/ or matrixes *tech* **1** (in MATHEMATICS, science, etc.) an arrangement of numbers, figures, or signs in a square made up of ordered lines **2** a MOULD (hollow container) into which melted metal, plastic, etc., is poured to form it into a shape **3** the rock in which hard stones or jewels have been formed **4** a living part in which something is formed or developed, such as the substance out of which the fingernails grow

ma·tron /ˈmeɪtrən/ n **1** *BrE* a woman in charge of the nurses in a hospital (now officially called a **senior nursing officer**) **2** *esp. BrE* a woman in a school where

children live who is in charge of medical care, repair of clothes, living arrangements, etc.: *Ask Matron to bandage your hand.* **3** *esp. AmE* a woman who is in charge of women and/or children, e.g. in a prison or police station **4** *esp. lit or old use* an older married woman

ma·tron·ly /ˈmeɪtrənli/ adj *euph* (of a woman) middle-aged and rather fat: *a matronly figure*

matron of hon·our /ˌ··· ˈ··/ n matrons of honour a married woman who helps the bride at a marriage ceremony —compare BRIDESMAID

matt , mat, also **matte** *AmE* /mæt/ adj of a dull, not shiny, surface: *matt paint* | *photographs with a matt finish* — compare GLOSS¹

mat·ted /ˈmæt‿d/ adj twisted in a thick mass: *matted hair/branches*

mat·ter¹ /ˈmætəʳ/ n **1** [C] a subject to which one gives attention; situation or affair: *There are several important matters we must discuss.* | *He went out on a business matter.* | *That's an interesting idea, but not relevant to the* **matter in/at hand.** (=the subject or situation we are talking about or dealing with) | *She's committed a serious offence, but since she's so young we've decided to* **let the matter drop.** (=take no further action about it) | *Looking after fifteen noisy children is* **no laughing matter.** (=is difficult) | *It's one thing to talk about climbing Mount Everest, but to actually do so is* **quite another matter/another matter altogether.** (=is very much more serious/difficult) | *Whether or not it's healthier to be a vegetarian is* **a matter of opinion.** | *I've lost my bag, and* **to make matters worse** *it had all my money in it.* | *They wouldn't ask for help unless it were* **a matter of life and death.** (=a dangerously serious matter) | *He's furious with her now, but he'll forgive her eventually. It's just* **a matter of time.** | *Your mother would never allow it, and* **for that matter** (=as further concerns the same subject), *neither would I.* **2** [*the* (**with**)] a trouble or cause of pain, illness, etc.: *What's the* **matter**; *why are you crying?* | *There's nothing the* **matter**/*Nothing's the* **matter** *with me.* (=nothing is wrong) | *What's the* **matter** *with the radio? Why isn't it working?* **3** [U] the physical material of which everything that we can see or touch is made, as opposed to thought or mind; solids, liquids, and gases: *Scientists have calculated the entire amount of matter in the universe.* **4** [U] a subject itself as opposed to the form in which it is spoken or written about: *He's such a lively and entertaining speaker that his lectures are worth going to, even if the* **subject matter** *sounds dull.* **5** [U] things of a particular kind or for a particular purpose: *I must take some suitable* **reading matter** (=books, magazines, etc.) *for the journey.* | *advertising matter* | *vegetable matter* | *waste matter* **6 a matter of:** **a** a little more or less than; about: *only a matter of (a few) pennies* **b** needing as a part or result: *Learning languages isn't just a matter of remembering words.* **7 a matter of course** a usual event; something natural: *When I go out of the house, I lock the door as a matter of course.* **8 as a matter of fact** really; in fact: *"I thought you wouldn't mind." "Well, as a matter of fact I don't. But you should have asked me first."* —see also MATTER-OF-FACT; see FACT (USAGE) **9 no matter** (**how, where, etc.**) it makes no difference; however, wherever, etc.: *I'll finish the job, no matter how long it takes.* —see also GREY MATTER, **mince matters** (MINCE¹)

matter² v [I (**to**)] *often in negatives*] to be important: *It doesn't matter (to me) if I miss my train, because there's another one later.* | *It had never mattered much to her that she had not had a formal education.* (=she did not mind) | *I wasn't able to speak to her before she left — not that it matters though, because I can phone her tonight.*

Mat·ter·horn /ˈmætəhɔːn‖-tərhɔːrn/ [*the*] a mountain in the Alps near the border between Italy and Switzerland. It has attracted many climbers, and is known for its shape, which is like a PYRAMID

matter-of-fact /ˌ··· ˈ·◂/ adj concerned with facts, not imagination or feelings; practical: *He talked about his experiences as a prisoner of war in a very matter-of-fact way.* —**~ly** adv —**~ness** n [U]

Mat·thau /ˈmæθaʊ/, **Wal·ter** /ˈwɔːltəʳ/ (1922–) an American actor in films and theatre, known esp. for his humorous ROLEs, e.g. in *The Odd Couple*

Matthew, Saint see SAINT MATTHEW

Mat·thews /ˈmæθjuːz/, **Sir Stanley** (1915–) an English football player who played as a professional for 33 years until he was 49. He played for England 54 times and was known esp. for his skill in running with the ball on the WING.

mat·ting /ˈmætɪŋ/ n [U] rough material for making mats: *coconut matting*

mat·tins /ˈmætɪnz‖ˈmætnz/ n [U+sing.|pl. v] (*often cap.*) MORNING PRAYER

mat·tress /ˈmætrɪs/ n the part of a bed that one lies on, consisting of a strong cloth cover filled with soft material or springs: *I'll have to get a new mattress for my bed — the springs have gone in this one.*

ma·tu·ra·tion /ˌmætʃ‿ˈreɪʃən/ n [U] the process or time of becoming mature

ma·ture¹ /məˈtʃʊər/ adj **1 a** fully grown and developed **b** *apprec* having or typical of a fully developed mind; sensible and reasonable: *She's very mature for her age.* | *a mature attitude* —opposite **immature** —see ADOLESCENT, ADULT **2** (of cheese, wine, etc.) old enough to be ready to be eaten or drunk **3** *fml* carefully decided, after a time of thought: *On mature reflection I've decided to go by train.* **4** *tech* (of a bill) ready to be paid **5** older than the usual age for something: *The Centre offers the mature learner opportunities to develop new skills.* — ~ **ly** adv

mature² v [I;T] to (cause to) become mature: *After six years, the wine will have matured.*

Mature, Victor (1916–) an American film actor

mature stu·dent /·ˌ· ˈ··/ n BrE a student at a university or college who is aged over 25. A growing number of people are now beginning to study after having worked for some years or brought up children. Most universities and colleges encourage them and some run special courses to help them learn to study.

ma·tu·ri·ty /məˈtʃʊərˌti/ n [U] the state or time of being mature

maud·lin /ˈmɔːdlɪn/ adj stupidly sad, esp. when drunk

Maugham /mɔːm/, **W Somerset** (1874–1965) a British writer considered to be one of the best short story writers in English. His best-known NOVEL is *Of Human Bondage.*

maul /mɔːl/ v [T] **1** (esp. of animals) to hurt badly by tearing the flesh: *The hunter was mauled by a lion.* **2** to handle roughly or in an unwelcome way: *If you don't stop mauling me* (=handling me roughly in a sexual way) *I'll slap your face!* | (fig.) *His speech sounded quite different when the newspapers had mauled it (about).*

Mau Mau /ˈmaʊ maʊ/ [*the*] a secret political organization established in Kenya in 1952 by the Kikuyu people with the aim of driving out the Europeans. It led a bloody struggle against the British colonial (COLONY) government. Kenya gained independence in 1963.

maun·der /ˈmɔːndər/ v [I (ON, about)] *often derog* to talk in an unclear and usu. complaining way

Maun·dy mon·ey /ˈmɔːndɪ ˌmʌnɪ/ n [U] specially-made coins given to chosen poor people by a British king or queen in a ceremony on **Maundy Thursday**, the Thursday before Easter

Mau·pas·sant /ˈməʊpæsɒn ‖ -ˌməʊpəˈsɑːn/, **Guy de** (1850–93) a French writer considered to be one of the great writers of short stories. He died after becoming mad owing to SYPHILIS.

Mau·ri·ac /ˈmɔːriˌæk‖mɔːriˈæk/, **Fran·çois** /ˈfrɒnswɑː‖ frɑːnˈswɑː/ (1885–1970) a French writer and winner of the Nobel prize for literature in 1952

Mau·ri·ta·ni·a /ˌmɒrˌˈteɪniə‖ˌmɔːr-/ a country in NW Africa on the Atlantic coast; capital Nouakchott; population 1,970,000 (1989) —**nian** n,adj

Mau·ri·tius /məˈrɪʃəs‖mɔː-/ an island and country in the SW Indian Ocean, an independent state within the COMMON-WEALTH (1); capital Port Louis; population 1,090,000 (1989) —**Mauritian** n,adj

mau·so·le·um /ˌmɔːsəˈliːəm/ n a large, often decorative stone building built over a grave or containing many graves; an important-looking TOMB

mauve /məʊv/ adj having a pale purple colour —**mauve** n [U]

ma·ven /ˈmeɪvən/ n AmE a person who knows a lot about a stated subject: *a cultural|Chinese-food maven*

mav·e·rick /ˈmævərɪk/ n derog in BrE someone, esp. a politician, who is determined to be different or act differently from the rest of their group

maw /mɔː/ n **1** an animal's throat or stomach **2** something which seems to swallow things up: *money disappearing into the maw of the national budget*

mawk·ish /ˈmɔːkɪʃ/ adj (of people or behaviour) expressing love and admiration in a silly perhaps false way — ~ **ly** adv — ~ **ness** n [U]

max¹ /mæks/ adj, n [U] *infml for* MAXIMUM: *We enjoyed the party to the max.*

max²

max out *phr v* [I] *AmE sl* to do or give the maximum amount possible: *I'd really maxed out that month at work, so I just slept for three days when I had time off.*

Max Fac·tor /ˌ·ˈ··/ *tdmk* a company which produces COSMETICS

max·im /ˈmæksˌm/ n a short saying that expresses a general truth or a rule for good and sensible behaviour: *"Waste not, want not" is her favourite maxim.*

max·i·mal /ˈmæksˌməl/ adj fml as great as possible: *of maximal educational value* —compare MINIMAL — ~ **ly** adv

max·i·mize also **-mise** BrE /ˈmæksˌmaɪz/ v [T] to increase to the greatest possible size or amount: *We must maximize output|our chances of success.* —compare MINIMIZE —**mization** /ˌmæksˌmaɪˈzeɪʃən‖-sˌmə-/ n [U]

Max·im's /ˈmæksˌmz/ a famous French restaurant and night club in Paris. They are expensive, and considered to be places where rich and famous people go.

max·i·mum /ˈmæksˌməm/ adj, n **-ma** /mə/ or **-mums** [A (of);C] (being) the largest number, amount, etc.: *What's the maximum amount of wine you're allowed to take through customs duty-free?* | *maximum speed|depth* | *He smokes (up to) a maximum of ten cigarettes a day.* | *Let me drive — you're over the maximum.* (=have more alcohol in your blood than is allowed by law when driving) —compare MINIMUM

Max·well /ˈmækswel/, **Rob·ert** /ˈrɒbət‖ˈrɑːbərt/ (1923–91) a British PUBLISHER, newspaper owner, and businessman, born in Czechoslovakia. He was head of MIRROR GROUP NEWSPAPERS. He was sometimes called "Captain Bob". He died suddenly, falling into the water from his boat. Since his death, it has been discovered that his financial dealings were not always honest and legal.

Maxwell House /ˌ·· ˈ·/ *tdmk* a type of INSTANT coffee

may¹ /meɪ/ v 3rd person sing. **may**, *negative short form (esp. BrE)* **mayn't** /*modal+to-v*/ **1** (used to show possibility) to be perhaps likely to: *He may come or he may not.* | *"Why hasn't he come?" "He may have missed the train."* (=perhaps he has missed it; we still do not know) | *He may have stopped to talk to someone – that's why he isn't here.* | *We will do whatever may be necessary.* —compare MIGHT¹ (1) **2** to have permission to; be allowed to (now less common than **can**): *"May I come in?" "Yes, you may."* | *May I leave this with you?* | *I may say I find your questions rather rude.* (=I think they are rude) | *May I give you a hand with the dishes?* —compare MIGHT¹ (3) **3** *fml* (used when expressing a wish, usu. with the subject after the verb): *May you have a very happy married life!* (=I|we very much hope that you will have this) **4** also **might** (used, followed by **but**, when admitting a point that goes against the main thing one is saying) perhaps; ADMIT-TEDLY: *He may be fat, but he can still run fast.* | *You may think you're clever, but that doesn't give you the right to order me about.* | (*although you think you're clever, that does not* ...) | *That coat may have cost a lot of money, but it's worth it.* **5** (in CLAUSES expressing hope or purpose) will; can: *Let's talk it over, so that we may come to a decision.* | *The doctor fears that she may die.* —compare MIGHT¹ (5) **6 may well (not)** to be very likely (not) to: *His appearance has changed so much that you may well not recognize him.* | *She may well refuse to speak to you, because she's in a very bad mood.* —compare **might well** (MIGHT) **7 may/might (just) as well** to have no strong reason not to: *It's late, so I may as well go to bed.* —see CAN (USAGE), COULD (USAGE), MIGHT (USAGE), NOT (USAGE)

may² n [U] HAWTHORN flowers

May n [C;U] the fifth month of the year, between April and June: *It happened on May the sixth|on the sixth of May|(AmE) on May sixth.* | *This office opened in May 1991.* | *She started work here last May|the May before last.*

▶CULTURAL NOTE May is a Spring month and the weather is often warm. May is sometimes referred to as the "merry month of May".◀

Ma·ya /ˈmaɪə/ n [C; *the* +P] (a member of) a Native American people chiefly of the Yucatan area who had developed an established civilization before the discovery of America by Europeans —**Maya** adj —**Mayan** n, adj: *Mayan civilization/inscriptions*

May Ball /ˌ· ˈ·/ n a formal dance held at the universities of Oxford and Cambridge every year in June. Students dress formally for a May Ball, and it is expensive to go to one.

may·be /ˈmeɪbi/ adv perhaps; possibly: *"Will they come?" "Maybe."* | *Maybe it's my imagination, but it seems rather cold in here — is the window open?*

▷ USAGE 1 **Maybe** is more informal than **perhaps.** 2 It can be used to make polite suggestions or requests: **Maybe** *we should meet sometime next week.* | **Maybe** *I could come to your place.* | **Maybe** *you could move that chair.* | *(You could) put it over here,* **maybe.** —see also PERHAPS (USAGE)◁

may·day /ˈmeɪdeɪ/ n (a radio signal used as) a call for help from a ship or plane: *the plane sent out a mayday (call)*

May Day /ˈ· ·/ n [C;U] the first day of May, when workers' associations and political parties of the LEFT² (2) in some countries march through the streets **May Day parades** and hold public meetings, and when in former times people welcomed spring with games and dances. It is not a public holiday in Britain. In Britain there are still some local customs and celebrations although these may not be held on May Day itself but on the May Day bank holiday, the first Monday in May. In the US young children often dance around a maypole at school, and often leave small baskets of flowers at a friend's door to be found on May Day morning. —see also MAY QUEEN

May·fair /ˈmeɪfeəʳ/ an area in W central London with many clubs and hotels. It is considered to be a fashionable area where only rich people can afford to live or stay in hotels.

May·flow·er /ˈmeɪflaʊəʳ/ [*the*] the ship that took a group of English settlers to Plymouth, Massachusetts in the US in 1620. Many of the settlers were religious and they are usually called the PILGRIM FATHERS. In the US people respect a person whose family "came over on the Mayflower," but since very few people can claim this, it is not unusual for people to make jokes about it.

may·fly /ˈmeɪflaɪ/ n a type of insect. The adults are very light and delicate and live for only a few days.

may·hem /ˈmeɪhem/ n [U] great disorder and confusion: *The escape of the monkeys from their cage created mayhem in the zoo.*

may·n't /ˈmeɪənt/ esp. BrE short for: may not

May·o /ˈmeɪəʊ/ a COUNTY in the W of the Republic of Ireland

Mayo Clin·ic /ˈ·· ˌ··/ [*the*] a medical institution and hospital in Rochester, Minnesota, famous in the US for its many excellent doctors, modern equipment, and successful treatments

may·on·naise /ˌmeɪəˈneɪz‖ˈmeɪəneɪz/ ‖ also **mayo** AmE infml— n [U] a thick cold pale yellow SAUCE made with eggs, oil, and VINEGAR, for eating with SALADs and other cold food. It is known to be difficult to make and many people buy it ready-made.

mayor /meəʳ‖ˈmeɪər/ n 1 BrE a person elected each year by a town council to be head of that city or town; the mayor often carries out duties such as opening new buildings, entertaining important visitors, and attending public ceremonies. A mayor can be a man or a woman and is addressed as "The Worshipful the Mayor of..." or "The Right Worshipful" and usu. wears a large chain of office. —compare PROVOST 2 AmE the head of government in a town or city. Mayors are usu. elected by popular vote and belong to one of the two main political parties. In large cities they are often very powerful, sometimes more so than the GOVERNOR of their state. — ~al adj

mayor·al·ty /ˈmeərəlti‖ˈmeɪərəlti/ n [U] the position of mayor or the time during which it is held

mayor·ess /ˈmeərˌs‖ˈmeɪərˌs/ n the wife of a mayor or a woman chosen to receive his guests

Mayor of Cas·ter·bridge /ˌmeɪər əv ˈkɑːstəbrɪdʒ‖ˌmeɪər əv ˈkæstər-/, **The** a NOVEL by Thomas Hardy (1886) describing the rise and fall of a farm worker who becomes Mayor of a town called Casterbridge but dies a poor and ruined man

maypole

may·pole /ˈmeɪpəʊl/ n a tall decorated pole round which people dance on May Day, each dancer holding a RIBBON tied to the top of the pole and making patterns with the ribbons as they danced. In former times most villages in England had a maypole, and now maypoles are sometimes seen as part of a FETE. The dancers are usu. children. —see also MAY DAY

May Queen /ˌ· ˈ·/ n a girl or young woman who is chosen and crowned as part of the May Day celebrations, usu. because she is judged to be very attractive. She wears a crown of flowers and is also called **Queen of the May.** —see also MAY DAY

Mays /meɪz/, **Willie** (1931–) an American BASEBALL player who was famous in the 1950s

mayst /meɪst/ v thou mayst old use or bibl (when talking to one person) you may

Maz·a·rin Bi·ble /ˌmæzərɪn ˈbaɪbəl/ [*the*] a BIBLE (=main religious book of Christians) printed in Germany around 1455 and the earliest European book printed from movable TYPE

Maz·da /ˈmæzdə/ tdmk a car made by the Japanese Mazda company

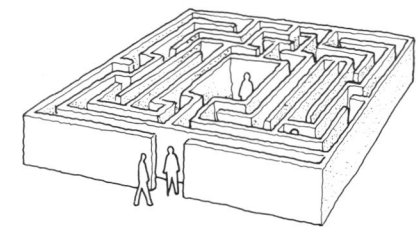

maze

maze /meɪz/ n a system of twisting and turning paths leading to a central point. The paths are usu. separated from each other by high HEDGEs, walls, etc., and are sometimes blocked off, so as to confuse someone who walks through them: *She was lost in the maze for several hours.* | (fig.) *a maze of narrow winding streets*

maz·el tov /ˈmæzəl tɒf‖ˈmɑːzəl tɔːf/ a Jewish expression meaning good luck or best wishes

Maze Pris·on /ˌ· ˈ··/ also **Maze—** [*the*] a prison in Northern Ireland where many prisoners, both Protestant and Catholic, are held for TERRORIST offences. In 1981 some IRA prisoners went on HUNGER STRIKE because they wanted to be regarded as political prisoners. One prisoner, Bobby Sands, was elected MP while on hunger strike. He and several others died.

Ma·zo·la /məˈzəʊlə/ also **Mazola Oil** /·ˌ·· ˈ·/— n tdmk [U] a kind of oil used in cooking, sold in Britain and the US

ma·zur·ka /məˈzɜːkə‖-ɜːr-/ n (a piece of quick lively music for) a Polish dance

MB /ˌem ˈbiː/ abbrev. for: Bachelor of Medicine: Jane Doe, MB

MBA /ˌem biː ˈeɪ/ Master of Business Administration; (a title for someone who has) a degree in which students learn the skills needed to be in charge of a business: He's thinking of doing an MBA.

Mba·ba·ne /əmbɑːˈbɑːni ‖ ˌembəˈbɑːn/ a town and business centre which is the capital of Swaziland

MBE /ˌem biː ˈiː/ n Member of the (Order of the) British Empire; an honour given to people for public service, esp. in industry or the arts

MBSc /ˌem biː es ˈsiː/ abbrev. for: Master of Business Science (a title for someone who has) a higher university degree in business science: Derek Jameson, MBSc

Mc to find a name which begins with **Mc**, look under **Mac**

MC /ˌem ˈsiː/ n MASTER OF CEREMONIES

MCAT /ˈem kæt/ n Medical College Admissions Test, an examination which must be taken by anyone who wants to attend MEDICAL SCHOOL in the US

MCC /ˌem siː ˈsiː/ [the] the **Marylebone Cricket Club**; a private CRICKET club established in 1787 and based at **Lord's** CRICKET ground in London. Until 1968 it arranged all foreign tours and the England team still wear the club colours of red and yellow. The club is still responsible for the Laws of Cricket. —see also CRICKET

MCP /ˌem siː ˈpiː/ BrE infml abbrev. for: male chauvinist pig; a man who behaves unreasonably towards women because he thinks them less able than men

Md written abbrev. for: MARYLAND

MD /ˌem ˈdiː/ abbrev. for: 1 Doctor of Medicine: John Snow, MD 2 Managing Director

MDS /ˌem diː ˈes/ n Master of Dental Surgery; a British QUALIFICATION obtained by someone who wants to become a DENTIST —compare DDS

MDT /ˌem diː ˈtiː/ abbrev. for: MOUNTAIN DAYLIGHT TIME

me /mi; strong miː/ pron (object form of I): He bought me a drink. | He bought a drink for me. | Show me your photos. | Show them to me again. | That's me on the left of the photograph. —see also ME GENERATION

▷ USAGE **Me, her, him, us**, and **them** are usually used in conversation after as, than, and be: I'm not as clever as **her**. | I'm fatter than **him**. | It's **me**. In formal writing it is possible to write **I, she, he, we**, and **they**: as clever as **she** | fatter than **he** | It is **I**. But, people usually try to express the idea in a different way: I'm not as clever as **she** is. | I'm fatter than **he** is. | I am the one/the person/etc.◁

ME¹ /ˌem ˈiː/ also **post viral fatigue syndrome**— n [U] myalgic encephalomyelitis, an illness which causes pain in one's muscles and which makes one feel tired, weak, and unhappy. It can last for a few months or years.

ME² written abbrev. for: 1 MAINE 2 MIDDLE ENGLISH

me·a cul·pa /ˌmeɪə ˈkʊlpə/ n, interj Lat a formal statement made in a Roman Catholic religious service by a person admitting that they have sinned (SIN²): (fig.) "Who forgot to file today's correspondence?" "Ah, mea culpa, old chap!"

mead /miːd/ n 1 [U] an alcoholic drink made from HONEY, drunk esp. formerly in England 2 [C] poet a meadow

Mead, Lake the largest RESERVOIR in the US, on the Colorado river behind the Hoover Dam

Mead¹, Margaret 2 (1901–78) an American anthropologist (ANTHROPOLOGY) who studied the ways in which different peoples, esp. those in the Pacific Islands, bring up children, and asked whether differences in behaviour between males and females were natural or learned. Her best-known books are Growing Up in New Guinea and Coming of Age in Samoa.

mead·ow /ˈmedəʊ/ n [C;U] a field or fields of wild grass and flowers on which cattle, sheep, etc., can feed —see also WATER MEADOW

mea·gre BrE ‖ **-ger** AmE /ˈmiːgər/ adj not enough in quantity, quality, strength, etc.: his meagre income | a meagre diet – ~**ly** adv – ~**ness** n [U]

meal¹ /miːl/ n 1 an amount of food eaten at one time, usu. consisting of two or more dishes: She usually

makes/cooks a hot meal in the evenings. | Breakfast is my favourite meal. 2 also **meal-time** /ˈmiːltaɪm/— the time of eating a meal: The family only meets at meals. 3 **make a meal of** derog to give (something) more effort, consideration, or time than it deserves —see also SQUARE MEAL

meal² n [U] grain which has been crushed into a powder, esp. for flour —see also BONE MEAL, CORN MEAL, OATMEAL

meals on wheels /ˌ·· ˈ·/ n [P] a service which provides hot meals to old or sick people in their homes, delivered by car by the SOCIAL SERVICES or the WRVS in Britain, and often by VOLUNTEERS in the US

meal tick·et /ˈ· ˌ··/ n infml a person or organization that can be depended upon to provide help and support without asking for anything in return (from the ticket given to workers in certain companies or the army that allows them to have a free meal)

meal·y /ˈmiːli/ adj 1 like or containing MEAL² 2 pale and powdery; FLOURY: mealy potatoes

mealy-mouthed /ˌ·· ˈ·◁/ adj derog (of people or speech) expressing things indirectly, not plainly, esp. when something unpleasant must be said: mealy-mouthed politicians/statements

mean¹ /miːn/ adj 1 [(with)] BrE unwilling to give or share what one has; ungenerous: He's very mean with his money. 2 [(to)] unkind; nasty: It was mean of you not to let the children play in the snow. | Don't be so mean to her! | He's got a mean streak in him. (=sometimes behaves unpleasantly) 3 esp. AmE bad-tempered; liking to hurt: That's a mean dog. Be careful it doesn't bite you. 4 [A] lit or old use of low social position: a man of mean birth 5 esp. lit (esp. of a place) poor or poor-looking: mean streets 6 sl, esp. AmE very good: She makes a mean chicken stew. 7 **no mean (something)** a very good (something): He's no mean cook. | Running ten miles is no mean achievement. – ~**ly** adv – ~**ness** n [U]

mean² v **meant** /ment/ [T not in progressive forms] 1 to represent or express (a meaning): What does this French word mean? | The red light means "Stop". [+that] The sign means that cars cannot enter. 2 to have in mind as a purpose; intend: She said Tuesday, but she meant Thursday. | He's very angry, and means trouble. (=intends to cause trouble) | I mean what I say. (=I am speaking seriously, and you should believe me.) [+to-v] I mean to go tomorrow. | I'm sorry; I didn't mean to imply that you were dishonest. [+(that)] He didn't express himself very clearly, but he means that he wants your help. | What do you mean, he's left? (=I can't believe he has really left) He said he'd stay till 6 o'clock. [obj(i)+obj(d)] Although she seems angry, she means you no harm. | This warning was meant for you. [+obj+to-v] How embarrassing! I never meant him to read what I wrote about him. | Is that blob in the corner of the picture meant to be a tree? 3 to be a sign of: The dark clouds mean rain. [+(that)] That expression means that she's angry. [+v-ing] Missing the train means waiting (=we will have to wait) for an hour. | A few marks can mean the difference between success and failure in an exam. 4 [(to)] to be of importance to the stated degree: In running a company, strict financial management means everything. | Her work means a lot/means everything to her. 5 **be meant to** esp. BrE to have to; be supposed to: You're meant to take your shoes off when you enter a Hindu temple. 6 **mean business** to act with serious intentions: Watch out. I think the guy with the gun means business. 7 **mean mischief** to have bad intentions 8 **mean well** to do or say what is intended to help, but often does not: I agree it was a bit tactless of her to say that, but she meant well. —see also WELL-MEANING, WELL-MEANT

▷ USAGE 1 The expression **I mean** /ə ˈmiːn/ is often used in conversation when you want to make something you have said clearer, by explaining it, repeating it in another way, or adding new information about it: He's really very rude. **I mean**, he never even says "Good morning". | My boss, **I mean** the person in charge of the office, left last week. It is also used to correct something you have just said: She plays the violin, **I mean** the viola, really well. 2 The expression **I mean to say** /· ·ˈ· · ·/ usually shows that you disapprove of something: He can't be allowed to behave like that. **I mean to say**, he's a grown man. | "She asked me to lend her my car." "Well, **I mean to say!**" (=I don't approve of her asking.) 3 The expression **What do you mean** … ? can be used to show annoyance or disagreement with something someone has just said: **What do you mean,** *you don't like my cooking?* | **What do you mean by** ... **?** can also introduce an angry protest: **What do you mean by** *coming home so late?*◁

mean³ *n* [*usu. sing.*] **1** an average amount, figure, or value: *The mean of 7, 9, and 14 is 10.* **2** a state or way of behaviour or course of action which is not too strong or too weak, too much or too little, but in between, in the middle position: *It's a question of finding the mean between too lenient treatment and too severe punishment.* –see also MEANS, GOLDEN MEAN

mean⁴ *adj* [A] (of measurements) average: *The mean yearly rainfall is 20 inches.* –see also GREENWICH MEAN TIME

me·an·der /mɪˈændəʳ/ *v* [I] **1** (of rivers and streams) to flow slowly, with many turns **2** to wander in a slow easy aimless way: *We usually meander down to the pub after dinner.* | (fig.) *She'd begun to meander on* (=speak in a long disordered way) *about some irrelevant topic, so the chairman shut her up.* – ~**ingly** *adv* – ~**ings** *n* [P]

mean·ie, meany /ˈmiːniː/ *n infml* a person who is unkind or ungenerous: *You old meanie.*

mean·ing¹ /ˈmiːnɪŋ/ *n* [C;U] **1** that which you are intended to understand by something spoken or written, or by something expressed in other ways, such as by signs: *One word can have several meanings.* **2** importance or value: *He says his life has lost its meaning (for him) since his wife died.* | *I can't quite grasp the meaning of these figures.* **3** an aim or intention, esp. a hidden one: *What's the meaning of this?* (often said when demanding an explanation of something that makes one angry) | *a look full of meaning*

meaning² *adj* [A] giving an effect of important (hidden) meaning or thought: *a meaning look* –see also WELL-MEANING

mean·ing·ful /ˈmiːnɪŋfəl/ *adj* having important meaning or value: *a meaningful statement* | *At such an advanced age they can no longer play a meaningful role in the company's affairs.* – ~**ly** *adv* – ~**ness** *n* [U]

mean·ing·less /ˈmiːnɪŋləs/ *adj* without meaning or purpose: *a meaningless existence* – ~**ly** *adv* – ~**ness** *n* [U]

means /miːnz/ *n* **means** **1** [C (**of**)+*sing./pl. v*] a method or way (of doing): *The quickest means of travel is by plane.* | *Use whatever means you can to persuade him.* | *I gave him a bicycle as* **a means to an end** (=a way of getting a result): *I want him to take more exercise.* | *Have you got any* **means of identification** (=a document showing your name and address)? **2** [P] money, income, or wealth, esp. large enough to afford all one needs: *Have you the means to support a family?* | *a man of means* (=a rich man) | *They have private means.* (=get income which they do not have to work for) | *to live* **beyond one's means** (=spend too much) **3** by **'all means** politely certainly; please do: *"May I borrow your paper?" "By all means."* **4** by **means of** by using: *We express our thoughts by means of words.* **5** by **'no means** *fml* not at all: *It is by no means certain.* –see also WAYS AND MEANS, **not by any manner of means** (MANNER)

means test /ˈ· ·/ *n* an inquiry into the amount of money someone has, esp. to find out if they have so little that they can be given money by the state –**means-test** *v* [T]: *means-tested benefits*

mean streets /ˈ· ˌ·/ *n* [P] areas in cities which are dangerous and difficult to live in: *a coming-of-age drama about young black men growing up on the mean streets of south-central Los Angeles*

meant /ment/ *past tense and participle of* MEAN

mean-time /ˈmiːntaɪm/ *n* **in the meantime** MEANWHILE (1): *The new secretary won't come until next week; in the meantime we've arranged for a temporary one.*

mean time /ˌ· ˈ·◁/ *n* see GREENWICH MEAN TIME

mean·while /ˈmiːnwaɪl/ *adv* **1** in the time between two events: *They'll be here soon. Meanwhile, let's have coffee.* **2** during the same period of time: *Eve was cutting the grass, (and) meanwhile Les was planting roses.* **3** **meanwhile, back at the ranch** a phrase used in old WESTERNS when the scene changes to show what is happening at the RANCH (=house) while some of the characters have been away from it. The phrase is often used humorously.

mea·sles /ˈmiːzəlz/ *n* [(*the*) U] an infectious illness in

which the sufferer has a fever and small red spots on the face and body –see also GERMAN MEASLES

meas·ly /ˈmiːzli/ *adj infml derog* of too small value, size, etc.: *a measly little gift* – ~**liness** *n* [U]

mea·su·ra·ble /ˈmeʒərəbəl/ *adj* large enough or not too large to be measured: *measurable progress* –see also IMMEASURABLE – ~**bly** *adv*: *Her temperature has not altered measurably over the last twelve hours.*

mea·sure¹ /ˈmeʒəʳ/ *n* **1** [C *often pl.*] an action taken to bring about a certain result: *The government has promised to take measures to help the unemployed.* | *If they won't go away quietly, we'll have to use stronger measures.* (=act more firmly) **2** [S;U (**of**)] *fml* an amount or quality: *He has not become rich, but he has had a certain measure of success/some measure of success.* | *There are no words to express the full measure of my gratitude.* | *His latest book is based in large measure* (=mostly) *on the work of Cohen.* | *His rudeness is beyond measure.* (=great; without limit) | *I don't trust them in that shop; they give you* **short measure** (=less than the correct amount of goods) **3** [C (**of**)] an amount or unit in a measuring system: *An hour is a measure of time.* **4** [C] an instrument or container used for calculating the stated amount, length, weight, etc.: *Pour the chemical mixture into a litre measure.* –see also TAPE MEASURE **5** [U] *tech* a system for measuring amount, size, weight, etc.: *An ounce in liquid measure is different from an ounce in dry measure.* **6** [C] *old-fash* a musical BAR or poetic METRE (=a pattern of repeated sounds) **7 for good measure** in addition: *After I'd weighed the apples, I put in another one for good measure.* **8 take someone's measure/get the measure of someone** to judge what someone is like –see also HALF MEASURES, MADE-TO-MEASURE, **tread a measure** (TREAD¹)

measure² *v* **1** [I;T] to find the size, length, amount, degree, etc., of (something) in standard units: *He measured the height of the cupboard.* | *The men measured the fence.* | *The dress designer measured her client for her new clothes.* **2** [T] to show or record (length, temperature, etc.): *A clock measures time.* **3** [L+*n*; *not in progressive forms*] to have the stated size: *That old tree must measure at least 30 metres from top to bottom.* | *He measures more round the waist than he used to.* **4 measure one's length** *BrE esp. lit* to fall flat on the ground

measure sbdy./sthg. **against** sbdy./sthg. *phr v* [T] to see if the size of (something) is right by comparing it with (something else): *I measured the coat against her and found it was too long.*

measure sthg. **off** *phr v* [T] to take (a measured length) from a longer length: *He measured off six yards of cloth.*

measure sthg. **out** *phr v* [T] to take (a measured quantity) from a larger quantity: *To make the cake, first measure out 250 grams of flour and 100 grams of butter.*

measure up *phr v* [I (**to**)] to have good enough qualities: *I'm afraid he just didn't measure up (to the job).*

mea·sured /ˈmeʒəd‖-ərd/ *adj* careful; exact; steady: *He spoke in measured tones.*

Measure for Measure /ˌ··· ˈ··/ a play (COMEDY) by William Shakespeare written in 1604

mea·sure·less /ˈmeʒələs‖-ʒər-/ *adj esp. lit* limitless; too great to be measured

mea·sure·ment /ˈmeʒəmənt‖-ʒər-/ *n* **1** [U] the act of measuring **2** [C *usu. pl.*] a length, height, etc., found by measuring, esp. by measuring part of the body: *What's your waist measurement?* | *I'll just take your measurements* (=measure you), *sir.*

measuring cup /ˈ··· ˌ·/ *n* a type of cup which holds an exact amount, used in American cooking: *a set of measuring cups consisting of ¼, ½, ¾, and 1 cup measures.*

measuring jug /ˈ··· ˌ·/ *n* a glass or plastic JUG marked down the side with measurements and used in cookery for measuring INGREDIENTS: *Pour a pint of milk into a measuring jug.* –see picture at JUG

meat /miːt/ *n* [U] **1** the flesh of four-footed animals and birds used for food: *His religion forbids the eating of meat.* | *There's not much meat on that bone/chicken.* | *What shall we have for the meat course?* –see also RED MEAT, WHITE MEAT **2** valuable material, ideas, etc.: *It was a clever speech, but there was no real meat in it.* **3** *old use* food (esp. in the phrase **meat and drink**) **4 be meat and drink to** to give great enjoyment to: *Football is meat and drink to him.* **5** *infml* **easy meat** someone or something that can easily be taken advantage of: *She was easy* *meat.* **6 one man's meat is another man's poison** *saying* things that are liked by one person may not be liked by another person

▷ USAGE The meat from some animals has a different name from the animal itself. For example, the meat from a **cow** is called **beef**, the meat from a **pig** is **pork** or **ham** or **bacon**, the meat from a **calf** (=a young cow) is **veal**, the meat from a **deer** is **venison**, and the meat from a **sheep** is **mutton**. But the meat from a **lamb** is **lamb**, and for birds the same word is used for both the meat and the creature: *Shall we have* **chicken** *or* **duck** *for dinner?*◁

meat and po·ta·toes /ˌ· · · ˈ·ˌ/ *n* [*the*] *AmE* the most important part of a matter or situation: *Let's get down to the meat and potatoes: how much are you going to pay me for this?*

meat and two veg /ˌ· · · ˈ·/ *n* [U] (what is considered to be) the typical British meal consisting of some meat and two different vegetables: *I prefer to stick to my meat and two veg.* | *I'm a meat and two veg man.*

meat·ball /ˈmiːtbɔːl/ *n* a small round ball of finely cut-up meat

Meath /miːð, miːθ/ a COUNTY in the NE of the Republic of Ireland, known for its good farming land

meat·head /ˈmiːthed/ *n* *AmE sl* a stupid person

meat·loaf /ˈmiːtləʊf/ *n* [C;U] a dish of meat and other INGREDIENTS, cut up very small, mixed, shaped into a loaf and cooked in an OVEN: *savoury meatloaf*

Meat Loaf /ˈ· ·/ (1948–) an American HEAVY METAL performer known for his very large size

meat-pack·ing /ˈ· ··/ *n* [U] *AmE* the preparation of dead animals for sale as meat: *the meat-packing industry* **—packer** *n*

meat wag·on /ˈ· ˌ··/ *n sl* **1** an AMBULANCE **2** a HEARSE **3** a police VAN

meat·y /ˈmiːti/ *adj* **1** full of meat **2** *infml* full of valuable ideas: *a meaty lecture* **—iness** *n* [U]

mec·ca /ˈmekə/ *n* [*usu. sing.*] (*sometimes cap.*) a place that many people wish to reach (from Mecca, the holiest city of Islam): *Lord's cricket ground is the cricketer's mecca.* | *This resort is a mecca for tourists in the summer.*

Mecca a city in Saudi Arabia where the PROPHET Muhammad was born, considered the holiest city of Islam. Non-Muslims are not allowed there, but every Muslim must try to go there in his or her lifetime.

Mec·ca·no /mɔˈkɑːnəʊ/ *n* [U] *BrE tdmk* a toy CONSTRUCTION set of small metal or plastic pieces used to build machines and models: *a battery-powered model crane made of Meccano*

me·chan·ic /mɪˈkænɪk/ *n* a person who is skilled in using, repairing, etc., machinery: *a motor mechanic*

me·chan·i·cal /mɪˈkænɪkəl/ *adj* **1** [*no comp.*] of or moved, worked, or produced by machinery: *a mechanical digger* **2** *often derog* (done) without thought or feeling; (done) from habit rather than will: *He was asked the same question so many times that the answer became mechanical.* **— ·ly** /kli/ *adv*

mechanical en·gi·neer·ing /ˌ·ˌ··· ··ˈ··/ *n* [U] the branch of ENGINEERING which includes the use of mechanical power, and the DESIGN and production of machines and tools **—mechanical engineer** *n*

me·chan·ics /mɪˈkænɪks/ *n* **1** [U] the science of the action of forces on objects **2** [(*the*) P (**of**)] the ways in which something works, produces results, etc.: *The subcommittee will work out the mechanics of setting up the scheme.*

mech·a·nis·m /ˈmekənɪzəm/ *n* (the arrangement and action of the parts of) a machine: *The clock doesn't go; there's something wrong with the mechanism.* | (fig.) *the mechanism of the brain* | (fig.) *the mechanism of local government*

mech·a·nis·tic /ˌmekəˈnɪstɪk◀/ *adj* tending to explain all actions of living things as if they were machines: *a mechanistic view of the universe* **— ·ally** /kli/ *adv*

mech·a·nize also **-nise** *BrE* /ˈmekənaɪz/ *v* [T] to use machines for (a job), instead of using the effort of human beings or animals: *to mechanize an industrial process* | *mechanized farming* **—nization** /ˌmekənaɪˈzeɪʃən‖-nə-/ *n* [U]

mechanized war·fare /ˌ·ˌ··· ˈ··/ *n* [U] the use of modern machines, esp. TANKs and HELICOPTERs, in war

M Econ *abbrev. for:* Master of Economics (a title for someone who has) a higher university degree in ECONOMICS: *Arnold Green, M Econ*

Med /med/ *infml*, **The** (the area surrounding) the Mediterranean Sea: *luxury holidays in the Med*

M Ed /ˌem ˈed/ *n* Master of Education; a higher university degree in teaching

med·al /ˈmedl/ *n* a round flat piece of metal, or a cross, with a picture and/or words marked on it, which is given to a person as an honour for an act of bravery or skill, or in memory of something important: *an Olympic gold medal*

me·dal·li·on /mɔˈdæliən/ *n* a round medal like a large coin, usu. worn round the neck for decoration

me·dal·li·on man /ˌ·ˈ··· ˌ·/ *n* *BrE infml derog* a type of man who wears a medallion, often with an open shirt, tight trousers, and other jewellery. The popular image of a medallion man is of a man with a hairy chest trying to look younger than he is. He thinks he is very MASCULINE and attractive to women, but most women think his appearance and the way he speaks to them is stupid.

medallion man

med·al·list *BrE* ‖ **medalist** *AmE* /ˈmedl-ɨst/ *n* a person who has won a medal in sport or in a competition: *He was the silver medallist in the 800 metres.*

Medal of Hon·or /ˌ··· · ˈ··/ see CONGRESSIONAL MEDAL OF HONOR

Me·dan /meɪˈdɑːn/ the largest city in Sumatra in Indonesia

Med·a·war /ˈmedəwəʳ/, **Sir Peter** (1915–87) a British ZOOLOGIST, known for his work on the understanding of the IMMUNE system. He shared the Nobel prize in 1960 and in 1959 gave the Reith Lectures on the future of man.

med·dle /ˈmedl/ *v* [I (**in, with**)] to take too much interest in, or take action about other people's private affairs; INTERFERE **—dler** *n*

med·dle·some /ˈmedlsəm/ *adj* (of people or behaviour) meddling: *a meddlesome old man* **— ~ness** *n* [U]

Me·dea /mɔˈdɪə/ in CLASSICAL MYTHOLOGY, a princess with magic powers, who helped Jason to win the Golden Fleece

Me·del·lin /ˌmedeɪˈiːn‖ˌmedəlˈiːn/ a city in the NW of Colombia which is known esp. as a drug centre and the home of DRUG BARONs

me·di·a /ˈmiːdiə/ also **mass media** *fml—* *n* [(*the*) +*sing./pl. v*] the newspapers, television, and radio: *The media have/has a lot of power today.* | *government control over the media* —see also MEDIUM¹ (1)

media cov·er·age /ˈ··· ˌ···/ *n* [U] the amount of time and space given to a subject or an event in the newspapers and on radio and television: *The Gulf War got massive media coverage.*

media e·vent /ˈ··· ·ˌ·/ *n* an event that is not very important but is widely reported by the media, esp. one that is deliberately made to happen only so that the media coverage makes someone or something involved in it seem important or interesting

media hype /ˌ··· ˈ·/ *n* [U] *infml, derog* a lot of attention given to a subject or an event by the newspapers or television, making the subject seem much more important than it really is: *People only went to see that film because of the media hype.*

med·i·ae·val /ˌmediˈiːvəl◀ˌmiː-/ *adj* MEDIEVAL

me·di·al /ˈmiːdiəl/ *adj* [A *no comp.*] *tech* in the middle position: *a medial consonant* (=between two vowels) **— ~ly** *adv*

me·di·an¹ /ˈmiːdiən/ *n tech* **1** a line passing from a point of a TRIANGLE to the centre of the opposite side **2** also **median strip**— *AmE for* a CENTRAL RESERVATION

median² *adj* [A *no comp.*] *tech* in or passing through the middle

me·di·ate /ˈmiːdieɪt/ *v* **1** [I (**between, in**)] to act as a peacemaker between opposing sides: *The government mediated between the workers and the employers.* **2** [T] to produce by mediating: *The army leaders have mediated a cease-fire/a settlement.* —**ator** *n* —**ation** /ˌmiːdɪˈeɪʃən/ *n* [U]

med·ic /ˈmedɪk/ *also* **medico**— *n infml* **1** a medical doctor or student **2** *AmE* a military person trained in medical treatment, esp. one working in time of war

med·ic·aid /ˈmedɪkeɪd/ *n* [U] (*often cap.*) (in the US) a system by which the government helps to pay the medical costs of people on low incomes. It is often criticized by its users and others and is generally thought to be not as good as private medical care. —compare MEDICARE and see also extra information on page 829

med·i·cal[1] /ˈmedɪkəl/ *adj* **1** of medicine and treating the sick: *a medical student* | *a medical examination* (=an examination of the body by a doctor) **2** of the treatment of disease by medicine rather than by operation: *the hospital's medical wards* —compare MEDICINAL, SURGICAL — ~**ly** /kli/ *adv* : *The soldier was pronounced medically fit (for active duty).*

medical[2] *also* **physical** *esp. AmE* — *n* a medical examination of the body: *I have to have a medical before going abroad.* | *his army medical*

medical card /ˈ··· ˌ·/ *n* (in Britain) an official card showing a person's name and address, their NHS number, and the name and address of their doctor

medical prac·ti·tion·er /ˌ··· ·ˈ···/ *n BrE fml* a doctor

Medical Re·search Coun·cil /ˌ··· ·ˌ· ·ˈ··, ˌ··· ·ˈ· ˌ·/ [the] a group which provides money from the government for medical RESEARCH in universities, research institutions, and hospitals in Britain

medical school /ˈ··· ·/ *also* **med school** *AmE infml*— *n* a school where people study to become doctors

me·dic·a·ment /mɪˈdɪkəmənt, ˈmedɪ-/ *n fml or tech* a substance used on or in the body to treat a disease; medicine

medical equipment

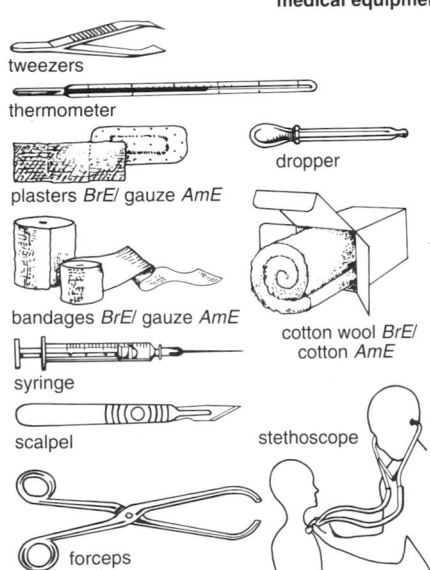

tweezers

thermometer

dropper

plasters *BrE*/ gauze *AmE*

bandages *BrE*/ gauze *AmE*

cotton wool *BrE*/ cotton *AmE*

syringe

scalpel

stethoscope

forceps

med·i·care /ˈmedɪkeəʳ/ *n* [U] (*often cap.*) (in the US and Canada) a system of medical care provided by the government, esp. for old people —compare MEDICAID —and see also extra information on page 829

med·i·cated /ˈmedɪkeɪtɪd/ *adj* including or mixed with a substance for diseased conditions: *medicated shampoo*

med·i·ca·tion /ˌmedɪˈkeɪʃən/ *n* [C;U] *esp. AmE* a medical substance, esp. a drug; medicine: *She's on medication for her heart.* | *I've tried several different medications and none of them work.*

Med·i·ci /ˈmedɪtʃiː/ the name of an Italian family that

owned a bank and that ruled Florence from the 15th to the 18th century and spent much of their wealth on the arts

me·di·ci·nal /məˈdɪsənəl/ *adj* **1** used as medicine: *medicinal alcohol* (=not for drinking) **2** used to encourage good health. Some people say that when they drink strong alcoholic drink, e.g. WHISKY, it is for medicinal purposes, but usu. they are saying it humorously: *I always keep brandy in the house, but purely for medicinal purposes.* —compare MEDICAL — ~**ly** *adv*

medi·cine /ˈmedsən‖ˈmedɪsən/ *n* **1** [C;U] a substance used for treating illness, esp. a liquid to be drunk: *a bottle/a dose of medicine* | *Have you taken your medicine?* | *the medicine cupboard* | (fig.) *The best medicine for you right now would be a good holiday.* —see picture at BOTTLE **2** [U] the science of treating and understanding illness: *preventative medicine* | *a doctor of medicine* —see also extra information on page 825 **3 give someone a taste/dose of their own medicine** *infml* to treat someone as (badly as) they have treated others, as a punishment **4 take one's medicine** to accept punishment or unpleasantness

medicine man /ˈ··· ·‖ˈ··· ·/ *also* **medicine wom·an** *fem.* /ˈ··· ˌ··/— *n* a person esp. among Native Americans who is recognized by the tribe as having knowledge and experience of medicinal plants and practices and as being able to help or cure people, often with the help of the spirit world —compare SHAMAN, WITCHDOCTOR

med·i·co /ˈmedɪkəʊ/ *n* -**cos** *infml* a MEDIC

med·i·e·val, **mediaeval** /ˌmedɪˈiːvəl‖ˌmiː-/ *adj* **1** of the period in history between about AD 1100 and 1500 (the Middle Ages) **2** *infml derog* very old or old-fashioned: *The plumbing in their house is positively medieval!*

Me·di·na /meˈdiːnə, mɪ-/ a city in Saudi Arabia that has the TOMB of Muhammad. To Muslims it is the most holy place except for Mecca. Non-Muslims are not allowed there.

me·di·o·cre /ˌmiːdiˈəʊkəʳ◄/ *adj* neither very good nor very bad, but usu. not good enough: *a mediocre story*

me·di·oc·ri·ty /ˌmiːdiˈɒkrɪti‖-ˈɑːk-/ *n* **1** [U] the state of being mediocre **2** [C] a person who is not very good at anything

med·i·tate /ˈmedɪteɪt/ *v* **1** [I (**on, upon**);T] to think seriously or deeply (about): *He meditated (on the matter) for two days before giving his answer.* [+*v-ing*] *I hear you're meditating giving up your job.* (=forming a possible intention to do so) **2** [I] to fix the attention on one idea or activity, having cleared the mind of thoughts, esp. for religious reasons and/or to gain a calm peaceful mind

med·i·ta·tion /ˌmedɪˈteɪʃən/ *n* **1** [U] *also* **meditations** *pl.*— the act or time of meditating: *He interrupted my meditations.* **2** [U] the practice of training the mind and body to become less active for certain regular periods, esp. so as to be able to control it better and use it more effectively

► CULTURAL NOTE In the 1960s and 1970s meditation as practised by the Indian Maharishi Mahesh Yogi became popular among young people who were not religious but were looking for a relaxed physical and mental state. It was thought of as part of the HIPPY movement and considered rather strange and silly by esp. older people. ◄

3 [C (**on, upon**) *often pl.*] a piece of deep thought on a subject, expressed in speech or writing

med·i·ta·tive /ˈmedɪtətɪv‖-teɪtɪv/ *adj* thoughtful; showing deep thought — ~**ly** *adv*

Med·i·ter·ra·ne·an /ˌmedɪtəˈreɪniən◄/ *also* **Mediterranean Sea** /ˌ······ ·ˈ·/, **Med** *infml*— [the] a large INLAND sea surrounded by the countries of southern Europe, N Africa and the Middle East. British people connect the Mediterranean with hot summers and warm winters. The area, esp. the European coasts and the islands, are popular places for holidays and are thought of as very ROMANTIC. —**Mediterranean** *adj* : *a Mediterranean climate*

me·di·um[1] /ˈmiːdiəm/ *adj* of middle size, amount, quality, value, etc.: *a medium-sized apple* | *of medium height* | *medium wine* (=not too sweet or too dry)

medium[2] *n* -**dia** /diə/ *or* -**diums** **1** a method for giving information; form of art: *He writes stories, but the theatre is his favourite medium.* | *Television can be a medium for giving information and opinions, for amusing people, and for teaching them.* —see also MEDIA **2** a substance in

Medicine in Britain

In Britain there is a NATIONAL HEALTH SERVICE (the NHS), which is paid for by taxes and national insurance, and in general people do not have to pay for medical treatment. Every person is registered (REGISTER(1)) with a doctor in their local area, known as a GENERAL PRACTITIONER or GP. This means that their name is on the GP's list, and they may make an appointment to see the doctor or may call the doctor out to visit them if they are ill. People do sometimes have to pay part of the cost of drugs that the doctor prescribes (PRESCRIBE). GPs are trained in general medicine but are not specialists in any particular subject. If a patient needs to see a specialist doctor, they must first go to their GP and then the GP will make an appointment for the patient to see a specialist at a hospital or clinic.

Although everyone in Britain can have free treatment under the NHS, it is also possible to have treatment done **privately**, for which one has to pay. Some people have private health insurance to help them pay for private treatment. Under the NHS, people who need to go to hospital (e.g. for an operation) may have to wait a long time on a waiting list for their treatment. If they pay for the treatment, they will probably get it more quickly.

Anyone who is very ill can call an AMBULANCE and get taken to hospital for free urgent medical treatment. Ambulances are a free service in Britain.

Medicine in the US

Unlike Britain, the US does not have a national health care service. The government does help pay for some medical care for people who are on low incomes (through the MEDICAID scheme) and for old people (through the MEDICARE scheme), but most people buy insurance to help pay for medical care. Some people cannot afford insurance but are not poor enough to get government help. The cost of medical insurance and the problems of those who cannot afford it are an important political subject.

When people are ill, they usually go first to a general practitioner (or INTERNIST). Unlike in Britain, however, people sometimes go straight to a specialist, without seeing their general practitioner first. Children are usually taken to a PEDIATRICIAN (=a doctor who is a specialist in the treatment of children). Many women make yearly appointments to see a gynecologist (=a doctor who is a specialist in women's health), as well as going to their general doctor when they are ill. As in Britain, if a patient needs to see a specialist doctor, their general doctor will usually give them the name of one.

Doctors do not go to people's homes when they are ill. People always make appointments to see the doctor in the doctor's office. In emergencies (EMERGENCY), people call for an ambulance. Hospitals must treat all emergency patients, even if the patient does not have medical insurance. The government would then help pay for some of the cost of the medical care.

Alternative medicine

Medical treatments which are used instead of drugs, surgery, and other officially accepted methods of treatment are known as ALTERNATIVE MEDICINE or COMPLEMENTARY MEDICINE. These more natural methods of treating illness include HOMEOPATHY, ACUPUNCTURE, OSTEOPATHY, AROMATHERAPY, CHIROPRACTIC, and REFLEXOLOGY. Alternative medicine is not available under the National Health service in Britain, and people who use it have to pay for it when they receive their treatment. Since the beginning of the 1980s, alternative medicine has become more and more popular with people and, although it is not officially accepted by the medical profession, some doctors do accept that such methods can be effective in treating some types of illness.

which objects or living things exist, or through which a force travels: *A fish in water is in its natural medium.* | *Sound travels through the medium of air.* **3** a middle position: *There's* **a happy medium** (=a correct average course of action) *between eating all the time and not eating at all!* **4 the medium is the message** *quote* a phrase used by Marshall McLuhan meaning that the way in which people receive information has more influence on what they think than the information itself

medium³ *n* **-diums** a person who claims to have the power to receive messages from the spirits of the dead

medium dry /ˌ··· ˈ·/ *adj* (of wine) having only slight sweetness and fruit taste —see also DRY¹ (6)

medium of ex·change /ˌ··· ··ˈ·/ *n* something commonly accepted in exchange for goods and services and representing a standard of value

medium wave /ˌ··· ˈ·◂/ *written abbrev.* **MW** *n* [U] radio broadcasting or receiving on waves of between about 150 and 550 metres in length —compare LONG WAVE, SHORT WAVE

med·lar /ˈmedləʳ/ *n* (a small tree with) a fruit like a wild apple, eaten when partly decayed

med·ley /ˈmedli/ *n* **1** [(of)] a mass or crowd of different types mixed together: *a medley of different nationalities* **2** a piece of music made up of parts of other musical works: *a medley of the Beatles' greatest hits* **3** a swimming race in which the swimmers swim distances in four different swimming STROKES (BACKSTROKE, BREASTSTROKE, BUTTERFLY, and FREESTYLE)

med school /ˈ· ·/ *n AmE infml for* MEDICAL SCHOOL

me·dul·la ob·lon·ga·ta /mʒˌdʌlə ˌɒblɒŋˈgɑːtə‖-ˌɑːblɔːŋ-/ *n* **medulla oblongatas, medullae oblongatae** /-liː, -tiː/ *med* the part of the BRAIN which continues from the SPINAL CORD into the back of the head and controls many important activities such as breathing

Me·du·sa /mʒˈdjuːzə‖-ˈduːsə/ *n* in CLASSICAL MYTHOLOGY, a woman who had snakes for hair and turned everyone who looked at her into stone. She was killed by Perseus, who protected himself by holding his shield in front of him so that Medusa could not see him. —see also GORGON and see colour picture on page 423

Med·way /ˈmedweɪ/ [*the*] a river in Kent in the SE of England which flows through the **Medway Towns** (Rochester, Gillingham and Chatham) and joins the river Thames near the sea

meek /miːk/ *adj* **1** (of people or behaviour) gentle and uncomplaining; accepting others' actions and opinions without argument: *She won't object – she's so* **meek and mild.** | *He's as* **meek as a lamb. 2** blessed are the **meek, for they shall inherit the earth** *saying from the Bible* (a phrase used when talking about quiet, gentle people achieving success, wealth or power): *Are the meek inheriting the earth?* | *Whether we like it or not, it is the swots who will inherit the earth. – ~ly* *adv* : *He nodded meekly.* *– ~ness* *n* [U]

meer·schaum /ˈmɪəʃəm‖ˈmɪər-/ *n* a pipe for smoking tobacco, made of hard white clay

meet¹ /miːt/ *v* **met** /met/ **1** [I;T] to come together (with), by chance or arrangement: *Let's meet for dinner.* | *You'll never guess who I met today – my old teacher! We haven't met for 20 years.* **2** [I;T] to get to know or be introduced (to) for the first time: *Come to the party and meet some interesting people.* | *We met at Ann's party, didn't we, but I don't remember your name.* **3** [I] to gather together: *The whole school met to hear the speech.* **4** [T] to be there at the arrival of: *I'll meet you off the train.* | *The taxi will meet the train.* **5** [I] to join: *My skirt won't meet round my waist.* | *The two roads meet just north of Birmingham.* **6** [I;T] to play against (an opponent in sport): *Germany and Spain will meet* (=play against each other) *in the soccer cup final.* **7** [I] to touch: *Their lips met in a kiss.* | *The two cars met* (=crashed) *head-on.* **8** [T] to experience (something unpleasant) by chance: *She met her death* (=was killed) *in a plane crash.* **9** [T (with)] to answer, esp. in opposition: *His speech was met with cries of anger.* | (fig.) *I couldn't* **meet his eyes.** (=look back at him) **10** [T] to satisfy (a need, demand, etc.): *Does the hotel meet your expectations?* | *Their new model of car is so popular that they have had to open a new factory to meet the demand.* **11** [T] to pay: *Can you meet your debts?* **12 meet someone halfway** to make an agreement which partly

satisfies the demands of both sides **13 more (in/to something) than meets the eye** hidden facts or reasons (in or for something): *The job seems easy, but there's more to it than meets the eye.* (=it is actually quite difficult) **14 when shall we three meet again, in thunder, lightning or in rain?** *quote* a phrase from Shakespeare's play *Macbeth*, said by the three WITCHES –see also MACBETH **15 We can't go on meeting like this** *quote* a phrase originally used by unhappy lovers in a play, and now used humorously –see also **make ends meet** 5 (END¹)
meet up *phr v* [I (with)] *infml* to meet, esp. by informal arrangement: *Let's meet up after the play.*
meet with sbdy./sthg. *phr v* [T] **1** to experience (esp. something unpleasant) by chance: *I met with some difficulties when I tried to enter the country.* | *They met with an accident on their way back.* **2** to have a meeting with: *Our representatives met with several heads of state to discuss the price of oil.*

meet² *n* **1** (in Britain) a gathering of people, esp. on horses with HOUNDS (=hunting dogs) to hunt foxes **2** *esp. AmE* a meeting of people, esp. for sports events: *a track meet*

meet³ *adj* [(for)] *old use or bibl* suitable; right

meet·ing /ˈmiːtɪŋ/ *n* **1** [C] a gathering of people for a purpose: *I was unable to attend the union meeting.* | *The chairman declared the meeting open.*

▶CULTURAL NOTE When someone telephones a business person, they may be told that they cannot speak to them because they are "in a meeting". This is also a well-known excuse used by people who do not wish to talk to the person asking for them.◀

2 [*the*+*sing./pl. v*] the people in such a gathering: *What has/have the meeting decided?* **3** [C *usu. sing.*] the coming together of two or more people, by chance or arrangement: *Our meeting in Tokyo was quite by chance.* **4 meeting of minds** agreement: *Let's see if we can have a meeting of minds about the schedule for the rest of the month.*

meet·ing·house /ˈmiːtɪŋhaʊs/ *n* **-houses** /ˌhaʊzɪz/ a place for religious meetings, esp. of NONCONFORMISTS such as Quakers. There is no leader in a meeting house and each person can say prayers or talk about the Bible as they wish, or pray silently. —compare CHURCH

mega- see WORD FORMATION

meg·a·bucks /ˈmegəbʌks/ *n* [P] *infml* a large amount of money: *The house has dry rot and needs a new roof – we're talking about megabucks.*

meg·a·death /ˈmegədeθ/ *n* [U] one million deaths, used when talking about the possible effects of a NUCLEAR war

meg·a·hertz /ˈmegəhɜːts‖-ɜːr-/ *written abbrev.* **MHz** also **meg·a·cy·cle** /ˈmegəˌsaɪkəl/— *n* **-hertz** a million HERTZ

meg·a·lith /ˈmegəlɪθ/ *n* a large tall stone usu. standing in an open place which was put up before historical times, perhaps as a religious sign. There are many megaliths or groups of megaliths in Britain. The most famous are the stone circles at Stonehenge and Avebury.

meg·a·lith·ic /ˌmegəˈlɪθɪk◂/ *adj* **1** of megaliths: *a megalithic monument* **2** of the time when these stones were put up: *the megalithic age*

meg·a·lo·ma·ni·a /ˌmegələʊˈmeɪniə/ *n* [U] the belief that one is more important, powerful, etc., than one really is —*ac* /nɪæk/ *adj, n*

meg·a·lop·o·lis /ˌmegəˈlɒpəlʒs‖-ˈlɑː-/ *n* a very large URBAN (=city) area, esp. one that has come about by nearby cities growing and meeting one another

meg·a·phone /ˈmegəfəʊn/ also **loudhailer** *BrE* ‖ **bullhorn** *AmE*— *n* an instrument shaped like a widening tube, often containing an AMPLIFIER, which is held to the mouth when speaking to make the sound of the voice louder: *The police chief addressed the huge crowd through a megaphone.* —compare BULLHORN, MICROPHONE

meg·a·star /ˈmegəstɑːʳ/ *n* a very famous performer, esp. in films or television; a SUPERSTAR

meg·a·ton /ˈmegətʌn/ *n* a measure of force of an explosion equal to that of a million TONS (about 1,016,000,000 kilograms) of TNT: *a five-megaton atomic bomb*

me gen·e·ra·tion /ˈ· ··ˌ·ˈ·/ *n* [*the*+*sing./pl. v*] (*often cap.* M) (esp. in the 1970s and 1980s) a group of young adults who are selfishly concerned only with their own affairs and interests, and pay no attention to the lives and problems of other people

Mein Kampf /ˌmaɪn ˈkæmpf/ a book written by Adolf Hitler while he was in prison in 1923, describing his political ideas and his plan for gaining power over the whole world

mei·o·sis /maɪˈəʊsɪs/ n [U] cell division in which the new cells produced each have half the characteristics of the two parent cells. Sex cells are produced this way, allowing children to be different from their parents and from each other —compare MITOSIS

Me·ir /meɪˈɪəʳ/, **Gol·da** /ˈgəʊldə/ (1898–1978) an Israeli politician and PRIME MINISTER (born in Russia). She resigned (RESIGN) after criticism that she had not prepared the country for the 1973 Arab–Israeli war.

Meis·sen /ˈmeɪsən/ also **Meissen ware** /ˈ··ˌ·/— n [C;U] a type of PORCELAIN developed in the town of Meissen, near Dresden, Germany in the 18th century. It is valuable and some people collect it.

Me·kong /ˌmiːˈkɒŋ◂‖ˌmeɪˈkɔːŋ◂/ [the] a river in the SE of Asia, which flows from Tibet through Cambodia and Laos to Vietnam. The Mekong Delta is one of the most important areas in Asia for growing rice.

mel·a·mine /ˈmeləmiːn/ n [U] a RESIN or plastic used e.g. to make a hard, decorative surface for shelves etc.

mel·an·cho·li·a /ˌmelənˈkəʊliə/ n [U] old-fash fml a condition in which one feels sad, hopeless, and worthless; DEPRESSION

mel·an·chol·ic /ˌmelənˈkɒlɪk◂‖-ˈkɑː-/ adj esp. fml or lit of or suffering from melancholia or melancholy

mel·an·chol·y¹ /ˈmelənkəli‖-kɑːli/ n [U] esp. fml or lit sadness, esp. over a period of time and not for any particular reason

melancholy² adj esp. fml or lit sad: a lone and feeling melancholy | melancholy news

Mel·a·ne·si·a /ˌmeləˈniːziə‖-ˈniːʃə/ a group of islands in the Pacific Ocean NE of Australia, including Vanuatu, the Solomon Islands, and Fiji

Mel·a·ne·si·an /ˌmeləˈniːziən◂‖-ˈniːʃən/ n 1 [C] a person of or from Melanesia 2 [U] the language of Melanesia ·**Melanesian** adj

mé·lange /meɪˈlɑːnʒ/ n [(of) usu. sing.] a mixture

mel·a·nin /ˈmelənɪn/ n [U] a natural dark brown colouring found in human skin, hair, and eyes

Mel·ba sauce /ˌmelbə ˈsɔːs/ n [C;U] a thick sweet liquid made with raspberries (RASPBERRY) used on ice cream — compare PEACH MELBA

Melba toast /ˌ·· ˈ·/ n [U] a kind of thin easily broken TOAST. In the US it is often given to people who are ill because it is easy to DIGEST. It is also given to babies who are growing teeth.

Mel·bourne /ˈmelbən‖-ərn/ a city in the state of Victoria in SE Australia, known as a business and industrial centre and for its famous RACECOURSE

mel·ee /ˈmeleɪ‖ˈmeɪleɪ, meɪˈleɪ/ n [usu. sing.] a struggling or disorderly crowd

mel·li·flu·ous /mɛˈlɪfluəs/ adj fml (of words, music, or a voice) having a sweet smooth flowing sound

mel·low¹ /ˈmeləʊ/ adj 1 (of fruit and wine) sweet and ripe or fully developed, esp. after being kept for a long time 2 (of a colour) soft and warm; not bright 3 (of people or behaviour) wise and gentle through age or experience: She used to have a fierce temper, but she's got mellower as she's got older. 4 infml (feeling) pleasantly calm and friendly, not nervous: The more wine he drank, the mellower he became. — ~ly adv — ~ness n [U]

mellow² v [I;T] to (cause to) become mellow as time passes: The colours mellowed as the sun went down. | The years have mellowed him. | She's mellowed over the years.
  mellow out phr v [I;T **mellow** sbdy ↔ **out**)] AmE infml to (cause to) relax: mellowing out in front of the fireplace | Would you give him something to mellow him out? He's getting on my nerves.

me·lod·ic /mɛˈlɒdɪk‖mɛˈlɑː-/ adj 1 of or having a melody 2 melodious

me·lo·di·ous /mɛˈləʊdiəs/ adj having a pleasant tune or sound; pleasing to listen to — ~ly adv — ~ness n [U]

mel·o·dra·ma /ˈmelədrɑːmə, ‖-drɑːmə, -dræmə/ n [C;U] a (type of) exciting play, full of sudden events, very good or very wicked characters, and (too) strong and simple feelings: (fig.) You've only cut your finger. Don't make such a melodrama out of it!

mel·o·dra·mat·ic /ˌmelədrəˈmætɪk◂/ adj showing, or intended to produce, strong and excited feelings; (too) EMOTIONAL: He says he's going to kill himself, but he's just being melodramatic. — ~ally /kli/ adv

mel·o·dy /ˈmelədi/ n 1 [C] a song or tune: a haunting melody 2 [C] the part which forms a clearly recognizable tune in a larger arrangement of notes: The sopranos have the melody while the others sing the accompaniment. 3 [U] the arrangement of music in a tuneful way; melodiousness

Melody Mak·er /ˈ··· ˌ··/ a British weekly magazine about popular music for young people

mel·on /ˈmelən/ n [C;U] a large rounded fruit, with a firm skin and juicy flesh which can be eaten. It is often eaten as a first course, but can also be eaten as a DESSERT. — see also CANTALOUP, HONEYDEW MELON, WATERMELON, and see picture at FRUIT

melt /melt/ v 1 [I;T] a to cause (a solid) to become liquid: The sun melted the snow. b (of a solid) to become liquid: The ice is melting in the sun. —compare FREEZE, THAW 2 [I;T] to (cause to) become gentle, sympathetic, etc.: He shouted at the little girl, but his heart melted when he saw her crying. 3 [I (AWAY)] to gradually disappear: I don't know where my money goes — it just seems to melt (away). | The crowd of demonstrators melted away when the police arrived. 4 [I (into)] (of a colour, sound, or sensation) to become lost in another by moving gently: The trumpet call melts gradually into the orchestral background. 5 **melt in the mouth** apprec (of solid food) to be easy and extremely pleasant to eat: These chocolates really melt in your mouth.
  ▷ USAGE The adjective **molten** means **melted,** but it is used only of things that melt at a very high temperature. Compare **molten** rock/metal and **melted** chocolate/butter.◁
  melt sthg. **down** phr v [T] to make (a metal object) liquid by heating, esp. so as to use the metal again

melt·down /ˈmeltdaʊn/ n [C;U] the melting of the material inside an atomic REACTOR, so that it burns through its container and allows dangerous RADIOACTIVITY to escape

melt·ing /ˈmeltɪŋ/ adj (esp. of a voice) gentle, soft, and pleasant — ~ly adv

melting point /ˈ·· ˌ·/ n the temperature at which a particular solid melts

melting pot /ˈ·· ˌ·/ n 1 a place where there is a mixing of people of different races and nations: America has been a melting pot since its beginnings. 2 **in the melting pot** not fixed; likely to be changed

Mel·ville /ˈmelvɪl/, **Her·man** /ˈhɜːmən‖ˈhɜːr-/ (1819–91) an American writer who wrote about his experiences as a SEAMAN. His most famous books are Moby Dick, and Billy Budd. —see also MOBY DICK

mem·ber /ˈmembəʳ/ n 1 [(of)] a person belonging to a club, group, etc.: a member of the family | a member of a political party | She became a member of the committee. | The club bar is open to members only. —see also PRIVATE MEMBER 2 a fml an organ or limb of the body b lit euph the male sexual organ

Member of Par·lia·ment /ˌ··· · ˈ···/ n an MP

mem·ber·ship /ˈmembəʃɪp‖-ər-/ n 1 [U (of)] the state of being a member of a club, society, etc.: I must renew my membership of the sailing club. | Have you applied for membership? 2 [C+sing./pl. v] all the members of a club, society, etc.: We're trying to increase our membership. | a small/large membership | The membership disagree/disagrees on the proposed change in the rules.

mem·brane /ˈmembreɪn/ n [C;U] (a) very soft thin skin, esp. in the body, covering or connecting parts of a structure: A vibrating membrane in the ear helps to convey sounds to the brain. —**branous** /ˈmembrənəs/ adj

me·men·to /mɛˈmentəʊ/ n -tos [(of)] a small object which reminds one of a holiday, a friend, etc.

mem·o /ˈmeməʊ/ n -os 1 also **memorandum** fml— a note from one person or office to another within the same firm or organization 2 a note of something to be remembered: I made a memo on my memo pad to buy more coffee.

mem·oir /ˈmemwɑːʳ/ n [(of)] fml a short piece of writing on a subject, esp. the story of someone else's life

mem·oirs /ˈmemwɑːz‖-ɑːrz/ n [P] a written account of one's own life and experiences, esp. one written by a person who has been active in politics or war; AUTOBIOGRAPHY: *The old general has started to write his memoirs.* — compare REMINISCENCES

mem·o·ra·bil·i·a /ˌmémərəˈbɪliə/ n [P] things that are interesting in connection with a famous person or event: *a collection of Shelley memorabilia, including several letters and a piece of his hair*

mem·o·ra·ble /ˈmemərəbəl/ adj [(for)] worth remembering; special in some way: *The film was memorable for* (=remembered because of) *its fine acting.* | *a memorable trip abroad* —**bly** adv : *a memorably awful performance*

mem·o·ran·dum /ˌmeməˈrændəm/ n -**da** /də/ or -**dums** 1 fml for MEMO (1) 2 fml or law a written agreement

Memorandum of As·so·ci·a·tion /··,····,··ˈ··/ n BrE a legal document which gives information about a new limited company, such as its title, address, business, capital, and shares

me·mo·ri·al /məˈmɔːriəl/ n [(to)] something, esp. a stone MONUMENT, in memory of a person, event, etc.: *a war memorial* (=in memory of dead soldiers) | *a memorial sculpture* | *The church service is a memorial to those killed in the war.*

Memorial Day /·ˈ···ˌ·/ a US legal holiday, the last Monday in May, when people remember those killed in wars: *Memorial Day weekend*

mem·o·rize also -**ise** BrE /ˈmeməraɪz/ v [T] to learn and remember (words, etc.) on purpose: *He memorized the list of dates.*

mem·o·ry /ˈmeməri/ n 1 [S (for);U] (an) ability to remember events and experiences: *She's got a good/bad memory for faces.* | *He played the tune from memory.* (=without written music) | *I've got a memory like a sieve!* (=I often forget things) | *I was sure I'd put my glasses down on this table* — **my memory is playing tricks on me.** (=I am remembering things incorrectly) 2 [C (of)] an event or experience that one remembers from the past: *One of my earliest memories is of playing in the garden.* 3 [C] the part of a computer in which information (DATA) can be stored until it is wanted: *The computer has a 256K memory.* 4 **if my memory serves me (well/correctly)** (used for showing that one is almost sure that one has remembered something correctly): *We first met in Egypt, if my memory serves me.* 5 **in memory of** as a way of remembering or reminding others of: *She set up the charitable trust in memory of her father.* 6 **someone's memory: a** the time during which things happened which someone can remember: *There have been two wars within the memory of my grandfather/*(**with)in living memory.** (=which can be remembered by people now alive) **b** someone as thought of after their death: *Her memory has always been held in the highest regard.* 7 **down memory lane** into the past, esp. when it is enjoyable to remember: *We had a little trip down memory lane last night, looking at all the old photographs.*

Mem·phis /ˈmemfɪs/ the largest city in the state of Tennessee, US, on the Mississippi river. Many people connect Memphis with music, esp. that of Elvis Presley. —see colour map on pages 1374–5

mem·sahib /ˈmemˌsɑːb‖-ˌsɑːhɪb, -ˌsɑːb/ n IndE & PakE a European woman, or an Indian woman of high social class —compare SAHIB

men /men/ n [P] 1 pl. of MAN 2 infml **separate the men from the boys** to separate those who have more skill or determination from those who are less able: *The run over the mountains will soon separate the men from the boys.* 3 **men in white coats/jackets** euph humor employees from a PSYCHIATRIC HOSPITAL who are mentioned in jokes as coming to take mentally ill people away to hospital: *If he goes on like this for much longer we'll have to send for the men in white coats!*

men·ace¹ /ˈmenɪs/ n 1 [C (to); U] a threat or danger: *He spoke with menace.* (=threateningly and frighteningly) | *The busy road is a menace to the children's safety.* 2 [C] infml an extremely troublesome person or thing: *The man's worse than irritating. He's a positive menace!* —see also DENNIS THE MENACE

menace² v [T] fml to threaten: *the pollution which is menacing our countryside* | *dark menacing clouds* (=threatening a storm) —**acingly** adv

mé·nage /ˈmeɪnɑːʒ‖meɪˈnɑːʒ/ n [C+sing./pl. v] a house and the people who live in it; HOUSEHOLD

ménage à trois /ˌmeɪnɑːʒ ɑː ˈtrwɑː‖məˌnɑːˈʒ-/ n [S] Fr a relationship in which two people and a lover of one of the pair live together

me·na·ge·rie /məˈnædʒəri/ n a collection of wild animals kept privately or for the public to see; ZOO

Men·ai Straits /ˌmenaɪ ˈstreɪts/ n [the+P] a CHANNEL in the Irish Sea between Anglesey and the Welsh mainland

MENCAP /ˈmenkæp/ the Royal Society for Mentally Handicapped Children and Adults; a British organization (CHARITY) which gives advice and practical help to people with learning difficulties and their families, and tries to get better conditions and services for them

mend¹ /mend/ v 1 [T] to repair (a break, fault, etc.) in (something): *to mend a hole in the pipe* | *to mend a shirt* 2 [I] infml **a** (of a part of the body) to become well or healthy again **b** (of a person) to regain one's health 3 **mend (one's) fences** to remove the bad effects of one's former actions, for example by becoming friendly with a person one has offended 4 **mend one's ways** to improve one's behaviour, work, etc. — —**er** n

mend² n 1 a repaired place: *These trousers have a mend* (=a PATCH or DARN) *on the knee.* 2 **on the mend** infml getting better after illness

men·da·cious /menˈdeɪʃəs/ adj fml (of a person or statement) not truthful; lying — —**ly** adv

men·da·ci·ty /menˈdæsɪti/ n [U] fml untruthfulness

Men·dels·sohn /ˈmendəlsən/, **Fe·lix** /ˈfiːlɪks/ (1809–47) a German COMPOSER (writer of music), who wrote five symphonies (SYMPHONY) and the OVERTURE *Fingal's Cave*. The *Wedding March* from his *Incidental Music to a Midsummer Night's Dream* is usu. played at church weddings as the newly-married man and woman leave the church.

men·di·cant /ˈmendɪkənt/ adj, n (a person) living as a beggar

mend·ing /ˈmendɪŋ/ n [U] clothes to be mended: *a basket of mending*

Men·dip Hills /ˌmendɪp ˈhɪlz/ also **Mendips**— [the + P] a range of hills in SW England, between the counties (COUNTY¹) of Avon and Somerset

Men·e·la·us /ˌmenɪˈleɪəs/ (in GREEK MYTHOLOGY) the king of Sparta, brother of Agamemnon and husband of Helen of Troy —see also HELEN OF TROY

men·folk /ˈmenfəʊk/ n [P] infml men, esp. one's male relatives

M Eng /ˌem ˈeŋ/ n Master of Engineering; (a title for someone who has) a higher university degree in ENGINEERING in the US

Men·em /ˈmenem/, **Car·los** /ˈkɑːlɒs‖ˈkɑːrləʊs/ (1930–) the president of Argentina since 1989, representing the Peronist party

Men·gis·tu /meŋˈɡɪstuː/, **Hai·le Ma·ri·am** /ˈhaɪli ˈmɑːriəm/ (1937–) an Ethiopian leader who established a Marxist government in 1977. He was driven out of power in 1991 by opposing forces after years of civil war and extreme lack of food in the country.

me·ni·al¹ /ˈmiːniəl/ adj (of work) not interesting or skilled, and done by unimportant people: *menial jobs like washing the floor* — —**ly** adv

menial² n derog someone who does menial work, esp. a servant in a house

men·in·gi·tis /ˌmenɪnˈdʒaɪtɪs/ n [U] a serious illness in which the outer part of the brain is swollen

Men·no·nite /ˈmenənaɪt/ n a member of various Protestant groups, mainly in the US, who refuse to join the ARMED FORCES, do not BAPTIZE their children, and have no formal church organization

Men of Har·lech /ˌmen əv ˈhɑːlɪk, -ˌlx ‖ -ˈhɑːr-/ the English title of an old Welsh song, originally sung by soldiers marching into battle, now often by groups protesting against unemployment in Wales

Men On·ly /ˌ·ˈ··/ a British magazine for men which contains articles on cars, men's fashions, and sex, and photographs of women with very few clothes on

men·o·pause /ˈmenəpɔːz/ also **change of life, change** euph— n the time when a woman's PERIODS stop, usu. between the ages of 45 and 50. Women are thought to behave strangely during the menopause, e.g. by having moods which often change. They may also suffer from physical problems, esp. HOT FLUSHes. —compare MALE MENOPAUSE —**pausal** /ˌmenəˈpɔːzəl◂/ adj

me·no·rah /mɪˈnɔːrə/ n a CANDLESTICK with space for usu. seven CANDLES, used in Chanukah celebrations in the Jewish religious year

Me·nor·ca /meˈnɔːkə‖-ɔːr-/ see MINORCA

MENSA /ˈmensə/ an international organization for people who are very clever. People take a test and are accepted into the organization if they are among the top 2 per cent in their country.

men's move·ment /ˈ· ˌ··/ [the] a movement thought to have begun in the late 1970s in which men, partly in reaction to FEMINISM, began to examine their emotions and behaviour in different ways. It is not regarded very seriously by many people. —see also NEW MAN

men's room /ˈ· ·/ n AmE for GENTS

mens sa·na in cor·po·re san·o /ˌmenz ˌsɑːnə ɪn ˌkɔːpəri ˈsɑːnəʊ‖-ˌkɔːr-/ phrase a Latin phrase meaning "a sound mind in a sound body", often used when encouraging people to take exercise to keep their bodies healthy

men·stru·al /ˈmenstruəl/ adj concerning a woman's PERIOD (4)

menstrual pe·ri·od /ˌ··· ˈ···/ n fml for PERIOD (4)

men·stru·ate /ˈmenstrueɪt/ v [I] tech to have a PERIOD (4) —**-ation** /ˌmenstruˈeɪʃən/ n [C;U]

men·su·ra·ble /ˈmenʃərəbəl‖-sərə-/ adj fml or tech for MEASURABLE

men·su·ra·tion /ˌmenʃəˈreɪʃən‖-səˈreɪ-/ n [U] fml or tech the measuring of length, area, and VOLUME (2)

mens·wear /ˈmenzweəʳ/ n clothing for men: a menswear shop | the menswear department

men·tal /ˈmentl/ adj **1** of the mind: a child's mental development | His problem is mental, not physical. | mental health **2** [A] done or made only in the mind: mental arithmetic | a mental picture | It's no use trying to explain your computer to me – I've got a **mental block** about them. **3** [A] concerning illness of the mind: a mental hospital | mental treatment | mental patients **4** [F] sl, offensive mad or stupid: Don't listen to him. He's mental! — **-ly** adv : mentally ill

mental age /ˌ·· ˈ·/ n a measure of someone's ability to use their mind, according to the usual age at which such ability would be found: The children in the special hospital are aged from seven to thirteen, but they all have a mental age of less than five.

mental de·fec·tive /ˌ··· ˈ···/ n derog a person who cannot learn or be independent because of **mental deficiency** (=weakness of the mind)

mental hand·i·cap /ˌ·· ˈ···/ n a state of low mental development, usu. from birth, caused by a variety of conditions —**mentally handicapped** adj, n (the+P): a special school for the mentally handicapped | My son is mentally handicapped.

mental hos·pi·tal /ˈ·· ˌ···/ old-fash, considered offensive by some people n a PSYCHIATRIC HOSPITAL

men·tal·i·ty /menˈtælɟti/ n **1** [U] the abilities and powers of the mind: a person of weak mentality **2** [C] a person's habitual way of thinking; character: I can't understand the mentality of anyone who says such callous things. | a get-rich-quick mentality

mental note /ˌ·· ˈ·/ n something fixed in the mind to be remembered: I must **make a mental note** to buy coffee/that we need more coffee. | When she mentioned her birthday casually he made a mental note of it.

men·thol /ˈmenθɒl‖-θɔːl, -θɑːl/ n [U] a white substance which smells and tastes of MINT³. It is used in some BRANDs of cigarettes to give them a special taste — ~**ated** /-θəleɪtɟd/ adj

men·tion¹ /ˈmenʃən/ v [T] **1** to tell about (something) in a few words, without giving details: We'd expected him to discuss the new scheme in his speech, but he hardly even mentioned it. [+(that)] She mentioned that she'd seen the film, but she didn't tell us anything about it. **2** to say the name of: He mentioned a useful book. | the **above-mentioned** person (=the one mentioned earlier) **3 Don't mention it** polite There is no need for thanks. I am glad to help: "Thank you very much." "Don't mention it." **4 not to mention** and in addition there is ... : They have three dogs to look after, not to mention the cat and the bird. —see also UNMENTIONABLE

mention² n [usu. sing.] a short remark about something

or naming of someone: The actor's wedding got a mention on television. | He was given a mention in the list of helpers. | (fml) He made no mention of having seen her. —see also HONOURABLE MENTION

men·tor /ˈmentɔːʳ/ n a person who gives advice to another over a period of time, esp. to help them in their working life

men·u /ˈmenjuː/ n **1** a list of dishes in a meal or to be ordered as separate meals, esp. in a restaurant: Is fish on the menu today? **2** a list of different choices shown on the SCREEN¹ (5) of a COMPUTER during a PROGRAM, from which the user must choose: a **menu-driven** program (=operated by using a menu)

Men·uh·in /ˈmenjuɟn/, **Sir Ye·hu·di** /jɟˈhuːdi/ (1916–) an American VIOLIN player, known for his music FESTIVAL in Gstaad in Switzerland and his school for children with special abilities in England

Men·zies /ˈmenziz/, **Sir Rob·ert Gor·don** /ˈrɒbət ˈgɔːdn‖ˈrɑːbərt ˈgɔːr-/ (1894–1978) an Australian politician and PRIME MINISTER who established the Liberal Party in Australia

me·ow /miˈaʊ/ n, v MIAOW

MEP /ˌem iː ˈpiː/ abbrev. for: Member of the European Parliament

Meph·i·stoph·e·les /ˌmefɟˈstɒfɟliːz‖-ˈstɑː-/ the Devil in the story of Faust, to whom Faust sold his soul —**lean** /ˌmefɪstəˈfiːliən◂/ adj

Merc /mɜːk‖mɜːrk/ infml abbrev for: **1** MERCEDES **2** MERCURY⁴

mer·can·tile /ˈmɜːkəntaɪl‖ˈmɜːrkəntiːl, -taɪl/ adj [A] fml of trade and business; COMMERCIAL: mercantile law

mercantile ma·rine /ˌ··· ·ˈ·/ n see MERCHANT NAVY

Mer·ca·tor pro·jec·tion /məˌkeɪtə prəˈdʒekʃən‖mərˌkeɪtər-/ also **Mercator's projection**— n [U] a way of drawing a map of the world so that it can be divided into regular squares, instead of getting thinner at the northern and southern edges

Mer·ce·des /mɜːˈseɪdiz‖mər-/ tdmk also **Mercedes Benz** /mɜːˌseɪdɪz ˈbenz ‖ mər-/, **Merc** infml a type of large, fast, comfortable car made by the German Mercedes-Benz company. It is regarded as a LUXURY car bought by very rich people.

mer·ce·na·ry¹ /ˈmɜːsɟnəri‖ˈmɜːrsəneri/ adj derog influenced by the wish for money

mercenary² n a soldier who fights for any country or group that pays him, not for his own country

mer·chan·dise¹ /ˈmɜːtʃəndaɪz, -daɪs‖ˈmɜːr-/ n [U] **1** things for sale; goods **2** goods such as records, BADGEs, T-SHIRTs, etc., connected with a popular performer or show, and sold at a performance: We make more from the merchandise than we do from ticket sales.

merchandise² v [T] to try to sell (goods or services): If this product is properly merchandised, it should sell very well.

mer·chant /ˈmɜːtʃənt‖ˈmɜːr-/ n a person who buys and sells goods, esp. of a particular sort, in large amounts: a timber/tea/coal merchant

merchant bank /ˌ·· ·ˈ·/ n a bank that provides banking services for businesses rather than for ordinary people. Merchant banks lend money, provide VENTURE CAPITAL, manage SHAREs¹ (2), and give advice to companies. Merchant banks are not found in the US, where the same banks deal with business and ordinary customers through different departments.

mer·chant·man /ˈmɜːtʃəntmən‖ˈmɜːr-/ also **merchant ship** /ˈ·· ·/— n -men /mən/ a ship carrying goods for trade

merchant na·vy /ˌ·· ˈ··/ also **mercantile marine** esp. BrE ‖ **merchant marine** /ˌ·· ·ˈ·/esp. AmE— n **1** all of a nation's ships which are used in trade, not war **2** [+sing./pl. v] the people who work on these ships

Merchant of Ven·ice /ˌ··· ·ˈ··/, **The** a play by Shakespeare, which includes the characters Shylock and Portia, and the argument over "a pound of flesh" —see also SHYLOCK

mer·ci·ful /ˈmɜːsɟfəl‖ˈmɜːr-/ adj **1** showing MERCY; forgiving or being kind rather than punishing or being cruel: The merciful king saved him from death. **2** happening by good luck and changing a bad situation: a merciful death (=it was fortunate to die, rather than suffer) — ~**ly** adv : Mercifully (=luckily), I remembered his name just in time. — ~**ness** n [U]

mer·ci·less /ˈmɜːsɪləs‖ˈmɜːr-/ *adj* showing no MERCY; punishing rather than forgiving: *a merciless judge* | (fig.) *merciless criticism* — ~**ly** *adv* — ~**ness** *n* [U]

mer·cu·ri·al /mɜːˈkjʊəriəl‖mɜːr-/ *adj esp. lit* quick, active, and often changing: *a mercurial temper* | *her mercurial mind* — ~**ly** *adv*

mer·cu·ry /ˈmɜːkjɒri‖ˈmɜːr-/ *n* [U] a heavy silver-white metal that is a simple substance (ELEMENT), is liquid at ordinary temperatures, and is used in THERMOMETERS, BAROMETERS, etc.

Mercury[1] in CLASSICAL MYTHOLOGY, the Roman messenger of the gods (Greek name Hermes). He is usu. shown with wings on his shoes and HELMET.

Mercury[2] the PLANET nearest to the sun —see picture at SOLAR SYSTEM

Mercury[3] an independent company which runs a TELECOMMUNICATIONS system in Britain, which the public can use in special blue telephone boxes. The system is also widely used by businesses.

Mercury[4] also **Merc** *infml*— an American car made by Ford

Mercury[5], **Fred·die** /ˈfredi/ (1946–91) a British popular music singer with the group **Queen**, known for his strange clothes and exciting performances on stage. He died of AIDS.

Mercury pro·gram /ˈ··· ˌ··/ [*the*] an American space programme of the early 1960s to put a man in ORBIT (=travelling in a large circle) around the earth

mer·cy /ˈmɜːsi‖ˈmɜːrsi/ *n* **1** [U] willingness to forgive, not to punish; kindness and pity: *The general showed no mercy, and killed all his prisoners.* **2** [S] *infml* a fortunate event: *It's a mercy the accident happened so close to the hospital.* **3 at the mercy of** powerless against: *They were lost at sea, at the mercy of wind and weather.* **4 leave to someone's (tender) mercies** *humor* to give to the cruel control of: *I'll teach him to ski myself, rather than leave him to the tender mercies of the skiing instructor.* **5 be thankful for small mercies** be grateful for what you have

mercy kill·ing /ˈ··· ˌ··/ *n* [C;U] EUTHANASIA

mere[1] /mɪəʳ/ *adj* **1** [A *no comp.*] nothing more than (a); only (a): *She lost the election by a mere 20 votes.* | *a mere child* **2 the merest** the smallest or most unimportant: *The merest little thing makes him nervous.*

mere[2] *n* **1** *lit.* a lake **2** (*in comb., as part of a name*): *Lake Windermere*

Mer·e·dith /ˈmerᵻdɪθ/, **George** (1828–1909) English writer and poet, whose works included the NOVEL *The Ordeal of Richard Feverel* and *Poems and Lyrics*

mere·ly /ˈmɪəli‖ˈmɪər-/ *adv* only; simply: *I merely suggested you should do it again; there's no need to get annoyed.* | *She's merely a child.*

mer·e·tri·cious /ˌmerᵻˈtrɪʃəs◂/ *adj fml* attractive on the surface, but false or of no real value: *a meretricious argument* — ~**ly** *adv* — ~**ness** *n* [U]

merge /mɜːdʒ‖mɜːrdʒ/ *v* [I;T (**into, with**)] to combine or cause (two or more things) to combine, esp. gradually, so as to become a single thing: *One colour merged into the other.* | *The two roads merge a mile ahead.* | *to merge two companies* —see MIX (USAGE)

merg·er /ˈmɜːdʒəʳ‖ˈmɜːr-/ *n* a joining together of two or more companies or firms

me·rid·i·an /məˈrɪdiən/ *n* **1** [C] an imaginary line drawn from the top point of the Earth (NORTH POLE) to the bottom (SOUTH POLE) over the surface of the Earth, one of several used on maps to show position **2** [(*the*) S] *fml* or *pomp* the highest point of success

me·ringue /məˈræŋ/ *n* [C;U] (a light round cake made of) a baked mixture of sugar and the white part of eggs

mer·it[1] /ˈmerᵻt/ *n* **1** [U] the quality of deserving praise, reward, etc.; personal worth: *There's little merit in passing the test if you cheated.* | *They recognized her merit and promoted her.* **2** [C] a good quality: *One of her many merits is absolute reliability.* | *We must judge each plan on its (own) merits.* (=by its own qualities, not by your opinions) | *The committee are looking at the merits and demerits of the proposal.* —compare DEMERIT

merit[2] *v* [T *not in progressive forms*] *fml* to deserve; have a right to: *Your suggestion merits serious consideration.*

mer·i·toc·ra·cy /ˌmerᵻˈtɒkrəsi‖-ˈtɑː-/ *n* **1** [C] a social system which gives the highest positions to those with the most ability **2** [*the*+S+*sing./pl. v*] the people who rule in this kind of system

mer·i·to·ri·ous /ˌmerᵻˈtɔːriəs◂/ *adj fml* deserving reward or praise — ~**ly** *adv*

Mer·lin /ˈmɜːlᵻn‖ˈmɜːr-/ (in the ARTHURIAN LEGEND) a MAGICIAN, adviser to King Arthur. He was imprisoned for all time by a woman to whom he told the secrets of his magic.

mermaid

mer·maid /ˈmɜːmeɪd‖ˈmɜːr-/ **mer·man** /-mæn/*masc.*— *n* (in stories) a creature with a woman's body from the head to the waist and a fish's tail instead of legs —see also LITTLE MERMAID

Mermaid Thea·tre /ˌ·· ˈ··/ [*the*] a theatre in London beside the river Thames

Mer·man /ˈmɜːmən‖ˈmɜːr-/, **Eth·el** /ˈeθəl/ (1909–84) an American singer and actress, most remembered for her loud and easily recognizable voice. People often copy the way she sang *There's No Business Like Show Business.*

mer·ri·ment /ˈmerᵻmənt/ *n* [U] laughter and (sounds of) fun and enjoyment: *His strange new hairstyle was the cause of much merriment.* (=made people laugh)

mer·ry /ˈmeri/ *adj* **1** cheerful; full of lively happiness, fun, etc.: *a merry fellow* | *a merry smile* **2** causing laughter and fun: *a merry prank* **3** [F] *BrE infml euph* rather drunk: *We got a bit merry at the party.* **4 make merry** *infml lit* to have fun, esp. eating and drinking for enjoyment **5 Merry Christmas!** Have a happy time at Christmas! **6 the more the merrier** a phrase used when saying that the more people join in an activity, the more enjoyable it will be —see also **eat, drink and be merry** (EAT) —**rily** *adv* —**riness** *n* [U]

Merry En·gland, **Mer·rie England** /ˌmeri ˈɪŋglənd/ *n* [U] an image of England in Elizabethan times when life was supposedly pleasant and joyful, with lots of singing and dancing

merry-go-round /ˈ··· ˌ·/ also **roundabout** *BrE* ‖ **carousel** *AmE*— *n* a machine in an amusement park on which esp. children can ride round and round sitting on model animals

mer·ry·mak·ing /ˈmeriˌmeɪkɪŋ/ *n* [U] *lit* fun and enjoyment, esp. eating, drinking, dancing, and games: *There was joy and merrymaking in the whole country when the king's son was born.* —**er** *n*

Merry Men /ˌ·· ˈ·/ *n* [P] (in the stories of Robin Hood) the companions of Robin Hood: *Robin Hood and his Merry Men* —see ROBIN HOOD and see colour picture on page 620

Merry Mon·arch /ˌ·· ˈ··/ [*the*] a NICKNAME for King Charles II of England, who was noted for his pleasure-loving way of life

Merry Wives of Wind·sor /ˌ·· ˌ· · ˈ··/, **The** a play (COMEDY) by William Shakespeare (1600), famous for the character of Sir John Falstaff —see also FALSTAFF

Mer·sey /ˈmɜːzi‖ˈmɜːr-/ [*the*] a river in the NW of England, which flows through Cheshire, Greater Manchester and Merseyside into the Irish Sea. The Mersey is often connected with Liverpool and the **Mersey sound** was the music of the Beatles in the 1960s. —see colour map on page 818

Mer·sey·side /ˈmɜːzisaɪd‖ˈmɜːr-/ a METROPOLITAN COUNTY in the NW of England, including Liverpool. It used to be an industrial area, with many DOCKS, but these have nearly all closed now. Its administrative centre is Liverpool.

Mer·thi·o·late /ˈmɜːθiəleɪt ‖ ˈmɜːr-/ *AmE tdmk* a bright red liquid medicine formerly used on small cuts in the skin to prevent infection

mes·ca·lin , -line /ˈmeskəliːn, -lᵻn/ *n* [U] a drug which is obtained from a type of CACTUS plant and causes HALLUCINATIONS (=imaginary things seen that seem real)

Mes·dames /ˈmeɪdæm‖meɪˈdɑːm/ *pl. of* MADAM, MADAME

Mes·de·moi·selles /ˌmeɪdəmwɑːˈzel/ *pl. of* MADEMOISELLE

mesh[1] /meʃ/ *n* [C;U] **1** (a piece of) material woven in a network with small holes between the threads: *We put some* wire mesh|*a fine wire mesh over the chimney so that the birds wouldn't fall in.* | *The fish were caught in the meshes of the net.* | (fig.) *caught in a mesh of lies* **2** the spaces of a certain size in a network: *a net of fine* (=small) *mesh* —see also MICROMESH **3 in mesh** (of the teeth of GEARs) held together

mesh² *v* [I (**with**)] **1** (of the teeth of GEARs) to connect; be held together: *The teeth on these two wheels mesh as the wheels revolve.* **2** (of qualities, ideas, etc.) to fit together suitably: *Their characters just don't mesh.* | *fast-food restaurants that don't really mesh with the atmosphere of old country towns*

mes·mer·is·m /ˈmezmərɪzəm/ *n* [U] *old use for* HYPNOTISM (from Franz Mesmer, an Austrian PHYSICIAN who developed the use of HYPNOTISM) —**·ist** *n*

mes·mer·ize also **-ise** *BrE* /ˈmezməraɪz/ *v* [T] **1** to hold the complete attention of, esp. so as to make speechless and unable to move; FASCINATE: *We stood by the lake, mesmerized by the flashing colours of the fish.* **2** *old use for* HYPNOTIZE: *a snake mesmerizing a rabbit* —**·ic** /mezˈmerɪk/ *adj*

me·son /ˈmiːzɒn‖-zɑːn/ *n* any of the ELEMENTARY PARTICLES in the centre of an atom that carry the STRONG FORCE

Mes·o·po·ta·mi·a /ˌmesəpəˈteɪmiə/ an area in W Asia around the Tigris and Euphrates rivers in modern Iraq, which was a centre of civilization in the ancient world

mess¹ /mes/ *n* **1** [S;U] (a state of) untidiness or dirt; dirty material: *This room's* **in a mess.** | *There's a lot of mess to clear up.* | *What an awful mess!* **2** [S] *infml* a situation full of difficulty and disorder; trouble: *The company's affairs are in a terrible mess.* **3** [C *usu. sing.*] *infml* someone or something untidy, disordered, etc.: *You look a mess — you can't go to the office like that.* | *That report you did's a real mess — do it again!* **4** [C] a room in which members of the armed forces eat together: *the officers' mess* **5** [C;U] *euph* a quantity of animal FAECES (=solid waste material): *The dog made a mess on the carpet.* **6 here's another fine mess you've gotten us in to** *quote* a phrase often used by the COMEDIANS Laurel and Hardy **7 make a mess of** *infml* to spoil, ruin, etc.: *This illness makes a mess of my holiday plans.*

mess² *v* **1** [I+*adv/prep*] to have meals in a MESS¹ (4) **2** [I (**with**)] *AmE* to argue with someone or annoy them by treating them badly: *Don't mess with me boy, or you'll be sorry!*

mess about esp. *BrE* ‖ **mess around** esp. *AmE* *phr v* **1** [I] *infml* to spend time lazily, doing things slowly with no plan: *He spent all day just messing about.* **2** [I] to act or speak stupidly: *Stop messing about and tell me clearly what happened!* **3** [I (**with**)] to work without speed or plan, but according to one's feelings at the time: *He's always enjoyed messing around with boats.* **4** [T] (**mess sbdy. about**) *infml* to treat badly or carelessly: *Don't mess me about; I want the money you promised me.*

mess around *phr v* [I (**with**)] *AmE euph* to make sexual advances, esp. when unwelcomed or forbidden: *arrested for messing around with young boys*

mess sthg. ↔ **up** *phr v* [T] *infml* to disorder, spoil, etc.: *Her late arrival messed up our plans.* —**mess-up** /ˈ· ·/ *n*

mess with sthg. *phr v* [T] to get involved with: *It's not a good idea to mess with stolen goods.*

mes·sage /ˈmesɪdʒ/ *n* **1** a spoken or written piece of information passed from one person to another: *There's an important message for you from your brother.* [+*to-v*] *Let's leave her a message to meet us at the station.* [+ *that*] *Did you get the message that your boss has cancelled the meeting?* **2** an important or main idea: *It's not just mindless entertainment — it's a film with a message.* [+*that*] *Christ's message was that God loved the world.* **3 get the message** *infml* to understand what is wanted or meant

mes·sen·ger /ˈmesɪndʒəʳ, -sʌn-/ *n* **1** a person who brings a message **2 blame/shoot the messenger** to be angry with someone who tells you that something is wrong, although it is not their fault

Mes·ser·schmitt /ˈmesəʃmɪt‖-sər-/ *n* a German plane used in the Second World War

mes·si·ah /mɪˈsaɪə/ *n* [*usu. sing.*] (*often cap.*) a great religious leader arriving suddenly to save the world, esp. (*cap.*) Christ in the Christian religion or the man still expected by the Jews —**·anic** /ˌmesiˈænɪk◂/ *adj*

Mes·sieurs /meɪˈsjɜːz‖-ɜːrz/ *pl. of* MONSIEUR

mess kit /ˈ· ·/ *n* a small box containing food and tools (UTENSILs) to eat it with, supplied to soldiers —see also MRE

Mes·srs /ˈmesəz‖-ərz/ (used chiefly in writing as the *pl.* of MR, esp. in the names of firms): *Messrs Ford and Dobson, piano repairers*

mess·y /ˈmesi/ *adj* **1** untidy: *a messy room* **2** needing a lot of cleaning up afterwards: *A kid's party is a messy business.* | (fig.) *a messy divorce* —**·ily** *adv* —**·iness** *n* [U]

mes·ti·zo /meˈstiːzəʊ/ *n* **-zos** a person with one Spanish parent and one Native American parent

met /met/ *past tense and participle of* MEET

Met [*the*] *infml short for:* **1** the METROPOLITAN OPERA COMPANY **2** the METROPOLITAN POLICE

me·tab·o·lis·m /mɪˈtæbəlɪzəm/ *n* the system of chemical activities by which a living thing gains power (ENERGY), esp. from food: *The metabolism is slowed down by extreme cold.* —**·lic** /ˌmetəˈbɒlɪk◂‖-ˈbɑː-/ *adj*

me·tab·o·lize also **-ise** *BrE*— /mɪˈtæbəlaɪz/ *v* [T] to break down (food) in the body by chemical activity

met·al¹ /ˈmetl/ *n* **1** [C;U] any usu. solid shiny mineral substance which can be shaped by pressure and used for passing an electric current: *Copper and silver are both metals.* | *They poured the molten metal into moulds.* | *a metal box* | *metal fatigue* —see also HEAVY METAL, METALLIC, WHITE METAL **2** [U] *old-fash BrE* small stones for making roads

metal² *v* **-ll-** *BrE* ‖ **-l-** *AmE* [T] *old-fash BrE* to cover (a road) with small stones: *a metalled road*

met·a·lan·guage /ˈmetəˌlæŋgwɪdʒ/ *n* [C;U] words used for talking about or describing language; the language of LINGUISTICS

metal de·tec·tor /ˈ·· ·ˌ··/ *n* a machine used to DETECT the presence of metal, usu. under the ground. Some people use metal detectors as a HOBBY, to try to find money, old coins, etc.

me·tal·lic /mɪˈtælɪk/ *adj* **1** of metal: *metallic alloys* **2** like a metal in appearance or sound: *a sharp metallic clink* | *a bright metallic blue*

met·al·lur·gy /mɪˈtælədʒi‖ˈmetələːrdʒi/ *n* [U] the scientific study of metals, their chemical structures, and the ways in which they behave and can be used —**·gist** *n* —**·gical** /ˌmetəˈlɜːdʒɪkəl◂‖-ɜːr-/ *adj*

met·al·work /ˈmetlwɜːk‖ -wɜːrk/ *n* [U] **1** shaped metal objects **2** the making of metal objects —**~ er** *n*

met·a·mor·phose /ˌmetəˈmɔːfəʊz‖-ɔːr-/ *v* [I;T (**from, into**)] *fml or tech* to (cause to) change into another form

metamorphosis

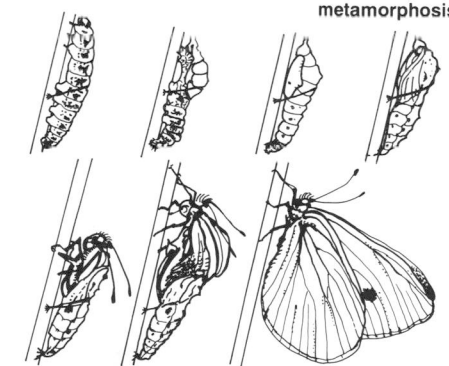

the metamorphis of a caterpillar into a butterfly

met·a·mor·pho·sis /ˌmetəˈmɔːfəsɪs‖-ɔːr-/ *n* **-ses** /siːz/ [C;U (**from, into**)] (a) complete change from one form to another: *A butterfly is produced by metamorphosis from a caterpillar.* | *I think you'll be pleasantly surprised; she's undergone quite a metamorphosis since you last saw her.*

met·a·phor /ˈmetəfəʳ, -fɔːʳ‖-fɔːr/ *n* [C;U] (the use of) an expression which means or describes one thing or idea using words usually used of something else with very similar qualities (as in *the sunshine of her smile* or *The rain came down in buckets.*) without using the words as or **like** —compare SIMILE; see also MIXED METAPHOR

met·a·phor·i·cal /ˌmetəˈfɒrɪkəl◀‖-ˈfɔː-, -ˈfɑː-/ adj using words to mean something different from their ordinary meaning: *It is a metaphorical phrase, Pierre; when I say he has green fingers, I mean he is good at gardening!* — ~**ly** /kli/ adv : *He's got a big head — metaphorically speaking, of course!*

met·a·phys·i·cal /ˌmetəˈfɪzɪkəl◀/ adj 1 [no comp.] of metaphysics 2 fml (of ideas or thinking) difficult to un- ·derstand; ABSTRACT (2) 3 [no comp.] (of British poetry) in a 17th century style which combined strong feelings with clever arrangements of words and ideas. The best-known metaphysical poetry is that of John Donne, George Herbert, and Andrew Marvell. — ~**ly** /kli/ adv

met·a·phys·ics /ˌmetəˈfɪzɪks/ n [U] a branch of PHILOSOPHY (=the study of thought) concerned with trying to under-stand and describe the nature of reality

mete /miːt/ v
mete sthg. ↔ **out** phr v [T (to)] fml or lit to cause some-one to suffer (punishment, bad treatment, etc.); ADMINISTER: *to mete out punishment to the offenders*

me·tem·psy·cho·sis /ˌmɛˌtemsaɪˈkəʊsɪs‖-sɪˈkəʊ-/ n [U] tech TRANSMIGRATION

me·te·or /ˈmiːtiəʳ/ n a small piece of matter floating in space that starts to burn if it falls into the Earth's air (AT-MOSPHERE), and can then be seen as a line of light

me·te·or·ic /ˌmiːtiˈɒrɪk◀‖-ˈɔːrɪk◀, -ˈɑːrɪk◀/ adj of or like a meteor, esp. in being very fast or in being bright and last-ing only a short time: *a meteoric rise to fame* — ~**ally** /kli/ adv

me·te·o·rite /ˈmiːtiəraɪt/ n a meteor that has landed on the Earth, without being totally burnt up

Meteorological Of·fice /·····‖···· ,··/ also **Met Office**— [the] the office which collects information on the weather in Britain and gives weather FORECASTs to the public, based at Bracknell in S England —compare NATIONAL WEATHER SERVICE

me·te·o·rol·o·gy /ˌmiːtiəˈrɒlədʒi‖-ˈrɑː-/ n [U] the scientific study of weather conditions —**gist** n —**gical** /ˌmiːtiərə-ˈlɒdʒɪkəl‖-ˈlɑː-/ adj

meters

electricity meter

parking meter

anemometer

micrometer

ammeter

me·ter¹ /ˈmiːtəʳ/ n (often in comb.) a machine which meas-ures the amount of something used: *The man from the gas board came to read the gas meter.* | *an altimeter* (=for measuring height) | *a coin (in the slot) meter* (=a meter which allows a measured amount of something, e.g. gas, to be used when the right coin is put into it) —see also PARKING METER

meter² n AmE for METRE

meter³ v [T] to measure or supply by means of a METER¹: *an instrument that meters rainfall* | *The water in our house is metered.*

-meter see WORD FORMATION

meter maid /··· ,·/ n old fash a woman whose job is to write PARKING TICKETS and put them on cars

meth·a·done /ˈmeθədəʊn/ n a drug which is often supplied to people trying to break their ADDICTION to HEROIN, usu. at a **methadone clinic**

me·thane /ˈmiːθeɪn‖ˈme-/ n [U] a gas which is formed from decaying matter, is often burned to give heat, and has re-cently come to public notice as a GREENHOUSE GAS

meth·a·nol /ˈmeθənɒl‖-nɔːl, -nɑːl/ n [U] AmE METHYL ALCOHOL

me·thinks /mɪˈθɪŋks/ **-thought** /ˈθɔːt/ old use I think

meth·od /ˈmeθəd/ n 1 [C (of, for)] a planned way of doing something: *The bank has introduced a new method of cal-culating the interest on loans.* | *outdated training methods* 2 [U] proper planning and arrangement: *There's not much method in the way they do their accounts.* —see also METHODOLOGY, SCIENTIFIC METHOD 3 cap a TECHNIQUE used by actors when they try to become the character they are playing, first introduced by Constantin Stanislavsky 4 **There's 'method in someone's madness** infml Even though someone seems to be behaving strangely, there's a sensible reason for what they're doing

me·thod·i·cal /mɪˈθɒdɪkəl‖məˈθɑː-/ adj doing things care-fully, using an ordered system: *a methodical person* — ~**ly** /kli/ adv : *He went through the thousands of books methodically, one by one.*

Meth·od·is·m /ˈmeθədɪzəm/ n [U] the beliefs of a Christian Protestant group which follows the teachings of John Wesley, who placed importance on personal and social MORALITY —**dist** adj, n

meth·o·dol·o·gy /ˌmeθəˈdɒlədʒi‖-ˈdɑː-/ n [C;U] tech the set of methods used for study or action in a particular sub-ject, as in science or education: *a new methodology of teaching/teaching methodology* —**gical** /ˌmeθədəˈlɒdʒɪ-kəl◀‖-ˈlɑː-/ adj —**gically** /kli/ adv

meths /meθs/ n [U] BrE infml for METHYLATED SPIRITS

Me·thu·se·lah /mɪˈθjuːzˌələ‖-ˈθuː-/ as old as **Methuselah** very old (from a man in the Bible who was said to have lived for 969 years)

meth·yl al·co·hol /ˌmeθl ˈælkəhɒl, tech ˌmiːθaɪl-‖-hɔːl/ also **wood alcohol, methanol**— n [U] poisonous alcohol found in some natural substances, such as wood — compare ETHYL ALCOHOL

meth·yl·at·ed spir·its /ˌmeθlˌleɪtd ˈspɪrɪts/ also **meths** BrE infml— n [U] a kind of alcohol for burning in lamps, heaters, etc. It is sometimes drunk by ALCOHOLICs be-cause it is cheap, but it is very harmful and dangerous.

me·tic·u·lous /mɪˈtɪkjᵿləs/ adj extremely careful; with great attention to detail: *meticulous drawings* | *a meticulous worker* — ~**ly** adv : *meticulously tidy* — ~**ness** n [U]

mé·ti·er /ˈmetieɪ, ˈmeɪ-‖ˈmeˈtjeɪ, ˈmetjeɪ/ n pomp the trade, profession, or type of work which one does, or to which one is suited

Met Of·fice /ˌ·· ,··/ [the] the METEOROLOGICAL OFFICE

me·too /ˌ·ˈ·/ adj [A] derog copying what others have done, without making an independent decision: *a car of me-too design, just like the ones other manufacturers have produced*

me·tre¹ BrE ‖ **meter** AmE /ˈmiːtəʳ/ (written abbrev. **m**) n a unit for measuring length: *It's three metres long.* | *an area of six square metres* —see TABLE 2

metre² BrE ‖ **meter** AmE n [C;U] (any type of) arrange-ment of words in poetry into strong and weak beats — compare RHYTHM

-metre see WORD FORMATION

met·ric /ˈmetrɪk/ adj of the system of weights and measures (**metric system**) based on the metre and kilogram — compare AVOIRDUPOIS, IMPERIAL (2)

► CULTURAL NOTE Although Britain officially uses the met-ric system, and children are taught only metric units in school, the IMPERIAL system, based on the pound and the mile is still widely used. Food in tins or packets usu. has the weight shown in kilograms, but fresh food such as fruit, vegetables and meat is usu. sold by the pound. Milk is sold in PINTs or litres, and BEER is sold in pints. Distances on road signs are shown in miles. People give their own weight in STONEs (a stone = 14 pounds) and pounds, and their height in feet and inches (INCH). ◄

The imperial system is used in the US for all usual weights and measures and the metric system is used only in scientific contexts. Note however that there are differ-ences between the British and American liquid meas-ures of OUNCE, PINT, and GALLON, the British ones being slightly larger. Americans use pounds rather than stone when talking about their own weight.

met·ri·cal /ˈmetrɪkəl/ also **metric**– adj tech written in the form of poetry, with regular beats: a metrical translation of Homer – –**ly** /kli/ adv

met·ri·ca·tion /ˌmetrɪˈkeɪʃən/ n [U] a change from standards of measurement used before (such as the foot and the pound) to metres, grams, etc.

met·ri·cize also -**cise** BrE– /ˈmetrɪˌsaɪz/ v [I;T] to change to the metric system

metric ton /ˌ·· ˈ·/ n a measure of weight –see TABLE 2

met·ro /ˈmetrəʊ/ n -ros [usu. sing.] (often cap.) an underground railway system in cities in France and various other countries: the Leningrad/Washington Metro | Can you get there by metro? –compare SUBWAY (2), UNDERGROUND³ (1)

Metro-Gold·wyn-May·er /ˌmetrəʊ ˌgəʊldwɪn ˈmeɪər/ see MGM

met·ro·nome /ˈmetrənəʊm/ n an instrument with an arm that moves from side to side to give the speed at which a piece of music should be played

me·trop·o·lis /məˈtrɒpəlɪs/ |mɪˈtrɑː-/ n 1 [(the) S] fml a chief city or the capital city of a country 2 [C] an important centre of a particular activity: a business metropolis

met·ro·pol·i·tan¹ /ˌmetrəˈpɒlɪtən/ ‖-ˈpɑː-/ adj 1 of a metropolis: London Transport serves the whole metropolitan area. 2 [A] being the central country of a system: Canadian French is different from the language of metropolitan France.

metropolitan² also **metropolitan bish·op** /ˌ····· ˈ··/– n (often cap.) the BISHOP (=chief priest of high rank) of an area, esp. in the Russian Orthodox Church

metropolitan county /····· ˈ··/– one of the six local government areas created in 1972 by the **Local Government Act**, which have similar powers to counties (COUNTY)

Metropolitan Mu·se·um of Art /ˌ····· ·ˌ·· ˈ·/ [the] the most important art MUSEUM in the US, in New York City –see colour map on page 1376

Metropolitan Op·e·ra Com·pa·ny /ˌ····· ˈ··· ˌ···/ also **Met**– [the] an American OPERA company based at the Lincoln Center for Performing Arts in New York. Their performances are often broadcast on the radio.

Metropolitan Po·lice /ˌ····· ·ˈ·/ also **Met**– n [the +sing./pl. v] the police force which is responsible for London, except for the City (central London)

met·tle /ˈmetl/ n [U] 1 the will to continue bravely in spite of difficulties: The runner fell and twisted his ankle badly, but he showed his mettle by continuing in the race. 2 be on one's mettle/put someone on their mettle rather old-fash to have to make/force someone to make the best possible effort

met·tle·some /ˈmetlsəm/ adj lit, usu. apprec (esp. of a horse) high-spirited and active

mew /mjuː/ v [I] to make the sound a cat makes; MIAOW – **mew** n

mews /mjuːz/ n mews BrE a back street or yard in a city, where horses were once kept, now partly rebuilt so that people can live there, cars can be stored there etc. Mews houses are quite small but are considered desirable and can be expensive to buy: They live at 6, Camden Mews. | a mews cottage

Mex·i·can /ˈmeksɪkən/ n a person who comes from or whose parents come from Mexico –**Mexican** adj

Mexican War /ˌ··· ˈ·/ [the] (1846–48) a war between the US and Mexico, which began when the US took over Texas, which had recently won its independence from Mexico. Mexico and the US disagreed over the Texas-Mexican border. The US also wanted to buy California and New Mexico, but Mexico did not want to sell. Led by General Zachary Taylor, the future president, the US won the war, and bought an extremely large area of land which included California, Nevada, and Utah, and parts of several other states. –see also ALAMO

Mexican wave /ˌ··· ˈ·/ n a wave-like movement made by a large number of seated people, e.g. in a sports STADIUM. They stand up and raise their arms, and then sit down, one after the other so that it looks like a continuous

movement (first seen at the football World Cup in Mexico City in 1986) –see colour picture on page 884

Mex·i·co /ˈmeksɪkəʊ/ the Spanish-speaking, mostly CATHOLIC country immediately south of the US; capital Mexico City; population 84,275,000 (1989). Its people are descended from NATIVE AMERICANS and Spanish COLONISTS of the 16th and 17th centuries. It has had a strong influence on American CULTURE, esp. in food and language. –see colour map on pages 1374–5

mez·za·nine /ˈmezəniːn, ˈmetsə-/‖ˈmezə-/ n 1 a floor that comes between two other floors of a building, esp. between the bottom floor and the next floor up, and usu. does not stretch all the way from one wall to the other 2 AmE (the first few rows of seats in) the lowest BALCONY in a theatre

mez·zo¹ /ˈmetsəʊ/ adv tech (in music) not very; MODERATELY (esp. in the phrases **mezzo forte** and **mezzo piano**)

mezzo² also **mezzo-soprano** /ˌ··· ·ˈ··/– n **mezzos, mezzo-sopranos** (a woman with) a voice that is not so high as a SOPRANO's nor so low as an ALTO's

mez·zo·tint /ˈmetsəʊˌtɪnt, ˈmedzəʊ-/ n a printed picture from a metal plate that is polished in places to produce areas of light and shade

MFI /ˌem ef ˈaɪ/ one of a group of British shops selling inexpensive furniture, usu. in the form of a kit (KIT¹ (3)) which the buyer puts together at home

mg written abbrev. for: MILLIGRAM

MG /ˌem ˈdʒiː/ n tdmk a popular British sports car. People who own these cars are often very proud of them.

M Glam written abbrev. for: Mid Glamorgan

MGM /ˌem dʒiː ˈem/ Metro-Goldwyn-Mayer; an American film company based in Hollywood which has made many famous films and CARTOONs

Mgr written abbrev for: 1 manager (MANAGER (1)) 2 MONSIGNOR

MHz written abbrev. for: MEGAHERTZ

mi /miː/ n [S;U] the third note in the (SOL-FA) musical SCALE

MI written abbrev. for: MICHIGAN

MI5 /ˌem aɪ ˈfaɪv/ the British organization responsible for protecting military secrets and catching foreign spies (SPY) (from Military Intelligence Section 5)

MI6 /ˌem aɪ ˈsɪks/ the British organization responsible for sending spies (SPY) into foreign countries (from Military Intelligence Section 6)

MIA /ˌem aɪ ˈeɪ/ n AmE short for **missing in action**; a soldier who is missing but not known to be dead or a PRISONER OF WAR. There are many American MIAs still unaccounted for from the VIETNAM WAR, and this is a continuing difficulty between the governments of the US and Vietnam. –compare AWOL

Mi·am·i /maɪˈæmi/ a city in the SE of Florida, US, known as a tourist centre, and connected in some people's minds with drug SMUGGLING. It has also become a centre for IMMIGRANTs from the Caribbean. –see colour map on pages 1374–5

Miami Vice /·ˌ·· ˈ·/ a popular American television SERIES, also shown in Britain, about policemen dealing with the problems of crime in Miami

mi·aow , meow /miˈaʊ/ also **mew** v [I] to make the crying sound a cat makes –compare PURR –**miaow** n

mi·as·ma /miˈæzmə, maɪ-/ n esp. lit 1 a thick poisonous mist 2 an evil and weakening influence: the miasma of hopelessness –**mal** adj

mi·ca /ˈmaɪkə/ n [U] a glasslike substance used in making electrical instruments

Mi·caw·ber /mɪˈkɔːbə/, **Wil·kins** /ˈwɪlkɪnz/ a character in the book David Copperfield by Charles Dickens. Mr Micawber is put in prison because he owes money and cannot pay it, but he is always happy and spends any money he gets on himself, confident that "something will turn up" to get him out of trouble. He is also remembered for saying "Annual income twenty pounds, annual expenditure nineteen pounds nineteen and six, result happiness. Annual income twenty pounds, annual expenditure twenty pounds ought and six, result misery." (meaning that if you spend slightly less than you earn you will be happy, but if you spend slightly more than you earn you will be unhappy).

mice /maɪs/ **1** *pl. of* MOUSE (1,2) **2 the best laid plans/ schemes of mice and men gang aft a-gley** a slightly changed phrase from a poem by Robert Burns, meaning that even very carefully made plans often go wrong

Mich·ael·mas /ˈmɪkəlməs/ *n* [C;U] 29th September, a Christian holy day in honour of Saint Michael. In some English universities, the TERM which starts just after Michaelmas is called the Michaelmas term.

Mi·chel·an·ge·lo /ˌmaɪkəl-ˈændʒələʊ/ (1475–1564) an Italian SCULPTOR, painter, and ARCHITECT considered to be one of the greatest of all time, known esp. for his painting of the CEILING of the Sistine Chapel in Rome

Michelangelo's David

Mich·e·lin Guide /ˈmɪtʃəlɪn ˌgaɪd, ˈmɪʃ-/ *n* also **Michelin**— a guide book (GUIDE¹ (3)) produced by the French Michelin company. The **red guides** contain maps and information on hotels and restaurants in towns and cities in European countries. The hotels and restaurants are graded (GRADE) according to their quality: *This restaurant has three stars in the Michelin.* The **green guides** contain maps and notes on places of interest in Europe and the US.

Michelin man /ˈ··· ˌ·/ *n* a drawing of a small, fat man who looks as if he is made of tyres, used in advertising by the French Michelin company

Mich·e·ner /ˈmɪtʃənər/, **James** (1907–) an American writer of stories whose many books, such as *Hawaii* and *Centennial*, look at the history of a place or people over a long period of time by following the events in one or more families for several GENERATIONs

Mich·i·gan /ˈmɪʃɪgən/ (*written abbrev.* **MI**) **1** a state in the N of the US, an industrial area, known esp. for car manufacturing (MANUFACTURE) **2** a lake in N central US, one of the Great Lakes —see colour map on pages 1374–5

Mick /mɪk/ *n BrE infml*, often *derog* a name used for someone from Ireland (a short form of **Michael**, a common first name in Ireland)

mick·ey /ˈmɪki/ *n* **1** also **mickey finn** /ˌmɪki ˈfɪn/— *sl* (*often cap.*) an alcoholic drink to which a drug has been added which will make the drinker unconscious **2 take the mickey (out of someone)** *infml, esp. BrE* to make someone feel foolish by copying them or laughing at them

Mickey Mouse¹ /ˌ·· ˈ·/ a character, based on a mouse, in the early CARTOONs of Walt Disney. Mickey Mouse and his female partner **Minnie Mouse** are famous all over the world and are recognized as a SYMBOL of Disney.

Mickey Mouse² *adj* [A] *infml, usu. derog* (esp. of a business firm or similar organization) small and unimportant; not to be taken seriously: *He calls himself the managing director but his company is just a Mickey Mouse operation that he runs from his own home.*

Mickey Mouse Club /ˌ··· ˈ· ˌ·/ [*the*] an American television programme for children during the 1950s. The show began with a group of children called **Mouseketeers** singing a song that spelled out the name of Mickey Mouse.

mi·cro /ˈmaɪkrəʊ/ *n* **-cros** *infml for* MICROCOMPUTER

micro- see WORD FORMATION

mi·crobe /ˈmaɪkrəʊb/ *n not tech* a living thing that is so small that it cannot be seen without a microscope, and that may cause disease; bacterium —compare VIRUS

mi·cro·bi·ol·o·gy /ˌmaɪkrəʊbaɪˈɒlədʒi‖-ˈɑːl-/ *n* [U] the scientific study of very small living things, such as bacteria —**-gist** *n* —**-gical** /-baɪəˈlɒdʒɪkəl‖-ˈlɑː-/ *adj*

mi·cro·chip /ˈmaɪkrəʊˌtʃɪp/ *n* a CHIP¹ (6)

mi·cro·com·put·er /ˌmaɪkrəʊkəmˈpjuːtər/ also **micro** *infml*— *n* the smallest type of computer, used esp. in the home, in schools, or by small businesses —compare MAINFRAME, MINICOMPUTER, PERSONAL COMPUTER

mi·cro·cos·m /ˈmaɪkrəʊkɒzəm‖-kɑː-/ *n* [(of)] something

small and self-contained that represents all the qualities, activities, etc., of something larger: *In this fish tank is a microcosm of life on the sea bed; it shows the sea bed in* **microcosm.** —compare MACROCOSM — **-~ic** /ˌmaɪkrəʊ-ˈkɒzmɪk◂‖-ˈkɑːz-/ *adj*

mi·cro·ec·o·nom·ics /ˌmaɪkrəʊekəˈnɒmɪks, -iːkə-‖-ˈnɑː-/ *n* [S] study of the economics of a single industry, product, or other feature within a larger system —compare MACROECONOMICS —**microeconomic** *adj*

mi·cro·e·lec·tron·ics /ˌmaɪkrəʊɪlekˈtrɒnɪks‖-ˈtrɑː-/ *n* [S] the branch of electronics which concerns the production of very small PRINTED CIRCUITs and COMPONENTs — **microelectronic** *adj*

mi·cro·fiche /ˈmaɪkrəʊfiːʃ/ *n* **-fiche** *or* **-fiches** [C;U] a sheet of film on which photographs of esp. printed pages can be stored in a very small size; the pages can be read by using a **microfiche reader**

mi·cro·film¹ /ˈmaɪkrəʊfɪlm/ *n* [C;U] (a narrow length of) film for photographing a page, a letter, etc., in a very small size so that it can be easily stored

microfilm² *v* [T] to photograph (something) on microfilm

mi·cro·light /ˈmaɪkrəʊlaɪt/ *n* [C] a very light and small aircraft usu. with a wing like a HANG GLIDER, for one or two people

mi·cro·mesh /ˈmaɪkrəʊmeʃ/ *n* [U] *BrE* very fine net material used esp. for making women's tights

mi·crom·e·ter /maɪˈkrɒmɪtər‖-ˈkrɑː-/ *n* an instrument for measuring very small objects —see picture at METER

mi·cron /ˈmaɪkrɒn‖-krɑːn/ *n* one millionth of a metre

Mi·cro·ne·si·a /ˌmaɪkrəʊˈniːziə‖-ʒə/ islands of the W Pacific Ocean, including the Caroline Islands and the Gilbert Islands —see map of the world

mi·cro·or·gan·is·m /ˌmaɪkrəʊˈɔːgənɪzəm‖-ˈɔːr-/ *n* a bacterium; MICROBE

mi·cro·phone /ˈmaɪkrəfəʊn/ also **mike** *infml*— *n* an instrument for receiving sound waves and changing them into electrical waves, used in broadcasting or recording sound (e.g. in radio, telephones, etc.) or for making sounds louder: *The singer used a microphone so that everyone in the hall could hear him.* —compare MEGAPHONE

mi·cro·pro·ces·sor /ˌmaɪkrəʊˈprəʊsesər/ *n* the central CHIP¹ (6) in a small computer which controls most of its operations —see also CENTRAL PROCESSING UNIT

mi·cro·scope /ˈmaɪkrəskəʊp/ *n* a scientific instrument that makes extremely small things look larger, so that they can be seen properly and examined scientifically: *He stained some slides and looked at them under the microscope.* —compare TELESCOPE; see INSTRUMENT (USAGE), and see picture at LABORATORY

mi·cro·scop·ic /ˌmaɪkrəˈskɒpɪk◂‖-ˈskɑː-/ *adj* **1** [A] by means of a microscope: *The scientist made a microscopic examination of the dust from the prisoner's clothes.* **2** *infml* very small: *It's impossible to read his microscopic handwriting.* — **-~ally** /kli/ *adv*

mi·cro·sec·ond /ˈmaɪkrəʊˌsekənd/ *n* one millionth of a second

mi·cro·wave¹ /ˈmaɪkrəweɪv/ *n* **1** a very short electric wave, used in sending messages by radio, in RADAR, and esp. in cooking food **2** also **microwave oven** a type of OVEN that uses microwaves to cook food. Microwave ovens are used in FAST FOOD restaurants as they cook food very quickly. They are also popular in the home for defrosting (DEFROST) and cooking food. —see picture at KITCHEN

microwave² *n* [T] to cook in a microwave oven

mi·cro·wave·a·ble , microwavable /ˈmaɪkrəweɪvəbəl/ *adj* (specially prepared to be) suitable for cooking in a microwave OVEN

mid /mɪd/ *prep poet* among; in the middle of

mid- see WORD FORMATION

mid·air /ˌmɪdˈeər◂/ *n* [U] a point up in the air or the sky, away from the ground: *The planes collided in midair.* | *a midair explosion caused by a terrorist bomb*

Mi·das /ˈmaɪdəs/, **King** in CLASSICAL MYTHOLOGY, a king who was given the power to turn everything he touched to gold. He was allowed to give up this power when he found that even his food and drink turned to gold as soon as he touched them.

midas touch /ˈ·· ˌ·/ n [the] (often cap.) the ability to make money out of any activity

Mid At·lan·tic /ˌ·· ·ˈ···◂/ adj, n a way of speaking halfway between American and British English: He's got a Mid Atlantic accent.

mid-day /ˌmɪdˈdeɪ◂‖ˈmɪd-deɪ/ n [U] the middle of the day; 12 o'clock NOON: a meal at midday | a midday meal | the full heat of the midday sun —compare MIDNIGHT

midday meal /ˌ·· ˈ·/ n a meal eaten in the middle of the day

mid·den /ˈmɪdn/ n esp. dial or tech a pile of waste matter, esp. from animals

mid·dle¹ /ˈmɪdl/ adj [A] in or nearly in the centre; at the same distance from two or more points, or from the beginning and end of something: Ours is the middle house in that row of five. | a country of middle size | middle-ranking army officers

middle² n [(the) S;U (of)] **1** the central part, point, or position: Here's a photo of him with his brothers; he's the one in the middle. | a rosetree in the middle of the garden | This bill must be paid not later than the middle of the month. **2** infml the waist or the part below the waist: He's getting fatter round the middle. **3 in the middle of** busy with: Can I call you back later − I'm in the middle of lunch.

▷ USAGE Compare **centre** and **middle**. Centre is similar to **middle²** but it usually suggests an exact physical point: the **centre** of the circle. Middle is used when you cannot be so exact: the **middle** of the forest. Middle is more usual when thinking of things as lines rather than areas: He was driving along the **middle** of the road and when talking about rows of objects or people: Eve was on the left, Bill was on the right and Tom was in the **middle**. Only **middle** can be used to talk about time: in the **middle** of the day/night.◁

middle³ v [T] to hit (a shot) properly with the middle of the BAT in cricket

Middle adj [A] (of a language) of a form that developed from an earlier stage, and into a later stage: Middle French was spoken from about AD 1300 to 1600. —compare MODERN¹ (3), OLD

middle age /ˌ·· ˈ·◂/ n [U] the period of life between youth and old age.

▶ CULTURAL NOTE Middle age is usually between about 40 to 60 years of age. Young people think of the middle-aged as being boring, dull, and unadventurous, and many people in their 30s do not want to become middle-aged. ◀

—compare MALE MENOPAUSE, MENOPAUSE, MID-LIFE CRISIS — **middle-aged** adj : He's only 24, but he behaves as if he's already middle-aged.

middle-aged spread /ˌ··· ˈ·/ **midriff bulge** esp. AmE— n [U] often humor the fatness round the waist which many people get as they grow older

Middle Ag·es /ˌ·· ˈ··/ n [the+P] the period in European history between about AD 1100 and 1500 or sometimes, in a wider sense, between AD 500 and 1500

▶ CULTURAL NOTE The Middle Ages are associated with the rise of Christianity and its influence on life and society, in such things as MONASTICISM, the Crusades, and FEUDALISM. They are also thought of as a time when people were not well educated, and there was little art, music, or literature. ◀

Middle A·mer·i·ca /ˌ·· ·ˈ···/ n [U] **1** the midwestern part of the US **2** the group of Americans who are neither very poor nor very rich and who usually hold TRADITIONAL values (=values that have not changed much over the years): political ideas unacceptable to Middle America

mid·dle·brow /ˈmɪdlbraʊ/ n sometimes derog a person who likes music, painting, poetry, etc., that is of quite good quality and is liked by lots of other people but is not too difficult to understand —compare HIGHBROW, LOWBROW — **middlebrow** adj

middle C /ˌ·· ˈ·/ n the musical note that is shown on the first additional line below the STAVE in the TREBLE CLEF and the first additional line above the stave in the BASS CLEF

middle class¹ /ˌ·· ˈ·◂/ also **middle classes** pl.— n [the+S;also+sing./pl. v] the social class to which people belong who are neither noble, very wealthy, etc., nor workers with their hands, usu. consisting of business or professional people, some farmers, and skilled workers: a mem-

ber of the middle class/classes —compare LOWER CLASS, UPPER CLASS, WORKING CLASS and see also extra information on page 1258

middle-class² adj **1** belonging to or typical of the middle class **2** derog MATERIALISTIC or unadventurous: bourgeois middle-class ideas

middle course /ˈ·· ·/ n [S] BrE a course of action which is halfway between two very different ones (esp. in the phrases **follow/take/steer a/the middle course**): a middle course between liberalism and conservatism

middle-dis·tance /ˌ·· ˈ···◂/ adj [A] (in sport) over a distance that is neither very short nor very long, specifically the 800 metres and 1500 metres runs and the 3000 metres STEEPLECHASE: a middle-distance race/runner

middle distance [the] the part of a picture or view between what is close to the looker (FOREGROUND) and what is farthest away (background)

Middle East /ˌ·· ˈ·◂/ [the] the countries of SW Asia and N Africa, around the eastern end of the Mediterranean, from Libya to Iran and including the Arabian Peninsula. Many countries in the Middle East are important oil producers, but people also often think of political problems, such as the Gulf War, when the Middle East is mentioned. —compare FAR EAST, NEAR EAST − ~ **ern** adj

Middle Eng·lish /ˌ·· ·/ (written abbrev. **ME**) n English from about 1150 to 1500 AD

middle fin·ger /ˌ·· ˈ··/ n the longest finger, in the middle of the five fingers of the hand —see picture at HAND

middle ground /ˌ·· ·/ n [U] a point of view that tries to account for two others that are very different from each other; COMPROMISE

mid·dle·man /ˈmɪdlmæn/ n -men /men/ a person who buys goods from a producer, and sells to a shopkeeper or directly to a user

middle man·age·ment /ˌ·· ˈ···/ n [U+sing.‖pl. v] (the level or rank of) people in a business company who are in charge of departments and groups within it, but are below those who make the main decisions about how the company is run

middle name /ˌ·· ·/ n **1** a name coming between the FIRST NAME and the SURNAME

▶ CULTURAL NOTE It is common in Britain and the US to have a middle name and it can be a FORENAME or a SURNAME (e.g. a married woman's MAIDEN NAME), sometimes written as an INITIAL. It is not related to the family name and can be taken from anywhere. People sometimes have more than one middle name: "What's your middle name?" "It's Michael."◀

2 one's middle name infml a main part of one's character: Generosity is her middle name. (−She is very generous.)

middle of no·where /ˌ·· ·· ˈ··/ n [the+S] infml derog a place far away from towns, cities, etc.: She lives in a little house out in the middle of nowhere.

middle-of-the-road /ˌ·· ·· ·ˈ·◂/ adj sometimes derog liking, holding, or being ideas, forms of expression, etc., that most other people like, and that do not make them angry or upset; not EXTREME: a middle-of-the-road candidate | middle-of-the-road music/political views

Mid·dles·brough /ˈmɪdlzbrə/ an industrial town in the NE of England on the river Tees, where the local government for Cleveland is based

middle school /ˈ·· ·/ n **1** [C;U] (in certain countries) a school for children between the ages of 9 and 13 or 11 and 14 **2** [the+S] (in Britain) a part of a SECONDARY school for children of about 14 and 15 **3** (in the US) a JUNIOR HIGH SCHOOL, which includes GRADES 7 and 8 (ages 12 and 13) and either grade 6 or grade 9 —compare JUNIOR HIGH SCHOOL, —see also HIGH SCHOOL

Mid·dle·sex Hos·pi·tal /ˌmɪdlseks ˈhɒspɪtl‖-ˈhɑː-/ [the] a large TEACHING HOSPITAL in central London

middle-sized /ˌ·· ˈ·◂/ adj neither very large nor very small

Middle Tem·ple /ˌ·· ˈ··/ [the] one of the four Inns of Court in London —see also INNS OF COURT

Mid·dle·ton /ˈmɪdltən/, **Thomas** (1580−1627) an English writer of plays who wrote SATIRICAL comedies (COMEDY¹) and tragedies (TRAGEDY¹), including Women Beware Women

mid·dle·weight /ˈmɪdlweɪt/ n a BOXER heavier than a

WELTERWEIGHT but lighter than a LIGHT HEAVYWEIGHT

Middle West /ˌ·· ˈ·/ [the] the MIDWEST — **-ern** adj

mid·dling /ˈmɪdlɪŋ/ adj infml between large and small, good and bad, etc.; average: *"How are you feeling now?" "Oh, fair to middling."* (=fairly well, but not very well)

mid·field /ˈmɪdfiːld/ n [U] **1** the middle part of a playing field, esp. in football, that is midway between the GOALs **2** the players on a team that usu. play in midfield

mid·field·er /ˈmɪdfiːldəʳ/ n (in sports such as football or LACROSSE) one of the players in a team who normally plays in midfield

midge /mɪdʒ/ n a very small flying and biting insect, like a MOSQUITO

midg·et¹ /ˈmɪdʒɪt/ n a very small or unusually small person —compare DWARF

midget² adj [A] very small: *a midget submarine*

Mid Gla·mor·gan /ˌmɪd ɡləˈmɔːɡən ‖ -ˈmɔːr-/ (written abbrev. **M Glam**) a COUNTY in the SE of Wales, known formerly for coal production

mid·i /ˈmɪdi/ n a woman's skirt that comes to between the knee and ankle

Mi·di /miːˈdiː/ [the] the S of France: *a holiday cottage in the Midi*

MIDI /ˈmɪdi/ n **1** Musical Instrument Digital Interface; a piece of ELECTRONIC equipment which allows electronic musical instruments, computers, and SYNTHESIZERs to be connected together and used at the same time **2** a kind of MUSIC CENTRE which includes a CD player

mid·land /ˈmɪdlənd/ adj [A] of the middle part of a country

Mid·land Bank /ˌ·· ˈ·/ also **Midland**— [the] one of the main British banks, branches of which can be found in many towns and cities in Britain —see also LISTENING BANK

Mid·land·er /ˈmɪdləndəʳ/ n a person who comes from the Midlands

Mid·lands /ˈmɪdləndz/ n [the+P] the central parts of England, between the N and the S. It is an important area for light ENGINEERING industries.

mid·life cri·sis /ˌ·· · ˈ··/ n a continuing feeling of unhappiness, lack of confidence, etc. suffered by someone in the middle years of their life, when they feel that their youth has ended, usually about the age of 40 —compare MALE MENOPAUSE, MENOPAUSE, MIDDLE AGE

Mid·lo·thi·an /mɪdˈləʊðiən/ a former COUNTY in E Scotland, now part of Lothian REGION

mid·most /ˈmɪdməʊst/ adj [A] lit in the exact middle: *in the midmost part of the forest*

mid·night /ˈmɪdnaɪt/ n [U] the middle of the night; 12 o'clock at night: *We close at midnight.* | *He didn't come in till after/past midnight.* | *The programme isn't on until a quarter to midnight.* | *The doctor received a midnight call.* —compare MIDDAY; see also **burn the midnight oil** (BURN¹)

midnight feast /ˌ·· ˈ·/ n a small amount of food eaten late at night, esp. sweet things eaten secretly by children at a BOARDING SCHOOL after they have gone to bed

Midnight Mass /ˌ·· ˈ·/ n [C;U] a special Christian religious service held at midnight on Christmas Eve, to celebrate Christmas and the birth of Christ

midnight sun /ˌ·· ˈ·/ [the] the sun seen in the middle of the night at midnight in the very far north or south of the world

mid·point /ˈmɪdpɔɪnt/ n [(of) usu. sing.] a point at or near the centre or middle: *We are now at the midpoint of this government's period of office.*

mid·rash /ˈmɪdrɑːʃ/ n [U] (often cap.) a collection of ancient Jewish writings on the Bible

mid·riff /ˈmɪdrɪf/ n **1** infml the part of the human body between the chest and the waist: *The punch caught him in the midriff.* **2 midriff bulge** (esp. AmE) MIDDLE-AGED SPREAD

mid·ship·man /ˈmɪdʃɪpmən/ n -men /mən/ The rank of someone who is training to become an officer in the Royal Navy —see TABLE 3

midst¹ /mɪdst/ n **in the midst of: a** in the middle of **b** lit among: *the enemy in our midst* (=among us) **c** lit surrounded by: *In the midst of all his troubles he managed to remain cheerful.*

midst² prep old use in the midst; among

mid·sum·mer /ˈmɪdˌsʌməʳ/ n [U] **1** the middle of summer **2** the summer SOLSTICE (21st or 22nd June)

Midsummer Day /ˌ··· ˈ·/ n [C;U] BrE 24th June —see also SUMMER SOLSTICE

midsummer mad·ness /ˌ··· ˈ··/ n [U] infml lit very foolish behaviour

Midsummer Night's Dream /ˌ··· ˌ· ˈ·/, **A** a COMEDY by William Shakespeare, which is famous for the characters Puck, a SPRITE, Oberon and Titania, the king and queen of the fairies (FAIRY), and **Bottom**, a weaver. Titania has a magic SPELL put on her while she is asleep, so that she falls in love with the first creature she sees when she wakes. This is Bottom, who has been given an ass's (ASS) head. She thinks he is beautiful, until Oberon frees her from the spell.

mid·term /ˈmɪdtɜːm‖-tɜːrm/ n AmE an examination in the middle of a (university) TERM: *The chemistry midterm was a real killer!*

midterm blues /ˌ·· ˈ·/ n [P] an expression used in newspapers etc. and by politicians to explain feelings of dissatisfaction expressed by the public midway through a government's or a President's time in office

mid·town /ˈmɪdtaʊn/ adj,adv AmE in the area of a city near the centre but which is not the main business area — compare DOWNTOWN

Midtown n AmE a central area of a city, esp. the part of Manhattan S of Central Park

mid·way /ˌmɪdˈweɪ◂‖ˈmɪdweɪ/ adj, adv halfway; in a middle position: *There's a small village midway between these two towns.* | *He was knocked out midway through the third round.*

Mid·way¹ /ˈmɪdweɪ/ two small islands in the Pacific Ocean NW of Honolulu used as an American air and navy base. In 1942 it was the scene of an important sea and air battle (**the Battle of Midway**).

Midway² an airport in Chicago, Illinois, used mostly for flights within the US

mid·week /ˌmɪdˈwiːk◂‖ˈmɪdwiːk/ adj, n [U] (happening during) the middle days of the week; Tuesday, Thursday, and esp. Wednesday: *a midweek match*

Mid·west /ˌmɪdˈwest/ also **Middle West**–, **The (American)** n an area of the US in the middle of the country, including the states of Ohio, Indiana, Illinois, Wisconsin, Minnesota, Kansas, Nebraska, Iowa, Missouri, Michigan, North Dakota, South Dakota, and Oklahoma. Much of the Midwest is known for its rich farm land. —compare NORTH, SOUTH, SOUTHWEST, WEST; see also EAST COAST, NEW ENGLAND, PACIFIC NORTHWEST, WEST COAST, WILD WEST

mid·wife /ˈmɪdwaɪf/ n -wives /waɪvz/ a person, usu. a woman, who is not a doctor but helps women when they are giving birth to children: *a male midwife*

mid·wif·e·ry /ˈmɪdˌwɪfəri‖-ˌwaɪfəri/ n [U] the skill or work of a MIDWIFE

mid·win·ter /ˌmɪdˈwɪntəʳ◂/ n [U] **1** the middle of winter **2** the winter SOLSTICE (21st or 22nd December)

mien /miːn/ n lit a person's expression or appearance, as showing a particular (stated) feeling: *a thoughtful and solemn mien*

Mies van der Ro·he /ˌmiːz væn də ˈrəʊə‖-dər-/, **Lud·wig** /ˈludwɪɡ/ (1886–1969) an American ARCHITECT, best known for his many glass SKYSCRAPERS. His buildings are very modern, plain and FUNCTIONAL, without decoration. People either like them very much or not at all.

miffed /mɪft/ adj [F] infml slightly angry

might¹ /maɪt/ v 3rd person sing. **might**, negative short form **mightn't** [modal+to-v] **1** (used to show very slight possibility): *He might come, but it's very unlikely.* | *That car nearly hit me; I might have been killed!* (=but I wasn't) —compare MAY¹ (1) **2** (describes may in the past): *I thought it might rain.* (=I thought, "It may rain.") | *They asked if they might go home.* (=They asked, "May we go home?") | (fml) *He said I might go if I wished.* **3** BrE (used instead of **may,** for asking permission politely) *"Might I come in?" "Yes, of course you may."* —compare MAY¹ (2) **4** (used like **ought** or **should**): *You might at least say "thank you" when someone helps you.* | *You might have offered to carry it!* (=I am angry because you did not offer) | *I* **might have known** *she'd refuse.* (=It was typical of her to refuse.) **5** (in CLAUSES expressing hope or purpose) would; could: *I'd have thought you might remember your mother's birthday.* | *The prisoner had hopes that he might be set free.* —compare MAY¹ (5) **6** also **may** *becoming rare– pomp or humor* (in questions) do/does: *And what might this mean?* (=What does this mean?) | *Who might you be?* (=Who are you?) **7** perhaps; MAY¹ (4): *You might think you're clever, but that doesn't give you the right to order me about!* **8 might well** to have been likely to: *We lost the football match, but we might well have won if one of our players hadn't been hurt.* **9 might (just) as well** to have no strong reason not to: *No one will eat this food; it might just as well be thrown away.*

▷ USAGE 1 When you are talking about possibility **might** sometimes suggests a smaller possibility than **may,** but often these words are used to mean the same thing: *I* **may/might** *see you tonight; I don't know yet.* 2 There can be a difference between *He* **may** *have* (=perhaps he has) *drowned,* and *He* **might** *have drowned* (=he was in danger of drowning, but he did not). But many people now use these words to mean the same thing. —see also CAN (USAGE), COULD (USAGE), NOT (USAGE)◁

might² *n* [U] **1** *esp. lit.* power; strength; force: *The army was crushed by the might of the enemy forces.* | *He pushed and pushed* **with all his might** *but it wouldn't move* **2 by/with might and main** *old-fash* by using all one's strength

might-have-beens /ˈ·· ˌ·/ *n* [*the*+P] *infml* desirable things that could have happened in the past, but did not: *The old lady would sit for hours, thinking sadly of all the might-have-beens.*

might·n't /ˈmaɪtənt/ *infml, esp. BrE short for:* might not: *They mightn't come.*

might·y¹ /ˈmaɪti/ *adj esp. lit. or bibl* very great in power, strength, size, etc.: *He raised the hammer and struck the rock a mighty blow.* | *mighty empires* | *a mighty king* | *the mighty Himalayas* —see also HIGH-AND-MIGHTY —**-ily** *adv* : *He swore mightily.* | *mightily* (=very) *amused*

mighty² *adv esp. AmE infml* very: *a mighty good meal*

mi·graine /ˈmiːɡreɪn, ˈmaɪ-‖ˈmaɪ-/ *n* [C;U] (a condition in which one has) a repeated severe headache, usu. with disorder of the eyesight

mi·grant /ˈmaɪɡrənt/ *n* a person, animal or esp. bird that migrates or is migrating: *Summer migrants nest here.* | *Migrant workers move from country to country in search of work.* | *cheap migrant labour* —see EMIGRATE (USAGE)

mi·grate /maɪˈɡreɪt‖ˈmaɪɡreɪt/ *v* [I (**from, to**)] **1** (of birds and fish) to travel regularly from one part of the world to another, according to the seasons of the year **2** to travel so as to change one's place of living, esp. for a limited period: *Some tribes migrate with their cattle in search of fresh grass.* —see EMIGRATE (USAGE) —**gratory** /maɪˈɡreɪtəri‖ˈmaɪɡrəˌtɔːri/ *adj* : *migratory birds*

mi·gra·tion /maɪˈɡreɪʃən/ *n* [C;U] (an example of) the act of migrating: *Scientists have studied the migration of fish over long distances.* | *Wars always cause great migrations of people.* —see EMIGRATE (USAGE)

mi·ka·do /mɪˈkɑːdəʊ/ *n* **-dos** (*often cap.*) (a former title for) the Emperor of Japan

Mikado, The a COMIC OPERA by Gilbert and Sullivan, perhaps the best known of their works. It is set in Japan and contains several well-known songs, including *The flowers that bloom in the spring tra-la* and *Three Little Maids from School.*

mike /maɪk/ *n infml for* MICROPHONE

Mike *n infml* **for the love of Mike!** an EXCLAMATION used to express annoyance or FRUSTRATION

mi·la·dy /mɪˈleɪdi/ *n* an Englishwoman of NOBLE birth, often used in the past as a form of address (from "my lady"): *yes, milady*

Mi·lan /mɪˈlæn/ a city in N Italy, an important financial and industrial centre, known for its CATHEDRAL and OPERA HOUSE, **La Scala**

milch cow /ˈmɪltʃ kaʊ/ *n BrE* **1** a cow kept for milking **2** *rare derog* a person or organization from whom it is easy to get money

mild¹ /maɪld/ *adj* **1** *usu. apprec* gentle; not violent: *He has*

too mild a nature to get angry, even if he has good cause.* | *a mild protest* **2** not causing a lot of discomfort or suffering; not severe; slight: *It's been a mild winter this year.* (=not a cold winter) | *only a mild fever* **3** (of food, drink, etc.) not strong or bitter in taste: *This is a very mild cheese; it has a delicate taste and hardly any smell.* — — **ness** *n* [U]

mild² *n* [U] *BrE infml* beer with a mild taste: *a glass of mild and bitter* (=a mixture of mild and bitter beer)

mil·dew /ˈmɪldjuː‖-duː/ *n* [U] a soft usu. whitish growth that forms on plants and on food, leather, etc., that has been kept for a long time in warm wet conditions — ~ **ed** *adj* : *mildewed old books* — ~ **y** *adj*

mild·ly /ˈmaɪldli/ *adv* **1** in a mild manner: *She complained loudly to the shopkeeper, who answered her mildly.* **2** slightly: *I suggested it to him, but he seemed only mildly interested.* **3 to put it mildly** (used when describing something less forcefully than one could do): *The minister didn't act very sensibly, to put it mildly.* (=he behaved very foolishly)

mild-man·nered /ˌ·· ˈ···◂/ *adj* (of a person) quiet, polite, not too easily excited or emotional

mile /maɪl/ *n* **1** [C] a unit for measuring length: *a five-mile drive* | *They walked for miles.* (=a very long way) | *She lives* **miles from nowhere** (=very far from anybody else) | *to drive at 70 miles per hour* —see TABLE 2 **2** [*the*+S] a race over this distance: *The mile was won by Coe.* —see also MILER **3** also **miles** *pl.*— *infml* a very large amount; a lot: *He was miles out in his calculations.* (=they were completely wrong) | *The exam was miles too difficult.* | *You* **can see/tell a mile away/off** (=it is very clear) *that she's used to getting her own way.* **4** *infml* **go the extra mile** to give more effort to something because it is important: *UN negotiators are going the extra mile in trying to calm the strife in Yugoslavia.* **5** *infml* **run a mile** to leave quickly to avoid someone or something: *I run a mile every time he comes into the room.* **6** *infml* **talk a mile a minute** to speak quickly without stopping: *She started to talk a mile a minute as soon as she arrived.* — see also NAUTICAL MILE

mile·age /ˈmaɪlɪdʒ/ *n* **1** [C *usu. sing.*;U] the distance that is travelled, measured in miles: *What mileage has your car done?* | *What mileage does your car do per gallon?* **2** [C *usu. sing.*;U] money paid for each mile that is travelled: *He uses his own car for business purposes, and is paid mileage/a* **mileage allowance.** **3** [U] *infml* an amount of use: *The newspapers are getting a lot of mileage out of the royal baby — there's a new story about him every day.*

mile·om·e·ter , **mil·om·e·ter** /maɪˈlɒmɪtəʳ‖-ˈlɑː-/ *BrE* ‖ **odometer** *AmE*— *n* an instrument fitted in a car, etc. to record the number of miles it travels

mil·er /ˈmaɪləʳ/ *n infml* a person or horse that runs in one-mile races

mile·stone /ˈmaɪlstəʊn/ *n* **1** a stone at the side of a road, on which is marked the number of miles to the next town **2** an important event which changes the course of someone's life, or of history: *The invention of the wheel was a milestone in human history.*

mi·lieu /ˈmiːljɜː‖miːˈljɜːr, -ˈljuː/ *n* **-s** *or* **-x** /ljɜːz, ljɜː‖ˈljɜːz, ˈljuːz, ˈljɜː, ˈljuː/ [*usu. sing.*] *fml* surroundings, esp. a person's social surroundings: *Meeting the local policeman in a completely different milieu, as a fellow member of the golf club, seemed somehow strange.*

mil·i·tant /ˈmɪlɪtənt/ *adj sometimes derog* (esp. of a person or a political group) ready to fight or use force; taking an active part in a struggle: *The more militant members of the group were in favour of expelling him.* | *a militant speech, designed to rouse the crowd's anger* | *a militant feminist* —compare MILITARY —**militant** *n* : *The disorders were caused by a few militants.* — ~ **ly** *adv* —**-tancy** *n* [U]

Militant *n* the newspaper of the Militant Tendency, often sold in the street

Militant Ten·den·cy /ˌ··· ˈ···/ [*the*] an extreme left-wing group formed in the British Labour Party. Its members have been made to leave the Labour Party because they were said to have formed "a party within a party" and to be no longer following Labour Party POLICY.

mil·i·ta·ris·m /ˈmɪlɪtərɪzəm/ *n* [U] *usu. derog* belief in the idea that a country should use armed force to get what it wants —**-rist** *n* —**-ristic** /ˌmɪlɪtəˈrɪstɪk◂/ *adj* —**-ristically** /kli/ *adv*

mil·i·ta·rize also **-ise** *BrE* /ˈmɪlɪtəraɪz/ *v* [T] **1** to supply (a country, area, etc.) with military forces and defences: *the militarized zone* **2** to give a military character to: *a militarized police force*

mil·i·ta·ry¹ /ˈmɪlᵻtəriǁ-teri/ *adj* of, for, or by soldiers, armies, or war: *the providing of military aid to friendly states | combined naval and military operations | His bearing was very military.* (=he looked and acted like a soldier) | *a military hospital | He comes of a military family.* (=his father, grandfather, etc., were soldiers) —compare MILITANT

military² *n* [*the*+P] soldiers; the army: *As the police could not keep order in the city, the military were called in to help.*

Military A·cad·e·my /ˌ··· ·ˈ···/ *n* **1** a state institution that offers higher military instruction, usually for officers, the best known in Britain being Sandhurst **2** a private secondary school in the US which includes military training and military uniforms

military band /ˌ···· ˈ·/ *n* a band of BRASS, WOODWIND, and PERCUSSION instruments connected to a military unit, which plays marching and concert music

Military Cross /ˌ···· ˈ·/ (*abbrev.* **MC**) [*the*] a MEDAL given to British army officers for bravery

military-in·dus·tri·al com·plex /ˌ···· ·ˈ··· ˌ··/ *n* the military forces and the large producers of weapons in a country or in the world, considered as a single, very powerful influence on governments

military po·lice /ˌ···· ·ˈ·/ *n abbrev* **MP** [*the*+P] (*often cap.*) a special police force formed of soldiers (**military policemen**), whose job is to deal with soldiers who break army rules

military ser·vice /ˌ···· ˈ··/ *n* [U] a system used in some countries by which young men (in some countries also young women) have to serve in the armed forces etc. for a period of time, often a year: *Did you have to do military service?* —see also DRAFT, NATIONAL SERVICE

mil·i·tate /ˈmɪlᵻteɪt/ *v*
  militate against sthg. *phr v* [T] *fml* to act as a reason against: *The fact that he'd been in prison militated against him when he applied for jobs.* [+*v-ing*] *The high risks involved in such a business venture militate against finding backers.*

mi·li·tia /mᵻˈlɪʃə/ *n* [(*the*) C+*sing./pl. v*] a body of men (**militiamen**) not belonging to a regular army, but trained as soldiers to serve only in their own country if it is attacked or in times when there is violence and disorder in towns, cities, etc.

milk¹ /mɪlk/ *n* [U] **1** a white liquid produced by women or female animals for the feeding of their young, and, (in the case of cows' and goats' milk) drunk by human beings or made into butter, cheese, etc.: *a bottle of milk | skimmed milk | pasteurized milk* —see picture at BOTTLE **2** a whitish liquid or juice obtained from certain plants and trees: *coconut milk* **3 a land of milk and honey** *lit* an imaginary place where life is easy and pleasant, with plenty of food **4 the milk of human kindness** *lit or pomp* the pity for the sufferings of others that should be natural to human beings —see also CONDENSED MILK, EVAPORATED MILK, SKIMMED MILK, **cry over spilt milk** (CRY¹)

milk² *v* **1 a** [T] to take milk from (a cow, goat, etc.) **b** [I] (of a cow, goat, etc.) to give milk: *This cow isn't milking very well.* **2** [T] to get money, knowledge of a secret, etc., from (someone or something) by clever or dishonest means **3** [T] to take the poison from (a snake) **4 milk something for all its worth** *esp. AmE* to take full advantage (of a situation) usu. in a way that is not approved of: *He's got a letter from a senator that he's milking for all its worth to get a job in the State Dept.*

milk choco·late /ˌ·ˈ···◂ ǁ ˌ·ˈ····◂/ *n* [U] solid chocolate made with the addition of milk —compare PLAIN CHOCOLATE

milk·er /ˈmɪlkəʳ/ *n* **1** a cow that gives milk: *This one is our best milker.* **2** a person who milks cows, goats, etc. **3** a milking machine

milk float /ˈ· ·/ *n BrE* a vehicle used by a milkman for delivering milk, now usu. driven by electricity

milking ma·chine /ˈ·· ·ˌ·/ also **milker** *AmE*— *n* a machine used for taking milk from cows. More than one cow may be connected to the machine at the same time.

milk lake /ˈ· ˌ·/ *n* a store of milk which is not needed or

used, esp. the one produced by the EC countries

milk·maid /ˈmɪlkmeɪd/ *n* (esp. in former times) a woman who milks cows; DAIRYMAID

milk·man /ˈmɪlkmən/ *n* -**men** /mən/ a person who sells milk, esp. one who goes on a regular journey from house to house each day to deliver it.

▶ CULTURAL NOTE In Britain milkmen are usually men and many jokes are made about them having sex with women who are at home alone while their husbands are at work. ◀

Milk Mar·ket·ing Board /ˌ· ˈ···· ˌ·/ [*the*] the organization in Britain that manages the sale of milk from farms to dairies (DAIRY) and finally to the public

milk of mag·ne·sia /ˌ· ·ˈ·ˌ··/ *n* [U] a thick white liquid containing MAGNESIUM, used to treat stomach problems and CONSTIPATION

milk pud·ding /ˌ· ˈ··/ *n* a dish made of RICE, TAPIOCA, or SAGO, baked in sweetened milk and eaten at the end of a meal

Milk Race /ˈ· ·/ [*the*] a bicycle race round Britain which lasts for 13 days and covers about 2410 km (the name comes from the SPONSOR of the race, the Milk Marketing Board)

milk round /ˈ· ˌ·/ *n* **1** [C] the regular journey a milkman makes every day to deliver milk to the same houses **2** [*the*] a number of visits to universities made by large companies who want to employ young people when they leave university

milk run /ˈ· ·/ *n infml* a familiar and frequently travelled journey or course

milk shake /ˌ· ˈ·ǁˈ· ·/ *n* a drink of milk and usu. ice cream shaken up and tasting of fruit, chocolate, etc.: *a strawberry milk shake*

milk·sop /ˈmɪlksɒpǁ-sɑːp/ *n old-fash derog* a boy or man who is too gentle and weak, and is afraid to do anything dangerous

milk tooth /ˈ· ·/ also **baby tooth** *esp. AmE*— *n* any of the first set of teeth developed by young children and animals, which come before the main set

Milk Tray /ˌ· ˈ·/ *n* [U] *tdmk* a selection of chocolates made by Cadbury's. In advertisements for Milk Tray, a man makes a dangerous and difficult journey, e.g. swimming across a lake or climbing a high mountain, to carry the chocolates to an attractive woman. At the end of his journey the advertisement says, "And all because the lady loves Milk Tray."

milk·weed /ˈmɪlkwiːd/ *n* [U] a common N American plant which lets out a bitter, milky-looking substance when its stem is broken, and which is said to cause much discomfort for people who suffer from HAY FEVER

milk·y /ˈmɪlki/ *adj* **1** made of, containing, or like milk: *milky coffee* (=made with a lot of milk) **2** (of water or other liquids) not clear; cloudy; having a milklike appearance —**iness** *n* [U]

Milky Bar /ˈ··· ·/ *n tdmk* a type of chocolate bar made by Nestlé; Milky Bars are made of white chocolate

▶ CULTURAL NOTE Milky Bars are advertised on television by a child character called the Milky Bar Kid ◀

Milky Way /ˌ··· ˈ·/ *n* **1** the pale white band of stars that can be seen across the sky at night **2** the GALAXY in which Earth and the SOLAR SYSTEM are found **3** *tdmk* in Britain, a chocolate bar with a well-known advertising phrase "a sweet you can eat between meals without ruining your appetite" **4** *tdmk* in the US, a chocolate bar with a soft centre and CARAMEL inside

mill¹ /mɪl/ *n* **1** also **flourmill**— (a building containing) a large machine for crushing grain into flour —see also MILLER, WATERMILL, WINDMILL **2** a factory: *a steel rolling mill | the cotton mills of Lancashire* (where cotton cloth was made) | *Paper is made in a paper mill.* —see also DARK SATANIC MILLS **3** a small machine for crushing or grinding (GRIND) the stated solid material: *a coffee mill | a pepper mill* **4 put someone/go through the mill** to (cause to) pass through a time of hard training, hard experience, or suffering —see also RUN-OF-THE-MILL

mill² *n AmE* a unit of money equal to 1/10 of a cent, used in setting taxes and other accounting purposes: *Three mills will be added to local property taxes to pay for the new school.*

mill³ *v* [T] **1 a** to crush (grain) in a mill **b** to produce (flour) by this means **2** to press, roll, or shape (metal) in a machine **3** to mark (the edge of a coin) with regularly placed lines

mill about/around *phr v* [I] *infml* (of a large number of people) to move about in a place with no fixed shared purpose, each person going in different directions: *There was a crowd of people milling about in the streets.*

Mill, John Stuart (1806–73) an English thinker who wrote about economics and had a great influence on modern economics, politics, and thought. His book *On Liberty* argued that people should be free to do as they wished as long as they did not harm others.

Mil·lais /ˈmɪleɪ/, **Sir John Ev·e·rett** /dʒɒn ˈevərɪt‖ˈdʒɑːn-/ (1829–96) an English painter, involved in the PRE-RAPHAELITE movement. His best-known works are *Christ in the Carpenter's Shop* and *The Boyhood of Raleigh*. — see picture at OPHELIA

Mill·bank /ˈmɪlbæŋk/ part of the N bank of the River Thames in London, on which stand the Tate Gallery and the **Millbank Tower**, a tall modern office building

mil·le·nar·i·an /ˌmɪlɪˈneəriən/ *n* a person who believes that the MILLENNIUM (2) will come —**millenarian** *adj*

mil·len·ni·um /mɪˈleniəm/ *n* **-nia** /niə/ **1** [C] a period of 1000 years **2** [*the* | S] a future age in which all people will be happy and satisfied. Some CHRISTIANS believe this time will come very soon.

mil·le·pede /ˈmɪlɪpiːd/ *n* a MILLIPEDE

mill·er /ˈmɪləʳ/ *n* a man who owns or works a flourmill

Miller *n* [C;U] *tdmk* a kind of beer made by a US company. They sell their low-CALORIE beer, **Miller Lite**, with the phrase "Tastes great; less filling," said by famous sports people in bars.

Miller, Arthur (1915–) an American writer of plays which deal with political or moral problems. His most famous works include *Death of a Salesman* and *The Crucible*. He was married for a time to Marilyn Monroe.

Miller, Glenn (1904–44) an American musician and bandleader whose dance music became popular during the Second World War. He is remembered esp. for his arrangement of the tune *In the Mood*.

Miller, Henry (1891–1980) an American writer best known for his NOVELS *Tropic of Cancer* and *Tropic of Capricorn* which were both banned (BAN¹) in the US until 1961 because of their descriptions of sexual activities. His books also contain scenes from his own life and thoughts on social and political subjects.

Miller, Jon·a·than /ˈdʒɒnəθən‖ˈdʒɑː-/ (1934–) an English director, actor, and writer, known for his imaginative direction of plays for the National Theatre and for television. He is also a doctor and has made television programmes on medicine and the human body.

mil·let /ˈmɪlɪt/ *n* [U] the small seeds of certain grasslike plants, used as food —see picture at CEREAL

mil·li·bar /ˈmɪlɪbɑːʳ/ *n* a measure of air pressure (ATMOSPHERE)

Mil·li·gan /ˈmɪlɪgən/, **Spike** (1918–) an Irish COMEDIAN and writer, born in India and living in England. A member of the Goons, he wrote much of their material. He has also appeared in films and on television and written humorous books and poetry.

mil·li·gram , **-gramme** /ˈmɪlɪgræm/ (*written abbrev.* **mg**) *n* a measure of weight —see TABLE 2

mil·li·li·tre *BrE‖* **-ter** *AmE* /ˈmɪlɪˌliːtəʳ/ (*written abbrev.* **ml**) *n* a liquid measure —see TABLE 2

mil·li·me·tre *BrE ‖* **-ter** *AmE* /ˈmɪlɪˌmiːtəʳ/ (*written abbrev.* **mm**) *n* a measure of length —see TABLE 2

mil·li·ner /ˈmɪlɪnəʳ/ *n old-fash or tech* a person who makes and/or sells women's hats

mil·li·ne·ry /ˈmɪlɪnəri‖-neri/ *n* [U] *old-fash or tech* **1** the articles made or sold by a milliner **2** the activity of making women's hats

mil·lion /ˈmɪljən/ *determiner, n, pron* **million** *or* **millions 1** (the number) 1,000,000; 10⁶: *three million pounds* | (*infml*) *There were millions of people* (=a very large number of people) *there.* | (*infml*) *You've told me that a million times.* (=very/too often) **2 a/one chance in a million** *infml* a very small chance **3 feel/look like a million dollars** *infml* to feel/look wonderful **4 in a million** *infml* one of the best possible; extremely good: *I've*

got a husband in a million. — ~ **th** *determiner, n, pron, adv*

mil·lion·aire /ˌmɪljəˈneəʳ/ **mil·lion·air·ess** /-ˈneərɪs‖fem.— *n* a person who has a million pounds or dollars; very rich person

mil·li·pede , **millepede** /ˈmɪlɪpiːd/ *n* a small animal rather like a worm, with a lot of legs

mill·pond /ˈmɪlpɒnd‖-pɑːnd/ *n* **1** an area of water used for driving the wheel of a WATERMILL **2 like a millpond** (of the sea) very calm

Mills /mɪlz/, **Sir John** (1908–) an English actor and director, best known for playing an English GENTLEMAN. His best-known films include *Ice Cold in Alex* and *Ryan's Daughter*.

Mills and Boon /ˌ·· ˈ·/ a British company that publishes (PUBLISH) stories about love and ROMANCE are very popular and sell in large numbers. The stories usu. concern a young woman who, after many problems and difficulties, falls in love and marries her IDEAL man.

mill·stone /ˈmɪlstəʊn/ *n* **1** either of the two circular stones between which grain is crushed into flour in a mill **2** a person or thing that gives someone great trouble, anxiety, etc., and prevents them from acting freely or successfully over a very long period (esp. in the phrase **a millstone round someone's neck**): *His lazy son is a* **millstone round his neck.**

mill·wheel /ˈmɪlwiːl/ *n* a large wheel that is turned by flowing water and is used for driving a mill

Milne /mɪln/, **A A** (1882–1956) an English writer, best known for his children's books such as *Winnie the Pooh*, and a collection of poems with the title *When We Were Very Young* —see also WINNIE THE POOH

milque·toast /ˈmɪlktəʊst/ *n, adj AmE* (of or being) a man who is too quiet, PASSIVE, or SHY

mil·om·e·ter /maɪˈlɒmɪtəʳ‖-ˈlɑː-/ *n* a MILEOMETER

milt /mɪlt/ *n* [U] (the organ containing) the seeds (SPERM) of a male fish

Mil·ton /ˈmɪltən/, **John** (1608–74) an English poet, famous for his EPIC poem *Paradise Lost*, which was followed by *Paradise Regained*, written after he had gone blind. He also wrote many articles in support of the Parliamentarians and of freedom for the INDIVIDUAL.

Milton Keynes /ˌmɪltən ˈkiːnz/ a town in Buckinghamshire, built as a NEW TOWN in 1967, which has many successful business companies. People in Britain connect Milton Keynes with the CONCRETE cows which were built in the town.

Mil·wau·kee /mɪlˈwɔːki/ the largest city of Wisconsin, US, an important Great Lakes port on Lake Michigan, known for its industries, esp. making beer —see colour map on pages 1374–5

mime¹ /maɪm/ *n* **1** [C;U] an act or the practice of using actions without language to show meaning: *I couldn't speak Chinese, but I showed in mime that I wanted a drink.* | *the art of mime* **2** [C] a simple theatrical play performed without words **3** [C] an actor who performs without using words

mime² *v* [I;T] to act (something) in mime: *The actor was miming the movements of a bird.* —compare MIMIC²

mim·e·o·graph¹ /ˈmɪmiəɡrɑːf‖-ɡræf/ *n AmE for* DUPLICATOR

mimeograph² *v* [T] *AmE* to make a copy of using a DUPLICATOR: *a mimeographed copy*

mi·met·ic /mɪˈmetɪk/ *adj usu. tech* copying; mimicking (MIMIC² (2)): *an insect's mimetic colouring*

mim·ic¹ /ˈmɪmɪk/ *n* **1** an actor who copies well-known people's speech, ways of behaving, etc. for entertainment **2** someone or something that copies the movement, appearance, etc. of other people or things

mimic² *v* **-ck-** [T] **1** to copy (someone or something), esp. in order to make people laugh: *She made us all laugh by mimicking the teacher/the teacher's voice.* **2** to look exactly like (something else) so as to deceive people: *pieces of paper that mimicked flowers* —compare IMITATE, MIME² — ~ **ry** *n* [U]

mimic³ *adj* [A] **1** *tech* giving protection by being like something else: *The mimic colouring of this moth protects them from predators.* **2** not real; pretended; MOCK

min *written abbrev. for:* **1** MINIMUM **2** minute(s)

min·a·ret /ˌmɪnəˈret, ˈmɪnəret/ *n* a tall thin tower on a

MOSQUE, from which Muslims are called to prayer

min·a·to·ry /ˈmɪnətəri‖-tɔːri/ *adj fml* showing an intention to hurt; threatening

mince¹ /mɪns/ *v* **1** [T] to make (esp. meat) into very small pieces, esp. with a knife or a MINCER: *minced chicken* **2** [I+*adv*|*prep*] *derog* to walk in an unnatural way, taking little short steps: *The actor minced across the stage.* **3 mince matters/one's words** [*usu. in negatives*] to speak of something unpleasant without using plain direct words: *We're in trouble ... Not to mince matters, we're ruined!*

mince² *n* [U] **1** *BrE* minced meat **2** *AmE* mincemeat

mince·meat /ˈmɪns-miːt/ *n* [U] **1** a mixture of apples, RAISINS, SUET, SPICES, etc., but no meat, used as a sweet filling to put inside pastry and eaten esp. at Christmas **2 make mincemeat of** *infml* to defeat or destroy (a person, belief, etc.) completely: *He made mincemeat of their arguments.*

mince pie /ˌ· ˈ·/ *n* a small round covered piece of pastry filled with mincemeat, eaten at Christmas

minc·er /ˈmɪnsər/ also **mincing ma·chine** /ˈ·· ·ˌ·/— *n* a machine for cutting food, esp. meat, into very small pieces esp. by forcing it through small holes

minc·ing·ly /ˈmɪnsɪŋli/ *adv* in a mincing (MINCE¹ (2)) way

mind¹ /maɪnd/ *n* **1** [C;U] a person's (way of) thinking or feeling; thoughts: *Her mind is filled with dreams of becoming a great actress.* | *Ever since I heard that song on the radio I've been unable to get it out of my mind.* (=I cannot stop thinking about it) | *Let's go to the cinema — that'll take your mind off the problem for a while.* | *She looks very worried; I wonder what's on her mind.* | *She has a very open mind and is always ready to consider new ideas.* | *It's better to avoid him when he's in this unpleasant frame/state of mind.* | *It's a good idea — I'll bear it in mind.* (=continue to consider the possibility of doing it) | *A number of possibilities come to mind.* (=I can think of several) | *It never crossed my mind to ask you.* (=I never even had the idea of asking you.) | *The election was due soon, and with this in mind* (=because of this) *we decided to step up our publicity campaign.* | *Knowing that she'd arrived safely restored my* **peace of mind.** **2** [C *usu. sing.*] the ability to think and reason; INTELLECT: *He has a very sharp mind.* (=He thinks and understands quickly.) | *She could do it if she tried — the trouble is she just doesn't use her mind half the time.* | *He's* **not** in his right mind/*He's* **(gone) out of his mind.** (=is/has gone mad) | *She is of perfectly sound mind.* (=is not mad) | *You paid £2000 for it? Are you out of your mind?/You must be out of your mind!* **3** [U] memory: *I couldn't quite call his name to mind.* (=remember it) | *You must bear in mind* (=remember) *that their customs are very different to ours.* | *It* **(completely) slipped my mind/It went (right) out of my mind.** (=I forgot it) | *Now what was it called? It's somewhere at the back of my mind, but I can't quite remember it.* | *I've told you time* **out of mind** (=more times than I can remember) *to turn off the lights when you go out.* | *You* **put** *me* **in mind of** (= remind me of) *my brother.* **4** [C] attention: *Keep your mind on your work.* | *You can do it if you give/put your mind to it.* | *Let us now turn our minds to* (=begin to consider) *tomorrow's meeting.* **5** [C;U] an intention: *I'll put up the shelves if you tell me exactly what you* **have in mind.** (=where you intend them to be, how many you want, etc.) | *Nothing was further from my mind.* (=that was not at all what I meant) | *Those boys have been stealing my apples again; I've* **got a good mind to**/*I've* **half a mind to** (=I think I may possibly) *report them to the police.* | *Have you* **made up your mind** (=decided) *what to do yet?* | *If he's* **set his mind on** *doing it* (=decided firmly to do it), *nothing will stop him.* **6** [C] an opinion: *Since getting to know him better, I've* **changed my mind** *about him.* | *Why don't you* **speak your mind** *plainly?* (=say what you think) | *We are of one mind/of the same mind on this matter.* (=we think the same about it) | *To* **my mind** (=in my opinion) *you're quite wrong.* | *John thinks we should go to Scotland for our holiday, but I'm still* **in two minds** *about it.* (=I cannot decide) | *He'll* **get**/*I'll* **give** *him* **a piece of my mind** (=I will tell him my low opinion of him) *if he dares come here again!* | *She's old enough to* **know her own mind.** (=to have her own opinions and make her own decisions) **7** [C] a person considered for their ability to think well: *She's among the best minds* (=cleverest people) *in the country.*

8 [C;U] the power of reason as opposed to feelings: *Her mind told her one thing and her heart another.* | *a campaign designed to appeal to the* **hearts and minds** (=feelings and reason) *of the electorate* **9** [U] the human spirit and power of reason as opposed to the body, the material world, etc.: *He believes in* **mind over matter.** (=the control of events or material objects by the power of the mind) **10 make up one's mind** to reach a firm decision —see also ABSENCE OF MIND, FRAME OF MIND, **meeting of minds** (MEETING), ONE-TRACK MIND, PRESENCE OF MIND, **blow someone's mind** (BLOW¹) **11 great minds think alike** *humor* people who are very clever have the same opinions, usually said by someone who finds that another person agrees exactly with their opinion or action. People sometimes answer this saying with "Fools never differ", meaning that stupid people also share the same opinions.

mind² *v* **1** [I (OUT);T] *esp. BrE* to be careful (of); pay close attention (to): *Mind that step; it's loose!* | *Mind out! There's a car coming.* | *Just get on with your work; don't mind me.* (=do not pay any attention to my presence) [+(*that*)] *Mind you don't drop it!* [+*wh-*] *Mind where you put your feet!* **2** [I;T *not in progressive forms*] (often used with **would**, in requests, and in negative sentences) to have a reason against or be opposed to (a particular thing); be troubled by or dislike (something): "*Which one would you like?*" "*I don't mind.*" (=I would be pleased with either.) | *I wouldn't mind a cup of tea.* (=I would rather like one) [+*v-ing*] *Would you mind opening the window?* (=please open it) [+*wh-*] *I don't mind where we go.* | *Do you mind if I smoke?* | "*Have some more beer?*" "*I don't mind if I do.*" (=yes, please) [+*obj*+*v-ing*] *Do you mind me smoking?* [+*obj*+*adj*] *Do you mind the window (being) open?* (=Does the window being open trouble you?) **3** [T] to take care or charge of; look after: *Our neighbour is minding our dog while we're on holiday.* | *Will you mind my bags while I make a telephone call?* **4 Do you mind?** (shows annoyance): *Do you mind? That's my foot you're standing on.* **5 mind one's own business** (*usu. imperative*) not to ask or take action about other people's private affairs: "*What has John sent you in that parcel?*" "*Mind your own business.*" (=I will not tell you.) **6 mind one's p's and q's** *infml* to be polite or careful in one's behaviour: *You'd better mind your p's and q's if you want to be invited again!* **7 mind you** also **mind**— also take this fact into account: *He spends a lot of time in bed now; mind you, he is 93!* | *He's a very nice bloke, mind (you), but I wouldn't want to marry him.* (=but even though he is nice, I would not want to) **8 never mind: a** don't worry: "*We've missed the train!*" "*Never mind, there'll be another in ten minutes.*" **b** it does not matter (about): "*Never mind your damaged gate; what about the front of my car!*" *said the angry driver.* **c** *AmE* said when the speaker has decided not to repeat what he has just said, because it was not important or incorrect: "*What did you say?*" "*Never mind.*" **9 never you mind** *infml* it is not your business, and you are not going to be told: *Never you mind what your father and I were talking about.*

▷ USAGE In conversation **mind you** can be used to introduce new information which suggests a different point of view, or even contradicts something which has just been said: *I'm afraid I failed my exam.* **Mind you,** *I didn't have much time to study.* | *He's very selfish,* **Mind you,** *he's good to his mother.* | "*She's very charming, isn't she?*" "*Yes. I wouldn't believe a word she says,* **mind you.**"◁

MIND /maɪnd/ a British organization (a CHARITY) that gives advice and practical help to people who are mentally ill and their families, and tries to make people understand more about mental illness

mind-bend·ing /ˈ· ˌ··/ *adj infml* (causing an experience) so strange and difficult that one cannot understand: *mind-bending drugs*

mind-blow·ing /ˈ· ˌ··/ *adj infml* very exciting, surprising, shocking, or strange —see also **blow someone's mind** (BLOW¹)

mind-bog·gling /ˈ· ˌ··/ *adj infml* very surprising; difficult to imagine because so big, unusual, etc.

mind·ed /ˈmaɪndᵻd/ *adj* **1** [F+*to-v*] *fml* having the will or desire: *He has enough money to travel, if he were minded to do so.* **2 -minded: a** having the stated kind of mind: *strong-minded* | *evil-minded* —see also ABSENT-MINDED, BLOODY-MINDED, BROADMINDED, CIVIC-MINDED, HIGH-MINDED,

LIKE-MINDED, NARROW-MINDED, OPEN-MINDED, SIMPLE-MINDED, SINGLE-MINDED **b** seeing the importance of the stated thing: *There'd be fewer accidents if all road-users were more safety-minded.*

mind·er /ˈmaɪndəʳ/ *n BrE* **1** someone employed to protect another person, often in the criminal world **2** (*usu. in comb.*) a person whose job it is to look after something: *a machine minder* —see also CHILDMINDER

Minder a British television series popular in the 1980s. It includes the character Arthur Daley.

mind·ful /ˈmaɪndfəl/ *adj* [F+of] *fml* giving attention (to); not forgetful (of): *Mindful of the need to maintain efficient communications, the committee makes the following proposals. . .* —**ness** *n* [U+of]

mind·less /ˈmaɪndləs/ *adj* **1** *derog* not having, needing, or using the power of thinking: *It's tiring and mindless work.* | *mindless cruelty* | *the mindless forces of nature* (=thunder, lightning, etc.) **2** [F+of] not giving attention (to); not thinking (about): *The fireman rushed into the burning house, mindless of the danger.* —~**ly** *adv* —~**ness** *n* [U]

mind read·er /ˈ· ˌ··/ *n often humor* a person who knows what another person is thinking without being told— **mind reading** *n* [U]

mind·set /ˈmaɪndset/ *n* **1** *AmE often derog* a fixed state of mind which can't be changed by new ideas or persuasion: *I tried to talk to him but he's got a real mindset about foreigners.* | *the mindset of a hardened criminal* **2** *BrE* a person's way of thinking and reasoning: *We are looking for someone with a logical and analytical mindset to develop computer programs.*

mind's eye /ˌ· ˈ·/ *n* [the+S] the mind as a means of imagining scenes or views: *The old lady can still see in her mind's eye the house where she lived as a child.*

mine[1] /maɪn/ *pron* (*possessive form of* I) the one(s) that belong to me: *That's your coat; mine* (=my coat) *is here.* | *That's mine! Give it back to me.* | *She borrowed a book of mine.* (=one of my books)

mine[2] *determiner old use* (before a vowel sound or *h*, or after a noun) my: *mine host*

mine[3] *n* **1** [C] (*often in comb.*) a deep hole or system of holes under the ground from which coal, gold, tin, or other mineral substances are dug: *a tinmine* | *Many of the workers were buried underground when there was an accident at the mine.* —compare QUARRY[1]; see also COALMINE, GOLDMINE **2** [S+of] a very full supply: *The old man was a mine of information* (=told us a lot) *about the history of the village.* **3** [C] a kind of bomb that is placed just below the ground or in the sea and is exploded electrically from far away or when touched or passed over **4** [C] *old use* a passage dug underground beneath an enemy position

mine[4] *v* **1** [I;T (for)] to dig or work a MINE[3] (1) (in): *mining for coal* | *They'd mined the hillside for diamonds.* **2** [T] to obtain by digging from a MINE[3] (1): *Tin used to be mined in south-western England.* **3** [T *often pass.*] to put MINES[3] (3) in or under: *All the roads leading to the city had been mined.* **4** [T *usu. pass.*] to destroy by MINES[3] (3): *Their ship was mined.* **5** [T] *old use* to dig a MINE[3] (4) under: *Parties of soldiers mined the walls of the castle.* —see also UNDERMINE

mine sthg. ↔ **out** *phr v* [T *usu. pass.*] to take all the minerals from (a place) by mining (MINE[4] (1)): *The whole area has been mined out.*

mine de·tec·tor /ˈ· ··ˌ··/ *n* an instrument for discovering the presence of a MINE[3] (3)

mine·field /ˈmaɪnfiːld/ *n* **1** an area of land or water in which MINES[3] (3) have been placed **2** something that is full of hidden dangers: *The legal system is a minefield for the ordinary person.*

min·er /ˈmaɪnəʳ/ *n* (*often in comb.*) a worker in a MINE[3] (1)

min·e·ral /ˈmɪnərəl/ *n* **1** any of various esp. solid substances that are formed naturally in the earth, such as stone, coal, and salt, esp. as obtained from the ground for human use: *Gold is a mineral.* | *The mineral wealth of a country* **2** [*usu. pl.*] *BrE for* MINERAL WATER (2)

min·e·ral·o·gy /ˌmɪnəˈrælədʒi‖-ˈrɑː-, -ˈræ-/ *n* [U] the scientific study of minerals —**gist** *n*

mineral oil /ˈ··· ·/ *n* [C;U] oil obtained from minerals, as opposed to from plants or animals

mineral wa·ter /ˈ··· ˌ··/ *n* [C *usu. pl.*;U] water that comes from a natural spring and contains minerals. People who are concerned to eat healthy foods often drink mineral water as they believe that it is more healthy than water from the tap.

Miners' Strike /ˈ·· ˌ·/ [*the*] the STRIKE by British coal MINERs in 1984–5 in protest at government decisions to close mines. It is remembered for violent fights between the miners, led by Arthur Scargill, and the police. The prime minister, Mrs Thatcher, called the miners "the enemy within" (=the enemy inside the country).

Mi·ner·va /mɪˈnɜːvə‖-ɜːr-/ in CLASSICAL MYTHOLOGY, the Roman goddess of WISDOM and learning (Greek name Athena)

min·e·stro·ne /ˌmɪnəˈstrəʊni◂/ *n* [U] an Italian soup containing vegetables and small pieces of PASTA

mine·sweep·er /ˈmaɪnˌswiːpəʳ/ *n* a naval ship fitted with apparatus for taking MINES[3] (3) out of the sea —**ing** *n* [U]

Ming Dyn·as·ty /ˈmɪŋ ˌdɪnəsti‖-ˌdaɪ-/ [*the*] a family which ruled China from 1368 to 1644. The Ming DYNASTY (line of rulers) is connected with improvements in the arts and politics in China. Ming VASEs (=pots made during the Ming rule) are famous for being beautiful and valuable.

min·gle /ˈmɪŋgəl/ *v* [I;T (**with,** TOGETHER)] to mix (with another thing or with people) so as to form an undivided whole, while keeping separate qualities: *He rushed out into the busy street and mingled with the crowd, hoping that the police wouldn't spot him.* | *a speech that contained praise mingled with blame*

Min·gus /ˈmɪŋgəs/, **Charles** (1922–79) American JAZZ player and influential COMPOSER who wrote the story of his own life, called *Beneath the Underdog*

min·gy /ˈmɪndʒi/ *adj BrE infml derog* not generous; STINGY: *a mingy person/present*

min·i /ˈmɪni/ *n infml* anything that is smaller than others of its kind, esp. **a** (*usu. cap., as tdmk*) a type of small British car, very popular among young people, esp. in the 1960s **b** a MINI SKIRT

mini- see WORD FORMATION

min·i·a·ture[1] /ˈmɪnətʃəʳ‖ˈmɪniətʃʊər/ *n* **1** a very small painting, usu. of a person **2 in miniature** very like the stated thing or person, but much smaller

miniature[2] *adj* [A] (esp. of something copied) very small: *The child was playing with his miniature railway.*

miniature golf /ˌ··· ˈ·‖ˌ···· ˈ·/ *n* [U] a GOLF game played on a miniature course having TUNNELs, bridges, sharp corners, and OBSTACLEs, usu. done for fun rather than as a serious sport. Miniature golf courses are typically found in seaside holiday towns in Britain.

min·i·a·tur·ist /ˈmɪnətʃərɪst‖ˈmɪniətʃʊə-/ *n* someone who paints MINIATUREs[1] (1)

min·i·a·tur·ize /ˈmɪnətʃəraɪz‖ˈmɪniətʃʊər-/ *v* [T] to make very small: *The movie is about a scientist who invents a machine to miniaturize things, and he accidentally shrinks his kids.*

mini-bud·get /ˈ·· ˌ··/ *n* an official statement from the government in order to make changes in a country's economy. It does not have as much detail as the main BUDGET.

min·i·bus /ˈmɪnibʌs/ *n* a small bus with seats for between six and 12 people: *The children go to school in a minibus/by minibus.*

min·i·cab /ˈmɪnikæb/ *n BrE* a taxi that can be called by telephone, but not stopped in the street —see picture at TAXI

min·i·com·put·er /ˈmɪnikəmˌpjuːtəʳ/ *n* a computer that is larger than a PERSONAL COMPUTER and smaller than a MAINFRAME, used by businesses and other large organizations

min·im /ˈmɪnɪm/ *BrE* ‖ **half note** *AmE*— *n* a musical note with a time value half as long as a SEMIBREVE —see picture at NOTATION

min·i·mal /ˈmɪnɪməl/ *adj fml* as little as possible; very little: *The storm did only minimal damage.* | *Her clothing was minimal.* —compare MAXIMAL —~**ly** *adv*

minimal art /ˌ··· ˈ·/ *n* [U] an art movement started in New York in the 1960s, involving esp. SCULPTUREs, consisting of simple forms in an IMPERSONAL style

mini-mall , minimall /ˈ·· ·/ *n* STRIP MALL

min·i·mize also **-mise** BrE— /ˈmɪnⱼmaɪz/ v [T]   **1** to lessen to the smallest possible amount or degree: *We had about twelve hours' warning, so we were able to minimize the effects of the flood.*   **2** to cause to seem little; treat as not serious: *It would be most unwise to minimize the dangers of this course of action.* —compare MAXIMIZE

min·i·mum /ˈmɪnⱼməm/ adj, n **-ma** /mə/ or **-mums** [A;C (of)] (being) the smallest number, amount, etc.: *This price is her minimum; she refuses to lower it any further.* | *minimum depth|temperature* | *He smokes a minimum of ten cigarettes a day.* | *He couldn't join the police, because he was below the minimum height allowed by the rules.* —compare MAXIMUM

minimum lend·ing rate /ˌ··· ˈ·· ·/ (abbrev. **MLR**) n the lowest rate of interest at which the Bank of England agrees to lend money, which influences the rate at which banks and building societies (BUILDING SOCIETY) lend money to the public

minimum wage /ˌ··· ˈ·/ n [usu. sing.] the lowest wage permitted by law or by agreement for certain work, introduced so that all workers will have a reasonable standard of living. There is no minimum wage in Britain or the US.

min·ing /ˈmaɪnɪŋ/ n [U] the action or industry of getting minerals out of the earth by digging: *coalmining* | *a mining company* —see also STRIP MINING

min·ion /ˈmɪnjən/ n derog or humor an employed person or helper who is too obedient: *He'll probably send one of his minions to buy the tickets.*

min·i·pill /ˈmɪnɪpɪl/ n a birth control PILL which contains only one kind of HORMONE, called PROGESTOGEN, while other types of birth control pills also contain OESTROGEN

mini-round·a·bout /ˌ··· ˈ···/ n BrE a small kind of ROUND-ABOUT (1), whose centre is a small painted circle on the road

min·is·cule /ˈmɪnⱼskjuːl/ adj MINUSCULE

mini skirt , miniskirt /ˈ··· ·/ n a very short skirt which was popular in the 1960s and has been fashionable at various times since then

min·is·ter[1] /ˈmɪnⱼstəʳ/ n **1** [(of)] a politician who is a member of the government and is in charge of a particular government department: *the Minister of Education* —see also PRIME MINISTER   **2** a MINISTER OF STATE or MINISTER WITHOUT PORTFOLIO   **3** a Christian leader like a priest in some branches of the church —see PRIEST (USAGE)   **4** a person of lower rank than an AMBASSADOR, who represents his/her government in a foreign country
▷ USAGE **Minister** (1) and (3) is not used for any US government officials, but it is used in American English for officials of other governments —compare SECRETARY (2)◁

minister[2] v
minister to sbdy. phr v [T] esp. lit to perform duties to help: *ministering to the sick*

min·is·ter·i·al /ˌmɪnⱼˈstɪəriəl◀/ adj of a MINISTER[1] (1,3) or ministers: *his ministerial duties* | *It's believed that ministerial changes will be made in the near future.* (=that some ministers will be dismissed, and new ones appointed) —**~ly** adv

ministerial re·spon·si·bil·i·ty /ˌ····· ···ˈ···/ n [U] the responsibility that government ministers should take for what happens in their departments

ministering an·gel /ˌ··· ˈ···/ n apprec, esp. BrE lit a person, usu. a woman, who helps those who are sick or in trouble

minister of state /ˌ··· · ˈ·/ BrE n a person whose job is to help the minister who is the head of a government department: *Mr. Christopher Gurney, minister of state at the Foreign Office*

minister with·out port·fo·li·o /ˌ··· ·ˌ· ·ˈ···/ n BrE a government minister with no specific departmental responsibilities (RESPONSIBILITY (3))

min·is·trant /ˈmɪnⱼstrənt/ n esp. lit a person who gives service to others

min·is·tra·tion /ˌmɪnⱼˈstreɪʃən/ also **ministrations** pl.— n [U] fml (a) giving of help and service, esp. to the sick or to those needing the services of a priest: *All the ministrations of the doctors and nurses couldn't save the child's life.*

min·is·try /ˈmɪnⱼstri/ n **1** [C (of)] (often cap.) a government department with a minister in charge of it: *The army, navy, and airforce are all controlled by the Ministry of Defence.*   **2** [the+S+sing.|pl. v] priests, considered as a group or profession; CLERGY: *He joined the ministry.* (=became a priest)

Ministry of Ag·ri·cul·ture, Fisheries and Food /ˌ···· · ˌ···· ˌ··· · ˈ·/ also **MAFF**— the British government department which controls farming and food

Ministry of De·fence /ˌ··· · ·ˈ·/ also **MOD**— [the] the British government department which is responsible for the army and other forces

Ministry of Sil·ly Walks /ˌ··· · ˌ·· ˈ·/ [the] an imaginary government department shown in the British television COMEDY programme *Monty Python's Flying Circus.* The ministers who worked there all walked in very silly ways, e.g. by kicking their legs right up into the air with each step. —see also MONTY PYTHON

ministry of the in·te·ri·or /ˌ··· · ·ˈ···/ n a government department which is responsible for public order inside a country and controls organizations such as the police and the fire service, as well as the movement of people into the country. In Britain this department is called the Home Office.

mink /mɪŋk/ n **mink**   **1** [C] a small fierce animal like a WEASEL   **2** [U] the valuable brown fur of this animal
▶ CULTURAL NOTE Mink is considered to be the finest and most expensive fur by many people. Others now consider using mink for coats as cruel and CAMPAIGN against it: *a mink coat*◀

Min·ne·ap·o·lis /ˌmɪniˈæpəlɪs/ a city in E Minnesota, US, on the Mississippi river, known as an important industrial centre and port. It is one of the Twin Cities, along with Saint Paul across the river. —see colour map on pages 1374–5

Min·ne·ha·ha /ˌmɪniˈhɑːhɑː/ according to NATIVE AMERICAN stories, the wife of Hiawatha

Min·nel·li /mɪˈneli/, **Li·za** /ˈlaɪzə/ (1946–) an American singer and actress, who is famous esp. for the film *Cabaret* (1972)

Liza Minnelli

Min·ne·so·ta /ˌmɪnⱼˈsəutə/ (written abbrev **MN**) a state in the north of the US, an industrial and farming area with many farms which produce milk —see colour map on pages 1374–5

Min·nie Mouse /ˌmɪni ˈmaus/ a CARTOON character, a female mouse who is the partner of Mickey Mouse —see also MICKEY MOUSE[1]

min·now /ˈmɪnəu/ n a very small fish of rivers and lakes: (fig.) *When they found the criminals the police arrested the minnows* (=unimportant ones) *but let the big fish* (=important ones) *go.*

Min·o·an /mɪˈnəuən/ adj of or about the civilization of ancient Crete (3000–1100 BC)

Mi·nogue /mɪˈnəug/, **Ky·lie** /ˈkaɪli/ (1968–) an Australian singer and actress who, with Jason Donovan, appeared in the Australian television SOAP OPERA, *Neighbours,* and then went on to become a successful singer, popular esp. with young TEENAGERS

Minolta /mɪˈnɒltə/ tdmk a camera made by the Japanese company Minolta

mi·nor[1] /ˈmaɪnəʳ/ adj **1** lesser or smaller in degree, size, number, or importance when compared with others: *He left most of his money to his sons; his daughter received only a minor share of his wealth.* | *The young actress was given a minor part in the new play.* | *The important thing is to finish it quickly; cost is only a relatively minor consideration.* | *a minor flaw|alteration* | *The infection|operation is fairly minor; nothing to worry about.* —opposite **major;** see MAJOR (USAGE)   **2** being or based on a musical SCALE on which there are SEMITONEs between different notes than those of the MAJOR SCALE: *in a minor key* | [after n] *a symphony in F minor*   **3** [after n] BrE old-fash being the younger of two boys of the same name in the same school: *Simkins minor* —opposite **major**

minor² *n law* a person below the age (now 18 in Britain and the US) at which they are fully responsible in law for their actions

Mi·nor·ca /mɪˈnɔːkə‖-ˈnɔːr-/ also **Menorca**— an island in the Spanish Balearic islands, popular with British tourists

mi·nor·i·ty /maɪˈnɒrᵻti‖mᵻˈnɔː-, mᵻˈnɑː-/ *n* **1** [(*the*) S+*sing.|pl. v*] the smaller number or part; less than half: *Most of the nation wants peace; only a minority wants the war to continue. | Boys are very much* **in the minority** *at the dancing class.* (=most of the pupils are girls) | *Three members of the committee disagreed with the main report, so they produced a minority report.* (=one that only represented the views of those three members) | *TV programmes that cater for minority interests* (=things that not many people are interested in) **2** [C+*sing.|pl. v*] a small part of a population which is different from the rest in race, religion, etc.: *a law to protect religious minorities|ethnic minorities* **3** [U] *law* the state or time of being a MINOR²: *The court appointed me as the boy's guardian during his minority.* —opposite **majority**

minority gov·ern·ment /·,··· ·,···/ *n* a government which has fewer seats in a parliament than the combined opposition parties have —see also extra information on page 412

minority lead·er /·,··· ·,··/ *n* **1** a person who represents a MINORITY group of people, esp. black and Asian citizens in Britain **2** *AmE* a leader of the political party in a LEGISLATURE which has fewer representatives than the leading party —compare MAJORITY LEADER

minor league /·,·· ·/ *n AmE* a group of professional sports clubs, esp. BASEBALL clubs, that are not in the large national LEAGUES: *a minor league pitcher*

minor plan·et /·,·· ·,··/ *n* an ASTEROID

minor suit /·,·· ·,·/ *n* (in the card game BRIDGE¹) either CLUBS¹ (6) or DIAMONDS (3), which have a lower value than the MAJOR SUITS

Min·o·taur /ˈmɪnətɔːʳ, ˈmaɪ-/ [*the*] in CLASSICAL MYTHOLOGY a creature which was half a man and half a BULL, which was kept in the LABYRINTH and fed on young men and women. It was killed by Theseus.

min·ster /ˈmɪnstəʳ/ *n BrE* (*often cap.*) (now usu. part of a name) a large or important church, esp. one that formed part of an ABBEY: *Westminster | York Minster*

min·strel /ˈmɪnstrəl/ *n* **1** a travelling musical entertainer in the Middle Ages **2** (esp. in former times) any of a group of performers who travel about giving amusing song and dance shows

min·strel·sy /ˈmɪnstrəlsi/ *n* [U] *rare* the art, songs, and music of a minstrel

mint¹ /mɪnt/ *n* **1** [U] a small plant whose leaves have a particular fresh smell and taste and are used in food and drinks. *mint tea | roast lamb with mint sauce* **2** [C;U] (a) PEPPERMINT or a sweet containing mint: *Have one of these mints! | after-dinner mints*

mint² *n* **1** [C] a place where coins are officially made by the government: *the Royal|Denver Mint* **2** [S] *infml* a large amount (of money): *He must be making a mint!* **3** **in mint condition** (of objects which people collect for pleasure, such as books, postage stamps, or coins) in perfect condition, as if new and unused

mint³ *v* [T] **1** to make (a coin) **2** to invent (a new word, phrase, etc.) —see also COIN² (3)

mint ju·lep /ˌ· ˈ··/ *n* see JULEP

Min·ton /ˈmɪntən/ *n* [U] a fine BONE CHINA made in Stoke-on-Trent in England (from Thomas **Minton** (1765–1836) who started the factory). The famous WILLOW PATTERN plates etc. are said to have been made first by the Minton company.

mint sauce /ˌ· ˈ·/ *n* [U] a mixture of VINEGAR, sugar, salt, and finely cut mint, eaten with ROAST lamb

min·u·et /ˌmɪnjuˈet/ *n* (a piece of music for) a type of slow graceful 17th- and 18th-century dance

mi·nus¹ /ˈmaɪnəs/ *prep* **1** made less by (the stated quantity): *17 minus 5 leaves|equals 12* (17 − 5=12). **2** being the stated number of degrees below the freezing point of water: *The temperature was minus 10 degrees* (=−10°). **3** *infml* without: *He won the fight, but when it ended he was minus two front teeth.* —opposite **plus**

minus² *n* **1** also **minus sign** /ˈ·· ·/— a sign (−) showing that a number is less than zero, or that the second number is to be taken away from the first **2** a disadvantage: *Traffic noise is one of the minuses of living on a main road.* —opposite **plus**

minus³ *adj* **1** [A] (of a number or quantity) less than zero **2** [A] disadvantageous: *He's very keen, but his youth is a minus factor.* **3** [after *n*] (of a mark) coming low in a range: *I got a B for my last essay, but only a B minus for this one.* —opposite **plus**

min·us·cule , miniscule /ˈmɪnᵻskjuːl/ *adj* extremely small: *a minuscule amount*

min·ute¹ /ˈmɪnᵻt/ *n* **1** any of the 60 parts into which an hour is divided: *The train arrived at four minutes past eight. | It's a ten minute walk|a few minutes' walk from here to the station.* **2** *infml* a very short period of time; MOMENT: *I'll be ready in a minute|a few minutes. | "Are you ready yet?" "No, but I won't be a minute."* (=I'll be ready very soon) | *Just a minute|Hang on a minute.* (=wait for a moment) − *I want to talk to you. | He can never make up his mind; one minute he says he wants to go, and the next he says he doesn't. | Have you got a minute?* (=Can I talk to you for a short time?) | *No; I'm* **not suggesting for a minute** (−certainly not suggesting) *that he's lying.* **3** any of the 60 parts into which a degree of angle is divided **4** a short official note asking for certain action to be taken, expressing an opinion, etc.: *The minister read the report and then added a minute expressing his complete agreement.* —see also MINUTES **5** **the minute (that)** as soon as: *I recognized him the minute (that) I saw him.* —see also LAST MINUTE, UP-TO-THE-MINUTE

minute² *v* [T] *BrE* to make a note of (something) in the MINUTES of a meeting: *I want my disagreement to be minuted.*

mi·nute³ /maɪˈnjuːt‖-ˈnuːt/ *adj* **1** very small: *His writing's minute. | a minute improvement* **2** *fml* giving attention to the smallest points; very careful and exact: *in minute detail* − −**ly** *adv* : *He examined the jewel minutely.* − −**ness** *n* [U]

minute bell /ˈmɪnᵻt bel/ *n* in Britain, a church bell that rings every minute while a funeral PROCESSION is going to or leaving a church

minute gun /ˈmɪnᵻt ɡʌn/ *n* in Britain, a gun fired every minute at funerals of very important people or COMMEMORATION ceremonies, or as a signal for help

minute hand /ˈmɪnᵻt hænd/ *n* the long hand that marks the minutes on a watch or a clock

min·ute·man /ˈmɪnᵻtmæn/ *n* **-men** /men/ *AmE* during the American Revolution, one of a group of men who were not official soldiers but who could be ready in one minute to fight against the government. Today the word is sometimes used in advertising by companies who want to show how quick their service is.

min·utes /ˈmɪnᵻts/ *n* [(*the*) P (**of**)] an official written record of what is said at a meeting, and what decisions are taken there: *Before the committee started its work, the minutes of the last meeting were read out. | to* **take** (=write) **minutes**

minute steak /ˈmɪnᵻt steɪk/ *n* a thin piece of STEAK that can be quickly cooked

mi·nu·ti·ae /maɪˈnjuːʃiaɪ, mᵻ-‖mᵻˈnuː-/ *n* [(*the*) P (**of**)] small exact details that often do not seem worth considering: *These are the broad outlines of what I want; I'll leave it to you to work out the minutiae.*

minx /mɪŋks/ *n old-fash derog, often humor* a disrespectful young girl

mips /mɪps/ *n* [S] *tech* millions of instructions per second; a unit for measuring the speed of a computer: *Their new range runs at 25 mips.*

mir·a·cle /ˈmɪrəkəl/ *n* **1** an action done by esp. a holy person that is impossible according to the ordinary laws of nature: *According to the Bible, Christ worked|performed many miracles, such as turning water into wine.* **2** a wonderful unexpected event: *It's a miracle you weren't killed! | It'll need a miracle to save the company from ruin. | an economic miracle | the miracles of modern science | a miracle cure* −**culous** /mɪˈrækjᵿləs/ *adj* : *a miraculous escape| recovery* −**culously** *adv* : *It was a terrible explosion but, miraculously, no one was killed.*

miracle play /ˈ·· ·/ also **mystery play**— *n* a theatrical play often performed in the Middle Ages, based on stories from the Bible or on the lives of holy men and women —compare MORALITY PLAY

mi·rage /ˈmɪrɑːʒ‖mɪˈrɑːʒ/ n **1** a strange effect of hot air conditions in a desert, in which objects appear which are not really there **2** a dream, hope, or wish that cannot come true: *pursuing the mirage of world peace*

Mi·ran·da /mɪˈrændə/, **Carmen** (1913–55) a star of musical films, who was known as "The Brazilian Bombshell". She is best remembered for her hats made of fruit.

Carmen Miranda

Miranda de·ci·sion /·ˈ·· ·ˌ··/ [*the*] a 1966 decision by the US SUPREME COURT that said it was necessary for police, when arresting (ARREST) people, to inform them of their legal rights, esp. the right to remain silent.

MIRAS /ˈmaɪræs, -rəs/ a system in Britain which allows a person who has a MORTGAGE to pay no tax on the interest payable on the money he/she has borrowed from a Building Society or bank. The Building Society can then claim the money from the government (the word stands for Mortgage Interest Relief at Source).

mire[1] /maɪər/ n [U] *esp. lit* deep mud: *like pigs in the mire* | (fig.) *His name was* **dragged through the mire**. (=talked about publicly in a way that brought shame on him) | (fig.) *With each probing question he was getting sucked deeper into the mire*. (=more and more caught up in difficulties) —**miry** *adj*

mire[2] *v* [T] *esp. lit, rare* **1** [(in)] to cause (a person) to be caught up in difficulties **2** to make dirty with mud

Mi·ró /mɪˈrəʊ/, **Jo·an** /ʒʊˈɑːn/ (1893–1983) a Spanish SURREALIST painter, famous for his use of bright colours and ABSTRACT shapes

mir·ror[1] /ˈmɪrər/ n **1** (*often in comb.*) a piece of glass, or other shiny or polished surface, that REFLECTS (=throws back) images: *The driver saw the police car in his mirror.* | *a shaving mirror* | *a full-length mirror* (=tall enough to REFLECT a standing person) **2** [(of)] an exact or close representation (of something): *This newspaper claims to be the mirror of public opinion.* (=claims to express what the people are really thinking) **3** **mirror, mirror on the wall, who's the fairest of them all?** a question asked by the wicked queen in the story of Snow White. The queen expects the mirror to say that she is the most beautiful of all, but the mirror tells her that Snow White is the most beautiful. This phrase is often used in jokes, advertising, newspapers, etc. —see also SNOW WHITE

mirror[2] *v* [T] **1** to give an exact or close representation of: *Do these opinion polls really mirror what people are thinking?* **2** to be similar to, esp. as if by copying: *My experience of working in this area closely mirrors your own.*

Mirror [*the*] the DAILY MIRROR

Mirror Group News·pa·pers /ˌ··· ˈ···/ *also* **the Mirror Group** /ˈ·· ·/— a company, formerly owned by Robert Maxwell, which publishes (PUBLISH) the Daily Mirror, the Daily Record, the People, the Sunday Mirror, and Sporting Life

mirror im·age /ˈ·· ˌ··/ n [(of)] **1** an image of something in which the right side appears on the left, and the left side on the right **2** something, such as an object or a situation, that looks like or is very similar to something else, but whose various parts may sometimes be arranged in a different or opposite way

mirth /mɜːθ‖mɜːrθ/ n [U] *esp. lit* happiness and laughter —~**ful** *adj* —~**fully** *adv* —~**less** *adj* —~**lessly** *adv*

MIRV /mɜːv‖mɜːrv/ n multiple independently-targeted reentry vehicle; a MISSILE (=a flying weapon) which has several bombs on it, each of which can be directed to hit a different place

mis- see WORD FORMATION

MIS /ˌem aɪ ˈes/ management information system; a group of computer PROGRAMs that arrange information in computers in a form that is useful to business managers

mis·ad·ven·ture /ˌmɪsədˈventʃər/ n [C;U] **1** *lit* (an) accident; (piece of) bad luck **2 death by misadventure** *BrE law* accidental death

mis·al·li·ance /ˌmɪsəˈlaɪəns/ n an unsuitable uniting of people, esp. an unsuitable marriage

mis·an·thrope /ˈmɪsənθrəʊp/ *also* **mis·an·thro·pist** /mɪsˈænθrəpɪst/— n *fml derog* a person who dislikes other people and would rather be alone —compare MISOGYNIST —**-thropic** /ˌmɪsənˈθrɒpɪk◀‖-ˈθrɑː-/ *adj* —**thropically** /kli/ *adv*

mis·an·thro·py /mɪsˈænθrəpi/ n [U] *fml derog* dislike of people in general

mis·ap·ply /ˌmɪsəˈplaɪ/ *v* [T] to use wrongly or for a wrong purpose —**-plication** /ˌmɪsæpləˈkeɪʃən/ n [C;U (of)] : *a misapplication of the law*

mis·ap·pre·hend /ˌmɪsæprɪˈhend/ *v* [T] *fml* to understand (something) wrongly: *The terms of the agreement must be quite explicit, so that there is no possibility of misapprehending them.*

mis·ap·pre·hen·sion /ˌmɪsæprɪˈhenʃən/ n *fml* a mistaken belief; misunderstanding: *He's not Mr Hart's brother? Then I've been* (**labouring**) **under a misapprehension.**

mis·ap·pro·pri·ate /ˌmɪsəˈprəʊprieɪt/ *v* [T] *fml or tech* to take dishonestly, esp. for one's own use: *The lawyer was sent to prison for misappropriating the money placed in his care.* —**ation** /-əprəʊpriˈeɪʃən/ n [C;U (of)]

mis·be·got·ten /ˌmɪsbɪˈgɒtn◀‖-ˈgɑː-/ *adj* [A] *derog or humor* **1** unlikely to succeed because badly planned or foolish: *his misbegotten scheme for selling fur coats during the summer* **2** (of a person) worthless; annoying: *Where's that misbegotten brother of yours?*

mis·be·have /ˌmɪsbɪˈheɪv/ *v* [I;T] to behave (oneself) badly: *Anyone in the crowd who misbehaves is quickly thrown out of the ground.*

mis·be·ha·viour *BrE* ‖ **-vior** *AmE* /ˌmɪsbɪˈheɪvjər/ n [U] bad behaviour

misc. *written abbreviation for:* MISCELLANEOUS

mis·cal·cu·late /ˌmɪsˈkælkjəleɪt/ *v* [I;T] **1** to calculate (figures, time, etc.) wrongly: *I missed the train because I'd miscalculated the time it would take me to reach the station.* **2** to form a wrong judgment (about): *If she thinks I'll agree to that she's miscalculated badly.* —**lation** /mɪsˌkælkjəˈleɪʃən/ n [C;U]

mis·call /ˌmɪsˈkɔːl/ *v* [T+obj (+n)] *fml* to call by a wrong name

mis·car·riage /ˌmɪsˈkærɪdʒ, ˈmɪskærɪdʒ/ n a case of accidentally giving birth to a child too early for it to live, esp. between the 12th and 28th weeks of PREGNANCY — compare ABORTION (1), STILLBIRTH

miscarriage of jus·tice /·ˌ··· ˈ··/ n [C;U] (a) failure to act justly, esp. in a court of law: *She was found guilty on a technical legal point, even though she was clearly innocent. What a miscarriage of justice!*

mis·car·ry /mɪsˈkæri/ *v* [I] **1** (of a woman) to have a miscarriage —compare ABORT (1,2) **2** *fml* (of an intention, plan, etc.) to be unsuccessful; fail to have the intended result

mis·cast /ˌmɪsˈkɑːst‖-ˈkæst/ *v* **miscast** [T *usu. pass.*] **1** [(as)] to give (an actor) an unsuitable part in a play, film, etc.: *He was badly miscast as Julius Caesar.* **2** to put an unsuitable actor or actors into (a part, play, etc.)

mis·ce·ge·na·tion /ˌmɪsɪdʒəˈneɪʃən‖-sedʒ-/ n [U] the production of children by a sexual union of people of different races, esp. when one of the partners is white

mis·cel·la·ne·ous /ˌmɪsəˈleɪniəs◀/ *adj* of several kinds or different kinds; too various to be called by a single name: *There are categories for all major areas of expenditure, and then one at the end for miscellaneous items.* —~**ly** *adv* —~**ness** n [U]

mis·cel·la·ny /mɪˈseləni‖ˈmɪsˌleɪni/ n [(of)] a mixture of various kinds, esp. a collection of writings on different subjects or by different writers: *a miscellany of American short stories*

mis·chance /ˌmɪsˈtʃɑːns‖-ˈtʃæns/ n [C;U] *fml* (an example of) bad luck: *By sheer mischance the letter was sent to the wrong address.*

mis·chief /ˈmɪstʃɪf/ n **1** [U] behaviour, esp. of children, that causes trouble and possibly damage, but no serious harm: *getting into mischief* | *She suspected the children* *were up to some mischief and she found them in the garden digging up the flowers.* | *We allowed the children to watch a film on television, to keep them out of mischief.* **2** [U] slightly wicked playfulness: *She gave her father a smile that was full of mischief.* **3** [U] *fml* damage or harm; wrong-doing: *The storm did a lot of mischief to the crops.* **4** [C] *infml, rather old-fash* a troublesomely playful child **5 do someone/oneself a mischief** *esp. BrE, usu. humor* to hurt someone/oneself: *If you try to lift that box you'll do yourself a mischief!* **6 make mischief (between)** *infml* to speak so as to cause quarrels, unfriendly feelings, etc., between people —see also **mean mischief** (MEAN²)

mis·chief-mak·er /'·· ‚··/ *n derog* a person who intentionally makes (sometimes serious) trouble or causes misunderstanding

mis·chie·vous /'mɪstʃɪvəs/ *adj* **1** *sometimes apprec* playfully troublesome: *One expects healthy children to be mischievous at times.* | *a mischievous grin/glance* **2** causing harm, often intentionally: *a mischievous remark* — ~**ly** *adv* — ~**ness** *n* [U]

mis·con·ceive /‚mɪskən'siːv/ *v* [T] **1** to plan (something) badly: *The government's plan to privatize the railways is wholly misconceived.* **2** *fml* to place a wrong meaning on; misunderstand

mis·con·cep·tion /‚mɪskən'sepʃən/ *n* [C;U] (an example of) understanding something wrongly: [+*that*] *the popular misconception that governments can guarantee full employment* (=many people think this, wrongly)

mis·con·duct¹ /‚mɪs'kɒndʌkt‖-'kɑːn-/ *n* [U] *fml* **1** intentional bad behaviour, esp. unacceptable sexual behaviour: *The doctor was found guilty of professional misconduct.* **2** [(of)] bad control, e.g. of a business company

mis·con·duct² /‚mɪskən'dʌkt/ *v* [T] *fml* to control (a business, etc.) badly; deal badly with: *The board has so misconducted the affairs of the company that it's deep in debt.*

mis·con·struc·tion /‚mɪskən'strʌkʃən/ *n* [C;U] *fml* (an example of) mistaken understanding: *A law must be stated in the clearest language, so that it is not* **open to misconstruction.** (=so that it cannot be misunderstood)

mis·con·strue /‚mɪskən'struː/ *v* [T] *fml* to understand or take (something said or done) wrongly: *Don't misconstrue what I am about to say …*

mis·count /‚mɪs'kaʊnt/ *v* [I;T] to count wrongly: *The teacher miscounted the number of boys.* —**miscount** /'mɪskaʊnt/ *n* : *a miscount in the election results*

mis·cre·ant /'mɪskriənt/ *n old use* a person of bad character

mis·deed /‚mɪs'diːd/ *n fml or lit* a wrong or illegal action; offence: *The selection committee decided to overlook his past misdeeds.*

mis·de·mea·nour *BrE* ‖ **-nor** *AmE* /‚mɪsdɪ'miːnər/ *n* **1** *law* a crime that is less serious than, for example, stealing or murder —compare FELONY **2** *fml* a bad or improper act that is not very serious

mis·di·rect /‚mɪsdɪ'rekt/ *v* [T] **1** to direct wrongly: *a misdirected letter* (=sent to the wrong address) **2** to use (one's efforts, abilities, etc.) in the wrong way, or for a wrong purpose: *misdirected energy* **3** (of a judge) to guide (a JURY) incorrectly on the law — ~**ion** /'rekʃən/ *n* [U (of)]

mise-en-scène /‚miːz ɒn 'sen, -'seɪn‖-ɑːn-/ *n* **mise-en-scènes** (*same pronunciation*) *Fr* **1** *tech* the arrangement of furniture, scenery, and other objects used on the stage in a play **2** *lit or pomp* the surroundings in which an event takes place

mi·ser /'maɪzər/ *n derog* a person who loves money and hates spending it, and often lives in very poor conditions in order to become wealthy by storing all his money — ~**liness** *n* [U] — ~**ly** *adj* : *a miserly attitude*

mis·e·ra·ble /'mɪzərəbəl/ *adj* **1** very unhappy: *The child's cold, hungry, and tired, so of course he's feeling miserable.* **2** causing unhappiness, discomfort, etc.: *a cold wet miserable day* | *miserable living conditions* **3** [A] *sometimes derog* very low in quality or very small in amount; CONTEMPTIBLE or PATHETIC: *All they offered us was a few miserable pounds.* | *a miserable failure* —**bly** *adv*

mis·e·ry /'mɪzəri/ *n* **1** [S;U] also **miseries** *pl.*— a condition of great unhappiness or great pain and suffering of body or mind: *the unspeakable misery of their existence, kept in tiny cages with no light and little food* | *The new neighbours play loud music all the time and it's making*

our lives a misery. **2** [C] *derog infml, esp. BrE* a person who is always complaining, esp. one who does not like others to enjoy themselves: *You old misery!* **3 put something/someone out of its/their misery: a** to kill an animal in order to end its suffering **b** *infml* to cause someone to stop feeling anxious, esp. by telling them something they are waiting to find out: *Let's put the interviewees out of their misery and tell them who's got the job.*

mis·field /‚mɪs'fiːld/ *v* [I;T] to make a mistake in fielding (FIELD² (1)) the ball in cricket, BASEBALL, etc.

mis·fire /‚mɪs'faɪər/ *v* [I] **1** (of a gun) to fail to send out the bullet when fired **2** (of the petrol mixture in a car engine) to fail to IGNITE at the proper time: *The engine misfired several times.* **3** (of a plan, joke, etc.) to fail to have the intended result —**misfire** *n*

mis·fit /'mɪs‚fɪt/ *n* someone whose character or behaviour makes them unsuited to the way they live, the people they work with, etc.: *a social misfit*

mis·for·tune /mɪs'fɔːtʃən‖-ɔːr-/ *n* [C;U] (an example of) bad luck, often of a serious kind: *His failure in business was due not to misfortune, but to his own mistakes.* | *I had the misfortune to have my driving licence taken away for a minor offence.*

mis·giv·ing /‚mɪs'gɪvɪŋ/ *n* [C;U] (a feeling of) doubt, distrust, or fear, esp. about a future event: *He looked with misgiving at the strange food on his plate.* | *I could see he had some misgivings about lending me his car.*

mis·guid·ed /‚mɪs'gaɪdᵻd/ *adj* (of a person or behaviour) directed by mistaken ideas; not sensible, esp. in trying to do something that will not work or will have bad results: *It was misguided of him to pay his daughter's debts again; she ought to learn to manage money.* | *her well-meaning but misguided attempts to reconcile the ex-lovers* — ~**ly** *adv*

mis·han·dle /‚mɪs'hændl/ *v* [T] to handle or treat roughly, without skill, or insensitively: *This detector is a very delicate instrument; it'll go wrong if it's mishandled.* | *Our company lost an important order because the directors mishandled the negotiations.*

mis·hap /'mɪshæp/ *n* [C;U] something that goes wrong; an often slight accident: *The long journey passed without mishap.*

mis·hear /‚mɪs'hɪər/ *v* -**heard** /'hɜːd‖'hɜːrd/ [I;T] to hear (someone or something) wrongly or mistakenly

Mish·i·ma /'mɪʃɪmə/, **Yu·ki·o** /'juːkiəʊ/ (1925–70) a Japanese writer who wrote about modern Japan and wanted to return to older, more traditional Japanese values. His best-known works include *Confessions of a Mask* and *The Sea of Fertility*. He killed himself after an unsuccessful military COUP by his private army.

mish·mash /'mɪʃmæʃ/ *n* [S (of)] *infml* an untidy disorderly mixture; HOTCHPOTCH: *This new book is an odd mishmash of ideas.*

Mish·nah /'mɪʃnə/ [*the*] a collection of Jewish TRADITIONs that form the Jewish law, on which the Talmud is based

mis·in·form /‚mɪsɪn'fɔːm‖-ɔːrm/ *v* [T (**about**) *often pass.*] to give (someone) wrong information: *I'm sorry, I thought they had already been sent; I must have been misinformed.*

mis·in·for·ma·tion /‚mɪsɪnfə'meɪʃən‖-fər-/ *n* [U] *often euph* wrong information, esp. given on purpose: *government propaganda and "misinformation"*

mis·in·ter·pret /‚mɪsɪn'tɜːprᵻt‖-ɜːr-/ *v* [T] to put a wrong meaning on (something said, done, etc.); explain or understood wrongly: *The driver misinterpreted the policeman's signal and turned in the wrong direction.* — ~**ation** /‚mɪsɪntɜːprᵻ'teɪʃən‖-ɜːr-/ *n* [C;U] : *a misinterpretation of the results of the experiment*

mis·judge /‚mɪs'dʒʌdʒ/ *v* [T] to judge (a person, action, time, distance, etc.) wrongly; form a wrong or unfairly bad opinion of: *What a very kind thing to do; I've clearly been misjudging him all these years.* | *The government misjudged the mood of the country when it decided to call an election.* —**judgment, judgement** *n* [C;U (of)]

Mis·ki·to /mɪs'kiːtəʊ/ *n* **1** [C] (a member of) a people of Nicaragua or Honduras **2** [U] the language of these people

mis·lay /mɪs'leɪ/ *v* -**laid** /'leɪd/ [T] to put (something) in a place and forget where; lose for a short time: *Oh dear, I've mislaid my glasses again.*

mis·lead /mɪs'liːd/ *v* -**led** /'led/ [T (**into**)] to cause (someone)

to think or act mistakenly; guide wrongly: *The car's shiny appearance misled me into thinking it was newer than it really was.* | *a misleading description/advertisement* – ~ingly *adv*

mis·man·age /ˌmɪsˈmænɪdʒ/ *v* [T] to control or deal with (private, public, or business affairs) badly, unskilfully, etc.: *It's not surprising the company's in debt – it's been completely mismanaged.* – ~ment *n* [U (of)]

mis·match /ˌmɪsˈmætʃ/ *v* [T *often pass.*] to match wrongly or unsuitably, esp. in marriage: *a mismatched couple* – mismatch /ˈmɪs·mætʃ/ *n*

mis·no·mer /mɪsˈnəʊməʳ/ *n* a wrong or unsuitable name: *To call it a hotel is a misnomer – it's more like a prison!*

mi·so /ˈmiːsəʊ/ *n* [U] a strong-tasting salty Japanese food made from fermented (FERMENT[1] (1)) rice or SOYA BEANS and used to add taste to soups, etc.

mi·so·gy·nist /mᵻˈsɒdʒᵻnᵻst‖mᵻˈsɑː-/ *n* a person who hates women –compare MISANTHROPE

mi·so·gy·ny /mᵻˈsɒdʒᵻni‖mᵻˈsɑː-/ *n* [U] *fml* hatred of women

mis·place /ˌmɪsˈpleɪs/ *v* [T *often pass.*] **1** to have (good feelings) for an undeserving person or thing: *Your trust in him is misplaced; he'll cheat you if he can.* **2** to MISLAY: *I've misplaced my glasses again.* **3** to put in an unsuitable or wrong place: *She's misplaced in that job; she ought to be doing something more creative.* – ~ment *n* [U (of)]

mis·print /ˈmɪs·prɪnt/ *n* a mistake in printing –misprint /ˌmɪsˈprɪnt/ *v* [T]

mis·pro·nounce /ˌmɪsprəˈnaʊns/ *v* to pronounce (a word) in a way that is usu. understood, but not correct: *People always mispronounce my last name.*

mis·quote /ˌmɪsˈkwəʊt/ *v* [T] to make a mistake in reporting (a person, or a person's words): *The minister complained that the newspapers had misquoted him/his speech.* –quotation /ˌmɪskwəʊˈteɪʃən/ *n* [C;U]

mis·read /ˌmɪsˈriːd/ *v* –read /ˈred/ [T] **1** to read (something) wrongly: *The letter was dated May 17th but I misread it as the 11th.* **2** to make a wrong judgment about: *The general misread the enemy's intentions, and didn't anticipate the attack.*

mis·re·port /ˌmɪsrɪˈpɔːt/ *v* [T *often pass.*] to give an incorrect or untrue account of: *The story in the newspaper isn't true; the facts have been misreported.*

mis·rep·re·sent /ˌmɪsreprɪˈzent/ *v* [T (as)] to give an intentionally untrue account or explanation of (someone, or someone's words or actions), esp. an unfavourable one: *The newspapers misrepresented him as a political extremist.* – ~ation /ˌmɪsreprɪzenˈteɪʃən/ *n* [C;U (of)] : *a gross misrepresentation of the truth*

mis·rule /ˌmɪsˈruːl/ *n* [U] **1** bad government **2** *esp. lit* disorder; confusion

Misrule, Lord of also **King of Misrule, Abbot of Misrule**– [*the*] formerly an officer at the court of the English king or queen who watched over the Christmas games and fun. At the Scottish court he was called the **Abbot of Unreason.**

miss[1] /mɪs/ *v* **1** [I;T] to fail to hit, catch, find, meet, touch, hear, see, etc.: *He shot at it, but missed.* | *The falling rock just missed my head.* | *I arrived too late and missed the train.* | *She went to the station to meet her husband, but missed* (=failed to meet) *him in the crowd.* | *We arrived late at the theatre, and missed* (=failed to see) *the first act of the play.* | *He's missed* (=failed to go to) *school three days this week.* | *I think you've missed* (=failed to understand) *the point.* | *an opportunity that is too good to miss* | *Yes, he's very observant; he doesn't miss much.* [+v-ing] *I don't want to miss seeing that film on television tonight.* **2** [T] to avoid or escape from (something unpleasant): *The two planes missed disaster by a matter of inches when they nearly collided.* | [+v-ing] *We narrowly missed being killed by the explosion.* **3** [T] to feel sorry or unhappy at the absence or loss of: *Her children have gone to Australia, and she misses them very much.* | *It's a rather ugly building; I don't think it would be missed.* [+v-ing] *I miss living in the country.* (=I wish I still lived there) **4** [T] to discover the absence or loss of: *I didn't miss the key until I got home and found it wasn't in my bag.* **5 miss the boat/the bus** *infml* to lose a good chance, esp. by being too slow **6 miss the/one's mark** to fail to reach the/one's intended result: *a joke that somewhat missed*

the mark (=failed to amuse anyone) –see also MISSING, HIT-OR-MISS

miss out *phr v* **1** [T] (**miss** sbdy./sthg. ↔ **out**) *BrE* to fail to include: *His account of the accident misses out one or two important facts.* | *When the waiter was pouring wine for everyone, he for some reason missed me out.* **2** [I (**on**)] to lose a chance to gain advantage or enjoyment: *You really missed out (on a lot of fun) by not coming to the office party.*

miss[2] *n* **1** a failure to hit, catch, hold, etc., whatever is aimed at –see also NEAR MISS **2 a miss is as good as a mile: a** a narrow escape from danger, defeat, etc., has the same result as an easy one **b** the smallest failure or mistake has the same result as a large one: *"I failed the exam by only 2%." "A miss is as good as a mile."* **3 give something a miss** *infml* not to do, take, etc., something: *I usually go swimming on Mondays, but I've decided to give it a miss this week.*

miss[3] *n* (*usu. cap.*) **1** a title placed **a** before the name of an unmarried woman or girl: *Miss Brown* | (*old-fash*) *The Misses Brown are sisters.* –compare MRS (1), MS **b** before the name of a place or activity which a young woman has been chosen to represent, usu. because she is beautiful: *Miss Brazil was voted Miss World 1986.* **2** a respectful form of address used **a** *esp. BrE* by pupils to a woman teacher: *Can we go now, Miss?* **b** *rather old-fash* by anyone to a young woman: *Excuse me, miss, is that your umbrella?* –compare MADAM (1), SIR (1) **3** *BrE often humor or derog, rather old-fash* a girl or young woman, esp. one who is playful or disrespectful

▶ CULTURAL NOTE In the US the title **Miss** is becoming rare in all senses except 1b above, unless it is referring (REFER) to very young girls. **Ms** is preferred for females from older TEENAGERS upwards. ◄

mis·sal /ˈmɪsəl/ *n* (*often cap.*) a book containing the complete religious service during the year for MASS in the Roman Catholic church

Miss A·mer·i·ca Pa·geant /ˌ·· ·ˈ··· ˌ··/ [*the*] a BEAUTY CONTEST held every year in Atlantic City, New Jersey, in which women who have won other competitions represent each of the 50 states. One of them is chosen to serve as **Miss America** for one year.

mis·shap·en /ˌmɪsˈʃeɪpən, mɪˈʃeɪ-/ *adj* (esp. of the body or a part of it) not of the usual or ordinary shape: *misshapen toes*

mis·sile /ˈmɪsaɪl‖ˈmɪsəl/ *n* **1** an explosive flying weapon with its own engine, which can be aimed at a distant object: *a nuclear missile* | *a missile base* –see also GUIDED MISSILE, ICBM **2** *fml* an object thrown as a weapon: *The angry football fans threw bottles and other missiles at each other.*

miss·ing /ˈmɪsɪŋ/ *adj* **1** that cannot be found; not in the proper or expected place; lost: *Some important figures are missing from this report.* | *He has a finger missing from his left hand.* **2** [F] (of a soldier, fighting vehicle, etc.) not returning after a battle, and therefore considered killed, destroyed, etc.: *Seven of our planes are missing.* | *He was reported* **missing in action**. –see also MIA

missing link /ˌ·· ·ˈ·/ *n* **1** [C] a fact that must be found in order to complete an argument, a proof, etc. **2** [*the*] *often humor* an animal halfway in the development of humans from monkey-like creatures, supposed to have existed long ago but never proved to have done so: *I've just met my new brother-in-law and I think he's the missing link.*

missing per·son /ˌ·· ˈ··/ *n* a person who has been reported lost to the police: *Hundreds of missing persons are reported to the police every week.* | *the Missing Persons Bureau*

mis·sion /ˈmɪʃən/ *n* **1** the usu. military duty or purpose for which people are sent somewhere: *A party of soldiers was landed secretly on the coast; their mission was to blow up the radio station.* | *a bombing mission* | *The astronauts reported the breakdown in* **mission control**. (=the people controlling the space flight) | *Mission accomplished!* (=I have done what I was sent to do.) **2** the particular work which one believes it is one's duty to do: [+to-v] *She felt that her mission in life was to help old people.* **3** [+*sing./pl. v*] a group of people sent abroad for a special reason, esp. to act for their country: *The British trade mission has just reached Leningrad.* **4** a place run by a religious organization where medical services, teaching, etc. are provided for the local people: *They come to the* *mission from many miles around to see the doctor.* **5 mission of mercy** an activity in which people are sent to help people in great need: *They went on a mission of mercy to feed starving children in Ethiopia.*

mis·sion·a·ry /ˈmɪʃənəri‖-neri/ *n* a person who is sent, usu. to a foreign country, to teach and spread religion, usu. the Christian religion: *She spent twenty years in East Africa as a missionary.*

► CULTURAL NOTE The STEREOTYPE of a missionary is of a white man wearing SHORTS and a PITH HELMET, working in usu. an African country. In CARTOONS missionaries are often shown being cooked in a large pot by CANNIBALS. The missionaries usu. seem to be cheerful and not to realize what is happening. In former times missionaries were often explorers, in some cases the first Europeans that people in many parts of the world had ever seen, and they were admired for their goodness and their bravery. Now many people question whether they were right to try to make people reject their own beliefs and accept a new religion. ◀

missionary po·si·tion /ˈˑˑˑˑ ·ˌ·/ *[the]* the sexual position in which the woman lies on her back with the man above and facing her (supposed to have been taught to PRIMITIVE peoples) by missionaries, who said it was the only correct position.

missionary zeal /ˈˑˑˑˑ ˈ·/ *n* [U] an eagerness to do something one believes to be important; from the idea that missionaries work very hard to persuade people to believe in Christianity: *He worked with missionary zeal on the project to clean up the river.*

Mission Im·pos·si·ble /ˈˑˑ ·ˈ·ˑ/ an American television programme of the 1960s and 1970s about a group of people who did secret work for their government. The programme always began with the words "Your mission, should you decide to accept it ..." on a TAPE which destroyed itself after it had been played.

mis·sis /ˈmɪsɪz/ *n* MISSUS

Mis·sis·sip·pi /ˌmɪsɪˈsɪpi◀/ *(written abbrev.* **MS)** **1** a state in the S of the US, an industrial area formerly producing COTTON, and a centre of the CIVIL RIGHTS MOVEMENT; —see also DEEP SOUTH **2** *[the]* the longest river in the US, flowing from Minnesota to the Gulf of Mexico, about 3779 km long —see colour map on pages 1374-5

mis·sive /ˈmɪsɪv/ *n humor or pomp* a letter, esp. a long one

Mis·sou·ri /mɔˈsuəri ‖ -ˈzuəri/ *(written abbrev.* **MO)** **1** a state in the central US, an industrial and AGRICULTURAL area; **2** *[the]* a long river in the US, flowing from the Rocky Mountains to join the Mississippi —see colour map on pages 1374-5

mis·spell /ˌmɪsˈspel/ *v* **-spelt** /ˈspelt◀/ *or* **-spelled** [T] to spell wrongly — ~**ing** *n* [C;U]

mis·spend /ˌmɪsˈspend/ *v* **-spent** /ˈspent◀/ [T] to spend (time, money, etc.) wrongly or unwisely; waste: *his misspent youth*

Miss Pig·gy /ˌ·ˈ·ˑ/ a PUPPET in the form of a pig from a television show *The Muppets* who thinks she is very beautiful and who is always trying to get her own way —see picture at KERMIT

mis·state /ˌmɪsˈsteɪt/ *v* [T] to state (a fact, argument, etc.) wrongly or falsely, esp. in order to deceive — ~**ment** *n* [C;U] : *several misstatements about the cost of the new aircraft*

mis·sus, **missis** /ˈmɪsɪz/ *n infml or humor, rather old-fash* (with **the, his, your,** etc.) a person's wife: *The missus will be angry if I'm home late.* | *How's your missus?*

Miss World /ˌ·ˈ·/ *n* [C;U] (the winner of) an international beauty competition

miss·y /ˈmɪsi/ *n infml, now rare* (used as a friendly way of addressing a young girl)

mist¹ /mɪst/ *n* **1** [C;U] (an area of) cloudy air near the ground, made up of very small floating drops of water; thin FOG: *The mountain top was covered in mist.* | (fig.) *a secret hidden in the mists of the past/lost in the mists of time* (=a time so long ago that it had been forgotten) — see also SCOTCH MIST **2** [S;U] a thin covering of small drops of water, through which it is hard to see: *She could hardly recognize her son through the mist of tears that filled her eyes.* —see also MISTY

mist² *v* [I;T (OVER, UP)] to (cause to) become covered with mist: *Their breath misted up the windows.* | *Her eyes misted over.* —see also DEMIST

mis·take¹ /mɪˈsteɪk/ *v* **-took** /mɪˈstʊk/, **-taken** /mɪˈsteɪkən/ [T] **1** to have a wrong idea about; MISUNDERSTAND: *He'd mistaken the address, and gone to the wrong house.* | *She mistook my meaning entirely.* **2** to fail to recognize: *You can't mistake his car; he's painted it bright red and yellow.* | **There's no mistaking** *his car.* (=it is always recognizable) —see also UNMISTAKABLE

    mistake sbdy./sthg. **for** sbdy./sthg. *phr v* [T] to think wrongly that (a person or thing) is (someone or something else): *They mistook him for his brother.* | *Don't mistake his silence for lack of interest.*

mistake² *n* [C;U] something done wrongly, or something that should not have been done: *You've made several spelling mistakes.* | *It was a mistake to tell him.* | *She put salt into her tea* **by mistake.** | *There must be some mistake in this bill; could you add it up again?* | (BrE) *He's an odd character* **and no mistake!** (=he's certainly very odd) | *If we don't finish the job today they won't pay us;* **make no mistake about it.** (=you can be quite certain) —see ERROR (USAGE)

mis·tak·en /mɪˈsteɪkən/ *adj* **1** [F (**about**)] (of a person) wrong; having understood incorrectly: *I think you must be mistaken about seeing him at the theatre; I'm sure he's been abroad all week.* | **Unless I'm (very much) mistaken,** *that's my watch you're wearing!* **2** (of an action, idea, etc.) incorrect; not properly formed or understood: *I was under the mistaken impression that they were French.* | *The police arrested her, but it turned out to be* **a case of mistaken identity.** (=they thought she was someone else) — ~**ly** *adv*

mis·ter /ˈmɪstər/ *n* **1** *esp. AmE infml* (used for addressing a man unknown to the speaker): *"What's the time, mister?", asked the little boy.* **2** *(cap.)* MR

mis·time /ˌmɪsˈtaɪm/ *v* [T] to do or say at a wrong time: *With the election only three days away, the government badly mistimed its announcement of tax increases.*

mis·tle·toe /ˈmɪsəltəʊ/ *n* [U] a plant with small white berries that grows and feeds on trees

► CULTURAL NOTE In British MYTHOLOGY mistletoe is connected with the DRUIDS who regarded it as a SACRED plant. Mistletoe is often hung in rooms at Christmas because there is a TRADITION that one may kiss anyone of the opposite sex who is under it. ◀

mis·took /mɪˈstʊk/ *past tense of* MISTAKE

mis·tral /ˈmɪstrɑːl/ *n* *[the]* a strong cold dry wind that blows from the north into southern France

mis·tress /ˈmɪstrɪs/ *n* **1** a woman who is in control: *She felt she was no longer mistress in her own house when her husband's mother came to stay.* | *The dog ran alongside his mistress.* **2** *often derog* a woman with whom a man has a sexual relationship, usu. not a socially acceptable one: *His wife left him when she discovered he had a mistress.* **3** *poet* a woman loved by a man: *He addressed many poems to his mistress, praising her beauty.* **4** *esp. BrE* a female teacher: *the new English mistress* —compare MASTER¹ (2)

Mistress *n old use* (a title for any woman or girl): *Mistress Quickly is a character in Shakespeare's plays.*

mis·tri·al /ˌmɪsˈtraɪəl/ *n law* a trial during which some mistake in law is made, so that judgments made in it have no legal effect and a new trial has to be held: *The High Court declared it a mistrial.*

mis·trust /mɪsˈtrʌst/ *v* [T] not to trust: *Why do you mistrust him so much? He seems honest enough to me.* —**mistrust** *n* [S;U (**of**)] : *He keeps his money at home because he has* **a great mistrust** *of banks.* — ~**ful** *adj* [(**of**)] — ~**fully** *adv* — ~**fulness** *n* [U]

mist·y /ˈmɪsti/ *adj* full of, covered with, or hidden by MIST: *a misty morning* | (fig.) *misty memories of her childhood* —**ily** *adv* —**iness** *n* [U]

mis·un·der·stand /ˌmɪsʌndəˈstænd‖-ər-/ *v* **-stood** /ˈstʊd/ [I;T] to understand wrongly; put a wrong meaning on: *He misunderstood what I said.* | *They pretended to misunderstand me/my complaint.*

mis·un·der·stand·ing /ˌmɪsʌndəˈstændɪŋ‖-ər-/ *n* **1** [C;U (**of**)] (an example of) the act of putting a wrong meaning on something: *I think there's been some misunderstanding: I meant nine in the morning, not nine at night.* **2** [C (**with**)] *often euph* a disagreement less serious than a quarrel: *a little misunderstanding with our neighbours*

mis·use¹ /ˌmɪsˈjuːz/ v [T] **1** to use (something) in a wrong way or for a wrong purpose: *I hate to see him misusing his time like that.* **2** *fml* to treat (something or someone) badly

▷ USAGE: Compare **abuse** and **misuse. Misuse** is often used about objects: *to misuse a tool.* **Abuse** is rarely used about objects, but when it is used in this way it is stronger than **misuse**, and suggests that there is damage: *You must have been abusing the knife I lent you — the blade is completely ruined.*◁

mis·use² /ˌmɪsˈjuːs/ n [C;U (of)] (an example of) bad, wrong, or unsuitable use: *(an) unforgivable misuse of power*

MIT /ˌem aɪ ˈtiː/ abbrev. for: Massachusetts Institute of Technology; a university in Cambridge, Massachusetts, in the US, famous for scientific education and study

Mitch·ell¹ /ˈmɪtʃəl/, **Jo·ni** /ˈdʒəʊni/ (1943–) a Canadian popular music singer, songwriter, and GUITAR player, best known for her FOLK songs in the 1960s

Mitchell², **Margaret** (1900–49) an American writer whose one NOVEL *Gone with the Wind* was very successful, as was the film based on it —see also GONE WITH THE WIND

Mitchell³, **Warren** (1926–) an English actor known esp. for playing the part of Alf Garnett in television's *Till Death Us Do Part*

Mitch·um /ˈmɪtʃəm/, **Rob·ert** /ˈrɒbət‖ˈrɑːbərt/ (1917–) an American film actor, who played leading parts in many films, esp. WESTERNs and films about criminals, from the 1940s onwards. Among his best-known films are *The Sundowners*, *Ryan's Daughter*, and *The Big Sleep*.

mite /maɪt/ n **1** [C] a very small insect-like creature **2** [C] *BrE* a small child, esp. one for whom one feels sorry: *The poor little mite!* **3** [S] *infml* a very small amount: *I couldn't eat a mite more.* **4** a **mite** *infml often humor* slightly: *I think he was a mite annoyed.*

Mit·ford /ˈmɪtfəd ‖ -fərd/, **Nan·cy** /ˈnænsi/ (1904–73) an English writer who wrote about the ARISTOCRACY. Her best known NOVELs include *The Pursuit of Love* and *Love in a Cold Climate*.

Mith·ras /ˈmɪθræs/ also **Mith·ra** /-rə/— the god of light or the sun in an ancient Persian religion (**Mithraism**) who was worshipped esp. by Roman soldiers

mit·i·gate /ˈmɪtɪɡeɪt/ v [T] *fml* to lessen the seriousness of (evil, harm, pain, etc.): *The judge said that nothing could mitigate the cruelty with which the mother had treated her child.* | *new economic measures to help mitigate the effects of the recession* | *Are there any **mitigating circumstances** in this case?* (=facts that make a crime less serious) —see also UNMITIGATED —-**gation** /ˌmɪtɪˈɡeɪʃən/ n [(in) U (of)]

mi·to·sis /maɪˈtəʊsɪs/ n [U] *tech* cell division in which one cell produces two that are exactly the same —compare MEIOSIS

mi·tre *BrE* ‖ **miter** *AmE* /ˈmaɪtər/ n **1** a tall pointed hat worn by BISHOPS and ARCHBISHOPS (=priests of high rank) **2** also **mitre joint** /ˈ··· ·/ a joint between two pieces of wood, in which each piece is cut at an angle as in the corners of a picture frame

Mit·su·bish·i /ˌmɪtsuːˈbɪʃi/ *tdmk* a car or other motor vehicle made by the Japanese company Mitsubishi

mitt /mɪt/ n **1** (*usu. in comb.*) a special type of mitten for protecting the hands: *an oven mitt* | *a catcher's mitt* (=used in BASEBALL) —see picture at GLOVE **2** *sl*, *often humor* a hand: *Those are my cigarettes; get your mitts off them!* (=don't take them)

mit·ten /ˈmɪtn/ n **1** a GLOVE with two parts, one for the thumb and the other for the fingers **2** a covering for the wrist and hand with holes for the fingers —see PAIR (USAGE), and see picture at GLOVE

Mit·ter·rand /ˈmiːtərɒŋ ‖ ˌmiːteˈrɑːn/, **Fran·çois** /ˈfrɒnswɑː‖frɑːnˈswɑː/ (1916–) a French Socialist leader who became President of France in 1981

Mit·ty /ˈmɪti/, **Wal·ter** /ˈwɔːltər/ a person who imagines that they are leading a different life in which they are an important or brave person; a DAYDREAMER (from the HERO of a story by James Thurber)

mix¹ /mɪks/ v **1** [I;T (UP, **with**)] to combine so that the parts no longer have a separate shape, appearance, etc., or cannot easily be separated: *Oil and water don't mix.* | *Oil doesn't mix with water.* | *You can't mix oil and water.* |

You can mix blue and yellow paint to make green. | *She put the butter and sugar into a bowl and mixed them up together.* | *to mix business with pleasure* **2** [T (**for**)] to make by combining substances: *to mix a cocktail* | *She mixed a hot drink for him.* [+obj(i)+obj(d)] *His wife mixed him a hot drink.* **3** [I (**with**)] (of a person) to be, or enjoy being, in the company of others: *She mixes well (with other children).* | *He's mixing with the wrong people.* **4** [T] *tech* to control the balance of (sounds in a record, film, etc.) **5** **mix it** *infml*, *esp. BrE* to fight or behave in a rough threatening way

▷ USAGE Compare **mix, blend, mingle, merge**, and **combine. Mix** in meaning 1 above is the most general word to use about substances: *to mix butter, eggs, and flour.* **Blend** is often used about the action of mixing in careful proportions to produce a particular taste, smell, or other good result: *to blend spices* | *blended whisky.* **Mingle** is usually intransitive and is used **a** of people: *I mingled with the crowd* **b** of flowing liquids of different origin, colour, temperature, etc.: *The fresh water of the Amazon mingles with the salt water of the South Atlantic.* **Merge** is intransitive and is used when one thing becomes lost in another, or two things become one: *an insect that merges with its surroundings* | *the place where two roads merge.* When two or more things **combine**, they join or stick to each other, but keep their own identities, and may be separated again under suitable conditions: *Hydrogen combines with oxygen to form water.*◁
mix sthg. ↔ **in** *phr v* [T] to combine (a substance) thoroughly with other substances: *Add the milk to the flour, and then mix in three eggs.*
mix sbdy./sthg. ↔ **up** *phr v* [T] **1** [(**with**)] to mistakenly think that (someone or something) is another rather similar person or thing: *It's easy to mix him up with his brother; they're so alike.* **2** to put into disorder: *If you mix up those papers we won't be able to find the one we need quickly enough.* —see also MIXED UP, MIX-UP

mix² n **1** [C;U] (*usu. in comb.*) a combination of all or most of the substances needed to make the stated thing: *cake mix* **2** [S (**of**)] a group of different things, people, etc.; mixture: *There was a strange mix of people at the party.* | *It's a question of getting the right mix of policies to appeal to the electorate.*

mixed /mɪkst/ adj **1** of different kinds: *He has **mixed feelings** about his daughter's marriage.* (=he likes it in some ways but not in others) **2** [no comp.] of or for both sexes: *a mixed school* | *mixed bathing* | *This joke isn't suitable to be told in mixed company.* (=isn't suitable for women to hear)

mixed-a·bil·i·ty /ˌ· ·ˈ···◁/ adj [A] containing pupils of many different levels of ability: *a mixed-ability school/class*

mixed bag /ˌ· ˈ·/ n [S] *infml* a collection of things of many different kinds, and usu. of different qualities: *The reviews the play got were a pretty mixed bag.* (=some were good, but many were bad too)

mixed bles·sing /ˌ· ˈ··/ n [S] something that is bad as well as good: *Getting that well-paid job was a bit of a mixed blessing; it means we'll have to live abroad for several years.*

mixed doub·les /ˌ· ˈ··/ n **mixed doubles** a match, esp. of tennis, in which a man and a woman play against another man and a woman

mixed e·con·o·my /ˌ· ·ˈ···/ n the operation of a country's money supply, industry, and trade by a mixture of CAPITALIST and SOCIALIST principles

mixed farm·ing /ˌ· ˈ··/ n [U] the raising of farm animals and the growing of crops on the same farm

mixed grill /ˌ· ˈ·/ n a dish of various kinds of meat grilled (GRILL¹) together, usually including STEAK, LIVER, SAUSAGEs, etc.

mixed herbs /ˌ· ˈ·/ n [P] a mixture of various kinds of dried HERB, sold ready mixed and used in cooking

mixed mar·riage /ˌ· ˈ··/ n a marriage between people of different races or religion

mixed met·a·phor /ˌ· ˈ···/ n a use of two different METAPHORs together with a foolish or funny effect: *"She is a tower of strength and is galloping ahead" is a mixed metaphor.*

mixed spice /ˌ· ˈ·/ n [U] a mixture of various kinds of SPICE, sold ready mixed and used esp. in making cakes

mixed up /ˌ· ˈ·◂/ adj 1 [F+in] connected with (something bad): *I didn't realize he was mixed up in that banking scandal.* | *Don't get mixed up in other people's quarrels.* 2 [F+with] connected with (someone undesirable): *Since we came to live on this housing estate he's been getting mixed up with a very rough crowd of boys.* 3 troubled and confused in one's mind: *He listened to so much conflicting advice that he got all mixed up.* | *a completely mixed-up kid* —see also MIX **up**, MIX-UP

mix·er /ˈmɪksəʳ/ n 1 (*often in comb.*) a machine by or in which substances are mixed: *a food mixer* | *a cement mixer* —see picture at KITCHEN 2 a non-alcoholic drink for mixing with an alcoholic drink, esp. a SPIRIT: *We've got tonic water or bitter lemon as mixers.* 3 tech a person who balances and controls the words, music, and sounds for a film 4 AmE (an organized activity at) a party whose purpose is to let people who have just met each other get to know each other better: *There's a mixer for new transfer students on Friday night.* 5 **good/bad mixer** a person who is happy/not happy in the company of people, likes/does not like talking to them, etc.: *a bad mixer who never talks to people at parties*

mixing bowl /ˈ·· ·/ n an esp. large bowl used in cookery for mixing materials, esp. for cakes

mix·ture /ˈmɪkstʃəʳ/ n 1 [C (**of**)] a set of substances mixed together so as to give a combined effect: *This tobacco is a mixture of three different sorts.* —compare COMPOUND¹ (1) 2 [S (**of**)] a combination of things or people of different types: *I listened to his excuse with a mixture of amusement and disbelief.* 3 [U] a usu. liquid substance made for the stated purpose by combining other substances: *a bottle of cough mixture* (=medicine for stopping coughs) 4 [U] *fml* the action of mixing or state of being mixed 5 BrE **the mixture as before** *infml, usu. derog* the same treatment or set of actions as before: *We were hoping for something original in this new film but it's the mixture as before.*

mix-up /ˈ·· ·/ n *infml* a state of disorder and confusion, as caused by bad planning, etc.: *There was a mix-up at the station and some of us got on the wrong train.* —see also MIXED UP, MIX **up**

Mk *written abbrev. for:* MARK¹ (7, 8)

ml *written abbrev. for:* MILLILITRE(s)

MLitt /ˌem ˈlɪt/ *abbrev. for:* Master of Letters; (a title for someone who has) a British university degree at a level higher than a BA but below a PHD: *Ms Poppy Catte, MLitt* | *She has an MLitt.*

MLR /ˌem el ˈɑːʳ/ *abbrev. for:* MINIMUM LENDING RATE

M'lud /məˈlʌd/ the title used to address a judge in a British court of law (from "My Lord")

mm *written abbrev. for:* MILLIMETRE(s)

MN *written abbrev. for:* MINNESOTA

M'Nagh·ten Rules /məkˈnɔːtn ˌruːlz/ see MCNAUGHTEN RULES

mne·mon·ic /nɪˈmɒnɪk‖nɪˈmɑː-/ adj, n (something, esp. a few lines of VERSE) used for helping one to remember: *The spelling guide "i before e except after c" is a mnemonic.* — ~ **ally** /kli/ adv

mo /məʊ/ n [S] BrE *infml* a very short space of time; MO-MENT: *Wait a mo.*

MO¹ /ˌem ˈəʊ/ n **MOs** *infml* 1 *esp. BrE* medical officer; an army doctor 2 a MODUS OPERANDI

MO² *written abbrev. for:* Missouri

moan¹ /məʊn/ n 1 a soft low sound of pain or grief: *From time to time there was a moan (of pain) from the sick man.* | (fig.) *the moan of the wind through the trees* 2 *infml, usu. derog* a complaint, expressed in a suffering discontented voice: *She's never satisfied; she's always got some moan or another.*

moan² v 1 [I] to make the sound of a moan: *The sick child moaned a little, and then fell asleep.* | (fig.) *The wind moaned round the house all night.* 2 [I (**about**);T] to complain annoyingly, esp. in a discontented voice without good reason: *Stop moaning; you've really got nothing to complain about.* | *"I'm hungry," he moaned.* [+*that*] *She's always moaning that she has too much work to do.* — ~ **er** n

Moaning Min·nie , moaning Minnie /ˌməʊnɪŋ ˈmɪni/ n 1 someone who is always complaining: *She's a real moaning Minnie.* 2 a German weapon used in the Second World War, which made a screaming (SCREAM) noise

when fired 3 the AIR RAID warning SIREN used in Britain during the Second World War

moat /məʊt/ n a long deep hole, usually filled with water, dug **a** for defence round a castle, fort, etc., in former times **b** round an area for animals in a modern ZOO, to stop them escaping —see picture at CASTLE — ~ **ed** adj : *lions in a moated enclosure*

mob¹ /mɒb‖mɑːb/ n [C+sing./pl. v] 1 *often derog* a large noisy crowd, esp. one which is violent: *An angry mob is attacking the palace.* | *mob violence/rule* 2 *usu. derog* a group of the stated sort of people: *the usual mob of freeloaders and hangers-on that attend first nights* 3 (*often cap.*) a powerful organization of criminals, esp. the MAFIA: *He told the police, and now the Mob's after him.*

mob² v **-bb-** [T] (of a group of people) to crowd around (someone) either because of interest or admiration, or in order to attack them: *The visiting pop star was mobbed by his excited fans.* | *The angry crowd mobbed the losing team as it left the football ground.*

Mo·bil /ˈməʊbəl/ also **Mobil Oil Company**— an international oil company which has petrol stations in many countries

mo·bile¹ /ˈməʊbaɪl‖-bəl, -biːl/ adj 1 able to move, or be moved, quickly and easily; not fixed in one position: *a mobile rocket-launcher* | *an actor with a very mobile face* (=able to change its expression a lot) | *She's much more mobile now she has a car.* | *I have a mobile telephone that I can take to the garden.* 2 [*no comp.*] contained, and driven from place to place, in a vehicle: *a mobile first aid room* — see also IMMOBILE, UPWARDLY-MOBILE

mo·bile² /ˈməʊbaɪl‖-biːl/ n a decoration or work of art made of small models, cards, etc., tied to wires or string and hung up so that it is moved by currents of air

mobile home /ˌ·· ˈ·/ also **trailer house** AmE— n 1 a kind of large CARAVAN in which people live all the time. Mobile homes have very small wheels and are rarely moved from their usual place which is usu. in a special area with other mobile homes, called a **mobile home park**. 2 a vehicle which is lived in as a home and has its own engine —compare MOTOR HOME —see colour picture on page 161

mobile li·bra·ry /ˌ·· ˈ···/ BrE ‖ **bookmobile** AmE— n a library that is kept, and driven from place to place, in a vehicle

mobile tel·e·phone /ˌ·· ˈ···/ also **mobile phone** /ˌ·· ˈ·/ ‖ usu. **carphone** AmE— n a telephone which one can carry with one

mo·bil·i·ty /məʊˈbɪləti/ n [U] *fml* the quality of being mobile: *job/labour mobility* (=the ability to move around the country to get work) | *a* **mobility allowance** (BrE) (=money from the government to help a person with a DISABILITY to move around) —see also SOCIAL MOBILITY

mo·bil·ize also **-ise** BrE /ˈməʊbəlaɪz/ v 1 [T] to prepare for war or a difficult situation by organizing: *to mobilize the army in an emergency* | *He's trying to mobilize all the support/supporters he can get for his new political party.* | *to mobilize one's resources* 2 [I] (of armed forces) to gather together and become ready for war —see also DEMOBILIZE —**-ization** /ˌməʊbəlaɪˈzeɪʃən‖-lə-/ n [C;U]

mob·ster /ˈmɒbstəʳ‖ˈmɑːb-/ n a GANGSTER

Mo·bu·tu /məˈbuːtuː/, **Ses·e Sek·o** /ˈseseɪ ˈsekəʊ/ (1930–) the President of Zaire who became president in 1967 after a COUP and established a one-party state

Mo·by Dick /ˌməʊbi ˈdɪk/ the name of the WHALE in the story *Moby Dick* by Herman Melville. The book tells the exciting story of a whaling captain's search for a great white whale.

moc·ca·sin /ˈmɒkəsɪn‖ˈmɑː-/ n a simple shoe made of soft leather —see PAIR (USAGE), and see picture at SHOE

moch·a /ˈmɒkə‖ˈməʊkə/ n [U] (*sometimes cap.*) 1 a type of fine coffee 2 AmE a combination of coffee and chocolate, used to give a pleasant taste to food

mock¹ /mɒk‖mɑːk/ v 1 [I (**at**);T] *fml* to laugh (at), esp. unkindly or unfairly; make fun (of): *You shouldn't mock (at) other people's religious beliefs.* | *mocking laughter* 2 [T] to make fun of (something) by copying it: *He made the other boys laugh by mocking the way the teacher spoke and walked.* 3 [T] *fml or lit* to cause to seem completely useless: *The continuing industrial unrest mocked the*

government's attempts to find a solution. — ~er n — ~ingly adv

mock sthg. ↔ **up** phr v [T] to make a MOCK-UP of

mock² adj [A] not real but very similar (to the real thing); pretended: The army training exercises ended with a mock battle. | She opened her eyes wide in mock disbelief. | mock exams

mock³ n **1** BrE a school examination taken as practice shortly before an official examination: He's taking his mocks in January; the A level exams are in May. **2 make a mock of** make a mockery of **3 make mock of** lit to laugh at; make fun of

mock- see WORD FORMATION

mock·ers /ˈmɒkəz‖ˈmɑːkərz/ n **put the mockers on** sl to put an end to (esp. a hope, plan, etc.), ruin

mock·e·ry /ˈmɒkəri‖ˈmɑː-/ n **1** [U] the act of laughing unkindly or unfairly at something, esp. to show that one thinks it foolish: He continued with his plans to build a flying machine, in spite of the mockery of his friends. | the humiliation of being held up to mockery (=made to seem foolish) in front of all my colleagues **2** [S] something that is not worthy of respect: The medical examination was a mockery; the doctor hardly looked at the child. **3 make a mockery of** to make or show to be useless or worthless: The violence and dishonesty of the election made a mockery of his claim to be restoring democracy.

mock·ing·bird /ˈmɒkɪŋbɜːd‖ˈmɑːkɪŋbɜːrd/ n an American bird that copies the songs of other birds

Mock Tur·tle /ˌ· ˈ··/ [the] a character from Lewis Carroll's book Alice in Wonderland

mock tur·tle soup /ˌ· ·· ˈ·/ n [U] soup made from meat, but tasting as if made from TURTLE

mock-up /ˈ· ·/ n a full-size model of something planned to be made or built: a mock-up of the film set/of the space shuttle —see also MOCK up

mods

mod /mɒd‖mɑːd/ n BrE (often cap.) a member of a group of young people following a fashion for neat clothes and/or esp. SOUL MUSIC, popular in Britain in the 1960s. Mods usu. drove motor SCOOTERS and often had fights with Rockers, esp. in seaside towns on Bank Holidays. —compare ROCKER²

Mod n a Gaelic FESTIVAL of music and poetry held in Scotland every year

MOD /ˌem əʊ ˈdiː/ abbrev. for: MINISTRY OF DEFENCE

mo·dal¹ /ˈməʊdl/ adj tech **1** [A] of the MOOD of a verb **2** of or written in a musical MODE — ~ly adv

modal² also **modal aux·il·i·a·ry** /ˌ·· ·ˈ····/, **modal verb** /ˌ·· ˈ·/— n tech any of the verb forms **can, could, may, might, shall, should, will, would, must, ought to, used to, need, had better** and **dare** —see also AUXILIARY VERB

mod con /ˌ· ˈ·/ n [often pl.] BrE infml (used esp. in house advertisements) a modern convenience; something that makes living easier and more comfortable, such as central heating: a desirable house with all mod cons

mode¹ /məʊd/ n **1** [(of)] fml a way of behaving, living, operating, etc.: He suddenly became wealthy, which changed his whole mode of life. | As the spacecraft came closer to the earth, it was put into its re-entry mode. | If you press this key the computer will go into its graphics mode. (=the system of operating in which pictures are produced) **2** tech any of various systems of arranging notes in music, such as MAJOR and MINOR in modern Western music

mode² n [the] fml what is fashionable: Long skirts were then the latest mode. —see also A LA MODE, MODISH

mod·el¹ /ˈmɒdl‖ˈmɑːdl/ n **1** [(of)] a small representation or copy of something: a model of the Eiffel Tower | a model aircraft/car | He made a working model of a steam engine out of old bits of metal. **2** a person, esp. a young woman, employed to model clothes, hairstyles, COSMETICS etc.: a fashion model | a male model **3** a person employed to be painted by a painter or photographed by a photographer **4** something on which a copy is based: building a new system of democracy, on the American model (=copying the American system) | Macho heroes in films are bad role models for children. —compare PATTERN¹ **5** [(of)] apprec a person or thing that is a perfect example to be followed or copied: She's a model student. | Her written work is a model of care and neatness. **6** a particular type of vehicle, weapon, machine, instrument, etc., as made by a particular maker: Volkswagen has produced two new models this year. | This dishwasher is the latest model. **7** euph, esp. BrE (used esp. in written advertisements) a PROSTITUTE

model² v -ll- ‖ -l- AmE **1** [T] **a** to shape (a soft substance) into an article: to model clay into little horses **b** to make a model of: to model little horses out of clay | to model a ship out of bits of wood —see also COMPUTER MODELLING **2** [T] to wear and show (clothes) to possible buyers: Angela is modelling an attractive blue silk dress. **3** [I] to work as a fashion model: She'd like to be a film actress, but at present she's modelling.

model sbdy./sthg. **on/upon** sbdy./sthg. phr v [T] to form as a copy of: Their railway system was modelled on the French one. | She modelled herself on her favourite film star. (=copied her character and behaviour)

Model T Ford /ˌ·· · ˈ·/ n a model of Ford car made between 1909 and 1927, the first car to be built on an ASSEMBLY LINE, and sold in very large numbers. The "Tin Lizzie", as the Model T was popularly known, was cheap, and almost always painted black. Henry Ford was talking about the Model T when he said the famous phrase "You can have any colour you like, so long as it's black."

mo·dem /ˈməʊdem, -dəm/ n tech an electronic apparatus for changing information from a form which a computer understands into a form which can be sent along a telephone line, allowing the information to be sent from one computer to another one a long way away

mod·e·rate¹ /ˈmɒdərɪt‖ˈmɑː-/ adj **1** not at either end of a range of size, force, etc. but perhaps nearer the lower end than the higher: The garden is of moderate size (=not very big). | travelling at a moderate speed **2** done or kept within sensible limits: The union's demands are very moderate; they're only asking for a small wage increase. | a moderate smoker **3** avoiding or not accepting ideas that are very different from those of most people; not politically extreme: a moderate politician | moderate views/opinions **4** often euph of average or less than average quality: a child of only moderate ability (=not very clever) | moderate success

mod·e·rate² /ˈmɒdəreɪt‖ˈmɑː-/ v [I;T] **1** rather fml to make or become less in force, degree, rate, etc.; reduce: The union decided to moderate their demands. | He should moderate his language when children are present. (=shouldn't use words not fit for them to hear) | Her fury moderated when she learned why he had done it. — compare MODIFY **2** to do the work of a MODERATOR (1) and (4)

mod·e·rate³ /ˈmɒdərɪt‖ˈmɑː-/ n a person whose opinions are MODERATE¹ (3)

moderate breeze /ˌ··· ˈ·/ n tech wind which has a speed of 20 to 28 kilometres per hour: Tomorrow will be sunny with a moderate breeze.

mod·e·rate·ly /ˈmɒdərɪtli‖ˈmɑː-/ adv to a moderate degree; not very: a moderately successful film

mod·e·ra·tion /ˌmɒdəˈreɪʃən‖ˌmɑː-/ n [U] **1** the ability to keep one's feelings, desires, and habits within reasonable limits; self-control: He showed great moderation in not responding angrily to the attacks on his character. **2** [(in)] fml reduction in force, degree, rate, etc.: Even after sunset there was little moderation in the temperature. **3 in moderation** within sensible limits: Some people say that smoking in moderation isn't harmful to health.

mod·e·ra·to /ˌmɒdəˈrɑːtəʊ‖ˌmɑː-/ n, adj -s (a piece of music) played at an average even speed —**moderato** adv

mod·e·ra·tor /ˈmɒdəreɪtəʳ‖ˈmɑː-/ n 1 a person who tries to help people to reach an agreement 2 (often cap.) a minister chosen to be in charge of a large meeting of the Presbyterian Church 3 BrE an examiner who makes sure that an examination paper arranged by someone else is fair, and also that the marks given by other examiners are of the right standard 4 a person who asks questions and keeps the marks of competing teams in a spoken game or competition

mod·ern¹ /ˈmɒdn‖ˈmɑːdərn/ adj 1 [no comp.] of the present time, or of the not far distant past; not ancient: The modern history of Italy dates from 1860, when the country became united. | What do you think of modern art? | modern times 2 often apprec typical of or developed in the most recent times; up to date: using the most modern surgical techniques | bright modern colours 3 [no comp.] (often cap.) (of a language) in use today: Modern English/Greek/Hebrew —compare MIDDLE, OLD; see also MODERN LANGUAGES, SECONDARY MODERN; see NEW (USAGE) — ~ity /mɒˈdɜːnɪti‖məˈdɜːr-/ n [U (of)]

modern² n [usu. pl.] lit or old-fash a person living in modern, as compared with ancient, times

modern art /ˌ·· ˈ·/ n [U] a general name for (work produced by) a variety of movements in art, mainly in the late 19th and early 20th centuries, which produced work extremely different from what had gone before, including Impressionism, Fauvism, Cubism, and Surrealism, as well as some more recent developments such as MINIMAL ART and Photorealism

modern dance /ˌ·· ˈ·/ n [U] a kind of dancing developed in Europe and the US in the early 20th century, which is performed in the theatre but is different from BALLET or the dancing which forms part of MUSICALs. Modern dance typically tried to avoid using the movements of ballet and to become independent of the structure of the music which goes with the dance.

modern-day /ˈ·· ·/ adj (typical) of the present time, esp. in the sense of being similar to something or someone from the past: She's a modern-day Joan of Arc, always finding a cause to martyr herself for.

mod·ern·is·m /ˈmɒdənɪzəm‖ˈmɑːdər-/ n [U] (sometimes cap.) (esp. in art and religion) a search for new forms of expression representative of modern times, esp. a tendency in the 1940s, 1950s, and 1960s to make a complete change from the past in using simple forms, artificial materials etc. in building, art decoration, etc. —compare POST-MODERNISM —**ist** adj, n : of the modernist school

mod·ern·ist·ic /ˌmɒdəˈnɪstɪk◂‖ˌmɑːdər-/ adj very noticeably and unusually modern: modernistic lampshades — ~**ally** /kli/ adv

mod·ern·ize also **-ise** BrE /ˈmɒdənaɪz‖ˈmɑːdər-/ v 1 [T] to make suitable for modern use, or for the needs of the present time: to modernize an old house by putting in a bathroom 2 [I] to start using more modern methods of operation: The business will lose money if it doesn't modernize. —**-ization** /ˌmɒdənaɪˈzeɪʃən‖ˌmɑːdərnə-/ n [C;U]

modern lan·gua·ges /ˌ·· ˈ···/ n [P] the study of one or more current foreign languages in a school or university

modern maths /ˌ·· ˈ·/ BrE ‖ **new math** AmE— n the MATHEMATICS which is currently taught in most schools in Britain and which includes such ideas as sets, SYMMETRY, and BASES (8)

mod·est /ˈmɒdəst‖ˈmɑː-/ adj 1 [(about)] apprec having or expressing a lower opinion of one's own ability than is probably deserved; hiding one's good qualities: The young actress is very modest about her success; she says it's as much the result of good luck as of her own talent. 2 not large in quantity, size, value, etc.: a modest rise in house prices | They were very modest in their demands. (=They didn't ask for too much.) | modest ambitions 3 old-fash apprec (esp. of a woman or her clothes or behaviour) avoiding or not showing anything that might excite sexual feelings: modest dress —see also IMMODEST — ~**ly** adv

mod·es·ty /ˈmɒdəsti‖ˈmɑː-/ n [U] often apprec 1 the quality, state, or fact of being modest: With commendable modesty, the editor has not included any of his own poems in the collection. 2 **in all modesty** euph without wishing to seem to praise oneself too much: I think I can say,

in all modesty, that we'd have lost the contract if I hadn't been there.

mod·i·cum /ˈmɒdɪkəm‖ˈmɑː-/ n [S (of)] usu. in negatives and questions] a small amount, esp. of a good quality such as truth, respect, etc.: If he had a modicum of sense, he wouldn't do such a thing.

mod·i·fi·ca·tion /ˌmɒdɪfɪˈkeɪʃən‖ˌmɑː-/ n 1 [U] the act of modifying or process of being modified 2 [C (to)] a small change made in something: A few simple modifications to this plan would greatly improve it.

mod·i·fi·er /ˈmɒdɪfaɪəʳ‖ˈmɑː-/ n tech (in grammar) a word or group of words that gives additional information about another word. Modifiers can be adjectives (such as fierce in the fierce dog), adverbs (such as loudly in The dog barked loudly), or phrases (such as with a short tail in the dog with a short tail).

mod·i·fy /ˈmɒdɪfaɪ‖ˈmɑː-/ v [T] 1 to change (a plan, an opinion, a condition, or the form or quality of something), esp. slightly: to modify one's views in the light of new evidence | The design has been modified to improve fuel consumption. 2 (of a word, esp. an adjective or adverb) to describe or limit the meaning of (another word): An adverb modifies the verb "talk" in the phrase "to talk quietly". —compare MODERATE⁷

Mod·i·glia·ni /ˌmɒdɪlˈjɑːni ‖ ˌmɔʊdiːl-/, **Am·e·de·o** /æməˈdeɪəʊ/ (1884–1920) an Italian painter and SCULPTOR influenced by Toulouse-Lautrec, Cézanne, and Picasso. He is known esp. for his pictures of people, in which their bodies and faces are much longer than in real life.

mod·ish /ˈməʊdɪʃ/ adj fashionable — ~**ly** adv

mod·u·lar /ˈmɒdjʊləʳ‖ˈmɑːdʒə-/ adj tech built or made using modules: modular furniture | a modular course in business studies

mod·u·late /ˈmɒdjʊleɪt‖ˈmɑːdʒə-/ v 1 [T] to vary the strength, nature, etc., of (a sound): He has a very monotonous voice; he should modulate it more. 2 [I+from, to] to pass by regular steps from one musical KEY to another: Here the music modulates from E to G. 3 [T] tech to vary the size or rate of (a radio wave or signal) —**lation** /ˌmɒdjʊˈleɪʃən‖ˌmɑːdʒə-/ n [C;U]

mod·ule /ˈmɒdjuːl‖ˈmɑːdʒuːl/ n tech 1 an independent part or unit which can be combined with others to form a structure or arrangement 2 a part of a spacecraft that can be used independently of the other parts for a particular purpose: While one of the astronauts went round the moon in the **command module**, the other went down to the surface in the **lunar module**.

mo·dus op·e·ran·di /ˌməʊdəs ˌɒpəˈrændi‖-ˌɑːpə-/ also **MO** infml— n [S] tech, Lat a method of doing something, esp. one that is typical of a particular person: His modus operandi is well-known to the police.

modus vi·ven·di /ˌməʊdəs vɪˈvendi/ n [S] Lat 1 [(with)] an arrangement between people of different opinions, habits, etc., to live or work together without quarrelling: They made a great effort to reach some kind of modus vivendi, for the sake of the children. 2 a way of living

mog·gy /ˈmɒgi‖ˈmɑːgi/, **mog·gie** /ˈmɒːgi/ also **mog** /mɒg‖mɑːg, mɔːg/— n BrE infml, esp. humor a cat

mo·gul /ˈməʊgəl/ n a person of very great power, wealth, and importance: the moguls of the film industry

mo·hair /ˈməʊheəʳ/ n [U] (cloth made from) the long fine silky hair of the ANGORA goat. Mohair is more expensive than most other types of woollen cloth: a mohair sweater

Mo·ham·med /məʊˈhæmɪd, mə-/ see MUHAMMAD

Mo·ham·me·dan /məʊˈhæmɪdən, mə-/ adj, n (a) Muslim (considered offensive by some Muslims)

Mo·ham·me·dan·is·m /məʊˈhæmɪdənɪzəm, mə-/ n [U] the Muslim religion; Islam (considered offensive by some Muslims)

Mo·ha·ve /məʊˈhɑːvi/ [the] see MOJAVE DESERT

Mo·hawk /ˈməʊhɔːk/ n [C; the+P] 1 (a member of) a Native American people of the Mohawk river valley in New York state —see NATIVE AMERICAN (CULTURAL NOTE) 2 AmE MOHICAN

mo·hi·can /məʊˈhiːkən/ BrE ‖ **mohawk** AmE— n a hairstyle in which the hair on the sides of the head is cut very short and the remaining hair is made to stand upright and is often brightly coloured. Mohicans were esp. popular among young people at the time of PUNK fashion, but are now becoming less common.

Mo·hi·can /məʊˈhiːkən/ n [C;the+P] (a member of) a Native American people of the upper Hudson river valley; invented by the writer James Fenimore Cooper for his stories

moi·e·ty /ˈmɔɪ‿ti/ n [(of) usu. sing.] law or lit a half share

moist /mɔɪst/ adj usu. apprec slightly wet: warm, moist air | This cake's nice and moist. | to plant flowers in the rich, moist earth —see DAMP (USAGE) — ~ly adv — ~ness n [U]

moist·en /ˈmɔɪsən/ v [I;T] to make or become moist: She moistened a tissue and gently wiped the dust off the necklace. | His eyes moistened slightly. (=he was perhaps going to cry)

mois·ture /ˈmɔɪstʃər/ n [U] water, or other liquids, in small quantities or in the form of steam or mist: The desert air contains hardly any moisture.

mois·tur·ize also **-ise** BrE /ˈmɔɪstʃəraɪz/ v [T] to remove the dryness from: to use moisturizing cream on one's hands —**izer** n

Mo·ja·ve Des·ert /məʊˌhɑːvi ˈdezət‖-zərt/ also **Mohave-** [the] a desert in southern California where DEATH VALLEY, the lowest point in the US, is found

moke /məʊk/ n BrE infml, esp. humor for horse or DONKEY

mo·lar /ˈməʊlər/ n any of the large teeth at the back of the mouth used for breaking up food —see also INCISOR, and see picture at TEETH

mo·las·ses /məˈlæs‿z/ n [U] **1** a thick dark sweet liquid produced from sugar plants **2** AmE for TREACLE

mold /məʊld/ n, v AmE for MOULD

Mol·da·vi·a /mɒlˈdeɪviə‖-mɑːl-/ a country in E Europe, bordering on Romania in the W and the Ukraine in the E and S; capital Kishinev; population 4,341,000 (1989) —**vian** n, adj

mol·der /ˈməʊldər/ v [I] AmE for MOULDER

mold·ing /ˈməʊldɪŋ/ n [C;U] AmE for MOULDING

mold·y /ˈməʊldi/ adj AmE for MOULDY —**iness** n [U]

mole[1] /məʊl/ n **1** a small, furry, almost blind animal that digs holes and passages underground to live in. One of the characters in The Wind in the Willows, a children's story by Kenneth Grahame, is a mole. **2** infml a person who works inside an organization, usu. for a long time, in order to provide secret information to the enemy: They've discovered a mole at the Foreign Office. —compare SPY[1]

mole[2] n a small, dark brown, slightly raised mark on a person's skin, usu. there since birth —compare FRECKLE

Mole, A·dri·an /ˈeɪdriən/ the main character in the book by Sue Townsend called The Growing Pains of Adrian Mole aged 13¾. Adrian Mole is a 13¾-year-old boy with spots, who writes an account of his daily life, thoughts, and worries. He describes many of the problems, esp. emotional problems, typical of ADOLESCENTS.

mol·e·cule /ˈmɒlɪkjuːl‖-ˈmɑː-/ n the smallest unit into which any substance can be divided without losing its own chemical nature, consisting usu. of two or more atoms: a hydrogen molecule —see picture at DIAGRAM —**-cular** /məˈlekjʊlər/ adj : molecular structure

mole·hill /ˈməʊlˌhɪl/ n a small pile of earth thrown up on the surface by a mole digging underground —see also **make a mountain out of a molehill** (MOUNTAIN)

mole·skin /ˈməʊlˌskɪn/ n [U] the fur of a mole, or a type of strong cotton cloth looking rather like this, used, esp. in former times, for making clothes: moleskin trousers

mo·lest /məˈlest/ v [T] **1** derog to attack and harm: A dog that molests sheep has to be killed. **2** sometimes euph to annoy or attack (esp. a woman or a child) sexually — ~ **er** n : The **child molester** was imprisoned for five years. — ~ **ation** /ˌməʊleˈsteɪʃən/ n [U]

Moles·worth /ˈməʊlzwəθ‖-wərθ/ a village in Cambridgeshire, E England, near which American CRUISE MISSILES were to have been based in the mid-1980s. There was a peace camp there, and a lot of government money was spent in putting a fence round the base, which was never used. —compare GREENHAM COMMON

Mol·i·ère /ˈmɒlieər ‖ məʊlˈjeər/ (1622–73) a French PLAYWRIGHT and actor whose real name was **Jean Baptiste Poquelin**. He was involved in many theatre activities but is best known as a writer of comedies (COMEDY(1)) of character which made fun of human be-

haviour, such as Le Misanthrope and Le Bourgeois Gentilhomme.

moll /mɒl‖mɑːl/ n sl a criminal's girlfriend: a gangster's moll

Moll Flanders see Moll FLANDERS

mol·li·fy /ˈmɒlɪfaɪ‖ˈmɑː-/ v [T] to make (a person or a person's feelings) less angry: He bought his angry wife some flowers, but she refused to be mollified. —**fication** /ˌmɒlɪf‿ˈkeɪʃən‖ˌmɑː-/ n [U]

mol·lusc ‖ also **mollusk** AmE /ˈmɒləsk‖ˈmɑː-/ n any of a class of animals which have soft bodies without a backbone or limbs and are usu. covered with a shell: Snails and octopuses are molluscs.

mol·ly·cod·dle /ˈmɒliˌkɒdl‖ˈmɑːliˌkɑːdl/ v [T] infml, usu. derog to take too much care of (a person or animal); show too much concern for the health and comfort of: My mother still tries to mollycoddle me.

Mol·ly Ma·guires /ˌmɒli məˈgwaɪəz‖ˌmɑːli məˈgwaɪərz/ n [P] a 19th-century secret organization of Irish Americans in the coal-producing area of Pennsylvania, US, which used often violent means to try to improve working conditions

Mo·loch /ˈməʊlɒk‖-lɑːk/ a god in an ancient religion for whom children were killed as an offering (SACRIFICE[2] (1))

Mol·o·tov cock·tail /ˌmɒlətɒf ˈkɒkteɪl‖ˌmɑːlətɔːf ˈkɑːk-, ˌmɔːl-/ n a simple bomb thrown by hand and made from a bottle filled with petrol, used mainly during RIOTs and often aimed at the police

molt /məʊlt/ v, n AmE for MOULT

mol·ten /ˈməʊltən/ adj (of metal or rock) turned to liquid by very great heat; melted: The volcano threw out molten lava. —see MELT (USAGE)

mol·to /ˈmɒltəʊ‖ˈməʊl-, ˈmɔːl-/ adv (in music) very: molto allegro (=very quickly)

Mo·luc·cas /məˈlʌkəz/ [the+P] a group of islands in E Indonesia, between Sulawesi and New Guinea, famous for producing SPICEs; capital Amboina

mo·lyb·de·num /məˈlɪbdənəm/ n [U] a silver-white metal that is a simple substance (ELEMENT) used esp. for strengthening steel

mom /mɒm‖mɑːm/ n AmE for MUM[1]

MOMA /ˈməʊmə/ n the MUSEUM OF MODERN ART

mom-and-pop /ˌ‿·‿·‿‿◂/ adj AmE (of a small business) owned and operated by a family or husband and wife: a mom-and-pop bakery

mo·ment /ˈməʊmənt/ n **1** [C] a very short period of time: Can I speak to you for a moment? | It will only take a moment/a few moments. | I'll be ready in a moment. (=very soon) | Just a moment (=wait); I want to have a word with you. | I wasn't fooled for a moment. (=at all) | He wrote the book at odd moments. (=short periods of free time) — see also MOMENTARY **2** [C] a particular point in time: Just at that moment, the door opened and the inspector walked in. | It's impossible to get a decision out of David; he changes his mind from one moment to the next. (=frequently) | He's only just this moment left the office, Mrs. Lee. (=he left a few seconds ago) | I cannot give you any answer at this moment in time. (=now) | one of those magic moments in a love affair **3** [C usu. sing.] the time for doing something: Choose your moment carefully if you want to ask her for a pay rise. [+to-v] This is not the (best) moment to tell him the news. **4** [of+U] old-fash fml importance: The president will speak to the nation tonight on a matter of the greatest moment. —see also MOMENTOUS **5** [C (of) usu. sing.] tech (a measure of) the turning power of a force **6 at any moment** at an unknown time only a little after the present: Be careful — he might come back at any moment! **7 at the last moment** only just in time; just before the start of an activity: He's never late, but he often arrives at the very last moment. **8 at the moment** at the present time; now: I'm busy at the moment, but I'll do it later. **9 for the moment** as far as the present time is concerned (although perhaps not later); for now: For the moment we are content to watch and wait. **10 have one's/its moments** infml to have times of being important, successful, happy, etc.: It was a dull film on the whole, though it had its moments. **11 the moment (that)** as soon as: I recognized her the moment (that) I saw her. —see also MOMENT OF TRUTH, **on the spur of the moment** (SPUR[1]) **12 the moment of truth** the moment that will show whether something is going to work or not

mo·men·tar·i·ly /ˈməʊməntərɪli‖ˌməʊmənˈterɪli/ adv **1** for just a very short time: *He was so surprised that he was momentarily unable to speak.* **2** AmE very soon; in a moment: *We will be landing at the airport momentarily.*

mo·men·ta·ry /ˈməʊməntəri‖-teri/ adj lasting for a very short time: *She hesitated in momentary confusion.*

mo·men·tous /məʊˈmentəs, mə-/ adj of very great importance or seriousness, esp. because of possible future effects: *the momentous news that war had begun* | *a momentous decision*

mo·men·tum /məʊˈmentəm, mə-/ n -ta /tə/ or -tums **1** [C;U] *tech* the quantity of movement in a body, measured by multiplying its mass by its speed: *As the rock rolled down the mountainside, it gathered momentum.* (=moved faster and faster) **2** [U] the force gained by the movement or development of events: *The struggle for independence is gaining momentum every day.*

MOMI /ˈməʊmi/ the MUSEUM OF THE MOVING IMAGE

mom·ma /ˈmɒmə‖ˈmɑːmə/ n AmE see MAMA[1], MUMMY[1]

mom·my /ˈmɒmi‖ˈmɑːmi/ n AmE infml for MUMMY[1]

Mon. *written abbrev. for:* Monday

Mon·a·co /ˈmɒnəkəʊ, məˈnɑːkəʊ‖ˈmɑːn-/ a small country, ruled by a prince, on the Mediterranean coast between France and Italy; population 28,000 (1989). Monaco is popular with tourists and attracts many to its CASINOs in Monte Carlo. Since 1927 Monaco has been ruled by the Grimaldi family, whose members are often written about in the popular newspapers. —**Monegasque** /ˌmɒnɪˈɡæsk ‖ˌmɑːn-/ n, adj

Mon·a·ghan /ˈmɒnəhən‖ˈmɑːn-/ a COUNTY in the NE of the Republic of Ireland

Mo·na Li·sa /ˌməʊnə ˈliːzə‖-ˈliːsə/ [the] a painting by Leonardo da Vinci of a woman with a mysterious smile. It is kept in the Louvre in Paris. —see colour picture on page 1016

mon·arch /ˈmɒnək‖ˈmɑːnərk, -ɑːrk/ n a ruler of a state, such as a king, queen, etc., who has a right to rule by birth, and does not have to be elected — ~ **ic** /məˈnɑːkɪk‖məˈnɑːr-/ adj : *monarchic rule*

mon·arch·is·m /ˈmɒnəkɪzəm‖ˈmɑːnər-/ n [U] (the principles of) monarchic government

mon·arch·ist /ˈmɒnəkɪst‖ˈmɑːnər-/ n a person in favour of the idea that kings, queens, etc., should rule, rather than elected leaders: *monarchist principles*

mon·ar·chy /ˈmɒnəki‖ˈmɑːnərki/ n **1** [U] (the system of) rule by a king or queen: *He's a staunch supporter of the monarchy.* **2** [C] a state ruled by a king or queen: *Britain is a constitutional monarchy.* —compare REPUBLIC

▶ CULTURAL NOTE Britain is a CONSTITUTIONAL MONARCHY. The monarch, at present Queen Elizabeth II, is the HEAD OF STATE (= the official ruler of the country) and has to agree to all new laws before they can come into force. Every year she performs the STATE OPENING OF PARLIAMENT, when she makes a speech which tells what the government intends to do. She appoints the Prime Minister and gives titles and other HONOURS to people who have done good things for the country. In practice she has very little power, and she may not express a political opinion in public. She cannot refuse to agree to a law which has been decided on by Parliament and she must appoint as Prime Minister the leader of the political party that has won the most Parliamentary seats. Most honours go to people chosen by the government. Her duties are mainly ceremonial. Some people think that the monarchy is old-fashioned and a waste of money, but others feel that it is a good thing to have someone to represent the country on important occasions who is not connected with any political party. ◀

mon·as·tery /ˈmɒnəstri‖ˈmɑːnəsteri/ n a building in which MONKs live —compare CONVENT

mo·nas·tic /məˈnæstɪk/ adj of or like monasteries or MONKs: *a monastic community* | *He lives a life of monastic simplicity.* — ~ **ally** /kli/ adv

mo·nas·ti·cis·m /məˈnæstɪsɪzəm/ n [U] the life, or way of life, of MONKs in a monastery

Mon·day /ˈmʌndi/ (*written abbrev.* **Mon.**)— n [C;U] the first day of the week, between Sunday and Tuesday: *He'll arrive on Monday.* | (*BrE infml or AmE*) *He'll arrive Monday.* | *It happened on Monday morning.* | *We do our shopping on Mondays.* | *My birthday is on a Monday this year.* | *It was in Monday's "Daily Express".* | *"What's the*

matter with you?" "Oh, nothing, just that Monday morning feeling|the Monday morning blues." (=I don't like returning to work after two days' holiday) —see DAY (CULTURAL NOTE)

Monday Club /ˈ·· ˌ·/ [the] a club of right-wing British Conservative politicians who formerly met on Mondays, started in 1961

Mon·dri·an /ˌmɒndriˈɑːn‖ˌmɔːn-/, **Piet** /piːt/ (1872–1944) a Dutch painter famous for his ABSTRACT work involving only straight lines and squares or RECTANGLEs of colour

Mon·et /ˈmɒneɪ ‖ məʊˈneɪ/, **Claude** /klɔːd/ (1840–1926) a French painter who was involved in starting Impressionism, best known for his pictures of the countryside in which he was concerned to show the effects of light —see colour picture on page 1016

mon·e·ta·ris·m /ˈmʌnɪtərɪzəm‖ˈmɑː-/ n [U] *tech* (in ECONOMICS) the belief that the best way of controlling the ECONOMY of a country is to control the MONEY SUPPLY — compare THATCHERISM —**·rist** n, adj

mon·e·ta·ry /ˈmʌnɪtəri‖ˈmɑːnɪteri/ adj esp. tech of or about money: *The monetary system of some countries used to be based on gold.*

mon·ey /ˈmʌni/ n [U] **1** a means of payment, esp. in the form of metal coins or paper notes: *His father makes|earns a lot of money as a pilot.* | *The repairs will cost a lot of money.* | *If it doesn't work, the shop should give you your money back.* (=repay its price to you) | *We enjoyed the film so much that we felt we'd had our money's worth.* (=full value for the price) | *"Have you got any cash?" "No, I don't usually carry much money on me."* (=with me) | *Don't throw that away; I paid good money* (=spent money that should not be wasted) *for it.* | *I want him to* **put (some) money into** (=INVEST in) *my business.* | *The school is holding a competition to* **raise** (=collect) **money for** *a new hall.* | *We needn't take a taxi* — *don't* **throw your money about/away.** (=spend it foolishly) | (*infml*) *I've never seen anyone spend so much in one evening; he must* **have money to burn**/*he must be* **rolling in money!** (=be very rich) **2** wealth: *He made his money in property speculation.* | *His business collapsed, and he lost all his money.* | (*infml*) *If this old picture is really by a famous artist, we're* **in the money.** (=rich) | (*infml*) *She intends to marry money.* (=a rich man) **3** for **'my money** *infml* in my opinion: *For my money, you were by far the best actor in the play.* **4 (the love of) money is the root of all evil** *saying from the Bible* the desire to have a lot of money is the cause of all crimes **5 'made of money** *infml* very rich: *I can't afford to buy you another car* — *do you think I'm made of money?* **6 money for jam/for old rope** *infml esp. BrE* money obtained or earned for very little effort **7 money makes the world go round** *saying* money is the most important thing in the world because most human activity depends on it **8 money talks** *infml* money can be used by those who have it to influence others **9 put one's money where one's mouth is** *infml, often humor* to support one's views with practical proof: *You say you're on the side of the workers: why don't you put your money where your mouth is and support the strike?* **10 your money or your life** give me your money or I will kill you — a threat that is supposed to have been made by highwaymen (HIGHWAYMAN) —see also MAD MONEY, MONEYS, BLOOD MONEY, HUSH MONEY, PIN MONEY, POCKET MONEY, READY MONEY, **a (good) run for one's money** (RUN[2]), **see the colour of someone's money** (SEE[1]), **throw good money after bad** (THROW[1]) — ~ **less** adj

▷ USAGE Compare **money, cash,** and **change. Money** is the most general term. **Cash** usually means "money in coins or notes": *"May I pay by cheque?" "I'm sorry, sir, we only take* **cash**", but it can be used informally to mean "money in any form": *I'm a bit short of* **cash/money** *at the moment.* When talking about the money returned when you have given more than the cost of something you have bought use **change:** *"Here you are, sir, 25 pence* **change.**" **Change** can also mean "money in low-value coins or notes": *"Can you give me* **change** *for 50 pence? I need some 5p pieces for the coffee machine."*◁

mon·ey·bags /ˈmʌnibæɡz/ n **moneybags** *infml derog* a very wealthy person

mon·ey·box /ˈmʌnibɒks‖-bɑːks/ n BrE a box for saving

money in, usu. used by children and with an opening into which coins can be put —compare PIGGYBANK

mon·ey·chang·er /ˈmʌniˌtʃeɪndʒəʳ/ n a person whose business is exchanging the money of one country for that of another

mon·eyed /ˈmʌnid/ adj [A] fml having a large amount of money; rich: the moneyed classes

money-grub·ber /ˈmʌniˌgrʌbəʳ/ n derog a person who is determined to gain money, often by dishonest means —-bing adj : a money-grubbing old skinflint

mon·ey·lend·er /ˈmʌniˌlendəʳ/ n sometimes derog a person whose business is lending money and charging interest on it, but who does not work for a bank

mon·ey·mak·er /ˈmʌniˌmeɪkəʳ/ n usu. apprec a product or business that brings in a lot of money —-ing adj

money mar·ket /ˈ·· ˌ·· / n banks, and other financial institutions taking part in buying, selling, lending, and borrowing money, esp. foreign money, for profit

money or·der /ˈ·· ˌ··/ n an official paper of a stated value which is bought from a post office, bank, etc., and sent to someone instead of money. In Britain this system is used for larger sums of money than a POSTAL ORDER.

mon·eys , monies /ˈmʌniz/ n [P] law or old use money: The moneys held in the trust fund cannot be paid to you until you are 18.

money spi·der /ˈ·· ˌ··/ n a small red or brown SPIDER which is thought by some people to bring good luck to any person it walks on

money-spin·ner /ˈ·· ˌ··/ n infml, esp. BrE something that brings in a large amount of money: This hotel's a real money-spinner in the summer months.

money sup·ply /ˈ·· ·ˌ·/ n [the] all the money that exists and is being paid and spent in a country, in the form of coins, notes, and CREDIT: a government plan to reduce the money supply

mon·gol /ˈmɒŋgəl‖ˈmɑːŋ-/ n now usu. taboo a person suffering from DOWN'S SYNDROME

Mongol n a person from Mongolia

Mon·go·li·a /mɒŋˈgəʊliə‖mɑːŋ-/ a country in N central Asia, officially called the **Mongolian People's Republic**, bordered by Russia to the N and China to the S; capital Ulaanbaatar; population 2,159,000 (1989) —-lian n, adj

mon·gol·is·m /ˈmɒŋgəlɪzəm‖ˈmɑːŋ-/ n [U] now usu. taboo for DOWN'S SYNDROME

mon·goose /ˈmɒŋguːs‖ˈmɑːŋ-/ n -gooses a small furry Indian animal that kills snakes and rats

mon·grel /ˈmʌŋgrəl‖ˈmɑːŋ-, ˈmʌŋ-/ n 1 an animal, esp. a dog, whose parents were of mixed breeds or different breeds —compare PEDIGREE² 2 infml something that is a mixture of two types of thing: The English word "television" is a mongrel because "tele" comes from Greek and "vision" from Latin.

mon·ies /ˈmʌniz/ n [P] MONEYS

mon·i·tor¹ /ˈmɒnɪtəʳ‖ˈmɑː-/ n 1 also **monitor screen** /ˈ··· ·/— a television set used in a television STUDIO to see the picture that a television camera is receiving 2 an instrument that receives and shows continuous information about the working of something, such as a body part: a heart monitor 3 a a VDU (=a SCREEN for use with a computer) b tech the parts of a computer operation (such as PROGRAMS, CIRCUITS, etc.) that make sure that the computer system is working properly —see picture at COMPUTER 4 a person whose work is to listen to news, messages, etc., from foreign radio stations and report their contents 5 a pupil chosen to help the teacher or school in various ways: The board monitor must clean the blackboard every morning. | a hall monitor

monitor² v [T] (of a person or machine) to watch or listen to (something) carefully over a certain period of time for a special purpose: This instrument monitors the patient's heartbeats. | We monitor the enemy's radio broadcasts for political information.

monk /mʌŋk/ n a member of an all-male religious group who lives a life of service, obedience, and prayer or MEDITATION, usu. in a MONASTERY, owning nothing and not marrying —compare FRIAR, NUN

▶ CULTURAL NOTE The STEREOTYPE of a monk is of a man wearing a black or brown HABIT (= a piece of clothing like a long dress with a HOOD, tied round the waist with rope)

and SANDALs, with no hair on top of his head (see TONSURE). In cartoons monks are usually simple and harmless, and are sometimes pictured with a HALO.◀

— ~ish adj sometimes derog

The Monkees

Mon·kees /ˈmʌŋkiːz/, **The** an American popular music group formed in 1966, who made a number of successful television programmes but separated in 1969

mon·key¹ /ˈmʌŋki/ n 1 a small tree-climbing animal with a long tail belonging to the class of animals most like humans

▶ CULTURAL NOTE Monkeys are thought of as being clever animals that enjoy playing tricks◀

monkey

2 infml a child who is full of annoying playfulness and tricks: Stop that, you little monkey! 3 BrE sl 500 pounds or dollars 4 make a monkey (out) of someone infml to make someone appear foolish 5 monkey on one's back AmE a serious and upsetting problem that one can't get rid of, esp. drug ADDICTION

monkey² v
monkey about/around phr v [I] infml to play foolishly: The boys were monkeying about in the playground, and one of them got hurt.
monkey with sbdy./sthg. phr v [T (ABOUT, AROUND)] infml to handle carelessly or irresponsibly: You'll break the TV if you don't stop monkeying about with it.

monkey bars /ˈ·· ·/ n [P] AmE for CLIMBING FRAME

monkey busi·ness /ˈ·· ˌ··/ n [U] infml behaviour which causes trouble: The children are being too good today; I think there's some monkey business going on.

monkey nut /ˈ·· ·/ n BrE old-fash for PEANUT

monkey-puz·zle /ˈ·· ˌ··/ also **monkey-puzzle tree** /ˈ·· ·· ·ˌ·/— n a tree with dark green prickly leaves growing very close together on long branches sometimes grown in gardens as a form of decoration

mon·key·shine /ˈmʌŋkiʃaɪn/ n AmE for PRACTICAL JOKE

monkey wrench /ˈ·· ·/ n a tool that can be used for holding or turning things of different widths

Monk·house /ˈmʌŋkhaʊs/, **Bob** (1928–) a British television entertainer known esp. for programmes such as The Golden Shot, Celebrity Squares, and Family Fortunes

mon·o¹ /ˈmɒnəʊ‖ˈmɑː-/ adj using a system of sound recording or broadcasting in which the sound appears to come from one direction only when played: a mono record/record player —compare QUADRAPHONIC, STEREO

mono² n [U] infml 1 mono sound 2 MONONUCLEOSIS

mono- see WORD FORMATION

mon·o·chrome /ˈmɒnəkrəʊm‖ˈmɑː-/ adj 1 using only black, white, and grey: a monochrome television 2 (of a painting, etc.) in only one colour: a monochrome study of trees by a pool | (fig.) a dull monochrome existence (=always the same)

mon·o·cle /ˈmɒnəkəl‖ˈmɑː-/ n an EYEGLASS for one eye only, worn in former times, esp. by UPPER-CLASS men

mo·nog·a·my /məˈnɒgəmi‖məˈnɑː-/ n [U] the custom or practice of having only one wife or husband at one time, the only legal form of marriage in most of the western

world —compare BIGAMY, POLYGAMY —**-mous** *adj*
—**-mously** *adv*

mon·o·gram /ˈmɒnəgræm‖ˈmɑː-/ *n* a figure formed of two or more combined letters, esp. a person's INITIALS, that is printed on writing paper, or sewn on clothes, TOWELS, etc. A monogram is considered to be a sign of a wealthy person. **— ~ med** *adj*

mon·o·graph /ˈmɒnəgrɑːf‖ˈmɑːnəgræf/ *n* [(**on**)] a serious article or short book on one particular subject that the writer has studied deeply

mon·o·ki·ni /ˈmɒnəʊkiːni ‖ ˈmɑː-/ *n* a piece of women's clothing for swimming which is in one piece and worn below the waist; a BIKINI without a top

mon·o·ling·ual /ˌmɒnəʊˈlɪŋgwəl◂‖ˌmɑːnə-/ *adj tech* speaking or using only one language: *a monolingual dictionary* —compare BILINGUAL

mon·o·lith /ˈmɒnəlɪθ‖ˈmɑː-/ *n* **1** a large block of stone, usu. taller than it is wide, standing by itself, esp. as put up in former times for religious purposes **2** something which is large and very difficult to change

mon·o·lith·ic /ˌmɒnəˈlɪθɪk◂‖ˌmɑː-/ *adj* **1** of or like a monolith: *a monolithic office building* **2** *often derog* forming a large unchangeable whole: *a monolithic totalitarian state* **— ~ ally** /kli/ *adv*

mon·o·logue ‖ also **monolog** *AmE* /ˈmɒnəlɒg‖ˈmɑːnələːg, -lɑːg/ *n* **1** a long speech for a single actor or actress, usu. alone on stage **2** *infml* a rather long period of talking by one person, which prevents others from taking part in the conversation —compare DIALOGUE (2), SOLILOQUY

mon·o·ma·ni·a /ˌmɒnəʊˈmeɪniə‖ˌmɑː-/ *n* [U] a condition of the mind in which a person keeps thinking of one particular idea or subject

mon·o·ma·ni·ac /ˌmɒnəʊˈmeɪniæk‖ˌmɑː-/ *n, adj* (a person) suffering from monomania

mon·o·nu·cle·o·sis /ˌmɒnəʊnjuːkliˈəʊsɪs‖ˌmɑːnəʊnuː-/ *n* [U] *esp. AmE for* GLANDULAR FEVER

mon·oph·thong /ˈmɒnəfθɒŋ‖ˈmɑːnəfθɔːŋ/ *n tech* a single vowel sound, in which the organs of speech remain in the same position while it is being pronounced: *The vowel sound in "me" is a monophthong.* —compare DIPHTHONG

mon·o·plane /ˈmɒnəʊpleɪn‖ˈmɑː-/ *n* an aircraft with only one wing on each side, as used today by most AIRLINEs —compare BIPLANE

Monopolies and Mer·gers Com·mis·sion /·ˌ··· · ˈ·· ·ˌ··/ [*the*] a British organization which examines planned MERGERs between companies to see whether they would have a damaging effect on the public. It can make suggestions to the government but the government is not forced to act upon them. —compare ANTITRUST LAWS

mo·nop·o·list /məˈnɒpəlɪst‖məˈnɑː-/ *n* a person who has a monopoly **— ~ ic** /məˌnɒpəˈlɪstɪk◂‖məˌnɑː-/ *adj* : *giant monopolistic corporations*

mo·nop·o·lize also **-lise** *BrE* /məˈnɒpəlaɪz‖məˈnɑː-/ *v* [T] to have or get complete control of: *The company eventually monopolized the entire cigarette industry.* | *Robert completely monopolized the conversation last night; Sally and I couldn't get a word in edgeways!* **—lization** /məˌnɒpəlaɪˈzeɪʃən‖məˌnɑːpələ-/ *n* [U (**of**)]

mo·nop·o·ly /məˈnɒpəli‖məˈnɑː-/ *n* **1** [C] control of all of the market for a product or service: *That airline has a monopoly on flights to Oslo.* | *The postal service is a government monopoly.* (=no one else is allowed to provide this service) **2** [S+**of**] possession of, or control over, something which is not shared by others: *He seems to think he has a monopoly of brains.* (=that he alone is clever) | *A university education shouldn't be the monopoly of the rich.*

Monopoly *n* [U] *tdmk* a board game in which players use IMITATION money to buy, rent, and sell squares on the board, and try to get more money than their opponents. The squares are marked with the names of real places, and the cost varies according to how valuable the real property would be. People sometimes use the expression **Monopoly money** to mean a very large, or too large, amount: *You know how much he's charging me to mend my roof? It's Monopoly money.*

mon·o·rail /ˈmɒnəʊreɪl‖ˈmɑː-/ *n* (a train travelling along the top of, or hanging from) a railway system with a single RAIL

mon·o·sod·i·um glu·tam·ate /ˌmɒnəʊˌsəʊdiəm ˈgluːtəmeɪt‖ˌmɑːnə-/ (*abbrev.* **MSG**) *n* [U] a chemical compound added to certain foods, esp. meat, to give a strong, savoury flavour, and considered by many people to be bad for the health

mon·o·syl·lab·ic /ˌmɒnəsɪˈlæbɪk◂‖ˌmɑː-/ *adj* **1** *tech* (of a word) having one SYLLABLE **2** (of a remark) short and rather rude: *He was sulking, and would give only monosyllabic replies, such as "yes" and "no".* **— ~ ally** /kli/ *adv*

mon·o·syl·la·ble /ˈmɒnəˌsɪləbəl‖ˈmɑː-/ *n tech* a word with one SYLLABLE: *"Can", "hot", and "neck" are monosyllables.*

mon·o·the·is·m /ˈmɒnəʊθiːɪzəm‖ˈmɑːnə-/ *n* [U] *tech* the belief that there is only one God —compare POLYTHEISM **—ist** *n* **—tic** /ˌmɒnəʊθiːˈɪstɪk◂‖ˌmɑːnə-/ *adj* : *Christianity is a monotheistic religion.*

mon·o·tone /ˈmɒnətəʊn‖ˈmɑː-/ *n* [S] a way of speaking or singing in which the voice neither rises nor falls, but continues on the same note: *to speak in a monotone*

mo·not·o·nous /məˈnɒtənəs‖məˈnɑː-/ *adj* having a tiring uninteresting sameness and lack of variety, dull: *He spoilt the poem by reading it in a monotonous voice.* | *My job is rather monotonous.* **— ~ ly** *adv*

mo·not·o·ny /məˈnɒtəni‖məˈnɑː-/ also **mo·not·o·nous·ness** /məˈnɒtənəsnəs‖məˈnɑː-/ — *n* [U] sameness; lack of variety: *the monotony of his voice/the job*

mon·o·un·sat·u·rate /ˌmɒnəʊʌnˈsætʃʊrɪt‖ˌmɑː-/ also **mon·o·un·sat·u·rat·ed fat** /ˌmɒnəʊʌnsætʃəreɪtɪd ˈfæt‖ˌmɑː-/— *n tech* a type of fat found esp. in vegetable foods which is less harmful than SATURATED fat, which is found in meat and DAIRY products

mo·nox·ide /məˈnɒksaɪd‖məˈnɑːk-/ *n* [C;U] *tech* a chemical compound containing one atom of oxygen to every atom of another ELEMENT: *carbon monoxide*

Mon·roe¹ /mənˈrəʊ/, **James** (1758–1831) the fifth president of the US (1817–25). He is most remembered for the **Monroe Doctrine** (1823) which opposed the influence of Europe in the affairs of countries in North and South America.

Monroe², **Mar·i·lyn** /ˈmærɪlɪn/ (1926–62) an American film actress whose real name was **Norma Jean Baker**, who played sexy characters in many successful films before she died as a result of taking too many SLEEPING PILLs. For many people she represents the attractions of the female sex. —see picture on page 228

Mon·ro·vi·a /mənˈrəʊviə/ a city and port which is the capital of Liberia, W Africa

Mon·sieur /məˈsjɜːʳ/ *n* **Messieurs** /meɪˈsjɜːz‖-ɜːrz/ (used as a title for a French-speaking man) Mr: *Monsieur Legrand*

Mon·si·gnor /mɒnˈsiːnjəʳ‖mɑːn-/ *n* (*written abbrev.* **Mgr—** *n* (used as a title for a priest of high rank in the Roman Catholic church): *I agree, Monsignor.* | *Monsignor Bruce Kent*

mon·soon /mɒnˈsuːn‖mɑːn-/ *n* **1** [*the*] **a** (the period or season of) heavy rains which fall in India and other Asian countries from about April to October **b** the wind that brings these rains **2** [C] *infml* a very heavy fall of rain

mon·ster /ˈmɒnstəʳ‖ˈmɑːn-/ *n*
1 a strange typically imaginary animal that is large, frightening, and usu. fierce: *a sea monster* | *She dreamt that terrible monsters with flaming eyes and sharp teeth were chasing her.* **2** a very evil person: *This monster murdered 15 women before the police caught him.* **3** *infml* an animal, plant, or thing of unusually great size: *His dog is huge — a real monster!* | *a monster potato*

monster

Monster Rav·ing Loon·y Par·ty /ˌ··· · ˈ·· ·ˌ··/ [*the*] a small British political party with ideas which are not intended to be taken seriously, but which some people vote for in order to show their dissatisfaction with the aims of all the other parties

mon·strance /ˈmɒnstrəns‖ˈmɑːn-/ *n* a cup usu. of silver or gold, and holding the holy bread, raised by the priest before the people during a service in a Roman Catholic church

mon·stros·i·ty /mɒnˈstrɒsᵻti‖maːnˈstrɑː-/ n infml something, esp. something large, that is very ugly: *Have you seen their new office building? What a monstrosity!*

mon·strous /ˈmɒnstrəs‖ˈmaːn-/ adj 1 extremely bad, improper, immoral, or shocking; DISGRACEFUL: *It's monstrous to charge £80 for a hotel room!* | *monstrous cruelty* | *a monstrous accusation* 2 of unnaturally large size, strange shape, etc. — ~ly adv

mons ven·e·ris /ˌmɒnz ˈvenərᵻs‖ˌmaːnz-/ n med the raised rounded area of flesh between the top of a woman's legs and just above the sex organs

mon·tage /ˈmɒntaːʒ‖maːnˈtaːʒ/ n 1 [C] a picture or a piece of writing or music made from separate parts combined together 2 [U] the choosing, cutting, and combining together of separate photographic material to make a connected film

Montagues /ˈmɒntəgjuːz‖-ˈmaːn/ see CAPULETS AND MONTAGUES

Mon·taigne /mɒnˈteɪn‖maːn-/, **Mi·chel Ey·quem de** /miːˈʃel iːˈkem də/ (1533–92) a French writer of ESSAYs (=short articles on real subjects) who influenced many writers with his informal but careful way of writing

Mon·ta·na /mɒnˈtaːnə ‖ maːnˈtæ-/ *(written abbrev. MT)*— a mountainous state in the NW of the US, the fourth largest of the states but with one of the smallest populations —see colour maps on pages 1374–5

Mont Blanc /ˌmɒŋ ˈblaːŋ ‖ məʊŋ-/ a mountain in the Alps which is the highest in Europe. A TUNNEL through Mont Blanc joins Italy and France.

Mon·te Car·lo /ˌmɒnti ˈkaːləʊ‖ˌmaːnti ˈkaːr-/ 1 a town in Monaco where many wealthy people live or visit. It has many CASINOs and is famous for a car RALLY and the Monaco Grand Prix car race which are held there every year. 2 **the man who broke the bank at Monte Carlo** the title of an old British popular song about a man who won a lot of money by gambling (GAMBLE) at Monte Carlo

Mon·te Cris·to /ˌmɒnti ˈkrɪstəʊ‖ˌmaːn-/, **Count of** a character in a book by the French writer Alexandre Dumas, who does not tell who he is as he wants to punish his enemies

Mon·te·go /mɒnˈtiːgəʊ‖maːn-/ n tdmk a middle-sized car built by the British Rover Group

Montego Bay /ˌ·ˌ·· ˈ·/ a city and port in NW Jamaica. It is a popular holiday resort and is the second largest town on the island

Mon·te·ne·gro /ˌmɒntᵻˈniːgrəʊ‖maːn-/ a republic in SW Yugoslavia with some Adriatic coastline

Mon·ter·rey /ˌmɒntəˈreɪ‖ˌmaːn-/ an industrial city in NE Mexico, the country's largest steel-making centre

Mon·tes·quieu /ˌmɒntəˈskjɜː‖ˌmaːntəˈskjuː/, **Charles Louis de Se·con·dat** /ˌsəkɒnˈdaː‖-kəʊn-/, **Baron de la Brède** /bred/ **et de** (1689–1755) a French political and social thinker whose book *The Spirit of the Laws* greatly influenced the system of laws and government of the US and other countries

Mon·tes·so·ri school /ˌmɒntᵻˈsɔːri ˌskuːl‖ˌmaːn-/ n a school for very young children in which they perform activities which allow them to develop freely and at their own speed (from the name of **Maria Montessori**, an Italian educator who developed the **Montessori method** now used in Montessori schools)

Mon·teux /mɒnˈtɜː‖məʊn-/, **Pi·erre** /piˈeəʳ/ (1875–1964) an American CONDUCTOR (=a person who directs the playing of a group of musicians) who was born in France. He was chief conductor of the London Symphony Orchestra from 1960.

Mon·te·vi·de·o /ˌmɒntᵻvɪˈdeɪəʊ‖ˌmaːn-/ a city and port in S Uruguay, the capital of the country

Mon·te·zu·ma /ˌmɒntᵻˈzuːmə‖ˌmaːn-/ (1480?–1520) the last Aztec ruler of Mexico, who was taken prisoner by the Spanish under Cortés, and later killed by his own people

Montezuma's re·venge /ˌ·····ˈ·/ n [U] humor DIARRHOEA and stomach upset experienced by travellers in tropical countries, esp. in Mexico and Latin America

Mont·gom·e·ry /məntˈgʌməri/, **Field Marshal** (1887–1976) an English military commander, known to the British people as Monty, who led the British army to victory at El Alamein in 1942 during the Second World War

Montgomery Ward & Com·pa·ny /ˌ·ˌ··· ˈ·· ˌ···/ also **Wards** infml— in the US, one of a group of large shops which sell many different kinds of goods. The company has stores in all 50 states and also sells goods by post.

month /mʌnθ/ n 1 any of the 12 named divisions of the (Western) year: *The month of January has 31 days.* | *He's coming home next month.* 2 a period of about four weeks: *The baby is six months old.* | *He got* (=was sent to prison for) *three months for dangerous driving.* | *I haven't seen him for months.* (=for a long time) 3 **in a month of Sundays** infml in a very long time: *I haven't seen her in a month of Sundays.* (=It's a very long time since I've seen her.) —see also CALENDAR MONTH, LUNAR MONTH

month·ly¹ /ˈmʌnθli/ adj, adv (happening, appearing, etc.) every month or once a month: *a monthly meeting*

monthly² n 1 a magazine appearing once a month 2 AmE infml a woman's PERIOD (4)

Mont·mar·tre /mɒnˈmaːtrə‖məʊn-/ an area of Paris in which the **Basilique du Sacré-Cœur**, a famous church, is found. Many people connect Montmartre with painters such as Toulouse-Lautrec, and think of it as a place where people lived as they wished and not how society said they ought to.

Mon·tre·al /ˌmɒntriˈɔːl‖ˌmaːn-/ a city and port on **Montreal Island** in the St. Lawrence river in S Quebec, in E Canada. Most people living in Montreal speak French as their main language.

Mon·treux Gold Rose /mɒnˌtrɜː gəʊld ˈrəʊz‖maːnˌtrəʊ-/ [the] a prize given to the winner of a competition for television programmes held every year in **Montreux**, W Switzerland

Mont·ser·rat /ˌmɒntsəˈræt‖ˌmaːnt-/ an island in the West Indies, one of the Leeward Islands, politically controlled by Britain; capital Plymouth —**Montserration** /-səˈreɪʃən/ n, adj

Mon·ty Py·thon /ˌmɒnti ˈpaɪθən‖ˌmaːnti ˈpaɪθaːn, -θən/ also **Monty Python's Flying Circus** a set of British television programmes produced in the 1970s by a team of British male actors and COMEDIANs who invented a type of SURREAL humour. The programmes were made up of short, humorous SKETCHes in which people often behaved in strange, silly, or rude ways: *Its the strangest meeting I've ever been to. It was like something out of Monty Python.* —see also PYTHONESQUE, John CLEESE, DEAD PARROT SKETCH, MINISTRY OF SILLY WALKS

mon·u·ment /ˈmɒnjᵿmənt‖ˈmaː-/ n 1 [(to)] a building, PILLAR, etc., built to preserve the memory of a person or event: *This statue is a monument to one of our greatest statesmen.* | (fig.) *Those empty office buildings are a monument to bad planning.* —compare MEMORIAL 2 a very old building or place, considered worth preserving for its historic interest or beauty: *The ruins of the castle are an ancient monument; there is a preservation order on them.* 3 **the Monument** a COLUMN built in E central London in memory of the Great Fire of London (1666), which began near where the Monument stands

mon·u·ment·al /ˌmɒnjᵿˈmentl◂‖ˌmaː-/ adj 1 [A] built as a monument: *a monumental pillar to commemorate a naval victory* 2 very large and causing great admiration: *The artist spent years on his monumental painting, which covered the whole ceiling of the church.* 3 infml (of something bad) very great in degree: *monumental stupidity* | *a monumental blunder*

mon·u·ment·al·ly /ˌmɒnjᵿˈmentəli‖ˌmaː-/ adv extremely: *a monumentally stupid action*

moo¹ /muː/ v [I] to make the sound that a cow makes

moo² n -s 1 the sound that a cow makes 2 BrE sl, becoming old-fash a stupid or worthless woman: *You silly moo!*

mooch /muːtʃ/ v [T] AmE sl to get by asking for it: *He tried to mooch a drink off me.*
　　mooch about/around phr v [I] infml to wander about with no purpose, and rather unhappily —**er** n usu. derog

mood¹ /muːd/ n 1 a state of the feelings at a particular time: *His moods change very quickly; one moment he's cheerful, and the next he's complaining about everything.* | *The beautiful sunny morning put him in a good mood.* | *The boss is in a bad mood today.* (=in a bad temper) | *The government had misjudged the mood of the public and was not prepared for the storm of anger which greeted its new measures.* [+to-v] *I'm very tired, and not in the mood to argue.* | *The management is* **in no mood for** (=not prepared for) *compromise over this issue.* 2 a state of feeling in which one is bad-tempered, silently angry or displeased, etc.: *Don't ask him to lend you money when he's in one of his moods.* (=in a bad temper, as he often is) | *She's in a mood this morning.*

mood² *n tech* (in grammar) any of the various sets of verb forms that express, for example **a** a fact or action (INDICATIVE²), **b** a command (IMPERATIVE² (1)), or **c** a doubt, wish, etc. (SUBJUNCTIVE). These are the only three moods in English, though others exist in other languages.

mood mu·sic /ˈ· ˌ··/ *n* [U] *AmE* music that is supposed to put the listener in a good mood

mood·y /ˈmuːdi/ *adj usu. derog* **1** having moods that change often and quickly: *a moody child* **2** bad-tempered, angry, displeased, or unhappy, esp. without good reason —**ily** *adv* —**iness** *n* [U]

Moody's In·vest·ors Ser·vice /ˌ··· ·ˈ·· ˌ··/ also **Moody's** *infml*— an American company with branches in various countries that offers advice about how dependable INVESTMENTs may be: *The bonds have a Moody's AAA rating.*

moo·la, moolah /ˈmuːlə/ *n* [U] *AmE sl* money

moon¹ /muːn/ *n* **1** [*the*] (*often cap.*) the body which moves round the Earth once every 28 days, and can be seen shining in the sky at night **2** [S] this body as it appears at a particular time: *There's no moon tonight.* (=it cannot be seen) | *a crescent moon* **3** [C] a body that moves round a PLANET other than the Earth: *the moons of Saturn* **4** [C *usu. pl.*] *esp. poet* a month: *many moons ago* **5 over the moon** *BrE infml* very happy: *She's over the moon about her new job.* —see also LUNAR, BLUE MOON, FULL MOON, HALF MOON, NEW MOON, **bay at the moon** (BAY⁴), **cry for the moon** (CRY¹), **promise someone the moon** (PROMISE²), **shoot the moon** (SHOOT¹)

moon² *v* also **throw a moon** ‖ **shoot the moon** *AmE* to bend over and show one's bare BUTTOCKs as a joke or a sign of disrespect. Mooning is usu. done by men: *The students mooned the governor's motorcade.*

moon about/around *phr v* [I] *BrE infml* to move about or pass time lazily or in a dreamlike state, with no purpose, interest, etc.: *Stop mooning about and do something useful for a change!*

moon over sbdy./sthg. *phr v* [T] *infml* to be in a dreamlike state of unsatisfied desire for (esp. a person): *She spent hours mooning over her favourite actor.*

moon·beam /ˈmuːnbiːm/ *n* a beam of moonlight: *moonbeams shafting through the trees*

moon boot /ˈ· ·/ *BrE n* a thick padded (PAD) boot worn in cold weather —compare MUCKLUCKS and see picture at SHOE

Moon·ie /ˈmuːni/ *n* (a member of) a religious group, the official name of which is the Unification Church, which was started in 1954 by **Sun Myung Moon**, a Korean industrialist. Many Moonies are young people who are thought to have been persuaded to leave their families and friends to live in groups with other Moonies: *to join the Moonies* | *After he became a Moonie we never saw him again.*

moon·less /ˈmuːnləs/ *adj* (of a night, or the night sky) dark, because the moon is not able to be seen: *a dark, moonless night*

moon·light¹ /ˈmuːnlaɪt/ *n* [U] the light of the moon: *The hills were bathed in pale/soft moonlight.* | *a moonlight walk* (=at night)

moonlight² *v* ~**ed** [I] *infml* **1** to have an additional job, esp. unofficially or without the knowledge of the government tax department **2** *BrE* ‖ **double-dip** *AmE*— to work although one is claiming money from the government for being unemployed: *He's been moonlighting for the past year as a plumber.* — ~**er** *n* — ~**ing** *n* [U]

moonlight flit /ˌ··· ·ˈ·/ *n BrE infml* an act of secretly escaping, esp. from someone to whom one owes something: *They did a moonlight flit and left the flat without paying the rent.*

moon·lit /ˈmuːnˌlɪt/ *adj* [A] given light by the moon: *a moonlit valley*

moon·scape /ˈmuːnskeɪp/ *n* a bare empty area which looks like the surface of the moon

moon·shine /ˈmuːnʃaɪn/ *n* [U] *infml* **1** foolish or impractical talk; nonsense **2** *esp. AmE* strong alcoholic drink produced illegally

moon shot /ˈ· ˌ·/ *n* a journey to the moon by a spacecraft

moon·stone /ˈmuːnstəʊn/ *n* a milky-white stone used in making jewellery

moon·struck /ˈmuːnstrʌk/ *adj infml* slightly mad

moon·y /ˈmuːni/ *adj infml* dreamy and purposeless

moor¹ /mʊəʳ/ also **moors** *pl.*— *n esp. BrE* a wide, open, often high, area of land, covered with rough grass or low bushes, that is not farmed because of its bad soil: *shooting grouse up on the moors* | *the Yorkshire moors*

moor² *v* [I;T (**to**)] to fasten (a ship, boat, etc.) to land, the bottom of the sea, etc., by means of ropes, an ANCHOR, etc.: *We moored in the estuary, waiting for high tide.*

Moore¹ /mʊəʳ/, **Bobby** (1941–93) an English footballer who was the captain of the English 1966 World Cup team

Moore², **Dud·ley** /ˈdʌdli/ (1935–) a British musician and COMEDIAN, famous esp. for his television partnership with Peter Cook. He has also made several films and is well-known as a PIANIST, particularly for playing JAZZ.

Moore³, **Henry** (1898–1986) an English SCULPTOR esp. famous for his works in wood and stone, in which the structure of the material influences the shape of the finished work

Moore⁴, **Mar·i·anne** /ˌmæriˈæn/ (1887–1972) an American poet and CRITIC, known for her clever and SATIRICAL poems

Moore⁵, **Ma·ry Ty·ler** /ˈmeəri ˈtaɪləʳ/ (1936–) an American actress who was in several popular humorous television programmes, esp. *The Mary Tyler Moore Show*, in which she played a woman who worked in a television news room

Moore⁶, **Pat·rick** /ˈpætrɪk/ (1923–) an English ASTRONOMER (=person who studies the stars) who has written books and has also appeared often on television. He is very popular, and famous for his fast speech and untidy hair.

Moore⁷, **Roger** (1928–) a British actor known esp. for playing James Bond in films

moor·hen /ˈmʊəhen‖ˈmʊər-/ *n* a black bird that lives beside streams and lakes

moor·ings /ˈmʊərɪŋz/ *n* [P] **1 a** the ropes, etc., used for mooring: *The ship's moorings broke during the storm.* **b** also **mooring**— a place where a ship or boat is moored **2** the means by which something is fastened to something else: *The big banner had become detached from its moorings.* | (fig.) *Children from broken homes tend to lose their emotional moorings.*

Moor·ish /ˈmʊərɪʃ/ *adj* of the Muslim peoples of mixed Arab race (**Moors**) who held power in Spain from 711 to 1492: *Moorish architecture*

moor·land /ˈmʊələnd‖ˈmʊər-/ also **moorlands** *pl.*— *n* [U] *esp. BrE* open country that is a moor

Moors Mur·der·ers /ˌ·· ˈ···/ *n* [*the* | P] Ian Brady and Myra Hindley, who murdered several children and buried them on moorland in N England in the early 1960s and were sent to prison for life

moose /muːs/ *n* **moose** a large deer with very large flat horns, that lives in North America and in Northern Europe

moot /muːt/ *v esp. BrE* [T *usu. pass.*] to state (a question, matter, etc.) for consideration; suggest: *The question of changing the club's rules was mooted at the last meeting.*

moot point /ˌ· ˈ·/ also **moot ques·tion** /ˌ· ˈ···/ — *n* [*usu. sing.*] **1** an undecided point; point on which there is more than one opinion: *"Will the government's measures really influence race relations in any way?" "It's a moot point."* (=I rather doubt that they will) **2** a point which is no longer important: *Since he's offered to pay for the damage, it's a moot point whether it was really him who caused it.*

mop¹ /mɒp‖mɑːp/ *n* **1** [C] a tool for washing floors, made up of a long stick with threads of thick string or a piece of SPONGE fastened to one end **2** [S (**of**)] *infml* a thick usu. untidy mass (of hair) looking as if it has not been brushed

mop² *v* -**pp**- [T] **1** to wash (esp. a floor) with a wet mop: *I mop the kitchen floor twice a week.* —see also CLEAN¹ (USAGE) **2** [(**with**)] to make dry by rubbing with a cloth or other soft material: *It was such a hot day that he had to keep mopping his forehead with his handkerchief.* **3**

[+*obj*+*adv*/*prep*] to remove (unwanted liquid) by rubbing with cloth or other soft material: *The nurse gently mopped the blood from the wound.*

mop sthg. ↔ **up** *phr v* [T]   **1** to remove (unwanted liquid, dirt, etc.) with a mop or cloth: *You spilt the milk, so you mop it up!*   **2** to finish dealing with: *The rebellion has been crushed, but* **mopping-up operations** *may take a few more weeks.*   **3** to use up; ABSORB: *The rebuilding programme soon mopped up all the allocated funds.* — **mop-up** /ˈ· ·/ *n infml*

mope /məʊp/ *v* [I] *derog* to continue to be sad without trying to become more cheerful
mope about/around *phr v* [I] *derog* to move about in a sad, lifeless way

mo·ped /ˈməʊped/ *n* a bicycle which has a small engine; a small MOTORCYCLE

mop·pet /ˈmɒpɪt‖ˈmɑː-/ *n infml, usu. apprec* a child, esp. a girl

Mop·sy /ˈmɒpsi‖ˈmɑːp-/ a rabbit who is one of the sisters of Peter Rabbit in the children's stories by Beatrix Potter

mo·quette /mɒˈket‖məʊ-/ *n* [U] a thick soft material used for making esp. furniture coverings

mo·raine /məˈreɪn/ *n* a mass of earth, pieces of rock, etc., left in a line at the edge or end of a GLACIER —see picture at MOUNTAIN

mor·al¹ /ˈmɒrəl‖ˈmɔː-/ *adj*   **1** [A *no comp.*] concerning or based on principles of right and wrong behaviour and the difference between good and evil: *a man of high moral principles/standards* | *He refused to join the army on moral grounds.* | *You don't know all the circumstances of their divorce, so don't make moral judgments about it.* | *Babies aren't born with a moral sense.* (=they cannot tell the difference between right and wrong) | *He ran away from the enemy; it's clear the fellow has no* **moral fibre**. (=is a coward) | *moral courage*   **2** based on the idea of what is right rather than on what is legal or effective in a practical way: *He isn't legally responsible for his nephew, but he feels he has a* **moral obligation/responsibility** *to help him.* | *I can't help your scheme with money, but I'll give you* **moral support**. (=encouragement) | *We lost the vote, but it was really a* **moral victory** *for our side.* (=we proved that we were right)   **3** good in character, behaviour, etc.; pure, esp. in matters of sex: *a very moral man* —compare AMORAL, IMMORAL

moral² *n* a piece of guidance on how to live one's life, how to act more effectively, etc., that can be learnt from a story or event: *The moral of this story is that crime doesn't pay.* —see also MORALS

mo·rale /məˈrɑːl‖məˈræl/ *n* [U] the condition of courage, determination, and pride in the mind(s) of a person, team, army, etc.; level of confidence: *The soldiers' morale was high/low.* | *The trapped men kept up their morale by singing together.* | *Simply telling him how valuable his work was boosted his morale a lot.*

mor·al·ist /ˈmɒrəlɪst‖ˈmɔː-/ *n*   **1** a teacher of moral principles   **2** *usu. derog* a person who tries to control other people's morals

mor·al·is·tic /ˌmɒrəˈlɪstɪk◂‖ˌmɔː-/ *adj derog* having very firm unchanging narrow ideas about right and wrong behaviour — ~ **ally** /kli/ *adv*

mo·ral·i·ty /məˈrælɪti/ *n* [U] rightness or honesty of behaviour, of an action, etc.: *One sometimes wonders if there's any morality in politics.* | *to question the morality of someone's actions* —opposite **immorality**

morality play /·ˈ··· ·/ *n* a theatrical play, often performed in the years 1400–1600, in which good and bad human qualities were represented as people —compare MIRACLE PLAY

mor·al·ize also **-ise** *BrE* /ˈmɒrəlaɪz‖ˈmɔː-/ *v* [I (**about, on**)] *usu. derog* to express one's thoughts on the rightness or, more usually, the wrongness of behaviour —**izer** *n*

mor·al·ly /ˈmɒrəli‖ˈmɔː-/ *adv*   **1** with regard to right behaviour: *What you did wasn't actually illegal, but it was morally wrong.*   **2** *apprec* in a MORAL¹ (3) way —opposite **immorally**   **3** *fml* most probably: *It's* **morally certain** *that she'll be the next Minister of Education.*

Moral Ma·jor·i·ty /ˌ··· ·ˈ···/ [*the*]   **1** *tdmk* a religious and political group started by the Rev. Jerry Falwell, which was an important force in the election of Ronald Reagan and

other CONSERVATIVE politicians to office in 1980   **2** *AmE* Americans whose views are right-wing and FUNDAMENTALIST Christian, and who believe, e.g. that ABORTION should be against the law

Moral Re·ar·ma·ment Move·ment /ˌ··· ·ˈ·· ˌ··/ [*the*] an organization begun in 1938 by the American EVANGELIST Frank Buchman (1878–1961) who had earlier begun the Oxford Group. Its aims were to act against the MATERIALISM of society by living according to high standards of morality, love, and religion.

mor·als /ˈmɒrəlz‖ˈmɔː-/ *n* [P] standards of behaviour, esp. in matters of sex: *How can you cheat your own family like that? Haven't you got any morals at all?* | *a woman of loose morals* (=of bad sexual behaviour)

mo·rass /məˈræs/ *n*   **1** [C] *esp. lit* a dangerous area of soft wet ground; MARSH   **2** [S (**of**)] a position from which it is almost impossible to free oneself: *They seemed to be bogged down in a morass of detail.*

mor·a·to·ri·um /ˌmɒrəˈtɔːriəm‖ˌmɔː-/ *n* **-ria** /riə/ [(**on**)] an official period of delay: *The council has declared a moratorium on the building of new houses.* (=it will not build any more for a particular time) | *a moratorium on arms sales* —compare EMBARGO¹

Mo·ray /ˈmʌri‖ˈmɜːri/ a former COUNTY in NE Scotland, now part of Grampian REGION

mor·bid /ˈmɔːbɪd‖ˈmɔːr-/ *adj*   **1** *derog* unhealthily interested in unpleasant subjects, esp. those concerning death: *a morbid fascination with the details of the murder*   **2** *med* connected with or caused by disease of body or mind — ~ **ly** *adv* — ~ **ity** /mɔːˈbɪdɪti‖mɔːr-/ *n* [U]

mor·dant /ˈmɔːdənt‖ˈmɔːr-/ *adj* (esp. of the way of expressing thoughts) cruel and cutting: *His political opponents feared his mordant wit.* — ~ **ly** *adv*

Mor·dred /ˈmɔːdred‖ˈmɔːr-/ in the ARTHURIAN LEGEND either the NEPHEW or son of King Arthur. He tries to take over the kingdom and is killed in battle by Arthur. —see also ARTHURIAN LEGEND

more¹ /mɔːʳ/ *adv* [(**than**)]   **1** (used for forming the COMPARATIVE of most adjectives and adverbs with more than two SYLLABLES, and of many that have only two): *The first question is more difficult than the second.* | *His illness was (much) more serious than we had thought.* | *Could you explain the problem (a bit) more simply?* | *We'd like to go there more often.* —opposite **less**   **2** to a greater degree: *He'll never play well if he doesn't practise more.* | *She seems to care (far/much) more for her dogs than for her children.* | *Businesses use computers a lot more than they used to.* | *It's her voice I dislike, more than what she says.* | *I couldn't agree more.* (=I completely agree.) —opposite **less**   **3** again (in the phrases **any more, once more, no more**): *They used to be good friends, but they don't like each other any more.* (=any longer) | *I'll repeat the question once more.* | (*lit*) *The ship sank below the waves, and was seen no more.* (=never again)   **4** **and what is more** also, and more importantly: *She admitted she'd spoken to them, and what's more had told them about our secret discussions.*   **5 more often than not** *infml* at most times; usually: *I like cooking, but more often than not I just open a tin of something when I get home.*   **6 more than a little** *pomp* very: *I was more than a little angry when I saw how they'd ruined it.*   **7 more than pleased/sorry/etc.** *fml* extremely pleased/sorry/etc.: *If you are not satisfied with your purchase, we will be more than happy to refund your money.* | *He was more than willing to help.*   **8 more ... than** ... it is more true to say ... than ... : *She's more thoughtless than stupid.*   **9 no more** *often pomp* neither: *She can't afford a car, and no more can I.*   **10 no more ... than** in no greater degree ... than: *He's no more fit to be a priest than I am!* (=is completely unfit)

more² *determiner, pron* (*comparative of* **many, much**) [(**of, than**)]   **1** a larger number or amount: *There are more cars on the roads in summer than in winter.* | *As he grows weaker, he spends more of his time in bed.* | **No more than** *five people applied for the job.* (=only five people, which was surprising) | *There were* **not more than** (=probably fewer than) *a hundred people at the rally.* | *It's no/not more than a mile to the sea.* | *More than one school has closed.* | *Wine costs more than beer.* —opposite **less** or **fewer** (see USAGE)   **2** an additional number or amount: *Have some more tea!* | *I have to write two more letters this morning.* (=besides those already written) | *There's no more milk left — I'd better go and buy some more.* | *A lot* of houses are being built, but many more are needed. | If you stay at that hotel, you'll have to pay a little more. | I'd like to know more about the job. | She's got a good job and plenty of money — what more does she want? (=surely she has everything she wants) | Tell me more! (= I'm interested in what you say.) —opposite **less** or **fewer** (see USAGE) **3 more and more** increasingly; (an amount) that continues to become larger: The questions get more and more difficult. | I seem to spend more and more on food every week! —opposite **less and less 4 more or less: a** almost; nearly: The job's more or less finished. **b** about; not exactly: The repairs will cost £50, more or less. **5** BrE **(the) more** the greater: "I'm slimming, so I haven't eaten for three days." "(The) more fool you!" (=you are very foolish) **6 the more ... , the more/less, etc.** (used to show that two things change together): The more I see of him, the less I like him. | The more he eats, the fatter he gets. | "Can I bring some friends to your party?" "Of course — **the more, the merrier!**" (=the more people there are, the better the party will be) —see also **more ... than** you've had hot dinners (DINNER), **more's the pity** (PITY[1])

▷ USAGE **More** is the opposite of both **less** (for amounts) and **fewer** (for numbers). Compare a few/three/many/a great many **more** (opposite **fewer**) friends and a bit/a little/much/a great deal **more** (opposite **less**) money. With both amounts and numbers you can use far, some, any, no, rather, and lots/a lot (infml): far **more** eggs/butter.◁

More, Sir Thomas (1478–1535) an English STATESMAN and writer. His most famous work is Utopia, about a perfect state governed by reason. He worked for King Henry VIII but refused to recognize him as head of the Church of England. For this he was put in prison and finally had his head cut off.

More·cambe and Wise /ˌmɔːkəm ənd ˈwaɪz‖ˌmɔːr-/ two British COMEDIANS, **Eric Morecambe** (1926–84) and **Ernie Wise** (1925–) who had a very popular television show which ran for more than 20 years. Many well-known people appeared as guests on the show although they often had to do things that made them look slightly silly. The shows are still repeated on British television, esp. around Christmas.

more·ish /ˈmɔːrɪʃ/ adj BrE infml (of food) very tasty, causing a desire for more: "I can't stop eating these chocolates — they're so moreish!"

more·o·ver /mɔːrˈəʊvər/ adv fml besides what has been said; in addition: The rent is reasonable, and moreover, the location is perfect.

mo·res /ˈmɔːreɪz/ n [P] fml or tech the moral customs of a particular group: current social mores

mor·ga·nat·ic /ˌmɔːgəˈnætɪk◂‖ˌmɔːr-/ adj tech (of a marriage) between a royal person and someone of lower rank, in which neither the person of lower rank, nor the children of the marriage, are allowed to take royal titles

Mor·gan le Fay /ˌmɔːgən lə ˈfeɪ‖ˌmɔːr-/ in the ARTHURIAN LEGEND, a sister of King Arthur with magic powers —see also ARTHURIAN LEGEND

morgue /mɔːg‖mɔːrg/ n **1** a MORTUARY[1] **2** derog a sad lifeless place: This pub's a bit of a morgue; let's liven it up with some dancing. **3** infml tech a collection of past copies of a newspaper, kept in the offices of the newspaper

MORI poll /ˈmɔːri ˌpəʊl/ n a special count of opinions in a country, done by a company called Market and Opinion Research International, who question a number of people chosen as being typical of the whole population: The Labour party has increased in popularity, according to a recent MORI poll.

mor·i·bund /ˈmɒrɪˌbʌnd‖ˈmɔː-, ˈmɑː-/ adj fml no longer operating effectively: A new manager was brought in to revive the moribund business. —compare OBSOLESCENT

Mor·mon /ˈmɔːmən‖ˈmɔːr-/ n a member of a religious organization, formed in 1830 in the US by Joseph Smith and officially called **The Church of Jesus Christ of Latter-Day Saints.**

▶ CULTURAL NOTE The largest groups of Mormons live in the W and NW states of the US, and esp. in Utah, where most of the people are Mormons. They have strict moral rules and do not drink alcohol or coffee. Many people associate POLYGAMY (= a man having more than one wife) with Mormons, although most of them no longer practise

this. They also have churches in Britain, and sometimes go from house to house trying to persuade people to join their church.◀
— ~ **ism** n [U]

morn /mɔːn‖mɔːrn/ n poet a morning

morn·ing /ˈmɔːnɪŋ‖ˈmɔːr-/ n [C;U] **1** the first part of the day, from the time when the sun rises, usu. until the time when the midday meal is eaten: a fine morning | tomorrow morning | on Tuesday mornings | mid-morning coffee | On Christmas morning we go to church. | It's very late; can't it wait until (the) morning? (=tomorrow morning) | The people next door play their radio from morning till night. (=all day) | the morning papers (=newspapers) **2** the part of the day from midnight until midday: He didn't get home until two o'clock in the morning. **3 in the morning** tomorrow morning: I haven't got what you want now, but I can get it for you in the morning. | I'll do it first thing in the morning. (=very early tomorrow) **4 morning, noon, and night** all and every day and night —see also COFFEE MORNING, GOOD MORNING, MORNINGS

morning-af·ter pill /ˌ··· ˈ··· ˌ·/ n a drug taken by mouth by a woman within 72 hours after having sex, in order to prevent her from having a baby. It is not intended to be a regular method of CONTRACEPTION.

morning coat /ˈ··· ·/ n a TAILCOAT worn as part of morning dress

morning dress /ˈ··· ·/ n **1** [U] esp. BrE formal clothes worn by a man at a ceremony in the daytime (such as a wedding) that include a morning coat, trousers, and a TOP HAT —see picture at EVENING DRESS **2** [C] AmE an informal dress worn by women esp. when doing work in the home

morning glo·ry /ˌ··· ˈ···‖ˈ··· ˌ··/ n [C;U] a climbing plant with blue, white, or pink flowers

Morning Prayer /ˌ··· ˈ·/ also **matins, mattins—** n [U] a morning church service in the Church of England and the Episcopal Church in the US —compare EVENSONG

morning room /ˈ··· ·/ n rather old-fash a room (usu. in a large house) for use in the morning, e.g. because it catches the morning light

morn·ings /ˈmɔːnɪŋz‖ˈmɔːr-/ adv esp. AmE in the morning; during any morning: She works mornings.

morning sick·ness /ˈ·· ˌ··/ n [U] a feeling of sickness in the early morning suffered by women in early PREGNANCY

morning star /ˌ··· ˈ·/ n [the] a bright PLANET, esp. Venus, seen in the eastern sky at sunrise —compare EVENING STAR

Morning Star n [the] a daily newspaper, no longer produced, which supported the ideas of the Communist Party of Great Britain

morning suit /ˈ··· ·/ n a man's formal suit, worn at formal occasions during the day, e.g. weddings

mo·roc·co /məˈrɒkəʊ‖məˈrɑː-/ n [U] fine soft leather made from goatskin, used esp. for covering books

Mo·roc·co a Muslim country in NW Africa bordered by the Mediterranean Sea and the Atlantic Ocean, whose people speak Arabic, Berber, and French; capital Rabat; population 24,522,000 (1989)— **Moroccan** n,adj

mo·ron /ˈmɔːrɒn‖ˈmɔːrɑːn/ n **1** derog a very stupid person: You've put salt in my tea, you moron! **2** tech for MENTAL DEFECTIVE — ~ **ic** /məˈrɒnɪk‖məˈrɑː-/ adj : a moronic grin/stare — ~ **ically** /kli/ adv

mo·rose /məˈrəʊs/ adj derog bad-tempered, unhappy, and silent: He came home tired and morose after a long and unsuccessful day's work. — ~ **ly** adv — ~ **ness** n [U]

mor·pheme /ˈmɔːfiːm‖ˈmɔːr-/ n tech the smallest meaningful unit in a language, consisting of a word or part of a word that cannot be divided without losing its meaning: "Gun" is one morpheme; "gun-s" contains two morphemes; "gun-fight-er" contains three morphemes.

Mor·phe·us /ˈmɔːfiəs, -fjuːs‖ˈmɔːr-/ n **1** in CLASSICAL MYTHOLOGY, the Greek god of dreams and sleep **2 in the arms of Morpheus** lit or pomp asleep

mor·phine /ˈmɔːfiːn‖ˈmɔːr-/ also **mor·phi·a** /-fiə/old-fash— n [U] a powerful and ADDICTIVE drug used for stopping pain and making people calmer

mor·phol·o·gy /mɔːˈfɒlədʒi‖mɔːrˈfɑː-/ n tech **1** [U] the study of the morphemes of a language, and of the way in which they are joined together to make words − compare SYNTAX **2** [U] the scientific study of the formation of animals, plants, and their parts **3** [C;U] the structure or formation of an object or system −**gical** /ˌmɔːfəˈlɒdʒɪkəl◂ ‖ ˌmɔːrfəˈlɑː-/ adj

Mor·ris[1] /ˈmɒrɪs‖ˈmɔː-, ˈmɑː-/ a former British company which made cars, VANs, and lorries (LORRY), now part of the Rover Group

Morris[2]**, Des·mond** /ˈdezmənd/ (1928−) a British ANTHRO-POLOGIST (=person who studies the human race) who has written popular books about human and animal behaviour, the best-known of which is *The Naked Ape*

Morris[3]**, Philip** see PHILIP MORRIS

Strawberry Thief by William Morris

Morris[4]**, William** (1834−96) an English CRAFTSMAN, writer, and supporter of social change, who designed (DESIGN[1]) and made his own furniture and materials and formed the Socialist League in 1884: *William Morris wallpaper* (=wallpaper with a pattern originally designed by William Morris)

morris dance /ˈ·· ·/ n any of various old English country dances usu. performed out doors in the summer by a group of men who wear special white clothes to which small bells are often fixed

Morris Mi·nor /ˌ·· ˈ··/ n tdmk a small British car built by Austin Morris from the 1950s to the 1970s which is still very popular and often sold for high prices today. The **Morris Minor Traveller**, the ESTATE CAR model of the Morris Minor, is connected in many people's minds with supporters of environmental or green organizations.

Mor·ri·son /ˈmɒrɪsən‖ˈmɔː-/**, Jim** /dʒɪm/ (1943−71) a singer with the ROCK[3] group the Doors, who died of taking too much of an illegal drug. Morrison is sometimes seen as an example of someone with many abilities who could not deal with the pressures of fame.

mor·row /ˈmɒrəʊ‖ˈmɑː-/ n **1** [the] lit **a** the day following today: *Let's hope that the morrow will bring better news.* | *We leave on the morrow.* (=tomorrow) **b** the time closely following an event; the future: *The war was at an end, and the nation was full of hopes for the morrow.* **2 good morrow** old use good morning!

Morse code /ˌmɔːs ˈkəʊd‖ˌmɔːrs-/ also **Morse**− n [U] a system of sending messages by radio, a lamp, etc., in which each letter is represented by a sign made up of one or more short signals (dots) and long signals (DASHes) in sound or light (named after Samuel Morse, an American who invented Morse code in 1844)

mor·sel /ˈmɔːsəl‖ˈmɔːr-/ n **1** [C (**of**)] a very small piece of food: *just a morsel of cake* | *a few choice|tasty morsels* **2** [S (**of**)] usu. in questions or negatives] a very small piece or quantity of anything: *If he had a morsel of* (=any) *sense he'd realize.*

mor·ta·del·la /ˌmɔːtəˈdelə‖ˌmɔːr-/ n [U] a kind of Italian SAUSAGE

mor·tal[1] /ˈmɔːtl‖ˈmɔːrtl/ adj **1** that will die; not living for ever: *all mortal creatures* −opposite **immortal** **2** [A] human; of human beings: *beyond mortal power* **3** causing or ending in death: *a mortal wound|injury* | *mortal combat* | *in mortal danger* −compare LETHAL **4** [A] (of an enemy) having a lasting hatred, that can never change into friendship **5** [A] (of fear, etc.) extremely great: *She lives in mortal terror of her husband's anger.* −see also MORTALLY, **shuffle off this mortal coil** (SHUFFLE[1] (4))

mortal[2] n [usu. pl.] esp. lit a human being as compared with a god, a spirit, etc.: *We're all mortals, with our human faults and weaknesses.*

mor·tal·i·ty /mɔːˈtælɪti‖mɔːr-/ n **1** [S;U] also **mortality rate** /ˈ··· ·/ − the rate or number of deaths caused by a particular thing, happening among a certain kind of people, etc.: *If this disease spreads, the doctors fear that there'll be a high mortality (rate).* | **Infant mortality** (=the rate at which babies die) *is still very high in some*

countries. **2** [U] the condition of being MORTAL[1] (1) − opposite **immortality**

mor·tal·ly /ˈmɔːtəli‖ˈmɔːr-/ adv **1** in a way that causes death: *He fell to the ground, mortally wounded.* **2** very greatly; deeply: *She was mortally offended by your remarks.*

mortal sin /ˌ·· ˈ·/ n [C;U] (in the Roman Catholic religion) (an act of) wrongdoing so great that it will bring EVER-LASTING punishment to the soul after death if it is not forgiven

mor·tar[1] /ˈmɔːtəʳ‖ˈmɔːr-/ n [U] a mixture of LIME, sand, and water, used in building, esp. for joining bricks together: *Put your money into bricks and mortar.* (=buy a house)

mortar[2] n **1** a heavy gun with a short barrel, firing an explosive that falls from a great height **2** a hard bowl in which substances are crushed with a PESTLE into very small pieces or powder −see picture at LABORATORY

mor·tar·board /ˈmɔːtəbɔːd‖ˈmɔːrtərbɔːrd/ n a usu. black cap with a flat square top, worn formerly by schoolteachers and still worn by members of some universities on formal occasions. Teachers in CARTOONS are often shown wearing mortarboards.

Morte d'Ar·thur /ˌmɔːt ˈdɑːθəʳ‖ˌmɔːrt ˈdɑːr-/, **Le** the death of Arthur; a work of literature written by Sir Thomas Malory in 1485 about King Arthur

mort·gage[1] /ˈmɔːgɪdʒ‖ˈmɔːr-/ n **1** an agreement to borrow money, esp. so as to buy a house, and pay interest on it to the lender over a period of years: *My mortgage is with a small building society.* | *to take out* (=start to have) *a mortgage* **2** the amount lent on a mortgage: *a mortgage of £23,000* **3** the amount of interest paid on a mortgage: *He's having a lot of trouble paying his mortgage every month.* | *Mortgage rates are going up again.*

mortgage[2] v [T] to give someone the right to the ownership of (a house, land, etc.) in return for money lent for a certain period: *His business is failing; he's mortgaged all his assets to try to save it.*

mort·gag·ee /ˌmɔːgəˈdʒiː‖ˌmɔːr-/ n tech a person who lends money in return for the right to own the borrower's property

mortgage re·pos·ses·sion /ˈ·· ··ˌ·•/ n the situation in which a house bought on a mortgage[1] (1) is taken back by a bank or BUILDING SOCIETY because the person buying it has not paid the interest on the money they borrowed: *The number of mortgage repossessions increased sharply when the interest rate went up.*

mort·ga·gor /ˈmɔːgɪdʒəʳ‖ˈmɔːr-/ n tech a person who borrows money from a mortgagee

mor·ti·cian /mɔːˈtɪʃən‖mɔːr-/ n AmE for UNDERTAKER

mor·ti·fy /ˈmɔːtɪfaɪ‖ˈmɔːr-/ v [T] **1** [usu. pass.] to hurt (a person's) feelings, causing shame or deep embarrassment: *I was somewhat mortified to be told that I was too old to join.* **2** to control natural human desires of (oneself or the body) by self-punishment: *Hermits of the Middle Ages rejected all the comforts of life, intent on mortifying the flesh.* −**fication** /ˌmɔːtɪfɪˈkeɪʃən‖ˌmɔːr-/ n [U]: *He discovered, to his mortification, that his son knew more about the subject than he did.* | *mortification of the flesh*

mor·tise /ˈmɔːtɪs‖ˈmɔːr-/ n tech a hole cut in a piece of wood or stone to receive the TENON (=the shaped end) of another piece, and form a joint

mortise lock /ˈ·· ·/ n a lock that fits into a hole cut in the edge of a door

Mor·ton /ˈmɔːtn‖ˈmɔːr-/, **Jelly Roll** (1885−1941) an American JAZZ piano player, bandleader, and writer of music who helped to develop New Orleans jazz

mor·tu·a·ry[1] /ˈmɔːtʃuəri‖ˈmɔːrtʃueri/ n **1** a building or room where a dead body is kept until the time of the funeral **2** AmE FUNERAL HOME

mortuary[2] adj [A] tech connected with death and funerals: *a mortuary urn*

mo·sa·ic /məʊˈzeɪ-ɪk/ n **1** [C;U] (a piece of decorative work produced by) the fitting together of small pieces of coloured stone, glass, etc., so as to form a pattern or picture **2** [C (**of**) usu. sing.] a number of small things seen together that seem to form a

mosaic

a mosiac of a fish

pattern: *The forest floor was a mosaic of autumnal colours.*

Mosaic *adj* of Moses: *Mosaic law*

Mosaic Law /·ₗ·· '·/ also **Law of Moses**— *n* [U] the rules and laws of the first five books of the Bible (the PEN-TATEUCH), believed to have been given by Moses

Mos·cow /ˈmɒskəʊ‖ˈmɑːskaʊ, -kəʊ/ the capital of the former USSR since 1918, which contains the Kremlin and is the political, COMMERCIAL, and industrial centre of the country

mo·selle /məʊˈzel/ *n* [U] (*often cap.*) a type of light German white wine originally made in the valley of the Moselle river

Moselle [*the*] a river which rises in E France and forms the border between Luxembourg and Germany before joining the Rhine at Koblenz in Germany

Mo·ses /ˈməʊzɪz/ a leader of the Jewish people in ancient times. According to the story in the Bible, he brought the Israelites out of Egypt. They were able to escape from the Egyptians when God parted (PART[2] (2)) the Red Sea so that they could walk across the sea bed. Moses received the TEN COMMANDMENTS (=God's laws) from God on Mount Sinai. see colour picture on page 424

Moses bas·ket /ˈ·· ˌ··/ *n BrE* a CRADLE with handles in which a baby can sleep and be carried, usu. a type of basket (from the Bible story in which Moses, as a baby, was left in a basket beside the river Nile)

Moses basket

mo·sey /ˈməʊzi/ *v* [I+*adv*/*prep*] *AmE infml* to walk in an unhurried way: *It's getting late; we'd better mosey along.*

Mos·lem /ˈmɒzləm‖ˈmɑːz-/ *n, adj* Muslim

Mos·ley /ˈməʊzli/, **Sir Oswald** (1896–1980) a British RIGHT-WING politician who set up the British Union of Fascists. He was an MP from 1918 to 1931.

mosque /mɒsk‖mɑːsk/ *n* a building in which Muslims worship

mos·qui·to /məˈskiːtəʊ/ *n* **-toes** *or* **-tos** a small flying insect, found esp. in hot countries, that sucks the blood of people and animals. A particular sort of mosquito can pass the illness MALARIA in this way. —see picture at INSECT

mosquito net /·ˈ·· ·/ *n* a net placed over a bed as a protection against mosquitoes, esp. in hot countries

moss /mɒs‖mɔːs/ *n* [U] a small flat green or yellow flowerless plant that grows in a thick furry mass on wet soil, or on a wet surface such as a rock —compare LICHEN

Moss, Stirling (1929–   ) a famous British racing driver who won 16 Grand Prix races and many other events in the 1950s and 1960s and is considered by many British people to be the best racing driver ever: *He thinks he's Stirling Moss.* (=he drives very fast like a racing driver)

Moss Bros /ˈmɒs brɒs‖ˈmɔːs brɔːs/ *tdmk* a shop in London, with branches around Britain, which sells men's clothing but is best known for hiring out suits, such as MORN-ING DRESS or DINNER JACKETS, for formal occasions

moss-grown /ˈ· ·/ *adj* covered with moss

Moss Side /ₗ· '·/ a poor area of central Manchester

moss·y /ˈmɒsi‖ˈmɔːsi/ *adj* **1** covered with moss: *a mossy bank* **2** like moss: *mossy green*

most[1] /məʊst/ *adv* **1** (used for forming the SUPERLATIVE of most adjectives and adverbs with more than two SYLLA-BLES, and of many that have only two): *the most comfortable hotel in this town* | *Which question did you think was most difficult?* | *All the girls are good at English, but Sue speaks it (the) most fluently.* —opposite **least** **2** to the greatest degree; more than anything else: *What annoyed me most was the way he laughed at me.* | *Geography is interesting, and English, but I like history most of all.* —opposite **least** **3** *fml* very: *It's most kind of you!* | *a most enjoyable party* | *I shall most certainly attend the meeting.* | *He'll most probably sell the house.* —see USAGE **4**

dial *or AmE infml* almost: *He plays cards most every evening.*

▷ USAGE **Most** can be used with the meaning "very" only before adjectives and adverbs that express the speaker's personal feeling or opinion. Compare *a* **most** *beautiful woman* | *a* **most** *amazing coincidence* | **Most** *certainly I can do it* and *a* **very** *tall woman* | *I can do it* **very** *quickly.*◁

most[2] *determiner, pron* (*superlative of* **many, much**) **1** [(of)] nearly all: *Most people take their holidays in the summer.* | *He spends most of his time travelling.* **2** [(the)] greatest in number or quantity: *The storm did (the) most damage to the houses on the cliff.* (=it damaged them more than any other houses) | *I didn't have any money to give him: the most I could do was offer him my support.* **3** at **(the) most** not more than; if not less: *She's 25 years old, at most.* | *The repairs will cost £35, at the very most.* —compare **at (the) least** (LEAST[2]) **4** for the '**most part** almost completely; mainly: *Summers in the south of France are for the most part dry and sunny.* **5 make the most of** to get the best advantage from: *We've only got one day in London, so let's make the most of it and see everything.*

-most see WORD FORMATION

most-fa·voured-na·tion sta·tus /ₗ· ₗ·· '·· ₗ··/ *n* [U] an arrangement which forms part of a trade agreement between several countries. A country which has signed the agreement is allowed to have any TARIFF reductions which may have been arranged between a country in the agreement and another country outside the agreement.

most·ly /ˈməʊstli/ *adv* mainly; in most cases or most of the time: *She uses her car mostly for driving to work.* | *He has the occasional cigarette, but mostly he smokes a pipe.*

MOT /ₗem əʊ ˈtiː/ *n infml* (in Britain) a regular official examination of cars more than three years old, carried out to make sure that they are in a good enough condition to be driven. In Britain it is illegal to drive a car which has not passed its MOT: *My car's failed its MOT (test).*

mote /məʊt/ *n esp. lit* a very small piece or grain, esp. of dust

mo·tel /məʊˈtel/ also **motor lodge** *AmE*— *n* a hotel for travelling motorists, usu. on a single level with space for a car near each room

mo·tet /məʊˈtet/ *n* a piece of church music for singers only

moth /mɒθ‖mɔːθ/ *n* **1** [C] an insect related to the BUTTER-FLY but usu. not so brightly coloured, that flies mainly at night and is attracted by lights —see picture at INSECT **2** [*the*] *BrE* the presence of young moths (**clothes moths**) in clothes, where they eat wool, fur, etc.

moth·ball /ˈmɒθbɔːl‖ˈmɔːθ-/ *n* [*usu. pl.*] **1** a small ball made of a strong-smelling chemical, used for keeping moths away from clothes **2 in mothballs** stored and not used: *With the end of the Cold War several warships were put into mothballs.*

moth-eat·en /ˈ· ˌ··/ *adj* **1** (of cloth) destroyed, or partly destroyed, by moths: *You're not going to wear that moth-eaten sweater!* **2** very worn out: *a moth-eaten old sofa* **3** *derog* no longer modern: *his moth-eaten ideas*

moth·er[1] /ˈmʌðəʳ/ *n* **1** [C] a female parent of a child or animal: *His mother and father are both doctors.* | *Can I borrow your car, please, mother?* | *We'd better ask (our) mother first.* | *a mother hen and her chicks* | *a mother-of-two* (=having two children) —see FATHER (USAGE) **2 be told/learn something at one's mother's knee** to learn something when one is very young **3 every mother's son** *lit* every man with none left out —see also **necessity is the mother of invention** (NECESSITY) — ~ **less** *adj*

moth·er[2] *v* [T] *sometimes derog* to care for or protect (someone) like a mother: *The old man mothered his beloved pigeons.* | *Tom's wife mothers him dreadfully.* —see also MOTHER'S BOY

Mother *n* **1** (a title of respect for the female head of a CON-VENT) —see also MOTHER SUPERIOR **2** *infml* (used esp. by a man, when speaking to an old woman): *Come along now, Mother, get into the ambulance.*

mother and tod·dler group /ₗ·· '·· ·/ *n* in Britain, a regular informal meeting for mothers with very young children. The mothers can sit and talk together while the children play with toys.

Moth·er·care /ˈmʌθəkeəʳ‖-ðər-/ *n tdmk* a British chain of stores which sells equipment, clothes, and toys for babies and young children and clothes for PREGNANT women. Mothercare is extremely successful and is the best-known shop in Britain for babies' clothes etc.

mother coun·try /ˈ·· ˌ·ˌ/ also **motherland**– n [(the)] **1** the country of one's birth; one's NATIVE land **2** the country from which a group of settlers in another part of the world originally came: *Some Australians still regard Britain as the|their mother country.*

Mother Earth /ˌ·· ˈ·/ the soil, or the Earth in general, seen as the mother of all living things: *The astronauts said they were glad to be back on Mother Earth. | Mother Earth will provide for all our needs.*

Mother Goose /ˌ·· ˈ·/ AmE (the imaginary writer of) NURSERY RHYMES (old poems or songs for children): *If you're good I'll read you some Mother Goose before you go to bed.*

moth·er·hood /ˈmʌðəhʊd‖-ər-/ n [U] the state of being a mother: *Motherhood doesn't suit her; she shouldn't have had children.*

Mother Hub·bard /ˌmʌðə ˈhʌbəd‖-ðər ˈhʌbərd/ **1** an old woman from a NURSERY RHYME (=old song or poem for children):
Old Mother Hubbard went to the cupboard
to get her poor dog a bone.
But when she got there
the cupboard was bare,
and so the poor dog had none.

2 a woman's long dress, worn without a belt

Mothering Sun·day /ˈ··· ˌ·ˌ/ n MOTHER'S DAY

mother-in-law /ˈ·· · ·/ n **mothers-in-law**, **mother-in-laws** the mother of a person's husband or wife

▶CULTURAL NOTE People often make jokes about mothers-in-law, because they are thought to give advice when it is not wanted and to always find fault with their SON-IN-LAW or DAUGHTER-IN-LAW. ◀

moth·er·land /ˈmʌðəlænd‖-ər-/ n see MOTHER COUNTRY

moth·er·ly /ˈmʌðəli‖-ər-/ adj like or typical of a good mother: *a motherly old teacher | a motherly kiss* – compare MATERNAL —**liness** n [U]

Mother May I /ˌ·· ˈ· ·/ n [U] esp. AmE a game played by children in which the leader does not face the other players but allows them to move towards the finish line when they ask to. If the leader catches players moving when he/she has not given permission, those players must begin at the starting line again: *"Mother may I take three giant steps?" "Yes you may."*

Mother Na·ture /ˌ·· ˈ··/ often humor NATURE seen as a force that controls the world and esp. the living things in it: *Cats are Mother Nature's way of limiting the number of mice.*

Mother of God /ˌ·· · ˈ·/ Mary, the mother of Jesus Christ in the Roman Catholic Church

mother-of-pearl /ˌ·· · ˈ·◂/ also **nacre**– n [U] a hard smooth shiny pale variously coloured substance inside the shell of certain SHELLFISH, used for making decorative articles: *a mother-of-pearl brooch*

mother's boy /ˈ·· ·/ BrE‖ **mama's boy** AmE– n [usu. sing.] infml derog a boy, or esp. a man, who allows his mother to protect him too much and is therefore considered weak

Mother's Day /ˈ·· ·/ n [C;U] a particular Sunday, in Britain the fourth Sunday in Lent, and in the US the second Sunday in May, on which people give cards and/or presents to their mothers to show their love for them – compare FATHER'S DAY

mother's help /ˌ·· ˈ·/ n a person, usu. a woman, who helps a mother with small children to do housework, and may also look after the children for short periods of time

mother ship /ˈ·· ·/ n a large ship travelling on the sea or in space, from which smaller boats or ships are sent out to fish, EXPLORE, etc., and to which they return

Mother Ship·ton /ˌmʌðə ˈʃɪptən‖-ðər-/ an old woman said to have been a WITCH from Yorkshire, England, who could tell the future and supposedly foretold (FORETELL) the Great Fire of London, although not everyone believes this

mother's ru·in /ˌ·· ˈ··/ n [U] old-fash humor, esp. BrE for GIN

Mothers' U·nion /ˌ·· ˈ··/ [the] a society of Christian women, set up by the Church of England, with the aim of support-

ing marriage, family life, and Christian values

mother su·pe·ri·or /ˌ·· ·ˈ··/ n (usu. caps.) the female head of a CONVENT (=a religious group of women)

Mother Te·re·sa /ˌmʌθə tə-ˈriːzə‖-θər-/ (1910–) a Roman Catholic NUN, born **Agnes Gouxha Bojaxhin** in Yugoslavia of Albanian parents and now a citizen of India, who works to help the poor and the sick, esp. in India. She started the Society of the Missionaries of Charity, now an international organization, and won the Nobel Prize for Peace in 1979.

Mother Teresa

mother-to-be /ˌ·· · ˈ·◂/ n **mothers-to-be** a PREGNANT woman

mother tongue /ˌ·· ˈ·/ n the language which one first learned to speak (and which one mainly speaks): *Yes, he speaks French excellently, but his mother tongue is actually Greek.*

moth·proof /ˈmɒθpruːf‖ˈmɔːθ-/ adj (of cloth, floor coverings, etc.) chemically treated against damage by MOTHS —**mothproof** v [T]

mo·tif /məʊˈtiːf/ also **motive**– n **1** a main subject, pattern, idea, etc., on which a work of art is based, or from which it is developed **2** a single or repeated pattern or colour: *a cat motif on the child's pyjamas* **3** an often-repeated arrangement of notes in a musical work —compare LEITMOTIV

mo·tion¹ /ˈməʊʃən/ n **1** [U] the act, way, or process of moving: *The gentle rolling motion of the ship made me feel sleepy. | Parts of the film were shown again* **in slow motion**. (=the movements appearing slower than in real life) **2** [C] a single or particular movement or way of moving: *With a motion of his hand he summoned the waiter.* **3** [C] a suggestion formally made at a meeting: *His motion was rejected.* [+to-v] *The motion to increase the club's membership charges was carried|defeated by 15 votes to 10.* [+that] *The committee passed a motion that the bar should remain open until midnight.* —see also MOVE¹ (7) **4** [C] esp. BrE fml an act of emptying the bowels: *The doctor asked if the child's motions were regular.* **5 go through the motions** infml to do something without care and interest, and only because one has to do it: *The doctor was sure the man wasn't really ill, but he went through the motions of examining him.* **6 put/set something in motion** to start a machine or a process: *Pull this handle to set the machine in motion. | If we're all agreed, we can put the plans in motion straight away.* – see also TIME-AND-MOTION

motion² v **1** [I (to, at)] to signal with a movement, usu. with the hand: *She motioned to the waiter.* **2** [T+obj+to-v|adv|prep] to direct (someone) with a movement, usu. with the hand: *He opened the door and motioned me to come in|motioned me into the room.*

mo·tion·less /ˈməʊʃənləs/ adj without any movement; completely still: *The cat remained motionless, waiting for the mouse to come out of its hole.* – **~ly** adv – **~ness** n [U]

motion pic·ture /ˌ·· ˈ··◂/ n AmE a cinema film – adj : *the motion picture industry*

motion sick·ness /ˈ·· ˌ··/ n [U] AmE for TRAVEL SICKNESS

mo·ti·vate /ˈməʊtɪˌveɪt/ v [T] **1** to provide (someone) with a (strong) reason for doing something: *He was motivated by love, and expected nothing in return. | We've got to try and motivate our salesmen.* (=make them try harder to sell things) [+obj+to-v] *There is little to motivate these kids to work hard at school.* **2** [often pass.] to be the reason why (something) is done: *This murder was motivated by hatred.*

mo·ti·va·tion /ˌməʊtɪˈveɪʃən/ n [U] the state of being motivated; need or purpose: *The stronger the motivation, the more quickly a person will learn a foreign language.* [+to-v] *His parents give him so much money that he's got no motivation to get a job.*

mo·tive /ˈməʊtɪv/ n a reason for action; that which urges a person to act in a certain way: *Jealousy was the motive for the murder|the murder motive. | What do you think his motives were in helping us? | We had begun to suspect his* *motives.* (=to think that he had acted for bad reasons) – ~**less** *adj*

motive² *adj* [A] *tech or fml* (of power, force, etc.) causing movement or action: *The wind provides the motive power that turns this wheel.* | *I think his wife was the motive force behind his resignation.* (=she made him leave his job)

mot juste /ˌmɔ̃ ˈʒuːst/ *n* **mots justes** (*same pronunciation*) [(*the*)] *Fr* exactly the right word or phrase

mot·ley¹ /ˈmɒtli‖ˈmɑːtli/ *adj* **1** *derog* of many different kinds: *His friends were a motley crew.* | *a motley collection of books on the shelf* **2** [A] *lit* (esp. of a garment) of different mixed colours, like the clothes worn by a JESTER

motley² *n* [U] *lit or tech* the clothes worn by a JESTER

mo·to·cross /ˈməʊtəʊkrɒs‖-krɔːs/ *n* [U] the sport of racing on motorcycles over a rough country track including steep hills, streams, etc.

mo·tor¹ /ˈməʊtə^r/ *n* **1** a machine that changes power, esp. electrical power, into movement, and is used for working other machines: *This lawn mower is driven by a small electric motor.* –see MACHINE¹ (USAGE) **2** *BrE infml* a car

motor² *adj* [A] **1** driven by an engine: *a motorboat* | *a motor scooter* | *a motor mower* **2** *esp. BrE* of or for cars or other vehicles driven by an engine, esp. those used on roads: *the motor industry/trade* | *a motor accident* | *motor racing* | *a motor magazine* **3** *tech* of or being a nerve that causes a muscle to move: *impaired motor functions*

motor³ *v* [I+*adv/prep*] *esp. BrE* becoming *rare* to travel by car, esp. for pleasure: *We motored over to Cambridge to see some friends.* – ~**ing** *n* [U] : *to go motoring in France* | *a motoring correspondent*

Mo·to·rail /ˈməʊtəreɪl/ *tdmk* a way of travelling by railway in which a passenger train also carries the passengers' cars

mo·tor·bike /ˈməʊtəbaɪk‖-tər-/ *n* **1** *BrE infml* a motorcycle **2** *AmE* a small light motorcycle –see TRANSPORT (USAGE)

mo·tor·boat /ˈməʊtəbəʊt‖-tər-/ *n* a boat, esp. a fast one, driven by an engine

mo·tor·cade /ˈməʊtəkeɪd‖-tər-/ *n* a procession of cars and other motor vehicles, esp. one in which an important person is travelling: *the president's motorcade*

mo·tor·car /ˈməʊtəkɑː^r‖-tər-/ *n BrE fml* a car

motor car·a·van /ˈ·· ‚···/ *BrE*‖**motor home** *AmE*– *n BrE* a large vehicle usu. used for holidays, which has beds, a table, and a kitchen area in the back

mo·tor·cy·cle /ˈməʊtəˌsaɪkəl‖-tər-/ *n* a large heavy bicycle driven by an engine –see TRANSPORT (USAGE) –-**clist** *n*

mo·tor·ing /ˈməʊtərɪŋ/ *n* [U] see MOTOR³

mo·tor·ist /ˈməʊtər‚st/ *n* a person who drives a car – compare PEDESTRIAN¹

mo·tor·ize also **-ise** *BrE* /ˈməʊtəraɪz/ *v* [T] **1** to provide (a vehicle) with a motor **2** to provide (soldiers, an army, etc.) with motor vehicles

motor lodge /ˈ·· ·/ *n AmE* a MOTEL

mo·tor·man /ˈməʊtəmæn‖-tər-/ *n* **-men** /men/ a driver of a vehicle driven by a motor, esp. an electric train

mo·tor·mouth /ˈməʊtəmaʊθ‖-tər-/ *n AmE infml derog* a person who talks too much and too loudly

motor rac·ing /ˈ·· ‚··/ *n* [U] the sport of racing fast cars on special courses, usu. outdoors –see also GRAND PRIX, STOCK CAR

motor scoot·er /ˈ·· ‚··/ also **scooter**– *n* a low vehicle with two small wheels, an enclosed engine, and usu. a wide curved part at the front to protect the legs

Motor Show /ˈ·· ·/ [*the*] an international show of new models of car, held every two years in Britain at the National Exhibition Centre in Birmingham

motor ve·hi·cle /ˈ·· ‚···/ *n* an official word for a vehicle which is powered by a motor, esp. an INTERNAL-COMBUSTION engine: *This road is closed to motor vehicles.* (=is open to people on foot or on bicycles)

mo·tor·way /ˈməʊtəweɪ‖-tər-/ *BrE* ‖ **freeway** *AmE*– *n* a very wide road built for fast long-distance travel: *The M1 is one of the longest motorways in Britain.* –see also EXPRESSWAY (USAGE)

motorway mad·ness /ˌ··· ˈ··/ *n* [U] *BrE* a dangerous situation in which people drive too fast or too close to other

cars on a motorway in bad weather conditions, esp. FOG: *Ten die in motorway madness.*

Mo·town /ˈməʊtaʊn/ *tdmk* **1** an American popular music record company based in Detroit **2** [U] a style of popular music connected with singers and groups recorded by the Motown company, esp. those who became successful in the 1960s and 1970s, e.g. Marvin Gaye, the Supremes, and Smokey Robinson the Miracles

mot·tled /ˈmɒtld‖ˈmɑː-/ *adj* having irregularly-shaped different-coloured markings: *mottled skin*

mot·to /ˈmɒtəʊ‖ˈmɑː-/ *n* **-tos** *or* **-toes** **1** a short sentence or a few words taken as the guiding principle of a person, of a school, etc.: *"Waste not, want not" was my mother's motto.* | *a school motto* –compare SLOGAN **2** *esp. BrE* an amusing or clever short printed phrase put esp. inside a CHRISTMAS CRACKER **3** a few words, or a short musical phrase, placed at the beginning of a book, or of a piece of music

mould¹ ‖ also **mold** *AmE* /məʊld/ *n* [U] **1** a soft greenish growth on bread, cheese, etc., that has been kept too long, or on objects that have been left for a long time in warm wet air **2** (*often in comb.*) loose soft soil full of decayed plant substances: *He planted the seeds in a box filled with leaf mould.*

mould

mould² ‖ also **mold** *AmE*– *n* **1** a hollow container of a particular shape, into which some soft substance is poured, so that when the substance becomes cool or hard, it takes this shape: *a jelly mould shaped like a rabbit* | *a candle mould* **2** *lit* a person's character or type: *We need to recruit more men of his mould.*

mould³ also **mold** *AmE*– *v* [T] **1** to make out of a material by changing its shape: *These huge presses mould the car bodies.* | *a figure of a man moulded in/out of clay* | (fig.) *His character has been moulded more by his experiences in life than by his education.* **2** to fit closely to the shape of something, esp. a body: *Her wet dress was moulded to her body.*

moul·der ‖ also **molder** *AmE* /ˈməʊldə^r/ *v* [I (AWAY)] *often lit* to decay slowly: *the mouldering walls of an ancient ruin* | (fig.) *The plans mouldered away in a forgotten corner of the office.* (=they were never put into practice)

mould·ing ‖ also **molding** *AmE* /ˈməʊldɪŋ/ *n* **1** [C;U] a decorative band of stone or wood round the edge of a wall, a piece of furniture, a picture frame, etc. **2** [C] an object, such as a piece of plastic, produced from a MOULD²

mould·y ‖ also **moldy** *AmE* /ˈməʊldi/ *adj* **1** of or covered with MOULD¹ : *mouldy cheese* | *a mouldy smell inside the cupboard* **2** *BrE sl* of little value; unpleasant: *Our mouldy old uncle won't let us play in his garden.* | *Only a mouldy five pounds for all that work?* **3** *AmE* out of date; OBSOLETE; no longer interesting or useful: *That radio station only plays oldy but moldies.* (=old songs no longer appreciated) –-**iness** *n* [U]

Mou·lin Rouge /ˌmuːlæŋ ˈruːʒ/ [*the*] a CABARET in Paris, famous esp. in the late 19th century but still popular today, esp. with tourists

moult¹ ‖ also **molt** *AmE* /məʊlt/ *v* [I;T] (of a bird or animal) to lose or throw off (most of its feathers, hair, or fur) at the season when a new covering for the body grows

moult² ‖ also **molt** *AmE*– *n* [C;U] the process or time of moulting

mound /maʊnd/ *n* [(of)] **1** a pile of earth, stones, etc., often one built in ancient times as a defence or over a grave; small hill: *a burial mound* **2** a large pile: *a mound of papers on my desk* **3** the small hill on which the PITCHER in the game of BASEBALL stands: *Lasorda walked slowly out to the mound to talk to the pitcher.* –see picture at BASEBALL

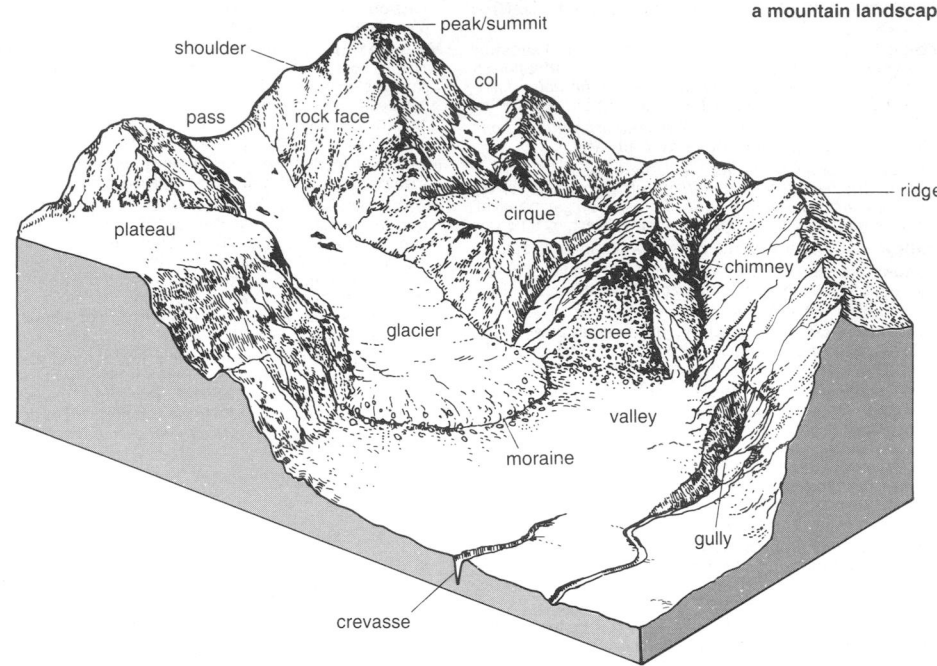

a mountain landscape

shoulder — peak/summit — col — ridge — chimney — cirque — scree — ridge — plateau — pass — rock face — glacier — valley — moraine — gully — crevasse

mount¹ /maʊnt/ v **1** [I;T] *rather fml* to get on (a horse, a bicycle, etc.): *The soldiers stood beside their horses, waiting for the order to mount.* | *He mounted his bicycle and rode away.* —opposite **dismount** **2** [T **(on)**] to provide (someone) with something to ride on, esp. a horse: *The soldiers were mounted on* (=rode) *fine black horses.* | *the mounted police* **3** [I (UP)] to rise in level or increase in amount: *Tension mounted as we waited for the decision.* | *Their debts continued to mount up.* **4** [T] to prepare and produce (an attack): *The opposition is getting ready to mount a powerful attack on the government.* | *They have too weak a team to mount a realistic challenge for the championship.* **5** [I (to);T] *fml* to go up; climb: *The old lady mounted the stairs with difficulty.* **6** [T] to fix on a support or in a frame: *The dead insect was mounted on a card by means of a pin.* **7** [T] *tech* (of a male animal, esp. a large one) to get up on (a female animal) in order to breed **8 mount guard (over)** to guard, esp. as a military duty **9 mount the throne** *fml* to become king, queen, etc.

mount² n **1** something on which or in which a thing is fixed and supported: *A silver cup on a wooden mount was presented to the winner.* **2** an animal on which one rides: *This old donkey is a good quiet mount for a child.*

mount³ n *old use, or (cap.) as part of a name* a mountain: *Mount Teide, Tenerife*

moun·tain /ˈmaʊntən/ n **1** a very high hill, usu. of bare or snow-covered rock: *He looked down from the top of the mountain to the valley far below.* | *a mountain chain/range* (=line of mountains) | *the mountain peaks* **2** [(of)] also **mountains** pl.— a very large amount: *mountains/a mountain of dirty clothes to wash* **3** *BrE* (usu. in comb.) a very large amount (of a food) that is stored to prevent prices falling: *the European Community's butter mountain* —compare LAKE¹ (2) **4 make a mountain out of a molehill** to make a matter or problem seem much more important or difficult than it really is

mountain bike /ˈ·· ˌ·/ also **mountain bi·cy·cle** /ˈ·· ˌ···/— n a strong bicycle with many GEARS, large wheels

mountain bike

with wide tyres, and powerful BRAKEs, which is used esp. on rough and hilly ground. Mountain bikes became very fashionable in the late 1980s and were bought by many people who only ever rode them in towns.

Mountain Day·light Time /ˌ··· ˈ·· ˌ·/ (abbrev. **MDT**) the time used in the summer months in the Mountain Time Zone of the US

moun·tain·eer /ˌmaʊntəˈnɪəʳ/ n a person who climbs mountains as a sport or profession — **~ing** n [U]

mountain li·on /ˈ·· ˌ··/ n a COUGAR

moun·tain·ous /ˈmaʊntənəs/ adj **1** full of mountains: *mountainous country* **2** very large or high: *mountainous waves*

mountain res·cue /ˌ·· ˈ··/ n an attempt to find help, or save people lost or hurt while in the mountains: *A mountain rescue team has been sent out to find the missing climbers.*

moun·tain·side /ˈmaʊntənsaɪd/ n [usu. sing.] the slope of a mountain: *The great rocks rolled down the mountainside.*

Mountain Stan·dard Time /ˌ··· ˈ·· ˌ·/ (abbrev. **MST**) the time used from autumn to spring in the Rocky Mountain area of N America (the **Mountain Time Zone**)

moun·tain·top /ˈmaʊntəntɒp‖-tɑːp/ n the top of a mountain —see also PEAK, SUMMIT

Mount Ar·a·rat /maʊnt ˈærəræt/ see ARARAT

Mount·bat·ten /maʊntˈbætn/, **Louis** (1900–79) an English ADMIRAL and STATESMAN, also known as **Prince Louis of Battenburg, Earl Mountbatten of Burma**. He was descended from Queen Victoria, led the Allies in Burma in the Second World War, and was the last British VICE-ROY. He was killed by an IRA bomb.

moun·te·bank /ˈmaʊntɪbæŋk/ n *lit derog* a dishonest, dishonourable, or deceiving man

Mount Etna see ETNA

Mount Eve·rest see EVEREST¹

Mount God·win Aus·ten /maʊnt ˌɡɒdwɪn ˈɒstɪn‖-ˌɡɑːdwɪn ˈɔːs-/ see K2, see picture on page 869

Mount·ie /ˈmaʊnti/ n *infml* a member of a special Canadian police force (the **Royal Canadian Mounted Police**) which often works on horseback. They wear bright red JACKETs and ride black horses, and are often regarded as one of the SYMBOLs of Canada. It is said that they "always get their man" (=always catch the man they are chasing).

Mountie

mount·ing /ˈmaʊntɪŋ/ n a fixed object to which other things, esp. parts of a machine, are fastened, and which keeps them in place: *The winch broke loose from its mountings.* | *The car's engine is supported by four rubberized mountings.*

Mount Kil·i·man·ja·ro /maʊnt ˌkɪlɪ̯mənˈdʒɑːrəʊ/ see KILIMANJARO

Mount Mc·Kin·ley /ˈmaʊnt məˈkɪnli/ also **Denali** a mountain in **Mount McKinley National Park** in central Alaska which is the highest point in North America

Mount of Ol·ives /ˌ· · ˈ·-/ [the] a mountain RIDGE E of Jerusalem, mentioned in the Bible esp. as the place of Jesus Christ's Ascension

Mount Olympus see OLYMPUS[1]

Mount Palomar see PALOMAR

Mount Rainier see RAINIER

Mount Saint Helens see ST HELENS

Mount Sinai see SINAI

Mount Ver·non /maʊnt ˈvɜːnən‖-ˈvɜːr-/ the home of George Washington between 1747 and 1799 and the place where he is buried. It is in NE Virginia, US and is now a MUSEUM.

Mount Vesuvius see VESUVIUS

mourn /mɔːn‖mɔːrn/ v [I (**for, over**);T] to feel and/or show grief (for), esp. because of someone's death: *The old woman still mourns her son's death|mourns for her son.* | *We all mourn the passing of the steam train.* (=wish that they had not stopped being used)

mourn·er /ˈmɔːnəʳ‖-ˈmɔːr-/ n a person who attends a funeral

mourn·ful /ˈmɔːnfəl‖ˈmɔːrn-/ adj sometimes derog sad; causing, feeling, or expressing sorrow: *a mournful occasion* | *a mournful expression on her face* — **~ly** adv — **~ness** n [U]

mourn·ing /ˈmɔːnɪŋ‖ˈmɔːr-/ n [U]   **1** (the expression of) grief, esp. for a death: *All the flags were at half-mast, as a sign of mourning for the dead president.*   **2** the clothes, black in Britain and some other countries, worn to show grief at the death of someone: *The royal court went into mourning* (=started to wear black) *when the queen died.* | *a widow dressed in deep* (=complete) *mourning*

mouse

mouse /maʊs/ n **mice** /maɪs/   **1** (*often in comb.*) a small furry animal with a long tail that lives in houses and in fields, related to but smaller than a rat: *I think we've got mice in the kitchen.* | *The children were as quiet as mice.* (=very quiet) | *a field mouse* —see picture at RODENT

▶ CULTURAL NOTE Mice are thought of as being quiet, TIMID animals. They are thought to like cheese in particular, though they eat many different things, and are thought by some people to frighten elephants, though this has certainly not been proved. Women are supposed to be frightened of mice, and CARTOONS often show a woman standing on a chair to escape from a mouse. ◀

2 infml a quiet nervous fearful person, esp. a girl or woman   **3** tech, pl **mouses**– a small box connected to a computer by a wire which, when moved by hand, causes a CURSOR to move around on a VDU so that choices can be made within the PROGRAM in use —see picture at COMPUTER; see also **play cat and mouse with** (CAT)

mous·er /ˈmaʊsəʳ/ n a cat that catches mice: *Our cat's a good mouser.*

mousetrap

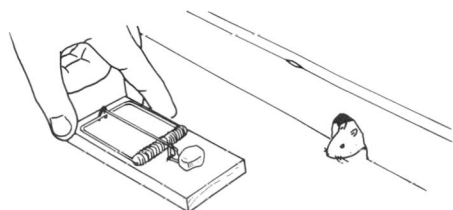

mouse·trap /ˈmaʊs-træp/ n   **1** a trap for catching mice, worked by a spring, and usu. supplied with a small piece of cheese for attracting the mice   **2** BrE infml mousetrap cheese

Mousetrap, The a play in London's WEST END which has been running continuously for longer than any other show in the world. It is a THRILLER by Agatha Christie, which opened in 1952 at the Ambassador Theatre, moved to St. Martin's Theatre in 1974, and has been performed over 16,000 times.

mousetrap cheese /ˌ·· ˈ·/ n [U] BrE infml cheese which is cheap and of poor quality

Mous·kou·ri /muːˈskuːri/, **Nan·a** /ˈnænə/ (1936–   ) an internationally-known Greek singer who sang freedom songs in other countries when Greece was ruled by a DICTATOR

mous·sa·ka /muːˈsɑːkə/ n [U] a Greek dish made from meat, cheese, and AUBERGINES

mousse /muːs/ n   **1** [C;U] (*often in comb.*) (a light usu. sweet dish made from) cream, eggs, and other substances mixed together and eaten cold: *chocolate mousse*   **2** a FROTHY substance usu. sold in an AEROSOL and put on hair to thicken it or to hold it in a particular style

mous·tache ‖ also **mustache** AmE /məˈstɑːʃ‖ˈmʌstæʃ/ n hair growing on the upper lip of a man: *He's shaved off his moustache.* —compare BEARD[1]

mous·y, **-ey** /ˈmaʊsi/ adj   **1** often derog (of hair) having a dull brownish-grey colour   **2** derog (of a person, esp. a girl or woman) unattractively plain and quiet; DRAB   **3** infml of or like mice: *a mousy smell* —**iness** n [U]

mouth[1] /maʊθ/ n **mouths** /maʊðz/   **1 a** the opening on the face through which a person or animal can take food into the body, and speak or make sounds: *The dentist told him to open his mouth wide.* | *They've got eight children; that's an awful lot of mouths to feed!* | *What beautiful chocolates! They really* **make my mouth water!** (=I want to eat them very much.) **b** infml (in certain phrases) the mouth when thought of as being used for speaking and making sounds: *Don't tell him any secrets; he's got* **a big mouth.** (=he talks too much, and will tell someone) | *I just mentioned Jim's girlfriend to his wife — me and my big mouth!* (=I said something I should not have said) | BrE *Don't worry, he won't report you to the headmaster; he's* **all mouth.** (=he says he will do things but doesn't have the courage to actually do them) | *Don't believe what he says about all the girlfriends he's had — he's all mouth and trousers.* (=he claims to be very attractive sexually but this is not true) | *You can tell him anything; he knows how* *to* **keep his mouth shut**. | *Shut your mouth, you fool!* (=stop talking) —see picture at HEAD **2** an opening, entrance, or way out: *the mouth of a river* (=where it joins the sea) | *the mouth of a cave* **3 down in the mouth** *infml* not cheerful; unhappy **4 out of the mouths (of babes and sucklings)** a phrase from the Bible, used when a child has just said something sensible or wise **5** **-mouthed** /maʊðd, maʊθt/: *a usu. derog* having the stated way of speaking: *loudmouthed* | *foul-mouthed* **b** having the stated kind of mouth: *a wide-mouthed jar* —see also **put one's foot in one's mouth** (FOOT¹ (19)), **look a gift horse in the mouth** (GIFT HORSE), **from hand to mouth** (HAND¹), **(straight) from the horse's mouth** (HORSE¹), **put one's money where one's mouth is** (MONEY), **shoot one's mouth off** (SHOOT¹), **by word of mouth, put words into someone's mouth, take the words out of someone's mouth** (WORD¹)

mouth² /maʊð/ *v* **1** [T] to move one's lips as if saying (words) but without making any sound: *The actor mouthed the words of the recorded song.* **2** [T] to say esp. repeatedly and without understanding or sincerity: *mouthing platitudes* | *mouthing curses* **3** [I (OFF)] *infml derog* to speak strongly or as if one knew more than anyone else: *mouthing off about the high price of fish*

mouth·ful /ˈmaʊθfʊl/ *n* **1** [C (**of**)] as much food or drink as fills the mouth; small quantity taken in the mouth: *I'm so full I couldn't eat another mouthful.* **2** [S] *infml, usu. humor* a big long word or phrase that is difficult to say: *Her name is a bit of a mouthful.* **3** [S] *infml, esp. AmE* a very important statement: *You said a mouthful!* —compare EARFUL

mouth·or·gan /ˈmaʊθˌɔːgən‖-ˌɔːr-/ *n infml for* HARMONICA

mouth·piece /ˈmaʊθpiːs/ *n* **1** the part of a musical instrument, a tobacco pipe, a telephone, etc., that is held in or near the mouth —see picture at BRASS **2** [(**of**) *usu. sing.*] *often derog* a person, newspaper, etc., that expresses the opinions of others: *This newspaper is the mouthpiece of the government.*

mouth-to-mouth re·sus·ci·ta·tion /ˌ· · · · ·ˌ·· ˈ·· ·/ also **kiss of life** *BrE*— *n* [U] the forcing of air into and out of the lungs of a person who has stopped breathing, by blowing into the mouth, then pressing the chest —see also FIRST AID; compare ARTIFICIAL RESPIRATION, CPR

mouth·wash /ˈmaʊθwɒʃ‖-wɔːʃ, -wɑːʃ/ *n* [C;U] (a) liquid used in the mouth, for making it feel and smell fresh, curing infection, etc.

mouth·wa·ter·ing /ˈ· ˌ··/ *adj* (of food) (looking as if it will be) very pleasant to eat: *mouth-watering chocolates*

mo·va·ble¹ , **moveable** /ˈmuːvəbəl/ *adj* that can be moved; not fixed in one place or position: *toy soldiers with movable arms and legs* —see also IMMOVABLE

movable² , **moveable** *n* [*usu. pl.*] *law* a personal possession, such as a piece of furniture, that can be moved from one house to another —opposite **fixture**

movable feast /ˌ·· ˈ·/ *n* a religious day, such as Easter, the date of which varies from year to year

move¹ /muːv/ *v* **1** [I;T] to (cause to) change place or position: *Don't get off the train while it's still moving.* (=before it has stopped) | *Please move your car; it's blocking the road.* | *Can you sit still without moving for ten minutes?* | *I can hear someone moving about upstairs.* | *He was trapped in the crashed car, and couldn't move his legs.* | *This student ought to be moved up to a higher class.* | (*infml*) *That car is really moving!* (=travelling very fast) —see SHIFT (USAGE) **2** [I] (of work, events, etc.) to advance; get nearer to an end: *Work on the new building is moving more quickly than was expected.* | *Let's get things moving.* (=make events advance more quickly) **3** [I] to change one's place of living or working: *Their present office is too small, so they've decided to move.* | *We can't move into the new flat until the other tenants have moved out.* | *They don't live here any longer — they've moved away.* —see also **move house** (MOVE¹) **4 a** [I;T] (in board games such as CHESS) to change the position of (a piece): *Haven't you moved yet?* **b** [I+adv/prep] (of a piece in such a game) to be able to travel to another position: *A castle only moves in straight lines.* **5** [T (**to**)] *fml* to cause (a person) to feel pity, sadness, anger, admiration, etc.: *The child's suffering moved us to tears.* | *I was very moved by her sad story.* —see also MOVING, UNMOVED **6** [T] *fml or pomp* to cause (a person) to act, change an opinion, etc.: *He can paint well only when the spirit moves him.* (=when

he feels a real desire to paint) [+*obj*+*to-v*] *Hearing so much nonsense talked, I felt moved to speak on the subject.* **7** [I (**for**); T] to make at a meeting (a formal suggestion on which arguments for and against are heard, and a decision taken, esp. by voting): *I wish to move an amendment to this law.* | *We moved for an adjournment of half an hour.* [+*that*] *Mr Chairman, I move that the meeting (should) be continued after dinner.* —see also MOTION¹ (3) **8** [I (**on**)] to (start to) take action: *When will the government move on this matter?* [+*to-v*] *The committee is moving to lift membership restrictions.* **9** [I;T] to sell (goods) or be sold: *The new line of stock is moving much too slowly.* **10** [I+*adv/prep*, esp. **among**, **in**] to spend one's time with people of the stated class or type: *a young writer who moves mostly in literary and artistic circles* (=among writers, painters, etc.) **11 move heaven and earth** to do everything one can (to cause or prevent something) **12 move house** *BrE* to take one's furniture and other property to a new home **13 move the goal-posts** *BrE infml* to change the limits within which action or talk concerning a particular matter can take place **14 move with the times** to change one's ways of thinking, living, etc., in accordance with the changes produced by the passing of time: *I don't really like all these computers in the office, but I suppose we must move with the times.* **15 not move a muscle** to stay completely still, esp. so as to show no feelings: *She screamed abuse at him but he didn't move a muscle.* **16 we shall not be moved** the title of a song sung by people who are protesting about something esp. by sitting in a public place and refusing to move

move along *phr v* **1** [I] to move further towards the front or back: *The people standing in the bus moved along, to make room for others.* **2** [I;T (=**move** sbdy. **along**)] to MOVE **on** (2)

move in *phr v* [I] **1** to take possession of a new home: *We've bought the house, but we can't move in until next month.* **2** [(**on**)] to (prepare to) take control, attack, etc.: *Our competitors have gone out of business, so now our company can move in.*

move off *phr v* [I] to leave: *The guard blew his whistle, and the train moved off.*

move on *phr v* **1** [I (**to**)] to change (to something different or new): *I think we've talked about that subject enough; let's move on.* | *In my day you could only get them in black-and-white, but things have moved on since then.* | (*humor*) *My boss has moved on to higher things; he's become a politician.* **2** [I;T (=**move** sbdy. **on**)] to (order to) go away to another place: *The drunk was annoying people, so the policeman moved him on.* | *"Come along, sir, move on,"* said the policeman.

move over *phr v* [I] to change position in order to make room for someone or something else: *Move over and let your grandmother sit down.* | (fig.) *He resigned his position as a director, as he felt he should move over in favour of someone younger.*

move² *n* **1** [S] an act of moving; movement: *If you make a move, I'll shoot.* | *She watched his every move like a hawk.* **2** [C] an act of going to a new home, office, etc.: *How did the move go?* **3** [C] (in games such as CHESS) **a** an act of taking a piece from one square and putting it on another **b** a way in which this may be done, according to the rules: *to learn all the different moves in chess* **c** a player's turn to do this: *It's your move.* **4** [C] a step in a course of action towards a particular result: [+*to-v*] *New moves to settle the strike have ended in failure.* | *The government is making a/no move to reduce international tension.* | *I know you're both proud and find it difficult to forgive each other after such a bad argument, but someone has to make the first move.* | *a good/bad/smart/shrewd move* **5 get a move on** *infml* (*often imperative*) to hurry up: *Tell Harry to get a move on.* **6 make a move** *infml* to start to leave: *It's getting late; we must be making a move soon.* **7 on the move: a** travelling around: *I don't know where Mike is this week; he's always on the move.* **b** beginning to move across land: *We have just received reports that the rebel army is on the move.*

move·a·ble /ˈmuːvəbəl/ *adj* MOVABLE¹,²

move·ment /ˈmuːvmənt/ *n* **1** [C; U] (an example of) the act of moving or condition of being moved: *He was so badly bruised that even the slightest movement was painful.* | *the movement of goods by road* | *the dancer's graceful movements* —see also MOVEMENTS **2** [C] a general feeling, way of thinking or acting, etc., towards something new:

the movement towards greater freedom for women | *a growing movement towards nuclear disarmament* **3** [C+*sing./pl. v*] a group of people who make united efforts for a particular purpose: *The trade union movement is concerned with working conditions.* | *the women's movement* **4** [C] a main division of a musical work, esp. of a SYMPHONY **5** [C] the moving parts of a piece of machinery, esp. a clock or watch **6** [C] *fml* an act of emptying the bowels

move·ments /ˈmuːvmənts/ *n* [P] the whole of a person's activities over a certain period: *The police think this man may be the thief they're looking for, so they're watching his movements carefully.*

mov·er /ˈmuːvəʳ/ *n* **1** a person who makes a formal suggestion at a meeting **2** a person who moves in the stated way: *She's a lovely mover.* (=moves very well) **3** *infml* a person, thing, idea, etc. that is being successful or advancing quickly: *These chocolate cakes are among our fastest movers.* (=we sell a lot of them) | *Talk to her if you want to see some action; she's one of the* **movers and shakers** (=people who have power) *in this company.* **4** *AmE* a person whose job is to help people MOVE¹ (3) —see also PRIME MOVER

mov·ie /ˈmuːvi/ *n esp. AmE for* FILM¹ (2): *There's a good movie on TV tonight.* —see also HOME MOVIE

mo·vie·go·er /ˈmuːviɡəʊəʳ/ *n* a person who visits the cinema, esp. regularly

mov·ies /ˈmuːviz/ *n* [*the*+P] *esp. AmE* the cinema: *We're going to the movies.*

movie star /ˈ··ˌ·/ *n AmE for* FILM STAR

mov·ing /ˈmuːvɪŋ/ *adj* **1** causing strong sympathetic feelings, esp. of pity: *The film about ill-treatment of animals was so moving that she almost wept.* | *a moving occasion/speech/appeal* **2** [A *no comp.*] producing movement or action: *She was the* **moving spirit** *behind the scheme.* (=the person who caused it to start) **3** [A *no comp.*] that moves; not fixed: *Oil the moving parts of this machine regularly.* − −**ly** *adv*

moving pic·ture /ˌ··· ˈ···◂/ *n fml, esp. AmE for* MOVIE

moving stair·case /ˌ··· ˈ···/ *n* an ESCALATOR

moving van /ˈ··· ˌ·/ *n* a REMOVAL VAN

mow /məʊ/ *v* **mowed, mowed** *or* **mown** /məʊn/ [I;T] to cut (grass, corn, etc.), or cut what grows in (a field or other area), with a mower or a SCYTHE: *to mow the grass/the lawn* | *new-mown hay* (=recently cut)
mow sbdy. **↔ down** *phr v* [T] to kill, destroy, or knock down, esp. in great numbers: *The soldiers were mown down by enemy gunfire.*

mow·er /ˈməʊəʳ/ *n* **1** a machine for mowing, esp. one for cutting grass in gardens; LAWNMOWER —see picture at GARDEN **2** *old use* a person who mows

Mow·gli /ˈmaʊɡli/ a character in *The Jungle Book*, by Rudyard Kipling, who is lost in the JUNGLE (a tropical forest) as a small child and is cared for and taught by the animals in the jungle, esp. the wolves (WOLF¹ (1))

Mo·zam·bique /ˌməʊzəmˈbiːk/ a republic in SE Africa, bordered by the Indian Ocean to the E, South Africa and Swaziland to the S, Zimbabwe, Zambia, and Malawi to the W, and Tanzania to the N; capital Maputo; population 15,326,000 (1989) —**biquean** *n,adj*

Mo·zart /ˈməʊtsaːt‖-aːrt/, **Wolf·gang Am·a·de·us** /ˈwʊlfɡæŋ æməˈdeɪəs/ (1756–91) an Austrian COMPOSER whose works include 41 symphonies (SYMPHONY), piano CONCERTOS and OPERAS. Mozart began to COMPOSE music before he was five years old and performed throughout Europe as a child. − −**ian** /məʊtˈsaːtiən‖-aːr-/ *adj*

moz·za·rel·la /ˌmɒtsəˈrelə ‖ ˌmɑːt-/ *n* [U] a soft white Italian cheese, often used on PIZZAS

MP /ˌem ˈpiː/ *n* **1** Member of Parliament; a person who has been elected to represent the people in a parliament (in Britain, in the House of Commons): *She's an MP.* | *Ken Newton, MP* —see also extra information on page 412 **2** *infml* (a member of) the MILITARY POLICE

MPAA /ˌem piː eɪ ˈeɪ/ *n* [U; *the*] the Motion Picture Association of America; the organization which determines to which age groups films may be shown: *An MPAA rating of 'X' (no persons under 18 allowed) is considered death to a commercial film.*

mpg *written abbrev. for:* miles per GALLON (esp. of petrol): *a car that does 35 mpg*

mph *written abbrev. for:* miles per hour: *driving along at 60 mph*

MPhil /ˌem ˈfɪl/ *n* Master of PHILOSOPHY; (a title for someone who has) a higher university degree at a lower level than a PhD: *Mary Jones, MPhil* | *He's studying for an MPhil.*

Mr /ˈmɪstəʳ/ *n* **1** (a title for a man who has no other title): *Mr Smith* | *Mr John Smith* —see also MESSRS
▶ CULTURAL NOTE **Mr** is the usual title for a man on a letter to him, and is more modern than **Esq**. When a man is married, he and his wife may be addressed formally as "Mr and Mrs Horace Bloggs", i.e. the man's FORENAME is used for both him and his wife, or his INITIALS may be used: "Mr and Mrs H J Bloggs". Many people consider this old-fashioned, and in less formal situations the couple might be called "Mr and Mrs Bloggs". ◀
2 (a title used when addressing certain men in official positions: *Mr Chairman* | (in the US) *Mr President* − compare MADAM **3** (used before the name of a place, profession, quality, etc., to form a title for a man representing that thing or quality): *Mr Universe* | *Mr Average*

Mr Big /ˌ· ˈ·/ *n sl esp. AmE* the male leader of an esp. criminal organization: *He thinks he's Mr Big.* | *Is he the Mr Big around here?*

MRE /ˌem aːr ˈiː/ *n* meal ready to eat, a meal supplied to a US soldier on active duty which does not need to be cooked

Mr Fix·it /ˌmɪstə ˈfɪksɪt‖-tər-/ see FIXIT

Mr. Good·bar /ˌmɪstə ˈɡʊdbaːʳ‖-tər-/ *n tdmk* a bar of chocolate with PEANUTS sold in the US

Mr. Kip·ling /ˌ·· ˈ···/ *n* [C;U] *tdmk* a range of cakes made by Manor Bakeries Ltd.: *Mr. Kipling's Cherry Bakewells. Mr. Kipling is my favourite.*

Mr Nice Guy /ˌ·· ˈ· ·/ *n* someone who is taken advantage of because he is too nice, esp. in the phrase **no more Mr Nice Guy**, which people use when they feel others have used them in spite of their kindness

MRP /ˌem aː ˈpiː‖-aːr-/ *n* manufacturer's recommended price; the price which the maker of a product says it should cost (often seen in advertisements): *Sale price £7.50, MRP £9.75*

Mr Right /ˌ·· ˈ·/ *humor* a man who would be the perfect husband or partner for a specific woman. Some people think that there is a Mr Right for every woman: *I'm waiting for Mr Right to come along before I consider marriage.* | *I haven't found Mr Right yet.*

Mr. Ro·gers' Neigh·bor·hood /ˌ·· ˌ·· ˈ···/ *n* an American television programme on PBS for very young children. Mr. Rogers, the host of the programme, is always very calm and nice.

Mrs /ˈmɪsɪz/ *n* **1** (a title for a married woman who has no other title)
▶ CULTURAL NOTE When a woman gets married she usu. takes the title Mrs and starts to use the family name of her husband: *Mrs Jones.* She usu. continues to use her own FORENAME with her husband's family name: *Mrs Sarah Jones*, but in formal esp. written language she may be addressed as Mrs with her husband's forename and family name: *Mrs Andrew Jones*; this practice is becoming rare. —compare MAIDEN NAME, MISS, MS ◀
2 (used before the name of a place, sport, profession, etc., to form a title for a married woman representing that thing): *Mrs 1988 in her modern kitchen*

Mr T. /ˌmɪstə ˈtiː‖-tər-/ an American actor whose real name is Lawrence Tureaud and who is best known for the part of B A Baracus in the American television programme *The A-Team*

ms, *pl.* **mss** (*often caps.*) *written abbrev. for:* MANUSCRIPT

Ms /mɪz, məz/ *n* (a title for a woman who does not wish to be called either "Miss" or "Mrs" or whose MARITAL STATUS is unknown by the person addressing her)
▶ CULTURAL NOTE The title Ms has been used widely since the 1970s, when it began to be used by women who did not want to be known according to whether or not they were married. Although Ms is now in common use, it still carries associations of FEMINISM. —compare MISS, MRS ◀

Ms. a leading FEMINIST magazine in the US: *I read it in an article in Ms.*

MS¹ /ˌem ˈes/ *abbrev. for:* MULTIPLE SCLEROSIS

MS² *written abbrev. for:* MISSISSIPPI

MSc /ˌem es ˈsiː/ *also* **MS** *AmE— n* Master of Science; (a title for someone who has) a university degree in science at the first level above the BSC: *John Smith, MSc* | *He has an MSc in astrophysics.* —compare MA, and see DEGREE (3) (CULTURAL NOTE)

MSF /ˌem es ˈef/ Manufacturing, Science, and Finance; a British TRADE UNION which represents a wide range of people who do professional, scientific, and technical work

MSG /ˌem es ˈdʒiː/ *n* [U] *abbrev. for:* MONOSODIUM GLUTAMATE

MST /ˌem es ˈtiː/ *abbrev. for*: MOUNTAIN STANDARD TIME

Mt *written abbrev. for:* MOUNT³: *Mt Everest*

MT *written abbrev. for* MONTANA

MTM /ˌem tiː ˈem/ an American company which makes television programmes, started by Mary Tyler Moore

MTV /ˌem tiː ˈviː/ music television; an American television company whose programmes are shown around the world. It broadcasts popular music, and pictures of the singers or groups performing it, 24 hours a day.

Mu·ba·rak /muːˈbɑːræk/, **Mu·ham·med Hos·ni** /muˈhæmɪd ˈhʊsni/ (1929–) an Egyptian politician, the president of Egypt from 1981

much¹ /mʌtʃ/ *adv* **1** by a large degree: *It was much worse than I thought.* | *He's getting much fatter.* | *He's much the fatter of the two.* | *much the quickest worker* | *much the most interesting story* | *It's much too cold.* | *I'd much rather not go.* —see MORE (USAGE) **2** (in the phrases **too much, so much, very much, how much?**) greatly: *Thank you very much.* | *I like him very much.* | *You've been doing too much — you should take a holiday.* | *She talks a great deal too much.* | *However much you hate cabbage, you must eat it all up.* | (*fml*) *He would so much like to go.* | *"It's dark!" "So much the better (for us)!* (=that's good) *They won't see us climbing the wall."* **3** [*usu. in negatives*] a to a great degree: *I don't much like that idea.* | *I don't like that idea much.* | *Much to my surprise/displeasure she forgot our meeting.* (=she forgot it, which surprised/displeased me greatly) | *The news was much the same as usual.* | *I'm not much good at tennis.* (=do not play it very well) | **Much as I** like her (=although I like her a lot), *I wouldn't like to be married to her.* b often: *We don't go out much.* **4** [(**like, as**)] almost the same: *I found the house much as I'd left it.* | *This sounds much like an argument I've heard before.* **5 much less** and certainly not: *I can hardly walk, much less run.* **6 not/nothing much** hardly anything: *There's nothing much we can do about it.* **7 not so much** ... **as** not ... but rather: *I don't so much dislike him as feel sorry for him!* **8 too/a bit much** *infml* unreasonable: *It really is too much of your father to bring guests home to dinner without letting me know in advance.* | *Well, that's a bit much!* **9 Not much!** *infml* (used to express firm disagreement or disbelief): *"He doesn't want to cheat you." "Not much (he doesn't)!"* (=I firmly believe he does want to cheat me.)

▷ USAGE 1 Use **much** with adjectives made from the passive form of verbs, in the same way as **very** is used with ordinary adjectives: *This picture is much admired/is very beautiful.* 2 Do not use **much** between a verb and its object, unless the object is a very long one. Compare *We very* **much** *enjoyed the party./We enjoyed the party very* **much** and *We enjoyed very* **much** *the party we went to at your house.*◁

much² *determiner, pron* **more, most 1** (used in questions and negatives about [U] nouns, and with **so** and **too**, but not usu. in simple statements) a large amount or part (of): *Hurry up; we haven't got very much time.* | *I've got far too much work to do.* | *How much is that dress?* (=what does it cost?) | *We haven't seen much of you* (=you haven't visited us) *recently.* | *You eat too much.* | (*fml*) *I have* **much** *pleasure in declaring this new factory open.* **2** something very good: *She's not much to look at, but she's very nice.* | *He's very good at tennis, but he's* **not much** *of a swimmer.* (=does not swim well) | *My French/This film is* **not up to much.** (=not very good) | **I don't think much of** *that idea.* (=I don't think it is very good) | *The new book is better than his last one, but* **that's not saying much.** (=the last one was so bad that almost anything would be better) **3 as much again** the same amount again: *It cost*

me *nearly £20 to have the TV aerial put up, and as much again to have it moved to the right place.* **4 as much as one can do** the most possible: *He was so rude, it was as much as I could do to keep my temper.* (=I nearly lost it) **5 I 'thought as much** I had expected that the stated usu. bad thing was so (and now I have been shown to be right): *So he's been cheating. I thought as much.* **6 make much of: a** to treat as important: *Why are you making so much of such a trifling matter?* **b** to understand well: *I couldn't make much of that new book.* **c** to treat with a show of fondness: *He always made much of his niece.* —compare **make little of** (LITTLE). **7 'so much for** that is the end of: *So much for past events; let me now move on to speculate about the future.* | *Now it's raining; so much for my idea of taking a walk.* (=it is no longer possible) **8 this/that much** the particular amount or words: *I'll say this much for him, he's a good worker.* (=although I don't like him) **9 too much for** too hard for: *Climbing the stairs is too much for my grandmother now.*

Much A·do a·bout Noth·ing /ˌ· ·ˌ· ·· ˈ··/ the title of a play by William Shakespeare. The phrase is now often used when someone is upset about something not very important.

much-her·ald·ed /ˌ· ˈ···/ *adj* [A] talked about a lot or for a long time before it actually comes or exists: *Ford today revealed their much-heralded new family car.*

much·ness /ˈmʌtʃnɪs/ *n* **much of a muchness** *BrE infml* the same in most ways; not very different from one another: *We found it hard to choose a carpet: they were all much of a muchness.*

mu·ci·lage /ˈmjuːsɪlɪdʒ/ *n* [U] sticky liquid obtained from plants and used esp. as glue

muck¹ /mʌk/ *n* [U] *infml or dial* **1** dirt or mud: *The kids were covered in muck.* **2** waste matter dropped from animals' bodies, esp. when used for spreading on the land; MANURE **3 make a muck of** *infml, esp. BrE* to spoil or do (something) wrongly or badly **4 where there's muck there's brass** *infml or dial* where there is dirt there is money; a phrase connected esp. with the North of England

muck² *v* [T] *infml* to spread muck on: *to muck the fields*
muck about/around *phr v infml, esp. BrE* **1** [I] to behave in a silly or aimless way: *Stop mucking about and listen to what I'm saying.* **2** [T] (**muck** sbdy. **about/around**) to treat without consideration: *My boss is mucking me about again; he keeps changing his mind.*
muck in *phr v* [I (**with**)] *infml, esp. BrE* to join in work or activity (with others): *If we all muck in we'll soon finish the job.*
muck (sthg. ↔) **out** *phr v* [I;T] **1** to clean (places where animals live): *to muck out the stable* **2** to do this for (an animal): *to muck out the horses*
muck sthg. ↔ **up** *phr v* [T] *infml, esp. BrE* **1** to make dirty: *I mucked up my shirt when I was working in the garden.* **2 a** to spoil (an arrangement): *The change in the weather has mucked up our sports timetable.* **b** to do (something) wrong: *to muck up an examination*

muck·heap /ˈmʌkhiːp/ *n* a pile of MANURE (=animal waste matter), esp. outside a farm

muck·lucks /ˈmʌklʌks/ *n* [P] *AmE* boots made from CANVAS with a thick SOLE, worn over thick socks or other shoes for walking in snow— see PAIR (USAGE)

muck·rak·ing /ˈmʌk-reɪkɪŋ/ *n* [U] the practice of searching out and telling unpleasant stories, which may or may not be true, about well-known people: *Those gossip columnists really enjoy muckraking.* —**muckraking** *adj* —**er** *n*

muck·spread·er /ˈmʌkspredəʳ/ *n* a machine used on a farm to spread MANURE (=animal waste matter) on fields

muck·spread·ing /ˈmʌkspredɪŋ/ *n* [U] the spreading of MANURE (=animal waste matter) on farm land to improve the goodness of the soil

muck·y /ˈmʌki/ *adj infml or dial* **1** dirty **2** *esp. BrE* (of weather) bad; stormy

mu·cous mem·brane /ˌmjuːkəs ˈmembreɪn/ *n* [U] the surface on certain inner parts of the body which is kept wet and smooth by producing mucus

mu·cus /ˈmjuːkəs/ *n* [U] a slippery liquid produced in certain delicate parts of the body, esp. the nose —**cous** *adj*

mud /mʌd/ *n* [U] **1** very wet earth in a sticky mass **2 someone's name is mud** *infml* someone is unpopular and spoken about with disapproval after causing trouble:

My name's mud in the office after what happened today. —see also **sling mud at** (SLING¹) **3 here's mud in your eye** *interj, infml* (used for expressing good wishes when drinking with someone; similar to CHEERS)

mud bath /¹· ·/ *n* a health treatment in which heated mud is put on the body, used esp. by people suffering from ARTHRITIS or RHEUMATISM to lessen pain —see also MUDPACK

mud·dle¹ /¹mʌdl/ *n* [*usu. sing.*] a state of confusion and disorder: *The papers are all in a muddle.* | *I was in such a muddle that I didn't even know what day it was.*

muddle² *v* [T (UP)] **1** to put into disorder: *Careful — you're muddling up the papers!* **2** to confuse in the mind: *That waitress gets muddled when she has to take a lot of orders at once.* **—dler** *n*
    muddle along *phr v* [I] to continue in a confused manner, without a clear plan
    muddle through *phr v* [I] to reach successful results without having a clear plan or using the best methods: *There were problems, but we muddled through somehow.*

muddle-head·ed /ˌ·· ¹···◂/ *adj* unable to think clearly — **~ness** *n* [U]

mud·dy¹ /¹mʌdi/ *adj* **1** covered with or containing mud: *the muddy waters of the river* | *Take off those muddy boots.* **2** (of colours) like mud; not bright: *a muddy brown* | *a muddy* (=dull and unhealthy) *complexion* **3** not clear; confused: *muddy thinking* **—diness** *n* [U]

muddy² *v* [T] to make dirty with mud: *Your dog's muddying my dress.*

mud·flap /¹mʌdflæp/ *BrE*‖ also **splash guard** *AmE*— *n* a piece of rubber or other heavy material hanging behind the wheel of a vehicle, esp. a TRUCK, to keep the mud from flying up —see picture at CAR

mud·flat /¹mʌdflæt/ *n* [*often pl.*] an area of muddy land, covered by the sea when it comes up and uncovered when it goes down

mud·guard /¹mʌdgɑːd‖-gɑːrd/ *BrE* ‖ **fender** *AmE*— *n* a cover over the wheel of a bicycle, etc. to keep the mud from flying up —see picture at BICYCLE

mud·pack /¹mʌdpæk/ *n* a MUD BATH for the face

mud pie /ˌ· ¹·/ *n* a little ball of wet mud made by children at play

mud·sling·er /¹mʌdslɪŋəʳ/ *n derog* a person who tells wicked, often untrue, stories about an opponent, esp. in politics **—ing** *n* [U]

mues·li /¹mjuːzli/ *n* [U] grain, nuts, dried fruits, etc., mixed together and eaten with milk as a breakfast food. Muesli is considered to be a healthy food and is often given as an example of the kind of food eaten by people interested in eating healthy foods.

mu·ez·zin /muː¹ezɪn, ¹mwezɪn/ *n* a man who calls Muslims to prayer from a MINARET

muff¹ /mʌf/ *n* a short tube of thick cloth or fur, into which one can put one's hands to keep them warm, used esp. in former times

muff² *v* [T] **1** (in games) to fail to hold; miss: *to muff a catch* **2** [(UP)] *infml* to spoil a chance to do (something) well; BUNGLE: *I had a chance to impress her with my efficiency and I muffed it (up).* **—muff** *n*

muf·fin /¹mʌfɪn/ *n* **1** *BrE* ‖ **English muffin** *AmE*— a small thick round breadlike cake, usu. eaten hot with butter —compare CRUMPET (1) **2** *AmE* a small sweetened cake which usu. has something particular added to give it an interesting taste: *blueberry/bran/chocolate chip muffins*

Muffin the Mule /ˌ··· · ¹·/ a wooden PUPPET shown on children's television in Britain in the 1950s

muf·fle /¹mʌfəl/ *v* [T *usu. pass.*] **1** to make (a sound) less easily heard: *The sound of the bell was muffled by the curtains.* | *muffled voices coming from the next room* **2** [(UP)] to cover (esp. oneself) thickly and warmly: *He went out into the snow muffled (up) in his scarf and heavy overcoat.*

muf·fler /¹mʌfləʳ/ *n* **1** a heavy SCARF worn to keep one's neck warm **2** *AmE for* SILENCER

muf·ti¹ /¹mʌfti/ *n* a person who officially explains Muslim law

mufti² *n* in **mufti** wearing ordinary clothes, not the uniform (esp. military uniform) which one usually wears

mug¹ /mʌg/ *n* **1** a round container for drinking esp. hot liquids such as tea and coffee, having straight sides and a handle, and used, without a SAUCER in the home or on

informal occasions but not at formal events. —compare CUP¹ and see picture at GLASS **2** also **mug·ful** /-fʊl/— the contents of a mug: *two mugs of coffee* **3** *BrE infml* a foolish person who is easily deceived —see also MUG'S GAME **4** *sl* the face or mouth: *his ugly mug*

mug² *v* **-gg-** [T] to rob (a person) with violence, esp. in a public place **—mugging** *n* [C;U]: *a big increase in the number of muggings in this area*
    mug up *phr v* [I;T (=**mug** sthg. ↔ **up**)] *infml, esp. BrE* to study with great effort, esp. when preparing for an exam

Mu·ga·be /muː¹gɑːbi/, **Rob·ert Ga·bri·el** /¹rɒbət ¹geɪbriəl‖ ¹rɑːbərt-/ (1924–) an African nationalist and politician who helped Zimbabwe to become independent. He became Prime Minister in 1980, when Zimbabwe became independent, and became its first president in 1988.

mug·ger /¹mʌgəʳ/ *n* a person who mugs people

Mug·ge·ridge /¹mʌgərɪdʒ/, **Malcolm** (1903–90) a British JOURNALIST, writer, and ACADEMIC, noted for his Christian views

mug·gins /¹mʌgɪnz/ *n BrE sl* a fool, esp. when used of oneself: *Everyone disappeared after dinner, leaving muggins* (=me) *to do the washing-up.*

mug·gy /¹mʌgi/ *adj infml* (of weather) unpleasantly warm with heavy wet air **—giness** *n* [U]

mug's game /ˈ· ₁·/ *n* [S] *BrE infml* a course of action that is unlikely to be rewarding or profitable: *Writing's a mug's game; you should get a proper job!* —see also MUG¹ (3)

mug·shot /¹mʌgʃɒt‖-ʃɑːt/ *n sl* a photograph of a person's face, esp. a photograph of a criminal taken by the police

mug·wump /¹mʌg-wʌmp/ *n AmE derog old-fash* a person who tries to be independent of the leaders in politics

Mu·ham·mad /muˈhæmʌd, mə-/ also **Mohammed**— (570?–632) an Arab holy man and the originator of Islam, born in Mecca, to whom God told many things which are recorded in the Koran

Muhammad, El·i·jah /ɪˈlaɪdʒə/ (1897–1975) the leader of the Black Muslims from the late 1930s until his death

Mu·ham·ma·dan /muˈhæmʌdən, mə-/ also **Mohammedan**— *adj, n* (a) Muslim (considered offensive by some Muslims)

Mu·ham·ma·dan·is·m /muˈhæmʌdənɪzəm, mə-/ also **Mohammedanism**— *n* [U] the Muslim religion; ISLAM (considered offensive by some Muslims)

Muir /mjʊəʳ/, **Frank** (1920–) a British writer for radio and television who also appears on television and is best known for the programme *Call My Bluff*

Muir, Jean /dʒiːn/ (1933–) a British dress DESIGNER, known for her CLASSIC clothes: *a Jean Muir dress*

mu·ja·hed·din /ˌmuːdʒəheˈdiːn/ *n* [P] Muslim soldiers who oppose the government in Afghanistan

mu·lat·to /mjuːˈlætəʊ‖mʊ-/ *n* **-tos** *or* **-toes** *now usu. considered derog* a person with one black parent and one white one

mul·ber·ry /¹mʌlbəri‖-beri/ *n* (a tree with) a dark purple fruit which can be eaten

mulch¹ /mʌltʃ/ *n* [S;U] a covering of material, often made from decaying plants, used to improve soil and protect the roots of plants

mulch² *v* [T] to cover with a mulch

mulct /mʌlkt/ *v* [T (**of**)] *fml or old use* to punish by taking away (money); to FINE

mule¹ /mjuːl/ *n* **1** the animal which is the young of a DONKEY and a usu. female horse. Mules are usu. thought of as being STUBBORN. **2** a sort of spinning-machine (SPIN¹ (2))

mule² *n* [*usu. pl.*] a shoe or SLIPPER with no back, but only a piece of material across the toes to hold it on —see PAIR (USAGE)

mu·le·teer /ˌmjuːlɪˈtɪəʳ/ also **mule·skin·ner** /¹mjuːlskɪnəʳ/ *AmE*— *n* a man who drives mules

mul·ish /¹mjuːlɪʃ/ *adj* unreasonably refusing to agree with the wishes of others; STUBBORN: *mulish obstinacy* **— ~ly** *adv* **— ~ness** *n* [U]

mull¹ /mʌl/ *v* [T] to heat (wine or beer) with sugar and SPICES: *mulled ale*
    mull sthg. ↔ **over** *phr v* [T] to think over; consider for

a time; PONDER: *I've been mulling over your advice but I still haven't decided what to do.*

mull² *n ScotE* an area of land standing out into the sea; PROMONTORY

Mull the largest island in the Inner Hebrides, NW Scotland, often visited by tourists

mul·lah /ˈmʌlə/ *n* a Muslim teacher of law and religion

mul·let /ˈmʌlɨt/ *n* **mullet** *or* **mullets** a fairly small sea fish which can be eaten

mul·li·ga·taw·ny /ˌmʌlɪgəˈtɔːni‖-ˈtɔːni, -ˈtɑːni/ *n* [U] a strong soup, containing hot SPICE*s*

mul·lion /ˈmʌljən/ *n* the wood, metal, or esp. stone part running up and down between the glass parts of a window − ~**ed** *adj* : *mullioned windows*

Mul·ro·ney /mʌlˈrəʊni/, **Bri·an** /ˈbraɪən/ (1939–   ) a Canadian politician who was Prime Minister from 1984 to 1993

multi- see WORD FORMATION

mul·ti-choice /ˌmʌlti ˈtʃɔɪs◂/ *adj* MULTIPLE CHOICE

mul·ti·cul·tu·ral /ˌmʌltiˈkʌltʃərəl◂/ *n* including people or teachings from several different CULTURES: *multicultural education*

multi-faith /ˌ·· ˈ·◂/ *adj* [A] including or involving people of several different religious faiths: *a multi-faith service of thanksgiving* | *a multi-faith society*

mul·ti·far·i·ous /ˌmʌltɨˈfeəriəs◂/ *adj* of many different types; showing great variety: *his multifarious business activities* − ~**ly** *adv* − ~**ness** *n* [U]

mul·ti·form /ˈmʌltɨfɔːm‖-fɔːrm/ *adj fml* having several different shapes or appearances

multi-func·tion /ˌ·· ˈ··◂/ *adj* [A] (of a machine, an apparatus, etc.) that has several different uses: *a multi-function clock, timer, and stop-watch* | *a multi-function tool which combines spanners, a screwdriver, and a saw*

mul·ti·lat·e·ral /ˌmʌltɨˈlætərəl◂/ *adj* concerning or including more than two groups or nations: *a multilateral agreement* | *multilateral trade* −compare BILATERAL, UNILATERAL − ~**ly** *adv*

mul·ti·lin·gual /ˌmʌltɨˈlɪŋgwəl◂/ *adj* **1** containing or expressed in many different languages: *a multilingual dictionary/advertisement* **2** able to speak many different languages: *a multilingual secretary* −compare POLYGLOT

mul·ti·mil·lio·naire /ˌmʌltɨˌmɪljəˈneəʳ/ *n* a person who has several million pounds or dollars

mul·ti·na·tion·al /ˌmʌltɨˈnæʃənəl◂/ *adj* (of a company) having factories, offices, or other operations in many different countries: *a multinational motor-manufacturing corporation* −**multinational** *n*

mul·ti·ple¹ /ˈmʌltɨpəl/ *adj* [no comp.] including many different parts, types, etc.: *The driver of the crashed car received multiple injuries.* | *multiple ownership* | *multiple births*

multiple² *n* [(of)] a number which contains a smaller number an exact number of times: *3×4=12, 2×6=12; so 12 is a multiple of 3* | *is a* **common multiple** *of 2, 3, 4, and 6.* | *These saving certificates are sold in multiples of £50.* −see also LOWEST COMMON MULTIPLE

multiple choice /ˌ··· ˈ·◂/ *also* **multi-choice**− *adj* (of a test) having several answers from which one is to be chosen. Many school examinations, such as GCSEs in the UK or SATs in the US, have multiple choice questions: *multiple choice exam*

multiple scle·ro·sis /ˌ··· ·ˈ··/ (*abbrev.* **MS**) *n* [U] a serious disease in which, over a period of time, an important covering around the nerves becomes reduced, and which may lead to a loss of feeling and an inability to control movements

multiple store /ˌ··· ˈ·/ *also* **multiple** *infml*− *n esp. BrE for* CHAIN STORE

mul·ti·plex /ˈmʌltɨpleks/ *adj tech* **1** having many parts: *the multiplex eye of the fly* **2** (of a cinema) having more than one SCREEN on which to show films: *If the film is a megahit, it may well be played on 2 of the 12 screens in a multiplex theatre.*

mul·ti·plex·er /ˈmʌltɨpleksəʳ/ *also* **mux** *infml n* an electronic DEVICE that allows many users to exchange information on a single CHANNEL (e.g. between computers)

mul·ti·pli·ca·tion /ˌmʌltɨplɨˈkeɪʃən/ *n* [U] **1** the method of combining two numbers by adding one of them to itself as many times as the other states: *2×4=8 is an example*

of multiplication. −compare DIVISION (5) **2** a big increase made by adding

multiplication ta·ble /ˌ···'·· ˌ··/ *a* TABLE¹ (5)

mul·ti·pli·ci·ty /ˌmʌltɨˈplɪsɨti/ *n* [S;U (of)] (a) large number or great variety: *a multiplicity of ideas* | *the stars in all their multiplicity*

mul·ti·ply /ˈmʌltɨplaɪ/ *v* **1** [I;T (by, TOGETHER)] to combine by multiplication: *to multiply 2 by 3* | *2 multiplied by 3 (2×3)=6* | *to multiply two numbers together* −compare DIVIDE¹ (4) **2** [I;T] to greatly increase in number or amount: *to multiply one's chances of success* | *Spending on military equipment has multiplied in the last five years.* **3** [I] to breed: *When animals have more food, they generally multiply faster.*

mul·ti·pur·pose /ˌmʌltɨˈpɜːpəs◂‖-ˈpɜːr-/ *adj* serving several different purposes: *a multipurpose cloth*

mul·ti·ra·cial /ˌmʌltɨˈreɪʃəl◂/ *adj* consisting of or including several races of people: *a multiracial community/school/ society*

mul·ti·sto·rey /ˌmʌltɨˈstɔːri◂/ *adj* [A] *BrE* (of a building) having several levels or floors: *a big multi-storey car park* −**multi-storey** *n* : *Let's park in the multi-storey.*

mul·ti·tude /ˈmʌltɨtjuːd‖-tuːd/ *n* **1** [C+*sing./pl. v*] a large number: *There is/are a multitude of reasons against it.* **2** [*the*] *also* **multitudes** *pl.*− **a** *old use or bibl* a large crowd **b** ordinary people, esp. considered as uneducated and easily influenced; the MASSES: *politicians who seek the approval of the multitude/the multitudes* **3 cover a** ᵗ**multitude of sins** *humor* to be a common and useful excuse: *Don't say you woke up late − say you were delayed. That covers a multitude of sins!*

mul·ti·tu·di·nous /ˌmʌltɨˈtjuːdɨnəs‖-ˈtuː-/ *adj fml or humor* very many; NUMEROUS: *all my wife's multitudinous relatives* − ~**ly** *adv* − ~**ness** *n* [U]

mum¹ /mʌm/ *BrE* ‖ **mom** *AmE*− *n infml* mother: *Can we go now, Mum?* | *I'll have to ask my mum and dad.* −see FATHER, MOTHER

mum² *adj* [F] not saying or telling anything; keeping silent, usu. about something secret (esp. in the phrase **keep mum**)

mum³ *interj* **mum's the word** this must not be talked about: *Remember it's a secret: mum's the word.*

mum·ble /ˈmʌmbəl/ *v* **1** [I;T] to speak or say unclearly: *Don't mumble − I can't hear what you're saying.* | *The old woman mumbled a prayer.* | *He mumbled something about a letter.* **2** [T] to bite (food) slowly as if without teeth: *an old dog mumbling a bone*

mum·bo jum·bo /ˌmʌmbəʊ ˈdʒʌmbəʊ/ *n* [U] *derog* mysterious talk or activity, esp. of a religious kind, which seems meaningless and confusing

mum·mi·fy /ˈmʌmɨfaɪ/ *v* [T] to preserve (a dead body) as a MUMMY² −**fication** /ˌmʌmɨfɨˈkeɪʃən/ *n* [U]

mum·ming /ˈmʌmɪŋ/ *n* **go mumming** (esp. formerly in Britain) to visit people at Christmas wearing special clothes, esp. to give a performance in a group according to an old custom −**mer** *n*

mum·my¹ /ˈmʌmi/ *BrE* ‖ **mommy, momma** *AmE*− *n* (used esp. by or to young children) mother −compare DADDY; see FATHER, MOTHER

mummy² *n* a dead body preserved from decay by treatment with special substances, esp. as in ancient Egypt

 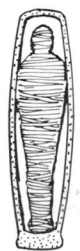

mummy

mum-to-be /ˌ·· · ˈ·/ *n infml* a MOTHER-TO-BE; a PREGNANT woman

mumps /mʌmps/ *n* [(the) U] an infectious illness in which the GLANDs (=organs which send substances into the bloodstream) swell, particularly those around the neck and mouth: *The child has (the) mumps.*

munch /mʌntʃ/ *v* [I (AWAY, at);T] to eat (something hard) with a strong movement of the jaw, making a noise: *munching an apple* | *The horse was munching away at my hat!*

Munch /moŋk/, **Ed·vard** /'edvɑːd‖-ɑːrd/ (1863–1944) a Norwegian painter famous for his pictures describing fear, death, or anxiety, such as *The Scream*

munch·ies /'mʌntʃiz/ *n AmE* **1** [*the*] slight hunger, esp. for a SNACK: *I've got the munchies.* **2** [P] SNACK foods: *I bought some munchies for the party.*

mun·dane /mʌn'deɪn/ *adj* **1** ordinary and uninteresting, with nothing exciting or unusual in it; BANAL: *a mundane existence* **2** of ordinary daily life when compared with that of religion and the spirit; WORLDLY – **– ly** *adv*

mung bean /ˌmʌŋ 'biːn/ *n* a small green bean which is usu. eaten as a bean SPROUT

Mu·nich /'mjuːnɪk/ an industrial city in S Germany; the German name is **München**

Munich A·gree·ment /ˌ··· ·'··/ [*the*] the agreement signed in 1938 between Adolf Hitler from Germany, Mussolini from Italy, Daladier from France, and Neville Chamberlain from Britain. The agreement gave Germany part of Czechoslovakia, and the other countries hoped that this would prevent Hitler from trying to take control of any other areas of land. Chamberlain returned to Britain saying that the agreement would give "peace in our time". In fact, Hitler's army attacked Poland soon afterwards, and the Second World War began. –see also APPEASEMENT, Neville CHAMBERLAIN

mu·ni·ci·pal /mjuː'nɪsɪpəl‖mjuː-/ *adj* concerning (the parts of) a town, city, etc., under its own government: *municipal affairs/buildings* – **– ly** /pli/ *adv*

municipal bond /·,··· ·'·/ *n AmE* a BOND¹ (3) sold by a local authority to raise money for public works such as roads, schools, parks, etc. Municipal bonds earn low interest, but income from them is not taxed.

mu·ni·ci·pal·i·ty /mjuː,nɪsɪ'pælɪti‖mjuː-/ *n* **1** a town, city, or other small area with its own government for local affairs **2** [+*sing./pl. v*] the group of people who manage the local affairs of a town: *The municipality has/have closed the swimming pool.*

mu·nif·i·cent /mjuː'nɪfɪsənt‖mjuː-/ *adj fml* very generous: *a munificent giver/gift* – **– ly** *adv* **––cence** *n* [U]

mu·ni·ments /'mjuːnɪmənts/ *n* [P] *law* legal papers which prove that one owns something, such as a house – **muniment** *adj* [A]

mu·ni·tions /mjuː'nɪʃənz‖mjuː-/ *n* [P] large arms for war; bombs, guns, etc. –**munition** *adj* [A]: *munition workers*

Mun·nings /'mʌnɪŋz/, **Sir Al·fred James** /'ælfrɪd dʒeɪmz/ (1878–1959) an English artist best known for his paintings of horses

Mun·ster /'mʌnstər/ a PROVINCE in the SW of the Republic of Ireland, containing the counties (COUNTY) of Clare, Cork, Kerry, Limerick, Tipperary, and Waterford

Mup·pets /'mʌpɪts/ [*the*] a popular American television show in which the characters are PUPPETS, notably Kermit the Frog and Miss Piggy, which perform along with well-known human entertainers. The characters also appear in a children's television show called *Sesame Street.* –see picture at KERMIT

mu·ral /'mjʊərəl/ *n* a painting which is painted on a wall, either indoors or outdoors – compare FRESCO –**mural** *adj* [A]

mural

mur·der¹ /'mɜːdər‖'mɜːr-/ *n* **1** [C;U] the crime of killing a person intentionally: *to commit murder* | *guilty of murder* | *There have been several murders this year.* | *the murder weapon* | *to read murder stories* –compare MANSLAUGHTER **2** [U] pointless death, esp. caused by carelessness: *It's little short of murder to send them out in the boat on a night like this.* **3** [U] *infml* a very difficult or tiring experience: *It was easy enough to find the fault in the engine, but it was murder putting all the pieces back together.* **4 murder most foul** *lit* very cruel murder –see also **get away with murder** (GET **away with**), **scream/shout blue murder** (BLUE)

murder² *v* [T] **1** to kill (a person) illegally and intentionally: *a murdered man* | (fig., *infml*) *She'll murder you* (=be very angry with you) *when she finds out what you've done!* –see KILL (USAGE) **2** *infml* to spoil or destroy, esp. to spoil (a play, a piece of music, etc.) by a bad performance – **– er** *n* **––ess** *n*

mur·der·ous /'mɜːdərəs‖'mɜːr-/ *adj* intending or likely to cause murder: *murderous intentions* | *a murderous expression on his face* | *a murderous looking knife* – **– ly** *adv* **– –ness** *n* [U]

murder week·end /'·· ·,·‖'·· ,·'·/ *n* an amusement in which people go away for a WEEKEND and see an actor who appears to die. Many small pieces of information (CLUES) are left for the people taking part, and they try to find out who the pretended criminal is.

Mur·doch /'mɜːdɒk‖'mɜːrdɑːk/, **Iris** (1919–) a British writer, born in Ireland, known for her clever, thoughtful and humorous NOVELs such as *The Sea, The Sea* and *The Book and The Brotherhood*

Murdoch, Ru·pert /'ruːpət‖-ərt/ (1931–) an Australian newspaper PUBLISHER and businessman who has established an international network of newspaper and broadcasting companies. In Britain he owns the Sun, News of the World, The Times, Sunday Times, and Today newspapers.

murk /mɜːk‖mɜːrk/ *n* [U] *esp. lit* darkness; GLOOM

murk·y /'mɜːki‖'mɜːr-/ *adj* **1** dark and unpleasant; GLOOMY: *a murky night* | *murky fog* **2** dishonourable; SHAMEFUL: *a murky secret* | *a criminal with a murky past* **––ily** *adv*

mur·mur¹ /'mɜːmər‖'mɜːr-/ *n* **1** [C] a soft low continuous sound: *the murmur of the stream* | *a murmur of voices* **2** [C;U] a sound made by the heart, which may show that it has an illness **3** [S] a complaint: *They obeyed me without a murmur.*

murmur² *v* **1** [I;T] to make a murmur or express in a murmur: *murmuring in her sleep* | *As she denounced the government's policy, the crowd murmured their approval.* **2** [I (**at, against**)] to complain, not officially but in private: *people murmuring against the government*

Mur·phy /'mɜːfi‖'mɜːr-/, **Ed·die** /'edi/ (1961–) an American actor and COMEDIAN who became known for his work on the television programme Saturday Night Live but now is known mostly for his films, such as *Trading Places* and *Beverly Hills Cop* –see colour picture on page 553

Murphy Brown /ˌ··· ·'·/ a US television programmes about an unmarried woman who has a very successful job

Mur·phy's law /ˌ·· ·'·/ *esp. AmE humor* SOD'S LAW

mur·rain /'mʌrɪn‖'mɜːr-/ *n* **1** [U] *not tech* a disease of cattle **2** [S] *old use* a curse: *A murrain on you!*

Mur·ray·field /'mʌrifiːld‖'mɜːr-/ the ground of the Scottish Rugby Union, in Edinburgh

Mur·row /'mʌrəʊ‖'mɜːr-/, **Edward R** (1908–65) an American television news reporter known for reporting from London during the BLITZ in the Second World War

Mus·ca·det /'mʌskədeɪ‖ˌmʌskə'deɪ/ *n* [C;U] a dry white wine from France

mus·ca·tel /ˌmʌskə'tel/ *n* [C;U] a sweet light-coloured wine made from a GRAPE of the same name

mus·cle¹ /'mʌsəl/ *n* **1** [C;U] (one of) the pieces of elastic material in the body which can tighten to produce movement, esp. bending of the joints: *He developed his arm muscles by lifting weights.* **2** [U] strength or power, esp. of the stated kind: *political/military/financial muscle* – see also **not move a muscle** (MOVE¹)

muscle² *v*
muscle in *phr v* [I (**on**)] to force one's way into a place or situation where one is not wanted, usu. so as to gain a share in what is produced

muscle-bound /'·· ·/ *adj* having large, stiff muscles usu. as a result of too much physical exercise

mus·cle·man /'mʌsəlmæn/ *n* **-men** /men/ **1** a man who has developed big muscles by special exercises **2** a man employed to use his size and strength to protect someone, esp. a criminal

Mus·co·vite /'mʌskəvaɪt/ *n* a person from Moscow

mus·cu·lar /'mʌskjŭlər/ *adj* **1** of or consisting of muscles: *a muscular disease* | *the muscular system* **2** having big muscles; strong-looking: *a muscular body* | *He's big and muscular.* — ~**ly** *adv*

muscular dys·tro·phy /ˌmʌskjʊlə ˈdɪstrəfi‖-lər-/ *n* [U] a serious illness in which the muscles become weaker over a period of time

muse[1] /mjuːz/ *v* [I (**over**, (**up**)**on**)] to think deeply, forgetting about the world around one: *She sat musing for hours.* —**musingly** *adv*

muse[2] *n* **1** (*sometimes cap.*) in CLASSICAL MYTHOLOGY, an ancient Greek goddess, one of nine, who each represented an art or science **2** a force or person that seems to help someone to write, paint, etc.; someone's INSPIRATION (2): *a musician whose muse has left him* (=who can no longer write music well)

Mu·sée d'Or·say /ˌmjuːzeɪ dɔːˈseɪ‖mjuːˌzeɪ dɔːr-/ [*the*] a museum in Paris, opened to the public in 1986 and built in a former railway station, which contains Impressionist and Post-Impressionist paintings, SCULPTUREs and Art Nouveau

mu·se·um /mjuːˈziːəm‖mjʊ-/ *n* a building or room where objects are kept and usu. shown to the public because of their scientific, historical, or artistic interest

Museum of Lon·don /·ˌ··· ·ˈ··/ [*the*] a large museum in central London which tells the history of London

Museum of Man·kind /·ˌ··· ·ˈ·/ [*the*] a museum in W central London of the lives and different CULTUREs of people around the world

Museum of Mod·ern Art /·ˌ··· ·ˌ·· ˈ·/ also **MOMA**— [*the*] a museum in New York City which contains one of the world's finest collections of modern art and photography

Museum of the Mov·ing Im·age /·ˌ··· · ·ˌ·· ˈ··/ also **MOMI** [*the*] a MUSEUM on London's South Bank, containing collections of equipment for producing moving pictures, and which has television and LASER shows

museum piece /·ˈ··· ·/ *n* **1** an object interesting enough to keep in a MUSEUM **2** *often humor* an old-fashioned person or thing

mush /mʌʃ/ *n* **1** [S;U] a soft mass of half-liquid, half-solid material, esp. food **2** [U] *AmE* a thick PORRIDGE made with CORN MEAL **3** [U] *infml* words, writing, etc., that are too sweet and sad; SENTIMENTALITY — ~**y** *adj* : *mushy peas* | *a mushy film*

mushroom

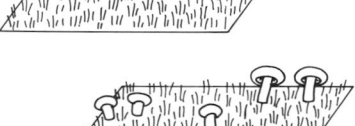

mush·room[1] /ˈmʌʃruːm, -rʊm/ *n* **1** any of several types of FUNGUS, some of which can be eaten, which grow and develop very quickly —compare TOADSTOOL **2** anything that grows and develops fast: *the mushroom development of new housing in this area* **3** the shape of the cloud that forms in the air above a NUCLEAR explosion: *a mushroom cloud* —see picture at NUCLEAR

mushroom[2] *v* [I] **1** to grow and develop fast: *New housing estates have mushroomed on the edge of the town.* **2** [+*adv*/*prep*] to form and spread in the shape of a mushroom: *The smoke mushroomed into the sky.*

mu·sic /ˈmjuːzɪk/ *n* [U] **1** the arrangement of sounds in patterns, esp. to produce a pleasing effect: *a beautiful piece of music* | *This music is by Beethoven.* | *an old poem set to music* (=for which music has been written) | *classical music* | (fig.) *Her voice was music to my ears.* **2** the art of making music: *to study music* | *a music student* **3** a written or printed set of notes: *Give me my music and I'll play it for you.* | *a sheet of music on a* **music stand** —see picture at NOTATION **4** **if music be**

the food of love, play on *quote* a phrase from Shakespeare's play *Twelfth Night* **5** **she shall have music wherever she goes** a line from the NURSERY RHYME *Ride a Cock-Horse* —see also **face the music** (FACE[2])

mu·sic·al[1] /ˈmjuːzɪkəl/ *adj* **1** [A *no comp.*] of or producing music: *musical instruments* | *We joined a musical society.* **2** skilled in and/or fond of music: *a very musical child* **3** like music; pleasant to hear: *her musical voice* —see also MUSICALLY

musical[2] also **musical com·e·dy** /·ˌ··· ·ˈ···/— *n* a play or film with spoken words, songs, and often dances: *a Broadway musical*

musical box /·ˈ··· ·/ *esp. BrE* ‖ also **music box** /·ˈ·· ·/*esp. AmE*— *n* a box containing a clockwork apparatus which plays music when the lid is lifted

musical chairs /·ˌ··· ·ˈ·/ *n* [U] a game often played at children's or family parties, in which music is played and whenever it stops, each person tries quickly to find a chair because there is always one chair too few

musical in·stru·ment /·ˌ··· ·ˈ···/ *n* an INSTRUMENT (2): *Do you play a musical instrument?*

mu·sic·ally /ˈmjuːzɪkli/ *adv* **1** in a musical way: *She laughed musically.* **2** with regard to music: *Musically it's a good song, but I don't like the words.*

music cen·tre /ˈ·· ·ˌ·/ *BrE* ‖ **stereo system** *AmE*— *n* a system containing typically a record player, a radio, a COMPACT DISC player, and a CASSETTE recorder in a single unit

music hall /ˈ··· ·/ *n* **1** [U] *BrE* ‖ **vaudeville** *AmE*— theatre entertainment, esp. in former times, with songs, jokes, acts of skill, etc. —compare VARIETY (4) **2** [C] (in Britain, esp. in former times) a theatre used for such performances

mu·si·cian /mjuːˈzɪʃən‖mjʊ-/ *n* a person who performs on, or writes music for, a musical instrument —compare COMPOSER and see colour picture on page 0000

mu·si·cian·ship /mjuːˈzɪʃənʃɪp‖mjʊ-/ *n* [U] skill in performing or writing music

music vid·e·o /ˈ·· ·ˌ···/ *n* a VIDEO[2] (1) in which the performance of a song is filmed, along with other images that express the ideas or feelings in the music

musk /mʌsk/ *n* [U] a strong smelling substance used in making PERFUMEs[1] (2) — ~**y** *adj* : *her musky perfume* — ~**iness** *n* [U]

mus·ket /ˈmʌskɪt/ *n* a type of gun used in former times

mus·ket·eer /ˌmʌskɪˈtɪər/ *n* a soldier who is armed with a musket —see also THREE MUSKETEERS

mus·ket·ry /ˈmʌskɪtri/ *n* [U] the skill of using small guns in battle

musk·rat /ˈmʌskræt/ also **mus·quash** /ˈmʌskwɒʃ ‖ -wɑːʃ, -wɔːʃ/— *n* a North American rat-like animal that lives in water and is hunted for its fur

Mus·lim /ˈmʌzlɪm, ˈmʊz-, ˈmʌs-/ also **Moslem** (*old-fash*)— *n* a follower of the religion started by Muhammad; a believer in Islam —see also BLACK MUSLIM —**Muslim** *adj* NOTE: **Mohammedan** and **Muhammadan** should not be used as they are considered very offensive by Muslims.

mus·lin /ˈmʌzlɪn/ *n* [U] a very fine thin cotton cloth, used (esp. formerly) for light dresses

muss /mʌs/ *v* [T (UP)] *infml, esp. AmE* to make (esp. the hair) untidy or disordered

mus·sel /ˈmʌsəl/ *n* a small sea animal living inside a shell made of two parts, whose soft body can be eaten as food

Mus·so·li·ni /ˌmʊsəˈliːni/, **Be·ni·to** /beˈniːtəʊ/ (1883–1945) an Italian Fascist DICTATOR, known as **Il Duce**, who led the Italian army during the Second World War. He was killed by the Italians after the war.

must[1] /məst; *strong* mʌst/ *v* 3rd person sing. **must**, *negative short form* **mustn't** [*modal*+*to*-*v*] **1** (*past* usu. **had to**) (shows what it is necessary for one to do, what one ought to do, or what one is forced to do): *I must leave at six today.* (compare *I had to leave at six yesterday.*) *You mustn't tell anyone about this – it's a secret.* | *This information must in no circumstances be given to the general public.* | *The notice says "Prams must be left outside the shop".* | *Must I take this horrible medicine?* | **I must admit** *I don't like her.* | (shows a firm intention) *I must write a letter to the bank.* | (used in making suggestions, etc.) *You must go and see that new film – you'd really enjoy it.* **2** (*past*

must have) to be likely or certain to: *You must feel tired after your long walk.* | *There's nobody here − they must have all gone home.* | *You must be* (=I suppose you are) *the new teacher.* (compare *You can't be the new teacher.*) | *£2000 for that old car?* **You must be joking!** (=Surely you are not serious!) **3** (*past* **must**) to do, in spite of being unwise or unwanted: *If you must drink so much, of course you'll feel sick.* | *Naturally, after I gave her my advice, she must go and do the opposite!* **4 must have** *old use* (in a sentence with **if**) would have had to: *If he had told me I must have helped him.* −see NOT (USAGE)

▷ USAGE 1 **Must** in senses 1 and 3 above is understood in American English, but most speakers find it formal or British-sounding, because **have to** is the more common form. 2 **Must** is used in two ways, to express **a** what is necessary, and **b** what is certain or probable. For sense **a** the past is usually **had to**: *I had to get up early yesterday.* The negative is either **mustn't** (=it is forbidden) or **needn't** (=it is unnecessary): *You* **mustn't** *smoke in the classroom.* | *You* **needn't** *arrive at the airport till 10.30.* −see also NEED[3] (USAGE). For sense **b** the past is **must have** and the negative **can't** (present) or **can't have/couldn't have** (past): *They* **must have** *known about it.* (=I'm sure they knew) | *They* **can't have** *known about it.* (=I'm sure they didn't know) 3 **Ought to** and **should** can be used as less strong forms of **must** in both these senses. Compare *The doctor told me I* **must** *stop smoking.* | *My friends told me I* **ought to/should** *stop smoking*, and in sense **b** *The meal* **must** *be ready by now.* (=I'm sure it is) | *The meal* **ought to/should** *be ready by now.* (=I expect it probably is)◁

must² *n* [S] something which it is necessary or very important to have or experience: *Warm clothes are a must in the mountains.*

must³ *n* [U] the liquid from which wine is made; GRAPE juice

mus·tache /məˈstɑːʃ‖ˈmʌstæʃ/ *n AmE for* MOUSTACHE

mus·ta·chi·o /məˈstɑːʃiəʊ‖ˈmʌˈstæ-/ *n* **-chios** [*usu. pl.*] a large curly MOUSTACHE −**-oed** *adj*

mus·tang /ˈmʌstæŋ/ *n* a small American wild horse; BRONCO

Mustang *n* a fast car built by the Ford company in the US, popular esp. in the 1960s and 1970s

mus·tard /ˈmʌstəd‖-ərd/ *n* [U] (a yellow-flowered plant whose seeds produce) a hot-tasting powder that is mixed with water and eaten in small quantities esp. with meat −see also **as keen as mustard** (KEEN[1])

mustard gas /ˈ··· ·/ *n* [U] a poisonous gas which burns the skin, sometimes used in the First World War

mustard plas·ter /ˈ·· ,··/ *n* a POULTICE containing mustard, used esp. in former times

mus·ter¹ /ˈmʌstər/ *v* [I;T (UP)] *esp. fml or lit* to gather or collect: *The troops mustered on the hill.* | *I mustered (up) my courage and walked onto the stage.* | *trying to muster support for her proposals*

muster² *n* **1** a gathering of people, esp. of soldiers **2 pass muster** to be accepted as satisfactory

Mus·tique /muˈstiːk/ a small island in the Caribbean. It is a popular place for very rich people, including members of the British Royal family, to take holidays.

must·n't /ˈmʌsənt/ *short for:* must not: *We must meet again, mustn't we/(fml) must we not?*

must·y /ˈmʌsti/ *adj* with an unpleasant smell as if old: *musty old books* −**-iness** *n* [U]

mu·ta·ble /ˈmjuːtəbəl/ *adj fml* able or likely to change −**-bility** /ˌmjuːtəˈbɪləti/ *n* [U]

mu·ta·gen /ˈmjuːtədʒən, -dʒen/ *n* a substance that causes a mutation (1) in a living thing

mu·tant /ˈmjuːtənt/ *n* a living thing which has a quality different from any of its parents' qualities and produced by a mutation

mu·ta·tion /mjuːˈteɪʃən/ *n* **1** [C;U] (an example or result of) a process of change in the cells of a living thing producing a new quality in the material or parts of the body, and sometimes causing illness **2** [U] *tech* change in a speech sound, esp. a vowel, because of the sound of the one next to it −see also UMLAUT

mu·ta·tis mu·tan·dis /muːˌtɑːtɪs muːˈtændɪs‖-ˈtɑːndɪs/ *adv*

Lat with or including necessary changes; taking into consideration differences in details

mute¹ /mjuːt/ *adj* **1** silent; without speech: *mute astonishment* **2** *tech* not pronounced: *The word "debt" contains a mute letter.* −−**ly** *adv* −−**ness** *n* [U]

mute² *n* **1** a person who cannot speak **2** *tech* an object used with a musical instrument to make it give a softer sound

mute³ *v* [I] *tech* (of a bird) to pass waste matter from the body

mut·ed /ˈmjuːtɪd/ *adj* **1** (of sound or colours) made softer than usual **2** (esp. of expressions of feeling) less forceful than usual or expected: *muted criticism/enthusiasm*

mu·ti·late /ˈmjuːtɪleɪt/ *v* [T *often pass.*] **1** to seriously damage (esp. a person's body) by removing a part; MAIM: *The kidnapper threatened to mutilate the child if his price was not paid soon.* | *a mutilated body* **2** to spoil completely: *You've mutilated the story by making such big changes.* −−**lation** /ˌmjuːtɪˈleɪʃən/ *n* [C;U]

mu·ti·neer /ˌmjuːtɪˈnɪər, -tən-/ *n* a person who takes part in a mutiny

mu·ti·nous /ˈmjuːtɪnəs, -tən-/ *adj* **1** taking part in a mutiny: *mutinous soldiers* **2** angrily disobedient; REBELLIOUS: *mutinous teenagers* | *the mutinous faces of the staff* −−**ly** *adv*

mu·ti·ny /ˈmjuːtɪni, -təni/ *n* [C;U] (an example of) the act of taking power from the person in charge, esp. from a captain on a ship: *There is talk of mutiny among the sailors.* −**mutiny** *v* [I]

Mutiny on the Boun·ty /ˌ··· ·· ˈ··/, **The** the title of a book and several films about the mutiny in 1789 of SAILORs on the ship *HMS Bounty*. They set their leader, **Captain Bligh**, out to sea in a small boat while they remained on a tropical island in the Pacific.

mutt /mʌt/ *n infml* **1** a fool **2** *esp. AmE* a dog of no particular breed

mut·ter /ˈmʌtər/ *v* [I;T] to speak (usu. angry or complaining words) in a low voice, not easily heard: *He muttered a threat/a complaint.* | *Some members of the government are beginning to mutter about the prime minister.* −**mutter** *n* [S] −−**er** *n*

mut·ton /ˈmʌtn/ *n* [U] **1** the meat from a sheep −see MEAT (USAGE) **2** *BrE* **mutton dressed as lamb** an older person, esp. a woman, trying too hard to look young

mut·ton·chops /ˌmʌtnˈtʃɒps◂‖ˈmʌtntʃɑːps/ also **mutton-chop whis·kers** /ˌ··· ˈ··/− *n* [P] a beard worn on the sides of the cheeks, but not on the chin

mu·tu·al /ˈmjuːtʃuəl/ *adj* **1** having or based on the same relationship one towards the other: *their mutual dislike* (=she dislikes him and he dislikes her) | *I like her and I hope the feeling is mutual.* (=I hope she likes me) **2** equally shared by each one: *mutual interests* | *our mutual friend John* (=who is a friend of yours, and a friend of mine, too) | *an agreement that will be for our mutual benefit* −−**ly** *adv*: *The two beliefs are* **mutually exclusive.** (=if you hold one of them it is impossible to hold the other) −−**ity** /ˌmjuːtʃuˈæləti/ *n* [U]

mutual fund /ˈ··· ·/ *n AmE for* UNIT TRUST

mux /mʌks/ *n infml* MULTIPLEXER

Muy·bridge /ˈmaɪbrɪdʒ/, **Ead·weard** /ˈedwəd‖-ərd/ (1830−1904) an English photographer who recorded the movement esp. of animals by taking sets of photographs with several cameras arranged in a row

mu·zak /ˈmjuːzæk/ *n* [U] *tdmk* (*often cap.*) recorded background music played continuously in airports, hotels, shops, etc.. Muzak is disliked by some people and the word is sometimes used for music which is unexciting and which people do not really pay attention to.

muz·zle¹ /ˈmʌzəl/ *n* **1** the front part of an animal's face, with the nose and mouth −see picture at HORSE **2** a covering fastened round an animal's mouth, to prevent it from biting **3** the front end of a gun barrel −see picture at GUN

muzzle² *v* [T] **1** to put a muzzle on (an animal) **2** to force to keep silent: *The newspapers that opposed the junta were effectively muzzled by strict censorship laws. See picture on page 878*

muz·zy /ˈmʌzi/ *adj* **1** not clear; blurred (BLUR[2]): *The television picture's muzzy.* **2** not thinking clearly, perhaps

muzzle

because of illness or alcohol: *a muzzy head* —**-zily** *adv*
—**-ziness** *n* [U]

MW *written abbrev. for:* MEDIUM WAVE

my /maɪ/ *determiner (possessive form of* I) **1** of or belong-
ing to me: *my car | my mother | You should take my ad-
vice. | That's my problem, not yours.* **2** (used to show sur-
prise or pleasure): *My (my)! What a clever boy you are!*
3 my dear *polite or humor* (a form of address): *My dear
sir, I'm so sorry. | Come in, my dear.*

Myan·mar /ˈmjænmɑːʳ/ also **Myanma** /-mɑː/— a country
on the Bay of Bengal in SE Asia, called **Burma** until 1988;
capital Yangon; population 40,810,000 (1989) —
Myanmarese /ˌmjænmɑːˈriːz◂/ *n, adj*

My·ce·nae /maɪˈsiːni/ a city in ancient Greece, where King
Agamemnon is supposed to have lived. In the late 19th
century many beautiful and ancient objects were found
in the place where the destroyed city had once been.

my·col·o·gy /maɪˈkɒlədʒi‖-ˈkɑː-/ *n* [U] the study of fungi
(FUNGUS)

My Coun·try 'Tis of Thee /· ˌ··· ˌ· · ˈ·/ a PATRIOTIC song
learned by American children. It has the same tune as
God Save the Queen and begins: *My country 'tis of thee,
sweet land of liberty, of thee I sing.*

My Fair La·dy /ˌ· · ˈ··/ a musical play and film about a
COCKNEY woman who is taught to speak and act in an
UPPER-CLASS way by a bad-tempered PROFESSOR. It is based
on the play *Pygmalion* by George Bernard Shaw.

My Lai mas·sa·cre /ˌmiː laɪ ˈmæsəkəʳ/ [the] an event in the
VIETNAM WAR in 1968 in which US soldiers cruelly killed
the people of the village of My Lai, mostly old people,
women, and children. The officer who ordered the killing was sentenced to life in prison, later reduced to 20
years.

my·nah , myna /ˈmaɪnə/ also **mynah bird** /ˈ··· ·/— a large
dark-coloured bird from Asia that can learn to make
sounds like words

MYOB /ˌem waɪ əʊ ˈbiː/ *v* [infinitive and imperative only]
AmE infml mind your own business; to avoid getting involved in other peoples' affairs: *He asked me where I got
the fifty bucks and I told him to MYOB.*

my·o·pi·a /maɪˈəʊpiə/ *n* [U] *fml* inability to see distant objects clearly —**pic** /maɪˈɒpɪk‖-ˈɑːpɪk/ *adj* : (fig.) *myopic
minds* —**pically** /kli/ *adv*

myr·i·ad /ˈmɪriəd/ *adj, n esp. lit* a great and varied number
(of): *a myriad stars | Myriads of followers joined Gandhi's
cause.*

myrrh /mɜːʳ/ *n* [U] a brown GUM² (1) obtained from trees,
which is used in making PERFUME and INCENSE —see also
gold, frankincense, and myrrh (GOLD¹ (5))

myr·tle /ˈmɜːtl‖ˈmɜːr-/ *n* a small tree with shiny green
leaves and sweet-smelling white flowers

my·self /maɪˈself/ *pron* **1** (*reflexive form of* I): *I hurt my-
self. | I'm pleased with myself.* **2** (*strong form of* I): *I'll
do it myself, if you won't. | My husband and myself are
both doctors. | I myself wrote it. | I'm afraid I can't help
you, I'm a stranger here myself.* (=like you) **3** *infml* (in)
my usual state of mind or body: *I feel more myself today.*
(=not so ill as before) **4 (all) by myself** alone, without
help: *I carried it all by myself.* **5 to myself** for my private use; not shared: *a bedroom to myself* —see YOURSELF
(USAGE)

mys·te·ri·ous /mɪˈstɪəriəs/ *adj* **1** full of mystery; not easily understood: *The mysterious disappearance of my
brother upset everyone.* **2** secret; hiding one's intentions:
He's being very mysterious about his future plans. — ~**ly**
adv — ~**ness** *n* [U]

mys·te·ry /ˈmɪstəri/ *n* **1** [C] something which cannot be
explained or understood: *Her sudden disappearance was
a complete mystery. | It's a mystery to me how she ever
passed that exam!* **2** [U] a strange secret nature or quality: *stories full of mystery* **3** [C *often pl.*] a religious teaching or belief that is beyond human understanding or that
is kept secret: *the ultimate mystery of God* **4** [C] an
invented story about crime and murder: *I enjoy (reading)
a good mystery.*

mystery play /ˈ··· ·/ *n* a MIRACLE PLAY

mystery tour /ˈ··· ·/ *n* a pleasure trip, usu. by bus, in which
the travellers do not know where they will be taken

mys·tic /ˈmɪstɪk/ *n* a person who practises mysticism

mys·tic·al /ˈmɪstɪkəl/ also **mystic**— *adj* **1** concerning
mysticism **2** of hidden religious or magic power: *mystical ceremonies* — ~**ly** /kli/ *adv*

mys·ti·cis·m /ˈmɪstɪsɪzəm/ *n* [U] the attempt to gain, or
practice of gaining, a knowledge of real truth and union
with God by prayer and MEDITATION

mys·ti·fy /ˈmɪstɪfaɪ/ *v* [T] to make (someone) unable to understand or explain something; fill with wonder; com-
pletely BEWILDER: *I'm quite mystified — where can it be? |
a strange case that mystified the police* —**fication**
/ˌmɪstɪfɪˈkeɪʃən/ *n* [U]

mys·tique /mɪˈstiːk/ *n* [*usu. sing.*] a special quality that
makes a person or thing seem mysterious and different,
esp. causing admiration: *the mystique of the film industry*

myth /mɪθ/ *n* **1** [C] an ancient story that is based on popular beliefs or that explains natural or historical events
2 [U] such stories generally: *an idea common in myth* **3**
[C] a widely believed but false story or idea: *the myth of
male superiority | This report should* **explode the myth**
(=show it to be false) *that high wages cause unemployment.* —compare LEGEND (1,2)

myth·i·cal /ˈmɪθɪkəl/ *adj* **1** of or in a myth: *mythical heroes
of ancient Greece* **2** not real; imagined or invented

myth·o·lo·gi·cal /ˌmɪθəˈlɒdʒɪkəl‖-ˈlɑː-/ *adj* **1** concerning
the study of myths **2** in a myth; MYTHICAL (1)

my·thol·o·gy /mɪˈθɒlədʒi‖-ˈθɑː-/ *n* [C;U] myths in general
and the beliefs which they contain: *He studies Greek and
Roman mythology.* —**gist** *n*

myx·o·ma·to·sis /ˌmɪksəməˈtəʊsɪs/ *n* [U] an illness which
infects rabbits, usu. killing them

N

N /en/ **N's, n's** *or* **Ns, ns**– the 14th letter of the English alphabet

n *written abbrev. for:* **1** noun **2** note

N *written abbrev. for:* north(ern)

'n' /ən/ *short for:* and: *rock 'n' roll*

N/A , n/a *abbrev.* **1** not APPLICABLE **2** not available

NAACP /ˌen dʌbəl ˌeɪ siː ˈpiː/ [*the*] National Association for the Advancement of Colored People; an American organization that defends and works for the improvement of CIVIL RIGHTS for black people

Naaf·i /ˈnæfi/ [*the*] a shop or eating place in any British military establishment in Britain or abroad –compare PX

naan /nɑːn/ *n* see NAN

nab /næb/ *v* **-bb-** [T] *infml* **1** to catch (a criminal) in an act of wrongdoing; ARREST: *He was nabbed while running out of the bank.* **2** to get or catch quickly: *Run with this letter and nab the postman.*

Na·bis·co /nəˈbɪskəʊ/ the largest American maker of processed (PROCESS² (1)) foods, known esp. for its breakfast foods and BISCUITs

na·bob /ˈneɪbɒb‖-bɑːb/ *n* **1** a governor of a part of India during the Mogul Empire **2** (in the 18th and 19th centuries) an Englishman who became rich in India and returned to Europe **3** *derog* a rich or powerful man

Na·bo·kov /nəˈbəʊkɒf‖-ˈbɔːkəf/, **Vlad·i·mir** /ˈvlædɪ̩mɪəʳ/ (1899–1977) an American writer, who was born in Russia and lived most of his life in Europe. He is best known for his NOVEL *Lolita*. –see also LOLITA

na·celle /nəˈsel, nə-/ *n tech* an enclosure containing one of the engines on an aircraft

na·chos /ˈnɑːtʃəʊz/ *n* [P] a hot-tasting Mexican dish of small pieces of fried (FRY) corn TORTILLAs covered with melted cheese and often beans and tomatoes (TOMATO)

na·cre /ˈneɪkəʳ/ *n* [U] *esp. BrE* MOTHER-OF-PEARL

Na·der /ˈneɪdəʳ/, **Ralph** /rælf/ (1934–) an American lawyer and political activist. He is best known for calling attention to government waste, environmental problems, and the rights of people who buy goods and services.

na·dir /ˈneɪdɪəʳ‖-dər/ *n* [*usu. sing.*] the lowest point of hope or fortune: *With this election defeat, the party's fortunes reached their nadir.*

naff¹ /næf/ *adj BrE sl* (of things, ideas, behaviour, etc.) foolish or worthless, esp. in a way that shows a lack of good judgment or good TASTE¹(1): *a really naff film*

naff² *v BrE sl*
naff off *phr v* [I, *usu. imperative*] to go away: *I just told him to naff off.*

nag¹ /næg/ *v* **-gg-** [I (at);T] **1** to annoy or try to persuade (someone) by continuously finding fault and complaining: *I wish you'd stop nagging (at me)!* | *The children are always nagging me for new toys.* | *They finally nagged me into taking them to the zoo.* (=persuaded me by nagging) [+obj+to-v] *He's been nagging me all week to mend his shirt.* **2** to cause to suffer continuous worry or discomfort: *a nagging headache* | *nagged by worries/doubts* – ~ger *n*

nag² *n infml* a person who has the habit of nagging

nag³ *n infml* a horse, esp. one that is old or in bad condition

Na·ga·sa·ki /ˌnægəˈsɑːki/ a city and port in W Kyushu, Japan, which suffered severe damage and loss of life when the second US atomic bomb was dropped there in 1945

Na·gor·no-Kar·a·bakh /nəˌgɔːnəʊ kərəˈbɑːk, -ɑːx‖-ɔːr-/ a REGION in S Azerbaijan, officially called the Nagorno-Karabakh Autonomous Region; capital Stepanakert. Many of its people are ETHNICALLY Armenian and there has been trouble between the different ethnic groups and between Azerbaijan and Armenia, which borders on it.

nai·ad /ˈnaɪæd‖ˈneɪæd, ˈnaɪ-, -əd/ *n* **-ads** *or* **-ades** /ədiːz/ a female spirit in ancient Greek stories who lived in a lake, stream, or river; water NYMPH –compare OREAD

nail¹ /neɪl/ *n* **1** a thin pointed piece of metal for hammering into a piece of wood, usu. to fasten the wood to something else **2** a fingernail or toenail: *Does your Mum let you paint your nails?* –see pictures at FOOT and HAND **3** **a nail in someone's coffin** something bad which will bring a person's ruin one step nearer **4 hard/tough as nails** *infml* **a** having a body in very good condition **b** without any tender feelings **5 (pay cash) on the nail** *infml* (to pay for something) at once –see also **hit the nail on the head** (HIT¹ (14)), **tooth and nail** (TOOTH)

nail² *v* [T] **1** [+*obj*+*adv/prep*] to fasten (as) with a nail or nails: *to nail a sign to the post* | *to nail the lid down* | *We nailed up the windows of the old house.* **2** *sl* to catch or trap: *They finally nailed the thief.* **3** *infml* to show clearly the falseness of (an idea or statement); EXPOSE (2) (esp. in the phrase **to nail a lie**)
nail sbdy. ↔ **down** *phr v* [T] **(to)** *infml* to force (a person) to state clearly their intentions or wishes: *Before they repair the car, nail them down to a price.* (=make them tell you how much it will cost)

nail-bi·ter /ˈ· ˌ·-/ *n* **1** a person who is unable to keep from biting his/her fingernails **2** *infml* a very exciting story, film, etc. which causes SUSPENSE: *That detective story was a real nail-biter – we never knew till the end who the murderer was.*

nail-bit·ing /ˈ· ··/ *adj* causing excitement and anxiety; full of SUSPENSE: *a nail-biting finish to the tennis final*

nail·brush /ˈneɪlbrʌʃ/ *n* a small stiff brush for cleaning hands, and esp. fingernails –see picture at BRUSH

nail file /ˈ· ·/ *n* a small instrument with a rough surface for shaping fingernails

nail pol·ish /ˈ· ˌ··/ *also* **nail var·nish** *BrE*– *n* [U] coloured or transparent liquid which is painted on women's nails, esp. fingernails, to give them a hard shiny surface and make them look attractive

nail scis·sors /ˈ· ˌ··/ *n* [P] a small pair of scissors for cutting fingernails or toenails –see PAIR (USAGE)

Nairn·shire /ˈneənʃəʳ‖ˈneərn-/ a former COUNTY in NE Scotland, now part of Highland REGION

Nai·ro·bi /naɪˈrəʊbi/ the capital of Kenya in E Africa

na·ive , **naïve** /naɪˈiːv‖nɑːˈiːv/ *adj* **1** without experience of social rules or behaviour, esp. because one is young: *The youngest boy was laughed at for his naive remarks.* **2** too willing to believe without proof: *He told her he was a close friend of the royal family, and she was naive enough to believe him.* – ~**ly** *adv*

na·i·ve·ty , **naivety**, **-eté** /naɪˈiːvəti‖nɑːˌiːvəˈteɪ/ *n* [U] the quality of being naive: *Her naivety is endearing/appalling.*

Na·ji·bul·lah /ˌnɑːdʒɪˈbʊlə/, **Dr** (1947–) the president of Afghanistan 1987–1992

na·ked /ˈneɪkɪd/ *adj* **1** (of a person's body, or part of it) not covered by clothes: *He was naked to the waist.* (=wore nothing above his waist) **2** not covered by the usual covering: *a naked hillside* (=without trees) | *a naked light* (=without glass over it) **3** [A] not hidden or made less clear; plain to see and perhaps shocking: *the naked truth* | *naked aggression* **4 with the naked eye** without any instrument to help one see: *too small/too far away to see with the naked eye.* – ~**ly** *adv* – ~**ness** *n* [U]

Naked Ape /ˌ·· ˈ·/, **The** [*the*] a book by Desmond Morris, examining similarities between the behaviour of humans and of APEs

NALGO /ˈnælgəʊ/ the National and Local Government Officers Association; one of the largest TRADE UNIONs in Britain

'Nam /nɑːm/ *AmE infml* (*short for*) VIETNAM

Na·math /ˈneɪməθ/, **Joe** /dʒəʊ/ (1943–) an American FOOTBALL (2) player who is also known for appearing in an advertisement for PANTY HOSE

nam·by-pam·by /ˌnæmbi ˈpæmbi◂/ *adj derog* too weak, childish, or easily frightened –**namby-pamby** *n*

name¹ /neɪm/ *n* **1** [C] the word(s) that someone or something is called or known by: *Her name is Mary Wilson; her first name is Mary.* | *What's the name of that river?* | *Do you know a boy by the name of* (=called) *David?* | *Although it's a big company, the director knows all the staff by name.* (=knows all their names) | *Please write your full name and address on the form.* –see also CHRISTIAN NAME, FIRST NAME, MIDDLE NAME, PEN NAME, SURNAME

2 [C] a usu. offensive title for someone, often connected with their character: *to call someone names* (=say bad or rude things about them) **3** [S (**for**)] the opinion others have of one; REPUTATION: *The company has a (good) name for reliability.* | *The restaurant got a bad name because of its slow service.* | *She* **made a name for herself**/**made her name** (=became famous) *as a painter.* **4** [C] *sl* a well-known person (esp. in the phrases **big name**, **famous name**, etc.): *A big-name band will play at the wedding.* | *There were several famous names in the audience.* **5 in name only** by title but not in fact: *She is his wife in name only; she lives abroad most of the time.* | *a democracy in name only* **6 in the name of** by the right of or for the advantage of: *Open the door, in the name of the law!* | *cruel animal experiments that are carried on in the name of science* **7 take someone's name in vain** *often humor* to speak disrespectfully about someone, without their knowledge, to another person **8 the name of the game** *sl* the most important quality or object: *In fishing, patience is the name of the game.* **9 to one's name** *infml* (esp. with **no**, **not**, etc.) (esp. of money) as one's property: *He hasn't a penny to his name.* **10 under the name (of)** using (a name) different from one's own: *H. H. Munro wrote under the name (of) Saki.* —see also **a rose by any other name** (ROSE² (4))

name² *v* [T] **1** to give a name to: *He was named after* (=given the same name as) *his father.* | *(AmE) The college is named for* (=given the same name as) *George Washington.* [+obj+n] *They named their daughter Sarah.* (=gave her the name Sarah) **2** to say what the name of (someone or something) is: *Can you name this plant?* | *The two murder victims have not yet been named (by the police).* | *Clothes, furniture, books —* **you name it**, *they sell it!* (=they sell everything that you could imagine) | *She has secret information about this scandal, and has threatened to* **name names.** (=give the actual names of people who have a part in it) **3** [(**as**, **for**)] to choose or appoint: *She's been named as the successor to the present manager.* | *We've named August 23rd for our wedding day.* | *"How much will you sell this for?" "Name your own price."* [+obj+n] *The President named him Secretary of State.*

Name *n* one of **the Names**, wealthy people who take the financial risk in an insurance contract set up by an UNDERWRITER at Lloyds of London. The Names usu. expect to make a profit, but in the early 1990s, owing to a number of very serious accidents, some of the Names lost a lot of money.

name day /ˈ· ·/ *n old use* the date each year when the Christian church honours the SAINT (=holy person) that one is named after —compare SAINT'S DAY

name-drop /ˈneɪmdrɒp‖-drɑːp/ *v* -**pp**- [I] *infml derog* to mention famous or important people's names in conversation to make it seem that one knows them personally — ~ **per** *n* — ~ **ping** *n* [U]

name-less /ˈneɪmləs/ *adj* **1** not known by name: ANONYMOUS: *the work of a nameless 13th century poet* | *It was given to me by a certain person* **who shall be nameless.** (=whose name I will not tell) **2** which has not been given a name: *some new and nameless plants* | *nameless fears* (=not clear enough to describe) **3** not marked by a name: *a nameless grave* **4** too terrible to name: *nameless crimes*

name-ly /ˈneɪmli/ *adv* (and) that is (to say): *Only one person can do the job, namely you.* | *There is one more topic to discuss, namely the question of your salary.* —compare I.E.; see VIZ. (USAGE)

▷ USAGE Compare **namely** and **that is to say** (often abbreviated to **i.e.**). Both terms can be used when you want to make clearer the meaning of something already said, but **namely** is the usual term before an expression which is more specific than what has already been said: *We visited two ancient cities,* **namely** *Nimes and Arles.* Before an expression which is less specific than what has already been said you can use only **i.e.**: *We visited Nimes and Arles, i.e. two ancient cities.* Use **i.e.** before an explanation which forms a complete sentence: *Arabic is written in the opposite direction to English, i.e. it is written from right to left.*◁

name-plate /ˈneɪmpleɪt/ *n* a piece of metal or plastic fastened to something, showing the name of the owner or maker, or the person who lives in a place — see also DOORPLATE

name-sake /ˈneɪmseɪk/ *n* **1** one of two or more people with the same name: *I often get letters meant for my namesake down the street; it's confusing that we're both called John Smith.* | *We're namesakes.* **2** a person who is named after someone else: *My niece is my namesake.*

Na-mib-i-a /nəˈmɪbiə/ a country in SW Africa, also known as **South West Africa**, bordered by Angola to the N, Zambia to the NE, Botswana to the E, South Africa to the SE, and the Atlantic Ocean to the W; capital Windhoek; population 1,300,000 (1990) —**bian** *n, adj*

nan , **naan** /nɑːn/ [U] *n* a type of bread eaten with Indian food

nan-ny /ˈnæni/ *n* **1** a woman employed to take care of the children in a family, usu. in the children's own home
▶ CULTURAL NOTE The STEREOTYPE of a nanny is a middle-aged woman employed by rich people. She is very firm, knows many old sayings and stories, calls the children "Master" or "Miss", and speaks to them in a particular way: *Now, Master James, if we* (= you) *don't eat our cabbage, we don't get any pudding, do we?* In stories she is often more important to the children than their mother. ◀
2 also **nan** /næn/ *BrE—* (used by or to children) a grandmother: *Give Nanny a kiss!* | *It's my nan's birthday tomorrow.*

nanny goat /ˈ· ·/ *n* (used esp. by or to children) a female goat —compare BILLY GOAT

nanny state /ˈ· ˌ·/ *n BrE derog* a government which controls the lives of its citizens while offering them a reasonable standard of living

nano- —see WORD FORMATION

nan-o-tech-nol-o-gy /ˌnænəʊtekˌnɒlədʒi‖-ˌnɑː-/ *n* [C;U] machinery, methods, etc. which can perform processes extremely quickly or make or measure objects which are extremely small: *Computer circuitry now includes advanced processes made possible by nanotechnology.*

Nan-tuck-et /nænˈtʌkɪt/ an island off the coast of Massachusetts, US, where many wealthy people have summer homes

nap¹ /næp/ *n* a short sleep, esp. during the day: *Father always takes/has a nap in the afternoon.* —compare SIESTA

nap² *v* -**pp**- [I] **1** to take a nap **2 catch someone napping** *infml* to find, or take advantage of, someone when they are unprepared or not doing their duty

nap³ *n* [*usu. sing.*] the soft furry surface on some cloth and leather, made by brushing the short fine threads or hairs in one direction —compare PILE³

na-palm /ˈneɪpɑːm‖-pɑːm, -pɑːlm/ *n* [U] a jelly made from petrol, which burns fiercely and is used in bombs

nape /neɪp/ *n* [*usu. sing.*] the back (of the neck)

naph-tha /ˈnæfθə/ *n* [U] any of various liquid HYDROCARBONs used for starting fires, removing spots of dirt from clothes, etc.

nap-kin /ˈnæpkɪn/ *n* **1** a usu. square piece of cloth or paper used for protecting one's clothes and for cleaning one's hands and lips during a meal —see picture at PLACE SETTING **2** *BrE fml* a baby's NAPPY

napkin ring /ˈ· ˌ·/ *n* a small ring in which a napkin is rolled and kept for the use of one particular person

Na-ples /ˈneɪpəlz/ an industrial city and port in S central Italy, on the Bay of Naples

Na-po-le-on /nəˈpəʊliən/ (1769–1821) the EMPEROR of France from 1804 to 1815, whose full name was Napoleon Bonaparte. He was a powerful military leader, defeating many other European countries in the Napoleonic Wars and building a European EMPIRE, and also a skilled politician, inventing the **Code Napoléon** which remains a guide to law in several European countries today. He attacked Russia in 1812 but was defeated. On his way back (the **Retreat from Moscow**) many soldiers died from cold and hunger. He was finally defeated at the Battle of Waterloo and died in EXILE. He is believed to have used the phrase "not tonight, Josephine" when refusing his

Napoleon

lover Josephine's desire for sex. —see colour picture on page 1015

Na·po·le·on·ic Wars /nə₁pəʊlɪɒnɪk ˈwɔːz‖-ɑːnɪk ˈwɔːrz/ [*the* + P] (1799–1815) the wars fought between France, under the control of Napoleon Bonaparte, and other European countries, esp. Austria, Prussia, Russia, and Britain

nap·py /ˈnæpi/ *BrE* ‖ **diaper** *AmE*— *n* a piece of soft cloth or paper worn between the legs and fastened around the waist of a baby to hold its EXCRETA (=liquid and solid waste)

nappy rash /ˈ·· ·/ *BrE* ‖ **diaper rash** *AmE*— *n* [U] soreness of the skin between a baby's legs caused by the contents of its nappy

narc /nɑːk ‖ nɑːrk/ *n AmE for* NARK[1]

nar·cis·sis·m /ˈnɑːsɪsɪzəm‖ˈnɑːr-/ *n* [U] too great love for one's own abilities or physical appearance —**-sist** *n* —**-sistic** /₁nɑːsɪˈsɪstɪk◂‖₁nɑːr-/ *adj*

nar·cis·sus /nɑːˈsɪsəs‖nɑːr-/ *n* **-suses** *or* **-si** /saɪ/ a white or yellow spring flower, such as the DAFFODIL

Narcissus in CLASSICAL MYTHOLOGY, a very attractive young man who fell in love with his own REFLECTION and died as a result. He was turned into a flower.

nar·cot·ic[1] /nɑːˈkɒtɪk‖nɑːrˈkɑː-/ *n* [*often pl.*] a drug which in small amounts causes sleep or takes away pain, and in large amounts is harmful and habit-forming: *He was sent to prison on a narcotics charge.* (=an offence concerning selling or using these drugs)

narcotic[2] *adj* **1** taking away pain or esp. causing sleep: *a narcotic drink* **2** [A *no comp.*] of or related to drugs: *narcotic addiction*

nark[1] /nɑːk‖nɑːrk/ *also* **narc** *AmE*— *n sl* a person who mixes with criminals and secretly reports on them to the police; a STOOLPIGEON

nark[2] *v* [T *usu. pass.*] *BrE sl* to annoy; make angry: *I was rather narked at|by what she said.*

nark·y /ˈnɑːki‖ˈnɑːr-/ *adj BrE sl* bad-tempered

Nar·ni·a /ˈnɑːniə‖ˈnɑːr-/ an imaginary land of magic people and animals visited by four children in *The Lion, the Witch and the Wardrobe* and other books written by C S Lewis

nar·rate /nəˈreɪt‖ˈnæreɪt, næˈreɪt, nə-/ *v* [T] *fml* to tell (a story); describe (an event or events) in order

nar·ra·tion /nəˈreɪʃən‖næ-, nə-/ *n* [C;U] *fml* (the telling of) a story

nar·ra·tive /ˈnærətɪv/ *n* **1** [C;U] *rather fml* that which is narrated; account of events: *a narrative of their exciting journey* | *Narrative makes up most of the book.* **2** [U] the art of narrating: *The writer had great skill in narrative.* —**narrative** *adj* : *a narrative poem*

nar·ra·tor /nəˈreɪtə‖ˈnæreɪ-, næˈreɪtər, nə-/ *n* **1** a person in some books, television shows, plays, etc., who tells the story or explains what is happening **2** *fml* a person who tells a story; STORYTELLER

nar·row[1] /ˈnærəʊ/ *adj* **1** small from one side to the other, esp. in comparison with length or with what is usual; not wide: *a narrow road|river* | *a gateway too narrow for a car to get through* —compare BROAD[1] (1) **2** limited in range or effect: *narrow ideas about religion* | *The decision was taken for narrow economic reasons, without considering its social effects.* —see also NARROW-MINDED **3** almost not enough or only just successful: *to win by a narrow majority* | *a narrow escape* —compare CLOSE[2] (7) **4** *fml* careful and thorough; PAINSTAKING: *a narrow examination of the facts* —see also NARROWLY, NARROWS, STRAIGHT AND NARROW; see THIN[1] (USAGE) —~**ness** *n* [U]

narrow[2] *v* **1** [I;T] to make or become narrower: *The river narrows at this point.* | *new tax laws that will narrow the gap between rich and poor* **2** [T (DOWN)] to limit the range of; RESTRICT: *The police have now narrowed down their list of suspects.* —compare WIDEN

narrow boat /ˈ·· ₁·/ *n BrE* a long narrow boat for use on CANALs

narrow gauge /ˈ·· ₁·/ *n* a size of railway track of less than standard width, the most famous British examples of which are in Wales, e.g. the Tal-y-Lyn and Ffestiniog Railways —see also GAUGE[1] (3)

nar·row·ly /ˈnærəʊli/ *adv* **1** only just; hardly: *We narrowly missed hitting the other car.* **2** *fml* in a thorough and usu.

doubting way: *The teacher questioned the boy narrowly about why he was late.*

narrow-mind·ed /₁·· ˈ···◂‖₁·· ₁··/ *adj derog* showing unwillingness to accept or understand new or different ideas, customs, etc.; PREJUDICED —opposite **broadminded**; compare SMALL-MINDED —~**ness** *n* [U]

nar·rows /ˈnærəʊz/ *n* [P] (*often cap. as part of name*) a narrow passage between two larger areas of water: *the Narrows of New York harbour*

narrow squeak /₁·· ˈ·/ *BrE* ‖ **narrow miss** *AmE*— *n infml* a situation in which something dangerous or very unpleasant is only just avoided: *The bus missed crashing into the cyclist by a narrow squeak.*

na·ry /ˈneəri/ *adv AmE infml* NOT (4); not one: *I looked all over the house but there was nary a soul* (=not a person) *anywhere.*

NASA /ˈnæsə/ National Aeronautics and Space Administration; a US government organization that controls space travel and the scientific study of space

na·sal[1] /ˈneɪzəl/ *n, adj tech* (a speech sound such as /m/, /n/, or /ŋ/) made through the nose

nasal[2] *adj* **1** of the nose: *to breathe through the nasal passage* **2** making nasal sounds: *His voice is very nasal.* —~**ly** /ˈneɪzəli/ *adv*

nas·cent /ˈnæsənt/ *adj fml* coming into existence or starting to develop: *nascent ability in music*

Nash /næʃ/, **John·ny** /ˈdʒɒni‖ˈdʒɑː-/ (1940–   ) an American singer and song-writer known for such songs as *I Can See Clearly Now*

Nash, Og·den /ˈɒgdən‖ˈɔːg-/ (1902–71) an American poet who wrote amusing poems

Nash·ville /ˈnæʃvɪl/ the capital city of the state of Tennessee, US, famous as the centre of the COUNTRY AND WESTERN music industry —see colour map on pages 1374–5

Nas·ser /ˈnæsər/, **Ga·mal Ab·dal** /gəˈmɑːl ˈæbdəl/ (1918–70) an Egyptian politician and army officer who was the first president of the republic of Egypt (1956–70)

Na·sta·se /nəˈstɑːzi/, **Il·ie** /ˈɪli/ (1946–   ) a tennis player originally from Romania

nas·tur·tium /nəˈstɜːʃəm‖-ɜːr-/ *n* a common garden plant with orange, yellow, or red flowers and circular leaves

nas·ty /ˈnɑːsti‖ˈnæsti/ *adj* **1 a** angry or threatening: *a nasty temper* | *He* **turned nasty** (=started to threaten me) *when I said I couldn't pay him.* **b** unkind; mean; MALICIOUS: *Don't be so nasty to her!* | *saying nasty things about their neighbours* **2** very ugly or unpleasant to see, taste, smell, etc.: *cheap and nasty furniture* | *nasty weather* | *a nasty smell* **3** dangerous or painful; severe: *a nasty accident with one person killed* | *a nasty cut on the head* | *It gave me a nasty shock.* | *a nasty situation* **4** morally bad or offensive; OBSCENE: *You've got a nasty mind.* —see also VIDEO NASTY —**·tily** *adv* —**·tiness** *n* [U]

na·tal /ˈneɪtl/ *adj* [A] (*esp. in comb.*) connected with someone's birth: (*pomp*) *her natal day* (=birthday) | *pre- and post-natal care* (=care before and after birth)

na·tion /ˈneɪʃən/ *n* [C+*sing./pl. v*] **1** a large group of people living in one area and usu. having an independent government: *The President spoke on radio to the nation.* | *The whole nation is|are rejoicing.* —compare COUNTRY[1] (1) **2** a large group of people with the same race and language: *the Cherokee|Kurdish nation* —see RACE (USAGE)

Nation, Car·rie /ˈkæri/ (1846–1911) an American social activist who believed that people should not drink alcohol because of its harmful effects. She often went to bars and damaged them.

na·tion·al[1] /ˈnæʃənəl/ *adj* **1** of or being a nation, esp. as opposed to **a** any of its parts: *a national newspaper* (=one read everywhere in the country) | *This is a local problem not a national one.* **b** another nation or other nations: *The national news comes after the international news.* | *trade protection policies that will safeguard our national interests* **2** owned or controlled by the central government of a country: *a national bank* | *the National Health Service* —~**ly** *adv*

national[2] *n* a person, esp. someone abroad, who belongs to another, usu. stated, country: *American nationals in England* | *Foreign nationals were asked to leave the country.* —compare ALIEN[2] (2), CITIZEN (2), SUBJECT[1] (5)

National 1 [*the*] the GRAND NATIONAL **2** [*the*] the NATIONAL

THEATRE **3** one of the airports serving the Washington DC area, used mostly for flights within the US

national an·them /ˌ··· ˈ··/ *n* the official song of a nation, to be sung or played on certain formal occasions. The British national anthem is *God Save the King (Queen)*; the American one is the STAR-SPANGLED BANNER

National As·so·ci·a·tion for the Ad·vance·ment of Col·ored Peo·ple /ˌ··· ···ˌ··· · ··ˌ· ˌ··/ NAACP

National Bas·ket·ball As·so·ci·a·tion /ˌ··· ˈ··· ···ˌ··/ NBA

National Can·cer In·sti·tute /ˌ··· ˈ·· ˌ···/ [*the*] an American organization that works to find the causes, treatments, and cures for cancer

National Child·birth Trust /ˌ··· ˈ·· ˌ·/ (*abbrev.* **NCT**) [*the*] a British organization which aims to educate people about how children are born and about the work of being a parent

National Coal Board /ˌ··· ˈ· ˌ·/ [*the*] the former name (1947–87) of British Coal

National Col·le·gi·ate Ath·let·ic As·so·ci·a·tion /ˌ··· ·ˌ··· ·ˈ·· ···ˌ··/ NCAA

national cos·tume /ˌ··· ˈ··/ *n* [C;U] also **national dress** /ˌ··· ˈ·/ [U]— clothing traditionally (TRADITIONAL) worn by the people of a country. In some parts of the world people still wear their national costume as their ordinary clothing, but in most places it is only worn on special occasions: *folk dancers in national dress* | *Unlike Scotland and Wales, England does not have a national costume.*—see picture at COSTUME

National Coun·cil for Civ·il Lib·er·ties /ˌ··· ˌ··· ˌ·· ˈ···/ [*the*] the name before 1989 of the organization now called Liberty

national cur·ric·u·lum /ˌ··· ·ˈ···/ [*the*] (*often cap.*) the CURRICULUM (=programme of study) which is meant to be followed by all STATE SCHOOLS in England and Wales. The government tells schools what subjects must be studied and what standards should be achieved by the pupils. All pupils have examinations in these subjects at the ages of 7, 11, 14 and 16. Schools must teach the national curriculum but may teach additional subjects if they wish and if they can afford to. The contents of the national curriculum have caused some disagreement between teachers and the government. —see also extra information on page 408

national debt /ˌ··· ˈ·/ *n* the total amount of money owed by the government of a country

National Ed·u·ca·tion As·so·ci·a·tion /ˌ··· ··ˈ·· ···ˌ··/ [*the*] see NEA¹

National En·dow·ment for the Arts /ˌ··· ·ˌ··· ˈ·/ (*abbrev.* **NEA**) [*the*] an American government organization which provides money for artists to help them in their work

National En·dow·ment for the Hu·man·i·ties /ˌ··· ·ˌ··· · ·ˈ···/ [*the*] an American government organization which provides money for writers and other people working in the HUMANITIES to help them with their work

National En·quir·er /ˌ··· ·ˈ··/ [*the*] a weekly American colour newspaper that features often unbelievable stories about famous people and the SUPERNATURAL

National Ex·ec·u·tive Com·mit·tee /ˌ··· ·ˈ··· ·ˌ·· / (*abbrev.* **NEC**) [*the*] the group elected by the Labour Party and the unions which makes decisions on the party's POLICY

National Ex·hi·bi·tion Cen·tre /ˌ··· ··ˈ·· ˌ··/ (*abbrev.* **NEC**) [*the*] a large centre in Birmingham, specially built as a place where CONFERENCES and EXHIBITIONS are held

National Ex·press /ˌ··· ·ˈ·/ a British company which runs coaches (COACH¹ (1), =a comfortable bus for making long journeys) connecting most towns in Britain

National Farm·ers U·nion /ˌ··· ˈ·· ˌ··/ (*abbrev.* **NFU**) [*the*] one of two British organizations, one in England and Wales and one in Scotland, which advise and support farmers but are not TRADE UNIONS

National Film Thea·tre /ˌ··· ˈ· ˌ··/ (*abbrev.* **NFT**) [*the*] a centre on London's South Bank which is run by the British Film Institute and contains two cinemas which show films of historical, CULTURAL, and artistic interest

National Foun·da·tion for the Arts and the Hu·man·i·ties /ˌ··· ·ˌ··· · ·· · ·ˌ···/ an American government organization which develops and supports arts and HUMANITIES. It works with the National Endowment for the Arts and the National Endowment for the Humanities.

National Front /ˌ··· ˈ·/ [*the*] an extreme RIGHT-WING political party in Britain which believes that white people should have more rights than black and Asian people who live in Britain

National Gal·le·ry /ˌ··· ˈ···/ [*the*] an art GALLERY in Trafalgar Square, London, which contains the largest permanent collection of western paintings in Britain, most of which were painted between 1200 and 1900 —see colour map on page 817

National Gal·le·ry of Art /ˌ··· ˌ··· · ˈ·/ [*the*] a large MUSEUM of paintings, SCULPTURE, and other art in Washington DC which is supported by the US government

National Gar·den Fes·ti·val /ˌ··· ˈ·· ˌ···/ [*the*] a show of garden plants and equipment held every two years in a different city or large town in Britain

National Ge·o·graph·ic /ˌ··· ··ˈ·/ [*the*] a popular American monthly magazine produced by the **National Geographic Society**. It has stories and pictures from interesting places around the world, and sometimes includes large maps.

national gov·ern·ment /ˌ··· ˈ···/ *n tech* a government formed by most or all of the political parties in a country, esp. during a war

national grid /ˌ··· ˈ·/ [*the*] **1** (in Britain) the NETWORK of electricity supply wires connecting power stations **2** the system of numbered squares printed on a map to show the exact position of a place

National Guard /ˌ··· ˈ·/ [*the*] a military force in each state of the US which can be called up for service by the state or the US government: *The governor* **called out the National Guard** *to help control the flooding/riots.* —compare TERRITORIAL ARMY

National Health Ser·vice /ˌ··· ˈ· ˌ··/ *abbrev.* **NHS**, also **Health Service**— [*the*] the British system of medical treatment for everyone, paid for by taxes —see also extra information on page 826

National Her·i·tage /ˌ··· ˈ···/ a British organization which gives money from the **National Heritage Memorial Fund**, provided by the government, to MUSEUMS and other institutions to help them buy things and keep buildings, etc. of historic interest in good condition

National In·sur·ance /ˌ··· ·ˈ··/ (*abbrev.* **NI**) *n* [U] (in Britain) a system of insurance run by the government, into which workers and employers make regular payments, and which provides money for people who are unemployed, old, or ill. Every adult in Britain has a National Insurance Number, and all people in employment and their employers have to make payments called **National Insurance Contributions**.

National In·sur·ance Num·ber /ˌ··· ·ˈ·· ˌ··/ *n* a number which everyone in Britain is given when they are old enough to work. It is used by the Department of Social Security and the Inland Revenue to IDENTIFY the person.

na·tion·al·is·m /ˈnæʃənəlɪzəm/ *n* [U] **1** *sometimes derog* love of and pride in one's own country, esp. believing it to be better than any other country **2** desire by a NATIONALITY (2) to form an independent country: *Scottish nationalism*

na·tion·al·ist¹ /ˈnæʃənəlɪst/ *n* **1** a person believing in NATIONALISM (2) **2** (*usu. cap.*) a member of a political group which wants national independence or strong national government: *Basque nationalists* | *In China the Nationalists were defeated by the Communists in 1949.*

nationalist² *adj* believing in NATIONALISM (2): *the nationalist party in Wales*

na·tion·al·is·tic /ˌnæʃənəˈlɪstɪk◂/ *adj often derog* of or showing (too) great love of one's country: *a nationalistic election speech* — ~**ally** /kli/ *adv*

na·tion·al·i·ty /ˌnæʃəˈnæl ti/ *n* **1** [C;U] the fact of being a citizen of a particular country: *She lives in France but has British nationality* (=she is legally a citizen of Britain, not France). | *people of many different nationalities/of the same nationality* | *His mother's French and his father's Spanish, so he has* **dual nationality** (=he is a citizen of France and Spain) **2** [C] a large group of people with the same race, origin, language, etc.: *the different nationalities of the USSR*

na·tion·al·ize also **-ise** *BrE* /ˈnæʃənəlaɪz/ *v* [T] (of a central government) to buy or take control of (a business, industry, etc.): *The British government nationalized the*

scoreboard

stadium

high jump

shot put

track

javelin

pole vault

long jump

...hletics *(BrE)* (or track and field *(AmE)*) is the general
...me given to the kind of sports and physical exercises
...own here. Athletics includes both track events
...running races) and field events (= sports involving
...mping, throwing things, etc. which are not races).
...ost field events are named according to distance, e.g.
...e's running in the 400 metres. (= running in a race over
...distance of 400 metres). The person who comes first in an
...ent wins a gold medal, the person who comes second wins a silver
...edal and the person who comes third wins a bronze medal. People
...ually talk about somebody winning 'the gold', 'the silver' or 'the bronze',
...g. He won the gold in the 100 metres. / She won a bronze in the javelin.

podium

basketball

rodeo

rugby

cricket

baseball

football (BrE) soccer (AmE)

a Mexican wave

American football (BrE) football (AmE)

railways in 1948. —opposites **denationalize, privatize**
—**-ization** /ˌnæʃənəlaɪˈzeɪʃən‖-nələ-/ *n* [U]

nationalized in·dus·try /ˌ··· ˈ···/ *n* an industry which is
owned by the state and controlled by the central government. Nationalized industries are usu. those which are
important to the country, and may be supported by the
government's money.

National La·bor Re·la·tions Board /ˌ··· ˈ· ··· ˌ·/ (*abbrev.*
NLRB) [*the*] a US government office that tries to settle
differences between unions and management, esp. in
large companies

National Lam·poon /ˌ··· ·ˈ·/ an American magazine read
mostly by young people which uses humour and SATIRE
that some esp. older or religious people find offensive

National League /ˈ··· ˌ·/ a group of professional US BASE-
BALL teams which play against each other —see also
BASEBALL

National Mar·i·time Mu·se·um /ˌ··· ˈ··· ·ˌ··/ [*the*] a MUSEUM
in Greenwich, S London, with models and pictures of
British ships, and things connected with the sea, sailing,
and famous seamen

national park /ˌ··· ˈ·/ *n* (*often caps.*) an area of natural,
historical, or scientific interest which is kept by the
government for people to visit: *Yosemite National Park*

National Or·gan·i·za·tion for Wom·en /ˌ··· ···ˌ··· ˈ··/ see
NOW

National Por·trait Gal·le·ry /ˌ··· ˈ·· ˌ··/ [*the*] an art GALLERY
in Trafalgar Square in London which contains many pictures of famous men and women in British history and
CULTURE

National Pow·er /ˌ··· ˈ··/ one of the two main companies
which produce electricity in Britain —see also POWERGEN

National Pub·lic Ra·di·o /ˌ··· ˌ··· ˈ···/ (*abbrev.* **NPR**) a network of independent US radio stations which is sup-
ported financially by people that listen to it; it is popular for its excellent and interesting programmes on news
and current affairs

National Ri·fle As·so·ci·a·tion /ˌ··· ˈ·· ···ˌ··/ (*abbrev.* **NRA**)
[*the*] an American organization which supports and defends people's rights to buy and keep guns. People connect the NRA with the GUN LOBBY and think it is responsible for ensuring that gun control laws are always
defeated in Congress.

National Sav·ings Bank /ˌ··· ˈ·· ·/ [*the*] a savings bank run
by the British Post Office, which offers National Savings
Certificates and Premium Bonds as ways of investing
(INVEST) money

National Sav·ings Cer·tif·i·cates /ˌ··· ˈ·· ·ˌ··/ *n* [P] CERTIFI-
CATES (=official papers) sold by the Post Office, which
show that the buyer has lent money to the National Savings Bank and will get interest on the money until the
certificates are sold back, usu. after a fixed period of
years

National Sci·ence Foun·da·tion /ˌ··· ˈ·· ·ˌ··/ [*the*] a US
government organization that provides money and
guidance for scientific study

national se·cu·ri·ty /ˌ··· ·ˈ···/ *n* [U] the safety of a nation
against its enemies. Providing for national security usu.
means having weapons and armies to defend the nation:
*Well over half of public money is spent on weapons for na-
tional security.*

National Se·cu·ri·ty Coun·cil /ˌ··· ·ˈ··· ˌ··/ [*the*] a council
in the US which controls the relationship between the
defence and foreign departments of the government

national ser·vice /ˌ··· ˈ·/ *n* BrE ‖ **draft** *AmE*— [U] (*often
caps.*) the system, no longer current in Britain or the US,
of making all men (and sometimes all women) serve in
the armed forces for a limited period: *He did his national
service in the navy.*

National Thea·tre /ˌ··· ˈ···/ *abbrev.* **NT**, full name **Royal
National Theatre**— [*the*] a modern building on London's
South Bank containing three theatres. It is the home of
the **Royal National Theatre Company**, who perform
a wide variety of old and new plays. The theatre is very
popular and attracts many tourists, although many people think the building is ugly. —see colour map on page
817

National Trust /ˌ··· ˈ·/ (*abbrev.* **NT**) [*the*] a British organization (CHARITY) which owns and takes care of many
beautiful places and historic buildings in England and

Wales, which people may visit. A similar organization,
the **National Trust for Scotland**, owns and takes care
of places in Scotland. —compare ENGLISH HERITAGE

National U·nion of Jour·nal·ists /ˌ··· ˌ··· · ˈ···/ (*abbrev.*
NUJ) [*the*] a British TRADE UNION which represents JOUR-
NALISTS (=writers of newspapers) and similar workers

National U·nion of Mine·work·ers /ˌ··· ˌ··· · ˈ···/ (*abbrev.*
NUM) [*the*] a British TRADE UNION which represents
many workers in the coal industry, well-known in Britain for arranging the Miners' Strike of 1984–85

National U·nion of Pub·lic Em·ploy·ees /ˌ··· ˌ··· · ˌ·· ·ˈ··,
ˌ··· ˌ··· · ˌ·· ·ˈ·/ (*abbrev.* **NUPE**) [*the*] a British TRADE
UNION which represents a wide range of people who work
for local authorities (LOCAL AUTHORITY) and the National
Health Service

National U·nion of Rail·way·men /ˌ··· ˌ··· · ˈ···/ (*abbrev.*
NUR) [*the*] a British TRADE UNION which represents railway workers

National U·nion of Stu·dents /ˌ··· ˌ··· · ˈ··/ (*abbrev.* **NUS**)
[*the*] a British organization that represents students in
universities and colleges. It campaigns (CAMPAIGN) nationally for students' rights, and also arranges entertainments, advice centres, etc. at colleges and universities
—compare STUDENTS' UNION

National U·nion of Teach·ers /ˌ··· ˌ··· · ˈ··/ (*abbrev.* **NUT**)
[*the*] a professional organization which is part of the TUC
and represents teachers in England and Wales, both in
state-run and private schools

National Weath·er Ser·vice /ˌ··· ˈ·· ˌ··/ [*the*] the US government office that makes weather maps, tells what the
weather will be like, and gives warnings when dangerous weather is on its way —compare METEOROLOGICAL
OFFICE

National West·min·ster Bank /ˌ··· ˌ··· ·ˈ·/ also **Nat West**—
[*the*] one of the main British banks, branches of which
are found in many towns and cities in Britain

National Youth Or·ches·tra /ˌ··· ˈ· ˌ··/ [*the*] an ORCHESTRA
for young musicians and music students in Britain

National Youth Thea·tre /ˌ··· ˈ· ˌ··/ [*the*] a theatre group
for young actors in London

Nation of Is·lam /ˌ·· · ˈ··/ [*the*] the official name of the Black
Muslims —see BLACK MUSLIMS

nation state /ˌ··· ˈ·/ *n* a nation forming a politically independent country —compare CITY-STATE

na·tion·wide /ˌneɪʃənˈwaɪd◂, ˈneɪʃənwaɪd/ *adj* (used esp.
in newspapers, on the radio, etc.) happening, existing,
etc., over a whole country; NATIONAL: *a nationwide search
for the criminals* | *a nationwide broadcast* (=heard every-
where in the country) —**nationwide** *adv* : *The President's
speech will be broadcast nationwide.*

Na·tion·wide /ˈneɪʃəwaɪd/ also **Nationwide An·gli·a** /ˌ···
ˈ···/— [*the*] a British BUILDING SOCIETY, branches of which
are found in many towns and cities in Britain

na·tive[1] /ˈneɪtɪv/ *adj* **1** [A] belonging to or being the place
of one's birth: *her native language* | *a visit by the Pope
to his native Poland* **2** [A] (of a person) belonging to a
place from birth: *a native New Yorker* **3** [(to)] growing,
living, produced, found, etc., in a place; not brought in
from another place; INDIGENOUS: *a plant native to the
eastern US* | *a house built of native stone* **4** [(to)] (of a
quality) belonging to someone from birth; not learned;
INNATE: *native ability* **5** [A] of or concerning the original people, esp. the non-Europeans, of a place: *a native
village* —see also NATIVE AMERICAN **6 go native** *infml,
often humor* (esp. of tourists) to live in the manner of the
people who usually live in a place: *In Scotland he tried
to go native by wearing a kilt.*

na·tive[2] *n* **1** [(of)] someone who was born in a place: *a native of California* **2** someone who lives in a place all the
time or has lived there a long time: *Are you a native here,
or just a visitor?* **3** [*often pl.*] (esp. used by Europeans
of non-Europeans) one of the original people living in a
place: *The government of the island treated the natives
badly.* **4** [(of)] a plant or animal living naturally in a
place: *The bear was once a native of Britain.*

Native A·mer·i·can /ˌ··· ·ˈ···/ also **American Indian,
Amerindian**— *n* a member of any of the original peoples
of America, esp. of the US and Canada. Native Americans
came from many different TRIBES (=groups of people who
are related), each having its own language and CULTURE.

▶CULTURAL NOTE Native Americans have often been shown, esp. in films, as cruel and warlike people, although recently books and films have tried to show them more favourably and to present their point of view. Most Native Americans suffered greatly from European settlers moving onto their lands, and fought to defend themselves and their way of life; this is still happening in parts of S America. In N America Native Americans were forced to leave their lands and live on RESERVATIONS (= areas of land set aside for them). Most still live on reservations, many are very poor and have problems resulting from unemployment and drinking alcohol. Many tribes are working to improve conditions on the reservations, and some are also trying to · bring back old customs and religious practices.◀

▷ USAGE **Native American** is now the preferred and usual term. **American Indian** and **Amerindian** are still used, esp. in British English and referring to Native Americans from S America. **Red Indian** is old-fashioned and usu. considered offensive.◁

native speaker /ˌ·· ˈ···◂/ n a person who has learned (a particular language) from birth, usu. as a result of having parents who speak it and living in a country where most people speak it: *a native speaker of English|an English native speaker|* native-speaker English

na·tiv·i·ty /nəˈtɪvᵻti/ n fml or pomp birth: *the place of my nativity*

Nativity n 1 [the] the birth of Jesus Christ, sometimes also called "the Christmas story". According to the story in the Bible, Mary and Joseph have to travel from Nazareth to Bethlehem for a CENSUS. There are no empty rooms in Bethlehem, so they have to stay in a STABLE. The phrase "no room at the INN" is often used when talking about this part of the story. Jesus is born in the stable, and he is laid in a MANGER (=a container for food for animals) instead of a bed. A bright star (the Star of Bethlehem) appears in the sky when Jesus is born, to show the way to the place of his birth. SHEPHERDS (=people who take care of sheep) nearby are told about the baby Jesus by an angel (=a messenger of God) and told to go to the stable to worship him. Three kings (also called "the Three Wise Men") from the East also come to worship him, following the bright star and bringing gifts of gold, FRANKINCENSE, and MYRRH. 2 [C] a picture of the scene of the birth of Jesus Christ. Pictures or models (CRIBS) of the Nativity scene usu. show the Holy Family (Jesus, Mary, and Joseph), animals in the stable (usu. an OX and an ASS), the shepherds, and the three kings. —see picture on page 224

nativity play /·ˈ··· ·/ n (often cap.) a play telling the story of the Nativity, esp. one performed by young children at school at Christmas time —compare PASSION PLAY

NATO /ˈneɪtəʊ/ the North Atlantic Treaty Organization; a group of countries including Britain, the US, and some Scandinavian and European countries, which give military help to each other: *our allies in NATO*

NATSOPA /nætˈsəʊpə/ National Society of Operative Printers, Graphical and Media Personnel; a trade union for people working in these jobs

nat·ter /ˈnætəʳ/ v [I (AWAY, ON)] BrE infml to talk continuously about unimportant things; CHATTER: *They nattered (away) all afternoon.* —**natter** n [S] : *a long natter*

NBA /ˌen biː ˈeɪ/ National Basketball Association; the American organization which arranges professional BASKETBALL matches in the US —see also BASKETBALL

nat·ty /ˈnæti/ adj old-fash infml neat in appearance; SMART: *He's a very natty dresser.* (=He dresses neatly and fashionably.) —**tily** adv

nat·u·ral¹ /ˈnætʃərəl/ adj 1 of or being what exists or happens ordinarily in the world, esp. a not caused, made, or controlled by people: *The country's natural resources include forests, coal, and oil.* | *death from natural causes* | *The town has a fine natural harbour.* —compare ARTIFICIAL (1,3), MAN-MADE b not concerning gods, fairies, or spirits: *a natural explanation for the strange event* —opposite **supernatural** 2 a expected from experience; usual: *It's very natural to feel nervous when you go to a new school.* | *It's only natural that you should be nervous.* —opposite **unnatural, abnormal** b generally expected and accepted, in accordance with the facts of a situation: *Her marketing background made her a natural choice for the job.* 3 not looking or sounding different from usual; not AFFECTED: *Try to look natural for your photograph.*

4 a belonging to someone from birth; not learned; INNATE: *a natural talent for music* | *Cats have a natural aversion to water.* b [A] (of a person) having a skill or quality from birth; not needing to be taught: *a natural musician|story-teller* 5 [A no comp.] (of a family member) a actually having the stated relation even if not in law: *John was adopted as a baby: he never knew his natural parents.* b euph, now rare ILLEGITIMATE (1): *She claimed to be the natural child of the king.* 6 [after n] (of a note in music) not SHARP or FLAT: *Don't sing C sharp, sing C natural!* —see also NATURALLY —compare FLAT² (8) —**~ness** n [U]

natural² n 1 [usu. sing.] infml someone or something well suited to a job, part in a play, etc., or certain to succeed: *As an actor, he's a natural.* 2 (in music) a a note which is not raised or lowered by a SHARP or FLAT b the sign (♮) for this —compare FLAT¹ (5)

natural child·birth /ˌ··· ˈ··/ n [U] a method of giving birth to a baby in which a woman chooses not to use drugs and uses breathing exercises to control pain

natural gas /ˌ··· ˈ·/ n [U] gas used esp. for heating and lighting taken from under the earth or under the bottom of the sea —compare COAL GAS

natural his·to·ry /ˌ··· ˈ···/ n [U] the study of plants, animals, and minerals, esp. as a subject of general interest — compare NATURAL SCIENCE

Natural His·to·ry Mu·se·um /ˌ··· ˈ··· ·ˌ··/ [the] a MUSEUM in London which is open to the public, contains articles related to the history of plants, animals, and minerals, and is famous for its collection of the bones of DINOSAURS

nat·u·ral·is·m /ˈnætʃərəlɪzəm/ n [U] 1 the showing, in art and literature, of the world and people exactly as they are 2 the system of thought which tries to explain everything by natural causes and laws —compare IDEALISM, REALISM

nat·u·ral·ist /ˈnætʃərəlᵻst/ n 1 a person who studies plants or animals, esp. outdoors and not in a LABORATORY 2 a person who believes in naturalism in art or literature

nat·u·ral·is·tic /ˌnætʃərəˈlɪstɪk◂/ also **naturalist**— adj showing or practising naturalism: *a naturalistic writer|painting* — **~ally** /kli/ adv

nat·u·ral·ize also **-ise** BrE /ˈnætʃərəlaɪz/ v [T often pass.] 1 to make (a person born elsewhere) a citizen of a country: *She became naturalized after living in Britain for ten years.* 2 to bring (a plant or animal) into a new place to live 3 to accept (a foreign word or phrase) as part of a language: *"Apropos" is a French phrase now naturalized into|in English.* —**-ization** /ˌnætʃərəlaɪˈzeɪʃən‖-lə-/ n [U]

nat·u·ral·ly /ˈnætʃərəli‖-tʃərəli, -tʃərli/ adv 1 by nature; as a natural quality: *Her cheeks are naturally red.* | *Swimming seems to come naturally to her.* (=she can easily learn to do it) 2 without trying to look or sound different from usual: *Try to speak naturally to the television camera.* 3 of course; as one could have expected: *"Did you win the game?" "Naturally."* | *Naturally you will want to discuss it with your wife.*

natural phi·los·o·phy /ˌ··· ·ˈ···/ n [U] old use science, esp. PHYSICS

natural re·sourc·es /ˌ··· ·ˈ··/ n [P] materials, land, and natural forces which exist in a place and can be used by humans: *The country's natural resources include coal, iron, and copper.* | *We plan to use the natural resources of the site, esp. wind and water power, to the full.*

natural sci·ence /ˌ··· ˈ··/ n 1 [U] BIOLOGY, chemistry, and PHYSICS considered together as subjects for study 2 [C usu. pl.] any of these: *Which of the natural sciences have you studied?* —compare NATURAL HISTORY, SOCIAL SCIENCE

natural se·lec·tion /ˌ··· ·ˈ··/ also **survival of the fittest**— n [U] tech the process by which plants and animals that are best suited to the conditions around them continue to live, while those less suited to these conditions die

natural wast·age /ˌ··· ˈ··/ n [U] a reduction in the number of people employed by a firm etc., which happens when people leave their jobs and are not replaced

na·ture /ˈneɪtʃəʳ/ n 1 [U] (often cap.) everything that exists in the world independently of people, such as plants and animals, earth and rocks, and the weather: *They stopped to admire the beauties of nature.* (=scenery) | *Farming on such bad land is a struggle against nature.*

—see also MOTHER NATURE   **2** [C;U] the qualities that make someone or something different from others; character: *What is the nature of the new chemical?* | *It's not in her nature to be rude; she's polite* **by nature.** (=she has a polite nature) | *It's his nature to be generous.* | *It's only* **human nature** *to like money.* (=everyone likes money) | *Owing to the sensitive nature of this case, the trial will be held in secret.*   **3** [S] a type; sort: *ceremonies of a solemn nature* | *I think he's a physicist or something of that nature.*   **4 in the 'nature of things** as is natural; as may be expected: *In the nature of things, there is bound to be the occasional accident.*   **5 in a state of nature: a** in the supposed unspoiled condition of people before civilization **b** *euph or humor* wearing no clothes; NAKED   **6 let nature take its course** *infml* to allow events to happen without help from anyone   **7 nature red in tooth and claw** *quote* a phrase from a poem by Alfred, Lord Tennyson, used when saying how cruel the natural world is —see also CALL OF NATURE, SECOND NATURE, GOOD-NATURED

Nature the title of a British scientific magazine about NATURE (1) which appears weekly

nature con·ser·va·tion /ˌ··· ··,·-/ *n* [U] work done to control, prevent, or repair damage done to nature esp. by humans

nature-nur·ture con·tro·ver·sy /ˌ,·· '·· ',····, ,·· '·· ·,··/ [the] a difference of opinions about which has a greater influence on people and animals: their GENETIC (=natural) system, or their environment. This argument is usu. connected with political and social questions, often about race.

nature re·serve /'·· ·,·/ *n* an area in which usu. rare animals and plants are protected from being damaged by humans, e.g. by limiting the movement of people through the area

nature stud·y /'·· ,··/ *n* [U] the study of plants, animals, etc., esp. purely for pleasure, or as a school subject: *a nature study class/lesson*

nature trail /'·· ·/ *n* a path in a country area where many plants, animals, etc. can be seen, esp. as laid out by a local group, farmer, etc. to keep visitors from walking everywhere and destroying wild life

na·tur·is·m /'neɪtʃərɪzəm/ *n* [U] NUDISM —**ist** *n*

na·tu·ro·path /'neɪtʃərəpæθ/ *n* a person who treats illness by trying to help the body to cure itself, using such means as changing the food that people eat, and not using dangerous drugs. This is regarded as a kind of ALTERNATIVE MEDICINE, —**pathic** /ˌneɪtʃərə'pæθɪk‖/ *adj* —**pathy** /ˌneɪtʃə'rɒpəθi‖-'rɑː-/ *n* [U]

Nat West /ˌnæt 'west/ [the] *BrE infml* National Westminster Bank

Nat-West Tro·phy /ˌ,·· '··/ [the] an English CRICKET competition in which one day matches are played and the losing team drops out of the competition

Nau·ga·hyde /'nɔːgəhaɪd/ *n* [U] *AmE tdmk* a plastic-coated fabric made to look like leather and used to cover furniture. It is often associated with bad taste, or pretensions of wealth.

naught /nɔːt‖nɔːt, nɑːt/ *n* [U]   **1** *old use or lit* nothing: *All his work* **came to naught** *when the storm destroyed his crops.*   **2 set at naught** *lit* not to care about or not fear

naugh·ty /'nɔːti‖'nɔːti, 'nɑːti/ *adj*   **1** (esp. of children or their behaviour) not obeying a parent, teacher, set of rules, etc.; DISOBEDIENT: *You naughty boy! I told you not to play in the road.* | *It's naughty to pull your sister's hair.* | (of adults) (*humor*) *It was rather naughty of you to deceive the tax inspector.* —see WICKED (USAGE)   **2** *euph* morally, esp. sexually, improper, in a not very serious way: *naughty pictures* | *a naughty joke*   **3 naughty but nice** (a phrase which was used in an advertisement for cakes, but which is used in speaking of many things which are enjoyable but which might be harmful esp. to the health)   **4 naughty bits** *euph, humor* the (esp. male) sexual organs; the phrase was first used on the television programme *Monty Python's Flying Circus* —**tily** *adv* —**tiness** *n* [U]

Na·u·ru /nɑː'uːruː, naʊ'ruː/ an independent republic, one of the smallest nations in the world, on an island in the Pacific Ocean near the Equator — ~ **an** *n, adj*

nau·se·a /'nɔːziə, -siə‖-ziə, -ʃə/ *n* [U] *fml* a feeling of sickness and desire to VOMIT (=to throw up the contents of the stomach through the mouth): *Early pregnancy is often*

accompanied by nausea. | *Do you experience any nausea?*

nau·se·ate /'nɔːzieɪt, -si-‖-zi-, -ʃi-/ *v* [T] to cause to feel nausea; SICKEN: *a nauseating smell* | (fig.) *The way he shouts at his wife nauseates me.* —**atingly** *adv*

nau·se·ous /'nɔːziəs, -siəs‖-ziəs, -ʃəs/ *adj*   **1** *fml* causing nausea: *nauseous medicine*   **2** *infml, esp. AmE* feeling great distaste; nauseated: *Violence in films makes me nauseous.* — ~ **ly** *adv* — ~ **ness** *n* [U]

nau·ti·cal /'nɔːtɪkəl/ *adj* of sailors, ships, or sailing — ~ **ly** /kli/ *adv*

nautical mile /ˌ,··· '·/ also **sea mile**— *n* a measure of distance used at sea, a little more than a land mile, equal to 1853 metres (=6080 feet)

Nav·a·jo /'nævəhəʊ/ *n* [C; *the*+P] (a member of) a Native American people of the southwestern US. They are the largest TRIBE in the US. —see NATIVE AMERICAN (CULTURAL NOTE)

na·val /'neɪvəl/ *adj* of a navy or ships of war: *a naval officer* | *naval battles* | *a naval base* (=a place where ships of a navy are kept)

nave /neɪv/ *n* the long central part of a church, often between two AISLES —see picture at CHURCH

na·vel /'neɪvəl/ *n* the small sunken place in the middle of a person's stomach, left when the UMBILICAL CORD was cut at birth —see also **contemplate one's navel** (CONTEMPLATE (3))

nav·i·ga·ble /'nævɪgəbəl/ *adj*   **1** (of a body of water) deep and wide enough to allow ships to travel: *The St Lawrence River is navigable from the Great Lakes to the Atlantic Ocean.*   **2** *fml* (of a ship, aircraft, etc.) able to be guided; steerable (STEER[1]) —**bility** /ˌnævɪgə'bɪlɪti/ *n* [U]

nav·i·gate /'nævɪgeɪt/ *v*   **1** [I;T] to direct the course of (a ship, plane, etc.): *to navigate by the stars* (=using the positions of stars for a guide) | (fig.) *I'll drive if you'll hold the map and navigate.*   **2** [T] to go by sea, air, etc. from one side or end to the other (of a place): *to navigate a river*

nav·i·ga·tion /ˌnævɪ'geɪʃən/ *n* [U]   **1** the act or practice of sailing a ship or piloting an aircraft: *Navigation is difficult on this river because of the hidden rocks.*   **2** the science of planning and keeping on a course on water or in the air from one place to another: *The compass is an instrument of navigation.*   **3** movement of ships or aircraft: *a passage open to navigation*

nav·i·ga·tor /'nævɪgeɪtəʳ/ *n* a person who is skilled in the art of navigation, esp. the officer on a ship or aircraft who plans and directs its course

Nav·rat·i·lo·va /ˌnævrætɪ'ləʊvə/, **Mar·ti·na** /mɑː'tiːnə‖mɑːr-/ (1956–) an American tennis player, born in Czechoslovakia, who has won the ladies' SINGLES title at Wimbledon eight times, and many other important competitions. She was generally considered to be the best woman tennis player in the world for most of the 1980s.

nav·vy /'nævi/ *n BrE* a LABOURER doing a heavy unskilled job in digging or building

na·vy /'neɪvi/ *n*   **1** [+*sing./pl. v*] the branch of a country's military forces that is concerned with attack and defence at sea: *to join the navy* | *The Navy wants/want more money for ships.*   **2** the ships of war belonging to a country: *a small navy of ten ships* —see also MERCHANT NAVY

navy blue /ˌ,·· '·◁/ also **navy**— *adj* a very dark blue colour —**navy blue** *n* [U]

nay[1] /neɪ/ *adv*   **1** *lit* not only this but also (something stronger than what has just been said): *a bright, nay (a) blinding light* (=not only bright but also blinding)   **2** *old use* no —opposite **yea** or **aye**; see also **say someone nay** (SAY[1] (16))

nay[2] *n* a vote or voter against an idea, plan, law, etc. —opposite **aye** or **yea**

Naz·a·reth /'næzərəθ/ a town in Galilee, N Israel, known for its associations with Jesus Christ and therefore visited by many people

Na·zi /'nɑːtsi/ *n* **Nazis** a person belonging to the political party of Adolf Hitler which controlled Germany from 1933 to 1945. The party's main ideas were the superiority (SUPERIOR) of the ARYAN master race, the establishment of a German THIRD REICH which would last a thousand years, and the removal of so-called enemies, mainly JEWS and COMMUNISTs. The policies (POLICY) were carried out by the GESTAPO (=secret police) and the SS, special soldiers who protected Adolf Hitler and were in charge of the CONCENTRATION CAMPs where millions of people died. —see also CONCENTRATION CAMP, **Adolf** HITLER, SECOND WORLD WAR, SS —**Nazi** adj : a Nazi officer | the Nazi party | Nazi Germany (=Germany between 1933–45) — **Nazism** n [U]

NB , **nb** Lat (used esp. in writing to begin a note) nota bene; take notice; note well

NBA /ˌen biː ˈeɪ/ [the] National Basketball Association; (the organization that includes) the main professional BASKETBALL teams in the US, which play games against each other

NBC /ˌen biː ˈsiː/ National Broadcasting Company; one of the four national American television networks supported by advertising: NBC News

NC written abbrev. for: NORTH CAROLINA

NCAA /ˌen siː dʌb əl ˈeɪ/ National Collegiate Athletic Association; an organization which sets rules for sports competitions between American colleges and universities

NCO /ˌen siː ˈəʊ/ n noncommissioned officer; a member of the army, navy, etc., such as a CORPORAL or SERGEANT, who is lower in rank than a COMMISSIONED OFFICER but has some responsibility to command others: He became an NCO at 18. —compare COMMISSIONED OFFICER

NCP /ˌen siː ˈpiː/ National Car Parks; a company which owns many car parks in Britain, and charges money for the number of hours a car is parked: There's an NCP car park a bit further down the road.

NCT /ˌen siː ˈtiː/ abbrev. for: NATIONAL CHILDBIRTH TRUST

ND written abbrev. for: NORTH DAKOTA

NE written abbrev. for: **1** northeast(ern) **2** NEBRASKA

NEA[1] /ˌen iː ˈeɪ/ [the] the National Education Association; an American organization that represents the interests of teachers and schools

NEA[2] [the] NATIONAL ENDOWMENT FOR THE ARTS

Neagh see LOUGH NEAGH

Ne·an·der·thal /niˈændətɑːl‖-dərtɔːl, -tɑːl/ n infml or humor (often not cap.) **1** a heavy, hairy, stupid man (as Neanderthal man is regarded) **2** esp. AmE a person who unthinkingly opposes all change; REACTIONARY

Neanderthal man /·ˈ··· ·/ n [U] an early type of human being who lived in Europe during the STONE AGE

ne·a·pol·i·tan /ˌniːəˈpɒlɪtən◂ ‖ -ˈpɑː-/ adj (of ice cream) having bands of different colours and tastes

neap tide /ˌniːp taɪd/ n a very small rise and fall of the sea at the times of the first and third quarters of the moon —compare SPRING TIDE

near[1] /nɪər/ adj **1** close; not at much distance away, in space, time, degree, or relationship: the near future | Go and pick an apple from the nearest tree. | My office is quite near. | They live 20 miles from the nearest town. | He's one of my nearest relations. (=is closely related to me) | Tell me how much it will cost, **to the nearest** £10/$10. **2** [A no comp.] **a** the closer one of two things: the near bank of the river —opposite **far** **b** the one on the left of a pair; NEARSIDE: the near wheel of a cart —opposite **off** **3** [A] only just missed or avoided; almost (the stated thing): a near disaster | The war led to a near doubling of oil prices. (=prices were almost doubled) —see also NEAR[2] (2) **4** **one's nearest and dearest** pomp or humor one's family —see also NEARLY — ~**ness** n [U]

▷ USAGE **Near** and **close** are almost the same in meaning, but there are certain phrases in which one must be used and not the other. Notice the **near** future | the **near** distance‖a **near** miss/disaster (not **close**); a **close** friend | **close** behind‖a **close** call/shave (not **near**). **Close** cannot be used alone as a preposition.◁

near[2] adv, prep **1** [(to)] not far (from); close (to): the tree nearest (to) the house | a house near the station | We want to find a house nearer (to) the station. | Move your chair a bit nearer (mine). | They live quite near (here). | Don't go too near the edge of the cliff; just near enough to see over it. | I came near to tears. (=almost cried) | Remind me again nearer (to) the time of the meeting. | The bus is **nowhere near as** fast as (=much slower than) the train. **2** almost: a near-perfect performance | The job is near impossible. —see also NEAR[1] (3)

near[3] v [I;T] to come closer in space or time (to); APPROACH:

The work is nearing completion. | He got more and more nervous as the day neared.

near·by /ˌnɪəˈbaɪ◂‖ˌnɪər-/ adj, adv near; close by: a nearby town | A football match was being played nearby.

Near East /ˌ· ˈ·/ [the] the Middle East —compare FAR EAST — ~**ern** adj

near let·ter qual·i·ty /ˌ· ˈ·· ˌ···/ adj [A] (of computer printers or PRINTOUT) producing or being nearly as good a quality of print as is produced by a good TYPEWRITER: an inexpensive dot-matrix printer producing near letter quality results

near·ly /ˈnɪəli‖ˈnɪərli/ adv **1** almost; not quite or not yet completely: He very nearly died. | It took nearly two weeks to get there. | The train was nearly full. | not nearly enough money (=far too little) | two nearly equal amounts | Is the job nearly finished? | The train was nearly full. —see ALMOST (USAGE) **2** fml rare closely: a question which concerns me nearly

near miss /ˌ· ˈ·/ n **1** a bomb, shot, etc., which does not hit exactly the right spot but comes close to it **2** an intention which fails but almost succeeds: I got there just after you'd left — such a near miss! —compare NEAR THING

near·side /ˈnɪəsaɪd‖ˈnɪər-/ adj [A no comp.] esp. BrE on the left-hand side, esp. of an animal or of a car or road: the nearside back light of a car —opposite **offside**

near·sight·ed /ˌnɪəˈsaɪtɪd◂‖ˈnɪərsaɪtɪd/ adj esp. AmE for SHORTSIGHTED — ~**ly** adv — ~**ness** n [U]

near thing /ˌ· ˈ·/ also **close thing**— n [usu. sing.] BrE infml **1** a situation in which something dangerous or very unpleasant is only just avoided: That was a near thing — we almost hit that car! —see also CLOSE CALL, CLOSE SHAVE, NARROW SQUEAK **2** a game, election, risk taken, etc., which comes close to failing before it succeeds: We won, but it was a near thing. —compare NEAR MISS

neat /niːt/ adj **1** in good order; showing care in appearance; tidy: neat handwriting | He keeps his office neat and tidy. **2** liking order and good arrangement: Cats are neat animals. **3** simple and effective: a neat trick|description | There are no neat solutions to this problem. **4** also **straight**— (of alcoholic drinks) without ice or water or other liquid: I like my whisky neat. **5** AmE infml very good; very pleasant; fine: The party was really neat — we had good fun. — ~**ly** adv — ~**ness** n [U]

'neath /niːθ/ prep poet beneath

Ne·bras·ka /nəˈbræskə/ written abbrev. **NE**— a state in the central US which is mainly farmland, producing corn, wheat, cattle, and pigs —see colour map on pages 1374–5 — ~**kan** n,adj

Neb·u·chad·nez·zar /ˌnebjʊkədˈnezə‖ˌnebəkəd-/, **King** (died 562 BC) a king of Babylonia who destroyed Jerusalem in 586 BC, as described in the Bible

neb·u·la /ˈnebjʊlə/ n **-lae** /liː/ or **-las** **1** a mass of gas and dust among the stars, appearing often as a bright cloud at night **2** a GALAXY (=mass of stars) which has this appearance — ~**lar** adj

neb·u·lous /ˈnebjʊləs/ adj lacking clear form or expression; VAGUE: his nebulous political ideas — ~**ly** adv — ~**ness** n [U]

NEC[1] /ˌen iː ˈsiː/ abbrev. for: **1** NATIONAL EXHIBITION CENTRE **2** NATIONAL EXECUTIVE COUNCIL

NEC[2] a large Japanese company that makes FAX machines, computers etc.

ne·ces·sa·ries /ˈnesɪsəriz‖-seriz/ n [P] esp. BrE things which are needed for a purpose, e.g. food and money for a journey

▷ USAGE **Necessaries** are things which you need; **necessities** is a stronger word that can mean "things which are needed in order to stay alive". Compare a few **necessaries** for the journey, like socks and a toothbrush | Water is a **necessity** of life.◁

ne·ces·sar·i·ly /ˈnesɪsərɪli, ˌnesɪˈserɪli‖ˌnesɪˈserɪli/ adv in a way that must be so; unavoidably: Food that looks good doesn't necessarily taste good. (=it might taste bad)

ne·ces·sa·ry[1] /ˈnesɪsəri‖-seri/ adj [(for)] that must be had, obtained, or done; needed; ESSENTIAL: Food is necessary for life. | Is it really necessary for me to attend the meeting? (=must I attend?) | It's not necessary to wear a tie. | This discussion can, if necessary, be continued tomorrow. | If we're agreed that the meeting should be next Friday, I'll *leave it to you to make the necessary arrangements.* — opposite **unnecessary**

necessary² *n* the **necessary** *infml or humor* what is needed, esp. money: *I suppose I'd better go and do the necessary — the dishes won't wash themselves.* | *We're not going on holiday, we haven't got the necessary.*

necessary e·vil /ˌ···· ˈ··/ *n* [S] something bad or unpleasant which is the only way to get a good result: *I don't like having two jobs, but it's a necessary evil if we want to buy a car.*

ne·ces·si·tate /nɪˈsesɪteɪt/ *v* [T] *fml* to cause a need for; make necessary: *Lack of money necessitated a change of plan.* [+v-ing] *This change would necessitate starting all over again.*

ne·ces·si·tous /nɪˈsesɪtəs/ *adj pomp or euph* poor; NEEDY: *a necessitous family* — ~**ly** *adv*

ne·ces·si·ty /nɪˈsesɪti/ *n* **1** [S;U (of, for)] the condition of being necessary or unavoidable; need: *Is there any necessity for another election?* | *We won't buy a car until the necessity arises.* (=until we really need one) | *We're faced with the necessity of buying* (=we have to buy) *a new car.* [+to-v] *There is no necessity to buy tickets in advance.* | *I walked home of|by necessity, because there was no bus.* **2** [C] something that is necessary: *Food and clothing are the* **bare necessities** *of life.* (=the very least that people need) —compare LUXURY; see NECESSARIES (USAGE) **3** [U] *fml* the condition of being in urgent need of money or food: *He was forced by necessity to steal a loaf of bread.* **4 necessity is the mother of invention** *saying* if people really need something they will find a way to get it or do it —see also **make a virtue of necessity** (VIRTUE)

neck¹ /nek/ *n* **1** [C] the part of the body by which the head is joined to the shoulders —see picture at HEAD **2** [C] the part of a garment that goes round the human neck: *the neck of a shirt* **3** [U] the neck of an animal, used as food: *neck of lamb* **4** [C] a narrow part that sticks out from a broader part: *the neck of a bottle|of a violin* | *a neck of land coming out from the coast* **5 by a neck** *infml* (to win or lose a race) by a very short distance from another: *Our horse won by a neck.* **6** *BrE* **get it in the neck** *infml* to be severely punished: *You'll get it in the neck if you wreck your father's car!* **7 neck and neck** *infml* (of two horses, people, etc., in a race or competition) equal so far; with an equal chance of winning: *The two parties are neck and neck in the opinion polls.* **8 neck of the woods** *infml* area or part of the country: *What are you doing in this neck of the woods?* **9 up to one's neck in** *infml* in or deeply concerned with (esp. a difficult situation): *I'm up to my neck in debt.* (=I owe a lot of money.) | *up to his neck in trouble as usual* **10 -necked** /nekt/ *also* **-neck** (of a piece of clothing) having a certain shape or style of neck: *a V-necked dress* | *an open-necked shirt* (=unbuttoned at the neck) —see also **pain in the neck** (PAIN¹), **risk one's neck** (RISK¹), **save one's neck** (SAVE¹), **stick one's neck out** (STICK out)

neck² *v* [I] *infml* to kiss, CARESS, etc., but without having full sexual relations: *a boy and girl necking in the back of a car*

neck·band /ˈnekbænd/ *n* a narrow piece which fits around the neck of a garment

neck·er·chief /ˈnekətʃɪf‖-ər-/ *n* **-chiefs** *or* **-chieves** /tʃiːvz/ a square of cloth which is folded and worn around the neck

neck·lace /ˈnek-lɪs/ *n* a decorative chain, or string of jewels, shells, BEADS, etc., worn around the neck

necklace kil·ling /ˈ··· ˌ··/ *n* a form of killing in which a tyre is placed around the VICTIM's neck and set on fire. It has been used in South Africa esp. for people who are thought to be disloyal to a particular group.

neck·let /ˈnek-lɪt/ *n* a short necklace

neck·line /ˈnek-laɪn/ *n* the line made by the neck opening of a woman's garment: *a dress with a* **low**/**plunging neckline** (=leaving part of the chest uncovered)

neck·tie /ˈnektaɪ/ *n esp. AmE for* TIE¹ (1)

nec·ro·man·cy /ˈnekrəmænsi/ *n* [U] *lit* **1** the practice which claims to learn about the future by talking with the dead **2** magic, esp. evil magic —**-mancer** *n*

nec·ro·phil·i·a /ˌnekrəʊˈfɪliə, -krə-/ *also* **ne·croph·i·lis·m** /nɪˈkrɒfɪlɪzəm‖-ˈkrɑː-/— *n* [U] *tech* sexual interest in dead bodies

nec·ro·phil·i·ac /ˌnekrəʊˈfɪliæk, -krə-/ *n tech* a person who suffers from necrophilia

ne·crop·o·lis /nɪˈkrɒpəlɪs‖-ˈkrɑː-/ *n lit* a large CEMETERY (=burial ground), esp. that of an ancient city

nec·tar /ˈnektəʳ/ *n* [U] **1** the sweet liquid collected by bees from flowers **2** in CLASSICAL MYTHOLOGY, the drink of the gods —compare AMBROSIA **3** a sweet and pleasant drink: (fig.) *to taste the nectar of success* (=enjoy one's success) **4** thick juice made from certain fruits: *peach|guava|apricot nectar*

nec·ta·rine /ˈnektəriːn/ *n* (a tree that produces) a variety of PEACH which has a smooth skin

Ned·dy /ˈnedi/ *BrE* a name for a DONKEY (used mainly by and to children)

NEDO /ˌen iː diː ˈəʊ/ *also* **Neddy** *infml* [*the*] the National Economic Development Office; a government organization which held meetings of government, company, and TRADE UNION representatives to try to improve Britain's economic performance. The NEDO was closed down in 1992.

née /neɪ/ *adv* (used after a married woman's name and before her original family name) formerly named; born with the name: *Mrs Robert Cook née Carol Williams* | *Mrs Carol Cook née Williams*

need¹ /niːd/ *n* **1** [S;U (of, for)] the condition in which something necessary, desirable, or very useful is missing, wanted: *There's a growing need for new housing in this area.* | *The doctor says I am in need of a holiday.* | *This accident shows the need for stricter safety regulations.* | *We take money from the bank* **as the need arises.** (=whenever it is necessary) **2** [S;U+to-v] (a) necessary duty; what must be done; OBLIGATION: *There's no need (for you) to come if you don't want to.* | (fig.) *There's no need to be so rude!* (=you shouldn't be) **3** [C usu. pl.] *fml* something one wants or must have: *The hotel staff will supply all your needs|your every need.* **4** [U] *fml or euph* the state of not having enough food or money: *We are collecting money for families* **in need.** **5 if need be** if it is necessary: *I'll work all night if need be.* —see also NEEDS, **a friend in need** (FRIEND (6))

need² *v* [T *not usu. in progressive forms*] to have a need for; want for some useful purpose; REQUIRE: *Children need milk.* | *This soup needs more salt.* | *She likes to feel needed.* | *You need a lot of patience to do this work.* | *I badly need a holiday.* (=need one very much) | *You can borrow my typewriter — I won't be needing it today.* [I v-ing|to v] *My coat needs mending|needs to be mended.* | | *You didn't need to tell him; it just upset him.* [+obj+to-v|v-ed|v-ing] *I need you to help me.* | *I need my coat mended|mending.* | (fig.) *What children need* (=should have) *is a bit of discipline!*

need³ *v, negative short form* **needn't** /modal+to-v; not in progressive forms; usu. in questions or negatives] to have to: *"Need we go so soon?" "No, we needn't."* (Compare *"Yes, we must."*) *You needn't talk so loud.* (=you shouldn't) | *Do you think I need to go to the meeting?* | *You needn't have told him the news; he knew it already.* | *I need hardly tell you* (=I am sure you already know) *that we are very disappointed with your work.* | *"Was he late for the meeting again?" "Need you ask!"* (=it is unnecessary to ask, because he is always late)

▷ USAGE 1 In questions you can say either **Need** *he study?* or *Does he* **need** *to study?* and in negative statements you can say either *He* **needn't** *study* or *He doesn't* **need** *to study.* In statements **need** is followed only by *to-v: He* **needs** *to study.* 2 Compare *I* **needn't have** *put on my thick coat.* (=but I did) and *I* **didn't need** *to put on my thick coat.* (=so I didn't *or* but I did) 3 All the remarks above describe the modal use of **need** in British English. In American it is much less common as a modal, esp. in speech, where **have to** is used instead; thus *Does he* **have**/**need** *to study?* is common, but not **Need** *he study? He* **needn't** *study.* The modal forms, though not widely used, are of course easily understood. —see also MUST (USAGE), OUGHT (USAGE)◁

need·ful /ˈniːdfəl/ *n* [*the*] **1** *BrE infml* whatever is necessary: *The baby's crying; I'd better go and* **do the need-ful.** **2** *BrE humor* money: *We're rather short of the needful this week.* — ~**ly** *adv*

nee·dle¹ /ˈniːdl/ *n* **1** [C] a long pointed metal pin with a hole in one end through which a piece of thread is passed, used in sewing: *to thread a needle* | *a darning needle* **2** [C] a thin pointed object that looks like this: *a pine needle* (=a thin leaf of this tree) **3** [C] a thin pointed rod used in knitting (KNIT): *a knitting needle* | *a pair of size eight needles* **4** [C] a very small pointed jewel or piece of metal used in a RECORD PLAYER to pick up sound from records; STYLUS **5** [C] a very thin hollow pointed tube, at the end of a HYPODERMIC, which is pushed into someone's skin to put a liquid (esp. medicine) into the body or take out blood: (fig.) *He's back on the needle.* (=he is taking ADDICTIVE drugs again) **6** [C] a long thin moving pointer in a scientific instrument: *the needle of a compass* **7** [U] *BrE* strong dislike or bad feeling between people, teams, etc., esp. as a result of competition: *the game between the two old rivals is always a real* **needle match** (=which each wants to win very much because of bad feeling between them) **8 needle in a haystack** *infml* something very small which is hard to find in a big place —see also CLEOPATRA'S NEEDLE, PINS AND NEEDLES

needle² *v infml* [T (**into**)] to annoy (someone) by repeated unkind remarks, stupid jokes, etc.; PROVOKE: *The boys always needled Jim about being fat.* | *She tried to needle me into losing my temper.*

nee·dle·point /ˈniːdlpɔint/ *n* [U] pictures made by sewing different coloured threads onto or into a material: *His mother does needlepoint.*

need·less /ˈniːdləs/ *adj* **1** not needed; unnecessary: *What a lot of needless trouble, preparing for guests who don't turn up!* **2 needless to say** of course; as was to be expected: *Needless to say, it rained when I left my window open.* – –**ly** *adv* : *She was needlessly worried.*

nee·dle·wom·an /ˈniːdlˌwumən/ *BrE* ‖ **seamstress** *AmE— n* -**women** /ˌwimɪn/ a woman who can sew: *a good needlewoman* | *I'm no needlewoman.*

nee·dle·work /ˈniːdlwɜːk‖-wɜːrk/ *n* [U] sewing, esp. fancy sewing, done with needle and thread: *tired eyes from doing fine needlework* | *chairs with needlework cushions*

need·n't /ˈniːdnt/ *short for:* NEED³ not: *You needn't go if you don't want to.* | *I needn't have put on this thick coat.* (=but I did) —see MUST (USAGE), OUGHT (USAGE)

needs /niːdz/ *adv* old use or humor necessarily (in the phrases **must needs** or **needs must**): *If those are his commands we must needs obey.* | *I can't really afford to take a taxi, but needs must.*

need·y /ˈniːdi/ *adj* [also *n, the*+P] poor; without food, clothing, etc.: *a needy family* | *money to help the needy* —**iness** *n* [U]

ne'er /neəʳ/ *adv poet* never: *Will he ne'er come home again?*

ne'er-do-well /ˈneə duː ˌwel‖-neər-/ *n derog* a useless lazy person

ne·far·i·ous /nɪˈfeəriəs/ *adj fml* very wicked; evil: *a nefarious crime/criminal* – –**ly** *adv* – –**ness** *n* [U]

neg. *written abbrev. for:* NEGATIVE

ne·gate /nɪˈgeɪt/ *v* [T] *rather fml* **1** to cause to have no effect: *This burst of terrorist activity could completely negate our efforts to expand tourism here.* **2** to declare untrue; DENY —**gation** /nɪˈgeɪʃən/ *n* [C;U]

neg·a·tive¹ /ˈnegətɪv/ *adj* **1 a** refusing, doubting, or disapproving; saying or meaning "no": *He gave a negative answer to my request.* **b** containing one of the words "no", "not", "nothing", "never", etc.: *"Not at all" is a negative expression.* | *"Can't" and "cannot" are negative forms of "can".* —opposite **affirmative 2** without any active, useful, or helpful qualities; not CONSTRUCTIVE: *I've had enough negative advice – it only tells me what not to do!* | *a negative attitude* **3** showing the lack of what was hoped for or expected: *I'm looking for a house, but with negative results so far.* (=I haven't found one) | *a negative return on our investment* | *(med) The test for bacteria was negative.* (=none were found) **4** [*no comp.*] (of electricity) of the type that is carried by ELECTRONS **5** [*no comp.*] (of a number) less than zero: *a negative profit* (=a loss) | *If x is positive then minus x (−x) is negative.* **6** [*no comp.*] *med* having no RHESUS FACTOR in the blood: *RH-negative blood* —opposite **positive** (for 2, 3, 4, 5, 6) – –**ly** *adv*

negative² *n* **1** a statement saying or meaning "no"; a refusal or DENIAL: *The answer to my request was a strong negative.* | *The answer was* **in the negative.** —opposite **affirmative 2** a photograph or film showing dark areas

in nature as light and light areas as dark —opposite **positive**

negative³ *v* [T] *infml* **1** [*often pass.*] to decide against; refuse to accept: *The plan was negatived by the committee.* **2** to disprove

negative pole /ˌ··· ˈ·/ *n* **1** the end of a MAGNET which turns naturally away from the Earth **2** a CATHODE

ne·glect¹ /nɪˈglekt/ *v* [T] **1** to give too little attention or care to: *a neglected garden* | *You've been neglecting your work.* **2** [+*to-v/v-ing; obj*] to fail (to do something), esp. because of carelessness or forgetfulness: *Don't neglect to lock the door/locking the door when you leave.*

neglect² *n* [U] **1** the action of neglecting: *The tenants are complaining about the council's neglect of their property.* **2** the condition of being neglected: *The garden has fallen into a state of neglect.*

ne·glect·ful /nɪˈglektfəl/ *adj* [(**of**)] in the habit of neglecting things; forgetful or careless: *a father who is neglectful of his children* (=doesn't give them enough attention and care) – –**ly** *adv* – –**ness** *n* [U]

neg·li·gee /ˈneglɪʒeɪ‖ˌneglɪˈʒeɪ/ *n* a woman's light and usu. fancy garment, worn over or in place of a NIGHTDRESS

neg·li·gent /ˈneglɪdʒənt/ *adj* **1** not taking enough care; neglectful: *The report said the doctor had been negligent in not giving the woman a full examination.* **2** *apprec* careless in a pleasant way; NONCHALANT: *to dress with negligent grace* – –**ly** *adv* —**gence** *n* [U] : *The accident was caused by the gross negligence of the driver.*

neg·li·gi·ble /ˈneglɪdʒəbəl/ *adj* too slight or unimportant to be worth any attention: *The damage to my car is negligible.* —**bly** *adv*

ne·go·ti·a·ble /nɪˈgəʊʃiəbəl, -ʃə-/ *adj* **1** able to be settled or changed by being negotiated: *a negotiable contract* | *He says the price is not negotiable.* **2** *tech* (of a cheque or order to pay money) that can be exchanged for money **3** *infml* that can be travelled through, along, etc.: *The road is only negotiable in dry weather.*

ne·go·ti·ate /nɪˈgəʊʃieɪt/ *v* **1** [I (**with, for**)] to talk with another person or group in order to try to come to an agreement or settle an argument: *The government says it will not negotiate with the terrorists.* | *negotiating for an improvement in the rate of pay* | *We are negotiating (with the council) to have this road closed to traffic.* **2** [T (**with**)] to produce (an agreement) or settle (a piece of business) in this way: *The trade union negotiated a new contract with the management.* **3** [T] *infml* to succeed in dealing with or getting past (something difficult): *to negotiate a steep hill/sharp bend in one's car* **4** [T] *tech* to get or give money for (a cheque, etc.) —**ator** *n* : *a skilful negotiator*

negotiating ta·ble /·ˈ····· ˌ··/ *[the]* a table (sometimes imaginary, but often real) where people meet to discuss their differences and agree what should be done: *No decisions have yet been taken on nurses' pay, as the parties have only just reached the negotiating table.*

ne·go·ti·a·tion /nɪˌgəʊʃiˈeɪʃən/ *n* **1** [C;U] also **negotiations** *pl.* — an act of negotiating: *The treaty was the result of long negotiations.* | *the negotiation of a new contract* | *The contract is still* **under negotiation.** (=in the process of being settled) **2** [U] the successful completion of a difficult trip or other activity: *Negotiation of the slippery road was not easy.*

Ne·gro /ˈniːgrəʊ/ **Ne·gress** /ˈniːgrəs/*fem.— n* -**groes** *tech or not polite* a person belonging to a dark-skinned esp. African race; black person —see also BLACK (USAGE)

▷ USAGE Black people now would rather be called **black** than **Negro.**◁

ne·groid /ˈniːgrɔɪd/ *adj tech or fml* like a Negro in appearance

Negro spir·i·tu·al /ˌ·· ˈ····/ *n* a SPIRITUAL²

Ne·gus /ˈniːgəs/, **Arthur** (1903–85) a British presenter of two television programmes about ANTIQUES (=very old, valuable objects)

Neh·ru /ˈneəruː/, **Ja·wa·har·lal** /dʒəˈwɑːhəˌlɑːl‖-hər-/ (1889–1964) an Indian politician and Prime Minister from 1947 who had the idea of NEUTRALITY towards the larger, more powerful countries. He was the father of Indira Gandhi.

neigh /neɪ/ *v* [I] to make the loud long cry that a horse or PONY makes —**neigh** *n*

neigh·bour *BrE* ‖ **-bor** *AmE* /ˈneɪbəʳ/ *n* **1** someone who lives near another: *my next-door neighbour* (=the person living in the next house) | *We're neighbours now.* | (fig.) *The country has always had good relations with its neighbours in the region.* **2 love thy neighbour** a phrase from the Bible, often used humorously or with IRONY

neigh·bour·hood *BrE* ‖ **-borhood** *AmE* /ˈneɪbəhʊd‖-ər-/ *n* **1** [C+*sing.|pl. v*] a group of people and their homes forming a small area within a larger place such as a town: *a quiet neighbourhood with good shops* | *a neighbourhood school* **2** [S] the area around a point or place: *somewhere in the neighbourhood (of the station)* | (fig.) *a price in the neighbourhood of £500*

neighbourhood watch /ˌ··· ˈ·/ *n* [U] a system by which people in an area keep watch on each other's houses in order to keep away thieves. The people involved are usually honest, respectable people with nice houses, living in good neighbourhoods. They report anything strange or anyone behaving badly to the police, who deal with it.

neigh·bour·ing *BrE* ‖ **-boring** *AmE* /ˈneɪbərɪŋ/ *adj* [A *no comp.*] (of places) near or close by: *a bus service between the town and the neighbouring villages*

neigh·bour·ly *BrE* ‖ **-borly** *AmE* /ˈneɪbəli‖-ər-/ *adj* friendly; like or typical of a good neighbour: *neighbourly help* —**liness** *n* [U]

Neigh·bours /ˈneɪbəz‖-bərz/ an Australian television SOAP OPERA shown in many countries around the world. It is very popular with people of all ages, partly because of its setting, and also because the characters are ordinary families living ordinary lives; some of the actors from the programme, such as Kylie Minogue and Jason Donovan, are now famous as singers and film stars.

Nei·man-Mar·cus /ˌniːmən ˈmɑːkəs‖-ˈmɑːr-/ a very expensive US chain department store with branches in many large cities. People associate Neiman-Marcus with rich people. Sometimes it is called "Needless Markup" because it is so expensive.

nei·ther¹ /ˈnaɪðəʳ‖ˈniː-/ *determiner, pron* not one and not the other of two: *Neither road|Neither of the roads is very good.* (=they are both bad) | *"Will you have tea or coffee?" "Neither thanks."* —compare NONE¹ (2)

neither² *conj* (used before the first of two or more choices separated by **nor**) not either: *He neither drinks, smokes, nor eats meat.* | *Neither my father nor I were there.*

neither³ *adv* (used with **no, not, never,** etc.) also not: *"I can't swim." "Neither can I." "Me neither."* (=I can't, either.) | *I wasn't there, and neither was Mary|neither were the children.* —compare EITHER⁴; see ALSO (USAGE)

▷ USAGE Notice the word order after **neither/nor,** which is the same as that of a question: **Neither/Nor** *can I* | **Neither/Nor** *does she.*◁

nel·ly¹ /ˈneli/ *n BrE sl* **not on your nelly** certainly not

nelly² *adj AmE infml* (of a man) EFFEMINATE; HOMOSEXUAL

Nelson

Nel·son¹ /ˈnelsən/, **Ho·ra·ti·o** /həˈreɪʃiəʊ/ (1758–1805) an English ADMIRAL who lost his right arm, and the sight in his right eye, during the wars against France in the 1790s, and he became a national HERO after winning several victories at sea, the most famous being the battle of Trafalgar in 1805. As he was dying after the battle of Trafalgar he is believed to have said "Kiss me, Hardy" to his friend, Sir Thomas Hardy.

Nelson², **Ozzie** see OZZIE AND HARRIET

Nelson³, **Willie** (1933–) an American singer and writer of COUNTRY MUSIC

Nelson's col·umn /ˌ·· ˈ··/ a very tall stone tower in Trafalgar Square, London, built in honour of Admiral Nelson, with a STATUE of him on the top —see colour map on page 817

nem con /ˌnem ˈkɒn‖-ˈkɑːn/ *adv Lat law* without any opposition: *The suggestion was accepted nem con by the committee.*

nem·e·sis /ˈneməsɪs/ *n* **-ses** /siːz/ [C;U] *lit* (*sometimes cap.*) just and esp. unavoidable punishment, often considered as a goddess or an active force

neo- see WORD FORMATION

ne·o·clas·sic·al /ˌniːəʊˈklæsɪkəl◄/ *adj tech* done or made recently, but in the CLASSICAL style of a former time, esp. in the style of ancient Greece and Rome

ne·o·co·lo·ni·al·is·m /ˌniːəʊkəˈləʊniəlɪzəm/ *n* [U] *derog* the trading and political practices by which a powerful country indirectly keeps or enlarges its control over esp. recently independent countries, without the need of military force —compare COLONIALISM

ne·o·lith·ic /ˌniːəʊˈlɪθɪk◄/ *adj* (*often cap.*) of the latest period of the STONE AGE, about 10,000 years ago, when people began to settle in villages, grow crops, keep animals, polish stone for tools, and use the wheel: *neolithic villages* —compare PALEOLITHIC

ne·ol·o·gis·m /niːˈɒlədʒɪzəm‖-ˈɑːl-/ *n* **1** [C] a new word or expression, or a new meaning for an older word: *The term "user-friendly" is a neologism that has come into everyday speech from the computer industry.* **2** [U] the use of such new words or meanings

ne·on /ˈniːɒn‖-ɑːn/ *n* [U] a chemically inactive gas that is a simple substance (ELEMENT)

Ne·o-Na·zi /ˌniːəʊ ˈnɑːtsi◄/ *adj* [A] (of modern politicians or political parties) having ideas similar to those of Adolf Hitler's Nazi Party —**Neo-Nazi** *n*

neon light /ˈ·· ·/ *n* a glass tube filled with neon which lights when an electric current goes through it, often shaped to form a **neon sign** advertising something

ne·o·phyte /ˈniːəfaɪt/ *n* **1** *fml* a new student of an art, skill, trade, etc.; BEGINNER **2** a new member of a religious group

Ne·pal /nɪˈpɔːl/ a country in S central Asia, in the Himalayan mountains, capital Katmandu; population 18,442,000 (1989). It is famous in Britain as the homeland of the Gurkha soldiers who serve in the British army, and now attracts many tourists who go there to walk and climb in the Himalayas.

Nep·al·ese /ˌnepəˈliːz◄/ *n* **1** [*the*·P] people of or from Nepal: *The Nepalese are very friendly people.* **2** [U] the language of Nepal; Nepali —**Nepalese** *adj* : *Nepalese baskets* | *He's Nepalese.*

Ne·pa·li /nɪˈpɔːli/ *n* **-lis** *or* **Nepali** **1** [C] a person who lives in or comes from Nepal **2** [U] the language of Nepal —**Nepali** *adj*

neph·ew /ˈnefjuː, ˈnev-‖ˈnef-/ *n* **1** the son of one's brother or sister **2** the son of one's wife's or husband's brother or sister —compare NIECE

ne·phri·tis /nɪˈfraɪtɪs/ *n* [U] *med* a disease of the KIDNEY

nep·o·tis·m /ˈnepətɪzəm/ *n* [U] the practice of giving one's relatives unfair advantages when one has power, esp. by giving them good jobs. Most disapprove of nepotism, although it is quite often done. —**tistic** /ˌnepəˈtɪstɪk◄/ *adj*

Nep·tune /ˈneptjuːn‖-tuːn/ **1** the PLANET eighth in order from the sun —see picture at SOLAR SYSTEM **2** in CLASSICAL MYTHOLOGY, the Roman god of the sea, similar to the Greek god Poseidon. He is usu. pictured with a beard, a fish's tail, and a TRIDENT (=a type of large fork with three points). —see colour picture on page 423

nerd /nɜːd‖nɜːrd/ *n derog sl* an unattractive or unpleasant person, esp. one who is thought to lack ordinary social skills

ner·e·id /ˈnɪəri·ɪd/ *n* a female spirit in CLASSICAL MYTHOLOGY who lived in the sea; sea NYMPH

Ne·ro /ˈnɪərəʊ/ (AD 37–68) a Roman EMPEROR, said to have killed his mother, wives, and many others. He blamed the Christians for causing the great fire of Rome in AD 64 and many were killed. He is also known for his performances as an actor and musician, and is usu. shown in pictures fiddling (=playing the VIOLIN) while Rome is on fire behind him. —see also **fiddle while Rome burns** (FIDDLE²)

nerve¹ /nɜːv‖nɜːrv/ n **1** [C] any of the threadlike parts of the body which form a system to carry feelings and messages to and from the brain –see picture at TEETH **2** [U] courage, determination, and self-control: *I wanted to tell her exactly what I thought, but I* **lost my nerve**. | *It must have taken a lot of nerve to risk so much money on one product.* **3** [S;U] *derog* disrespectful rudeness; CHEEK; EF-FRONTERY: *He's the dirtiest man I know, and he has the nerve to tell me my shoes need cleaning!* | *What (a) nerve!* –see also NERVES, **strain every nerve** (STRAIN)

nerve² v [T (UP)] *fml* to give courage to (someone, esp. oneself) before doing something difficult or dangerous: [+obj+to-v/for] *The parachutist nerved himself to jump/for the jump.*

nerve cen·tre /'· ˌ···/ n the place from which a system, organization, etc., is controlled

nerve gas /'· ˌ·/ n [C;U] a gas, used as a weapon but forbidden by many countries, which attacks the central nervous system of anyone who breathes it in

nerve·less /'nɜːvləs‖'nɜːr-/ adj **1** weak or without courage **2** not nervous; COOL¹ (2) – ~ **ly** adv – ~ **ness** n [U]

nerve-rack·ing /'· ˌ··/ adj *infml* difficult to do or bear calmly because frightening and dangerous: *a nerve-racking journey on a narrow mountain road*

nerves /nɜːvz‖nɜːrvz/ n [P] *infml* **1** a condition of great nervousness; ANXIETY: *She gets nerves before every exam.* | *His nerves are very bad.* (=he is habitually nervous) | *I'm just a bundle of nerves today.* | *Before making the speech I had a drink to steady my nerves.* **2 get on someone's nerves** to make someone annoyed or bad-tempered: *That man/music gets on my nerves.* –see also WAR OF NERVES

ner·vous /'nɜːvəs‖'nɜːr-/ adj **1** [(of)] rather frightened; worried about what might happen: *Don't be nervous – the doctor won't hurt you.* | *I've got to give a speech and I'm a bit nervous about it.* | *a nervous smile* | *He's nervous of strangers.* **2** of the nervous system of the body, or the feelings: *a nervous disorder* **3 not suitable for people of a nervous disposition** a phrase used as a warning before a violent or frightening television or radio programme – ~ **ly** adv – ~ **ness** n [U]

▷ USAGE Compare **nervous, concerned,** and **anxious.** You can be **nervous** (=rather afraid) before or during an event: *I'm always nervous when I have to speak in public.* You can be **concerned** (=worried) about something that is happening now, and often about another person: *We're rather concerned about your father's health.* **Anxious** usually means "worried about something which might happen": *Your father will be anxious until he knows that you're safe.*◁

nervous break·down /ˌ·· ˈ···/ n a serious medical condition of deep anxiety, tiredness, and uncontrollable crying, which makes the sufferer unable to do his/her usual work or activities

nervous sys·tem /'·· ˌ··/ n the system (=the brain, nerves, etc.) in people and animals which receives and passes on feelings, messages, and other such information from inside and outside the body –see also CENTRAL NERVOUS SYSTEM

nerv·y /'nɜːvi‖'nɜːr-/ adj sl **1** BrE nervous and anxious **2** AmE disrespectfully rude; having NERVE¹ (3)

Nes·caf·é /'neskæfeɪ‖ˌneskæ'feɪ/ n [C;U] *tdmk* (a cup of) a make of INSTANT coffee, which is used as a word meaning instant coffee: *a cup of Nescafé* | *Do you want real coffee or Nescafé?*

Nes·quik /'neskwɪk/ n [C;U] *tdmk* a type of powder made by Nestlé and mixed with milk to make MILK SHAKE; there are different FLAVOURS of Nesquik, which is esp. popular with children

Nes·sie /'nesi/ n a familiar name for the Loch Ness Monster –see LOCH NESS MONSTER

nest¹ /nest/ n **1** a hollow place built or found by a bird for use as a home and a place to keep its eggs **2** the settled and protected home of certain other animals or insects: *an ants' nest* | (fig.) *The husband and wife built themselves a comfortable nest.* **3** [+of] a place that provides favourable conditions for a particular usu. bad activity:

The palace was a nest of intrigue. **4** (of)] a group of similar objects which fit closely inside one another: *a nest of tables/boxes* **5** a protected position for one or more weapons (esp. in the phrase **machinegun nest**)

nest² v **1** [I] to build or use a nest: *Most birds nest in trees.* **2** [I;T] to (cause to) fit closely inside another thing or each other: *nested cooking pots*

nest egg /'· ·/ n an amount of money saved for special future use

nes·tle /'nesəl/ v [I+adv/prep;T+obj+adv/prep] to (cause to) settle or lie in a close comfortable position: *She nestled her head on/against his shoulder.* | *villages nestling among the mountains* | *to nestle down in a big chair with a book*

Nest·lé /'nesəl, 'nesleɪ/ tdmk a large company which makes milk-based products such as baby milk, chocolate, and other foods; it is the maker of Nescafé. It has been the object of many BOYCOTTS (=people refusing to buy its products) because of the way it sells baby milk in poor countries.

nest·ling /'nestlɪŋ, 'neslɪŋ/ n a young bird who has not left the nest

net¹ /net/ n **1** [C;U] a material of strings, wires, threads, etc., twisted, tied, or woven together with regular equal spaces between them – compare MESH **2** [C] any of various objects made from this, such as **a** a large piece of net spread out under water to catch fish **b** a bag of net on a frame with a handle, for catching things: *a butterfly net* **c** a length of net dividing the two sides of the court in tennis, BADMINTON, etc. – see picture at TENNIS **d** an enclosure at the back of the goal in football, HOCKEY, etc. **e** the bag-like net on the GOAL in NETBALL and BASKETBALL –see also HAIRNET **3** [C] a network (esp. in the phrases **radio net, communication(s) net**) **4** [C] a piece of material in a frame, in which firemen catch someone falling or jumping –see also NETS, **cast one's net wide** (CAST¹)

net

net² v -tt- [T] **1** to catch (as if) in a net: *We netted three fish.* [+obj(i)+obj(d)] *She's netted herself a rich husband.* **2** to cover with a net: *Net the fruit trees to protect them from birds.* **3** *infml* to hit or kick (the ball) into the net in a game

net³ also **nett** BrE– adj [A;after n] (of an amount) when nothing further is to be subtracted: *net profit* (=after tax, rent, etc. are paid) | *net weight* (=of an object without its packet) | *This jar of coffee weighs 250 grams net.* | (fig.) *The* **net result** (=the result when everything has been considered) *of our efforts was one small basket of strawberries.* –compare GROSS¹

net⁴ v -tt- [T (for)] to gain as a profit: *The sale netted a fat profit (for the company).* [+obj(i)+obj(d)] *It netted us a large profit.*

net·ball /'netbɔːl/ n [U] a game that is related to BASKETBALL but usu. played by women, in which teams make points by making a ball fall through one of the two high rings at the opposite ends of a court. It is one of the sports played by girls of school age in Britain, but not usu. by boys.

Net Book A·gree·ment /ˌ· ˈ· ·ˌ··/ [the] an agreement between booksellers in Britain to sell books at the prices decided by the PUBLISHERS. There has been much discussion of whether this agreement is good for the public and the book industry. Some booksellers would like to stop it, but others believe that small bookshops would be forced out of business by the competition.

net cord /'· ·/ n a shot in tennis that hits the top edge of the net but lands correctly on the opponent's side of the court

neth·er /'neðəʳ/ adj [A] *lit or humor* in a lower place or position: *his nether garments* (=trousers) | *nether regions*

Neth·er·lands /'neðələndz‖-ðər-/ [the] a country in NW Europe. The capital is Amsterdam but the government is at The Hague; population 14,835,000 (1989). Most of the country is flat and much of it is below the level of the sea.

Its people (the **Dutch**) have enclosed and drained (DRAIN) parts of the sea to get more land. Although Holland is only one part of the Netherlands, most people say Holland when they mean the whole country. People connect the Netherlands with WINDMILLS, TULIPS, and wooden shoes (CLOGS).

Netherlands An·til·les /ˌneðələndz ænˈtɪliːz ‖ -ðər-/ a group of islands in the West Indies, esp. Bonaire and Curacao; capital Willemstad; population 193,000 (1989)

neth·er·most /ˈneðəməʊst‖-ðər-/ adj [A] lit lowest: the nethermost point on the map

nets /nets/ n [(the) P] (in cricket) one or more WICKETs surrounded by a net, in which players can practise

nett /net/ adj BrE for NET³

net·ting /ˈnetɪŋ/ n [U] string, wire, etc., made into a net: a fence of wire netting

net·tle¹ /ˈnetl/ n a wild plant with hairy leaves which may sting and make red marks on the skin —see also **grasp the nettle** (GRASP¹)

nettle² v [T] to make (someone) angry or impatient, esp. for only a short time; IRRITATE: I was rather nettled by his rude questions.

nettle rash /ˈ·· ·/ n [C;U] an area of stinging red spots on one's skin: I sometimes get (a) nettle rash from eating fish.

net·work¹ /ˈnetwɜːk‖-wɜːrk/ n **1** a large system of lines, tubes, wires, etc., that cross one another or are connected with one another: Britain's railway network | the network of blood vessels in the body | (fig.) a network of friends in different cities **2** a group of radio or television stations in different places using many of the same broadcasts **3** a set of computers that are connected to each other and can be used as a means of sending and sharing information or messages —see also LAN, OLD-BOY NETWORK

network² v [I;T] to connect (computers) to form a NETWORK¹ (3)

net·work·ing /ˈnetwɜːkɪŋ‖-ɜːr-/ n [U] the establishing of professional connections with the aim of sharing information, advice, or support. In Britain the word is used esp. by women working at home, or in areas which do not give them the advantages enjoyed by people in other businesses or professions. In the US the word is used generally about anyone improving their professional connections. —compare OLD-BOY, NETWORK

Network South-East /ˌ·· ·ˈ·/ an area within the British railway system, including London and SE England but also stretching as far N as Oxford, Northampton, and Cambridge, and as far W as Exeter.

neu·ral·gia /njʊˈrældʒə‖nʊ-/ n [U] med sharp pain along the length of one or more nerves —**gic** adj : neuralgic pain

neuro- see WORD FORMATION

neu·rol·o·gy /njʊˈrolədʒi‖nʊˈraː-/ n [U] the scientific study of the NERVOUS SYSTEM and its diseases —**gist** n

neu·ro·sis /njʊˈrəʊsɪs‖nʊ-/ n -ses /siːz/ [C;U] med a disorder of the mind in which a person suffers from strong unreasonable fears and ideas about the outside world, troubled relations with other people, and often physical illness

neu·rot·ic /njʊˈrotɪk‖nʊˈraː-/ adj **1** of or suffering from neurosis: neurotic fears **2** not tech unreasonably anxious or sensitive: She's neurotic about getting fat! —**neurotic** n

neu·ter¹ /ˈnjuːtəʳ‖ˈnuː-/ adj tech **1** (in grammar) for or belonging to the class of words that usu. includes most of the words for things rather than males or females: a neuter noun/ending **2** (of plants or animals) with no or undeveloped sexual organs: Worker bees are neuter. —compare FEMININE, MASCULINE

neuter² v [T usu. pass.] euph to remove part of the sex organs of (an animal) by an operation, to prevent (the animal) producing young —compare CASTRATE, SPAY, ALTER (2)

neu·tral¹ /ˈnjuːtrəl‖ˈnuː-/ adj **1** without strong feelings or opinions on either side of a question or argument: neutral reporting of a political issue **2** being or belonging to a country which is not fighting or helping either side in a war: a neutral country | neutral waters **3** without strong or noticeable qualities, esp. of the stated kind, such as a very weak or colourless: a neutral colour **b** (in chemistry) neither acid nor BASE¹ (5) **c** with no electrical charge — ~**ly** adv

neutral² n **1** [U] (in a car or other machine) the position of the GEARS in which no power is carried from the engine to the wheels: When you start the engine, be sure the car is in neutral. **2** [C] a NEUTRAL¹ (2) person or country

neu·tral·i·ty /njuːˈtrælɪti‖nuː-/ n [U] the condition or quality of being neutral, esp. in a war

neu·tral·ize also **-ise** BrE /ˈnjuːtrəlaɪz‖ˈnuː-/ v [T] **1** to cause to have no effect; destroy the value, force, or activity of: to neutralize an acid with a base | Rising prices tend to neutralize increased wages. —compare COUNTERACT **2** to make (a country) neutral by international agreement —**-ization** /ˌnjuːtrəlaɪˈzeɪʃən‖ˌnuːtrələ-/ n [U]

neu·tron /ˈnjuːtron‖ˈnuːtraːn/ n a very small piece of matter that carries no electricity and that together with the PROTON forms the NUCLEUS (=central part) of an atom — see also ELECTRON

neutron bomb /ˈ·· ˌ·/ n a kind of NUCLEAR bomb that destroys life but which causes little damage to property

Ne·va·da /nɪˈvɑːdə‖-ˈvæ-/ written abbrev. NV— a state in the western US, between California and Utah. Much of it is desert, but it is also known for legalized gambling (GAMBLE) and PROSTITUTION, and for the city of Las Vegas. —see colour map on pages 1374-5 — ~ **n** n, adj

nev·er /ˈnevəʳ/ adv **1** not ever; not at any time: I've never been to Paris. | I've never been so annoyed in all my life! (=I was extremely annoyed) | I'll never forget that night. | Never leave your car unlocked. | Never (before) have I met with such great kindness. | "Have you ever eaten snails?" "No, and I hope I never will!" **2** (in certain phrases) not: Never fear! (=don't worry) | He never so much as said "Thanks". (=didn't even thank me) | This dirty shirt will never do for your interview. (=isn't good enough to wear) | (shows surprise) I never knew you were interested in football! | (BrE) You're never eighteen! (=surely not) **3** (Well) I never (did)! I've never seen/heard anything like this! —see also **never mind** (MIND²)

▷ USAGE Compare these sentences which describe how often something happens. Notice that things happen more often as you go down the list: 1 The sun never shines at night. 2 I rarely/hardly ever/seldom (fml) work at the week-end. 3 I occasionally/sometimes work late on Fridays. 4 They often/frequently eat out at a restaurant. 5 She usually/nearly always comes to work by train. 6 The sun always rises in the east.◁

never-end·ing /ˌ·· ˈ··/ adj continuous, never stopping, or at least not for a very long time: a never-ending catalogue of all his illnesses

nev·er·more /ˌnevəˈmɔːʳ‖-vər-/ adv poet never again — compare EVERMORE

never-never /ˌ·· ˈ··/ n on the never-never BrE humor sl by HIRE PURCHASE: to buy a car on the never-never

never-never land /ˌ·· ˈ·· ·/ an imaginary and wonderful place; a FANTASY or dream land (from the imaginary country in the story of Peter Pan, by J M Barrie, in which children always remain children and never grow up)

nev·er·the·less /ˌnevəðəˈles‖-vər-/ also **nonetheless** — adv in spite of that; yet: What you said was true but (it was) nevertheless unkind. | I can't go. Nevertheless, I appreciate the invitation. | This year's fall in profits was not unexpected. Nevertheless, it is very disappointing.

Ne·vis /ˈniːvɪs/ **1** an island in the Caribbean, one of the Leeward Islands and part of the state of St Kitts-Nevis **2** see BEN NEVIS

new /njuː‖nuː/ adj **1** having existed for only a short time; recently begun, made, built, etc.: a new film | a new government | the newest fashions | This idea isn't new. | Have you seen their new baby? [also n, the)] The new is sometimes more attractive than the old. **2** [no comp.] not used or owned by anyone before: They sell new and secondhand books. | a **brand new** bicycle **3** [A] only recently found or known: the discovery of a new star | important new evidence in the murder trial **b** having been in the stated position or state for only a short time: a new member of the club | the new nations of Africa **4** [A no comp.] different from an earlier one of the same kind; (an)other: Our teacher got a new job, so our class had to have a new teacher. (=another teacher) | They've gone to Australia to start a new life. | The company is moving into new markets. **5** first picked of a crop: delicious little new peas **6** [F+to] **a** just beginning to know about or do; still unfamiliar with: a young clerk new to the job **b** unfamiliar

to: *Her name is new to me: I've never heard of her before.*
7 new- newly; recently: *a newborn baby* | *a new-laid egg*
—see also NEWLY, NEWS **8 What's new?** *AmE infml*
(friendly greeting) *— ~ness n* [U]
▷ USAGE **New** is a general word for something that exists now but has been in existence for only a short time:
a new road/law/book. **Recent** describes something
that happened or came into existence a short time ago,
and is used esp. of events: *our recent holiday* | *The re-*
cent *election produced a new government.* **Modern**
covers a longer period of time than **new,** and means
"belonging to the present time or the not too distant
past": *an examination in modern history, from 1550 to
the present day.* | **Modern** *medical science has con-
quered many diseases.* **Contemporary** means "belonging to the present": contemporary *art/music.* **Current**
describes something that exists now, but was different
before and may be different again: *The* current *fashion
is for men to have short hair.*◁

New Age Move·ment /ˌ· ˈ· ˌ··/ [*the*] a development of
popular interest in esp. spiritual and MYSTICAL ideas,
ways of life, products, etc. which appeared in the 1980s
in Britain and America. It is deeply distrusted by many
FUNDAMENTALIST Christians in the US, who think the
devil is behind it. —**New Age** /ˌ· ˈ·◂/ *adj* : *New Age
music/jewellery*

New Age trav·el·ler /ˌ· · ˈ···/ *n* [*usu.* P] *BrE* a person who
has rejected (REJECT) the values of ordinary society and
goes from place to place living in a vehicle (sometimes
a CARAVAN, often an old bus or LORRY). They are disliked
and distrusted by many people, who believe that they
steal things and use drugs. —compare GIPSY

New·ark /ˈnjuːək‖ˈnuːərk/ **1** a large city and port in New
Jersey, US, across the Hudson River from New York **2**
also **Newark International Airport**—one of the main
airports serving the New York area **3** a town in Nottinghamshire, central England, officially called
Newark-on-Trent

new blood /ˌ· ˈ·/ *n* [U] new members of a group, esp. when
thought of as bringing new ideas, ENERGY, etc.: *What we
need in this company is (some) new blood.*

new·born /ˈnjuːbɔːn‖ˈnuːbɔːrn/ *adj* [A] (of a baby) recently
born —**newborn** *n* : *clothes for newborns*

new broom /ˌ· ˈ·/ *n esp. BrE* a newly appointed person who
is eager to make changes, not necessarily approved of by
people already there

New Bruns·wick /njuː ˈbrʌnzwɪk‖nuː-/ a PROVINCE of
Canada on the Gulf of St. Lawrence

New·burg /ˈnjuːbɜːg‖ˈnuːbɜːrg/ *adj* [F] (of seafood) cooked
or served in a thick liquid made from cream, eggs, butter, wine, and NUTMEG: *lobster Newburg*

New·cas·tle /ˈnjuːkɑːsəl‖ˈnuːkæsəl/ a city, port, and important industrial centre in New South Wales, SE Australia, near the mouth of the Hunter river

Newcastle Brown /ˌ···· ˈ·/ *n* [C;U] *tdmk* a type of strong ALE
that is made in N England by Newcastle Breweries
▶ CULTURAL NOTE Many people from N England, esp. from
Newcastle, are proud of Newcastle Brown and say that it
is the best English beer◀

New·cas·tle upon Tyne /ˌ····· ·· ˈ·/ also **Newcastle**— a city
and port in Tyne and Wear, NE England, where the local
government for that COUNTY is based. It is mainly industrial, including a large shipbuilding area and coalfields,
but also has a university, castle, and CATHEDRAL. —see
colour map on page 818

new·com·er /ˈnjuːkʌməʳ‖ˈnuː-/ *n* [(to)] a person who has
only recently arrived or only recently started an activity:
a newcomer to the city (=visiting or living there for the
first time) | *I'm a newcomer to teaching.*

new deal /ˌ· ˈ·/ *n* **1** a new and fairer plan of esp. social
or political action: *a new deal for farmers with higher
meat and milk prices* **2** (*caps.*) the programme of economic and social reform introduced in the US by President Roosevelt in the 1930s

New Del·hi /ˌ· ˈ··/ the capital city of India, built to the south
of the old city of Delhi by the British in 1912

New Dem·o·crat·ic Par·ty /ˌ· ··· ˈ·· ˌ··/ [*the*] a political party
in Canada which supports SOCIALIST ideas

New En·gland /ˌ· ˈ··/ the states of the northeast corner of
the US: Maine, New Hampshire, Vermont, Mas-

sachusetts, Rhode Island, and Connecticut. New England
is connected with well-educated and fairly wealthy people, New England ACCENTS, IVY LEAGUE colleges, very neat
houses, small towns aħd cities, long, snowy winters, and
the leaves changing to bright colours in the autumn. —
see colour map on pages 1374–5

New En·gland·er /ˌ· ˈ···/ *n* a person who lives or was born
in New England

New England Jour·nal of Medi·cine /ˌ· ˌ·· ˌ·· · ˈ··/ [*the*]
the title of a highly-respected American magazine which
reports recent discoveries or ideas in medicine, drugs,
etc. Its technical language is generally suitable only for
doctors and other medical professionals. —see also
LANCET

New En·glish Bi·ble /ˌ· ·· ˈ··/ [*the*] a modern English translation of the Bible, which was introduced in 1970

new·fan·gled /ˌnjuːˈfæŋɡəld◂‖ˌnuː-/ *adj derog* or *humor* (of
ideas, machines, etc.) new but neither necessary nor better: *We need better teachers, not newfangled ideas about
education!* | *ridiculous newfangled gadgets for chopping
vegetables*

New For·est /ˌ· ˈ··/ [*the*] an area with many OAK and BEECH
trees, in Hampshire, southern England. Many people
spend holidays there, riding horses or walking in the
woods.

New For·est po·ny /ˌ· ·· ˈ··/ *n* a type of PONY (=small horse)
which lives half-wild in the New Forest

new-found /ˈ· ·/ *adj* newly discovered or obtained: *British industry has a new-found optimism now the election
is over.*

New·found·land¹ /ˈnjuːfəndlənd‖ˈnuː-/ a PROVINCE of eastern
Canada consisting of the island of Newfoundland and the
coast of Labrador. It is important for fishing.

Newfoundland² *n* a type of large dog originally from Newfoundland. Newfoundlands are good swimmers and very
strong, and are famous for saving people who are
drowning.

New·gate /ˈnjuːɡeɪt‖ˈnuː-/ also **Newgate pris·on** /ˌ·· ˈ··/—
a prison in London from about 1200 to about 1900, known
for its terrible conditions and for holding some of the
most famous criminals of the time

New Guin·ea /ˌ· ˈ··/ *n* see PAPUA NEW GUINEA

New Hamp·shire /ˌ· ˈ··/ *written abbrev.* **NH**— a state in the
NE US, known for its beautiful lakes and mountains. It
was the first state to declare its independence from Britain (1776). —see colour map on pages 1374–5

New·ha·ven /ˈnjuːheɪvən‖ˈnuː-/ a port and town on the S
coast of England, from which ferries (FERRY¹) sail to
France

New Ha·ven /ˌ· ˈ··/ a city and port in S Connecticut, US,
an early settlement of the English Puritans (1638), and
the home town of Yale University

New Heb·ri·des /ˌ· ˈ···/ [*the*] see VANUATU

Ne Win /ˌneɪ ˈwɪn/ (1911–) the PRIME MINISTER of Myanmar from 1958 to 1960 and president from 1962 to 1981

New Jer·sey /ˌ· ˈ··/ *written abbrev.* **NJ** also **Jersey** *infml*—
a state in NE US, with a large population and much in-
dustry. It was one of the 13 original British colonies
(COLONY). —see colour maps on pages 1374–5 and page
1376

New Je·ru·sa·lem /ˌ· ·ˈ···/ [*the*] *bibl* a Christian name for
heaven

New Kids On The Block /ˌ· ˌ· · · ˈ·/ an American popular
music group, first successful in the late 1980s

New Left /ˌ· ˈ·/ [*the*] a left-wing political movement, esp.
among students, that began in many countries in the
1960s *— ~ist n*

new·ly /ˈnjuːli‖ˈnuːli/ *adv* (used before a past participle) re-
cently; freshly: *a newly built house* | *a newly qualified
teacher* | *the newly industrialized nations*

new·ly·wed /ˈnjuːliwed‖ˈnuː-/ *n* [*usu. pl.*] a person recently
married: *Mr and Mrs Smith are newlyweds/are a
newlywed couple.*

New·man¹ /ˈnjuːmən‖ˈnuː-/, **Cardinal John Henry**
(1801–90) an English religious leader and writer

Newman², Paul (1925–) an American actor and director, leading male star of Hollywood films in the 1960s and
1970s and considered very attractive. His films include

Butch Cassidy and the Sundance Kid, The Sting, and *The Color of Money.* —see picture at BUTCH CASSIDY AND THE SUNDANCE KID

New Man /ˌ·ˈ·/ *n* a man who is interested in spending time with his family and sharing the care of children and home with his partner. Such men were supposed to be more common in the 1980s and 1990s, showing less concern for making money and doing well in their CAREERS, and more for enjoying and taking responsibility for the family, esp. so that the woman in the family had time for her own career: *"The New Man – does he exist?"* | *Oh, he's a New Man, he does all the cooking and looks after the baby.* —see also MEN'S MOVEMENT

New·mar·ket /ˈnjuːmɑːkɪt‖ˈnuːmɑːr-/ a market town in Suffolk, SE England, a centre for horse racing, and breeding and training horses for racing, for more than 300 years

new math /ˌ·ˈ·/ *AmE* ‖ **modern maths** *BrE*— *n* a new way of teaching and understanding MATHEMATICS, introduced into schools in the early 1970s

New Mex·i·co /ˌ·ˈ···/ (*written abbrev.* NM) a state in the SW US with a strong Hispanic influence. It is mostly desert or mountain forests. —see colour map on pages 1374–5

New Mod·el Ar·my /ˌ·ˈ·· ˈ··/ [*the*] the British army as reorganized (ORGANIZE) during the English Civil War of 1645 by the Parliamentarians —see CIVIL WAR

new mon·ey /ˌ·ˈ··/ also **new rich**— *n* [U+*sing./pl. v*] *AmE infml* for NOUVEAU RICHE

new moon /ˌ·ˈ·/ *n* **1** the time when the moon is between the Earth and the sun, and cannot be seen **2** the bright thin edge of the moon seen a few days after this — compare FULL MOON, HALF MOON

New Mu·sic·al Ex·press /ˌ·ˌ··· ·ˈ·/ *abbrev.* NME— a British weekly newspaper, read esp. by young people, which has news about popular music

New Or·le·ans /ˌnjuː ɔːˈliːənz‖ˌnuː ˈɔːrliənz/ *n* a city in Louisiana in the southern US, on the Mississippi river. It is famous for the French influences on its streetlife and nightlife, the **Mardi Gras** CARNIVAL every year, and the JAZZ and BLUES music made there. —see colour map on pages 1374–5

New·port /ˈnjuːpɔːt‖ˈnuːpɔːrt/ **1** a city and port in Gwent, SE Wales, where the local government for that COUNTY is based. It is known for the making of steel and the shipping (SHIP² (1)) of coal. **2** a town in the Isle of Wight in S England, where the local government for the island is based **3** a wealthy city in Rhode Island, US; an important naval port

Newport Jazz Fes·ti·val /ˌ·· ˈ· ˌ···/ [*the*] a gathering of JAZZ¹ (1) musicians, originally held in 1954 at Newport, Rhode Island, and now held yearly in three places in New York State

new po·ta·to /ˌ·ˈ···/ *n* a potato from one of the first crops of a year, rather than one which has been stored from the previous year

new rich /ˌ·ˈ·/ *n* [U+*sing./pl. v*] *AmE* for NOUVEAU RICHE — **new rich** *adj* : *new rich behaviour*

New Right /ˌ·ˈ·/ [*the*] (in the 1980s) (a movement of) people supporting a system in which the state does not have control over education, health, industrial activity, etc.

news /njuːz‖nuːz/ *n* **1** [U (**of, about**)] facts that are reported about a recent event or events; new information: *a piece/item of news* | *What's the latest* (=most recent) *news about the election?* | *News is just coming in of a serious plane crash.* | *Have you heard any news from your son lately?* (=received a letter or telephone call, etc.) | *You'd better* **break the news** (=tell it) *to her gently that her daughter has left home.* **2** [*the*] a regular report of recent events broadcast on radio and television: *I heard it on the 9 o'clock news.* **3** **All the news that's fit to print** the MOTTO of the New York Times **4 bad news travels fast** *saying* people very quickly hear about bad news **5 news to someone** *infml* something which one has not heard before: *There's no class tomorrow? That's news to me!* (=no one told me) **6 no news is good news** *saying* if you are waiting for news about something, and you have not heard anything yet, it is probably the case that the news will be good when it arrives

news a·gen·cy /ˈ· ˌ···/ *n* a company that supplies informa-

tion to newspapers, radio, and television

news·a·gent /ˈnjuːzˌeɪdʒənt‖ˈnuːz-/ *BrE* ‖ **news deal·er** /ˈ· ˌ··/*AmE*— *n* a person who owns or works in a shop (**newsagent's**) which sells newspapers and magazines: *Is there a newsagent's near here?*

News at Ten /ˌ·· ·ˈ·/ [*the*] in Britain, a television news programme broadcast by ITN at 10 p.m. every weekday —compare NINE O'CLOCK NEWS

news bul·le·tin /ˈ· ˌ···/ *n* a short report about events which have happened very recently, made public without delay: *a television news bulletin about the rapidly-changing situation in Georgia*

news·cast·er /ˈnjuːzˌkɑːstəʳ‖ˈnuːzˌkæ-/ also **newsreader** *esp. BrE*— *n* a person who broadcasts news on radio or television

New Sci·en·tist /ˌ·ˈ···/ [*the*] a British weekly magazine which has news about recent developments in science and TECHNOLOGY

news con·fer·ence /ˈ· ˌ···/ *n* a PRESS CONFERENCE

New Scot·land Yard /ˌ·· ·· ·ˈ·/ the official name for SCOTLAND YARD

news·flash /ˈnjuːzflæʃ‖ˈnuːz-/ *n* a short news broadcast, usu. in the middle of another television programme, when something very important has happened: *I've just seen a newsflash saying that Margaret Thatcher has resigned.*

News from No·where /ˌ·· ·ˈ··/ a Utopian SOCIALIST FANTASY by William Morris, written in 1890

news·hound /ˈnjuːzhaʊnd‖ˈnuːz-/ *n* a very eager newspaper reporter, who is always looking for new stories

news·let·ter /ˈnjuːzˌletəʳ‖ˈnuːz-/ *n* a small sheet of printed news sent regularly to a particular group of people: *the company newsletter*

News·night /ˈnjuːznaɪt‖ˈnuːz-/ a British television programme broadcast on BBC2 in the late evening, in which there is discussion about the news and current affairs

News of the World /ˌ·· · ·ˈ·/ [*the*] a popular TABLOID Sunday newspaper sold in Britain, known esp. for printing stories about the marriage problems, sexual SCANDALS, and details of the private lives of the rich and famous — see extra information on page 896

New South Wales /ˌ·· ·ˈ·/ a state in SE Australia bordering on the Pacific Ocean; economically the most important state, producing steel, coal, grain and wool

news·pa·per /ˈnjuːzˌpeɪpəʳ‖ ˈnuːz-/ *n* **1** [C] also **paper**— set of large folded sheets of paper containing news, articles, advertisements, etc., printed and sold usu. daily or weekly: *an evening newspaper* | *the Sunday papers* | *the editor of a well-known national newspaper* see also EXTRA information on page 896 **2** [U] paper on which these have been printed: *Wrap it up in newspaper.* —compare NEWSPRINT **3** [C] a company which produces a newspaper: *One of our oldest newspapers has just gone out of business.*

news·pa·per·man /ˈnjuːzpeɪpəmæn‖ˈnuːzpeɪpər-/ *n* **-men** /men/ a person who has worked, usu. for many years, as a reporter on a newspaper

newspaper stand /ˈ··· ˌ·/ *n* a   **newspaper stand**
NEWSSTAND

new·speak /ˈnjuːspiːk‖ˈnuː-/ *n* [U] *derog* language whose meanings are slightly changed to make people believe things that are not quite true (from the language used in the book *Nineteen Eighty-Four* by George Orwell, which describes life in the future when the government controls everyone's lives completely)

news·print /ˈnjuːzˌprɪnt‖ˈnuːz-/ *n* [U] *tech* cheap paper used mostly for printing newspapers on

news·read·er /ˈnjuːzˌriːdəʳ‖ˈnuːz-/ *n esp. BrE* for NEWSCASTER

news·reel /ˈnjuːzriːl‖ˈnuːz-/ *n* a short cinema film of news

Newspapers in Britain

National and local newspapers

In Britain there are 11 national daily newspapers and most people read one of them every day. There are two kinds of newspaper. One is large in size and has many detailed articles about national and international events. These newspapers are called the serious papers or the QUALITY PAPERS. The other kind, called the TABLOIDs are smaller in size, have more pictures, often in colour, and shorter articles, often about less important events or about the private lives of well-known people. Although some people disapprove of the tabloids, more people buy them than buy the serious newspapers. The *Sun*, for example, which is a tabloid, is the biggest-selling newspaper in Britain. People who disapprove of the tabloids very strongly sometimes call them the GUTTER PRESS.

There are daily or weekly newspapers in all parts of Britain which cover local news as well as some national and international stories. Local papers give information about films, concerts, and other things that are happening in the local neighbourhood, including, for example, information about local people who have been married or died recently. National papers generally give information about film, concerts and other events happening in London. In Scotland, many people read the *Glasgow Herald* or the *Scotsman* (serious newspapers) and there are Scottish EDITIONs (=newspapers with special news for Scotland) of the tabloids.

There are also many free local newspapers which are delivered to people's homes whether they ask for them or not These contain a lot of advertisements and also some news.

Politics

Most national newspapers in Britain express a political opinion and people choose the newspaper that they read according to their own political beliefs. Most of the newspapers are RIGHT-WING. These are the *Daily Telegraph* (serious newspaper), the *Daily Express*, *Daily Mail*, *Daily Star*, the *Sun* and *Today* (all tabloids). Of the other serious newspapers, *The Times*, the oldest newspaper in Britain, did not formerly have one strong political view but it is now more right-wing.The *Guardian* is slightly left-wing. The *Independent* does not support any one poltical party, and neither does the *Financial Times*, which concentrates on business and financial news. The *Daily Mirror* (tabloid) is left-wing. —see also SUN-READER, GUARDIAN-READER.

Daily and Sunday newspapers

Daily newspapers are published on every day of the week except Sunday. Sunday newspapers are larger than daily newspapers, often having 2 or 3 sections. There is also often a magazine, called the COLOUR SUPPLEMENT. All the Sunday newspapers are national. Serious newspapers include the *Observer* (which is slightly left-wing), the *Sunday Times*, the *Sunday Telegraph* and the *Independent on Sunday*, the *Sunday Mirror*, the *Sunday Express*, the *News of the World* (right-wing and known for containing stories abut sex and SCANDAL) and the *Sunday Sport* which is considered to lack much serious information.

Newspapers in the US

National and local newspapers

There are more than 1500 daily newspapers in the US. Each one is usually sold only in one part of the country, e.g. in a city, but they cover national and international news. In larger cities, there is often more than one newspaper and the different ones express different political opinions. Some newspapers are sold in nearly all parts of the US, e.g. *USA Today*, the *Wall Street Journal*, and the national edition of the *New York Times*. Two other newspapers, the *Los Angeles Times* and the *Washington Post* are known and respected all over the US but cannot be bought everywhere. Other important newspapers are : the *Boston Globe*, sold in New England, the *Chicago Tribune*, sold in the Midwest, the *Rocky Mountain News*, sold in the mountain states, and the *Christian Science Monitor*, sold in cities nationally.

There are also weekly newspapers in all parts of the US which cover local news, such as what is happening in the local neighbourhood. Fewer people read these than read the daily newspapers.

Daily and Sunday newspapers

Daily newspapers are published (PUBLISH) on every day of the week except Sunday. Sunday newspapers are very big, often having several separate parts (SECTIONs(1)). They contain many longer articles and a lot of advertisements. Each section deals with a different subject, e.g. national and international news, sport, travel, etc. One section, the CLASSIFIEDs has advertisements for jobs and things for sale. Another section has CARTOONs and COMIC STRIPs (=humorous drawings) and is called the FUNNIES. There is often also a magazine which is in colour.

Alternative newspapers

In the 1960s a group of newspapers began to appear that were later called the 'alternative press'. They expressed extreme political opinions, especially LEFT-WING opinions. Many of the newspapers which were part of this movement, such as the *Village Voice* in New York or the *Reader* in Chicago, are less extreme today and more widely read.

news·room /ˈnjuːzrʊm, -ruːm‖ˈnuːz-/ *n* the office in a newspaper or broadcasting station where news is received and news reports are written

news·sheet /ˈnjuːzʃiːt‖ˈnuːz-/ *n* a small newspaper, usu. of one or two pages

news·stand /ˈnjuːzstænd‖ˈnuːz-/ *n* a table or STALL, e.g. on a street or in a station, from which newspapers and sometimes magazines and books are sold

New States·man and So·ci·e·ty /· ˌ· · · ·ˈ···/ a serious British weekly magazine which contains news articles and opinions, political argument, and arts reviews. It is thought to represent an independent view and often criticizes the government.

news·ven·dor /ˈnjuːzˌvendəʳ‖ˈnuːz-/ *n esp. BrE* a person who sells newspapers

News·week /ˈnjuːzwiːk‖ˈnuːz-/ an American weekly magazine containing articles about news and current affairs

news·wor·thy /ˈnjuːzˌwɜːði‖ˈnuːzˌwɜːrði/ *adj* important or interesting enough to be reported as news

news·y /ˈnjuːzi‖ˈnuːzi/ *adj* filled with not very serious news: *a newsy letter*

newt /njuːt‖nuːt/ *n* a small four-legged animal, similar to a FROG but with a tail, living on land and in water

new tech·nol·o·gy /ˌ· ·ˈ···/ *n* [*(the)* U] the production and use, esp. in business and industry, of computers and systems that use computers: *I can't cope with all the new technology we've got at work now.*

New Ter·ri·to·ries /ˌ· ·····/ *n* [*the* + P] the part of Hong Kong leased (LEASE) by Great Britain from China. The lease runs for 99 years from 1898.

New Tes·ta·ment /ˌ· ·····/ [*the*] the second part of the Bible, containing the earliest Christian writings. It includes the four Gospels, describing the teachings and life of Jesus. —compare OLD TESTAMENT

New·ton /ˈnjuːtn‖ˈnuːt-/, **Isaac** (1642–1727) an English PHYSICIST and MATHEMATICIAN who discovered the law of GRAVITY and many other laws and scientific theories (THEORY) which helped to shape the study of PHYSICS. Newton is often shown in pictures holding an apple, because he is supposed to have discovered the law of gravity when an apple fell on his head while he was sitting under a tree.

Newton-John /ˌ·· ·ˈ·/, **O·liv·i·a** /əˈlɪviə/ (1948–   ) an Australian popular music singer, born in Britain, who was successful esp. in the 1970s and popular with people of all ages. She appeared with John Travolta in the films *Saturday Night Fever* and *Grease*.

new town /ˈ· ·/ *n* any of several towns built in Britain since 1946, each planned and built as a whole with factories, houses, shops, etc.: *Harlow New Town* —compare GARDEN CITY

new wave /ˌ· ˈ·/ *n (often caps.)* (a group of people making) a conscious effort to change the styles of art, filmmaking, etc., esp. **a** in the French cinema of the 1960s, using new methods of photography **b** in the popular music of the late 1970s, using a strong beat and expressing strong social opinions

New World /ˌ· ˈ·/ [*the*] North, Central, and South America; the Western Hemisphere —compare OLD WORLD

new year /ˌ· ˈ·/ *n* [*(the)* U] *(often caps.)* the year which has just begun or will soon begin: *Let's hope things will improve in the new year.*

▶ CULTURAL NOTE The beginning of a new year is regarded as a time for celebrating and for making a new start. Around the time of the new year people wish each other "Happy New Year" and some send special greeting cards. Many people make **New Year's resolutions**, when they promise that they will improve their behaviour and give up bad habits, e.g. they will lose weight or give up smoking; no one really expects these promises to last for very long. On **New Year's Eve** (December 31st) many people in the US, Britain, and esp. in Scotland, go to parties or get together with their families, neighbours or friends, and stay up until midnight to "see the New Year in". They sing a special song, **Auld Lang Syne**, and some get very drunk. In London people gather to celebrate in Trafalgar Square; from there they can hear Big Ben, the large clock at the Houses of Parliament. When it is nearly midnight everyone is very quiet, but when Big Ben strikes they all cheer, sing, hug and kiss each other and shout "Happy New Year"; some kiss the

police who are there to control the crowd. **New Year's Day** (January 1st) is a public holiday in Britain and the US. — see also AULD LANG SYNE, FIRST FOOTING, HOGMANAY ◀

New Year's Hon·ours /ˌ· · ·ˈ··/ [*the*] a list (made public on January 1st each year) in which various people in Britain are given honours, such as OBEs, MBEs, etc., for service to the country in some way

New York Cit·y /ˌ· · ·ˈ··/ also **New York**—; written abbrev. **NYC** the largest city and richest port in the US, on the SE coast in NEW YORK STATE. —see colour maps on pages 1376 and 1374–5

▶ CULTURAL NOTE New York City is an international leader in trade, finance, and the performing arts. The city is divided into five BOROUGHS: MANHATTAN, the BRONX, BROOKLYN, QUEENS, and RICHMOND. Though many people avoid and fear the city for its crime and crowds, others love it for its entertainment and CULTURE (2) —see also BIG APPLE, BROADWAY, CENTRAL PARK, MADISON AVENUE, WALL STREET — compare NEW YORK STATE ◀

New York Dra·ma Crit·ics Cir·cle A·ward /ˌ· · ˌ·· ·· ˌ·· ·ˈ·/ a group of newspaper writers on the theatre which gives prizes for excellent work in the theatre each year

New York·er[1] /njuː ˈjɔːkəʳ‖nuː ˈjɔːr-/ *n* a person who lives or was born in New York City. esp. New York City

New Yorker[2] [*the*] a popular weekly arts magazine mostly about New York City, but also with articles that cover many interesting subjects, and short stories. It is a highly respected magazine read by educated people and it is considered an achievement for writers to get their work into the **New Yorker**. It is also well known for its very funny CARTOONS.

New York State /ˌ· · ·ˈ·/ also **New York**—; *written abbrev.* **NY** a state in the NE US. Its capital is Albany and its largest city is NEW YORK CITY. New York State is famous for its beauty, esp. its trees, mountains, and rivers. It was one of the 13 original British colonies (COLONY) — compare NEW YORK CITY

New York Stock Ex·change /ˌ· · ·ˈ· ·ˌ·/ *(abbrev.* **NYSE)** [*the*] a market where shares in companies are bought and sold. It is one of the three main such markets in the world, the others being in Tokyo and London.

New York Times /ˌ· · ·ˈ·/ [*the*] a serious newspaper printed in New York which is read around the world as a guide to American opinion. It is one of only two daily newspapers that are available almost everywhere in the US, and it is highly respected for the quality of its reporting. —see extra information on page 893

New Zealand

Auckland
NORTH ISLAND
Wellington
SOUTH ISLAND
Christchurch
Dunedin

New Zea·land /njuː ˈziːlənd‖nuː-/ a country consisting of two main islands (North Island and South Island) and some smaller ones, in the Pacific Ocean SE of Australia; capital Wellington; population 3,312,000 (1989). It is known mainly for its farming, esp. lamb, meat, and butter. The population is mainly of British origin, with some Maori people who were the first settlers there. — ~**er** *n*

next[1] /nekst/ *determiner* **1** closest in space, order, or degree; without anything coming before or between: *The next house to ours is a mile away.* | *Take the next left turn after the school.* | *When you've finished this chapter go on to the next one.* | *Japan is the main market for our products, and the next biggest market is Germany.* | *The quickest way is by train; the* **next best** *way is to go by road.* **2** immediately following in time; the one after the one mentioned or after the present: *Where will you be during the next few weeks?* | *Will you be at our next* *meeting?* | *How long will it be till the next election?* | *The law was passed in 1962, but three years later it was repealed by the next government.* | (without **the**) *Next time you see her, give her my best wishes.* | *the week after next* | *We went there last Sunday and we're going again next Sunday.* —compare LAST[1] (3)   **3 (the) next day** the day after: *She rang me and we arranged to meet the next day.* —compare **the other day** (OTHER)   **4 Next (please).** Will the next person waiting please speak/come forward? — see also **next of kin** (KIN)

next² *adv*   **1** just afterwards: *What will you do next?* | *I like tennis best of all and swimming next.* | *First, you heat the fat; next, you add the onions.*   **2** at the first time after this or that: *I'll tell you the answer when we next meet.* — compare LAST² (2)   **3 next to: a** closest to; beside: *the table next to the door* | *I sit next to you?* **b** closest to, in order, degree, etc.: *Next to biology, I like physics best.* | *the next-to-last name on the list* **c** almost: *He earns next to nothing.* | *It's next to impossible to drive in this weather.*

Next one of a group of shops in Britain which sell fashionable clothes for adults and children as well as furnishings. They sell some of their products in a CATALOGUE, the **Next Directory.**

next-door /ˌ· ˈ·◂/ *adj* [A] in or being the next building, esp. in a row: *next-door neighbours*

next door /ˌ· ˈ·/ *adv* [(to)]   **1** in or being the next building: *the people next door* | *We live next door to a restaurant.*   **2 next door to** almost the same as: *Knocking someone down in your car when you're drunk is next door to murder.*

nex·us /ˈneksəs/ *n* a connection or network of connections between objects, ideas, etc.

NF /ˌen ˈef/ *abbrev. for:* NATIONAL FRONT

NFL /ˌen ef ˈel/ [*the*] National Football League; the group of US professional football teams whose games are shown on television —see also FOOTBALL (2)

NFT /ˌen ef ˈtiː/ *abbrev for:* NATIONAL FILM THEATRE

NFU /ˌen ef ˈjuː/ *abbrev. for:* NATIONAL FARMERS UNION

NH *written abbrev. for:* NEW HAMPSHIRE

NHL /ˌen eɪtʃ ˈel/ [*the*] National Hockey League; the group of US and Canadian ICE HOCKEY teams who play games against one another

NHS /ˌen eɪtʃ ˈes/ *abbrev for:* National Health Service: *NHS hospitals* | *Can I get my glasses on the NHS?*

NHS num·ber /ˌ· · ˈ· ˌ··/ *n* National Health Service number; a number which everyone in Britain is given when they are born or when they come to live in Britain. It is used by the National Health Service to IDENTIFY the person.

NI /ˌen ˈaɪ/ *abbrev. for:* NATIONAL INSURANCE

Ni·ag·a·ra Falls /naɪˌægərə ˈfɔːlz/ [*the* + P] very large waterfalls on the border between Canada and the US, popular with tourists and used to supply electricity. Americans often joke about newly-married people going to Niagara Falls on their HONEYMOON, but not many people really go there for that reason —see colour map on pages 1374–5

nib /nɪb/ *n* the pointed piece from which the ink flows at the end of a pen —see also NIBS

nib·ble¹ /ˈnɪbəl/ *v*   **1** [I (AWAY, **at, on**);T] to eat with small repeated bites: *Aren't you hungry? You're only nibbling at your food.* | *nibbling (on) a bit of bread* | (fig.) *Food and rent bills nibbled (away) at their savings.*   **2** [T+*obj*+*adv/prep*] to make (a hole) in this way: *The mice have nibbled a hole in the cheese.* | *The mice nibbled their way through the wooden door.*   **3** [I (**at**)] to show slight interest in something, esp. an offer or suggestion

nibble² *n infml*   **1** [(**at**)] an act of nibbling: *I haven't sold my car yet but I've had a few nibbles.* (=some people have shown interest)   **2** a very small amount of food

nibs /nɪbz/ *n humor* **his** or **her nibs** *sl* an important person, or one who thinks he/she is important: *His nibs has wine with his meal, but we only get water.*

Nic·a·rag·u·a /ˌnɪkəˈrægjuə‖-ˈrɑːgwə/ the largest republic of Central America between the Caribbean Sea and the Pacific Ocean which has a small population and produces cotton, coffee, rice, sugar, and tobacco; capital Managua; population 3,745,000 (1989). In the 1980s it suffered CIVIL WAR between the left-wing Sandinista government and the Contras, who were helped by the US.

—see also CONTRA, SANDINISTA —**Nicaraguan** *n,adj*

nice /naɪs/ *adj*   **1 a** kind or friendly: *She's the nicest person I know.* | *I know you don't like him but try to be nice to him.* | *It was nice of you to help us.* **b** giving pleasure; good: *a nice day* (=with good weather) | *This soup tastes very nice.* | *How nice to see you!* | *Have a nice time at the party!* | *It'd be nice if we could meet soon.*   **2** *fml* showing or needing careful understanding or decision; delicate; SUBTLE: *a nice point of law* | *a nice distinction between two meanings*   **3** *becoming rare* having (too) high standards of moral or social behaviour; RESPECTABLE: *Nice girls don't go there!*   **4** *infml derog* bad; unpleasant: *That's a nice way to welcome your aunt, staring at the television!*   **5 have a nice day** *esp. AmE* a phrase used when saying goodbye to someone during the day, esp. by people in shops, restaurants etc. to their customers.   **6 nice ...**, **pity/shame about the** ... *infml humor.* a phrase used when saying that a person or thing has something that is good, but is spoilt by something that is bad: *nice face, shame about the body* | *nice cinema, shame about the film*   **7 nice and** *infml* (used before adjectives and adverbs to give a favourable meaning): *The soup is nice and hot.* | *I didn't like the speech, but at least it was nice and short.* — ~ **ness** *n* [U]

▷ USAGE **Nice** is very commonly used in speech, but in formal writing it is better to avoid it, and to use **amusing, beautiful, interesting,** etc., according to the meaning.◁

Nice /niːs/ a city on the Mediterranean coast of France, famous as a fashionable place for tourists to stay, and also a port and industrial area

nice·ly /ˈnaɪsli/ *adv*   **1** well; in a good, pleasant, kind, or skilful way: *to smile nicely* | *The injured man is doing nicely* (=his condition is all right) *in hospital.*   **2** exactly; delicately: *a nicely calculated distance*

ni·ce·ty /ˈnaɪsɪti/ *n*   **1** [U] the quality of being NICE (2); delicateness   **2** [C *usu. pl.*] a fine or delicate point or difference; detail: *Let's answer the question in general: we haven't time to consider all the niceties.*   **3** *BrE* **to a nicety** exactly: *She calculated the amount to a nicety.*

niche¹ /nɪtʃ, niːʃ‖nɪtʃ/ *n*   **1** a hollow place in a wall, usu. made to hold a piece of art such as a BUST or STATUE   **2** [(**in**)] a suitable place, job, etc.: *He's found a niche (for himself) in the book trade.*

niche

niche² *n* (of a product or a company) aimed at a particular group of people: *a niche travel operator*

Nicholas, Saint see SAINT NICHOLAS

Nich·o·las I /ˌnɪkələs ðə ˈfɜːst‖ -ˈfɜːrst/ (1796–1855) the TSAR of Russia from 1825 who fought against Turkey and also in the Crimean War

Nicholas II /ˌnɪkələs ðə ˈsekənd/ (1868–1918) the TSAR of Russia from 1894–1917, whose bad management of foreign and home affairs led to the Revolution of 1905. He was also responsible for taking Russia into the First World War. During the Russian Revolution of 1917 he was forced to ABDICATE (=stop being ruler), and was shot with his family in 1918.

Nicholas Nick·le·by /ˌnɪkələs ˈnɪkəlbi/ a character in a book of the same name by Charles Dickens. The story was also made into a long play which was very successful.

Nich·ol·son /ˈnɪkəlsən/, **Jack** (1937–   ) an American film actor who started appearing in films in the 1960s, such as *Easy Rider*, which represented the feelings of young Americans, and has now become a big Hollywood star, in films including *One Flew over the Cuckoo's Nest* and *Batman* —see colour picture on page 228

nick¹ /nɪk/ *n*   **1** [C] a small often accidental cut in a surface or edge   **2** [*the*] *BrE infml* prison or police station: *ten years in the nick*   **3 in the nick of time** just in time; at the necessary moment: *I saw the baby was about to fall off and I caught it just in the nick of time.*

nick² *v* [T]   **1** to cut a nick in: *A bullet nicked his leg.*   **2** *infml, esp. BrE* to steal: *Someone's nicked my bicycle.*

3 *BrE sl for* ARREST: *The police nicked him for stealing my bicycle.* **4** [(for)] *infml, esp. AmE* to charge too much: *They nicked me for $30 just to have my hair cut!*

nick³ *n* [U] *BrE sl* a stated physical condition; SHAPE¹ (3): *The doctor says my heart is still in good nick.* | *The house is in excellent nick.* (=in very good repair)

nick·el¹ /ˈnɪkəl/ *n* **1** [U] a hard silver-white metal that is a simple substance (ELEMENT) and is used in the production of other metals **2** [C] a coin of the US or Canada worth five cents —compare CENT

nickel² also **nickel-plate** /ˌ·· ˈ·/— *v* -**ll**-*BrE* ‖ -**l**- *AmE*— [T] to put a thin surface of nickel over: *nickelled/nickel-plated steel*

nickel-and-dime /ˌ··· · ˈ·/ *adj AmE* unimportant; not involving much money: *a nickel-and-dime operation/theory*

nick·er /ˈnɪkəʳ/ *n* nicker *BrE old-fash sl* a pound; £1: *You can have it for 50 nicker.*

Nick·laus /ˈnɪklaʊs/, **Jack** (1940–) an American GOLF player who has won many important titles

Nickleby, Nicholas see NICHOLAS NICKLEBY

nick·nack /ˈnɪknæk/ *n infml* a KNICK-KNACK

nick·name /ˈnɪkneɪm/ *n* a name used informally instead of a person's own name, usu. a short form of the actual name or a name connected with one's character or history. Nicknames are often given at school to annoy or upset other children, and many last into adult life. – **nickname** *v* [T+obj+n] : *They nicknamed him "Lofty" because he was so tall.*

Nic·o·si·a /ˌnɪkəˈsiːə/ the capital city of Cyprus, important for producing leather goods, POTTERY, and TEXTILES

nic·o·tine /ˈnɪkətiːn/ *n* [U] a poisonous chemical which provides the taste and effect of tobacco

nicotine patch /ˈ··· ˌ·/ *n* a small piece of a material containing nicotine which is stuck on to the skin of a person who wants to give up smoking. The nicotine gradually gets into their blood through their skin, so that they do not need to smoke to get it.

niece /niːs/ *n* **1** the daughter of one's brother or sister **2** the daughter of one's wife's or husband's brother or sister —compare NEPHEW

Niel·sen Rat·ings /ˈniːlsən ˌreɪtɪŋz/ [*the* + P] also **Nielsens**— information produced by **Nielsen Media Research**, an American company that finds out how many people watch different television programmes. The ratings are used to decide how much companies have to pay to advertise their products during a particular programme.

Nietz·sche /ˈniːtʃə/, **Fried·rich** /ˈfriːdrɪk, -ɪx/ (1844–1900) a German thinker and writer whose most famous books are *Thus Spake Zarathustra* and *The Antichrist*. He writes that "God is dead", meaning that the values which support Christian culture have come to an end. He announces the coming of the "Ubermensh" (=Superman), who creates his own values and enjoys the highest freedom. The idea of the Superman was misused by the Nazis to support their racist beliefs. — ~ **an** /ˈniːtʃiən/ *adj*

niff /nɪf/ *n* [S] *BrE infml* a bad smell — ~ **y** *adj*

nif·ty /ˈnɪfti/ *adj infml* very good, attractive, or effective: *a nifty little gadget for squeezing oranges*

Ni·ger /ˈnaɪdʒəʳ, niːˈʒeəʳ‖ˈnaɪdʒər/ **1** a country in W Africa bordered by Burkino Faso and Mali in W and by Nigeria and Benin in S; capital Niamey; population 6,895,000 (1989) **2** [*the*] the third longest river in Africa, running through Mali, Niger, and Nigeria —**Nigerian** /niːˈʒeəriən/ *n, adj*

Ni·ge·ri·a /naɪˈdʒɪəriə/ an oil producing country in W Africa bordered by Benin in W, Niger in N, and Chad and Cameroon in E; capital Abuja; largest city Lagos; population 109,175,000 (1989) —**Nigerian** *n,adj*

nig·gard /ˈnɪgəd‖-ərd/ *n derog* a niggardly person

nig·gard·ly /ˈnɪgədli‖-ər-/ *adj derog* **1** (of a person) not willing to spend money, time, etc.; STINGY **2** spent or given unwillingly; MEAGRE: *a niggardly offer for such a good car* | *niggardly praise* —**liness** *n* [U]

nig·ger /ˈnɪgəʳ/ *n* **1** *taboo derog* a black person (considered extremely offensive)

▶ CULTURAL NOTE The various words used in Great Britain and the US to describe people of African or Asian origin are used in different situations, and with different meanings, by people with particular views. Offensive words, marked *taboo* in this dictionary, such as **nigger**, **coon**, **wog**, **nignog**, or **darkie**, are not considered acceptable when used by white people, showing a dislike of black people and a lack of awareness of the racist nature of these words. **Nigger**, however, may be used inoffensively by a black person about himself or another person, and is sometimes even a positive word, used to show pride. The word **coloured** was once considered inoffensive, but is now mostly used by older people, and is not acceptable today. It is also used in *SAfrE* as a technical term for a person of mixed race, under the system of APARTHEID where these classes affect people's position and rights in society.◄

In Britain and the US now, the most common word is black (*sometimes cap.*) as in the phrases the **black community/black theatre** etc. However, people of Asian descent do not always like being included in this group so care should be taken with its use. In the US, **black** refers only to people of African origin, never to Asians. —see also AFRICAN-AMERICAN **2 nigger in the woodpile** *now taboo* (someone who causes) an unexpected problem

nig·gle /ˈnɪgəl/ *v* [I] **1** [(about, over)] to pay too much attention to small details, esp. when finding fault: *She niggled over every detail of the bill.* **2** [(at)] to annoy someone slightly but continually: *There's still a doubt niggling at my brain.* —**gler** *n*

nig·gling /ˈnɪgəlɪŋ/ *adj* [A] **1** slightly and continually annoying: *a niggling doubt* **2** (of a piece of work) needing too much attention to detail: *a niggling job*

nigh /naɪ/ *adv, prep* **1** *poet or old use* near: *The time has drawn nigh.* (=it has nearly come) **2 nigh on/onto/unto** *dial or old use* almost —see also WELL-NIGH

night /naɪt/ *n* **1** [C;U] the dark part of each 24-hour period, when the sun cannot be seen: *The nights are longer in winter.* | *Nurses often have to work at night.* | *The moon gives light by/at night.* | *Night began to fall.* (=it started to get dark) | *a few nights ago* | *The hotel charges $60 a night.* | *Where were you on the night of January 16th?* **2** [C;U] the earlier part of this period; the evening: *We'll be out tomorrow night.* | *to go dancing on Saturday night(s)* | *Is that programme at 10 o'clock in the morning or 10 o'clock at night?* **b** the period after bedtime: *to sleep well all night* | *The baby woke up twice in the night.* | *Where did you stay last night?* **3** [C] a special occasion taking place in the evening: *We saw the show on its first night.* (=first performance) | *It was a great night – everyone was there.* **4** [C *usu. sing.*] the evening of a stated holiday, etc.: *Christmas night* —compare EVE (1) **5** [C (of)] *lit* a sad period or experience: *through the night of doubt and sorrow* | *the dark night of the soul* **6 by night** during the night (esp. when compared with by day): *He works in an office by day and drives a taxi by night.* **7 it ain't a fit night out for man nor beast** a phrase used in old films, meaning that it is a very cold, stormy night; now often used humorously. **8 it'll be all right on the night** *BrE* a phrase used in the theatre, meaning that a play or show will be performed in public without mistakes, even though there are difficulties while it is being prepared **9 make a night of it** *infml* to spend the night in enjoyment **10 night after night** *infml* regularly every night: *He goes out drinking night after night.* **11 night and day** also **day and night**— *infml* all the time; continuously: *I worry about it night and day.* **12 the other night** a few nights ago: *I saw David the other night.* —see also NIGHTS, NOCTURNAL, morning, noon, and night (MORNING)

Night Before Christ·mas /ˌ· ·· ˈ··/, **The** a poem by Clement Moore which contains many of the popular ideas and images that Americans connect with Santa Claus. It has been set to music, made into a television film, and appears printed in newspapers and magazines at Christmastime.

night blind·ness /ˈ· ˌ··/ *n* [U] inability to see things in bad light

night·cap /ˈnaɪtkæp/ *n* **1** a usu. alcoholic drink taken before going to bed **2** a soft cloth cap worn in bed in former times

night·clothes /ˈnaɪtkləʊðz, -kləʊz/ *n* [P] any variety of clothes worn in bed by men, women, or children

night·club /ˈnaɪtklʌb/ *n* a place of entertainment open late at night where people can eat, drink, dance, and often see a show

night·club·bing /ˈnaɪtˌklʌbɪŋ/ *BrE*, also **clubbing** *n* [U] the visiting of nightclubs

night crawl·er /ˈ· ˌ··/ *n AmE* a large worm that lives in the soil (EARTHWORM) and comes out at night, often used as BAIT in fishing

night de·pos·i·to·ry /ˈ· ·ˌ····/ *n AmE for* NIGHT SAFE

night·dress /ˈnaɪtdres/ also **nigh·tie** /ˈnaɪti/ *infml*, **night·gown** /-gaʊn/*AmE–* *n* a piece of women's clothing like a loose dress, made to be worn in bed —compare NIGHTSHIRT

night·fall /ˈnaɪtfɔːl/ *n* [U] the beginning of night; DUSK: *We gave up the search at nightfall.*

night·hawk /ˈnaɪthɔːk/ *n AmE for* NIGHT OWL

nigh·tin·gale /ˈnaɪtɪŋɡeɪl/ *n* a bird (a kind of THRUSH) known for its beautiful song

Nightingale, Florence
(1820–1910) an English nurse who became a national HEROINE during the Crimean War when she set up a hospital for soldiers at Scutari. She became known as the *Lady with the Lamp* because she used to walk round the hospital in the evenings with a lamp, to check that everything was in order. She established nursing as a profession, and as a respectable job for women.

Florence Nightingale

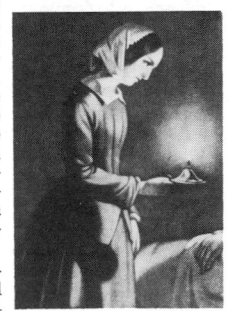

night·life /ˈnaɪtlaɪf/ *n* [U] evening entertainment or social activity, e.g. in BARS, NIGHTCLUBs, etc.: *a holiday resort with good nightlife*

night·light /ˈnaɪtlaɪt/ *n* a not very bright light or small candle which is kept burning through the night, e.g. in a child's room

night·long /ˈnaɪtlɒŋ‖-lɔːŋ/ *adj, adv esp. lit* (lasting) through the whole night: *a nightlong vigil*

night·ly /ˈnaɪtli/ *adj, adv* (happening, done, etc.) every night: *a play performed nightly* | *a nightly news broadcast*

night·mare /ˈnaɪtmeəʳ/ *n* 1 a terrible dream 2 a terrible experience or event: *the nightmare of a nuclear war* | *Driving on that ice was a real nightmare.* —**marish** *adj* —**marishly** *adv* —**marishness** *n* [U]

nightmare sce·na·ri·o /ˈ·· ·ˌ···/ *n* a description of a possible situation or course of action which would be terrible if it happened: *Citizens living near the proposed waste site fear the nightmare scenario of a radiation leak.*

night owl /ˈ· ·/ also **nighthawk** *AmE–* *n infml* a person who likes to stay awake most of the night to read, work, go out, etc.

nights /naɪts/ *adv esp. AmE* at night repeatedly; during any night: *He works nights.* | *I lie awake nights.*

night safe /ˈ· ·/ *BrE* ‖ **night depository** *AmE–* *n* a special opening in the outside wall of a bank in which a customer can put money, etc. when the bank is closed

night school /ˈ· ·/ *n* [U] a school or set of classes meeting in the evening, esp. for people who have jobs during the day: *She wants to learn French at night school*‖(*AmE*) *in night school.*

night·shade /ˈnaɪtʃeɪd/ *n* see DEADLY NIGHTSHADE

night shift /ˈ· ·/ *n* 1 [C] a period of time beginning at night and ending in the morning, during which people regularly work in a factory, hospital, or other place of work: *to work (on) the night shift* 2 [*the+sing./pl.* v] this group of workers: *The night shift is*‖*are just coming off duty.* —see also SHIFT[2] (2)

night·shirt /ˈnaɪt-ʃɜːt‖-ʃɜːrt/ *n* a piece of men's clothing like a long loose shirt, made to be worn in bed —compare NIGHTDRESS

night soil /ˈ· ·/ *n* [U] *euph* waste matter from the human bowels which is collected and used for growing crops

night·stand /ˈnaɪtstænd/ also **night ta·ble** /ˈ· ˌ··/– *n AmE* a small table beside a bed

night·stick /ˈnaɪtˌstɪk/ *n AmE for* TRUNCHEON

night·time /ˈnaɪt-taɪm/ *n* [(*the*) U] the time when it is dark;

NIGHT: *animals that hunt in the nighttime* —opposite **daytime**

night watch /ˈ· ·/ *n* WATCH[2] (5)

night watch·man /ˌ· ˈ··/ *n* 1 a man with the job of guarding a building at night 2 (in cricket) one of the less good batsmen (BATSMAN) in a team who is sent to BAT at the end of a day's play so that the better batsmen do not need to face the BOWLING until the next day

night·wear /ˈnaɪtweəʳ/ *n* [U] clothes worn in bed at night

nig·nog /ˈnɪɡnɒɡ‖-nɑːɡ/ *n BrE, taboo derog* a black person (considered extremely offensive)

ni·hil·is·m /ˈnaɪɪlɪzəm/ *n* [U] 1 the belief that nothing has meaning or value 2 the belief that social and political organization should be destroyed, even if nothing better can take its place —**ist** *n* —**istic** /ˌnaɪɪˈlɪstɪk‖/ *adj*

Ni·jin·sky /nɪˈdʒɪnski/, **Vas·lav** /ˈvɑːtslɑːf/ (1890–1950) a Russian BALLET dancer known for his powerful but graceful movement and his use of free expression

Niké /naɪk, ˈnaɪki/ *tdmk* an American company which makes sports clothes and shoes which have become very fashionable

Nik·kei in·dex /ˌnɪkeɪ ˈɪndeks/ also **Nikkei–** [*the*] an INDEX (=a system for comparing levels) of the prices of some typical shares (SHARE[1] (2)) on the Tokyo Stock Exchange, operated by a Japanese financial newspaper

Ni·kon /ˈnɪkɒn ‖ -ɑːn/ a camera made by the Japanese company Nikon

nil /nɪl/ *n* [U] nothing; zero: *The new machine reduced labour costs to almost nil.* | (*BrE*) *Our team won by four goals to nil.* —see ZERO (USAGE)

Nile /naɪl/ [*the*] a river in NE Africa, the longest in the world, which has supported most of the farming in Egypt, and also Sudan, since the early Egyptian civilization began there in about 4000 BC —see picture at DELTA

Ni·lot·ic /naɪˈlɒtɪk‖-ˈlɑː-/ *adj tech* of the River Nile, the peoples living around it, or their languages

nim·ble /ˈnɪmbəl/ *adj apprec* 1 quick, light, and neat in movement; AGILE: *a nimble climber* 2 quick in thinking or understanding: *a nimble mind*‖*imagination* —**bly** *adv* — **~ness** *n* [U]

nim·bus /ˈnɪmbəs/ *n* **-buses** *or* **-bi** /baɪ/ 1 [U] a dark spreading cloud that may bring rain or snow —compare CIRRUS, CUMULUS 2 [C] a HALO

nim·by /ˈnɪmbi/ *n sometimes all caps.* a person who does not want a particular building or activity to be carried out near their own house, but to be put somewhere else (from the first letters of the words "not in my back yard") — **nimby** *adj* : *a nimby attitude* — **~ism** *n*

Nim·mo /ˈnɪməʊ/, **Derek** (1933–) an English actor known for playing funny parts esp. priests

Ni·ña /ˈniːnə/ [*the*] one of the three ships which sailed to America with Christopher Columbus in 1492 –see also PINTA, SANTA MARIA

nin·com·poop /ˈnɪŋkəmpuːp/ *n old-fash infml* a stupid person; fool

nine /naɪn/ *determiner, n, pron* 1 (the number) 9 –see TABLE 1 2 **nine times out of ten** *infml* almost always –see also CLOUD NINE, **dressed up to the nines** (DRESS[1] (10))

nine days' won·der /ˌ· · ˈ··/ *n* a thing or event that causes excitement for a short time and then is forgotten

911 /ˌnaɪn wʌn ˈwʌn/ *the* telephone number used in the US to call the fire or police department or for an AMBULANCE in an EMERGENCY: *Call 911! The house is on fire!*

999 /ˌnaɪn naɪn ˈnaɪn/ *the* telephone number used in Britain to telephone the fire, police, or AMBULANCE services in an EMERGENCY: *Quick, dial 999* | *a 999 call*

Nine O'Clock News /ˌ· · ·ˈ·/ [*the*] a British television news programme broadcast on BBC1 at 9 p.m. each weekday —compare NEWS AT TEN

nine·pins /ˈnaɪnˌpɪnz/ *n* [U] an early form of the game of BOWLING using nine instead of ten bottle-shaped objects (**ninepins**) —**ninepin** *adj* [A] : *a ninepin alley* (=place for playing the game)

nine·teen /ˌnaɪnˈtiːn◂/ *determiner, n, pron* 1 (the number) 19 –see TABLE 1 2 **nineteen to the dozen** *infml* (speaking) quickly and continually, never stopping: *They were* *chatting away nineteen to the dozen.* — ~ **th** *determiner, n, pron, adv*

Nineteen Eigh·ty-Four /ˌ··· ··· ˈ·/ a book written by George Orwell in 1948, which looked into the future and imagined Britain in the year 1984 as a place where the government controls everyone's lives completely and watches what everyone is doing all the time. The title of the book, or the date "1984", are sometimes used to describe a society which is like this in some way. —see also BIG BROTHER, NEWSPEAK

nineteenth hole /ˌ·· ˈ·/ *[the] humor* a place where people playing GOLF can relax and have a drink after a game; the club bar

1922 Com·mit·tee /ˌnaɪntiːn ˌtwenti ˈtuː kəˌmɪti/ *[the]* the group of British Conservative members of parliament who are not ministers (BACKBENCHERS)

nine·ties /ˈnaɪntiz/ *n [P]* **1** *[the]* also **'90s** the 1990s (=the years from 1990 to 1999): *in the early nineties | the car for the nineties* **2** in **his/her/their nineties** aged from 90 to 99: *my grandparents are both in their nineties* **3** *[the]* the numbers from 90 to 99, esp. when used to measure temperature: *another hot day, with temperatures expected to reach the nineties.*

nine-to-five /ˌ·· · ˈ·◂/ *adj, adv* from nine o'clock in the morning until five o'clock in the evening, the typical working hours of an office worker: *a nine-to-five job | to work nine-to-five*

nine·ty /ˈnaɪnti/ *determiner, n, pron* (the number) 90 —see TABLE 1 —**tieth** /ˈnaɪntiˌθ/ *determiner, n, pron, adv*

ninety-nine /ˌ·· ˈ·◂/ *determiner, n, pron* **1** (the number) 99 —see TABLE 1 **2** **ninety-nine times out of a hundred** *infml* almost always

Nin·e·veh /ˈnɪnɪvə/ the capital of the ancient Assyrian EMPIRE, on the east bank of the river Tigris, in what is now Iraq. The remains of very fine buildings have been found buried there.

nin·ja /ˈnɪndʒə/ *n* (a member of) a Japanese class of professional killers, in former times. Toys and computer games involving Ninja warriors were popular in the early 1990s. Ninjas are always shown in dark clothes with a scarf covering the face and have special fighting skills. —see also TEENAGE MUTANT HERO TURTLES: *ninja warriors*

nin·ny /ˈnɪni/ *n infml* a silly foolish person

Nin·ten·do /nɪnˈtendəʊ/ *tdmk* a computer games machine made by the Japanese company Nintendo, esp. a small one that can be held in the hand

ninth /naɪnθ/ *determiner, adv, n, pron* 9th —see TABLE 1

nip¹ /nɪp/ *v* **-pp-** **1** [I (**at**);T] to catch in a tight sharp hold between two points or surfaces: *The little dog nipped my ankles* (=bit them)/*nipped at my ankles.* | (=tried to bite them) | *I nipped my finger in the door.* | *to nip off* (=cut off) *the corner of the page with scissors* **2** [I+prep] *BrE infml* to go quickly or for a short time: *I'll nip out and buy a newspaper.* | *She won't be long — she's just nipped down to the shops.* **3** [T] *fml* to stop the growth of (plants): *The frost has nipped the fruit trees.* **4** **nip (something) in the bud** to stop (something) before it has properly started: *Her plans to go to bed with a book were nipped in the bud when visitors arrived unexpectedly.*
nip in *phr v* [I] *BrE infml* to move quickly sideways in traffic or in a race: *I had to stop when another car nipped in in front of me.*

nip² *n* [S] **1** a coldness: *There's a nip in the air today: winter's coming.* **2** the act or result of nipping; PINCH: *I gave my fingers a nasty nip in the door.*

nip³ *n* [(**of**)] *infml* a small amount of a strong alcoholic drink, (not beer or wine): *a nip of whisky*

nip and tuck /ˌ·· · ˈ·/ *adv, adj AmE infml* **1** (of two or more competing things) nearly equal: *nip and tuck in the last lap of the race* **2** (of a situation) having barely what is needed to get a result: *I might make it to New York in this old beater, but it's going to be nip and tuck.*

nip·per /ˈnɪpəʳ/ *n infml, esp. BrE* a child, esp. a small boy

nip·pers /ˈnɪpəz/ *n* [P] any of various tools like PLIERS —see PAIR (USAGE)

nip·ple /ˈnɪpəl/ *n* **1 a** the dark part of a woman's breast, through which a baby can suck milk **b** the dark part of a man's chest —compare TEAT **2** *AmE* the piece of rubber shaped like this on the end of a baby's bottle; TEAT

(1) **3** a small opening shaped like this on a machine, for oil or GREASE

nip·py /ˈnɪpi/ *adj* **1** (of weather) cold; CHILLY: *a nippy winter morning* **2** quick in movement: *You'll have to be nippy if you want to catch the bus.* —**piness** *n* [U]

Ni·rex /ˈnaɪəreks/ see UK NIREX

nir·va·na /nɪəˈvɑːnə, nɜː-‖nɪər-, nɜːr-/ *n* [U] (*sometimes cap.*) (in Buddhism and Hinduism) ENLIGHTENMENT (2); a state of knowledge or understanding reached while meditating (MEDITATE) which is beyond life and death, suffering and change, and is the aim of all believers in these religions

nisi see DECREE NISI

Nis·san /ˈnɪsæn‖-sɑːn/ a car or other vehicle made by the Japanese company Nissan

Nis·sen hut /ˈnɪsən hʌt/ *n* (in Britain) a shelter whose roof and side walls are made in one round piece from iron sheets —compare QUONSET HUT

nit¹ /nɪt/ *n* an egg of an insect (usu. a LOUSE) that is sometimes found in people's hair

nit² *n BrE derog infml* a NITWIT

nit·pick·ing /ˈnɪtˌpɪkɪŋ/ *n* [U] *infml derog* the habit of paying too much attention to small and unimportant points or faults —**nitpicking** *adj* —**nitpicker** *n*

ni·trate /ˈnaɪtreɪt, -trᵻt/ *n* [C;U] any of several chemicals used mainly as FERTILIZER in improving soil for growing crops

ni·tre *BrE* ‖ **niter** *AmE* /ˈnaɪtəʳ/ *n* [U] any of certain nitrates, including SALTPETRE, esp. as substances found in nature

ni·tric ac·id /ˌnaɪtrɪk ˈæsᵻd/ *n* [U] a powerful acid (HNO_3) which eats away other substances and is used in explosives and other chemical products

ni·tro·gen /ˈnaɪtrədʒən/ *n* [U] a gas that is a simple substance (ELEMENT), without colour or smell, that forms most of the Earth's air

nitrogen ox·ides /ˌ··· ˈ··/ *n* [P] compounds of nitrogen and oxygen which are produced by the process of burning and are POLLUTANTS (=substances which are harmful to the environment)

ni·tro·gly·ce·rine , **-rin** /ˌnaɪtrəʊˈglɪsərᵻn, -trə-, -riːn‖-rᵻn/ *n* [U] a powerful liquid explosive —see also DYNAMITE

nit·ty-grit·ty /ˌnɪti ˈgrɪti/ *n* **get down to/come to the nitty-gritty** *sl* to deal with the difficult and practical part of a situation, e.g. when making an agreement or a decision: *Let's get down to the nitty-gritty: exactly how much do you intend to pay me for this?* —*adj* : *nitty-gritty details*

nit·wit /ˈnɪt·wɪt/ *n infml* a silly foolish person: *Open it, you nitwit!*

Niv·e·a /ˈnɪviə/ *n tdmk* a range of skin care products made by Smith and Nephew

Niv·en /ˈnɪvən/, **David** (1909–83) a British actor who appeared in many films, including *The Guns of Navarone*, and is known esp. for playing a particular sort of ELEGANT English gentleman. He also wrote two books about his life, containing many humorous stories about other famous people.

nix¹ /nɪks/ *adv AmE infml* no: *Dad said nix to our plan.*

nix² *v* [T] *AmE infml* (esp. in newspapers) to answer no to; forbid; REJECT: *The city nixed the plan.*

Nix·on /ˈnɪksən/, **Richard** (1913–) an American Republican politician who was president from 1969 to 1974, responsible for American soldiers leaving Vietnam, and for improving the country's relationship with China. He is now remembered esp. for his part in the Watergate affair which caused his downfall. —see also WATERGATE

NJ *written abbrev. for:* NEW JERSEY

N·ko·mo /əŋˈkaʊməʊ/, **Joshua** (1917–) a Zimbabwean politician, leader of the black nationalist movement against the white Rhodesian government of Ian Smith, and an important minister in the Zimbabwean government after independence

N·kru·mah /əŋˈkruːmə/, **Kwa·me** /ˈkwɑːmi/ (1909–72) a Ghanaian politician, Prime Minister from 1952–60 (before and after independence) and President from 1960–66; a believer in African unity and SOCIALISM. Many people regarded him as a DICTATOR and he was removed from power by the army.

NLRB /ˌen el ɑː ˈbiː‖-ɑːr-/ n abbrev. for: National Labor Relations Board

NM written abbrev. for: NEW MEXICO

NME /ˌen em ˈiː/ abbrev. for: NEW MUSICAL EXPRESS

no¹ /nəʊ/ adv **1** (used as an answer expressing refusal or disagreement): "Have you finished yet?" "No, I haven't." | "Is it raining?" "No, it's snowing." | "Will you post this letter for me?" "No, it's too cold to go out." —opposite **yes** **2** not any: I'm feeling no worse (=feeling the same or better) than yesterday. | There were no fewer than (=at least) 150 people at the party. | They no longer live here. — compare NOT (1); see MORE (USAGE) **3** often pomp (used before an adjective to give the opposite meaning): She had no small part (=had a large part) in its success. | a question of no great importance (=of little importance) | for no particular reason | "Did you have good weather?" "No such luck; it rained the whole time." **4** (used for expressing great surprise): "I bought this bicycle for £5." "No!" **5** BrE nonstandard **or no** or not: You'll have to do it, whether or no you want to. | Like it or no, you'll have to do it.

no² determiner **1** not a; not one; not any: no sugar in the bowl | no telephone in our house | no buses in this part of town | You can't lie to me; I'm no fool! | Her refusal came as no surprise. (=I expected it) —see SOME (USAGE); NO WAY **2** (used in warnings and road signs to express what is not allowed): No smoking | No parking **3** infml very little; hardly any: We're almost home; we'll be there **in no time.** (=very soon) | It's no distance at all to the school, only a short walk. **4** infml **there's no knowing/saying/telling, etc.** it's not possible to know/say/tell, etc.: He's such a strange person: there's no knowing what he'll do next.

▷ USAGE 1 Compare **no** and **not.** You can use **no** where the meaning is "not any": **no** money | **no** smoking | **no** thick shoes | **no** faster | **no** good. Otherwise use **not**: **not** a chance | **not** all of us | **not** enough | **not** often | **not** on Sunday | I'm **not** coming. | She's **not** stupid. 2 When answering questions remember that your choice of "yes" or "no" depends on whether what you are going to say is positive or negative and not on whether or not you agree with the speaker: "She's not very clever." "**No,** she isn't." (=you are right, she isn't)./"**Yes,** she is." (=you are wrong, she is clever).◁

no³ n noes **1** [usu. sing.] an answer or decision of no: a clear no to my request for money —opposite **yes** **2** [usu. pl.] a vote or voter against a question to be decided, esp. in a parliament —opposite **aye**

No , Noh /nəʊ/ n [U] a type of traditional Japanese DRAMA (2), which involves music and dance, and is based on religious or old stories

no. nos. written abbrev. for: NUMBER¹ (2)

No. 10 Number Ten /ˌnʌmbə ˈten ‖ -bər-/ No. 10 Downing Street ‖ No. 10 Downing Street; the address of the official home of the British Prime Minister; also used to mean the views held by the Prime Minister: This suggestion won't be welcomed at No. 10. | sources close to Number 10 —see colour picture on page 950

No. 10 Downing Street

No. 11 Number Eleven /ˌnʌmbər ɪˈlevən/ No. 11 Downing Street; the address of the official home of the British Chancellor of the Exchequer

no-ac·count /ˈ· ·ˌ·/ also **no-count**— n, adj [A] AmE dial derog (a person who is) completely worthless: his no-count, good-for-nothing nephew

No·ah /ˈnəʊə/ n in the Bible, the man chosen by God to build an ARK (a very large boat) in which he saved his family and two of every kind of animal from a terrible flood which covered the Earth. There are many songs and stories about **Noah's ark,** and the images from it (esp. the animals being chosen, and going into the ark "two by two") are very well known even by children. —see also FLOOD

Noah, Yan·nick /ˈjænɪk/ (1960–) a popular French tennis player known esp. for his exciting play and his DREADLOCKS

nob /nɒb‖nɑːb/ n infml derog or humor, esp. BrE a rich person with a high social position: The nobs live in the big houses on the hill.

no ball /ˈ· ·/ n (in cricket and other similar games) an act of bowling (BOWL² (1b)) the ball in a way that is not allowed by the rules

nob·ble /ˈnɒbəl‖ˈnɑː-/ v [T] BrE sl **1** to prevent (a racehorse) from winning, esp. by giving it drugs: They nobbled the favourite. **2** to get the attention of (someone), esp. in order to persuade or ask for a favour: I nobbled him at the party and told him about the book I was writing **3** to get dishonestly: He nobbled the free ticket for himself.

No·bel /nəʊˈbel/, **Al·fred** /ˈælfrɨd/ (1833–96) a Swedish engineer and CHEMIST who invented DYNAMITE. He is known for establishing the Nobel prizes, for which purpose he left his large fortune made from selling explosives.

No·bel prize /nəʊˌbel ˈpraɪz, ˌnəʊbel-/ n any of several prizes given in Sweden each year to people from any country for important work in science, medicine, economics and literature and towards world peace

no·bil·i·ty /nəʊˈbɪlɨti, nə-/ n **1** [the+sing./pl. v] the group of people in certain countries who are of the highest social class and have titles such as (in Britain) DUKE and EARL, the ARISTOCRACY: Most of the nobility fled during the revolution. **2** [U] also **no·ble·ness** /ˈnəʊbəlnɨs/— the quality of being noble in character or appearance

no·ble¹ /ˈnəʊbəl/ adj **1** deserving praise and admiration because of unselfishness and high moral quality: noble and generous feelings | It was very noble of you to look after your old neighbour when she was sick. | fighting for a noble cause —opposite **ignoble** **2** admirable in appearance; grand; IMPRESSIVE: this noble monument to our war heroes **3** of or belonging to the nobility: a noble family | a man of noble birth **4** [no comp.] (of metals like gold and silver) not chemically changed by air —compare BASE METAL; see also NOBLY **5** this was the **noblest** Roman of them all quote a phrase from Shakespeare's play Julius Caesar, said by Mark Antony about Brutus

noble² n [usu. pl.] (esp. in FEUDAL times) a person of the highest and most powerful social class outside the royal family —compare COMMONER

no·ble·man /ˈnəʊbəlmən/ **no·ble·wom·an** /-ˌwʊmən/fem.— n **-men** /mən/ a member of the nobility; PEER

noble sav·age /ˌ·· ˈ··/ [the] a person who is uneducated but has a lot of natural good qualities. The idea of the noble savage was invented by the French writer and thinker, Jean-Jacques Rousseau, who believed that people were naturally good and kind, but were corrupted (CORRUPT) by society, which taught them to be evil.

no·blesse o·blige /nəʊˌbles əˈbliːʒ/ n [U] the principle that people with high social class, money, good education, etc., should use these advantages to help people who do not have them

no·bly /ˈnəʊbli/ adv **1** in a noble way, esp. generously and unselfishly: She nobly did my work as well as hers while I was ill. **2** with a noble rank (in the phrase **nobly born**)

no·bod·y¹ /ˈnəʊbədi‖-ˌbɑːdi, -bədi/ pron no person; no one: I knocked on the door but nobody answered. —see also **like nobody's business** (BUSINESS (10)); see EVERYONE (USAGE), SOMETHING (USAGE)

nobody² n a person of no importance or influence: I want to be famous — I'm tired of being a nobody!

no-claims bo·nus /· ˈ· ·ˌ··/ n a reduction in the regular payments made to an insurance company (esp. for motor vehicles), given to someone who has not made any claims within a particular period

no con·test /ˌ· ˈ··/ see NOLO CONTENDERE

no-count /ˈ· ·/ see NO-ACCOUNT

noc·tur·nal /nɒkˈtɜːnl‖nɑːkˈtɜːr-/ adj fml or tech of, happening, or active at night: a nocturnal visit | nocturnal creatures such as owls and badgers — -ly adv

noc·turne /ˈnɒktɜːn‖ˈnɑːktɜːrn/ n a piece of music related to the night, esp. a soft beautiful piece of piano music

nod¹ /nɒd‖nɑːd/ v -dd- **1** [I;T] to bend (one's head) forward and down, esp. to show agreement or give a greeting or sign: *She nodded (her head) when she passed me in the street.* | *I asked her if she was ready to go, and she nodded.* | *The committee members nodded in agreement with him.* | (fig.) *flowers nodding in the wind* —compare **shake one's head** (SHAKE¹) **2** [T] to show in this way: *They nodded their agreement.*

nod off *phr v* [I] to fall asleep, esp. unintentionally, letting one's head drop: *I nodded off in my chair and missed the end of the film.*

nod² *n* **1** [*usu. sing.*] an act of nodding: *She greeted us with a nod (of the head).* | *He gave a slight nod.* **2** approval: *The governor gave the new bill a nod on Thursday.* **3 a nod's as good as a wink** *infml, often humor* (used to show that the speaker understands a situation without needing a full explanation) **4 on the nod** *BrE infml* (approved or accepted) by general agreement and without being talked about: *The chairman's proposals are usually passed on the nod at the shareholders' meetings.*

no·dal /'nəʊdl/ *adj fml* of or near one or more nodes

nod·ding ac·quaint·ance /ˌ·· ·'··/ *n* [S (**with**)] a very slight familiarity with a person or subject: *She and I have a nodding acquaintance.*

nod·dle /'nɒdl/ /'nɑːdl/ *n old-fash sl* a person's head or brain

Nod·dy /'nɒdi/ /'nɑː-/ a character in many children's books by the English writer Enid Blyton. He wears a little blue cap with a bell on the top, and drives a yellow and red car around Toytown, with his friend Big Ears.

node /nəʊd/ *n* **1** *tech* a place where branches or parts of a system or network meet or join **2** a swelling or roundish lump, as on a tree trunk or a person's body

nod·ule /'nɒdjuːl/ /'nɑːdʒuːl/ *n* a small round mass or lump, esp. a small round swelling on a plant or a person's body —**ular** /'nɒdjʊlər/ /'nɑːdʒə-/ *adj*

No·el /nəʊ'el/ *n* [U] *poet* (the season of) Christmas: *the first Noel*

noes /nəʊz/ *pl. of* NO³

no-fault /'·· ·/ *adj tech, esp AmE* of a point of view in which the determination of blame or responsibility is not important: *no-fault insurance laws* | *a no-fault divorce case*

no-fly zone /ˌ· '· ˌ·/ *n* an AIR EXCLUSION ZONE

nog·gin /'nɒgɪn/ /'nɑː-/ *n* [*usu. sing.*] **1** *sl* a person's head or brain: *Think! Use your noggin.* **2** *BrE* a small amount (usu. a GILL) of an alcoholic drink

no-go ar·e·a /ˌ· '· ·ˌ···/ *n infml, esp. BrE* an area, esp. in a city, controlled by one of two opposed groups and dangerous for anyone else to enter: *Since the invasion of the southern part of the town has become a no-go area.*

Noh /nəʊ/ *n* [U] see NO

no-hit·ter /ˌ· '··/ *n* (in BASEBALL) a game in which the PITCHER² does not allow anyone on the opposing team to hit the ball successfully: *Cy Young was the first pitcher ever to throw a no-hitter.*

no·how /'nəʊhaʊ/ *adv nonstandard or humor* in no way; not at all

noise¹ /nɔɪz/ *n* **1** [C;U] sound, esp. (an) unwanted or meaningless unmusical sound: *I heard a noise outside.* | *Try not to make a noise when you go upstairs; the baby's asleep.* | *There's so much noise in this restaurant I can hardly hear you talking.* | *What's wrong with the car? The engine's making funny noises.* **2** [U] *tech* **a** unwanted signals produced by an electrical CIRCUIT **b** meaningless information produced by a computer **3 make noises** *infml* to express feelings or intentions of the stated kind: *My teacher made encouraging noises when I said I wanted to go to university.* —see also BIG NOISE — ~**less** *adj* — ~**lessly** *adv* — ~**lessness** *n* [U]

▷ USAGE Compare **sound, voice,** and **noise.** A **sound** is anything that you hear: *the* **sound** *of voices/of music/of breaking glass.* A **voice** is the sound of a person speaking or singing: *She has a loud/high/charming* **voice.** | *a song for male* **voices.** A **noise** is usually a loud, unpleasant **sound:** *Stop making so much* **noise!**◁

noise² *v esp. BrE*

noise sthg. **about/abroad/around** *phr v* [T *often pass.*] to make public (a piece of news that is perhaps untrue): *Rumours of an election are being noised abroad.* | *It's being noised around that the factory is going to close.*

noise pol·lu·tion /'·· ·ˌ··/ *n* [U] (the making of) a very loud

noise which is unpleasant to people near it and which is viewed as a type of POLLUTION: *People living opposite the factory complained that it was a source of noise pollution.*

noi·sette /nwɑː'zet/ *n often pl.* a small round boneless piece of usu. lamb meat: *noisettes of lamb*

noi·some /'nɔɪsəm/ *adj esp. lit* very unpleasant (esp. of a smell)

nois·y /'nɔɪzi/ *adj* full of noise; making a lot of noise: *a noisy car* | *It's very noisy in this office.* —**ily** *adv* —**iness** *n* [U]

no·lo con·ten·de·re /ˌnəʊləʊ kɒn'tendəri‖-kən'tendəreɪ/ *also* **no contest** *infml adv, adj, n Lat* (in US law) (of) a PLEA in a court case that means the person being tried does not admit guilt, but also does not defend himself: *The former governor was convicted after a nolo contendere plea on charges of corruption.* | *She pleaded nolo contendere to the homicide charge.*

no·mad /'nəʊmæd/ *n* a member of a tribe which travels from place to place, esp. to find grass for its animals: *the nomads of the desert* — ~**ic** /nəʊ'mædɪk/ *adj* : *a nomadic people*

no-man's-land /'·· ˌ·/ *n* [S;U] an area of land which no one owns or controls, esp. between two borders or two opposing armies: *He was shot crossing no-man's-land.*

nom de plume /ˌnɒm də 'pluːm‖ˌnɑːm-/ *n* **noms de plume** (*same pronunciation*) a PEN NAME

no·men·cla·ture /nəʊ'menklətʃər‖'nəʊmənkler-/ *n tech* [C;U] a system of naming things, esp. in science: *medical nomenclature* | *the nomenclature of chemical compounds*

nom·i·nal /'nɒmɪnəl‖'nɑː-/ *adj* **1** in name or form but usu. not in reality: *The old man is only the nominal head of the business: his daughter makes all the decisions.* | *His position as chairman is purely nominal.* **2** (of an amount of money) very small; NEGLIGIBLE: *sold for a nominal sum* (=a price far below the real value) **3** *tech* (in grammar) of or used as a noun: *a nominal phrase* | *nominal endings such as "-ness" and "-ation".* — ~**ly** *adv* : *He is nominally the head of the firm.*

nom·i·nate /'nɒmɪneɪt‖'nɑː-/ *v* [T] **1** [(**for, as**)] to suggest or name (someone) officially for a position, office, duty, honour, etc.: *I wish to nominate Jane Morrison for/as president of the club.* [+*obj*+*to-v*] *I nominate John to represent us at the meeting.* **2** [(**as**)] to appoint (someone) to such a position, office, etc., without election: *The director nominated me as his official representative at the conference.*

nom·i·na·tion /ˌnɒmɪ'neɪʃən‖ˌnɑː-/ *n* [C;U (**for, as**)] the act of nominating or a case of being nominated: *The club agreed to all the committee's nominations.* | *Who will get the Republican nomination for president?* | *His nomination as chief executive was approved/rejected by the board.*

nom·i·na·tive /'nɒmɪnətɪv, 'nɒmnə-‖'nɑː-/ *n tech* a particular form of a noun in certain languages, such as Latin, Greek, and German, which shows that the noun is the subject of a verb —**nominative** *adj*

nom·i·nee /ˌnɒmɪ'niː‖ˌnɑː-/ *n* a person who has been nominated

non- see WORD FORMATION

no·na·ge·nar·i·an /ˌnəʊnədʒɪ'neəriən/ *n* a person who is between 90 and 99 years old

non·ag·gres·sion /ˌnɒn-ə'greʃən‖ˌnɑːn-/ *n* [U] the avoidance of fighting, esp. between countries: *a nonaggression pact* (=with each side promising not to attack the other)

non·a·ligned /ˌnɒn-ə'laɪnd◂‖ˌnɑːn-/ *adj* (of a country) not dependent on or supporting any particular one of the world powers —**lignment** *n* [U]

non·bi·o·lo·gi·cal /ˌ·· ··'····◂/ *adj* (of a cleaning product) not containing ENZYMES or other products made by living cells

nonce¹ /nɒns‖nɑːns/ *adj* [A] *tech* (esp. of a word or phrase) invented for a particular occasion only

nonce² *n lit or humor* **for the nonce** for the present time; for this occasion

non·cha·lant /'nɒnʃələnt‖ˌnɑːnʃə'lɑːnt/ *adj* showing calmness, lack of anxiety, and often lack of interest; UNCONCERNED; COOL: *a nonchalant attitude to his debts* —**lance** *n* [U] : *She received the prize with an air of nonchalance.* — ~**ly** *adv*

non·com·ba·tant /ˌnɒnˈkɒmbətənt‖ˌnɑːnkəmˈbætənt/ n a person, esp. in the armed forces (such as a CHAPLAIN or doctor), who does not take part in actual fighting: *He served in the war as a noncombatant.* | *noncombatant duty*

non·com·mis·sioned of·fi·cer /ˌnɒnkəˌmɪʃənd ˈɒfɪsəᵣ‖ˌnɑːn-; -ˈɔːf-, -ˈɑːf-/ also **non·com** /ˌnɒnˈkɒm‖ˌnɑːnˈkɑːm/ esp. AmE— n see NCO

non·com·mit·tal /ˌnɒnkəˈmɪtl◂‖ˌnɑːn-/ adj not expressing (or refusing to express) a clear opinion or intention: *I asked him to vote for me but he was noncommittal.* —see also COMMIT (2) — ~**ly** adv : *She answered noncommittally.*

non com·pos men·tis /ˌnɒn ˌkɒmpəs ˈmentɪs‖ˌnɑːn ˌkɑːm-/ adj [F] *Lat, law or humor* unable to think clearly or be responsible for one's actions: *The court judged him to have been non compos mentis when he committed the murder.* —opposite **compos mentis**

non·con·duc·tor /ˌnɒnkənˈdʌktəᵣ‖ˌnɑːn-/ n a substance which allows little or no sound, heat, or esp. electricity to pass through it —compare INSULATOR

non·con·form·ist /ˌnɒnkənˈfɔːmɪst◂‖ˌnɑːnkənˈfɔːr-/ adj, n (of or being) a person who does not follow generally accepted way(s) of living, thinking, etc.: *a political nonconformist* | *nonconformist attitudes* —**ity**, **-ism** n [U]

Nonconformist adj, n (a member) of any of several Christian religious groups which have separated from the Church of England: *a Nonconformist minister|chapel* —**ity** n [U]

non·con·trib·u·to·ry /ˌnɒnkənˈtrɪbjʊtəri◂‖ˌnɑːnkənˈtrɪbjʊtɔːri/ adj (of a PENSION or insurance plan) paid for by the employer only and not by the worker —opposite **contributory**

non·cus·to·di·al /ˌnɒnkʌˈstəʊdiəl◂‖ˌnɑːn-/ adj 1 (of a person) who does not have legal CUSTODY of his or her children: *child support obligations of noncustodial parents* 2 (of a form of punishment) which does not involve being kept in prison or some other institution: *She was given a noncustodial sentence for the crime in light of her previous clean record.*

non·dai·ry /ˌ· ˈ··◂/ adj not containing milk or milk products: *a new non-dairy dessert topping*

non·de·script /ˈnɒndɪˌskrɪpt‖ˌnɑːndɪˈskrɪpt/ adj without any noticeable or interesting qualities; very ordinary-looking; not DISTINCTIVE: *Her clothes were so nondescript I can't remember what she was wearing.*

non·dis·crim·i·na·tion /ˌ· ···ˈ··/ n [U] the action of not discriminating against (=not treating unfairly) particular groups of people, esp. when done by a public organization in order to be fair to people who may be at a disadvantage in society: *The council has a policy of nondiscrimination.* —**tory** adj

none¹ /nʌn/ pron [(of)] 1 not any; no amount or part: *"Have you any money?" "No, none at all|none whatever."* | *She had none of her mother's beauty.* | *I'm afraid we can't have coffee; there's none left.* | *None of your foolishness, please!* (=Stop being foolish.) 2 not any of a group of more than two: *None of my friends* (=I have more than two) *ever come(s) to see me.* | *None of the telephones is|are working.* | *None of their promises have been kept.* —compare NEITHER¹ 3 not any one: *Even an old car is better than none at all.* 4 **have none of** fml to take no part in; not accept: *He was offered a job in a weapons factory but he said he would have none of it.* 5 **none but** *often lit* only: *None but the best ingredients are used in our products.* 6 **none other (than)** (shows surprise) no one else (but): *The mystery guest on the show was none other than Prince Charles!* —see also NONETHELESS, **second to none** (SECOND¹), **bar none** (BAR³)

▷ USAGE When **none** of is followed by a plural noun, it usually takes a plural verb in ordinary speech: **None of** *us are ready yet.* But in formal writing a singular verb is used: **None** *of our factories is in operation yet.* —see also EITHER² (USAGE)◁

none² adv 1 **none the** (used before a comparative) not; in no way: *He explained it to me, but I'm none the wiser.* (=I still don't understand it) | *My car is none the worse for* (=is no worse because of) *the accident.* 2 **none too** not very: *The service in this restaurant is none too fast and the food is none too good, either.*

non·en·ti·ty /nɒˈnentɪti‖nɑː-/ n *derog* a person without

much ability, character, or importance: *a weak government, full of complete nonentities*

none·such /ˈnʌnsʌtʃ/ n [*usu. sing.*] *lit* a NONPAREIL (1)

none·the·less /ˌnʌnðəˈles◂/ adv in spite of that; NEVERTHELESS

non-e·vent /ˌ· ·ˈ·/ n *infml* an event that is much less important, interesting, etc., than expected: *The demonstration was a bit of a non-event; only a few people turned up.* —compare MEDIA EVENT

non-ex·ec·u·tive di·rec·tor /ˌ· ·ˌ··· ·ˈ··/ n a person who sits on the BOARD¹ (4) of directors of a company and gives advice but who does not have responsibility for how the company is run

non-ex·ist·ent /ˌnɒnɪgˈzɪstənt◂‖ˌnɑːn-/ adj not existing: *Their government is bankrupt, and public services are now practically nonexistent.*

non-fic·tion /ˌnɒnˈfɪkʃən‖ˌnɑːn-/ n [U] writing that is about real facts or events rather than imagined things; not poetry, plays, stories, or NOVELS —compare FICTION

non-fi·nite /ˌ· ˈ··/ adj 1 not FINITE; having no end or limit 2 *tech* (of a verb form) not marked to show a particular tense or subject: *"Being" and "been" are non-finite forms of the verb "to be", but "am" and "was" are finite.*

non·flam·ma·ble /ˌnɒnˈflæməbəl‖ˌnɑːn-/ also **non·in·flam·ma·ble** /ˌnɒnɪnˈflæməbəl‖ˌnɑːn-/ adj difficult or impossible to set on fire or burn: *The firemen's uniforms are made of nonflammable material.* —opposite **inflammable**; see FLAMMABLE (USAGE)

non·in·ter·ven·tion /ˌnɒnɪntəˈvenʃən‖ˌnɑːnɪntər-/ also **non·in·ter·fer·ence** /ˌnɒnɪntəˈfɪərəns‖ˌnɑːnɪntər-/— n [U] the practice, esp. by a government, of not taking part in or trying to influence the affairs or disagreements of other people, countries, etc.: *a nonintervention policy* | *a policy of nonintervention* —see also INTERVENE

non-i·ron /ˌ· ˈ··◂/ adj not needing to be ironed after washing: *a non-iron fabric*

no-no /ˈ· ·/ n *infml* 1 something which one refuses to consider, or cannot take, as a possible course of action, etc.: *They might consider letting us borrow a little money, but a million pounds is a definite no-no.* 2 something that a child is forbidden to touch, esp. by their parents

no-non·sense /ˌ· ˈ··◂/ adj [A] practical and direct; BUSINESSLIKE: *Her no-nonsense approach soon solved the problem.*

non·pa·reil /ˈnɒnpərəl, -pəreɪl‖ˌnɑːnpəˈrel/ n 1 *lit* a person or thing so excellent as to have no equal 2 *AmE* for HUNDREDS AND THOUSANDS 3 *AmE* a flat round piece of chocolate covered with nonpareils (2)

non·par·ti·san /ˌnɒnpɑːtɪˈzæn◂‖ˌnɑːnˈpɑːrtɪzən, -sən/ n, adj (a person) lacking interest in the arguments or ideas of a particular political party: *a nonpartisan approach to the housing problem*

non·pay·ment /ˌnɒnˈpeɪmənt‖ˌnɑːn-/ n [U (of)] failure to pay (bills, tax, etc.): *The landlord took them to court for nonpayment of rent.*

non·plus /ˌnɒnˈplʌs‖ˌnɑːn-/ v **-ss-** [T *usu. pass.*] to cause (someone) to be surprised and not know what to think or do: *The speaker seemed completely nonplussed (by my question).*

non·prof·it-mak·ing /ˌ· ˈ·· ˌ··/ adj 1 *BrE* ‖ usu. **non-profit** or **not-for-profit** *AmE*— not run in order to make a profit: *This charity is a non-profit-making organization.* 2 not successful in making a profit; unprofitable

non·pro·lif·e·ra·tion /ˌnɒnprəˌlɪfəˈreɪʃən‖ˌnɑːn-/ n [U] the act or aim of limiting NUCLEAR weapons to the same amounts and the same countries as at the (present) time: *a nonproliferation agreement* —see also PROLIFERATE

non·res·i·dent /ˌnɒnˈrezᵻdənt‖ˌnɑːn-/ n, adj (a person) not living in a certain place, esp. in a a country: *Are nonresidents entitled to vote?* b a hotel: *The hotel restaurant is open to nonresidents.*

non·res·i·den·tial /ˌ· ··ˈ··◂/ adj not staying overnight at the place where a certain activity is carried out: *nonresidential students pay a reduced fee* | *non-residential care for the elderly* (=they are looked after during the day, and go home at night)

non·re·stric·tive /ˌnɒnrᵻˈstrɪktɪv◂‖ˌnɑːn-/ adj *tech* (of a CLAUSE) giving additional information about a person or thing, rather than saying which person or thing is meant:

*In "My father, who collects stamps", the phrase "who col-
lects stamps" is a nonrestrictive clause, because it does not
tell us which father is meant but tells us something else
about him.* —compare RESTRICTIVE (2)

non·sense /ˈnɒnsəns‖ˈnaːnsens/ *n* [U] **1** speech or writing
with no meaning: *She left out three words when she copied the sentence and the result was nonsense.* **2** statements, ideas, etc., that go against good sense; RUBBISH[1]:
*"I can't go out dressed like this." "Nonsense!|What non-
sense! You look fine." | You're talking complete|utter non-
sense. | Her speech was full of the usual nonsense about
"Victorian values".* [also S, BrE] *To say that this law will
not affect our profits is a nonsense.* **3** foolish behaviour:
*Stop that nonsense, children! | a strict teacher who would
stand no nonsense* **4** *apprec* humorous imaginative
poetry usu. telling a rather meaningless story: *a collection of nonsense verse* **5** BrE **make (a) nonsense of** to
spoil or cause to fail: *Your tactless remarks made nonsense
of our attempts to reassure them.*

non·sen·si·cal /nɒnˈsensɪkəl‖naːn-/ *adj* full of nonsense;
foolish; ABSURD: *nonsensical opinions* — ~**ly** /kli/ *adv*

non seq·ui·tur /ˌnɒn ˈsekwɪtər‖ˌnaːn-/ *n* **non sequiturs** *Lat
fml* a statement which does not follow from the facts or
arguments which have gone before; an incorrect piece
of reasoning

non-shrink /ˌ· ˈ·◄/ *adj* (of a material or piece of clothing)
not likely to get smaller if treated according to the washing instructions

non·smok·er /ˌnɒnˈsməʊkər‖ˌnaːn-/ *n* **1** a person who does
not smoke **2** BrE a railway carriage where smoking is
not allowed — **·ing** *adj*

non·spe·cif·ic u·re·thri·tis /ˌnɒnspɪˌsɪfɪk ˌjʊriˈθraɪtɪs‖
ˌnaːn-/ *n* see NSU

non·stan·dard /ˌnɒnˈstændəd◄‖ˌnaːnˈstændərd◄/ *adj* **1** not
standard: *nonstandard shoe sizes* —compare SUBSTAN-
DARD **2** (of words, expressions, pronunciations, etc.) not
usu. regarded as correct by educated speakers of a language: *Lots of people say "I gotta go", but "gotta" is still
considered nonstandard.*

non·start·er /ˌnɒnˈstaːtər‖ˌnaːnˈstaːr-/ *n* [usu. sing.] *infml*
a person or idea that has no chance of success and so cannot be seriously considered: *We wanted to buy a house,
but that was a nonstarter because we didn't have nearly
enough money.*

non·stick /ˌnɒnˈstɪk◄‖ˌnaːn-/ *adj* (of a cooking pan) having
a specially treated smooth inside surface to which food
will not stick

non-stop /ˌnɒnˈstɒp◄‖ˌnaːnˈstaːp◄/ *adj, adv* without a
pause or interruption: *a nonstop flight from London to
Singapore | music playing nonstop all night*

non-U /ˌnɒn ˈjuː◄‖ˌnaːn-/ *adj* BrE old-fash *infml* (esp. of a
word or action) not used by or typical of the upper class:
*wall-to-wall patterned carpets – distinctly non-U | He said
"settee" – that's a bit non-U, isn't it?* —opposite U

non·u·nion /ˌnɒn-ˈjuːnjən◄‖ˌnaːn-/ *adj* **1** not belonging to
a trade union: *nonunion employees* **2** not giving official
recognition to a trade union: *a nonunion firm*

non·ver·bal /ˌnɒnˈvɜːbəl◄‖ˌnaːnˈvɜːr-/ *adj* not using words:
nonverbal means of expression — ~**ly** *adv*

non·vi·o·lence /ˌnɒnˈvaɪələns‖ˌnaːn-/ *n* [U] political opposition without fighting, shown esp. by not obeying laws
or orders: *Gandhi was an advocate of nonviolence.* —**lent**
adj : *nonviolent protest* —**lently** *adv*

non·white /ˌnɒnˈwaɪt◄‖ˌnaːn-/ *n, adj esp.* SAfrE (a person
who is) not white by race

noo·dle /ˈnuːdl/ *n* [usu. pl.] a usu. long thin food substance
made from flour, water, and eggs, and cooked in soup or
boiling water: *chicken noodle soup | beef with noodles*

nook /nʊk/ *n* **1** a small space in a corner of a room: *sitting in the chimney nook* (=the space in a corner beside
the chimney) **2** a sheltered private place: *a shady nook
in the garden* **3** **nooks and crannies** hidden or little-
known places: *to search every nook and cranny* (=look
everywhere)

noon /nuːn/ also **noon·day** /ˈnuːndeɪ/*lit* — *n* [U] 12 o'clock
in the daytime; MIDDAY: *We left home at noon.* —see also
morning, noon, and night (MORNING)

▷ USAGE **Noon** is used in almost all contexts in American English where **midday** is found in British
English.◁

no one /ˈ· ·/ also **nobody**— *pron* not anyone; no person:
*There's no one here apart from me. | a surprise result that
no one expected | Can you help me? No one else* (=no other
person) *can. | No one likes being criticized. | No one has
phoned me this morning, have they?* –see also **no one's
fool** (FOOL[1] (9)), **like no one's business** (BUSINESS (10));
see EVERYONE (USAGE), SOMETHING (USAGE)

noose /nuːs/ *n* **1** [C] a ring formed by the end of a cord,
rope, etc., which closes more tightly as it is pulled **2** [*the*]
a rope with such a ring in it, used to hang a person; death
by hanging

NOP /ˌen əʊ ˈpiː/‖ National Opinion Polls; a British organization which tries to find out what people in general
think about a particular subject, esp. who will win an
election

nope /nəʊp/ *adv sl* no: *"Hungry?" "Nope. I just ate."*

no place /ˈ· ·/ *adv infml, esp. AmE* nowhere: *There's no
place left to hide.*

no-quib·ble guar·an·tee /ˌ· ˌ·· ··ˈ·/ *n infml* a GUARANTEE (1)
in which the maker or seller of goods says they will
replace any faulty goods willingly, without arguing over
small details which might prevent the guarantee from
being used

nor /nɔːr/ *conj* **1** (used between the two or more choices
after **neither**): *just pleasantly warm, neither too cold nor
too hot* **2** (used before the second, third, etc., choices
after **not**) and/or not: *The job cannot be done by you nor
(by) me nor (by) anyone else.* **3** *esp.* BrE (used at the beginning of an expression just before a verb) and also not:
*"I don't like it." "Nor do I." | I'm not going to work today
and nor is Susie.* | (*fml*) *I have never been dishonest, nor
do I intend to start being so now.* —see NEITHER[1] (USAGE)

Nor·den /ˈnɔːdn‖ˈnɔːr-/, **Den·is** /ˈdenɪs/ (1922–) an English writer for television and radio and a broadcaster
who is best-known for the television programme *It'll be
alright on the night*

Nor·dic /ˈnɔːdɪk‖ˈnɔːr-/ *adj* of the Germanic peoples of
northern Europe, esp. Norway, Sweden, Denmark,
Iceland, and Finland

Nor·folk /ˈnɔːfək‖ˈnɔːr-/ a COUNTY in eastern England,
mainly farmland with some marshes (MARSH). It is
known for the lakes called **the Norfolk Broads**, where
many people take boating holidays.

Norfolk jack·et /ˌ·· ˈ··/ *n* a man's short coat with a belt and
with PLEATS (=flat folds) in the front and at the back,
worn esp. in former times

Nor·i·e·ga /ˌnɒriˈeɪgə‖ˌnɔːr-/, **Man·u·el** /ˈmænuˈel‖ˈmænˈwel/
(1940–) a soldier and politician, ruler of Panama from
1982 until 1989, when he was taken to the US and imprisoned for drug dealing, after President Bush had ordered
American soldiers to INVADE Panama

norm /nɔːm‖nɔːrm/ *n* a standard e.g. of behaviour or ability, that is regarded as average or generally acceptable:
*terrorists who violate the norms of civilized society | devi-
ation from the norm | a pay increase that is well below the
national norm*

nor·mal /ˈnɔːməl‖ˈnɔːr-/ *adj* **1** according to what is expected, usual, or average: *normal working hours from
nine to five | It's perfectly normal to get depressed some-
times. | Rainfall has been above|below normal this July.|
Train services are now back to normal after last week's
strike.* **2** (of a person) developing in the expected way;
without any disorder in mind or body: *a normal child in
every way* —compare ABNORMAL; see also NORMALLY

nor·mal·i·ty /nɔːˈmælɪti‖nɔːr-/ also **nor·mal·cy** /ˈnɔːməlsi
‖ˈnɔːr-/*AmE*— *n* [U]*fml* the quality or fact of being normal; the usual state of affairs: *We're hoping for a return
to normality in our international relations.*

nor·mal·ize also **-ise** BrE /ˈnɔːməlaɪz‖ˈnɔːr-/ *v* [I;T] to (cause
to) become normal; esp. to bring or come back to a nor-
mal friendly state: *After a period of international tension,
the two countries are now trying to normalize relations
with each other.* —**ization** /ˌnɔːməlaɪˈzeɪʃən‖ˌnɔːrmələ-/
n [U]

nor·mal·ly /ˈnɔːməli‖ˈnɔːr-/ *adv* **1** in the usual way or to
the usual degree: *behaving quite normally in spite of anxi-
ety | The factory is now running normally again. | a nor-
mally active child* **2** in the usual conditions; ordinarily:
*I normally go to bed early, but I stayed up late last night.|
Normally, the disease lasts about five days.*

Nor·man[1] /ˈnɔːmən‖ˈnɔːr-/ *adj* **1** of the northern French people who took control of England in the 11th century **2** (of buildings in Britain) built in the style (**Norman architecture**) of this period typically with thick, strong walls, tall, narrow windows and doors with rounded tops, and GEOMETRIC patterns decorating the stonework; ROMANESQUE: *a Norman church* | *a Norman arch* –see colour picture on page 227 –**Norman** *n*

Norman[2], **Greg** /greg/ (1955–) an Australian GOLF player who has won the world match-play title three times

Norman[3], **Jes·sye** /ˈdʒesi/ (1945–) an American OPERA singer known for her beautiful and powerful voice

Norman[4], **Bar·ry** /ˈbæri/ (1933–) an English writer and broadcaster known esp. for his programmes of film reviews

Norman Con·quest /ˌ·· ˈ··/ [*the*] the period in English history following the Battle of Hastings in 1066, when the Normans, led by William the Conqueror, ruled England, introducing French as the language spoken by the upper classes, and Norman ARCHITECTURE and customs. For no clear reason, the date of the Battle of Hastings is one of the few dates in history which most British people know, esp. in connection with a book, *1066 and all that* which describes the history of Britain in a very humorous way.

Nor·man·dy /ˈnɔːməndi‖ˈnɔːr-/ a part of northern France, on the English Channel, known for production of cheeses, as well as the ports of Cherbourg and Le Havre where boats carrying passengers from England arrive. In 1944 it was the scene of the **Normandy Landings**, when the Allies landed on the Normandy shore and began to drive Adolf Hitler's forces out of France. The day on which they landed is called **D-Day**. –see also D-DAY

nor·ma·tive /ˈnɔːmətɪv‖ˈnɔːr-/ *adj fml* urging obedience to a rule; stating a NORM: *normative judgments about how people should behave* | *normative grammar*

Norse /nɔːs‖nɔːrs/ *adj* of the ancient Scandinavian people, esp. the VIKINGS

Norse·man /ˈnɔːsmən‖ˈnɔːrs-/ *n* **-men** /mən/ *lit* a VIKING

north[1] /nɔːθ‖nɔːrθ/ (*abbrev.* **N**) *n* (*often cap.*) **1** [*the*;U] the direction which is up from the centre line of the Earth (EQUATOR); the direction which is on the left of a person facing the rising sun: *I'm lost – which direction is North?* | *A strange light appeared in the north.* | *Cheshunt is a few kilometres (to the) north of London.* **2** [*the*] the northern part of a country: *The North will be dry and bright.* | *unemployment in the north of England.* | *the frozen North* –see also NORTH-SOUTH DIVIDE, TRUE NORTH

north[2] (*abbrev.* **N**) *adj* [A] **1** (*sometimes cap.*) in the north or facing the north: *The north side of the building doesn't get much sun.* | *He lives in North Korea.* **2** (of a wind) coming from the north: *a cold north wind*

▷ USAGE For clear divisions of the Earth's surface, especially political ones, we usually say **North, South, East,** or **West.** For more uncertain ones we usually say **Northern, Southern, Eastern** or **Western.** Compare **South** *Africa* | **Southern** *England* | *the* **North** *Pole* | **Northern** *Europe* | **East Sussex** | **Eastern** *countries.* But these words are often part of a name, and there is no clear rule about which form will be correct.◁

north[3] (*abbrev.* **N**) *adv* (*often cap.*) **1** towards the north: *The room faces north, so it gets rather cold.* | *The birds fly north in summer.* | *Edinburgh is (a long way) north of London.* **2 up north** *infml* to or in the north of the country: *They've moved up north.*

North[1] *n* [*the*] **1** the northeastern states of the US, esp. during the CIVIL WAR, when they fought the SOUTH. Today, the NEW ENGLAND states and New York, New Jersey, and Pennsylvania are usu. called the **Northeast**, while the states to the west of these are called the MIDWEST. –compare SOUTH; –see also WEST (2) **2** the northern part of Britain –see also NORTH/SOUTH DIVIDE **3** the richer countries of esp. northern parts of the world, such as Europe and North America –see also NORTH/SOUTH DIVIDE (2)

North[2], **Ol·i·ver** /ˈɒlɪ̈vəʳ‖ˈɑːl-/ (1943–) an American Marine Lieutenant-Colonel, who was in charge of the US bombing of Libya in 1986. He was also tried for his involvement in a deal with Iran in 1985 in which the US gave weapons to Iran in exchange for the release of American HOSTAGES. The charges against Oliver North were later dropped. –see also IRANGATE

North·al·ler·ton /nɔːθˈælətən‖nɔːrθˈælər-/ a market town in North Yorkshire, NE England, where the local government for that COUNTY is based

North A·mer·i·ca /ˌ· ·ˈ···/ the third largest CONTINENT in the world, consisting of Canada and the United States of America, as well as Mexico, Central America, Greenland, and other smaller islands –**-can** *n,adj*

Nor·thamp·ton /nɔːˈθæmptən ‖ nɔːr-/ a town in Northamptonshire, central England, where the local government for that COUNTY is based. It is famous for its shoe-making industry.

Nor·thamp·ton·shire /nɔːˈθæmptənʃəʳ‖nɔːr-/ *abbrev.* **Nor·thants.** /ˈnɔːθænts‖ˈnɔːr-/– a COUNTY in central England. It is mainly farmland but has some industries including engineering, iron and steel-making, and shoe-making.

North At·lan·tic Treat·y Or·ga·ni·za·tion /ˌ· ··· ˈ·· ···ˌ··/ [*the*] see NATO

north·bound /ˈnɔːθbaʊnd‖ˈnɔːrθ-/ *adj* travelling or leading towards the north: *northbound traffic* | *the northbound side of the motorway*

North Car·o·li·na /ˌnɔːθ kærəˈlaɪnə‖ˌnɔːr-/ *written abbrev.* **NC**– a state on the eastern coast of the US, known mainly for production of tobacco. It was one of the 13 original British colonies (COLONY) –see colour map on pages 1374–5

North Cir·cu·lar /ˌ· ˈ···/ [*the*] an important road, the A406, which goes through N London in a SEMICIRCLE and connects with the South Circular Road on the east and the west sides of London

North·cliffe /ˈnɔːθklɪf‖ˈnɔːrθ-/, **Lord** (1865–1922) an Irish writer for newspapers and a leading man in this field who helped to increase their spread and started three important British newspapers with his brothers

North Da·ko·ta /ˌnɔːθ dəˈkəʊtə ‖ ˌnɔːrθ-/ *written abbrev.* **ND** a state in the north central US, on the border with Canada, with a small population but sizeable mineral and farming interests –see colour map on pages 1374–5

North Downs /ˌ· ˈ·/ [*the*+P] a range of hills to the S of London, running across S England. The white cliffs of Dover are at the eastern end. –compare SOUTH DOWNS

north·east[1] /ˌnɔːθˈiːst◂‖ˌnɔːrθ-/ (*abbrev.* **NE**) *n* (*often cap.*) **1** [*the*;U] the direction which is half-way between north and east: *The wind's in* (=is coming from) *the northeast.* **2** [*the*] the northeastern part of a country, esp. the northeastern part of England, from Humberside to the Scottish border

northeast[2] (*abbrev.* **NE**) *adj* [A] (of a wind) coming from the northeast –**northeast** *adv* : *to sail northeast* | *Burma is northeast of Sri Lanka.*

Northeast Cor·ri·dor /ˌ·· ˈ···/ [*the*] the area of the northeast US, roughly between Boston and Washington DC, which has the highest population DENSITY in the country

north·east·er /ˌnɔːθˈiːstəʳ‖ˌnɔːrθ-/ *n* a strong wind or storm coming from the northeast

north·east·er·ly /ˌnɔːθˈiːstəli‖ˌnɔːrθˈiːstərli/ *adj* **1** towards or in the northeast: *Rain will spread to northeasterly regions during the day.* **2** (of a wind) coming from the northeast

north·east·ern /ˌnɔːθˈiːstən‖ˌnɔːrθˈiːstərn/ (*abbrev.* **NE**) *adj* (*often cap.*) of the northeast part, esp. of a country

Northeast Pas·sage /ˌ·· ˈ··/ [*the*] a way by sea along the N coast of Europe and Asia, between the Atlantic and Pacific Oceans, discovered by the Swedish EXPLORER Nils Nordenskjöld in 1878–79

north·east·ward /ˌnɔːθˈiːstwəd‖ˌnɔːrθˈiːstwərd/ *adj* going towards the northeast: *in a northeastward direction* –**northeastwards, northeastward** *adv* : *sailing northeastwards*

nor·ther·ly /ˈnɔːðəli‖ˈnɔːrðərli/ *adj* **1** towards or in the north: *We set off in a northerly direction.* **2** (of a wind) coming from the north: *strong northerly winds*

nor·thern /ˈnɔːðən‖ˈnɔːrðərn/ (*abbrev.* **N**) *adj* (*often cap.*) of or belonging to the north part of the world or of a country: *In the northern hemisphere, spring is in March and April.* | *a Northern accent* –see NORTH[2] (USAGE) –see picture at GLOBE

nor·thern·er /ˈnɔːðənəʳ‖ˈnɔːrðər-/ *n* (also *cap.*) a person who lives in or comes from the northern part of a country

Northern Ire·land /ˌˈ·· ˈ·ˈ/ the northern part of Ireland, which is politically part of the United Kingdom and consists of six counties (COUNTY) of the ancient region of Ulster; capital Belfast. Most of the people who live there are PROTESTANT, and usually UNIONISTS who want it to remain part of the United Kingdom, but many ROMAN CATHOLICS who live there are REPUBLICANS and think it should join with the Republic of Ireland and become part of an Irish state. Both sides use violence, including bombing and shooting people, and the British government keeps a force of armed soldiers there to try to control the situation. Repeated attempts to find a political settlement have failed, and few people can see any answer to Northern Ireland's problems. When people talk about **the Northern Ireland situation**, or **the troubles** in Northern Ireland, this is what they mean. —see also BELFAST, IRA¹

Northern Ireland As·sem·bly /ˌˈ·· ˈ···ˈ·ˈ/ [the] the governing authority of Northern Ireland between 1921 and 1986, ended by the British government in 1986 because Unionist Party members in the Assembly, in a protest against the Anglo-Irish Agreement, were preventing the Assembly from operating

northern lights /ˌˈ·· ·ˈ/ n [the+P] (usu. caps.) see AURORA

nor·thern·most /ˈnɔːðənməʊst‖ˈnɔːrðərn-/ adj furthest north: the northernmost parts of Norway

Northern Ter·ri·to·ry /ˌˈ·· ˈ····ˈ/ [the] an area of N central Australia, the chief city of which is Darwin

North Is·land /ˈ· ˌ·ˈ/ n [the] the further north of the two main islands of New Zealand

North Ko·re·a /ˌˈ· ·ˈ··ˈ/ a republic in NE Asia; capital Pyongyang —see also KOREA

north of Wat·ford /ˌnɔːθ əv ˈwɒtfəd‖ˌnɔːrθ əv ˈwɑːtfərd/ adv [no comp.] often humor the northern part of Britain, esp. in its distance from London: I don't know where that town is, it's north of Watford somewhere.

▶ CULTURAL NOTE Watford is a town northwest of London, just outside the boundaries of Greater London. One of London's Underground railway lines ends there. People often make jokes saying that the cultural life associated with London does not extend any further than Watford: He won't have seen that new film yet — he lives north of Watford!◀

North Pole /ˌ· ˈ·ˈ/ [the] (the lands around) the most northern point on the surface of the Earth —see also MAGNETIC POLE, SOUTH POLE —see picture at GLOBE

North-Ri·ding /ˌnɔːθ ˈraɪdɪŋ/ [the] a former local government division of Yorkshire, N England, which after 1974 became part of the COUNTY of North Yorkshire

North Sea /ˌ· ˈ·◄/ [the] an arm of the Atlantic Ocean, between Great Britain and NW Europe. It is economically important because of its fish, and also for oil and gas which were discovered in 1970 under the sea. – see colour map on page 818

North Sea gas /ˌ· · ·ˈ/ n [U] gas which is found along with the oil under the North Sea. Most of the gas used in British homes and businesses is North Sea gas.

North Sea oil /ˌ· · ·ˈ/ n [U] oil which is found under the North Sea. Britain has gained a lot of money from sales of North Sea oil since its discovery in 1970.

North/South di·vide /ˌ· · · ·ˈ·ˈ/ n [(the)] **1** the difference between the north of a country and the south, as shown e.g. in the employment situation, standard of living, wages, health and CULTURE: The government was accused of creating a North/South divide.

▶ CULTURAL NOTE In Britain the North/South divide is between northern England and Scotland, and southern England, esp. the south-east. People in the South generally have better pay than people in the North; there is less unemployment and people are healthier and have better services. In the North the cost of living is lower and housing, in particular, is cheaper. Although the term North/South divide expresses general differences, some areas in the South, particularly Wales and south-west England, also have high rates of unemployment, while some parts of north-east England and Scotland are comparatively wealthy. —see also NORTH OF WATFORD◀

2 the difference between the richer countries of the northern parts of the world and the poorer countries of the south, as shown by living standards and levels of industrial and economic development —see also NORTH¹ (2), SOUTH (3)

North·um·ber·land /nɔːˈθʌmbələnd‖nɔːrˈθʌmbər-/ a COUNTY in NE England, bordering on Scotland and the North Sea, known mainly for its historical remains, esp. the Roman wall which is well preserved and enjoyed by walkers

Nor·thum·bri·a /nɔːˈθʌmbriə‖nɔːr-/ a former Anglo-Saxon kingdom in England and southern Scotland, formed in the seventh century and becoming part of the kingdom of Wessex after 920. The name is sometimes used unofficially when talking about this area, esp. the English part of it.

Northumbrian Wa·ter /·ˌ··· ˈ··ˈ/ a water company in NE England that deals with the supply of water to people and businesses and the removal and treatment of SEWAGE

North Wales /ˌ· ˈ·ˈ/ the N part of Wales, including Anglesey and Snowdonia —see also WALES

North Wa·li·an /ˌnɔːθ ˈweɪliən‖ˌnɔːrθ-/ n infml **1** [C] a person born or living in North Wales **2** [U] the variety of English spoken in North Wales, noted for its special INTONATION

north·ward /ˈnɔːθwəd‖ˈnɔːrθwərd/ adj going towards the north: in a northward direction

north·wards /ˈnɔːθwədz‖ˈnɔːrθwərdz/ also **northward**— adv towards the north: We sailed northwards. | It's further northward than you might think. —see also NORTH³

north·west¹ /ˌnɔːθˈwest◄‖ˌnɔːrθ-/ (abbrev. NW) n (often cap.) **1** [the;U] the direction which is half-way between north and west: The wind is in (=is coming from) the northwest. **2** [the] the northwestern part of a country

northwest² (abbrev. NW) adj [A] (of a wind) coming from the northwest —**northwest** adv : to sail northwest | The town is northwest of Washington D.C.

north·west·er /ˌnɔːθˈwestəʳ‖ˌnɔːrθ-/ n a strong wind or storm coming from the northwest

north·west·er·ly /ˌnɔːθˈwestəli‖ˌnɔːrθˈwestərli/ adj **1** towards or in the northwest **2** (of a wind) coming from the northwest

north·west·ern /ˌnɔːθˈwestən‖ˌnɔːrθˈwestərn/ (abbrev. NW) adj (often cap.) of the northwest part, esp. of a country

Northwestern U·ni·ver·si·ty /·ˌ·ˌ·· ··ˈ···ˈ/ also **Northwestern**— a private university in Evanston, Illinois near Chicago, US

Northwest Pas·sage /ˌ·· ˈ··ˈ/ [the] a way by sea along the N coast of North America, between the Atlantic and Pacific Oceans, first sailed over by Roald Amundsen in 1903–06

Northwest Ter·ri·to·ries /ˌ·· ˈ····ˈ/ [the+P] the large area in NW Canada E of the Yukon. It covers a third of the area of Canada but it has a very small population and very cold weather.

north·west·ward /ˌnɔːθˈwestwəd‖ˌnɔːrθˈwestwərd/ adj going towards the northwest: in a northwestward direction **northwestwards, northwestward** adv : sailing northwestwards

North West Wa·ter /ˌ· · ·ˈ/ a water company in NW England that deals with the supply of water to people and businesses and the removal and treatment of SEWAGE

North York Moors /ˌ· · ·ˈ/ [the+P] an area of high, open land, a National Park, in NE Yorkshire, N England

North York·shire /ˌ· ˈ··ˈ/ a COUNTY in NE England. It consists mainly of farmland. The centre of local government is at Northallerton but the main city is York —see YORKSHIRE

Nor·way /ˈnɔːweɪ‖ˈnɔːr-/ a county of northern Europe, in W Scandinavia; capital Oslo; population 4,227,000 (1989). It is known esp. for its beautiful FJORDS.

Nor·we·gian /nɔːˈwiːdʒən‖nɔːr-/ n **1** [C] a person who comes from or whose parents come from Norway **2** [U] the language spoken in Norway —**Norwegian** adj

Nor·wich /ˈnɒrɪdʒ, -ɪtʃ‖ˈnɔː-/ a city in Norfolk, E central England, where the local government for that COUNTY is based. It has a university, the University of East Anglia, an important market, and a CATHEDRAL.

nos. written abbrev. for: numbers

nose¹ /nəʊz/ n **1** [C] the part of the face above the mouth which is the organ of smell and through which air is breathed: a broken nose | He punched me on the nose. | to **blow one's nose** (=clear it by blowing strongly into a handkerchief) | a baby with a **runny nose** (=with MUCUS coming out of the nose) —see also ROMAN NOSE, and see picture at HEAD **2** [C] the narrow or pointed front end of something, such as a car, plane, tool, or gun: *The nose of the plane dipped as we came in to land.* | *The instruments are in the nose section of the rocket.* —see picture at AIRCRAFT **3** [S (**for**)] **a** a sense of smell: *a dog with a good nose* **b** the ability to find (out) or recognize things: *a newspaper reporter with a good nose for a story* (=a special ability to find one) | *Turn left at the corner, then just* follow your nose *and you're sure to find it.* **4** [C] *infml* the nose thought of as representing a too great interest in things which do not concern one: *Keep your (big) nose out of this.* | *Stop* poking your nose into *my affairs!* —see also NOSY **5 get up someone's nose** *BrE infml* to annoy someone very much **6 keep one's 'nose clean** *infml* to avoid getting into trouble, breaking the law, etc. **7 one's nose to the grindstone** *infml* working very hard, without interruption: *We'll have to keep our noses to the grindstone to finish this by six o'clock.* **8 poke/stick one's nose in (where it's not wanted)** *infml* to INTERFERE in someone else's business **9 put someone's 'nose out of joint** *infml* to make someone jealous, esp. by taking their place as the centre of attention **10 turn one's nose up (at)** *infml* to consider (something) not good enough or important enough to be enjoyed or taken seriously: *My children turn up their noses at fresh vegetables/at classical music.* **11 under someone's (very) nose** *infml* right in front of someone; quite openly: *They stole the jewels from under the very nose(s) of the police.* **12 -nosed** /nəʊzd/ having a certain shape or kind of nose: *red-nosed* | *long-nosed* —see also HARD-NOSED, **cut off one's nose to spite one's face** (CUT off), **lead someone by the nose** (LEAD[1]), NOSE JOB, **pay through the nose** (PAY[1]), **powder one's nose** (POWDER[2]), **rub someone's nose in (the dirt)** (RUB[1])

nose[2] *v* **1** [I+*adv/prep*;T+*obj/adv/prep*] to move or push ahead slowly and carefully: *a ship nosing its way through the narrow channel* | *I nosed the car (out)/The car nosed (out) into the traffic.* **2** [I+*adv/prep*] *infml* to try to find out esp. things that do not concern one; search; PRY: *The old lady was nosing about (the house), looking for dust.* | *Stop nosing into my affairs!*
nose sthg. ↔ **out** *phr v* [T] *infml* to discover by careful and continuous searching: *The reporters have nosed out some interesting facts about the political scandal.*

nose·bag /'nəʊzbæg/ usu. **feedbag** *AmE—* *n* a bag hung around a horse's head to hold its food

nose·bleed /'nəʊzbliːd/ *n* a case of bleeding from the nose: *He often has nosebleeds.*

nose·cone /'nəʊzkəʊn/ *n* the CONE-shaped front part of a spacecraft or MISSILE, which may separate from the rest

nose·dive /'nəʊzdaɪv/ *v* [I] **1** (of an aircraft) to drop suddenly with the nose pointing (almost) straight down **2** to fall or drop suddenly and by a great deal: *Prices have nosedived in the last year.* —**nosedive** *n*

no-see-um /nəʊ 'siː əm/ *n* *AmE* a very small summer insect that is difficult to see but easy to feel when it bites

nose·gay /'nəʊzgeɪ/ *n* *lit* a small bunch of flowers, usu. to be carried or worn on a dress —compare CORSAGE

nose job /'· ·/ *n* a medical operation on the nose to change its appearance: *Michael Jackson sure looked different after his nose job.*

nosh[1] /nɒʃ‖nɑːʃ/ *v* [I] *BrE sl* to eat

nosh[2] *n* *BrE sl* **1** [S] a meal: *a quick nosh* **2** [U] food: *They serve good nosh there.*

no-show /ˌ· '·/ *n* a person who is expected to appear (at a theatre or restaurant, or on an aircraft) and doesn't: *Those three seats in the front are no-shows.*

nosh-up /'· ·/ *n* [S] *BrE sl* a big satisfying meal: *What a nosh-up we had on my birthday!*

nos·tal·gia /nɒ'stældʒə‖nɑː-/ *n* [U] a feeling of fondness for something in the past, often mixed with a kind of pleasant sadness: *nostalgia for the clothes of the 1920s* | *The old song filled me with nostalgia.* —**-gic** *adj*: *The film was a nostalgic re-creation of 19th century America.* —**-gically** /kli/ *adv*

Nos·tra·da·mus /ˌnɒstrə'dɑːməs‖ˌnɑː-/ (1503–66) a French doctor and ASTROLOGER who gave advice to the French royal family, and wrote a book of prophesies (PROPHESY) in RHYME which has been considered very meaningful by various people who believe that what he said will happen in the future

nos·tril /'nɒstrₗl‖'nɑː-/ *n* either of the two openings at the end of the nose, through which one breathes and smells —see picture at HEAD

nos·trum /'nɒstrəm‖'nɑː-/ *n* *derog* a medicine of unknown contents (not one given by a doctor), which is claimed to be effective, perhaps falsely: (fig.) *There is no simple nostrum for the problem of unemployment.* —compare PANACEA

nos·y, **nosey** /'nəʊzi/ *adj* *derog* *infml* interested in things that do not concern one; tending to PRY: *Our nosy neighbours are always watching us.* —see also NOSE[1] (4) —**-iness** *n* [U]

nosy park·er /ˌ·· '··/ *n* *BrE derog infml* a nosy person

not /nɒt‖nɑːt/ *adv* **1** (used for changing a word or expression to one with the opposite meaning): **a** (with verbs): *We're not coming/We aren't coming.* | *If you didn't like it you were wrong not to say so.* —see USAGE **b** (with other words and expressions): *not thirsty* | *not on Sundays* | *It's a cat, not a dog.* | *It's not a cat, but a dog.* | *Not everyone likes this book.* (=some people don't like it) | *The question is not at all easy to answer.* | *"Do you want to go?" "Not me!"* (=I don't, though others may want to) | *Not all her books have been as successful as this one.* (=some have been unsuccessful) —compare NO[1] **2** (used in place of a whole expression, often after verbs marked [+*that*]): *Are you coming or not?* | *"Will it rain?" "I hope not."* (=I hope that it won't rain) | *"Have you got £5 to lend me?" "I'm afraid not."* | *I'll try to come by nine, but if not, start the meeting without me.* —compare SO[1] (2) **3** *esp. pomp* (used with negative words, esp. those beginning with **un-** and words meaning "small", "slow", etc., to give force to the opposite meaning): *a not uncommon problem* (=a very common one) | *not slow to complain, and not without good reason* | *He drank not a little* (=drank a lot) *of the wine.* | *It was not without its problems.* **4 not** a not even one: *"How much did this cost?" "Not a penny!"* (=nothing) | *Not a (single) house was left standing after the earthquake.* —see also NARY **5 Not at all** *rather fml* (an answer to thanks or polite praise): *"Thanks for coming." "Not at all: I enjoyed it."* **6 not only** ... **but (also)** (used to show a second choice as well as the first one): *Shakespeare was not only a writer but (also) an actor.* **7 not that** although it is not true that: *Where were you last night? Not that I care, of course.* —see also **not half** (HALF[3]), **not to say** (SAY[1])

▷ USAGE **Not** can be shortened to **n't** after *is, are, was, were, has, have, had, do, does, did, can, could, would, should, must, ought, need, may (BrE), might, dare (BrE), used (BrE).* **Shall not** and **will not** can be shortened to **shan't** (*BrE*) and **won't**. Otherwise **not** is never shortened. —see also NO (USAGE), AIN'T◁

no·ta·ble[1] /'nəʊtəbəl/ *adj* [(**for**)] deserving to be noticed or given attention; important or excellent; OUTSTANDING: *notable events* | *a notable improvement* | *The area is notable for its pleasant climate.* | *Most of the directors are men, but Ms Parker is a notable exception.* —**-bility** /ˌnəʊtə'bɪlₗti/ *n* [U]

notable[2] *n* [*usu. pl.*] a famous or important person

no·ta·bly /'nəʊtəbli/ *adv* **1** especially; particularly: *Many members were absent, notably the vice-chairman.* **2** noticeably: *notably higher sales*

no·ta·rize also **-rise** *BrE* /'nəʊtəraɪz/ *v* [T *often pass.*] *fml* (of a notary) to make (a written statement) official: *to have a will notarized*

no·ta·ry /'nəʊtəri/ also **notary pub·lic** /ˌ··· '··/— *n* a public official with the power in law to witness the signing of written statements and make them official

no·ta·tion /nəʊ'teɪʃən/ *n* [C;U] the use of a system of written signs to describe the stated kinds of things and represent things, e.g. musical notes or ideas in: *a page covered with musical/mathematical notation.* See picture on page 909

notch[1] /nɒtʃ‖nɑːtʃ/ *n* **1** a V-shaped cut in a surface or edge: *He cut a notch in the stick with a sharp knife.* **2** *infml* a degree on a scale: *a good book, several notches above anything else by this writer* **3** *AmE* a narrow passage between mountains —see also TOP-NOTCH

notch[2] *v* [T] **1** to make a notch in **2** [(UP)] *infml* to win or record (a victory or gain): *The team notched up their third victory in a row.*

note[1] /nəʊt/ *n* **1** [C] also **notes** *pl.—* a record or reminder

notation

mathematical notation		musical notation
=	is equal to	‖O‖ breve
≠	is not equal to	O semibreve *BrE*/ whole note *AmE*
>	is greater than	♩ minim *BrE*/ half note *AmE*
<	is less than	♩ crotchet *BrE*/ quarter note *AmE*
≥	is greater than or equal to	♪ quaver *BrE*/ eighth note *AmE*
≤	is less than or equal to	♫ semiquaver *BrE*/ sixteenth note *AmE*

in writing: *Make notes/Make a note of how much money you spend on the trip.* | *students* **taking notes** *in a lecture* | *The speaker forgot his notes so he had to talk from memory.*   **2** [C] a remark added to a piece of writing and placed outside the main part of the writing, e.g. at the side or bottom of a page, esp. to give more information: *I made some notes in the margin.* | *I really couldn't understand the text — I had to refer to the notes at the back.* —see also FOOTNOTE   **3** [C] **a** a short usu. informal letter: *a thank-you note* **b** a formal letter between governments: *a diplomatic note*   **4** [C] also **bill** *AmE*— a piece of paper money: *a £5 note* —see also BANK NOTE   **5** [C] also **tone** *AmE*— (a written sign representing) a single musical sound of a particular length and degree of highness or lowness: *I can't sing the high notes.*   **6** [S (**of**)] a stated quality or feeling: *There was a note of anger in her voice.* | *Although the company still has some difficulties, the director's report ended on an optimistic note.* (=showing a hopeful feeling)   **7 of note** *fml* a of fame or importance: *a writer of (some/great) note* **b** worth noticing or paying attention to: *Did anything of note happen at the meeting?*   **8 take note of** to pay careful attention to: *The committee has taken note of objections.* —see also CLIFF'S NOTES, CREDIT NOTE, DEBIT NOTE, DELIVERY NOTE, MENTAL NOTE, **compare notes** (COMPARE¹), **strike a note (of)** (STRIKE¹)

note² *v* [T] *fml*   **1** to notice and remember; OBSERVE: *Note the way this writer uses the present tense for dramatic effect.* [+that] *Please note that this bill must be paid within ten days.* [+wh-] *Note how he operates the machine and try to copy him.*   **2** to call attention to; remark: *The report notes with approval the government's efforts to resolve this problem.*

note·book /ˈnəʊtbʊk/ *n* a book of plain paper in which NOTES can be written: *When I use my dictionary I jot down all the new words I learn in this little notebook.*

not·ed /ˈnəʊtɪd/ *adj* [(**for**)] well known, esp. because of a special quality or ability: *a noted authority on American history* | *a town noted for its cheeses* | (*humor*) *He's not exactly noted for his generosity.* (=He is very mean.)

note·let /ˈnəʊtlɪt/ *n* a small folded card usu. with a picture on the front, used for writing a short letter

note·pad /ˈnəʊtpæd/ *n* a small PAD¹ (2) for writing lists, messages, etc.

note·pa·per /ˈnəʊtˌpeɪpəʳ/ *n* [U] paper for writing letters on; WRITING PAPER

note·wor·thy /ˈnəʊtˌwɜːði‖-ɜːr-/ *adj* (esp. of things and events) deserving attention; NOTABLE: *There's nothing particularly noteworthy in this report.*

not-for-prof·it /ˌ·· ·ˈ··/ *adj* *AmE for* NON-PROFIT MAKING

noth·ing¹ /ˈnʌθɪŋ/ *pron*   **1** not any thing; no thing: *There's nothing in this box: it's empty.* | *I've got nothing to do.* | *Nothing ever happens in this town.* | *You'll have to have bread—there's* **nothing else** (=no other thing) *to eat.* | *We want you to tell us the truth — nothing more, nothing less.* | *There's nothing in these rumours* (=they are not true). | *"What's the food like at your school?" "Nothing special."* (=not very good) | *It cost* **next to nothing.** (=almost nothing)   **2** something of no importance: *She's nothing to me.* | *They think nothing of walking 20 miles.* | *"Is there anything good on the telly tonight?" "Nothing in particular."*   **3** *AmE* zero (esp. in sports results): *We beat them*

ten *to nothing.*   **4 for nothing: a** for no money; free: *I got this bicycle for nothing: my friend gave me it when she bought a new one.* **b** for no purpose; with no good result: *All our preparations were/went for nothing because the exam was cancelled.* —see also GOOD-FOR-NOTHING   **5 nothing but** only: *He's nothing but a criminal.*   **6 nothing doing** *sl* no; I won't: *"Will you lend me £5?" "Nothing doing."*   **7 nothing 'for it** no other way possible: *With the bridge destroyed, there was nothing for it but to swim.*   **8 nothing if not** (used to add force to an expression) very: *He's nothing if not determined.* (=He's very determined.)   **9 nothing much** *infml* not much; very little: *There's nothing much happening this week.*   **10 nothing to do with** (having) no connection with: *My affairs have/are nothing to do with you.*   **11 nothing to it** no difficulty in it: *Anyone can ride a bike — there's nothing to it.* —see also SWEET NOTHINGS, **to say nothing of** (SAY¹ (21)); see SOMETHING (USAGE)

nothing² *adv* (in certain phrases) in no way; not at all: *Your house is nothing like ours.* | *A hundred dollars for a room — that's* **nothing short of** (=it's almost the same as) *robbery.* | *(BrE) He failed the test six times but,* **nothing daunted** (=not at all discouraged), *he decided to take it again.*

noth·ing·ness /ˈnʌθɪŋnɪs/ *n* [U] the state of being nothing; not being: *Is there only nothingness after death?*

no·tice¹ /ˈnəʊtɪs/ *n*   **1** [C] a written or printed statement giving information or directions to the public: *They announced the birth of their baby by putting a notice in the newspaper.* | *The notice on the wall says "No smoking".* | *The workers put up a notice announcing a mass meeting.*   **2** [U] a warning or information about something that is going to happen: *These rules are subject to change without notice.* | *Can you be ready at ten minutes' notice?* (=if I tell you only ten minutes before) | *The office is closed* **until further notice.** (=from now until another change is made) | *If you want to reserve a room you have to give them a few days' notice.* **b** formal warning of the end of an agreement: *I'm fed up with this job, I'm giving in my notice tomorrow.* | *The landlady has given me* **notice to quit.** (=has told me I will have to leave my house, room, etc.) | *If the company wants to dismiss me, they have to give me three months' notice.*   **3** [U] attention: *Don't* **take any notice** *of* (=pay no attention to) *what he says.* | *It has come to my notice/not escaped my notice* (=I have noticed or been told) *that some of you have been missing classes.*   **4** [C *often pl.*] a statement of opinion, esp. in a newspaper, about a new book, play, etc.; REVIEW: *The new play got mixed notices.* (=some good, some bad)

notice² *v* [I;T *not in progressive forms*] to pay attention (to) with the eyes, other senses, or mind; OBSERVE: *She was wearing a new dress, but he didn't even notice (it).* [+obj+v-ing] *Did you notice anyone leave/leaving the house?* [+wh-] *Did you notice whether I locked the door?* [+(that)] *"I noticed (that) he was looking very nervous." "Yes, so I noticed."* | *a young actress trying to get herself noticed* (=to become publicly known)

no·tice·a·ble /ˈnəʊtɪsəbəl/ *adj* worth noticing or easily noticed; SIGNIFICANT: *a noticeable drop in the amount of crime* | *The damage to my car is hardly noticeable.* **—bly** *adv* : *noticeably fewer people* | *Crime has decreased noticeably.*

notice board /ˈ·· ˌ·/ *BrE* ‖ **bulletin board** *AmE*— *n* a board on a wall which notices may be fixed to: *If you look on the notice board, you'll find details of tomorrow's classes.*

no·ti·fi·a·ble /ˈnəʊtɪfaɪəbəl/ *adj* *tech, esp. BrE* (esp. of certain diseases) needing by law to be reported to an office of public health: *Typhoid, cholera, etc., are notifiable diseases.*

no·ti·fi·ca·tion /ˌnəʊtɪfɪˈkeɪʃən/ *n fml* [C *usu. sing.*;U] (the act of giving) warning or information: *If you decide to go ahead with the rebuilding scheme, can you give us some notification?*

no·ti·fy /ˈnəʊtɪfaɪ/ *v* [T (**of**)] to tell (someone), esp. formally; INFORM: *to notify the police of a crime* [+obj+that] *Please notify all staff that the inspectors will be here on Monday.*

no·tion /ˈnəʊʃən/ *n*   **1** an idea, belief, or opinion in someone's mind; CONCEPT: *an education system based on the old-fashioned notion of women as home-makers* | *the old notion that the sun moved round the Earth* [+wh-] *I haven't the faintest notion* (=I have no idea at all) *what you're talking about.*   **2** a sudden desire; WHIM: [+to-v]

She took/had a sudden notion to visit all her relatives. – see also NOTIONS

no·tion·al /ˈnəʊʃənəl/ adj 1 existing only in the mind, not in practice; THEORETICAL: *to give the object a notional price* 2 tech (of a word) having an actual meaning in a sentence: *"Have" in "I have an apple" is notional; it means "possess".* —compare RELATIONAL

no·tions /ˈnəʊʃənz/ n [P] esp. AmE small things for sewing or other useful purposes, sold in one part of a large shop: *You'll find that in notions, on the third floor.*

no·to·ri·e·ty /ˌnəʊtəˈraɪəti/ n [U] the state of being notorious: *His daring escape from prison gained him a certain notoriety.*

no·to·ri·ous /nəʊˈtɔːriəs, nə-/ adj [(for)] derog famous or widely known for something bad: *a notorious murderer | This airport is notorious for its bad security.* —see FAMOUS (USAGE) — ~ly adv : *a notoriously inefficient company* — ~ness n [U]

Not·re Dame /ˌnɒtrə ˈdɑːm‖ˌnəʊtər-/ also **Notre Dame de Pa·ris** /ˌnɒtrə ˌdɑːm də pæˈriː‖ˌnəʊtər-/ fml— a CATHEDRAL (large church) in Paris which is a beautiful Gothic building —see also HUNCHBACK OF NOTRE DAME

Notre Dame /ˌnɒtrə ˌdɑːm ‖ ˌnəʊtər ˈdeɪm/, **University of** a private Catholic university in Indiana, US, noted esp. for its football team

Not·ting·ham /ˈnɒtɪŋəm‖ˈnɑː-/ a city in Nottinghamshire, in central England where the local government for that COUNTY is based. It has long been a centre for the making of LACE —see colour map on page 818

Nottingham For·est /ˌ·· ˈ··/ a leading English football team from Nottingham

Not·ting·ham·shire /ˈnɒtɪŋəmʃəʳ‖ˈnɑː-/ abbrev. **Notts.** a COUNTY in central England; consisting mainly of farmland and some coalfields

Not·ting Hill Car·ni·val /ˌnɒtɪŋ hɪl ˈkɑːnɪvəl‖ˌnɑː-, -ˈkɑːr-/ [the] a street CARNIVAL that takes place in the Notting Hill area of west London in August every year, mostly involving black people and known for the colourful COSTUMES worn and the steel band music played

Notts. /nɒts‖nɑːts/ abbrev. for: Nottinghamshire; an area of central England

not·with·stand·ing /ˌnɒtwɪθˈstændɪŋ, -wɪð-‖ˌnɑːt-/ prep fml in spite of (used after its object): *They are determined to go ahead with the plan, notwithstanding widespread public opposition. | They went ahead, public opposition notwithstanding.* —**notwithstanding** adv

nou·gat /ˈnuːgɑː‖-gət/ n [C;U] (a small piece of) a sticky pink or white sweet made of sugar, nuts, bits of fruit, etc.

nought /nɔːt/ n 1 [C] BrE (the figure) 0; zero: *0.6 is usually read "nought point six", and .06 is usually read "point nought six".* —see ZERO (USAGE) 2 [U] esp. old use or lit nothing; NAUGHT

noughts and cross·es /ˌ·· ˈ··/ BrE ‖ **tick-tack-toe** AmE— n [U] a game in which two players take turns to write O or X in a pattern of nine squares, trying to win with a row of three Os or three Xs

noun /naʊn/ n a word or group of words that is the name of a person (such as *Mary* or *teacher* or *police officer*), a place (such as *France* or *school*), a thing or activity (such as *coffee* or *football*), or a quality or idea (such as *danger* or *happiness*). Nouns can be used as the subject or object of a verb (as in *The teacher arrived* or *We like the teacher*) or as the object of a PREPOSITION (as in *good at football*). —see also COMMON NOUN, COUNT NOUN, PROPER NOUN, VERBAL NOUN

nour·ish /ˈnʌrɪʃ‖ˈnɜːrɪʃ, ˈnʌ-/ v [T] 1 to give (someone) what is needed in order to live, grow, and stay healthy: *Milk is a nourishing drink. | a well-nourished baby* —see also UNDERNOURISHED 2 (of a person) to keep (a feeling, plan, etc.) alive; ENTERTAIN (3): *to nourish the hope of a trip abroad*

nour·ish·ment /ˈnʌrɪʃmənt‖ˈnɜːrɪʃ-, ˈnʌ-/ n [U] esp. fml something that nourishes; food: *The child took no nourishment all day. | Plants get nourishment from the soil.*

nous /naʊs‖nuːs/ n [U] BrE infml practical good judgment; COMMON SENSE

nou·veau riche /ˌnuːvəʊ ˈriːʃ/ also **new rich, new money** AmE— n **nouveaux riches** (same pronunciation) [usu.

pl.] usu. derog a person or people having only recently become rich and tending to spend a lot of money in order to prove one's wealth, esp. in a way that is thought of as lacking in good TASTE —**nouveau riche** adj

nou·velle cui·sine /ˌnuːvel kwɪˈziːn/ n [U] a style of cooking, originally from France, that uses a lot of fresh fruit and vegetables cooked in a simple way, without using a lot of cream and SAUCES

Nov. written abbrev. for: NOVEMBER

no·va /ˈnəʊvə/ n **-vas** or **-vae** /ˈnəʊviː/ a star which explodes and suddenly becomes much brighter, and then gradually fainter —compare SUPERNOVA

No·va Sco·tia /ˌnəʊvə ˈskəʊʃə/ a PROVINCE of SE Canada which sticks out into the Atlantic Ocean east of New Brunswick. It consists mainly of farmland and forests, and also produces minerals.

No·va·ya Zem·ly·a /ˌnəʊviə ˈzemliə/ a group of islands in the Arctic Ocean off the NE coast of Russia

nov·el[1] /ˈnɒvəl‖ˈnɑː-/ n a long written story, not in poetry, dealing with invented people and events: *"War and Peace", the great novel by Leo Tolstoy*

nov·el[2] adj often apprec not like anything known before; new and perhaps clever; original: *a novel idea/suggestion*

nov·el·ette /ˌnɒvəˈlet‖ˌnɑː-/ n often derog a short, not very serious novel, usu. about love

nov·el·ist /ˈnɒvəlɪst‖ˈnɑː-/ n a writer of novels: *a great novelist | a romantic novelist*

no·vel·la /nəʊˈvelə/ n **novellas** or **novelle** /nəʊˈveliː/ a story between the length of a novel and a SHORT STORY

nov·el·ty /ˈnɒvəlti‖ˈnɑː-/ n 1 [U] the quality of being NOVEL[2]; interesting newness: *the novelty of his ideas | At first I enjoyed all the parties, but the novelty soon wore off.* 2 [C] something new, unusual, and interesting: *It was quite a novelty to spend my holidays working on a boat.* 3 [C usu. pl.] an unusual small cheap object, usu. not very useful but suitable to be given as a present: *a novelty pen | Christmas novelties*

No·vem·ber /nəʊˈvembəʳ, nə-/ (written abbrev. **Nov.**) n [C;U] the 11th month of the year, between October and December: *It happened on November the fifth/on the fifth of November/(AmE) on November fifth. | This office opened in November 1991. | He started work here last November/the November before last.*

▶ CULTURAL NOTE November is a cold, often wet, month and in Britain is associated with FOG. In Britain, November 5th is GUY FAWKES NIGHT. In the US, the fourth Thursday in November is THANKSGIVING. ◀

nov·ice /ˈnɒvɪs‖ˈnɑː-/ n 1 [(at)] a person with no experience in a skill or subject; beginner: *a novice swimmer | a novice at skiing* 2 a person who has recently joined a religious group to become a MONK or NUN

no·vi·ti·ate, -ciate /nəʊˈvɪʃiət, nə-, -ʃieɪt‖-ˈvɪʃət/ n tech the period of being a novice, esp. in a religious group

no·vo·caine /ˈnəʊvəkeɪn/ n [U] tdmk a drug used for stopping pain during a small operation, esp. on the teeth

now[1] /naʊ/ adv 1 a at this time; at present: *I had a headache this morning, but I'm all right now. | We used to live in Bristol but now we live in London. | A journey that used to take several weeks can now be made in a few hours.* b at the time just mentioned, e.g. in a story or an account of past events: *He opened the door. Now the noise was very loud.* 2 at the time just following the present; at once: *We've finished our dinner so now let's have some coffee. | Now for (=now we will have) the next question. | They'll be here any time now.* 3 a (used to introduce a statement or question): *Now, I don't know if you'll agree with this, but I'd like to make a suggestion.* b (used to add force to a command, warning, etc.): *Now then, what's going on here? | Be careful, now! | Now, now, stop crying!* —compare THERE[3] 4 (used after an expression of time) calculating from or up to the present: *It hasn't been working properly for three weeks now. | It's now 27 years/It's 27 years now since he died.* 5 (every) **now and then/now and again** at times; sometimes: *She meets her old boyfriend for a drink now and then. | I like to visit art galleries now and again.* 6 **now ... now** sometimes ... and sometimes: *The market is very unstable, with prices now rising, now falling.*

now[2] n [U] the present time or moment: *Now is the time to tell him the truth. | The time for action is now! | Up* *to|Until now we've had no problems. | He should have finished by now. | As of now|From now on* (=starting now) *the bank will close at 3.30 pm. | Goodbye for now.*

now³ also **now that**— *conj* because (something has happened): *Now (that) John's arrived, we can begin.*

NOW /ˌen əʊ ˈdʌbəljuː/ the National Organization for Women, a large American organization started in 1966 which works for legal, economic, and social equality between men and women. Its first president was Betty Friedan.

now·a·days /ˈnaʊədeɪz/ *adv* (esp. in comparisons with the past) at the present time; in these modern times: *We used to listen to the radio a lot, but nowadays we mostly watch television.*

no way /ˌ· ˈ·/ *adv, interj sl* no; certainly not: *"Did you agree to work at the weekend?" "No way!" | No way will we be finished by 5 o'clock.*

no·where /ˈnəʊweəʳ/ *adv* **1** also **no place** *AmE infml*— not anywhere; (in, at, or to) no place: *The book was nowhere to be found. | The poor old man has nowhere to live. | There's nowhere else* (=no other place) *I really want to go to. | (fml) Nowhere are the effects of these policies more evident than in the inner cities. | (fig.) That kind of talk will* **get you nowhere.** (=won't do you any good) *| Five dollars goes nowhere now.* (=will hardly buy anything) *| (fig.) In the last few seconds of the race, Ovett came* **from nowhere** (=from a seemingly hopeless position) *and won.* **2 nowhere near** not at all near or nearly: *She's nowhere near as clever as her sister. | We're nowhere near finding a cure yet.* —see SOMETHING (USAGE)

no-win sit·u·a·tion /ˌ· ˈ· ··ˌ··/ *n* a state of affairs which will end badly whichever choice one makes

no·wise /ˈnəʊwaɪz/ *adv lit old use* not at all

nox·ious /ˈnɒkʃəs‖ˈnɑːk-/ *adj fml or tech* harmful; poisonous: *noxious fumes | noxious chemicals in the river water* — ~**ly** *adv* — ~**ness** *n* [U]

noz·zle /ˈnɒzəl‖ˈnɑː-/ *n* a short tube fitted to the end of a HOSE, pipe, etc., to direct and control the stream of liquid or gas pouring out: *Point the nozzle of the fire extinguisher at the flames.*

NPR /ˌen piː ˈɑːʳ/ *abbrev. for:* NATIONAL PUBLIC RADIO

NRA /ˌen ɑːr ˈeɪ/ *abbrev. for:* **1** *AmE* NATIONAL RIFLE ASSOCIATION **2** *BrE* NATIONAL RIVERS AUTHORITY

NRC /ˌen ɑː ˈsiː‖-ɑːr-/ *abbrev. for* NUCLEAR REGULATORY COMMISSION

NSB /ˌen es ˈbiː/ *abbrev. for:* NATIONAL SAVINGS BANK

NSC /ˌen es ˈsiː/ *abbrev. for:* NATIONAL SECURITY COUNCIL

NSPCC /ˌen es ˌpiː siː ˈsiː/ *[the]* National Society for the Prevention of Cruelty to Children; a British organization which looks after the interests of children who are being badly treated or are in danger of being harmed

NSU /ˌen es ˈjuː/ *n* [U] non-specific urethritis; an infection of the URETHRA —compare CYSTITIS

NT /ˌen ˈtiː/ *abbrev. for:* **1** NATIONAL THEATRE **2** NATIONAL TRUST

-n't /ənt/ *short for:* not: *hadn't | didn't | wouldn't | isn't* —see NOT (USAGE)

nth /enθ/ *adj* **1** (used to suggest a very large number): *I've reminded him for the nth time, but he still never remembers to do it.* **2 to the nth degree** *infml* as much as possible; extremely: *It was boring to the nth degree.*

nu·ance /ˈnjuːɑːns‖ˈnuː-/ *n* a slight delicate difference in meaning, colour, etc.: *nuances of taste which are hard to describe | There is a nuance of greater uncertainty in "I might do it" than in "I may do it".*

nub /nʌb/ *n* **1** [(of) *usu. sing.*] the most important point; CRUX: *This is the nub of the argument|matter.* **2** *rare* a lump or piece

nu·bile /ˈnjuːbaɪl‖ˈnuːbəl/ *adj fml or humor* (of a girl) young and sexually attractive: *his nubile companions*

nu·cle·ar /ˈnjuːkliəʳ‖ˈnuː-/ *adj* [*no comp.*] **1** of, concerning, or using NUCLEAR ENERGY **2** of or being a NUCLEUS: *nuclear fission* (=the breaking up of atoms)

nuclear bomb /ˌ··· ˈ·/ *n* a bomb which explodes because of the ATOMIC reactions inside it. Nuclear bombs are feared by people because of the terrible destruction they can cause.

nuclear ca·pa·bil·i·ty /ˌ··· ··ˈ···/ *n* [U] the fact of whether a country has NUCLEAR WEAPONs or not: *Iraq's nuclear capability was not known.*

nuclear ca·pa·ci·ty /ˌ··· ·ˈ···/ *n* [S] the number of NUCLEAR WEAPONs possessed by a country: *The enemy's nuclear capacity has risen over the last few months.*

nuclear dis·ar·ma·ment /ˌ··· ·ˈ··/ *n* [U] the giving up of NUCLEAR WEAPONs, either by agreement between nations (**multilateral disarmament**) or by a single nation on its own (**unilateral disarmament**)

nuclear en·er·gy /ˌ··· ˈ···/ *n* [U] the powerful force that is produced when the NUCLEUS (=central part) of an atom is either split or joined to another atom

nuclear fa·cil·i·ty /ˌ··· ·ˈ···/ *n* a factory or other place where NUCLEAR WEAPONs might be made

nuclear fam·i·ly /ˌ··· ˈ···/ *n* a family unit that consists only of husband, wife, and children, without grandmothers, uncles, etc. —compare EXTENDED FAMILY

nuclear fis·sion /ˌ··· ˈ··/ also **fission**— *n* [U] the splitting of the NUCLEUS (centre) of an atom, which results in much power being RELEASED (let go). Nuclear fission is used in NUCLEAR WEAPONs.

nuclear-free /ˌ··· ˈ·/ *adj* (of places) in which the use, carrying, and storing of NUCLEAR materials is not allowed: *a nuclear-free zone*

nuclear fu·sion /ˌ··· ˈ··/ also **fusion**— *n* [C;U] a NUCLEAR reaction in which the nuclei (NUCLEUS) of light atoms join with the nuclei of heavier atoms. Nuclear fusion may be used in bombs, such as the HYDROGEN BOMB.

nuclear in·dus·try /ˌ··· ˈ···/ *n* a branch of industry which produces machinery and FUEL¹ connected with the use of nuclear power, and/or NUCLEAR WEAPONs: *The nuclear industry is strongly in favour of the phasing-out of coal-fired power stations.*

nuclear phys·i·cist /ˌ··· ˈ···/ *n* a person who studies or works in nuclear physics

nuclear phys·ics /ˌ··· ˈ··/ *n* [U] the branch of PHYSICS which is concerned with the structure and properties of the NUCLEUS (=central part) of atoms

nuclear pow·er /ˌ··· ˈ··/ *n* [U] power, usu. electricity, from NUCLEAR ENERGY

▶CULTURAL NOTE Many people worry about the risks associated with nuclear power, and do not want more nuclear power stations to be built. They worry about accidents such as the one at Chernobyl, and about the safe disposal of RADIOACTIVE waste products. They also fear that people, esp. children, living near nuclear processing plants have a great risk of getting some kinds of CANCER. Some people feel that the nuclear industry and the government do not always tell the truth about nuclear power.◀

nuclear re·ac·tion /ˌ··· ·ˈ··/ *n* a process in which the parts of the NUCLEUS (=centre) of an atom are rearranged to form new substances —see FISSION, FUSION; compare CHEMICAL REACTION

nuclear re·ac·tor /ˌ··· ·ˈ··/ also **reactor, atomic pile**— *n* a large machine that produces NUCLEAR ENERGY, esp. as a means of producing electricity

Nuclear Reg·u·la·to·ry Com·mis·sion /ˌ··· ˈ····· ·ˌ··/ (*abbrev. for:* NRC) an American government organization that checks on the safety of NUCLEAR power stations

nuclear re·pro·ces·sing /ˌ··· ·ˈ···/ *n* [U] a process in which waste from NUCLEAR POWER stations is cleaned so that some of it may be used again

nuclear sub·ma·rine /ˌ··· ˈ···, ˌ··· ··ˈ·/ *n* a submarine (=a ship which can stay under water) which is driven by power from a nuclear reactor

nuclear war /ˌ··· ˈ·/ *n* [C;U] a war fought using nuclear weapons: *all-out nuclear war*

nuclear waste /ˌ··· ˈ·/ *n* [U] waste material which is RADIOACTIVE, esp. used FUEL¹ from NUCLEAR REACTORs: *the problem of nuclear waste disposal*

a mushroom cloud from a nuclear explosion

nuclear weap·on /ˌ··· ˈ··/ *n* a very powerful weapon which uses atomic power to cause mass destruction and death

nuclear win·ter /ˌ··· ˈ··/ *n* the period which, according to many scientists, would follow a nuclear war or a large nuclear explosion, when there would be no light, warmth, or growth because the sun would be hidden by dust

nu·cle·ic ac·id /njuːˌkliːɪk ˈæsˌd, -ˌkleɪ-‖nuː-/ *n* [U] see DNA, RNA

nu·cle·us /ˈnjuːkliəs‖ˈnuː-/ *n* **-clei** /klaɪ/ **1** the central part of an atom, made up of NEUTRONS, PROTONS, and other ELEMENTARY PARTICLES **2** the central part of almost all cells of living matter —see picture at CELL **3** an original or central point, part, or group inside a larger thing, group, organization, etc.: *These 100 books will form the nucleus of the new school library.*

nude¹ /njuːd‖nuːd/ *adj* **1** not wearing clothes; NAKED **2** [A *no comp.*] of, for, or by people not wearing clothes: *a nude party* | *a nude beach* | *nude swimming*

nude² *n* **1** [C] (a piece of art showing) a person, usu. a woman, without clothes **2** [*the*] the state of being nude: *They went swimming* **in the nude.**

nudge /nʌdʒ/ *v* **1** [T] to push gently, usu. with one's elbow, esp. in order to call a person's attention: *He nudged his friend to let him know it was time to leave.* **2** [I+*adv/prep*;T] to move by gently pushing: *He nudged me out of the way.* | *a ship nudging (its way) through the ice* | (fig.) *During the meeting we tried to nudge them towards* (=gently help them to find) *a practical solution.* **3** **nudge, nudge, (wink, wink)** *infml humor* a phrase, first used in the British television programme *Monty Python's Flying Circus,* used when suggesting that there may be a sexual meaning to something that someone has just said —**nudge** *n*

nud·is·m /ˈnjuːdɪzəm‖ˈnuː-/ *n* [U] the practice of being nude as much as possible, esp. in a group, in a special holiday camp, and for reasons of health —**ist** *adj, n* : *a nudist camp* | *a beach for nudists*

nu·di·ty /ˈnjuːdˌti‖ˈnuː-/ *n* [U] the state of being nude: *a lot of nudity in recent films*

nu·ga·to·ry /ˈnjuːgətəri‖ˈnuːgətɔːri/ *adj fml* without value; TRIFLING

nug·get /ˈnʌgˌt/ *n* [(**of**)] a small rough lump of a precious metal, found in the earth: *a gold nugget* | (fig.) *nuggets of information/wisdom*

nui·sance /ˈnjuːsəns‖ˈnuː-/ *n* **1** a person, thing, or situation that causes annoyance or inconvenience: *Sit down, and stop being a nuisance/making a nuisance of yourself.* | *What a nuisance! I've forgotten my ticket.* | *It was a nuisance having to go back home to get my ticket.* **2** *law* the use of a place or property in a way that causes public annoyance (esp. in the phrase **Commit no nuisance,** on a notice in a public place)

nuisance val·ue /ˈ··· ˌ··/ *n* [S;U] the quality of being valuable as a cause of trouble and inconvenience to one's opponents: *A small political group may not be able to defeat the government, but it may still have some/a certain nuisance value.*

NUJ /ˌen juː ˈdʒeɪ/ *abbrev. for:* NATIONAL UNION OF JOURNALISTS

nuke¹ /njuːk‖nuːk/ *v* [T] *infml* to attack with NUCLEAR weapons

nuke² *n infml* a NUCLEAR weapon

null /nʌl/ *adj* [A *no comp.*] *tech* of, being, or concerning zero: *a null result* (=one giving the answer 0) | *a null set/sequence*

null and void /ˌ·· · ˈ·/ *adj* [F] *fml or law* having no legal force; INVALID: *The court declared the contract null and void.*

nul·li·fy /ˈnʌlˌfaɪ/ *v* [T] *fml or law* **1** to cause or declare to have no legal force: *a claim nullified by the court* **2** to cause to have no effect or value; NEGATE: *a rise in prices nullifying a rise in wages* —**fication** /ˌnʌlˌfˌˈkeɪʃən/ *n* [U]

nul·li·ty /ˈnʌlˌti/ *n fml or law* **1** [U] (esp. of a marriage) the state of being null and void in law: *a decree of nullity* — see also ANNUL **2** [U] nothingness: *a feeling of the nullity of life* **3** [C] *rare* a NONENTITY

null set /ˌ· ˈ·/ also **empty set**— *n tech* (in MATHEMATICS) a SET³ (10) with no members, usu. written { }

NUM /ˌen juː ˈem/ *abbrev. for:* NATIONAL UNION OF MINEWORKERS

numb¹ /nʌm/ *adj* [(**with**)] (of part of the body) unable to feel anything: *My hands are numb with* (=because of) *cold.* | *The anaesthetic made my arm go numb.* | (fig.) *numb with shock/fear* — **~ly** *adv* — **~ness** *n* [U]

numb² *v* [T *often pass.*] to cause to feel nothing or no pain; make numb: *fingers numbed with cold* | *the numbing effect of the drug* | *He was numbed by his wife's death.*

num·ber¹ /ˈnʌmbərʳ/ *n* **1** [C] (a written sign representing) a member of the system used in counting and measuring: *1, 2, and 3 are numbers.* | *Choose any number between one and ten.* | *What is your phone number?* | *Six is my lucky number.* —see also CARDINAL NUMBER, ORDINAL NUMBER **2** [C] (*written abbrev.* **No., no.,** or (*esp. AmE*) **#**) a number used to show the position of something in an ordered set or list: *a number 9* (=size 9) *shoe* | *We live at no. 107 Church Street.* (=our house has the number 107) | *question number four* —see also NUMBER ONE, BOX NUMBER, E NUMBER **3** [C (**of**);U] also **numbers** *pl.* — (a) quantity or amount: *Large numbers of/A large number of vehicles had to be abandoned because of the heavy snow.* | *This killing brings the number of deaths this year to 25.* | *The governing party, though few in number, held all the power.* | *a small number of/small numbers of visitors* | *A number of* (=several) *well-qualified people have recently left the company.* | *efforts to reduce the number(s) of people in prison* | *I've told you* **any number of times** (=very often) *to shut the door.* | *grains of sand* **beyond number** (=too many to count) **4** [S] a group of people: *The whole school went on a trip to France, but only three of our number could speak French.* **5** [C] *BrE* ‖ **issue** *AmE* a (copy of a) magazine printed at a particular time; ISSUE: *the latest number of "Vogue" magazine* | *back* (=past) *numbers of "Punch"* **6** [C] a piece of music (esp. popular music or JAZZ), usu. forming part of a longer performance: *She sang several numbers from her latest album.* **7** [C *usu. sing.*] *infml* a piece of clothing, esp. a woman's dress: *a chic little black number for evening wear* **8** [C *usu. sing.*] *infml* any person, object, situation, etc., of the stated type: *That new job of hers is a real* **cushy number.** (=something very easy) | *That new waitress sure is a hot number.* (=very attractive) **9** [U] *tech* change in the form of words, esp. (in English) of nouns and verbs, depending on whether one or more than one thing is talked about: *"Horses" is plural in number, "horse" is singular.* **10 have someone's number** *infml* to have knowledge about someone, esp. when useful in annoying or defeating them: *Our team couldn't do anything right: the opposing team had their number.* **11 someone's number is up/has come up** *infml* it is someone's turn, esp. to suffer, be punished, etc. —see also NUMBERS, OPPOSITE NUMBER

▷ USAGE Usually plural nouns after a number take a plural verb: *73 dogs/people* **are** *coming,* but if you are giving an opinion about the size of the number itself, use a singular verb. Compare *25 bottles of wine* **were** *drunk at the office party* and *£25 pounds* **is** *too much to pay.* —see also ABOUT (USAGE)◁

number² *v* **1** [T] to give a number to: *They forgot to number the pages.* | *All seats in the theatre are numbered.* [+*obj+n*] *Number the questions (from) 1 to 10.* | *a numbering system* **2** [I+*prep*;L+*n*] to reach as a total; be in number: *The people at the meeting numbered several thousand/numbered in the thousands.* **3** [I;T (**among, with**)] *fml* to include or be included as one of a particular group: *He numbers/is numbered among the best modern writers.* | *I'm glad to number her with my friends/as a friend.* **4** [T] *poet* to find the number of; count: *Who can number the stars?* —see also **his/her/its days are numbered** (DAYS¹)

number off *BrE* ‖ **count off** *AmE*— *phr v* [I] (in military use) to call out one's number when one's turn comes: *The soldiers numbered off from left to right.*

number crunch·er /ˈ·· ˌ··/ *n infml* a person or machine that works with numbers, such as an ACCOUNTANT, ECONOMIST, or STATISTICIAN

number crunch·ing /ˈ·· ˌ··/ *n* [U] the process of working with numbers and calculating many results: *Financial analysts spend their days number crunching.* —**number-crunching** *adj* : *number-crunching computers used by statisticians*

Number 11 /ˌnʌmbər ɪˈlevən/ see NO. 11

num·ber·less /ˈnʌmbələs‖-bər-/ adj esp. lit too many to count: numberless possibilities

number one /ˌ‥ ˈ‥/ n [U] **1** infml oneself and no one else: She only ever thinks of number one. (=herself) **2** the most important person or thing: George is number one in this organization and I'm his **number two.** (=second in command) | Solving this problem is our number one priority. [after n] public enemy number one

num·ber·plate /ˈnʌmbəpleɪt‖-ər-/ BrE ‖ **license plate** AmE‖**registration plate** AustrE, NZE— n either of the signs on a vehicle (usu. at the front and back ends), showing its REGISTRATION NUMBER —see picture at CAR, and note at LICENSE PLATE

num·bers /ˈnʌmbəz‖-ərz/ n **1** [P;U] the study of ARITHMETIC **2** [U] the state of having more supporters, soldiers, etc., than an opponent (esp. in the phrases **by sheer force/weight of numbers**): Our small army was defeated by sheer weight of numbers. **3** [the+S] (in the US) a usu. ILLEGAL game in which people risk money on the appearance of a combination of numbers in a newspaper: to play the numbers | the numbers game

Number 10 /ˌnʌmbə ˈten‖-bər-/ see NO. 10

numb·skull /ˈnʌmskʌl/ n a NUMSKULL

nu·me·ral /ˈnjuːmərəl‖ˈnuː-/ n a sign that represents a number —see also ARABIC NUMERAL, ROMAN NUMERAL — **numeral** adj

nu·me·rate /ˈnjuːmərət‖ˈnuː-/ adj esp. BrE having a general understanding of calculations with numbers; able to do ARITHMETIC and MATHEMATICS —opposite innumerate; compare LITERATE —**·racy** n [U]

nu·me·ra·tion /ˌnjuːməˈreɪʃən‖ˌnuː-/ n [C;U] tech a system or the process of counting

nu·me·ra·tor /ˈnjuːməreɪtər‖ˈnuː-/ n tech the number above the line in a FRACTION: 2 is the numerator in ⅔ and $\frac{2}{(x+y)}$ —compare DENOMINATOR

nu·mer·i·cal /njuːˈmerɪkəl‖nuː-/ adj of or using numbers: numerical ability (=skill with numbers) | a numerical code | Their army has numerical superiority over ours (=is greater in numbers) but it is less well trained. — ~ ly /kli/ adv : numerically greater

nu·me·rol·o·gy /ˌnjuːməˈrɒlədʒi‖ˌnuːməˈrɑː-/ n [U] the study of the magic meaning of numbers. This is not taken seriously by most people, but is used as a game or amusement, e.g. to give a meaning to the dates in a person's life, or to use the numerical value of the letters in their name as a guide to their character or future.

nu·me·ro u·no /ˌnuːmərəʊ ˈuːnəʊ/ n AmE NUMBER ONE, esp. sense (2)

nu·me·rous /ˈnjuːmərəs‖ˈnuː-/ adj rather fml many: numerous reasons | for reasons too numerous to mention — ~ ly adv — ~ ness n [U]

nu·mi·nous /ˈnjuːmɪnəs‖ˈnuː-/ adj tech or lit causing or filled with a sense of the presence of God; holy and mysterious — ~ ness n [U]

nu·mis·mat·ics /ˌnjuːmɪz'mætɪks‖ˌnuː-/ n [U] tech or fml the study or collection of coins, money, and MEDALS; coin-collecting —**numismatic** adj [A] : an old penny of great numismatic value —**·ist** /njuːˈmɪzmətɪst‖nuː-/ n

num·skull , numbskull /ˈnʌmskʌl/ n infml a stupid person: Can't you see what you've done, you numskull?

nun /nʌn/ n a member of an all-female religious group who live together in a CONVENT and wear a long dress (HABIT) and also a head covering. Nuns do not get married, thinking of themselves as being married to Jesus Christ, and they lead a very severe and demanding religious life, working and praying together, often also helping other people by nursing or teaching. —compare MONK

nun·ci·o /ˈnʌnsiəʊ/ n -cios a representative of the Pope in a foreign country

nun·ne·ry /ˈnʌnəri/ n esp. lit a building in which nuns live together; CONVENT —compare MONASTERY

NUPE /ˈnjuːpi/ abbrev. for: NATIONAL UNION OF PUBLIC EMPLOYEES

nup·tial /ˈnʌpʃəl/ adj [A] pomp or tech of marriage or the marriage ceremony: the nuptial day | a nuptial mass | (humor) nuptial bliss

nup·tials /ˈnʌpʃəlz/ n [P] pomp a wedding: The nuptials were performed by the local priest.

NUR /ˌen juː ˈɑːr/ abbrev. for: NATIONAL UNION OF RAILWAYMEN

Nu·rem·berg /ˈnjuərəmbɜːg‖ˈnurəmbɜːrg/ a city in Bavaria, Germany (formerly in W Germany), known for its associations with the Nazis. From 1933–38 the Nazis held their party meetings there each year, and in 1945–46 the Nazi war criminals were tried there (**the Nuremberg trials**) and some were given death sentences.

Nu·re·yev /ˈnjuərief, njuˈreɪef‖nuˈreɪef/, **Ru·dolf** /ˈruːdɒlf‖-dɑːlf/ (1938–93) an Austrian dancer, born in Russia, who came to the West in 1961 and worked with the Royal Ballet, and esp. with Margot Fonteyn. He was known as a great CLASSICAL dancer but also worked in MODERN DANCE.

nurse¹ /nɜːs‖nɜːrs/ n **1** a person, typically a woman, who is trained to take care of sick, hurt, or old people, esp. as directed by a doctor in a hospital: Our daughter is a nurse. | a student nurse (=a person learning to be a nurse) | a male nurse | a private nurse taking care of him at home | Nurse Jones | Nurse will do it. | Thank you, Nurse. —see LANGUAGE NOTE: Addressing People

▶CULTURAL NOTE In Britain, nurses are very well liked. The popular image of a nurse is of a young woman who is hardworking, caring, and badly-paid. They are sometimes called "angels".◀

2 a woman employed to take care of a young child; NANNY —see also WET NURSE

nurse² v **1** [T] **a** to take care of as or like a nurse: He nursed her back to health. | She spends her time nursing her old father. | (fig.) He nursed the company through a difficult period. **b** to try to cure: I stayed in bed and nursed my cold. **2** [I] to be a professional nurse: She spent some time nursing in a military hospital. | to take up nursing (=become a nurse) **3** [I (at);T] **a** (of a baby) to suck milk from a woman's breast: nursing at its mother's breast **b** (of a woman) to feed (a baby) with milk from the breast: a nursing mother —compare BREAST-FEED, SUCKLE **4** [T] to hold lovingly: a child nursing a kitten | He nursed his glass of beer all evening. (=kept it in his hand without drinking it) **5** [T] infml to handle carefully so as to preserve, keep going, etc.: He nursed his delicate plants. | They nursed the damaged plane home. **6** [T] to hold (a feeling, esp. a bad feeling) in the mind: She still nursed a grudge against (=continued to feel anger towards) her husband's new wife. | to nurse a hope

nurse·ling /ˈnɜːslɪŋ‖ˈnɜːrs-/ n old use a NURSLING

nurse·maid /ˈnɜːsmeɪd‖ˈnɜːrs-/ n a NURSE¹ (2)

nur·se·ry /ˈnɜːsəri‖ˈnɜːr-/ n **1** also **day nursery, day care center** AmE — a place where small children, but not usu. babies, are taken care of while their parents are at work, etc. —compare CRECHE (1), NURSERY SCHOOL, PLAYGROUP **2** esp. old use a small child's bedroom or playroom in a private house **3** also **nursery garden** /ˈ‥‥ ˌ‥/— BrE an area where plants and trees are grown to be sold or planted in other places

nur·se·ry·man /ˈnɜːsərimən‖ˈnɜːr-/ n -men /mən/ a person who grows plants in a plant nursery

nursery nurse /ˈ‥‥ ˌ‥/ n BrE a nurse who works with, and has taken a special course in the care of, young children

nursery rhyme /ˈ‥‥ ˌ‥/ also **Mother Goose rhyme** esp. AmE— n a short usu. old and well-known song or poem for small children

nursery school /ˈ‥‥ ˌ‥/ n [C;U] a school for young children of two or three to five years of age, where the children learn such things as numbers, letters, colours, etc., and may begin to read and write —compare KINDERGARTEN, NURSERY (1), PLAYGROUP and see also extra information on page 407

nursery slope /ˈ‥‥ ˌ‥/ n a gentle mountain slope where people of any age are first taught how to SKI²

nurs·ing /ˈnɜːsɪŋ‖ˈnɜːr-/ n the work of being a hospital nurse: a career in nursing

nursing home /ˈ‥‥ ˌ‥/ n **1** a usu. private establishment where people (esp. old people) who cannot take care of themselves can live and be looked after **2** BrE a small private hospital

▶CULTURAL NOTE It is common in the US and Britain for people to put their parents in a nursing home when the parents are too old or ill to take care of themselves.◀

nursing moth·er /ˌ·· ˈ··/ n a mother who is breast-feeding her child

nurs·ling , nurseling /ˈnɜːslɪŋ‖ˈnɜːr-/ n old use a baby who is being fed from the breast, or taken care of by a nurse

nur·ture¹ /ˈnɜːtʃəʳ‖ˈnɜːr-/ n [U] esp. lit education, training, and care (given e.g. by parents), esp. as these concern development

nurture² v [T often pass.] lit **1** to give care and food to: nurtured by loving parents | plants nurtured in the greenhouse **2** to cause or encourage to develop: ideas that are nurtured in the universities | nurturing a hatred

NUS /ˌen juː ˈes/ abbrev. for: NATIONAL UNION OF STUDENTS

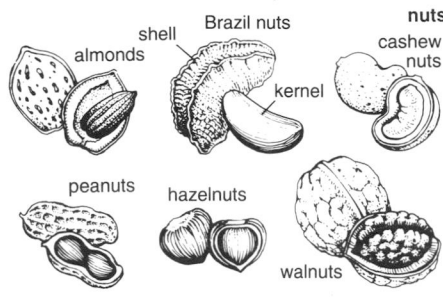

shell — Brazil nuts — nuts — almonds — cashew nuts — kernel — peanuts — hazelnuts — walnuts

nut /nʌt/ n **1 a** a dry fruit with a KERNEL (=seed) surrounded by a hard shell: to crack open|shell a nut **b** this seed, which can be eaten **2** a small piece of metal with a hole through it for screwing onto a BOLT in order to fix or fasten something —see picture at BOLT **3** infml a person who is or seems to be mad: He's a bit of a nut. **4** infml a person who is very keen on the stated thing; FREAK: She's a Clark Gable nut: she's seen all his films. **5** infml one's head: You must be **off your nut**! (=mad) **6** [usu. pl.] BrE a small lump of coal **7** [usu. pl.] taboo sl, esp. AmE a TESTICLE **8 a hard/tough nut to crack** infml a difficult question, person, etc., to deal with **9 do one's nut** BrE sl to suddenly become very angry or worried: I told him what she had said about him and he did his nut. **10 for nuts** BrE infml (esp. after **can't**) at all: She can't sing for nuts! —see also NUTS, NUTS AND BOLTS, GINGER NUT

NUT /ˌen juː ˈtiː/ abbrev. for: National Union of Teachers

nut-brown /ˌ· ˈ·◁/ adj lit having a pleasant dark red-brown colour: nut-brown ale|complexion

nut·case /ˈnʌtkeɪs/ n infml humor a mad person; NUT (3)

nut·crack·er /ˈnʌtˌkrækəʳ/ also **nutcrackers** pl.— n a tool for cracking the shell of a nut: Have we got a nutcracker|a pair of nutcrackers in the house?

Nutcracker, The the title of a BALLET (1), with music (the **Nutcracker Suite**) written by the COMPOSER Tchaikovsky in 1892

nut·house /ˈnʌthaʊs/ n -houses /ˌhaʊzɪz/ sl for PSYCHIATRIC HOSPITAL

nut·meg /ˈnʌtmeg/ n **1** [C] a small hard seed of a tropical tree, which is usu. made into a powder used (as a SPICE) to give a particular taste to food **2** [U] this powder: a pinch of nutmeg

Nu·tra-Sweet /ˈnjuːtrə swiːt‖ˈnuː-/ tdmk an artificial sweetener, used, esp. in drinks, instead of sugar

nu·tri·a /ˈnjuːtriə‖ˈnuː-/ n [U] (the fur of the) COYPU: a nutria coat

nu·tri·ent /ˈnjuːtriənt‖ˈnuː-/ n, adj, tech (a chemical or food) providing what is needed for life and growth: This soil contains valuable nutrients.

nu·tri·ment /ˈnjuːtrɪˌmənt‖ˈnuː-/ n [U] fml food needed for life and growth; NOURISHMENT

nu·tri·tion /njuːˈtrɪʃən‖nuː-/ n [U] the process of giving or getting food; NOURISHMENT: Good nutrition is essential for good health. | the science of nutrition —see also MALNUTRITION

nu·tri·tion·ist /njuːˈtrɪʃənɪst ‖ nuː-/ n a person with special knowledge about foods and how they affect health, growth, and disease

nu·tri·tious /njuːˈtrɪʃəs‖nuː-/ adj valuable to the body as food; nourishing (NOURISH): Milk is very nutritious. | a nutritious meal — ~ly adv

nu·tri·tive /ˈnjuːtrɪˌtɪv‖ˈnuː-/ adj **1** [no comp.] fml or tech of nutrition: What is the nutritive value of potatoes? **2** fml nutritious

nuts¹ /nʌts/ adj [F] infml **1** mad; CRAZY: I'll go nuts if I have to wait much longer! **2** [+on/about/over] very keen on: She's nuts about flying|the boy next door.

nuts² interj sl, esp. AmE (an expression of annoyance, anger, or fearless refusal): Nuts to you and your friends!

nuts and bolts /ˌ·· ˈ·/ n [(the) P] the simple facts or skills of a subject or job: to learn the nuts and bolts of cooking

nut·shell /ˈnʌt-ʃel/ n **1** the hard outer covering of a nut **2 in a nutshell** infml described in as few words as possible: There's a lot I could say about the show but to put it in a nutshell, it was terrible.

nut·ty /ˈnʌti/ adj **1 a** tasting like nuts: wine with a nutty taste **b** filled with nuts: a nutty cake **2** sl mad; CRAZY: another of his nutty ideas | She's **as nutty as a fruitcake**. (=completely mad) —**-tiness** n [U]

Nuuk /nuːk/ the capital city and main port of Greenland (formerly called Godthaab)

nuz·zle /ˈnʌzəl/ v **1** [I;T (UP, **against**)] (esp. of an animal) to rub, touch, or push gently with the nose: The horse nuzzled (up) against me. | The dog nuzzled the sleeping child. **2** [T+obj+adv/prep] to press close, usu. with repeated short movements: She nuzzled her head against his shoulder.

NV written abbrev. for: NEVADA

NW written abbrev. for: northwest(ern)

NY written abbrev. for: NEW YORK (City or State)

NYC written abbrev. for: NEW YORK CITY

Nye·re·re /njəˈreəri/, **Jul·i·us** /ˈdʒuːliəs/ (1922–) a Tanzanian SOCIALIST politician. He became PRIME MINISTER of Tanganyika in 1961 and helped to bring about its union with Zanzibar to form the new republic of Tanzania. He was Tanzania's first president from 1964 to 1985, and became head of the Organization of African Unity in 1984.

ny·lon /ˈnaɪlɒn‖-lɑːn/ n [U] a strong man-made substance made into cords, plastics, and material for clothes: nylon thread/thread made of nylon | a nylon shirt

ny·lons /ˈnaɪlɒnz‖-lɑːnz/ n [P] women's nylon STOCKINGs: a pair of nylons

nymph /nɪmf/ n **1** (in CLASSICAL MYTHOLOGY) any of the less important goddesses of nature, represented as young girls living in trees, streams, mountains, etc. **2** lit a girl or young woman

nym·phet /nɪmˈfet, ˈnɪmfɪt‖nɪmˈfet/ n humor a young girl of about 10–14 years old, regarded as sexually desirable; the word became popular after it was used in Vladimir Nabokov's book Lolita.

nym·pho·ma·ni·a /ˌnɪmfəˈmeɪniə/ n not tech [U] strong sexual desire in a woman to a degree considered as unhealthy or socially unacceptable

nym·pho·ma·ni·ac /ˌnɪmfəˈmeɪniæk◁/ also **nym·pho** /ˈnɪmfəʊ/ sl— adj, n, derog (of or being) a woman with nymphomania

NYSE /ˌen waɪ es ˈiː/ abbrev. for: NEW YORK STOCK EXCHANGE

NZ written abbrev. for: NEW ZEALAND

O, o /əʊ/ **O's, o's** or **Os, os** 1 the 15th letter of the English alphabet 2 (in speech) a zero —see ZERO (USAGE) 3 one of the major blood groups

o /əʊ/ interj esp. poet (usu. cap.) OH: *O wild West Wind!*

o' /ə/ prep lit or old use 1 of 2 on

oaf /əʊf/ n a stupid ungraceful person, esp. male: *You clumsy oaf!* — ~ **ish** adj — ~ **ishly** adv — ~ **ishness** n [U]

oak /əʊk/ n 1 [C] a large tree with hard wood, common in northern countries: *an ancient oak (tree)* —see picture at TREE 2 [U] the wood of this: *an oak door | polished oak* 3 **great oaks from little acorns grow** *saying* small things can grow into very big things over time

oak·en /'əʊkən/ adj [A] esp. lit made of oak

Oak·ley /'əʊkli/, **An·nie** /'æni/ (1860–1926) an American SHARPSHOOTER, member of Buffalo Bill's **Wild West Show**. The musical show and film, *Annie Get Your Gun*, is loosely based on her life and character.

Oaks /əʊks/ [the] a horse race held every year at Epsom, for three-year-old female horses

oa·kum /'əʊkəm/ n [U] small pieces of old rope used for filling up small holes in the sides of wooden ships

OAP /,əʊ eɪ 'piː/ n BrE old age pensioner; a person who is old enough to receive an OLD AGE PENSION from the state. In Britain, this means a woman over 60 or a man over 65: *Tickets are £6, or £3 for students and OAPs.* —compare SENIOR CITIZEN

oar /ɔːʳ/ n 1 a long pole with a wide flat blade at one end, used for rowing a boat, usu. while held in position by ROWLOCKS on the boat: *He pulled hard on the oars.* 2 BrE **put/shove/stick one's oar in** infml to give opinions about other people's affairs without being asked to: *This is our business — nobody asked you to stick your oar in!*

oar·lock /'ɔːlɒk∥'ɔːrlɑːk/ n AmE for ROWLOCK

oars·man /'ɔːzmən∥'ɔːrz-/ **oars·wom·an** /-ˌwʊmən/fem.— n -**men** /mən/ a person who rows a boat, esp. in races

oars·man·ship /'ɔːzmənʃɪp∥'ɔːrz-/ n [U] skill in rowing

OAS /,əʊ eɪ 'es/ [the] the Organization of American States; its members include the US and most Latin American countries, who work together on social, political, and economic matters

OASDHI /,əʊ eɪ ,es ,diː eɪtʃ 'aɪ/ old age, survivors, disability, and hospital insurance; the SOCIAL SECURITY insurance programme provided by the American government to people who have worked in the US for a certain number of years. The programme provides PENSIONS (money for old people who have stopped working), money for people who have been permanently injured (INJURE), and MEDICARE.

o·a·sis /əʊ'eɪsɪs/ n -**ses** /siːz/ 1 a place with water and trees in a desert: *The caravan stopped for the night at an oasis.* 2 a place or situation that is different from its surroundings, usu. in a pleasant or comforting way: *Her bedroom is an oasis of calm in the noisy house.*

oast house /'əʊst haʊs/ n BrE a building, usu. with a pointed top, for drying HOPS (=the plant used in making beer)

oat·cake /'əʊtkeɪk/ n a flat cake made of oatmeal

Oates /əʊts/, **Laur·ence** /'lɒrəns∥'lɔː-/ (1880–1912) a British EXPLORER (also known by his NICKNAME, Titus Oates), who went with Scott on his journey to the South Pole, and on the way back, suffering from FROSTBITE, he went out into the snow to die rather than delay the other members of the team. The words he used, "I may be gone some time" are now often said humorously by someone about to do something dangerous or uncertain.

oath /əʊθ/ n **oaths** /əʊðz/ 1 a solemn promise: *to swear an oath | Repeat the oath after me.* 2 an expression of strong feeling using religious or sexual words improperly: *oaths and curses* 3 **be on/under oath** law to have made a solemn promise to tell the truth: *The judge reminded the witness that she was under oath.* 4 **take the oath** to make a solemn promise to tell the truth in a court of law

▶CULTURAL NOTE In Britain and the US the oath is a religious promise. The person taking the oath holds or touches a Bible and promises to tell "the truth, the whole truth, and nothing but the truth". Someone who does not wish to make a religious promise may AFFIRM (=make a solemn promise, but without mentioning God or using a Bible). Everyone who gives EVIDENCE must take the oath or affirm; if they then tell a lie they can be charged with PERJURY. —see also HIPPOCRATIC OATH◀

oat·meal /'əʊtmiːl/ n [U] 1 crushed oats used for making cakes and PORRIDGE 2 AmE for PORRIDGE

oats /əʊts/ n [P] 1 a grain that provides food for people and animals —see picture at CEREAL 2 OATMEAL 3 **be off one's oats** BrE infml to have lost the wish to eat 4 **feel one's oats** infml to feel full of life and ready for action —see also WILD OATS

OAU /,əʊ eɪ 'juː/ [the] Organization of African Unity; an organization which aims to end COLONIALISM in Africa, and agree on political, economic, defence and health plans etc. among member countries

ob·du·rate /'ɒbdʒ₃ˈr₄t∥'ɑːbdə-/ adj fml, usu. derog refusing to change one's beliefs or feelings, esp. in spite of people's attempts to persuade one; STUBBORN: *Despite all my pleas she remained obdurate.* — ~ **ly** adv —**racy** n [U]

OBE /,əʊ biː 'iː/ n Order of the British Empire; an honour given to someone as a title, to thank them or show respect for the work they have done in various fields, including sport, entertainment, politics, business, etc.. The MEDAL marking the title is given by the Queen in a special ceremony: *John Smith, OBE | You deserve an OBE/to be given/awarded an OBE.*

o·be·di·ent /ə'biːdiənt/ adj [(to)] doing what one is ordered to do; willing to obey the orders of someone in a position of power, such as a parent or teacher: *an obedient dog/child* —opposite **disobedient** — ~ **ly** adv —**ence** n [U (to)]

o·bei·sance /əʊ'beɪsəns/ n [C;U (to)] fml a show of respect and obedience, esp. by bending the head or upper part of the body: *He made a deep obeisance to the queen.*

ob·e·lisk /'ɒbəlɪsk∥'ɑː-, 'əʊ-/ n 1 a tall pointed stone PILLAR built usu. in honour of a person or event 2 (in printing) a DAGGER (2)

O·ber·am·mer·gau /,əʊbər'æməgaʊ∥-mər-/ a town in Bavaria, Germany, known for the PASSION PLAYS, held every ten years since 1634 as a way of giving thanks for being saved from the Black Death

O·be·ron /'əʊbərɒn∥-rɑːn/ the king of the fairies (FAIRY) and the husband of Titania in Shakespeare's play *A Midsummer Night's Dream*

o·bese /əʊ'biːs/ adj fml very fat; unhealthily fat —see FAT (USAGE) —**obesity** n [U]

o·bey /əʊ'beɪ, ə-/ v 1 [I;T] to do what one is told to do (by someone in a position of power), or act in accordance with (orders, laws, etc.): *Soldiers are expected to obey (their officers/their orders) without question. | to obey the law* 2 **She who must be obeyed** infml humor a phrase used for a woman (for example, one's wife) who one does not wish to displease: *"Are you coming for a drink tonight?" "Better not. She who must be obeyed wants to go to the pictures."* —opposite **disobey**

ob·fus·cate /'ɒbfəskeɪt∥'ɑːb-/ v [T] fml to confuse or make difficult to understand, perhaps intentionally: *The report obfuscates the principal points.* —**cation** /,ɒbfə'skeɪʃən ∥,ɑːb-/ n [U]

ob/gyn /,əʊbi 'gaɪn/ n short for OBSTETRICS and GYNAECOLOGY, two branches of medicine that are often combined in medical schools and hospitals

O·bie A·ward /'əʊbi ə,wɔːd∥-ɔːrd/ also **The Village Voice Off-Broadway Awards**— n a prize given to plays produced OFF-BROADWAY

ob·i·ter dic·tum /,ɒbɪtə 'dɪktəm∥,ɑːbɪtər-, ,əʊb-/ n obiter dicta /-tə/ Lat, law or fml a remark which is related to the main argument but not necessary to it

o·bit·u·a·ry /ə'bɪtʃʊəri∥-tʃueri/ also **o·bit** /'əʊbɪt/ infml— n a formal report, esp. in a newspaper, that someone has died, usu. with an account of the dead person's life: *an obituary notice/column*

ob·ject¹ /'ɒbdʒɪkt∥'ɑːb-/ n 1 a thing that can be seen or felt: *What's that little black object? | an unidentified object* 2 [+of] something or someone that produces interest, at tention, or some other stated feeling: *an object of admiration|of fear* | *She has become an object of pity|contempt.* **3** purpose; aim: *The object of his visit was to open the new hospital.* | *The new law turned public opinion against the government, which was not* **the object of the exercise.** (=not the intended result) **4** *tech* (in grammar) a noun, noun phrase, or PRONOUN, etc., representing **a** the person or thing (the **direct object**) that something is done to, such as *house* in *We built a house*, or **b** the person (the **indirect object**) who is concerned in the result of an action, such as *her* in *I gave her the book* or in *I gave the book to her*, or **c** the person or thing that is joined by a PREPOSITION to another word or phrase, such as *table* in *He sat on the table.* —compare SUBJECT¹ (4) **5 no object** not a difficulty: *I want the best you can find — money (is) no object.* (=I don't care what it costs)

ob·ject² /əbˈdʒekt/ v **1** [I (to)] to be against something or someone; feel or show opposition or disapproval: *I'd like to open the window, if no one objects.* | *I strongly object to being treated like a child|to his treating me like a child.* | *They object on religious grounds* (=for religious reasons) *to this new law.* **2** [T+(that);obj] to give as an argument against something: *I wanted to climb the hill, but Bill objected that he was too tired.* — ~ **or** n

object code /ˈ·· ˌ·/ n [U] MACHINE CODE

ob·jec·tion /əbˈdʒekʃən/ n **1** [(to)] a statement or feeling of opposition or disapproval: *If no one has any objections, I'll declare the meeting closed.* **2** [(to, against)] a reason or argument against: *The only objection (to|against hiring her) is that she can't drive.*

ob·jec·tio·na·ble /əbˈdʒekʃ∂nəbəl/ adj likely to be objected to; unpleasant; offensive: *his objectionable behaviour* —**bly** adv

ob·jec·tive¹ /əbˈdʒektɪv/ adj **1** [no comp.] existing outside the mind; real: *objective facts|reality* **2** not influenced by personal feelings or opinions; fair: *an objective analysis of the political situation* | *Try to be more objective about it.* —opposite **subjective 3** *tech* (in grammar) of the object — ~ **ly** adv : *Objectively (speaking), he can't possibly succeed.* —**-tivity** /ˌɒbdʒekˈtɪvˌti||ˌaːb-/ n [U]

objective² n an aim, esp. one that must be worked towards over a long period; GOAL: *Our objective is (to achieve) full employment.* | *We have succeeded in our main objectives.*

object les·son /ˈ·· ˌ·/ n [(in)] an event or story from which one can learn how or how not to behave: *Her career is an object lesson in determination.*

ob·jet d'art /ˌɒbʒeɪ ˈdɑːr||ˌaːb-/ n **objets d'art** (*same pronunciation*) an object, usu. small, of some value as art

ob·late sphere /ˌɒbleɪt ˈsfɪər||ˌaːb-/ n *tech* a ball which, like the Earth, is not quite round but slightly flattened at the top and bottom

ob·la·tion /əˈbleɪʃən/ n [(to) often pl.] *fml or tech* a religious offering

ob·li·gate /ˈɒblɪˌɡeɪt||ˈaːb-/ v [T+obj+to-v;usu. pass.] *AmE or fml* to make (someone) feel it necessary (to do something), esp. because of a sense of duty: *He felt obligated to visit his parents.*

ob·li·ga·tion /ˌɒblɪˈɡeɪʃən||ˌaːb-/ n [C;U] **1** a condition or influence that makes it necessary for someone to do something; duty: [+to-v] *You can look around the shop with no obligation to buy.* | *Everyone has a legal obligation to provide the tax office with details of their earnings.* | *to fulfil one's obligations* **2 under an obligation (to): a** having a duty (to): *We are invited, but we are under no obligation to go.* **b** having to be grateful (to): *Her kindness has placed me under an obligation to her.*

ob·lig·a·to·ry /əˈblɪɡətəri||-tɔːri/ adj fml which must be done by law, rule, etc.; COMPULSORY: *If you are a member, attendance at the meeting is obligatory.* —opposites **optional, voluntary**

o·blige /əˈblaɪdʒ/ v **1** [T+obj+to-v;often pass.] to make it necessary for (someone) to do something: *Falling profits obliged them to close the factory.* | *I felt obliged to leave after such an unpleasant quarrel.* **2** [I;T] to do (someone) a favour; fulfil the wishes (of): *Could you oblige me by opening the window?* | *Could you oblige me with a match?* (=please give me a match) | *I'd be obliged if you would stop interfering.* (=please stop) | *They asked her for more information, and she willingly obliged.* **3 (I'm) much obliged (to you)** *polite* (I'm) very grateful (to you)

o·blig·ing /əˈblaɪdʒɪŋ/ adj willing and eager to help — ~ **ly** adv

o·blique¹ /əˈbliːk/ adj **1** indirect: *oblique hints* | *an oblique reference* **2** having a sloping direction or position: *an oblique line* **3** (of an angle) either more or less than 90 degrees

oblique² also **oblique stroke** /·ˈ· ·/, **slash (mark)**, **solidus; stroke** — n a mark (/) used for writing FRACTIONS, for separating numbers, etc. In this dictionary it is used for separating two or more possible choices of words, and in pairs for enclosing pronunciations.

o·blit·er·ate /əˈblɪtəreɪt/ v [T] **1** to remove all signs of; destroy completely: *The village was obliterated in the bombing raid.* **2** to cover completely; BLOT out: *Storm clouds obliterated the sun.* —**-ation** /əˌblɪtəˈreɪʃən/ n [U]

o·bliv·i·on /əˈblɪviən/ n [U] **1** the state of being completely forgotten: *The ancient civilization fell|sank into oblivion.* | *The unsuccessful candidate was consigned to (political) oblivion.* **2** the state of being unconscious or not noticing one's surroundings; obliviousness: *This drug promises instant oblivion.*

o·bliv·i·ous /əˈblɪviəs/ adj [(to, of)] not noticing; UNAWARE: *He was quite oblivious of|to the danger.* — ~ **ly** adv — ~ **ness** n [U]

ob·long /ˈɒblɒŋ||ˈaːblɔːŋ/ n, adj of or being a shape with four straight sides that is longer than it is wide: *an oblong room|circle* —compare RECTANGLE, SQUARE —**oblong** adj

ob·lo·quy /ˈɒbləkwi||ˈaːb-/ n [U] fml **1** strong words spoken against someone; ABUSE **2** loss of respect and honour; DISGRACE

ob·nox·ious /əbˈnɒkʃəs||-ˈnaːk-/ adj fml very unpleasant or offensive; extremely DISAGREEABLE: *an obnoxious smell|person* — ~ **ly** adv — ~ **ness** n [U]

o·boe /ˈəʊbəʊ/ n a musical instrument of the WOODWIND family, with a double REED, played by blowing —see picture at WOODWIND

o·bo·ist /ˈəʊbəʊˌɪst/ n an oboe player

O·bo·te /əʊˈbəʊti/, **Milton** (1924–) a Ugandan politician who led the movement for independence from 1961, becoming Prime Minister in 1962 and President from 1966 to 1971 and 1980 to 1985

ob·scene /əbˈsiːn/ adj (esp. of ideas, books, etc., usu. about sex) offensive to accepted ideas of morality; INDECENT: *The police seized a quantity of obscene publications.* | *It is obscene* (=shocking) *that people should still be dying of starvation in the 1980s.* — ~ **ly** adv

ob·scen·i·ty /əbˈsenˌti/ n **1** [U] obscene language or behaviour **2** [C] an obscene word or action: *to shout obscenities*

ob·scu·ran·tis·m /ˌɒbskjʊˈræntɪzəm||ˌaːb-/ n [U] fml derog the practice of intentionally stopping ideas and facts from being known; hiding the truth

ob·scure¹ /əbˈskjʊər/ adj **1** hard to understand; not clear: *a speech full of obscure political jokes* **2** not well known: *an obscure poet* — ~ **ly** adv

obscure² v [T] to hide; make difficult to see or understand: *The clouds obscured the moon.* | *The report obscures the fact that taxes have actually risen.*

ob·scu·ri·ty /əbˈskjʊərˌti/ n **1** [U] the state of being obscure: *After a 20-year break from acting, the new film rescued her from obscurity.* **2** [C] something which is obscure: *His poems are full of obscurities.*

ob·se·quies /ˈɒbsˌkwiz||ˈaːb-/ n [P] fml funeral ceremonies

ob·se·qui·ous /əbˈsiːkwiəs/ adj fml too eager to obey or serve; having too little self-respect; SERVILE: *obsequious servants|behaviour* — ~ **ly** adv — ~ **ness** n [U]

ob·ser·va·ble /əbˈzɜːvəbəl||-ɜːr-/ adj that can be seen or noticed: *no observable improvement* —**bly** adv

ob·ser·vance /əbˈzɜːvəns||-ɜːr-/ n **1** [U] behaviour in accordance with a law, ceremony, or custom: *strict observance of the rules* | *the observance of Christmas* **2** [C often pl.] a part of a religious ceremony: *ritual observances*

ob·ser·vant /əbˈzɜːvənt||-ɜːr-/ adj **1** quick at noticing things: *Luckily an observant passerby noticed the fire.* —opposite **unobservant 2** [(of)] *rare* acting in accordance with esp. religious law or custom

ob·ser·va·tion /ˌɒbzəˈveɪʃən||ˌaːbzɜːr-/ n **1** [C;U] (an) action of noticing or watching: *She's in hospital* **under**

observation. (=being watched to see if she is ill) | *He left by the back door to* **escape observation.** (=to avoid being noticed) | *to make scientific observations* (=record what one has noticed) | *powers of observation* (=ability to notice things) **2** [C] *fml* a spoken or written remark (about something noticed): *She made some interesting observations on the current political scene.* **3** [U] observance

observation post /ˌ·ˈ·· ·/ *n* a position from which something, for example the movements of an enemy, can be watched

ob·ser·va·to·ry /əbˈzɜːvətəri‖əbˈzɜːrvətɔːri/ *n* a place from which scientists watch natural objects and events (esp. the moon, stars, etc.)

ob·serve /əbˈzɜːv‖-ˈɜːrv/ *v* [T] **1 a** to see and notice: *Did you observe anything unusual in his behaviour?* [+*that*|*wh-*] *I observed that they were late*|*where they went.* [+*obj+to-v*|*v-ing*] *The police observed him enter*|*entering the bank with a shotgun.* **b** to watch with careful attention: *to observe the stars* | *The police have been observing his movements.* **2** to act in accordance with (law, custom, etc.): *to observe the speed limit*|*a cease-fire* | *Do you observe Christmas?* **3** to make a remark; say: *"That's odd," he observed.* [+*that*] *He observed that it was odd.*

ob·serv·er /əbˈzɜːvəʳ‖-ɜːr / *n* **1** someone who observes. *an observer of nature* | *an impartial observer of the current political scene* **2** someone who attends meetings, classes, etc., only to listen, not to take part: *The United Nations sent a team of observers to the peace talks.*

Observer [*the*] a serious British newspaper which is printed and sold every Sunday —see also extra information on page 896

ob·sess /əbˈses/ *v* [T *usu. pass.*] to completely fill the mind of (someone) so that no attention is given to other matters; PREOCCUPY to an extreme degree: *She's obsessed by the thought of another war*|*with the desire to become a great scientist.*

ob·ses·sion /əbˈseʃən/ *n* [(**about, with**)] a fixed and often unreasonable idea with which the mind is continually concerned: *He has an unhealthy obsession with death.*

ob·ses·sion·al /əbˈseʃənəl/ *adj* **1** [(**about**)] (of a person) having obsessions: *She's obsessional about cleanliness.* **2** causing or connected with obsessions: *His obsessional behaviour is beginning to annoy me.* | *an obsessional idea*|*illness*

ob·ses·sive[1] /əbˈsesɪv/ *adj* of or being an obsession: *his obsessive interest in sex* | *an obsessive hatred of women*

obsessive[2] *n* a person who has obsessions

ob·sid·i·an /əbˈsɪdiən/ *n* [U] a type of dark rock which looks like glass

ob·so·les·cent /ˌɒbsəˈlesənt◄‖ˌɑːb-/ *adj* becoming obsolete: *This type of computer is obsolescent.* —compare MORIBUND; see also PLANNED OBSOLESCENCE —**cence** *n* [U]

ob·so·lete /ˈɒbsəliːt‖ˌɑːbsəˈliːt/ *adj* no longer used; completely out of date: *obsolete machinery*|*ideas*|*words*

ob·sta·cle /ˈɒbstəkəl‖ˈɑːb-/ *n* [(**to**)] something which prevents action, movement, or success: *She felt that her family were an obstacle to her work.* | *They tried to* **put obstacles in the way of** (–to prevent) *our marriage.*

obstacle course /ˈ··· ·/ *n* **1** a line of objects which runners in an **obstacle race** have to jump over|climb through, etc.: (fig.) *Claimants face an obstacle course of forms, interviews, and assessments which seem designed to stop them getting their rights.* **2** *AmE* ASSAULT COURSE

ob·ste·tri·cian /ˌɒbstɪˈtrɪʃən‖ˌɑːb-/ *n* a doctor who is a specialist in obstetrics

ob·stet·rics /əbˈstetrɪks/ *n* [U] the branch of medicine concerned with the birth of children —**ric** *adj*

ob·sti·nate /ˈɒbstɪnɪt‖ˈɑːb-/ *adj* **1** refusing to change one's opinion or behaviour, in spite of argument or attempts to persuade one: *She's so obstinate – she won't let anyone help her.* | *an obstinate child* **2** difficult to deal with, control, or defeat: *obstinate resistance* | *an obstinate cough* (=hard to cure) — **ly** *adv* —**nacy** *n* [U]

ob·strep·e·rous /əbˈstrepərəs/ *adj fml or humor* (of people or behaviour) noisy, bad-tempered, and uncontrollable — **ly** *adv* — **ness** *n* [U]

ob·struct /əbˈstrʌkt/ *v* [T] **1** to block up (a road, passage, etc.): *The broken-down truck obstructed the road*|*the traffic.* **2** to put difficulties in the way of: *to obstruct a plan* | *to obstruct the course of justice by withholding vital information*

ob·struc·tion /əbˈstrʌkʃən/ *n* **1** [U] the process of obstructing: *The opposition tried to stop the law being passed by deliberate obstruction.* **2** [C] something that obstructs: *an obstruction in a pipe*|*in the throat* **3** [U] (in football, HOCKEY, etc.) a FOUL in which a player gets between an opponent and the ball so as to prevent the opponent from playing the ball

ob·struc·tion·is·m /əbˈstrʌkʃənɪzəm/ *n* [U] the act of intentionally obstructing something, esp. the passing of a law —**ist** *n*

ob·struc·tive /əbˈstrʌktɪv/ *adj* intentionally obstructing: *obstructive behaviour*|*policy* — **ly** *adv* — **ness** *n* [U]

ob·tain /əbˈteɪn/ *v* **1** [T] *rather fml* to become the owner of, esp. by means of effort or planning; get: *I haven't been able to obtain that record anywhere.* | *He said the police had obtained this information by illegal means.* | *Further information can be obtained from our head office.* **2** [I not in progressive forms] *fml* to be established; remain in or come into existence: *Those conditions no longer obtain.*

ob·tain·a·ble /əbˈteɪnəbəl/ *adj* that can be obtained: *I'm sorry sir, that type of camera is no longer obtainable.* — opposite **unobtainable**

ob·trude /əbˈtruːd/ *v* [I;T] *fml* **1** to (cause to) stick out: *The snail's horns obtruded.* | *The snail obtruded its horns.* **2** [(**on, upon**)] to (cause to) be noticed, esp. when unwanted: *Unfortunately, in this essay his personal opinions keep obtruding (themselves).* —compare EXTRUDE, INTRUDE, PROTRUDE

ob·tru·sive /əbˈtruːsɪv/ *adj* unpleasantly noticeable: *rather obtrusive smells* /*music* /*behaviour* —opposite **unobtrusive** — **ly** *adv* — **ness** *n* [U]

ob·tuse /əbˈtjuːs‖-ˈtuːs/ *adj* **1** *fml* annoyingly slow in understanding: *Is he stupid or is he being deliberately obtuse?* **2** (of an angle) between 90 and 180 degrees —see picture at ANGLE — **ly** *adv* — **ness** *n*

ob·verse /ˈɒbvɜːs‖ˈɑːbvɜːrs/ *n* [*the*] **1** *tech* the front side of a coin or MEDAL —opposite **reverse** **2** [(**of**)] *fml* a necessary opposite: *Defeat is the obverse of victory.*

ob·vi·ate /ˈɒbvieɪt‖ˈɑːb-/ *v* [T] *fml* to clear away (a difficulty); make unnecessary: *The use of a credit card obviates the need to carry a lot of money.*

ob·vi·ous /ˈɒbviəs‖ˈɑːb-/ *adj* [(**to**)] easy to see and understand; clear; which must be recognized: *There are obvious disadvantages in this plan.* | *I've got my exams tomorrow, so for obvious reasons I won't be able to come out tonight.* | *It was obvious to everyone that he was lying.* | *To say we are disappointed would be* **stating the obvious.** (=saying what is too clear to need saying) — — **ness** *n* [U]

ob·vi·ous·ly /ˈɒbviəsli‖ˈɑːb-/ *adv* it can be easily seen (that); plainly: *This key is obviously the wrong one.* | *"Is she sorry?" "Obviously not! Look at her."* —compare APPARENTLY, EVIDENTLY

oc·a·ri·na /ˌɒkəˈriːnə‖ˌɑː/ *n* a type of small musical instrument played by blowing

oc·ca·sion[1] /əˈkeɪʒən/ *n* **1** [C] a time when something happens: *on several occasions* | *On that occasion I was not at home.* **2** [S (**for**)] a suitable or favourable time: *This is hardly the occasion for a family argument.* | *You should go there* **if the occasion** (=the chance) **arises.** **3** [C] a special event or ceremony: *The opening of a new school is always a great occasion.* | *I wear a tie only on special occasions.* **4** [S (**of**)] *fml* a direct cause or reason: *His remark was the occasion of a bitter quarrel.* [+*to-v*] *There was no occasion to be so rude.* **5 on occasion** *fml* from time to time; occasionally —see also SENSE OF OCCASION, **rise to the occasion** (RISE[1]); see CHANCE (USAGE)

occasion[2] *v* [T] *fml* to cause: *What occasioned this outburst of temper?* [+*obj(i)+obj(d)*] *Your behaviour has occasioned us a lot of trouble.*

oc·ca·sion·al /əˈkeɪʒənəl/ *adj* **1** happening from time to time; not regular: *occasional showers* | *I'm not a heavy drinker, but I like the occasional glass of wine.* **2** [A] *fml or tech* written or intended for a special occasion: *occasional poems* —see NEVER (USAGE) — **ly** *adv*

Oc·ci·dent /ˈɒksɪdənt‖ˈɑːksɪdənt, -dənt/ *n* [*the*] *esp. fml or*

lit the western part of the world, esp. Europe and the Americas —compare ORIENT

oc·ci·den·tal /ˌɒksɪˈdentəl◄‖ˌɑːk-/ *n, adj esp. fml or lit* (*sometimes cap.*) (a person) of the Occident —compare ORIENTAL

oc·cult /ˈɒkʌlt, əˈkʌlt‖əˈkʌlt, ˈɑː-/ *adj* magical and mysterious; hidden from the knowledge or understanding of ordinary people: *occult powers/ceremonies* —**occult** *n* [*the*]: *She's fascinated by black magic and the occult.*

oc·cu·pan·cy /ˈɒkjɵpənsi‖ˈɑːk-/ *n* [U] *fml* the act or period of actually using a building, piece of land, or other space: *five years' occupancy* | *commercial occupancy*

oc·cu·pant /ˈɒkjɵpənt‖ˈɑːk-/ *n* [(of)] *fml* **1** a person who lives in a place, though without necessarily owning it: *the occupant of the flat upstairs* **2** a person who is in a place or space: *The car plunged into the river, killing all its occupants.*

oc·cu·pa·tion /ˌɒkjɵˈpeɪʃən‖ˌɑːk-/ *n* **1** [C] a job; employment: *Please state your name, address, and occupation.* —see JOB (USAGE) **2** [C] a way of spending time; PASTIME: *Knitting is a peaceful occupation.* **3** [U] the act of occupying a place, or the state or period of being occupied, esp. of one country occupying another

Occupation also **German Occupation**– [*the*] the period during the Second World War when German soldiers occupied France

oc·cu·pa·tion·al /ˌɒkjɵˈpeɪʃənəl◄‖ˌɑːk-/ *adj* of, about, or caused by one's job: *For professional footballers, injuries are an occupational hazard.* (=a risk connected with their work) — ~**ly** *adv*

occupational ther·a·py /ˌ····· ˈ···/ *n* [U] the treatment of illness by giving people special help and special work to do to keep them active while their bodies recover after an illness or accident —**pist** *n*

oc·cu·pi·er /ˈɒkjɵpaɪəʳ‖ˈɑːk-/ *n esp. BrE* a person who occupies a place, esp. an OCCUPANT of a house —see also OWNER-OCCUPIER

oc·cu·py /ˈɒkjɵpaɪ‖ˈɑːk-/ *v* [T] **1** to move into and hold possession of (a place), e.g. by military force: *The workers occupied the factory and refused to leave.* | *The enemy occupied the town.* | *an occupying army* **2** to fill (a position, space, or time): *Writing occupies most of my free time.* | *The story occupied most of the front page of the paper.* **3** [*usu. pass.*] to be in (a place): *The house is no longer occupied.* | *Is that seat occupied?* (=Is it free?) **4** [(in, with)] to cause to spend time (doing something); keep busy: *This game will keep the children occupied.* | *I occupied myself in writing letters.*

oc·cur /əˈkɜːʳ/ *v* **-rr-** [I] **1** *rather fml* (esp. of unplanned events) to take place; happen: *Many accidents occur in the home.* | *The tragedy occurred only minutes after takeoff.* —see HAPPEN (USAGE) **2** [+*adv/prep*] (esp. of something not alive) to be found; exist: *That sound doesn't occur in his language so it's difficult for him to pronounce.*

occur to sbdy. *phr v* [T *no pass.*] (of an idea) to come to (someone's) mind: *Didn't it occur to you that he might be late?* | *The possibility that she might be wrong never even occurred to her.* | *It suddenly occurred to me that we could use a computer to do the job.*

oc·cur·rence /əˈkʌrəns‖əˈkɜː-/ *n* **1** [C] an event; happening: *This sort of incident is an everyday occurrence.* **2** [U] the process of happening: *the occurrence of violent storms*

o·cean /ˈəʊʃən/ *n* **1** [(*the*) U] the great mass of salt water that covers most of the Earth's surface **2** [C] (*often cap. as part of a name*) any of the great seas into which this mass is divided: *the Pacific Ocean* **3 oceans of** *infml* a great mass or amount of: *oceans of flowers* —see also **a drop in the ocean** (DROP²) — ~**ic** /ˌəʊʃiˈænɪk◄/ *adj*

o·cean·go·ing /ˈəʊʃənˌgəʊɪŋ/ also **seagoing**– *adj* (esp. of a ship) built to travel on the sea rather than on rivers or in HARBOURS

o·cean·og·ra·phy /ˌəʊʃənˈɒgrəfi‖-ˈɑːg-/ *n* [U] the scientific study of the ocean —**pher** *n*

oc·e·lot /ˈɒsɪlɒt‖ˈɑːsɪlɑːt, ˈəʊ-/ *n* a large spotted American wild cat

o·chre ‖ *usu.* **ocher** *AmE* /ˈəʊkəʳ/ *n* [U] **1** a fine reddish-yellow earth used as a colouring substance in paints **2** the colour of ochre —**ochre** *adj*

o'clock /əˈklɒk‖əˈklɑːk/ *adv* (used with the numbers from 1 to 12 in telling time) exactly the hour stated according

---

to the clock: *"What time is it?" "It's 9 o'clock."*

▷ USAGE In modern English, **o'clock** is used only when saying the exact hour, not an hour and a number of minutes: *9 o'clock,* but *5 past 9* (*5 after 9* in American English), *half past 9,* etc.◁

O Come All Ye Faith·ful /ˌ· ˌ· · · ˈ··/ the title and first line of a well-known Christmas CAROL (=religious song sung at Christmas)

O'Con·nell /əʊˈkɒnl‖-ˈkɑː-/, **Daniel** (1775–1847) an Irish politician who forced the government to give rights to Roman Catholics, and worked for an end to the union with Britain

O'Con·nor /əʊˈkɒnəʳ‖-ˈkɑː-/, **Des** /dez/ (1932–) an English popular music singer and television PERSONALITY, popular esp. with older people. He is sometimes mentioned by British people in jokes as being a bad singer.

O'Connor, San·dra Day /ˈsændrə deɪ/ (1930–) the first woman JUSTICE (judge) on the American Supreme Court

OCR /ˌəʊ siː ˈɑːʳ/ *n* [U] optical character recognition; a method by which a machine can read words and store them directly on a computer, without the use of a typist

Oct. *written abbrev. for*: OCTOBER

oc·ta·gon /ˈɒktəgən‖ˈɑːktəgɑːn/ *n tech* a flat shape with eight sides and eight angles — ~**al** /ɒkˈtægənəl‖ɑːk-/ *adj*

oc·tal /ˈɒktəl‖ˈɑːk-/ *adj tech* based on the number 8; using the numbers 0-7 in combination. Octal numbers have many uses in computers.

oc·tane /ˈɒkteɪn‖ˈɑːk-/ *n* a chemical compound added to petrol. Sometimes an **octane number** shows the power and quality of petrol, the higher the better: *100-octane petrol* | *high octane fuel*

oc·tave /ˈɒktɪv, -teɪv‖ˈɑːk-/ *n tech* **1 a** a space of eight degrees between musical notes: *two notes an octave apart* | *a singer with a range of three octaves* **b** a set of eight musical notes, with the highest and lowest notes eight degrees apart **2** a group of eight lines of poetry, esp. the first eight of a SONNET (=poem of 14 lines)

oc·ta·vo /ɒkˈteɪvəʊ‖ɑːk-/ *n* [U] *tech* the (size of) paper produced by folding a large sheet of paper three times so as to give eight sheets or sixteen pages in all. In Britain and Europe the metric measures for paper are now more often used. —see also FOLIO (2), QUARTO

oc·tet /ɒkˈtet‖ɑːk-/ *n* **1** [+*sing./pl. v*] eight singers or musicians performing together **2** a piece of music for an octet —compare SEXTET, SEPTET

Oc·to·ber /ɒkˈtəʊbəʳ‖ɑːk-/ *n* (*written abbrev.* **Oct.**) *n* [C;U] the tenth month of the year, between September and November: *It happened on October the third/on the third of October/(AmE) on October third.* | *This office opened in October 1991.* | *She started work here last October/the October before last.*

▶ CULTURAL NOTE October is connected in people's minds with autumn, leaves falling off trees, and Hallowe'en, which is on October 31st. ◀

oc·to·ge·nar·i·an /ˌɒktəʊdʒɪˈneəriən, -tə-‖ˌɑːk-/ *n* a person who is between 80 and 89 years old

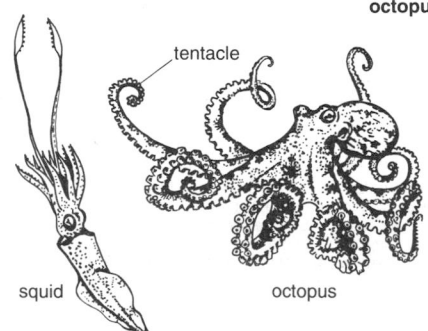

octopus

tentacle

squid   octopus

oc·to·pus /ˈɒktəpəs‖ˈɑːk-/ *n* **-puses** *or* **-pi** /paɪ/ **1** [C] a deep-sea creature with eight TENTACLES (=arms) —see also SQUID **2** [U] octopus meat as food; it is a rare food in

Britain, eaten mainly in restaurants, e.g. as part of a SEAFOOD SALAD

oc·u·lar /'ɒkjʊlə^r‖'ɑːk-/ *adj fml or tech* of the eyes: *ocular muscles*

oc·u·list /'ɒkjʊlɪst‖'ɑːk-/ *n* a doctor who examines and treats people's eyes —compare OPTICIAN (USAGE)

OD /ˌəʊ 'diː/ *v* [I (**on**)] *sl* to take too much of a drug; take an OVERDOSE; used esp. when speaking of dangerous drugs: *He O.D.ed on heroin.*

o·da·lisque /'əʊdəlɪsk/ *n lit* an Eastern female slave in former times, esp. one used for sexual purposes

odd /ɒd‖ɑːd/ *adj* **1** different from what is ordinary or expected; unusual; PECULIAR: *odd behaviour|people | It's very odd that she didn't reply to our letter.* **2** [A] separated from its pair or set: *an odd shoe* **3** (of a number) that cannot be divided exactly by two: *1, 3, 5, 7, etc., are odd.* —opposite **even** **4** [A] not regular; OCCASIONAL: *He does odd jobs for me from time to time. | We get the odd complaint but most of our customers seem quite satisfied.* **5** [after *n*] *infml* (after numbers) rather more than the stated number: *20-odd years* (=a little more than 20 years) —see also ODDLY

odd·ball /'ɒdbɔːl‖'ɑːd-/ *n infml, esp. AmE* a person who behaves in an odd way

Odd Cou·ple /'·ˌ··/ [the] a play, film, and television programme made in the US about two men, Felix and Oscar, who share a flat with each other and who are very different from each other. Felix is very tidy and clean, but Oscar is lazy and dirty.

odd·i·ty /'ɒdɪti‖'ɑː-/ *n* **1** [C] a strange or unusual person, thing, etc. **2** [U] strangeness

odd-job man /·ˈ·ˈ·/ *n* a man who is employed to do various small pieces of work (**odd jobs**) for pay, usu. in people's houses

odd·ly /'ɒdli‖'ɑːdli/ *adv* **1** in an odd way: *behaving rather oddly* **2** it is odd that: **Oddly enough,** *the letter never arrived.*

odd man out /ˌ·· '·/ also **odd one out**– *n* **odd men/ones out** **1** a (male or female) person or thing that is different from, or left out of, a group: *Which of these three shapes is the odd one out?* **2** *infml* someone (male or female) who does not mix easily with others: *I was always the odd man out in my class at school.* —see MAN (USAGE)

odd·ment /'ɒdmənt‖'ɑːd-/ *n* [often *pl.*] *infml* something remaining; REMNANT: *a few oddments of cloth*

odds /ɒdz‖ɑːdz/ *n* [P] **1** a the probability that something will or will not happen: *She may pass but the odds are* (=it is likely that) *she will fail. | Against all the odds* (=very unexpectedly) *he recovered from his illness. | They are fighting against heavy odds.* **b** such probability expressed in numbers when making a BET: |+(*that*)| *The odds are 10 to 1 that her horse will win. | I laid him* (=offered him) **odds** *of 50 to 1. | to back a horse at* **long/short odds** (=odds that are/are not strongly against its winning) **2 at odds (with)** in disagreement (with): *Those two have been at odds (with one another) for ages. | This new evidence is at odds with their earlier statement.* **3 it/that makes no odds** *BrE* it/that makes no difference; has no importance: *It makes no odds whether we go or stay.*

odds and ends /ˌ·· '·/ also **odds and sods** *BrE sl*– *n* [P] **1** small articles of various kinds, without much value **2** small jobs of various kinds, of no great importance

odds-on /·ˈ·◂/ *adj* very likely (to win): *The* **odds-on favourite** (=the horse that everyone thought would win) *came in last, to everyone's surprise. | It's odds-on that she won't come.*

ode /əʊd/ *n* a usu. long poem addressed to a person or thing

O·de·on /'əʊdiən/ *n* [C;U] (a cinema run by) a company which operates cinemas in most British cities

O·din /'əʊdɪn/ also **Woden**– in Norse MYTHOLOGY, the highest god and maker of the universe; the God of wisdom, poetry, farming, war, and the dead

o·di·ous /'əʊdiəs/ *adj fml* hateful; very unpleasant — ~ **ly** *adv*

o·di·um /'əʊdiəm/ *n* [U] *fml* widespread hatred: *to be exposed to/held in public odium*

o·dom·e·ter /əʊ'dɒmɪtə^r‖-'dɑː-/ *n AmE for* MILEOMETER

o·do·rif·er·ous /ˌəʊdər'ɪfərəs◂/ *adj fml or humor* having a smell, esp. a pleasant one

o·do·rous /'əʊdərəs/ *adj fml* having a smell —compare MALODOROUS

o·dour *BrE* ‖ **-dor** *AmE* /'əʊdə^r/ *n* **1** *rather fml* a smell, esp. an unpleasant one **2** *BrE* **in bad odour (with)** *fml* badly thought of (by): *I've been in bad odour with the boss since he discovered that I had criticized him.* — ~ **less** *adj*: *an odourless deodorant*

O·dys·se·us /ə'dɪsiəs‖əʊ-/ also **Ulysses**– in CLASSICAL MYTHOLOGY, the King of Ithaca, husband of Penelope, and leader of the Greeks in the Trojan War, noted for his bravery and cleverness

od·ys·sey /'ɒdɪsi‖'ɑː-/ *n esp. lit* **1** [*the* + cap.] the story of Odysseus' ten-year journey home after the Trojan War, as told by Homer **2** a long adventurous journey marked by many changes of fortune

OECD /ˌəʊ iː siː 'diː/ [the] the Organization for Economic Cooperation and Development; an international group of wealthy countries who work together for developing trade and economic growth. Most western European countries are members, along with Australia, Canada, Japan, New Zealand and the US.

OED /ˌəʊ iː 'diː/ *abbrev. for:* Oxford English Dictionary

oe·di·pal /'iːdɪpəl‖'ed-/ *adj* related to an Oedipus complex: *Oedipal longings/fantasies*

Oe·di·pus /'iːdɪpəs‖'ed-/ in CLASSICAL MYTHOLOGY, the son of King Laius and Queen Jocasta of Thebes, who was adopted (ADOPT (1)) by the King of Corinth. As an adult, Oedipus returned to Thebes and, without knowing who they were, killed his father and married his mother. His story is told in the play *Oedipus Rex* by Sophocles.

Oe·di·pus com·plex /'iːdɪpəs ˌkɒmpleks‖'ed-pəs ˌkɑːm-/ *n* (in Freudian PSYCHOLOGY) an unconscious sexual desire by a child for the parent of the opposite sex, esp. by a young boy for his mother combined with hatred of his father

OEM /ˌəʊ iː 'em/ *n tech* original equipment manufacturer; a company that makes esp. computer equipment and sells it to other companies who use it in their own products which are sold to the public: *Our firm is an OEM for several hardware vendors.*

o'er /əʊə^r/ *adv, prep poet* over

oe·soph·a·gus *esp. BrE* ‖ usu. **esophagus** *AmE* /ɪ'sɒf-əgəs‖ɪ'sɑː-/ *n med* the food tube leading from the mouth down into the stomach —see picture at RESPIRATORY

oes·tro·gen *BrE* ‖ **es-** *AmE* /'iːstrədʒən‖'es-/ *n* [U] a substance produced in the female OVARY, which causes certain changes in the body in preparation for the production of young. It is widely used in ORAL CONTRACEPTIVES and HORMONE REPLACEMENT THERAPY, usu. with PROGESTERONE.

oeu·vre /'ɜːvrə/ *n Fr* all the works of an artist, such as a painter, writer, etc.: *Picasso's/Forster's oeuvre*

of /əv, ə; *strong* ɒv‖əv, ə; *strong* ɑːv/ *prep* **1** belonging to: *the colour of her dress | the roots of your hair | the size of the wings | the leg of the table* (compare *John's leg, the dog's leg*) —see USAGE **2** made from: *a dress of silk | a crown of gold* **3** containing: *a bag of potatoes | a book of poems | a glass of beer* **4** (shows a part in relation to a whole): *two pounds of sugar | much of the night | two kilometres of bad road | lots of money | a blade of grass | a drop of oil* **5** from the group that includes: *members of the team | one of his last poems | the two of us | both of us | the older of the two | the most important of all | a sort of basket* **6 a** (used in dates): *the 27th of February* **b** *AmE* (used in telling time) before: *It's five (minutes) of two.* (=1.55) **c** during: *They always like to go there of an evening.* **7** that is/are; being: *the City of New York | the art of painting | at the age of eight | the problem of unemployment | a price increase of 15 per cent | some fool of a boy* (=some foolish boy) **8 a** directed towards; felt for or done to: *the villagers' fear of an earthquake | the killing of innocent civilians* **b** felt by or done by: *the fear of the villagers | the howling of the dogs | the attacks of her opponents* **9** (of works of art or literature) **a** written, painted, etc., by: *the plays of Shakespeare* **b** about; having as a subject: *a picture of John* **10** in relation to; connected with: *the King of England | the results of the meeting | a teacher of English | the time of arrival | east of Suez | the advantages of using a computer | slow of speech |*

to die of hunger | fond of swimming | to cure him of a dis-
ease | within a mile of here (=not more than a mile from
here) | a lover of music **11** with; having: an area of low
rainfall|high unemployment | a woman of ability | a mat-
ter of no importance **12** (showing origin) coming from:
a man of the people | Jesus of Nazareth **13** (showing
cause) by; through: She did it of her own free will. | It
didn't happen of itself. **14** (used in the pattern adj+of,
for making a judgment about behaviour): How kind of
John to buy the tickets! | It was typical of the government
to raise the tax on beer.

▷ USAGE Use **'s** rather than **of** to mean "belonging to a
person or something alive": Compare John**'s** aim | the
dog**'s** leg | my father**'s** character | the girls**'** dresses with
the arm **of** the chair | the leg **of** the table | the character
of the new building. **'s** is used in expressions of time
like a day**'s** work | Let's meet in a year**'s** time. It is some-
times used with place-names, especially in
newspapers, to save space: London**'s** traffic | Britain**'s**
athletes.◁

off¹ /ɒf‖ɔːf/ adj, adv [F] **1** away from or no longer in a
place or position: They got into the car and drove off. |
Catch this bus and get off (=out of the bus) at the station. |
We turned off (=aside) into a side road. | Goodbye! I'm off
now. (=I'm leaving) | They're off! (=the race has started) |
(old-fash) Be off with you! (=go away) | The show got **off**
to a good start. (=started well) **2** to or at a particular
distance away in time or space: two miles off | several
years off **3** in or into a state of being disconnected or re-
moved: The door handle fell off. | Take off your shoes.|
How do you get this lid off? | to cut off a branch from a
tree | If you buy more than ten, they knock 20p off the price.
4 (esp. of a machine or electrical apparatus) not work-
ing; not operating: Turn the light/the tap off. | The TV is
off. | Switch off the engine before you put any petrol in.
—opposite **on** **5** so as to be completely finished or no
longer there: Finish the work off before you go home. |
They killed off all the mosquitoes. **6** (of food) **a** esp. BrE
no longer good to eat or drink: The milk is off/has gone
off. **b** no longer being served in a restaurant: Sorry,
madam, strawberries are off. **7** away or free from regu-
lar work: have Monday off | I'm taking a week off over
Christmas. | The maid is off today. —see also DAY OFF **8**
(of behaviour) not quite right; not as good as usual: Her
work has gone off lately. | (infml) I thought it was a bit
off, not even answering my letter! **9** not going to happen
after all: I'm afraid the party's off. | Their engagement's
off. —compare ON² (6) **10** [(for)] having a stated amount
of something, esp. money: They're **badly off**/not **well off.**
(=They're poor.) | You'd be **better off** with a bicycle
rather than that old car. | How are you off for clean socks?
(=have you enough?) —see also BADLY-OFF, WELL-OFF **11**
(of actors) not on the stage but able to be heard in the
theatre; OFFSTAGE: voices off **12 off and on** also on and
off— from time to time; sometimes **13 off the top of
one's head** without thinking or preparation **14 right
off**/(esp. BrE) **straight off** at once

off² prep **1** not on; away from (a surface that is touched
or rested on): Get off my foot! | Keep off the grass. | She
jumped off the bus. **2** from (something that supports or
holds up): Take the curtains off their hooks. | to eat off
golden plates **3 a** disconnected or removed from: A button has come off my shirt. **b** subtracted or taken away
from: cut a piece off the loaf | knock five dollars off the
price | (infml) He borrowed a pound off me. **4** to or at a
particular distance away from in time or space: The ship
was blown off course. | We're going (right) off the subject. |
(fig.) We're a long way off understanding this yet. **5** (esp.
of a road) turning away from (a larger one): a narrow
street off the High Street | Our house is just off/50 metres
off the main road. **6** in the sea near: an island off the
coast of France | six miles off Portsmouth **7** (of a person)
a BrE no longer wanting: He's off his food. | I've gone
off/I'm right off her books for some reason. **b** no longer
taking (esp. medicine): The doctor took her off the pills.

off³ adj [A] **1** (of a period) **a** marked by lower than usual
standards of performance: I'm afraid this is one of his off
days; he usually plays better. **b** with less than usual activity; quiet: Tickets are cheaper during the off season. **2**
[no comp.] of a pair, the one on the right; OFFSIDE: the off
wheel of a cart —opposite **near**

off⁴ also **off side**— n [the] that part of a cricket field in front
and to the right of the (right-handed) player who hits the

ball (BATSMAN) as he faces the player who BOWLs it —
opposite **leg**

off⁵ v [T] AmE sl to kill

off- —see WORD FORMATION

of·fal /'ɒfəl‖'ɔː-, 'ɑː-/ BrE ‖ **variety meats** AmE— n [U]
the heart, head, brains, etc., of an animal, used as food

Of·fa's Dyke /ˌɒfəz 'daɪk‖ˌɔːf-/ a long bank of earth put up
between Wales and the Anglo-Saxon kingdom of Mercia,
by King **Offa** of Mercia in the eighth century. Parts of
it can still be seen, and it is followed by a public path.

off·beat /ˌɒf'biːt◀‖ˌɔːf-/ adj infml unusual; not CONVEN-
TIONAL: offbeat clothes/tastes/ideas

off-break /'· ·/ n (in cricket) a slow ball that turns from the
off (OFF⁴) side to the leg (LEG (7)) side when it bounces
(BOUNCE)

off Broad·way /ˌ· '···◀/ adv AmE **1** (of theatre in new York)
not in the main professional group of theatres, but more
unusual or EXPERIMENTAL in nature: His new play about
life in a women's prison is opening off Broadway. **2 off-
off Broadway** more unusual, or perhaps extreme, than
off Broadway —**off-Broadway** adj : an off-Broadway
production of Hamlet

off-chance /'· ·/ n a very unlikely possibility: I'm just waiting here on the off-chance that the Queen will walk past.

off col·our /ˌ· '···◀/ adj **1** BrE not well: She's been feeling
a bit off colour for the last day or two. **2** sexually improper: The nightclub comedian told some rather off-
colour jokes.

off-du·ty /ˌ· '···/ adj (of someone in a profession or armed
service) not working: an off-duty policeman

of·fence BrE ‖ **offense** AmE /ə'fens/ n **1** [C (**against**)] an
act of wrongdoing, esp. of breaking the law; crime: Driv-
ing while drunk is a serious offence/is not a minor offence. |
They won't imprison him for a **first offence.** (=his first
crime) | The defendant asked for ten similar offences to
be taken into consideration. (=asked for his/her sentence
to be made less severe because he/she had admitted to
the ten other crimes) | His evil crimes were an offence
against the whole of humanity. **2** [U] cause for hurt feel-
ings: to give/cause offence to someone | I hope you won't
take offence (=feel offended) if I ask you not to smoke. |
Don't be upset by what he said — he **meant no offence.**
(=did not intend to offend you) **3** [C (**to**)] something that
causes displeasure: That dirty old house is an offence to
the eye|to everyone who lives in the street.

of·fend /ə'fend/ v **1** [T often pass.] to hurt the feelings of;
upset: I was very offended that you forgot my birthday. |
I hope you won't be offended if I don't finish this cake. **2**
[T] to cause displeasure to; be offensive to: Cruelty to
animals offends many people. **3** [I (**against**)] fml to do
wrong: to offend against good manners|good taste

of·fend·er /ə'fendər/ n someone who offends, esp. a criminal: They don't usually imprison **first offenders.**
(=people found guilty for the first time)

of·fend·ing /ə'fendɪŋ/ adj [A] often humor causing displeasure, discomfort, or inconvenience: I had bad toothache
and decided to have the offending tooth removed.

of·fense /'ɒfens‖'ɔː-fens, 'ɑː-/ n AmE **1** OFFENCE (1), (2),
and (3) **2** the part of a game concerned with making
points and winning: He plays offense for the Bears.‖We'll
never win if we don't improve our offense. —opposite
defense

of·fen·sive¹ /ə'fensɪv/ adj **1** causing offence; unpleasant:
offensive remarks|smells | I found him extremely offen-
sive. | crude jokes that are offensive to women —opposite
inoffensive **2** of or for attacking: offensive weapons |
The troops took up offensive positions. —opposite **defensive** **3** AmE of the offense in a game: an offensive play
—**-ly** adv —**-ness** n [U]

offensive² n **1** a continued military attack: The enemy
launched a full-scale offensive. **2 on the offensive** making an attack or ready to attack **3 take the offensive**
to attack first

of·fer¹ /'ɒfər‖'ɔː-, 'ɑː-/ v **1** [T (**to**)] to hold out (to a person) for acceptance or refusal: The police are offering a
big reward for any information about the murder. | May
I offer a suggestion? | Offer some coffee to the guests.
[+obj(i)+obj(d)] They've offered us £60,000 for the house.
Shall we take it? | I've been offered a job in advertising.
2 [I;T+to-v;obj] to express willingness (to do something):

She offered to drive me to the station. | *I don't need any help, but it was kind of you to offer.* **3** [T] to provide; give: *This agreement does not offer much hope of a lasting peace.* | *The booklet offers practical advice to people with housing problems.* **4** [T (UP, **to**)] to give (to God): *He offered (up) a prayer|a sacrifice.*

offer² *n* **1** a statement offering (to do) something: *an offer of assistance* | *a firm offer* (=a promise, esp. to pay a certain amount of money) | *They made us an offer we couldn't refuse.* **2** something which is offered: *an offer of £5* | *He made a generous offer for the house.* —see also OFFERING **3 on offer** *BrE*||**on sale** *AmE* for sale, esp. cheaply: *They've got cornflakes on offer|on special offer this week.* **4 under offer** *BrE* (of a house, flat, etc., for sale) already having a possible buyer who has offered money —see REFUSE (USAGE)

of·fer·ing /ˈɒfərɪŋ||ˈɔː-, ˈɑː-/ *n* something offered, esp. to God —see also BURNT OFFERING, PEACE OFFERING

of·fer·to·ry /ˈɒfətəri||ˈɔːfətɔːri, ˈɑː-/ *n* (the collection of) the money people give during a religious service

off guard /ˌ· ˈ·◄/ *adj* not paying attention, not ALERT: *These comments were made when she was off guard.* | *an off-guard moment*

off·hand /ˌɒfˈhænd◄||ˌɔːf-/ *adv, adj* **1** careless or disrespectful in manner; CASUAL: *She was rather offhand (with me).* **2** at once; without time to think or prepare: *I can't give you the exact figures offhand.* – ~**edly** *adv* – ~**edness** *n* [U]

of·fice /ˈɒfɪs||ˈɒː-, ˈɑː-/ *n* **1** [C] a room or building where written work, accounts, etc., are done (esp. in connection with a business or organization): *the manager's office* | *"Where's Dad?" "He's gone to the office."* | *The company is moving to new offices in central London.* | *Their new head office is in Tokyo.* | *during office hours* (=between about nine and five o'clock) | *office equipment* —see picture at OPEN PLAN **2** [C] a place where a particular service is provided: *a ticket office* —see also BOX OFFICE, POST OFFICE **3** [C] *BrE* (*usu. caps.*) a government department: *the Foreign Office* **4** [C;U] a position of responsibility and power, esp. in government: *the office of President* | *to hold (public) office* | *Our party has been in|out of office for three years.* —see also GOOD OFFICES

office block /ˈ·· ·/ *BrE* ‖ **office build·ing** *AmE* /ˈ·· ··/– *n* a large building divided into offices

office boy /ˈ·· ·/ **office girl** *fem.*– *n* a young person employed to do the less important work in an office

of·fice·hold·er /ˈɒfɪsˌhəʊldəʳ||ˈɔː-, ˈɑː-/ *n* one who holds a position, esp. in government

Office of Fair Trad·ing /ˌ··· · ˈ··/ (*abbrev.* **OFT**) [*the*] a British government organization whose job is to protect the public against unfair business practices

Office of Man·age·ment and Bud·get /ˌ··· · ˌ··· · ˈ··/ (*abbrev.* **OMB**) [*the*] an American organization used by the president and his staff to help organize government departments and activities and to prepare the BUDGET (plan for using money)

office par·ty /ˈ··· ˈ··/ *n* a party held esp. on or just before Christmas Eve in the office of a firm or a government organization or at a place nearby. It is usu. a relaxed occasion in which employers and workers alike drink a lot of alcohol and behave less formally than usual towards each other. People sometimes make jokes about office parties because it is said that there is often a lot of sex and drunkenness.

of·fi·cer /ˈɒfɪsəʳ||ˈɔː-, ˈɑː-/ *n* **1** a person in a position of command in the armed forces: *The officers live here, and the enlisted men over there.* —see also FLYING OFFICER, NCO **2** a person who holds a position of some importance, esp. in government, a business, or a club: *a local government officer* | *the Public Health Officer* | *a customs officer* —see also RETURNING OFFICER **3** a policeman: *Certainly, officer!* | (*AmE*) *Officer Jones will help you.*

▷ USAGE **Civil servants** are people who work for the government, and an **official** is someone who works for a government or other large organization in a position of responsibility: *a meeting between* **civil servants** *from the Department of Transport and important railway* **officials**. An **officer** is usually a member of the armed forces in a position of command, or a member of the police force, but the word is sometimes used like **official**. A **clerk** is an office worker of fairly low rank.

This word is also used in American English for someone who works in a shop (a **sales clerk**), but in British English **shop assistant** is used.◁

officers' quar·ters /ˈ··· ˌ··/ *n* [P] buildings or rooms in a military camp etc. where officers live

of·fi·cial¹ /əˈfɪʃəl/ *n* a person who holds an OFFICE (4): *a union|government official* —see OFFICER (USAGE)

official² *adj* **1** of, from, or about a person in a position of power and responsibility: *an official position* | *official duties* | *You have to get official permission to build a new house.* | *an official inquiry into the cause of the accident* **2** made known publicly: *Their engagement is not official yet.* —opposite **unofficial** —see also OFFICIALLY

▷ USAGE Compare *an* **official** *letter about my income tax* and *a rather* **officious** *letter from my neighbour, complaining about the noise from my radio.*◁

Official Birth·day /ˌ·· ˈ··/ [*the*] the day (the second Saturday in June) when the Queen or King of England's birthday is officially celebrated; it is not her/his real birthday. The ceremonies of Trooping the Colour and giving the Birthday Honours take place on the Official Birthday.

of·fi·cial·dom /əˈfɪʃəldəm/ *n* [U] *often derog* officials as a group

of·fi·cial·ese /əˌfɪʃəˈliːz/ *n* [U] *infml derog* the language of government officials, considered unnecessarily hard to understand

official list /ˌ··· ˈ·/ *n* a list of current prices of STOCKS¹ (3) and SHARES¹ (2), printed daily by the London STOCK EXCHANGE

of·fi·cial·ly /əˈfɪʃəli/ *adv* **1** publicly and/or formally: *They have officially announced their engagement.* | *The new hospital was officially opened last week.* **2** according to what is stated publicly (but may not be true): *Officially, he's on holiday; actually, he's in hospital.* —opposite **unofficially**

official re·ceiv·er /ˌ··· ·ˈ··/ *n* (*often caps.*) a RECEIVER (3)

Official Se·crets Act /ˌ··· ˈ·· ˌ·/ [*the*] a law passed by the British Parliament which forbids people who work for the government to discuss their work with anyone who is not covered by the Act. Workers must sign a document in agreement to this, which is known as 'signing the Official Secrets Act', and they can be put in prison if they break this promise. —compare FREEDOM OF INFORMATION ACT

of·fi·ci·ate /əˈfɪʃieɪt/ *v* [I (**at**)] to perform official duties: *Two priests officiated at the wedding.*

of·fi·cious /əˈfɪʃəs/ *adj derog* too eager to give orders or to offer advice: *An officious little guard came and told me not to whistle in the museum garden.* —see OFFICIAL (USAGE) – ~**ly** *adv* – ~**ness** *n* [U]

off·ing /ˈɒfɪŋ||ˈɔː-, ˈɑː-/ *n* **in the offing** coming soon: *I think in her case a promotion is in the offing.*

off·li·cence /ˈ·· ··/ *n BrE* a shop where alcohol is sold to be taken away. It may also sell other things, e.g. newspapers and chocolates: *If you're going past the off-licence could you get me some beer and some crisps?*

off lim·its /ˌ· ˈ··◄/ *adj* not open to anyone who does not have permission to enter, take part, etc.: *Off-limits areas of discussion* | *The officers' quarters are off limits to non-army personnel.*

off·line /ˈɒflaɪn||ˈɔːf-/ *adj, adv* not directly connected to and/or controlled by a computer: *an offline terminal*‖ *Your job just knocked the printer offline.* –opposite **online**

off·load /ˌ·· ˈ·/ *v* [T (**onto**)] to get rid of (something unwanted): *We managed to off-load all those old typewriters (onto a friend of mine).*

off·peak /ˌ·· ˈ·◄/ *adj* **1** less busy: *Telephone charges are lower during off-peak periods.* **2** used or in effect during less busy periods: *off-peak electricity* | *Big reductions for off-peak holidays.* —compare PEAK¹ (3)

off·print /ˈɒfprɪnt||ˈɔːf-/ *n* a separately printed article from a magazine: *offprints of articles about physics from "Scientific American"*

off·put·ting /ˈ·· ··/ *adj* unpleasantly surprising and/or causing dislike: *I found his aggressive manner rather off-putting.* —see also PUT off

off·road ve·hi·cle /ˌ·· · ˈ···/ *n* a vehicle which is built very strongly, so that it may be used over rough ground where there are no proper roads or none at all. In Britain, many people who spend most of their time in towns and cities still buy off-road vehicles because they are fashionable and look impressive.

off·set[1] /ˈɒfset, ˌɒfˈset‖ˈɔːfset, ˌɔːfˈset/ v offset; present participle offsetting [T] to make up for; balance: The cost of getting there was offset by the fact that the hotels are so cheap. | He offset his travel expenses against tax.

off·set[2] /ˈɒfset‖ˈɔːf-/ n, adj of or being a method of printing in which ink is moved onto rollers before it goes on the paper. Very many books, magazines, and newspapers are printed this way in Western countries.

off·shoot /ˈɒfʃuːt‖ˈɔːf-/ n a new stem or branch: (fig.) an offshoot of a large organization

off·shore /ˌɒfˈʃɔːʳ‖ˌɔːf-/ adv, adj 1 in the water, at a distance from the shore: Britain's offshore oil [after n] two miles offshore 2 (of financial matters) based abroad in countries where the tax system is more favourable than in the home country: offshore banking | an offshore account/fund

▶CULTURAL NOTE This word has a negative meaning for some people who think that firms using offshore banks etc. are dishonestly avoiding paying tax in Britain.◀

3 (coming or moving) away from the shore: an offshore wind —compare INSHORE, ONSHORE

off·side /ˌɒfˈsaɪd◀‖ˌɔːf-/ adj, adv 1 (in certain sports) in a position in which play is not allowed: That player is offside. [after n] She's two yards offside. —opposite onside 2 [A no comp.] esp. BrE on the right-hand side, esp. of an animal or of a car or road: the offside rear light of a car —opposite nearside

off side /ˈ· ·/ n [the] the OFF[4]

off spin /ˈ· ·/ n [U] (in cricket) SPIN that makes a ball turn from the off (OFF[4]) side towards the leg (LEG (7)) side when it bounces

off·spring /ˈɒfˌsprɪŋ‖ˈɔːf-/ n offspring fml or humor (not with an) a child or children from particular parents, of a particular number, etc.: They have several offspring. | Is this your offspring?

off·stage /ˌɒfˈsteɪdʒ◀‖ˌɔːf-/ adv, adj not on the open stage; out of sight of those watching a play: He ran offstage. | a loud crash offstage

off-street /ˈ· ·/ adj [A] away from the main streets (often in the phrase off-street parking)

off-the-cuff /ˌ· · ˈ·◀/ adj, adv (said) without thinking deeply before speaking, unprepared: an off-the-cuff speech | remarks made off-the-cuff

off-the-peg /ˌ· · ˈ·◀/ BrE ‖ off-the-rack AmE adj, adv (of clothes, etc.) made to standard sizes and so easy to find: She's slim and of average height, so she can buy her dresses off the peg. | (fig.) There are several off-the-peg forms for making your own will. —compare MADE-TO-MEASURE, OFF-THE-SHELF

off-the-rec·ord /ˌ· · ˈ···◀/ adj, adv (given or made) unofficially and not to be written down in the notes of the meeting, publicly reported, etc.: The Prime Minister's remarks were strictly off-the-record. | Off the record, I agree with your criticisms.

off-the-shelf /ˌ· · ˈ·◀/ adj, adv AmE READY-MADE and available: an off-the-shelf software package

▷ USAGE AmE uses off-the-rack for clothes and off-the-shelf for most other things; BrE uses off-the-peg for both. —compare OFF-THE-PEG◁

off-the-wall /ˌ· · ˈ·◀/ adj infml, esp. AmE amusingly foolish; ZANY: This idea is really off-the-wall.

off·track /ˈɒftræk‖ˈɔːf-/ adj AmE away from a RACETRACK: Only a few states allow offtrack betting.

off-white /ˌ· ˈ·◀/ adj having a colour that is not a pure white but has some grey or yellow in it —off-white n [U]

Of·gas, **OFGAS** /ˈɒfgæs‖ˈɔːf-/ a British government organization which aims to make sure that there are no unfair or bad practices, and controls prices, in the gas industry —compare OFTEL, OFWAT

OFT /ˌɒu ef ˈtiː/ abbrev. for: OFFICE OF FAIR TRADING

oft /ɒft‖ɔːft/ adv poet (usu. in comb.) often: oft-repeated advice

Of·tel, **OFTEL** /ˈɒftel‖ˈɔːf-/ the Office of Telecommunications; a British government organization which aims to

make sure that there are no unfair or bad practices, and controls prices, in the telecommunications industry — compare OFGAS, OFWAT

of·ten /ˈɒfən, ˈɒftən‖ˈɔːf-/ adv 1 many times: "How often do you go there?" "Once a month, but I'd like to go more often." | I've often heard it said that he is the cleverest person in the government. 2 in many cases: Americans are often very tall. | It's often difficult to translate poems. 3 as often as not quite often; at least half of the time 4 do you come here often? humor a phrase used by a man as a way of introducing himself to a woman he is interested in sexually. The humorous answer is "only in the mating (MATE[2]) season". 5 every so often from time to time 6 more often than not more than half of the time; usually: More often than not she misses the bus. —see NEVER (USAGE)

Of·wat, **OFWAT** /ˈɒfwɒt‖ˈɔːfwɔːt, -wɑːt/ a British government organization which aims to make sure that there are no unfair or bad practices, and controls prices, in the water supply industry —compare OFGAS, OFTEL

Og·den /ˈɒgdən‖ˈɑːg-/, **Hil·da** /ˈhɪldə/ a character from British television's Coronation Street who is considered to be a STEREOTYPE of a British WORKING-CLASS woman. She always wears CURLERS and a SCARF on her head, and is known for being very interested in what other people are doing and wanting to talk about it and give her opinions.

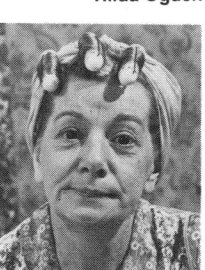

Hilda Ogden

o·gle /ˈəʊgəl/ v [I (at);T] derog to look (at) with great interest, esp. sexual interest: old men ogling young girls

O grade /ˈəʊ greɪd/ n 1 [U] the lower level of the Scottish Certificate of Education 2 an examination of this standard in a particular subject: She took eight O grades. —compare HIGHER, O LEVEL

o·gre /ˈəʊgəʳ/ **o·gress** /ˈəʊgrɪs/ fem.— n 1 a fierce creature in children's stories, like a very large person, who is thought to eat children 2 a frightening person: Our boss is a bit of an ogre.

oh /əʊ/ interj 1 (expressing surprise, fear, etc.): Oh, how dreadful! | Oh no, not again! 2 (used before a name when calling someone): Oh, David, come here a moment!

OH written abbrev. for: OHIO

O'Ha·ra /əʊˈhɑːrə‖-ˈhæ-/, **Scar·lett** /ˈskɑːlɪt‖ˈskɑːr-/ the main female character (HEROINE) in the book and film Gone With the Wind, who was very clever and often cruel in getting the men and other things she wanted —see also SOUTHERN BELLE —see colour picture on page 685

O'Hare /əʊˈheəʳ/ O'Hare International Airport; the airport which serves Chicago, in the US. It is the busiest airport in the world.

O·hi·o /əʊˈhaɪəʊ/ written abbrev. **OH** state in the MIDWEST of the US, known for its engineering and farming —see colour map on pages 1374–5

ohm /əʊm/ n tech the standard unit of electrical RESISTANCE, which allows one AMP to flow under a pressure of one VOLT

OHMS /ˌəʊ eɪtʃ em ˈes/ abbrev. On Her (or His) Majesty's Service; (on letters, etc.) sent officially by the Civil Service, or government departments

o·ho /əʊˈhəʊ/ interj lit or old use (expressing surprise or joy at success)

Oh Su·san·na /ˌəʊ suːˈzænə/ an old popular American song

oil[1] /ɔɪl/ n [U] 1 (often in comb.) any of several types of thick fatty liquid (from animals, plants, or under the ground) used for burning, making machines run easily, cooking, etc.: olive oil | coconut oil | hair oil 2 PETROLEUM: The price of oil has gone up. | After drilling for several weeks they finally struck oil. (=found it underground) | the oil industry —see also OILS, OILY, burn the midnight oil (BURN[1] (15)), pour oil on troubled waters (POUR)

oil[2] v [T] 1 to put or rub oil on or into: to oil a bicycle | to oil the hinges to stop them squeaking 2 oil the wheels *infml* fig. to make things go more smoothly, esp. in business, sometimes by offering people illegal gifts of money, etc.

oil-bear·ing /ˈ·ˌ··/ *adj* (esp. of areas underground) containing oil: *oil-bearing rock/strata*

oil-can /ˈɔɪlkæn/ *n* an oil container (usu. with a long thin neck) used for oiling machinery

oil-cloth /ˈɔɪlklɒθ‖-klɔːθ/ *n* [U] cloth treated with oil and used for covering tables, shelves, etc. because it is easy to WIPE clean

oil-field /ˈɔɪlfiːld/ *n* an area under which there is oil: *oilfields in the desert/under the North Sea*

oil-fired /ˈ·ˌ·/ *adj* (esp. of a heating system) burning oil to produce heat

oil·man /ˈɔɪlmən/ *n* **-men** /mən/ a worker or businessman in the oil industry

oil paint /ˈ·ˌ·/ *n* [C;U] OILS

oil paint·ing /ˈ·ˌ··/ *n* **1** [U] the art or activity of painting in OILS **2** [C] a picture painted in OILS —compare WATER-COLOUR (3) **3** *BrE* **no oil painting** *infml, often humor* (someone or something that is) not at all beautiful

oil pan /ˈ·ˌ·/ *n AmE for* SUMP

oil·rig /ˈɔɪlrɪg/, also **oil plat·form** /ˈ·ˌ··/— *n* a large piece of equipment for getting oil from underground, esp. from under the sea

oils /ɔɪlz/ *n* [P] paints (esp. for pictures) containing oil: *to paint in oils* —compare WATERCOLOUR

oil-skin /ˈɔɪl-skɪn/ *n* [C;U] (a garment made of) cloth treated with oil so that water will not pass through it: *a fisherman in oilskins*

oil slick /ˈ·ˌ·/ also **slick**— *n* a usu. long, wide sheet of oil floating on water, esp. as a result of accident to an oil-carrying ship

oil tank·er /ˈ·ˌ··/ *n* a ship with large containers for carrying oil

oil well /ˈ·ˌ·/ *n* a hole made in the ground from which oil is obtained —see picture at DIAGRAM

oil·y /ˈɔɪli/ *adj* **1** of, about, or like oil: *an oily liquid* **2** covered with or containing oil: *oily fried food/hair* **3** *derog* unpleasantly polite; UNCTUOUS: *an oily manner*

oink /ɔɪŋk/ *v* [I] *infml* to make the sound that a pig makes —**oink** *n*

oint·ment /ˈɔɪntmənt/ *n* [C;U] an oily substance, often medicinal, to be rubbed on the skin —see also **fly in the ointment** (FLY³ (5))

OJ /ˌəʊ ˈdʒeɪ/ *n* [U] *AmE infml* orange juice: *Eggs over easy, hashbrowns, and a glass of OJ, please.*

O·jib·wa, Ojibway /əʊˈdʒɪbweɪ, -wə/ *n* [C; *the*+P] see CHIPPEWA

OK *written abbrev. for* OKLAHOMA

o·kay¹, OK /əʊˈkeɪ/ *adj, adv infml* **1 a** all right: *The car's going okay now.* | *Is my hair okay?* | *Is it OK with/by you if I borrow this book?* | *"Sorry I'm late." "That's OK."* **b** satisfactory, but not wonderful: *"What was the film like?" "Oh, OK, I suppose."* **2** (asking for or expressing agreement, or giving permission) all right; agreed: *Let's go there, okay?* | *"Can I use your car?" "OK."* **3 OK, yah** (an expression of agreement thought to be typically said by YUPPIEs and HOORAY HENRYs)

okay², OK *v* **okayed, OKed; okaying, OKing** [T] *infml* to agree to; give permission to: *Has the bank okayed your request for a loan?*

okay³, OK *n* **okays, OKs** *infml* approval; permission: *I got the OK to leave early.*

OK Cor·ral /ˌəʊ keɪ kəˈrɑːl‖-ˈræl/ a CORRAL (an enclosure for horses) in the town of Tombstone, Arizona, in 1881 the scene of a famous gunfight in which the SHERIFF, Virgil Earp, with his brothers Wyatt and Morgan, and Doc Holliday, fought against the Clanton GANG. Three of the Clanton gang were killed but the leader, Ike, and another escaped. The people of Tombstone dismissed Virgil Earp as sheriff because they believed that the Earps were not fighting crime but had murdered the Clantons, with whom they had had many disagreements. The story was made into a well-known film, *Gunfight at the OK Corral*, and this phrase is sometimes used humorously by someone talking about a fight involving several people: *It was*

more like the gunfight at the OK Corral than a football match

O·kee·cho·bee /ˌəʊkɪˈtʃəʊbi/, **Lake** a large lake of fresh water in S Florida, US. Water flows from it into the Atlantic Ocean through the Everglades.

O'Keeffe /əʊˈkiːf/, **Georgia** (1887–1986) an American artist most remembered for her large, beautiful paintings of flowers and animal bones

O·ke·fe·no·kee Swamp /ˌəʊkɪfɪnəʊki ˈswɒmp‖-ˈswɑːmp/ a large area of SWAMP land in the US, in SE Georgia and NE Florida. It is the home of many ALLIGATORs and many kinds of snake and bird. Most of the area is now included in the **Okefenokee National Wildlife Refuge.**

o·key-doke /ˌəʊki ˈdəʊk/ also **okey-do·key** /-ˈdəʊki/— *adj, adv infml* OKAY¹

O·kie /ˈəʊki/ *n AmE infml often derog* **1** a person from Oklahoma **2** an uneducated person with narrow opinions; HICK

Ok·i·na·wa /ˌɒkɪˈnɑːwə‖ˌəʊ-/ an island in the W Pacific Ocean, SW of Kyushu, Japan, the scene of fierce fighting between American and Japanese forces during 1945

O·kla·ho·ma /ˌəʊkləˈhəʊmə/ *written abbrev.* **OK** a state in the Great Plains of the US, noted for its minerals and its large Native American population. Its farm lands became part of the DUST BOWL in the 1930s. —see colour map on pages 1374–5

Oklahoma! the title of a MUSICAL² by Rodgers and Hammerstein. It was a great success in the US and Britain in the 1950s and was also made into a film.

Oklahoma Cit·y /ˌ···· ˈ··/ the state capital of Oklahoma, US, established in one night in 1889 —see colour map on pages 1374–5

o·kra /ˈɒkrə, ˈəʊ-‖ˈəʊ-/ also **lady's fingers**— *n* [U] a long thin green vegetable which is the seed POD of a flower thought of by many Britons as an unusual vegetable

old /əʊld/ *adj* **1** having lived or existed for a long time: *an old man* | *a big old house* | *old and young people* | *old and new books/ideas* | *an old British tradition* [also *n*, *the*+P] *The old* (=old people) *and the young do not always understand each other.* **2** (of things) having existed or been in use long enough to show signs of use or be no longer fresh: *old shoes* | *an old car* | *This bread is a bit old.* | *She always gives the same old speech.* **3** having a particular age; of age: *You're old enough to dress yourself now.* | *Is your car as old as/older than mine?* [latter *n*] *"How old is the baby?" "She's eight months old."* | *a 16-year-old girl* **4** [A] having continued in the relationship for a long time: *We are (very) old friends.* | *She's an old schoolfriend of mine.* **5** [A *no comp.*] former: *He got his old job back.* **6** [A] known for a long time: *an old joke* | *the old familiar routine* | *Good old John!* **7** [A *no comp.*] *infml* (used for making **any** stronger): *Come any old time.* **8 (as) old as the hills** very old **9 for 'old times' sake** because of or as a reminder of happy times in the past **10 of old: a** *lit* long ago; in the past: *days of old* **b** *rare* since a long time ago: *I know him of old.* **11 you're as old as you feel** a phrase often used to make someone feel happier if they are sad because they think they are getting too old **12 you're never too old to learn** an old saying

▷ USAGE When speaking of people, **elderly** is a polite way of saying old. Compare *an old church* and *an old/elderly lady.* —see also ELDER (USAGE)◁

Old *adj* [A] (of a language) of an early period in the history of the language: *Old English* | *Old Irish* —compare MIDDLE, MODERN¹ (3)

old age /ˌ· ˈ·◂/ *n* [U] the part of one's life when one is old: *He was still active in (his) old age.* | *The effects of old age.*

old age pen·sion /ˌ· · ˈ··/ also **retirement pension**— *n* [(*the*) U] *esp. BrE* money paid regularly by the state to old people —see also OAP — ~ **er** *n*

Old Bai·ley /ˌəʊld ˈbeɪli/ also **Central Criminal Court**— [the] the CROWN COURT (=the court above the MAGISTRATES' COURT for trying criminal cases) for Greater London, actually named after the street (**Old Bailey**) in which it is to be found. Many famous criminals, including murderers and TRAITORs, have been tried at the Old Bailey, and most British people are familiar with the name and with the figure of JUSTICE on top of the building. —see picture on page 751 and colour map on page 817

Old Bill /ˌ· '·/ also **the Bill**— n [the+P] BrE infml; often derog the police

old boy /'· ·(for 1), · '· (for 2,3)/ n 1 BrE a man who is a former pupil of a school 2 also **oldchap/fellow/man**—old-fash infml (used as a form of address to a male friend): I say, old boy, could you lend me a fiver? 3 infml an old man: the old boy from down the road

old-boy net·work /'·· ˌ·/ [the] often derog 1 the system by which men who are former pupils of the same school, the same education system (esp. of the English PUBLIC SCHOOLS), or the same wealthy families favour each other in later life and help each other to get jobs, etc., usu. in an unofficial way: He got where he is through the old-boy network. 2 [+sing./pl. v] the people who operate this system —compare OLD SCHOOL TIE (2)

Old Bull and Bush /ˌ· ˌ· · '·/, **The** a pub in Hampstead, N London, well known because it is mentioned in an old popular song called Down at the Old Bull and Bush

old·e /'əʊldi/ adj often humor a spelling of **old** used (to give the feeling of being) in former times: ye olde tea shoppe

old·en /'əʊldən/ adj [A] esp. old use past; long ago: in olden times

Ol·den·burg /'əʊldəbɜːg‖-bɜːrg/, **Claes** /klɔːs/ (1929–) an American SCULPTOR, born in Sweden, important in the POP ART movement and famous for his large SCULPTURES of small, ordinary objects, often made of soft materials

Old En·glish Sheep·dog /ˌ· ·· '··/ BrE‖**English Sheepdog** AmE— n a breed of dog formerly used to control sheep, with a grey and white coat, and thick hair which is usu. allowed to grow long and cover the eyes. In Britain, the Old English Sheepdog appears in advertisements for Dulux paint and is sometimes called the "Dulux dog" because of this. —see picture at DOG

Old E·to·ni·an /ˌəʊld iː'təʊniən/ n BrE a man who was a schoolboy from Eton College, usu. thought of as from a wealthy and PRIVILEGED background

old·e world·e /ˌəʊldi 'wɜːldi‖-ɜːr-/ adj BrE infml, sometimes derog too consciously old-fashioned; QUAINT: an olde worlde country pub —compare old-world

Old Faith·ful /ˌ· '··/ a large GEYSER in Yellowstone National Park, US, that sends a JET of hot water into the air at regular times

old-fashioned

an old-fashioned radio

old-fash·ioned /ˌ· '··◂/ adj 1 once usual or fashionable but now less common: old-fashioned equipment/ideas | "Wireless" is an old-fashioned word for "radio". 2 [A] BrE infml (of a look, expression, etc.) suggesting disapproval: She gave me one of those old-fashioned looks.

old flame /ˌ· '·/ n someone with whom one used to be in love: Edward's an old flame of mine.

old folk /'· ˌ·/ n [P] infml old people considered as a group, esp. when speaking of them in a SENTIMENTAL way: We always try and do something for the old folk at Christmas.

old folk's home /ˌ· '· ˌ·/ n an OLD PEOPLE'S HOME

old girl /· '· (for 1), '· · (for 2)/ n 1 infml an old woman: She's a nice old girl. 2 a woman who is a former pupil of a school: a reunion for old girls

Old Glo·ry /ˌ· '··/ n AmE the flag of the US —see also STARS AND STRIPES, STAR-SPANGLED BANNER

old guard /'· ˌ·/ n [the+S+sing./pl. v] (a group of) old-fashioned people within an organization or society who are against new ideas, change, etc.: The old guard very much dislike(s) his new sculpture.

old hand /ˌ· '·/ n [(at)] a very experienced person: an old hand at fishing

old hat /ˌ· '·/ adj [F] infml derog familiar, old-fashioned, and unexciting: My children say loud rock 'n' roll is old hat.

old·ish /'əʊldɪʃ/ adj rather old

old la·dy /ˌ· '··/ also **old woman**— n [(the) S] sl 1 one's wife: Have you met the/my old lady? 2 one's mother

Old La·dy of Thread·nee·dle Street /ˌəʊld ˌleɪdi əv 'θredniːdl ˌstriːt/ [the] a NICKNAME for the Bank of England, from Threadneedle Street in London where it stands

old lag /ˌ· '·/ n infml, esp. BrE an old or former prisoner

old maid /ˌ· '·/ n derog 1 an unmarried woman who is no longer young. The STEREOTYPE of an old maid is of an unpleasant, unattractive woman who is too concerned with unimportant details. She is typically thought of as being shocked by anything to do with sex, but there are also many jokes about old maids having sex with men who are not willing. 2 infml a person who is very careful about small matters: He was a real old maid about picking up litter. – –**ish** adj

old man /ˌ· '·/ n 1 [(the) S] sl one's husband: Have you met the/my old man? 2 [(the) S] sl one's father: My old man wants me to be an engineer, like him. 3 also **old boy/ chap/fellow**— old-fash infml (used as a form of address to a friend): Hello, old man. How's the wife?

Old Man of the Sea /· ˌ· · · '·/, **The** a character in the story of Sindbad the Sailor, who persuades Sindbad to carry him on his back then twists his legs around so that Sindbad cannot get him off. Sindbad makes the old man drunk with wine, drops him, and kills him.

old mas·ter /ˌ· '··/ n (a picture by) an important painter of former times, esp. of the 15th to 18th century: a priceless collection of old masters

Old Moth·er Hub·bard /ˌ· ·· '··/ a character in a NURSERY RHYME (=an old poem or story for children):
Old Mother Hubbard, she went to the cupboard
To get her poor dog a bone;
But when she got there, the cupboard was bare,
And so the poor dog had none.

Old Nick /ˌ· '·/ infml humor the devil

old peo·ple's home /ˌ· '·· ˌ·/ also **old folks' home** infml— n a place where old people can live together and receive special care —see also RESIDENTIAL CARE (CULTURE NOTE)

old po·ta·to /ˌ· ·'·· ˌ·/ n a potato kept in store from the previous year's crop

Old Pre·tend·er /ˌ· ·'··/ [the] see James Francis Edward STUART

old school /'· ·/ n of the old school old-fashioned; keeping to old ideas: parents of the old school who don't let their children stay up late

old school tie /ˌ· · '·/ n esp. BrE 1 [C] a special TIE that is worn by someone who has been at a certain school, esp. a PUBLIC SCHOOL 2 [the+S] often derog a support system among former pupils of the same school in later life: He's not very clever but he got the job – I'm afraid it's a case of the old school tie. —compare OLD-BOY NETWORK

Olds·mo·bile /'əʊldzməʊbiːl/ n [C;U] (a vehicle made by) an American company producing large, comfortable cars, a part of General Motors

old·ster /'əʊldstər/ n infml, often humor an old person

Old Tes·ta·ment /ˌ· '···/ [the] the first part of the Bible, containing ancient Hebrew writings about events before the birth of Christ —compare NEW TESTAMENT

old-tim·er /ˌ· '··/ n 1 a person who has been in a particular place, job, etc., for a long time: Jackson's one of the old-timers in this department. 2 esp. AmE an old man

Old Traf·ford /əʊld 'træfəd‖-fərd/ a football and cricket ground in SW Manchester, N England, the home of the football team Manchester United and the Lancashire Cricket Club

Old Un·cle Tom Cob·bleigh /əʊld ˌʌnkəl tɒm 'kɒbli‖ -tɑːm 'kɑː-/ BrE see Old Uncle Tom COBBLEIGH

Old Vic /ˌəʊld 'vɪk/ [the] a London theatre originally opened in 1818, the full name of which is the Royal Victoria Theatre

old wives' tale /ˌ· '· ·/ n an ancient and not necessarily true belief: They say carrots are good for your eyesight, but it's just an old wives' tale.

old wom·an /ˌ· '··/ n sl 1 [(the) S] OLD LADY 2 [C] derog a person (usu. a man) who is too careful about small matters and/or easily frightened —**old-womanish** adj

Old Wom·an Who Lived in a Shoe /· ˌ··· ˌ· · · ˈ·/, **The** a character in a NURSERY RHYME (=old song or poem for children):

> There was an old woman who lived in a shoe,
> Who had so many children
> she didn't know what to do...

old-world /ˈ··/ adj [A] apprec (of places, qualities, etc.) attractively old; QUAINT: old-world charm/streets —compare OLDE WORLDE

Old World /ˌ·ˈ·◄/ [the] Europe, Asia, and Africa; the Eastern Hemisphere —compare NEW WORLD

o·le·ag·i·nous /ˌəʊliˈædʒᵻnəs/ adj tech oily; fatty

o·le·an·der /ˌəʊliˈændəʳ/ n [C;U] a green bush from the Mediterranean area with white, red, or pink flowers

o·le·o /ˈəʊliəʊ/ also **o·le·o·mar·ga·rine** /ˌəʊliəʊməˈdʒɑːriːn, -mɑːgə- ‖ -ˈmɑːrdʒərᵻn/ fml— n [U] AmE infml MARGARINE

O lev·el /ˈ· ˌ··/ also **ordinary level**— n 1 [U] (before 1988) the lower of the two standards of examination in the British GCE 2 [C] an examination of this standard in a particular subject: She took six O levels. | He's got O level maths. —compare A LEVEL, GCSE, O GRADE

ol·fac·to·ry /ɒlˈfæktəri‖ɑːl-, əʊl-/ adj med or humor of or about the sense of smell: the olfactory organ (=the nose)

ol·i·garch /ˈɒlᵻgɑːk‖ˈɑːlᵻgɑːrk, ˈəʊ-/ n a member of an OLIGARCHY (3)

ol·i·gar·chy /ˈɒlᵻgɑːki‖ˈɑːlᵻgɑːrki, ˈəʊ-/ n 1 [U] government by a small group of people, often for their own interests 2 [C] a state governed by a small group 3 [C+sing./pl. v] the group who govern such a state

O Lit·tle Town of Beth·le·hem /· ˌ··· · ˈ···/ the title and first line of a well known Christmas CAROL (=a religious song sung at Christmas):

> O little town of Bethlehem,
> How still we see thee lie,
> Above thy deep and dreamless sleep,
> The silent stars go by.

ol·ive /ˈɒlᵻv‖ˈɑː-/ n 1 [C] a tree grown in Mediterranean countries, which has a small bitter-tasting egg-shaped fruit: an olive grove 2 [C] the fruit of this tree, used for food and also for its oil —see picture at FRUIT 3 [U] also **olive green** /ˌ·· ˈ·◄/— dull pale green

olive branch /ˈ··· ·/ n [S] a sign of peace; esp. in the phrase **hold out an/the olive branch** (=to make a sign of peace).

▶CULTURAL NOTE In the Bible story of the Flood, Noah let out a DOVE which came back with a small piece of an olive tree. This showed that the water was beginning to go down. The olive branch was therefore regarded as a sign that the loving relationship between God and man had been reestablished. The dove is also a sign of peace, and is often pictured carrying a small olive branch. —see also FLOOD◄

olive drab /ˌ·· ˈ·/ adj esp. AmE having a greyish-green colour, used esp. for military uniforms —**olive drab** n [U]

olive oil /ˌ·· ˈ·/ n [U] a pale greenish-yellow oil obtained from olives, used in cooking and for making SALAD DRESSINGS

Ol·i·ver Twist /ˌɒlᵻvə ˈtwɪst‖ˌɑːlᵻvər-/ a book by Charles Dickens. Oliver Twist is a poor boy brought up in the WORKHOUSE. The most famous scene in the book is when he holds out his bowl and asks for more food, for which he is punished. He escapes and is taken in by Fagin, a thief who has a group of young boys, led by the Artful Dodger, who steal for him. Oliver will not steal, but is forced by Bill Sikes, a cruel thief, to help him get into a house. Finally Sikes is killed, Fagin is caught and Oliver is brought up by a good man, Mr Brownlow. The MUSICAL² Oliver was based on this story. —see colour picture on page 1145

Laurence Olivier as Hamlet

Ol·ives /ˈɒlᵻvz‖ˈɑː-/, **Mount of** see MOUNT OF OLIVES

Ol·iv·i·er /əˈlɪvieɪ‖əʊ-/, **Sir Laur·ence** /ˈlɒrəns‖ˈlɔː-/, also **Lar·ry** /ˈlæri/ (1907–89) English actor thought of by many people as the greatest of the 20th century. He

appeared in the theatre and in many films. He was the first director of the National Theatre, and the first actor to be made a LIFE PEER. Most people know his films of Shakespeare's plays Hamlet, Henry V, and Richard III.

O·lym·pi·a /əˈlɪmpiə/ 1 a set of large buildings in W London, used for EXHIBITIONS 2 an ancient Greek religious centre in the W Peloponnese, S Greece, where the OLYMPIC GAMES were held

O·lym·pi·ad /əˈlɪmpi·æd/ n fml a particular occasion of the modern Olympic Games: The 14th Olympiad was held in London.

O·lym·pi·an¹ /əˈlɪmpiən/ n in CLASSICAL MYTHOLOGY, one of the ancient Greek gods —see OLYMPUS

Olympian² adj [no comp.] 1 in CLASSICAL MYTHOLOGY, like or of the ancient Greek gods 2 (often not cap.) like a god, esp. in being calm and untroubled by ordinary affairs: He cultivates an olympian detachment. —see OLYMPUS

O·lym·pic /əˈlɪmpɪk/ adj [A no comp.] of the Olympic Games: an Olympic runner

Olympic Games /·ˌ·· ˈ·/ also **O·lym·pics** /əˈlɪmpɪks/— n **Olympic Games** [(the) C+sing./pl. v] 1 a modern international sports event in which people of all nationalities compete in various sports, held once every four years in different countries. It is seen by many people as a symbol of countries coming together to compete with each other in a friendly way. —see also colour picture on page 883 2 (In ancient times) a sports event held at Olympia in Greece once every four years

O·lym·pus /əˈlɪmpəs/ also **Mount Olympus**— in CLASSICAL MYTHOLOGY, the mountain on which the ancient Greek gods were said to live, the highest place that could be imagined: (fig.) Come down off Mount Olympus and have a look at the real world of ordinary people!

Olympus² tdmk a camera made by the Japanese company Olympus

om /əʊm/ a MANTRA (religious word) used in MEDITATION (the act of thinking deeply and calmly for religious reasons), esp. in the Hindu religion

OM /ˌəʊ ˈem/ abbrev. for: ORDER OF MERIT

O·man /əʊˈmɑːn/ an independent SULTANATE in the SE of Arabia, bordering on the Arabian Sea; capital Muscat; population 1,422,000 (1989) —**Omani** n, adj

O·mar Khay·yám /ˌəʊmɑː kaɪˈæm‖-ɑːr kaɪˈjɑːm/ (1048?–1123?) a Persian MATHEMATICIAN and poet known for his poem Rubaiyat, which is mainly about love and nature

OMB /ˌəʊ em ˈbiː/ OFFICE OF MANAGEMENT AND BUDGET

om·buds·man /ˈɒmbʊdzmən‖ˈɑːm-/ n **-men** /mən/ a person appointed by an institution (such as a government or a university) to receive and report on complaints made by ordinary people against the the services of that institution. In Britain the government Ombudsman is officially called the **Parliamentary Commissioner for Administration**, and examines complaints against government organizations, including the National Health Service. There is also a Local Ombudsman who examines complaints against local authorities.

o·me·ga /ˈəʊmᵻgə‖əʊˈmegə, -ˈmiː-, -ˈmeɪ-/ n the last letter (Ω, ω) of the Greek alphabet —see ALPHA AND OMEGA

ome·lette, **-let** /ˈɒmlᵻt‖ˈɑːm-/ n 1 eggs beaten together and cooked in hot fat, sometimes with other foods added: a cheese omelette 2 **you can't make an omelette without breaking eggs** saying it is impossible to do or achieve anything, esp. something new, without hurting or offending someone or causing some kind of difficulty

o·men /ˈəʊmən/ n [(of)] a sign that something is going to happen in the future: When it rained on their wedding day she took it as a bad omen. —see also ILL-OMENED

om·i·nous /ˈɒmᵻnəs‖ˈɑː-/ adj giving a warning of something bad that is going to happen: ominous black clouds | an ominous silence —~ly adv

o·mis·sion /əʊˈmɪʃən, ə-/ n 1 [U] the act of omitting: She complained about the omission of her name from the list. 2 [C] something or someone omitted: There are some surprising omissions in this report/this list of candidates.

o·mit /əʊˈmɪt, ə-/ v **-tt-** [T] 1 to not include, by mistake or on purpose; leave out: In writing this report I have omitted all unnecessary details. 2 [+to-v/v-ing; obj] to fail to do something, by mistake or on purpose: *He omitted to tell me when he was leaving.*

omni- see WORD FORMATION

om·ni·bus¹ /'ɒmnɪbəs, -ˌbʌs‖'ɑːm-/ *n* **1** a book containing several works, esp. by one writer, which have already been printed separately: *a Dickens omnibus | the omnibus edition of the soap opera* (=more than one show seen together) —compare ANTHOLOGY **2** *old use for* BUS¹ (1)

omnibus² *adj* doing, providing, or dealing with many different things at once: *an omnibus training program for teachers, translators and guides*

om·nip·o·tent /ɒm'nɪpətənt‖ɑːm-/ *adj fml* (esp. of God) having unlimited power; able to do anything **—tence** *n* [U]

om·ni·pres·ent /ˌɒmnɪ'prezənt◀‖ˌɑːm-/ *adj fml* present everywhere **—ence** *n* [U]

om·nis·ci·ent /ɒm'nɪʃənt, -'nɪsiənt‖ɑːm'nɪʃənt/ *adj fml* (esp. of God) knowing everything **—ence** *n* [U]

om·niv·o·rous /ɒm'nɪvərəs‖ɑːm-/ *adj fml or tech* **1** (esp. of animals) eating everything, esp. both plant and animal food —compare CARNIVORE, HERBIVORE, INSECTIVORE **2** interested in everything, esp. in all books: *an omnivorous reader*

on¹ /ɒn‖ɔːn, ɑːn/ *prep* **1** also **upon** *fml*— (showing position in relation to a surface or supported by a surface): *a lamp on the table|the wall | a ring on my finger | You've got mud on your shoes. | He jumped on|onto the horse. | The ball hit me on the head. | on page 23* (not *upon page 23*) | (fig.) *I wonder what's on his mind?* (=what is worrying him) (compare *I wonder what's in his mind?*) **2** also **upon** *fml*— supported by, hanging from, or connected to: *to stand on one foot | a ball on a string | the wheels on my car | We aren't on the telephone.* (=we have no telephone *BrE*‖we aren't using the telephone *AmE*) **3** also **upon** *fml*— **a** to; towards; in the direction of: *on my right | to march on Rome | to make an attack on the enemy* **b** concerning or influencing: *a tax on cigarettes* **4** also **upon** *fml*— **a** at the edge of; along: *a town (right) on the river|on the border | trees on both sides of the street*‖(*AmE*) *He lives on Mulberry Street.*‖(*AmE*) *What street did you say you lived on?*‖(*AmE*) *I met her on the street the other day.* **b** (used with words about travelling): *on a journey | I'm on my way to school.* **5** during; at the time of: *They arrive on Tuesday.* (*AmE* also *They arrive Tuesday.*) | *on July 1st | on the morning of July 1st | was rushed to hospital but was dead on arrival. | on the hour* (=every hour at exactly 2 o'clock, 3 o'clock, etc.) (compare *in the morning, in 1985, at 6 o'clock*) **6** also **upon** *fml*— directly after (and often as a result of): *acting on your advice | On hearing the news, she burst into tears. |* **On second thoughts** (=after some consideration), *let's not bother going out.* —compare IN¹ (19) **7** also **upon** *fml*— with regard to; about: *a book on India | a lecture on philosophy | new evidence on the matter | keen on football* —see USAGE **8** using as a means of travelling: *on foot|horseback | on a ship | on the 9 o'clock train* (compare *in a car, by ship, by train*) **9** by means of: *They live on potatoes. | A car runs on petrol. | to hear it on the radio | to speak on the telephone* (compare *by telephone*) | *He cut his foot on* (=against) *a piece of glass.* **10** supported by: *He went round the world on the money his aunt gave him. | on the dole|on welfare. | (infml) She's on drugs.* (=uses them and depends on them) **11** (before a noun or **the**) in a state or process of: *on fire | on sale | on holiday | Unemployment is on the increase.* (=is increasing) | *on offer | on purpose* (compare *by accident*) **12** working for; belonging to: *to serve on a committee | a job on a newspaper | Which side was he on in the game?* **13** also **upon** *fml*— (between repeated words for unpleasant things) added to; after: *to suffer defeat on defeat | Wave upon wave of enemy soldiers poured into the town.* **14** by comparison with: *a big improvement on your last essay | Sales are up on last year's figures.* **15** *infml* (before PRONOUNS) with: *Have you any money on you?* **16** *infml* paid for by: *Drinks are on me!* **17** *infml* causing difficulty or inconvenience to: *I'd just got through to her when the phone went dead on me. | The car broke down on us.* **18 have|get something on someone** *sl* to have|get information that can be used against someone: *The police have nothing on me.*

▷ USAGE A book **on** rabbits is probably more formal and scientific than a book **about** rabbits which might, for example, be a children's story.◁

on² *adv, adj* [F] **1** continuously; not stopping: *We worked*

on (and on) all night. | He just kept on talking. **2** further in space or time; forward: *If you walk on you'll come to the church. | If any letters come, shall I send them on?* (=to your new address) | *It's time to move on. | I'll do it later* **on.** (=afterwards) | (*BrE*) *to put the clock on* (=so that it shows a later time) **3** (so as to be) connected or in place: *with his coat on | He had nothing* (=no clothes) *on. | The bus stopped, and we got on. | I fixed the handle back on.* **4** with the stated part in front: *The two cars crashed head on.* **5** (esp. of a machine or electrical apparatus) working; operating: *Turn the light|the taps on. | Is the TV on?* (fig.) *He has only two speeds, on and off.* —opposite **off**; compare IN³ (4) **6** (of something that has been arranged) happening or going to happen: *There's a new film on at the cinema. | I've nothing on tonight, so let's go out.* —compare OFF¹ (9) **7** (of actors) actually performing on the stage: *You're on in two minutes!* **8 be on about** *BrE infml & usu. derog* to keep talking, esp. in a dull way and for too long, about: *What's he on about now?* **9 be on at (someone)** *infml* to keep trying to persuade someone in a complaining way: *She's always on at me to have my hair cut.* **10 not on** *infml, esp. BrE* impossible; not acceptable or reasonable: *You can't refuse to help her now — it's just not on!* **11 on and off** also **off and on**— from time to time; sometimes **12 on and on** without stopping — see also ONTO, **and so on** (AND)

on³ also **on side**— *n* [*the*+S] (in cricket) LEG¹ (7)

on-air /'· ·/ *adj* [A] broadcast while actually happening: *an on-air interview*

O·nas·sis /əʊ'næsₔs/, **Aristotle (Socrates)** (1906?–75) a Greek, the best known member of the largest and richest family of ship owners in the world, who in 1968 married the WIDOW of President John F Kennedy

once¹ /wʌns/ *adv* **1** one time and no more: *We've met only once. | They go there once a week.* **2** at some time in the past; formerly: *He once lived in Rome. | The town isn't as big as it was once|(fml) as once it was. | this once-great nation* **3 once again** now again, as in the past: *With this new book she has once again proved her remarkable talent.* **4 once and for all** for the last time: *Let's try to solve this problem once and for all.* **5 once in a while** sometimes, but not often: *I still see my ex-wife once in a while.* **6 once more: a** one more time **b** now again as before: *John's back home once more.* **7 once or twice** several times; a few times: *I've been there once or twice.* **8 once upon a time** (used to begin a story for small children) at some time in the past: *Once upon a time there was a little girl, and her name was Alice.* —see also **all at once** (ALL²)

once² *n* **1** [*this|the*+S] one time; one occasion: *Do it just this once. | She did it just the once, and once was enough.* **2 at once: a** now; without delay: *Do it at once!* **b** at the same time; together: *Don't all talk at once!* **3 (just) for once** for this one time only: *For once he was telling the truth.*

once³ *conj* from the moment that; when: *Once she arrives, we can start. | Once in bed, the children usually stay there.*

Once in Roy·al Da·vid's Cit·y /ˌ· · ˌ·· ˌ·· '··/ the title and first line of a very well-known Christmas CAROL (=a religious song sung at Christmas)

once-o·ver /'· ˌ··/ *n* give something a|the once-over *infml* to look at something quickly: *He gave the car the once-over and decided not to buy it.*

on·com·ing /'ɒnˌkʌmɪŋ‖'ɔːn-, 'ɑːn-/ *adj* [A] coming towards one; advancing: *facing the oncoming traffic |* (fig.) *the oncoming winter*

one¹ /wʌn/ *determiner, n* **1** (the number) 1: *Only one person came. | twenty-one | one thousand six hundred* (1600) | *one o'clock | page one | one pound fifty pence* (=£1.50) | *to combine two substances into one* (substance) | *There were three letters and one* (of them) *was for you. | one third* (=⅓) *of the Earth's surface is land and two thirds is sea.* | *one of your friends* (=a friend of yours) **2** a certain, esp. **a** (before times): *I met her one day|one afternoon in June.* | *early one morning* **b** *fml* (before a name, esp. of a person not known to the speaker): *The victim of the crime was one Arthur Nesbitt.* **3** (esp. before past or future dates) some: *Come again one day soon.* (=some day soon) **4** [(with)] the same: *Do you think we can all fit into the one room? | They are of one mind.* (=of the same opinion) | *I am one with you|of one mind with you on this.* **5** (the) only: *She's the one person I trust. | He's my one and only*

(=my only) *friend.* **6** (as opposed to **another, the other,** etc.) a particular example or type (of): *He can't tell one tree from another.* | *One (of them) went North, the other went South.* | *Are we taking all these children? One or other is sure to be sick!* **7** *AmE infml* certainly a(n); an unusually: *I tell you, she's one wonderful girl!* **8** also **single** *AmE* a one-dollar bill: *Have you got five ones for five?*‖*Give me the five back, I'll give you three ones and the right change.* **9 a one** old *infml, esp. BrE* (expressing shocked admiration) an amusingly disrespectful person: *Oh, you are a one!* **10 a** '**right one** old *infml, esp. BrE* a fool: *You're a right one, losing the tickets again!* **11 as one (man)** *fml* all together; with the agreement of everyone **12 at one (with)** *fml* in agreement (with): *We, the opposition, are at one with the government on this (issue).* **13 be one up (on someone)** to have the advantage (over someone) —see also ONE-UPMANSHIP **14 for one** as one (person, reason, etc.) of perhaps several: *I for one think he's guilty.* | *For one thing, it costs too much.* **15 in one:** a also **all in one**— combined; together: *She's president and secretary in one.* **b** *infml* in only one attempt: *She did it in one!* **16 in ones and twos** a few at a time **17 one after the other/after another** singly; first one, then the next, etc. **18 one and all** every one: *The bride was cheerfully welcomed by one and all.* **19 one and the same** exactly the same: *In fact the soldier and the priest were one and the same person.* **20 one for all and all for one** *quote* the phrase used by the Three Musketeers in the book by Alexandre Dumas to show that they would all support and protect each other **21 one for the road** *infml* a last drink (usu. alcoholic) before going home **22 one of** a member of (a group): *Our dog is like one of the family.* **23 one or two** a few: *I've invited one or two friends round this evening.* **24 one-** having only one: *one-armed* | *one-eyed* | *a one-parent family* (=with either a mother or father, but not both) | *a one-man boat* —see also ONE-TO-ONE

one² *pron* **1** (*pl.* **ones**) (used instead of a noun or noun phrase that describes a single thing or person): *Have you any books on farming? I'd like to borrow one.* (=a book on farming) | *I've got several books: which one/which ones would you like?* (compare *I know you've got a lot of books and I'd like to borrow some.*) | *"Which key do you want?" "The one that's lying on the table."* | *There are only hard chocolates left; we've eaten all the soft ones.* | *This one's a bit small — have you got a slightly bigger one?* | *The officer is the one who gives the orders.* | *The problem is one that has caused us a lot of trouble.* —see USAGE 1 **2** (*no pl.*) *fml or pomp* any person; YOU: *One should do one's duty/(AmE) his duty.* | *It makes one wonder if the government know what they are doing.* | *If necessary, one can always consult a dictionary.* —see USAGE 3 **3 one who/that/to, etc.** the sort of person who/that/to, etc.: *I'm not usually one to complain, but ...* **4 the/one's little/young ones** *pomp or humor* the/one's children: *My little ones are grown up, with young ones of their own.* **5 the one about** *infml* the joke about: *Have you heard the one about the travelling salesman and the farmer's daughter?*

▷ USAGE 1 In formal writing avoid the use of **ones** when two adjectives are used for comparison: *He buys German man rather than British cars* (*fml*) and *He buys German cars rather than British* **ones** (*infml*). 2 In American English and formal British English **ones** is not used after *these* or *those*: *Shall we adopt these methods or those?* 3 In British English **one** meaning "any person" is usually followed by **one's** and **oneself: One** *should wash* **oneself**/*wash* **one's** *hair regularly.* In American English it is also correct to say: **One** *should wash himself/wash his hair regularly.* 4 American speakers are more used to using and hearing **you** in sense 2, meaning "any person", and **one** therefore sounds formal and British. Thus: (*AmE and infml*) *You can't always get what you want.*‖(*BrE and fml*) *One can't always get what one wants.*◁

one an·oth·er /ˌ· ·ˈ·-/ *pron* each other: *They hit one another.* | *They often stay at one another's houses.*

one-armed ban·dit /ˌ· · ˈ··/ also **fruit machine** *BrE*‖**slot machine** *AmE*— *n* a machine with one long handle, into which people put money to try to win more money

one-day crick·et /ˌ· · ˈ··/ *n* [U] a game of CRICKET with a limited number of OVERs which must be completed within one day. Each team receives the same number of

balls and the team that gets the most runs is the winner.

one-horse /ˈ· ·/ *adj* [A] **1** pulled by only one horse **2** *humor* small and uninteresting: *a one-horse town*

O'Neill /əʊˈniːl/, **Eu·gene** /ˈjuːdʒiːn/ (1888–1953) American writer of plays who won the NOBEL PRIZE for literature in 1936, known esp. for *Long Day's Journey into Night*

one-lin·er /ˌ· ˈ··/ *n* very short joke or humorous remark: *new play full of snappy one-liners*

one-man /ˈ· ·/ *adj* [A] operated, worked, or run by one person: *a one-man show* (with only one person performing) | *the buses are one-man operated* (the driver also takes the passengers' money and gives out tickets)

one-man band /ˌ·· ˈ·/ *n* **1** a street musician who carries several different instruments and plays them all at once, with the hands, mouth, knees, feet, etc. **2** *infml* an activity which someone does without accepting help from other people: *This firm is really a one-man band.*

one-night stand /ˌ·· ˈ·/ *n* **1** a performance of music or a play that is given only once in each of a number of places: *The rock group played a series of one-night stands in the North.* **2** *infml* (a person involved in) a (sexual) relationship which lasts only one night or a very short time

one-off /ˌ· ˈ·◂/ *adj BrE* [A] **1** happening or done only once: *Yours for a one-off payment of £200.* **2** made as a single example —**one-off** *n* : *the car's a one-off; it's worth a fortune* | (fig.) *He's a one-off, a real character.* —see also ONE-SHOT

one-pa·rent fam·i·ly /ˌ· ··· ˈ···/ *n* a family of at least one dependent child and a mother or father who has no partner. Many councils in Britain make special efforts to find places for one-parent families to live, although some people, who think that the parents should stay together, disapprove of this.

one-piece /ˈ· ·/ *adj* [A] made in one piece only; not having separate parts: *a one-piece swimsuit*

o·ner·ous /ˈɒnərəs, ˈəʊ-‖ˈɑː-, ˈəʊ-/ *adj* difficult; BURDENSOME: *an onerous task/duty* —~ly *adv* —~ness *n* [U]

one·self /wʌnˈself/ *pron esp. BrE* **1** (*reflexive form of* **one**): *to wash oneself* | *One can't enjoy oneself if one/if he* (*AmE*) *is too tired.* **2** (*strong form of* **one**): *To do something oneself is often easier than getting someone else to do it.* **3** *infml* (in) one's usual state of mind or body: *One isn't quite oneself in the early morning.* **4 (all) by oneself** alone; without help: *One can't play tennis by oneself.* **5 to oneself** for one's own private use; not to be shared: *One would rather have a bedroom to oneself.* —see ONE (USAGE), YOURSELF (USAGE)

one-shot /ˈ· ·/ *adj AmE* (complete after) happening only once; ONE-OFF: *He claims it's a one-shot solution to our problem.*‖*Is this a* **one-shot deal** *or do I have to pay again every year?*

one-sid·ed /ˌ· ˈ···◂/ *adj* **1** seeing only one side (of a question); unfair: *a one-sided attitude* **2** with one side much stronger than the other: *The football match was rather one-sided.* —~ly *adv* —~ness *n* [U]

one-star /ˈ· ·/ *adj* [A] of the lowest rank in a system which shows quality by a number of stars: *a one-star hotel providing clean, simple accommodation*

one·time /ˈwʌntaɪm/ *adj* former: *the onetime President*

one-to-one /ˌ·· ˈ·◂/ *adj, adv* **1** matching one another exactly: *a one-to-one correspondence between the ranks in two different navies* **2** between only two people: *one-to-one teaching* (=with one teacher and one student)

one-track mind /ˌ·· ˈ·/ *n* a mind that thinks of only one thing at a time or that is continually concerned with one particular thing: *All you ever talk about is sex — you've got a one-track mind!*

one-two /ˌ· ˈ·/ *n* **1** (in boxing) a combination of two quick blows with different hands **2** (in football) a combination of two quick passes between two players

one-up·man·ship /wʌnˈʌpmənʃɪp/ also **one-ups·man·ship** /-ˈʌpsmən-/ *AmE n* [U] the art of getting an advantage over others or showing that one is better than them without actually cheating

one-way /ˌ· ˈ·◂/ *adj* **1** moving or allowing movement in only one direction: *one-way traffic* | *a one-way street* **2** *esp. AmE* for SINGLE¹ (6)

one-wom·an /ˈ· ··/ *adj* [A] operated, worked, or run by one woman: *a one-woman show* (=with only one woman performing)

on·go·ing /ˈɒnˌgəʊɪŋ‖ˈɑːn-/ *adj* continuing, or continuing to develop: *an ongoing process* | *ongoing negotiations* —see also GO **on** (6)

on·ion /ˈʌnjən/ *n* **1** [C] a strong-smelling round vegetable made up of one skin within another, used in cooking —see picture at VEGETABLE **2** [C;U] this vegetable as food: *fried onions* | *onion soup* —see also **know one's onions** (KNOW¹)

on·ion·skin /ˈʌnjənskɪn/ *n, adj AmE* of or being very thin, light writing paper, used esp. for AIRMAIL *letters*

on·line /ˈɒnlaɪn‖ˈɔːn-, ˈɑːn-/ *adj* directly connected to and/or controlled by a computer: *an online printer* | *an online database* (=a store of information on a central computer, to which other computers can be connected in order to use the information) —**online** *adv*

on·look·er /ˈɒnˌlʊkəʳ‖ˈɔːn-, ˈɑːn-/ *n* a person who watches something happening without taking part in it: *After the accident the police asked the onlookers to move back.* —see also LOOK **on**

on·ly¹ /ˈəʊnli/ *adj* [A] **1** with no others in the same group or of the same type: *John and I were the only people in the room.* | *the only person in the office who smokes* | *The only problem is that it's rather expensive.* | *an* **only child** (=one with no brothers or sisters) **2** the best: *She's the only person for this job.* | *This is the only way to convince him.*

only² *adv* **1** nothing more than; with no one or nothing else added or included: *only five minutes more* | *Ladies only!* | *I saw him only yesterday.* (=and no longer ago) | *Don't eat it — it will only make you ill.* (=that will certainly be the result) | *made only from the finest ingredients* | *Their decision will affect not only our class but the whole school.* | *Only a doctor can do that.* **2 if only** (expressing a strong wish): *If only he wouldn't eat so noisily.* | *If he would only learn to eat quietly!* **3 only just:** *esp. BrE* **a** a moment before: *They've*|*They had only just (now) arrived.* **b** almost not: *I've only just enough money.* **4 only too** very; completely: *It's only too true.*

▷ USAGE 1 In writing, put **only** in front of the part of the sentence which it is about: **Only** *John saw the lion.* (=no one else saw it) | *John* **only** *saw the lion.* (=he didn't shoot it) | *John saw* **only** *the lion* (=he didn't see the tiger). In speech **only** is not usually put after the verb. The way the sentence is said makes it clear what is meant. 2 In formal language **only** may come at the beginning of a sentence. Notice the word order: **Only** *in Paris can you buy shoes like that.*◁

only³ *conj infml* except that; but: *She wants to go, only she hasn't got enough money.*

Only Fools and Hors·es /ˌ·· ·‿· ‿·/ a popular British television programme about the humorous problems of two brothers Derek, (also DEL BOY) and Rodney Trotter, who live in a WORKING-CLASS area of London and who try to make money without getting jobs or paying tax

o.n.o. *written abbrev for:* (*BrE*) or near offer: *"Man's bicycle for sale, hardly used: £35 o.n.o."* (advertisement)

O·no /ˈəʊnəʊ/, **Yo·ko** /ˈjəʊkəʊ/ (1933–) a Japanese artist, now working in America, who was the second wife of John Lennon. She made several records with Lennon and as part of the group, the Plastic Ono Band, including the song *Give Peace A Chance.*

on·o·mat·o·poe·ia /ˌɒnəmætəˈpiːə‖ˌɑː-/ *n* [U] the formation of words that are like natural sounds (as when the word CUCKOO is used to name the bird that makes that sound) —**ic** *adj*

on·rush /ˈɒnrʌʃ‖ˈɔːn-, ˈɑːn-/ *n* [(of)] *usu. sing* a strong movement forward: *There was a sudden onrush of demonstrators, and the police withdrew.* — ~ **ing** *adj* [A] : *the onrushing tide*

on-screen /ˌ· ‿·/ *adj, adv* so as to be actually seen on the SCREEN of a computer: *The text is edited on-screen.*

on·set /ˈɒnset‖ˈɔːn-, ˈɑːn-/ *n* [(*the*) S (**of**)] the first attack or beginning (of something bad): *the onset of a fever*

on·shore /ˌɒnˈʃɔːʳ◂‖ˌɔːn-·,ɑːn-/ *adj, adv* **1** on(to) or near the shore, not in the water: *onshore oil production* **2** (coming or moving) towards the shore: *The wind was blowing onshore.* —compare OFFSHORE

on·side /ˌɒnˈsaɪd◂‖ˌɔːn-, ˌɑːn-/ *adj, adv* (in certain sports) not OFFSIDE (1)

on side /ˌ· ·/ *n* [*the*+S] the ON³

on·slaught /ˈɒnslɔːt‖ˈɔːn-, ˈɑːn-/ *n* [(**on**)] a fierce attack: *Our army tried to withstand the enemy onslaught.* | *The politician made a violent onslaught* (=attacking speech) *on the unions.*

on·stream /ˈɒnstriːm‖ˈɔːn-, ˈɑːn-/ *adj, adv* [F] (of an industrial process, a piece of equipment, etc.) in operation or ready to go into operation

On·ta·ri·o /ɒnˈteəriəʊ‖ɑːn-/ a PROVINCE in the east of central Canada, containing the country's largest city, Toronto, and over a third of its population

Ontario, Lake the smallest of the five Great Lakes, between the US and Canada —see colour map on pages 1374-5

on the job /ˌ· · ·‿·/ *adj, adv* while working: *on-the-job training*‖*He was fired for sleeping on the job* (=while he should have been working)

On the Or·i·gin of Spe·cies /ˌ· ·‿· ‿·‿·/ the title of a book by Charles Darwin in which he explained his ideas about EVOLUTION (1)

on-the-spot /ˌ· · ·‿·/ *adj* see SPOT¹ (12)

on·to /ˈɒntə; *before vowels* ˈɒntʊ‖ˈɔːn-, ˈɑːn-/ *prep* **1** to a position or point on: *He jumped onto the train.* **2 be onto a good thing** *infml* to have found a good, easy or profitable situation **3 be onto someone** *infml* **a** to have found out about someone's illegal activities: *The police are onto us!* **b** *esp. BrE* to get in touch with someone: *I've been onto the local authorities about the drains.*

on·tol·o·gy /ɒnˈtɒlədʒi‖ɑːnˈtɑː-/ *n* [U] the branch of PHILOSOPHY concerned with the nature of existence —**gical** /ˌɒntəˈlɒdʒɪkəl◂‖ˌɑːntəˈlɑː-/ *adj* —**gically** /kli/ *adv*

o·nus /ˈəʊnəs/ *n* [*the*+S] *fml* the duty or responsibility of doing something: *The onus is on you to complete this report.*

on·ward /ˈɒnwəd‖ˈɔːnwərd, ˈɑːn-/ *adj* [A] forward in space or time: *the onward march of events* —**onwards**, usu. **onward** *AmE* — *adv* : *from breakfast onwards* | *From now onward we'll do things my way.*

on·yx /ˈɒnɪks‖ˈɑː-/ *n* [U] a precious stone with lines of various colours

oo·dles /ˈuːdlz/ *n* [P (**of**)] *old-fash infml* lots: *oodles of cream*

oof /uːf/ *interj often humor* (a word like the sound that people make when hit in the stomach)

ooh la la, ooh là là /ˌuː ˌlɑː ˈlɑː/ words said when one hears about someone or something surprising or beautiful. It is thought to sound like a French expression.

oomph /ʊmf/ *n* [U] *sl* the power of forceful activity; ENERGY: *It's not a bad song, but it needs more oomph.*

oops /ʊps/ **also whoops**— *interj infml* (said when someone has fallen, dropped something, or made a mistake): *Oops! I nearly dropped my cup of tea!*

oops-a-dai·sy /ˈ· ·‿ˌ·/ **also ups-a-daisy** – *interj infml* or *humor* (used to encourage someone who falls down or when helping someone to sit up, stand up, or climb): *Are you ready Grandma? Come on then* – *oops-a-daisy!*

ooze¹ /uːz/ *v* **1** [I+*adv/prep*] (of liquid, esp. a thick liquid) to pass or flow slowly: *Blood was oozing out of the wound on his leg.* | (fig.) *Their courage oozed away.* **2** [T] to allow (liquid) to pass slowly out: *The meat oozed blood.* | (fig.) *He simply oozes charm.*

ooze² *n* [U] mud or thick liquid, as at the bottom of a river —**oozy** *adj*

op¹ /ɒp‖ɑːp/ *n BrE infml for* OPERATION (3)

op² [A] *written abbrev for:* (*usu. cap.*) OPUS

o·pac·i·ty /əʊˈpæsˌti/ *n* [U] the quality of being opaque

o·pal /ˈəʊpəl/ *n* [C;U] (a) precious stone which looks like milky water with colours in it

o·pa·les·cent /ˌəʊpəˈlesənt◂/ *adj* like an opal; having softly-shining quickly-changing colours —**cence** *n* [U]

o·paque /əʊˈpeɪk/ *adj* **1** not able to be seen through: *opaque glass* **2** hard to understand —compare TRANSPARENT — ~ **ly** *adv* — ~ **ness** *n* [U] —see also OPACITY

op art /ˈ· ·/ also **optical art**— *n* [U] a form of modern art using patterns that play tricks on your eyes —compare POP ART

op. cit. /ˌɒp ˈsɪt‖ˌɑːp-/ abbrev opere citato (Lat.), in the work (usu. a book) mentioned before

ope /əʊp/ v [I;T] poet to open

OPEC /ˈəʊpek/ Organization of Petroleum Exporting Countries; an organization which includes representatives of most of the countries that produce oil. They plan together how much to produce and at what price to sell it: OPEC has/have decided to raise the price of oil.

op-ed page /ˌ· ˈ· ˌ·/ n AmE the page opposite the EDITORIAL page in many American newspapers, which usu. contains interesting feature articles on current subjects

O·pel /ˈəʊpəl/ tdmk a German company producing cars, part of the American company General Motors

o·pen¹ /ˈəʊpən/ adj **1** not shut: She pushed/held/propped the door open. | The window was **wide open**. (=completely open) | An open book lay on the table. | I was so tired I could hardly keep my eyes open. | Her mouth fell open in astonishment. | Is the road open? (=not blocked) | We must try to keep all lines of communication open. **2** [A] not surrounded by walls, etc.; not enclosed: the open country | open fields | open space | the open sea (=the sea far from land) | It felt good to be out in **the open air** (=to be outside) at last. **3** without a roof: an open boat **4** not fastened or folded: His shirt was open at the neck. | The flowers are open. **5** not completely decided or answered: an open question | Let's leave it open. (=let's not decide yet) | I like to keep my options open. | Try and keep **an open mind** on the subject until you have heard all the facts. **6** [F] **a** ready to provide a service to customers: The bank isn't open yet. **b** officially ready to start being used: I declare the new bridge open. **7** [F] (esp. of a job) not filled: Is the teaching vacancy still open? **8 a** (of a feeling, system, etc.) not hidden or limited: open hostility/rivalry | I didn't have to bribe anyone – it was all **open and above board**. (=completely honest) | The house should fetch £40,000 on the **open market**. **b** (of people) very willing to talk honestly: Let's be open with each other. | an extremely frank and open person **9** [(to)] that anyone can enter: an open competition | These gardens are open to the public. **10** BrE (of a cheque) payable in actual money to the person whose name is written on it; not CROSSED —compare CROSS² **11** tech (in PHONETICS, of a vowel) pronounced with the tongue low in the mouth —opposite **close 12** [F+to] **a** not safe from: This book is open to criticism. | His truthfulness is open to question.| That statement is open to being misinterpreted. **b** willing to receive: I'm always open to suggestions. **c** possible for: It's the only course of action open to you. **13 with open arms** in a very friendly way: They welcomed us with open arms. —see also OPENLY, lay someone/oneself open to (LAY²)

open² v **1** [I;T] to (cause to) become open: This door opens inwards. | Open your mouth. | (fig.) The decision opened the door to a flood of appeals for help from other organizations. **2** [I;T (UP, OUT)] to (cause to) spread or unfold: to open a book/an umbrella | (fig.) A split has opened up in the committee. | (fig.) A new life was opening up before her. **3** [I;T] to (cause to) start: He opened the conference with a speech of welcome. | to open an investigation/a debate **4** [I;T] to (cause to) begin business: The shop opens at nine o'clock. | to open Parliament/a new hospital **5** [T] to make (a passage) usable by removing the things that are blocking it: They cleared away the rocks to open the tunnel. **6** [I] (in cricket) to be one of the two batsmen (BATSMAN) who take the first turn at batting (BAT) for one's team: Gooch and Stewart opened for England. **7 open fire (at/on)** to start shooting (at) **8 open one's mouth** to start talking: I knew she was French the moment she opened her mouth. **9 open someone's eyes (to)** to make someone know or understand: The way he deceived me really opened my eyes to his true character.

▷ USAGE You **open** or **shut** (**close** sometimes fml) doors, windows, or boxes. You **undo** or **do up** a shirt, etc. You **turn** water or gas TAPs on or **off**. You **turn** or **switch** electrical things **on** or **off**.◁

open into/onto sthg. phr v [T] to provide a means of entering or reaching: The bedroom has French windows opening onto the garden.

open out phr v [I] to speak more freely; OPEN up

open up phr v **1** [T (to)] (**open** sthg. ↔ **up**) to make possible the development of: They opened the country up

(to trade). **2** [I often imperative] infml to open a door: Open up or we'll break the door down! **3** [I] to speak more freely: When she felt she could trust me, she began to open up.

open³ n [the+S] **1** the outdoors: life in the open **2** a (sporting) competition that anyone can enter **3 in(to) the open** (of opinions, secrets, etc.) in(to) the consciousness of the people around one

Open [the] one of the Open GOLF championship games, e.g. the British Open

open-air /ˌ·ˈ· ◄/ adj of or in the outdoors: an open-air concert/swimming pool —opposite **indoor**

open-and-shut /ˌ·· ˈ·◄/ adj easy to prove; without mystery: an open-and-shut case of murder

open bar /ˌ·· ·/ n AmE a bar where drinks are served free: They had an open bar at the mayor's reception.

o·pen·cast /ˈəʊpənkɑːst‖-kæst/ adj where minerals, esp. coal, are dug from an open hole in the ground and not from a deep passage: opencast mines/mining —compare STRIP MINING

Open Col·lege /ˌ·· ˈ·◄/ [the] a British organization which teaches adults in their own homes by means of radio and television programmes and CORRESPONDENCE COURSES (courses of study in which work is sent between teachers and students by post). It teaches courses on business and the skills needed to work in many jobs and industries — compare OPEN UNIVERSITY

open day /ˈ·· ·/ also **open house** AmE— n a day on which a college, theatre, organization, etc. opens its doors to the public to allow them to see what work is done in places to which they are not usually admitted

open-end·ed /ˌ·· ˈ··◄/ adj without any clear end, aim, or time limit set in advance: an open-ended discussion | an open-ended housing policy (=which may change according to needs)

o·pen·er /ˈəʊpənər/ n **1** (usu. in comb.) a person or thing that opens something: a bottle opener **2** an opening (OPEN (6)) BATSMAN in cricket

open-eyed /ˌ·· ˈ·◄/ adj, adv with one's eyes wide open, esp. as an expression of surprise: to stare open-eyed in disbelief

open gov·ern·ment /ˌ·· ˈ···/ n [U] a system of government in which there is little secrecy and where information is freely available

open-hand·ed /ˌ·· ˈ··◄/ adj generous: an open-handed offer of help — -**ly** adv — -**ness** n [U]

o·pen-heart·ed /ˌəʊpən'hɑːtɪd◄‖-ɑːr-/ adj generous; freely giving or given — -**ly** adv — -**ness** n [U]

open-heart sur·ge·ry /ˌ··· ˈ···/ n [U] a medical operation in which the heart is caused to stop pumping blood for a time and is cut open to be examined and treated

open house /ˌ·· ˈ·/ n [U] **1** a state of always welcoming visitors at any time: It's always open house round at the Collinses. | We keep open house at Christmas for the children's friends. **2** [C] AmE for OPEN DAY

o·pen·ing¹ /ˈəʊpənɪŋ/ n **1** the act of becoming or making open, esp. officially: the opening of a new university | shop opening hours **2** [(in)] a hole or clear space; GAP: an opening in the fence/in the clouds **3** [(for)] a favourable set of conditions (for); OPPORTUNITY: good openings for business **4** [(at, in)] an unfilled job position; VACANCY: There are no openings for secretaries at the bank at present.

opening² adj [A] first; beginning: her opening words | the opening night of a new play‖the opening lineup (=starting players) for today's game

opening hours /ˈ··· ·ˌ·/ n [P] the time during which a building, esp. a PUB or restaurant, is open to the public: What are your opening hours? — 10.30 a.m. to 11 p.m.

opening time /ˈ··· ·/ n [C;U] the time at which a business opens, esp. the time at which a bar or PUB starts serving drinks

opening-up /ˌ··· ˈ·/ n [U] **1** the action of making possible the development of a place: New roads and railways paved the way for the opening-up of the interior of Australia. **2** the situation of becoming more free or less limited: We hope to see an opening-up of relations between Albania and the EC.

open let·ter /ˌ·· ˈ··/ n a letter addressed to a particular person but meant for the general public to see, and often printed in a newspaper. People write open letters when they want others to know about a situation that they think is important, or they want to answer publicly a charge that has been made against them. Open letters are usu. written by and to well-known people.

o·pen·ly /ˈəʊpənli/ adv not secretly: *They talked openly about their plans.* | *He openly admits that he misled the public.* | *a speech openly attacking the government* —**-ness** n [U]

open mar·ket /ˌ··ˈ···/ n [the] on the open market available for anyone to buy: *We'll have to put it on the open market.*

open-mind·ed /ˌ···ˈ···◄/ adj willing to consider new arguments, ideas, opinions, etc.: *open-minded parents* | *I'm quite open-minded about this subject.* —compare NARROW-MINDED — **~ly** adv — **~ness** n [U]

open-mouthed /ˌ··ˈ·◄/ adj, adv with one's mouth wide open, esp. in surprise or shock

open-plan

partition

an open-plan office

open-plan /ˌ··ˈ·◄/ adj (of a large room) not divided into a lot of little rooms: *modern open-plan offices*

open pri·ma·ry /ˌ··ˈ···/ also **crossover primary**— n an election in the US, held to determine who will represent each party in the final election, in which voters may vote for a CANDIDATE (a person running for political office) from either party: *Bush supporters fear that Democrats voting in the State's open primary will vote for the opposing Republican candidates in an effort to weaken Bush's position.* —compare CLOSED PRIMARY

open pris·on /ˌ··ˈ···/ n a prison which does not restrict prisoners as much as ordinary prisons, and which takes only those who are less violent and less likely to try to escape

open sand·wich /ˌ··ˈ···/ n a single piece of bread with various foods on top of it

open sea·son /ˈ·· ˌ··/ n [(for, on)] the period of each year when certain animals or fish may by law be killed for sport: *the open season for fishing* —opposite **close season**

open se·cret /ˌ··ˈ···/ n something supposed to be a secret but in fact known to everyone

open ses·a·me /ˌ··ˈ···/ n [(to)] often humor a completely certain way to a desired end that would otherwise be beyond one's reach (from the magic words used for opening a hidden door in the *Arabian Nights* stories): *A university degree is no longer the open sesame to a good job.*

open shop /ˌ··ˈ·/ n a place of work where it is not necessary to belong to a TRADE UNION —opposite **closed shop**

open so·ci·e·ty /ˌ··ˈ···/ n a SOCIETY (2) in which people have considerable freedom in political and religious matters: *In an open society it ought to be possible for citizens to criticize the government without being imprisoned.*

Open Soft·ware Foun·da·tion /ˌ··ˈ·· ˌ··/ (abbrev. **OSF**) [the] a group of large computer makers and others who are trying to set international standards for the UNIX operating system and PROGRAMS that run under it

open sys·tem /ˈ·· ˌ··/ n tech a computer system made according to set standards and which can be connected with similar systems made by other companies

Open U·ni·ver·si·ty /ˌ··ˈ··◄···/ (abbrev. **OU**) [the] a British university based in Milton Keynes, central S England, which teaches adult students in their own homes by

means of television and radio programmes, CORRESPONDENCE COURSES (=courses of study in which work is sent between teachers and students by post), and summer courses, where the students spend a short time together studying away from home. Students can be of any age and do not have to have passed examinations before they start their course. Both science and arts subjects are taught —compare OPEN COLLEGE

open ver·dict /ˌ·· ˈ···/ n (in a British CORONER's court) a decision that records a death, but not how it was caused, esp. because this is not known: *The jury returned an open verdict.*

o·pen·work /ˈəʊpənˌwɜːk‖-wɜːrk/ n [U] a pattern with spaces in between thread, metal, etc.: *openwork stockings*

op·e·ra /ˈɒpərə‖ˈɑː-/ n 1 [C] a musical play in which many or all of the words are sung: *Mozart's operas* 2 [U] such musical plays as a form of art, a business, etc.: *I'm fond of opera.* | *an opera house* —compare OPERETTA; see also COMIC OPERA, GRAND OPERA, HORSE OPERA, SOAP OPERA — **~tic** /ˌɒpəˈrætɪk◄‖ˌɑː-/ adj : *an operatic voice* — **~tically** /kli/ adv

op·e·ra·ble /ˈɒpərəbəl‖ˈɑː-/ adj med (of a disease or medical condition) able to be treated by means of an operation —opposite **inoperable** —**bly** adv

opera glass·es /ˈ··· ˌ··/ n [P] small BINOCULARS to be used in a theatre —see PAIR (USAGE)

opera house /ˈ··· ·/ n a theatre in which OPERAS are performed

op·e·rate /ˈɒpəreɪt‖ˈɑː-/ v 1 [I;T] to (cause to) work or be in action; (cause to) FUNCTION: *Do you know how to operate the heating system?* | *The machine is not operating at maximum efficiency.* | *controls on the way the committee operates in future* | *one-man operated trains* 2 [I+adv/prep] to carry on trade or business: *Our company operates in several countries/out of Rome.* | *operating losses/costs* | *a gang of thieves operating in the city* 3 [I+adv/prep] to produce effects: *The new law operates against us/doesn't operate in our favour.* 4 [I (on, for)] to cut the body in order to set right or remove a diseased part, usu. in an operating theatre in a hospital: *I'm afraid we'll have to operate.* | *to operate on a patient for appendicitis*

operating sys·tem /ˈ···· ˌ··/ n a set of PROGRAMS inside a computer that controls the way it works and helps it to handle other programs

operating thea·tre /ˈ···· ˌ··/ BrE ‖ **operating room** /ˈ···· ˌ·/ AmE— n a room in a hospital where OPERATIONS (3) are done

op·e·ra·tion /ˌɒpəˈreɪʃən‖ˌɑː-/ n 1 [U] the condition or process of working: *The operation of a new machine can be hard to learn.* | *When does the new law* **come into operation**? 2 [C] a thing (to be) done; an activity: *The company's overseas operations include banking and insurance.* | *Getting the glue off the rug was a difficult/major operation.* | *to finance a mining/hotels operation* | *to organize a search/famine relief operation* 3 [C (on, for)] also **op** BrE infml— the cutting of the body in order to set right or remove a diseased part: *The surgeon is performing a delicate operation/a hip operation.* | *She's going into hospital to have a minor operation on her knee.* 4 [C] a planned, esp. military, movement: *the army's operations in Northern Ireland* | *It's code-named Operation Sunshine.* | *to mount/coordinate a major security operation* 5 [C] tech **a** a process used to get one MATHEMATICAL expression or figure from others **b** a single step performed by a computer

op·e·ra·tion·al /ˌɒpəˈreɪʃənəl◄‖ˌɑː-/ adj 1 [F] ready to be used: *The new machines are not yet fully operational.* 2 [A] of or about operations: *operational costs* —compare OPERATIVE — **~ly** adv

operational re·search /ˌ····· ·ˈ·, ˌ····· ···/ also **operations research** /ˌ····· ·ˈ·, ˌ····· ···/— n [U] tech the study of how best to build and use machines or plan organizations

Operation Des·ert Shield /ˌ··· ˌ·· ·ˈ·/ the military operation carried out by the ALLIES to move men and equipment into the Middle East and protect Saudia Arabia and Israel after Iraq had moved into Kuwait in 1990

Operation Des·ert Storm /ˌ··· ˌ·· ·ˈ·/, also **Desert Storm** the military operation carried out by the ALLIES to take back control of Kuwait from Iraq during the GULF WAR of 1990–91

Operation O·ver·lord /ˌ··· '···/ the secret name given to the Allied INVASION of NW Europe, on D Day 1944

op·e·ra·tive¹ /ˈɒpərətɪv‖ˈɑːpərə-, ˈɑːpəreɪ-/ *adj* **1** [F] (of plans, laws, etc.) in operation; producing effects — opposite **inoperative**; compare OPERATIONAL **2** [A] most suitable: *"We should push him for a decision." "Yes, "push" is the* **operative word!"**

operative² *n often euph* a worker

op·e·ra·tor /ˈɒpəreɪtəʳ‖ˈɑː-/ *n* **1** a person who works a machine, apparatus, etc. **2** a person who works a telephone SWITCHBOARD: *Operator! I've been cut off.* —see TELEPHONE (USAGE) **3** *infml, often derog* a person who is (rather too) clever at dealing with difficulties: *a clever|smooth operator*

op·e·ret·ta /ˌɒpəˈretə‖ˌɑː-/ *n* a short cheerful musical play that includes dancing and in which many of the words are spoken —compare OPERA

Ophelia by Sir John Everett Millais

O·phe·li·a /əˈfiːliə‖əʊ-/ a female character in Shakespeare's play *Hamlet*. She loves Hamlet and dies by killing herself after he stops courting her. —see also HAMLET

oph·thal·mi·a /ɒfˈθælmiə‖ɑːf-/ *n* [U] *med* an illness of the eyes causing redness and swelling

oph·thal·mic /ɒfˈθælmɪk‖ɑːf-/ *adj med* of or concerning the eyes: *an ophthalmic surgeon*

oph·thal·mol·o·gy /ˌɒfθælˈmɒlədʒi‖ˌɑːfθælˈmɑː-/ *n* [U] *med* the study of the eyes and their diseases —**-gist** *n* —see OPTICIAN (USAGE)

o·pi·ate /ˈəʊpiɪt, -eɪt/ *n* a sleep-producing drug containing OPIUM

o·pine /əʊˈpaɪn/ *v* [T+*that;obj*] *pomp* to express an opinion: *He opined that it was too dangerous.*

o·pin·ion /əˈpɪnjən/ *n* **1** [C;U (**of, about**)] what a person thinks about something, based on personal judgment rather than actual facts: *Her recent behaviour confirms my opinion that she is not happy here.* | *What's your opinion of this wine?* | *to give|express one's opinion* | *In my opinion you're wrong.* | *George is of the opinion that* (=he thinks) *they should close the factory.* | *I can't stomach my son's political opinions.* | *to form strong opinions* | *We had a slight* **difference of opinion** (=disagreement) *about which car to buy.* | *It's my* **considered opinion** *that he is a liar and a cheat.* (=I say this after careful thought about it) | *Is French food better than English food? It's all* **a matter of opinion.** (=not something that can be clearly proved or decided) **2** [U] what people in general think about something: **Public opinion** *is against him.* **3** [C] professional judgment or advice: *You should get a* **second opinion** *from another doctor.* **4 have a good** or **high/bad** or **low opinion of** to think well/badly of: *They have a very high opinion of his work.*

o·pin·ion·at·ed /əˈpɪnjəneɪtɪ̣d/ *adj derog* too sure of the rightness of one's opinions

opinion poll /·ˈ··· ·/ *n* a POLL¹ (1)

o·pi·um /ˈəʊpiəm/ *n* [U] **1** an ADDICTIVE drug made from the seeds of the white POPPY that lessens pain and makes one sleep **2 the opium of the people** *quotation* a phrase used by Karl Marx to describe religion

o·pos·sum /əˈpɒsəm‖-ˈpɑː-, ˈpɑːsəm/ *n esp. BrE and fml* for POSSUM

Op·pen·hei·mer /ˈɒpənhaɪməʳ‖ˈɑːp-/, **J Robert** (1904–67) American scientist who was head of the team which built the first ATOM BOMB in 1945

op·po·nent /əˈpəʊnənt/ *n* **1** a person who takes the oppo-

site side in a game, competition, etc.: *His opponent did not stand a chance.* **2** a person who opposes someone or something: *She is one of the strongest opponents of tax reform.* —see also OPPOSITION; compare PROPONENT

op·por·tune /ˈɒpətjuːn‖ˌɑːpərˈtuːn/ *adj* **1** (of times) right for a purpose: *I picked an opportune moment to ask a favour of her.* **2** coming at the right time: *an opportune remark* —opposite **inopportune** — **~ ly** *adv*

op·por·tun·is·m /ˌɒpəˈtjuːnɪzəm‖ˌɑːpərˈtuː-/ *n* [U] *usu. derog* the tendency to take advantage of every chance for success, sometimes to other people's disadvantage: *blatant opportunism* —**-ist** *n* : *a political opportunist*

op·por·tu·ni·ty /ˌɒpəˈtjuːnɪti‖ˌɑːpərˈtuː-/ *n* [C;U (**for, of**)] a favourable moment or occasion (for doing something): *You should go and see this film if you get the opportunity.* | *My flight was delayed so it was a good opportunity for doing some shopping.* | *I took the opportunity of visiting Ann while I was in London.* | *I'd like to|May I take this opportunity to thank everyone for their hard work on the project.* [+*to-v*] *You shouldn't miss the opportunity to see the play — it's rarely put on.* —see CHANCE (USAGE)

Opportunity Knocks /ˌ····· ˈ·/ a British television programme popular in the 1950s, 60s, and 70s, in which ordinary people were given the chance to perform on television, usu. by singing, dancing, telling jokes, etc.

opposable thumb /·ˌ··· ˈ·/ *n* a thumb that is set at an angle facing the other fingers, such as on the human hand, which makes it possible to use the hands in many more ways than animals can use their PAWS

op·pose /əˈpəʊz/ *v* [T] to regard (esp. a suggestion or planned course of action) with strong disapproval, and esp. to take action to try to prevent it from happening or succeeding: *The proposed new airport will be vigorously|strongly opposed by the local residents.* [+*v-ing*] *The President opposes giving military aid to this country.* | *an attempt to reconcile their opposing views on this question*

op·posed /əˈpəʊzd/ *adj* [(**to**)] opposite; against: *Their opinions are* **diametrically opposed.** (=completely opposed) | *I am strongly opposed to your suggestion.* | *This is a book about business practice* **as opposed to** *theory.* | *Our members are definitely opposed to making concessions on the health and safety question.*

op·po·site¹ /ˈɒpəzɪt‖ˈɑː-/ *n* [C;*the*+S (**of**)] a person or thing that is as different as possible from another: *Black and white are opposites.* | *Black is the opposite of white.* | *She's rather quiet, but her sister is completely|just the opposite.*

opposite² *adj* [(**to**)] **1** as different as possible from: *He turned and walked in the opposite direction.* | *the opposite sex* | *They are at opposite ends of the political spectrum.* (=their political views are completely different) **2** facing: *He lives opposite (me|to me).* | *on the opposite page* [after *n*] *I live in the houses opposite.*

opposite³ *prep* facing: *the houses opposite the station*

opposite num·ber /ˌ··· ˈ··/ *n BrE* a person in the same job as oneself but in a different organization: *Our Safety Officer will discuss the problem with his opposite number in your firm.* —compare COUNTERPART

op·po·si·tion /ˌɒpəˈzɪʃ*ə*n‖ˌɑː-/ *n* **1** [U (**to**)] the act or state of being opposed to or fighting against: *There was a lot of opposition to the new road.* | *His proposals met with fierce opposition.* **2** [U] the people who are fighting or competing against (someone): *Our team will be a good match for the opposition.* **3** [(*the*) C+*sing.|pl. v*] (*often cap.*) the political parties opposed to the government, esp. the most important of these parties, in Britain the LABOUR or CONSERVATIVE party: *The Opposition is|are voting against this bill.*

▶ CULTURAL NOTE In Britain the Opposition, esp. the main opposition party, is very important. The Leader of the Opposition is a Privy Councillor, and members of the Opposition take part in committees set up by parliament to examine various problems. The official title of the Opposition is **Her** or **His Majesty's Loyal Opposition**, showing that the Opposition is considered loyal to the Queen or King and to the country, although it does not agree with the government's ideas. ◀

op·press /əˈpres/ *v* [T] **1** to rule in a hard and cruel way: *The oppressed peasants rose up against the dictator.* **2** [*usu. pass.*] *esp. lit* to cause to feel ill or sad: *oppressed by|with worry*

op·pres·sion /əˈpreʃən/ n [U] the condition of oppressing or being oppressed

op·pres·sive /əˈpresɪv/ adj **1** cruel; unjust: *oppressive taxation* **2** causing feelings of illness or sadness **3** with no wind and very hot, as if there is about to be a storm: *We've had really oppressive weather today.* — ~ly adv — ~ness n [U]

op·pres·sor /əˈpresər/ n a person or group that oppresses

op·pro·bri·ous /əˈprəʊbriəs/ adj fml (esp. of words) showing great disrespect — ~ly adv

op·pro·bri·um /əˈprəʊbriəm/ n [U] fml public shame or hatred

O·pren /ˈəʊprən/ n [U] tdmk a drug for ARTHRITIS which was removed from sale in 1982 after it was claimed that people taking the drug had suffered severe and unpleasant side effects

opt /ɒpt‖ɑːpt/ v [I+for/to-v] to make a choice (esp. of one thing or course of action instead of another): *You can opt to receive your pension in small regular amounts or in a single lump sum. | The voters opted for higher taxes rather than any reduction in services.*
  opt out phr v **1** [I (of)] to choose not to do something or take part in something: *You promised to help us, so please don't opt out (of it) now! | Employees may choose to opt out of the company pension scheme and to make their own arrangements.* **2** BrE (of a hospital or school) to choose to leave local authority control and to receive money to run the organization direct from the government

op·tic /ˈɒptɪk‖ˈɑːp-/ adj of or belonging to the eyes: *the optic nerve* —see picture at EYE

op·ti·cal /ˈɒptɪkəl‖ˈɑːp-/ adj **1** of or about the sense of sight; VISUAL: *optical instruments | an optical illusion* (=something that deceives the sense of sight) —see picture at ILLUSION **2** of or using light, esp. for the purpose of recording and storing information for use in a computer system: *optical character recognition | optical storage | an optical disk* —compare MAGNETIC (2) — ~ly /kli/ adv

optical art /ˌ··· ˈ·/ n [U] OP ART

optical fi·bre /ˌ··· ˈ··/ n a thread-like piece of glass or plastic which can carry light, and is used in many modern technical situations where electricity was formerly used

op·ti·cian /ɒpˈtɪʃən‖ɑːp-/ n a person who makes glasses and/or CONTACT LENSes and sells them in a shop (**optician's**): *I've got an appointment at the optician's today.*
  ▷ USAGE Compare **oculist, optician, optometrist** and **ophthalmologist. Oculist** is an old-fashioned word and not much used. In Britain, people associate eyetests and glasses with an **optician**; in the US, **optometrist** is more common. Technically, an **optician** is qualified only to make glasses, not to test the eyes, but an **ophthalmologist** holds a regular medical degree and specializes in the eyes. He or she can test the eyes, and also perform SURGERY on them, or PRESCRIBE drugs.◁

op·tics /ˈɒptɪks‖ˈɑːp-/ n [U] the scientific study of light

op·ti·mal /ˈɒptɪməl‖ˈɑːp-/ adj OPTIMUM

op·ti·mis·m /ˈɒptɪmɪzəm‖ˈɑːp-/ n [U] a tendency to give more attention to the good side of a situation or to expect the best possible result —opposite **pessimism**

op·ti·mist /ˈɒptɪmɪst‖ˈɑːp-/ n a person who thinks that whatever happens will be good: *Tom, an eternal optimist/ever the optimist, hadn't bothered to bring his umbrella.* —opposite **pessimist** — ~ic /ˌɒptɪˈmɪstɪk◄‖ˌɑːp-/ adj : *The experts are optimistic about our chances of success/optimistic that we will succeed.* — ~ically /kli/ adv

op·ti·mize also **-mise** BrE /ˈɒptɪmaɪz‖ˈɑːp-/ v [T] to make as perfect or effective as possible: *to tune up a racing car engine in order to optimize its performance*

op·ti·mum /ˈɒptɪməm‖ˈɑːp-/ also **optimal**— adj [A] most likely to bring success or advantage; most favourable: *optimum conditions for growing rice*

op·tion /ˈɒpʃən‖ˈɑːp-/ n **1** [(the) U] the freedom to choose: *You will have to pay them; you have no option.* **2** [C] one of a number of courses of action that are possible and may be chosen: *The government has two options: to reduce spending or to increase taxes. | I want to keep my options open for the moment.* (=not choose too soon) | *There are various options open to you.* (=possible for you) | *The stu-dents regard this subject as a soft option.* (=easier than others that could be chosen) **3** [C] something that is offered as well as standard equipment: *The car includes air-conditioning among its options.* **4** [C (on)] the right to buy or sell something in the future: *Jones has taken an option on shares in the company.*

op·tion·al /ˈɒpʃənəl‖ˈɑːp-/ adj which may be freely chosen or not chosen: *optional subjects at school | The car radio is an optional extra.* —opposites **compulsory, obligatory** — ~ly adv

op·tom·e·trist /ɒpˈtɒmɪtrɪst‖ɑːpˈtɑː-/ n esp. AmE a specialist who tests the eyes and PRESCRIBEs glasses for people who cannot see properly without them —see OPTICIAN (USAGE)

Op·trex /ˈɒptreks‖ˈɑːp-/ n [U] tdmk a type of liquid made by Optrex Ltd and used for washing the eyes to stop them being sore

op·u·lence /ˈɒpjʊləns‖ˈɑːp-/ n [U] very great and splendid wealth

op·u·lent /ˈɒpjʊlənt‖ˈɑːp-/ adj **1** having or showing great wealth: *opulent surroundings* **2** fml in good supply; PLENTIFUL: *an opulent beard* — ~ly adv

o·pus /ˈəʊpəs/ n [usu. sing.] **1** (often cap.) a work of music by a particular musician, numbered according to when it was written: *Beethoven's Opus 106* **2** often pomp or derog any work of art —see also MAGNUM OPUS

Opus mag·num /ˌ··· ˈ··/ MAGNUM OPUS

or /ər; strong ɔːr/ conj **1** (often with **either**; used before the last of a set of possibilities): *Would you prefer coffee or tea? | She's either 21 or 22. | I don't care whether I get it or not. | Did you or didn't you? | She's going to spend the summer in London or Paris or Rome/in London, Paris, or Rome.* —see EITHER³ (USAGE) **2** (after a negative) and not: *He never smokes or drinks.* **3** if not; otherwise: *Wear your coat or (else) you'll be cold. | He can't be ill, or he wouldn't have come. | Either say you're sorry or get out!* **4** (used when giving a second name for something) that is; that means; it would be better to say: *She was born in Saigon, or Ho Chi Minh City as it is now called.* **5** or **so** about; at least; or more: *a minute or so | five dollars or so* **6** or **two** (used after singular nouns) about; at least; or more: *a minute or two | a dollar or two* —see also **or else** (ELSE)
  ▷ USAGE **Or** can be used when you want to limit or correct something you have said: *It's going to snow tomorrow,* **or** *that's what the forecast says. | He is,* **or** *was, a very famous writer.*◁

OR written abbrev. for: OREGON

or·a·cle /ˈɒrəkəl‖ˈɔː-, ˈɑː-/ n **1** (in ancient Greece) **a** a person through whom a god was thought to speak **b** a place where a god was believed to answer people's questions through such a person **2** humor or derog a very wise person who can give the best advice: *I suppose before we do anything we'd better consult the oracle.* **3** work the oracle BrE infml to succeed in doing something difficult —see also DELPHIC ORACLE

Oracle the TELETEXT (=television broadcasting of written information) system operated by the IBA in Britain

o·rac·u·lar /ɒˈrækjʊlər, ə-‖ɔː-, ə-/ adj **1** of an oracle **2** (of a statement) solemn and hard to understand

o·ral /ˈɔːrəl/ adj **1** spoken, not written: *He passed his French oral (examination).* **2** esp. med of, about, or taken in by the mouth: *oral hygiene* — ~ly adv
  ▷ USAGE Compare **aural** which means "of or received through hearing": *an aural test* (=a test where students listen) | *an oral test* (=a test where students speak).◁

oral con·tra·cep·tive /ˌ··· ···ˈ···/ n fml or tech a combination of drugs (usu. OESTROGEN and PROGESTERONE) which can be swallowed to prevent a woman becoming PREGNANT —see also MORNING-AFTER-PILL, PILL (2)

oral sex /ˌ·· ˈ·/ n [U] the practice of touching the sex organs with the lips and tongue in order to give sexual pleasure —see also CUNNILINGUS, FELLATIO

oral sur·geon /ˈ··· ˌ··/ n a DENTIST who can perform operations in the mouth —compare DENTIST

or·ange /ˈɒrɪndʒ‖ˈɔː-, ˈɑː-/ n **1** [C] a round reddish-yellow bitter-sweet fruit grown in tropical areas, with a thick skin and divided into parts (SEGMENTs) inside: *to peel an orange* —see picture at FRUIT **2** [U] the colour of an orange —**orange** adj : *an orange glow in the sky*

or·ange·ade /ˌɒrˌndʒ'eɪd‖ˌɔː-, ˌɑː-/ n [U] a drink containing or tasting of orange juice

orange blos·som /'··· ˌ··/ n [U] the small white flowers of the orange tree

Orange Free State /ˌ··· '·/ [the] a former British COLONY in southern Africa which is now part of South Africa

Or·ange·man /'ɒrɪndʒmən‖'ɔː-, 'ɑː-/ n -men /mən/ a member of a Northern Ireland society of PROTESTANTS, with branches also in Scotland, named after WILLIAM OF ORANGE; also known as the **Orange Order** or the **Loyal Orange Institution**

Orangemen's Day /'··· ˌ·/ July 12, celebrated by Protestants in Northern Ireland with the **Orangemen's Day Parade**, which remembers the Protestant success over James II and his Catholic supporters at the Battle of the Boyne

oranges and lem·ons /ˌ··· · '··/ a British NURSERY RHYME (an old song for children) based on the names of places, esp. churches, in London:

"Oranges and lemons"
  say the bells of St. Clements.
"You owe me five farthings"
  say the bells of St. Martins.
"When will you pay me?"
  say the bells of Old Bailey.
"When I grow rich"
  say the bells of Shoreditch.
"When will that be?"
  say the bells of Stepney.
"I do not know"
  says the great bell at Bow.

Young children play a game to this song. Two children join hands and hold their arms up to form an arch: they sing the song while the other players go underneath. At the end of the song they say: *"Here comes a candle to light you to bed, here comes a chopper to chop off your head. Chip chop, chip chop, the last man's dead"*, and as they say the last word they bring their arms down quickly to catch a child going underneath.

o·rang·u·tang /ɔːˌræŋuː'tæŋ‖ə'ræŋətæŋ/ also **o·rang·u·tan** /-tæn/— n a large monkey with reddish hair and no tail —see picture at APE

o·ra·tion /ə'reɪʃən, ɔː-/ n a formal and solemn public speech: *to deliver an oration*

or·a·tor /'ɒrətə‖'ɔː-, 'ɑː-/ n a person who speaks in public, esp. strongly and to a large crowd of people

or·a·to·ri·o /ˌɒrə'tɔːriəʊ‖ˌɔː-, ˌɑː-/ n -los a long musical work with singing but without acting, usu. telling a story from the Bible or about a religious subject —compare CANTATA

or·a·tory[1] /'ɒrətri‖'ɔːrətɔːri, 'ɑː-/ n [U] **1** the art of making good speeches **2** *sometimes derog* language highly decorated with long or formal words **-rical** /ˌɒrə'tɒrɪkəl‖ˌɔːrə'tɔː-, ˌɑːrə'tɑː-/ adj **--rically** /kli/ adv

oratory[2] n (esp. in the Roman Catholic Church) a small room or building for prayer

orb /ɔːb‖ɔːrb/ n **1** a ball decorated with gold, etc., carried by a king or queen on formal occasions as a sign of power **2** [usu. pl.] poet an eye

Or·bi·son /'ɔːbɪsən‖'ɔːr-/, **Roy** /rɔɪ/ (1936–88) a singer and songwriter who is best remembered for his 1964 song *Pretty Woman*

or·bit[1] /'ɔːbɪt‖'ɔːr-/ n **1** the curved path of something moving round something else, esp. of the Earth going round the sun, or the moon or a spacecraft going round the Earth: *a satellite in orbit round the Earth* **2** an area of power or influence: *countries within the Soviet orbit* ~ **al** adj : *an orbital road* (=round a city)

orbit[2] v [I;T] to move in an orbit (round): *The satellite orbits the Earth every 48 hours.*

or·chard /'ɔːtʃəd‖'ɔːrtʃərd/ n a place where certain, esp. non-CITRUS, fruit trees are grown: *an apple orchard* —compare GROVE (2)

or·ches·tra /'ɔːkɪstrə‖'ɔːr-/ n [C+sing./pl. v] a large group of musicians who play music for combinations of different instruments: *He plays the violin in a symphony orchestra/a string orchestra.* —compare BAND[2] (2), ENSEMBLE

or·ches·tral /ɔː'kestrəl‖ɔːr-/ adj of, by, or written for an orchestra: *orchestral music*

orchestra pit /'··· ·/ n the space below and in front of a theatre stage where musicians sit and play —see picture at THEATRE

or·ches·trate /'ɔːkɪstreɪt‖'ɔːr-/ v [T] **1** to arrange (music) so that it can be performed by an orchestra **2** *sometimes derog* to plan (something with many parts) for the best effect: *to orchestrate a political campaign | Someone is trying to orchestrate our downfall.* —**-tration** /ˌɔːkɪ'streɪʃən‖ˌɔːr-/ n [C;U]

or·chid /'ɔːkɪd‖'ɔːr-/ also **or·chis** /'ɔːkɪs‖'ɔːr-/tech— n (a tropical plant with) an often big bright flower divided into three parts of which the middle one is larger and like a lip

or·dain /ɔː'deɪn‖ɔːr-/ v [T] **1** to make (someone) a priest or religious leader: *He was ordained in 1984.* [+obj+n] *She was ordained the first woman priest of her church.* —see also ORDINATION **2** [+that;obj] (of God, the law, etc.) to order; DECREE

or·deal /ɔː'diːl, 'ɔːdiːl‖ɔːr'diːl, 'ɔːrdiːl/ n a difficult or painful experience: *The parents went through a terrible ordeal when their child was kidnapped.*

or·der[1] /'ɔːdə‖'ɔːr-/ n **1** [U] the special way in which a group of people, objects, etc., are put on a list or arranged in connection with each other; SEQUENCE: *The words in a dictionary are shown in alphabetical order. | The items are listed in order of importance. | in chronological order* **2** [U] the state in which things are carefully arranged in their proper place; neatness: *Just give me five minutes to put my desk in order.* | (fig.) *He put his business affairs in order before he died.* —opposite **disorder** **3** [U] fitness for use or operation: *The telephone's* **out of order.** (=does not work) | *This car is in good working/running order.* **4** [U] the condition in which laws and rules are obeyed: *That young teacher can't keep order in her classroom. | The chairman* **called him to order** *at the meeting.* (=told him to stop disobeying the rules) | *Order! Order!* (=Stop breaking the rules of the meeting.) | *Your question is* **out of order.** (=against the rules) —see also POINT OF ORDER, **law and order** (LAW (9)), **in order** (ORDER[1]) **5** [C] also **orders** pl.— a command or direction, given by a person who has the right to command: *You must obey my orders.* [+to-v/that] *I have orders* (=I have been commanded) *to search your room/that your room must be searched. | The general gave the order to advance. | I'm here by order of the general. | The ship left* **under orders** *to sail to the Pacific.* (=having been commanded to do this) | (infml) *Take your medicine: it's* **doctor's orders.** **6** [C (**for**)] a request (esp. by a customer) to supply goods. *We placed* (=made) *an order for a newspaper to be delivered daily.* | *"Shall I take your orders now?" asked the waiter.* —see also MAIL ORDER, SIDE ORDER, **on order, to order** (ORDER[1]) **7** [C] the goods supplied in accordance with such a request: *He collected his order from the shop.* **8** [C] a written or printed paper which allows the holder to do something, e.g. to be paid money —see also MONEY ORDER, POSTAL ORDER **9** [C+sing./pl. v] (often cap. as part of a name) **a** a society of people who lead a holy life according to a particular set of religious rules: *an order of monks/nuns* **b** a (secret) society of people who allow others to join them through an INITIATION ceremony: *a Masonic order/the Benevolent and Protective Order of Elks* —see also ORDERS **10** [(the) C (of)] (often cap. as part of a name) **a** a group of people who have received any of several special honours given by a king, queen, etc., for service, bravery, etc.: *a member of the Order of the Garter* **b** a piece of metal, silk, etc., worn to show that one belongs to such a group: *wearing his orders* **11** [C] fml a kind; sort: *intelligence of the highest order* **12** [C usu. sing.] fml the way things usually happen at a particular time in history: *the present economic order* **13** [C] also **orders** pl.— a special group or rank in a society: *the military order | (now rare or humor) the lower orders* (=workers, servants, etc.) **14** [U] the stated kind of clothing worn or equipment carried, or the stated arrangement of soldiers, machines, etc.: *troops in full marching order | The aircraft flew in* **close order.** (=with little space between them) **15** [C] tech a division of animals or plants (or languages), below a CLASS[1] (6) and above a FAMILY (5) **16** [C] tech a division of any group of things: *Greek pillars of the Doric and Ionic orders* **17 in order** fml acceptable; properly arranged or according to accepted rules: *It'll be quite in order for you to speak now. | Is your passport in order?* **18 in order that** fml so that: *He sold it in order that we might live more comfortably.* **19 in order to** with the purpose or intention of; so that one may: *He stood on a chair in order to reach the top shelf.* | *I sent the plans in order for you to study them fully before the meeting.* **20 last orders** *BrE* the phrase used in PUBS to warn people that the pub is about to close and people should order their last drinks **21 of/in the order of** *BrE* || **on the order of** *AmE*– about; about as much or as many as: *Her income is of the order of £17,000 a year.* **22 only obeying orders** a phrase used by many German soldiers charged with WAR CRIMES after the Second World War. They defended their actions by saying that they had no choice because they were "only obeying orders". **23 on order** asked for from the maker or supplier but not yet supplied: *The textbook you require is temporarily out of stock, but it's on order.* **24 out of order: a** not working properly **b** not in accordance with the rules of a parliament, court, or similar body **c** *sl* behaving in a wrong or unacceptable way **25 to order** made to fit a particular person's body or according to the exact needs of a particular person: *We supply handmade shoes to order.* –see also COURT ORDER, MARCHING ORDERS, STANDING ORDER, TALL ORDER, **call to order** (CALL[1])

order[2] *v* **1** [T] to give an order (to or for); command: *The general ordered an attack.* [+that] *He ordered that the men (should) fire the guns/that the guns (should) be fired.* [+obj+to-v] *The doctor ordered her patient to take a month's rest.* | *If you make any more noise I shall order you* (=command you to go) *out of the room.* **2** [I;T (**for**)] to ask for (something) to be brought, made, etc., in return for payment: *"Have you ordered yet, Madam?" asked the waiter.* | *I've ordered new curtains for the bedroom.* | *Don't forget to order a taxi.* | *I've ordered a beer for you.* [+obj(i)+obj(d)] *I've ordered you a beer.* **3** [T] to arrange; put in order: *Take time to order your thoughts before you write the essay.* | *a well-ordered existence*

▷ USAGE People whose position gives them a right to be obeyed can **order** or give **orders**, but **command** is usually used only in a military sense: *The doctor ordered me to rest for a week.* | *The general ordered/commanded his men to advance.* **Direct**, **instruct**, **tell** and **ask** are similar to **order** but not as strong.◁
order sbdy. **about/around** *phr v* [T] to annoy (someone) by giving many orders, esp. unpleasantly; BOSS[2] about: *His big brother is always ordering him about.*

order book /'··· ·/ *n BrE* (a book in which are written) all the orders which remain to be dealt with by a particular company, etc.: *Order books in the shipping industry remain generally much below normal.*

or·der·ly[1] /'ɔːdəli||'ɔːrdərli/ *adj* **1** well-arranged: *an orderly office* **2** loving good arrangement; of a tidy nature and habits **3** peaceful and well-behaved: *an orderly crowd* –opposite **disorderly** —**·liness** *n* [U]

orderly[2] *n* **1** a person who helps in a hospital, usu. without special professional training **2** a soldier who attends an officer

Order of Mer·it /,·· · · '··/ (*abbrev.* OM) [*the*] a special honour given to British people who have done something unusually good in military or CIVILIAN life. Only 24 people have the Order of Merit at any one time. –compare COMPANION OF HONOUR

Order of the Bath /,·· · · '·/ [*the*] one of the highest degrees of British KNIGHTHOOD. There are three classes of the Order, and each is divided into military and CIVIL (1) varieties.

Order of the Gar·ter /,·· · · '··/ [*the*] the highest degree of British KNIGHTHOOD, together with the Order of the Thistle (from the GARTER said to have been lost by the Countess of Salisbury at a royal event, and picked up by King Edward III, whose action saved her embarrassment)

Order of the This·tle /,·· · · '··/ [*the*] the highest degree of British KNIGHTHOOD, together with the Order of the Garter. Only 16 people have the Order of the Thistle at any one time, and they are mainly Scottish men of high rank.

order pa·per /'·· ··/ *n* a list of what is to be talked about, esp. in the British parliament

or·ders /'ɔːdəz||'ɔːrdərz/ *n* [P] *tech* the state of being a priest or other person permitted to perform Christian services and duties: *He took holy orders.* (=became a priest)

or·di·nal[1] /'ɔːdɨnəl||'ɔːr-/ *adj* showing position in a set of numbers

ordinal[2] also **ordinal num·ber** /,··· '··/– *n* one of the numbers (1st, 2nd, 3rd, etc.) that show order rather than quantity –compare CARDINAL NUMBER

or·di·nance /'ɔːdɨnəns||'ɔːrdənəns/ *n fml* **1** an order given by a ruler or governing body: *an ordinance of the council* **2** *AmE* a law, usu. of a city or town, that forbids or controls some activity: *an ordinance to prevent loitering in the park*

or·di·na·ri·ly /'ɔːdənərɨli, ,ɔːdən'eərɨli||,ɔːrdən'erɨli/ *adv* **1** in an ordinary way: *He was behaving quite ordinarily.* **2** usually: *Ordinarily, she's back by five o'clock.*

or·di·na·ry /'ɔːdənri||'ɔːrdəneri/ *adj* **1** not unusual; common: *I've got an ordinary sort of car, nothing special.* | *Visiting old people is part of her ordinary routine.* | *I think this artist's paintings are rather ordinary.* (=not particularly good) **2 in the 'ordinary way** if nothing unusual happens **3 out of the ordinary** unusual; uncommon: *We'll be there by six, as long as nothing out of the ordinary happens.* –see also EXTRAORDINARY —**·iness** *n* [U]

ordinary lev·el /'··· ,··/ *n* [C;U] see O LEVEL

ordinary sea·man /,··· '··/ *n* a naval rank –see TABLE 3

ordinary shares /,··· '·/ also **equities**– *n* [P] the largest part of a company's capital. People who own the ordinary shares of a company choose the directors, vote at meetings, and have the right to receive part of the company's profits if these are given out.

or·di·na·tion /,ɔːdɨ'neɪʃən||,ɔːr-/ *n* [C;U] the act or ceremony of ordaining (ORDAIN) a priest

▶CULTURAL NOTE Until 1992 there were no Anglican women priests in England, but in 1992, after much discussion, the Church of England decided to allow the ordination of women priests. Many people in the Church of England disagreed with this decision, and are still opposed to the idea of women priests.◀

ord·nance /'ɔːdnəns||'ɔːr-/ *n* [U] **1** big guns on wheels; ARTILLERY **2** weapons, explosives, and vehicles used in fighting

Ordnance Sur·vey /,·· '··/ also **OS**– [*the*] an official organization which makes very detailed and correct maps of Britain and Ireland. The maps are used by people walking in the country, and each map has its own OS number. –compare US GEOLOGICAL SURVEY

or·dure /'ɔːdjuə[r]||'ɔːrdʒər/ *n* [U] *fml* dirt, esp. waste matter from the bowels

ore /ɔː[r]/ *n* [C;U] rock, earth, etc., from which metal can be obtained: *iron/copper ore*

o·re·ad /'ɔːriæd/ *n* in ancient stories, a female spirit of the mountains –compare NAIAD, DRYAD

o·reg·a·no /,ɔːrɪ'gɑːnəʊ||ə'regənəʊ/ *n* [U] a plant used in cooking to add a special taste to food

Or·e·gon /'ɒrɨgən||'ɔː-, 'ɑː-/ *written abbrev* **OR** a state in the NW of the US known for its fruit, fish, and scenery –see colour map on pages 1374-5

Oregon Trail /'··· ,·/ [*the*] the path that early American settlers followed to reach the Northwest. It crossed the Great Plains and the Rocky Mountains before turning towards Idaho, Washington, and Oregon.

O·re·o /'ɔːriəʊ/ *n tdmk* **1** a very popular American COOKIE that is chocolate outside and white ICING inside **2** *usu. derog* a black person who thinks like and has the values of a white person

or·gan /'ɔːgən||'ɔːr-/ *n* **1** a part of an animal or plant that has a special purpose: *The liver is a vital organ.* (=an organ without which life cannot continue) | *the sexual organs/organs of reproduction* **2** an organization, usu. official, that has a special purpose: *Parliament is an organ of government.* **3** [(**of**)] a newspaper, radio station, etc., that supplies information to, or represents the views of, a particular group: *This paper is the official organ of the Socialist party.* **4 a** a musical instrument made of many pipes of different lengths through which air is forced, played rather like a piano and often found in churches –see also ORGANIST **b** a similar instrument without pipes: *an electric organ* –see also BARREL ORGAN, MOUTHORGAN **5** *euph* (esp. in the phrase **male organ**) a PENIS

or·gan·die ‖ also **-dy** *AmE* /ˈɔːɡəndi‖ˈɔːr-/ *n* [U] very thin rather stiff cotton material, used esp. for women's dresses

organ grind·er /ˈ··ˌ··/ *n* **1** a street musician who plays a BARREL ORGAN and often has a monkey dressed like a human **2** *BrE sl* the person in charge: *I've come to speak to the organ grinder, not his monkey!*

or·gan·ic /ɔːˈɡænɪk‖ɔːr-/ *adj* **1** of or for living things or the organs of the body: *chemistry/diseases/architecture* — opposite **inorganic 2 a** made of parts with specialized purposes: *an organic system* **b** [(to)] being one of these parts; necessary: *The music is organic to the story.* **3** (of food) produced without the help of artificial chemicals: *organic vegetables | beef | bread*
▶ CULTURAL NOTE Organic food is usu. more expensive than non-organic food, and is bought by people interested in eating healthy foods.◀
— ~ally /kli/ *adv*

organic farm·ing /·ˌ·· ˈ··/ *n* [U] a method of farming in which food is grown without the help of artificial chemicals

or·gan·is·m /ˈɔːɡənɪzəm‖ˈɔːr-/ *n* **1** a living being **2** a whole system made of specialized parts

or·gan·ist /ˈɔːɡənɪst‖ˈɔːr-/ *n* a musician who plays an ORGAN (4a)

or·gan·i·za·tion also **-sation** *BrE* /ˌɔːɡənaɪˈzeɪʃən‖ˌɔːrɡənə-/ *n* **1** [C] a group of people with a special purpose, such as a club or business: *to set up/found/run a charity organization* **2** [U] the arrangement or planning of parts so as to form an effective whole: *Efficiency depends on good organization.* — ~al *adj* : *organizational ability* — ~ally *adv*

Organization of A·mer·i·can States /·····ˌ··· ··ˌ···· ˈ·/ [*the*] see OAS

or·gan·ize also **-ise** *BrE* /ˈɔːɡənaɪz‖ˈɔːr-/ *v* **1** [T] to arrange into a good working system: *to organize one's facts in order to make a speech | I must try to organize my life a bit better.* **2** [T] to make the necessary arrangements for: *Who is organizing this year's office party? | I'll try and organize a lift for you.* **3** [I;T] *esp. AmE for* UNIONIZE — **-izer** *n*

or·gan·ized also **-ised** *BrE* /ˈɔːɡənaɪzd‖ˈɔːr-/ *adj* having good and effective organization: *I'm afraid I'm not very organized this morning. | a well-organized house* — opposite **disorganized**

organized crime /ˌ··· ˈ·/ *n* [U] (the activities of) professional criminals operating in large well-organized groups: *Most of the trade in hard drugs is now controlled by organized crime.* —see also MAFIA

or·gas·m /ˈɔːɡæzəm‖ˈɔːr-/ *n* [C;U] the highest point of sexual pleasure —**-mic** /ɔːˈɡæzmɪk‖ɔːr-/ *adj*

or·gi·as·tic /ˌɔːdʒiˈæstɪk◄‖ˌɔːr-/ *adj* **1** of or like an orgy **2** full of excitement or wild activity

or·gy /ˈɔːdʒi‖ˈɔːr-/ *n* **1** a wild party, usu. with large quantities of food, alcohol, etc., and esp. with sexual activity: *a drunken orgy* **2** [(of)] *infml* an activity or set of activities done too much, or without control: *They embarked on an orgy of sightseeing/of spending.*

o·ri·el win·dow /ˈɔːriəl ˌwɪndəʊ/ *n tech* an upper window that is built out from a wall

o·ri·ent¹ /ˈɔːriənt, ˈɒri-‖ˈɔː-/ *v* [T] *esp. AmE* to ORIENTATE

orient² ** *adj* [A] *poet* **1 eastern **2** (of the sun) rising

Orient *n* [*the*] *esp. fml or lit* the eastern part of the world; Asia —compare OCCIDENT, EAST

o·ri·en·tal /ˌɔːriˈentl◄, ˌɒ-‖ˌɔː-/ *n, adj* (*sometimes cap.*) (a person) of or from the Orient —compare OCCIDENTAL, and see SUBCONTINENTAL (USAGE NOTE)

o·ri·en·tal·ist /ˌɔːriˈentəlɪst, ˌɒ-‖ˌɔː-/ *n* a specialist in the languages, civilizations, etc., of the countries of the Orient, including the Middle East

o·ri·en·tate /ˈɔːriənteɪt, ˈɒ-‖ˈɔː-/ also **orient** *esp. AmE*— *v* [T] **1** [*often pass.*] to arrange or direct with a particular purpose: *an English language course that is orientated towards the needs of businessmen | an export-oriented company* (=which deals mostly in EXPORTS) *| a text-oriented microcomputer* **2** to establish the position of (oneself or something else), esp. in relation to a map or COMPASS: *The climbers stopped to orientate themselves before descending the mountain.* —see also DISORIENTATE

o·ri·en·ta·tion /ˌɔːriənˈteɪʃən, ˌɒ-‖ˌɔː-/ *n* [C;U] **1** a position or direction: (fig.) *a new orientation in life* **2** [U] *AmE* preparation for a new, usu. long-lasting activity: *The new students have three days of orientation before classes begin.‖an orientation meeting for the workshop*

o·ri·en·teer·ing /ˌɔːriənˈtɪərɪŋ, ˌɒ-‖ˌɔː-/ *n* [U] a sport in which people have to find their way quickly across unknown country, using a map and COMPASS

Orient Ex·press /ˌ··· ·ˈ·/ [*the*] a railway train for the rich which became famous for making the journey from Europe (starting in London) all the way across Asia. It now runs regularly only between London and Venice.

or·i·fice /ˈɒrɪfɪs‖ˈɔː-, ˈɑː-/ *n fml or humor* an opening; hole, esp. in the body

o·ri·ga·mi /ˌɒrɪˈɡɑːmi ‖ ˌɔː-/ *n* [U] the Japanese art of folding paper to make decorative objects such as birds, animals, etc.

or·i·gin /ˈɒrɪdʒɪn‖ˈɔː-, ˈɑː-/ *n* **1** [C;U] a starting point: *the origin of a river/of a belief | a word of unknown origin* **2** [U] also **origins** *pl.*— parents and conditions of early life: *a woman of humble origin(s)* (=from a low social class or a poor family)

o·rig·i·nal¹ /əˈrɪdʒɪnəl, -dʒənəl/ *adj* **1** [A *no comp.*] first; earliest: *The original owner of the house was a Frenchman.* **2** *often apprec* new and different; unlike others: *an original idea/invention | a very original thinker | How original of you!* —opposite **unoriginal 3** [A] not copied: *an original (painting by) Picasso* —see also ORIGINALLY

original² *n* **1** [C] (of a painting, official paper, etc.) the one from which copies have been or can be made: *Which museum is the original in?* **2** [*the*+S] the language in which something was originally written: *They are studying Arabic in order to read the Koran in the original.* **3** [C] *infml, sometimes humor or derog* a person whose behaviour, clothing, etc., are unusual

o·rig·i·nal·i·ty /əˌrɪdʒɪˈnælɪti/ *n* [U] *often apprec* the quality of being ORIGINAL¹ (2): *Her book shows great originality.*

o·rig·i·nal·ly /əˈrɪdʒɪnəli, -dʒənəli/ *adv* **1** in the beginning; formerly: *The family originally came from France. | It was originally conceived as a biography, but became a novel.* **2** in a new and different way: *a very originally written play*

original sin /·ˌ··· ˈ·/ *n* [U] the state of disobedience to God which everyone is in from birth, according to Christian teaching, because Adam picked the fruit in the garden of Eden —see also FALL

o·rig·i·nate /əˈrɪdʒɪneɪt/ *v* **1** [I+*adv/prep*] to have as an established starting point: *This TV series originated in/from a short story.* **2** [T] to be the first person to establish: *She originated a discussion group.* —**-nator** *n*

Origin of Species [*the*] see ON THE ORIGIN OF SPECIES

o·ri·son /ˈɒrɪzən‖ˈɔː-, ˈɑː-/ *n old use* a prayer

Ork·ney /ˈɔːkni‖ˈɔːr-/ a group of islands, also known as the **Orkney Islands** or the **Orkneys**, off the N coast of Scotland; mainly farmland but also serving as a base for the North Sea oil industry. The main town is Kirkwall. —see colour map on page 818

Or·lan·do /ɔːˈlændəʊ‖ɔːr-/ a city in Florida, US which claims that it attracts more tourists than anywhere else in the world, mainly because of DISNEY WORLD and other large amusement parks —see colour map on pages 1374-5

Or·ly Air·port /ˌɔːli ˈeəpɔːt‖ˌɔːrli ˈeərpɔːrt/ also **Orly**— an international airport SE of Paris, France

or·mo·lu /ˈɔːməluː‖ˈɔːr-/ *n* [U] a gold-coloured mixture of metals, not containing real gold: *an ormolu clock*

or·na·ment¹ /ˈɔːnəmənt‖ˈɔːr-/ *n* **1** [C] an object possessed because it is (thought to be) beautiful rather than because it is useful: *little ornaments on the mantelpiece* **2** [U] something that is added to make something else more beautiful: *very plain architecture, with little ornament* **3** [C (to)] *fml sometimes derog* a person or thing that adds honour, importance, or beauty (but not necessarily usefulness or cleverness): *She is an ornament to her profession. | Her escort is strictly an ornament, he doesn't seem to have a brain cell working.*

or·na·ment² /ˈɔːnəmənt‖ˈɔːr-/ *v* [T (**with**)] to add ornament to: *a finely ornamented ceiling*

or·na·men·tal /ˌɔːnəˈmentl◄‖ˌɔːr-/ *adj* providing or used as ornament; DECORATIVE: *a photograph in an ornamental frame* | *The buttons on this dress are only ornamental.* (=you cannot unfasten them) | *an ornamental bush –* **– ly** *adv*

or·na·men·ta·tion /ˌɔːnəmenˈteɪʃən‖ˌɔːr-/ *n* [U] the quality of having or adding ornament

or·nate /ɔːˈneɪt‖ɔːr-/ *adj sometimes derog* having a great deal of decoration; not simple: *an ornate style –* ~ **ly** *adv* **– ~ ness** *n* [U]

or·ne·ry /ˈɔːnəri‖ˈɔːr-/ *adj humor, esp. AmE* bad-tempered

or·ni·thol·o·gy /ˌɔːnɪˈθɒlədʒi‖ˌɔːrnɪˈθɑː-/ *n* [U] the scientific study of birds **–gist** *n* **–gical** /ˌɔːnɪˈθɒlɒdʒɪkəl‖ˌɔːrnɪˈθɑː-/ *adj*

o·ro·tund /ˈɒrəʊtʌnd‖ˈɔːrə-/ *adj fml* **1** full and strong in sound **2** foolishly solemn

or·phan[1] /ˈɔːfən‖ˈɔːr-/ *n* a person, esp. a child, whose parents are both dead; sometimes used of a person who has one parent only left alive

orphan[2] *v* [T *usu. pass.*] to cause to be an orphan: *She was orphaned when her parents died in a plane crash.*

or·phan·age /ˈɔːfənɪdʒ‖ˈɔːr-/ *n* a place where orphan children live

Or·phe·us and Eu·ry·di·ce /ˌɔːfiəs ənd juːˈrɪdɪsi‖ˌɔːr-/ in CLASSICAL MYTHOLOGY, a loving husband and wife. Orpheus was a wonderful musician, and even wild animals and birds would stay and listen to him. When Eurydice died he followed her down into HADES and sang to the king and queen there, who allowed Eurydice to leave as long as Orpheus did not look round to see if she was following him. He did look round and so he lost her.

Orr /ɔːʳ/, **Bobby** (1948–) a Canadian ICE HOCKEY player

or·re·ry /ˈɒrəri‖ˈɔː-, ˈɑː-/ *n* an apparatus used for showing the positions and movements of bodies in the SOLAR SYSTEM

Or·te·ga /ɔːˈteɪɡə ‖ ɔːr-/, **Daniel** (1945–) a Nicaraguan Socialist politician, a member of the Sandinista Liberation Front, and head of state from 1981. His government was opposed by the Contras.

or·tho·don·tics /ˌɔːθəˈdɒntɪks‖ˌɔːrθəˈdɑːn-/ *n* [U] *tech* the skill or process of causing teeth that are not growing correctly to grow straight **–orthodontist** *n* : *My orthodontist has made my teeth much straighter.* **–orthodontic** *adj*

or·tho·dox /ˈɔːθədɒks‖ˈɔːrθədɑːks/ *adj* **1** generally or officially accepted: *orthodox ideas* **2** holding accepted (esp. religious) opinions: *an orthodox Muslim* –see also UNOR·THODOX **– –doxy** *n* [U] : *I would question the orthodoxy of his research methods.*

Orthodox Church /ˌ··· ˈ·/ also **Eastern Orthodox Church–** [*the*] any of several Christian churches esp. in eastern Europe and parts of Asia. The Orthodox churches regard the Communion as the central part of their worship. The LITURGY is always sung.

Orthodox Jew /ˌ··· ˈ·/ *n* a believer in **Orthodox Judaism**, which says that God's law must be followed exactly rather than used only as a set of principles to live by. Orthodox Jews sometimes dress in a particular way, the men being noticeable for their long beards and large black hats.

or·thog·ra·phy /ɔːˈθɒɡrəfi‖ɔːrˈθɑː-/ *n* [U] **1** spelling in general **2** correct spelling **–phic(al)** /ˌɔːθəˈɡræfɪk-(əl)◂‖ˌɔːr-/ *adj* **–phically** /kli/ *adv*

or·tho·pae·dic , **-pedic** /ˌɔːθəˈpiːdɪk◂‖ˌɔːr-/ *adj* of the branch of medicine (**orthopaedics**) that deals with making bones grow straight: *an orthopaedic hospital/ specialist*

Or·well /ˈɔːwel‖ˈɔːr-/, **George** (1903–50) an English writer best known for his NOVELs about TOTALITARIAN government, *Nineteen Eighty-Four* and *Animal Farm* –see also ANIMAL FARM, NINETEEN EIGHTY-FOUR

OS /ˌəʊ ˈes/ *abbrev. for:* **1** ORDNANCE SURVEY **2** OUTSIZE

O·sa·ka /əʊˈsɑːkə/ a city in Japan, the second largest in Japan

Os·borne /ˈɒzbɔːn‖ˈɑːzbɔːrn/, **John** (1929–) an English

writer of plays whose most famous works are *Look Back in Anger* and *The Entertainer* –see also ANGRY YOUNG MAN

Os·car /ˈɒskəʳ‖ˈɑːs-/ *n* **1** (a small STATUE given as) an American cinema prize each year: *She won the Oscar for Best Actress.* | *The film was nominated for two Oscars.* *the Oscars* (=the prize-giving ceremony) –see also ACADEMY AWARD; compare EMMY **2** a character from the children's television programme *Sesame Street*, who lives in a DUSTBIN and is dirty and rude, but still lovable

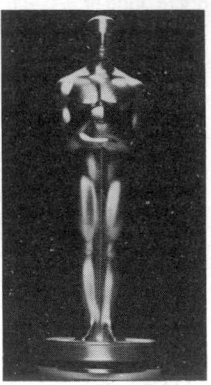
an Oscar

os·cil·late /ˈɒsɪleɪt‖ˈɑː-/ *v* [I] **1** *tech* to keep moving regularly from side to side, between two limits: *an oscillating pendulum* **2** [(**bet·ween**)] to vary between opposing choices; VACILLATE

os·cil·la·tion /ˌɒsɪˈleɪʃən‖ˌɑː-/ *n* **1** [U] the action of oscillating **2** [C] a single movement of something that is oscillating

os·cil·la·tor /ˈɒsɪleɪtəʳ‖ˈɑː-/ *n* **1** a person or thing that oscillates **2** *tech* a machine that produces electrical oscillations

os·cu·la·tion /ˌɒskjʊˈleɪʃən‖ˌɑː-/ *n* [U] *pomp & humor* the act of kissing

OSF /ˌəʊ es ˈef/ *abbrev. for:* OPEN SOFTWARE FOUNDATION

OSHA /ˈəʊʃə/ the Occupational Safety and Health Administration; a US government office that looks after the safety and health conditions of people at work

OSI /ˌəʊ es ˈaɪ/ open systems interconnection; an international plan to make different types of computers able to exchange information over wires or telephone lines by setting standards for the way it is organized (ORGANIZE) and sent

o·si·er /ˈəʊziəʳ‖ˈəʊʒəʳ/ *n* a tree (a type of WILLOW) whose branches are used for making baskets

O·si·ris /əʊˈsaɪərɪs/ an ancient Egyptian god-king of the sun and the dead, husband and brother of Isis

Os·lo /ˈɒzləʊ‖ˈɑːz-/ a city in SE Norway, the country's capital and chief port

Os·mond /ˈɒzmənd‖ˈɑːz-/ the name of a family of American entertainers who are known esp. for being clean, morally good, and religious, esp. singers **Donny Osmond** (1957–) and his sister **Marie Osmond** (1959–)

os·mo·sis /ɒzˈməʊsɪs‖ɑːz-/ *n* [U] *tech* the gradual passing of liquid through a MEMBRANE (=a skinlike wall): (fig.) *If you don't tell me, how am I supposed to know – by osmosis?* (=TELEPATHY) **–tic** /ɒzˈmɒtɪk‖ɑːzˈmɑː-/ *adj* **–tically** /kli/ *adv*

os·prey /ˈɒspri, -preɪ‖ˈɑː-/ *n* a type of large fish-eating bird

OSS /ˌəʊ es ˈes/ the Office of Strategic Services; a department of the US government established in 1942 to collect information about foreign enemies (SPY). It was replaced by the CIA in 1947.

os·se·ous /ˈɒsiəs‖ˈɑː-/ *adj med* bony

os·si·fy /ˈɒsɪfaɪ‖ˈɑː-/ *v* [I;T] **1** *tech* to (cause to) change into bone **2** to (cause to) become hard and unchanging in one's ideas **–fication** /ˌɒsɪfɪˈkeɪʃən‖ˌɑː-/ *n* [U]

Os·tend /ɒstˈend‖ɑːst-/ a town and port in NW Belgium, on the North Sea, known to many British people because of the ferries (FERRY) that go there from SE England

os·ten·si·ble /ɒˈstensɪbəl‖ɑː-/ *adj* [A] (esp. of reasons) seeming or pretended, but perhaps not really true: *Her ostensible reason for failing the exam was illness.* **–bly** *adv* : *ostensibly for love, but really for money*

os·ten·ta·tion /ˌɒstənˈteɪʃən, -ten- ‖ ˌɑː-/ *n* [U] *derog* unnecessary show of wealth, knowledge, etc. **–tious** *adj* : *an ostentatious lifestyle* **–tiously** *adv*

os·te·o·path /ˈɒstiəpæθ‖ˈɑː-/ *n* a person who treats illness and physical problems by the system (**osteopathy** /ˌɒstiˈɒpəθi‖ˌɑːstiˈɑː-/) of moving and pressing muscles and bones

▶ CULTURAL NOTE In Britain osteopaths receive training in osteopathy but are usu. not qualified in medicine and do not usu. work for the National Health Service. In the US, osteopaths have the same training as Doctors of Medicine, and their professional standing is the same. —compare CHIROPRACTOR ◀

os·tler /ˈɒslər/ also **hostler** esp. AmE— n (in former times) a man who took care of guests' horses at a small hotel

os·tra·cize also **-cise** BrE /ˈɒstrəsaɪz‖ˈɑː-/ v [T] (of a group of people) to stop accepting (someone) as a member of the group: The people who refused to join the strike have been ostracized by their workmates. — ~ **cism** /sɪzəm/ n [U]

os·trich /ˈɒstrɪtʃ‖ˈɔː-, ˈɑː-/ n 1 a very large African bird with beautiful feathers, which runs very quickly but cannot fly 2 infml a person who hides away from unpleasant reality (from the belief that the ostrich puts its head in the sand and then thinks that all of its body is hidden): It's no good playing ostrich. You have to face up to things.

ostrich

Os·wald /ˈɒzwəld‖ˈɑːz-/, **Lee Harvey** (1939–63) the man who is said to have shot the US President John F Kennedy in 1963

OTC /ˌəʊ tiː ˈsiː/ see OVER-THE-COUNTER (1)

O·thel·lo /əˈθeləʊ/ the black MOORISH main character in Shakespeare's play of the same name who killed his faithful wife, Desdemona, because he was made to believe that she had a lover

oth·er /ˈʌðər/ determiner, pron 1 the second of two; the remaining one of a set; what is left as well as that mentioned: She was holding the wheel with one hand and waving with the other (one). | She's cleverer than (any of) the others|than the other girls in her class. | Mary's here. Where are all the others? | These trousers are wet — I'll change into my others|my other ones. (=I have only two pairs) | We go to Europe every other year. (=every two years) 2 an additional person or thing; more as well: Are there any other problems? | There are plenty of other ways of getting there than by car. | I saw John with some other boys. (compare John with some girls) | A few of them are red; others are brown. (=some of the remaining ones are brown) | A few of them are red; the others are brown. (=all the rest are brown) 3 not the same; not this, not one-self, not one's own, etc.: He enjoys spending other people's money. (=not his own) | You should try to be more sensitive to the needs of others. (=other people) | He came here for other reasons (than the food and the beer). | I'm busy tonight — can I meet you some other time? | The company says it has to reduce its labour costs — in other words (=this means) — some of us are going to lose our jobs. 4 [usu. in negatives] other than: a except; apart from: There was nothing we could do other than wait. | You can't get there other than by boat. b anything but: She can hardly be other than annoyed about it. (=she is certain to be annoyed) 5 the other end/side the far or opposite of two ends/sides from this one: a voice at the other end of the telephone | a car parked on the other side of the street | They live on the other side of town. —opposite this end/side 6 the other day/afternoon/evening/night on a recent day/afternoon/evening/night —see also EACH OTHER, every other (EVERY), on the other hand (HAND¹), one after the other/after another (ONE), this, that, and the other (THIS); compare one day (ONE), next day (NEXT)

▷ USAGE Other is not used after an. The word is then **another**: They need another ticket|some other tickets. | Would you like another|some others?◁

other half /ˌ··· ˈ·/ n infml humor 1 a person's wife or husband: I've met Bert, but I haven't met his other half yet. 2 see how the other half lives to see how very wealthy people live

oth·er·wise /ˈʌðəwaɪz‖ˈʌðər-/ adv 1 in a different way;

differently: She says it's genuine, but we think otherwise. | You are presumed to be innocent until proved otherwise. (=proved not to be) | I was unable to attend the conference because I was **otherwise engaged**. (=busy with something else) 2 apart from that; in other ways: The soup was cold, but otherwise the meal was excellent|but it was an otherwise excellent meal. 3 if not: You'd better go now, otherwise you'll miss your train. 4 **or otherwise:** a or in some other way: We'll get there somehow, by train or otherwise. b or not: mothers, whether married or otherwise

oth·er·world·ly /ˌʌðəˈwɜːldli◂‖ˌʌðərˈwɜːr-/ adj sometimes derog more concerned with things of the spirit or mind than with material things —compare WORLDLY (2)

o·ti·ose /ˈəʊʃiəʊs, ˈəʊti-/ adj fml (of ideas, words, etc.) unnecessary; REDUNDANT

OTT /ˌəʊ tiː ˈtiː/ adj BrE OVER-THE-TOP

Ot·ta·wa /ˈɒtəwə‖ˈɑːt-/ the capital city of Canada, in the SE of the country, and its seat of government. One third of its people are French-speaking.

ot·ter /ˈɒtər‖ˈɑː-/ n a swimming fish-eating animal with beautiful brown fur

ot·to·man /ˈɒtəmən‖ˈɑː-/ n 1 a long soft seat without back or arms, sometimes hollow and used for storing things 2 AmE a piece of soft furniture, usu. half a metre high and round or square, which sits in front of a chair for resting the feet

Ottoman Em·pire /ˌ··· ˈ··/ [the] a large state which was begun by the Turks in the 13th century and lasted until after the First World War. The land which is now Turkey was only part of the Ottoman Empire, which included parts of modern Asia, Europe, and Africa.

OU /ˌəʊ ˈjuː/ abbrev. for: OPEN UNIVERSITY

ou·bli·ette /ˌuːbliˈet/ n (esp. in old castles) a small room that could be entered only from above, where prisoners could be kept

ouch /aʊtʃ/ interj (a cry expressing sudden pain): "Ouch! You hit my finger!"

ought /ɔːt/ v 3rd person sing. **ought** present tense negative short form **oughtn't** /ˈɔːtənt/ [modal+to-v] 1 to have the moral duty to do something; should: She ought to look after her children better. | You ought to be ashamed of yourself. | I wonder whether I oughtn't to speak to him about it. | He ought to be punished, oughtn't he? (=someone should punish him) | He oughtn't to have said that (but he did). 2 (shows that some action would be right or sensible): You ought to be more careful, you know.| Oughtn't he|(fml) ought he not to see a doctor? | We really ought to buy a new car, oughtn't we? | This old coat ought to have been thrown away years ago. | You ought to (=I wish you could) hear her play the piano! 3 will probably; can be expected to do something: Prices ought to come down soon. | They ought to win easily. — see NOT (USAGE)

▷ USAGE 1 **Ought** and **should** are similar in meaning but **ought** is slightly stronger in British English. In American English there is no significant difference in force or sense, and any differences in usage are dialectical (DIALECT). 2 **Oughtn't** and **shouldn't** are used to warn that an action is wrong or unwise: You **oughtn't to/shouldn't** talk so loud; you'll wake the baby. Compare **needn't** which means that something is unnecessary: You **needn't** talk so loud; I can hear you. 3 The past form of **ought** is **ought to have:** You **ought to have/should have** helped him. (=but you did not) | You **oughtn't to have/shouldn't have** hit him. (=but you did) —see also MUST (USAGE)◁

oui·ja board /ˈwiːdʒə bɔːd‖ˈwiːdʒiː bɔːrd/ n tdmk (often cap. O) a board with letters and signs on it, which people use to try to receive messages from the spirits of the dead

▶ CULTURAL NOTE Most people in Britain and the US do not believe that ouija boards work, but they are sometimes used for fun at parties. However, some people believe that it is very dangerous to use them, because the spirits of the dead may be harmful. ◀

ounce /aʊns/ (written abbrev. oz)— n 1 [C] either of two units of weight: Six ounces of cheese, please. —see TABLE 2 2 [S+of] (even) a small amount: Haven't you got an ounce of sense?

our /aʊər/ determiner (possessive form of WE) of or belonging to us: We told him that our daughter was in France.|

Have you seen our new car? | It was our happiest moment.| our modern world | one of our (=this country's) *most famous actors*

Our Fa·ther /ˌ·ˈ·-/ *n* [*the*] the LORD'S PRAYER

Our La·dy /ˌ·ˈ·-/ Mary, the mother of Christ

Our Lord /ˌ·ˈ·/ God or Christ, in the Christian religion

Our Man in Ha·van·a /ˌ·ˌ·ˈ·-·/ a book written in 1958 by Graham Greene about a man who was the British government's SECRET AGENT in Havana

Our Mu·tu·al Friend /ˌ·ˌ···ˈ·/ a book written in 1864–65 by Charles Dickens

ours /aʊəz‖aʊərz/ *pron* (*possessive form of* WE) (the one or ones) of or belonging to us: *This is your room, and ours* (=our room) *is next door. | Ours is|are on the table. | She said it was hers, but we insisted it was ours. | He's a friend of ours.*

our·selves /aʊəˈselvz‖aʊər-/ *pron* **1** (*reflexive form of* WE):*We saw ourselves on television. | We bought ourselves a car.* **2** (*strong form of* WE): *We built the house ourselves.* **3** *infml* (in) our usual state of mind or body: *We soon came to ourselves.* (=regained consciousness) **4** (all) by ourselves: **a** alone; without help: *We did it all by ourselves.* **b** alone; without anyone else: *We walked home by ourselves.* −see YOURSELF (USAGE) **5 to ourselves** for our private use; not shared: *a bathroom to ourselves*

Ouse /uːz/ [*the*] **1** also **Great Ouse**− a river in E England which begins in Northamptonshire and flows NE to join the Wash near the town of King's Lynn **2** a river in NE England, formed by the joining of the Rivers Swale and Ure in Yorkshire, which flows SE to the Humber

oust /aʊst/ *v* [T (**from**)] to force (someone) out, and perhaps take their place: *She ousted him as manager|from his position.*

ous·ter /ˈaʊstəʳ/ *n AmE* an act of ousting

out¹ /aʊt/ *adj, adv* [F] **1** away from the inside; in or to the outdoors, the outside, etc.: *Open the bag and take the money out. | Blood poured out from the wound. | It's not in my pocket − it must have fallen out. | Shut the door to keep the wind out. | He put his tongue out at her. | She opened the cage and let the bird out.* (=let it go free) | *I went to the bank and drew out £100.* (=took it from my account) | *I opened the box and out jumped a mouse.* (note word order) −see OUTSIDE (USAGE) **2 a** away from home or from a building: *Let's have an evening out at the theatre. | It's rather cold out. | They've invited me out for dinner. | She stays out late at nights. | tramps sleeping out (in the park)* **b** not in one's usual place; absent: *I'm afraid Mr Jones is out|has just gone out. | (BrE) The dockers came out* (=on STRIKE) *in sympathy with the miners.* **3** away from land, a town, or one's own country: *They live right out in the country. | to go out to Africa* **4 a** away from a surface or edge: *I tore my coat on a nail that was sticking out from the wall. | a piece of land jutting out into the sea* **b** away from a set of things: *Pick out the best of the apples.* **5** to a number of people or in all directions: *to hand out drinks|exam papers | to spread out the cloth | to share out the profits* **6 a** so as to be clearly seen, shown, understood, etc.: *Think|Plan it out properly. | Their secret is out. | The sun came out. | Are the daffodils out yet?* (=fully open) | *The black trees stood out against the snow. | When does his new book come out?* (=when will it be on sale in the shops?) | *A quarrel broke out.* **b** *esp. AmE* open and not secretive, esp. about homosexuality (HOMOSEXUAL): *He isn't out to his parents yet.* (=They don't know he's homosexual) | *Her husband sympathizes with our cause, but he isn't very out about it.* −see also OUT² (2); compare CLOSET² **7** in a loud voice; aloud: *Read|Call out the names. | (fig.) If you disagree you should speak out.* (=say what you think) **8** completely; so as to be finished: *to clean out the room | I'm tired out. | He'll be back before the month is out.* (=is ended) | *Let's try and sort out this mess.* **9** so as to no longer exist: *to wash out the dirty marks | They had to cut short their holiday when their money ran out.* **10 a** (of a fire or light) no longer burning: *The fire's gone out. | Please put your cigarette out.* **b** *infml* (of a machine) no longer working; not in ORDER¹ (3): *The elevator's out again.* **11** (so as to be) no longer conscious or awake: *He was knocked out in the second round of the fight. | I went out like a light* (=fell asleep) *as soon as I got into bed.* **12** no longer in a position of power: *The Republicans are out. | They were voted out at the last election.* **13** no longer fashionable: *Long skirts*

went out last year. **14** completely unsuitable or impossible: *That suggestion's absolutely out.* **15** (of a guess or sum, or the person responsible for it) wrong: *The bill was £4 out. | You're badly out in your calculations.* **16 a** (of a player or team in a game such as cricket or BASEBALL) no longer allowed to take part, according to the rules: *Sussex are all out for 351. | Andrews is out at second base.| Gooch was 84 not out.* **b** (of the ball in a game such as tennis or BASKETBALL) outside the line −opposite **in**; see also OUT-OF-BOUNDS **17** (of the TIDE) away from the coast; low **18** *BrE* (*after a superlative*) ever; existing: *He's the stupidest man out.* | *He's out and away* (=much) *the stupidest man I know.* **19 out and about** (of someone who has been ill) able to get up and leave the house − compare **up and about** (UP³) **20** out for trying to get: *Don't trust him − he's only out for your money.* **21** out to trying to: *Be careful: he's out to get* (=harm) *you. | They're out to win.* **22** out to lunch *AmE humor* slightly mad; confused: *Sometimes he's really out to lunch with his reorganization ideas. | She wasn't just out to lunch, this woman was out to every meal.* (=quite mad) **23** Out with it! *infml* Say it! **24** Out you go! *infml* Go out!

out of /ˈ·-·/ *prep* **1** from inside; away from: *We're moving out of our flat. | to jump out of bed | to walk out of the room* **2** from a state of: *to wake up out of a deep sleep | We're out of danger* (=safe) *now. | The car went out of control.* **3** beyond the limits of: *out of sight|earshot* (=to where a thing cannot be seen|heard) **4** from among: *Three out of four people choose "Silver Fox" soap!* **5** not having; without: *We're nearly out of petrol. | He's been out of work|out of a job* (=unable to get a job) *for six months.* **6** because of: *I came out of interest.* **7** (shows what something is made from): *made out of wood* **8** *tech* having (the stated female animal, esp. a horse) as a mother: *Golden Trumpet, by Golden Rain out of Silver Trumpet* − compare BY¹ (18) **9 out of it** (all): **a** lonely and unhappy because one is not included in something: *I felt rather out of it in France because I can't speak French.* **b** *infml* not thinking clearly **10 out of one's head|mind** *infml* mad −see also **out of the blue** (BLUE² (5)), **out of the question** (QUESTION¹), **out of sorts** (SORT¹), **out of this world** (WORLD)

out² *prep infml* (used for showing an outward movement): *He went out the door.*

out³ *adj* **1** [A] directed outwards; used for sending or going out: *Put the letter in the out tray* (*BrE*)*|out box* (*AmE*). −opposite **in** **2 out-and-out** complete; total: *an out-and-out lie*

out⁴ *v* [T] *infml* **1** to throw out; EJECT **2** to tell something that a person would rather keep secret, esp. to declare (a person) publicly to be HOMOSEXUAL: *Gay activists threatened to out several MPs* **3** [I] to become known: *Murder will out.* (=cannot be kept secret) | *Truth will out.*

out⁵ *n* **1** [S] an excuse for leaving an activity or for avoiding blame −see also INS AND OUTS **2** [C] (in games such as BASEBALL) an act of a player becoming out: *Is that one out or two? | That isn't an out, he dropped the ball.*

out- see WORD FORMATION

out·age /ˈaʊtɪdʒ/ *n* a period when something normally supplied is missing, esp. electricity: *a power outage*

out·back /ˈaʊtbæk/ *n* [*the*+S] the part of Australia that is far away from cities

out·bal·ance /aʊtˈbæləns/ *v* [T] to be of greater weight or importance than; OUTWEIGH

out·bid /aʊtˈbɪd/ *v* **-bid**, *present participle* **-bidding** [T] to offer a higher price than (someone else) esp. at an AUCTION: *We badly wanted the cottage but I'm afraid we were outbid.*

out·board mo·tor /ˌaʊtbɔːd ˈməʊtəʳ‖-bɔːrd-/ *n* a motor fixed to the back end of a small boat −compare INBOARD

out·bound /ˈaʊtbaʊnd/ *adj* moving away from the speaker or the starting point: *outbound traffic at the beginning of a holiday weekend* − opposite **inbound** (*esp. AmE*)

out·brave /aʊtˈbreɪv/ *v* [T] to fight bravely against, usu. with success

out·break /ˈaʊtbreɪk/ *n* [(**of**)] a sudden appearance or beginning of something bad: *an outbreak of disease | sporadic outbreaks of fighting* −see also BREAK out

out·build·ing /ˈaʊtˌbɪldɪŋ/ also **outhouse** *BrE*− *n* a smaller building forming part of a group with a larger main building: *the farm and its outbuildings*

out·burst /ˈaʊtbɜːst‖-ɜːr-/ n [(of)] a sudden powerful expression of a activity: *outbursts of gunfire* b feeling: *outbursts of laughter/weeping* —compare OUTPOURINGS; see also BURST **out**

out·cast /ˈaʊtkɑːst‖-kæst/ n, adj (a person) forced from his/her home or without friends: *an outcast from society* —see also CAST **out**

out·caste /ˈaʊtkɑːst‖-kæst/ n, adj (a person) not, or no longer, a member of a fixed social class (CASTE) in India

out·class /aʊtˈklɑːs‖-ˈklæs/ v [T] to be very much better than: *She outclasses all of us at tennis.*

out·come /ˈaʊtkʌm/ n [(of) usu. sing.] an effect; result: *We are anxiously awaiting the outcome of their discussion.* —see also COME **out**

out·crop /ˈaʊtkrɒp‖-krɑːp/ n a rock or group of rocks which appears at the surface of the ground

out·cry /ˈaʊtkraɪ/ n a public expression of anger: *There'll be a great outcry if they try to close the railway.*

out·dat·ed /ˌaʊtˈdeɪtꜝd◂/ adj no longer in general use; out of date: *outdated ideas/customs*

out·dis·tance /aʊtˈdɪstəns/ v [T] to go further or faster than (esp. in a race)

out·do /aʊtˈduː/ v **-did** /ˈdɪd/, **-done** /ˈdʌn/, *3rd person sing. present tense* **-does** /ˈdʌz/ [T] to do or be better than (someone else): *She outdid him in running and in swimming.| The Smiths built a swimming pool in their back garden and, not to be outdone, their neighbours built an even bigger one.*

out·door /ˈaʊtdɔːʳ/ adj [A] existing, happening, done, or used outside: *outdoor shoes | to lead an outdoor life | a teacher of outdoor activities* —opposite **indoor**

out·doors¹ /ˌaʊtˈdɔːz‖-ɔːrz/ also **out of doors**— adv outside; in the open air: *I haven't been outdoors all day. | children playing outdoors* —opposite **indoors** —**outdoorsy** adj infml : *She's a real outdoorsy person, she goes camping every chance she gets.*

outdoors² n [the+S] the open air, esp. far away from any buildings: *hunting in the great outdoors*

out·draw /aʊtˈdrɔː/ v [T] AmE **1** to attract more (people): *The jazz festival outdrew the Puerto Rico Day parade.* **2** to draw (a gun) faster

out·er /ˈaʊtəʳ/ adj [A no comp.] on the outside; at a greater distance from the middle: *the outer walls | outer London | outer space* (=where the stars are) —opposite **inner**

Outer He·br·i·dee /ˌ ' / also **Western Isles** [the] a group of islands, part of the Hebrides, off the NW coast of Scotland, further west than the Inner Hebrides. The most important islands are Lewis with Harris, North Uist and South Uist. Many people there still speak Gaelic. The main industries are fishing, farming and making TWEED. Stornoway is the largest town.

Outer Mon·go·li·a /ˌ·· ·ˈ···/ another name for MONGOLIA

out·er·most /ˈaʊtəməʊst‖-tər-/ also **outmost**— adj [A no comp.] furthest outside or furthest from the middle: *the outermost stars* —opposite **inmost, innermost**

outer space /ˌ·· ˈ·/ n [U] SPACE¹ (4)

out·er·wear /ˈaʊtəweəʳ‖-tər-/ n [U] tech clothes, such as coats and JACKETS, worn over ordinary clothes when outdoors

out·face /aʊtˈfeɪs/ v [T] **1** to meet and deal with bravely —compare FACE² **out 2** also **outstare**— to cause (someone) to look away by looking at them steadily

out·fall /ˈaʊtfɔːl/ n a place where water (e.g. a river or DRAIN) flows out

out·field /ˈaʊtfiːld/ n [the+S] **1** the part of a cricket or BASEBALL field furthest from the player who is to hit the ball —see picture at BASEBALL **2** [+sing./pl. v] the players in this part of the field —compare INFIELD — **~ er** n

out·fight /aʊtˈfaɪt/ v **-fought** /ˈfɔːt/ [T] to fight better than

out·fit¹ /ˈaʊtˌfɪt/ n **1** a set of things needed for a particular purpose or of clothes worn together: *a child's cowboy outfit* **2** [+sing./pl. v] infml a group of people working together

outfit² -tt- [T (with)] to provide with an outfit, esp. of clothes or equipment for camping —see also FIT **out** — **~ ter** n : *a firm of men's outfitters* (=selling men's clothes) | *expedition outfitters*

out·flank /aʊtˈflæŋk/ v [T] **1** to go round the side of (an enemy) and attack from behind **2** to gain an advantage over (someone) by doing something unexpected

out·flow /ˈaʊtfləʊ/ n a flowing out: *the outflow of currency from a country*

out·fox /aʊtˈfɒks‖-ˈfɑːks/ v [T] to defeat by being cleverer; OUTWIT

out·gen·e·ral /aʊtˈdʒenərəl/ v -ll- BrE ‖ -l- AmE [T] to defeat by being a better general or by better planning

out·go·ing /ˌaʊtˈgəʊɪŋ◂/ adj **1** [A] leaving; going out; finishing a period in office: *the outgoing president* —compare INCOMING **2** eager to mix socially with others; friendly: *We need an outgoing person to receive our foreign visitors.*

out·go·ings /ˈaʊtˌgəʊɪŋz/ n [P] esp. BrE amounts of money that are spent —compare INCOME

out·grow /aʊtˈgrəʊ/ v **-grew** /ˈgruː/, **-grown** /ˈgrəʊn/ [T] **1** to grow too big or too old for; GROW **out of**: *to outgrow one's clothes/one's childish habits* **2** to grow faster than: *a population outgrowing its resources*

out·growth /ˈaʊtgrəʊθ/ n **1** a natural but perhaps undesirable result: *Crime is often an outgrowth of poverty.* **2** something that grows out: *an outgrowth of hair*

out·guess /aʊtˈges/ v [T] to OUTWIT, esp. in a situation where knowledge of future events is important

out-Her·od /ˌ· ·ˈ··/ v BrE **out-Herod Herod** to be more cruel, violent, etc., than anyone else (from King **Herod** in the Bible, who killed all the children under a certain age in his attempt to kill the baby Jesus)

out·house /ˈaʊthaʊs/ n -houses /ˌhaʊzꜝz/ **1** BrE for OUT BUILDING **2** AmE an outside LAVATORY

out·ing /ˈaʊtɪŋ/ n **1** a short pleasure trip, esp. for a group of people: *a school outing to the seaside* **2** [U;C] the activity (or an example) of publicly naming people as HOMOSEXUALs, when they do not want anyone to know this

out·land·ish /aʊtˈlændɪʃ/ adj strange and not pleasing: *outlandish clothes/notions* – **~ ly** adv – – **~ ness** n [U]

out·last /aʊtˈlɑːst‖-ˈlæst/ v [T] to last longer than

out·law¹ /ˈaʊtlɔː/ n (esp. in former times) a person who has broken the laws of society and now lives outside society, esp. in lonely areas, trying to avoid punishment —see colour picture on page 385

outlaw² v [T] **1** to declare (someone) to be an outlaw; take the protection of the law from **2** to declare (something) not legal or not socially acceptable: *Drinking and driving has been outlawed.*

out·lay /ˈaʊtleɪ/ n [(on, for)] money spent for a purpose: *House buyers usually have a large initial outlay on carpets and furniture.* —**outlay** /aʊtˈleɪ/ v **-laid** /ˈleɪd/ [T] esp. AmE : *to outlay $200 on/for videotapes* —see also LAY **out**

out·let /ˈaʊtlət, lꜝt/ n [(for)] **1** a way through which something (usu. a liquid or a gas) may go out: (fig.) *an outlet for his feelings* —compare INLET; see also LET **out 2** shops, companies, etc., through which products are sold: *retail outlets* **3** AmE for POINT¹ (13)

out·line /ˈaʊtlaɪn/ n [(of)] **1** a line showing the shape of something: *the outline of her face in the candlelight | to sketch a rough outline map of Europe* **2** the main ideas or facts of something, without details: *an outline of world history/of the main points of the talk* —**outline** v [T] : *He outlined their responsibilities.*

out·live /aʊtˈlɪv/ v [T] to live longer than: *to outlive one's wife* | (fig.) *The machine has outlived its usefulness.* (=is no longer useful)

out·look /ˈaʊtlʊk/ n [usu. sing.] **1** a view from a particular place: *a pleasing outlook from the bedroom window onto the garden* —see also LOOK **out 2** future probabilities: *The weather outlook for the weekend is bad. | a poor outlook for the tourist trade* **3** [(on)] one's general point of view: *He has a very strange outlook on life.*

out·ly·ing /ˈaʊtˌlaɪ-ɪŋ/ adj [A] distant; far (from a city, etc.): *outlying villages*

out·ma·noeu·vre BrE ‖ **-neuver** AmE /ˌaʊtməˈnuːvəʳ/ v [T] **1** to make more effective movements than (an opponent); put in a position of disadvantage

out·mod·ed /aʊtˈməʊdꜝd/ adj no longer in fashion or use: *outmoded thinking*

out·most /ˈaʊtməʊst/ adj [A no comp.] OUTERMOST

out·num·ber /aʊtˈnʌmbəʳ/ v [T] to be more in numbers than: *We were completely outnumbered by the enemy.*

out-of-bounds /ˌ·· ˈ·◄/ *adj, adv* **1** outside the permitted border or limit (of a game, activity, etc.): *kick the ball out-of-bounds* | *His behaviour at the party was really out-of-bounds.* (=unacceptable) **2** *BrE* not open to certain people who do not have permission to go there: *The laboratories are out-of-bounds to all pupils unless a teacher is present.*

out-of-date /ˌ·· ˈ·◄/ *adj* no longer in use or in fashion; OUTDATED

out of doors /ˌ·· ˈ·/ *adv* OUTDOORS

out-of-pock·et ex·pens·es /ˌ···· ·ˈ··/ *n* [P] what one has to pay with one's own money for small additional needs, such as meals and travel costs, when doing a job, usu. for someone else —see also **out of pocket** (POCKET¹)

out-of-the-way /ˌ··· ˈ·◄/ *adj* **1** distant; far away from people and places: *an out-of-the-way restaurant* **2** not known by most people; unusual —see also **out of the way** (WAY¹)

out·pa·tient /ˈaʊtˌpeɪʃənt/ *n* a person who goes to a hospital for treatment while continuing to live at home — compare IN-PATIENT

out·per·form /ˌaʊtpəˈfɔːm‖-pərˈfɔːrm/ v [T] to perform better than: *The new Chevette outperforms the Vega in all road tests.*

out·play /aʊtˈpleɪ/ v [T] to defeat in a game

out·point /aʊtˈpɔɪnt/ v [T] to defeat (an opponent in BOXING) by gaining more points

out·post /ˈaʊtpəʊst/ *n* [(of)] a small town or collection of buildings established esp. by settlers in a distant lonely place: *the last outpost of the British Empire*

out·pour·ings /ˈaʊtˌpɔːrɪŋz/ *n* [P] continuous strong expressions of feelings —compare OUTBURST; see also POUR out

out·put /ˈaʊtpʊt/ *n* [C;U] **1** production: *The car factory hopes to increase its output by 30% next year.* | *an output of 36 tons a day* **2** the product of a computer operation —opposite INPUT; see also I/O —**output** v: *The file is too big to output to the printer.*

out·rage¹ /ˈaʊtreɪdʒ/ *n* **1** [C (**against**)] a very wrong or cruel act: *an outrage against public dignity* | *to commit outrages* **2** [U] anger caused by such an act: *a sense of outrage*

outrage² v [T] to offend greatly: *The closing of the hospital has outraged public opinion.*

Outrage a British organization which works to defend and increase the rights of HOMOSEXUALs by organizing (OR-GANIZE) marches and DEMONSTRATIONS —compare STONEWALL

out·ra·geous /aʊtˈreɪdʒəs/ *adj* **1** very offensive: *outrageous language/prices* **2** wildly unexpected and unusual: *her outrageous hats* – ~**ly** *adv*

out·ran /aʊtˈræn/ v past tense of OUTRUN

out·rank /aʊtˈræŋk/ v [T] to have a higher rank than (usu. a member of the same group)

ou·tré /ˈuːtreɪ‖uːˈtreɪ/ *adj fml or pomp; usu. derog* (of ideas, behaviour, etc.) very strange and unusual

out·reach /ˈaʊtriːtʃ/ *n, adj esp. AmE* of or being a service to people not usu. included: *counselling outreach for shut-ins/disabled*

out·ride /aʊtˈraɪd/ v -**rode** /ˈrəʊd/, -**ridden** /ˈrɪdn/ [T] to ride faster or further than

out·rid·er /ˈaʊtˌraɪdəʳ/ *n* a guard or attendant riding on a motorcycle or horse, beside or in front of a vehicle usu. containing a very important person

out·rig·ger /ˈaʊtˌrɪgəʳ/ *n* **1** a piece of wood shaped like a small narrow boat which is fixed to the side of a boat (esp. a CANOE) to prevent it from turning over in the water **2** a boat to which this is fixed, used esp. in the South Pacific

out·right¹ /aʊtˈraɪt/ *adv* **1** completely: *He bought the house outright – he doesn't have a mortgage.* | *She won outright.* **2** without delay: *to be killed outright* **3** openly: *Tell him outright just what you think.*

out·right² /ˈaʊtraɪt/ *adj* [A] complete and clear; without any doubt: *the outright winner* | *an outright refusal*

out·ri·val /aʊtˈraɪvəl/ v -**ll**- *BrE* ‖ -**l**- *AmE* [T] to defeat in a competition

out·rode /aʊtˈrəʊd/ v past tense of OUTRIDE

out·run /aʊtˈrʌn/ v -**ran** /ˈræn/, -**run** /ˈrʌn/, *present participle* -**running** [T] **1** to run or go faster or further than **2** to go beyond; OVERRUN: *The TV programme outran its time.*

outs /aʊts/ *n* see INS AND OUTS

out·sell /aʊtˈsel/ v [T] to sell or be sold in larger quantities than

out·set /ˈaʊtset/ *n* [the+S] the beginning: *There was trouble at/from the outset.*

out·shine /aʊtˈʃaɪn/ v -**shone** /ˈʃɒn‖ˈʃəʊn/ [T] **1** to shine more brightly than **2** to be much better than: *She outshines all the other competitors.*

out·side¹ /aʊtˈsaɪd, ˈaʊtsaɪd/ *n* **1** [(the) S] the outer part of a solid object; the part that is furthest from the centre, or that faces away towards other people or towards the open air: *It looked tiny from the outside, but inside it was nice and roomy.* | *to paint the outside of the house* | *a coat with fur on the outside* —opposite **inside 2** [the+S] the side furthest from the buildings on a road: *Always overtake other vehicles on the outside.* —opposite **inside 3** a place or situation different from one's own: *An observer from the outside would think we were quite strange.* | *After being in prison, being on the outside is like a holiday.* **4 at the (very) outside** at the most; and not more: *It'll cost £100 at the outside.*

out·side² /ˈaʊtsaɪd/ *adj* [A] **1** on or of the outside: *the outside wall* | *an outside lavatory* | *outside repairs* | *driving fast in the outside lane* —opposite **inside**; see also OUT-DOOR, OUTER **2 a** from elsewhere: *We can't do it ourselves — we must get outside help.* | *an outside broadcast* (=not from the STUDIO) **b** not belonging to one's regular work: *outside interests* **3** (of a chance or possibility) slight; distant: *There's just an outside chance we'll get the contract after all.* **4** (of things that can be measured) the most that can be allowed or accepted: *an outside figure of £100*

out·side³ /aʊtˈsaɪd/ *adv* **1** to or on the outside: *Come outside a minute.* | *There were some children playing outside in the street.* | *It's quite dark outside – there's no moon.* —opposite **inside**; see also OUTDOORS¹ **2** outside of *infml, esp. AmE* **a** except for: *Outside of Jane, there's no one who could do this job.* **b** outside: *shouts coming from outside of the building*

▷ USAGE Compare **outside** and **out**. If we go **outside** a room or building we remain near it: *Go outside if you want to smoke.* (=you cannot smoke inside the room) If we go **out**, we go from a building to a different place: *Let's go out for a drink/drive.*◁

out·side⁴ /aʊtˈsaɪd, ˈaʊtsaɪd/ *prep* **1** to or on the outside of (something solid): *to wait just outside the door* — opposite **inside 2** beyond the limits of; not in: *to stay somewhere outside New York* | *It's quite outside my experience.* | *a job to be done outside working hours* — opposite **within**

out·sid·er /aʊtˈsaɪdəʳ/ *n* **1** a person who is not accepted as a member of a particular social group —compare IN-SIDER **2** a person or animal not expected to win a race or competition: *The woman who actually got the job was a* **rank** (=complete) **outsider**.

out·size /ˈaʊtsaɪz/ *adj* (esp. of clothing) larger than the standard sizes

out·skirts /ˈaʊtskɜːts‖-ɜːr-/ *n* [P (of)] the outer areas or limits: *on the outskirts of Paris* | *He hovered shyly on the outskirts of the group.* —compare PERIPHERY (1)

out·smart /aʊtˈsmɑːt‖-ɑːr-/ v [T] to defeat by behaving more cleverly; OUTWIT

out·spo·ken /aʊtˈspəʊkən/ *adj not derog* expressing openly what is thought or felt; FRANK —see also SPEAK out – ~**ly** *adv* – – ~**ness** *n* [U]

out·spread /ˌaʊtˈspred◄/ *adj* spread out flat or to full width: *with arms/wings outspread*

out·stand·ing /aʊtˈstændɪŋ/ *adj* **1** much better than most others; very good: *an outstanding young musician* —see also STAND out **2** not yet done, settled, or paid: *some problems/debts still outstanding* – ~**ly** *adv*

out·stare /aʊtˈsteəʳ/ v [T] to OUTFACE

out·stay /aʊtˈsteɪ/ v [T] to stay longer than (other people) —see also **outstay one's welcome** (WELCOME¹)

out·stretched /ˌaʊtˈstretʃt◄/ *adj* stretched out to full length: *She welcomed them with outstretched arms.*

out·strip /aʊtˈstrɪp/ v -pp- [T] **1** to pass in running **2** to do better than: *to outstrip our competitors in selling computers*

out·take /ˈ··/ n a piece of a film or television show that is removed before it is shown or broadcast, esp. because it contains a mistake

out·talk /aʊtˈtɔːk/ v [T] to talk better or longer than

out tray /ˈ··/ n a box used to hold work, letters, etc. which have been dealt with and are ready to be sent out or put away —compare IN TRAY

out·vote /aʊtˈvəʊt/ v [T] to vote in larger numbers than; defeat by having a larger number of votes

out·ward /ˈaʊtwəd‖-wərd/ adj [A] **1** going away: *the outward voyage* | *an outward bound* (=going away) *ship* —opposite **homeward** or **return** **2** on the outside, though perhaps not really true: *outward cheerfulness* | *To all outward appearances* (=as things seem), *she's happy.* —compare **inward** – ~ **ly** adv : *outwardly happy*

Outward Bound /ˌ··ˈ·/ (a course run by) an organization which teaches school children or adults how to SURVIVE in difficult country or situations and tries to build character

out·wards /ˈaʊtwədz‖-wərdz/ also **outward** AmE— adv away from the centre; towards the outside: *This door opens outwards.* | *Fold the petals outwards.* —opposite **inwards**

out·weigh /aʊtˈweɪ/ v [T] fml to be more important than: *In this case the disadvantages far outweigh the advantages.*

out·wit /aʊtˈwɪt/ v -tt- [T] to defeat by behaving more cleverly

out·with /ˌaʊtˈwɪθ◂/ prep ScotE outside of: *Outwith normal working hours, please contact me at home.*

out·work /ˈaʊtwɜːk‖-wɜːrk/ n **1** [C usu. pl.] a militarily strong position at some distance from a larger one **2** [U] work for a business that is done outside the usual place of business, esp. by people at home; many types of outwork are very poorly paid – ~ **er** n

out·worn /ˌaʊtˈwɔːn◂‖-ˈwɔːrn◂/ adj (of an idea, custom, etc.) no longer useful or used; OUTMODED: *an outworn social system* —compare WORN-OUT

ou·zo /ˈuːzəʊ/ n [U] a Greek alcoholic drink, drunk with water —compare PERNOD

o·va /ˈəʊvə/ pl. of OVUM

o·val /ˈəʊvəl/ n, adj (anything which is) egg-shaped: *an oval face*

Oval [the] a famous cricket ground in S London, one of the largest in England and the home of the Surrey County cricket club. The last game of a test match SERIES is usu. played there.

Oval Of·fice /ˌ·· ˈ··/ [the] the office of the US president, in the White House, Washington, D.C.: *We're awaiting a decision from the Oval Office.*

O·val·tine /ˈəʊvəltiːn/ n tdmk **1** [U] a sweet brown powder containing COCOA, MALT, and dried milk, used in drinks **2** [C;U] (a cupful of) a drink made from hot water mixed with this powder, usu. with milk added afterwards. It is usu. drunk before going to bed at night.

o·var·i·an /əʊˈveəriən/ adj of an ovary

o·va·ry /ˈəʊvəri/ n **1** the part of a female that produces eggs **2** the part of a female plant that produces seeds —see picture at FLOWER

o·va·tion /əʊˈveɪʃ ən/ n a joyful expression of public approval, esp. by means of APPLAUSE: *The crowd gave him a standing ovation.*

ov·en /ˈʌvən/ n **1** a closed box used for cooking, baking clay, etc.: *Cook the meat in a slow* (=not very hot) *oven for two hours.* —see COOK (USAGE), and see picture at KITCHEN **2 like an oven** infml uncomfortably hot: *It's like an oven in here; open the window!* —see also DUTCH OVEN, **have a bun in the oven** (BUN)

ov·en·proof /ˈʌvənpruːf/ adj (of dishes, plates, etc.) made to be unharmed by the heat inside an oven, so that food can be cooked on them

oven-read·y /ˌ·· ˈ···◂/ adj (of food) already prepared to be cooked in an oven: *oven-ready chickens* | *our new range of oven-ready frozen meals*

ov·en·ware /ˈʌvənweəʳ/ n [U] cooking pots that can be put in a hot oven without cracking

o·ver¹ /ˈəʊvəʳ/ prep **1** directly above; higher than, but not touching: *The lamp hung over/above the table.* | *The doctor leaned over the sick child.* —opposite **under;** see ABOVE (USAGE), ACROSS (USAGE), UNDER (USAGE) **2** so as to cover; resting on top of: *He put the newspaper over his face.* —opposite **under** **3** from side to side of, esp. by going up and then down again: *to jump over the wall/the ditch* | *If we can't go over the mountain we must go round it.* | *The car ran over a dog and killed it.* | *a bridge over/across the river* | *The ball rolled over/across the grass.* **4** down the edge of: *to fall over a cliff* **5** on the far side of: *They live (just) over/across the street.* | *(fig.) We're over* (=past) *the worst of our troubles now.* **6** in many parts of; everywhere in: *They travelled (all) over Europe.* **7** commanding; in control of: *He ruled over a large kingdom.* | *I don't want anyone over me, telling me what to do.* —opposite **under** **8** more than; above: *over 30 books* | *over ten years ago* | *children over* (=older than) *seven* | *over the legal limit* —opposite **under** **9** during; through (a period): *Will you be at home over Christmas?* | *Over the years he's become lazier and lazier.* **10** while doing, eating, etc.: *to hold a meeting over dinner* | *relaxing over a glass of wine* | *He's taking a long time over it.* (=in doing it) **11** by means of; using: *I don't want to say it over the telephone.* | *I heard it over the radio.* **12** in connection with: *problems over his income tax* **13 over and above** as well as; besides: *Over and above his teaching duties, he is the chairman of two committees.*

over² adv **1** downwards from an upright position: *He pushed me and I fell over.* **2** across an edge, a distance, or an open space: *The milk's boiling over!* | *We flew over to the US.* (=across the Atlantic) | *Come and sit over here.* (=on this side of the room) | *Come over* (= to our house) *and see us later.* **3** from one person or group to another: *Hand it over!* | *He signed over the money to his son.* **4** so as to be in each other's positions: *Let's change these two pictures over.* **5** so that another side is shown: *Turn the page over.* | *dogs rolling over and over on the grass* **6** beyond a quantity or limit: *children of seven and over* (=older) | *The programme ran two minutes over.* (=beyond the time limit) —opposite **under** **7** (in comb.) (before an adjective or adverb) too much; too: *Don't be over-anxious about it.* | *Rather over-enthusiastically, he tried to do it all himself.* **8** remaining; not used when part has been taken: *Was there any money over?* | *three into seven goes twice and one over* **9** so as to be covered and not seen: *Let's paint it over in green.* | *The windows are boarded over.* **10** completely through from beginning to end: *You'd better read/think/talk it over carefully.* **11** (showing that something is repeated): *I've told him over and over.* | *I made so many mistakes that I had to do it* **(all) over again.** (=once more) **12** AmE again: *My sums were wrong and I had to do them over.* **13** esp. AmE during or beyond a certain period: *Don't leave now; why not stay/stop over until Monday?* **14 Over!** also **Over to you!**— (in radio signalling) You speak now! **15 over against** rare compared to

over³ adj [F (with)] **1** (of an event or period of time) finished; ended: *I'm sorry, the party's over; they've all gone home.* | *Let's do it now and* **get it over (with). 2 over and done with** infml (of an unpleasant event) completely finished: *Thank goodness the exams are over and done with!*

over⁴ n (in cricket) a set of six or eight balls in the same direction from one BOWLER

over- see WORD FORMATION

over-a·chiev·er /ˌəʊvərəˈtʃiːvəʳ/ n **1** a person who works hard for success and becomes very unhappy if they do not achieve everything they want to **2** a person who performs better than expected in an examination etc. —compare UNDERACHIEVE

o·ver·act /ˌəʊvərˈækt/ v [I;T] to act (a part in a play) in a way that goes beyond what is natural

o·ver·age /ˌəʊvərˈeɪdʒ◂/ adj too old for some purpose: *The army wouldn't have him because he was overage.* —opposite **underage**

o·ver·all¹ /ˌəʊvərˈɔːl◂/ adj, adv **1** including everything: *My overall impression of his work is good.* | *The fish measured 1.7 metres overall.* | *What will it cost overall?* **2** on the whole; generally: *Overall, prices are still rising.* **3** of or for overalls: *my overall pockets*

overalls

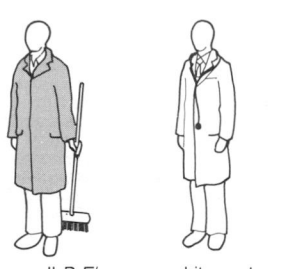

an overall *BrE*/
a work coat *AmE*

a white coat

a lab coat

overalls or a
boiler suit *BrE*/
an overall *AmE*

dungarees *BrE*/
overalls *AmE*

jeans *BrE*/
dungarees
AmE

jeans

o·ver·all² /ˈəʊvərɔːl/ *n BrE* ‖ **work coat** *AmE*— a loose-fitting coat-like garment worn over other clothes to protect them

o·ver·alls /ˈəʊvərɔːlz/ *n* [P] **1** *BrE*‖**jump suit** *AmE*— a garment made in one piece to cover the whole body, worn esp. by workers over other clothes to protect them — compare BOILER SUIT, DUNGAREES **2** *AmE for* DUNGAREES —see PAIR (USAGE)

o·ver·arch /ˌəʊvərˈɑːtʃ‖-ˈɑːrtʃ/ *v* [I;T] *esp. lit* to form an arch (over)

o·ver·arm /ˈəʊvərɑːm‖-ɑːrm/ also **overhand**— *adj, adv* (in sport) with the arm moving above the shoulder: *He bowled overarm.* | *an overarm throw* —opposite **underarm**

o·ver·awe /ˌəʊvərˈɔː/ *v* [T] to make quiet because of respect and fear: *They were completely overawed by his powerful speech.*

o·ver·bal·ance /ˌəʊvəˈbæləns‖-vər-/ *v* [I;T] to (cause to) lose one's balance and fall over

o·ver·bear /ˌəʊvəˈbeər‖-vər-/ *v* -**bore** /ˈbɔːr/ -**borne** /ˈbɔːn ‖ ˈbɔːrn/ [T *usu. pass.*] *fml* to force into obedience

o·ver·bear·ing /ˌəʊvəˈbeərɪŋ◄‖-vər-/ *adj derog* frequently trying to tell other people what to do without regard for their ideas or feelings: *an overbearing manner/personality* — ~ **ly** *adv*

o·ver·bid /ˌəʊvəˈbɪd‖-vər-/ *v* -**bid**, *present participle* -**bidding** **1** [I (**for**)] (esp. in an AUCTION) to offer too high a price **2** [T] to offer more than **3** [I;T] (in the card game BRIDGE) to offer more than (the value of one's cards) — **overbid** /ˈəʊvəbɪd‖-vər-/ *n*

o·ver·blown /ˌəʊvəˈbləʊn◄‖-vər-/ *adj* using too many words and movements of the hands; PRETENTIOUS: *vastly overblown compliments*

o·ver·board /ˈəʊvəbɔːd‖ˈəʊvərbɔːrd/ *adv* **1** over the side of a ship or boat into the water: *He fell overboard and drowned.* | *Man overboard!* **2 go overboard for/about** *infml* to become extremely keen on (someone or something): *She's gone overboard about her new boyfriend.* **3 throw overboard** *infml* to throw away as useless; REJECT

o·ver·book /ˌəʊvəˈbʊk‖-vər-/ *v* [I;T] to sell more places for (a theatre, holiday, etc.) than are available

o·ver·bur·den /ˌəʊvəˈbɜːdn‖ˌəʊvərˈbɜːrdn/ *v* [T (**with**)] to make (someone or something) carry or do too much: *overburdened students/vehicles*

o·ver·came /ˌəʊvəˈkeɪm‖-vər-/ *v past tense of* OVERCOME

o·ver·cap·i·tal·ize also -**ise** *BrE* /ˌəʊvəˈkæpɪtəlaɪz‖-vər-/ *v* [I;T] **1** to supply too much money for (a business) — opposite **undercapitalize** **2** to put too high a value on (a business) —-**ization** /ˌəʊvəkæpɪtəlaɪˈzeɪʃən‖-vərkæpɪtələ-/ *n*

o·ver·cast /ˌəʊvəˈkɑːst◄‖ˌəʊvərˈkæst◄/ *adj* dark with clouds: *an overcast sky/day*

o·ver·charge /ˌəʊvəˈtʃɑːdʒ‖ˌəʊvərˈtʃɑːrdʒ/ *v* **1** [I;T] to charge too much: *They overcharged for the wine.* | *They overcharged me (by 25p).* [+obj(i)+obj(d)] *They overcharged me 25p.* —opposite **undercharge** **2** [T (**with**)] to fill or load too much: *to overcharge the electrical apparatus* | (fig.) *overcharged with feeling* —**overcharge** /ˈəʊvətʃɑːdʒ‖-vərtʃɑːrdʒ/ *n*

o·ver·cloud /ˌəʊvəˈklaʊd‖-vər-/ *v* [T] **1** [*usu. pass.*] to cover with clouds **2** to fill with sadness or worry

o·ver·coat /ˈəʊvəkəʊt‖-vər-/ *n* a long warm coat worn over other clothes in cold weather

o·ver·come /ˌəʊvəˈkʌm‖-vər-/ *v* -**came** /ˈkeɪm/, -**come** /ˈkʌm/ **1** [I;T] to fight successfully (against); defeat: *to overcome the enemy/one's fear/difficulties* **2** [T *usu. pass.*] to make helpless; defeat, esp. by smoke or FUMES, or by feelings: *She was overcome by the smoke/overcome with emotion.*

o·ver·com·pen·sate /ˌəʊvəˈkɒmpənseɪt, -pen-‖-vərˈkɑːm/ *v* [I (**for**)] to try to correct one's weaknesses by taking too strong an action in the opposite direction: *She overcompensated for her shyness by talking too much.* —-**sation** /ˌəʊvəkɒmpənˈseɪʃən, -pen- ‖ -vər kɑːm-/ *n* [U]

o·ver·crop /ˌəʊvəˈkrɒp‖ˌəʊvərˈkrɑːp/ *v* -**pp**- [T] *tech* to spoil (farmland) by growing too many crops

o·ver·crowd /ˌəʊvəˈkraʊd‖-vər-/ *v* [T (**with**)] to put or allow too many people or things in (one place): *an overcrowded room*

o·ver·crowd·ing /ˌəʊvəˈkraʊdɪŋ‖-vər-/ *n* [U] the condition of living too close together, with too many people or animals in too few rooms, houses, or buildings: *overcrowding is a major cause of stress in families* | *overcrowding encourages the spread of disease in farm animals*

o·ver·de·vel·op /ˌəʊvədɪˈveləp‖-vər-/ *v* [T] to develop too much: *overdeveloped films* | *an overdeveloped sense of his own importance*

o·ver·do /ˌəʊvəˈduː‖-vər-/ *v* -**did** /ˈdɪd/, -**done** /ˈdʌn/ [T] **1** [*often pass.*] to do, decorate, perform, etc., too much: *The love scenes in the film were a bit overdone.* | *I've been rather* **overdoing it** (=working too much) *lately.* **2** to use too much: *Don't overdo the salt.*

o·ver·done /ˌəʊvəˈdʌn◄‖-vər-/ *adj* cooked too much — opposite **underdone**

o·ver·dose /ˈəʊvədəʊs‖-vər-/ *n* too much of a drug: *He took a massive overdose of heroin and died.* —**overdose** /ˌəʊvəˈdəʊs‖-vər-/ *v* [I (**on**)]

o·ver·draft /ˈəʊvədrɑːft‖ˈəʊvərdræft/ *n* the sum owed to a bank by a person who has overdrawn: *We are paying off a large overdraft.*

overdraft fa·cil·i·ty /ˈ··· ·,···/ *n* an agreement with the bank that the customer may overdraw by a fixed amount, at an agreed rate of interest, usu. with no PENALTY (=charge made for overdrawing). The customer does not have to borrow all the money that they are allowed to.

o·ver·draw /ˌəʊvəˈdrɔː‖-vər-/ *v* -**drew** /ˈdruː/, -**drawn** /ˈdrɔːn/ [I;T] to take more money from one's bank account than it contains: *I'm/My account is £300 overdrawn.* | *overdrawn by £300*

o·ver·dress /ˌəʊvəˈdres‖-vər-/ *v* [I;T] to (cause to) dress in clothes that are too formal —**overdressed** *adj* : *I felt distinctly overdressed—everyone else was in jeans.*

o·ver·drive /ˈəʊvədraɪv‖-vər-/ *n* [U] a GEAR that allows a car to go fast while its engine produces the least power necessary: (fig.) *His imagination is in overdrive.* (=working very hard)

o·ver·due /ˌəʊvəˈdjuː◄‖ˌəʊvərˈduː◄/ *adj* **1** left unpaid too long: *an overdue gas bill* **2** later than expected: *Her baby* is overdue. [after n] *The train is 15 minutes overdue.* **3** [F+**for**] having been in need (of something) for some time: *The car is overdue for a service.* **4** (of a library book, etc.) not returned to the library by the date expected: *These books are two weeks overdue.* | *A charge of 3 c per day is made on all overdue books.*

over ea·sy /ˌ··ˈ···/ *adj, adv AmE* (of eggs) cooked in hot fat and turned over to cook on the other side only for a moment: *Two eggs over easy, please.* —compare SUNNY-SIDE UP

o·ver·egg /ˌəʊvərˈeg/ *v* **overegg the pudding** *BrE infml* to make something too complicated or ELABORATE by adding something that is not needed: *We sent her a birthday card and some flowers; to send champagne as well would just be overegging the pudding.*

o·ver·es·ti·mate[1] /ˌəʊvərˈestɪmeɪt/ *v* **1** [I;T] to guess too high a value for (an amount): *We overestimated the bill.* **2** [T] to have too high an opinion of: *I think you're overestimating his abilities.* —opposite **underestimate**

o·ver·es·ti·mate[2] /ˌəʊvərˈestɪmɪt/ *n* an ESTIMATE which is too large

o·ver·ex·pose /ˌəʊvərɪkˈspəʊz/ *v* [T] to give too much light to (a film or photograph) —opposite **underexpose**

o·ver·flow[1] /ˌəʊvəˈfləʊ‖-vər-/ *v* **1** [I;T] to flow over the edges (of): *The river overflowed (its banks).* | *The bath is overflowing; who left the water running?* **2** [I;T (into)] to go beyond the limits (of): *The crowd overflowed (the theatre) into the street.* **3** [I (with)] to be very full: *His heart overflowed with gratitude.*

o·ver·flow[2] /ˈəʊvəfləʊ‖-vər-/ *n* **1** something that overflows: *The water butt catches the overflow from this pipe.* **2** a pipe or passage for carrying away water that is more than is needed **3** an act of overflowing

o·ver·fly /ˌəʊvəˈflaɪ‖-vər-/ *v* **-flew** /ˈfluː/, **-flown** /ˈfləʊn/ [T] (of a pilot or aircraft) to fly over (a place), esp. in a group on a ceremonial occasion

o·ver·grown /ˌəʊvəˈgrəʊn‖-vər-/ *adj* **1** [(**with**)] covered esp. with plants growing uncontrolled: *a garden overgrown with weeds* **2** [A] *derog* grown too large: *He's just like an overgrown schoolboy.*

o·ver·hand /ˈəʊvəhænd‖-vər-/ *adj, adv* OVERARM

o·ver·hang[1] /ˌəʊvəˈhæŋ‖-vər-/ *v* **-hung** /ˈhʌŋ/ [I;T] to hang over (something) or stick out over (something): *The rock overhung the path.* | *overhanging cliffs*

o·ver·hang[2] /ˈəʊvəhæŋ‖-vər-/ *n* [*usu. sing.*] **1** a rock, roof, etc., that overhangs **2** the amount by which something overhangs

o·ver·haul[1] /ˌəʊvəˈhɔːl‖-vər-/ *v* [T] **1** to examine thoroughly and perhaps repair if necessary: *to overhaul a car* **2** to come up to from behind and pass; OVERTAKE

o·ver·haul[2] /ˈəʊvəhɔːl‖-vər-/ *n* a thorough examination and repair if necessary: *I gave the van a complete overhaul.*

o·ver·head /ˌəʊvəˈhed‖-vər-/ *adj, adv* above one's head: *electricity carried by overhead wires* (=not underground) | *A plane flew overhead.* —compare **over someone's head** (HEAD[1] (42))

overhead pro·jec·tor /ˌ··· ·ˈ··/ *n* a lamp which makes images on a flat transparent surface larger and throws them, by means of a mirror, onto a white wall or SCREEN

o·ver·heads /ˈəʊvəhedz‖-vər-/ [P] *BrE* ‖ **overhead** [U] *AmE*— *n* money spent regularly (e.g. on insurance or heating) to keep a business running: *Their office is in central London, so their overheads are very high.* —compare PRIME COST

o·ver·hear /ˌəʊvəˈhɪər‖-vər-/ *v* **-heard** /ˈhɜːd‖ˈhɜːrd/ [T] to hear (what others are saying) without their knowledge and by accident: *I overheard some cruel remarks about my husband.* [+to-v/v-ing] *I overheard them say/saying they were dissatisfied.* —compare EAVESDROP

o·ver·heat·ed /ˌəʊvəˈhiːtɪd‖-vər-/ *adj* **1** at too high a temperature **2** (of e.g. economic conditions) showing too much activity to be healthy

o·ver·hung /ˌəʊvəˈhʌŋ ‖ -vər-/ *v* past tense & participle of OVERHANG[1]

o·ver·in·dulge /ˌəʊvərɪnˈdʌldʒ/ *v* [I (**in**);T] to let (oneself or another person) have too much of what is wanted: *to overindulge in chocolates/television* (=eat too many/watch too much) | *She overindulges her children.* —**dulgence** *n* [U] : *suffering from last night's overindulgence*

o·ver·joyed /ˌəʊvəˈdʒɔɪd‖-vər-/ *adj* [F] extremely pleased;

full of joy: [+*to-v/that*] *We were overjoyed (to hear) that they were safe.*

o·ver·kill /ˈəʊvəkɪl‖-vər-/ *n* [U] **1** more than enough (esp. atomic) weapons to kill everyone in a country **2** something that goes beyond the desirable or safe limits: *a propaganda overkill that stops people from believing it*

o·ver·la·den /ˌəʊvəˈleɪdn‖-vər/ *past participle of* OVERLOAD

o·ver·laid /ˌəʊvəˈleɪd‖-vər-/ *v* past tense & participle of OVERLAY[1]

o·ver·land /ˌəʊvəˈlænd‖-vər-/ *adj, adv* across land, not by sea or air: *an overland route* | *going overland to China*

o·ver·lap[1] /ˌəʊvəˈlæp‖-vər-/ *v* **-pp-** [I;T] to cover (something) partly and go beyond it: *Roofs are often made with overlapping tiles.* | (fig.) *Economics and politics are best studied together as the two subjects overlap.*

overlap[2] /ˈəʊvəlæp‖-vər-/ *n* [C;U] the amount by which two or more things overlap each other

o·ver·lay[1] /ˌəʊvəˈleɪ‖-vər-/ *v* **-laid** /ˈleɪd/ [T (**with**) *usu. pass.*] to cover usu. thinly: *wood overlaid with silver*

o·ver·lay[2] /ˈəʊvəleɪ‖-vər-/ *n* something laid over something else: (fig.) *sad stories with an overlay of humour*

o·ver·leaf /ˌəʊvəˈliːf‖ˈəʊvərliːf/ *adv* on the other side of the page

o·ver·lie /ˌəʊvəˈlaɪ‖-vər-/ *v* **-lay** /ˈleɪ/, **-lain** /ˈleɪn/ [T] *tech* **1** to lie over: *The rock overlies the coal.* **2** to cause the death of (a baby or young animal) by lying on it

o·ver·load /ˌəʊvəˈləʊd‖-vər-/ *v* **-loaded, -loaded** *or* **-laden** /ˈleɪdn/ [T (**with**)] **1** to load too heavily **2** to put too much electricity through: *Don't overload the electrical system by using too many machines.* —**overload** /ˈəʊvələʊd‖-vər-/ *n*

o·ver·long /ˌəʊvəˈlɒŋ‖-vərˈlɔːŋ/ *adj, adv* too long, esp. in time: *The performance was overlong.*

o·ver·look /ˌəʊvəˈlʊk‖-vər-/ *v* [T] **1** to have or give a view of from above: *Our room/We overlooked the sea.* | *We're overlooked here.* (=the neighbours can see into our house) **2** not to notice; miss: *These little details are easily overlooked.* **3** to pretend not to see; forgive: *I'll overlook your mistake this time.*

o·ver·lord /ˈəʊvələːd‖ˈəʊvərlɔːrd/ *n* (in former times) a lord who ruled over other lords; highest ruler

o·ver·ly /ˈəʊvəli‖-vər-/ *adv* (*usu. in negatives*) too; very much: *I'm not overly interested.*

o·ver·manned /ˌəʊvəˈmænd‖ -vər-/ *adj* having more workers than are needed for a job, etc.; OVERSTAFFED — opposite **undermanned** —**manning** *n* [U]

o·ver·mas·ter /ˌəʊvəˈmɑːstər‖-vərˈmæstər/ *v* [T] *fml* to defeat (a feeling or a person) by greater power

o·ver·much /ˌəʊvəˈmʌtʃ◄‖-vər-/ *adv, determiner, pron* **1** *fml* too much: *overmuch work* **2** (*usu. in negatives*) very much: *He doesn't like me overmuch.*

o·ver·night /ˌəʊvəˈnaɪt◄‖-vər-/ *adj, adv* **1** for or during the night: *an overnight journey* | *an overnight bag* | *to stay overnight* **2** sudden(ly): *The actor became famous overnight.* | *an overnight success*

over·op·ti·mis·tic /ˌ··· ··ˈ··/ *adj* foolishly or unreasonably OPTIMISTIC, expecting that things will be better than is actually possible or likely: *His estimate that they could do the job twice as quickly as the previous firm did, seems rather over-optimistic.* | *Maybe you will get paid as quickly as you think, but don't be over-optimistic.*

o·ver·pass /ˈəʊvəpɑːs‖ˈəʊvərpæs/ *n AmE for* FLYOVER

o·ver·pay /ˌəʊvəˈpeɪ‖-vər-/ *v* **-paid** /ˈpeɪd/ [T] to pay (someone) too much —opposite **underpay**

o·ver·play /ˌəʊvəˈpleɪ‖-vər-/ *v* [T] **1** to make (something) appear more important than it really is —opposite **underplay** **2** **overplay one's hand** to promise or try to do more than one can really do

o·ver·pop·u·lat·ed /ˌəʊvəˈpɒpjʊleɪtɪd‖ˌəʊvərˈpɑːp-/ *adj* (of a city, etc.) having too many people —**ion** /ˌəʊvəpɒpjʊˈleɪʃən‖ˌəʊvərpɑː-/ *n* [U]

o·ver·pow·er /ˌəʊvəˈpaʊər‖-vər-/ *v* [T] **1** to defeat (someone) by greater power **2** (of feelings) to make helpless; OVERCOME

o·ver·pow·er·ing /ˌəʊvəˈpaʊərɪŋ‖-vər-/ *adj* **1** very strong; INTENSE: *an overpowering desire/smell* **2** (of a person) having a character that is too forceful; OVERBEARING — **~ly** *adv*

o·ver·proof /ˌəʊvəˈpruːf‖-vər-/ adj containing more alcohol than PROOF SPIRIT does: [after n] 10 degrees overproof

o·ver·ran /ˌəʊvəˈræn/ n past tense of OVERRUN

o·ver·rate /ˌəʊvəˈreɪt/ v [T] to put too high a value on (quality, ability, etc.): I think that film is overrated. | an overrated pleasure —opposite **underrate**

o·ver·reach /ˌəʊvəˈriːtʃ/ v [T] to defeat (oneself) by trying to do or get too much

o·ver·re·act /ˌəʊvəriˈækt/ v [I (to)] to act too strongly as a result of (something): She tends to overreact to criticism. — ~ion /ˈækʃən/ n [C;U]

o·ver·ride /ˌəʊvəˈraɪd/ v -rode /ˈrəʊd/ -ridden /ˈrɪdn/ [T] to take no notice of (another person's orders, claims, etc.): He overrode their objections.

o·ver·rid·ing /ˌəʊvəˈraɪdɪŋ◄/ adj [A] more important than anything else: a question of overriding importance

o·ver·rule /ˌəʊvəˈruːl/ v [T] to decide against (something already decided) by official power: The boss overruled me/my decision.

o·ver·run /ˌəʊvəˈrʌn/ v -ran /ˈræn/, -run 1 [T] (of something unwanted) to spread over in great numbers: The stables are overrun with rats. 2 [I;T] to continue beyond (a time limit or a previously decided stopping place): Sorry I'm late; the meeting overran.

o·ver·seas /ˌəʊvəˈsiːz◄‖-vər-/ adj, adv to, at, or in somewhere across the sea; foreign: overseas markets | They've gone to live overseas.

▷ USAGE 1 **Overseas** students‖**foreign students** have come to one's own country from abroad in order to study; the same idea is expressed by students from overseas. But students overseas are people studying in other countries. 2 Compare **overseas** and **foreign**. **Overseas** as an adjective can only be used before a noun, and, in British English, is slightly more polite than **foreign**: You're foreign, aren't you? | You're one of our foreign/overseas students, aren't you?◁

Overseas De·vel·op·ment Ad·min·is·tra·tion /ˌ··· ·ˈ··· ···,··/ abbrev. **ODA** [the] a British government department which controls financial and technical help for developing countries (=poor countries that are trying to build up their industry)

o·ver·see /ˌəʊvəˈsiː‖-vər-/ v -saw /ˈsɔː/, -seen /ˈsiːn/ [T] to watch to see that work is properly done: to oversee the work/the workers —**-seer** /ˈəʊvəsɪər‖-vər-/ n

o·ver·sell /ˌəʊvəˈsel‖-vər-/ v -sold /ˈsəʊld/ [T] infml to praise too much

o·ver·sexed /ˌəʊvəˈsekst◄‖-vər-/ adj having unusually strong sexual desire —opposite **undersexed**

o·ver·shad·ow /ˌəʊvəˈʃædəʊ‖-vər-/ v [T] 1 to throw a shadow over: (fig.) The threat of war overshadowed the nation. (=made it worried and unhappy) 2 to make appear less important: Her new book will overshadow all her earlier ones.

o·ver·shoe /ˈəʊvəʃuː‖-vər-/ n a rubber shoe worn over an ordinary shoe; GALOSH —see PAIR (USAGE)

o·ver·shoot /ˌəʊvəˈʃuːt‖-vər-/ v -shot /ˈʃɒt‖ˈʃɑːt/ [I;T] to go or shoot too far or beyond, and miss: The train overshot the station.

o·ver·side /ˌəʊvəˈsaɪd◄‖-vər-/ adv AmE over the side of a ship into the water

o·ver·sight /ˈəʊvəsaɪt‖-vər-/ n 1 [C;U] (an) unintended failure to notice or do something: The mistake was the result of (an) oversight. 2 [S;U] fml watchfulness

o·ver·sim·pli·fy /ˌəʊvəˈsɪmplɪˌfaɪ‖-vər-/ v [I;T] to express (something) too simply —**-fication** /ˌəʊvəˌsɪmplɪˌfɪˈkeɪʃən/-vər-/ n [C;U]

over-six·ties /ˌ·· ˈ··/ [the+P] people who are over 60 years old: moderately-paced cycling holidays for the over-sixties | an over-sixties club

o·ver·sized /ˌəʊvəˈsaɪzd◄‖-vər-/ also **o·ver·size** /-ˈsaɪz◄/— adj bigger than usual; too big: oversized ears

o·ver·sleep /ˌəʊvəˈsliːp‖-vər-/ v -slept /ˈslept/ [I] to sleep longer than one intended: I overslept this morning and was late for work. —compare SLEEP in

o·ver·spill /ˈəʊvəˌspɪl‖-vər-/ n [usu. sing.] esp. BrE people who leave a city because too many people live there, and settle on the edges or beyond: A new town was built for London's overspill.

o·ver·staffed /ˌəʊvəˈstɑːft◄ ‖ ˌəʊvərˈstæft◄/ adj having more workers than are needed; OVERMANNED —opposite **understaffed**

o·ver·state /ˌəʊvəˈsteɪt‖-vər-/ v [T] to state too strongly, making things appear better, worse, or more important than they really are: She overstated her case, so we didn't believe her. —opposite **understate** — ~ ment n [C;U]

o·ver·stay /ˌəʊvəˈsteɪ‖-vər-/ v [T] to stay beyond the end of (a period of time) —see also **overstay one's welcome** (WELCOME⁴)

o·ver·step /ˌəʊvəˈstep‖-vər-/ v -pp- [T] to go beyond (a limit of what is wise or proper): to overstep the limits/boundaries of good taste | She overstepped her authority. | I've been very patient so far, but he's really overstepped the mark this time!

o·ver·stock /ˌəʊvəˈstɒk‖ˌəʊvərˈstɑːk/ v [I;T (with)] to keep more supplies than are needed in (a place): We'd overstocked (the shop) with copies of an unpopular textbook.

o·ver·strung /ˌəʊvəˈstrʌŋ‖-vər-/ adj too sensitive and nervous; HIGHLY-STRUNG

o·ver·sub·scribed /ˌəʊvəsəbˈskraɪbd‖-vər-/ adj with more wanted than is on sale: This play is very popular; seats in the theatre are oversubscribed. —opposite **undersubscribed**

o·vert /ˈəʊvɜːt, əʊˈvɜːt‖-ɜːrt/ adj fml (of beliefs or actions) public; not secret: overt moves to undermine his authority —opposite **covert** — ~ ly adv

o·ver·take /ˌəʊvəˈteɪk‖-vər-/ v -took /ˈtʊk/, -taken /ˈteɪkən/ 1 [I;T] to come up to from behind, and pass: Don't overtake on a corner. | We overtook the slow lorry. | Smith has overtaken Jones's record. 2 [T] (of something unpleasant) to reach suddenly and unexpectedly: overtaken by misfortune

o·ver·tax /ˌəʊvəˈtæks‖-vər-/ v [T] 1 a to put too great a tax on (goods) b to demand too much tax from (people) 2 to force beyond a limit: Don't overtax your strength/yourself!

over-the-coun·ter /ˌ··· ˈ···◄/ adj 1 AmE also **OTC**— (of certain business shares) not LISTED on an official STOCK EXCHANGE list: over-the-counter securities 2 (of a drug) available without a doctor's PRESCRIPTION

over the top /ˌ··· ˈ·/ also **OTT**— adj BrE extreme or exaggerated (EXAGGERATE): That's a bit over the top, isn't it? He's right-wing, but I wouldn't call him a fascist. | Just look at her hat—all those feathers! Completely OTT!

over-the-tran·som /ˌ··· ˈ···◄/ adj AmE received without having been asked for: the company often gets over-the-transom manuscripts from unpublished writers.

o·ver·throw¹ /ˌəʊvəˈθrəʊ‖-vər-/ v -threw /ˈθruː/, -thrown /ˈθrəʊn/ [T] to defeat, esp. using force; remove from a position of power: Rebels have overthrown the government.

o·ver·throw² /ˈəʊvəθrəʊ‖-vər-/ n 1 [usu. sing.] defeat; removal from power: the violent overthrow of the government 2 (in cricket) a poor return of the ball from a FIELDER that allows further runs to be scored (SCORE)

o·ver·time /ˈəʊvətaɪm‖-vər-/ n, adv [U] 1 (time) beyond the usual time, esp. working time: They're working overtime to finish the job. | He's on overtime tonight. 2 payment for working more than the usual time. The amount people are paid for each hour of overtime is usu. much more than they are paid for working their usual hours: to pay/earn overtime 3 AmE time added to the end of a game (of football, etc.) when time has been lost during the game, e.g. because a player was hurt, or when the points total of the teams are level at the end of ordinary time

o·ver·tone /ˈəʊvətəʊn‖-vər-/ n tech 1 a musical note higher than a main note and sounding together with it 2 a colour that one thinks one can see when looking at another colour

o·ver·tones /ˈəʊvətəʊnz‖-vər-/ n [P (of)] things that are suggested but not shown or stated clearly: His words were polite, but there were overtones of anger in his voice. —compare UNDERTONE (2)

o·ver·took /ˌəʊvəˈtʊk ‖ -vər-/ v past tense of OVERTAKE

o·ver·top /ˌəʊvəˈtɒp‖ˌəʊvərˈtɑːp/ v -pp- [T] fml to be higher or better than

o·ver·ture /ˈəʊvətjʊər, -tʃʊər, -tʃər‖-vər-/ n 1 a musical introduction to a long musical piece, esp. an OPERA 2 a short musical piece for playing at the beginning of a concert

o·ver·tures /ˈəʊvətjʊəz, -tʃʊəz, -tʃəz‖ˈoʊvərtjʊərz, -tʃʊərz, -tʃərz/ n [P] an offer to begin talks with someone in the hope of reaching an agreement: *Their government is making overtures for/of peace.*

o·ver·turn /ˌəʊvəˈtɜːn‖ˌoʊvərˈtɜːrn/ v 1 [I;T] to (cause to) turn over: *The boat overturned.* | *They overturned the boat/lamp;* CAPSIZE 2 [T] to bring (esp. a government) to an end suddenly 3 to decide that (an original result, etc.) was wrong: *The judges overturned the decision of the lower court.*

o·ver·view /ˈəʊvəvjuː‖-vər-/ n 1 a usu. short account (of something) which gives a general picture but no details; SUMMARY: *The managing director gave us an overview of the company's marketing plans for the coming year.* 2 an examination of something, e.g. a company system or plan, that does not go into detail but considers it as a whole: *We need someone to take an overview and plan the company's long-term strategy.*

o·ver·ween·ing /ˌəʊvəˈwiːnɪŋ◂‖-vər-/ adj fml derog too proud and too sure of oneself: *overweening pride* – ~ **ly** adv

o·ver·weight /ˌəʊvəˈweɪt◂‖-vər-/ adj weighing more than is expected or usual: *This parcel is overweight by two kilos.* [after n] *He's two kilos overweight.* | *an overweight person* —opposite **underweight**; see FAT (USAGE)

o·ver·whelm /ˌəʊvəˈwelm‖-vər-/ v [T] 1 to defeat or make powerless (usu. a group of people) by much greater force of numbers: *to overwhelm the opposing army* 2 [often pass.] (of feelings) to make (someone) completely helpless, usu. suddenly: *to be overwhelmed by grief* 3 (of water) to cover completely and usu. suddenly

o·ver·whelm·ing /ˌəʊvəˈwelmɪŋ‖-vər-/ adj very large; too great to oppose: *overwhelming generosity* | *An over-whelming majority voted against the proposal.* – ~ **ly** adv

o·ver·win·ter /ˌəʊvəˈwɪntəʳ‖-vər-/ v [I] (usu. of plants) to live through the winter: *This variety of spinach will over-winter if it is well mulched.*

o·ver·work¹ /ˌəʊvəˈwɜːk‖ˌoʊvərˈwɜːrk/ v [I;T] to (cause to) work too much

overwork² n [U] too much work; working too hard

o·ver·wrought /ˌəʊvəˈrɔːt◂/ adj too nervous and excited at the moment, esp. because of anxiety —compare WROUGHT-UP

O·vett /əʊˈvet/, **Steve** /stiːv/ (1955–) a British MIDDLE-DISTANCE runner who has broken several world records and won Olympic and other titles

Ov·id /ˈɒvɪd‖ˈɑːv-/ (43 BC–17? AD) a Latin poet whose Roman name was **Publius Ovidius Naso**, famous for the *Metamorphoses*, a set of poems telling ancient stories (MYTHS)

o·vip·a·rous /əʊˈvɪpərəs/ adj tech egg-laying

o·void /ˈəʊvɔɪd/ adj, n fml or tech (an object that is) egg-shaped

ov·u·late /ˈɒvjʊleɪt‖ˈɑːv-/ v [I] to produce eggs from the OVARY —**lation** /ˌɒvjʊˈleɪʃən‖ˌɑːv-/ n [C;U]

o·vum /ˈəʊvəm/ n ova /ˈəʊvə/ tech an egg, esp. one that develops inside the mother's body

ow /aʊ/ interj (an expression of sudden slight pain)

owe /əʊ/ v [T not in progressive forms] 1 [(to, for)] to have to pay, for something already done or given: *I still owe the garage for those repairs.* [+obj(i)+obj(d)] *I owe the garage £20 (for the new tyre).* | (fig.) *We owe loyalty to our country.* | *He seems to think the world owes him a living.* (=he doesn't want to make any effort at anything) 2 [(to)] to feel grateful: *We owe a lot to our parents.* [+obj(i)+obj(d)] *We owe our parents a lot.* 3 **owe some-one one** infml to be prepared to do someone a favour, in return for a favour that they have done for oneself —see also IOU

owe sthg. **to** sthg./sbdy. phr v [T not in progressive forms] to have (something good) because of: *She owes her success to good luck.*

Ow·en /ˈəʊɪn/, **Lord David** (1938–) a British politician, Labour Foreign Secretary 1977–79. He was one of the GANG OF FOUR, Labour ministers who left the party in 1981 to form a centre party, the Social Democratic Party

(SDP). He became its leader in 1983, gave up the leader-ship in 1987 when most of its members joined with the Liberal Party, and was elected leader of a separate, smaller SDP in 1988. This was not a success, and he left British party politics in 1992.

Owen, Rob·ert /ˈrɒbət‖ˈrɑːbərt/ (1771–1858) a Welsh leader in the COOPERATIVE movement who started settlements in Scotland and the US

Owen, Wil·fred /ˈwɪlfrəd/ (1893–1918) an English poet who wrote about the terrible events of the First World War. He was killed in the fighting just before the end of the war, and his poems were published (PUBLISH) after his death.

Ow·ens /ˈəʊɪnz/, **Jes·se** /ˈdʒesi/ (1914–80) an African-American who won several GOLD MEDALS (=first prizes) at the 1936 Olympics. His victories were seen as impor-tant because they disproved Hitler's ideas about white people from Northern Europe being better than people of other races.

ow·ing /ˈəʊɪŋ/ adj 1 [F (to)] still to be paid: *How much is owing to you?* | *There is still £5 owing.* 2 **owing to** be-cause of: *Our flight was delayed, owing to the bad weather.* —see DUE (USAGE)

owl /aʊl/ n a night bird with large eyes and a loud call, *tu-wit tu-whoo.* According to old stories, owls are very wise. —see also NIGHT OWL

owl

Owl and the Pus·sy·cat /ˌaʊl ənd ðə ˈpʊsikæt/, **The** a NON-SENSE poem by Edward Lear, which begins:

> *The owl and the pussycat*
> *went to sea*
> *In a beautiful*
> *pea-green boat.*
> *They took some honey*
> *and plenty of money,*
> *Wrapped up*
> *in a five-pound note...*

owl·et /ˈaʊlət/ n a young owl

owl·ish /ˈaʊlɪʃ/ adj (of a person) having a round solemn face and usu. glasses

owl·ish·ly /ˈaʊlɪʃli/ adv solemnly; in a wise manner

own¹ /əʊn/ determiner, pron 1 belonging to oneself and to no one else: *It was (all) her own idea.* | *I only borrowed the book; it's not my own.* | *They treated the child as if she were their own.* | *The country has its own oil and doesn't need to import any.* | *For reasons of my own, I don't want to see him just yet.* | *Mind your own business!* (=Pay at-tention to your own affairs, not mine!) | *I didn't believe it till I saw it* **with my own eyes.** 2 **have/get one's own back (on someone)** to succeed in doing harm (to someone) in return for harm done to oneself; get one's REVENGE 3 **(all) on one's own: a** alone: *How do you like living on your own?* **b** without help: *I can't carry it on my own; it's too heavy.* —see also **come into one's own** (COME¹), **hold one's own** (HOLD¹), **one's own man** (MAN¹ (27))

▷ USAGE **Own** is used only after possessive words like *my, John's, the company's,* etc: *He has his own room/a room of his own.* It can be made stronger by adding **very:** *He has his very own room/a room of his own.*◁

own² v [T not in progressive forms] 1 to possess (some-thing), esp. by lawful right: *Who owns this house/this dog?* | *Do you own a car, sir?* —see also DISOWN 2 [+(that);obj] fml to admit: *He owns (that) he was wrong.*

own to sthg. phr v [T] fml to admit: *I must own to a feel-ing of anxiety.* [+v-ing] *I must own to feeling rather anxious.*

own up phr v [I (to)] to admit a fault or crime: *He owned up to the robbery.* | *She finally owned up to having taken the money.*

own·er /ˈəʊnəʳ/ n a person who owns something, esp. by lawful right: *He is now the proud owner of a new car.* – ~**ship** n [U] : *the ownership of the means of production* | *a dispute over ownership* | *home ownership*

owner-driv·er /ˌ·· ˈ··/ n esp. BrE a person who drives their own car

owner-oc·cu·pi·er /ˌ·· ˈ····/ n esp. BrE a person who owns the house or flat in which they live —compare TENANT —**pied** /ˌ·ˈ·◂/ adj : owner-occupied flats

own goal /ˌ· ˈ·/ n esp. BrE **1** (in football) a GOAL against one's own team scored (SCORE) by mistake by one of one's own players **2** infml a mistake that makes one look foolish, esp. a remark or action that is against one's own interests: the minister's spectacular own goal in his speech to parliament

own la·bel /ˌ· ˈ··◂/ also **own brand** /ˌ· ˈ·◂/ BrE ‖ **store brand** AmE— n goods produced for and sold by certain shops, carrying the name of the shop rather than the producer: Have you tried Sainsbury's own label tomato ketchup? It's very good. —compare TRADE NAME

ox /ɒks‖ɑːks/ n **ox·en** /ˈɒksən‖ˈɑːk-/ **1** also **bullock**— a fully-grown male of the cattle family with its sexual organs removed, often used for heavy work on farms — compare HEIFER, STEER² **2** any large animal of the cattle type

Ox·bridge /ˈɒksˌbrɪdʒ‖ˈɑːks-/ (of, from, or typical of) the universities of Oxford and/or Cambridge: Oxbridge students —compare REDBRICK

▶ CULTURAL NOTE Oxford and Cambridge are the two oldest and most highly-regarded universities in Britain. Although both have tried in recent years to take more students from state schools, many Oxbridge students come from private or PUBLIC SCHOOLS, and Oxbridge GRADUATES often go on to become influential and powerful in British society. Because of this, people regard the two universities as being part of the British ESTABLISHMENT and class system, and use the word Oxbridge to refer to values and beliefs which they consider EXCLUSIVE, ELITIST, and out of touch with ordinary people. Others use the word to refer to TRADITIONAL values and high standards in learning and teaching. ◀

ox·cart /ˈɒkskɑːt‖ˈɑːkskɑːrt/ n a cart pulled by oxen

Ox·fam , OXFAM /ˈɒksfæm‖ˈɑːks-/ Oxford Committee for Famine Relief; a British CHARITY organization that helps people in poor countries, esp. by training them in farming methods, providing medicines, etc.. It raises some of its money through sales of new and used goods in its **Oxfam shops**: He always looks as if he buys his clothes from Oxfam.

Ox·ford /ˈɒksfəd‖ˈɑːksfərd/ **1** a town on the river Thames in Oxfordshire, S England, where the local government for that COUNTY is based. It has many beautiful old buildings and is famous for its university. —see colour map on page 818 **2** Oxford University: He went to/was educated at Oxford.

Oxford Cir·cus /ˌ·· ˈ··/ the place in London where Regent Street and Oxford Street cross, also the name of a nearby underground station

Oxford En·glish /ˌ·· ˈ··/ n [U] one of the names for the form of the English language which is thought by many people to be the desirable standard —see also BBC ENGLISH, RP

Oxford En·glish Dic·tion·a·ry /ˌ··· ˌ·· ˈ·····/ abbrev. **OED** a very large dictionary of English produced by Oxford University Press, famous for its completeness and for its explanation of the origins of words

Oxford Group /ˈ·· ˌ·/ [the] a group started by the American EVANGELIST Frank Buchman (1878–1961) which had many supporters at Oxford University in the 1920s. It was concerned with social, industrial, and international problems and later developed into the Moral Rearmament movement.

Oxford Move·ment /ˈ·· ˌ··/ [the] a religious movement within the Anglican Church in the 1800s, started by people at Oxford University, which tried to bring new life to Anglican religious practices by bringing in some TRADITIONs and beliefs of the Roman Catholic Church

Ox·fords /ˈɒksfədz ‖ ˈɑːksfərdz/ n [P] AmE (a pair of) men's leather shoes that tie with SHOELACEs —compare LOAFERS

Ox·ford·shire /ˈɒksfədʃər ‖ ˈɑːksfərd-/ abbrev. **Oxon** a COUNTY in S central England, in and around the Thames valley. It is mainly farmland, with some fine old market towns.

Oxford Street /ˈ·· ·/ one of the main streets of central London, famous for its shops —see colour map on page 817

Oxford U·ni·ver·si·ty /ˌ·· ···ˈ····/ also **Oxford**— one of the oldest and most highly regarded British universities.

Students must pass a special examination before they are accepted by the university, and the students who go there often come from PUBLIC SCHOOLS. —see also CAMBRIDGE UNIVERSITY, OXBRIDGE (CULTURAL NOTE)

ox·ide /ˈɒksaɪd‖ˈɑːk-/ n [C;U] a chemical compound in which something else is combined with oxygen: iron oxide

ox·i·dize also **-dise** BrE /ˈɒksˌdaɪz‖ˈɑːk-/ v [I;T] to (cause to) combine with oxygen, esp. in such a way as to make or become RUSTY —**dization** /ˌɒksˌdaɪˈzeɪʃən‖ˌɑːksˌdə-/ also **oxidation** /ˌɒksˌˈdeɪʃən‖ˌɑːk-/ n [U]

Ox·o /ˈɒksəʊ‖ˈɑːk-/ n [U] tdmk a type of meat STOCK (4) made by Brooke Bond Foods Ltd and sold usu. in the form of dried STOCK CUBEs

Ox·on /ˈɒksɒn‖ˈɑːksɑːn/ written abbrev. for: **1** Oxfordshire **2** (used esp. after the title of a degree) of Oxford University: David Jones, BA Oxon

Ox·o·ni·an /ɒkˈsəʊniən‖ɑːk-/ n,adj (a person) of or from Oxford or Oxfordshire

ox·y·a·cet·y·lene /ˌɒksiəˈsetˌliːn‖ˌɑːk-, -lən, -liːn/ n [U] tech a mixture of oxygen and another gas (ACETYLENE) that produces a hot white flame: an oxyacetylene torch

ox·y·gen /ˈɒksɪdʒən‖ˈɑːk-/ n [U] a gas present in the air that is a simple substance (ELEMENT), is without colour, taste, or smell, and is necessary for all forms of life on Earth

ox·y·gen·ate /ˈɒksɪdʒəneɪt‖ˈɑːk-/ v [T] tech to add oxygen to (esp. the blood): The heart pumps oxygenated blood through the arteries.

oxygen mask /ˈ··· ·/ n an apparatus placed over the nose and mouth to supply oxygen

oxygen tent /ˈ··· ·/ n a tent-like apparatus inside which oxygen can be supplied to people who are ill

ox·y·mo·ron /ˌɒksiˈmɔːrɒn‖ˌɑːksiˈmɔːrɑːn/ n tech a combination of words which seem to CONTRADICT (=disagree with) each other, such as "cruel kindness"

o·yez /əʊˈjez‖ˈəʊjez/ interj (a word used by a law official or, esp. in former times, by TOWN CRIERs giving news in the streets, to get people's attention)

oy·ster /ˈɔɪstəʳ/ n **1** a flat shellfish, eaten cooked or raw, which can produce a jewel called a PEARL. Some people think that eating oysters makes one better at sex. **2 the world is your oyster** saying you can go anywhere or do anything that you like: I've got my degree now, so the world's my oyster!

oyster bed /ˈ··· ·/ n an area at the bottom of the sea where oysters are bred

oy·ster·catch·er /ˈɔɪstəˌkætʃəʳ‖-tər-/ n a black and white seabird that eats shellfish

oz written abbrev. for: OUNCE (1) or OUNCEs

Oz /ɒz‖ɑːz/ **1** sl another name for Australia **2** a magical land in the children's story The Wizard of Oz

O·zal /əʊˈzɑːl/, **Tur·gut** /ˈtɜːgʊt‖ˈtɜːr-/ (1927–93) the president of Turkey since 1989, representing the Motherland Party

O·zarks /ˈəʊzɑːks‖-zɑːrks/ n [the+P] a high area of forest land mainly in the states of Missouri and Arkansas, US

O·za·wa /əʊˈzɑːwə/, **Sei·ji** /ˈseɪdʒi/ (1935–) an American CONDUCTOR (=a person who directs the playing of a group of musicians), born in China

o·zone /ˈəʊzəʊn/ n [U] **1** tech a poisonous blue gas; type of oxygen **2** infml air that is pleasant to breathe, esp. near the sea: a breath of ozone

ozone-friend·ly /ˈ·· ˌ··/ adj not containing chemicals which are harmful to the ozone layer: an ozone-friendly aerosol/propellant

ozone lay·er /ˈ·· ˌ··/ [the] a layer in the earth's ATMOSPHERE in which ozone is formed, preventing harmful RADIATION from the sun reaching the earth. Recently it has been found that there are holes in the ozone layer, and scientists believe that the ozone layer is being damaged by the use of certain chemicals.

Oz·zie and Har·ri·et /ˌɒzi ənd ˈhæriət‖ˌɑː-/ Ozzie Nelson (1906–75) and his wife Harriet (1914–), who were in an American programme called The Adventures of Ozzie and Harriet which was on during the 1950s and 1960s. The programme was about their family life and many people considered them to be a perfect American family.

P

P , **p** /piː/ P's, p's or Ps, ps the 16th letter of the English alphabet —see also **mind one's p's and q's** (MIND²)

p¹ BrE infml penny/pence: *This newspaper costs 25p.* —see PENNY (USAGE)

p² written abbrev for: **1** page —see also PP **2** participle **3** population **4** (in music) PIANO² **5** BrE penny/pence

P written abbrev for: PARKING (2)

P45 /ˌpiː fɔːti 'faɪv‖-fɔːrti-/ n in Britain, an official document given to a person when they leave a job to show how much money they have earned and how much tax and NATIONAL INSURANCE they have paid during their period of employment. This document must be given to their employer when the person starts a new job.

P60 /ˌpiː 'sɪksti/ n in Britain, an official document given to a person by their employer each year, which shows how much money they have earned and how much tax and NATIONAL INSURANCE they have paid during that year

pa /paː/ n infml & becoming rare (used to address one's father)

PA¹ /ˌpiː 'eɪ/ n **1** [C] BrE personal assistant; a senior secretary employed to look after and take responsibility for the affairs of just one person: *She's my PA.* —compare SECRETARY **2** [the+S] public-address system; an electrically controlled apparatus used for making a speaker clearly heard by large groups of people, e.g. in airports or outside: *The message came over loud and clear over the PA.*

PA² written abbrev. for: PENNSYLVANIA

p.a. written abbrev. for: PER ANNUM

PAC /pæk/ n see POLITICAL ACTION COMMITTEE

PAC 10 /ˌpæk 'ten/ n see PAC TEN

pace¹ /peɪs/ n **1** [S] rate or speed in walking, running, advance of a plan, etc., usu. continued over a period of time: *to walk at a slow pace* | *The faster runner* **set the pace**, (=fixed the speed) *and the others followed.* | *She works so fast I can't* **keep pace** *with her.* (-go as fast as her) **2** [C] a single step in running or walking, or the distance moved in one step: *She finished only a few paces behind the winner.* —compare STEP¹ **3** [C usu. sing.] a way that a horse walks or runs: *The natural paces of the horse include the walk, the trot, and the gallop.* **4** **put someone through their paces** to make someone do something in order to show their abilities: *The film director put the new actor through his paces.* **5** **show one's paces** to show one's abilities

pace² v **1** [I+adv/prep;T] to walk (across) with slow, regular, steady steps, esp. backwards and forwards: *The policeman paced up and down.* | *The lion paced the floor of his cage restlessly.* **2** [T (OFF, OUT)] to measure by taking steps of an equal and known length: *I think the hall is 80 metres long: I'll pace it (out).* **3** [T] to set the speed of movement for: *She knew how fast she was running, because her trainer was pacing her on a bicycle.*

pa·ce³ /'peɪsiː, 'paːkeɪ, 'paːtʃeɪ/ prep Lat fml, rare giving proper respect to, but in a polite way disagreeing with: *My own view, pace the last speaker, is that we should sell the property.*

pace bowl·er /'· ·,··/ also **pace man** /'·· ·/— n a player who bowls (BOWL²) the ball fast in cricket

pace·mak·er /'peɪsˌmeɪkər/ n **1** also **pace·set·ter** /-ˌsetər/ AmE— a person or animal that sets a speed that others in a race try to equal **b** a person who sets an example for others **2** a small machine fixed inside the heart in order to make weak or irregular heartbeats regular

pach·y·derm /'pækɪdɜːm‖-dɜːrm/ n tech a thick-skinned animal, e.g. the elephant and the RHINOCEROS

pa·cif·ic /pə'sɪfɪk/ adj fml **1** helping to cause peace **2** calm; peace-loving — ~ **ally** /kli/ adv

Pacific Day·light Time /·,·· '·· ·/ (abbrev. PDT) the time used in the summer months in the Pacific Time Zone of the US

Pacific North·west /·,·· '·· ·/ [the] the area of the US which

includes Washington State, Oregon, and northern California, esp. along the Pacific coast. The area is known for its wild beauty, cliffs, and forests. —compare WEST, WEST COAST

Pacific Ocean /·,·· '····/ also **Pacific**— [the] the world's largest ocean, covering one third of the Earth's surface between the CONTINENTS of America to the E and Asia and Australia to the W —see colour map on pages 1374-5

Pacific Stan·dard Time /·,·· '·· ·/ the time used from autumn to spring in the Pacific Time Zone of the US

Pacific Ten /·,·· '·· ·/ n see PAC TEN

pac·i·fi·er /'pæsɪfaɪər/ n **1** a person who pacifies **2** AmE for DUMMY (3)

pac·i·fist /'pæsɪfɪst/ n a person who believes that all wars are wrong and refuses to fight in them —**fism** n [U]

pac·i·fy /'pæsɪfaɪ/ v [T] **1** to make calm, quiet, and satisfied: *to pacify a crying baby* **2** to bring peace to; end war in (a place) —**fication** /ˌpæsɪfɪ'keɪʃən/ n [U]

Pa·ci·no /pə'tʃiːnəʊ/, **Al** /æl/ (1940–) an American actor known for films such as *The Godfather* and *Scarface*

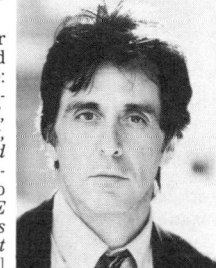

Al Pacino

pack¹ /pæk/ n **1** [C] a number of things wrapped or tied together, or put in a case: *Your membership pack includes a membership card, window sticker, rule book, and list of addresses.* | *Send away for your free information pack today.* —see also SIX-PACK **2** [C (**of**)] esp. AmE a PACKET: *a pack of cigarettes* —see USAGE NOTE at PACKET (1) **3** [C+sing./pl. v] **a** a group of wild animals that hunt together, or a group of dogs trained together for hunting: *The pack of hounds was baying loudly.* | *a ferocious pack of wolves* **b** a group of fighting machines that fight together as one force, esp. SUBMARINES and aircraft **c** (in RUGBY football) the group of players (FORWARDS⁵) whose job is to get possession of the ball for their side **d** a group of CUB SCOUTS or BROWNIE GUIDES **e** derog any collection or group: *a pack of thieves* | *a pack of lies* **4** [C] BrE‖**deck** AmE a complete set of playing cards: *He dealt the pack.* (-divided the cards among the players) **5** [C] a thick mass of soft cloth pressed to a wound to stop bleeding, etc.; COMPRESS —see also ICE PACK **6** [C] a substance, often a special mud or clay, used on the face as a beauty treatment —see also FACE PACK, MUDPACK **7** [C;U] PACK ICE

pack² v **1 a** [I;T (UP)] to put (things, esp. one's belongings) into cases, boxes, etc., for taking somewhere or storing: *We leave tomorrow but I haven't begun to pack yet!* | *He remembered to pack his toothbrush.* | *She takes a packed lunch to school every day.* | *They packed up the contents of their house.* [+obj(i)+obj(d)] *Have you packed me a razor?* —opposite **unpack b** [T] to put things into (a case, box, etc.): *He packed a case/an overnight bag.* | *to pack a tea chest* **c** [I] to be suitable for putting into a container: *This dress packs without creasing.* —see also PACKING **2** [I+adv/prep;T+obj+adv/prep] to fit, crush, or push into a space: *When the door was opened, people began to pack into the hall.* | *The bus was packed with noisy schoolchildren.* | (fig.) *They tried to pack too much into the holiday* (=do too many things) *and returned exhausted.* —see also PACKED **3** [T] to cover, fill, or surround closely with a protective material: *Pack this cloth round the picnic cups so they won't break.* —see also PACKING **4** [I;T+obj +adv/prep] to settle or be driven into a mass: *The wind packed the snow against the wall.* **5** [T] to prepare and put (food) into containers for preserving or selling **6** [T] derog to choose members of (a committee or a JURY) favourable to one's own purpose: *He packed the meeting with his own supporters.* **7** [T] AmE infml to carry regularly: *to pack a gun* **8 pack a (hard) punch** infml **a** (of a fighter) to be able to hit hard **b** to use very forceful direct language, esp. effectively —see also **send someone packing** (SEND (7)) **9 pack up your troubles in your old kit-bag** the title and first line of a song sung by British soldiers during the First World War: *Pack up your troubles in your old kit-bag and smile, smile, smile…*

pack sbdy./sthg. ↔ **in** phr v [T] infml **1** to attract (people) in large numbers: That film is really packing them in. **2** esp. BrE to stop doing; used esp. of something one finds unpleasant, annoying, etc.: I decided to pack in my university studies and get a job. | Pack it in you two; I'm tired of hearing you arguing!

pack sbdy./sthg. **off** phr v [T (**to**)] infml to send away quickly, esp. to avoid trouble: She packed her son off to school.

pack up phr v **1** [I] infml to finish work: As business was slack she packed up early. **2** [I] infml, esp. BrE (of a machine) to stop working: The engine's packed up! **3** [T] to stop: He packed up his job after three months. [+v-ing] She's packed up smoking at long last.

package

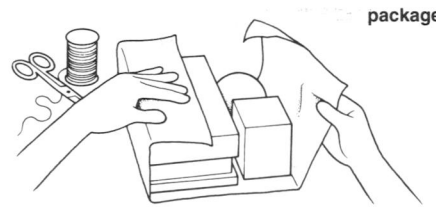

pack·age[1] /ˈpækɪdʒ/ n [(**of**)] **1** an amount or esp. a number of things packed together firmly; a parcel: She sent him a large package of books. **2** a set of related things sold or offered as a unit: The union has negotiated a new package of benefits with the management. | a new software package

package[2] v [T] **1** [(UP)] to make into or tie up as a package: She packaged up the old clothes and put them in the cupboard. **2** to place in a special package before selling: Those chocolates have been packaged very attractively. —**ager** n

package deal /ˈ·· ·/ n infml an offer or agreement that includes a number of things all of which must be accepted together

package tour /ˈ·· ·/ also **package hol·i·day** /ˈ·· ˌ···/ n a completely planned holiday arranged by a company at a fixed price, which includes travel, hotels, meals, etc. —see also extra information on page 632

▶CULTURAL NOTE Many people take package holidays abroad, and there are all kinds of tours to suit different people. However, the popular image of a package tour is of a cheap holiday to a place by the sea in southern Europe (esp. Spain). Many jokes are made about package holidays, esp. about delayed flights, poor quality hotels which serve poor food, and hotels which are a long way from the sea and are not finished: We went on a package tour this year; a fortnight in Gatwick Airport. It was miles from the beach, but at least it had a roof!◀

pack·ag·ing /ˈpækɪdʒɪŋ/ n [U] material used for packing products: Complicated packaging increases the price of food.

pack an·i·mal /ˈ· ˌ···/ n an animal, such as a horse (**packhorse**), used for carrying things on its back

packed /pækt/ adj (of a room, building, etc.) full of people; CROWDED: a packed theatre

packed lunch /ˌ· ˈ·/ n a cold midday meal of sandwiches (SANDWICH[1]), fruit, sweets or other things, packed into a box or parcel and taken with you in the morning to be eaten later. Packed lunches are often given to school children, or people staying at a hotel who are going out on a full day trip.

packed-out /ˌ· ˈ·◄/ adj [F] infml, esp. BrE (of a room, building, etc.) completely full of people

pack·er /ˈpækər/ n a person who packs, such as **a** a person who works where food is put into tins, etc., for preserving **b** a person employed to pack the furniture, clothing, etc., of people moving from one house to another

pack·et /ˈpækɪt/ n **1** [(**of**)] also **pack** esp.AmE— a small parcel; a number of things tied or put together into a small container: a packet of envelopes/cigarettes/sugar

▷ USAGE Both **pack** and **packet** are used in AmE; packets are usu. smaller than packs: a packet of seeds | a packet of sugar (containing one serving); a pack of cigarettes◁

2 [usu. sing.] sl a large amount of money: That car cost me a packet. **3** also **packet boat** /ˈ·· ˌ·/— a boat that carries mail and usu. passengers at regular times between places **4 catch/cop/get/stop a packet** BrE sl to get into serious trouble or receive a heavy punishment

packet of three /ˌ··· ˈ·/ n BrE infml a small packet containing three CONDOMS

packet-switch·ing /ˈ·· ˌ··/ n [U] a method of sending DATA (=information stored on a computer) on telephone lines that breaks long messages into pieces (packets) and puts them together again when they are received. It is faster than older methods, and allows many users on a network at the same time.

pack ice /ˈ· ·/ n [U] sea ice crushed together into a large floating mass

pack·ing /ˈpækɪŋ/ n [U] **1** the act of putting things in cases or boxes: I'll do my packing the night before we leave. **2** protective material for packing things: The price of the books includes **postage and packing.**

packing case /ˈ·· ·/ n a large strong wooden box in which heavy articles are packed to be sent elsewhere

pack rat /ˈ· ·/ n **1** a large RAT which collects and stores various things, carrying them in its fat cheeks **2** AmE someone who collects and stores things for a long time, esp. unneeded things

pact /pækt/ n a solemn agreement, esp. between opposing groups or nations: The two opposition parties made an electoral pact. (=agreed to work together in the election) [+to-v] a pact between the management and the union leaders to restrict salary increases —compare CONVENTION (3), TREATY (1)

Pac Ten /ˌpæk ˈten/ also **Pacific Ten, Pac 10**— n [U] a group of ten university FOOTBALL (2) teams from the area of the US along the Pacific coast who play against each other

pad[1] /pæd/ n **1** anything made of or filled with soft material to protect something or make it more comfortable, or to fill out a shape: Put a clean pad of cotton over the wound. —see also SHOULDER PAD; see picture at CRICKET **2** a number of sheets of paper fastened together, used for writing letters, drawing pictures, etc.: a writing pad **3** a piece of material made wet with ink for pressing onto a marker; INKPAD **4** the usu. thick-skinned fleshy underpart of the foot of some four-footed animals: The dog had a thorn in its pad. **5** tech the large floating leaf of certain water plants such as the WATER LILY **6** a LAUNCH PAD **7** AmE a SANITARY TOWEL **8** rather old-fash sl one's house or flat: I'm going over to his pad this evening.

pad[2] v -dd- [T] **1** to protect, shape, or make more comfortable by covering or filling with soft material. In cricket, batsmen (BATSMAN) wear special pads to protect their legs: a coat with padded shoulders | a **padded cell** (=room with soft walls) in a psychiatric hospital **2** [(OUT)] to make (a sentence, speech, etc.) longer by adding unnecessary words: a speech padded (out) with amusing anecdotes

pad[3] v -dd- [I+adv/prep] to walk steadily and usu. softly, with the foot flat on the ground: John's dog padded patiently along beside him as he walked. | The little boy padded down the hall to his parents' bedroom.

pad·ding /ˈpædɪŋ/ n [U] material used to PAD[2] something: the padding in my coat/in your speech

Pad·ding·ton[1] /ˈpædɪŋtən/ one of the mainline railway stations in London —see colour map on page 817

Paddington[2] also **Paddington Bear** /ˌ···· ˈ·/— the main character in the stories for children about a toy bear from Peru who is lost at Paddington Station and goes to live with an English family.

Paddington Bear

pad·dle[1] /ˈpædl/ n **1** [C] a short pole with a wide flat blade at one end or (if a **double paddle**) at both ends, used for moving a small boat (esp. a CANOE) along. It is used freely and not held in position on the side of the boat. —compare OAR **2** [C] anything shaped like this, such as **a** a tool like a flat

the House of Lords

the House of Commons

the House of Representatives in the US

Every year a ceremony called the STATE OPENING OF PARLIAMENT takes place at the Houses of Parliament where the Queen officially opens Parliament

John Major outside 10 Downing Street, the official home of the British Prime Minister

A British politician talking to people in the street to try to get their votes during an election campaign

Bill Clinton at a US political rally in 1992

George Bush throwing a baseball onto the field to start the first game of the World Serie

The US President, Bill Clinton, and his wife Hillary

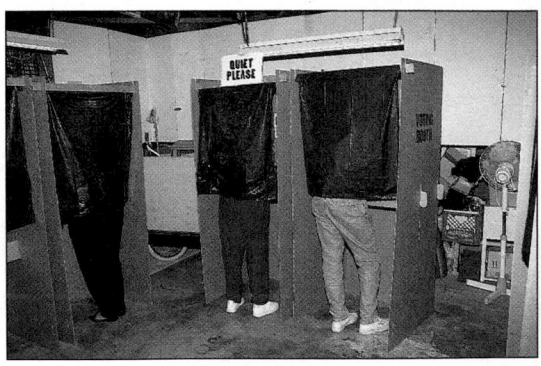

polling booths (places where people go to vote in an election) (voting booths AmE)

spoon, used for mixing food **b** one of the wide blades used on the wheel of a PADDLE STEAMER **3** *AmE* a small wide flat BAT¹ (1), used esp. in TABLE TENNIS **4** [S] an act or period of walking about in water which is not at all deep: *to go for a paddle in the sea* —see also DOG PADDLE

paddle² *v* **1** [I+*adv*/*prep*;T+*obj*+*adv*/*prep*] to move (a small light boat, esp. a CANOE) through water, using one or more paddles —compare ROW¹ **2** [I] to swim as a dog or duck does **3** [I] to walk about in water which is not at all deep: *children paddling in the sea* —compare WADE **4** [T] *AmE infml* to strike with the open hand in punishing **5 paddle one's own canoe** *infml* to depend on oneself and no one else

paddle steam·er /ˈ··ˌ··/ *BrE* ‖ **side-wheeler** or **stern-wheeler** *AmE*— *n* a steamship which is pushed forward by a pair of large wheels (**paddle wheels**) at the sides or one large wheel at the back

padd·ling pool /ˈ·· ·/ ‖ usu. **baby pool** *or* **wading pool** *AmE*— *n* **1** a small area of water which is not at all deep, where children paddle, usu. in a park **2** a plastic container that can be filled with water, for children to play in

pad·dock /ˈpædək/ *n* **1** a small field near a house or STABLES where horses are kept or exercised **2** a grassy place where horses are brought together before a race so that people may see them

pad·dy¹ /ˈpædi/ *also* **paddy field** /ˈ·· ·/, **rice paddy**— *n* a field where rice is grown in water

paddy² *n* [S] *BrE infml* a state of bad temper

Paddy *n infml, sometimes derog* an Irishman (a short form of Patrick, a common name in Ireland)

paddy wag·on /ˈ·· ˌ··/ *n infml AmE* PATROL WAGON

Pad·e·rew·ski /ˌpædəˈrefski/, **Jan** /jæn‖jɑːn/ (1860 1941) a Polish piano player of CLASSICAL music who became the first PRIME MINISTER of Poland after the First World War

pad·lock /ˈpædlɒk‖-lɑːk/ *n* a lock that can be put on and removed, by means of a U-shaped metal bar, used for locking gates, bicycles, cupboards, etc. —**padlock** *v* [T]: *to padlock the gate*

pa·dre /ˈpɑːdri, -rei/ *n infml (often cap.)* a priest, esp. one in the Armed Forces; CHAPLAIN: *Hello, Padre!* —see PRIEST (USAGE)

pae·an /ˈpiːən/ *n lit* a joyous song of praise, thanks, or victory

paed·e·rast *BrE* ‖ **pederast** *AmE* /ˈpedəræst/ *tech n* a man who has sex with a boy — ~**rasty** *n* [U]

pae·di·a·tri·cian *BrE* ‖ **pediatrician** *AmE* /ˌpiːdiəˈtrɪʃən/ *n* a doctor who specializes in paediatrics

pae·di·at·rics *BrE* ‖ **pediatrics** *AmE* /ˌpiːdiˈætrɪks/ *n* [U] the branch of medicine concerned with children and their illnesses

pae·do·phile *BrE* ‖ **pedophile** *AmE* /ˈpiːdəfaɪl/ *n* a person who is sexually attracted to young children

pa·el·la /paɪˈelə‖pɑː-/ *n* [U] a Spanish dish of rice cooked with pieces of meat, fish, and vegetables

pae·o·ny /ˈpiːəni/ *n* a PEONY

pa·gan /ˈpeɪgən/ *n* **1** *derog* a person (esp. in ancient times) who is not a believer in any of the chief religions of the world, and esp. not in one's own religion; HEATHEN: *They regard us all as pagans.* —compare ATHEIST, HEATHEN **2** (used esp. of the ancient Greeks and Romans) a person who believes in many gods —**pagan** *adj* : *pagan tribes*/*beliefs* — ~**ism** *n* [U]

Pag·a·ni·ni /ˌpægəˈniːni/, **Nic·co·lò** /ˈnɪkələʊ/ (1782–1840) Italian VIOLIN player and writer of music, of international fame

page¹ /peɪdʒ/ *n* **1** one side or both sides of a sheet of paper in a book, newspaper, etc.: *Turn over; there's a picture on the next page.* | *Turn to page 44.* | *Someone has torn a page out of this book.* | *I took*/*made several pages of notes on his talk.* | *a dog-eared page* | *a blank*/*fresh*/*new page* | *the front page*/*sports pages of the newspaper* **2** *lit* an important event or period: *These years will be remembered as some of the finest pages in our country's history.*

page² *n* **1** *also* **pageboy**— **a** a boy servant in a hotel, club, etc., usu. uniformed **b** a boy attendant on the BRIDE at a wedding **2** a boy in former times who was in training to be a KNIGHT (noble soldier) **3** *now rare* a boy in service to a person of high rank

page³ *v* [T] (in a public place) to call aloud for (someone

who is wanted for some reason), esp. through a LOUD-SPEAKER: *I couldn't find my friend at the airport, so I had her paged.*

pag·eant /ˈpædʒənt/ *n* **1** [C] a splendid public show or ceremony, usu. out of doors, in which there is a procession of people in rich dress or in which historical scenes are acted: *a village pageant moving through the streets on floats* | (fig.) *the rich pageant of history* **2** [U] splendid show that looks grand but has no meaning or power

pag·eant·ry /ˈpædʒəntri/ *n* [U] splendid show of ceremonial grandness with people in beautiful dress: *the pageantry of a royal wedding*

page·boy /ˈpeɪdʒbɔɪ/ *n* **1** a PAGE² (1) **2** a style of cutting women's hair, in which the hair reaches down to the neck, has its ends turned under, and is cut in a long FRINGE¹ (2) at the front

pa·ger /ˈpeɪdʒəʳ/ *n AmE for* BLEEPER

page three girl /ˌ· ˈ· ·/ *n BrE* a young and attractive woman, usu. with large breasts, whose photograph appears on the third page of the *Sun*, a British newspaper

pa·go·da /pəˈgəʊdə/ *n* a temple (esp. Buddhist or Hindu) often built on several floors or levels with a decorative roof at each level

Pah·la·vi /ˈpɑːləvi‖ˈpæl-/, **Mo·ham·med Re·za** /məʊˈhæm‖d ˈriːzə‖-riːˈzɑː/ (1918–80) the Shah of Iran from 1941 to 1979. He was forced to leave his country during a period of political trouble and died soon afterwards.

paid /peɪd/ *written abbrev.* **pd** *past tense and participle of* PAY

paid po·lit·i·cal broad·cast /ˌ· ·ˌ··· ˈ··/ *AmE for* PARTY POLITICAL BROADCAST

paid-up /ˌ· ˈ·◂/ *adj* having paid in full, esp. so as to continue being a member: *a paid-up member of the club* —compare PAY **up**

pail /peɪl/ *n esp. AmE* **1** *esp. AmE* a bucket for carrying liquids: *a milk pail* | *a slop pail* (=for dirty water and liquid waste) **2** *also* **pail·ful** /-fʊl/— the amount a pail will hold: *two pailfuls of water*

pail·lasse /ˈpæliæs‖ˌpæliˈæs/ *n* a PALLIASSE

pain¹ /peɪn/ *n* **1** [U] suffering; great discomfort of the body or mind: *He was in great pain*/*crying with pain after he broke his arm.* | *His behaviour caused his parents a great deal of pain.* | *The pain eased slightly.* | *to inflict pain on someone* **2** [C] an esp. sharp feeling of suffering or discomfort in a particular part of the body: *a stabbing*/*severe*/*nagging pain in my back* | *slight stomach pains* | *She's always complaining of* **aches and pains**. | (fig., *sl*) *You give me a pain!* (=You annoy me.) —compare ACHE²; see also GROWING PAINS **3** [S] *also* **pain in the neck** /ˌ· · ˈ·/— *sl* a person, thing, or situation that makes one angry and tired, but is difficult to avoid; NUISANCE: *She's a real pain.* | *It's a pain in the neck having to meet them at the airport.* **4 on**/**under pain of** *fml* at the risk of suffering (some punishment): *They were forbidden to leave, on pain of death.* —see also PAINS

pain² *v* [T] **1** *lit or fml* to cause to feel pain in the mind; hurt: *It pains me to have to leave, but I must.* **2** [*no pass.*] *fml* (of a part of the body) to cause pain to; hurt

Paine /peɪn/, **Thomas** (1737–1809) an American political thinker and writer, born in England. He supported the French Revolution and had to escape from England to France because of this. His most famous books are *The Rights of Man* and *The Age of Reason.*

pained /peɪnd/ *adj* [(at)] displeased or hurt in one's feelings: *She looked rather pained at your remarks.* | *After they had quarrelled there was a pained silence.*

pain·ful /ˈpeɪnfəl/ *adj* causing pain, esp. physical pain: *a painful cut on his thumb* | *Does it still feel painful?* | *It must have been very painful for you tell her about the accident.* | (fig.)*That singer is*/*sounds absolutely painful!* (=terrible) — ~**ly** *adv* : *It is painfully clear that Tom will fail his exam.* — ~**ness** *n* [U]

pain·kill·er /ˈpeɪnˌkɪləʳ/ *also* **analgesic** *med*— *n* a medicine which lessens or removes pain

pain·less /ˈpeɪnləs/ *adj* **1** causing no pain: *painless childbirth* **2** *infml* needing no effort or hard work: *a painless way of learning a foreign language* — ~**ly** *adv*

pains /peɪnz/ *n* [P] **1** trouble; effort: *We gave the taxi driver*

something extra for his pains. | *She* went to great pains/took pains *with her work.* (=made an effort) **2** be at pains to do something: a to take great trouble about something: *The teacher was at (great) pains to make sure that we all understood.* b to be particularly careful to do something: *He was at pains to point out my mistake.*

pains·tak·ing /ˈpeɪnzˌteɪkɪŋ/ *adj* very careful and thorough: *painstaking care* | *She is not very clever but she is painstaking.* — ~**ly** *adv*

paint¹ /peɪnt/ *n* [U] **1** liquid colouring matter which can be put or spread on a surface to make it a certain colour: *a tin/a tube of green paint* | *oil paint* | *gloss paint* | *Wet Paint* (=a warning sign placed near a freshly painted surface) **2** *old use* colouring matter used on the face; MAKE-UP —see also GREASEPAINT, PAINTS; compare DYE

paint² *v* **1** [I;T] to put paint on (a surface): *I wear old trousers when I'm painting.* | *The ceiling needs painting.* [+*obj*+*adj*] *I painted the door blue.* **2 a** [T] to make by using paint: *to paint pictures* **b** [T] to make a picture of: *She painted the view from her hotel window.* **c** [I] to paint pictures: *His wife paints.* | *She paints in oils/in water-colours.* **3** [I;T] *old use derog* to colour (the face) with MAKE-UP: *painted prostitutes* **4** [T] to describe in clear well-chosen words: *His letters paint a wonderful picture of his life in Burma.* **5** [T] to put medicine on (esp. the throat) with a brush **6 paint the town red** *infml* to go out and have an extremely good time, usu. to CELEBRATE something —see also **not as black as one is painted** (BLACK¹)

paint·box /ˈpeɪntbɒks‖-bɑːks/ *n* a (usu. metal) box containing hard blocks of paint which can be mixed with water, often used by children

paint·brush /ˈpeɪntbrʌʃ/ *n* a brush for spreading paint on a surface —see picture at BRUSH

Painted Des·ert /ˌ·· ˈ···/ [*the*] an area in the American state of Arizona, east of the Little Colorado River, known for its red, brown, and purple rock surfaces on small and large PLATEAUS (=stretches of level land higher than the surrounding land)

paint·er¹ /ˈpeɪntəʳ/ *n* **1** a person whose job is painting houses, rooms, etc. **2** a person who paints pictures; ARTIST: *a portrait/landscape painter* | *a good painter*

painter² *n tech* a rope for tying a small boat to a ship or to a post on land

paint·ing /ˈpeɪntɪŋ/ *n* **1** [U] the act of painting **a** houses, rooms, etc. **b** pictures: *I've always admired Monet's early painting.* **2** [C] a painted picture: *to hang a painting*

paints /peɪnts/ *n* [P] a set of small tubes or CAKES (=dry flat pieces) of paint of different colours, usu. in a paintbox, used for making pictures: *a set of oil paints*

paint·work /ˈpeɪntwɜːk‖-wɜːrk/ *n* [U] a painted surface: *some damage to the paintwork on my car*

pair¹ /peəʳ/ *n* **pairs** *or* **pair** **1** [(of)] something made up of two parts that are alike and are joined and used together: *There's a clean pair of trousers on your bed.* | *a pair of scissors* —see USAGE **2** [(of)] two things that are alike or of the same kind, and are usu. used together: *Is that a new pair of shoes?* | *a beautiful pair of candlesticks* | *a pair (of kings)* (=two playing cards of the same value) | *I've lost my gloves – have you got a spare pair?* | *I've only got one pair of hands!* (=I can't do all this work) **3** [+*sing./pl. v*] two people closely connected, esp. a COUPLE¹ (2): *a pair of dancers* | *The* **happy** **pair** *is/are going to Spain after their wedding.* | *The children walked* **in pairs.** (=in twos) **4** [+*sing./pl. v*] **a** two animals, male and female, that stay together for a long time **b** two horses that pull a cart, etc.: *to drive a carriage and pair* —see also TEAM¹ (2) **5** *taboo sl* a woman's breasts

▷ USAGE Some words like **trousers** and **scissors** are used like plural nouns, but they are not thought of as having number. So you can say *These scissors/My other trousers are old,* but the actual number of items (one or more) can only be known from the situation. You cannot use words to show the number of these items unless you also use **pair** or **pairs**: *a* **pair** *of* scissors | *both* **pairs** *of* trousers | *three* **pairs** *of* trousers. **Pair** is also used for things like **shoes** which can be talked about separately or two at a time. You can say *one* shoe/*both* shoes as well as *a* **pair** *of* shoes/*five* **pairs** *of* shoes. Any word in this dictionary which is followed by the note "see PAIR (USAGE)" can be used

in the expression *a* **pair** *of X.* —compare BRACE; see COUPLE (USAGE)◁

pair² *v* [I;T (OFF, UP)] to (cause to) form into one or more pairs: *Birds often pair in the spring.* | *We tried to pair Jane and David off/to pair Jane off with David.* | *He was paired (up) with my sister in the tennis tournament.*

pais·ley /ˈpeɪzli/ *n* [U] (*sometimes cap.*) cloth with curved coloured patterns (from the town **Paisley** in Scotland, where the pattern was first made on a large scale): *a paisley skirt*

Paisley, the Reverend I·an /ˈiːən/ (1926–) Northern Irish PROTESTANT political leader who speaks very strongly in favour of Northern Ireland remaining part of the United Kingdom, and against the IRA. He is known for his strong, emotional way of speaking about religious and political matters.

Pai·ute /paɪˈuːt/ *n* [C; *the* +P] (a member of) a Native American people living in the SW of the US —see also NATIVE AMERICAN (CULTURAL NOTE)

pa·ja·mas /pəˈdʒɑːməz‖-ˈdʒæ-, -ˈdʒæ-/ *n* [P] *esp. AmE for* PYJAMAS —see PAIR (USAGE) —**pajama** *adj* [A]

Pak·i /ˈpæki/ *n BrE derog* a person from Pakistan, or one born in Britain whose parents were from Pakistan; an offensive word

Paki bash·ing /ˈ·· ˌ··/ *n* [U] *BrE infml* attacks and other violence against people of Asian origin in Britain, usu. by young people with RIGHT-WING opinions

Paki shop /ˈ·· ·/ *n BrE derog* a small local shop, often on a street corner, run by Asians of any country

Pa·kis·tan /ˌpɑːkɪˈstɑːn, ˌpækɪˈstæn/ a country, officially called the Islamic Republic of Pakistan, bordered by India to the E, Afghanistan to the N and W, Iran to the SW, and the Arabian Sea to the S; capital Islamabad; population 108,678,000 (1989) —**tani** /ˌpɑːkɪˈstɑːni◂, pæk-‖-ˈstɑːni◂, -ˈstæni◂/ *n,adj*

pal¹ /pæl/ *n infml* **1** a close friend: *an old pal of mine* | *We've been pals for years!* **2** *esp. AmE, ScE* (often used in unfriendly speech to a man): *Listen, pal, I don't want you talking to my sister any more, see?* —see also PALLY

pal² *v*

pal up *phr v* -ll- [I (**with**)] *BrE infml* to become friends

Pal *n* [U] *tdmk* a type of food for dogs, made by Pedigree Petfoods

pal·ace /ˈpæləs/ *n* **1** [C] (*often cap. as part of a name*) a large grand house where a ruling king or queen, or a British BISHOP or ARCHBISHOP, officially lives: *Buckingham Palace* —see HOUSE (USAGE) **2** [C] any large splendid house: *The nobles of Florence built splendid palaces.* | *His home is a palace compared to ours!* —compare STATELY HOME **3** [C] *esp. BrE* a large building used for public amusement: *Some cinemas used to be called Picture Palaces.* —see also PALATIAL

Palace [*the*] *BrE* **1** *infml* Buckingham Palace **2** the Queen (or King) and the royal officials: *a Palace spokesman* | *The Palace won't like all this gossip.*

Palace of West·min·ster /ˌ·· · ˈ··/ [*the*] the official name of the Houses of Parliament, London. The full title, not so frequently used, is the **New Palace of Westminster** (from the name of a royal palace which used to stand where the Houses of Parliament are now).

palace rev·o·lu·tion /ˌ··· ··ˈ··/ *n* the removal from office of a king, president, etc., usu. by those just beneath him/her in rank

pal·a·din /ˈpælədɪn/ *n* **1** any of 12 men of high rank under Charlemagne (742–814) **2** *lit* someone who is strongly in favour of something, esp. in politics

pal·ais /ˈpæleɪ, *infml* ˈpæli‖pæˈleɪ/ *also* **palais de danse** /ˌpæleɪ də ˈdɑːns‖pæˈleɪ də dæns/— *n* **palais** /ˈpæleɪz‖pæˈleɪz/ *BrE* (*often cap.*) a large public hall used for dancing

pal·an·quin /ˌpælənˈkiːn/ *n* a vehicle like a box with a seat or bed inside it for one person, carried on poles, formerly used in India and other eastern countries; the person carried would probably be rich or important

pal·a·ta·ble /ˈpælətəbəl/ *adj* **1** pleasant to taste, though not special: *a palatable meal* **2** pleasant: *She didn't find my suggestion at all palatable.* —opposite **unpalatable** —**bly** *adv*

pal·a·tal /ˈpælətl/ *n, adj tech* (a consonant sound) made by putting the tongue against or near the HARD PALATE

pal·ate /ˈpælət/ n **1** [C] the ROOF (=top inside part) of the mouth —see also CLEFT PALATE, HARD PALATE, SOFT PALATE **2** [C (**for**)] *usu. sing.*] the ability to judge good food or wine: *She has a good palate for wine.* **3** [C;U (**for**)] a taste or liking: *His novels are too sad for my palate.* | *Spicy food suits my palate best.*

▷ USAGE Many people would use **taste** or **liking** rather than **palate**, as **palate** is a more formal word.◁

pa·la·tial /pəˈleɪʃəl/ adj (usu. of buildings) like a palace; grand and splendid: *a palatial hotel* – – ~**ly** adv

pa·lat·i·nate /pəˈlætɪnɪt/ n *old use (often cap.)* an area formerly ruled over by a man of high rank (**Palatine, Count Palatine**) who was the representative of a higher ruler: *the Rhine Palatinate*

pa·la·ver /pəˈlɑːvər‖-ˈlæ-/ n **1** [U] *infml* continuous foolish meaningless talk: *What's all the palaver about?* **2** [U] *infml* trouble, inconvenience, or anxiety (over small matters); BOTHER; FUSS: *all the palaver of booking tickets and renewing my passport* **3** [C] *rare* a long talk about something important, esp. between opposing leaders

pale¹ /peɪl/ adj **1** (of a person's face or skin) having less than the usual amount of colour; rather white: *You're looking rather pale; are you ill?* | *a pale complexion* **2** (of colours or light) not bright: *pale blue* | *pale sunshine* —compare DEEP¹ (5), LIGHT³ (2) – – ~**ly** /ˈpeɪl-li/ adv – ~**ness** n [U]

pale² v [I] **1** to become pale: *He paled at the sight of the blood.* **2** [(**before, beside**)] to seem less important, clever, beautiful, etc., when compared with: *All other anxieties paled into insignificance beside the possibility of war.* | *This year's profits pale by/in comparison with the huge profits we made last year.*

pale³ n **1** a PALING **2 beyond the pale** beyond the limit of proper behaviour: *She went a bit beyond the pale bringing six uninvited people to my party!*

pale ale /ˌ· ˈ·/ n [U] LIGHT ALE

pale·face /ˈpeɪlfeɪs/ n *derog & humor* (the name said to have been used formerly by Native Americans for) a white person

pal·e·og·ra·phy /ˌpæliˈɒɡrəfi‖ˌpeɪliˈɑː-/ n [U] the study of ancient writing —**pher** n

pal·e·o·lith·ic /ˌpæliəʊˈlɪθɪk◂‖ˌpeɪ-/ adj *(often cap.)* of the earliest period of the STONE AGE, when people made stone weapons and tools: *a paleolithic axe* —compare NEOLITHIC

pal·e·on·tol·o·gy /ˌpæliɒnˈtɒlədʒi‖ˌpeɪliɑːnˈtɑː-/ n [U] the study of FOSSILs —**gist** n

Pal·es·tine /ˈpæləstaɪn/ an area covering parts of modern Israel, holy to Christians, Jews, and Muslims. It has been the cause of fierce argument and fighting for many years between Israel and the Arab states.

Palestine Lib·e·ra·tion Or·ga·ni·za·tion /ˌ··· ··ˈ··· ···ˌ··/ [the] see PLO

Pal·es·tin·i·an /ˌpæləˈstɪniən◂/ adj a usu. Muslim person from Palestine. Most Palestinians are Muslims, but some are Christians.

pal·ette /ˈpælɪt/ n **1** a board with a curved edge and a hole for the thumb, on which a painter mixes colours **2** *tech* the particular colours used by a painter or for a picture

palette knife /ˈ··· ·/ n a thin bendable knife with a rounded end, used by painters to mix colours, and in cookery

pal·frey /ˈpɔːlfri/ n *old use & poet* a horse trained for riding, esp. for use by a woman

Pa·li Can·on /ˌpɑːli ˈkænən/ [the] all of the teachings of the Buddha, as written down in the Pali language, starting in the first century BC.

pal·i·mo·ny /ˈpælɪməni‖-məʊni/ n [U] *AmE* money that a man or woman has been ordered to pay regularly to a former partner when they separate after having lived together without being married

pal·imp·sest /ˈpælɪmpsest/ n an ancient piece of writing material on which the original writing was rubbed out, not always completely, so that it could be used again

pal·in·drome /ˈpælɪndrəʊm/ n a word, phrase, etc., that reads the same backwards as it does forwards: *The words "deed" and "level" are palindromes.*

pal·ing /ˈpeɪlɪŋ/ n **1** [C *usu. pl.*] also **pale**– a pointed piece of wood used with others in making a fence **2** [U] palings

pal·ings /ˈpeɪlɪŋz/ n [P] a fence made out of palings: *He jumped over the palings.*

pal·i·sade /ˌpælɪˈseɪd/ n **1** a fence made of strong pointed iron or wooden poles, usu. used for defence in past centuries **2** also **palisades** *pl.*– *esp. AmE* a line of high straight cliffs esp. along a river or beside the sea

pal·ish /ˈpeɪlɪʃ/ adj rather pale

pall¹ /pɔːl/ v [I (**on, upon**)] to become uninteresting or unattractive, esp. through being done, used, heard, etc., too often or for too long: *I find his books begin to pall (on me) after a while – they're all very similar.*

pall² n **1** [S (**of**)] something heavy or dark which covers or seems to cover: *a pall of darkness* | *A pall of smoke hung over the burning city.* **2** [C] a large piece of cloth spread over a COFFIN (=a box in which a dead body is carried) **3** [C] *AmE* a COFFIN with a body inside

Pal·la·di·an /pəˈleɪdiən/ adj *tech* **1** of an Italian 16th-century style of building **2** of an English 18th-century CLASSICAL (1) style of building

Pal·la·di·um /pəˈleɪdiəm/ [the] the LONDON PALLADIUM

pall-bear·er /ˈpɔːlˌbeərər/ n a person who walks beside or helps to carry a COFFIN at a funeral

pal·let /ˈpælɪt/ n **1** a large metal plate or flat wooden frame for lifting and storing heavy goods, used with a FORKLIFT TRUCK and having a hole into which the fork can be fixed **2** *AmE, old-fash* a STRAW MATTRESS (=part of a bed that one sleeps on) or temporary bed **3** *AmE* for SKID² (3)

pal·li·asse , **paillasse** /ˈpæliæs‖ˌpæliˈæs/ n *old-fash or lit* a thin cloth case filled with STRAW for sleeping on

pal·li·ate /ˈpælieɪt/ v [T] *fml* **1** to lessen the unpleasant effects of (illness, suffering, etc.) without removing the cause **2** to make (something) seem less wrong by giving excuses —**ation** /ˌpæliˈeɪʃən/ n [U]

pal·li·a·tive /ˈpæliətɪv/ n [(**for**)] *fml* something that palliates: *The government's new economic measures are merely palliatives; they don't get to the root of the trouble.*

pal·lid /ˈpælɪd/ adj (of the face, skin, etc.) unusually or unhealthily pale; WAN: *a pallid complexion* | (fig.) *She gave a pretty pallid* (=dull and lifeless) *performance.* – – ~**ly** adv – – ~**ness** n [U]

Pall Mall /ˌpæl ˈmæl/ a broad road in central London, between Trafalgar Square and St James's Palace, known formerly as a fashionable place

pal·lor /ˈpælər/ n [S] unhealthy paleness of the skin or face

pal·ly /ˈpæli/ also **palsy-walsy**– adj [F (**with**)] *infml* having a friendly relationship (with); FRIENDLY sometimes used in a disapproving way: *They are very pally.* | *I didn't know you were pally with her.*

palm¹ /pɑːm‖pɑːm, puːlm/ n **1** also **palm tree** /ˈ· ·/– any of a large family of mainly tropical trees which are usu. very tall and have branchless stems and a mass of large leaves at the top —see also COCONUT, DATE³ **2 bear/ carry off the palm** *fml* to be judged to be the best of all, esp. in some kind of sport, study, or skill

palm

palm² n **1 a** the surface of the hand between the base of the fingers and the wrist on the side that can be bent inwards —see picture at HAND **b** the part of a GLOVE that covers the inside of the hand **2 hold/have someone in the palm of one's hand** to have complete power over someone —see also ITCHY PALM, **cross someone's palm (with silver)** (CROSS²), **grease someone's palm** (GREASE²)

palm³ v [T] to hide in the palm of one's hand, esp. when performing a trick or stealing something: *The magician palmed the coin and suddenly produced it from a boy's ear.*

palm sthg./sbdy. **off** *phr v* [T] *infml* **1** [(**on, onto, as**)] to get rid of (something bad or unwanted) by persuading someone that it is acceptable: *The fruit seller palmed off some bad oranges onto the old lady.* | *He tried to palm the painting off as a real Renoir.* —compare FOB off/on, PASS off (2) **2** [(**with**)] to persuade (someone) to accept something worthless by lying or some other deception: *They tried to palm me off with an obsolete computer/with some excuse.* —compare FOB off with

Palm Beach /ˌ· ˑ·/ a town in SE Florida, US, which is a tourist centre popular esp. with rich people

Pal·me /ˈpælmə/, **O·lof** /ˈəʊləf/ (1927–86) the Prime Minister of Sweden from 1982 until he was killed by an unknown man who shot him in the street in Stockholm

Palm·er /ˈpɑːmərʳ/, **Arnold** (1929–) American GOLF player, one of the best of modern times

pal·met·to /pælˈmetəʊ/ n -tos or -toes a small palm tree with deeply cut leaves, found esp. in the south-eastern US

palm·ist /ˈpɑːmₘɪst‖ˈpɑːm-, ˈpɑːlm-/ ‖ usu. **palm read·er** /ˈ· ˌˑˑ/ AmE— n a person who claims to be able to tell what someone is like, or what their future is, by examining the lines on the palm of their hand —compare FORTUNE-TELLER

palm·ist·ry /ˈpɑːmₘstri‖ˈpɑːm-, ˈpɑːlm-/ also **palm read·ing** /ˈ· ˌˑˑ/— n [U] the art or practice of a palmist

palm oil /ˈ· ·/ n [U] oil obtained from the nut of an African palm tree

Palm Springs /ˌ· ˑ·/ a city in the US state of California, east of Los Angeles, known esp. for attracting rich and famous people, and for its GOLF COURSES

Palm Sun·day /ˌ· ˑˑ/ n [C;U] (in the Christian church) the Sunday before Easter (from the palm leaves that were spread on the ground in front of Jesus as he entered Jerusalem). In some churches people who attend the service on Palm Sunday are given a piece of palm leaf folded into the shape of a cross.

palm·y /ˈpɑːmi‖ˈpɑːmi, ˈpɑːlmi/ adj (esp. of a period in the past) active and successful; PROSPEROUS

Pal·o·mar /ˈpæləʊmɑːʳ/, **Mount** a mountain near San Diego, CA, where the **Mount Palomar Observatory** is. It has a very large TELESCOPE and other instruments for studying things in space.

pal·o·mi·no /ˌpæləˈmiːnəʊ◂/ n -nos (sometimes cap.) a horse of a golden or cream colour, with a white MANE and tail

pal·pa·ble /ˈpælpəbəl/ adj fml **1** (esp. of something bad) easily and clearly known by the senses or the mind; OBVIOUS: a palpable lie **2** that can be touched or physically felt; TANGIBLE: an almost palpable atmosphere of mistrust. —opposite **impalpable** —**bly** adv : What you say is palpably false.

pal·pate /pælˈpeɪt‖ˈpælpeɪt/ v [T] med to examine by touching: The doctor palpated his abdomen. —**pation** /pælˈpeɪʃən/ n [C;U]

pal·pi·tate /ˈpælpₘteɪt/ v [I] **1** med (of the heart) to beat fast and irregularly **2** [(with)] fml (of a person or the body) to tremble: He was positively palpitating with excitement.

pal·pi·ta·tions /ˌpælpₘˈteɪʃənz/ n [P] med irregular or unusually fast beating of the heart, caused by illness, too much effort, etc.

pal·sied /ˈpɔːlzid/ adj old use weakened by or suffering from palsy: The cup slipped from his palsied grasp.

pal·sy /ˈpɔːlzi/ n [U] **1** old use or med for PARALYSIS **2** a disease causing trembling of limbs —see CEREBRAL PALSY

pal·sy-wal·sy /ˌpælzi ˈwælzi/ adj infml PALLY

pal·try /ˈpɔːltri/ adj **1** worthless or worthlessly small; DERISORY: The management offered us a paltry 3% salary increase. **2** showing a nasty or ungenerous character; PETTY (2): What a paltry trick that was to play.

pam·pas /ˈpæmpəz, -pəs/ n [(the) S] the large wide treeless plains in parts of South America

pampas grass /ˈ·· ·/ n [U] tall grass with sharp-edged blades and feathery silver-white flowers

pam·per /ˈpæmpəʳ/ v [T] to pay too much attention to making (someone) comfortable and happy; treat too kindly: a pampered cat | (fig.) Pamper your skin with this new luxurious soap.

Pam·pers /ˈpæmpəz‖-pərz/ n [P] tdmk a type of DISPOSABLE NAPPY

pam·phlet /ˈpæmflₜt/ n a small thin book with paper covers, often dealing with a matter of public interest: a political pamphlet

pam·phle·teer /ˌpæmflₜˈtɪəʳ/ n a person who writes pamphlets, esp. political pamphlets

pan¹ /pæn/ n **1** (often in comb.) a round metal container usu. with one long handle and sometimes with a lid, used esp. in cooking: Cook the pasta in a large pan of boiling water. | a frying pan —compare POT; see also SAUCEPAN

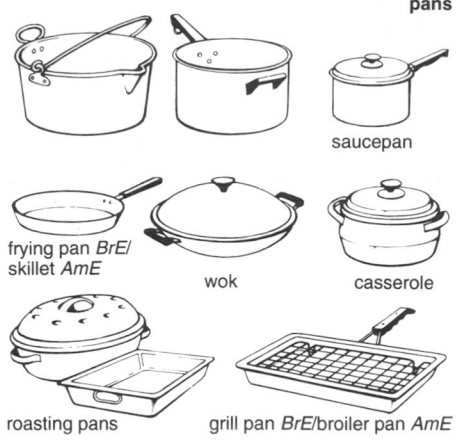
pans

saucepan

frying pan BrE/
skillet AmE

wok

casserole

roasting pans

grill pan BrE/broiler pan AmE

2 either of the two dishes on a small weighing machine **3** esp. BrE the bowl of a LAVATORY **4** a container with holes or a wire net in the bottom used for separating precious metals, such as gold, from other substances by washing them in water **5 (go) down the pan** BrE sl (to become) no longer worth using or keeping —see also BEDPAN, DUSTPAN, SALTPAN, WARMING PAN, **flash in the pan** (FLASH²)

pan² v -nn- **1** [I (for);T (OFF, OUT)] to wash (soil or GRAVEL) in a PAN¹ (4) looking for or trying to separate a precious metal **2** [T (OFF, OUT)] to get or separate (a precious metal) in this way **3** [T] infml to express a very unfavourable judgment of; CRITICIZE very severely: His new play was really panned by the critics.

pan out phr v [I usu. in questions or negatives] to happen in a particular way; develop, esp. successfully: I thought it was a good idea, but now I don't think it will pan out. | I wonder how it will pan out.

pan³ v -nn- **1** [I;T] to move (a film or still camera) from side to side, up and down, etc., following action which is being recorded on film or television **2** [I] (of a camera) to be moved in this way: The camera panned slowly across to the door.

Pan in CLASSICAL MYTHOLOGY, the god of fields, forests, and SHEPHERDS. Pictures of Pan show him as a smiling, ugly man with goat's horns and legs, playing the PANPIPES, and ancient stories often mention his love affairs.

Pan, Peter see PETER PAN

pan- see WORD FORMATION

pan·a·cea /ˌpænəˈsɪə/ n [(for)] often derog **1** something that will put right all troubles: Higher public spending is not a panacea for all our social problems. **2** a medicine or other treatment that is supposed to cure any illness —compare NOSTRUM

pa·nache /pəˈnæʃ, pæ-/ n [U] apprec a stylish manner of doing things that causes admiration and seems to be without any difficulty: With great panache he pulled the tablecloth off the table without disturbing any of the plates and glasses.

pan·a·ma /ˌpænəˈmɑː◂, ˈpænəmɑː/ also **panama hat** /ˌˑˑˑ ˈ·/– n a lightweight hat for men made from the dried undeveloped leaves of a South American PALM tree —see picture at HAT

Panama a country on the **Istmus of Panama**, a narrow piece of land connecting Central and South America; capital Panama City; population 2,370,000 (1989). The official name of the country is the **Republic of Panama** and it is known for the **Panama Canal**, an artificial waterway crossing the country and connecting the Atlantic and Pacific Oceans. —**Panamanian** /ˌpænəˈmeɪniən◂/

Pan A·mer·i·can Games /ˌ· ·ˌˑˑˑ ˈ·/ n [P] a number of sports competitions which take place every four years in which the countries of South, Central, and North America take part —see also OLYMPIC GAMES

Pan·a·son·ic /ˌpænəˈsɒnɪk‖-ˈsɑː-/a Japanese maker of televisions, home electronic equipment etc.

pan·a·tel·a , **-tella** /ˌpænəˈtelə/ n a long thin CIGAR

pan·cake /ˈpæŋkeɪk/ n **1** ‖**crepe** AmE— a thin, soft, flat cake made of BATTER (=a mixture of flour, milk, and eggs), cooked in a flat pan, and usu. eaten hot, often with a sweet or SAVOURY filling **2** ‖ also **flapjack, hotcake** AmE— a similar but thicker cake that is often served in a pile with three or four others, usu. for breakfast. Pancakes are eaten with **maple syrup** (MAPLE), butter, or JAM.

Pancake Day /ˈ·· ·/ also **Pancake Tues·day** /ˌ·· ˈ··/— n [C;U] BrE infml the popular name for SHROVE TUESDAY, on which, according to custom, pancakes are eaten. In some places **pancake races** are held in which each runner has to carry a pancake in a FRYING PAN, throwing it into the air and catching it again as they run along.

pancake land·ing /ˌ·· ˈ··/ n a landing in which an aircraft drops flat to the ground from a low height, made usu. because it is in some trouble

pancake roll /ˌ·· ˈ·/ n BrE for SPRING ROLL

pan·cre·as /ˈpæŋkriəs/ n a part (GLAND) inside the body, near the stomach, which produces INSULIN and a liquid (**pancreatic juice** /ˌpæŋkriætɪk ˈdʒuːs/) that helps in changing food chemically for use by the body

pan·da /ˈpændə/ n **pandas** or **panda 1** a GIANT PANDA **2** a small bearlike animal with red-brown fur and a long tail, found chiefly in the south-eastern Himalayas

Panda car /ˈ·· ·/ n BrE a police car that is driven continuously through the streets of a town so that the police can look out for crimes (so called because it was originally painted black and white like a GIANT PANDA)

pan·dem·ic /pænˈdemɪk/ adj, n med (of) a disease which is widespread over a large area or among a population —compare ENDEMIC, EPIDEMIC

pan·de·mo·ni·um /ˌpændɪˈməʊniəm/ n [U] a state of wild and noisy disorder: *There was sheer pandemonium in the dance hall when someone shouted "Fire!"*

pan·der /ˈpændəʳ/ v
pander to sthg./sbdy. phr v [T] derog to provide something that satisfies (the unpleasant or undesirable wishes) of (a person or group): *The newspapers here pander to people's interest in sex scandals. | Don't pander to such people!*

pan·dit /ˈpʌndɪt, ˈpæn-/ n (often cap.) (used in India as) a title of respect for a wise man: *Pandit Nehru*

P & O /ˌpiː ənd ˈəʊ/ n a British shipping and TRANSPORT company known esp. for its comfortable CRUISE ships, esp. in the 1920s, and now for its ferries (FERRY)

Pan·do·ra's box /pænˈdɔːrəz ˈbɒks‖-ˈbɑːks/ n open **Pandora's box** to unintentionally cause, by taking some action, a large number of problems that did not exist or were not known about before. In CLASSICAL MYTHOLOGY, Pandora opened the box containing all the world's evils.

p & p written abbrev. for: postage and packing (PACKING (2))

pane /peɪn/ n a single sheet of glass for use in a frame, esp. of a window

pan·e·gyr·ic /ˌpænɪˈdʒɪrɪk/ n [(on, upon)] fml a speech or piece of writing praising someone or something highly, perhaps too highly

pan·el¹ /ˈpænl/ n **1** a separate usu. four-sided division of the surface of a door, wall, or other structure, which is different in some way to the surface round it **2** a board on which controls or instruments of various kinds are fixed: *an aircraft's control panel* **3** [+sing./pl. v] **a** a group of people with special skills who are chosen to perform a particular service: *a panel of experts/advisers* **b** a group of usu. well-known speakers or entertainers who answer questions to inform or amuse the public, usu. on a radio or television show: *a panel game | What does/do the panel think?* —see also PANELLIST **4** a piece of cloth of a different colour or material, set in an article of clothing **5** a thin board with a picture painted on it —see also SOLAR PANEL

panel² v **-ll-** BrE ‖ **-l-** AmE [T (**in, with**)] to decorate with PANELS¹ (1): *a panelled room | The walls were panelled in/with oak.*

pan·el·ling BrE ‖ **paneling** AmE /ˈpænəl-ɪŋ/ n [U] PANELS¹ (1): *oak panelling*

pan·el·list BrE ‖ **panelist** AmE /ˈpænəl-ɪst/ n a member of a PANEL¹ (3b)

pan·el pin /ˈ·· ·/ n a short thin type of nail used for fastening thin pieces of wood together

pang /pæŋ/ n [(of)] a sudden sharp feeling of pain: *pangs of hunger | She left her children with a pang of regret.*

Pan·gae·a /pænˈdʒiːə/ the very large mass of land that existed as the only land on earth before it broke apart and started to form the CONTINENTS as they exist today —see also LAURASIA, GONDWANALAND

pan·han·dle¹ /ˈpænˌhændl/ n esp. AmE a thin stretch of land joined to a larger area like the handle of a pan

panhandle² v [I] AmE infml to beg, esp. in the streets —**dler** n

pan·ic¹ /ˈpænɪk/ n **1** [C. usu. sing.;U] (a state of) sudden uncontrollable quickly-spreading terror or anxiety: *The audience were thrown into a panic when the fire started. | She got into a panic when she thought she'd forgotten the tickets. | Panic spread quickly on the Stock Exchange, and millions of pounds were knocked off the value of shares. | panic selling* (=done is a state of panic) **2** [S] AmE old fash, sl a very funny thing; SCREAM² (2) **3 push the 'panic button** infml to take quick, often careless or violent action as the result of a sudden unexpected and possibly dangerous situation

panic² v **-ck-** [I (**at**);T] to (cause to) feel panic: *Don't panic! | The crowd panicked at the sound of the explosion. | The thunder panicked the horses. | a crisis that panicked the government into taking rash measures*

pan·ic·ky /ˈpænɪki/ adj infml (resulting from) feeling sudden great fear

panic sta·tions /ˈ·· ˌ··/ n [U] a state of confused anxiety because something needs to be done in a hurry

panic-strick·en /ˈ·· ˌ··/ adj filled with panic

pan·jan·drum /pænˈdʒændrəm/ n humor a powerful person, esp. one who has a high opinion of his/her own importance

Pank·hurst /ˈpæŋkhɜːst‖-hɜːrst/, **Mrs Em·me·line** /ˈeməliːn/ (1858–1928) a famous member of the British SUFFRAGETTES, who fought for women's rights, esp. the vote. She was put in prison many times for her actions. Her daughters, **Christobel** and **Sylvia**, were also suffragettes and worked for the rights of poor women.

pan·ni·er /ˈpæniəʳ/ n a basket, esp. **a** either of a pair carried by a horse, on a bicycle, etc. **b** one used to carry a load on a person's back

pan·ni·kin /ˈpænɪkɪn/ n BrE & AustrE old-fash (the amount held by) a small metal drinking cup

pan·o·ply /ˈpænəpli/ n [U] splendid ceremonial show or dress: *the whole panoply of a royal funeral* —**plied** adj

pan·o·ra·ma /ˌpænəˈrɑːmə‖-ˈræmə/ n [(of)] **1** a complete view of a wide stretch of land: *a breathtaking panorama from the top of the hill* **2** a general representation in words or pictures: *This book gives a panorama of life in England 400 years ago.* —**mic** /-ˈræmɪk◂/ adj : *From here you get a panoramic view of the whole valley.* —**mically** /kli/ adv

Panorama 1 a British television programme about politics and current affairs, esp. matters which cause disagreement, broadcast weekly on BBC1 **2** an American television programme which includes serious discussions, usu. about current affairs

pan·pipes /ˈpænpaɪps/ n [P] a simple musical instrument made of a number of short pipes and played by blowing across their open ends (from Pan, in CLASSICAL MYTHOLOGY, the Greek god who is supposed to have invented them)

pan·sy /ˈpænzi/ n **1** a small garden plant with wide flat flowers in many different colours **2** infml derog **a** an EFFEMINATE young man **b** old-fash, offensive a male HOMOSEXUAL

pant¹ /pænt/ v **1** [I] to breathe quickly, taking short breaths, esp. after great effort or in great heat: *He stood panting at the top of the stairs.* **2** [T (OUT)] to say while panting: *She panted out her message and then collapsed.* **3** [I (**for**)] esp. lit to have a strong eager desire; YEARN: *She was panting for a chance to speak.*

pant² n a short quick breath —see also PANTS

pan·ta·loons /ˌpæntəˈluːnz/ n [P] men's close-fitting trousers worn in former times —see PAIR (USAGE)

pan·tech·ni·con /pænˈteknɪkən‖-kɑːn/ n BrE old-fash a very large VAN, esp. a REMOVAL VAN

pan·the·is·m /ˈpænθi-ɪzəm/ n [U] 1 the religious idea that God and the universe are the same thing and that God is present in all natural things 2 belief in and worship of all gods known to a society —ist n —istic /ˌpænθiˈɪstɪk◂/ adj : pantheistic religions

pan·the·on /ˈpænθiən‖-θiɑːn/ n 1 all the gods of a society or nation thought of together: Mars, Jupiter, and Vulcan were gods of the Roman pantheon. 2 a temple built in honour of all gods 3 a building in which the famous dead of a nation are buried and/or given honour

pan·ther /ˈpænθər/ n panthers or panther 1 a LEOPARD, esp. a black one 2 AmE for COUGAR or JAGUAR

pan·ties /ˈpæntiz/ also pants BrE‖usu. underpants, underwear AmE— n [P] a short undergarment worn below the waist by women and girls; KNICKERS (BrE) — see PAIR (USAGE); compare UNDERPANTS

pan·tile /ˈpæntaɪl/ n [usu. pl.] a TILE (=a piece of baked clay) shaped as a double curve, used in making roofs

pan·to·graph /ˈpæntəɡrɑːf‖-ɡræf/ n 1 an instrument used to make a smaller or larger exact copy of a drawing, plan, etc. 2 the metal structure on top of an electric railway engine for gathering power from the wires hung above the line

pan·to·mime /ˈpæntəmaɪm/ n 1 [C;U] also pan·to /ˈpæntəʊ‖BrE infml— a kind of British play for children, usu. performed at Christmas, with music, humorous songs, etc.

▶ CULTURAL NOTE Pantomimes are based on TRADITIONAL stories such as Cinderella, Jack and the Beanstalk, Aladdin, and Peter Pan. The chief male character, called the **Principal Boy**, is played by a young woman. There is also usu. an ugly old woman, the **Dame**, played by a man, who is meant to be very funny, and a comic animal such as the pantomime horse. The children are encouraged to join in the songs, to shout out to the actors, and to give warning when the bad characters appear, although the good characters pretend not to believe them: "I haven't seen the villain. Do you know where he is, children?" "Behind you!" "Oh no he isn't!" "O yes he is!" Most towns and cities have a pantomime of some kind at Christmas. In large towns and cities it may be performed for several weeks before and after Christmas, and famous singers, COMEDIANs, and celebrities (CELEBRITY) may take part. —see picture at WIDOW TWANKEY◄

2 [U] MIME¹ (1,2)

pantomime horse /ˈ··· ·/ n BrE an artificial horse which appears esp. in pantomimes and is operated by two people. One person's legs become the front legs, and the other person's legs become the back legs of the horse.

pan·try /ˈpæntri/ n 1 a small room in a house, with shelves and cupboards for keeping food; LARDER 2 a room in a big house, hotel, ship, etc., where glasses, dishes, spoons, etc., are kept

pantomime horse

pants /pænts/ n [P] 1 BrE for PANTIES or UNDERPANTS 2 esp. AmE trousers 3 put one's pants on one leg at a time AmE infml to be an ordinary person: He puts his pants on one leg at a time, just like we do – go ahead, ask him for his autograph! 4 with one's 'pants down humor awkwardly unprepared —see also beat the pants off someone (BEAT¹), by the seat of one's pants (SEAT¹); see PAIR (USAGE)

pant·suit /ˈpæntsuːt, -sjuːt‖-suːt/ n AmE for TROUSER SUIT

panty hose /ˈ·· ·/ n esp. AmE for TIGHTS (1) which are flesh-coloured and SHEER (=can be seen through)

pan·ty·lin·er /ˈpæntilaɪnər/ n a small SANITARY TOWEL which has a band of sticky material on the back, which sticks to the inside of a woman's pants

pan·zer /ˈpænzər/ n (sometimes cap.) a German TANK (2) or

similar armoured vehicle: a Panzer regiment

pap /pæp/ n 1 [S;U] often derog soft almost liquid food, esp. for babies or sick people 2 [U] derog, esp. AmE reading matter or entertainment intended only for amusement, which does not instruct or contain ideas of any value: I don't know how you can watch all that pap on the television.

pap·a¹ /ˈpɑːpə/ also poppa— n AmE infml a father (used esp. in the South)

pa·pa² /pəˈpɑː/ n BrE old use a father: Good morning, Papa.

pa·pa·cy /ˈpeɪpəsi/ n 1 [the+S] the power and office of the POPE 2 [C] the time during which a particular pope holds office

Papa Doc /ˌpɑːpə ˈdɒk‖-ˈdɑːk/ , also Papa Doc Du·val·i·er /ˌ·· · ·ˈ···/— another name for François Duvalier (DUVALIER)

pap·a·dum /ˈpæpədəm‖ˈpɑː-/ n a POPADUM

pa·pal /ˈpeɪpəl/ adj of the POPE or the papacy: papal authority | the papal legate

Pap·an·dre·ou /ˌpæpənˈdreɪ-uː/, An·dre·as /ænˈdreɪəs/ (1919–) a Greek Socialist politician, Prime Minister from 1981 to 1989

pap·a·raz·zo /ˌpæpəˈrætsəʊ/ n -zi /si/ a newspaper writer or photographer who follows famous people about hoping to find out interesting or shocking stories about them

pa·pa·ya /pəˈpaɪə/ also pawpaw esp. BrE & CarE— n the large yellow-green fruit of a tall tropical tree —see picture at FRUIT

pa·per¹ /ˈpeɪpər/ n 1 [U] a material in the form of thin flat sheets used esp. for writing or printing on, and also for covering parcels, decorating walls, etc., and made from very thin threads of wood or cloth: a piece/sheet of paper | You write letters on writing paper. | a paper bag | a paper handkerchief | a brown paper parcel 2 [C] a newspaper: Have you seen today's paper? | It was in all the papers. | She works as a reporter on the local paper. 3 [C] also examination paper fml— a set of printed questions used as an examination in a particular subject: The history paper was really easy. 4 AmE a piece of writing which is part of the work required for school, university, or another course of study: I can't go out this weekend. I have a paper to write on the Civil War. 5 [C (on)] a piece of writing for specialists, often read aloud: At this year's conference, the professor will be giving/reading a paper on her latest research. 6 [C;U] WALLPAPER 7 TOILET PAPER 8 not worth the paper it is printed/written on (of something written, such as a contract) completely worthless 9 on paper as written down or printed, but not yet tested by experience; in THEORY: The plans look good on paper, but there is no guarantee that they will work. —see also DAILY PAPER, PAPERS, GREEN PAPER, WHITE PAPER, put pen to paper (PEN¹)

paper² v [T] 1 (in, with)] to cover (a wall) or the walls of (a room) with WALLPAPER: This room needs papering. | She papered the room green/in green/with green paper. 2 [(OVER, UP)] to hide (disagreements or difficulties) quickly or imperfectly, in order to provide an appearance of agreement, etc. (often in the phrase paper over the cracks)

paper³ adj [A] often derog existing only as an idea; unreal: paper profits | paper promises

pa·per·back /ˈpeɪpəbæk‖-pər-/ n a book with a thin cardboard cover. Paperbacks are usu. cheaper than books with hard covers, and many books are produced with hard covers first and only later in paperback form: This bookshop only sells paperbacks. | a paperback novel | Has this book come out in paperback yet? —compare HARDBACK

pa·per·boy /ˈpeɪpəbɔɪ‖-ər-/ pa·per·girl /-ɡɜːl‖-ɡɜːrl/fem.— n a young person who delivers newspapers to people's houses, usu. before going to school

paper chase /ˈ·· ·/ n a race across open country in which a runner drops pieces of paper which others, running some distance behind, follow

paper clip /ˈ·· ·/ n a small piece of curved wire used for holding sheets of paper together

pa·per·hang·er /ˈpeɪpəˌhæŋər‖-pər-/ n a person whose job is to stick WALLPAPER on the inside walls of a room

paper knife /ˈ·· ·/ BrE ‖ letter opener AmE— n a knife that is only slightly sharp, usu. used for opening envelopes

paper mon·ey /ˈ·· ˌ··/ n [U] money in the form of NOTES (=small sheets of paper), rather than coins

paper round /ˈ·· ·/ n 1 a job, usu. done by children, delivering newspapers to a group of houses 2 the particular group of houses delivered to

pa·pers /ˈpeɪpəz‖-ərz/ n [P] 1 pieces of paper with writing on them: *I think I've left my papers on the table.* 2 official pieces of paper with writing on them, esp. that one carries to show who or what one is; DOCUMENTS: *naturalization papers | "Can I see your papers, please?" said the policeman.*

paper shop /ˈ·· ˌ·/ BrE‖**newsstand** AmE— n a shop selling newspapers and usu. sweets, cigarettes, and other similar things; a NEWSAGENT

paper ti·ger /ˌ·· ˈ··/ n derog an enemy that seems or wishes to seem powerful or threatening, but is really not so

paper tow·el /ˌ·· ˈ··/ n 1 a small square of thick paper used for drying one's hands, usu. in a public toilet 2 KITCHEN ROLL

pa·per·ware /ˈpeɪpweəʳ‖-pər-/ n [U] plates, cups, etc. made of thick paper and intended to be thrown away after use: *a colourful range of picnic paperware*

pa·per·weight /ˈpeɪpəweɪt‖-ər-/ n a heavy object placed on top of loose papers to keep them from being scattered

pa·per·work /ˈpeɪpəwɜːk‖-pərwɜːrk/ n [U] regular work of writing reports, letters, keeping records, lists, etc., esp. as a less important part of a job: *I've finished the job, but I've still got to catch up on the paperwork.*

pa·per·y /ˈpeɪpəri/ adj thin or stiff like paper: *dry papery skin*

pa·pi·er-mâ·ché /ˌpæpieɪ ˈmæʃeɪ, ˌpeɪpə-‖ˌpeɪpər məˈʃeɪ/ n [U] paper boiled into a soft mass, mixed with a stiffening substance, and used for making boxes, models, etc.

pa·pist /ˈpeɪpɪst/ n derog a member of the Roman Catholic Church

pa·poose /pəˈpuːs‖pæ-/ n 1 a young child of Native American parents 2 a sort of bag fixed to a frame, used for carrying a baby on a person's back

pap·py /ˈpæpi/ n AmE infml, esp. dial a father

pap·ri·ka /ˈpæprɪkə‖pəˈpriːkə/ n [U] a red powder made from a type of SWEET PEPPER and used in cooking to give a special hot taste to food

Pap smear /ˈ·· ·/ also **Pap test**— n AmE for SMEAR TEST

Pap·u·a New Guin·ea /ˌpæpuə njuː ˈgɪni‖ˌpæpjuə nuː-/ an independent country in the SW Pacific Ocean, N of Australia, including the eastern half of the island of New Guinea, and various small islands; capital Port Moresby; population 3,593,000 (1989) —**Papuan** /ˈpæpuən‖ˈpæpjuən/

Pap·worth Hos·pi·tal /ˌpæpwəθ ˈhɒspɪtl‖-wərθ ˈhɑː-/ a hospital near Cambridge, E England, which specializes in heart TRANSPLANT[1] (1) operations

pa·py·rus /pəˈpaɪərəs/ n -ruses or -ri /raɪ/ 1 [U] a grass like water plant formerly common in Egypt, used in ancient times esp. for making paper 2 [U] a type of paper made from this plant 3 [C] a piece of ancient writing on this paper

par[1] /pɑːʳ/ n 1 [S] a level which is equal or almost the same; PARITY: *As far as size goes, these two cities are on a par (with each other).* (=are equally big) 2 [U] infml the usual or average standard or condition (of health, activity, etc.): *I'm feeling a bit below/under par* (=slightly unwell) *today. | Your latest piece of work isn't up to par.* (=is not as good as usual) | *(humor) The train was 20 minutes late again today — which I suppose is about par for the course.* (=what can be expected to happen) 3 [U] also **par value**— the original value written on a share of ownership in a business: *He bought the shares at par and sold them above par, making a profit.* 4 [U] (in GOLF) the number of strokes a good player should take to hit the ball into a hole or all of the holes

par[2] also **par·a** /ˈpærə/— abbrev. for: PARAGRAPH

para- see WORD FORMATION

par·a·ble /ˈpærəbəl/ n a short simple story which teaches a moral or religious lesson, esp a story from the Bible

pa·rab·o·la /pəˈræbələ/ n tech a curve like the line made by a ball when it is thrown high in the air to a person some distance away —**lic** /ˌpærəˈbɒlɪk◂‖-ˈbɑː-/ adj —**lically** /kli/ adv

par·a·ce·ta·mol /ˌpærəˈsiːtəmɒl‖-mɑːl/ n [C;U] BrE an important and common drug for killing pain, reducing headaches, etc. which does not contain ASPIRIN

par·a·chute[1] /ˈpærəʃuːt/ n a large usu. circular piece of cloth fastened by thin ropes to people or objects that are dropped from aircraft in order to make them fall slowly: *a parachute jump* —see also PARATROOPER

parachute[2] v [I+adv/prep;T+obj+adv/prep] to (cause to) drop from an aircraft by means of a parachute: *We parachuted to safety. | They parachuted behind enemy lines. | We parachuted the supplies to them.*

par·a·chut·ist /ˈpærəʃuːtɨst/ n a person who drops from an aircraft using a parachute

pa·rade[1] /pəˈreɪd/ n 1 a public procession: *The Olympic Games began with a parade of all the competing nations.*

▶ CULTURAL NOTE Parades are a regular feature of American celebrations from the smallest towns to the biggest cities. They usu. include MARCHING BANDS, MAJORETTES, FLOATS[2] (3), and well-known people who ride in big cars waving and smiling.◀

2 a ceremonial gathering together of soldiers for the purpose of being officially looked at: *The general inspected the parade. | The soldiers are on parade today.* 3 often derog an act of showing one's skill, knowledge, feelings, etc., with the intention of attracting people's attention or gaining admiration: *I hate the way he makes a parade of his knowledge.* 4 esp. BrE (written abbrev. **Pde**) a row of local shops in an area consisting mainly of houses

parade[2] v 1 [I+adv/prep] to walk in a public procession: *The circus paraded through the town to advertise its forthcoming performance.* 2 [I;T] to gather or cause (soldiers) to gather together in a PARADE[1] (2): *Parade the men, sergeant-major!* 3 [I+adv/prep;T] often derog to walk about in (a room or area) with the aim of attracting attention or admiration: *She paraded (through) the corridors in her new dress. | (fig.) old ideas parading as the latest information* 4 [T] often derog to show publicly in order to attract attention or admiration; FLAUNT: *He is always parading his knowledge/his wealth.*

parade ground /·ˈ·· ˌ·/ n a large flat area where soldiers PARADE[2] (2)

par·a·digm /ˈpærədaɪm/ n 1 [(of)] fml a very clear or typical example of something 2 tech an example or pattern of a word, showing all its forms in grammar: *"Child, child's, children, children's" is a paradigm.*

par·a·dig·mat·ic /ˌpærədɪgˈmætɪk◂/ adj tech or fml of, like, or by means of a paradigm — ~**ally** /kli/ adv

par·a·dise /ˈpærədaɪs/ n 1 [U] (usu. cap.) Heaven 2 [U] (usu. cap.) (in the Bible) the Garden of Eden, home of the first humans Adam and Eve 3 [U] a place, state, or condition of perfect happiness: *It's sheer paradise to relax in a hot bath after a hard day's work.* 4 [S] infml a favourite place in which there is everything needed for a particular activity: *These forests are a hunter's paradise.* (—there are lots of animals for them to shoot) —see also BIRD OF PARADISE, FOOL'S PARADISE

Paradise Lost /ˌ··· ˈ·/ a long poem by John Milton telling the story of Adam and Eve. A later poem, which continued the story, was called **Paradise Regained**

par·a·dox /ˈpærədɒks‖-dɑːks/ n 1 a statement which seems impossible, because it says two opposite things, but which has some truth in it: *"More haste, less speed" is a paradox.* 2 an improbable combination of opposing qualities, ideas, etc.: *It is a paradox that in such a rich country there should be so many poor people.* —compare IRONY — ~**ical** /ˌpærəˈdɒksɪkəl◂‖-ˈdɑːk-/ adj

par·a·dox·i·cally /ˌpærəˈdɒksɪkli‖-ˈdɑːk-/ adv 1 in a paradoxical way 2 it is a paradox that: *Paradoxically (enough), the faster he tried to finish, the longer it seemed to take him.* —compare IRONICALLY

par·af·fin /ˈpærəfɨn/ n [U] 1 BrE ‖ **kerosene** AmE— an oil made from PETROLEUM, coal, etc., burnt for heat and in lamps for light 2 also **paraffin wax** /ˌ··· ˈ·/— a soft white substance obtained from PETROLEUM, coal, etc., used esp. in making candles

par·a·gon /ˈpærəgɒn‖-gɑːn/ n [(of)] a person or thing that is or seems to be a perfect model to copy: *He behaves as if he were a **paragon of virtue**, but I could tell you a thing or two about him!*

par·a·graph /ˈpærəgrɑːf‖-græf/ n 1 a division of a piece of writing which is made up of one or more sentences and begins a new line   **2** a short news report in a newspaper

Par·a·guay /ˈpærəgwaɪ/ *a country in S central South America, bordering on Bolivia to the N and W, Brazil to the E, and Argentina to the S and W; capital Asunción; population 4,157,000 (1989)* —**Parguayan** /ˌpærə-ˈgwaɪən◄/

par·a·keet /ˈpærəkiːt/ *n* a kind of small PARROT, usu. with a long tail, found in tropical countries

par·a·le·gal /ˌpærəˈliːgəl◄/ *n AmE* someone who does legal work but who is not a lawyer

par·al·lel¹ /ˈpærəlel/ *adj* **1** (of two or more lines or rows) running side by side but never getting nearer to or further away from each other   **2** [(to, with)] (of one line or row) running side by side with another line but never getting nearer to or further away from it: *Draw a line parallel to|with this one.* | *The railway line runs parallel to|with the road.*   **3** [(to)] of the same type and happening or done at the same time; CORRESPONDING: *As well as the inquiry in London, there is a parallel investigation going on in New York into the cause of the disaster.*

parallel² *n*   **1** [C (to, with)] a parallel line or surface   **2** [C (to, with);U] a person or thing that is closely similar or comparable to another person or thing: *The doctor knew of no parallel to his patient's case, and was unsure what treatment to prescribe.* | *Such disgraceful behaviour is without parallel in my experience.* (=I have never heard of any so bad)   **3** [C (between, with)] (a point of) similarity: *There are some interesting parallels between the educational systems of these two countries.* | *The present famine is almost* **on a parallel** *with the disastrous one of ten years ago.* (=is almost as bad, severe, etc.)   **4** [C (between)] a comparison that shows similarity: *She* **drew a parallel** *between the events leading up to the previous war and the current political situation.*   [C] also **parallel of lat·i·tude** /ˌ··· ˈ···/— any of a number of lines on a map drawn parallel to the EQUATOR: *the 49th parallel*   **6 in parallel** *tech* (of a number of electrical apparatuses) connected between two points in such a way that each may receive electrical power whether or not the others are being used —compare **in series** (SERIES)

parallel³ *v* **-l-** ‖ also **-ll-** *BrE* [T]   **1** to be similar to: *Your experience parallels my own.*   **2** *fml* to equal; match: *a level of economic prosperity that has been paralleled by few other countries* —see also UNPARALLELED

parallel bars /ˌ··· ˈ·/ *n* [(the) P] a pair of parallel bars supported by four upright posts, used for swinging on to exercise the body

par·al·lel·is·m /ˈpærəlelɪzəm/ *n*   **1** [U] the state or quality of being PARALLEL¹ (1,3)   **2** [C] *fml* a point of similarity; PARALLEL² (3)

par·al·lel·o·gram /ˌpærəˈleləgræm/ *n* a flat four-sided shape with opposite sides equal and parallel —see picture at QUADRILATERAL

parallel pro·ces·sing /ˌ··· ˈ···/ *n* [U] a very efficient method of using a computer, which uses a lot of PROCESSORS working together at the same time, instead of one after the other

par·a·lyse *BrE* ‖ **-lyze** *AmE* /ˈpærəlaɪz/ *v* [T]   **1** to cause paralysis to: *After the accident she was paralysed from the waist down.* | (fig.) *He stood paralysed by fear.*   **2** to make ineffective; cause to stop working: *The electricity failure paralysed the train service.*

pa·ral·y·sis /pəˈrælɟsɟs/ *n* **-ses** /siːz/ [C;U]   **1** (a) loss of feeling in, and loss of control of, all or some of the body muscles: *The disease can cause temporary paralysis of the arm.*   **2** (a) loss or lack of ability to move, operate, think, etc.: *The transport strike caused total paralysis in the capital.*

par·a·lyt·ic¹ /ˌpærəˈlɪtɪk◄/ *adj*   **1** suffering from paralysis   **2** *infml, esp. BrE* very drunk — ~**ally** /kli/ *adv*

paralytic² *n* a paralysed person

par·a·med·ic /ˌpærəˈmedɪk/ *n esp. AmE* someone, such as an AMBULANCE driver, who is trained to help in the care of sick people but is not a doctor or nurse

pa·ram·e·ter /pəˈræmɟtər/ *n* [usu. pl.] any of the established limits within which something must operate: *There is plenty of scope for experimentation, provided we remain within the parameters of the budget.*

par·a·mil·i·tary /ˌpærəˈmɪlɟtri◄ ‖ -teri◄/ *adj*   **1** connected

with and helping a regular military force: *In some countries the police have paramilitary duties.*   **2** like a regular military force, or intended for use as an irregular military force, esp. illegally: *the paramilitary organizations of Northern Ireland*

par·a·mount /ˈpærəmaʊnt/ *adj fml* greater than all others in importance or influence; PRIMARY: *This matter is of paramount importance.* | *The interests of the consumer should be paramount.* — ~**cy** *n* [U]

Paramount *a film company* (STUDIO) *in Hollywood, California*

par·a·mour /ˈpærəmʊər/ *n lit or old use* a lover, esp. a MISTRESS (2) —compare INAMORATA

par·a·noi·a /ˌpærəˈnɔɪə/ *n* [U]   **1** a serious disease of the mind in which the sufferer believes that he or she is hated and being purposely mistreated, or is a person of great power or importance   **2** *infml* an unreasonable lack of trust in other people, sometimes amounting to fear

par·a·noi·ac /ˌpærəˈnɔɪæk◄/ also **pa·ra·no·ic** /-ˈnɔɪ-ɪk◄/— *adj, n* (of or being) a person suffering from paranoia — ~**ally** /kli/ *adv*

par·a·noid /ˈpærənɔɪd/ *adj* (as if) suffering from paranoia: *My father locks every door and window in the house — he's paranoid about being robbed.*

par·a·nor·mal /ˌpærəˈnɔːməl◄ ‖ -ˈnɔːr-/ *adj* impossible to explain by science; SUPERNATURAL

par·a·pet /ˈpærəpɟt, -pet/ *n*   **1** a low wall at the edge of a roof, bridge, etc.   **2** a protective wall of earth or stone built in front of the TRENCHes used by soldiers in war

par·a·pher·na·li·a /ˌpærəfəˈneɪliə ‖ -fər-/ *n*   **1** [U] small articles of various kinds, esp. personal belongings or those needed for a particular activity; usu. used of things which are complicated or many in number: *I keep all my photographic paraphernalia in that cupboard.*   **2** [S] *infml, esp. BrE* unwanted, annoying, or difficult activity, esp. that is necessary for doing or getting something; PALAVER: *all the paraphernalia of getting a new passport*   **3** *AmE* the things used in taking illegal drugs, such as pipes, containers, etc.: *In some states it is not illegal to sell (drug) paraphernalia.*

par·a·phrase /ˈpærəfreɪz/ *n* [(of)] a re-statement in different words of (something written or said), esp. in words that are easier to understand —**paraphrase** *v* [T]

par·a·ple·gi·a /ˌpærəˈpliːdʒiə, -dʒə/ *n* [U] PARALYSIS of the lower part of the body, including both legs

par·a·ple·gic /ˌpærəˈpliːdʒɪk◄/ *n, adj* (a person) suffering from paraplegia

par·a·psy·chol·o·gy /ˌpærəsaɪˈkɒlədʒi ‖ -ˈkɑː-/ *n* [U] the scientific study of PSYCHIC powers, such as the ability to see into the future, to see into another person's mind, etc.

par·a·quat /ˈpærəkwɒt ‖ -kwɑːt/ *n* [U] *tdmk* a very powerful liquid poison used to kill unwanted plants. In the US, paraquat is remembered for having been used on CANNABIS plants by the government, which led to cannabis users being poisoned.

par·as /ˈpærəz/ *n* [(the) P] *BrE infml for* PARATROOPS

par·a·site /ˈpærəsaɪt/ *n* [(on, of)]   **1** a plant or animal that lives on or in another and gets food from it: *The mistletoe plant is a parasite on|of trees.*   **2** *derog* a useless person who is supported by the generosity or efforts of others

par·a·sit·ic /ˌpærəˈsɪtɪk◄/ also **par·a·sit·i·cal** /-ɪkəl/— *adj*   **1** [(on)] of, like, or being a parasite: *a parasitic plant*   **2** caused by a parasite: *a parasitic disease* — ~**ally** /kli/ *adv*

par·a·sol /ˈpærəsɒl ‖ -sɔːl, -sɑːl/ *n* a SUNSHADE

par·a·thy·roid /ˌpærəˈθaɪrɔɪd/ also **parathyroid gland** /ˌ··ˈ·· ˌ·ˈ/— *n* any of four small bodily parts (GLANDS) in the throat which control the use of two chemicals, CALCIUM and PHOSPHORUS, by the body

par·a·troop·er /ˈpærəˌtruːpər/ *n* a soldier trained to drop from an aircraft using a PARACHUTE

par·a·troops /ˈpærətruːps/ *n* [P] paratroopers, esp. as formed into a military unit to fight together

par·a·ty·phoid /ˌpærəˈtaɪfɔɪd/ *n* [U] a disease that attacks the bowels, and is very similar to, but less serious than, TYPHOID

par·boil /ˈpɑːbɔɪl ‖ ˈpɑːr-/ *v* [T] to boil until partly cooked

par·cel¹ /ˈpɑːsəl‖ˈpɑːr-/ n [(of)] **1** esp. BrE ‖ also **package** esp. AmE– a thing or collection of things wrapped in paper and tied or fastened in some other way for easy carrying, posting, etc.: *She tied up the parcel with string.* | *He undid/unwrapped the parcel.* | *a parcel of clothes* **2** esp. law or AmE a piece of land, esp. part of a larger piece that has been divided –compare PACKET; see also **part and parcel of** (PART¹)

parcel² v -ll- BrE ‖ -l- AmE
  parcel sthg. ↔ **out** phr v [T] to divide into parts or shares for giving out
  parcel sthg. ↔ **up** phr v [T] to make into a parcel by wrapping and tying: *We parcelled up the clothes for Oxfam.*

Parcel Force /ˈ·· ˌ·/ a branch of the British postal service which deals with parcels: *A Parcel Force van drew up outside the house.*

parcel post /ˈ·· ·/ n [U] BrE the system or method of sending or carrying parcels by post

parch /pɑːtʃ‖pɑːrtʃ/ v [I;T] to (cause to) become completely dry as a result of great heat: *The fierce sun had parched the landscape.* | *The plants will parch if the hot weather continues.* | *I'm parched; I could do with a drink!*

par·chee·si /pɑːˈtʃiːzi‖pɑːr-/ n tdmk AmE for LUDO

parch·ment /ˈpɑːtʃmənt‖ˈpɑːr-/ n **1** [U] a writing material used esp. in ancient times, made from the skin of a sheep or goat: *The old man's skin was like parchment.* **2** [C] an ancient piece of writing on this material **3** [C;U] (an official piece of writing on) any of various types of paper of good quality

pard·ner /ˈpɑːdnəʳ‖ˈpɑːr-/ n AmE infml partner, used as a greeting, often to someone you do not know: *Howdy, pardner!*

par·don¹ /ˈpɑːdn‖ˈpɑːrdn/ n **1** [C] an action of a court or ruler forgiving a person for an illegal act and giving freedom from punishment: *His pardon came through only three hours before he was due to be executed.* –see also FREE PARDON **2** [C;U (for)] fml (an act or example of) forgiving: *If I have offended you, I ask your pardon.* **3** **Pardon my French** infml, humor (said before or after using bad or impolite language (SWEARING)): *The bloody car's broken down–pardon my French.* **4** **I beg your pardon** also **Pardon** ˈme– a polite Please excuse me (said when you accidentally touch or push someone) **b** also **Pardon** infml– (said with the voice rising at the end) I did not hear/understand what you said and would like you to repeat it **c** polite Please excuse me (said when one accidentally does something (e.g. BELCH noisily) that could be offensive to another person) **d** (said in a firm unfriendly voice) I'm afraid I think that what you have just said is not true or not acceptable –see EXCUSE (USAGE); see also **excuse me** (EXCUSE¹);

pardon² v [T] **1** [(for)] to forgive or excuse: *Pardon my strong language.* [+obj(i)+obj(d)] *We must pardon him (for) his little outbursts of temper.* [+obj+v-ing] *Pardon me interrupting, but …* | *It seems to me like a bit of a cock-up, if you'll pardon the expression.* (=excuse my use of this phrase) **2** to give an official pardon to or for **3** **Pardon** ˈme –see PARDON¹ (4)

par·don·a·ble /ˈpɑːdənəbəl‖ˈpɑːr-/ adj that can be forgiven: *a pardonable mistake/weakness* –opposite **unpardonable** —**bly** adv

par·don·er /ˈpɑːdənəʳ‖ˈpɑːr-/ n (in former times) a person who went about the country selling official religious INDULGENCES (4)

pare /peəʳ/ v [T] **1** [(DOWN)] to cut away the thin outer covering, edge, or skin of (something), usu. with a sharp knife; PEEL: *to pare one's fingernails* | (fig.) *We must pare down* (=reduce) *costs to improve our profitability.* | *Spending on education has been pared to the bone.* (=reduced to the lowest possible level) **2** [(AWAY, OFF)] to cut away (the thin outer covering, edge, or skin of something), usu. with a sharp knife: *She pared off the apple peel.* –see also CHEESEPARING, PARING

par·ent /ˈpeərənt/ n **1** the father or mother of a person or animal: *my parents* | *Being a parent* (=having children) *can be hard work.* | *a single-parent family* | (fig.) *Our club is the parent organization, and there are now four others like it.* **2** **to lose one parent may be regarded as a misfortune; to lose both looks like carelessness** quote a slightly changed phrase from the play *The Importance*

of Being Earnest by Oscar Wilde – – **al** /pəˈrentl/ adj : *parental responsibilities* | *to get married without parental consent*

par·ent·age /ˈpeərəntɪdʒ/ n [U] the fact of being descended from particular parents: *a child of unknown parentage* (=we do not know who its parents are)

parent com·pa·ny /ˌ··· ˈ···/ n a business company that controls one or more others

parent governor /ˌ·· ˈ···/ n a person whose child attends a particular school, and who, with other people, has the power to make certain decisions about how the school is run

pa·ren·the·sis /pəˈrenθəsɪs/ n -theses /θɪsiːz/ **1** [usu. pl.] BrE fml or AmE for BRACKET⁴ (2) **2** one or more words introduced as an added explanation or thought, and in writing usu. enclosed at both ends by a parenthesis, as in the following sentence: *This class (and I speak from long experience) is the worst I have ever known.*

par·en·thet·ic /ˌpærənˈθetɪk◀/ also **par·en·thet·i·cal** /-ɪkəl/– adj introduced as an added explanation or thought: *If I may add a few parenthetic remarks of a personal nature here …* – ~**ally** /kli/ adv

par·ent·hood /ˈpeərənthʊd/ n [U] the state or condition of being a parent

par·ent·ing /ˈpeərəntɪŋ/ n [U] parental care of children: *the problems of parenting*

parent-teach·er as·so·ci·a·tion /ˌ·· ˈ·· ···ˌ·ˌ·/ n see PTA

par ex·cel·lence /ˌpɑːr ˈeksəlɑːns‖-eksəˈlɑːns/ adj [after n] Fr, apprec without equal, as the best and/or most typical of its kind: *"Wuthering Heights" is surely the romantic novel par excellence.*

par·he·li·on /pɑːˈhiːliən‖pɑːr-/ n -lia /liə/ tech an image of the sun sometimes seen at the side of the sun at sunset

pa·ri·ah /pəˈraɪə, ˈpæriə‖pəˈraɪə/ n fml derog a person who is not accepted by society; social OUTCAST

par·i·mu·tu·el /ˌpæri ˈmjuːtjuəl‖-tʃuəl/ n Fr a system of risking money, esp. on a horse race, in which the money risked by the losers is taken and divided up among the winners

parimutuel ma·chine /···ˈ··· ·ˌ·/ n AmE TOTE² (1)

par·ing /ˈpeərɪŋ/ n [usu. pl.] something thin that has been pared off (PARE (2)): *vegetable parings*

Par·is¹ /ˈpærɪs/ the capital city of France, in the N central part of the country on the River Seine, often thought of as a city for lovers and honeymooners (HONEYMOON²) –see also EIFFEL TOWER, LEFT BANK, MONTMARTRE

Paris² in CLASSICAL MYTHOLOGY, a prince of Troy who took Helen away from Greece, causing the Trojan War, and who killed Achilles in this war

Paris-Dak·ar Ral·ly /ˌpærɪs ˈdækɑː ˌræli‖-dəˈkɑːr-/ [the] a motor race over public roads from Paris, France to Dakar, Senegal, including the crossing of the Sahara Desert. The Paris-Dakar Rally is open to all kinds of motor vehicles.

par·ish /ˈpærɪʃ/ n **1** (esp. in the Anglican and Roman Catholic Churches) an area in the care of a single priest and served by one main church: *a parish priest* –see also PAROCHIAL **2 a** also **civil parish**– (in England) a small area, esp. a village, having its own local government; the smallest unit of local government **b** (in the American state of Louisiana) COUNTY¹: *Vermilion Parish* **3** infml, esp. BrE an area of knowledge or work that is the special responsibility of a particular person

Parish, Max·field /ˈmæksfiːld/ (1870–1966) an American artist famous for his ILLUSTRATIONS (=pictures in book), which are ROMANTIC and colourful and show light in a slightly SURREAL way

parish church /ˌ·· ˈ·/ n the main church in a PARISH (1)

parish clerk /ˌ·· ˈ·/ n a church official in a PARISH (1) who performs various duties in or for the church

parish coun·cil /ˌ·· ˈ··/ n in Britain, a group of elected people which manages the affairs of a PARISH (2a), but has not as much power as a DISTRICT COUNCIL

pa·rish·io·ner /pəˈrɪʃənəʳ/ n a person living in a particular PARISH (1), esp. one who regularly attends the parish church

parish-pump /ˌ·· ˈ·◀/ adj [A] BrE, often derog of local interest only: *parish-pump politics*

parish re·gis·ter /ˌ·· ˈ···/ n a large book, or a number of books, in which are written details of all the births, deaths, and marriages in a parish

Pa·ris·i·an /pəˈrɪziən‖pəˈrɪʒən, -ˈriː-/ *n, adj* (a person) of or from Paris

par·i·ty /ˈpærⱸti/ *n* **1** [U (**with**)] the state or quality of being equal, e.g. in level, position, amount, etc.: *We have worked hard to achieve parity with our commercial competitors.* **2** *tech* a system by which computer DATA (=stored information) sent from one place to another can be tested for mistakes

park¹ /pɑːk‖pɑːrk/ *n* **1** [C] a large usu. grassy enclosed piece of land in a town, used by the public for pleasure and rest: *children playing in the park* | *a park bench* **2** [C] *BrE* a large enclosed stretch of land with grass, trees, etc., round a large country house —compare PARKLAND **3** [*the+*S] *BrE sl* a field on which esp. professional SOC-CER is played: *the best player on the park* —see also AMUSE-MENT PARK, BALL PARK, CAR PARK, LORRY PARK, NATIONAL PARK, SCIENCE PARK, THEME PARK

park² *v* **1** [I;T] to put or place (a car or other vehicle) in a particular place for a time: *You're not allowed to park (the car) in this street.* | *I'm parked over there.* (=My car is parked over there.) —see PARKING (USAGE) **2** [T+*obj*+*adv/prep*] *infml* to leave or place (something or someone) in a particular position for a certain time, often in a way that causes annoyance: *Don't park your books on top of my papers!* | *They parked their children on us while they went shopping.*

par·ka /ˈpɑːkə‖ˈpɑːrkə/ *n* **1** a coat down to the knees with a HOOD (=a protective cover) for the head, usu. with fur inside —compare ANORAK **2** *esp. AmE for* ANORAK

Par·ker¹ /ˈpɑːkəʳ‖ˈpɑːrr-/, **Charlie "Bird"** (1920–55) a black American JAZZ musician and writer of music who played the SAXOPHONE and invented BEBOP with Dizzy Gillespie

Parker², **Dor·o·thy** /ˈdɒrəθi‖ˈdɔː-/ (1893–1967) an American writer of criticism, poetry, and short stories, best remembered for her clever sayings and her association with the Algonquin Round Table

Park·hurst pris·on /ˌpɑːkhɜːst ˈprɪzən‖ˌpɑːrkhɜːrst-/ also **Parkhurst** a British prison on the Isle of Wight for men who have received long prison sentences for serious crimes

park·ing /ˈpɑːkɪŋ‖ˈpɑːr-/ *n* [U] **1** the leaving of a car or other vehicle in a particular place for a time **2** space in which vehicles may be left like this: *There is plenty of parking behind the cinema.*

▷ USAGE You **park** (your car) in a **car park** *BrE*‖**parking lot** *AmE or* **parking place**. When it is standing there it is **parked.** The signs *Parking/No Parking* mean "**Parking** is permitted/not permitted here".◁

parking ga·rage /ˈ·· ˌ··‖ˈ·· ˌ·/ *n AmE for* CAR PARK (2)

parking light /ˈ·· ˌ·/ *n AmE for* SIDELIGHT (1) —see picture at CAR

parking lot /ˈ·· ·/ *n AmE for* CAR PARK (1)

parking me·ter /ˈ·· ˌ··/ *n* an apparatus at the side of a street, into which one puts a coin to pay for parking a car beside it for a certain time —see picture at METER

parking tick·et /ˈ·· ˌ··/ *n* an official notice fixed to a vehicle by a TRAFFIC WARDEN or a policeman, stating that the vehicle has been parked in a way which is against the law, and that a FINE⁴ will be made: *He's had ten parking tickets this month, and hasn't paid any of the fines yet.*

Par·kin·son¹ /ˈpɑːkɪnsən‖ˈpɑːr-/, **Lord Ce·cil** /ˈsesⱸl/ (1931–) an English Conservative politician. In 1983 he left the Cabinet because it was made public that he had a MISTRESS (2) who was going to have a child by him. In 1987 he was brought back into the Cabinet.

Parkinson², **Mi·chael** /ˈmaɪkəl/ (1935–) an English television PRESENTER and INTERVIEWER (=a person who asks others questions in a television programme)

Parkinson's dis·ease /ˈ··· ·ˌ·/ —also **Par·kin·son·is·m** /ˈpɑːkɪnsənɪzəm‖ˈpɑːr-/ *n* [U] a kind of PARALYSIS, esp. of old people, in which the muscles become stiff and the limbs continually shake

Parkinson's law /ˈ··· ˌ·/ *n* [S] *esp. humor* the idea that work increases to fill the time allowed for it (from the name of its inventor, British writer Cyril Northcote Parkinson

park keep·er /ˈ· ˌ··/ *BrE* ‖ **park ranger** *AmE*— *n* a person

who is in charge of a park or whose job it is to help look after a park

park·land /ˈpɑːk-lænd‖ˈpɑːrk-/ *n* [U] **1** *BrE* grassy land, esp. that surrounding a large country house, covering a large area and having trees growing in it —compare PARK¹ (2) **2** land used as or fit for use as a park

Park Lane /ˌ· ˈ·/ a wide street in central London between Marble Arch and Hyde Park Corner. It is famous for its hotels and houses for the rich.

Parks /pɑːks‖pɑːrks/, **Ro·sa** /ˈrəʊzə/ (1913–) a black American woman who in 1955 refused to give up her seat at the front of a bus to a white man. This was against the law and she was arrested (ARREST) by the police. This is seen as one of the most important events at the beginning of the CIVIL RIGHTS MOVEMENT. In 1956, the US Supreme Court said that SEGREGATION (keeping black people separate from white people) on buses was not legal under the American Constitution.

park·way /ˈpɑːkweɪ‖ˈpɑːrk-/ *n esp. AmE* a wide road divided by or bordered with an area of grass and trees

par·ky /ˈpɑːki‖ˈpɑːrki/ *adj BrE infml* (of the air, weather, etc.) rather cold

par·lance /ˈpɑːləns‖ˈpɑːr-/ *n* [U] *fml* a particular manner of speech or use of words: *In naval parlance, a kitchen is a "galley".* | *in legal/common parlance*

par·ley /ˈpɑːli‖ˈpɑːrli/ *n* a talk, esp. with an enemy or other opponent, in order to make peace —**parley** *v* [I (**with**)]

par·lia·ment /ˈpɑːləmənt‖ˈpɑːr-/ *n* (*often cap.*) **1** [C] (in some countries) the main law-making body, made up of members wholly or partly elected by the people of the country **2** (in Britain) the main law-making body, consisting of both the elected representatives of the people (the House of Commons) and the House of Lords. When people talk about Parliament, they often mean only the House of Commons. **3** [C] a parliament as it exists for the time between its ceremonial opening and its official closing: *Several new laws have been passed in/during the present parliament.* —see also HOUSES OF PARLIAMENT, ACT OF PARLIAMENT and see extra information on page 566

par·lia·men·tar·i·an /ˌpɑːləmənˈteəriən‖ˌpɑːr-/ *n* **1** a person who is a skilled and experienced member of a parliament **2** [*often pl.*] (*usu. cap.*) a ROUNDHEAD

par·lia·men·ta·ry /ˌpɑːləˈmentəri◂‖ˌpɑːr-/ *adj* of or suitable for a parliament: *parliamentary procedure* —see also UN-PARLIAMENTARY

Parliamentary Com·mit·tee /ˌ······ ·ˈ··/ *n* any of several groups of British MPs who have particular Parliament business to do. Parliamentary Committees are divided into **Standing Committees**, which mainly examine suggestions for new laws, and **Select Committees**, which check on how well government departments are working and on how much money they are spending.

parliamentary ma·jor·i·ty /ˌ····· ·ˈ··/ *n* (in Britain) the amount by which the number of MPs belonging to the ruling party is greater than the number of MPs belonging to all other parties: *For some time Wilson's government had a parliamentary majority of only three.*

parliamentary priv·i·lege /ˌ····· ˈ···/ *n* (in Britain) any of several special rights which are given to MPs e.g. freedom of speech, and not having to serve as a member of a JURY (1)

parliamentary sec·re·ta·ry /ˌ····· ˈ·····/ *n* a British MP who usu. has the title Junior Minister and who helps a minister of high rank with the work of his/her department

parlor car /ˈ·· ·/ *n AmE for* PULLMAN

par·lour *BrE* ‖ **parlor** *AmE* /ˈpɑːləʳ‖ˈpɑːr-/ *n* **1** *esp. AmE* (*in comb.*) a shop for some kind of personal service or for selling a particular type of article: *an ice-cream parlour* | *a massage parlour* **2** *old-fash* a room in a private house used by the family for meeting guests, reading, and other amusements **3** *old-fash* a room in certain public buildings where guests are received: *the mayor's parlour* **4** "**Will you walk into my parlour?**" said a spider to a fly *quote* the first line of a poem by Mary Howitt, often mentioned when saying that a person will pretend to be friendly in order to get something that they want —see also BEAUTY PARLOUR, MILKING PARLOUR

parlour game /ˈ·· ·/ *n old-fash* a game which can be played indoors, usu. sitting down, such as a guessing game or a word game

par·lour·maid *BrE* ‖ **parlormaid** *AmE*– /ˈpɑːləmeɪd‖ ˈpɑːlər-/ *n old-fash* a female servant employed in a large house to serve guests in the parlour

par·lous /ˈpɑːləs‖ ˈpɑːr-/ *adj fml or humor* in danger of failing; uncertain and dangerous: *My finances are in a pretty parlous condition.* (=I haven't much money.) | *the parlous state of international relations*

Par·me·san /ˌpɑːmᵻˈzæn◂‖ˈpɑːrmᵻzɑːn, -zæn/ also **Parmesan cheese** /ˌ···ˈ·/– *n* [U] a hard strong-tasting Italian cheese. It is usu. grated (GRATE) finely and put on top of PASTA dishes

Par·nas·sus /pɑːˈnæsəs‖pɑːr-/ a high mountain in central Greece, the modern name of which is **Parnassós**. In ancient times it was thought to be a holy place of the gods Apollo and Dionysus, and of the Muses (=goddesses of the arts).

Par·nell /pɑːˈnel‖pɑːr-/, **Charles Stewart** (1846–91) Irish politician who wanted HOME RULE (=self-government) in Ireland, and became leader of the Home Rule party in the House of Commons. He lost political power when it became known that he was the lover of a married woman.

pa·ro·chi·al /pəˈrəʊkiəl/ *adj* **1** *derog* limited or narrow in range; interested in or dealing only with things close to oneself: *Local newspapers tend to be very parochial.* —compare INSULAR **2** of a PARISH (1) – ~**ly** *adv* – ~**ism** *n* [U]

parochial school /·ˈ··· ˌ·/ *n* a private school which is run by, or connected with, a church

par·o·dy¹ /ˈpærədi/ *n* **1** [C;U (**of**, **on**)] (a piece of) writing or music intended to amuse, which recognizably copies the style of a known writer or musician –compare SATIRE **2** [C (**of**)] *derog* a weak and unsuccessful copy; TRAVESTY: *The trial was a parody of justice.* —**dist** *n*

parody² *v* [T] to make a parody of

pa·role¹ /pəˈrəʊl/ *n* [U] **1** the letting out of a prisoner for a limited time, on condition that they return: *He was released* **on parole** *to go to his daughter's wedding.* **2** the letting out of a prisoner before the official period of their imprisonment has ended, on condition that they behave well: *The sentence was for fifteen years but he was released on parole after ten years.*

parole² *v* [T] to set free on parole

par·ox·ysm /ˈpærəksɪzəm/ *n* 1(**of**) **1** a sudden uncontrollable expression of strong feeling: *a paroxysm of rage/laughter* **2** a sudden but passing attack (of a sharp pain or a disease that comes regularly): *paroxysms of pain/of coughing*

par·quet /ˈpɑːkeɪ, ˈpɑːki‖pɑːrˈkeɪ/ *n* [U] small flat blocks of wood fitted together in a pattern and stuck onto the floor of a room: *a parquet floor*

par·ri·cide /ˈpærᵻsaɪd/ *n* **1** *fml* the crime of killing one's father, mother, or a close relative **2** [C] *tech* a person guilty of this crime —compare MATRICIDE, PATRICIDE

par·rot¹ /ˈpærət/ *n* **1** any of a large group of usu. tropical birds that have a curved beak and usu. brightly coloured feathers. Some of these birds can be taught to copy human speech. They are sometimes taken to other countries and kept as pets. Polly is a TRADITIONAL name for a parrot, and parrots are often taught to say "pretty Polly". In stories, PIRATES often have a parrot which sits on their shoulder and says "pieces of eight" (=old, valuable coins). —see also LONG JOHN SILVER, PIRATE **2** *usu. derog* a person who copies, often without understanding, the words or actions of another **3** ¹**parrot fashion** *usu. derog* by means of continuous repeating, but usu. without real understanding: *The children learnt the poem parrot fashion.* —see also DEAD PARROT SKETCH, **sick as a parrot** (SICK)

parrot

parrot² *v* [T] *usu. derog* to repeat (the words or actions of someone else) without thinking or understanding

par·ry¹ /ˈpæri/ *v* [T] to turn aside or keep away (an attacking blow or a weapon); DEFLECT: (fig.) *He parried the unwelcome question very skilfully.*

parry² *n* an act of parrying; movement of defence in some sports, esp. FENCING

parse /pɑːz‖pɑːrs/ *v* [T] *tech* (in grammar) **1** to state the PART OF SPEECH, the form in grammar, and the use in a particular sentence of (a word) **2** to give this information about all the words in (a sentence) –**parser** *n* : *an automatic parser that uses a computer program*

Par·see , Parsi /pɑːˈsiː‖ˈpɑːrsiː/ *n, adj* (a member) of an ancient Persian religious group in India

par·si·mo·ni·ous /ˌpɑːsᵻˈməʊniəs◂‖ˌpɑːr-/ *adj fml, usu. derog* extremely careful with money; unwilling to spend; STINGY: *a parsimonious person/gift* – ~**ly** *adv* – ~**ness** *n* [U]

par·si·mo·ny /ˈpɑːsᵻməni‖ˈpɑːrsᵻməʊni/ *n* [U] *fml, usu. derog* the quality of being parsimonious; failure to be generous

pars·ley /ˈpɑːsli‖ˈpɑːr-/ *n* [U] a small plant (HERB) with curly strong-tasting leaves, grown in gardens and used in cooking or as a decoration on food

parsley sauce /ˌ··ˈ·/ *n* [U] a WHITE SAUCE (=a thick white liquid cooked with flour) with finely cut up parsley in it, eaten in Britain esp. with fish

pars·nip /ˈpɑːsnɪp‖ˈpɑːr-/ *n* [C;U] (a plant with) a thick white or yellowish root that is used as a vegetable

par·son /ˈpɑːsən‖ˈpɑːr-/ *n* **1** a priest of the Church of England who is in charge of a PARISH (1) **2** *AmE* a Protestant priest who is in charge of a local church or PARISH **3** *infml* any Christian priest

par·son·age /ˈpɑːsənɪdʒ‖ˈpɑːr-/ *n* the house where a parson lives

Par·sons /ˈpɑːsənz‖ˈpɑːr-/, **Nich·o·las** /ˈnɪkələs/ (1928–) an English actor now known esp. as a QUIZMASTER

parson's nose /ˌ··ˈ·/ *BrE* ‖ **pope's nose** *AmE*– *n infml humor* the piece of flesh at the tail end of a cooked bird, such as a chicken

part¹ /pɑːt‖pɑːrt/ *n* **1** [C;U (**of**)] any of the pieces into which something is divided or may be considered as being divided, whether separated from a whole or connected with it, and which is therefore less than the whole: *This is only (a) part of it; where's the rest?* | *I didn't like the first part of the book.* | *Which part of the town do you live in?* | *Divide the mixture into two equal parts.* | *A large part of the house was/Large parts of the house were destroyed by the fire.* | *The best part of my job is all the travel it involves.* | *She lived there for the greater part* (=most) *of her life.* | *We waited for* **the best part/the better part of** *an hour.* (=almost an hour) **2** [C] a division of a story or other work which appears regularly on radio or television, in a newspaper, as a PART WORK, etc.: *You can see part two of the serial at the same time next week.* | *a book by Charles Dickens, adapted for radio in 14 parts* **3** [C] **a** a necessary or important piece of a machine or other apparatus: *This machine has over a hundred moving parts.* **b** a SPARE PART **4** [C] any of several equal divisions which make up a whole: *This mixture is one part wine and two parts water.* | (*infml*) *The work's three parts* (=three quarters; nearly) *finished.* **5** [S;U (**in**)] a share or responsibility in some activity: *to* **take part** *in a race/a debate* | *Luck* **played a part** *in* (=helped to cause) *his success.* | *The question of cost will play an important part in our decision.* | *He was the host, so it wasn't my part to tell him who should be invited.* | *This is a dishonest plan, and I want no part in it.* **6** [U] a side or position **a** in an argument: *Tom* **took my part** *in the disagreement.* (=supported my side) **b** *law* in an agreement or contract **7** [C] (the words and actions of) a character acted by an actor in a play, film, etc.: *Have you learnt your part yet?* | *She's been offered a marvellous part in the new film.* | *In the play, I take/play the part of a policeman.* | (fig.) *He's a very successful businessman, but he doesn't really* **look/dress the part.** (=look/dress like someone in that position) —see also BIT PART **8** [C] *AmE for* PARTING¹ (2) **9 for** ¹**my part** as far as I am concerned; speaking for myself: *For my part, I don't care who wins.* **10 for the** ¹**most part: a** mostly: *This orange drink is for the most part water.* **b** most of the time; in most cases: *For the most part the children are very healthy.* **11** *BrE* **in good part** without being offended: *I hope you will take my advice* **in good part. 12 in part** in some degree; partly: *The accident was due in part to carelessness, but mainly to bad luck.* **13 on the part of someone** of or by someone: *It was a* *mistake on the part of Jones|on Jones's part* (=Jones was mistaken) *to sign the contract without reading it.* **14 part and parcel of** a necessary or important part that cannot be separated from the whole of: *Working irregular hours is part and parcel of being a journalist.* —see also PARTS, PRIVATE PARTS

part² v 1 [I (**from, as**); T (**from**)] *esp. fml or lit* to (cause to) separate or no longer be together: *I hope we can part (as) friends.* (=remain friends even though we part) | *The war parted many men from their families.* | *We tried to part the two angry dogs.* (=stop them fighting) | *She refused to be parted from her beloved cat.* **2** [I;T] to (cause to) separate into parts or spread apart: *The clouds parted and the sun shone.* | *She parted the curtains and looked out.* **3** [T] to separate (hair on the head) along a line with a comb **4 part company (with): a** to end a relationship (with): *I hear he and his wife have parted company.* **b** to no longer be together (with): *I'm getting off the train here, so we must part company.* **c** to disagree (with): *I'll have to part company with you on that point.* **5 parting is such sweet sorrow** *quote* a phrase from Shakespeare's play *Romeo and Juliet*, often used humorously
 part with sthg. *phr v* [T] to give away; stop having: *It's not easy to part with one's favourite possessions.*

part³ *adv* partly: *The medical exams are part written, part practical.*

part⁴ *adj* [A] not complete; PARTIAL: *I gave them a pound in part payment.* | *They are part owners of the house.* (=they share ownership of it)

par·take /pɑːˈteɪk‖pɑːr-/ *v* partook /pɑːˈtʊk‖pɑːr-/, par·taken /pɑːˈteɪkən‖pɑːr-/ [I] *old use or fml* **1** [(**in**)] to take part (in an activity); PARTICIPATE **2** [(**of**)] *often humor* to eat or drink esp. something offered: *"Will you partake of a little wine?" "No, thank you; I don't partake."* (=don't drink alcohol)
 partake of sthg. *phr v* [T] *fml* to have the qualities, to some degree, of: *a self-confident manner that partakes of arrogance*

par·terre /pɑːˈteəʳ‖pɑːr-/ *n* a level space in a garden, with an area of grass and decorative areas of flowers in a formal pattern

part ex·change /ˌ· ·ˈ·/ *BrE* ‖ **trade-in** *AmE*— *n* [C;U] (an example of) the system of paying for something partly in money and partly in goods, esp. with a used object of the same kind as the thing one is buying: *When you buy a new car you can often give your old one in part exchange.*

par·the·no·gen·e·sis /ˌpɑːθɪnəʊˈdʒenɪsɪs‖ˌpɑːr-/ *n* [U] *tech* the production of a new plant or animal from a female without sexual union with a male

Par·the·non /ˈpɑːθɪnən‖ˈpɑːrθənɑːn/ [*the*] a temple to the goddess Athena on the ACROPOLIS in Athens; the most famous example of a Greek temple, and visited by many people

par·tial /ˈpɑːʃəl‖ˈpɑːr-/ *adj* **1** not complete: *a partial success|recovery* **2** *derog* showing special favour to one person, side, etc., esp. in a way that is unfair —opposite **im·partial** **3** [F+**to**] *infml* having a strong liking or taste for: *I'm very partial to cream cakes.* —see also PARTIALLY

par·ti·al·i·ty /ˌpɑːʃiˈælɪti‖ˌpɑːr-/ *n* **1** [U] *derog* being PARTIAL (2); BIAS —opposite **impartiality** **2** [S (**for**)] a special liking or fondness: *a partiality for cream cakes*

par·tial·ly /ˈpɑːʃəli‖ˈpɑːr-/ *adv* **1** not completely; partly: *He was (only) partially to blame for the accident.* **2** *derog* in a PARTIAL (2) way

par·tic·i·pant /pɑːˈtɪsɪpənt‖pɑːr-/ *n* [(**in**)] a person who takes part or has a share in an activity or event: *All participants in the race should give their names to the starter.*

par·tic·i·pate /pɑːˈtɪsɪpeɪt‖pɑːr-/ *v* [I (**in**)] *rather fml* to take part or have a share in an activity or event: *Everyone in the class is expected to participate in these discussions.* —**pation** /pɑːˌtɪsɪˈpeɪʃən‖pɑːr-/ *n* [U (**in**)] : *They want greater participation in the decision-making process.*

par·ti·cip·i·al /ˌpɑːtɪˈsɪpiəl◂‖ˌpɑːr-/ *adj tech* (in grammar) being or using a participle: *"Singing" in "a singing bird" is a participial adjective.* —**ly** *adv*

par·ti·ci·ple /ˈpɑːtɪsɪpəl‖ˈpɑːr-/ *n tech* (in grammar) a NON-FINITE verb form that can be used in compound forms of the verb or as an adjective. English has two participles, the PAST PARTICIPLE and the PRESENT PARTICIPLE.

par·ti·cle /ˈpɑːtɪkəl‖ˈpɑːr-/ *n* **1** [(**of**)] a very small piece:

dust particles floating in the sunlight | (fig.) *There wasn't a particle of truth in what he said.* —see also ELEMENTARY PARTICLE **2** (in grammar) any of a number of usu. short words that are not as important in a sentence as the subject, verb, etc.: *Prepositions and conjunctions are particles.*

particle ac·cel·e·ra·tor /ˈ··· ·ˌ·····/ *n* ACCELERATOR (2)

particle phys·ics /ˈ··· ˌ··/ *n* [U] the study of the formation and behaviour of ELEMENTARY PARTICLES (=very small bits of matter inside atoms)

par·ti·col·oured /ˌpɑːti ˈkʌləd◂‖ˌpɑːrti ˈkʌlərd◂/ *adj* having different colours in different parts

par·tic·u·lar¹ /pəˈtɪkjʊləʳ‖pər-/ *adj* **1** [A *no comp.*] deserving special notice or attention; unusual: *There was nothing in the letter of particular importance.* | *There's no particular reason why you shouldn't go.* **2** [A *no comp.*] single and different from others; considered separately: *This particular case is an exception to the rule.* | *Shall I just order beer, or is there some particular type you prefer?* **3** [(**about, over**)] showing (too) much care or interest in small matters: *He's very particular about having his breakfast at exactly 8 o'clock.* | *She's very particular about her food.* (=chooses it carefully and will not eat certain kinds) [+*wh-*] *I'm not particular* (=do not care) *how you do it as long as it gets done.* **4** [A] *fml* careful and exact: *a full and particular account of what happened*

particular² *n* **1** *fml* a small single part of a whole; detail: *This work must be correct* **in every particular/in all particulars.** **2** **in particular** especially: *I noticed his eyes in particular, because they were such an unusual colour.* —see also PARTICULARS

par·tic·u·lar·i·ty /pəˌtɪkjʊˈlærɪti‖pər-/ *n fml* **1** [U] exactness; attention to detail **2** [C] a particular **3** [C] something strange or unusual; PECULIARITY

par·tic·u·lar·ize also **-ise** *BrE* /pəˈtɪkjʊləraɪz‖pər-/ *v* [I;T] *fml* to give the details of (something) one by one; ITEMIZE —**-ization** /pəˌtɪkjʊləraɪˈzeɪʃən‖pərˌtɪkjʊlərə-/ *n* [U]

par·tic·u·lar·ly /pəˈtɪkjʊləli‖pərˈtɪkjʊlərli/ *adv* especially; in a way that is special and different from others: *I particularly like this one.* | *He isn't particularly clever.* | *Watch that horse particularly — it bites!*

par·tic·u·lars /pəˈtɪkjʊləz‖pərˈtɪkjʊlərz/ *n* [P (**of**)] detailed information or facts: *The policeman took down her particulars.* (=wrote down her name, address, etc.) | *I'd like you to give us full particulars of the incident.*

part·ing¹ /ˈpɑːtɪŋ‖ˈpɑːr-/ *n* **1** [C;U] (an example of) the action of parting (PART² (1, 2)) **2** [C] *BrE* ‖ **part** *AmE*— the line on a person's head where the hair is parted (PART² (3)): *a centre parting* **3 the parting of the ways** the point at which two people must separate or a choice must be made

parting² *adj* [A] done or given at the time of parting (PART² (1)): *a parting kiss*

parting shot /ˌ·· ˈ·/ *n* a last remark, special look, etc., made at the moment of leaving, esp. as the last reply in an argument

Par·ti Qué·bé·cois /ˌpɑːti keɪbeˈkwɑː‖ˌpɑːr-/ a political party in the PROVINCE of Quebec, Canada, which wants Quebec to become a separate country

par·ti·san¹ , **-zan** /ˌpɑːtɪˈzæn‖ˈpɑːrtɪˌzən, -sən/ *adj* usu. *derog* showing strong often unreasoning support of a particular party, group, plan, etc., and dislike of any others: *a very partisan speech|newspaper*

partisan² , **-zan** *n* **1** a member of an armed group that fights in secret against an enemy that has defeated its country —compare TERRORIST **2** usu. *derog* a partisan person — **~ship** *n* [U]

par·ti·tion /pɑːˈtɪʃən‖pər-, pɑːr-/ *n* **1** [C] something that separates, esp. a thin wall inside a building that divides a larger room: *You could hear what he was saying on the phone through the partition.* | *a glass partition* —see picture at OPEN-PLAN **2** [U (**into**)] division, esp. of a country, into two or more parts: *India before partition* (=division into India and Pakistan)

partition² *v* [T (**into**)] to divide into two or more parts
 partition sthg. ↔ **off** *phr v* [T] to make (esp. a part of a room) separate by means of a partition

par·ti·tive /ˈpɑːtɪtɪv‖ˈpɑːr-/ *n, adj tech* (a word) which expresses a part of a whole: *"Some" is a partitive word, as in the phrase "some of the cake".* — **~ly** *adv*

part·ly /ˈpɑːtli‖ˈpɑːr-/ adv in some way or in some degree; not completely: *What you say is partly true.* | *We are all partly to blame.* | *a partly-finished building.*

part·ner¹ /ˈpɑːtnər‖ˈpɑːr-/ n **1** either of two people sharing an activity, such as dancing together or playing together against two others in certain games **2** any of the owners of a business, who share the profits and losses rather than receiving regular pay: *She's a partner in a law firm.* —see also SLEEPING PARTNER **3** a person who shares and helps in the same stated activity: *They were* **partners in crime.** —compare COMPANION (1,2) **4** either of two people who have a relationship that is both sexual and social, esp. if they are living together (—see also COHABIT): *This is John, my partner.*

partner² v [T] **1** to act as partner to: *John partnered Jane at the dance.* **2** [(UP, with)] to provide (someone) with a partner or bring (two people) together as partners
  partner up phr v [I (with)] to become a partner or partners: *John and Mary have partnered up for the dance.*

part·ner·ship /ˈpɑːtnəʃɪp‖ˈpɑːrtnər-/ n **1** [U] the state of being a partner, esp. in business: *We've been in partnership for five years.* | *She's gone into partnership with two of the other local doctors.* **2** [C] a business owned by two or more partners **3** [C] (in cricket) the total number of runs scored by two batsmen (BATSMAN) batting together in a match

part of speech /ˌ·· ˈ·/ n tech (in grammar) any of the classes into which words are divided according to their use: *"Noun", "verb", and "adjective" are parts of speech.* —see also PRINCIPAL PARTS

Par·ton /ˈpɑːtn‖ˈpɑːr-/, **Dolly** (1946–) an American popular music singer, songwriter and GUITAR player who started as a COUNTRY AND WESTERN singer and has become an actress and well-known television personality in the US. She is known for her unusually large breasts, her thick white hair, her bright personality and her attractive singing voice.

Dolly Parton

par·took /pɑːˈtʊk‖pɑːr-/ past tense of PARTAKE

par·tridge /ˈpɑːtrɪdʒ‖ˈpɑːr-/ n **partridges** or **partridge** any of various middle-size birds, with a round body and short tail, shot for sport and food. In Britain partridge is one of the more expensive foods and shooting them is a generally UPPER-CLASS sport.

parts /pɑːts‖pɑːrts/ n [P] **1** a general area or division of a country, without fixed limits: *We don't have much rain in these parts.* | *She lives in* **foreign parts.** (=abroad) **2** **of parts** lit or pomp of many different abilities (in the phrase **a man/woman of parts**) **3** infml SPARE PARTS —see also PRIVATE PARTS

part-song /ˈ· ·/ n a song which is made up of three or more musical lines sung together

part-time /ˌ· ˈ·◂/ adj, adv working or giving work during only a part of the regular working time: *a part-time secretary/student* | *He got a part-time job washing dishes.* —compare FULL-TIME —**part-timer** n : *We have three full-time staff, and a part-timer who works mornings.*

par·tu·ri·tion /ˌpɑːtjʊˈrɪʃən‖ˌpɑːrtə-, -tʃə-/ n [U] med the act of giving birth

part-way /ˌ· ˈ·◂/ adv infml slightly, a little: *If he were only part-way competent, I'd be satisfied.*

part work /ˈ· ·/ n BrE a set of magazines on one particular subject that are produced usu. once a week and can be put together to form a book

par·ty¹ /ˈpɑːti‖ˈpɑːrti/ n **1** an occasion when people meet together, usu. by invitation and often in a private home, to enjoy themselves, e.g. by eating and drinking, dancing, etc.: *We're having/giving/throwing a party on New Year's Eve.* | *a tea party* | *a birthday party* | *a garden party* | *a party dress* —compare FESTIVAL, HOLIDAY, see also HEN PARTY, HOUSE PARTY, STAG PARTY **2** [+sing./pl. v] a group of people **a** doing something together: *A party of schoolchildren is going to France.* **b** given a special duty together: *a search party* —see also WORKING PARTY **3** [+sing./pl. v] an association of people having the same

political aims, esp. as formed to try to win elections: *the Labour party* | *party politics* | *an all-party committee* | *Politicians shouldn't put party before country.* | *He always* **follows the party line.** (=acts according to its official opinion) | *one of* **the party faithful** (=loyal members of the party) **4** a person or group of people concerned or taking part in an agreement, argument, or other activity, esp. a legal matter: *the two parties* (=groups of people) *in the quarrel* | *Are you (a) party to the agreement?* | *I could never be a party to such dishonesty.* | *We know he is the* **guilty party,** *because we saw him take the money.* —see also THIRD PARTY

party² v [I] infml, esp. AmE to enjoy oneself, esp. at a party or parties

Party Con·fe·rence /ˌ·· ˈ···/ n (in Britain) the yearly meeting of a political party when plans for the coming year are discussed

party game /ˈ·· ˌ·/ n a game played at esp. a children's party

party line /ˈ·· ·/ n a telephone line connected to two or more telephones belonging to different people —see also PARTY¹ (3)

party piece /ˈ·· ˌ·/ n usu. humor a song, poem, etc. that is someone's usual choice when they are asked to give a performance, e.g. at a party

party-po·lit·i·cal /ˌ··· ·ˈ····◂/ adj [A] esp. BrE connected or concerned with party politics: *fruitless party-political wranglings* | *an issue of purely party-political interest*

party-political broad·cast /ˌ··· ···· ˈ··/ BrE ‖ **paid political broadcast** AmE— n a television programme, broadcast esp. before a General Election, in which a politician asks the public to vote for his/her party and gives reasons why he/she thinks they should do so. Party political broadcasts last only a few minutes, and in Britain all parties making these broadcasts are allowed the same amount of time.

party pol·i·tics /ˌ·· ˈ···/ n [U+sing./pl.v] political activity done by a party in order to improve its own structure, to gain more power, etc., rather than for the good of other organizations or the public: *She wanted to change society but found herself bogged down in party politics.*

party poop·er /ˈpɑːti ˌpuːpər‖ˈpɑːr-/ n infml a dull or unfriendly person who does not enjoy being with other people, spoils their fun, etc.

party wall /ˌ·· ˈ·/ n a dividing wall between two houses, belonging to the owners of both houses

par val·ue /ˈ· ˌ·/ n [U] PAR¹ (3)

par·ve·nu /ˈpɑːvənjuː‖ˈpɑːrvənuː/ n usu. derog a person of a low social position who suddenly gains power or wealth

Pas·cal /pæˈskæl/, **Blaise** /blɛɪz/ (1623–62) a French scientist and religious thinker (PHILOSOPHER), noted for his work in MATHEMATICS and PHYSICS and for his religious writings in which he argues that faith is needed to understand the universe

PASCAL /ˈpæskæl‖pæˈskæl/ n [U] a computer language used esp. when teaching computer studies and with small computers in business: *Do you use PASCAL?*

pas·chal /ˈpæskəl/ adj [A] (often cap.) **1** of the Jewish holiday of Passover **2** lit or old use of Easter: *the Paschal lamb*

pas de deux /ˌpɑː də ˈdɜː‖-ˈduː/ n pas de deux a dance, esp. in BALLET, for two people dancing together

Pas·o·li·ni /ˌpæsəˈliːni/, **Pier Pao·lo** /pjeə ˈpaʊləʊ/ (1922–75) an Italian film director who was murdered. His films include *The Gospel According to St. Matthew, Medea,* and *Oedipus Rex*

pass¹ /pɑːs‖pæs/ v **1** [I (BY);T] to reach and move beyond (a person or place): *She waved at me as she passed (by).* | *It's dangerous to* **pass** (=OVERTAKE other cars) *on this narrow road.* | *I passed the pub on my way to the library.* | (fig.) *It* **passes my understanding/comprehension** (=I cannot understand) *how he could have done such a stupid thing.* **2** [I+adv/prep;T+obj+adv/prep] to go, move, or place, esp. in or for a short space of time: *A cloud passed across the sun.* | *She passed amongst the crowd distributing leaflets.* | *We pass through Germany on our way to Austria.* | *The news quickly passed round the hall.* | *His famous exploits have passed into folklore.* | *She passed the rope round the tree.* | (fig.) *Angry words passed between them.* **3** [I;T] to get or go through, across, over, or between: *The crowd parted to let the coach pass.* | *The smugglers passed the frontier without being searched.* | *Sales of the book have now passed the million mark.* (=more than a million have been sold) **4** [I (AWAY)] to come to an end or disappear: *The storm soon passed (away).* | *Your sorrow will soon pass.* **5** [T (**to**)] to move (something) from one person to another, esp. by hand; give: [+*obj(i)*+*obj(d)*] *Pass me the salt, please − I can't quite reach it.* | *He passed her the bread*|*passed the bread to her.*| *Could you pass (me) that book down from the top shelf?* **6** [I;T (**to**)] (in various sports) to kick, throw, hit, etc. (esp. a ball), esp. to a member of one's own side: *He passed (the ball) back to the goalkeeper.* **7** [I;T] **a** (of time) to go by: *The hours passed slowly.* **b** to spend (time), esp. in a way that does not seem too long or dull: *On the train journey, we played cards to pass the time.* **8** [I+*adv*|*prep*, esp. **from, to, into**] to change: *When you melt ice, it passes from a solid to a liquid state.* **9** [I;T] **a** to officially approve or be approved, esp. after a vote: *Parliament has passed a law to restrict immigration.* **b** to accept or be accepted as satisfactory, esp. after an examination: *I can't pass this bad piece of work!* | *The doctor wouldn't pass him (as) fit*|*ready for work.* | *You might be able to get into a disco in those clothes, but they won't pass in this office!* **10** [I;T] to succeed in (an examination): *"Did you pass your driving test?" "No, I failed."* **11** [T] to cause (money) to be accepted, esp. by illegal or dishonest means: [+*obj(i)*+*obj(d)*] *Someone tried to pass me a forged £10 note.* **12** [T (**on, upon**)] to give or express (a judgment, opinion, remark, etc.): *I wouldn't like to pass an opinion on such a complicated subject.* | *The judge passed a heavy sentence on her.* | *He passed some comment or other, but I didn't hear what it was.* | *He stopped to* **pass the time of day** (=to have a short conversation) *with a neighbour.* **13** [I+*adv*|*prep*, esp. **to, into**] to go from the control or possession of one person to that of another: *On his death, the farm will pass to his son*|*into the hands of the state.* **14** [I] (in card games) to let one's turn go by without playing a card, putting down money, or making a BID² (3) **15** [I] to give no answer to a question because you do not know the answer: *I think I'll pass on that one.*| *"Who was the President of the US in 1956?" "Pass."* **16** [T] *fml* to send out from the bowels or BLADDER: *to pass water* (=to URINATE) **17** [I] *fml or bibl* to happen: *How can such a terrible state of affairs have* **come to pass** (=happened); *what can have* **brought it to pass? 18 let something pass** to leave (a wrong statement, mistake, etc.) without putting it right: *He said Shakespeare was an American and I couldn't let that pass.* −see also PASS·ING, **pass the hat round** (HAT), **pass muster** (MUSTER²); see PAST (USAGE)

pass as sbdy./sthg. *phr v* [T] to PASS **for**

pass away/on *phr v* [I] *euph* (esp. of a person) to die: *She passed away in her sleep.* −see DEAD¹ (CULTURAL NOTE)

pass sbdy. ↔ **by/over** *phr v* [T] to pay no attention to; take no notice of: *The voters passed him by.* | *Life has passed me by.*

pass sthg. ↔ **down/on** *phr v* [T (**to**) *often pass.*] to give or leave to people who are younger or live later: *a skill that has been passed down from father to son*

pass for/as sbdy./sthg. *phr v* [T] to be (mistakenly) accepted or considered as: *His English is so good he could pass as a native.* | *I can't imagine how this place passes for a five-star hotel! The service is dreadful.*

pass off *phr v* **1** [I+*adv*|*prep*] to take place and be completed: *The meeting passed off well.* **2** [T (**as**)] (**pass** sbdy./sthg. ↔ **off**) to present falsely: *She passed herself off as an experienced actress.* −compare PALM **off** (1)

pass on *phr v* **1** [I] *euph* to die; PASS **away 2** [T] to PASS **down 3** [I] to move on: *Let us now pass on to the next subject.* **4** [T] (**pass** sthg. ↔ **on**) to give to another person: *Read the note then pass it on.*

pass out *phr v* **1** [I] to faint: *He always passes out at the sight of blood.* **2** [I] *esp. BrE* to finish a course esp. at a military school: *a passing-out parade* **3** [T] (**pass** sthg. ↔ **out**) to give out: DISTRIBUTE (3)

pass over *phr v* [T] **1** (**pass** sbdy. ↔ **over**) to PASS **by**: *He was passed over for promotion*|*in favour of a younger man.* **2** (**pass over** sthg.) to try not to notice or mention: *Let us pass over his rude remarks in silence.*

pass sthg. ↔ **up** *phr v* [T] to fail to take advantage of; miss: *I had a chance to go to America, but I passed it up.*

pass² *n* **1** [C] an act of moving past: *The aircraft made a*

few passes over the enemy camp, but didn't drop any bombs. **2** [C] an official piece of paper with writing on it which shows that one is allowed to do a certain thing, such as travel on a train or bus without paying, enter a building, etc.: *We had to show our passes to the security guard.* −see also FREE PASS **3** [C] **a** a successful result in an examination: *a pass in geography* **b** (esp. in Britain) the completing of a university course with an examination standard that is acceptable but not good enough for HONOURS (2): *a pass degree* **4** [C] (in various sports) an act of passing (PASS¹ (6)) a ball **5** a way by which one may move or travel through or over a place, esp. over a range of mountains: *the Brenner Pass* | *the landslide blocked the pass.* −see picture at MOUNTAIN **6** [S] *BrE infml* a difficult state or condition: *Things have* **come to a pretty/fine/sorry pass** *if we can't even afford beer!* **7** [C] a single complete stage in a process of dealing with something: *This is just the first pass, when we discard the most unsuitable candidates.* **8 make a pass at** *sl* (esp. of a man) to invite or attempt sexual activity, either with words or by trying to touch (a member of the opposite sex)

pass. *abbrev. for:* PASSIVE¹ (2)

pass·a·ble /ˈpɑːsəbəl‖ˈpæ-/ *adj* **1** (just) good enough to be accepted; satisfactory but not very good: *a passable piece of work* **2** (of a road or river) that can be travelled along or across −opposite **impassable** −**bly** *adv*

pas·sage /ˈpæsɪdʒ/ *n* **1** [C] *also* **pas·sage·way** /ˈpæsɪdʒweɪ/ *BrE* || *also* **hall, hallway** *AmE*− a long narrow connecting way, esp. inside a building; CORRIDOR: *Her room is just along the passage.* **2** [C (**through**)] *esp. BrE* a usu. narrow way through; opening: *We forced a passage through the crowd.* **3** [U (**of**)] *fml* the action of going across, by, over, through, etc., something: *The old bridge is not strong enough to allow the passage of heavy vehicles.* | *(fig.) The bill was amended several times during its passage through Parliament.* **4** [U (**of**)] the course (of time): *With the passage of time the incident was forgotten.* **5** [S (**from, to**)] (the cost of) a journey, esp. by sea or air: *He couldn't afford the passage, and so he had to* **work his passage** *by doing jobs on the ship.* | *We had a rough passage.* **6** [C] a usu. short part of a speech or a piece of writing or music, considered by itself −see also PURPLE PASSAGE, **rites of passage** (RITE)

Passage to In·di·a /ˌ··· ··ˈ····/, **A** a NOVEL by E M Forster about misunderstandings between people of different countries, in this case, Britain and India. It has been made into a successful film.

pas·sant /ˈpæsɒn‖pɑːˈsɑːn/ see EN PASSANT

pass·book /ˈpɑːsbʊk‖ˈpæs-/ *n* **1 a** a book in which a record of the money one puts into and takes out of a BUILDING SOCIETY is kept **b** *AmE* for BANKBOOK **2** (in S Africa before 1987) a small book which non-white people had to carry which allowed them to be in a certain area

pas·sé /ˈpɑːseɪ, ˈpæseɪ‖pæˈseɪ/ *adj* [F] *derog* no longer considered modern; old-fashioned

pas·sen·ger /ˈpæsɪndʒəʳ, -sən-/ *n* **1** a person, not the driver, travelling in a public or private vehicle: *This bus can carry 60 passengers.* | *a passenger train* | *The driver and both passengers were unhurt in the accident.* **2** *BrE derog* a member of a team or other group who does not do his or her share of the group's work

Passe·par·tout /ˌpæspɑːˈtuː‖-pɑːr-/ a character in Jules Verne's story *Around the World in 80 Days*, Phileas Fogg's servant and travelling-companion −see also Phileas FOGG

pass·er·by /ˌpɑːsəˈbaɪ‖ˌpæsər-/ *n* **passersby** /-səz-‖-sərz-/ a person who (by chance) is walking, driving, etc. past a place: *A few passersby saw the accident.*

pas·sim /ˈpæsɪm/ *adv tech* (of a phrase, idea, etc., that appears in a book, a writer's work, etc.) frequently; in many places: *For further information, see chapter six passim.*

pass·ing¹ /ˈpɑːsɪŋ‖ˈpæ-/ *n* [U (**of**)] **1** the act of going by: *With the passing of the years he grew more and more ill-tempered.* **2 a** ending; disappearance: *The old government was voted out, and few people mourned its passing.* **b** *euph* death **3 in passing** in the course of a statement, esp. one about a different matter: *He was talking about his holiday in Spain, and he mentioned in passing that you were thinking of going there next year.*

passing[2] *adj* [A] **1** moving or going by: *He watched the passing cars.* | *With every passing day she grew stronger.* | *a passing shot in tennis* (=that passes one's opponent) **2** not lasting very long; BRIEF: *She did not give the matter even a passing thought.* | *a passing reference*

passing[3] *adv old use very*: *passing strange*

passing shot /'·· ¸·/ *n* (in TENNIS) a shot that hits the ball to one side and beyond the reach of an opponent who is coming towards the net

pas·sion /'pæʃən/ *n* **1** [C;U (**for**)] (a) strong, deep, often uncontrollable feeling, esp. of sexual love, hatred, or anger: *The poet expressed his burning passion for the woman he loved.* | *a political meeting where passions ran high* (=people expressed strong feelings) **2** [S] a sudden show of anger or bad temper: *She gets into a passion if you contradict her.* **3** [S+**for**] *infml* a strong liking: *a passion for (collecting) antiques* —see also CRIME OF PASSION — ~less *adj* — ~lessly *adv*

Passion [*the*] *n tech* the suffering and death of Christ

pas·sion·ate /'pæʃənət/ *adj* **1** able to feel strongly with passion: *a passionate woman* **2** showing or filled with passion: *a passionate speech in defence of freedom* **3** very eager; INTENSE: *a passionate interest in sports* — ~ly *adv*: *He believes passionately in the justice of his cause.*

pas·sion·flow·er /'pæʃən¸flaʊəʳ/ *n* any of various types of climbing plant with large flowers, usu. growing in warm countries, some of which produce an egg-shaped fruit (**passionfruit**) which is good to eat

passion play /'·· ·/ *n* (*often cap. first* P) a play telling the story of the Passion —compare NATIVITY PLAY

Passion Sun·day /¸·· '··/ the second Sunday before Easter in the Christian church, when special prayers are said

pas·sive[1] /'pæsɪv/ *adj* **1** *sometimes derog* accepting what happens or what other people do to one, but not doing anything in return; suffering without opposition: *They received the news of their defeat with passive resignation.* | *How can you be so passive? Why don't you retaliate?* | *They mounted a campaign of passive resistance against the occupiers.* (=opposing them without using violence) **2** [*no comp.*] *tech* (of a verb or sentence) having as the subject the person or thing to which an action is done (as in *The boy was thrown from his horse*) —compare ACTIVE[1] (3) — ~ly *adj*

passive[2] *also* **passive voice** /¸·· '·/— *n* [*the*+S] *tech* the passive form of a verb: *"The ball was kicked by the boy" is in the passive.* —compare ACTIVE[2]

passive smok·ing /¸·· '··/ *n* [U] the breathing in of smoke from the cigarettes, PIPEs, etc. that other people are smoking, now considered to be almost as harmful to health as actually smoking yourself

pas·siv·i·ty /pæ'sɪv¸ti/ *also* **pas·sive·ness** /'pæsɪvn¸s/— *n* [U] *sometimes derog* the quality of being PASSIVE[1] (1)

pas·siv·ize *also* **-ise** *BrE* /'pæsɪvaɪz/ *v* [I;T] *tech* to (cause to) become PASSIVE[1] (2) —**-ization** /¸pæsɪvaɪ'zeɪʃən‖ -və-/ *n* [U]

pass·key /'pɑːskiː‖'pæs-/ *n* **1** a key made to open a particular door or gate, and given only to those few people allowed to use that door or gate **2** a key that will open a number of different locks, all of which have keys of their own

pass laws /'· ·/ *n* [P] South African laws which formerly controlled or prevented the movement of black people from place to place. The pass laws were stopped as part of the end of APARTHEID.

Pass·o·ver /'pɑːsəʊvəʳ‖'pæs-/ *n* [(*the*)] (in the Jewish religion) a religious holiday in memory of the escape of the Jews from being slaves in Egypt. Passover is one of the most important Jewish holidays and takes place in the spring.

pass·port /'pɑːspɔːt‖'pæspɔːrt/ *n* **1** a small official book given by a government to a citizen, which proves who that person is and allows them to leave their country and enter foreign countries: *She holds* (=has) *a French passport.* **2** [(**to**)] something, such as a quality or possession, that makes it possible for a person to do or get something desirable: *He thought that money was a passport to happiness/to high society*

passport con·trol /'·· ·¸·/ *n* where one's passport is checked when leaving and entering a country

pass the par·cel /¸· · '··/ *n* [U] a British game played esp. at children's parties, in which a parcel wrapped in many sheets of paper is passed from player to player while music is played. When the music stops, the player holding the parcel tries to unwrap as much paper as possible from the parcel before the music starts again. The game ends when a player unwraps the parcel completely and receives a prize which was inside it.

pass·word /'pɑːswɜːd‖'pæswɜːrd/ *n* **1** a secret word or phrase which must be spoken by a person before they are allowed to enter a building, camp, etc. <> they are used as a safety measure to prevent the wrong people from entering **2** a secret group of letters, numbers, etc., which must be used by a person before they can operate a computer system

past[1] /pɑːst‖pæst/ *adj* **1** [A;after *n*] (of time) much earlier than the present: *In years past/past years they never would have done that.* **2** [A;after *n*] (*with perfect tenses*) (of time) a little earlier than the present; up until now or until the time of speaking: *I've not been feeling very well for the past few days.* | *I've been meaning to speak to you for some time past.* **3** finished; ended: *The time for talking is past — we need action!* | *Winter is past and spring has come.* **4** [A] former; PREVIOUS: *Judging by past performance, I expect her to do well.* | *a past president of our club* **5** [A] *tech* being the form of a verb used to show a past act or state: *the past tense* —compare FUTURE[1]

  ▷ USAGE The past participle of **pass** is **passed**, but the adjective is **past.** Compare *The week has* **passed** quickly *and the* **past** *week.*◁

past[2] *prep* **1 a** farther than: *The hospital is about a mile past the school.* **b** up to and beyond: *The boys rushed past us.* **2** beyond in time or age: *The time is half past three.* | *The trains leave at ten past (the hour).* | *It's past my bedtime.* | *She must be past 50.* **3** beyond the possibility of: *The sick man's condition is past hope.* | *Frankly, I'm past caring.* (=I no longer care) **4** **past it** *infml* no longer able to do the things one could formerly do: *This old car's past it; we'll have to get a new one.* **5** **wouldn't put it past someone** (**to do something**) *infml* to regard someone as likely (to do something bad, unusual, etc.): *I'm not sure if he actually cheated in the exam, but I wouldn't put it past him!*

past[3] *n* **1** [(*the*) S] (what happened in) time before the present: *In the past he has been a bricklayer and a milkman, and now he's a farmer.* | *Good manners seem to have become a thing of the past.* (=something that no longer exists) | *a country with a glorious past* (=history) —compare FUTURE[1] **2** [*the*+S] *tech* (in grammar) the form of a verb that shows that the act or state described by the verb happened or existed at some time before the present moment **3** [S] *old-fash derog* a former life, esp. a secret one containing wrong-doing of some kind: *a woman with a past*

past[4] *adv* by; to and beyond a point in space or time: *Children came running past.* | *Days went past without any news.*

pas·ta /'pæstə‖'pɑː-/ *n* [U] food made, in various different shapes, from flour paste, and often covered with SAUCE and/or cheese: *Macaroni, spaghetti, and vermicelli are all types of pasta.*

  ▶CULTURAL NOTE Pasta is generally thought of as Italian food, but is widely eaten in Britain and the US at home and in restaurants. ◀

paste[1] /peɪst/ *n* [C;U] **1** a soft sticky mixture of powder and liquid that is easily shaped or spread: *Add water, mix it into a paste, and fill the cracks with it.* | *Marzipan is made from almond paste.* —see also TOOTHPASTE **2** a thin mixture, esp. of flour and water, used for sticking paper together or onto other surfaces —compare GLUE **3** a food made by crushing solid foods into a smooth soft mass, used for spreading on bread: *meat paste* | *fish paste* —compare PÂTÉ **4** a shining material made of lead and glass, used to copy the appearance of real jewels: *They're not diamonds, they're only paste.*

paste[2] *v* [T+*obj*+*adv*/*prep*] to stick or fasten (paper) with paste: *A notice was pasted to/on the door.* | *Paste down the edge of the paper.* | *Notices about the demonstration were pasted up (on walls) all over the university.* —see also PASTE-UP, PASTING

paste·board[1] /'peɪstbɔːd‖-bɔːrd/ *n* [U] flat stiff cardboard made by pasting sheets of paper together

pasteboard[2] *adj* [A] *derog* lacking strength or reality; CARDBOARD[2] (2): *a play full of pasteboard characters*

pas·tel[1] /'pæstl‖pæ'stel/ *n* **1** [C;U] (a small stick of) a solid chalklike substance made of powdery colouring matter used for drawing **2** [C] a picture drawn using this substance **3** [C] any soft light colour

pastel[2] *adj* [A] **1** drawn in pastels **2** soft and light in colour: *pastel shades | pastel blue*

pas·tern /'pæstɜːn‖-ɜːrn/ *n* the narrow upper part of a horse's foot, above the HOOF —see picture at HORSE

Pas·ter·nak /'pæstənæk‖-tər-/, **Bor·is** /'bɒrɪs‖'bɔː-/ (1890–1960) a Russian poet, NOVELIST, and translator who wrote *Doctor Zhivago*, which was banned (BAN) in the USSR. In 1958 he won the Nobel Prize, but the Soviet government of the time did not approve and he did not accept it.

paste-up /'· ·/ *n* pieces of printed matter, pictures, etc., stuck in position (as if) on a page, either to be photographed for a real page or to show what the page will look like when the book, newspaper, etc., is produced

Pas·teur /pæ'stɜːʳ/, **Louis** (1822–95) a French scientist known for his studies of FERMENTATION and bacteria; inventor of the process of pasteurization

pas·teur·ize also **-ise** *BrE* /'pæstʃəraɪz, 'pɑː-, -stə-‖'pæstʃə-, -stə-/ *v* [T] to heat (a liquid) in a certain way in order to destroy bacteria: *pasteurized milk* —**ization** /ˌpæstʃəraɪ'zeɪʃən, ˌpɑː-, -stə-‖ˌpæstʃərə-, -stərə-/ *n* [U]

pas·tiche /pæ'stiːʃ/ *n* **1** [C (**of**)] a work of art, such as a piece of writing or music, that is purposely made in the style of a another writer, musician, etc. **2** [C] a work of art made up of pieces of various other works put together **3** [U] the style or practice of making works of art in either of these ways

pas·tille /pæ'stiːl/ ‖ also **lozenge** *esp. AmE*— *n* a small round hard sweet, esp. one containing a medicine for a sore throat

pas·time /'pɑːstaɪm‖'pæs-/ *n* something done to pass one's time in a pleasant way: *Listening to music is my favourite pastime.*

past·ing /'peɪstɪŋ/ *n* [*usu. sing.*] *infml* **1** a hard beating: *You'll get a real pasting if the teacher finds out what you've done!* **2** (in sport or other sorts of competition) a severe defeat

past mas·ter /ˌ· '··/ *n* [(**at, in, of**)] a person who is very clever or skilled in a particular subject or action: *He's a past master at getting free drinks/in the art of conversation.*

pas·tor /'pɑːstəʳ‖'pæ-/ *n* a Christian religious leader in charge of a church and its members, esp. in a Protestant church, other than the Church of England

pas·tor·al[1] /'pɑːstərəl‖'pæ-/ *adj* **1** of the members of a religious group, or its leader's duties towards them: *The priest/rabbi makes pastoral visits every Tuesday. | a teacher's pastoral duties* (=giving advice on personal matters rather than educational matters) **2** *esp. lit* concerning simple peaceful country life: *a charming pastoral scene of cows drinking from a stream | pastoral poetry* **3** (of land) grassy; suitable for feeding sheep and cattle

pastoral[2] also **pastoral let·ter** /ˌ··· '··/— *n tech* an official letter sent by a BISHOP to the church members in his area

past par·ti·ci·ple /ˌ· '·····/ also **perfect participle**— *n tech* (in grammar) a PARTICIPLE that can be used in compound forms of the verb to show the PASSIVE or the PERFECT[1] (6) tenses (such as *broken* in *The cup was broken by John* or *I have broken the cup*) or sometimes as an adjective (such as *broken* in *a broken cup*)

past per·fect /ˌ· '··/ also **pluperfect**— *n* [*the*] *tech* (in grammar) the form of a verb that shows that the action described by the verb was completed before a particular time in the past (stated or understood), formed in English with **had** and a past participle —**past perfect** *adj*

pas·tra·mi /pə'strɑːmi/ *n* [U] (esp. in the US) very strong-tasting BEEF dried in smoke

pas·try /'peɪstri/ *n* **1** [U] a mixture of flour, fat, milk or water, and sometimes sugar, eaten when baked, used esp. to enclose other foods: *The pie crust is made of pastry.* **2** [C] an article of food, esp. a small sweet cake, made wholly or partly of this —see also DANISH PASTRY

pas·tur·age /'pɑːstʃərɪdʒ‖'pæs-/ *n* [U] **1** the right to use land for feeding one's cattle, horses, etc. **2** also **pas·ture·land** /'pɑːstʃəlænd‖'pæstʃər-/— (natural) grassland suitable for feeding cattle on

pas·ture[1] /'pɑːstʃəʳ‖'pæs-/ **pas·ture·land** /'pɑːstʃəlænd‖'pæstʃər-/ *n* [C;U] **1** (a piece of) grassy land where farm animals feed: *the rolling pastures of southern England | We're putting our cattle* **out to pasture**. (=to feed on grass) | (fig.) *It's about time this old sewing machine was* **put out to pasture**. (=got rid of) —compare ARABLE **2 fresh fields and pastures new** *quote* a slightly changed phrase from a poem by John Milton, used when saying that someone is moving on to a new place or a new activity

pasture[2] *v* **1** [T] to put (farm animals) in a pasture to feed: *He's pasturing his cattle on the top meadow.* **2** [I(**on**)] (of cattle, sheep, etc.) to feed on an area of growing grass; GRAZE[1]

pas·ty[1] /'pæsti/ *n BrE* a small case of pastry, filled usu. with meat —see also CORNISH PASTY

past·y[2] /'peɪsti/ *adj* (of the face) white and unhealthy in appearance

pasty-faced /'peɪsti feɪst/ *adj usu. derog* having a white and unhealthy-looking face

pat[1] /pæt/ *n* **1** [C] a light stroke with the flat hand, usu. showing friendliness and not intended to hurt: *He gave the dog a pat as he walked past.* **2** [S] a sound made by hitting something lightly with a flat object **3** [C (**of**)] a small shaped mass, esp. of butter **4 a pat on the back** *infml* an expression of praise or satisfaction for something done: *We don't want a pat on the back from the management — we want more money!*

pat[2] *v* **-tt-** [T] **1** to touch or strike gently and repeatedly with the flat hand or a flat object, often to show, friendliness, sympathy, etc.: *He patted the dog. | She patted her hair to make sure it was tidy.* **2 pat someone/oneself on the back** *infml* to praise someone/oneself for doing something well

pat[3] *adv often derog* **1** without delay, as if already prepared: *The answer came pat.* **2 have/know something (off) pat** *BrE* ‖ **have something down pat** *AmE*— to know something thoroughly and have it ready in one's mind so that one can say it or write it immediately and without having to think

pat[4] *adj often derog* (esp. of words) coming (too) easily or readily, as if already prepared: *His explanation was too pat to be convincing.*

patch[1] /pætʃ/ *n* **1** an often irregularly shaped part of a surface or space that is different, esp. in colour, from the surface or space round it: *The dog's coat is white with black patches. | wet patches on the wall | Patches of mist can be expected at dawn.* **2** a usu. small piece of material used to cover a hole or a damaged place: *He had a patch on the elbow of his jacket.* **3** a usu. small piece of ground, esp. as used for growing vegetables: *a potato patch* **4** a period of experience of the stated kind, esp. a time of trouble or misfortune: *Art in Britain is* **going through a bad patch** *at the moment. | Their marriage seems to have* **hit a difficult patch. 5** also **eyepatch**— a protective piece of material worn over an eye that has been hurt **6** *BrE infml* a usu. small area in which someone, esp. a policeman, always works and which he/she knows very well **7** also **beauty patch, beauty spot**— (in the 17th and 18th centuries) a small round usu. black piece of silk or other material worn on the face, to show up the beauty of the skin **8** *AmE* a small piece of cloth with words or a picture on it: *a windbreaker with patches on it from all the places they had visited* **9 in patches** in parts; not completely: *This film was good in patches, but I didn't like all of it.* —see also PATCHY (2) **10 not a patch on** *BrE infml* not nearly as good as: *This Algerian wine isn't a patch on the French.*

patch[2] *v* [T] to put a PATCH[1] (2) on (a hole, worn place, etc.), esp. in (a garment): *patched trousers*
patch sbdy./sthg. ↔ **up** *phr v* [T] **1** to settle (a quarrel or disagreement): *We managed to patch up our quarrel.* **2** to mend or repair quickly or roughly, esp. with a PATCH[1] (2): *patched-up jeans* | (fig.) *The doctors patched up the wounded soldiers and sent them back to the front again.*

patch·ou·li , patchouly /'pætʃʊli, pə'tʃuːli/ *n* the ESSENTIAL OIL from an E Indian heavy-smelling plant

patch pock·et /ˌ·ˈ··/ n a pocket made by sewing a square piece of material onto the outside of a garment

patch·work /ˈpætʃwɜːk‖-wɜːrk/ n [C;U] (a piece of) sewn work made by joining together a number of pieces of cloth of different colours, patterns, and shapes: *a patchwork quilt|blanket* | (fig.) *From the aircraft we could see a patchwork of fields of different shapes and colours.*

patch·y /ˈpætʃi/ adj **1** made up of or appearing in patches (PATCH¹ (1)): *The sun has faded the curtains so the colours are rather patchy.* | *There will be patchy fog at dawn.* **2** usu. derog **a** incomplete: *My knowledge of science is patchy.* **b** only good in parts: *The concert was patchy.* —**ily** adv —**iness** n [U]

pate /peɪt/ n old use or humor the top of the head: *his bald pate*

pât·é /ˈpæteɪ‖pɑːˈteɪ, pæ-/ n [U] a food made by crushing solid foods, esp. LIVER, into a smooth soft mass —compare PASTE¹ (3)

pâté de foie gras /ˌpæteɪ də ˌfwɑː ˈɡrɑː‖pɑːˌteɪ-, pæ-/ also **foie gras** infml— n [U] Fr pâté made from the LIVER of a GOOSE which has been fed a lot to make it fat. The best types are expensive and it is considered a LUXURY food.

pa·tel·la /pəˈtelə/ n med for KNEECAP¹ (1) —see picture at SKELETON

pa·tent¹ /ˈpeɪtnt, ˈpæ-‖ˈpæ-/ adj **1** fml (esp. of feelings or qualities) easy and plain to see; OBVIOUS: *his patent lack of honesty* **2** [A] protected, by a PATENT² (1), from being copied or sold by those who do not have a right to do so: *a patent lock* **3** [A] infml (of some act or skill invented by a particular person) cleverly made or done: *his patent way of making mayonnaise*

patent² n **1** a paper from the Patent Office of a government giving someone the right to make or sell a new invention for a certain number of years: *This new machine is protected by patent; the inventor has taken out a patent on it.* **2** the right given in such a paper: *The patent runs out in two years' time.*

patent³ v [T] to obtain a PATENT² (1) for: *If you don't patent your invention, someone might steal the idea.*

pa·tent·ee /ˌpeɪtnˈtiː‖ˌpæ-/ n esp. law a person to whom a PATENT² (1) is given

patent leath·er /ˌpeɪtnt ˈleðər◂‖ˌpæ-/ n [U] fine thin very shiny leather, usu. black: *patent-leather shoes*

pa·tent·ly /ˈpeɪtntli‖ˈpæ-/ adv fml (of something bad) clearly and plainly: *He was patently lying.* | *It was patently obvious that he was lying.* | *a patently false statement*

patent medi·cine /ˌ·· ·ˈ··/ n a medicine which can be bought without a PRESCRIPTION (=a written order from a doctor saying that a person needs a particular medicine)

Patent Of·fice /ˈ·· ˌ··/ [the] the British or American government department that decides which new inventions can be given patents. In the US the official name is the Patent and Trademark Office.

pa·ter /ˈpeɪtər/ n BrE (sometimes cap.) father: *Good morning, pater.* The word was formerly used by young UPPER-CLASS people, esp. by boys at PUBLIC SCHOOL; now rarely used except humorously —compare MATER

pa·ter·fa·mil·i·as /ˌpeɪtəfəˈmiːliæs‖ˌpɑːtərfəˈmiːliəs/ n **patresfamilias** /ˌpɑːtreɪz-/ fml or pomp (a person acting as) the father or male head of a family

pa·ter·nal /pəˈtɜːnl‖-ɜːr-/ adj **1** of, like, or natural to a father: *paternal love* —compare FATHERLY **2** derog protecting people and satisfying their needs but without allowing them any freedom or responsibility: *The employees resented the bosses' paternal attitude.* **3** [A] related through the father's side of the family: *my paternal grandmother* (=my father's mother) —compare MATERNAL —**ly** adv

pa·ter·nal·is·m /pəˈtɜːnəl-ɪzəm‖-ɜːr-/ n [U] derog a PATERNAL (2) way of controlling people, managing a company, etc. —**ist** n —**istic** /pəˌtɜːnəlˈɪstɪk◂‖-ɜːr-/ adj —**istically** /kli/ adv

pa·ter·ni·ty /pəˈtɜːnə̣ti‖-ɜːr-/ n [U] **1** esp. law origin from the male parent: *Tests are being made to establish the paternity of the child.* (=to find out who its father is) **2** fml fatherhood: *Paternity suits you!* —compare MATERNITY¹ (1)

paternity leave /·ˈ··· ˌ·/ n [U] time off work for the father of a new baby to help with its care. Very few British or American employers give paternity leave. —compare MATERNITY LEAVE

pa·ter·nos·ter /ˌpætəˈnɒstər‖-tərˈnɑː-/ n (usu. cap.) (in the Christian religion) the LORD'S PRAYER, esp. in Latin (from the Latin for the first two words of the prayer which begins "Our Father…")

path /pɑːθ‖pæθ/ **paths** /pɑːðz‖pæðz/ n **1** also **pathway**— a track or way made by or for people walking over the ground: *They strolled along|down the garden path.* | *Walk on the path, not on the grass|in the road.* | (fig.) *Hard work is the pathway to success.* | (fig.) *I will withdraw my objections, because I don't want to stand in your path.* (=block your possible success) **2** [(through)] an open space made to allow forward movement: *They used axes to clear a path through the forest.* **3** [(of)] a line along which something moves: *The path of an arrow is a curve.* —see also beat a path (BEAT¹), lead someone up the garden path (LEAD¹); see WAY (USAGE) — ~less adj

Pa·than /pəˈtɑːn/ n, adj (a member) of a group of people living esp. in Afghanistan and the western part of Pakistan

pa·thet·ic /pəˈθetɪk/ adj **1** causing a feeling of pity or sorrow; full of PATHOS: *the little dog's pathetic cries of pain* **2** derog hopelessly unsuccessful; useless: *my pathetic attempts to learn French* | *He's a pathetic actor.* — ~ally /kli/ adv : *pathetically inadequate*

pathetic fal·la·cy /·ˌ·· ·ˈ··· ·/ n [the+S] tech (esp. in a work of literature) the describing of non-living things, such as rocks, the sea, the weather, etc., as if they were human, e.g. by calling them "cruel", "happy", etc.

path·find·er /ˈpɑːθˌfaɪndər‖ˈpæθ-/ n **1** a person who goes on ahead of a group and finds the best way through unknown land **2** a person who discovers new ways of doing things

path·o·log·i·cal /ˌpæθəˈlɒdʒɪkəl◂‖-ˈlɑː-/ adj **1** med of PATHOLOGY **2** med caused by disease, esp. of the mind **3** infml unreasonable and unnatural; going on for a long time and out of control: *a pathological fear of the dark* | *a pathological liar* — ~ly /kli/ adv : *pathologically jealous*

pa·thol·o·gist /pəˈθɒlədʒ̣ɪst‖-ˈθɑː-/ n med a person, esp. a doctor, who is a specialist in pathology

pa·thol·o·gy /pəˈθɒlədʒi‖-ˈθɑː-/ n [U] med the study of the causes and effects of illnesses

pa·thos /ˈpeɪθɒs‖-ɑːs/ n [U] esp. lit the quality in a situation, a person, or in something said or written that causes a feeling of pity and sorrow

path·way /ˈpɑːweɪ‖ˈpæθ-/ n a PATH (1)

pa·tience /ˈpeɪʃəns/ n [U] **1 a** the ability to wait calmly for a long time and not be made angry by delay: *You need patience if you want to get served in this shop.* **b** the ability to accept pain, trouble, or anything that causes annoyance, without complaining or losing one's self-control: *The teacher had no patience with the less intelligent pupils.* | *The continual noise from the road repairs is beginning to try my patience.* (=make me lose my patience) **2** (the power of showing) care and close attention to work that is difficult or tiring: *I wouldn't have the patience to sit mending watches all day.* **3** ‖ also **solitaire** AmE— a card game for one player

pa·tient¹ /ˈpeɪʃənt/ adj [(with)] having or showing patience —opposite impatient — ~ly adv

patient² n a person receiving medical treatment from a doctor and/or in a hospital —see CUSTOMER (USAGE)

Patient's Char·ter /ˌ·· ˈ··/ [the] a British government-written statement of the rights of people who use the National Health Service. Most parts of it became effective in 1992

pat·i·na /ˈpætȷ̣nə/ n [S;U] **1** a usu. green surface covering formed naturally on copper or BRONZE **2** a pleasingly smooth shiny surface that gradually develops on wood, walls, etc.: (fig.) *the patina of wealth*

pat·i·o /ˈpætiəʊ/ n -os an open space with a stone floor next to a house, used for sitting on or eating on in fine weather —compare TERRACE, VERANDA

patio doors /ˈ··· ˌ·/ n [P] sliding doors which are usu. made of glass and open from a living room onto a patio

pa·tis·se·rie /pəˈtiːsəri/ n [C;U] (a shop that sells) French-style cakes, etc.

pa·tois /ˈpætwɑː/ n -tois /twɑːz/ [C;U] a form of spoken language used by the people of a small area, which is different from the national language, esp. if felt to be non-standard

Pa·ton /ˈpeɪtn/, **Al·an** /ˈælən/ (1903–88) a South African writer and politician best known for the NOVEL *Cry, the Beloved Country*

pa·tri·al /ˈpeɪtriəl, ˈpæ-/ n esp. BrE someone who for special reasons, esp. because one of their parents or their grandfather or grandmother was born in the United Kingdom, has a legal right to settle in the United Kingdom

pa·tri·arch /ˈpeɪtriɑːk‖-ɑːrk/ n 1 an old and much-respected man, esp. one who is the head of a family —compare MATRIARCH 2 a a BISHOP in the early Christian church b (usu. cap.) a chief bishop of the Eastern churches: *the Patriarch of Jerusalem*

pa·tri·arch·al /ˌpeɪtriˈɑːkəl◂‖-ˈɑːr-/ adj 1 ruled or controlled only by men: *a patriarchal society* 2 of or like a patriarch —compare MATRIARCHAL

pa·tri·arch·y /ˈpeɪtriɑːki‖-ɑːr-/ n [C;U] 1 (an example of) a social system in which the oldest man is head of the family, and passes power and possessions on to his sons 2 (an example of) a social system in which men hold all the power and use it only for their own advantage — compare MATRIARCHY

pa·tri·cian[1] /pəˈtrɪʃən/ n 1 a member of the governing classes in ancient Rome 2 sometimes derog or apprec a nobleman; ARISTOCRAT —compare PLEBEIAN

patrician[2] adj 1 belonging to the governing classes in ancient Rome 2 sometimes derog of or like a PATRICIAN[1] (2): *patrician aloofness*

pat·ri·cide /ˈpætrɪˌsaɪd/ n 1 [U] fml the murder of one's father 2 [C] tech a person guilty of this crime —compare MATRICIDE, PARRICIDE

Patrick, Saint see SAINT PATRICK

pat·ri·mo·ny /ˈpætrɪˌməni‖-məuni/ n [S;U] fml property inherited (INHERIT) from one's father, grandfather, etc. —compare MATRIMONY —**·nial** /ˌpætrɪˈməuniəl◂/ adj

pat·ri·ot /ˈpætriət, -trɪɒt, ˈpeɪ-‖ˈpeɪtriət, -triɑːt/ n usu. apprec someone who loves and is willing to defend their country

Patriot n a MISSILE system used against Iraqi missiles in the Gulf War: *Patriot missiles*

pat·ri·ot·ic /ˌpætriˈɒtɪk◂, ˌpeɪ-‖ˌpeɪtriˈɑːtɪk◂/ adj usu. apprec having or expressing the qualities of a patriot: *He's very patriotic.* | *patriotic songs* —**~ally** /kli/ adv

pat·ri·ot·is·m /ˈpætriətɪzəm, ˈpeɪ-‖ˈpeɪ-/ n [U] usu. apprec love for and loyalty to one's country

pa·trol[1] /pəˈtrəul/ n 1 [U] the act of patrolling or a period of patrolling: *Warships were on patrol in the North Atlantic.* | *During the night, security guards make regular patrols of the factory premises.* 2 [C+sing./pl. v] a small group, esp. of soldiers, aircraft, warships, etc., sent out to search for the enemy or to protect a place from the enemy: *The patrol has/have reported that all is quiet.* 3 [C+sing./pl. v] a small group of SCOUTS[1] (1) or GUIDES[1] (5) within the TROOP[1] (3) 4 ‖ AmE also **safety patrol**— a child given responsibility for the safety of other children on the school bus and on the walk to and from school. Safety patrols usu. wear bright orange belts. 5 AmE (in some states of the US) a police force: *the Illinois State Patrol*

patrol[2] v -ll- [I+adv/prep;T] to go at regular times round (an area, building, etc.) to see that there is no trouble, that no one is trying to get in or out illegally, etc.: *Guards patrolled the prison's perimeter fence.* | *The grounds of the presidential palace are patrolled by soldiers with guard dogs.* | (fig.) *Gangs of youths patrol (=walk threateningly along) the streets on Saturday nights.*

patrol car /·ˈ· ·/ n a car used by the police for patrolling roads

pa·trol·man /pəˈtrəulmən/ n -men /mən/ 1 esp. AmE a policeman who regularly patrols a particular area 2 BrE a person working for a car-owners' association who drives along roads to give help to motorists who need it: *an AA patrolman*

patrol wag·on /·ˈ· ˌ··/ also **paddy wagon** infml— n AmE a police vehicle used to carry prisoners, e.g. to and from court; BLACK MARIA

pa·tron /ˈpeɪtrən/ **pat·ron·ess** /-nɪs/ fem.— n 1 [(of)] a person or group that supports and gives money to an

organization or activity that is regarded as valuable and deserving support: *a patron of the arts* 2 fml or polite a person who uses a particular shop, hotel, etc., esp. regularly: *a special offer for our regular patrons* —compare CUSTOMER (1)

pat·ron·age /ˈpætrənɪdʒ/ n [U] 1 the support given by a PATRON (1) 2 fml the trade and support received from a PATRON (2) 3 sometimes derog the right to appoint people to important positions, esp. without regard to their ability

pat·ron·ize also **-ise** BrE /ˈpætrənaɪz‖ˈpeɪ-, ˈpæ-/ v [T] 1 derog to behave towards (someone) as if one were better or more important than them: *Don't patronize me; I know just as much about it as you do.* | *a patronizing remark/smile* 2 fml to use or visit (a shop, theatre, etc.): *I won't patronize this shop any more; the assistants are so rude.*

patron saint /ˌ·· ˈ·/ n [(of)] a Christian SAINT who is regarded as giving special protection to a particular place, activity, etc.: *Saint Christopher is the patron saint of travellers.*

pat·ro·nym·ic /ˌpætrəˈnɪmɪk/ n, adj tech (a name) formed from the name of one's father, grandfather, etc.

pat·sy /ˈpætsi/ n esp. AmE infml derog a person who is tricked or deceived, esp. into taking all the blame or punishment for something

pat·ten /ˈpætn/ n a CLOG (=a wooden shoe), with pieces of iron on the bottom worn, esp. formerly, when walking over wet or muddy ground

Patten, Chris /krɪs/ (1944–) a British Conservative politician who became Environment Secretary in 1989 and then Chairman of the Conservative Party. He lost his seat in Parliament in the 1992 general election and became GOVERNOR of Hong Kong later that year.

pat·ter[1] /ˈpætər/ v [I+adv/prep] to make, or move while making, the soft sound of something hitting a surface lightly, quickly, and repeatedly: *The dog pattered down the stairs/across the hall.* | *The falling leaves pattered against the window panes.*

patter[2] n 1 [S (of)] a sound of something pattering: *the patter of the rain on the tent* | *They will soon be hearing* **the patter of tiny feet.** (=they are going to have a baby) 2 [S;U] very fast continuous often amusing talk, esp. as used by someone trying to sell something, a magician while doing tricks, or someone telling jokes; one would not trust this talk: *She wasn't taken in by the salesman's patter.* 3 [U] the language, words, etc., used by a particular class of people, esp. criminals: *thieves' patter*

patterns

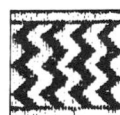

herringbone   checked   zigzag

pat·tern[1] /ˈpætən‖ˈpætərn/ n 1 a a regularly repeated arrangement of lines, shapes, or colours on a surface, that has, or is intended to have, a decorative or pleasing effect: *The cloth has a pattern of red and white squares.* | *snowflakes forming a pattern on the windowpane* b any regularly repeated arrangement, e.g. of sounds or words —compare DESIGN 2 the way in which something happens or develops: *The illness is not following its usual pattern.* | *a strange pattern of events* | *behavioural patterns that are typical of this social group* 3 a small piece of cloth, paper, etc., that shows what a large piece (of usual size) will look like; SAMPLE **4** a shape used as a guide for making something, esp. a piece of paper used to show the shape of a part of a garment: *a dress pattern* **5** [*usu. sing.*] a person, thing, or form that is an example to copy: *The success of the course* **set a pattern** *for the training of new employees.* —compare MODEL¹ (4)

pattern² *v* [T] **1** [(with)] to make a decorative pattern on: *patterned curtain material* | *patterned with roses* **2** [+*obj*+*adv*/*prep*, esp. **after, on, upon**] *fml* to form the character, qualities, etc., of (esp. oneself) by copying: *He patterned himself upon a man he admired.*

Pat·ton /ˈpætn/, **George Smith** (1885–1945) an American army general. He was an important commander during the First World War and the Second World War and was sometimes called "Old Blood and Guts".

pat·ty /ˈpæti/ *n* **1** *BrE* a small PIE or PASTY **2** food cut into very small pieces, formed into small flat shapes, and cooked: *beef patties*

patty melt /ˈ·· ˌ·/ *n AmE* a flat round piece of finely cut BEEF, cooked with cheese on top and served on bread

pau·ci·ty /ˈpɔːsɨ̩ti/ *n* [S (**of**)] *fml* less than is needed; a lack; DEARTH: *a paucity of good ideas*

Paul —see SAINT PAUL

Pau·ling /ˈpɔːlɪŋ/ **Li·nus** /ˈlaɪnəs/ (1901–   ) an American scientist noted for his work on how chemicals join together and for his opposition to the testing of NUCLEAR weapons. He won the Nobel prize for chemistry and the Nobel Peace Prize.

paunch /pɔːntʃ/ *n derog or humor* a fat stomach, esp. a man's: *He seems to be developing a paunch.* —**~y** *adj* — **~iness** *n* [U]

pau·per /ˈpɔːpəʳ/ *n* a very poor person, esp. one who in former times received official help

pause¹ /pɔːz/ *n* **1** [(in)] a short but noticeable break in activity, speech, etc.: *a pause in the conversation* | *They worked for almost six hours without a pause.* **2** a mark ( ) over a musical note, showing that the note is to be played or sung longer than usual **3** **give someone pause** to cause someone to stop and consider carefully what they are doing

pause² *v* [I] to make a pause; stop for a short time before continuing: *I had to pause for breath/to get my breath back.*

pa·vane /pəˈvæn, ˈpævən‖pəˈvɑːn, pəˈvæn/ *n* (the music for) a formal COURTLY dance of the 16th and 17th centuries

Pav·a·rot·ti /ˌpævəˈrɒti‖-ˈrɑː-/, **Lu·cia·no** /luːˈtʃɑːnəʊ/ (1935–   ) an Italian OPERA singer, considered to be one of the world's leading TENORs (–men with high singing voices), who has also given many concerts   see colour picture on page 554

pave /peɪv/ *v* [T (**with**) *usu. pass.*] **1** to cover (a path, area, etc.) with a hard level surface, esp. of PAVING STONES: *a paved courtyard* | *country boys who thought the streets of London were* **paved with gold** (=that London was a place of wealth and success) **2 pave the way for/to** to prepare for or make possible: *The agreement paves the way for a lasting peace.*

pave·ment /ˈpeɪvmənt/ *n* **1** *BrE* a paved surface or path at the side of a street for people to walk on; SIDEWALK – see picture at HOUSE **2** *AmE* the hard surface of a street **3** a paved surface of any sort; PAVING (2)

pavement art·ist /ˈ·· ˌ··/ *BrE* ‖ **sidewalk artist** *AmE* – *n* a person who draws pictures on a pavement with coloured chalk, hoping that people passing will give money

pavement caf·é /ˈ·· ˌ··‖ˈ·· ˌˌ·/ *BrE* ‖ **sidewalk cafe** *AmE* – *n* a CAFE (=restaurant serving light meals and drinks) with tables outside

pa·vil·ion /pəˈvɪljən/ *n* **1** *esp. BrE* a building beside a sports field, esp. a cricket field, for the use of the players and those watching the game **2** a large structure, lightly built and intended to be used for only a short time, used for public amusements or EXHIBITIONs: *the British pavilion at the World Trade Fair*

pav·ing /ˈpeɪvɪŋ/ *n* **1** [U] material used to pave a surface **2** [U] a paved surface of any sort; PAVEMENT (3) **3** [C *usu. pl.*] a paving stone —see also CRAZY PAVING

pavement café

paving stone /ˈ·· ·/ *n* a piece of flat stone, fitted close to other such stones to form a pavement

Pav·lov /ˈpævlɒv‖-lɑːv/, **I·van Pet·ro·vich** /ˈaɪvən ˈpetrəvɪtʃ/ (1849–1936) a Russian scientist best known for his work which proved the existence of the CONDITIONED REFLEX. Whenever he was going to feed the dogs he rang a bell, and the dogs soon started to get excited and want food when they heard the bell. —**Pavlovian** /pævˈləʊviən/ *adj*

pav·lo·va /pævˈləʊvə‖pɑːv-/ *n* a light cake made of MERINGUE, cream, and fruit esp. popular in Australia. It is thought to have been invented to celebrate a visit to Australia or New Zealand by Anna Pavlova.

Pavlova, An·na /ˈænə/ (1885–1931) a Russian BALLET dancer esp. remembered for her dancing of *The Dying Swan.* She is considered by many to have been the world's greatest ballet dancer.

paw¹ /pɔː/ *n* **1** an animal's foot that has nails or CLAWS: *a lion's paw* —compare HOOF **2** *infml, esp. humor* a human hand: *Go and wash your dirty paws!*

paw² *v* [I (**at**);T] **1** (of an animal) to touch or rub (a surface), esp. repeatedly, with a paw or HOOF, showing anger, fear, impatience, etc.: *The dog was pawing (at) the door, trying to get out.* | *an angry bull pawing the ground* **2** *infml* (of a person) to feel or touch with the hands, esp. in a rough and sexually improper manner: *She wanted to watch the film, but he kept pawing her.*

paw·ky /ˈpɔːki/ *adj esp. BrE* amusing in an odd clever way, so that one cannot tell whether the thing said was meant to be funny or serious: *The Scots are famous for their pawky humour.* —**kily** *adv* —**kiness** *n* [U]

pawn¹ /pɔːn/ *v* [T] to leave (something of value) with a pawnbroker as a promise that one will repay the money he has lent one: *He had to pawn his watch to pay for a meal.*

pawn² *n* [U] the state of having been pawned: *My watch is in pawn.*

pawn³ *n* **1** any of the eight smallest and least valuable playing pieces in the game of CHESS –see picture at CHESS **2** [(in)] an unimportant person used by someone else for their own advantage: *I was merely a pawn in his cunning stratagem.*

pawn·bro·ker /ˈpɔːnˌbrəʊkəʳ/ *n* a person to whom people bring valuable articles so that he will lend them money, and who has the right to sell the articles if the money is not repaid within a certain time. Pawnbrokers usu. lend less money than the value of the article and sell it at a profit if the owner cannot REDEEM it (=get it back by paying the money lent, with some extra money charged by the pawnbroker).

Paw·nee /pɔːˈniː/ *n* [C;*the*+P] (a member of) a Native American people who live on the PLAINS of the US, mainly now in Oklahoma —see NATIVE AMERICAN (CULTURAL NOTE)

pawn·shop /ˈpɔːnʃɒp‖-ʃɑːp/ *n* a pawnbroker's place of business. The sign for a pawnshop is three golden balls. In former times every town had a pawnshop, but they are now much less common. The pawnshop was the only place where poor people could borrow money, and poor families would sometimes have something such as a piece of furniture or clothing that was regularly pawned when money was needed.

paw·paw /ˈpɔːpɔː/ *n esp. BrE and CarE for* PAPAYA

Pax A·mer·i·ca·na /ˌpæks əmerɨ̩ˈkɑːnə/ the peace supposed to be established in the world by the presence of the power of the United States

Pax Bri·tan·ni·ca /ˌpæks brɪˈtænɪkə/ [(the)] the peace supposed to be established by British rule in the days of the British Empire

PAXO /ˈpæksəʊ/ n [U] tdmk (in Britain) a type of dried STUFFING, cooked and eaten esp. with turkey at Christmas

pay¹ /peɪ/ v **paid** /peɪd/ **1** [I;T (**for, to**)] to give (money) to (someone) in exchange for goods that one has bought, services that have been provided, or work that has been done: *She tried to leave the shop without paying (for the dress).* | *How soon can you pay me (for the work)?* | *The bank pays interest of 9% on savings.* | *We get paid by the hour|on Friday.* | *How much did you pay for that car?* | *"Are you paying cash?" "No, I'll pay by cheque."* | **I paid £200 for the painting.** [+obj(i)+obj(d)] *I paid him £200 (for this painting).* | *I paid it to him in instalments.* | *I'll pay you (£3) to clean my car.* | (fig.) *This washing machine should pay for itself within a year.* (=will make it possible to save the same amount of money as was needed to buy it) —see also PAY **for** **2** [T] to give (money that is owed); settle (a bill, debt, etc.): *Have you paid the electricity bill yet?* | *to pay one's taxes|train fare* **3** [T (IN, into)] to put (money, a cheque, etc.) into a bank, an account, etc., to be kept safe: *Have you paid the cheque in yet|paid it into your account yet?* **4** [I;T] to be profitable (to); produce advantage or gain that is worth the trouble or cost (to): *We must make the farm pay, or we'll have to sell it.* | *Crime doesn't pay.* | *It won't pay (you) to argue with her.* **5** [I+adv] (of work, something done, etc.) to bring or give one money or something of value in return: *This job pays well.* | *a poorly-paid job* **6** [T (**to**)] to give, offer, or make: *I shall* **pay a call** *on you tomorrow.* | **Pay attention** *to what I'm saying!* | *He certainly knows how to* **pay a compliment.** | *He* **paid his respects** *to the bishop.* [+obj(i)+obj(d)] *I'll* **pay you a visit** *next week.* **7 pay one's way** to pay money for things as one buys them so as not to get into debt **8 he who pays the piper calls the tune** *saying* the person who is paying for something can choose what it will be like **9 pay through the nose (for)** *infml* to pay far too much (for) − ~**er** n

pay sbdy./sthg. ↔ **back** phr v [T (**for**)] **1** to return (what is owing) to (someone); REPAY: *I'll pay you back tomorrow.* | *They can't pay back the loan.* [+obj(i)+obj(d)] *Have I paid you back the £10 I borrowed|paid the £10 back to you?* **2** also **pay out** BrE old-fash− to return bad treatment, rudeness, etc., to (someone who has done something wrong to oneself): *I'll pay him back for what he did to me!*

pay for sthg. phr v [T] to receive punishment or suffering for: *These people must be made to pay for their crimes.* | *He* **paid dearly** *for his unfaithfulness to her.* | (fig.) *We are paying for the fine summer with a wet winter.* [+v-ing] *I'll make him pay for ruining my chances.*

pay (sbdy./sthg. ↔) **off** phr v **1** [T] to pay the whole of (a debt) **2** [T] to pay and dismiss from a job: *His work was most unsatisfactory, so we paid him off at the end of the week.* **3** [T] to pay (someone) to keep silent about a wrong or illegal act **4** [I] to be successful: *Did your plan pay off?* —see also PAYOFF

pay (sbdy./sthg. ↔) **out** phr v **1** [I;T (=**pay** sthg. ↔ **out**)] to make a usu. large payment in return for (goods or services): *I paid out a lot of money for that car.* | *It's always me who has to pay out.* **2** [T] (**pay** sthg. ↔ **out**) to allow (esp. a rope) to be pulled out gradually to a greater length **3** [T] (**pay** sbdy. ↔ **out**) BrE old-fash for PAY **back** (2) —see also PAYOUT

pay sthg. ↔ **over** phr v [T (**to**)] to make formal payment of (money)

pay up phr v [I] to pay money that is owed, esp. unwillingly or late —compare PAID-UP

pay² n [U] **1** money received in exchange for work: *He gets his pay each Thursday.* | *They are negotiating for a pay increase|rise.* | *It's interesting work but the pay isn't very good.* | *holiday|sick pay* (=money given by an employer when one is on holiday or ill) **2 in the pay of** esp. derog employed by or working for: *an informer who is in the pay of the police*

▷ USAGE **Pay** is a general word for the money you receive for work, but **income** means any money you receive regularly, whether from work or from rents, etc.: *Have you any* **income** *apart from your pay?* A

salary is paid monthly into the bank (especially to professional people) and **wages** are paid weekly in cash (especially to people who work with their hands). Money paid for certain professional services (e.g. to a lawyer) is a **fee.**◁

pay·a·ble /ˈpeɪəbəl/ adj [F] **1** (of a bill, debt, etc.) that must or may be paid: *This bill is payable now.* | *payable in advance* —compare RECEIVABLE (2) **2** [+**to**] (of a cheque) having written on it the name of a particular person to whom the stated amount of money will be paid

pay·bed /ˈpeɪbed/ n BrE a hospital bed in a publicly-owned hospital used by a person who does not pay for their treatment but who pays to have better conditions, e.g. a private room

pay·cheque BrE ‖ **paycheck** AmE /ˈpeɪtʃek/ n **1** [C] a cheque for a person's wages **2** [U] esp. AmE the amount of wages a person earns —compare PAY PACKET

pay·day /ˈpeɪdeɪ/ n [U] the day on which wages are paid

pay dirt /ˈ· ·/ n [U] AmE **1** earth found to contain valuable minerals, such as gold **2** a valuable or useful discovery

PAYE /ˌpiː eɪ waɪ ˈiː/ n [U] pay as you earn; a system by which income tax and National Insurance Contributions are taken away from wages before the wages are paid

pay·ee /peɪˈiː/ n tech a person to whom money, esp. a cheque, is or should be paid

pay en·ve·lope /ˈ· ˌ···/ n AmE for PAY PACKET (1)

paying guest /ˌ·· ˈ·/ n a person who lives in a private house and pays rent to the owner; a LODGER

paying-in book /ˌ·· ˈ· ˌ·/ BrE ‖ **deposit book** AmE− n a book of forms used when paying money into one's account at a bank, or when making regular payments through the bank to another organization

pay·load /ˈpeɪləʊd/ n **1** (the weight of) the part of a load of a load-carrying vehicle for which payment is received **2** the amount of explosive in the head of a MISSILE **3** instruments and equipment carried in a spacecraft

pay·mas·ter /ˈpeɪˌmɑːstəʳ‖-ˌmæ-/ n **1** an official in a factory, the armed forces, etc., who pays wages to people **2** [often pl.] derog a person who pays someone to do usu. illegal work, and who therefore has control over the other person's actions: *He was forced by his paymasters in the secret service to keep quiet about these murders.*

Paymaster Gen·e·ral /ˌ··· ˈ···/ [the] the head of a British government department, the Paymaster General's Office, which provides bank services for other government departments

pay·ment /ˈpeɪmənt/ n **1** [U] the act of paying (PAY¹ (1,2,3)): *Here is a cheque* **in payment of** (=to pay) *my account.* | *We expect prompt payment.* | *The room can be reserved on payment of a small deposit.* | (fig.) *All the payment I got for my trouble was insults.* —see also NONPAYMENT **2** [C] an amount of money that has been or must be paid: *monthly mortgage payments of £300* —see also BALANCE OF PAYMENTS, DOWN PAYMENT

Payne /peɪn/, **Cyn·thi·a** /ˈsɪnθɪə/ (1933−) a British woman who was tried, but found not guilty in 1987, for running a house of PROSTITUTES (=women who have sex for money). She was said to have had wild parties in her London home in which police took part, and the newspapers called her "Madame Cyn."

pay·off /ˈpeɪɒf‖-ɔːf/ n [(the) S] infml **1** the act or time of paying wages, debts, money won at cards, etc.: *He got a big payoff for agreeing to lose the game deliberately.* **2** the end of a number of connected acts, esp. the end of a story someone has been telling, when everything is explained —see also PAY **off**

pay·o·la /peɪˈəʊlə/ n [S;U] infml, esp. AmE (the practice of making) a secret or not direct payment in return for a business favour: *That disc jockey expects some payola for agreeing to plug a record on his radio show.*

pay·out /ˈpeɪaʊt/ n infml (an act of making) a usu. large payment of money: *a big payout on this month's lottery.* —see also PAY **out**

pay pack·et /ˈ· ˌ··/ n BrE **1** ‖ **pay envelope** AmE− an envelope containing a person's pay. People who are given their pay in this way are usu. BLUE-COLLAR WORKERS —see PAY² (USAGE) **2** ‖ **paycheque** AmE −the amount of wages a person earns: *a large pay packet*

pay phone /ˈ· ·/ n a public telephone inside a public building which one can use only after putting in a coin

pay rise /ˈ· ·/ BrE ‖ **pay raise** AmE— n an increase in the amount one is paid for one's job

pay·roll /ˈpeɪrəʊl/ n **1** [C] a list of workers employed by a company and the amount of wages each person is to be paid: He's no longer **on their payroll**. (=no longer works for them) **2** [S] the total amount of wages paid to all the workers in a particular company

pay set·tle·ment /ˈ· ·ˌ····/ n an agreement on pay reached between unions and managers usu. after long argument

pay·slip /ˈpeɪslɪp/ n a piece of paper showing the amount paid to an employed person and the amount remaining after tax, etc.

Pay·ton /ˈpeɪtn/, **Wal·ter** /ˈwɔːltər/ (1954–) an American FOOTBALL (2) player who set records for running with the ball

PBS /ˌpiː biː ˈes/ n Public Broadcasting System; an American television company which is not run to make money and which broadcasts no advertising. It aims to put on good quality television programmes and is supported with money from people who watch these programmes, from the government, and from large companies. Two programmes for which PBS is known are Sesame Street and Masterpiece Theatre.

PC /ˌpiː ˈsiː/ abbrev. for: PERSONAL COMPUTER

P.C. /ˌpiː ˈsiː◂/ n BrE police constable; a policeman having the lowest rank: P.C. Johnson | Two P.C.'s were attacked. —see also W.P.C.

PCAS /ˈpiːkæs/ Polytechnics Central Admissions System; a British official organization which deals with people's requests to study at POLYTECHNICS

PCB /ˌpiː siː ˈbiː/ n POLYCHLORINATED BIPHENYL; one of several chemical compounds used in industry which are poisonous in the environment

PCC /ˌpiː siː ˈsiː/ abbrev. for: PAROCHIAL CHURCH COUNCIL

pcm abbrev per calendar month; used when stating e.g. the amount of rent payable on a house, etc.

PCP /ˌpiː siː ˈpiː/ n [U] AmE phencyclidine hydrochloride; an ANAESTHETIC drug for animals which some people take illegally because it produces HALLUCINATIONS (=experiences of seeing things which are not really there)

pd written abbrev. for: PAID

Pde written abbrev. for: PARADE¹ (4)

PDQ /ˌpiː diː ˈkjuː/ adv sl pretty damn (or darn) quick; immediately: If he doesn't get back here pdq there's going to be trouble.

PDSA /ˌpiː diː es ˈeɪ/ [the] the People's Dispensary for Sick Animals; a British organization (CHARITY) which provides free treatment for sick animals, esp. pets, whose owners cannot afford to pay to take the animal to a VET

PDT /ˌpiː diː ˈtiː/ abbrev. for: PACIFIC DAYLIGHT TIME

PE /ˌpiː ˈiː/ n [U] physical education; PT

pea /piː/ n **1** a large round green seed which is cooked and eaten as a vegetable: to shell peas —see picture at VEGETABLE **2** a climbing plant which produces long green PODs containing these seeds **3** **as like as two peas (in a pod)** infml (esp. of people) exactly the same in appearance —see also SWEET PEA

peace /piːs/ n **1** [S;U] a condition or period in which there is no war between two or more nations: Both warring nations longed for peace. | a peace treaty (=to end a war) | a dangerous situation that threatens world peace | The peace movement campaigns for the banning of nuclear weapons. **2** [the+S] a state of freedom from disorder within a country, with the citizens living according to the law: The job of the police is to **keep the peace**. | The youths were arrested for a **breach of the peace**. (=something, e.g. fighting, that breaks the public peace) **3** [U] **a** freedom from anxiety or troubling thoughts: Knowing that she had arrived safely restored my **peace of mind**. **b** freedom from unwanted noise or activity; calmness: Please let me get on with my work in peace. | All I want is a bit of **peace and quiet**. **4 at peace**: **a** in a state of quiet or calm **b** euph dead **5 hold one's peace** to remain silent even though one has something to say: In spite of his provocative remarks, I held my peace. **6 make one's peace with** to settle one's disagreements

with **7 peace in our time** quote a phrase used by the British politician Neville Chamberlain after his meeting with Adolf Hitler in Munich in 1938, when he thought he had prevented war from breaking out —see also MUNICH AGREEMENT **8 peace with honour** quote a phrase made popular by the 19th-century British politician Disraeli **9 rest in peace** a phrase used to bless the dead, said during a funeral service or written on a GRAVESTONE

peace·a·ble /ˈpiːsəbəl/ adj **1** disliking argument or quarrelling **2** calm; free from disorder or fighting: a peaceable agreement —**bly** adv : The two tribes live peaceably together.

peace camp /ˈ· ·/ n a camp set up outside a military base, esp. one having NUCLEAR weapons, by people protesting against military activities

Peace Corps /ˈ· ·/ [the] an American government organization which sends VOLUNTEERS (=people who give their services without payment), esp. young people, with technical knowledge to help DEVELOPING COUNTRIES (=poor countries which are trying to build up their industry)

peace div·i·dend /ˈ· ˌ····/ n the money saved on weapons and available for other purposes when a government reduces its military strength

peace·ful /ˈpiːsfəl/ adj **1** quiet and calm; untroubled: a peaceful afternoon by the river **2 a** without war: The best we can hope for is a state of **peaceful coexistence** between East and West. **b** without disorder: a peaceful demonstration —~**ly** adv —~**ness** n [U]

peace·keep·ing /ˈpiːskiːpɪŋ/ n the preserving of peace esp. between states or peoples who were recently at war or are about to go to war: a peacekeeping force/attempt

peace·mak·er /ˈpiːsmeɪkər/ n Bibl a person who tries to achieve peace between others who are fighting. In the Bible, it says "Blessed are the peacemakers: for they shall be called the children of God."

peace march /ˈ· ·/ n a march or other DEMONSTRATION by people who are protesting against violence or military activities: The Campaign for Nuclear Disarmament are organizing a peace march. | Protestants and Catholics united in a peace march and prayed for an end to violence in Northern Ireland.

peace of·fer·ing /ˈ· ˌ···/ n infml something offered to show that one wants to be friendly, esp. with someone whom one has annoyed

peace pipe /ˈ· ·/ also **pipe of peace**— n a ceremonial tobacco pipe smoked by Native Americans as a sign of peace —see colour picture on page 358

peace·time /ˈpiːstaɪm/ n [U] a time when a nation is not at war: Their armed forces have returned to peacetime levels. —opposite **wartime**

peace wom·en /ˈ· ˌ···/ n pl a name given to the women at the peace camp at GREENHAM COMMON

peach /piːtʃ/ n **1** [C] (a tree that produces) a round fruit with soft yellowish-red skin, sweet juicy flesh, and a large rough seed in its centre —see picture at FRUIT **2** [U] a light-yellowish pink colour **3** [S] infml a person or thing that is greatly admired: a peach of a hat (=a very fine or attractive one)

Peach Mel·ba /ˌpiːtʃ ˈmelbə/ n [C;U] half a peach served with ice cream and RASPBERRY juice

pea·cock /ˈpiːkɒk ‖ -kɑːk/ n **1** a large bird (a male peafowl), which has long tail feathers that can be spread out showing beautiful colours and patterns **2** also **peacock but·ter·fly** /ˌ·· ˈ···/— a BUTTERFLY with large wings which have patterns on them like those on the tail of a peacock **3** not tech a peahen

Peacock, Thomas Love (1785–1866) an English SATIRICAL writer and poet whose works include Headlong Hall and Nightmare Abbey

peacock blue /ˌ·· ˈ·◂/ adj having a bright shiny blue colour

pea·fowl /ˈpiːfaʊl/ n peafowl or peafowls a peacock or peahen

pea green /ˌ· ˈ·◂/ adj having a light bright green colour like that of PEAs

pea·hen /ˈpiːhen/ n a large brownish bird, the female peafowl

peak¹ /piːk/ n **1 a** a sharply pointed mountain top: The *(mountain) peaks are covered with snow all the year.* **b** a whole mountain with a pointed top: *Here the high peaks begin to rise from the plain.* —compare SUMMIT and see picture at MOUNTAIN **2** a part that curves to a point above a surface: *The wind blew the waves into great peaks.* **3** the highest point, level, etc., esp. of a varying amount, rate, etc.: *Sales have reached a new peak.* | *Demand for coal is at its peak in January and February.* —compare OFF-PEAK **4** the flat curved part of a cap which sticks out in front above the eyes —see picture at HAT

peak² *v* [I] to reach a PEAK¹ (3): *Sales have now peaked, and we expect them to decrease soon.*

peak³ *adj* [A] at the point of greatest activity, value, power, etc.: *The factory is running at peak productivity.* | *Athletes have to train continuously to stay in peak condition.*

Peak Dis·trict /ˈ·ˌ··/ *[the]* a hilly area and national park, mostly in N Derbyshire, N Central England. It is popular for climbing, walking, and POT HOLING.

Peake /piːk/, **Mer·vyn** /ˈmɜːvɪn‖ˈmɜːr-/ (1911–68) an English writer and ILLUSTRATOR born in China. His NOVELS include the strange fantasies (FANTASY) *Titus Groan, Gormenghast,* and *Titus Alone.*

peaked /piːkt/ *adj* having a PEAK¹ (4): *a peaked cap* —see picture at HAT

peak time /ˈ· ˌ·/ *n BrE* **1** a time when a stated activity, value, power, etc. is at its greatest level: *Peak times for electricity consumption are in the early evening.* | *We found that the peak time at this junction is 5.20 p.m.* **2** [U] *BrE,* also **peak viewing hours** *BrE* ‖ **prime time** *AmE—* the time when the number of people watching television is at its greatest. Television companies charge more during this time to put their advertisements on television. In Britain, peak time is between 7.30 and 10.30 at night, and in the US it is between 8 and 11 at night.

pea·ky /ˈpiːki/ *adj infml, esp. BrE* rather pale or ill: *I'm feeling a bit peaky this morning.* | *She's been looking rather peaky lately.*

peal¹ /piːl/ *n* **1** [(of)] a loud long sound or number of sounds one after the other: *a peal of thunder* | *peals of laughter* **2** the sound of the loud ringing of bells **3** *tech* **a** a musical pattern made by the ringing of a number of bells one after another **b** a set of bells on which these patterns can be played

peal² *v* [I (OUT);T] to (cause to) ring out or sound loudly: *The bells pealed out.*

pea·nut /ˈpiːnʌt/ also **groundnut** *BrE tech,* **monkey-nut** *old-fash— n* a nut which grows in a shell under the ground, and can be eaten —see also PEANUTS, and see picture at NUT

peanut but·ter /ˌ·· ˈ··‖ˈ·· ˌ··/ *n* [U] a soft substance made of crushed peanuts, usu. eaten on bread

peanut gal·le·ry /ˈ·· ˌ···/ *n AmE humor* the rows of seats at the back of a theatre or cinema, usu. on a raised platform, where the seats are cheap

pea·nuts /ˈpiːnʌts/ *n* [U] *infml* a sum of money so small that it is not worth considering: *He pays his workers peanuts.*

Peanuts a COMIC STRIP by the American CARTOONIST (=person who makes humorous drawings) Charles Schultz featuring a group of children. The main character is Charlie Brown, and other characters include Snoopy, Lucy, Linus, Pigpen, Sally, Peppermint Patty, and Schroeder.

pear /peəʳ/ *n* (a tree that produces) a sweet juicy fruit, which has a round base and usu. becomes narrower towards the stem —see picture at FRUIT

pearl /pɜːl‖pɜːrl/ *n* **1** [C] a hard round small silvery-white mass formed inside the shell of OYSTERS and similar creatures, very valuable as a jewel: *a pearl necklace* | *a string of pearls* | *(fig.) pearls of wisdom* **2** [U] the colour of this; silvery-white **3** [U] MOTHER-OF-PEARL: *a knife with a pearl handle* **4** **do not cast/throw pearls before swine** (=pigs) (a slightly changed saying from the Bible) do not give something valuable to someone who cannot understand its value: *The children were too young to understand the Shakespeare read to them; it was like casting pearls before swine.* | *Trying to explain to the fur traders why these animals should be preserved was like casting pearls before swine.*

pearl bar·ley /ˌ· ˈ··/ *n* [U] a variety of BARLEY with small round grains

pearl div·er /ˈ· ˌ··/ *n* a person who swims under water in the sea, looking for shells containing pearls

Pearl Har·bor /ˌ· ˈ··/ an American naval base in Hawaii which was the scene of a surprise Japanese air attack in 1941 which brought the US into the Second World War

pearl·y /ˈpɜːli‖ˈpɜːrli/ *adj* like or decorated with pearls: *pearly teeth* | *a pale pearly grey* —**iness** *n* [U]

pearly gates /ˌ·· ˈ·/ *n* *[the+P]* *often humor* the gates of heaven

pearly king /ˌ·· ˈ·/ **pearly queen** *fem— n* a person chosen from certain London families who has the right, on certain special occasions, to wear clothes richly decorated with patterns of **pearl buttons** (buttons made of, or looking like MOTHER-OF-PEARL)

pear·main /ˈpeəmeɪn‖ˈpeər-/ *n (usu. in comb.)* a type of apple

Pears /peəz‖peərz/ *n tdmk* a type of soap made by A & F Pears Ltd; Pears is generally considered to be good for the skin

▶ CULTURAL NOTE Pears is known in the UK for holding a competition every year to find the little girl with the prettiest face and the softest skin ◀

Pears /pɪəz‖pɪərz/, **Sir Peter** (1910–86) an English singer; a TENOR who started the ALDEBURGH FESTIVAL with Benjamin Britten in 1948

Pears Cy·clo·pae·di·a /ˌpeəz saɪklə'piːdiə‖ˌpeərz-/ a British book produced every year, containing information on politics, music, science, famous people, etc. in Britain and the US

pear-shaped /ˈ· ·/ *adj* shaped like a pear; wider at the bottom and narrower at the top. It is often said that this is the typical shape of a British woman.

peas·ant /ˈpezənt/ *n* **1** (now used esp. in connection with developing countries or former times) a person who works on the land, esp. one who owns and lives on a small piece of land **2** *infml derog* a person without education or good manners: *Don't be such a peasant!*

peas·ant·ry /ˈpezəntri/ *n [the+S+sing.|pl. v]* all the PEASANTS (1) of a particular country

Peasants' Re·volt /ˌ·· ·ˈ·/ *[the]* a mostly unsuccessful movement of English poor people (PEASANTS) in 1381 against unfair social and economic conditions

pease pud·ding /ˌpiːz ˈpʊdɪŋ/ *n* [U] *BrE* a dish made of dried PEAS, boiled to a soft yellow mass

pea·shoot·er /ˈpiːˌʃuːtəʳ/ *n* a small tube used by children for blowing small objects, esp. dried PEAS, at people or things

pea soup·er /ˌ· piː 'suːpəʳ/ *n infml old-fash* a thick heavy yellow FOG, often thought to be typical of London in the 19th and early 20th century

peat /piːt/ *BrE* ‖ *usu.* **peat moss** /ˌ· ·/ *AmE— n* **1** [U] partly decayed vegetable matter which takes the place of ordinary soil in certain areas (**peat bogs**), and is used for burning instead of coal or for making plants grow well **2** [C] a piece of this cut out to be used for making fires —**peaty** *adj*

Peat Mar·wick Mc·Lin·tock /ˌpiːt ˌmɑːwɪk məˈklɪntək ‖-ˌmɑːr-/ a very large international ACCOUNTANCY firm

peb·ble /ˈpebəl/ *n* **1** a small roundish smooth stone found esp. on the seashore or on a riverbed **2** **not the only pebble on the beach** not the only person who has to be considered; only one out of many others who deserve attention —**bly** *adj* : *a pebbly beach*

peb·ble·dash /ˈpebəldæʃ/ *n* [U] *BrE* CEMENT with lots of small pebbles set in it, used for covering the outside walls of a house

pe·can /pɪˈkæn, ˈpiːkən‖pɪˈkɑːn, pɪˈkæn/ *n* a nut with a long thin reddish shell. **Pecan pie** is a favourite sweet dish in the US.

pec·ca·dil·lo /ˌpekəˈdɪləʊ/ *n* -loes *or* -los a small unimportant fault or bad action: *His wife seems willing to overlook his little peccadilloes with other women.*

pec·ca·ry /ˈpekəri/ *n* peccaries *or* peccary a wild hairy piglike animal found esp. in Central and South America

peck¹ /pek/ *v* **1** [I (at);T] (of a bird) to strike with the beak: *Don't get too near that bird; it might peck you.* | *The hens were pecking at the corn.* (=picking it up with their beaks) | *It had pecked a hole in the bottom of its cage.* (=made a hole by pecking) | (fig.) *She seemed upset, and* *just pecked at her food.* (=ate it in small bites, without interest) **2** [T **(on)**] *infml* to kiss quickly, lightly, and without much feeling: *He pecked her on the cheek.* —see also HENPECKED

peck² *n* **1** a stroke or mark made by pecking **2** [(**on**)] *infml* a hurried kiss

peck³ *n* a measure of amount for dry substances such as fruit and grain —see TABLE 2

Peck, Greg·o·ry /ˈɡreɡəri/ (1916–) an American film actor whose many films include *Moby Dick* and *To Kill a Mockingbird*

peck·er /ˈpekəʳ/ *n* **1** *AmE sl for* PENIS **2 keep one's pecker up** *BrE infml* to remain cheerful even when it is difficult to do so

pecking or·der /ˈ·· ˌ··/ *n often humor* the social order of a particular group of people or animals, by means of which the members of the group know who is more important and who is less important than themselves

Peck·in·pah /ˈpekɪnpɑː/, **Sam** /sæm/ (1925–84) a US film director known for the violence of his films which include *The Wild Bunch* and *Straw Dogs*

peck·ish /ˈpekɪʃ/ *adj* [F] *infml, esp. BrE* slightly hungry

pec·tic /ˈpektɪk/ *adj* [A] *tech* of or from pectin

pec·tin /ˈpektɪn/ *n* [U] *tech* a sugar-like chemical substance found in certain fruits, which is important in making JAMS and jellies

pec·to·ral /ˈpektərəl/ *adj tech* of the chest: *pectoral muscles*

pectoral cross /ˌ··· ˈ·/ *n tech* a decorative cross worn on the chest by BISHOPS

pe·cu·li·ar /pɪˈkjuːliəʳ/ *adj* **1** strange or unusual, esp. in a troubling or displeasing way: *What a peculiar thing to say! | This meat tastes peculiar; I hope it's all right. | It's rather peculiar that we were not given this information until now.* **2** [F+**to**] belonging only (to a particular person, place, time, etc.); EXCLUSIVE: *This style of cooking is peculiar to the south-west of the country. | a plant species peculiar to the Scilly Islands* **3** *euph* rather mad; ECCENTRIC **4** [F] *infml* rather ill: *I'm feeling a bit peculiar — I think I'll go and lie down.* —see also PECULIARLY

pe·cu·li·ar·i·ty /pɪˌkjuːliˈærɪti/ *n* **1** [U] the quality of being peculiar **2** [C] something which is PECULIAR (2) to a particular person, place, time, etc.: *The lack of a written constitution is a peculiarity of the British political system.* **3** [C] a strange or unusual habit, quality, etc.

pe·cu·li·ar·ly /pɪˈkjuːliəli‖-ər-/ *adv* **1** especially: *a peculiarly difficult question.* **2** strangely: *He's been behaving most peculiarly.* **3** in a way that is PECULIAR (2) to a particular person, place, time, etc.: *a peculiarly British phenomenon* (=found only in Britain)

pe·cu·ni·a·ry /pɪˈkjuːniəri‖-nieri/ *adj fml or pomp* connected with or consisting of money: *pecuniary gain/motives*

ped·a·gogue /ˈpedəɡɒɡ‖-ɡɑːɡ/ *n* **1** *derog* a teacher who is too concerned with rules **2** *old use or humor* a teacher

ped·a·go·gy /ˈpedəɡɒdʒi‖-ɡəʊ-/ *n* [U] *tech* the practice of teaching or the study of teaching methods —**gic** /ˌpedəˈɡɒdʒɪk◂‖-ˈɡɑː-, -ˈɡəʊ-/, —**gical** *adj* —**gically** /kli/ *adv*

ped·al¹ /ˈpedl/ *n* a barlike part of a machine which can be pressed with the foot in order to control the working of the machine or to drive it: *One of the pedals has come off my bicycle. | the accelerator pedal on a car | an organ pedal | a pedal boat* (=worked by pedals) —see picture at BICYCLE

pedal² *v* [I;T] **-ll-** *BrE* ‖ **-l-** *AmE* **1** to work the pedals of (a machine): *I pedalled like mad but nothing happened.* **2** [(+*obj*)+*adv/prep*] to ride (a bicycle): *He pedalled the bicycle up the hill. | I was just pedalling along.* —see also SOFT-PEDAL

pedal bin /ˈ·· ·/ *n* a container for waste, esp. in a kitchen, which stands on the floor and has a lid which is opened by pressing a pedal with your foot

pedal steel gui·tar /ˌ·· · ·ˈ·/ *n* see STEEL GUITAR

ped·ant /ˈpednt/ *n derog* a person who pays too much attention to small details and unimportant rules — **~ic** /pɪˈdæntɪk/ *adj* : *a pedantic teacher* — **~ically** /kli/ *adv*

ped·ant·ry /ˈpedntri/ *n* **1** [U] the quality of being a pedant **2** [C *usu. pl.*] a pedantic expression or action

ped·dle /ˈpedl/ *v* [T] *usu. derog* **1** to try to sell by going

from place to place: *She was sent to prison for peddling drugs.* **2** to try to spread (opinions, false information, etc.): *I don't know who's been peddling these nasty rumours about me.*

ped·dler /ˈpedləʳ/ *n* **1** *old-fash* a person who peddles dangerous or illegal drugs **2** *AmE for* PEDLAR

ped·e·rast /ˈpedəræst/ *n AmE for* PAEDERAST

ped·es·tal /ˈpedɪstəl/ *n* **1** the base on which a PILLAR or STATUE stands —see picture at STATUE **2** a position of (too) great respect: *However much you admire her, you shouldn't try and* **put her on a pedestal.** (=treat her as if she is perfect or better than anyone else)

pe·des·tri·an¹ /pɪˈdestriən/ *n* a person travelling on foot, esp. in a street or other place used by cars —compare MOTORIST

pedestrian² *adj* **1** *derog* lacking in imagination or any special qualities; dull: *a rather pedestrian student | a pedestrian performance* **2** [A] of or for pedestrians: *a pedestrian precinct* (=an area where motor traffic is not allowed)

pedestrian cross·ing /ˌ···· ˈ··/ *BrE* ‖ also **crosswalk** *AmE*— *n* a special place for pedestrians to cross the road —see also PELICAN CROSSING, ZEBRA CROSSING

pe·di·a·tri·cian /ˌpiːdiəˈtrɪʃən/ *n AmE for* PAEDIATRICIAN

pe·di·at·rics /ˌpiːdiˈætrɪks/ *n* [U] *AmE for* PAEDIATRICS

ped·i·cure /ˈpedɪkjʊəʳ/ *n* [C;U] (a) treatment of the feet and toenails, to make them more comfortable or more beautiful —compare MANICURE¹ —**-curist** *n*

ped·i·gree¹ /ˈpedɪɡriː/ *n* [C;U] (an official description of) the set of people or animals from whom a person or animal is descended; ANCESTRY: *Examine its pedigree carefully before you buy such an expensive cat. | a dog of unknown pedigree | a young woman of impeccable pedigree* (=from an ancient family)

pedigree² *adj* [A] (of an animal) descended from a long, recorded, and usu. specially chosen family of animals, and therefore of high quality: *a pedigree dog* —compare MONGREL (1), PUREBRED, THOROUGHBRED

Pedigree Chum /ˌ··· ·ˈ·/ *n* [U] *tdmk* a range of different types of food for dogs, made by Pedigree Petfoods; it is generally considered to be high quality food which is good for dogs

ped·i·ment /ˈpedɪmənt/ *n* a three-sided piece of stone or other material placed above the entrance to a building, found esp. in the buildings of ancient Greece

ped·lar ‖ also **peddler** *AmE* /ˈpedləʳ/ *n* a person who, in the past, went from place to place trying to sell small articles

pe·do·phile /ˈpiːdəfaɪl/ *n AmE for* PAEDOPHILE

pee¹ /piː/ *v* [I] *infml for* URINATE

pee² *n infml* **1** [S] an act of urinating (URINATE): *I must go for/have a pee.* **2** [U] URINE

Pee·bles·shire /ˈpiːbəlʒəʳ/ a former COUNTY in S Scotland, now part of the Borders REGION

peek /piːk/ *v* [I (**at**)] *infml* to take a quick look at something, esp. when one should not: *They caught him peeking through the keyhole at what was going on in the room.* —compare PEEP¹, PEER² —**peek** *n* [S (**at**)] : *to take/have a peek*

peek·a·boo /ˌpiːkəˈbuː/ *also* **peepbo**— *interj, n* [U] (a shout used in) a game played to amuse babies, in which you repeatedly hide your face and then bring it back into view, saying "peek-a-boo"

peel¹ /piːl/ *v* **1** [T] to remove the outer covering from (a fruit, vegetable, etc.): *a machine that peels potatoes* **2** [T+*obj*+*adv/prep*] to remove (the outer covering) from something: *She peeled the skin off the banana. | He peeled away the outer layers of the onion. |* (fig.) *They peeled off their clothes and jumped into the water.* **3** [I] **a** to lose an outer covering or surface: *The walls were damp and were peeling.* **b** (of an outer covering or surface) to come off, esp. in small pieces: *Wallpaper was peeling off the damp walls. | My skin always peels when I've been in the sun.* **4 keep one's 'eyes peeled** *infml* to keep careful watch for anything dangerous or unusual which may happen — **~er** *n* : *a potato peeler*

peel off *phr v* [I] (of an aircraft) to turn and move away from other aircraft in the air

peel² *n* [U] the outer covering of certain fruits and vegetables, esp. of those which one usu. peels before eating: *One*

speaks of *orange peel* and *apple peel*, but of *tomato skin*.
—compare RIND (1); see also PEELINGS; see RIND (USAGE),
and see picture at FRUIT

Peel, Rob·ert /ˈrɒbət‖ˈrɑːbərt/ (1788–1850) a British Conservative politician who established the first official British police force and introduced freedoms for Roman
Catholics. He was PRIME MINISTER from 1834 to 1835 and
1841 to 1846.

peel·er /ˈpiːləʳ/ n **1** a special type of knife for peeling fruit
or vegetables **2** *BrE old-fash* (*often cap.*) a policeman
(from Sir Robert Peel, who began the London police force
in 1829)

peel·ings /ˈpiːlɪŋz/ n [P] parts peeled off, esp. from potatoes

peep[1] /piːp/ v [I] **1** [(at)] to look at something quickly and
secretly, esp. through a hole or other small opening: *I
caught him peeping at my work.* | *peeping through the cur-
tains* **2** [+adv/prep] to begin slowly to appear; come
partly into view: *The flowers are beginning to peep
through the soil.* | *strands of hair peeping out from under
her hat* —compare PEEK, PEER[2]

peep[2] n [S (at)] a quick, incomplete, or secret look: *He took
a peep at the back of the book to find out the answers to
the questions.*

peep[3] n **1** [C] a short weak high sound as made by a young
bird or a mouse **2** [S] *infml* a sound, esp. something
spoken: *I don't want to hear a peep out of you until din-
nertime.* (=be quiet!) | *We haven't* **had a peep out of**
(=haven't heard from) *them for over a month.* **3** [C] *BrE*
also **beep** (used esp. by or to children) the sound of a car's
horn

peep[4] v [I] to make a PEEP[3] (1)

peep·bo /ˈpiːpbəʊ/ *interj, n* [U] PEEKABOO

peep·er /ˈpiːpəʳ/ n **1** [*usu. pl.*] *infml* an eye: *Keep your
peepers open!* (=watch carefully!) **2** *usu. derog* someone
who PEEPS[1] (1), esp. a PEEPING TOM

peep·hole /ˈpiːphəʊl/ n a small hole, esp. in a door or wall,
through which one can peep at something. They are often
found in doors for safety reasons so that the person inside can check who is outside before opening the door.

peeping Tom /ˌpiːpɪŋ ˈtɒm‖-ˈtɑːm/ n derog a person who
secretly looks at others who think they are not being
watched, esp. when they are undressing (from the story
of Peeping Tom who is said to have been a TAILOR from
the city of Coventry in central England, who peeped at
Lady Godiva as she rode through the city with no clothes
on and was struck blind)

peep show /ˈ· ·/ n **1** an esp. sexy entertainment (e.g. a
film) or object (e.g. a photograph) seen through a small
hole usu. fitted with glass to make the image bigger **2**
a live show with sexy entertainment

peer[1] /pɪəʳ/ n **1** *fml or tech* a person of the same age, class,
position, etc., as oneself: *The opinions of his peers are
more important to him than his parents' ideas.* | *Children
are very susceptible to peer pressure.* —see also PEERLESS
2 also **peer of the realm**— (in Britain) a member of any
of five noble ranks, BARON, VISCOUNT, EARL, MARQUIS, and
DUKE, who has the right to sit in the House of Lords —
see also LIFE PEER, PEERESS

peer[2] v [I+adv/prep] to look very carefully or hard, esp. as
if not able to see clearly: *She peered through the mist, try-
ing to find the right path.* | *He peered at me over the top
of his glasses* —compare PEEK, PEEP[1]

peer·age /ˈpɪərɪdʒ/ n **1** [(*the*) C] the rank of a PEER[1] (2):
*After ten years in the government she was given a peer-
age*|*was* **raised to the peerage. 2** [*the*+S+*sing.|pl.*] all
the peers, considered as a group **3** [C] a book containing a list of peers and the families from which they are
descended

peer·ess /ˈpɪərɪs/ n **1** a female PEER[1] (1) **2** the wife of
a PEER[1] (1)

peer group /ˈ· ·/ n a group of people of the same age, class,
background, etc. (as oneself): *Children are very susceptible to* **peer-group pressure**/*pressure from their peer
group.*

peer·less /ˈpɪələs‖ˈpɪər-/ adj fml apprec without an equal;
better than any other: *peerless beauty*

peer pres·sure /ˈ· ˌ··/ n the pressure to be the same as one's
peers. This phrase usu. means the pressure on young
people to smoke, drink, take drugs, etc., when they feel
they must do such things to have friends.

peeve /piːv/ v [T *often pass.*] *infml* to make (someone) feel
angry and offended: *I was very peeved by his refusal to
cooperate.*

peev·ish /ˈpiːvɪʃ/ adj bad-tempered; easily annoyed by
unimportant things – ~**ly** adv – ~**ness** n [U]

pee·wit /ˈpiːwɪt/ n a LAPWING

peg[1] /peg/ n **1** a short piece of wood, metal, etc., usu. thinner at one end than at the other, used for fastening things,
hanging things on, etc: *Hang your coat on the peg in the
hall.* | *First hammer the tent pegs into the ground, then
tie the ropes onto them.* | (fig.) *He'll use anything as a peg
to hang an argument on.* **2** also **clothes peg**
BrE ‖ **clothespin** *AmE*— a small piece of plastic or wood
with two points, or two rounded ends held together by
a spring, used for fixing washed clothes to a line to dry
3 also **tuning peg**— a wooden screw used to tighten or
loosen the strings of certain musical instruments **4**
BrE, becoming rare a small amount of a strong alcoholic
drink, esp. WHISKY or BRANDY **5 off the peg**‖**off the rack**
(of clothes) not specially made to fit a particular person's
measurements: *He buys his suits off the peg.* | *Off-the-peg
clothes are usually cheaper.* | (fig.) *off-the-peg computer
software* (=not specially written for a particular user) –
compare BESPOKE, **off the shelf** (SHELF) **6 take someone 'down a peg (or two)** *infml* to show someone that
they are not as important as they thought they were –
see also **square peg in a round hole** (SQUARE[2])

pegs

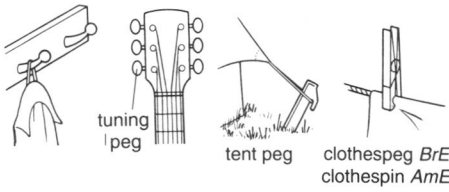

tuning peg | tent peg | clothespeg *BrE*/
clothespin *AmE*

peg[2] v -gg- [T] **1** to fasten with a peg **2** [(OUT, UP)] *BrE*
to fasten (wet clothes) to a rope with a peg for drying **3**
to fix or hold (prices, wages, etc.) at a certain level
peg away at sthg. *phr v* [T *no pass.*] *infml* to work hard
and steadily at
peg out *phr v* **1** [T] (**peg** sthg. ↔ **out**) to mark (a piece
of ground) with wooden sticks **2** [I] *infml, esp. BrE* to die

Peg·a·sus /ˈpegəsəs/ in CLASSICAL MYTHOLOGY, a horse with
wings

peg·board /ˈpegbɔːd‖-bɔːrd/ n **1** a small RECTANGULAR
board with holes in it used to record a player's points in
certain esp. card games **2** [U] material (e.g. FIBREBOARD)
with holes in it into which one puts PEGs or hooks for
hanging articles on

peg leg /ˈ· ·/ n *infml* an artificial leg, esp. a wooden one

Peirce /pɪəs‖pɪərs/, **Charles San·ders** /ˈtʃɑːlz ˈsɑːndəz‖
tʃɑːrlz ˈsændərz/ (1838–1914) an American thinker
(PHILOSOPHER), who said that the meaning of an idea depended on the results that idea would have. His most important writings were put together after his death in a
book called *Chance, Love and Logic.*

pe·jo·ra·tive /pɪˈdʒɒrətɪv‖-ˈdʒɔː-, -ˈdʒɑː-/ adj fml (of a word,
phrase, etc.) expressing disapproval or suggesting that
someone or something is of little value or importance:
*Many women now consider "housewife" a pejorative ex-
pression, because it patronizes them.* – ~**ly** adv

pe·kin·ese, pekingese /ˌpiːkɪˈniːz◂/ also **peke** /piːk/*infml*—
n pekinese or pekineses (often cap.) a very small dog
with a short flat nose and long silky hair –see picture
at DOG

Pe·king /ˌpiːˈkɪŋ◂/ another name for Beijing, now regarded
as old-fashioned

Peking duck /ˌ·· ˈ·/ n a special Chinese dish of ROAST duck
served with SPRING ONIONS and a special SAUCE (=liquid
with a particular taste)

pe·koe /ˈpiːkəʊ/ n [U] a kind of tea made from the BUD
(=youngest part) of the tea plant. It is esp. popular in the
US.

pe·lag·ic /pɪˈlædʒɪk/ adj fml or tech connected with or living in the deep sea far from the shore

Pel·é /ˈpeleɪ‖peˈleɪ/ (1940–) a Brazilian footballer considered by many to be the greatest footballer ever. He played for Brazil in three World Cups and then went to the US, where he helped to make football more popular.

pel·i·can /ˈpelɪkən/ n **pelicans** or **pelican** a large water bird which catches fish for food and stores them in a deep baglike part under its beak —see picture at WATER BIRD

pelican cross·ing /ˌ···ˈ··/ n (in Britain) a PEDESTRIAN CROSSING where someone wishing to cross the road can stop the traffic by working special TRAFFIC LIGHTS. Pelican crossings are known by the figures of a standing red man which appears on the lights when it is not safe to cross and a walking green man which appears when it is safe. —compare ZEBRA CROSSING

pel·lag·ra /pɪˈlægrə/ n [U] a disease which is caused by a lack of a type of B VITAMIN, and produces great tiredness and disorder of the skin and CENTRAL NERVOUS SYSTEM

pel·let /ˈpelɪt/ n **1** [(of)] a small ball of any soft substance made (as if) by rolling between the fingers: *hens fed on pellets of food* **2** a small ball of metal made to be fired from a gun

pell-mell /ˌpel ˈmel◂/ adv old-fash in a disorderly hurry: *children running pell-mell down the street*

pel·lu·cid /pɪˈluːsɪd/ adj lit very clear; TRANSPARENT: *a pellucid stream* – ~ly adv

pel·met /ˈpelmɪt/ esp. BrE ‖ **valance** esp. AmE– n a narrow piece of wood or cloth above a window that hides the rod on which curtains hang

Pel·o·pon·nese /ˌpeləpəˈniːs◂/ a mountainous area forming S Greece

Pel·o·pon·ne·sian Wars /ˌpeləpəniːʃən ˈwɔːz‖-ˈwɔːrz/ [the+P] wars between two powers, Sparta and Athens, which are today in Greece, between 431 and 404 BC. Their history was recorded by Thucydides.

pe·lot·a /pəˈlɒtə‖-ˈloʊ-/ n [U] a ball game played esp. in Spain, America, and the Philippines, in which a long basket tied to the wrist is used to hit the ball against a wall

pelt¹ /pelt/ v **1** [T (with)] to attack (someone) by throwing a lot of things at them, quickly and repeatedly: *They pelted the speaker with rotten tomatoes.* | (fig.) *The children pelted him with questions about his journey.* **2** [I (DOWN)] (of rain) to fall heavily and continuously: *I'm not going out there – it's really pelting (down)!* | (esp. BrE) *It's pelting with rain.* **3** [I+adv/prep] to run very fast: *The boys came pelting down the hill.*

pelt² n **(at) full pelt** (moving, running, etc.) as fast as possible

pelt³ n **1** the skin of a dead animal **a** with the fur or hair still on it **b** with the fur or hair removed and ready to be prepared as leather **2** the fur or hair of a living animal

pel·vic /ˈpelvɪk/ adj med of or near the pelvis: *the pelvic bones*

pel·vis /ˈpelvɪs/ n **-vises** or **-ves** /viːz/ the bowl-shaped frame of bones at the base of the SPINE, to which the leg bones are joined —see picture at SKELETON

Pem·broke /ˈpembruk‖-brəuk/ a market town in Dyfed, SW Wales

Pem·broke·shire /ˈpembrukʃər ‖ -brəuk-/ a former COUNTY in SW Wales now forming part of Dyfed

pem·mi·can , pemican /ˈpemɪkən/ n [U] dried meat beaten into small pieces and pressed into flat round shapes, used by travellers in distant places where food cannot be found

pen¹ /pen/ n **1** an instrument for writing or drawing with ink: *a ballpoint pen* | *a fountain pen* | *a felt-tip pen* **2 the pen is mightier than the sword** quote words and books can have a stronger influence on events than the use of force (from a poem by Edward Bulwer-Lytton) **3 put/set pen to paper** to start to write

pen² v **-nn-** [T (to)] pomp to write with a pen

pen³ n (often in comb.) a small piece of land enclosed by a fence, used esp. for keeping animals in: *a sheep pen* – see also PLAYPEN

pen⁴ v **-nn-** [T (UP, in, IN)] **1** to shut (animals) in a pen **2** to shut (people) in a small space

pen⁵ n AmE sl a prison (short for PENITENTIARY)

pe·nal /ˈpiːnl/ adj **1** [A] of or for legal punishment: *the government's penal policy* (=how it runs prisons, punishes criminals, etc.) | *a* **penal colony/settlement** (=place where prisoners are kept) *on an island* | *He was sentenced to 12 years'* **penal servitude.** (=imprisonment with hard physical work) **2** [A] punishable by law: *a penal offence* **3** very severe; severely unpleasant: *penal rates of taxation* – ~ly adv

penal code /ˈ·· ˌ·/ n a system of laws and statements of the punishments for breaking them

pe·nal·ize also **-ise** BrE /ˈpiːnəl-aɪz‖ˈpiː-, ˈpe-/ v [T (for)] **1** to put (someone) in a very unfavourable or unfair position: *The new tax laws penalize people who earn less than £7000 a year.* **2** (in sports) to punish (a team or player) by giving an advantage to the other team, esp. by giving the other team a PENALTY (3b): *England were penalized for wasting time.* —**ization** /ˌpiːnəl-aɪˈzeɪʃən‖ˌpiːnəl-ə-, ˌpe-/ n [U]

penal sys·tem /ˈ·· ˌ··/ n a system of legal punishment. In Britain this includes FINES (=a payment of money), PROBATION (=going free under certain conditions), and imprisonment, but does not include the DEATH PENALTY.

pen·al·ty /ˈpenlti/ n **1** [(for)] a punishment for breaking a law, rule, or legal agreement: *She has paid* (=suffered) **the penalty** *for her reckless drive five years in prison.* | *The law imposes tough penalties on advertisers who do not tell the truth.* | *Some politicians would like to restore the* **death penalty** *for people convicted of terrorism.* | *The maximum penalty for murder is life imprisonment.* | *Fishing in this river is forbidden – penalty £5.* **2** [(of)] suffering or loss that is the result of one's unwise action or of one's condition or situation: *One of the penalties of fame is that people point at you in the street.* **3** (in sports) **a** a disadvantage given to a player or team for breaking a rule: *If you pick up the ball with your hand in golf, you suffer a penalty.* **b** an advantage given to a team because the other team have broken a rule: *Liverpool were given/awarded a penalty (kick) when one of their opponents handled the ball.* **c** also **penalty goal** /ˈ··· ·/– (in football) a GOAL gained by this means

penalty ar·e·a /ˈ··· ˌ···/ also **penalty box** infml– n (in football) a space in front of the GOAL where the breaking of a rule means that the opposing team gets a PENALTY (3b)

penalty box /ˈ··· ˌ·/ n **1** (in ICE HOCKEY) a box in which a player must sit for several minutes if he has broken the rules while playing: *The referee sent him to the penalty box for two minutes for high sticking (holding his stick in a way that is dangerous to other players).* **2** (in football) the penalty area

penalty clause /ˈ··· ˌ·/ n part of a contract which places penalties on the person(s) doing the work if it is not completed on time

penalty goal /ˈ··· ˌ·/ n a GOAL scored by a penalty kick in RUGBY

penalty kick /ˈ··· ˌ·/ also **penalty–** n **1** (in football) a free kick at the GOAL given to a team because the other team have broken a rule in the penalty area. The GOAL is defended only by the GOALKEEPER. **2** (in RUGBY) a FREE KICK

penalty points /ˈ··· ˌ·/ BrE ‖ **points** AmE– n [usu. pl.] points given as penalties for certain driving offences and which appear on the driver's licence. When the points reach a certain total the driver is forbidden to drive for a set period.

penalty shoot-out /ˌ··· ˈ· ·/ n an additional competition played at the end of some football matches to decide who wins, when the match has ended in a draw. Players from each team take penalty kicks, and the team that scores (SCORE (1)) the most wins the match.

pen·ance /ˈpenəns/ n [U (for)] the action of willingly making oneself suffer, esp. for religious reasons, to show that one is sorry for having done wrong: *do penance for one's sins*

► CULTURAL NOTE In some Christian churches, esp. the Roman Catholic church, penance takes the form of saying prayers and is given by a priest after telling him what one has done wrong and being forgiven for it. ◄

pen-and-ink¹ /ˌ·· ˈ·◂/ adj (of a drawing) produced using a pen and (usu. black) ink, rather than brush and paint, and therefore using lines and shading rather than solid colours

pen-and-ink² /ˌ·· '·/ n BrE humor sl an unpleasant smell, a STINK² (1)

pence /pens/ BrE **1** (often in comb.) pl. of PENNY: twopence | eleven pence | a few pence —see PENNY (USAGE), compare CENT **2** -pence also p— having the value of the stated number of pennies: a 13-pence stamp | a 5p piece (=coin) **3** not have two pence to rub together infml to be very poor: He couldn't possibly afford a holiday abroad—he hasn't got two pence to rub together!

pen·chant /'pɒnʃɒn, 'pentʃənt‖'pentʃənt/ n [(for) usu. sing.] Fr a liking, esp. for something that is slightly disapproved of by other people: a penchant for fast cars

pen·cil¹ /'pensəl/ **1** a narrow pointed usu. wooden instrument used for writing or drawing, containing a thin stick of a black or coloured material: written with a pencil/in pencil | a pencil sketch | to sharpen a blunt pencil **2** [(of)] a narrow beam (of light) beginning from or ending in a small point —see also EYEBROW PENCIL

pencil² v -ll- BrE ‖ -l- AmE
pencil sbdy./sthg. **in** phr v [T] to include for the present time, e.g. on a list or in an arrangement, with the possibility of being changed later: I've pencilled you in for the match on Saturday; tell me as soon as you know for certain if you can play.

pencil push·er /'·· ˌ·/ n AmE a PEN PUSHER

pen·dant, -dent /'pendənt/ n a hanging piece of jewellery, esp. a long chain worn round the neck with a small decorative object hanging from it

pen·dent /'pendənt/ adj fml or tech **1** hanging supported from above: a pendent lamp **2** hanging over; sticking out beyond a surface: pendent rocks

pend·ing¹ /'pendɪŋ/ prep fml while waiting for; until: We delayed our decision pending his return from Europe.

pending² adj **1** [F] fml not yet decided or settled: The letter's in the pending file/tray (=a FILE/TRAY where papers are kept which cannot be dealt with yet, e.g. because they are about something which has not yet happened, or because more information is needed) **2** [A] soon to happen; IMPENDING

pen·du·lous /'pendjʊləs‖-dʒə-/ adj fml hanging down loosely so as to swing freely: pendulous breasts — — ly adv

pen·du·lum /'pendjʊləm‖-dʒə-/ n **1** a weight that hangs from a fixed point and swings freely **2** a rod with a weight at the bottom, used to control the working of a clock **3** something that tends to change regularly from one position to an opposite one: Since the last election, the pendulum of public opinion has swung back against the government.

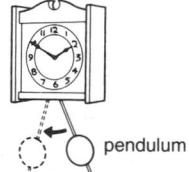
pendulum
pendulum

Pe·nel·o·pe /pə'neləpi/ in CLASSICAL MYTHOLOGY, the wife of Odysseus who remained faithful to him during his long absence

pen·e·trate /'penɪtreɪt/ v **1** [I (into, through);T] to enter, pass, cut, or force a way (into or through): The knife penetrated his stomach. | The rain had penetrated right through (his clothes) to his skin. | The noise of the explosion penetrated the thickest walls. | They are hoping to penetrate the Japanese market (=begin selling goods there) with their latest product. **2** [T] to see into or through: My eyes couldn't penetrate the gloom. | (fig.) the scientists who first penetrated the mystery of the atom | He had a false beard on, but we soon penetrated his disguise. (=recognized that it was him) **3** [I] infml to come to be understood: I heard what you said, but it didn't penetrate. —compare PIERCE; see also IMPENETRABLE —-trable /trəbəl/ adj —-trability /ˌpenɪtrə'bɪlɪti/ n [U]

pen·e·trat·ing /'penɪtreɪtɪŋ/ adj **1** (of the eye, sight, a question, etc.) sharp and searching: his penetrating gaze **2** (of a person, the mind, etc.) able to understand clearly and deeply; ACUTE **3** (of a sound) sharp and loud: a penetrating whistle **4** spreading and reaching everywhere: penetrating dampness — — ly adv

pen·e·tra·tion /ˌpenɪ'treɪʃən/ n [U] **1** the act or process of penetrating: The company has had a successful first year at home but penetration of the international market has been slow. **2** fml apprec the ability to understand quickly

and clearly; INSIGHT **3** tech the putting of the male sex organ into the female sex organ when having sex

pen·e·tra·tive /'penɪtrətɪv‖-treɪtɪv/ adj **1** able to penetrate easily **2** (of a person, their mind, etc.) keen; INTELLIGENT: her penetrative observations — — ly adv

pen friend /'· ·/ ‖ **pen pal** esp. AmE— n a person, esp. in a foreign country, with whom one has made friends by writing letters, but whom one has probably never met. Students learning a foreign language are often encouraged to find a pen friend, and this can be done through organizations established for this purpose.

pen·guin /'peŋgwɪn/ n an often large black-and-white seabird, esp. of the Antarctic, which cannot fly but uses its wings for swimming —see picture at WATER BIRD

Penguin tdmk a PAPERBACK book produced by Penguin Books. Probably the best known name of paperbacks, Penguin were the first good books to appear as paperbacks at a reasonable price.

pen·i·cil·lin /ˌpenɪ'sɪlɪn/ n [U] a substance used as a medicine to destroy certain bacteria in people and animals; a powerful ANTIBIOTIC. It was the first antibiotic and although others are now more often used it is the best-known. Some people, esp. older people, use the word to mean any antibiotic.

pe·nin·su·la /pɪ'nɪnsjʊlə‖-sələ/ n a piece of land almost completely surrounded by water but joined to a larger mass of land: Italy is a peninsula. ---**lar** adj

Peninsular War /·ˌ··· '·/ [the] a war fought in Spain and Portugal between France and Britain, which began in 1808 when Napoleon I INVADED Spain, and continued until he was defeated in 1814

pe·nis /'piːnɪs/ n the outer sex organ of male animals that is used for passing water from the body and in sexual activity

pen·i·tent¹ /'penɪtənt/ adj fml feeling or showing that one is sorry for having done wrong and that one intends not to do so again; REPENTANT —opposite **impenitent** — — ly adv —-**tence** n [U (for)]

penitent² n a person who is doing or suffering religious PENANCE

pen·i·ten·tial /ˌpenɪ'tenʃəl◁/ adj of penitence or PENANCE — — ly adv

pen·i·ten·tia·ry /ˌpenɪ'tenʃəri/ n a prison, esp. in the US: the state penitentiary

pen·knife /'pen-naɪf/ also **pocketknife**— n -**knives** /naɪvz/ a small knife with usu. two blades that fold into the handle, usu. carried in the pocket —compare SWISS ARMY KNIFE

pen·man·ship /'penmənʃɪp/ n [U] fml the art of writing by hand, or skill in this art: his flawless penmanship

Penn /pen/, **William** (1644–1718) an English leader of the Quaker religious movement, who began the Quaker COLONY (2) of Pennsylvania, now part of the US

pen name /'· ·/ n a name used by a writer instead of his/her real name —see also PSEUDONYM

pen·nant /'penənt/ n **1** a usu. long narrow pointed flag, esp. as used on ships for signalling or by schools, sports teams, etc. **2** (in BASEBALL) the prize given to the best team in both the American and National Leagues; these two teams then go on to play in the World Series: The Cubs are in the **pennant race** for the first time in years (they have a chance to win the pennant).

Penney, J. C. see J. C. PENNEY

pen·nies /'peniz/ pl. of PENNY —see PENNY (USAGE)

pen·ni·less /'penɪləs/ adj having no money; very poor: The debt-collectors took all his money, and he was left completely penniless.

Pen·nines /'penaɪnz/ [the] a mountain range running down the centre from the north to N central England. Because of its position it is also called the BACKBONE of England.

Pennine Way /ˌ·· '·/ [the] a very long path (250 miles) along the Pennines, opened to walkers in 1965

pen·non /'penən/ n a long narrow pointed flag, esp. as carried on the end of a LANCE (=spear) by soldiers on horseback

pen·n'orth /'penəθ‖-ərθ/ BrE **pen·ny·worth** /'peniwəθ‖ -wərθ/ AmE, BrE fml— n [(of)] old-fash as much as can be bought for a penny: a penn'orth/six penn'orth of sweets

Penn·syl·va·ni·a /ˌpensəlˈveɪniə◂, -sɪl-/ *written abbrev.* **PA** a state in the NE of the US, known as an important producer of steel and coal. It was one of the 13 original British colonies (COLONY) and was a former centre of the AMERICAN REVOLUTION —see colour map on pages 1374-5

Pennsylvania Dutch /ˌ····· ˈ·/ *n, adj* (of or being) a group of people living in Pennsylvania who are descended from German settlers that went there in the 1600s and 1700s to find religious freedom. The Pennsylvania Dutch are Protestants who still wear clothes of that period, do not have cars, etc. They include the AMISH and the MENNONITES.

pen·ny /ˈpeni/ *n* **pennies** *or* **pence** /pens/ *BrE—* **1** [C] **a** also **p** /piː/ — (in Britain since 1971) a unit of money equal to one hundredth ($^1/_{100}$) of a pound: *That'll be 75p, please.* | *a 20p/50p piece* | *It only costs a few pence.* **b** a small BRONZE coin worth one penny: *a stack of pennies* **2** [C] (in Britain before 1971) a unit of money equal to one 12th ($^1/_{12}$) of a SHILLING: *The book cost two and sixpence.* **3** [C] (in the US and Canada) (a coin worth) a cent **4** [S *usu. in negatives*] a small amount of money: *The journey won't cost you a penny if you come in my car.* **5 a penny for them/for your thoughts** (usu. said to someone who has been silent for a while or appears deep in thought) tell me what you are thinking about **6 be two/ten a penny** *infml* to be very cheap and/or easy to obtain, and therefore of little value: *Brilliant students are ten a penny at that college.* **7 in for a penny, in for a pound** *BrE* if something has been started it should be finished, whatever the cost may be **8 the penny (has) dropped** *BrE infml* the meaning (of something said) was/has been at last understood: *He puzzled over her remark for a moment, and then at last the penny dropped.* **9 -penny** /pəni; *strong* peni/worth the stated number of pence: *a fourpenny stamp* | *a sixpenny piece* (=coin) —see also HALFPENNY, PRETTY PENNY, **spend a penny** (SPEND)

▷ USAGE In Britain, the US, and Canada, the plural **pennies** is used when speaking or writing of the coins themselves: *He had some coins in his pocket, but no* **pennies.** In Britain, when writing about an amount of money, use **pence** (in the US, **cents**): *It will only cost a few* **pence** or (in prices) **p**: *30 p a packet.* When saying an amount of money use **pence**, or **p** (*infml*): *six* **pence**/*ten* **p** (ˌ· ˈ·). The singular form for an amount of money is *a*/*one* **penny**, *one* **pence**, *one* **p** (in informal speech) or *1*p (when writing prices).◁

Penny Black /ˌ·· ˈ·/ *n* the first British postage stamp, introduced in 1840, and the first in general use with ADHESIVE. It is highly valued by collectors although not the rarest British stamp.

penny dread·ful /ˌ·· ˈ··/ *n BrE* a book about exciting adventures or violent crime, originally costing one penny, of a type that was common in the 19th century

penny-far·thing /ˌ·· ˈ··/ *n* a bicycle with a very large front wheel and a very small back wheel, used in the late 19th century

penny-half·penny /ˌ·· ˈ··/ *n BrE* THREE-HALFPENCE

penny pinch·er /ˈ·· ˌ··/ *n derog* a person who is unwilling to spend or give money —**penny-pinching** *adj, n* [U]

penny whis·tle /ˌ·· ˈ··/ *n* a simple tubelike musical instrument, played by blowing and moving the fingers. Penny whistles are commonly used in Irish music.

pen·ny·worth /ˈpeniwəθ‖-wərθ/ *n* [(of)] *BrE fml or AmE* a PENN'ORTH

pe·nol·o·gy /piːˈnɒlədʒi‖-ˈnɑːl-/ *n* [U] the scientific study of the punishment of criminals, the operation of prisons, etc.

pen pal /ˈ· ·/ *n esp. AmE for* PEN FRIEND

pen push·er /ˈ· ˌ··/ ‖ *usu.* **pencil pusher** *AmE— n humor or derog* a clerk

pen·sion¹ /ˈpenʃən/ *n* an amount of money paid regularly, esp. by a government or company, to someone who can no longer earn (enough) money by working, esp. when they are old or ill. Money is previously paid regularly, usu. for many years, into the pension system by the person, and the amount they pay decides the size of the pension: *She went to the post office to* **draw** (=collect) **her pension.** | *He retired on a company pension.* | *a war/retirement pension* | *a pension scheme* —see also OLD AGE PENSION

pension² *v*

   pension sbdy. ↔ **off** *phr v* [T] to dismiss from work, esp. because of old age or illness, but continue to pay a pension to: *She was pensioned off at 55.* | (fig., *infml*) *It's time your rusty old bike was pensioned off.* (=got rid of)

pen·si·on³ /ˈpɒnsiɒn‖ˌpɑːnsiˈəʊn/ *n* a house in a non-English-speaking country where one can get a room and meals; BOARDINGHOUSE

pen·sion·a·ble /ˈpenʃənəbəl/ *adj* giving one the right to receive a pension: *She is of pensionable age.* | *a pensionable job*

pension book /ˈ·· ·/ *n* (in Britain) a book of forms which a person signs each week when they go to collect their OLD AGE PENSION

pen·sion·er /ˈpenʃənər/ *n BrE* ‖ **senior citizen** *AmE—* a person who is receiving a pension esp. an OLD AGE PENSION: *an old age pensioner* —see also CHELSEA PENSIONER, OAP

pension fund /ˈ·· ·/ *n* a FUND (=a sum of money for a special purpose) which is invested (INVEST¹). The money which is gained from the investment is used to pay pensions to people who have paid money, usu. a fixed amount each month, into the fund.

pension plan /ˈ·· ˌ·/ ‖ also **retirement plan** *AmE— n* a system by which a person who will not get a pension from an employer pays money, usu. a fixed amount each month, to an insurance company which INVESTs the money to provide the person with a pension

pension scheme /ˈ·· ·/ ‖ also **retirement plan** *AmE— n* a system in many companies in which both the company and the workers pay money into a pension fund for the workers

pen·sive /ˈpensɪv/ *adj* deeply or sadly thoughtful: *a pensive smile* | *You're looking very pensive — is anything wrong?* — ~**ly** *adv* — ~**ness** *n* [U]

pen·ta·gon /ˈpentəgən‖-gɑːn/ *n* a flat shape with five esp. equal sides and five angles — ~**al** /penˈtægənəl/ *adj*

The Pentagon

Pentagon [*the*] the large five-sided building near Washington D.C. which contains the main offices of the US Department of Defense, and from which the armed forces of the US are directed: *The Pentagon is planning a massive air-strike.*

Pentagon Pa·pers /ˈ···· ˌ··/ [*the*] papers taken from the Pentagon which discussed American involvement in Vietnam and were printed in the *New York Times*. The president and the people who worked for him tried to prevent the papers being printed, but the US Supreme Court said that the newspaper had a right to print them under the First Amendment. The case looked at the government's right to keep important things secret against the public's right to know what its government is doing.

pen·ta·gram /ˈpentəgræm/ *n* a five-pointed star, used as a magic sign

pen·tam·e·ter /penˈtæmɪtər/ *n* a line of poetry with five main beats

Pen·ta·teuch /ˈpentətjuːk‖-tuːk/ [*the*] the first five books of the OLD TESTAMENT

pen·tath·lon /penˈtæθlən/ *n* a sports event in which those taking part have to compete against each other in five different sports: running, swimming, riding, shooting, and FENCING —compare DECATHLON

Pen·tax /ˈpentæks/ *tdmk* a camera made by the Japanese company Pentax

Pen·te·cost /ˈpentɪkɒst‖-kɔːst, -kɑːst/ **1** also **Shabuoth, Shavuot**— (in the Jewish religion) a holiday 50 days after Passover, which celebrates Moses receiving the Ten

Commandments from God on Mount Sinai **2** (in the Christian religion) the seventh Sunday after Easter; Whitsunday

Pen·te·cos·tal /ˌpentɪ'kɒstəl◂‖-'kɔːs-, -'kɑːs-/ *adj* **1** of or suggesting Pentecost **2** concerning any of various Christian groups with particular interest in the gifts of the HOLY SPIRIT e.g. FAITH HEALING and SPEAKING IN TONGUES: *Pentecostal church/service*

Pen·te·cos·ta·list /ˌpentɪ'kɒstəl-ɫst‖-'kɔːs-, -'kɑːs-/ *n* a member of a Pentecostal (2) group − ~ **ism** *n* [U]

pent·house /'penthaʊs/ *n* **-houses** /ˌhaʊz̩z/ a small house or set of rooms built on top of a tall building, often considered very desirable to live in: *the film star's luxury penthouse* | *the hotel's penthouse suite*

Penthouse an American magazine for men which has serious articles but is known esp. for its pictures of young women with few clothes on and its articles about sex

Pen·ton·ville /'pentənvɪl/ also **Pentonville prison** /ˌ···
'··/− a large prison for men, in N London

pent up /ˌ·· '·◂/ *adj* shut up within narrow limits; not allowed to be free or freely expressed: *I don't like being pent up in the house all the time.* | *A good argument allows you to release your pent-up emotions.*

pe·nul·ti·mate /pɪ'nʌltɫm̩ɫt/ *adj* [A] next to the last

pe·num·bra /pɫ'nʌmbrə/ *n tech* a slightly dark area between full shadow or darkness and full light

pe·nu·ri·ous /pɫ'njʊəriəs/ *adj fml* very poor − ~ **ly** *adv*

pen·u·ry /'penjɫri/ *n* [U] *fml* the state of being very poor; POVERTY: *living in utter penury*

pe·on /'piːən/ *n AmE* **1** a person who works at a boring or physically hard job for low pay: *I worked and saved to go back to college and escape the peon job market.* **2** (in Mexico and South America) a person who works as a kind of slave to pay his debts

pe·o·ny /'piːəni/ *n* a garden plant with large round white, pink, or esp. dark red flowers

peo·ple¹ /'piːpəl/ *n* **1** [P] persons; human beings: *Were there many people at the meeting?* | *buses crammed with people* | *Most people seem to like her.* | *People in the south of England speak in a different way from people in the north.* | *I like theatre people.* (=people connected with the theatre) **2** [P] persons in general; persons other than oneself: *If you do that, people will start to talk.* (=about your behaviour) | *People enjoy reading about the rich and famous.* **3** [(the) P] all the ordinary members of a state; all those persons in a society who do not have special rank or position: *Abraham Lincoln spoke of "government of the people, by the people, for the people".* | *The Prime Minister claimed he had a mandate from the people.* | *Like many politicians, he likes to be thought of as a **man of the (common) people.*** **4** [C+*sing./pl. v*] a race; nation: *The Chinese are a hard-working people.* | *the peoples of Africa* **5** [P] **a** the persons from whom one is descended and/or to whom one is related: *Her people have lived in this valley for over 200 years.* **b** *old-fash infml* one's close relatives, esp. parents: *One day I'll take you home to meet my people.* **6** **of** '**all people: a** especially; more than anyone else: *You of all people ought to have been able to understand what he was saying.* **b** surprisingly, out of all those who might be expected to be present, to take action, etc.: *For her, of all people, to complain about you being late for work!* (=she is often late herself) −see also LITTLE PEOPLE; see FOLK (USAGE), MAN (USAGE), PERSON (USAGE)

people² *v* [T *usu. pass.*] **1** to live in (a place); INHABIT: *a desert peopled only by wandering tribes* **2** [(with)] *usu. derog* to fill or supply with people of the stated type: *This office is peopled with petty-minded bureaucrats.*

People¹ a US magazine with many short articles about and pictures of well-known people, esp. people known from television and film

People², **The** a British popular Sunday newspaper

people's re·pub·lic /ˌ··· ·'··/ *n* **1** [*cap.*] a name or title taken by some SOCIALIST or COMMUNIST states: *the People's Republic of China* **2** *BrE humor, usu. derog* a place which has a left-wing local council: *the people's republic of Lambeth*

pep¹ /pep/ *n* [U] *infml* keen activity and forcefulness; VIGOUR: *Put a bit more pep into your work!* −see also PEP PILL, PEP TALK

pep² *v* **-pp-**
pep sthg./sbdy. ↔ **up** *phr v* [T] *infml* to make more active or interesting; ENLIVEN: *A holiday is just what you need to pep you up.* | *The food tasted rather bland, so she added some spices to pep it up a little.*

PEP /ˌpiː iː 'piː/ *n BrE* a Personal Equity Plan; a government proposal allowing people to buy relatively small amounts of SHARES in British companies without having to pay certain taxes

pep·per¹ /'pepəʳ/ *n* **1** [U] **a** a hot-tasting greyish or pale yellowish powder made from crushed peppercorns, used for making food taste better −see also BLACK PEPPER, WHITE PEPPER **b** a powder like this, esp. CAYENNE PEPPER or PAPRIKA, made from certain other plants **2** [C] also **bell pepper** *AmE* (a plant with) a large round or long narrow red, green, or yellow fruit used esp. as a vegetable, with a special, sometimes hot taste: *I bought some green peppers for the salad.* −see also SWEET PEPPER, and see picture at VEGETABLE

pepper² *v* [T] **1** [(with)] *infml* **a** to hit repeatedly, esp. with small shots: *I'll pepper his behind with buckshot if he comes on my land again!* **b** to cause to appear repeatedly in: *The report was peppered with mistakes/statistics.* **2** to add or give the taste of pepper to (food)

pepper-and-salt /ˌ··· ·'·◂/ *adj* [A] having small spots of black and white mixed together to give a greyish appearance: *a pepper-and-salt beard*

pep·per·corn /'pepəkɔːn‖'pepərkɔːrn/ *n* the seedlike fruit of a tropical plant, which is dried and crushed to make pepper

peppercorn rent /ˌ··· '·/ *n BrE* a very small amount of money (much less than one would expect) paid as rent

pep·per mill /'·· ·/ also **pepper grind·er** /'·· ˌ··/− *n* a small apparatus worked by hand and used for crushing peppercorns into powder

pep·per·mint /'pepəˌmɪnt‖-ər-/ *n* **1** [U] **a** a MINT³ (1) plant with a special strong taste, used esp. in making sweets and medicine **b** the taste of this plant: *peppermint liqueur/flavouring* **2** [C] also **mint**− a sweet with this taste

pepper pot /'·· ·/ *BrE* ‖ **pepper shak·er** /'·· ˌ··/ *AmE*− *n* a container with small holes in the top, used for shaking pepper onto food −compare SALTCELLAR

pep·per·y /'pepəri/ *adj* **1** (of food) like or tasting of pepper **2** (of a person) easily made angry; IRRITABLE

pep pill /'· ·/ *n infml* a PILL containing a drug which is taken to make one quicker in thought and action or happier, for a short time; STIMULANT

pep ral·ly /'· ˌ··/ *n* (in the US) a meeting of all of the students in a HIGH SCHOOL, before a school sports event, to encourage the team to win, and to encourage the students to support their team and their school. At most pep rallies, CHEER LEADERS lead the school in loud, happy cheers for the team. Often the school's song is sung at the end of the pep rally.

Pep·si /'pepsi/ *tdmk* the name of an American COLA drink, one of the two best known colas in the world

pep·sin /'pepsɫn/ *n* [U] a liquid in the stomach that changes food into a form that can be used by the body

pep talk /'· ·/ *n infml* a usu. short talk intended to encourage the listener(s) esp. to work harder or win: *The manager gave his team a pep talk at half time.*

pep·tic ul·cer /ˌpeptɪk 'ʌlsəʳ/ *n* a sore painful place inside the stomach caused by the action of pepsin

Pep·to-bis·mol /ˌpeptəʊ'bɪzmɒl‖-mɔːl/ *tdmk AmE* an American medicine for the stomach which is a thick, pink, sweet-tasting liquid

Pepys /piːps/, **Sam·u·el** /'sæmjuəl/ (1633−1703) an English writer who was an official in the navy, best known for his DIARY which records full details of social life and conditions at the time

per /pəʳ; *strong* pɜːʳ/ *prep* **1** (esp. of amounts, prices, etc.) for each: *These apples cost 40 pence per pound.* | *My car does about 12 miles per litre.* (=for each litre of petrol) | *How much beer will they drink **per head**?* (=how much will each person drink) **2** (of time) during each: *How many of these can you do per day/a day?* **3** *infml* according to: *The work has been done **as per** your instructions.* **4** **as per usual** *infml* (esp. of something that one disapproves of) as usual: *He was late, as per usual.*

—see also PER ANNUM, PER CAPITA, PER CENT

per·ad·ven·ture /ˌperədˈventʃəʳ/ adv old use　**1** perhaps　**2** (after **if** or **lest**) by chance

per·am·bu·late /pəˈræmbjǔleɪt/ v [I+adv/prep;T] fml to walk about, round, or up and down (a place) without hurry —**-lation** /pəˌræmbjǔˈleɪʃən/ n [C;U]

per·am·bu·la·tor /pəˈræmbjǔleɪtəʳ/ n fml for PRAM

per an·num /pər ˈænəm/ written abbrev. **p.a.** esp. tech for or in each year: a salary of £11,000 per annum

per cap·i·ta /pə ˈkæpǐtə‖pər-/ adj, adv fml or tech for or by each person: What is the average per capita income in this country?

per·ceive /pəˈsiːv‖pər-/ v [T not in progressive forms] fml to (come to) have knowledge of (something) through one of the senses (esp. the sight) or through the mind; become conscious of or understand: He perceived a subtle change in her manner. [+(that)] They perceived that they were unwelcome and left. [+wh-] We were unable to perceive where the problem lay. [+obj+v-ing] I perceived a small trickle of blood coming from the patient's ear. —see also PERCEPTIBLE, PERCEPTION

▷ USAGE You **perceive** (=notice, become conscious of) something that exists outside your thoughts: I perceived a change in the tone of her voice. You **conceive** (=form in the mind) a completely new idea: She conceived a bold plan of escape.◁

per cent¹, **percent** /pəˈsent‖pər-/ adj, adv (calculated) in or for each 100: This restaurant has a 10 percent (=10%) service charge. | (fig.) I am a hundred per cent (=totally) in agreement with you.

per cent² n **per cent** one part in or for each 100: This company can only supply 30 per cent (=30%) of what we need. | to charge interest at fourteen per cent (=14%)

per·cen·tage /pəˈsentɪdʒ‖pər-/ n　**1** [C (**of**) usu. sing.] an amount stated as if it is part of a whole which is 100; PROPORTION: a high/large/small percentage | What percentage of babies die of scarlet fever every year? | The numbers are small, in percentage terms, but significant.　**2** [C usu. sing.] infml a share of profits: She gets a percentage on every copy they sell.　**3** [U usu. in negatives] infml advantage; profit: There's **no percentage in** being unadventurous; you've got to think big.

per·cep·ti·ble /pəˈseptǐbəl‖pər-/ adj fml that can be perceived; noticeable: a barely perceptible difference —opposite **imperceptible** —**-bly** adv

per·cep·tion /pəˈsepʃən‖pər-/ n [U] fml　**1** the action of perceiving: a drug which alters one's perception of visual stimuli　**2** also **perceptiveness** /pəˈseptɪvnǎs‖pər-/— the ability to perceive well; keen natural understanding: a man of great perception

per·cep·tive /pəˈseptɪv‖pər-/ adj apprec showing an unusually good ability to notice and understand: a perceptive woman | perceptive comments —compare SENSITIVE —**~ly** adv

perch¹ /pɜːtʃ‖pɜːrtʃ/ n　**1** a branch, rod, etc., where a bird rests, often specially provided for the purpose　**2** infml a high position in which a person or building is placed: From our perch up there on top of the cliff we can see the whole town. | (fig.) I'm glad to see someone has **knocked him off his perch** at last. (=shown that he is not as important, clever, etc., as he thought himself to be)

perch² v [esp. **on, upon**]　**1** [I+adv/prep] (of a bird) to come to rest, esp. on a thin, raised object such as a branch: The birds perched on the telephone wires.　**2** [I+adv/prep; T+obj+adv/prep] infml to (cause to) go into or be in the stated position, esp. unsafely or on something narrow or high: She perched (herself) on a tall stool. | a house perched on the edge of a cliff

perch³ n perch or perches a popular food fish with prickly FINS that lives in lakes and rivers

per·chance /pəˈtʃɑːns‖pərˈtʃæns/ adv old use or lit　**1** perhaps　**2** (after **if** or **lest**) by chance

per·cip·i·ent /pəˈsɪpiənt‖pər-/ adj fml quick to notice and understand; PERCEPTIVE —**-ence** n [U]

per·co·late /ˈpɜːkəleɪt‖ˈpɜːr-/ v　**1** [I+adv/prep] to pass slowly through a material that has small holes in it: The water gradually percolated down through the rock. | (fig.) News from the war eventually percolated through to us.　**2** [I;T] also **perk** infml— a (of coffee) to be made in a special pot by the passing of hot water through crushed

coffee beans **b** to make (coffee) by this method —**-lation** /ˌpɜːkəˈleɪʃən‖ˌpɜːr-/ n [C;U]

per·co·la·tor /ˈpɜːkəleɪtəʳ‖ˈpɜːr-/ n a pot in which coffee is percolated

percussion instruments

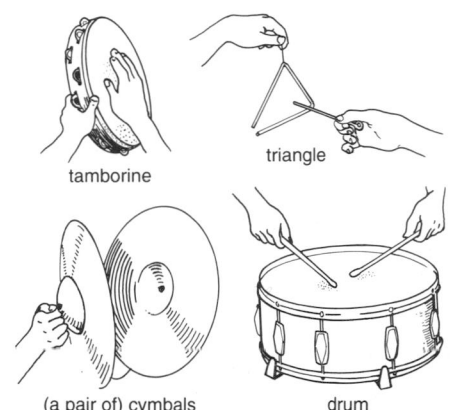

tamborine　triangle

(a pair of) cymbals　drum

per·cus·sion /pəˈkʌʃən‖pər-/ n　**1** [the+S+sing./pl. v] musical instruments that are played by being struck by the hand or by an object such as a stick or hammer, esp. as a division (**percussion section**) of a band: The drum is a percussion instrument. | The percussion is too loud.　**2** [U] tech (the effect or sound produced by) the forceful striking together of two hard objects —**-sive** /pəˈkʌsɪv‖pər-/ adj

percussion cap /·ˈ··· ·/ n　**1** a small container holding an explosive, used formerly in firing guns　**2** fml for CAP¹ (7)

per·cus·sion·ist /pəˈkʌʃənǎst‖pər-/ n a person who plays percussion instruments

per di·em¹ /pə ˈdiːem‖pər-/ n esp. AmE money paid by an employer to EMPLOYEES travelling on business, based on what it is thought they need for one day: What's the per diem rate?

per diem² adv every day or by the day: We are paid per diem.

per·di·tion /pəˈdɪʃən‖pər-/ n [U] fml　**1** punishment that goes on forever　**2** complete destruction

per·e·gri·na·tion /ˌperǎgrǐˈneɪʃən/ also **peregrinations** pl.— n lit or humor a long and wandering journey, esp. in foreign countries

per·e·grine fal·con /ˌperǎgrǎn ˈfɔːlkən‖-ˈfɔːl-, -ˈfɑːl-/ also **peregrine**— n a hunting bird with a black and white spotted front

pe·remp·to·ry /pəˈremptəri/ adj fml　**1** derog (of a person, their manner, etc.) showing an expectation of being obeyed at once and without question; impolitely quick and unfriendly: in a peremptory tone of voice　**2** (of a command) that must be obeyed —**-rily** adv

pe·ren·ni·al¹ /pəˈreniəl/ adj　**1** lasting forever or for a long time; CONSTANT: a perennial problem/worry.　**2** [no comp.] (of a plant) that lives for more than two years —**~ly** adv

perennial² n a perennial plant: hardy perennials | (fig.) That joke is a **hardy perennial**! (=keeps being told)

Per·es /ˈperes/, **Shi·mon** /ʃɪˈmɒn‖-ˈməʊn/ (1923–) an Israeli Socialist politician, Prime Minister from 1984 to 1986

per·es·troi·ka /ˌperǎˈstrɔɪkə/ n [U] a Russian word meaning rebuilding; the term used to describe the economic, political, and social changes started by Mikhail Gorbachev in the USSR, including reduction of state controls on trading and making politicians more responsible for their actions —compare GLASNOST

Per·ez de Cuel·lar /ˌperes də ˈkweɪjɑːʳ/, **Jav·i·er** /ˈhæviei ‖hɑːˈvjeəʳ/ (1920–) a Peruvian DIPLOMAT and SECRETARY-GENERAL to the UN from 1982 to 1991

per·fect¹ /ˈpɜːfɪkt‖ˈpɜːr-/ adj　**1** of the very best possible kind, degree, or standard: The weather was absolutely *perfect.* | *a perfect wife* | *a perfect crime* (=one in which the criminal is never discovered) **2** agreeing in every way with an example accepted as correct: *His technique is almost perfect.* | *Yes, Pedro's English is excellent, but I think it's almost too perfect.* (=not showing the natural freedom shown by someone using their first language) **3** [(for)] suitable; having everything that is needed in every way: *This big house is perfect for our large family.* **4** complete and without fault; with nothing missing, spoilt, etc.: *She still has a perfect set of teeth.* **5** [A] complete; thorough; UTTER: *a perfect stranger* | *perfect nonsense* **6** [A] *tech* being the form of a verb that shows a period of time up to and including the present (**present perfect**), past (**past perfect**), or future (**future perfect**) (as in "He *has gone*", "He *had gone*", "He *will have gone*") —see also IMPERFECT, PERFECTLY

per·fect² /pəˈfekt‖pərˈ-/ *v* [T] to make perfect: *He practised hard to perfect his technique.*

perfect³ /ˈpɜːfɪkt‖ˈpɜːr-/ *also* **perfect tense** /ˌ·· ˈ·/, **present perfect**— *n* [the+S] *tech* (in grammar) the form of a verb that shows a period of time up to and including the present, and in English is usu. formed with **have** and a past participle —see also PAST PERFECT

per·fec·ti·ble /pəˈfekt‿bəl‖pər-/ *adj* that can be improved or made perfect —**·bility** /pəˌfekt‿ˈbɪl‿ti‖pər-/ *n* [U]

per·fec·tion /pəˈfekʃən‖pər-/ *n* [U] **1** the state of being perfect: *The meat was cooked* **to perfection.** (=perfectly) **2** [(of)] the process of making something perfect: *He worked hard at the perfection of his technique.* (=worked hard to make it perfect) **3** the perfect example: *His performance was sheer perfection.* (=could not have been better)

per·fec·tion·ist /pəˈfekʃən‿st‖pər-/ *n sometimes derog* someone who is not satisfied with anything that is not completely perfect: *It takes him hours to cook a simple meal because he's such a perfectionist.* —**perfectionist** *adj* —**·ism** *n* [U]

per·fect·ly /ˈpɜːfɪktli‖ˈpɜːr-/ *adv* **1** in a perfect way: *She speaks French perfectly.* | *The colours match perfectly.* **2** very; completely (esp. in expressions of annoyance or disapproval): *What a perfectly ridiculous thing to say!* | *I'm perfectly capable of running my own life, thank you!* (=don't tell me how to behave)

perfect par·ti·ci·ple /ˌ·· ˈ····/ *n* PAST PARTICIPLE

perfect pitch /ˌ·· ˈ·/ *n* [U] the ability to sing or play a note at exactly the right level when it is heard, or named by someone

per·fid·i·ous /pəˈfɪdiəs‖pər-/ *adj fml, esp. lit* disloyal; TREACHEROUS — ~**ly** *adv* — ~**ness** *n* [U]

per·fi·dy /ˈpɜːf‿di‖ˈpɜːr-/ *n* [C;U] *fml, esp. lit* (an example of) disloyalty; TREACHERY

per·fo·rate /ˈpɜːfəreɪt‖ˈpɜːr-/ *v* [T] **1** to make a hole or holes through (something): *They sent the dog in a perforated box so that it could breathe.* | *Her broken ribs had perforated her lung.* **2** to make a line of small holes in (paper), so that a part may be torn off: *This machine perforates the sheets of stamps.* | *perforated edges*

per·fo·ra·tion /ˌpɜːfəˈreɪʃən‖ˌpɜːr-/ *n* **1** [C *often pl.*] a small hole or line of holes made by perforating something: *the perforations in a sheet of stamps* **2** [U] the act of perforating or state of being perforated

per·force /pəˈfɔːs‖pərˈfɔːrs/ *adv old use or lit* because it is necessary

per·form /pəˈfɔːm‖pərˈfɔːrm/ *v* **1** [T] to do; carry out (a piece of work, duty, ceremony, etc.), esp. according to a usual or established method: *The surgeon has performed the operation.* | *to perform a miracle* **2** [I (**on, at**);T] to give, act, or show (a play, a part in a play, a piece of music, tricks, etc.), esp. in the presence of the public: *I've never seen "Othello" performed so brilliantly.* | *The magician performed some astonishing tricks.* | *He will be performing on the clarinet/at the piano.* | *a performing bear* **3** [I] **a** (of a machine) to work (in the proper or intended way): *This car performs well on hills.* **b** *infml* (of a person) to carry out a particular activity, esp. well and with great skill: *Our team performed very well in the match yesterday.*

per·form·ance /pəˈfɔːməns‖pərˈfɔːr-/ *n* **1** [C] the action or an act of performing (a character in a) play, a piece of music, tricks, etc., esp. in the presence of the public: *His performance of/as Othello was very good.* | *The orchestra*

will give two more performances before leaving Britain.| *tickets for the evening performance* | *the band's first public performance* **2** [U] the action or manner of carrying out an activity, piece of work, etc.: *Her performance in the exams was rather disappointing.* | *(fml) the performance of one's official duties* **3** [U] the ability of a person or machine to do something well: *The car's performance on corners needs to be improved.* **4** [S] *infml, esp. BrE* **a** something that needs a lot of work, effort, or preparation: *I enjoy this dish, but it's too much of a performance to cook it often.* **b** *derog* an example of bad and socially unacceptable behaviour (esp. in the phrase **What a performance!**)

performance art /·ˈ·· ˌ·/ *n* [U] art having some theatre and something to see and/or hear e.g. a SCULPTURE of which the artist forms a part —performance **artist** *n*

performance pay /·ˈ·· ˌ·/ *n* [U] additional payment given by an employer to a worker, where the amount given depends on how successful the worker has been

performance-re·lat·ed /·ˈ·· ··,··/ *adj* (of wages, etc.) depending on how successfully work is done: *The salary is performance-related.* (=the greater the success, the more money will be paid) | *a performance-related amount*

per·form·er /pəˈfɔːmər‖pərˈfɔːr-/ *n* a person who performs, esp. an actor, musician, etc.: *The audience booed some of the performers.* | *He's their star performer.*

performing arts /·,·· ˈ·/ *n* [the + P] the arts, e.g. dance, DRAMA, and music, which are usu. performed in front of a group of people listening or watching

per·fume¹ /ˈpɜːfjuːm‖ˈpɜːr-/ *also* **scent** *BrE— n* [C;U] **1** a sweet or pleasant smell: *the roses' heady perfume* **2** a sweet-smelling liquid, often made from flowers, for use esp. on a woman's face, wrists, and body

per·fume² /ˈpɜːfjuːm‖pərˈfjuːm/ *v* [T (**with**)] **1** *fml or poet* to fill with a sweet or pleasant smell: *a garden perfumed with flowers* **2** to put a sweet-smelling liquid on: *a perfumed handkerchief*

per·fum·er·y /pəˈfjuːməri‖pər-/ *n* [U] (the process of making) sweet-smelling liquids: *a shop's perfumery counter*

per·func·to·ry /pəˈfʌŋktəri‖pər-/ *adj fml* **1** (of an action) done hastily and without thought, interest, or care: *a perfunctory kiss/wave/glance* **2** (of a person) acting in this manner —**·rily** *adv* —**·riness** *n* [U]

per·go·la /ˈpɜːɡələ‖ˈpɜːr-/ *n* an arrangement of posts built for climbing plants to grow over in a garden

per·haps /pəˈhæps, præps‖pər-, præps/ *adv* **1** possibly; MAYBE: *Perhaps she's in the other office.* | *This is perhaps his finest novel yet.* | *"Do you think it'll rain?" "Perhaps."* | *"Will he come with us?" "Perhaps not."* **2** (used in making polite requests): *Perhaps you would be* (=Would you be) *good enough to explain this for me?*

▷ USAGE **1 Perhaps** is similar to **maybe,** but **maybe** is more informal. **2 Perhaps** can be used to make suggestions or requests or to give orders in a polite manner: **Perhaps** *you would like to join us for lunch.* | **Perhaps** *you could bring me the report tomorrow.* | *You'd better go now,* **perhaps.** —see also MAYBE (USAGE)◁

per·i·gee /ˈper‿dʒiː/ *n tech* the point where the path of an object through space is closest to the Earth —compare APOGEE (1)

per·i·he·li·on /ˌper‿ˈhiːliən/ *n tech* the point where the path of an object through space is closest to the sun

per·il /ˈper‿l/ *n esp. lit* **1** [U] (great) danger, esp. of being harmed or killed: *a prayer for those in peril on the sea* **2** [C] something that causes danger: *the perils of motor racing* **3 at one's peril** (used when advising someone not to do something) with the near certainty of meeting great danger: *You ignore this warning at your peril.*

per·il·ous /ˈper‿ləs/ *adj esp. lit* very dangerous; risky: *a perilous journey across the mountains* — ~**ly** *adv* — ~**ness** *n* [U]

pe·rim·e·ter /pəˈrɪm‿tər/ *n* **1** the border round any enclosed flat space or special area of ground, esp. a camp or airfield: *The perimeter of the airfield is protected by guard-dogs.* | *a perimeter fence* **2** the length of this border: *What is the perimeter of this circle/square?* —compare CIRCUMFERENCE

pe·ri·na·tal /ˌper‿ˈneɪtl◂/ *adj med* (happening) at about the time of birth: *a high rate of perinatal mortality*

pe·ri·od /ˈpɪəriəd/ *n* **1** a stretch of time with a beginning and an end, but not always of measured length: *There were long periods when we had no news of him.* | *Tomorrow's weather will be dry with sunny periods.* | *a period of international tension* | *She was taken on for a three-month trial period before being accepted as a permanent member of staff.* **2** a particular stretch of time during the development of a person, a civilization, the Earth, an illness, etc.: *His teenage son is going through a difficult period at the moment.* | *"Which period (of history) are you studying?" "The Romans."* | *They put on a play about the French Revolution, with all the actors wearing period costume.* (=the clothes of that period) —see picture at COSTUME **3** a division of a school day; lesson: *three periods of chemistry a week* | *a double period* **4** also **menstrual period** *fml*— a monthly flow of blood from the body of a woman: *a heavy period* | *period pains* **5** *esp. AmE* a FULL STOP —see picture at PUNCTUATION MARK **b** (used at the end of a sentence to express completeness, or firmness of decision): *I'm not going, period!*

pe·ri·od·ic /ˌpɪəriˈɒdɪk◀‖-ˈɑː-/ also **periodical**— *adj* happening repeatedly, usu. at regular times: *periodic bouts of fever|fits of coughing* —compare SPASMODIC — **~ally** /kli/ *adv* : *She looked in on the baby periodically to check that it was all right.*

pe·ri·od·i·cal /ˌpɪəriˈɒdɪkəl‖-ˈɑː-/ *n* a magazine, esp. one of a serious kind, that comes out at regular times, such as every month

periodic ta·ble /ˌ···· ˈ··/ *n* [*the*+S] a list of simple chemical substances (ELEMENTS) arranged according to their atomic weights

period piece /ˈ···· ·/ *n* **1** a fine example of a piece of furniture, work of art, etc., of a certain period in history **2** *infml, esp. humor* something very old-fashioned

per·i·pa·tet·ic /ˌperɪpəˈtetɪk◀/ *adj fml* travelling about; going from place to place, esp. to work: *a peripatetic music teacher who works at several schools* — **~ally** /kli/ *adv*

pe·riph·e·ral[1] /pəˈrɪfərəl/ *adj rather fml* **1** [(to)] of slight importance by comparison; not central or closely related: *matters of peripheral interest* | *peripheral to the main argument* **2** of or in a periphery: *peripheral areas* | *peripheral nerves* (=outside the CENTRAL NERVOUS SYSTEM) —compare OUTSKIRTS **—rally** *adv*

peripheral[2] *n* a piece of equipment, such as a VDU or printer, which is connected to a computer to help in using the computer —compare ADD-ON

pe·riph·e·ry /pəˈrɪfəri/ *n* **1** [(of) *usu. sing.*] a line or area that surrounds or encloses (something); outside edge: *a factory built on the periphery of the town* | (fig.) *people on the periphery of our movement who have less influence than they would like to think* —compare OUTSKIRTS **2** *med* the places outside the brain and the SPINAL CORD where the nerves end, e.g. in the fingers or toes

pe·riph·ra·sis /pəˈrɪfrəsɪs/ *n* -ses /siːz/ [C;U] **1** *fml* (an example of) the use of long words or phrases, or of unclear expressions, when short simple ones are all that is needed **2** *tech* (in grammar) (an example of) the use of AUXILIARY words instead of inflected (INFLECT) forms

per·i·phras·tic /ˌperɪˈfræstɪk◀/ *adj fml or tech* using or expressed in periphrasis — **~ally** /kli/ *adv*

per·i·scope /ˈperɪskəʊp/ *n* a long tube with mirrors fitted in it so that people who are lower down, esp. in SUBMARINES, can see what is above them

per·ish /ˈperɪʃ/ *v* **1** [I] (esp. in writing or in newspapers) to die, esp. in a terrible or sudden way: *Hundreds perish in aircrash disaster!* (=a newspaper HEADLINE) **2** [I;T] *esp. BrE* to (cause to) decay or lose natural qualities: *The chlorine in the swimming pool has perished the rubber in this swimsuit.* **3 Perish the thought!** (said as an answer to an unwelcome suggestion) I hope that this will not happen!

per·ish·a·ble /ˈperɪʃəbəl/ *adj* (esp. of food) likely to decay quickly if not kept in proper conditions: *perishable goods such as butter, milk, fruit, and fish* —**perishables** *n* [P] : *a cargo of perishables*

per·ish·er /ˈperɪʃər/ *n infml, often humor, BrE* a troublesome person, esp. a child: *Come out of there, you little perisher!*

per·ish·ing /ˈperɪʃɪŋ/ *adj infml, esp. BrE* **1** [F (with)] also **perished**— (of a person) feeling very cold: *Let's get indoors — I'm perishing|perished (with cold).* **2** [F] (of weather) very cold: *It's really perishing this morning!* **3**

[A] *old-fash* annoying; DAMN[3]: *Tell those perishing kids to shut up!* — **~ly** *adv* : *perishingly cold*

per·i·style /ˈperɪstaɪl/ *n* **1** a row of PILLARS round an open space next to a building, a temple, etc. **2** the space surrounded by a row of pillars

per·i·to·ne·um /ˌperɪtəˈniːəm/ *n* -neums *or* -nea /ˈniːə/ *med* the inside wall of the ABDOMEN (=the lower part of the body)

per·i·to·ni·tis /ˌperɪtəˈnaɪtɪs/ *n* [U] *med* an INFLAMMATION (=a poisoned and sore condition) of the peritoneum

per·i·wig /ˈperɪwɪg/ *n* a white WIG for men, with rolls of curls at the sides, fashionable in the 18th century and now worn by male and female lawyers in British courts

per·i·win·kle[1] /ˈperɪwɪŋkəl/ *n* a small plant with light blue or white flowers that grows along the ground

periwinkle[2] *n* a WINKLE[1]

per·jure /ˈpɜːdʒər‖ˈpɜːr-/ *v* **perjure oneself** to tell a lie intentionally after promising solemnly to tell the truth, esp. in a court of law

per·jur·er /ˈpɜːdʒərər‖ˈpɜːr-/ *n* a person who perjures himself/herself

per·ju·ry /ˈpɜːdʒəri‖ˈpɜːr-/ *n* **1** [U] the act of perjuring oneself: *to commit perjury* **2** [C] a lie told on purpose, esp. in a court of law. Perjury is an offence under British and American law.

perk[1] /pɜːk‖pɜːrk/ also **perquisite** *fml*— *n* [*usu. pl.*] *infml* money, goods, or an advantage that one gets regularly and legally from one's work in addition to one's pay: *With all the perks, such as free meals and a car, she's really earning over £15,000 a year.* | *"Surely you shouldn't take all that stationery home?" "Oh, it's one of the perks of the job."*

perk[2] *v*

perk up *phr v* [I;T (=**perk** sbdy. ↔ **up**)] *infml* to (cause to) become more cheerful, show interest, etc.: *She perked up when her boyfriend's letter arrived.* | *I need a drink to perk me up.*

perk[3] *v* [I;T] *infml for* PERCOLATE (2)

perk·y /ˈpɜːki‖ˈpɜːrki/ *adj infml apprec* confidently cheerful; full of life and interest: *a perky little chap* **—ily** *adv* **—iness** *n* [U]

perm[1] /pɜːm‖pɜːrm/ || also **permanent wave** *fml* || also **permanent** *AmE*— *n* the putting of waves or curls into straight hair by chemical treatment so that they will last for several months

perm[2] *v* [T] *infml* to give a perm to: *I'm having my hair permed today.*

perm[3] *v* [T (from)] *BrE infml* (in the POOLS) to pick out and combine a specific number of (the names of football teams) from a larger number, in order to get the best SCORE

per·ma·frost /ˈpɜːməfrɒst‖ˈpɜːrməfrɔːst/ *n* [U] a thickness of soil, esp. below the Earth's surface, that is frozen all the time

per·ma·nence /ˈpɜːmənəns‖ˈpɜːr-/ also **per·ma·nen·cy** /-nənsi/— *n* [U] the state of being permanent —opposite **impermanence**

per·ma·nent[1] /ˈpɜːmənənt‖ˈpɜːr-/ *adj* lasting or intended to last for a long time or for ever: *This car wax gives permanent protection against heavy rain.* | *Is this your permanent address, or are you only staying there for a short time?* | *a permanent job* | *I think he's a permanent fixture in her life now.* (=they will be together for a long time) —compare IMPERMANENT, TEMPORARY — **~ly** *adv* : *permanently incapacitated*

permanent[2] *n* *AmE for* PERM[1]

Permanent Sec·re·ta·ry /ˌ··· ˈ·····/ also **Permanent Un·der-Secretary** /ˌ··· ˈ·· ˌ···/— *n* the non-political head (the chief CIVIL SERVANT) of a British government department

permanent wave /ˌ··· ˈ·/ *n fml a* PERM[1]

permanent way /ˌ··· ˈ·/ *n BrE* a railway track and the stones and beams on which it is laid

per·man·ga·nate /pəˈmæŋgənət‖pərˈmæŋgəneɪt/ also **permanganate of pot·ash** /ˌ··· ˈ·· ˌ··/ *n* [U] a dark purple chemical compound used for disinfecting (DISINFECT)

per·me·a·ble /ˈpɜːmiəbəl‖ˈpɜːr-/ *adj fml or tech* that can be permeated, esp. by water —opposite **impermeable** —**bility** /ˌpɜːmiəˈbɪləti‖ˌpɜːr-/ n [U]

per·me·ate /ˈpɜːmieɪt‖ˈpɜːr-/ v [I+adv/prep, esp. **into**, **through**;T] to spread or pass through or into every part of (a thing, place, etc.): *Water permeated through the cracks in the wall.* | *The smell of her perfume permeated the room.* | *A feeling of sadness permeates all his music.* —**ation** /ˌpɜːmiˈeɪʃən‖ˌpɜːr-/ n [U]

per·mis·si·ble /pəˈmɪsəbəl‖pər-/ adj fml allowed; that is permitted: *a permissible stretching of the rules* —**bly** adv

per·mis·sion /pəˈmɪʃən‖pər-/ n [U] an esp. formal act of allowing; written or spoken agreement; CONSENT: *With your permission* (=if you allow me) *I'll leave now.* [+to-v] *Did he give you permission to take that?* | *The company has applied to court for permission to renegotiate the contract.* —see also PLANNING PERMISSION; see REFUSE (USAGE)

per·mis·sive /pəˈmɪsɪv‖pər-/ adj allowing people a great deal of freedom (perhaps too much freedom), esp. in sexual matters: *My parents were permissive and let me make my own mistakes* | *We live in a permissive age.* — **ly** adv — **ness** n [U]

permissive so·ci·e·ty /·ˌ···· ·ˈ··ˌ·/ [the] often derog society, such as in Britain and the US in the 1960s and 1970s, in which there is a lot of freedom, esp. in sexual behaviour, and many different kinds of relationships and LIFESTYLES are accepted. Some people connected the permissive society with the use of drugs for pleasure and a lack of moral standards, esp. in relation to sex.

per·mit¹ /pəˈmɪt‖pər-/ v -tt- rather fml **1** [T] to allow, esp. by a formal written or spoken agreement: [+obj(i)+obj(d)] *You are not permitted access to* (=you are not allowed to see or use) *the confidential files.* [+v-ing] *The rules of the club do not permit smoking.* [+obj+to-v] *Will you permit us to leave now?* | (fml) *Permit me to say how pleased I am that...* **2** [T+obj+adv/prep] to allow to be or to come: *She won't permit dogs in the house.* **3** [I] to make it possible (for a stated thing to happen): *I'll come after the meeting if time permits.* (=if it finishes early enough) | *The party will be held in the garden,* **weather permitting**. (=if the weather is good enough to allow it) **4** [T no pass.] also **permit of** fml— to allow as possible; admit: *The facts permit* (of) *no other explanation.*

per·mit² /ˈpɜːmɪt‖ˈpɜːrmɪt, pərˈmɪt/ n an official written statement giving one the right to do something: *You can't work here without a* (work) *permit.* | *a travel permit* | *an import/export permit*

per·mu·ta·tion /ˌpɜːmjʊˈteɪʃən‖ˌpɜːr-/ n any of the ways in which a number of things can be arranged in order: *The six possible permutations of two letters chosen from ABC are AB, BA, CB, BC, AC, and CA.* | *to try various permutations* —compare COMBINATION (4)

per·mute /pəˈmjuːt‖pər-/ v [T] tech to rearrange in a different order

per·ni·cious /pəˈnɪʃəs‖pər-/ adj fml very harmful, often in a way that is not easily noticeable; having or being an evil influence: *the pernicious effect of these horror videos on young children* | *a pernicious lie* — **ly** adv — **ness** n [U]

pernicious a·nae·mi·a /·ˌ··· ·ˈ···/ n [U] med ANAEMIA that will kill the sick person if it is not treated

per·nick·e·ty /pəˈnɪkəti‖pər-/ BrE‖**persnickety** AmE— adj infml, often derog **1** worrying (too much) about small or unimportant things; FUSSY **2** detailed and needing a lot of attention; FIDDLY: *a pernickety job*

Per·nod /ˈpɜːnəʊ, ˈpeə-‖peərˈnəʊ, pər-/ tdmk a clear alcoholic drink tasting of ANISEED, which turns cloudy when water etc. is added; a product of France —compare OUZO

Pe·rón /peˈrɒn, pə-‖-ˈrəʊn/, **E·va** /ˈeɪvə/ (1919–52) the second wife of Juan Domingo Perón, who had a very large personal and political following. Her life story is known esp. through the show *Evita*.

Perón, Juan Do·min·go /wɑːn dəˈmɪŋgəʊ‖hwɑːn-/ (1895–1974) an army officer who became president of Argentina in 1946. He and his wife **Eva Perón** were very popular but after she died he lost a lot of his popularity and had to leave the country in 1955. He returned and became president again in 1973.

per·o·ra·tion /ˌperəˈreɪʃən/ n **1** tech the last part of a speech, esp. the part in which the main points are

repeated in a shorter form **2** fml derog a grand, long, but meaningless speech

Pe·rot /pəˈrəʊ/, **Henry Ross** (1930–) a wealthy American who entered the 1992 presidential election and enjoyed a lot of popular support, even though he was not connected with either of the main political parties. Voters thought he was more honest and direct than other politicians.

per·ox·ide /pəˈrɒksaɪd‖-ˈrɑːk-/ also **hydrogen peroxide** tech— n [U] a chemical liquid used to take the colour out of dark hair and to kill bacteria

peroxide blonde /·ˌ·· ·ˈ·/ n usu. derog a woman who has made her naturally dark hair very light yellow, by using peroxide —compare PLATINUM BLONDE

per·pen·dic·u·lar¹ /ˌpɜːpənˈdɪkjˠləʳ‖ˌpɜːr-/ adj tech **1** exactly upright; not leaning to one side or the other; VERTICAL: *a perpendicular line* | (humor) *He'd drunk so much he found it hard to remain perpendicular.* **2** [F+to] (of a line or surface) at an angle of 90 degrees to another line or surface **3** (often cap.) of the style of 14th and 15th century English buildings, esp. churches, in which there was decoration by the use of straight upright lines — **ly** adv

perpendicular² n [C;(the) U] tech a perpendicular line or position

per·pe·trate /ˈpɜːpˠtreɪt‖ˈpɜːr-/ v [T] fml to do (something wrong or criminal); be guilty of: *to perpetrate a crime/a fraud* | (fig., humor) *It was the managing director who perpetrated that frightful statue in the reception area.* —**trator** n —**tration** /ˌpɜːpˠˈtreɪʃən‖ˌpɜːr-/ n [U]

per·pet·u·al /pəˈpetʃuəl‖pər-/ adj **1** often derog **a** continuing endlessly; uninterrupted: *the perpetual noise of the machines* **b** repeating or being repeated many times: *I'm tired of your perpetual complaints.* **2** lasting for ever or for a long time: *the perpetual snows of the mountaintops* — **ly** adv

perpetual mo·tion ma·chine /·ˌ···· ·ˈ·· ·ˌ·/ n an imaginary machine that could operate on its own power without the use of outside force or FUEL. Natural laws make such a machine impossible.

per·pet·u·ate /pəˈpetʃueɪt‖pər-/ v [T] fml to make (something) continue to exist for a long time; preserve: *They put up a statue to perpetuate her memory.* (=so that she would always be remembered) | *an education system that perpetuates the divisions of our society* —**ation** /pəˌpetʃu-ˈeɪʃən‖pər-/ n [U]

per·pe·tu·i·ty /ˌpɜːpˠˈtjuːˠti‖ˌpɜːrpˠˈtuː-/ n **in perpetuity** fml for ever

per·plex /pəˈpleks‖pər-/ v [T] fml to make (someone) feel confused and worried by being difficult to understand or answer: *a perplexing problem* | *He was perplexed by her contradictory behaviour.* — **edly** /ˈpleksˠdli, ˈplekstli/ adv

per·plex·i·ty /pəˈpleksˠti‖pər-/ n [U] fml the state of being perplexed

per·qui·site /ˈpɜːkwˠzɪt‖ˈpɜːr-/ n fml for PERK¹

Per·ri·er /ˈperieɪ/ n [C;U] tdmk a very well known type of MINERAL WATER which is bottled and exported (EXPORT) from Vergeze in France; Perrier is CARBONATED

Per·rin /ˈperˠn, Re·gin·ald /ˈredʒˠnəld/ a character played by the actor Leonard Rossiter in the popular British television SITUATION COMEDY *The Fall and Rise of Reginald Perrin*. He was a businessman who planned his own disappearance because of the boredom of his life.

per·ry /ˈperi/ n [U] esp. BrE an alcoholic drink made from PEARS

Perry¹, Fred /fred/ (1909–) an English tennis player who won the men's SINGLES title at WIMBLEDON three times and who also produces sports clothes —see also FRED PERRY

Perry², William (19 –) an American FOOTBALL player well-known because he is very large. He is sometimes called "the Refrigerator" because it is said that he can drink as many cans of beer as a REFRIGERATOR can hold.

per se /ˌpɜː ˈseɪ‖ˌpɜːr ˈsiː, ˌpɜːr ˈseɪ, ˌpeər ˈseɪ, ˌpɜːr ˈseɪ/ adv Lat considered alone and not in connection with other things; in, of, or by itself; as such: *It's a very beautiful piece of furniture per se, but it doesn't go with* (=look good with) *the rest of the room.*

per·se·cute /'pɜːsɪkjuːt‖'pɜːr-/ v [T] **1** to treat cruelly and cause to suffer, esp. for religious or political beliefs: *The Romans persecuted the Christians.* **2** to try to harm (someone) by continually annoying them or causing trouble for them; HARASS: *People who think they're always being persecuted may be suffering from a mental illness.* —**-cutor** n —**-cution** /ˌpɜːsɪ'kjuːʃən‖ˌpɜːr-/ n [C;U] : *the persecution of the Jews* | *a persecution complex* (=feeling that people are always persecuting you)

Per·se·phone /pɜː'sefəni‖pɜːr-/ in CLASSICAL MYTHOLOGY, the daughter of Zeus and Demeter who was taken to the UNDERWORLD by Pluto and made queen there. Zeus finally allowed her to return, but only for six months a year, beginning in the spring. She represents death and rebirth, the yearly cycle of summer and winter (Roman name Proserpine).

Per·se·us /'pɜːsiəs‖'pɜːr-/ in CLASSICAL MYTHOLOGY, the man who killed Medusa, who could turn people to stone by looking at them. Perseus used his shield as a mirror and cut off her head without looking at her directly

per·se·ver·ance /ˌpɜːsɪ'viərəns‖ˌpɜːr-/ n [U] *usu. apprec* continual steady effort made to fulfil some aim: *He's slow to learn, but shows great perseverance.*

per·se·vere /ˌpɜːsɪ'viəʳ‖ˌpɜːr-/ v [I (at, in, with)] *usu. apprec* to continue steadily and with determination in spite of difficulties: *If you persevere (with the work), you'll succeed in the end.* | *a persevering student* —compare PERSIST

Pershing mis·sile /ˌpɜːʃɪŋ 'mɪsaɪl‖ˌpɜːrʃɪŋ 'mɪsəl/ n a nuclear BALLISTIC MISSILE (=flying bomb) developed by the US and used in W Europe

Per·sia /'pɜːʃə, -ʒə‖'pɜːrʒə/ the former name of IRAN

Per·sian¹ /'pɜːʃən, -ʒən‖'pɜːrʒən/ adj of the people, language, art, etc. of Persia (now called Iran): *a Persian carpet*

Persian² n also **Farsi**— [U] the language spoken in Iran

Persian cat /ˌ·· '·/ n a kind of cat with long silky hair

Persian Gulf [*the*] GULF

per·si·flage /'pɜːsɪflɑːʒ‖'pɜːr-/ n [U] *fml or pomp* light amusing talk, esp. concerned with laughing at the small weaknesses of others

Per·sil /'pɜːsɪl‖'pɜːr-/ n [U] *tdmk* a powder or liquid for washing clothes

Persil-white /ˌ·· '·◂/ adj BrE *infml* (of clothes) extremely white and clean (from the advertisement for Persil washing powder, which says that "Persil washes whiter")

per·sim·mon /pə'sɪmən‖pər-/ n an orange-coloured soft fruit

per·sist /pə'sɪst‖pər-/ v [I] **1** [(in, with)] to continue in a course of action or way of behaving, firmly and perhaps unreasonably, in spite of opposition or warning: *If you persist in causing trouble, the company may be forced to dismiss you.* | *Must you persist in misunderstanding me?* (=you seem to be intentionally trying not to understand me) **2** to continue to exist: *The bad weather will persist all over the country.* | *Despite official denials, the rumours persisted.* —compare PERSEVERE

per·sis·tent /pə'sɪstənt‖pər-/ adj *often derog* **1** continuing in a course of action or way of behaving, esp. in spite of opposition or warning: *his persistent attempts to annoy me* | *I kept telling him I wasn't interested in his offer, but he was most persistent.* | *a persistent offender* **2** continuing to exist, happen, or appear for a long time, esp. for longer than is usual or desirable: *a persistent cough* | *persistent rumours* —compare INSISTENT — ~ **ly** adv —**-tence** n [U]

per·snick·e·ty /pə'snɪkɪ̱ti‖pər-/ adj AmE for PERNICKETY

per·son /'pɜːsən‖'pɜːr-/ n **1** [C] (*pl.* **people**) a human being considered as having a character of his or her own, or as being different from all others: *I like her as a person, but not as a secretary.* | *Would you call a week-old baby a person?* | *You're just the person I wanted to see.* | *She's a difficult person to deal with.* | *Our new neighbours seem nice people.* **2** [C] esp. *fml or law* (*pl.* **persons**) someone unknown or not named: *Any person wishing to lodge a complaint should contact the manager in writing.* | *The police have a department dealing with missing persons.* | *murder by a person or persons unknown* **3** [C *usu. sing.*] (*pl.* **persons**) *fml* someone's body or outward appearance, sometimes including their clothes: *I think he had a gun concealed about his person.* **4** [C;U] (*pl.* **persons**)

tech (in grammar) any of the three special forms of verbs or PRONOUNs that show the speaker (**first person**), the one who is being spoken to (**second person**), or the one that is being spoken about (**third person**): *The third person singular of the verb "go" is "goes".* | *"I", "me", and "we" are all first person pronouns.* **5 in person** *personally*; *oneself*: *I can't attend the meeting in person, but I'm sending someone to speak for me.* **6 in the person of** *fml* namely; he or she is: *The club has a faithful supporter in the person of Jim Brown.* **7 -person** someone who does the stated thing or has the stated job: *These days it is fashionable to say "spokesperson" rather than "spokesman" or "spokeswoman".* | *a chairperson* | *a salesperson* —see also PERSON-TO-PERSON

▷ USAGE 1 The usual plural of **person** is **people**: *Only one person|A lot of people replied to our advert.* **Persons** is formal, and is often used in official writings, notices, etc.: *He was murdered by a person or persons unknown.* 2 Many people, especially women, do not like the use of words such as **chairman** or **spokesman** to refer to both sexes. They also dislike the use of these words to refer to women. They prefer to use words which can refer to both men and women: *She/he is our new chairperson.* | *She/he agreed to act as spokesperson.*◁

per·so·na /pə'səʊnə‖pər-/ n (in PSYCHOLOGY) the outward character a person takes on in order to persuade other people that he or she is a particular type of person —see also PERSONA NON GRATA

per·son·a·ble /'pɜːsənəbəl‖'pɜːr-/ adj attractive in appearance or character: *a personable young man* —**bly** adv

per·son·age /'pɜːsənɪdʒ‖'pɜːr-/ n *fml or pomp* **1** a famous or important person **2** a character in a play or book, or in history

per·son·al¹ /'pɜːsənəl‖'pɜːr-/ adj **1** [*no comp.*] concerning, belonging to, or for the use of a particular person; private: *the President's personal bodyguard* | *a letter marked "Personal"* | *I'd like to speak to Mr Davis about a personal matter.* | *If you want my personal opinion, I think it's a load of rubbish.* | *On his release the police returned all his personal effects.* (=small articles belonging to him) | *It was a simple recipe, but he had added one or two personal touches to make the meal more interesting.* **2** [*no comp.*] done or made directly by a particular person, not by a representative: *The manager will give you his personal attention, Madam.* | *He made a personal appeal to the kidnappers to return his child.* | *I have a personal stake in his success.* **3** *derog* (making remarks) directed against (the appearance or character of) a particular person; rude: *Don't be so personal!* | *They made some highly personal remarks about the size of his nose.* **4** [A *no comp.*] *fml* of the body or appearance: *Personal hygiene is important for health.* —compare IMPERSONAL; see also PERSONALLY

personal² n AmE a short personal advertisement placed in a newspaper or magazine by someone who wishes to find a friend or lover —see PERSONAL COLUMN

personal al·low·ance /ˌ··· ·'··/ BrE‖**exemption** AmE— n BrE the income below a set limit on which one does not pay INCOME TAX. It is different for e.g. a married or single person.

personal as·sis·tant /ˌ··· ·'··/ n see PA¹

personal col·umn /'··· ·ˌ··/ n a part of a newspaper that gives or asks for messages, information, etc., about particular people. People can also advertise in the personal column to find a person to start a relationship with: *to put an ad in the personal column*

personal com·pu·ter /ˌ··· ·'··/ abbrev. **PC** n a small computer for use by one person at a time in business or in the home, used for WORD PROCESSING, business accounts, or COMPUTER GAMES —see picture of COMPUTER

personal eq·ui·ty plan /ˌ··· '··· ˌ·/ n see PEP

personal es·tate /ˌ··· ·'·/ n [U] *law* PERSONAL PROPERTY

personal hy·giene /ˌ··· '··/ n [U] *fml* keeping one's own body clean: *Personal hygiene is important for good health.*

personal i·den·ti·fi·ca·tion num·ber /ˌ··· ·····'·· ˌ··/ n see PIN

per·son·al·i·ties /ˌpɜːsə'nælɪ̱tiz‖ˌpɜːr-/ n [P] BrE unkind or rude remarks directed against someone's appearance, character, etc.: *Let's keep personalities out of the conversation, shall we!*

per·son·al·i·ty /ˌpɜːsəˈnælɪti‖ˌpɜːr-/ n 1 [C;U] the whole nature or character of a particular person: *He has a strong/dynamic/weak personality.* | *The drug changed her whole personality.* —compare CHARACTER (1) 2 [C;U] (a person with) forceful, lively, and usu. attractive qualities of character: *She has a lot of/She is quite a personality.* 3 [C] a person who is well known to the public or to people connected with some particular activity: *a television personality*

personality cult /ˈ··· ·/ n usu. derog the officially encouraged practice of giving too great admiration, praise, love, etc., to a particular person, esp. a political leader: *a personality cult surrounding the Prime Minister*

per·son·al·ize also **-ise** BrE /ˈpɜːsənəlaɪz‖ˈpɜːr-/ v [T] 1 to make personal, esp. by adding one's address or (the first letters of) one's name: *personalized handkerchiefs/stationery* 2 often derog to change so as to be concerned with personal matters or relationships rather than with facts: *Let's not personalize this argument.* —**ization** /ˌpɜːsənəlaɪˈzeɪʃən‖ˌpɜːrsənələ-/ n [U]

per·son·al·ly /ˈpɜːsənəli‖ˈpɜːr-/ adv 1 directly and not through someone acting for one: *The director is personally in charge of all the arrangements.* 2 speaking for oneself only; to give one's own opinion: *She said she didn't like it, but personally I thought it was very good.* 3 as a person; with regard to personal qualities: *She may be personally very charming, but will she be a good secretary?* 4 derog as directed against oneself in a PERSONAL¹ (3) way: *You mustn't take her criticisms of your plan personally.* 5 privately: *May I speak to you personally about this problem, sir?*

personal or·ga·ni·zer /ˌ··· ˈ···/ n a small RING BINDER holding sheets of specially shaped paper for information, addresses, a DIARY, etc. —compare FILOFAX

personal pen·sion plan /ˌ··· ˈ·· ˌ·/ n a PENSION PLAN which is a private agreement between a person and an insurance company, rather than with the government or an employer

personal pro·noun /ˌ··· ˈ··/ n tech (in grammar) a PRONOUN used for the one who is being spoken to, or the one that is being spoken about: *"I", "you", and "they" are personal pronouns.* —see also PERSON (4)

personal prop·er·ty /ˌ··· ˈ···/ also **personal estate**— n [U] law all the things owned by a person except land and buildings —compare REAL ESTATE (1)

personal ster·e·o /ˌ··· ˈ···/ also **walkman** tdmk— n a small CASSETTE PLAYER and/or radio which is carried and listened to through small speakers that fit in or over the ears

persona non gra·ta /pəˌsəʊnə nɒn ˈɡrɑːtə‖pərˌsəʊnə nɑːn ˈɡrætə/ n [U] Lat a person who is not acceptable or welcome, esp. in someone's house or to a government: *He was declared persona non grata and thrown out of the country.*

per·son·i·fi·ca·tion /pəˌsɒnɪfɪˈkeɪʃən‖pərˌsɑː-/ n 1 [C (of)] a person or thing considered as a perfect example of some quality, either good or bad: *the personification of evil* —compare INCARNATION (3) 2 [C;U] (an act of) personifying something that is without life

per·son·i·fy /pəˈsɒnɪfaɪ‖pərˈsɑː-/ v [T] 1 to be a (perfect) example of; be the living form of (some quality): *He is evil/patience personified.* 2 to think of or represent (something that is without life) as a human being or as having human qualities: *A ship is often personified as "she".*

per·son·nel /ˌpɜːsəˈnel‖ˌpɜːr-/ n 1 [P] all the people employed by a company, in the armed forces, or working in any organization: *army personnel* | *The company's main problem is the shortage of skilled personnel.* | *She is studying personnel management.* 2 [U+sing./pl. v] the department in an organization that deals with (the complaints and difficulties of) these people: *She works in personnel.* | *Personnel has/have lost my tax forms.* | *Speak to the personnel officer about it.*

person-to-person /ˌ··· ˈ···◂/ adj esp. AmE (of a telephone call) made to one person in particular, and not needing to be paid for if they are not there and someone else answers

per·spec·tive /pəˈspektɪv‖pər-/ n 1 [U] (the rules governing) the art of drawing solid objects on a flat surface so that they give a natural effect of depth, distance, and so-lidity: *The picture looks strange because it has no perspective. In those days artists didn't understand perspective.* | *The objects in the background are in/out of perspective.* 2 [C;U (on)] the way in which a situation or problem is judged, so that (proper) consideration and importance is given to each part: *We must get/keep the problem in perspective; it's not really that serious.* | *The company's results need to be looked at in perspective/in their proper perspective; our profits have fallen but it's been a difficult year for our competitors, too.* | *The new evidence put an entirely different perspective on the case.* | *a historical perspective* 3 [C (of)] a view, esp. one stretching far into the distance

per·spex /ˈpɜːspeks‖ˈpɜːr-/ BrE tdmk ‖ **plexiglass** tdmk AmE— n [U] (sometimes cap.) a strong plastic material that can be seen through and is used instead of glass

per·spi·ca·cious /ˌpɜːspɪˈkeɪʃəs◂‖ˌpɜːr-/ adj fml having or showing very clever judgment and understanding: *a perspicacious comment* — ~**ly** adv —**city** /ˈkæsɪti/ n [U]

per·spi·ra·tion /ˌpɜːspəˈreɪʃən‖ˌpɜːr-/ n [U] euph or tech SWEAT² (1) or the act of sweating (SWEAT¹ (1))

per·spire /pəˈspaɪəʳ‖pər-/ v [I] euph or tech for SWEAT¹ (1)

per·suade /pəˈsweɪd‖pər-/ v [T] 1 [(into, out of)] to make (someone) willing to do something by reasoning, arguing, repeatedly asking, etc.: *Despite all my efforts to persuade him, he wouldn't agree.* | *He persuaded her into/out of going* (=to go/not to go) *to the party.* [+obj+to-v] *Try to persuade them to come with us.* | (fig.) *I persuaded the piece of wood* (=made it go gradually) *into the little crack.* 2 [(of)] rather fml to cause to believe or feel certain; CONVINCE: *She was not persuaded of the truth of his statement.* [+obj+(that)] *He was unable to persuade the police that he had been elsewhere at the time of the crime.* —**suadable** adj

per·sua·sion /pəˈsweɪʒən‖pər-/ n 1 [U] the act or skill of persuading: *In spite of my efforts at persuasion, he wouldn't agree.* | *She used all her powers of persuasion on them.* 2 [C] fml or humor a particular belief: *people of many different political persuasions* 3 [C usu. sing.] fml or derog the stated kind or sort: *an artist of the modern persuasion* 4 [S] fml a strongly held belief or opinion: [+that] *It is my persuasion that such people should not be allowed to enter this country.*

per·sua·sive /pəˈsweɪsɪv‖pər-/ adj having the power to influence others into believing or doing what one wishes: *a persuasive talker* | *very persuasive arguments* — ~**ly** adv — ~**ness** n [U]

pert /pɜːt‖pɜːrt/ adj 1 (esp. of a girl or young woman) slightly disrespectful in a rather amusing way; SAUCY: *a pert young miss* 2 neat and stylish in a cheerful way: *She wore a pert little hat.* — ~**ly** adv — ~**ness** n [U]

per·tain /pəˈteɪn‖pər-/ v
pertain to sthg. phr v [T] fml to have a connection with; concern: *Any inquiries pertaining to the granting of planning permission should be addressed to the Town Hall.*

Perth /pɜːθ‖pɜːrθ/ 1 a city in SW Australia, capital of the state of Western Australia 2 a city in central Scotland on the river Tay

Perth·shire /ˈpɜːθʃəʳ‖ˈpɜːrθ-/ a former COUNTY in central Scotland, now part of Tayside REGION

per·ti·na·cious /ˌpɜːtɪˈneɪʃəs◂‖ˌpɜːr-/ adj fml holding to an opinion, course of action, etc., in a very determined way; STUBBORN — ~**ly** adv —**city** /ˈnæsɪti/ n [U]

per·ti·nent /ˈpɜːtɪnənt‖ˈpɜːr-/ adj [(to)] fml connected directly with something that is being considered; RELEVANT: *She asked several highly pertinent questions.* | *Your remarks are not pertinent to our discussion.* —opposite **irrelevant**; see also IMPERTINENT — ~**ly** adv —**nence** n [U]

per·turb /pəˈtɜːb‖pərˈtɜːrb/ v [T] fml to cause to worry greatly; DISTURB: *I am deeply perturbed by the alarming way the situation is developing.* —**turbation** /ˌpɜːtə-ˈbeɪʃən‖ˌpɜːrtər-/ n [U]

Pe·ru /pəˈruː/ a country in W South America bordering the Pacific Ocean; capital Lima; population 21,792,000 (1989). People connect Peru with the Incas and often think of it as a REMOTE and mysterious place: *darkest Peru*

pe·ruse /pəˈruːz/ v [T] 1 fml to read through carefully 2 often humor to read: *After breakfast he perused the newspapers.* —**rusal** n [C;U]

Pe·ru·vi·an /pəˈruːviən/ adj, n (a person who comes or whose parents come) from Peru

per·vade /pəˈveɪd‖pər-/ v [T] fml or lit (of smells and of ideas, feelings, etc.) to spread through every part of: *The smell of cooking pervaded the house.* | *A spirit of hopelessness pervaded the country.*

per·va·sive /pəˈveɪsɪv‖pər-/ adj tending to pervade; widespread: *the pervasive influence of television* | *pervasive doubts* — ~ly adv — ~ness n [U]

per·verse /pəˈvɜːs‖pərˈvɜːrs/ adj **1** (of a person, behaviour, etc.) purposely continuing to do, believe in, etc. something that one knows to be wrong, unreasonable, or unacceptable: *She gets a perverse satisfaction from making other people embarrassed.* **2** (of a person or event) unreasonably opposed to the wishes of (other) people; awkward and annoying: *We all wanted to go tomorrow, but she had to be perverse and insisted on going today.* — ~ly adv : *Perversely, it started to rain just as the match was due to start.*

per·ver·sion /pəˈvɜːʃən, -ʒən‖pərˈvɜːrʒən/ n **1** [C (**of**)] a perverted or twisted form of what is true, reasonable, etc.: *a newspaper story full of perversions of the truth* **2** [C] a form of sexual behaviour that is (considered) unnatural **3** [U] the action of perverting or the state of being perverted

per·ver·si·ty /pəˈvɜːsɪti‖pərˈvɜːr-/ n **1** [U] also **per·verse·ness** /pəˈvɜːsnəs‖pərˈvɜːr-/— the quality or state of being perverse: *the perversity of the British weather* **2** [C] a perverse act

per·vert¹ /pəˈvɜːt‖pərˈvɜːrt/ v [T] **1** to lead into ways of thinking or forms of behaviour (esp. sexual behaviour) that are considered wrong or unnatural; DEPRAVE: *All this violence on TV is perverting the minds of our young children.* | *perverted sexual practices* **2** to use for a bad purpose: *Scientific knowledge was perverted to help cause destruction and war.* | *To* **pervert the course of justice** *is to try to prevent justice being done.* **3** to change or twist (the meaning of words)

per·vert² /ˈpɜːvɜːt‖ˈpɜːrvɜːrt/ n derog a person whose sexual behaviour is not (considered) natural

pe·se·ta /pəˈseɪtə/ n a Spanish coin, on which the Spanish money system is based

pes·ky /ˈpeski/ adj [A] infml, esp. AmE annoying and causing trouble

pe·so /ˈpeɪsəʊ/ n **pesos** a small coin on which the money systems of many Spanish American countries are based

pes·sa·ry /ˈpesəri/ n **1** a medicine in solid form put into the female sex organ (VAGINA) —compare SUPPOSITORY **2** an instrument put into the VAGINA to support the WOMB or as a means of birth control

pes·si·mis·m /ˈpesᵻmɪzəm/ n [U] a tendency to give more attention to the bad side of a situation or to expect the worst possible result —opposite **optimism**

pes·si·mist /ˈpesᵻmɪst/ n a person who thinks that whatever happens will be bad: *Don't be such a pessimist — I'm sure you'll pass.* —opposite **optimist** — ~ic /ˌpesᵻˈmɪstɪk◂/ adj : *The experts are pessimistic about our chances of success.* — ~ically /kli/ adv

pest /pest/ n **1** a usu. small animal or insect that harms or destroys food supplies: *Rabbits are great pests to farmers.* | *garden pests* | *pest control* **2** infml an annoying person or thing: *That child's a real pest; he's continually asking questions.*

pes·ter /ˈpestəʳ/ v [T (**for**, **with**)] infml to annoy (someone) continually, esp. with demands: *The beggars pestered the tourists for money.* [+obj+to-v] *My daughter has been pestering me to take her with me.*

pes·ti·cide /ˈpestᵻsaɪd/ n [C;U] a chemical substance used to kill PESTS (1)

pes·ti·lence /ˈpestᵻləns/ n [C;U] esp. old use a disease that causes death and spreads quickly to large numbers of people, esp. BUBONIC PLAGUE

pes·ti·lent /ˈpestᵻlənt/ also **pes·ti·len·tial** /ˌpestᵻˈlenʃəl◂/— adj **1** esp. old use of or causing pestilence **2** often humor continually annoying and unpleasant

pes·tle /ˈpesəl, ˈpestl/ n an instrument with a heavy rounded end, used for crushing substances in a special bowl (MORTAR) —see picture at LABORATORY

pet¹ /pet/ n **1** an animal kept in the home as a compan-

ion. Pets are much loved in Britain and the US and treated as members of the family: *Have you got any pets?* | *He keeps a monkey as a pet.* | *a pet dog/rabbit* | *pet food* **2** often given esp. a child, or thing given special and perhaps unfairly favourable treatment: *She is the* **teacher's pet**. | *his pet theory* **3** [usu. sing.] a person who is specially loved or lovable: *Come here, (my) pet!* —see also PET NAME

pet² v **-tt-** **1** [T] to touch kindly with the hands, showing love: *She petted the little dog.* **2** [I;T] infml to kiss and touch (someone else or each other) in sexual play —see also HEAVY PETTING

pet³ n old-fash a sudden show of childish bad temper and impatience, esp. about something unimportant: *It's nothing to get* **in a pet** *about.* —see also PETTISH

Pé·tain /peˈtæŋ/, **Marshal Hen·ri** /ˈɒnriˈɑːnˈriː/ (1856–1951) a French soldier who fought for France in the First World War and was made Prime Minister in 1940. He became head of the Vichy government which collaborated (COLLABORATE (2)) with the Nazis. After the war he was imprisoned for TREASON. —see also VICHY

pet·al /ˈpetl/ n **1** any of the usu. coloured leaflike divisions of a flower: *rose petals* **2 -petalled** also **-petaled** AmE /ˈpetld/ having petals of the stated number or kind —see picture at FLOWER

pe·tard /pᵻˈtɑːd‖-ɑːrd/ n see hoist with one's own petard (HOIST)

pet·er¹ /ˈpiːtəʳ/ v
peter out phr v [I] to come gradually to an end: *Interest in the project has petered out.* | *The road became narrower and rougher and eventually petered out.*

peter² n see BLUE PETER

Peter¹ robbing Peter to pay Paul to borrow money in order to pay someone else, or use money meant for one purpose for some other purpose: *To increase funding for universities at the expense of primary education is simply robbing Peter to pay Paul.*

Peter², Simon see SAINT PETER

Peter Dom·i·nic /ˌpiːtə ˈdɒmᵻnɪk‖-tər ˈdɑː-/ one of a group of British shops selling wines, beer, and spirits

Peter Jones /ˌ‥ ˈ‥/ a large department store in Sloane Square, central London

Peter Pan /ˌ‥ ˈ‥/ **1** the main character in a story by J M Barrie, a young boy who never grows up but lives in a magic land called **Never-Never Land**. In the story, three children, Michael, John, and Wendy, go with Peter Pan and the FAIRY, Tinkerbell to stay in the Never Never Land, where they have many adventures. Peter Pan's enemy in the story is Captain Hook, an evil PIRATE who has a metal hook in the place of one of his hands. Captain Hook lost his hand in a fight with Peter Pan, and Peter Pan threw the hand into some water. It was eaten by a crocodile, who liked the taste so much that it then followed Captain Hook around trying to catch and eat the rest of him. —see colour picture on page 619 **2** a man whose body or attitudes never seem to change as the years pass; a man who never seems to grow up: *the Peter Pan of the music business*

Peter Pan col·lar /ˌ‥ ˈ‥ ‥/ n a type of usu. small collar with rounded ends, used esp. on women's clothes

Peter Pan collar

Peter, Paul, and Ma·ry /ˌ‥ ˌ‥ ‥ ˈ‥/ a group of American popular music singers who were popular esp. in the 1960s and 1970s

Peter prin·ci·ple /ˈ‥ ˌ‥ ‥/ n [S] infml, often humor the idea that each person in an organization is given higher rank with more responsibility until they reach their **level of incompetence** (=the level at which they cannot do the job properly). They then stay at this level, having a bad effect on the organization as a whole (from the name of its inventor, American educator **Laurence Peter**).

Peter Rab·bit /ˌ‥ ˈ‥/ a character in children's stories by Beatrix Potter, a young rabbit who behaved badly but was still lovable

Pe·ter·son /ˈpiːtəsən‖-tər-/, **Oscar** (1925–) a Canadian JAZZ piano player, famous for his original and inventive music

Peter's pence /ˌ·· ˈ·/ [S] **1** a one-penny tax paid in England until 1534 for the Pope **2** money freely given by Catholics in some countries to pay for the running of the Vatican

Peter the Great /ˌ··· ·ˈ·/ also **Peter I** /ˌpiːtə ðə ˈfɜːst ‖ -tər ðə ˈfɜːrst/ (1672–1725) the TSAR (=ruler) of Russia from 1682–1725

pet food /ˈ· ·/ n food prepared specially for pets, esp. cats and dogs, and usu. preserved in tins

pet hate /ˌ· ˈ·/ n BrE‖also **pet peeve** esp. AmE infml— something that one finds particularly annoying, even when others do not find it so: *Small dogs are my pet peeve.* | *My pet hate is those stupid car horns that play a tune.*

pet·it bour·geois /ˌpeti ˈbʊəʒwɑː, -bʊəˈʒwɑː‖ˌpeti bʊərˈʒwɑː, pəˌtiː-/ also **petty bourgeois**— n, adj Fr **1** (a person, such as a small shopkeeper or skilled worker) of the lower middle class **2** BOURGEOIS[1] (2),[2]

pe·tite /pəˈtiːt/ adj apprec (of a woman or girl) having a small and neat figure: *a petite blonde*

petit four /ˌpeti ˈfʊər, -ˈfɔːr/ n Fr a kind of small sweet cake or BISCUIT served with coffee, esp. at the end of a meal

pe·ti·tion[1] /pɪˈtɪʃən/ n **1** [(for, against)] (a piece or pieces of paper containing) a request or demand made to a government or other body, usu. signed by many people: *Will you sign our petition against using animals in scientific experiments?* | *to get up* (=arrange) *a petition* **2** an official letter to a court of law, asking for consideration of one's case **3** fml a solemn prayer or request to God, a ruler, etc.

petition[2] v [I;T (for, against)] to make or send a petition or official request: *We're petitioning for a new playground for the village children.* [+to-v] *The people petitioned to be allowed to return to their island.* [+obj+to-v] *They petitioned the government to reconsider its decision.*

pe·ti·tion·er /pɪˈtɪʃənər/ n **1** someone who makes or signs a petition **2** law someone asking for their marriage to be legally ended

petit mal /ˌpeti ˈmæl/ n [U] Fr a slight form of the disease of EPILEPSY —compare GRAND MAL

petit pain /ˌpeti ˈpæn/ n **petits pains**, (same pronunciation) Fr a small rich loaf for one person, often eaten warm with coffee at breakfast, esp. in France

pet name /ˌ· ˈ·/ n a name given to someone whom one specially likes or loves, used instead of that person's real name

Pet·o In·sti·tute /ˈpetəʊ ˌɪnstɪtjuːt‖-tuːt/ an institution in Budapest, Hungary, set up by **Dr Andras Peto** in 1945, which teaches children who cannot control their bodies properly to lead more independent lives by means of CONDUCTIVE EDUCATION

pet peeve /ˌ· ˈ·/ n see PET HATE

Pet·ra /ˈpetrə/ the ruins of an ancient civilization in Jordan, where houses are cut into rock

pet·rel /ˈpetrəl/ n a black and white seabird —see also STORMY PETREL

Petrified For·est /ˌ··· ˈ··/ [the] a large national park in E Arizona, USA, where the rock surfaces show FOSSILs of very old trees

pet·ri·fy /ˈpetrɪfaɪ/ v **1** [T] to put (someone) into a state of extreme shock or fear so that they are unable to think or take action: *He sat there petrified as the ghost glided across the room.* | (fig.) *My new boss absolutely petrifies me.* —see FRIGHTENED (USAGE) **2** [I;T] to turn into stone: *petrified wood* —**faction** /ˌpetrɪˈfækʃən/ n [U] fml

pet·ro·chem·i·cal /ˌpetrəʊˈkemɪkəl‑/ n a chemical substance obtained from PETROLEUM or natural gas: *the petrochemical industry* | *a petrochemical plant* (=factory)

pet·ro·dol·lar /ˈpetrəʊˌdɒlər‖-ˌdɑːl-/ n tech an American dollar earned by the sale of oil, esp. by the oil-producing countries of the Middle East

Pet·ro·grad /ˈpetrəgræd/ the modern Russian name for St Petersburg, also used from 1914–24

pet·rol /ˈpetrəl/ BrE ‖ **gas, gasoline** AmE— n [U] a liquid obtained esp. from petroleum, used mainly for producing power in the engines of cars, aircraft, etc.: *We filled (the car) up with petrol before the long journey.* | *Six gallons/litres of petrol, please.* | *the petrol tank* | *petrol fumes* | *a petrol pump* | *two star/four star petrol* (=the number of

stars showing the quality of the petrol) —see picture at PUMP

petrol bomb /ˈ··· ·/ n a type of bomb made by putting petrol inside a container, e.g. a bottle, attaching a piece of cloth, and lighting the cloth. Petrol bombs are thrown usu. by TERRORISTs or people involved in RIOTs.

pe·tro·le·um /pɪˈtrəʊliəm/ n [U] a mineral oil obtained from below the surface of the Earth, and used to produce petrol, PARAFFIN, and various chemical substances: *petroleum-based products*

petroleum jel·ly /·ˌ···ˈ··/ also **Vaseline** tdmk ‖ also **pet·ro·la·tum** /ˌpetrəˈleɪtəm/AmE— n [U] a thick GREASE (2) substance made from petroleum, used esp. on cut or broken skin

pe·trol·o·gy /pɪˈtrɒlədʒi‖-ˈtrɑː-/ n [U] the scientific study of rocks —**gist** n

petrol sta·tion /ˈ··· ˌ··/ BrE‖**filling station, gas station** AmE— n a place where you take your car and fill it with petrol. Most petrol stations also sell oil and small SPARE PARTs, and other goods such as cigarettes and sweets. Some will also do simple repairs.

Pet Shop Boys /ˈ·· ˌ·/, **The** two British popular singers popular among young people in the 1980s and 1990s. They are known esp. for their electronic music and their flat, unemotional style.

pet·ti·coat /ˈpetikəʊt/ also **slip** BrE old-fash ‖ **slip** AmE— n a woman's undergarment which hangs from the shoulders or waist

Petticoat Lane /ˌ··· ˈ·/ a street in the East End of London, officially called Middlesex Street, where a market is held every week on Sunday morning

pet·ti·fog·ging /ˈpetiˌfɒgɪŋ‖-ˌfɑː-, -ˌfɔː-/ adj BrE derog **1** needlessly concerned with small unimportant details: *I'm sick to death of those pettifogging bureaucrats!* **2** too small to be worth considering

pet·tish /ˈpetɪʃ/ adj derog impatiently angry; showing childish bad temper, esp. over something unimportant —see also PET[3] —~**ly** adv —~**ness** n [U]

pet·ty /ˈpeti/ adj **1** of (relatively) little importance; on a small scale: *Our problems seem petty when compared to those of people who never get enough to eat.* | *petty crime* **2** derog having or showing a mind that is limited, narrow, and ungenerous; SMALL-MINDED: *petty spite* | *Don't be so petty/petty-minded.* —**tily** adv —**tiness** n [U]

petty bour·geois /ˌ··· ·ˈ·/ n, adj (a) PETIT BOURGEOIS

petty cash /ˌ··· ˈ·/ n [(the) U] an amount of money kept ready in an office for making small payments

petty lar·ce·ny /ˌ··· ˈ···/ n [C;U] law the stealing of articles of a value below a certain amount

petty of·fi·cer /ˌ··· ˈ···◂/ n a naval rank —see TABLE 3

pet·u·lant /ˈpetʃʊlənt/ adj showing childish bad temper over unimportant things, or for no reason at all —~**ly** adv : *"I won't!" she said petulantly.* —**lance** n [U (at)]

pe·tu·ni·a /pɪˈtjuːniə‖pɪˈtuː-/ n a garden plant with colourful flowers shaped like a widening tube

Peu·geot /ˈpɜːʒəʊ‖pjuːˈʒəʊ/ also **Peugeot Tal·bot** /ˌ·· ˈ··/ a French company that makes cars and bikes: *He works for Peugeot.* | *I've just bought a new Peugeot.*

pew /pjuː/ n **1** a long seat (BENCH (1)) with a back to it, for people to sit on in church. Pews are generally thought of as hard and uncomfortable. **2** humor a seat: *Take a pew!* (=sit down)

pew·ter /ˈpjuːtər/ n [U] **1** a greyish metal made by mixing lead and tin: *a pewter tankard* **2** also **pewter ware** /ˈ·· ˌ·/— dishes, cups, etc., made from this

pey·ote /peɪˈəʊti/ n a kind of CACTUS plant which is used by NATIVE AMERICANs in Mexico and the American southwest in religious ceremonies and for making sick people well. The plant contains a drug called MESCALIN which is HALLUCINOGENIC (=causes dream-like thoughts which seem real).

Pey·ton Place /ˌpeɪtn ˈpleɪs/ a NOVEL by Grace Metalious, later made into a film. It takes place in a small town among a few people who have difficult emotional relationships and treat each other badly. People sometimes say that a situation is like Peyton Place, meaning that there are many secrets, BETRAYALs, and emotional upsets.

Pfeif·fer /ˈfaɪfər/, **Mi·chelle** /miːˈʃel/ (1959–) an

American film actress, regarded as one of the most beautiful. Her films include *Dangerous Liaisons* and *The Fabulous Baker Boys.* —see colour picture on page 228

pfen·nig /ˈfenɪg/ *n* a small German coin worth one hundredth (¹/₁₀₀) of a MARK³

PG /ˌpiː ˈdʒiː/ *n* 'parental guidance; (of a film) which may in parts be unsuitable for children under 15. Children may watch PG films only if they are with an adult. —compare U³

PGA /ˌpiː dʒiː ˈeɪ/ *[the]* Professional Golfers' Association; an American organization for those who make money from GOLF either by playing it, running golf courses, or teaching. The organization runs the **PGA Championship**, a golfing competition.

PGCE /ˌpiː dʒiː siː ˈiː/ *n* (in Britain) postgraduate certificate of education; a qualification that allows people who have been to university to teach in state schools: *I'm planning to do a PGCE next year.* | *Have you got a PGCE?*

PG Tips /ˌpiː dʒiː ˈtɪps/ *tdmk* a kind of tea sold in Britain, known for its advertisements which feature CHIMPANZEES dressed to look like humans

pH /piː ˈeɪtʃ/ *n [usu. sing.]* a number which represents the degree to which a substance, esp. soil, is acid or ALKALINE (ALKALI): *to test the pH of the soil*

phae·ton /ˈfeɪtn‖ˈfeɪətn/ *n* a light open carriage used in former times, usu. pulled by two horses

phag·o·cyte /ˈfæɡəsaɪt/ *n med* a blood cell, such as a LEUCOCYTE, which protects the body by destroying harmful bacteria, etc.

pha·lanx /ˈfælæŋks‖ˈfeɪ-/ *n* **-lanxes** *or* **-langes** /fəˈlændʒiːz/ **1** [+*sing./pl. v*] a group of men or animals packed closely together, esp. for attack or defence: *A phalanx of police men bore down on the rioters.* **2** [+*sing./pl. v*] (esp. in ancient Greece) a group of soldiers packed closely together for better protection **3** *med* a bone in a finger or toe

phal·lic /ˈfælɪk/ *adj* or like a phallus: *a phallic symbol*

phal·lus /ˈfæləs/ *n* an image of the male sex organ (PENIS), esp. as used in some forms of religion as a sign of the power of man to produce children

phan·tas·m /ˈfæntæzəm/ *n esp. lit* something that exists only in the imagination; an ILLUSION —**phantasmal** /fænˈtæzməl/ *adj*

phan·tas·ma·go·ri·a /ˌfænˌtæzməˈɡɔːriə, ˌfæntæz-/ *n [(of)]* a confused dreamlike changing scene of different things, real and/or imagined —**ric** /ˈɡɒrɪk‖ˈɡɑː-, ˈɡɔː-/, **-rical** *adj*

phan·ta·sy /ˈfæntəsi/ *n [C;U] old use for* FANTASY

phan·tom /ˈfæntəm/ *n* **1** a shadowy likeness of a dead person that seems to appear on earth; GHOST: *phantom riders passing by in the night* | (fig., humor) *The phantom letter-writer has been here again; all my stationery has disappeared!* **2** something that exists only in one's imagination: *the phantoms that troubled his dreams*

Phantom of the Op·e·ra /ˌ··· · ˈ···/ *[the]* a story about a man wearing a MASK who KIDNAPS an OPERA singer. There are many different films and plays based on the story.

phantom preg·nan·cy /ˌ··· ˈ···/ *also* **hysterical pregnancy** *AmE*- *n* a condition in which a woman seems to be PREGNANT but in fact is not

pha·raoh /ˈfeərəʊ/ *n (often cap.)* a ruler of ancient Egypt: *Pharaoh Rameses II*

phar·i·sa·ic /ˌfærəˈseɪ-ɪk/ *also* **phar·i·sa·i·cal** /-ɪkəl/— *adj fml derog* making a show of being good and religious —**ism** /ˈfærɪseɪ-ɪzəm/ *n [U]*

phar·i·see /ˈfærɪsiː/ *n fml derog* a person who in a self-satisfied way values too highly the outward form of something, esp. a religion, rather than its true meaning

Pharisee *n* a member of a group of Jews in ancient Jerusalem who were very careful and serious in obeying religious laws, and considered themselves very holy because of this. In the Bible, Jesus criticized them for being HYPOCRITEs.

phar·ma·ceu·ti·cal /ˌfɑːməˈsjuːtɪkəl◂‖ˌfɑːrməˈsuː-/ *adj* connected with (the making of) medicine: *the large pharmaceutical companies* —**cally** /kli/ *adv*

phar·ma·cist /ˈfɑːməsɪst‖ˈfɑːr-/ *n* ‖*also* **druggist** *AmE*— a skilled person who owns or runs a pharmacy; CHEMIST (3)

phar·ma·col·o·gy /ˌfɑːməˈkɒlədʒi‖ˌfɑːrməˈkɑː-/ *n [U]* the scientific study of medicines and drugs —**gist** *n*

phar·ma·co·poe·ia /ˌfɑːməkəˈpiːə‖ˌfɑːr-/ *n tech* **1** an official book describing medicines, what they contain, the amount to be given to a sick person, etc. **2** all the medicines that are (officially permitted to be) used in a particular country

phar·ma·cy /ˈfɑːməsi‖ˈfɑːr-/ *n* **1** [C] a (part of a) shop where medicines are sold: *an all-night pharmacy* —compare DISPENSARY, DRUGSTORE **2** [U] (the study of) the making and/or giving out of medicine

phar·yn·gi·tis /ˌfærɪnˈdʒaɪtɪs/ *n [U] med* a medical condition that includes soreness of the throat

phar·ynx /ˈfærɪŋks/ *n med* the tube at the back of the mouth that leads from the back of the nose to the point where the air-passage and food-passage divide —see picture at RESPIRATORY

phase¹ /feɪz/ *n* **1** [(in, of)] a stage of development: *The new weapons system is still in the research phase.* | *The election campaign has now entered a critical phase|its final phase.* | *Don't worry about your son's shyness; it's just a phase he's going through.* —compare STAGE¹ (2) **2** [(of)] any of a fixed number of changes in the appearance of the moon or a PLANET as seen from the Earth at different times during their ORBIT: *the phases of the moon* **3 in/out of phase (with)** *tech* working|not working or going together (with another or each other): *The carrier wave has got out of phase with the signal wave.*

phase² *v* [T] to plan or arrange in separate phases: *The army is making a phased withdrawal from the occupied territory.*
phase sthg. ↔ **in** *phr v* [T] to introduce (something) in stages or gradually: *The government is going to phase in the new pension scheme over five years.*
phase sthg. ↔ **out** *phr v* [T] to stop or remove (something) in stages or gradually: *The bus service to country areas is being phased out.* —**phase-out** /ˈ· ·/ *n*

PhD /ˌpiː eɪtʃ ˈdiː/ *also* **D Phil**— *n* Doctor of Philosophy; (a title for someone who has) a university degree of very high rank, above an MA or MSc, which takes about three years and usu. involves doing research. Someone who has a PhD is said to have a **doctorate** and is often given the title of **Dr**: *Jacqueline Hope, PhD* | *Dr Jacqueline Hope*

pheas·ant /ˈfezənt/ *n* **pheasants** *or* **pheasant** a large long-tailed bird shot for food, the male of which is usu. brightly coloured. Pheasants can legally be shot in certain seasons in Britain and the US, and in Britain shooting them is a generally UPPER-CLASS sport. —see picture at BIRD

phe·no·bar·bi·tone /ˌfiːnəʊˈbɑːbɪtəʊn‖-ˈbɑːr-/ *BrE* ‖ **phe·no·bar·bi·tal** /-bɪtl‖-bɪtɔːl/ *esp. AmE*— *n [U]* a powerful calming drug that helps a person to sleep

phe·nom·e·nal /fɪˈnɒmɪnəl‖-ˈnɑː-/ *adj* **1** *usu. apprec* very unusual; EXTRAORDINARY: *phenomenal strength* | *a phenomenal* (=very powerful) *memory* **2** [*no comp.*] *fml* known through the senses: *a phenomenal experience* —**ly** *adj*: *phenomenally strong*

phe·nom·e·non /fɪˈnɒmɪnən‖fɪˈnɑːmɪnɑːn, -nən/ *n* **-na** /nə/ **1** a fact, event, type of behaviour, etc., that exists and can be experienced by the senses, esp. one that is unusual and/or of scientific interest: *Magnetism is a natural phenomenon.* | *Snow in Egypt is an almost unknown phenomenon.* | *International terrorism is not just a recent phenomenon.* **2** a very unusual person, thing, event, etc.: *A child who could play the piano at the age of two would indeed be a phenomenon.*

phew /fjuː/ *also* **whew** *interj* (a quick short whistling breath, either in or out, expressing tiredness, shock, or RELIEF)

phi·al /ˈfaɪəl/ *also* **vial**— *n* a small bottle, esp. for liquid medicines: *a phial of morphine*

Phi Be·ta Kap·pa /ˌfaɪ ˌbiːtə ˈkæpə/ *n* (someone who is a member of) an American society for the recognition of ACADEMIC high achievement in university and college students. This **honor society** was started in 1776. Students are elected for this highly-respected honour in their third or fourth year of college.

Phil·a·del·phi·a /ˌfɪləˈdelfiə/ *also* **Philly** *infml* a city in the US state of Pennsylvania, where the Declaration of Independence from Britain was signed in 1776. Philadelphia is the fifth largest city in the US. —see colour map on pages 1374–5

phi·lan·der·er /fɪˈlændərəʳ/ *n old-fash derog* a man who amuses himself by having (sexual) relations with (many) women, with no serious intentions —**dering** adj, n [A;U]

phil·an·throp·ic /ˌfɪlənˈθrɒpɪk◀‖-ˈθrɑː-/ adj of or showing philanthropy: a philanthropic attitude | our philanthropic institutions — ~ **ally** /kli/ adv

phi·lan·thro·pist /fɪˈlænθrəp⌄st/ n a person who helps those who are poor or in trouble, esp. a rich person who gives generous gifts of money

phi·lan·thro·py /fɪˈlænθrəpi/ n [U] a feeling of kindness and love for all people, esp. as shown in an active way by giving help or money to people who are poor or in trouble

phi·lat·e·ly /fɪˈlætəli/ n [U] tech stamp collecting —**list** n —**lic** /ˌfɪləˈtelɪk◀/ adj

Phil·by /ˈfɪlbi/, **Kim** /kɪm/ (1911–88) an English SPY who was already working for the Soviet Union when he was employed by the British government. He went to the Soviet Union to live in 1963 before he could be caught. —see also Anthony BLUNT, Guy BURGESS, Donald MACLEAN

Phil·har·mo·ni·a Or·ches·tra /ˌfɪləməʊniə ˈɔːk⅃⌄strə, ˌfɪlhɑː-‖-hɑːrməʊniə ˈɔːr-/ n [the] an important London ORCHESTRA, begun in 1945

phil·har·mon·ic /ˌfɪlɑːˈmɒnɪk◀, ˌfɪlhɑː-‖ˌfɪlərˈmɑː-, ˌfɪlhɑːr-/ adj [A] (usu. cap.) (used in names of musical organizations): the Royal Philharmonic Orchestra

Phil·ip /ˈfɪl⅃p/, **Prince** (1921–) DUKE OF EDINBURGH and husband of the British queen, ELIZABETH II. Prince Philip was born into the Greek royal family but became a British citizen in 1947. He has no official position but is involved in many public organizations and charities (CHARITY).

Phil·ip Mor·ris /ˌfɪl⅃p ˈmɒr⅃s‖-mɔːr-/ an American MANUFACTURING company known mostly for tobacco products

phi·lip·pic /f⅃⌄ˈlɪpɪk/ n lit or fml a bitter angry speech attacking someone in public

Phil·ip·pines /ˈfɪl⅃piːnz‖ˌfɪlə'piːnz/ [the] a country made up of a group of over 7,000 islands off the SE coast of Asia; capital Manila; population 60,097,000 (1989). Much of its foreign trade is with the US, and there are important US military bases there.

phil·is·tine /ˈfɪl⅃staɪn‖-stiːn/ n derog a person who does not understand and actively dislikes art, literature, music, beautiful things, etc., and is proud to remain in this condition —**tinism** /stɪnɪz⅃m/ n [U]

Philistine a member of a race of people, the **Philistines**, who lived in the area of Palestine in Biblical times

Phil·lips /ˈfɪl⅃ps/, **Captain Mark** (1949–) an English army officer who was the husband of Princess Anne from 1973 until they separated in 1989 and divorced (DIVORCE) in 1992

Philly /ˈfɪli/ see PHILADELPHIA

phi·lol·o·gy /f⅃⌄ˈlɒlədʒi‖-ˈlɑː-/ n [U] old-fash tech the study of the nature and esp. development of words or language —compare LINGUISTICS —**gist** n —**gical** /fɪləˈlɒdʒɪkəl‖-ˈlɑː-/ adj —**gically** /kli/ adv

phi·los·o·pher /f⅃⌄ˈlɒsəfər‖-ˈlɑː-/ n 1 a person who studies, has much knowledge of, and usu. teaches philosophy: Plato, Aristotle, and the other Greek philosophers 2 a PHILOSOPHICAL (2) person: If you've had as much trouble as I've had in my life, you need to be a bit of a philosopher.

philosopher's stone /·,··· ˈ·/ n an imaginary substance that was thought in former times to have the power to change any other metal into gold

phil·o·soph·i·cal /ˌfɪləˈsɒfɪkəl◀‖-ˈsɑː-/ also **phil·o·soph·ic** /ˌfɪləˈsɒfɪk◀‖-ˈsɑː-/ adj 1 of or about philosophy: the philosophical writings of Sartre 2 [(about)] apprec accepting difficulty or unhappiness with calmness and quiet courage: a philosophical nature | She was quite philosophical about failing her driving test. — ~ **ly** /kli/ adv : He took his defeat philosophically.

phi·los·o·phize also **-phise** BrE /f⅃⌄ˈlɒsəfaɪz‖-ˈlɑː-/ v [I (about)] to reason in a PHILOSOPHICAL (1) way

phi·los·o·phy /f⅃⌄ˈlɒsəfi‖-ˈlɑː-/ n 1 [U] the study of the nature and meaning of existence, reality, knowledge, goodness, etc. 2 [C] any of various systems of thought having this as its base: the philosophy of Aristotle | (fig.) Eat, drink, and be merry — that's my philosophy! (=my rule for living life) —see also NATURAL PHILOSOPHY

phil·tre ‖ also **-ter** AmE /ˈfɪltərˈ/ n esp. lit a magic drink intended to make a person fall in love

phiz·og /ˈfɪzɒg‖-zɑːg/ n [usu. sing.] old-fash humor, esp. BrE the face

phle·bi·tis /fl⅃'baɪt⅃s/ n [U] a diseased swollen condition of the tubes carrying blood through the body (VEINS)

phlegm /flem/ n [U] 1 the thick jelly-like substance (MUCUS) produced in the nose and throat, esp. when one has a cold 2 fml, often apprec slowness in showing feeling, interest, or activity; calmness

phleg·mat·ic /fleg'mætɪk/ adj fml, often apprec calm and unexcitable: He's a very phlegmatic character. — ~ **ally** /kli/ adv

phlox /flɒks‖flɑːks/ n 1 a tall garden plant which produces groups of brightly coloured flowers 2 AmE a low, spreading plant which has flowers in the spring

Phnom Penh /ˌnɒm 'pen, pəˌnɒm-‖ˌnɑːm-/ capital of Cambodia, taken by the KHMER ROUGE in 1975, when most of the population was sent out to work in the country

pho·bi·a /ˈfəʊbiə/ n [(about)] a strong, unnatural, and usu. unreasonable fear and dislike; common phobias are fear of water, flying, heights, and closed spaces: He needs help in overcoming his phobias. —**phobic** n, adj

phoe·nix /ˈfiːnɪks/ n in CLASSICAL MYTHOLOGY, a bird believed to live for 500 years and then burn itself and be born again from the ashes: We all thought the airline was finished when it went bankrupt, but it rose phoenix-like/**like a phoenix from the ashes**.

Phoenix the capital and largest city of Arizona —see colour map on pages 1374–5

phone¹ /fəʊn/ n a telephone: Are you **on the phone**? (=Do you own a telephone?) | I spoke to him **by phone**. | The phone was ringing so she answered it. | a long-distance phone call | What's your phone number? | He picked up the phone. (=the part into which one speaks; RECEIVER) | I was so angry I slammed down the phone.

phone² ‖ also **call** AmE— v [I;T (UP)] to telephone: Has she phoned yet? | I phoned him (up) last night. | He phoned (me) to say he couldn't come. | I'll phone the result of the test to you. —see TELEPHONE (USAGE)
  phone (sthg. ↔) **in** phr v [I;T] to telephone (one's place of work) to report something or receive new instructions, esp. regularly: How many of our salesmen have phoned in so far? | He phoned in the results of the poll. —see also PHONE-IN

-phone see WORD FORMATION

phone book /'· ·/ also **telephone directory** fml— n a book containing an alphabetical list of the names, addresses, and telephone numbers of all the people who have a telephone in a certain area except for those who wish these details to remain private: Are you in the phone book? —see TELEPHONE (USAGE), compare YELLOW PAGES

phone box /'· ·/ also **call box, phone booth, telephone box, telephone booth**‖usu. **phone booth** or **telephone booth** AmE— n a small building or structure containing a telephone for use by the public —see TELEPHONE (USAGE). See picture on page 989

phone·card /ˈfəʊnkɑːd‖-kɑːrd/ n (in Britain) a plastic card bought from certain shops which is used in some pay telephones instead of money

phone-in /'· ·/ BrE ‖ **call-in** AmE— n a radio or television show in which telephoned questions, statements, etc., from the public are broadcast. A particular subject is usu. discussed each time and there may be one or more people in the STUDIO answering questions and giving information.

pho·neme /ˈfəʊniːm/ n tech the smallest unit of speech that can be used to make a word different from another that is the same in every other way: In English, the "b" in "big" and the "p" in "pig" represent two different phonemes. —**nemic** /fə'niːmɪk/ adj —**nemically** /kli/ adv

pho·ne·mics /fə'niːmɪks/ n [U] tech the study and description of the phonemes of languages

phone-tap·ping /'· ˌ··/ n [U] listening secretly to other people's telephone conversations by means of special ELECTRONIC equipment

pho·net·ic /fə'netɪk/ adj tech 1 of or about the sounds of human speech 2 using special signs, often different from ordinary letters, to represent the actual sounds of speech: *This dictionary uses a phonetic alphabet as a guide to pronunciation.* | *These are phonetic symbols/characters:* ə, ɪ, ʃ, ʊ. *– ~* **ally** /kli/ *adv*

pho·ne·ti·cian /ˌfəunɬˈtɪʃən/ *n tech* a person who has special knowledge of phonetics

pho·net·ics /fəˈnetɪks/ *n* [U] *tech* the study and science of speech sounds

pho·ney also -ny *AmE* /ˈfəuni/ *n, adj infml, usu. derog* (someone or something) pretended, false, unreal, or intended to deceive; FAKE: *He's such a phoney.* | *a phoney accent* | *I gave the police a phoney address.* *—*-**niness** *n* [U]

phoney war /ˌ·· ˈ·/ *n infml* a period during which a state of war officially exists but there is no actual fighting

phon·ic /ˈfɒnɪk, ˈfəu-‖ˈfɑ:-/ *adj tech* **1** of sound **2** of speech sounds

pho·no·graph /ˈfəunəgrɑ:f‖-græf/ *n old-fash AmE for* RECORD PLAYER

pho·nol·o·gy /fəˈnɒlədʒi‖-ˈnɑ:-/ *n* [U] *tech* the study of speech sounds of a language or languages, and the laws governing these *—*-**gist** *n* *—*-**gical** /ˌfɒnəˈlɒdʒɪkəl◂‖ˌfɑ:nə-ˈlɑ:-/ *adj* *—*-**gically** /kli/ *adv*

phoo·ey /ˈfu:i/ *interj infml* (used for expressing strong disbelief or disappointment)

phos·phate /ˈfɒsfeɪt‖ˈfɑ:s/ *n* [C;U] **1** any of various forms of a SALT[1] (2) of PHOSPHORIC acid, widely used in industry **2** [*usu. pl.*] a material containing a phosphate, used for making plants grow better

phos·pho·res·cence /ˌfɒsfəˈresəns‖ˌfɑ:s-/ *n* [U] **1** the giving out of light with little or no heat **2** faint light that is only noticeable in the dark, such as that given out by decaying fish and some insects and sea creatures

/fəˌnetɪk ˈsɪmbəlz/

phos·pho·res·cent /ˌfɒsfəˈresənt◂‖ˌfɑ:s-/ *adj* shining faintly in the dark with little or no heat: *You can see a strange phosphorescent light at night on tropical seas.* *– ~* **ly** *adv*

phos·phor·ic /fɒsˈfɒrɪk‖fɑ:sˈfɔ:-, fɑ:sˈfɑ:-, ˈfɑ:sfərɪk/ *adj* of or containing phosphorus: *phosphoric acid*

phos·pho·rus /ˈfɒsfərəs‖ˈfɑ:s-/ *n* [U] a poisonous yellowish simple substance (ELEMENT) that shines faintly in the dark and starts to burn when brought out into the air

pho·to /ˈfəutəu/ *n* -**tos** *infml* a photograph: *She showed him her photos of Spain.* | *to take a photo* | *a photo album*

photo- see WORD FORMATION

pho·to·cop·i·er /ˈfəutəuˌkɒpiə r‖-təˌkɑ:-/ *n* a machine that makes photocopies

---

phone boxes

an old British phone box

a new British phone box

an American phone booth

---

pho·to·cop·y[1] /ˈfəutəuˌkɒpi‖-təˌkɑ:pi/ *n* a photographic copy, esp. of something printed, written, or drawn: *I made/took two photocopies of the report.* –compare PHOTOSTAT[1], XEROX

photocopy[2] *v* [T] to make a photocopy of –compare PHOTOSTAT[2], XEROX

pho·to·e·lec·tric /ˌfəutəu-ɪˈlektrɪk◂/ *adj* of or using an electrical effect which is controlled by light

photoelectric cell /ˌ·· ·· ˈ·/ *n* **1** an instrument that changes light into electricity **2** also **electric/magic eye** *infml—* an instrument by which light is made to start an electrical apparatus working, often used in BURGLAR ALARMS

photo fin·ish /ˌ·· ˈ··/ *n* the end of a race, esp. a horse or dog race, in which the leaders finish so close together that a photograph has to be taken to show which is the winner: (fig.) *The election resulted in a photo finish.* (=the winner only had a few more votes than the loser)

Pho·to·fit /ˈfəutəufɪt/ *adj* [A] *tdmk* a collection of photographs of parts of the face which can be fitted together to produce complete pictures of different faces, so that witnesses to a crime can help the police to make the face that looks most like that of the criminal: *The police have issued a Photofit picture of the attacker.* –compare IDENTIKIT

pho·to·gen·ic /ˌfəutəuˈdʒenɪk◂, ˌfəutə-/ *adj* (esp. of a person) having an appearance that looks pleasing or effective when photographed

pho·to·graph[1] /ˈfəutəgrɑ:f‖-græf/ also **photo, picture** *infml—* *n* a picture obtained by using a camera and film sensitive to light: *a black and white/colour photograph* | *He* **took a photograph of** (=photographed) *his son.* | *Did you see John's photograph* (=a photograph of John) *in the local paper?* | *an aerial photograph* (=taken from the air)

photograph[2] *v* **1** [T] to make a picture of (someone or something) by using a camera and film sensitive to light: *He enjoys photographing mountain landscapes.* **2** [I+adv] to produce an effect, likeness, or picture of the stated kind when used as the subject of a photograph: *She photographs well.*

pho·tog·ra·pher /fəˈtɒgrəfə r‖-ˈtɑ:-/ *n* a person who takes photographs, esp. as a business or an art: *a portrait photographer* | *a fashion photographer* | *a keen amateur photographer*

pho·to·graph·ic /ˌfəutəˈgræfɪk◂/ *adj* **1** [*no comp.*] of, got by, or used in producing photographs; *photographic equipment* | *a photographic studio* **2** (of a person's memory) able to keep an image of things that one has seen with very great exactness *—~* **ally** /kli/ *adv*

pho·tog·ra·phy /fəˈtɒgrəfi‖-ˈtɑ:-/ *n* [U] the art, system, or business of producing photographs or films: *Photography is one of his hobbies.* | *There was some marvellous wildlife photography in the documentary.*

pho·to·jour·nal·is·m /ˌfəutəuˈdʒɜːnəl-ɪzəm‖-ˈɜːr-/ *n* [U] the use of photographs to record and make statements about news events

pho·ton /ˈfəutɒn‖-tɑːn/ *n* a unit of ENERGY with no mass that carries light

Pho·to·rea·lis·m /ˌfəutəuˈrɪəlɪzəm/ *n* [U] an art movement in the 1960s and 1970s which gave great importance to making very exact images of objects, esp. by painting

pho·to·sen·si·tive /ˌfəutəuˈsensɪtɪv◂‖-təˈsen-/ *adj* changing under the action of light: *photosensitive paper*

pho·to·sen·si·tize also -**tise** *BrE* /ˌfəutəuˈsensɪtaɪz‖-təˈsen-/ *v* [T] to make photosensitive: *photosensitized paper* *—*-**tization** /ˌfəutəusensɪtaɪˈzeɪʃən‖-təˈzeɪ-/ *n* [U]

pho·to·stat[1] /ˈfəutəstæt/ *n tdmk* (*sometimes cap.*) (a type of machine used for making) a PHOTOCOPY *—~* **ic** /ˌfəutəˈstætɪk◂/ *adj*

photostat[2] *v* -**tt-** [T] to PHOTOCOPY, esp. using a photostat

pho·to·syn·the·sis /ˌfəutəuˈsɪnθɪsɬs‖-təˈsɪn-/ *n* [U] the production of special sugar-like substances that keep plants alive, caused by the action of sunlight on CHLOROPHYLL (=the green matter in leaves); the way green plants make their own food

pho·to·type·set·ter /ˌfəutəuˈtaɪpsetə r/ *n* a TYPESETTER that works like a camera, using light to print images of characters on photographic paper *—*-**ting** *n* [U]

phras·al /ˈfreɪzəl/ adj made up of or connected with a phrase or phrases

phrasal verb /ˌ··ˈ·/ n a group of words that acts like a verb and consists usu. of a verb with an adverb and/or a PREPOSITION. *"Set off"* and *"put up with"* are phrasal verbs. In this dictionary phrasal verbs are marked *phr v*

phrase[1] /freɪz/ n 1 (in grammar) a group of words without a FINITE verb, esp. when they are used to form part of a sentence: *"Walking along the road"* and *"a packet of cigarettes"* are phrases. —compare CLAUSE (1), SENTENCE[1] (1) 2 a short expression, esp. one that is clever and very suited to what is meant: *He was — what is the phrase I'm looking for — not intimately acquainted with his subject.* —see also **to coin a phrase** (COIN[2]), **turn a phrase** (TURN[1]) 3 a short independent passage of music that is part of a longer piece

phrase[2] v [T+obj+adv|prep] 1 to express in the stated way: *He phrased his criticisms carefully|in careful terms.| a politely-phrased refusal* 2 to perform (music) so as to give full effect to separate PHRASES[1] (3)

phrase·book /ˈfreɪzbʊk/ n a book giving and explaining phrases of a particular (foreign) language, for people to use when they go abroad

phra·se·ol·o·gy /ˌfreɪziˈɒlədʒi‖-ˈɑː-/ n [U] the way in which words are chosen, arranged, and/or used, esp. in the stated subject or field: *I don't understand all this scientific phraseology.*

phre·no·lo·gy /frəˈnɒlədʒi‖-ˈnɑː-/ n [U] the study of the shape of the human head, claimed to show a subject's character and mental ability, esp. popular in the 19th century —**phrenologist** n

phut /fʌt/ n infml 1 BrE a dull sound like something bursting 2 **go phut‖go kaput** to break down completely: *The television's gone phut.*

phy·lum /ˈfaɪləm/ n **phyla** /ˈfaɪlə/ tech a main division of animals or plants (or languages), above a CLASS[1] (6)

Phys. Ed. /ˌfɪz ˈed/ n AmE abbrev. for: PHYSICAL EDUCATION

phys·ic /ˈfɪzɪk/ n [C;U] old use or humor (a) medicine, esp. a LAXATIVE: *a dose of physic* —see also PHYSICS

phys·i·cal[1] /ˈfɪzɪkəl/ adj 1 of or for the body: *physical exercise | physical strength | people with mental or physical disabilities | a complete physical examination* —see also PHYSICAL[2] 2 of or being matter or material things, as opposed to things of the mind, spirit, etc.: *the physical world* 3 of or according to the laws of nature: *There must be a physical explanation for these strange happenings.* 4 [A] concerning the natural formation of the Earth's surface: *physical geography* 5 [A] (of certain sciences) of the branch that is connected with physics: *physical chemistry* 6 euph (esp. in sports) using violence; rough: *That tackle was rather physical!* —see also PHYSICALLY

physical[2] also **medical, physical ex·am·i·na·tion** /ˌ··· ···ˈ···/— n a thorough examination of the body and general health of a person by a doctor, esp. in order to discover whether they are fit to do a particular job: *The company insisted that he had a complete physical. | to pass|fail the physical* —compare CHECKUP

physical ed·u·ca·tion /ˌ··· ···ˈ···/ (abbrev. **P.E., Phys. Ed.** AmE) n [U] the time spent in school at sports and exercise

physical jerks /ˌ··· ˈ·/ n [P] humor bodily exercises

phys·i·cal·ly /ˈfɪzɪkli/ adv 1 with regard to the body: *He's all right physically, but mentally he's rather confused.* 2 infml completely: *It's physically impossible to finish all this work by the end of the week.*

physically chal·lenged /ˌ··· ˈ··/ adj AmE euph physically HANDICAPPED

physical sci·ence /ˌ··· ˈ··/ n [U] those branches of science which are concerned mainly with non-living things, e.g. PHYSICS, chemistry, and ASTRONOMY

physical train·ing /ˌ··· ˈ··/ also **physical education**— n see PT

phy·si·cian /fɪˈzɪʃən/ n old-fash 1 a doctor, esp. one who treats diseases with medicines (as opposed to a SURGEON, who performs operations) 2 **physician, heal thyself** a phrase from the Bible, used when saying that a person should deal with their own problems or weaknesses before they begin to advise others

phys·i·cist /ˈfɪzɪsɪst/ n a person who studies or works in physics

phys·ics /ˈfɪzɪks/ n [U] the science concerned with the study of matter and natural forces, such as light, heat, movement, etc.

phys·i·o /ˈfɪziəʊ/ n -s infml a physiotherapist

phys·i·og·no·my /ˌfɪziˈɒnəmi‖-ˈɑːg-, -ˈɑːg-/ n fml or tech the general appearance of the face, esp. as showing the character and the mind

phys·i·ol·o·gy /ˌfɪziˈɒlədʒi‖-ˈɑː-/ n [U] a science concerned with the study of how the bodies of living things, and their various parts, work —compare ANATOMY —**gist** n —**gical** /ˌfɪziəˈlɒdʒɪkəl◂‖-ˈlɑː-/ adj : *The doctors could find no physiological cause for his illness, and decided it must be psychosomatic.*

phys·i·o·ther·a·py /ˌfɪziəʊˈθerəpi/ n [U] the use of exercises, rubbing, heat, etc., in the treatment of sick people —**pist** n

phy·sique /fɪˈziːk/ n the form and appearance of a human body, esp. a male body: *He has a magnificent physique.* (=has large muscles and is not at all fat)

pi /paɪ/ n a letter (Π, π) of the Greek alphabet, used in GEOMETRY to represent the fixed RATIO of the CIRCUMFERENCE of a circle to its DIAMETER: *Pi equals|The value of pi is about* $^{22}/_7$, *or 3·14159.*

Pi·af /ˈpiːæf‖piːˈɑːf/, **E·dith** /ˈiːdɪθ/ n (1915–63) a popular French CABARET singer and songwriter, sometimes called the **Little Sparrow**. She had many problems in her life and her music has a feeling of strength and sadness. Her best-known songs are *Milord* and *Je ne regrette rien.*

pi·a·nist /ˈpiːənɪst, ˈpjɑː-‖ˈpiːænɪst, ˈpiːə-/ n a person who plays the piano, esp. with skill: *a concert pianist*

pi·an·o[1] /piˈænəʊ/ also **pi·an·o·for·te** /piˌænəʊˈfɔːti‖ -ˈfɔːrteɪ/fml— n -os a large musical instrument, played by pressing narrow black or white bars (KEYS) which cause small hammers to hit wire strings: *to play the piano | to have piano lessons | a piano stool* —see also GRAND PIANO, UPRIGHT PIANO, see INSTRUMENT (USAGE)

pi·an·o[2] /piˈænəʊ, piˈɑː-‖piˈænəʊ/ adj, adv (of music) played quietly —compare FORTE[2]

Pi·a·no·la /ˌpiːəˈnəʊlə/ n tdmk (often not cap.) a type of PLAYER PIANO

piano stool /ˈ·· ˌ·/ n a seat the height of which can be changed to suit different heights of people playing a piano

pi·as·tre ‖ also **-ter** AmE /piˈæstər/ n a small coin or banknote in Egypt, Syria, the Lebanon, and the Sudan, worth one hundredth $^1/_{100}$ of the units on which their money systems are based

pi·az·za /piˈætsə/ n a public square or market place, esp. in Italy

pic·a·dor /ˈpɪkədɔːr/ n (in a BULLFIGHT) a man on horseback who annoys and weakens the BULL by sticking a long spearlike weapon into it —compare MATADOR

pic·a·resque /ˌpɪkəˈresk◂/ adj tech telling the story of the adventures and travels of a character of whom one rather disapproves but who is usu. not really wicked: *a picaresque novel*

Pi·cas·so /pɪˈkæsəʊ‖-ˈkɑː-/, **Pab·lo** /ˈpæbləʊ‖ˈpɑː-/ (1881–1973) a Spanish painter who worked in France; one of the FOUNDERS of CUBISM. His work is usu. divided into periods e.g. his **blue period**. One of his most famous paintings is *Guernica,* a criticism of war and FASCISM. —see picture at CUBISM

Pic·ca·dil·ly /ˌpɪkəˈdɪli◂/ a central London street that runs beside GREEN PARK between Hyde Park Corner and Piccadilly Circus. Buildings on Piccadilly include expensive hotels, clubs, and offices.

Piccadilly Cir·cus /ˌ··· ˈ··/ a busy square in central London known for the figure of EROS in the middle and for its lively night-life — see colour map on page 817.

pic·ca·lil·li /ˌpɪkəˈlɪli/ n [U] a hot-tasting food made with cut-up vegetables, usu. eaten with meat

pic·ca·nin·ny , pick·a- /ˌpɪkəˈnɪni, ˈpɪkənini/ n old-fash, now taboo a small child of a black-skinned race

pic·co·lo /ˈpɪkələʊ/ n -los a small musical instrument of the WOODWIND family; small FLUTE

Piccadilly Circus

pick¹ /pɪk/ v [T] **1** to take (what one likes or considers best or most suitable) from among a group or number; choose: *The students have to pick three courses from a list of 15.* | *He was picked for the England team.* [+obj+to-v] *She's been picked to head the planning committee.* | *You've really* **picked a winner** (=made a very good choice) *this time!* —see also PICK **out** (1) **2** [(for)] to pull or break off (part of a plant) from a tree or plant; gather: *They've gone fruit-picking today.* | *She picked some flowers from the garden.* [+obj(i)+obj(d)] *He picked her a rose.* **3** [(from, out of)] to take up or remove (something) separately or bit by bit using the fingers, a beak, a pointed instrument, etc.: *The vultures were picking the meat from the carcass.* | *picking bits of glass out of the carpet* | *The dog picked the bone clean.* (=removed all the meat from it) **4** to remove unwanted pieces from, esp. with a finger or a pointed instrument: *Don't pick your nose!* | *She was picking her teeth.* **5** to cause intentionally; PROVOKE: *He's so argumentative; he's always trying to* **pick quarrels/fights** *with people.* **6** to steal or take from, esp. in small amounts: *It's easy to* **have your pocket picked** *in a big crowd.* | (fig.) *I hear you're a mechanic; can I* **pick your brains** *about repairing my car?* (=make use of your knowledge) —see also PICKPOCKET **7** to unlock (a lock) with any instrument other than a key, esp. secretly and for an illegal purpose **8** *AmE for* PLUCK¹ (3) **9 pick and choose** *sometimes derog* to choose very carefully from a number of objects, possibilities, etc., taking only those one particularly likes or that are particularly good, etc. **10 pick holes in** to find fault with; find the weak points in: *It was easy to pick holes in his flimsy argument.* **11 pick one's way/steps** to walk carefully, choosing the places to put one's feet down: *After the explosion I picked my way through the rubble.* **12 pick someone/something to pieces** *infml* to examine the nature of a person or thing closely in order to find fault: *She's very polite to him when he's there, but picks him to pieces behind his back.* —see also **have (got) a bone to pick with someone** (BONE¹)

pick at sthg. *phr v* [T] to eat only in small quantities and with little effort or interest

pick sbdy./sthg. ↔ **off** *phr v* [T] to shoot (people or animals) one by one, by taking careful aim

pick on sbdy./sthg. *phr v* [T] *infml* to choose for punishment, blame, or an unpleasant job, esp. repeatedly and unfairly: *Why are you always picking on me?* | *I'm tired of being picked on.*

pick sbdy./sthg. ↔ **out** *phr v* [T] **1** to choose specially or carefully from among others: *She picked out a scarf to wear with the dress.* | *The witness picked out the wrong man in the identification parade.* **2** to see (someone or something) among others, esp. with difficulty; DISCERN: *Can you pick out your sister in this crowd?* **3** [*often pass.*] to make (something) clear to see: *The houses in the painting were picked out in white.* **4** to play (a tune) on a stringed musical instrument, usu. slowly or with difficulty

pick sthg. ↔ **over** *phr v* [T] *infml* to examine (too) carefully in order to choose the best or remove the unwanted: *He was picking over the tomatoes on the stall.*

pick up *phr v* **1** [T] (**pick** sthg./sbdy. ↔ **up**) to take hold of (esp. something small or light) and lift it up from a surface: *I picked up a magazine that was lying on the table.* | *She picked up a stone and threw it at the window.* **2** [T] (**pick** sthg. ↔ **up**) to gather together; collect: *Please pick up all your toys when you've finished playing.* | (fig.) *It was a bad setback, but we must* **pick up the pieces** *and start again.* | *Angrily, he broke off their engagement, but some months later they were able to* **pick up the threads** *of their relationship.* (=begin it again) **3** [T] (**pick** sbdy. ↔ **up**) to raise (oneself) after a fall or failure: *She picked herself up and started running again.* **4** [I;T (**pick** sthg. ↔ **up**)] to (cause to) start again: *Let's* **pick up where we left off.** | *We picked up the conversation after an interruption.* **5** [T] (**pick** sthg. ↔ **up**) to come to have; gain, buy, learn, etc.; ACQUIRE: *Where did you pick up that book/your English/that habit/such ideas?* | *The system looks difficult at first, but you'll soon pick it up.* (=begin to understand it) | *He picked up a bug* (=an illness) *while he was abroad.* **6** [T] (**pick** sbdy./sthg. ↔ **up**) to collect; arrange to go and get: *Pick me up at the hotel.* | *I'm going to pick up my coat from the cleaner's.* **7** [T] (**pick** sbdy. ↔ **up**) to allow to enter a vehicle: *We picked up a hitchhiker.* **8** [T] (**pick** sbdy. ↔ **up**) *infml* to become friendly with after a short meeting, usu. with sexual intentions: *I didn't like him; he was just trying to pick me up.* **9** [T] (**pick** sbdy. ↔ **up**) to catch (a criminal); ARREST: *He was picked up by the police as he tried to leave the country.* **10** [T] (**pick** sthg. ↔ **up**) to be able to hear or receive: *We picked up radio signals for help from the damaged plane.* **11** [T] (**pick** sthg. ↔ **up**) to be prepared to pay: *The football club should* **pick up the bill/tab** *for the damage, since their fans are responsible for it.* **12** [T] (**pick** sthg. ↔ **up**) to cause to increase: *We picked up speed as we went downhill.* **13** [I] to improve; return to a former good state: *Trade is picking up again.* **14** [I;T (**pick** sbdy. ↔ **up**)] to (cause to) improve in health: *This tonic should pick you up.* —see also PICK-ME-UP, PICK-UP

pick up on sthg. *phr v* [T] **1** to be sensitive to: *I was trying to indicate I didn't want to go, but they didn't pick up on it.* **2** to notice: *Did you pick up on those things that were crawling in her hair?* **3** to call attention to or begin speaking about (something already mentioned): *Now I'd like to pick up on your objections to funding the project through the summer.*

pick² *n* **1** [U] choice: *Which one do you want —* **take your pick!** (=choose whichever one you want) | *She could have had her pick of all the eligible young men.* **2** [*the*+S+*of*] the best (of many): *It's the pick of this month's new films.* | *It's not much good, but it's the* **pick of the bunch.**

pick³ *n* **1** (*usu. in comb.*) a sharp-pointed usu. small instrument —see also ICE PICK, TOOTHPICK **2** *infml* a pick-axe **3** *AmE or infml for* PLECTRUM

pick·axe *BrE*‖**pickax** *AmE* /ˈpɪk-æks/ *also* **pick** *infml* — a large steel tool with a wooden handle fitted into a curved iron bar with two sharp points, used for breaking up roads, rock, etc. —see picture at AXE

picked /pɪkt/ *adj* [A] *often apprec* chosen as very suitable for a special purpose: *The assault group consisted of six picked men.* —see also HANDPICKED

pick·er /ˈpɪkəʳ/ *n* (*usu. in comb.*) a person or instrument that picks things, esp. crops: *The cotton pickers want more money.*

pick·et¹ /ˈpɪkɪt/ *n* **1** someone placed, esp. by a trade union, at the entrance to a factory, shop, etc., to prevent anyone, esp. other workers, from going in until a quarrel with the employers is over. The number of pickets allowed in one place is limited by law in Britain: *The pickets persuaded the truck driver not to enter the factory.* —see also FLYING PICKET **2** [+*sing./pl. v*] a group or line of pickets: *The union placed a large picket at the factory gates.* | *Don't* **cross the picket line!** | *There were over a hundred men* **on the picket line** *this morning.* **3** a soldier with the special job of guarding a camp: *on picket duty* **4** [+*sing./pl. v*] a small group of such soldiers **5** [*often pl.*] a strong pointed stick fixed into the ground, esp. used with others to make a fence (**picket fence**)

picket² *v* **1** [T] to surround as PICKETS¹ (1) and stop the work or activity of: *The men picketed the factory/picketed all the people who wanted to go inside to work.* **2** [I] to act as a picket: *picketing miners* **3** [T+*obj+adv/prep*] to place (soldiers) in position as PICKETS¹ (3)

Pick·ford's /ˈpɪkfədz‖-fərdz/ a company which stores people's furniture and moves belongings for people who are moving to a new house

pick·ings /'pɪkɪŋz/ n [P] infml additional money or profits taken dishonestly or regarded as a right: There are some easy/rich pickings to be made in this job.

pick·le¹ /'pɪkəl/ n **1** [U] a liquid, esp. VINEGAR or salt water, used to preserve vegetables or sometimes meat **2** [U] esp. BrE a substance eaten with food, esp. cold food, consisting of pieces of vegetable preserved in this: sweet pickle (=with added sugar) | cheese and pickle sandwiches **3** [C] AmE a vegetable, esp. a CUCUMBER, preserved in this **4** [S] infml a difficult or confused condition; MESS: You are in a (pretty) pickle, aren't you! Let me help you out. **5** [C] BrE infml a child who playfully does bad but not very harmful things

pickle² v [T] to preserve (food) in pickle: pickled onions

pick·led /'pɪkəld/ adj [F] infml drunk

pick-me-up /'·· ·,·/ n infml something, esp. a drink or medicine, that makes one feel stronger and more cheerful — see also PICK **up** (14)

pick·pock·et /'pɪk₁pɒkჳt‖-₁pɑːk-/ n a person who steals things from people's pockets, esp. in a crowd

pick·up /'·· ·/ n **1** the part of a record player, esp. the needle and arm, which receives and plays the sound from a record **2** also **pick-up truck** /'·· ₁·/— a light VAN having an open body with low sides —see picture at TRUCK and at VAN **3** infml a person, esp. a woman, who is picked up (PICK **up** (8)) **4** [U] AmE rate of increasing speed; ACCELERATION: a car with good pick-up

Pick·wick /'pɪkwɪk/, **Mr Sam·u·el** /'sæmjuəl/ the chief character in the **Pickwick Papers**, a story by Charles Dickens. Pickwick is kind and good-tempered and thinks well of everyone. He is sometimes thought of as a typical Victorian English gentleman.

Pickwick Pa·pers /₁·· '··/ a book written in 1836–37 by Charles Dickens about the members of the Pickwick Club. They were Samuel Pickwick, Tracy Tupman, Augustus Snodgrass, and Nathaniel Winkle and the book is about their adventures.

pick·y /'pɪki/ adj derog, esp. AmE for CHOOSY: She's such a picky eater. —**-iness** n [U]

pic·nic¹ /'pɪknɪk/ n **1** [C] **a** an occasion when food, usu. cold food, is taken to be eaten somewhere outdoors, esp. in the country: They went on/for a picnic. | a picnic lunch **b** BrE the food taken: What a delicious picnic! **2** [S usu. in negatives] infml something especially easy or pleasant to do: It's no picnic having to look after six small children all day, you know!

picnic² v -ck- [I] to go on or have a picnic — ~ **ker** n

picnic ar·e·a /'·· ₁···/ n an area near a road, with space to park cars, and tables where motorists can sit and have picnics

picnic bas·ket /'·· ₁··/ also **picnic hamper**— n a strong basket used to carry food etc. for a picnic, esp. one that contains its own special plates, cups, knives, etc.

picnic ta·ble /'·· ₁··/ n a table used to have a picnic on, esp. one built near a road in the country and used by motorists

Pict /pɪkt/ n one of the group of people who lived in north and central Scotland from the 3rd to the 9th century and who often fought against the English

pic·to·ri·al /pɪk'tɔːriəl/ adj having, or expressed in, PIC-TURES¹ (1,2): pictorial magazines | a pictorial record of the event — ~ **ly** adv

pic·ture¹ /'pɪktʃəʳ/ n **1** [C (of)] a painting or drawing: Draw a picture of that tree/those children. | She painted a picture of the church. | Where shall I hang this picture? | You look **as pretty as a picture** (=very pretty) in that dress. —compare PORTRAIT and see picture at LIVING ROOM **2** [C (of)] a photograph: He took her picture/took a picture of her. **3** [C usu. sing.] what is seen on a television or cinema SCREEN: You can't get a clear picture on this TV set. **4** [C] esp. BrE a cinema film —see also PICTURES **5** [C (of) usu. sing.] an image in the mind, esp. an exact image produced by a skilful description: This book gives a vivid picture of life in England 200 years ago. | He painted a grim picture of the company's financial problems. **6** [S] a situation: The present political picture gives much cause for anxiety. | We'll fool him; you come in five minutes after me — **get the picture?** (=do you understand?) **7** [the+S+of] the perfect example: That baby is the picture of health. (=looks very healthy) **8** [S] a person or thing

that is beautiful or unusual to look at: This garden is a picture in the summer. | His face was a picture when we told him! **9** in/out of the picture infml a in/not in the position of knowing all the facts: I haven't heard about the latest developments; perhaps you could put me in the picture. **b** receiving/not receiving one's share of attention: She always wants to be in the picture. **10** picture in the attic in the book The Picture of Dorian Gray by Oscar Wilde, a way of talking about the picture in the title —see PICTURE OF DORIAN GRAY

picture² v [T] **1** to imagine: Just picture the scene — it must have been a terrible experience. | I can't quite picture myself as a father. [+wh-] Can't you picture how she must feel? **2** [+obj+adv/prep] to paint or draw; make a picture of: The artist has pictured him as a young man in riding dress. —compare DEPICT

picture book /'·· ·/ n a book for young children, made up mostly of pictures

picture card /'·· ·/ n a COURT CARD (‖FACE CARD)

Picture of Do·ri·an Gray /₁pɪktʃəʳ əv ₁dɔːriən 'greɪ/, **The** a story by Oscar Wilde about a young, attractive man who has a picture of himself that he keeps in a room at the top of his house. As he gets older, he becomes an evil and immoral person, but his own face does not change with age. Instead, the picture of him changes to show how old and unpleasant he has become.

picture post·card /₁·· '··/ n fml for POSTCARD (2)

picture-postcard /₁·· '··◄/ adj [A] very pretty; picturesque: a picture-postcard village

picture rail /'·· ·/ n a long, narrow piece of wood, plastic, etc. fixed to the upper part of living-room walls in older houses, for hanging pictures from

pic·tures /'pɪktʃəz‖-əʳz/ BrE ‖ **movies** esp. AmE— n infml **1** [the+P] old-fash the cinema: Are you going to the pictures tonight? **2** [P] the business of producing or acting in cinema films: He's in pictures.

pic·tur·esque /₁pɪktʃə'resk◄/ adj **1** (esp. of a place) charming and interesting enough to be made into a picture: a picturesque scene/village **2** (of a person or their manner, clothes, etc.) rather strange and unusual: He was a picturesque figure with his long beard and strange old clothes. **3** often euph (of language) unusually clear, strong, and descriptive — ~ **ly** adv — ~ **ness** n [U]

picture win·dow /'·· ₁··/ n a large window made of a single piece of glass, usu. placed so that it looks out over an attractive view

pid·dle /'pɪdl/ v [I] infml **1** BrE for URINATE **2** AmE to waste time; DAWDLE —**piddle** n [U]

pid·dling /'pɪdlɪŋ/ adj derog small and unimportant: piddling details

pid·gin /'pɪdჳn/ n [C;U] a language which is a mixture of two or more other languages, esp. as used between people who do not speak each other's language: pidgin English —compare CREOLE (1), LINGUA FRANCA

pie /paɪ/ n [C;U] **1** (often in comb.) a pastry case, esp. a round one, filled with meat or fruit and covered with pastry, baked in a deep dish (**pie dish**): a cherry pie | a meat pie. —compare TART¹ (1) **2** pie in the sky infml a hopeful plan or suggestion that has not been, or has little chance of being, put into effect —see also APPLE PIE, CUSTARD PIE, MUD PIE, PIE CHART, as easy as pie (EASY¹), have a finger in every pie (FINGER¹)

▷ USAGE In British English a **pie** usually has a pastry cover; if there is no cover it is called a **tart** (if it is filled with fruit) or a **flan**. In American English a **pie** may or may not have a cover.◁

pie and mash /₁·· · '·/ n [C;U] BrE (a serving of) a small PIE (=meat covered with pastry) served with mashed (MASH¹) potatoes, typically served in cheap restaurants

pie·bald /'paɪbɔːld/ n, adj (a horse) coloured with large black and white PATCHes —compare SKEWBALD

piece¹ /piːs/ n **1** [C (of)] a bit, such as: **a** a part of anything solid which is separated, broken, or marked off from a larger part or a whole body: a piece of chalk/sellotape/string/cake | pieces of broken glass **b** a single object that is an example of a kind or class, or that forms part of a set: a piece of paper (=a whole sheet) | a piece of furniture (=a chair, table, bed, etc.) | a piece of sculpture (=a STATUE, etc.) | a piece of music (=a song, SYMPHONY, etc.) | (fig.) Let me give you a piece of (=some) advice. **2** [C] a

piece

There are many words available to talk about a piece of something in English. The table below shows some of them and gives an idea of which substance they can refer to.

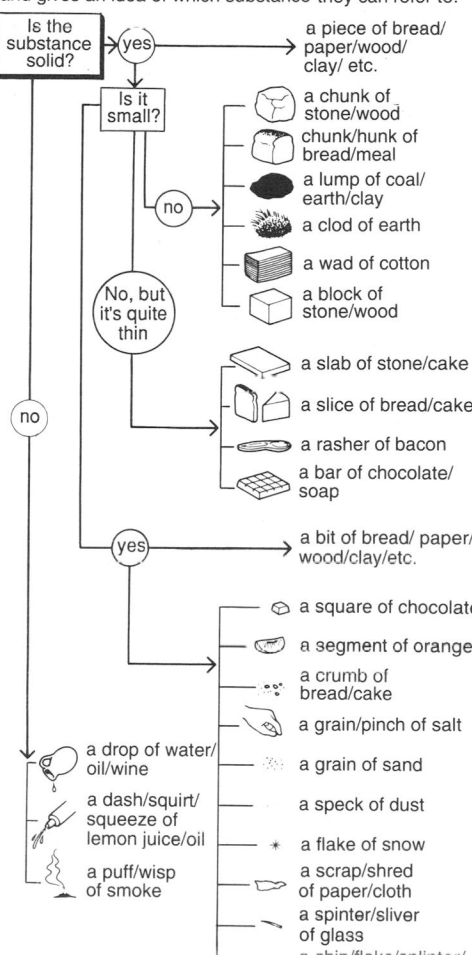

| Is the substance solid? | →yes | → a piece of bread/ paper/wood/ clay/ etc. |

a chunk of stone/wood

Is it small? — chunk/hunk of bread/meal

a lump of coal/ earth/clay

no — a clod of earth

a wad of cotton

No, but it's quite thin — a block of stone/wood

a slab of stone/cake

a slice of bread/cake

a rasher of bacon

a bar of chocolate/ soap

no — yes — a bit of bread/ paper/ wood/clay/etc.

a square of chocolate

a segment of orange

a crumb of bread/cake

a grain/pinch of salt

a drop of water/ oil/wine — a grain of sand

a dash/squirt/ squeeze of lemon juice/oil — a speck of dust

a flake of snow

a puff/wisp of smoke — a scrap/shred of paper/cloth

a spinter/sliver of glass

a chip/flake/splinter/ sliver of stone/wood

any of many parts made to be fitted together: *This jig-saw had 2000 pieces, but some are missing.* | *This chair* **comes to pieces.** (=can be taken apart) | *I'm going to* **take** *the engine* **to pieces** (=separate it into parts) *to see what's wrong with it.* | *It just* **fell to pieces** *in my hands.* (=came apart) **b** (*usu. in comb.*) an object or person forming part of a set: *a 36-piece dinner service* | *an 80-piece orchestra* (=one with 80 players or instruments) **3** [C] any of a set of small round objects or figures used in playing certain board games, esp. CHESS: *Which piece moves diagonally?* **4** [C] something whole and complete made by an ARTIST or other skilful person: *This is one of Rodin's finest pieces.* (=STATUES) | *This piece* (=of music) *should be played very slowly.* **5** [C *usu. sing.*] a short written statement in a newspaper, magazine, etc.: *Did you see the piece in the paper about Mrs Smith's accident?* **6** [C] a coin, esp. of the stated value: *a 50-penny piece* | *a ten-cent piece* | *30 pieces of silver* **7** [(*the*) S] an amount of work (to be) done: *We pay our workers by the piece here, not by the time they take to do the work.* —see also PIECEWORK **8** (**all**) **in one piece** *infml* **a** (of a thing) undamaged; still whole **b** (of a person) unharmed, esp. after an accident: *She was lucky to survive the crash all in one piece.* **9 give someone a piece of one's mind** *infml* to tell someone angrily what one thinks of them: *I'm going to give that little rascal a piece of my mind when I catch him!* **10 go (all) to pieces** *infml* to lose the ability to think or act clearly because of fear, sorrow, etc.: *Under the pressure*

of police questioning she went to pieces and confessed everything. **11 of a piece: a** like each other in character: *They're all of a piece.* **b** in agreement: *His action is of a piece with what he has been saying he will do for the past few months.* **12 piece by piece** one by one; one part at a time **13 pull someone/something to pieces** to say or show that someone/something is worthless by pointing at the weak points or faults: *The committee pulled my proposal to pieces.* **14 say one's piece** to say what one wants to or has planned to say, esp. in a way that is annoying or unwelcome to others: *I've said my piece, so I'll be going now.* —see also MUSEUM PIECE, PARTY PIECE, SET PIECE, **the villain of the piece** (VILLAIN)

piece² *v*

piece sthg. ↔ **together** *phr v* [T] to make (something, esp. a story or an account of events) complete by gradually finding all the parts and adding them to each other: *The detectives tried to piece together the facts.*

pi·èce de ré·sis·tance /piːˌes də reziːˈstɑːns/ *n* **pièces de résistance** (*same pronunciation*) *Fr* the best or most important thing or event among a number, esp. one that comes or is shown after all the others

piece·meal /ˈpiːsmiːl/ *adj, adv* (done, made, etc.) bit by bit; only one part at a time: *The college buildings were put together piecemeal.*

piece of cake /ˌ· · ˈ·/ *n* [S] *infml* something very easy to do: *That exam was a piece of cake!*

piece of eight /ˌ· · ˈ·/ *n* [*usu. pl.*] (esp. in stories) a silver coin formerly used in Spain. In humorous stories about PIRATEs, the pirate often has a PARROT on his shoulder who says "pieces of eight" repeatedly.

piece of work /ˌ· · ˈ·/ *n* **1** something made or done, esp. of the stated quality: *This watch is a fine piece of work.* **2** *infml* someone who is disliked or disapproved of in the stated way: *Look out for him; he's a nasty piece of work.*

piece rate /ˈ· ·/ *n* a fixed amount of money paid for each thing that a worker produces: *dressmakers working on a piece rate*

piece·work /ˈpiːswɜːk‖-wɜːrk/ *n* [U] work paid for by the amount done rather than by the hours worked

pie chart /ˈ· ˌ·/ *n* a circle divided into several parts that shows the way in which something, such as a population or an amount of money, is divided up: *The students drew up a pie chart of government spending/the racial composition of their school/the uses of local land.* —see picture at CHART

pie·crust /ˈpaɪkrʌst/ *n* [C;U] the baked pastry of a PIE

pied /paɪd/ *adj* [A] (esp. of certain types of bird) irregularly coloured with two or more colours, esp. black and white: *a pied wagtail*

pied-à-terre /ˌpjeɪd æ ˈteəʳ‖ˌpiˌed ɑː ˈteɑr/ *n* **pieds-à-terre** (*same pronunciation*) *Fr* a small set of rooms or second home which one keeps for use when needed. *They live in the country but they've got a pied-à-terre in London.*

the Pied Piper

Pied Pip·er /ˌ· ˈ···/ *n* **1** [*the*] the main character in an old fairy story about a man who freed the town of Hamelin in Germany from rats by playing his FLUTE and making the rats follow him to the river and drown. When he was not paid for this job, the Pied Piper led away all the town's children too. **2** a person who attracts followers: *a great leader, a Pied Piper of politics*

pie-eyed /ˌpaɪ ˈaɪd◂/ *adj infml, usu. humor* drunk

pier /pɪəʳ/ *n* **1** a bridgelike structure of wood, metal, etc., built out into the sea at places where people go for holidays, with small buildings on it where people can eat and amuse themselves: *Brighton pier* | *a variety show on the end of the pier* —compare BOARDWALK **2** a similar structure at which boats can stop to take in or land their passengers or goods, usu. larger than a JETTY **3** a thick post of stone, wood, metal, etc., esp. as used to support a bridge or the roof of a high building

pierce /pɪəs‖pɪərs/ *v* [T] *rather fml* **1** to make a hole in or through (something) with a point: *The nurse pierced the skin covering his vein with the syringe and injected the medicine.* | *Many women have got* **pierced ears.** (=holes made in their ears for EARRINGS) | (fig.) *He couldn't pierce* (=find a way through) *her unfriendly manner.* **2** (of light, sound, pain, etc.) to be suddenly seen, heard, or felt in or through (someone or something): *The first shafts of sunlight pierced the gloom.* | *A sudden scream pierced the silence.* —compare PENETRATE

Pierce, Franklin (1804–69) the 14th president of the US (1853–57)

pierc·ing /ˈpɪəsɪŋ‖ˈpɪər-/ *adj* **1** (of wind) very strong and cold; BITING **2** (of sound) very sharp and clear, esp. in an unpleasant way: *A piercing cry rang out across the moor.* | *a very piercing voice* **3** going straight to the centre or the main point; PENETRATING: *a piercing look/question* | *piercing blue eyes* — ~ly *adv*

Pier·rot /ˈpɪərəʊ/ a silent PANTOMIME character, usu. a fool or musician with a sad white face and loose, white, fancy clothes

Piers Plow·man /ˌpɪəz ˈplaʊmən‖ˌpɪərz-/ a religious poem written in Middle English by William Langland (1330?–86)

pi·e·ty /ˈpaɪəti/ also **piousness**— *n* [U] *fml* the showing and feeling of deep respect for God and religion —opposite **impiety**; see also PIOUS

pie·zo·e·lec·tric /ˌpiːzəʊ-ɪˈlektrɪk◂, ˌpiːtsəʊ-‖piˌeɪzəʊ-/ *adj* worked by electricity produced by pressure on a small piece of a certain type of stone (CRYSTAL): *a piezoelectric cigarette lighter*

pif·fle /ˈpɪfəl/ *n* [U] *BrE infml, old-fash* foolish talk; nonsense

pif·fling /ˈpɪflɪŋ/ *adj BrE infml* useless; meaningless; TRIVIAL: *some piffling excuse or other*

pig[1] /pɪg/ *n* **1** ‖ also **hog** *AmE*— a fat short-legged animal with a usu. curly tail and thick skin with short stiff hairs, often kept on farms for its meat. Pigs are usu. thought to be GREEDY, dirty, and noisy. —see also GUINEA PIG; see MEAT (USAGE) **2** *infml derog* **a** an unpleasant person, esp. one who eats too much, behaves in an offensive way, or refuses to consider others: *You greedy pig!* | *He* **made a (real) pig of himself** *at the restaurant.* **b** something difficult or nasty: *This passage is a real pig to translate.* **3** *derog sl* a policeman **4 a pig in a poke** *infml* something one has bought without seeing or examining it, and that one may then find to be worthless **5 make a pig's ear of** *infml, esp. BrE* to do something awkwardly or wrongly: *I'd been practising the speech for days, but I made a real pig's ear of it anyway.* **6 pigs might fly**‖**If pigs could fly we could shoot for bacon!** *esp. humor* What you have just said is not possible: *"The management might offer us a decent pay rise." "Pigs might fly!"* **7 This little piggy went to market** the first line of an old poem for children, said while counting the child's toes

pig[2] *v* -gg- [I;T] to eat (food) greedily (GREEDY): *He's pigged all the cake!* | *We pigged ourselves on/with ice cream and jelly.*

pig out *phr v* [I (on)] *sl, esp. AmE* to eat food greedily (GREEDY) and in large amounts; gorge oneself (GORGE[2]): *We really pigged out last night. I feel sick!*

pi·geon /ˈpɪdʒɪn/ *n* pigeons *or* pigeon **1** [C] a fairly large grey short-legged bird

▶ CULTURAL NOTE Trafalgar Square in London is known as a place where people go to feed the pigeons, but they are generally disliked because of the mess they make. Farmers dislike them because of the amount of corn they eat, and in the country they are often shot and eaten. A tame pigeon that is taken away from its home will always fly back, and some people race them against each other to see which bird gets home first.◄

2 [S] *BrE infml* someone's responsibility or affair: *It's not my pigeon — someone else can deal with it.* —see also CAR-

RIER PIGEON, CLAY PIGEON, **put/set the cat among the pigeons** (CAT), and see picture at BIRD

pigeon-chest·ed /ˌ··ˈ···◂‖ˈ··ˌ··/ *adj* (of a person) having a chest that is narrow and sticks out unnaturally

pi·geon·hole[1] /ˈpɪdʒɪnhəʊl/ *n* **pigeonhole** **1** any of a set of boxlike divisions in a frame, e.g. on a wall or on top of a desk, for putting esp. papers or letters in **2** a neat division (of ideas, feelings, etc.) which separates things too simply: *You shouldn't put people in pigeonholes.*

pigeonhole[2] *v* [T] **1** to put aside and keep for possible future use or attention; SHELVE: *That's a good idea, but we'll have to pigeonhole it until we know whether we can afford it.* **2** to put into the proper class or group: *It's the sort of job you can't pigeonhole — he seems to do different things every week.*

pigeon-toed /ˈ··ˌ·/ *adj* (of a person) having the feet pointing inwards

pig·ge·ry /ˈpɪgəri/ *n* **1** [C] a pig farm **2** [C] a PIGSTY (1) or a large building for pigs **3** [U] *derog* the behaviour of a PIG (2): *the supreme example of male chauvinist piggery*

pig·gish /ˈpɪgɪʃ/ *adj derog* (of a person) like a pig, esp. in being dirty or eating too much — ~ly *adv* — ~ness *n* [U]

Pig·gott /ˈpɪgət/, **Les·ter** /ˈlestər/ (1935–) an English JOCKEY (=a person who rides horses in races), regarded by many as the best there has ever been. He won over 4000 races, including the Derby 8 times. He was imprisoned in 1987 for not paying his taxes, and began racing again in 1990.

pig·gy[1] /ˈpɪgi/ *n infml* **1** (used esp. by or to children) a (little) pig **2 piggy in the middle** *esp. BrE* someone who is caught between two opposing sides but is unable to influence either of them (from the ball game in which one person tries to catch the ball as it is thrown between two others)

piggy[2] *adj infml derog* **1** (esp. of a child) GREEDY **2** like a pig: *little piggy eyes*

pig·gy·back /ˈpɪgibæk/ *n* a ride on someone else's back or shoulders, esp. given to a child: *Give me a piggyback!* — **piggyback** *adv*

pig·gy·bank /ˈpɪgibæŋk/ *n* a small container, often in the shape of a pig, used for saving coins

pig·head·ed /ˌpɪgˈhedɪd◂/ *adj derog* determinedly holding to an opinion or course of action in spite of argument, reason, etc.; STUBBORN — ~ly *adv* — ~ness *n* [U]

pig i·ron /ˈ·ˌ··/ *n* [U] an impure form of iron obtained directly from a BLAST FURNACE

pig·let /ˈpɪglɪt/ *n* a young pig

Piglet a loyal friend of Pooh Bear in stories by A. A. Milne. Piglet looks a little like a small pig, but he walks on two legs and has no tail.

pig·ment /ˈpɪgmənt/ *n* **1** [C;U] (a) dry coloured powder that is mixed with oil, water, etc., to make paint **2** [U] natural colouring matter of plants and animals, such as in leaves, hair, skin, etc.

pig·men·ta·tion /ˌpɪgmənˈteɪʃən/ *n* [U] **1** the spreading of colouring matter in parts of living things **2** the colouring of living things

pig·my /ˈpɪgmi/ *n* a PYGMY

pig·pen /ˈpɪgpen/ *n AmE for* PIGSTY

Pigpen *n* a character in the Peanuts COMIC STRIP, who is very dirty and always has a cloud of dirt all around him

Pigs, Bay of *n* see BAY OF PIGS

pig·skin /ˈpɪgˌskɪn/ *n* [U] leather made from pig's skin: *a pigskin bag*

pig's trot·ters /ˌ· ˈ···/ *n* [P] pigs' feet, cooked and eaten as food

pig·sty /ˈpɪgstaɪ/ also **pig·pen** *esp. AmE*— *n* **1** also **sty**— an enclosure with a small building in it, where pigs are kept **2** *derog* a very dirty room or house, esp. that is also in bad repair: *How can you live in this pigsty?*

pig·swill /ˈpɪgˌswɪl/ *n* [U] **1** waste food, such as vegetable skins, given to pigs   2 *derog* tasteless or bad-tasting food

pig·tail /ˈpɪɡteɪl/ *n* **1** one of two bunches of hair worn on either side of the face, either plaited (PLAIT²) or loose, esp. by young girls: *a little girl with her hair in pigtails.* **2** *BrE*‖**braid** *AmE*– a length of hair that has been twisted together in a short PLAIT and hangs down the back of the neck and shoulders, esp. worn by young girls –compare PONYTAIL – **– ed** *adj*

pike¹ /paɪk/ *n* **pikes** *or* **pike** a large fish-eating fish that lives in rivers and lakes

pike² *n* a long-handled spear formerly used by soldiers fighting on foot – **– man** /mən/ *n*

pike³ *n* a TURNPIKE

Pike, Zeb·u·lon /ˈzebjʊlən/ (1779–1813) an American army general and EXPLORER

Pike's Peak /ˌ· ˈ·/ a mountain in the Rockies, Colorado, US

pike·staff /ˈpaɪkstɑːf‖-stæf/ *n* the long wooden handle of a PIKE² –see also **as plain as a pikestaff** (PLAIN¹)

pi·laf , pilaff /ˈpiːlæf ‖ pɪˈlɑːf/ also **pi·lau** /ˈpiːlaʊ ‖ pɪˈlaʊ/– *n* [C;U] (*often in comb.*) a dish made from rice and sometimes vegetables, and often served with meat: *chicken pilaf*

pi·las·ter /pɪˈlæstər/ *n* a square post that usu. sticks out only partly beyond the wall of a building and is usu. only decorative

Pi·late /ˈpaɪlət/, **Pon·tius** /ˈpɒnʃəs, ˈpɒntiəs‖ˈpɑːntʃiəs/ (1st century) the Roman governor of Judaea at the time when Jesus Christ was tried and put to death. According to the Bible, Pilate offered to free Jesus, but the Jewish leaders would not accept this. Pilate washed his hands and said that he was not to blame for Jesus's death. People mention Pilate when they are talking about a person who is not strong enough to do what they think is right.

pil·chard /ˈpɪltʃəd‖-ərd/ *n* a small sea fish like the HERRING, often preserved in tins as food

pile

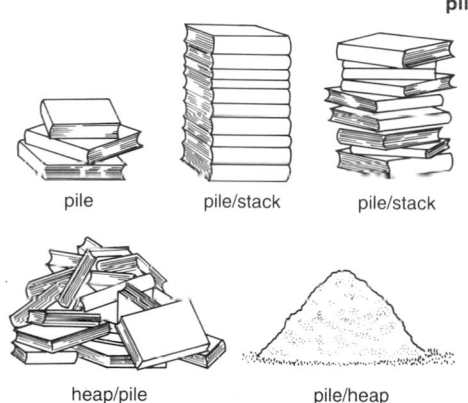

pile   pile/stack   pile/stack

heap/pile   pile/heap

pile¹ /paɪl/ *n* **1** [(of)] a tidy collection of objects, esp. when made of a number of things of the same kind placed on top of each other: *a pile of books/plates* | *We put the newspapers in piles on the floor.* –see USAGE   **2** a PYRE   **3** [(of)] also **piles** *pl.*– *infml* a lot: *I've got piles of work to do today.*   **4** [*usu. sing.*] *infml* a very large amount of money; fortune: *He made a/his pile and retired to the Bahamas.*   **5** *pomp* a large tall building or group of buildings: *They live in a rambling Victorian pile.* –see also PILES, ATOMIC PILE

▷ USAGE Compare **pile, stack,** and **heap,** which can all mean "a mass of things placed one on top of the other". A **pile** is a usually tidy collection of objects, usually of the same kind: *a pile of books/papers/leaves.* A **stack** is a carefully arranged **pile** usually made up of a lot of things of the same shape and size: *a stack of books/coins/cassettes.* A **heap** is a large disorderly pile of things, not necessarily of the same kind: *a heap of toys/books/dirty washing.* Both **pile** and **heap** can also be used with uncountable nouns: *a pile/heap of sand/straw/manure.*◁

pile² *v* **1** [T (**on, UP**)] to make a pile of: *He piled the boxes one on top of the other.* | *The little boy was piling up his building blocks.* **2** [T (**onto, with**)] to fill or cover plentifully; load: *He piled the spaghetti onto his plate.* | *The cart was piled high with fruit and vegetables.* **3** [I+*adv/prep*] *infml* (of people) to come or go in a (disorderly) crowd: *He opened the doors and they all piled in.* | *The boat arrived and hordes of people piled off.*

pile on *phr v infml* **1 pile it on** to say too much; EXAGGERATE: *She was trying to impress the interviewer, so she really piled it on.* | *Giving someone a compliment is one thing, but you were piling it on!* **2 pile on the agony** to enjoy making something seem worse than it really is

pile up *phr v* [I] **1** to form into a mass or large quantity; ACCUMULATE: *My work is piling up.* | *The clouds are piling up.* **2** (of a number of vehicles) to crash into each other –see also PILEUP

pile³ *n* [C;U] the soft surface of short threads on CARPETS and some cloths, esp. VELVET: *a deep pile carpet* – compare NAP³

pile⁴ *n* a heavy wooden, metal, or CONCRETE post hammered upright into the ground as a support for a building, bridge, etc.

pile driv·er /ˈ· ˌ··/ *n* **1** a machine for hammering PILES⁴ into the ground   **2** *infml* a very hard blow (PUNCH), esp. in BOXING

piles /paɪlz/ *n* [P] *infml for* HAEMORRHOIDS. Piles are often treated by non-sufferers as a rather humorous complaint.

pile·up /ˈpaɪlʌp/ *n* *infml* a traffic accident in which a number of vehicles crash into each other: *a bad pileup on the motorway* –see also PILE³ **up** (2)

pil·fer /ˈpɪlfər/ *v* [I;T] to steal (small amounts or things of little value): *He was found pilfering from other children's desks.* | *Petty pilfering is on the increase in department stores.* – **– er** *n*

pil·grim /ˈpɪlɡrɪm/ *n* a person who travels esp. a long way to a holy place as an act of religious love and respect

pil·grim·age /ˈpɪlɡrɪmɪdʒ/ *n* [C;U (**to**)] (a) journey made by a pilgrim: *Aziz is planning to go on/make a pilgrimage to Mecca.* | (fig.) *Many music-lovers make pilgrimages to Mozart's birthplace.*

Pilgrim Fa·thers /ˌ·· ˈ··/ also **Pilgrims**– [*the*+P] the group of English PURITANS who sailed to America to escape from England and make a new kind of society based on their religious beliefs. They arrived on their ship *Mayflower* at Plymouth, Massachusetts, US in 1620 – compare FOUNDING FATHER and see colour picture on page 1015

Pilgrim's Pro·gress /ˌ·· ˈ··/, **The** a book by the 17th century English writer John Bunyan. It is an ALLEGORY of the difficult journey of the human soul through life to Heaven. The main character, Christian, leaves his family and travels through the **Slough of Despond**, the **Valley of the Shadow of Death**, **Vanity Fair**, the land of **Beulah**, etc. meeting many dangers, until he reaches the **Celestial City**. Later his wife and children follow him.

Pilgrim's Way /ˌ·· ˈ·/ [*the*] the name of an old path from Winchester to Canterbury, which religious PILGRIMS travelled along in the past

Pil·king·ton /ˈpɪlkɪŋtən/ a British company which specializes in glass products

pill /pɪl/ *n* **1** [C] a small solid piece of medicine, made to be swallowed whole: *to take* (=swallow) *a sleeping pill* – see also **a bitter pill (to swallow)** (BITTER), MORNING-AFTER PILL, **sugar the pill** (SUGAR²) **2** [*the*+S] (*often cap.*) a pill taken regularly, usu. every day, by women as a means of birth control: *Is she on the pill?* (=taking the pill) | *She went on/came off the pill on her doctor's advice.*

pills

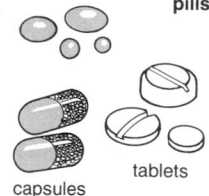

capsules   tablets

▶CULTURAL NOTE The Pill was the first method of CONTRACEPTION that was simple, reliable, and not difficult to use. Although there have been health problems associated with taking the Pill, and some women cannot use it at all, it is the most popular method in most Western countries. Because its use is controlled by the woman herself, making her able to choose when, or whether, to have children, it has helped to change women's attitude to themselves and their place in the world, e.g. by enabling a woman to delay having children until she is established in a career. It has also increased the freedom of unmarried people to have sex, and some people blame the Pill for what they regard as the evils of the PERMISSIVE SOCIETY. ◀

pil·lage¹ /ˈpɪlɪdʒ/ n [U] old use the act of pillaging

pillage² v [I;T] old use to steal things violently from (a place taken in war); PLUNDER: *The Vikings raped and pillaged all along the coast.* —compare LOOT —**-lager** n

pil·lar /ˈpɪləʳ/ n 1 a tall upright round post made usu. of stone a used as a support for a roof: *the graceful pillars of the Roman Forum* b standing alone in memory of some person or event 2 [(of)] something tall, narrow, and upright: *a pillar of smoke* 3 [(of)] *apprec* an important member and active supporter: *a pillar of the community/church* 4 (**be driven**) **from pillar to post** (to be chased or hunted) from one place or difficulty to another —compare COLUMN¹

pillar box /ˈ·· ·/ n (in Britain) a large tube-shaped type of POSTBOX that stands in the street and is usu. painted red —compare LETTERBOX, POST² (3)

pillar of salt /ˌ··· ˈ·/ n pillars of salt a rock-like upright piece of salt. In the Bible, Lot's wife is said to have become a pillar of salt after she disobeyed advice and looked back on the destruction of Sodom and Gomorrah.

Pillars of Her·cu·les /ˌ··· ˈ···/ [the +P] the two pieces of high land coming out into the water on either side of the Strait of Gibraltar which in former times marked the end of the civilized world at the western end of the Mediterranean and which, in CLASSICAL MYTHOLOGY, were separated by Hercules

pill·box /ˈpɪlbɒks‖-bɑːks/ n 1 a small round box for holding PILLs (1) 2 a small usu. circular CONCRETE shelter with a gun inside it, built as a defence esp. along a shore

pil·lion /ˈpɪljən/ n a seat for a second person on a motorcycle, placed behind the driver: *a pillion passenger* | *He was riding pillion.* (=on the pillion)

pil·lock /ˈpɪlək/ n BrE sl a foolish worthless person

pil·lo·ry¹ /ˈpɪləri/ n a wooden post with a bar at the top into which in former times the neck and wrists of wrongdoers were locked as a public punishment —compare STOCKS (1)

pillory

pillory² v [T] 1 to attack with words, esp. so as to cause to be treated with disrespect by the public: *The education secretary was pilloried in the press for his ridiculous decision.* 2 to punish by putting in a pillory

pil·low¹ /ˈpɪləʊ/ n 1 a cloth bag, usu. longer than it is wide, filled with a soft substance such as feathers and used for supporting the head in bed: *The children were having a marvellous pillow fight.* (=hitting each other with pillows) —compare CUSHION¹ (1) 2 any object used for supporting the head, esp. while sleeping: *She used her saddlebag as a pillow.* —see also PILLOW TALK

pillow² v [T+obj+adv/prep] to rest (esp. one's head) on something, esp. in order to go to sleep: *She pillowed her head on his shoulder.*

pil·low·case /ˈpɪləʊkeɪs/ also **pillow slip** /ˈ·· ·/— n a baglike cloth covering for a pillow

pillow talk /ˈ·· ·/ n [U] infml conversation in bed between lovers

Pills·bu·ry /ˈpɪlzbəri‖-beri/ an American maker of PROCESSED FOODs and flour. Their advertising personality is a small man made of DOUGH, called the **Pillsbury Doughboy**.

pi·lot¹ /ˈpaɪlət/ n 1 a person who controls an aircraft or spacecraft, esp. one who has been specially trained: *an airline pilot* 2 a person with a special knowledge of a particular stretch of water, esp. the entrance to a HARBOUR, who is employed to go on board and guide ships that use it: *a harbour pilot* 3 a television programme which is made to see if people like it and whether they would watch such a programme regularly if it were on

every week —see also AUTOMATIC PILOT, **drop the pilot** (DROP¹)

pilot² v [T] 1 to act as pilot of (an aircraft, spacecraft, or ship) —see BOAT (USAGE), DRIVE (USAGE), PLANE (USAGE) 2 [+obj+adv/prep, esp. **through**] to help and guide; show the way: *She piloted the old man through the crowd to his seat.* | (fig.) *The minister has piloted several useful bills through Parliament.* (=made sure they came successfully through and were made into laws)

pilot³ adj [A] acting as a trial for something: *We're doing a pilot survey on this product; if it sells well, we'll go into full production.* | *a pilot scheme*

pilot light /ˈ·· ·/ n 1 also **pilot burn·er** /ˈ·· ˌ··/— a small gas flame kept burning all the time, used for lighting larger gas burners when the gas in them is turned on 2 a small electric light on a piece of electrical apparatus that shows when it is turned on

pilot of·fi·cer /ˈ·· ˌ···/ n an airforce rank —see TABLE 3

Pilt·down Man /ˌpɪltdaʊn ˈmæn/ a supposed race of early people, bones of whom were thought to have been found in England in 1912. Later tests proved that the bones were not old and it was decided that Piltdown Man never existed.

Pi·ma /ˈpiːmə/ n [C; *the* + P] (a member of) a Native American people living in Arizona, US —see NATIVE AMERICAN (CULTURAL NOTE)

pi·men·to /pɪˈmentəʊ/ n -tos or -to [C;U] a small PEPPER¹ (2), often used for putting inside OLIVEs

Pim·li·co /ˈpɪmlɪkəʊ/ an area of London N of the Thames and SW of the City

Pimms /pɪmz/ n [U] tdmk a make of alcoholic drink based usu. on GIN, called in full **Pimms Number One Cup**. Pimms is often drunk in summer at fashionable and/or UPPER-CLASS events such as the Henley Regatta or Wimbledon.

pimp /pɪmp/ n a man who controls and makes a profit from the activities of PROSTITUTEs —**pimp** v [I (**for**)]

pim·per·nel /ˈpɪmpənel‖-ər-/ n a small low-growing wild plant with flowers that are blue, white, or esp. SCARLET

pim·ple /ˈpɪmpəl/ also **spot** BrE n a small raised infected spot on the skin (esp. of the face), usu. containing PUS — see also GOOSE FLESH —**-pled** adj —**-ply** adj : *pimply skin* | *a pimply youth*

pins

pin

brooch/pin AmE

safety pin

tie pin

drawing pin BrE/ thumbtack AmE

hairpin

bobbypin AmE/ hairgrip BrE

pin¹ /pɪn/ n 1 a short thin piece of metal that looks like a small nail, used for fastening together pieces of cloth, paper, etc., used e.g. when making clothes —see also PIN-CUSHION 2 (*often in comb.*) a quite short thin piece of metal, pointed at one end and with a decoration at the other, used esp. as a form of jewellery: *a hat pin* | *a tie pin* 3 AmE for BROOCH 4 a short piece of wood or metal used as a support, for fastening things together, etc.; PEG: *The doctor put a steel pin in his wrist.* 5 [usu. pl.] BrE infml a leg: *He's a bit unsteady on his pins.* 6 any of the bottle-shaped objects which a player tries to knock down by rolling a ball at them in the game of BOWLING: *He knocked down four pins with his first ball.* 7 BrE **for two pins** infml without needing to be persuaded very hard: *He's just stepped on my clean floor — for two pins I'd hit him!* —see also DRAWING PIN, NINEPINS, PINS AND NEEDLES, ROLLING PIN, SAFETY PIN

pin² *v* **-nn-** [T+*obj*+*adv*/*prep*] **1** to fasten or join with a pin or pins: *She pinned the front and back pieces of the dress together and tried it on for size.* | *She pinned the notice to the board.* | *He pinned the medal on the soldier's chest.* **2** to keep in one position, esp. by weight from above: *The wrestler pinned his opponent to the canvas.* | *In the accident she was pinned under the car.* **3** **Pin your** ˈ**ears back!** *infml, esp. BrE* Listen carefully!

pin *sbdy.*/*sthg.* ↔ **down** *phr v* [T (**to**)] **1** to force to give clear details, make a firm decision, etc.; NAIL **down**: *I won't pin you down to a particular day; just come whenever you're free.* **2** to know or understand clearly (who or what something is); IDENTIFY: *We know there is corruption in the organization but it is difficult to pin it down.*

pin *sthg.* **on** *sbdy. phr v* [T] **1** to fix (guilt, blame, etc.) on: *Don't try and pin the blame on me; I didn't do it!* **2** **pin one's hopes on someone** to depend on someone or something for success, help, a favour, etc.

PIN /pɪn/ *also* **PIN number** *n* personal identification number; a special number which is only known to the owner of a special card and which allows the owner to use his card to get money from a CASH POINT (=a machine which gives money from one's bank account). PIN numbers are kept secret so that a thief who steals the card cannot use it to get money.

pi·ña col·a·da /ˌpiːnjə kəʊˈlɑːdə/ *n* [C;U] *Sp* (a glass of) an alcoholic drink made from COCONUT juice, PINEAPPLE juice, and RUM

pin·a·fore /ˈpɪnəfɔːr/ *n BrE* **1** *also* **pinny** *infml*— a loose garment that does not cover the arms or usu. the back, worn over a dress to keep it clean **2** *also* **pinafore dress** /ˈ··· ·/ *BrE*‖**jumper** *AmE*— a dress that does not cover the arms, and under which a BLOUSE or other garment is worn

pin·ball /ˈpɪnbɔːl/ *n* [U] a game played on a machine with a sloping board down which a rolling ball is guided by various means: *a pinball machine*

pince-nez /ˌpæns ˈneɪ, ˌpɪns-/ *n* **pince-nez** /-ˈneɪz/ [C+*sing.*/*pl. v*] glasses, used esp. in former times, that are held in position on the nose by a spring, instead of by pieces fitting round the ears —see PAIR (USAGE)

pin·cer /ˈpɪnsər/ *n* [*usu. pl.*] either of the pair of footlike parts, made up of two pieces of pointed shell-like material, at the end of the legs of a CRAB, LOBSTER, etc., used for taking hold of food —see also PINCERS, and see picture at LOBSTER — ~ **like** *adj*

pincer move·ment /ˈ·· ˌ··/ *n* an attack by two groups of soldiers advancing from opposite directions to trap the enemy between them

pin·cers /ˈpɪnsəz‖-ərz/ *n* [P] a tool made of two crossed pieces of metal with curved parts at one end, used for holding tightly and pulling small things, such as a nail from wood —compare PLIERS; see PAIR (USAGE), and see picture at TOOL

pinch¹ /pɪntʃ/ *v* **1** [I;T] to press (esp. a person's flesh) tightly and usu. painfully between two hard surfaces or between the thumb and a finger: *He pinched his fingers in the car door.* | *She pinched me on the arm.* | *I had to pinch myself to make sure I wasn't dreaming.* | *Stop pinching (me)!* **2** [I] to give pain by being too tight: *Don't buy the shoes if they pinch.* **3** [T] *infml* to take without permission; steal: *My car's been pinched!* **4** [T (**with**) *usu. pass.*] **a** to cause pain to: *They came in pinched with cold and hunger.* **b** to make (the face) thin or tired-looking: *Her face was pinched and drawn with anxiety.* **5** [T (**for**) *often pass.*] *infml for* ARREST (1): *She got pinched for speeding.* **6** **pinch and scrape** to spend only what is necessary (or even less) —see also PENNY PINCHER

pinch² *n* **1** [C] an act of pinching someone: *She gave him a pinch to wake him up.* | *a playful/spiteful pinch* **2** [C (**of**)] an amount that can be picked up between the thumb and a finger: *a pinch of salt/snuff* —see picture at PIECE **3** [*the*+S] suffering caused by lack of necessary things, esp. money: *It's six months since he lost his job, so he's beginning to feel the pinch.* **4 at a pinch** *BrE* ‖ **in a pinch** *AmE*— if necessary: *It's more than I really want to spend, but at a pinch I suppose I could manage £60.* —see also **take something with a pinch of salt** (SALT¹)

pinched /pɪntʃt/ *adj* [F (**for**)] without enough (money);

SHORT¹ (4): *We're rather pinched (for money) these days.* —see also PINCH² (3)

pin·cush·ion /ˈpɪnˌkʊʃən/ *n* a filled bag like a small CUSHION into which PINs are stuck until they are needed, used esp. by dressmakers

pin·down /ˈpɪndaʊn/ *n* [U] (in Britain) a method of dealing with difficult children in special homes for them which was judged to be against the law. It involved separating the children from others, allowing them to wear few clothes, and giving them little food.

pine¹ /paɪn/ *n* **1** [C] *also* **pine·tree**— a tall tree with thin sharp leaves (**pine needles**) that do not drop off in winter and woody fruits (**pinecones**), that grows esp. in colder parts of the world: *a pine forest* | *pine-fresh disinfectant* (=smelling of pine) —see picture at TREE **2** [U] the white or yellowish soft wood of this tree: *a pine table*

pine² *v* [I] **1** [(AWAY)] to become thin, less active, and lose strength and health slowly, through disease or esp. grief: *He pined away after his wife died.* **2** [(for)] to desire very strongly over a long period of time, and to grieve for: *The dog was pining for its dead master.* | *She pined for her lost love until he finally returned.* **3** [(for)] to have a strong desire, esp. that is impossible to fulfil: *They were pining for their homeland back in Europe.*

Pine, Court·ney /ˈkɔːtni‖ˈkɔːr-/ (1964–) an English JAZZ musician and COMPOSER known esp. for playing the SAXOPHONE

pin·e·al gland /ˈpɪniəl glænd‖ˈpaɪn-/ *n* a small growth in the brain, the exact purpose of which is not known, but which may be sensitive to light in some way

pine·ap·ple /ˈpaɪnæpəl/ *n* **1** [C;U] (the sweet juicy yellow flesh of) a large dark yellow tropical fruit with a mass of thin stiff leaves on top; pineapples are sold fresh or in tins: *pineapple rings/chunks* | *pineapple juice* —see picture at FRUIT **2** [C] *sl for* HAND GRENADE

pine mar·ten /ˈ· ˌ··/ *n* a small European animal that lives in forests

pine nee·dles /ˈ· ˌ··/ *n* the leaves of the pine tree, which are like needles (long, thin, and sharp)

pine straw /ˈ· ·/ *n AmE infml* dried, brown pine needles which have fallen to the ground. Pine straw becomes very deep in a pine forest.

pine·tree /ˈpaɪntriː/ *n* a PINE¹ (1)

pine·wood /ˈpaɪnwʊd/ *n* **1** [C] *also* **pinewoods** *pl.*— a pine forest **2** [U] the wood of the pine tree

Pinewood Stu·di·os /ˌ·· ˈ···/ *n* [*the* + P] a large film STUDIO (=place where films are made) near Slough, W of London, which opened in 1936

pin·ey /ˈpaɪni/ *adj* PINY

ping¹ /pɪŋ/ *n* [S] *infml* a short sharp ringing sound, such as the sound made by hitting a glass with something hard

ping² *v* [I] **1** *infml* to make a ping: *a pinging sound* **2** *AmE for* PINK³

ping-pong /ˈ· ·/ *n* [U] *infml for* TABLE TENNIS

pin·head /ˈpɪnhed/ *n* **1** the head of a pin **2** *infml derog* a rather stupid person

pin·ion¹ /ˈpɪnjən/ *v* [T] *fml* **1** to hold or tie up (the arms or legs) in order to prevent movement **2** [(to)] to prevent the movement of (a person or animal) by holding or tying up the arms or legs: *The wrestler pinioned his opponent to the floor.*

pinion² *n* a small wheel, with teeth on its outer edge, that fits into a larger wheel and turns it or is turned by it —compare COGWHEEL, RACK¹ (3)

pinion³ *n* **1** *poet* a bird's wing **2** *tech* the joint or part of a bird's wing furthest away from the body

pink¹ /pɪŋk/ *adj* **1** pale red: *salmon pink* | *a pink carnation/rose* **2** *often derog* giving some slight support to SOCIALIST political parties and ideas —compare RED¹ (1); see also PINKO, **tickled pink** (TICKLE¹)

pink² *n* **1** [C;U] a pale red colour

▶CULTURAL NOTE Pink is often thought of as a colour for females. Girl babies are sometimes given pink clothes and boy babies, blue.◀

2 [C] a garden plant with sweet-smelling pink, white, or red flowers **3 in the pink** *usu. humor* in perfect health; very well

pink³ *BrE* ‖ **ping** *AmE*— *v* [I] (of a car engine) to make knocking sounds as a result of not working properly

pink-col·lar /ₗˈ···/ adj esp. AmE of or concerning jobs of fairly low rank such as those of secretaries, waitresses (WAITRESS), typists (TYPIST), clerks, etc. that are usu. taken by women —compare WHITE COLLAR, BLUE-COLLAR

pink el·e·phant /ₗ· ˈ···/ n [often pl.] humor an imaginary thing supposed to be seen by someone who is drunk

pink·eye /ˈpɪnkaɪ/ n [U] infml for CONJUNCTIVITIS

Pink Floyd /ₗpɪŋk ˈflɔɪd/ a British rock music group famous for its FUTURISTIC music. Its most well-known ALBUM is *The Wall*.

pink gin /ₗ· ˈ·/ n [C;U] esp. BrE (a glass of) an alcoholic drink made of GIN, with ANGOSTURA added to give it a pink colour

pink·ie, **pinky** /ˈpɪŋki/ n ScotE or AmE the smallest finger of the human hand —see picture at HAND

pink·ing shears /ˈ·· ·/ also **pinking scis·sors** /ˈ·· ₗ··/— n [P] a special type of scissors with blades that have V-shaped teeth, used to cut cloth in such a way that the threads along the cut edge will not come out easily —see PAIR (USAGE)

pink·ish /ˈpɪŋkɪʃ/ adj slightly pink

pink·o /ˈpɪŋkəʊ/ n -oes or -os infml derog a person who gives some slight support to SOCIALIST political parties and ideas —compare RED²; see also PINK¹ (2)

Pink Pan·ther /ₗ· ˈ···/ [the] **1** the name of the thief in humorous films about a police officer of middle rank called Inspector Clousseau, usu. played by Peter Sellers **2** a CARTOON character, based on this, who is really pink and really a PANTHER

pink slip /ₗ· ˈ·/ n AmE official notice from an employer that one's employment is ended: *We're going to give him the pink slip tomorrow.* —see MARCHING ORDERS, WALKING PAPERS

Pink·y and Perk·y /ₗpɪŋki ənd ˈpɜːki‖-ˈpɜːr-/ two pig PUPPETs that were popular on British children's television in the 1950s and 60s and are remembered esp. for singing songs in high squeaky voices

pin mon·ey /ˈ· ₗ··/ n [U] infml a small amount of (additional) money that is earned, esp. by a married woman, and that can be spent on oneself, e.g. on clothes

pin·nace /ˈpɪnɪs/ n a small boat used for taking goods and esp. people to and from a ship —compare LIGHTER²

pin·na·cle /ˈpɪnəkəl/ n **1** [(of)] usu. sing.] the highest point or degree: *She had reached the pinnacle of success/fame.* **2** esp. lit a pointed stone decoration like a small tower, built on a roof esp. in old churches and castles: *the towers and pinnacles of the ancient city*

pin·nate /ˈpɪneɪt/ adj tech (of a leaf) made of little leaves arranged opposite each other in two rows along a stem

Pin·no·chi·o /pɪˈnəʊkiəʊ/ a character from a story and film of the same name. Pinnochio was a boy PUPPET made of wood who came to life and whose nose grew longer when he told lies.

PIN num·ber /ˈpɪn ₗnʌmbəʳ/ n see PIN

pin·ny /ˈpɪni/ n infml for PINAFORE (1)

Pi·no·chet /ˈpiːnəʊʃeɪ‖ˌpiːnəʊˈtʃet/, **Au·gus·to** /aʊˈgʊstəʊ/ (1915–) a Chilean general who became president of the country after the elected government of Salvador Allende was removed in 1973. He was defeated and removed from office in 1989, but remains head of the armed forces.

piñ·on, pinyon /ˈpɪnjən/ n [U;C] a short PINE tree common in western N America, which produces eatable seeds (**piñon nuts**)

pin·point¹ /ˈpɪnpɔɪnt/ v [T] **1** to find or describe exactly (the nature or cause of something): *Investigators are trying to pinpoint the causes of the crash.* **2** to show the exact position of: *Can you pinpoint it on the map for me?*

pinpoint² n [(of)] a very small area or point: *a pinpoint of light at the end of the tunnel*

pinpoint³ adj [A] **1** very exact: *The radar enables us to*

locate the target with pinpoint accuracy. **2** (of a TARGET to be hit by gunfire, bombs, etc.) very small, esp. as seen from a distance, and needing great care and exactness of aim

pin·prick /ˈpɪnprɪk/ n **1** a small mark or hole made (as if) by a pin: *Don't make such a fuss; it's only a pinprick!* **2** something that causes slight annoyance or difficulty

pins and nee·dles /ₗ· · ˈ··/ n [P] infml **1** slight continuous sharp pains in a part of the body, esp. a limb, to which the supply of blood is returning after having been stopped by pressure; pins and needles are usu. the result of sitting in one position for too long: *I've got pins and needles in my right leg.* **2 on pins and needles** AmE in a state of anxious expectation

pin·stripe /ˈpɪnstraɪp/ n any of a number of thin usu. white lines repeated at regular spaces along usu. dark cloth to form a pattern —**-striped** adj

pin·stripe suit /ₗ·· ˈ·/ n a suit made of cloth that has a pattern of pinstripes. There is a strong association in people's minds between pinstripe suits and men who work in London's financial institutions —see also CITY GENT

pint /paɪnt/ n **1** [(of)] a measure for liquids, esp. milk or beer: *a pint of milk* | *Two pints today, please.* (=a note to the MILKMAN) —see TABLE 2, and see picture at LITRE **2** BrE infml a drink of beer of this amount: *We're going for a quick pint.* | *Let me buy you a pint.*

pint·a /ˈpaɪntə/ n BrE infml a pint of milk. A well-known advertisement for milk in Britain said that people should "drink a pinta milk a day".

Pin·ta /ˈpɪntə/ one of the three ships which sailed to America with Christopher Columbus in 1492 —see also NINA, SANTA MARIA

pin·ta·ble /ˈpɪnₗteɪbəl/ n BrE a machine for playing PINBALL

Pin·ter /ˈpɪntəʳ/, **Harold** (1930–) a British writer best known for plays like *The Caretaker*, which show the strangeness of ordinary lives and family relationships

pin·to bean /ˈpɪntəʊ ₗbiːn/ n a small, light brown bean

pint-size /ˈ· ·/ also **pint-sized**— adj usu. derog small and unimportant: *her pint-size boyfriend*

pin·up /ˈpɪnʌp/ n **1** a picture of an attractive or admired person, esp. of a woman wearing no clothes, esp. as stuck up on a wall by the admirer **2** the person in such a picture

pin·wheel /ˈpɪnwiːl/ n AmE for WINDMILL (2)

pin·y , piney /ˈpaɪni/ adj like or containing PINE trees: *a piny smell*

Pin·yin /ₗpɪn ˈjɪn◂/ n [U] a system of writing the Chinese language in the Roman alphabet officially recognized in China since 1958 and used in Western newspapers and other public documents

pin·yon /ˈpɪnjən/ n see PIÑON

pi·o·neer¹ /ₗpaɪəˈnɪəʳ◂/ n **1** any of the first settlers in a new or unknown land, who are later followed by others: *log cabins built by the early pioneers* **2** [(of)] a person who does something first and so makes it possible or easier for others to do it later: *He was a pioneer of heart transplant operations.*

pioneer² v [T] to begin or help in the early development of: *This company pioneered the use of the silicon chip.*

pi·o·neer·ing /ₗpaɪəˈnɪərɪŋ◂/ adj apprec introducing new ways of doing things, which others later follow: *She did pioneering work in the field of genetic engineering.* | *a pioneering firm* | *a pioneering novel*

pi·ous /ˈpaɪəs/ adj fml **1** showing and feeling deep respect for God and religion —see also PIETY **2** derog pretending to have deep respect and sincere feelings: *Despite his pious expressions of regret, we could see that the outcome was quite satisfactory to him.* **3** [A] unlikely to be fulfilled: *I suppose some of them may not have been destroyed, but it's a rather pious hope.* — ~ly adv

pi·ous·ness /ˈpaɪəsnₗs/ n [U] PIETY

pip¹ /pɪp/ ‖ usu. **seed** AmE— n a small fruit seed, esp. of an apple, orange, etc.: *He spat out the pips.* —compare STONE¹ (4), and see picture at FRUIT

pip² n a short high-sounding note, esp. as given on the radio to show the exact time, or as used in the operation of public telephones

pip³ *n infml* **1** any of the small marks on playing cards, DICE, and dominoes (DOMINO), showing their values **2** *BrE* any of the stars on the shoulders of the coats of army officers of certain ranks: *Captains have three pips.*

pip⁴ *v* **-pp-** [T] *BrE infml* to beat narrowly in a race, competition, etc.: *I nearly got the job, but I was* **pipped at the post** (=right at the end of the choosing process) *by the other candidate.*

pip⁵ *n* [the+S] *old-fash infml, BrE* a feeling of annoyance or lack of cheerfulness: *This rainy weather really* **gives me the pip.**

pi·pal /ˈpiːpəl/ *n* a large Indian tree

pipe¹ /paɪp/ *n* **1** a tube used for carrying liquids or gas, often underground: *a gas/water/sewage pipe | a burst/blocked/broken pipe | to lay pipes under the road | to lag the pipes in the loft* **2** a small tube with a bowl-like container at one end, used for smoking tobacco: *He filled and lit his pipe. | He's a pipe-smoker. | the stem/bowl of a pipe | pipe tobacco* **3 a** a simple tubelike musical instrument, played by blowing **b** any of the tubelike metal parts through which air is forced in an ORGAN **4 Put 'that in your pipe and smoke it** *infml* You'll have to accept what I've just said, whether you like it or not —see also PIPES

pipe² *v* **1** [T (**into, to**) *often pass.*] to carry (esp. liquid or gas) through pipes: *Water is piped to all the houses.* **2** [I; T] *esp. lit* **a** (of a bird) to sing (high notes) **b** (of a person) to speak or sing in a high childish voice —see also PIPE UP **3** [T+obj+adv/prep] *tech* to welcome onto a ship by blowing a special whistle: *The admiral was piped aboard.* **4** [T (**with**)] to decorate (a dress, cake, etc.) with PIPING¹ (2b)
  pipe down *phr v* [I] *infml* to stop talking or making a noise: *Pipe down! I'm trying to listen to the news.*
  pipe up *phr v* [I] *infml* to begin to speak or sing, esp. unexpectedly and in a high voice: *The smallest child piped up with the answer.*

pipe and slip·pers /ˌ· · ˈ··/ *n* [P] two things which it is thought a man enjoys after a hard day at work. They often appear in jokes and CARTOONS: *Shall I bring your pipe and slippers, dear?*

pipe clean·er /ˈ· ˌ··/ *n* a length of wire covered with soft threads, used to unblock the stem of a tobacco pipe. Pipe cleaners are also used by children to make shapes and models.

piped mu·sic /ˌ· ˈ··/ also **canned music**— *n* [U] *often derog* quiet recorded music played continuously in a public place, such as a shop, hotel, or restaurant. The expression is often used as criticism by people who would prefer a higher quality of music or none at all. —see also ELEVATOR MUSIC, MUZAK

pipe dream /ˈ· ·/ *n* an impossible hope, plan, idea, etc.: *His scheme for building a perpetual-motion machine is just a pipe dream.*

pipe fit·ter /ˈ· ˌ··/ *n* **1** *BrE* a person who puts in and repairs PIPING¹ (1) **2** *AmE for* GAS FITTER

pipe·line /ˈpaɪp-laɪn/ *n* **1** a line of connected pipes, often underground, esp. for carrying liquids or gas a long distance **2 in the pipeline** about to happen but still in the process of being prepared or produced: *Some important changes in this law are now in the pipeline.*

pipe of peace /ˌ· · ˈ·/ *n* a PEACE PIPE

pip·er /ˈpaɪpəʳ/ *n* a musician who plays on a PIPE¹ (3a) or BAGPIPES

pipe rack /ˈ· ·/ *n* a small frame for holding several tobacco pipes

Piper Al·pha /ˌ·· ˈ··/ an oil RIG in the North Sea which caught fire in 1988. 167 workers died in the fire. The accident caused criticism of safety standards on oil rigs and the methods of inspecting rigs and making sure that proper safety measures were taken.

pipes /paɪps/ *n* [(the) P] *BrE infml for* BAGPIPES

pi·pette /pɪˈpet/ /paɪ-/ *n* a thin glass tube used in chemistry, into which exact amounts of liquid can be sucked, then held and/or allowed to flow out —see picture at LABORATORY

pip·ing¹ /ˈpaɪpɪŋ/ *n* [U] **1** PIPES¹ (1) in general or a system of pipes: *outdoor piping | a length of copper/plastic piping* **2 a** a narrow often tubelike band of cloth used for decorating the edges of clothes, furniture, etc.: *blue sofa*

covers with white piping **b** thin lines of ICING used for decorating cakes **3** the action or skill of a PIPER

piping² *adv* **piping hot** *apprec* (esp. of liquids or food) very hot; a word usu. used by someone who is feeling very cold: *piping hot soup*

pip·it /ˈpɪpɪt/ *n* (*usu. in comb.*) a small usu. brown or greyish bird: *the meadow pipit*

pip·pin /ˈpɪpɪn/ *n* (*usu. cap. as part of a name*) a kind of sweet apple

pip·squeak /ˈpɪpskwiːk/ *n derog* someone who is not really worth one's attention or respect, but who behaves as if he/she is important, esp. a child

pi·quant /ˈpiːkənt/ *adj* **1** having a pleasant sharp taste: *a piquant sauce* **2** pleasantly interesting and exciting, and giving one a feeling of satisfaction: *a particularly piquant situation when my old enemy asked for my help* — **~ly** *adv* **—quancy** *n* [U]

pique¹ /piːk/ *n* [U] a feeling of annoyance and displeasure, esp. caused by the hurting of one's pride: *He left* **in a fit of pique.**

pique² *v* [T *often pass.*] to make (someone) angry by hurting their pride; offend: *He was piqued by her indifference.*

pi·ra·cy /ˈpaɪərəsi/ *n* **1** [U] robbery by pirates **2** [U] the action of pirating **3** [C] an example of either of these

Pir·an·del·lo /ˌpɪrənˈdeləʊ/, **Lu·i·gi** /luˈiːdʒi/ (1867–1936) an Italian writer known for plays which examine the relationship between the real and the unreal, who won the NOBEL PRIZE for literature in 1934

pi·ra·nha /pɪ̥ˈrɑːnjə, -nə/ *n* a fierce South American flesh-eating river fish

pi·rate¹ /ˈpaɪərət/ *n* **1** (esp. formerly) a person who sails the seas stopping and robbing ships at sea. Pirates in stories often speak roughly, drink a lot, esp. RUM, and have a PARROT on their shoulder. They sometimes wear a black PATCH over one eye and have a wooden leg. They also use phrases which are connected esp. with pirates, e.g. "Shiver me timbers" (=used as a phrase showing great surprise). —see also LONG JOHN SILVER and see picture at LONG JOHN SILVER

pirates

2 a person who pirates the work of other people —**-ratical** /paɪˈrætɪkəl, pɪ̥-/ *adj* : *a large piratical beard* **—-ratically** /kli/ *adv*

pirate² *v* [T] to copy and sell (the work of other people, such as a book, a new invention, etc.) without permission or payment, when the COPYRIGHT (=the right to do so) belongs to someone else. It is against the law to pirate books, CASSETTEs, VIDEOs, etc. in Britain and in many other countries: *pirated video tapes*

pirate ra·di·o /ˌ··· ˈ···/ *n* [U] radio broadcasts, or the stations sending them out, which are not legal because they do not have a LICENCE (1) to operate

Pirates of Pen·zance /ˌpaɪərəts əv penˈzæns/, **The** an OPERETTA by Gilbert and Sullivan, about a band of pirates who never succeed in robbing anyone. It contains the humorous songs *The Very Model of a Modern Major General* and *A Policeman's Lot is Not a Happy One.*

Pi·rel·li cal·en·dar /pɪˌreli ˈkælɪ̥ndəʳ/ *n* any of the CALENDARS (=table of days arranged in weeks and months) produced yearly by the Pirelli company. Each month shows a photograph of a woman with few clothes on and some people consider the photographs to be artistic.

pir·ou·ette /ˌpɪruˈet/ *n* a very fast turn made on one toe or the front part of one foot, esp. by a BALLET dancer: *to dance/do a pirouette* **—pirouette** *v* [I]

Pi·sa /ˈpiːzə/ a city in N central Italy, famous for its CATHEDRAL and the Leaning Tower —see also LEANING TOWER OF PISA

pis·ca·to·ri·al /ˌpɪskəˈtɔːriəl◂/ *adj fml or pomp* connected with fishing or fishermen

Pis·ces /ˈpaɪsiːz/ *n* **1** the 12th sign of the ZODIAC represented by two fish **2** [C] a person born between February 20 and March 20 —see ZODIAC (USAGE) and see picture at ZODIAC

pish /pɪʃ/ interj old use (used to express feelings of not very strong anger or impatience)

piss[1] /pɪs/ v taboo sl **1** [I] to URINATE **2** [it+I (DOWN)] esp. BrE (of rain) to fall heavily: It's pissing down. **3 piss oneself** esp. BrE to laugh uncontrollably
  piss about/around phr v [I] taboo sl to act in a foolish irresponsible way; waste time
  piss off phr v **1** [I usu. imperative] taboo sl to go away **2** [T] (**piss** sbdy. ↔ **off**) sl, not taboo **a** BrE [usu. pass.] to cause to lose interest; BORE: She's rather pissed off with her job. **b** to annoy: The way he insults his friends behind their backs really pisses me off.

piss[2] n taboo sl **1** [U] URINE **2** [S] an act of urinating (URINATE): to have|take a piss **3 take the piss out of** BrE to make fun of —see also PISS-TAKE

Pis·sar·ro /pɪˈsɑːrəʊ/, **Ca·mille** /kæˈmiːl/ (1830–1903) a French IMPRESSIONIST artist

pissed /pɪst/ adj [F] **1** BrE taboo sl drunk **2** AmE sl, not taboo annoyed or angered **3 pissed as a newt, pissed out of one's head/mind** BrE taboo sl very drunk

piss-take /ˈ· ·/ n [usu. sing.] taboo sl an act of making fun of someone —see also **take the piss out of** (PISS[2])

piss-up /ˈ· ·/ n taboo sl, esp. BrE an occasion of drinking lots of alcohol

pis·ta·chi·o /pɪˈstɑːʃiəʊ‖pɪˈstæ-/ n **-chios** a small green nut: pistachio ice cream

pis·til /ˈpɪstl/ n tech the female seed-producing part of a flower

pis·tol /ˈpɪstl/ n a small gun held in one hand: to draw|aim|fire a pistol —see picture at GUN

pis·ton /ˈpɪstən/ n a part of an engine consisting of a short solid pipe-shaped piece of metal that fits tightly into a CYLINDER (=a tube). It is moved up and down in the tube by means of pressure or explosion, and causes other parts of the engine to move.

piston ring /ˈ··· ·/ n a circular metal spring used to stop gas or liquid escaping from between a piston and its CYLINDER (3)

pit[1] /pɪt/ n **1** [C] a hole in the ground: They dug a pit to bury the rubbish. —compare PITS (2) **2** [C] a coal mine: plans for the closure of uneconomic pits | He worked all his life down the pit. (=in the coal industry) **3** [(the) C usu. sing.] also **orchestra pit**— the space below and in front of a theatre stage where musicians play the music for a performance **4** [(the) C usu. sing.] the seats at the back of the ground floor of a theatre, behind the STALLS **5** [C often pl.] a small hollow mark or place in the surface of something, esp. as left on the face after certain diseases, esp. SMALLPOX **6** AmE for PITS (1) **7** [C usu. sing.] BrE humor one's bed: in my pit **8** [the+S] esp. bibl for HELL (1) **9 pit of one's stomach** the hollow place just below the chest, esp. thought of as being the place where fear is felt —see also PITS, ARMPIT, SANDPIT

pit[2] v **-tt-** [T] to mark with PITS[1] (5): the deeply|heavily pitted surface of the metal
  pit sbdy./sthg. **against** sbdy./sthg. phr v [T] to set against in a competition to see which is better, who will win, etc.: pitting his strength against that of a man twice his size | In the quiz she had to **pit her wits** (=match her mental ability) against some very clever people.

pit[3] n AmE for STONE[1] (4) —see picture at FRUIT

pit[4] v **-tt-** [T] AmE for STONE[2] (2)

pit·a bread /ˈpɪtə bred ‖ ˈpiːtə-/ AmE for PITTA BREAD

pit-a-pat /ˈ· ·ˌ·/ also **pitter-patter**— adv infml with many quick light beats or steps: His heart went pit-a-pat. | The rain fell pitter-patter against the window. —**pit-a-pat, pitter-patter** n [(the) S], adj [A]

pit bull ter·ri·er /ˌ· · ˈ···/ also **pit bull** /ˌ· ˈ·◄/— n an American fighting dog considered very dangerous when its owner is unable to control it. Pit bull terriers have caused terrible injuries to children and adults. In Britain they may no longer be sold, bred, or brought into the country, and they must wear a MUZZLE (=a covering round the mouth to prevent the dog from biting) when they are in a public place. —see picture at DOG

pitch[1] /pɪtʃ/ v **1** [T] to set up (a tent, camp, etc.), esp. for a short time: They pitched camp by the river. —opposite **strike 2** [T+obj+adv/prep] to set the degree or highness or lowness of (a sound, music, etc.): This song is pitched too high for my voice. —see also HIGH-PITCHED, LOW-PITCHED

3 [T+obj+adv/prep] to express in a way suitable to be understood by particular people: He pitched his speech at a very simple level so that even the children could understand. **4** [I+adv/prep; T+obj+adv/prep] to (cause to) fall heavily or suddenly forwards or outwards: His foot caught in a rock and he pitched forwards. **5** [I] (of a ship or aircraft) to move along with the back and front going up and down: The ship pitched violently in the stormy sea. —compare ROLL[1](6), YAW **6** [T+obj+adv/prep] to throw, esp. in a way that shows dislike or annoyance; TOSS: He screwed up the letter and pitched it into the fire. **7** [I] (of a ball in cricket or GOLF) to hit the ground **8** (in GOLF) to hit (the ball) in a high ARC **9** [T] (of a cricketer) to make (a ball) hit the ground when bowling (BOWL) **10** [I;T] (in the game of BASEBALL) to aim and throw (a ball) **11** [I+adv/prep] to slope downwards: The roof of this house pitches sharply. —see also PITCHED
  pitch in phr v [I] infml **1** to start to work or eat eagerly, esp. in a group: If we all pitch in and help we should get the job finished this afternoon. **2** [(with)] to add one's help or support: The local council pitched in with an offer of a free van.

pitch[2] n **1** [C] BrE ‖ **field** AmE— (in sport) a special marked-out area of ground on which football, HOCKEY, NETBALL, etc., are played: The crowd invaded the pitch at the end of the match. **2** [C] the degree of highness or lowness of a musical note or speaking voice —see also CONCERT PITCH **3** [S (of);U] degree; level: Disagreement reached such a pitch that we thought a fight would break out. | Speculation about the forthcoming election was **at fever pitch** (=at the highest degree). **4** [C] a place in a public area, such as a street or market, where someone regularly tries to get money from people who are passing, e.g. by performing, selling things, etc. **5** [S] a backward and forward movement of a ship or aircraft —compare ROLL[2](1) **6** [S;U (of)] (esp. in building) amount or degree of slope, esp. of a roof **7** [C] infml for SALES PITCH —see also **queer someone's pitch** (QUEER[3])

pitch[3] n [U] a black substance that is melted into a sticky material used for making protective coverings or for filling cracks, esp. in a ship, to stop water coming through: It's **as black as pitch** (=very dark) in here; has anyone got a torch?

pitch-and-putt /ˌ· · ˈ·/ n [U] a game of GOLF on a special course where the holes (HOLE[1] (5b)) are shorter than on a full-size golf course

pitch-black /ˌ· ˈ·◄/ also **pitch-dark**— adj completely black or dark: a pitch-black moonless night — — **ness** n [U]

pitch·blende /ˈpɪtʃblend/ n [U] a dark shiny substance dug from the earth, from which URANIUM and RADIUM are obtained

pitched /pɪtʃt/ adj (of a roof) sloping rather than flat —see also HIGH-PITCHED, LOW-PITCHED

pitched bat·tle /ˌ· ˈ··/ n **1** (in former times) a battle at a chosen place between armies with positions already prepared —compare SKIRMISH **2** infml a fierce and usu. long quarrel or argument: We had a pitched battle with the council before they'd agree to repair the road.

pitch·er[1] /ˈpɪtʃər/ n **1** BrE a large container for holding and pouring liquids, usu. made of clay and having two ear-shaped handles **2** AmE for JUG[1] (1) —see picture at JUG

pitch·er[2] n (in BASEBALL) a player who throws the ball towards the BATTER —see picture at BASE BALL

pitch·fork[1] /ˈpɪtʃfɔːk‖-fɔːrk/ n a long-handled farm tool with two long curved metal points, used esp. for lifting and throwing HAY (=dried cut grass)

pitchfork[2] v [T] **1** to lift and throw (HAY) using a pitchfork **2** [+obj+adv/prep] to put (a person) suddenly or unexpectedly into a place or situation for which they are not properly prepared: He was pitchforked into the post of manager without any training.

pit·e·ous /ˈpɪtiəs/ adj esp. lit expressing suffering in a sad way, so that one feels pity: the piteous cries of the starving children — — **ly** adv — — **ness** n

pit·fall /ˈpɪtfɔːl/ n an unexpected difficulty or danger; mistake that can easily be made: English spelling presents many pitfalls for foreign students.

pith /pɪθ/ n [U] **1** a soft white SPONGE-like substance that fills the stems of certain plants **2** a white material just under the coloured outside skin of oranges and similar fruit **3** the central most important part of an argument, idea, etc.

pit·head /ˈpɪt-hed/ n the entrance to a coal mine and the buildings around it: *pithead baths*

pith hel·met /ˈ· ··/ also **topee**– n a large light hat worn in the tropics, esp. formerly, to protect the head from the sun

pith·y /ˈpɪθi/ adj **1** (of something said or written) strongly and cleverly stated without wasting any words: *pithy advice* **2** of, like, or having a lot of pith —**·ily** adv —**·iness** n [U]

pit·i·a·ble /ˈpɪtiəbəl/ adj rather fml pitiful —**bly** adv

pit·i·ful /ˈpɪtɪfəl/ adj **1** causing or deserving pity: *The sick animals were in a pitiful condition.* **2** derog not deserving respect or serious consideration: *You don't expect me to believe that pitiful excuse, do you?* —**ly** adv : *She had become pitifully thin.* — ~**ness** n [U]

pit·i·less /ˈpɪtɪləs/ adj showing no pity or MERCY; cruel and unforgiving: *a pitiless tyrant* | *pitiless cruelty* | (fig.) *The pitiless* (=unbearably severe) *north wind blew for weeks on end.* — ~**ly** adv — ~**ness** n [U]

pit·man /ˈpɪtmən/ n **-men** /mən/ a coal miner

Pi·tot tube /ˈpiːtəʊ tjuːb‖-tuːb/ n an instrument used in measuring the speed of an aircraft

pit po·ny /ˈ· ˌ··/ n a small horse used esp. formerly for moving coal in a coal mine

pit prop /ˈ· ·/ n a support for the roof of an underground passage in a coal mine

pits /pɪts/ n [the+P] **1** (in motor racing) a place beside a track where cars can come during a race to be quickly examined and repaired **2** infml derog the worst possible example of something: *That new film is the pits!*

pit stop /ˈ· ·/ n the action of stopping in the pits during a car race to get more petrol or have repairs done: (fig.) *We'll make a pit stop in Butte to get something to eat and use the restrooms.*

pit·ta bread /ˈpɪtə bred‖ˈpiːtə-/ BrE ‖ **pita bread** AmE– n [U] a type of bread, originally from the Middle East, which is flat and hollow: *For a healthy lunch, fill a piece of pitta bread with lettuce, tomatoes, cucumbers, and slices of avocado.*

pit·tance /ˈpɪtəns/ n [usu. sing.] a very small ungenerous amount of pay or money. *She gets paid a (mere) pittance in her present job.*

pit·ted /ˈpɪtɪd/ adj esp. AmE for STONELESS: *pitted dates*

pit·ter-pat·ter /ˈpɪtə ˌpætəʳ‖ˈpɪtər-/ adj, adv, n PIT-A-PAT

Pitts·burgh /ˈpɪtsbɜːg‖-bɜːrg/ also **Pitt** /pɪt/ infml– an industrial city in the US state of Pennsylvania —see colour map on pages 1374–5

pi·tu·i·ta·ry /pɪˈtjuːɪtəri‖pɪˈtuːɪteri/ also **pituitary gland** /·ˈ···· ˌ·/– n a small organ at the base of the brain which produces various HORMONEs that influence the growth and development of the body

pit·y¹ /ˈpɪti/ n **1** [U] sympathy and sorrow for someone's suffering or unhappiness: *We had/took pity on* (=felt sorry for and decided to help) *the homeless family and took them into our house.* **2** [S] a sad, unfortunate, or inconvenient state of affairs; SHAME¹ (4): *"We've got to leave now." "What a pity!"* [+(that)] *It's a pity you can't come to the party.* | *"I can't afford to run this car." "(It's a) pity you didn't think of that before you bought it."* (=you should have thought of it) **3 for pity's sake** (used to add force to a request, esp. showing impatience) please: *For pity's sake be quiet and let me get on with my work.* —see SAKE (USAGE) **4** BrE **more's the pity** infml unfortunately: *I won't be able to come this evening, more's the pity.* —see also SELF-PITY

pit·y² v [T] to feel pity for (and perhaps give help to): *Pity us in our distress.* | *I pity anyone who has to feed a family on such a low income.*

piv·ot¹ /ˈpɪvət/ n a fixed central point or pin on which something turns: (fig.) *Capturing the enemy-held towns is the pivot of our plans.* (=our plans depend on this, and if we can't do it they won't work)

pivot² v **1** [I (on)] to turn round (as if) on a pivot: *a pivoting gate* **2** [T] to provide with or fix by means of a pivot **pivot on** sthg. phr v [T] to depend on

piv·ot·al /ˈpɪvətəl/ adj **1** of or being a pivot **2** of main

importance and influence; CRUCIAL: *a pivotal event in the country's struggle for independence*

pix /pɪks/ n [P] sl pictures or photographs

pix·el /ˈpɪksəl/ n tech the smallest unit of an image on a computer SCREEN¹ (4)

pix·ie , pixy /ˈpɪksi/ n a small FAIRY believed to enjoy playing tricks on people

Pi·zar·ro /pɪˈzɑːrəʊ/, **Fran·cis·co** /frænˈsɪskəʊ/ (about 1475–1541) a Spanish EXPLORER of South America who took control of Peru and established the city of Lima

piz·za /ˈpiːtsə/ n [C;U] a plate-shaped piece of DOUGH or pastry baked with a mixture of cheese, TOMATOes, etc., on top. Pizza is originally an Italian food but is now very popular in Britain and the US. Some restaurants specialize in pizzas and will deliver them hot to your door when you make your order by telephone.

Pizza Hut /ˈ·· ˌ·/ any branch of a group of pizza restaurants found in the US and Britain

Pizzaland /ˈpiːtsəlænd/ a company which runs restaurants in many British towns, selling pizzas

piz·za par·lour /ˈ·· ˌ··/ n a restaurant whose speciality is pizza

piz·ze·ri·a /ˌpiːtsəˈriːə/ n a restaurant which specializes in pizzas

piz·zazz /pəˈzæz/ n [U] sl apprec, esp. AmE an excitingly forceful quality; DASH² (5): *This song and dance show needs more pizzazz.*

piz·zi·ca·to /ˌpɪtsɪˈkɑːtəʊ◂/ adj, adv played by picking the strings of a VIOLIN, CELLO, etc. with one's finger instead of using a BOW³ (2)

pj's , PJ's /ˌpiːˈdʒeɪz/ n [P] AmE infml PYJAMAS— **pj** adj : *pj bottoms*

pl. written abbrev. for: plural

plac·ard¹ /ˈplækɑːd‖-ərd/ n a large notice or advertisement put up or carried in a public place: *The demonstrators carried placards attacking the government.*

plac·ard² /ˈplækɑːd‖-ɑːrd/ v [T] to stick placards on or all over

pla·cate /pləˈkeɪt‖ˈpleɪkeɪt/ v [T] to cause to stop feeling angry; APPEASE: *I tried to placate her by offering to pay for the repairs.* —**catory** /pləˈkeɪtəri, ˈplækətəri‖ˈpleɪkətɔːri/ adj : *placatory words*

place¹ /pleɪs/ n **1** [C] a particular area or position in space in relation to others: *This is the place where the accident happened.* | *Where would be the best place to put this new clock?* | *Put it back in its place.* (=the position where it usually is) | *I've got a sore place* (=area) *on my lip.* | (fig.) *I dropped the book and lost my place.* (=could not find the point I had reached in reading it) | (fig.) *Could you keep my place in the queue* (=make sure no one comes and stands where I have been standing) *while I go and get a paper?* | (fig.) *People with racist views have no place in our union.* (=we will not accept them) **2** [C] a particular part of the Earth's surface, such as a stretch of land, a town, a building, etc.: *Moscow is a very cold place in winter.* | *What a desolate place the moon must be.* | *Is London a nice place to live?* | *a place of worship* (=a church, temple, etc.) | *This restaurant is one of the best places to eat in London.* | *They've bought a little place* (=house) *in the country.* | *Come over to my place* (=home) *tomorrow.* **3** [C usu. sing.] a position that can be used by someone for a particular purpose: *There were still some empty places* (=seats) *on the coach.* | *He's been offered a place at university.* (=as a student) | *They* **laid a place** *for him at the table.* (=put a knife, fork, spoon, etc. in position) **4** [C] a proper or suitable occasion or moment: *A business meeting isn't the place at which to talk about one's private life.* **5** [C usu. sing.] a (numbered) position in the result of a competition, race, etc.: *John took first place in the history exam.* | *I finished in third place.* | (fig.) *Our personal wishes* **take second place to** (=are less important than) *the needs of the children.* **6** [C] social position; rank: *This has been talked about* **in high places.** (=by people of high rank and influence) | *He thought he was being very clever, but she soon* **put him in his place.** (=showed that he was not) **7** [S] a usu. numbered point in an argument, explanation, etc.: **In the first place** *I don't want to go, and* **in the second place** *I can't afford to.* **8** [C] the position of a figure in a row of figures, to the right of a decimal point: *If you divide 11 by 9 and* calculate the division to four decimal places, the answer is 1.2222. **9** [S] duty; what one should or must do: *It's not your place to tell me what to do.* **10** [C *usu. sing.*] tech any of the first three positions in the result of a horse race, esp. the second (*BrE* or third) position: *£5 on Not So Fast for a place, please* (=to come second or third) **11 all over the place** *infml* **a** everywhere **b** in disorder: *She's left her books spread all over the place.* **12 a place for everything (and everything in its place)** (usu. said to express the idea that things should be returned to where they belong, so they can be easily found) **13 click/fall/slot into place** (of a set of events, facts, etc.) to be seen in its proper order or position, esp. so that the whole thing can be understood: *When the newspaper published his photo, everything fell into place: he was the man I'd seen at the scene of the crime.* **14 ¹go places** *infml* (*usu. in progressive forms or in future tenses*) to be increasingly successful: *That girl's got a lot of talent; she's really going to go places.* **15 in place: a** in the proper or usual position:*As soon as all the chairs are in place, we can let the people in.* **b** in existence and ready to be used: *The new regulations are now in place.* **16 in place of** instead of: *In place of our advertised programme we will be showing a film.* | *Jane couldn't go so I attended the conference in her place.* **17 out of place:a** not in the proper or usual position **b** unsuitable(for the occasion or situation): *The luxurious furnishings would not have been out of place in a palace.* **18 place in the sun** *infml* a position that is favourable to someone's future development **19 take one's place: a** to go to one's special position for some activity: *Take your places for the next dance.* **b** to be considered as being: *This new work will take its place among the most important paintings of this century.* **20 take place** to happen, esp. by arrangement: *the peace talks currently taking place in Geneva* —see HAPPEN (USAGE) **21 take the place of** to act or be used instead of; REPLACE: *Electric trains have now taken the place of steam trains in England.* | *I can't come to the meeting myself, so my deputy will take my place.* —see also PRIDE OF PLACE

▷ USAGE **Room** [U] and **place** [C] can both mean free space that can be used for a purpose; but **place** is used for a single particular piece of space, while **room** means space in general: *"Is there (any)* **room** *for me to sit down in here?" "Yes, there's a* **place** *in the corner."* | *This is the* **place** *where we keep the coal.* | *There's no* **room** *for any more coal in here.* —see also POSITION¹ (USAGE)◁

place² *v* [T] **1** [+*obj*+*adv/prep*] *rather fml* to put or arrange in the stated position: *He placed the book carefully on the shelf.* | *Her request places me in a very difficult position.* | *Place the ten wines in order of preference.* | (fig.) *A politician should place his loyalty to the people above party interest.* **2** to give to a person, firm, etc., who can do the needed action: *We placed an order with them for 500 pairs of shoes.* (=we ordered these shoes from them) | *to place* (=make) *a bet* **3** [+*obj*+*adj/adv/prep*; *usu. pass.*] to state the position of (a runner) at the end of a race: *He was placed second.* **4** [*usu. in questions and negatives*] to remember fully the name or other details of (someone or something), and where and when one last saw or heard them or it: *I'm sure I've met her before somewhere, but I can't quite place her.* **5** to find a suitable job for **6** (of a horse in a race) **a** *BrE* [*pass*] to come in second or third: *Last season Freda's Boy won once and was placed twice.* **b** *AmE* [I] to come in second: *Seadog placed in the last race.* | *$10 on Bengal Lady to place, please.*

pla·ce·bo /pləˈsiːbəʊ/ *n* **-bos** or **-boes** a substance given instead of real medicine, without the person who takes it knowing that it is not real. Often a person will become well simply because they know they've been given a medicine, whether or not the medicine works. This is called the **placebo effect.**

place card /ˈ· ·/ *n* a small card with someone's name on it, put on a table to show where they are to sit at a formal dinner

placed /pleɪst/ *adj esp. BrE* **1** [F (**for**)] in the stated situation: *How are you placed for money?* (=Have you got enough money?) **2 be placed** see PLACE² (6)

place kick /ˈ· ·/ *n* a kick at a ball, esp. in RUGBY, placed or held in position on the ground

place mat /ˈ· ·/ *n* a mat for a single PLACE SETTING at a table

place·ment /ˈpleɪsmənt/ *n* [C;U] the act or an example of placing someone or something in position: *The univer-*

sity offers a placement service for its graduates. (=a service to find jobs for them)

pla·cen·ta /pləˈsentə/ *n* **-tas** or **-tae** /tiː/ a thick mass of flesh containing many blood tubes, which forms inside the WOMB to join an unborn child to its mother —compare AFTERBIRTH

place of work /ˌ· · ˈ·/ *n* **places of work** tech the place where a person goes to work

place of wor·ship /ˌ· · ˈ·/ *n* **places of worship** a building where people worship or practise their religion: *mosques, synagogues, and other places of worship*

place settings

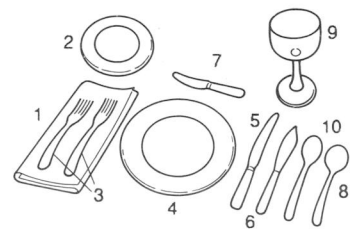

an American place setting

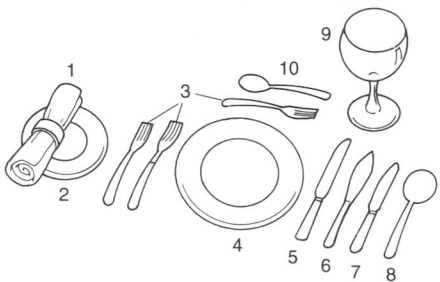

a British place setting

1 napkin/serviette	6 fish knife
2 side plate	7 butter knife
3 fork	8 soup spoon
4 plate	9 wine glass
5 knife	10 dessertspoon

place set·ting /ˈ· ˌ·/ *n* an arrangement of knives, forks, spoons, glasses, etc., to be used by one person when eating at a table

places of in·terest /ˌ· · ˈ·/ *n* [P] the places, such as MUSEUMs, historic buildings, etc., in an area which tourists go to see: *There are many places of interest in and around Oxford, including the Botanical Gardens, the Colleges and, a short distance away, the historic market town of Abingdon.*

plac·id /ˈplæsɪd/ *adj* **1** (of a person or animal) not easily made angry or excited: *a placid child/disposition* **2** (of a thing) calm; peaceful: *the placid surface of the lake* — ~**ly** *adv* — ~**ness**, ~**ity** /pləˈsɪdɪti/ *n* [U]

plac·ing /ˈpleɪsɪŋ/ *n* tech a sale of shares, STOCKs, or BONDs by a company to people or institutions who have agreed in advance to buy them

pla·gia·ris·m /ˈpleɪdʒərɪzəm/ *n* **1** [U] the action of plagiarizing **2** [C] a plagiarized idea, phrase, story, etc.: *an article full of plagiarisms* —**rist** *n*

pla·gia·rize also **-rise** *BrE* /ˈpleɪdʒəraɪz/ *v* [I;T] to take (words, ideas, etc.) from (someone else's work) and use them in one's own work without admitting one has done so. If you plagiarize at university in Britain or the US you may be refused a degree: *Half the ideas in his talk were plagiarized from an article I wrote last year.*

plague¹ /pleɪg/ *n* **1** [C] an attack of disease causing death and spreading quickly to a large number of people: *Europe suffered many plagues in the Middle Ages.* **2** [(*the*) U] a very infectious disease that produces high fever, swellings on the body, and death, esp. BUBONIC PLAGUE — see also BLACK DEATH **3** [C+of] a widespread, uncontrollable, and harmful mass or number: *a plague of rats/insects* **4 a plague on someone/something** *lit* (used as a curse to express the wish that someone/something will suffer)

plague² *v* [T] **1** to cause continual discomfort, suffering, or trouble to: *She's been plagued by back pain all her life.* **2** [(**with**)] to annoy, esp. by some repeated action: *He's been plaguing me with silly questions all day!*

plaice /pleɪs/ *n* **plaice** [C;U] a flat sea fish commonly eaten

plaid /plæd/ *n* **1** [U] thick material having a pattern of squares formed by brightly coloured crossing bands, esp. of a sort (TARTAN) originally from Scotland **2** [C] a piece of plaid worn over the shoulder and across the chest by Scotsmen as part of their NATIONAL COSTUME

Plaid Cym·ru /ˌplaɪd ˈkʌmri/ a political party in Wales representing people who want a separate Welsh state and more use of the Welsh language

plain¹ /pleɪn/ *adj* **1** simple; without anything added; without decoration: *plain food* | *You should wear a plain blouse with this checked skirt.* | (fig.) *The plain fact is that we just can't afford it.* **2 a** clear, easy to see, hear, or understand: *It's quite plain (to me) that you haven't been paying attention.* | *Explain it in plain English.* **b** showing clearly, honestly, and exactly what is thought or felt; FRANK: *plain speaking* | *I hope I've made myself plain on this issue.* **3** (of paper) without lines **4** *euph* (esp. of a woman) not pretty or good-looking; rather ugly **5** [A] complete; undoubted: *It's just plain foolishness to spend all your pay as soon as you get it!* **6 as plain as day/as a pikestaff/as the nose on your face** *infml* very noticeable or clearly understandable; OBVIOUS — see also PLAINLY — **~ness** *n* [U]

plain² also **plains** *pl.* — *n* a large stretch of flat land: *the Great Plains of the US* — see GREAT PLAINS

plain³ *adv infml* completely: *That's just plain stupid!*

plain⁴ also **knit** — *n* [U] *tech* the ordinary stitch in knitting (KNIT): *three plain, two purl* — compare PURL¹

plain·chant /ˈpleɪntʃɑːnt‖-tʃænt/ *n* [U] PLAINSONG

plain choc·o·late /ˌ·ˈ··‖ˌ·ˈ···/ *BrE* ‖ **dark chocolate** *AmE* — *n* [U] dark chocolate made without milk and with little sugar — compare MILK CHOCOLATE

plain-clothes /ˌ·ˈ·◂/ *adj* (of a policeman) wearing ordinary clothes while on duty, rather than a uniform: *a plain-clothes detective investigating a murder*

plain flour /ˌ·ˈ·/ *BrE* ‖ **all-purpose flour** *AmE* — *n* [U] flour that contains no BAKING POWDER — compare SELF-RAISING FLOUR

plain·ly /ˈpleɪnli/ *adv* **1** in a PLAIN¹ (1,2) way: *Their conversation could be quite plainly heard by the neighbours.* | *plainly dressed* | *I told her plainly what I thought of her scheme.* **2** it is clear that; OBVIOUSLY: *The door's locked, so plainly they must be out.*

plain sail·ing /ˌ·ˈ··/ *n* [U] a situation or course of action that is free from difficulty or trouble: *We've got over the difficult part, so it will be plain sailing from now on.*

plain·song /ˈpleɪnsɒŋ‖-sɔːŋ/ also **plainchant** *n* [U] a type of old Christian church music for voices that has no HARMONY and sounds rather like sung speech

plain-spo·ken /ˌpleɪnˈspəʊkən◂/ *adj* direct and honest in what one says, sometimes in a rude way; BLUNT¹ (2) — compare OUTSPOKEN

plaint /pleɪnt/ *n poet* an expression of great sorrow

plain·tiff /ˈpleɪntɪf/ also **complainant** — *n* a person who brings a charge against someone (the DEFENDANT) in a court of law

plain·tive /ˈpleɪntɪv/ *adj* **1** (usu. of a sound) expressing suffering or sorrow: *We heard a plaintive whimpering coming from the kitchen — it was the dog, who'd been locked in.* **2** expressing gentle sadness: *a plaintive love song* — **~ly** *adv* — **~ness** *n* [U]

plait¹ /plæt‖pleɪt/ *esp. BrE* ‖ **braid** *esp. AmE* — *n* [often pl.] a length of something, esp. hair, made by plaiting: *The little girl wore plaits/wore her hair in plaits.* — compare PIGTAIL, PONYTAIL

plait² *esp. BrE* ‖ **braid** *esp. AmE* — *v* [T] to form (hair, dried stems of grass, etc.) into a ropelike length by twisting

three or more lengths of it over and under each other: *plaited hair* | *a plaited leather belt*

She studied the plan of the house.

plan¹ /plæn/ *n* [(**for, of**)] **1 a** an arrangement, esp. one that has been carefully considered, for carrying out some (future) activity: *new government plans for reducing inflation* | *If we keep to the plan, the work should be completed in two weeks.* [+to-v] *They devised* (=made) *a plan to rob a bank.* | *I'm glad to say the meeting* **went according to plan.** (=as we expected) **b** a future course of action that has been decided on; aim or intention: *His plan is to get a degree in economics and work abroad for two years.* | *What are your plans for the weekend?* **c** a way of doing something or bringing something about: *Your best plan would be to catch a taxi; that's the only way you'll get there in time.* — see REFUSE (USAGE) **2 a** an arrangement of the parts of a group or system: *What's the seating plan for the guests at dinner?* **b** a maplike drawing showing this: *a street-plan of London* | *The spy stole the secret plans for the new submarine.* **3** a drawing of a building or room as it might be seen from above, showing the shape, measurements, position of the walls, etc. — compare ELEVATION (3), SECTION¹ (3); see also GROUND PLAN

plan² *v* **-nn-** **1** [I (**for, on**);T (OUT)] to make a plan for (something); arrange (carefully) in advance: *He never plans (ahead) — he just waits to see what will happen.* | *We hadn't planned for/on so many guests, so there wasn't enough food.* | *We've been planning this visit for months; it's all planned out.* | *I'd planned on doing some work this afternoon.* (=that's what I had intended to do) [+to-v] *Where do you plan* (=intend) *to spend your holiday?* **2** [T] to make drawings, models, or other representations of (something to be built or made); DESIGN: *the architect who planned the new shopping centre*

Plan B /ˌ·ˈ·/ *infml* the action which is planned if a main plan fails, or if anything goes wrong

Planck /plæŋk‖plɑːŋk/, **Max** (1858–1947) a German scientist who developed the ideas on which QUANTUM THEORY is based

plane¹ /pleɪn/ *n* **1** an AEROPLANE: *The next plane to New York departs in 20 minutes.* | *It's quicker by plane.* **2 a** level; standard: *Let's keep the conversation on a friendly plane.* | *You can't really compare the two newspapers — they're on completely different intellectual planes.* **3** *tech* (in GEOMETRY) a completely flat surface

▷ USAGE If you are in control of a plane you **fly** it or **pilot** it. As a passenger, you travel **by** plane, and **in** or **on** a particular plane. At the beginning of your journey you **get on** or **board** a plane and at the end of your journey you **get off** it. — see also DRIVE¹ (USAGE), TRANSPORT¹ (USAGE), STEER (USAGE)◁

plane² *adj* [A] *tech* **1** completely flat and smooth: *a plane surface* **2** about or being lines and figures with only length and width; two-DIMENSIONAL: **Plane geometry** *is the study of plane figures, angles, measurements, etc.*

plane³ *n* a tool with a blade that takes very thin pieces off wooden surfaces to make them smooth — see picture at TOOL

plane⁴ *v* [T] to use a PLANE³ on: *He planed the door.* | *He planed the door smooth.* | *Try to plane down those bumps in the wood.*

plane⁵ *n* a PLANE TREE

plan·et /ˈplænɪt/ *n* a large body in space that moves round a star, esp. round the sun: *The Earth is a planet.* | *the planet Mars* | *Is there life on other planets?* — **~ary** *adj*: *planetary motion* — see also INTERPLANETARY

plan·e·tar·i·um /ˌplænɟ'teəriəm/ n -riums or -ria /riə/ a building containing an apparatus that throws spots of light onto the inside of a curved roof to show the movements of planets and stars. Members of the public pay to visit a planetarium and to watch the images while listening to a talk.

Planet of the Apes /ˌ··· '·/ an American film, set in an imaginary future where monkeys rule the world and control humans

plane tree /'·· ·/ also **plane**— n a broad-leaved wide-spreading tree that commonly grows in towns in Britain

plan·gent /'plændʒənt/ adj lit (of a sound) having an expressive and sorrowful quality — ~ly adv —-gency n [U]

plank /plæŋk/ n 1 a long narrow usu. heavy piece of wooden board, esp. used for making structures to walk on: a small bridge made of planks 2 any of the main principles of a political party's stated set of aims: The main plank in their election programme is the promise to cut taxes. —see also **as thick as two planks** (THICK¹ (12)), **walk the plank** (WALK¹)

plank·ing /'plæŋkɪŋ/ n [U] planks, esp. put down as a floor

plank·ton /'plæŋktən/ n [U] the very small forms of plant and animal life that live in water, esp. the sea, and are eaten by many fish

planned ob·so·les·cence /ˌ··· '·· '··/ n [U] (an act of) making a product with a feature that will become unfashionable or unusable in a short time, so that the person who bought the product will soon have to buy something to replace it

Planned Pa·rent·hood /ˌ·· '····/ an American private organization which gives free advice on FAMILY PLANNING (=the controlling of the number of children born in a family)

plan·ner /'plænə²/ n (often in comb.) a person who plans, esp. one who plans the way in which towns develop — see also TOWN PLANNING

planning per·mis·sion /'·· ·,··/ n [U] official permission to put up a new building or change an existing one. Planning permission must be obtained from the local authority or, in some cases, the government before work begins: The garage was built without planning permission.

plant¹ /plɑːnt‖plænt/ n 1 [C] a living thing that has leaves and roots, and grows usu. in earth, esp. the kind smaller than trees: All plants need water and light. | a potato plant —see also HOUSEPLANT 2 [C] (often in comb.) a factory or other place where an industrial process is carried out: a water-softening plant | They've just built a new chemical plant. —see also POWER PLANT 3 [U] heavy machinery, esp. used for industrial processes: investing in new plant for our factory 4 [C usu. sing.] infml something, esp. stolen goods, that has been hidden on someone so that it will be found, and they will seem guilty

plant² v [T] 1 to put (plants or seeds) in the ground to grow: We've planted a tree/some tomatoes in the garden. | (fig.)The propaganda had planted the seeds of doubt in their minds. 2 [(with)] to put seeds or growing plants in the ground in (a place): We're planting a small garden. | The hillside was planted with trees. 3 [(on)] infml to hide (esp. stolen or illegal goods) on someone so that they will be found and the person will seem guilty: These drugs aren't mine — they must have been planted on me! 4 [+obj+adv/prep] infml to put in position secretly or so as to deceive: Plain-clothes policemen had been planted at all the exits. | bombs planted in the railway station | She suspected the stories had been planted in the newspapers by her enemies, to discredit her. 5 [+obj+adv/prep] infml to fix or place firmly or forcefully: He planted a knife in her back. | She planted herself in a chair by the fire. | She planted a kiss on his cheek. (=kissed his cheek firmly) **plant** sthg. ↔ **out** phr v [T] to place (a plant grown in a pot) in soil outdoors with enough room for growth

Plan·ta·ge·nets /plæn'tædʒənəts/ [the + P] the royal family of England from 1154 to 1399 which included Henry II, Richard II, and Richard III

plan·tain¹ /'plæntɟn/ n [C;U] (the fruit of) a treelike tropical plant with yellowish-green fruit that are like BANANAs but are cooked before being eaten

plantain² n a common wild plant with small green flowers and wide leaves growing close to the ground

plan·ta·tion /plæn'teɪʃən, plɑːn-‖plæn-/ n 1 (often in comb.) a large piece of land, esp. in tropical countries, on which crops such as tea, cotton, sugar, and rubber are grown: a rubber plantation 2 (in the Southern US) such a large piece of land, growing cotton or other crops, esp. before the CIVIL WAR, when plantation-owners could own many black SLAVEs to do the work. Plantations are remembered for their large, expensive, white, COLUMNed houses, the wealth of their owners, and because they exploited (EXPLOIT) slaves. 3 a large group of trees planted esp. to produce wood: a plantation of fir trees

plant·er /'plɑːntə²‖'plæn-/ n 1 (often in comb.) a person who owns or is in charge of a plantation: a tea planter 2 (usu. in comb.) a machine for planting: a potato planter 3 a container in which plants are grown for decorative purposes

plant hire /'·· ·/ n [U] BrE ‖ **equipment rental** AmE— the borrowing for money of heavy equipment such as diggers. Builders often borrow equipment rather than buy it

plant pot /'·· ·/ BrE‖**flower pot** AmE— n a usu. plastic pot in which a plant or plants are grown, in the house or for replanting in the garden

plaque /plɑːk, plæk‖plæk/ n 1 [C] a flat decorative metal or stone plate that is fixed to a wall esp. one that has writing on it describing a famous person who once lived at that place, an event that happened near there, etc. 2 [U] med a substance that forms on teeth, and in which bacteria can live and breed —compare TARTAR¹ (1)

plas·ma /'plæzmə/ n [U] 1 also **blood plasma**— the yellowish liquid which contains the blood cells; liquid part of blood 2 a gaslike substance that is found inside stars, in flashes of electricity, etc.

plas·ter¹ /'plɑːstə²‖'plæ-/ n 1 [U] a mixture of LIME, water, sand, etc., which hardens when dry and is used, esp. on walls, to give a smooth surface 2 [C;U] BrE‖**Bandaid** tdmk AmE— (a thin band of) material that can be stuck to the skin to protect small wounds 3 **in plaster** in a PLASTER CAST (2): with his leg in plaster

plaster² v [T] 1 to put wet plaster on; cover with plaster: to plaster the walls in a new house | (fig.) The government thinks the cracks in its policies can be plastered over (=that their faults can be hidden) with fine-sounding promises. 2 to spread (something), perhaps too thickly, on (a surface); cover: [+obj+with] They plastered the wall with posters. [+obj+on, over] They plastered posters on the wall/all over the wall. | a child completely plastered with mud 3 [+obj+adv/prep] to cause to lie flat or stick to another surface with a sticky substance: He'd plastered his hair down with grease.

plas·ter·board /'plɑːstəbɔːd‖'plæstərbɔːrd/ n [U] board made of large sheets of cardboard held together with plaster, used instead of plaster to cover walls and CEILINGs

plaster cast /ˌ··· '·, '··· ·/ n 1 a copy, esp. of a STATUE, made from plaster of paris 2 a case made from plaster of paris, placed round a part of the body to protect or support a broken bone

plas·tered /'plɑːstəd‖'plæstərd/ adj [F] sl drunk

plas·ter·er /'plɑːstərə²‖'plæ-/ n a person whose job is to PLASTER² walls, CEILINGs, etc.

plaster of par·is /ˌplɑːstər əv 'pærɟs‖ˌplæ-/ n [U] (often cap. 2nd P) a quick-drying whitish mixture of GYPSUM (=a chalklike powder) and water, used for plaster casts, in decorative building work, etc.

plas·tic¹ /'plæstɪk/ n 1 [C;U] a light artificial material produced chemically, which can be made into different shapes when soft, keeps its shape when hard, and is commonly used for making various objects: a plastic spoon | These spoons are plastic/are made of plastic. | He packed his sandwiches in a plastic bag. 2 [U] see PLASTIC MONEY

plastic² adj 1 tech (of a substance) easily formed into various shapes by pressing, and able to keep the new shape: Clay and wax are plastic substances. 2 infml derog artificial; SYNTHETIC: plastic food (=food containing artificial substances)

plastic art /ˌ··· '·/ n [C usu. pl.;U] tech (an) art concerned with representing things in a form that can be seen, esp. painting, SCULPTURE, or making films

plastic bul·let /ˌ··· '··/ n a large bullet made of hard plastic that is meant to hurt but not kill people and is used for controlling violent crowds

plastic card /ˌ·· ˈ·/ n a CREDIT CARD, DEBIT CARD, CHARGE CARD, etc.

plastic ex·plo·sive /ˌ·· ·ˈ··/ n [C;U] (a small bomb made from) an explosive substance that can be shaped by hand

plas·ti·cine /ˈplæstɬsiːn/ BrE tdmk ‖ **play dough** AmE— n [U] a soft claylike substance made in many different colours, used by young children for making small models, shapes, etc.

plas·tic·i·ty /plæsˈtɪsɬti/ n [U] tech the quality of being PLASTIC[2] (1)

plastic mac /ˌ·· ˈ·/ n BrE a usu. cheap RAINCOAT made from plastic

plastic mon·ey /ˌ·· ˈ··/ also **plastic**— n [U] infml small plastic cards used instead of money for making payments; CREDIT CARDS: *Does the restaurant take plastic money?* | *Can I put it on the plastic?* (=can I use a credit/DEBIT/ CHARGE card to pay for it)

plas·tics /ˈplæstɪks/ n [U] the producing of plastic: *the plastics industry*

plastic sur·ge·ry /ˌ·· ˈ···/ n [U] the repairing or improving of damaged, diseased, or unsatisfactorily shaped parts of the body with pieces of skin or bone taken from other parts of the body. In Britain and the US plastic surgery must be paid for if it is not considered necessary for medical reasons: *She had plastic surgery on her face after the car accident.* —compare COSMETIC SURGERY —**plastic sur·geon** /ˌ·· ˈ··/ n

plastic wrap /ˌ·· ˈ·/ also **saran wrap** tdmk— n AmE for CLING FILM

plat du jour /ˌpla: du ˈʒuər/ n **plats du jour** (same pronunciation) Fr the special dish to which the owner of a restaurant draws people's attention on a particular day

plate[1] /pleɪt/ n **1** [C] **a** also **dish** AmE— a flat usu. round dish with a slightly raised edge, from which food is eaten or served: *The plates were piled high with rice.* | *a dinner plate* **b** also **plate·ful** /-ful/— the amount of food that this will hold: *a plate of meat and potatoes* —see picture at PLACE SETTING **2** [C] (often in comb.) a flat, thin, usu. large piece of something hard: *The reptile's body is covered with protective horny plates.* | *The surgeon inserted a metal plate into the damaged skull.* | *The Earth's crust is made up of vast interlocking sheets of rock, known as plates.* —see also ARMOUR PLATE, FOOTPLATE **3** [U] articles made of valuable metal: *All the church plate has been locked up.* **4** [C] (often in comb.) a small sheet of metal with letters, information, etc. on it: *the numberplate on a car* —see also L-PLATE, NAMEPLATE **5** [U] (often in comb.) ordinary metal with a thin covering of gold or silver; it looks like gold or silver but is less valuable: *gold plate* **6** [C] tech a picture in a book, printed on different paper from the written part and often coloured: *a book with ten full-colour plates* **7** [C] a sheet of metal treated so that words or a picture can be printed from its surface **8** [C usu. sing.] also **dental plate**— a thin piece of plastic shaped to fit inside a person's mouth, into which false teeth are fixed **9** [C] a thin sheet of glass used esp. formerly in photography, having on one surface chemicals that are sensitive to light **10** [the+S] a metal dish or small bag used to collect money in church: *The plate was passed around.* **11** HOME PLATE **12 on a plate** infml with too little effort: *They just handed the game to the other team on a plate.* (=allowed them to win it too easily) **13 on one's plate** infml to deal with (and giving one a lot of problems): *I can't possibly take a holiday at the moment; I've got far too much on my plate.*

plate[2] v [T (with)] to cover (a metal article) thinly with another metal, esp. gold, silver, or tin: *The ring wasn't solid gold — it was only plated (with gold)/gold-plated.*

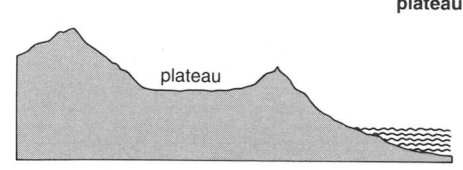

plateau

plat·eau /ˈplætəʊ‖plæˈtəʊ/ n **-teaus** or **-teaux** /-təʊ/ **1** a large stretch of level land that is higher than the land around it on at least one side —see picture at MOUNTAIN **2** a steady unchanging level, period, or condition: *House prices seem to have reached a plateau, but they may start rising again soon.*

plate glass /ˌ· ˈ·◄/ n [U] fine clear glass made in large, quite thick sheets for use esp. in shop windows —**plate-glass** adj [A]

plate·lay·er /ˈpleɪtˌleɪər/ BrE ‖ **tracklayer** AmE— n a workman who builds or repairs railway tracks

plate·let /ˈpleɪtlɬt/ n any of the very small plate-shaped cells in the blood that help to make it go solid when bleeding takes place

plate rack /ˈ· ·/ n a frame for storing plates, or where plates, cups, etc., are put to dry after washing —see picture at RACK

plate tec·ton·ics /ˌpleɪt tekˈtɒnɪks‖-ˌtɑːn-/ n [U] the study of the formation, movement, and destruction of the plates which form the surface of the earth under the ocean, and on which the land rests

plat·form[1] /ˈplætfɔːm‖-fɔːrm/ n **1** a raised flat surface built along the side of the track at a railway station for travellers getting on or off a train: *The Edinburgh train will depart from platform six.* **2 a** a tall or high structure built so that people can stand or work above the surrounding area: *an oil exploration platform in the sea.* | *They built a platform in the trees from which they could watch the animals unobserved.* **b** a raised floor or stage for speakers, performers, etc.: *This is the young pianist's first appearance on the concert platform.* | *Please address your remarks to the platform.* (=to the people on the platform) | (fig.) *Television should not provide a platform for terrorists' views.* (=a place where they can express their views publicly) **3** BrE the open part at the end of a DOUBLE-DECKER bus, where passengers enter and leave. Open platforms are increasingly being replaced by double doors. **4** [usu. sing.] the main ideas and aims of a political party, esp. as stated before an election: *What will be the main plank* (=principle or promise) *in your party's platform?*

platform[2] adj [A] (of a shoe or part of a shoe) unusually high because of an additional thickness of material: *platform soles*

Plath /plæθ/, **Syl·vi·a** /ˈsɪlviə/ (1932–63) an American poet, famous for poems about women and about death, and for her NOVEL (=story) *The Bell Jar*. She killed herself after many years of unhappiness.

plat·i·num /ˈplætɬnəm/ n [U] a greyish-white metal that is a simple substance (ELEMENT) that does not become dirty or impure and is used esp. in very valuable jewellery and in chemical industries: *a platinum ring* | *This ring is (made of) platinum.*

platinum blonde /ˌ··· ˈ·/ n infml a young woman having light silver-grey hair, often not natural but coloured with chemicals —compare PEROXIDE BLONDE

plat·i·tude /ˈplætɬtjuːd‖-tuːd/ n derog a statement that is true but not new, interesting, or clever: *a very uninspiring speech full of platitudes* —compare CLICHE, COMMONPLACE[2] —**tudinous** /ˌplætɬˈtjuːdɬnəs‖-ˈtuː-/ adj

Pla·to /ˈpleɪtəʊ/ (427–347 BC) a Greek think (PHILOSOPHER) who explained his ideas in the form of written conversations. His most famous work is the *Republic*, about the perfect state and form of government.

pla·ton·ic /pləˈtɒnɪk‖-ˈtɑː-/ adj (of a relationship between a man and woman) just friendly, not sexual — ~ **ally** /kli/ adv

pla·toon /pləˈtuːn/ n [C+sing./pl. v] a small group of soldiers which is part of a COMPANY and is commanded by a LIEUTENANT

plat·ter /ˈplætər/ n **1** AmE for a large PLATE[1] (1) **2** old use a flat dish, usu. made of wood **3** AmE infml RECORD[2] (4): *Your favourite DJ will be spinning the platters from 4 to 6 this afternoon.*

plat·y·pus /ˈplætɬpəs/ also **duckbilled platypus**— n a small furry Australian animal that has a beak and feet like a duck's, lays eggs, and gives milk to its young

plau·dit /ˈplɔːdɬt/ n [usu. pl.] fml or pomp praise: *Her performance won/earned the plaudits of the critics.* (=they praised it)

plau·si·ble /ˈplɔːzɪbəl/ adj often derog 1 (of a statement, argument, etc.) seeming to be true or reasonable: *Your explanation sounds plausible, but I'm not sure I believe it.* —compare FEASIBLE 2 (of a person) skilled in producing statements that seem reasonable, but which may not be true: *a plausible rogue* —opposite **implausible** —**bly** *adv* —**bility** /ˌplɔːzɪˈbɪlɪti/ n [U]

play[1] /pleɪ/ n 1 [U] activity for amusement only, esp. among children: *the happy laughter of children* **at play** | *She only did it* **in play** – **she didn't really mean it. 2** [C] a piece of writing (to be) performed by actors in a theatre or on television or radio: *one of Shakespeare's best-known plays* | *He has written a new TV play.* | *The college drama society are going to put on* (=perform) *a play.* **3** [U] the action in a sport: *We've had an interesting day's play in the cricket match.* | *Rain stopped play.* | *unfair play* **4** [U] *fml* the state of being in effect or operation: *He had to* **bring** *all his experience* **into play** (=use all his experience) *to beat this difficult opponent.* | *Now that television has become important in elections, a new set of circumstances has* **come into play. 5** [U] freedom of movement given by slight looseness: *There's too much play in the steering wheel.* | (fig.) *He gave full/free play to his feelings and began to shout angrily.* **6** [S] an act intended to bring about a particular result: *He decided to* **make a play for** *the girl.* (=to try to attract her) **7** [(the) S] *esp. lit* light, quick, not lasting movement: *the play of sunshine and shadow among the trees* **8 in/into/out of play** (of the ball in football, cricket, etc.) in/into/not in a position where the rules of the game allow it to be played: *The defender kicked the ball out of play.* —see also CHILD'S PLAY, FAIR PLAY; see RECREATION (USAGE)

play[2] v 1 [I (**with**)] (esp. of children) to amuse oneself with a game, using toys, running and jumping, etc.: *Can Bob come out to play (with me)?* | *The children were playing with their train set.* **2** [I;T (**on, for, to**)] **a** to produce sounds (from): *The radio was playing very loudly.* | *He just sits in his room playing records on his stereo.* **b** to perform (a piece of music) on (a musical instrument): *A world-famous violinist is playing at tonight's concert.* | *She plays the piano well.* | *He'd written a tune, and played it for/to us on the piano.* [+obj(i)+obj(d)] *He played us a tune on the piano.* **3** [I;T (**against, for**)] to take part in (a sport or game): *Our best defender is injured and won't be able to play today.* | *He plays cricket for England.* | *Can you play chess?* | *England are playing France* (=playing against them) *at football tomorrow.* **4** [T (**on**)] to plan and carry out for one's own amusement or gain: *They played a joke on me.* | (fig.) *I thought my eyes must be* **playing tricks on** *me.* (=deceiving me) **5** [I+adv/prep;T] **a** (of an actor or theatre group) to perform (in): *(The part of) Othello was played by Olivier.* | *Olivier is playing in "Othello" at the National Theatre.* | (fig.) *The United States played a key role in getting the hostages released.* **b** (of a play or film) to be performed or shown: *"Gone with the Wind" is playing at the Odeon.* **6** [L] to pretend to be: *She likes to play the great lady.* (=behave in a very grand way) | *The children are playing doctors and nurses.* | *He played dead.* | (fig.) *You're always* **playing the fool.** (=behaving in a silly way) **7** [T+obj+adv/prep] to hit and send (a ball): *She played the ball just over the net.* **8** [T] to place (a playing card) face upwards on the table: *Shall I play my jack or my queen?* **9** [I+adv/prep] *often lit* to move quickly, irregularly, or continuously: *A smile played across her lips.* | *She watched the sunlight playing on the water.* **10** [T+obj+adv/prep] to aim or direct, esp. continuously: *The firemen played their hoses on the burning buildings.* **11** [T+obj+adv/prep] *infml* to deal with; handle: *"I don't know how you want to play this meeting." "It could be rather tricky, so we'd better play it carefully."* **12 play ball** *infml* to agree to do what someone else has suggested; COOPERATE: *We wanted to get the union's agreement on the new procedures, but they wouldn't play ball (with us).* **13 play for time** to cause delay, in order to gain more time **14 play hard to get** *infml* to pretend one is not sexually interested in someone in order to make them more interested **15 play hooky/hookey** —see HOOKY **16 play into someone's hands** to behave in a way that gives someone an advantage over one **17 play it again, Sam** *quote* a slightly changed phrase from the film *Casablanca*, now used humorously when asking someone to play a piece of music again **18 play it by ear** to act according to changing conditions, rather than making fixed plans in advance

19 play it cool *infml* to behave in a calm and unexcited way; not lose one's temper **20 play (it) safe** *infml* to act in such a way that one has the best chance of avoiding trouble: *It may not rain, but you'd better play (it) safe and take a raincoat.* **21 play one's cards right/properly** *infml* to use well whatever chances, conditions, facts, etc., one has: *If you play your cards right you could make a nice little profit out of this job.* **22 play the devil with** to do a lot of harm to: *Snow storms are playing the devil with food deliveries to the area.* **23 play the field** *infml, esp. AmE* to have social and perhaps sexual relations with more than one partner of the opposite sex **24 play the game** *infml* to be fair, honest, and honourable **25 play the market** to buy and sell business shares in order to try to make money **26 play to the gallery** to do what will please most people in order to gain popularity, even if it is not the most sensible course of action

play about/around *phr v* [I] 1 to spend time having fun 2 [(**with**)] to have a non-serious sexual relationship: *He's always playing around with other men's wives.*

play along *phr v* 1 [I (**with**)] to pretend to agree (with someone or someone's ideas), esp. so as to gain an advantage or avoid trouble 2 [T] (**play sbdy. along**) to deceive (someone) by making them think one is soon going to do something for them

play at *sthg. phr v* [T+obj/v-ing] 1 (of children) to pretend to be or do for fun: *little boys playing at (being) soldiers* 2 to do in a way that is not very serious: *His parents are so rich that he can just play at business/at being a businessman.* | (showing annoyance or impatience) *What (the hell) do you think you're playing at?* – *You can't change a wheel that way!*

play *sthg.* ↔ **back** *phr v* [T] to play (something that has just been recorded on a machine) so as to listen to it or look at it —see also PLAYBACK

play *sthg.* ↔ **down** *phr v* [T] to make (something) seem less important: *The government is trying to play down its role in the affair.* (=trying to make it seem that it did not take an important part in it) —opposite **play up**

play *sbdy.* **in** *phr v* [T] to get (oneself) used to playing at the beginning of a game: *I need a few more minutes to play myself in.* | (fig.) *She's still playing herself into her new job as sales director.*

play off *phr v* 1 [T (**against**)] (**play** *sbdy./sthg.* ↔ **off**) to set (people or things) in opposition, esp. for one's own advantage: *She played her two boyfriends off (against each other).* 2 [I] to play another match in order to decide who wins: *The losing semifinalists will play off for third place.* —see also PLAY-OFF

play on/upon *sthg. phr v* [T] to try to use or encourage (esp. the feelings of others) for one's own advantage; EXPLOIT: *This film about handicapped people is just playing on people's sympathy.*

play *sthg.* ↔ **out** *phr v* [T] to continue (a game or struggle) until a result is gained: *Shall we call it a draw, or play it out?* —see also PLAYED OUT

play up *phr v* 1 [T] (**play** *sthg.* ↔ **up**) to give special importance to; EMPHASIZE: *In the interview you should play up your experience of working abroad.* —opposite **play down** 2 [I;T (=**play** *sbdy.* ↔ **up**)] to cause trouble or suffering (to): *My bad leg has been playing up again.*

play up to *sbdy. phr v* [T] *often derog* to behave so as to win the favour of: *She's always playing up to the boss.*

play with *sbdy./sthg. phr v* [T] 1 to consider (an idea) not very seriously: *She's been playing with the idea of starting her own business.* 2 **play with oneself** *euph for* MASTURBATE 3 **to play with** that one can use; AVAILABLE: *We haven't got a lot of time to play with, so we'd better hurry up.* —see also PLAY[2] (1), **play with fire** (FIRE[1])

play·a·ble /ˈpleɪəbəl/ adj 1 (of a piece of ground used for sports) fit to be played on —see also UNPLAYABLE 2 (of music) not too difficult to be played

play·act /ˈ· ·/ v [I] *often derog* to behave in a non-serious way, esp. by pretending things that are not true – **~ing** n [U]

play·back /ˈpleɪbæk/ also **replay**– n a recording of something heard or seen, esp. on television, that is played at once after it is made, so that one can study it carefully: *a video playback machine* —see also PLAY **back**

play·boy /ˈpleɪbɔɪ/ n *sometimes derog* a wealthy man who lives a life of expensive pleasure, doing no work. Playboys are thought of as enjoying fast cars and the company of many beautiful women: *a middle-aged playboy* | *his playboy lifestyle*

Playboy a magazine for men which has serious articles but is known esp. for its pictures of women wearing very few clothes and its articles on sex

Play-Doh /ˈpleɪ dəʊ/ n [U] tdmk a kind of play dough

play dough /ˈ· ·/ n [U] AmE a soft clay-like substance which children use to make brightly coloured models

played-out /ˌ· ˈ·◂/ adj **1** having lost one's former powers, ability, etc. **2** derog of no further use; old-fashioned: played-out ideas −see also PLAY out

play·er /ˈpleɪəʳ/ n **1** a person taking part in a game or sport **2** a person playing a musical instrument **3** esp. old use or pomp an actor −see also RECORD PLAYER

player pi·an·o /ˌ··· ·ˈ··◂/ also **Pianola** tdmk− n a piano that is played by machinery, the music being controlled by a continuous roll of paper (**piano roll**) with holes cut into it for the notes

Play·er's /ˈpleɪəz‖-ərz/ tdmk the name of a kind of cigarette

play·fel·low /ˈpleɪˌfeləʊ/ n BrE a PLAYMATE

play·ful /ˈpleɪfəl/ adj **1** happily active; full of fun: a playful little dog **2** not intended seriously: a playful kiss on the cheek − −**ly** adv − −**ness** n [U]

play·go·er /ˈpleɪˌɡəʊəʳ/ n a person who goes to see plays, esp. regularly

play·ground /ˈpleɪɡraʊnd/ n **1** a piece of ground kept for children to play on, esp. at a school or in a park. Playgrounds in parks usu. contain SWINGS, ROUNDABOUTS and slides. −compare PLAYING FIELD **2** an area where esp. the stated people go for enjoyment: The South of France is the playground of the rich. **3** AmE for RECREATION GROUND

play·group /ˈpleɪɡruːp/ also **pre-school playgroup, playschool**− n esp. BrE a group in which children aged 2–5 meet to learn through playing. Playgroups started in Britain in the 1960s because the British government did not provide many schools for children this age: Robert's at playgroup today. −compare CRECHE, NURSERY, NURSERY SCHOOL and see also extra information on page 408

play·house /ˈpleɪhaʊs/ n **-houses** /ˌhaʊzˌz/ **1** (often cap. as part of a name) a theatre: the Oxford Playhouse **2** a hut built to look like a small house, for children to play in

playing card /ˈ··· ·/ n fml for CARD³ (1)

playing field /ˈ··· ·/ n a large piece of ground with particular areas marked out for playing such games as football and cricket

play·mate /ˈpleɪmeɪt/ also **playfellow** BrE− n old-fash a friend who shares in children's games and play: The little boy's chief playmate was his dog. | We were childhood playmates.

play-off /ˈ· ·/ n a second match played to decide who wins, when the first has not done so −compare RUN-OFF; see also PLAY² **off** (?)

play on words /ˌ· · ˈ·/ n plays on words [usu. sing.] a PUN¹

play·pen /ˈpleɪpen/ n a frame enclosed by bars or a net and placed on the floor for a small child to play safely in

play·room /ˈpleɪrʊm, -ruːm/ n a room for children to play in

play·school /ˈpleɪskuːl/ n BrE a PLAYGROUP

play·thing /ˈpleɪˌθɪŋ/ n **1** fml a toy **2** esp. lit a person who is treated without seriousness or consideration by another: He was just her plaything. | Are we the playthings of fate? (=Are we not free to decide our own actions?)

play·time /ˈpleɪtaɪm/ n [U] a (short) period of time, esp. at a school, when children can go out to play

play·wright /ˈpleɪraɪt/ n a writer of plays

pla·za /ˈplɑːzə‖ˈplæzə/ n **1** a public square or marketplace, esp. in towns in Spanish-speaking countries **2** a group of shops and other COMMERCIAL buildings in a town: a shopping plaza

Plaza [the] a common name for a cinema, esp. in the past

plc /ˌpiː el ˈsiː/ abbrev. for: PUBLIC LIMITED COMPANY: Marks & Spencer plc −compare INC, LIMITED (2)

plea /pliː/ n **1** [C (for)] fml an urgent or serious request: a plea for mercy/forgiveness **2** [C (of) usu. sing.] law a statement by someone in a court of law, saying whether or not they are guilty of a charge: The accused entered a plea of "not guilty". **3** [S] rare an excuse: She left early on the plea of having a headache.

plea bar·gain·ing /ˈ· ˌ···/ n [U] the practice of agreeing to say in a court of law that one is guilty of a small crime in exchange for not being charged with a greater one

plead /pliːd/ v **pleaded** or **pled** /pled/ esp. ScotE & AmE− **1** [I (for)] to ask very strongly and seriously and in a begging way: They wept and pleaded until we agreed to do as they wished. | She pleaded for more time to pay. [+with+to-v] He pleaded with them to release his daughter. **2** [T] to give as an excuse for an action: I'm sorry I didn't answer your letter − I can only plead forgetfulness. **3** [I] law to answer a charge in court: The woman charged with murder was said to be mad and unfit to plead. **4** [T no pass.] law to declare in official language that one is (in a state of): "Prisoner at the bar, how do you plead?" "I plead not guilty." | He pleaded insanity in the hope of getting a shorter sentence. **5** [T] to speak or argue in support of: The poor and unemployed have no one to plead their case for them. −see also SPECIAL PLEADING

pleas·ant /ˈplezənt/ adj **1** giving one a feeling of enjoyment or happiness: What a pleasant surprise! | a flower with a pleasant smell **2** (esp. of a person) likeable; friendly: She seems a pleasant woman. | I know you're annoyed, but please make an effort to be pleasant to him. | a pleasant smile **3** (of weather) fine: It's quite pleasant today, though the wind is rather cool. −opposite **unpleasant** − −**ly** adv

pleas·ant·ry /ˈplezəntri/ n fml an amusing or not very serious remark made esp. in order to be polite: They exchanged the usual pleasantries before getting down to discussing business.

please¹ /pliːz/ v [not in progressive forms] **1** [I;T] to make (someone) happy; give satisfaction (to): The girl in the shop is always eager to please (everyone). | I didn't want it myself; I only got it to please you. | He wasn't at all pleased (=was angry) when he found out. | There's no pleasing some people. (=It is impossible to satisfy certain people.) −opposite **displease** **2** [I+adv/prep] (not as the main verb of a sentence) to want; like: You can have wine, beer, fruit juice − whichever you please. | He just does what he pleases and never thinks about anyone else. | They can appoint whoever they please. **3 if you please**: a fml (used to give force after a request) PLEASE² (1): Come this way, if you please. b old-fash can you believe this?: He's broken my bicycle, and now, if you please, he wants me to get it mended so that he can use it again! **4 please God** fml I hope: Please God they'll all return safely. **5 please oneself**: a to do whatever one likes, without having to obey others: We don't have to be back in the hotel by a certain time; we can just please ourselves. b [imperative] infml (esp. showing annoyance) Do whatever you like, it doesn't matter to me

please² interj **1** (used when asking politely for something). It is considered rude not to say "please" if one does not know the other person very well indeed: A cup of tea, please. | Can we go now, please? **2** (used to give force to a request or wish): Please, sir, I don't understand! | Will you please keep quiet! **3** usu. **yes, please**− yes I accept and am grateful: "Would you like a cup of coffee?" "Please, I'd love one."

pleased /pliːzd/ adj **1** [(with, about)] happy or satisfied: I always feel pleased when I've finished a piece of work. | She had a pleased look on her face. | Are you pleased with your new car? (=is it satisfactory) | "She's given up that boyfriend of hers." "I'm pleased about that." [+(that)] I'm very pleased you've decided to come. [+to-v] We were pleased to hear about your new job. | "(I'm) pleased to meet you." (=said when meeting someone for the first time) **2 be pleased to (do something)**: a polite to be very willing to; be glad to: We will be pleased to offer any assistance you need. b fml to have decided (as an act of favour) to: The Queen is graciously pleased to invite you to next month's garden party. **3 pleased with oneself** often derog (too) satisfied with what one has done: He was looking very pleased with himself so I guessed he'd passed his driving test.

pleas·ing /ˈpliːzɪŋ/ adj [(to)] fml or pomp **1** likeable; giving delight or enjoyment; pleasant: a pleasing young man | This wine is most pleasing to the taste. **2** giving satisfaction: We have made pleasing progress in our talks. − −**ly** adv

plea·sur·a·ble /ˈpleʒərəbəl/ adj fml enjoyable: I trust that you had a pleasurable journey. −−**bly** adv : feeling pleasurably mellow after a good meal

plea·sure /'pleʒəʳ/ n 1 [U] the state or feeling of happiness or satisfaction resulting from an experience that one enjoys: *small gifts that give a lot of pleasure and don't cost much* | *how to get more pleasure out of sex* | *It gave me no pleasure to have to tell them they were fired; I* **take no pleasure in** (=do not enjoy) *such things.* —opposite **displeasure** 2 [U] doing things for fun rather than as work: *Are you here on business or for pleasure?* | *a pleasure cruise* 3 [C] a cause of happiness, enjoyment, or satisfaction: *It's been a great pleasure to talk to you.* | *Some old people have very few pleasures in life.* 4 [S (of)] *polite* enjoyment gained by doing or having something: *May I* **have the pleasure of** *the next dance with you?* | *I had the pleasure of meeting your parents yesterday.* 5 [S] *polite* something that is not inconvenient and that one is happy to do; an expression often used to be polite even if the speaker is not happy: *"Thank you for helping me."* *"My pleasure|It was a pleasure."* 6 [S] *fml or polite* desire; wish: *These arrangements can be changed* **at your pleasure.** (=as you wish or decide) | *Is it your pleasure that I sign the minutes of the last meeting as correct?* 7 **during his/her majesty's pleasure** *BrE law* with no fixed limit on the time one is kept in prison 8 **with pleasure** *polite* willingly: *"Would you take this along to the office for me?" "With pleasure."*

pleasure beach /'··· ·/ n *BrE* a place of outdoor entertainment at the seaside, with large machines to ride on and other amusements —compare FAIR

pleasure seek·er /'··· ‚··/ n somebody who does something for enjoyment without considering other people

pleat¹ /pliːt/ n a flattened narrow fold in cloth

pleat² v [T] to make pleats in: *a pleated skirt*

pleb /pleb/ n [*often pl.*] *infml derog* a member of the lower social classes **– – by** *adj*

plebe /pliːb/ n *AmE infml* a first-year student at a military or naval college or university

ple·be·ian /plɪ'biːən/ n, adj 1 *derog* (a member) of the lower social classes: *plebeian tastes in food* 2 (in ancient Rome) (a member) of the common people —compare PATRICIAN

pleb·is·cite /'plebₔsₔt‖-saɪt/ n a direct vote of the people of a country to decide a matter of national importance: *The choice of whether to join the federation was decided by plebiscite.* —compare REFERENDUM

plec·trum /'plektrəm/ also **pick** *BrE infml BrE*‖**pick** *AmE*– n a small thin piece of plastic, metal, etc. held between the fingers and used for playing certain stringed instruments, such as the GUITAR, by quickly pulling at the strings

pled /pled/ *ScotE & AmE past tense & participle of* PLEAD

pledge¹ /pledʒ/ n 1 [C] (esp. in newspapers) a solemn promise or agreement: [+to-v] *They made a firm pledge to support us.* | *an election pledge to reduce taxes* [+that] *The government has given a pledge that it will halt the bombing.* 2 [C (of)] something given or received as a sign of faithful love or friendship: *Take this ring as a pledge of our friendship.* 3 [C] something valuable left with someone else as proof that one will fulfil an agreement: *She borrowed £50 and left her gold bracelet as a pledge.* 4 **sign/take the pledge** *old-fash* to promise never to drink alcohol

pledge² v [T] 1 (esp. in newspapers) to make a solemn promise of: *They have pledged their support for our case.*| *The firm has most generously pledged* (=promised to give) *£10,000 as its contribution to the charity.* | *a nation pledging allegiance* (=loyalty) *to the flag* [+to-v] *The government pledged to re-house the refugees.* [+that] *They have pledged that any details given to them will remain confidential.* 2 [(to)] *fml* to make (someone) give a solemn promise: *I was pledged to secrecy.* [+obj+to-v] *They pledged themselves never to tell the secret.* 3 [(for)] *rare* to leave (something) with someone as a PLEDGE¹ (3)

Pledge of Al·le·giance /‚· ·····/ [*the*] a solemn promise to respect and be loyal to the United States of America. Most schoolchildren in the US say the Pledge of Allegiance every morning while putting their hands over their hearts and facing the flag.

Plei·a·des /'plaɪədiːz‖'pliː-/ [*the* +P] 1 a group of stars in the CONSTELLATION Taurus 2 in CLASSICAL MYTHOLOGY, the seven daughters of Atlas who were changed into stars by Zeus

pleis·to·cene /'plaɪstəsiːn/ adj of the period in the Earth's history which started about 1,000,000 years ago and lasted about 800,000 years, when much of the Earth was covered with ice

ple·na·ry /'pliːnəri/ adj [*no comp.*] *fml or tech* 1 (of a meeting) attended by everyone who has the right to attend: *Will you be at the* **plenary session** *of the conference?* 2 (of power of government) complete; without limit: *The envoy was given* **plenary powers** *to negotiate with the rebels.*

plen·i·po·ten·tia·ry /‚plenₔpə'tenʃəri‖-ʃieri/ n, adj *fml or tech* (someone) having full power to take action or make decisions, esp. as a representative of their government in a foreign country: [after n] *a minister plenipotentiary*

plen·i·tude /'plenₔtjuːd‖-tuːd/ n [U] *pomp* 1 completeness; fullness 2 plenty; a great amount

plen·te·ous /'plentiəs/ adj esp. poet plentiful: *a plenteous harvest* **– –ly** *adv* **– –ness** *n* [U]

plen·ti·ful /'plentɪfəl/ adj (more than) enough in quantity: *a plentiful supply of cheap fuel* **– –ly** *adv* : *a cupboard plentifully stocked with food*

plen·ty¹ /'plenti/ pron often apprec a large quantity or number; enough or more than enough: *"Do you need any more money?" "No, we have £100 and that's plenty."* | *Make sure there is plenty* (of food) *for everyone.* | *If you want some chairs, there are plenty more in here.* | *I gave the boys plenty to eat.* | *Plenty of foreign firms have set up factories here.* | *There's plenty of room for everyone inside.* –compare FEW, LOT¹ (1)

plenty² n [U] *fml* 1 the state of having a large supply of something, esp. of what is needed for life: *In years of plenty everyone has enough to eat.* 2 **in plenty** in large supply; enough: *It was boom time, and there was work in plenty for everyone.* —see also HORN OF PLENTY

plenty³ adv *infml* 1 quite: *There's no need to add any more – it's plenty big enough already.* 2 *AmE infml* to quite a large degree; very: *I'm plenty hungry, you guys.*

ple·o·nas·m /'pliːənæzəm/ n [C;U] *tech* (a) use of more words than are needed to express an idea: *The phrase "an apple divided into two halves" is a pleonasm.* **––nastic** /‚pliə 'næstɪk◂/ adj

Ples·sy vs. Fer·gu·son /‚plesi vɜːsəs 'fɜːɡəsən‖-vɜːrsəs 'fɜːr-/ law (the court case which resulted in) a decision by the American SUPREME COURT in 1896 that SEGREGATION (=separation) of blacks from whites was legal, as long as they were given SEPARATE BUT EQUAL services. The decision related specifically to segregation on trains, but led in some states to separate schools, hotels, restaurants, seats in theatres, buses, etc. The Plessy vs. Ferguson decision was changed in 1955 by BROWN VS BOARD OF EDUCATION OF TOPEKA. –see also CIVIL RIGHTS MOVEMENT

pleth·o·ra /'pleθərə/ n [S (of)] *fml* an amount or supply much greater than is needed or than one can deal with: *a plethora of suggestions* | *a plethora of classical music on the radio*

pleu·ri·sy /'plʊərₔsi/ n [U] a disease of the thin inner covering of the chest that surrounds the lungs, causing pain in the chest and sides

plex·i·glass /'pleksi‚ɡlɑːs‖-‚ɡlæs/ n [U] *tdmk, AmE for* PERSPEX

pli·a·ble /'plaɪəbəl/ adj 1 easily bent without breaking: *pliable metal* 2 able and willing to change or to accept new ways and ideas; ADAPTABLE 3 *usu. derog* easily influenced; pliant **––bility** /‚plaɪə'bɪlₔti/ n [U]

pli·ant /'plaɪənt/ adj 1 *usu. derog* easily influenced; accepting the wishes or commands of others 2 PLIABLE (1,2) **– –ly** *adv* **––ancy** *n* [U]

pli·ers /'plaɪəz‖-ərz/ n [P] a small tool made of two crossed pieces of metal with long flat jaws at one end, used to hold small things or to bend and cut wire —compare PINCERS; see PAIR (USAGE), and see picture at TOOL

plight¹ /plaɪt/ n [*usu. sing.*] a (bad, serious, or sad) condition or situation: *We are all moved by the plight of these poor homeless children.*

plight² v **plight one's troth** *old use* to make a promise of marriage

plim·soll /'plɪmsəl, -səʊl/ also **gymshoe** *BrE* ‖ **sneaker** *AmE*– n a light shoe with a top made of heavy cloth and a flat rubber bottom, used esp. for games and sports – see PAIR (USAGE), and see picture at SHOE

Plimsoll line /ˈ·· ·/ also **Plimsoll mark**— n a line painted on the outside of a ship showing the depth to which it can be allowed to go down in the water when loaded

plinth /plɪnθ/ n a square block, usu. of stone, which forms the base of a PILLAR or STATUE

Plin·y the El·der /ˌplɪni ði ˈeldəʳ/ (23–79 AD) a Roman writer on the study of plants, animals, and minerals

Pliny the Young·er /ˌ··· ˈ··/ (72?–?113) a Roman politician known for his letters, which give a picture of Roman life in his time

pli·o·cene /ˈplaɪəsiːn/ adj of the period in the Earth's history which started about 13,000,000 years ago and lasted about 12,000,000 years

PLO /ˌpiː el ˈəʊ/ [the] the Palestine Liberation Organization; a political association of Palestinians who believe that the Israeli controlled land that used to be Palestine should be returned to them

plod /plɒd‖plɑːd/ v -dd- **1** [I+adv/prep] to walk slowly along, esp. with difficulty and great effort; TRUDGE: *The carthorse plodded along/plodded up the hill pulling the load behind it.* **2** [I+adv/prep, esp. AWAY, ON] to work steadily, esp. at something uninteresting: *She plods away quietly in her corner.* | *I'll plod on* (=continue to work) *for another hour and then take a break.*

Plod, P.C. BrE a name used in jokes and CARTOONS for an old-fashioned British policeman who is not very clever

plod·der /ˈplɒdəʳ‖ˈplɑː-/ n usu. derog a slow, not very clever, but steady worker who often succeeds in the end

plonk¹ /plɒŋk‖plɑːŋk, plɔːŋk/ n [S] infml a sound like something dropping onto or into a metal object —**plonk** adv [+prep] : *It fell plonk onto the floor.*

plonk² v [T+obj+adv/prep] infml to put, esp. heavily or with force: *Just plonk those parcels down over there.* | *She plonked herself in the chair and refused to move.*

plonk³ n [U] infml, esp. BrE & Austr E cheap wine

plop¹ /plɒp‖plɑːp/ n [S] infml a sound like something solid dropping smoothly into liquid: *There was a loud plop as the soap fell into the bath.* —**plop** adv [+prep] : *The soap fell plop into the bath.*

plop² v -pp- [I+adv/prep, esp. **into**] infml to fall with or make a plop: *The stone plopped into the stream.*

plo·sive /ˈpləʊsɪv/ adj, n tech (a consonant sound such as /t/ or /g/) made by stopping the air completely and then suddenly letting it out of the mouth

plot¹ /plɒt‖plɑːt/ n **1** the set of connected events on which a story, play, film, etc., is based: *The plot was so complicated that I couldn't follow it.* **2** a secret plan to do something harmful, needing combined action by several people: *an IRA bomb plot* [+to-v] *The police have uncovered a plot to assassinate the president.* **3** a small marked or measured piece of ground for building or growing things: *I grow potatoes on my little plot of land.* | *a vegetable plot* **4** AmE for GROUND PLAN **5 the plot thickens** humor a phrase used when events seem to be becoming more difficult to understand

plot² v -tt- **1** [I (**against**);T] (of a group of people) to make a secret plan for (something harmful): *They're plotting against him.* | *They're plotting his murder.* [+to-v] *They're plotting to kill him.* **2** [T] to mark, calculate, or follow (the position of a moving aircraft or ship) on a map or using RADAR: *The captain plotted a new course.* **3** [T] to draw (a line or curve showing certain facts) on paper marked with small squares: *We've plotted (a graph showing) the increase in sales this year.* **4** [T (OUT)] to make a PLOT¹ (1) for (a story) — ~**ter** n [usu. pl.]

plough¹ ‖ usu. **plow** AmE /plaʊ/ n a farming tool with a heavy cutting blade for breaking up and turning over the earth in fields, esp. so that seeds can be planted: *Ploughs are pulled by tractors, or in some countries by oxen.* —see also SNOWPLOUGH

plough² ‖ usu. **plow** AmE— v **1** [I;T (UP)] to break up or turn over (land) with a plough: *Farmers plough (their fields) in autumn or spring.* **2** [I+adv/prep] to force a way or make a track, sometimes violently: *The great ship ploughed across the ocean.* | *The van's brakes failed, and it ploughed into a crowd of people.* | (fig.) *He ploughed through the book to the end.* (=He finished the book although it was dull and difficult to read.) **3 We plough the fields and scatter** the first line of a religious song

sung at Harvest Festival to celebrate the gathering in of the year's crops

plough → back phr v [T (**into**)] to put (money earned) back into a business so as to make the business more successful: *They ploughed the profits back into the firm in order to buy new equipment.*

Plough esp. BrE ‖ usu. **Big Dipper** AmE— [the] a group of seven bright stars (=CONSTELLATION) seen only from the northern part of the world

plough·boy /ˈplaʊbɔɪ/ n (esp. in former times) a boy who leads a horse pulling a plough

plough·man /ˈplaʊmən/ n -men /mən/ a man whose job is to guide a plough, esp. of the type pulled by animals

plough·man's lunch /ˌ·· ˈ·/ also **ploughman's**— n BrE a simple midday meal, usu. bread, cheese, and onion eaten in a PUB

plough·share /ˈplaʊʃeəʳ/ also **share**— n the broad curved metal blade of a plough which turns over the soil

plov·er /ˈplʌvəʳ/ n plovers or plover a type of small bird that usu. lives near the sea

plow /plaʊ/ n, v AmE for PLOUGH

ploy /plɔɪ/ n something done in order to gain an often unfair advantage; TACTIC: *His usual ploy is to pretend to be ill, so that people will feel sorry for him.* | *The offer was widely viewed as a management ploy to weaken support for the union among the workforce.*

PLR /ˌpiː el ˈɑːʳ/ abbrev. for: PUBLIC LENDING RIGHT

pluck¹ /plʌk/ v **1** [T] to pull the feathers off (a dead hen, duck, etc., being prepared for cooking) **2** [T (OUT, **from**, **off**)] to pull off (esp. something unwanted) out sharply: *Do you pluck your eyebrows?* (=remove hairs to improve their shape) | *She tried to pluck out some of her grey hairs.* | (fig.) *He was plucked from obscurity to star in the new musical.* **3** [I(**at**);T] ‖ also **pick** AmE— to play (a stringed instrument) by quickly pulling (the strings) **4** [T] esp. poet to pick (a flower, fruit, or leaf): *He plucked a rose for his lover.*

pluck at sthg. phr v [T] to pull quickly and repeatedly with the fingers: *The little boy plucked at her sleeve to try and get her attention.*

pluck up phr v **pluck up (one's) courage** to show bravery in spite of fear: *He couldn't pluck up enough courage to ask her to go out with him.*

pluck² n [U] infml apprec courage and determination: *She showed a lot of pluck to leave a safe job and set up her own business.*

pluck·y /ˈplʌki/ adj infml apprec brave and determined, esp. in an unexpected way —**ily** adv —**iness** n [U]

plugs

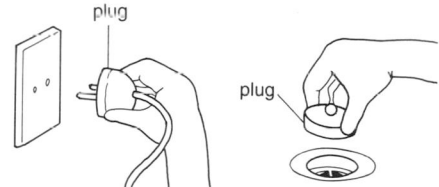

plug

plug

plug¹ /plʌg/ n **1** a small usu. round piece of rubber, wood, metal, etc., used for blocking a hole, esp. in something that contains liquid: *She pulled the plug out of the bath and the dirty water ran away.* **2 a** a small plastic object with two or three metal pins that are pushed into an electric SOCKET to connect an apparatus with the electricity supply **b** not tech an electric SOCKET; POINT¹ (15) **3** infml a publicly stated favourable opinion about a record, a product, a book, etc., that is intended to make people want to buy it, hear it, read it, etc.: *The TV compere gave her new record a plug.* —see also PLUG² (2) **4** infml for SPARK PLUG **5 pull the plug on** infml to discontinue suddenly; prevent from continuing: *The government pulled the plug on the project when it became too expensive.*

plug² v -gg- [T] **1** [(UP)] to block, close, or fill with a PLUG¹ (1): *Use this wad of cloth to plug (the hole in) the barrel.* —opposite **unplug** **2** infml to advertise (something) by continually or repeatedly mentioning it: *He's been* *plugging his new book on the radio.* **3** *AmE old-fash sl* to shoot (someone) with a gun

plug away at sthg. *phr v* [T *no pass.*] *infml* to work determinedly to complete (a difficult job)

plug sthg. ↔ **in** *phr v* [T] to connect to a supply of electricity with a PLUG¹ (2a): *"The television doesn't work." "Have you plugged it in?"* —opposite **unplug**

plug into sthg. *phr v* [T] to gain the use of (a system) by making an electrical connection with it: *You can plug into the national computer network.*

plug·hole /ˈplʌɡhəʊl/ *BrE* ‖ **drain** *AmE*— *n* a hole into which a PLUG¹ (1) is fitted, esp. where water flows away

plum /plʌm/ *n* **1** [C] a roundish sweet juicy smooth-skinned fruit, usu. dark red or yellow, with a single hard nutlike STONE (=seed): *stewed plums* | *plum trees* —see picture at FRUIT **2** [C] *infml* something very desirable or the best of its kind, esp. a good or easy well-paid job: *This new job that he's got is a real plum.* | *She landed* (=got) *a plum job at the United Nations.* **3** [U] a dark reddish-blue colour

plum·age /ˈpluːmɪdʒ/ *n* [U] a bird's covering of feathers

plumb¹ /plʌm/ *v* [T] **1** to examine very carefully in order to try to fully understand: *Psychoanalysts plumb the deep mysteries of the human mind.* **2 plumb the depths (of)** to reach the lowest point (of): *This new play really plumbs the depths of unpleasantness.*

plumb sthg. ↔ **in** *phr v* [T] *esp. BrE* to fix in place and connect to a supply of water: *When's the man coming to plumb in the washing machine?*

plumb² *adv infml* **1** [+*adv/prep*] exactly: *The bullet hit him plumb between the eyes.* **2** *esp. AmE* completely: *He's just plumb stupid.*

plumb³ *adj* [F] *tech* **1** exactly upright or level: *Is this wall plumb?* **2 out of plumb** not exactly upright

plumb·er /ˈplʌməʳ/ *n* a person whose job is to fit and repair water pipes, bathroom apparatus, etc.

plumber's friend /ˌ·· ˈ·/ also **plumber's help·er** /ˌ·· ˈ··/— *n esp. AmE infml for* PLUNGER (1)

plumb·ing /ˈplʌmɪŋ/ *n* [U] **1** all the water pipes, containers for storing water, etc., in a building: *an old house with noisy plumbing* **2** the work of a plumber

plumb line /ˈ· ·/ *n* a piece of string with a piece of lead tied to one end, used for measuring the depth of water or for finding out whether a wall is built exactly upright

plume¹ /pluːm/ *n* **1** [*usu. pl.*] a feather, esp. a large or showy one worn as a (ceremonial) decoration **2** [(of)] something that rises into the air in a shape rather like that of a feather: *a plume of smoke*

plume² *v* [T] (of a bird) to clean or make smooth (its feathers)

plumed /pluːmd/ *adj* [A] having or decorated with plumes: *a plumed hat*

plum·met /ˈplʌmɪt/ *v* [I] to fall steeply or suddenly: *The damaged aircraft plummeted towards the earth.* | *Prices have plummeted.* —compare PLUNGE

plum·my /ˈplʌmi/ *adj BrE* **1** *usu. derog* having or being an (unattractively) full-sounding and rich voice, of a type considered typical of the upper class **2** desirable; very good: *a plummy part in the play*

plump¹ /plʌmp/ *adj usu. apprec or euph* pleasantly fat; nicely rounded: *a baby with plump little arms and legs* | *a nice plump chicken in the butcher's window* | *I'm too plump to wear this dress.* —see FAT (USAGE) — **~ness** *n* [U]

plump² *v*

plump (sthg./sbdy. ↔) **down** *phr v* [I;T (**in, on**)] *infml* to (cause to) fall suddenly, heavily, or carelessly: *She plumped (herself) down in a chair.*

plump for sthg. *phr v* [T] *BrE infml* to decide in favour of; choose: *We finally plumped for the red car rather than the black one.*

plump sthg. ↔ **up** *phr v* [T] to make (esp. bed coverings) rounded and soft by shaking: *He plumped up the pillows.*

plum pud·ding /ˌ· ˈ··/ *n* [C;U] *BrE old-fash for* CHRISTMAS PUDDING

plun·der¹ /ˈplʌndəʳ/ *v* [I (**from**);T] (esp. of an army, etc.) to take (things) by force and usu. violently from (a place) esp. in time of war or disorder: *They plundered the cap-*

tured town/plundered all the valuable things they could find. — **~er** *n*

plunder² *n* [U] **1** (things taken in the course of) plundering **2** stolen goods; LOOT: *The thieves hid their plunder in the cave.*

plunge¹ /plʌndʒ/ *v* **1** [I+*adv/prep*;T+*obj*+*adv/prep*] to (cause to) move or be thrown suddenly forwards and/or downwards: *The car suddenly stopped and he plunged forward/through the windscreen.* | *She fell from the cliff and plunged to her death.* | *We ran to the edge of the lake and plunged in.* | *He snatched off the lid and plunged his hand in.* | (fig.) *The price of oil has plunged to a new low.* —compare PRECIPITATE¹ (2) **2** [I] (of a ship) to move with the forward end going violently up and down: *The ship plunged dangerously in the rough sea.* **3** [I] (of the neck of a woman's garment) to have a low curve or V-shape that shows a quite large area of the chest: *a plunging neckline*

plunge into *phr v* [T] **1** (**plunge** (sthg.) **into** sbdy./sthg.) to push, jump, or rush suddenly or violently all the way into (something deep, thick, etc.): *He plunged into the water.* | *Firemen plunged into the burning building to rescue the child.* | *She plunged the knife into his back.* **2** (**plunge** sbdy./sthg. **into** sthg.) to bring or force suddenly into (the stated esp. unpleasant condition): *The room was plunged into darkness.* | *These dangerous policies could plunge Europe into a new war/plunge the country into chaos.* **3** (**plunge into** sthg.) to begin suddenly or hastily: *She plunged into a description of her latest illness.*

plunge² *n* [S] **1** an act of plunging, esp. head first into water **2 take the plunge** to decide on and do something determinedly, after having delayed through uncertainty or nervousness: *After going out together for two years, they decided to take the plunge and get married.*

plung·er /ˈplʌndʒəʳ/ *n* **1** a rubber cup on the end of a handle, used for unblocking kitchen or bathroom pipes by means of SUCTION **2** a part of a machine that moves up and down

plu·per·fect /pluːˈpɜːfɪkt‖-ɜːr-/ *adj, n* [*the*+S] PAST PERFECT

plu·ral /ˈplʊərəl/ *n, adj* (a word or form) that expresses more than one: *"Dogs" is a plural noun.* | *"Dogs" is the plural of "dog" and "mice" is the plural of "mouse".* | *The third person plural, present tense, of the verb "have" is "they have".* —compare SINGULAR¹ (1)

plu·ral·is·m /ˈplʊərəlɪzəm/ *n* [U] **1** *usu. apprec* the principle that people of different races, religions, and political beliefs can live together peacefully in the same society **2** *usu. derog* the holding of more than one job at a time, esp. in the Church —**ist** *n, adj* —**istic** /ˌplʊərəˈlɪstɪk◂/ *adj*

plu·ral·i·ty /plʊəˈrælɨti/ *n* **1** [U] *fml* (in grammar) the state of being plural **2** [S (**of**)] *tech, esp. AmE* the largest number of votes in an election, esp. when less than a MAJORITY

plus¹ /plʌs/ *prep* **1** made m·re by (the stated quantity); with the addition of: *3 plus 6 is 9.* (3+6=9) | *The cost is a pound plus 50 pence for postage.* —opposite **minus 2** *infml* and also: *This work needs experience plus care.*

plus² *n* **1** also **plus sign** — a sign (+) showing that two or more numbers are to be added together, or that a number is greater than zero **2** *infml* a welcome or favourable addition; advantage: *Knowledge of French or Spanish could be a plus in this job.* —opposite **minus**

plus³ *adj* **1** [A] (of a number or quantity) greater than zero **2** [A] *infml* additional and desirable: *Her previous experience in social work is a plus factor.* **3** [after *n*] and above (a stated number or mark): *All the children here are twelve plus.* (=are 12 or more years old) | *She earns $20,000 a year plus.* | *a B plus for my homework* —opposite **minus**

plus⁴ *conj* in addition to this: *I've got to finish reading this book by Friday, plus I've got two essays to write!*

plus fours /ˌ· ˈ·/ *n* [P] trousers with loose wide legs drawn in to fit closely just below the knee, used esp. in former times in playing GOLF —see PAIR (USAGE)

plush¹ /plʌʃ/ also **plush·y** /ˈplʌʃi/— *adj infml, usu. apprec* seeming expensive, comfortable, and of good quality: *a plush hotel*

plush² *n* [U] silk or cotton cloth with a surface like short fur

plus sign /ˈ· ·/ *n* see PLUS² (1)

Plu·tarch /ˈpluːtɑːk‖-ɑːrk/ (46?–120 AD) a Greek writer who wrote about famous Greeks and Romans such as Julius Caesar

Plu·to¹ /ˈpluːtəʊ/ in CLASSICAL MYTHOLOGY, the Greek god of the UNDERWORLD, Hades

Pluto² the most distant PLANET, ninth in order from the Sun —see picture at SOLAR SYSTEM

Pluto³ a dog in Walt Disney's CARTOONs for children

plu·toc·ra·cy /pluːˈtɒkrəsi‖-ˈtɑːk-/ *n* a ruling class of wealthy people

plu·to·crat /ˈpluːtəkræt/ *n* **1** someone who has power because of their wealth **2** *infml, often derog* a very rich person — ~ **ic** /ˌpluːtəˈkrætɪk◂/ *adj*

plu·to·ni·um /pluːˈtəʊniəm/ *n* [U] a simple substance (ELEMENT) that is used esp. in the production of atomic power

ply¹ /plaɪ/ *n* [U] (*usu. in comb.*) **1** a measure of the thickness of woollen thread, rope, etc., according to the number of single threads or lengths of material it is made from: *four-ply wool* **2** a measure of the thickness of plywood, according to the number of single thin sheets of wood it is made from. *three-ply wood*

ply² *v* **1** [I+*adv/prep*] *esp. BrE* (esp. of a taxi driver) to drive around or wait at a particular place looking for passengers: *You won't find many taxis plying for hire at this time of night.* **2** [I+*adv/prep*, esp. **between**;T] (of a taxi, bus, or esp. boat) to travel regularly (in or on): *This ship plies between London and Australia.* | *schooners plying the old trade routes* **3** [T] *lit or old use* **a** to work at (one's trade), esp. regularly: *the streets where flowersellers once plied their trade* **b** to use or work steadily with (a tool): *She sat plying her needle.* (=sewing)

ply sbdy. with sthg. *phr v* [T] to keep supplying (someone) with (esp. food, drink, or questions): *They plied their guests with wine and snacks.* | *The children plied the teacher with questions.*

Plym·outh¹ /ˈplɪməθ/ a port and naval base in Devon, SW England

Plymouth² *tdmk* an American car made by Chrysler

Plymouth Breth·ren /ˌ·· ˈ··/ also **Brethren**— [*the*+P] a Christian religious organization which is opposed to religious ceremony and to having a group of priests. The Plymouth Brethren are also known for having a family life which is very correct according to severe moral rules.

Plymouth Col·o·ny /ˈ·· ˌ···/ the second permanent English settlement in America (the first was in JAMESTOWN, Virginia), in what is now Plymouth, Massachusetts in 1620. The settlers were PURITANs who sailed on the ship *Mayflower* from Plymouth, England. Only half of them were still alive after the first winter in America, but they were then helped by the NATIVE AMERICANS and the settlement grew until Massachusetts was established. According to old stories, the settlers' first steps when they landed were on a large rock, today called **Plymouth Rock**. —see THANKSGIVING

Plymouth Rock /ˌ·· ˈ·/ a rock on the coast at **Plymouth**, Massachusetts, where the Pilgrims are said to have landed in 1620

ply·wood /ˈplaɪwʊd/ *n* [U] a material made of several thin sheets of wood stuck together to form a strong board

pm, **PM** /ˌpiː ˈem/ *abbrev. for:* post meridiem=(*Lat*) after midday (used after numbers expressing time): *the 8 pm (train) to London* —see also AM

PM /ˌpiː ˈem◂/ *n infml, esp. BrE for:* PRIME MINISTER: *an urgent meeting with the PM*

PMS /ˌpiː em ˈes/ *n* [U] *AmE abbrev. for:* PREMENSTRUAL SYNDROME —see PREMENSTRUAL TENSION

PMT /ˌpiː em ˈtiː/ *n* [U] *BrE abbrev. for:* PREMENSTRUAL TENSION

pneu·mat·ic /njuːˈmætɪk‖nʊ-/ *adj* **1** worked by air pressure: *a pneumatic pump* **2** containing air: *a pneumatic tyre* — ~ **ally** /kli/ *adv*

pneumatic drill /·ˌ·· ˈ·/ *esp. BrE* ‖ **jackhammer** *esp. AmE— n* a powerful hand-held tool (a type of DRILL) that is worked by air pressure and is used for breaking up hard materials, esp. road surfaces —see picture at DRILL

pneu·mo·co·ni·o·sis /ˌnjuːməʊkəʊniˈəʊsᵻs‖ˌnuː-/ *n* [U] a disease of the lungs caused by breathing in dust, powder, etc. —compare SILICOSIS

pneu·mo·ni·a /njuːˈməʊniə‖nʊ-/ *n* [U] a serious disease of the lungs with INFLAMMATION and difficulty in breathing: *You'll catch pneumonia if you go out in the snow without a coat!*

Po /pəʊ/ [*the*] the main river of N Italy

PO /ˌpiː ˈəʊ◂/ *abbrev. for:* **1** POST OFFICE **2** POSTAL ORDER **3** PETTY OFFICER

poach¹ /pəʊtʃ/ *v* [T] to cook (esp. eggs or fish) in gently boiling water or other liquid: *poached eggs on toast*

poach² *v* **1** [I;T] to catch or shoot (animals, birds, or fish) without permission on private land: *The gamekeeper caught him poaching (pheasants).* **2** [I (**on**);T (**from**)] to take or use unfairly (an idea, person, etc. belonging to or claimed by someone else): *A rival company poached our ideas and marketed them very successfully.* | *One of our key employees had been poached by a competitor.* (=they had persuaded him/her to go and work for them) — ~ **er** *n*

PO Box /ˌpiː əʊ ˈbɒks◂‖-ˈbɑːks/ also **post office box** *fml— n* a numbered box in a post office, to which someone's mail can be sent and from which they can collect it: *For further details, write to P.O. Box 179.*

Poc·a·hon·tas /ˌpɒkəˈhɒntəs‖ˌpəʊkəˈhɑːn-/ (1595?–1617) a Native American woman, daughter of Chief Powhatan of the **Powhatan** tribe. Pocahontas saved the life of Captain John Smith, leader of the British settlers at Jamestown, Virginia, when he was about to be killed by her father. Later, Chief Powhatan made friends with the settlers (=the English), and Pocahontas married an Englishman and moved to England, where she died of SMALLPOX.

pocked /pɒkt‖pɑːkt/ *adj* POCKMARKED

pock·et¹ /ˈpɒkᵻt‖ˈpɑːkᵻt/ *n* **1** a small flat cloth bag sewn into or onto a garment, for keeping small articles in: *standing with his hands in his pockets* | *My keys are in my coat pocket.* | *The policeman made me turn out my pockets.* (=empty them and show him what was inside) **2** [*usu. sing.*] (a supply of) money; income: *He paid for it out of his own pocket.* | *A lot of demands have been made on my pocket* (=I have had to spend a lot) *recently.* | *a range of family holidays* **to suit every pocket** (=for people of all incomes) **3** a container for small or thin articles made by fitting a piece of cloth, net, etc., into the inside of a case or a car door, onto the back of an aircraft seat, etc. **4** [(**of**)] a small area or group that exists separated from others like it: *Pockets of mist could be seen down by the river.* | *The invaders met pockets of resistance* (=small groups of people who fought against them) *in some cities.* —see also AIRPOCKET **5** any of the six small net bags round the table used in BILLIARDS, into which a ball can roll **6 be/live in each other's pockets** *esp. BrE infml* (of two people) to be together too much **7 have someone in one's pocket** to have complete influence over someone **8 have something in one's pocket** to be (almost) certain of gaining something or being successful in something: *The Democrats have got the election in their pocket.* **9 in pocket** *BrE* having made a profit: *I bought it for £500 and sold it for £550, so I was in pocket on the deal/I ended up £50 in pocket.* **10 out of pocket** *BrE* having paid a certain amount, usu. without good results: *I bought a new cigarette lighter and it broke; now I'm £10 out of pocket.* —see also OUT-OF-POCKET EXPENSES **11 put one's hand in one's pocket** to spend or give money —see also **line one's pockets** (LINE³)

pocket² *v* [T] **1** to put into one's pocket: *He pocketed his wallet and car keys.* **2** to take or get (money), esp. dishonestly: *We gave him £10 to buy presents for the children, but he pocketed most of it.* **3** (in games like BILLIARDS) to hit (a ball) into a POCKET¹ (5)

pocket³ *adj* [A] **1** small enough to be carried in the pocket: *a pocket camera* **2** smaller than the usual size: *a pocket battleship*

pock·et·book /ˈpɒkᵻtbʊk‖ˈpɑː-/ *n* **1** a small notebook **2** *AmE old-fash* a woman's HANDBAG, esp. one without a shoulder STRAP

pocket cal·cu·la·tor /ˌ·· ˈ··ˌ····/ *n* a small piece of electronic equipment which a person can carry with them and with which they can do calculations. People use them at school, college, work, and in the shops.

pock·et·ful /ˈpɒkɪtfʊl‖ˈpɑː-/ n [(of)] the amount that a pocket will hold

pocket-hand·ker·chief¹ /ˌ··· ˈ···/ n fml a handkerchief made of material, not paper

pocket-handkerchief² adj [A] infml, esp. BrE square and very small: a pocket-handkerchief garden

pock·et·knife /ˈpɒkɪtnaɪf‖ˈpɑː-/ n -knives /naɪvz/ a small knife with one or more blades that fold into the handle; PENKNIFE

pocket mon·ey /ˈ·· ˌ··/ n [U] **1** esp. BrE ‖ **allowance** AmE— money given weekly to a child by its parents **2** infml a little money to buy oneself things

pocket ve·to /ˈ·· ˌ··/ n AmE a VETO (disapproval) of a BILL¹ (2) by the President in which he takes no action on the bill. The President has ten days to either sign or refuse to accept a bill. If he takes no action and Congress is not working when the bill is returned to them at the end of the ten days, then the bill fails and does not become law and this is called a pocket veto.

pock·mark /ˈpɒkmɑːk‖ˈpɑːkmɑːrk/ n a hollow mark left on the skin where a small diseased area has been, esp. one caused by the disease SMALLPOX

pock·marked /ˈpɒkmɑːkt‖ˈpɑːkmɑːrkt/ also **pocked**— adj [(with)] covered with pockmarks: a pockmarked face | (fig.) The metal surface was pockmarked with little holes.

pod¹ /pɒd‖pɑːd/ n **1** a long narrow seed container of various plants, esp. beans and PEAs: a pea pod **2** a long narrow container for petrol or other substances, esp. one carried under an aircraft wing **3** a part of a space vehicle that can be separated from the main part

pod² v -dd- [T] to take (beans, PEAs, etc.) from their pod before cooking

podg·y /ˈpɒdʒi‖ˈpɑː-/ also **pudgy**— adj infml, usu. derog (of a person or part of the body) short and fat: his podgy little hands —iness n [U]

po·di·a·trist /pəˈdaɪətrɪst/ n esp. AmE for CHIROPODIST —-try n [U]

po·di·um /ˈpəʊdiəm/ n -diums or -dia /diə/ **1** a small raised area for a performer, speaker, musical CONDUCTOR, etc., to stand on —see colour picture on page 883 **2** AmE for LECTERN

po·dunk /ˈpəʊdʌŋk/ adj AmE infml derog (usu. of a town) small and in the country: I went to a podunk little school in a podunk town.

Poe /pəʊ/, Ed·gar Al·lan /ˈedgər ˈælən/ (1809–49) an American poet and writer of short stories. He wrote DETECTIVE stories such as The Murders in the Rue Morgue, but is most famous for writing stories about death and the SUPERNATURAL including The Fall of the House of Usher.

po·em /ˈpəʊɪm/ n a piece of writing, arranged in patterns of lines and of sounds, expressing some thought, feeling, or human experience in language full of imagination

po·e·sy /ˈpəʊɪzi‖-si/ n [U] old use or poet poetry

po·et /ˈpəʊɪt/ n a person who writes (good or serious) poems: (fig.) She is a poet amongst pianists. (=plays the piano with great feeling and imagination)

po·et·as·ter /ˌpəʊɪˈtæstər/ n derog, esp. lit a writer of bad poems

po·et·ess /ˌpəʊɪˈtes‖ˈpəʊɪtɪs/ n now rare a female poet

po·et·ic /pəʊˈetɪk/ adj **1** of or like poets or poetry: poetic language|drama —compare PROSE (1) **2** apprec having qualities of deep feeling and effortless expression: The dancer moved with poetic grace. —~ally /kli/ adv

po·et·i·cal /pəʊˈetɪkəl/ adj **1** [A] written in the form of poems: the complete poetical works of Wordsworth **2** poetic

poetic jus·tice /ˌ·,·· ˈ···/ n [U] a result in which someone is punished or made to suffer for something bad they have done in a way that seems particularly suitable or right: The rumours he had spread led to my dismissal, so it was poetic justice when he too was fired soon after.

poetic li·cence /ˌ·,·· ˈ···/ n [U] the freedom to change facts, not to obey the usual rules, etc. as allowed to poets, painters, etc.

poet lau·re·ate /ˌ··· ˈ····/ n (often caps.) a poet appointed by a country or a state, who writes poems on important occasions

po·et·ry /ˈpəʊɪtri/ n [U] **1** poems: a book of poetry | the

poetry of Dryden —compare PROSE **2** the art of writing poems **3** apprec a quality of beauty, grace, and deep feeling: This dancer has poetry in her movements.

Poets' Cor·ner /ˌ·· ˈ··/ a part of Westminster Abbey in London where many famous English poets are buried, including Chaucer

po-faced /ˌpəʊ ˈfeɪst◂/ adj BrE infml derog having a silly solemn expression on the face, esp. showing disapproval

po·go stick /ˈpəʊgəʊ stɪk/ n a pole with a spring and a bar near the bottom on which one can place one's feet, holding the top, and then jump about for fun

pogo stick

pog·rom /ˈpɒgrəm‖pəˈgrɑːm/ n a planned killing of large numbers of people, esp. Jews, carried out for reasons of race or religion

poi·gnant /ˈpɔɪnjənt/ adj fml **1** producing a sharp feeling of sadness or pity: poignant memories of an unhappy childhood | a poignant farewell **2** (of sorrow, grief, etc.) painful and deeply felt — ~ly adv —gnancy n [U]

Poin·ca·ré /ˈpwæŋkæreɪ‖ˌpwæŋkɑːˈreɪ/, Hen·ri /ˈɒnri‖ɑːnˈriː/ (1854–1912) a French MATHEMATICIAN, one of the greatest of his time

Poin·dex·ter /ˈpɔɪndekstər/, John (1936–) an American REAR ADMIRAL and Republican government official. He was forced to RESIGN after the Irangate affair and was found guilty of selling arms to Iran.

poin·set·ti·a /pɔɪnˈsetiə‖-ˈsetə, -ˈsetiə/ n a tropical plant with flowerlike groups of large bright red leaves, popular for Christmas decoration

point¹ /pɔɪnt/ n **1** [C (of)] a sharp end: She pricked herself with|on the point of a needle. | These thorns have sharp points. | (fig.) I won't make concessions at the point of a gun. (=when I have a gun aimed at me) **2** [C] a particular real or imaginary place: The bus stops at four or five points along this road. | (fig.) The only point of contact between them was their love of fishing. —see also TURNING POINT **3** [C] a particular noticeable quality or ability of a person or thing; FEATURE: What are the points to look for when you are buying a new computer? | I can't see any weak points in your plan. —see also STRONG POINT **4** [C;U] an exact moment; particular time or state: I'll resume the story at the point where the hero is about to rescue them. | At one point in the meeting she nearly lost her temper. | the **melting point** of gold (=the temperature at which it melts) | My patience had reached **breaking point**, and I'm afraid I was very rude to him. | She's always threatening to leave, but when **it comes to the point** (=when the moment comes for her to take action) she never does. — see also BOILING POINT, FREEZING POINT, HIGH POINT **5** [C] any of the units used for recording the SCORE in various sports and games: We won the rugby match by 12 points to 3. | The first player to get 21 points is the winner. **6** [C] a single particular idea, fact, or part of an argument or statement: There were two or three points in your speech that I didn't understand. | a five-point plan | Yes, I **take your point.** (=I think that what you have just said is quite reasonable) | You've **got a point** there. (=What you have said seems to be right.) | By skilful argument she succeeded in **carrying/gaining her point.** (=making others agree) | All right, you've **made your point** (=I understand what you are trying to say); there's no need to go on about it. | He didn't seem keen to accept the offer, so I didn't **press the point.** (=I did not continue to try to make him accept) **7** [the] the main idea contained in something said or done, which gives meaning to all of it: I didn't **see the point** of his last remark. (=did not understand it, or why he made it) | He seems to have missed (=failed to understand) the whole point of the book. | I know he's a nice person but **that's not the point.** (=not really important to or connected with the thing being talked about) | I'm in a hurry, so **come/get to the point.** (=come to the most important or urgent part of what you have to say) | The fact that he's your brother is **beside the point.** (=has nothing to do with the main subject) | The chairman made a few rambling remarks, which were rather **off the point**. | Your suggestion is very much to **the point**. (=is highly RELEVANT) **8** [U (**in, of**)] purpose; advantage; use: There's not much point in repairing that old car again. | What's the point of locking all the doors? | I can't see the point in trying to persuade him – he'll never change his mind. **9** [C] also **decimal point**– a sign (·) used for separating a whole number from any following decimals: When we read out 4.23 we say "four point two three". **10** [C] tech a FULL STOP **11** [C] **a** a measure of increase or decrease in cost, value, etc.: The dollar has fallen a few points on the money markets today. | The cost of living has risen by three percentage points. (=by 3%) **b** AmE an amount of money equal to 1% of a MORTGAGE (=money borrowed to buy a house or other property): If I refinance now I can knock two points off my mortgage. **12** [C (**of**)] a very small area or spot: We could just make out a **point of light** at the end of the tunnel. **13** [C] a COMPASS POINT **14** [C] a sharply angled piece of land that stretches out into the sea: The ship rounded the point. **15** [C] also **power point** BrE ‖ **electric socket** AmE– a piece of plastic or other material with holes in it, in Britain usu. three square holes which is fixed into a wall and to which electrical equipment can be connected for the electricity supply **16** [C usu. pl.] tech the end of an electrical instrument or wire across which, or from which, a small amount of electricity is sent: If the engine isn't working properly the points may need cleaning. **17** at the point of just before: at the point of death|collapse **18** case in point something that proves or is an example of the subject under consideration: I'm always ill when I go abroad; what happened on our last holiday is a case in point. **19** in point of fact actually; in reality: He makes great claims about being an experienced traveller, but in point of fact he's only been abroad once. **20** make a point of to take particular care about: She always makes a point of being punctual. **21** on the point of just starting to; just about to: I was on the point of leaving when the phone rang. **22** point of no return a particular moment at which one has to decide whether to stop what one is doing or go on, because if one continues any further one will not be able to stop **23** to the point of to a degree that can be described as: Her manner of speaking is direct to the point of rudeness. –see also POINTS, **stretch a point** (STRETCH[1])

point² v **1** [T (**at, to**)] to draw attention to something, or show where it is or how to get there, by holding out a finger or a long pointed object towards it: She pointed to the house on the corner and said, "That's where I live." | It's rude to point at people. **2** [T (**at, towards**)] to aim or direct: You should never point a gun if you don't mean to fire it. | Their missiles are pointed at targets in enemy countries. | She pointed the boat upstream. **3** [I+adv/prep] to be aimed in or show the stated direction: The arrow points north. **4** [T] to fill in and make smooth the spaces between the bricks of (a wall, house, etc.) with cement **5** point the finger (at) infml to blame (someone) publicly; ACCUSE **6** point the way to show how to gain a particular result: This new discovery points the way forward in the search for a cure.
point sbdy./sthg. ↔ **out** phr v [T] **1** [(**to**)] to show who or what (a particular person or thing) is, esp. by pointing: You've never met her? Well she's here somewhere, so I'll point her out to you if I see her. [wh-] I pointed out to him where I used to live. **2** [+that] to draw attention to the fact: May I point out that if we don't leave now we shall miss the bus.
point to/towards sbdy./sthg. phr v [T] to suggest the strong possibility of; be a sign of: All the evidence points towards Randall as the murderer.
point sthg. ↔ **up** phr v [T] fml to make clearer or more urgent; EMPHASIZE: The increasing number of accidents points up the need for stricter road-safety measures.

point-blank /ˌ · ˈ·◂/ adj, adv **1** (fired) from a very close position: He shot the animal point-blank|at point-blank range. **2** (in a way that is) forceful and direct: a point-blank refusal | I told him point-blank what I thought of his ridiculous idea.

point du·ty /ˈ· ··/ n [(**on**) U] BrE the controlling of traffic by a policeman standing usu. at a point where two roads cross each other

point·ed /ˈpɔɪntɪd/ adj **1** shaped to a point at one end: long pointed fingernails **2** done in a noticeable way and intended to express a particular message or meaning: She looked in a pointed manner at the clock and I understood that it was time to leave. **3** (of something said) aimed noticeably and unfavourably at a particular person: a few pointed remarks about the length of his hair – –ly adv

point·er /ˈpɔɪntə[r]/ n **1** a thin piece of metal that moves and points to the numbers on a measuring apparatus **2** [(**to**)] infml a helpful piece of advice or information: I'm new to this job, so I'd be grateful if you could give me a few pointers. **3** a stick used for pointing at things on a large map, board, etc. **4** a hunting dog that points its nose towards a hunted animal or bird that it has smelt

poin·til·lis·m /ˈpwæntɪlɪzəm, ˈpɔɪn-/ n [U] a style of painting which uses dots of colour to get its effect, developed in the late 19th century by artists who did not agree with the ideas of IMPRESSIONISM. The most famous painter to use this style was Seurat. –see also IMPRESSIONISM, SEURAT –**list** n, adj : the 19th-century French pointillist Seurat | a pointillist painting

point·less /ˈpɔɪntləs/ adj often derog **1** done for no reason; meaningless: pointless violence **2** that cannot have any result; useless; FUTILE: It's pointless to try to negotiate with them because they'll never change their minds. – –ly adv – –ness n [U]

point man /ˈ· ·/ n AmE a person, esp. a soldier, who goes ahead of a group to see if there is any danger

point of or·der /ˌ· · ˈ··/ n fml a matter connected with the organization of an official meeting: to raise a point of order | On a point of order, Mr Chairman, shouldn't the minutes be read first?

point of ref·e·rence /ˌ· · ˈ···/ n something one knows about already which helps one when one thinks about something else

point of view /ˌ· · ˈ·/ also **viewpoint**– n a particular way of considering or judging a situation, person, event, etc.: We need someone with a fresh point of view, who can suggest changes. | From the government's point of view it would be better if this information were kept secret. | Try to look at it from their point of view. (=to see the situation as they see it)

points /pɔɪnts/ n [P] **1** BrE ‖ **switches** AmE– a pair of short RAILs that can be moved to allow a train to cross over from one track to another **2** the ends of the toes, as used to dance on in BALLET **3** the gaining of more points than one's opponent in BOXING, rather than knocking him down: Smith beat Jones **on points**. | a points victory

points·man /ˈpɔɪntsmən/ BrE ‖ **switchman** AmE– n pl -men /mən/ **1** a person who operates railway POINTS (1) **2** a police or traffic officer controlling and directing traffic where two roads cross

point-to-point /ˌ· · ˈ·/ n point-to-points BrE a horserace across country from one place to another, usu. with points along the way marked with flags. This sport is especially popular with upper-class people who live in the country.

Poi·rot /ˈpwɑːrəʊ‖pwɑːˈrəʊ/, **Her·cule** /ˈeəkjuːl‖eərˈkjuːl/ an imaginary DETECTIVE from the books of the English writer Agatha Christie. Hercule Poirot is a small, BALD man with a large MOUSTACHE and a very neat appearance. He is Belgian and thinks the English are strange, while the English think that his way of speaking English is funny. He is very clever and always discovers who the criminal is.

Hercule Poirot

poise¹ /pɔɪz/ n [U] apprec **1** good judgment and self-control in one's actions, combined with a quiet confidence in one's abilities; COMPOSURE **2** a well-balanced way of holding or moving one's body: the dancer's graceful poise

poise² v [T+obj+adv/prep] to hold or place in a carefully balanced position: He poised the glass on the edge of the shelf.

poised /pɔɪzd/ adj **1** [F+between] in a condition of (dangerous) uncertainty: The sick man is poised between life *and death.* **2** [F (**for**/*to-v*)] in a state of readiness to act or move: *The army was poised for a major attack/poised to attack.* **3** [F+*adv*/*prep*] not moving, as if hanging in the air: *The bee hung poised above the flower.* **4** [F+*adv*/*prep*] carefully balanced: *She sat poised on the edge of her chair as if ready to go.* **5** *apprec* having or showing poise

poi·son[1] /ˈpɔɪzən/ *n* **1** [C;U] (a) substance that can cause illness or death if taken into the body: *These mushrooms contain a deadly poison.* | *a bottle of rat poison* (=for killing rats) | *Arsenic is a poison.* | *They* **hate each other like poison.** (=very much) | (fig.) *the poison* (=extremely harmful influence) *of pornography* **2** [U] *humor sl* alcoholic drink: *What's your poison?* (=What would you like to drink?)

poison[2] *v* [T] **1** to harm or kill with poison: *Someone tried to poison our dog.* **2** to put poison into or onto (something): *Someone tried to poison our dog's food.* | *a poisoned arrow/water supply* **3** to make dangerously impure: *Exhaust fumes from cars are poisoning the air of our cities.* **4** to have a damaging influence on: *Their minds have been poisoned by propaganda.* | *His insensitive remarks will poison relations between the two superpowers.* —see also FOOD POISONING **5** *esp. BrE* to infect (esp. a part of the body): *a poisoned foot* *— ~ er n*

poison gas /ˌ··ˈ·/ *n* [U] gas used in war to kill or harm an enemy

poison i·vy /ˌ··ˈ···/ *n* [U] a North American climbing plant that causes painful spots on the skin when touched

poi·son·ous /ˈpɔɪzənəs/ *adj* **1** containing poison: *poisonous snakes* | *Some plants have poisonous berries.* **2** having the effects of poison: *This medicine is poisonous if taken in large quantities.* | (fig.) *the poisonous* (=extremely harmful) *influence of their lies* **3** *derog* nasty; very unpleasant: *She gave him a poisonous look.* *— ~ ly adv*

poison-pen let·ter /ˌ·· ·· ˌ··/ *n* a usu. unsigned letter saying bad things about someone

Poi·ti·er /ˈpwɒtieɪ‖ˈpwaːtjeɪ/, **Sid·ney** /ˈsɪdni/ (1927–) a black American film actor and DIRECTOR, who was one of the first black actors to play serious parts rather than black STEREOTYPES

poke[1] /pəʊk/ *v* [I;T] **1** [(+*obj*)+*adv*/*prep*] to stretch out sharply or suddenly through or beyond a particular place or opening: *His elbow was poking (out) through his torn shirt sleeve.* | *She poked her head round the corner.* **2** [(**in, with**)] to push a pointed thing into (someone or something; PROD: *You nearly poked me in the eye with your pencil.* | *She poked the fire to make it burn better.* **3 poke fun at** to laugh or cause others to laugh rather unkindly at; make fun of —see also **poke one's nose in** (NOSE[1] (8))
   poke about/around *phr v* [I] *infml* to move things about when looking for something: *She poked about in her bag for her ticket.* | *Who's been poking about in my private drawer?*

poke[2] *n* an act of poking with something pointed: *I gave her a poke in the ribs with my elbow to wake her up.* —see also **pig in a poke** (PIG[1])

pok·er[1] /ˈpəʊkər/ *n* a metal rod used to poke a fire in order to make it burn better —see picture at FIREPLACE

poker[2] *n* [U] a card game usu. played for money

poker face /ˈ·· ·/ *n* [S] a face that shows nothing of what a person is thinking or feeling (from the game of poker in which players try not to show what they are feeling because they do not want other players to know if their cards are good or bad) —**poker-faced** *adj*

po·ker·work /ˈpəʊkəwɜːk‖-kərwɜːrk/ *n* [U] (the art of making) pictures or decoration on wood or leather made by burning the surface with hot tools

pok·y , pokey /ˈpəʊki/ *adj infml derog* **1** (of a place) uncomfortably small and unattractive: *a poky little house with a poky little garden in front* **2** ‖ **pokey** *AmE* annoyingly slow *—*iness *n* [U]

Po·lack /ˈpəʊlæk/ *n AmE taboo* a POLE (=a person from Poland). In the US, jokes are made about the Polish, in which they appear to be quite stupid. These jokes are considered offensive, esp. by Polish people themselves —compare IRISH JOKE

Po·land /ˈpəʊlənd/ a country in central Europe; capital Warsaw; population 37,854,000 (1989). In 1939 Germany

invaded (INVADE) Poland and during the Second World War many Polish people were killed by the Germans. From 1945 the USSR controlled the Polish government and the Communist party was the only political party allowed. In 1980, a new political party, Solidarity, led by Lech Walesa, began to oppose the Communist government and finally, in 1989, was elected as the new government. —see also EASTERN BLOC, SOLIDARITY, Lech WALESA

Po·lan·ski /pəˈlænski/, **Roman** (1933–) a Polish film DIRECTOR, who has made his films in English since the mid 1960s. His films are often about madness and violence and include *Repulsion* and *Rosemary's Baby*. He was married to the actress Sharon Tate who was killed by Charles Manson and his followers. He is no longer able to work in America because he was said to have had sex with girls who were too young to do this legally.

po·lar /ˈpəʊlər/ *adj* [A] **1** of, near, like, or coming from lands near the North or South Poles: *the polar ice-cap* **2** *fml or tech* exactly opposite in kind, quality, etc.: *The two systems of government are* **polar opposites.**

polar bear /ˌ·· ˈ·/ *n* a large white bear that lives near the North Pole —see picture at BEAR

Po·la·ris /pəˈlɑːrɪs‖-ˈlæ-/ *n* an American NUCLEAR weapon fired from a SUBMARINE, developed in the 1950s and 60s and used by the US and Britain as a nuclear DETERRENT

po·lar·i·ty /pəˈlærəti/ *n* [C;U] **1** *fml* the state of having or developing two opposite qualities: *a growing polarity between the opinions of the government and those of the trade unions* **2** *tech* **a** the state of having two opposite POLES[3] (3,4,5) **b** either of the two states of electricity possessed by POLES[3] (4) (in the phrases **negative polarity, positive polarity**)

po·lar·ize also **-ise** *BrE* /ˈpəʊləraɪz/ *v* **1** [I;T (**into**)] to divide into groups based on two completely opposite principles, political opinions, etc.: *a highly controversial issue which has polarized the country* **2** [T] *tech* **a** to give POLARITY (2a) to **b** to cause (light waves) to VIBRATE (=move up and down) in a single particular pattern *—*ization /ˌpəʊləraɪˈzeɪʃən‖-rə-/ *n* [U]

Po·lar·oid /ˈpəʊlərɔɪd/ *n tdmk* **1** [U] a material with which glass is treated in order to make light shine less brightly through it, used in making SUNGLASSES, car windows, etc. **2** [C] also **Polaroid camera** a camera that produces a finished photograph from inside itself only seconds after the picture has been taken

Po·lar·oids /ˈpəʊlərɔɪdz/ *n* [P] SUNGLASSES treated with Polaroid —see PAIR (USAGE)

pole[1] /pəʊl/ *n* **1** (*often in comb.*) a long straight round rather thin stick or post, esp. one stuck upright or nearly upright into the ground as a support: *The hut was made of poles covered with grass mats.* | *a tent pole* | *a flagpole* | (fig.) *climbing the greasy/slippery pole of promotion* (=where it is easy to fail and go backwards) **2 up the pole** *infml, esp. BrE* slightly mad

pole[2] *v* [I] to use a pole or poles to move along, e.g. in a flat-bottomed boat or when sliding over snow on SKIs

pole[3] *n* **1** (the area around) the most northern and southern points on the surface of a PLANET, esp., on Earth, the NORTH POLE or SOUTH POLE or the cold areas around them: *the rigours of life at the poles* | (fig., *lit*) *from pole to pole* (=all over the world) —see also MAGNETIC POLE **2** either of two positions that are as far apart or different as possible: *Our opinions on this subject are at opposite poles.* **3** either of the two points in the sky to the north and south round which stars seem to turn **4** either of the points at the ends of a MAGNET where its power of pulling iron towards itself is strongest **5** either of the two points at which wires can be fixed onto an electric BATTERY in order to use the electricity (often in the phrases **negative pole, positive pole**) **6** either end of an imaginary straight line (AXIS) round which a solid round mass turns **7 poles apart** widely separated; having no shared quality, idea, etc.: *They are poles apart in their political attitudes.*

Pole *n* a person who comes or whose parents come from Poland

pole-axe /ˈpəʊlæks/ *v* [T] to knock down (as if) with a very hard hit; *The boxer was poleaxed by a savage punch to the jaw.*

pole·cat /ˈpəʊlkæt/ *n* **1** a small fierce dark brown animal

Scenes from History

Christopher Columbus discovers America
In 1492 Christopher Columbus was the first European to discover America.

'Not tonight, Josephine.'

Napoleon Bonaparte, the French military leader, is supposed to have said this to Josephine one evening when she was feeling romantic but he was resting before battle. People sometimes use this phrase in a joking way when they refuse an invitation or an offer.

The Boston Tea Party
In 1773 a group of American men, dressed as Native Americans, went onto English ships in Boston Harbour because they were angry that the English government, which ruled America, had introduced a new tax on tea. The men threw all the tea that the ships were carrying into the water.

The Charge of the Light Brigade
During the Crimean War, British soldiers were sent into a battle which they could not win because they had only swords and were fighting against cannons. Many were killed.

The Pilgrim Fathers
The Pilgrim Fathers sailed to America because they wanted to escape from England to make a new kind of society based on their own religious beliefs.

The Mona Lisa
by Leonardo Da Vinci

The Haywain
by John Constable

Sunflowers
by Vincent Van Gogh

View on the Grand Canal
by Canaletto

Waterlily Pond
by Claude Monet

The Laughing Cavalier
by Frans Hals

American Gothic
by Grant Wood

Le Moulin de la Galette
by Renoir

that lives in northern Europe and has a very unpleasant smell **2** *AmE infml for* SKUNK (1)

po·lem·ic /pəˈlemɪk/ *n fml or tech* **1** [C] a fierce attack on or defence of an opinion **2** [U] also **polemics**— the art or practice of attacking or defending opinions, ideas, etc.

po·lem·i·cal /pəˈlemɪkəl/ also **polemic**— *adj fml or tech* written or said with the main purpose of attacking or defending opinions, ideas, etc. as if in an argument, rather than simply expressing or explaining them — ~ **ly** /kli/ *adv*

pole po·si·tion /ˈ· ·ˌ·ˌ··/ *n* [C;U] the front position at the beginning of a car race: *By doing the fastest practice lap Senna got (the) pole position.*

pole star /ˈ· ·/ also **North Star**— *n* [the] (often cap.) the rather bright star that is nearest to the centre of the sky in the northern part of the world

pole vault /ˈ· ·/ *n* **1** [C] a jump made over a high raised bar with the help of a long pole **2** [the+S] the sport of doing this —see colour picture on page 883 —**pole-vault** *v* [I] — ~ **er** *n*

po·lice¹ /pəˈliːs/ *n* [(the) P] an official body of men and women whose job is to protect people and property, to make everyone obey the law, to catch criminals, etc. In Britain, people can call the police quickly by dialling (DIAL²) 999; in the US, the number is 911: *The police have caught the murderer.* | *Have you reported the incident to the police?* | *Extra police were rushed to the scene of the trouble.* | *She wants to join the police force.* | *a police car* —see also MILITARY POLICE, SECRET POLICE

police² *v* [T] **1** to control (a place) (as if) using police: *increased policing of the inner cities* | *The army policed the riot-torn city.* **2** to control; keep a watch on: *A new body has been set up to police the nuclear power industry.*

Police, The a British popular music group successful in the 1970s and 1980s, whose lead singer was called Sting

police con·sta·ble /·ˌ· ˈ···ˌ/ *n BrE fml* see P.C.

police dog /·ˈ· ·/ *n* **1** a dog, usu. an Alsatian, which is trained to help the police find drugs or catch criminals **2** *AmE* ALSATIAN

policemen

an American policeman　　　　a British policeman

po·lice·man /pəˈliːsmən/ *n* -men /mən/ **1** a male police officer

► CULTURAL NOTE In Britain and the US, the old-fashioned STEREOTYPE of a policeman is of a friendly man who helps people, for example by telling them how to get to a place or by telling them what time it is.

2 a policeman's lot is not a happy one *quote* a slightly changed phrase from an OPERA by Gilbert and Sullivan, often used when saying how difficult the job of the police is

police of·fi·cer /·ˈ· ·ˌ···/ *n* a member of a police force

police state /·ˈ· ·/ *n derog* a country in which most activities of the citizens are controlled by (secret) political police

police sta·tion /·ˈ· ·ˌ··/ *n* the local office of the police in a town, part of a city, etc.

po·lice·wom·an /pəˈliːsˌwʊmən/ *n* -women /ˌwɪmɪn/ a female police officer

policewomen

an American policewoman　　a British policewoman

pol·i·cy¹ /ˈpɒlɪsi‖ˈpɑː-/ *n* [C;U] **1** a course of action for dealing with a particular matter or situation, esp. as chosen by a political party, government, business company, etc.: *The government must evolve new policies to reduce unemployment.* | *The nationalization of industries is not government policy.* (=they do not intend to do it) | *What is the company's policy on employing disabled people?* | *economic policy* | *a policy statement* **2** a course or principle of action, esp. one that is to one's own advantage: *It's bad policy to smoke too much; it may harm your health.* | *As they say, honesty is the best policy.*

policy² also **insurance policy**— *n* a written statement of the details of an agreement with an insurance company: *an all-risks policy* | *policy-holders*

po·li·o /ˈpəʊliəʊ/ also **po·li·o·my·e·li·tis** /ˌpəʊliəʊmaɪəˈlaɪtɪs/tech— *n* [U] a serious infectious disease of the nerves in the SPINE, often resulting in a lasting PARALYSIS (=inability to move certain muscles)

pol·ish¹ /ˈpɒlɪʃ‖ˈpɑː-/ *v* [T(UP)] to make smooth, bright, and shiny by continual rubbing: *Polish your shoes with a brush.* | *He polished up the old copper coins.* — ~ **er** *n* : *an electric floor polisher*
　　polish sthg. ·· **off** *phr v* [T] *infml* to finish (food, work, etc.), esp. quickly or easily: *He polished off a plate of fish and chips in no time at all.*
　　polish sthg. ↔ **up** *phr v* [T] to improve by practising: *I'll need to polish up my French if I'm going to France for my holidays.*

polish² *n* **1** [U] (often in comb.) a liquid, powder, PASTE, etc., used in polishing a surface: *a tin of brown shoe polish* | *floor polish* —see also FRENCH POLISH **2** [S] a smooth shiny surface produced by rubbing: *A hot plate will spoil the table's polish.* **3** [S] an act of polishing: *These shoes need a polish!* **4** [U] the quality of being POLISHED: *His writing has potential but lacks polish.*

Pol·ish /ˈpəʊlɪʃ/ *adj* of Poland, its people, or their language

pol·ished /ˈpɒlɪʃt‖ˈpɑː-/ *adj* **1** (of a piece of artistic work, a performance, etc.) done with great skill and control **2** (of manners, etc.) polite and graceful

po·lit·bu·ro /pəˈlɪtbjʊərəʊ, ˈpɒlɪt-‖ˈpɑːlɪt-, pəˈlɪt-/ *n* -ros (often cap.) the chief decision-making committee of a Communist party or Communist government

po·lite /pəˈlaɪt/ *adj apprec* **1** having or showing good manners, sensitivity to other people's feelings, and/or correct social behaviour: *What polite well-behaved children!* | *It's not considered polite to talk with your mouth full.* | *a polite refusal* | *I know he said he liked it, but he was only being polite.* (=in fact, he didn't like it) —opposite **rude, impolite 2** *old-fash pomp* showing fineness of feeling, good education and manners, etc.; REFINED: *polite society* — ~ **ly** *adv* — ~ **ness** *n* [U]

polite so·ci·e·ty /·ˌ· ·ˈ···/ *n* [U] (the company of) the set of people who are considered to have a good education, good manners, and fine feelings: *That's not the kind of word you'd use in polite society.* | *an ex-farmer who felt ill at ease in polite society*

pol·i·tic /ˈpɒlətɪk‖ˈpɑː-/ *adj fml* (of behaviour or actions) well-judged and likely to bring advantage; PRUDENT: *It would be politic to agree with him.* —see also BODY POLITIC

po·lit·i·cal /pəˈlɪtɪkəl/ *adj* **1** [*no comp.*] of public affairs and/or the government of a country and its relations with other countries: *the loss of political freedoms | a country's political institutions* (=its law-making bodies, systems of government, etc.) | *attempts to find a political solution* (=not a military one) *to the problems of the region* **2** [*no comp.*] of (party) politics: *She has very strong political opinions.* | *the newspaper's political editor* **3** [*no comp.*] charged with or being an act harmful to a government: *a political offence* **4** very interested in or active in politics: *The students in this university are very political.* **5** *usu. derog* connected with, influenced by, or done for reasons of personal, group, or governmental advantage rather than for the reasons officially given: *a political decision* | *The tax cuts were made for purely political reasons.* — **–ly** /kli/ *adv* : *politically motivated strikes*

political ac·tion com·mit·tee /·ˌ··· ˈ··· ·ˌ··/ also **PAC**– *n AmE* an organization formed by a business, INTEREST GROUP, or TRADE UNION to raise money to help people who support their ideas to run for CONGRESS

political ac·tiv·ist /·ˌ··· ˈ··/ *n sometimes derog* a person taking a very active part in a political movement

political a·sy·lum /·ˌ··· ·ˈ··/ *n* [U] the right to remain safely in another country, for a person who cannot live safely in their own because of the political situation: *a Tamil refugee seeking political asylum*

political e·con·o·my /·ˌ··· ·ˈ···/ *n* [U] the study of the way nations manage the making and use of wealth

political ge·og·ra·phy /·ˌ··· ·ˈ···/ *n* [U] the study of the Earth's surface as it is divided up into different countries, rather than as marked by rivers, mountain ranges, etc.

politically cor·rect /·ˌ··· ·ˈ·/ also **PC**– *adj* correct according to a set of LIBERAL opinions, e.g. that black people and women should have equal chances to get jobs, education, etc.: *His politically correct speech stated that university students should study literature written by blacks and women as well as Shakespeare and Homer.*

political ma·chine /·ˌ··· ·ˈ·/ *n AmE, usu. derog* the way in which a politician, esp. a MAYOR or GOVERNOR runs his office so that he is in control of everything that happens

political par·ty /·ˌ··· ˈ··/ *n* a group of people with similar political ideas who try to gain power in a country: *Which of the main political parties is most likely to win the election?*

political pris·on·er /·ˌ··· ˈ···/ *n* a person who is put in prison because they oppose the government of a country, or because the government does not agree with their ideas

political sci·ence /·ˌ··· ˈ··/ *n* [U] the scientific study of politics and government **political scientist** *n*

pol·i·ti·cian /ˌpɒləˈtɪʃən‖ˌpɑː-/ *n* **1** a person whose business is politics, esp. one who has been elected to a parliament or to a position in government. Politicians are often mentioned in jokes as being people you cannot trust. — see colour picture on page 950 **2** someone who is skilled at dealing with people in a way that is advantageous to himself or herself or at using a system to his or her own advantage: *You need to be a bit of a politician to succeed in this company.*

po·lit·i·cize also **-cise** *BrE* /pəˈlɪtɪsaɪz/ *v* [T] *often derog* **1** to give a political character to **2** to cause to develop an interest in, and understanding of politics —**-cization** /pəˌlɪtɪsaɪˈzeɪʃən‖-sə-/ *n* [U] : *opposition to the politicization of the civil service*

pol·i·tick·ing /ˈpɒlətɪkɪŋ‖ˈpɑː-/ *n* [U] *usu. derog* taking part in political activity or talk, esp. for personal advantage

po·lit·i·co /pəˈlɪtɪkəʊ/ *n* **-cos** or **-coes** *usu. derog* a politician or other person who is active in politics: *politicos and party hacks, trying to get into comfortable jobs in the government*

pol·i·tics /ˈpɒlətɪks‖ˈpɑː-/ *n* **1** [U+*sing.*/*pl. v*] political affairs, esp. considered as a profession and/or as a means

of winning and keeping governmental control: *Politics has/have never interested me.* | *She wants to* **go into politics.** (=become a politician) | *local politics* | *I was active in student politics when I was at college.* **2** [U] the art or science of government: *Tom is studying politics at university.* **3** [P] political opinions; the political ideas or party that one favours: *What are her politics?* **4** [U] activity within a particular group or organization by which some members of the group try to gain an advantage over others: *Try not to get involved in* **office politics.** | *sexual politics*

pol·i·ty /ˈpɒlɪti‖ˈpɑː-/ *n* [C;U] *fml* (a particular form of) political or governmental organization

Polk /pəʊk/, **James** (1795–1849) the 11th president of the US (1845–49)

pol·ka /ˈpɒlkə, ˈpəʊlkə ‖ ˈpəʊl-/ *n* (a piece of music for) a very quick simple dance for people dancing in pairs. In the US, the polka is seen as rather old-fashioned and amusing.

polka dot /ˈ·· ·/ *n* [*usu. pl.*] any of a number of circular spots forming a pattern, used esp. on dress material: *a polka-dot skirt*

poll¹ /pəʊl/ *n* **1** [C] also **opinion poll**– **a** an attempt to find out the general opinion about something, esp. about a political matter, by questioning a number of people chosen by chance: *We're conducting a poll to find out how many people are in favour of nuclear power.* **b** a record of the result of this: *The latest poll gives the Republicans a 5% lead.* —see also DEED POLL, GALLUP POLL, STRAW POLL **2** [U] also **polls** *pl.*– the giving of votes in writing at an election: *The result of the poll won't be known until midnight.* | *The Conservatives were defeated at the polls.* | *The British public will* **go to the polls** (=vote in an election) *in the autumn.* **3** [S] the number of votes recorded at an election: *They expected a heavy poll.* (=expected that a large number of people would vote) **4** [U] *AmE* POLLS (2)

poll² *v* [T] **1** to question (people) in making a poll: *Almost three-quarters of those who were polled said they opposed the government's policy.* **2** to receive (the stated number of votes) at an election: *She polled 10,372 votes.*

pol·lard¹ /ˈpɒləd‖ˈpɑːlərd/ *n* **1** a tree from which the top has been cut in order to make the branches below the cut place grow more thickly **2** a hornless kind of sheep, goat, etc.

pollard² *v* [T] to cut the top off (a tree) in order to make lower branches grow more thickly

pol·len /ˈpɒlən‖ˈpɑː-/ *n* [C] fine dust on the male part of a flower that causes other flowers to produce seeds when it is carried to them

pollen count /ˈ·· ·/ *n* a measure of the amount of pollen floating in the air, esp. as a guide for people who are made ill by it: *a very high pollen count* —see also HAY FEVER

pol·li·nate /ˈpɒləneɪt‖ˈpɑː-/ *v* [T] to cause (a flower or plant) to be able to produce seeds by adding or bringing pollen: *Flowers are often pollinated by bees.* —**-nation** /ˌpɒlə-ˈneɪʃən‖ˌpɑː-/ *n* [U]

poll·ing /ˈpəʊlɪŋ/ *n* [U] voting at an election: *Polling was quite heavy.* (=A lot of people voted.)

polling booth /ˈ·· ·/ *n esp. BrE* ‖ **voting booth** *AmE*– a partly enclosed place inside a polling station where someone marks their voting paper secretly —see colour picture on page 950

polling day /ˈ·· ·/ *n BrE* ‖ **election day** *AmE*– the day on which people go to vote in an election

polling sta·tion /ˈ·· ·ˌ··/ *n esp. BrE* ‖ **polling place, the polls** *AmE*– a building or other place where people go to vote at an election: *Our local library is used as a polling station during elections.*

Pol·lock /ˈpɒlək‖ˈpɑː-/, **Jackson** (1912–56) an American ARTIST whose large ABSTRACT paintings are full of colour and are often made with DRIPs of paint. Pollock was one of the first artists to try and express his feelings through this type of painting.

polls /pəʊlz/ *n* [*the*+P] **1** POLL¹ (2) **2** *AmE* the place where one goes to vote: *"Where are the polls this year?" "At the school."*

poll·ster /ˈpəʊlstər/ *n infml* a person who carries out POLLs¹ (1), or who explains the meaning of the results of polls

poll tax /ˈ· ·/ [*the*] **1** a tax of a fixed amount collected from every citizen **2** also **Community Charge** a British tax of a fixed amount to be paid by each person in each area of the country, introduced by the Conservative government of Margaret Thatcher as a way of paying for local government services. The amount to be paid was fixed separately by each area. Many people protested against this tax, and it was decided to replace it with the **council tax**, based mainly on the value of people's houses.

pol·lut·ant /pə'luːtənt/ n [C;U] a substance that pollutes, esp. a waste product of an industrial process: *Pollutants are constantly being released into the atmosphere.*

pol·lute /pə'luːt/ v [T] to make (air, water, soil, etc.) dangerously impure or unfit for use: *The river has been polluted by waste products from the factory.* | (fig.) *violent films that pollute* (=make impure) *young minds*

pol·lu·tion /pə'luːʃən/ n [U] **1** the action of polluting or the state of being polluted: *pollution of tourist beaches* | *anti-pollution laws* **2** (an area or mass of) a substance that pollutes: *The men were clearing all the pollution off the beach.*

Pollux see CASTOR AND POLLUX

poll watch·er /'· ··/ n a person who goes to a POLLING STATION to make sure that the voting is fair and honest: *Poll watchers were sent to observe the country's first democratic elections but were unable to prevent some abuses.*

Pol·ly /'pɒli‖'pɑː-/ a popular name for a PARROT

Pol·ly·an·na /ˌpɒli'ænə‖ˌpɑː-/ n a person who is always OPTIMISTIC and cheerful, esp. when seen as having little experience of the world (from the book *Pollyanna* by Eleanor Porter, whose main character is a young girl who always believes something good will happen): *She's a real Pollyanna, she's sure someone will send her the money.*

po·lo /'pəʊləʊ/ n [U] a game played between two teams of players on horseback, who hit a small ball with long-handled wooden hammers. Polo is a game which is played and watched esp. by very rich and fashionable people, including the Prince of Wales, and is seen as a GLAMOROUS and exciting sport. —see also WATER POLO

Polo[1] also **Polo mint** /'·· ·/ — BrE tdmk a round white sweet which tastes of MINT and has a hole in the middle

Polo[2] **, Mar·co** /'mɑːkəʊ‖'mɑːr-/ (1254?–1324) an Italian TRAVELLER who wrote about his stay at the court of Kublai Khan in China and his travels in India and SE Asia

pol·o·naise /ˌpɒlə'neɪz‖ˌpɑː-/ n a piece of music of a slow ceremonial kind, esp. written for the piano

polo neck /'·· ·/ esp. BrE ‖ **turtleneck** esp. AmE— n a round rolled collar, usu. woollen: *a polo-neck sweater*

po·lo·ni·um /pə'ləʊniəm/ n [U] a heavy metal that is a simple substance (ELEMENT) and is RADIOACTIVE

polo shirt /'·· ·/ n a shirt with short SLEEVEs and a collar made out of soft knitted (KNIT[1]) cotton material

Pol Pot /ˌpɒl 'pɒt‖ˌpɒ:l 'pɑːt/ (1920?   ) the Prime Minister of Kampuchea (formerly Cambodia) from 1975 to 1979 during which time very many people were killed. Pol Pot is a member of the Communist political group the Khmer Rouge. —see also KHMER ROUGE

pol·ter·geist /'pɒltəgaɪst‖'pəʊltər-/ n a troublesome spirit that is believed to make noises, throw objects about, etc., esp. in a home. Not everyone believes that poltergeists really exist.

pol·troon /pɒl'truːn‖pɑːl-/ n derog old use a coward

pol·y /'pɒli‖'pɑːli/ n **polys** BrE infml for POLYTECHNIC

poly- see WORD FORMATION

pol·y·an·dry /ˌpɒli'ændri, 'pɒliændri‖ˌpɑː-/ n [U] tech the custom or practice of having more than one husband at the same time. In Britain and the US it is against the law for women to do this. —compare BIGAMY, POLYGAMY —**drous** adj

pol·y·an·thus /ˌpɒli'ænθəs‖ˌpɑː-/ n [C;U] a small garden plant with a group of round brightly-coloured flowers at the top of each stem

pol·y·es·ter /'pɒliestər, ˌpɒli'estər‖'pɑːliestər/ n [U] a man-made material used to make cloth. Polyester is not usu. as expensive or as fashionable as natural materials such as wool or cotton.

pol·y·eth·y·lene /ˌpɒli'eθəliːn‖ˌpɑː-/ n [U] esp. AmE for POLYTHENE

po·lyg·a·mist /pə'lɪgəmɪst/ n tech a man who has more than one wife in a society where this is allowed —see also POLYGAMY

po·lyg·a·my /pə'lɪgəmi/ n [U] tech the custom or practice of having more than one husband or wife at the same time in a society where this is allowed. In Britain and the US it is against the law for men or women to do this. —compare BIGAMY, MONOGAMY —**mous** adj : *Many ancient societies were polygamous.*

pol·y·glot /'pɒliglɒt‖'pɑːliglɑːt/ adj tech **1** (of a person, book, etc.) speaking or using many languages; MULTILINGUAL **2** including groups that speak different languages: *a polyglot population/society* —**polyglot** n

pol·y·gon /'pɒligən‖'pɑːligɑːn/ n (in GEOMETRY) a figure on a flat surface having five or more straight sides

pol·y·graph /'pɒligrɑːf‖'pɑːligræf/ n tech for LIE DETECTOR

pol·y·math /'pɒlimæθ‖'pɑː-/ n fml apprec a person who has a wide range of knowledge in many subjects

pol·y·mer /'pɒlimər‖'pɑː-/ n a chemical compound having a simple structure of large MOLECULEs

pol·y·mor·phous /ˌpɒli'mɔːfəs◂‖ˌpɑːli'mɔːr-/ also **pol·y·mor·phic** /-fɪk◂/— adj fml or tech having or passing through many stages of growth, development, etc.

Pol·y·ne·si·a /ˌpɒli'niːziə‖ˌpɑːli'niːʒə/ the islands in the central and southern Pacific Ocean, including the Hawaiian islands, Tonga, and the islands of French Polynesia

Pol·y·ne·si·an /ˌpɒli'niːziən◂‖ˌpɑːli'niːʒən◂/ n **1** a person who comes from or whose parents come from Polynesia **2** [U] a group of languages spoken in Polynesia — **Polynesian** adj

pol·yp /'pɒlip‖'pɑː-/ n **1** a very simple small water animal, having the form of a tubelike bag **2** a small unnatural growth in the body, caused by an illness — **~ous** adj

po·lyph·o·ny /pə'lɪfəni/ n [U] a form of musical writing in which several different patterns of notes are sung or played together, fitting in with each other musically, according to certain rules; COUNTERPOINT —**nic** /ˌpɒli'fɒnɪk‖ˌpɑːli'fɑːnɪk/ adj

pol·y·pro·py·lene /ˌpɒli'prəʊpəliːn‖ˌpɑː-/ n [U] a lightweight plastic material used for wrapping, in floor coverings, etc.

po·lys·e·mous /ˌpə'lɪsɪməs, ˌpɒlɪ'siːməs‖pə'lɪsɪməs/ adj tech (of a word) having many different meanings

pol·y·sor·bate /ˌpɒli'sɔːbeɪt‖ˌpɑːli'sɔːr-/ n [U] a kind of EMULSIFIER used in preparing PROCESSED FOODS to keep liquids and solids from separating; a food ADDITIVE

pol·y·sty·rene /ˌpɒli'staɪəriːn‖ˌpɑː-/ ‖ also **Styrofoam** AmE tdmk— n [U] a light plastic that prevents the escape of heat, used esp. for making containers

pol·y·syl·la·ble /'pɒliˌsɪləbəl‖'pɑː-/ n tech a word that contains more than three SYLLABLEs —**bic** /ˌpɒliˈsɪˌlæbɪk◂‖ˌpɑː-/ adj : *"Unnecessary" is polysyllabic.* —**bically** /kli/ adv

pol·y·tech·nic /ˌpɒli'teknɪk‖ˌpɑː-/ also **poly** infml— n (esp. in Britain) a place of higher education, similar to a university, providing training and degrees in many subjects, esp. those which prepare people for particular jobs in science, industry, etc. Although degrees from polytechnics are as good as those from universities, they are considered by some people to be less PRESTIGIOUS than university degrees. —compare TECHNICAL COLLEGE, UNIVERSITY and see also extra information on page 408

pol·y·the·is·m /'pɒliθiːɪzəm‖'pɑː-/ n [U] the belief that there is more than one god —compare MONOTHEISM —**ist** adj, n —**istic** /ˌpɒliθiːˈɪstɪk◂‖ˌpɑː-/ adj

pol·y·thene /'pɒliθiːn‖'pɑː-/ ‖ also **polyethylene** esp. AmE— n [U] a strong light bendable plastic used esp. as a protective covering, for making many common articles: *a polythene bag*

pol·y·un·sat·u·rate /ˌpɒliʌn'sætʃərət‖ˌpɑː-/ n a polyunsaturated FATTY ACID: *This vegetable oil is high in polyunsaturates.*

pol·y·un·sat·u·rat·ed /ˌpɒliʌn'sætʃəreitɪd◂‖ˌpɑː-/ adj (of a fat or oil) having chemicals combined in a way that is thought to be good for the health when eaten: *Most vegetable oils contain polyunsaturated fats.* —compare SATURATED FAT

pol·y·u·re·thane /ˌpɒlɪˈjʊərₔθeɪn◂‖ˌpɑː-/ n [U] a plastic used esp. in making paints and VARNISH

pom /pɒm‖pɑːm/ also **pommy**– n AustrE, NZE sl, often derog an English person, esp. one who has gone to live in Australia or New Zealand. In Australia and New Zealand the popular image of an English person is of someone who is lazy and who complains all the time (a "whinging Pom").

po·made /pəˈmɑːd, pəˈmeɪd‖pəʊˈmeɪd/ n [U] a sweet-smelling oily substance rubbed on men's hair to make it smooth, esp. in former times

po·man·der /pəʊˈmændə‖r/ n a box or ball-shaped container holding sweet-smelling substances, HERBs, etc., used for giving a room or cupboard a pleasant smell

pom·e·gran·ate /ˈpɒmₔgrænₔt‖ˈˈpɑːm-/ n a round thick-skinned reddish fruit containing a mass of small seeds in a red juicy flesh

pom·mel /ˈpʌməl/ n **1** the rounded part at the front of a horse's SADDLE –see picture at HORSE **2** the ball-shaped end of a sword handle

pommel horse /ˈ·· ˌ·/ n AmE for VAULTING HORSE

pom·my /ˈpɒmi‖ˈpɑː-/ n a POM

pomp /pɒmp‖pɑːmp/ n [U] solemn and splendid ceremonial show, esp. on a public or official occasion: all the pomp of an imperial coronation

Pom·pa·dour /ˈpɒmpəduə‖r‖ˈpɑːmpədɔːr/, **Madame de** (1721–64) a MISTRESS (2) of King Louis XV of France, from 1745, who had an influence on his choice of government ministers

Pom·pei·i /pɒmˈpeɪ-i‖pɑːm-/ an ancient city in southern Italy, SE of Naples, which was buried when the VOLCANO Mount Vesuvius erupted (ERUPT) in AD 79. Pompeii was preserved underneath the volcanic ash and LAVA and has helped us to learn many things about Roman civilization.

Pom·pey /ˈpɒmpi‖ˈpɑːm-/ (106–48 BC) a Roman GENERAL (=military leader) and politician who opposed Julius Caesar but was defeated by him in 48 BC

Pomp·id·ou /ˈpɒmpₔduː‖ˈpɑːm-/, **Georges** /ʒɔːʒ‖ʒɔːrʒ/ (1911–74) a French politician who was president of France from 1969 until his death

Pompidou Cen·tre /ˈ··· ˌ··/ [the] a MUSEUM in Paris which has paintings by important 20th century artists. The museum building, which is very modern, is made of glass and of metal tubes in bright colours.

pom·pom /ˈpɒmpɒm‖ˈpɑːmpɑːm/ n **1** a small woollen ball used as a decoration on garments, esp. hats **2** also **pom-pon** /-pɒn ‖ -pɑːn/ a round ball made of loose plastic strings used by CHEERLEADERs, who used to be called pompom girls

pom·pous /ˈpɒmpəs‖ˈpɑːm-/ adj derog foolishly solemn and thinking oneself to be important. Pompous words or phrases are marked pomp in this dictionary: The railway guard was a pompous little official, who acted as though he controlled the whole railway system. – ~ly adv – ~ness, -posity /pɒmˈpɒsₔti‖pɑːm-/ n [U]

ponce¹ /pɒns‖pɑːns/ n BrE **1** derog sl a man who acts in an EFFEMINATE way **2** a man who lives with, and on the money earned by, a PROSTITUTE; a PIMP

ponce² v
  ponce about/around phr v [I] BrE derog sl (of a man) to act like a PONCE¹ (1), or in a foolish time-wasting way

Ponce de Le·ón /ˌpɒns də ˈliːən‖ˌpɑːns-/, **Juan** /wɑːn‖hwɑːn/ (1460–1521) a Spanish man who discovered Florida when he was searching for the FOUNTAIN OF YOUTH (a flow of water which was supposed to make people young forever)

pon·cho /ˈpɒntʃəʊ‖ˈpɑːn-/ n -chos a garment for the top half of the body consisting of a single piece of usu. thick woollen cloth, rather like a BLANKET, with a hole in the middle for the head

ponc·y, **-ey** /ˈpɒnsi‖ˈpɑː-/ adj BrE derog sl like or typical of a PONCE¹ (1): wearing a poncy little pale blue bow tie

pond /pɒnd‖pɑːnd/ n an area of still water smaller than a lake, esp. one that has been artificially made: The farm has a pond from which cattle can drink. | a duck pond – compare LAKE¹ (1), POOL

pon·der /ˈpɒndə‖r‖ˈpɑːn-/ v [I (on, over);T] to spend time in carefully considering (a fact, difficulty, etc.): She pon-

dered for some minutes before giving an answer. | Successive committees have pondered over this problem without finding a solution. | The cabinet would do well to ponder the advisability of such a course of action. [+v-ing] They're pondering moving their offices outside London. [+wh-] We pondered whether to tell him.

pon·der·ous /ˈpɒndərəs‖ˈpɑːn-/ adj fml **1** slow and awkward because of great size and weight; UNWIELDY: The elephant lowered its ponderous body into the water. | (fig., derog) the ponderous government machinery of Whitehall **2** derog dull and solemn; lacking lightness or grace: a ponderous style of writing | the city's ponderous architecture – ~ly adv – ~ness n [U]

pone /pəʊn/ n [U] CORN PONE

pong /pɒŋ‖pɑːŋ/ v, n [I] BrE infml derog (to make) an unpleasant smell – ~y adj : pongy socks

pon·iard /ˈpɒnjəd‖ˈpɑːnjərd/ n a small pointed knife used in former times as a weapon

Pon·ti·ac /ˈpɒntiæk‖ˈpɑːn-/ tdmk an American car made by General Motors

pon·tiff /ˈpɒntₔf‖ˈpɑːn-/ n tech for POPE

pon·tif·i·cal /pɒnˈtɪfɪkəl‖pɑːn-/ adj tech **1** with a priest of high rank in charge: a pontifical high mass **2** of or from a POPE: a pontifical letter

pon·tif·i·cate¹ /pɒnˈtɪfₔkeɪt‖pɑːn-/ v [I (about, on)] derog to give one's opinion or judgment as if it were the only correct one: Why must Father always pontificate about the duties of women?

pon·tif·i·cate² /pɒnˈtɪfɪkₔt‖pɑːn-/ n tech the position or period of office of a POPE: during the pontificate of John XXIII

Pon·tins /ˈpɒntɪnz‖ˈpɑːn-/ tdmk the name of several holiday villages in Britain where people go in the summer and where lots of entertainment is provided at a reasonable price, which made them popular with families and other less wealthy sections of British society: We always go to Pontins for our holidays.–see also BUTLINS

Pontius Pilate see Pontius PILATE

pon·toon¹ /pɒnˈtuːn‖pɑːn-/ n a floating hollow metal container or flat-bottomed boat that is fastened to others side by side to support a floating bridge (**pontoon bridge**) across a river

pontoon² n [U] BrE for BLACKJACK (1)

po·ny /ˈpəʊni/ n **1** a small horse –see also PIT PONY, SHANKS'S PONY, SHETLAND PONY **2** AmE infml a very small bottle of an alcoholic drink: Could I have a pony of gin, please?

Pony Club /ˈ·· ·/ [the] a British club which arranges horse riding activities for children

pony ex·press /ˌ··· ·ˈ·/ n an American postal service in the 1860s which used horses and riders to take the post from Missouri to California. It moved the post much more quickly than any other way.

po·ny·tail /ˈpəʊniteɪl/ n hair tied in a bunch high at the back of the head and falling like a horse's tail: She has a ponytail/wears her hair in a ponytail. –compare PIGTAIL, PLAIT

pony-trek·king /ˈ·· ˌ··/ n [U] BrE a holiday activity or sport in which people ride across the country on ponies

poo also **pooh** /puː/ ‖ also **poo-poo** /ˈ· ·/, **poop** AmE– infml **1** [U] (used esp. by and to children) solid waste from the bowels; EXCREMENT **2** [S] (used esp. by and to children) an act of passing this waste from the body: Mummy, Lucy's done a poo. –poo v [I;T] infml : Bobby's pooed his pants.

pooch /puːtʃ/ n infml, usu. humor a dog

poo·dle /ˈpuːdl/ n **1** a dog with thick curling hair, often cut in special shapes –see picture at DOG **2** be someone's poodle BrE humor derog to be too ready to obey someone or support them in whatever they do

poof, **pouf** /puːf, pʊf/ also **poof·ter** /ˈpuːftə‖r, ˈpʊf-/– n BrE & AustrE derog sl a male HOMOSEXUAL – ~y adj

pooh /puː/ interj infml (used for expressing dislike of an unpleasant smell)

Pooh also **Pooh Bear** /ˌ· ˈ·/ see WINNIE THE POOH

pooh-pooh /ˌ· ˈ·/ v [T] infml to express a very low opinion of (an idea, suggestion, effort, etc.) and say that one does not think it will work: I thought it was quite a good idea, but she pooh-poohed it.

Pooh·sticks /ˈpuːstɪks/ n [U] a game played by children (and some adults) in which sticks are thrown into a stream above a bridge, after which the players watch to see which stick appears at the other side of the bridge first (from the stories of Winnie the Pooh, in which the game is described).

pool¹ /puːl/ n **1** a small area of still water in a hollow place, usu. naturally formed: *a rock pool* (=among rocks on the sea shore) **2** [(of)] a small amount of any liquid poured or dropped on a surface: *The wounded man was lying in a pool of blood.* **3** a SWIMMING POOL: *They had a dip in the hotel pool before lunch.* **4** a deeper part of a river where the water is almost still —compare POND

pool² n **1** [C] a supply of money, goods, workers, etc., which is shared between and may be used by a number of people: *a pool of skilled labour* —see also CAR POOL, TYPING POOL **2** [C] an amount of money collected from all the players in certain card games, which forms the winner's prize **3** [U] an American game of BILLIARDS played usu. with 15 numbered balls on a table that has six holes —compare SNOOKER¹; see also POOLS

pool³ v [T] to combine; share; bring together for the advantage of everyone in a group: *If we pool our ideas, we may be able to produce a really good plan.* | *None of us can afford it separately, so let's pool our resources.*

Poole /puːl/ a town and port on the SW coast of England, on **Poole Harbour**, a large natural sheltered area of water with an opening to the sea.

pool hall /ˈ· ·/ n AmE POOLROOM

pool·room /ˈpuːlruːm, -rʊm/ n a place where one can play pool. Poolrooms are often dark and filled with smoke and used mostly by men.

pools /puːlz/ also **football pools** fml— n [the+P] (esp. in Britain) an arrangement by which people risk smallamounts of money on the results of certain football matches, and those who guess the results correctly win large shares of the collected money. Many people do this, even people who are not particularly interested in football: *He's just won £1000 on the pools.*

poop /puːp/ n **1** tech the back end of a ship **2** also **poop deck** /ˈ· ·/— the raised floor level at this end **3** AmE sl information, esp. with a dependable but unofficial origin: *Who can give me the poop on this new computer?* **4** AmE for POO

pooped /puːpt/ also **pooped out** /ˌ· ˈ·/— adj [F] infml, esp. AmE very tired

pooper n see PARTY POOPER

poo-poo /ˈ· ·/ AmE for POO

poop-scoop /ˈ· ·/ also **poop·er-scoop·er** /ˈpuːpə ˌskuːpəʳ ‖-pər-/— n infml a small spade-like device used by dog owners for removing dog EXCREMENT from the streets. In many towns and cities it is a crime for people not to clean up after their dogs, so they take a poop-scoop with them when they take their dogs for a walk.

poor /pʊəʳ/ adj **1** having very little money and therefore a low standard of living: *He was too poor to buy shoes for his family.* | *a poor neighbourhood with high unemployment* [also n, the+P] *This government has helped the rich but done nothing to improve the condition of the poor.* **2** rather fml far below the usual standard; low in quality; INFERIOR: *The weather has been very poor this summer.* | *They blamed the situation on poor management.* | *My German is rather poor, and I couldn't make myself understood.* **3** rather fml less than is needed or expected; small in size or quantity: *We had a poor crop of beans this year.* **4** rather fml (of health) weak; not good: *He's still in poor health after his illness.* **5** [A] derog (of someone who loses) showing displeasure instead of praising one's opponent: *He gets angry when he loses a game — he's a poor loser.* **6** [A] deserving or causing pity; unlucky: *Poor David has failed his driving test again.*

poor boy /ˈ· ·/ n AmE for SUBMARINE SANDWICH

poor·house /ˈpʊəhaʊs ‖ˈpʊər-/ n -houses /ˌhaʊzz/ (in former times) a building provided by public money where poor people could live and be fed —see also WORKHOUSE

poor law /ˈ· ·/ n **1** [the] (in Britain in former times) a group of laws concerning help for poor people **2** [C] any of these laws

poor·ly¹ /ˈpʊəli ‖ˈpʊərli/ adv rather fml **1** badly; not well:

poorly dressed | *poorly paid* | *They did poorly in the exam.* **2 think poorly of** to have a bad or low opinion of

poorly² adj [F] infml, esp. BrE ill: *I'm feeling rather poorly today.*

poorly off /ˌ·· ˈ·◂/ adj [F] **1** having very little money **2** [(for)] not having enough (of): *The school is poorly off for textbooks.* —opposite **well-off**

poor-mouth /ˈ· ·/ v [I;T] AmE to say that something or someone is not as good as it really is: *He poor-mouths his achievements because he thinks other people don't like really clever people.*

poor·ness /ˈpʊənɪs ‖ˈpʊər-/ n [U (of)] rather fml lowness (of quality); lack of a desired quality: *the poorness of the quality of the materials* —compare POVERTY

poor re·la·tion /ˌ· ·ˈ···/ n a person or thing that is the lowest or least important one among similar people or things: *Theatre musicians are often treated like the poor relations of the musical profession.*

poor-spir·it·ed /ˌ· ˈ····◂/ adj lit derog not brave; lacking confidence or courage —~ly adv

poor white trash /ˌ· · ˈ·/ n [U] AmE derog poor white people who are not well educated and of the lowest social level

pop¹ /pɒp ‖pɑːp/ v -pp- **1** [I;T] to (cause to) make a short sharp explosive sound: *The champagne cork popped when I pulled it out.* | *He blew the bag up and then popped it between his hands.* **2** [I+adv/prep] infml to move quickly or suddenly away from a surface; spring: *The child's eyes almost popped out of her head with excitement.* | *A button popped off my shirt when I sneezed.* **3** [I+adv/prep] infml to go or come suddenly, quickly, or unexpectedly: *I've just popped in to return your book.* | *I'm afraid she's just popped out for a few minutes.* | *Pop down to the shops and get a bottle of milk.* **4** [T+obj+adv/prep] infml to put quickly and lightly: *He popped his head round the door.* | *I'll just pop this cake in the oven.* **5** [T] BrE infml to use (PILLS) too often: *He was popping pills all afternoon, trying to calm his nerves.* **6** [T] BrE old-fash sl for PAWN¹ **7 pop one's clogs** BrE infml humor to die, esp. unexpectedly **8 pop the question** infml to ask someone to marry you

pop off phr v [I] infml to die, esp. unexpectedly

pop up phr v [I] infml **1** to happen or appear suddenly or unexpectedly —see also POP-UP **2** (in BASEBALL) to hit a ball into the air so that it does not travel very far away from the hitter: *He popped up to first* (=he hit the ball in the air towards the player at first base)

pop² n **1** [C] a sound like that of a slight explosion: *When he opened the bottle it went pop.* (=made this sound) **2** [U] also **soda** esp. AmE— infml, a sweet FIZZY drink, usu. made to taste of a particular fruit: *a bottle of pop*

pop³ n [U] modern popular music of a simple kind with a strong beat and not usu. of lasting interest, liked esp. by younger people: *I don't like classical music; I prefer pop.* | *pop music* | *a pop concert* —compare ROCK³, ROCK 'N' ROLL

pop³ n [U] POP MUSIC: *I don't like classical music; I prefer pop.*

pop⁴ n esp. AmE infml a father: *Can I borrow the car, pop?*

pop⁵ abbrev. for: population

pop·a·dum /ˈpɒpədəm ‖ˈpɑː-/ also **papadum, poppadum**— n a very thin flat Indian bread cooked in hot fat

pop art /ˌ· ˈ·◂/ n [U] a form of modern art which shows common objects from everyday life, such as advertisements, articles found around the house, etc., rather than the usual subjects of art —compare OP ART

pop·corn /ˈpɒpkɔːn ‖ˈpɑːpkɔːrn/ n [U] a type of MAIZE that swells and bursts open when heated, usu. eaten warm with salt and butter or sweetened with sugar. People often eat popcorn while they are watching a film at the cinema.

pope /pəʊp/ n (often cap.) **1** the head of the Roman Catholic Church: *The Pope will visit Britain next year.* | *Pope John XXIII* —compare PAPAL **2 Is the Pope Catholic?** infml humor (said to show that something is thought to be true or clear to everybody): *"Bill got stopped by the police for drunken driving." "Will he lose his licence?" "Is the Pope Catholic?"* (=he most certainly will lose it). See picture on page 1022

Pope, Al·ex·an·der /ˌælɪg-ˈzɑːndəʳ‖-ˈzæn-/ (1688–1744) a British SATIRICAL poet who wrote the *Rape of the Lock*, which describes the foolishness of fashionable people

the Pope

pop·e·ry /ˈpəʊpəri/ *n* [U] *derog, esp. old use* the teachings and forms of worship of the Roman Catholic Church

pope's nose /ˈ· ·/ *n AmE for* PARSON'S NOSE

Pop·eye /ˈpɒpaɪ‖-ˈpɑː-/ a popular American CARTOON character. Popeye is a SAILOR who smokes a pipe and when he eats SPINACH his muscles grow bigger and he becomes very strong.

pop-eyed /ˌ· ˈ·◄/ *adj infml* having the eyes wide open, esp. with surprise or excitement

pop fly /ˈ· ·/ *n* (in BASEBALL) a ball which is hit into the air and travels only a short distance: *a pop fly to first base*

Pop Goes the Wea·sel /ˌ· · · ˈ··/ the title of an old children's song:
> *Half a pound of tuppenny rice,*
> *Half a pound of treacle;*
> *That's the way the money goes,*
> *Pop goes the weasel!*

pop group /ˈ· ·/ *n* a group of people who sing and/or play POP³

pop·gun /ˈpɒpgʌn‖ˈpɑːp-/ *n* a toy gun that fires small objects, esp. CORKS¹ (2), with a loud noise

pop·in·jay /ˈpɒpɪndʒeɪ‖ˈpɑː-/ *n derog old use* a showily-dressed young man who is full of self-admiration

pop·ish /ˈpəʊpɪʃ/ *adj derog, esp. old use* Roman Catholic – **~ness** *n* [U]

pop·lar /ˈpɒpləʳ‖ˈpɑːp-/ *n* a very tall straight thin tree

pop·lin /ˈpɒplɪn‖ˈpɑːp-/ *n* [U] a strong shiny cotton cloth: *a poplin shirt*

Pop·o·cat·é·pet·l /ˌpɒpəkætəˈpetl‖ˌpəʊ-/ a mountain in Mexico, known in Britain esp. because its name is difficult to say

pop·o·ver /ˈpɒpəʊvəʳ‖ˈpɑː-/ *n AmE* a light hollow cake made with eggs, milk, and flour and often filled with fruit: *an apple popover* —compare TURNOVER (4)

pop·pa /ˈpɒpə‖ˈpɑːpə/ *n AmE infml* a father

pop·pa·dum /ˈpɒpədəm‖ˈpɑː-/ *n* a POPADUM

pop·per /ˈpɒpəʳ‖ˈpɑː-/ *n infml for* PRESS-STUD

Popper, Sir Karl /kɑːl‖kɑːrl/ (1902–) a British thinker (PHILOSOPHER) who thought that ideas about the world must be able to be shown scientifically to be true or false

pop·pet /ˈpɒpɪt‖ˈpɑː-/ *n BrE infml* a child or animal that one loves or that pleases one: *Come here, poppet.* | *Look at that little dog. Isn't he a poppet!*

Poppy Day

pop·py /ˈpɒpi‖ˈpɑːpi/ *n* a plant that has brightly coloured flowers, esp. red ones

▶ CULTURAL NOTE For British people the poppy represents

the soldiers who died in the two World Wars (particularly the First World War) because these flowers grew in the fields of France where many were buried. At the beginning of November, near Remembrance Day (often called **Poppy Day**), many people buy red poppies made of paper to show that they remember the men who died. —see also REMEMBRANCE DAY ◀

pop·py·cock /ˈpɒpikɒk‖ˈpɑːpika:k/ *n* [U] *infml* foolish nonsense: *He's talking pure poppycock!*

pop·py·seed /ˈpɒpisiːd‖ˈpɑː-/ *n* the small black seeds of the poppy plant used in food, esp. bread or cakes: *poppyseed rolls*

pops /pɒps‖pɑːps/ *adj AmE* (of music) being or connected with familiar CLASSICAL music or popular music played by an ORCHESTRA: *a pops concert* | *Arthur Fiedler and the Boston Pops Orchestra*

Pop·si·cle /ˈpɒpsɪkəl‖ˈpɑː-/ *n AmE tdmk for* ICE LOLLY

pop sing·er /ˈ· ˌ··/ *n* a person who sings pop songs

pop song /ˈ· ·/ *n* a modern popular song usu. of a simple kind with a strong beat, liked esp. by young people

pop·star /ˈpɒpstɑːʳ‖ˈpɑːp-/ *n* a famous and successful POP³ musician

pop·u·lace /ˈpɒpjʊləs‖ˈpɑː-/ *n [the+sing./pl. v] fml* all the people of a country, esp. those without high social position, wealth, etc.; the MASSES: *Panic had spread among the populace as a result of the rumours.*

pop·u·lar /ˈpɒpjʊləʳ‖ˈpɑː-/ *adj* **1** [(with)] liked by many people: *a popular holiday resort* | *a popular decision that almost everyone approved of* | *That teacher's very popular with her pupils.* | (*humor*) *You'll be popular when they find out you've broken their window!* (=they will be angry with you) —opposite **unpopular** **2** general; common; widespread: *"Mary" used to be quite a popular name for a girl.* **3** [A] *sometimes derog* suited to the understanding, liking, or needs of most ordinary people: *popular science* | *The popular newspapers take a great interest in the royal family.* **4** [A *no comp.*] of or from the general public: *popular opinion* | *The TV series was brought back* **by popular demand.** (=because lots of people wanted it) | *a policy that enjoys wide popular support* | *It's a popular misconception* (=lots of people think, wrongly) *that nearly all snakes are poisonous.* —see also POPULARLY

popular cap·i·tal·is·m /ˌ··· ˈ·····/ *n* [U] a RIGHT-WING political and economic system where the aim is for people to pay lower taxes and for the government to spend less money on houses, hospitals etc. The government also encourages people to buy their own homes and to start their own small businesses. These ideas were particularly fashionable in Britain during the 1980s.

pop·u·lar·i·ty /ˌpɒpjʊˈlærɪti‖ˌpɑː-/ *n* [U] the quality of being well liked, approved of, or admired: *the President's declining popularity* —opposite **unpopularity**

pop·u·lar·ize also **-ise** *BrE* /ˈpɒpjʊləraɪz‖ˈpɑː-/ *v* [T] **1** to cause to be well known and generally liked or used: *Reggae music was popularized by Bob Marley in the 1970s.* **2** to make (a difficult subject or idea) easily understandable to ordinary people —**-ization** /ˌpɒpjʊləraɪˈzeɪʃən‖ˌpɑːpjʊlərə-/ *n* [U]

pop·u·lar·ly /ˈpɒpjʊləli‖ˈpɑːpjʊlərli/ *adv* generally; by most people: *It's popularly believed that taking large amounts of vitamin C cures colds.*

popular press /ˌ··· ˈ·/ *[the]* newspapers read by less educated people and which are more concerned with sex, violence, funny events, and the private lives of film or TV stars than with national and international news – see also GUTTER PRESS, TABLOID; compare QUALITY PAPER

pop·u·late /ˈpɒpjʊleɪt‖ˈpɑː-/ *v* [T] **1** [*often pass.*] (of a group) to live in (an area); INHABIT: *This side of the island is populated mainly by fishermen.* | *a densely-populated area* **2** (of a group) to come and live in (an area): *The new land was quickly populated by settlers from abroad.*

pop·u·la·tion /ˌpɒpjʊˈleɪʃən‖ˌpɑː-/ *n [usu sing.]* **1** the number of people living in a particular area, country, etc.: *What was the population of Europe in 1900?* | *There's been a real* **population explosion** *here over the last decade.* (=the population has become very much larger) | *a city with a population of almost two million* **2** [+*sing./pl. v*] the people living in an area: *Half the world's population doesn't get enough to eat.* **3** [+*sing./pl. v*] a particular group or type of people or animals living in a particular place: *He has a lot of support among the country's white population.* | *the elephant population of Kenya*

pop·u·list /ˈpɒpjᵿlᵻst‖ˈpɑː-/ n **1** *often derog* a person who claims to believe in the wisdom and judgment of ordinary people, esp. in political matters **2** *(often cap.)* (esp. in the US) a member of a political party that claims to represent ordinary people —**lism** n [U]

pop·u·lous /ˈpɒpjᵿləs‖ˈpɑː-/ adj (of a place) having a large population, esp. when compared with size: *London is the most populous area of Britain.* — ~ **ness** n [U]

pop-up /ˈ· ·/ adj [A] made in such a way that what is inside can spring up or out: *a pop-up toaster* | *a pop-up book*

Pop War·ner /ˌ· ˈ··/ an American organization which teaches children to play FOOTBALL (2) in teams

porce·lain /ˈpɔːslᵻn‖ˈpɔːrsᵊlᵻn/ also **china**— n [U] (articles made of) a hard white substance made by baking a special sort of fine clay at a high temperature: *a porcelain figure* —compare EARTHENWARE

porch /pɔːtʃ‖pɔːrtʃ/ n **1** a roofed entrance built out from a house or church —see pictures at CHURCH and HOUSE **2** *AmE for* VERANDA

por·cine /ˈpɔːsaɪn‖ˈpɔːr-/ adj *tech or derog* of or like a pig

por·cu·pine /ˈpɔːkjᵿpaɪn‖ˈpɔːr-/ n a short-legged animal that has long sharp QUILLs all over its back and sides —compare HEDGEHOG

pore¹ /pɔːʳ/ n a very small opening, esp. in the skin, through which liquids, esp. SWEAT² (1), can pass

pore² v

porcupine

pore over sthg. *phr v* [T] to study or give close attention to (usu. something written or printed): *many hours spent in the library poring over musty documents*

pork /pɔːk‖pɔːrk/ n [U] meat from pigs: *a pork chop* —compare BACON, HAM¹ (1); see MEAT (USAGE)

pork bar·rel /ˈ· ˌ··/ n *AmE sl* a government plan to spend a lot of money in an area in order to gain political advantage: *The party won a great increase in votes as a result of its pork-barrel politics.*

pork·er /ˈpɔːkəʳ‖ˈpɔːr-/ n **1** a young pig, made specially fat before being killed for food **2** *humor* a pig

pork pie /ˌ· ˈ·/ n **1** [C;U] (esp. in Britain) a small usu. round baked pastry case containing small pieces of cooked pork **2** [C] *BrE infml humor* a lie: *He told quite a few pork pies at that interview!*

pork·pie hat /ˌpɔːkpaɪ ˈhæt‖ˌpɔːrk-/ n *BrE* a hat shaped like a pork pie, popular with followers of SKA music

pork rinds /ˈ· ˌ·/ n [P] *AmE* for SCRATCHINGS

pork·y /ˈpɔːki‖ˈpɔːrki/ adj *infml* (esp. of a person) fat

Porky Pig /ˌ·· ˈ·/ an American television CARTOON character

porn /pɔːn‖pɔːrn/ n [U] *infml* pornography —**porn, por·no** /ˈpɔːnəʊ‖ˈpɔːr-/ adj: *a porno movie* | *the porn king/queen of Soho* (=the most important man or woman in the pornography business in Soho)

por·nog·ra·phy /pɔːˈnɒɡrəfi‖pɔːrˈnɑːɡ-/ n [U] **1** *derog* the treatment of sexual subjects in pictures, writing or film in a way that is meant to cause sexual excitement **2** books, photographs, films, etc., containing this: *Police have seized several consignments of pornography.*

▶CULTURAL NOTE Although people are often too embarrassed or ashamed to admit that they read pornographic magazines, you can find them in most shops which sell newspapers and many people buy them, esp. men. The type of pornography that you see in newspaper shops is called soft pornography and shows NAKED people, esp. women. It is considered much more acceptable than HARD-CORE pornography, which is usu. sold in special sex shops and is offensive to a great many people because it shows sex in more detail and may show violent acts. Many women do not like pornography because they think it encourages bad treatment of or violence against women. There are laws about what you can show in this type of book, film etc. and people can go to prison for selling illegal pornographic materials. ◀

—**pher** n —**phic** /ˌpɔːnəˈɡræfɪk◀‖ˌpɔːr-/ adj —**phically** /kli/ adv

po·rous /ˈpɔːrəs/ adj allowing liquid to pass slowly through: *porous soil* | *This clay pot is porous.* — ~ **ness**, -**rosity** *tech*— /pɔːˈrɒsᵻti‖-ˈrɑː-, pə-/ n [U]

por·poise /ˈpɔːpəs‖ˈpɔːr-/ n a fishlike sea animal rather like a DOLPHIN that swims about in groups —see picture at DOLPHIN

por·ridge /ˈpɒrɪdʒ‖ˈpɑː-, ˈpɔː-/ *BrE* ‖ **oatmeal** *AmE*— n [U] **1** a soft breakfast food made by boiling OATMEAL (=crushed grain) in milk or water. Porridge used to be typical of Scotland but is now eaten everywhere in Britain and the US. **2** *BrE sl* a period of time spent in prison: *"Where's Mick got to?" "He's doing porridge."*

Porridge a British television COMEDY programme about life in prison, with Ronnie Barker as the main actor

Porsche /pɔːʃ, ˈpɔːʃə‖-ɔːr-/ n *tdmk* a very expensive type of car, often associated with rich young men

port¹ /pɔːt‖pɔːrt/ n **1** [C;U] a place where ships can load and unload people or goods; HARBOUR: *The main problem is getting the food from the ports to the interior of the country.* | *ships coming into/leaving port* **2** [C] *(sometimes cap. as part of a name)* a town with a HARBOUR or DOCKs, on a sea coast or on a river: *London used to be Britain's largest port.* | *Port Said* **3** *any port in a storm* any means of escape from trouble must be accepted, even if it has some disadvantages —see also AIRPORT, FREE PORT, PORT OF CALL, PORT OF ENTRY

port² n [U] the left side of a ship or aircraft as one faces forward: *The damaged ship was leaning over to port.* | *on the port side* —compare STARBOARD

port³ n [U] strong usu. sweet dark Portuguese wine, usu. drunk after a meal. In Britain in the past, after formal dinner parties, the men would stay behind to have a glass of port while the women went into another room.

port⁴ v **port arms** *(usu. imperative)* (of a soldier) to hold a RIFLE in a sloping position across the body, so that it can be examined by an officer

port⁵ n *tech* an opening on a computer by which connections can be made with other pieces of equipment such as printers or DISK DRIVEs

por·ta·ble /ˈpɔːtəbəl‖ˈpɔːr-/ adj that can be (easily) carried or moved; quite small and light: *a portable television/typewriter* | (fig.) *a portable pension* (=that can be moved from one job to another) —**bility** /ˌpɔːtəˈbɪlᵻti‖ˌpɔːr-/ n [U]

por·ta·crib /ˈpɔːtəkrɪb‖ˈpɔːr-/ n *AmE tdmk* a CARRYCOT —see picture at BED

Por·ta·kab·in /ˈpɔːtəkæbᵻn‖ˈpɔːr-/ n *tdmk* a small hut which can be moved by LORRY and used as a temporary office, etc., esp. while a new building is being built

por·tals /ˈpɔːtlz‖ˈpɔːrtlz/ n [P] **(of)** *fml or pomp* **1** a very large and important-looking entrance to a building, esp considered as representing the organization, company, etc., that uses that building **2** a beginning; THRESHOLD (2): *standing at the portals of happiness*

port·cul·lis /pɔːtˈkʌlᵻs‖pɔːrt-/ n (in old castles, forts, etc.) a strong gatelike structure of bars with points at the bottom, hung above an entrance and lowered as a protection against attack —see picture at CASTLE

por·tend /pɔːˈtend‖pɔːr-/ v [T] *fml or lit* to be a sign or warning of (a future unpleasant event): *What do these strange events portend?*

por·tent /ˈpɔːtent‖ˈpɔːr-/ n *fml or lit* [(of)] a clear sign or warning, esp. of something strange or unpleasant; OMEN: *Dark clouds are gathering, portents of war.*

por·ten·tous /pɔːˈtentəs‖pɔːr-/ adj esp. *lit* **1** *fml derog* solemnly self-important; POMPOUS **2** that warns or tells of future unpleasant events; threatening — ~ **ly** adv

por·ter¹ /ˈpɔːtəʳ‖ˈpɔːr-/ n **1** a person employed to carry travellers' bags at railway stations, airports, etc. Most people now carry their own bags or use a TROLLEY. **2** a person employed to carry loads at markets **3** esp. *BrE* a person in charge of the entrance to a hotel, school, hospital, etc. —compare JANITOR (2) **4** *AmE* an attendant employed in a sleeping-carriage in a train

porter² n [U] (esp. in former times) a dark brown bitter beer

Porter, Cole /ˈkəʊl/ (1891–1964) an American COMPOSER who wrote many famous songs including *Night and Day* and *Let's Do It.* He also wrote MUSICALs and some of these, such as *Kiss Me Kate* and *Can-Can* were made into films. The words of Cole Porter's songs are considered to be WITTY and clever and when people imagine a Cole Porter musical they think of a world of fashionable and SOPHISTICATED people.

Porter, Kath·e·rine Anne /ˈkæθərɪn æn/ (1890–1980) an American short story writer

por·ter·house /ˈpɔːtəhaʊs‖ˈpɔːrtər-/ also **porterhouse steak** /ˌ···ˈ·/— n [C;U] (a) STEAK of high-quality BEEF

port·fo·li·o /pɔːtˈfəʊliəʊ‖pɔːrt-/ n -lios 1 a large flat case like a very large book cover, for carrying drawings, business papers, etc. 2 a collection of drawings or other papers contained in this: *The artist showed us a portfolio of her drawings.* 3 a collection of different business shares owned by a particular person or company: *an investment portfolio* 4 the job of a particular government minister: *The Prime Minister offered him the foreign affairs portfolio.* | *a minister* **without portfolio** (=who is not responsible for any particular government department)

port·hole /ˈpɔːthəʊl‖ˈpɔːrt-/ n a small usu. circular window in the side of a ship or aircraft

por·ti·co /ˈpɔːtɪkəʊ‖ˈpɔːr-/ n -coes or -cos a covered entrance to a building, sometimes consisting of a roof supported by PILLARS

por·tion[1] /ˈpɔːʃən‖ˈpɔːr-/ n [(of)] 1 [C] a part of something larger, considered separately from the rest: *the front portion of the train* | *The computer factory represents only a small portion of the company's business.* | *the first portion of the book* 2 [C] a share of something that is divided among two or more people: *The driver must bear a portion of the blame for the accident* 3 [C] a standard amount of a particular food for one person as served in a restaurant: *He was hungry and ordered an extra portion of potatoes.* 4 [S] *fml or lit* a person's fate or fortune; LOT[2] (6): *Sorrow has always been her portion.*

portion[2] v

portion sthg. ↔ **out** *phr v* [T (**among, between**)] to divide and give; share: *The money was portioned out among the four children.*

Port·land /ˈpɔːtlənd‖ˈpɔːrt-/ an inland port in NW Oregon, USA and the largest city in the state

port·ly /ˈpɔːtli‖ˈpɔːr-/ adj euph or humor (esp. of a rather old man) round and fat; STOUT: *a portly old gentleman* —**liness** n [U]

port·man·teau /pɔːtˈmæntəʊ‖pɔːrt-/ n -teaus or -teaux /təʊz/ old-fash a very large case for a traveller's clothes, esp. one that opens into two equal parts

portmanteau word /ˌ···ˌ·/ n an invented word that combines the meaning and sound of two words; BLEND: *"Motel" is a portmanteau word, made up from "motor" and "hotel".*

Port·mei·ri·on /pɔːtˈmeriən‖pɔːrt-/ a small village in the Italian style in N Wales, all planned by Clough Williams-Ellis and popular with tourists

Port·o·bel·lo Road /ˌpɔːtəbeləʊ ˈrəʊd‖ˌpɔːr-/ [(the)] a street in W London known for its Saturday market for ANTIQUES (=furniture, jewellery, etc. made in an earlier period)

port of call /ˌ··ˈ·/ n ports of call 1 a port where a ship stops (regularly) for travellers, supplies, repairs, etc. 2 *infml* a place which one visits or stops at during a journey or set of activities: *My next port of call is the library.*

port of en·try /ˌ··ˈ··/ n ports of entry a place such as a HARBOUR or airport where people or goods may enter a country

Port of Lon·don Au·thor·i·ty /ˌ·· ·ˌ·· ·ˈ···/ also **PLA** abbrev.— [the] the organization which controls the port of London

Por·ton Down /ˌpɔːtn ˈdaʊn‖ˌpɔːr-/ a place in the S of England with a government LABORATORY formerly used for studying GERM WARFARE (=the use of disease-producing bacteria in war)

Por·to Ri·co /ˌpɔːtəʊ ˈriːkəʊ‖ˌpɔːr-/ see PUERTO RICO

por·trait /ˈpɔːtrɪt‖ˈpɔːr-/ n 1 [(of)] a painting, drawing, or photograph of a real person or group of people: *I commissioned her to paint my portrait.* (=a picture of me) | *a portrait painter* | (fig.) *His book gives/paints a very convincing portrait* (=description) *of life in medieval England.* —see picture at CARICATURE 2 PORTRAIT MODE

portrait mode /ˈ·· ˌ·/ n [U] tech in portrait mode (of paper, or a picture on a page) with the shorter edge from left to right (HORIZONTAL) and the longer edge from top to bottom (VERTICAL): *I can't get my file to print out in portrait mode.* —compare LANDSCAPE MODE

Portrait of the Ar·tist as a Young Man /ˌ·· ·· ·ˌ·· ·· ·· ˈ·/ a book by James Joyce based on the story of his own life

por·trai·ture /ˈpɔːtrɪtʃəʳ‖ˈpɔːr-/ n [U] the art of making portraits

por·tray /pɔːˈtreɪ‖pɔːr-/ v [T] 1 to be or make a representation or description of: *This painting portrays the death of Nelson.* | *The writer portrays life in a refugee camp very vividly.* 2 [(**as**)] to describe according to one's opinion: *In British history books Richard III is usually portrayed as a wicked man.* 3 to act the part of (a particular character) in a play — — **al** n [C;U (**of**)] : *The actor's portrayal of Othello was superb.*

Ports·mouth /ˈpɔːtsməθ‖ˈpɔːr-/ a town and port on the S coast of England, known for its navy base and as a place from which ferries (FERRY[1]) go to France

Port Stan·ley /ˌ·ˈ··/ the capital of the Falkland Islands. It was the centre of attention during the Falklands War of 1982 as the place where the war started and ended.

Port Tal·bot /pɔːt ˈtɔːlbət‖pɔːrt-/ a port and industrial town in S Wales

Por·tu·gal /ˈpɔːtʃʊgəl‖ˈpɔːr-/ a country in SW Europe, W of Spain, bordering the Atlantic; capital Lisbon; population 10,467,000 (1989). Portugal is a popular holiday place for British people.

Por·tu·guese /ˌpɔːtʃʊˈgiːz◂‖ˌpɔːr-/ n 1 [the +P] people from Portugal 2 [U] of the language of Portugal, Brazil, etc. —**Portuguese** adj : *I'm Portuguese.|Portuguese wine*

Portuguese man-of-war /ˌ··· · ·ˈ·/ n a large JELLYFISH with long poisonous parts (TENTACLES) hanging beneath its floating body

pose[1] /pəʊz/ v 1 [I (**for**); T] to (cause to) sit or stand in a particular position, esp. in order to be photographed, painted, etc.: *After the wedding we all posed for a photograph.* 2 [T] to be the cause of (something difficult to deal with); PRESENT: *The high cost of oil poses serious problems for industry.* | *Pollution poses a threat to the continued existence of this species.* 3 [T] to ask (a question that is difficult or needs to be carefully thought about) 4 [I] *derog* to behave unnaturally or pretend to be cleverer, more artistic, etc. than one really is, in order to attract interest or admiration: *Stop posing!* —compare POSTURE[2]

pose as sthg. *phr v* [T] to pretend to be: *The spy posed as an office worker to get into the building.*

pose[2] n 1 a position in which someone stands, sits, etc., esp. in order to be photographed, painted, etc.: *The photographer stood his model in various poses.* 2 *derog* an unnatural way of behaving, or the act of pretending to be cleverer, more artistic, etc. than one really is, in order to attract (undeserved) interest or admiration; AFFECTATION: *He's always talking about his deep interest in literature, but it's just a pose.* —compare POSE[1]

Po·sei·don /pəˈsaɪdn/ the Greek name for NEPTUNE

pos·er /ˈpəʊzəʳ/ n infml 1 a difficult or awkward question 2 a matter that is awkward to deal with 3 derog esp. BrE a poseur

po·seur /pəʊˈzɜːʳ/ n derog somone who behaves unnaturally or pretends to be cleverer, more artistic, etc. than they really are, in order to attract attention or admiration —compare POSE[2] (2)

pos·ey /ˈpəʊzi/ adj infml of, or typical of, a poseur; PRETENTIOUS: *She disliked his posey remarks about how his work had influenced modern art.* | *a posey wine bar*

posh /pɒʃ‖pɑːʃ/ adj infml, esp. BrE 1 usu. apprec fashionable, splendid, and usu. expensive: *a posh hotel* 2 sometimes derog for or typical of people of high social class: *a posh part of town* | *a posh accent* —**posh** adv BrE nonstandard : *Doesn't she talk posh!*

pos·it /ˈpɒzɪt‖ˈpɑː-/ v [T] fml to suggest for the purpose of argument; POSTULATE

po·si·tion[1] /pəˈzɪʃən/ n 1 [C] a place where someone or something is or stands, esp. in relation to other objects, places, etc.: *The castle occupies a strategic position overlooking the valley.* | *This footballer usually plays in an attacking position.* | *Can you find our position on this* map? | *The army will attack the enemy's positions.* (=places where they have placed soldiers and guns) **2** [U] the place where someone or something is supposed to be; the proper place: *The shelves are held in position by metal brackets.* | *The rocket puts the satellite into position high above the Earth.* | *The guard took up his position outside the hospital door.* **3** [C] the way in which someone or something is placed or moves, stands, sits, etc.: *He had to work in a most uncomfortable position under the car.* | *in a sitting position* **4** [C (**in**)] a particular place or rank in an organization, competition, etc.: *She finished in second position in the race.* | *This sort of scandal could be disastrous to a man in my position.* (=of my high rank in society) **5** [C *usu. sing.*] a situation; state: *It was supposed to be secret; by telling everyone, you've put me in a very difficult position.* | *In the company's present position, they can't afford to offer higher wages.* [+to-v] *I'd like to help you, but I'm afraid I'm not in a position|I'm in no position to do so.* (=I can't) **6** [C (**on**)] an opinion or judgment on a matter; ATTITUDE: *What's your position on this question?* [+that] *He* **takes the position** *that what his sister does is no concern of his.* **7** [C (**with, in**)] *fml* a job; employment: *to apply for a position with|in an oil company* | *a position of responsibility* **8 jockey/manoeuvre/jostle for position** to compete keenly in order to gain an advantage over others who are trying to get the same thing as oneself: *They knew the director's job was going to become vacant soon, and they were both jockeying for position.* —see JOB (USAGE)

▷ USAGE Compare **place**, **position**, and **location**. **Place** is the ordinary word when talking about where something is or happens: *I'll show you the* **place** *where I was born.* **Position** is used to talk about the place where something is or should be in relation to other places: *He drew a plan showing the* **position** *of all the furniture in the room.* **Location** is a formal or technical word for **place** or **position**: *The company has found a suitable* **location** *for its new headquarters.*◁

position² *v* [T+*obj+adv|prep*] to put in the stated position: *He positioned himself just by the window so he could see what was going on outside.*

po·si·tion·al /pə'zɪʃənəl/ *adj* concerning position, esp. (in sports) the position that a player takes up on the field: *The manager made some positional changes for the next game.* (=kept the same players, but they played in different positions)

pos·i·tive¹ /'pɒzˌʒtɪv‖'pɑː-/ *adj* **1** [F (**of, about**)] (of a person) having no doubt; sure: *"Are you sure?" "Positive."* (=Yes, I am sure.) | *It seemed unlikely to me, but she seemed absolutely positive of|about it.* [+(*that*)] *Are you positive (that) you've never seen that man before?* **2** often *apprec* leading to practical action; CONSTRUCTIVE: *positive advice* | *positive thinking* **3** showing confidence and hope: *a positive attitude to life* **4** leaving no possibility of doubt; DEFINITE: *It's no use giving the police all these vague times and dates; they need something positive to go on.* | *These fingerprints are positive proof|proof positive that he used the gun.* **5** [*no comp.*] (in grammar) of the simple form of an adjective or adverb, which expresses no COMPARISON: *"Good" is the positive form of the adjective, "better" is the comparative.* —compare COMPARATIVE¹ (1), SUPERLATIVE¹ (1) **6** [*no comp.*] (in MATHEMATICS) (of a number or quantity) greater than zero: *Twelve is a positive amount.* **7** [*no comp.*] (of electricity) of the type that is carried by PROTONs **8** [*no comp.*] (of a photograph) having light and dark as they are in nature, not the other way around **9** (of a medical test) showing signs of the presence of a substance or growth: *The test was positive; you're pregnant!* **10** [*no comp.*] *med* having RHESUS FACTOR in the blood: *RH-positive blood* **11** [A *no comp.*] (used for giving force to a noun) complete; real: *It was a positive delight to hear her sing.* —opposite **negative** (for 2, 3, 6, 7, 8, 9, 10) — ~**ness** *n* [U]

positive² *n* **1** (in grammar) the POSITIVE¹ (5) form of an adjective or adverb: *The positive of "prettiest" is "pretty".* **2** a POSITIVE¹ (8) photograph

positive dis·crim·i·na·tion /ˌ··· ···'···/ *BrE* ‖ also **affirmative action**— *n* [U] the practice or principle of favouring people who are often treated unfairly, esp. because of their sex or race —compare REVERSE DISCRIMINATION

pos·i·tive·ly /'pɒzˌʒtɪvli‖'pɑː-/ *adv* **1** in a POSITIVE¹ (1,4) way, esp. (as if) with certainty: *He said quite positively*

that he would come, and we were all surprised when he didn't. **2** *infml* (used for adding force to an expression) really; in fact: *She's not just pretty, she's positively beautiful!* **3** *tech* in a POSITIVE¹ (7) way (esp. in the phrase **positively charged**)

positive pole /ˌ··· '·/ *n* **1** the end of a MAGNET which turns naturally towards the Earth **2** an ANODE

positive vet·ting /ˌ··· '··/ *n* [U] in Britain, the practice of checking certain government workers, before telling them official secrets, to make sure that they are not working against the state

pos·i·tiv·is·m /'pɒzˌʒtɪvɪzəm‖'pɑː-/ *n* [U] a PHILOSOPHY (=a system of thought) based on real facts that can be experienced and proved, rather than on ideas formed in the mind —**ist** *n*

pos·i·tron /'pɒzˌʒtrɒn‖'pɑːzˌʒtrɑːn/ *n* a very small piece of matter (ELEMENTARY PARTICLE) that is like an ELECTRON but is positively charged

poss. /pɒs‖pɑːs/ **1** *BrE infml abbrev. for:* possible: *Do it by Monday if poss.* **2** *written abbrev. for:* POSSESSIVE¹ (2) —compare PASS.

pos·se /'pɒsi‖'pɑːsi/ also **posse com·i·ta·tus** /ˌpɒsi kɒmɪ-'teɪtəs‖ˌpɑːsi kɑːm-/ *fml*— *n* [(*of*)] (in the US) a group of men gathered together by a SHERIFF (=local law officer) to help find a criminal or keep order: (fig.) *The film star was pursued all over the country by a posse* (=group) *of reporters.*

pos·sess /pə'zes/ *v* [T *not in progressive forms*] **1** *fml* to have as one's property, as a quality, etc.; own: *The police asked me if I possessed a gun.* **2** (of a feeling or idea) to influence (someone) so completely as to make them do esp. something foolish: [I *obj+to-v*] *I don't know what possessed him to* (=made him) *drive so fast down that busy street.*

pos·sessed /pə'zest/ *adj* **1** wildly mad, (as if) controlled by an evil spirit: [after *n*] *He was waving the knife and screaming like a man possessed.* **2** [F+**of**] *fml or lit* having: *He's never been possessed of* (=had) *much sense.* —see also SELF-POSSESSED

pos·ses·sion /pə'zeʃən/ *n* **1** [U (**of**)] the state of having, holding, or owning something; ownership: *Dangerous drugs were found in her possession|She was found in possession of dangerous drugs.* | *When her father died, she came into possession of a large fortune.* | *While our team is in possession|has possession* (=has the ball) *the other team can't score.* | *The police arrested him and took* **possession** *of certain substances found in his house.* (=they took the substances from him) | (*fml or pomp*) *According to facts in my possession* (=facts that I know about) *he cannot possibly be guilty.* **2** [U (**of**)] *esp. law* actual control and use: *We've bought the house, but we take|get possession (of it) before July.* **3** [C *often pl.*] a piece of personal property: *The people had to gather up their few possessions and escape to the hills.* **4** [C] a country controlled or governed by another: *Britain's former overseas possessions* **5** [U] the condition of being under the control of an evil spirit **6 possession is nine tenths/nine points of the law** a person who actually possesses a thing is in a better position to keep it than someone else who may have a better claim to own it

pos·ses·sive¹ /pə'zesɪv/ *adj* **1** *derog* **a** unwilling to share one's own things with other people **b** wanting someone to have feelings of love or friendship only for oneself: *a possessive father who resents his daughter's boyfriends* **2** (in grammar) of or being a word that shows ownership or connection: *"My" and "its" are possessive adjectives.* — ~**ly** *adv* — ~**ness** *n* [U]

possessive² *n* (in grammar) a possessive word or form: *"Hers" is the possessive of "she".* —compare GENITIVE

pos·ses·sor /pə'zesər/ *n* [(**of**)] *usu. sing.] fml* a person who owns or has something (often a quality rather than a piece of property): *He is the (proud) possessor of* (=he has) *a fine singing voice.*

pos·set /'pɒsˌʒt‖'pɑː-/ *n* a drink made from warm milk mixed with wine or beer, taken in former times to cure colds

pos·si·bil·i·ties /ˌpɒsˌʒ'bɪlˌʒtiz‖ˌpɑː-/ *n* [P] ability to be developed, improved, or made useful in the future; POTENTIAL: *The flat's in a poor condition but it has distinct possibilities if you can decorate it and clean it up a bit.*

pos·si·bil·i·ty /ˌpɒsˌʒ'bɪlˌʒti‖ˌpɑː-/ *n* **1** [S;U (**of**)] a (degree of) likelihood: *The fire looked like an accident, but the police are still considering the possibility of* (=considering whether it could have been) *arson.* [+*that*] *"Is there any possibility that you'll be back by the weekend?" "There's a strong possibility I won't."* **2** [U] the fact of being possible: *Travel outside our solar system is not within* **the realms of possibility** (=is not possible) *at present.* **3** [C] something that is possible: *The general would not accept that defeat was a possibility.*

pos·si·ble¹ /ˈpɒsɪbəlǁˈpɑː-/ *adj* **1** that can exist, happen, or be done: *It's no longer possible to find a cheap flat in London.* | *I'll do everything possible to help you. I'll help you* **if (at all) possible.** (=if it is possible) | *Do it* **as soon as possible.** (=as soon as you can) **2** [F] that may or may not be, happen, or be expected: *It is possible that the doctor may want you to have an X-ray.* | *The supermarket is probably closed by now, but it's possible that it's still/it will still be open.* **3** acceptable; suitable: *This is only one of many possible answers.*

possible² *n* **1** [*the*] that which can exist or can be done: *That's quite beyond the bounds of the possible!* (=that is completely impossible) **2** [C] a person or thing that might be suitable: *Emma's a possible for the job.*

pos·si·bly /ˈpɒsɪbliǁˈpɑː-/ *adv* **1** in accordance with what is possible: *I'll do all I possibly can.* | *You can't possibly walk 20 miles in an hour!* (=it's impossible) **2** perhaps: *"Will you come with us tomorrow?" "Possibly, I'm not sure yet."* | (in polite requests) *Could you possibly lend me £10?: Requests, Tentativeness*

pos·sum /ˈpɒsəmǁˈpɑː-/ also **opossum** *esp. BrE— n* **pos·sums** *or* **possum 1** any of various types of a small treeclimbing animal found in either America or Australia **2 play possum** *infml* to pretend to be asleep or inattentive in order to deceive someone

post¹ /pəʊst/ *n* **1** [C] (*often in comb.*) a strong thick upright pole or bar made of wood, metal, etc., fixed into the ground or some other base, esp. as a support: *The fence was made of wooden posts and barbed wire.* | *a gatepost* | *a signpost* **2** [*the*] the finishing place in a race, esp. a horse race: *The horses galloped towards the* **winning/finishing post.** | *My horse got beaten* **at the post.** (=when it was very close to finishing the race) **3** [C] *infml for* GOALPOST: *The ball hit the post.* —see also FIRST PAST THE POST, **from pillar to post** (PILLAR), **pipped at the post** (PIP⁴)

post² *esp. BrE* ǁ **mail** *esp. AmE— n* **1** [*the*;U] the official system for carrying letters, parcels, etc., from the sender to the receiver: *I sent the parcel by post.* | *My reply is in the post and you will probably receive it tomorrow.* | *The parcel got lost in the post.* —see also **by return (of post)** (RETURN² (6)) **2** [(*the*) S;U] (a single official collection or delivery of) letters, parcels, etc., sent by this means: *Has the post arrived?* | *A letter has come for you in the second post.* (=the second delivery of the day) | *Has any post come for me today?* **3** [*the*] *infml* an official place, box, etc., where stamped letters are left for sending: *I've just taken her birthday card down to the post.* —compare PILLAR BOX, POSTBOX, POST OFFICE; see also STAGING POST; see MAIL (USAGE)

post³ *v* [T(OFF, **to**)] **1** *esp. BrE* ǁ **mail** *esp. AmE—* to send (a letter, parcel, etc.) by post: *I must post off all my Christmas cards this week.* | *Could you post this letter for me please?* | *I posted it (to you) on Friday.* [+*obj(i)+obj(d)*] *Did you post John the book?* | (fig.) *Bring me back the key. If I'm not in when you call you can post it through my letterbox.* **2 keep someone posted** to continue to give someone all the latest news about something

post⁴ *n* **1** a job: *The vacant post was advertised in today's paper.* —see JOB (USAGE) **2 a** a special place of duty, esp. on guard or on watch: *The soldier was punished for falling asleep at his post.* **b** a military base or camp —see also LAST POST, TRADING POST

post⁵ ǁ also **station** *esp. AmE— v* [T] **1** to place (soldiers, policemen, etc.) on duty in a special place, esp. as a guard: *Pickets were posted at the factory gate.* **2** [+*obj+adv/prep*] *esp. BrE* to send or appoint to a particular army group, a place or duty with a company, etc.: *Jackson has been posted to Hong Kong/posted overseas.*

post⁶ *v* [T] **1** [(UP)] to put up a notice about (something) on a wall, board, post, etc., so as to make it public: *The names of the members of the team will be posted up today.* **2** [+*obj+adj;usu pass.*] to make known as being, by put-

ting up a notice: *The ship was posted missing.*

Post¹ [*the*] **1** see SUNDAY POST **2** see WASHINGTON POST

Post², Em·i·ly /ˈemɪliǁ/ (1872–1960) an American writer of books and newspaper articles on ETIQUETTE (=correct behaviour)

post- see WORD FORMATION

post·age /ˈpəʊstɪdʒ/ *n* [U] the money charged for carrying a letter, parcel, etc., by post: *Please enclose £5.50 plus 99p postage.*

postage me·ter /ˈ··ˌ··/ *n AmE* a machine which puts a mark on letters and packages to show that postage has been paid and which is used mostly by businesses

postage stamp /ˈ··ˌ·/ *n fml for* STAMP² (1)

post·al /ˈpəʊstl/ *adj* [A] *esp. BrE* **1** connected with the public letter service: *Postal charges have gone up again.* **2** sent by post: *a postal reminder*

postal or·der /ˈ··ˌ··/ *n* (in Britain) an official paper of a particular value which can be sent by post. The receiver can change it for money of the same value at a post office: *a 50p postal order* —compare MONEY ORDER

Postal Ser·vice /ˈ··ˌ··/ also **US Postal Service** [*the*] *AmE* the official name for the US government department responsible for collecting and delivering post

postal vote /ˈ··ˌ·/ *n* a vote sent through the post, esp. by a person who cannot be present to vote on the day of an election

post·bag /ˈpəʊstbæg/ *n esp. BrE* **1** [C] a postman's bag for carrying letters; MAILBAG **2** [S] *infml* all the letters received by someone at one particular time: *The magazine's advice column always gets a big postbag.*

post·box /ˈpəʊstbɒksǁ-bɑːks/ *esp. BrE* ǁ **mailbox, mail drop** *AmE— n* an official metal box in a public place, fixed to the ground or on a wall, into which people can put letters to be collected and sent by post —compare POST² (3); see also LETTERBOX, PILLAR BOX

post boxes

a British post box

post·card /ˈpəʊstkɑːdǁ-kɑːrd/ *n* **1** a card of a fixed size for sending messages by post without an envelope **2** also **picture postcard** *fml—* a card like this with a picture or photograph on one side

▶ CULTURAL NOTE People on holiday often send postcards to friends and to people in their family who are not on holiday. The words "Wish you were here" are often mentioned in jokes as being a typical thing to write on a postcard. In many seaside towns in Britain, there are **saucy postcards** on sale. These are usu. CARTOONS, often showing a large woman with big breasts, and a small, weak-looking man, and almost always involving a joke about sex. ◀

an American mailbox

post·code /ˈpəʊstkəʊd/ *BrE* ǁ **zip code** *AmE— n* a group of letters and/or numbers that mean a particular small area, and can be added to a postal address so that letters, etc. can be delivered more quickly

post·date /ˌpəʊstˈdeɪt/ *v* [T] **1** to write a date later than the actual date of writing on (a letter, cheque, etc.): *My rent's due on Monday and I'm not paid until Friday – I'll have to postdate the rent cheque.* —compare ANTEDATE, BACKDATE **2** to happen later in history than

post·doc·tor·al /ˌpəʊstˈdɒktərəlǁ-ˈdɑːk-/ also **post·doc** /ˌpəʊstˈdɒkǁ-ˈdɑːk/ *AmE infml— adj* of or related to ACADEMIC or professional work following a PHD

post·er /ˈpəʊstəʳ/ *n* a large printed notice, picture, or photograph: *They put up posters all round the town advertising the circus.*

poster col·our /ˈ··ˌ··/ *n* POSTER PAINT

poste res·tante /ˌpəʊstˈrestɒnt‖-resˈtɑːnt/ *BrE* ‖ **general delivery** *AmE*— *n* [U] a post office department to which letters for a traveller can be sent and where they will be kept until the person collects them

pos·te·ri·or¹ /pɒˈstɪəriəʳ‖pɑː-/ *adj* [*no comp.*] **1** [F+**to**] *fml* later (than); after **2** [A] (in BIOLOGY) nearer the back — opposite **anterior**

posterior² *n humor* the part of the body a person sits on; BOTTOM

pos·ter·i·ty /pɒˈsterɪti‖pɑː-/ *n* [U] (people of) the future: *His fame will* **go down to posterity.** (=He will be famous long after he is dead.) | *These wonderful paintings should be preserved for posterity.*

poster paint /ˈ··· ·/ also **poster colour**— *n* [C;U] brightly coloured paint that contains no oil, used e.g. for painting pictures, advertisements, etc.

post ex·change /ˈ· ·ˌ·/ *n AmE* PX

post·fem·i·nist /ˌpəʊstˈfemᵻnᵻst◂/ *adj* developing from and including the ideas and beliefs of FEMINISM (=a movement supporting equality for women): *a postfeminist book/writer/artist/approach*

post-free /ˌ·ˈ· ·◂/ *esp. BrE* ‖ **postpaid** *esp. AmE*— *adj, adv* without any (further) charge to the sender for posting: *Send £2 for our post-free catalogue.* —compare FREEPOST

post·grad·u·ate /ˌpəʊstˈgrædjuᵻt◂‖-ˈgrædʒuᵻt◂/ also **post·grad** *infml* ‖ **graduate** *esp. AmE*— *n, adj* (a person doing studies that are) done at a university after one has received one's first degree: *a postgraduate course*

post·haste /ˌpəʊstˈheɪst/ *adv lit* at very great speed; in a great hurry

post horn /ˈ·· ·/ *n* (in the 18th and 19th centuries) a horn blown by a person riding on a carriage as a warning

post·hu·mous /ˈpɒstjᵿməs‖ˈpɑːstʃə-/ *adj* — **~ly** *adv* happening after someone has died: *The medal was awarded posthumously.*

post·ie /ˈpəʊsti/ *n esp. ScotE, CanE, & AustrE infml* a postman

pos·til·ion , -till- /pəˈstɪljən/ *n* (in former times) a servant who rides on any of the horses pulling a carriage when there is no driver on or in the carriage. The words "my postilion has been struck by lightning" are sometimes mentioned in jokes as being a typical, nearly useless phrase found in an old-fashioned PHRASEBOOK for English people travelling abroad.

post-im·pres·sion·is·m /ˌ·· ·ˈ····/ *n* [U] a late 19th-century style of painting in which paintings have strong colour and a strong plan — **~ist** *n, adj*

post-in·dus·tri·al /ˌ·· ·ˈ·····◂/ *adj* of the period in the late 20th century when heavy industries (HEAVY INDUSTRY) have become less important, computers and ELECTRONICS more important, and people have more free time

post·ing /ˈpəʊstɪŋ/ *n* [(to)] *esp. BrE* an appointment to a POST⁴, esp. in the armed forces: *He wasn't very pleased about his posting to a remote northern town.*

postman

post·man /ˈpəʊstmən/ *esp. BrE* ‖ **mailman** *esp. AmE*— *n* **-men** /mən/ a person whose job is to collect and deliver letters, parcels, etc. People often make jokes about postmen being chased and bitten by fierce dogs while they are delivering letters.

Postman Pat /ˌ··· ·ˈ·/ a character in British books and television programmes for children. Postman Pat is a happy postman who drives around in his van delivering letters and parcels with his cat, Jess.

postman's knock /ˌ··· ·ˈ·/ *BrE* ‖ **post office** *AmE*— *n* [U] a children's game in which a player pretends to deliver a letter to another player and gets a kiss as a reward

post·mark /ˈpəʊstmɑːk‖-mɑːrk/ *n* an official mark made on a letter, parcel, etc., usu. over the stamp, showing when and from where it is sent —**postmark** *v* [T *usu. pass.*] : [+*obj*+*n*] *The parcel was postmarked Brighton.*

post·mas·ter /ˈpəʊstˌmɑːstəʳ‖-ˌmæ-/ **post·mis·tress** /-ˌmɪstrəs/ *fem.*— *n* a person in charge of a post office

Postmaster Gen·e·ral /ˌ··· ·ˈ···/ *n* Postmasters General a person who is in charge of a national postal system

post me·rid·i·em /ˌpəʊst məˈrɪdiəm/ *adv fml rare for* PM

post·mod·ern·is·m /ˌ·· ·ˈ····/ a style of building, decoration, art, etc., esp. in the 1980s, which uses an unusual mixing of old and new forms —compare MODERNISM (2) — **post-modernist** *n, adj*

post·mor·tem /ˌpəʊstˈmɔːtəm‖-ˈmɔːr-/ *n* **1** also **postmortem ex·am·i·na·tion** /·ˌ··· ···‖·/ *fml, autopsy*— an examination of a dead body to discover the cause of death **2** an examination of a plan or event that failed in order to discover the cause of failure: *They held a postmortem on the company's poor sales results.*

post·na·tal /ˌpəʊstˈneɪtl◂/ *adj tech* of or for the time after a birth, or of a recently born child: *postnatal care for mother and baby* —compare ANTENATAL

post-natal de·pres·sion /ˌ·· ··· ·ˈ···/ *n* [U] an illness in which a woman feels DEPRESSED after her baby has been born

post of·fice /ˈ· ˌ··/ *n* **1** [C] a building, office, shop, etc., which sells stamps, deals with the post, and does certain other government business, such as (in Britain) selling television LICENCES and paying PENSIONS **2** [U] *AmE for* POSTMAN'S KNOCK

Post Of·fice also **GPO** *old-fash*— [*the*] the government organization responsible for the post in Britain

post office box /ˈ· ·· ˌ·/ *n fml for* P O BOX

Post Office Tow·er /ˌ·· ·· ˈ··/ [*the*] a former name for the TELECOM TOWER

post·paid /ˌpəʊstˈpeɪd◂/ *adj, adv esp. AmE for* POST-FREE

post·pone /pəʊsˈpəʊn/ *v* [T (**until, to**)] to delay; move to some later time: *We're postponing our holiday until August.* [+*v-ing*] *to postpone making a decision* —compare ADJOURN, CANCEL (1) — **~ment** *n* [C;U]

post·pran·di·al /ˌpəʊstˈprændiəl◂/ *adj humor or pomp* happening just after dinner: *a postprandial snooze.*

post·script /ˈpəʊsˌskrɪpt/ also **PS** *infml*— *n* a short addition to a letter, below the place where one has signed one's name: (fig.) *He added a brief postscript to his speech, giving the latest figures.*

post-trau·mat·ic stress dis·or·der /ˌ·· ·ˌ·· ·ˈ· ·ˌ··/ *n* [U] a PSYCHOLOGICAL illness which somebody suffers as a result of a terrible experience such as a plane crash

pos·tu·lant /ˈpɒstjᵿlənt‖ˈpɑːstʃə-/ *n tech* a person who is preparing to enter a religious ORDER¹ (9)

pos·tu·late¹ /ˈpɒstjᵿleɪt‖ˈpɑːstʃə-/ *v* [T] *fml* to suggest (something) as being likely or as a base for further reasoning, even though it has not been proved: *Scientists have postulated a missing link to account for the development of human beings from apes.* [+*that*] *Even if we postulate that she had a motive for the murder, that still doesn't mean that she did it.*

pos·tu·late² /ˈpɒstjᵿlᵻt‖ˈpɑːstʃə-/ *n esp. tech* something supposed or known (but not proved) to be true, on which an argument or piece of scientific reasoning is based

pos·ture¹ /ˈpɒstʃəʳ‖ˈpɑːs-/ *n* **1** [S;U] the general way of holding the body when standing, walking, and sitting: *Humans have a naturally erect posture.* | *good/bad posture* **2** [C] a particular bodily position; POSE: *I had to bend over in a rather uncomfortable/embarrassing posture.* **3** [C (**on**) *usu. sing.*] a way of behaving or thinking on a particular occasion; ATTITUDE: *The government's posture on this new trade agreement seems very unhelpful.* —compare STANCE

posture² *v* [I] *often derog* to talk or behave unnaturally or insincerely, esp. in order to attract attention or admiration —compare POSE¹ (4) — **~ing** *n* [C;U] : *Despite their posturings, the politicians still haven't solved the problem.*

post-vi·ral syn·drome /ˌ·· ·ˌ·· ·ˈ··/ *n* [U] see ME¹

post·war /ˌpəʊstˈwɔːʳ◂/ *adj, adv* (happening or existing)

after a war, esp. the First or Second World War — compare PREWAR

po·sy¹ /ˈpəʊzi/ *n esp. lit* a small bunch of flowers

posy² *adj infml* POSEY

pots

a teapot   a coffeepot   a flowerpot

a pot of paint   a pot of jam

see also picture at **pan**

pot¹ /pɒt‖pɑːt/ *n* **1** [C] a round container made of metal, baked clay, glass, etc., with or without a handle or cover, made to contain liquids or solids, esp. for cooking: *a pot of jam | a plant pot | a coffeepot | Will you help me wash up all these* **pots and pans**? (=cooking containers) **2** [C (of)] also **pot·ful** /-fʊl/— the amount that a pot will hold: *A pot of tea for two, please.* **3** [C] *infml* a dish, bowl, or other container made by hand out of clay: *learning to make/throw pots* —see also POTTER, POTTERY **4** [C] a POT-TY² **5** [C (**of**)] also **pots** *pl.— infml* a large amount (of money): *They're very rich; they've got pots of money.* **6** [(*the*) S] all the money risked on one card game, esp. in POKER, and taken by the winner **7** [C] *BrE* a hit which sends the ball into any of the six small bags at the edge of the table in BILLIARDS or SNOOKER **8** [U] *sl for* MARI-JUANA **9** [C] *usu. derog or humor* POTBELLY **10** [C (**at**)] *infml* a POTSHOT **11** **go to pot** *infml* to become ruined or worthless, esp. from lack of care **12** **the pot calling the kettle black** *infml* a person who is criticizing another person for faults that they also have themselves

pot² *v* **-tt-** **1** [I (**at**);T] to shoot and (try to) kill, esp. for food or sport: *potting (at) rabbits in the field* **2** [T (UP)] to put (a young plant) in a pot filled with earth —see also POT-TED **3** [T] *BrE* to hit (a ball) into any of the six bags at the edge of a billiard table (BILLIARDS)

po·ta·ble /ˈpəʊtəbəl/ *adj fml or humor* (of a liquid, esp. water) suitable for drinking; drinkable

pot·ash /ˈpɒtæʃ‖ˈpɑː-/ *n* [U] a sort of potassium used esp. in farming to make the soil produce better crops, and in making soap, strong glass, and various chemical compounds

po·tas·si·um /pəˈtæsiəm/ *n* [U] a silver-white soft easily melted metal that is a simple substance (ELEMENT). It is found in nature in large quantities, but only in combination with other substances, such as in plants and rocks, and is necessary to the existence of all living things.

po·ta·tion /pəʊˈteɪʃən/ *n rare pomp or humor* **1** [*usu. pl.*] an act of drinking a lot, esp. of alcoholic drink **2** an (al-coholic) drink

po·ta·to /pəˈteɪtəʊ/ *n* **-toes** **1** [C;U] a roundish root vegeta-ble with a thin brown or yellowish skin, that is cooked

and served in many different ways: *Would you like some more roast potatoes/mashed potato?* —see also CHIP¹ **2** [C] a plant which has potatoes growing on its roots: *a field of potatoes* —see also HOT POTATO, SWEET POTATO, and see picture at VEGETABLE

potato bee·tle /·ˈ··· ˌ··/ *n* a COLORADO BEETLE

potato chip /·ˈ··· ·/ *n* **1** *BrE for* CHIP¹ (3) **2** also **chip**— *AmE Austr E for* CRISP¹

potato crisp /·ˌ·· ˈ·/ *n* a CRISP¹

Potato Fam·ine /·ˈ··· ˌ··/ [*the*] the failure of the potato crop in Ireland in 1845, which led to the deaths of many Irish people, and the movement of others to England and the US

potato pee·ler /·ˈ··· ˌ··/ *n* a special piece of equipment, usu. similar to a knife, used for removing the skin of potatoes

pot·bel·ly /ˈpɒtˌbeli‖ˈpɑːt-/ also **pot**— *n usu. derog or humor* a large rounded noticeable stomach. In Britain and the US, a potbelly is not considered to be attractive. **—lied** *adj*

pot·boil·er /ˈpɒtˌbɔɪləʳ‖ˈpɑːt-/ *n derog* a book, article, paint-ing, etc. of low quality produced quickly in order to get money

pot·bound /ˈpɒtbaʊnd‖ˈpɑːt-/ usu. **rootbound** *AmE— adj* (of a plant growing in a pot) having roots that have grown to fill the pot, and therefore are unable to grow any further

po·teen , **po·theen** /pəˈtʃiːn, -ˈtiːn/ *n* [U] Irish WHISKEY made secretly and illegally to avoid paying government tax

po·ten·cy /ˈpəʊtənsi/ *n* [U] **1** the quality of being potent; power: *Alcohol increases the drug's potency.* **2** the abil-ity of a man to have sex —see also IMPOTENCE

po·tent /ˈpəʊtənt/ *adj* **1** (of a medicine, drug, drink, etc.) having a strong and/or quick effect on the body or mind **2** *fml* (of arguments, reasoning, etc.) very effective; caus-ing one to agree; CONVINCING **3** *lit or fml* having great power: *a potent new weapons system* —see also IMPOTENT **— ~ ly** *adv*

po·ten·tate /ˈpəʊtənteɪt/ *n* someone with very great or un-limited power, esp., in former times, a ruler with direct power over his or her people, not limited by a law-making body: *the despotic rule of Eastern potentates*

po·ten·tial¹ /pəˈtenʃəl/ *adj* [*no comp.*] that may happen or become so, although not actually existing at present: *a potential danger | weighing up the potential benefits and disadvantages of investing in new industries* — ~ **ly** *adv*: *She's potentially our best tennis player, but she needs to practise much harder.*

potential² *n* [S;U] **1** [(for)] (the degree of) possibility for developing or being favourably developed: *This new in-vention has (an) enormous sales potential.* (=could be sold in very large quantities) | *a young player with great potential | the potential for expansion* **2** the degree of electricity or electrical force, usu. measured in VOLTS

po·ten·ti·al·i·ty /pəˌtenʃiˈælɪti/ *n* [(for)] **1** [C *usu. pl.*] *fml* a hidden unused power of mind or character: *potentiali-ties for either good or evil* **2** [U] POTENTIAL² (1)

pot·ful /ˈpɒtfʊl‖ˈpɑːt-/ *n* a POT¹ (2)

pot·head /ˈpɒthed‖ˈpɒːt-/ *n AmE sl derog* a person who smokes MARIJUANA

po·theen /pəˈtʃiːn, -ˈtiːn/ *n* [U] POTEEN

pot·hold·er /ˈpɒthəʊldəʳ‖ˈpɑːt-/ *n AmE* a piece of padded (PAD²) material used to hold hot cooking pans

pot·hole /ˈpɒthəʊl‖ˈpɑːt-/ *n* **1** a large hole which goes deep underground in rocky country **2** a hole in the surface of a road which makes driving, etc. difficult or dangerous

pot·hol·ing /ˈpɒtˌhəʊlɪŋ‖ˈpɑːt-/ *n* [U] the sport of climbing down inside POTHOLES (1) **—er** *n*

pot·hun·ter /ˈpɒtˌhʌntəʳ‖ˈpɑːt-/ *n BrE infml derog* a person who competes in races or competitions only in order to win prizes

po·tion /ˈpəʊʃən/ *n esp. lit* a liquid mixture intended as a medicine, poison, or magic charm: *a potion supposed to cure baldness*

pot·luck /ˌpɒtˈlʌk◀‖ˌpɑːt-/ *n* **take potluck: a** to choose without enough information; take a chance: *I don't know anything about any of these films, so let's just go to the nearest cinema and take potluck.* **b** (esp. of an unexpected guest) to have whatever meal has been prepared : *Come home with us and have supper, if you don't mind taking potluck.*

potluck² *adj AmE* with dishes of food brought by many different people: *a potluck supper | Will you bring a salad to the potluck lunch next Sunday?*

Pot Noo·dle /ˈ· ˌ··/ *n tdmk* a type of SNACK meal made by Golden Wonder and consisting of dried PASTA, meat and vegetables; it is mixed with hot water to make it ready to eat

Po·to·mac /pəˈtəʊmæk/ [*the*] a river in the E of the US which separates Maryland and Washington DC from Virginia and West Virginia

pot plant /ˈ· ·/ *n* **1** *BrE* ‖ **potted plant** /ˌ·· ˈ·/ *AmE*– a usu. decorative plant grown in a pot indoors **2** *AmE infml* a MARIJUANA plant

pot·pour·ri /pəʊˈpʊəri‖-pʊˈriː/ *n* **1** a mixture of dried pieces of sweet-smelling flowers and leaves, kept in a bowl to give a pleasant smell to a room **2** [(**of**)] a mixed collection, esp. of pieces of music or writing of a popular sort; MISCELLANY

pot roast /ˈ· ˌ·/ *n* a piece of meat, usu. BEEF, cooked in a pan on top of the cooker, usu. with potatoes and vegetables

Pots·dam A·gree·ment /ˌpɒtsdæm əˈgriːmənt ‖ ˌpɑːts-/ [*the*] an agreement by the countries that won the Second World War (the US, Britain, the USSR, and France) to divide control of Germany between them

pot·sherd /ˈpɒt-ʃɜːd‖ˈpɑːt-ʃɜːrd/ *n tech* (in ARCHAEOLOGY) a piece of a broken pot

pot·shot /ˈpɒt-ʃɒt‖ˈpɑːt-ʃɑːt/ also **pot**– *n* [(**at**)] *infml* a carelessly aimed shot: *I took a potshot at the rabbit.*

pot·ted /ˈpɒtᵻd‖ˈpɑː-/ *adj* [A] **1** (of meat, fish, or chicken) made into a PASTE to be eaten esp. spread on bread **2** (of a plant) grown in a pot: *potted palms* **3** *esp. BrE, sometimes derog* (of a book) produced in a shorter simpler form: *a potted history of the world*

pot·ter¹ /ˈpɒtə‖ˈpɑː-/ *n* a person who makes pots, dishes, etc., out of baked clay, esp. by hand –see also POTTERY

potter² *BrE* ‖ **putter** *AmE*– *v* [I+*adv*/*prep*] *infml* **1** to go in an unhurried way: *I was just pottering along in my little car when two motorbikes roared past.* **2** to spend time moving about a place slowly doing unimportant activities that need little effort: *Granny just potters about the house. | pottering in the garden* –**potter** *n* [S]

Potter¹, Bea·trix /ˈbɪətrɪks‖ˈbɪər-/ (1866–1943) an English writer who wrote animal stories for young children and also drew the pictures for her books. Her books include *The Tale of Peter Rabbit* and *The Tailor of Gloucester* and are still very popular with British children and their parents

Potter², Den·nis /ˈdenᵻs/ (1935–) an English writer of plays, best-known for his television SERIES *Pennies from Heaven* and *The Singing Detective*

Pot·ter·ies /ˈpɒtəriz‖ˈpɑː-/ [*the*] a part of Staffordshire in the midlands of England which is a centre for the CHINA and pottery industry

potter's field /ˈ·· ˌ·/ *n* (formerly) a place where poor people were buried

potter's wheel /ˌ·· ˈ·/ *n* a round flat spinning plate on which wet clay is placed to be shaped into a pot

pot·ter·y /ˈpɒtəri‖ˈpɑː-/ *n* [U] **1** the work of a potter **2** (pots and other objects made out of) baked clay: *a collection of medieval pottery | a pottery dish | a pottery class*

potting com·post /ˈ·· ˌ··/ *n* [U] a mixture of earth, sand, decayed plant material, and plant foods which is put into pots in which plants are grown

pot·ting shed /ˈ·· ·/ *n esp. BrE* a small building for the use of a gardener, in which garden tools, seeds, etc. are kept

pot·ty¹ /ˈpɒti‖ˈpɑːti/ *adj BrE infml* **1** silly; slightly mad: *What a potty idea! | That noise is driving me potty.* **2** [F+**about**] having an extremely strong, or too strong interest in or admiration for: *He's potty about the girl next door/about sailing.* –**tiness** *n* [U]

potty² also **pot**– *n* **1** a CHAMBER POT for children, now usu. made of plastic –compare BEDPAN **2** *AmE* (used by or to children) the toilet: *Have you been to the potty?*

potty-trained /ˈ·· ·/ also **toilet-trained**– *adj* (of a child) trained to use a potty or TOILET –**potty-training** *n* [U]

pouch /paʊtʃ/ *n* **1** a small leather bag used for holding esp. tobacco or, in former times, explosive powder, money, etc. **2** a pocket of skin in the lower half of the body, in which MARSUPIAL animals carry their young –see picture at KANGAROO **3** a baglike fold of skin inside each cheek, in which certain animals carry and store food

pouf /puːf/ *n* **1** also **pouffe** /puːf/ *BrE* ‖ **hassock** *AmE*– a soft drum-shaped object used as a seat or for resting the feet on –see picture at LIVING ROOM **2** *BrE derog sl for* a male HOMOSEXUAL. This word is used only by people who do not approve of homosexual men. –see HOMOSEXUAL

poul·ter·er /ˈpəʊltərər/ *n old-fash* a person who sells poultry

poul·tice /ˈpəʊltᵻs/ *n* a heated wet mass of a soft substance, spread on a thin cloth and laid against the skin to lessen pain, swelling, etc.: *a mustard poultice*

poul·try /ˈpəʊltri/ *n* [P;U] (meat from) farmyard birds such as hens, ducks, etc., kept for supplying eggs and meat: *Poultry is cheaper than meat* (=meat from cattle, pigs, etc.) *at the moment.*

pounce¹ /paʊns/ *v* [I (**on**)] to jump suddenly in order to take hold of something firmly, esp. so as to kill and eat it: *The cat pounced on the unsuspecting mouse.* | (fig.) *Policemen were hiding in the bank, ready to pounce on the thieves.*
pounce on sbdy./sthg. *phr v* [T] **1** to accept eagerly: *He pounced on my offer.* **2** to notice at once and make a sharp remark about: *If you make a single mistake, Vernon will pounce on it/you and say you're a fool.*

pounce² *n* [*usu. sing.*] an attack made by pouncing

pound¹ /paʊnd/ *n* **1** [C] (*written abbrev.* **lb**) a unit of weight equal to 0·454 kilograms: *This weighs seven pounds.* (=7 lbs) | *Two pounds of apples, please.* | *Sugar is still sold by the pound here.* –see TABLE 2 **2** [C] a also **pound sterling** *fml or tech*– the standard unit of money in Britain, divided into 100 pence. The pound used to be in the form of paper money called a pound note, but in 1985 this was replaced by a coin (called a pound coin): *Five pounds can also be written £5.* | *The floods caused damage estimated at over a million pounds.* **b** the standard unit of money in various other countries, such as Egypt and the Sudan **3** [*the*] the value of British money in relation to the money of other countries: *The pound has fallen again (against the dollar).* **4** –**pounder**: **a** something, esp. a fish, that weighs the stated number of pounds: *I caught a five-pounder.* **b** a large gun that fires a shot weighing the stated number of pounds: *a 32-pounder* **5** **one's pound of flesh** the exact amount that one owes esp. when its payment will cause great pain or trouble to the person who owes it

pound² *v* **1** [T (UP)] to crush into a soft mass or powder by hitting repeatedly with a heavy object: *Pound the tomatoes into a paste.* **2** [I;T] to beat or hit repeatedly, heavily, and noisily: *My heart pounded (with excitement).* | *He pounded the table angrily.* | (fig.) *Our guns pounded away at the enemy positions.* (=kept firing heavily at them) **3** [I+*adv*/*prep*] to move with heavy quick steps that make a dull sound: *The runaway cattle pounded down the hill.*

pound³ *n* a place where lost dogs and cats, or cars that have been illegally parked, are kept by the police until claimed by the owner –see also IMPOUND

Pound, Ez·ra /ˈezrə/ (1885–1972) an American poet who lived mostly in Europe and whose poems include the *Cantos*. He supported FASCISM during the Second World War and after the war he was accused (ACCUSE) of TREASON and sent to an American mental hospital.

pound·age /ˈpaʊndɪdʒ/ *n* [U (**on**)] *tech* an amount charged for every pound in weight, or for every British £1 in value

pound cake /ˈ· ·/ *n AmE* a heavy cake made from almost equal parts of flour, sugar, and butter

pound·ing /ˈpaʊndɪŋ/ *n* **1** [C;U] the act or sound of someone or something that POUNDS²: *the pounding of my heart* **2** [C] *infml* a severe defeat: *Our football team took a real pounding from Brazil.*

pour /pɔː/ *v* **1** [T+*obj*+*adv*/*prep*] to cause (something) to flow (out of or into a container): *Pour some wine into my glass.* | *Pour away the dirty water.* | *The chimney was pouring out black smoke.* | (fig.) *The government has been pouring money into the steel industry.* (=supporting it with large amounts of money) [+*obj*(*i*)+*obj*(*d*)] *Can I pour* you (out) another cup of tea? **2** [I+*adv/prep*] to flow steadily and rapidly: *Blood poured from the wound.* | *Smoke was pouring from the window.* | (fig.) *At five o'clock workers poured out of the factories.* **3** [I] *infml* to fill cups of tea, coffee, etc., and serve them to others: *Shall I pour or will you?* **4** [I+*adv*] (of a container) to be suitable for pouring: *This teapot doesn't pour very well.* **5** [I (DOWN)] (of rain) to fall hard and steadily: *The rain is really pouring down.* | *She spoilt her new shoes in* **the pouring rain.** [*it*+I] *It's pouring down/pouring with rain.* —see RAIN (USAGE) **6 pour cold water over/on** *infml* to speak discouragingly about; dismiss as not being sensible: *Don't pour cold water on the scheme: it has some good points.* **7 pour oil on troubled waters** to try to stop trouble, a quarrel, etc. by making the people who are causing it calmer **8 pour scorn on** to speak with unkind disrespect about

pour sthg. ↔ **out** *phr v* [T (**to**)] to tell (a story, news, one's troubles, etc.) in an uncontrolled way so that the words rush out, esp. after keeping them unexpressed for a long time: *She poured out her worries to the doctor.*

Pous·sin /ˈpuːsæn‖puːˈsɑːn/, **Nic·o·las** /ˈnɪkələs/ (1594–1665) a French painter known esp. for his LANDSCAPE paintings

pout¹ /paʊt/ *v* [I;T] to push (the lips or the lower lip) forward, esp. to show displeasure or to attract sexual interest: *The spoilt child sat there pouting.* | *The film star pouted provocatively.*

pout² *n* an act of pouting: *a sullen/sensual pout*

pov·er·ty /ˈpɒvəti‖ˈpɑːvərti/ *n* **1** [U] the state of being poor: *They live in abject poverty/below* **the poverty line.** (=their income is less than is needed to buy enough food, pay for a proper place to live, etc.) **2** [S;U (**of**)] *fml derog* (a) lack: *His later stories show (a) surprising poverty of imagination.* —compare POORNESS

poverty line /ˈ··· ˌ·/ [*the*] a level of income under which a person or family is considered to be very poor and able to receive government help. In the US the poverty line in the late 1980s was set at about $12,000 a year for a family of four, and the amount is changed each year because of INFLATION.

poverty-strick·en /ˈ··· ˌ··/ *adj* extremely poor

poverty trap /ˈ··· ˌ·/ *n* a situation in which the amount of money earned by a poor person or family increases slightly so that they are no longer allowed to receive special government payments and as a result they have even less money than before

pow /paʊ/ *interj* a word used in children's COMICS (=magazines of picture stories) to show that somebody has hit another person hard

POW /ˌpiː əʊ ˈdʌbəljuː/ *n* a PRISONER OF WAR: *a POW camp*

pow·der¹ /ˈpaʊdəʳ/ *n* **1** [C;U] (a) dry substance in the form of extremely small grains: *On examination, the white powder turned out to be heroin.* | *milk powder* **2** [U] a pleasant-smelling often flesh-coloured substance in this form, for use on the skin: *baby powder* | *face powder* — see also TALCUM POWDER **3** [C] *old use* a medicine in the form of powder: *a stomach powder* **4** [U] GUNPOWDER **5 take a powder** *AmE sl* to be hurt and usu. to fall down in a fight: *He took a powder in the third round.*

powder² *v* **1** [T] to put powder on: *She powdered the baby after its bath.* **2 powder one's nose** *euph* (of a woman) to go to the TOILET

pow·dered /ˈpaʊdəd‖-ərd/ *adj* **1** produced or dried in the form of powder: *powdered egg* **2** covered with powder: *powdered hair*

powdered milk /ˌ··· ˈ·/ also **dried milk**— *n* [U] milk which has been dried for easy keeping —see also BABY MILK

powder keg /ˈ·· ·/ *n* something dangerous that might explode: (fig.) *That country is a political powder keg; revolution could break out at any time.*

powder puff /ˈ·· ·/ *n* a small thick piece or ball of soft material for spreading POWDER on the face or body

powder room /ˈ·· ·/ *n euph* a women's public TOILET in a theatre, hotel, restaurant, big shop, etc.

pow·der·y /ˈpaʊdəri/ *adj* **1** like or easily broken into powder: *powdery snow* **2** covered with powder

Pow·ell /ˈpəʊəl/, **An·tho·ny** /ˈæntəni/ (1905–) a 20th century English writer who wrote *A Dance to the Music of Time*

Powell /ˈpaʊəl/, **E·noch** /ˈiːnɒk‖-nɑːk/ (1912–) an English politician who is famous for opposing IMMIGRATION, esp. in the 1960s, and for being against Britain joining the Common Market. In 1968 he made a famous speech, now referred to as the "Rivers of Blood" speech, in which he said that if Britain allowed too many black people to come and live in this country, there would be fighting and "rivers of blood" in the streets. Many people think that he is a RACIST because of this.

pow·er¹ /ˈpaʊəʳ/ *n* **1** [S;U (**over**)] control over others; influence: *The power of governments has increased greatly over the past century.* | *The chairman was forced to resign following a boardroom power struggle.* | *a religious cult which seems to exercise a strange power over the people who join it* | *Now I've got him in* **my power**, *I can make him do anything I want.* **2** [U] governmental control: *Which party is* **in power** (=is the government) *now?* | *The Progressive Party was* **returned to power**, *with an increased majority in the election.* | *The rebels have seized power.* **3** [C;U] (a) right to act, given by law, rule, or official position: [+*to-v*] *Only certain directors in the company have the power to sign company cheques.* | *The police and the army have been given special powers to deal with the situation.* **4** [(*the*) U (**of**)] also **powers** *pl.*— what one can do; (natural) ability: *Humans are the only animals with the power of speech.* [+*to-v*] *She claims to have the power to see into the future.* | *He did everything in* **his power** (=did all he could) *to comfort her.* | *I'm afraid it's not (with)in my power to help you.* | *She's nearly 80 and very ill, and her* **powers are failing.** (=she no longer has all her natural abilities) | *When he wrote that book, he was* **at the height of his powers** *as a writer.* **5** [U] ability to have physical effect; force; strength: *So enormous was the hurricane's power that it carried away whole buildings.* | (fig.) *We plan to increase our air power.* (=get more military aircraft) | (fig.) *Japan's industrial power* **6** [U] force that can be used for doing work, driving a machine, or producing electricity: *nuclear power* | *The engine is being specially adapted to increase its power.* | *"This drill isn't working." "You haven't turned on the power."* (=electricity) —see also HORSEPOWER, MANPOWER **7** [U] a measure of the degree to which a microscope, TELESCOPE, etc. is able to make things seen through it look larger **8** [C] (*sometimes cap.*) a person, group, nation, spirit, etc., that has influence or control: *People say that Britain is no longer a world power.* | *He was only an ordinary MP when I first knew him, but these days he's quite* **a power in the land.** (=someone with a lot of power and influence) | **the powers of darkness** (=the forces of the devil) —see also SUPERPOWER **9** [C] (in MATHEMATICS) the number of times that an amount is to be multiplied by itself: *The amount 2 to the power of 3 is written 2^3, and means $2 \times 2 \times 2$.* **10** [S+**of**] *infml* a large amount; lot: *Your visit while I was ill* **did me a power of good. 11 more power to someone's elbow!** *infml, esp. BrE* good luck to someone! may someone's efforts succeed!: *She's trying to get the boss to arrange a firm's party? Well, more power to her elbow!* **12 power behind the throne** someone who, though having no official position, has great private influence over a ruler or leader **13 power tends to corrupt and absolute power corrupts absolutely** *quote* a phrase used by the English HISTORIAN Lord Acton **14 the power and the glory** a phrase from the LORD'S PRAYER **15 the powers that** '**be** *infml, often humor* the unknown people in important official positions who make decisions that have an effect on one's life **16 power trip** *AmE derog* an eagerness to use the power one has been given: *Ever since he got that promotion he's been on a real power trip.* **17 -powered** /paʊəd‖-ərd/ using, producing, or having the stated type or amount of POWER (6,7): *a low-powered engine* | *a high-powered telescope* — see also BALANCE OF POWER, BLACK POWER, HIGH-POWERED, PURCHASING POWER, STAYING POWER

power² *v* **1** [T *usu. pass.*] to supply power to (esp. a vehicle): *The aircraft is powered by three jet engines.* **2** [I + *adv/prep*] *infml* to move powerfully and fast: *The racing car powered down the home straight.*

power³ *adj* [A] driven by a motor: *a power saw/mower*

power base /ˈ··· ·/ *n* an area, group, etc. that provides someone with a means of having influence: *For the first time we have a president whose political power base is in the west of the country.*

pow·er·boat /ˈpaʊəbəʊt‖ˈpaʊər-/ *n* a powerful MOTORBOAT, esp. one for racing

power bro·ker /'·· ·/ n someone who controls the degree to which others have political influence, esp. in affairs between nations

power cut /'·· ·/ also **power failure**— n a failure of the electricity supply: *We got the gas stove because we were always getting power cuts.*

power dive /'·· ·/ n a steep downward movement of an aircraft with the engines working

power dres·sing /'·· ·/ n [U] a way of dressing used esp. in the 1980s by women to show that they are as able as men to have positions of power in society

power fail·ure /'·· ·/ n [C;U] power cut

pow·er·ful /'pauəfəl‖'pauɔr-/ adj 1 able to produce great physical force: *powerful muscles* | *a powerful engine* | *a powerful swimmer* (=who can swim fast and/or a long way) 2 great in degree or effect: *a powerful electric current.* | *a powerful telescope* | *powerful drugs* | *Onions have a powerful smell.* | *a powerful imagination* 3 having much control and influence: *Powerful nations sometimes try to control weaker ones.* | *a powerful position in the government* — ~ **ly** *adv : He's very powerfully built.* (=has a big strong body)

Pow·er·Gen /'pauədʒen‖-ər-/ one of the two main companies, which produce electricity in Britain —see also NATIONAL POWER

pow·er·house /'pauəhaus‖-ər-/ n -houses /ˌhauzɪz/ *infml, usu. apprec* 1 a very strong person 2 [(of)] a person or place that acts, behaves, or produces things with great forcefulness: *an intellectual powerhouse* | *the idea of a university as a powerhouse of ideas*

pow·er·less /'pauələs‖'pauɔr-/ adj lacking power, strength, or ability: [F+to-v] *I was powerless to* (=could not) *prevent the accident.* — ~ **ly** *adv* — ~ **ness** *n* [U]

power line /'·· ·/ n a large wire carrying electricity over land or underground from where the electricity is produced to where it is used

power of at·tor·ney /ˌ·· ··'··/ n [C;U] *law* (a signed official paper giving) the right to act for someone else in business or law

power plant /'·· ·/ n 1 an engine and other parts which supply power to a factory, an aircraft, a car, etc. 2 *esp. AmE* a POWER STATION

power point /'·· ·/ also **point, socket** *BrE* ‖ **electric socket** *AmE*— n *esp. BrE* a piece of plastic or other material with holes in it, in Britain usu. three square holes, in the US usu. two, which is fixed into a wall and to which electrical equipment can be connected for the electricity supply

power pol·i·tics /'·· ˌ···/ n [U] *often derog* (in international politics) the use or threat of armed force instead of peaceful argument

power shar·ing /'·· ˌ···/ the sharing of political power by different groups in a society, esp. a political arrangement in Northern Ireland in 1973 in which Catholics and Protestants shared in government. The arrangement did not end the troubles there, and ended in 1976.

power show·er /'·· ˌ···/ n a SHOWER¹ (3h) which has a very forceful flow of water

power sta·tion /'·· ˌ···/ ‖ also **power plant** *esp. AmE*— n a large building in which electricity is made

power steer·ing /'·· ˌ···/ n [U] (in a vehicle) a system for steering (STEER²) which uses power from the vehicle's engine and therefore needs less effort from the driver

power work·er /'·· ˌ···/ n a worker in the electricity-producing industry

pow·wow /'pauˌwau/ n 1 a meeting or council of Native Americans 2 *humor* a meeting or discussion

Pow·ys /'pauɪs/ a COUNTY in central Wales

pox /pɒks‖pɑːks/ n 1 [the+S] *infml* the disease SYPHILIS 2 [U] *old use* the disease SMALLPOX 3 **a pox on** *old use* (used for expressing complete disrespect for someone or something worthless): *A pox on our enemies!* —see also CHICKEN POX, COWPOX

pp *abbrev. for:* 1 pages: *see pp 15–37* —see also P² 2 (written before the name of another person, when one is signing a letter for them)

PPS /ˌpiː piː 'es/ n 1 (in Britain) Parliamentary Private Secretary; a member of parliament who is appointed to help a minister 2 also **p.p.s.**— *abbrev. for:* post postscriptum; a note added after a P.S. in a letter or message

PR¹ /ˌpiː 'ɑːr/ n [U] 1 PUBLIC RELATIONS: *an expert in PR* 2 PROPORTIONAL REPRESENTATION

PR² *written abbrev. for:* PUERTO RICO

prac·ti·ca·ble /'præktɪkəbəl/ adj that can be successfully done or used, though not yet tried: *Is it practicable to try to develop agriculture in desert regions?* —opposite **impracticable** — **·bly** *adv* — **·bility** /ˌpræktɪkə'bɪlɪti/ n [U]

▷ USAGE People are beginning to use **practical** with the same meaning as **practicable**; a **practical/practicable** plan or suggestion is one that will work. **Practicable** is not used of people.◁

prac·ti·cal¹ /'præktɪkəl/ adj 1 concerned with action, practice, or actual conditions and results, rather than with ideas: *They've agreed to store the furniture; but we still have the practical problem of how to transport it over there.* | *She lacks practical experience.* 2 *apprec* effective or convenient in actual use; suited to actual conditions: *a practical uniform which is comfortable and doesn't show the dirt* 3 *usu. apprec* sensible; clever at doing things and dealing with difficulties: *Be practical — we can't afford both a car and a holiday.* | *She's a very practical person.* 4 practicable 5 **for all practical purposes** actually; in reality: *He does so little work in the office that for all practical purposes it would make no difference if he didn't come.* —opposite **impractical** (for 2,3); see also PRACTICALLY; see PRACTICABLE (USAGE) — ~ **ity** /ˌpræktɪ'kælɪti/ n [C;U] : *I'm not sure about the practicality of that suggestion.* | *Please stick to practicalities.*

practical² n *infml* a PRACTICAL lesson, test, or examination, esp. in science: *a chemistry practical*

practical joke /ˌ··· '·/ n a trick played on someone to amuse others: *She glued the teacher's book to the desk as a practical joke.* —compare PRANK, TRICK¹ (3)

prac·ti·cally /'præktɪkli/ adv 1 in a practical way 2 very nearly; almost: *The holidays are practically over; there's only one day left.*

▷ USAGE **Practically** can be used in the same way as **almost,** but is less common. It cannot be used in exactly the same way as **nearly.** —see also ALMOST (USAGE)◁

prac·tice /'præktɪs/ n 1 [C;U] (a) regular or repeated performance or exercise in order to learn to do something well: *You need to get some more practice at reversing round corners before you take your driving test.* | *He's gone to football practice.* | *We have three choir practices a week.* | *The student teachers are now doing their teaching practice.* | *I haven't played tennis for years, so I'm really out of practice.* (=I lack the practice needed to play well) | *He took a couple of practice swings with his club before playing the shot.* 2 [U] the actual doing of something (rather than the idea of it): *It sounded like a good idea, but in* **practice** *it didn't work.* | *We've made our plans, and now we must put them into practice.* (=actually carry them out) —compare THEORY (2) 3 [C] the business of a doctor or lawyer: *He has a large practice* (=many people to look after) *in London.* —see also GROUP PRACTICE, PRIVATE PRACTICE 4 [C;U] a repeated, habitual, or standard act or course of action: *unfair business practices* | *religious practices* | *I'll lend you the money this time, but I don't intend to make a practice of it.* (=lend you money regularly) | *It is the practice in English law to consider someone innocent until they have been proved guilty.* (=that is what is done in English law) | *It is now quite common practice for married women not to take their husband's second name.* —see also SHARP PRACTICE; see HABIT (USAGE) 5 **practice makes perfect** *saying* if you do something repeatedly, you will learn to do it perfectly

prac·tise *BrE* ‖ **-tice** *AmE* /'præktɪs/ v 1 [I;T] to do (an action) or perform on (esp. a musical instrument) regularly or repeatedly in order to gain skill: *You'll never learn to ride a bike if you don't practise.* | *She's been practising the same tune on the piano for nearly an hour.* | *You mustn't practise the drums while the baby is sleeping.* [+v-ing] *You need to practise parking the car in a small space.* 2 [I (as);T] to do (the work of a doctor, lawyer, etc.): *She passed her law examinations and is now practising (as a lawyer).* | *a practising doctor* 3 [T] to act in accordance with (the ideas of one's religion): *a practising Jew* 4 [T] *fml* to make continuous use of (a course of action): *Our income has decreased and now we must practise economy.* (=must avoid spending money) 5 [T] *fml* to do; perform:

to practise magic **6 practise what one preaches** to do oneself what one advises others to do

prac·tised *BrE* ‖ **-tice** *AmE* /ˈpræktˌst/ *adj* **1** [(in)] (of a person) skilled through practice: *a practised liar | thoroughly practised in the skills of politics | practised at avoiding difficult questions* **2** [A] *apprec* gained by practice: *The dancer moved with practised grace.* **3** *usu. derog* used so often that it is no longer natural: *The hotel manager welcomed the guests with a practised smile.*

prac·ti·tion·er /prækˈtɪʃənəʳ/ *n* **1** a person who works in a profession, esp. a doctor or lawyer: *medical practitioners* **2** *sometimes derog* a person who performs a skill or art: *practitioners of magic* —see also GENERAL PRACTITIONER

Pra·do /ˈprɑːdəʊ/ [*the*] the national Spanish MUSEUM of painting and SCULPTURE which is in Madrid and has many very important works of art by painters such as El Greco, Goya, and Rubens

prae·sid·i·um /prɪˈsɪdiəm, -ˈzɪ-/ *n* **-iums** *or* **-ia** /-diə/ a PRESIDIUM

prae·tor·i·an guard /prɪˌtɔːriən ˈɡɑːd‖-ˈɡɑːrd/ *n* [*the*] **1** the soldiers who defended the life of the Roman EMPEROR **2** a group of people who are supposed to defend a person in power against people who want to take power from them, but who are often more to do them interested in their own aims

prag·mat·ic /præɡˈmætɪk/ *adj usu. apprec* dealing with matters in the way that seems best under the actual conditions, rather than following a general principle; concerned with practical results —**~ally** /kli/ *adv*

prag·mat·ics /præɡˈmætɪks/ *n* [U] *tech* (in the study of language) the study of the way words and phrases are used in conversation to express meanings, feelings, and ideas which are sometimes different from the actual meaning of the words used

prag·ma·tis·m /ˈpræɡmətɪzəm/ *n* [U] *usu. apprec* pragmatic ways of considering and dealing with things —**tist** *n*

Prague /prɑːɡ/ the capital city of Czechoslovakia, a port and industrial centre with many beautiful buildings

Prague spring /ˌ·ˈ·/ a short time in 1968 when the Communist government of Czechoslovakia, under Alexander Dubcek, allowed people to have more freedom than before. The Soviet Union did not agree with these changes and invaded (INVADE) Czechoslovakia and forced the government to return to the way things were before.

prai·rie /ˈpreəri/ also **prairies** *pl.*— *n* a wide treeless grassy plain, esp. in N America

prairie dog /ˈ·· ·/ *n* a small animal with a short tail which is found in the prairies in N America. Prairie dogs live in large groups under the ground, and are often seen standing on their back legs looking for danger.

prairie oy·ster /ˈ·· ˌ·/ *n infml* **1** a type of drink made with raw egg which is supposed to be a cure for a HANGOVER (1) **2** *AmE* also **Rocky Mountain oyster**— the TESTICLEs of a CALF (=male young of a cow), eaten as food

prairie schoo·ner /ˌ·· ˈ··/ *n AmE infml* a small COVERED WAGON

praise¹ /preɪz/ *v* [T (**for**)] **1** to speak of with admiration and approval: *The doctor praised her for her courage.* **2** *fml or lit* to offer thanks and honour to (God), esp. by singing religious songs in a church service **3 praise someone/something to the skies** to express very strong praise for someone or something

praise² *n* [U] **1** expression of admiration: *The new film received high praise from everyone. | All sides of the community joined together in praise of the police's prompt action.* **2** *fml or lit* worship: *Let us give praise to God.* **3 praise be** *old-fash* thank God: *At last I've found you, praise be!* —see also **damn with faint praise** (DAMN⁴)

prais·es /ˈpreɪzɪz/ *n* [P (**of**)] words that praise someone or something: *Everyone's singing the praises of* (=praising) *his new film, but I didn't think much of it.*

praise·wor·thy /ˈpreɪzwɜːði‖-ɜːr-/ *adj apprec* deserving praise, esp. even though not successful; COMMENDABLE: *a praiseworthy attempt to simplify the complex laws in this area* —**thily** *adv* —**thiness** *n* [U]

pra·line /ˈprɑːliːn/ *n* a sweet made of nuts cooked in boiling sugar, used esp. as a filling for chocolates

pram /præm/ also **perambulator** *old-fash or fml, esp.*

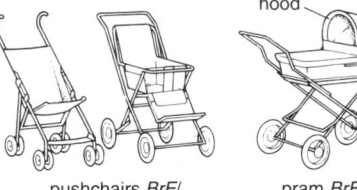

pushchairs *BrE/* strollers *AmE* pram *BrE/* baby buggy *AmE*

BrE ‖ **baby buggy, baby carriage** *AmE*— *n* a four-wheeled carriage, pushed by hand, in which a baby can sleep or be taken about —compare PUSHCHAIR

prance /prɑːns‖præns/ *v* [I+*adv/prep*] **1** (of an animal, esp. a horse) to jump high or move quickly by raising the front legs and springing forwards on the back legs **2** *sometimes derog* to move quickly, happily, or proudly with a springing or dancing step: *The children were prancing about with delight. | That cheeky new secretary just pranced up to me and asked if I worked here!*

prank /præŋk/ *n* a playful but foolish trick, not intended to harm: *Children like to play pranks on people. | a schoolboy prank* —compare PRACTICAL JOKE

prank·ster /ˈpræŋkstəʳ/ *n infml* a person who plays pranks

prat /præt/ *n BrE derog sl* a worthless stupid person

prate /preɪt/ *v* [I (**ON, about**)] *old-fash derog* to talk foolishly

prat·fall /ˈprætfɔːl/ *n AmE infml* a fall on one's BUTTOCKS, often on purpose to cause laughter: *The comedian slipped on a banana skin and did a pratfall.*

prat·tle¹ /ˈprætl/ *v* [I (**ON, about**)] *infml, often derog* to talk continually in a childish or foolish way about matters of no importance: *The children prattled on about their presents.* —**tler** *n*

prattle² *n* [U] *infml, often derog* childish, unimportant, or meaningless talk

Prav·da /ˈprɑːvdə/ a Russian newspaper, formerly the official newspaper of the Communist party of the USSR

prawn /prɔːn/ *BrE* ‖ **shrimp** *AmE*— *n* a small ten-legged sea animal used for food, like a SHRIMP, but larger

prawn cock·tail /ˌ· ˈ··/ *n* a British dish served before the main course of a meal and consisting of prawns in MAYONNAISE on a bed of LETTUCE leaves

pray¹ /preɪ/ *v* **1** [I (**for, to**);T] to speak, often silently, to God or a god, privately or with others, to show love, give thanks, or ask for (something): *They went to the mosque to pray. | I will pray to God for your safety. | We pray God's forgiveness.* [+*to-v*] *Many times when he was in terrible pain he had prayed to be allowed to die.* [+(that)] *They prayed that their enemies might be defeated.* | (fig.) *The school picnic is on Saturday, so we're praying* (=hoping very strongly) *for a fine day.* | (fig.) *I pray to God* (=hope very strongly) *nothing like that ever happens again.* **2** [T] *lit or old use* to ask or beg seriously and with strong feeling: *Take great care, I pray you!*

pray² *adv fml or lit* (used for giving force to a request) please: *Pray be seated!*

prayer /preəʳ/ *n* **1** [C] (a fixed form of words used in making) a solemn request to God or a god: *a special prayer for Easter Sunday | He says his prayers every night before he goes to bed. | Her prayer was answered and her husband came home safely.* **2** [U] the act or regular habit of praying to God or a god: *The congregation knelt in prayer.* **3** [U] (*often cap.*) a fixed form of church service including prayers: *Evening Prayer* —see also PRAYERS

Prayer Book /ˈ· ·/ [*the*] the BOOK OF COMMON PRAYER

prayer meet·ing /ˈ· ˌ··/ *n* (in Protestant churches) a public meeting at which people offer personal prayers to God

prayer rug /ˈ· ·/ also **prayer mat**— *n* a small mat knelt on by Muslims when they are praying

prayers /preəz‖-ərz/ *n* [P] a daily religious service among a group of people, mainly consisting of praying: *school prayers | family prayers*

prayer wheel /ˈ· ·/ *n* a drum-shaped piece of wood or metal that turns round on a pole, and on which prayers are written, used by Buddhists in Tibet

pray·ing man·tis /ˌ·· '··/ also **mantis**— *n* a large insect that eats other insects and holds out its front legs pressed together —see picture at INSECT

pre- see WORD FORMATION

preach /priːtʃ/ *v* **1** [I (**to**);T] to speak or say (a religious speech) in public: *Christ preached to large crowds.* | *The priest preached a sermon on the need for charity.* [+*that*] *Christ preached that we should love each other.* **2** [T] *often derog* to advise or urge others to accept (something one believes in): *These misguided people go around preaching revolution.* **3** [I (**at, to, about**)] *derog* to offer unwanted advice on matters of right and wrong: *My sister has been preaching at me again about my untidy habits.* **4 preach to the converted** to explain one's ideas or beliefs to people who already share them — ~ **er** *n*

Preak·ness /'priːknəs/ [*the*] a race for three-year-old horses held in Maryland —see also TRIPLE CROWN

pre·am·ble /priː'æmbəl‖'priːæmbəl/ *n tech or derog* **1** a statement at the beginning of a speech or piece of writing, giving its reason and purpose: *a preamble to the treaty* **2** *usu. cap, AmE* the statements at the beginning of the American CONSTITUTION

pre·ar·range /ˌpriːə'reɪndʒ/ *v* [T] to arrange in advance: *At a prearranged signal, everyone stood up.* — ~ **ment** *n* [U]

preb·end /'prebənd/ *n tech* a small regular payment made to a priest of quite high rank for services connected with a CATHEDRAL or special church

preb·en·da·ry /'prebəndəri‖-deri/ *n* a priest who receives a prebend

pre·car·i·ous /prɪ'keəriəs/ *adj* unsafe; not firm or steady; full of danger: *The climber had only a precarious hold on the slippery rock.* | *Our financial situation is still precarious.* — ~ **ly** *adv* : *She had a cup of tea balanced precariously on her knee.* — ~ **ness** *n* [U]

pre·cast /ˌpriːˈkɑːst◂‖-ˈkæst◂/ *adj* (of CONCRETE²) formed into blocks ready for use in building

pre·cau·tion /prɪ'kɔːʃən/ *n* [(**against**)] an action done to avoid possible danger, discomfort, etc.: *Equipment is always carefully sterilized as a precaution against infection.* | *It would be a wise precaution to lock all the doors.* — ~ **ary** *adj* : *a precautionary X-ray*

pre·cede /prɪ'siːd/ *v* [T] **1** *fml* to come, go, or happen (just) before: *The flash of lightning preceded the sound of thunder by two seconds.* | *He came in, preceded by his wife.* **2** [+*obj*+*adv*/*prep*, esp. **with**] to introduce (an activity) in the stated way; PREFACE: *He preceded his speech with a few words of welcome to the special guests.* —compare PROCEED

pre·ce·dence /'presɪdəns/ *n* [U (**over**)] the right to be put or dealt with before others, esp. because of greater importance: *The hospital building programme will have to have/take precedence over the road building programme.* | *In the dispute over custody of the child, the court decided to give precedence to the mother's claims.* | *Let's deal with the questions in order of precedence.* (=the important ones first) —compare PRIORITY

pre·ce·dent /'presɪdənt/ *n* **1** [U] use of former customs or decisions as a guide to present actions: *The Queen has broken with precedent by sending her children to ordinary schools.* **2** [C] a former action or case that may be used as an example or rule for present or future action: *This intervention in another nation's affairs has set a precedent which we hope other countries will not follow.* | *This course of action is quite without precedent.* (=has never happened before) —see also UNPRECEDENTED

pre·ced·ing /prɪ'siːdɪŋ/ *adj* [A] *fml* coming just before in time or place: *the preceding day*

pre·cen·tor /prɪ'sentə/ *n* (in some English CATHEDRALs) an official who deals with the musical arrangements for the religious services, and sometimes directs the trained singers

pre·cept /'priːsept/ *n* a guiding rule on which behaviour, a way of thought or action, etc., is based: *Just follow these few basic precepts and you won't go far wrong in life.*

pre·cep·to·ri·al /ˌpriːsep'tɔːriəl, ˌpriːsep-/ *n AmE* a lesson at a university or college which is a small discussion group and for which students usu. do independent reading or study

pre·ces·sion /prɪ'seʃən/ *n* [C;U] **1** also **precession of the**

eq·ui·nox·es /ˌ·· · · '····/— a slow westward change in the slope at which the earth turns round daily, which causes the times of the year at which day and night are both exactly 12 hours long to be slightly earlier each year **2** *tech* a sideways or circular movement of the slope of a spinning object — ~ **al** *adj*

pre·cinct /'priːsɪŋkt/ *n* **1** *BrE* a part of a town planned for or limited to the stated use: *a new shopping precinct* (=an area containing only shops) **2** *AmE* a division of a town or city for election or police purposes

pre·cincts /'priːsɪŋkts/ *n* [P (**of**)] **1** the space, often enclosed by walls, that surrounds an important building or group of buildings: *It's quiet within the precincts of the old college.* **2** *rare* the area around a particular place; neighbourhood

pre·ci·os·i·ty /ˌpreʃi'ɒsɪti‖-'ɑː-/ *n* [U] *fml derog* unnatural perfection of detail, esp. in speech or pronunciation

pre·cious¹ /'preʃəs/ *adj* **1** of great value, esp. because very expensive or much loved: *some of our country's most precious military secrets* | *He poured a few drops of the precious liquid into the glass.* | *That old toy is my most precious* (=dearly loved) *possession.* | *My time is precious; I can only give you a few minutes.* **2** *derog* (of manners, use of words, etc.) too concerned with perfection or unimportant details; unnaturally delicate **3** [A] *infml* (used for giving force to an expression of annoyance) worthless: *"Stop using that pen — it's mine!" "Take your precious pen, then!"* — ~ **ly** *adv* — ~ **ness** *n* [U]

precious² *adv infml* very: *You'll get precious little sympathy from her.* | *There were precious few left.*

precious³ *n infml becoming rare* (used when speaking to someone you love): *Come here, (my) precious!*

precious met·al /ˌ·· '··/ *n* [C;U] a rare and valuable metal: *Gold and silver are precious metals.* —compare BASE METAL

precious stone /ˌ·· '·/ *n* a rare and valuable jewel: *Diamonds and emeralds are precious stones.* —compare SEMI-PRECIOUS

pre·ci·pice /'presɪpɪs/ *n* a dangerously steep side of a high rock, mountain, or cliff: (fig.) *In 1939 everyone felt Europe was* on the edge of the precipice. (=in very great danger)

pre·cip·i·tate¹ /prɪ'sɪpɪteɪt/ *v* **1** [T] *fml* to make (an unwanted event) happen sooner; HASTEN: *Fears about the solvency of the banks precipitated the great economic crash.* **2** [T+*adv*/*prep*, esp. **into**] *fml* **a** to throw forwards or downwards with great force: *The cart overturned and precipitated us into the ditch.* **b** to force suddenly into the stated condition or situation: *The border incident precipitated the two countries into war.* —compare PLUNGE¹ (1) **3** [I;T (**OUT**)] *tech* (in chemistry) to separate or cause (solid matter) to separate from a liquid by chemical action

pre·cip·i·tate² /prɪ'sɪpɪtət/ *n* [C;U] *tech* (in chemistry) solid matter that has been separated from a liquid by chemical action —compare PRECIPITATION (4)

precipitate³ also **precipitous**— *adj fml* acting or done with too much hurry or without care or thought; IMPULSIVE: *They acted with precipitate haste.* | *She made a rather precipitate departure.* — ~ **ly** *adv*

pre·cip·i·ta·tion /prɪˌsɪpɪ'teɪʃən/ *n* **1** [U] *fml or tech* the act of precipitating or state of being precipitated **2** [U] *tech* (the amount of) rain, snow, etc. which has fallen onto the ground: *There will be precipitation on northern hills tonight.* **3** [U] *fml derog* unwisely hurried action **4** [C;U] *tech* (in chemistry) matter that has precipitated (PRECIPITATE¹ (3)) naturally —compare PRECIPITATE²

pre·cip·i·tous /prɪ'sɪpɪtəs/ *adj* **1** dangerously high or steep: *A precipitous path led down the cliff.* **2** PRECIPITATE³ — ~ **ly** *adv* — ~ **ness** *n* [U]

pré·cis¹ /'preɪsiː‖preɪ'siː/ *n* précis /'preɪsiːz‖preɪ'siːz/ [(**of**)] a shortened form of a piece of writing or of what someone has said, giving only the main points

précis² *v* précised /'preɪsiːd‖preɪ'siːd/, *present participle* précising /'preɪsiːɪŋ‖preɪ'siːɪŋ/ [T] to make a précis of

pre·cise /prɪ'saɪs/ *adj* **1** exact in form, detail, measurements, time, etc.: *very precise calculations* | *Our train leaves at about half past nine — 09.33 to be precise.* **2** [A] particular; exact; VERY: *At the precise moment that I put my foot on the step, the bus started.* **3** *sometimes derog*

careful and correct about small details: *A lawyer needs a precise mind.* | *a very precise old lady* —opposite **imprecise**

pre·cise·ly /prɪˈsaɪsli/ *adv* **1** exactly: *The train leaves at ten o'clock precisely.* **2** yes, that is correct; you are right: *"So you think we ought to wait until autumn?" "Precisely."*

pre·ci·sion¹ /prɪˈsɪʒən/ also **pre·cise·ness** /prɪˈsaɪsnəs/— *n* [U] exactness: *Scientific instruments have to be made with great precision.* —opposite **imprecision**

precision² *adj* [A] **1** made or done with great exactness: *a precision landing* | *precision bombing* **2** used for producing very exact results: *Precision instruments are used to help pilots in guiding their aircraft.*

pre·clude /prɪˈkluːd/ *v* [T (from)] *fml* to prevent; make impossible: *The temporary cease-fire agreement does not preclude possible retaliatory attacks later.* | *I wouldn't want to preclude the possibility of a small payment being made.* (=I wouldn't want to say that that could not happen.) —compare PREEMPT **—·clusion** /ˈkluːʒən/ *n* [U]

pre·co·cious /prɪˈkəʊʃəs/ *adj* showing unusually early development of mind or body: *a precocious child who could already talk well at the age of one* | *Her precocious mathematical ability astounded her parents.* — ~ **ly** *adv* — ~ **ness** also **-city** *fml* /prɪˈkɒsəti/—ˈkɑː-/— *n* [U]

pre·cog·ni·tion /ˌpriːkɒgˈnɪʃən/—kɑːg-/ *n* [U (of)] *tech* knowledge of something that will happen in the future, esp. as received in the form of a direct message to the mind which cannot be explained

pre·con·ceived /ˌpriːkənˈsiːvd◄/ *adj* (of an idea, opinion, etc.) formed in advance, without (enough) knowledge or experience: *To appreciate his work you have to put aside any preconceived notions about how paintings should look.*

pre·con·cep·tion /ˌpriːkənˈsepʃən/ *n* [(about)] an opinion formed in advance, without actual knowledge: *Most of my preconceptions about Jane were proved wrong when I eventually met her.*

pre·con·di·tion /ˌpriːkənˈdɪʃən/ *n* [(of)] something that must be agreed to in advance if something else is to happen: *He made it a precondition of the talks that they should be held in a neutral country.*

pre·cook /ˌpriːˈkʊk/ *v* [T] to cook (food) partly or completely in advance, esp. so as to be heated up again later for eating

pre·cur·sor /prɪˈkɜːsəʳ/—ˈkɜːr-/ *n* [(of, to)] *fml* something that comes before another and leads to it or is developed into it: *The precursor of the modern car was a horseless carriage with a petrol engine.* | *Rapidly rising inflation has traditionally been a precursor to recession.*

pre·date /priːˈdeɪt/ *v* [T (by)] to be earlier in history than; ANTEDATE: *This coin predates the Roman occupation.*

pred·a·tor /ˈpredətəʳ/ *n* **1** a predatory animal or bird **2** a predatory person

pred·a·to·ry /ˈpredətəri/—tɔːri/ *adj* **1** also **pre·da·ceous, pre·da·cious** /prɪˈdeɪʃəs/ *fml rare*— (esp. of a wild animal) that kills and eats other animals **2** having the habit of trying to take other people's property: (fig.) *Watch out for that predatory female — she's after everyone else's husband!*

pre·de·cease /ˌpriːdɪˈsiːs/ *v* [T] *law* to die before (someone): *If you should predecease your wife …*

pre·de·ces·sor /ˈpriːdɪˌsesəʳ/—ˈpre-/ *n* [(of)] **1** a person who held a position before someone else: *Our new doctor is much younger than his predecessor.* **2** something formerly used, but which has now been changed for something else: *This is the fifth plan we've made and it's no better than any of its predecessors.* —compare SUCCESSOR

pre·des·ti·na·tion /prɪˌdestɪˈneɪʃən, ˌpriːdes-/ *n* [U] **1** the belief that God has decided everything that will happen, and that no human effort can change things —compare FREE WILL (2) **2** the belief that by God's wish some souls will go to heaven after death, and others will go to HELL

pre·des·tine /prɪˈdestɪn/ *v* [T (to) *often pass.*] *fml* to settle in advance, esp. as if by fate or the will of God: *The plan seemed predestined to failure.* [+obj+to-v] *It seemed predestined to fail.* | *It was as if we were predestined to meet.*

pre·de·ter·mine /ˌpriːdɪˈtɜːmɪn/—ˈtɜːr-/ *v* [T *usu. pass.*] *fml* **1** to fix unchangeably from the beginning: *The colour of a person's eyes is predetermined by those of his parents.*

2 to arrange in advance; PREARRANGE: *We met at a predetermined spot a few miles out of town.* **—·mination** /ˌpriːdɪˌtɜːmɪˈneɪʃən/—ˈtɜːr-/ *n* [U]

pre·de·ter·min·er /ˌpriːdɪˈtɜːmɪnəʳ/—ˈtɜːr-/ *n tech* a word that can be used before a DETERMINER (=word such as **the, that, his,** etc.): *In the phrases "all the boys" and "both his parents", the words "all" and "both" are predeterminers.*

pre·dic·a·ment /prɪˈdɪkəmənt/ *n* a difficult or unpleasant situation in which one does not know what to do, or must make a difficult choice

pred·i·cate¹ /ˈpredɪkət/ *n* the part of a sentence which makes a statement about the subject: *In "Fishes swim" and "She is an artist", "swim" and "is an artist" are predicates.*

pred·i·cate² /ˈpredɪkeɪt/ *v* [T] *fml* **1** [(on) *often pass.*] to take something as a reason for doing (something else); base: *The company's plans to increase production were predicated on the growing demand for computer products.* **2** [(of)] to state that (a particular quality) belongs to (someone or something): *We predicate rationality of man.*

pre·dic·a·tive /prɪˈdɪkətɪv/—ˈpredɪkeɪ-/ *adj* (esp. of an adjective or phrase) coming after a verb: *In "He is alive", "alive" is a predicative adjective.* —compare ATTRIBUTIVE — ~ **ly** *adv*

pre·dict /prɪˈdɪkt/ *v* [T] to see or describe (a future happening) in advance as a result of knowledge, experience, thought, etc.: *The economists predicted an increase in the rate of inflation.* [+that] *The fortune-teller predicted that I would marry a doctor.* [+wh-] *It's hard to predict when it will happen.* —compare FORECAST¹

pre·dic·ta·ble /prɪˈdɪktəbəl/ *adj* **1** that can be predicted **2** *derog* not being or doing anything unexpected or showing any imagination: *You're so predictable!* —opposite **unpredictable** **—·bly** *adv* : *Predictably, he came late.* (=it could be expected because he always does) **—·bility** /prɪˌdɪktəˈbɪləti/ *n* [U]

pre·dic·tion /prɪˈdɪkʃən/ *n* [C;U] the act of predicting or something predicted: *Her prediction turned out to be correct.* [+that] *He made a prediction that the government would be defeated at the general election.* **—·tive** /ˈdɪktɪv/ *adj* **—·tively** *adv*

pre·di·gest /ˌpriːdaɪˈdʒest, ˌpriːdɪ-/ *v* [T] **1** to make (food) easier for sick people or babies to take, esp. by chemical treatment **2** *infml, often derog* to make simpler, for easy use: *predigested facts*

pre·di·lec·tion /ˌpriːdɪˈlekʃən/—ˌpredlˈek-/ *n* [(for)] *fml* a special liking that has become a habit: *a predilection for dangerous sports*

pre·dis·pose /ˌpriːdɪsˈpəʊz/ *v* [T+obj+adv/prep/to-v] *rather fml* to influence (someone) in the stated way, esp. in advance: *Her father is of course predisposed in her favour.* (=tends to think favourably of her) | *His weak chest predisposes him to* (=makes him tend to have) *winter illnesses.* | *After all the bad things I'd heard about her I wasn't predisposed to like her.* (=I thought I would dislike her) —compare PREJUDICE²

pre·dis·po·si·tion /ˌpriːdɪspəˈzɪʃən/ *n* [(to, towards)] a state of body or mind that is favourable to something, often something bad: *a predisposition to arthritis* | *an unhealthy predisposition towards violence*

pre·dom·i·nant /prɪˈdɒmənənt/—ˈdɑː-/ *adj* [(over)] most powerful, noticeable, or important, or largest in number: *Bright red was the predominant colour in the room.* **—·nance** *n* [S;U (of)] *fml*: *There is a predominance of black people* (=more of them than other races) *in the population of Jamaica.* —compare PREPONDERANCE

pre·dom·i·nant·ly /prɪˈdɒmənəntli/—ˈdɑː-/ *adv rather fml* mostly; mainly: *Jamaica's population is predominantly black.*

pre·dom·i·nate /prɪˈdɒməneɪt/—ˈdɑː-/ *v* [I (over)] **1** to have the main power or influence: *The views of the left wing have tended to predominate within the party.* **2** to be greater or greatest in numbers, force, etc.; be most noticeable: *In northern areas pine forests predominate (over deciduous woodland).*

pree·mie /ˈpriːmi/ *n AmE infml* a PREMATURE (2) baby

pre·em·i·nent /priːˈemənənt/ *adj* [(in, among, at)] *fml apprec* above all others in having some usu. good quality, ability, or main activity: *This country has always been* *preeminent in the field of medical research.* — ~**ly** *adv* —**·nence** *n* [U]

pre·empt /priː'empt/ *v* [T *often pass.*] to make (something) ineffective, or remove any reason for doing (something), by taking action in advance: *The council found that their traffic plans had been preempted by a government decision.* —compare PRECLUDE — ~**ion** /'empʃən/ *n* [U]

pre·emp·tive /priː'emptɪv/ *adj* done before other people have a chance to act, and in order to prevent them from doing so: *a preemptive offer for the property our competitors wanted to buy* | *The army launched a preemptive strike (=attack) against the enemy.* — ~**ly** *adv*

preen /priːn/ *v* [I;T] (of a bird) to clean or smooth (itself or its feathers) with its beak: (fig.) *He was preening himself in front of the mirror.*
   preen *sbdy.* **on/upon** *sthg. phr v* [T] *derog rare* to feel proud of or satisfied with (oneself) because of (an action or quality)

pre·ex·ist /ˌpriːɪg'zɪst/ *v* [I] *fml* to exist before, esp. as a soul before uniting with the present body — ~**ence** *n* [U] — ~**ent** *adj*

pre·fab /'priːfæb‖ˌpriː'fæb/ *n* *infml* a small prefabricated house, esp. of the type put up in Britain and elsewhere after the Second World War. Prefabs were intended as temporary homes to replace houses which were destroyed in the war, though some prefabs are still in use in Britain now.

pre·fab·ri·cate /priː'fæbrɪkeɪt/ *v* [T] to make (the parts of a building, ship, etc.) in a factory in large numbers and standard sizes, ready for fitting together in any place chosen for building —**cation** /ˌpriːˌfæbrɪ'keɪʃən/ *n* [U]

pre·fab·ri·cat·ed /priː'fæbrɪkeɪtɪd/ *adj* (of a building, ship, etc.) built out of prefabricated parts

pref·ace¹ /'prefɪs/ *n* [(to)] **1** an introduction to a book or speech **2** an action that is intended to introduce something else more important

▷ USAGE A **preface**, a **foreword**, and an **introduction** all come in the first pages of a book before the main contents. An **introduction** is usually longer than a **preface** or **foreword**. A **foreword** is sometimes more informal than a **preface** or **introduction**, or written from a more personal point of view The **beginning** of the book is the early part of the actual contents, after the **preface**.◁

preface² *v* [T] *fml* **1** to act as a preface to: *Several pages of closely reasoned argument preface her account of the war.* **2** [+obj+adv/prep, esp. **with**] to introduce (speech or writing) in the stated way: *She prefaced her remarks with a few words of welcome to the guest speaker.* — compare PREFIX² (2)

pret·a·to·ry /'prefətəri‖-tɔːri/ *adj fml* acting as a preface or introduction: *a few prefatory remarks*

pre·fect /'priːfekt/ *n* **1** (in some British schools) an older pupil with certain powers to control and punish other pupils **2** (*sometimes cap.*) (in certain countries) a public officer or judge with duties in government, the police, or the army: *the Prefect of Police of Paris*

pre·fec·ture /'priːfektʃʊəʳ‖-tʃər/ *n* **1** a governmental division or area of certain countries, such as France and Japan **2** (in France) the official home or place of work of a prefect

pre·fer /prɪ'fɜːʳ/ *v* -**rr**- [T *not in progressive forms*] **1** [(to)] to choose (one thing or action) rather than another; like better: *"Would you like meat or fish?" "I'd prefer meat, please."* | *I much prefer dogs to cats.* [+v-ing] *I prefer singing to acting.* [+to-v] *He chose Spain, but personally I'd prefer to go to Greece.* [+obj+to-v] *"Let me wash the dishes — or would you prefer me to dry them?"* [+that] *Would you prefer that we reschedule the meeting for next week?* **2** *law* to officially make (a charge) against someone: *Since they are so young, the police have decided not to prefer charges/a charge.* **3** [(to)] *fml or tech* to appoint to a higher position, esp. in the church

pref·e·ra·ble /'prefərəbəl/ *adj* [(to)] better, esp. because more suitable; that one should or would prefer: *A dark suit is preferable to a light one for evening wear.* | *Anything is preferable to having her stay for the whole week!* —**bly** *adv* : *I can meet you at any time tomorrow, but preferably not before 11 o'clock.* (=I would prefer not before 11 o'clock)

pref·e·rence /'prefərəns/ *n* [C;U] **1** [(for, to)] (a) liking for one thing rather than another: *Of the two, my preference is for the smaller car.* | *I don't know your preferences, so please help yourself.* (=choose the things you prefer) | *"Would you like tea or coffee?" "Either; I've no strong preference."* | *He always drinks red wine in preference to* (=rather than) *white.* **2** [(over, to)] (a) special favour or consideration shown to a person, group, etc., esp. in business matters: *We've granted that country special trade preferences.* | *In considering people for jobs, we give preference to those with some experience.* | *Teachers try not to show preference to any particular student.*

preference share /'··· ·/ *BrE*‖**preferred stock** *AmE*— *n* a SHARE¹ (2) in a public company that usu. pays a fixed rather than a variable DIVIDEND, and which would be worth more than an ordinary share if the company were to fail

pref·e·ren·tial /ˌprefə'renʃəl◀/ *adj* [A] of, giving, receiving, or showing PREFERENCE (2): *The theatre gives preferential booking privileges to its regular patrons.* | *a controversial new law that gives preferential treatment to certain minority groups* — ~**ly** *adv* : *Don't expect to be treated preferentially.*

pre·fer·ment /prɪ'fɜːmənt‖-ɜːr-/ *n* [U (**to**)] *fml or tech* appointment to a higher rank or position, esp. in the church

preferred stock /·ˌ· '·/ *n* [U;C] *AmE for* PREFERENCE SHARE

pre·fig·ure /ˌpriː'fɪgəʳ‖-gjər/ *v* [T] *fml* to be a sign of (something that will come later): *This meeting may prefigure an improvement in relations between the two countries.* —**uration** /prɪˌfɪgə'reɪʃən‖-gjə-/ *n* [C;U]

pre·fix¹ /'priːfɪks/ *n* **1** (in grammar) an AFFIX added to the beginning of a word (as in *un*tie, *mis*understood) — compare SUFFIX **2** a title used before a person's name: *"Mr" and "Dr" are prefixes.* **3** a CODE¹ (3)

prefix² *v* [T] **1** to add a prefix to (a word or name) **2** [(to)] to add (something) to the beginning (of): *She prefixed a few complimentary remarks to her speech.* —compare PREFACE²

preg·nan·cy /'pregnənsi/ *n* [C;U] (an example of) the condition of being pregnant: *You are advised not to smoke during pregnancy.* | *This is her third pregnancy.*

pregnancy test /'··· ·/ *n* a test performed on a woman's URINE to find out whether she is pregnant or not. In many countries women can buy pregnancy test materials at the CHEMIST's and do the test themselves.

preg·nant /'pregnənt/ *adj* **1** (of a woman or female animal) having an unborn child or unborn young in the body: *She was pregnant with her second child.* | *How long has she been pregnant?* [after *n*] *She's five months pregnant.* **2** [A] full of important but unexpressed or hidden meaning: *His words were followed by a pregnant pause.* **3** [F+**with**] *fml* filled with something not yet fully known, understood, or developed; giving signs or warnings of some future development: *Every phrase in this poem is pregnant with meaning.* | *a situation pregnant with several interesting possibilities* — ~**ly** *adv*

pre·heat /ˌpriː'hiːt/ *v* [T] to heat up (an OVEN) to a particular temperature before using it for cooking

pre·hen·sile /prɪ'hensaɪl‖-səl/ *adj tech* (of a part of the body) able to curl round things and hold on to them: *The monkey was hanging from the branch by its prehensile tail.*

pre·his·tor·ic /ˌpriːhɪ'stɒrɪk◀‖-'stɔː-, -'stɑː-/ *adj* of a time before recorded history: *prehistoric man* | *prehistoric burial grounds* | (fig.) *His ideas on morals are really prehistoric.* (=very old-fashioned) —compare HISTORIC — ~**ally** /kli/ *adv*

pre·his·to·ry /priː'hɪstəri/ *n* [U] the time in human history before there were any written records

pre·judge /ˌpriː'dʒʌdʒ/ *v* [T] *derog* to form an opinion about (someone or something) before knowing or examining all the facts: *Try not to prejudge the issue.* —**judgment, -judgement** *n* [C;U]

prej·u·dice¹ /'predʒʊdɪs/ *n* **1** [C;U (**against, in favour of**)] (an) unfair and often unfavourable feeling or opinion formed without thinking deeply and clearly or without enough knowledge, and sometimes resulting from fear or distrust of ideas different from one's own: *They accused him of having a prejudice against his women employees.* | *A judge must be free from prejudice.* | *A new law has been brought in to discourage racial prejudice.*

(=prejudice against members of other races) **2** [U] *fml* **a** harm caused to something or someone by the action or judgment of another: *He continued to smoke, to the prejudice of his health.* **b** harm to one's own right or claim in law: *We accept this interim settlement,* **without prejudice to** *our claim for a full settlement later on.* (=we still keep our right to such a claim)

prejudice² *v* [T] **1** [(**against/in favour of**) *often pass.*] to cause to have a prejudice; influence unfairly: *She's prejudiced against French wine because she's Italian.* | *His pleasant voice and manner prejudiced the jury in his favour.* **2** to weaken or harm (someone's case, expectations, etc.): *Your bad spelling may prejudice your chances of getting the job.* —compare PREDISPOSE

prej·u·diced /'predʒʊdɪst/ *adj derog* feeling or showing prejudice; unfair: *Don't ask him; he's prejudiced.* | *a prejudiced judgment* | *racially prejudiced* —opposite **unprejudiced**

prej·u·di·cial /ˌpredʒʊˈdɪʃəl◂/ *adj* [F+**to**] *rather fml* harmful: *Too much smoking is prejudicial to health.*

prel·ate /'prelɪt/ *n* a priest of high position in the church, such as a BISHOP or ABBOT

pre·lim·i·na·ry¹ /prɪˈlɪmɪnəri‖-neri/ *adj* [A] coming before and introducing or preparing for something more important: *The students take a preliminary test in March, and the main exam in July.* | *Our team got beaten in the preliminary rounds of the competition.* | *May I make a few preliminary remarks before we start the interview?*

preliminary² *n* [*usu. pl.*] something done first, to introduce or prepare for later things: *There are a lot of preliminaries to be gone through before you can visit certain foreign countries.*

pre·lit·e·rate /ˌpriːˈlɪtərɪt/ *adj tech* not having a written language or keeping written records: *ancient preliterate societies* —compare ILLITERATE

prel·ude /'preljuːd/ *n* [(**to**)] **1** [*usu. sing.*] something that is followed by something larger or more important: *The fighting in the streets may be a prelude to more serious trouble.* **2 a** a short piece of music that introduces a large musical work: *the prelude to Wagner's "Mastersingers"* **b** a short separate piece of music for piano or ORGAN

pre·mar·i·tal /priːˈmærɪtəl/ *adj* happening or existing before marriage — ~**ly** *adv*

premar·i·tal con·tract /ˌ·ˈ·· ˈ··/ also **prenuptial agreement**— *n AmE* an agreement made by two people getting married about how to divide up their property if they decide to separate. Premarital contracts are common in the US but not in Britain.

premarital sex /ˌ·ˈ·· ˈ·/ *n* [U] sexual relations between a man and a woman before marriage. In Britain, the US, and many other Western countries, this is thought to be quite common and it is not generally considered to be as immoral or shocking as it was in former times, though some groups are strongly against it, e.g. the Catholic Church.

pre·ma·ture /'premətʃər, -tʃʊər, ˌpremə'tʃʊər‖ˌpriːmə'tʃʊər/ *adj* **1** developing or happening before the natural or proper time: *His premature death at the age of 32 is a great loss.* **2** (of a baby or birth) born or happening after less than the usual period of time inside the mother's body: [*after n*] *The baby was two months premature.* (=was born two months earlier than expected) **3** *derog* done too early or too soon: *I think your criticism of the new law is a bit premature, as we don't yet know all the details.* — ~**ly** *adv*

pre·med /priːˈmed/ *n,adj AmE abbrev. for:* premedical; the university course a student takes before entering medical school: *premed studies* | *She's premed* (she is taking premedical studies).

pre·med·i·tat·ed /priːˈmedɪteɪtɪd‖prɪ-/ *adj often derog* planned in advance and done on purpose: *premeditated murder* | *a premeditated attack on my reputation* — opposite **unpremeditated** —**ion** /priːˌmedɪˈteɪʃən‖ prɪ-/ *n* [U] *fml: The jury has to decide if the act was committed with premeditation.*

pre·men·stru·al /priːˈmenstruəl/ *adj tech* happening just before a PERIOD (4)

premenstrual ten·sion /ˌ·ˈ·· ˈ··/ also **PMT, premenstrual syndrome**— *n* [U] the unpleasant feelings including tiredness, headaches and bad temper felt by many women during the days before a PERIOD (4), that are caused by changes in the levels of HORMONES in the body. In the past, many people did not take women seriously when they complained about these feelings. It is now generally accepted that PMT is quite common and can cause real suffering and upsetting changes in behaviour.

prem·i·er¹ /'premiər‖prɪˈmɪər/ *n* (*often cap.*) (esp. in newspapers) PRIME MINISTER: *The Irish premier is paying an official visit to Britain.* | *"Premier Wilson resigns"* (news story title) — ~**ship** *n*

premier² *adj* [A] *fml apprec* finest or most important: *She attended Britain's premier university.*

Premier Di·vi·sion /ˌ··· ·ˈ··‖ˌ·,· ·ˈ··/ [*the*] the top division in Scottish football —compare PREMIER LEAGUE; see also FOOTBALL (1)

prem·i·ere¹, **-ère** /'premieər‖prɪˈmɪər/ *n* the first public performance of a play or film

premiere², **-ère** *v* [T *often pass.*] to give a premiere of (a play or film): *His film was premiered in New York.*

Premier League /ˌ··· ˈ·‖ˌ·,· ˈ·/ [*the*] the top division in English football —compare PREMIER DIVISION; see also FOOTBALL (1)

Prem·in·ger /'premɪndʒər/, **Ot·to** /'ɒtəʊ‖ˈɑː-/ (1906–86) an American film DIRECTOR, born in Austria. His films include *Anatomy of a Murder* and *Exodus*.

prem·ise /'premɪs/ *n* **1** *fml* a statement or idea on which reasoning is based: [+*that*] *British and American justice works on the premise that an accused person is innocent until he's proved guilty.* **2** also **prem·iss** /'premɪs/— *tech* (in LOGIC) either of two statements (**major premise** and **minor premise**) from which a third statement can be proved to be true

prem·is·es /'premɪsɪz/ *n* [P] a building with any surrounding land, considered as a particular piece of property: *Taxes on business premises are higher than those on private premises.* | *Food bought in this shop may not be eaten* **on the premises.** (=must be taken away and eaten somewhere else)

pre·mi·um /'priːmiəm/ *n* **1** [C] a payment made to buy insurance: *The annual premium on my policy is £50.* **2** [C] an additional amount of money (above a standard rate) **3** [U] *AmE* HIGH-OCTANE petrol **4 at a premium: a** (of a business share) at a rate above the usual value **b** rare or difficult to get, and therefore worth more than usual: *During the holiday months hotel rooms are at a premium.* **5 put a premium on** to cause (a quality or action) to be advantageous: *Work paid according to the amount done puts a premium on speed and not on quality.*

premium bond /ˈ··· ·/ *n* (*often caps.*) (in Britain) a numbered piece of paper bought from the government, that gives the buyer the chance of a monthly prize of a small or large amount of money —see also ERNIE

pre·mo·ni·tion /ˌpreməˈnɪʃən, ˌpriː-/ *n* [(**of**)] a feeling that something, esp. something unpleasant, is going to happen; forewarning: *The day before her accident, she had a premonition of danger.*

pre·mon·i·to·ry /prɪˈmɒnɪtəri‖-ˈmɑːnɪtɔːri/ *adj fml* giving a warning

pre·na·tal /ˌpriːˈneɪtl◂/ *adj AmE for* ANTENATAL — ~**ly** *adv*

pre·nup·tial a·gree·ment /priːˌnʌpʃəl əˈgriːmənt/ *n* see PREMARITAL CONTRACT

pre·oc·cu·pa·tion /priːˌɒkjʊˈpeɪʃən‖-,ɑːk-/ *n* **1** [S;U] (**with**)] the state of being preoccupied: *Such an excessive preoccupation with one's health can't be normal.* **2** [C] something that takes up one's attention: *He's got so many preoccupations at the moment that he ignores his family completely.*

pre·oc·cu·pied /priːˈɒkjʊpaɪd‖-ˈɑːk-/ *adj* [(**with**)] with the mind fixed on something, esp. something worrying, so that one pays no attention to anything else: *a preoccupied expression* | *Come and see me next week, when I'm not so preoccupied with the annual accounts.*

pre·oc·cu·py /priːˈɒkjʊpaɪ‖-ˈɑːk-/ *v* [T] to fill the thoughts of (someone or someone's mind) almost completely, esp. so that not enough attention is given to other things: *Something's been preoccupying you lately — what is it?*

pre·or·dain /ˌpriːɔːˈdeɪn‖-ɔːr-/ *v* [T (**to**) *usu. pass.*] *fml* (esp. of God or fate) to fix or decide in advance or from the beginning: *I sometimes think our failure was preordained.*

[+(*that*)] *Perhaps it was preordained that we should fail.* [+*obj*+*to-v*] *We seemed preordained to fail.* — ~ **ment,** **-dination** /ˌpriːɔːˈdeɪʃən‖-ɔːr-/ *fml n* [C;U]

prep¹ /prep/ *n* [U] *BrE infml* school work that is done at home. This word is more often used by children in private schools than in STATE SCHOOLS, where the usual word is HOMEWORK.

prep² *v* **-pp-** *AmE infml* **1** [I] to attend PREPARATORY school: *My little brother's still prepping.* **2** [I] to do school work at home **3** [T] to prepare (someone) for an operation or examination: *The nurse prepped the patient for surgery.*

prep³ *n written abbrev. for:* PREPOSITION

pre·pack /ˌpriːˈpæk/ *also* **pre·pack·age** /-ˈpækɪdʒ/— *v* [T] to wrap up (food or other articles) before offering it for sale

pre·paid /ˌpriːˈpeɪd◂/ *adj* already paid for: *Return the film in the prepaid envelope.* (=the user does not have to put a stamp on)

prep·a·ra·tion /ˌprepəˈreɪʃən/ *n* **1** [U (**for, of**)] the act or process of preparing: *He didn't do enough preparation for his exam, and failed.* | *Plans for the new school are now in preparation.* (=being prepared) **2** [C (**for**) *usu. pl.*] an arrangement for a future event: *Preparations for the queen's visit are almost complete.* **3** [C] something that has been made by mixing a number of (chemical) substances, usu. for use as a medicine, COSMETIC, etc.: *a new preparation for cleaning the skin*

pre·par·a·to·ry /prɪˈpærətəri‖-tɔːri/ *adj* [A] **1** done in order to get ready for something: *preparatory talks to clear the way for a settlement* **2** **preparatory to** *fml* as a preparation for; before: *several meetings preparatory to signing the contract*

preparatory school /-ˈ···· ·/ *also* **prep school** *infml— n* **1** (in Britain) a private school for children between the ages of 8 and 13, where they are made ready to attend a school for older pupils, usu. a PUBLIC SCHOOL. Only a small PERCENTAGE of school-age children attend these schools. Most preparatory schools are for boys only or girls only. **2** (in the US) a private school that makes pupils ready for college

pre·pare /prɪˈpeəʳ/ *v* **1** [T (**for**)] to put into a suitable state for a purpose, event, or experience: *First prepare the rice by washing it, then cook it in boiling water.* | *a course that prepares students for the English exams* [+*obj*+*to-v*] *preparing the city to withstand an attack* **2** [T (**for**)] to put together or make, e.g. by combining things: *The defence lawyers asked for another week to prepare their case.* | *John is preparing a meal for us.* [+*obj(i)*+*obj(d)*] *John is preparing us a meal.* **3** [I;T (**for**)] to get ready or make by collecting supplies, making necessary arrangements, planning, studying, etc.: *Will you help me prepare for the party?* | *Who prepared these building plans?* [+*to-v*] *They are busy preparing to go on holiday.* **4** [I;T (**for**)] to put (oneself) into a suitable state of mind for something: *Prepare (yourself) for a shock.* [+*to-v*] *Prepare to die, you cowardly traitor!* [+*obj*+*to-v*] *He prepared himself to accept defeat.*

pre·pared /prɪˈpeəd‖-ˈpeərd/ *adj* **1** made in advance: *The chairman read out a prepared statement.* **2** [F+*to-v*] willing: *I'm not prepared to listen to all your weak excuses.* **3** [F+**for**] expecting: *I wasn't prepared for such a large bill.* **4** **Be prepared** the MOTTO of the BOY SCOUTS, often used humorously when saying that a person should carry a particular thing with them because it might be useful

pre·pared·ness /prɪˈpeədnəs, -ˈpeəʳd-‖-ˈpeərəd-, -ˈpeərd-/ *n* [U] (the state of) being ready for something: *the country's lack of military preparedness*

pre·pay /ˌpriːˈpeɪ/ *v* **-paid** [T] to pay for (something) in advance: *All accommodation must be prepaid.*

pre·pon·de·rance /prɪˈpɒndərəns‖-ˈpɑːn-/ *n* [S (**of**)] *fml* the state of being greater in amount, number, etc.: *There was a preponderance of female students in the music department.* (=there were more females than males) —compare PREDOMINANT — **rant** *adj* [(**over**)] — **rantly** *adv*

pre·pon·de·rate /prɪˈpɒndəreɪt‖-ˈpɑːn-/ *v* [I (**over**)] *fml* to be greater in quantity, importance, influence, etc.

prep·o·si·tion /ˌprepəˈzɪʃən/ *n* a word used with a noun, PRONOUN, or *-ing* form to show its connection with another word: *In "a house made of wood" and "We opened it by breaking the lock", "of", and "by" are prepositions: Words followed by Prepositions — ~ **al** adj — ~ **ally** adv: In "He went out of the door", "out" is being used prepositionally.*

prepositional phrase /ˌ····· ·ˈ·/ *n tech* a phrase consisting of a preposition and the noun following it (such as *in bed, in his bed, in the bed*)

pre·pos·sessed /ˌpriːpəˈzest/ *adj* [F] *fml* **1** [+**by**] favourably influenced **2** PREOCCUPIED — **session** /ˈzeʃən/ *n* [C;U]

pre·pos·sess·ing /ˌpriːpəˈzesɪŋ◂/ *adj fml apprec* producing a favourable effect at once; attractive: *a prepossessing smile* —opposite **unprepossessing**

pre·pos·ter·ous /prɪˈpɒstərəs‖-ˈpɑːs-/ *adj fml* **1** completely unreasonable; ABSURD: *What a preposterous suggestion!* **2** foolish in a way that makes people laugh: *Look at that preposterous car — 25 feet long and covered in chromium!* — ~ **ly** *adv*

prep·py /ˈprepi/ *adj AmE infml* typical of students or former students of expensive private schools in the US, esp. in being neat and well-dressed: *a preppy girl* | *preppy clothes* | *a bar that caters for the rich preppy set*

preppies

prep school /ˈ· ·/ *n infml for* PREPARATORY SCHOOL

Pre-Raph·ael·ite /ˌpriː-ˈræfəlaɪt‖-fiəlaɪt/ *n* a person belonging to the group of late 19th-century English painters (**Pre-Raphaelite Brotherhood**) who based their work on the supposed artistic principles and practices of the late Middle Ages, turning away from industrialized Britain to look for the beauty of the past. Their paintings had many small details and often used bright colours on a white background. One of the best-known Pre-Raphaelites was D G ROSSETTI and one of the most famous followers of the group was William Morris. —**Pre-Raphaelite** *adj*

pre·re·cord /ˌpriːrɪˈkɔːd‖-ˈkɔːrd/ *v* [T] to record (music, a play, a speech, etc.) on a machine for later use

pre·req·ui·site /priːˈrekwɪzɪt/ *n* [(**of, for, to**)] *fml* something that is necessary before something else can happen or be done: *A reasonable proficiency in English is a prerequisite of/for joining this advanced course.*

pre·rog·a·tive /prɪˈrɒgətɪv‖-ˈrɑː-/ *n* [*usu. sing.*] a special right belonging to a particular person, esp. because of the official position they hold: *The President may use his prerogative to pardon a criminal.* —compare PRIVILEGE (1); see also ROYAL PREROGATIVE

pres. *written abbrev. for:* **1** present **2** (*usu. cap.*) president

pres·age¹ /ˈpresɪdʒ, prɪˈseɪdʒ/ *v* [T *not in progressive forms*] *fml or lit* to be a warning or sign of (a future event)

pres·age² /ˈpresɪdʒ/ *n* [(**of**)] *lit* a warning feeling or sign that something, esp. something bad, will happen

Pres·by·te·ri·an /ˌprezbɪˈtɪəriən◂/ *n, adj* (a member) of a Protestant church governed by a body of official people all of equal rank and following the principles of Calvinism including severe rules of behaviour and morals. John Knox established Presbyterianism in Scotland where it has had a great influence on society, and there are also Presbyterian churches in other parts of the UK, the US, and other countries. — ~ **ism** *n* [U]

pres·by·te·ry /ˈprezbɪtəri‖-teri/ *n* **1** (in the Presbyterian Church) (the area controlled by) a local court or ruling body **2** (in the Roman Catholic Church) the house in which a local priest lives **3** the eastern part of a church, behind the place where the CHOIR (=trained singers) sit

pre·school¹ /ˌpriːˈskuːl◂/ *adj* [A] of or in the time in a child's life before it goes to school

pre·school² /ˈpriːskuːl/ *n AmE for* NURSERY SCHOOL

pre-school play-group /ˌ· · ·ˈ··/ *n* PLAYGROUP

pre·sci·ent /ˈpresiənt/ *adj lit or fml* able to imagine or guess what will probably happen — **ence** *n* [U]

pre·scribe /prɪˈskraɪb/ *v* [I;T (**for**)] **1** to say (what medicine or treatment) a sick person should or must have:

What can you prescribe for the pain in my back, doctor? **2** *fml* to state (what must happen or be done in certain conditions): *What punishment does the law prescribe for this crime?* [+*wh-*] *Someone who does such foolish things as you has no right to prescribe how others should behave.* —compare PROSCRIBE

pre·scribed /prɪˈskraɪbd/ *adj* fixed (as if) by rule: *It's quite an informal job; you don't have to work a prescribed number of hours.*

pre·script /ˈpriːˌskrɪpt/ *n fml* an order or rule that is prescribed (PRESCRIBE (2))

pre·scrip·tion /prɪˈskrɪpʃən/ *n* **1** [C (**for**)] **a** a particular medicine or treatment ordered by a doctor for a person's illness: (fig.) *What's your prescription for a happy marriage?* (=What do you suggest is needed to make a marriage happy?) **b** a written order describing this, which is given to a person by his or her doctor (in Britain, a GP) and is then taken to a CHEMIST (*BrE*) or PHARMACIST (*AmE*) who will supply the medicine described in it. There are certain drugs and medicines which chemists are not allowed to sell to people without prescriptions. **2** [U] the act of prescribing

prescription charge /·ˈ··· ·/ *n* [*usu. pl.*] (in Britain) an amount of money that has to be paid (usu. to a CHEMIST) when getting medicine through the National Health Service. These charges increased in the 1980s but still do not represent the full cost of the medicine. Certain groups of people, e.g. children, old people, and the unemployed, do not have to pay. In the US, people have to pay the full amount for any medicine that they need.

pre·scrip·tive /prɪˈskrɪptɪv/ *adj* **1** *tech, sometimes derog* saying how a language ought to be used, rather than simply describing how it is used: *prescriptive grammar* — compare DESCRIPTIVE (2) **2** *fml* saying how something should be done or what someone should do —**-tivism** *n* [U] —**-tivist** *n* — ~**ly** *adv*

prescriptive right /·ˌ··· ·ˈ·/ *n law* a right to do something which has existed for so long by custom that it has the force of law

pres·ence /ˈprezəns/ *n* **1** [U] the fact of being present: *She was so quiet that her presence was hardly noticed.* | *Your presence is requested at the club meeting on Thursday.* | *He never seemed at ease in my presence.* (=when I was there; when we were together) | *The concert will be performed in the presence of the Queen.* (=she will attend it) | *The police scientists detected the presence of poison in the dead woman's blood.* —opposite **absence 2** [S] a group of people of the stated type in a place, regarded as a sign that they or their country are active or have influence there: *He advocated the withdrawal of the American presence in the Lebanon.* | *There was a strong police presence at the anti-nuclear rally.* **3** [S;U] *apprec* personal qualities and ways of behaving that have a strong effect on others: *a man of great presence* **4** [C *usu. sing.*] a spirit or an influence that cannot be seen but is felt to be near: *I could feel a strange presence in the room.* **5 make one's presence felt** to have a strong noticeable effect (on the people around one): *Since she joined the team last season she has really made her presence felt.* (=by playing well)

presence of mind /ˌ··· ·ˈ·/ *n* [U] *apprec* the ability to act calmly, quickly, and wisely in conditions of sudden danger or surprise: *When the fire started in the kitchen, John had the presence of mind to turn off the gas.*

pres·ent¹ /ˈprezənt/ *n* **1** something that is given willingly, without the expectation that anything will be given in return; a gift: *They unwrapped their Christmas presents.* —see colour picture on page 1212 **2 make someone a present of something: a** to give someone something as a gift: *I don't want all these old books; I'll make you a present of them.* **b** *infml* to give something away to someone carelessly: *They made the other team a present of a goal by careless play.*

pre·sent² /prɪˈzent/ *v* **1** [T (**to, with**)] to give (something) away, esp. at a ceremonial occasion: *to present the prizes at the annual flower show* | *When Mr. Brown left the firm, the director presented a gold watch to him*/*presented him with a gold watch.* | (fig.) *His wife presented him with a brand-new baby girl.* **2** [T (**to, with**)] to be the cause of: *He's clever with computers; they present no problems to him.* | *His sudden resignation presents us with a tricky situation.* **3** [T (**to**)] to offer for consideration or acceptance: *When are the committee presenting their report?* **4**

[T (**to**)] to be when looked at; show: *The grim walls of the prison present a forbidding picture to a new inmate.* **5** [T] to provide for the public to see or hear in a theatre, cinema, etc.: *The National Theatre is presenting "King Lear" next month.* **6** [T] to introduce and take part in (a television or radio show): *And here to present the show tonight is Bob Hope.* **7** [T (**to**)] *fml* to offer politely: *Mrs Gottlieb presents her apologies, but she won't be able to attend.* | *Mr Cox* **presents his compliments** (=greets you politely), *and asks if you will join him.* **8** [T (**to**)] *fml* to introduce (someone) formally, esp. to someone of higher rank: *He had the honour of being presented to the Queen.* | *May I present Mr. Jobbings?* **9 present arms** (used esp. in giving a military order) to hold a weapon upright in front of the body as a ceremonial greeting to an officer or person of high rank **10 present itself: a** (of an idea) to arrive in the mind, esp. unexpectedly **b** (of something possible) to happen: *If the chance to buy this farm presents itself, buy it.* **11 present oneself** *fml* (of a person) to attend; arrive; be present: *He was ordered to present himself at the chairman's office at nine o'clock next morning.*

pres·ent³ /ˈprezənt/ *adj* **1** [F] in this/that place; here/there: *How many people were present at the meeting?* | *Small amounts of the gas are present in the atmosphere.* | *It was unfair to discuss his case if he wasn't present.* —opposite **absent 2** [A] existing or being considered now: *What's your present address?* | *It's usually best to wait, but in the present case* (=in this case) *I'd advise you to act without delay.* **3** [A] being the form of a verb that shows an existing state or act: *"He wants" and "They are coming" are examples of verbs in the present tense.* **4** [F] *fml* strongly felt, remembered, or imagined: *The tragic death of her son last year is still present in her mind.* **5 all present and correct** *humor* a phrase said by someone who is reporting that all the people or things that should be in a place are now there **6 present company (always) excepted** (used when making unfavourable or rude remarks about people) not including anyone now here in this place —see also PRESENTLY (USAGE)

present⁴ *n* [*the*] **1** the PRESENT³ (2) time: *encouraging them to live in the present and not have regrets over lost opportunities in the past* | *"I'm thinking of asking her to marry me." "Well, there's* **no time like the present."** (=you should ask her now) **2** *tech* (in grammar) the form of a verb that shows what exists or is happening now —see also HISTORIC PRESENT **3 at present: a** now; at this time; at this moment: *She's busy at present and can't speak to you.* **b** during this period of time: *At present he's Professor of Chemistry at Oxford.* —see PRESENTLY (USAGE) **4 for the present** now but not necessarily in the future: *Let's leave things as they are for the present; we can always make changes later on if we have to.*

pre·sen·ta·ble /prɪˈzentəbəl/ *adj apprec* suitable to be shown, heard, etc., in public; fit to be seen and judged: *He looked very presentable in his new suit.* | *I'm just going upstairs to* **make myself presentable** (=make my appearance tidy) *before the guests arrive.* | *The children made quite a presentable snowman.* —**bly** *adv*

pre·sen·ta·tion /ˌprezənˈteɪʃən‖ˌpriːzen-, -zən-/ *n* **1** [C;U (**of**)] the act of presenting something: *There are two presentations of the cabaret each night.* | *The presentation of prizes will begin at three o'clock.* **2** [U (**of**)] the way in which something is said, offered, shown, explained, etc., to others: *It's this product's attractive presentation* (=the way it is wrapped up, advertised, etc.) *that makes it sell so well.* **3** [C (**on**)] a talk, usu. to a group of people, in which information is given: *The sales director will give a short presentation on the new sales campaign.* **4** [C;U] *med* the position in which a baby is lying in the mother's body just before birth — ~ **al** *adj*: *Our party's policies are right; our only problems are presentational.* (=we do not explain them in a way that makes them seem attractive)

presentation cop·y /···ˈ·· ˌ··/ *n* a book given away free, esp. by the writer

pres·ent-day /ˌprezənt ˈdeɪ◂/ *adj* [A *no comp.*] modern; existing now

pre·sent·er /prɪˈzentəʳ/ *esp. BrE* ‖ **announcer, host** *AmE*— *n* a person who PRESENTS² (6) a television or radio show

pre·sen·ti·ment /prɪˈzentᵻmənt/ *n* [(**of**)] *fml* an unexplained uncomfortable feeling that something, esp. something bad, is going to happen; PREMONITION: *a presentiment of danger*

pres·ent·ly /'prezəntli/ *adv* **1** in a short time; soon: *The doctor will be here presently.* **2** *esp. AmE & ScotE* at present; now: *The doctor is presently writing a book.*
▷ USAGE British speakers are beginning to use **presently** to mean "now", as the Americans do, rather than "soon". **At present** always means "now".◁

present par·ti·ci·ple /ˌ··· ˈ····/ *n tech* (in grammar) a PARTICIPLE that is formed in English by adding **-ing** to the verb and can be used in compound forms of the verb to show PROGRESSIVE tenses (such as *sleeping* in *She's sleeping*), or sometimes as an adjective (such as *sleeping* in *a sleeping child*) −compare VERBAL NOUN

present per·fect /ˌ··· ˈ··/ also **present perfect tense** /ˌ··· ˌ·· ˈ·/− *n* [*the*+S] *fml or tech for* PERFECT[3]

pres·er·va·tion /ˌprezəˈveɪʃ*ə*n‖-zər-/ *n* [U] the act of preserving or state of being preserved: *The police are responsible for the preservation of law and order.* | *The old building is in a good state of preservation* (=in good condition after a long time) *except for the wooden floors.* −see also SELF-PRESERVATION

preservation or·der /·····‖·······/ *n esp. BrE* an official order that something, esp. a historical building, must be preserved and not destroyed

pre·ser·va·tive /prɪˈzɜːvətɪv‖-ɜːr-/ *n, adj* [C;U] (a usu. chemical substance) that can be used to PRESERVE[1] (3) foods. In many countries, there are now rules about the use of preservatives because of the dangers to health −see E NUMBER

pre·serve[1] /prɪˈzɜːv‖-ɜːrv/ *v* [T] **1** [(**from**)] to prevent (someone or something) from being harmed or destroyed: *The ancient Egyptians knew ways to preserve dead bodies (from decay).* | *I think these interesting old customs should be preserved.* | (*humor*) *Lord preserve us from these so-called experts!* **2** to cause (a condition) to last; keep unchanged: *He's managed to preserve his independence.* | *It's the duty of the police to preserve public order.* **3** [(**in**)] to treat (food) in such a way that it can be kept a long time: *preserved fruit* | *figs preserved in brandy* −see also WELL-PRESERVED —**servable** *adj* —**server** *n*

preserve[2] *n* **1** [C *usu. pl.*]; U] (*often in comb.*) *becoming old-fash* a substance made from fruit boiled in sugar, used esp. for spreading on bread; JAM: *strawberry preserve* **2** [C] a stretch of land or water kept for private hunting or fishing **3** [C] something that belongs to or is for the use of only a certain person or limited number of people: *She considers the arranging of flowers in the church to be her own personal preserve.* | *In the past, fire-fighting/child-care has always been a male/female preserve.*

pre·set /ˌpriːˈset/ *v* **preset**, *present participle* **presetting** [T] to set in advance: *You can preset the video to record programmes while you are out.*

pre·shrunk /ˌpriːˈʃrʌŋk◂/ *adj* (of cloth) made to SHRINK before being sold in order to prevent shrinking after use

pre·side /prɪˈzaɪd/ *v* [I (**at, over**)] *fml* to be in charge (of); lead: *Who is presiding at this meeting?* | *the presiding officer* | *As prime minister, she presided over the biggest ever rise in unemployment.*

pres·i·den·cy /'prezɪdənsi/ *n* **1** [(**of**)] the office of president: *Roosevelt was elected four times to the presidency of the US.* **2** the period during which a person is president

pres·i·dent /'prezɪdənt/ *n* [(**of**)] **1** (*often cap.*) the leader, and often also ruler or chief governing official, of many modern states that do not have a king or queen: *the President of France* | *President Bush* −see extra information on page 568 and see colour picture on page 950
▶CULTURAL NOTE In the US, an election for president is held every four years. Presidents cannot serve more than two TERMS (periods of time), which means that no president can remain in power for longer than eight years. This rule only started in the 1940s, but President Franklin Roosevelt is the only president to have served more than two terms. It is often said that any child born in the US can grow up to become president, because one does not need to come from the upper class or have an important family to become president, although these things sometimes help. Women may run for president, but so far no woman has become president.◀

2 (*sometimes cap.*) the head of a club or society, some universities or colleges, some government departments, etc.: *the President of the Royal Academy* | *I was invited to become president of the local camera club.* **3** *esp. AmE*

(*sometimes cap.*) the head of a business company, bank, etc.: *the president of General Motors* −~**ial** /ˌprezɪ-ˈdenʃ*ə*l◂/ *adj* : *presidential government* | *a presidential election* | (*AmE*) *Next year will be a presidential year.* (=there will be an election to choose a president)

president pro tem·po·re /ˌprezɪdənt prəʊ 'tempəreɪ/ also **president pro tem** /ˌ··· · ˈ·/ *infml*− *n* a member of the US Senate who is elected by the other members of the Senate to control the course of its business when the US Vice-President, who is usu. responsible, is away

President's Day /ˈ··· ˌ·/ *n* an American public holiday in February which celebrates the birthdays of presidents George Washington and Abraham Lincoln

pre·sid·i·um, praes- /prɪˈsɪdiəm, -ˈzɪ-/ *n* ~**s** *or* -**ia** /-diə/ (esp. in Communist countries) a committee chosen to represent and act for a larger body, esp. a political body: *the presidium of the Supreme Soviet*

Pres·ley /'prezli/, **El·vis** /ˈelvɪs/ (1935–77) an American singer and GUITAR player who made ROCK 'N' ROLL (later called ROCK) popular in the 1950s. From 1956–63, he was the most successful and influential person in popular music. He was sometimes called "Elvis the Pelvis" because of the way he moved the lower half of his body during his performances. His many successful records include *Heartbreak Hotel* and *Don't be Cruel*, and he also appeared in films including *Loving You* and *G I Blues*. −see also ELVIS SIGHTING and see colour picture on page 554

press[1] /pres/ *v* **1** [T] to push firmly and steadily: *Press this button to start the engine.* | *I pressed a coin into the little girl's hand.* | *The little boy pressed his nose against the shop window.* **2** [T] to put weight onto (something) in order to crush, flatten, shape, pack tightly, or get liquid out: *To make wine, first you must press the grapes.* | *pressed flowers* | *Before cooking, the pastry must be pressed flat and thin.* **3** [T] to give (a garment) a smooth surface and a sharp fold by using a hot iron; IRON[2] **4** [T] to take hold of (a part of the body) firmly as a sign of friendship, love, pity, etc.: *He pressed my hand warmly when we met.* **5** [I+*adv/prep*] to push one's way roughly, esp. in a mass: *Crowds pressed round her trying to get her autograph.* **6** [T+*obj+to-v*] to urge strongly: *She pressed her guests to stay a little longer.* −see also PRESS **for 7** [T] to continue to try to gain acceptance of: *In view of their limited financial resources, we shall not press our claim for compensation.* (=we shall stop making the claim) | *I suggested we make a joint appeal, but he didn't seem very keen, so I didn't press the point.* **8** [I] *infml* to make quick action or attention necessary: *Work presses/Time presses* (=there is not much time), *so I can't stop to talk.* −see also PRESS **on**, PRESSING[1] **9** [T] *tech* to make a copy of (a GRAMOPHONE record, etc.) −see also PRESSING[2] **10 press home: a** to get the greatest possible effect from (an advantage) **b** to continue (an attack) forcefully and successfully **11 press the flesh** *infml humor* to shake hands. This phrase is often used in connection with political CANDIDATEs, who meet many people and try to influence them in the weeks before an election: *I've had a busy day walking round the ward, kissing babies, pressing the flesh, and all that.*
    press (sbdy.) **for** sthg. *phr v* [T] to demand urgently (from): *I don't know whether to accept this new job, and the firm is pressing (me) for a decision.*
    press on *phr v* **1** [I (**with**)] also **press ahead**− to continue with determination or without delay: *Let's press on with our work.* | *Shall we stop here or press on to the next town?* **2** [T] (**press** sthg. **on** sbdy.) to force (someone) to accept (something): *He tried to press another drink on me.*

press[2] *n* **1** [(*the*) U+*sing./pl. v*] (writers and reporters working for) newspapers and magazines, and usu. also the news-gathering services of radio and television: *The minister invited the press to a meeting to explain his actions.* | *It's vital to protect the freedom of the press.* (=their freedom to print news and fair opinion without being stopped by the government) | *a press photographer* −see also GUTTER PRESS **2** [S] treatment of the stated kind given by newspapers, etc. when reporting about a person or event: *The play had a good press* (=the newspapers said it was good) *but very few people went to see it.* **3** [C] a PRINTING PRESS: *Stop the presses! A piece of late news has come in.* | *When does the paper* **go to press?** (=start being printed) | *The new book is* **in (the) press.** (=being printed) −see also STOP PRESS **4** [C] (*usu. cap.*) a business for printing (and sometimes also for selling) books, magazines, etc.: *the Clarendon Press* **5** [S] an act of pushing steadily against something small: *Give the button another press.* **6** [C] *infml* an act of making a garment smooth with a hot iron: *Could you give my trousers a quick press?* **7** [C] (*often in comb.*) an apparatus used for putting weight onto something: *She keeps her tennis racket in a press to stop it from getting out of shape.* | *a wine/garlic press* —see also TROUSER PRESS

press³ *v* **press someone/something into service** to use someone or something in a time of urgent need, even though they may not be completely suitable

press a·gen·cy /'· ,···/ *n* the office or business of a press agent

press a·gent /'· ,···/ *n* a person whose job is to keep an actor, musician, sportsman, etc., in favourable public notice by supplying photographs, interesting facts, etc., to newspapers

Press As·so·ci·a·tion /'· ···,···/ (*abbrev.* **PA**) an organization which provides news about Britain to newspapers and radio and television stations in other countries, and which informs industry and the government of the news as it happens

press bar·on /'· ,···/ *n* esp. *BrE infml sometimes derog* a person who owns and controls one or more important national newspapers. In Britain, Robert Maxwell was, and Rupert Murdoch is, sometimes described as a press baron. —compare DRUG BARON

press box /'· ·/ *n* an (enclosed) space at some outdoor events, esp. sports events, that is kept for the use of newspaper reporters

Press Com·plaints Com·mis·sion /ₗ· '· ·,··/ [*the*] a British organization which is supposed to make sure that the British PRESS¹ (1) keeps high professional standards, and which deals with complaints about the press

press con·fer·ence /'· ,···/ also **news conference**— *n* a meeting during which an important person gives a statement to news reporters or answers questions

press corps /'· ·/ *n* **press corps** a group of news reporters from different newspapers who gather for a NEWS CONFERENCE, where something important is happening, or where an important statement will be made

Press Coun·cil /'· ,··/ [*the*] a British organization which dealt with complaints about the PRESS¹ (1). It was replaced in 1991 by the Press Complaints Commission.

press cut·ting /'· ,··/ *n* [*usu. pl.*] a CUTTING¹ (2)

pressed /prest/ *adj* **1** [F+*for*] not having enough: *I'm pressed for time this morning so it will have to wait until this afternoon.* **2** (of food) given a firm shape by being packed into a container so as to be easily cut for eating cold: *pressed duck*

press gal·le·ry /'· ,···/ *n* (esp. in the British parliament) a space with seats above or at the back of the main level of a hall, kept for the use of news reporters

press·gang¹ /'presgæn/ *n* (in former times, esp. in the 18th century) a group of sailors employed to take men away by force and make them join the navy

pressgang² *v* [T (*into*)] *infml* (esp. of a group) to force (someone) to do something unwillingly: *I was press-ganged into playing in the charity cricket match.*

press·ing¹ /'presɪŋ/ *adj* **1** that must have attention, action, etc., now; urgent: *Pressing business matters prevented him from taking a holiday.* **2** asking for something strongly, in a way that is hard to refuse; INSISTENT: *a pressing invitation* — **~ly** *adv*

pressing² *n* **1** an act of pressing: *olive oil from the first cold pressing* **2** any of the copies of a GRAMOPHONE record made at any one time

press·man /'presmæn/ *n* **-men** /men/ *BrE infml* a newspaper reporter

press of·fice /'· ,··/ *n* an office of an organization, esp. a government department, from which information about the organization's activities is given to the press, often in the form of a **press release** (=a written description of a news story designed to encourage newspapers to write about it) —**press officer** *n*

press re·lease /'· ·,·/ *n* a prepared statement given out to news services and newspapers

press sec·re·ta·ry /'· ,····/ *n* a secretary to an important

person or organization who gives news about them to newspapers

press-stud /'· ·/ *BrE*, also **popper** *infml, esp. BrE* ‖ **snap fastener** *AmE*— *n* a small metal fastener for a garment, in which one part is pressed into a hollow in another — see picture at FASTENER

press-up /'· ·/ *esp. BrE* ‖ **push-up** *esp. AmE*— *n* a form of exercise in which someone lies face down on the ground, keeping their back straight, and pushes their body up with their arms: *She does twenty press-ups every morning.*

pres·sure¹ /'preʃəʳ/ *n* **1** [U] the action of putting force or weight onto something: *The pressure of the water turns this wheel, and this is used to make electric power.* **2** [C;U] the strength of this force: *These gas containers will burst at high pressures.* | *Low (atmospheric) pressure often brings rain.* | *a pressure of ten pounds to the square inch* | *a pressure gauge* **3** [U] forceful influence; strong persuasion: *He only agreed to do it under pressure from his parents.* [+*to-v*] *We're trying to* **put pressure on/bring pressure to bear on** *the government to change the law.* | *The government is coming under increasing pressure to change the law.* | *He only agreed to leave the country* **under pressure.** (=after being forcefully persuaded to do so) **4** [C;U] conditions in one's work, one's style of living, etc. that cause anxiety and difficulty: *I'd like to help out, but I really haven't got time*—**pressure of work**, *you know!* | *the pressures of modern life* | *He works best* **under pressure.** —see also BLOOD PRESSURE, HIGH-PRESSURE

pressure² *v* [T (*into*)] *esp. AmE for* PRESSURIZE (1)

pressure cook·er /'· ·,·/ *n* a tightly covered metal cooking pot in which food can be cooked very quickly by the pressure of hot steam —see picture at KITCHEN

pressure group /'· ·/ *n* [C+*sing./pl. v*] a group of people that actively tries to influence public opinion and government action —compare INTEREST GROUP

pressure point /'· ·/ *n* **1** a point on the human body where a blood-carrying tube (ARTERY) runs near a bone, so that it can be closed off by pressing on it, for example to stop blood loss **2** a point used in ACUPRESSURE

pres·sur·ize also **-ise** *BrE* /'preʃəraɪz/ *v* [T] **1** [(*into*)] *esp. BrE* ‖ **pressure** *esp. AmE*— to (try to) make (someone) do something by using strong or unfair influence: *The government have pressurized the farmers into producing more milk.* [+*obj+to-v*] *I'm being pressurized to make a statement.* **2** to control the air pressure inside (something) so that it does not become much lower than the pressure on Earth: *an aircraft's pressurized cabin* —**·ization** /ₗpreʃəraɪ'zeɪʃən‖-rə'zeɪ-/ *n* [U]

Pres·tel /'prestel/ *tdmk* a service provided by British Telecom which carries information (e.g. weather, news, sports results) on television to people who have paid for this service. The information is received by calling it up on the telephone.

pres·ti·di·gi·ta·tion /ₗprestₗdɪdʒᵻ'teɪʃən/ *n* [U] *humor or fml* the performing of tricks by quick clever use of the hands; conjuring (CONJURE)

pres·tige¹ /pre'stiːʒ/ *n* [U] general respect or admiration felt for someone or something because they have (or are connected with) high quality, social influence, success, etc.: *The old universities of Oxford and Cambridge still have a lot of prestige.* | *the prestige conferred in many cultures by having a professional job, such as that of a doctor or lawyer*

prestige² *adj* [A] *usu. apprec or derog* causing admiration because of being an outward sign of wealth or success: *Some people say the country should spend its money on really important things, not on prestige developments like new airports.* | *a prestige car* (=big, expensive, and important-looking)

pres·ti·gious /pre'stɪdʒəs‖-'stiː-, -'stɪ-/ *adj usu. apprec* having or bringing prestige: *a very prestigious address in the best part of town*

pres·to /'prestəʊ/ *n, adj, adv* **-tos** (a piece of music) played very quickly —see also HEY PRESTO

Pres·ton /'prestən/ a town in NW England, where the local government for Lancashire is based

pre·stressed /ₗpriː'strest◄/ *adj* (of CONCRETE²) strengthened by having stretched wires put inside

Prest·wick /'prestwɪk/ a town in SW Scotland

pre·su·ma·bly /prɪ'zjuːməbli‖-'zuː-/ *adv* it may reasonably be supposed that; probably: *If you've already eaten, you presumably won't want dinner.* | *Presumably you've read this notice.* (=I suppose/hope that you have)

pre·sume /prɪˈzjuːm‖-ˈzuːm/ v **1** [T] to take (something) as true or as a fact without direct proof but with some feeling of being certain; suppose: [+(that)] *John didn't say when he'd return, but I presume (that) he'll be back for dinner.* | *"Will he be back for dinner?" "I presume so."* [+obj+to-v] (*fml*) *From the way they talked I presumed them to be married.* **2** [T] to accept as true until proved untrue, esp. in a matter of law, justice, etc.: *We must presume innocence until we have evidence of guilt.* [+(that)] *We must presume they are innocent.* [+obj+adj] *The soldier was* **missing, presumed dead.** [+obj+to-v] *Anyone not replying within 28 days is presumed to have given up his or her claim.* **3** [I *usu. in questions and negatives*] *fml* to behave without enough respect or politeness; dare to do something which one has no right to do: *I don't wish to presume, sir, but don't you think you need a larger size?* [+to-v] *Are you presuming to tell me how to drive my car?* **4** [T] *fml* to be a reasonable sign or proof of; PRESUPPOSE: *An answer, by its nature, presumes a question.* **5 Dr Livingstone, I presume** a phrase believed to have been used by Sir Henry Stanley when he found Dr Livingstone, an EXPLORER, who had been lost in Africa. The phrase is now sometimes used humorously. —see also Dr LIVINGSTONE

presume on/upon sthg. *phr v* [T] *fml* to (try to) take unfair advantage of (someone's kindness or connection with oneself): *I feel it would be presuming on our rather brief friendship to ask him to lend me that much money.*

pre·sump·tion /prɪˈzʌmpʃən/ n **1** [C;U] **a** an act of supposing **b** *law* an act of supposing that is reasonable and sensible: *the presumption of innocence* **2** [U] *fml derog* disrespectful behaviour that shows too high an opinion of oneself

pre·sump·tive /prɪˈzʌmptɪv/ *adj* [A] *fml, esp. law* based on a reasonable belief; probable: *presumptive proof* —see also HEIR PRESUMPTIVE — ~ **ly** *adv*

pre·sump·tu·ous /prɪˈzʌmptʃuəs/ *adj derog* showing disrespect towards others as a result of having too high an opinion of oneself — ~ **ly** *adv*

pre·sup·pose /ˌpriːsəˈpəʊz/ v [T *not in progressive forms*] *fml* **1** to suppose or take to be true in advance and without proof; ASSUME: [+that] *All these plans presuppose that the bank will be willing to lend us the money.* **2** to show that (that stated thing) must exist: *A child presupposes a mother.*

pre·sup·po·si·tion /ˌpriːsʌpəˈzɪʃən/ n [C;U] *fml* (an example of) supposing that something is true without proof: [+that] *Your judgment of the case is based on the presupposition that the witness is telling the truth.*

pre·tence ‖ also **-tense** *AmE* /prɪˈtens‖ˈpriːtens/ n **1** [S;U] a false appearance intended either to deceive people or as a game: *He didn't like the food, but as he was a guest he made a pretence of eating* (=pretended to eat) *some of it.* | *She isn't really ill; it's only pretence.* [+that] *How much longer are you going to keep up this pretence that you're ill?* **2** [U+to; *usu. in questions and negatives*] a claim to possess some desirable quality: *a simple man, with little pretence to education* —see also FALSE PRETENCES

pre·tend[1] /prɪˈtend/ v **1** [I;T] to give an appearance of (something that is not true), with the intention of deceiving: *She wasn't really crying; she was only pretending.* | *He often pretends deafness when you ask him an awkward question.* [+(that)/to-v] *She pretended she didn't know me/pretended not to know me when we met in the street.* **2** [I;T *obj*] (usu. of a child) to imagine as a game: [+(that)/to-v] *Let's pretend we're on the moon/pretend to be on the moon.* **3** [T+to-v; *obj; usu. in questions and negatives*] to make a claim, esp. one that cannot be supported: *I don't pretend to understand these technical terms.* (=I admit that I do not understand them)

pretend to sthg. *phr v* [T] *fml* to claim to possess: *I don't pretend to much expertise in these matters, but ...*

pretend[2] *adj infml* (used esp. by or to children) imagined; imaginary: *That's my pretend friend.* | *a pretend monster*

pre·tend·ed /prɪˈtendɪd/ *adj often derog* false or unreal in spite of seeming true or real; insincere: *pretended sympathy*

pre·tend·er /prɪˈtendər/ n [(to)] a person who makes a claim

(which is doubtful or not proved) to some high position, such as to be the rightful king

pre·ten·sion /prɪˈtenʃən/ n **1** [C (to) *often pl.*] a claim to possess skill, qualities, etc.: *I make no pretensions to skill as an artist, but I enjoy painting.* | (fig.) *a house of modest pretensions* (=not very large and expensive-looking) **2** [U] *fml* pretentiousness

pre·ten·tious /prɪˈtenʃəs/ *adj* claiming (in an unpleasant way) to have importance, artistic value, or social rank that one does not really possess: *one of those pretentious films that claim to be "art"* —opposite **unpretentious** — ~ **ly** *adv* — ~ **ness** *n* [U]

pret·er·ite, -it /ˈpretərɪt/ n, *adj* [*the*] *tech* (a tense or verb form) that expresses a past action or condition: *"Sang"* is the preterite (form) of "sing".

pre·ter·nat·u·ral /ˌpriːtəˈnætʃərəl◂‖-tər-/ *adj fml* **1** beyond what is usual: *a warrior of preternatural strength* **2** strange; beyond what is natural or can be explained naturally: *In former times people believed that thunder and lightning were signs of preternatural forces.* — ~ **ly** *adv* : *preternaturally strong*

pre·text /ˈpriːtekst/ n [(of, for)] a reason given for an action in order to hide the real intention; excuse: *He came to the house* **under/on the pretext** *of seeing Mr Jackson, but he really wanted to see Jackson's daughter.* | *The riots were used by the government as a pretext for banning all political activity.* —see EXCUSE[2] (USAGE)

Pre·to·ri·a /prɪˈtɔːriə/ a city and the ADMINISTRATIVE capital of South Africa

pret·ti·fy /ˈprɪtɪfaɪ/ v [T] *usu. derog* to make pretty without serious intention or effect

pret·ty[1] /ˈprɪti/ *adj* **1** *apprec* (esp. of a woman, a child, or a small thing) pleasing to look at, listen to, etc.; charming and attractive without being very beautiful or important-looking: *She looks much prettier with long hair than with short hair.* | *a pretty dress* | *What a pretty little garden!* —see BEAUTIFUL (USAGE) **2** [A] *derog* (of a young man) graceful and/or charming but rather EFFEMINATE **3** [A] *derog, rather old-fash* not nice; displeasing: *It's a pretty state of affairs when I can't afford the price of a pint of beer any more!* —**tily** *adv* —**tiness** *n* [U]

pretty[2] *adv infml* **1** quite, though not completely; rather: *It's pretty cold today.* | *I'm pretty sure he'll say yes.* **2** very: *This work of yours is a pretty poor effort. You'd better do it again.* **3 pretty much** also **pretty well, pretty nearly—** very nearly; almost: *"How is she feeling today?" "Pretty much the same as yesterday."* | *It's pretty well impossible to travel over these mountains in winter.* —see also **be sitting pretty** (SIT (12))

pretty pen·ny /ˌ·· ˈ··/ n [S] *infml* a rather large amount of money: *That car cost a pretty penny, I can tell you!*

pret·ty-pret·ty /ˈ·· ˌ··/ *adj infml derog, esp. BrE* pretty in a silly or weak way

pret·zel /ˈpretsəl/ n **1** a hard salty BISCUIT or CRACKER baked in the shape of a stick or a loose knot, very popular in the US: *beer and pretzels* **2** *AmE* also **soft pretzel—** a salty bread baked in the shape of a knot and eaten while warm. It is often bought at a sports event or from a person selling them on the street.

pre·vail /prɪˈveɪl/ v [I] *fml* **1** [(among, in)] to (continue to) exist or be widespread: *A belief in magic still prevails among some tribes.* **2** [(against, over)] to gain control or victory; win a fight: *Justice has prevailed; the guilty man has been punished.*

prevail upon/on sbdy. *phr v* [T+obj+to-v] *fml* to persuade: *I'm late for my train — could I prevail upon you to drive me to the station?*

pre·vail·ing /prɪˈveɪlɪŋ/ *adj* [A] **1** (of a wind) that blows over an area most of the time: *The prevailing winds here are from the west.* **2** *fml* existing or most widely accepted at a particular time or in a particular place; CURRENT: *the prevailing fashion* | *the prevailing economic climate*

prev·a·lent /ˈprevələnt/ *adj* [(among, in)] *fml* existing commonly, generally, or widely in a particular place or at a particular time: *Eye diseases are prevalent in some tropical countries.* — ~ **lence** *n* [U]

pre·var·i·cate /prɪˈværɪkeɪt/ v [I] *fml* **1** to try to hide the truth by not answering questions clearly or completely truthfully **2** *euph* to tell lies —**cator** *n* —**cation** /prɪˌværɪˈkeɪʃən/ n [C;U]

pre·vent /prɪˈvent/ v [T (**from**)] to stop (something) happening or stop (someone) doing something: *These rules are intended to prevent accidents.* [+obj+v-ing] *What can we do to prevent this disease spreading?* | *Unless we get more funding we'll be prevented from finishing our experimental programme.* — ~**able** adj : *preventable cancer*

pre·ven·tion /prɪˈvenʃən/ [U] the act of preventing: *the prevention of crime/disease*

Prevention of Ter·ror·is·m Act /·ˌ·· · ˈ···· ˌ·/ [the] a British law passed in 1989 giving the army, police, and government more powers to deal with TERRORISTS, such as being able to prevent someone who is thought to be or have been involved in terrorist activities from entering the country. It is used mainly against people who are thought to be in the IRA.

pre·ven·tive /prɪˈventɪv/ also **pre·ven·ta·tive** /-tətɪv/— n, adj (something) that helps to prevent something undesirable: *The government is taking preventative measures to safeguard law and order.* — ~**ly** adv

preventive de·ten·tion /·ˌ·· ·ˈ··/ n [U] *BrE tech* imprisonment for a long time for habitual criminals over 30 years old

preventive medi·cine /·ˌ·· ˈ·· ‖ ·ˌ·· ˈ···/ n [U] medicine that helps prevent illness, e.g. VACCINATION. This expression is also used to describe measures taken to improve public health (e.g. providing pure water), and to educate people about personal health (e.g. eating habits, physical exercise).

pre·view¹ /ˈpriːvjuː/ n [(of)] **1** a private showing of paintings, a cinema film, etc., before they are shown to the general public **2** a short description of something that will soon happen, esp. a film or television show soon to be shown: *I don't want to see it — I read the previews and they weren't very enthusiastic.* | *This book gives us a preview of life in the 25th century.* —see also SNEAK PREVIEW **3** *AmE* short pieces from a film or television programme which are shown sometime before it as an ADVERTISEMENT —see TRAILER

preview² v [T] to give a preview of (a play, film, etc.)

Prev·in /ˈprevɪn/, **An·dré** /ˈɒndreɪ ‖ ˈɑːn-/ (1929–) an American CONDUCTOR (=a person who directs the playing of a group of musicians), COMPOSER, and piano player, who, through his television appearances, brought CLASSICAL music to a wider public. He was made Conductor LAUREATE of the London Symphony Orchestra in 1992.

pre·vi·ous /ˈpriːviəs/ adj **1** [A] happening or existing before the one mentioned: *On Sunday he denied all knowledge of it, but on the previous day* (=Saturday) *he'd admitted to me that he knew all about it.* | *Have you had any previous experience of this kind of work?* | *on a previous occasion* —see AGO (USAGE), LAST (USAGE) **2** [F] *now rare* acting too soon; PREMATURE: *He was a little previous in thanking her for something she had not yet given him.* **3** previous to *fml* before; PRIOR to: *Women are now in a majority on the committee, although previous to 1976 there were no women members at all.* — ~**ly** adv : *This record was previously held by Sebastian Coe.*

pre·vi·sion /ˌpriːˈvɪʒən/ n [C;U (of)] *fml* (a case of) knowledge of something before it happens

pre·war /ˌpriːˈwɔːʳ ◂/ adj, adv (happening or existing) before a war, esp. the First or Second World War: *conditions in pre-war Europe* —compare POSTWAR

prey¹ /preɪ/ n [U] **1** an animal that is hunted and eaten by another animal: *lions pursuing their prey* | (fig.) *Gullible people like him are easy prey for/to clever salesmen.* (=can easily be deceived by them) | (fig., rather *fml*) *Left on her own, she* **was/fell prey to** (=was troubled by) *all sorts of strange fears.* **2** habit or way of life based on killing and eating other animals: *The tiger is a* **beast of prey.**| *The eagle is a* **bird of prey.**

prey² v
prey on/upon sthg./sbdy. *phr v* [T] **1** (of an animal) to hunt and eat as prey: *Cats prey on birds and mice.* **2** (of unhappiness, troubles, etc.) to trouble greatly: *This problem has been preying on my mind all day.* **3** *derog* (of a person) to live by getting money from (someone who is weak, trusting, helpless, etc.) by influence, deceit, etc.: *He's very charming and preys on rich widows.*

prez·zie /ˈprezi/ n *infml* a present

price¹ /praɪs/ n **1** an amount of money for which a thing is offered, sold, or bought: *What price did you pay for the house?* | *What is the price of this suit?* | *Eggs are selling at a high price.* | *House prices are rising/going up.* | *big price reductions* | (fig.) *Isn't bad health a high price to pay for the pleasure you get from smoking?* | (fig.) *Good friendship is above/beyond/without price.* (=cannot be bought) *You can't* **put a price** *on it.* (=because it is too valuable) | (fig.) *Everyone* **has their price.** (=will accept a BRIBE if it is large enough) **2** (in risking money, e.g. on a horse in a race) the difference in amount between the money risked and the sum of the money one will get if one wins; ODDS: *"What price are you offering on 'Lucky Shot'?" "Seven to four."* —see also STARTING PRICE **3 a price on someone's head** a reward for catching or killing someone: *The escaped prisoner fled across the border because he knew there was a price on his head.* **4 at a price** for a lot of money: *You can buy excellent wine here — at a price!* **5 not at** ¹**any price** not on any condition, even if favourable: *I wouldn't travel by air at any price.* —see also ASKING PRICE, CLOSING PRICE, COST PRICE, LIST PRICE, MARKET PRICE; see COST (USAGE)

price² v [T] **1** [+obj+adv/prep; often pass.] to fix the price of (something for sale): *The new car is priced very competitively.* (=at a price that makes people willing to buy it) | *high-priced goods* | *This hat is priced at £27, madam.* **2** *infml* to find out the price of: *I have been pricing radios in the London shops.* **3 price out of the market** to make the price of (oneself or one's goods) so high that people are unwilling to pay: *You'll price yourself out of the market if you ask that much.*

Price, Le·on·tyne /liˈɒntiːn, ˈliːən-‖liˈɑːn-/ (1927–) an American OPERA singer

price-fix·ing /ˈ· ˌ··/ n [U] **1** the setting of prices by the government **2** an agreement between two or more producers, sellers, etc. to fix the price of a product at a level favourable to them. In many countries, including Britain and the US, this is illegal.

price in·dex /ˈ· ˌ··/ n a system of numbers by which prices can be compared to a former level —see also RETAIL PRICE INDEX

price·less /ˈpraɪsləs/ adj **1** of such a high value that it cannot be calculated: *a priceless collection of paintings* | *Good health is priceless.* —see VALUABLE (USAGE) **2** *infml* very funny or laughably foolish

prices and in·comes pol·i·cy /ˌ··· · ˈ·· ˌ···/ n a course of action taken by a government and intended to prevent prices and incomes increasing, in order to stop or limit INFLATION

price sup·port /ˈ· ·ˌ·/ n the practice of keeping prices of a product or food at a fixed level, even though the price should go down or up, by giving the producer government money or having the government buy the product

price tag /ˈ· ·/ n **1** a small ticket put onto an article, showing its price **2** *infml* (esp. in newspapers) a fixed or stated price: *The government was asked to* **put a price tag on** *its new building plans.* (=say what they would cost)

price war /ˈ· ˌ·/ n a period during which companies reduce the prices of their products or services to win a larger share of the market or get rid of competition: *Oil companies are entering a price war over the cost of unleaded fuel.*

Price Wa·ter·house /ˌpraɪs ˈwɔːtəhaʊs‖-ˈwɔːtər-, -ˈwɑː-/ an international firm of ACCOUNTANTS and MANAGEMENT CONSULTANTS

pric·ey, pricy /ˈpraɪsi/ adj **pricier, priciest** *infml derog, esp. BrE* expensive: *These new cars are a bit pricey.* | *That shop's too pricey for me.* —**iness** n [U]

prick¹ /prɪk/ n **1** a small sharp pain: *She felt a prick when the needle went into her finger.* | (fig.) *the pricks of conscience* (=uncomfortable thoughts because one knows one has done something wrong) **2** a small mark or hole made by pricking **3** a prickle **4** *taboo* the male sex organ; PENIS **5** *taboo derog sl* a stupid or very unpleasant man: *You stupid prick!* —see also PINPRICK, **kick against the pricks** (KICK¹ (6))

prick² v **1** [T (**with, on**)] to make a very small hole in (one's) skin or surface of (something) with a sharp-pointed object: *When I was pruning the roses I pricked myself/my finger on a thorn.* **2** [I;T] to (cause to) feel a sensation of light sharp pain on the skin: *The pepper in the food pricked the back of his throat.* | (fig.) *Her conscience pricked her.* **3 prick up its ears** (of an animal) to raise the ears so as to listen attentively **4 prick up one's ears** (of a person) to listen carefully; be ready to hear information: *He pricked up his ears when they began to talk about him.*

    prick sthg. ↔ **out** *phr v* [T] to place (a young plant) in a hole specially made in the earth

prick·le¹ /'prɪkəl/ *n* **1** [C] any of a number of small, esp. long and thin, sharp-pointed growths on the skin of some plants or animals: *a hedgehog's prickles* —see picture at HEDGEHOG **2** [(*the*) S] a pricking sensation on the skin

prickle² *v* [I;T] to give or feel a pricking sensation: *This rough shirt prickles my skin.*

prick·ly /'prɪkli/ *adj* **1** covered with prickles: *prickly bushes* **2** that has or gives a pricking sensation: *prickly woollen underclothes* **3** *infml* difficult to deal with: *Nuclear defence policy is bound to be one of the prickliest issues at the party conference.* | *He's a prickly character.* (=easily made angry) —**liness** *n* [U]

prickly heat /ˌ·· '·/ *n* [U] an uncomfortable hot PRICKLY (2) condition of the skin with painful red spots, common in tropical countries

prickly pear /ˌ·· '·/ *n* (the roundish PRICKLY (1) eatable fruit of) a CACTUS with yellow flowers

pric·y /'praɪsi/ *adj* PRICEY

pride¹ /praɪd/ *n* **1** [S;U (**in**)] (a feeling of) satisfaction or pleasure in what one can do or has done, or in someone or something connected with oneself: *They* **take** *great* **pride** *in their daughter, who is now a famous scientist.* **2** [U] reasonable self-respect; proper high opinion of oneself: *I think you* **hurt his pride** *by laughing at the way he speaks English.* **3** [U] *derog* too high an opinion of oneself because of one's position, wealth, abilities, etc. Pride is one of the Seven Deadly Sins according to the Christian religion: *Pride was his downfall.* (=caused his ruin) —see also SEVEN DEADLY SINS **4** [S (**of**)] the most valuable person or thing: *This fine picture is the pride of my collection.* | *My garden is my* **pride and joy.** (=something that I think has great value) **5** [C+*sing./pl. v*] a group (of lions) **6 pride goes before a fall** *saying* someone who behaves too proudly will soon suffer a defeat or misfortune

pride² *v* [T] **pride oneself on** to feel satisfied with oneself about: *She prided herself on her ability to speak eight languages/on knowing eight languages.*

Pride and Prej·u·dice /ˌ· · '···/ a book by Jane Austen in which the most important characters are the Bennett family and Mr Darcy

pride of place /ˌ· · '·/ *n* [U (**in**)] *esp. BrE* the highest or best position: *Amongst all our playwrights, Shakespeare has/takes pride of place.* (=is considered the best) | *A poster of Elvis Presley had pride of place in her room.*

priest /priːst/ *n* **1** (in the Christian church, and esp. in the Roman Catholic Church) a specially trained person, usu. a man, who performs various religious duties and ceremonies for a group of worshippers **2** also **priest·ess** /'priːstes/ *fem.*— a specially-trained person with religious duties and responsibilities in certain non-Christian religions —see also HIGH PRIEST

priest·hood /'priːsthʊd/ *n* [(*the*) U] **1** the office or position of a priest: *He entered the priesthood.* (=became a priest) **2** [+*sing./pl. v*] all priests, usu. of a particular religion or country

Priest·ley /'priːstli/, **J B** (1894–1984) a British writer and broadcaster who took a humorous view of English life in his NOVELS, e.g. *The Good Companions.* His many plays include *Dangerous Corner.* He also wrote about literature, travel, and society and was noted for his radio talks during the Second World War.

priest·ly /'priːstli/ *adj fml* of a priest: *his priestly duties*

prig /prɪg/ *n derog* someone who is very careful about obeying rules of correct behaviour and therefore thinks himor herself morally better than other people — ~ **gish** *adj* — ~ **gishness** *n* [U]

prim /prɪm/ *adj* -**mm**- **1** *usu. derog* (of a person) very formal or exact in behaviour, and easily shocked by anything rude: *She's much too* **prim and proper** *to enjoy such a rude joke.* **2** neat: *prim little blouses* — ~ **ly** *adv* — ~ **ness** *n* [U]

Pri·ma /'priːmə/ a monthly women's magazine, which has articles on fashion, cookery, etc.

pri·ma bal·le·ri·na /ˌ·· ··'··/ *n* the main woman dancer in a BALLET company

pri·ma·cy /'praɪməsi/ *n* [U] **1** [(of, over)] *fml* the state, quality, or position of being first in position, importance, etc.: *We should insist on the primacy of practical skill over theoretical knowledge.* **2** the position of a PRIMATE²

prima don·na /ˌpriːmə 'dɒnə||-'dɑːnə/ *n* **1** the main woman singer in an OPERA company **2** *derog* an excitable self-important person who is always changing her or his mind and expects everyone to do as she or he wishes: *He's a bit of a prima donna, which makes him hard to work with.*

pri·mae·val /praɪ'miːvəl/ *adj esp. BrE for* PRIMEVAL

pri·ma fa·cie /ˌpraɪmə 'feɪʃi||-ʃə/ *adj, adv* [A *no comp.*] *Lat, esp. law* based on what seems to be true, even though it may be disproved later: *Unless there is a prima facie case against him, the trial cannot proceed.*

pri·mal /'praɪməl/ *adj fml* **1** [A] (as if) belonging to the earliest time in the world; original: *man's primal innocence* —compare PRIMORDIAL **2** PRIMARY (1): *a primal need*

primal scream ther·a·py /ˌ·· '· ˌ···/ also **primal therapy** /'·· ˌ···/, **scream therapy**— *n* [S] a form of treatment for mental disorders in which it is thought that if a person can be taken back to a much earlier time of his or her life and re-experience very difficult emotions and SCREAM about them, they will be able to manage better in their lives. People who do not take this seriously sometimes make jokes about it.

pri·ma·ri·ly /'praɪmərəli||praɪ'merəli/ *adv fml* mainly; chiefly: *Ten years ago it was primarily a fishing village, but now it's a thriving tourist centre.*

pri·ma·ry¹ /'praɪməri||-meri/ *adj* **1** chief; main; PRINCIPAL: *The primary purpose of his visit is to improve trading relations.* | *a matter of primary importance* **2** [A] also **elementary** *AmE* (of education, a teacher, etc.) for children between 5 and 11 years old —compare SECONDARY (1) **3** [A] earliest in time or order of development: *In the primary stages of their civilization, they had no metal tools.*

primary² *n* (esp. in the US) an election at which the members of a political party in a particular area vote for the person that they would like to see as their party's CANDIDATE for a political office

primary col·our /ˌ··· '··/ *n* any of three colours (red, yellow, and blue) from which all other colours can be made by mixing

primary health care /ˌ··· '· ·/ also **primary med·i·cal care** /ˌ··· '··· ·/— *n* [U] the first kind of official medical care which a person receives. In Britain and the US, this is usu. care from the local or family doctor (GP) or the CASUALTY department of a hospital: *Training programmes for doctors ensure that advice about a healthy diet and lifestyle will be available from primary health care.*

primary school /'··· ˌ·/ *n* **1** *BrE* a school for children between 5 and 11 years old in England and Wales, often divided into an INFANT SCHOOL (5–7) and a JUNIOR SCHOOL (7–11) —compare SECONDARY SCHOOL and see also extra information on page 408 **2** *AmE* an ELEMENTARY SCHOOL

primary stress /ˌ··· '·/ also **primary ac·cent** /ˌ··· '··/— *n* [C;U] *tech* the strongest force (STRESS) given in speech to part of a compound or long word, and shown in this dictionary by the mark ': *In the word "primary", the primary stress falls on the first syllable ("pri-").*

pri·mate¹ /'praɪmeɪt/ *n* a member of the most highly developed group of MAMMALS, which includes human beings, monkeys, and related animals

pri·mate² /'praɪmət/ *n* (*often cap.*) a priest with the highest office in esp. the Church of England, e.g. the Archbishop of Canterbury is called the **Primate of All England**

prime¹ /praɪm/ *n* **1** [(*the*) S] the state or time of someone's or something's greatest perfection, strength, or activity: *He was about 40 years old, and* **in the prime of life.** | *She is still good-looking, but she's* **past her prime.** | *Many young soldiers have been* **cut off in their prime.** (=killed in battle while still young) **2** [C] *tech* a PRIME NUMBER

prime² *adj* **1** [A] first in position or importance; chief: *A prime reason for our economic decline is lack of investment.* | *This is a matter of prime importance.* **2** [A] of the very best quality or kind: *This is a prime* (=very clear)

example of the waste I've been talking about. | *a succulent piece of prime beef* **3** *tech* being a prime number: *7 and 13 are prime, but 12 isn't.* **4** connected with a standard of meat in the US, set by the FDA: *a roast labelled prime beef*

prime³ *v* [T] **1** to cover (a surface) with a first spreading of esp. paint, as a base for the main painting —see also PRIMER¹ (1) **2** [(**with**)] to instruct in advance, esp. in how to ask or answer difficult questions: *The witness at the trial had been carefully primed by defence lawyers.* **3** to put explosive powder into (a gun of the old-fashioned type) so that it can be fired —see also PRIMER¹ (2) **4** [(**with**)] to prepare (a machine) for working by filling it with water, oil, etc. **5 prime the pump** *infml* to encourage the growth of an inactive business or industry by putting money into it

prime cost /ˌ· ˈ·/ *n* [U] the actual cost of producing an article, as opposed to money spent on selling it, on renting factories, etc. —compare OVERHEADS

prime me·rid·i·an /ˌ· ·ˈ···/ *[the]* the imaginary line drawn from north to south on the earth, which passes through Greenwich, England, and from which east and west are measured on a map in degrees

prime min·is·ter /ˌ· ˈ···◂/ *also* **P M** *infml*— *n (often caps.)* the chief minister and leader of the government in certain countries esp. those with a parliamentary system of government. In Britain, the prime minister is the leader of the political party which has the most members in the House of Commons and is an elected member of the House. If the prime minister loses support in the House of Commons, they are expected to RESIGN, as Margaret THATCHER did in 1990. —see also extra information on page 412 and see colour picture on page 950 — ~**ship** *n*

Prime Minister's ques·tion time /ˌ· ··· ˈ·· ·/ a certain period of time during each week (on Tuesday and Thursday afternoons) when the British Prime Minister must be in the House of Commons to answer questions from other members of that House. During Prime Minister's question time strong, often very noisy, disagreement is expressed between the Prime Minister and the Opposition, and it is often broadcast on radio and television. Some people disapprove of the way Members of Parliament shout and interrupt each other during this time, although it is probably not typical of the usual work of Parliament.

prime mov·er /ˌ· ˈ··/ *n* **1** *tech* a natural force, such as wind or moving water, which can be used directly or to produce a more useful form of power **2** [(**of, in**)] a person or thing that has great influence in the development of something important

prime num·ber /ˌ· ˈ··/ *also* **prime**— *n tech* a number that can be divided exactly only by itself and the number one: *23 is a prime number.*

prim·er¹ /ˈpraɪmə^r/ *n* **1** [C;U] a paint or other substance for spreading over the bare surface of wood, metal, etc. before the main painting —see also PRIME³ (1) **2** [C] a tube containing explosive, used to fire a gun, explode a bomb, etc. —see also PRIME³ (3)

prim·er² /ˈpraɪmə^r‖ˈprɪmər/ *n old-fash* a simple beginner's book in a school subject

prime rate /ˈ· ˌ·/ *n* the lowest rate of interest at which money can be borrowed at a particular time and place, offered by banks to certain borrowers: *US prime rates are edging downwards.* —compare BASE RATE, DISCOUNT RATE

prime rib /ˌ· ˈ·/ *also* **prime fore rib** /ˌ· ˈ· ·/, **fore rib**— *n* [U] an expensive piece of BEEF which is usu. roasted (ROAST¹)

prime time /ˈ· ˌ·/ *n* [U] *esp. AmE* PEAK TIME

pri·me·val *also* **-mae-** *esp. BrE* /praɪˈmiːvəl/ *adj* **1** very ancient; having been in existence for a very long time: *primeval forests* **2** of the earliest period in the existence of something, such as the Earth, the universe, etc.: *Primeval clouds of gas formed themselves into stars.*

prim·i·tive¹ /ˈprɪmɪtɪv/ *adj* **1** [A] of the earliest stage of development, esp. of life or of human beings: *Primitive man made himself primitive tools from sharp stones and animal bones.* | *primitive art on the walls of caves* **2** simple; roughly made or done; not greatly developed or improved: *Small seashells were often used as a primitive kind of money.* **3** *derog* old-fashioned and inconvenient:

primitive living conditions, without electricity or running water — ~**ly** *adv* — ~**ness** *n* [U]

primitive² *n* **1** a painter, SCULPTOR, etc. of the time before the Renaissance: *an Italian primitive* **2** a modern painter who paints simple and rather flat-looking pictures

pri·mo·gen·i·ture /ˌpraɪməʊˈdʒenɪtʃə^r/ *n* [U] *tech* the system according to which property owned by a father goes after his death to the eldest son

pri·mor·di·al /praɪˈmɔːdiəl‖-ɔːr-/ *adj fml* existing from or at the beginning (of time): *Scientists used to believe that all the stars developed from a primordial mass of gases.* — compare PRIMAL (1) — ~**ly** *adv*

primordial soup /ˌ·ˌ··· ˈ·/ *n* [S] *infml* the mixture of substances, gases, etc. thought to have existed before the BIG BANG (=the explosion that began the universe)

primp /prɪmp/ *v* [I;T] to do one's hair, put on MAKE-UP, dress carefully, etc., so that one looks nice (used esp. of women): *She's primping in front of the mirror upstairs.*

prim·rose /ˈprɪmrəʊz/ *n* **1** [C] (a flower of) a common wild plant that produces light yellow flowers in the spring **2** [U] *also* **primrose yel·low** /ˌ·· ˈ··/— a light yellow colour **3 primrose path** *lit* a way of life full of physical pleasure but damaging to the soul

prim·u·la /ˈprɪmjʊlə/ *n* a plant of the primrose family which is grown in gardens for its brightly coloured flowers

pri·mus /ˈpraɪməs/ *also* **primus stove** /ˈ·· ·/— *n tdmk* an oil-burning metal apparatus for cooking, heating water, etc., that can be easily carried about

prince /prɪns/ *n* **1** (*often cap.*) a son or other near male relation of a king or queen: *Prince Rupert* **2** (*often cap.*) a ruler of a usu. small country: *Prince Rainier of Monaco* | *In former times parts of India were ruled by princes.* **3** [(**among, of**)] *usu. sing.] lit or pomp* a very great, successful, or powerful man of the stated kind: *the merchant princes of Venice*

Prince¹, The a book by Machiavelli which discusses the importance of the state and how a ruler should use any means possible to preserve it —see also MACHIAVELLI

Prince² (1958–) an American singer and writer of popular music whose songs include *Dirty Minds*, and *Controversy*. Prince was one of the most successful popular music singers of the 1980s, though his songs were considered shocking by some people

Prince Albert see Prince ALBERT

Prince Andrew see Prince ANDREW

Prince Charles see Prince CHARLES —see picture at ROYAL WEDDING

Prince Charm·ing /ˌ· ˈ··/ *n infml or humor* a man who as a lover fulfils the dreams of a young girl (from the story of Cinderella in which Prince Charming was the perfect answer to Cinderella's dreams) —see CINDERELLA and see colour picture on page 357

prince con·sort /ˌ· ˈ··/ *n* **princes consort** /ˌ·· ˈ··/ (*often caps.*) a special title sometimes given to the husband of a ruling queen, esp. to Prince Albert, the husband of Queen Victoria of Britain —compare QUEEN CONSORT

prince·dom /ˈprɪnsdəm/ *n fml* a country ruled by a PRINCE (2); PRINCIPALITY

Prince Edward see Prince EDWARD

Prince Ed·ward Is·land /ˌ· ˈ·· ˌ··/ a PROVINCE in SE Canada that is an island in the Gulf of St Lawrence

Prince Henry see Prince HENRY

prince·ly /ˈprɪnsli/ *adj* **1** of a PRINCE (1,2): *the princely courts of Europe* **2** *fml apprec* fine; splendid; generous: *a princely gift* | *He offered us a* **princely sum** (=a lot of money) *for it.*

Prince of Dark·ness /ˌ· · ˈ··/ *[the] poet* SATAN

Prince of Peace /ˌ· · ˈ·/ *n [the] poet* CHRIST

Prince of Wales /ˌ· · ˈ·/ *[the]* a title given to the first son of a British king or queen. Prince Charles was given this title in a ceremony at Caernarvon Castle in 1969 —see also Prince CHARLES

Prince Philip see Prince PHILIP

Prince Re·gent /ˌ· ˈ··/ *[the]* the son of George III of Britain who acted as king from 1811 to 1820 because his father was mad. This period in British history is known as the

Regency. The Prince Regent later became King George IV.

Princes in the Tow·er /ˌ··· ˈ··/ [the +P] the boy king Edward V and his brother Richard who were murdered in 1483 in the Tower of London

prin·cess /ˌprɪnˈses◂‖ˈprɪnsəs/ n (often cap.) **1** a daughter or other near female relation of a king or queen: *Princess Anne* **2** the wife of a PRINCE (1,2): *Princess Diana*

Princess and the Pea /ˌ··· ˈ·/, **The** a story by Hans Andersen in which any woman wishing to marry a particular prince must sleep on 20 MATTRESSes under which there is a PEA (=small hard round green vegetable). Only the real princess is so delicate that she feels the pea and cannot sleep.

Princess Anne see Princess ANNE

Princess Diana also **Princess Di** *infml*– see Princess DIANA

Princess Margaret see Princess MARGARET

Princess of Wales /ˌ··· ˈ·/ [the] the wife of the Prince of Wales. Lady Diana Spencer became the Princess of Wales when she married Prince Charles, the Prince of Wales, in 1981. –see also Princess DIANA

Princess Roy·al /ˌ·· ˈ··/ [the] a title given to the first daughter of a British king or queen. Princess Anne was given this title by her mother, Queen Elizabeth II, in 1987.

Princes Street /ˈ·· ·/ an important street in Edinburgh, Scotland, with many shops and banks

Prince·ton U·ni·ver·si·ty /ˌprɪnstən juːnˌˈvɜːsˌti�‖-ɜːr-/ one of the oldest (1746) and most respected American universities. Princeton, in Princeton, New Jersey, is one of the Ivy League. –see also IVY LEAGUE

Prince William see Prince WILLIAM

prin·ci·pal¹ /ˈprɪnsˌpəl/ adj [A] rather fml highest in importance or position; chief; main: *The Nile is one of the principal rivers of Africa.* | *my principal source of income* | *Our principal problem was lack of time.* –see also PRINCIPALLY

principal² n **1** [C] (often cap.) the head of some universities, colleges, and schools **2** [S] *tech* an amount of money lent, put into a business, etc., and on which interest is paid **3** [C often pl.] a leading performer in a play, group of musicians, etc. **4** [C often pl.] *fml* a person for whom someone else acts as a representative, esp. in a piece of business: *I will have to consult my principals before I can give you an answer on that.*

principal boy /ˌ··· ·/ n BrE the chief male character in a PANTOMIME, usu. played by a young woman

prin·ci·pal·i·ty /ˌprɪnsˌˈpælˌti/ n a country ruled by a PRINCE (2), or from which he takes his title

Principality [the] BrE pomp Wales

prin·ci·pally /ˈprɪnsˌpli/ adv mainly; mostly: *The money is invested principally in government stock.*

principal parts /ˌ··· ˈ·/ n [(the) P] *tech* the parts of a verb from which other parts are formed or can be guessed, in English usu. the INFINITIVE, past tense, present participle, and past participle: *The principal parts of the verb "sing" are "sing", "sang", "singing", and "sung".*

prin·ci·ple /ˈprɪnsˌpəl/ n **1** [C] a truth or belief that is accepted as a base for reasoning or action: *the principle of free speech* [+ that] *One of the principles of this dictionary is that definitions should be in simple language.* | *They agreed to the plan* **in principle** (=agreed to the general idea of it) *but there were several details they didn't like.* | *All these expensive new refinements are a waste of money. We must get back to* **first principles.** (=the most simple and important truths) **2** [C;U] a moral rule or set of ideas which guides behaviour: *It's not that I object to him using my car; it's* **the principle** *of the thing.* (=morally, he should not have borrowed it without asking) | *She resigned on a matter of principle.* | *I never buy South African goods* **on principle.** (=because I believe it would be morally wrong) [+that] *I usually follow the principle that it's better not to get involved in other people's quarrels.* –compare PRINCIPLES (2) **3** [U] *apprec* strong belief in, and practice of, honourable behaviour: *a man of principle* –compare PRINCIPLES (2) **4** [C] (a statement of) the way in which natural objects and forces work in the universe, esp. as it influences the workings of e.g. a machine: *Archimedes' principle* | *the principle of the internal combustion engine* | *A bicycle and a motorcycle are built on the same princi-*

ple, though the force that moves them is different.

prin·ci·pled /ˈprɪnsˌpld/ adj **1** [A] (usu. in comb.) having or based upon PRINCIPLES (1,2): *I have no principled objection* (=no OBJECTION on principle) *to it.* **2** having PRINCIPLES (2): *a high-principled man* –see also UNPRINCIPLED

prin·ci·ples /ˈprɪnsˌplz/ n [P] **1** the general rules on which a skill, science, etc., is based, and which a beginner must understand: *This course teaches the principles of cooking.* **2** high personal standards of what is right and wrong, used as a guide to behaviour: *He has no principles; he'll do anything, however bad, as long as it's profitable* –compare PRINCIPLE (2,3)

Principles one of a group of British shops selling women's clothes

prints

fingerprint   footprint

print¹ /prɪnt/ n **1** [U] letters, words, or language in printed form: *I can't read small fine print without my glasses.* | *I wouldn't have believed it if I hadn't seen it* **in print.** –see also FINE PRINT, SMALL PRINT **2** [C] (often in comb.) a mark made on a surface showing the shape, pattern, etc., of the thing pressed into or onto it: *a thumbprint* | *These deep marks in the wet ground look like the prints of a bicycle tyre.* –see also FOOTPRINT **3** [C usu. pl.] *infml for* FINGERPRINT: *The thief had left his prints on the handle.* **4** [C] (a copy of) a photograph printed after treatment of a photographic film: *Lend me the negatives and I'll order some extra prints.* **5** [C] a picture printed from a small sheet of metal or block of wood: *a set of rare old Chinese prints* **6** [C;U] cloth, usu. cotton, on which a coloured pattern has been printed: *cheap print dresses* **7** **in/out of print** (of a book) that can still/no longer be obtained from the PUBLISHER: *His books haven't been in print for twenty years.*

print² v **1** [I;T] to press (letters or pictures) onto (paper) by using shapes covered with ink or paint, or copy (letters or pictures) onto (paper) by using photographic methods: *The bottom line on this page hasn't been properly printed.* | *This machine can print 60 pages in a minute.* | *The photocopier isn't printing well.* **2** [I;T] to make (a book, magazine, etc.) by pressing or copying letters or pictures onto paper: *a book printed in Hong Kong* –compare PUBLISH **3** [T] to make or copy (a photograph) on paper sensitive to light, from a specially treated sheet of photographic film **4** [T] to record in a book, newspaper, etc.: *All today's newspapers have printed the minister's speech in full.* **5** [T] to decorate (cloth or wallpaper) with a coloured pattern pressed or rubbed on the surface: *printed fabrics* **6** [I;T] to write without joining the letters: *Please print your name and address clearly in capital letters.* **7** [T] to press (a mark) onto a soft surface: *The mark of a man's shoe was clearly printed in the mud.* **8** **print money** *often derog* (esp. of a government) to produce a large supply of money so that people can afford to pay for goods whose cost has increased

    print (sthg. ↔) **out** *phr v* [I;T] (of a computer) to produce (a printed record of information) –see also PRINTOUT

prin·ta·ble /ˈprɪntəbəl/ adj [usu. negative] fit to be printed; suitable for reading by anyone: *Her remarks were scarcely printable.* (=were very rude) –opposite **unprintable**

printed cir·cuit /ˌ··· ˈ··/ n a set of connections between points in an electrical apparatus which uses not wire but a continuous thin line of metal laid down on a surface to CONDUCT (=carry) the electricity. Printed circuits are important for electrical equipment because they are small, easily made, and do not develop faults.

printed mat·ter /ˈ·· ˌ··/ n [U] *tech* printed articles, such as official advertisements, that can be sent by post at a special cheap rate

printed word /ˌ·· ˈ·/ [the] magazines, newspapers, books, etc.: *The government was accused of putting a tax on the printed word.*

print·er /ˈprɪntəʳ/ n 1 a person employed in the trade of printing 2 a machine for making copies, esp. photographs 3 a machine which is connected to a computer and makes a printed record of computer information – compare PRINTING PRESS, and see picture at COMPUTER

print·ing /ˈprɪntɪŋ/ n 1 [U] the act or art of printing: *The invention of printing made it possible for many more people to learn to read.* | *a printing error* 2 [C] an act of printing a number of copies of a book; IMPRESSION: *This is the third printing of the book.* 3 [U] letters printed by hand

printing ink /ˈ··· ·/ also **printer's ink**– n [U] a quick-drying ink used in printing books, newspapers, etc. –compare PRINTER (2,3)

printing press /ˈ··· ·/ also **press, printing ma·chine** /ˈ··· ·ˌ·/– n a machine that prints books, newspapers, etc.

print·out /ˈprɪntˌaʊt/ n [C;U] a sheet or length of paper containing printed information produced by a computer

pri·or¹ /ˈpraɪəʳ/ adj [A] 1 coming or planned before: *I was unable to attend the meeting because of a prior engagement.* (=before I was asked to the meeting, I had arranged to do something else which would prevent me from going to the meeting) 2 more important; coming first in importance: *I stopped playing football because my work had a prior claim on my time.* 3 **prior to** fml before: *All the arrangements should have been completed prior to our departure.*

prior² n 1 also **pri·or·ess** /ˈpraɪərɪs/ fem.– the head of a priory 2 the priest next in rank below the head of an ABBEY (=a large religious house)

pri·o·ri·tize also **-tise** BrE /praɪˈɒrɪtaɪz‖-ˈɔːr-/ v [T] 1 to give (something) priority: *The public wants to see the fight against crime prioritized.* 2 to arrange (a number of things, problems, etc.) in the order in which they will be dealt with: *We need to prioritize all these jobs before we can start working on them.*

pri·or·i·ty /praɪˈɒrɪti‖-ˈɔːr-/ n 1 [U (over)] the state or right of coming before others in position or time: *The badly wounded take/have priority for medical attention over those only slightly hurt.* | *We have a priority booking scheme for members of our supporters' club.* (=they can get tickets before anyone else) 2 [C] something that needs attention, consideration, service, etc., before others: *The arranging of this business agreement is a* **top priority**. | *You must learn to get your priorities right.* (=deal with the most important things first) 3 [U] the right of a vehicle to go forward while others must wait: *Vehicles coming from the left have priority.* –compare PRECEDENCE

pri·o·ry /ˈpraɪəri/ n (often cap.) a Christian religious house or group of men (MONKS) or women (NUNS) living together, which is smaller and less important than an ABBEY –compare ABBEY

prise /praɪz/ v [T] esp. BrE for PRIZE⁵

pris·m /ˈprɪzəm/ n 1 (in GEOMETRY) a solid figure with a flat base and parallel upright edges 2 a transparent three-sided block, usu. made of glass, that breaks up white light into different colours –see picture at SPECTRUM

pris·mat·ic /prɪzˈmætɪk/ adj 1 using a PRISM (2): *a prismatic compass* 2 (of a colour) very bright, clear, and varied

pris·on /ˈprɪzən/ n 1 [C;U] a large building (usu. owned by the state) where people are kept as a punishment after being found guilty of a crime or while waiting to be tried: *The thief was sent to prison for a year.* –see picture at CELL 2 [U] the state or condition of being kept in such a place; imprisonment: *Many people believe that prison isn't a cure for crime.* 3 **stone walls do not a prison make** quote a phrase from a poem by Richard Lovelace, meaning that people can still feel free even if they are locked up

prison camp /ˈ··· ·/ n a guarded camp, usu. surrounded by a wire fence, for prisoners of war

pris·on·er /ˈprɪzənəʳ/ n 1 a person kept in a prison for a crime or while waiting to be tried: *The prisoners are allowed an hour's exercise every day.* | *"Prisoner at the bar* (=on trial), *how do you plead?"* 2 a person or animal (taken and) held with limited freedom of movement: *He was captured and* **taken prisoner** (=was made a prisoner) *by enemy soldiers.* | *The guerillas held/kept her*

prisoner for three months. | (fig.) *We are all prisoners of our past.*

prisoner of con·science /ˌ··· · ˈ··/ n a person who is put in prison because people in power do not like their political ideas

prisoner of war /ˌ··· ˈ·/ also **POW** infml– n a member of the armed forces caught by the enemy during a war and kept as a prisoner, usu. until the war is over

Prisoner of Zen·da /ˌprɪzənər əv ˈzendə/, **The** a story by Anthony Hope about the adventures of an Englishman in the imaginary kingdom of Ruritania

prison vis·i·tor /ˌ·· ˈ···/ n (in Britain) a person who visits prisoners in order to help them with their difficulties or complaints, to keep them cheerful, etc.

pris·sy /ˈprɪsi/ adj infml annoyingly exact or proper in behaviour –**sily** adv –**siness** n [U]

pris·tine /ˈprɪstiːn/ adj fml or lit pure; undamaged; fresh and clean: *an old book still in pristine condition* | *the pristine whiteness of newly-fallen snow*

Pritch·ett /ˈprɪtʃɪt/, V S (1900–) a British writer known esp. for his short stories; his works include *Collected Stories* (1982) and *The Spanish Temper*, a travel book

prith·ee /ˈprɪði/ interj old use please

priv·a·cy /ˈprɪvəsi, ˈpraɪ-‖ˈpraɪ-/ n [U] 1 the (desirable) state of being away from other people, so that they cannot see or hear what one is doing, interest themselves in one's affairs, etc. In many western countries, this is usu. given particular value and people expect to have their privacy respected by others: *There's not much privacy in these flats because of the large windows and thin walls.* 2 secrecy; avoidance of being noticed or talked about publicly

pri·vate¹ /ˈpraɪvɪt/ adj 1 personal; secret; not (to be) shared with others: *It's wrong to read people's private letters without permission.* | *Don't tell anyone else what I told you; it's private.* 2 not intended for everyone, but for a particular person or chosen group; not public: *A well-known singer gave a private performance at the party.* | *The directors have their own private plane.* | *private land* 3 independent; not connected with government, public service, etc.: *Treatment in government hospitals is free, but if you go to a private hospital you must pay.* 4 unofficial; not connected with one's business or official position, or with one's public life: *The president is paying a private visit to Europe.* | *I don't like the way newspapers snoop into people's* **private lives**. 5 where other people are not present, or cannot see or hear one: *Is there some private corner where we can sit and talk by ourselves?* 6 (of a person) (liking to be) away from other people, on one's own *She's a very private person.* –compare PUBLIC¹ – –**ly** adv : *May I speak to you privately?* (=with no one else present) | *a privately printed book* (=not produced by a PUBLISHER)

private² n 1 (written abbrev. **Pte**) also **private soldier** fml– (often cap.) a soldier of the lowest rank 2 **in private** secretly; not in the presence of other people – opposite **in public**

private bill /ˌ·· ˈ·/ n a BILL¹ (2) that has an effect on a particular person or class, rather than the general public

private de·tec·tive /ˌ··· ·ˈ···/ also **private eye** /ˌ·· ˈ·/ infml, **private in·ves·ti·ga·tor** /ˌ·· ·ˈ····/, **gumshoe** AmE sl– n a person, not a policeman, who can be hired to do certain sorts of police work, such as following people and reporting on their actions

private ed·u·ca·tion /ˌ·· ···ˈ··/ n [U] education provided privately and not by the government. Quite a large number of people in Britain are against private education because they think it strengthens class differences and makes people less equal, but some people in Britain and the US are willing to pay for private education because they feel it gives their children a better standard of education.

private en·ter·prise /ˌ··ˈ···/ n 1 [U] the economic system in which private businesses operate in free competition with each other and the government does not control industry 2 [C] a business set up by an individual person or group of people

pri·va·teer /ˌpraɪvəˈtɪəʳ/ n (in former times) (the commander of, or a sailor on) an armed ship, owned and commanded by private people, that had government permission to attack and rob enemy ships carrying goods

Private Eye /ˌ··ˈ·/ a British humorous magazine known for making fun of well-known people, including politicians and the royal family, and for uncovering secrets. It has often been taken to court by people who claim to have been damaged by things which have been written about them.

private in·come /ˌ··ˈ··/ n money which one gets regularly, usu. enough to live on, not from working but because one has money in a business or bank, which earns INTEREST¹ (5)

private law /ˈ·· ˌ·/ n [U] law the part of the law concerned with private people, property, and relationships — compare PUBLIC LAW (2)

private medi·cine /ˌ··ˈ·· ‖ ˌ·· ˈ··/ n [U] BrE HEALTH CARE which is not provided by the government but paid for by private insurance or directly. Most people in Britain are proud of the National Health Service, mainly paid for by the government, which provides free health care for all. Some people feel that the growth of private medicine will reduce standards in the public service. The people who have private medicine often do so because they are treated more quickly.

private mem·ber /ˌ··ˈ··/ n (esp. in Britain) a member of a parliament who is not a minister in the government

private member's bill /ˌ··ˈ·· ˌ·/ n (esp. in Britain) a parliamentary law introduced by a member of parliament who is not a minister in the government. Most parliamentary laws are introduced by the government but some private member's bills have been important e.g. in introducing laws concerning DIVORCE and CAPITAL PUNISHMENT.

private mon·ey /ˌ··ˈ··/ n [U] money used to pay for business plans, e.g. the Channel Tunnel, which comes from private people and not from the government

private parts /ˌ··ˈ·/ also **pri·vates** /ˈpraɪvɪts/ infml— n [P] euph the outer sexual organs

private pa·tient /ˌ··ˈ··/ n BrE somebody who pays for HEALTH CARE rather than receiving free care provided by the government

private prac·tice /ˌ··ˈ··/ n [U] 1 the practice of a professional person which is independent of an organization; esp. the practice of doctors and DENTISTS in Britain outside the National Health Service (NHS). It is quite common for doctors and dentists in Britain to have private PATIENTS, who pay, in addition to their NHS patients. 2 AmE the practice of a professional person, esp. a doctor or lawyer, who works alone rather than with a group of others: He set up a private practice when he got tired of the firm's politics.

private school /ˌ··ˈ·/ n a school not supported by government money, where education must be paid for. In Britain a private school is often called a PREP SCHOOL or a PUBLIC SCHOOL. Only a fairly small number of school-age children attend private schools; most attend STATE SCHOOLS.

private sec·re·ta·ry /ˌ··ˈ····/ n a secretary who is employed to help one person esp. with CONFIDENTIAL business matters

private sec·tor /ˌ··ˈ···/ n [the] those industries and services in a country that are owned and run by private companies, not by the state: pay increases in the private sector | private sector employees —compare PUBLIC SECTOR

private sol·dier /ˌ··ˈ··/ n fml for PRIVATE² (1)

private treat·y /ˌ··ˈ··/ n BrE law by private treaty by private arrangement between buyer and seller and not

in a public meeting: For sale by private treaty, a 4-bedroomed country house overlooking the Wye Valley.

private view /ˌ··ˈ·/ also **private view·ing** /ˌ··ˈ··/— n an occasion on which certain people are able to see a public show of objects such as paintings before it opens to the general public

pri·va·tion /praɪˈveɪʃən/ n fml [C;U] (a) lack or loss of the necessary things or the main comforts of life: Everyone suffered privations during the war, when there wasn't enough food in the country.

pri·vat·i·zation /ˌpraɪvətaɪˈzeɪʃən‖-tə-/ n [U] the selling (of a government-owned industry or organization) into private ownership. Margaret Thatcher was strongly in favour of this and during the 1980s, her Conservative government sold many state-run companies into private ownership e.g. British Telecom, British Gas, British Airways etc.

pri·vat·ize also **-ise** BrE /ˈpraɪvətaɪz/ v [T] esp. BrE to sell (a government-owned industry or organization) into private ownership: Cleaning services in state-run hospitals have been privatized. —compare NATIONALIZE

priv·et /ˈprɪvɪt/ n [U] a bush with leaves that stay green all the year, often grown in gardens to form a HEDGE

priv·i·lege /ˈprɪvɪlɪdʒ/ n 1 [C] a special advantage limited to a particular person or group: He had his privileges withdrawn as a punishment. | Education is a privilege, not a right, in many countries. —compare PREROGATIVE 2 [U] often derog advantage possessed by a person or group because of their wealth, social rank, etc.: The British public schools are bastions of privilege. 3 [S] a special favour; advantage that gives one great pleasure: He's a fine musician; it's a privilege to hear him play. 4 [C;U] (a) right to do or say things without risk of punishment, esp. in a parliament: A member of parliament mustn't hit a fellow member; that would be **a breach of privilege**. (=a breaking of the rules about what a member can do or say)

priv·i·leged /ˈprɪvɪlɪdʒd/ adj 1 having a special favour or honour: [F+to-v] We are privileged tonight to have as our main speaker the Foreign Minister of France. 2 often derog having advantage because of wealth, social rank etc.: the privileged classes 3 that a court of law cannot force one to make known: a privileged communication

priv·y¹ /ˈprɪvi/ adj 1 [F+to] fml sharing secret knowledge (of): I was not privy to the discussions, so I cannot tell you what was decided. 2 [A] old use secret; private —**ily** adv

privy² also **outhouse** AmE— n old use a TOILET, esp. an outdoor one

Privy Coun·cil /ˌ··ˈ··/ [the] (in Britain) a body of people of high rank in politics and public life who can be asked to advise the king or queen on certain state affairs — ~**lor** n

Privy Purse /ˌ··ˈ·/ [the] (sometimes not cap.) (in Britain) money given by the government to a king or queen for their personal use

Privy Seal /ˌ··ˈ·/ [the] see LORD PRIVY SEAL

prize¹ /praɪz/ n [(for)] something, typically valuable or desirable, given to someone who is successful in a game, race, competition, game of chance, etc., or given as a reward for some good action or work: Hundreds of prizes can be won in our newspaper competition. | **First** (=main) **prize** in the raffle is a holiday for two in Paris. | Lady Browne will present the prizes after the school sports. | I will now announce the **prizewinning** entry in the competition. | (fig.) To some men wealth is the greatest prize in life, and to others, fame. | (fig.) There are no prizes for guessing who told them. (=it is easy to guess)

prize² adj [A] 1 that has won a prize: prize cattle | a prize rose 2 given as a prize: prize money 3 infml, often humor complete; UTTER: She always makes a mess of things; she's a prize idiot!

prize³ v [T] to value highly: The boy's bicycle was his most prized possession. | This sort of hen is much prized for its high egg yield.

prize⁴ n 1 (esp. in former times) (the goods contained in) an enemy ship taken possession of at sea 2 something caught and taken away: The fox raided the henhouse and ran off with its prize. (=a chicken)

prize⁵ also **prise** esp. BrE ‖also **pry** esp. AmE— v [T+obj+adv/prep] to move, lift, or force with a tool or metal bar: *We prized the top off the box|prized the box open with a lever.*

prize sthg. ↔ **out** *phr v* [T (**of**)] to get (information) from someone with difficulty or by force: *At last we managed to prize the secret out of him with the offer of a bribe.*

prize day /'· ·/ *n esp. BrE* (*often cap.*) (in a school) a yearly giving of prizes for good work done during the year

prize-fight /'praɪzfaɪt/ *n* **1** (in former times) a public BOX-ING match for a money prize, in which the two men fought with bare hands **2** *AmE* as PROFESSIONAL BOXING match — ~ **er** *n* — ~ **ing** *n* [U]

pro /prəʊ/ *n* **pros 1** *infml for* PROFESSIONAL² (2): *a pro football-baller* | *That actor's a real pro, and always gives a good performance!* **2** *BrE old-fash infml for* PROSTITUTE¹ —see also PROS AND CONS

PRO /ˌpiː ɑːr 'əʊ/ *n* a public relations officer; a person whose job is to supply information about an organization and keep a good relationship between it and the public

pro- see WORD FORMATION

pro-am /ˌprəʊ 'æm◄/ *n, adj* [A] (a competition, esp. in GOLF) in which those taking part include both PROFESSIONALS (people who play for money) and AMATEURS (those who just play for pleasure)

prob·a·bil·i·ty /ˌprɒbə'bɪlɪti‖ˌprɑː-/ *n* **1** [S;U (**of**)] the state of being probable or the degree to which something is probable; likelihood: *There's very little probability of an agreement being reached.* [+(*that*)] *There is a strong probability that the tumour is operable.* | **In all probability** (=almost certainly) *they will simply get a strong warning not to do it again* **2** [C] a probable event or result: *A peace agreement is now a real probability.* —opposite **improbability** (for 1,2) **3** [C] (in MATHEMATICS) the chance of an event happening, expressed as a calculation based on known numbers: *a probability of one in four*

prob·a·ble¹ /'prɒbəbəl‖'prɑː-/ *adj* that may be expected to happen; that has a good chance of being true or correct; likely: *It's possible that they will win, but judging by their recent performances it doesn't seem very probable.* | *The probable outcome of the talks is a compromise.* [+*that*] *It is highly probable that there will be an election this year.* —opposite **improbable**

▷ USAGE Although it means the same as **likely**, **probable** cannot be used with *to-v*. You cannot use **probable** instead of **likely** in this type of sentence: *It is* **likely** *to happen.*◁

probable² *n infml* a person who is likely to be chosen for a team, to win a race, etc.

probable cause /ˌ··· '·/ *n* [U] *law* a reason to believe that someone has committed (COMMIT) a crime and should go to court for a TRIAL

prob·a·bly /'prɒbəbli‖'prɑː-/ *adv* almost (but not quite) certainly; according to what is likely: *John probably told his father all about the matter; he usually tells him everything.* | *We're going on holiday soon, probably next month.* | *"Will you be able to come tomorrow?" "Probably not."*

pro·bate¹ /'prəʊbeɪt, -bɪt‖-beɪt/ *n law* [U] the legal process of deciding that someone's WILL² (5) has been properly made and can be carried out

probate² *v* [T] *AmE law* to prove (a WILL² (5)) to be legal

pro·ba·tion /prə'beɪʃən‖prəʊ-/ *n* [U] **1** the process of testing, for a usu. fixed length of time, the suitability of a person's character, abilities, etc. (e.g. for a job or for membership of a society): *You'll be* **on probation** *for the first two months.* **2** *law* the system of allowing certain law-breakers not to go to prison, etc., if they behave well and report regularly to a PROBATION OFFICER for a fixed period of time: *The young offender was* **put on probation** *for two years.* — ~ **ary** *adj* : *a probationary period*

pro·ba·tion·er /prə'beɪʃənər‖prəʊ-/ *n* **1** a person who is being tested for membership of a church or religious group **2** a young hospital nurse during the early part of training **3** a law-breaker who has been put on probation

probation hos·tel /·'·· ˌ··/ *n* a place operated by local authorities in Britain, providing temporary housing and support for people who are on BAIL (1) —compare BAIL HOSTEL

probation of·fi·cer /·'·· ˌ···/ *n* a person whose job is to

watch, advise, and help law-breakers who are on probation

probe¹ /prəʊb/ *n* **1** a long thin metal instrument, usu. with a rounded end, esp. one used to search inside a wound, a hole in a tooth, etc. **2** also **space probe**— a spacecraft without humans on board, sent to examine conditions in outer space and send information back to Earth **3** [(**into**)] (esp. in newspapers) a careful and thorough inquiry: *a probe into police corruption*

probe² *v* [I (**into**);T] to search or examine (as if) with a probe: *He probed the mud with a stick, looking for the ring he had dropped.* | (fig.) *a newspaper report probing (into) the activities of drug dealers* | *probing questions* — **probingly** *adv*

pro·bi·ty /'prəʊbɪti/ *n* [U] *fml* perfect honesty; the quality of being completely honourable and trustworthy

prob·lem /'prɒbləm‖'prɑː-/ *n* **1** a difficulty that needs attention and thought: *The biggest problem we face is the shortage of trained staff.* | *The shortage of trained staff poses* (= causes us to have) *a serious problem.* | *The problem is that we need the director's approval, but the director is on holiday.* | *"I've left my money at home." "That's* **no problem***. I can lend you what you need."* | *a policy that will solve the unemployment problem* | *a conference to discuss the pressing* (=serious) *problem of drought in East Africa* **2** a question, esp. connected with numbers, facts, etc., for which an answer is needed: *to solve a mathematical problem* **3** [*usu. sing.*] *infml* a person who causes difficulty: *a problem child* **4** **no problem** *AmE* it was no trouble; it doesn't matter (said when someone thanks you or says they are sorry for something)

prob·lem·at·ic /ˌprɒblə'mætɪk◄‖ˌprɑː-/ also **prob·lem·at·i·cal** /-kəl/— *adj* full of problems or causing problems: *Putting this policy into effect could be very problematic.* — **-ically** /kli/ *adv*

problem solv·ing /'·· ˌ··/ *n* [U] the activity of finding answers to difficulties: *It's really a job for someone with good problem-solving abilities*

pro bo·no pub·li·co /ˌprəʊ ˌbəʊnəʊ 'pʊblɪkəʊ‖-ˌbɔːnəʊ 'puː-/ also **pro bono**— *adj Lat* for the public good; of or about work that is done for the help of the public and not for money, esp. work done by a lawyer or group of lawyers: *Some law firms have a policy of taking on pro bono cases when possible.*

pro·bos·cis /prə'bɒsɪs‖-'bɑː-/ *n* **-cises** /sɪsiːz/*or* **-cides** /sɪdiːz/ *tech* **1** the long movable nose of certain animals, esp. the elephant **2** a long tube-like part of the mouth of some insects and worms

pro·ce·du·ral /prə'siːdʒərəl/ *adj* of procedure, esp. in a court of law: *procedural difficulties*

pro·ce·dure /prə'siːdʒər/ *n* **1** [U] the method and order of directing business in an official meeting, a law case, etc.: *So much time was spent on agreeing procedure at our first meeting that we didn't start any actual business until our second.* **2** [C (**for**)] a set of actions necessary for doing something: *Writing a cheque is quite a simple procedure.* | *What's the correct procedure for renewing your car tax?* —compare PROCESS¹

pro·ceed /prə'siːd/ *v* [I] *rather fml* **1** [(**to, with**)] to begin or continue in a course of action or set of actions: *The work is proceeding according to plan.* | *We can now proceed to the main business of the meeting.* | *He paused to consult his notes, and then proceeded with his questions.* [+*to-v*] *The director said he liked my scheme very much, and then proceeded to tear it to bits!* (=destroy it completely) **2** [+*adv/prep*] to advance; move in a particular direction: *According to the policeman's report, the stolen car was proceeding in a northerly direction.* | *Passengers for the New York flight should now proceed to Gate 25.* —compare PRECEDE

proceed against sbdy. *phr v* [T *pass. rare*] *fml* to take an action in law against

proceed from sthg. *phr v* [T *no pass.*] *fml* to happen or exist as a result of: *diseases that proceed from poverty*

pro·ceed·ing /prə'siːdɪŋ/ *n* [*often pl.*] **1** an act of business: *the necessary proceedings for the merger of the two banks* **2** *fml* an event or course of action, esp. one that is unusual or undesirable: *He watched the proceedings with interest.*

pro·ceed·ings /prə'siːdɪŋz/ *n* [P] **1** an action taken in law (esp. in the phrases **start/take (legal) proceedings**) **2** (*often cap.*) the records of business, activities, etc., at the meetings of an association or club: *the Proceedings of the London Historical Society*

pro·ceeds /ˈprəʊsiːdz/ *n* [P] money gained from the sale of something, or as the result of some activity for getting money: *The proceeds of the sale amounted to £500.*

pro·cess¹ /ˈprəʊses‖ˈprɑː-/ **1** a connected set of natural actions or events that produce continuation or gradual change, and over which humans have little control: *Coal was formed out of dead forests by a long slow process of chemical change.* | *the process of breathing* | *the ageing process* (=by which people grow old) **2** a connected set of human actions or operations that are performed intentionally in order to reach a particular result or as part of an official system or established method of doing something: *the process of learning to read* | *the electoral/democratic process* | *The company is still* **in the process** (=performing the operation) *of moving to a new factory.* | *They are trying to extend the range of goods they sell and, in the process, to appeal to a new type of customer.* | *The police established the identity of the dead man* **by a process of elimination. 3** a particular system or treatment of materials used esp. in producing goods: *an advanced industrial process* **4** *tech* part of a plant or animal that grows standing out and is easily seen **5** *tech* a legal action in all its stages —compare PROCEDURE

process² *v* [T] **1** to treat and preserve (a substance, esp. a food) by a particular PROCESS¹ (3): *processed cheese* **2** to print a picture from (a photographic film) **3** to put (information, numbers, etc.) into a computer for examination **4** to examine or deal with, esp. by means of an established system or process: *Your application for a mortgage is now being processed.*

pro·cess³ /prəˈses/ *v* [I+ *adv/prep*] to walk (as if) in a procession

processed food /ˌ··· ˈ·/ *n* [C;U] *usu. derog* food which has been prepared for sale and specially treated so that it can be stored, and so that it is attractive to the buyer, e.g. by adding extra colour to it. Processed foods are generally considered to be less healthy than fresh foods.

pro·ces·sion /prəˈseʃən/ *n* **1** [C (**of**)] a line of people, vehicles, etc., moving forward in an orderly way, e.g. as part of a religious ceremony or public entertainment: *a carnival procession* | (fig.) *interrupted by a procession of unwelcome visitors* **2** [C;U] a continuous onward movement of people or things: *The workers marched in procession.* | *to hold a procession*

pro·ces·sion·al /prəˈseʃənəl/ *adj* [A] connected with or used in a solemn religious procession: *a processional march/banner*

pro·ces·sor /ˈprəʊsesəʳ‖ˈprɑː-/ *n* a MICROPROCESSOR —see also FOOD PROCESSOR, WORD PROCESSOR

pro-choice /ˌ·ˈ·/ *adj euph* favouring ABORTION being available to those who want it. In the US, people who are pro-choice often LOBBY Congress and walk in DEMONSTRATIONS. —compare PRO-LIFE; see also ABORTION (CULTURAL NOTE)

pro·claim /prəˈkleɪm‖prəʊ-/ *v* [T] **1** *fml* to make (esp. news of national importance) known publicly, esp. using speech rather than writing; declare officially: *The ringing bells proclaimed the birth of the prince.* | *A national holiday was proclaimed.* | *He proclaimed his intention of attending, despite their opposition.* [+*obj+n*] *The boy was proclaimed king.* **2** *lit* to show clearly; be an outward sign of: [+*obj*/(*that*)] *His accent proclaimed his American origins/proclaimed that he was American.*

proc·la·ma·tion /ˌprɒkləˈmeɪʃən‖ˌprɑː-/ *n* **1** [C] an official public statement: *a royal proclamation* **2** [U] the act of proclaiming

pro·cliv·i·ty /prəˈklɪvəti‖prəʊ-/ *n* [(**to, towards**)] *fml* a strong natural liking or tendency, esp. towards something bad

pro·con·sul /prəʊˈkɒnsəl‖-ˈkɑːn-/ *n* a governor of a part of the ancient Roman Empire – –**ar** /prəʊˈkɒnsjʊləʳ‖-ˈkɑːnsələr/ *adj* [A]

pro·con·su·late /prəʊˈkɒnsjʊlət‖-ˈkɑːnsəl-/ also **pro·con·sul·ship** /prəʊˈkɒnsəlʃɪp‖-ˈkɑːn-/– *n* the rank or period of office of a proconsul

pro·cras·ti·nate /prəˈkræstəneɪt/ *v* [I] *fml* to delay repeatedly and without good reason in doing something that must

be done: *Stop procrastinating – just sit down and do it.* – –**nation** /prəˌkræstəˈneɪʃən/ *n* [U]

pro·cre·ate /ˈprəʊkrieɪt/ *v* [I;T] *esp. fml or tech* to produce or give life to (young) – –**ation** /ˌprəʊkriˈeɪʃən/ *n* [U]

Procter & Gam·ble /ˌ··· ˈ··/ *tdmk* an American company which makes washing powder and many different cleaning products

proc·tor¹ /ˈprɒktəʳ‖ˈprɑːk-/ *n* **1** (esp. at Oxford and Cambridge) a university officer whose duties include making students keep university rules **2** *AmE* a person appointed to make sure students do not cheat in an examination

proctor² *v* [T] *AmE for* INVIGILATE

pro·cu·ra·tor fis·cal /ˌprɒkjʊreɪtə ˈfɪskəl‖ˌprɑːkjʊreɪtər-/ also **fiscal** *infml*– *n* an official in Scotland who is in charge of deciding whether there is enough evidence against a person for them to be sent to court for a TRIAL –see also extra information on page 739

pro·cure /prəˈkjʊəʳ‖prəʊ-/ *v* [(**for**)] **1** [T] *fml* to obtain, esp. by effort or careful attention: *I managed to procure two tickets for the final.* [+*obj(i)+obj(d)*] *Somehow he had procured us an invitation.* **2** [I;T] *derog, esp. lit* to provide (a woman) for someone else's sexual satisfaction – ~**ment** *n* [U]

pro·cur·er /prəˈkjʊərəʳ/ **pro·cur·ess** /-rɪs/ *fem.*– *n* a person who procures (esp. PROCURE (2))

prod¹ /prɒd‖prɑːd/ *v* -**dd**- **1** [I (**at**); T] to push or press (something or someone) with a pointed object; POKE: *He prodded (at) the snake with his toe to make sure it was dead.* | *She prodded him in the ribs.* **2** [T (**into**)] to urge sharply into action or thought: *The announcement prodded us into action.* | *He's not lazy, but he needs prodding.*

prod² *n* **1** an act of prodding: *You'd better give her memory a prod.* (=remind her) **2** an instrument used for prodding

prod·i·gal¹ /ˈprɒdɪgəl‖ˈprɑː-/ *adj* **1** *derog* carelessly wasteful, esp. of money: *his prodigal lifestyle* **2** [F+**of**] *fml approc* giving or producing large amounts freely and generously: *a mind prodigal of ideas* – –~**ly** *adv* – –~**ity** /ˌprɒdɪˈgæləti‖ˌprɑː-/ *n* [U]

prodigal² *n infml, often humor* a person who leads a life of careless wasteful spending and perhaps immoral pleasure

prodigal son /ˌ··· ˈ·/ [*the*] (often *cap.*) a young man in a story in the Bible who leaves home and wastes his time and money but then feels sorry and returns home, where he receives a joyful welcome from his family –see also **kill the fatted calf** (KILL)

pro·di·gious /prəˈdɪdʒəs/ *adj* wonderfully large, powerful, etc.: *a prodigious memory* – –~**ly** *adv*

prod·i·gy /ˈprɒdɪdʒi‖ˈprɑː-/ *n* **1** a person who has unusual and very noticeable abilities: *a* **child prodigy** (=an unusually clever child) **2** a wonder in nature: *Mount Everest is one of nature's prodigies.*

pro·duce¹ /prəˈdjuːs‖-ˈduːs/ *v* **1** [T] to grow or bring into existence naturally: *These trees produce rubber.* | *The pancreas is an organ in the body that produces insulin.* | *Canada produces high-quality wheat.* **2** [I;T] to make (goods for sale), esp. in large quantities: *They produce over 250 cars a week.* | *Gas can be produced from coal.* | *The factory hasn't begun to produce yet.* –see also MASS PRODUCE **3** [T] to make by using skill and imagination: *to produce a work of art* | *She can produce a delicious meal from simple ingredients.* **4** [T] to give birth to (a young animal): *Female sheep produce one or two lambs at a time.* | (*humor*) *Mrs Dobson has just produced twins.* **5** [T] to show, bring out, or offer for examination or consideration: *The magician produced a rabbit from a hat.* | *Can you produce any proof of your date of birth?* | *He suddenly produced a gun.* **6** [T] to prepare and bring before the public: *The book/The play was produced on a very small budget.* **7** [T] to cause; have as a result or effect: *The election did not produce a clear victory for any party.* | *The two lasers combine to produce a powerful cutting tool.* **8** [T] *tech* (in GEOMETRY) to lengthen or continue (a line) to a point —see PRODUCTION

prod·uce² /ˈprɒdjuːs‖ˈprɑːduːs/ *n* [U] something that has been produced, esp. by growing or farming: *The wine bottle was marked "Produce of Spain".* —see PRODUCTION (USAGE)

pro·duc·er /prə'djuːsəʳ‖-'duː-/ n 1 a person, company, or country that produces goods, foods, or materials: *one of the world's leading oil producers* —compare CONSUMER 2 a person who has general control esp. of the money for a play, film, or broadcast, but who does not direct the actors —compare DIRECTOR (2), IMPRESARIO; see PRODUCTION (USAGE)

prod·uct /'prɒdʌkt‖'prɑː-/ n 1 something useful produced by growth or from the ground, or made in a factory: *The country's main products are cocoa and gold.* | *a decline in our exports of manufactured products* | *to market new products* | *the finished product coming off the assembly line* —see also BY-PRODUCT, END PRODUCT, GNP 2 something that is produced as a result of thought, will, planning, conditions, etc.: *Today's housing problems are the product of years of neglect.* 3 [(of)] *tech* (in MATHEMATICS) the number got by multiplying two or more numbers: *The product of 3 multiplied by 2 multiplied by 6 is 36.* 4 *tech* a new chemical compound produced by chemical action —see PRODUCTION (USAGE)

pro·duc·tion /prə'dʌkʃən/ n 1 [U (of)] the act of producing something: *Entrance is permitted only on production of a ticket.* | *She has been involved in the production of several well-known films.* 2 [U] the process of making products: *one of the stages in the production of paper* | *When will the new range of computers* **go into (full) production?** (=begin to be produced in large numbers) | *a factory's production manager* | *to stimulate production* 3 [U] the amount produced: *Production of steel has increased in the last few weeks.* | *a cut in production* 4 [C] something produced by skill or imagination, esp. a work of art or a play, film, or broadcast: *This theatre is known for its imaginative productions.* —see also MASS PRODUCTION

▷ USAGE Compare **production, product, produce,** and **producer. Production** [U] is the process in which things are made: *a good rate of* **production.** A **production** [C] is a play, film, etc. made for the theatre, television, etc.: *a new* **production** *of "Hamlet".* A **product** [C] is something made by industry: *various industrial* **products. Produce** [U] ('·,·) is the general word for things got from a farm, such as milk, potatoes, or wool: *a large quantity of agricultural* **produce.** If you **produce** (·'·) any of the things mentioned above you are a **producer.**◁

production line /·'·· ·/ n an arrangement of workers and machines in a factory so that the stages of work follow each other in order; ASSEMBLY LINE

production num·ber /·'·· ,·-/ n (in a MUSICAL²) a scene involving many people singing and usu. dancing on the stage all at once

production plat·form /·'·· ,·-/ n a large piece of equipment standing on very long legs used for getting oil out of the ground under the sea

pro·duc·tive /prə'dʌktɪv/ adj 1 that produces well or in large quantities: *a very productive writer* | *productive land* | *a productive meeting* (=bringing useful results) — opposite **unproductive** 2 of or resulting in the production of goods or wealth: *Office work is necessary, but most of it is not directly productive.* | *the factory's productive capacity* — ~ **ly** adv — ~ **ness** n [U]

pro·duc·tiv·i·ty /ˌprɒdʌk'tɪvɪti, -dək-‖ˌprɑː-/ n [U] the rate of producing goods, crops, etc.; the relationship between the amount that is produced and the work, money, etc., that is needed to produce it: *new production methods that have led to high/increased productivity* | *a productivity bonus*

prof /prɒf‖prɑːf/ n sl for PROFESSOR (1,2)

Prof *written abbrev. for:* PROFESSOR (1,2): *Prof Peter Smith*

pro·fane¹ /prə'feɪn/ adj 1 showing disrespect for God or for holy things: *To smoke in a church or mosque would be a profane act.* 2 (esp. of language) socially shocking, esp. because of improper use of religious words — compare OBSCENE 3 *fml* not religious or holy; concerned with human life in this world; SECULAR: *profane art* — opposite **sacred** — ~ **ly** adv

profane² v [T] to treat (esp. something holy) disrespectfully —**-fanation** /ˌprɒfə'neɪʃən‖ˌprɑː-/ n [C;U]

pro·fan·i·ty /prə'fænɪti/ n [C;U] (an example of) being profane, esp. in language: *Their conversation was full of pro-*

fanities. (=shocking words) —compare BLASPHEMY, OBSCENITY

pro·fess /prə'fes/ v [T] *fml* 1 to make a (usu. false or insincere) claim of or about: *She professed ignorance of their intentions.* [+to-v] *I don't profess to know anything about poetry.* 2 to declare openly or freely (a personal feeling, belief, etc.): *The president has professed his enthusiasm for the scheme.* [+obj+n/adj] *She professed herself (to be) completely satisfied with the arrangements.* 3 to have (a religion or belief)

pro·fessed /prə'fest/ adj 1 [A] plainly self-declared: *She is a professed man-hater.* 2 pretended: *a professed sorrow* — ~ **ly** /prə'fesɪdli/ adv

pro·fes·sion /prə'feʃən/ n 1 [C] a form of employment, esp. one that is possible only for an educated person and after training (such as law, medicine, or teaching) and that is respected in society as honourable: *He is a lawyer* **by profession.** | *to pursue a profession* —see JOB (USAGE) 2 [*the+sing./pl. v*] the whole body of people in a particular profession: *The teaching profession claim(s) to be badly paid.* | *Dr Wilde is well-respected by leading members of the (medical) profession.* 3 [C (of)] *fml* a declaration of one's belief, opinion, or feeling: *professions of regret* 4 **the oldest profession in the world** *humor* the profession of being a PROSTITUTE

pro·fes·sion·al¹ /prə'feʃənəl/ adj 1 [A *no comp.*] of or working in one of the professions: *I'm not sure about your legal position in this matter: I think you should take professional advice.* (=from a lawyer) | *Our doctor has been accused of professional misconduct.* 2 *usu. apprec* showing the qualities of training of a member of a profession: *You made a good job of painting the kitchen — very professional!* | *professional standards* | *Don't wear those old clothes to work; try to look more professional.* 3 [*no comp.*] doing for money what others do **a** for enjoyment: *a professional photographer* | *a footballer who has just* **turned professional** (=started to play football as a job) **b** themselves, in order to save money: *a professional painter and decorator* —compare AMATEUR (1) 4 [*no comp.*] done by people who are paid: *professional football* —compare AMATEUR 5 [A *no comp.*] *BrE euph* (of a breaking of rules in sport) intentional: *If a footballer handles the ball to stop another player getting it, it is often called a professional foul.* — ~ **ly** adv : *She was professionally trained.*

professional² also **pro** *infml* — n 1 *apprec* a person who has great experience and high professional standards: *She's a real professional.* 2 a person who earns money by practising a particular skill or sport —compare AMATEUR 3 (*often in comb.*) a sportsman employed by a private club to play for it and to teach its members: *a tennis professional*

Professional Golf·ers' As·so·ci·a·tion of A·mer·i·ca /·,··· ,·· ···,·· · ·'···/ n see PGA

pro·fes·sion·al·is·m /prə'feʃənəlɪzəm/ n [U] 1 *often apprec* the behaviour, skill, or qualities shown by a professional 2 (in sports) the practice of using professional players

professional per·son /·,··· '··/ n an educated man or woman who usu. has a job in an office and who is often seen by other people as someone who has high standards of behaviour: *Professional person wanted to rent small house.*

pro·fes·sor /prə'fesəʳ/ n 1 *BrE* a teacher of the highest rank in a university department: *Professor Ward* | *a history professor/a professor of history* | *Certainly, professor.* —see also ABSENT-MINDED PROFESSOR 2 *AmE* any full member of the teaching body at a university or college 3 a title taken by those who teach or claim various skills: *Madame Clara, professor of dancing*

pro·fes·so·ri·al /ˌprɒfə'sɔːriəl‖ˌprɑː-/ adj of a university professor: *professorial rank* —**-ally** adv

pro·fes·sor·ship /prə'fesəʃɪp‖-sər-/ n the position of a university professor

prof·fer /'prɒfəʳ‖'prɑː-/ v [T (to)] *fml* to offer, esp. by holding out in the hands for acceptance: *She refused the proffered drink.* [+obj(i)+obj(d)] *He proffered me a cigar.*

pro·fi·cient /prə'fɪʃənt/ adj [(at, in)] thoroughly skilled; well practised: *She is proficient at/in operating the computer.* | *a proficient typist* — ~ **ly** adv —**-ciency** n [U (at, in)] : *a maths proficiency test*

pro·file¹ /ˈprəʊfaɪl/ n **1** a side view, esp. of someone's head: *He drew her profile.* | *She photographed him in profile.* **2** an edge or shape of something seen against a background: *the sharp profile of the hills against the sky* **3** the state of being noticed by other people around one: *He is attracting most of the criticism, partly because of his* high *political* **profile** *at the moment.* | *The government is trying to keep a* **low profile** *on this issue.* **4** [(of)] a short description, esp. of a person's life and character, esp. as given on television or in a newspaper: *an exclusive profile of the new tennis champion*

profile

profile² v [T] to draw, write, or show a profile of: *an article profiling the new Soviet leader*

prof·it¹ /ˈprɒfɪt/ n **1** [C;U] money gained by trade or business: *There's very little profit in selling newspapers at present.* | *The company announced a trading profit|a pre-tax profit of £2 million for 1986, after making a loss in 1985.* | *We sold our house* **at a profit**. (=sold it for more than it had cost) | *They* **made a profit** *of £6000 on the deal.*| *I made a handsome* (=very good) *profit from the sale of my car.* | *a non-profit-making organization* | *a for-profit hospital chain* | *hoping to bring the system into profit this year* | *net|gross profit* **2** [U] *fml* advantage gained from some action: *reading for profit and pleasure* — ~**less** *adj* — ~**lessly** *adv*

profit² v [T +obj(i)+obj(d)] *fml or old use* to be of advantage to (someone): *It will profit you nothing to do that.* **profit by/from** *sthg. phr* v [T] to learn or gain advantage from (an experience, activity, etc.): *You can profit by my mistakes and avoid them yourself.* [+v-ing] *She has certainly profited from spending a year in England.*

prof·it·a·bil·i·ty /ˌprɒfɪtəˈbɪlɪti/ n [U] the state of being profitable or the degree to which a business or operation is profitable: *The company hopes to return to profitability this year.* | *high profitability*

prof·it·a·ble /ˈprɒfɪtəbəl/ adj producing or resulting in profit or advantage: *a profitable deal* | *It's a very profitable little business.* | *We spent a profitable day cleaning out the cupboards.* —opposite **unprofitable** —~**bly** adv

profit and loss ac·count /ˌ··· ˈ·· ·ˌ·/ n a financial statement showing a company's income, spending, and profit over a certain period

prof·it·eer /ˌprɒfɪˈtɪəʳ/ n derog a person who makes unfairly large profits, esp. by selling things at very high prices when much-needed goods are difficult to get: *black market profiteers* —**profiteer** v [I] — ~**ing** n [U] : *arrested for profiteering*

profit mar·gin /ˈ·· ˌ·/ n the difference between the cost of production and the selling price: *a high profit margin*

profit shar·ing /ˈ·· ˌ··/ n [U] a system according to which the workers share in the profits of a factory, business, etc.

prof·li·gate¹ /ˈprɒflɪgɪt/ adj **1** [(of)] carelessly and foolishly wasteful, esp. of money: *profligate spending by our local council* **2** fml wicked; shamelessly immoral —**gacy** n [U] fml

profligate² n fml a profligate person

pro·found /prəˈfaʊnd/ adj **1** deep; very strongly felt; IN-TENSE: *There was a profound silence in the empty church.* | *The incident made a profound impression on me.* **2** often apprec having or using thorough knowledge and deep understanding: *a profound thinker* | *a very profound remark* **3** [A] lit or fml deep; far below the surface: *in the profound depths of the ocean* **4** tech complete: *profound deafness* — ~**ly** adv : *I am profoundly grateful.*

Pro·fu·mo Scan·dal /prəʊˈfjuːməʊ ˌskændl/ [the] also **Profumo Af·fair** /·ˈ·· ·ˌ·/— the sexual relationship, which became public in 1963, between John Profumo, the Minister of War in the Conservative government, and a young woman, Christine Keeler, and the activities of others connected with this. After first lying in Parliament about the affair, Profumo later admitted to it and was forced to RESIGN. It was discovered that Keeler had also had an affair with a Russian naval officer but an official report later said that no national secrets had been given away. Newspaper reports of wild parties and sexual behaviour involving important public figures mixing with criminals shocked the nation and severely em-

barrassed the government. —see also Mandy RICE-DAVIES

pro·fun·di·ty /prəˈfʌndɪti/ n fml **1** [U] the quality of being profound, esp. in feeling or understanding **2** [C usu. pl.] something profound, esp. a profound thought or idea

pro·fuse /prəˈfjuːs/ adj **1** produced, flowing, or poured out freely and in great quantity: *a profuse mass of curls* | *profuse tears* | *profuse apologies* **2** [F (in, of)] (too) eager, free, or generous in giving (praise, thanks, etc.): *She was profuse in her thanks.* — ~**ly** adv — ~**ness** n [U]

pro·fu·sion /prəˈfjuːʒən/ n fml [S (of);U] large supply; great or too great amount: *flowers growing* **in profusion** | *The room was spoilt by a profusion of ugly little ornaments.*

pro·gen·i·tor /prəʊˈdʒenɪtəʳ/ n [(of)] tech or fml a person or thing from the distant past, from which someone or something is descended; ANCESTOR or PRECURSOR: *Schoenberg was a progenitor of modern music.*

prog·e·ny /ˈprɒdʒɪni/ /ˈprɑː-/ n [U+sing.|pl. v] **1** tech or lit the descendants of a person, animal, or plant form **2** sometimes humor a person's children or an animal's young: *Her numerous progeny were all asleep.*

pro·ges·ter·one /prəʊˈdʒestərəʊn/ n [U] a substance in the female organs that prepares the UTERUS (=the childbearing part) for its work. Because it stops the production of eggs from the OVARY, it is widely used in making the PILL (2).

prog·na·thous /prɒgˈneɪθəs/ /prɑːg-/ adj tech having or being a jaw that sticks out

prog·no·sis /prɒgˈnəʊsɪs/ /prɑːg-/ n **-ses** /siːz/ **1** med a doctor's opinion, based on medical experience, of what course a disease will probably take —compare DIAGNOSIS **2** fml judgment about the future based on information or experience

prog·nos·ti·cate /prɒgˈnɒstɪkeɪt/ /prɑːg ˈnɑː-/ v [T] fml or humor to say or be a sign of (what is going to happen) —**cator** n —**cation** /prɒgˌnɒstɪˈkeɪʃən/ /prɑːgˌnɑː-/ n [C;U]

pro·gram¹ /ˈprəʊgræm/ n **1** a list of instructions that must be given to a computer in order to make it perform an operation: *to write a program* | *a new program for forecasting our sales figures* **2** AmE a programme

program² v **-mm-** or **-m-** [T] **1** to supply (a computer) with a program: *a programming language* [+obj+to-v] *The computer can be programmed to list all the French words in the dictionary* **2** AmE to programme

pro·gram·er /ˈprəʊgræməʳ/ n a PROGRAMMER

pro·gram·ma·ble /ˈprəʊgræməbəl/ adj controllable by means of a program: *a programmable heating system*

pro·gramme¹ BrE || **-gram** AmE /ˈprəʊgræm/ n **1** a (printed) list of performers or things to be performed at a concert, a theatre, a sports competition, etc.: *According to the programme, the first race starts at two.* **2** a complete show or performance, esp. one made up of several different parts: *What is your favourite TV programme?* | *a current affairs programme on the radio* **3** a list of planned activities; plan for future action: *The hospital building programme has been delayed by lack of money.* | *(esp. AmE) The Republican Party's election program promises big tax cuts.* **4** BrE a set of actions performed in order by a machine such as a washing machine or MICROWAVE: *I think it would be best to do it on the wool programme.* | *The microwave has a separate programme for defrosting.*

programme² BrE || **-gram** AmE— v **-mm-** [T] to plan or arrange: [+obj+to-v] *The central heating system| washing machine|microwave is programmed to start working at six o'clock.*

programmed course /ˌ·· ˈ·/ n an educational course in which the material is arranged in a book or a machine to be seen in small amounts, each of which must be learnt and tested before passing on to the next

programmed learn·ing /ˌ·· ˈ··/ n [U] an educational system in which one teaches oneself by means of a PROGRAMMED COURSE

programme mu·sic /ˈ·· ˌ··/ n [U] descriptive music, using sound to suggest a story, picture, etc.

pro·gram·mer , programer /ˈprəʊgræməʳ/ n a person who writes computer programs

pro·gress¹ /ˈprəʊgres/ /ˈprɑː-/ n **1** [U] forward movement in space; advance: *The ship made slow progress through*

the rough sea. **2** [U] continual improvement or development towards an intended or desired result: *Jane is still in hospital, but she's making (good|rapid) progress.* (=is getting better) | *He's not making much progress with his English.* | *Progress in the peace talks has been rather disappointing.* **3** [U] the process of continuing or being done: *Please do not enter the classroom while a lesson is in progress.* **4** [C] *old use* an official ceremonial journey, esp. of a king or queen

pro·gress² /prə'gres/ *v* [I] **1** to move forward in space or time; advance: *It became hotter and hotter as the day progressed.* | *Later he progressed to more difficult tasks.* **2** to improve; develop favourably: *Work on the new road is progressing quite well.* | *"Your father is progressing nicely," said the nurse.* —compare REGRESS

pro·gres·sion /prə'greʃən/ *n* **1** [S;U] (the action of) progressing, esp. by stages **2** [C] *tech* (in MATHEMATICS) a set of numbers that vary in a particular way —see also ARITHMETIC PROGRESSION, GEOMETRIC PROGRESSION

pro·gres·sive¹ /prə'gresɪv/ *adj* **1** [*no comp.*] moving forward or developing continuously or by stages: *a progressive decline in exports* | *progressive loss of sight in old age* **2** *usu. apprec* favouring change or new ideas, e.g. in politics or education: *a progressive thinker|school* | *This is a progressive firm that uses the most modern systems.* **3** [*no comp.*] *tech* (of a verb form) showing action that is continuing. Progressive forms are shown in English by be+PRESENT PARTICIPLE, as in "They *are waiting* for a bus" or "She *was reading* a book". Verbs that cannot be used like this, such as "know", are marked [*not in progressive forms*] in this dictionary. – – **ly** *adv* : *It got progressively worse|better.* – – **ness** *n* [U]

progressive² *n* a person with progressive ideas, esp. about social change

Progressive Con·ser·va·tive Par·ty /·,··· ·'··· ,··/ [*the*] one of the main political parties in Canada: *Prime Minister Mulroney's Progresssive Conservatives have tried to placate the separatist Québécois.*

Progressive Par·ty /·'··· ,··/ [*the*] any of three separate political organizations in the US that were active in the presidential elections of 1912, 1924, and 1948 and were in favour of social REFORM

progressive tax /·'·· ,·/ *n* a tax that takes a larger PERCENTAGE of money from people with higher incomes than from those with low incomes —compare REGRESSIVE TAX

progress re·port /'·· ·,·/ *n* a statement about how something, esp. work, is advancing or developing

pro·hib·it /prə'hɪbɪt‖prəʊ-/ *v* [T (**from**)] *fml* **1** to forbid by law or rule: *Smoking in this railway carriage is (strictly) prohibited.* | *We are prohibited from drinking alcohol during working hours.* **2** to prevent; make impossible: *The price prohibited us from buying it.*

pro·hi·bi·tion /ˌprəʊhɪ'bɪʃən/ *n* **1** [U (**of**)] the act of prohibiting something **2** [C (**against**)] *fml* an order forbidding something **3** [U] (*usu. cap.*) the forbidding by law of the making or sale of alcoholic drinks

Prohibition the period from 1919 to 1933 in the US when the making, sale, and TRANSPORT of alcoholic drinks were forbidden by law. It was impossible to make people obey the law and there was a lot of criminal activity. Prohibition is the subject of many American films. —see also BOOTLEG, SPEAKEASY

pro·hi·bi·tion·ist /ˌprəʊhɪ'bɪʃənɪst/ *n* a person who supports PROHIBITION (3)

pro·hib·i·tive /prə'hɪbɪtɪv‖prəʊ-/ *adj* preventing or tending to discourage something: *The government has put a prohibitive tax* (=higher than anyone can pay) *on foreign goods.* – – **ly** *adv* : *prohibitively expensive*

pro·hib·i·to·ry /prə'hɪbɪtəri‖prəʊ'hɪbɪtɔːri/ *adj fml* intended to prohibit something: *a prohibitory gesture*

proj·ect¹ /'prɒdʒekt‖'prɑː-/ *n* **1** a piece of work that needs skill, effort, and careful planning, esp. over a period of time: *In their geography class, the children are doing a special project on Native Americans.* | *The new dam is a major construction project, funded by the government.* **2** *AmE* a HOUSING PROJECT

pro·ject² /prə'dʒekt/ *v* **1** [I;T] to (cause to) stick out beyond an edge or surface: *a signpost projecting from the wall* **2** [T (**at, into**)] to throw through the air with force; PROPEL: *to project a missile into space* | (fig.) *Try to project your*

mind into the future and imagine what life will be like then. **3** [T *usu. pass.*] to think about as a likely course of action; plan: *our projected visit to Australia* | *projected cuts in government expenditure* **4** to judge or calculate, using the information one has: *projected sales figures* **5** [T (**into, onto**)] to cause (heat, sound, light, or shadow) to be directed into space or onto a surface: *I had no screen, so I projected the slides onto an old white sheet.* | *A singer must learn to project his voice so as to be heard in a large hall.* —see also PROJECTOR **6** [I;T] to express or represent (oneself or one's qualities) outwardly, esp. in a way that has a favourable effect on others: *to project oneself in order to make a good impression on an interviewer* **7** [I;T (**on, onto**)] to imagine (one's own esp. bad feelings or thoughts) as being experienced by others: *Don't project your guilt feelings onto me!* **8** [T] *tech* **a** to make a picture of (a solid, esp. curved, object) on a flat surface **b** to make (a map) by this means

pro·jec·tile /prə'dʒektaɪl‖-tl/ *n fml or tech* an object or weapon that is thrown or shot forward, esp. from a gun

pro·jec·tion /prə'dʒekʃən/ *n* **1** [C] something that sticks out from a surface: *small projections from the wall of the cave* **2** [C (**of**)] something planned, esp. a guess of future possibilities, based on the general direction of events at a particular time: *These figures show our projection of the town's population increase over the next ten years.* **3** [C] an image, sound, etc., that has been projected **4** [U] the act of projecting **5** [C] *tech* a figure, esp. a map, that has been projected —see also MERCATOR PROJECTION

pro·jec·tion·ist /prə'dʒekʃənɪst/ *n* a person who works a cinema projector

pro·jec·tor /prə'dʒektər/ *n* an apparatus for projecting films or pictures onto a surface —see also OVERHEAD PROJECTOR

Pro·kof·i·ev /prə'kɒfief‖-'kɔː-/, **Ser·gei** /'seəgei‖seər'gei/ (1891–1953) a Russian COMPOSER, whose works include the *Classical Symphony*, the BALLET *Romeo and Juliet*, and the musical story *Peter and the Wolf*

pro·lapse /prəʊ'læps/ *v* [I] *med* (of an inner body organ, such as the bowel) to slip or fall down out of the proper place: *a prolapsed uterus* —**prolapse** /'prəʊlæps‖prəʊ-'læps/ *n*

prole /prəʊl/ *n derog* a member of the proletariat

pro·le·gom·e·na /ˌprəʊlɪ'gɒmɪnə‖-'gɑː-/ *n* -**ena** /ʒnə/ *fml* a written introduction to a serious book

pro·le·tar·i·an /ˌprəʊlɪ'teəriən◂/ *n, adj often derog* (a member) of the proletariat

pro·le·tar·i·at /ˌprəʊlɪ'teəriət/ *n* [*the*+*sing.|pl. v*] the class of workers who own little or no property and have to work for wages, esp. at unskilled jobs in the city. This word is used esp. by Karl Marx who believed that in time the industrial proletariat would win their struggle against CAPITALISM.

pro-life /ˌ·· '·/ *adj euph* opposed to ABORTION

▶CULTURAL NOTE In the US, pro-life groups are very active and LOBBY Congress. Some **pro-lifers** have even used violence, such as throwing bombs at CLINICS that perform abortions. Pro-life groups will often protest at such hospitals and clinics by walking in front of them holding signs with pro-life SLOGANS on them. —see also LIFE; compare PRO-CHOICE; see also ABORTION (CULTURE NOTE)◄

pro-lif·er /ˌ·· '··/ *n* a person who is opposed to ABORTION

pro·lif·e·rate /prə'lɪfəreɪt/ *v* [I] to increase rapidly in numbers or by producing new parts: *During the 1980s, computer companies proliferated.*

pro·lif·e·ra·tion /prəˌlɪfə'reɪʃən/ *n* **1** [S;U] a rapid increase or spreading: *the proliferation of nuclear weapons* —see also NONPROLIFERATION **2** [C] *tech* (in BIOLOGY) a part formed by the division of cells

pro·lif·ic /prə'lɪfɪk/ *adj* **1** producing many young, fruit, etc.: *Rats are very prolific.* | *prolific plants* **2** *usu. apprec* producing many works: *a prolific writer* | *During their most prolific years, this research team was publishing new evidence every month.* – – **ally** /kli/ *adv*

pro·lix /'prəʊlɪks‖prəʊ'lɪks/ *adj fml* (of a speech, writer, etc.) using too many words and therefore tiringly and uninterestingly long; WORDY – – **ity** /prə'lɪksˌti‖prəʊ-/ *n* [U]

Pro·log /'prəʊlɒg‖-lɔːg, -lɑːg/ *n* [U] *tdmk* a computer language often used for educational purposes

pro·logue ‖ also **prolog** *AmE* /'prəʊlɒg‖-lɔːg, -lɑːg/ *n* [(**to**))]

1 (*sometimes cap.*) an introduction to a play, long poem, etc. —compare EPILOGUE (1)   **2** an act or event that leads up to and causes another more important set of events: *The border incident proved to be just the prologue to a full-scale invasion.*

pro·long /prə'lɒŋ||-'lɔːŋ/ *v* [T] to make longer; lengthen: *She tried desperately to prolong the conversation.* | *He prolonged his visit by two weeks.* —compare PROTRACT

pro·lon·ga·tion /ˌprəʊlɒŋ'geɪʃən||-lɔːŋ-/ *n* **1** [U] the action of prolonging something   **2** [C (**of**)] something added that prolongs something

pro·longed /prə'lɒŋd||-'lɔːŋd/ *adj* continuing for a long time: *a prolonged silence/absence*

prom /prɒm||prɑːm/ *n* **1** *AmE* a formal dance party given for students in a HIGH SCHOOL or college class

▶ CULTURAL NOTE The most important prom in high school is the **Senior Prom**, which is held at the end of the school year for the students who are in their last (SENIOR) year of high school. It is often held either in the high school GYM-NASIUM or in a room with a dance floor at a hotel. Usually boys ask girls to go with them, but sometimes people go as a group of friends. There are usu. parties after the prom is over. ◀

2 *BrE infml for* PROMENADE[1] (1): *sitting on the prom, smelling the fresh sea air*   **3** (*often cap.*) *BrE infml for* PROMENADE CONCERT

prom·e·nade[1] /ˌprɒmə'nɑːd◄, 'prɒmənɑːd||ˌprɑːmə'neɪd◄/ *n* **1** a wide path beside a road along the coast in a holiday town —compare FRONT[1] (3)   **2** *fml* an unhurried walk, ride, or drive for pleasure or exercise

promenade[2] *v fml* **1** [I; T] to walk slowly up and down along (a place, street, etc.)   **2** [T] *sometimes derog* to take on an unhurried walk, ride, or drive, esp. for show

promenade con·cert /·'··· ,·'·/ *n* (*sometimes caps.*) (esp. in Britain) a concert at which parts of the hall have no seats and are used by listeners who stand. A number of these CLASSICAL MUSIC concerts are held over a period of several weeks every summer in the Royal Albert Hall and are usu. called the Proms. Established by Henry Wood in 1895 and conducted (CONDUCT[1] (4)) for many years by Sir Malcolm Sargent, they have become a well-known national event. In particular, the last night of the Proms is a special occasion. —see also LAST NIGHT OF THE PROMS

promenade deck /·'··· ,·/ *n* an upper DECK of a passenger ship, usu. open at the sides, where people may walk

Pro·me·the·us /prə'miːθiəs, -θjuːs/ in CLASSICAL MYTHOLOGY, a GIANT who stole fire from heaven to give to men. He was kept in chains and punished by Zeus, and was finally freed by Hercules. He is the subject of many works of literature.

prom·i·nence /'prɒmɪnəns||'prɑː-/ *n* **1** [U] the fact or quality of being prominent or noticeable; importance. *The newspapers gave the story undue prominence.* | *This young fashion designer is rising to/coming into prominence.* (=attracting more and more attention)   **2** [C] *fml* a part or place that is PROMINENT (1)

prom·i·nent /'prɒmɪnənt||'prɑː-/ *adj* **1** sticking or stretching out beyond a surface: *She has prominent teeth.*   **2** noticeable; easily seen: *Our house is in a prominent position.*   **3** of great importance, fame, etc.: *a prominent musician/citizen/critic of the government* – ~ly *adv*

pro·mis·cu·ous /prə'mɪskjuəs/ *adj* **1** *derog* having many sexual partners: *a promiscuous girl/life*   **2** *fml* of many sorts mixed together in a disorderly way   **3** *fml* not choosing carefully; INDISCRIMINATE – ~ly *adv* – **-ity** /ˌprɒmɪ'skjuːɪti||ˌprɑː-/ *n* [U] : *the dangers of promiscuity*

prom·ise[1] /'prɒmɪs||'prɑː-/ *n* **1** [C] a statement, which someone else has a right to believe and depend on, that one will or will not do something, give something, etc.: *If you make a promise you shouldn't break it.* | *Do politicians ever keep their promises?* (=do what they say they will do) [+*to-v/that*] *Despite their promise to bring down inflation/that they would bring down inflation, prices have gone on rising.* | *a promise of help/support* | *a solemn promise* | *campaign promises* | *a government that can deliver its promises*   **2** [S;U] expectation or signs of future success, good results, etc.: *The news brings little promise of peace.* | *My son is showing great promise as a cricketer.*

promise[2] *v* **1** [I;T (**to**)] to make a promise to do or give

(something) or that (something) will be done: *They have promised their support.* | *"She's not coming tonight." "But she promised!"* | *"I'll do it tomorrow." "Promise?" "Yes, I promise."* [+*to-v*] *I promise not to be late again.* [+*(that)*] *They promised (that) the work would all be finished by next week.* [+*obj*+*(that)*] *I promised my mother (that) I'd write to her.* | *I can't give you the book; I've promised it to Susan.* [+*obj(i)*+*obj(d)*] *Her parents have promised her a new bike if she passes the exam.* | *She's been promised a new bike.* | **I promise you**, (=I warn you), *the work won't be easy.*   **2** [T] to cause one to expect or hope for (something): *The clear sky promises fine weather.* [+*to-v*] *It promises to be a fine day.*   **3 promise someone the moon/the earth** *infml* to promise to give someone something that is beyond one's ability to give

Promised Land /ˌ··· '·/ *n* **1** [*the*] (in the Bible) the land of Canaan promised by God to Abraham and his people   **2** [(*the*) S] a place or condition not yet experienced which one believes will bring happiness

prom·is·ing /'prɒmɪsɪŋ||'prɑː-/ *adj apprec* showing signs of likely future success; full of PROMISE[1] (2): *a promising young singer* —opposite **unpromising** – ~ly *adv*

prom·is·sory note /ˌprɒmɪsəri 'nəʊt||ˌprɑːmɪsɔːri-/ *n* a written promise to pay a certain sum of money on demand or on a stated date

pro·mo /'prəʊməʊ/ *n* **-s** *infml* something, such as a short film, intended to advertise a product or activity

prom·on·to·ry /'prɒməntəri||'prɑːməntɔːri/ *n* a long narrow point of land stretching out into the sea; HEADLAND

pro·mote /prə'məʊt/ *v* [T] **1** [(**to**)] **a** to give (someone) a higher position or rank: *My daughter's just been promoted.* | *The young army officer was promoted to (the rank of) captain.* [+*obj*+*n*] (*esp. BrE*) *They promoted him captain.* —opposite **demote** **b** *esp. BrE* to put (a team) up to a higher level in a sports competition: *After this win, Manchester United were promoted to the First Division.* —compare RELEGATE   **2** to help actively in forming or arranging (a business, concert, play, etc.): *to promote a boxing match* | *to promote a bill in Parliament* (=introduce and support it)   **3** to bring (goods) to public notice in order to encourage people to buy: *a big advertising campaign to promote our new toothpaste*   **4** *fml* to help in the growth or development of: *Milk promotes health.* | *new efforts to promote the cause of world peace*

pro·mot·er /prə'məʊtər/ *n* a person whose job is to promote events, activities, goods, etc. (PROMOTE (2,3))

pro·mo·tion /prə'məʊʃən/ *n* **1** [C;U] (an) advancement in rank or position: *Congratulations on your promotion!* | *There are good chances of promotion in this firm.*   **2** [C;U] (an) activity intended to help the development or success of something, esp. of a product for sale: *This year's sales promotions haven't been very successful.* | *a video promotion of a pop record*   **3** [C] a product that is being promoted: *one of our latest promotions* – ~**al** *adj*

prompt[1] /prɒmpt||prɑːmpt/ *v* **1** [T] to cause or urge: *The sight of the ships prompted thoughts of his distant home.* | *What prompted that remark?* [+*obj*+*to-v*] *His evasive reply prompted me to ask another question.*   **2** [I; T] to remind (an actor) of the next words in a speech —see also PROMPT[4]   **3** [T] to help (a speaker who pauses) by suggesting how to continue: *to prompt a witness in court*

prompt[2] *adj* **1** (of an action) done quickly, at once, or at the right time: *Prompt payment of bills is greatly appreciated.*   **2** [F] (of a person) **a** arriving at the right time; PUNCTUAL: *I can't understand it; she's usually very prompt.* **b** quick to take action: *She's always prompt to criticize other people's ideas.* | *He is always prompt in answering letters.* – ~ly *adv* : *The performance will begin promptly at nine o'clock.* – ~**ness** *n* [U] – ~**itude** *fml*

prompt[3] *adv infml* exactly in regard to time: *The performance will start at seven o'clock prompt.*

prompt[4] *n* **1** a word or words spoken in prompting an actor   **2** also **prompt·er** /'prɒmptər||'prɑːmp-/– a person who prompts actors

Proms /prɒmz||prɑːmz/ [*the*+P] *BrE* see PROMENADE CONCERT

prom·ul·gate /'prɒməlgeɪt||'prɑː-/ *v* [T] *fml* **1** to cause (a law or religious rule) to be brought into effect by official public declaration   **2** to spread (a belief, idea, etc.) widely – **-gator** *n* – **-gation** /ˌprɒməl'geɪʃən||ˌprɑː-/ *n* [U]

pron *written abbrev. for:* PRONOUN

prone /prəʊn/ adj **1** [F+to-v/to] likely to suffer (usu. something undesirable): *People are more prone to make mistakes when they are tired.* | *Women are especially prone to this disease.* | *strike-prone industries* | *Mary's always hurting herself; she's very* **accident-prone**. **2** *fml* lying on one's front, face downwards: *They stepped over his prone body.* —compare PROSTRATE, SUPINE (1) — ~ **ness** *n* [U (**to**)]

prong /prɒŋ‖prɔːŋ/ *n* **1** a thin sharp-pointed piece or part, such as part of a fork or one of the branched horns of a deer **2** -**pronged** /prɒŋd‖prɔːŋd/a having the stated number of prongs: *a four-pronged fork* **b** (of an attack) coming from a stated number of different directions at the same time: *a two-pronged attack*

pro·nom·i·nal /prəʊˈnɒmɪnəl‖-ˈnɑː-/ adj tech of or like a pronoun — ~ **ly** adv : *a word used pronominally*

pro·noun /ˈprəʊnaʊn/ n a word that is used in place of a noun or a noun phrase, such as **he** instead of "Peter" or instead of "the man" —see also DEMONSTRATIVE PRONOUN, PERSONAL PRONOUN

pro·nounce /prəˈnaʊns/ v **1** [T] to make the sound of (a letter, a word, etc.): *In the word "knew", the "k" is not pronounced.* | *How do you pronounce your name?* **2** [T+obj+adj/n] to declare, esp. officially or after consideration: *The doctor pronounced the man dead.* | *The priest said, "I now pronounce you man and wife."* **3** [I+prep] esp. law to give judgment: *The court pronounced against my claim to the land.* | (fig.) *She's too ready to pronounce on/upon matters of which she really knows very little.*

pro·nounce·a·ble /prəˈnaʊnsəbəl/ adj (of a sound, a word, etc.) that can be pronounced —opposite **unpronounceable**

pro·nounced /prəˈnaʊnst/ adj very strong or noticeable: *He has very pronounced ideas on everything.* | *a pronounced limp* — ~ **ly** /prəˈnaʊnsɪdli/ adv

pro·nounce·ment /prəˈnaʊnsmənt/ n a solemn declaration or statement: *The Pope made a pronouncement on the subject of the war.*

pron·to /ˈprɒntəʊ‖ˈprɑː-/ adv infml at once; very quickly: *Bring the ladder over here(, and) pronto!*

pro·nun·ci·a·tion /prəˌnʌnsiˈeɪʃən/ n **1** [C;U] the way in which a language or a particular word is pronounced: *the right pronunciation* **2** [S;U] a particular person's way of pronouncing words or a language: *excellent pronunciation*

proof¹ /pruːf/ n **1** [C;U (**of**)] (a) way of showing that something is true; facts, information, documents, etc., that prove something: *I believe what you say; I don't need any proof.* [+that] *Have you got any proof that you own this car/proof of ownership?* | *to produce conclusive/definite proof* | *scientific proof* —see also BURDEN OF PROOF **2** [C] a test or trial of quality, strength, etc.: *A soldier's courage is* **put to the proof** *in battle.* **3** [C] tech a test copy made of something printed, so that mistakes can be put right before the proper printing is done **4** [U or after n] tech the standard of strength of some kinds of alcoholic drink (compared with that of PROOF SPIRIT): *This gin is 15 per cent under proof.* **5** [C] tech **a** (in MATHEMATICS) a test made of the correctness of a calculation **b** (in GEOMETRY) the reasoning that shows a statement (THEOREM) to be true **6** **the proof of the pudding is in the eating** it is only possible to tell if something is good or bad by testing, using, or experiencing it

proof² adj **1** [F+**against**] giving or having protection against something harmful or unwanted: *His honesty is proof against any temptation.* | (in comb.) *a bullet-proof vest* | *a waterproof coat* | *a soundproof room* | *an inflation-proof pension* —see also FOOLPROOF **2** [after n] (of certain types of alcoholic drink) of the stated alcoholic strength in comparison with some standard: *In the US, whiskey of 90 proof is 45% alcohol.*

proof³ v [T (**against**)] to treat (esp. cloth) in order to give protection against something unwanted, esp. water

-proof see WORD FORMATION

proof·read /ˈpruːfˌriːd/ v -**read** /red/ [I;T] to read and correct the printer's proofs of (a book, etc.) — ~ **er** n

proof spir·it /ˌ·ˈ·/ n [U] a standard mixture of alcohol and water with which the strength of certain alcoholic drinks is compared for the purposes of taxation

Proops /pruːps/, **Mar·jo·rie** /ˈmɑːdʒəri ‖ ˈmɑːr-/, **Marje**

/mɑːdʒ ‖ mɑːrdʒ/ a well known English AGONY AUNT who writes regularly in the DAILY MIRROR

prop¹ /prɒp‖prɑːp/ n a support placed to hold up something heavy: *The roof of the tunnel was supported by wooden props.* | (fig.) *Her daughter was a prop to her during her illness.* —see also PIT PROP

prop² v -**pp**- [T+obj+adv/prep] to support or keep in a leaning or resting position: *She propped up the baby's head by putting a pillow behind it.* | *Prop the gate open with a brick.* | *He propped his bicycle (up) against the fence.* **prop** sthg. ↔ **up** phr v [T] sometimes derog to help or give support to (often with money): *It is not the government's policy to prop up declining industries.*

prop³ also **property** fml— n [usu. pl.] a small article, such as a weapon or piece of furniture, that is used on the stage in the acting of a play

prop⁴ n infml an aircraft's PROPELLER

prop·a·gan·da /ˌprɒpəˈɡændə‖ˌprɑː-/ n [U] usu. derog information that is spread in a planned or official way, esp. by a government, in order to influence public opinion: *Their speeches have been exposed as pure propaganda.* | *a massive propaganda campaign* | *anti-French propaganda* | *propaganda films/slogans*

prop·a·gan·dist /ˌprɒpəˈɡændɪst‖ˌprɑː-/ n usu. derog a person who plans or spreads esp. political propaganda

prop·a·gan·dize also -**dise** BrE /ˌprɒpəˈɡændaɪz‖ˌprɑː-/ [I;T] usu. derog to spread propaganda in (a place) or to (people)

prop·a·gate /ˈprɒpəɡeɪt‖ˈprɑː-/ v **1** [I] (of living things) to increase in number by producing young: *Most plants propagate by seed.* **2** [T] to cause to continue or increase by producing descendants: *Human beings propagate their species by sexual reproduction.* **3** [T] to cause to spread to a great number of people: *They started a newspaper to propagate their ideas.* —-**gator** n —-**gation** /ˌprɒpəˈɡeɪʃən‖ˌprɑː-/ n [U]

pro·pane /ˈprəʊpeɪn/ n [U] a colourless gas used for cooking and heating

pro·pel /prəˈpel/ v -**ll**- [T] to move, drive, or push forward: *A sailing boat is propelled by wind.* | *a rocket-propelled grenade* —see also PROPULSION

pro·pel·lant, -**lent** /prəˈpelənt/ n [C;U] **1** (an) explosive for firing a bullet or ROCKET **2** (a) gas pressed into a small space in a bottle, which drives out the contents of the bottle when the pressure is taken away —**propellant**, **propellent** adj

pro·pel·ler /prəˈpelər/ n an apparatus for producing movement in a ship or aircraft, consisting of two or more blades fixed to a central bar that is turned at high speed by an engine —see picture at WINDMILL

pro·pel·ling pen·cil /·ˌ·· ˈ··/ n a pencil in which the stick of LEAD⁴ (2) is pushed forward by an apparatus inside the pencil as the lead is used up

pro·pen·si·ty /prəˈpensɪti/ n [(**for, to, towards**)] fml a natural tendency towards a particular usu. undesirable kind of behaviour: *a propensity for upsetting people* [+to-v] *a propensity to spend too much money*

prop·er¹ /ˈprɒpər‖ˈprɑː-/ adj **1** [A no comp.] right; suitable; correct: *She's too ill to be nursed at home; she needs proper medical attention at a hospital.* | *That's not the proper way to stop the machine.* | *without proper authorization* | *the proper role of the press* **2** sometimes derog (paying great attention to what is) socially correct or acceptable: *That short dress isn't really proper for wearing to a funeral.* | *Why are you surprised? It's only* **right and proper** *that his wife should inherit all his money.* —see also IMPROPER, PROPRIETY **3** [A] BrE infml real; actual: *The little boy wanted a proper dog, not a toy dog.* **4** [after n] in its actual, most limited meaning; itself: *Many people call themselves Londoners though they live outside the city proper.* **5** [A no comp.] infml, esp. BrE (often of something unpleasant or undesirable) thorough; complete: *We've got ourselves into a proper mess.* | *I felt a proper fool.* **6** [F+**to**] fml belonging only or especially to; natural to: *to wear clothes proper to a tropical climate* —see also PROPERLY

prop·er² adv sl, esp. dial very; completely: *He drove the car into a wall and wrecked it, good and proper!*

proper frac·tion /ˌ··· ˈ··/ n a FRACTION in which the number above the line is smaller than the one below it: *¼ and*

⅕ *are proper fractions.* —compare IMPROPER FRACTION

prop·er·ly /ˈprɒpəli‖ˈprɑːpərli/ *adv* **1** suitably; correctly: *I'm learning Italian, but I still can't speak it properly.* | *She'd only just got out of bed, and wasn't properly dressed.* **2** really; actually; exactly: *I'm not, properly speaking, a nurse, as I haven't been trained, but I've looked after many sick people.* **3** *infml, esp. BrE* completely; thoroughly: *I'm properly muddled!*

proper noun /ˌ·· ˈ·/ also **proper name**– *n* (in grammar) a noun that is the name of a single particular thing or person, and is spelt with a CAPITAL letter: *"James", "London", and "China" are proper nouns in English.* —compare COMMON NOUN

prop·er·tied /ˈprɒpətid‖ˈprɑːpər-/ *adj* [A] owning a lot of property, esp. land: *the propertied classes*

prop·er·ty /ˈprɒpəti‖ˈprɑːpərti/ *n* **1** [U] something which is owned; possession(s): *That car is my property; you mustn't use it without my permission.* | *The police found some stolen property in the thief's house.* | *This machine is the property of the government|is government property.* **2** [U] land, buildings, or both together: *The city is growing and property in the centre is becoming more expensive.* | *a property developer* (=someone who makes money by buying and selling property) **3** [C] a building, a piece of land, or both together. This word is used esp. by lawyers and ESTATE AGENTS: *Several properties in this street are for sale.* **4** [C] a stated quality, power, or effect that belongs naturally to something: *Many plants have medicinal properties.* | *Oil has the property of floating on water.* **5** [C *usu. pl.*] *fml for* PROP³ **6** [U] ownership, with its rights and duties according to the law: *Most societies have accepted the idea of private property.* —see also LOST PROPERTY, PERSONAL PROPERTY, REAL PROPERTY

property tax /ˈ··· ˌ·/ *n* a tax based on the value of someone's house

proph·e·cy *BrE* ‖ also **prophesy** *AmE* /ˈprɒfɪsi‖ˈprɑː-/ *n* **1** [C] a statement telling something that will happen in the future, esp. one based on one's personal feelings rather than on any proof: *to make a prophecy* [+that] *The teacher's prophecy that the boy would become famous was later fulfilled.* **2** [U] the telling of things that will happen in the future

proph·e·sy /ˈprɒfɪsaɪ‖ˈprɑː-/ *v* [I;T] to make a statement expressing one's beliefs about (what will happen in) the future; FORECAST: *The soothsayers prophesied war.* [+that] *She prophesied that there would be a bad winter.* [+wh-] *I wouldn't like to prophesy who will win the election*

proph·et /ˈprɒfɪt‖ˈprɑː-/ *n* **1** (in the Christian, Jewish, and Muslim religions) a man who believes that he is directed by God to make known and explain God's will and/or to lead or teach a religion: *the prophet Isaiah* **2** *sometimes* **proph·et·ess** /ˈprɒfɪtes ‖ˈprɑːfɪtəs/ *fem.*– a person who introduces and teaches some new idea: *a prophet of monetarist economics* **3** a person who claims to be able to tell the course of future events: *a prophet of doom* (=someone who always says that bad things will happen)

Prophet [*the*] Muhammad, who formed the Muslim religion: *followers of the Prophet* (=Muslims)

pro·phet·ic /prəˈfetɪk/ also **pro·phet·i·cal** /-kəl/– *adj* [(of)] correctly telling of things that will happen in the future; like or being a prophecy: *a prophetic remark* —**ically** /kli/ *adv*

Proph·ets /ˈprɒfɪts‖ˈprɑː-/ *n* [*the*+P] **1** the Jewish holy men whose writings form part of the Bible **2** the writings themselves, which together with certain other writings form the second and last part of the Old Testament

pro·phy·lac·tic¹ /ˌprɒfɪˈlæktɪk◂‖ˌprɑː-/ *adj fml or tech* intended to prevent disease —**ally** /kli/ *adv*

prophylactic² *n tech esp. AmE, often euph* something prophylactic, esp. a CONDOM sold supposedly for the prevention of VENEREAL DISEASE

pro·phy·lax·is /ˌprɒfɪˈlæksɪs‖ˌprɑː-/ *n* **-laxes** /ˈlæksiːz/ [C;U] *tech* (a) treatment for preventing disease

pro·pin·qui·ty /prəˈpɪŋkwɪti/ *n* [U (of, to)] *fml* nearness in space or relationship

pro·pi·ti·ate /prəˈpɪʃieɪt/ *v* [T] *fml* to win the favour of (someone who is angry or unfriendly) by some pleasing act —**ation** /prəˌpɪʃiˈeɪʃən/ *n* [U (for)]

pro·pi·ti·a·to·ry /prəˈpɪʃiətəri‖-tɔːri/ *adj fml* intended to propitiate: *a propitiatory gift of flowers*

pro·pi·tious /prəˈpɪʃəs/ *adj fml* [(for, to, towards)] advantageous; favourable: *a propitious sign* | *It wasn't really a propitious moment to raise the subject of my pay rise.* —~**ly** *adv*

pro·po·nent /prəˈpəʊnənt/ *n* [(of)] a person who supports or argues in favour of something; ADVOCATE: *an enthusiastic proponent of yoga* | *one of its keenest proponents* —compare OPPONENT (2)

pro·por·tion¹ /prəˈpɔːʃən‖-ɔːr-/ *n* **1** [U] the correct relationship between the size, position, and shape of the different parts of a whole: *This drawing isn't in proportion; the man is larger than the house.* —opposite **disproportion** **2** [C;U] the compared relationship between two things in regard to size, amount, importance, etc.: *The proportion of men to women in the population has changed in recent years.* | *The tax increases in proportion to the amount you earn.* | *Mix the paint in the proportion of one part of paint to two parts of water.* | (fig.) *Don't panic about it; try not to lose your sense of proportion.* (=ability to judge what is most important) —compare RATIO **3** [C (of)] a part or share, esp. when measured and compared with the whole: *"What proportion of your wages do you spend on rent?" "About a quarter."* | *A large|high|increasing proportion of the children come to school by train.* **4** [U] *tech* (in MATHEMATICS) equalness of relationship between two sets of numbers: *The statement "as 6 is to 4, so is 24 to 16" is a statement of proportion.* **5 in/out of proportion** (not) according to real importance; (not) sensibly: *When you're angry you don't always see things in proportion.* **6 out of (all) proportion to** (much) too great as compared with: *The price of this article is out of all proportion to its value.* —see also PROPORTIONS

proportion² *v* [T (to)] *fml* to make in or put into correct or suitable PROPORTION¹ (1,2): *to proportion one's expenditure to one's income* | *a well-proportioned room*

pro·por·tion·al /prəˈpɔːʃənəl‖-ɔːr-/ *adj* **1** [(to)] in PROPORTION (2): *The payment he will have to make will be proportional to the amount of damage he has done.* **2** concerning PROPORTION¹ (2) —opposite **disproportional** —~**ly** *adv*

proportional rep·re·sen·ta·tion /·ˌ··· ···ˈ··/ also **PR** *infml*– *n* [U] a system of voting in elections by which all political parties, small as well as large, are represented in the governing body according to the proportion of votes they receive, rather than having to get more votes than any other party, in each voting area. In Britain, the SOCIAL AND LIBERAL DEMOCRAT party is strongly in favour of changing to this system. —compare FIRST PAST THE POST

pro·por·tion·ate /prəˈpɔːʃənət‖-ɔːr-/ *adj* [(to)] in PROPORTION¹ (1,2): *You will have to work an extra three days, but there will be a proportionate increase in your pay.* —opposite **disproportionate** —~**ly** *adv*

pro·por·tions /prəˈpɔːʃənz‖-ɔːr-/ *n* [P] the size and shape of something: *The church is a building of fine proportions.* | (*humor*) *Mary finds it difficult to fit her ample proportions into my little car!* (=she is rather fat)

proposal

pro·pos·al /prəˈpəʊzəl/ *n* **1** [C;U] a plan or suggestion; (an) act of proposing: *The French have put forward a proposal for a joint project.* | *peace proposals* [+to-v|that] *The proposal to close the hospital|that the hospital should be closed was rejected by a large majority.* **2** [C] an offer of marriage —compare PROPOSITION¹ (4); see REFUSE (USAGE)

pro·pose /prə'pəʊz/ v 1 [T] to put forward for consideration (a possible course of action, a plan to be voted on by a meeting, etc.); suggest: *What do you propose we do?* | *The company has proposed a new formula for settling the dispute.* | *I wish to propose Charles Robson for membership of the club.* | *to propose a motion* [+v-ing/that] *I propose delaying our decision until the next meeting/that we delay our decision until the next meeting.* —see also SECOND⁴ 2 [T] *fml* to have formed a plan for; intend: *We propose an early holiday in the spring.* [+to-v] *I propose to go to London on Tuesday.* | *How do you propose to finance this venture?* 3 [I (to);T] (usu. of a man) to make an offer of (marriage). In Britain and the US it is the custom for a man to propose to a woman. The man is supposed to kneel in front of the woman and ask her to marry him. On the 29th of February (the last day in February in a LEAP YEAR), however, a woman may by custom propose to a man. These customs are not followed as much as they used to be. 4 [T] *fml* to ask a social gathering to offer (a wish for success, happiness, etc.) to someone, while raising a glass of wine which is afterwards drunk (usu. in the phrases **propose a toast/propose someone's health**) —**poser** n

prop·o·si·tion¹ /ˌprɒpə'zɪʃən/ˌprɑː-/ n 1 [C] an unproved statement in which an opinion or judgment is expressed 2 [C] a suggested (business) offer, arrangement, or settlement: *We made him a proposition: he would join us, and we would support his company.* | *I have a proposition to put to you ...* 3 [S] *infml* a person or situation of the stated type that must be dealt with: *We could build a tunnel instead of a bridge, but that's a much more difficult proposition.* 4 [C] *euph* a suggested offer to have sex with someone: *He made me a proposition.* —compare PROPOSAL (2) 5 [C] *tech* (in GEOMETRY) a truth that must be proved, or a question to which the answer must be found — ~ **al** *adj*

proposition² v [T] *infml* to make a PROPOSITION¹ (esp. 4) to (someone)

Proposition 13 /ˌprɒpəzɪʃən θɜː'tiːn‖ˌprɑːpəzɪʃən θɜːr-/ also **Prop 13**— a law which was voted on directly and passed by California voters in 1978 rather than by California state LEGISLATURE (law-making body), which reduced taxes on property. The passage of Proposition 13 in California led voters in other states to vote for similar laws and is seen by some people as the first of many tax cuts introduced by the state and national government in the 1980s.

pro·pound /prə'paʊnd/ v [T] *fml* to put forward as a question or matter for consideration: *to propound a problem/a theory*

pro·pri·e·ta·ry /prə'praɪətəri‖-teri/ *adj* 1 privately owned or controlled: *proprietary brands of toothpaste* 2 of or like an owner: *Jane has rather a proprietary manner with her boyfriend.*

pro·pri·e·ties /prə'praɪətiz/ n [the+P] *fml* the accepted rules of proper social behaviour: *to observe the proprieties*

pro·pri·e·tor /prə'praɪətər/ **pro·pri·e·tress** /prə'praɪətrəs/ *fem.*— n an owner of a business, an invention, etc.: *newspaper proprietors* (=people who own the businesses that produce newspapers) | *I've written a complaint to the proprietor of the hotel.* — **ial** /prəˌpraɪə'tɔːriəl/ *adj* : *proprietorial rights* — ~ **ially** *adv*

pro·pri·e·ty /prə'praɪəti/ n [U] *fml* 1 correctness of social or moral behaviour, esp. between men and women or between people of different social ranks, age, etc.: *to behave with complete propriety* 2 rightness or reasonableness: *I doubt the propriety of making a public statement on the matter before we have studied the official reports.* —see also IMPROPRIETY

pro·pul·sion /prə'pʌlʃən/ n [U] *tech* the force that PROPELS (=drives forward) something, esp. a vehicle: *This aircraft works by jet propulsion.* (=has JET engines) —**sive** /prə'pʌlsɪv/ *adj* : *propulsive force*

pro ra·ta /ˌprəʊ 'rɑːtə‖-'reɪtə/ *adj, adv tech* calculated according to the rate, fair share, etc., of each: *a pro rata increase*

pro·rate /prəʊ'reɪt/ v [T] *AmE* to calculate (a charge, price, etc.) according to a larger amount divided into parts: *Your rent will be prorated from the 21st of the month, since that's when you moved in.*

pro·rogue /prəʊ'rəʊg, prə-/ v [T] *tech* to bring to an end a

set of meetings of (a parliament) until a stated day —**rogation** /ˌprəʊrə'geɪʃən‖ˌprəʊrəʊ-/ n [C;U]

pro·sa·ic /prəʊ'zeɪ-ɪk, prə-/ *adj* 1 dull; uninteresting: *a prosaic job/speech* 2 lacking feeling and imagination: *He's too prosaic to think of sending me flowers.* — ~ **ally** /kli/ *adv*

pros and cons /ˌprəʊz ən 'kɒnz‖-'kɑːnz/ n [the+P] the reasons for and against something: *to consider all the pros and cons of a matter before reaching a decision*

pro·sce·ni·um /prə'siːniəm, prəʊ-/ n 1 the front arch of a theatre stage, where a curtain may be lowered 2 the part of a stage that comes forward beyond this

pro·scribe /prəʊ'skraɪb/ v [T] 1 *fml* to forbid (esp. something dangerous or harmful), esp. by law 2 *old use* to state publicly that (a citizen) is outside the protection of the law —compare PRESCRIBE —**scription** /prəʊ'skrɪpʃən, prə-/ n [C;U]

prose /prəʊz/ n 1 [U] written language in its usual form, as opposed to POETRY: *Newspapers are written in prose.* | *He writes a very clear simple prose.* | *a prose translation of Homer's epic poems* —compare POETIC 2 [C] *BrE* a student's exercise in translating a piece of writing into a foreign language: *I've got two French proses to do.* —see also PROSY

pros·e·cute /'prɒsɪkjuːt‖'prɑː-/ v 1 [I;T (**for**)] to bring a criminal charge against (someone) in a court of law: *He was prosecuted for stealing.* | *The police have decided not to prosecute (him).* 2 [I] (of a lawyer) to represent in court the person who is bringing a criminal charge against someone —compare DEFEND (3) 3 [T] *fml* to continue steadily (esp. something that needs effort); carry out: *to prosecute an investigation*

pros·e·cu·tion /ˌprɒsɪ'kjuːʃən‖ˌprɑː-/ n 1 [C;U] (an example of) prosecuting or being prosecuted by law 2 [the+sing./pl. v] the group of people who represent the person bringing a criminal charge against someone in court: *a witness for the prosecution* | *The prosecution is/are trying to show that he was seen near the scene of the crime.* —compare DEFENCE (4) 3 [U] *fml* the carrying out of something that needs to be done: *She has to travel a great deal in the prosecution of her duties.*

pros·e·cu·tor /'prɒsɪkjuːtər‖'prɑː-/ n a person (often a lawyer) who prosecutes someone —see also PUBLIC PROSECUTOR

pros·e·lyte /'prɒsɪlaɪt‖'prɑː-/ n *fml* a person who has just been persuaded to join a religious group, political party, etc.

pros·e·lyt·ize also **-ise** *BrE* /'prɒsələtaɪz‖'prɑː-/ v [I; T] *fml, sometimes derog* to (try to) persuade (someone) to join a religious group, political party, etc. —**izer** n

Pros·er·pine /'prɒsəpaɪn‖'prɑːsər-/ see PERSEPHONE

pros·o·dy /'prɒsədi‖'prɑː-/ n [U] (the study of) the rules by which the patterns of sounds and beats are arranged in poetry —**dic** /prə'sɒdɪk‖-'sɑː-/ *adj* [A no comp.]

pros·pect¹ /'prɒspekt‖'prɑː-/ n 1 [C;U (**of**)] reasonable hope of something happening: *I'm afraid there's not much/I don't see much prospect of this being finished before the weekend.* | *a job with excellent prospects* (=chances of future success) 2 [S;U (**of**)] something which is probable soon: *She doesn't like the prospect of having to live alone.* | *not a very cheerful prospect* | *a lot of hard work* **in prospect** (=going to be necessary) 3 [C *usu. sing.*] a wide distant view: *From the top of the hill there's a beautiful prospect over the valley.* 4 [C] a person who may perhaps buy one's goods, accept a job one is offering, etc.: *I interviewed three likely prospects.* —see also PROSPECTIVE

pros·pect² /prə'spekt‖'prɑːspekt/ v [I;T (**for**)] to examine (land, an area, etc.) in order to find gold, silver, oil, etc. — ~ **or** n : *Thousands of prospectors flocked to the Klondike during the great Gold Rush.*

pro·spec·tive /prə'spektɪv/ *adj* expected or intended; likely to be or become: *a prospective buyer for the house*

pro·spec·tus /prə'spektəs/ n a printed statement describing the advantages of a college, a new business, etc. —compare LISTING PARTICULARS

pros·per /'prɒspər‖'prɑː-/ v 1 [I] to become successful and esp. rich: *He/His business prospered.* 2 [I] to develop favourably or in a healthy way; grow well; THRIVE: *The children seem to be prospering under their care.* 3 [T] *old use* to cause to succeed: *May the gods prosper our city!*

pro·sper·i·ty /prɒˈspɛrɪti‖prɑː-/ n [U] good fortune and success, esp. in money matters: *We wish you health, happiness, and prosperity.*

pros·per·ous /ˈprɒspərəs‖ˈprɑː-/ adj successful and rich − **~ly** adv

Prost /prɒst‖prəʊst/, **Al·ain** /ˈælæn‖æˈlæŋ/ (1955–) a French racing driver who was world CHAMPION in 1985–86 and has had more GRAND PRIX (=an international car race) wins than any other driver ever

pros·tate /ˈprɒsteɪt‖ˈprɑː-/ also **prostate gland** /ˈ·· ·/− n an organ in the body of male animals that produces a liquid in which SPERMATOZOA (seeds) are carried

pros·the·sis /prɒsˈθiːsɪs‖prɑːs-/ n tech an artificial limb, tooth, or other body part to take the place of a missing one

pros·ti·tute¹ /ˈprɒstɪtjuːt‖ˈprɑːstɪtuːt/ **male prostitute** *masc.*− n a person, esp. a woman, who earns money by having sex with anyone who will pay for it. The STEREO-TYPE of a prostitute is of a woman wearing a short skirt, FISHNET STOCKINGS, HIGH HEELS, and a lot of MAKE-UP.

prostitute² v [T] *fml* **1** to put to a dishonourable use for money: *He never prostituted his great acting talent by appearing in television advertisements.* **2** to give the services of (oneself) as a prostitute

pros·ti·tu·tion /ˌprɒstɪˈtjuːʃən‖ˌprɑːstɪˈtuːʃən/ n [U] **1** the act or trade of being a prostitute. In Britain, since 1959, the law allows the practice of prostitution but it does not allow a person to openly offer him or herself as a prostitute, or to provide a prostitute for someone else. In the US, prostitution is legal only in the state of Nevada, but it is practised everywhere. Prostitution is sometimes described as "the oldest profession in the world": *a police clampdown on prostitution* **2** [(of)] *fml* dishonourable misuse, esp. for money

pros·trate¹ /ˈprɒstreɪt‖ˈprɑː-/ adj **1** lying on one's front, face downwards, esp. in obedience or worship −compare PRONE (2) **2** having lost all strength, courage, and ability to act: *She was prostrate with grief.* | *a prostrate* (=defeated and powerless) *nation* −**tration** /prɒˈstreɪʃən‖prɑː-/ n [C;U] : *Ceremonial prostration is part of Muslim prayer.*

pros·trate² /prɒˈstreɪt‖ˈprɑːstreɪt/ v [T] **1** to put in a prostrate position· *They prostrated themselves before the king.* **2** [*usu. pass.*] to cause to lose strength, courage, etc.; make PROSTRATE¹ (2): *a prostrating illness*

pros·y /ˈprəʊzi/ adj saying too much in a dull, tiring manner −**ily** adv −**iness** n [U]

pro·tag·o·nist /prəʊˈtæɡənɪst/ n **1** [(of)] the leader or a noticeable supporter of some (new) idea or purpose: *Friedman was one of the chief protagonists of monetarist economic policies.* **2** the chief character in a play or story **3** someone taking part esp. in a sports competition −compare ANTAGONIST

pro·te·an /ˈprəʊtiən, prəʊˈtiːən/ adj *lit* continually changing; able to appear in various forms or characters (from Proteus, a Greek sea god who could change his shape)

pro·tect /prəˈtekt/ v [T] **1** [(against, from)] to keep safe, esp. by guarding or covering: *The hard shell of a nut protects the seed inside it.* | *A line of forts was built along the border to protect the country against attack.* | *He raised his arm to protect his face from the blow.* | *These rare birds are protected by special laws − they are a* **protected species.** | *to protect one's reputation* **2** to help (industry) by taxing foreign goods −see also PROTECTIONISM **3** [(against)] to guard (property, etc.) against possible future loss, damage, etc., by means of insurance −see also PROTECTIVE

pro·tec·tion /prəˈtekʃən/ n **1** [U] the act of protecting or state of being protected: *Her thin coat gave/provided little protection against the cold.* | *After the threat on her life, she was offered police protection.* | *consumer protection* **2** [S] something that protects: *Shoes are a protection for the feet.* **3** [U] also **protection mon·ey** /·ˈ·· ,·/− *infml euph* money paid to people who run a protection racket

pro·tec·tion·is·m /prəˈtekʃənɪzəm/ n [U] *often derog* the system of protecting one's own country's trade, esp. by TARIFFS −**ist** n

protection rack·et /·ˈ·· ,·/ n *infml* a system by which criminals demand money from the owners of shops, restaurants, etc., for protection against damage that would be caused by the criminals themselves if the owners refused to pay

pro·tec·tive /prəˈtektɪv/ adj **1** [A *no comp.*] that gives protection: *protective clothing* | *protective colouring on an insect's body* (=making it difficult for enemies to see) | *a protective tariff* (=tax on foreign goods) **2** [(towards)] wishing to protect: *She's too protective/overprotective towards her children; she should let them be more independent.* − **~ly** adv − **~ness** n [U]

protective cus·to·dy /·,·· ˈ···/ n [U] the state of being kept by the police for one's own safety

pro·tec·tor /prəˈtektər/ n **1** a person or thing that protects: *a chest protector* **2** (*usu. cap.*) (in former times) a prince or nobleman appointed to govern England during the childhood or illness of the king

Protector [*the*] the official title of Oliver Cromwell and Richard Cromwell during the period (the **Protectorate**) when they ruled Britain (1653–1659)

pro·tec·tor·ate /prəˈtektərət/ n **1** a country controlled and protected by a more powerful nation that takes charge esp. of its defence and foreign affairs **2** also **pro·tec·tor·ship** /prəˈtektəʃɪp‖-ˈtektər-/− the time during which a PROTECTOR (2) governs

prot·é·gé /ˈprɒtɪʒeɪ‖ˈprəʊ-/ **protégée** (*same pronunciation*) *fem.*− n a person who is guided and helped by someone of influence or power: *This young politician is the prime minister's protégé.*

pro·tein /ˈprəʊtiːn/ n [C;U] any of many substances present in such foods as meat, eggs, and beans that help to build up the body and keep it healthy: *a high-protein diet*

pro tem /ˌprəʊ ˈtem/ adv now but only for a short time; for the present only

pro·test¹ /ˈprəʊtest/ n [C;U] **1** (a) complaint or strong expression of disapproval, disagreement, opposition, etc.: *The local people have made a strong protest to/registered their protest with the minister about the new airport.* | *a protest march/vote* | *They refused to buy the company's goods in protest against/as a protest against the way it treated its workers.* | *He went to bed* **without protest.** (=calmly) **2 under protest** unwillingly and feeling that something is not just: *I would like it on record that I signed under protest.*

pro·test² /prəˈtest/ v **1** [I (about, against, at)] to express one's disagreement, feeling of unfairness, annoyance, etc.: *The footballers all protested bitterly to the referee (about his decision).* | *There was a large crowd in the square, protesting against the war.* | *He protested vehemently as they took him away.* **2** [T] to declare in complaint or opposition: *She protested her innocence.* [+*that*] *She protested that she knew nothing about the stolen goods.* **3** [T] *AmE* to make a protest against: *a large crowd protesting the war* **4 the lady doth protest too much, methinks** *quote* a phrase from Shakespeare's play *Hamlet*, used when saying that someone seems to be denying (DENY) something too strongly, which suggests that it might be true − **~er** n : *Police arrested several of the peace protesters.*

Prot·es·tant /ˈprɒtɪstənt‖ˈprɑː-/ n, adj (a member) of a part of the Christian church that separated from the Roman Catholic Church in the 16th century. There are many divisions within the church but in general Protestants believe in the authority of the Bible, rather than in the authority of TRADITION or of the Pope. They also believe in the importance of preaching (PREACH) and studying God's word in the Bible. Protestant services are rather plain compared to Catholic services. In Britain and the US most Christians are Protestant. −compare ROMAN CATHOLIC − **~ism** n [U]

prot·es·ta·tion /ˌprɒtɪˈsteɪʃən, ˌprəʊ-‖ˌprɑː-, ˌprəʊ-/ n *fml* **1** [C (of)] a solemn declaration: *protestations of friendship* **2** [U (against)] the expression of disagreement

protest march /·ˈ· ,·/ n a march usu. by a large number of people made to express disapproval, disagreement or opposition, usu. concerning a political subject. In London, protest marches often end with a large meeting in Hyde Park where people make speeches. In the US, protest marches usu. take place near a building or place which people think of in connection with what they are protesting about, e.g. an EMBASSY or government building. Protest marches held in Washington, D.C., often go to the Capitol or the White House. −see also VIETNAM WAR

protest song /ˈ·· ˌ·/ n a song written and sung to express disapproval, disagreement or opposition, usu. concerning a social or political subject, e.g. the songs against war of the 1960s by Bob Dylan and others —see also VIETNAM WAR

proto- see WORD FORMATION

pro·to·col /ˈprəʊtəkɒl‖-kɔːl/ n 1 [U] the ceremonial system of fixed rules and accepted behaviour used esp. by representatives of governments on official occasions: *Protocol demands that the queen meet him at the airport.* | *a breach of* (=failure to follow) *diplomatic protocol* 2 [C] *tech* an established method of connecting computers or electronic equipment so that they can exchange DATA: *We have to use a different protocol with this new modem.*

pro·ton /ˈprəʊtɒn‖-tɑːn/ n a very small piece of matter that carries POSITIVE electricity and that together with the NEUTRON forms the NUCLEUS (=central part) of an atom — see also ELECTRON

pro·to·plas·m /ˈprəʊtəplæzəm/ n [U] the colourless jelly-like living substance from which all plants and creatures are formed

pro·to·type /ˈprəʊtətaɪp/ n [(of)] the first form of something, esp. of a machine or industrial product, from which all later forms develop, sometimes with improvements: *the prototype of a new car*

pro·to·zo·a /ˌprəʊtəˈzəʊə/ n [P] very small single-celled living things that can be seen only under a microscope

pro·to·zo·an, **-on** /ˌprəʊtəˈzəʊən/ n a single member of the protozoa —**protozoan** adj

pro·tract /prəˈtrækt‖prəʊ-/ v [T] to make the time during which (something) lasts long or longer, often without good reason: *a protracted argument* | *protracted pay negotiations* —compare PROLONG — ~**ion** /ˈtrækʃən/ n [U]

pro·trac·tor /prəˈtræktər‖prəʊ-/ n an instrument, usu. in the form of a half-circle, used for measuring and drawing angles —see picture at MATHEMATICS

pro·trude /prəˈtruːd‖prəʊ-/ v [I (**from**)] to stick out from a place or through a surface: *He glimpsed a gun protruding from the man's pocket.* | *protruding teeth* —compare OBTRUDE

pro·tru·sion /prəˈtruːʒən‖prəʊ-/ n 1 [C] something that protrudes 2 [U] the act of protruding

pro·tu·ber·ance /prəˈtjuːbərəns‖prəʊˈtuː-/ n fml a swelling; BULGE: *protuberances on a flower stem*

pro·tu·ber·ant /prəˈtjuːbərənt‖prəʊˈtuː-/ adj swelling or curving outwards: *a protuberant stomach* — ~**ly** adv

proud /praʊd/ adj 1 apprec showing proper and reasonable respect for oneself: *They're poor but proud.* | *too proud to accept money from the state* 2 derog having too high an opinion of oneself and one's own importance; ARROGANT: *Lord Ponsonby is so proud he won't even speak to people like us.* | *You're really proud of yourself, aren't you?* 3 [(of)] having, expressing, or causing personal satisfaction and pleasure in something connected with oneself: *Tom is very proud of his new car.* | *The factory's safety record is something it can be proud of.* [F+to-v] *She was proud to be invited to speak.* [F+(that)] *We are very proud that a pupil from our school has won the prize.* | *It was a proud day for her parents when she qualified as a doctor.* —see also HOUSE-PROUD 4 tech, esp. BrE sticking out above a surface or surrounding area 5 **do someone proud** infml to treat someone, esp. a guest, splendidly —see also PRIDE — ~**ly** adv

Proust /pruːst/, **Mar·cel** /ˈmɑːsel‖mɑːrˈsel/ (1871–1922) a French writer, considered to be one of the greatest writers of modern times. His great work, translated into English, is *Remembrance of Things Past* (1922–32), which consists of seven NOVELs and is a detailed study of society.

prove /pruːv/ v **proved** /pruːvd/, **proved** also **proven** /ˈpruːvən/ esp. AmE 1 [T] to show to be true by means of facts, documents, information, etc.; give proof of: *evidence that proves his innocence* | *In order to prove her point, she showed them the latest sales figures.* [+(that)] *The fingerprints on the gun prove conclusively that she was the murderer.* [+obj+adj] *They prove her (to be) guilty.* —see also DISPROVE 2 [L;T] to show (oneself or itself) afterwards or in the course of time or experience, etc., to be: [+adj/n] *These revelations could prove highly embarrassing for the government.* | *Perhaps the book will prove*

(to be) useful, after all. | *On the long journey, he proved a most amusing companion.* [+obj+n|adj] *He proved himself (to be) an amusing companion.* 3 [T] *law* to show that (a WILL² (5)) has been properly made —**provable** adj — **provably** adv

prov·en /ˈpruːvən; ScotE ˈprəʊvən/ adj 1 [A] also **proved**— apprec tested and shown to be true: *a man of proven ability* —opposite **unproven** 2 **not proven** (in the Scottish legal system) when it has not been proved beyond doubt that someone has broken the law and they are therefore set free

prov·e·nance /ˈprɒvənəns‖ˈprɑː-/ n [U] fml or tech (the stated place of) origin: *Gunpowder is now considered to be of Chinese provenance.*

Pro·ven·çal /ˌprɒvɒnˈsɑːl‖ˌprɑːvɑːn-/ n, adj (a person or language) of Provence, SE France

Provençale, **Provençal** /ˌprɒvɒnˈsɑːl◂‖ˌprɑːvɑːn-/ adj [after n] *cooked with oil, GARLIC, HERBS and usu. TOMATOes*

Pro·vence /prɒˈvɒns, prə-‖prəˈvɑːns/ an area in SE France on the Mediterranean Sea known for producing wine, fruit and vegetables, and for tourism. Its main towns are Nice and Marseilles.

prov·en·der /ˈprɒvəndər‖ˈprɑː-/ n [U] 1 old-fash dry food for horses and cattle 2 infml, often humor food for people

prov·erb /ˈprɒvɜːb‖ˈprɑːvɜːrb/ n a short well-known, supposedly wise, saying usu. in simple language: *"Don't put all your eggs in one basket"* is a proverb.

pro·ver·bi·al /prəˈvɜːbiəl‖-ɜːr-/ adj 1 of a proverb: *a proverbial expression* 2 [A] infml spoken of in a popular saying or comparison: *He's got more lives than the proverbial cat!* (cats are often said to have nine lives, meaning that they often narrowly escape death) 3 very widely known and spoken of; undoubted: *His generosity is proverbial.*

pro·ver·bi·al·ly /prəˈvɜːbiəli‖-ɜːr-/ adv as is widely known or believed: *The Scots are proverbially careful with money.*

Prov·erbs /ˈprɒvɜːbz‖ˈprɑːvɜːrbz/ in the Bible a collection of proverbs believed to be the work of Solomon, forming part of the Old Testament

pro·vide /prəˈvaɪd/ v [T] 1 [(**for**)] to cause or arrange for (someone) to have or use (something needed or useful); supply: *The course is free but you have to provide your own books.* | *The hotel provides a shoe-cleaning service for its residents.* [+obj+**with**] *These letters should provide us with all the information we need.* | *Senior members of the government are provided with research assistants.* —see SPREAD (USAGE) 2 [+that; obj] fml (of a law, rule, agreement, etc.) to state a special arrangement that must be fulfilled: *The law provides that ancient buildings must be preserved by the government.*

provide against sthg. phr v [T] 1 to make arrangements in order to avoid (a danger) 2 fml (of a law, rule, etc.) to forbid

provide for sbdy./sthg. phr v [T] 1 to support; supply with the things necessary for life: *He has five children to provide for.* 2 to make the necessary future arrangements for: *to provide for every eventuality* (=for whatever might happen) [+obj+v-ing] *The plans provide for road traffic increasing to twice its present volume.* 3 (of a law, rule, etc.) to allow; make possible: *The possibility of the book being translated is provided for in your contract.*

pro·vid·ed /prəˈvaɪdɪd/ also **provided that**, **providing**, **providing that**— conj 1 if: *Provided (that) there is no opposition, we shall hold the meeting here.* 2 and only if; on condition that: *I will go, (always) provided|providing (that) you go too.*

prov·i·dence /ˈprɒvɪdəns‖ˈprɑː-/ n 1 [S;U] (often cap.) an act or event showing God's care or the kindness of fate (often in the phrase **divine providence**): *It seemed like providence that the doctor happened to be passing just at the time of the accident.* 2 [U] old use the quality of being provident

Providence the capital city of the state of Rhode Island, NE US

prov·i·dent /ˈprɒvɪdənt‖ˈprɑː-/ adj apprec careful and sensible in providing for future needs, esp. by saving or storing —opposite **improvident** — ~**ly** adv

prov·i·den·tial /ˌprɒvɪˈdenʃəl◂‖ˌprɑː-/ adj fml happening just when needed; lucky —**tially** adv

pro·vid·er /prə'vaɪdə^r/ n a person who provides, esp. one who supports a family

pro·vid·ing /prə'vaɪdɪŋ/ also **providing that** /·'·· ·/— conj PROVIDED

prov·ince /'prɒvɪns‖'prɑː-/ n **1** [C] any of the main divisions of some countries, and formerly of some EMPIRES (groups of countries) that forms a separate whole for purposes of government control **2** [S] an area of knowledge, activity, etc., esp. one that is regarded as belonging to a particular person: *Sales forecasts are outside my province – you should discuss them with the sales manager.* | *Everything to do with our finances is my wife's province.* **3** [C] an area under the charge of an ARCH-BISHOP (=a priest of the highest rank) —compare DIOCESE

prov·inc·es /'prɒvɪnsɪz‖'prɑː-/ n [the+P] the parts of a country that are distant from the main city: *I saw the new film in London; it's not yet being shown in the provinces.*

pro·vin·cial¹ /prə'vɪnʃəl/ adj **1** [no comp.] of a province or the provinces: *provincial government* | *a provincial newspaper* **2** *often derog* having the manners, speech, opinions, rather limited or old-fashioned customs, etc., that are sometimes regarded as typical of people from the PROVINCES: *her narrow-minded provincial attitudes* – ~ly adv – ~ism n [C;U] : *provincialism(s) of dress and manner*

provincial² n **1** a PROVINCIAL¹ (esp. 2) person **2** *tech* the head of a PROVINCE (3)

prov·ing ground /'·· ·/ n **1** a place for scientific testing, esp. of vehicles **2** a place or situation in which something new is tried out: *The school was a proving ground for his educational theories.*

pro·vi·sion¹ /prə'vɪʒən/ n **1** [U+of] the act of providing: *The provision of a new library has been of great benefit to the students.* **2** [U+against, for] preparation against future risks or for future needs: *They spend all their money and make no provision for the future.* **3** [C] a condition in an agreement or law; PROVISO: *According to the provisions of the agreement the interest on the loan must be paid monthly.* [+that] *The doctor agreed to go to Africa, with the provision that he could take his family with him.* —see also PROVISIONS

provision² v [T (for)] to provide with food and supplies in large quantities for a long time: *to provision a ship/an army*

pro·vi·sion·al /prə'vɪʒənəl/ adj for the present time only; suitable now, but likely to be changed: *a provisional government until we can hold an election* | *a provisional arrangement* —compare TEMPORARY – ~ly adv : *Provisionally, we've arranged the meeting for Tuesday, but we can change it if that doesn't suit you.*

Provisional IRA /·,··· ··'·/ also **Provisionals, Provos**— [the] a group within the IRA that uses violence and TERRORISM to achieve its aim of a united Ireland. It is separate from the official IRA.

provisional li·cence /·'··· ,··/ BrE ‖ *learner's permit* AmE— n an official paper which is given to a person who is learning to drive. It is temporary and lasts for one year.

pro·vi·sions /prə'vɪʒənz/ n [P] food supplies, esp. for a particular purpose such as a journey —**provision** adj [A] : *a provision merchant*

pro·vi·so /prə'vaɪzəʊ/ n -sos a necessary condition in an agreement that is made in advance: [+that] *I agree to do the work, with one proviso – that I'm paid in advance.*

prov·o·ca·tion /,prɒvə'keɪʃən‖,prɑː-/ n **1** [U] the act of provoking or reason for being provoked: *It's true that he hit her, but he was acting under severe provocation – she was hurting his child.* | *They attacked our border guards without the slightest provocation.* **2** [C] something that tests one's powers of self-control: *the provocations of teaching a class of badly-behaved children*

pro·voc·a·tive /prə'vɒkətɪv‖-'vɑː-/ adj likely to cause strong feelings, e.g. of anger or sexual interest: *his provocative remarks about unemployed people being lazy* | *Amanda is looking very provocative in those tight jeans.* – ~ly adv

pro·voke /prə'vəʊk/ v [T] **1** [(into, to)] to make (a person or animal) angry or bad-tempered, esp. by continually annoying them: *That dog is very dangerous when provoked.* | *The students tried to provoke the teacher into losing her temper.* (=make her lose her temper by provoking her) [+obj+to-v] *His refusal to answer provoked me*

to shout at him. —see ANNOY (USAGE) **2** to be the sudden cause of (a usu. unpleasant feeling or action): *Her insensitive speech provoked an angry reaction.* | *Don't throw one bone to two dogs; you'll only provoke a fight.* **3** **enough to provoke a saint** so annoying that it would make even the calmest and most patient person angry

Pro·vos /'prəʊvəʊz/ [the+P] *infml* the PROVISIONAL IRA

prov·ost /'prɒvəst‖'prəʊvəʊst/ n *(usu. cap.)* **1 a** the head of certain colleges: *the Provost of King's College* **b** AmE a university official of high rank **2** the head of a Scottish town council —compare MAYOR **3** the head of the CHAPTER in a CATHEDRAL in Britain, usu. also the PARISH priest where the cathedral is the parish church

pro·vost court /prə'vəʊ kɔːt‖'prəʊvəʊ ˌkɔːrt/ n a military court usu. for small offences in a country held by an army

provost mar·shal /prə,vəʊ 'mɑːʃəl‖,prəʊvəʊ 'mɑːr-/ n an officer who is in charge of military police

prow /praʊ/ n *esp. lit* the pointed front part of a ship or boat; BOW⁵

prow·ess /'praʊɪs/ n *usu. fml or lit* [U (**as, at, in**)] great ability, skill, or bravery. This word is usu. used in a military or sexual context: *The tribesmen sang a song of victory, describing their prowess in battle.* | *boasting about his sexual prowess*

prowl¹ /praʊl/ v [I;T] (esp. of an animal looking for food, or of a thief looking for a chance to steal) to move about (an area) quietly, trying not to be seen or heard: *I heard someone prowling about in the garden.* | *rough-looking men who prowl the streets after dark* – ~er n : *to report a prowler to the police*

prowl² n [S] an act of prowling: *a hungry lion on the prowl* (=prowling) | (fig., *infml*) *I'm going for a prowl round the bookshops.* (=looking for books to buy)

prowl car /'· ·/ n AmE a police car that is driven round the streets of a city looking for crime —see also PATROL CAR

prox /prɒks‖prɑːks/ BrE *fml, becoming rare* (used after a date in business letters) of next month: *The meeting will be held on the 24th prox.*

prox·i·mate /'prɒksɪmɪt‖'prɑːk-/ adj [no comp.] *fml* **1** [(to)] nearest in time, order, or family relationship **2** [A] (of a cause) direct – ~ly adv

prox·im·i·ty /prɒk'sɪmɪti‖prɑːk-/ n [U (**to, of**)] *fml* nearness: *Proximity to a good shopping centre is important.* | *a monument to be erected* **in the proximity of** (=somewhere near) *the town hall*

prox·y /'prɒksi‖'prɑːksi/ n **1** [U] the right given to a person to act for or represent another person on a single occasion, esp. a voter at an election, because the person is not able to go because of illness or absence from the country. Official permission must be given before this right can be used: *to vote* **by proxy** (=by sending someone else) **2** [C] a person whom one chooses to act for or represent one

proxy vote /'·· ,·/ n a vote made by a person acting as a proxy (2) for another. The person represented either tells the proxy which way to vote, or allows him/her to vote as they think best.

prude /pruːd/ n *derog* a person who is, or claims to be, easily shocked by improper or rude things, esp. of a sexual nature. This word is usu. used for a woman, esp. a very CONSERVATIVE older woman. —**prudish** adj —**prudishly** adv : *"I never laugh at dirty jokes," she said prudishly.* —see also PRUDERY

pru·dent /'pruːdənt/ adj thinking carefully before taking action; careful to avoid risks, unpleasantness, difficulties, etc.: *I think it would be prudent to hear the other side of the argument before you make your decision.* —opposite **imprudent** – ~ly adv —**dence** n [U] : *financial prudence*

pru·den·tial /pruː'denʃəl/ adj *fml* resulting from prudence, esp. in business matters – ~ly adv

Prudential also **Pru** /pruː/ *infml* – [the] tdmk a British and American insurance company

prud·er·y /'pruːdəri/ also **prud·ish·ness** /'pruːdɪʃnɪs/— n [U] *derog* the behaviour of a prude

prune¹ /pruːn/ v [T] **1** [(BACK)] to cut off or shorten some of the branches of (a tree or bush) in order to improve the shape and growth: *to prune roses with a pruning knife* —see picture at GARDEN **2** [(AWAY, BACK)] to remove (branches, stems, etc.) in this way **3** [(AWAY, DOWN)] to reduce or remove (anything useless or unwanted) from (something) by making careful choices: *You should prune the speech down; it's too long.* | *pruning waste in the health service to reduce government spending*

prune² *n* **1** a dried PLUM, sometimes gently boiled before eating **2** *BrE infml* a silly person

pruning hook /'··.··/ *n* a hook-shaped knife on a usu. long pole, used for cutting branches of trees etc.

pru·ri·ent /'prʊəriənt/ *adj fml* having an unpleasantly strong and unhealthy interest in sex – ~ **ly** *adv* —**ence** *n* [U]

Prus·sia /'prʌʃə/ a former German state, divided between W Germany, E Germany, the USSR, and Poland in 1947. British people think of the typical Prussian as being very proud and military in their way of behaving. —**Prussian** *n,adj*

Prus·sian blue /ˌprʌʃən 'bluː/ *n* [U] a deep blue colour or paint —**Prussian blue** *adj*

prus·sic ac·id /ˌprʌsɪk 'æsɪd/ *n* [U] a very poisonous acid that quickly causes death

pry¹ /praɪ/ *v* [I (**into**)] *derog* to try to find out about someone else's private affairs: *I don't wish to pry, but is it true that you've sold your house?* | *prying newspaper reporters* | *He put a cover over it to discourage prying eyes.*

pry² *v* [T] *esp. AmE for* PRIZE⁵: *We used an iron bar to pry open the box.*

Pry·or /'praɪər/, **Richard** (1940–) an American COMEDIAN who has appeared in films and made several records. He is black and often makes jokes about situations involving black and white people together.

P.S. /ˌpiː 'es/ *n* **1** a postscript; a note added at the end of a letter: *She added a P.S. asking me to send some money.* | *Yours, J. Smith. P.S. If Thursday is not convenient for you, please let me know.* **2** PRIVATE SECRETARY

psalm /sɑːm‖sɑːm, sɑːlm/ *n* (*sometimes cap.*) a song or poem in praise of God, esp. one of those in the Bible (from the **Book of Psalms**, in the OLD TESTAMENT, a collection of songs (HYMNS) often sung at church services on Sundays)

psalm·ist /'sɑːmɪst‖'sɑːm-, 'sɑːlm-/ *n* a writer of psalms

psal·ter /'sɔːltər/ *n* (*often cap.*) a book of the psalms in the Bible, often with music, for use in church services

psal·ter·y /'sɔːltəri/ *n* an ancient musical instrument with strings stretched over a board, played with the fingers

PSAT /ˌpiː es eɪ 'tiː/ *n* Preliminary Scholastic Aptitude Test; an examination which students in the US take to prepare for the SAT. Students who do well on the PSAT may win a National Merit Scholarship. —see also SAT

PSBR /ˌpiː es biː 'ɑːr/ *abbrev. for* PUBLIC SECTOR BORROWING REQUIREMENT

pse·phol·o·gy /se'fɒlədʒi‖siː'fɑː-/ *n* [U] the study of how people vote at elections —**gist** *n*

pseud /sjuːd‖suːd/ *n BrE infml derog* someone who pretends to have especially great knowledge or especially good judgment, esp. in matters such as art or literature. British people tend to dislike this kind of person and would use this word to show their disapproval and CONTEMPT. —**pseudy** *adj*

pseudo- see WORD FORMATION

pseu·do·nym /'sjuːdənɪm‖'suːdənɪm/ *n* an invented name used instead of one's real name, esp. by a writer: *Charlotte Brontë wrote under the pseudonym of Currer Bell.*

pseu·don·y·mous /sjuː'dɒnɪməs‖suː'dɑː-/ *adj* written or writing under a pseudonym: *the pseudonymous writer of this newspaper column*

pshaw /pʃɔː‖ʃɔː/ *interj* a sound used to express annoyance, disapproval, disbelief, or when you think someone or something is worthless or wrong

psit·ta·co·sis /ˌsɪtə'kəʊsɪs/ *n* [U] a serious disease of certain birds, that can also be caught by people

pso·ri·a·sis /sə'raɪəsɪs/ *n med* an illness of the skin which makes the skin dry, red, and FLAKY (1)

psst /ps/ *interj* (a sound used for getting a person's attention while asking for secrecy): *Psst! Put your shoes on before he comes in!*

PST /ˌpiː es 'tiː/ *abbrev. for:* PACIFIC STANDARD TIME

PSTN /ˌpiː es tiː 'en/ *n* [U] Public Switched Telephone Network; the system of telephone lines around the world used for voice calls, or for DATA calls when proper equipment is used —see also ISDN

psych /saɪk/ *v*

psych sbdy./sthg. ↔ **out** *phr v* [T] *sl, esp. AmE* **1** to frighten, using only the power of one's mind: *The boxer stared hard at his opponent before the match, trying to psych him out.* **2** to understand by INTUITION: *I psyched him out at once, and knew I couldn't trust him.*

psych sbdy. **up** *phr v* [T] *sl, esp. AmE* to make (esp. oneself) keen and ready: *She'd got herself all psyched up for the exam, so it was a big letdown when it was postponed.*

psy·che /'saɪki/ *n* [*usu. sing.*] *tech or fml* the human mind, soul, or spirit

psyched /saɪkt/ also **psyched up** /ˌ· '·/— *adj sl* excited: *He was pretty psyched about his bike trip in Europe.*

psy·che·del·ic /ˌsaɪkɪ'delɪk◄/ *adj* **1** (of a mind-influencing drug) causing strange and powerful sensations of happiness, understanding, hopelessness, etc. These drugs became popular in the 1960s and 70s, and now have a strong association with this period. —see also HIPPIE **2** (of a form of art) producing an effect on the brain by means of strong patterns of noise, colour, lines, moving lights, etc., like the effects produced by psychedelic drugs – ~ **ally** /kli/ *adv*

psychiatric hos·pi·tal /ˌ···· '····/ *n* a hospital where people with illnesses of the mind are treated

psy·chi·a·trist /saɪ'kaɪətrɪst‖sə-/ *n* a doctor trained in psychiatry: *a session on the psychiatrist's couch* —compare PSYCHOLOGIST (1)

psy·chi·a·try /saɪ'kaɪətri‖sə-/ *n* [U] the study and treatment of diseases of the mind, esp. when considered as a branch of medicine, that deals with mental, emotional, or behavioural problems —**tric** /ˌsaɪki'ætrɪk◄/ *adj* : *psychiatric treatment/disorders* —**trically** /kli/ *adv*

psy·chic¹ /'saɪkɪk/ also **psy·chi·cal** /-kɪkəl/— *adj* **1** (of a person) having powers that cannot be scientifically explained, e.g. the ability to see into the future: *How did you know I was here? You must be psychic!* —compare CLAIRVOYANT **2** [*no comp.*] concerning the soul or the spirits of the dead: *psychic experiences* **3** [*no comp.*] (of an illness) of the mind as opposed to the body: *psychic disorders* – ~ **ally** /kli/ *adv*

psychic² *n* a PSYCHIC¹ (1) person, esp. one who is believed to receive messages from the dead (a MEDIUM²). Many people do not believe in psychics and consider them to be strange, although they are often interested in what psychics say and do.

psychic re·search /ˌ·· '··, ˌ·· ·'·/ *n* [U] the study of the PARANORMAL, esp. the powers of the mind and also the existence of such things as GHOSTS, POLTERGEISTS, etc. This is a subject which causes a lot of argument and disagreement. People are often very interested in the more sensational forms of the paranormal, such as TELEKINESIS (=moving objects by the power of the mind alone), and these often appear in films or are mentioned in newspapers. —see also ESP, Uri GELLER

psy·cho /'saɪkəʊ/ *n infml* a PSYCHOPATH.

Psycho an American HORROR film made in 1960 directed by Alfred HITCHCOCK. It is esp. known for a scene in which the character Marion (Janet Leigh) is stabbed (STAB) in a SHOWER by Norman BATES (Anthony Perkins). —see picture on page 685

psycho- see WORD FORMATION

psy·cho·an·a·lyse also **-lyze** *AmE* /ˌsaɪkəʊ'ænəlaɪz/ *v* [T] to treat by psychoanalysis

psy·cho·a·nal·y·sis /ˌsaɪkəʊ-ə'næləsɪs/ *n* [U] a way of treating certain nervous disorders of the mind by examination of the sufferer's memories of past life, experiences, dreams, etc., in an effort to find hidden causes of the illness. It was developed by Sigmund Freud. Psychoanalysis is fairly common in the US, but British people often have a negative view of it and are not certain that it is effective. —**tic** /ˌsaɪkəʊ-ænə'lɪtɪk◄/, **-tical**— *adj* —**tically** /kli/ *adv*

psy·cho·an·a·lyst /ˌsaɪkəʊ'ænə-lɪst/ also **analyst** *AmE*— *n* a person who is trained in psychoanalysis. The STEREOTYPE of a psychoanalyst is of a very serious, unemotional man who sounds German, who sits next to the person being treated (who lies on a COUCH¹), and writes things in a NOTEBOOK but says very little.

psy·cho·bi·ol·o·gy /ˌsaɪkəʊbaɪˈɒlədʒi‖-ˈɑːl-/ n the study of the body in relation to the mind: *His speciality is the psychobiology of manic-depressives.*

psy·cho·dra·ma /ˈsaɪkəʊˌdrɑːmə‖-ˌdrɑːmə, -ˌdræmə/ n the playing of ROLEs in events from a person's life as a method in PSYCHOTHERAPY or education

psy·cho·ki·ne·sis /ˌsaɪkəʊkaɪˈniːsɪs‖-kɪˈniː-/ n [U] the moving of solid objects by the power of the mind alone. There is very little scientific proof for psychokinesis and most people do not believe in it. However, it causes great interest, and people like to watch shows which supposedly prove that it exists. —see also Uri GELLER **—tic** /-ˈnetɪk/ adj **—tically** /kli/ adv

psy·cho·log·i·cal /ˌsaɪkəˈlɒdʒɪkəl◄‖-ˈlɑː-/ adj **1** of or connected with the way that the mind works: *a psychological play about a mother's power over her son's mind | There could be some psychological explanation for his bad health.* **2 at the psychological moment** *infml* just at the right time: *If you ask him at the psychological moment, he may say yes.* **—cally** /kli/ adv : *psychologically unstable/disturbed*

psychological war·fare /ˌ····· ˈ··/ n [U] action taken to lessen enemy courage and loyalty by spreading fear, anxiety, different political beliefs, etc.

psy·chol·o·gist /saɪˈkɒlədʒɪst‖-ˈkɑː-/ n **1** a person who is trained in psychology: *police psychologists* —compare PSYCHIATRIST **2** *infml* a person who understands people's characters: *He fancies himself as a bit of a psychologist. | a good psychologist*

psy·chol·o·gy /saɪˈkɒlədʒi‖-ˈkɑː-/ n **1** [U] the study or science of the mind and the way it works and influences behaviour: *educational psychology* **2** [C;U] *infml* a particular person's character and the way this influences their behaviour **3** [U] *infml* cleverness in understanding people: *You'll have to use a bit of psychology if you want to persuade them.*

psy·cho·path /ˈsaɪkəpæθ/ n a person who has a serious disorder of character that may cause violent or criminal behaviour —compare SOCIOPATH **— ~ ic** /ˌsaɪkəˈpæθɪk◄/ adj **— ~ically** /kli/ adv

psy·cho·sis /saɪˈkəʊsɪs/ n **-ses** /siːz/ [C;U] a serious disorder of the mind that may produce character changes and makes one lose touch with reality —see also PSYCHOTIC

psy·cho·so·mat·ic /ˌsaɪkəʊsəˈmætɪk◄‖-kəsə-/ adj **1** (of an illness) caused by fear or anxiety in the mind rather than by a physical disorder **2** concerning the relationship between the mind and the body in illness: *psychosomatic medicine* **— ~ally** /kli/ adv

psy·cho·ther·a·py /ˌsaɪkəʊˈθerəpi/ n [U] *tech* the treatment of DEPRESSION, anger, and other strong feelings, as well as disorders of the mind using psychology rather than drugs, operations, etc. **—pist** n

psy·chot·ic /saɪˈkɒtɪk‖-ˈkɑː-/ adj, n tech (of or being) a person suffering from psychosis: *psychotic behaviour | He became (a) psychotic.* **— ~ally** /kli/ adv

pt *written abbrev. for:* **1** part **2** payment **3** PINT(s) **4** point **5** (*often cap.*) port: *Pt Moresby*

PT /ˌpiː ˈtiː/ n [U] *esp. BrE* physical training; development of the body by games, exercises, etc.: *I enjoy PT. | a PT lesson* —compare GYM

PTA /ˌpiː tiː ˈeɪ/ n Parent-Teacher Association; an organization of teachers and parents that works for the improvement of a school —compare PTO²

PT boat /ˌpiː ˈtiː bəʊt/ n a small, fast boat used by the US armed forces, esp. during the Second World War. Many Americans remember that President John F Kennedy fought during the Second World War in a PT boat, PT 109, and that when it was sunk, Kennedy led the men to safety.

Pte *BrE written abbrev. for* PRIVATE² (1)

pter·o·dac·tyl /ˌterəˈdæktɪl‖-tl, -tɪl/ n a flying animal that lived many millions of years ago

PTO¹ /ˌpiː tiː ˈəʊ/ abbrev. for (written at the bottom of a page) please turn over; look at the next page

PTO² n esp. AmE Parent-Teacher Organization; a PTA

Ptol·e·ma·ic sys·tem /ˌtɒlɪ ˈmeɪ-ɪk ˌsɪstəm‖ˌtɑːl-/ [the] the system according to which, in former times, the Earth

was believed to be at the centre of the universe, with the sun, stars, and PLANETs travelling round it (from **Ptolemy** (2nd century AD), a Greek-Egyptian scientist —compare COPERNICAN SYSTEM

Ptol·e·my¹ /ˈtɒləmi‖ˈtɑː-/ a Greek-Egyptian scientist who studied the stars, and thought that the stars, the sun, and the PLANETs went round the earth. This idea is known as the Ptolemaic System.

Ptolemy² the name of five kings of Egypt from the 3rd to the 1st century BC

pto·maine /ˈtəʊmeɪn, təʊˈmeɪn/ adj [A] concerning or caused by poisonous substances formed by bacteria in decaying meat: *ptomaine poisoning*

pty *written abbrev. for:* PROPRIETARY (used in Australia, New Zealand, and South Africa after the name of a business company): *Australian Wine Growers Pty*

▶ Pubs

the inside of a pub   the outside of a pub

Pubs are an important part of British life. Even very small villages nearly always have a pub. People, especially men, will often go to the pub for a drink in the evenings and at weekends. A man will usually go to the same pub, one which is close by and which is called the LOCAL (2 2): *I'm just nipping down to the local for a pint.* Women now go to pubs more than they used to, but usually do not like to go to a pub on their own. Children under 16 are not usually allowed into pubs, although some pubs have a children's room or a garden where children can sit.

Until 1988, pubs were only allowed to be open from 12:00 am to 2:00 pm and from 6:00 pm to 11:00 pm. The laws which say when alcoholic drink can be sold in a public place are called the LICENSING LAWS. Even though the law was changed so that alcohol can now be sold all day, many pubs still only open at lunchtime and in the evening. When it is nearly time for the pub to close, the LANDLORD (=man who runs the pub) or LANDLADY (=woman who runs the pub) shouts '**last orders**' (=buy your last drinks) and then '**time**' (=no more drinks will be served and people should now finish their drinks and leave the pub).

Pubs often sell food or SNACKs as well as drinks. Food that is considered typical pub food is SCAMPI (=kind of shellfish) and CHIPS (=fried potatoes), PIE and chips, chicken and chips, and PLOUGHMAN's LUNCH (=bread with cheese).

Pubs have names, e.g. *The Angel, The Black Swan, The Crown, The King's Arms, The Red Lion, The White Horse,* etc. and people usually refer to the pub by its name: *Turn left at the Rose and Crown.* There is often a sign outside the pub showing the name with a picture.

a pub sign

GREENE KING

THE CROWN

Many pubs have two or more different bars. The PUBLIC BAR is usually plainly furnished and often has a POOL table and DARTBOARD. It is the bar usually used by the LOCALs (=people, especially men, from nearby who use the pub regularly). The SALOON BAR is comfortable and well-furnished and is the bar that is usually used by men and women drinking together.

pub /pʌb/ also **public house** BrE fml— n (esp. in Britain) a building, not a club or hotel, where alcohol may be bought and drunk during fixed hours: *They've gone down to the pub.* | *the landlord of the pub* | *a pub lunch* —see also LOCAL² (2); compare BAR¹ (3a)

pub-crawl /ˈ·ˌ·/ n esp. BrE sl a visit to several pubs one after another, usu. having a drink at each place. People who **go on a pub-crawl** are usu. young men and often get drunk: *Taxi-drivers dislike picking up people who have been on a pub-crawl.* —**pub-crawl** v [I]

pu-ber-ty /ˈpjuːbəti‖-ər-/ n [U] the stage of change in the human body from childhood to the adult state in which it is possible to produce children. In Western countries people do not celebrate puberty and it is not usu. discussed openly. Parents usu. inform their children about the changes at puberty and it is also taught at school.

pu-bic /ˈpjuːbɪk/ adj [A] of or near the sexual organs: *pubic hair*

pub-lic¹ /ˈpʌblɪk/ adj **1** [no comp.] of, for, or concerning people in general: *The rise in drug-taking is a matter of public concern.* | *The regulations were changed as a result of public pressure.* | *The government's attitude to this is a public disgrace/scandal.* **2** [no comp.] for the use of everyone; not private: *a public fountain* | *Is this garden public?* **3** [no comp.] connected with the government and the services it provides for the people: *a new policy on public spending* | *to hold public office* (=be a government minister, etc.) **4** (able to be) known to all or to many; not secret: *The news was not made public for several days.* | *Don't talk about it here; this place is too public.* | *a public inquiry into the causes of the accident* **5 go public** to become a PUBLIC COMPANY **6 in the public eye** (of a person) often seen in public or on television, or mentioned in newspapers —compare PRIVATE¹ — ~**ly** adv : *publicly humiliated*

public² n **1** [the +sing./pl. v] people in general: *The town gardens are open to the public/to members of the public daily.* | *The British public is/are not really interested in this issue.* —see also JOE BLOGGS **2** [S; U+sing./pl. v] any group considered in terms of its relation to a particular person, activity, etc.: *The singer tried to please his public by singing old songs.* | *Is there a public for that sort of book?* (=will people be interested in it?) **3 in public** in the presence of strangers or of many people —opposite **in private**

public ac-cess /ˌ·· ˈ··/ n [U] the right of people in general to go on to certain land: *The Ramblers Association is protesting about the lack of public access to parts of the North Yorkshire moors.*

public ac-cess chan-nel /ˌ·· ˈ·· ˌ·/ n COMMUNITY CHANNEL

public-ad-dress sys-tem /ˌ·· ·ˈ· ˌ·/ n see PA (2)

public af-fairs /ˌ·· ·ˈ·/ n [P] events and questions, esp. political ones, which concern most people: *There's a programme on TV every week which discusses public affairs in a non-partisan manner.*

pub-li-can /ˈpʌblɪkən/ n **1** fml, esp. BrE a person who runs a PUB —compare INNKEEPER **2** a tax collector in ancient Rome

pub-li-ca-tion /ˌpʌblɪˈkeɪʃən/ n **1** [U] the act of making something known to the public: *the publication of the election results* **2** [U] the offering for sale to the public of something printed: *The book is ready for publication.* **3** [C] something published (PUBLISH), such as a book or magazine: *The library gets the usual monthly publications.*

public bar /ˌ·· ˈ·/ n BrE a plainly furnished room in a PUB, hotel, etc., where lower prices are charged for drinks than in the SALOON BAR. The public bar is usually the most popular room in a pub and also the place where games are played. —see also PUB

public bill /ˌ·· ˈ·/ n BrE a BILL¹ (2) that has an effect on the general public rather than a particular person or class —compare PRIVATE BILL

public com-pa-ny /ˌ·· ˈ···/ n a business company that offers its shares for sale on the STOCK EXCHANGE

public con-ve-ni-ence /ˌ·· ·ˈ···/ also **convenience**— n BrE euph a public TOILET provided by local government —see TOILET (USAGE)

public cor-po-ra-tion /ˌ·· ··ˈ··/ n **1** an organization set up by the British government to run a state-owned business e.g. British Rail **2** AmE a company whose shares are bought and sold on a STOCK EXCHANGE and which is therefore owned by a large number of people

public de-fend-er /ˌ·· ·ˈ··/ n AmE a lawyer provided by the state, COUNTY, or city government to defend poor people in law cases —compare DISTRIC ATTORNEY

public do-main /ˌ·· ·ˈ·/ law **in the public domain** (of a work of art, literature, an invention, or a piece of information) no longer the property of the artist, writer, or inventor. When a work is in the public domain, anyone can use it without asking permission: *Many famous pieces of classical music are in the public domain and are used in advertisements.*

public en-e-my /ˌ·· ˈ···/ n **1** a person, esp. a wanted criminal, who is a danger to the public and who is usually being hunted by the police. Pictures of the person are often put up in public places. **2 public enemy number one** a phrase used in speaking of a criminal, an illness, etc. that is regarded as the most serious threat to people's safety or health: *For a few weeks, pitbull terriers became public enemy number one in the popular press.*

public ex-pen-di-ture /ˌ·· ·ˈ···/ n [U] spending by the government on e.g. schools, roads, hospitals, the army, SOCIAL SECURITY, and wages

public foot-path /ˌ·· ˈ···/ n BrE a footpath which is open to the public and which people have a right to use, as opposed to a PRIVATE footpath

public fund-ing /ˌ·· ˈ···/ also **public funds** /ˌ·· ·ˈ·/— n [U] money given by the government for activities or organizations for the public use: *Public funding for the arts is lower in Britain than in Germany.*

public health /ˌ·· ·ˈ·/ n [U] HEALTH CARE for the public, provided by the government or local authority and including PREVENTIVE MEDICINE, SANITATION, and HYGIENE in public places

public hol-i-day /ˌ·· ˈ···/ n a general holiday when most people are off work and shops are usu. closed

public house /ˌ·· ·ˈ·/ n BrE fml for PUB

public hous-ing /ˌ·· ˈ···/ n [U] AmE flats or houses built by the US government for very poor people. It is usu. in cities, of poor quality, and strongly disliked by everyone, esp. those who live in it. —compare COUNCIL HOUSE

public in-quir-y /ˌ·· ·ˈ···‖ˌ·· ˈ···, ˌ·· ·ˈ··/ n an official INVESTIGATION into the reasons for something happening, esp. an accident: *They are going to conduct a public inquiry into the causes of the disaster.* | *the subject of a public inquiry*

pub-li-cist /ˈpʌblɪsɪst/ n a person whose business is to bring something, esp. products for sale, to the attention of the public: (fig.) *He's a good self-publicist.* (=he is good at making himself well-known)

pub-lic-i-ty /pʌˈblɪsɪti/ n [U] **1** public notice or attention: *The film star's marriage got a lot of publicity.* | *unwelcome publicity* **2** the business of bringing someone or something to the attention of the public: *Who is in charge of publicity for our show?* | *a big publicity campaign to highlight the dangers of smoking*

pub-li-cize also **-cise** BrE /ˈpʌblɪsaɪz/ v [T] to bring to public notice: *to publicize a new policy*

public law /ˌ·· ·ˈ·/ n law **1** [C] a law which concerns the general public **2** [U] the part of law concerned with the relations of the state with people and the activities, rights, and duties of the government and its departments —compare PRIVATE LAW

public lend-ing right /ˌ·· ˈ·· ˌ·/ n (in Britain) an arrangement which provides payment for writers depending on how often their books are borrowed from certain public libraries

public li-bra-ry /ˌ·· ˈ···/ n a building paid for out of taxes where people can go and borrow books free of charge

public lim-it-ed com-pa-ny /ˌ·· ˈ··· ˌ·· ˈ···/ also **plc** abbrev.— n a company in Britain which has at least two members and SHARES¹(2) available to the public. Public limited companies must print their accounts and include **plc** in their name.

public nui-sance /ˌ·· ˈ··/ n **1** law an act or failure to act which is harmful to everyone: *He committed a public nuisance by blocking the road.* **2** infml a person who makes trouble

public o·pin·ion /ˌ·· ·'··/ n [U] the opinions, views, or beliefs held by the general public on subjects of national interest or importance: *public opinion says that politicians can never make the mistake of having an affair.*

public own·er·ship /ˌ·· '···/ n [U] the owning of businesses, property, etc., by the state. In Britain several companies in public ownership have been privatized (PRIVATIZE), esp. during Mrs Thatcher's government.

public pros·e·cu·tor /ˌ·· '·····/ n (*often caps.*) (in Britain) a government lawyer who acts for the state in bringing charges against criminals in a court of law —compare DISTRICT ATTORNEY

Public Rec·ord Of·fice /ˌ·· '·· ˌ··/ [the] an office in London that holds all the government records, some of historical value. Most of the records can be examined by the general public after 30 years.

public re·la·tions /ˌ·· ·'··/ also **PR** — n **1** [U] the work of forming in the minds of the general public a favourable opinion of an organization: *She's a public relations officer in a big oil company.* **2** [P] good relations between an organization and the public: *Giving money to the local theatre would be good for (our company's) public relations.*

public relations ex·er·cise /ˌ·· ·'·· ˌ··/ n an action that is done only to gain favour with the public and not because of any real feeling or interest: *The parades come down to one thing: a public relations exercise for the Bush Administration.*

public school /ˌ·· '·/ n **1** a private FEE-PAYING British and esp. English SECONDARY school where children usu. live as well as study. Public schools are known for their high ACADEMIC standards and are considered PRESTIGIOUS. They are expensive and attended usu. by people of high social STATUS or with a lot of money. The most famous British public schools include Eton, Harrow, and Winchester. **2** (esp. in the US and Scotland) a free local school, controlled and paid for by the state, for children who study there but live at home —compare PRIVATE SCHOOL

public sec·tor /ˌ·· '··/ [the] those industries and services in a country that are owned and run by the state, such as (in many countries) the education service and the railways: *a job in the public sector | public-sector employees* —compare PRIVATE SECTOR

public sector bor·row·ing re·quire·ment /ˌ·· ˌ·· '·· ·ˌ··/ also **PSBR** *abbrev.*— [the] the difference between the money the government collects and the money it spends, when this is greater

public serv·ant /ˌ·· '··/ n a person who works for the government, esp. one who is elected

public serv·ice /ˌ·· '··/ n [C;the] **1** the supply of a COMMODITY, such as gas or electricity, or service, such as TRANSPORT, to the general public **2** a service performed in the public interest **3** [employment in the government or its departments; CIVIL SERVICE

public speak·ing /ˌ·· '··/ n [U] the practice of making speeches in public

public spend·ing /ˌ·· '··/ n [U] the money spent by local and central government and public organizations on things such as roads, schools, HOUSING, etc.

public spir·it /ˌ·· '··/ n [U] *apprec* willingness to do what is helpful for everyone, without regard for personal advantage —**public-spirited** /ˌ·· '····/ adj : *Thank you for volunteering; that's very public-spirited of you!*

public tel·e·vi·sion /ˌ·· '····, ˌ·· ··'··/ n [U] a television service in the US which is supported by money given by the government, large companies, and people who watch public television stations. Public television is thought of by many people as making good quality programmes that are both educational and entertaining. —see also PBS

public trans·port /ˌ·· '··/ , **public trans·por·ta·tion** /ˌ·· ··'··/ AmE— n [U] means of TRANSPORT open to the general public; bus, train, UNDERGROUND³, etc.

public works /ˌ·· '·/ n [P] buildings, roads, ports, etc., provided by the government for public use

pub·lish /ˈpʌblɪʃ/ v **1** [I;T] (of a business firm) to choose, arrange, have printed, and offer for sale to the public (a book, magazine, newspaper, etc.): *This firm publishes educational books/software.* | *to get a job in publishing* **b** (of a newspaper or magazine) to print for the public to

read: *We can't publish all the letters we receive.* **2** [I;T] (of a writer or musician) to have (one's work) printed and put on sale: *She's just published her fourth novel.* **3** [T *often pass.*] to make known generally; bring to the knowledge of the public: *The latest unemployment figures will be published tomorrow.* **4 publish and be damned** *quote* a phrase which is believed to have been used by the Duke of Wellington, now used when saying that people should publish a book even if it will cause disagreement or protest **5 publish or perish** *AmE* a saying used about university teachers, meaning that if they do not publish something new each year they may lose their jobs. The publish or perish system is often criticized and blamed for causing teachers to spend less time with their students.

pub·lish·er /ˈpʌblɪʃər/ n a person or firm (also **publishing house**) whose business is to PUBLISH (1) books, newspapers, etc., or (sometimes) to make and sell records

Puc·ci·ni /puˈtʃiːni/, **Gia·co·mo** /ˈdʒækəməʊ‖ˈdʒɑː-/ (1858–1924) an Italian COMPOSER famous for his OPERAS, esp. *La Bohème* and *Tosca*

puce /pjuːs/ adj dark brownish purple

puck /pʌk/ n a hard flat circular piece of rubber used instead of a ball in the game of ICE HOCKEY

Puck 1 an imaginary creature that enjoys playing tricks on people **2** a character who behaves in this way in Shakespeare's play *A Midsummer Night's Dream*

puck·er /ˈpʌkər/ v [I;T (UP)] to tighten into uneven or unattractive folds: *Her little mouth puckered up and tears filled her eyes.* —**pucker** n

puck·ish /ˈpʌkɪʃ/ adj lit harmlessly playful; CHEEKY (from Puck, a playful FAIRY in *A Midsummer Night's Dream* by William Shakespeare): *a puckish grin* — **-ly** adv

pud /pʊd/ n [C;U] *BrE infml for* PUDDING

pud·ding /ˈpʊdɪŋ/ n [C;U] **1** *BrE* a sweet food served at the end of a meal: *What's for pudding?* —see DESSERT (USAGE) **2** *esp. BrE* (*usu. in comb.*) a usu. solid hot sweet dish based on pastry, rice, bread, etc., with fat and fruit or other substances added. Puddings are very TRADITIONAL British food and are very popular: *a helping of rice pudding* | *(a) bread and butter pudding* **3** *BrE* (*usu. in comb.*) an unsweetened dish of a mixture of flour, fat, etc., either covering or enclosing meat and boiled with it: *(a) steak and kidney pudding* **4** *AmE* a thick, soft, sweet DESSERT usu. made with milk, eggs, sugar, and a little flour, and served either hot or cold: *chocolate pudding* —see also BLACK PUDDING, CHRISTMAS PUDDING, MILK PUDDING, PLUM PUDDING, YORKSHIRE PUDDING, **the proof of the pudding is in the eating** (PROOF¹)

pudding ba·sin /ˈ·· ˌ··/ n *BrE* **1** a deep round dish narrower at the bottom than the top, in which puddings are cooked **2** a haircut for straight hair in which the hair is cut round in a straight line and looks like a pudding basin

pud·dle¹ /ˈpʌdl/ n a small amount of water, esp. rain, lying in a hollow place in the ground

puddle² v [T] *tech* to mix (sand, clay, and water) into a mass

pu·den·dum /pjuːˈdendəm/ n -**da** /də/ *old-fash fml* the sexual organs (esp. of a woman)

pudg·y /ˈpʌdʒi/ adj PODGY —**-iness** n [U]

pueb·lo /ˈpwebləʊ/ n *Sp* a town; used esp. of towns in the SW US

Pueblo n [C;U] (a member of) a group of TRIBES of Native Americans, including the Hopi, living in the southwestern part of the US. They are known esp. for their ADOBE buildings. —see NATIVE AMERICAN (CULTURAL NOTE)

pu·er·ile /ˈpjʊəraɪl‖-rəl/ *adj fml* childish; silly; IMMATURE: *his puerile sense of humour* —**-ility** /pjʊəˈrɪlˌti/ n [U]

pu·er·per·al /pjuːˈɜːpərəl‖-ˈɜːr-/ *adj* [A] *med* of, after, or caused by giving birth (esp. in the phrase **puerperal fever**)

Puer·to Ri·co /ˌpwɜːtəʊ ˈriːkəʊ‖ˌpɔːrtə-, ˌpweərtə-/ an island SE of the US; capital San Juan; population 3,658,000 (1989). People who live in Puerto Rico are US citizens but Puerto Rico is not a US state and governs itself. Many people from Puerto Rico move to the US in order to earn more money. —**Puerto Rican** /ˌpwɜːtəʊ ˈriːkən◄‖ˌpɔːrtə-, ˌpweərtə-/ n, adj

Puerto Val·lar·ta /ˌpwɜːtəʊ vaɪˈɑːtə‖ˌpɔːrtə vaɪ-ˈɑːrtə, pweərtə-/ a town in western Mexico on the Pacific Ocean. Many Americans go on holiday to Puerto Vallarta.

puff¹ /pʌf/ v 1 [I] to breathe rapidly and with effort, usu. during or after hurried movement: *Running makes him puff heavily.* | *He puffed up the steep slope.* (=climbed while breathing fast) 2 [I+*adv/prep*] to breathe in and out while smoking a cigarette, pipe, etc.: *He puffed (away) at his pipe as he talked.* | *She puffed at a cigarette nervously.* 3 [I;T (OUT)] a (of smoke or steam) to blow or come out repeatedly, esp. in small amounts b to cause to come out in this way: *Don't puff cigarette smoke in my face.* 4 [I+*adv/prep*] to move along while sending out little clouds of smoke: *The old engine puffed along/puffed into the station.* 5 [T] *old-fash infml* to praise (esp. something for sale) more than is deserved: *critics puffing a new film* 6 *infml* **puff and blow** to show signs of making a great physical effort: *he was puffing and blowing carrying the heavy box up the stairs*
  puff sthg. ↔ **out** *phr v* [T] 1 [(with)] to make larger, esp. with air: *The bird puffed out its feathers.* | *He puffed his chest out proudly.* 2 to put out the flame of (something) by blowing lightly: *to puff out a candle*
  puff up *phr v* [I; T (=**puff** sthg. ↔ **up**)] to (cause to) swell: *Mustard makes my eyes puff up.* | (fig.) *He is puffed up (with pride).* (=too proud)

puff² n 1 [C] an act of puffing: *He took a puff at his cigarette.* 2 [C] a sudden light rush of air, smoke, etc.: *a puff of wind* —see picture at PIECE 3 [C] a decorative part of a garment that swells out in the middle: *puff sleeves* 4 [C] (*usu. in comb.*) a hollow piece of light pastry (**puff pastry**) that is filled with a soft usu. sweet mixture: *a lemon puff* 5 [U] *infml humor* breath 6 [C] *infml* a piece of writing praising a person or an entertainment —see also POWDER PUFF

puff·ball /ˈpʌfbɔːl/ n a type of FUNGUS that looks like a ball and bursts when ripe, giving off a cloud of SPORES (=seeds)

puffball skirt /ˈˌ‥ ˈ‥/ n a short skirt which becomes wider between the waist and the lower edge, giving a rounded shape gathered at the lower edge

puffed /pʌft/ *adj* [F] *infml* (esp. of a person) breathing with difficulty; out of breath

puffed sleeve /ˌ‥ ˈ‥/ n a short SLEEVE which becomes wider in the middle and is gathered at the top and lower edge

puffed wheat /ˌ‥ ˈ‥/ n grains of wheat that are PUFFed up and eaten with milk (and sugar) as a breakfast CEREAL

puf·fin /ˈpʌfɪn/ n a North Atlantic seabird that has a very large brightly coloured beak —see picture at WATER BIRD

Puffin n *tdmk* a PAPERBACK book for children and young people produced by Penguin Books

Puff the Ma·gic Drag·on /ˌ‥ ‥ ˌ‥ ˈ‥/ an imaginary DRAGON in a children's song with the same name

puff·y /ˈpʌfi/ *adj* rather swollen: *puffy eyes* —**iness** n [U]

pug /pʌg/ n a small fat short-haired dog with a wide flat face and a short flat nose

Pu·get Sound /ˌpjuːdʒɪt ˈsaʊnd/ n a body of water leading from the Pacific Ocean into the US state of Washington. The cities of Seattle and Tacoma are on its shores.

pu·gi·lis·m /ˈpjuːdʒɪlɪzəm/ n [U] *fml* (in former times) the art or sport of BOXING —**tic** /ˌpjuːdʒɪˈlɪstɪk◂/ *adj*

pu·gi·list /ˈpjuːdʒɪlɪst/ n *fml or pomp* a BOXER (1)

pug·na·cious /pʌgˈneɪʃəs/ *adj fml* (of people or behaviour, but not countries) fond of quarrelling and fighting — compare BELLIGERENT¹ (1) — ~ **ly** *adv* —**nacity** /pʌgˈnæsⱅi/, -**naciousness** /-ˈneɪʃəsnⱅs/ n [U] *fml*: *known for his pugnacity/pugnaciousness*

pu·is·sance¹ /ˈpjuːⱅsəns, ˈpwɪsəns/ n [U] *poet or old use* power or strength, esp. of a king

puis·sance² /ˈpwiːsəns/ n a competition in which riders have to make their horses jump over very high fences

pu·is·sant /ˈpjuːⱅsənt, ˈpwɪsənt/ *adj poet or old use* powerful

puke¹ /pjuːk/ v [I;T (UP)] *sl* to be sick; VOMIT

puke² n [U] *sl* food brought back from the stomach through the mouth; VOMIT

puk·ka /ˈpʌkə/ *adj esp. IndE & PakE* 1 good; of high quality 2 real; GENUINE 3 *humor* stiff and formal (from the

fixed social manners supposed to be typical of the British in India during the period of British rule there)

pul·chri·tude /ˈpʌlkrⱅtjuːd‖-tuːd/ n [U] *fml or pomp* beauty, esp. of a woman —**tudinous** /ˌpʌlkrⱅˈtjuːdⱅnəs◂‖-ˈtuː-/ *adj*

Pul·it·zer Prize /ˈpʊlɪtsə ˌpraɪz/-sər-/ n one of the eight prizes given every year for newspaper writing (JOURNALISM) and for LITERARY achievement (from Joseph Pulitzer (1847–1911), an American newspaper PUBLISHER who provided money for the prizes)

pull¹ /pʊl/ v 1 [I;T] to bring (something) along behind one while moving: *The horse was pulling a cart.* | *The train is pulled by a powerful engine.* —compare DRAG 2 [I;T] to use force on (something), esp. with the hands, in order to move it towards oneself or in the direction of the force: *Help me move the piano over here; you push and I'll pull.* | *In an emergency pull the cord to stop the train.* | *sailors pulling on a rope* [+*obj+adv/prep*] *She pulled her chair up to the table.* | *He pulled his socks on.* | *The cupboard door is stuck and I can't pull it open.* | *She pulled the fence apart/to pieces with her bare hands.* 3 [T] to bring or press towards one in order to make an apparatus work: *To fire the gun, just pull the trigger.* 4 [T (OUT, UP)] to take (something out of a place where it is fixed or enclosed), usu. with force: *The decayed tooth should be pulled (out).* | *to pull the cork from a bottle* | *She went into the garden to pull (up) a few onions for dinner.* 5 [T] to stretch and damage, by using force; STRAIN: *He's pulled a muscle trying to lift the piano.* 6 [T] to win, gain, or attract: *The big match pulled in an enormous crowd.* | *She's unlikely to pull many votes at the election.* | (*infml*) *He's hoping to pull the girls with his flashy new car.* 7 [T (on)] to bring out (a small weapon) ready for use: *He pulled a gun on me.* (=took out a gun and aimed it at me) 8 [T] *esp. BrE* to get (beer) out of a barrel by pulling a handle: *to pull a pint* 9 [I] (of a horse) to struggle and press the mouth hard against the BIT² 10 [T] *sl, esp. AmE* to succeed in doing (a crime, something daring, something annoying or deceiving, etc.): *They pulled a bank robbery.* | *What are you trying to pull?* (=What trick are you trying to play?) 11 [T] *tech* to hold back (a horse in a race, or a blow being aimed in BOXING) with the intention of avoiding victory —see also **pull one's punches** (PUNCH²) 12 [I;T] *tech* to hit (the ball in cricket or GOLF) away from a straight course and away from the side of the player's stronger hand 13 [I] *old-fash* to row —compare PUSH¹; see also **pull a fast one** (FAST¹), **pull one's finger out** (FINGER¹), **pull someone's leg** (LEG¹), **pull something out of the bag** (BAG¹), **pull to pieces** (PIECE¹), **pull rank** (RANK¹), **pull the rug out from under** (RUG), **pull one's socks up** (SOCK¹), **pull strings** (STRING¹), **pull one's weight** (WEIGHT¹), **pull the wool over someone's eyes** (WOOL)
  pull ahead *phr v* [I (of)] to get in front by moving faster: *The taxi soon pulled ahead of the bus.*
  pull at sthg. *phr v* [T] 1 to seize and pull sharply and repeatedly: *She pulled at the thread until it came out of the cloth.* | *The child pulled at his mother's coat, wanting to be lifted up.* 2 *old-fash* to cause tobacco smoke to flow from (a pipe) 3 *old-fash* to take a long drink from (a container)
  pull away *phr v* [I (from)] (esp. of a vehicle or its driver) to start to move away a from the side of the road b from another moving vehicle: *He jumped onto the bus just as it was pulling away.* | *The thieves steadily pulled away from the police car.*
  pull sbdy./sthg. ↔ **down** *phr v* [T] 1 to break in pieces and destroy (something built): *They are pulling down those houses to make room for a new hotel.* 2 to weaken in health
  pull in *phr v* 1 [I] (of a train) to arrive at a station 2 [I] (of a vehicle or its driver) to move to one side and perhaps stop —compare PULL over; see also PULL-IN 3 [T] (**pull** sbdy. ↔ **in**) to take (a possible criminal) to a police station: *The police have pulled him in for questioning.* 4 [T] (**pull** sthg. ↔ **in**) *infml* to earn (a lot of money): *She's pulling in quite a bit in her new job.*
  pull sthg. ↔ **off** *phr v* [T] *infml* to succeed in (a difficult attempt): *The trick looked impossible, but she pulled it off.*
  pull out *phr v* 1 [I] (of a train) to leave a station — compare PULL away 2 [I] (of a vehicle or its driver) to move a away from the side of the road b in front of another moving vehicle 3 [I;T (=**pull** sbdy. ↔ **out**)

(**of**)] to (cause to) leave a place or time of trouble: *The general pulled his troops out of the area.* | *Jim saw that the firm was going to be ruined, so he pulled out.* —see also **pull out all the stops** (STOP²)

   pull over *phr v* [I;T (=**pull** sthg. ↔ **over**)] **a** (of a vehicle or its driver) to move over to one side of the road: *The policeman signalled to him to pull over.* **b** to drive (one's vehicle) to the side of the road —compare PULL **in** (2)

   pull through *phr v* [I;T (=**pull** sbdy. **through**)] **1** also **pull round**— to (cause to) live in spite of illness or wounds: *He's very ill, but with careful nursing he'll pull through.* —compare BRING **through** **2** to (help to) succeed in spite of difficulties: *Margaret had difficulty with her work for the examinations, but her teacher pulled her through.*

   pull together *phr v* **1** [I] (of a group of people) to work so as to help a shared effort **2** [T *no pass.*] (**pull** sbdy. **together**) to control the feelings of (oneself): *Stop acting like a baby!* **Pull yourself together!** **3** [T] (**pull** sthg. **together**) to cause to improve through proper organization: *We need an experienced man to pull the department together.*

   pull up *phr v* **1** [I;T (**pull** sthg. **up**)] to (cause to) come to a stop: *The car pulled up at the traffic lights.* | *His unexpected criticism rather pulled me up short.* (=made me stop and think) **2** [I (**to, with**)] to come level (with another competitor in a race) **3** [T (**on, for**)] (**pull** sbdy. **up**) to stop (someone who is making mistakes) and express disapproval

pull² *n* **1** [C;U] (an act of) pulling: *Give the rope a good/gentle pull.* | *the moon's pull on the sea* —compare TUG **2** [S] a difficult steep climb: *It's a long pull up this hill.* **3** [C (**at**)] *old-fash* an act of taking in tobacco smoke or of taking a long drink: *He took a pull at his pipe/at his beer.* **4** [C] (*usu. in comb.*) a rope, handle, etc., used for pulling something: *a bellpull* **5** [S;U] *infml* special influence; (unfair) personal advantage: *The importance of his family's name gives him a certain pull/lots of pull in this town.* **6** [C] a stroke in cricket or GOLF that PULLS¹ (12) the ball

pul·let /ˈpʊlɪt/ *n* a young hen during its first year of laying eggs

pul·ley /ˈpʊli/ *n* an apparatus consisting of a wheel over which a rope or chain can be moved, mainly used for lifting heavy things: *a system of pulleys*

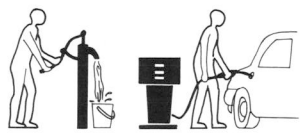
pulley

pull-in /ˈ· ·/ *n BrE infml* a place by the roadside where vehicles may stop and the drivers can get drinks and light meals —see also PULL **in** (2)

Pull·man /ˈpʊlmən/ also **sleeping car** *AmE*— *tdmk n* a specially comfortable railway carriage, esp. for sleeping in (from George Mortimer Pullman (1831–97), an American inventor who fitted railway COACHes with beds for overnight travel)

pull-on /ˈ· ·/ *adj* [A] (of a garment) that is pulled on and fits tightly, without any fastenings: *a pull-on shirt*

pull-out /ˈpʊlaʊt/ *n* a part of a book, magazine, etc., that is complete in itself and may be taken out separately

pull·o·ver /ˈpʊlˌəʊvəʳ/ *n* a SWEATER that is pulled on over the head

pul·lu·late /ˈpʌljʊleɪt/ *v* [I] *fml* to breed or multiply quickly and in great numbers —**lation** /ˌpʌljʊˈleɪʃən/ *n* [U]

pull-up /ˈ· ·/ also **chin-up** *AmE*— *n* an exercise in which one takes hold of a bar above one's head and uses one's arms to pull up the body until one's head is over the bar: *How many pull-ups can you do?*

pul·mo·nary /ˈpʊlmənəri, ˈpʌ-‖-neri/ *adj tech* of or having an effect on the lungs

pulp¹ /pʌlp/ *n* **1** [S;U] a soft almost liquid mass, such as the soft inside part of many fruits or vegetables: *A banana is mainly pulp, except for its skin.* | *These vegetables have been boiling too long; they're cooked to a pulp.* | (fig.) *I'll beat/mash him (in) to a pulp if I catch him!* | (fig.) *a terrifying teacher who could always reduce me*

to (a) **pulp** (=make me helplessly afraid and unable to act) **2** [U] wood or other vegetable materials, such as cotton cloth, softened and used for making paper —**pulpy** *adj*

pulp² *v* [T] to cause (esp. books, etc.) to become pulp

pulp³ *adj* [A] *derog* (of books and magazines) cheaply produced on rough paper and containing matter of bad quality, esp. shocking stories about sex and violence: *pulp novels*

pul·pit /ˈpʊlpɪt/ *n* **1** [C] a small raised enclosure of wood or stone in a church, from which the priest speaks to the worshippers —see picture at CHURCH **2** [*the*] *fml* (the Christian priesthood as a profession which includes) religious teaching in church

pulp·wood /ˈpʌlpwʊd/ *n* [U] crushed wood that is used to make paper

pul·sar /ˈpʌlsɑːʳ/ *n* a star-like object that usu. cannot be seen, but is known to exist because of the regular radio signals that it gives out —compare QUASAR

pul·sate /pʌlˈseɪt‖ˈpʌlseɪt/ *v* [I (**with**)] **1** to shake very regularly; VIBRATE: *The air seemed to pulsate with the bright light.* | *the pulsating beat of Latin American dance music* **2** to PULSE² (1)

pul·sa·tion /pʌlˈseɪʃən/ *n* **1** [C] *esp. tech* a beat of the heart or any regular beat that can be measured **2** [U] pulsating movement

pulse¹ /pʌls/ *n* **1** [*usu. sing.*] the regular beating of blood in the main blood tubes carrying blood from the heart, esp. as felt at the wrist: *The doctor felt/took the woman's pulse.* (=counted the number of beats per minute) | *His pulse quickened/raced.* (=his heart beat very quickly) | *Her pulse was strong/weak.* **2** a strong regular beat as in music, on a drum, etc. **3 a** a short sound as sent by radio **b** a small change in the quantity of electricity going through something, esp. that in a telephone which makes it able to ask for connection with another telephone

pulse² *v* [I] **1** [(**through, with**)] to beat steadily as the heart does; move or flow with a steady rapid beat and sound: *He could feel the blood pulsing through his veins as he waited for the signal to attack.* | *One could feel the excitement pulsing through the crowd.* **2** (of a machine) to send out signals in regular PULSES¹ (3)

pulse³ *n* [*usu. pl.*] (the seeds of) beans, PEAS, LENTILS, etc., used as food

pul·ver·ize also **-ise** *BrE* /ˈpʌlvəraɪz/ *v* [T] **1** to crush into a fine grain of powder or dust **2** *infml* to defeat thoroughly —**ization** /ˌpʌlvəraɪˈzeɪʃən‖-rə-/ *n* [U]

pu·ma /ˈpjuːmə/ *n* **pumas** or **puma** a COUGAR

pum·ice /ˈpʌmɪs/ also **pumice stone** /ˈ··· ·/— *n* [U] a very light, silver-grey rock, used in pieces or in powder form for cleaning and for rubbing surfaces smooth

pum·mel /ˈpʌməl/ ‖ also **pommel** *esp. AmE*— *v* **-ll-** *DrE* ‖ **-l-** *AmE* [T] to hit repeatedly, esp. with two FISTs (closed hands): *When he picked up his small daughter she pummelled him angrily on the chest.*

pump¹ /pʌmp/ *n* **1** [C] (*often in comb.*) a machine for forcing liquids, air, or gas into or out of something: *an old-fashioned pump for drawing water from a well* | *The heart is a kind of natural pump that moves the blood around the body.* | *He blew up his car tyres with a foot pump.* | *to operate a petrol pump* | *a bicycle pump* —see also STOMACH PUMP and see picture at BICYCLE **2** [S] an act of pumping —see also HEAT PUMP, **prime the pump** (PRIME³), and see picture at ENGINE

pumps

petrol pump   bicycle pump

pump² *v* **1** [T+*obj*+*adv/prep*] **a** to empty or fill (a

container) using a pump: *She pumped up her car tyres.*
b to move (liquids, air, or gas) with a pump: *The doctor pumped the poison out of the child's stomach.* | (fig.) *The government has been pumping money into new road-building schemes.* (=spending a lot of money on them) **2** [I (AWAY)] **a** to work a pump: *He pumped away furiously.* **b** to work like a pump: *My heart was pumping very fast.* **3** [I+ *adv/prep*] (of a liquid) to come out in short bursts as if from a pump: *blood pumping from a wound* **4** [T] to move (something) up and down like the handle of an old-fashioned pump: *He pumped his friend's hand up and down, saying how glad he was to see him.* **5** [T] *infml* to repeatedly ask (someone) questions, esp. indirect ones, in the hope of finding out something: *I tried to pump him for details of their other contracts.*

pump³ *n* a flat light shoe for dancing, etc. —see PAIR (USAGE)

pump-ac·tion /ˈ·ˌ··/ *adj* using the action of a pump to force something in or out: *a pump-action shotgun/can* (e.g. of HAIRSPRAY)

pum·per·nick·el /ˈpʌmpənɪkəl‖ˈpʌmpər-/ *n* [U] a heavy dark brown bread, usu. cut into thin pieces before being sold

pump·kin /ˈpʌmpkɪn/ *n* [C;U] (a plant with) a very large dark yellow roundish fruit that grows on the ground, often used in PIES and also to make LANTERNS at Hallowe'en. In the US, **pumpkin pie** is usu. eaten as part of Thanksgiving Day dinner. In the story of Cinderella, the FAIRY GODMOTHER changed a pumpkin into a COACH to take Cinderella to the BALL, and people sometimes make jokes about turning into a pumpkin at midnight, esp. if they have been out late at a party etc., because this is what happened to Cinderella's coach. —see also CINDERELLA and see colour picture on page 357

pump room /ˈ·ˌ·/ *n* a room at a SPA where people come to drink the water

pun¹ /pʌn/ also **play on words**— *n* an amusing use of a word or phrase that has two meanings, or of words with the same sound but different meanings: *He made this pun: "Seven days without water make one weak."* (=1 week) | *to groan at a bad pun*

pun² *v* **-nn-** [I (**on, upon**)] to make puns: *He punned on the two meanings of "one" and the similarity of "weak" and "week".* —see also PUNSTER

punch¹ /pʌntʃ/ *v* **1** [T (**in,on**)] to hit (someone or something) hard with the FIST (closed hand): *He punched the man in the chest/on the nose.* —see SLAP² (USAGE) **2** [T] to use a PUNCH³ to cut (a hole) in (something): *The ticket-collector punched my ticket/punched a hole in my ticket.* **3** *AmE* to move (cattle) from one place to another — **~er** *n*
punch in, punch out *phr v* [I] *AmE for* CLOCK in, CLOCK out
   punch sbdy. **↔ up** *phr v* [T] *BrE infml* to hit (someone) repeatedly —see also PUNCH-UP

punch² *n* **1** [C (**in, on**)] a quick strong blow made with the FIST (closed hand): *I'd like to give that man a punch on the nose.* | *a straight punch to the jaw* —see also **pack a punch** (PACK²) **2** [S;U] *apprec* forcefulness; effective power: *His speech lacked punch.* —see also PUNCHY **3 pull one's punches** to express one's bad opinion more gently than is deserved

punch³ *n* a metal tool for cutting holes: *a ticket punch*

punch⁴ *n* [C *usu. sing.*;U] (*often in comb.*) a drink made from fruit juice, sugar, water, etc., and usu. wine or other alcohol: *a bowl of rum punch*

Punch¹ a British weekly magazine (1841–1992) known for its humorous articles and its LITERARY criticism

Punch² *n* **as pleased/proud as Punch** extremely pleased/proud

Punch and Ju·dy show /ˌpʌntʃ ən ˈdʒuːdi ʃəʊ/ *n* (esp. in Britain) a PUPPET show for children in which the main character Punch (sometimes called Mr Punch) fights humorously with his wife Judy. Punch is an ugly character with a long nose who enjoys hitting people,

Punch and Judy

esp. Judy or their baby, with his stick. Punch and Judy shows are TRADITIONAL events in British life and are usu. performed at seaside and holiday towns in summer.

punch ball /ˈ·ˌ·/ also **punch·bag** /ˈpʌntʃbæg/ ‖ also **punching bag** /ˈ·ˌ··/*AmE*— *n* a large leather ball or bag, fixed on a spring or hung from a rope, which is punched (PUNCH¹) for exercise

punch bowl /ˈ·ˌ·/ *n* a large bowl in which PUNCH⁴ is served

punch-drunk /ˈ·ˌ·/ *adj* **1** (of a professional fighter) suffering brain damage from repeated blows on the head in BOXING **2** *infml* very confused, esp. by continual misfortune or bad treatment

punched card /ˌ·ˈ·/ also **punch card** /ˈ·ˌ·/— *n* a card with a pattern of holes in it for putting into a computer, each of which carries a particular piece of information to the computer

punch line /ˈ·ˌ·/ *n* the last few words of a joke or story, that give meaning to the whole and cause amusement or surprise

punch-up /ˈ·ˌ·/ *n* *BrE infml* a fight —see also PUNCH up

punch·y /ˈpʌntʃi/ *adj sl* having a forceful, effective quality; INCISIVE — **-iness** *n* [U]

punc·til·i·o /pʌŋkˈtɪliəʊ/ *n* **-os** [C;U] *fml* (an example of) careful attention paid to every small exact detail of ceremonial behaviour, performance of duties, etc.

punc·til·i·ous /pʌŋkˈtɪliəs/ *adj fml, usu. apprec* (of a person or behaviour) very exact and particular about details of behaviour or duty — **~ly** *adv* — **~ness** *n* [U]

punc·tu·al /ˈpʌŋktʃuəl/ *adj* not late; happening, doing something, etc., at the exact time; PROMPT: *She's never punctual for appointments so you can expect to be kept waiting.* | *The cat makes a punctual appearance at mealtimes.* — **~ly** *adv* : *Be there punctually at ten o'clock.* — **~ity** /ˌpʌŋktʃuˈæləti/ *n* [U]

punc·tu·ate /ˈpʌŋktʃueɪt/ *v* [T] **1** to divide (written matter) into sentences, phrases, etc., with PUNCTUATION MARKS **2** [(**with**) *usu. pass.*] to break the flow of, repeatedly: *The tense silence was punctuated by bursts of gunfire.* | *He punctuated his solemn remarks with a few well-chosen jokes.*

punc·tu·a·tion /ˌpʌŋktʃuˈeɪʃən/ *n* [U] the marks used in punctuating a piece of writing: *A piece of writing without any punctuation is difficult to understand.*

punctuation marks

.	full stop *BrE*/ period *AmE*	?	question mark
,	comma	!	exclamation mark *BrE*/ exclamation point *AmE*
;	semi-colon	( )	bracket
:	colon	" "	quotation marks

punctuation mark /ˌ··ˈ··ˌ·/ *n* a sign used in punctuating, e.g. a COMMA a QUESTION MARK, or a HYPHEN: *Make sure you put the proper punctuation marks in your essay.*

punc·ture¹ /ˈpʌŋktʃər/ *n* a small hole made with a sharp point through a soft surface, esp. in a tyre: *I'm sorry I'm late; my car/I had a puncture.* | *to mend a puncture*
▷ USAGE In the US, most people would use FLAT¹ (4) to mean a puncture as well as not having enough air in the tyre: *She ran over some glass on her bicycle and got a flat.*◁

punc·ture² *v* **1** [I; T] to (cause to) get a puncture: *A nail on the road punctured the tyre.* | *Her rubber ball punctured when it fell on a prickly bush.* | *He's in hospital with a punctured lung.* **2** [T] to destroy as if by bursting: *His unexpected failure punctured his self-importance.*

pun·dit /ˈpʌndɪt/ *n sometimes humor* a person who knows a great deal about a particular subject, esp. one whose opinion is asked for by others: *political pundits*

pun·gent /ˈpʌndʒənt/ *adj* **1** (of a taste or smell) strong, sharp, and stinging: *the pungent aroma of garlic* **2** (of speech or writing) producing a sharp direct effect: *pungent remarks about my lateness* — **~ly** *adv* — **-gency** *n* [U]

pun·ish /ˈpʌnɪʃ/ v [T] **1 a** [(for)] to cause (someone who has broken the law or done something wrong) to suffer, e.g. by sending them to prison or making them do something that they do not want to do: *Motorists should be severely punished for dangerous driving.* | *Their mother punished them for their rudeness.* | *It wasn't your fault; stop punishing yourself!* (=stop blaming yourself) **b** to cause someone to suffer for (a crime or fault): *Dangerous driving should be severely punished.* **2** to deal roughly with: *to punish one's opponent at golf* | *to punish an engine*

pun·ish·a·ble /ˈpʌnɪʃəbəl/ adj [(by)] that may be punished by law: *a punishable offence* | *Murder is punishable by death in some countries.*

pun·ish·ing¹ /ˈpʌnɪʃɪŋ/ adj infml that makes one thoroughly tired and weak: *a long, punishing climb* | *a punishing workload* —~ly adv

punishing² n [S] infml a case of rough or damaging treatment: *Your car seems to have taken a punishing.*

pun·ish·ment /ˈpʌnɪʃmənt/ n **1** [U] the act of punishing or process of being punished: *We are determined that the terrorists will not escape punishment.* | *capital punishment* (=punishment by being officially killed) **2** [C (for)] a way in which a person is punished: *She sent her son to bed early as a punishment (for breaking the window).* | *He took his punishment like a man.* (=bravely) | *to mete out punishments* | *a harsh|severe|unjust punishment* **3** [U] infml rough treatment; damage: *With five active children in the house, the furniture had taken a lot of punishment.* **4** **Let the punishment fit the crime** quote a phrase from the OPERA *Mikado* by Gilbert and Sullivan, often used when saying that a person should be punished very severely for a serious crime —compare PENALTY

pu·ni·tive /ˈpjuːnɪtɪv/ adj **1** intended as punishment: *to take punitive action against offenders* **2** very severe; causing hardship: *punitive taxation* —~ly adv

Pun·jab /pʌnˈdʒɑːb/ [the] an area in Pakistan and NW India which contains the city of Amritsar, a holy place for followers of the Sikh religion. Many Sikhs would like to have independence from India, and there has been fighting in the Punjab about this.

Pun·ja·bi, **Panjabi** /pʌnˈdʒɑːbi/ n **1** [C] a person from the main group of people living in the Punjab in India **2** [U] their language —**Punjabi, Panjabi** adj

punk¹ /pʌŋk/ adj **1** [A] of a movement among certain young people in the 1970s and 1980s who were opposed to the values of money-based society and who expressed this esp. in loud violent music (**punk rock**), strange clothing, and hair of unusual colours **2** AmE rare sl in poor health

punk² n **1** also **punk rock·er** /ˌ· ˈ··/— someone who follows punk styles in music, dress, etc. **2** AmE derog sl an esp. young man or boy, esp. one who fights and breaks the law (often in the phrase **young/little punk**) **3** AmE a substance that will burn without a flame, used to light FIREWORKS etc.

pun·kah /ˈpʌŋkə/ n IndE & PakE a FAN hung across a room and swung backwards and forwards by pulling a rope, used, esp. formerly, in hot countries

punk rock /ˌ· ˈ·/ n [U] a style of ROCK³ music played very fast and loud with often violent and offensive words, made popular in the 1970s by groups such as the Sex Pistols

pun·net /ˈpʌnɪt/ n esp. BrE (the amount contained in) a small square basket in which soft fruits are sold: *a punnet of strawberries*

pun·ster /ˈpʌnstər/ n a person who makes PUNs

punt¹ /pʌnt/ n **1** a long narrow flat-bottomed river boat with square ends, moved by someone standing on it and pushing a long pole against the bottom of the river **2** (in FOOTBALL (2)) a kick in which the ball is kicked after being dropped from the hands: *a punt which went wide of the goalposts*

punt² v **1** [I;T] to go or take by punt: *to punt (the family) up the river* **2** [T] to move (a boat) by pushing a pole against the bottom of the river **3** [I;T] (in FOOTBALL (2)) to kick a ball that has been dropped from the hands: *He punted the ball forty yards.*

punt·er /ˈpʌntər/ n esp. BrE **1** someone who punts **2** infml a person who makes a BET on the result of a horse race **3** infml the user of a product or service; customer: *We've got to cater for the needs of the punter.* **4** BrE infml ‖ **john** AmE sl —a PROSTITUTE's customer

pu·ny /ˈpjuːni/ adj derog small and weak; poorly developed: *puny little arms and legs* —~**iness** n [U]

pup¹ /pʌp/ n **1** a young SEAL¹ or OTTER **2** a PUPPY —see also **sell someone a pup** (SELL¹)

pup² v -pp- [I] esp. tech to give birth to pups

pu·pa /ˈpjuːpə/ n -pas or -pae /piː/ (the state or form of) an insect in the middle stage of its development to a full-grown form, contained in and protected by a hard or soft covering —compare CHRYSALIS, COCOON¹ —**pal** adj : *in the pupal stage*

pu·pil¹ /ˈpjuːpəl/ n a person, esp. a child, who is being taught: *The school has about 500 pupils.* | *one of my best pupils* —see STUDENT (USAGE)

pupil² n the small black round opening in the middle of the coloured part of the eye, through which light passes —see picture at EYE

pup·pet /ˈpʌpɪt/ n **1** also **marionette**— a toylike jointed figure of a person or animal that is made to move by someone pulling wires or strings at a theatre performance (a **puppet show**) **2** also **glove puppet**— a toy-like hollow cloth figure of a person or animal moved by putting one's hand inside it **3** often derog a person or group that is controlled by someone else: *Are we the puppets of fate?* | *a puppet government*

pup·pe·teer /ˌpʌpɪˈtɪər/ n an entertainer who performs with puppets

pup·py /ˈpʌpi/ also **pup**— n **1** a young dog **2** old-fash a foolish self-important young man

puppy fat /ˈ·· ·/ BrE ‖ **baby fat** AmE— n [U] infml, often euph fatness in boys and girls that usually disappears as they grow older

puppy love /ˈ·· ·/ also **calf love**— n [U] sometimes derog a young boy's or girl's love for esp. an older person of the opposite sex, which does not last long or lead to sexual relations

pup tent /ˈ· ·/ n a tent for two people, with ends shaped like an ∧ and using poles and ropes to hold it up

pur·blind /ˈpɜːblaɪnd‖ˈpɜːr-/ adj fml or lit dull; stupid

Pur·cell /ˈpɜːsəl‖ˈpɜːr-/, Henry (1659–95) an English COMPOSER who is remembered esp. for his OPERA *Dido and Aeneas*

Purcell Room /ˈ·· ˌ·/ [the] a room in the South Bank Arts Centre in London, used esp. for performances of CHAMBER MUSIC and named after Henry Purcell

pur·chase¹ /ˈpɜːtʃəs‖ˈpɜːr-/ v [T] fml **1** to buy: *to secure a loan to purchase a new car* | *The purchasing power of the dollar* (=the amount it will buy) *has declined.* **2** to gain at the cost of effort or loss: *They purchased life at the expense of honour.* —**chasable** adj —**chaser** n

purchase² n **1** [U] fml the act of buying: *He gave his son some money for the purchase of his school books.* —see also HIRE PURCHASE **2** [C often pl.] fml **a** an act of buying: *She made several purchases in the dress shop.* **b** an article that has just been bought: *Do you wish us to deliver your purchases?* **3** [S;U] a firm hold for pulling or raising something: *The climber tried to gain a purchase with his foot on a narrow ledge.*

purchase tax /ˈ·· ·/ n [U] (in Britain) a tax charged on all goods except those necessary for life, such as food, and collected by being added to the price in shops (after 1973 changed to VAT in Britain) —compare SALES TAX

pur·dah /ˈpɜːdə, -dɑː‖ˈpɜːr-/ n [U] IndE & PakE (esp. among Muslims) the system of keeping women out of public view

pure /pjʊəʳ/ adj **1** not mixed with anything else: *"Is this sweater made of pure wool?" "No, it's 60% wool and 40% acrylic."* | *pure silver* | *a horse of pure Arab breed* **2** clean; free from dirt, dust, bacteria, or any harmful matter: *The air by the sea is pure and healthy.* | *pure drinking water* **3** free from evil, and esp. without sexual thoughts or experience: *I'm sure his motives were pure.* | *a pure young girl* **4** (of colour or sound) clear; unmixed with other colours or sounds: *a cloudless sky of the purest blue* **5** [A *no comp.*] *infml* complete; thorough; only: *By pure chance/coincidence my boss was flying on the same plane as me.* | *The error was due to carelessness* **pure and simple**. (=only carelessness) **6** [A] (of an art or branch of study) considered only for its own nature as a skill or exercise of the mind, separate from any use that might be made of it: *pure science* —compare APPLIED; see also IM-PURE, PURELY, PURIFY **7 as pure as the driven snow** very pure in character or moral behaviour, sometimes used to mean the opposite in conversation: *He makes himself out to be as pure as the driven snow, but some of his dealings have been, quite simply, dishonest.* **8 to the pure all things are pure** *saying from the Bible, usu. humor* people who are sexually INNOCENT do not understand rude things —~ **ness** n [U]

pure·blood·ed /ˌpjʊəˈblʌdˌd◂‖ˌpjʊər-/ adj descended from one race with no mixture of other races: *pureblooded Native Americans* —compare PEDIGREE (1), THOROUGHBRED

pure·bred /ˈpjʊəbred‖ˈpjʊər-/ n, adj (an animal) descended from one breed with no mixture of other breeds: *purebred hens* —compare THOROUGHBRED

pu·ree¹, purée /ˈpjʊəreɪ‖pjuˈreɪ/ n [C;U] (*often in comb.*) food boiled to a soft half-liquid mass: *an apple puree*

puree², purée v [T] to make into a puree: *She pureed the vegetables for the baby.*

pure·ly /ˈpjʊəli‖ˈpjʊərli/ adv completely; wholly; only: *I helped him* **purely and simply** *out of friendship.* | *a decision that was taken for purely political reasons*

pure math·e·mat·ics /ˌ·· ···‖···/ also **pure maths** /ˌ· ·/ *BrE infml*— n the science of numbers treated as a subject of interest in its own right and not originally developed for practical purposes —compare APPLIED MATHEMATICS

pur·ga·tion /pɜːˈɡeɪʃən‖pɜːr-/ n [U] *fml* the act of purging (PURGE¹)

pur·ga·tive /ˈpɜːɡətɪv‖ˈpɜːr-/ n, adj (a medicine) that causes the bowels to empty: *This fruit often has a purgative effect.*

pur·ga·to·ry /ˈpɜːɡətəri‖ˈpɜːrɡətɔːri/ n [U] **1** (*often cap.*) (esp. according to the Roman Catholic religion) a state or place in which the soul of a dead person must be made pure by suffering for wrong-doing on Earth, until it is fit to enter Heaven —compare LIMBO¹ **2** *often humor* a place, state, or time of great suffering: *It's purgatory listening to Tim's attempts to play the guitar.* —**rial** /ˌpɜːɡəˈtɔːriəl◂‖ˌpɜːr-/ adj

purge¹ /pɜːdʒ‖pɜːrdʒ/ v [T] **1** to get rid of (unwanted people) in (a state, political party, etc.) by removal from office, driving out of the country, killing, etc.: *to purge a political party* [+obj+of] *to purge the party of dissidents* [+obj+from] *to purge dissidents from the party* **2** [(of, from)] *esp. lit* to make clean and free from (something evil): *to purge one's soul from sin* | *to purge one's spirit of hatred* **3** *law* to remove the bad effects of (an act of wrong-doing) for oneself: *The judge ordered him to purge his contempt by apologizing to the court.* **4** *tech or old-fash* to clear waste matter from (the bowels)

purge² n **1** an act or set of actions intended to get rid of unwanted members of a group suddenly, often unjustly, and often by force: *The new president carried out a purge of disloyal army officers.* **2** *tech or old-fash* a medicine that clears the bowels of waste matter

pu·ri·fy /ˈpjʊərˌfaɪ/ v [T (of)] to make PURE (esp. 2): *This salt has been purified for use in medicine.* —**fier** n : *an air purifier* —**fication** /ˌpjʊərˌfˌˈkeɪʃən/ n [U] : *ritual purification*

Pu·rim /ˈpʊərɪm/ n a JEWISH holiday in memory of the Jews' escape from the destruction planned for them after Mordecai (a Jew) refused to lie on the floor in front of his Persian ruler. The story is told in the book of Esther in the Bible.

pur·ist /ˈpjʊərˌst/ n someone who is always (too) careful to practise and preserve what they regard as the correct way of doing something, esp. in matters of grammar, use of words, etc.: *A purist would say "To whom does this belong?", but nowadays "Who does this belong to?" is much more common.* —**ism** n [U]

pu·ri·tan /ˈpjʊərˌtən/ adj, n usu. derog (of or being) a person who has rather hard fixed standards of behaviour and self-control, and thinks pleasure is unnecessary or wrong: *his puritan beliefs* | *He's too much of a puritan to enjoy dancing.*

Puritan n, adj (a member) of a PROTESTANT religious group in the 16th and 17th centuries who wished to make religion simpler and less ceremonial. Most broke away from the Church of England. They were treated badly in England at the end of the 17th century and many went to America to find religious freedom. In the US, Puritan beliefs have had a strong influence on the American way of life.

pu·ri·tan·i·cal /ˌpjʊərˌˈtænɪkəl◂/ adj derog like a puritan: *a puritanical father who wouldn't let his children watch television* —**cally** /kli/ adv

pu·ri·tan·is·m /ˈpjʊərˌtənɪzəm/ n [U] **1** (*cap.*) the beliefs and practices of the Puritans **2** *often derog* living according to severe and demanding rules, esp. in matters of religion and morals: *She went to live with her boyfriend as a protest against her family's puritanism.*

pu·ri·ty /ˈpjʊərˌti/ n [U] the quality or state of being pure —opposite **impurity**

purl¹ /pɜːl‖pɜːrl/ n [U] *tech* the second of the two main stitches in knitting (KNIT), made by doing an ordinary stitch backwards: *a purl stitch* | *three plain, two purl* —compare KNIT², PLAIN⁴

purl² v [I; T] *tech* (usu. in instructions) to use the purl stitch (on): *Knit one, purl one.* | *Purl (for) three rows.* —compare KNIT¹

purl³ v [I] *lit* (of a small stream) to flow with a low gentle continuous noise

purl·er /ˈpɜːləʳ‖ˈpɜːr-/ n [S] *BrE old-fash infml* a heavy fall, usu. head first: *He* **came a purler**. (=fell heavily)

pur·lieus /ˈpɜːljuːz‖ˈpɜːrluːz/ n [(the) P (of)] *lit or pomp* the area in and around a place

pur·loin /pɜːˈlɔɪn, ˈpɜːrlɔɪn‖-ɜːr-/ v [T] *fml or humor* to steal (esp. something of small value)

pur·ple¹ /ˈpɜːpəl‖ˈpɜːr-/ adj of the colour purple

purple² n **1** [U] a dark colour made of a mixture of red and blue —compare MAUVE, VIOLET **2** [the] *esp. lit* (in former times) dark red or purple garments worn only by people of very high rank: *He was* **born to the purple**. (=born into a royal family)

purple heart /ˌ·· ·/ n *BrE infml* a small PILL containing a drug (AMPHETAMINE) that causes excitement, often taken by drug ADDICTS

Purple Heart n a MEDAL (=a coinlike piece of metal) given as an honour to be worn by soldiers of the US wounded in battle

purple pas·sage /ˌ·· ·/ also **purple patch** /ˌ·· ·/— n a splendid or too grand-sounding part in the middle of a piece of writing

pur·plish /ˈpɜːplɪʃ‖ˈpɜːr-/ adj slightly purple: *purplish blue*

pur·port¹ /pɜːˈpɔːt‖pɜːrˈpɔːrt/ v [T+to-v;obj] *fml* to claim to be; have an (intended) appearance of being: *The orders, which purported to be signed by the general, were an enemy trick.*

pur·port² /ˈpɜːpɔːt, -pət‖ˈpɜːrpɔːrt/ n [U (of)] *fml* the general meaning or intention of someone's words or actions: *The purport of the message seemed to be this: Work harder or find another job.*

pur·pose¹ /ˈpɜːpəs‖ˈpɜːr-/ n **1** [C] an intention or plan; a person's reason for an action: *What was the purpose of her visit?* | *Did you come to London to see your family, or for business purposes?* | *He's registered as a single parent, for tax purposes.* **2** [C] a use; effect; result: *Don't waste your money; put it to some good purpose.* | *I haven't got a pen, but a pencil will* **answer/serve the same purpose**. (=will do what is needed) | *This computer is not quite as powerful as the other one, but* **for all practical purposes** (=in most cases) *it is just as good.* **3** [U] steady determined following of an aim: *a man of purpose* | *a sense of purpose* **4 on purpose: a** intentionally: *"I'm sorry I stepped on your toe; it was an accident." "It wasn't! You did it on purpose."* **b** with a particular stated intention:

I came here on purpose to see you. **5 to little/no/some/ good purpose** with little/no/some/good result **6 to the purpose** *old-fash* useful; very much connected with the subject —see also PURPOSELY **7 accidentally on purpose** *BrE infml* with conscious intention but also making something appear to be an accident: *He dropped the vase accidentally on purpose because he hated it.*

purpose² *v* [T] *fml* to have as one's intention: [+to-v/v-ing] *He purposes to visit America/visiting America.*

purpose-built /ˌ·· ˈ·◂/ *adj esp. BrE* originally made for a particular use: *The architect has designed purpose-built flats for old people.*

pur·pose·ful /ˈpɜːpəsfəl‖ˈpɜːr-/ *adj* (of people or behaviour) having a clear aim; determined: *He went out with a purposeful air.* — ~ly *adv*

pur·pose·less /ˈpɜːpəsləs‖ˈpɜːr-/ *adj* aimless; meaningless — ~ly *adv* — ~ness *n* [U]

pur·pose·ly /ˈpɜːpəsli‖ˈpɜːr-/ *adv* intentionally: *I purposely left it where he would see it.*

purr /pɜːʳ/ *v* **1** [I] to make the low continuous sound produced by a pleased cat: *The cat purred loudly.* | (fig) *The big car purred along the road.* **2** [I] (of a person) to show quiet happiness in a pleasant low voice **3** [T] to express or say in this way: *"Come again, won't you?" she purred.* —**purr** *n*

purse

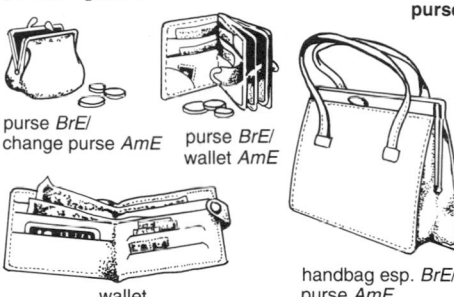

purse *BrE*/ change purse *AmE*

purse *BrE*/ wallet *AmE*

wallet

handbag esp. *BrE*/ purse *AmE*

purse¹ /pɜːs‖pɜːrs/ *n* **1** *BrE* a small flattish bag, usu. made of leather or plastic, used esp.by women **a** for carrying coins (*AmE* **coin purse**) **b** (esp. divided into two parts) for carrying both coins and paper money (*AmE* **wallet**) **2** [C] *AmE* a woman's HANDBAG **3** [S] an amount of money to spend: *That beautiful picture is* **beyond my purse.** (=I can't afford it) | *The first prize will be a purse of $1000.* —see also PRIVY PURSE **4 you can't make a silk purse out of a sow's ear** you cannot make something good from material that is of bad quality

purse² *v* [T (UP)] to bring (esp. the lips) together in little folds: *She pursed (up) her lips with disgust.*

purs·er /ˈpɜːsəʳ‖ˈpɜːr-/ *n* an officer on a ship who keeps the ship's accounts and is also in charge of the travellers' rooms, comfort, etc.

purse strings /ˈ· ·/ *n* **hold the purse strings** to control the spending of the money of a family, a firm, etc.

pur·su·ance /pəˈsjuːəns‖pərˈsuː-/ *n* **in (the) pursuance of** *fml* in the process of performing: *He was wounded in the pursuance of his duty.*

pur·sue /pəˈsjuː‖pərˈsuː/ *v* [T] **1** to follow, esp. in order to catch, kill, or defeat: *The police are pursuing an escaped prisoner.* | *The tourists were pursued by beggars.* | (fig.) *Bad luck has pursued us all through the year.* **2** to continue steadily with; carry on: *She is pursuing her studies at the university.* | *He was losing the argument, so he said, "I'd rather not pursue the matter".* | *The government is pursuing a policy of non-intervention.*

pur·su·er /pəˈsjuːəʳ‖pərˈsuːər/ *n* a person or animal that PURSUES (1): *The deer ran faster than its pursuers.*

pur·suit /pəˈsjuːt‖pərˈsuːt/ *n* **1** [U] the act of pursuing: *The police car raced through the streets in pursuit of another car.* | *The pop stars ran from the theatre to their car, with dozens of fans* **in hot pursuit.** (=close behind them) | *a pursuit vehicle* (=used for chasing the enemy) | (fig.) *The government is selling off the railways, in pursuit of* (=following) *its policy of privatization.* **2** [C] *fml* an activity to which one gives one's time, whether as work or for pleasure

pu·ru·lent /ˈpjʊərələnt/ *adj med* containing or producing PUS (=poisonous yellow matter) in the body —**lence** *n* [U]

pur·vey /pɜːˈveɪ‖pɜːr-/ *v* [T (**to**)] *fml or tech* to supply (food or other goods) as a trade — ~ **or** *n*

pur·view /ˈpɜːvjuː‖ˈpɜːr-/ *n* [U (**of**)] *fml or lit* the limit of one's concern, activity, or knowledge: *facts which fall outside the purview of this inquiry.*

pus /pʌs/ *n* [U] a thick yellowish liquid produced in an infected wound or poisoned part of the body

push¹ /pʊʃ/ *v* **1** [I;T] to use sudden or steady pressure in order to move (someone or something) forward, away from oneself, or to a different position: *He pushed me, and I fell into the water.* | *She pushed the chairs out of the way.* | *You stop the machine by pushing this button.* | *Don't push: wait for your turn to get on the bus.* | *You push it from behind, and I'll pull it.* | *Please push the door shut/push the door to.* (=into a shut position) **2** [I+adv/prep;T+obj+ adv/prep] to make (one's way) by pushing: *She pushed past me.* | *He pushed his way to the front of the crowd.* **3** [T (**into**)] to try to force (someone) to do something by continual urging; put pressure on: *I'm not pushing you; if you don't want the job, don't take it.* | *He pushed her into making a decision.* | *Don't push yourself too hard* (=work too hard) *or you'll get ill.* [+obj+to-v] *His parents are pushing him to study medicine.* **4** [T] *infml* to try to draw attention to (someone or something) e.g. by advertising, in order to gain customers, support, approval, etc.: *The company are pushing their new product.* | *He used the sales conference to push his latest ideas.* **5** [T] *infml* to sell (drugs that are not legal) —see also PUSHER **6 be pushing** *infml* to be nearly (a stated age): *You wouldn't think so to look at her, but she's pushing 60.* **7 push one's luck** *infml* to take a risk, esp. because of a previous success **8 push the 'boat out** *BrE infml* to make a special effort to make something enjoyable, esp. by spending more money than usual: *They really pushed the boat out for their daughter's wedding.* —compare PRESS¹, PULL¹; see also PUSHED

push ahead/forward/on *phr v* [I (**with**)] **1** to continue one's journey or march; ADVANCE **2** to continue with a plan or activity, esp. in a steady determined way: *Despite opposition, they are pushing ahead with their scheme for a new airport.*

push along *phr v* [I] *infml* to leave: *It's getting late; we must be pushing along.*

push sbdy. **around** *phr v* [T] *infml* to treat roughly and unfairly, esp. in order to force obedience; ORDER **about**

push for sthg. *phr v* [T *pass. rare*] to demand urgently and forcefully; try to get: *People living near the airport are pushing for new restrictions on night flights.*

push forward *phr v* **1** [T] (**push** sbdy. **forward**) *often derog* to try to attract attention to (someone, esp. oneself) **2** [I] to PUSH ahead

push in *phr v* [I] *infml* **1** to join a line in front of other people already waiting **2** to interrupt rudely

push off *phr v* [I] **1** [*usu. imperative*] *infml* to go away: *What are you doing in my garden? Push off!* **2** to start a journey in a small boat

push on *phr v* [I] to PUSH ahead

push sbdy. ↔ **out** *phr v* [T *often pass.*] to dismiss or get rid of, often unfairly

push sbdy./sthg. **through** (sthg.) *phr v* [T] to cause the acceptance or success of (a person or thing) by means of forceful pressure or effort: *They pushed the legislation through (Parliament) without much discussion.* | *The teacher pushed the student through the examination.*

push sthg. ↔ **up** *phr v* [T] **1** to cause to increase at a steady rate: *War in the Gulf pushed up the price of oil.* **2 push up the daisies** *humor* to be dead and buried

push² *n* **1** [C] an act of pushing: *They gave the car a push to start it.* **2** [C] a forceful, often planned effort to gain a desired result: *a big advertising push to publicize our new product* **3** [U] *infml, usu. apprec* the active will to succeed, esp. by forcing oneself and one's wishes on others —see also PUSHY **4 at a push** *infml, esp. BrE* if really necessary: *I can finish the work by next month at a push.* **5 give/get the push** *sl* to dismiss/be dismissed from a job **6 if/when it comes to the push** if/when there is a moment of special need: *If it came to the push we could always borrow a bit more money from the bank.* —compare PULL²

push·bike /ˈpʊʃbaɪk/ *n BrE infml* a bicycle

push-but·ton /ˈ· ˌ··/ *adj* [A] operated by a button (**push**

button) that one presses with the finger: *This machine has a push-button starter.* | *a push-button car radio* | (fig.) *push-button warfare* (=by means of explosives that can be fired over very long distances, not by soldiers fighting with ordinary weapons)

push·cart /ˈpʊʃkɑːt‖-kɑːrt/ *n* a small cart pushed by hand, used e.g. by a street trader

push·chair /ˈpʊʃ-tʃeəʳ/ *BrE* ‖ **stroller** *esp.AmE— n* a small chair on wheels for pushing a small child about —see picture at PRAM

pushed /pʊʃt/ *adj* [F] *infml* **1** [(for)] having difficulty in finding enough (money, time, etc.): *I'm always rather pushed for money by the end of the month.* [+to-v] *You'll be pushed to finish the job by this evening.* **2** having no free time; busy: *I'd like to stop for a chat, but I'm rather pushed today.*

push·er /ˈpʊʃəʳ/ *n derog* **1** a person who sells illegal drugs **2** *infml* a PUSHY person **3** *BrE* a small tool for pushing food onto a spoon at meals, used by very young children

Push·kin /ˈpʊʃkɪn/, **Al·ek·san·dr** /ˌælɪgˈzɑːndəʳ‖-ˈzæn-/ (1799–1837) a Russian poet considered to be the FOUNDER of modern Russian poetry, whose best-known work is *Eugene Onegin*

push·o·ver /ˈpʊʃˌəʊvəʳ/ *n* [S] *infml* **1** something that is very easy to do or win: *The exam was a pushover* **2** [(for)] someone who is easily influenced or defeated (by): *Charles is a pushover for girls with blue eyes.*

push-start /ˈ· ·/ *n* the act of pushing a vehicle to turn the engine and so make the vehicle go —**push-start** *v* : *The battery was flat so we had to push-start the car.*

push-up /ˈ· ·/ *n AmE for* PRESS-UP

push·y /ˈpʊʃi/ also **push·ing** /ˈpʊʃɪŋ/— *adj usu. derog* showing forceful determination to get things done and make people accept one's wishes; ASSERTIVE: *He's not really pushy enough to succeed in business.* —**ily** *adv* —**iness** *n* [U]

pu·sil·lan·i·mous /ˌpjuːsɪˈlænə̥məs/ *adj fml* cowardly and weak; frightened of taking the slightest risk — ~**ly** *adv* —**mity** /ˌpjuːsɪləˈnɪmə̥ti/ *n* [U]

puss /pʊs/ *n infml* (a name for) a cat: *Here puss, puss, puss!*

Puss in Boots /ˌ· · ˈ·/ a children's story, also a PANTOMIME, about a clever cat who wore BOOTS and who made his owner rich

pus·sy[1] /ˈpʊsi/ also **pus·sy·cat** /ˈpʊsiˌkæt/— *n infml* (a name for) a cat (used esp. by or to children)

pussy[2] *n taboo sl* **1** the female sex organs **2** *AmE* SISSY

pus·sy·foot /ˈpʊsifʊt/ *v* [I (ABOUT, AROUND)] *infml derog* to be too careful and frightened to express one's opinions, take strong action, etc.: *It's no good pussyfooting around — they should just lock these people up!*

pussy wil·low /ˈ·· ˌ··/ *n* [C;U] (a tree with) bunches of small soft furry white or greyish flowers on stems, often used for decoration

pus·tule /ˈpʌstjuːl‖-tʃuːl/ *n med* a small raised spot on the skin containing poisonous matter

put[1] /pʊt/ *v* **put**, *present participle* **putting** [T] **1** [+obj+adv/prep] to move, set, place, lay, or fix in, on, or to a stated place: *Put the box on the table.* | *Put the chair nearer the fire.* | *You put too much salt in this soup.* | *Put the toy back in its box.* | *Put your hand over your mouth when you cough.* | *Put that newspaper down while I'm talking to you!* | *They were put on a plane and sent back to their own country.* | *He put the children to bed.* | *He put a match to his cigarette.* (=lit it) | *She put her head round the door* (=looked into the room) *and asked if we were coming.* | (fig.) *The prisoner was* **put on trial/put to death.** (=killed) | (fig.) *Whatever put that idea into your* **head***?* | (fig.) *Their generosity* **put us to shame.** (=made us feel ashamed) | *I know it was a dishonest thing to do, but* **put yourself in my place/position.** (=imagine being me) *What would you have done?* **2** [+obj+adv/prep] to cause to be in the stated condition: *He put his books in order.* | *"You've made a mistake." "I'll* **put it right** *at once."* | *She's put her knowledge of French to good use.* | *His boring lessons always put me to sleep.* | *The unexpected delay put me in a bad mood.* **3** [+obj+adv/prep] to cause (something) to have an effect or influence; APPLY: *They are intending to put pressure on the government to change its mind.* | *Don't try to* **put the blame on me** — *it wasn't my fault.* | *It's time we* **put an end/a stop to** *these*

ridiculous rumours. | *I'm sure you'll be able to do it if you* **put your mind to** *it.* | *They ought to put more money into the business/more effort into their work.* **4** [+obj+adv/prep] to express something in words: *She is — how shall I put it? — not exactly fat, but rather well-built.* | *His ideas were cleverly put.* | *She was trying to put her feelings into words.* | *There is — as today's papers put it — no satisfactory explanation for his outrageous comments.* | *It's a dangerous job,* **to put it mildly.** (=it is extremely dangerous) **5** [(to, before)] to express officially for judgment or decision: *The lawyer put several questions to the witness.* | *I'll put your suggestion before the management committee.* **6** [+obj+adv/prep] to write down; make (a written mark of some kind): *Put a cross opposite each mistake.* | *"What shall I put at the end of the sentence?" "Put a question mark."* **7** [+obj+adv/prep] to make busy; set to regular work: *Put all the boys to work.* | *We're putting extra staff on the job to make sure it gets finished.* **8** [+obj+adv/prep] *tech* to guide or direct (a boat or horse) in a stated direction: *The captain put the ship into port for repairs.* **9** to throw a heavy metal ball (SHOT) as a form of sports competition **10 Put it there** *infml* (used esp. in coming to an agreement) Please shake hands with me **11 put paid to** *BrE* to ruin; finish completely: *The accident has put paid to his chances of taking part in the race.* —see also **keep/put something on ice** (ICE[1] (5)), **stay put** (STAY[1])

put about *phr v* **1** [T] (**put** sthg. ↔ **about**) *BrE infml* to spread (bad or false news); CIRCULATE: *They've been putting rumours about.* | *It's being put about that she was secretly married.* **2** [I;T (=put** sthg. **about**)] *tech* **a** (of a ship) to change direction **b** to cause (a ship) to change direction **3 put oneself about** *BrE infml* to be very active, esp. sexually

put sthg. ↔ **across/over** *phr v* [T] to cause (one's ideas, feelings, etc.) to be understood, esp. by listeners; COMMUNICATE: *an inexperienced teacher who doesn't put his ideas/himself across very well*

put sthg. **across** sbdy. *phr v* [T] *infml, esp. BrE* to deceive into believing or accepting (something): *You can't put that old excuse across your boss.* (=make him/her believe it)

put sthg. ↔ **aside** *phr v* [T] **1** [(for)] to save (esp. money), for later use or a special purpose: *We have some money put aside for a holiday.* **2** to pay no attention to; DISREGARD: *They have agreed to put aside their differences in the interests of winning the election.*

put sthg. **at** sthg. *phr v* [T] to guess to be (a certain number or amount): *I'd put her age at 33.* | *Official estimates put the damage done by the storm at over $10 million.*

put sbdy./sthg. ↔ **away** *phr v* [T] **1** to remove (something) to the place where it is usually kept: *Put the books away in the cupboard.* **2** to save (money) for later use; PUT **by 3** *infml* to eat (a lot of food) **4** *euph* to place (someone) in prison or in a hospital for mad people: *People like that ought to be put away!* **5** *bibl* to end one's marriage to (one's wife) by law

put back *phr v* **1** [T] (**put** sthg. ↔ **back**) to delay: *The fire in the factory has put back production.* | *The meeting has been put back* (=its date has been moved) *to next week.* —compare PUT **forward** (2) **2** [T] (**put** sthg. ↔ **back**) to cause (a clock or watch) to show an earlier time — compare PUT **forward** (3) **3** [I;T (=put** sthg. ↔ **back)** *tech* **a** (of a ship) to return: *The ship put back to port.* **b** to cause (a ship) to return

put sthg. ↔ **by** *phr v* [T] to save (money) for later use: *Try to put a little bit by each week.*

put down *phr v* **1** [T] (**put** sthg. ↔ **down**) to bring to an end or bring under control; QUELL: *The army put down all opposition.* | *to put down a riot* **2** [T] (**put** sbdy. ↔ **down**) *infml* to make (someone) feel unimportant; HUMILIATE —see also PUT-DOWN **3** [T] (**put** sthg. ↔ **down**) *euph* to kill (an animal), esp. because it is old or ill **4** [T] (**put** sthg. ↔ **down**) to record in writing: *Let me put down your telephone number.* **5** [T] (**put** sbdy. ↔ **down**) *BrE* to allow to leave a vehicle: *You needn't drive the car up to the house; just put me down here/at the gate.* **6** [T] (**put** sthg. ↔ **down**) to pay (an amount) as part of the cost of something, with a promise to pay the rest later —see also DOWN PAYMENT **7** [I;T] (=put** sthg. ↔ **down**) **a** (of an aircraft) to land **b** to land (an aircraft): *The engine failed and the pilot had to put (the plane) down in the sea.*

put sbdy. **down as** sthg. *phr v* [T] to guess (someone) to be or do (something): *I'd put him down as an ex-army man.*

put sbdy. **down for** sthg. *phr v* [T] to put (someone's name) on a list of people who **a** want to join (a competition, school, etc.): *She put her name down for the 100 metres race.* or **b** will give (money): *Put me down for £5.*

put sthg. **down to** sthg. *phr v* [T] to state or think that (something) is caused or explained by (something else): *I put his bad temper down to his recent illness.*

put sthg. ↔ **forth** *phr v* [T] *fml or lit* **1** to produce and send out: *In spring the bush put forth new leaves.* **2** to PUT **forward** (1)

put sbdy./sthg. ↔ **forward** *phr v* [T] **1** to offer for consideration; suggest: *They have put forward a plan for reducing the level of traffic.* | *May I put your name forward as a possible chairman of the committee?* **2** to move to an earlier date or time; advance: *The warm weather has put the harvest forward.* | *The meeting has been put forward to this week.* —compare PUT **back** (1) **3** to cause (a clock or watch) to show a later time: *The plane will soon be landing in Bombay – please remember to put your watches forward by five hours.* —compare PUT **back** (2) **4** to bring (someone) to public attention

put in *phr v* **1** [I (**at**)] (of a ship) to enter a port: *The ship puts in at Singapore and remains there for a day.* **2** [T] (**put** sthg. ↔ **in**) to make or send (a request or claim); SUBMIT: *If the goods were damaged in the post, you can put in a claim to the post office.* | *to put in an application* **3** [T] (**put** sthg. ↔ **in**) to do (work) or spend (time), esp. for a purpose: *She put in an hour's work on her project.* **4** [T] (**put** sthg. ↔ **in**) to interrupt by saying: *"Don't forget us," she put in.* **5** [T] (**put** sbdy. ↔ **in**) to elect (a government) —see also INPUT

put in for sthg. *phr v* [T] to make a formal request for; APPLY for: *They've put in for a pay rise|a government grant.*

put into sthg. *phr v* [T] (of a ship) to enter (a port): *The boat put into Sydney for supplies.*

put off *phr v* [T] **1** (**put** sthg./sbdy. ↔ **off**) to move to a later date; delay: [+*obj|v;ing*] *I'll have to put off my visit|put off going until next month.* | *We've invited them to dinner, but we'll have to put them off because the baby's sick.* **2** (**put** sbdy. ↔ **off**) to make excuses to (someone) in order to avoid a duty: *I put him off with a promise to pay him next week.* —see also PUT-OFF **3** (**put** sbdy. **off** (sthg.)) to discourage (someone) (from something): *She was trying to make a serious point, but people kept putting her off (her speech) by shouting.* | *Don't talk, it puts her off her game.* | *Their interruptions put **him off his stride/stroke.*** (=upset him, so that he stopped what he was doing or did it wrong) [+*v ing*] *The smell put me off eating for a week!* **4** (**put** sbdy. **off** (sthg./sbdy.)) to cause (someone) to dislike (someone or something); REPEL: *His bad manners|bad breath put me right off (him).* —see also OFF-PUTTING **5** (**put** sbdy. ↔ **off**) to stop and allow (someone) to leave a vehicle or boat

put on *phr v* [T] **1** (**put** sthg. ↔ **on**) to cover (part of) the body with (esp. clothing); get dressed in: *She put her hat and coat on.* | *He put on his glasses to read the letter.* —opposite TAKE **off** (1); see DRESS (USAGE) **2** (**put** sthg. ↔ **on**) to cause (a light, an electrical apparatus, etc.) to operate by pressing or turning a button, SWITCH, etc.: *Put on the light|the radio.* | *Have you put the heating on?* **3** (**put** sthg. ↔ **on**) (of a person) to increase in (weight) and grow fatter: *I put on six pounds|a lot of weight while I was on holiday.* **4** (**put** sthg. **on** sthg.) to add (an amount) to the cost or rate of: *a tax increase that will put another 10p on the price of petrol* **5** *BrE* (**put** sthg. ↔ **on**) to provide in addition to existing services: *So many people wanted to go to the match that another train had to be put on.* **6** (**put** sthg. **on** sthg.) to guess or guess (the price, value, etc.) of: *What price would you put on this fine old silver cup?* **7** (**put** sthg. **on** sthg.) to risk (something, esp. money) on; BET on **8** (**put** sthg. ↔ **on**) to pretend to have (an opinion, quality, etc.): *She's not really ill; she puts it on to get people's sympathy.* **9** (**put** sthg. ↔ **on**) to arrange for the performance of (a play, show, etc.); STAGE **10** (**put** sbdy. **on**) *infml, esp. AmE* to play a trick on; deceive: *"My dog can sing." "No, you're putting me on!"* —see also PUT-ON

put sbdy. **onto** sbdy./sthg. *phr v* [T] *infml* to give information about (someone or something good): *I can't help you myself, but I can put you onto a good lawyer.*

put out *phr v* **1** [T] (**put** sthg. ↔ **out**) to cause to stop burning: *It took them six hours to put the fire out.* | *She put out the light.* **2** [T] (**put** sbdy. **out**) **a** to upset or annoy: *She was so put out by his rudeness that she didn't*

know what to say. **b** to cause inconvenience to: *Will it put you out if I bring another guest?* | *She never **puts herself out** (=takes trouble) to help people.* **3** [T] (**put** sthg. ↔ **out**) to produce, broadcast, or print; ISSUE: *The government has put out a statement denying these rumours.* **4** [T] (**put** sthg. ↔ **out**) to put (part of the body) out of place; DISLOCATE: *I can't play tennis today, I've put my shoulder out.* **5** [I (**to**)] to begin sailing; move away from the shore or coast: *We put out to sea at high tide.* **6** [T] (**put** sbdy. **out**) (esp. of a doctor, etc.) to make (someone) unconscious **7** [I (**for**)] *AmE sl* (of a woman) to be willing to have sex with someone **8** [T] (**put** sbdy. **out**) (in BASEBALL and CRICKET) to prevent (a player) from scoring (SCORE[2]) by removing him/her from play

put sthg. ↔ **over** *phr v* [T] to PUT **across**: *He can't put his ideas over clearly enough.*

put sthg. **over on** sbdy. *phr v* [T] *infml* to deceive into believing or accepting (something worthless): *He tried to **put one over on** me* (=cheat me) *by selling me a car that didn't work.*

put through *phr v* [T] **1** (**put** sbdy./sthg. **through**) **a** to connect (a telephone caller) by telephone: *If she's not in, can you put me through to her secretary?* **b** to make (a telephone call): *I have to put through a call to our Madrid office.* **2** (**put** sthg. ↔ **through**) to complete (a piece of work or business) successfully: *Production will start up again when these changes have been put through.* **3 put someone through it/through the mill** *infml* to give someone a severe test of courage or ability

put sbdy./sthg. **to** sbdy./sthg. *phr v* [T] **1** to ask (a question) of or make (an offer) to: *I'd like to put a question to the speaker.* **2** to test (something or someone) by (the stated means): *Let's put the matter to a vote|to a full discussion.* **3 put it to someone (that)** to suggest; invite someone to consider (that): *I put it to you that you haven't told us the full facts.* —see also **be hard put (to it) to** (HARD[2] (5))

put sbdy./sthg. ↔ **together** *phr v* [T] **1** to form by combining parts or members: *to put a team together* | *to put together a proposal* **2** [*usu. pass.*] to combine: *His share was more than all the others' put together.*

put up *phr v* [T] **1** [T] (**put** sthg. ↔ **up**) to build or raise into position: *Have you put up the tent?* | *They're putting up a new office block.* **2** [T] (**put** sthg. ↔ **up**) to fix (esp. a notice) in a public place where people can see it: *She put up the exam results.* —opposite **take down 3** [T] (**put** sthg. ↔ **up**) to increase in amount: *They've put the price up.* **4 a** [T] (**put** sbdy. ↔ **up**) to provide food and lodging for: *I'm afraid I can't put you up; you'll have to go to a hotel.* **b** [I+*adv|prep*] *esp. BrE* to get food and lodging; stay: *We'll put up at a hotel|with friends for the night.* **5** [T] (**put up** sthg.) to show, or give in a fight or competition: *They put up a lot of resistance.* | *What a coward; he didn't put up much of a fight!* **6** [T] (**put up** sthg.) to offer for sale: *She's putting her house up (for sale).* **7** [T] (**put** sthg. ↔ **up**) to supply or lend (money needed): *The plans for the new sports centre are all prepared, but someone will have to put up £50,000.* **8** [T] (**put** sbdy. ↔ **up**) to suggest as being a suitable person for a job, etc.: *Will you put Tom up for the cricket club?* (=suggest him as a member) **9** [T] (**put** sthg. ↔ **up**) *tech* to make (a hunted animal or bird) leave a hiding place —see also **put someone's back up** (BACK[1])

put upon sbdy. *phr v* [T] *esp. BrE* to be a cause of inconvenience to: *You're sure I won't be putting upon you if I stay to dinner?* —see also PUT-UPON

put sbdy. **up to** sthg. *phr v* [T] to give the idea of (doing esp. something bad): *It's not like David to cause trouble: someone must have put him up to it.*

put up with sbdy./sthg. *phr v* [T *pass. rare*] *infml* to suffer (something annoying or unpleasant) without complaining: *I can't put up with your rudeness any more; leave the room.* | *That woman has a lot to put up with.* (=has many troubles)

put[2] *n tech* the right to sell a certain quantity of something (e.g. SHARES[1] (2)) at a fixed price within a given time – compare **call**[2] ( )

pu·ta·tive /ˈpjuːtətɪv/ *adj* [A] *fml* generally accepted or supposed to be or become: *the putative father of her child*

put-down /ˈ· ·/ *n infml* words, esp. as an answer, that make someone feel unimportant or hurt; SNUB —see also PUT **down** (2)

put-off /ˈ· ·/ *n infml, esp. AmE* a pretended reason for not doing something; excuse —see also PUT **off**

put-on /ˈ·ˌ·/ n AmE infml something not intended seriously or sincerely —see also PUT **on**

put op·tion /ˈ· ˌ··/ n the right to sell an ASSET at an agreed price by a particular date

pu·tre·fac·tion /ˌpjuːtrɪˈfækʃən/ n [U] fml or tech   **1** the process of becoming putrid   **2** putrid matter

pu·tre·fy /ˈpjuːtrɪfaɪ/ v [I;T] to decay; (cause to) become putrid

pu·tres·cent /pjuːˈtresənt/ adj fml or tech beginning to decay and smell bad: putrescent fish —**-cence** n [U]

pu·trid /ˈpjuːtrɪd/ adj   **1** (esp. of an animal or plant substance) very decayed and bad-smelling   **2** infml worthless; very much disliked: That play last night was really putrid!

putsch /pʊtʃ/ n a sudden secretly planned attempt to remove a government by force

putt /pʌt/ v [I;T] (in the game of GOLF or PUTTING) to strike (the ball) gently along the ground towards or into the hole —**putt** n

put·ter¹ /ˈpʊtər/ n [(of)] a person who puts something

put·ter² /ˈpʌtər/ n (in the game of GOLF)   **1** a GOLF CLUB used in putting (PUTT) the ball —see picture at GOLF   **2** a person who PUTTS: an expert putter

put·ter³ /ˈpʌtər/ n, v AmE for POTTER²

put·ting /ˈpʌtɪŋ/ n [U] a simple game of GOLF played on a PUTTING GREEN (2) in public parks and seaside towns. Putting is popular with British people and is played esp. on holiday.

putting green /ˈ·· ˌ·/ n   **1** one of the smooth grassy areas on a GOLF course containing the hole where the ball must be played   **2** a smooth grassy area in a public park etc. with a number of holes where the game of putting is played

Putt·nam /ˈpʌtnəm/, **David** (1941–) an English film producer known esp. for the films Chariots of Fire and The Killing Fields

put·ty /ˈpʌti/ n [U] a soft pale oily substance, used esp. in fixing glass to window frames: He was **like putty in her hands**. (=very easily influenced by her)

put-up job /ˈ·· ˌ·/ n [usu. sing.] infml something dishonestly arranged in advance

put-up·on /ˈ·· ·ˌ·/ adj [F] (of a person) used for someone else's advantage: The way his neighbour always borrows things from him makes him feel put-upon. —see also PUT **upon**

puz·zle¹ /ˈpʌzəl/ v   **1** [T often pass.] to make (someone) feel helpless and uncertain in the effort to explain or understand something: Her illness has puzzled all the doctors. | What puzzles me is why they didn't take her advice. | a puzzling situation | You look puzzled.   **2** [I+prep, esp. **about, over, as to**] to make a great effort of the mind in order to find the answer to a question: I've been puzzling over all the figures, trying to find what happened to the missing money.
   puzzle sthg. ↔ **out** phr v [T] to find the answer to (a problem) by thinking hard: I'm trying to puzzle out the meaning of his words. [+wh-] We finally puzzled out how to open the box.

puzzle² n   **1** (often in comb.) a game, toy, or apparatus in which parts must be fitted together correctly, intended to amuse or exercise the mind: a crossword puzzle | a book of puzzles —see also JIGSAW   **2** [usu. sing.] something that one cannot understand or explain: We can't find what happened to him exactly — it's a bit of a puzzle.

puz·zle·ment /ˈpʌzəlmənt/ n [U] the state of being puzzled: He gazed at the strange writing in puzzlement.

puz·zler /ˈpʌzlər/ n infml a person or thing that puzzles one: That last question was a real puzzler.

PVC /ˌpiː viː ˈsiː◂/ n [U] a type of plastic: This raincoat is (made of) PVC.

pw written abbrev. for: per week: The jobholder may earn up to £200 pw.

P.W. /ˌpiː ˈdʌbəljuː◂/ abbrev. for: policewoman

PWA /ˌpiː dʌbəljuː ˈeɪ/ abbrev. for: person with AIDS

PWR /ˌpiː dʌbəljuː ˈɑːr/ abbrev. for: pressurized water reactor; a type of NUCLEAR REACTOR

PX /ˌpiː ˈeks/ also **post exchange** fml— n **PXs** /ˌpiː ˈeksↄz/ tdmk a shop at a US military base —compare NAAFI

Pyg·ma·li·on /pɪgˈmeɪliən/ a famous play by George Bernard Shaw in which a COCKNEY woman, Eliza Doolittle, is taught to speak and behave in an UPPER-CLASS way by Professor Higgins. Pygmalion was made into a popular MUSICAL called My Fair Lady

pyg·my, **pigmy** /ˈpɪgmi/ n   **1** (usu. cap.) a member of a race of very small people in Africa   **2** a very small person or animal: a pygmy elephant   **3** derog a person with very little skill or importance: a political pygmy

py·ja·mas /pəˈdʒɑːməz‖-ˈdʒæ-, -ˈdʒɑː-/ also **jammies** BrE ‖ **pajamas**, **Pj's** AmE n [P]   **1** a soft loose-fitting pair of trousers and top worn in bed, esp. by men   **2** loose trousers tied round the waist, worn by Muslim men and women —see PAIR (USAGE) —**pyjama** adj [A] : Where are my pyjama trousers?

py·lon /ˈpaɪlən‖-lɑːn, -lən/ n   **1** a tall structure of steel bars used for supporting wires that carry electricity over land   **2** a high tower or post used as a guiding mark for aircraft   **3** tech a gateway to an ancient Egyptian temple

PYO written abbrev. for: Pick Your Own; (a sign put up at farms where people can pick their own fruit and vegetables. Food picked in this way is usu. cheaper than in the shops.)

py·or·rhoe·a, **-rhea** /ˌpaɪəˈriːə/ n [U] a disease of the flesh round the teeth, which may cause them to become loose

pyr·a·mid /ˈpɪrəmɪd/ n   **1** (in GEOMETRY) a solid figure with a flat usu. square base and straight flat three-angled sides that slope upwards to meet at a point   **2** (often cap.) a very large stone structure in this shape, used in ancient Egypt as the burial place of an important person, e.g. a king   **3** a building or pile of objects in this shape: A pyramid of stones marked the spot.

the Pyramids

Pyr·a·mids /ˈpɪrəmɪdz/ [the] the pyramids in Egypt where the kings of Egypt were buried. Many stories are told of the opening of the pyramids, often by British ARCHAEOLOGISTs, who found many important and valuable things inside.

pyramid sell·ing /ˈ··· ˌ··/ n [U] tech an unfair system by which a person buys a right to sell a company's goods and then sells part of that right to other people

Pyr·a·mus and This·be /ˌpɪrəməs ənd ˈθɪzbi/ in CLASSICAL MYTHOLOGY, a pair of lovers who killed themselves because each thought the other person was dead

pyre /paɪər/ n a high mass of wood for the ceremonial burning of a dead body: a funeral pyre

Pyr·e·nees /ˌpɪrəˈniːz‖ˈpɪrəniːz/ [the +P] a mountain range between France and Spain

Py·rex /ˈpaɪreks/ n [U] tdmk a kind of glass that does not crack in great heat, and so is used in making cooking containers: a Pyrex bowl

py·rites /paɪˈraɪtiːz‖pə-/ n [U] (usu. in comb.) a natural compound of SULPHUR with a metal, esp. iron (**iron pyrites**), found in the earth and having a shiny yellow appearance, like gold

py·ro·ma·ni·a /ˌpaɪərəʊˈmeɪniə‖-rə-/ n [U] tech an illness of the mind causing an uncontrollable desire to start fires

py·ro·ma·ni·ac /ˌpaɪərəʊˈmeɪniæk‖-rə-/ n tech a person suffering from pyromania

py·ro·tech·nics /ˌpaɪərəʊˈtekniks‖-rə-/ n   **1** [U] tech the making of bright explosive lights, as used for amusement (FIREWORKs) or as signals for ships, aircraft, etc.   **2** [P] fml or tech a public show of FIREWORKs   **3** [P] a splendid show of skill in words, music, etc.: the pianist's pyrotechnics in the scherzo —**pyrotechnic** adj

Pyr·rhic vic·to·ry /ˌpɪrɪk ˈvɪktəri/ *n* a victory in which the winner suffers such great losses that the victory is worthless (from Pyrrhus, whose army suffered heavy losses in defeating the Romans)

Py·thag·o·ras /paɪˈθægərəs‖pə-/ (582?–?507 BC) a Greek thinker and MATHEMATICIAN, known for **Pythagoras's Theorem**, a way of finding the length of the third side of a TRIANGLE with one angle of 90°

py·thon /ˈpaɪθən‖-θɑːn, -θən/ *n* **pythons** *or* **python** a large non-poisonous tropical snake that kills animals for food by winding round them and crushing them

Py·thon·esque /ˌpaɪθənˈesk◂/ *adj* humorous in a silly, strange, and SURREAL way (from the television COMEDY programme *Monty Python's Flying Circus*) —see also MONTY PYTHON

pyx /pɪks/ *n tech* a container in which the holy bread used for the Christian service of COMMUNION is kept, esp. a small round metal dish used for carrying Communion to the sick

Q

Q /kjuː/ **Q's, q's** or **Qs, qs** the 17th letter of the English alphabet

Qad·daf·i, Qadhafi /gə'dæfi ‖ -'dɑː-/ see GADDAFI

Qa·tar /kʌ'tɑːʳ‖'kɑːtər/ a country in E Arabia, whose economic life is based on oil; capital Doha; population 1,220,000 (1989)

QC /ˌkjuː 'siː/ n Queen's Counsel; (the title given, while a queen is ruling, to) a British BARRISTER (=lawyer) of high rank: *Sir John is a leading QC.* | *Sir John Smithers, QC* —compare KC

QED /ˌkjuː iː 'diː/ *abbrev. for:* (*Lat*) quod erat demonstrandum; there is the proof of my argument

QE2 /ˌkwjuː iː 'tuː/ [*the*] a large passenger ship owned by the Cunard company operating between Southampton and New York, and also taking people on sea journeys all over the world, for pleasure. The QE2 is considered to be a very comfortable and expensive way of travelling.

QPR /ˌkjuː piː 'ɑːʳ/ *abbrev. for* QUEEN'S PARK RANGERS

qr *written abbrev. for:* quarter

qt *written abbrev. for:* QUART

q.t. /ˌkjuː 'tiː/ n **on the q.t.** *infml* secret; secretly: *Don't say I told you; it's supposed to be on the q.t.*

Q-tip /'kjuː tɪp/ n AmE tdmk COTTON BUD

qu *written abbrev. for:* question

qua /kweɪ, kwɑː‖kwɑː/ *prep fml* when thought of particularly in the character of; by itself: *Money, qua money, cannot provide happiness.*

Quaa·lude /'kweɪluːd/ also **lude—** n tdmk a drug used to help people sleep

quack¹ /kwæk/ v [I] to make the sound that ducks make — **quack** n

quack² n *infml* **1** *derog* a person dishonestly claiming to have medical knowledge or skills: *a quack doctor* — compare CHARLATAN **2** *esp. BrE* a doctor

quack·er·y /'kwækəri/ n [U] *derog* the behaviour or methods of a QUACK² (1)

quad /kwɒd‖kwɑːd/ n *infml* **1** a square open place with buildings round it, esp. in a school or college **2** a QUADRUPLET

Quad·ra·ges·i·ma /ˌkwɒdrə'dʒesɪmə‖ˌkwɑː-/ n [U] the first Sunday in LENT (from Latin quadraginta, meaning 40, since Quadragesima is about 40 days before Easter)

quad·ran·gle /'kwɒdræŋɡəl‖'kwɑː-/ n **1** *tech* a QUADRILATERAL, such as a square **2** *fml for* QUAD (1)

quad·ran·gu·lar /kwɒ'dræŋɡjʊləʳ‖kwɑː-/ adj having the shape of a quadrangle

quad·rant /'kwɒdrənt‖'kwɑː-/ n **1** a quarter of a circle **2** an instrument for measuring angles, when sailing or when looking at the stars

quad·ra·phon·ic /ˌkwɒdrə'fɒnɪk◂‖ˌkwɑːdrə'fɑː-/ adj using a system of sound recording, broadcasting, or receiving in which sound comes from four different places — compare MONO¹, STEREO²

quad·rat·ic e·qua·tion /kwɒˌdrætɪk ɪ'kweɪʒən‖kwɑː-/ n *tech* an EQUATION, such as $ax^2+bx+c=y$, which includes numbers or quantities multiplied by themselves once

quad·ri·lat·er·al /ˌkwɒdrɪ'lætərəl◂‖ˌkwɑː-/ n, adj (a flat figure) with four straight sides

qua·drille /kwə'drɪl‖kwɑː-/ n a dance, popular esp. formerly, in which the dancers form a square

qua·dril·lion /kwɒ'drɪljən‖kwɑː-/ n, determiner, pron **quadrillion** or **quadrillions 1** *BrE* the number one followed by 24 zeros; 10^{24} **2** *AmE* the number one followed by 15 zeros; 10^{15}

quad·ru·ped /'kwɒdrʊped‖'kwɑː-/ n *tech* a four-legged animal —compare BIPED

quad·ru·ple¹ /'kwɒdrʊpəl, kwɒ'druː-‖kwɑː'druː-/ v **1** [T] to multiply (a number or amount) by four **2** [I] to become four times as great: *Profits have quadrupled.*

quadruple² adj, predeterminer *fml* four times as big or many: *quadruple the amount of profit* —**ply** adv

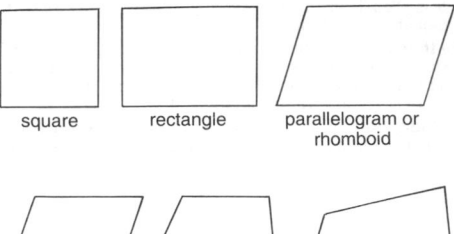

square   rectangle   parallelogram or rhomboid

rhombus   trapezium *BrE*/   trapezoid *BrE*/
            trapezoid *AmE*   trapezium *AmE*

quad·ru·plet /'kwɒdrʊplɪt‖kwɑː'druːp-/ also **quad** *infml— n* [*usu. pl.*] any of four children born of the same mother at the same time

quaff /kwɒf, kwɑːf‖kwɑːf, kwæf/ v [T] *esp. lit* to drink deeply

quag·mire /'kwægmaɪəʳ, 'kwɒg-‖'kwæg-/ n an area of soft wet ground: *After the rain, the football pitch is a real quagmire.* | (fig.) *They'd allowed themselves to get bogged down in a quagmire of unnecessary details.*

quail¹ /kweɪl/ n *quail* or *quails* [C;U] (the meat of) a small bird like the PARTRIDGE, expensive, and eaten esp. by rich people. **Quail's eggs** are also considered a LUXURY food.

quail² v [I (**with, at**)] *lit or fml* to be afraid; tremble: *I quailed (with fear) at the thought of telling her the bad news.*

quaint /kweɪnt/ adj unusual and attractive, esp. in an old-fashioned way: *a quaint old village custom* — ~**ly** adv — ~**ness** n [U]

quake¹ /kweɪk/ v [I (**with, at**)] to shake or tremble, esp. in a violent way and usu. because of fear: *He was quaking in his boots at the thought.*

quake² n *infml for* EARTHQUAKE

Qua·ker /'kweɪkəʳ/ n,adj (a member) of a Christian religious group called the Society of Friends. Quakers believe in "inner light", have no ministers or organized service, and often spend their religious services (called **Meetings**) in silence. Quakers are known for their opposition to violence and war, and are active in helping other people and in education. —see also FRIEND

qual·i·fi·ca·tion /ˌkwɒlɪfɪ'keɪʃən‖ˌkwɑː-/ n **1** [C *often pl.*] a proof that one has passed an examination and gained a certain level of knowledge or skill: *to gain a medical qualification* | *academic qualifications* **2** [C (**for**)] an ability, quality, or record of experience that makes a person suitable for a particular job or position: *Previous experience is not an essential qualification for this job.* [+*to-v*] *She has all the right qualifications to be a good manager.* **3** [C] something that limits the force of a statement: *I agree, with certain qualifications.* [+*that*] *We support the plan, with the qualification that it should be done more cheaply.* **4** [U] the act of qualifying

qual·i·fied /'kwɒlɪfaɪd‖'kwɑː-/ adj **1** having suitable knowledge or qualifications, esp. for a job: *a highly qualified engineer* [+*to-v*] *He's not qualified to teach young children.* **2** limited; not complete: *qualified agreement*

qual·i·fi·er /'kwɒlɪfaɪəʳ‖'kwɑː-/ n **1** someone who has qualified or had to qualify, esp. by passing a test, winning a match, etc. **2** *tech* (in grammar) a word or phrase, esp. an adjective or adverb, which limits the meaning of another word or phrase

qual·i·fy /'kwɒlɪfaɪ‖'kwɑː-/ v **1** [I;T (**as, for**)] to (cause to) reach a necessary standard, e.g. of knowledge, ability, or performance, or get a QUALIFICATION: *She qualified as a doctor this year.* | *Will our team qualify for the second round of the competition?* | *Her teaching experience qualifies her admirably for the job.* | *People on low incomes may qualify for a special heating allowance.* [+*obj+to-v*] *Spending a week in Russia doesn't qualify you to talk about it as an expert.* | *a qualifying match* (=the team/person that wins it will be allowed to go on to the next stage of the competition) **2** [T] to limit the force or meaning of (something stated); MODIFY: *I'd like to qualify my last statement—it was too strong.* | *(tech) Adjectives qualify nouns.*

qual·i·ta·tive /ˈkwɒlɪtətɪv‖ˈkwɑːlɪtɪtcɪ-/ *adj* of or about quality: *a qualitative judgment* —compare QUANTITATIVE — ~**ly** *adv*

qual·i·ty /ˈkwɒlɪti‖ˈkwɑː-/ *n* **1** [U] **a** the degree to which something is excellent; standard of goodness: *material of low/poor quality* | *The quality of the service here has improved a lot.* | *high-quality goods* **b** a high standard: *It is difficult to recruit teachers of quality.* | *an actor of real quality* (=a very good actor) **2** [C] something typical of a person or thing; CHARACTERISTIC: *Sympathy is his best quality.* | *She shows qualities of leadership.* | *This music has a rather sinister quality.*

quality as·sur·ance /ˈ··· ·ˌ··/ *n* [U] management of the quality of production according to a system

quality con·trol /ˈ··· ·ˌ·/ *n* [U] the practice of checking examples of goods produced to make sure that the quality of all the goods is what it should be

quality of life /ˌ··· · ˈ·/ *n* [U] the level of health, comfort, and pleasure in a (person's) life: *A government which says it is concerned about the quality of life cannot then ignore the weakest members of our society.* | *Our quality of life has already been affected by this latest nuclear disaster.*

quality pa·per /ˈ··· ˌ··/ *n* a British daily or Sunday newspaper aimed at educated readers. Quality papers are sometimes called the serious papers. They contain detailed news articles, FEATURES, and REVIEWS written in a serious style. —compare POPULAR PRESS, TABLOID and see also extra information on page 0000

quality time /ˈ··· ˌ·/ *n* [U] time spent with e.g. one's children when one is relaxed and has got nothing else to do. This is supposed to be good for parent and child, esp. because the parent is at work for most of the day: *She took comfort in the idea that her uninterrupted hour with the children at bedtime was quality time.*

qualm /kwɑːm‖kwɑːm, kwɑːlm/ *n* [(**about**) *often pl.*] an uncomfortable feeling of uncertainty, esp. as to whether something is right: *He had no qualms about cheating the tax inspector.*

quan·da·ry /ˈkwɒndəri‖ˈkwɑːn-/ *n* [(**about, over**)] a feeling of not knowing what to do: *I was in a quandary about whether to go.*

quan·go /ˈkwæŋgəʊ/ *n* -**gos** *usu. derog* (in Britain) an independent body, such as the Race Relations Board, set up by the government but having its own separate legal powers in a particular area of activity (from quasi-autonomous non-governmental organization)

Quant /kwɒnt‖kwɑːnt/, **Mary** (1934   ) an English fashion DESIGNER, popular in the 1960s, who is best known for her GEOMETRIC clothes and the MINI SKIRT

quan·ta /ˈkwɒntə‖ˈkwɑːn-/ *pl. of* QUANTUM

quan·ti·fi·er /ˈkwɒntɪfaɪəʳ‖ˈkwɑːn-/ *n* *tech* (in grammar) a word or phrase that is used with a noun to show quantity, such as **much, few,** and **a lot of**

quan·ti·fy /ˈkwɒntɪfaɪ‖ˈkwɑːn-/ *v* [T] *fml* to measure (an amount or quantity): *It is difficult to quantify the value of space exploration.* —**-fiable** *adj* —**fication** /ˌkwɒntɪfɪ-ˈkeɪʃən‖ˌkwɑːn-/ *n* [U]

quan·ti·ta·tive /ˈkwɒntɪtətɪv‖ˈkwɑːntɪteɪ-/ *adj* of or about quantity: *a quantitative difference* —compare QUALITA-TIVE — ~**ly** *adv*

quan·ti·ty /ˈkwɒntɪti‖ˈkwɑːn-/ *n* **1** [U] the fact of being measurable; amount: *It was a bad year for new films, in terms of both quantity and quality.* (=there were not many, and they were not very good) **2** [C (**of**)] also **quan·tities** *pl.* **a** an amount or number: *A large/vast quantity of beer was sold.* | *expensive cars that are manufactured in small quantities* **b** *old-fash* a large amount or number: *Quantities of food were spread out on the table.* —see also UNKNOWN QUANTITY

quantity sur·vey·or /ˈ··· ·ˌ··/ *n* a person who calculates the amount of materials needed for a future building, and what they will cost

Quan·tocks /ˈkwɒntɒks‖ˈkwɑːntɑːks/ also **Quantock Hills** /ˌ··· ˈ·ˌ·/ —[*the*+P] a range of hills in Somerset, SW England

quan·tum /ˈkwɒntəm‖ˈkwɑːn-/ *n* **-ta** /tə/ *tech* (esp. in PHYSICS) a fixed amount which varies from the next pos-

---

sible smaller or larger amount by a specific degree

quantum leap /ˌ··· ˈ·/ *n* a very large and important advance or improvement: *The concept of sixth generation computers represents a quantum leap in communications systems.*

quantum me·chan·ics /ˌ··· ·ˈ··/ [P+*sing./pl.v*] the study of ELEMENTARY PARTICLEs, which behave according to the rules of quantum theory but unlike larger objects which obey the laws of ordinary PHYSICS

quantum the·o·ry /ˈ··· ·ˌ··/ *n* [(*the*) U] a 20th century development in PHYSICS which says that ENERGY and mass, esp. at the atomic level and smaller, show properties in quantum divisions only

quar·an·tine[1] /ˈkwɒrəntiːn‖ˈkwɔː-/ *n* [S;(**in**) U] a period of time when a person or animal that may be carrying disease is kept separate from others so that the disease cannot spread: *Animals entering Britain from abroad are put in quarantine for six months.*

quarantine[2] *v* [T *often pass.*] to put in quarantine

quark /kwɑːk, kwɔːk‖kwɔːrk, kwɑːrk/ *n* **1** *tech* an extremely small piece of matter that forms the substances of which atoms are made **2** *BrE* a low fat cream cheese

quar·rel[1] /ˈkwɒrəl‖ˈkwɔː-, ˈkwɑː-/ *n* [(**with**)] **1** an angry argument, often about something not very important: *I got involved in a quarrel about the price.* | *He seems to enjoy picking* (=causing) **quarrels** *with people.* **2 have no quarrel with** to have no cause for or point of disagreement with: *I have no quarrel with what the minister says.*

quarrel[2] *v* -**ll**- *BrE* ‖ -**l**- *AmE* [I (**about, over, with**)] to have a quarrel: *They were quarrelling furiously (with each other) about whose turn it was to cook the dinner.*

▷ USAGE Compare **quarrel** and **argue**. Both words can mean "to have an unpleasant disagreement in which people feel angry": *Jack and Jill* **argued/quarrelled** *about who should get the money, and stopped speaking to each other.* However you can also **argue** with someone (=have a discussion in which there are differences of opinion) without feeling angry: *Jill and I often have a drink together and* **argue** *about modern art.*◁

quarrel with *sthg. phr v* [T] to disagree with or complain about: *I don't quarrel with what you say, but with how you say it.*

quar·rel·some /ˈkwɒrəlsəm‖ˈkwɔː-, ˈkwɑː-/ *adj derog* (of a person) likely to quarrel; often arguing — ~**ness** *n* [U]

quar·ry[1] /ˈkwɒri‖ˈkwɔː-, ˈkwɑː-/ *n* a place from which stone, sand, etc., are dug out —compare MINE[3] (1)

quarry[2] *v* [T (**from**)] to dig out (stone, sand, etc.) from a quarry

quarry[3] *n* [S] the person or animal that one is hunting or chasing: *The policeman followed his quarry into the park to arrest him.*

quart /kwɔːt‖kwɔːrt/ *n* **1** a unit of liquid and dry measure: *a quart of milk* —see TABLE 2 **2 put a quart into a pint pot** *BrE infml* [*usu. in negatives*] to do something impossible

quar·ter[1] /ˈkwɔːtəʳ‖ˈkwɔːr-/ *n* **1** [C] a fourth part of a whole; $\frac{1}{4}$: *a quarter of a mile* | *a mile and a quarter* | *A quarter* (=$\frac{1}{4}$ *of a POUND) of sweets, please.* | *a quarter of a million* (=250,000) | *The currency has been reduced to a quarter of its former value.* **2** [C] 15 minutes before or after the hour: *It's a quarter to ten‖(AmE) after ten.* (=10.15) | *a quarter to ten‖(AmE) of ten* (=9.45) | *in three quarters of an hour* (=45 minutes) | *This clock strikes the quarters.* **3** [C] a period of three months, used esp. for making payments: *I pay my rent by the quarter.* | *The company's profits rose by 11 per cent in the first quarter.* —see also QUARTERLY[1] **4** [C] (in the US and Canada) a coin worth 25 cents (=$\frac{1}{4}$ of a dollar) **5** *AmE* a period of 10 to 12 weeks into which the teaching year is divided in some American colleges and universities: *What classes are you taking fall quarter?* **6** any of the four equal periods of time into which some sports matches are divided: *At the end of the first quarter, the Lakers led 26-22.* **7** [C *often pl.*] a place or person from which something comes or may be expected: *Help is arriving from all quarters.* | *The best advice came from a most unexpected quarter.* | *This decision is seen in some quarters* (=by some people) *as a change of policy.* **8** [C] a part of a town lived in or worked in by the stated people: *the student quarter* | *the Arab quarter* **9** [C] a unit of weight

—see TABLE 2 **10** [U *usu. in negatives*] *fml* the giving of life to a defeated enemy; MERCY: *They are ferocious fighters, who neither give nor expect any quarter.* **11** [C] (*often in comb.*) a piece of meat from a large animal, including a leg: *a quarter of beef* **12** [C] the period twice a month when the moon shows a quarter of its surface: *In the first week the moon is in its first quarter, in the third it is in its last quarter.* —see also QUARTERS, **at close quarters** (CLOSE²)

quarter² *v* [T] **1** to cut or divide into four parts **2** [(on)] to provide lodgings for (esp. soldiers): *He quartered his men on families in the town.*

quar·ter·back /ˈkwɔːtəbæk‖ˈkwɔːrtər-/ *n* (in FOOTBALL²) the player who decides how the team will play and who passes the ball to the other players

quarter day /ˈ·· ·/ *n* BrE a day which officially begins a three-month period of the year, and on which payments are made

quar·ter·deck /ˈkwɔːtədek‖ˈkwɔːrtər-/ *n* [*the*] *tech* part of the highest level of a ship, used only by officers

quar·ter·fi·nal /ˌkwɔːtəˈfaɪnl‖ˌkwɔːrtər-/ *n* any of four matches in a competition, whose winners will play in the two SEMIFINALS

quarter horse /ˈ·· ·/ *n* (in the US) a strong horse bred (BREED¹) to run short races, usu. races of a quarter of a mile

quar·ter·ly¹ /ˈkwɔːtəli‖ˈkwɔːrtər-/ *adj, adv* (happening, appearing, etc.) four times a year: *quarterly payments | a quarterly newsletter*

quarterly² *n* a magazine appearing four times a year

quar·ter·mas·ter /ˈkwɔːtəˌmɑːstəʳ‖ˈkwɔːrtərˌmæ-/ *n* a military officer in charge of provisions

quarter note /ˈ·· ·/ *n* AmE for CROTCHET —see picture at NOTATION

quar·ters /ˈkwɔːtəz‖ˈkwɔːrtərz/ *n* [P] lodgings: *Married quarters are houses where soldiers live with their families.*

quarter ses·sions /ˈ·· ˌ··/ also **sessions**— *n* [P] a law court held every three months formerly in England

quar·ter·staff /ˈkwɔːtəstɑːf‖ˈkwɔːrtərstæf/ *n* **-staffs** or **-staves** /steɪvz/ a long wooden pole used as a weapon, esp. in former times

quar·tet , **-tette** /kwɔːˈtet‖kwɔːr-/ *n* esp. BrE **1** [+*sing./pl. v*] four singers or musicians performing together: *A quartet is/are playing tonight.* **2** a piece of music for four performers —compare QUINTET, TRIO

quar·to /ˈkwɔːtəʊ‖ˈkwɔːr-/ *n* **-tos** *tech* the (size of) paper produced by folding a large sheet of paper twice so as to give four sheets or eight pages in all: *In most libraries, quarto books are kept separately because they are so big.* —compare FOLIO (2), OCTAVO

quartz /kwɔːts‖kwɔːrts/ *n* [U] a hard mineral substance, now used in making very exact watches and clocks

qua·sar /ˈkweɪzɑːʳ/ *n* tech a very bright very distant object like a star, whose exact nature is unknown —compare PULSAR

quash /kwɒʃ‖kwɑːʃ, kwɔːʃ/ *v* [T] *fml* **1** to officially refuse to accept (something already decided): *The high court judge quashed the decision of the lower court.* **2** to bring to an end by force; CRUSH: *The army quashed the rebellion.*

quasi- see WORD FORMATION

Qua·si·mo·do /ˌkwɑːzɪˈməʊdəʊ/ a character in Victor Hugo's *The Hunchback of Notre Dame*, an ugly HUNCH-BACK whose job is to ring the bells of Notre Dame (a CATHEDRAL in Paris)

quat·er·cen·te·na·ry /ˌkwætəsənˈtiːnəri‖ˌkwɑːtərsenˈte-/ *n* the day or year exactly 400 years after a particular event: *1964 was the quatercentenary of Shakespeare's birth.*

quat·rain /ˈkwɒtreɪn‖ˈkwɑː-/ *n* a group of four lines which is a whole poem, or part of a poem

qua·ver¹ /ˈkweɪvəʳ/ *v* **1** [I] (of a voice or music) to shake; TREMBLE **2** [T] to say in a shaky voice — ~ **y** *adj*: *a quavery voice*

quaver² *n* **1** a shaking in the voice **2** BrE ‖ **eighth note** AmE— a musical note with a time value half as long as a CROTCHET —see picture at NOTATION

quay /kiː/ *n* a place where boats can stop to load and un-

load, usu. built of stone and usu. forming part of a HARBOUR

Quayle /kweɪl/, **John Dan·forth** /dʒɒn ˈdænfəθ‖dʒɑːn ˈdænfərθ/ **(Dan)** (1947–) VICE-PRESIDENT of the US since 1989 under President George Bush. Many Americans think that Quayle does not really have enough experience to be vice-president, and jokes are sometimes made about mistakes he has made.

quea·sy /ˈkwiːzi/ *adj infml* **1** feeling that one is going to VOMIT: *I felt a little queasy on the ship. | a queasy stomach* **2** [(about, at)] unwilling to do something; UNEASY — **-sily** *adv* — **-siness** *n* [U]

Que·bec /kwɪˈbek/ **1** a PROVINCE in E Canada. Quebec is an industrial and farming area, and the centre of French Canadian CULTURE and language. Quebec has sometimes considered whether it should separate from the rest of Canada and become a nation by itself. Some people in Canada see Quebec as a troublemaker for this reason and do not like some of the things the government has allowed Quebec to do in order to keep it as part of Canada, for example, making French the official language of business and education in Quebec. **2** capital city of Quebec province, the centre of French Canadian nationalism

Qué·bé·cois /ˌkeɪbeˈkwɑː◂/ *n* **Québécois** a person who lives in Quebec, Canada

queen¹ /kwiːn/ *n* **1** [(of)] (*sometimes cap.*) (the title of) a a female ruler of a country, usu. the daughter of a former ruler: *Queen Elizabeth the Second | She became queen in 1952.* **b** the wife of a king —see KINGDOM (USAGE) **2** [(of)] the leading female, often chosen in a competition: *a beauty queen | (fig.) London is the queen of British cities.* —see also MAY QUEEN **3** (*often in comb.*) the leading female insect of a group: *the queen ant/bee* **4 a** the most powerful piece in CHESS **b** [(of)] any of the four playing cards with a picture of a queen —see CARDS (USAGE), and see picture at CHESS **5** *derog sl* a male HOMOSEXUAL. This word is used by homosexuals among themselves, but they consider it offensive when it is said by other people.

queen² *v* [T] **1** (in CHESS) to change (a PAWN) into a queen **2 queen it** BrE *infml derog* (of a woman) to behave in an unpleasantly proud way

Queen¹ [*the*] Her Majesty the Queen; the official title of the queen of the United Kingdom of Great Britain and Northern Ireland. The Queen is the official head of state of Britain and of other countries in the COMMONWEALTH (1), but has little real political power. She has to give her official agreement (Royal Assent) to all new laws before they can actually become laws but in fact she does not have the right to refuse this agreement. —see also ELIZABETH II

Queen² a British popular music group, successful in the 1970s and 1980s, whose LEAD³ singer was Freddie Mercury

Queen Anne /ˌ· ˈ·/ *adj* **1** a style of furniture popular in the 18th century: *a Queen Anne chair | Queen Anne legs* (=legs on a table, chair, etc. that are curved) **2** a style of ARCHITECTURE known by its CLASSICAL (1) detail and red BRICKWORK (from Queen Anne of Britain (1665–1714))

queen con·sort /ˌ· ˈ··/ *n* **queens consort** (*often caps.*) (a special title sometimes given to) the wife of a ruling king —compare PRINCE CONSORT

Queen Elizabeth I see ELIZABETH I

Queen Elizabeth II¹ see ELIZABETH II —see colour picture on page 752

Queen Elizabeth II² see QE2

Queen E·liz·a·beth Hall /ˌ· ·ˌ··· ˈ·/ [*the*] a concert hall in London, part of the South Bank Arts Centre, known as a place for performances of CLASSICAL music

Queen E·liz·a·beth Is·lands /ˌ· ·ˈ··· ˌ··/ [*the* +P] a group of islands off the N coast of Canada

Queen Elizabeth, the Queen Mother see QUEEN MOTHER

queen·ly /ˈkwiːnli/ *adj apprec* like or suitable for a queen: *her queenly dignity*

Queen Mab /kwiːn ˈmæb/ the queen of the fairies (FAIRY (1)) in various old stories

queen moth·er /ˌ· ˈ··/ *n* the mother of a ruler

Queen Moth·er /ˌ· ˈ··/ also **Queen Mum** /ˌ· ˈ·/ BrE *infml*— [*the*] (1900–) **Queen Elizabeth, the Queen Mother**, mother of Elizabeth II and WIDOW of King George VI. She is popular with the British people and is seen as a caring person who gives support and sympathy to ordinary people.

Queen of She·ba /ˌkwiːn əv ˈʃiːbə/ n a person who is very rich or who spends money as if they were very rich (from the Bible story of the wealth of the Queen of Sheba who visited Solomon)

Queen of the May /ˌ··· ˈ·/ n see MAY QUEEN

Queens /ˈkwiːnz/ one of the five BOROUGHs of New York City, on the W end of Long Island —see colour map on page 1376

Queen's Bench /ˌ·· ˈ·/ also **Queen's Bench Di·vi·sion** /ˌ·· ·ˌ··/— n [the] (the name given, while a queen is ruling, to) a division of the High Court of Justice in England — compare KING'S BENCH

Queens·ber·ry rules /ˌkwiːnzbəri ˈruːlz‖-beri-/ n [the+P] the rules of fair fighting in BOXING (from the Marquess of Queensberry who made up the rules)

Queen's birth·day /ˌ·· ˈ··/ [the] either April 21, the Queen's actual birthday, or her Official Birthday, the second Saturday in June —see also OFFICIAL BIRTHDAY

Queen's Coun·sel /ˌ·· ˈ··/ n see QC

Queen's En·glish /ˌ·· ˈ··/ n [the+S] (the expression sometimes used, while a queen is ruling, to describe) good correct English as spoken in Britain —compare KING'S ENGLISH

queen's ev·i·dence /ˌ·· ˈ···/ also **king's evidence** BrE‖**state's evidence** AmE— n (often caps.) **turn queen's evidence** BrE (of a criminal) to give information in a court of law against other criminals, esp. in order to get less punishment oneself

queen-size /ˈ· ·/ adj AmE (of a bed, sheets, etc.) being larger than standard size: a queen-size mattress

Queens·land /ˈkwiːnzlənd/ a state in NE Australia, known for its sugar EXPORT and mines and also the Great Barrier Reef, a popular tourist attraction

Queens-Mid·town Tun·nel /ˌ·· ˈ·· ·ˌ··/[the] a traffic tunnel under the East River that connects Manhattan and Queens —see colour map on page 1376

Queen's Own High·land·ers /ˌ·· · ˈ···/ [the +P] a Scottish REGIMENT (=large division of men) in the British army

Queen's Park Ran·gers /ˌ·· · ˈ··/ also **QPR** infml— a London football team

Queen's speech /ˌ·· ˈ·/ [the] the speech made by the Queen at the opening of the British Parliament each year. It is prepared by the government and gives details of the government's programme for the next year, and their political ideas.

queer¹ /kwɪəʳ/ adj rather old-fash **1** strange or difficult to explain: What a queer story! | It's queer that she never answered. **2** infml slightly unwell: I'm feeling a little queer; I think I'll go home. **3** infml derog for HOMOSEXUAL **4** infml slightly mad: She's a bit **queer in the head**. **5 in ¹queer street** BrE sl in debt; in trouble over money matters — ~ly adv — ~ness n [U]

queer² n old-fash infml derog a male HOMOSEXUAL

queer³ v **queer someone's pitch** to spoil someone's plans or chances

queer bash·ing /ˈ· ˌ··/ n [U] the act of attacking people because they are HOMOSEXUALs

quell /kwel/ v [T] to bring to an end, esp. by force: "Army Quells Rebellion" (in newspaper) | The government's reassurances have done nothing to quell the doubts of the public.

quench /kwentʃ/ v [T (**with**)] **1** to satisfy (one's thirst) by drinking: She quenched her thirst with a glass of cold milk. | a thirst-quenching drink **2** lit to put out (flames, a light, etc.)

quer·u·lous /ˈkwerʉləs/ adj fml derog habitually complaining, esp. in a weak self-pitying way: querulous voices/old ladies — ~ly adv — ~ness n [U]

que·ry¹ /ˈkwɪəri/ n a question or doubt: I'd like to raise a few queries here.

query² v [T] to express doubt or uncertainty about: I would like to query the speaker's last point. [+wh-] He queried whether the law allowed this sort of procedure.

quest /kwest/ n [(**of, for**)] esp. lit a long search; an attempt to find something: the continuing quest for a cure for the disease | They travelled in quest of gold. —quest v [I (**for, after**)]

ques·tion¹ /ˈkwestʃən/ n **1** [C] a sentence or phrase which asks for information: I asked you a question and you didn't answer. | The question is: how was he killed? | In response to your last question, no, I do not intend to resign. | Answer three out of the five questions on the exam paper **2** [C] a matter that needs to be settled or dealt with; ISSUE: The government is examining the energy question closely. | It's a question of finding enough time. | At the end of the meeting, a number of important questions were still unresolved. **3** [C;U (**about**)] (a) doubt or uncertainty: There's no question about it: she did it. | This incident raises further questions about the effectiveness of airport security. | His honesty is **beyond question** (=cannot be doubted)/is **open to question**. (=may be doubted) [+that] There's no question about her sincerity/that she is sincere. (=she is certainly sincere) **4 in question** under consideration; being talked about: That is not the point in question. **5 out of the question** impossible: You can't go to the wedding in that old shirt; it's quite out of the question. **6 pop the question** infml to ask someone to marry you: It took him months to pluck up enough courage to pop the question. **7 there's no question** of there's no possibility of: There's no question of our dismissing you. (=we certainly will not) —see also LEADING QUESTION, VEXED QUESTION, **beg the question** (BEG), **call into question** (CALL¹)

question² v [T] **1** [(**about**)] to ask (someone) questions: Two men are being questioned by the police in connection with the robbery. **2** to have or express doubts about: I would never question his honesty/his ability. [+wh-] I question whether this policy will be effective. —see ASK (USAGE) — ~er n

ques·tion·a·ble /ˈkwestʃənəbəl/ adj **1** not certain: It's questionable whether she told him. **2** perhaps not true, right, or honest: highly questionable behaviour in money matters —-bly adv

ques·tion·ing /ˈkwestʃənɪŋ/ adj appearing to have doubts or want information: She gave him a questioning look. — ~ly adv

question mark /ˈ·· ·/ n the mark (?) used at the end of a sentence that asks a question: (fig.) There's a big question mark over the future of this football club. (=it may soon no longer exist) see picture at PUNCTUATION MARK

question mas·ter /ˈ·· ˌ··/ esp. BrE ‖ usu. **quizmaster** AmE— n the person who asks the questions in a QUIZ game

ques·tion·naire /ˌkwestʃəˈneəʳ, ˌkes-/ n a written set of questions which a large number of people are asked to answer in order to provide information, e.g. for a government or company

question tag /ˈ·· ·/ n TAG¹ (4)

question time /ˈ·· ·/ n [U] the period of time in a parliament when ministers answer members' questions. Question time is shown on television and can be interesting to watch because of the loud, sometimes angry discussions which take place. —see also PRIME MINISTER'S QUESTION TIME

Quet·zal·co·at·l /ˌketsəl-kəuˈætl/ a NATIVE AMERICAN nature god shown in pictures as a snake with feathers on its head

queue¹ /kjuː/ BrE ‖ **line** AmE— [(**of**)] n **1** a line of people, cars, etc., waiting to move, to get on a vehicle, to enter a building, etc.: There was a long queue outside the cinema/at the bus stop. | (fig.) There's a queue of people waiting for new houses. | (fig) policies aimed at reducing the **dole queues** (=the number of people without work) —see also **jump the queue** (JUMP¹ (14)) **2** tech a computer feature that allows similar operations of different users to be dealt with one at a time: There are four jobs in the queue. | Shut down that queue as soon as it's empty.

queue² v [I (**UP, for**)] BrE **1** to form or join a line while waiting: We queued (up) for the bus. | People are queueing to buy tickets. **2** [I;T (**up**)] tech to put into a QUEUE¹ (2): I corrected the mistakes but I haven't queued the file yet. | Your job's queued up and should print out in a couple of minutes.

queue-jump /ˈ· ·/ v [I] BrE derog to join a queue at a point in front of other people who have been waiting longer than oneself —**jumper** n

quib·ble /ˈkwɪbəl/ v [I (**about, over, with**)] derog to argue about small unimportant points or details: Don't quibble (with her) over the money; pay her what she asks.— **quibble** n : I have just one quibble (=small complaint): there's not enough salt. —**bler** n

quiche /kiːʃ/ n [C;U] a flat open pastry case filled with a mixture of eggs and cream and such things as cheese, BACON, and vegetables. In Britain and the US, there is an association of quiche with weakness, esp. in men, as in the saying "Real men don't eat quiche", used in a humorous way.

quick[1] /kwɪk/ adj **1 a** performing an action in an unusually short time; acting with speed; fast: a quick worker | He's quick with his hands. [F+to-v] She's quick to learn|quick at learning. | His opponents were quick to take advantage of his mistake. | Bring me that book, and **be quick about it**! (=hurry up) **b** done in a short time; soon finished: a quick journey | a quick drink **2** easily showing anger (in the phrases **a quick temper, quick tempered**) **3** old use living; alive: [also n, the+P] the quick and the dead **4** clever and able to learn or understand fast: a quick learner | She's very quick. —see CLEVER (USAGE) — **~ ly** adv : You got here quickly; did you come by car? | Come quickly; he's drowning! | The report was quickly prepared for publication. — **~ ness** n [U]

quick[2] adv quickly; fast: Come quick; something terrible has happened! | Everyone wants to get rich quick. | a quick-acting drug

quick[3] n [(the) U] the flesh to which the fingernails and toenails are joined: (fig.) He cut me to the quick (=upset me deeply) with his unkind remark.

quick bread /ˈ· ·/ n [U] AmE any of several kinds of bread which do not use YEAST so can be baked immediately: a selection of quick bread recipes

quick-change /ˌ· ˈ·◂/ adj [A] (of an actor) frequently changing clothes during a performance: a quick-change artist

quick·en /ˈkwɪkən/ v [I;T] **1** to (cause to) become quicker: the quickening pace of technological change **2** old use or lit to (cause to) show life: The seeds are quickening in the soil. | The recent television series has quickened (=increased) interest in this subject.

quick·fire /ˈkwɪkfaɪəʳ/ adj sharp and lively, usu. of speech or conversation

quick·freeze /ˈkwɪkfriːz/ ‖ also **flashfreeze** AmE— v [T] to freeze food rapidly so that the quality is not damaged

quick·ie /ˈkwɪki/ n infml something done or made in a hurry: a quickie divorce

quick·lime /ˈkwɪk-laɪm/ n [U] LIME[1] (1)

quick·sand /ˈkwɪksænd/ n also **quicksands** pl.— [C;U] wet sand which sucks in anyone or anything that tries to cross it

quick·sil·ver /ˈkwɪkˌsɪlvəʳ/ n [U] old use for MERCURY

quick·step /ˈkwɪkstep/ n (music for) a dance with fast steps

quick-wit·ted /ˌ· ˈ···◂/ adj clever; quick to understand and take action

quid /kwɪd/ n quid BrE infml **1** a pound in money; £1: She earns at least 200 quid a week. **2 to be quids in** to be in a fortunate position: If you can sell your car for the same price as you bought it, you'll be quids in.

quid pro quo /ˌkwɪd prəʊ ˈkwəʊ/ n quid pro quos [(for)] Lat something given or received in exchange for something else: We let them have a discount on purchases as a quid pro quo for the use of their computer.

qui·es·cent /kwiˈesənt, kwaɪ-/ adj fml at rest; in a state of inactivity, esp. one that will not last — **~ ly** adv —**cence** n [U]

qui·et[1] /ˈkwaɪət/ adj **1** with little noise: a quiet voice | Be quiet! I'm telephoning. | The latest model has a new quieter engine. **2** without unwanted activity or excitement; untroubled; calm: a quiet life | The situation at the border is fairly quiet at the moment. (=without fighting, shooting, etc.) **3** not attracting attention: Can I have a quiet word with you? | her quiet confidence **4 All Quiet on the Western Front** the title of a book about the First World War. The phrase is now sometimes used humorously when talking about a period of calm and peace during an argument. — **~ ly** adv — **~ ness** n [U]

quiet[2] n [U] **1** the state of being quiet; quietness: Calm down, children; give your father some **peace and quiet**.

2 on the quiet infml without telling anyone; secretly

qui·et·en /ˈkwaɪətn/ BrE ‖ **quiet** AmE— v **1** [I;T (DOWN)] to (cause to) become quiet: The children were shouting, but they soon quietened down. **2** [T] to make (fears, worries, etc.) less severe; ALLAY

qui·et·is·m /ˈkwaɪətɪzəm/ n [U] **1** a religious system which teaches that one should give up all desires, and gain peace by thinking quietly about God and holy things **2** often derog calm acceptance of things as they are, without any effort to change them: political quietism —**ist** n

qui·e·tude /ˈkwaɪətjuːd‖-tuːd/ n [U] fml calmness; stillness

qui·e·tus /kwaɪˈiːtəs, kwiˈeɪtəs‖kwaɪˈiːtəs/ n [usu. sing.] lit or fml rare **1** death, or the act which brings it **2** the settlement of something by bringing it to an end: She gave the false rumour its quietus.

quiff /kwɪf/ n BrE the part of a man's hairstyle where the hair stands up at the front over the forehead

quill /kwɪl/ n **1** a bird's feather, esp. a long stiff one in the wing or tail **2** also **quill pen** /ˌ· ˈ·/— a pen made from this, used in former times **3** a sharp pointed growth on some animals —see picture at PORCUPINE

quilt /kwɪlt/ n a cloth cover for a bed filled with soft warm material such as feathers: a patchwork quilt —see also CONTINENTAL QUILT

quilt·ed /ˈkwɪltɪd/ adj made with cloth containing soft material with stitching across it: a quilted housecoat

quilting bee /ˈ··· ˌ·/ n AmE old-fash a group of women who get together to make QUILTs

quin /kwɪn/ BrE ‖ **quint** /kwɪnt/ AmE— n infml for QUINTUPLET

quince /kwɪns/ n a hard fruit related to the apple, used esp. for making jelly

quin·ine /ˈkwɪniːn‖ˈkwaɪnaɪn/ n [U] a drug used for treating fevers, esp. MALARIA

quinine wa·ter /ˈ··· ˌ··/ n [U] AmE TONIC WATER

Quin·qua·ges·i·ma /ˌkwɪŋkwəˈdʒesɨmə/ n [U] tech the Sunday before Lent (from Latin quinquaginta, meaning 50, since Quinquagesima is about 50 days before Easter)

quin·tes·sence /kwɪnˈtesəns/ n [the+S+of] fml the perfect type or example: John is the quintessence of good manners. —**sential** /ˌkwɪntɨˈsentʃəl◂/ adj : This film is the quintessential horror movie. —**sentially** adv

quin·tet , -tette /kwɪnˈtet/ n **1** [+sing./pl. v] five singers or musicians performing together: A quintet is/are playing tonight. **2** a piece of music for five performers — compare QUARTET, SEXTET

quin·tu·plet /ˈkwɪntjʊplɨt, kwɪnˈtjuːp-‖kwɪnˈtʌp-/ also **quin** BrE ‖ **quint** AmE— n [usu. pl.] any of five children born of the same mother at the same time

quip[1] /kwɪp/ n a clever amusing remark made without planning it in advance

quip[2] v -pp- [I] to make a quip

quire /kwaɪəʳ/ n 24 sheets of paper —compare REAM[1] (1)

quirk /kwɜːk‖kwɜːrk/ n **1** a strange happening or accident: By some quirk of fate the two of us were on the same train. **2** a strange little habit or part of a person's character; FOIBLE: One of his quirks is that he refuses to travel by train. — **~ y** adj — **~ ily** adv — **~ iness** n [U]

quis·ling /ˈkwɪzlɪŋ/ n derog someone who helps an enemy country that has taken control of his/her own country (from Vidkun Quisling, a Norwegian politician who helped the Germans in Norway during the Second World War)

quit[1] /kwɪt/ v quit (also **quitted** BrE) present participle **quitting 1** [I;T] infml to stop (doing something) and leave: I've quit my job. [+v-ing] I've quit working. | I'd had enough, so I quit. **2** [T] old use to leave (a place)

quit[2] adj [F+of] becoming rare finished with; free of: We're quit of all our difficulties.

quite /kwaɪt/ predeterminer, adv **1** completely; perfectly: quite different | I'm not quite ready to go. | "Are you ready?" "Not quite." | You're quite right. | If you want to go, that's quite all right with me. | not quite all|enough|so much | It's quite the best thing in the area. | I just don't know what to say. | (shows annoyance) If you've quite finished interrupting, perhaps I can continue. **2** esp. BrE to some degree; rather: quite a good story | quite small | quite a lot of people | It takes quite a|some time. | It was *quite good, but not perfect.* **3** *esp. BrE* (used as an answer) I agree; that's true: *"It's unreasonable to expect any improvement at this stage." "Quite (so)."* **4** *AmE* very: *That meal was quite good.* **5 quite a/an** (*esp. AmE*) *often apprec* an unusual; an above average: *That was quite a party/quite some party.* (=it was unusually noisy or nice or long or wild) | *She's quite a girl.* **6 quite something** *infml* unusual, esp. very good: *It's quite something to be made a government minister at the age of 29: Criticism and Praise, Tentativeness*

▷ USAGE In American English, **quite** can be used to mean "very" in sentences where in British English it means "fairly": *That dress is* **quite** *nice* means "very nice" in American English and "fairly nice" in British English. —see also FAIRLY (USAGE)◁

quits /kwɪts/ *adj* [F (**with**)] *infml* back on an even level with someone after an argument, after repaying money which is owed, etc.: *Now we're quits.* | *I'm quits with him.* | *Give me £5 and we'll* **call it quits**. (=agree that nothing more is owed) —see also **double or quits** (DOUBLE[2])

quit·tance /ˈkwɪtəns/ *n law* a statement freeing someone from repayment of money or from performing a duty

quit·ter /ˈkwɪtər/ *n infml derog* a person who lacks the courage to finish things when they meet difficulties

quiv·er[1] /ˈkwɪvər/ *v* [I (**with, at**)] to make a slight trembling movement, esp. from fear or excitement: *I quivered (with fear) at the sound.* | *Her voice was quivering with anger.* —**quiver** *n* : *I felt a quiver of excitement.*

quiver[2] *n* a container for carrying ARROWS

qui vive /ˌkiː ˈviːv/ *n Fr* **on the qui vive** *infml* watchful; careful to notice

quix·ot·ic /kwɪkˈsɒtɪk‖-ˈsaː-/ *adj* trying to do the impossible, often so as to help others, while getting oneself into danger (from Don Quixote, HERO of the NOVEL *Don Quixote de la Mancha*): *His behaviour was very quixotic.* —see also DON QUIXOTE — ~**ally** /kli/ *adv*

quiz[1] /kwɪz/ *n* **-zz-** **1** a competition or game in which competitors have to answer questions: *a TV quiz show* **2** *esp. AmE* a short examination: *The teacher gave us a quiz at the end of the lesson.*

quiz[2] *v* **-zz-** [T (**about**)] to ask questions of (someone), esp. repeatedly: *He quizzed me about where I'd been last night.*

quiz·mas·ter /ˈkwɪzmɑːstər‖-mæ-/ *n esp. AmE for* QUESTION MASTER

quiz·zi·cal /ˈkwɪzɪkəl/ *adj* (of a smile or look) suggesting that one is asking a question without saying anything or that one is laughing at the other person: *a quizzical glance* —~**cally** /kli/ *adv*

quod /kwɒd‖kwɑːd/ *n* [(**in**) U] *BrE old-fash sl* a prison

quoit /kwɔɪt, kɔɪt/ *n* a ring that is thrown over a small upright post in a game (**quoits**) often played on ships

quon·dam /ˈkwɒndəm, -dæm‖ˈkwɑːn-/ *adj* [A] *pomp* (at) one time; former: *a quondam friend*

Quon·set hut /ˈkwɒnset ˌhʌt‖ˈkwɑːn-/ *n AmE tdmk* a large shelter with a round roof made of iron sheets —compare NISSEN HUT

quo·rate /ˈkwɔːrɪt/ *adj tech* (of a meeting) having a quorum present —opposite **inquorate**

Quorn /kwɔːn‖kwɔːrn/ *n* [U] *BrE tdmk* a vegetable PROTEIN used in cooking, esp. by non-meat eaters, instead of meat

quo·rum /ˈkwɔːrəm/ *n* a stated number of people, without whom a meeting cannot be held: *As soon as John arrives we will have a quorum, and the meeting can begin.*

quo·ta /ˈkwəʊtə/ *n* [(**of**)] a number or amount that has been officially fixed as someone's share, e.g. of goods that must be produced, people that can be allowed in a place, etc.: *The factory has fulfilled its production quota.* | *The university has exceeded its quota of science students.*

quo·ta·ble /ˈkwəʊtəbəl/ *adj* worthy of being quoted: *He uttered the very quotable remark "Never...have so many owed so much to so few".* —**bility** /ˌkwəʊtəˈbɪlɪti/ *n* [U]

quo·ta·tion /kwəʊˈteɪʃən/ *n* **1** [C] also **quote** *infml*— a sentence or phrase taken from a work of literature or other piece of writing and repeated, esp. in order to prove a point or support an argument **2** [U] the act of quoting **3** [C] also **quote** *infml*— the calculated cost of a piece of work: *They gave me a quotation for mending the roof.* (=told me how much it would cost) —compare ESTIMATE[2] (2)

quotation mark /·ˈ·· ·/ also **inverted comma**– *n* either of a pair of marks (" ") or (' ') showing the beginning and end of words quoted —see picture at PUNCTUATION MARK

quote[1] /kwəʊt/ *v* **1** [I (**from**);T] to repeat in speech or writing the words of (a person, a book, etc.): *She asked the newspaper reporter not to quote her remark.* | *The president was quoted as saying that he would not stand for re-election.* | *She quoted (from) the report to support her point.* | *Don't quote me on this* (=don't publicly repeat what I am saying), *but I think the company is in serious difficulties.* **2** [T] to mention (an example) to add force to one's argument: *She quoted several cases of unjust imprisonment.* **3** [T] to state (a price), e.g. for services offered: *He quoted £100 for mending the roof.* | *The company's shares are currently quoted at 84 pence.* —compare ESTIMATE[1] (2)

quote[2] *n infml* **1** a QUOTATION (1,3) **2 in quotes** in quotation marks

quote[3] *adv* (used in speech to show that one is starting to quote): *The figures given are (quote) "not to be trusted" (unquote), according to this writer.*

quoth /kwəʊθ/ *v* **quoth I/he/she** *old use* I/he/she said: *"Here shall I stay for ever" quoth the magic bird.*

quo·tid·i·an /kwəʊˈtɪdiən/ *adj* [A] *old use or fml* daily: *quotidian duties*

quo·tient /ˈkwəʊʃənt/ *n* a number which is the result when one number is divided by another

Qu·r'an /kɔːˈrɑːn, kə-‖kəˈræn, -ˈrɑːn/ *n* [*the*] the KORAN

q.v. *abbrev. for:* (*Lat*) quod vide; (used for telling readers to look in another place in the same book to find some thing out)

qwert·y /ˈkwɜːti‖ˈkwɜːrti/ *adj BrE* (of the KEYBOARD of a TYPEWRITER or computer) of the ordinary sort, whose top line begins with the letters Q, W, E, R, T, and Y

R

R /ɑːʳ/ **R's, r's** *or* **Rs, rs** **1** the 18th letter of the English alphabet **2** *AmE* (of a film) which children under 17 may not see except with an adult **3 unless there is an R in the month** except during the winter months (used when saying that certain foods should only be eaten during the winter months) —see also THREE R'S

R **1** *abbrev. for:* royal, as in R.A.F. **2** *written abbrev. for:* (on a map) river **3** *abbrev. for:* REX *or* REGINA: *Elizabeth R*

RA /ˌɑːr ˈeɪ/ *abbrev. for:* **1** REAR ADMIRAL **2** ROYAL ACADEMY **3** ROYAL ARTILLERY

RAA /ˌɑːr eɪ ˈeɪ/ *abbrev. for:* ROYAL ACADEMY OF ARTS

Ra·bat /rəˈbɑːt/ the capital city of Morocco, on the Atlantic coast

rab·bi /ˈræbaɪ/ *n* a Jewish priest —see FATHER (USAGE)

rab·bin·i·cal /rəˈbɪnɪkəl/ *adj* of or being the writings, teaching, etc., of Jewish religious leaders and teachers

rabbit

hare   rabbit

rab·bit¹ /ˈræbɪ̣t/ *n* **1** [C] a common small long-eared animal that lives in a BURROW (=a hole it makes in the ground), and which is often kept as a pet. In the past some country people used to carry a rabbit's foot with them because they thought it would bring them luck. Rabbits are also known for producing large numbers of young very quickly and jokes are sometimes made about this. —compare HARE¹ **2** [U] the fur or meat of this animal **3** [C] *BrE infml* someone who plays a game badly: *I'm just a rabbit at tennis.*

rabbit² *v* **-tt-** *or* **-t-** [I (ON)] *infml derog, esp. BrE* to talk continuously, esp. in an uninteresting or complaining way: *He keeps rabbitting (on) about his health.*

rabbit ears /ˈ··· ·/ *n* [P] *AmE* (a plastic holder with) two movable rods in the shape of a V which sit on top of a television set and are connected to it by a wire. They serve as an AERIAL¹: *We don't get very good reception with these rabbit ears.*

rabbit hole /ˈ··· ·/ *n* a hole where a rabbit lives. In the story of *Alice's Adventures in Wonderland*, Alice goes down a rabbit hole and finds herself in a strange place where many surprising things happen. —see also ALICE IN WONDERLAND

rabbit hutch /ˈ··· ·/ *n* a wooden cage for pet rabbits

rabbit punch /ˈ··· ·/ *n* a quick blow on the back of the neck

rabbit war·ren /ˈ··· ˌ··/ *n* an area where wild rabbits live in their BURROWs (=holes): *The old city is a real rabbit warren.* (=consists of many narrow winding streets)

rab·ble /ˈræbəl/ *n* **1** [C+*sing./pl. v*] a noisy disorderly crowd of people; MOB **2** [*the*+S] *derog* the lower classes; the common people

rabble-rous·ing /ˈ··· ˌ··/ *adj* (of a speaker or speech) exciting people to hatred and violence: *a rabble-rousing speech* —**rabble-rouser** *n*

Rab·e·lais /ˈræbəleɪ/, **Fran·çois** /ˈfrɒnswɑːǁfrɑːnˈswɑː/ (1490–1553) a French writer whose books *Gargantua* and *Pantagruel* contain a mixture of often sexual humour, good sense, and sharp SATIRE

Ra·be·lai·si·an /ˌræbəˈleɪziən◂, -ʒən◂/ *adj* (of stories, writings, etc.) full of jokes about sex and the body that are shocking but harmless, like the work of the French writer Rabelais: *Rabelaisian humour*

rab·id /ˈræbɪ̣d/ *adj* **1** [*no comp.*] *tech* suffering from rabies:

a rabid dog **2** *derog* (of people or their opinions) violently and unreasoningly keen; fanatical (FANATIC): *a rabid Tory*

ra·bies /ˈreɪbiːz/ also **hydrophobia** *tech—* *n* [U] a disease of certain animals, including humans, passed on by the bite of an infected animal and causing madness and death

Ra·bin /ræˈbiːn/, **Itz·hak** /ˈjɪtshɑːk/ (1922–   ) an Israeli soldier and politician who became PRIME MINISTER in 1992

RAC /ˌɑːr iː ˈsiː/ [*the*] Royal Automobile Club; a British organization for car owners which repairs or moves cars that have broken down: *I joined the RAC at the weekend.*

rac·coon, **racoon** /rəˈkuːn, ræ-ǁræ-/ also **coon** *AmE infml—* *n* **1** [C] a small meat-eating North American animal with a long black-ringed tail **2** [U] the thick fur of this animal: *a raccoon coat*

race¹ /reɪs/ *n* **1** [(against, between, with)] a competition in speed: *to have/run/lose/win a race* | *a ten-mile race* | *a boat race* | *a horse race* | (fig.) *a race against time* (=an attempt to complete something before it is too late) **2** *tech or lit* a strong flow of water: *A mill-race is the stream of water driving a water-mill.* —see also ARMS RACE, RAT RACE

race² *v* **1** [I;T] to compete in a race (against): *She's a very good swimmer and often races.* | *I'll race you to the end of the road.* **2** [I;T+*obj*+*adv/prep*] to (cause to) move or go very fast; RUSH: *He came racing across the road.* | *We raced the sick woman to hospital.* | *We really had to race to get the work finished in time.* | (fig.) *The holidays raced by.* —see RUN (USAGE) **3** [T] to cause (an animal or vehicle) to run a race: *My horse has hurt his foot so I can't race him.* **4** [I] (of an engine) to run too fast, esp. because the machine that it drives is disconnected

race³ *n* **1** [C] any of the main groups into which human beings can be divided according to their physical type: *the black/white/brown races* **2** [U] the fact of belonging to one of these groups: *The law forbids discrimination on the grounds of race or religion.* | *race relations* (=relations between different races) | *a person of mixed race* (=with parents who each belong to a different race) **3** [C] a group of people with the same history, language, customs, etc.: *the German race* **4** [C] *tech* a breed or type of animal or plant: *They bred an improved race of cattle.* —see also RACISM, HUMAN RACE

▷ USAGE **Race, nation, state,** and **tribe** are all words for large groups into which human beings may be divided. The largest of these groups is a **race**, a group of people of the same colour and/or physical type. A **nation** is a group of people who share a common history and usually a language, and usually but not always live in the same area: *the Native American* **nations**. A **state** is either a politically independent country, or one of the **states** making up a country such as the US: *The German* **nation** *was divided into two* **states,** *East Germany and West Germany.* A **tribe** is a social group, smaller than a **nation,** sharing the same customs and usually the same language, and often following an ancient way of life: *a wandering* **tribe** *of hunters in the Amazon forest.*◁

race car /ˈ· ·/ *AmE for* RACING CAR

race·course /ˈreɪs-kɔːsǁ-kɔːrs/ *n* **1** *BrE* a track round which horses race **2** *AmE* a racetrack

race·horse /ˈreɪshɔːsǁ-hɔːrs/ *n* a horse specially bred and trained for racing

race meet·ing /ˈ· ˌ··/ *n BrE* an occasion when horse races are held at a particular place

race norm·ing /ˈreɪs ˌnɔːmɪŋǁ-ɔːr-/ *n* [U] *BrE* the practice of giving people of different races equal chances by giving employment, HIGHER EDUCATION, etc. to a certain number of each race according to their relative numbers in the society

rac·er /ˈreɪsəʳ/ *n* an animal bred and trained for racing, or a vehicle planned for use in races

race re·la·tions /ˈ· ·ˌ··/ *n* [P] relations between people of different racial origin in a country. Britain has many different racial groups, including Indians, Pakistanis, and West Indians. Their interests are looked after by the Commission for Racial Equality. The US also has many different racial groups, including blacks, Hispanics, and Asians, as well as whites. Race relations, esp. in the large cities, are often a problem.

Race Re·la·tions Act /ˌ· ·ˈ·· ˌ·/ [the] an Act of Parliament passed in 1976 to protect the legal rights of racial minorities (MINORITY) in Britain and to make sure that people are treated fairly whatever their colour, race, or nationality —see also COMMISSION FOR RACIAL EQUALITY

rac·es /ˈreɪsɪz/ n [the+P] a race meeting: *a day at the races*

race·track /ˈreɪs-træk/ n a track round which runners, cars, horses, etc., race

Rach·man·i·noff /rækˈmænɪnɒf‖rɑːkˈmɑːnɪnɔːf/, **Ser·gei Was·sil·ie·vitch** /ˈseəgeɪ væˈsɪləvɪtʃ‖seərˈgeɪ-/ (1873–1943) Russian COMPOSER, best known for his piano CONCERTOS and symphonies (SYMPHONY)

ra·cial /ˈreɪʃəl/ adj **1** of or connected with a person's race: *racial pride/customs* **2** existing or happening between different races of people: *racial violence/harmony/segregation*

racial dis·crim·i·na·tion /ˌ·· ···ˈ··/ n [U] the unfair treatment of people because of their race. Racial discrimination is illegal in Britain and the US, and people and companies can be PROSECUTEd (=brought before a court of law) for practising it. Racial discrimination can be difficult to prove, however, as it can be very SUBTLE (=existing, but hard to recognize). —see also COMMISSION FOR RACIAL EQUALITY, RACE RELATIONS ACT

racial en·gi·neer·ing /ˌ·· ··ˈ··/ n BrE [U] the practice of doing things to give people of different races in a society equal chances in employment, education, etc. — compare AFFIRMATIVE ACTION

racial e·qual·i·ty /ˌ·· ·ˈ···/ n [U] the state in which all the races in a society have the same chances of employment, education, etc.

ra·cial·is·m /ˈreɪʃəlɪzəm/ n BrE [U] RACISM —-ist n, adj

ra·cial·ly /ˈreɪʃəli/ adv from the point of view of race: *a racially mixed population*

Ra·cine /ræˈsiːn/, **Jean** /ʒɒn‖ʒɑːn/ (1639–99) a French writer for the theatre, noted for his powerful plays based on CLASSICAL MYTHOLOGY and history

rac·ing /ˈreɪsɪŋ/ adj [A] **1** used for racing in competitions: *a racing car* | *a racing pigeon* **2** interested in or concerned with racing: *a racing club* —see also FLAT RACING

racing car /ˈ·· ·/ BrE ‖ **racecar** AmE

ra·cis·m /ˈreɪsɪzəm/ n [U] **1** the belief that racial differences between people are the main influence on their characters and abilities, and esp. that one's own race is the best **2** dislike or unfair treatment of people based on this belief —compare XENOPHOBIA —-**cist** n, adj : *racist policies* | *a racist attack*

racks

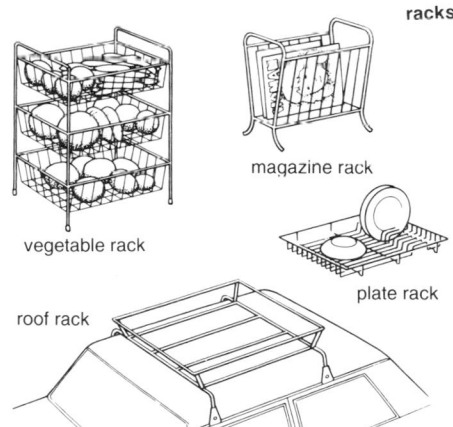

vegetable rack

magazine rack

roof rack

plate rack

rack¹ /ræk/ n **1** [C] (*often in comb.*) a frame or shelf with bars, hooks, etc., for holding things: *Wash the dishes then put them in the plate rack to dry.* —see also LUGGAGE RACK, ROOF RACK **2** [the] an instrument formerly used to TORTURE people (=to cause them great pain) by stretching their bodies **3** [C] a part of a machine consisting of a bar with teeth on one edge, moved along by a PINION (=a wheel with teeth round its edge) **4 on the rack** suffering from severe pain or anxiety

rack² v [T] **1** [(by, with)] to cause great pain or anxiety to; TORMENT: *He was racked with pain/by doubts.* **2 rack one's brains** to think very deeply or for a long time: *I really had to rack my brains to remember his name.*

rack sthg ↔ **up** phr v AmE infml **1** to gain (points, etc.) in a competition **2** to hurt; INJURE: *I've racked up my knee, so I can't play.*

rack³, wrack n [U] **rack and ruin** a ruined state, esp. of a building, caused by lack of care: *The house was unoccupied for several years and went to rack and ruin/is in rack and ruin.*

rack⁴, wrack n [C;U] lit (a) floating cloud

rack·et¹, racquet /ˈrækɪt/ n an instrument consisting of a network usu. of nylon stretched in a frame with a handle, used for hitting the ball in games such as tennis — see also RACKETS and see picture at TENNIS

racket² n infml **1** [S] a loud noise: *Stop making such a racket! I can't sleep.* **2** [C] **a** dishonest way of getting money, for example by threatening people or selling them goods which are useless or illegal: *a drugs racket* **b** humor any business or trade —see also PROTECTION RACKET

rack·e·teer /ˌrækɪˈtɪəʳ/ n derog someone who works a RACKET² (2a): *Al Capone was a famous racketeer in Chicago.*

rack·ets , racquets /ˈrækɪts/ n [U] a fast ball game for two or four players, played with rackets and a hard ball in an enclosed court that is smaller than for SQUASH² (2)

Rack·ham /ˈrækəm/, **Arthur** (1867–1939) an English artist who drew pictures for books, esp. fairy stories

rac·on·teur /ˌrækɒnˈtɜːʳ‖-kɑːn-/ n someone who is good at telling stories in an interesting and amusing way

ra·coon /rəˈkuːn, ræ-‖ræ-/ n a RACCOON

rac·quet /ˈrækɪt/ n a RACKET¹

racquetball

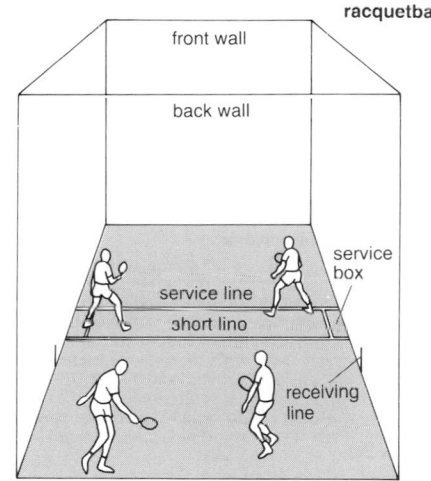

front wall

back wall

service box

service line

short line

receiving line

see also picture at squash

rac·quet·ball /ˈrækɪtbɔːl/ n [U] a game played in a four-walled court by two or four people following the rules of HANDBALL but using a short-handled RACKET¹. It is popular esp. in the US. —compare SQUASH

rac·quets /ˈrækɪts/ n [U] RACKETS

rac·y /ˈreɪsi/ adj (of speech or writing) amusing, full of life, and perhaps dealing with sex: *racy stories* —-**ily** adv —-**iness** n [U]

RADA /ˈrɑːdə/ Royal Academy of Dramatic Art; a school in London for people who want to become actors

ra·dar /ˈreɪdɑːʳ/ n [U] a method of finding the position of solid objects by receiving and measuring the speed of radio waves returning from them: *There are enemy aircraft on the radar screen.*

radar trap /ˈ·· ·/ n a method, using radar, employed by police to catch motorists who are driving faster than the legal speed

ra·di·al¹ /ˈreɪdiəl/ adj arranged like a wheel; with bars, lines, etc., coming from the centre — **~ly** adv

radial² also **radial tyre** /ˌ…ˈ·/— n a car tyre with cords inside the rubber that go across the edge of the wheel rather than along it, so as to give better control —compare CROSS-PLY

ra·di·ant /ˈreɪdiənt/ adj 1 [A] sending out light or heat in all directions; shining: the radiant sun 2 [(with)] (of a person or his/her appearance) showing love and happiness: her radiant face | She was radiant with joy. 3 [A] tech sent out by radiation: radiant heat — **~ly** adv **—ance** n [C;U]

ra·di·ate /ˈreɪdieɪt/ v [T] to send out (light or heat) in all directions: (fig.) She radiated happiness/confidence.
radiate from sthg. phr v [T no pass.] to come out or spread in all directions from: A system of roads radiates from the town centre.

ra·di·a·tion /ˌreɪdiˈeɪʃən/ n 1 [U] the radiating of heat, light, etc. 2 [C] something which is radiated: This apparatus produces harmful radiations. 3 [U] RADIOACTIVITY (2): an escape of low-level radiation from the nuclear power plant

radiation sick·ness /ˌ…ˈ·ˌ…/ n [U] sickness that results from strong radiation (3), marked by NAUSEA, vomiting (VOMIT¹) and hair and teeth loss

ra·di·a·tor /ˈreɪdieɪtəʳ/ n 1 an apparatus, esp. one consisting of pipes with steam or hot water passing through them, used for heating buildings —see picture at LIVING ROOM 2 an apparatus which keeps the engine of a motor vehicle cool —see pictures at CAR, ENGINE

rad·i·cal¹ /ˈrædɪkəl/ adj 1 (of a change) having wide and important effects; thorough and complete: a radical reform of our tax system | The talks are aimed at radical reductions in the level of weapons. 2 (of a person or his/her opinions) in favour of thorough and complete political change: radical views | the radical wing of the party | the radical right —compare REACTIONARY 3 AmE sl very good: a radical wave to surf — **~ly** /kli/ adv

radical² n a person who is in favour of radical changes, esp. social and political changes — **~ism** n [U]

radical chic /ˌ…ˈ·/ n [U] derog LEFT WING political opinions which are not sincere but are held because of a desire to appear fashionable

ra·dic·chi·o /ræˈdɪkiəʊ‖rɑːˈdiː-/ n [C] a variety of CHICORY with red leaves, usu. eaten in a mixture of raw vegetables. Radicchio is expensive and has become fashionable in Britain and the US.

rad·i·i /ˈreɪdiaɪ/ pl. of RADIUS

ra·di·o¹ /ˈreɪdiəʊ/ n -os 1 [C] an apparatus for receiving sounds broadcast through the air by means of electrical waves: to turn/switch the radio on/off | a transistor radio —see pictures at LIVING ROOM and at OLD-FASHIONED 2 [U] the sending or receiving of sounds through the air by electrical waves: Air traffic controllers were in radio contact with the aircraft. | a radio signal 3 [U] the radio broadcasting industry: a radio producer | a local radio station 4 **on the radio** broadcast or broadcasting by radio: I heard it on the radio. | John was on the radio again today. —see also AM, FM

radio² -oed, -oing v 1 [I;T] to send (a message) through the air by means of electrical waves: The ship radioed for help. | We must radio the message at once. 2 [T] to send a message to (a place or person) in this way: They radioed London for permission to land.

Radio 1 /ˌreɪdiəʊ ˈwʌn/ n [U] a BBC radio station which broadcasts mostly POP³ music and is listened to mostly by young people

Radio 2 /ˌreɪdiəʊ ˈtuː/ n [U] a BBC radio station which broadcasts mostly music and ENTERTAINMENT programmes and is listened to esp. by older people

Radio 3 /ˌreɪdiəʊ ˈθriː/ n [U] a BBC radio station which broadcasts mostly CLASSICAL music

Radio 4 /ˌreɪdiəʊ ˈfɔːʳ/ n [U] a BBC radio station which broadcasts programmes on news and current affairs as well as plays and arts programmes. Radio 4 is considered to be a quality station and listened to by educated people.

Radio 5 /ˌreɪdiəʊ ˈfaɪv/ n [U] a BBC radio station which broadcasts a variety of programmes

radio- see WORD FORMATION

ra·di·o·ac·tive /ˌreɪdiəʊˈæktɪv◂/ adj possessing or produced by radioactivity: a highly radioactive material | radioactive contamination

radioactive dat·ing /ˌ…ˈ……ˈ·/ n [U] AmE CARBON DATING

radioactive waste /ˌ……ˈ·/ also **radwaste** AmE— n [U] the radioactive BY-PRODUCTS from a NUCLEAR REACTOR, which are difficult to get rid of safely and are usu. buried

ra·di·o·ac·tiv·i·ty /ˌreɪdiəʊækˈtɪvˌti/ n [U] 1 the quality, harmful to living things, that some simple substances (ELEMENTs) have of giving out force (ENERGY) by the breaking up of atoms 2 the ENERGY given out in this way: Some of the workers were exposed to radioactivity.

radio a·larm /ˌ…ˈ·ˌ·/ also **clock radio**— n a clock that can be set to turn on a radio to wake someone who is asleep —compare ALARM CLOCK

radio bea·con /ˈ…ˈ·ˌ…/ also **beacon**— n a station that sends out radio signals to help planes to find their way

radio car /ˈ…ˈ·/ n a car fitted with radio for speaking to people away from the car

ra·di·o·car·bon dat·ing /ˌreɪdiəʊkɑːbən ˈdeɪtɪŋ‖-kɑːr-/ n [U] CARBON DATING

Radio Cit·y Mu·sic Hall /ˌ…ˈ… …ˈ… ·/ a large theatre in New York City, which often had shows with lots of singing and dancing —see also ROCKETTES

radio fre·quen·cy /ˈ…ˈ·ˌ…/ n the FREQUENCY of the radio waves commonly used in broadcasting

ra·di·o·gram /ˈreɪdiəʊgræm/ n 1 BrE a piece of furniture, popular esp. formerly, combining a radio and a record player 2 a message that has been radioed

ra·di·og·ra·pher /ˌreɪdiˈɒgrəfəʳ‖-ˈɑːg-/ n a person who makes or studies X-RAY photographs, esp. of people's bodies, or who treats illnesses with X-RAYs

ra·di·og·ra·phy /ˌreɪdiˈɒgrəfi‖-ˈɑːg-/ n [U] the taking of photographs made with short waves (X-RAYs), usu. for medical reasons

ra·di·ol·o·gy /ˌreɪdiˈɒlədʒi‖-ˈɑː-/ n [U] the study and medical use of RADIOACTIVITY **—gist** n

radio tel·e·scope /ˌ…ˈ… …ˈ…/ n a radio receiver used for following the movements of the stars and of spacecraft

ra·di·o·ther·a·py /ˌreɪdiəʊˈθerəpi/ n [U] the treatment of illnesses by RADIOACTIVITY **—pist** n

Radio Times /ˌ…ˈ·/ [the] a weekly magazine which gives details of programmes on radio and television

rad·ish /ˈrædɪʃ/ n a small vegetable whose red or white sometimes hot-tasting root is eaten raw: a bunch of radishes —see picture at VEGETABLE

ra·di·um /ˈreɪdiəm/ n [U] a rare shining white metal that is a simple substance (ELEMENT), is RADIOACTIVE, and is used in the treatment of certain illnesses, esp. CANCER

ra·di·us /ˈreɪdiəs/ n -dii /diaɪ/ 1 (the length of) a straight line going from the side of a circle to the centre — compare DIAMETER (1) 2 a stated circular area measured from its centre point: This tax affects every household within a ten-mile radius of the town. 3 the outer bone of the lower arm —see picture at SKELETON

ra·don /ˈreɪdɒn‖-dɑːn/ n [U] tech a RADIOACTIVE gas, usu. harmless but harmful in large amounts. Sometimes the gas will get into houses, where it is thought to cause health problems.

rad·waste /ˈrædweɪst/ n [U] AmE for RADIOACTIVE WASTE

RAE /ˌɑːr eɪ ˈiː/ [the] the Royal Aircraft Establishment; a centre at Farnborough, England, under the control of the Royal Air Force for the planning and testing of new planes

R.A.F. /ˌɑːr eɪ ˈef, infml ræf/ [the] Royal Air Force; the British airforce: He joined the R.A.F.

raf·fi·a /ˈræfiə/ n [U] a soft stringlike substance from the leaf stems of a PALM tree, used for making hats, baskets, etc.

raf·fish /ˈræfɪʃ/ adj usu. derog (of a person or his/her behaviour or appearance) happy, wild, and not very respectable; DISREPUTABLE: a raffish young man | raffish parties — **~ly** adv — **~ness** n [U]

raf·fle /ˈræfəl/ n a way of making money, esp. for some good public purpose, by selling numbered tickets, some of which win prizes: a raffle ticket | He won a car in the raffle. —compare DRAW² (2), LOTTERY

raffle² v [T (OFF)] to offer as the prize in a raffle: They're raffling (off) a colour TV.

Raf·fles /ˈræfəlz/ [the] the name of a famous hotel in Singapore, where English people stayed in COLONIAL times

Raf·san·ja·ni /ˌræfsænˈdʒɑːni/, **Ho·ja·tol·es·lam Al·i Ak·bar Hash·e·mi** /ˈhəʊdʒætɒlɪˌslɑːm ˈæli ˈækbɑːʳ ˈhæʃemi ‖ ˈɑːli-/ (1934–) an Iranian religious teacher and politician who became state President after the death of Ayatollah Khomeini in 1989

raft¹ /rɑːft‖ræft/ n 1 [C] a flat floating structure, usu. made of wood, used as a boat or as a landing place for swimmers 2 [C] also **life raft**– a small flat rubber boat that can be filled with air, for the use of passengers on a sinking ship or crashed aircraft 3 [S+of] infml, esp. AmE a large number or amount: A whole raft of people came for drinks.

raft² v [I;T] to travel or carry on a raft: They rafted (the stores) down the river.

raf·ter /ˈrɑːftəʳ‖ˈræf-/ n any of the large sloping esp. wooden beams that hold up a roof

rag¹ /ræg/ n 1 [C;U] (a small piece of) old cloth: He cleaned the machine with an oily rag|a piece of oily rag. | (fig.) I feel **like a wet rag**. (=very tired) 2 [C usu. pl.] an old worn-out garment: The beggar was dressed in rags. –see also GLAD RAGS 3 [C] infml, usu. derog a newspaper, esp. one of low quality: the local rag 4 **from rags to riches** from being very poor to being very rich: a brilliant young footballer whose talent took him from rags to riches 5 **on the rag** AmE sl having a PERIOD (4)

rag² n esp. BrE 1 an amusing procession of college students through the streets on a special day (**rag day**) or during a special week (**rag week**) each year, collecting money for CHARITY 2 old-fash a rough but harmless trick: They pushed him into the river for|as a rag.

rag³ v -gg- [T] old-fash, esp. BrE to play rough tricks on or make fun of: They ragged him about his big ears.

rag⁴ n a piece of music written in RAGTIME

ra·ga /ˈrɑːɡə/ n 1 any of the many ancient patterns of notes in Indian music 2 a piece of music based on one of these patterns: an evening raga

rag·a·muf·fin /ˈræɡəˌmʌfən/ n esp. lit a dirty young child in torn clothes

rag-and-bone man /ˌ· · ˈ· ·/ n BrE a man who goes round the streets with a LORRY or a horse and CART¹ buying things such as old clothes that people do not want

rag·bag /ˈræɡbæg/ n [(of)] often derog a confused mixture

rag doll

rag doll /ˌ· ˈ·/ n a soft DOLL made out of cloth. Rag dolls are known for being FLOPPY, and a very tired, or hurt, person is sometimes compared to one.

rage¹ /reɪdʒ/ n 1 [C;U] (a sudden feeling of) wild uncontrollable anger: His suggestions have been greeted with rage by his opponents. | He **flies into a rage** every time I mention money. | (fig.) the rage of the storm 2 [C] infml a very popular fashion: the latest rage | Dresses like this used to be **all the rage**. (=very fashionable)

rage² v [I] 1 [(about, against, at)] to be in a RAGE¹ (1) 2 to spread or continue with great force or violence: a raging storm | The disease raged through the city. | The argument over the new airport is still raging.

rag·ged /ˈræɡəd/ adj 1 also **raggedy** AmE–old and torn: a ragged shirt 2 dressed in old torn clothes: a ragged boy 3 (of work) seeming unfinished and imperfect: The musicians gave a ragged performance. 4 with uneven edges or surfaces: a ragged beard 5 **ragged edge** AmE a difficult or dangerous position: So many horrible things have happened to him recently that he feels like he's **on the ragged edge**. – –**ly** adv : raggedly dressed – –**ness** n [U]

Rag·ged·y Ann /ˌræɡədi ˈæn/ n AmE tdmk a toy DOLL made from rags. She usu. has red hair and red spots on her cheeks. The male doll which looks like this is called **Raggedy Andy**.

rag·lan /ˈræɡlən/ adj [A] (of an arm of a garment) joined with two sideways lines of sewing from the arm to the neck, instead of being sewn on at the shoulder: a coat with raglan sleeves | a raglan sweater

ra·gout /ræˈɡuː, ˈræɡuː‖ræˈɡuː/ n [C;U] Fr (a) mixture of vegetables and pieces of meat boiled together; STEW

rags-to-rich·es /ˌ· · ˈ··/ adj [A] (of a story, a CAREER, etc.) about a person who comes from a poor background and becomes very successful and wealthy: Her life is a rags-to-riches story.

rag·time /ˈræɡtaɪm/ n [U] a type of music, song, and dance of black US origin, popular in the 1920s, in which the strong note of the tune is syncopated (SYNCOPATE): a ragtime band | a song in ragtime

rag trade /ˈ· ·/ [the] infml the garment industry, esp. the making and selling of women's clothes

raid¹ /reɪd/ n [(on)] 1 a quick attack on an enemy position, not to take control of the place but to do damage: a bombing raid. | a cross-border raid | (fig., humor) The hungry children made a raid on the kitchen and took all the cakes. –see also AIR RAID, DAWN RAID 2 a sudden visit by the police, in search of criminals or illegal goods: As a result of the raid three people were charged with possessing illegal drugs.

raid² v [I;T] to visit or attack (a place) on a raid: Police raided the club. – –**er** n

rail¹ /reɪl/ n 1 [C] a fixed bar, esp. one to hang things on or for protection: Keep your hand on the rail as you climb the steps. | a towel rail 2 [C] either of the pair of metal bars fixed to the ground, along which a train runs: Passengers must not cross the rails. 3 [U] the railway: We'll travel by rail. | rail travel 4 **go off the rails** to start to behave in a strange, confused way, as if mad **b** in a dishonest or criminal way

rail² v [T (IN, OFF)] to enclose or separate (a place) with rails: They've railed off the garden.

rail³ v [I (against, at)] fml to express angry disapproval or complaint: railing against these injustices

Rail·card /ˈreɪlkɑːd‖-kɑːrd/ n a card that can be bought by certain groups of travellers, such as students and PENSIONERS and then used to buy British Rail tickets at lower prices than usual

rail·head /ˈreɪlhed/ n the end of a railway track

rail·ing /ˈreɪlɪŋ/ n [often pl.] any of a set of rails making up a fence: The dog got its head stuck between the railings. –compare BANISTER, HANDRAIL

rail·le·ry /ˈreɪləri/ n [U] fml friendly joking at someone's weakness; teasing (TEASE)

rail·road¹ /ˈreɪlrəʊd/ n AmE a railway

railroad² v [T] 1 [(into)] to hurry (someone) with unfair pressure: The workers were railroaded into signing the agreement. 2 [(through)] to pass (a law) or carry out (a plan) quickly in spite of opposition: The chairman railroaded the plan through the committee. 3 AmE to send (goods) quickly

rail·way /ˈreɪlweɪ/ BrE ‖ **railroad** AmE– n 1 a track for trains: a railway locomotive 2 also **railways** pl.– a system of these tracks, with its engines, stations, etc.: I got a job on the railway(s) as a booking clerk.

railway line /ˈ·· ·/ also **railway track** BrE ‖ **railroad** AmE– n BrE a stretch of railway going between one place and another: the London to Leeds railway line | a disused railway line

rail·way·man /ˈreɪlweɪmən/ n -men /mən/ BrE a man who works on the railways

railway sta·tion /ˈ·· ˌ··/ BrE ‖ **railroad station** AmE– n a STATION (1)

rai·ment /ˈreɪmənt/ n [U] lit clothes

rain¹ /reɪn/ n 1 [U] water falling in separate drops from the clouds; the fall of these drops: The rain fell continuously. | The crops need rain. | She went out in the rain without a coat. | **It looks like rain**. (=there will probably be rain) | a rain cloud | (BrE) It's **pouring with rain**. (=raining very hard) 2 [C] a fall of rain of the stated type: A heavy rain began to fall. 3 [S+of] a thick fall: a rain *of arrows/of questions* **4 as right as rain** *infml* in perfect health: *Jane's been ill, but she's as right as rain now.* **5 (come) rain or shine** whatever happens; whether things are good or bad: *She's always there, come rain or shine.* —see also RAINS, ACID RAIN **— ~ less** *adj*

▷ USAGE 1 Compare **rain, hail, snow,** and **sleet. Rain** is water falling from the clouds. **Hail** is rain which falls as hard, frozen drops. **Snow** is frozen rain that falls in soft, white pieces. **Sleet** is rain falling as snow but partly melted. 2 If it is raining very heavily we say it is **pouring,** but if it is raining very lightly we say it is **drizzling.** 3 A **shower** is a fall of rain that does not last very long. A **downpour** is a heavy fall of rain. A **blizzard** is a heavy fall of snow, with strong winds.◁

rain² *v* **1** [*it*+I] (of rain) to fall: *It's raining.* | *It began to rain hard.* **2** [I+*adv/prep*;T+*obj*+*adv/prep*] to (cause to) fall like rain: *Tears rained down her cheeks.* | *Their rich uncle rained gifts on the children.* | *to rain (down) insults on someone* **3 it never rains but it pours** *saying* when one thing goes wrong, everything starts to go wrong **4 rain cats and dogs** *infml* to rain very heavily **rain** sthg. **↔ off** *BrE* ‖ **rain** sthg. **↔ out** *esp. AmE— phr v* [T *usu. pass.*] *infml* to cause (an event or activity) to stop because of rain: *The game was rained off.*

rain·bow /'reɪnbəʊ/ *n* an arch of different colours that sometimes appears in the sky after rain: (fig.) *They've painted their house (in)* **all the colours of the rainbow.** (=in many bright colours)

▶ CULTURAL NOTE People think of the rainbow in connection with the Bible story of the FLOOD, in which God sent a rainbow as a promise that there would not be another great flood like the one Noah had lived through. In another old story, a CROCK (= a large container) of gold (*AmE* pot of gold) is found where a rainbow meets the ground, and phrases like "at the rainbow's end" are sometimes used in speaking of people who find (or hope to find) what they always wanted, as if by magic.◀

rainbow co·a·li·tion /ˌ·· ··ˌ··/ *n AmE* a group of people of different races who work together on social and political problems, esp. problems of CIVIL RIGHTS

rainbow guide /'·· ˌ·/ *n* a member of an association, the youngest branch of the **Guides,** for training girls aged five to seven to be independent

Rainbow War·ri·or /ˌ··· ·ʹ···/ [*the*] a ship belonging to the organization Greenpeace which is used to get information about actions which harm the environment, and to prevent them

rain check /'· ·/ *n infml, esp. AmE* a ticket which can be used another time, given to the holder of a ticket for an event (such as a game, play, or CONCERT) which is not going to take place: *Rainchecks were issued to the fans and the game was rescheduled for tomorrow night.* | (fig.) *"Can I buy you a cup of coffee?" "No thanks, but I'll take a rain-check."* (=I'll accept your invitation at another time)

rain·coat /'reɪnkəʊt/ *n* a light coat worn to keep the wearer dry when it rains

rain·drop /'reɪndrɒp‖-drɑːp/ *n* a single drop of rain

rain·fall /'reɪnfɔːl/ *n* [C;U] the amount of rain or snow that falls in an area in a certain time: *This area has (a) very low rainfall.*

rain for·est /'· ˌ··/ *n* a tropical forest with tall trees growing thickly together and with a high rainfall. People usu. think of the rain forest of South America, known for its many different SPECIES of plant and animal life. There is a lot of discussion about the destruction of the rain forest and the effect this has on the world CLIMATE, and many people feel that the rain forest must be preserved.

rain gauge /'· ·/ *n* an instrument for measuring the rainfall

Rai·ni·er /'reɪniəʳ ‖ rəˈnɪəʳ/, **Mount** a mountain in the W of Washington State, US, the highest mountain in the Cascade Range

Rai·ni·er III /ˌreɪnieɪ ðə ʹθɜːd ‖ rəˌnɪər ðə ʹθɜːrd/ (1923–) the Prince of Monaco, who married the American film actress Grace Kelly

rain·proof /'reɪnpruːf/ *adj* able to keep rain out: *The roof is no longer rainproof.*

rains /reɪnz/ *n* [*the*+P] the season in tropical countries when rain falls continually; MONSOON: *The rains have started early this year.*

rain·storm /'reɪnstɔːm‖-ɔːrm/ *n* a sudden heavy fall of rain

rain·wa·ter /'reɪnwɔːtəʳ‖-wɔː-, -wɑː-/ *n* [U] water that has fallen as rain

rain·wear /'reɪnweəʳ/ *n* [U] clothes to be worn in the rain which do not allow water through

rain·y /'reɪni/ *adj* **1** having a lot of rain: *a very rainy day/place* | *the rainy season* (=the rains) **2 for a rainy day** for a (future) time when money may be needed: *to save up for a rainy day.*

raise¹ /reɪz/ *v* [T] **1** to lift, push, or move upwards: *He raised the lid of the box.* | *I raised my hat.* | *She raised her finger to her lips as a sign for silence.* | *He raised the fallen child to its feet.* (=helped it to stand) —opposite **lower 2** [(to)] a to increase in amount, size, etc.: *to raise the rent/the temperature/someone's pay* **b** to bring to a higher level, rank, or degree: *The builders raised the ceiling by six inches.* | *He was raised to the rank of captain.* | *to raise one's voice* (=shout) *in anger* | *I don't want to raise your hopes unduly.* (=make you too hopeful) —opposite **lower 3** to collect together: *The king raised an army.* | *an appeal to raise money for victims of the disaster* **4** to produce, cause to grow or develop, and look after (living things): *I've raised five children.* | *They raise horses/ wheat.* —compare REAR² (1) **5** to mention or introduce (a subject) for consideration: *There's an important point I want to raise.* | *to raise a question/issue* **6 a** to make (a noise): *The men raised a cheer/a shout.* | *to raise the alarm* **b** to cause people to make (a noise): *Her joke raised a laugh.* **7** to cause to appear or exist: *The car raised a cloud of dust as it rushed past.* | *His long absence raised doubts/fears about his safety.* **8** *fml* to build (something high and noticeable): *to raise a monument* **9** to bring to an end (something that controls or forbids): *to raise a siege/an embargo* **10** to bring (a dead person) back to life **11** to make a higher BID than (a player in a game of cards): *I'll raise you!* **12** to get in touch by radio with: *I can't raise Melbourne.* **13 raise a number to the power of another number** to multiply a number by itself the stated number of times: *2 raised to the power of 3* (=2³) *is 8.* **14 raise Cain/the devil/hell/the roof** *infml* to become very angry: *Mother will raise hell if you wake the baby.* **15 raise one's eyebrows (at)** to express surprise, doubt, displeasure, or disapproval (at), (as if) by raising the two lines of hair above one's eyes: *There were a lot of raised eyebrows/a lot of eyebrows raised at the news of the minister's dismissal.* **16 raise one's hand to/against someone** to make a movement to hit someone —see RISE¹ (USAGE)

raise² *n AmE for* RISE² (4): *a salary raise*

rais·er /'reɪzəʳ/ *n* (*usu. in comb.*) **1** a person who raises esp. money or animals: *a fund-raiser* | *a cattle-raiser* **2** a person who causes: *A fire-raiser is someone who sets fire to buildings on purpose.* —see also CURTAIN RAISER

rai·sin /'reɪzən/ *n* a sweet dried GRAPE used in cakes, etc.

rai·son d'e·tre /ˌreɪzɒn ʹdetrə‖-zəʊn-/ *n Fr* a reason for existing

raj /rɑːdʒ/ [*the*] (*often cap.*) the period of British rule in India before 1947: *life during/under the Raj*

ra·jah , raja /'rɑːdʒə/ *n* an Indian ruler —see also RANEE

Raj·neesh /rɑːdʒʹniːʃ/, **Bag·wan** /'bɑːgwɑːn/ (1931–1990) an Indian religious man whose ideas came from a number of Eastern religions and who became well-known for owning 93 ROLLS ROYCES and encouraging his followers to have group sex

rake¹ /reɪk/ *n* **1** a gardening tool consisting of a row of points at the end of a long handle, used for making the soil level, gathering up dead leaves, etc. —see picture at GARDEN **2** any similar tool, such as one used to draw together the money on the table during a game of chance

rake² *v* **1** [I;T] to gather, loosen or level with a rake: *He raked the garden paths.* | *She raked over the soil to loosen the weeds.* | *They raked up the dead leaves.* **2** [I+*adv/prep*] to search carefully by turning over a pile of things: *I'll rake about/around among my papers and see if I can find it.* **3** [T (**with**)] to examine or fire at (an area) in a continuous sweeping movement along its whole length: *The police raked the hillside with powerful binoculars but did not see the escaped prisoner.* **4 rake someone over the coals** *AmE for* haul someone over the coals (HAUL¹ (4)) **rake** sthg. **↔ in** *phr v* [T] *infml* to earn as income (a lot of money): *He must be raking in at least £800 a week!* | *They're raking it in!*

rake sthg. ↔ **out** *phr v* [T] *infml* to find by searching: *The reporter had raked out some interesting facts.* | *I'll try and rake out something for you to wear.*

rake sthg. ↔ **up** *phr v* [T] *infml* **1** to remember and talk about (something that should be forgotten): *Don't rake up that old quarrel again.* **2** to collect together with difficulty: *Can we rake up some players for the team|enough money for the rent?*

rake³ *n old use* a man, esp. rich and of high social class, who has led a wild life with regard to drink and women

rake⁴ *n* [S] the angle of a slope: *the rake of the stage|of a ship's funnels* **–rake** *v* [I;T] : *the raked wings of an aircraft*

rake-off /'·· ·/ *n infml* a usu. dishonest share of profits: *The taxi-driver gets a rake-off from the hotel if he takes tourists there.*

rak·ish /'reɪkɪʃ/ *adj* **1** wild and irresponsible, like (that of) a RAKE³; DISSOLUTE: *He's led a rakish life.* **2** showing a cheerful informal self-confidence; JAUNTY: *She wore her cap at a rakish angle.* (=sideways on her head) **– ~ly** *adv* **– ~ness** *n* [U]

Ra·leigh¹ /'rɑːli, 'rɔː-/ a British company which makes bicycles

Sir Walter Raleigh

Raleigh², **Sir Wal·ter** /'wɔːltəʳ/ (1552?–1618) an English traveller and HISTORIAN who was a favourite of Elizabeth I. He is known as the person who introduced the potato and tobacco into Britain and who put his CLOAK over a PUDDLE so that Elizabeth I could walk over it.

ral·len·tan·do /ˌrælən'tændəʊ‖ˌrɑːlən'tɑːndəʊ/ *n, adj, adv* **-dos** (a piece of music) getting slower

ral·ly¹ /'ræli/ *v* **1** [I;T **(to)**] to come or bring together (again) for a shared purpose or effort: *Her supporters rallied to her defence when she was attacked by her critics.* | *The general rallied his tired soldiers and they drove the enemy back.* | *The rail workers have rallied support for the strike from other unions.* **2** [I] to return to a former good state, e.g. after illness or difficulty: *He soon rallied after the shock of his father's death.* | *Prices on the stock market rallied this afternoon after earlier falls.*

rally round *phr v* [I] *infml* (esp. of a group) to come to someone's help at a time of difficulty: *Her friends all rallied round when she was ill.*

rally² *n* **1** a large esp. political public meeting –compare DEMONSTRATION; see colour picture on page 950 **2** a motor race over public roads **3** (in tennis and similar games) a long struggle to gain a point, with each player hitting the ball again and again over the net **4** an act of rallying

rally³ *v* [T **(about, on)**] *old use* to make fun of (a person) in a friendly way; TEASE: *They rallied him about|on his strange appearance.*

ram¹ /ræm/ *n* **1** an adult male sheep that can be the father of young –compare EWE **2** a BATTERING RAM **3** a machine that repeatedly drops or pushes a weight onto or into something, or that uses water pressure for lifting

ram² *v* **-mm-** [T] **1** to run or drive into (something) very hard: *His car rammed mine.* **2** [+obj+adv/prep] to force

into place with heavy pressure: *I rammed down the earth round the newly planted bush.* | (fig.) *The terrorist attack rammed home the need for tighter security.* (=forced people to recognize this need) **3 ram something down someone's throat** to force an unwanted idea or plan on someone: *I hate the way he rams his political views down everyone's throat.*

RAM¹ /ˌɑːr eɪ 'em/ *abbrev. for* ROYAL ACADEMY OF MUSIC

RAM² /ræm/ Random Access Memory; a memory in a computer system, used as a temporary store for information which can be changed by the user. It can be searched in any order the user likes.

Ram·a·dan /'ræmədæn, -dɑːn, ˌræmə'dɑːn, -'dæn/ *n* [U] the ninth month of the Muslim year, during which no food or drink may be taken between sunrise and sunset. The Muslim year is based on the movements of the moon, and Ramadan takes place at different times each year.

Ra·ma·krish·na /ˌrɑːmə'krɪʃnə/ (1834–86) an Indian HINDU religious man who helped to change people's thinking by saying that all religions are of equal value because they are all different paths to God

Ram·bert Dance Com·pa·ny /ˌrɒmbeə 'dɑːns ˌkʌmpəni‖ rɑːmˌbeər 'dæns-/ [the] a BALLET company based in London and known for performing modern ballet (from Marie Rambert, dancer and teacher, who started the company in 1930)

ram·ble¹ /'ræmbəl/ *v* [I] **1** [(ABOUT, **through**, **among**)] to go on a ramble: *They rambled through the woods.* **2** [(ON, **about**)] *usu. derog* to talk or write at great length in a disordered wandering way: *The old lady was rambling (on) about her youth.* **3** (of a plant) to grow loosely in all directions: *a rambling rose* – see also RAMBLER (2)

ram·ble² *n* a (long) walk for enjoyment, often in the country: *We went for|on a ramble through the woods.*

ram·bler /'ræmbləʳ/ *n* **1** a person who rambles **2** a rose bush that rambles

Rambler a popular small car once made by the American Motor Company

Ramblers' As·so·ci·a·tion /'·· ···,·/ [the] a British association which supports ramblers and makes sure public footpaths are kept open

ram·bling /'ræmblɪŋ/ *adj* **1** *usu. derog* (of speech or writing) disordered and wandering: *a long and very rambling letter* **2** (of a house, street, etc.) of irregular shape and covering a large area: *a rambling old house*

Ram·bo /'ræmbəʊ/ *n* a character in several films played by Sylvester Stallone. He is strong and violent and is always seen fighting against evil forces, esp. COMMUNISM. Though very popular, educated people do not take him seriously: *There is no need for Rambo-style politics here.*

Sylvester Stallone as Rambo

ram·bunc·tious /ræm'bʌŋkʃəs/ *adj humor* (of a person or behaviour) noisy, uncontrollable, and full of life; BOISTEROUS **– ~ly** *adv* **– ~ness** *n* [U]

ram·e·kin /'ræmɪkɪn, 'ræmkɪn/ *n* a small container in which a quantity of food large enough for one person can be baked and served

ram·ie /'ræmi/ *n* a plant from which a type of cloth is made: *a ramie-and-cotton blouse*

ram·i·fi·ca·tion /ˌræmɪfɪ'keɪʃən/ *n* [usu. pl.] *fml* **1** a branch of a system that has many parts; part of a network: *the ramifications of a business|of a railway system* **2** any of a large number of results that follow from an action or decision; IMPLICATION: *What are the ramifications of our decision to join the union?*

ram·i·fy /'ræmɪfaɪ/ *v* [I;T] to (cause to) branch out in all directions; form (into) a network

ramp /ræmp/ *n* **1** an artificial slope that connects two levels: *Drive the car up the ramp.* **2** *BrE* a place in a road that is higher or lower than the main road surface, esp. a raised part built to force people to drive slowly **3** *AmE for* SLIP ROAD

ram·page¹ /ræm'peɪdʒ, 'ræmpeɪdʒ/ *v* [I (ABOUT, **through**)] to rush about wildly or angrily: *The elephants rampaged through the forest.*

ram·page² /ˈræmpeɪdʒ, ræmˈpeɪdʒ/ *n* [(the) S] excited and violent behaviour: *Football crowds went on the rampage through the town, breaking windows and damaging cars.* —**pageous** /ræmˈpeɪdʒəs/ *adj*

ram·pant /ˈræmpənt/ *adj* **1** (of crime, disease, wrong beliefs, etc.) widespread and impossible to control: *Sickness was rampant in the area.* | *rampant lawlessness* **2** (of a plant) growing and spreading uncontrollably **3** [after *n*] *tech* (of an animal drawn in HERALDRY) standing on the back legs with the front legs raised as if to strike: *two lions rampant* — ~**ly** *adv*

ram·part /ˈræmpɑːt‖-pɑːrt/ also **ramparts** *pl.*— *n* a wide bank of earth or a stone wall built to protect a fort or city esp. in former times

Ramp·ton /ˈræmptən/ a heavily-guarded British prison for men who have committed (COMMIT) serious crimes and are thought to be violent and dangerous

ram·rod /ˈræmrɒd‖-rɑːd/ *n* a stick for pushing the GUNPOWDER into an old-fashioned gun or for cleaning a small gun: *He may be 82, but the old general still has a back as straight/stiff as a ramrod.*

Ram·sey /ˈræmzi/, **Sir Alf** /ælf/ (1920–) an English footballer who later became a football manager and was manager of the England team when it won the World Cup in 1966

ram·shack·le /ˈræmʃækəl/ *adj* (of a building or vehicle) badly made or needing repair; falling to pieces: *a ramshackle old house*

ran /ræn/ *past tense of* RUN

ranch /rɑːntʃ‖ræntʃ/ *n* **1** (in the western US and Canada) a very large farm where sheep, cattle, or horses are bred **2** *AmE* a farm that produces the stated thing: *a fruit/chicken ranch* —see also **meanwhile, back at the ranch** (MEANWHILE) **3** RANCH HOUSE (1): *a 3-bed ranch with 2-car garage*

ranch·er /ˈrɑːntʃər‖ˈræn-/ *n* a person who owns or works on a ranch: *a cattle rancher*

ranch house /ˈ· ·/ *n AmE* **1** a house built on one level, usu. with a roof that does not slope much **2** a house on a ranch in which the rancher and his/her family live —see colour picture on page 161

ran·cid /ˈrænsɪd/ *adj* (of oily food or its taste or smell) not fresh; tasting or smelling unpleasant: *rancid butter* | *This smells/tastes/has gone rancid.* — ~**ity** /rænˈsɪdɪti/ *n* [U]

ran·cour *BrE* ‖ **-cor** *AmE* /ˈræŋkər/ *n* [U] *fml* a feeling of bitter unforgiving hatred: *Can we not conduct these negotiations without rancour?* —**corous** *adj* —**corously** *adv*

rand /rænd/ *n* **rand** the standard money unit of South Africa, divided into 100 cents

R and A /ˌɑːr ənd ˈeɪ/ [the] ROYAL AND ANCIENT

R and B /ˌɑːr ən ˈbiː/ *n* [U] RHYTHM AND BLUES

R and D /ˌɑːr ən ˈdiː/ *n* [U] research and development; the part of esp. a business concerned with studying new ideas, planning new products, etc.: *The company has a large R and D budget.*

ran·dom¹ /ˈrændəm/ *adj* without any plan, aim, or pattern: *He fired a few random shots.* | *a random choice* | *a random sample of people* (=people chosen in such a way that anyone is equally likely to be chosen) — ~**ly** *adv* — ~**ness** *n* [U]

random² *n* **at random** in a random way; aimlessly: *The people for the experiment were chosen completely at random.*

random ac·cess mem·o·ry /ˌ··· ˈ·· ˌ···/ *n* see RAM²

R and R /ˌɑːr ənd ˈɑːr/ *n* [U] *AmE* rest and relaxation; a holiday given to people in the armed forces to allow them to relax after a long time of hard work or during wartime: *a week's R and R in Seoul*

rand·y /ˈrændi/ *adj infml, esp. BrE* (of a person or his/her feelings) full of sexual desire —**iness** *n* [U]

ra·nee , rani /ˈrɑːni, rɑːˈniː/ *n* a female RAJAH or the wife of a RAJAH

rang /ræŋ/ *past tense of* RING³

range¹ /reɪndʒ/ *n* **1** [S (of)] the (measurable) limits within which variable amounts or qualities are included: *a* country with a wide range of temperature | *Several cars are available within this price range.* | *I'm afraid that high note is beyond my range.* | *a wide range of different options* **2** [S (of)] the limits within which something operates, exists, or is effective; SCOPE: *matters which lie outside the range of this inquiry* | *a medium-range weather forecast* (=covering the future, but not the distant future) **3** [S;U] the distance at which one can see or hear: *Shout as soon as she comes within range.* **4** [S (of);U] the distance that a gun can fire: *a hunting rifle with a range of 200 metres* | *He shot the rabbit at short/close/point-blank range.* | *He's still out of/beyond/in/within range (of my gun).* **5** [C] an area where shooting is practised, or where MISSILES are tested: *a rifle range* **6** [C (of)] a connected line of mountains, hills, etc.: *a high mountain range* **7** [the] (in N America) a wide stretch of grassy land where cattle feed **8** [C (of)] a set of different objects of the same kind, esp. for sale in a shop: *a complete range of gardening tools* **9** *AmE* a HOB (1) and OVEN combined together for use in a home kitchen: *a new electric range* **10** [C] an old-fashioned iron fireplace for cooking, built into a chimney in a kitchen —see also FREE-RANGE

range² *v* **1** [I+prep;not in progressive forms] to vary between limits; reach from one limit to another: *The children's ages range from 5 to 15/between 5 and 15.* | *a wide-ranging programme of reforms* **2** [I+adv/prep, esp. over;T] *esp. lit* to wander freely: *We ranged (over) the hills and valleys.* | (fig.) *Our conversation ranged over many topics.* **3** [T+obj+adv/prep] to put in position or order, esp. in lines or rows; arrange: *She ranged the goods neatly in the shop window.*

range find·er /ˈ· ˌ···/ *n* an instrument for finding the distance of an object when shooting or taking photographs

rang·er /ˈreɪndʒər/ *n* **1** the keeper of a forest or area of country, such as a NATIONAL PARK **2** (in N America) a policeman who rides through country areas to see that the law is kept —see also LONE RANGER **3** (in the US) a COMMANDO **4** an older member of the GUIDES¹ (5), aged from 14 to 19

Range Rov·er /ˈ· ˌ···/ *n tdmk* a large expensive car made by the Rover group, which can be driven on rough ground. Range Rovers are popular with wealthy farmers and upper-class people who live in the country. Many people think that a Range Rover is a STATUS SYMBOL. — compare LAND ROVER

Ran·gers /ˈreɪndʒəz‖-ərz/ also **Glasgow Rangers** *fml*— a Scottish football team based in Glasgow. There is much competition between Rangers and Celtic, the other main Glasgow football team.

Ran·goon /ræŋˈguːn/ the former name for **Yangon**, the capital city of Myanmar (Burma)

Ran·jit Singh /ˌrændʒɪt ˈsɪŋ/, **Maharaja** (1780–1839) the former ruler of Lahore, who established the Sikh kingdom of the Punjab

rank

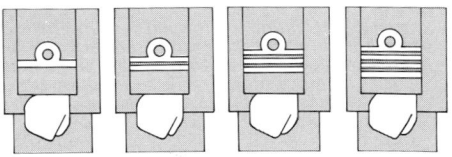

sub-lieutenant   lieutenant   commander   captain

rank¹ /ræŋk/ *n* **1** [C;U] a level of relative value, ability, importance, etc., on a scale, esp. the official position someone holds in the army, navy, etc.: *to attain the rank of general* | *He's above me in rank.* | *a writer of the* **first/front/top rank** (=among the best) **2** [C;U] (high) social class: *a person of rank* | *people of all ranks* **3** [C] a line of soldiers, policemen, etc., standing side by side **4** [C (of)] a line of people or things: *Rank upon rank of ancient elms stretched away to the horizon.* —see also TAXI RANK **5 keep/break rank(s)** (of soldiers) to stay/fail to stay in line: *The enemy broke rank(s) and ran.* **6 close ranks** (of a group of people) to join together to face difficulties: *When their business failed, the family closed ranks and worked to pay off the debts.* **7 pull rank** *infml* to use the advantage of one's higher position, perhaps unfairly: *When my assistant became obstinate I had to pull rank (on him) and insist that he obey.* —see also RANKS

rank² *v* **1** [I+*adv*/*prep*;T+*obj*+*adv*/*prep*] to have or regard as having a certain rank or relative position: *This result ranks as one of their most successful election performances of the last ten years.* | *a tennis player who is ranked third in the world* (=officially regarded as the third-best player) | *a high-ranking diplomat* **2** [T *often pass.*] to arrange in regular order: *The cups were ranked neatly on the shelf.* **3** [T] *AmE* (of an officer) to be of higher rank than: *A general ranks a captain.*

rank³ *adj* **1** (of a plant) too thick and widespread: *rank grass* **2** (of smell or taste) very strong and unpleasant: *rank tobacco* **3** [A] (esp. of bad things) complete: *He's a rank beginner at the job.* | *It was rank bad luck.* — ~**ly** *adv* — ~**ness** *n* [U]

rank and file /ˌ· · ˈ·/ *n* [*the*+*sing.*/*pl. v*] **1** the ordinary members of an organization as opposed to the leaders: *The rank and file is/are getting discontented.* | *the rank-and-file members of a trade union* **2** the ordinary soldiers who are not officers

rank·er /ˈræŋkəʳ/ *n BrE* an officer who has risen from being an ordinary soldier

rank·ing /ˈræŋkɪŋ/ *adj* [A] *AmE* (of an officer) of highest rank: *Who's the ranking officer here?*

ran·kle /ˈræŋkəl/ *v* [I (**with**)] to continue to be remembered with bitterness and anger: *Their defeat still rankles (with them).*

Rank Or·ga·ni·sa·tion /ˈ· ···ˌˈ··/ [*the*] a highly successful British organization started by Joseph Rank (1888–1972) which began in the film business and moved into hotel ownership and other profitable areas

ranks /ræŋks/ *n* **1** [P (**of**)] *pomp or humor* the stated class or group: *She's joined the ranks of the* (=become) *unemployed.* | *a brilliant speech that helped to swell* (=increase) *the ranks of his supporters* **2** *the*/*other* **ranks** ordinary soldiers below the rank of SERGEANT: *He was reduced to the ranks as a punishment for drinking.* | *an officer who has risen from the ranks*

ran·sack /ˈrænsæk/ *v* [T] **1** to search (a place) thoroughly and roughly, causing disorder: *The police ransacked the house, looking for drugs.* **2** to go through (a place) stealing and causing widespread damage: *Enemy soldiers ransacked the town.*

ran·som¹ /ˈrænsəm/ *n* **1** a sum of money paid to free a prisoner who is being held illegally: *We had to pay a large ransom.* **2 hold someone to ransom** to keep someone prisoner so as to demand payment: *The terrorists kidnapped the boy and held him to ransom.* | (fig.) *We will not allow these strikers to hold the country to ransom.*

ransom² *v* [T] to set (someone) free by paying a ransom — ~**er** *n*

Ran·some /ˈrænsəm/, **Arthur** (1884–1967) an English writer best known for his books for children, esp. *Swallows and Amazons*, about children's sailing adventures

rant /rænt/ *v* [I (ON)] *usu. derog* to talk in a loud excited way, using grand but meaningless phrases: *The priest ranted (on) about the devil.* | *He's been ranting and raving about the way they insulted him.* —**rant** *n* [U]

Ran·tzen /ˈræntsən/, **Es·ther** /ˈestəʳ/ (1940–) a British woman who produces and introduces television programmes for the BBC programme *That's Life*. More recently, she has worked with the CHARITY Childline to help children who have been abused (ABUSE).

rap¹ /ræp/ *n* **1** [C] (the sound of) a quick light blow: *I heard a rap on the door.* | *The teacher gave me a rap over the head with her pencil.* | (fig.) *The newspaper received an official* **rap over the knuckles** *from the palace for the way it reported the story about the princess.* (=angry disapproval was expressed) **2** [S *usu. in negatives*] *infml* the least bit: *I don't care a rap for him.* **3** [U] a type of POP³ music in which the words of a song are spoken in time with music with a steady beat. Rap is performed esp. by black people. **4 beat the rap** *AmE sl* to escape punishment **5 take the rap (for)** *sl* to receive the punishment (for someone else's crime)

rap² *v* **-pp-** **1** [I+*prep*;T] to strike quickly and lightly: *Someone was rapping loudly at the door/on the table.* | *She rapped her pen on the table and called for silence.* **2** [T] *BrE* (esp. in newspapers) to speak to or about with severe disapproval: *The judge rapped the police for their treatment of the witness.* **3** [T (OUT)] to say sharply and suddenly: *The officer rapped out an order.* **4** [I] *old-fash sl, esp. AmE* to talk; CHAT **5** [I] to speak the words of a song to music with a steady beat —see also RAP¹ (3)

ra·pa·cious /rəˈpeɪʃəs/ *adj fml* taking everything one can, esp. by force: *a rapacious band of robbers* — ~**ly** *adv* — ~**ness**, **-city** /rəˈpæsˌti/— *n* [U]

rape¹ /reɪp/ *v* [T] (esp. of a man) to have sex with (someone, esp. a woman) against their will. Rape is illegal in most countries. In the past in Britain, a man could not be charged with raping his wife, because he had CONJUGAL RIGHTS (=the right to have sex with his wife). However, rape within marriage is now a crime.

rape² *n* [C;U] **1** (a case of) the crime of raping someone: *a rape victim* | *to commit rape* —see also RAPIST **2** *fml* spoiling: *the rape of our beautiful forests*

rape³ also **canola** *AmE n* [U] a European plant with yellow flowers, grown as animal food and for the oil produced from its seeds

Raph·a·el /ˈræfeɪəl/ (1483–1520) an Italian painter and ARCHITECT whose full name was **Raffaello Santi** or **Sanzio**, one of the leading figures of the Italian RENAISSANCE

Raphael, Sally Jessy /ˈdʒɛsi/ (1943–) an American radio and television personality whose programmes are mostly of interest to women

rap·id /ˈræpˌd/ *adj* happening, moving, or doing something at great speed; fast: *The patient made a rapid recovery.* | *They asked their questions in rapid succession.* | *The school promises rapid results in language learning.* | *a rapid growth in population* — ~**ly** *adv* : *the rapidly changing world of computer technology* — ~**ity** /rəˈpɪdˌti/, ~**ness** /ˈræpˌdnˌs/ *n* [U]

rapid eye move·ment /ˌ·· ˈ· ˌ··/ *n* [U] rapid movement of the eyes during sleep, thought to happen during periods when the sleeper is dreaming

rapid-fire /ˈ·· ·/ *adj* [A] **1** (of a gun) able to fire shots quickly one after the other **2** (of questions, jokes, etc.) spoken quickly one after the other

rapid re·ac·tion force /ˌ·· ·ˈ·· ˌ·/ *n* a military force formed to act quickly in answer to a sudden threat to peace

rap·ids /ˈræpˌdz/ also **whitewater** *AmE*— *n* [P] a part of a river where the water moves very fast over rocks: *The canoe* **shot the rapids.** (=passed quickly over them)

rapid tran·sit /ˌ·· ˈ··/ *adj AmE* of a way of moving people around a city quickly, such as by UNDERGROUND³, trains, etc.: *Los Angeles is building a subway downtown as part of its rapid transit system.*

ra·pi·er /ˈreɪpiəʳ/ *n* a long thin sharp two-edged sword —see picture at SWORD

rap·ine /ˈræpaɪn/ˈræpˌn/ *n* [U] *lit* the carrying away of property by force; PLUNDER

rap·ist /ˈreɪpˌst/ *n* a man guilty of RAPE² (1)

rap·pel /ræˈpel/ *v* [I] *AmE for* ABSEIL -**rappel** *n*

rap·port /ræˈpɔːʳ/ *n* [S;U (**between, with**)] close agreement and understanding: *to have/develop a good rapport with someone*

rap·proche·ment /ræˈprɒʃmɒŋ, ræˈprəʊʃ-‖ˌræprəʊʃˈmɑːŋ/ *n* [(**between, with**)] *fml, Fr* a coming together again in friendship of former enemies: *At last there are signs of a rapprochement between our two countries.*

rap·scal·lion /ræpˈskæljən/ *n old use or humor* a worthless man or boy whom one is rather fond of

rap sheet /ˈ· ·/ *n AmE sl* a paper which has a list of someone's criminal record

rapt /ræpt/ *adj* giving one's whole mind; engrossed (ENGROSS): *We listened to her amazing story with rapt attention.* — ~**ness** *n* [U]

rap·ture /ˈræptʃəʳ/ also **raptures** *pl.*— *n* [U (**at, about, over**)] *fml* great joy and delight: *She went into/was in* **raptures** *at the news.* —**turous** *adj* : *a rapturous welcome* | *rapturous applause* —**turously** *adv*

Ra·pun·zel /rəˈpʌnzəl/ a female character in a FAIRY TALE who is kept locked up at the top of a tower but who is freed when she lets down her very long hair through the window and a HANDSOME PRINCE climbs up —see picture on page 1088

rare¹ /reəʳ/ *adj* **1** extremely unusual or uncommon: *the preservation of rare species* | *It's very rare for him to be*

late. | *a rare disease* **2** (esp. of air) thin; light: *the rare air of the mountains* **3** [A] *infml* unusually good or extreme: *You gave them a rare fright.* | *We had a* **rare old** *time at the party.* —see also RARELY, RARITY — **~ ness** *n* [U]

▷ USAGE Compare **rare** and **scarce.** Things that are uncommon, and perhaps valuable, are **rare**: *a* **rare** *bird/coin.* Ordinary useful things that we have not got enough of are **scarce**: *Potatoes were* **scarce** *last winter.* We can use **rare**, but not **scarce**, about time: *one of my* **rare** (=not happening often) *visits to Paris.* Note that **rarely** means "not often" while **scarcely** means "hardly, only just".◁

rare² *adj* (of meat, esp. STEAK) lightly cooked —compare WELL-DONE

rare·bit /ˈreəbɪt‖ˈreər-/ *n* [U] see WELSH RAREBIT

rare earth /ˌ· ˈ·/ *n tech* any of a group of rare metal substances (ELEMENTS)

rar·e·fied /ˈreərɪˌfaɪd/ *adj* **1** (of air in high places) light; thin, with less oxygen than usual **2** *often humor* limited to people who are special in some way; EXALTED: *He moves in very rarefied circles; his friends are all lords.*

rare·ly /ˈreəli‖ˈreərli/ *adv* not at all often: *I have rarely seen/(fml) Rarely have I seen such a beautiful sunset.* | *He rarely, if ever, goes out.* | *a rarely-shown silent movie* —compare SCARCELY

▷ USAGE The word order of a sentence beginning with **rarely** or **seldom** is like that of a question: **Rarely/Seldom** *have I heard such a strange story.* — see also NEVER (USAGE)◁

rar·ing /ˈreərɪŋ/ *adj* [F+*to-v*] *infml* very eager: *The children were raring to get out into the snow.* | *They were* **raring to go.** (=eager to start)

rar·i·ty /ˈreərˌti/ *n* **1** [U] the state or quality of being RARE¹ (1): *These stamps have great rarity value.* **2** [C] something uncommon: *People who bake their own bread have become a rarity/something of a rarity.*

ras·cal /ˈrɑːskəl‖ˈræs-/ *n* **1** a dishonest person **2** *humor* a person, esp. a child, who plays tricks or misbehaves but is regarded with fondness: *You little rascal! Where have you hidden my shoes?* — **~ ly** *adj old use*: *a rascally trick*

rash¹ /ræʃ/ *adj* foolishly confident and not thinking enough of the results: *a rash decision* | *I promised in a rash moment to buy the children a pet monkey.* | *It was rather rash of you to agree to lend them your car.* — **~ ly** *adv* — **~ ness** *n* [U]

rash² *n* a set of red spots on the skin, caused by illness: *a heat rash* | *He* **came out in** (=became covered with) **a rash** *today.* | (fig.) *a rash of* (=a sudden large number of) *complaints/accidents*

rash·er /ˈræʃər/ *n BrE* a thin piece of BACON or HAM —see picture at PIECE

rasp¹ /rɑːsp‖ræsp/ *v* **1** [T] to rub with something rough: *The cat's tongue rasped my hand.* **2** [I] **(on, upon)**;T] (of a sound) to have a rough annoying effect (on): *Her loud voice rasped (on) the sick man's nerves.* | *a rasping sound/accent* — **~ ingly** *adv*

rasp² *n* **1** [C] a metal tool for shaping wood, metal, etc.; rough FILE¹ **2** [S] a sound that might be made by this tool: *The rasp of metal on stone could be heard.*

rasp·ber·ry /ˈrɑːzbəri‖ˈræzberi/ *n* **1** a soft sweet usu. red berry (or its bush): *raspberries and cream* | *raspberry jam* —see picture at BERRY **2** *sl* a rude sound made by putting one's tongue out and blowing: *He* **blew a raspberry** *at the General.*

Ras·pu·tin /ræˈspjuːtɪn/, **Gri·go·ri E·fim·o·vich** /grɪˈgɔːri eˈfiməvɪtʃ/ (1872–1916) a Russian holy man from Siberia who had great influence over Czarina Alexandra and, through her, over Czar Nicholas. Rasputin caused many ministers to be dismissed, while some people connected with him gained high government positions. He was finally assassinated (ASSASSINATE).

ras·ta·fa·ri·an /ˌræstəˈfeəriən◂/ also **ras·ta** /ˈræstə/— *n (often cap.)* a follower of a religion from Jamaica which teaches that black West Indians will return to Africa and that Haile Selassie, the former EMPEROR of Ethiopia, is to be worshipped. Rastafarians often wear their hair in DREADLOCKS. — **~ ism** *n*

ras·ta·man /ˈræstəmæn/ *n infml* **-men** /men/ a male rastafarian

rat¹ /ræt/ *n* **1** a long-tailed animal related to but larger than the mouse: *rat poison* | *He looks like a drowned rat.* (=wet and cold and uncomfortable)

▶ CULTURAL NOTE Rats are generally feared and disliked, as they are thought to be dirty and to spread diseases. — see picture at RODENT◀

2 *infml* a worthless disloyal person: *But you promised to help us, you rat!* **3** like **rats deserting a sinking ship** a phrase used when people are leaving a person or company that is having a lot of difficulties. Like the rats on an old ship, they want to leave before it finally sinks. **4** **you dirty rat** *quote* a slightly changed phrase used as an insult by James Cagney in an American film —see also RAT RACE, RATS, RAT TRAP, **smell a rat** (SMELL¹)

rat² *v* **-tt-** [I] **1** [(on)] *infml* to act in a disloyal way; break a promise: *They said they'd help but they've ratted (on us).* **2** to hunt rats: *The dogs went ratting.*

rat-a-tat /ˌræt ə ˈtæt/ also **rat-a-tat-tat** /ˌræt ə tæt ˈtæt/— *n* [S] RAT-TAT

rat·a·tou·ille /ˌrætəˈtuːi, -ˈtwiː/ *n* [U] a French dish of vegetables esp. onions, tomatoes, COURGETTES, and AUBERGINES, cooked in oil

rat·bag /ˈrætbæg/ *n BrE & AustrE derog sl* an unpleasant or worthless person

ratch·et /ˈrætʃt/ *n* a toothed wheel or bar provided with a piece of metal that fits between its teeth to allow movement in one direction but not the other, used in machinery

rate¹ /reɪt/ *n* **1** [(of)] a quantity such as value, cost, or speed, measured by its relation to some other amount: *The* **birth rate** *is the number of births compared to the size of the population.* | *a fall in the rate of inflation* | *We drove at a steady rate.* | *The drug has a high success rate in curing the disease.* **2** a charge or payment fixed according to a standard scale: *The big banks have put up interest rates for borrowers to 15%.* | *They're demanding higher rates of pay.* | *What's the* **going rate** (=the usual or average rate,e.g.of pay) *for computer programmers?* | *an hourly rate of £10* (=a payment or charge of £10 for each hour) —see also BANK RATE **3** [*usu. pl.*] a local tax formerly paid in Britain by owners of buildings, for locally provided services. It was replaced by the COMMUNITY CHARGE —see also RATE-CAP **4** **at this/that rate** if events continue in the same way as now/then: *At this rate we won't be able to afford a holiday.* **5** *BrE* **at a rate of knots** very fast: *He's getting through the ironing at a rate of knots.* **6** **-rate** of the stated level of quality: *a first-rate* (=very good) *performer* | *a very second-rate team* —see also **at any rate** (ANY¹)

rate² *v* **1** [T] [+*obj*+*adv/prep*] to have the stated opinion about; value: *The company seem to rate her very highly.* | *She is generally rated as one of the best modern poets.* **2** [T] to deserve: *an unimportant news story that didn't rate a mention on the national news* **3** *AmE* to be thought very good, valuable, etc.: *George liked the film but didn't think it rated.* **4** [T *usu. pass.*] *BrE* to fix a RATE¹ (3) on (a building): *a house rated at £500* **5** [T] to give a letter to (a film) showing who may see it: *The film has been rated PG.*

rate³ *v* [I;T] *old use* to speak angrily (to); BERATE

rate·a·ble val·ue, ratable value /ˌreɪtəbəl ˈvæljuː/ also **RV** *abbrev.*— *n BrE* a value formerly given to a building for the purpose of calculating the RATE¹ (3) to be charged: *What's the rateable value of this shop?*

rate-cap /ˈ· ·/ *v* **-pp-** [T] *BrE* (of a central government) to

rastafarian

Rapunzel

limit the amount of RATE¹ (3) that could be charged by (a local council) —**capping** n [U]

rate of ex·change /ˌ· · ·ˈ·/ n the EXCHANGE RATE

rate of re·turn /ˌ· · ·ˈ·/ n a company's profit for a year expressed as a PERCENTAGE of the capital employed during the year

rate·pay·er /ˈreɪtpeɪəʳ/ n BrE a person who pays for locally provided services, formerly by paying a RATE¹ (3) and after that by paying the COMMUNITY CHARGE: *The ratepayers always have to pay for the council's mistakes.*

rate sup·port grant /ˌ· ·ˈ· ˌ·/ n BrE money paid by the government to a LOCAL AUTHORITY which forms part of the money that the local authority can spend

ra·ther /ˈrɑːðəʳ‖ˈræðər/ *predeterminer, adv* **1** to some degree; QUITE (2): *It's rather cold today.* | *a rather cold day* | *rather a cold day* | *rather cold weather* | *She's driving rather fast.* | *These shoes are rather too big.* | *I'm feeling rather better.* | *It's rather like a potato.* | *She's getting rather fat.* | *It's rather a pity.* | *He earns rather a lot of money.* | *It rather surprised me.* | *I rather like him.* | *I rather stupidly agreed to do it.* (=I agreed to do it, and this was rather stupid) —see MORE (USAGE) **2** (often with **would** and sometimes with **had**) more willingly: *I'd rather play tennis than swim.* | *"Have a drink?" "No thanks, I'd rather not."* | *Rather than cause trouble, he left.* **3** more exactly; more truly: *He came home very late last night, or rather very early this morning.* | *The job will take months rather than weeks.* **4** to a greater degree or with better reasons: *The parents should be blamed rather than the children.* | *It was what he meant rather than what he said that annoyed me.* | *The decision was taken for political rather than military reasons.* **5** infml, esp. BrE (used as an answer) yes, certainly: *"Would you like a swim?" "Rather!"*

▷ USAGE Compare **fairly** and **rather**. **Fairly** is often used for qualities that are neither good nor bad: *The weather was* **fairly** *cold* (=cold, but not very cold) | *I was driving* **fairly** *fast* (=fast, but not very fast). **Rather** is stronger than **fairly**, and often suggests that a quality is bad or unsuitable: *It's* **rather** *cold* (=colder than I would like) | *I was driving* **rather** *fast* (=too fast for the conditions on the road). But British speakers may use **rather** about things they like very much: *I was* **rather** *pleased when I won the prize.* The use of **rather** in senses 1 and 5 above is rare in American English, and sounds typically British to most Americans. They would use **fairly, somewhat**, or infml **pretty** instead for sense 1, and a simple answer such as "yes" for sense 5. —see also FAIRLY (USAGE)◁

Rather, Dan (1931–   ) an American reader of the news for CBS television

rat·i·fy /ˈrætɪfaɪ/ v [T] fml to approve (a written agreement) and make it official by signing it: *The heads of the two governments met to ratify the treaty.* —**-fication** /ˌrætɪfɪˈkeɪʃən/ n [U]

rat·ing /ˈreɪtɪŋ/ n **1** [C] the position that someone or something has on a scale of values or amounts: *The President has a favourable rating in the opinion polls.* **2** [C;U] the value of a building for local tax (RATES¹ (3)): *The rating officer came to look at the farm.* **3** [C] the class in which a ship or machine is placed according to its size: *a ship with a rating of 500,000 tons* **4** [C] a sailor in the British navy who is not an officer **5** [the +P] the number of people who watch or listen to a television or radio programme: *This show has done badly in the ratings.* — see also NIELSEN RATINGS **6** [C] the system of giving a letter to a film, showing who may see it: *The film has been given an X rating.*

ra·ti·o /ˈreɪʃiəʊ‖ˈreɪʃəʊ/ n -os [(of, to)] a figure showing the number of times one quantity contains another, used to show the relationship between two amounts: *The ratio of 10 to 5 is 2 to 1.* | *The ratio of nursing staff to doctors is 2:1.* —compare PROPORTION (2)

ra·ti·o·ci·na·tion /ˌrætiɒsɪˈneɪʃən‖ˌræʃiɑːs-, ˌræti-əʊs-/ n [U] fml or pomp exact and careful thinking

ra·tion¹ /ˈræʃən‖ˈræ-, ˈreɪ-/ n [(of)] a share of food, petrol, etc., allowed to one person for a time, esp. during a war or at a time of short supply: *the weekly meat ration* | *The soldiers were given their rations (of food).* | (fig.) *We've had our ration (=lots) of bad luck this year.* —see also IRON RATIONS

ra·tion² v [T] **1** [(to)] to limit (someone) to a fixed ration: *We were rationed to two eggs a week.* **2** to limit and control (supplies). In Britain many people remember the period during and after the Second World War when many goods were rationed, esp. food, clothes and petrol. —see also SECOND WORLD WAR
ration sthg. ↔ **out** phr v [T] to give out (supplies) as rations: *He rationed out the water to the sailors.*

ra·tion·al /ˈræʃənəl/ adj **1** (of a person) having the ability to think, understand, and make decisions; having reason **2** (of ideas and behaviour) sensible; based on or according to reason: *a rational explanation/decision* —opposite **irrational** — ~ **ly** adv — ~ **ity** /ˌræʃəˈnælɪti/ n [U]

ra·tio·nale /ˌræʃəˈnɑːl‖-ˈnæl/ n [C;U] fml the reasons and principles on which a system or practice is based

ra·tion·al·ist /ˈræʃənəlɪst/ adj, n (typical of) someone who bases their opinions and actions on reason, rather than on feelings or on religious belief —**-ism** n [U] — ~ **ic** /ˌræʃənəˈlɪstɪk◂/ adj

ra·tion·al·ize also **-ise** BrE /ˈræʃənəlaɪz/ v [I;T] **1 a** to explain (something) in a rational way **b** to find a reasonable but perhaps untrue explanation for (one's own behaviour or opinions): *He rationalized his dislike of authority.* **2** esp. BrE to make (a method or system) more modern and effective and less wasteful: *We're rationalizing the organization of the company to make it more efficient.* —**-ization** /ˌræʃənəlaɪˈzeɪʃən‖-lə-/ n [C;U]

ration book /ˈ·· ·/ n BrE a book of stamps representing necessary articles such as food, clothes, petrol etc. given out by the government during the Second World War and for a time afterwards in order to share out these limited articles fairly. The number of stamps in the book showed the amount of a particular thing that people were allowed to buy.

Rat·ners /ˈrætnəz‖-ərz/ one of a group of shops in Britain known esp. for selling a range of inexpensive jewellery

rat race /ˈ· ·/ [the] infml derog the endless competition to succeed, esp. in business, in spite of the pressures of modern city life: *I moved to the country to get out of the rat race.*

rats /ræts/ interj infml (used to express annoyance or slight anger)

rat·tan /rəˈtæn/ n [U] a plant from which WICKER furniture is made: *a rattan chair*

rat-tat /ˌræt ˈtæt/ also **rat-a-tat**— n [S] a sound of knocking, esp. on a door: *I heard a loud rat-tat at the door.*

Rat·ti·gan /ˈrætɪgən/, **Sir Ter·ence** /ˈterəns/ (1911–77) an English writer of plays, best known for *The Winslow Boy* and *Separate Tables*

rat·tle¹ /ˈrætl/ v **1** [I;T] to (cause to) make a number of quick sharp noises like small hard objects hitting each other repeatedly: *The windows rattled in the wind.* | *The beggar rattled the coins in his tin.* **2** [I+adv/prep] to move quickly while making these noises: *The cart rattled along the stony road.* **3** [T] BrE infml to make anxious and cause to lose confidence; UNNERVE: *She was badly rattled by her failure in the exam.* —see also SABRE-RATTLING
rattle sthg. ↔ **off** phr v [T] infml to repeat quickly and easily from memory: *He rattled off the poem.*
rattle on phr v [I] infml to talk quickly and continuously, esp. about things of no importance
rattle through sthg. phr v [T] infml to perform quickly: *She rattled through her speech/her work.*

rattle² n **1** [S] a rattling noise: *the rattle of milk bottles* **2** [C] a baby's toy that rattles **3** [C] an instrument that rattles, used esp. by people watching a football match **4** [C] the hard rings in a rattlesnake's tail that make a rattling noise —see also DEATH RATTLE

Rattle, Simon (1955–   ) the musician who directs the playing of the City of Birmingham Symphony Orchestra

rat·tle·snake /ˈrætlsneɪk/ also **rat·tler** /ˈrætləʳ/esp. AmE— n a poisonous American snake that makes a rattling noise with its tail when it is angry

rat·tle·trap /ˈrætltræp/ n infml a noisy old vehicle, esp. a car

rat·tling /ˈrætlɪŋ/ adv old-fash infml, apprec very: *a rattling good story*

rat trap /ˈ· ·/ n AmE a dirty old building that is in very bad condition

rat·ty /ˈræti/ adj **1** BrE infml bad-tempered; IRRITABLE **2**

AmE infml untidy and in bad condition; SHABBY: *a ratty old coat* **3** like or full of rats

Ratty a character in *The Wind in the Willows*, a children's story by Kenneth Grahame. He is a water rat, known esp. for his enjoyment of "messing about in boats" (=spending time lazily in boats).

rau·cous /'rɔːkəs/ *adj* (of voices) rough and unpleasant: *raucous shouts | the raucous behaviour of drunken teenagers* — ~**ly** *adv* — ~**ness** *n* [U]

raunch·y /'rɔːntʃi/ *adj infml* suggesting thoughts of sex; sexy: *a raunchy dance* —**ily** *adv* —**iness** *n* [U]

rav·age /'rævɪdʒ/ *v* [T *often pass.*] to ruin and destroy; DEVASTATE: *crops ravaged by storms | The whole area was ravaged by forest fires.*

rav·ag·es /'rævɪdʒɪz/ *n* [*the*+P+of] damage caused (as if) by ravaging; destroying effects: *the ravages of fire|war|inflation*

rave¹ /reɪv/ *v* [I (**about, against, at**)] to talk wildly as if mad: *He raved all night in his fever. | Father's raving at|against the government again.* —see also RAVING
  rave about sthg. *phr v* [T] *infml* to speak about with extreme praise or admiration: *Everyone was raving about the new singer.*

rave² *adj* [A] *infml* full of very eager praise, esp. in a newspaper: *His new play has been getting* **rave notices/reviews** *in the papers.*

rave³ *n* (in Britain) a very large dance for young people which may last all night. Raves take place in large empty buildings, sometimes without the owner's permission, and are associated in people's minds with HOUSE MUSIC and drugs such as ECSTASY. The police often try to prevent raves —see also ACID HOUSE PARTY

rav·el /'rævəl/ *v* -ll- *BrE* ‖ -l- *AmE* [I;T] **1** [(UP)] to (cause to) become twisted and knotted **2** to UNRAVEL

Ra·vel /ræ'vel/, **Mau·rice** /mɒ'riːs‖mɔː-/ (1875–1937) a French COMPOSER, known esp. for his *Boléro*

ra·ven /'reɪvən/ *n* a large shiny black bird with a black beak which makes a deep unmusical sound (CROAK). Some ravens live outside the Tower of London and it is said that something terrible will happen to England if they leave. A well-known poem by Edgar Allan Poe called *The Raven* features a raven who repeats the word "nevermore".

raven-haired /ˌ··'·◂/ *adj lit* with shiny black hair

rav·en·ing /'rævənɪŋ/ *adj* [A] *esp. lit* fierce and dangerous because of hunger: *ravening tigers*

rav·en·ous /'rævənəs/ *adj* very hungry: *a ravenous appetite | Have a sandwich; you must be ravenous!* — ~**ly** *adv*

rav·er /'reɪvəʳ/ *n infml, esp. BrE* a person who leads an exciting life of social and sexual freedom

rave-up /'· ·/ *n infml, esp. BrE* a wild exciting party

ra·vine /rə'viːn/ *n* a deep narrow valley with steep sides — see VALLEY (USAGE)

rav·ing /'reɪvɪŋ/ *adj, adv infml* **1** talking or behaving wildly: *a raving lunatic | He's (stark) raving mad.* **2** [A] very great; attracting great admiration: *a raving beauty* (=a very beautiful woman) *| The concert was not a raving success.*

rav·ings /'reɪvɪŋz/ *n* [P] wild uncontrolled talk: *the ravings of a madman*

rav·i·o·li /ˌrævi'əʊli/ *n* [U] Italian PASTA (=food made from a flour and water mixture) in the form of small cases filled with meat, cooked in boiling water

rav·ish /'rævɪʃ/ *v* [T] *esp. lit* **1** [*often pass.*] to fill with delight: *I was ravished by her beauty.* **2** to seize or rob with violence **3** to RAPE — ~**ment** *n* [U]

rav·ish·ing /'rævɪʃɪŋ/ *adj* very beautiful; causing great delight: *a ravishing sight|blonde* — ~**ly** *adv* : *ravishingly beautiful*

raw¹ /rɔː/ *adj* **1** (of food) not cooked: *raw vegetables* **2** in the natural state; not yet treated for use: *raw sugar|cotton|sewage* **3** (of a person) not yet trained; not experienced: *a raw recruit who has just joined the army* **4** (of a part of the skin) painful; sore: *hands raw with cold* **5** (of weather) cold and wet: *a raw winter day* — ~**ly** *adv* — ~**ness** *n* [U]

raw² *n* **in the raw: a** in an original natural state, without civilization: *life in the raw* **b** *infml* without clothes

Rawal·pin·di /ˌrɔːl'pɪndi‖ˌrɑːwəl-/ a city in NE Pakistan which was formerly the capital of Pakistan

raw-boned /ˌ· '·◂/ *adj* having large bones that show under the skin

raw deal /ˌ· '·/ *n infml* a case of unfair or cruel treatment: *The employees who were sacked got (rather) a raw deal*

raw·hide /'rɔːhaɪd/ *n* [U] natural untreated cow's leather: *a rawhide belt*

Rawl·plug /'rɔːlplʌg/ *n tdmk* a special piece of material put into a hole in a wall before a screw is put in to make the screw stay firmly in place

raw ma·te·ri·als /ˌ· ·'···/ *n* [P] things such as minerals, metals, wood, oil, or skins which are the starting point for many manufacturing (MANUFACTURE¹) processes: *Coal and oil are important raw materials for the manufacture of plastics.*

ray¹ /reɪ/ *n* [(**of**)] **1** a narrow beam of light, esp. one of a group going out from the same centre: *a ray of light | (fig.) Her visit brought a* **ray of sunshine** *into the old man's life.* **2** a beam of heat, electricity, or some other form of ENERGY (3): *a gun that fires invisible rays* —see also COSMIC RAY, X-RAY **3** a very small bit (of hope or comfort): *There isn't a ray of hope left for us.*

ray² *n* a large flat sea fish with a long pointed tail

Ray, Sat·ya·jit /'sætjədʒɪt/ (1921–92) an Indian film director known for films such as *Pather Panchali* and *The Chess Players*

Ray·ner /'reɪnəʳ/, **Claire** /kleəʳ/ (1931–) a well known English AGONY AUNT

ray·on /'reɪɒn‖-ɑːn/ *n* [U] a smooth silk-like material made from plant substances, often used to make clothes

raze /reɪz/ *v* [T] *fml* to destroy (buildings, towns, etc.) completely, so that no part is left standing: *The air attack* **razed the city to the ground.**

razors

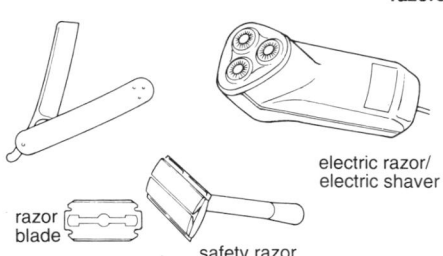

electric razor/
electric shaver

razor
blade

safety razor

ra·zor /'reɪzəʳ/ *n* a sharp instrument for removing hair, esp. the hair that grows on a man's face: *I shave with an electric razor. | (fig.) his* **razor-sharp** (=very fine and quick) *wit* —compare SHAVER; see also CUTTHROAT¹ (2), SAFETY RAZOR

razor blade /'·· ·/ *n* a flat blade with a very sharp cutting edge, used in a SAFETY RAZOR —see picture at RAZOR

razor edge /ˌ·· '·◂/ also **razor's edge** — *n* [S] a difficult or dangerous position between two opposite states: *Edward nearly died after the accident — his life was on a razor edge for days.*

raz·zle /'ræzəl/ *n infml, esp. BrE* **on the razzle** having a wild enjoyable time: *After they won the match they all went on the razzle.*

razzle-daz·zle /ˌ·· '··/ *n* [U] noisy, colourful activity which is meant to excite and impress: *That advertising campaign uses a lot of razzle-dazzle to hide the fact that the product isn't very good.*

razz·ma·tazz /ˌræzmə'tæz/ *n* [U] *infml* noisy showy activity intended to attract attention and admiration: *all the razzmatazz of the presidential election campaign*

RBI /ˌɑː biː 'aɪ‖ˌɑːr-/ *n* (in BASEBALL) runs batted in; the total number of runs (RUN² (10)) which a player helps to make by hitting the ball: *He had six R.B.I.'s this game alone and sixty-two for the season so far.*

RC /ˌɑː 'siː‖ˌɑːr-/ *abbrev. for:* ROMAN CATHOLIC

RCMP /ˌɑː siː em 'piː‖ˌɑːr-/ Royal Canadian Mounted Police; a police force of Canada —see also MOUNTIE

Rd *written abbrev. for:* ROAD

RD /ˌɑː ˈdiː/ǁˌɑːr-/ *n AmE* rural delivery; a postal service which delivers the post in country areas; the letters R.D. are part of someone's address

re¹ /reɪ/ *n* [S;U] the second note in the SOL-FA musical SCALE¹ (5)

re² /riː/ *prep* (esp. in business letters) on the subject of; with regard to: *re your inquiry of the 19th October*

RE /ˌɑːr ˈiː/ *abbrev. for:* RELIGIOUS EDUCATION

re- see WORD FORMATION

're /ər/ *short for:* are: *We're ready but they're not.* (compare They're not ready but we are (not *we're*))

reach¹ /riːtʃ/ *v* **1** [T] to arrive at or come as far as; get to, often after much time or effort: *After several changes of plane, we finally reached London on Tuesday morning.| Have you reached the end of the book yet? | The news only reached me yesterday. | She's reached the age of 50. | Our sales to Germany have reached record levels. | The two sides failed to reach (an) agreement after several hours of discussion.* **2** [I+adv/prep] to stretch out a hand or arm for some purpose: *He reached across the table and picked up the book. | The shopkeeper reached for a packet of tea.* **3** [I;T *not in progressive forms*] to be able to touch (something) by stretching out a hand or arm: *Are you tall enough to reach that apple on the tree? | (fig.) We could see nothing but houses as far as the eye could reach.* (=to the horizon) **4** [I+adv/prep;T *not in progressive forms*] (of a thing or place) to be big enough to touch; stretch out as far as: *The ladder won't quite reach (as far as) the window. | The garden reaches down to the lake.* **5** [T (**for**)] to get or give by stretching out a hand or arm: *I reached down the child's cap from the hook. [+obj(i)+obj(d)] Could you reach me that book from the top shelf?* **6** [T] to get a message to; get in touch with; CONTACT: *You can usually reach him on this phone number ...* **7 reach for the stars** to try to gain something far away and seemingly impossible to reach

reach sthg. ↔ **out** *phr v* [T (**for**)] to stretch out (a hand or arm): *The monkey reached out a hand for the banana.*

reach² *n* **1** [U (**of**)] **a** the distance that one can touch by stretching: *The bottle was within/out of (his) reach.* (=he could/could not reach it) **b** the distance that can be (easily) travelled: *We live within easy reach of the shops.* **c** the limit to which something can have effect or influence: *It's beyond the reach of my imagination.* **2** [S] the length of one's arm: *a boxer with a long reach* **3** [C] a straight stretch of water between two bends in a river: *the upper reaches of the river* (=the part of the river farthest from the sea)

reach-me-down /ˈ· · ˌ·/ *n [usu. pl.] BrE for* HAND-ME-DOWN

re·act /riˈækt/ *v* [I] **1** [(**to**, **against**)] to act or behave in a particular way in answer or opposition: *The government has reacted to the outbreak of violence by sending army patrols to police the area. | How did he react to your suggestion? | She reacted angrily to these accusations. | Children tend to react against their parents by going against their wishes. | The patient reacted badly to the drug.* (=was made ill by it) **2** [(**with**, **on**)] *tech* (of a substance) to change when mixed with another: *An acid can react with a base to form a salt.* —see also REAGENT, RESPOND (USAGE)

re·ac·tion /riˈækʃ∂n/ *n* **1** [C;U (**to**)] (a case or way of) reacting; RESPONSE: *What was your reaction to the news?* (=what did you think about it?) | *The news of the planned closure of the factory provoked a hostile reaction from the union.* **2** [C;U (**on**, **to**, **against**)] *tech* (in science) **a** (a) force exercised by a body in reply to another force, which is of equal strength and acts in the opposite direction **b** (a) change caused in a chemical substance by the action of another **3** [S;U (**from**, **against**)] **a** (a) change back to a former condition: *The popularity of these old-fashioned views reflects a reaction against the permissiveness of the 1960s.* **b** sudden weakness, tiredness, low spirits, etc., coming after unusual activity, esp. of the mind: *She may suffer a reaction when the drug wears off.* **4** [U] *derog* the quality of being reactionary: *The revolution was defeated by the forces of reaction.* —see also CHAIN REACTION

re·ac·tion·a·ry /riˈækʃ∂n∂riǁ-ʃ∂neri/ *n, adj derog* (a person) strongly opposed to social or political change: *a diehard reactionary | reactionary views* —compare LIBERAL¹, RADICAL¹ (2)

re·ac·tiv·ate /riˈæktɪ̱veɪt/ *v* [I;T] to make or become active again: *We reactivated the machine. | The chemicals reactivate when heated.*

re·ac·tive /riˈæktɪv/ *adj tech* (of a chemical substance) that REACTS (2) – **~ly** *adv* – **~ness** *n*

re·ac·tor /riˈæktər/ *n* **1 a** NUCLEAR REACTOR **2** a container for a chemical reaction

read¹ /riːd/ *v* **read** /red/ **1** [I;T] to look at and understand (something printed or written): *The little boy can read quite well now. | He reads well for a six-year-old. | to read a book|music|a map | Read the instructions before you start the machine. | I can read French but I can't speak it.* **2** [I;T] to learn (the stated information) from print or writing: *I read about the murder|read an account of the murder in the paper. [+that] I read that the new director is Spanish.* **3** [I+adv/prep; L+n; *not in progressive forms*] (of written words) to have a particular form or produce a particular effect when read: *The name should read "Benson", not "Fenton". | Her letter reads as follows ... | I rewrote the last paragraph because it didn't read very well.* **4** [I;T (**to**)] to say (printed or written words) to others: *The teacher read the poem aloud to the class.| She read (a story) to the children. [+obj(i)+obj(d)] She read the children a story.* —compare READ **out 5** [T] (of a measuring instrument) to show: *The thermometer reads 33 degrees.* **6** [T] *BrE* to study (a subject) at university: *Helen's reading history|law at Oxford.* —compare READ **for 7** [T (**as**)] **a** to understand the meaning or nature of (a statement, event, experience, person, etc.) in a particular way; INTERPRET: *His speech about unity showed that he had accurately read the mood of the conference. | I read her reply as a refusal. | How do you read the latest trade figures? | I can read your thoughts from the look on your face. | It's hard to read him when he's in one of his moods.* **b** to tell what will happen in the future from (various visible objects): *Have you ever had your palm read? | I know a woman who reads tea leaves. | His wife reads tarot cards.* **8** [T (**as, for**) *usu. imperative*] *fml* to understand the (stated printed or written words) to be a mistake for: *For £50 please read £15. | Please read £50 as £15.* **9** [T] to obtain and use (information) from a computer STORAGE system: *The disk drive reads data from the disk into the computer's memory.* **10 read all about it!** (a phrase typically said by people selling newspapers on the street): *Big fire in city warehouse – read all about it!* **11 read between the lines** to find hidden meanings: *If you read between the lines, this letter is really a request for money.* **12 read the tea leaves** to look at the pattern of tea leaves left in the bottom of the cup in order to know the future **13 take something as read** esp. *BrE* to accept something as true or right without the need to hear it, talk about it, etc.: *We didn't have time to hear the secretary's report, so we took it as read. | We can take it as read that the newspapers will support our opponents.* **14 -read** /red/ (of a person) having a stated amount of knowledge gained from books: *a well-read woman | He's widely-read.* **b** (of a book, newspaper, etc.) read by a stated number of people: *a little-read novel* —see also **read the riot act** (RIOT ACT)

read for sthg. *phr v* [T] esp. *BrE* to study in order to gain (esp. a university degree): *She's reading for a degree in physics.* —compare READ¹ (6)

read sthg. **into** sthg. *phr v* [T] to believe (something) to be meant though not expressed by (something else): *Don't read more into her letter than she intended. | It was only a casual remark – don't read too much into it.*

read sthg. ↔ **out** *phr v* [T] to read aloud for others to hear: *The announcer read out the football results.* —compare READ¹ (4)

read sthg. ↔ **over/through** *phr v* [T] to read completely, from beginning to end –**read-through** /ˈ· ·/ *n* [S]

read up *phr v* [I (**on**);T (=**read** sthg. ↔ **up**)] *infml* to study (a subject) thoroughly; find out about by reading: *I need to read up (on) the tax laws.*

read² *n* [S] **1** an act or period of reading: *Can I have a read of your paper?* **2** something of the stated kind to be read: *It's not great literature but it's a good read.*

rea·da·ble /ˈriːdəbəl/ *adj* **1** *apprec* interesting or enjoyable to read **2** LEGIBLE –opposite **unreadable**; see also MACHINE-READABLE –**-bility** /ˌriːdəˈbɪlɪ̱ti/ *n* [U]

re·ad·dress /ˌriːəˈdres/ *BrE* ‖ **forward** *AmE*– *v* [T (**to**)] to write a different address on (a letter that has been delivered wrongly to one's own address); REDIRECT: *I asked*

them to readdress my letters (to my new house).

read·er /ˈriːdəʳ/ n **1** a person who reads a stated thing or in a stated way: *Are you a fast reader?* | *My brother's a great reader|an avid reader.* (=he reads a lot) | (in a newspaper) *We have received many letters on this subject from our readers.* **2** a person who reads books to put mistakes right before printing, or to decide whether to print (PUBLISH) them **3** |(in)| (*often cap.*) a British university teacher just below the rank of PROFESSOR: *She's a reader in French.* **4** a schoolbook for beginners, usu. containing short passages or stories for reading **5** a book containing a collection of writings by one writer, or about a particular subject

Reader, The a weekly US newspaper printed in Chicago. It is known esp. for news about entertainment. —see also extra information on page 896

Reader's Di·gest /ˌ·· ˈ··/ a popular magazine for the general reader, printed in many different languages and containing a variety of information and stories about many different subjects. It is delivered to readers by post. The American and British magazines of this name are produced separately.

read·er·ship /ˈriːdəʃɪp‖-ər-/ n **1** [S] the particular number or type of people who read a newspaper or magazine: *The paper has a readership of 80,000|a very well-educated readership.* **2** [C (**in**)] the position of a READER (3)

read·ies /ˈrediːz/ n [P] *BrE* READY³ (1)

read·i·ly /ˈredɪli/ adv **1** quickly and willingly: *He readily agreed to their suggestion.* **2** with no difficulty: *This type of plug is readily available.*

read·i·ness /ˈredinɪs/ n fml **1** |(in)| U (**for**)] the state of being ready or prepared: *The defences are kept in readiness for an enemy attack.* **2** [S;U] (a) willingness: [+to-v] *She shows (a) great readiness to learn.* **3** [S;U+of] (a) quickness and ability to do something easily: *readiness of understanding* —see also READY¹ (3)

read·ing¹ /ˈriːdɪŋ/ n **1** [U] the act or practice of reading: *Children learn reading and writing at school.* **2** [C (**of**)] an opinion about the meaning of (a statement, set of events, etc.); INTERPRETATION: *My reading of the law is that we needn't pay.* | *What's your reading of the latest trade figures?* **3** [C] a figure shown by a measuring instrument: *What are the temperature readings for the week?* **4** [U] something of the stated type to be read: *Books like this are unsuitable|difficult reading for children.* | *The report makes interesting reading.* (=is interesting to read) | *reading matter* (=books, newspapers, etc.) **5** [C] a gathering of people at which literature is read aloud: *a poetry reading* **6** [C] any of the official occasions in the British Parliament or US Congress on which a BILL (=a suggested new law) is read aloud and considered before it can actually become law: *the third reading of the Industrial Relations Bill*

reading² adj [A] for reading: *the reading room at the library* | *a reading lamp*

Read·ing /ˈredɪŋ/ a university town on the River Thames in Berkshire, S England, where the local government for that COUNTY is based

re·ad·just /ˌriːəˈdʒʌst/ v [I;T (**to**)] to get or put back into the proper state or position: *Readjust the driving mirror.* | *It's hard to readjust (oneself) to school life after the holidays.* — ~ **ment** n [C;U] : *a period of readjustment* | *The mechanic made a few minor readjustments.*

read·on·ly mem·o·ry /ˌ··· ˈ····/ see ROM

read·out /ˈriːd-aʊt/ n a showing, e.g. in printed form or on a SCREEN, of information that has been processed by a computer: *Using this program, you can get a readout of all the areas where sales have increased.* —see also PRINTOUT

read·y¹ /ˈredi/ adj **1** [F (**for**)] prepared and fit (for use or action): *Is breakfast ready?* | *Come on — aren't you ready yet?* | *Is everything ready for the party?* [+to-v] *I'm not ready to go yet.* | *These apples are ready to eat* (=ready to be eaten) | *We'd better get ready to leave.* | (*fml*) *They* **made ready** (=prepared) *for the attack.* **2** [F] (of a person) willing to give or do something: [+**with**] *She's always ready with advice|with an excuse.* [+to-v] *You're too ready to criticize.* **3** [A] *fml, usu. apprec* (of the powers of the mind) quick: *a man of ready wit* | *a ready understanding of the problem* **4** [F+to-v] likely to do something: *I felt ready to cry with frustration.* | *We marched*

until we were ready to drop. —see also READILY, READINESS

ready² adv (used before a past participle) in advance; already: *You can buy the bread ready cut.* | *a ready-cooked dinner*

ready³ n [*the*] **1** also **readies** pl.— *BrE infml for* READY MONEY: *I'm a bit short of the ready this week.* **2** **at|to the ready** in|to the state of being ready: *Have your guns at the ready men!*

ready⁴ interj *BrE* **ready, steady, go!** also **on your mark(s), get set, go!** *esp. AmE* (used when telling people to begin a race)

ready⁵ v [T] *fml* to make ready; prepare

ready-made /ˌ·· ˈ·◂/ adj **1** (esp. of clothes) not made specially for the buyer; able to be worn at once: *a ready-made suit* | (fig.) *His second wife had three children already, so when he married her he had a ready-made family.* **2** useful and suitable for a purpose; convenient: *The rain gave us a ready-made excuse for not going out.* **3** *derog* not original: *ready-made opinions*

ready meal /ˌ·· ˈ·/ n a prepared meal bought in a shop and which only needs to be heated before eating

ready-mix¹ /ˈ·· ·/ adj (of food powder) ready to cook after adding water or milk: *a ready-mix cake*

ready-mix² n tdmk CONCRETE which has been mixed before or during delivery to a place where building is being done

ready mon·ey /ˌ·· ˈ··/ also **ready cash** /ˌ·· ˈ·/— n [U] money that can be paid at once in actual coins and notes, and not owed

ready-to-wear /ˌ·· · ˈ·◂/ adj (of clothes) ready-made: *a ready-to-wear suit*

re·af·firm /ˌriːəˈfɜːm‖-ˈɜːrm/ v [T] to declare again, or in answer to a question or doubt: *The conference overwhelmingly reaffirmed its commitment to nuclear disarmament.* [+that] *The statement reaffirmed that the government would never make concessions to terrorists.* — ~ **ation** /ˌriːæfəˈmeɪʃən‖-fər-/ n [C;U]

re·af·for·est /ˌriːəˈfɒrəst‖-ˈfɔː-, -ˈfɑː-/ esp. *BrE*‖**reforest** esp. *AmE* — v [T] to plant (land) again with forest trees for industrial use or to improve the environment — ~ **ation** /ˌriːəfɒrɪˈsteɪʃən‖-fɔː-, -fɑː-/ n [U]

Rea·gan¹ /ˈreɪgən/, **Nan·cy** /ˈnænsi/ (1923–) the wife of the former American president Ronald Reagan, known for her belief in the power of ASTROLOGY and her strong influence on her husband while he was president

Reagan², Ron·ald Wil·son /ˈrɒnəld ˈwɪlsən‖ˈrɑː-/ (1911–) an American Republican politician who was the 40th president of the US (1981–89). Reagan was a popular president among many Americans, partly because of his policies (POLICY) and partly because he seemed likeable. People also connect him with SDI, a programme of defence in space, and with the Iran-Contra affair (IRANGATE), though he said that he knew nothing about it. He is also known for having been a film actor before he became a politician.

Ronald and Nancy Reagan

Rea·gan·om·ics /ˌreɪgəˈnɒmɪks‖-ˈnɑː-/ n [P+sing.|pl.v] the economic ideas and policies (POLICY) of the US between 1981 and 1989, when Ronald Reagan was president

re·a·gent /riːˈeɪdʒənt/ n tech a substance that by causing a chemical REACTION (2) in a compound shows the presence of another substance

real¹ /rɪəl/ adj **1** not pretended, artificial, or false; actual or true: *Is your ring real gold?* | *What was the real reason for your absence?* | *He didn't start the club purely as a business venture — he's got a real* (=sincere) *interest in jazz music.* | *The director got all the credit for the new product, but it was his assistant who was the real brain behind it.* (=who did the important work) | *The real* (=most important) *lesson of this tragedy is that safety regulations must be made more strict.* | *The money spent on education has gone up by 10%* **in real terms.** (=after taking account of general rises in price) **2** actually existing; not imaginary: *a story of real life* **3** [A] (used to add force) complete; great: *You're a real idiot!* | *That cake was a real treat.* **4** [A] *apprec* (esp. of a drink or food) made in the proper old way rather than by modern artificial methods: *real mashed potatoes* **5 for real** *infml, esp. AmE* serious or seriously: *They were fighting for real.* | *We didn't believe their threats were for real.* — see also REALITY, REALLY — ~**ness** *n* [U]

real² *adv infml, esp. AmE* very: *I'm real sorry!*

real ale /ˌ· ˈ·/ *n* a type of beer made by TRADITIONAL methods, which ferments (FERMENT¹) in the BARREL and which is not FIZZY

real es·tate /ˈ· ·ˌ·/ *n* [U] **1** also **real property**— *fml or law* property in the form of land and houses —compare PERSONAL PROPERTY **2** *esp. AmE* houses to be bought: *He sells real estate.*

real estate a·gent /ˈ· ·· ˌ··/ also **Realtor** *tdmk*— *n AmE for* ESTATE AGENT

re·a·lign /ˌriːəˈlaɪn/ *v* [I;T] to form into new groups, new types of organization or arrangement, etc: *The general realigned his forces to mount a fresh attack.* — ~**ment** *n* [C;U] : *a realignment of political parties*

rea·lis·m /ˈrɪəlɪzəm/ *n* [U] **1** *apprec* accepting and dealing with life and its problems in a practical way, without being influenced by feelings or false ideas **2** (*often cap.*) (in art and literature, esp. following ROMANTICISM in the 19th century) the showing of things as they really are — compare CLASSICISM (1,2), ROMANTICISM —**·list** *n*

rea·lis·tic /rɪəˈlɪstɪk/ *adj apprec* **1** showing REALISM (1); sensible and reasonable: *It would be nice to have another holiday, but we've got to be realistic (about it) — we can't really afford one.* | *Faced with the realities of the country's economy, the new government has had to moderate its aims.* | *It's not really worth £1000; a more realistic estimate would be £600.* | *a realistic assessment of their prospects* —opposite **unrealistic** **2** (of art or literature) showing or describing things as they appear to most people: *a realistic drawing of a horse* — ~**ally** /kli/ *adv* : *She drew the horse very realistically.* | *Realistically, it's only worth about £600.*

re·al·i·ty /riˈæləti/ *n* **1** [U] the quality or state of being real: *She believes in the reality of God.* | *We thought they had come to repair the phone, but in reality* (=in actual fact) *they were burglars.* **2** [C;U] something or everything that is real: *Her dream of being a film star became a reality.* | *Many people go to the cinema as an escape from reality.* | *We were promised a trouble-free holiday, but the reality* (=what actually happened) *was rather different.*

rea·li·za·tion also **-sation** *BrE* /ˌrɪəlaɪˈzeɪʃən‖-lə-/ *n* **1** [S;U] (an experience of) understanding and believing; being or becoming conscious (of): *(a) full realization of his guilt* [+that] *the sudden realization that we had been wrong all the time* **2** [the+of] the becoming real of a hope, plan, fear, etc.: *The next year saw the realization of my hopes.* **3** [the+of] *tech* the act of selling ASSETS or of getting money for property: *the realization of the house|of £1000|of their shares*

rea·lize also **-lise** *BrE* /ˈrɪəlaɪz/ *v* [T *not usu. in progressive forms*] **1** to understand and believe (a fact); be or become conscious of: *He didn't realize his mistake|the risks he was taking.* [+(that)] *She spoke English so well that I never realized she was German.* [+wh-] *I didn't realize how late it was.* | (in making requests) *I realize you're very busy, but could I talk to you for a few minutes?* | (shows annoyance) *Do you realize you're half an hour late?* **2** to make (a hope, purpose, fear, etc.) real: *She realized her ambition of becoming an actress.* | *My worst fears were realized when I saw what the exam questions were.* **3** *fml* **a** to change into money by selling: *We realized all our assets.* **b** to get (money by selling): *We realized a profit (on the house).* **c** (of something sold) to bring (an amount of money): *The car realized £3000.* —**-lizable** *adj* : *realizable hopes|property*

real·ly /ˈrɪəli/ *adv* **1** in fact; actually: *Did she really say that?* | *I really don't|I don't really want any more coffee.* | *The report describes things as they really are.* | *He's really rather a nice boy|He's quite a nice boy, really.* **2** very (much); thoroughly: *It's really cold today.* | *a really cold day* | *I really can't stand him.* **3** (used esp. with **ought** or **should**) correctly; properly: *You ought really (BrE)* | *really ought (AmE) to have asked me first.* | *I'll let you use the phone this time, but you're not really supposed to.* **4**

(shows interest, doubt, surprise, or slight displeasure): *"I collect rare coins." "Really?"* | *Well, really! What a stupid thing to do.*

▷ USAGE In informal American speech, **really** is used in most cases where a British speaker would use **quite**: *It was quite (BrE)‖really (AmE) nice of you.* | *I thought the film was quite (BrE)* | *really (AmE) good.*◁

realm /relm/ *n* **1** (*often cap.*) *lit or law* a country ruled over by a king or queen: *the defence of the Realm* **2** [(of)] also **realms** *pl.*— an area of activity, study, etc.: *the realm of science* | *Such a thing is not within the realms of possibility.* (=is not possible)

re·al·pol·i·tik /reɪˈɑːlpɒliːtiːk‖-pɑː-/ *n* [U] politics based on practical facts or possibilities rather than on moral aims, and directed towards the success and advantage of one's own country, political group, etc.

real prop·er·ty /ˌ· ˈ···/ *n* [U] *fml, esp. law for* REAL ESTATE (1)

real ten·nis /ˌ· ˈ··/ *n* [U] a game played by two or four people using rackets (RACKET (1)) and a ball in an indoor court of an irregular shape, divided by a net. This game was the original form of tennis.

real-time /ˈ· ·/ *adj* [A] *tech* of or being a computer's handling of a requested operation immediately and without interruption until it is finished: *a real-time interactive database* **real time** *n* [U] : *These schedule updates have to happen in real time.* —compare TIME-SHARING

Real·tor /ˈrɪəltər, -tɔːʳ/ *n AmE tdmk for* ESTATE AGENT

real·ty /ˈrɪəlti/ *n* [U] *AmE for* REAL ESTATE

real world /ˌ· ˈ·/ *n* [the] the world, life, conditions, situations, etc. as they really exist, not as in someone's imagination of how they should be: *You suggest that we should abolish income tax altogether, but that's not living in the real world.*

ream¹ /riːm/ *n* **1 a** (in Britain) 480 pieces of paper **b** (in the US) 500 pieces of paper —compare QUIRE **2** [(of)] also **reams** *pl.*— *infml* a lot of writing: *She wrote reams of notes.*

ream² *v* [T] *esp. AmE* **1** to make (a hole or opening) larger **2** *infml* to treat badly, esp. by cheating

ream·er /ˈriːməʳ/ *n esp. AmE* a tool used to make a hole or opening larger

re·an·i·mate /riːˈænəmeɪt/ *v* [T] *fml* to fill with new strength or courage; bring back to life: *The new leader reanimated the political party.*

reap /riːp/ *v* [I;T] to cut and gather (a crop of grain): *The men were all out reaping.* | *Nowadays machines are used to reap the corn.* | (fig.) *She invested cleverly, and* **reaped a rich reward.** | (fig.) *He finally* **reaped the benefit** *of all his years of hard work.* —compare HARVEST² — ~**er** *n* —see also GRIM REAPER

re·ap·pear /ˌriːəˈpɪəʳ/ *v* [I] to appear again after an absence — ~**ance** *n* [U]

re·ap·praise /ˌriːəˈpreɪz/ *v* [T] *fml* to examine (something) again to see whether one should change one's opinion of it: *The time had come for them to reappraise their economic strategy.* —**·praisal** *n* [C;U]

rear¹ /rɪəʳ/ *n* **1** [the] *rather fml* the back: *a garden at the rear of the house* | *The engine is in the rear.* —compare FRONT¹ (1) **2** [C] *euph* the part of the body on which one sits; BUTTOCKS **3 bring up the rear** to be the last, e.g. in a line of people or a race —**rear** *adj* [A] : *a rear window* | *The rear light of a car* —see picture at CAR

▷ USAGE British speakers say **at the rear** for something that is behind: *a garden* **at the rear** *of the house*, and **in the rear** for the back part of something: *to walk* **in the rear** *of the procession*. American speakers generally say **in the rear** for both.◁

rear² *v* **1** [T (on)] to care for until fully grown: *She's reared a large family.* | *a hand-reared goat* (=fed by a human being) —compare RAISE¹ (4) **2** [I] (of a four-legged animal) to rise upright on the back legs: *The horse reared and threw me off.* —compare BUCK² (2) **3** [T] to lift up (a part of oneself, esp. the head), esp. so as to be noticed: *The lion reared its head.* | (fig.) *The threat of war|of a big price rise|once again has* **reared its ugly head.** (=appeared)

rear ad·mi·ral /ˌ· ˈ···◄/ *n* (*often cap.*) a rank in the navy: *Rear Admiral Jones* —see TABLE 3

Rear·don /ˈrɪədən‖ˈrɪər-/, **Ray** (1932–) a Welsh SNOOKER player who has been world snooker CHAMPION six times

rear·guard /ˈrɪəgɑːd‖ˈrɪərgɑːrd/ n [C+sing./pl. v] a formation of soldiers protecting the rear of an army —compare VANGUARD

rearguard ac·tion /ˌ·· ˈ··/ n a fight by the rearguard of an army that is being driven back by a victorious enemy: (fig.) *They fought a rearguard action against political changes that were almost inevitable.*

re·arm /riːˈɑːm‖-ˈɑːrm/ v [I;T (**with**)] to provide (oneself or others) with weapons again, or with new weapons: *If we want to fight we must rearm.* | *They rearmed their allies with modern missiles.* —compare DISARM (2)

re·ar·ma·ment /riːˈɑːməmənt‖-ˈɑːr-/ n [U] the rearming of a nation —compare DISARMAMENT

rear·most /ˈrɪəməʊst‖ˈrɪər-/ adj [A] furthest back; last: *the rearmost carriage of the train*

re·ar·range /ˌriːəˈreɪndʒ/ v [T] to put into a different (and better) arrangement: *Let's rearrange the room and have the desk by the window.* — **~ ment** n [C;U] : *various rearrangements* | *a lot of rearrangement*

rear·view mir·ror /ˌrɪəvjuː ˈmɪrər‖ ˌrɪər-/ n a mirror in a vehicle, such as a car or a bus, which lets the driver see the area behind the vehicle —see picture at CAR

rear·ward /ˈrɪəwəd‖ˈrɪərwərd/ adj, n [A; the] (in or towards) the REAR¹ (1) —**·wards, -ward** adv

rea·son¹ /ˈriːzən/ n **1** [C;U (**for**)] the cause of an event or situation; a fact, event, or statement that provides an explanation or excuse for something: *She just suddenly left without giving any reason.* | *He decided not to accept the job, but wouldn't tell us his reasons.* | *The reason for the flood was all that heavy rain.* [+to-v] *They have said the new product will be a success, and I see no reason to doubt it.* | *There is reason to believe she was murdered.* | *In view of her behaviour, you had* **every reason** (=good reason) *to be suspicious.* [+(that)] *The reason I didn't tell you was that I wanted it to be a surprise.* [+why] *The reason why she didn't get the job was that her English was not very good.* | (fml) *He escaped punishment,* **by reason of** (=because of) *his youth.* | *He thinks,* **with reason** (=rightly), *that I don't like him.* | *She decided,* **for reasons best known to herself** (=no one else knew her reasons), *to move to another job.* | *For safety reasons/For reasons of safety, the doors are kept locked.* **2** [U] the ability to think, understand, and form opinions or judgments that are based on facts: *People are different from animals because they possess the power of reason.* **3** [U] good sense: *There's a great deal of reason in his advice.* | *Their demands are/go* **beyond all reason!** (=are more than is acceptable or reasonable) | *I told him not to be so stupid, but he wouldn't* **listen to reason.** (=be persuaded by sensible advice) **4** [U] a healthy mind that is not mad: *to* **lose/regain one's reason 5 within reason** within reasonable limits: *The bank will lend you as much as you need, within reason.* —see also **stand to reason** (STAND¹ (32))

▷ USAGE 1 Some people think a sentence such as *The* **reason** *for my absence was* **because** *I was ill* is bad English. It is better to say *The* **reason** *for my absence was that I was ill.* 2 Compare **cause** and **reason.** A **cause** is something which produces a result: *The* **cause** *of the accident was the fact that he was driving too fast.* A **reason** is something which explains or excuses an action: *The* **reason** *he was driving so fast was that he was late for an important meeting* . —see also EXCUSE² (USAGE)◁

reason² v **1** [I] to use one's REASON¹ (2): *the ability to reason* **2** [T+*that; obj*] to form an opinion based on REASON¹ (2): *We reasoned that the terrorists would not negotiate unless we made some concessions.* **3** [T+*obj*+**into/out of**] to persuade (someone) to do/not to do: *Try to reason him out of that idea/into going away quietly.* **4 Their's not to reason why, Their's but to do and die** *quote* a phrase from the poem *The Charge of the Light Brigade* by Tennyson, used now to say that someone should not ask questions but should just do as they are told —see also CHARGE OF THE LIGHT BRIGADE — **~ er** n : *a clever reasoner* **reason with** sbdy. *phr* v [T] to talk or argue with (someone) in order to persuade them to be more sensible: *There's no point in trying to reason with him — he'll never change his mind.*

rea·so·na·ble /ˈriːzənəbəl/ adj **1** (of a person or their behaviour) showing fairness and good sense: *a reasonable man* | *a reasonable request* | *Be reasonable — you can't*

expect her to do all the work on her own! | *a perfectly reasonable thing to do* | *It's reasonable to expect that prices will come down soon.* —opposite **unreasonable;** see LOGICAL (USAGE) **2** a not too much, too many, or too great: *We live a reasonable distance away from the station.* **b** (of a price) fair; not expensive: *Bananas are quite reasonable this week.* **3** not bad; quite good: *"What's the food in the canteen like?" "It's quite reasonable."* — **~ ness** n [U]

rea·son·a·bly /ˈriːzənəbli/ adv **1** sensibly: *to behave reasonably* **2** quite; fairly: *The car is in reasonably good condition.* | *They live reasonably close.* | *a reasonably-priced car*

rea·soned /ˈriːzənd/ adj [A] apprec (of a statement, argument, etc.) clearly thought out; based on reason: *a (well-)reasoned statement/explanation*

rea·son·ing /ˈriːzənɪŋ/ n [U] the use of one's REASON¹ (2): *According to their reasoning lower oil prices will stimulate business activity in the poorer countries.*

re·as·sure /ˌriːəˈʃʊər/ v [T (**about**)] to comfort and make free from fear or worry; bring back confidence to: *I was worried that my work wasn't good enough, but the teacher reassured me (about it).* | *She was reassured by our offer of support.* [+that] *The chairman tried to reassure the shareholders that the company's bad results would not be repeated.* —see INSURE (USAGE) —**surance** n [C;U] : *She won't believe it in spite of all our reassurance(s).* —**suringly** adv : *"You'll be all right," he said reassuringly.*

re·bar·ba·tive /rɪˈbɑːbətɪv‖-ɑːr-/ adj fml very unattractive or offensive; REPELLENT

re·bate /ˈriːbeɪt/ n an official return of part of a payment: *You can claim a rebate on your tax because you didn't work for a full year.* —compare DISCOUNT¹ (1)

reb·el¹ /ˈrebəl/ n **1** a person who rebels: *Anti-government rebels have seized the radio station.* | *Tom's always been a bit of a rebel; he hates conforming.* | *rebel tribesmen* | *a rebel stronghold* **2** *AmE* a supporter of the Confederacy in the American Civil War

re·bel² /rɪˈbel/ v **-ll-** [I (**against**)] to oppose or fight against someone in a position of control: *The people have rebelled against their foreign rulers.* | *children who rebel against authority/against their parents*

re·bel·lion /rɪˈbeljən/ n [C;U (**against**)] (an act of) rebelling: *The slaves rose in rebellion against their masters.* | *an armed rebellion* | *The rebellion was ruthlessly put down.* (=stopped) | *The president's determination to pursue this policy led to a rebellion among his own ministers.* —compare REVOLUTION (1)

re·bel·lious /rɪˈbeljəs/ adj disobedient and hard to control; tending to rebel: *rebellious teenagers/behaviour* — **~ ly** adv — **~ ness** n [U]

Rebel With·out a Cause /ˌ·· ·ˌ·· ˈ·/ an American film with James Dean as a young man from a good home who gets into trouble with the police. James Dean's performance has provided an image of the typical REBEL (=someone who opposes authority) since the film first came out in 1955.

re·bind /ˌriːˈbaɪnd/ v **-bound** /ˈbaʊnd/ [T] to put a new BINDING (=cover) onto (a book)

re·birth /ˌriːˈbɜːθ‖-ɜːrθ/ n [S] fml a renewal of life or existence: *The firm had gone bankrupt, but the following year saw its rebirth under a new name.*

re·boot /ˌriːˈbuːt/ v [I;T] to start up (a computer), usu. from a state of not working, or not working properly: *That problem should go away as soon as you reboot.* | *We normally reboot our systems only once every 24 hours.* **-reboot** /ˈriːbuːt/ n

re·born /ˌriːˈbɔːn‖-ɔːrn/ adj [F] fml or lit (as if) born again: *Our hopes of success were reborn.*

re·bound¹ /rɪˈbaʊnd/ v [I] **1** to fly back after hitting something: *The ball rebounded from the wall and I caught it.* **2** (esp. of prices, amounts, etc.) to move quickly back to a former level after falling: *Share prices rebounded today after last week's falls.*
rebound on/upon sbdy. *phr* v [T *no pass.*] (of a harmful action) to have a bad effect on (the person who did it): *His lies rebounded on him in the end because no one trusted him any more.*

re·bound² /ˈriːbaʊnd/ n **on the rebound: a** while rebounding: *I caught the ball on the rebound.* **b** (while) in an unsettled state of mind as a result of unhappiness or a disappointment: *He married her on the rebound, only a few weeks after his previous girlfriend left him.*

re·buff /rɪ'bʌf/ *n,fml* an unkind or unfriendly answer to a suggestion, request, or offer of help or friendship; SNUB: *Our request for support met with an unexpected rebuff.* — **rebuff** *v* [T] : *She rebuffed all my offers of friendship.*

re·build /ˌriː'bɪld/ *v* **-built** /'bɪlt/ [T] to build again or build new parts to: *The house was rebuilt after the fire.* | (fig.) *a political party that wants to rebuild our manufacturing industry* | (fig.) *to rebuild one's confidence after a setback*

re·buke /rɪ'bjuːk/ *v* [T (**for**)] *fml* to speak to (someone) severely, esp. officially: *The judge rebuked the police for their treatment of the prisoner.* —**rebuke** *n* : *to administer a rebuke*

re·bus /'riːbəs/ *n* a word game or PUZZLE in which words have to be guessed from pictures or letters that suggest the sounds that make them: *"R U 18" is a rebus for "Are you 18?"*

re·but /rɪ'bʌt/ *v* **-tt-** [T] *fml* to prove the falseness of (a statement or charge); REFUTE — ~ **tal** *n* [C;U]

re·cal·ci·trant /rɪ'kælsɪtrənt/ *adj,fml* refusing to obey or be controlled, even after being punished: *recalcitrant children/behaviour* —**trance** *n* [U]

re·call¹ /rɪ'kɔːl/ *v* [T] **1** [*not in progressive forms*] *rather fml* **a** to bring back to the mind; remember: *I can't recall the exact details of the report.* [+*v·ing/that*] *I don't recall ever meeting her/that I ever met her.* [+*wh-*] *Do you recall why she left?* **b** to make one remember (someone or something) by being similar: *a style of film-making that recalls Alfred Hitchcock* **2** [(**from, to**)] to send for or take back: *The government recalled its ambassador after the diplomatic row.* | *The makers have recalled a lot of cars that were unsafe.* — ~ **able** *adj*

re·call² /rɪ'kɔːl‖'riːkɔːl, riː'kɔːl/ *n* **1** [S;U (**from, to**)] (a) call to return: *the recall of our ambassador* **2** [U] the power to remember something learned or experienced: *John has* **total recall** *and never forgets anything.* **3 beyond/past recall** impossible to be changed

re·cant /rɪ'kænt/ *v* [I;T] *fml* to say publicly that one no longer holds (a former political or religious belief): *He recanted (his faith) and became a Muslim/Christian.* | *She recanted her testimony that she had never met the accused man.* — ~ **ation** /ˌriːkæn'teɪʃən/ *n* [C;U]

re·cap¹ /'riːkæp/ *v* **-pp-** [I;T] *infml* to recapitulate: *He recapped on what the teacher had said.* —**recap** *n*

re·cap² /ˌriː'kæp/ *v* [T] *AmE infml for* RETREAD —**recap** /'riːkæp/ *n*

re·ca·pit·u·late /ˌriːkə'pɪtʃʊleɪt/ *v* [I;T] to repeat (the chief points of something that has been said); SUMMARIZE: *So, to recapitulate, here again are the main reasons why I think we should proceed with the project.* —**lation** /ˌriːkəpɪtʃʊ'leɪʃən/ *n* [C;U]

re·cap·ture /riː'kæptʃəʳ/ *v* [T] **1** to get into one's power again; CAPTURE¹ (1,2) again: *The police recaptured the escaped criminal.* **2** *lit* to bring back into the mind; cause to be experienced again: *a book that recaptures perfectly the flavour of the period*

re·cast /ˌriː'kɑːst‖ˌriː'kæst/ *v* **-cast** [T] **1** to give a new shape to: *to recast a statue/a sentence* **2** to change the actors in (a play): (fig.) *The cabinet* (=most important ministers) *has been completely recast in the latest government changes.*

recd *written abbrev. for:* received

re·cede /rɪ'siːd/ *v* [I (**from**)] **1** (of a thing) to move back or away: *His hair is beginning to recede from his forehead.* | (fig.) *Hopes for their safety are receding fast.* **2** to slope backwards: *a receding chin*

re·ceipt /rɪ'siːt/ *n* **1** [C] a written statement that one has received money (or sometimes goods): *Ask the shop for a receipt when you pay the bill.* | *The assistant will* **make out** (=write) **a receipt.** **2** [U (**of**)] *fml* the fact of receiving: *Did you write to acknowledge receipt of their cheque?* | **On receipt of** (=when we receive) *your instructions, we will send the goods.* **3** [C] *old use for* RECIPE **4 be in receipt of** *pomp* to have received: *We are in receipt of your letter of the 17th.*

re·ceipts /rɪ'siːts/ *n* [P] money received by a business, bank, etc.: *The bank's receipts have increased since last year.*

re·cei·va·ble /rɪ'siːvəbəl/ *adj* **1** able or fit to be received **2** *tech* (of a bill or debt) on which money is to be received —compare PAYABLE (1)

re·ceive /rɪ'siːv/ *v* [T] **1** to come into possession of (something that is given or sent to one); get: *to receive a letter/some good news/a lot of attention* | *The lake receives the water from this river.* | *Are you entitled to receive unemployment benefit?* | *We've received a lot of complaints about the new radio programme.* **2** to experience; be the subject of; UNDERGO: *to receive a nasty shock/a blow on the head from a falling stone* | *He is receiving specialist medical treatment at a private clinic.* **3 a** to accept as a visitor or member; welcome: *He was received into the Church.* | *She only receives guests on Monday afternoons.* **b** to act in reply to: *How did they receive your suggestion?* (=did they like it, dislike it, accept it, refuse it, etc.?) **4 a** (of a radio or television set) to turn (radio waves) into sound or pictures **b** to be able to hear a radio message sent by: *"Are you receiving me?" "Receiving you loud and clear!"* **5 For what we are about to receive, may the Lord make us truly thankful** *quote* a prayer sometimes said before a meal **6 on the re'ceiving end (of)** *infml* suffering (something unpleasant done by someone else): *We were on the receiving end of several complaints.*

re·ceived /rɪ'siːvd/ *adj* [A] *fml or tech* generally accepted or regarded as standard: *The* **received wisdom** (=general opinion) *in Washington is that the Defense Secretary will resign.*

Received Pro·nun·ci·a·tion /ˌ·ˌ ··· ˈ·ˌ/ *n* [U] RP

re·ceiv·er /rɪ'siːvəʳ/ *n* **1** the part of a telephone that is held to one's ear —see TELEPHONE (USAGE) **2** *fml or old-fash* a radio or television set **3** (*often cap.*) (in British law) someone officially appointed to take charge of affairs of someone who is BANKRUPT (1): *Their business has failed and is* **in the hands of the (official) receiver. 4** a person who buys and sells stolen property **5** (in American football) an offensive player in a position to catch a pass: *wide receiver* (=one near the border of the playing area)

re·ceiv·er·ship /rɪ'siːvəʃɪp‖-vər-/ *n* [U] the duty of the (official) receiver (3): *Due to the recession this company will* **go into receivership** (=be managed by the receiver) *as from Monday.*

re·ceiv·ing /rɪ'siːvɪŋ/ *n* [U] the crime of being a RECEIVER (4): *The police charged him with receiving.*

re·cent /'riːsənt/ *adj* having happened or come into existence only a short time ago: *recent history* | *a news report on the most recent developments in the court case* | *one of the most exciting elections of recent years* | *during his recent visit to China* —see NEW (USAGE) — ~ **ness** *n* [U]

re·cent·ly /'riːsəntli/ *adv* not long ago; lately: *I've only recently started learning French.* | *I lived in London until quite recently.* | *her recently published autobiography*

re·cep·ta·cle /rɪ'septəkəl/ *n tech or fml* a container for keeping things in

re·cep·tion /rɪ'sepʃən/ *n* **1** [C *usu. sing.*] a particular kind of welcome: *I got a warm/a very friendly reception.* | *The Senator was given a cool/hostile reception by the crowd.* **2** [C] a large formal party: *They're giving/holding a reception to welcome the new ambassador.* **3** [U] the office, desk, or department that receives visitors to a hotel or large organization: *Leave your key at reception/at the reception desk.* | *I'll wait for you in reception.* **4** [U] the quality of radio or television signals: *Radio reception isn't very good here.* **5** [C] a large party after a marriage ceremony held at the BRIDE's house, in a restaurant, or in a hotel —see also extra information on page 1402

reception class /·'·· ˌ·/ *also* **reception**— *n BrE* a class for children aged four or five who have just started at a school

re·cep·tion·ist /rɪ'sepʃənɪst/ *n* a person who welcomes or deals with people arriving in a hotel or place of business, visiting a doctor, etc.

reception room /·'·· ·/ *n tech, esp. BrE* a room, esp. a LIVING ROOM in a private house that is not a kitchen, bedroom, or bathroom: *According to the estate agent's ad, the house has three bedrooms and two reception rooms.*

re·cep·tive /rɪ'septɪv/ *adj* [(**to**)] willing to consider new ideas: *a receptive mind* | *He's not very receptive to my suggestions.* — ~ **ly** *adv* — ~ **ness, -tivity** /ˌriːsep'tɪvⱥti/ *n* [U]

re·cess¹ /rɪ'ses‖'riːses/ *n* **1** [C;U] a pause for rest during the working day or the working year: *Parliament is in*

recess *now.* | *the summer recess* **2** [U] *AmE* a short pause between classes in a GRADE SCHOOL **3** [C] a space in the wall of a room for shelves, cupboards, etc.; ALCOVE **4** [C *often pl.*] *lit* a secret inner part or place, that is hard to reach: *the inmost recesses of the cave|of her mind*

re-cess² /rɪ'ses/ *v* **1** [T] to make into or put into a RECESS¹ (3): *a recessed bookshelf* **2** [I] *esp. AmE* to take a RECESS¹ (1)

re-ces-sion /rɪ'seʃən/ *n* a period of reduced trade and business activity —compare DEPRESSION (2)

re-ces-sion-al /rɪ'seʃənəl/ *n* a HYMN (=holy song) sung at the end of a church service

re-ces-sive /rɪ'sesɪv/ *adj tech* (of groups of physical qualities passed on from parent to child) only appearing in the child if also in the GENEs of both parents: *Blue eyes are recessive and brown eyes are dominant.*

re-charge /ˌriː'tʃɑːdʒ‖-ɑːr-/ *v* [T] to put a new charge of electricity into (a BATTERY): *The holiday has really recharged my batteries* (=has made me feel much better). —**recharge** *n* : *These batteries need a recharge.* — ~ **able** *adj* : *a rechargeable torch*

re-cher-ché /rə'ʃeɪʃeɪ‖rə'ʃeər-, rəˌʃeər'ʃeɪ/ *adj* rare and strange; EXOTIC: *His ideas were too recherché for his audience.*

re-cid-i-vist /rɪ'sɪdɪvɪst/ *n tech* a person who keeps going back to a life of crime, even after being punished; an incurable criminal —**-vism** *n* [U]

re-ci-pe /'resɪpi/ *n* [(for)] a set of instructions for cooking a particular type of food: *a recipe for (making) chocolate cake* | *He didn't follow the recipe and the cake came out all wrong.* | *a recipe book* | (fig.) *a recipe for a happy marriage* —compare FORMULA (2)

re-cip-i-ent /rɪ'sɪpiənt/ *n* [(of)] *fml* a person who receives something: *the recipient of the letter|of the news|of a grant*

re-cip-ro-cal /rɪ'sɪprəkəl/ *adj fml* given and received in return; exchanged between two people or groups; MUTUAL: *a reciprocal trade agreement between two nations* | *They have a reciprocal loathing for|of each other.* — ~ **ly** /kli/ *adv*

re-cip-ro-cate /rɪ'sɪprəkeɪt/ *v* **1** [I;T] *fml* to give or do something in return (for): *They invited us to their party, and we reciprocated (their invitation) by inviting them to ours.* | *His dislike of me is entirely reciprocated.* (=I dislike him too.) **2** [I] *tech* (of a machine part) to move backwards and forwards in a straight line, like a PISTON: *a reciprocating engine* —**-cation** /rɪˌsɪprə'keɪʃən/ *n* [U]

re-ci-pro-ci-ty /ˌresɪ'prosɪti‖-'prɑː-/ *n* [U] *fml or tech* the exchange of advantages between two groups: *reciprocity in trading rights between two nations*

re-cit-al /rɪ'saɪtl/ *n* [(of)] **1** a performance of poetry or esp. music, given by one performer, or the students of one teacher, or written by one writer: *a piano recital* — compare CONCERT (1) **2** *fml* an account or description: *He gave us a terrible recital of his experiences.*

re-ci-ta-tion /ˌresɪ'teɪʃən/ *n* **1** [U] the act of reciting **2** [C] a piece of literature that is recited: *He gives recitations from Shakespeare.*

re-ci-ta-tive /ˌresɪtə'tiːv/ *n* [C;U] *tech* (a) speech set to music that continues the story of an OPERA (=a musical play) between the songs

re-cite /rɪ'saɪt/ *v* **1** [I;T] to say (something learned) aloud from memory: *to recite a poem* **2** [T] to give a detailed account or list of; ENUMERATE: *He recited his complaints.* **3** [I] *AmE* to answer a teacher's questions about a lesson —**-citer** *n*

reck /rek/ *v* [T] *BrE lit* (usu. with **not** or **little**) to care; mind: *They recked nothing|little of the danger.* | *He little recked what might happen.*

reck-less /'rekləs/ *adj* [(of)] (of a person or their behaviour) not caring or worrying about the possible bad or dangerous results of one's actions; hasty and careless: *It was reckless of him to leave his job before he had another one.* | *reckless driving* | *a reckless disregard of the consequences of their action* | (*fml*) *reckless of danger* — ~ **ly** *adv* — ~ **ness** *n* [U]

reck-on /'rekən/ *v* [T] **1** to guess; believe as a result of calculating roughly but not exactly: [+*that*] *The experts reckon that about 10,000 tonnes of grain will be needed.* | *How much do you reckon (that) she earns?* [+*obj+to-v*] *The likely cost of the system is reckoned to be about $100*

million. **2** [+(*that*); *obj*] *infml* to think; suppose: *I reckon (that) he'll come soon.* | *"Can you do it?" "I reckon so."* **3** [*often pass; not in progressive forms*] *rather fml generally* to consider or regard: [+*obj+to-v|n|adj*] *She was reckoned (to be) a great actress|to have the greatest talent of her generation.* [+*obj+adv|prep*, esp. **among, as**] *I reckon him as a friend|among my friends.* **4** [(UP)] *fml* to calculate; add up (an amount, cost, etc.): *My pay is reckoned from the 1st of the month.* | *She reckoned up the cost.*

reckon sthg. ↔ **in** (sthg.) *phr v* [T] *fml* to include (in); take (an amount) into account in (a sum): *Have you reckoned in the cost of postage?* | *Have you reckoned the cost of postage in the total?*

reckon on sbdy./sthg. *phr v* [T] to expect or depend on (something happening or having something); make plans in expectation of: *We're reckoning on a large profit|on your support.* [+*v-ing*] *We didn't reckon on spending so much money on the repairs.*

reckon with sbdy./sthg. *phr v* [T] **1** to be faced with or opposed by; have to deal with: *If you do that again you'll have the head teacher to reckon with.* **2** to take account of in one's plans: *We hadn't reckoned with the possibility that it might rain.* **3 to be reckoned with** to be taken into account seriously as a possible opponent, competitor, danger, etc.: *She's a woman to be reckoned with.* | *The new company is already a force to be reckoned with.*

reckon without sbdy./sthg. *phr v* [T] to fail to take account of (possible problems) when making a plan; not consider: *When he decided to change his job, he reckoned without the difficulty of selling his house.*

reck-on-ing /'rekənɪŋ/ *n* **1** [U] calculation, esp. rough rather than exact calculation: *By my reckoning, it must be 60 kilometres from here to the coast.* | *I think you're out* (=mistaken) *in your reckoning.* **2** [C] *old use* a bill: *We paid our reckoning and left.* **3** [U] the calculation of a ship's position —compare DEAD RECKONING; see also DAY OF RECKONING

re-claim /rɪ'kleɪm/ *v* [T (**from**)] **1** to ask for the return of: *You may be entitled to reclaim some of the tax you paid last year.* **2** to make (land) fit for use: *This land was reclaimed from the sea.* **3** to obtain (useful materials) from a waste product: *a firm that reclaims metal from old cars* **4** *fml* to help to behave in a more socially acceptable way, lead a better life, etc.: *Her mission was to reclaim former criminals.* —**reclamation** /ˌreklə'meɪʃən/ *n* [U] : *land reclamation*

re-cline /rɪ'klaɪn/ *v* **1** [I+*adv*|*prep*] *fml* to lie back or down; be or put oneself in a position of rest: *She reclined lazily on the cushions.* | *in a reclining position* **2** [T+*obj*+*adv*|*prep*] *fml* to lean (a part of oneself): *She reclined her head against my shoulder.*

re-cluse /rɪ'kluːs‖'rekluːs/ *n* a person who lives alone away from the world and avoids other people; HERMIT

rec-og-ni-tion /ˌrekəg'nɪʃən/ *n* **1** [U] the fact of knowing someone or something; recognizing or being recognized: *She hoped she would avoid recognition by wearing dark glasses and a hat.* | *Illness and age had changed her* **beyond recognition/out of all recognition.** (=made her impossible to recognize) | *a voice recognition system for a computer* **2** [U] the state of being accepted as legal, real, or valuable: *The new government has not yet received recognition from other countries.* | *a young writer struggling for recognition* **3** [S;U (of)] *fml* (a) reward given to show gratefulness: *Please accept this cheque* **in recognition of/as a recognition of** *your services.*

re-cog-ni-zance /rɪ'kɒgnɪzəns‖ -'kɑːg-/ *n* [U] *law* **on one's own recognizance** with the promise that one will do what has been asked by a court, e.g. to appear at one's TRIAL: *After the arraignment the men were released on their own recognizance until the trial next month.* —compare BAIL¹ (1)

rec-og-nize also **-nise** *BrE* /'rekəgnaɪz, 'rekən-/ *v* [T *not in progressive forms*] **1** to know again (someone or something one has seen, heard, or experienced before): *I recognized Mary in the photograph.* | *Dogs recognize people by their smell.* | *The town has changed so much you wouldn't recognize it.* | *The doctor immediately recognized the child's symptoms; she had measles.* **2** [(**as**)] to accept as being legal or real, or as having value: *They refused to recognize our government/to recognize the union.* | *She is a recognized authority on teaching English* **3** to see clearly though perhaps unwillingly; be prepared to admit: *You must recognize the difficult position the* company is in. [+(that)] *We recognize that this is an un-pleasant choice to have to make.* **4** to show official grate-fulness for: *The government recognized his services by making him a lord.* —**nizable** *adj* —**nizably** *adv*

re·coil¹ /rɪˈkɔɪl/ *v* [I] **1** [(from)] to move back suddenly in fear or dislike: *She recoiled at the sight of the snake|recoiled from the snake.* | (*fig.*) *He tends to recoil from making difficult decisions.* **2** (of a gun) to spring back (when fired)
    recoil on/upon sbdy. *phr v* [T *no pass.*] *fml* (of a harm-ful action) to have a bad effect on (the person who did it): *Their dishonest business methods recoiled on them be-cause no one would do business with them any more.*

re·coil² /ˈriːkɔɪl, rɪˈkɔɪl/ *n* [S;U] (a) sudden backward move-ment, esp. of a gun after firing

rec·ol·lect /ˌrekəˈlekt/ *v* [T *not in progressive forms*] *rather fml* to call back to mind (something formerly known); remember: *Do you recollect her name?* [+*v-ing|wh-*] *I don't recollect meeting her|where she lives|how to get there.* [+(*that*)] *I recollect (that) she had red hair.* | *As far as I (can) recollect, her name is Juliet.*

rec·ol·lec·tion /ˌrekəˈlekʃən/ *n rather fml* **1** [U (of)] the power or action of remembering the past; memory: *I have no recollection of* (=do not remember) *meeting him.* | *Her recollection of the events is rather patchy.* **2** [C] some-thing in one's memory of the past: *That evening together is one of my happiest recollections.* **3 to the best of my recollection** if I remember right; I think, but am not sure: *To the best of my recollection she drives a Mercedes.*

re·com·bi·nant DNA /riːˌkɒmbɪnənt diː en ˈeɪ||-ˌkɑːm-/ *n* [U] DNA that has been taken out of one cell and combined with the DNA of another cell. The cells may come from completely different kinds of living things, such as animals and plants —see also GENETIC ENGINEERING

rec·om·mend /ˌrekəˈmend/ *v* [T] **1** [(for, as, to)] to praise as being good for a purpose; provide information about (someone or something good): *They recommended her for the job|as a good lawyer.* | *Can you recommend a good hotel (to me)?* [+*obj(i)+obj(d)*] (*BrE*) *Can you recommend me a good hotel?* **2** to advise or suggest as a correct or suitable course of action: *I recommend caution in deal-ing with this matter.* [+*v-ing*] *He recommends wearing safety equipment.* [+*that*] *The committee has recom-mended that the training programme (should) be im-proved.* | *You shouldn't exceed the recommended dose of the medicine.* **3** [(to)] (of a quality) to make (someone or something) attractive: *This hotel has nothing to recom-mend it (to travellers) except cheapness.*

rec·om·men·da·tion /ˌrekəmenˈdeɪʃən/ *n* **1** [C;U] the act of recommending or something (esp. a course of action) that is recommended; advice or suggestion: *We bought the car on Paul's recommendation.* (=he recommended it) | *The government has agreed to implement* (=carry out) *the recommendations in the report.* | *We agreed to make a recommendation to the board.* **2** [C] a letter or state-ment that recommends, esp. someone for a job: *I wrote him a good recommendation.*

rec·om·pense¹ /ˈrekəmpens/ *v* [T (for)] *fml* to give a recom-pense to: *We ought to recompense them (for their trouble).*

recompense² *n* [S;U (for)] *fml* a reward or payment (for trouble, loss, inconvenience, etc.): *They received £1000 in recompense|as a recompense for the damage to their house.* —compare COMPENSATION, CONSOLATION

rec·on·cile /ˈrekənsaɪl/ *v* [T (with)] **1** to find agreement between (two ideas, situations, etc. that seem to be in op-position): *How do you reconcile your political principles with your religious beliefs?* | *the problem of reconciling all the different versions of this event* **2** to bring back friendly relations between; make friendly again: *They quarrelled, but now they're completely reconciled.* —**cilable** /ˌrekənˈsaɪləbəl/ *adj*
    reconcile sbdy. **to** sthg. *phr v* [T] to cause (someone) to accept (something unwanted or unpleasant): *He never became reconciled to the loss of his wife.*

rec·on·cil·i·a·tion /ˌrekənsɪliˈeɪʃən/ also **rec·on·cile·ment** /ˈrekənsaɪlmənt/— *n* [S;U (between, with)] (a) bringing back of friendly relations: *There was no hope of a recon-ciliation between the two families.* | *a spirit of reconcilia-tion* | *to effect a reconciliation*

rec·on·dite /ˈrekəndaɪt, rɪˈkɒn-||ˈrekən-, rɪˈkɑːn-/ *adj fml* (of ideas, knowledge, etc.) not commonly known; difficult

to understand; ABSTRUSE: *a recondite subject* — ~**ness** *n* [U]

re·con·di·tion /ˌriːkənˈdɪʃən/ *v* [T] to repair and bring back into working order: *A reconditioned engine is cheaper than a new one.*

re·con·nais·sance /rɪˈkɒnɪsəns||rɪˈkɑː-/ *n* [C;U] (an act of) reconnoitring: *The patrol made a reconnaissance.* | *a reconnaissance flight|aircraft*

re·con·noi·tre *BrE* || **-ter** *AmE* /ˌrekəˈnɔɪtər||ˌriː-/ *v* [I;T] (of soldiers, ships, or aircraft) to go near (the place where an enemy is) in order to find out the enemy's numbers, position, etc.

re·con·sid·er /ˌriːkənˈsɪdər/ *v* [I;T] to think again about (a subject) with the possibility of changing one's mind: *She was asked to reconsider her decision to resign.* — ~**ation** /ˌriːkənsɪdəˈreɪʃən/ *n* [U]

re·con·sti·tute /riːˈkɒnstɪtjuːt||riːˈkɑːnstɪtuːt/ *v* [T] **1** to bring back into existence, usu. in a changed form: *We decided to reconstitute the committee under a new chair-man.* **2** to bring back (dried food) into its former condi-tion by adding water: *Milk powder has to be reconstituted.* | *reconstituted potato*

re·con·struct /ˌriːkənˈstrʌkt/ *v* [T] **1** to rebuild after des-truction or damage **2** to build up a complete description or picture of (something only partly known): *The police are trying to reconstruct the crime from the few clues they have.*

re·con·struc·tion /ˌriːkənˈstrʌkʃən/ *n* **1** [C;U] the action, or an example of reconstructing: *a reconstruction of an 18th-century village* **2** [U] (*cap.*) (1865–77) the period of American history after the Civil War when the southern states, under government and military control, rejoined the US. Slavery was **abolished** (ABOLISH), black people were given the right to vote, and a few universities were established for black people. Many white southerners strongly opposed these measures and some formed the KU KLUX KLAN. Military control ended in 1877. —see also CIVIL RIGHTS MOVEMENT, CIVIL WAR

re·cord¹ /rɪˈkɔːd||-ɔːrd/ *v* **1** [T] to write down (a descrip-tion or piece of information) so that it will be known in the future: *I recorded the score in a notebook.* | *The coroner recorded a verdict of accidental death.* [+*wh-*] *What be-came of him|How he died is not recorded.* | *This is the first recorded case of anyone surviving this disease.* **2** [I;T] to preserve (sound or a television broadcast) so that it can be heard and/or seen again: *The machine is recording now.* | *The broadcast was recorded, not live.* | *Their con-versation was secretly recorded.* | *She has recorded several albums.* (=several records of her music have been made) **3** [T] (of an instrument) to show by measuring: *The ther-mometer recorded a temperature of 28 degrees.* | *Winds of up to 100 kph have been recorded.*

rec·ord² /ˈrekɔːd||-ərd/ *n* **1** [C (of)] a written statement of facts, events, etc.: *Keep a record of how much you spend.* | (*fig.*) **To set the record straight** (=so that the true facts will be known), *it was not my decision to do this.* **2** [C] the known or recorded facts about the past behaviour or performance of a person, group, company, etc.: *John and Peter both have fine military records.* | *He has a long criminal record.* | *She's new to the sales department, but her* **track record** (=list of successes) *as publicity direc-tor is excellent.* **3** [C (for)] the best yet done, esp. in sport; the highest/lowest figure ever reached: *She set|estab-lished a record|broke the record for long distance swim-ming.* | *the British long-jump record* | *She holds the world record for discus throwing.* **4** [C (of)] also **gramophone record, disc, LP, album**– a circular piece of plastic on which sound is stored by MECHANICAL means so that it can be played back at any time (on a RECORD PLAYER): *Put on|Play another record.* | *She has made several records of Schubert songs.* | *a record collection* —compare COM-PACT DISC **5** [C (of)] something that provides information about the past: *Archaeologists dig up the records of an-cient civilizations.* **6** *tech* a unit of stored DATA on a com-puter that can be handled in a single operation **7** [U] *fml* the state of being recorded in writing and therefore es-tablished as fact: *It is a* **matter of record** (=known to be true) *that no one has ever failed this examination.* **8 for the record** declared openly and formally, esp. so as to make known one's disagreement: *Just for the record, I think we're making a grave mistake.* **9 off the record** *infml* unofficial(ly); speaking/spoken privately: *My*

remarks were off the record and are not to be printed. |
Strictly off the record (=I am speaking unofficially), *the
company is in serious trouble.* —see also OFF-THE-RECORD
10 on record: a (of a fact or event) ever recorded: *the coldest winter on record* **b** (of a person) having publicly said,
as if for written records: *He is/went on record as hav-
ing opposed this law.* | *I'd like to put on record my oppo-
sition to this law.* (=state it clearly and have it recorded)

record³ *adj* [A] more, faster, better, etc., than ever before:
a record crop of corn | *They finished in record time.* | *Sales
have reached record levels/a record high.*

record-break·ing /ˈ·· ˌ··/ *adj* (usu. in sport) going beyond
the former RECORD² (3): *a record-breaking speed* —**record-
breaker** *n*

recorded de·liv·er·y /·ˌ·· ·ˈ···/ *n* [U] *BrE* a method of sending mail by which one can get official proof that it has
been delivered: *I sent it (by) recorded delivery.* —compare
CERTIFIED MAIL

re·cord·er /rɪˈkɔːdəʳ‖-ɔːr-/ *n* **1** a simple musical instrument of the WOODWIND family, with no REED (2), played
by blowing into it; a kind of whistle **2** a TAPE RECORDER
3 (*often cap.*) a judge in some city courts both in Britain
and in the US

re·cord·ing /rɪˈkɔːdɪŋ‖-ɔːr-/ *n* [(of)] (esp. in broadcasting)
a performance, speech, or piece of music that has been
recorded: *They made a recording of her voice.* | *some
recordings of early Italian music* | *We listened to his latest
recording.*

record li·bra·ry /ˈ·· ˌ···/ *n* a collection of RECORDS² (4) for
people to borrow, usu. for a small charge

record play·er /ˈ·· ˌ··/ also **gramophone** *old-fash BrE* ‖
phonograph *old-fash AmE— n* a piece of equipment
which can turn the information stored on a RECORD² (4)
back into the original sounds, music, etc. —see also
STEREO¹ (1)

re·count¹ /rɪˈkaʊnt/ *v* [T] *fml* to tell (a story): *She recounted
her adventures.*

re·count² /ˌriːˈkaʊnt/ *v* [T] to count again: *They had to recount the votes.*

re·count³ /ˈriːkaʊnt/ *n* a second or fresh count, esp. of votes:
The defeated candidate demanded a recount.

re·coup /rɪˈkuːp/ *v* [T] **1** to get back; regain (what one has
lost or spent): *I recoup my travelling expenses from my employer.* **2** to provide (oneself) again with money: *He stole
the diamonds to recoup himself for his gambling losses.*

re·course /rɪˈkɔːs‖ˈriːkɔːrs/ *n* [U] *fml* the use of someone
or something as a means of help: *The company hopes to
solve this problem without recourse to* (=without making use of) *further borrowing.* —compare RESORT¹ (2)

re·cov·er /rɪˈkʌvəʳ/ *v* **1** [T] to get back or bring back (esp.
something lost or taken away): *The police recovered the
stolen jewellery.* | *She recovered consciousness soon after
the accident.* | *The company hopes to recover the cost of de-
veloping this product within about two years.* | *They are
still trying to recover bodies from the wrecked building.*
(=find them and get them out) **2** [I (from)] to return to
the proper state of health, strength, ability, etc.: *He is very
ill and unlikely to recover.* | *recovering from a bad cold* |
(fig.) *The country had not yet recovered from the effects of
the war.* **3** [T] *fml* to get (oneself or one's senses, powers,
etc.) back into a proper or favourable state or position:
He almost fell, but managed to recover himself. | *She soon
recovered herself/her control and went on with her lecture.*
— **·able** *adj*

re·cov·er /ˌriːˈkʌvəʳ/ *v* [T] to put a new cover on: *They recovered all the chairs in purple silk.*

re·cov·er·y /rɪˈkʌvəri/ *n* **1** [U] the getting back of something: *the recovery of the stolen jewels* **2** [S (from)] a
return to good health, a strong condition, etc.: *She made
a quick/speedy recovery from her illness and was soon back
at work.* | *Will the government's policies lead to an eco-
nomic recovery?*

recovery pro·gram /·ˈ··· ˌ··/ *n AmE* a programme that
helps people with difficult problems of ADDICTION (=being
unable to stop doing or using something harmful e.g.
drugs, alcohol, etc.). Recovery programmes, also called
12-step programs, are very common in the US. Many
of the programmes are free and are operated by the
people who take part in them.

rec·re·ant /ˈrekriənt/ *n old use* a cowardly and disloyal
person

re·cre·ate /ˌriːkriˈeɪt/ *v* [T] **1** to make a copy of: *a Spanish
bar which tries to recreate the atmosphere of a typical English pub* **2** to cause to be seen, heard, or experienced
again, esp. in the mind: *to recreate the past in one's imagination*

rec·re·a·tion /ˌrekriˈeɪʃən/ *n* [C;U] (a form of) amusement
and enjoyment; way of spending free time: *His only recre-
ations are drinking beer and working in the garden.* | *a
recreation programme for senior citizens* — **~al** *adj* :
recreational activities/facilities

▷ USAGE **Recreation** [U] is a general word for what people do in their spare time for amusement and enjoyment. A **recreation** [C] is any particular activity
which is done for amusement. Forms of recreation include **sport,** which needs physical effort and is usually
played according to rules: *I'm not interested in* **sport.** |
My favourite **sports** *are tennis and football.* A **game**
is either an example of a sport, or an activity in which
people compete with each other using their brains :
Let's have a **game** *of tennis/cards.* An important public game is a **match:** *Have you got a ticket for the football* **match** *on Saturday?* A **hobby** is a form of recreation which people do on their own, not in order to
compete: *Her* **hobbies** *are gardening, stamp-collecting,
and playing the piano.*◁

recreation ground /·ˈ·· ·/ *BrE*‖**playground** *AmE— n* a
piece of public land set aside for games: *The children were
playing football on the recreation ground.*

recreation room /·ˈ·· ·/ *n* **1** a public room, for example
in a hospital, used for social activities **2** *AmE* also **rec
room** *infml* a room in a house used for playing games in

recreational ve·hi·cle /···ˌ··· ˈ···/ also **RV**— *n AmE tech* a
motor vehicle made esp. for recreation, such as camp-
ing or travelling with a family. Many states require special LICENSE PLATES for such vehicles, which usu. carry
the letters **RV.**

re·crim·i·nate /rɪˈkrɪmɪˌneɪt/ *v* [I (against)] *fml* to make a
charge of lying, dishonesty, or other bad behaviour
against a person who has already made a charge against
oneself —**natory** /nətəriˈ-tɔːri/ *adj*

re·crim·i·na·tion /rɪˌkrɪmɪˈneɪʃən/ *n* [C usu. pl.;U (against)]
(an act of) quarrelling and blaming one another: *Let's
make friends, instead of wasting our time on recrimina-
tions (against each other).* | *The negotiations broke down
in an atmosphere of recrimination.*

rec room /ˈrek ruːm, -rʊm/ *n AmE infml for* RECREATION
ROOM (2)

re·cru·des·cence /ˌriːkruːˈdesəns/ *n* [+of] *fml* a sudden
fresh reappearance, esp. of something unpleasant: *a
recrudescence of urban violence*

re·cruit¹ /rɪˈkruːt/ *n* **1** someone who has just joined one
of the armed forces, esp. without being forced to, and is
still being trained: *a squad of* **raw** (=completely un-
trained) **recruits 2** [(to)] a new member of an organization: *New recruits to our music club are always welcome.*

recruit² *v* **1** [T] to find in order to employ; get the services of: *We are having difficulties in recruiting well-
qualified staff.* | *Most of the teachers there are recruited
from abroad.* **2** [I;T] **a** to get (recruits) for the armed
forces **b** to form (an army, etc.) by doing this: *The King
recruited an army.* —compare CONSCRIPT¹ **3** [T] to attract
and obtain (someone) as a new member: *to recruit new
members to the party/the club* | *a recruiting drive* **4** [I;T]
old use or fml to regain (one's health, strength, etc.), e.g.
by rest and good food — **~ment** *n* [U]

recruitment a·gen·cy /·ˈ·· ˌ···/ *n* a business that makes its
money by finding suitable people for employers who
need new workers, esp. WHITE-COLLAR workers

rec·tal /ˈrektəl/ *adj med* of the RECTUM — **~ly** *adv*

rec·tan·gle /ˈrektæŋgəl/ *n* a flat shape with four straight
sides forming four RIGHT ANGLES —compare SQUARE¹ (1),
and see picture at QUADRILATERAL

rec·tan·gu·lar /rekˈtæŋgjʊləʳ/ *adj tech* in the shape of a
rectangle

rec·ti·fi·er /ˈrektɪˌfaɪəʳ/ *n* **1** someone or something that rectifies (RECTIFY (1,2)) **2** *tech* an instrument that rectifies
(RECTIFY (3))

rec·ti·fy /ˈrektɪˌfaɪ/ *v* [T] **1** *fml* to put right: *Please rectify
the mistakes in my bill.* **2** *tech* to make pure: *rectified
alcohol* **3** *tech* to change (an ALTERNATING CURRENT, or

flow of electricity backwards and forwards along a wire) so that it flows only one way (DIRECT CURRENT) —**fiable** adj —**fication** /ˌrektɪfɪˈkeɪʃən/ n [C;U]

rec·ti·lin·e·ar /ˌrektɪˈlɪniəʳ ◄/ adj fml or tech forming or moving in a straight line; having or made of straight lines

rec·ti·tude /ˈrektɪtjuːd‖-tuːd/ n [U] fml honesty of character; moral correctness

rec·to /ˈrektəʊ/ adj, n -tos [A;C] tech (being) a right-hand page of a book: written on the recto (side) —compare VERSO

rec·tor /ˈrektəʳ/ n **1** (in the Church of England and the Episcopal church) a priest in charge of an area (PARISH) from which he receives his income directly —compare VICAR (1) **2** the head of certain colleges and schools, esp. in Scotland

rec·to·ry /ˈrektəri/ n the house where a RECTOR (1) lives or used to live

rec·tum /ˈrektəm/ n med the lowest end of the bowels (the LARGE INTESTINE) through which solid food waste passes from the COLON to the ANUS —see also RECTAL

re·cum·bent /rɪˈkʌmbənt/ adj fml lying down on the back or side: a recumbent statue/posture

re·cu·pe·rate /rɪˈkjuːpəreɪt, -ˈkuː-/ v [I;T] to get well again after illness or difficulty; get back (one's health, strength, etc.): He went to the mountains to recuperate (his strength). | (fig.) to recuperate one's financial losses —**ration** /rɪˌkjuːpəˈreɪʃən, -ˌkuː-/ n [U]

re·cu·pe·ra·tive /rɪˈkjuːpərətɪv, -ˈkuː-‖-pəreɪtɪv/ adj helping one to recuperate: a recuperative holiday

re·cur /rɪˈkɜːʳ/ v -rr- [I] **1** (esp. of something unpleasant or unwelcome) to happen or appear again, or more than once; return: If the pain recurs, take these tablets. | The memory of the accident often recurs to me. (=returns to my mind) | a recurring dream/problem **2** tech (of a DECIMAL) to be repeated for ever in the same order: In 5·1515 … the figures 15 recur, and the number can be read "5·15 recurring".

re·cur·rence /rɪˈkʌrəns‖-ˈkɜːr-/ n [C;U] (an example of) recurring: the frequent recurrence/several recurrences of the disease/of a technical fault

re·cur·rent /rɪˈkʌrənt‖-ˈkɜːr-/ adj happening again and again; repeated: a recurrent problem | recurrent pains in the head — ~**ly** adv

re·cu·sant /ˈrekjʊzənt/ n, adj old use fml (someone) refusing to obey official rules or esp. to accept official religious beliefs: recusant priests

re·cy·cla·ble /ˌriːˈsaɪkləbəl/ n, adj (being) a thing that can be recycled: recyclable plastic bags | Separate the recyclables in those boxes over there.

recyclable

re·cy·cle /ˌriːˈsaɪkəl/ v [T] to treat (a substance that has already been used) so that it is fit to use again. People who care about the environment like to recycle things they have finished with to help preserve the earth's natural RESOURCES: The glass from bottles can be recycled. | a bag made of recycled paper

re·cy·cling /ˌriːˈsaɪklɪŋ/ n, adj [U] (of) the activity of reusing things that have already been used: The children are very enthusiastic about recycling. | Is there a **recycling centre** =place to take recyclables) around here?

recycling plant /·ˈ·· ˌ·/ n a workplace where materials such as glass or paper which have been used once are prepared for re-use

red¹ /red/ adj -dd- **1** of the colour of blood or fire: a red rose/dress | We painted the door red. **2** (of human hair) of a bright brownish orange or copper colour **3** (of the human skin) pink, usu. for a short time: I turned red with embarrassment/anger. | The child's eyes (=the skin round the eyes) were red from crying. **4** (of wine) of a dark pink to dark purple colour **5 be like a red rag** (BrE)/**a red flag** (AmE) **to a bull** infml to be likely to cause uncontrollable anger: She's an ardent feminist, so jokes about women are like a red rag to a bull to her. — ~**ness** n [U]

red² n **1** [C;U] (a) red colour: the reds and yellows of the evening sky | You mix red and yellow to make orange. |

The colour red is often used as a sign of danger, and in signs on roads meaning "stop". **2** [U] red clothes: dressed in red **3** in/into/out of the red in/into/out of debt: Your account is in the red. —opposite **in the black** —see also **paint the town red** (PAINT²), **see red** (SEE¹)

Red¹ adj **1** derog (esp. in newspapers) supporting LEFT-WING political ideas; Socialist or Communist: "Red Ken wins seat in Parliament." (newspaper report) —compare PINK¹ (2) **2** [no comp.] of Communist countries; esp. formerly the Communist countries of Eastern Europe **3 better Red than dead** a phrase used during the Cold War by some people opposed to NUCLEAR weapons, meaning that it would be better to be controlled by a Communist government than to be killed in a nuclear war

Red² n derog **1** for COMMUNIST **2 Reds under the beds** the unreasonable idea that there are secret Communists in public life who are a threat to the state. This phrase was used esp. after the Second World War by those opposed to Joseph McCarthy's unreasonable charges against many people in American public life that they were Communists. —see also McCARTHYISM

red ad·mi·ral /ˌ· ˈ···/ n a BUTTERFLY with bright red marks on its black wings, common in Europe and America

red a·lert /ˌ· ·ˈ·/ n [C;U] (a condition of readiness to deal with) a situation of sudden great danger: The hospital services have been put on red alert.

Red Ar·my /ˌ· ˈ···/ [the] **1** the Soviet army formed by the COMMUNIST government of the former USSR in 1918, the idea of which was to make a people's army, the soldiers coming from the workers and the officers being good Communist party men. The word Red was dropped in 1946. **2** a Japanese politically very LEFT-WING TERRORIST group formed in the 1960s

Red Ar·my Fac·tion /ˌ· ˈ·· ˌ··/ [the] see BAADER-MEINHOF GANG

Red Arrows

Red Ar·rows /ˌ· ˈ··/ [the+P] a team of British fighter aircraft which fly at shows to entertain people

Red Bar·on /ˌ· ˈ··/ [the] (1882–1918) a German airman, the **Baron von Richthofen**, who commanded a group of fighter planes during the First World War. The planes were known as Richthofen's Flying Circus because they were red and highly decorated. He shot down more planes (80) than any other pilot and was finally shot down behind enemy lines.

Red Ber·ets /ˌ· ˈ··‖ˌ· ·ˈ·/ [the+P] the popular name for the PARACHUTE division of the British army, so called because of their red hats

red blood cell /ˌ· ˈ· ·/ also **red cor·pus·cle** /ˌ· ˈ···/— n any of the cells in the blood which carry oxygen to every part of the body —compare WHITE BLOOD CELL

red-blood·ed /ˌ· ˈ···◄/ adj apprec (of a person or their behaviour) confident and strong; VIRILE: a few red-blooded curses | red-blooded males

red·breast /ˈredbrest/ n lit for ROBIN

red·brick /ˈredˌbrɪk/ n (often cap.) any of the British universities started in the late 19th century in cities outside London: Manchester and Leeds are redbricks/are redbrick universities. —compare OXBRIDGE

Red Bri·gades /ˌ· ·ˌ·/ [the] a LEFT-WING extremist TERRORIST group operating in Italy from the early 1970s

red card /ˌ· ˈ·/ n a piece of red card held up by the REFEREE of a football match to show that a player is to be sent off the field for carrying out a FOUL: The referee has given/shown him the red card. | It's a red card for their top goalscorer.

red car·pet /ˌ· ˈ··/ n [the] a special ceremonial welcome to an important guest, sometimes involving laying a red carpet on the ground for the guest to walk on: *We'll roll out the red carpet when the President comes.* | *We'll give him the* **red-carpet treatment.**

red cent /ˌ· '·/ n [S] *AmE infml* a very small amount of money: *I wouldn't give you a red cent for that old clunker.* | *not worth a red cent*

Red Chi·na /ˌ· '··/ *infml for* The People's Republic of CHINA

red·coat /'redkəʊt/ n **1** a worker at a HOLIDAY CAMP who helps entertain holidaymakers **2** a British soldier during the 18th and 19th centuries

Red Cres·cent /ˌ· '··/ [the] part of the International Red Cross and Red Crescent Movement whose aim is to offer protection and help to people suffering as a result of wars, natural disasters, etc. National Red Crescent Societies are found in many Muslim countries. Its sign, a red CRESCENT, is recognized under the Geneva Conventions and protects the people using it from being attacked or harmed —compare RED CROSS

the symbol for the **Red Crescent**

Red Cross /ˌ· '·/ n [the] part of the International Red Cross and Red Crescent Movement whose aim is to offer protection and help to people suffering as a result of wars, natural disasters, etc. Its sign, a red cross on a white background, is recognized under the Geneva Conventions and protects the people using it from being attacked or harmed: *The Red Cross is/are sending medical supplies.* —compare RED CRESCENT

the symbol for the **Red Cross**

a red cross on a white background: *The Red Cross is/are sending medical supplies.*

red·cur·rant /ˌred'kʌrənt◄‖-'kɜːr-/ n a small red berry that grows in bunches on a bush: *redcurrant wine*

red deer /ˌ· '·/ n **red deer** a large deer common in northern Europe and Asia, with a reddish brown coat

red·den /'redn/ v [I;T] to (cause to) turn red: *She reddened with embarrassment.* | *The sunset reddened the clouds.*

Red Dev·ils /ˌ· '··/ [the+P] a special British army team who give public performances of SKYDIVING

Red·ding /'redɪŋ/, **O·tis** /'əʊtɪs/ (1941–67) an American popular music singer and songwriter considered to be one of the best SOUL singers. After his death in a plane crash, his records continued to be successful, esp. *Dock Of The Bay.*

red·dish /'redɪʃ/ adj slightly red

re·dec·o·rate /riː'dekəreɪt/ v [I;T] to put new paint, paper, etc., on (the inside of a building): *We must redecorate the bathroom.*

re·deem /rɪ'diːm/ v [T] *fml* **1** to carry out; fulfil: *Has the government redeemed all its election promises?* **2** to make free of blame or bring back into favour: *She redeemed herself/her reputation with a powerful speech to the party convention.* **3** to make (something bad) slightly less bad: *Olivier's performance redeems an otherwise second-rate production.* | *He's a thoroughly unpleasant man; his one* **redeeming feature** *is his honesty.* **4** [(from)] to buy back (something one has given in return for being lent money): *I redeemed my watch from the pawnshop.* **5** *fml* to buy or gain (someone's) freedom: *Christ came to Earth to redeem us from sin.* **6** to exchange for goods or other things of value: *Redeem this coupon for 10p off your next purchase.* **– –able** adj

Re·deem·er /rɪ'diːmə^r/ [the, our] *lit* Jesus Christ

re·demp·tion /rɪ'dempʃən/ n [U] **1** the action of redeeming or state of being redeemed **2 beyond/past redemption** *fml* too bad to be saved or improved

redemption cen·ter /·'·· ˌ·/ n *AmE* a place where TRADING STAMPS can be redeemed

Red En·sign /ˌ· '··/ [the] the flag of the British Merchant

Navy, a red flag with the Union Jack in the top left corner

re·de·ploy /ˌriːdɪ'plɔɪ/ v [T] to rearrange (workers, soldiers, equipment, etc.) in a more effective way: *This small school is being closed, but the teachers will be redeployed* (=given new jobs) *in other schools.* **– ~ment** n [U]

re·de·vel·op /ˌriːdɪ'veləp/ v [T] to rebuild (a building or esp. an area): *The old city centre has been completely redeveloped since the war.* **– ~ment** n [C;U]

red eye /'· ·/ n [U] **1** an unwanted effect in a photograph taken with a flash, in which a person's eyes appear to be red **2** *AmE sl* cheap WHISKEY or other strong spirits **3** *AmE infml* a passenger aircraft making a long-distance flight at night: *He's travelling on the red-eye from New York.*

red-faced /ˌ· '·◄/ adj (having red cheeks because of being) embarrassed or ashamed about something: *After their predictions of easy success, the actual election result left them very red-faced.*

red flag /ˌ· '·/ n **1** [C] a flag of a red colour, used as a danger signal **2** [the] (*often cap.*) **a** the flag of the political LEFT² (2) **b** the party song of the political LEFT² (4)

Red·ford /'redfəd‖-fərd/, **Rob·ert** /'rɒbət‖'rɑːbərt/ (1937–) an American film actor and DIRECTOR who was in films such as *Butch Cassidy and the Sundance Kid*, *The Sting*, and *Out of Africa*. He is popular for his good looks as well as his acting. —see pictures at BUTCH CASSIDY AND THE SUNDANCE KID, GREAT GATSBY

red gi·ant /ˌ· '··/ n a coolish star, near to the middle of its life, larger and less solid than the sun —compare WHITE DWARF

Red·grave /'redgreɪv/, **Sir Mi·chael** /'maɪkəl/ (1908–1985) an English film and theatre actor

Redgrave, Va·nes·sa /və'nesə/ (1937–) an English actress, the daughter of Sir Michael Redgrave. She is active in LEFT-WING politics.

red-hand·ed /ˌ· '··◄/ adj [F] in the act of doing something wrong: *They caught him red-handed while he was just putting the diamonds in his pocket.*

red·head /'redhed/ n *infml* a person, esp. a woman, with RED¹ (2) hair: *He married a beautiful redhead.*

red her·ring /ˌ· '··/ n a fact or subject which is introduced to draw people's attention away from the main point

red-hot /ˌ· '·◄/ adj (of metal) so hot that it shines red: *red-hot iron* | (fig.) *red-hot enthusiasm* —compare WHITE-HOT

Re·dif·fu·sion /ˌriːdɪ'fjuːʒən/ *BrE* a system for sending radio and television programmes to listeners and viewers by using CABLES

Red In·di·an /ˌ· '···/, also **Indian**— n *taboo* a NATIVE AMERICAN

re·di·rect /ˌriːdaɪ'rekt, -dɪ-/ *BrE* ‖ **forward** *AmE*— v [T] to send in a new direction, esp. to send (a letter) to a different address

re·dis·trib·ute /ˌriːdɪ'strɪbjuːt/ v [T] to share out again in a different way **– –ution** /ˌriːdɪstrɪ'bjuːʃən/ n [U] : *the redistribution of wealth in the country*

Red Leices·ter /ˌ· '··/ n [U] a type of English cheese

red-let·ter day /ˌ· '·· ·/ n a specially happy day that will be remembered: *It was a red-letter day for us when Paul came home from the war.*

red light /ˌ· '·/ n a red light used as a danger signal or as a sign that vehicles should stop —compare GREEN LIGHT

red-light dis·trict /ˌ· '· ˌ··/ n the part of a town where one can hire women for sexual pleasure (PROSTITUTES)

Red Light Green Light /ˌ· '· · ·/ n [U] a game played by children in which the leader does not face the other players but calls out "green light" when they are allowed to move towards the finish line and shouts "red light" and turns around when they must stop. If the leader sees anyone moving after he or she has said "red light", that player must go back to the starting line.

Red List /'· ˌ·/ n *BrE* a government list of dangerous objects: *It is on the Red List of toxic substances dangerous in water.*

red meat /ˌ· '·/ n [U] meat from four-legged animals, such as BEEF or LAMB¹ (2) —compare WHITE MEAT

red·neck /'rednek/ n *infml derog*, esp. *AmE* a man who lives in a country area, esp. one who is uneducated or poor and has strong, unreasonable opinions

redneck

▶CULTURAL NOTE Rednecks are an American STEREO-TYPE. People think of them as driving PICK-UP TRUCKS, owning and using guns (esp. RIFLES), having SEXIST and RACIST attitudes, and drinking beer.◀

Red Nose Day /ˌ·ˈ·ˌ·/ BrE the day in the year on which activities organized by COMIC RELIEF are carried out to raise money for charities (CHARITY). Many people in Britain wear plastic red noses on this day and some people put large red noses on the front of their cars to show their support. —see also COMIC RELIEF

re·do /riːˈduː/ v **-did** /ˈdɪd/, **-done** /ˈdʌn/ [T] to do again: We redid (=repainted) the bathroom in pink. | She redid her hair. | You'll have to redo this piece of work.

red·o·lent /ˈredələnt/ adj [F+of] fml **1** smelling of: The kitchen was redolent of onions. **2** making one think of; suggesting: an old house redolent of mystery **—lence** n [U+of]

re·dou·ble /riːˈdʌbəl/ v [T] to increase (esp. activity) greatly: The police **redoubled their efforts** to find the missing child.

re·doubt /rɪˈdaʊt/ n tech a small fort

re·doubt·a·ble /rɪˈdaʊtəbəl/ adj lit or humor deserving to be respected and feared: a redoubtable opponent

re·dound /rɪˈdaʊnd/ v
    redound to sthg. phr v [T] fml (of an event or action) to have the effect of increasing (fame, honour, etc.): Any help you can give us will redound to your credit. (=make people admire you)

red pep·per /ˌ·ˈ··/ n **1** [U] a hot-tasting powder made from the dried red seed cases of a plant of the pepper family (tho CAYENNE PEPPER), used for giving taste to food **2** [C] the red fruit of the CAPSICUM plant, used as a vegetable

re·dress¹ /rɪˈdres/ v [T] fml **1** to put right (a wrong, injustice, etc.) **2 redress the balance** to make things equal or fair (again): Most of the films in this series were directed by men, so in order to redress the balance they are now showing some films by women directors.

re·dress² /rɪˈdres‖ˈriːdres/ n [U] fml payment for a wrong that has been done; COMPENSATION: You must **seek redress** in the law courts for the damage to your car.

Red Riding Hood see LITTLE RED RIDING HOOD

Red River /ˌ·ˈ··/ [the] a long river in the S of the US, which forms part of the border between the states of Oklahoma and Texas. There is a popular American FOLK SONG called The Red River Valley which begins: From this valley they may say you are going …

red route /ˈ· ˌ·/ n BrE a road in a city in Britain, esp. London, where all vehicles are forbidden to park. Red routes were introduced in 1991 to speed up the flow of traffic in busy areas.

Red Rum /ˌ·ˈ·/ a famous British race horse

Red Scare /ˈ· ˌ·/ [the] an American government action in 1919 and 1920 that deported (DEPORT) foreigners who had recently settled in the US, for fear that they were Communists and would persuade others of the worth of their ideas

Red Sea /ˌ·ˈ·/ [the] a sea between NE Africa and the Arabian Peninsula, joined with the Mediterranean Sea (by the Suez Canal) and the Indian Ocean. It is an important

passage for many shipping companies. The Bible tells a story of God parting (PART² (2)) the Red Sea, allowing Moses and the Jews who had been in Egypt to escape by walking across the sea bed. —see colour picture on page 424

red shift /ˌ·ˈ·ˌ/ n [U;C] a change in the light pattern given off by stars as they are seen from the Earth, which shows that the stars are moving away, and supporting the BIG BANG THEORY of the universe

Red Shoes /ˌ·ˈ·/, **The** a FAIRY STORY by Hans Andersen in which an ungrateful little girl is punished when she cannot remove her red shoes, and has to dance in them night and day

red·skin /ˈredˌskɪn/ n old use, now taboo for NATIVE AMERICAN

Red Square /ˌ·ˈ·/ the large square (=broad, open space in a town) in Moscow, known for its processions on May Day when Moscow was the capital of the USSR

red squir·rel /ˌ·ˈ···/ n a reddish-brown SQUIRREL which lives in North America and Britain, where it is becoming rare

Red Star /ˌ·ˈ·/ a British parcel and letter delivery service which uses trains to transport the parcels and letters

red tape /ˌ·ˈ·/ n [U] derog silly detailed unnecessary official rules that delay action: It took a long time to **cut through the red tape** of the planning regulations and get the building started.

re·duce /rɪˈdjuːs‖rɪˈduːs/ v **1** [T (**from, to**)] to make less in size, amount, price, degree, etc.: a promise to reduce taxes | a defence policy that reduces the risk of war | I bought this shirt because it was reduced (from £12 to £6). | He won't reduce the rent of our house. | Reduce the sauce by boiling it for ten minutes. | The plague reduced the population to half its previous level. —compare INCREASE; see also REDUCTION **2** [T] old use to defeat and take control of (a place): By constant bombardment we reduced the citadel. **3** [I] esp AmE lose weight: The doctor told me I had to reduce. | She won't eat any dessert, she's reducing. —**reducible** adj
    reduce sbdy./sthg. **to** sthg. phr v [T] **1** to change (something) to (its parts): We can reduce the report to three main points. | The explosion reduced the house to rubble. **2** [usu. pass.] to bring or force (someone) to (esp. a weaker or less favourable state): His extraordinary reply reduced me to silence. | The captain was **reduced to the ranks** (=made an ordinary soldier) for his disobedience. | The child was **reduced to tears**. (=made to cry) [+v-ing] She was reduced to begging for a living.

reduced cir·cum·stanc·es /·ˌ· ˈ·····/ n [P] old-fash euph a poorer way of life than one formerly had: living in reduced circumstances

re·duc·ti·o ad ab·sur·dum /rɪˌdʌktiəʊ æd əbˈsɜːdəm‖-ɜːr-/ n [U] Lat the disproof of a piece of reasoning by showing that it must lead in the end to a silly or unacceptable result

re·duc·tion /rɪˈdʌkʃən/ n **1** [C;U (**in**)] (a case of) making or becoming smaller; the amount taken off in reducing something: some reduction|a slight reduction in the price of food | price reductions —compare INCREASE **2** [C] a smaller copy of a picture, map, or photograph —opposite enlargement

re·dun·dan·cy /rɪˈdʌndənsi/ n **1** [C;U] BrE (a case of) being made redundant: The closure of the export department led to a lot of redundancy|led to over 200 redundancies. **2** [C;U] fml or tech (esp. of words) (a case of) being REDUNDANT (2) **3** [U] tech (of something made up of many parts) the quality of containing additional parts that will make the system work if other parts fail: the redundancy of the English language|of computerized systems

redundancy pay·ment /·ˈ··· ˌ··/ BrE‖**severance pay** AmE— n a sum of money given by an employer to a worker who is being made redundant. In Britain the amount is usually calculated according to how long the person has worked for the employer. There is a legal MINIMUM redundancy payment for workers who have worked continuously for the same employer for two years.

re·dun·dant /rɪˈdʌndənt/ adj **1** BrE (of a worker) no longer employed because there is not enough work: Seventy men at the factory were **made redundant** because of falling demand for our products. **2** not needed; more than is necessary: In the sentence "She lives alone by herself", the word "alone" is redundant. | redundant information/ machine parts — ~·ly adv

re·du·pli·cate /rɪˈdjuːplᵻkeɪt‖rɪˈduː-/ v [T] fml to make or do again; repeat —·**cation** /rɪˌdjuːplᵻˈkeɪʃən‖rɪˌduː-/ n [U]

red·wood /ˈredwʊd/ also **sequoia**— n a CONIFEROUS tree that grows in California. Redwoods attract many tourists because they can grow to more than 100 metres high, and live for many hundreds of years. They are also important for their wood.

Ree·bok /ˈriːbɒk‖-baːk/ n [P] tdmk a kind of expensive and fashionable sports shoe —see PAIR (USAGE)

re·ech·o /riːˈekəʊ/ v [I;T] to (cause to) be repeated again and again as an ECHO: Their cries echoed and reechoed among the lonely hills.

reed /riːd/ n **1** a grasslike plant that grows in wet places: a roof made of dried reeds **2** a thin piece of wood or metal in a musical instrument that produces sound by shaking (VIBRATION) when air is blown over it: **reed instruments** such as the oboe and bassoon

Reed, Sir Carol (1906–1976) an English film DIRECTOR, best known for the film The Third Man

Reed In·ter·na·tion·al /ˌ·· ··ˈ····/ a British company that produces books, magazines, newspapers, travel industry information etc.

re·ed·u·cate /riːˈedjᵿkeɪt‖-dʒə-/ v [T] to train or educate (someone) again: We should reeducate young criminals (to take their place in society). —·**cation** /ˌriːedjᵿˈkeɪʃən ‖-dʒə-/ n [U]

reed·y /ˈriːdi/ adj **1** (of a sound) thin and high: a reedy voice **2** (of a place) full of REEDS (1): a reedy lake —·**iness** n [U]

reef¹ /riːf/ n a line of sharp rocks, often made of CORAL, or a bank of sand on or near the surface of the sea: The ship was wrecked on a reef.

reef² v [T] naut to tie up (part of a sail) so as to make it smaller

reef³ n naut a reduction in the area of a sail made by reefing

ree·fer /ˈriːfəʳ/ n old-fash infml a cigarette containing the drug MARIJUANA

reefer jack·et /ˈ··‚ ‚··/ n BrE a man's short close-fitting coat made of thick material

reef knot /ˈ· ·/ esp. BrE ‖ usu. **square knot** AmE— n a double knot that will not come undone easily

reek¹ /riːk/ n [S] **1** a strong unpleasant smell: a reek of tobacco and beer **2** lit or ScotE a thick smoke

reek² v [I] **1** [(of, with)] to smell strongly and unpleasantly: His breath reeks of onions. | (fig.) That whole transaction reeks of/with dishonesty. **2** dial to give out smoke: a reeking chimney

reel¹ /riːl/ n **1** BrE ‖ **spool** AmE— a round object on which a length of sewing thread, wire, fishing line, recording TAPE (2a), etc., can be wound —compare BOBBIN **2** [(of)] the amount that any of these will hold: two whole reels of cotton **3** one of several parts of a cinema film contained on a reel: They get married at the end of the eighth reel.

reel² v [T+obj+adv/prep] to bring, take, etc. by winding: He reeled in his fishing line. | Reel some more thread off the machine.
reel sthg. ↔ **off** phr v [T] infml to repeat (usu. a lot of information) quickly and easily from memory; RATTLE **off**: He could reel off the dates of all the kings of England.

reel³ v [I] **1** [+adv/prep] to walk unsteadily, moving from side to side, as if drunk: He came reeling up the street. **2** [(BACK)] to step away suddenly and unsteadily (as if) after being hit or receiving a shock: When I hit him he reeled (back) and almost fell. **3** to be in a state of shock, confusion, or uncertainty: All these statistics make my head reel. | The party is still reeling from its recent election defeat. **4** to seem to go round and round: The room reeled before my eyes and I became unconscious.

reel⁴ n (the music for) a quick cheerful Scottish or Irish dance

re·e·lect /ˌriːᵻˈlekt/ v [T] to elect again: He has been reelected to Parliament. — ~·**ion** /ˈlekʃən/ n [C;U]: She is seeking reelection for a third term of office.

re·en·try /riːˈentri/ n [C;U] (an act of) entering again: The spacecraft made a successful reentry into the Earth's atmosphere.

Reese's Pea·nut But·ter Cup /ˌriːsᵻz ‚piːnʌt bʌtə ˈkʌp ‖-bʌtər-/ n tdmk a round CANDY made of chocolate and sweet PEANUT BUTTER

reeve /riːv/ n **1** an English law officer in former times **2** the president of a modern Canadian town council

Reeves /riːvz/, **Jim** /dʒɪm/ (1923–64) a soft-voiced American COUNTRY singer known as "Gentleman Jim Reeves", best remembered for his recording of He'll Have to Go

ref¹ /ref/ n infml for REFEREE¹ (1): Hey, ref, that was a foul!

ref.² abbrev. for: REFERENCE (4)

re·face /riːˈfeɪs/ v [T] to put a new surface on (a wall): The worn stonework on this building must be refaced.

re·fec·to·ry /rɪˈfektəri/ BrE‖**cafeteria** AmE— n a large room in a school, college, etc. in which meals are served and eaten

re·fer /rɪˈfɜːʳ/ v **-rr-**
refer to phr v [T] **1** (**refer to** sbdy./sthg.) to mention or speak about: The scientist referred to the discovery as the most exciting new development in this field. | Which companies was she referring to when she spoke of competing firms? | The figures in the left-hand column refer to our overseas sales. **2** (**refer to** sthg.) to look at for information: to refer to a dictionary | Let me just refer to my notes to find the exact figures. **3** (**refer to** sbdy./sthg.) to concern; be directed towards or be RELEVANT to: The new law does not refer to land used for farming. **4** (**refer** sbdy./sthg. **to** sbdy.) to send or direct to (another place or person) for information, decision, or action: The shop referred the complaint (back) to the makers of the articles. | The professor referred me to an article she had written on this subject. | The proposal will have to be referred to the Finance Committee. —see also CROSS-REFER — ~**able to** adj

ref·er·ee¹ /ˌrefəˈriː/ n **1** a judge in charge of some games **2** BrE for REFERENCE (3b) **3** a person who is asked to settle a disagreement
▷ USAGE **Referee** is used in connection with **basketball, boxing, football, hockey, lacrosse, rugby, snooker, squash,** and **wrestling. Umpire** is used in connection with **badminton, baseball, cricket, swimming, tennis,** and **volleyball.**◁

referee² v [I;T] to act as referee for (a game): Who's going to referee (the football match)?

ref·er·ence /ˈrefərəns/ n **1** [C;U (to)] (an example of) mentioning: When I spoke to him about the expedition, he didn't make any reference to (=mention) your coming with us. | King William II was known as "Rufus", a reference to his (=because he had) red hair. | Her speech contained only a passing reference to (=a quick mention of) the problem of unemployment. **2** [C;U (to)] (an example of) looking at something for information: Use this dictionary for easy reference. **3** [C] **a** a piece of written information about someone's character, ability, etc., esp. when they are looking for employment: We will need to have references from your former employers. | We will lend you the money if you can provide a **banker's reference**. (=a note from the bank to say that you are a trustworthy customer) **b** a person who provides such information: Ask your teacher to act as one of your references. **4** [C] something that tells a reader where the information came from that is used in a piece of writing: a list of references at the end of the article **5** **in/with reference to** fml in connection with; about: With reference to your recent letter, I am instructed to inform you … —see also CROSS-REFERENCE, FRAME OF REFERENCE, TERMS OF REFERENCE

▷ USAGE A **testimonial** is usually shown to the person it describes, or made public. A **reference** is not usually shown to the person, and may be negative. A **recommendation** is more informal, not always written, usually positive, and made known to the person it describes.◁

reference book /ˈ···· ·/ n a book, such as a dictionary, that is looked at when one needs information rather than read from beginning to end

reference li·bra·ry /ˈ··· ‚···/ n a collection of books that cannot be taken away but must be studied in the place where they are kept

ref·er·en·dum /ˌrefəˈrendəm/ n **-da** /də/ or **-dums** [C;U] a direct vote by all the people to decide about something on which there is strong disagreement, instead of the government making the decision. Referendums are legal in Britain but are very rarely used. In the US there is rarely a national referendum, but states hold them regularly, usu. at the same time as other elections, to test public opinion on sensitive matters: *The government will hold a referendum on whether the electoral system should be changed.* | *The question was decided by referendum.* — compare PLEBISCITE

re·fer·ral /rɪˈfɜːrəl/ n [C;U (to)] (a case of) referring or being referred: *a referral of the matter to the Finance Committee*

re·fill¹ /ˌriːˈfɪl/ v [T] to fill again: *I'll refill my teapot.* — ~**able** adj : *a refillable cigarette lighter*

re·fill² /ˈriːfɪl/ n (a container holding) a quantity of ink, petrol, etc., to refill something: *I bought two refills for my pen.* | (*infml*) *I can see your glass is empty; would you like a refill?* (=another drink)

re·fine /rɪˈfaɪn/ v [T] to make pure: *Oil has to be refined before it can be used.* —**finer** n

  refine on/upon sthg. *phr v* [T] to improve (a method, plan, etc.), esp. in details; make refinements to

re·fined /rɪˈfaɪnd/ adj **1** [no comp.] made pure: *refined oil/sugar* **2** *sometimes derog* (of a person or their behaviour) showing, or intending to show education, delicate feeling, and gentleness of manners; GENTEEL: *a refined way of speaking* | *She's so refined that she always eats cake with a little fork.* —opposite **unrefined**

re·fine·ment /rɪˈfaɪnmənt/ n **1** [C (on)] an addition or improvement to an existing product, system, etc.: *The new car has many added refinements such as air-conditioning and anti-locking brakes.* **2** [U] the process of making something pure: *the refinement of sugar* **3** [U] the quality of being REFINED (2): *a woman of great refinement*

re·fin·e·ry /rɪˈfaɪnəri/ n a building and apparatus for refining metals, oil, sugar, etc.: *a sugar refinery*

re·fit¹ /ˌriːˈfɪt/ v -tt- [I;T] **a** (esp. of a ship) to be made ready for further use: *We sailed into port to refit.* **b** to make (esp. a ship) ready for further use, e.g. by doing repairs and putting in new machinery

re·fit² /ˈriːfɪt/ n [C;U] the process of being refitted: *The yacht needs a refit/is under refit.*

re·flate /riːˈfleɪt/ v [I;T] to increase the supply of money in (a money system) to a former or desirable level

re·fla·tion /riːˈfleɪʃən/ n [U] a POLICY of increasing the amount of money being used in a system, usu. leading to more demand for goods and more industrial activity —compare DEFLATION, INFLATION — ~**ary** adj

re·flect /rɪˈflekt/ v **1** [T] to throw back (heat, light, sound, or an image): *The mirror reflects my face.* | *The mountains were reflected in the lake.* **2** [T *not usu. in progressive forms*] to express, make clear, or be a sign of; show: *His behaviour reflects his lazy attitude to work.* | *The low value of the dollar reflects growing concern about the US economy.* | *Concern about the economy is reflected in the low value of the dollar.* [+wh-] *Does this letter reflect what you really think?* **3** [I (on)] to think carefully: *After reflecting for a time (on the problem) he decided not to go.*

  reflect on/upon *phr v* [T] **1** (**reflect on** sbdy./sthg.) (of an action or event) to cause to be seen or considered in a particular, usu. unfavourable, way: *The unemployment figures reflect badly on the government's policies.* | *an incident that reflects on* (=causes doubts about) *their honesty* **2** (**reflect** sthg. **on** sbdy./sthg.) (of an action or event) to bring (CREDIT¹ (5) or DISCREDIT²) on: *Their prompt action in the emergency reflects great credit on them.*

reflecting tel·e·scope /·ˈ·· ˌ···/ n a TELESCOPE (=an instrument for seeing distant objects) in which the image is reflected in a mirror and made bigger —compare REFRACTING TELESCOPE

re·flec·tion /rɪˈflekʃən/ n **1** [C] an image reflected in a mirror or similar surface: *We looked at our reflections in the lake.* **2** [U] the reflecting of heat, light, sound, or an image: *The moon looks bright because of the reflection of light.* **3** [C;U (on)] (an idea or statement resulting from) deep and careful thought: *It was interesting to hear her reflections on Indian politics.* | *At first I thought it was a bad idea, but on reflection I realized she was right.* **4** [C (of)] something that shows the effects of, or is a sign of, a particular condition, situation, etc.: *The rising rate of crime is a reflection of an unstable society.* | *Do you think this opinion is an accurate reflection of the public mood?* **5** [S+on] disapproval or an unfavourable judgment, esp. expressed in an indirect way; CRITICISM: *The fact that*

we're dismissing you is no reflection on the quality of your work — we simply can't afford to employ you any more.

re·flec·tive /rɪˈflektɪv/ adj **1** (esp. of a person) thoughtful **2** (of clothing or a material) reflecting light: *The cyclist wore a reflective belt/waistcoat so that cars could see her more easily at night.*

re·flec·tor /rɪˈflektər/ n a surface that reflects light. Reflectors are often worn or carried for safety reasons by people riding bicycles or walking at night, so that they will be seen by the drivers of vehicles with HEADLIGHTS —see picture at BICYCLE

re·flex /ˈriːfleks/ n an unintentional movement that is made in reply to some outside influence: *The doctor hit my knee with a hammer to test my reflexes.* | *I can't help shivering when I'm cold — it's a* **reflex action.** —see also CONDITIONED REFLEX

re·flex·ive /rɪˈfleksɪv/ n, adj tech (a word) showing that the action in the sentence has its effect on the person or thing that does the action: *In "I enjoyed myself", "enjoy" is a reflexive/is a* **reflexive verb,** *and the pronoun "myself" is a* **reflexive pronoun.**

re·flex·ol·o·gy /ˌriːflekˈsɒlədʒi‖-ˈsɑː-/ n [U] a kind of ALTERNATIVE MEDICINE, in which particular areas of the feet and hands are touched in order to help certain medical conditions

re·for·est /riːˈfɒrɪst‖-ˈfɔː-, -ˈfɑː-/ v [T] esp. AmE for REAFFOREST — ~**ation** /riːˌfɒrɪˈsteɪʃən‖-ˌfɔː-, -ˌfɑː-/ n [U]

re·form¹ /rɪˈfɔːm‖-ɔːrm/ v [I;T] to improve, e.g. by changing behaviour or by removing undesirable qualities: *a plan to reform the tax system and make it simpler and fairer* | *Harry has completely reformed/is a completely* **reformed character** *now — he's stopped taking drugs.* — ~**er** n : *a famous social reformer*

reform² n [C;U] (a) change made, esp. to a system or organization, that is intended to improve it, remove unfairness, etc.: *The President has proposed* **sweeping** (=very big) **reforms** *of the tax system.* | *a programme of social/economic/educational reform*

re-form /ˌriːˈfɔːm‖-ɔːrm/ v [I;T] to (cause to) form again, esp. into ranks: *The army re-formed, ready to attack again.*

ref·or·ma·tion /ˌrefəˈmeɪʃən‖-fər-/ n [C;U] (an) improvement; the act of reforming or state of being reformed: *a complete reformation in his character*

Reformation [*the*] the religious movement in Europe in the 16th century leading to the establishment of the Protestant churches

re·for·ma·to·ry¹ /rɪˈfɔːmətəri‖rɪˈfɔːrmətɔːri/ also **reform school**— n old use or AmE for COMMUNITY HOME

reformatory² also **re·for·ma·tive** /rɪˈfɔːmətɪv‖-ˈfɔːr-/ adj fml intended to produce reform

Reform Club /·ˈ· ·/ [*the*] (in Britain) a gentleman's CLUB¹ (3) in Pall Mall, London, which has a strong association with the Liberal Party

re·form·ist /rɪˈfɔːmɪst‖-ɔːr-/ adj, n (a person) in favour of, or suggesting (esp. political) REFORM

reform school /·ˈ· ·/ n AmE for COMMUNITY HOME

re·fract /rɪˈfrækt/ v [T] (of water, glass, etc.) to cause (light) to change direction when passing through at an angle — ~**ion** /rɪˈfrækʃən/ n [U] : *Refraction makes a straight stick look bent if it is partly in water.*

refracting tel·e·scope /·ˈ·· ˌ···/ n a TELESCOPE (=an instrument for seeing distant objects) in which the image is refracted by passing through a LENS (a piece of glass) — compare REFLECTING TELESCOPE

re·frac·to·ry /rɪˈfræktəri/ adj fml derog disobedient and troublesome: *a refractory horse*

re·frain¹ /rɪˈfreɪn/ v [I (from)] fml to hold oneself back from doing something; not do: *Please refrain from smoking.*

refrain² n **1** a part of a song that is repeated, esp. at the end of each VERSE **2** often derog a remark or idea that is often repeated: *Our proposal met with the familiar refrain that the company could not afford such a big investment.*

re·fresh /rɪˈfreʃ/ v **1** [T] to make less hot or tired; bring back strength and freshness to: *A hot bath will refresh you.* | *He refreshed himself with a glass of beer.* **2** [I;T] (of computer OUTPUT) to provide again; UPDATE: *This display will not refresh (itself) till you repeat the command.* **3 refresh one's memory** to cause oneself to remember again: *I looked at the map to refresh my memory of the route.* **4 refreshes the parts other beers cannot reach** a phrase used in advertisements for Heineken LAGER, now often used humorously

re·fresh·er course /·'·· ·/ *n* a training course given to bring someone's knowledge up to date, esp. knowledge needed for a job: *They're holding/attending a refresher course on modern teaching methods.*

re·fresh·ing /rɪˈfreʃɪŋ/ *adj apprec* **1** producing a feeling of comfort and new strength: *a very refreshing sleep* **2** pleasantly new and interesting: *It's refreshing to see a film that isn't full of sex and violence.* — ~**ly** *adv*

re·fresh·ment /rɪˈfreʃmənt/ *n* [U] **1** (the experience of) being refreshed **2** food and drink: *We worked all day without refreshment.*

re·fresh·ments /rɪˈfreʃmənts/ *n* [P] food and drinks served as a light meal: *Refreshments will be served after the meeting.*

re·fried beans /ˈriːfraɪd ˈbiːnz/ *n* [P] PINTO BEANS which have been boiled and then crushed and fried (FRY), often with onions; usu. eaten with Mexican food

re·fri·ge·rant /rɪˈfrɪdʒərənt/ *n* a substance that is used to refrigerate, such as solid CARBON DIOXIDE

re·fri·ge·rate /rɪˈfrɪdʒəreɪt/ *v* [T] to make (food, liquid, etc.) cold as a way of preserving it: *refrigerated meat* —**ration** /rɪˌfrɪdʒəˈreɪʃən/ *n* [U] : *The meat was kept under refrigeration.*

re·fri·ge·ra·tor /rɪˈfrɪdʒəreɪtər/ *n BrE fml or AmE for* FRIDGE —see picture at KITCHEN

refrigerator-freez·er /·,····· '··/ *n BrE fml & AmE for* FRIDGE-FREEZER

re·fuel /ˌriːˈfjʊəl/ *v* -ll- *BrE* ‖ -l- *AmE* [I;T] to (cause to) fill up again with FUEL: *The aircraft refuelled/They refuelled the aircraft at Cairo.* | *a refuelling stop*

ref·uge /ˈrefjuːdʒ/ *n* [C;U (from)] (a place that provides) protection or shelter from danger: *a mountain refuge for climbers* | *The political dissidents sought/took refuge abroad.*

ref·u·gee /ˌrefjʊˈdʒiː/ *n* someone who has been forced to leave their country for political reasons or during a war. Refugees are becoming a political problem in many European countries. Some governments think that many people wanting to become refugees are coming to Europe for economic reasons, and not for their personal safety.

re·ful·gent /rɪˈfʌldʒənt‖rɪˈfʊl-/ *adj lit* (of light) very bright; BRILLIANT —**gence** *n* [U]

re·fund¹ /ˈriːfʌnd/ *n* a repayment; a sum of money refunded: *She took the faulty radio back to the shop and demanded a refund.* | *(esp. AmE) a tax refund*

re·fund² /rɪˈfʌnd/ *v* [T (to)] to give (money) in repayment, in return for loss or damage, in order to balance accounts, etc.: *They refunded the cost of the damaged book.* [+obj(i)+obj(d)] *They refunded us our money when the play was cancelled.* —compare REIMBURSE

re·fur·bish /ˌriːˈfɜːbɪʃ‖-ɜːr-/ *v* [T] to make bright, clean and fresh again: *to refurbish an old theatre* | *(fig.) He's going to Paris to refurbish his French.* — ~**ment** *n* [U]

re·fus·al /rɪˈfjuːzəl/ *n* [C;U] (a case of) refusing: *My offer met with (=was answered with) a cold/a polite refusal.* [+to-v] *Their refusal to negotiate with us made progress impossible.* —see also FIRST REFUSAL

re·fuse¹ /rɪˈfjuːz/ *v* **1** [I;T] to state one's strong unwillingness to accept; say no (to): *He asked her to marry him but she refused.* | *She refused his offer.* **2** [T+obj(i)+obj(d)] to not give or allow: *We were refused entry/refused permission to enter.* **3** [T+to-v; obj] to show or state strong unwillingness (to do something): *She flatly refused to have anything to do with the plan.* | *The engine refused to start.* | *I told him to come back but he refused to.* | *I refuse to answer that question.*

▷ USAGE 1 **Refuse, decline, reject,** and **turn down** all mean that you do not do something that you are asked to do (opposite **agree to**), or do not take something that you are offered (opposite **accept**). You can **refuse** or **decline** an invitation; **refuse** permission; **decline, reject,** or **turn down** a suggestion; **refuse, decline, reject,** or **turn down** an offer; **reject** or **turn down** a plan or proposal. 2 **Decline** is more polite than **refuse** and not so firm. Compare *I'm afraid I must decline your invitation/decline to answer that question* and *The*

prisoner refused to give his name. 3 You must **decline** in words: *The horse refused* (not *declined*) *to jump the fence.* You need not **reject** or **refuse** something in words: *The horse rejected/refused the apple.*◁

ref·use² /ˈrefjuːs/ *n* [U] *fml* waste material; RUBBISH: *a heap of kitchen refuse* | *a refuse dump* (=where a town's waste material is put)

re·fuse·nik /rɪˈfjuːznɪk/ *n* a Jew in the former USSR who has been refused permission to EMIGRATE, especially to Israel

refuse work·er /·'·· ,··/ *n BrE fml or euph* a DUSTMAN

re·fute /rɪˈfjuːt/ *v* [T] to prove that (someone or something) is mistaken or incorrect: *I was able to refute him/his argument.* | *to refute the proposition that the world is flat* —**refutation** /ˌrefjʊˈteɪʃən/ *n* [C;U]

▷ USAGE **Refute** is often used simply with the meaning "say (not prove) that an argument or statement is mistaken": *I refute the allegation entirely.* But some people think this is bad English.◁

re·gain /rɪˈɡeɪn/ *v* [T] **1** to get or win back: *The football club regained the trophy it had lost the previous year.* | *She is slowly regaining her strength/confidence after the accident.* | *She was unable to regain her balance, and she fell off the wall.* | *The government is fighting to regain control of the rebel-held areas.* **2** *lit* to reach (a place) again: *Shall we regain the shore alive?*

re·gal /ˈriːɡəl/ *adj fml apprec* very splendid; of, like, or suitable for a king or queen: *regal manners* | *a regal old lady* —compare ROYAL¹ (1) — ~**ly** *adv* : *We were regally entertained.*

re·gale /rɪˈɡeɪl/ *v*
  regale sbdy. **with** sthg. *phr v* [T] to entertain with: *He regaled us with some stories about his youth.*

re·ga·li·a /rɪˈɡeɪliə/ *n* [U+*sing./pl. v*] ceremonial clothes and decorations, esp. those used on official occasions: *royal regalia* | *a mayor's regalia*

re·gard¹ /rɪˈɡɑːd‖-ɑːrd/ *n* [U] *usu. fml* **1** respect; ESTEEM: *I hold her in high/low/the greatest regard.* **2** [+for, to] respectful attention; consideration: *You have no regard for my feelings!* | *The report pays little regard/scant regard to the facts of the case.* **3** connection or relation (in phrases like **in this regard, with regard to**): *The company is owned by its staff, and in that regard it is rather unusual.* | *With regard to your recent application, I am afraid we are unable to offer you the job.* **4** *lit* a long look without moving one's eyes —see also REGARDS

regard² *v* [T *not in progressive forms*] **1** [+obj+adv/prep] to consider in the stated way: *I have always regarded him highly/with the greatest admiration.* | *She is generally regarded as one of the best writers in the country.* | *We regard these developments with grave concern.* **2** [+obj+adv/prep] *fml* to look at in the stated way: *She regarded him thoughtfully/with suspicion.* **3** [*usu. negative*] *fml* to pay attention to (thoughts, ideas, etc.): *If you fail to regard my warning, you may be sorry.*

re·gard·ful /rɪˈɡɑːdfəl‖-ɑːr-/ *adj* [F+of] *fml* full of respectful attention

re·gard·ing /rɪˈɡɑːdɪŋ‖-ɑːr-/ also **as regards, re** — *prep fml* (esp. in business letters) on the subject of; in connection with; concerning: *Regarding your recent inquiry* ... .

re·gard·less /rɪˈɡɑːdləs‖-ɑːr-/ *adv* **1** *infml* in spite of everything: *They knew it was too expensive, but they went ahead regardless and bought it.* **2 regardless of** without worrying about or taking account of: *They decorated the house regardless of cost.* | *All our proposals were rejected, regardless of their merits.* —compare IRRESPECTIVE

re·gards /rɪˈɡɑːdz‖-ɑːr-/ *n* [P] **1** good wishes: *Give him my (best) regards.* **2 with kind/best/warm regards** (a friendly but rather formal way of ending a letter)

re·gat·ta /rɪˈɡætə/ *n* a meeting for races between rowing or sailing boats

re·gen·cy /ˈriːdʒənsi/ *n* [C;U] (a period of) government by a regent

Regency¹ *adj* of the British style (in buildings, furniture, etc.) of the period 1811–1830: *a graceful Regency chair*

Regency² [*the*] the period of British history between 1811 and 1820, when the Prince Regent acted as king —see also PRINCE REGENT

re·gen·e·rate /rɪˈdʒenəreɪt/ *v* [I;T] to give or obtain new life;

form, grow again: *This creature's tail will regenerate if it is cut off.* —see also UNREGENERATE —**-ration** /rɪˌdʒenə-ˈreɪʃən/ *n* [U] : *the regeneration of agriculture after the war*

re·gent /ˈriːdʒənt/ *n* (*often cap.*) a person who governs in place of a king or ruling queen who is ill, absent, or still a child —**regent** *adj* [after *n*] : *the Prince Regent*

Regent Street /ˈ··ˌ·/ a street in the WEST END of London which runs between Oxford Circus and Piccadilly Circus and is a popular place for shopping.

Regent's Park /ˌ·· ˈ·/ a park in NW London, open to the public. It is the home of London Zoo and has an open-air theatre where Shakespeare plays are performed in the summer. —see colour map on page 817

reg·gae /ˈreɡeɪ/ *n* [U] (*often cap.*) a kind of popular music from the West Indies with a strong regular beat, which developed in Jamaica in the 1960s. The songs often have a political message or are about Rastafarianism (RASTAFARIAN). The best known, most successful reggae singer was Bob Marley.

re·gi·cide /ˈredʒɪˌsaɪd/ *n* **1** [U] the crime of killing a king or queen **2** [C] a person who does this

re·gime /reɪˈʒiːm/ *n* **1** *often derog* a particular (system of) government: *a fascist/military regime* | *Things will change under the new regime.* **2** a regimen

re·gi·men /ˈredʒɪmən/ *n fml* a fixed plan of food, exercise, etc., in order to improve one's health: *I followed a strict regimen.* | *the daily regimen of a ballet dancer*

re·gi·ment[1] /ˈredʒɪmənt/ *n* [C+*sing./pl. v*] **1** a large military group, commanded by a COLONEL: *a cavalry regiment* **2** [(**of**)] a very large number of living creatures: *a whole regiment of ants*

re·gi·ment[2] /ˈredʒɪment/ *v* [T *often pass.*] *derog* to control (people) firmly, forcing them to obey orders: *Modern children don't like being regimented.* | *a regimented society* —**~ation** /ˌredʒɪmenˈteɪʃən‖-mən-/ *n* [U]

re·gi·ment·al /ˌredʒɪˈmentl◂/ *adj* of a regiment: *the regimental band*

re·gi·ment·als /ˌredʒɪˈmentlz/ *n* [P] the uniform of a particular regiment: *an officer in full regimentals*

Re·gi·na /rɪˈdʒaɪnə/ *n Lat* **1** [after *n*] (the title used in official writing after the name of a ruling British queen): *Elizabeth Regina* **2** *law* (used, when a queen is ruling, in titles of British law cases) the governing power of the State: *in the action Regina v Smith* (=the state against Smith) —compare REX

re·gion /ˈriːdʒən/ *n* **1** a particular fairly large area or part, usu. without exact limits: *the southern region of England* | *a tropical region* | *a pain in the region of the heart* | *America's main ally in this region* —see AREA (USAGE) **2** a local government division of Scotland There are nine mainland regions: Borders, Central, Dumfries and Galloway, Fife, Grampian, Highland, Lothian, Strathclyde, and Tayside, and three island regions: Orkney, Shetland, and Western Isles. —compare COUNTY[1] **3** **in the region of** about: *It will cost (somewhere) in the region of $500.*

re·gion·al /ˈriːdʒənəl/ *adj* of or in a particular region: *the regional authorities* | *a regional accent* | *regional differences in temperature* —**~ly** *adv*

re·gions /ˈriːdʒənz/ *n* [*the*+P] eight areas into which Britain is divided, mainly for statistical (STATISTICS) purposes. The regions are South East, East Anglia, South West, West Midlands, East Midlands, Yorkshire and Humberside, North West, and North. The regions play no part in local government.

re·gis·ter[1] /ˈredʒɪstəʳ/ *n* **1** [C] (a book containing) an official record or list: *By law we are required to keep a register of births and deaths.* | *a school attendance register* | *The electoral register lists everyone who is entitled to vote.* —see also CASH REGISTER **2** the book kept in a church or REGISTRY OFFICE, which a man and woman sign at the end of their marriage ceremony **3** [C] *tech* the range of a human voice or musical instrument: *That note is outside my register/is in the upper register of this instrument.* **4** [C;U] *tech* the words, style, and grammar used by speakers and writers in particular conditions: *Official documents are written in (a) formal register.* **5** *AmE* a movable metal plate that controls the flow of air in a heating or cooling (COOL[2] (1)) system

register[2] *v* **1** [T] to put into an official list or record: *Have you registered the birth of your baby?* | *The car is registered in my name.* | *registered voters* **2** [I] **a** to enter one's name on a list: *Newly arrived guests must register at the hotel's reception desk.* | *He went to register as unemployed.* **b** to join officially: *Students must register before they attend classes.* **3** [T] *fml* (of a machine or instrument) to show; record: *The thermometer registered 35°C.* **4** [T] *fml* (of a person or face) to express (a feeling): *She/Her face registered anxiety/surprise.* **5** [T] *fml* to state officially and cause to be recorded: *I wish to register my total opposition to these proposals.* **6** [T] to send by REGISTERED POST: *You'd better register this parcel.* | *a registered letter* **7** [I *usu. negative*] *infml* to have an effect (on a person); be noticed or remembered: *She told me her name but I'm afraid it didn't register.* (=I have forgotten it)

registered dis·a·bled /ˌ··· ·ˈ··/ *adj BrE* on a local authority list of HANDICAPPED people. People who are registered disabled may be given special financial or other help by the government.

Registered Gen·e·ral Nurse /ˌ··· ˌ··· ˈ·/ *n* (in Britain) a fully-trained person who is officially allowed to practise as a nurse —compare STATE ENROLLED NURSE, STATE REGISTERED NURSE

Registered Nurse /ˌ··· ˈ·/ also **RN** *abbrev.* —*n* (in the US) a fully-trained person who is officially allowed to practise as a nurse

registered of·fice /ˌ··· ˈ··/ *n* the office of a company to which all letters and notices must be addressed. Every British company must have a registered office, even if it is not based in Britain.

registered post /ˌ··· ˈ·/ *BrE* ‖ **registered mail** *AmE*— *n* [U] a postal service which, for an additional charge, protects the sender of a valuable letter or parcel against loss

register of·fice /ˈ··· ˌ··/ *n* a REGISTRY OFFICE

re·gis·trar /ˌredʒɪˈstrɑːʳ◂‖ˈredʒɪstrɑːr/ *n* **1** a person who is in charge of official records, e.g. in a REGISTRY OFFICE or a college **2** a British hospital doctor who has finished his/her training but is of a lower rank than a CONSULTANT (2)

re·gis·tra·tion /ˌredʒɪˈstreɪʃən/ *n* **1** [U] the act of registering: *The registration of students for the course will begin on Thursday morning.* | (*BrE*) *My car is a C registration.* (=was registered in 1985-6) **2** [C] a person or thing that is registered

registration doc·u·ment /·····ˈ·, ····/ *BrE* ‖ **registration** *AmE*— *n* an official piece of paper containing details about a motor vehicle and naming its owner: *The registration's in the glove box, in case you get stopped by the police.*

registration num·ber /····ˈ·, ····/ *n* **1** a number that is connected with a particular registration (2). *We can't find your name without your registration number.* **2** *BrE* the official set of numbers and letters that must be shown on the front and back of a motor vehicle (on the vehicle's NUMBERPLATE)

registration plate /····ˈ·, ·ˈ·/ *n AustrE, NZE for* NUMBERPLATE

re·gis·try /ˈredʒɪstri/ *n* a place where records are kept

registry of·fice /ˈ··· ˌ··/ also **register office**— *n* (esp. in Britain) an office where marriages can legally take place and where births, marriages, and deaths are officially recorded. Many people who do not want a church wedding get married in a registry office instead, esp. if they want the wedding to be a small, private event. Practising Christians usu. get married in a church.

reg·nant /ˈreɡnənt/ *adj* [after *n*] *fml or tech* ruling, esp. (of a queen) in her own right and not as the wife of a king: *queen regnant*

re·gress /rɪˈɡres/ *v* [I] *fml or tech* to go back to a former and usu. worse or less developed condition, way of behaving, etc.: *For a while the boy's disturbed behaviour seemed to be improving, but he regressed when his parents divorced.* —compare PROGRESS[2] (2) —**~ion** /rɪˈɡreʃən/ *n* [U] : *Most people show signs of regression* (=losing memory, sight, etc.) *when they grow old.*

re·gres·sive /rɪˈɡresɪv/ *adj fml or tech* tending to regress or showing regression

regressive tax /·ˈ·· ˌ·/ *n* a tax that takes a larger PERCENTAGE of money from people with low incomes

than from those with high incomes —compare PROGRES-SIVE TAX

re-gret¹ /rɪˈgret/ v -tt- [T]   **1** to feel sorry about (a sad fact or event, a mistake one has made, etc.), and wish it had not happened or was not true: *Later on, I regretted my decision not to take the job.* [+v-ing] *We've always deeply regretted selling the farm.* [+that] (*polite*) *I regret that I will be unable to attend.* | (in making threats) *Don't tell the police about this — or you'll regret it!*   **2** *fml* to be sorry that one has lost; miss very much: *I don't mind living in the city, but I do regret my horse!*   **3** I/We **regret to say/to inform you/to tell you** *fml* (used when bad news is to follow): *We regret to inform you that you owe the bank £100.*   **4 I only regret that I have but one life to lose for my country** *quote* a phrase used by the American Nathan Hale

regret² *n* [U (**at**)] a feeling of sorrow or unhappiness, often mixed with disappointment (at the loss of something, at a sad event, etc.): *We decided, with some regret/with great regret that we could not offer him the job.* | *I feel no regret at her absence.* | *The prime minister expressed her regret at the failure of the talks.* | **Much to my regret** (=I am sorry to say), *I am unable to accept your invitation.* —see also REGRETS —-**ful** *adj* : *She said goodbye to her old home with many regretful glances.* —-**fulness** *n* [U]

re-gret·ful·ly /rɪˈgretfəli/ *adv*   **1** in a regretful way   **2** REGRETTABLY (2)

▷ USAGE **Regretfully** is often used to mean "it is regrettable that", but many people think this is bad English.◁

re-grets /rɪˈgrets/ *n* [P]   **1** (used in polite expressions of refusal) a note or message refusing an invitation: *Philip sends his regrets.* | *I can't come — please give them my regrets.*   **2 have no regrets** not to feel sorry about what has happened: *He said he had no regrets about leaving the university.*

re-gret·ta·ble /rɪˈgretəbəl/ *adj euph* (often used when a stronger word is really meant) that one should feel sorry about; causing regret: *His behaviour at the party was most regrettable.* (=very bad) | *It is regrettable that the government has found it necessary to use such secretive methods.*

re-gret·ta·bly /rɪˈgretəbli/ *adv*   **1** in a regrettable manner; to a regrettable degree   **2** it is regrettable that: *Regrettably, the cancellation of this order will lead to some job losses.* —see REGRETFULLY (USAGE)

re-group /ˌriːˈgruːp/ v [I;T] to (cause to) form into new groups or into groups again

reg·u·lar¹ /ˈregjʊləʳ/ *adj*   **1** happening or appearing with the same amount of time or space between each one and the next; not varying: *the regular tick of the clock* | *His pulse is not very regular.* | *Plant the seeds at regular intervals.*   **2 a** happening, coming, or doing something again and again at the same times each day, week, etc.: *regular readers of this newspaper/users of this bus service* | *regular working hours* | *We hold regular planning meetings.* | *We meet* **on a regular basis.** | *They* **keep regular hours.** (=get up and go to bed at the same times each day) **b** (of a person) getting rid of waste food from the bowels often enough: *Eating fruit will keep you regular.*   **3** happening (almost) every time: *regular attendance at church* | *his regular failure to meet the deadlines*   **4** *usu. apprec* evenly shaped: *He has very regular features.* (=of the face) | *A cube is a* **regular solid.** (=all its sides are the same)   **5** proper; correct: *It's not the regular way of spelling this word.*   **6** *esp. AmE* ordinary; average: *Do you want the regular size or this big one?*   **7** (in grammar) following a common pattern: *The verb "dance" is regular, but the verb "be" is not.* —opposite **irregular** (for 1 to 7)   **8** [A *no comp.*] professional; not just employed for a time: *the* **regular army** | *a regular soldier*   **9** [A] *old-fash infml* complete; thorough: *He's always ordering us about — he's a regular little dictator.*   **10** [A] *esp. AmE apprec* pleasant and honest: *a regular guy*   **11** [*no comp.*] *tech* living under a particular religious rule of life: *Ordinary Roman Catholic priests are not members of the* **regular clergy,** *but monks are.* —compare SECULAR (3); see also REGULARLY, **regular as clockwork** (CLOCKWORK) —-**ity** /ˌregjʊˈlærˌti/ *n* [U]

regular² *n*   **1** *infml* a regular visitor, customer, etc.: *a group of regulars drinking in the bar*   **2** a soldier who is a member of an army kept by a country all the time   **3** [U] *AmE* **a** petrol that contains LEAD (4) **b** petrol of the

ordinary kind, not HIGH-OCTANE —compare UNLEADED

reg·u·lar·ize also **-ise** *BrE* /ˈregjʊləraɪz/ v [T] to make (a state of affairs that has already gone on for some time) legal and official: *After living together for several years they regularized the position and got married.* —-**ization** /ˌregjʊləraɪˈzeɪʃən‖-lərə-/ *n* [U]

reg·u·lar·ly /ˈregjʊləli‖-ərli/ *adv*   **1 a** at regular times: *Take the medicine regularly three times a day.* | *We meet regularly to discuss business.* **b** often and repeatedly: *I regularly get letters from people who have read my books.*   **2** evenly: *Her nose is regularly shaped.*

reg·u·late /ˈregjʊleɪt/ v [T]   **1** to control, esp. by rules; bring order or method to: *There are strict rules regulating the use of chemicals in food.* | *a well-regulated family*   **2** to make (a machine) work at a certain speed, etc.; ADJUST: *You can regulate the radiator by turning this little dial.* —see also DEREGULATE

reg·u·la·tion /ˌregjʊˈleɪʃən/ *n*   **1** [C] an esp. official rule or order: *regulations governing the sale of guns* | *She was fined for driving above the regulation speed.* | *tax/safety regulations* | *I'm fed up with* **rules and regulations.**   **2** [U] control; the bringing of order: *the regulation of public spending*

reg·u·la·tor /ˈregjʊleɪtəʳ/ *n* an instrument that controls something, such as the part of a clock that controls its speed —see picture at TYPEWRITER

reg·u·la·to·ry /ˈregjʊlətəri‖-tɔːri/ *adj fml* having the purpose of regulating

reg·u·lo /ˈregjʊləʊ/ *n BrE* a degree of heat in a gas cooker, shown by the stated number: *Cook this meat on regulo 4.*

re-gur·gi·tate /rɪˈgɜːdʒɪteɪt‖-ɜːr-/ v [I;T] *fml* to bring back (food already swallowed) into the mouth: *Some birds and animals regurgitate (food) to feed their young.* | (fig.) *She just regurgitates everything the teacher says, instead of thinking for herself.* —-**tation** /rɪˌgɜːdʒɪˈteɪʃən‖-ɜːr-/ *n* [U]

re-hab /ˈriːhæb/ v -bb- *AmE* rehabilitate, esp. sense 2: *He makes a living rehabbing old houses.* —**rehab** /riːˈhæb/ *n, adj* : *a rehab program for drug addicts* | *We live in a rehab.* (=rehabbed house)

re-ha·bil·i·tate /ˌriːhəˈbɪlɪteɪt/ v [T]   **1** to make (a person) able to live a healthy, useful, or active life again, esp. after being ill or in prison, e.g. by training: *The social services do their best to rehabilitate criminals once they've left prison.*   **2** to put back into good condition: *a plan to rehabilitate inner-city areas*   **3** to bring back to a former high level, e.g. of rank or in public opinion: *He left the presidency in disgrace, but he/his reputation has now been rehabilitated.* —-**tation** /ˌriːhəbɪlɪˈteɪʃən/ *n* [U] : *a rehabilitation centre/clinic for drug addicts*

re-hash /riːˈhæʃ/ v [T] *infml, usu. derog* to use (the same ideas) again in a new form which is not really different or better: *a politician who keeps rehashing the same old speech* —**rehash** /ˈriːhæʃ/ *n* : *a rehash of an old idea*

re-hears·al /rɪˈhɜːsəl‖-ɜːr-/ *n* [C;U]   **1** (an occasion of) rehearsing a play, concert, etc.: *This play still needs a lot of rehearsal(s).* —see also DRESS REHEARSAL   **2** [(**of**)] *fml* the telling of events or a story

re-hearse /rɪˈhɜːs‖-ɜːrs/ v   **1** [I;T] **a** to practise (a play, concert, etc.) in order to prepare for a public performance: *The actors were rehearsing (the play) until 2 o'clock in the morning.* **b** to cause (someone) to do this: *She rehearsed the musicians.*   **2** [T] *fml* to tell fully (events or a story); RECOUNT

Rehn·quist /ˈrenkwɪst/, **William H** (1924–) the Chief Justice (=most important judge) of the US Supreme Court since 1986. He has been a member of the Supreme Court since 1972 and is thought to be a CONSERVATIVE judge.

re-house /ˌriːˈhaʊz/ v [T] to put (someone) into a new or better home

Reich /raɪk, raɪx/ *Ger* [*the*] the German state or kingdom, esp. during any of three particular periods: *The* **Third Reich** *lasted from 1933 to 1945.*

Reid /riːd/, **Beryl** (1920–) an English COMEDIENNE (=a woman who makes people laugh) and actress, well-known for playing character parts

reign¹ /reɪn/ *n* a period of reigning: *during the reign of George IV*

reign² v [I]   **1** (**over**)] to be the king or queen, esp. without holding real power: *The British Queen reigns but does not* *rule.* | *He reigned over a small kingdom.* **2** *esp. lit* (of a state or situation, often an undesirable one) to exist noticeably; PREVAIL: *Silence reigned once more after the thunder.* | *After the dictator's death, anarchy and confusion reigned for several years.*

reign·ing /ˈreɪnɪŋ/ *adj* [A] being the most recent winner of a competition: *the reigning Miss World/Wimbledon champion*

reign of ter·ror /ˌ··ˈ··/ *n* a period of political cruelty and widespread official killing of opponents of those in power

re·im·burse /ˌriːɪmˈbɜːs‖-ɜːrs/ *v* [T (**to, for**)] *fml* to pay (money) back to (esp. someone who has had to spend money in connection with their work): *We will reimburse you for your travelling expenses.* | *Your expenses will be reimbursed.* [+*obj(i)+obj(d)*] *We will reimburse you your expenses.* —compare REFUND² — ~**ment** *n* [C;U]

rein¹ /reɪn/ *also* **reins** *pl.*— *n* **1** a long narrow band usu. of leather, by which a horse, or sometimes a young child, is controlled and guided: *Pull on the reins/the left rein.* —see picture at HORSE **2 give (free) rein to** to give freedom to (feelings or desires): *He gave free rein to his imagination.* **3 keep a tight rein on** to control firmly: *The finance director keeps a very tight rein on our spending.* —see also REINS

rein² *v*

    rein sthg. ↔ **back** *phr v* [T] to cause (a horse) to stop by pulling the reins

    rein sthg. ↔ **in** *phr v* [T] to cause (a horse) to go more slowly by pulling the reins; RESTRAIN: (fig.) *The government is reining in public expenditure.*

re·in·car·nate /ˌriːɪnˈkɑːneɪt‖-ɑːr-/ *v* [T (**as**) *usu. pass.*] to cause to return to life in a new body, after death: *Perhaps you will be reincarnated as a snake.*

re·in·car·na·tion /ˌriːɪnkɑːˈneɪʃən‖-ɑːr-/ *n* **1** [U] the act or fact of being reincarnated: *Hindus believe in reincarnation.* **2** [C (**of**)] the person or animal that results: *She thinks she is a reincarnation of Cleopatra.*

rein·deer /ˈreɪndɪəʳ/ *n* **reindeer** a large deer with long branching horns.

▶ CULTURAL NOTE Reindeer are wild and plentiful in northern Canada and Alaska, where they are sometimes called **caribou**. They are used in the coldest parts of Europe for pulling carriages (SLEDGES) across the snow, and many children believe that at CHRISTMAS Santa Claus travels in a sledge pulled by reindeer. ◄

re·in·force /ˌriːɪnˈfɔːs‖-ˈfɔːrs/ *v* [T] **1** to strengthen (a group, esp. an army) by the addition of men, equipment, etc. **2** to add strength or support to; make stronger or firmer: *to reinforce the elbows of a jacket with leather patches* | *Their arguments are strongly reinforced by the latest trade figures.* | *Newspapers like this tend to reinforce people's prejudices* —**forcement** *n* [U] : *The wall needs some reinforcement.*

reinforced con·crete /ˌ··· ˈ··/ *also* **ferroconcrete**— *n* [U] stonelike material (CONCRETE) strengthened by metal rods placed in it before it hardens, and used in building

re·in·force·ments /ˌriːɪnˈfɔːsmənts‖-ˈfɔːrs-/ *n* [P] more soldiers sent to reinforce an army

Rein·hardt /ˈraɪnhɑːt‖-ɑːrt/, **Djan·go** /ˈdʒæŋɡəʊ/ (1910–53) a Belgian JAZZ musician who played the GUITAR with Stephane Grappelli and with many famous American jazz musicians

reins /reɪnz/ *n* [*the*+P] a means or position of control: *Who will take the reins while the boss is in hospital?* | *to* **hold/take over the reins** *of government* —see also REIN

re·in·state /ˌriːɪnˈsteɪt/ *v* [T (**as, in**)] to put back into a former job or position: *He was dismissed, but was later reinstated (as head teacher in his former job).* — ~**ment** *n* [C;U]

re·in·sure /ˌriːɪnˈʃʊəʳ/ *v* [T] *tech* to insure again with another insurance company, so that the risk of loss will be shared —**surance** *n* [U]

re·is·sue /ˌriːˈɪʃuː, -ˈɪsjuː‖-ˈɪʃuː/ *v* [T] to print again after a time: *The book was reissued in a new cover.* —**reissue** *n* : *a reissue of stamps*

re·it·e·rate /riːˈɪtəreɪt/ *v* [T] *fml* to repeat several times, in order to make one's position or opinions as clear as possible: *They reiterated their demands for an official inquiry into the accident.* [+*that*] *Let me reiterate that we have absolutely no plans to increase taxation.* —**ration** /riːˌɪtəˈreɪʃən/ *n* [C;U]

Reith /riːθ/, **Lord** (1889–1971) the first manager of the BBC, known for his high standards

Reith lec·tures /ˌ· ˈ··/ [*the*+P] a yearly set of talks broadcast on the BBC, given by a person who is very knowledgeable about an important subject

re·ject¹ /rɪˈdʒekt/ *v* [T] **1** to refuse to accept, consider, or use: *She rejected my suggestion.* | *He was rejected for the army because of his bad eyesight.* | *If people are unkind to him he feels rejected.* | *The patient rejected* (=his body failed to accept) *the transplanted heart.* | *The teachers voted to reject the government's pay offer.* **2** to throw away as useless or imperfect: *Choose the good apples and reject the bad ones.* —see REFUSE (USAGE)

re·ject² /ˈriːdʒekt/ *n* something rejected, esp. because it is not good enough to be sold

re·jec·tion /rɪˈdʒekʃən/ *n* [C;U] (an example of) rejecting or being rejected: *the rejection of an application* | *I've had so many rejections I've stopped offering to help her.*

re·jig /riːˈdʒɪɡ/ *BrE* ‖ **re·jig·ger** /riːˈdʒɪɡəʳ/ *AmE*— *v* -**gg**- [T] to supply with new equipment or new systems; rearrange, esp. so as to perform different work or to work more effectively: *The factory had to be rejigged to accommodate the new machinery.* —**rejig** /ˈriːdʒɪɡ/ *n*

re·joice /rɪˈdʒɔɪs/ *v* [I (**at, over**)] *fml or lit* to feel or show great joy: *We rejoiced at/over the good news.* [+*to-v*] *They all rejoiced to hear the happy news.*

    rejoice in sthg. *phr v* [T *no pass.*] **1** to have (something that brings happiness): *They rejoiced in their good fortune.* **2** *BrE humor* (of a person) to have (a particular name or title, esp. one that is silly or amusing): *He rejoices in the name of Pigg.*

re·joic·ing /rɪˈdʒɔɪsɪŋ/ *also* **rejoicings** *pl.*— *n* [U (**at, over**)] *fml or lit* great and uncontrolled joy, esp. shown by a number of people: *great rejoicing(s) over the victory*

re·join¹ /ˌriːˈdʒɔɪn/ *v* [T] **1** to join together again: *Rejoin the two wires.* **2** to go back to (a group, organization, etc.): *He rejoined his regiment after a week's leave.*

re·join² /rɪˈdʒɔɪn/ *v* [T] to say (something) in reply, esp. rudely or angrily: *"No, I won't!" he rejoined rudely.* —see ANSWER (USAGE)

re·join·der /rɪˈdʒɔɪndəʳ/ *n* an answer, esp. a rude one: *a sharp rejoinder*

re·ju·ve·nate /rɪˈdʒuːvəneɪt/ *v* [T *often pass.*] to make (someone) feel or look young and strong again: *The mountain air will rejuvenate you.* | (fig.) *They have restored and rejuvenated the derelict theatre.* —**nation** /rɪˌdʒuːvəˈneɪʃən/ *n* [S;U]

re·kin·dle /riːˈkɪndl/ *v* [T] to light (esp. a fire) again: (fig.) *The accident rekindled the public debate on this issue.* (=made it active again)

re·laid /ˌriːˈleɪd/ *past tense & participle of* RELAY³

re·lapse /rɪˈlæps‖ˈriːlæps/ *v* [I (**into**)] to fall back into a bad state of health or way of life, after an improvement; return: *He soon relapsed into his old bad habits.* —**relapse** *n* : *She can't return to work because she's had a relapse.* (=is ill again)

re·late /rɪˈleɪt/ *v* [T (**to**)] *fml* **1** [(**to**)] to tell (a story): *He related (to us) the story of his escape.* | **Strange to relate** (=this is surprising), *they never met again.* **2** to show or establish a connection between: *The police are still trying to relate these two pieces of evidence.* | *The report seeks to relate the rise in crime to the increase in unemployment.*

    relate to sbdy./sthg. *phr v* [T] **1** to concern; be about or be directed towards: *These proposals relate only to agricultural land.* | *secret documents relating to the conduct of the war* **2** to have a connection with: *The cost relates directly to the amount of time spent on the job.* **3** to have a satisfactory relationship with; understand and accept: *She doesn't relate very well to her mother.* | (fig.) *I can't relate to his ideas/music at all.*

Relate a British organization which helps those who have problems with relationships such as marriage. It used to be called the Marriage Guidance Council.

re·lat·ed /rɪˈleɪtɪd/ *adj* [(**to**)] **1** [F] connected by a family relationship: *She and I are related.* | *I am related to her by marriage.* **2** connected in some way: *The programme deals with drug addiction, juvenile crime, and related issues.* | *The fall in the cost of living is directly related to the drop in the oil price.* —opposite **unrelated** — ~**ness** *n* [U]

re·la·tion /rɪ'leɪʃən/ n 1 [C] also **relative** esp. AmE– a member of one's family: close/distant relations | They invited all their relations to stay at Christmas. | My husband's relations are my **relations by marriage.** –see also BLOOD RELATION 2 [C;U (**between, to**)] RELATIONSHIP (2): The actual cost **bears no/little/some relation to** (=matches not at all/not much/partly) what we expected. 3 [U (**of**)] fml the act of telling a story 4 **in/with relation to** fml or pomp about; with regard to –see RELATIONSHIP (USAGE); see also POOR RELATION, PUBLIC RELATIONS

re·la·tion·al /rɪ'leɪʃənəl/ adj tech (of a word) used as part of a sentence but without a meaning of its own: "Have" in "I have gone" is a relational word. –compare NOTIONAL (2)

relational da·ta·base /·,··· '··/ n a computer DATABASE which allows a user to find and work with the same information in many different ways

re·la·tions /rɪ'leɪʃənz/ n [P (**between, with**)] 1 way of treating and thinking of each other: We had/enjoyed friendly relations with the Soviet Union. | The relations between our two countries are not good just now. 2 connections; affairs together: They have business relations with our firm. | After this incident we broke off diplomatic relations with their country. | It is believed he had **sexual relations with** (=had sex with) her. | the relations between landlord and tenant –see RELATIONSHIP (USAGE)

re·la·tion·ship /rɪ'leɪʃənʃɪp/ n 1 [C (**between, with**)] a friendship or connection between people: My relationship with my boyfriend has lasted six months now. | the good relationship between the police and the local people 2 [C;U (**between, to**)] (a) connection: the relationship between wages and prices 3 [U (**between**)] the state of being of the same family: They're both called Smith, but there's no relationship between them.

▷ USAGE Compare **relationship, relation,** and **relations.** All three words can be used to suggest a connection between people or things. **Relationship,** when used of people, suggests a close connection with strong feelings: her **relationship** with her husband. Both **relationship** and **relation** can be used of things that depend on each other: the **relationship/relation** between temperature and humidity. **Relations** can be used of a more formal or distant **relationship** between people or groups: The local community has good **relations** with the police. | **Relations** between our countries are improving.◁

rel·a·tive¹ /'relətɪv/ n esp. AmE a RELATION (1): My uncle is my nearest/closest living relative.

relative² adj 1 compared to each other or to something else: the relative costs of building in stone and in brick | After his money troubles, he's now living in relative comfort. | an atmosphere of relative calm after the recent upheavals –opposite **absolute** 2 [F+to] fml connected (with); on the subject (of); RELEVANT (to): facts relative to this question –see also RELATIVELY

relative clause /,··· '·/ n tech (in grammar) a part of a sentence that has a verb in it, and is joined to the rest of the sentence by **who, which, where,** etc.: In "The man who lives next door is a doctor" the words "who lives next door" form a relative clause.

relative hu·mid·i·ty /,··· ·'···/ n [U] the amount of water VAPOUR present in the air, expressed as a PERCENTAGE of the greatest possible amount that could be present. In the US it is often given in weather reports. Very high relative humidity (over 90%) causes discomfort for most people.

rel·a·tive·ly /'relətɪvli/ adv quite; when compared to others of the same kind: The exam was relatively easy. | a relatively warm day for the time of year | Relatively speaking it's not important.

relative pro·noun /,··· '··/ n tech a PRONOUN such as **who, which, that,** etc., by which a relative clause is connected to the rest of the sentence

rel·a·tiv·i·ty /,relə'tɪvəti/ n [U] (often cap.) a THEORY about the relationships between time, ENERGY, and mass, which change with increased speed: Einstein's Theory of Relativity

re·lax /rɪ'læks/ v 1 [I;T] to make or become less active and worried: Sit down and relax! | The music will help to relax you. 2 [I;T] to make or become less stiff or tight: His muscles relaxed. | She relaxed her hold on the wheel. 3 [T]

to make (effort or control) less severe: You must not relax your efforts for a moment. | a proposal to relax immigration controls

re·lax·a·tion /,riːlæk'seɪʃən/ n 1 [C;U] (something done for) rest and amusement: He plays the piano for a bit of relaxation. It's one of his favourite relaxations. 2 [U (**of, in**)] the act of making or becoming less stiff or severe: the relaxation of controls on government spending

re·laxed /rɪ'lækst/ adj 1 (of a person) free from worry; easy in manner: He was lying in the sun looking very relaxed and happy. 2 (esp. of a group situation or surroundings) comfortable and informal; restful: a relaxed atmosphere

re·lax·ing /rɪ'læksɪŋ/ adj making one feel relaxed: a relaxing afternoon in the garden

re·lay¹ /'riːleɪ/ n 1 [C;U] a part of a team or organization, that takes its turn in keeping an activity going continuously, a fresh group replacing a tired one: Groups of men worked **in relays** to clear the blocked railway line. 2 a relay race 3 a [U] an electrical arrangement or apparatus that receives and passes on messages by telephone, radio, etc.: The concert was broadcast **by relay.** b [C (**of**)] a broadcast sent out in this way: We listened to a relay of the concert.

relay² /'riːleɪ ‖ rɪ'leɪ, 'riːleɪ/ v -**layed** [T (**to**)] 1 to send out by RELAY¹ (2): The broadcast was relayed to Europe. 2 to pass (a message) from one person to another: Could you relay the news to the other teachers?

re·lay³ /,riː'leɪ/ v -**laid** /'leɪd/ [T] to lay (esp. a CARPET or CABLE¹ (2)) again

relay race /'··· ,·/ n a running or swimming race between two or more teams in which each member of each team runs or swims part of the total distance

re·lease¹ /rɪ'liːs/ v [T] 1 [(**from**)] to set free; let go: She released the rabbit from the trap. | The hijackers released three of the hostages. | The aircraft released its bombs. | He released (his hold on) her arm. 2 to press (a handle) so as to allow something to move: She released the handbrake of the car. 3 to allow **a** (a new film or record) to be shown or sold publicly **b** (a news story or piece of government information) to be known and printed: The new trade figures have just been released.

release² n 1 [S;U (**from**)] the act of setting free or being set free: After his release from prison he came home. | After my examination I had a feeling of release. 2 [C] a new film, record, or piece of information that has been released: On this show they play the latest releases. –see also PRESS RELEASE 3 [C] a letter or message that sets someone free: The governor of the prison signed the release. 4 [C] a handle, button, etc. that can be pressed to allow part of a machine to move –see picture at TYPEWRITER 5 **on general release** (of a film) able to be seen at all the cinemas in an area –see also DAY RELEASE COURSE

rel·e·gate /'relɪgeɪt/ v [T (**to**)] to put into a lower or worse place: We relegated the old furniture to the children's room. | (esp. BrE) Everyone was surprised when the football team was relegated (to the second division). –compare PROMOTE – -**gation** /,relɪ'geɪʃən/ n [U (**to**)]

re·lent /rɪ'lent/ v [I] to have or show pity; become less severe or cruel: At first she threatened to dismiss us all, but later she relented. | (fig.) In the morning the storm relented a little.

re·lent·less /rɪ'lentləs/ adj continuously severe: the relentless fury of the waves | relentless pain | He was relentless in questioning the suspect. – –**ly** adv : He beat the dog relentlessly. | We worked relentlessly to finish the job. – ~**ness** n [U]

rel·e·vant /'relɪvənt/ adj [(**to**)] 1 directly connected with the subject: His nationality isn't relevant to whether he's a good lawyer/isn't a relevant point. 2 having practical value or importance: This type of university course is no longer relevant (to today's problems). –opposite **irrelevant** – –**ly** adv –-**vance, -vancy** n [U (**to**)] : What you say has no relevance to the subject. –opposite **irrelevance**

re·li·a·ble /rɪ'laɪəbəl/ adj that may be trusted; dependable: She may forget to come – she's not very reliable. | I have it on reliable evidence (=I have heard it from someone trustworthy) that the hospital is going to be closed down. | a reliable car | a reliable source of information –opposite **unreliable** – -**bly** adv : (pomp) I am reliably informed (=a reliable person told me) that he's deep in debt. – -**bility**

/rɪˌlaɪəˈbɪlɪti/ n [U] —opposite **unreliability**

re·li·ance /rɪˈlaɪəns/ n [U **(on)**] **1** trust: *I place complete reliance on his judgment.* **2** the state of being materially supported; dependence: *our country's reliance on imported oil* —see also RELY ON

re·li·ant /rɪˈlaɪənt/ adj [F+**on**] depending on; relying on (RELY **on**): *We should not be so reliant on imported oil.* — see also SELF-RELIANT

rel·ic /ˈrelɪk/ n **1** [(**of**)] something old that reminds us of the past: *This stone axe is a relic of ancient times.* | (*humor*) *How much longer are you going to drive around in that old relic?* **2** a part of the body or clothing of a holy person, or something that belonged to them which is kept and respected after their death —see also RELIQUARY

rel·ics /ˈrelɪks/ n [P] *lit* someone's dead body: *His relics are buried at Winchester.*

rel·ict /ˈrelɪkt/ adj [A] *tech* remaining in existence after most others of the same type no longer exist

re·lief /rɪˈliːf/ n **1** [S;U] (a) feeling of comfort at the ending of anxiety, pain, or dullness: *This medicine will give/bring you some relief.* | *a drug for the relief of pain* | *I* **heaved a sigh of relief** *when I heard he was safe.* | *You're safe! What a relief!* | *Much to my relief/To my great relief, her injuries were only slight.* | *The funny scenes in Shakespeare provide a little* **light relief.** (=a pleasant and amusing change) **2** [U] help for people in trouble: *The government sent relief* (=money, food, clothes) *to the people who lost their homes in the flood.* | *They've started a relief fund for the refugees.* **3** [U] *BrE* ‖ **benefit** *AmE—* a part of one's income on which one does not have to pay tax for some special reason: *He gets tax relief because he supports his old mother.* **4** [U] *AmE* money given by the government to help people who are poor, old, unemployed, etc. **5** [C+*sing.|pl. v*] a person or group taking from another the responsibility for a duty: *The relief for the military guard is/are expected soon.* | *a relief driver* | *They had to provide a relief bus because there were so many passengers.* | *The Yankees are bringing in their* **relief** *pitcher.* **6** [U+**of**] the act of driving away an enemy: *the relief of the city* **7** [U] *tech* a legal way of dealing with a problem: *seek relief by taking the matter to court* **8** [C;U] (a shape or) decoration cut so that it sticks out above the rest of the surface it is on, as on a coin: *a carving in* **high/low relief** (=sticking out a long way/a little) | (fig.) *black trees standing out* **in bold/sharp relief** (=seeming to stick out) *against the snow* —compare BAS-RELIEF, HIGH RELIEF

relief map /·ˈ· ·/ n a map with the mountains and high parts shown differently from the low parts, esp. by being printed in a different colour

relief road /·ˈ· ·/ n *esp. BrE* a road made in order to take away heavy traffic from another road

re·lieve /rɪˈliːv/ v [T] **1** to lessen (pain, anxiety, or trouble): *a drug that relieves headaches* **2** to take a duty from (someone) as a RELIEF (5): *The guard will be relieved at midnight.* **3** to give variety to; make more interesting: *I went for a walk to relieve the boredom of the day.* **4** to drive away the enemy from (a town, fort, etc.) **5 relieve oneself** *fml euph* to URINATE or empty the bowels **6 relieve one's feelings** to cry, shout, etc., in order to make oneself feel better: *He relieved his feelings by throwing his boots at the cat.*

  relieve sbdy. **of** sthg. *phr v* [T] **1** to free (someone) of (something heavy to carry or hard to do): *Let me relieve you of that heavy parcel/of some of the housework.* | (*humor*) *A thief relieved me of my watch.* (=stole it) **2** [*often pass.*] *euph* to dismiss from (a position): *He was relieved of his employment/his duties.*

re·lieved /rɪˈliːvd/ adj no longer worried; feeling relief: *Your mother will be very relieved (at the news).* | *She had a relieved look on her face.* [F+*to-v/that*] *I was relieved (to hear) that they were safe.*

re·li·gion /rɪˈlɪdʒən/ n **1** [U] belief in the life of the spirit and usu. in one or more gods, esp. the belief that it/they made the world and can control it **2** [C] a particular system of this belief and the worship, behaviour, etc., connected with it: *the Christian religion* | *Islam and Buddhism are two of the great religions of the world.* | (fig.) *Music is a religion with John; he* **makes a religion of** *it.*

re·li·gi·ose /rɪˈlɪdʒiəʊs/ adj (of a person) unreasonably or too noticeably religious —**-osity** /rɪˌlɪdʒiˈɒsəti‖-ˈɑːs-/ n [U]

re·li·gious /rɪˈlɪdʒəs/ adj **1** of religion: *a religious service* | *religious liberty* (=freedom to choose one's religion) **2** (of a person or their behaviour) obeying the rules of a religion very carefully; PIOUS: *a very religious man —* opposite **irreligious 3** [A] performing duties very carefully, as a matter of conscience: *She washes the floor with religious care every morning.*

religious ed·u·ca·tion /·ˌ··· ··ˈ···/ also **religious in·struc·tion** /·ˌ·· ·ˈ··/, **RE** *abbrev.—* n [U] the study of religion at school. In Britain, all children receive some religious education at school. In the US, state schools are not allowed to teach religion on the principle of the SEPARATION OF CHURCH AND STATE.

re·li·gious·ly /rɪˈlɪdʒəsli/ adv in a careful and thorough way: *They followed the instructions quite religiously.*

religious ob·serv·ance /·ˌ··· ·ˈ··/ n **1** [U] the practice of performing the formal act of one's religion **2** [C] a formal act of religion

religious tol·er·ance /·ˌ··· ·ˈ···/ n [U] the idea that other people have a right to practise a religion which is not one's own

re·line /ˌriːˈlaɪn/ v [T] to put a new LINING (=inside covering) into: *She relined the old coat.*

re·lin·quish /rɪˈlɪŋkwɪʃ/ v [T **(to)**] *fml* to give up (power, position, a claim, etc.): *to relinquish power* | *He relinquished his claim to the land/his hold on my arm.* | *She relinquished all control over the family business to her daughter.*

rel·i·qua·ry /ˈrelɪkwəri‖-kweri/ n a container for religious RELICS (2)

rel·ish¹ /ˈrelɪʃ/ n **1** [S;U **(for)**] great enjoyment, esp. of food; pleasure and satisfaction: *He drank up the wine with relish.* **2** [C;U] (a) substance eaten with a meal, such as PICKLES or SAUCE, to add taste and interest

relish² v [T] to enjoy; be pleased and satisfied with: *He didn't relish the prospect of having to explain his behaviour.* [+*v-ing*] *Hilary won't relish having to wash all those dishes.*

re·live /ˌriːˈlɪv/ v [T] to experience again, esp. in the imagination: *She relived her school days in conversation with an old friend.*

re·load /ˌriːˈləʊd/ v [I;T] to load (a gun) again

re·lo·cate /ˌriːləʊˈkeɪt‖riːˈləʊkeɪt/ v [I,T] to move to or establish in a new place: *The factory has been relocated into the Bristol area.* | *We're relocating into the Bristol area.* —**-cation** /ˌriːləʊˈkeɪʃən/ n [U]

re·luc·tant /rɪˈlʌktənt/ adj unwilling, and therefore perhaps slow to act: *reluctant helpers* | *He gave a reluctant promise.* [F+*to-v*] *They were very reluctant to help.* (=but probably did help) —**-ly** *adv* : *She reluctantly accepted the money.* —**-tance** n [S;U (+*to-v*)] : *He agreed, but with great reluctance/with a certain reluctance.*

re·ly /rɪˈlaɪ/ v
  rely on/upon sbdy./sthg. *phr v* [T] **1** to trust (esp. that something will happen or someone will do something); have confidence in: *You can't rely on the weather.* (=it may well be bad) | *I think I can come, but don't rely on it.* | *We're relying on your discretion.* [+*v-ing*] *Don't rely on going to India.* (=perhaps you won't) [+*obj+v-ing*] *Rely on my/me doing it.* | *Don't rely on the bank lending you the money.* (=perhaps they won't) [+*obj+to-v*] *You can rely on me to help you.* **2** [(**for**)] to be materially supported by; depend on: *They have to rely on the river for their water.*

REM /rem/ n [U] *abbrev. for* RAPID EYE MOVEMENT

re·main /rɪˈmeɪn/ v [*not usu. in progressive forms*] **1** [I] *rather fml* to stay or be left behind after others have gone, been lost, etc.: *She remained at home to look after the children when her husband went out.* | *Little of the original architecture remains.* | *The only remaining question is whether or not we can raise the money.* [+*to-v*] *Several things remain to be done.* | *It only remains for me to say that ...* (=All that is left for me to say is ...) | *It sounds a good idea, but* **it remains to be seen** (=we shall know later on) *whether it will succeed.* **2** [I+*adv/prep*;L] to continue to be (in an unchanged state): *He remained a prisoner for the rest of his life.* | *The situation remains unchanged.* | *Despite the danger, she remained calm/she remained in complete control.* | *I'm sorry you're tired, but* **the fact remains** (=in spite of that) *that the job has to be done, so hurry up!* —see STAY (USAGE)

re·main·der¹ /rɪˈmeɪndəʳ/ n [(the) S+sing./pl. v] **1** what is left over; the rest: *The remainder of the food will do for tomorrow.* | *Ten people in our class are Arabs and the remainder are Germans.* **2** in DIVISION (5), the number undivided that is smaller than the DIVISOR: *Fifteen divided by six equals two, with a remainder of three.*

remainder² v [T usu. pass.] to sell (esp. books) cheap so as to get rid of them quickly

re·mains /rɪˈmeɪnz/ n [P] **1** [(of)] parts which are left: *the remains of dinner|of an old castle* **2** fml a dead body: *His remains lie in the churchyard.*

re·make /ˌriːˈmeɪk/ v -made /ˈmeɪd/ [T] to make (esp. a film) again —**remake** /ˈriːmeɪk/ n : *They're doing a remake of "Gone with the Wind".*

re·mand /rɪˈmɑːnd‖rɪˈmænd/ v [T usu. pass.] BrE to send back to prison from a court of law, to be tried later after further inquiries have been made (often in the phrase **remanded in custody**) —**remand** n [C;U] : *He's on remand.* (=in prison waiting for a trial). One of the problems of the prison service in Britain is that remand prisoners have to live in the same conditions as people who have already been convicted (CONVICT) of a crime, often for quite a long time, even though they may be completely INNOCENT.

remand home /·ˈ·ˌ·/ n BrE an institution, also called a **remand centre**, where JUVENILE offenders wait to appear in court, esp. formerly —see also COMMUNITY HOME

re·mark¹ /rɪˈmɑːk‖-ɑːrk/ v [T+that; obj] to say esp. something that one has just noticed; give as an opinion: *He remarked that it was getting late.* | *"It's getting late," he remarked.*

remark on/upon sthg. phr v [T] fml to notice and say or write something about: *Everyone remarked on his absence.*

remark² n **1** [C (about, on)] a spoken or written opinion; COMMENT: *Don't make/pass rude remarks about her appearance.* **2** [U] fml notice; attention: *Her strange appearance could hardly escape remark/was worthy of remark.*

re·mar·ka·ble /rɪˈmɑːkəbəl‖-ɑːr-/ adj [(for)] esp. apprec worth mentioning, esp. because unusual or noticeable: *a most remarkable sunset/coincidence* | *Finland is remarkable for the large number of its lakes.* —opposite **unremarkable**

re·mar·ka·bly /rɪˈmɑːkəbli‖-ɑːr-/ adv (used esp. with adjectives and adverbs) unusually; noticeably: *He sings remarkably well.* | *a remarkably fine day* | *Remarkably, he's never been abroad.*

re·mar·ry /ˌriːˈmæri/ v [I;T] to marry again: *He decided to remarry after his wife's death.* | *She remarried her former husband.*

re·mas·ter /riːˈmɑːstəʳ‖-ˈmæs-/ v to make a new and better original (MASTER¹ (5)) from which copies can be made: *remaster an old recording*

Rem·brandt /ˈrembrænt/ (1606–69) a Dutch painter, considered to be one of the greatest painters of all time, who drew many pictures of himself and other people, as well as religious subjects, and is known esp. for his use of light and shade — ~**esque** /ˌrembrænˈtesk◂/ adj

re·me·di·a·ble /rɪˈmiːdiəbəl/ adj fml or tech that can be put right or cured —opposite **irremediable**

re·me·di·al /rɪˈmiːdiəl/ adj curing or helping; providing a remedy: *He had to do remedial exercises for his weak back.* | *remedial teaching* — ~**ly** adv

remedial class /·ˈ···ˌ·/ n a class in some schools where children who have difficulty with reading, writing, or other skills are given special help

rem·e·dy¹ /ˈremɪdi/ n [C;U (for, against)] a way of curing something: *A good night's sleep would be the best remedy for your headache.* | *herbal remedies* | *Such evils are beyond/past remedy.* | *The law provides no remedy for this injustice.* (=cannot put it right)

remedy² v [T] to put or make (something bad) right: *How can we remedy this situation/injustice/mistake/loss?*

re·mem·ber /rɪˈmembəʳ/ v [not usu. in progressive forms] **1** [I;T (as)] to (be able to) bring back to one's mind (information, past events, etc.); keep in the memory: *"What's her name?" "I can't remember."* | *I'll always remember that wonderful day.* | *I remember her as* (=I think she was, if my memory is correct) *rather a tall*

woman. [+(that)] *She suddenly remembered that she had not locked the door.* [+wh-] *Can you remember where he lives/how to get there?* [+v-ing] *I don't remember agreeing to that.* | *Certainly I posted your letter — I remember posting it.* [+obj+v-ing] *Do you remember me asking you that same question?* **2** [I(about);T] to take care not to forget: *Did you remember that book I asked you for?* (=have you got it for me?) | *You will remember about watering the plants, won't you?* [+to-v] *"You will remember to post my letter, won't you?" "Yes, I'll remember."* | *Please remember to water the plants while I'm away.* —opposite **forget** (for 1,2) **3** [T] often euph to give money or a present to: *She always remembers me at Christmas.* | *He remembered me in his will.* (=left me some money after his death) **4** [T] to think about with special respect and honour: *On this day we remember the dead of two world wars.* | *I'll remember you in my prayers.* (=pray for you) **5** **Remember, remember, the fifth of November, gunpowder, treason, and plot** quote the first lines of a children's poem about the plan by Guy Fawkes and others to destroy the Houses of Parliament by an explosion — see also GUY FAWKES NIGHT **6** **we will remember them** a phrase used esp. during the religious service on Remembrance Day in Britain, when people remember those who died in the two world wars

▷ USAGE Note the difference between **remember** +v-ing and **remember** +to-v. I **remember** *locking the door as I left the house.* (=I locked the door and can call this event to mind now.) | I **remembered** *to lock the door as I left the house.* (=It was in my mind then that I must lock the door, and I locked it.)◁

remember sbdy. **to** sbdy. phr v [T] infml to send greetings from (someone) to: *Please remember me to your mother.* | *He asked to be remembered to you.*

re·mem·brance /rɪˈmembrəns/ n [(of)] **1** [U] the act of remembering: *A church service was held in remembrance of those killed in the war.* **2** [C] old-fash something kept or given to remind one: *He gave me his photograph as a remembrance (of him).*

Remembrance Day /·ˈ··· ˌ·/ also **Remembrance Sun·day** /·ˌ·· ˈ··/— n [C;U] the Sunday nearest to November 11th, when people in Britain remember those killed in the two world wars. Services are held in churches, and at war MEMORIALS, and the custom is to wear a red paper POPPY (=a type of flower) in one's buttonhole, as a sign of remembering. The money raised by the sale of these poppies is given to charities (CHARITY) involved with people who suffered in the wars. A few people think that these customs make war seem GLORIOUS, rather than being a reminder of the deaths and the damage that was done, and these people wear a white poppy as a sign of peace. —compare VETERANS DAY; see also ARMISTICE DAY

re·mind /rɪˈmaɪnd/ v [T (of)] to tell or cause (someone) to remember (a fact, or to do something): *I must write to Mother — will you remind me? | I've forgotten his name — will you remind me of it? | Don't remind me of that awful day — I made such a fool of myself! | Will you remind me about that appointment.* [+obj+to-v] *Remind me to write to Mother.* [+obj+that] *She reminded me that I hadn't written to Mother.* | *The sight of the clock reminded me that I was late.*

remind sbdy. **of** sbdy./sthg. phr v [T] to appear to (someone) to be similar to: *This hotel reminds me of the one we stayed in last year.*

re·mind·er /rɪˈmaɪndəʳ/ n something that makes one remember: *He hadn't paid the bill, so the shop sent him a reminder.* (=a letter reminding him to pay)

rem·i·nisce /ˌremɪˈnɪs/ v [I (about)] to talk or think about past experiences, esp. pleasant ones: *The two old friends were reminiscing (about their youth).* — -**niscence** n [U] : *to enjoy the pleasures of reminiscence*

rem·i·nis·cenc·es /ˌremɪˈnɪsənsɪz/ n [P (of)] a spoken or written account of one's own life: *We had to listen to his reminiscences of the war.* —compare MEMOIRS

rem·i·nis·cent /ˌremɪˈnɪsənt/ adj **1** [F+of] that reminds one of; like: *This hotel is reminiscent of the one we stayed in last year.* | *a taste reminiscent of chicken* **2** [A] thinking about the past; remembering something: *a reminiscent smile.*

re·miss /rɪˈmɪs/ adj [F] fml careless about a duty; showing lack of care or attention: *It was remiss of me not to* (=I was remiss because I did not) *answer your letter.* | *He has been remiss in his work.* — ~**ness** n [U]

re·mis·sion /rɪˈmɪʃən/ n 1 [C;U] BrE (a) lessening of the time a person has to stay in prison. This is possible in Britain because prison sentences are often only ADVISORY, and even people who are guilty of very serious crimes such as RAPE may be allowed out of prison before they have served the full amount of time advised by the court: *The prisoner was given six months' remission for good behaviour.* 2 [C; U] a period when an illness is less severe for a time: *He|The disease* **went into remission** *last month.* 3 [U] fml the remitting (REMIT¹ (1)) of a debt or punishment: *Christians pray for* **the remission of sins.** (=that their SINs will be forgiven)

re·mit¹ /rɪˈmɪt/ v -tt- fml 1 [T] to free someone from (a debt or punishment) 2 [I;T (**to**)] to send (money) by post: *Please remit payment|remit by cheque immediately.* — compare UNREMITTING

    remit sthg. to sbdy./sthg. phr v [T] fml to send back to for a decision or other action: *The proposal has been remitted to the executive committee.*

re·mit² /ˈriːmɪt‖ˈriːmɪt, ˈriːmɪt/ n [U] BrE fml the area over which one has judgment or control: *It is not part of the committee's remit to investigate government policy.*

re·mit·tance /rɪˈmɪtəns/ n 1 [C] an amount of money remitted: *He sends her a small remittance each month.* 2 [U] fml the remitting of money: *We will forward the goods on remittance of £10.*

rem·nant /ˈremnənt/ n 1 [(**of**)] a part that remains: *We fed the remnants of the feast to the dogs.* 2 a small piece of cloth left over from a larger piece and sold cheap: *a remnant sale*

re·mod·el /ˌriːˈmɒdl‖ˌriːˈmɑːdl/ v -ll- BrE ‖ -l- AmE [T] to change the shape of: *an actress who had her nose remodelled*

re·mon·strance /rɪˈmɒnstrəns‖rɪˈmɑːn-/ n [C;U (**at, against**)] fml (a) complaint: *loud cries of remonstrance*

rem·on·strate /ˈremənstreɪt‖rɪˈmɑːn-/ v [I (**against, with**)] fml to complain; express disapproval: *I remonstrated against his behaviour.* | *She remonstrated with him* (=complained to him) *about his behaviour.*

re·morse /rɪˈmɔːs‖-ɔːrs/ n [U] great sorrow and a feeling of guilt for having done wrong: *He felt|was filled with remorse after hitting the child.* – ~**ful** adj – ~**fully** adv

re·morse·less /rɪˈmɔːsləs‖-ɔːr-/ adj 1 showing no remorse: *remorseless cruelty* 2 threateningly unstoppable: *The avalanche continued its remorseless descent down the mountainside.* – ~**ly** adv – ~**ness** n [U]

re·mote /rɪˈməʊt/ adj [(**from**)] 1 distant in space or time: *remote stars* | *the remote future* 2 quiet and lonely; far from the city: *a remote village in the hills* 3 widely separated (from); not close: *remote cousins* | *The connection between these two ideas is very remote.* 4 (esp. of a chance or possibility) slight: *I haven't the remotest idea* (=don't know at all) *what you mean.* | *I'm afraid your chances of success are rather remote.* 5 (of behaviour) not showing interest in others: *Her manner was polite but remote.* – ~**ness** n [U]

remote con·trol /·ˌ· ·ˈ·/ n 1 [U] a system for controlling machinery from a distance by radio signals 2 [C] an apparatus that does this: *Pass me the remote control so I can change the TV channel.* –**remote-controlled** adj : *a remote-controlled model car*

re·mote·ly /rɪˈməʊtli/ adv [usu. in negatives] to a very small degree; at all: *She isn't remotely interested in what you're saying.*

re·mould /ˌriːˈməʊld/ v [T] BrE to RETREAD –**remould** /ˈriːməʊld/ n

re·mount¹ /ˌriːˈmaʊnt/ v 1 [I;T] to get onto (a horse or bicycle) again; climb (a ladder, hill, etc.) again: *He remounted (his horse) and rode away.* 2 [T] to fix (a picture, photograph, etc.) on a new piece of cardboard (MOUNT² (1))

re·mount² /ˈriːmaʊnt/ n a fresh horse

re·mov·al /rɪˈmuːvəl/ n [C;U] (an act of) removing: *a charity organizing the removal of supplies to famine-stricken areas* | (fml) *our removal* (=change of house) *to London* | *No one could account for the removal of the desk from the room.*

removal van /·ˈ· ·/ also **moving van** AmE– n a large covered vehicle (VAN) used for moving furniture when moving from one house to another

re·move¹ /rɪˈmuːv/ v 1 [T (**from**)] to take away (from a place) or take to another place: *Remove* (=take off) *your hat.* | *He removed the child from the class.* 2 [T (**from**)] to get rid of: *He removed the mud from his shoes.* | *an operation to remove the tumour* 3 [T (**from**)] fml to dismiss: *That officer must be removed (from his position).* 4 [I (**from, to**)] fml to go to live or work in another place: *Our office has removed to Harlow from London.* 5 **once|twice|etc., removed** (of COUSINs) different by one, two, etc., GENERATIONs (2): *My second cousin once removed is the child of my second cousin.* 6 **removed from** distant from: *What you say is far removed from what you said before.* –**removable** adj : *Are the spots removable?*

re·move² n 1 [C] (always with a statement of number) a stage or degree (in phrases like (**at**) **only one remove from, several removes from**): *Their action was only* (at) *one remove from* (=was very nearly) *revolution.* 2 [the] (often cap.) a class in some British schools into which pupils are put because they have not made enough progress to go into the next higher one. Pupils at British schools usually go up to the next class each September, when the new school year starts, the system being based on age, not ability. It is only in some independent or private schools that pupils must reach a certain standard before moving up.

re·mov·er /rɪˈmuːvər/ n [C;U] (usu. in comb.) a chemical for cleaning off an unwanted substance: *a bottle of paint-remover* | *fingernail polish remover*

re·mu·ne·rate /rɪˈmjuːnəreɪt/ v [T (**for**)] fml to reward; pay (someone) for work or trouble –**-ration** /rɪˌmjuːnəˈreɪʃən/ n [S;U] : *You will receive (a small) remuneration.*

re·mu·ne·ra·tive /rɪˈmjuːnərətɪv‖-nəreɪtɪv/ adj fml (of work) well-paid; profitable – ~**ly** adv

Remus see ROMULUS AND REMUS

re·nais·sance /rɪˈneɪsəns‖ˌrenəˈsɑːns◂/ also **re·nas·cence** /rɪˈnæsəns/– n a renewal of interest in some particular kind of art, literature, etc.

Renaissance [the] the period in Europe between the 14th and 17th centuries, when the art, literature, and ideas of ancient Greece were discovered again and widely studied, causing a rebirth of activity in all these things –compare MIDDLE AGES

Renaissance man /·ˌ·· ˈ·‖ˌ··· ˈ·/ **Renaissance wom·an** /·ˌ·· ˈ·‖ˌ··· ˈ··/ fem.– n a person with interests and skills in many subjects, esp. in both the arts and the sciences

re·nal /ˈriːnl/ adj med of the KIDNEYs

re·name /riːˈneɪm/ v [T+obj (+n)] to give a new name to: *The street has been renamed (Silver Lane).*

re·nas·cent /rɪˈnæsənt/ adj fml (of an idea or feeling) starting again after being absent

Ren·ault /ˈrenəʊ‖rəˈnɔːlt/ tdmk a French company that makes cars that are sold in many countries and are quite popular in Britain, such as the **Renault 5**: *I'm thinking of buying a Renault.*

rend /rend/ v **rent** /rent/ [T] lit 1 [(APART)] to divide by force; split: *She wept and rent her garments.* | (fig.) *A terrible cry rent the air.* 2 [+obj+adv|prep] to pull violently: *She was rending her hair out in anger.* –see also HEARTRENDING

Ren·dell /ˈrendl/, **Ruth** (1930–) an English writer whose short stories and NOVELs are often about the reasons for murder. Some of her books have been filmed for television.

ren·der /ˈrendər/ v [T] fml 1 [+obj+adj] to cause to be: *His fatness renders him unable to touch his toes.* 2 [(**to**)] to give: *You will be expected to render an account of money that is owed.* | *Let us render thanks unto God.* [+obj(i)+obj(d)] *You have rendered me a service.* 3 to perform: *She rendered the song beautifully.* 4 tech to put PLASTER or cement onto (a wall)

    render sthg. ↔ **down** phr v [T] to make (fat) pure by melting

    render sthg. **into** sthg. phr v [T] fml to translate into (a language): *a copy of the Bible rendered into Gujarati*

    render sthg. ↔ **up** phr v [T (**to**)] 1 fml to say (a prayer) 2 old use to give up to an enemy: *They rendered up their city to the conqueror.*

ren·der·ing /ˈrendərɪŋ/ n 1 [C] esp. BrE for RENDITION 2 [U] a material made mainly of cement and sand, used to protect outside walls of buildings

ren·dez·vous[1] /'rɒndₐvuː, -deɪ-‖'rɑːndeɪ-/ n **-vous** /vuːz/ **1** [(**with**)] (an arrangement for) a meeting at a certain time and place: *He made a rendezvous with his girlfriend.* **2** [(**for**)] a popular place for people to meet: *This club is a rendezvous for writers.*

rendezvous[2] v **-voused** /vuːd/ [I (**with**)] to meet by arrangement: *The two spacecraft rendezvoused successfully.*

ren·di·tion /ren'dɪʃən/ also **rendering** esp. BrE— n **1** a performance of a play or piece of music: *She gave a splendid rendition of the song.* **2** a translation of a piece of writing: *an English rendition of a Greek poem.*

ren·e·gade /'renₐgeɪd/ n derog, esp. lit a person who deserts one country or belief to join another; TRAITOR

re·nege, **renegue** /rɪ'niːg, rɪ'neɪg‖rɪ'nɪg, rɪ'niːg/ v [I] **1** [(**on**)] fml to break a promise: *He reneged on his contract.* **2** (in card games) to REVOKE (2)

re·new /rɪ'njuː‖rɪ'nuː/ v [T] **1** to repeat (an action): *In the morning the enemy renewed their attack.* **2** to give new life and freshness to; make as good as new again: *I came back from my holiday with renewed strength.* **3** to replace (something old) with something new of the same kind: *I must renew my library ticket.* **4** to obtain a further period of lending for (something borrowed from a library): *I must renew these books.* — ~**al** n [C; U]

re·new·a·ble /rɪ'njuːəbəl‖rɪ'nuː-/ adj **1** that can be renewed, esp. by natural processes or good management: *Sun, wind, and waves are* **renewable sources** *of energy.* **2** that must be renewed: *This ticket is renewable after 12 months.*

Ren·frew·shire /'renfruːʃəʳ/ a former COUNTY in central Scotland, now part of Strathclyde REGION

ren·net /'renₐt/ n [U] a substance used for thickening milk to make cheese, etc.

Re·no /'riːnəʊ/ a city in Nevada, US, known for gambling (GAMBLE), legalized PROSTITUTION, and the fact that it is easy to obtain a DIVORCE there without living there for any great length of time

Re·no, Janet /'dʒænₐt/ (1938–) a government lawyer from Florida who became US Attorney General in 1993

Ren·oir /'renwɑːʳ‖rən'wɑːr/, **Jean** /ʒɒn‖ʒɑːn/ (1894–1979) a French film DIRECTOR whose films include *La Grande Illusion* and *Le Règle du Jeu*

Renoir, Pi·erre Au·guste /piˈeəʳ ɔːˈgjuːst/ (1841–1919) a French painter who helped to form the IMPRESSIONIST movement. He is known for his bright, colourful style of painting –see colour picture on page 1016

re·nounce /rɪ'naʊns/ v [T] rather fml **1** to give up (a claim); say formally that one does not own: *He renounced his claim to the property.* **2** to say formally that one has no more connection with: *He renounced his religion and became a Muslim.* –see also RENUNCIATION

ren·o·vate /'renəveɪt/ v [T] to put back into good condition by repairing, rebuilding, etc.: *The old house is being renovated.* –**vation** /ˌrenə'veɪʃən/ n [C;U]

re·nown /rɪ'naʊn/ n [U] fame: *He won renown as a painter.* | *a painter of some/great/high renown*

re·nowned /rɪ'naʊnd/ adj [(**as, for**)] well known to the general public or to a limited group of people for a particular quality, skill, invention, etc.: *Edison was renowned as an inventor/renowned for his inventions/was a renowned inventor.*

rent[1] /rent/ n [C;U] **1** (a stated sum of) money paid regularly for the use of a room, building, television set, piece of land, etc.: *They let the house to a young man.* | *We pay a high/low rent.* | *They'll have to pay more/less rent.* | *a rent collector* –see also GROUND RENT **2** esp. AmE money paid in this way for the use of a car, boat, clothes, etc.

rent[2] v **1** [T (**from**)] to pay rent for the use of: *I rent a room from Mrs Jones.* **2** [T (**to, out**)] esp. AmE‖**let** esp. BrE— to give the use of (a room, building, etc.) in return for rent: *She rents (out) rooms to students.* | *We've rented our house to some French people.* **3** [I+**at, for**] (of a building, land, etc.) to bring in rent: *This house rents at £100 a month.* **4** [T] esp. AmE to pay money for the use of (a car, boat, etc.) for a short time; HIRE: *I'll need to rent a tuxedo/car.* **5** **Rent-a**... used in the names of companies whose business is renting things to people: *Rent-a-van* | *Rent-a-tent* – ~**able** adj – ~**er** n

rent[3] n a large tear (as if) in cloth: *several great rents in the curtains*

rent[4] past tense & participle of REND

rent·al /'rentl/ n **1** a sum of money fixed to be paid as rent: *Have you paid this month's television rental?* **2** AmE something rented: *These cars are for sale and those over there are rentals.* | *Are there any summer rentals* (=houses to rent) *in this area?*

rent book /'· ·/ n a book stating the amounts and times of payment of RENT[1] (1) for a property, etc., usu. kept by the person paying it

rent boy /'· ·/ BrE ‖ **hustler** AmE– n a young male PROSTITUTE, often a boy who is homeless and needs to earn money for food

rent con·trol /'· ·ˌ·/ n [U;C] laws, usu. local, that limit how often and how much LANDLORDs may increase rent

rent-free /ˌ· '·◂/ adv, adj (used) without payment of rent: *He lives there rent-free.* | *a rent-free house*

ren·ti·er /'rɒntieɪ‖'rɑːntjeɪ/ n Fr, often derog a person who lives without working, on INVESTMENTS (=money lent and bringing in an income)

Ren·to·kil /'rentəʊkɪl/ a company in Britain which works on buildings esp. to protect them from harmful insects or decay of the wooden parts

rent strike /'· ·/ n a refusal to pay rent by all the people living in a block of flats or group of houses, usually as a protest against the amount of rent charged, or to complain about conditions

re·nun·ci·a·tion /rɪˌnʌnsi'eɪʃən/ n [C;U] (an act of) renouncing (RENOUNCE) something

re·o·pen /riː'əʊpən/ v [I;T] to (cause to) open or begin again: *School reopens next week.* | *New evidence has come to light, so the police will have to reopen the case.* | *Talks between the two countries have reopened.*

re·or·gan·ize also **-ise** BrE /riː'ɔːgənaɪz‖-'ɔːr-/ v [I;T] to ORGANIZE (something) again, perhaps in a new way: *She reorganized the room.* (=changed the position of the furniture) | *The managing director reorganized the department and made several promotions.* –**ization** /riːˌɔːgənaɪ'zeɪʃən‖riːˌɔːrgənə-/ n [U]

rep[1] /rep/ n infml for SALES REPRESENTATIVE: *Our rep will call on Monday.*

rep[2] n infml **1** [C] a REPERTORY theatre or company: *the local rep* **2** [U] REPERTORY: *She acts in rep.*

rep[3] n AmE infml REPUTATION: *Showing up drunk blew my rep with Linda's parents.*

Rep written abbrev. for: REPUBLICAN

re·paid /riː'peɪd/ past tense & participle of REPAY

re·pair[1] /rɪ'peəʳ/ v [T] **1** to make (something worn or broken) work again; mend: *a crew of workmen repairing the road* | *My watch has broken – I'll have to have it repaired.* | *We'll have to get a new car – the gear box can't be repaired.* **2** fml to put right (a wrong, mistake, etc.): *How can I repair the wrong I have done her?* –see also IRREPARABLE – ~**able** adj – ~**er** n
  repair to sthg. phr v [T] fml to go to (a place), often or in large numbers: *We all repaired to a restaurant and drank coffee together.*

repair[2] n **1** [C often pl.;U] (an act of) mending something: *The garage is carrying out repairs to my damaged car.* | *The road is* **under repair.** (=being mended) | *I'm afraid this old radio is* **beyond repair.** (=too badly broken to be mended) **2** [C] a mended place: *a neat repair on the elbow of the coat* **3** in (a) **good/bad (state of) repair** in good/bad condition

rep·a·ra·ble /'repərəbəl/ adj [usu. in negatives] (of a wrong, mistake, etc.) that can be put right –opposite **irreparable**

rep·a·ra·tion /ˌrepə'reɪʃən/ n [U (**to, for**)] fml repayment for loss or wrong: *You must* **make reparation** *for the damage.*

rep·a·ra·tions /ˌrepə'reɪʃənz/ n [P] money paid by a defeated nation after a war

rep·ar·tee /ˌrepɑː'tiː‖ˌrepər'tiː/ n [U] (the ability to make) quick amusing answers in conversation: *I enjoy listening to their witty repartee.*

re·past /rɪ'pɑːst‖rɪ'pæst/ n fml a meal

re·pat·ri·ate /riː'pætrieɪt‖riː'peɪ-/ v [T (**to**)] to bring or send (someone) back to their own country –**ation** /ˌriːpætri'eɪʃən‖ˌriːpeɪ-/ n [U]

re·pay /rɪˈpeɪ/ v **-paid** /ˈpeɪd/ [T] **1** [(to)] to return (what is owed) to (someone); pay back: *I've repaid the loan (to the bank).* | *When will you repay me?* [+obj(i)+obj(d)] *I repaid her the £10 she lent me.* **2** [(by, for, with)] to reward: *We must repay their hospitality|them for their hospitality.* | *He repaid their kindness with insults|by stealing their camera.*

re·pay·a·ble /rɪˈpeɪəbəl/ adj (of money) that can or must be paid back: *The debt is repayable in 30 days.*

re·pay·ment /rɪˈpeɪmənt/ n [C;U] paying back; something paid back: *a|some small repayment for all you have done* | *The repayments of the loan are spread over 25 years.*

re·peal /rɪˈpiːl/ v [T] to put an official end to (a law) —**repeal** n [U]

re·peat¹ /rɪˈpiːt/ v **1** [T] to say or do again: *Please repeat that word.* [+(that)] *He repeated several times that he was busy.* | *"I'm busy", he repeated.* | *Repeat after me, "I must not be a naughty boy."* | *Can you repeat this experiment?* | *to repeat a course|a year in school* (=remain in the same class) | *to repeat an order in business* (=supply the same article again) **2** [T] to say (something heard or learnt) to others: *She repeated the poem.* | *Don't repeat what I told you.* **3** [I] *BrE infml* (of food that one has eaten) to be tasted afterwards in the mouth: *I find that onions repeat.* **4 not bear repeating** (of words) to be too bad to say again **5 repeat oneself** to say or be the same thing again and again: *History seems to be repeating itself.* —see also REPE·TITION, REPETITIOUS

repeat² n **1** a performance shown or broadcast a second time: *I wish we could see more new programmes on television, not repeats all the time.* **2** (in music) a sign (:‖) showing that a passage is to be played again

re·peat·ed /rɪˈpiːtɪd/ adj [A] done again and again: *repeated failure* — **-ly** adv : *He repeatedly fails to pass the exam.* | *I've told you repeatedly* (=very often) *not to do that.*

re·peat·er /rɪˈpiːtəʳ/ n a repeating gun, watch, or clock

re·peat·ing /rɪˈpiːtɪŋ/ adj [A] **1** (of a gun) able to be fired several times without reloading **2** (of a watch or clock, esp. in former times) striking the latest hour and quarter-hours when a spring is pressed

re·pel /rɪˈpel/ v **-ll-** [T] **1** to drive away (as if) by force: *The crew repelled the attack.* | *a fabric that repels moisture* **2** to cause strong feelings of dislike in: *She was repelled by the dirty room.*

re·pel·lent /rɪˈpelənt/ adj causing strong dislike; nasty: *a plate of repellent cold potatoes* | *The sight of blood is repellent to some people.*

repellent², **-lant** n [C;U] (a) substance that drives something, esp. insects, away: *a mosquito repellent*

re·pent /rɪˈpent/ v [I (of)] fml to be sorry for and wish one had not done (something bad): *He repented his wickedness.* | *I have nothing to repent of.* [+v-ing] *He repented having shot the bird.*

re·pen·tant /rɪˈpentənt/ adj sorry for wrongdoing: *If you are truly repentant you will be forgiven.* —opposite **unrepentant** — **-ly** adv —**-tance** n [U]

re·per·cus·sion /ˌriːpəˈkʌʃən‖-pər-/ n [often pl.] a far-reaching effect of some action or event: *The president's death had unexpected repercussions all over the world.*

rep·er·toire /ˈrepətwɑːʳ‖-ər-/ n the collection of plays, pieces of music, etc., that a performer or theatre company can perform: (fig.) *He has a large repertoire of funny stories.*

rep·er·to·ry /ˈrepətəri‖ˈrepərtɔːri/ also **rep** infml— n [U] the practice of performing several plays, with the same actors and in the same theatres, one after the other on different days: *a job in repertory* | *a repertory theatre|company*

rep·e·ti·tion /ˌrepɪˈtɪʃən/ n [C;U] the act of repeating, or something repeated: *This accident is a repetition of one that happened here three weeks ago.*

rep·e·ti·tious /ˌrepɪˈtɪʃəs◂/ also **re·pet·i·tive** /rɪˈpetɪtɪv/— adj derog containing parts that are said or done too many times: *a repetitious speech* | *a repetitive job* — **-ness** n [U]

repetitive strain in·ju·ry /·ˌ··· ˈ·· ˌ···/ also **RSI**— n [U] med a condition caused by doing certain types of work in an uncomfortable position, leading to pain in the arms, legs, or back

re·phrase /riːˈfreɪz/ v [T] to express (something) in different words, esp. so as to make the meaning clearer or less offensive: *Let me rephrase that.*

re·pine /rɪˈpaɪn/ v [I (against, at)] fml or lit to feel or express sadness or dissatisfaction

re·place /rɪˈpleɪs/ v [T] **1** to take the place of: *George has replaced Edward as captain of the team.* **2** [(with, by)] to change (one person or thing) for another, often better, newer, etc.: *You'll have to replace those tyres; they're badly worn.* | *We've replaced the old adding machine with|by a computer.* **3** fml to put (something) back in the right place: *He replaced the book on the shelf.* — **-able** adj

▷ USAGE Compare the patterns in these sentences: *We* **replaced** *apples with oranges.* (=we put oranges in the place of apples) | *We* **substituted** *apples for oranges.* (=we put apples in the place of oranges)◁

re·place·ment /rɪˈpleɪsmənt/ n **1** [U] the act of replacing, esp. with something better, newer, etc.: *These worn tyres are badly in need of replacement.* **2** [C (for)] someone or something that replaces: *We need a replacement for the secretary who left.*

re·play¹ /ˌriːˈpleɪ/ v **1** [I;T] to play (a match) again: *The game ended in a draw, so they'll replay it on Wednesday.* **2** [T] **a** to play (something that has been recorded on a machine); PLAY **back b** to play (a recording, piece of music, etc.) again

re·play² /ˈriːpleɪ/ n **1** a match played again **2** a recording; PLAYBACK: *They showed an action replay of the goal.* | *I wish they'd show us an instant replay (AmE) of that fumble.*

re·plen·ish /rɪˈplenɪʃ/ v [T (with)] fml to fill up again; put new supplies into: *We need to replenish the food cupboard|our stocks of coal.* | *Let me replenish your glass.* — **~ment** n [U]

re·plete /rɪˈpliːt/ adj [F (with)] fml fully provided or filled, esp. with food: *He sat back replete at the end of the meal.* | *a book replete with maps and diagrams*

rep·li·ca /ˈreplɪkə/ n [(of)] a close copy, esp. of a painting or other work of art: *They built a replica of a Second World War plane.*

rep·li·cate /ˈreplɪkeɪt/ v [T] tech to do or make again, esp. so as to get the same result or make an exact copy: *Can the experiment be replicated?* | *These tissue cells replicate themselves.* —**-cation** /ˌreplɪˈkeɪʃən/ n [C;U] : *The material inside our genes reproduces itself by replication.*

re·ply¹ /rɪˈplaɪ/ v [I (to);T] to answer; say or do as an answer: *I asked him where he was going, but he didn't reply.* | *Have you replied to him|to his letter?* | *What did she reply?* [+(that)] *She replied that she couldn't come.* | *"Of course not," she replied.* —see ANSWER (USAGE)

reply² n [(to)] something said, written or done as a way of replying: *I asked him, but he gave no reply.* | *What did you say in reply to his suggestion?* | *Her criticisms brought an immediate reply from a government spokesman.*

reply-paid /·ˌ· ˈ·◂/ adj (of a TELEGRAM, postcard, etc.) with the cost of the answer paid by the sender

re·po man /ˈriːpəʊ ˌmæn/ n AmE infml a person whose job is to take away (REPOSSESS) property, esp. cars, which the owners are unable to finish paying for

re·port¹ /rɪˈpɔːt‖-ɔːrt/ n **1** [C (of, on)] an account or description of events, experiences, business records, etc., which is prepared in order to provide people with information: *Did you read the newspaper reports of the accident?* | *the company's annual report* | *a weather report* | *an interim report on the progress of the arms control talks* **2** [C;U] (a piece of) talk that spreads without official support; RUMOUR: *According to report he's not coming back.* **3** [C] BrE ‖ **report card** /·ˈ· ·/AmE— a written statement by teachers about a child's work at school, sent to his or her parents **4** [C] fml the noise of an explosion or shot: *a loud report* **5 The report of my death was an exaggeration** quote a phrase from a letter written by Mark Twain

report² v **1** [I (on);T (to)] to provide information (about) or give an account (of); make (something) known: *The committee of inquiry will not report until next year.* | *Any case of stealing should be reported immediately to the proper authorities.* | *They came back after a week to report (on) progress.* (=to say what had been done up to then) | *He reported sick.* (=said he could not work because he was sick) [+v-ing/that] *They reported having seen him in Brighton|that they had seen him in Brighton.* [+obj+to-v; pass.] *He is reported to have been seen in Brighton.*

[+obj+adj] *The ship was reported lost with all hands.* **2** [I (**on**)T] (of a reporter) to write or give an account of (a piece of news): *She reported the president's speech for the newspaper.* | *He cabled to say he had nothing to report, but hoped to get more information later.* | *Here is our Far East correspondent reporting from Japan on the earthquake.* **3** [T (**for, to**)] to make a complaint about: *He reported the boy (to the head teacher) (for smoking on the school premises).* **4** [I (**for, to**)] to go or be present: *While she's out on bail she has to report to the police every day.* | *They report for work at 8.0 a.m.* | *What time do you have to report at the airport?*

report (sthg. ↔) **back** *phr v* [I;T (**to**)] to bring or send back an account (of): *Go and find out what's happened and report back (to me) quickly!* [+that] *They reported back that enemy forces were moving towards the border.*

re·port·age /rɪˈpɔːtɪdʒ, ˌrepɔːˈtɑːʒ‖-ˈpɔːr-, ˌrepərˈtɑːʒ/ *n* [U] **1** the act of reporting news **2** the style in which this is usually done **3** writing, photographs, or film in this style, intended to give an account of an event

re·port·ed·ly /rɪˈpɔːtɪdli‖-ɔːr-/ *adv* according to what is said: *He is reportedly not intending to return to this country.*

reported speech /·,·· ·ˈ·/ *n* [U] INDIRECT SPEECH

re·port·er /rɪˈpɔːtər‖-ɔːr-/ *n* a person who finds out and writes about news events for a newspaper, or for radio or television —compare JOURNALIST; see also COURT REPORTER

re·pose¹ /rɪˈpəʊz/ *n* [U] *fml* **1** (a state of) calm or comfortable rest; peace **2** calmness of manner; COMPOSURE — **~ful** *adj*

repose² *v fml or pomp* **1** [I+*adv/prep*, esp. **on**] **a** to lie or be placed (on) **b** to lie dead: *His body reposed in state in the cathedral.* **2** [T+*obj+adv/prep*, esp. **on**] to place (an object or part of the body) on

repose sthg. **in** sthg./sbdy. *phr v* [T] *fml* to place (trust, hopes, etc.) in: *We do not repose much confidence in his judgment.*

re·pos·i·to·ry /rɪˈpɒzɪtəri‖rɪˈpɑːzɪtɔːri/ *n* a place where things are stored or found in large quantity: *a furniture repository* | (fig.) *He's a repository of* (=has lots of) *all sorts of out-of-the-way knowledge.* | *The Black Hills are a rich repository of minerals.*

re·pos·sess /ˌriːpəˈzes/ *v* [T] to regain possession of (property), esp. when necessary payments have not been made: *The rental company are threatening to repossess the television.* —see also REPO MAN, MORTGAGE REPOSSESSION — **~ion** /ˈzeʃən/ *n* [U] : *The landlord has applied for a* **repossession order.**

rep·re·hend /ˌrepriˈhend/ *v* [T] *fml rare* to express disapproval of: *His conduct deserves to be reprehended.*

rep·re·hen·si·ble /ˌrepriˈhensəbəl/ *adj fml* (of a person or their behaviour) deserving to be blamed; extremely bad: *a reprehensible action* | *His conduct was reprehensible.* **—bly** *adv*

rep·re·sent /ˌrepriˈzent/ *v* **1** [T] **a** to act or speak officially for (another person or group of people): *She represented her fellow-workers at the union meeting.* | *He was represented in court by John Stevens, the famous criminal lawyer.* **b** to be the member of Parliament or Congress for (a place): *Does Mr Walker still represent Worcester?* | *She represents the 8th congressional district of Illinois.* **2** [T] to be a picture or STATUE of; DEPICT: *This painting represents the death of Nelson/represents Nelson dying at Trafalgar.* | *a tall stone figure representing the god of war* **3** [T] to be a sign of; SYMBOLIZE: *The red lines on the map represent railways.* **4** [L+*n; not in progressive forms*] to be; have the character of; CONSTITUTE: *This essay represents a considerable improvement on your recent work.* **5** [T *usu. pass.*] (of a member of a group) to be present as an example of (that group): *All the different races of the country were represented* (=were present) *at the parade.* **6** [T+*obj+as/to-v*] to describe or declare, perhaps falsely: *He represented himself as/to be a friend of the workers, but now we know the truth.*

represent sthg. **to** sbdy. *phr v* [T] *fml* to express or point out to, often angrily or complainingly: *You should represent your grievances/complaints to the management.*

re·pre·sent /ˌriːprɪˈzent/ *v* [T] to give or offer again; send in again: *They re-presented the bill for payment.*

rep·re·sen·ta·tion /ˌreprɪzenˈteɪʃən/ *n* **1** [U] the act of representing or state of being represented (REPRESENT

(1)): *"No taxation without representation" means that if people pay taxes they should be represented in a parliament.* | *She appeared in court without representation.* (=without a lawyer) **2** [C (**of**)] something that REPRESENTS (2,3) something else: *This painting is a representation of a storm at sea.* | *the representation of speech sounds by phonetic symbols* —see also REPRESENTATIONS, PROPORTIONAL REPRESENTATION

rep·re·sen·ta·tion·al /ˌreprɪzenˈteɪʃənəl◂/ *adj* (of a style of art, a painting, etc.) showing things as they actually appear in real life —compare ABSTRACT¹ (3)

rep·re·sen·ta·tions /ˌreprɪzenˈteɪʃənz/ *n* [P (**about, to**)] *esp. BrE* official complaints made in a formal way: *They* **made representations** *to the college authorities about the bad accommodation.*

rep·re·sen·ta·tive¹ /ˌreprɪˈzentətɪv/ *adj* **1** [(**of**)] typical; being an example of what other members of the same group or type are like: *a representative sample* | *Are your opinions representative of those of the other students?* | *If this is representative of the general quality of your work, I'm not very impressed.* —opposite **unrepresentative 2** (of a system of government) in which the people and their opinions are represented

representative² *n* [(**of**)] a person who has been chosen to act in place of one or more others: *I couldn't be present myself, but I sent my representative to the meeting.* | *an elected representative of the people* —see also HOUSE OF REPRESENTATIVES, SALES REPRESENTATIVE

Representative *n* a member of the House of Representatives, the lower house of Congress in the United States, usu. called a Congresswoman or Congressman

re·press /rɪˈpres/ *v* [T] to control, hold back, or prevent the natural expression of (a feeling, desire, action, etc.): *a repressed child* | *repressed desires* | *I could hardly repress my laughter.* —compare SUPPRESS

re·pres·sion /rɪˈpreʃən/ *n* [C;U] the act of repressing or state of being repressed, esp. **a** the forcing of feelings or desires of which one is ashamed out of the conscious mind into the unconscious mind, often with strange effects upon one's behaviour: *sexual repression* **b** cruel and severe control: *political repression* —compare SUPPRESSION

re·pres·sive /rɪˈpresɪv/ *adj* (of a law, system of government, etc.) hard and cruel: *Under the general's repressive regime, thousands of people were imprisoned without trial.* — **~ly** *adv* — **~ness** *n* [U]

re·prieve¹ /rɪˈpriːv/ *v* [T *often pass.*] to give a reprieve to: *The prisoner was reprieved.* | (fig.) *The government was going to discontinue the youth training programme, but it's been reprieved.*

reprieve² *n* an official order delaying or stopping the punishment of a prisoner who was to die: *The Home Secretary granted him a reprieve the day before he was due to be hanged.* | *a last-minute reprieve*

rep·ri·mand /ˈreprɪmɑːnd‖-mænd/ *v* [T] to express strong official disapproval of: *The military court ordered him to be reprimanded for failing to do his duty.* —**reprimand** *n* : *She received a severe reprimand.*

re·print¹ /ˌriːˈprɪnt/ *v* [I;T] to print (a book) or be printed again when supplies have run out: *The book is reprinting — you'll be able to buy one soon.* | *The new dictionary has sold so well that it's had to be reprinted.*

re·print² /ˈriːˌprɪnt/ *n* a reprinted book

re·pri·sal /rɪˈpraɪzəl/ *also* **reprisals** *pl.*— *n* [C;U] (an act of) punishing others for harm done to oneself, esp. of a political or military kind: *Our government has threatened theirs with reprisals/threatened to* **carry out/take reprisals** *if they continue to infringe our fishing limits.* | *They bombed the enemy village in reprisal for/as a reprisal for the killing of some of their own troops.* | *a reprisal raid*

re·prise /rɪˈpriːz/ *n* a repeating of all or part of a piece of music

re·proach¹ /rɪˈprəʊtʃ/ *n* **1** [U] blame; the expression of disapproval: *She gave me a look of reproach.* | *His behaviour was* **above/beyond reproach.** (=perfect) **2** [C] *fml* a word or words of blame: *When he came home drunk his wife greeted him with loud reproaches.* **3** [S+**to**] *fml* something that deserves blame or brings shame; DISGRACE: *These derelict houses are a reproach to the city.* — **~ful** *adj* : *a reproachful glance* — **~fully** *adv*

reproach² v [T (**for, with**)] to blame (someone), usu. not angrily but sadly and in a way that shows disappointment: *It wasn't your fault – you have nothing to reproach yourself with.* (=to blame yourself for)

rep·ro·bate /ˈreprəbeɪt/ n fml or humor a person of bad character: *He's an old reprobate who spends all his money on beer.*

re·pro·cess /riːˈprəʊses‖-ˈprɒ:-/ v [T] to treat (something that has been used) so that it can be used again: *the reprocessing of nuclear fuel*

re·pro·duce /ˌriːprəˈdjuːs‖-ˈduːs/ v [I;T] **1** to produce the young of (oneself or one's own kind): *Most fish reproduce (themselves) by laying eggs.* **2** to produce a copy (of); (cause to) be seen, heard, or done again: *This photograph of the painting reproduces the colours of the original extremely well.* | *They were unable to reproduce the results of the first experiment when they repeated it.* —**-ducer** n —**-ducible** adj

re·pro·duc·tion /ˌriːprəˈdʌkʃən/ n **1** [U] the act or process of producing young: *human reproduction* | *a biology lesson on the reproduction of the rabbit* **2** [U] the process of producing a copy: *The quality of reproduction isn't very good on this recording.* **3** [C (**of**)] a copy, esp. of a work of art, less exact than a REPLICA: *a cheap reproduction of a famous painting*

re·pro·duc·tive /ˌriːprəˈdʌktɪv◂/ adj **1** concerned with producing young: *the female reproductive system* **2** concerned with copying: *The reproductive quality of audio tapes has improved enormously.*

re·proof /rɪˈpruːf/ n [C;U] fml (an expression of) blame or disapproval: *You can scarcely expect to escape reproof for such irresponsible behaviour.*

re·prove /rɪˈpruːv/ v [T (**for**)] fml to talk to angrily or express disapproval of: *She reproved him for telling lies.*

re·prov·ing /rɪˈpruːvɪŋ/ adj fml expressing reproof: *a reproving glance* – ~**ly** adv

rep·tile /ˈreptaɪl‖ˈreptl/ n an animal whose blood changes temperature according to the temperature around it and that usu. lays eggs: *Snakes, lizards, and crocodiles are reptiles.*

rep·til·i·an¹ /repˈtɪliən/ adj **1** [no comp.] of, like, or being a reptile **2** derog (of a person) very unpleasant, dishonest, or untrustworthy; REPULSIVE

reptilian² n tech a reptile

re·pub·lic /rɪˈpʌblɪk/ n a nation, usu. governed by elected representatives, whose head of state is not a king or queen but a president: *Ireland is a republic.* | *The People's Republic of China* —compare MONARCHY (2); see also BANANA REPUBLIC, PEOPLE'S REPUBLIC

re·pub·li·can¹ /rɪˈpʌblɪkən/ adj belonging to or supporting a republic: *a republican system of government*

republican² n a person who disapproves of kings and queens, and believes in government by elected representatives only

Republican¹ adj **1** of or supporting the **Republican Party**, one of the two largest political parties of the US —compare DEMOCRATIC **2** of or supporting SINN FEIN

Republican² n **1** a member or supporter of the Republican Party of the US —compare DEMOCRAT **2** a member or supporter of SINN FEIN

Republican Guard /·ˌ··· ·ˈ·/ [the] (in Iraq) a special group of soldiers who were involved in the GULF WAR in 1990, as part of Saddam Hussein's army

re·pub·li·can·is·m /rɪˈpʌblɪkənɪzəm/ n [U] the beliefs or practices of republicans

Republicanism n [U] the beliefs or practices of the Republican Party of the US

Republican Par·ty /·ˈ··· ˌ··/ [the] one of the two main political parties in the US, also known as **the Republicans**. It was established in 1854 to oppose SLAVERY, and won its first presidential election with Abraham Lincoln in 1860. It is sometimes called the **Grand Old Party** or **GOP**, and is thought of as the party of big business and CONSERVATIVE politics but actually represents a wide range of views. —see also DEMOCRATIC PARTY

Republic of Ire·land /·ˌ·· · ˈ··/ also **Ireland, Irish Republic, Eire, Southern Ireland**— n [the] the country that forms the larger part of the island of Ireland, capital Dublin; population 3,515,000 (1989). The main industries are

farming and tourism, and the main religion is Roman Catholicism. English and Gaelic are the official languages. The national SYMBOL of the Republic of Ireland is the SHAMROCK and the PATRON SAINT is Saint Patrick. —see also NORTHERN IRELAND and see colour map on page 818

re·pu·di·ate /rɪˈpjuːdieɪt/ v [T] fml **1** to state that (something) is untrue or unjust: *I repudiate emphatically any suggestion that I have acted dishonourably.* **2** to refuse to accept; REJECT: *He repudiated all offers of friendship.* **3** old-fash to refuse to meet or recognize; state that one has no connection with (someone); DISOWN: *He repudiated his daughter when she married without his consent.* **4** tech to refuse to pay (a debt) —**-ation** /rɪˌpjuːdiˈeɪʃən/ n [U]

re·pug·nance /rɪˈpʌgnəns/ n [S;U (**for**)] fml a feeling of strong dislike, often mixed with moral disapproval: *She turned away from the disgusting sight in/with repugnance.*

re·pug·nant /rɪˈpʌgnənt/ adj fml very unpleasant and offensive; causing repugnance: *I find his opinions repugnant.*

re·pulse¹ /rɪˈpʌls/ v [T] fml **1** to refuse in a cold, unfriendly, or impolite way; push away (a friendly person, or an offer of friendship) **2** to drive back (an enemy attack)

repulse² n **1** the military defeat of an attack **2** a rude refusal of friendship; REBUFF

re·pul·sion /rɪˈpʌlʃən/ n **1** [S;U] very strong dislike; REPUGNANCE: *For a lot of people, the sight of blood produces a feeling of repulsion.* **2** [U] tech (in science) the force by which one object drives another away from it —opposite **attraction**

re·pul·sive /rɪˈpʌlsɪv/ adj **1** very unpleasant; causing repulsion: *repulsive skin diseases* | *What a repulsive man!* **2** [no comp.] tech (in science) having REPULSION (2): *repulsive forces* – ~**ly** adv – ~**ness** n [U]

rep·u·ta·ble /ˈrepjṵtəbəl/ adj having a good reputation, esp. for being honest and dependable: *a reputable firm of builders* —opposite **disreputable** —**-bly** adv

rep·u·ta·tion /ˌrepjṵˈteɪʃən/ also **rep** AmE infml— n [C;U (**for**)] (an) opinion held about someone or something, esp. by people in general; the degree to which one is trusted or admired: *This restaurant has a good/bad reputation.* | *It has gained/acquired a reputation for good/bad food.* | *He has the reputation of being a tough manager.* | *If people find out what you're doing it will ruin your reputation.* | *It can be hard to live up to one's reputation.* (=to behave in the way people have come to expect) —compare CHARACTER (4)

re·pute /rɪˈpjuːt/ n [U] fml or pomp **1** reputation: *a man of good/evil repute* | *He is held in high repute.* (=people have a good opinion of him) **2** good reputation: *a hotel of (some) repute* **3** house of ill repute old fash or humor a BROTHEL

re·put·ed /rɪˈpjuːtɪd/ adj generally supposed or considered (to be), but with some doubt: *the reputed father of her baby* [F+to-v] *She is reputed to be extremely wealthy.*

re·put·ed·ly /rɪˈpjuːtɪdli/ adv according to what people say: *Reputedly, she is very rich.*

re·quest¹ /rɪˈkwest/ n **1** [C (**for**)] an act of asking for something, esp. politely: *They have made an urgent request for international aid.* | *The President's request for an increase in the defense budget has been turned down by Congress.* [+that] *Despite repeated requests that they should make less noise, they persisted in playing their music at full volume.* **2** [U] the fact of being asked for, esp. politely: *The name of the murder victim was not published in the newspapers,* **at the request of** *the judge.* (=because the judge requested that it should not be PUBLISHED) | *Full details will be sent* **on request.** (=if you ask for them) **3** [C] something that has been asked for: *Do they play requests on this radio show?* (=records that have been asked for by listeners) | *I'm going to the coffee shop—any requests?* (=Does anyone want anything from there?)

request² v [T (**of**)] rather fml to ask (for), esp. politely; make a request (for): *Your presence is requested at the meeting.* | *This record has been requested by Mrs Simpson of Potters Bar.* (=she has asked for it to be played on the radio) [+obj+to-v] *All members of the club are requested to attend the annual meeting.* [+that] *The teaching staff requested (of the head teacher) that he should reconsider his decision.*

▷ USAGE Compare **ask (for)**, **request**, and **demand**. **Ask** is the usual word for speaking or writing to someone in order to get something done: *I asked one of my friends to help me*, and **ask for** the expression for trying to get something: *I asked for help.***Request** is more formal and stronger; if you **request** something you usually have the right to get what you want: *The letter requested us to leave the house within six weeks.* | *I requested assistance.* **Demand** is even stronger; if you **demand** something, you feel strongly that you have the right to get it, and will not take "no" for an answer. *The dissatisfied customer* **demanded** *to see the manager of the store.* | *I demand my rights.*◁

request stop /·'· ·/ *BrE*‖**flag stop** *AmE*— *n* a place where buses stop only if they are asked to do so, esp. by someone signalling with their hand

req·ui·em /'rekwiəm, 'rekwiem/ also **requiem mass** /'··· '·/— *n* (a piece of music written for) a Christian religious ceremony (MASS) for a dead person, at which people pray for his or her soul; these are performed on ALL SOULS DAY and at FUNERALS, or on request

re·quire /rɪ'kwaɪəʳ/ *v* [T *not in progressive forms*] **1** *rather fml* to need or make necessary: *This suggestion will require careful thought.* | *Is there anything further you require, sir?* [+*v-ing*] *To carry out this plan would require increasing our staff by 50%.* [+*that*] *The urgency of the situation requires that we (should) make an immediate decision.* **2** [(**of**)]*fml* to demand by right; give an order (for or to), with the expectation that it will be obeyed: *Silence is required of all examination candidates.* [+*obj+to-v*] *All passengers are required to show their tickets.* [+*that*] *The regulations require that all students shall attend at least 90 per cent of the lectures.* | *This book is* **required reading** *for our course.* (=you must read it)

re·quire·ment /rɪ'kwaɪəmənt‖-'kwaɪər-/ *n* something that is needed or that is demanded as necessary: *The refugees' main requirements are food and shelter.* | *Can this computer handle the requirements of the wages department?* | *Candidates who fail to meet* (=satisfy) *these requirements will not be admitted to the University.*

req·ui·site¹ /'rekwɪzɪt/ *adj* [(**for**)]*fml* needed for a purpose; necessary: *He hasn't got the requisite qualifications for this job.*

requisite² *n* [*usu. pl.*]*fml* something needed for or used in connection with the stated thing: *toilet requisites* (=soap, SHAMPOO, COLOGNE, etc.)

req·ui·si·tion¹ /ˌrekwɪ'zɪʃən/ *n* [C;U (**for**)] an official demand or request, esp. one made by a military body: *The school authorities have made a requisition for more computing equipment.* | *to fill in a requisition form*

requisition² *v* [T] to make a requisition for: *The army requisitioned all our stores of petrol.*

re·quit·al /rɪ'kwaɪtl/ *n* [U]*fml* **1** repayment for something done or given: *I have made full requital.* **2** something given or done in return for something else

re·quite /rɪ'kwaɪt/ *v* [T (**with**)]*fml* to pay back (something): *Our kindness and trust was requited only with dishonesty on their part.* —see also UNREQUITED

rere·dos /'rɪədɒs‖'rɪərdɑːs, 'reərədəːs/ *n* a decorative wall or large wall-like work of art behind an ALTAR in a church

re·route /ˌriː'ruːt‖-'ruːt, -'raʊt/ *v* [T] to send (usu. vehicles) another way: *Traffic is being rerouted.*

re·run¹ /riː'rʌn/ *v* **-ran** /'ræn/, **-run** *present participle* **-running** [T] **1** to show (a film or recorded broadcast) again: *They rerun so many old films on television.* **2** to arrange for (a race or competition) to be held again: *One of the competitors was found to have cheated, so the race had to be rerun.*

re·run² /'riːrʌn/ *n* **1** a film or recorded broadcast that is rerun **2** something that happens again in the same way as before: *These measures were taken in order to avert a rerun of the Three Mile Island disaster.*

re·sale shop /'riːseɪl ˌʃɒp‖-ˌʃɑːp/ *n AmE* a shop that sells used goods, usu. to raise money for a CHARITY

re·sched·ule /ˌriː'ʃedjuːl‖-'skedʒʊl, -dʒəl/ *v* [T] *tech* to arrange for (money which one has been lent) to be paid back at a later time than was originally agreed

re·scind /rɪ'sɪnd/ *v* [T] *law* to put an end to (a law, decision, or agreement); ANNUL or REPEAL

res·cue¹ /'reskjuː/ *v* [T (**from**)] to save or set free from harm, danger, or loss: *He rescued the man from drowning*|*the cat from the high tree*|*his stamp collection from the burning house.* | *She clung to the floating wreckage for hours before she was rescued.* | *a final attempt to rescue the company from bankruptcy* —**cuer** *n*

rescue² *n* an act of rescuing: *a daring rescue carried out at sea* | *A rescue team is trying to reach the trapped miners.*| *We were about to close down the business, but the bank* **came to our rescue** (=saved us) *with a huge loan.* | *a rescue attempt*

re·search¹ /rɪ'sɜːtʃ, 'riːsɜːtʃ‖-ɜːr-/ also **researches** *pl.*— *n* [U (**in, into, on**)] serious and detailed study of a subject, that is aimed at learning new facts, scientific laws, testing ideas, etc.: *a very interesting piece of research* | *They are carrying out*|*doing some research into*|*on the effects of brain damage.* | *Will they publish the results of their research*|*researches?* | *research students*|*workers* | *a research laboratory* —see also MARKET RESEARCH, R AND D

re·search² /rɪ'sɜːtʃ‖-ɜːr-/ *v* **1** [I (**in, into, on**)] to do research: *I'm researching in medieval history.* | *They're researching on*|*into the effects of cigarette smoking.* **2** [T] to do research on or for: *to research a subject* | *This book has been very well researched.* — ~**er** *n*

research and de·vel·op·ment /·ˌ·· ·'···, ˌ··· ·'···/ *n* [U] see R AND D

re·sem·blance /rɪ'zembləns/ *n* [C;U (**between, to**)] (a) similarity, esp. in appearance; likeness: *There's a strong resemblance between Susan and Robert.* | *He didn't* **bear much resemblance** *to the man whose photo I'd seen.* | *a certain resemblance between the styles of the two writers*

re·sem·ble /rɪ'zembəl/ *v* [T (**in**) *not in progressive forms*; *no pass.*] to look like or be like: *She resembles her sister in appearance but not in character.*

re·sent /rɪ'zent/ *v* [T] to feel anger and dislike about (something that hurts, offends, or annoys one): *I strongly*|*bitterly resent her attempts to interfere in my work.* [+*v-ing*] *I resent having to get his permission for everything I do.* — ~**ful** *adj* : *She gave him a resentful look.* — ~**fully** *adv* — ~**fulness** *n* [U]

re·sent·ment /rɪ'zentmənt/ *n* [U (**at, against, towards**)] the feeling of resenting something; feeling that one has been badly treated: *There is widespread resentment against the management over the way they have ignored all our demands.*

res·er·va·tion /ˌrezə'veɪʃən‖-zər-/ *n* **1** [C;U] (a) feeling of doubt or uncertainty, esp. when one's agreement with something is in some way limited: *Some members of the committee expressed reservations about these proposals.*| *We accept their offer*|*condemn their action* **without reservation.** (=completely) | *I have some reservations about the truth of these claims.* (=I find it hard to believe them) **2** [C *often pl*] an arrangement made in advance to have something, such as a place in a hotel, restaurant, or on a plane; BOOKING: *Have you made the reservations for our holiday yet?* | *a hotel reservation* | *They are only seating people with reservations.* **3** [C] (in the US) a piece of land set apart for Native Americans to live on; these have been a problem since they were established. Many Native Americans died because of the change of lifestyle, and there are still arguments about ownership of the land. —also NATIVE AMERICAN **4** [C] *esp. AmE* an area of land set apart for animals to live unharmed, without being hunted: *a game*|*wildlife reservation* —see also CENTRAL RESERVATION

re·serve¹ /rɪ'zɜːv‖-ɜːrv/ *v* [T] **1** [(**for**)] to set apart, set aside, or keep for a special purpose: *These seats are reserved for old and sick people.* | *He reserved his rudest comments for the boss.* **2** to make a RESERVATION (2): *Have you reserved our seats on the plane?*

reserve² *n* **1** [C (**of**);U] also **reserves** *pl.*— a quantity of something kept for future use; store: *We must keep back a reserve*|*some reserves of food.* | *We always keep some money* **in reserve.** (=ready for use if needed) **2** [C] a piece of land set aside for wild animals, plants, etc.: *a nature*|*wildlife reserve* **3** [C] a player who will play in a team game if any other member of the team is hurt or cannot play **4** [U] the quality of being RESERVED (1): *behaving with typical British reserve* **5** [*the*] also **reserves** *pl.*— (*often cap.*) a military force that a country keeps, in addition to its regular forces, for use if needed: *to call up the reserve(s)* —see also RESERVIST **6** [C] also **reserve**

price /·ˌ· ˈ·/‖upset price AmE— a price limit below which something is not to be sold, esp. in an AUCTION: *They put a reserve of £30,000 on the house.* 7 **without reserve** *fml* freely and openly: *She told me all about it without reserve.*

re·served /rɪˈzɜːvd‖-ɜːr-/ adj 1 (typical of people) who do not like to talk about themselves or to show their feelings; SHY: *Bob is very reserved – you never know what he's thinking.* 2 kept for the future or special use: *reserved seats/tables* —see also UNRESERVED — — ly adv

Reserve Of·fi·cer Train·ing Corps /·ˌ· ··· ˈ·· ·/ [the] AmE see ROTC

re·serv·ist /rɪˈzɜːvʌ̩st‖-ɜːr-/ n a soldier who can be called at any time of difficulty to serve in a country's army

res·er·voir /ˈrezəvwɑːʳ‖-ərvwɑːr, -vɔːr/ n 1 a place where liquid is stored, esp. an artificial lake to provide water for an area 2 [+of] also **reservoirs** pl.— a large supply, esp. one that has not yet been used: *We must make use of our untapped reservoirs of talent.* (=useful and clever people)

re·set¹ /ˌriːˈset/ v -set, present participle -setting [T] 1 to change so as to show a different number, time, etc.: *She reset her watch when her flight from London arrived in New York.* | *Reset the dial at zero.* 2 to put (a broken bone) back in place for a second time 3 to make up TYPE¹ (2) again for (something to be printed): *The book had to be reset because there were so many mistakes in the first printing.* 4 to put (a jewel) into a new arrangement of jewellery 5 to BOOT³ (a small computer)

reset² /ˈriːset/ adj causing to reset (1 and 5): *Next time that happens just push the reset button.*

re·set·tle /ˌriːˈsetl/ v [I;T] to (help to) go to live in a new country or area: *Many Ugandan Asian families resettled in Canada in the 1970s.* | *tribespeople who were forcibly resettled by the government* — ~ ment n [U] : *a land resettlement programme*

re·shuf·fle¹ /ˌriːˈʃʌfəl/ v 1 [I;T] to SHUFFLE (playing cards) again 2 [T] to carry out a reshuffle of: *The prime minister reshuffled her cabinet.*

reshuffle² n a process of changing around the positions of the people who work in an organization, esp. in government: *a cabinet reshuffle*

re·side /rɪˈzaɪd/ v [I+adv/prep] fml to have one's home: *They reside abroad.* | *The defendant resides at 8, New Road.* —see LIVE (USAGE)
reside in sthg./sbdy. phr v [T no pass.] fml (of a power, right, etc.) to belong to: *The power to change the law resides in Parliament.*

res·i·dence /ˈrezˌdəns/ n fml 1 [C] the place where one lives; a house, esp. a large important one: *the ambassador's official residence* | *desirable residence for sale* (advertisement) | *(humor) How nice of you to visit me at my humble residence!* 2 [U] the state of residing: *He took up residence* (=went to live) *in Jamaica.* 3 in **residence** actually living in a place, esp. **a** (of an official) in the official house **b** (of a student) at the university: *The students are not in residence during the holidays.* —see also HALL OF RESIDENCE, IN-RESIDENCE

res·i·dent¹ /ˈrezˌdənt/ adj [(in)] living (in a place): *The ex-chairman, now resident in Spain, is accused of embezzling company funds.* | *a resident doctor* (=living in the hospital) | *(humor) He's our resident expert on horse racing.*

resident² n a person who lives in a place, such as a house, hotel or particular area, all the time or just while working, studying, or visiting: *This hotel serves meals to residents only.* (=only to people who sleep there)

res·i·den·tial /ˌrezˌˈdenʃəl◂/ adj 1 (of part of a town) consisting of private houses, without offices or factories: *a quiet residential street/area in Leeds* 2 for which one must live or stay in a place for a certain period: *It's a residential course, so bring your pyjamas.* | *You can't vote in this country unless you've got residential qualifications.*

residential care /ˌ···· ˈ·/ n [U] a system of care for old or ill people who are unable to look after themselves at home, and need nursing or other professional care which their families cannot provide

residential treat·ment fa·cil·i·ty /ˌ···· ˈ·· ·ˌ···/ n AmE tech or euph for MENTAL HOSPITAL

resident's as·so·ci·a·tion /ˈ··· ···ˌ··/ n [+sing./pl.v] an association of people who all live in the same building or

local area, formed to deal with matters which concern them

re·sid·u·al /rɪˈzɪdʒuəl/ adj fml left over; remaining: *There was still some residual unrest after the rebellion had been crushed.* | *one's residual income, after all taxes have been paid*

residual cur·rent de·vice /·ˌ·· ˈ·· ·ˌ·/ also **circuit breaker**— n a safety DEVICE used with certain electrical APPLIANCES such as LAWNMOWERS, which cuts off the supply of electricity in the event of an accident such as the wires being cut, to prevent electrocution (ELECTROCUTE)

res·i·due /ˈrezˌdjuː‖-duː/ n [(of) usu. sing.] tech what is left, esp. **a** (in law) after a dead person's debts and gifts have been settled: *The residue of the estate goes to his daughter.* **b** (in science) after chemical treatment: *a sticky residue in the bottom of the test tube*

re·sign /rɪˈzaɪn/ v [I (from); T] 1 to give up (a job or position): *If Paul resigns, who will get the job?* | *She resigned from the committee/resigned as a member of the committee.* | *He resigned his post because he had been offered a better job.* —compare RETIRE 2 **resign oneself to** to cause or allow (oneself) to accept (something unpleasant which cannot be avoided) calmly or patiently: *He seems quite resigned to his fate.* | *You must resign yourselves to waiting a bit longer.* —see also RESIGNED

res·ig·na·tion /ˌrezɪgˈneɪʃən/ n 1 [C;U] (an act or written statement of) resigning: *You have the choice between resignation and dismissal.* | *He handed/sent in his resignation.* 2 [U] the state of being resigned: *He accepted his fate with resignation.*

re·signed /rɪˈzaɪnd/ adj typical of a person who has resigned himself/herself to something unpleasant: *"I didn't really want it anyway," he said with a resigned sigh.* — ~ ly /rɪˈzaɪnˌdli/ adv : *"I suppose it was bound to happen," she said resignedly.*

re·sil·i·ent /rɪˈzɪliənt/ adj 1 (of a substance) able to spring back to the former shape or position when pressure is removed: *Rubber is more resilient than wood.* 2 apprec able to return quickly to usual health or good spirits after going through difficulty, disease, change, etc.: *It's been a terrible shock, but she's very resilient and will get over it soon.* — ~ ly adv —**ence, -ency** n [U] : *Rubber has more resilience than wood.*

res·in /ˈrezˌn/ n 1 [U] a thick sticky liquid that comes out of certain trees such as the FIR, and later becomes a hard yellow substance. It is used for making paint, in medicine, and as ROSIN. 2 [C] any of various artificial plastic substances, produced chemically and used in industry — ~ ous adj

res·in·at·ed /ˈrezˌneɪtˌd/ adj mixed with or tasting of RESIN (1): *Resinated wine is drunk in Greece.*

re·sist /rɪˈzɪst/ v 1 [I;T] to oppose; fight against (something): *The city resisted the enemy onslaught for two weeks.* | *The government are resisting the nurses' wage demands.* | *He was charged with resisting arrest.* 2 [T] to remain unchanged or unharmed by: *Lack of proper nourishment reduces their power to resist disease.* | *You need a roof that will resist the weather.* 3 [I;T usu. in negatives] to force or allow oneself not to accept: *I can't resist chocolate mints.* (=I like them very much) | *She's such a charming girl; it's hard to resist her.* (=to refuse to give her what she wants) [+v-ing] *I couldn't resist telling him the secret.* (=I had to tell him) — ~ er n

re·sist·ance /rɪˈzɪstəns/ n 1 [S;U (to)] an act of resisting or the ability to resist: *The defenders put up (a) strong resistance.* | *There has been a lot of resistance* (=opposition) *to this new law.* | *We took the line of least resistance* (=the easiest way) *and paid the money instead of arguing.* | *the baby's resistance to disease* | *The escaped criminal offered no resistance when the police caught up with him.* —see also SALES RESISTANCE 2 [U] the stated force opposed to anything moving: *The aircraft is streamlined to cut down wind resistance.* 3 [U] the power of a substance to RESIST (2) the passing through it of an electric current: *Copper has less resistance than lead.* —compare VOLTAGE 4 [(the) U+sing./pl. v] (often cap.) an organization that fights secretly against an enemy that has defeated and now controls its country, esp. that of France in the Second World War 5 [C] a RESISTOR

re·sis·tant /rɪˈzɪstənt/ adj [(to)] (often in comb.) having or showing resistance: *This new type of infection is resistant*

to antibiotics. | *a disease-resistant variety of wheat*

re·sis·tor /rɪˈzɪstəʳ/ n a piece of wire or other material used for increasing electrical RESISTANCE (3)

re·sit /ˌriːˈsɪt/ v -sat /ˈsæt/, *present participle* -sitting [T] *esp. BrE* to take (an examination) again —**re·sit** /ˈriːsɪt/ n

res·o·lute /ˈrezəluːt/ adj fml, apprec (of a person or their character) firm; determined in purpose: *a resolute optimist* | *Be resolute (in your efforts).* —opposite **irresolute** — ~**ly** adv : *They defended the city resolutely.*

res·o·lu·tion /ˌrezəˈluːʃən/ n 1 [C] a formal decision or statement made by the vote of a group: *All those in favour of the resolution should raise their hands.* [+to-v/that] *The committee have passed|carried|adopted|rejected a resolution to build a new library|a resolution that a new library (should) be built.* 2 [C] a firm decision; something one makes up one's mind to do or stop doing: *She's always making good resolutions but she never carries them out.* [+to-v] *I've made a* **New Year** (*BrE*)‖**Year's** (*AmE*) **resolution** (=one made on January 1st for the year ahead) *to stop smoking.* —compare RESOLVE² (1) 3 also **res·o·lute·ness** /ˈrezəluːtnɪs/— [U] apprec the quality of being resolute; DETERMINATION: *She lacks resolution.* 4 [U] the action of resolving (RESOLVE¹ (1)) something: *The lawyer's advice led to the resolution of this difficult problem.* 5 [U+of, into] (in science) the process of breaking up into parts: *the resolution of a chemical mixture into simple substances* 6 [C;U] (a measure of) the power of a scientific instrument to give a clear picture of things that are very small or close together: *a high-resolution microscope|computer screen*

re·sol·va·ble /rɪˈzɒlvəbəl‖-ˈzɑːl-, -ˈzɔːl-/ adj 1 that can be resolved: *This difficulty should be easily resolvable.* 2 [F+into] that can be resolved into parts: *This mixture is resolvable into two simple substances.*

re·solve¹ /rɪˈzɒlv‖rɪˈzɑːlv, rɪˈzɔːlv/ v 1 [T] to find a satisfactory way of dealing with (a difficulty); settle: *to resolve a dispute* | *There weren't enough beds, but the matter was resolved by George sleeping on the sofa.* 2 [I+on; T+to-v/ that; obj] to make a determined decision; decide firmly: *Once she has resolved on doing it, you won't get her to change her mind.* | *He resolved to work harder/that he would work harder.* 3 [I+adv/prep; T+to-v/that; obj] (of a committee or public body) to make a RESOLUTION: *The committee resolved on/against appointing a new secretary.* | *Parliament has resolved that ...* | *The Senate resolved, by 70 votes to 30, to accept the President's budget proposals.*
resolve (sthg.) **into** sthg. phr v [T] to separate or become separated into (parts): *The problem can be resolved into two areas of misunderstanding.* | *This mixture will resolve into two separate compounds.*

resolve² n fml 1 [C] a RESOLUTION (2): [+to-v] *He made a firm resolve to give up drinking and smoking.* 2 [U] apprec RESOLUTION (3): *Her encouragement and support strengthened our resolve.*

res·o·nance /ˈrezənəns/ n 1 [U] the quality of being RESONANT (1): *the resonance of his voice* 2 [C;U] (a) sound produced or increased in one object by sound waves from another: *Playing the piano sets up resonance(s) in those glass ornaments.*

res·o·nant /ˈrezənənt/ adj 1 (of a sound) deep, loud, clear, and continuing: *the resonant note of a bell* | *a resonant voice* 2 producing RESONANCE (2) 3 [F+with] (of a place) filled with the stated sound: *The air was resonant with the shouts of children.* — ~**ly** adv

res·o·nate /ˈrezəneɪt/ v [I] 1 to produce RESONANCE (2) 2 (of a sound) to be RESONANT (1)

res·o·na·tor /ˈrezəneɪtəʳ/ n an apparatus for increasing the RESONANCE (2) of sound, as in a musical instrument

re·sort¹ /rɪˈzɔːt‖-ɔːrt/ n 1 [C] a place where people regularly go for holidays: *Brighton is one of the most popular resorts on the south coast of England.* | *skiing resorts* | *a health resort* (=place considered good for the health) 2 [U+(to)] fml the action of resorting to something: *If this can't be settled reasonably, it may be necessary to* **have resort to** *force.* | *He couldn't have passed the exam without resort to cheating.* | **As a‖In the last resort** (=if everything else fails) *we could borrow more money from the bank.* —compare RECOURSE

resort² v
resort to sthg. phr v [T] to make use of; turn to (often

something bad) for help: *When polite requests failed he resorted to threats.* [+v-ing] *She resorted to stealing when she had no more money.*

re·sound /rɪˈzaʊnd/ v [I] 1 [(with)] (of a place) to be filled with sound; ECHO: *The hall resounded with laughter and whistles.* 2 [(through, throughout)] (of a musical instrument, a sound, etc.) to be loudly and clearly heard: *The (notes of the) hunting horn resounded through the forest.* —compare REVERBERATE

re·sound·ing /rɪˈzaʊndɪŋ/ adj 1 [A] (of a sound) loud and clear; echoing (ECHO²): *They all gave three resounding cheers.* 2 very great; complete: *a resounding victory/defeat/failure* — ~**ly** adv

re·source¹ /rɪˈzɔːs, -ˈsɔːs‖-ɔːrs, ˈriːsɔːrs/ n 1 [C usu. pl.] any of the possessions or qualities of a person, an organization, or esp. a country: *Oil is Kuwait's most important natural resource.* | *a country rich in mineral resources* (=such as metal, coal, oil, etc. in the ground) | *The job called for all my resources of energy and patience.* | *This country is wasting its resources and manpower on building old-fashioned ships.* | *Resource management is an important business skill.* 2 [C] a means of comfort or help; something one turns to when one is in difficulty: *Religion is her only resource now.* | *She has* **inner resources** *of courage.* 3 [U] also **re·source·ful·ness** /rɪˈzɔːsfəlnɪs, -ˈsɔːs-‖-ɔːr-/ [U] apprec cleverness in finding a way to avoid difficulties; practical ability: *a man of great resource* 4 **leave someone to their own resources** to leave someone to act as they wish or to do the best they can, esp. in a difficult situation

re·source² /rɪˈzɔːs, -ˈsɔːs‖-ɔːrs/ v [T] to provide (money or other resources) for: *The FTC will resource the new study.* | *The program failed because it wasn't adequately resourced.* —see also UNDERRESOURCE

re·source·ful /rɪˈzɔːsfəl, -ˈsɔːs-‖-ɔːr-/ adj apprec good at finding ways to deal with difficult situations: *It was very resourceful of her to make that shelter out of old packing cases.* — ~**ly** adv — ~**ness** n [U]

re·spect¹ /rɪˈspekt/ n 1 [U (for)] the feeling that one admires someone or something very much and that they or it should be treated well and honourably: *Show some respect to/Have some respect for your parents.* | *He* **commands the respect of** (=has earned the respect of) *all who know him well.* | (used formally to introduce an expression of disagreement) **With (the greatest) respect/With due respect,** *I think you're wrong.* — opposite **disrespect**; see also RESPECTS, SELF-RESPECT 2 [U (for)] consideration or care: *Out of respect for the wishes of her family, the affair was not reported in the newspapers.* | *If they had any respect for human life they wouldn't do such terrible things.* 3 [in+C] a detail; particular point: *This room is fine except in one respect — what can I sit on?* | *In many respects the new version is less good than the old one.* 4 **in respect of** fml a concerning; with regard to **b** (esp. in business letters) in payment for: *He will be paid £100 in respect of the work he has done.* 5 **without respect to** without considering; without regard to: *Anyone can join the club, without respect to class, race, or sex.* —see also IRRESPECTIVE 6 **with respect to** (used esp. to introduce a new subject or one that has been mentioned earlier) concerning: *With respect to your other proposals, I am not yet able to tell you our decision.*

respect² v [T] 1 to feel respect for (esp. a person or their qualities): *He's a man much respected by all his colleagues.* | *I deeply respect her courage.* 2 to show careful consideration for: *I promise to respect your wishes.* | *Please respect* (=obey) *the no smoking sign as long as it appears.* —see also SELF-RESPECTING

re·spec·ta·bil·i·ty /rɪˌspektəˈbɪləti/ n [U] the quality of being RESPECTABLE (1): *They got married for the sake of respectability.*

re·spec·ta·ble /rɪˈspektəbəl/ adj 1 showing standards of behaviour, appearance, etc. that are socially acceptable, but may be thought of as boring and lacking in excitement, unwilling to take risks etc.: *What an outrageous suggestion, young man — I'm a respectable married woman!* | *It's not respectable to be drunk in the street.* | *I must go and put on a clean shirt and make myself look respectable!* | (derog) *I'd never marry her; she's too respectable!* 2 infml quite good; enough in amount or quality: *England's football team won three matches out of five*

— quite a respectable total. | *a respectable income* —**-bly** *adv* — ~**ness** *n* [U]

re·spect·er /rɪ'spektə^r/ *n* [(of) *usu. in negatives*] someone or something that shows RESPECT¹ (1,2): *He's* **no respecter of persons.** (=does not respect rich or important people any more than ordinary people) | *A hurricane is no respecter of property.*

re·spect·ful /rɪ'spektfəl/ *adj* [(to)] feeling or showing RESPECT¹ (1): *The crowd stood in respectful silence as the funeral procession went by.* —opposite **disrespectful** — ~**ly** *adv* — ~**ness** *n* [U]

re·spect·ing /rɪ'spektɪŋ/ *prep fml* concerning; in respect of (RESPECT¹ (4a))

re·spec·tive /rɪ'spektɪv/ *adj* [A] of or for each one; particular and separate: *The two friends said goodbye and went to their respective homes.*

re·spec·tive·ly /rɪ'spektɪvli/ *adv* each separately in the order mentioned: *The nurses and the miners got pay rises of 5% and 7% respectively.* (=the nurses got 5% and the miners got 7%)

re·spects /rɪ'spekts/ *n* [P] **1** one's polite formal greetings; good wishes: *Give my respects to your wife.* | *Please send them my respects when you write.* **2 pay one's respects to** *fml* to pay a polite visit to (a person): *I've come to pay my respects to the countess.*

res·pi·ra·tion /ˌrespɪ'reɪʃən/ *n* [U] *fml or tech* breathing: *Respiration becomes difficult at great heights.* —see also ARTIFICIAL RESPIRATION

res·pi·ra·tor /'respɪreɪtə^r/ *n* an apparatus that is worn over the nose and mouth, to help people to breathe in spite of gas, smoke, etc.: *The firemen wore respirators.*

the respiratory system

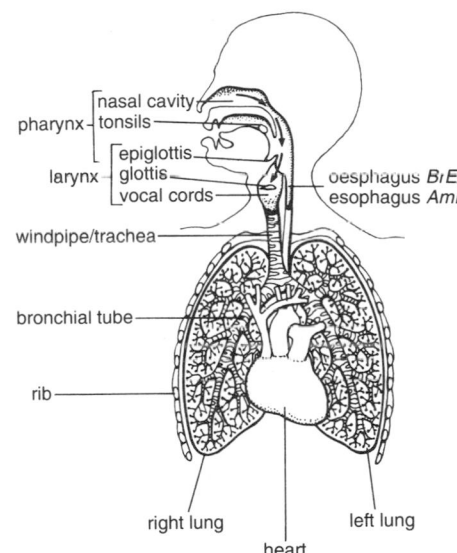

pharynx — nasal cavity
tonsils
epiglottis
larynx — glottis
vocal cords
oesophagus *BrE*/
esophagus *AmE*
windpipe/trachea
bronchial tube
rib
right lung　left lung
heart

re·spi·ra·to·ry /rɪ'spɪrətəri, 'respəreɪtəri, rɪ'spaɪərə-‖ 'respərətɔːri, rɪ'spaɪərə-/ *adj fml or tech* connected with breathing: *respiratory diseases/difficulties* | *the respiratory system* (=the lungs and the tubes leading to them)

re·spire /rɪ'spaɪə^r/ *v* [I] *tech* to breathe

res·pite /'respɪt, -paɪt‖-pɪt/ *n* [C *usu. sing.*;U] **1** [(from)] (a short period of) pause or rest, during a time of great effort, pain, or trouble: *a welcome/much needed respite from the continual hard work* | *The noise went on all night* **without (a moment's) respite.** **2** a welcome period of delay before doing or suffering something unpleasant; REPRIEVE: *The office will be shut until Monday, so we have a few days' respite before we need to pay the rent.*

re·splen·dent /rɪ'splendənt/ *adj fml or pomp* bright and shining; splendid in appearance: *the resplendent colours of the New England woods in autumn* | (fig.) *George*

arrived, resplendent in a new white suit. — ~**ly** *adv* : *resplendently dressed in purple silk* —**-dence** *n* [U]

re·spond /rɪ'spɒnd‖rɪ'spɑːnd/ *v* **1** [I (**to**);T] to say or write (something) in reply: *They still haven't responded to my letter.* | *"Yes, I'd love to come," he responded.* [+*that*] *He responded that he would come.* —see ANSWER (USAGE) **2** [I (**by, to, with**)] to do something in answer; REACT: *He responded (to my suggestion) with a laugh/by laughing.* **3** [I (**to**)] (esp. of a disease or a part of the body that is hurt) to get better as a result of treatment; REACT favourably: *The disease failed to respond to the drugs.* | *Is her leg responding to treatment?*

▷ USAGE Compare **respond** and **react**. In many contexts they are used with the same meaning but **react** has a sense of being more immediate and sometimes resulting from feeling more than thought, while **respond** suggests that some consideration has been involved. We may want to know someone's **reaction** simply from CURIOSITY but if we want to know their **response** it is because we need the information in order to make a decision, etc.◁

re·spon·dent /rɪ'spɒndənt‖rɪ'spɑːn-/ *n law* a person who has to answer a charge in a law court, esp. in a DIVORCE case —compare CORRESPONDENT

re·sponse /rɪ'spɒns‖rɪ'spɑːns/ *n* **1** [C (**to**)] a reply: *I asked him a question but he made/gave no response.* | *There have been several responses to our advertisement.* **2** [C;U (**to**)] (an) action done in answer: *There's been a generous response/a lukewarm response to the appeal on behalf of the earthquake victims.* | *Our call for new suggestions evoked* (=produced) *very little response.* | *She opened the door* **in response** *to the knock.* **3** [C *usu. pl.*] any of the parts of a religious service that are said or sung by the CONGREGATION (=people in a place of worship) in answer to the parts sung by the priest —see RESPOND (USAGE)

re·spon·si·bil·i·ty /rɪˌspɒnsɪ'bɪlɪti‖rɪˌspɑːn-/ *n* **1** [U (**for**)] the condition or quality of being responsible: *I take* **(full) responsibility** *for losing the money.* (=I admit that it was my fault) | *The defence secretary has responsibility for* (=is responsible for) *the upkeep of the armed forces.* | *A terrorist organization has* **claimed responsibility for** *the bombing.* | *a position of great responsibility in the government* | *We have joint responsibility* (=we share the responsibility) *for the running of the company.* **2** [U] the quality of being sensible and trustworthy: *Now that you're 13 you should have more sense of responsibility.* —opposite **irresponsibility** **3** [C] something for which one is RESPONSIBLE (2): *The head of a large company has many responsibilities.* | *It's your responsibility to make the decision.* **4 do something on one's own responsibility** to do something without being told or officially allowed to

re·spon·si·ble /rɪ'spɒnsəbəl‖rɪ'spɑːn-/ *adj* **1** [F (**for**)] having done or been the cause of esp. something bad; guilty: *Who's responsible for this terrible mess?* | *These tax laws are responsible for a lot of hardship.* | *It was your idea, so if anything goes wrong I shall hold you personally responsible.* **2** [F (**for, to**)] having the duty of looking after someone or something, so that one can be blamed if things go wrong: *The teacher made me responsible (to her) for keeping the class in order while she went out.* **3** *apprec* sensible, trustworthy, and able to make good moral and practical judgments: *You can leave the children with him — he's very responsible.* —opposite **irresponsible** **4** (of a job) needing a trustworthy person to do it: *She holds a very responsible position in the firm.*

re·spon·si·bly /rɪ'spɒnsəbli‖rɪ'spɑːn-/ *adv* in a RESPONSIBLE (3) way: *I'll trust you to behave responsibly while I'm out.* —opposite **irresponsibly**

re·spon·sive /rɪ'spɒnsɪv‖rɪ'spɑːn-/ *adj* **1** [(**to**)] giving the hoped-for response or result quickly or willingly: *This car's steering isn't very responsive.* (=you have to turn it hard to get the car to change direction) | *The disease isn't proving responsive to treatment.* | *I think you'll find she's more responsive to praise than to criticism.* **2** giving answers willingly: *He wasn't very responsive, so I asked her instead.* —opposite **unresponsive** — ~**ly** *adv* — ~**ness** *n* [U]

rest¹ /rest/ *n* **1** [C;U (**from**)] (a period of) freedom from activity or from something tiring or worrying: *I'm tired; let's* **take/have a rest.** | *a well-earned rest after her exams* | *You need a good night's rest.* (=sleep) | *She needs*

rest (=peace, quiet, and little activity) *after her long illness.* | *I need a rest from all this hard work.* | (fig., *infml*) **Give it a rest,** *can't you!* (=stop being annoying, esp. by talking or making a noise) | (fig., *euph*) *She was* **laid to rest** (=buried) *in the village churchyard.* | (fig.) *I'm glad that ridiculous plan has finally been* **laid to rest.** (=got rid of) | *The letter from her daughter* **set her mind at rest.** (=freed her from anxiety) **2** [U] the condition of not moving: *The ball rolled down the hill and* **came to rest** (=stopped) *at the bottom.* | *Measure the mass of the body while it is* **at rest. 3** [C] (*often in comb.*) a support, esp. for the stated thing: *an armrest* | *This wall will do as a rest for your camera.* —see also HEADREST, and see picture at CAR **4** [C] (in music) **a** a period of silence of a fixed length **b** any of a set of signs, such as ♪, that mark the length of these periods

rest[2] *v* **1** [I (**from**);T] to (allow to) take a rest: *I always rest for an hour after dinner.* | *Sit down and rest your feet.* | (fig., *euph*) *Let him* **rest** (=lie buried) **in peace.** | (fig., *euph*) *She's lying in her* **last resting-place.** (=grave) **2** [I+*adv/prep*;T+*obj*+*adv/prep*] to (allow to) lean or be supported: *Rest your bicycle against the wall/your head on my shoulder.* | *The ladder rested on/against the wall.* — see also REST **on/upon. 3** [I *only in negatives*] to stop being active; be calm: *The police said they wouldn't rest until all the criminals were caught.* | *I will not rest until I know he's safe.* **4** [I+*adv/prep*] to be discontinued; not be talked about further: *We decided to let the matter/the argument rest, because it was obvious we would never agree.* **5** [I;T] *law* **a** (of a case in a law court) to have been fully explained: *My case rests.* **b** to stop explaining (one's case) to the court, because enough has been said: *I rest my case, my lord.* | *The prosecution rested (its case) after three days of testimony.* | *The defense rests, your Honor.* **6 rest assured** *usu. imperative* to be certain: *Rest assured/You can rest assured that we will do all we can.*

rest on/upon sthg. *phr v* [T] **1** to lean on; be supported by: *The bridge rests on stone arches.* —see also REST[2] (2) **2** (of sight or the eyes) to be directed on; fall on: *His eyes rested on the empty seat.* **3** *fml* (esp. of a proof, argument, etc.) to depend on esp. be based on: *Your argument rests on a statement that can't be proved.* | *We've tried everything: now it all rests on him.* **4 rest on one's laurels** *derog* to be satisfied with what one has done already, and therefore not do any more

rest with sbdy. *phr v* [T *no pass.*] *fml* to be the responsibility of: *The decision rests with you.* | *The fate of these prisoners rests with the judge.*

rest[3] *n* [*the*+S+*sing./pl. v*] **1** what is left; the ones that still remain: *We'll eat some of the butter and keep the rest (of it) for breakfast.* | *Only ten students attended the class because all the rest (of them) were off sick.* | *John's Scottish and the rest of us are Welsh.* **2 for the rest** apart from what has already been mentioned; as for everything else

Re·start /ˈriːstɑːt‖-ɑːrt/ the name of a British government SCHEME for people who have been unemployed for six months or more. It is intended to help them find work by providing advice, information, and TRAINING.

re·state /ˌriːˈsteɪt/ *v* [T] to state again or in a different way: *Do I have to restate my objections to this ridiculous plan?* | *Seeing his look of confusion, she tried to restate her opinion more clearly.* — ~ment *n* [C;U]

res·tau·rant /ˈrestərɒnt‖-rɒnt, -rɑːnt/ *n* a place where meals are prepared, sold, and eaten

restaurant car /ˈ··· ·/ *n* a DINING CAR

res·tau·ra·teur /ˌrestərəˈtɜːr/ also **res·tau·ran·teur** /ˌrestɒrɒnˈtɜːr‖-rɑːn-/ *esp. AmE*— *n* the owner of a restaurant, esp. one who runs it himself or herself

rest cure /ˈ· ·/ *n* a course of treatment, often for people with illnesses of the mind, consisting of rest from one's usual activities: *Make an effort; this is a battle training course, not a rest cure!*

rest·ful /ˈrestfəl/ *adj* peaceful and quiet; giving one a feeling of rest: *Pale greens and yellows make a restful colour scheme for a room.* | *a restful holiday/atmosphere* — ~ly *adv* — ~ness *n* [U]

rest home /ˈ· ·/ *n* an establishment where old or ill people are looked after —see RESIDENTIAL CARE (CULTURAL NOTE)

res·ti·tu·tion /ˌrestɪˈtjuːʃ*ə*n‖-ˈtuː-/ *n* [U (**to**)] *fml* the act of returning something lost or stolen to its owner, or of paying for damage: *The court ordered him to make full*

restitution of the money to the people he had stolen it from.

res·tive /ˈrestɪv/ *adj* unwilling to keep still or be controlled; nervous: *The horses are restive tonight; there must be wolves about.* — ~ly *adv* — ~ness *n* [U]

rest·less /ˈrestləs/ *adj* **1** giving no rest: *I spent a very restless night.* (=could not sleep) **2** unwilling or unable to stay still, esp. because of anxiety or lack of interest: *After listening to him for three hours the audience became restless.* | *He's been feeling very restless lately and is applying for jobs abroad.* | *the restless sea* — ~ly *adv* — ~ness *n* [U]

re·stock /ˌriːˈstɒk‖ˌriːˈstɑːk/ *v* [I;T (**with**)] to get a new supply of things (for): *to restock the shelves in a supermarket* | *The lake has been restocked with fish.*

res·to·ra·tion /ˌrestəˈreɪʃ*ə*n/ *n* [C;U] (an example of) the act of restoring or condition of being restored: *The army's task was the restoration of public order.* | *We gave money to the church restoration fund.* | *This restoration of a prehistoric village shows what it must have looked like.*

Restoration [*the*] (the period in Britain following) the return of Charles II as king in 1660. The period was characterized by advances in trade, opposition to the ROMAN CATHOLIC religion, the establishment of the WHIG and TORY political parties, and new developments in poetry and the theatre.

Restoration com·e·dy /ˌ···· ˈ···/ *n* a type of play that was popular in England at the time of the Restoration, characterized by its SATIRICAL humour and jokes about society, e.g. *She Stoops to Conquer* written by Oliver Goldsmith

re·sto·ra·tive /rɪˈstɔːrətɪv/ *n, adj fml or old-fash* (a food, medicine, etc.) that brings back health and strength

re·store /rɪˈstɔːr/ *v* [T] **1** to bring back into use or existence; introduce again: *The army was called in to restore law and order.* | *This proposal would restore the tax advantages that small business used to enjoy.* **2** [(**to**)] to put back into a former position: *The new manager's job is to restore the company to profitability.* **3** [(**to**) *usu. pass.*] to bring back to a good or desirable state, esp. of health: *I feel quite restored (to health) after my holiday.* **4** to put (esp. an old building, piece of furniture, or work of art) back into its original state: *The old painting was damaged in the flood and had to be painstakingly restored.* **5** [(**to**)] *rather fml* to give back: *The stolen property must be restored to its owner.* —**storer** *n* [C;U] : *He's a picture restorer.* | *a bottle of hair restorer* (=for people whose hair is falling out)

re·strain /rɪˈstreɪn/ *v* [T (**from**)] to control or prevent from doing something, esp. by use of force: *If you can't restrain your dog (from biting people) you must lock it up.* | *I had to restrain myself from telling him what I thought of him.*

re·strained /rɪˈstreɪnd/ *adj* **1** (of a person or their behaviour) calm and controlled; not showing strong feelings: *a restrained and cool-headed response to their unfair criticisms* —*opposite* **unrestrained 2** not bright or highly decorated: *a room painted in restrained colours*

re·straint /rɪˈstreɪnt/ *n* **1** [U] *often apprec* the quality of being restrained or restraining oneself: *I think you showed great restraint in not hitting him after what he said.* | *a policy of wage restraint* (=holding back from giving or asking for higher wages) **2** [C (**on**) *usu. pl.*] something that restrains; restriction: *government restraints imposed on foreign trade* | *constitutional restraints on the power of the president* | *She was put in restraints after her violent attack.* **3** [U] the condition of having no freedom of action or movement: *He went mad and had to be* **kept under restraint. 4** [C] a SEAT BELT in a car: *Children from four to 14 years old travelling in the back of a car must use a restraint specifically designed for them or an adult safety belt.*

re·strict /rɪˈstrɪkt/ *v* [T (**to**)] to keep within limits of size or number or to a certain limit: *I restrict myself to (smoking) two cigarettes a day.* | *laws to restrict the sale of alcohol* | *We had to restrict the number of students on this course.* —compare CONSTRICT

re·strict·ed /rɪˈstrɪktɪd/ *adj* **1** [(**to**)] controlled or limited in some way, esp. by law: *The sale of alcohol is restricted in Britain.* | *Membership of the club is restricted to people under 30.* (=only people under 30 can join) **2** for a particular purpose, or for the use of a particular group only: *a restricted area, where only the army are allowed to go* | *This information is restricted.* (=secret) **3** *sometimes* *derog* limited in space; narrow and shut in: *I need a bigger kitchen — it's hard to work in such a restricted space.* | (fig.) *He leads a very restricted life.*

re·stric·tion /rɪˈstrɪkʃən/ *n* [C;U (**on**)] the act of restricting, or something that restricts: *The law imposes restrictions on the export of high-technology goods.* | *speed/currency restrictions*

re·stric·tive /rɪˈstrɪktɪv/ *adj* **1** tending to restrict; limiting: *He finds life in a small town too restrictive.* | *an attempt to get rid of* **restrictive practices** (=rules or ways of working that limit the freedom of workers or employers) **2** *tech* (of a CLAUSE) saying which person or thing is meant, rather than giving additional information: *In "the man who came to dinner" the words "who came to dinner" are a restrictive clause, because they tell us which man is meant.* —compare NONRESTRICTIVE — ~**ly** *adv* — ~**ness** *n* [U]

restrictive prac·tice /·,·· '··/ *n* **1** a trading agreement which is against the public interest **2** a limitation on what work a union will allow workers from other unions to do

rest room /'· ·/ *n AmE euph* a public TOILET in a hotel, restaurant, etc. —see TOILET (USAGE)

rest stop /'· ·/ *n* a place near an American road or HIGH-WAY where there are TOILETs and where people can eat in the open air

re·struc·ture /ˌriːˈstrʌktʃər/ *v* [T] to arrange (a system or organization) in a new way; give a new structure to: *the restructuring of local government*

re·sult¹ /rɪˈzʌlt/ *v* [I (**from**)] to happen as an effect or result; be the CONSEQUENCE (of): *If these two substances are combined, an enormous explosion will result.* | *His illness resulted from* (=was caused by) *eating contaminated food.*

result in sthg. *phr v* [T *no pass.*] to have as a result; cause: *The accident resulted in the death of two passengers.* [+*obj+v-ing*] *The accident resulted in two passengers dying.*

result² *n* **1** [C;U (**of**)] something that happens because of an action or event: *His illness is a/the result of eating contaminated food.* | *She was late* **as a result of** (=because of) *the snow.* | *These problems are the result of years of bad management.* | *(fml) I was away on business, with the result that* (=so that) *I missed the vital meeting.* | *The* **net result** (=the result at the end) *of all our discussions was that she agreed to take the job.* **2** [C;U] (a) noticeable good effect: *Your hard work is beginning to show results.* **3** [C (**of**)] (a report of) the success or failure of a person, team, organization, etc. in an examination, sports match, etc.: *The football results are broadcast on the radio.* | *The result (of the match) was 1–0 to England.* | *When will you get your exam results?* | *The company's annual results show a profit of over $5 million.* **4** [C] the answer to a sum: *Let's both add it up and see if we get the same result.* **5** [C] *BrE infml* (esp. in football) a win: *If we don't get a result tonight we'll be put down into a lower division.*

re·sul·tant /rɪˈzʌltənt/ *adj* [A] *fml* happening as an effect; resulting: *He was arrested for drunkenness and the resultant publicity ruined his career.*

re·sume /rɪˈzjuːm‖rɪˈzuːm/ *v* **1** [I;T] *rather fml* to begin again after a pause: *Let us resume where we left off.* | *We resumed our journey/our discussions after a short rest.* [+*v-ing*] *We'll stop now and resume working at two o'clock.* **2** [T] *fml* to take again: *Kindly resume your seats, ladies and gentlemen.*

ré·su·mé /ˈrezjuːmeɪ, ˈreɪ-‖ˌrezʊˈmeɪ/ *n* **1** [(**of**)] a shortened form of a speech, book, etc.; SUMMARY **2** *AmE for* CURRICULUM VITAE

re·sump·tion /rɪˈzʌmpʃən/ *n* [U] *fml* the act of resuming: *the resumption of business after a holiday*

re·sur·face /ˌriːˈsɜːfɪs‖-ɜːr-/ *v* **1** [T] to put a new surface on (a road) **2** [I] to come back to the surface: *The children watched as the submarine resurfaced.* | (fig.) *Old rivalries are beginning to resurface.*

re·sur·gence /rɪˈsɜːdʒəns‖-ɜːr-/ *n* [S;U] the return of ideas, beliefs, etc. to a state of being active and noticeable: *There has been a resurgence of interest in her work after a period of neglect.* | *a resurgence of terrorist activity* —**gent** *adj* : *resurgent interest*

res·ur·rect /ˌrezəˈrekt/ *v* [T] **1** *often derog* to bring back into use, existence, or fashion; REVIVE: *The government resurrected an ancient law in order to punish the ringleaders.* |

It's a mistake to resurrect old quarrels. **2** *rare* to bring back to life

res·ur·rec·tion /ˌrezəˈrekʃən/ *n* **1** [U] *fml* the act of resurrecting something; renewal: *The plan has now been dropped, with little hope of resurrection.* **2** **I am the resurrection and the life** *phrase from the Bible* one of the most important phrases said by Jesus, a promise that people who believe in him will live forever

Resurrection [*the*] **1** the return of Christ to life after his death as described in the Bible, which is remembered with ceremonies at Easter, and is one of the main beliefs on which Christianity is based **2** the return of all dead people to life at the end of the world. Christians believe that, as a result of Christ's resurrection, the souls of people who believe in him will be united with their bodies on JUDGMENT DAY, in the form that will last for ever.

re·sus·ci·tate /rɪˈsʌsɪteɪt/ *v* [T] to bring (a person or animal that is almost dead) back to life: *They tried to resuscitate the drowned man.* —**tation** /rɪˌsʌsɪˈteɪʃən/ *n* [U] : *Despite our attempts at resuscitation, she died.*

re·tail¹ /ˈriːteɪl/ *n* [U] the sale of goods in shops to customers, for their own use and not for selling to anyone else: *the retail of goods* | *retail prices* | *a retail outlet* (=a shop) — compare WHOLESALE¹

retail² *adv* by retail; from a retailer: *I bought it retail.*

re·tail³ /rɪˈteɪl/ *v* **1** [I+*at/for*;T] *tech* to sell or be sold by retail: *In this shop they retail tobacco and sweets.* | *These socks retail at £5 a pair.* **2** [T] *fml* to tell (esp. unpleasant facts about a person) to other people: *Who is responsible for retailing these rumours about him?*

retail bank /'·· ,·/ *n BrE* a bank which has branches in many towns and provides services to ordinary people and small companies

re·tail·er /ˈriːteɪlər/ *n* someone who sells things by retail; shopkeeper

retail price in·dex /ˌ·· '· ,··/ also **RPI**— [*the*] an official system (in Britain) which is a monthly measure of the prices of goods and services bought by an average person, to show changes in the cost of living —see also CONSUMER PRICE INDEX

retail trade /'·· ,·/ *n* **1** [U] the business of selling goods to the public in shops **2** [C] a particular kind of business that sells goods to the public in shops

re·tain /rɪˈteɪn/ *v* [T] *rather fml* **1** to keep possession of; avoid losing: *She tried to retain her self-control/her balance.* | *This village still retains its old-world character.* | *His business has been taken over by a big corporation, but he still retains some control over it.* | *Lead retains heat well.* | *a heavy soil that retains water* —see also RETENTION **2** to hold in place: *The dam retains the waters of the lake.* | *A* **retaining wall** *holds the earth in place.* **3** to employ (esp. a lawyer or adviser) to act for one, by paying in advance

re·tain·er /rɪˈteɪnər/ *n* **1** a sum of money paid to someone, esp. a lawyer, for their advice and help **2** *old-fash* a servant, esp. one who has always worked for a particular person or family: *an old and trusted retainer*

re·take¹ /ˌriːˈteɪk/ *v* **-took** /ˈtʊk/, **-taken** /ˈteɪkən/ [T] **1** to regain possession of (a place lost in war): *We retook the city after severe fighting.* **2** to record or film again

re·take² /ˈriːteɪk/ *n* an act of filming or recording something again: *I forgot my lines, so they had to do a retake.*

re·tal·i·ate /rɪˈtælieɪt/ *v* [I (**against**)] to do something bad to someone who has done something bad to you: *One of their players kicked me, so I retaliated and kicked him back.* | *When they refused to allow our exports into their country, we retaliated by putting a tax on goods from their country.* —**ation** /rɪˌtæliˈeɪʃən/ *n* [U] : *The government decided against military retaliation for the terrorist attack.* | *a tax imposed* **in retaliation for** *their import restrictions*

re·tal·i·a·to·ry /rɪˈtæliətəri‖-tɔːri/ *adj fml* done in retaliation: *a retaliatory kick* | *a retaliatory bombing raid*

re·tard¹ /rɪˈtɑːd‖-ɑːrd/ *v* [T] *esp. fml or tech* to delay, esp. in development, cause to happen later than usual or expected: *Cold weather retards the growth of the crops.* — ~**ation** /ˌriːtɑːˈdeɪʃən‖-ɑːr-/ *n* [U]

re·tard² /ˈriːtɑːd‖-ɑːrd/ *n AmE infml derog* a person with a mental disability; an offensive word used esp. by children

re·tard·ed /rɪ'tɑːdᶾd‖-ɑːr-/ *adj* (esp. of a child) slower in development or less able than others: *Lucy is very retarded and can't read yet.* | *mentally retarded*

retch /retʃ/ *v* [I] to try to VOMIT (=be sick) esp. without success

retd *written abbrev. for:* RETIRED (1): *Captain Percy Truscott RN (retd)*

re·tell /ˌriː'tel/ *v* -**told** /'təʊld/ [T] to tell (a story) again in a new way or different language: *German fairy stories retold in English*

re·ten·tion /rɪ'tenʃən/ *n* [U] *fml* the state or action of retaining (RETAIN): *Retention of urine is the inability to pass urine from the body.* | *The swelling is due to water retention.* | *They advocate the retention of our nuclear power plants.* (=that they should be kept)

re·ten·tive /rɪ'tentɪv/ *adj* able to RETAIN things, esp. facts in the mind: *She has a very retentive memory.* — ~ **ly** *adv* — ~**ness** *n* [U]

re·think¹ /ˌriː'θɪŋk/ *v* -**thought** /'θɔːt/ [I;T] to think (about) again; reconsider (an idea, plan, etc.), esp. with the likelihood of changing it: *We'd better rethink our whole strategy.* | *If that's what he wants, he'll have to rethink.*

re·think² /'riːθɪŋk/ *n* [S] an act of rethinking: *It's clearly not going to work in the way we'd originally intended; we'll have to have a rethink.*

ret·i·cent /'retᶾsənt/ *adj* (of a person or their behaviour) unwilling to speak; not expressing as much as is known or felt: *He was reticent about the reasons for the quarrel.* — ~**ly** *adv* —**cence** *n* [U]

re·tic·u·la·ted /rɪ'tɪkjᵿleɪtᶾd/ also **re·tic·u·late** /-kjᵿlᶾt/— *adj tech* forming or covered with a netlike pattern of squares and lines: *a reticulated leaf*

re·tic·u·la·tion /rɪˌtɪkjᵿ'leɪʃən/ *n* [C *often pl.*;U] *tech* (a) netlike pattern: *a snake covered with beautiful orange and black reticulations*

ret·i·cule /'retɪkjuːl/ *n old use or humor* a small handbag

ret·i·na /'retᶾnə/ *n* -**nas** *or* -**nae** /niː/ an area at the back of the eye that receives light and sends an image of what is seen through nerves to the brain —see picture at EYE

ret·i·nue /'retɪnjuː‖-nuː/ *n* [C+*sing.|pl. v*] a group of helpers and followers travelling with an important person: *Two whole floors of the hotel were booked for the president's retinue.*

re·tire /rɪ'taɪəʳ/ *v* **1** [I;T] to (cause to) stop working at one's job, profession, etc., usu. because of age: *My father retired (from his job in the Civil Service) at the age of 60.* | *They retired her on full pay.*

▶CULTURAL NOTE In Britain the age at which people retire depends on the company they work for and the type of work they do, but on average women retire at 60 and men retire at 65 as this is when they are allowed to receive the state retirement PENSION. In the US workers can get their full SOCIAL SECURITY payments at age 65, or they can get a part of them if they wish to retire earlier. —compare RE-SIGN (1)◀

2 [I (**from, to**)] *fml* to go away to a quiet or less central place: *Members of the jury, you must now retire to consider your verdict.* **3** [I] *fml or humor* to go to bed —compare RISE¹ (5) **4** [I] (esp. of an army) to move back intentionally, without being forced to: *Our armies have retired to regroup for a fresh attack.* —compare RETREAT² **5 light the blue touchpaper and retire immediately** a phrase used in the directions printed on FIREWORKs, meaning that one should light the firework and then move away immediately

re·tired /rɪ'taɪəd‖-'taɪərd/ *adj* **1** [*no comp.*] (of a person) having stopped working, usu. because of age: *My father is retired|is a retired doctor.* **2** *old-fash fml* (of a place) far from crowds and large towns

re·tire·ment /rɪ'taɪəmənt‖-'taɪər-/ *n* **1** [C;U] (a case of) retiring (RETIRE (1)): *His employers gave him a gold watch on his retirement.* | *We've had two retirements in our office this year.* | *a retirement present* —see also EARLY RETIREMENT

▶CULTURAL NOTE In the past, workers who had worked for a company for a long time were given a gold watch by the company when they retired. People still mention this, although it does not often happen now.◀

2 [S;U] the period after one has retired: *What will you do*

to pass your time during your retirement? | *a long and happy retirement* | *a retirement pension*

retirement pen·sion /·'·· ˌ·./ *n* OLD AGE PENSION

retirement plan /·'·· ˌ·/ *n AmE for* PENSION PLAN

re·tir·ing /rɪ'taɪərɪŋ/ *adj* (typical of a person) who generally avoids the company of others; SHY and RESERVED: *Jane is a shy retiring girl|has a retiring nature, and hates parties.*

re·tort¹ /rɪ'tɔːt‖-ɔːrt/ *v* [T] to make a RETORT²: *"Of course not," she retorted.* [+(*that*)] *He retorted that it was all my fault.* —see ANSWER (USAGE)

retort² *n* a quick, angry, rude, or amusing answer

retort³ *n* a bottle with a long narrow bent neck, used for heating chemicals

re·touch /ˌriː'tʌtʃ/ *v* [T] to improve (a picture or photograph) by adding small strokes with a brush or pencil

re·trace /rɪ'treɪs, riː-/ *v* [T] to go back over (esp. a journey or a course of events): *The police have succeeded in retracing his movements on the night of the crime.* | *She* **re·traced her steps** (=went back exactly the way she had come) *to try to find her lost ring.*

re·tract /rɪ'trækt/ *v* [I;T] *fml* **1** to state, esp. officially, that (a statement or offer that one has made) is not true or can no longer be accepted; WITHDRAW: *At the trial, the prisoner retracted his confession.* **2** to (cause to) draw back or in: *The aircraft's undercarriage retracted as it climbed into the air.* | *A cat can retract its claws, but a dog can't.* — ~**able** *adj* : *an aircraft with a retractable undercarriage* — ~**ion** /'trækʃən/ *n* [C;U] : *The newspaper was forced to publish a retraction of all the allegations they had made against her.*

re·trac·tile /rɪ'træktaɪl‖-tl/ *adj tech* (esp. of a CLAW) that can be retracted (RETRACT (2))

re·train /ˌriː'treɪn/ *v* [I;T] to learn, or teach, the skills of a different job, esp. because one is (about to become) unemployed —**retraining** *n* [U]

re·tread¹ /ˌriː'tred/ also **remould** *BrE* ‖ **recap** *AmE*— *v* [T] to renew the rubber covering on the bare surface of (a worn tyre)

re·tread² /'riːtred/ *n* **1** also **remould** *BrE* ‖ **recap** *AmE*— a retreaded tyre **2** *AmE* RETARD **3** *AmE* a person, esp. an older one, who has been trained to do a kind of work which is different from what they did before

re·treat¹ /rɪ'triːt/ *n* **1** [C;U (**from, to**)] (an act of) retreating: *Napoleon's retreat from Moscow* | *The army fell back* **in full retreat.** | (fig.) *The latest concessions mark a significant retreat from the President's hard-line policy.* —compare ADVANCE² (1) **2** [*the*+S] a military signal for retreating: *The general ordered the bugler to* **sound the retreat.** **3** [C] a place into which one can go for peace and safety: *He has a little retreat in the mountains.* **4** [C;U] (the practice of spending) a period of prayer, thought, and religious study, with a group: *They spent a week in retreat|on a retreat.* —see also **beat a retreat** (BEAT¹ (8))

retreat² *v* [I (**from, to**)] to move back or leave a centre of fighting or other activity, esp. when forced to do so: *The defeated army had to retreat hastily (from the field of battle to the coast).* | *firefighters retreating from an uncontrollable forest fire* | (fig.) *The opposition groups forced the government to retreat on their proposed pay legislation.* —compare ADVANCE¹ (1), RETIRE (4)

re·trench /rɪ'trentʃ/ *v* [I] *fml* (of a government, business, etc.) to arrange to spend less; cut costs — ~**ment** [C;U] : *The worsening economic situation has forced the government into a policy of retrenchment.*

re·tri·al /'riːtraɪəl/ *n* an act of trying a law case again; new trial: *Some members of the jury had been bribed, so the judge ordered a retrial.*

ret·ri·bu·tion /ˌretrᶾ'bjuːʃən/ *n* [S;U (**for**)] *fml* (a) severe deserved punishment: *The public are demanding swift and effective retribution for this act of terrorism.*

re·trib·u·tive /rɪ'trɪbjᵿtɪv/ *adj fml* done as a deserved punishment: *retributive measures*

re·triev·al /rɪ'triːvəl/ *n* [U] *fml* the act or process of retrieving: *The court ordered the retrieval of the confiscated funds.* | *a computerized* **retrieval system** *that will enable you to find the information you want within a few* *seconds.* | *I'm afraid the situation is* **beyond/past retrieval.** (=cannot now be put right)

re·trieve /rɪˈtriːv/ v **1** [T (**from**)] *usu. fml or tech* to find and bring back; regain: *I went and retrieved the bag I had left on the train.* | *This computer can retrieve stored information in a matter of seconds.* | *Wreckage from the crashed plane was retrieved from the ocean.* **2** [T] to put right; make up for (a mistake, loss, defeat, etc.): *She tried to retrieve the situation by making profuse apologies.* **3** [I;T] (of a dog) to bring back (shot birds) —**retrievable** *adj*

re·triev·er /rɪˈtriːvəʳ/ *n* a type of middle-sized hunting dog trained to bring back shot birds

retro- see WORD FORMATION

ret·ro·ac·tive /ˌretrəʊˈæktɪv◂/ also **retrospective**— *adj fml* (esp. of a law) having effect on the past as well as on the future: *a retroactive pay increase* — ~**ly** *adv*

ret·ro·flex /ˈretrəfleks/ also **ret·ro·flexed** /-flekst/— *adj* **1** *tech* (of a speech sound) made with the TIP (=point) of the tongue curled upwards and backwards **2** *fml* turned or bent sharply backwards

ret·ro·grade /ˈretrəgreɪd/ *adj fml derog* seeming to show a return to an earlier and worse state: *Selling off all our nationalized companies to private ownership is a very retrograde step.*

ret·ro·gress /ˌretrəˈgres/ v [I (**to**)] *fml or tech* to go back to an earlier and worse state — ~**ion** /ˈgreʃən/ *n* [U]

ret·ro·gres·sive /ˌretrəˈgresɪv◂/ *adj fml derog* retrograde: *retrogressive changes to the tax laws* — ~**ly** *adv*

ret·ro·rock·et /ˈretrəʊ ˌrɒkɪt‖-ˌrɑː-/ *n* a ROCKET that is used for slowing down or changing the direction of an aircraft or spacecraft by firing forwards

ret·ro·spect /ˈretrəspekt/ *n* **in retrospect** thinking back to the past from the present: *My school life seems happier in retrospect than it seemed at the time.* | *In retrospect, it is now clear that this battle was a turning point in the war.*

ret·ro·spec·tion /ˌretrəˈspekʃən/ *n* [U] thought about the past: *the pleasures of retrospection*

retro·spec·tive¹ /ˌretrəˈspektɪv◂/ *adj* **1** concerned with or thinking about the past: *in a retrospective mood* **2** (esp. of a law) RETROACTIVE — ~**ly** *adv*

retrospective² also **retrospective ex·hi·bi·tion** /ˌ····
··ˈ···/— *n* a show of the work of a painter, SCULPTOR, etc. from his or her earliest years up to the present time

re·trous·sé /rəˈtruːseɪ‖rəˌtruːˈseɪ/ *adj Fr, often apprec* (of a nose) turned up at the lower end

ret·si·na /retˈsiːnə/ *n* [U] a Greek wine that tastes of the RESIN (=juice) of certain trees

re·turn¹ /rɪˈtɜːn‖-ɜːrn/ v **1** [I (**from, to**)] to come or go back to a former place, condition, or activity: *When are you returning home/returning to London?* | *What time does your wife return from work?* | *The dispute between transport workers and management has been settled and services will return to normal tomorrow.* | *He gave up drinking for a while, then soon returned to his old ways.* | *Let's return to the main point of the discussion.* —see also RETURNER **2** [T (**to**)] to give, put, or send back: *I'm going to the library to return my books.* | *Fortunately the hostages were returned unharmed.* [+obj(i)+obj(d)] *Don't forget to return me my keys!* | *We returned the empty bottles to the shop.* **3** [T] to give or do in exchange; REPAY: *She wondered whether he would* **return the/her visit.** (=go to see her after she had been to see him) | *He told her she was very clever and she* **returned the compliment.** (=said something nice about him in return) **4** [T (**to**)] to elect to a political position: *At the general election she was returned (to Parliament) with an increased majority.* **5** [T] (of a JURY) to give (a VERDICT): *They returned a verdict of "Not Guilty".* **6** [T] to produce as a profit; YIELD: *These shares return a good rate of interest.* **7** [T] *fml* to give an official account of, esp. in answer to a demand: *He returned his earnings as £9000 on the tax declaration.* **8 return to work** (of a woman) to go back to work after having children and looking after them for a few years: *She's thinking of returning to work.*

return² *n* **1** [C;U (**from, to**)] the act or an example of returning (RETURN¹ (1)): *We look forward to your return (from China).* | **On his return** (=when he came back) *he found her asleep.* | *Keep some food to eat on the return journey.* | *This cold weather has brought a return of the flu epidemic.* | *The army has promised a return to civilian*

rule within two years. **2** [U] the act of giving, putting, or sending something back: *The library is demanding the return of the books.* | *The spectators cheered the tennis champion's return of service.* | *After the game the players arranged a return match.* (=to play each other again) **3** also **returns** *pl.*— [C] an amount of money produced as a profit: *These shares* **have brought in** *good returns.* | *We guarantee a high return on your investment.* **4** [C] an official account, esp. of money earned or spent: *Make sure you put in all your earnings on your tax return.* **5** [C] *BrE* a RETURN³ ticket **6 by return (of post)** *esp. BrE* by the next post: *Please let us know your answer by return.* **7 in return (for)** in exchange or as payment (for): *He agreed to give evidence against the terrorists in return for a guarantee of protection.* | *They are letting us use their computer, and in return we are giving them the results of our research.* **8 many happy returns (of the day)** (used as a birthday greeting)

return³ *BrE‖***round-trip** *AmE*— *adj* (of a ticket or its cost) for a trip from one place to another and back again: *The price is £1 single and £1.80 return.* —compare SINGLE¹ (6); see also DAY RETURN

re·tur·na·ble /rɪˈtɜːnəbəl‖-ɜːr-/ *adj* **1** that can be given or sent back, often to be used again: *returnable bottles* — opposite **nonreturnable** **2** *fml* that must be given or sent back: *The writ is returnable immediately.*

re·turn·er /rɪˈtɜːnəʳ‖-ɜːr-/ *n BrE* a person who goes back to work after a long time away, esp. a woman who returns to a job after spending time at home with her children: *government plans to help returners*

returning of·fi·cer /·ˈ·· ˌ···/ *n* (in Britain) the official in each town or area who arranges an election to Parliament and gives out the result

Reu·ben sand·wich /ˈruːbɪn ˌsænwɪdʒ‖-ˌsændwɪtʃ, -ˌsænwɪtʃ/ *n* (in the US) a popular sandwich made of salt beef, SWISS CHEESE, and SAUERKRAUT usu. on RYE bread

re·u·ni·fy /riːˈjuːnɪfaɪ/ v [T] to join the parts of (e.g. a divided country) again —compare REUNITE —**reunification** /riːˌjuːnɪfɪˈkeɪʃən/ *n* [U] : *the reunification of Germany*

re·u·nion /riːˈjuːnjən/ *n* **1** [C] a meeting of friends or fellow-workers after a separation: *We hold an annual reunion of former students of the college.* **2** [U] the state of being brought together again

re·u·nite /ˌriːjuːˈnaɪt/ v [I;T (**with**)] to (cause to) come or join together again: *Do you think the two parts of Ireland will ever reunite?* | *After the hijacking, the hostages were reunited with their families.*

re·up·hol·ster /ˌriːʌpˈhəʊlstəʳ/ v [T] to replace the coverings and fillings of (a seat): *I'd like to have that chair reupholstered.*

re·use /ˌriːˈjuːz/ v [T] **1** to use again **2** to RECYCLE — **reusable** *adj*

Reu·ters /ˈrɔɪtəz‖-ərz/ a British company which employs journalists in many different countries to send news from all over the world to sell to newspapers, etc.

rev¹ /rev/ *n infml for* REVOLUTION (4): *The engine is on low revs.* (=is turning slowly)

rev² v **-vv-** *infml* **1** [T (**up**)] to increase the speed of (an engine): *Don't rev (up) your engine so loudly — you'll wake the baby.* | (fig.) *We need to rev up production if we're going to reach our target for this year.* **2** [I (**up**)] (of an engine) to increase speed: *We could hear a car revving (up) in the driveway.*

Rev also **Revd** *BrE‖***Rev.** *AmE written abbrev for:* REVEREND: *the Rev D. Macleod*

re·val·ue /riːˈvæljuː/ v [T] **1** to find out or state the latest or real value of; make a new VALUATION of: *We're having all the contents of our house revalued for insurance purposes.* **2** to increase the exchange value of (a country's money): *The dollar is being revalued.* —compare DEVALUE (1) —**uation** /riːˌvæljuˈeɪʃən/ *n* [C;U]

re·vamp /riːˈvæmp/ v [T] *infml* to give a new (and better) form or structure to (something old): *a radical plan to revamp the whole system of secondary education*

re·veal /rɪˈviːl/ v [T] **1** to show or allow (something previously hidden) to be seen: *The curtains opened, to reveal a darkened stage.* **2** to make known (something previously secret or unknown): *Do you promise not to reveal my secret?* | *The investigation has revealed some serious*

faults in the system. [+*that*] *I can now reveal that the new director is to be James Johnson.*

re·veal·ing /rɪˈviːlɪŋ/ *adj* **1** allowing parts to be seen which are usually kept covered: *a very revealing dress* **2** giving some esp. interesting or unexpected information which had been unknown: *She made some very revealing comments when I had a private chat with her.*

re·veil·le /rɪˈvæli‖ˈrevəli/ *n* [(*the*) S] music played as a signal to waken soldiers in the morning: *When (the) reveille sounds|is sounded, we all leap out of bed.*

rev·el /ˈrevəl/ *v* -ll- *BrE‖*-l- *AmE* [I] *old use or humor* to pass the time in dancing, eating, drinking, etc. esp. wildly at a party or celebration: *They were revelling all night.* – ~**ler** *BrE‖* – **er** *AmE n* : *We were kept awake by crowds of noisy revellers.*
  revel in sthg. *phr v* [T] to enjoy greatly; get pleasure from (esp. something unpleasant or something that most other people do not enjoy): *to revel in scandal | She revels in all the attention she gets from the media.* [+*v-ing*] *He seems to revel in inflicting pain.*

rev·e·la·tion /ˌrevəˈleɪʃən/ *n* **1** [U] the making known of something secret: *The revelation of his scandalous past led to his resignation.* **2** [C] an often surprising fact that is made known, esp. one that explains or makes something clear: *Have you read the ex-minister's amazing revelations in the newspaper?* [+*that*] *The revelation that he was her father astonished her.* **3** [C;U] (an example of) the making known of the truth by God

Rev·e·la·tions /ˌrevəˈleɪʃənz/ the final book of the New Testament in the Bible in which the story of the end of the world is told

rev·el·ry /ˈrevəlri/ also **revelries** *pl.*– *n* [U] wild noisy dancing, eating, drinking, etc.; revelling

re·venge¹ /rɪˈvendʒ/ *n* [U (**for, on**)] punishment given to someone in return for harm done to oneself: *We bombed their cities* **in revenge** *for their attacks on ours. | We* **took revenge** *on them by bombing their cities. | a revenge attack | After I'd beaten him at chess I gave him a chance to get his revenge.* (=by beating me) – ~**ful** *adj*

revenge² *v* [T] **1** to do something in revenge for (harm done to someone, esp. to oneself): *to revenge a defeat|an injustice* **2 revenge oneself on** to take revenge on (a person or group)

rev·e·nue /ˈrevₐnjuː‖-nuː/ also **revenues** *pl.*– *n* [U] income, esp. that which the government receives as tax: *The government was short of money because of falling oil revenues.* –see also INLAND REVENUE, INTERNAL REVENUE SERVICE

re·ver·be·rate /rɪˈvɜːbəreɪt‖-ɜːr-/ *v* [I] (of sound) to be thrown back again and again: ECHO² repeatedly: *The thunder reverberated across the valley.* | (fig.) *The shocking news reverberated round the world.* –compare RESOUND –~**rant** *adj*

re·ver·be·ra·tion /rɪˌvɜːbəˈreɪʃən‖-ɜːr-/ *n* [C *usu. pl.*;U] (a) sound heard again and again: *The reverberation(s) of the shot died away slowly.*

re·vere /rɪˈvɪəʳ/ *v* [T] *fml* to give great respect and admiration to; regard with reverence: *to revere the memory of a great leader | a much revered institution*

Revere, Paul (1735–1818) an American HERO who is known for his ride to warn the people of Massachusetts that British soldiers were coming, during the AMERICAN REVOLUTION. This is the subject of a poem by Longfellow.

rev·e·rence¹ /ˈrevₐrₐns/ *n* **1** [U (**for**)] *fml* great respect and admiration mixed with love: *The old queen was held in great reverence.* **2** [C] *old use, humor, or IrE* (used when speaking to or of a priest): *Will you take a glass of sherry,* **your reverence**?

reverence² *v* [T] *fml rare* to revere

rev·e·rend /ˈrevₐrₐnd/ *adj* [A] *fml* being a priest: *A reverend gentleman is here to see you, sir!*

Reverend *n* (a title of respect for) a Christian priest: *the Reverend Donald Jones | When will the new church be finished, Reverend?*

Reverend Moth·er /ˌ··· ˈ··/ *n* (a title of respect for) the MOTHER SUPERIOR of a CONVENT

rev·e·rent /ˈrevₐrₐnt/ *adj* showing a feeling of reverence: *They all maintained a reverent silence.* –opposite **irreverent** – ~**ly** *adv*

rev·e·ren·tial /ˌrevəˈrenʃəl◂/ *adj fml* respectful; expressing reverence: *a reverential bow of the head* – ~**ly** *adv*

rev·e·rie /ˈrevəri/ *n* [C;U] *fml* (a state of) pleasant thoughts and dreams while awake; DAYDREAM: *She fell into a reverie about the past. | He was sunk in reverie and did not hear me.*

re·vers /rɪˈvɪəʳ/ *n* -**vers** /ˈvɪəz‖ˈvɪərz/ [*usu. pl.*] a part of a coat or dress turned back at the neck to show the inside, which may be a different colour from the rest –compare LAPEL

re·vers·al /rɪˈvɜːsəl‖-ɜːr-/ *n* **1** [C;U] (a case of) being reversed: *In a complete reversal of his previous decision, he gave permission for the project to go ahead.* **2** [C] a defeat or piece of bad luck: *They were finally successful in spite of a number of reversals. | We experienced a* **reversal of fortune** *in the second half of the game.*

re·verse¹ /rɪˈvɜːs‖-ɜːrs/ *adj* [A] opposite to the usual or former, esp. in position or direction: *Please read the names on this list* **in reverse order**. (=from the end to the beginning) | *the reverse side* (=back) *of the cloth*

reverse² *v* **1** [I;T] to go or cause (a vehicle) to go backwards: *The car reversed through the gate. | I reversed (the car) through the gate.* **2** [T] to change round (usual order or positions): *They reversed the normal order of the ceremony and had the prayers at the beginning.* **3** [T] to change (e.g. a decision or judgment) to the opposite: *The appeal court reversed the original verdict and set the prisoner free. | The company's profits have been steadily falling, and his job is to reverse this trend.* **4** [T] to turn (something) over, so as to show the back: *She reversed the sheet of paper.* **5 reverse the charges** *BrE ‖* also **call collect** *AmE*– to make a telephone call to be paid for by the person receiving it –~**versible** *adj* : *This coat is reversible; you can wear it inside out.* –~**versibility** /rɪˌvɜːsɪˈbɪlɪti‖rɪˌvɜːr-/ *n* [U]

reverse³ *n* **1** [*the* (**of**)] the opposite; the other way round: *He did the reverse of what we expected: instead of being angry, he bought us a drink. | "Are you pleased?" "Quite the reverse, I'm very disappointed."* **2** [U] also **reverse gear** /·ˌ· ˈ·/– the position of the controls that causes backward movement, esp. in a car: *Put the car into reverse.* **3** [C] *fml* a defeat or change to a worse condition; SETBACK: *The defeat of these proposals was a serious reverse for the President. | After several reverses the enemy was forced to retreat.* **4** [*the*] the side of a coin that does not show a person's head: *The British ten-pence piece has a lion on the reverse.* –opposite **obverse**; see also HEADS, TAILS

reverse di·scrim·i·na·tion /·ˌ· ···ˈ··/ *n* [U] the act or idea of treating a usu. favoured group in an unfair way in order to give advantage to a group which is usu. treated unfairly: *Bakke claimed that he was a victim of reverse discrimination because he, a white man, was denied entry to medical school so that the school could admit more black people.* –compare POSITIVE DISCRIMINATION

reversing light /·ˈ·· ˌ·/ also **back-up light** *AmE*– *n* a light on the back of a car which comes on when the car is going backwards

re·ver·sion /rɪˈvɜːʃən‖rɪˈvɜːrʒən/ *n* [S;U+**to**] *fml* **1** a return to a former (usu. undesirable) condition or habit: *the danger of a reversion to anarchy in the region* **2** *law* the reverting of property to an owner

re·vert /rɪˈvɜːt‖-ɜːrt/ *v*
  revert to sbdy./sthg. *phr v* [T] **1** to go back to (a former, usu. undesirable condition or habit): *After the settlers left, the area soon reverted to desert. | We thought he was a reformed character, but he soon* **reverted to type** *and started stealing again.* [+*v-ing*] *He's stopped taking drugs now, but he may revert to taking them again.* **2** to talk about or consider again; go back to (a former subject of conversation): *I'd like to revert to your earlier point about our export trade.* **3** *law* (esp. of land) to become the property of (a former owner) again: *When he dies his land will revert to the state.*

re·vet·ment /rɪˈvetmₐnt/ *n tech* a surface of stone or other building material added for strength to a wall that holds back loose earth, water, etc.

re·view¹ /rɪˈvjuː/ *n* **1** [C;U] (an act of) reviewing (REVIEW² (1)): *an annual review of the department's expenditure | The state medical service has been|come very much* **under review** *recently. | All prices are subject to review.* (=may be changed) **2 a** [C] a magazine or newspaper article that gives a judgment on a new book, play, television show, etc.: *I hope your new book gets good|favourable reviews.* **b** [U] the writing of these articles: *A* **review copy** *of a book is one that is sent to a magazine for review|for review purposes.* **3** [C] an official show of the armed forces in the presence of a king, president, officer of high-rank, etc.: *a naval review* **4** [C] a REVUE

review[2] *v* **1** [T] to consider and judge carefully (an event or situation): *The committee is reviewing its decision.* | *The airport authorities have promised to review their security arrangements.* **2** [I;T] to write a REVIEW[1] (2) of (a play, book, etc.): *The play was very well reviewed.* (=was praised by the reviewers) | *Susan has been doing some reviewing for "The Times".* **3** [T] to hold a REVIEW[1] (3) of (armed forces) **4** [I;T] *AmE for* REVISE (3)

re·view·er /rɪˈvjuːəʳ/ *n* a person who writes REVIEWS[1] (2)

re·vile /rɪˈvaɪl/ *v* [T] *fml* to express hatred of; speak very strongly and angrily to or about: *Their much reviled system in fact works far better than many highly praised ones elsewhere.* —**viler** *n*

re·vise /rɪˈvaɪz/ *v* **1** [T] to change (opinions, intentions, etc.) because of new information or more thought: *I can see I'll have to revise my ideas about Tom — he's really quite clever after all.* | *Our original forecast of this year's profits has now been* **revised upwards.** (=we now think profits will be higher) **2** [T] to read through (a piece of writing) carefully, making improvements and putting mistakes right: *He revised the manuscript of his book before sending it to the publisher.* **3** [I (**for**);T] *BrE‖*review *AmE—* to study again (lessons or a subject already learnt), usu. before an examination: *I'm revising my history notes for the exam on Monday.* —**reviser** *n*

Revised Stan·dard Ver·sion /·ˌ·ˈ··/ *also* **RSV—** *n* a revision of the Bible prepared by American SCHOLARS which came out in 1952

Revised Ver·sion /·ˌ· ˈ··/ [*the*] a British revision of the Authorized Version of the Bible printed in 1881 and 1885

re·vi·sion /rɪˈvɪʒən/ *n* **1** [C;U] (an act of) revising something, esp. a piece of writing: *That book needs a lot of revision|has already had three revisions.* **2** [C] a piece of writing that has been revised **3** [U (**for**)] *BrE* the work of studying again lessons already learnt: *She did some revision for the exam.*

re·vi·sion·is·m /rɪˈvɪʒənɪzəm/ *n* [U] *often derog* the questioning of the main beliefs of an already existing political system, esp. a Marxist one —**ist** *adj, n*

re·vi·tal·ize *also* **-ise** *BrE* /riːˈvaɪtəl-aɪz/ *v* [T] to put new strength or power into: *The discovery of vast new coalfields has revitalized our mining industry.* —compare DEVITALIZE —**ization** /riːˌvaɪtəl aɪˈzeɪʃən‖-tələ-/ *n* [U]

re·viv·al /rɪˈvaɪvəl/ *n* **1** [C;U] a case of something being brought back into use or existence; renewal: *There has been a|some revival of interest in this composer's music.| a revival in consumer demand after a period of slow business* **2** [C] a performance of an old play after many years: *She starred in a revival of "West Side Story".* **3** [C] *also* **revival meeting** /·ˈ·· ˌ··/— a public religious meeting, with music, famous speakers, etc., intended to waken and increase people's interest in Christianity

re·viv·al·ist /rɪˈvaɪvəlɪ̆st/ *n* a person who holds revival meetings

revival tent /·ˈ·· ˌ·/ *n AmE* a large tent which is moved from place to place for the holding of REVIVALS (3): *a revival tent preacher*

re·vive /rɪˈvaɪv/ *v* **1** [I;T] to become or make conscious or healthy again: *That rose will revive if you water it.* | *He felt rather faint but the fresh air soon revived him.* **2** [I;T] to come or bring back into use or existence: *Interest in this composer's music has revived recently.* | *It's nice that these old customs are being revived.* | *The company are going to revive an old musical for their next production.| Seeing her old schoolfriend again revived memories of her childhood.*

re·viv·i·fy /riːˈvɪvɪ̆faɪ/ *v* [T] *fml* to give new life and health to

rev·o·ca·tion /ˌrevəˈkeɪʃən/ *n* [C;U] (an act of) revoking (REVOKE (1)): *the revocation of an order*

re·voke /rɪˈvəʊk/ *v* **1** [T] to put an end to (a law, decision, permission, etc.); CANCEL: *The government has revoked its permission for them to enter the country.* —see also IR-

REVOCABLE **2** [I] (in card games such as BRIDGE) to break the rules by playing a card of the wrong kind (SUIT) when one has a card of the right kind

re·volt[1] /rɪˈvəʊlt/ *v* **1** [I (**against**)] (esp. of a large number of people) to take strong and often violent action against those in power, usu. with the aim of taking power from them; REBEL: *The people revolted against the military government.* **2** [I+*prep*;T] to (cause to) feel sick and shocked; (cause to) turn away with violent dislike: *We were revolted by their cruelty.* | *All civilized people will revolt at|from|against this terrible crime.* —see also REVULSION

revolt[2] *n* **1** [C;U (**against**)] (an example of) the act of revolting (REVOLT[1] (1)): *They seized power in a revolt.* | *The whole nation is in (a state of)* **revolt** *against the tyrannical regime.* | (fig.) *The president faces a revolt among his own supporters in the Senate if he persists with this plan.* (=they will refuse to support him) **2** [(**in**) U] REVULSION

re·volt·ing /rɪˈvəʊltɪŋ/ *adj* extremely unpleasant; DISGUSTING: *a revolting smell of bad eggs* | *Their sexual practices were revolting to her.* —**ly** *adv* : *Your socks are revoltingly dirty.*

rev·o·lu·tion /ˌrevəˈluːʃən/ *n* **1** [C;U] (a time of) great, usu. sudden, social and political change, esp. the changing of a ruler and/or political system by force: *the French revolution* | *The constant oppression of the workers led inevitably to strife and revolution.* —see also AMERICAN REVOLUTION, COUNTER-REVOLUTION, CULTURAL REVOLUTION, FRENCH REVOLUTION, INDUSTRIAL REVOLUTION, PALACE REVOLUTION, RUSSIAN REVOLUTION **2** [C (**in**)] a complete change in ways of thinking, methods of working, etc.: *The invention of air travel caused a revolution in our way of living.| the computer revolution* **3** [C;U (**round**)] (one complete) circular movement round a fixed point: *the revolution of the moon round the Earth* | *The Earth makes one revolution round the sun each year.* **4** [C] *also* **rev** *infml—* (in a machine) one complete circular movement on a central point, e.g. of a wheel: *a speed of 100 revolutions per minute* —see also REVOLVE (1)

rev·o·lu·tion·a·ry[1] /ˌrevəˈluːʃənəri◂‖-ʃəneri◂/ *adj* **1** [A] connected with or being a REVOLUTION (1): *a revolutionary leader* | *He suffered for his revolutionary principles.* **2** *usu. apprec* completely new and different: *a revolutionary new way of growing rice*

revolutionary[2] *n* a person who joins in or supports a REVOLUTION (1): *The revolutionaries are attacking the palace.*

Revolutionary War /ˌ·····ˈ·/ [*the*] another name for the AMERICAN REVOLUTION

rev·o·lu·tion·ize *also* **-ise** *BrE* /ˌrevəˈluːʃənaɪz/ *v* [T] to cause a complete change in; cause a REVOLUTION (2) in: *The discovery of the new drug has revolutionized the treatment of many diseases.*

re·volve /rɪˈvɒlv‖rɪˈvɑːlv/ *v* **1** [I;T (**on**)] to (cause to) spin round on a central point: *The Earth revolves on its own axis once every 24 hours.* | *The hotel has revolving doors.* **2** [I+*adv*|*prep*,T] *fml rare* to consider or be considered carefully: *He revolved the main points in his mind.* | *All sorts of mad ideas revolved in|around my mind.*

revolve around sthg. *phr v* [T *no pass.*] **1** [*not in progressive forms*] to have as a centre or main subject: *A baby's life revolves mainly around its mother.* | *He thinks the whole world revolves around him.* (=He thinks he is more important than anyone|anything else.) **2** *esp. AmE for* REVOLVE **round**

revolve round/about sthg. *phr v* [T *no pass.*] to move in circles round: *The moon revolves round the Earth.*

re·volv·er /rɪˈvɒlvəʳ‖rɪˈvɑːl-/ *n* a PISTOL (=a small gun) which has a revolving container for bullets, allowing several shots to be fired without reloading —see picture at GUN

revolving door

revolving door /·ˌ·· ˈ·/ *n* a door that has four pieces of wood or glass set at RIGHT ANGLES to each other and which move in a circle around a central point. This type of door is usu. used as an entrance to large buildings and not houses and allows people to come in without losing all the heat inside the building.

re·vue, **review** /rɪ'vjuː/ n a light theatrical show with short acts, songs, dances, and jokes, esp. about the events and fashions of the present time

re·vul·sion /rɪ'vʌlʃən/ n [S;U (**against**)] (a) feeling of being deeply shocked and revolted (REVOLT¹ (2)): *The scenes of torture produced a feeling of revulsion in most viewers.* | *They turned away in revulsion.*

re·ward¹ /rɪ'wɔːd‖-ɔːrd/ n **1** [C;U] (something gained or received as) a return for doing something good or valuable: *As a reward for passing her exams, she got a new bike from her parents.* | *A pension of £3000 a year is not much of a reward for a lifetime's service.* | *I don't expect anything in reward; I did it because I enjoyed it.* | *They will expect some reward after working so hard.* | *The job isn't well paid, but there are rewards.* (=it brings advantages in other ways) **2** [C (**for**)] an amount of money given to someone who helps the police or brings back lost property: *The police are offering a big reward for information about the robbery.*

reward² v [T (**for, with**)] to give a reward to (someone) or for (an action): *He was generously rewarded.* | *They rewarded the boy with £5 for bringing back the lost dog.* | *How can I reward your kindness?* | *After hours of searching, their patience was rewarded and they found what they were looking for.*

re·ward·ing /rɪ'wɔːdɪŋ‖-ɔːr-/ adj (of an experience or action) worth doing or having; giving satisfaction, but perhaps not much money: *Nursing can be a very rewarding career.*

re·wind¹ /ˌriː'waɪnd/ v [I;T] to (cause to) wind backwards or in an opposite direction: *Rewind the tape and play that song again.* | *When it reaches the end the tape will rewind automatically.*

re·wind² /'riːwaɪnd/ n **1** an act of rewinding: *These tapes tend to fall apart after a dozen rewinds.* **2** also **rewind but·ton** /'·· ˌ··/— a button on a tape player or computer that causes a tape to rewind: *Push the rewind till the counter is back at zero.*

re·wire /ˌriː'waɪər/ v [T] to put new electric wires into (a building)

re·word /ˌriː'wɜːd‖-'wɜːrd/ v [T] to say or write again in different words: *This section of the contract should be reworded to make its meaning clearer.*

re·work /ˌriː'wɜːk‖-'wɜːrk/ v [T] to put (music, writing, etc.) into a new and different form (in order to use again): *a reworking of familiar ideas*

re·write /ˌriː'raɪt/ v -**wrote** /'rəʊt/, -**written** /'rɪtn/ [T] to write again in a different, esp. more suitable way: *He had to rewrite the article when the lawyers pointed out the danger of libel.* —**rewrite** /'riːraɪt/ n : *a modern rewrite of an old story*

Rex /reks/ n Lat **1** [after n] (the title used in official writing after the name of a ruling British king): *Georgius Rex* **2** law (used, when a king is ruling, in titles of British law cases) the governing power of the state: *in the action Rex v Jones* (=the state against Jones) —compare REGINA

Reye's syn·drome /'raɪz ˌsɪndrəʊm, 'reɪz-/ n [U] med a rare and dangerous illness which occurs usu. in children, and often after they have taken ASPIRIN. For this reason it is now not recommended (RECOMMEND) that children under 12 be given aspirin as a painkiller.

Rey·kja·vik /'reɪkjəvɪk/ the capital city and main port of Iceland. It is the centre of the COD-fishing industry.

Rey·nard the Fox /ˌrenɑːd ðə 'fɒks, ˌreɪ-‖-ɑːrd ðə 'fɑːks/ BrE a FOX in various old stories, which represents a man who, while breaking certain of society's rules, always escapes punishment by his cleverness

Rey·nolds /'renəldz/, **Burt** /bɜːt‖bɜːrt/ (1936–) an American film actor known for adventure films and comedies (COMEDY) such as *Deliverance*, *City Heat*, and *Smokey and the Bandit*

Reynolds, Sir Joshua (1723–92) an English painter who became the first president of the ROYAL ACADEMY. He is famous esp. for his PORTRAITs.

RFD /ˌɑːr ef 'diː/ n [U] AmE rural free delivery; used for postal addresses outside towns: *Our address is R.F.D.3, Mayberry, Arkansas.*

rhap·so·dize also -**dise** BrE /'ræpsədaɪz/ v [I (**about, over**)] to express eager and excited approval: *Mother rhapsodized about/over your beautiful kitchen.*

rhap·so·dy /'ræpsədi/ n **1** [(**about, over**)] an expression of eager and excited approval: *They all* **went into** (=expressed) **rhapsodies** *over the beauty of the scenery.* **2** a dreamy piece of music written as if made up as one plays it, not in any regular form —**dic** /ræp'sɒdɪk‖ -'sɑː-/ adj : *a rhapsodic passage in the slow movement of the symphony*

rhea /'rɪə, 'riːə/ n a large South American bird like the OSTRICH but smaller

rheo·stat /'rɪəstæt/ n an instrument that controls the loudness of radio sound or the brightness of electric light, by limiting the flow of electric current

rhe·sus /'riːsəs/ also **rhesus mon·key** /'·· ˌ··/— n a small short-tailed pale brown North Indian monkey, often used in scientific tests

Rhesus fac·tor /'·· ˌ··/ also **Rh factor**— [the] tech a substance whose presence (**Rhesus positive**) or absence (**Rhesus negative**) in the red blood cells may have dangerous effects when a person receives the blood of another person during medical treatment

rhet·o·ric /'retərɪk/ n [U] **1** the art of speaking or writing in a way that is likely to persuade or influence people **2** the language used, esp. by politicians, in doing this: *Despite their tough anti-American rhetoric, the government is privately trying to maintain good relations with the US.* **3** derog speech or writing that sounds fine and important, but is really insincere or without meaning

rhe·tor·i·cal /rɪ'tɒrɪkəl‖-'tɔː-, -'tɑː-/ adj **1** (of a question) asked only to gain an effect, and not expecting any answer: *a* **rhetorical question**, *such as "Who knows how long the war will last?"* **2** of, connected with, or showing rhetoric: *The speaker showed great rhetorical skill.* —~**ly** /kli/ adv : *I was only asking rhetorically; I didn't really expect an answer.*

rhet·o·ri·cian /ˌretə'rɪʃən/ n fml a person trained and skilled in RHETORIC (1)

rheu·mat·ic /ruː'mætɪk/ adj **1** of or connected with RHEUMATISM: *a rheumatic condition of the joints* **2** suffering from rheumatism: *a rheumatic old woman who can't walk very fast* —see also RHEUMATICS

rheumatic fe·ver /ˌ·,·· '··/ n [U] a serious infectious disease, esp. in children, with fever, swelling of the joints, and possible damage to the heart

rheu·mat·ick·y /ruː'mætɪki/ adj infml for RHEUMATIC (2)

rheu·mat·ics /ruː'mætɪks/ n [P] infml, esp. BrE rheumatism

rheu·ma·tis·m /'ruːmətɪzəm/ n [U] a disease causing pain and stiffness in the joints or muscles of the body

rheu·ma·toid /'ruːmətɔɪd/ adj tech of rheumatism or a long-continuing disease (**rheumatoid arthritis**) causing pain and stiffness in the joints of the legs and arms and often making them lose their proper shape

Rh fac·tor /ˌɑːr 'eɪtʃ ˌfæktər/ n the RHESUS FACTOR

Rhine /raɪn/ [the] the longest river in W Europe, which is used to carry coal and other products used in industry

rhine·stone /'raɪnstəʊn/ n [C;U] a shining colourless jewel made from glass or a transparent rock and intended to look like a diamond

Rhine wine /ˌ· '·/ n [C;U] any of several white wines produced in the Rhine valley

rhi·no·ce·ros /raɪ'nɒsərəs‖ -'nɑː-/ also **rhi·no** /'raɪnəʊ/ infml— n **rhinoceros** or **rhinoceroses** a large heavy thick-skinned animal of Africa or Asia, with either one or two horns on its nose

rhinoceros

rhi·no·plas·ty /'raɪnəʊˌplæsti/ n [U] plastic SURGERY of the nose, performed to improve the shape of a person's nose, usu. for reasons of appearance rather than any medical reason —see also NOSE JOB —**plastic** adj

rhi·zome /'raɪzəʊm/ n tech the thick stem of some plants such as the IRIS, which lies flat along the ground with roots and leaves growing from it

Rhode Is·land /ˈrəʊd ˌaɪlənd‖rəʊd ˈaɪlənd/ *written abbrev:* **RI** the smallest of the US states, in New England. It was one of the 13 original British colonies (COLONY). −see colour map on pages 1374−5

Rhode Island Red /ˌ‧ ‧‧ ‧‖‧ ‧‧ ‧‧/ *n* a type of American hen which has dark red-brown feathers

Rhodes /rəʊdz/ a large Greek island near the coast of Turkey. This island was known for one of the Seven Wonders of the World, the **Colossus of Rhodes**, which was destroyed by an EARTHQUAKE in about 224 BC.

Rhodes, Ce·cil /ˈsesɪl/ (1853−1902) a South African politician who was born in Britain and was PRIME MINISTER of the Cape Colony in 1890−96. He was responsible for the formation of Rhodesia, now Zimbabwe.

Rhodes, Zan·dra /ˈzɑːndrə/ (1940−   ) an English fashion DESIGNER who is known for her expensive and strange dresses

Rho·de·si·a /rəʊˈdiːsʃə‖-ʒə/ a former name for Zimbabwe —**·sian** *n,adj*

Rhodes Schol·ar·ship /ˌ‧ ‧‧‧/ *n* a SCHOLARSHIP available to students from America, the British COMMONWEALTH, and Germany to allow them to study at Oxford University − **Rhodes scholar** *n*

rho·do·den·dron /ˌrəʊdəˈdendrən/ *n* a large bush which has large bright flowers and which keeps its leaves in winter

rhom·boid[1] /ˈrɒmbɔɪd‖ˈrɑːm-/ *n tech* (in GEOMETRY) a four-sided shape whose opposite sides are equal; PARALLELO GRAM −see picture at QUADRILATERAL

rhomboid[2] *also* **rhom·boid·al** /rɒmˈbɔɪdl‖rɑːm-/− *adj [no comp.] tech* in the shape of a rhombus

rhom·bus /ˈrɒmbəs‖ˈrɑːm-/ *n tech* (in GEOMETRY) a shape with four equal straight sides, esp. one that is not square −see picture at QUADRILATERAL

Rhon·dda /ˈrɒndə‖ˈrɑː-/ a DISTRICT in Wales, sometimes called **the Rhondda valley**, and mainly known for coalmining, although this is no longer so important in the area

Rhône /rəʊn/ an important river in Europe, used for HYDROELECTRIC power in France

rhu·barb /ˈruːbɑːb‖-ɑːrb/ *n* **1** [U] a broad-leaved garden plant whose thick red juicy stems are eaten, often having been stewed (STEW[1] (1)) and served with CUSTARD **2** [U] *infml* the sound made by actors to suggest many people talking at the same time **3** [C] *AmE old fash* a noisy argument

rhyme[1] /raɪm/ *n* **1** [C] a short and not serious piece of writing, using words that rhyme: *He made up funny rhymes to amuse the children.* −see also NURSERY RHYME **2** [C (for)] a word that rhymes with another: *"Fold" and "cold" are rhymes.* | *I can't find a rhyme for "donkey".* **3** [U] (the use of) words that rhyme at the ends of the lines in poetry: *Shakespeare sometimes wrote in rhyme.* **4** **rhyme or reason** [*usu. in negatives*] (any) sense or meaning: *There doesn't seem to be any rhyme or reason in his demands − is he mad?*

rhyme[2] *v* [*not in progressive forms*] **1** [I (**with**)] (of words or lines of poetry) to end with the same sound, including a vowel: *"House" rhymes with "mouse".* | *"School" and "fool" rhyme.* | *The last two lines of this poem don't rhyme properly.* **2** [T (**with**)] to put together (words or one word with another) ending with the same sound, including a vowel: *You can rhyme "duty" with "beauty" but you can't rhyme "box" and "backs".* | *a rhyming couplet* (=two lines of poetry that rhyme)

rhyme·ster /ˈraɪmstəʳ/ *n old use derog* a writer of poems, esp. bad ones

rhyming slang /ˌ‧‧ ‧‧/ *n* [U] (the use, esp. by some people from London (COCKNEYS), of) words and phrases that rhyme with those which are really meant: *"Plates of meat" is rhyming slang for "feet".*

rhyth·m /ˈrɪðəm/ *n* [C;U] (a) regular repeated pattern of sounds or movements: *This music is written in a rhythm of three beats to a bar.* | *the rhythm of his heartbeats* | *the exciting rhythms of African drum music* | **the rhythm section** *of a band* (=drums and other instruments that provide a strong beat) | (fig.) *the rhythm of the seasons* −compare METRE[2]; see also BIORHYTHMS

rhythm and blues /ˌ‧‧ ‧ ‧‧/ *also* **R and B**− *n* [U] a type of popular music which is a mixture of BLUES and JAZZ and often uses amplified (AMPLIFY) instruments to make a powerful beat. It was first developed by black musicians, who greatly influenced many ROCK musicians.

rhyth·mic /ˈrɪðmɪk/ *also* **rhyth·mi·cal** /-kəl/− *adj* having rhythm: *the rhythmic beating of one's heart* −see also EU-RHYTHMICS − − **ally** /kli/ *adv*

rhythmic gym·nas·tics /ˌ‧‧ ‧‧‧/ *n* [U] a kind of GYMNASTICS in which people perform with long RIBBONS, balls, and HOOPS (ring-like objects) to music

rhythm meth·od /ˈ‧‧ ˌ‧/ *n* [*the*] a method of BIRTH CONTROL which depends on having sex only at a time when the woman is not likely to CONCEIVE

▶CULTURAL NOTE This is a method commonly used by people such as ROMAN CATHOLICS who believe that any other form of birth control is wrong, because they think that the purpose of sex is to have children and that it is wrong to do anything to interfere with this process.◀

RI /ˌɑːr ˈaɪ/ **1** *abbrev. for:* RELIGIOUS INSTRUCTION **2** *written abbrev. for:* RHODE ISLAND

ri·al /riˈɑːl‖riˈɔːl, -ˈɑːl/ *n* a RIYAL

rib[1] /rɪb/ *n* **1** any of the 12 pairs of bones running round the chest of a person or animal, from the SPINE to where they join at the front: *He suffered three cracked ribs in the accident.* | *We're having roast ribs of beef for dinner.* −see picture at SKELETON

▶CULTURAL NOTE According to the Bible, God made Eve, the first woman, from one of the ribs of Adam, the first man.◀

2 a curved piece of wood, metal, etc. used for forming or strengthening a frame: *the ribs of a boat|an umbrella* **3** one of a group of long thin raised lines in a pattern: *the ribs of a leaf* **4** **dig/poke someone in the ribs** to push someone with a finger or the elbow so as to attract attention

rib[2] *v* **-bb-** [T] *infml* to make fun of in a friendly way; laugh at: *All the boys ribbed him for keeping a pet pig.*

rib·ald /ˈrɪbəld/ *adj fml* rudely humorous in a loud, insensitive, and disrespectful way: *ribald jokes* | *the ribald laughter of the drunken men* | *a crowd of ribald soldiers*

rib·ald·ry /ˈrɪbəldri/ *n* [U] *fml* ribald language or jokes: *We've had enough of this ribaldry − this is a serious occasion.*

ribbed /rɪbd/ *adj* having a pattern of long thin raised lines: *a ribbed fabric* | *ribbed socks*

Rib·ben·trop /ˈrɪbəntrɒp‖-trɑːp/, **Jo·a·chim von** /ˈjəʊəkɪm vɒn‖-vɑːn/ (1893−1946) a German leader in the NAZI PARTY who advised Hitler on foreign affairs and was German AMBASSADOR to Britain from 1936−38. He was tried and hanged at Nuremberg as a war criminal.

rib·bing /ˈrɪbɪŋ/ *n* [U] a pattern of long thin raised lines in knitting (KNIT): *the ribbing round the tops of his socks*

rib·bon /ˈrɪbən/ *also* **rib·and** /ˈrɪbənd/*old use*− *n* **1** [C;U] (a piece of) silk or other material woven in a long narrow band and used for tying things, for decoration, etc.: *She wore red ribbons in her hair.* | *I must get some more typewriter ribbon.* **2** [C] a piece of ribbon in a special colour or pattern, worn to show that one has received a particular military honour **3** [C] a long irregular narrow band; STRIP: *The old torn curtains hung in ribbons.* | *The cat has torn my scarf to ribbons.* | *His coat was in ribbons.* (=very badly torn) | (fig.) *a ribbon of mist along the river bank*

ribbon de·vel·op·ment /ˈ‧‧ ‧ˌ‧‧/ *n* [U] *usu. derog* (the practice of building) long lines of houses along the sides of main roads leading out of a city

rib cage /ˈ‧ ‧/ *n* the arrangement of RIBs in the body that encloses and protects the lungs −see picture at RESPIRATORY

Ri·be·na /raɪˈbiːnə/ *n* [U] *tdmk* a drink made from BLACK-CURRANTS and sugar which is very popular in Britain with young children, mixed with cold or hot water

ri·bo·fla·vin /ˌraɪbəʊˈfleɪvɪn‖ˌraɪbə-/ *n* [U] *tech* a substance (VITAMIN B2) that exists naturally in meat, milk, and certain vegetables, and is important for human health

rice /raɪs/ *n* [U] **1** a plant grown in wet warm places for its seed **2** the seed of this plant, which is cooked and eaten everywhere in the world: *a plate of boiled rice* |

chicken and fried rice —see also BROWN RICE, WILD RICE, and see picture at CEREAL

Rice, An·ne·ka /ˈænɪkə/ (1958–) a woman, popular on British television, who became known through the programme *Treasure Hunt* in which she had to do a lot of running and travelling by HELICOPTER to try to find hidden TREASURE

Rice-Da·vies /ˌ· ˈ··/, **Mandy** (1944–) an English model known for her involvement in the Profumo SCANDAL in 1963 because of her friendship with Christine Keeler — see PROFUMO SCANDAL

Rice Kris·pies, rice crispies /ˌraɪs ˈkrɪspiz/ *n* [P] *tdmk* a breakfast food made from rice and usu. eaten with milk and sugar. In advertising, Rice Krispies are sold with the phrase "snap, crackle, and pop" because this is supposed to describe the noise they make when you pour milk onto them.

rice pad·dy /ˈ· ˌ··/ *n* a PADDY[1]

rice pa·per /ˈ· ˌ··/ *n* [U] **1** a thin paper made esp. in China and used by ARTISTs there **2** a special form of this that can be eaten, and is used in cooking, esp. on the bottom of certain BISCUITs to stop them sticking to the tin while they cook

rice pud·ding /ˌ· ˈ··/ *n* [U] a sweet dish made of rice, milk, and sugar which is cooked for a long time in an OVEN. In Britain it is considered to be TRADITIONAL British food, but is not very common now.

rich /rɪtʃ/ *adj* **1** [also *n*, *(the)*P] wealthy; possessing a lot of money or other valuable goods or property: *a rich banker* | *Times are hard for* **rich and poor** *alike.* | *The rich get richer and the poor get poorer.* **2** [F+**in**] also **-rich**— possessing or containing a lot of the stated thing: *Sardines are rich in oil.* | *The canal had been receiving nitrogen-rich run off from agricultural lands for years.* | *a city rich in ancient buildings* **3** expensive, valuable, and beautiful: *The walls were hung with rich silks.* **4** (of food) containing a lot of cream, sugar, eggs, etc.: *a very rich Christmas cake* **5** (of land) good for growing plants in; FERTILE: *rich soil* | (fig.) *This subject offers a rich field for advanced study.* **6** (of a sound or colour) deep, strong, and beautiful: *the rich notes of the church organ* | *a rich dark red* **7** [F] *infml* amusing but often rather annoying: *"They've made John the captain."* *"That's rich! Even I can play football better than him!"* —opposite **poor** (for 1,5) **8 for richer for poorer** *quote* part of the Christian marriage service, in which the people getting married promise to love each other whether they are rich or poor —see also MARRIAGE — ~ **ness** *n* [U] : *the richness of the furnishings/the soil/the food*

Rich·ard /ˈrɪtʃəd‖-ərd/, **Cliff** (1940–) an English popular music singer who has been making popular music since the 1950s, originally with his group The Shadows. His hit songs include *Living Doll, Move It,* and *We Don't Talk Anymore.* He is well known for his youthful appearance and his Christian faith.

Cliff Richard

Richard I /ˌrɪtʃəd ðə ˈfɜːst‖-ərd ðə ˈfɜːrst/ (1157–99) see RICHARD THE LIONHEART

Richard II /ˌrɪtʃəd ðə ˈsekənd‖-ərd-/ **1** (1367–1400) the king of England from 1377 to 1399, who had many of his opponents killed so that he had complete power. He was removed by PARLIAMENT and died mysteriously after being imprisoned in 1399. **2** a play by William Shakespeare about the life of Richard II

Richard III /ˌrɪtʃəd ðə ˈθɜːd‖-ərd ðə ˈθɜːrd/ **1** (1452–85) the king of England from 1483 to 1485 thought to have ordered the killing of his NEPHEWs. He was killed at the battle of Bosworth Field after losing his horse. **2** a play by William Shakespeare about the life of Richard III. It includes the line: **A horse! a horse! my kingdom for a horse!**, said by Richard III when he has lost his horse during the battle of Bosworth Field.

Rich·ards /ˈrɪtʃədz‖-ərdz/, **Viv** /vɪv/ (1952–) a West Indian CRICKETER

Richard Shops /ˈ·· ˌ·/ (the name of) a group of shops found in large towns in Britain which sell women's fashions

Rich·ard·son /ˈrɪtʃədsən‖-ərd-/, **Sir Ralph** /rælf/ (1902–83) an English actor known for his Shakespearean ROLES on stage, as well as films such as *Our Man in Havana* and *O Lucky Man!*

Richardson, Sam·u·el /ˈsæmjuəl/ (1689–1761) an English writer who influenced the development of the modern NOVEL, with such books as *Pamela* and *Clarissa*, written in the form of letters

Richard the Lionheart /ˌ··· ˈ ···/ also **Richard Coeur de Li·on** /-ˈkɜː də ˈliːɒn‖-ˌkɜːr də ˈlaɪən/— (1157–99) Richard I, the King of England from 1189 to 1199, who spent a long time fighting in the CRUSADEs (=holy wars) and who was popular for his gentlemanly behaviour and his bravery

Riche·lieu /ˈriːʃljɜː‖ˈriːʃəluː/, **Cardinal** (1585–1642) a French CARDINAL who was very powerful and had a lot of influence with the French King Louis XIII. He is remembered esp. for destroying the political power of the Huguenots in France.

rich·es /ˈrɪtʃɪz/ *n* [P] *esp. lit* wealth: *His success had brought him vast riches.*

rich·ly /ˈrɪtʃli/ *adv* **1** splendidly; in a large quantity: *The queen's dress was richly decorated with jewels.* **2** fully: *They got the punishment they so* **richly deserved.**

Rich·mond /ˈrɪtʃmənd/ **1** a market town in N Yorkshire, England **2** the capital city of Virginia, in the East of the US, known for producing tobacco. It was the capital of the CONFEDERACY during the American CIVIL WAR. **3** a COUNTY of New York City which includes Staten Island

Richmond-u·pon-Thames /ˌ··· ˈ·/ a BOROUGH of SW Greater London, England, containing Kew Gardens and Hampton Court Palace

Rich Tea /ˌ· ˈ·/ the name of a plain sweet BISCUIT made by McVities

Rich·ter scale /ˈrɪktə ˌskeɪl, ˈrɪx-‖-tər-/ [*the*] a scale used to measure the strength of EARTHQUAKEs; the range is from one to ten, ten being the strongest

Richt·ho·fen /ˈrɪkthəʊfən, ˈrɪxt-/, **Baron von** /ˈbærən vɒn ‖ -vɑːn/ (1892–1918) a German aircraft pilot, known as **the Red Baron**. He shot down 80 aircraft in the First World War before being killed in action.

rick[1] /rɪk/ *n* a large pile of wheat stems or dried grass that stands out in the open air until it is needed: *a hay rick*

rick[2] *v* [T] *esp. BrE* to twist (a joint or part of the body) slightly: *I've ricked my back/my ankle.*

rick·ets /ˈrɪkɪts/ *n* [U] a children's disease caused by lack of the VITAMIN D provided by sunshine, butter, fresh milk, etc., which makes the bones become soft and bent

rick·et·y /ˈrɪkɪti/ *adj infml* weakly joined and likely to break; unsteady: *rickety old stairs* | *a rickety chair*

rick·rack /ˈrɪkræk/ *n* [U] *AmE* a narrow piece of cloth (a RIBBON) in a ZIGZAG shape used to decorate clothing, etc.

rick·shaw /ˈrɪkʃɔː/ *n* a small two-wheeled vehicle used in parts of East Asia for carrying one or two passengers and powered by a man either pulling or cycling

ric·o·chet[1] /ˈrɪkəʃeɪ/ *n* **1** a sudden sharp change in the direction of a moving object such as a stone or bullet when it hits a surface at an angle **2 a** an object to which this has happened: *She was wounded by a ricochet, not by a direct hit.* **b** the sound made by a ricochet

ricochet[2] *v* **-cheted** /ʃeɪd/ *or* **-chetted** /ʃetɪd/ [I (**off**)] to change direction in a ricochet: *The bullet ricocheted off the metal girder.*

ri·cot·ta /rɪˈkɒtə‖-ˈkɔː-/ *n* [U] a type of Italian cheese made from sheep's milk, and often used in PASTA dishes, esp. with SPINACH

rid /rɪd/ *v* **rid** *or* **ridded**, **rid**, *present participle* **ridding** **rid** sbdy./sthg. **of** sthg. *phr v* [T] **1** to make (esp. a place) free of (something harmful or unwanted): *One day we will manage to rid the world of this terrible disease.* | *You must rid yourself of these old-fashioned ideas.* | *He's gone, and I'm glad to be rid of him.* **2 get rid of: a** to free oneself from (something unwanted): *I've tried all sorts of medicines to get rid of this cold.* **b** to drive, send, throw, or give away or destroy: *How can we get rid of all these flies in the kitchen?* | *He just sat there talking all evening and I couldn't get rid of him.*

rid·dance /ˈrɪdəns/ *n infml* **good riddance** (said rudely when one is glad that someone or something has gone): *"They've gone at last." "Good riddance (to them)!"*

-ridden see WORD FORMATION

rid·dle¹ /ˈrɪdl/ n **1** a difficult and often amusing question to which one must guess the answer: *Christmas crackers with a gift and a riddle inside* | (fig.) *You're speaking in riddles; why can't you just say what you mean in an uncomplicated way?* **2** a mystery; something one cannot understand: *Robert's disappearance is a complete riddle.*

riddle² n a large SIEVE, as used for separating earth from stones in the garden

riddle³ v [T] to pass (earth, corn, ashes, etc.) through a RIDDLE²

    riddle sbdy./sthg. **with** sthg. *phr v* [T usu. pass.] **1** to make many holes in (a person or thing) by means of: *The gunman riddled the car with bullets.* **2** to make full of, and so damage: *The tent's riddled with holes and the rain's coming in.* | *The whole report is riddled with* (=full of) *errors.*

ride¹ /raɪd/ v **rode** /rəʊd/, **ridden** /ˈrɪdn/ **1** [T] to travel along, controlling and sitting on (a horse or other animal, a bicycle, or a motorcycle): *Can you ride a bicycle?* | *I'll ride the old horse and you ride the pony.* | *The winning horse was ridden by Willie Carson.* —compare DRIVE¹ (1); see DRIVE (USAGE) **2** [I] *esp. BrE* to travel along controlling and sitting on a horse, for exercise and pleasure: *Who taught you to ride?* | *We're going riding on Saturday.* | *a riding school* (=a place where people are taught to ride horses) **3** [I+*adv/prep*] to go somewhere controlling and sitting on a horse, bicycle, etc.: *We rode across the fields.* | *He got on his bicycle and rode slowly off down the road.* **4** [I (**on, in**)] to be carried along on an animal, on or in a vehicle, etc.; travel: *His dog likes to ride with him on his motorbike.* | *riding on a camel in the desert* | *The little boy rode on his father's shoulders.* | *riding in an open carriage* **5** [T] *esp. AmE* to travel in, esp. on horseback: *riding the freight trains* **b** to travel across, usu. on horseback: *The cowboy rode the range.* **6** [I+*adv*] (of a vehicle) to travel over a surface in the stated manner: *This car rides smoothly.* **7** [I+*adv/prep*; T] *lit* (of a ship) to move or float (on): *The boat rode at anchor in the channel.* | *The ship rode the rough sea.* **8** [T] *esp. AmE* to cause intentional and continual difficulty to; annoy: *Leave her alone and stop riding her — she's doing her best!* **9** [T] to move back so as to lessen the force of (a blow): *The boxer managed to ride the punch.* **10 let something ride** *infml* to let something continue, even if one does not really approve of it; take no action about something **11 ride for a fall** *infml* to behave in a risky way: *She's riding for a fall, investing all her money in that shaky company.* **12 ride high** to have great success, be in a top position, etc.: *The England team are riding high at the moment; they've won their last five matches.* **13 ride roughshod over** to act in an insensitive and hurtful way towards: *You can't just ride roughshod over people's feelings like that.*

    ride sbdy. ↔ **down** *phr v* [T] **1** to chase and reach on one's horse **2** to knock down with one's horse

    ride on sthg. *phr v* [T] *infml* to depend on: *It's vital that we win this contract; the whole future of the company is riding on it.*

    ride sthg. ↔ **out** *phr v* [T] (of a ship) to keep floating until the end of (a period of bad weather): *We decided to try to ride out the storm rather than attempt to get back to harbour.* | (fig.) *With good financial management we should be able to ride out our current economic difficulties.*

    ride up *phr v* [I] (of clothing) to move upward out of place: *This tight skirt rides up when I sit down.*

ride² n **1** [(**on, in**)] a journey on an animal, in a vehicle, etc.: *Shall we go for a ride in the car?* | *The town centre is only a short bus ride away.* | *Give me a ride on your back!* | *a ride on a donkey* **2** travel of the stated type on an animal or in a vehicle: *The champion jockey had an easy ride in the Derby* | (fig.) *I hear they gave you a pretty rough ride in the interview.* (=asked you very difficult questions, etc.) **3** a path, esp. through a wood, with a soft surface suitable for riding a horse on but not for vehicles **4 along for the ride** *infml* present with others but not taking part seriously: *They were going on a geology field trip, and as I had nothing better to do I said I'd come along for the ride.* **5 in for a bumpy ride** *infml*: likely to meet difficulties ahead **6 take someone for a ride** *infml* to deceive or cheat someone: *This contract*

is worthless; you've been taken for a ride! see also **free ride** (FREE¹ (15))

Ride a Cock-Horse /ˌ·· ·ˈ·/ a NURSERY RHYME (=an old song or poem for children):
    Ride a cock-horse to Banbury Cross,
    To see a fine lady upon a white horse,
    With rings on her fingers, and bells on her toes,
    She shall have music wherever she goes.

rid·er /ˈraɪdəʳ/ n **1** a person who rides or is riding esp. a horse **2** a statement, opinion, or piece of advice added esp. to an official declaration or judgment: [+*v-ing/that*] *The coroner decided that the child had been drowned, and added a rider (advising) that the lake should be filled in.* — **~less** *adj* : *a riderless horse*

ridge¹ /rɪdʒ/ n a long narrow raised part of a surface, such as the top of a range of mountains or of a sloping roof where the two sloping surfaces meet: *We walked along the mountain ridge.* | *The sea left a pattern of ridges and hollows on the sand.* | (fig.) *A* **ridge** (=long area) **of high pressure** *is approaching from the Atlantic and will bring sunny weather.* —see picture at MOUNTAIN

ridge² v [T] to make a ridge or ridges in: *The sea had ridged the sand with rippling patterns.*

ridge·pole /ˈrɪdʒpəʊl/ n **1** the pole along the top of the roof of a long tent **2** the piece of wood, etc., to which the sloping RAFTERs of the roof are joined

rid·i·cule¹ /ˈrɪdɪkjuːl/ n [U] language or behaviour intended to make someone or something appear foolish or worthless; unkind expression of amusement: *Her paintings, which were once* **held up to ridicule** (=made fun of as being silly), *are now widely acknowledged as masterpieces.* | *You* **lay yourself open to ridicule** (=will make people laugh at you) *by suggesting such an outlandish plan.* | *The minister declined to be interviewed on the television as he did not want to risk being* **exposed to public ridicule.**

ridicule² v [T] to laugh unkindly at; declare the foolishness of: *They all ridiculed my suggestion.*

ri·dic·u·lous /rɪˈdɪkjʊləs/ *adj derog* deserving ridicule; silly or unreasonable: *The fat old man looked ridiculous in his tight pink trousers.* | *What a ridiculous suggestion!* | *It's ridiculous that we should have to queue, when we've already got our tickets.* — **~ly** *adv* : *The exam was ridiculously* (=extremely) *easy.* — **~ness** n [U]

Ri·ding /ˈraɪdɪŋ/ n one of the three former parts of Yorkshire: *We've always lived in the West Riding of Yorkshire.*

riding hab·it /ˈ·· ˌ··/ n a woman's set of clothing worn in former times for riding a horse in, usu. with a long skirt for riding with both legs on the same side of the horse

Rie·fen·stahl /ˈriːfənʃtɑːl/, **Le·ni** /ˈleɪni/ (1902–) a German film maker known for her association with Hitler. She made a film of the NAZI meetings at Nuremberg, and one about the 1936 Berlin OLYMPIC GAMES.

Ries·ling /ˈriːzlɪŋ/ n [C;U] a sweet or dry white wine with a light, flowery taste, made esp. in Germany

rife /raɪf/ *adj* [F] *esp. lit* **1** (of something bad) widespread; common: *Disease and violence were rife in the city.* **2** [+**with**] full (of something bad): *The whole system is rife with corruption.*

riff /rɪf/ n a repeated phrase in popular or JAZZ music

rif·fle /ˈrɪfəl/ v
    riffle through sthg. *phr v* [T] *infml* to turn over (papers, pages, etc.) quickly with one's finger

riff·raff /ˈrɪfræf/ n [U+*sing./pl. v*] *derog* worthless badly-behaved people: *Why did she invite all this/these riffraff to her party?*

ri·fle¹ /ˈraɪfəl/ n a gun with a long rifled barrel, which is fired from the shoulder —compare HANDGUN, and see picture at GUN

rifle² v [T] to make GROOVEs (curved cuts) inside (the barrel of a gun) so as to make the bullets spin

rifle³ v [T] to search through and steal everything valuable from (e.g. a desk, drawers, handbag, etc.): *The drawers had been rifled and several valuable documents taken.*

rifle range /ˈ·· ·/ n a place where people practise shooting with rifles

ri·fling /ˈraɪflɪŋ/ n [U] the cuts (GROOVEs) inside the barrel of a rifled gun

rift /rɪft/ n [(**between, in**)] a crack or narrow opening in a large mass: *The sun appeared through a rift in the clouds.* | (fig.) *I hope we can heal the rift between them — they used to be such good friends.*

rift val·ley /ˈ· ˌ··/ n a valley with very steep sides, formed by the cracking and slipping of the Earth's surface

rig[1] /rɪg/ v **-gg-** [T] to provide (a ship) with the necessary ropes, sails, etc.: *a fully-rigged vessel*
  rig sbdy. ↔ **out** phr v [T (**as, in**)] to dress (someone) in special or funny clothes; DRESS **up** (1,2): *She was rigged out/She rigged herself out in a bright orange uniform.* | *They rigged the little boy out as a sailor.* —see also RIG-OUT
  rig sthg. ↔ **up** phr v [T] infml to put together for a short time out of materials easily found: *We can rig up an aerial from these pieces of wire.*

rig[2] n **1** the way a ship's sails and the MASTS that carry them are arranged: *Most modern yachts have a fore and aft rig, but the old galleons were square-rigged.* **2** (*usu. in comb.*) a piece of apparatus used for the stated purpose: *a drilling rig* —see also OILRIG **3** infml a set of clothes; the way a person is dressed: *He looked rather out of place when he turned up in full ceremonial rig.* —see also RIG-OUT **4** infml, esp. AmE a large TRUCK, esp. when fully loaded

rig[3] v **-gg-** [T] to arrange (an event) dishonestly for one's own advantage: *They complained that the election had been rigged.*

Ri·ga /ˈriːgə/ the capital city of Latvia

rig·a·ma·role /ˈrɪgəmərəʊl/ n RIGMAROLE

rig·a·to·ni /ˌrɪgəˈtəʊni/ n [P] a type of PASTA in the shape of short RIBBED tubes

Rigg /rɪg/, **Diana** (1938–) an English actress known for her appearances on television in the television SERIES *The Avengers*

rig·ging /ˈrɪgɪŋ/ n [(*the*) U] all the ropes, chains, etc., that hold up a ship's sails: *The sailor climbed up the rigging to see if he could sight land.* —see picture at YACHT

right[1] /raɪt/ adj **1** [A] on, for, or belonging to the side of the body away from the heart: *one's right arm/eye* | *my right shoe* **2** [A] on, by, or in the direction of one's right side: *the right bank of the river* | *Take a right turn at the crossroads.* **3** belonging to, connected with, or supporting the RIGHT[2] (2) in politics; RIGHT WING: *She's very right.* | *a small far-right party* (=with strong RIGHT WING views) —opposite **left**

right[2] n **1** [(*the*) U] the RIGHT[1] side or direction: *Keep to the right!* | *He doesn't know his left from his right.* | *Take the next turning on/to your right.* (=the next one you come to on your right side) | *The Conservative party is* to the **right of** *the Liberals.* **2** [*the*+*sing./pl. v*] (*often cap.*) political parties or groups, such as the Conservatives in Britain and the Republicans in the US, that have NATIONALISTIC views and are in favour of less state control and more FREE ENTERPRISE and choice. They generally support the employers or those in official positions rather than the workers: *The election results mean that the Right has/have gained control of the Senate.* —see also RIGHT WING **3** [C] a blow struck with the right hand: *He got me with a right to the jaw.* —opposite **left 4 be somewhere to the right of Ghengis Khan/Attila the Hun** to have very strong RIGHT-WING political opinions

right[3] adj **1** just, proper, or morally correct; in accordance with accepted ideas of what is good: *I'll try to do whatever is right.* | *It's difficult to know what is the right thing to do in this situation.* | *It's not right to tell lies.* | *It's* **only right** *that you should know.* (=You ought to know.) | *I thought it right to tell you.* [+*to-v*] *You were quite right to report the matter to the police.* [+(**in**)] correct or true; in accordance with the facts: *Is that the right time?* | *He gave the right answer.* | *Would I be right in thinking that you come from Australia?* | *"Is this Piccadilly Circus?" "Yes, that's right."* **3** most suitable; best for a particular purpose: *Are we going in the right direction?* | *I think he's the right person for the job.* | *She's the sort of woman who always says the right things and knows the right* (=socially important) *people.* | *a newspaper with just the right mixture of serious comment and entertaining articles* **4** in a correct, satisfactory, or healthy state, position, etc.: *The wiring is all wrong — you'll have to call an electrician to put it right.* | *That picture isn't quite right — could you straighten it?* | *I'm sorry about all the trou-*

ble I've caused — I'll do my best to put/set things right. | *A week by the sea will soon put you right again.* (=cure you or make you feel better) | *You've got a mild case of food poisoning, but don't worry — you'll be* **right as rain** (=perfectly healthy) *in a couple of days.* | *Don't pay any attention to what she says — she's not* (**quite**) **right in the head/in her right mind.** (=she's mad) **5** [A] BrE infml (esp. of something bad) complete; to a great degree: *That man's a right idiot!* **6 Right you are!** also **Right oh!**— BrE infml yes; I will; I agree: *"Shut the window, please." "Right you are!"* —opposite **wrong** (for 1,2,3) —see also RIGHTLY, **see someone right** (SEE[1] (22)) **7 right?** infml is that right?: *You're Mrs Smith's daughter, right?* — ~**ness** n [U] : *They believe in the rightness of what they're doing.*

right[4] n **1** [U] what is RIGHT[3] (1): *You're old enough to know the difference between right and wrong.* **2** [C;U (**to, of**)] (a) morally just or legal claim: *She has a/the right to half your money.* | *the right to a fair trial* | *We fought for the right of access to government information.* [+*to-v*] to exercise one's right to vote | *You have no right to* (=should not) *treat me like this.* | *I know he's the boss, but that doesn't give him the right to order us around.* | *I've got every right to be annoyed.* (=it is quite reasonable that I am) | (*fml*) *Every shareholder will receive an invitation to the meeting* **as of right.** (=because they are SHAREHOLDERS, without any further special claim) | *She is British* **by right of** *birth.* | *You'd be quite* **within your rights** (=not going beyond your just claims) *to refuse to work on Sundays.* **3 in one's own right** because of a personal claim that does not depend on anyone else: *Elizabeth II is queen of England in her own right.* (=rather than through marriage to a king) **4 in the right** having justice on one's side; not deserving blame: *We must find out which of them was in the right.* —opposite **in the wrong** —see also RIGHTS

right[5] adv **1** towards the RIGHT[2] (1,2): *Turn right at the crossroads.* —opposite **left 2** properly or correctly: *Luckily I guessed right.* | *Did I do it right?* —opposite **wrong 3** [+*adv/prep*] exactly: *She was standing right in the middle of the room.* | *Do it right now.* | *The police arrived right at the moment of the explosion.* **4** [+*adv/prep*] directly; straight: *Go right home at once; don't stop off anywhere on the way.* | *There's the house, right in front of you.* | *right after breakfast* **5** [+*adv/prep*] completely; all the way: *Go right to the end of the road.* | *Go right back to the beginning.* | *I haven't read the book right through.* | *I'm* **right behind** *you there.* (=support you completely) **6** BrE sl, NEngE, old use very: *He's a right argumentative little brat.* | *I'm right glad to see you, lad!* | (in some titles) *the Right Honourable John Jones* | *the Right Reverend Bishop Jenkins* **7** (used in answer to a suggestion or order) yes; I will; ALL RIGHT: *"Come tomorrow." "Right! What time?"* —see also ALL RIGHT **8 right and left** also **right, left, and centre**— infml everywhere or in every way: *We're losing money right and left.* **9 right away** also **right off** esp. AmE— at once; without delay **10 right 'on** sl (used to express agreement or approval) exactly correct **11 Too right** esp. AustrE You are correct; I agree

right[6] v [T] to put (something) right or upright again; bring back to a correct position or condition: *The boat capsized but we soon righted it.* | *to* **right the wrongs** *that have been done to these people*

right an·gle /ˈ· ˌ··/ n an angle of 90 degrees, e.g. at any of the four corners of a square: *Put the tables at right angles to each other.* —see picture at ANGLE

right-an·gled /ˈ· ˌ··/ adj (of a TRIANGLE) with one angle of 90 degrees —see picture at TRIANGLE

right-brain /ˈ· ·/ adj concerned with or resulting from the right side of the brain, which controls the left side of the body and also ARTISTIC and IMAGINATIVE thinking

right·eous /ˈraɪtʃəs/ adj **1** esp. lit or bibl (of a person or their behaviour) (doing what is) morally good and just: *a righteous man* [also n, the+P] *The righteous shall go to Heaven.* | *"I never drink or smoke," he said in a righteous tone.* —see also SELF-RIGHTEOUS **2** (of feelings) morally blameless; having just cause: *righteous indignation* — ~**ly** adv — ~**ness** n [U]

right field /ˈ· ·/ n **1** (in BASEBALL) the area of the playing field outside the DIAMOND and to the right **2** the position of the player (the **rightfielder**) who plays in this area

right·ful /ˈraɪtfəl/ adj [A] fml in accordance with what is just or legally correct: *He regained his rightful place on the English throne.* (=as king of England) | *Who is the rightful owner of this car? —* ~ **ly** adv : *The legacy is rightfully yours; she always intended you to have it. —* ~ **ness** n [U]

right-hand /ˌ·ˈ·◂/ adj [A] **1** on or to the right side: *the right-hand page* **2** of, for, with, or done by the right hand: *a right-hand stroke* **3** turning or going to the right: *a right-hand bend* | *Take the right-hand lane.* —opposite **left-hand**

right-hand-drive /ˌ·· ·ˈ·◂/ adj (of a car) having the driver's wheel and foot controls on the right-hand side, being intended for driving on the left-hand side of the road

right-hand·ed /ˌ·· ˈ···◂/ adj **1** using the right hand for most actions rather than the left: *a right-handed tennis player* **2** made for use by a right-handed person: *right-handed scissors* —opposite **left-handed —** ~ **ness** n [U]

right-hand·er /ˌ·· ˈ···/ n **1** a hit or stroke given with the right hand **2** ‖ also **righty** AmE infml— someone who usu. uses their right hand for most actions rather than their left —opposite **left-hander**

right-hand man /ˌ·· · ˈ·/ also **right-hand—** n one's most useful and valuable helper

Right Hon·our·a·ble /ˌ·· ·ˈ····/ adj (in Britain, a title of respect used when mentioning important government ministers or certain lords): *the Right Honourable Edward Heath, M.P.* | *my Right Honourable friend, the Member for Croydon South*

right·ist /ˈraɪtɪst/ n, adj (often cap.) sometimes derog (a supporter) of the RIGHT² (2) in politics: *a rightist government* —opposite **leftist**

right·ly /ˈraɪtli/ adv **1** [no comp.] correctly, truly, or with good reason: *If I am rightly informed …* | *He believed, rightly or wrongly, that she was guilty.* | *They argue, quite rightly, that this measure will do nothing to solve the problem.* **2** justly: *He was punished, and (very|quite) rightly so.* **3** [usu. in negatives] infml for certain; without any doubt: *I can't rightly say|don't rightly know whether it was Tuesday or Wednesday.*

right-mind·ed /ˌ·ˈ···◂/ also **right-thinking—** adj [A] having correct and acceptable opinions, principles, or standards of behaviour: *All right-minded people will support this change in the law. —* ~ **ness** n [U]

right of ap·peal /ˌ· · ·ˈ·/ n rights of appeal the legal right to ask for a court's decision to be re-examined

right-of-centre , right of centre /ˌ·· · ˈ···◂/ adj to the CONSERVATIVE¹ (1) (right) side of political thinking, but not very far —compare LEFT-OF-CENTRE

right of way /ˌ·· · ˈ·/ n rights of way **1** [(the) U] the right of traffic to drive, cross, pass, etc., before other vehicles: *It's our right of way at this road junction.* (=we can go first) **2** [C] **a** a right to follow a path across a piece of private land: *We have a right of way across his field to our house.* **b** a path over which someone holds this right: *a public right of way through the forest*

Right Rev·er·end /ˌ·· ·ˈ···/ adj (used as a title of respect when mentioning a BISHOP)

rights /raɪts/ n [P] **1** the political, social, and other advantages to which someone has a just claim, morally or legally: *The suffragettes led the fight for women's rights.* | *a prisoners' rights campaign* **2 by rights** if things were done properly or correctly: *I shouldn't by rights be at this party at all — I'm on duty tonight!* **3 set|put someone|something to rights** to bring someone|something (back) to a healthy, correct, or satisfactory condition: *This medicine will soon put you to rights.* | *We need a new leader to set the country to rights again.* **4 the rights and wrongs of** the true facts about: *We are determined to find out the rights and wrongs of this matter.* —see also BILL OF RIGHTS, CIVIL RIGHTS, HUMAN RIGHTS

rights is·sue /ˈ· ˌ··/ n tech an offer by a company to sell shares at a favourable price to those people who already hold shares in it

right-think·ing /ˌ·· ˈ···◂/ adj RIGHT-MINDED

right to life /ˌ· · · ˈ·/ n the right to live, esp. the right of an unborn child to be born. This phrase is used by people who are opposed to ABORTION.

right-to-lif·er /ˌ· · ˈ··/ n a person who supports the idea of the unborn child's right to be born, and is opposed to ABORTION

right tri·an·gle /ˌ· ˈ···/ n AmE for a RIGHT-ANGLED TRIANGLE

right·ward /ˈraɪtwəd‖-wərd/ adj on or towards the right — opposite **leftward**

right·wards /ˈraɪtwədz‖-wərdz-/ esp. BrE‖usu. **rightward** AmE— adv on or towards the right —opposite **leftwards**

right wing /ˌ· ·ˈ·◂/ n, adj [the] **1** [+sing. v] (the members) of a group or political party that favour either fewer political changes or less state control, and who are usu. rather NATIONALISTIC: *He is on the right wing of his party.* **2** [+sing.|pl. v] (of) the RIGHT² (2): *right-wing ideas|newspapers* | *She's very right-wing.* **3** (on) the right-hand side of the field in games such as football: *He centred the ball from the right wing.* —opposite **left wing** **—right-winger** n

ri·gid /ˈrɪdʒɪd/ adj **1** stiff; not easy to bend: *a tent supported on a rigid framework* | *She was rigid with fear.* **2** often derog firm or fixed in behaviour, views, or methods; difficult to change or unwilling to change: *He's very rigid in his ideas.* | *the rigid discipline of army life* | *rigid distinctions between social classes* | *rigid adherence to the regulations —* ~ **ly** adv : *rigidly opposed to all new ideas* | *rigidly orthodox —* ~ **ity** /rɪˈdʒɪdɪti/ n [U]

rig·ma·role /ˈrɪgmərəʊl/ ‖ also **rigamarole** AmE— n infml derog **1** [U] a long, confusing, and often meaningless set of actions: *I had to go through the whole rigmarole of swearing in front of the judge and kissing the Bible.* **2** [S;U] a long confused story without much meaning: *She told me some rigmarole or other about having lost her keys.*

rig·or mor·tis /ˌrɪgə ˈmɔːtɪs, ˌraɪgɔː-‖ˌrɪgər ˈmɔːr-/ n [U] Lat the stiffening of the muscles after death: *Bury him before rigor mortis sets in.* (=before his body becomes stiff)

rig·or·ous /ˈrɪgərəs/ adj **1** often apprec careful, thorough, and exact: *The planes have to undergo rigorous safety checks.* **2** severe; painful: *the rigorous hardships of the journey —* ~ **ly** adv

rig·our BrE ‖ **-or** AmE /ˈrɪgər/ n [U] **1** firmness or severity; lack of pity: *He deserves to be punished with the full rigour of the law.* **2** also **rigours** pl.— severe conditions: *The expedition suffered all the rigour(s) of a Canadian winter.* **3** often apprec (in a subject of study) exactness that demands clear thinking: *the rigour of a scientific proof*

rig-out /ˈ· ·/ n BrE infml, often derog a set of clothes of a particular, esp. unusual, type: *You can't go to the party in that rig-out!* —see also RIG out

Rig-Ve·da /ˌrɪg ˈveɪdə/ [the] the first of the four holy books of the VEDA, which contains prayers and HYMNs to gods in the Hindu religion

rile /raɪl/ v [T] infml to annoy; make very angry: *His patronizing manner really riles me.* —see ANNOY (USAGE)

Ri·ley /ˈraɪli/ n see **lead the life of Riley** (LEAD¹ (13))

Ril·ke /ˈrɪlkə/, **Rai·ner Ma·ri·a** /ˈraɪnəʳ məˈriːə/ (1875–1926) a German writer, born in Prague, known for his poetry including *Sonnets to Orpheus*

rill /rɪl/ n poet a small stream

rim¹ /rɪm/ n **1** the outside edge or border of esp. a round or circular object: *the rim of a cup* | *You fit the tyre round the rim of the wheel.* | *military bases on the rim of the Pacific* **2 -rimmed** /rɪmd/ having a rim or rims of the stated type or material —see also HORN-RIMMED — ~ **less** adj : *She wore rimless glasses.*

rim² v **-mm-** [T] to be round the edge of (esp. something round or circular): *Trees rimmed the pool.*

Rim·baud /ˈræmbəʊ‖ræmˈbəʊ/, **Arthur** (1854–91) a French poet known for dream-like poetry including *Les Illuminations*

rime /raɪm/ n [U] lit white FROST¹ (1)

Rime of the Ancient Mariner see ANCIENT MARINER

Rim·i·ni /ˈrɪmɪni/ a city on the Adriatic coast of Italy. It is a market town and tourist centre.

Rim·sky-Kor·sa·kov /ˌrɪmski ˈkɔːsəkɒf‖-ˈkɔːrsəkɔːf/, **Nik·o·lai An·drey·e·vich** /ˈnɪkəlaɪ ænˈdreɪəvɪtʃ/ (1844–1908) a Russian COMPOSER who used the RHYTHMs of Russian FOLK SONGs in his music. His works include *The Snow Maiden* and *Scheherazada*.

rind /raɪnd/ n [C;U] **1** (a piece of) the thick rather hard outer covering of certain fruits, esp. of the MELON and LEMON: *grated lemon rind* —compare PEEL² **2** (a piece of) the thick outer skin of certain foods: *cheese rind | bacon rind*

▷ USAGE Although the skin of the orange is of this type, it is called "peel". In the US, the skin of the lemon is also often called "peel".◁

rind·less /ˈraɪndləs/ *adj* (of BACON) having the rind removed

ring¹ /rɪŋ/ *n* **1** [C] a small circular piece of metal, esp. gold or silver, that is worn on the finger as an ITEM of jewellery, or to show that a person is ENGAGED or married: *a gold ring | a diamond ring* (=decorated with one or more diamonds) —see also ENGAGEMENT RING, WEDDING RING **2** [C] a circular band or shape, esp. of the stated substance or for the stated purpose: *He puffed at his pipe and blew smoke rings into the air. | The little girl was supported in the water by an inflatable rubber ring. | the rings of the planet Saturn | a bull with a metal ring through its nose | Rings are put round birds' legs to identify them.* —see also KEY RING **3** [C] a circular line, mark, or arrangement: *There was a ring of troops round the building. | They danced around in a ring. | You can tell how old a tree is by cutting it across and counting the rings inside.* | (fig.) *You must have been having too many late nights – you've got rings round your eyes.* (=dark marks from too little sleep) **4** [C] *esp. BrE* a circular arrangement of metal that can be heated up by gas or electricity to cook things on: *a gas ring* —see picture at KITCHEN **5** [*the*] an enclosed usu. circular central space in a CIRCUS where the performances take place — see also RINGMASTER **6** [*the*+S] the small square space closed in with ropes in which people BOX or WRESTLE: *The challenger climbed into the ring. | He retired from the ring* (=from BOXING) *at 34.* **7** [C] a group of people who work together, often dishonestly in business or crime for their own advantage: *a drug ring|spy ring | The auctioneers organized a secret ring to control the sales.* **8 make/run rings round someone** to do things much better and faster than someone **9 with rings on her fingers and bells on her toes** a line from a NURSERY RHYME (=an old song or poem for children) —see RIDE A COCK-HORSE **10 with this ring, I thee wed** a phrase from the Christian marriage service, said at the point where the man gives the woman (and sometimes the woman gives the man) a wedding ring —see also **throw one's hat into the ring** (THROW¹ (22))

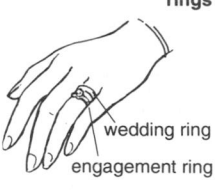
wedding ring
engagement ring

boxing ring

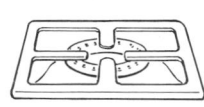
gas ring

ring² *v* [T (with)] **1** to make, form, or put a ring round; ENCIRCLE: *Police ringed the building. | The old house was ringed (about) with trees. | Ring the spelling mistakes with red ink.* **2** to put a ring round the leg of (a bird)

ring³ *v* **rang** /ræŋ/, **rung** /rʌŋ/ **1** [T (for)] to cause (a bell) to sound: *The cyclist rang his bell loudly. | I rang the doorbell but no one answered.* **2** [I (at, for)] to ring a bell as a sign that one wants something: *She rang for service|for a drink.* **3** [I] (of a bell, telephone, etc.) to sound: *The telephone's ringing. | The bell rang loudly.* **4** [I;T (UP)] *esp. BrE* ‖ call *esp. AmE*– to telephone (someone): *I'm expecting my mother to ring. | I think we should ring for an ambulance.* (=call one by telephoning) *| Please ring the doctor. | I'll ring you (up) tomorrow. | I tried to ring you but you weren't in.* —see TELEPHONE (USAGE) **5** [I] to make a continuous high or loud hollow sound: *The glass should ring if you hit it gently.* | (fig.) *His cruel laughter rang in my ears.* **6** [I (with, to)] to be filled with this sort of sound: *The courtyard rang with|to their shouts. | The crash really made my ears ring.* **7 ring a bell** *infml* to remind one of something: *Her name rings a bell but I can't remember whether I've ever met her.* **8 ring hol-**

low to sound untrue or insincere: *I knew he didn't really care, so his words of sympathy rang hollow.* **9 ring the changes (on)** to introduce variety (esp. in something where there is a limited range of possibilities) **10 ring the curtain up/down** to start/end a play by signalling for the theatre curtain to go up/down **11 ring true/false** to sound true/untrue: *It was a clever excuse but it didn't really ring true.*

ring (sbdy. ↔) **back** *phr v* [I;T] *esp. BrE* to telephone again, esp. after a first unsuccessful attempt: *I told him you weren't in, so he said he'd ring (you) back later.*

ring in *phr v* **1** [I] esp. AmE to make a telephone call to a place, such as one's office, a radio station, etc.: *Jane has rung in to say she'll be late today.* **2** [T] (=**ring** sthg. ↔ **in**) to mark the beginning of (the New Year) by ringing church bells —compare RING **out** (2)

ring off *phr v* [I] *esp. BrE* to end a telephone conversation: *I'd better ring off now — the baby's crying.*

ring out *phr v* **1** [I] (of a voice, bell, etc.) to sound loudly and clearly: *The word of command rang out.* **2** [T] (=**ring** sthg. ↔ **out**) to mark the end of (the old year) by ringing church bells —compare RING **in** (2)

ring round (sbdy.) *phr v* [I;T] *esp. BrE* to make telephone calls to (a number of people): *She rang round to tell all her friends the news|rang round all her friends to tell them the news.*

ring sthg. ↔ **up** *phr v* [T] to record (money paid) on a CASH REGISTER: *The cashier rang up £20 instead of 20p by mistake.* —see also RING³ (4)

ring⁴ *n* **1** [C (of)] (an act of making) the sound of a bell or a bell-like sound: *He gave several loud rings at the door. | the ring of church bells* **2** [S (of)] a certain quality, esp. in something said: *Her story had the ring of truth about it.* (=sounded true) *| His excuse had a familiar ring.* (=I had heard it before) **3 have a ring of confidence** appearing to have a calm unworried manner or strong belief in one's abilities: *Tommy's ring of confidence. School caretaker Tommy Joyce knows how to deal with bullies – he puts on boxing gloves and teaches victims how to fight back.* **4** [S] *infml, esp. BrE* a telephone call: *I'll give you a ring tonight.* —see TELEPHONE (USAGE)

Ring also **Ring of the Ni·be·lung·en** /ˌrɪŋ əv ðə ˈniːbəlʊŋən/, **Ring Cy·cle** /ˈ· ˌ··/– [*the*] four OPERAS by Richard Wagner based on German MYTHOLOGY

Ring a ring o'ros·es /ˌ· · ˌ· · ˈ··/ *n* a children's singing game in which the children join hands and dance round in a circle singing:
> *Ring a ring o' roses*
> *A pocket full of posies*
> *A-tishoo! A-tishoo!*
> *We all fall down*

Ring-a-round-the-ros·y /ˌ· ·ˌ· · ˈ··/ an American children's singing game:
> *Ring-around-the-rosy,*
> *Pocket full of posy,*
> *Ashes, Ashes,*
> *All fall down*

ring bind·er /ˈ· ˌ··/ *n* a notebook whose loose pages are held in position by metal rings fastened to a firm back

ring·er /ˈrɪŋəʳ/ *n* **1** a person who rings bells, esp. in a church **2** *AmE* a person who enters a sports competition against the rules —see also DEAD RINGER

ring fin·ger /ˈ· ˌ··/ *n* the third finger of the left hand (or, in some parts of the world, the right hand), on which a WEDDING RING is usually worn —see picture at HAND

ringing /ˈrɪŋɪŋ/ *adj* emotional, definite and expressed openly: *He praised her in ringing tones. | a ringing condemnation of human rights abuses*

ring·lead·er /ˈrɪŋ ˌliːdəʳ/ *n* a person who leads others to do wrong or make trouble: *Police arrested the ringleaders, but let the rest go free.*

ring·let /ˈrɪŋlɪt/ *n* a long hanging curl of hair: *a pretty child with golden ringlets*

ring·mas·ter /ˈrɪŋ ˌmɑːstəʳ‖-ˌmæ-/ *n* a person, esp. a man, whose job is directing performances in a CIRCUS

ring-pull /ˈ· ·/ *n* a ring on a tin of drink which is pulled to open it: *It comes in a ring-pull can.*

ring road /ˈ· ·/ *BrE* ‖ **beltway** *AmE*– *n* a road that goes round the edge of a large town so that traffic does not have to pass through the centre

ring·side /ˈrɪŋsaɪd/ adj, n [the] (at) the edge of a RING¹ (5,6): *We had **ringside seats**/seats by the ringside for the big fight, and saw it all.*

ring span·ner /ˈ· ˌ··/ BrE ‖ **box end wrench** AmE— n a type of SPANNER with a hollow end that fits over the NUT to be screwed or unscrewed —see picture at TOOL

ring·way /ˈrɪŋweɪ/ n (a name for) a main road which goes round a town rather than through it

ring·worm /ˈrɪŋwɜːm‖-wɜːrm/ n [U] a skin disease passed on by touch, causing red rings often on the head

rink /rɪŋk/ n a specially prepared surface of **a** ice, for skating (SKATE) **b** any hard material, for using ROLLER SKATES

rin·ky-dink /ˈrɪŋki dɪŋk/ adj AmE sl small, worn, and without much to interest one

rinse¹ /rɪns/ v [T] **1** [(OUT)] to clean using fresh water, esp. to put (clothes or hair) in clean water in order to remove soap after washing: *I'll just rinse (out) these shirts.* | *Rinse your mouth (out) with this mouthwash.* **2** [+adv/prep, esp. OUT] to remove (soap, dirt, etc.) from something by rinsing: *Rinse the soap out of these shirts/out of your hair.* | *She rinsed out the sea water from her swimming-costume.*

rinse² n **1** [C] an act of rinsing: *Give the shirts at least three rinses.* **2** [C;U] (a) pale liquid for colouring the hair: *a (bottle of) blue rinse for grey hair*

rinse aid /ˈ· ·/ n [U] a liquid put into a dishwasher to stop the rinsing water leaving marks on the plates, etc.

rinse hold /ˈ· ˌ·/ n a washing machine control which prevents clothes from becoming creased (CREASE) by leaving them in water until the user is ready to take them out

Ri·o de Ja·nei·ro /ˌriːəʊ də ʒəˈnɪərəʊ‖-deɪ ʒəˈncɑːrəʊ/ a port and former capital of Brazil, also known as **Rio**. It is famous for its beaches (BEACH) such as the COPACABANA, and the SUGAR LOAF MOUNTAIN. The Earth Summit was held there in 1992.

Ri·o Grande /ˌriːəʊ ˈɡrænd/ [the] a river in the south of the US which forms a border between the US and Mexico. The Mexican name for it is **Rio Bravo**. —see colour map on pages 1374–5

ri·ot¹ /ˈraɪət/ n **1** [C] a scene of noisy, uncontrolled, often violent behaviour by a large disorderly crowd of people: *The sudden increase in the price of bread led to riots in the streets.* | *The army had to be called in to put down the riot.* | *The **riot police** used teargas to control the mob.* **2** [S] infml a very funny and successful occasion or person: *You should go and see the new show — it's a riot.* **3** [S+of] a bright and splendid show: *The garden is a **riot of colour** in summer.* **4 run riot: a** to become violent and uncontrollable: *The football supporters ran riot through the town after their team lost the match.* **b** (of a plant) to grow thickly and uncontrollably

ri·ot² v [I] to take part in a riot: *crowds rioting in the streets* — ~**er** n

riot act /ˈ··· ·/ n **read the riot act** usu. humor to severely warn (a person or group) to stop making trouble: *If the children don't quieten down and go to sleep, I'll go upstairs and read (them) the riot act.*

ri·ot·ous /ˈraɪətəs/ adj **1** (of people or behaviour) wild, uncontrolled, and disorderly: *a riotous crowd* | *They were charged with **riotous assembly**.* (=taking part in a riot) | *riotous laughter* **2** (of an occasion) noisy and exciting: *They spent a riotous night drinking and singing.* — ~**ly** adv — ~**ness** n [U]

rip¹ /rɪp/ v -pp- [I;T] **1** to tear or be torn quickly and violently: *The sail ripped under the force of the wind.* | *I ripped my tights on a nail.* | *Impatiently, he ripped the letter open.* | *The cat's ripped the cushion cover* **to pieces/into shreds.** | (fig.) *He ripped my argument to pieces.* —see also RIPPER **2 let something rip** infml to let something start or continue without any controls or limits: *OK, driver — open the throttle and really let her rip!*

rip sbdy./sthg. ↔ **off** phr v [T] **1** infml derog to charge too much: *They really ripped us off at that hotel!* **2** sl to steal: *Someone's ripped off my new bicycle!* —see also RIP-OFF

rip sthg. ↔ **up** phr v [T] to tear violently into pieces: *She ripped the letter up angrily.*

rip into sbdy. phr v [T] to angrily attack someone with words or physically: *He really ripped into Sue for not showing up when she was supposed to.*

rip² n a long tear or cut: *There was a rip in the tyre caused by a sharp stone.*

RIP /ˌaːr aɪ ˈpiː/ abbrev. for: rest in peace (=words written on gravestones)

rip·cord /ˈrɪpkɔːd‖-kɔːrd/ n **1** the cord that one pulls to open a PARACHUTE after jumping from an aircraft **2** the cord that one pulls to let gas out of a BALLOON (1)

ripe /raɪp/ adj **1** (esp. of fruit and crops) fully grown and ready to be eaten: *These apples aren't ripe; they'll give you indigestion.* | *a field of ripe corn* | *a ripe old Stilton cheese* | (fig.) *her ripe red lips*—opposite **unripe** **2** [F (for)] in a suitable condition (for something, esp. a change or new development): *This land is ripe for industrial development.* | *The **time was ripe** for a challenge to the power of the government.* **3** old-fash infml shocking in an amusing way: *That joke was rather ripe.* **4 a ripe old age** a very great age: *He lived to a ripe old age.* | (humor) *She first appeared on stage at the ripe old age of six.* — ~**ness** n [U]

rip·en /ˈraɪpən/ v [I;T] to become or make ripe: *The corn ripens in the sun.* | *The sun ripens the corn.*

rip-off /ˈ· ·/ n **1** infml derog an act of charging too much: *They charged you £5 for a coffee? What a rip-off!* **2** sl an act of stealing —see also RIP off

Rip·on /ˈrɪpən/ a market town in N Yorkshire, England, which is famous esp. for its CATHEDRAL

ri·poste¹ /rɪˈpɒst, rɪˈpəʊst‖rɪˈpəʊst/ n **1** a quick, clever, and often unfriendly reply; RETORT **2** (in FENCING) a quick return stroke with a sword

riposte² v **1** [I;T] to reply as a RIPOSTE¹ (1) **2** [I] to make a RIPOSTE¹ (2)

Rip·per /ˈrɪpəʳ/ [the] a name given to a person (usu. a man) who kills several times in a very unpleasant way which shocks and worries the public. The name is usu. given by the TABLOID newspapers as the killer becomes famous and the police search for him. —see also JACK THE RIPPER, YORKSHIRE RIPPER

rip·ple¹ /ˈrɪpəl/ v **1** [I;T] to (cause to) move in small waves: *The lake rippled gently.* | *The wind rippled the surface of the cornfield.* | (fig.) *Laughter rippled through the audience.* **2** [T] to form RIPPLES² (2) on: *the rippled surface of the sand* **3** [I] to make a sound like gently running water: *a rippling stream* | *The water rippled over the stones.*

ripple² n **1** [C] a very small wave or gentle waving movement: *The light wind caused ripples to appear on the pool* | (fig.) *There was a **ripple of applause**.* | (fig.) *A ripple of excitement ran through the crowd as the princess approached.* **2** [C] a wavelike mark: *The sea leaves ripples on the sand.* **3** [S (of)] a sound of or like gently running water: *I heard the ripple of the stream.* **4** [U] a type of ice cream with bands of white VANILLA ice cream and another type of usu. coloured ice cream: *raspberry ripple* | *strawberry ripple*

Rip·pon /ˈrɪpən/, **An·ge·la** /ˈændʒ‿lə/ (1944–   ) an English reader of the news on television who now works mostly on the radio. She is famous for being one of the first women to read the television news.

rip-roar·ing /ˌ· ˈ··◄/ adj infml noisy, exciting, and uncontrolled: *a rip-roaring party* | *They had a rip-roaring time spending all their wages in one night.* | *The new play was a rip-roaring* (=very great) *success.*

rip·saw /ˈrɪpsɔː/ n a large-toothed SAW that cuts wood along the direction of growth (GRAIN (4))

rip·snort·er /ˌrɪpˈsnɔːtəʳ‖-ɔːr-/ n AmE old fash sl something which is very exciting: *The roller coasters there are real ripsnorters.*

rip·tide /ˈrɪptaɪd/ n a TIDE (=regular rise and fall of the sea) that makes rough water and currents

Rip van Win·kle /ˌ· · · ˈ··/ a person who is completely UNAWARE of new ideas and fashions (from a character in a story by Washington Irving, who slept for 20 years and found the world very changed when he woke up)

rise¹ /raɪz/ v **rose** /rəʊz/, **risen** /ˈrɪzən/ [I] **1** to move from a lower to a higher level or position; go up; get higher: *Smoke rose from the factory chimneys.* | *The river is rising after the rain.* | *Their voices rose higher and higher with excitement.* | *The price of bread has risen sharply/has risen by 15%.* | *The road rises steeply from the village.* | *The house was built on rising ground.* | *She eventually*

rose to an important position in the firm. | *He rose from captain to colonel in five years.* | *My spirits rose* (=I became happier) *when I heard the news.* | *Tension in the region is rising.* (=increasing) | *rising prices/unemployment* —opposite **fall**; see also RISING² **2** (of the sun, moon, or stars) to come up; appear above the horizon: *The sun rises in the east.* —opposite **set** **3** [+*adv/prep*; *not in progressive forms*] to show above the surroundings: *The trees rose above the roof-tops.* **4** [(UP)] also **arise** *fml*— to stand up from a lying, kneeling, or sitting position: *He rose from his knees.* | *She rose to greet her guests.* **5** *fml* to get out of bed; get up: *She rises before it is light.* — compare RETIRE (3) **6** *fml* (of a group of people) to formally end a meeting: *The court will rise at 4.30.* **7** (of wind or storms) to get stronger **8** [(UP, **against**)] to begin to be active in opposition; REBEL: *The people rose up against their cruel oppressors.* —see also RISING¹ **9** *lit or bibl* to come back to life after being dead: *According to the Bible, Jesus rose/rose again/rose from the dead on the third day after his death.* **10** [+*adv/prep*; *not in progressive forms*] (esp. of a river) to come into being; begin; have origin: *The River Rhine rises in Switzerland.* | *The quarrel rose from/out of a misunderstanding.* **11** (of fish) to come up to the surface of water: *The fish are rising; perhaps we'll catch one.* | (fig.) *He made some stupid remarks about women drivers, but she didn't* **rise to the bait.** (=she refused to become angry) **12** (of uncooked bread) to swell as the YEAST works **13 rise to the occasion** to show that one can deal with a difficult situation when it happens: *When the guest speaker failed to arrive, the chairman rose to the occasion and made a very amusing speech himself.*

▷ USAGE Compare **rise** and **raise**. If you **raise** [T] something you lift it to a higher position: *We* **raised** *the ship from the sea bed.* If you yourself move to a higher position you **rise** [I]: *I* **rose** *from my seat.* If more effort is needed you **raise** yourself: *He* **raised** *himself from the ground.*◁

rise above sthg. *phr v* [T *no pass.*] to deal successfully with (a problem, disadvantage, etc.); OVERCOME: *to rise above one's misfortunes.*

rise² *n* **1** [C (**in**)] an increase in quantity, price, demand, etc.: *There's been a sharp rise in the cost of living.* | *The rise in her temperature is giving cause for concern.* | *a 25% rise in the price of oil* —opposite **fall** **2** [U] the act of growing more powerful, more active, or more widespread; development: *the rise and fall of the Roman Empire* | *The rise of computer technology has transformed industry.* **3** [C] an upward slope: *There's a slight rise in the road just before our house.* | *We sat at the top of a small rise.* **4** [C] *BrE* ‖ **raise** *AmE*— an increase in wages: *We all got a £6-a-week (pay) rise last month.* **5 get/take a rise out of someone** *infml* to intentionally make someone show annoyance: *You can always get a rise out of John by making jokes about his hair.* **6 give rise to** to be the cause of; lead to (something bad or undesirable): *Unhygienic conditions give rise to disease.*

▷ USAGE Note the fixed phrase **rise and fall**: *The* **rise and fall** *of the temperature during the day.*◁

ris·er /ˈraɪzəʳ/ *n* **1** a person who gets out of bed at the stated time in the morning: *She's an* **early/late riser.** **2** the upright part of a step, between two TREADS (=flat parts)

ris·ers /ˈraɪzəz‖-ərz/ *n* [U] a temporary set of steps which people can stand on so that each row is standing higher than the next: *The choir mounted the risers quietly.*

ris·i·ble /ˈrɪzɪbəl/ *adj fml, usu. derog* causing laughter or deserving to be laughed at: *His suggestion was so stupid as to be risible.* —**·bility** /ˌrɪzɪˈbɪlɪti/ *n* [U]

ris·ing¹ /ˈraɪzɪŋ/ also **uprising**— *n* an occasion of sudden violent opposition to a government or ruler

rising² *adj* moving to a position of greater importance, fame, etc.: *the rising generation* | *a rising tennis star* | *a rising young politician*

rising³ *prep esp. BrE* nearly (the stated age): *My daughter is rising seven.*

rising damp /ˌ·· ˈ·/ *n* [U] water that comes up from the ground into the walls of a building

rising fives /ˌ·· ˈ·/ *n* [P] in Britain, children who will soon be five years old, the age by which they must start school. Sometimes INFANT SCHOOLs take children when they are rising fives.

risk¹ /rɪsk/ *n* **1** [C;U (**of**)] (a) danger; (a) possibility that something harmful or undesirable may happen: *The firemen wouldn't allow anyone back into the building because there was a risk/some risk of the fire breaking out again.* [+(*that*)] *There was a risk that the fire would break out again.* | *Fishermen face a lot of risks in their daily lives.* | *Are you insured against all risks?* | *This window is a security risk; you should have a lock put on it.* | *The disease is spreading, and all young children are* **at risk.** (=in danger) | *You have to* **take/run** *a lot of* **risks** *if you want to succeed in business.* | *I don't want to* **run the risk of** (=take the chance of) *meeting George, so I'll stay here.* | **At the risk of** *seeming rude* (=even if this seems rude), *I must admit that I don't really like the painting.* | *a high-risk investment* (=with a high danger of loss) **2** [C] (in insurance) a person or thing that has the stated likelihood of making the insurance company pay a claim: *Because of his high blood pressure, he's not a very good risk for life insurance.* **3 at one's own risk** agreeing to accept any loss or danger: *"Anyone swimming in this lake does so at his own risk."* (notice)

risk² *v* [T] **1** to put in danger; take the chance of losing: *You're risking your health by smoking.* | *She risked her life trying to save the drowning child.* **2** to take the chance of (a possible unpleasant result): *They will be risking a serious defeat if they hold an election now.* | *He realized that the police might find out but decided to risk it.* [+ *v-ing*] *By criticizing the boss he risked losing his job.* **3** [+*obj/v-ing*] to take (an action that may lead to danger or loss) in the hope that things will go well: *In the present circumstances they are unlikely to risk an election/risk holding an election.* (=because they may lose it) **4 risk one's neck** to endanger one's life

risk·y /ˈrɪski/ *adj* (esp. of an action) having a high degree of risk; rather dangerous: *You drove too fast round that corner — it was a risky thing to do.* | *a risky journey/operation/business investment* —**ily** *adv* —**iness** *n* [U]

ri·sot·to /rɪˈzɒtəʊ‖-ˈsɔː-/ *n* -**tos** [C;U] a dish made of rice cooked with cheese, onions, chicken, etc.

ris·qué /ˈrɪskeɪ‖rɪˈskeɪ/ *adj* (of a joke, story, etc.) slightly rude and shocking, esp. because concerned with sex

ris·sole /ˈrɪsəʊl/ *n* a small round flat mass of cut-up meat cooked in hot fat

rite /raɪt/ *n* [*usu. pl.*] a ceremonial act with a fixed pattern, usu. for a religious purpose: *funeral rites* | *The priest performed the* **last rites** *over the dying woman.* | *Anthropologists have described* **rites of passage** (=ceremonies marking a new stage in one's life) *practised by certain societies.* | *Satanic rites*

rit·u·al¹ /ˈrɪtʃuəl/ *adj* [A] done as (part of) a rite or ritual: *ritual dances* | *ritual murder* — ~ **ly** *adv* : *ritually killed*

ritual² *n* [C;U] one or more ceremonies or customary acts which are often repeated in the same form: *Christian ritual(s)* (=the form of church services) | (fig., *humor*) *She went through her usual ritual of making sure all the doors were locked before she went to bed.*

rit·u·al·is·m /ˈrɪtʃuəlɪzəm/ *n* [U] *often derog* great interest in or obedience to ritual —**istic** /ˌrɪtʃuəˈlɪstɪk◂/ *adj* —**istically** /kli/ *adv*

ritz /rɪts/ *n AmE infml* **put on the ritz** to show that one is wealthy by living in a large house, giving parties, etc.: *He really puts on the ritz to try to impress people.*

Ritz [*the*] one of an international group of expensive hotels: *We stay at the Ritz wherever we can.*

ritz·y /ˈrɪtsi/ *adj infml apprec* fashionable and expensive; GLAMOROUS (from the **Ritz** hotel chain, which is very comfortable and expensive, esp. **The Ritz** in London)

ri·val¹ /ˈraɪvəl/ *n* [(**for, in**)] a person, group, or organization with whom one competes: *Who will be his main rival in the presidential election?* | *Bob and I were friendly rivals for the job/rivals in love.* | *These two companies are* **arch-rivals** (=very great rivals) *in the computer industry.* | *She left her job and went to work for a rival company.* | *a clash between rival football supporters*

rival² *v* **-ll-** *BrE* ‖ **-l-** *AmE* [T] to equal; be as good as or reach the same standard as: *Ships can't rival aircraft for speed.* | *As a tourist centre, it rivals anywhere in Europe.* —see also UNRIVALLED

ri·val·ry /ˈraɪvəlri/ *n* [C;U (**with, between**)] competition; (a case of) being rivals: *There was a friendly rivalry between the two women.* | *There was fierce/intense rivalry* between the two companies to get the contract.

Ri·vals /ˈraɪvəlz/, **The** a play by Richard Sheridan, in which the character Mrs Malaprop appears —see also Mrs MALAPROP

riv·en /ˈrɪvən/ adj [F] fml split violently apart: The whole community was riven by the strike, which some men had joined and others had not.

riv·er /ˈrɪvəʳ/ n **1** a wide natural stream of water flowing between banks into a lake, into another wider stream, or into the sea: Let's go swimming in the river|sailing on the river. | the river Amazon | the Mississippi River | a river steamer | a river delta | the mouth of a river | sail up|down the river | (fig.) Rivers of blood flowed during the war. —compare STREAM¹ (1); see also **sell someone down the river** (SELL¹) **2 rivers of blood** quote a phrase used by the British politician Enoch Powell in a speech saying that Britain should not allow IMMIGRANTS to enter the country. He said that if too many black people were allowed in, there would be fighting and "rivers of blood" in the streets of Britain. —see also Enoch POWELL

river ba·sin /ˈ·· ˌ··/ n an area from which all the water flows into the same river

riv·er·bed /ˈrɪvəbed‖-ər-/ n the ground over which a river flows between its banks

Riv·ers /ˈrɪvəz‖-vərz/, **Joan** /dʒəʊn/ (1933–) an American COMEDIENNE (=a woman who makes people laugh) and writer, known esp. for making rude jokes about sex and important people

Joan Rivers

riv·er·side /ˈrɪvəsaɪd‖-ər-/ n [the] the land on or near the banks of a river: Let's go for a picnic by the riverside. | an old riverside inn

riv·et¹ /ˈrɪvɪt/ n a metal pin used for fastening metal plates together by putting it through a hole in the plates and then hammering one end flat, so that it spreads and holds firmly

rivet² v [T] **1** to fasten with rivets: The metal plates used in making ships used to be riveted together, but now they're usually welded. | (fig.) I stood **riveted to the spot** (=unable to move) as the lions escaped from the cage and charged towards me. **2** to attract and hold (someone's attention) strongly: My attention was riveted by a slight movement in the bushes; could it be the murderer?
rivet sthg. on sbdy./sthg. phr v [T often pass.] to fix (eyes or attention) firmly on: He riveted his eyes on her.| Public attention was riveted on the nuclear accident

riv·et·er /ˈrɪvɪtəʳ/ n a person whose job is fastening rivets —see also ROSIE THE RIVETER

riv·et·ing /ˈrɪvɪtɪŋ/ adj apprec very interesting and exciting; holding one's attention: This is an absolutely riveting book; I can hardly put it down!

ri·vi·e·ra /ˌrɪviˈeərə/ n [the] **1** a warm stretch of coast that is popular with holidaymakers: the Cornish Riviera **2 the (French) Riviera** the Mediterranean coast of France and Italy including Nice, Cannes, St Tropez, the Côte d'Azur, and Monaco. People think of the Riviera as being fashionable and expensive, and a place where rich and famous people go. —see also SOUTH OF FRANCE

riv·u·let /ˈrɪvjʊlɪt/ n lit a very small stream: (fig.) rivulets of sweat

Riy·adh /ˈriːæd/ the capital city of Saudi Arabia

ri·yal , rial /riˈɑːl‖riˈɔːl, -ˈɑːl/ n a unit of money in Saudi Arabia and certain other Arab countries

RN /ˌɑːr ˈen/ abbrev. for: **1** Royal Navy; the British navy: Captain Anstruther, RN **2** REGISTERED NURSE

RNA /ˌɑːr en ˈeɪ/ n [U] ribonucleic acid; an important chemical found in all living cells

RNIB /ˌɑːr en aɪ ˈbiː/ [the] abbrev. for: ROYAL NATIONAL INSTITUTE FOR THE BLIND

RNLI /ˌɑːr en el ˈaɪ/ [the] Royal National Lifeboat Institution; a British organization (a CHARITY) of unpaid workers who raise money for the LIFEBOAT service around the coast of Britain

roach¹ /rəʊtʃ/ n roach or roaches a European fresh-water fish related to the CARP

roach² n **1** AmE infml for COCKROACH **2** sl the unsmoked end of a MARIJUANA cigarette

road /rəʊd/ n **1** [C] a prepared track or way, usu. with a smooth hard surface, along which wheeled vehicles can travel: a busy road | Follow the road round to the right and you'll find his house. | a main road | a side road | a bumpy dirt road (=without a hard surface) | It takes three hours by train and four **by road** (=driving). | a road map of Western Europe | He hasn't got much **road sense**. (=drives/walks carelessly and is likely to have accidents) | a road accident (=car crash, etc.) | a **road safety** campaign (=to make people drive more safely. Cross the road more carefully, etc.) | My address is 21 Princess Road. (written abbrev. **Rd**) —see also HIGH ROAD; see STREET (USAGE) **2** [S] dial one's way: You're in my road|Get out of my road; I want to pass. **3** [C] also **roads** pl.— tech an open stretch of deep water, such as at the mouth of a river, where ships can be kept **4 all roads lead to Rome** any opinions formed, or decisions made, etc. will take one to the same place in the end: All roads lead to Bryant quality homes. | For Lendl all roads lead to Wimbledon. **5 on the road: a** on a car journey; travelling, esp. for one's work: I've been on the road since five o'clock this morning and I'm really tired. | **b** moving towards (a desirable result): He finally felt he was **on the road to success** after they agreed to publish his first book. | Scientists have not yet found a cure for the disease, but they believe they're **on the right road**. (=getting close to finding one) **c** (of a group of performers, esp. a theatrical company or popular music band) giving a number of planned performances at different places: When will the band be going **on the road** again? | (fig., infml) Let's **get this show on the road**. (=get this activity started) —compare **be on the streets** (STREET) **6 hit the road** AmE infml to begin travelling: We hit the road bright and early. **7 one for the road** infml one last drink before leaving a party. This is now discouraged because drinking and driving is considered dangerous. **8 the road to hell is paved with good intentions** saying a phrase used to criticize someone who has promised to do a good action or to behave better but who is unlikely to actually do this **9 ye'll tak the high road and I'll tak the low road, and I'll be in Scotland afore you** a phrase from the popular song The bonny, bonny banks of Loch Lomond

road·block /ˈrəʊdblɒk‖-blɑːk/ n a bar or other object(s) placed across a road, esp. by the police, to stop traffic: roadblocks put up to trap the fleeing terrorists | (fig.) American investors are growing restive over roadblocks to their projects.

road haul·age /ˈ· ˌ··/ n [U] the business of taking goods from one place to another by road

road haul·i·er /ˌ· ˈ···/ n a person whose business is the carriage of goods by road

road hog /ˈ· ·/ n infml derog a fast, selfish, and careless car driver

road·house /ˈrəʊdhaʊs/ n -houses /ˌhaʊzɪz/ a restaurant or bar on a main road outside a city, to which one goes to eat, drink, dance, etc.

road·ie /ˈrəʊdi/ n infml a person whose job is moving equipment, driving, etc. for entertainers, esp. ROCK³ musicians, when they are travelling

road kill /ˈ· ·/ n AmE infml an animal that has been killed by a vehicle on the road

road·man /ˈrəʊdmən/ also **road mend·er** /ˈ· ˌ··/— n -men /mən/ a man whose job is mending roads

road man·a·ger /ˈ· ˌ···/ n a person whose job is making arrangements for entertainers, esp. ROCK³ musicians, when they are travelling

road rol·ler /ˈ· ˌ··/ n a heavy machine with very wide wheels for driving over and flattening road surfaces —see also STEAMROLLER¹

road·run·ner /ˈrəʊdˌrʌnəʳ/ n **1** a small bird which runs very fast and lives in the central and western areas of the US **2** (cap.) a CARTOON character on television like this bird, which always escapes when a COYOTE (called Wiley Coyote) tries to catch it

road safe·ty /ˌ· ˈ··/ n [U] the prevention of people being killed or hurt by road traffic: *the Government's new road safety campaign*

road·show /ˈrəʊdʃəʊ/ *n* a group that travels around the country giving public performances for the purpose of entertainment, advertising, etc.

road·side /ˈrəʊdsaɪd/ *n* [*the*] the edge of the road: *We ate our meal by the roadside/at a roadside pub.*

road·sign /ˈrəʊdsaɪn/ *n* a sign by a road which gives information about the way ahead or instructions to road users

road·ster /ˈrəʊdstər/ *n old-fash* an open sports car with two seats

road tax /ˈ· ·/ *n* [C;U] a tax (esp. in Britain) which the owner of a vehicle must pay to be allowed to drive it on the road: *Always display your (road) tax disc on the vehicle.*

road test /ˈ· ·/ *n* a test of a vehicle on public roads to see if it is fit to be on the road —**road-test** *v* [T]

road·way /ˈrəʊdweɪ/ *n* [*the*] the middle part of a road where vehicles drive: *Don't stop on the roadway; move in to the side.*

road·work /ˈrəʊdwɜːk‖-wɜːrk/ *n* [U] the running done by sportsmen, e.g. BOXERS to prepare for a match

road works /ˈrəʊdwɜːks‖-ɜːr-/ *n* [P] (often seen in Britain on a warning sign for motorists) road repairs being done

road·wor·thy /ˈrəʊd,wɜːði‖-ɜːr-/ *adj* (of a vehicle) in proper and safe condition to be driven —**-thiness** *n* [U]

roam /rəʊm/ *v* [I+adv/prep;T] to wander with no very clear purpose: *The lovers roamed across the fields in complete forgetfulness of the time.* | *Crowds of youths roamed the streets looking for trouble.* — ~**er** *n*

roan /rəʊn/ *n, adj* (a horse) of a mixed colour, esp. brown with white hairs in it

roar¹ /rɔːr/ *n* a deep loud continuing sound: *the roar of an angry lion/of a football crowd/of an aircraft engine/of the wind and waves* | *roars of laughter*

roar² *v* **1** [I] to give a roar: *The lion/The football crowd roared.* | *I turned the key and the engine roared into life.* | *The traffic roared past.* | *He roared with pain/anger.* **2** [T (OUT)] to say or express loudly or with force: *The crowd roared (out) their approval.* | *"Come here, you horrible little man!" he roared.* **3** [I] *infml* to laugh long and loudly: *His jokes made us all roar (with laughter).* **4** [I] *infml* (of a child) to cry noisily: *Billy began to roar when I took the chocolate away.*

roaring /ˈrɔːrɪŋ/ *adv, adj* [A] *infml* (in certain phrases) to a very great degree: *He came home roaring drunk.* | *The film was a roaring success.* | *The new restaurant is doing a roaring trade.* (=doing very good business)

roaring for·ties /ˌ·· ˈ··/ *n* [*the*+P] the part of the Atlantic Ocean about 40 degrees north of the Equator where storms are very common

Roaring Twen·ties /ˌ·· ˈ··/ *n* [*the*] the 1920s, esp. in the US, where life was thought to be very adventurous because of Prohibition, GANGSTERS, and FLAPPERS

roast¹ /rəʊst/ *v* **1** [I; T] to cook (esp. meat) or be cooked by dry heat, either in front of an open fire or in an OVEN: *Roast the chicken at about 200°C.* | *The beef is roasting nicely on the spit.* | *roasted coffee beans* | (fig.) *They sat in the sun roasting themselves.* —see COOK (USAGE) and see picture at PAN **2** *AmE infml* to say funny things about a person whom a group has gathered to honour: *Don Rickles got up and roasted Alan King.* — ~**er** *n*

roast² *n* **1** a large piece of roasted meat: *Let's have a nice roast for Sunday dinner.* | *Roast beef and Yorkshire pudding is a common British meal.* | *Roast lamb and mint sauce are often eaten as a Sunday lunch.* **2** *AmE infml* an occasion when a group of people honour a person by saying funny and then kind things about him: *a celebrity roast on TV* **3** *AmE* an outdoor party at which the stated kind of meat is roasted and eaten: *a pig/hot dog roast*

roast³ *adj* [A] roasted: *a roast chicken* | *roast potatoes* | *medium roast coffee*

roast beef /ˌ· ˈ·/ *n* [U] the meat of farm cattle which has been roasted. Roast beef, esp. served with YORKSHIRE PUDDING for Sunday lunch, is thought of as the most typical English food. —see also SUNDAY LUNCH

roast·ing¹ /ˈrəʊstɪŋ/ *adv, adj* very (hot): *a roasting (hot) summer day* | *I'm roasting out here; let's go into the shade.*

roasting² *n infml* an act of expressing strong angry disap-

proval: *He got a real roasting from the teacher for being insolent.*

rob /rɒb‖rɑːb/ *v* -bb- [T (of)] **1** to take the property of (a person or organization) illegally, esp. using violence, threats, etc.: *I've been robbed!* | *The brothers planned to rob a bank.* | *They knocked him down and robbed him of his watch.* (compare *They stole his watch.*) | (fig.) *The silly ending robs the plot of any credibility.* —see STEAL (USAGE) **2 rob Peter to pay Paul** to take or get something from one person in order to pay another **3 we was/wuz robbed!** *sl humor* a phrase typically said by supporters of a sports team who feel that the team lost a match unfairly

rob·ber /ˈrɒbər‖ˈrɑː-/ *n* a person who robs or has robbed: *a gang of robbers* —compare BURGLAR, THIEF

robber bar·on /ˌ·· ˈ··/ *n AmE* one of a group of mostly late 19th century American businessmen who made very large fortunes without regard to fairness or honesty

rob·ber·y /ˈrɒbəri‖ˈrɑː-/ *n* [C;U] (an example of) the crime of taking someone else's property; robbing: *He had committed several robberies in the neighbourhood.* | *He was charged with robbery with violence.* —see also DAYLIGHT ROBBERY

robe¹ /rəʊb/ *n* **1** also **robes** *pl*— a long loose garment worn for official or ceremonial occasions: *a judge's black robes* **2** *esp. AmE* a long loose garment worn informally indoors —see also BATHROBE

robe² *v* [I;T (in)] *rare* to dress (oneself or someone else) in robes; put on a robe: *The king and queen were robed in red.*

Rob·erts /ˈrɒbəts‖ˈrɑːbərts/, **Oral** (1918–) a television preacher (PREACH) in the US who started a university in Oklahoma. He is remembered for saying on television that God would take him up to heaven if more than a million dollars was not raised for his university by a certain date.

Robert the Bruce see Robert BRUCE

Robe·son /ˈrəʊbsən/, **Paul** (1898–1976) an American singer and actor whose wide success in Britain and the US was unusual for a black person at that time. He left the US during the time of MCCARTHY because of his COMMUNIST beliefs. His most popular song was *Ol' Man River* from the musical *Showboat.*

Robes·pierre /ˈrəʊbspɪər/, **Max·i·mil·i·en** /ˌmæksɪˈmɪliən/ (1758–94) one of the leaders of the FRENCH REVOLUTION, whose head was cut off at the GUILLOTINE after his short period in power

rob·in /ˈrɒbɪn‖ˈrɑː-/ *n* **1** a common small European bird with a brown back and wings and a red breast **2** any of various larger birds that look like this, in the US and other English-speaking countries —see picture at BIRD, and see also ROUND ROBIN

Robin¹ Batman's young partner, who helps him to fight criminals. Robin is also known as the "Boy Wonder". —see also BATMAN

Robin², **Christopher** see Christopher ROBIN

Robin Hood /ˌ·· ˈ·/ according to old stories, a man who lived as an OUTLAW in Sherwood Forest, near Nottingham, with a group of companions (the "Merry Men"), including Little John, Friar Tuck, and his lover Maid Marion. Robin Hood is remembered esp. for stealing money from rich people and giving it to poor people. His main enemy was the Sheriff of Nottingham, who was always trying to catch and punish him. Robin Hood is usu. shown dressed in green clothes and holding a BOW³ (1): *Labour MPs deem him a Robin Hood in reverse, robbing the poor to give to the rich.* —see colour picture on page 620

Rob·in·son /ˈrɒbɪnsən‖ˈrɑː-/, **Edward G.** (1893–1973) an American film actor famous for character parts and playing GANGSTERS

Robinson, Jackie (1919–72) an American who was the first black man to be allowed to play BASEBALL in the MAJOR LEAGUE

Rob·in·son, Smok·ey /ˈsməʊki/ (1940–) an American popular music singer, songwriter, and businessman who first became successful in the 1960s with the group The Miracles and the record company Motown, of which he later became Vice-President

Robinson, Sugar Ray (1920–89) an American BOXER, winner of six world titles

Robinson Cru·soe /ˌrɒbɪ̩nsən ˈkruːsəʊ‖ˌraː-/ a character from a story of the same name by Daniel Defoe. Robinson Crusoe's boat sinks and he finds himself alone on an island. He manages to live by using whatever he can find by his own cleverness. He also meets a black man whom he calls Man Friday who becomes his servant and companion. They are both finally discovered by a British ship and taken home. —see colour picture on page 1145

robots

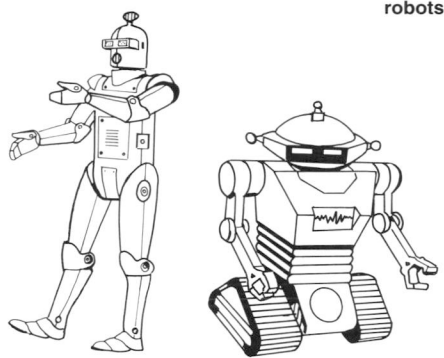

industrial robots

ro·bot /ˈrəʊbɒt‖-baːt, -bət/ n a machine that can move and do some of the work of a human being and is usu. controlled by a computer: *These cars were built by robots.* | (fig.) *They were so brainwashed that they worked like robots, with no thought or initiative of their own.*

ro·bo·tics /rəʊˈbɒtɪks‖-ˈbɑː-/ n [U] the study of the making and use of robots

Rob Roy /ˌrɒb ˈrɔɪ‖ˌraːb-/ (1671–1734) a Scottish OUTLAW, known as the "Robin Hood of Scotland", who lived largely by stealing cows and selling protection against thieves. He was ordered to leave Scotland as punishment but was later forgiven. He is remembered mainly through Sir Walter Scott's NOVEL of the same name.

Rob·son¹ /ˈrɒbsən‖ˈraːb-/, **Bobby** (1933–) a former English football player at club and national level and a former manager of Ipswich football club and the England football team

Robson², Bry·an /ˈbraɪən/ (1957–) an English football player who has played for Manchester United since 1981 and was the captain of England for a long time

Robson³, Dame Flora (1902–84) an English actress

ro·bust /rəˈbʌst, ˈrəʊbʌst/ adj 1 apprec having or showing good health or strength: *a very robust child who never gets ill* | *a robust company* | *That chair's not very robust; don't sit on it!* 2 euph using strong arguments; forceful and effective: *rather robust criticism* | *a robust defence of the Administration's record* — ~**ly** adv — ~**ness** n [U]

Roc /rɒk‖raːk/ [the] in ancient Eastern stories, a bird of great size and strength which, in the story of Sindbad the Sailor, carried Sindbad out of the valley of diamonds

Roch·dale /ˈrɒtʃdeɪl‖ˈraːtʃ-/ a town in NW England near Manchester formerly known esp. for its cotton MILLS¹ (2)

rock¹ /rɒk‖raːk/ v 1 [I;T] to (cause to) move regularly backwards and forwards or from side to side: *The boat rocked (to and fro) on the water.* | *She rocked the child in her arms.* | *He rocked the baby to sleep in the cradle.* 2 [T] to cause great shock and surprise to: *The news of the President's murder rocked the nation.* 3 **Rock-a-bye baby on the tree top** the first line of a song sung to get children to go to sleep 4 **rock the boat** derog to spoil the good or comfortable situation that exists: *We've been doing it this way for years; don't rock the boat by trying to introduce new methods.*

rock² n 1 [C;U] (a type of) stone forming part of the Earth's surface: *To build this tunnel we had to cut through (the) solid rock.* | *They go rock-climbing every weekend.* | *an interesting rock formation* | *igneous rocks* | *The house is as solid as a rock.* (=very strong and well built) 2 [C] a large separate piece of stone: *There's danger from falling rocks.* 3 [C] AmE any stone, large or small: *They threw rocks at her car.* 4 [U] BrE a hard sticky kind of sweet made in long round bars and sold esp. at the seaside in Britain with the name of the place marked in it: *a stick of (Brighton) rock* 5 [C usu. pl.] sl, esp. AmE a diamond 6 **between a rock and a hard place** having two possible courses of action open to one, both of which are dangerous, unpleasant, etc. 7 **Rock of ages, cleft for me, let me hide myself in thee** the first words of a famous HYMN (=religious song) written in 1775 by the Reverend Toplady, who had the idea for the hymn while sheltering from a storm, in a CAVE within a large rock

rock³ also **rock music**— n [U] 1 any of several styles of popular modern music which are based on ROCK 'N' ROLL, usu. played on electrical instruments: *a rock concert* — compare POP³ 2 ROCK 'N' ROLL

rock bot·tom /ˌ· ˈ···◂/ n [U] the lowest point; the bottom: *Prices have reached rock bottom.* | *Performance standards have fallen to rock bottom.* | *rock-bottom prices at the sales*

rock·bound /ˈrɒkbaʊnd‖ˈraːk-/ adj (of a coast) bordered with rocks

rock cake /ˈ· ·/ also **rock bun**— n BrE a small hard cake with a rough surface

rock climb·ing /ˈ· ˌ··/ n [U] the sport of climbing up large rocks and parts of mountains which are impossible to walk up

rock dash /ˈ· ·/ n [U] AmE for PEBBLEDASH

Rock·e·fel·ler /ˈrɒkəfelər‖ˈraːk-/, **John D** (1839–1937) a very wealthy American bank owner who gave away millions of dollars, esp. for medical studies and to start the University of Chicago. His son, **John D Rockefeller II**, gave the land for the United Nations HEADQUARTERS and built the **Rockefeller Center** in New York City, a large group of buildings which includes offices, shops, and various places of entertainment. —see colour map on page 1376

rock·er¹ /ˈrɒkər‖ˈraː-/ n 1 either of the curved pieces of wood fixed to the underside of a ROCKING CHAIR, ROCKING HORSE, or CRADLE¹ (1) which allow movement backwards and forwards when pushed 2 ROCKING CHAIR 3 **off one's rocker** infml, often humor mad

rockers

rocker² n (often cap.) a member of a group of young people, in Britain esp. in the 1960s, following a fashion for leather clothes, motorcycles, and ROCK 'N' ROLL —compare MOD

rock·e·ry /ˈrɒkəri‖ˈraː-/ also **rock garden**— n a (part of a) garden laid out as a pile of rocks with low-growing plants growing between them

rock·et¹ /ˈrɒkɪt‖ˈraː-/ n 1 a usu. tube-shaped object that is driven through the air by burning gases and is used for travelling into space, for helping aircraft to take off, etc.: *The space rocket was launched and went into orbit.* | *a two-stage rocket* —see also RETRO-ROCKET   **2** a similar object used as a weapon, esp. one that carries a bomb: *an anti-tank rocket* | *a rocket base*   **3** also **skyrocket**— a small tube that has a stick fixed to it, is driven through the air by burning explosive powder, and is used as a FIREWORK   **4** *BrE infml* a case of being severely spoken to because one has done something wrong: *You'll really get a rocket if you're late again!*

rocket² *v* [I]   **1** [(UP)] also **skyrocket**— (esp. of an amount, price, etc.) to rise quickly and suddenly: *The price of sugar has suddenly rocketed (up).*   **2** [+*adv/prep*] to move at very great speed: *The train rocketed through the station at 90 miles an hour.* | (fig.) *After his amazing success in the film he rocketed to stardom.*

rocket launch·er /ˈ·· ˌ··/ *n* a machine, carried by hand or on a vehicle, for sending up military rocket-type bombs

Rock·ettes /rɒˈkets‖ˈrɑː-/ [*the* +P] a group of women who perform at Radio City Music Hall, singing and dancing, usu. while in a line across the stage

rock·fall /ˈrɒkˌfɔːl‖ˈrɑːk-/ *n* a mass of falling or fallen rocks

rock gar·den /ˈ· ˌ··/ *n* a ROCKERY

rock hard /ˌ· ˈ·◂/ *adj* as hard as a rock

rock hound /ˈ· ·/ *n AmE infml*   **1** a GEOLOGIST   **2** a collector of rocks and minerals

Rock·ies /ˈrɒkiz‖ˈrɑː-/ see ROCKY MOUNTAINS

rock·ing chair /ˈ·· ·/ also **rocker**— *n* a chair fitted with ROCKERS so that it moves backwards and forwards when a person sits in it

▶ CULTURAL NOTE Rocking chairs are often thought of as used by old people or country people or for sitting in while calming a baby. —see picture at CHAIR◀

rocking horse /ˈ·· ·/ *n* a wooden horse for a child to ride on fitted with ROCKERS so that it moves backwards and forwards

rock mu·sic /ˈ· ˌ··/ *n* [U] see ROCK³

Rock·ne /ˈrɒkni‖ˈrɑːk-/, **Knute** /nuːt/ (1888–1931) an American FOOTBALL (2) COACH (teacher) who helped improve the standards of the game. When one of his players was ill, Rockne told his team to win the game for "the Gipper". President Ronald Reagan, who as an actor played in a film about Rockne, often used the phrase "do it for the Gipper."

rock 'n' roll /ˌrɒk ən ˈrəʊl‖ ˌrɑːk-/ also **rock**, **rock and roll**— *n* [U] a style of music that was popular esp. in the 1950s but is still played now, which has a strong loud beat and is usu. played on electrical instruments and repeats a few simple phrases. It was first made popular by Bill Haley and Elvis Presley. —compare POP³

rock 'n' roll

Rock of Gi·bral·tar /ˌ·· · ··ˈ··/ [*the*] a mountainous cliff at the NW end of the Mediterranean Sea. British people sometimes mention it when they want to give an idea that something is very solid: *"That tree house doesn't look very safe to me." "Oh, it's like the Rock of Gibraltar."*

rock plant /ˈ· ·/ *n* a plant that grows naturally among rocks and can be planted in a ROCKERY

rocks /rɒks‖rɑːks/ *n* [P]   **1** a line of ROCK² (1) under or beside the sea: *The ship was driven onto the rocks during the storm.*   **2 on the rocks:** *infml* **a** in difficulties; likely to fail soon: *The business/Their marriage is on the rocks.* **b** (of an alcoholic drink) with ice but no water: *Scotch on the rocks*

rock sal·mon /ˌ·· ˈ··/ *n* [U] *BrE* (the trade name for) any of several inexpensive types of fish, such as DOGFISH, when sold as food

rock salt /ˈ· ·/ *n* [U] common salt of the type found in mines, not in the sea

rock sol·id /ˌ· ˈ··/ *adj* very firm and safe: *The reserves of the Building Society are rock solid.* | *Support for the Tory candidate was rock solid.*

Rock·well /ˈrɒkwəl‖ˈrɑːk-/, **Norman** (1894–1978) an American artist who drew many pictures of ordinary small-town people for popular magazines, often showing the American way of life in an idealistic (IDEALIST) way. His style of painting is very well known in the US.

rock·y¹ /ˈrɒki‖ˈrɑːki/ *adj*   **1** full of rocks or made of rock: *a rocky path up the mountain* | *rocky soil*   **2** hard like rock —**iness** *n* [U]

rocky² *adj infml* unsteady; not firm: *I feel a bit rocky (on my legs) after that fall.* | *After the recent problems, the company faces a rocky road ahead.* (=an uncertain future)

Rocky the first of a group of films (later ones were called **Rocky II**, **Rocky III**, etc.) starring Sylvester Stallone as a determined boxer called Rocky. In each of the films the main character overcomes difficulties and wins a fight against a strong opponent. The films are esp. popular with young people. —see colour picture on page 685

Rocky Hor·ror Show /ˌ··· ˈ·· ˌ·/ [*the*] a play and a film (**Rocky Horror Picture Show**) about a young man and woman who become involved with a strange man who dresses wildly. The film and the music from it are very popular with some people and these people can often say all the lines from the film and perform the dances.

Rocky Moun·tain oy·ster /ˌ··· ˌ·· ˈ··/ *n AmE* PRAIRIE OYSTER (2)

Rocky Moun·tains /ˌ·· ˈ··/ also **Rockies**— *n* [*the*+P] a range of high mountains lying between the W coastal plains of N America and the rest of the US and Canada from Alaska down to New Mexico —see colour map on pages 1374–5

Rocky Moun·tain spot·ted fe·ver /ˌ··· ˌ·· ˌ·· ˈ··/ *n* [U] a serious illness caused by the bite of a TICK³ in which one has a high fever and pain in the muscles, bones, and joints. The illness is found in the areas of the US near the Rocky Mountains. If untreated, it may cause death.

ro·co·co /rəˈkəʊkəʊ/ *adj* (of buildings, furniture, etc.) in a style fashionable in Europe from the late 17th to the 18th century, with a great deal of curling decoration —compare BAROQUE

rod /rɒd‖rɑːd/ *n*   **1** (*often in comb.*) a long thin pole or bar of any firm material such as wood, metal, or plastic, used for various purposes: *a fishing-rod* | *The piston-rods connect the pistons to the parts of the engine which they move.* | *The concrete walls are reinforced with steel rods.* | *fuel rods in a nuclear reactor*   **2** *old-fash* a stick used for beating people   **3 make a rod for one's own back** to prepare trouble for oneself in the future —see also HOT ROD, **rule with a rod of iron** (RULE²), **spare the rod** (SPARE¹)

Rod·dick /ˈrɒdɪk‖ˈrɑː-/, **A·ni·ta** /əˈniːtə/ (1942–   ) a successful British businesswoman who established the group of Body Shops which sell soap and beauty products. She is known for her concern for the environment.

rode /rəʊd/ *past tense of* RIDE

rodents

beaver

rat

mouse   lemming   squirrel

ro·dent /ˈrəʊdənt/ *n fml or tech* a small plant-eating animal with strong sharp long front teeth: *Rats, mice, and rabbits are rodents/members of the rodent family.*

ro·de·o /ˈrəʊdi-əʊ, rəʊˈdeɪ-əʊ/ *n* **-os** (esp. in Canada and the western US) a public entertainment at which COWBOYS ride wild horses, catch cattle with ropes, etc. —see colour picture on page 884

Ro·de·o Drive /rəʊˌdeɪəʊ ˈdraɪv/ a street in Beverly Hills, California, which has many expensive shops

Rod·gers /ˈrɒdʒəz‖ˈrɑːdʒərz/, **Richard** (1902–79) an American songwriter and COMPOSER who wrote many songs for musical plays and films with Lorenz Hart, including *My Funny Valentine* and *The Lady Is a Tramp*, and then with Oscar Hammerstein, such as *Oklahoma!*, *The King and I*, and *The Sound of Music*

Ro·din /ˈrəʊdæn‖rəʊˈdæn/, **Au·guste** /əʊˈgjuːst/ (1840–1917) French SCULPTOR whose best known works are *The Thinker* and *The Kiss*

The Thinker
by Auguste Rodin

ro·do·mon·tade /ˌrɒdəmɒnˈteɪd, -ˈtɑːd‖ˌrɑːdəmən-/ n [U] *fml derog* claiming to be specially brave or clever; BOASTFUL talk or behaviour

roe /rəʊ/ n [C;U] (a) mass of eggs in a female fish **(hard roe)** or SPERM in a male fish **(soft roe)**, often eaten as food, esp. as a less expensive choice than CAVIAR: *smoked cod's roe*

roe·buck /ˈrəʊbʌk/ n **roebucks** or **roebuck** a male roe deer

Roe·dean /ˈrəʊdiːn/ an expensive English private school for girls

roe deer /ˈ· ·/ n a small European and Asian forest deer

roent·gen[1], **röntgen** /ˈrɒntɡən‖ˈrentɡən/ adj [A] *tech* (often *cap.*) of or being X-RAYS (from **William Conrad Roentgen** or **Röntgen** who discovered the X-ray)

roentgen[2], **röntgen** n *tech* the international measure for X-RAYS

Roe vs. Wade /ˌ· ·· ˈ·/ n a court case decided by the US Supreme Court in 1973 which said that the states cannot prevent a woman from having an ABORTION

▶CULTURAL NOTE This decision has caused CONTROVERSY and despite what the court decided many states have tried to make laws against abortion or have tried to prevent abortions in other ways, such as by saying that CLINICS which receive government money cannot discuss abortion with their patients. Many PRO-LIFE supporters would like another abortion case to go to the Supreme Court because they believe a different decision might be made now.◀

ro·ger /ˈrɒdʒəʳ‖ˈrɑː-/ interj (used in radio and signalling to say that a message has been received and understood): *"Roger, control. Over and out."*

Roger n see JOLLY ROGER

Ro·gers /ˈrɒdʒəz‖ˈrɑːdʒərz/, **Buck** a HERO in a COMIC who had many adventures in space

Hogers, Ginger (1911–) an American film actress and dancer best known as Fred Astaire's partner in 1930s musicals —see picture at Fred ASTAIRE

Rogers, Richard (1933–) a leading British ARCHITECT who designed (DESIGN) the Pompidou Centre in Paris and the Lloyd's Building in London

Rogers, Roy /rɔɪ/ (1912–) an American actor who usu. played a COWBOY. With his wife **Dale Evans** (1912–) and his horse **Trigger** he appeared in a television programme in the 1950s and 1960s. At the end of their programme he and his wife always sang the song "Happy Trails to You," which is still associated with them. —see also ROY ROGERS

Rogers, Will (1879–1935) an American actor and HUMORIST. Rogers sometimes told jokes while spinning a LASSO (a rope) and often made fun of politics and politicians. People believe that Rogers once said "I never met a man I didn't like," though what he really said was slightly different.

Ro·get /ˈrɒʒeɪ‖rəʊˈʒeɪ/, **Peter Mark** (1779–1869) a British scientist and writer of *Roget's Thesaurus*, now a standard work on the English language

Roget's The·sau·rus /ˌ·· ·ˈ·‖ˌ·, ·ˈ·/ *tdmk* the original THESAURUS (=a book of words arranged in groups according to connections between their meanings) written in English by Roget and printed in 1852

rogue[1] /rəʊɡ/ n **1** a dishonest person, esp. a man: *Don't buy a used car from that rogue.* **2** *not derog, often humor* a person who enjoys making trouble, but usu. in a harmless and playful way; MISCHIEVOUS person

rogue[2] adj [A] **1** (of a wild animal) living apart from the rest and very easily made angry: *a rogue elephant* **2** not following the usual or accepted standards, esp. in an uncontrollable or troublesome way: *rogue politicians who go against the party line*

rogu·e·ry /ˈrəʊɡəri/ n [C;U] (a piece of) behaviour typical of a rogue

rogues' gal·ler·y /ˌ· ˈ···/ n a collection of (pictures of) bad or unpleasant people, esp. criminals

rogu·ish /ˈrəʊɡɪʃ/ adj *often humor* playful, perhaps slightly dishonest, and fond of playing tricks or making trouble: *a roguish grin* – –ly adv – –ness n [U]

rois·ter·er /ˈrɔɪstərəʳ/ n *old-fash* a rough cheerful noisy person: *a crowd of drunken roisterers*

role /rəʊl/ n **1** the part or character taken by an actor in a play, film, etc.: *Olivier played/took the role of Hamlet.* | *She prefers to play comic roles.* **2** the duty or purpose of a person or group in a particular activity or area of life: *The local priest played a leading role in settling the dispute.* | *the increasingly important role of the media in political life* | *The success of her business made it difficult for her to fulfil her role as wife and mother.* –see also TITLE ROLE

role mod·el /ˈ· ˌ··/ n a person whose behaviour in a particular ROLE (2) is copied or is likely to be copied by others, esp. because he or she is admired

role play·ing /ˈ· ˌ··/ n [U] the act of behaving in a way typical of someone else or of an imaginary person, either unconsciously or for the purpose of learning a job, learning how to behave in certain social situations, etc. –**role play** n, v

role reversal /ˈ· ·ˌ··/ n [C;U] (an act of) doing what the opposite sex usu. does esp. in areas such as work, care of children, jobs in the house etc.

Ro·lex /ˈrəʊleks/ n *tdmk* a very expensive type of watch

rolf·ing /ˈrɒlfɪŋ‖ˈrɑː-/ also **Structural Integration**– n [U] *tdmk* a method of improving the body's shape and balance by moving and reshaping the deep muscles and TISSUES. Rolfing was developed by Ida P Rolf (1896–1979), an American doctor (PhD) of PHYSIOLOGY. The method is better-known in the US than in Britain, but is still new to the public. As it is not practised by an ordinary doctor, but by a trained **rolfer**, it is considered a kind of ALTERNATIVE MEDICINE:*He's going to try rolfing.*

roll[1] /rəʊl/ v **1** [I+adv/prep; T+obj+adv/prep] to turn over and over or from side to side, or move by doing this: *The dog rolled on the floor/in the mud.* | *The ball rolled into the hole.* | *They rolled the logs down the hill into the river.* | *Roll up your sleeves/trousers before putting your arms/legs in the water.* | *The driver rolled down his window* (=opened it by turning the handle) *to speak to the policeman.* **2** [T (UP)] to form into a tube or other (stated) shape by curling round and round: *to roll up a carpet* | *He rolled (up) his umbrella.* | *The cat rolled itself into a ball and went to sleep.* | *He rolled a cigarette.* (=made one by wrapping paper round tobacco) –opposite **unroll**; see also ROLL **out** (2) **3** [I] to move steadily and smoothly along (as if) on wheels: *The train rolled slowly into the station.* | *The waves rolled over the sand.* | *Tears were rolling down her cheeks.* | *Time rolled on.* **4** [I;T] to move or cause (the eyes) to move round and round: *She rolled her eyes in disbelief.* **5** [I;T] to throw (DICE): *Have you rolled (the dice) yet?* **6** [I] (of a ship) to swing from side to side with the movement of the waves: *The ship rolled so heavily that we were all sick.* | (fig.) *The drunken man rolled home to bed.* –compare PITCH[1] (5), YAW **7** [T] to make flat by pressing with a ROLLER (1) or ROLLING PIN: *The lawn should be well rolled.* | *Roll the pastry as flat as you can.* | *rolled oats* –compare ROLL **out** (1) **8** [I] to make a long deep sound like that of a lot of quick strokes: *The thunder/The drums rolled.* **9** [I] (of a machine, esp. a film camera) to work or begin working: *Are the cameras rolling?* | *The presses* (=for printing a newspaper) *are ready to roll.* | (fig.) *He hopes to get his new venture rolling by July.* **10** [T] *AmE sl* to rob someone when he is drunk or asleep: *He got some change by rolling a drunk.* **11 a rolling stone gathers no moss** a person who frequently changes his/her job, place of living, etc. will not

become tied to anything that limits their freedom **12 rolled into one** (of something with different parts or qualities) in a single thing, activity, etc.: *Breakfast TV is like a chat show and a news programme rolled into one.* **13 roll in the aisles** (esp. of people at the theatre) to laugh uncontrollably **14 roll one's r's** to pronounce the sound /r/ with the tongue beating rapidly against the roof of the mouth, as is common e.g. in Scotland **15 roll one's own** *infml* to make one's own cigarettes instead of buying them —see also **set/start/keep the ball rolling** (BALL), **heads will roll** (HEAD¹), **rolling in it** (ROLLING) **16 roll out of bed** *AmE infml* to get out of bed
roll around/round to come again, esp. as part of a pattern: *School will soon be rolling around again, the summer's nearly over.*
roll sthg. ↔ **back** *phr v* [T] **1** to force (opponents) to move back; push back: *We rolled back the enemy forces on all fronts.* | (fig.) *to roll back the frontiers of science/the powers of central government* **2** *AmE* to reduce (prices)
roll in *phr v* [I] to come or arrive in large quantities: *Invitations kept rolling in.* —compare ROLL **up**
roll on *phr v* [I *imperative*] *BrE infml* (used to express a wish that a time or event will come quickly): *I really need a break — roll on Christmas!* —see also ROLL-ON
roll sthg. ↔ **out** *phr v* [T] **1** to spread (a piece of material) out flat and thin by pressing with a ROLLER or a ROLLING PIN: *Roll out the pastry.* —compare ROLL¹ (7) **2** to UNROLL: (fig.) *We rolled out the red carpet* (=we made special preparations) *for the important visitor.*
roll up *phr v* [I] **1** *infml* to arrive, esp. late or in some unacceptable way: *I might have known you wouldn't roll up until the meeting had nearly finished.* **2** [*usu. imperative*] (used esp. when asking people to come inside and see a show at a CIRCUS, FAIR, etc.) to come in: *Roll up, roll up, the show's about to begin!* —compare ROLL **in**; see also ROLL (1,2)

rolls

roll of film

hair rollers/
hair curlers

bread rolls

rolling pin

roller skate

roller towel *BrE*/
towel roll *AmE*

garden roller *BrE*/
lawn roller *AmE*

roll² *n* **1** [C] an act of rolling; a rolling movement, over and over or from side to side: *a young horse having a roll on the grass* | *the slow roll of a ship on the rough sea* | *another roll of the dice* —compare PITCH² (5) **2** [C (**of**)] a piece of flat material that has been rolled into a tube: *a roll of film/of paper/of cloth* —see picture at ROLL¹ **3** [C] something in this shape: *She was disgusted by the rolls of fat on his stomach.* **4** [C] a small loaf for one person, either long or round: *crusty/soft rolls* | *a cheese roll* (=cut and filled with cheese) —see also SAUSAGE ROLL, SPRING ROLL, and picture at ROLL¹ **5** [(*the*) +**of**] a long deep sound (as if) of a lot of quick strokes: *a roll of thunder/of drums* | *We heard the distant roll of the big guns.* **6** [C] an official list of names: *The teacher called the roll.*

(=read the list aloud to see if everyone was there) **7** [C] the act of throwing DICE: *Come on, it's your roll!* | *I had doubles so I get another roll.*
roll bar /ˈ· ·/ *n* a metal bar on the top of a car, to protect the people inside if the car turns over
roll call /ˈ· ·/ *n* [C;U] (the time for) an act of reading out an official list of names to see who is there: *They had a roll call to check that no one was missing.* | *I'll see you after roll call.*
rolled gold /ˌ· ˈ·/ also **gold plate**‖**filled gold** *AmE*— *n* [U] a thin covering of gold on the surface of another metal: *My watch is only rolled gold* (=has a covering of gold), *not solid gold.*
rolled oats /ˌ· ˈ·/ *n* [P] a kind of grain which has been rolled to make it thinner and so quicker to cook and easier to eat. Rolled oats are used for MUESLI and PORRIDGE.
roll·er /ˈrəʊləʳ/ *n* **1** a tube-shaped piece of wood, metal, hard rubber, etc., that rolls over and over, esp. one that is used **a** in a machine, for crushing, pressing, printing, etc. **b** for making the surface of grass or roads smooth: *a garden roller* —see also STEAMROLLER **c** for moving heavy things that have no wheels: *They pushed the boat down to the water on rollers.* **d** also **curler** for shaping: *She put her hair in rollers to make it curl.* —see picture at ROLL¹ **2** a rod round which something is rolled up: *a big map on a roller* **3** a long heavy wave on the coast: *The great Atlantic rollers surged in.* **4** a person or thing that rolls something
roller blind /ˈ·· ·/ *BrE* ‖ **blind**, **shade** *AmE*— *n* a piece of cloth or other material that can be rolled up and down over a window to reduce the amount of light entering — compare LOUVRE BLIND, VENETIAN BLIND and see picture at BLIND
roller coast·er /ˈ·· ˌ··/ *n* a small railway with steep slopes and sharp curves, found in amusement parks: (fig.) *a roller coaster of successes and disasters*
roller dis·co /ˈ·· ˌ··/ *n* a dance to recorded music at which people dance while wearing roller skates
roller skate /ˈ·· ·/ *n* a frame with four wheels for fitting under a shoe, or a shoe with wheels fixed on it, allowing the wearer to move quickly on a road or smooth surface: *a boy on roller skates* —compare ICE SKATE, SKATEBOARD; see PAIR (USAGE), and see picture at ROLL¹ —**roller-skate** *v* [I] —**roller-skater** *n*
roller tow·el /ˈ·· ˌ··/ *n* a cloth (TOWEL) that has its ends joined to form a circle so that a dry part can be pulled out for drying the hands on; mainly used in public places, not in ordinary houses —see picture at ROLL¹
rol·lick·ing¹ /ˈrɒlɪkɪŋ‖ˈrɑː-/ *adj* [A] noisy and merry; BOISTEROUS: *We had a rollicking time.*
rollicking² *n BrE infml* an act of expressing angry disapproval of someone: *He arrived several hours late and got a right rollicking from the boss.*
roll·ing /ˈrəʊlɪŋ/ *adj* **1** [A] (of land) rising and falling in long gentle slopes: *rolling hills* **2** [A] happening continuously by stages rather than all at once: *rolling devolution of power to local government* **3 rolling in it** *infml* extremely rich: *He's bought another new car — he must be absolutely rolling in it!*
rolling mill /ˈ·· ·/ *n* a factory or machine in which metal is rolled out into large flat thin pieces
rolling pin /ˈ·· ·/ *n* a long tube-shaped piece of wood or other material for spreading pastry out flat and thin before cooking
▶ CULTURAL NOTE In humorous stories and jokes, a wife is sometimes shown hitting her husband with a rolling pin when he arrives home late or drunk. ◀
rolling stock /ˈ·· ·/ *n* [U] everything on wheels that belongs to a railway, such as engines and carriages
rolling stone /ˌ·· ˈ·/ *n infml* a person who travels around a lot and has no fixed address or responsibilities
Rolling Stone an American magazine that reports esp. on people and events in the popular music industry
Rolling Stones /ˌ·· ˈ·/, **The** also **Stones** *infml*— British popular music group which was formed in the 1960s and became one of the most successful ever. The group still sometimes plays together, and the best known member is Mick Jagger. —see colour picture on page 554

roll·mop /ˈrɒlmɒp‖ˈrɑːlmɑːp/ *n BrE* a piece of HERRING that has been rolled up and pickled (PICKLE²)

roll of hon·our /ˌ· · ˈ··/ *BrE* ‖ **honor roll** *AmE–* *n* a list of the names of people who have earned praise, e.g. by passing an examination, showing bravery in battle, etc.

roll-on /ˈ·· ·/ *n* **1** a liquid that is put on, esp. onto the body, by means of a rolling ball in the neck of its container: *roll-on deodorants* **2** a woman's elastic GIRDLE that is pulled on in one piece, worn esp. formerly

roll-on roll-off /ˈ·· ˌ· ·/ also **ro-ro** *infml–* *adj* [A] allowing vehicles to drive on and off: *a roll-on roll-off car ferry*

roll·o·ver /ˈrəʊləʊvəʳ/ *adj AmE* (of an amount of money such as a PENSION or INVESTMENT) continuing to be invested (INVEST) or lent (LOAN) without stopping, to avoid financial PENALTY: *a rollover investment account which prevents tax demands on the interest*

Rolls-Royce /ˌrəʊlz ˈrɔɪs◂/ also **Rolls** *infml–* *n tdmk* **1** a company which produces very expensive and comfortable cars and is also well-known for aircraft engines: *That pop singer down the road has just bought a Rolls Royce!* **2** *infml* a product that is regarded as the highest quality example of a particular type of product: *This is the Rolls-Royce of video recorders—it has everything.*

roll·top desk /ˌrəʊltɒp ˈdesk‖-tɑːp-/ *n* a desk whose cover rolls back out of the way when it is opened

ro·ly-po·ly¹ /ˌrəʊli ˈpəʊli◂/ also **roly-poly pud·ding** /ˌ·· ·· ˈ··/– *n* [C;U] (in Britain) (a) sweet dish made of JAM that is rolled up in pastry and then baked or boiled

roly-poly² *adj infml humor* (of a person) fat and round: *a roly-poly little man*

ROM /rɒm‖rɑːm/ *n* read-only memory; a computer memory holding information that is continuously needed by the computer, such as the instructions for the language it uses. Information in this form cannot usually be changed or removed: *a ROM chip/circuit | a programmable ROM* —compare RANDOM ACCESS MEMORY; see also CD ROM

ro·maine let·tuce /rəʊˌmeɪn ˈletᵻs/ *n esp. AmE for* COS LETTUCE

ro·man /ˈrəʊmən/ *n* [U] (the ordinary style of) printing with upright letters like the ones used for printing these words —compare ITALICS

Roman *n, adj* (a citizen) **a** of ancient Rome or its EMPIRE: *the Roman emperors | Roman roads | a book about Roman history* **b** of the city of Rome —see also HOLY ROMAN EMPIRE, ROMAN EMPIRE

Roman

Roman al·pha·bet /ˌ·· ˈ···/ [the] the alphabet beginning A, B, C, used in English and many other languages, as opposed to those of Greek, Arabic, the Cyrillic languages, etc.

Roman can·dle /ˌ·· ˈ··/ *n* a tube-shaped FIREWORK that shoots out burning coloured stars

Roman Cath·o·lic /ˌ·· ˈ···◂/ also **Catholic–** *n, adj* (a member) of the branch of the Christian religion (the **Roman Catholic Church**) whose leader (the POPE) rules from Rome. Services usu. involve more ceremony and RITUAL than Protestant services. Roman Catholic priests are not allowed to marry: *Her family are Roman Catholic/are all Roman Catholics. | a Roman Catholic bishop* —compare PROTESTANT **—licism** /ˌ·· ·ˈ····/ *n* [U]

ro·mance¹ /rəʊˈmæns, rə-/ *n* **1** [C] a love affair: *She thought it was going to be the big romance of her life, but he left her after only a few weeks.* **2** [U] a ROMANTIC¹ (2) quality: *the romance of life in the Wild West* **3** [C] a story of love, adventure, mystery, etc., often set in a distant time or place, whose events are happier or grander or more exciting than those of real life: *a romance about a king who married a beggar girl* **4** [U] love between a man and a woman, represented in Britain by boxes of chocolates, red roses, dinners by CANDLELIGHT, love letters, and walks by the light of the moon: *She went on holiday in search of romance.*

romance² *v* [I] *rare* **1** [(about)] to tell improbable stories **2** [(with)] to carry on a love affair

Romance *adj* [A] (of a language) having grown out of Latin, the language of ancient Rome: *French and Portuguese are Romance languages.*

Roman Em·pire /ˌ·· ˈ··/ [the] the countries of Europe and the Near East which were ruled from Rome from around 44 BC until around AD 395, when it was split into two. The W Roman Empire lasted until around 476 and the E Roman Empire until the 15th century. The Romans are remembered for being brave, but rather cruel fighting men, who liked to watch men or animals and men fighting to the death as a form of entertainment. In particular they persecuted (PERSECUTE) people of the Christian religion and liked to watch them being killed by lions.

Ro·man·esque /ˌrəʊmə ˈnesk◂/ *adj* in the style of building with round arches and thick PILLARs that was common in Western Europe in about the 11th and 12th centuries

Ro·ma·ni·a /rəʊˈmeɪniə/ also **Rumania, Roumania–** *n* a country in SE Europe bordering on the Black Sea; capital Bucharest; population 23,152,000 (1989). It was formerly a COMMUNIST country, but in 1989 the people killed their leader, Nicolae Ceauşescu, in a violent REBELLION. **—nian** *n, adj*

Roman law /ˌ·· ˈ·/ *n* [U] CIVIL LAW (2)

Roman nose /ˌ·· ˈ·/ *n* a nose that curves out near the top

Roman nu·me·ral /ˌ·· ˈ···/ *n* any of the signs (such as I, II, V, X, L, D) used for numbers in ancient Rome and sometimes now —compare ARABIC NUMERAL (1)

Romano- see WORD FORMATION

Roman road /ˌ·· ˈ·/ *n* a road built by the Romans. Roman roads are known for being very straight.

ro·man·tic¹ /rəʊˈmæntɪk, rə-/ *adj* **1** showing strong feelings of love: *"Tom always sends me red roses on my birthday." "How romantic!"* **2** dealing with or suggesting love, adventure: *writers of romantic fiction | The old abbey ruins look very romantic in the moonlight.* **3** sometimes *derog* showing a lot of imagination or impractical: *She has romantic notions about becoming a famous actress. | middle-class intellectuals with their romantic back-to-nature ideas* **4** [no comp.] (often cap.) (of art, literature, and music) marked by romanticism: *romantic poetry* **—ally** /kli/ *adv*

romantic² *n* **1** a romantic person **2** (often cap.) a writer, painter, etc., whose work shows romanticism, or who was a member of the ROMANTIC MOVEMENT

ro·man·ti·cis·m /rəʊˈmæntᵻsɪzəm, rə-/ *n* [U] (often cap.) (in art and literature, esp. in the late 18th and early 19th centuries) the quality of admiring feeling rather than thought, and wild natural beauty rather than things made by people: *the romanticism of Wordsworth's poetry* —compare CLASSICISM (1,2), REALISM (3) **—cist** *n*

ro·man·ti·cize also **-cise** *BrE* /rəʊˈmæntᵻsaɪz, rə-/ *v* [I;T] *derog* to make (something) seem more interesting or ROMANTIC¹ (2, 3) than it really is: *He tends to romanticize his past. | The film gives a rather romanticized picture of life during the war.*

Romantic Move·ment /·ˈ·· ˌ··/ [the] (in English and European poetry, literature, art, and music) a group of writers, artists, etc. who followed their feelings and emotions rather than LOGICAL thought or reason, and who preferred wild, natural beauty to things made by man. It first became popular in the late 18th century. —see ROMANTICISM

Ro·ma·ny /ˈrəʊməni‖ˈrɑː-/ *n* **1** [C] a GIPSY **2** [U] the language of the GIPSY people

Rome /rəʊm/ **1** the capital city of Italy, famous for its art, history, and centres of learning, religion, etc., and for containing the state within which the Pope lives, Vatican City —see also ROMULUS AND REMUS, TREATY OF ROME **2 Rome was not built in a day** a job cannot be done properly if it is done in a hurry **3 When in Rome, do as the Romans do** one should follow the customs of the people one is visiting or living with —see also **to fiddle while Rome burns** (FIDDLE)

Ro·me·o /ˈrəʊmiəʊ/ *n* **-os** *often humor or derog* a ROMANTIC male lover, esp. one who tries to attract all the women he meets in a romantic or sexual way: *the office Romeo | A Romeo solicitor masterminded a £3.8 million mortgage fraud to pay for his mistress and high life.*

Romeo and Ju·li·et /ˌ··· · ˈ···/ a play by William Shakespeare about the love of two people, Romeo and Juliet, from families who are enemies. They marry secretly, but they are prevented from being together and they both kill themselves. They are seen as typical examples of unfortunate, unhappy lovers. Many lines from the play are well known, esp. "Romeo, Romeo, wherefore art thou Romeo?" which Juliet says while looking down from a BALCONY. —see colour picture on page 1146

Rom·mel /ˈrɒməl‖ˈrɑː-/, **Er·win** /ˈɜːwɪn‖ˈɜːr-/ (1891–1944) one of Hitler's generals in the Second World War, remembered for his CAMPAIGNS in North Africa and Egypt. He attempted with others to kill Hitler and failed, later taking his own life.

romp¹ /rɒmp‖rɑːmp/ v (I (ABOUT, AROUND)) **1** to play noisily and roughly with a lot of running and jumping: *We could hear the children romping (about) upstairs.* **2** **romp home** (esp. of an animal) to win a race easily: *The favourite romped home.*

romp through phr v (T) BrE infml to succeed in, quickly and without effort: *She simply romped through her exams.*

romp² n **1** an occasion of romping **2** infml a piece of amusing entertainment with plenty of action: *The new film is an enjoyable romp, but with no intellectual content.*

Romp·er Room /ˈ·· ˌ·/ an American television programme of the 1950s and 1960s for young children

romp·ers /ˈrɒmpəz‖ˈrɑːmpərz/ also **romper suit** /ˈ·· ·/— n [P] a one-piece garment for babies combining a top and short trouser-like bottom: *a pair of rompers*

Rom·u·lus and Re·mus /ˌrɒmjə̆ləs ənd ˈriːməs‖ˌrɑːm-/ TWIN brothers in an ancient Roman story, nursed by a WOLF and brought up by a SHEPHERD. They started up the city of Rome, and Romulus later killed Remus after a quarrel. —see colour picture on page 423

Ro·nay /ˈrəʊneɪ/, **E·gon** /ˈiːɡɒn‖-ɑːn/ a CHEF and writer of food and restaurant guides. He came to Britain from Hungary in 1946.

ron·do /ˈrɒndəʊ‖ˈrɑːn-/ n -dos a piece of music that repeats the main tune several times, and may sometimes form part of a longer musical work such as a CONCERTO

Ron·nie Scott's /ˌrɒni ˈskɒts‖ˌrɑːni ˈskɑːts/ a London club opened by Ronnie Scott in 1959 and well-known as a place where leading JAZZ musicians have always played —see also Ronnie SCOTT

Ron·stadt /ˈrɒnstæt‖ˈrɑːn-/, **Lin·da** /ˈlɪndə/ (1946–) an American singer of many different kinds of popular music

rönt·gen, Röntgen /ˈrɒntɡən‖ˈrentɡən/ adj, n ROENTGEN¹ʼ²

rood /ruːd/ n old use or tech a Christian cross or CRUCIFIX, usu. in a church

rood screen /ˈ· ·/ n a wooden or stone decorative wall in a Christian church which divides the part containing the singers (CHOIR) from the part where the other worshippers sit —see picture at CHURCH

roof¹ /ruːf‖ruːf, rʊf/ n **1** the outside covering on top of a building, closed vehicle, tent, etc.: *The rain's coming in — the roof must be leaking.* | *She carries her sailboard on the roof of her car.* | *roof tiles* | *a tiled/thatched roof* | *She and I can't live* **under the same roof.** (=in the same house) —compare CEILING (1), and see picture at CAR and HOUSE **2** a/no **'roof over one's head** somewhere/nowhere to live: *I may not have a job, but at least I've got a roof over my head.* **3** **go through the roof** infml a (of a price) to rise to a very high level **b** to express great anger **4** **hit the roof** AmE infml to express great anger: *Dad will hit the roof when he finds out you've taken the car without asking first.* **5** **raise the roof** AmE infml to complain loudly: *If I don't get my money back on this piece of worthless junk I'll raise the roof!* **6** **the roof of one's mouth** the bony upper part of the inside of the mouth

roof² v (T (with)) to put a roof on or be a roof for: *a house roofed with slates*

roof sthg.↔**in/over** phr v (T) to enclose by putting a roof on (an open place): *We're going to roof in the yard to make a garage.*

roof gar·den /ˈ· ˌ··/ n a garden on a flat roof

roof·ing /ˈruːfɪŋ‖ˈruːf-, ˈrʊf-/ n (U) material for making or covering roofs

roofing felt /ˈ·· ˌ·/ n (U) material which is unrolled over

supports to make a cheap roof that does not last many years. It is used on flat-roofed additions to houses and on SHEDS.

roof·less /ˈruːfləs‖ˈruːf-, ˈrʊf-/ adj with no roof

roof rack /ˈ· ·/ n a metal frame fixed on top of a car roof, for carrying things —see picture at RACK

roof·top /ˈruːftɒp‖ˈruːftɑːp, ˈrʊf-/ n a roof —see also **shout something from the rooftops** (SHOUT¹)

rook¹ /rʊk/ n a large black European bird like a CROW

rook² also **castle**— n (in the game of CHESS) a piece that can move any number of squares but only in a straight line parallel to a side of the board —see picture at CHESS

rook³ v (T) infml to cheat (someone), esp. by charging a very high price or by winning money at card games: *Five pounds for that! You've been rooked!*

rook·e·ry /ˈrʊkəri/ n a collection of rooks' nests, high up in a group of trees

rook·ie /ˈrʊki/ n AmE infml **1** someone who is new to and has no experience of an activity, esp. a new soldier or policeman: *a rookie cop* **2** a player in his first year of professional sports: *As a rookie he batted 386.*

room¹ /ruːm, rʊm/ n **1** [C] (often in comb.) a division of a building, which has its own walls, floor, and CEILING and is usu. used for a particular purpose: *There are three rooms on the first floor and two on the top floor.* | *the bathroom/bedroom/dining room* | *a changing room* | *the billiard room* | *I'd like* **a single/a double room** (=for one/two people in a hotel) *with a bath.* | *I could hear a telephone in the next room/the adjoining room.* | *She locked the bedroom door.* | *Room 107* (=the people in this room in a hotel) *have asked for coffee.* —see picture at LIVING ROOM **2** [U (for)] space that could be filled, or that is enough for the stated purpose: *There's room for three on the back seat.* | *Move along and* **make room for** *me!* | *A piano* **takes up** *a lot of room.* [+to-v] *There's hardly room to breathe in here!* | (fig.) *He needs room* (=a chance) *to develop his skill as a painter.* —see also ELBOWROOM, LEGROOM; see PLACE¹ (USAGE) **3** [U+for] the need or possibility for something to happen or be done; SCOPE: *His work isn't bad but there's still plenty of* **room for improvement.** | *I'm afraid the facts leave little* **room for** *doubt as to her guilt.* | *They want to reduce taxes, but the bad state of the economy has left them little* **room for manoeuvre.** —see PLACE¹ (USAGE) **4** [U] the people in a room: *The speaker held the room enthralled.* **5** **no room at the inn** humor no room in a place, esp. one open to the public (from the Bible story in which Mary and Joseph are told that there is no room at the INN in Bethlehem): *We got to the cinema only ten minutes late, and already there was no room at the inn.* **6** **not enough room to swing a cat** infml very little space **7** **-roomed** /ruːmd, rʊmd/ having the stated number or size of rooms: *a six-roomed house* —see also ROOMS, COMMON ROOM, DRAWING ROOM, FRONT ROOM — ~ **ful** /fʊl/ n [(of)] : *a roomful of noisy children*

room² v [I+adv/prep] AmE to have lodgings; have a room or rooms: *He's rooming at our house/with us.*

room and board /ˌ· · ˈ·/ n [U] AmE for BED AND BOARD

Room at the Top /ˌ· · · ˈ·/ a NOVEL by John Braine

room·er /ˈruːməʳ, ˈrʊm-/ n AmE for LODGER

rooming house /ˈ·· ·/ n AmE a LODGING HOUSE

room·mate /ˈruːmˌmeɪt, ˈrʊm-/ n **1** BrE a person, not a member of one's family, with whom one shares a bedroom for a period of time, for example at school or on holiday: *Bill and Ben are roommates.* | *My roommate is very untidy.* **2** AmE a person with whom one shares a room, APARTMENT, or house —compare FLATMATE

rooms /ruːmz, rʊmz/ n [P] old-fash, esp. BrE a rented set of rooms in a building; LODGINGS

room ser·vice /ˈ· ˌ··/ n [U] **1** a service provided by a hotel, by which food, drink, etc., are sent up to a person's room: *Does this hotel have/provide room service?* **2** [+sing./pl. v] the people who provide this service: *She called room service and ordered some champagne.*

Room With a View /ˌ· · · ˈ·/, **A** a NOVEL by E M Forster

room·y /ˈruːmi, ˈrʊmi/ adj apprec with plenty of space inside it; SPACIOUS: *a roomy house/cupboard/car* —**iness** n [U]

Roo·se·velt¹ /ˈrəʊzəvelt/, **El·ea·nor** /ˈelɪnəʳ/ (1884–1962) the wife of Franklin Delano Roosevelt. She was a writer who was involved in politics and social questions, esp. those concerning women and minorities (MINORITY(2))

Roosevelt²,   **Frank·lin Del·a·no** /ˈfræŋklɪn ˈdelənəʊ/ (1882–1945) the 32nd president of the US serving from 1933 to 1945. He was president during the Great Depression and was responsible for his country's efforts during the Second World War, during which he was elected for the third and fourth times. —see picture on page 752

Franklin D. Roosevelt

►CULTURAL   NOTE
Roosevelt is the only president to have served more than two TERMs (= periods of time in power). He was a popular and respected president, and many people listened to his "**fireside chats**" on the radio, in which he told people what was happening in the country and what he was doing. He was the first president to appear on television. Roosevelt was often called **FDR.◄**

Roosevelt³, The·o·dore /ˈθiːədɔːʳ/ (**Teddy**) (1858–1919) the 26th president of the US, from 1901 to 1909. Roosevelt became famous during a war between the US and Spain when he went to Cuba and formed the ROUGH RIDERS. He was a popular president and people remember that he had a large MOUSTACHE and said things were "bully" when he liked them.

roost¹ /ruːst/ n **1** a bar, branch, etc., on which birds settle at night, esp. one for hens in a HEN HOUSE **2 come home to roost** (of a bad or unwise action) to have a bad effect on the doer, esp. after a period of time: *Their lack of financial planning is now coming home to roost.* —see also **rule the roost** (RULE²)

roost² v [I] (of a bird) to sit and sleep for the night

roost·er /ˈruːstəʳ/ n esp. AmE for COCK¹ (1)

root¹ /ruːt/ n **1** [*often pl.*] the part of a plant that grows down into the soil in search of food and water. *Pull the plant up by the|its roots.* | *Do you think the new rosebush has* **taken root?** (=started to grow) | (fig.) *How did these strange ideas take root?* (–become established) —compare STEM¹ (1) **2** the part of a tooth, hair, fingernail, etc., that holds it to the rest of the body —see picture at TEETH **3** [(**of**)] the fact or condition from which something begins, or by which something is caused; origin: *Let's try to* **get to the root of** *this problem.* | *Unhappiness is the* **root cause** *of his illness.* | *His illness* **has its roots in** *unhappiness.* **4** [(**of**)] *tech* (in MATHEMATICS) a number that when multiplied by itself a stated number of times gives another stated number: *2 is the fourth root of 16* (because 2 x 2 x 2 x 2=16) —see also CUBE ROOT, SQUARE ROOT **5** [(**of**)] *tech* the base part of a word, from which it originally comes or to which other parts can be added: *The Latin word "videre", meaning "to see", is the root of the English words video, vista, vision, visionary, and revision.* —compare STEM¹ (4) **6 root and branch** *fml* (of something bad that must be got rid of) thoroughly: *This evil system must be destroyed root and branch.* —see also ROOTS, GRASS ROOTS

root² v **1** [I;T] to (cause to) form roots: *Do roses root easily?* **2** [I+adv/prep] also **roo·tle** /ˈruːtl/ BrE— (esp. of a pig) to search for food by digging with the nose **3** [I+adv/prep] *infml* to search for something by turning things over: *Who's been rooting about among my papers?* —see also ROOTED
  root for sbdy./sthg. *phr v* [T] *esp. AmE* to give strong support to (someone who is competing): *Good luck – we'll all be rooting for you.*
  root sthg.↔**out** *phr v* [T] **1** to destroy or get rid of completely (something bad); ERADICATE: *This disease is the scourge of Africa, and scientists doubt if it can ever be altogether rooted out.* | *a promise to root out corrupt officials* —see also UPROOT **2** *infml* to find by searching: *I'll try and root out something suitable for you to wear.*

root beer /ˈ· ·/ n [U] (esp. in the US) a sweet gassy non-alcoholic drink made from the roots of various plants

root bound /ˈ· ·/ adj AmE for POTBOUND

root cel·lar /ˈ· ˌ··/ n AmE an underground room, usu. away from the house, used for keeping vegetables such as potatoes and CARROTs

root crop /ˈ· ·/ also **root vege·ta·ble** /ˈ· ˌ···/— n a vegetable grown for its roots, such as potatoes or CARROTs

root·ed /ˈruːtɪd/ adj **1** [F(to)] fixed as if by roots: *He stood* **rooted to the spot** *in terror|fascination.* **2** (of an idea, principle, etc.) firmly fixed and unchangeable: *(deep-) rooted prejudices* **3** [F+in] having as its origin or cause: *an economic policy that is rooted in Marxist theory*

root·less /ˈruːtləs/ adj having no home or sense of belonging anywhere – ~**ness** n [U]

roots /ruːts/ n [P] **1** (one's connection with and feeling of belonging to) a place, esp. the place in which one was born and brought up: *Her roots are in Scotland where she was born.* | *We've been here a year now, and we're beginning to* **put down (new) roots.** (=make new friends, join in local activities, etc.) —see also GRASS ROOTS **2** (one's connection with and feeling of belonging to) a family: *She's searching for her roots by tracing her family tree.*

Roots an American television programme shown in 1977 which followed the history of a black family from Kunta Kinte, a man born in Africa and caught to be a slave in the US, through his children and their children until the Civil War. The programme, which was based on Alex Haley's book about his family, was on every night for a week and was very popular. Several years later another programme followed the family from the Civil War until the present time.

rope¹ /rəʊp/ n **1** [C;U] (a piece of) strong thick cord made by twisting together threads of cotton, HEMP, etc.: *They tied their prisoner up with ropes|with a piece of rope.* | *to coil up a rope* —compare STRING¹ (1) **2** [C+of] a fat twisted string, esp. of the stated jewels: *a rope of pearls* **3** [*the*+S] hanging as a punishment **4 give someone enough rope to hang himself|herself** to give a bad or foolish person freedom of action in the hope that they will cause their own ruin or failure in the end **5 give someone (plenty of) rope** to allow someone (plenty of) freedom to act —see also ROPES, TIGHTROPE. **jump rope** (JUMP), **money for old rope** (MONEY)

rope² v [T] **1** [+obj+adv/prep] to tie with a rope: *He roped his horse to a nearby tree.* | *Make sure you're properly roped together before you begin to climb.* **2** esp. AmE to catch (an animal) with a rope; LASSO
  rope sbdy.↔**in** *phr v* [T] *infml* to persuade or force (esp. someone who is unwilling) to help in one's plans or join an activity: *I've been roped in to help sell the tickets.*
  rope sthg.↔**off** *phr v* [T] to separate or enclose (an area) with ropes: *They've roped off one end of the room.*
  rope up *phr v* [I] (of two or more mountain climbers) to get fastened together with the same rope: *We'd better rope up for this difficult bit.*

rope lad·der /ˈ· ˌ··/ n a ladder made of two long ropes connected by cross pieces of wood, rope, or metal

ropes /rəʊps/ n [*the*+S] **1** the rope fence that surrounds a sports ring, esp. a BOXING ring **2** *infml* the rules, customs, and ways of operating in some place or activity: *I've been to China before so I* **know the ropes**; *can I help you?* | *Shirley's only joined the firm today, so will you* **show her the ropes?**

rop·y , ropey /ˈrəʊpi/ adj BrE infml in bad condition or of bad quality: *We stayed in a really ropy hotel.* | *I'm feeling a bit ropy* (=not very well) *this morning.* —**iness** n [U]

Roque·fort /ˈrɒkfɔːʳ‖ˈrəʊkfərt/ n [U] a strong French cheese with blue lines in it, made from sheep's milk

Ror·schach test /ˈrɔːʃæk test‖ˈrɔːr-/ n a method of testing someone's mind and character by making them say what various irregular spots of ink remind them of

ro·sa·ry /ˈrəʊzəri/ n **1** [C] a string of BEADS (=small decorative balls) used esp. by Roman Catholics for counting prayers **2** [*the*] (*often cap.*) a Roman Catholic religious practice that consists of repeating the set of prayers that are counted in this way

rose¹ /rəʊz/ past tense of RISE

rose² n **1** [C] (the usu. red, pink, white, or yellow sweet-smelling flower of) any of various wild or cultivated bushes with strong prickly stems. In Britain, it is thought of as a typically English flower: *He sent her a* *dozen red roses on their anniversary.* | *a rosebed* (=where roses grow) | *a rose bush* | *rose petals* —see picture at FLOWER **2** [U] a pale to dark pink colour **3** [C] a circular piece of metal with holes in it that is fitted to the end of a pipe or WATERING CAN for watering gardens **4 a rose by any other name would smell as sweet** *quote* a phrase from Shakespeare's play *Romeo and Juliet*. People use the phrase when saying that the nature of a thing is important, not what it is called. **5 a rose is a rose is a rose** *quote* a slightly changed phrase from a poem by Gertrude Stein, often changed further and used when someone is saying that there can only be one kind of a particular thing: *I don't care whether he's unhappy at home—a bully is a bully is a bully, and he shouldn't be allowed to make others miserable!* **6 be not all roses** *infml* (of a job, situation, etc.) to include some unpleasant things: *A lot of people envy the royal family, but their life isn't all roses, you know.* **7 come up roses** [*usu. in progressive forms*] to happen or develop in the best possible way —see also BED OF ROSES, WARS OF THE ROSES

rose³ *adj* (*usu. in comb.*) (of a colour) pale to dark pink: *rose pink*

Rose, Pete /piːt/ (1942–) an American BASEBALL player and team manager who in the 1990s was found to have illegally BET (put money on the result of a game) on baseball games

ro·sé /ˈrəʊzeɪ‖rəʊˈzeɪ/ n [U] a light pink wine

Rose·anne /rəʊˈzæn/ a humorous American television show about a WORKING-CLASS family in which the actress Roseanne Arnold appears as the main character

Roseanne

ro·se·ate /ˈrəʊziɪt/ *adj lit* pink: *the roseate hues of the evening sky*

Rose Bowl /ˈ·ˌ·/ n a FOOTBALL (2) game held on January 1st each year in Pasadena, California, between the winners of the two main college CONFERENCEs

rose·bud /ˈrəʊzbʌd/ n the young tightly rolled-up flower (BUD¹) of a rose before it opens: *She's as pretty as a rosebud.*

rose·col·oured /ˈ· ·ˌ·/ also **rose·tinted**— *adj* **look at/see/view the world through rose-coloured spectacles/glasses** *usu. derog* to see the world, life, etc., as better and more pleasant than they really are

rose hip /ˈ· ·/ n the red fruit of some kinds of rose bush, used in medicines and juices

rose·ma·ry /ˈrəʊzməri‖-meri/ n [U] a low bush whose sweet-smelling leaves are used in cooking

Rosemary's Ba·by /ˌ··· ˈ··/ a NOVEL by American writer Ira Levin, made into a film in 1968, in which a man agrees to let Satan be the father of a baby with his wife

Rose Pa·rade /ˈ· ·ˌ·/ n a PARADE held every year in Pasadena, California, on January 1st with many large vehicles covered with flowers, marching bands, and horse riders. The parade is shown on television all over the US.

Roses, War of the SEE WARS OF THE ROSES

Ro·set·ta Stone /rəʊˈzetə ˌstəʊn/ [*the*] the stone, found in Egypt in 1799, on which was written the passage that provided the key to translating HIEROGLYPHICS

ro·sette /rəʊˈzet/ n **1** a bunch of RIBBONs (=narrow silk bands) made up in the form of a broad flat flower and worn for decoration or as a sign of something: *She won a rosette in the riding competition.* **2** a shape like this in stone or wood, cut on a building as a decoration

rosette

rose·wa·ter /ˈrəʊz ˌwɔːtəʳ‖ -ˌwɔː-, -ˌwɑː-/ n [U] a liquid made from roses and used for its pleasant smell

rose win·dow /ˈ· ·ˌ··/ n a circular decorative window in a church, usu. containing a pattern of small divisions spreading out from a centre and filled in with coloured glass

rose·wood /ˈrəʊzwʊd/ n [U] a valuable hard dark red tropical wood, used for making fine furniture

Rosh Ha·sha·nah , Rosh Hashana /ˌrɒʃ həˈʃɑːnə‖ ˌrəʊʃ həˈʃɑːnə/ n the first day of the Jewish new year, a holy day, usu. beginning some time in September

Ro·si·cru·cians /ˌrəʊzɪˈkruːʃənz/ n [P] a 17th century secret society whose members claimed that they had SPIRITUAL knowledge from studying science. They still advertise for new members in the US, and are now based in San Jose, California.

Rosie the Riv·et·er /ˌrəʊzi ðə ˈrɪvɪtəʳ/ (a name invented to represent) any of the American women who worked in arms or aircraft factories during the Second World War

ros·in¹ /ˈrɒzɪn‖ˈrɑː-/ n [U] RESIN, esp. as used in a solid form on the strings of musical instruments

rosin² *v* [T] to rub with rosin

Ross /rɒs‖rɔːs/, **Bet·sy** /ˈbetsi/ (1752–1836) the woman who is supposed to have made the first American flag

Ross, Diana (1944–) an American popular music singer who was with the group The Supremes until 1970

Ross and Crom·ar·ty /ˌrɒs ənd ˈkrɒməti‖ˌrɔːs ənd ˈkrɑːmərti/ a former COUNTY in northern Scotland, now part of Highland REGION

Ros·set·ti /rəˈzeti‖rəʊ-/, **Chris·ti·na Geor·gi·na** /krɪˈstiːnə dʒɔːˈdʒiːnə‖-dʒɔː-/ (1830–94) an English poet whose poems include *Goblin Market*

Rossetti, Dante Gabriel (1828–82) an English poet and artist who helped to form the PRE-RAPHAELITES

Ros·si·ni /rɒˈsiːni‖rəʊ-/, **Gio·ac·chi·no** /ˌdʒəʊəˈkiːnəʊ/ (1792–1868) an Italian musician who wrote many OPERAs, including *The Barber of Seville*

ros·ter /ˈrɒstəʳ‖ˈrɑː-/ n a list of people's names, esp. giving the jobs they have to do or the times at which they have to do them: *a duty roster*

ros·trum /ˈrɒstrəm‖ˈrɑː-/ n **-trums** or **-tra** /trə/ a raised place (PLATFORM) for a public speaker, music CONDUCTOR, etc.

ros·y /ˈrəʊzi/ *adj* **1** *apprec* (esp. of the human skin) pink and healthy-looking: *rosy cheeks* **2** giving hope, esp. without good reason: *He painted a rosy picture of the company's prospects.* (=described them in a very hopeful way, perhaps without good cause) —**iness** n [U]

rot¹ /rɒt‖rɑːt/ *v* **-tt-** [I;T] (AWAY, DOWN)] to (cause to) decay by a gradual natural process; (cause to) go bad: *The meat will rot if it isn't kept cool.* | *The damp has rotted (away) the roof beams.* | *rotting vegetables* | *You can rot garden waste down to make a fine compost.* | (fig.) *They left him to rot in prison for twenty years.* | (fig.) *Too much television rots your brain.* —see also ROTTEN

rot² n **1** [U] the process of rotting or an area of rotten growth; decay: *an old hollow tree full of rot* —see also DRY ROT **2** [*the*+S] *infml* the process by which everything goes wrong or gets worse: *He thinks the* **rot set in** (=started) *when the country was opened up to tourists.* | *It was tourism that really* **started the rot.** | *Their profits are going down and down, and they don't know how to* **stop the rot.** **3** [U] *BrE old-fash infml* foolish remarks or ideas: *Don't talk such rot!*

ro·ta /ˈrəʊtə/ n *esp. BrE* a list giving details of things which are to be done in a particular order, esp. by different people taking turns: *We organized the cleaning on a rota basis.* (=according to a list) | *to draw up a rota*

Ro·tar·i·an /rəʊˈteəriən/ n a member of the Rotary Club

ro·ta·ry /ˈrəʊtəri/ *adj* **1** also **rotatory**— (of movement) turning round a fixed point, like a wheel: *the rotary movement of the blades* **2** being or having a moving part that does this: *a rotary lawn mower* | *a rotary clothes line*

Rotary Club /ˈ··· ˌ·/ also **Rotary In·ter·na·tion·al** /ˌ···· ··ˈ···/— [*the*] an organization of men from different businesses in a town who work together for the good of the town, often by raising money for the poor and sick

rotary til·ler /ˌ··· ˈ··/ n *AmE for* DISC HARROW

ro·tate /rəʊˈteɪt‖ˈrəʊteɪt/ *v* [I;T] **1** to (cause to) turn round a fixed point or AXIS: *The Earth rotates once every 24 hours.* | *a rotating mirror* —compare REVOLVE **2** to (cause to) take turns or come round in regular order: *We rotate the crops, sowing wheat one year, sugar beet the*

Robinson Crusoe by Daniel Defoe
After his ship is destroyed, Robinson Crusoe has to live on a desert island. At first he thinks he is alone, but one day he finds a black man living there who he calls Man Friday because he meets him on a Friday.

Around the World in Eighty Days by Jules Verne.

Phileas Fogg and his servant Passepartout use many different forms of transport in their attempt to travel around the world in eighty days.

The Grapes of Wrath by John Steinbeck

A poor American family have to leave their land because it is too dry for farming and travel to look for work during the Depression.

The Adventures of Tom Sawyer by Mark Twain
Tom Sawyer and his friend Huckleberry Finn

Wuthering Heights by Emily Brontë
Wuthering Heights is the story of the passionate love between Cathy and Heathcliffe, set in the wild countryside of the Yorkshire Moors.

Oliver Twist by Charles Dickens
There is a famous scene where Oliver asks for more food by saying 'Please, sir, I want some more' because he is still hungry.

'O Romeo, Romeo! Wherefore art thou Romeo?'

(*Romeo and Juliet*, Act II, Scene II)

The balcony scene from the play *Romeo and Juliet*

'Alas, poor Yorick! – I knew him, Horatio'

(*Hamlet, Prince of Denmark*, Act V, Scene I)

Hamlet picks up the skull of his dead friend Yorick

'Double, double, toil and trouble; Fire burn and cauldron bubble'

(*Macbeth*, Act IV, Scene I)

The three witches who use magic to tell Macbeth what is going to happen in the future.

'Friends, Romans, countrymen, lend me your ears I come to bury Caesar, not to praise him'

(*Julius Caesar*, Act III, Scene II)

Mark Antony speaking to the crowd after Caesar has been killed

'Once more unto the breach, dear friends, once more'

(*Henry V*, Act III, Scene I)

King Henry V leading his soldiers into battle

next, and so on. | *The chairmanship of the department rotates annually.*

ro·ta·tion /rəʊˈteɪʃən/ n **1** [U] the action of rotating: *the rotation of the Earth on its axis* | *The rotation of crops keeps the soil healthy and fertile.* **2** [C] one complete turn round a fixed point **3 in rotation** (of events) coming round one after the other in regular order: *The seasons follow each other in rotation.*

ro·ta·to·ry /rəʊˈteɪtəri‖ˈrəʊtətɔːri/ adj ROTARY (1)

ROTC /ˈrɒtsi‖ˌrɑːt-/ [the] AmE Reserve Officer Training Corps; a programme run by the American army to train students at colleges and university in military leadership. The army will often pay for the student's education in return for two to four years of service in the army after finishing university. During the 1960s students tried to get ROTC programmes to stop running on CAMPUS, but in the 1980s many students saw the ROTC as a good way of getting an education at a low cost.

rote /rəʊt/ n [U] fml repeated study using memory rather than understanding. Learning by rote is not fashionable in British schools: *to learn poetry* **by rote** | *rote-learning*

rot·gut /ˈrɒtɡʌt‖ˈrɑːt-/ n [U] sl strong cheap alcohol that is bad for the stomach

Roth /rɒθ‖rɔːθ/, **Philip** (1933–) an American writer, whose most famous book *Portnoy's Complaint* deals humorously with middle-class Jewish life in the US

Roth·ko /ˈrɒθkəʊ‖ˈrɑːθ-/, **Mark** (1903–70) an American painter famous esp. for paintings of squares and RECTANGLES

Roth·man's /ˈrɒθmənz‖ˈrɔːθ-, ˈrɑːθ-/ tdmk the name of a type of cigarette

Roths·child /ˈrɒθs-tʃaɪld‖ˈrɔːθs-/, **N M** the London MERCHANT BANK

ro·tis·ser·ie /rəʊˈtɪsəri/ n an apparatus for cooking meat by turning it over and over on a bar (SPIT³ (1)) under direct heat

ro·tor /ˈrəʊtəʳ/ n **1** a part of a machine that turns round on a fixed point: *The giant turbine rotors began to turn.* **2** the system of blades that raise a HELICOPTER into the air by turning round and round

Ro·to-root·er /ˈrəʊtəʊ ˌruːtəʳ/ tdmk (an American company which makes) a machine that unblocks pipes and DRAINS by use of a power-driven, quickly turning snake-like tube. Because of the unusual nature of the machine it is often the subject of jokes: *My dentist doesn't use a drill, he uses a Roto-rooter.* | *Clogged drain? Call Roto-rooter!* (advertisement)

ro·to·va·tor /ˈrəʊtəveɪtəʳ/ BrE ‖ **Ro·to·til·ler** /ˈrəʊtəʊˌtɪləʳ/ AmE— n tdmk a tool with blades that turn round to break up esp. soil

rot·ten /ˈrɒtn‖ˈrɑːtn/ adj **1** decayed; gone bad: *rotten eggs/fruit* | *a rotten branch* **2** infml nasty, unpleasant, or unsatisfactory: *What rotten weather!* | *Paul's a rotten driver.* | *What a rotten thing to do to her!* **3 feel rotten** infml to feel ill or unhappy: *I feel rotten this morning; it must have been something I ate.* | *I felt rotten about having to sack him, but I had no alternative.* **4 one rotten apple spoils the barrel** one bad person or thing can have a bad effect on others which are good but which may easily be spoilt **5 Something is rotten in the state of Denmark** quote a phrase from Shakespeare's play *Hamlet*, often used in speaking of a bad state of affairs in any country: *The number of violent crimes in Britain is on the increase; clearly, something is rotten in the state of Denmark.* — ~ **ly** adv — ~ **ness** n [U]

rotten bor·ough /ˌ·· ˈ··/ n (in Britain before 1832) any of a number of places (BOROUGHS) which elected a Member of Parliament although they had very few voters

rot·ter /ˈrɒtəʳ‖ˈrɑː-/ n BrE old-fash infml a worthless or dishonourable person

Rot·ter·dam /ˈrɒtədæm‖ˈrɑːtər-/ a city in the W Netherlands, one of the world's largest and most modern ports

rott·wei·ler /ˈrɒtwaɪləʳ‖ˈrɑːt-/ n a German breed of dog which has a large body and head and very strong muscles, used to guard property, people, or (originally) animals. Rottweilers became feared by many people after a series of violent attacks on adults and children in the late 1980s and early 1990s. In Britain rottweilers must now be registered (REGISTER² (1)) and wear a covering

around their mouth when outside to prevent them from biting. —see picture at DOG

ro·tund /rəʊˈtʌnd/ adj fml or humor (of a person) fat and round — ~ **ity** n

ro·tun·da /rəʊˈtʌndə/ n a round building or hall, esp. one with a DOME (=rounded bowl-shaped roof)

rou·ble , ruble /ˈruːbəl/ n (a coin or note worth) the standard unit of money in the former USSR

rou·é /ˈruːeɪ‖ruːˈeɪ/ n old use a RAKE³

rouge¹ /ruːʒ/ n [U] a red substance used for colouring the cheeks to give a healthy appearance, esp. by women and actors

rouge² v [T] to put rouge on (one's face)

rough¹ /rʌf/ adj **1** having an uneven surface; not smooth: *The rough road made the car vibrate.* | *A cat's tongue is rough.* | *rough hands* **2** (of weather, the sea, or a sea journey) stormy and violent; not calm: *rough winds* | *We had a very rough crossing to France.* **3** usu. derog (esp. of a person or their behaviour) showing a lack of gentleness, good manners, or consideration, and perhaps a readiness to use force or violence: *a rough boy* | *He's a rough-looking character.* | *They complained of rough handling by the police.* | *a rough neighbourhood* (=full of rough people) | *Don't be so rough with that box – it's got eggs in it.* **4** (of a sound) not gentle or tuneful: *a rough voice* **5** done or made without attention to detail or exactness; APPROXIMATE: *a rough translation* | *She did a rough drawing to show me what she meant.* | *Could you give me* **a rough idea** *when you'll be back?* (–tell me, without needing to be too exact) | *At a rough guess I'd say he was about 45.* —see also ROUGH PAPER **6** (of food and living conditions) not delicate or comfortable; simple: *Life was rough out in the American West in the last century.* | *a rough country wine* **7 (on)** infml unfortunate and/or unfair: *She's had a very rough time recently.* | *My boss realized I was unprepared for the meeting, and gave me a bit of* **a rough ride.** (=a difficult time) | *It's a bit rough on* (=unfortunate for) *him, losing his job.* **8** [F] infml unwell: *I'm feeling pretty rough; I think I'll go to bed.* **9 rough and ready** simple and without comfort: *The living conditions in the camp were a bit rough and ready.* **10 the rough side of one's tongue** old-fash infml an act of speaking angrily to someone: *You'll get the rough side of my tongue if you're cheeky again.* —see also ROUGHLY — ~ **ness** n [U]

rough² n **1** [(the) U] the uneven ground with long grass on a GOLF course: *I lost my ball in the rough.* —see picture at GOLF **2** [C] old use a violent noisy man: *A crowd of young roughs was fighting at the football game.* **3** [C] a quick drawing not showing all details **4 in rough** in an incomplete, untidy, or undetailed form: *Write it out in rough first and then copy it out neatly.* **5 take the rough with the smooth** to accept bad things as well as good things without complaining

rough³ v **rough it** infml to live in a simple and not very comfortable way: *Living in a tent's not for me – I don't like roughing it.*

    rough sthg. ↔ **in** phr v [T] to put in (a few practice lines in a drawing): *I'll just rough in the shape of the head and you can paint the sky round it.*

    rough sthg. ↔ **out** phr v [T] to make (a first plan of a drawing or piece of writing): *I'll just rough out the whole picture and you can do the details.*

    rough sbdy. ↔ **up** phr v [T] infml to attack roughly, usu. as a threat

rough⁴ adv **1** BrE in uncomfortable conditions, esp. out of doors: *When you're a tramp, you get used to* **sleeping rough.** **2** not in a gentle way; using (too much) force: *Those boys certainly play rough!* —see also ROUGHLY

rough·age /ˈrʌfɪdʒ/ n [U] FIBRE (=string-like vegetable material) contained in food, that does not actually feed the eater, but helps the bowels to work: *Wholemeal bread provides valuable roughage.*

rough-and-tum·ble /ˌ· ·ˈ··/ n [C;U] (an occasion of) noisy fighting: *The kids were having a bit of a rough-and-tumble when one of them banged his head.* | (fig.) *the rough-and-tumble of politics*

rough·cast /ˈrʌfkɑːst‖-kæst/ n [U] a rough surface on the outside of a building, made of PLASTER mixed with little stones or broken shells —**roughcast** adj [A]

rough di·a·mond /ˌ· ˈ···/ BrE‖**diamond in the rough**

AmE— *n infml* a person who has a kind and generous nature and/or great ability, but whose outward manner is rather rough

rough·en /ˈrʌfən/ *v* [I;T] to make or become rough: *Constant washing of clothes had roughened her hands.*

rough-hewn /ˌ· ˈ·◂/ *adj* (of wood or stone) roughly cut; not made smooth: *a wall of rough-hewn blocks*

rough·house[1] /ˈrʌfhaʊs/ *n* [S] *BrE old-fash infml* a noisy disorderly fight, not usu. with weapons

roughhouse[2] *v* [I] *AmE* to play roughly, to WRESTLE: *The children were roughhousing in the living room and knocked over a lamp.*

rough·ly /ˈrʌfli/ *adv* **1** in a rough manner: *He pushed her roughly away.* | *"Get out!" he said roughly.* **2** about; not exactly: *There were roughly 200 people there.* | *How many people, roughly?* | *Roughly speaking, I'd say 200.* | *The cost of the two systems is roughly equal/roughly the same.*

rough·neck /ˈrʌfnek/ *n* **1** a member of the team of men who make or operate an oil well **2** *infml, esp. AmE* a rough bad-tempered person

rough pa·per /ˌ· ˈ··/ *n* [U] paper (to be) used for making an incomplete or undetailed drawing, piece of writing, etc.

Rough Rid·ers /ˈ· ˌ··/ *n* [P] an American CAVALRY group led by Teddy Roosevelt and made up of COWBOYS and RANCHERS who fought in a war against Spain in 1898

rough·shod /ˈrʌfʃɒd‖-ʃɑːd/ *adv* see **ride roughshod over** (RIDE[1])

rough sleep·er /ˈ· ˌ··/ *n BrE* a homeless person who sleeps out on the street

rough stuff /ˈ· ·/ *n* [U] *infml* violence; violent behaviour

rou·lette /ruːˈlet/ *n* [U] a game of chance in which a small ball is spun round a moving wheel and falls into a hole marked with a number —see also RUSSIAN ROULETTE

Rou·ma·ni·a /ruːˈmeɪniə/ *n* ROMANIA

round[1] /raʊnd/ *adj* **1** shaped like a circle; circular: *a round plate/table* | *The little boy's eyes grew round with delight.* **2** shaped like a ball; SPHERICAL: *The Earth is round, not flat.* **3** (of a part of the body) fat and curved: *the child's round red cheeks* **4** [A] (of a number) full; complete: *a round dozen* **5 in round figures** (of a number) not expressed exactly, but to the nearest 10, 100, 1000, etc., without paying attention to small amounts: *The car cost £9878 — that's £10,000 in round figures.* —see also ROUNDLY —~ness *n* [U]

round[2] ‖ usu. **around** *AmE*— *adv* **1** with a circular movement; (as if) spinning in a circle: *The Earth turns round once in 24 hours.* | *The wheels went round and round.*| *His head was spinning round with all the excitement.* | (fig.) *Your birthday will soon come round again.* | (fig.) *This plant flowers all (the) year round.* (=during the whole year) **2** in a circular position or arrangement; surrounding a central point: *The field has a fence all round.* | *The children gathered round to hear the story.*| *The tree trunk is two metres round.* **3** to various places: *They travel round together.* **4** to a particular place: *They invited us round* (=to their house) *for drinks.* | *He came round* (*to our place*) *at 6.00 and we went out together.* **5** all over the place; in or into all parts; everywhere or to everyone in a place: *Hand/Pass round the wine glasses.*| *Let me show you round.* | *A nasty rumour has been going round.* | *Let's go into the palace and have a look round.*| *There weren't enough books* **to go round.** (=enough for each person to have one) **6** so as to face the other way or the stated way: *Turn the picture round to face the wall.*| *He's got his hat on* **the wrong way round.** (=with the back of the hat in front) **7** (of a journey) not going the straightest way: *Let's walk/drive round by the park instead of going straight home.* **8 round about** *infml* a little bit more or less than; about: *It'll cost you round about £300.* —see also ROUNDABOUT **9 the other/opposite way round** in the opposite order: *The dog didn't bite the boy. It was the other way round — the boy bit the dog!* —see also ALL ROUND

round[3] ‖ usu. **around** *AmE*— *prep* **1** with a circular movement about (a central point): *The Earth goes round the sun.* | *Drake sailed* (*right/all*) *round the world and came back to England.* **2** in a circular position on all or some sides of (a central point): *We sat round the table.* | *Tie the belt round your waist.* | *Put something round your shoul-*

ders — *it's cold.* **3** into all parts of; all over (a place): *Have a look round the shop.* | *Let me show you round the castle.*| *They danced round and round the room.* | *We travelled round Europe.* **4** to or at the other side of, not going straight but changing direction: *He disappeared round the corner.* | *The car's round the back of the house.* **5** in the neighbourhood of; near (a place): *Do you live round here?* **6** a little bit more or less than; about: *It'll cost somewhere round £50.* **7** *BrE nonstandard* to; round to: *I'm just going round the shops for some sugar.* —see also **round the bend** (BEND[2]), **around/round the clock** (CLOCK[1])

▷ USAGE Some people use **round** (*adv* and *prep*) or **about** (*adv*) while others, especially Americans, use **around.** People who use both often make a difference between **round** for "circular movement" or "measurement": *He turned* **round.** | *a tree five feet* **round,** and **around** meaning "in a general area" or "moving to different places": *He lives somewhere* **around.** | *I was just walking* **around.** Compare: *The spaceship travelled right* **round** *the world in 40 minutes* (=in one complete circle) and *I travelled all* **around** *the world for a few years* (=all over the place).◁

round[4] *n* **1** [(of)] a number or set of connected events: *We hope the next round of arms-limitation talks will be more successful.* | *Life was one continual round of parties.* **2** a regular journey to a number of houses, offices, etc., in a town: *She does a paper round.* (=delivers newspapers to houses) —see also MILK ROUND, ROUNDS, ROUNDSMAN **3** a number of esp. alcoholic drinks bought for everyone present: *to buy a round of drinks* | *What'll you have? It's my round.* (=I'm paying) **4** (in GOLF) a complete game including all the holes **5 a** (in BOXING, WRESTLING, etc.) any of the periods of fighting in a match, separated by short rests: *He was knocked out in the second round.* | *a 12-round contest* **b** (in tennis, football, etc.) any of the stages in a competition: *Becker will play Cash in the next round of the US Open Championships.* **6** one single shot from a gun: *He fired round after round.* | *I've only got two rounds (of ammunition) left.* (=bullets for two shots) **7** [+of] a long burst: *Let's have a big round of applause for that very fine performance!* **8** *esp. BrE* **a** a SANDWICH made with two whole pieces of bread: *I'll have two rounds of cheese sandwiches.* **b** one whole piece of bread: *two rounds of toast* **9** [(of)] something that has a circular shape: *Put a little round of butter on each steak.* **10** a song for three or four singers, in which each sings the same tune, one starting a line after another has just finished it **11 the/one's daily round** the/one's duties that must be done every day: *the daily round of cooking and cleaning* —see also THEATRE IN THE ROUND

round[5] *v* [T] **1** to go round: *She rounded the corner at top speed.* | *We rounded the cape and sailed for home.* **2** to make round: *He rounded his lips as if about to whistle.*

round sthg. ↔ **down** *phr v* [T (to)] to reduce (an exact figure) to the nearest whole number: *If your income is £12,386.46, it will be rounded down to £12,386 for tax purposes.* —compare ROUND off (2), ROUND up (2)

round sthg. ↔ **off** *phr v* [T] **1** [(by, with)] to end suitably and satisfactorily: *We rounded off the meal with some brandy.* **2** to change (an exact figure) into the nearest whole number —compare ROUND **down,** ROUND **up** (2)

round on sbdy./sthg. *phr v* [T] to turn and attack, angrily and unexpectedly: *The lion suddenly rounded on the hunters.* | *Then for no reason she rounded on me and started screaming.*

round out *phr v* **1** [T] (**round** sthg.↔**out**) to complete: *He rounded out his education by spending a year in Paris.* **2** [I] (esp. of a woman) to become rounder in shape, esp. in an attractive way

round sbdy./sthg. ↔ **up** *phr v* [T] **1** to gather or bring together (scattered things, people, or animals, esp. cattle): *The shepherd's dog rounded up some stray sheep.* | *Round up a few friends to help you!* | *Two of the thieves were arrested outside the bank, and the rest of the gang was rounded up later.* —see also ROUNDUP **2** [(to)] to increase (an exact figure) to the next highest whole number —compare ROUND **down,** ROUND **off** (2)

round·a·bout[1] /ˈraʊndəbaʊt/ *n* **1** *BrE* ‖ **traffic circle** *AmE*— a place where three or more roads meet, which has a usu. circular area in the middle round which the traffic must go, rather than straight across **2** *BrE* for

MERRY-GO-ROUND —see also **what you lose on the swings you gain on the roundabouts** (SWING²)

roundabout² adj indirect; not in the shortest possible way: *We took a roundabout route to avoid the floods.* | *a round-about way of saying something*

round brack·et /ˌ· ˈ··/ n BrE for BRACKET¹ (2c)

round·ed /ˈraʊndɪd/ adj round, esp. pleasingly curved: *her pleasantly rounded figure* —see also WELL-ROUNDED (1)

roun·del /ˈraʊndl/ n 1 a small raised circle cut into wood or stone as a decoration 2 a coloured circle showing the nationality of a military aircraft

roun·ders /ˈraʊndəz‖-ərz/ n [U] a British ball game like BASEBALL, usu. played by children, in which a player hits the ball and then runs round the edge of a square area

Round·head /ˈraʊndhed/ n (usu. cap.) a supporter of Parliament against the King in the English Civil War in the 17th century. The Roundheads fought against the CAVALIERS. —see pictures at CAVALIER and at CROMWELL

round·ish /ˈraʊndɪʃ/ adj fairly or rather round in shape

round·ly /ˈraʊndli/ adv fml 1 completely: *We were roundly defeated.* 2 strongly and forcefully: *The new tax law has been roundly condemned by the Opposition.*

round rob·in /ˌ· ˈ··/ n 1 a letter expressing opinions or complaints, signed by many people and sent in to an official body 2 AmE a competition in which each player or team plays against each of the other players or teams

rounds /raʊndz/ n 1 the tour or usual visits one makes as part of one's job: *The doctor is doing his rounds/out on his rounds.* (=visiting sick people) 2 **go the rounds** BrE ‖ **do the rounds** AmE infml (esp. of news or illness) to be passed on; CIRCULATE: *There's a very nasty kind of flu going the rounds this winter.*

round-shoul·dered /ˌ· ˈ··◂/ adj derog having shoulders that are bent forwards or slope downwards

rounds·man /ˈraʊndzmən/ n -men /mən/ esp. BrE a man employed by a shop to go round delivering goods to people's houses: *the baker's roundsman*

round-ta·ble /ˌ· ˈ··◂/ adj [A] at which all the people present meet in an equal way and have equal importance: *a round-table discussion/conference*

Round Table [the] 1 the table at which King Arthur and his KNIGHTS sat, according to old stories. As it was round, all the places at it were equal. —see ARTHURIAN LEGEND 2 an organization for young business and PROFESSIONAL people which holds meetings and does work for the community, eg. CHARITY work

round-the-clock /ˌ·· ˈ·◂/ adj [A] done or happening all the time, both day and night: *The police kept a round-the-clock watch on the house.* —see also **around/round the clock** (CLOCK¹)

round-trip /ˌ· ˈ·◂/ adj AmE (of a ticket or its cost) for a round trip; RETURN³: *a round-trip ticket*

round trip n a journey to a place and back again: *The round trip took just over an hour.*

round·up /ˈraʊndʌp/ n a gathering or bringing together of scattered things, animals, or people: *There's been a police roundup of all the suspects.* | *a cattle roundup* (=by men on horses) | *There'll be a news roundup* (=giving the main points of the news) *before the station goes off the air.* —see also ROUND **up** (1)

rouse /raʊz/ v [T] 1 [(**from, out of**)] fml to waken: *The noise roused me (from/out of a deep sleep).* 2 [(**from, out of, to**)] to make more active, interested, or excited: *The speaker tried to rouse his listeners to action/from their apathy.* | *I warn you, he's dangerous when he's roused!* (=when something makes him angry) —see also AROUSE

rous·ing /ˈraʊzɪŋ/ adj that makes people excited and eager; STIRRING: *a rousing speech about freedom* | *a rousing chorus of "Rule Britannia"*

Rous·seau /ˈruːsəʊ‖ruːˈsəʊ/, **Jean Jacques** /ʒɒn ʒæk‖ ʒɑːn ʒɑːk/ (1712–78) a French writer and thinker who introduced the phrase "Liberty, Equality, Fraternity", later to become the MOTTO of the French Revolution, in his book *The Social Contract*. He is also remembered for writing about the NOBLE SAVAGE

Rous·sos /ˈruːsɒs‖-səʊs/, **Dem·is** /ˈdemɪs/ (1947–) a Greek singer, esp. popular in the 1970s. He is remembered esp. for his rather high voice and for his large size.

roust /raʊst/ v [T] to get someone out of a place: *Go roust your brother out of bed.*

rous·ta·bout /ˈraʊstəbaʊt/ n AmE a man who does heavy unskilled work, esp. **a** at a seaport or in an oil field, or **b** in a CIRCUS

rout¹ /raʊt/ n a complete defeat and disorderly running away: *the total rout of the enemy forces* | *We put the enemy to rout.* (=beat them and drove them away) | (fig.) *The match was an utter rout; we lost 15–0.*

rout² v [T] to defeat completely and drive away: *They routed the enemy.* | (fig.) *Our party was routed at the election.*
rout sbdy. ↔ **out** phr v [T (**of**)] infml to force or drive (someone) out of somewhere they ought not to be: *Harry's been in the bath long enough — go and rout him out!*

route /ruːt‖ruːt, raʊt/ n a chosen direction or line of travel between one place and another: *What's the shortest route from London to Cambridge?* | *The school is on a bus route.* (=buses go past and stop) | *to plan one's route* | *the busy Transatlantic air routes* | (fig.) *the surest route to disaster/to success* —see also EN ROUTE, RED ROUTE, SNOW ROUTE, TRADE ROUTE

route² v [T+obj+adv/prep] to send by a particular route: *They routed the goods through Italy/by way of Germany.*

route march /ˈ· ·/ n a long march by soldiers in training

rou·tine¹ /ruːˈtiːn/ n 1 [C;U] (a) regular and habitual way of working or doing things: *The security men changed their usual routine and collected the money at a different time.* | *She longed to escape from the same old familiar routine.* | *the stultifying routine of housework* 2 [C] a set of steps learnt and practised by a dancer for public performance: *a dance routine* 3 [C] a set of instructions given to a computer to carry out a particular operation

rou·tine² /ˌruːˈtiːn◂/ adj 1 regular; according to what is always habitually done; not special: *It's just a routine medical examination, nothing to get worried about.* | *routine maintenance* | *routine police inquiries* 2 derog not unusual or exciting: *a dull, routine job* — **~ly** adv

roux /ruː/ n roux /ruːz/ [C;U] (a) liquid mixture of fat and flour used for thickening soups and SAUCES

rove /rəʊv/ v [I;T] esp. lit to wander; move continually (around): *His eyes roved about the crowded room, looking for the mysterious stranger.* | *a roving reporter*

rov·er /ˈrəʊvəʳ/ n lit a wanderer

Rover tdmk a British company that makes good quality cars

roving com·mis·sion /ˌ··· ·ˈ··/ n 1 tech permission, given to a person who is inquiring (officially) into a matter, to travel when necessary 2 infml a job or piece of work that takes one to many places

roving eye /ˌ·· ˈ·/ n [S] infml sexual interests that pass quickly from one person to another: *Her husband's got a roving eye.*

row¹ /rəʊ/ n 1 [(of)] a neat line (of people or things) side by side: *a row of houses* | *a row of cups on a shelf* | *We sat in the third row of the stalls.* (=in a theatre, etc.) | *The children stood in a row.* | *Plant the seedlings in parallel rows.* 2 **in a row** one after the other without a break: *She won the competition three times in a row.*

row² /rəʊ/ v [I;T] 1 to move (a boat) through the water with OARS (=long poles with flat ends): *Can you row (a boat)?* | *a rowing club* —see BOAT¹ (USAGE) 2 [(+obj)+adv/ prep] to travel or carry in this way: *We rowed down to the island.* | *He rowed us across the lake.* — **~er** n

row³ /rəʊ/ n [usu. sing.] a trip or journey in a ROWING BOAT

row⁴ /raʊ/ n BrE infml 1 [C] **a** a noisy quarrel: *He's always having rows with his wife.* **b** a public argument in which charges of wrongdoing and opposing views are exchanged; a DISPUTE or CONTROVERSY: *The Prime Minister is at the centre of a new row concerning government secrets.* | *Her speech provoked a bitter row.* 2 [S] derog a noise: *Stop making such a row; I can't sleep!*

row⁵ /raʊ/ v [I (**about, with**)] BrE infml to quarrel, often noisily or violently: *They were rowing about money, as usual.*

row·an /ˈrəʊən, ˈraʊən/ n (the bright red berry of) a small tree of the rose family

row·dy /ˈraʊdi/ adj infml derog noisy and rough: *We don't let Timothy play with those rowdy children.* | *a rowdy party* — **-dily** adv — **-diness** n [U]

row·dy·is·m /ˈraʊdi-ɪzəm/ n [U] derog rowdy behaviour: *rowdyism at football matches*

row house /ˈrəʊ haʊs/ *n AmE for* TERRACED HOUSE —see picture at HOUSE and see colour picture on page 161

rowing boat /ˈrəʊɪŋ bəʊt/ *BrE* ‖ also **row·boat** /ˈrəʊbəʊt/ *esp. AmE—* *n* a small boat that is moved through the water with OARs (=long poles with flat ends)

Row·land /ˈrəʊlənd/, **Tiny** the CHIEF EXECUTIVE of Lonrho, a British based MULTINATIONAL company with interests in trade in every part of the world

row·lock /ˈrɒlək/ˈrɑː-; *not tech* ˈrəʊlɒk‖-lɑːk/ *BrE* ‖ **oarlock** *AmE— n* a pin or U-shaped rest on the side of a boat, for holding an OAR in place

Rown·tree Mack·in·tosh /ˌraʊntriː ˈmækɪntɒʃ‖-tɑːʃ/ *tdmk* one of Britain's largest makers of sweets, chocolates, etc.

Rox·burgh·shire /ˈrɒksbərəʃərˈ‖ˈrɑːk-/ a former COUNTY in SE Scotland, now part of the Borders REGION

roy·al¹ /ˈrɔɪəl/ *adj* [A *no comp.*] **1** (*often cap.*) for, belonging to, or connected with a king or queen: *the royal family* | *The new law has received the royal assent.* (=the approval of the king or queen) —compare REGAL **2** splendid; MAGNIFICENT: *They gave us a* **right royal** (=very splendid) *welcome.* —see also BATTLE ROYAL — **~ly** *adv*

royal² *n* [*usu. pl.*] *infml* a member of the Royal Family: *The papers are full of stories about the royals.*

Royal A·cad·e·my /ˌ.··ˈ·—·/ also **Royal Academy of Arts** /ˌ.··ˌ.··ˈ·/— [*the*] **1** the British society of artists whose members can use the title **RA** after their name. They run a POSTGRADUATE school for artists and hold many EXHIBITIONS. Anyone can put forward a piece of art for their Summer Exhibition each year but only the best paintings are shown. There is fierce competition to take part. **2** the building in London where their work is shown

Royal A·cad·e·my of Dra·mat·ic Arts /ˌ.··ˌ.···ˌ.··ˈ·/ see RADA

Royal Academy of Mu·sic /ˌ.··ˌ.··ˈ·/ [*the*] an important London music college

Royal Air·craft Es·tab·lish·ment /ˌ.··ˈ·ˌ.···/ see RAE

Royal Air Force /ˌ.··ˈ·/ see RAF

the Royal Albert Hall

Royal Al·bert Hall /ˌ.··ˌ.··ˈ·/ [*the*] see ALBERT HALL

Royal and An·cient /ˌ.··ˈ·/ also **R and A—** [*the*] the organization which decides on the rules of GOLF for most countries except the US. Its full name is the **Royal and Ancient Golf Club of St Andrews.**

Royal An·gli·a Re·gi·ment /ˌ.··ˈ·ˌ.···/ [*the*] a REGIMENT (a large division of men) in the British army

Royal As·cot /ˌ.··ˈ·/ a four-day horse-racing event at Ascot, England, every June. It is one of the most important race meetings in Britain and members of the royal family always attend. One of the days is called Ladies' Day and some of the women like to wear unusual and usu. big hats. It is popular esp. with UPPER-CLASS people.

royal as·sent /ˌ.··ˈ·/ [*the*] the signing of a law by the British king or queen, the final stage of its passing through Parliament. The signing is purely formal and has no connection with the king or queen's personal wishes.: *The Channel Tunnel bill today received the royal assent.*

Royal Bal·let /ˌ.··ˈ·‖ˌ.··ˈ·/ [*the*] Britain's national BALLET company, which includes many dancers of international quality, and has its base at Covent Garden in London

Royal Bank of Scot·land /ˌ.··ˌ.··ˈ·/ [*the*] one of the main Scottish banks which is now often also found in England. Like other Scottish banks, it prints its own banknotes.

royal blue /ˌ.··ˈ·◂/ *adj* of a purplish-blue colour

Royal Brit·ish Le·gion /ˌ.··ˌ.··ˈ·/ [*the*] see BRITISH LEGION

Royal Ca·na·di·an Mount·ed Police /ˌ.··ˌ.··ˌ.··ˈ·/ (*abbrev.* **RCMP**) [*the*] a Canadian police force —see also MOUNTIE

Royal Col·lege of Art /ˌ.··ˌ.··ˈ·/ also **RCA** — [*the*] a leading London art college

Royal College of Mu·sic /ˌ.··ˌ.··ˈ·/ [*the*] a London school for musicians who show the promise of great ability

Royal College of Nurs·es /ˌ.··ˌ.··ˈ·/ [*the*] an association of British nurses which represents them when this is necessary

royal com·mis·sion /ˌ.··ˈ·/ *n* a group of people chosen to look carefully at a subject which the British government thinks may need new laws, and to make suggestions: *the royal commission on the future of broadcasting*

Royal Court /ˌ.··ˈ·/ [*the*] a London theatre known for its production of serious new plays

Royal Doul·ton /ˌrɔɪəl ˈdəʊltən/ *tdmk* a type of high quality fine CHINA (2) made in England

Royal En·clos·ure /ˌ.··ˈ·/ [*the*] a special area at Ascot, open to ticket holders only

the royal family

royal fam·i·ly /ˌ.··ˈ·/ [*the*] **1** the family of the king or queen of a country **2** (*often caps.*) (in Britain) Queen Elizabeth II and her family. There are many colourful ceremonies involving the Royal Family and they visit towns and institutions. A lot of British people are very fond of the Royal Family and like to read about them. The popular newspapers often write about them.

Royal Fes·ti·val Hall /ˌ.··ˌ.··ˈ·/ [*the*] see FESTIVAL HALL

royal flush /ˌ.··ˈ·/ *n* (in card games) a set of cards dealt to a person which are the five highest cards in one of the four different types (SUITS¹ (2))

Royal Green Jackets /ˌ.··ˈ·ˌ.··/ also **Green Jackets—** [*the*] a REGIMENT (=a large division of men) in the British army

Royal Green·wich Ob·ser·va·to·ry /ˌ.··ˌ.··ˈ·ˌ.···/ [*the*] an OBSERVATORY which sets the time in Britain, and the TIME ZONES in the world —see also GREENWICH MEAN TIME

Royal High·land Re·gi·ment /ˌ.··ˌ.··ˈ·/ [*the*] see BLACK WATCH

Royal High·ness /ˌ.··ˈ·/ *n* (used for speaking to or about a royal person, esp. a prince or princess): *Good morning, Your Royal Highness.* | *Their Royal Highnesses have graciously consented to attend.*

Royal Horse Guards /ˌ.··ˈ·ˌ.·/ also **The Blues—** [*the*+P] a former REGIMENT (=large division of men) of the British army, called The Blues because of their blue uniform, which joined with the Royal Dragoons in 1969 to form the Blues and Royals —see also HOUSEHOLD CAVALRY

Royal Hor·ti·cul·tur·al So·ci·e·ty /ˌ.··ˌ.··ˌ.··/ [*the*] a British society of garden lovers which arranges the CHELSEA FLOWER SHOW each year

Royal In·sti·tu·tion /ˌ.··ˌ.··ˈ·/ [*the*] a British institution which encourages science

Royal I·rish Ran·gers /ˌ.··ˌ.··ˈ·/ [*the*] an Irish REGIMENT (=a large division of men) in the British army. In 1992 they joined with the UDR to become the **Royal Irish Regiment.**

roy·al·ist /ˈrɔɪəlˌɪst/ *adj, n* (*sometimes cap.*) (typical of) someone who supports a king or queen, or who believes that a country should be ruled by kings and queens: *an ardent royalist*

royal jel·ly /ˌ·· ˈ··/ *n* [U] a substance produced by bees which, it is claimed, has the effect of increasing health and helping humans to live longer. It is used in cosmetics (COSMETIC¹) and eaten.

Royal Mail /ˌ·· ˈ·/ [*the*] the official name of the part of the POST OFFICE which deals with delivering letters, parcels, and selling stamps

Royal Ma·rines /ˌ··· ·ˈ·/ [*the*] the part of the British army trained to fight at sea

Royal Mile /ˌ·· ˈ·/ [*the*] a line of streets in Edinburgh which runs from the Castle to Holyrood House, a royal palace

Royal Mil·i·ta·ry A·cad·e·my /ˌ··· ·ˌ···· ·ˈ···/ [*the*] see SANDHURST

Royal Mint /ˌ·· ˈ·/ [*the*] **1** a British government department which is responsible for making paper money and coins **2** the building where this work is done

Royal Na·tion·al In·sti·tute for the Blind /ˌ·· ˌ··· ˌ····· ·ˈ·/ also **RNIB** − [*the*] an association which helps blind people in Britain

Royal National Institute for the Deaf /ˌ·· ˌ··· ˌ····· ·ˈ·/ [*the*] a British organization which gives help and support to people who cannot hear

Royal National Life·boat In·sti·tu·tion /ˌ·· ˌ··· ˈ·· ··ˌ··/ [*the*] see RNLI

Royal Na·val Col·lege /ˌ·· ˈ·· ˌ··/ also **Britannia Royal Naval College**− [*the*] a training college at Dartmouth, SW England, where young men in the Royal Navy learn to be officers

Royal Na·vy /ˌ·· ˈ··/ [*the*] the men and ships of Britain's armed forces at sea −compare MERCHANT NAVY

Royal Op·e·ra House /ˌ··· ˈ··· ·/ [*the*] one of the two important London theatres where OPERAS and BALLET are performed, often called **Covent Garden** because it is in Covent Garden

Royal Pa·vil·ion /ˌ·· ·ˈ··/ [*the*] a building in an exciting and unusual ORIENTAL style built in Brighton in 1817 for the Prince of Wales

Royal Phil·har·mon·ic Or·ches·tra /ˌ·· ··ˈ·· ˌ··/ also **RPO, Royal Philharmonic** − [*the*] a leading London ORCHESTRA

royal pre·rog·a·tive /ˌ·· ·ˈ··/ *n* [*the*] (*often caps.*) (any of) the special rights of a king or queen: *In Britain it is the royal prerogative to order Parliament to meet.*

Royal Re·gi·ment of Fu·si·liers /ˌ·· ˌ··· · ··ˈ·/ [*the*] a REGIMENT (=a large division of men) in the British army

Royal Scot /ˌ·· ˈ·/ [*the*] the most famous British steam train

Royal Scots /ˌ· ˈ ·/ [*the*] a Scottish REGIMENT (=a large division of men) in the British army. It is the oldest regiment.

Royal Scots Dra·goon Guards /ˌ··· ·ˈ· ˌ·/ [*the*+P] a part of the British army which is involved with ARMOURED vehicles

Royal Shakes·peare Com·pa·ny /ˌ·· ˈ·· ˌ··/ [*the*] a British theatre company of high quality actors who perform works by Shakespeare and other writers; also called the **RSC**

Royal Show /ˌ·· ˈ·/ [*the*] a yearly British farming show

Royal So·ci·e·ty /ˌ··· ·ˈ···/ [*the*] Britain's oldest scientific society, whose members (FELLOWS) are elected because of the high standard of their work in their particular fields

Royal Society for the Pro·tec·tion of Birds /ˌ·· ·ˌ···· · ·ˌ··· · ˈ·/ [*the*] see RSPB

Royal Society of Arts /ˌ·· ·ˌ··· ·ˈ·/ [*the*] see RSA

Royal Tour·na·ment /ˌ·· ˈ···/ [*the*] a yearly public show produced by the British army, air force, and navy in which they show their skills with displays of GYMNASTICS etc.

roy·al·ty /ˈrɔɪəlti/ *n* **1** [U+*sing./pl. v*] also **the Royals**− members of the Royal Family: *The flag is only raised when royalty is/are present.* **2** [C] a payment made to the writer of a book, piece of music, etc., out of the money made from selling that work: *The writer gets a 10% royalty on each copy (sold) of his book.*

Royal Ul·ster Con·stab·u·la·ry /ˌ·· ·ˌ·· ·ˈ····/ [*the*] see RUC

Royal Va·ri·e·ty Show /ˌ·· ·ˈ··· ˌ·/ [*the*] a yearly show of

singing, dancing, etc. in the London Palladium, which raises money for CHARITY and at which members of the British royal family are present

royal we /ˌ·· ˈ·/ *n* [*the*] *sometimes humor* the use of we (by a king or queen) when it really means I

Royal Welsh Fu·si·liers /ˌ·· ·ˌ ··ˈ·/ [*the*] a Welsh REGIMENT (=large division of men) in the British army

Royal Worces·ter /ˌ·· ˈ··/ a type of high quality fine CHINA (2) made in England

Royal Yacht /ˌ·· ˈ·/ [*the*] a boat belonging to the British Royal Family. They sometimes travel in it when they make official visits to other countries. It is called **Britannia.**

Roy Ro·gers /ˌrɔɪ ˈrɒdʒəz‖-ˈrɑːdʒərz/ also **Shirley Temple**− *n* [C;U] (in the US) a glass of) a drink for children made of LEMONADE and GRENADINE (a sweet juice) with a CHERRY floating in it

rozz·er /ˈrɒzəʳ‖ˈrɑː-/ *n BrE old-fash sl* a policeman

RP /ˌɑː ˈpiː‖ˌɑːr-/ *n* [U] Received Pronunciation; the form of British English pronunciation which is used by many educated people in every part of Britain and is typical of many people in the South of England. It is thought of as a standard form and is often used by the BBC, esp. by NEWSREADERS. −see also BBC ENGLISH, OXFORD ENGLISH

rpm /ˌɑː piː ˈem‖ˌɑːr-/ *abbrev. for:* revolutions per minute; a measure of the speed of an apparatus that goes round or of an engine: *Play this record at 33¹/₃ rpm.*

RPO /ˌɑː piː ˈəʊ‖ˌɑːr-/ [*the*] *abbrev. for* ROYAL PHILHARMONIC ORCHESTRA

RSA /ˌɑːr es ˈeɪ/ [*the*] Royal Society of Arts; a British association which encourages education for the arts and trade. It sets examinations in English as a Foreign Language together with the University of Cambridge Local Examinations Syndicate.

RSI /ˌɑːr es ˈaɪ/ *abbrev. for:* REPETITIVE STRAIN INJURY

RSPB /ˌɑːr es piː ˈbiː/ [*the*] Royal Society for the Protection of Birds; an organization (CHARITY) in Britain which tries to protect birds

RSPCA /ˌɑːr es piː siː ˈeɪ/ [*the*] Royal Society for the Prevention of Cruelty to Animals; an organization (a CHARITY) in Britain which is concerned with the protection of animals

RS232 /ˌɑːr es ˌtuː θriː ˈtuː/ also **RS232C** /ˌ·· ·ˌ··· ·ˈ·/− *tech* (the name usually used for) the standard connector between a computer and a MODEM or between a computer and various kinds of equipment that are connected to it. It is a PLUG with (holes for) 25 pins, arranged in two rows, one with 13 pins and one with 12 pins.

RSV /ˌɑːr es ˈviː/ *n abbrev. for:* REVISED STANDARD VERSION

RSVP /ˌɑːr es viː ˈpiː/ *abbrev. for:* répondez s'il vous plait (*Fr*); please reply (written on invitations)

Rt Hon *written abbrev. for* Right Honourable −see RIGHT⁵ (6)

rub¹ /rʌb/ *v* **-bb-** **1** [I;T] to press one's hand or another surface against (something), usu. with a repeated up-and-down or round-and-round movement: *He rubbed his itchy skin.* | *I rubbed the window with a cloth.* | *She rubbed the rude words off the board.* | *I accidentally rubbed against the wet paint, and ruined my jacket.* **2** [T (TOGETHER)] to slide (two surfaces) against each other in this way: *He rubbed his hands (together) with pleasure/to warm them.* **3** [I (**against, on**)] (of a surface) to slide up and down or round and round, esp. so as to cause pain or damage: *My shoe's rubbing.* (=against my heel, toe, etc.) | *This tyre seems badly worn; it must be rubbing against/on something.* **4** [T+*obj+adv/prep*] to put on, over, or into a surface by rubbing: *Rub salt into the meat before cooking it.* | *Rub the ointment in well.* | *Spray the polish onto the table and rub it well in with a soft cloth.* **5** [T+*obj+adj/adv/ prep*] to make or put in the stated condition by rubbing: *Rub your hair dry with this cloth.* | *You've rubbed a hole in the elbow of your coat.* **6 rub it in** *infml* to keep talking about something that another person wants to forget, such as a past mistake: *"I told you it would never work like that." "All right − there's no need to rub it in!"* **7 rub salt into the/someone's wound(s)** to make someone's suffering or annoyance even worse **8 rub shoulders with** *infml* to meet socially and treat as equals (esp. people of a different type or social class): *In my job I rub shoulders with all sorts of interesting people.* **9 rub**

someone's nose in it/in the dirt *infml* to punish someone by reminding them of the bad results of their actions **10 rub someone (up) the wrong way** *infml* to annoy someone, esp. by dealing with them without proper care or thought: ANTAGONIZE

rub along *phr v* [I] *BrE infml* **1** [(by, on)] to continue to live or to do what is necessary, but with difficulty; SURVIVE: *We haven't got much money, but we rub along somehow.* **2** [(with, TOGETHER)] to have a fairly good relationship; remain quite friendly: *My boss and I seem to rub along (together) all right.*

rub down *phr v* **1** [I;T (=**rub** sbdy./sthg. ↔ **down**)] to dry (oneself or an animal) by rubbing: *She rubbed her horse down after her ride.* **2** [T] (**rub** sthg.↔**down**) to clean or make smooth (a surface) by rubbing: *Rub the door down before you paint it.* −see also RUBDOWN

rub off *phr v* [I (**on, onto**)] to come off a surface by rubbing: *The paint marks will rub off quite easily.* | (fig.) *I hope that some of her good qualities will rub off onto you.* (=that you will get some of her good qualities as a result of working or spending time with her)

rub out *phr v* **1** [I;T (=**rub** sthg.↔**out**)] *BrE*‖**erase** *AmE*− to remove (esp. pencil writing) or be removedwith a RUBBER¹ (2): *He pencilled in his name, then changed his mind and rubbed it out.* | *These marks won't rub out properly.* **2** [T] (**rub** sbdy.↔**out**) *AmE sl* to murder

rub² *n* **1** [S] *infml* an act of rubbing: *Give the table a good rub with this cloth.* **2 there's the rub** there's the difficulty or cause of trouble: *We need to borrow more money to save the company, but there's the rub: no one will lend us any.* **3 the rub of the green** *BrE infml* (the influence of) a piece of good or bad luck

rub·ber¹ /ˈrʌbəʳ/ *n* **1** [U] a substance, made either naturally from the juice of a tropical tree or artificially, which keeps out water and springs back into position when stretched: *Tyres are made of rubber.* | *a rubber plantation* | *a rubber ball* **2** [C] *esp. BrE* a piece of rubber used for removing pencil marks; ERASER **3** [C] *esp. BrE* ‖ **eraser** *AmE*− a piece of material used for rubbing surfaces to clean them: *a board rubber* (=for cleaning BLACKBOARDS) **4** [C] *infml for* CONDOM **5** [C *usu. pl.*] *AmE for* GALOSH −see also RUBBERY **6** (in BASEBALL) the piece of material placed where the PITCHER stands: *Niekro consults with the catcher before going back to the rubber and preparing for the next pitch.*

rubber² *n* a competition, esp. in cards or international cricket, which usu. consists of an odd number of games: *Shall we have/play a few rubbers of bridge after dinner?*

rubber band /ˌ·· '·/ also **elastic band**− *n* a thin circular piece of rubber used for fastening things together: *Put a rubber band round this bunch of flowers.*

rubber boot /'·· ·/ *n AmE for* a WELLINGTON −see picture at SHOE

rubber ce·ment /ˌ·· '·/ *n* [U] *AmE* a very sticky kind of glue which dries slowly

rubber din·ghy /ˌ·· '··/ *n* a small rubber boat blown up with air −see picture at DINGHY

rub·ber·neck /ˈrʌbənek‖-ər-/ *v* [I] *AmE infml derog* **1** to look about or watch something with too much interest, esp. an accident **2** to go on a pleasure trip as one of a group with a guide −−**er** *n* : *The accident on the 405 has been moved to the side, but rubberneckers are still causing traffic to slow down.* (people looking at the accident as they drive past are slowing the traffic).

rubber plant /'·· ·/ *n* a decorative house plant with large shiny dark green leaves

rubber-stamp /ˌ·· '·/ *v* [T] *often derog* to give official approval to (a decision) without really thinking about it: *The divorce proceedings are a formality; the court will just rubber-stamp them.*

rubber stamp *n* **1** a small object used for printing the date, the name of an organization, etc., consisting of a piece of rubber on a handle, with raised letters or figures, which is pressed onto an INKPAD and then onto the printing surface **2** *usu. derog* a person or body that acts only to make official the decisions already made by another

rubber tree /'·· ·/ *n* a tropical tree from which rubber is obtained

rub·ber·y /ˈrʌbəri/ *adj* strong and slightly elastic like rubber: *The meat's a bit rubbery − you cooked it too long!*

rub·bing /ˈrʌbɪŋ/ *n* a copy of a raised shape or pattern in

stone or metal (esp. brass), made by rubbing a piece of paper laid over the shape with WAX, chalk, etc.: *She did a brass rubbing of the medieval knight in the old church.*

rubbing al·co·hol /'·· ˌ···/ *n* [U] *AmE for* SURGICAL SPIRIT

rub·bish¹ /ˈrʌbɪʃ/ *n* [U] *BrE* **1** also **garbage, trash** *AmE*− things or material of no use or value that will be or have been thrown away: *The dustmen come on Thursdays to collect the rubbish.* | *Throw it on the rubbish heap.* | *household rubbish* **2** something worthless that does not deserve serious attention; nonsense: *He's talking a load of rubbish.* | *That new TV show is absolute rubbish.*

rubbish² *v* [T] *infml, esp. BrE & AustrE* to say that (someone or something) is bad or worthless; severely CRITICIZE: *The government's plan was rubbished by the opposition parties.*

rubbish bin /'·· ·/ *BrE*‖**trash can, garbage can** *AmE*− *n* **1** a DUSTBIN **2** a container for rubbish

rub·bish·y /ˈrʌbɪʃi/ *adj infml, esp. BrE* worthless and silly; TRASHY: *a rubbishy love story*

rub·ble /ˈrʌbəl/ *n* [U] (a mass of) broken stones or bricks, esp. from a building that has been destroyed: *After the bombing her house was just a heap of rubble.*

rub·down /ˈrʌbdaʊn/ also **rub down** /ˌ· '·/− *n* **1** an act of rubbing something down (RUB **down**): *Give the wall a rubdown with some sandpaper.* **2** *AmE* a MASSAGE, esp. after exercise

rube /ruːb/ *n AmE derog sl* a person, usu. from the country, who does not understand the ways of the world and lacks taste: *Those rubes wouldn't know a good show if they saw one!*

ru·bel·la /ruːˈbelə/ *n* [U] *med for* GERMAN MEASLES

Ru·bens /ˈruːbɪnz/, **Peter Paul** (1577−1640) a Flemish artist regarded as one of the great artists, responsible for over 2000 paintings

Ru·bi·con /ˈruːbɪkən, -kɒn‖-kɑːn/ *n* see **cross the Rubicon** (CROSS² (12))

ru·bi·cund /ˈruːbɪkənd/ *adj fml or humor* (of a person or esp. their face) fat, red, and healthy-looking: *a jolly, rubicund farmer*

Ru·bik's Cube /ˈruːbɪks ˌkjuːb/ also **Rubik Cube**− *n tdmk* a toy consisting of a CUBE with nine smaller coloured cubes forming each face. The small cubes must be turned so that each face of the large cube shows one colour only. Rubik's Cube was a very popular toy in the 1970s.

ru·ble /ˈruːbəl/ *n* a ROUBLE

ru·bric /ˈruːbrɪk/ *n fml* a set of rules or explanations on an examination paper, in a book, etc. which is printed in a different way to the main body of the writing and which tells one what to do

ru·by /ˈruːbi/ *n* **1** [C] a deep red precious stone **2** [U] the colour of this stone

Ruby, Jack (1911−67) the man who killed Lee Harvey Oswald, who is believed to have killed President John F Kennedy. Ruby's killing of Oswald led some people to believe that there was a CONSPIRACY (=secret plan) to kill Kennedy and that Oswald was shot so that he could not say anything about it.

RUC /ˌ aː juː 'siː‖ˌ aːr-/ [*the*] Royal Ulster Constabulary; the police force of Northern Ireland

ruck¹ /rʌk/ *n BrE* **1** [*the*] the ordinary level of life: *She dreamed of getting out of the (common) ruck and becoming famous as a singer.* **2** [S] (esp. in the game of RUGBY) a loose disordered group of players

ruck² *v*

ruck up *phr v* [I] (of cloth) to form unwanted folds: *Your coat has rucked up at the back.*

ruck·sack /ˈrʌksæk/ *esp. BrE*‖usu. **backpack** *AmE*− *n* a bag fastened to the shoulders and usu. fixed to a light frame, used by climbers and walkers for carrying their belongings

ruck·us /ˈrʌkəs/ *n* [*usu. sing.*] *infml, esp. AmE* a noisy argument or a noisy confused situation; RUMPUS

ruc·tion /ˈrʌkʃən/ also **ructions** *pl.*− *n* [S] *infml, esp. BrE* noisy complaints and anger: *There'll be ructions if you don't give him some more chocolate!*

rud·der /ˈrʌdəʳ/ *n* a wooden or metal blade at the back of a ship or aircraft that is swung from side to side to control the direction in which it moves −see picture at

► **Rugby**

rugby

There are two forms of rugby football played in Britain, rugby union and rugby league.

Rugby union is played by AMATEURs (=they are not paid). There are 15 players on each team. Rugby union is played internationally between many countries including Australia, Fiji, France, South Africa, Argentina, England, Ireland, Wales, Scotland, and New Zealand. In Britain it is played especially in public schools.

Rugby league is a professional game, played mainly in the N of England (and in Australia). There are 13 players on each team, and the rules are slightly different from rugby union. It is thought to be a rough, hard game.

scrum

AIRCRAFT and YACHT – ~ **less** *adj* : (fig., *fml*) *The death of our leader has left the country rudderless.*

Rud·dles /ˈrʌdlz/ *n* [C;U] *tdmk* a type of British beer

rud·dy[1] /ˈrʌdi/ *adj* **1** *apprec* (of the face) pink and healthy-looking: *the children's ruddy cheeks* **2** *esp. lit* red or reddish: *The fire cast a ruddy glow over the city.* **3** [A] *BrE euph* (used to add force, esp. to an expression of anger) BLOODY[2]: *You're standing on my ruddy foot!* – **diness** *n* [U]

ruddy[2] *adv BrE euph* BLOODY[2]: *There's no need to be so ruddy rude!*

rude /ruːd/ *adj* **1** (of a person or their behaviour) not at all polite; intentionally bad-mannered; offensive: *It's rude to tell someone you don't like them.* | *Don't be so rude to your father!* | *It was very rude of her to leave without telling us.* | *a rude remark|letter* –see IMPOLITE (USAGE) **2** (used esp. by or to children) concerned with sex: *She told a rather rude joke, and everyone looked embarrassed.* **3** [A] sudden and unpleasant: *We had a rude shock when we discovered who he really was.* | *The staff had* a **rude awakening** *when they learned that the company was in serious trouble.* **4** [A] *old use or lit* simple and roughly made: *a rude hut* **5** in **rude health** *fml or pomp* very healthy – ~ **ness** *n* [U]

rude·ly /ˈruːdli/ *adv* **1** in a RUDE (1) way: *"Go away!" he said rudely.* **2** *old use or lit* in a RUDE (4) way: *a rudely constructed shelter*

ru·di·men·ta·ry /ˌruːdɨˈmentəri◂/ *adj fml* **1** (of facts, knowledge, etc.) at the simplest level; coming or learnt first: *I have only a rudimentary knowledge|grasp of chemistry.* **2** simple and incomplete; PRIMITIVE: *Their road-building equipment is fairly rudimentary* | *a rudimentary airfield* **3** *esp. tech* small and not fully usable, either because not yet developed or because of gradual disappearance: *Ostriches have rudimentary wings.*

ru·di·ments /ˈruːdɨmənts/ *n* [the+P+of] the simplest parts (of a subject), learnt at the very beginning: *It didn't take me long to pick up|learn the rudiments of the language.*

Ru·dolph, the Red-nosed Rein·deer /ˌruːdɒlf ðə ˌred nəʊzd ˈreɪndɪəʳ‖ˌruːdɑːlf-/ a character in a children's song, a REINDEER called Rudolph who had a shiny red nose. The other reindeer thought his nose looked silly, but in spite of this Santa Claus chose (CHOOSE) him to pull his SLEDGE. In the US he is a character in a children's television CARTOON and has a nose that lights up. –see colour picture on page 1212

rue /ruː/ *v* [T] *esp. old use or humor* to be very sorry about (something one has done or not done); REGRET: *He'll* **rue the day** *(=will always be sorry that) he married her.*

rue·ful /ˈruːfəl/ *adj* feeling or showing that one is sorry about something: *"If only I hadn't agreed to do it," he thought with a rueful smile.* – ~ **ly** *adv*

ruff /rʌf/ *n* **1** a stiff wheel-shaped white collar worn in Europe in the 16th century **2** a ring of hair or feathers round the neck of an animal or bird

ruf·fi·an /ˈrʌfiən/ *n old-fash derog* an unpleasant violent man: *a gang of ruffians* – ~ **ly** *adj*

ruf·fle[1] /ˈrʌfəl/ *v* [T] **1** [(UP)] to move the smooth surface of; make uneven: *He fondly ruffled the child's hair.* | *The*

bird *ruffled (up) its feathers.* **2** to trouble or upset, esp. causing a loss of confidence: *Her taunts ruffled his pride|composure.* | *Some of the audience were shouting at him, and you could see he was getting a bit ruffled.* **3 ruffle someone's feathers** *infml* to make someone slightly angry or upset

ruffle[2] *n* a band of fine cloth sewn in folds as a decoration round the edge of something, esp. at the neck or wrists of a garment; FRILL

rug /rʌg/ *n* **1** a thick usu. woollen mat, smaller than a CARPET, used to cover the floor or for decoration: *a rug in front of the fire* | *a hearthrug* –compare MAT[1] (1) –see picture at LIVING ROOM **2** *esp. BrE* a large warm woollen covering to wrap round oneself, esp. when travelling or camping: *Put this rug over your knees.* **3** *humor, esp. AmE for* TOUPEE **4 pull the rug (out) from under** *infml* to suddenly stop supporting or helping

rug·by /ˈrʌgbi/ *also* **rugby foot·ball** /ˌ·· ˈ··/ *fml n* [U] (sometimes *cap.*) a type of football in which the ball can be handled, played with an OVAL (=egg-shaped) ball by two teams of either 13 players (**Rugby League** which is played by people who are paid to play rugby as their job) or 15 players (**Rugby Union** which is a non-professional game and has slightly different rules) –see picture on page 884

Rugby a town in central England best known for the PUBLIC SCHOOL (Rugby School) where rugby football was first played

rugby shirt /ˈ·· ˌ·/ *n* a shirt, usu. with wide bands of two different colours worn by rugby football players and also as a fashion

rug·ged /ˈrʌgɨd/ *adj* **1** having a rough uneven surface: *rugged hills* | *rugged terrain* **2** strongly built; STURDY: *You need a fairly rugged vehicle for crossing the desert.* | (fig.) *She admired his rugged good looks.* – ~ **ly** *adv* – ~ **ness** *n* [U]

rug·ger /ˈrʌgəʳ/ *n* [U] Rugby Union football. Many people think of this word as UPPER CLASS or used only in the British PUBLIC SCHOOLs.

ru·in[1] /ˈruːɨn/ *n* **1** [U] (something that causes) complete failure or loss of one's money, position, moral standards, etc.; DOWNFALL: *His rashness led ultimately to his ruin.* | *With the collapse of grain prices the small farmers are on the brink of (financial) ruin.* | *The country is going to* **rack and ruin.** **2** [U] a condition of destruction and decay: *The ancient temple had fallen into ruin.* **3** [C] *also* **ruins** *pl.* – the remains of a building that has fallen down or been (partly) destroyed: *There's an interesting old ruin at the top of that hill.* | *We picked our way through the ruins of the bombed building.* **4 in ruins** (of a building) ruined: *The castle now lies in ruins.* | (fig.) *His life|career is in ruins.* –see also MOTHER'S RUIN

ruin[2] *v* [T] **1** to destroy or spoil (completely): *an ancient ruined city* | *The rain ruined my painting|our holiday|her hairstyle.* | *You'll ruin your chances of the job if you wear that shirt to the interview!* | *disclosures that ruined her reputation* **2** to cause total loss of money to: *I was (financially) ruined by that law suit. See picture on page 1154*

ru·in·a·tion /ˌruːɨˈneɪʃən/ *n* [U] (the cause of) being ruined: *You'll be the ruination of me, spending all that money!*

ru·in·ous /ˈruːɨnəs/ *adj* causing or likely to cause

ruins

destruction or total loss of money: *The cost will be ruinous.* | *a ruinous war* – ~**ly** *adv* : *ruinously expensive*

rule¹ /ruːl/ *n* **1** [C] **a** an official or accepted principle or order which guides behaviour, says how things are to be done, etc.: *It's* **against the rules** *to handle the ball in football.* | *You must obey/observe the rules.* | *There's a penalty if you* **break the rules.** | *the rules of tennis* | *the club rules* [+that] *We have a rule that the loser of the game buys everyone a drink.* | *I get so annoyed by all these petty* **rules and regulations.** | *You're not really allowed to do that, but perhaps on this occasion we can* **bend/stretch the rules.** (=break the rules slightly) **b** the usual way that something happens: *the rules of grammar* | *Snow here in April is* **the exception, not the rule.** (=is unusual) | **As a rule** (=usually) *I get home by seven o'clock.* **2** [U] a period or way of ruling: *The country prospered under her wise rule.* | *Our nation is under foreign rule.* (=governed by foreigners) | *Everyone is subject to the* **rule of law.** | *mob rule* **3** [C] a RULER (2): *a two-foot rule* –see also GOLDEN RULE, GROUND RULE, HOME RULE, QUEENSBERRY RULES, RULE OF THUMB, SLIDE RULE, **work to rule** (WORK²)

rule² *v* **1** [I (**over**); T] to control or be the person in charge of (a country, people, etc.): *Alexander the Great ruled (over) a large empire.* **2** [T] to have a controlling influence over: *Don't let the desire for money rule your life.* | *He* **let his heart rule his head.** (=made decisions according to his feelings rather than his judgment) | *Be ruled by me* (=take my advice); *don't give to do it.* **3** [I+adv/prep; T] (esp. in law) to give an official decision (on): *It is up to the courts to rule on this matter.* | *The court has ruled in favour of the sacked employee.* [+that] *The judge ruled that she must pay the money back.* [+obj+adj/adv/prep] *The judge ruled him out of order/in contempt of court.* | *The company's behaviour has been ruled unlawful.* –see also RULING¹ **4** [T] to draw (a line) using a ruler or similar straight edge **5** ...**rules OK** a phrase used with names esp. of football teams or GANG's of youths, usu. written on walls etc. as GRAFFITI and meaning that the team/gang mentioned is considered to be the best by its supporters/members: *Arsenal rules OK.* | *Gelderd Boot Boys rule OK.* **6 rule the roost** *infml* to be in charge: *It's his wife who really rules the roost in that house.* **7 rule someone with a rod of iron/with an iron hand** to govern (esp. a group) in a very severe way

rule sthg./sbdy.↔**out** *phr v* [T] **1** to say that (something or someone) is not under consideration as a possibility: *The police have ruled out foul play.* | *We can't rule out the possibility that she was murdered by her husband.* **2** to make it impossible for (something) to happen, (someone) to do something, etc.: *Rain ruled out further play.* | *An ankle injury ruled him out for the big match.*

rule-book /ˈruːlbʊk/ *n* **1** [C] a book of rules, esp. one given to workers on a job **2** [the+S] the set of all the rules of a particular activity: *He always goes by* (=obeys) *the rulebook.*

Rule Bri-tan-nia /ˌ··ˈ··/ a song about Britain's command of the seas in former years, sung on PATRIOTIC occasions in the belief that Britain is still great: *Thousands of people had gathered in the Mall and sung Rule Britannia.*

ruled /ruːld/ *adj* (of paper) having parallel lines drawn on it

rule of thumb /ˌ··ˈ·/ *n* [C;U] a principle or method based on practical sense and experience rather than exact rules or calculations: *As a rough rule of thumb, each £1000 you borrow will cost you £10 a month in repayments.*

rul-er /ˈruːlər/ *n* **1** a person who rules **2** a long narrow flat piece of wood, plastic, or metal with straight edges, which is marked with INCHes or centimetres and used for measuring things or for drawing straight lines: *a 12-inch ruler* –compare TAPE MEASURE, and see picture at MATHEMATICS

rul-ing¹ /ˈruːlɪŋ/ *n* [(**on**)] an official decision, esp. of a court: *We're anxiously awaiting the court's ruling on this matter.* [+that] *The judge gave a ruling that they should pay all the money back.* –see also RULE²

ruling² *adj* [A] most powerful; in control: *the ruling classes* | *the ruling party in the national assembly* | *His garden is his* **ruling passion.** (=main interest in life)

rum¹ /rʌm/ *n* [C;U] (a glass of) a strong alcoholic drink made from the juice of the SUGARCANE plant

▶ CULTURAL NOTE Rum is the TRADITIONAL drink of sailors, and is associated esp. with PIRATEs, who are often shown drinking rum in stories.◀

rum² *adj* **-mm-** *old-fash infml, esp. BrE* unusual; strange

Ru-ma-ni-a /ruːˈmeɪniə/ ROMANIA

rum-ba /ˈrʌmbə/ *n* (the music for) a popular dance originally from Cuba

rum-ble¹ /ˈrʌmbəl/ *v* **1** [I] to make or move with a deep rolling sound: *The thunder/The big guns rumbled in the distance.* | *The heavy cart rumbled down the street.* | *I'm hungry – my stomach's rumbling.* **2** [T] *BrE infml* to find out or make known the true facts about (esp. a dishonest person or activity): *We've been rumbled; someone must have told the police.*

rumble² *n* **1** [S] a rumbling sound: *a rumble of thunder* **2** [C] *AmE old fash sl* a street fight

rum-bling /ˈrʌmblɪŋ/ *n* **1** [S] a rumbling sound **2** [C *usu. pl.*] widespread unofficial talk or complaint: *rumblings of dissent/discontent*

rum-bus-tious /rʌmˈbʌstʃəs/ *adj* *infml, esp. BrE* noisy, lively, and cheerful: *The new film is a rumbustious farce that all the family will enjoy.*

ru-mi-nant /ˈruːmɪnənt/ *n, adj* (an animal) that RUMINATEs (2): *The cow is a ruminant.*

ru-mi-nate /ˈruːmɪneɪt/ *v* [I] **1** *fml* (of a person) to think deeply and repeatedly; PONDER: *He ruminated over/on the problem.* **2** *tech* (of cattle, deer, etc.) to bring back food from the stomach and bite it over and over again –**-nation** /ˌruːmɪˈneɪʃən/ *n* [C;U]

ru-mi-na-tive /ˈruːmɪnətɪv‖-neɪ-/ *adj* (of a person or their behaviour) seeming thoughtful: *a ruminative frown* – ~**ly** *adv*

rum-mage¹ /ˈrʌmɪdʒ/ *v* [I+adv/prep] *infml* to turn things over and look into all the corners while trying to find something, esp. causing disorder: *Who's been rummaging (about) through my papers?*

rummage² *n* *infml* **1** [S (ABOUT, AROUND)] an act of rummaging: *I'll have a good rummage (around) and see what I can find.* **2** [U] *esp. AmE* old clothes and other things found by rummaging about

rummage sale /ˈ·· ·/ *n* *AmE for* JUMBLE SALE

rummy /ˈrʌmi/ *n* [U] a simple card game for two or more players

ru-mour *BrE* ‖ **rumor** *AmE* /ˈruːmər/ *n* **1** [U] unofficial news or information, perhaps untrue, which is spread from person to person; HEARSAY: *The whole article was based on rumour.* | **Rumour has it** (=people are saying) *that Jean's getting married again.* **2** [C (**about, of**)] a story or opinion based on rumour, which may or may not be true: *All sorts of rumours are going round the office about him and his secretary.* | *His illness led to rumours of an early election.* [+that] *There's a rumour circulating* (=being spread) *that the factory's going to shut down.* – compare GOSSIP¹

ru-moured *BrE* ‖ **rumored** *AmE* /ˈruːməd‖-ərd/ *adj* reported unofficially: *The rumoured marriage between the prince and the dancer did not in fact take place.* [F+ to-v] *He is rumoured to have left the country.* [+that] *It's rumoured that there'll be an election this year.*

ru-mour-mon-ger /ˈruːməˌmʌŋgər‖-mərˌmɑːŋ-, -ˌmʌŋ-/ *n* *derog* a person who spreads rumours

rump /rʌmp/ *n* **1** the part of an animal at the back just above the legs: *She ordered a juicy* **rump steak.** (=cut from this part of a cow) **2** *humor* the part of the body one sits on; BOTTOM **3** the remaining small, often worthless part of something that used to be larger, such as a public body or organization: *After the election the party was reduced to a rump.*

Rum·pel·stilt·skin /ˌrʌmpəlˈstɪltskɪn/ a character in a fairy story of the same name by the brothers Grimm. Rumpelstiltskin teaches a young girl how to spin STRAW into gold for the king and demands her first child as a reward. She becomes queen, but forgets her promise. Rumpelstiltskin gives her three days to discover his name. A servant happens to hear him saying his name, and when the girl tells him what it is, he destroys himself in his anger.

rum·ple /ˈrʌmpəl/ v [T] to disarrange (hair, clothes, etc.); make untidy: *We could see from the rumpled sheets that the bed had been slept in.*

rum·pus /ˈrʌmpəs/ n [S] *infml* a noisy angry argument or disagreement: *They're bound to* **kick up** (=make) **a rumpus** *about all this damage.*

rumpus room /ˈ··· ·/ n AmE a room, usu. below ground level in a house, used for active games and parties

run¹ /rʌn/ v **ran** /ræn/, **run** /rʌn/, *present participle* **running** ■ to move fast on foot **1** [I] (of people and some animals) to move on one's legs at a speed faster than walking: *I had to run to catch the bus.* | *The children came running when she called them.* | *The insect ran up my leg.* | *The little boy ran off to get his brother.* | *He's got a gun!* **Run for it/Run for your lives!** (=to save yourselves) **2** [T] **a** to move (a distance) by running: *He ran a mile in four minutes.* **b** to do or complete (as if) by running: *My son often* **runs errands** *for me.* (=goes on a short journey to get something) | (fig.) *The illness/rioting* **ran its course**. (=started, developed, and ended in the expected way) **3** [T] **a** to take part in (a race) by running: *Ovett ran a fine race but only finished second.* **b** to cause (an animal) to take part in a race: *We won't run this horse in any more races this season.* **c** to cause (a race) to happen: *The Derby will be run at three o'clock.* —see also ALSO-RAN ■ to move or travel in some other way **4** [I+adv/prep; T+obj+adv/prep] (to cause to) move quickly or freely: *The car ran downhill out of control/ran off the road/ran into a tree.* | *An alarming thought kept running through my mind.* | *A shudder ran through his body as he died.* | *He ran his fingers through his hair in confusion.* | *Run the videotape back to the point where the ball bounces.* | *Could you* **run your eyes over** *this list?* (=examine it quickly) **5** [I; T] **a** (of a public vehicle) to travel as arranged: *The trains don't run on Sundays/aren't running today.* | *This bus runs between Manchester and Liverpool/from here to the station.* **b** to cause (a public vehicle) to travel: *They're running a special train to the football match.* **6** [I+adv/prep; T+obj+adv/prep] *infml* to go or take in a vehicle: *Can I run you home?* ■ to flow or make something flow **7** [I] (of liquid, sand, etc.) to flow freely: *The tears run down his face.* | *The salt won't run out if it's too damp.* *The terrible scream* **made my blood run cold**. (=frightened me) **8** [T] to cause (liquids, sand, etc.) to flow, esp. from a TAP: *Run the water until it gets hot.* [+obj(i)+obj(d)] *Please run me a nice hot bath.* (=fill the bath with water for me) **9** [I] (esp. of a container) to pour out liquid: *Have you left the tap/bath running?* | *The baby's nose is running.* **10** [I] to melt and spread by the action of heat or water: *The butter will run if you put it near the fire.* | *I'm afraid the colours ran when I washed this shirt.* ■ to operate or be in charge of **11** [I;T (on, by)] to (cause to) work or be in operation: *Don't touch the engine while it's running.* | *This machine runs on/by electricity.* | *to run a computer program* | *Can you just run the projector to check that it's working?* | *Despite the shortage of drugs and trained staff, they managed to keep the hospital running.* | *This is an expensive car to run.* (=it costs a lot to keep it working, buy petrol for it, etc.) | (fig.) *Is everything running smoothly at the office?* | *The new computer has arrived but it won't be* **up and running** (=in full operation) *until next week.* **12** [T] to control (an organization or system); be in charge of and cause to work: *Who's running this company/contest?* | *They run a small hotel.* | *Don't try and run my life!* | *a well-run/badly-run company* | *the state-run national airline* ■ to continue in a particular direction or state **13** [I+adv/prep; *not in progressive forms*] to pass or continue in the stated direction, way, etc.: *The boundary runs to the south of that forest.* | *The road runs along the river bank/over the mountains/through a tunnel.* **14** [I+adv/prep, esp. **for**] to have official force during a period of time; remain VALID: *The*

licence runs for a year. | *The insurance has only another month to run.* **15** [I+adv/prep] to continue without interruption: *The play ran* (=was performed regularly) *for two years in New York.* | *The story/poem runs like this ...* | *I can't remember how the rest of Hamlet's speech runs.* | *Good looks* **run in their family**. (=tend to be passed from the parents to the children) **16** [I (**at**) *usu. in progressive forms*] to be or remain at the stated level: *The factory's output is currently running at 50 cars a day.* ■ other meanings **17** [L+adj] to develop or pass into the stated (usu. undesirable) condition: *The well has run dry.* | *Our supply of coal is running short/low.* | *Several people shouted at the chairman; feelings were* **running high**. (=people were getting excited and angry) | *Since their parents divorced those children have been* **running wild**. (=allowed to do what they like, without any control) | *Disease is* **running rife** (=spreading quickly) *in the shanty towns.* **18** [T] to give in a newspaper, magazine, etc.; print: *"The Sunday Times" ran a story about the discovery of Hitler's diaries.* **19** [I (**against, for, in**)] *esp. AmE* to be or become a CANDIDATE (=a person trying to get elected) in an election; STAND¹ (17): *Johnson didn't run a second time.* | *The Democrats chose Mondale to run against Reagan/to run for President.* **20** [T] to bring into a country illegally and secretly: *to run drugs/guns across the border/into Ireland* —see also RUNNER **21** [I] *esp. AmE* (of a hole in woven cloth) to spread; LADDER: *This hole in my tights is starting to run.* **22** [T *usu. in progressive forms*] to have an unusually high (body temperature): *Johnny's running a temperature today; he may have flu.* **23 run a mile** *infml* to run away quickly to avoid someone or something: *She's so shy, I think if a man spoke to her she'd run a mile.* —see also RUNNING, **run amok** (AMOK), **cut and run** (CUT), **run to earth** (EARTH), **run it fine** (FINE), **run the gauntlet** (GAUNTLET), **run one's head against a brick wall** (HEAD), **run rings round** (RING), **run riot** (RIOT), **run to seed** (SEED)

▷ USAGE **Run** is the general word for moving quickly on one's legs. **Race, dash**, and **sprint** all suggest running very fast for a short distance: *I raced/dashed/sprinted down the road to catch the bus.* To **jog** is to run in a steady unhurried way as a form of exercise: *She goes* **jogging** *every morning.*◁

■ phrasal verbs

run across sbdy./sthg. *phr v* [T] to find or meet (esp. someone or something pleasant) by chance: *I ran across an old friend in the street.* —compare COME **across** (1)

run after sbdy./sthg. *phr v* [T] **1** to chase: *My dog was running after a rabbit.* **2** *derog* to try to gain the attention and company of: *If you didn't run after her so much, she might be more interested in you.* **3** *infml* to perform the duties of a servant for: *I can't keep running after you all day!*

run along *phr v* [I *often imperative*] *infml* (used esp. to a child) to leave; go away: *Run along now, all of you! I'm busy.*

run around *phr v* [I+adv/prep, esp. **with**] to go about habitually in company (together or with): *Her husband found she'd been running around with another man.* —see also RUN-AROUND

run away *phr v* [I (**from**)] to go away (as if) to escape: *He ran away to sea/from home at the age of fourteen.* | *They ran away together to get married.* —see also RUNAWAY

run away with sbdy./sthg. *phr v* [T] **1** to take and carry off secretly or illegally: *Someone's run away with all my jewels.* | *He ran away with his boss's wife.* **2** (of ideas, feelings, etc.) to gain control of and carry away: *Don't let your temper/enthusiasm run away with you.* **3** [*usu. in negatives*] to believe too easily (a false idea): *Don't run away with the idea that you needn't do any work, just because you're working for your father.* **4** *infml* to win (a game or competition) easily

run down *phr v* [T] (**run** sbdy./sthg.↔**down**) to knock down and hurt (a person or large animal) with a motor vehicle, perhaps intentionally —compare RUN **into** (1), RUN **over** (1) **2** [I] (esp. of a clock or an electric BATTERY) to lose power and stop working **3** [I;T] (=**run** sthg.↔**down**) to (allow to) gradually stop working or be reduced in size; (allow to) DECLINE: *The coal industry is running down/is being run down.* **4** [T] (**run** sbdy./sthg.↔**down**) *infml* to say rude or unfair things about; DENIGRATE: *She's jealous of your success; that's why she's always running you down.* **5** [T] (**run**

sbdy./sthg. ↔ **down**) to find by searching: *See if you can run down that book in the library for me.* —see also RUNDOWN, RUN-DOWN

run sbdy./sthg. **in** *phr v* [T] **1** to bring (esp. an engine) gradually and carefully into full use **2** *infml* (of the police) to catch (a criminal); ARREST

run into sbdy./sthg. *phr v* [T] **1** to hit forcefully with one's vehicle: *We went too fast round the corner and ran into a lamppost.* —compare RUN **down** (1), RUN **over** (1) **2** *infml* to meet (someone) by chance: *Guess who I ran into in town today?* **3** to begin to experience (difficulty); get into (a difficult or unpleasant situation): *After a promising start, the company ran into trouble/into debt.* **4** to add up to; reach (a length or amount): *They had debts running into thousands of pounds.*

run sthg. ↔ **off** *phr v* [T] **1** to make up, perform, or repeat (a piece of music, poem, speech, etc.) quickly or easily. **2** to print (copies): *I'll run off a hundred of these notices for you.* **3** to get rid of (unwanted weight) by running: *You're too fat; try and run off all those excess pounds.* —see also RUN-OFF

run off with sbdy./sthg. *phr v* [T] to RUN **away with**

run on *phr v* [I] **1** to continue, esp. beyond the arranged time: *The concert ran on until eleven o'clock.* **2** *infml* to talk without stopping: *He'll run on for hours about his computer if you let him.*

run out *phr v* **1** [I] to come to an end, so that there is no more; be completely used up: *Our food soon ran out.* | *Have you nearly finished? Time is running out.* **2** [I (**of**)] to use all one's supplies; have no more: *"Can you give me a cigarette?" "Sorry, I've run out."* | *I'm afraid we've run out of petrol.* | *I'm running out of patience.* **3** [T *usu. pass.*] (**run** sbdy. ↔ **out**) (in cricket) to cause (a player who is in the middle of making a RUN² (10a)) to have to leave the field by hitting with the ball the WICKET towards which he is running

run sbdy. **out of** sthg. *phr v* [T] *infml* to force to leave (a place): *They ran him out of town.*

run out on sbdy./sthg. also **walk out on** sbdy./sthg.— *phr v* [T] *derog* to leave or desert (someone or something one is responsible for): *He ran out on his wife.*

run over *phr v* **1** [T] (**run** sbdy./sthg. ↔ **over**) (of a vehicle or its driver) to knock down and pass over the top of: *He was run over and killed by a bus.* | *I ran over a rabbit this morning.* —compare RUN **down** (1), RUN **into** (1) **2** [T] (**run over** sthg.) to RUN **through** (1) **3** [I] (of a liquid or its container) to overflow: *The water/bath/bucket ran over.*

run through *phr v* [T] **1** (**run through** sthg.) also **run over**— to repeat for practice: *Let's run through the first scene again.* —see also RUN-THROUGH **2** (**run through** sthg.) to read or examine quickly: *I'll just run through this list of figures with you.* **3** (**run through** sthg.) to spend (money) fast and esp. wastefully: *He soon ran through all his father's money.* **4** [*no pass.*] (**run through** sthg.) to be part of; spread right through: *A feeling of sadness runs through his poetry.* **5** (**run** sbdy. **through**) *esp. lit* to push one's sword right through

run to sthg. *phr v* [T *not in progressive forms*] *esp. BrE* to be or have enough to pay for: *My wages won't run to a car/to buying a car.*

run sthg. ↔ **up** *phr v* [T] **1** to raise (a flag): *They ran up the national flag on the queen's birthday.* **2** to cause oneself to have (bills or debts): *She ran up a large phone bill.* **3** to make quickly, esp. by sewing: *I ran this dress up in one evening.* —see also RUN-UP

run up against sthg. *phr v* [T] *infml* to meet or be forced to deal with (something difficult): *We ran up against some unexpected opposition.*

run² *n* **1** [C] an act of running: *She usually goes for a run/takes the dog for a run before breakfast.* | *A cross-country run is a run across the fields.* | *a five-mile run* **2** [S] a short journey in a car, esp. for pleasure: *Let's go for a run in the car.* **3** [C *usu. sing.*] a journey of the stated kind made regularly by a train, ship, TRUCK, etc.: *It's a 55-minute run from London to Brighton.* | *This old ferry used to be on the Felixstowe to Stockholm run.* **4** [C] a continuous set of performances of a play, film, etc.: *The play had a run of three months.* **5** [S+**of**] a continuous set of similar events; SEQUENCE: *I've had a run of bad luck recently.* (=lots of unlucky things have happened to me) **6** [*the* (**of**)] the usual or average sort: *She's different from the common/general run of students.* —see also RUN-OF-THE-MILL **7** [S+**on**] **a** an eager demand: *There's*

been a big run on ice cream during this hot weather. **b** a general desire to sell money or to take one's money out: *The run on the pound forced the government to act.* | *a run on the bank* **8** [*the*+**of**] the freedom to visit or use (a place): *He's given our children the run of his garden.* | *I have the run of his extensive library.* **9** [C] an enclosed but usu. uncovered area where animals are kept: *a chicken run* | *a sheep run* **10** [C] a point won **a** in cricket, by two players running from one WICKET to the other, passing each other on the way: *England scored/made 301 runs.* **b** in BASEBALL, by a player reaching the home base safely: *a home run* **11** [C] a sloping course for a downhill sport: *a ski run* **12** [C] (in card games) a set of cards dealt to a person, in which the numbers on all the cards follow on from each other —compare FLUSH⁵ **13** [C] (in music) a set of notes played or sung quickly up or down the SCALE¹ (5) without a break **14** [C] *AmE for* LADDER¹ (2): *I've got a run in my new panty hose.* **15 a** (**good**) **run for one's money** *infml* **a** plenty of opposition in a competition: *They may be a better team than us, but we'll give them a run for their money.* **b** good or satisfactory results, treatment, etc., (esp. in return for one's time, money or effort): *He lived to be 92, so I think he had a good run for his money.* **16 at a run** running: *She left the house at a run.* **17 in the ˈlong run** after a long period; in the end: *It'll be cheaper in the long run to use real leather because it will last longer.* **18 in the ˈshort run** for the near future: *Of course plastic's cheaper than leather in the short run, but it won't last as long.* **19 on the run** trying to escape or hide, esp. from the police: *The escaped murderer has been on the run for three weeks.* —see also RUNS, DUMMY RUN, FUN RUN, MILK RUN, TRIAL RUN

run-a-bout /ˈ··ˌ·/ *n infml* a small light car

run-a-round /ˈ··ˌ·/ *n* [*the*] *infml* delaying or deceiving treatment: *They've been giving me the run-around for six months now; they just won't give me a straight answer to a straight question.* | *He's been giving his wife the run-around.* (=making love to another woman) —see also RUN **around**

run-a-way¹ /ˈrʌnəweɪ/ *adj* [A] **1** out of control: *a runaway horse/train* | *We're suffering from runaway inflation.* **2** having run away: *a runaway child* **3** done by running away: *a runaway marriage*

runaway² *n* a person or animal that has run away —see also RUN **away**

Run-cie /ˈrʌnsi/, **Ro-bert** /ˈrɒbət‖ˈraːbərt/ (1921–) a minister of the church who was ARCHBISHOP OF CANTERBURY and head of the Anglican church from 1980 to 1990

run-down¹ /ˈrʌndaʊn/ *n* **1** [(*the*) S (**of**)] the (process of running something down (RUN **down** (3)): *the phased rundown of the steel industry* **2** [C (**on**)] *infml* a detailed report of a set of events: *I want a complete rundown on everything that happened while I was away.*

run-down² /ˌ·ˈ·◄/ *adj* **1** (esp. of a place) old and broken or in bad condition; DILAPIDATED: *an old run-down hotel* **2** [F] (of a person) tired and weak and in poor health: *You need a holiday; you look a bit run-down.*

rune /ruːn/ *n* **1** any of the letters of an alphabet cut on stone, wood, etc., once used by the peoples of Northern Europe **2** a magic charm written or spoken mysteriously —**runic** *adj* : *the runic alphabet*

rung¹ /rʌŋ/ *past participle of* RING

rung² *n* **1** any of the cross-bars that form the steps of a ladder: *a broken rung* | (fig.) *The director made his son start* **on the bottom/first rung of the ladder** (=the lowest level in the organization) *as an office boy.* **2** a bar like this between the legs of a chair

run-in /ˈ·· ·/ *n infml* a quarrel or disagreement, esp. with the police or an official body: *to have a run-in with the law*

run-nel /ˈrʌnl/ *n esp. lit* a small stream

run-ner /ˈrʌnəʳ/ *n* **1 a** a person or animal that runs, esp. **a** in a race or as a sport: *Bannister was the first runner to achieve the four-minute mile.* | *a long-distance runner* | *There are six runners* (=horses that will run) *in the 3.30 at Epsom.* | *the runner at first base* **b** (esp. in former times) to carry messages: *The general sent a runner from Marathon to Athens to carry the news.* **2** (*usu. in comb.*) someone who SMUGGLES the stated goods (=takes them illegally into a country): *a dope-runner* **3** either of the two thin blades on which a SLEDGE slides over the snow or the single blade on which a SKATE slides over the ice **4**

the supporting bars on which a shelf, drawer, etc. slides **5** any of the stems with which a plant like the STRAW-BERRY spreads itself along the ground —see also FRONT-RUNNER, RUNNERS

runner bean /ˌ·· '·/ *BrE* ‖ **string bean** *AmE*— *n* a climbing bean with long green PODS (=seed containers) which are used as food —see picture at VEGETABLE

run·ners /'rʌnəz‖-ərz/ also **trainers** *BrE* ‖ **running shoes** *AmE*— *n* [P] a pair of shoes for running in or for other sports

runner-up /ˌ·· '·/ *n* **runners-up** *or* **runner-ups** the person or team that comes second in a race or competition

run·ning[1] /'rʌnɪŋ/ *n* [U] **1** the act or sport of running **2** direction; control: *He left the running of the company in the hands of his son.* **3** **in/out of the running** with some/no hope of winning: *Charles is still in the running for the directorship/as a possible director.* **4** **make the running** *BrE* to set the speed at which a race is run, at which a relationship develops, etc.; set a standard or be a leader: *If you want to be friends with her you'll have to make (all) the running.*

running[2] *adj* [A] **1** (of water) **a** flowing: *These fish prefer to live in running water.* **b** flowing from TAPS: *This hotel has hot and cold running water in every room.* **2** **a** continuing over a long period: *For five years we had a* **running battle** *with the council over who was responsible for repairing the road.* **b** made during a process or activity: *a running commentary on the football match* (=describing it as it happens) | *Keep a running total of your expenses as you go along.* | *He couldn't stop to overhaul the engine properly, so he just made a few* **running repairs.** (=so as to be able to finish his journey) **3** for or concerned with running as a sport: *running shoes* | *a running track* **4** giving out PUS (=liquid matter) from the body: *a running sore* —compare RUNNY (2) **5** **in 'running order** (of a machine) working properly —see also RUN[1] (11)

running[3] *adv* (after a plural noun with a number) one after the other without a break; in a row: *She won the prize three times running.* | *For the third year running the company has made a big loss.*

running costs /'··· ·/ *n* [P] the amount of money needed for operating a business or other activity: *The running costs of the helpline are met by donations.* | *We're trying to reduce our running costs.*

running jump /ˌ·· '·/ *n* **1** a jump made by running to the point at which one takes off **2** **take a 'running jump** [*often imperative*] *infml* to go away and stop being annoying: *If he asks you any more personal questions, tell him to take a running jump.*

running mate /'··· ·/ *n* (in US politics) a person with whom another is trying to get elected to a pair of political positions of greater and less importance, esp. those of President and Vice-President: *Reagan has yet to choose his running mate.*

run·ny /'rʌni/ *adj infml* **1** in a more liquid form than is usual or expected: *runny butter* (of the nose or **eyes**) producing liquid, as when one has a cold: *She wiped the baby's runny nose.* —compare RUNNING[2] (5)

Run·ny·mede /'rʌnimiːd/ a field near the River Thames at Egham, S England, where King John is said to have signed the Magna Carta in 1215 —see MAGNA CARTA

run-off /'· ·/ *n* **1** [C] a last race or competition to decide the winner, because two or more people have won an equal number of points, races, etc. —compare PLAY-OFF; see also RUN **off 2** [U] liquid which flows off or from (something): *nitrogen-rich run-off from agricultural land* **3** **run-off election** *AmE* a state election held if in the first election no person got more than half of the vote. The two people with most votes compete against each other to be elected.

run-of-the-mill /ˌ··· '·◂/ *adj usu. derog* ordinary; not special in any way: *a run-of-the-mill office job/performance* —see also RUN[2] (6)

run-on sen·tence /'·· ·ˌ··/ *n AmE* a sentence that contains too many CLAUSES to be read or understood easily and which is better made into two or more sentences

runs /rʌnz/ also **trots**— *n* [*the*+P] *infml for* DIARRHOEA

runt /rʌnt/ *n* **1** a small badly developed animal, esp. the smallest of a set of baby pigs **2** *derog* a small unpleasant person

run-through /'· ·/ *n* an act of running through something for practice (RUN **through**): *We need one more run-through before the performance.*

run-up /'· ·/ *n esp. BrE* **1** [C] (in sports) an act or distance of running in order to gain enough speed for a particular action: *a bowler's run-up* **2** [*the*+(**to**)] (the activities in) the period of time leading up to an event: *During the run-up to the election the polls showed the Democrats in the lead.* **3** [C] *AmE* a sudden increase

run·way /'rʌnweɪ/ *n* an area with a specially prepared hard surface, on which aircraft land and take off —compare AIRSTRIP

Run·yon /'rʌnjən/, **Da·mon** /'deɪmən/ (1884–1946) an American writer of stories about GANGSTERS. Runyon's characters talk and act in a rough and violent way, and people will say that someone is behaving or talking like someone out of Damon Runyon if they are acting like this.

ru·pee /ruːˈpiː/ *n* (a note or coin worth) a unit of money in India, Pakistan, Sri Lanka, and some other countries

Ru·pert Bear /ˌruːpət 'beəʳ‖-pərt-/ (in Britain) a little bear dressed in a red jumper and yellow checked trousers and a SCARF, who is the main character in a popular collection of children's stories by Mary Tourtel

rup·ture[1] /'rʌptʃəʳ/ *n* **1** [C;U] *tech or fml* (a) sudden breaking apart or bursting: *the rupture of a blood vessel* | (fig.) *It is sad to see the rupture of friendly relations between our two countries.* **2** [C] a lump in the front wall of the stomach; HERNIA

rupture[2] *v tech* **1** [I;T] to (cause to) break or burst: *They reported that the pipeline had ruptured.* **2** [T] to cause (oneself) to have a RUPTURE[1] (2): *He ruptured himself lifting a heavy weight.*

ru·ral /'rʊərəl/ *adj* of or like the COUNTRYSIDE; concerning country or village life: *Rural bus services are often inadequate.* | *a peaceful rural setting* | *rural areas* —opposite **urban**; compare RUSTIC[1] (1)

rural free de·liv·er·y /ˌ·· ·ˌ· ·'···/ *n AmE* RFD

Ru·ri·ta·ni·an /ˌrʊərɪˈteɪniən◂/ *adj* typical of Ruritania, an imaginary small European kingdom of former times, full of exciting but clearly unreal adventures

ruse /ruːz‖ruːs, ruːz/ *n* a trick to deceive an opponent

rush[1] /rʌʃ/ *v* **1** [I+*adv/prep*; T+*obj+adv/prep*] to (cause to) go or move suddenly and with great speed or violence: *They rushed up the stairs/out into the street/towards the door.* | *The fire engine rushed past us as we waited at the traffic lights.* | *Doctors and medical supplies were rushed to the scene of the accident.* | *We'll try to rush your order through* (=deal with it especially quickly) *before Saturday.* **2** [I;T (**into**)] to (cause or force to) hurry or act (too) quickly: *There's plenty of time; we needn't rush.* | *Don't rush into marriage; you might regret it later.* | *You shouldn't rush this sort of work* | *Don't rush your breakfast; you'll get indigestion.* **3** [T (**into**)] to force (someone) to act or decide hastily: *Don't rush me; let me think about it.* | *I was rushed into buying these fur boots.* **4** [T] to attack suddenly and all together: *We rushed the guards and captured their guns.* **5** [I;T] (in FOOTBALL[3]) to carry the ball forward: *The home team rushed for seven yards in the last play.* **6** [T] *AmE* **a** to entertain someone or a group of people before deciding who may become a member of a FRATERNITY or SORORITY **b** to go to parties or events of a sorority or fraternity in order to try to become a member: *Which fraternity are you going to rush?* **7** **be rushed off one's feet** to be so busy that one has no time to stop or rest

rush[2] *n* **1** [C] a sudden rapid and often violent movement: *There was a rush for* (=towards) *the exits when the film ended.* | *When the new space programme was agreed, there was a big rush for the valuable government contracts.* **2** [S;U] (need for) (too much) hurrying: *We needn't leave yet; what's all the rush?* | *There's no rush.* | *I've got to write a report for my boss before tomorrow; it'll be a bit of a* **rush job.** (=I haven't enough time to do it properly) **3** [U] great activity and excitement: *I hate shopping during the Christmas rush when the shops are crowded.* **4** [S+**on/for**/*to-v*] a sudden great demand: *There's been a rush on/a rush for/a rush to get tickets for the big football game.* **5** *AmE sl* a sudden strong feeling of excitement —see also GOLD RUSH **6** [U] *AmE* a period of time at American colleges during which students who wish to join fraternities (FRATERNITY) or sororities (SORORITY)

must attend their many social activities in order to be considered for membership. In the past, rush has involved too much alcoholic drinking, leading to accidents. Now **dry rush** (=no alcohol) is popular at many colleges.

rush³ *n* a grasslike water plant whose long thin hollow stems are often dried and made into mats, baskets, and the seats of chairs: *a rush mat* − − **y** *adj*

rush·es /ˈrʌʃɪz/ also **dailies** *AmE− n* [P] (in film-making) the first prints of a film before it has been edited (EDIT): *Most directors like to see the rushes of the previous day's shooting.*

rush hour /ˈ· ·/ also **peak hour, peak time** *BrE− n* [C;U] either of the two periods in the day (usu. longer than an hour) when people are travelling to and from work in a city and the streets are crowded. The images people have of rush hour is of a lot of tired unsmiling faces crowded into buses and trains and long lines of cars trying to get to or from work as fast as possible: *I like to get to work before the rush hour.* | *rush hour traffic* | *There's a train every half hour, or every 20 minutes at peak time.*

rush·light /ˈrʌʃlaɪt/ *n* a kind of candle made by dipping the inside part of a RUSH³ into melted fat, used esp. in former times

Mount Rushmore

Rush·more /ˈrʌʃmɔːʳ/, **Mount** also **Mount Rushmore National Memorial** *fml− n* a mountain face in South Dakota which has been carved (CARVE) into the faces of four US presidents: Washington, Jefferson, Lincoln, and Theodore Roosevelt

rush week /ˈ· ·/ *n AmE* the week, usu. in the autumn, in which fraternities (FRATERNITY) and sororities (SORORITY) hold parties and other events to attract new members

rusk /rʌsk/ *n esp. BrE* a hard dry BISCUIT for babies, often made from a piece of bread baked hard

Rus·sell /ˈrʌsəl/, **Ber·trand** /ˈbɜːtrənd‖ˈbɜːr-/ (1872−1970) a British PHILOSOPHER and MATHEMATICIAN, born the 3rd **Earl Russell**, who for most of his life also fought for the cause of peace. He received the NOBEL PRIZE for literature in 1950.

Russell, Charles (1864−1926) an American who painted scenes of COWBOYS and of NATIVE AMERICANS

Russell, Ken (1927−) a film director best known for DOCUMENTARY films and for the film *Women in Love*

rus·set /ˈrʌsɪt/ *n* [U] *esp. lit* of a reddish brown or golden brown colour −**russet** *adj*

Rus·sia /ˈrʌʃə/ also **the Russian Fed·er·a·tion** /ˌ··· ··ˈ··/ *fml− a* country in E Europe stretching from the far North and the Arctic to the Black Sea in S; capital Moscow; population 147,350,000 (1989). It is part of the Commonwealth of Independent States (CIS) which was formerly the USSR. −see CIS, **from Russia with love** (FROM)

Rus·sian /ˈrʌʃən/ *n* **1** [C] a person who comes from or whose parents come from Russia **2** [U] the language of Russia −**Russian** *adj*

Russian dolls /ˌ··· ˈ·/ *n* [P] a Russian toy which is a set of wooden figures of a woman of different sizes, the largest one having all the others inside

Russian Or·tho·dox Church /ˌ··· ˌ··· ˈ·/ [the] the leading Russian Christian church −**Russian Orthodox** *adj*

Russian Rev·o·lu·tion /ˌ··· ···ˈ··/ [the] the events of 1917, when the Russian people overthrew (OVERTHROW) their TSAR and then a government before the COMMUNISTS took over under the leadership of Lenin

Russian dolls

Russian rou·lette /ˌ··· ·ˈ·/ *n* [U] a dangerous game in which one shoots at one's own head a gun with a bullet in only one of the CHAMBERS (=set of spaces for bullets), without knowing whether it will fire or not

Russo- see WORD FORMATION

rust¹ /rʌst/ *n* [U] **1** the reddish brown surface that forms on iron and some other metals when they are attacked by water and air: *patches of rust on the bicycle frame* | *a tin of rust remover* | *rust-coloured upholstery* **2** a plant disease causing reddish brown spots: *wheat rust* −see also RUSTPROOF, RUSTY

rust² *v* [I;T] to (cause to) become covered with rust: *Stainless steel does not rust.* | *The rain will rust the iron roof.*
    rust away *phr v* [I;T] (=**rust** sthg.↔**away**)) to (cause to) disappear through the action of rust: *The ancient lock had completely rusted away so the door opened easily.*

Rust Belt /ˈ· ·/ *AmE* an area in the northern US consisting of states which are suffering economically because their large industries, esp. the steel and car industries, have become smaller or stopped doing business: *This race will be all over by Illinois, one of the two big Rust Belt primaries (Michigan is the other) held on March 17.*

rus·tic¹ /ˈrʌstɪk/ *adj* **1** *often apprec* typical of the country, esp. in being simple and unspoiled by modern developments: *The village has a certain rustic charm.* −compare RURAL **2** [A] (of furniture and wooden objects) roughly made out of wood with its BARK (=outer skin) left on: *a rustic garden seat* − −**ity** /rʌˈstɪsɪti/ *n* [U]

rustic² *n old-fash, often derog* a person from the country, esp. a farm worker

rus·ti·cate /ˈrʌstɪkeɪt/ *v* [T] *BrE fml* to send (a student) away from university for a period as a punishment

rus·tle¹ /ˈrʌsəl/ *v* **1** [I;T] to (cause to) make slight sounds like paper, dry leaves, silk, etc., moving or being rubbed together: *Her long silk skirt rustled as she walked.* | *Stop rustling that newspaper!* **2** [T] *esp. AmE* to steal (cattle or horses that are left loose in open country)
    rustle sthg.↔**up** *phr v* [T] *infml* to provide or find quickly: *I'll try and rustle up something for you to eat.*

rustle² *n* [S] a sound of rustling: *a rustle of leaves*

rus·tler /ˈrʌsləʳ/ *n esp. AmE* a cattle thief; person who rustles cattle

rust·proof /ˈrʌstpruːf/ *adj* (of metal) protected from RUST by special treatment −**rustproof** *v* [T]

rust·y /ˈrʌsti/ *adj* **1** (of metal) covered with RUST: *a rusty nail* **2** [F] *infml* (of one's knowledge of a subject, language, etc.) mostly forgotten: *My French is a bit rusty.* **3** [F] *infml* unable to perform well because of lack of recent practice: *I agreed to play in the cricket match, although I'm very rusty.* **4** *old-fash* (of black cloth) having become brown with age −−**iness** *n* [U]

rut¹ /rʌt/ *n* **1** [C] a deep narrow track left in soft ground by a wheel: *The farm carts have worn ruts in the lane.* **2** [S] a fixed and dull way of life: *I felt I was getting into a rut/stuck in a rut, so I decided to change my job. See picture on page 1159*

rut² *v* -**tt**- [T] to form ruts in: *the rutted surface of the road*

rut³ *n* [(the) U] *tech* (the season of) sexual excitement in an animal, esp. a male deer

rut⁴ *v* -**tt**- [I] *tech* (of an animal, esp. a male deer) to be in a state of sexual excitement: *rutting stags*

ru·ta·ba·ga /ˌruːtəˈbeɪgə/ *n AmE for* SWEDE

Ruth /ruːθ/, **Babe** (1895−1948) an American BASEBALL

player, the most famous in the game's history, who set HOME RUN records which stood for almost 40 years, and was known as the Sultan of Swat

Babe Ruth

Ruth, Doctor see DOCTOR RUTH

Ruth·er·ford /ˈrʌðəfəd‖ -ðərfərd/, **Er·nest** /ˈɜːnɪst‖ ˈɜːr-/ (1871–1937) a British scientist who suggested a THEORY about the changes made in atoms by RADIOAC- TIVITY. He was the first to split the atom.

Rutherford, Dame Margaret (1892–1972) an English ac- tress famous for playing EC- CENTRIC old ladies, and known esp. for playing the Agatha Christie character, Miss Marple

ruth·less /ˈruːθləs/ adj **1** (of a person or their behaviour) showing no human feelings; without pity or forgiveness: *The enemy killed women and children with ruthless cruelty.* **2** *not always derog* firm in taking unpleasant decisions: *We'll have to be ruthless if we want to eliminate unnecessary waste.* − −**ly** adv − −**ness** n [U]

Rut·land /ˈrʌtlənd/ the smallest English COUNTY until 1974, when it became part of Leicestershire

RV /ˌɑː ˈviː‖ˌɑːr-/ n AmE see RECREATIONAL VEHICLE

Rw·an·da /ruˈændə‖-ˈɑːn-/ a country in E central Africa bordered by Zaire, Uganda, Tanzania, and Burundi; cap- ital: Kigali; population 6,989,000 (1989) −**Rwandan** n,adj

Rx. n AmE written abbrev. for PRESCRIPTION

Ry·an /ˈraɪən/, **No·lan** /ˈnəʊlən/ (1947–) a BASEBALL player known for his pitching (PITCH¹ (9))

Ry·der Cup /ˈraɪdə ˌkʌp‖-dər-/ [the] a GOLF competition be- tween the best players in Europe and the US, held every other year

rye /raɪ/ n [U] a grass plant grown in cold countries for its grain, which is used esp. for making flour: *rye bread* | *rye whisky* −see picture at CEREAL

S

S , **s** /es/ **S's, s's** or **Ss, ss** the 19th letter of the English alphabet

S *written abbrev. for:* south(ern)

-'s¹ /'|z, s/ *short for:* **1** is: *Father's here.* | *What's that?* **2** has: *Mother's gone out.* | *It's got six legs.* **3** *nonstandard (in questions after* **who, what, when,** etc.) does: *How's he plan to do it?* —compare **-'D** (2) **4** us (only in the phrase **let's**)

-'s² **1** (forms the possessive case of singular nouns and of plural nouns that do not end in *-s*): *the dog's bone* | *yesterday's lesson* | *the children's bedroom* —see OF (USAGE) **2** *esp. BrE* (forms a word for a shop or someone's home): *I bought it at the baker's.* (=at the baker's shop) | *I met him at Mary's.* (=at Mary's house)

-s' (forms the possessive case of most [C] nouns in the plural): *a boys' club* —see OF (USAGE)

Saab /saːb/ *n tdmk* a Swedish company that makes cars: *We're hoping to get a Saab next time we buy a new car.*

Saa·tchi and Saa·tchi /ˌsaːtʃi ənd 'saːtʃi/ a British advertising and public relations company

Sa·bah /'saːbaː/ a state of East Malaysia which used to be the British PROTECTORATE of North Borneo

Sab·a·ti·ni /ˌsæbə'tiːni/, **Gab·ri·el·a** /ˌgæbri'elə/ (1970–   ) an Argentinian tennis player of international standard, winner of the US Open in 1990 and a Wimbledon finalist in 1991

sab·ba·tar·i·an /ˌsæbə'teəriən◂/ *adj, n (often cap.)* (of or being) a person who believes in keeping the Sabbath as a holy day

Sab·bath /'sæbəθ/ also **Sabbath day** /ˌ·· '·/— *[the]* **1** *oldfash* Sunday, kept as a day of rest and worship by most Christian churches **2** Saturday, kept as a day of rest and worship by Jews and some Christians **3 keep/break the Sabbath** to keep/break the religious rules which limit work and play on this day: *Remember the Sabbath day, to keep it holy.*

sab·bat·i·cal /sə'bætɪkəl/ *n* a period, often one year in each seven, when someone, esp. a university teacher, does not do their ordinary job and may travel, study, etc., but still gets paid as usual: *She's* **on sabbatical** *this year.* | *to take a sabbatical*

sabbatical² *adj* [A] of or being a sabbatical: *a sabbatical year/term* | *sabbatical leave*

sa·ber /'seɪbəʳ/ *n AmE for* SABRE —see picture at SWORD

sa·ble¹ /'seɪbəl/ *n* [C;U] (the dark fur of) a small animal of northern Europe and Asia: *an artist's sable brush* (=made from this fur)

sable² *adj poet* black or very dark

sab·o·tage¹ /'sæbətaːʒ/ *n* [U] **1** intentional damage to machines, buildings, etc., usu. carried out secretly to weaken a government, an enemy country in wartime, or a business competitor: *an act of sabotage* **2** intentional indirect or secret action to prevent or ruin a plan

sabotage² *v* [T] to damage, destroy, or cause to fail by means of sabotage: *Someone had sabotaged the railway line by blowing up a tunnel.* | *a deliberate attempt to sabotage the country's economy*

sab·o·teur /ˌsæbə'tɜːʳ/ *n* a person who practises sabotage

sa·bra /'saːbrə/ *n infml, esp. AmE (often cap.)* a citizen of Israel who was born there

sa·bre *BrE* ‖ **saber** *AmE* /'seɪbəʳ/ *n* **1** a heavy military sword with a curved blade used in former times **2** a light sharp-pointed sword with one sharp edge used in FENCING —compare EPEE, FOIL³ and see picture at SWORD

sabre-rat·tling /'·· ˌ·/ *n* [U] *derog* threats of the use of military power

sabre-toothed ti·ger /ˌ·· '··/ *n* a large tiger that lived very long ago, and had two long curved teeth in its upper jaw

sac /sæk/ *n tech* a part shaped like a bag inside a plant or animal, usu. containing a particular liquid

Sac·a·ja·we·a /ˌsækədʒə'wiːə/ (1784?–1884?) a Native American woman who acted as a guide on Lewis and Clark's travels from St. Louis to the Pacific Ocean

sac·cha·rin /'sækərɪn/ *n* [U] a very sweet-tasting chemical used instead of sugar, usu. in drinks, esp. by people who want to reduce their weight or must not eat sugar

sac·cha·rine /'sækəriːn/ *adj* **1** very sweet or unpleasantly sweet **2** *derog* too friendly, nice, kind, happy, etc.: *a saccharine love story*

sac·er·do·tal /ˌsækə'dəʊtl◂-kər-/ *adj tech* of or like a priest or priests

sach·et /'sæfeɪ‖sæ'ʃeɪ/ *n* a small usu. plastic bag or packet containing a liquid or powder, esp. enough to be used all at one time: *a sachet of sugar/shampoo* | *She put a perfumed sachet in her drawers to scent her clothes.*

sack¹ /sæk/ *n* **1** [C] **a** a large bag, usu. of strong rough cloth, strong paper, or plastic used for storing or carrying flour, coal, vegetables, grain, etc.: *a sack of potatoes* **b** also **sack·ful** /'fʊl/— the amount that a sack contains **2** *[the] BrE infml* dismissed from one's job: *If you're late again the boss will* **give** *you* **the sack/***you'll* **get the sack.** **3** [C] *infml, esp. AmE* a bed **4 hit the sack** *infml* to go to bed

sack² *v* **1** [T] *BrE infml* to dismiss from a job: *I've just been sacked.* **2** [T] (in American football) to knock down a player: *sack the quarterback*
sack out *phr v* [I] *AmE infml* to go to sleep, esp. for the night: *I'm ready to sack out.*

sack³ *v* [T] (esp. of an army in former times) to destroy buildings, take things of value, and usu. harm or kill people in (a defeated city) —**sack** *n* [(the)] S **(of)** : *the sack of Rome by the barbarians*

sack⁴ *n* [U] a white wine brought to England esp. from Spain in the 16th and 17th centuries

sack·cloth /'sæk-klɒθ‖-klɔːθ/ also **sack·ing** /'sækɪŋ/— *n* [U] rough cloth for making sacks

sackcloth and ashes /ˌ·· ·· '··/ *n* [P] **wear sackcloth and ashes** to do something publicly to show that one has done something wrong (from a custom described in the Bible of wearing sackcloth and ashes to show that one was sorry about something one had done wrong): *I know I've done something wrong, but I'm not going to walk around wearing sackcloth and ashes!*

sack race /'· ·/ *n* a race in which the competitors have to run or jump forwards with both legs inside a sack, usu. performed by younger children, e.g. at a school sports day.

sac·ra·ment /'sækrəmənt/ *n* (used esp. in the Roman Catholic Church) an important Christian ceremony, such as BAPTISM, the EUCHARIST, or marriage, considered as bringing God's blessing to those who receive it — **~al** /ˌsaekrə'mentl◂/ *adj*

Sacrament *[the]* (used esp. in the Roman Catholic Church) the holy bread eaten at the EUCHARIST

sa·cred /'seɪkrɪd/ *adj* **1** [A *no comp.*] religious in nature or use: *sacred music* | *sacred history* (=the history of the church or religion) —opposite **secular** **2** holy because connected with God or a god: *Cows are sacred to Hindus.* **3** serious, solemn, and important in the way religious things are: *a sacred oath* | (*esp. humor*) *Tennis players are wearing coloured clothes at Wimbledon –* **is nothing sacred any more?** – **~ly** *adv* – **~ness** *n* [U]

sacred cow /ˌ·· '·/ *n derog* an idea, practice, etc. that is so much accepted that not even honest doubts about it are allowed: *You can't attack free enterprise at the Republican convention; it's one of the party's sacred cows.*

sac·ri·fice¹ /'sækrɪfaɪs/ *n* [C;U] **1** (a) religious offering to God or a god, in the hope of gaining favour or preventing something bad from happening, esp. of an animal by killing it in a ceremony **2** (a) loss or giving up of something of value, esp. for what is believed to be a good purpose: *Success in your job is not worth the sacrifice of your health.* | *another speech by the Prime Minister about the need for economic sacrifice* | *His parents* **made** *a lot of* **sacrifices** *to make sure he got a good education.* **3** (in BASEBALL) a hit which allows a runner on BASE to move to the next base but which puts the BATTER out **4 the final/supreme sacrifice** *fml* the act of giving one's life esp. for a good cause: *a war hero who made the final sacrifice to save his fellow soldiers*

sacrifice² *v* [I;T] to make an offering of (something or someone) as a sacrifice, esp. by killing it in a ceremony: *The high priest sacrificed the goat on the altar.* **2** [T **(for,**

to)] to lose or give up, esp. for a good purpose or to gain a desirable result: *It is the company's policy to sacrifice short-term profits for the sake of long-term growth.* | *to increase production without sacrificing quality* **3** [T;I] to make a sacrifice¹ (3)

sac·ri·fi·cial /ˌsækrɪˈfɪʃəl◀/ *adj* of or being a sacrifice: *a sacrificial lamb/victim* – – **ly** *adv*

sac·ri·lege /ˈsækrɪlɪdʒ/ *n* [C;U] (an example of) the act of treating a holy place or thing without respect: (fig.) *I think it would be (a) sacrilege to pull down this beautiful old building.* –compare BLASPHEMY –**legious** /ˌsækrɪˈlɪdʒəs◀/ *adj* –**legiously** *adv*

sac·ris·tan /ˈsækrɪstən/ *n* a person in a church whose job is to take care of the articles used in worship, and sometimes of the whole church building

sac·ris·ty /ˈsækrɪsti/ *n* a VESTRY (1)

sac·ro·il·i·ac /ˌsækrəʊˈɪliæk◀/ *n* the area of the body at the bottom of the BACKBONE where it meets the HIPs

sac·ro·sanct /ˈsækrəʊsæŋkt/ *adj often derog or humor* too holy or important to be allowed to suffer any harm or disrespect: *I never take any work home at the weekends – they are sacrosanct.*

sad /sæd/ *adj* -**dd**- **1** feeling, showing, or causing grief or sorrow; unhappy: *I was sad to hear that you're leaving.* | *It was a sad day for our team when we lost the final.* | *sad eyes* | *sad news* | *the saddest moment in the whole book* **2** [A] unsatisfactory or unacceptable; DEPLORABLE: *It's a sad state of affairs when children aren't taught to read properly.* **3 sadder but wiser** *infml* having learned from unpleasant experience **4 sad to say** unfortunately: *Sad to say, the weather here has been nothing but rain all week.* –opposite **happy**; see also SADLY – ~**ness** *n* [U]

Sa·dat /səˈdæt/, **An·war al-** /ˈænwɑːʳ æl/ (1918–81) the president of Egypt from 1970 to 1981, who helped the cause of peace between the Arabs and Israel, for which he received a share in the Nobel Peace Prize with Menachem Begin. He was killed by some of his own officers.

Sad·dam /sæˈdæm/, **Hussein** see Sadam HUSSEIN

sad·den /ˈsædn/ *v* [T *often pass.*] *fml* to make sad: *We were very saddened to hear of the death of your mother.*

sad·dle¹ /ˈsædl/ *n* **1** [C] a usu. leather seat made to fit over the back of an animal, esp. a horse, for a rider to sit on: *After many hours in the saddle* (=riding) *he was very weary.* –see picture at HORSE **2** [C] a seat on a bicycle, motorcycle, etc. –see picture at BICYCLE **3** [C;U+of] *esp. BrE* (a piece of) meat cut from the back of a sheep or deer just in front of the back legs: *roast saddle of lamb* **4 in the saddle** *infml* in control: *It's good to have an experienced man in the saddle again.*

saddle² *v* [T (UP)] to put a saddle on (an animal): *He saddled (up) his horse and rode away.*

saddle up *phr v* [I] to put a saddle on a horse: *He saddled up and rode away.*

saddle sbdy. with sthg./sbdy. *phr v* [T] to cause (someone) to have (a difficult or unpleasant duty, responsibility, etc.): *They saddled me with all the secretarial work because I was the only one who could type.* [+v-ing] *I got saddled with taking the children to school again!*

sad·dle·bag /ˈsædlbæg/ *n* **1** either of a joined pair of bags placed over an animal's back so that one hangs on each side below a saddle **2** a bag fixed to a bicycle, motorcycle, etc., behind the seat or in a pair over the back wheel

saddle blan·ket /ˈ·· ˌ··/ *n AmE* a thick piece of cloth which one puts beneath the saddle on a horse

sad·dler /ˈsædləʳ/ *n* a maker of saddles and other leather articles for horses

sad·dler·y /ˈsædləri/ *n* **1** [U] goods made by a saddler **2** [C] a saddler's shop

saddle shoe /ˈ·· ·/ *n AmE* a shoe on which the toe and heel are of one colour and the middle part is of another colour. They are usu. black and white, and were fashionable in the 1950s, esp. worn with BOBBY SOCKs and full skirts.

saddle-sore /ˈ·· ·/ *adj* (of a person) sore and painfully stiff from riding a horse or bicycle

Sade /sɑːd/, **Mar·quis de** /ˈmɑːki də/ (1740–1814) a French soldier and writer who was put in prison for sexual offences. He wrote plays and books about gaining sexual pleasure from causing pain, now known as **sadism**.

sa·dhu /ˈsɑːduː/ *n* an ASCETIC wandering Hindu holy man

Sa·die Haw·kins Day /ˌseɪdi ˈhɔːkɪnz ˌdeɪ/ *AmE* a day on which women ask men to go out with them, usu. to a special dance (a **Sadie Hawkins dance**)

sa·dis·m /ˈseɪdɪzəm/ *n* [U] **1** the gaining of pleasure from being cruel **2** the gaining of sexual pleasure from causing pain to someone –compare MASOCHISM, see Marquis de SADE –**sadist** *n* : *The headmaster's a bit of a sadist; he loves to keep boys waiting outside his office in fear.* –**distic** /səˈdɪstɪk/ *adj* : *"I'm afraid you will never see your children again,"* *he said with a sadistic smile.* –**distically** /kli/ *adv*

Sad·ler's Wells /ˌsædləz ˈwelz‖-lərz-/ a theatre in London. OPERA, BALLET, and DRAMA were performed here and the theatre gave its name to the Sadler's Wells Royal Ballet which has now become the Birmingham Royal Ballet.

sad·ly /ˈsædli/ *adv* **1** in a sad manner: *He walked sadly away.* **2** unfortunately: *Sadly, our plan failed.* **3** in a way that is wrong or unacceptable: *The garden was beautiful once, but has been sadly neglected.* | *If you think you can get money from him you're sadly mistaken* (=completely wrong); *he never lends anything to anyone.*

sa·do·mas·o·chis·m /ˌseɪdəʊˈmæsəkɪzəm/ *n* [U] the gaining of pleasure from being cruel to others (SADISM) and also from being hurt (MASOCHISM) –**chist** *n* –**chistic** /ˌseɪdəʊmæsəˈkɪstɪk◀/ *adj*

s.a.e., S.A.E. /ˌes eɪ ˈiː/ *BrE– abbrev. for:* **1** stamped addressed envelope; one often has to send an s.a.e. to get a reply from e.g. an advertiser **2** self-addressed envelope –compare SASE

sa·fa·ri¹ /səˈfɑːri/ *n* a trip through wild country, esp. in east or central Africa, hunting or photographing big animals: *They went on safari searching for the rare black rhinoceros.*

safari² *adj* [A] (of clothes) made of light material, usu. with two pockets on the chest and a belt, originally made to be suitable for the weather in Africa: *a safari suit/jacket*

safari park /·ˈ·· ·/ *n* a park in which large groups of wild animals are kept, so that one can drive round in a car and look at them

safe¹ /seɪf/ *adj* **1** [F (from)] out of danger; not threatened by harm; not able to be hurt; protected: *We were safe from attack in the underground shelter.* | *Don't cry; you're safe now.* | *Your money will be as safe as houses* (=completely safe) *with me.* **2** not hurt; unharmed: *They prayed for the safe return of the kidnapped child.* | *The fragile china survived the bumpy journey* **safe and sound.** (=completely undamaged) **3** not allowing or likely to cause danger or harm: *Flying is one of the safest forms of travel.* | *Don't walk on that old roof – it isn't safe.* | *Keep these papers in a safe place.* | *a safe form of energy* | *Is this water safe for drinking?* [+to-v] *Is this a safe place to swim? | Is it safe to swim here?* –opposite **unsafe** **4** not likely to cause disagreement: *Don't mention his divorce; stick to safe subjects.* **5** not involving any risk: *a safe investment/decision* | *It's safe to say/a safe bet that house prices will continue to rise.* | *a safe method of birth control* **6** (of a person) fit to be trusted; unlikely to take risks; RELIABLE: *a safe driver* | *She wouldn't agree to the children going until she felt satisfied they would be in safe hands.* (=carefully looked after) **7** (of a seat in a parliament) certain to be won in an election by the present holder: *a safe Labour seat* **8 better safe than sorry** it is wiser to take care in advance than to risk loss, danger, etc. when doing something: *I've checked that the safety harness is in good condition – better safe than sorry!* **9 on the 'safe side** taking no risks; being more careful than may be necessary: *Let's be on the safe side and take more money than we think we'll need.* –see also **play it safe** (PLAY² (20)), FAIL-SAFE – ~**ly** *adv* : *Drive safely! | I think we can safely assume* (=without much risk of being wrong) *that she will pass the exam.* – ~**ness** *n* [U]

safe² *n* a box or cupboard with thick metal sides and a lock, sometimes built as part of a wall, used for protecting valuable things from thieves and fire: *to break into/crack a safe*

safe·break·er /ˈseɪfˌbreɪkəʳ/ *BrE* ‖**safe·crack·er** /ˈseɪfˌkrækəʳ/*esp. AmE*– *n* a person who opens safes by force to steal

safe-con·duct /ˌ·ˈ··/ *n* [C;U] (a written order for) official protection given to a person, such as an enemy in wartime, who is passing through a particular area

safe·de·pos·it box /¹· ·,·· ,·/ also **safety-deposit box**– n a small box for the safe storing of small valuable things, usu. in a special room in a bank: *I've lost the key to my safe-deposit box.*

safe·guard¹ /ˈseɪfgɑːd‖-gɑːrd/ n [(against)] a means of protection against possible dangers: *This clause in the contract is a necessary safeguard against our losing money on the deal.* | *The law contains new safeguards to protect customers who buy used cars.*

safeguard² v [T (from, against)] to be a safeguard for; protect: *This agreement will safeguard the newspapers from government interference.*

safe ha·ven /,· ¹··/ n **1** a place where one is protected from dangers **2** an area within a country where a group of people can live without fear of attack or PERSECUTION on e.g. religious grounds

safe house /,· ¹·/ n a house where someone can hide or take shelter, e.g. when enemies are looking for them or when they are planning an illegal activity. Safe houses are esp. thought of in connection with spies (SPY¹).

safe·keep·ing /,seɪfˈkiːpɪŋ/ n [U] the action or state of protection from harm or loss for things of value: *Put your important documents in the bank for safekeeping.* | *They were left in my safekeeping, so I can't really lend them to you.*

safe seat /,· ¹·/ n a political seat which is always won by the same political party and is in no danger of being won by another

safe sex /,· ¹·/ n [U] sex which reduces the risk of the spread of AIDS and other infections, e.g. by using a CONDOM

safe·ty /ˈseɪfti/ n **1** [U] the condition of being safe; freedom from danger, harm, or risk: *The safety of the ship is the captain's responsibility.* | *She led the children to a place of safety.* | *There are fears for the safety of the climbers.* (=they might be hurt or dead) | *The management took all reasonable safety precautions.* | *Safety checks are carried out on all industrial machinery.* | *Let's try to stay together as a group: there's* **safety in numbers**. | *It's very important to teach children about* **road safety**. **2** (in FOOTBALL (2)) two points gained by making the opposing team set the ball down in its own GOAL. This usu. happens by tackling (TACKLE¹ (3)) the player with the ball.

safety belt /¹·· ·/ n a SEAT BELT, esp. in an aircraft

safety catch /¹·· ·/ n a lock on a gun to prevent it from being fired accidentally

safety cur·tain /¹·· ,··/ n a theatre curtain made of material that will not burn, which may be lowered in front of the stage

safety-de·pos·it box /¹·· ·,·· ,·/ n a SAFE-DEPOSIT BOX

safety-first /,·· ¹·/ adj [A] *sometimes derog* showing a wish to take no risks; CAUTIOUS: *a safety-first attitude*

safety glass /¹·· ·/ n [U] strong glass that breaks only into small pieces which are not sharp, used, for example, in car windows

safety is·land /¹·· ,··/ n AmE for ISLAND (2)

safety lamp /¹·· ·/ n a miner's lamp made so that its flame cannot explode the gases found underground

safety match /¹·· ·/ n a match which can be lit only by rubbing it along a special surface on its box or packet

safety mea·sure /¹·· ,··/ n action taken to prevent something dangerous from happening: *The wearing of hard hats on building sites has been an important safety measure.*

safety net /¹·· ·/ n a large net stretched out below someone performing high above the ground to catch them if they fall: *A safety net was spread below the tightrope walker.* | (fig.) *What happens to the poor people who are not caught by the government's safety net of welfare payments?*

safety pin /¹·· ·/ n a wire pin that has a cover at one end and is bent round so that its point can be held safely inside the cover; used e.g. to fasten babies' nappies (NAPPY) –see picture at PIN

safety ra·zor /¹·· ,··/ n a RAZOR with a cover fitting over the thin blade to protect the skin from being cut –see picture at RAZOR

safety valve /¹·· ·/ n a part of a machine, esp. of a steam

engine, which allows gas, steam, etc., to escape when the pressure becomes too great: (fig.) *Vigorous exercise is a good safety valve if you're under a lot of pressure at work.*

Safe·way /ˈseɪfweɪ/ one of a group of SUPERMARKETS in Britain and the US, selling mainly food but also other goods

saf·fron /ˈsæfrən/ n [U] **1** powder of a deep orange colour obtained from a flower and used for colouring and giving a special taste to food, esp. rice **2** an orange-yellow colour: *a Buddhist monk's saffron robes*

sag¹ v **-gg-** [I] **1** to sink, settle, or bend downwards, esp. away from the usual or correct position: *The branch sagged under the weight of the apples.* | *the old man's sagging cheeks* | (fig.) *My spirits sagged* (=I became less happy) *when I saw the amount of work I had to do.* **2** to fall in value, amount, or level, esp. for a short time: *the sagging demand for gas during the summer months.* **3** (of a book, performance, etc.) to become uninteresting during part of the length: *I finished the book even though it sagged a bit in the middle and I almost stopped reading.*

sag² n [S;U (in)] **1** (a) downward bending or sinking: *We need to do something about the sag in the ceiling.* **2** fall in value, amount, or level: *a sag in the price of oil.*

SAG /sæg/ Screen Actors' Guild; an American TRADE UNION for actors and actresses whose performances are filmed for television or films –compare AFTRA, EQUITY

sa·ga /ˈsɑːgə/ n **-gas 1** any of the stories written from the 12th to the 14th century about the Vikings of Norway and Iceland **2** a long story about a particular place, time in history, group of people, etc.: *This new novel is an absorbing family saga.* **3** *derog* (a detailed account of) a set of usu. not very interesting events happening over a long period: *She told me the saga of all her operations.*

sa·ga·cious /səˈgeɪʃəs/ adj fml or lit having or showing deep understanding and good judgment; wise – **~ ly** adv

sa·ga·ci·ty /səˈgæsɪti/ n [U] fml or lit good judgment and understanding; wisdom

sage¹ /seɪdʒ/ adj esp. lit wise, esp. as a result of long thinking and experience: *I was grateful for the old man's sage advice.* – **~ ly** adv : *He nodded sagely.*

sage² n [often pl.] esp. lit someone, esp. an old man or historical person, well known for their wisdom and long experience

sage³ n [U] a plant with grey-green leaves which are used in cooking to give a special taste to food: *sage and onion stuffing*

sage·brush /ˈseɪdʒbrʌʃ/ n [U] a short bushy plant very common on the dry plains of the western US

sag·gy /ˈsægi/ adj usu. derog that sinks or drops downwards, esp. having lost its original firmness: *a saggy mattress* | *saggy cheeks/breasts*

Sa·git·tar·i·us /,sædʒɪˈteəriəs/ n **1** [U] the ninth sign of the ZODIAC, represented by an animal that is half-horse and half-human shooting an ARROW **2** [C] a person born between November 22 and December 22 –see ZODIAC (USAGE) and see picture at ZODIAC

sa·go /ˈseɪgəʊ/ n [U] a white food substance (STARCH) made from the stems of certain PALM trees and used in the form of grains or powder for making sweet dishes with milk

sa·gua·ro /səˈgwɑːrəʊ/ n a large desert plant which has arms branching off the main body. It grows mainly in the southwestern US and parts of Mexico.

Sa·ha·ra /səˈhɑːrə‖-ˈhæ-/ also **Sahara Des·ert** /·,·· ¹··/ [the] the world's largest desert, in N Africa

sahib /sɑːb‖ˈsɑː-ɪb/ n IndE & PakE (usu. cap.) (used in India in former times as a title of respect for a European man): *Good morning, sahib!* | *The colonel sahib is not in his office.* –compare MEMSAHIB

said¹ /sed/ past tense & participle of SAY

said² adj [(the)] A] law the particular (person, thing, etc.) spoken of before: *John James Smith is charged with stealing. The said John Smith was seen leaving the shop at the times stated.*

Sai·gon /,saɪˈgɒn‖-ˈgɑːn/ the former name of Ho Chi Minh City in southern Vietnam. It was the capital of South Vietnam when the country was divided in two, and it was badly damaged during the VIETNAM WAR.

sail¹ /seɪl/ n **1** [C;U] a piece of strong cloth, such as NYLON or CANVAS, fixed in position on a ship to move it through the water by the force of the wind: *We hoisted/lowered the*

sails. | *a ship* **in full sail** (=with all its sails spread) **2**
[S] a short trip, usu. for pleasure, in a boat with sails: *Let's
go for a sail this afternoon.* **3** [C] any of the broad wind-
catching blades of a WINDMILL —see picture at WINDMILL
4 set sail to begin a journey by ship or change course
at sea: *We set sail for home.* **5 under sail** being driven
by sails and wind

sail² *v* **1** [I+*adv/prep*; T] to travel on water or across (a
body of water) in a ship or boat (not only one with sails):
The great ships sailed past. | *We sailed (across) the Atlan-
tic in five days.* —see BOAT (USAGE) **2** [T] to direct or
command (a ship or boat) on water: *Do you know how to
sail this boat?* | *The captain sailed his ship through the
narrow channel.* **3** [I+*adv/prep*] to begin a journey
across water: *We sail with the tide.* | *Our ship sails tomor-
row for New York.* **4** [I+*adv/prep*] to move proudly,
smoothly, or easily: *The actress sailed into the room in
her flowing dress.* | *He simply sailed through the difficult
exam.* (=passed it easily) **5 sail under false colours** to
express feelings or opinions in favour of something
which one really opposes —see also **(sail) close to the
wind** (CLOSE³)

sail into sthg./sbdy. *phr v* [T] to attack forcefully: *She
sailed into her critics.*

sail·board /ˈseɪlbɔːd||-bɔːrd/ *n* a flat floating board with a
sail fixed to it which is used by one person standing up
in the sport of WIND-SURFING

sail·cloth /ˈseɪlklɒθ||-klɔːθ/ *n* [U] a type of heavy CANVAS (1)
cloth used mainly for making sails for boats or ships

sail·ing /ˈseɪlɪŋ/ *n* **1** [U] the skill of directing the course
of a ship **2** [U] the sport of riding in or directing a small
boat with sails **3** [C] an occasion of a ship leaving a port:

sailing ships

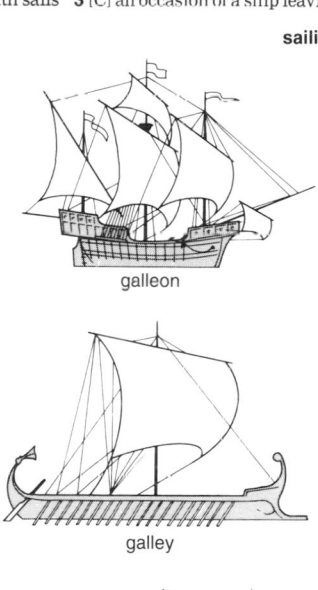

galleon

galley

clipper

When is the next sailing to Ostend? —see also PLAIN
SAILING

sailing boat /ˈ·· ·/ ‖ also **sail·boat** /ˈseɪlbəʊt/*AmE*— *n* a boat
driven by one or more sails, esp. a small boat used for
racing and pleasure trips —see also YACHT

sailing ship /ˈ·· ·/ *n* a large ship which gets its power only
from the action of the wind on its sails, having either no
motor or only a small one for helping it in making certain movements

sail·or /ˈseɪləʳ/ *n* **1** a person with a job on a ship, esp. one
who is not a ship's officer **2** a member of a navy —
compare SOLDIER

▶ CULTURAL NOTE Sailors are thought, esp. in jokes, to
have a different woman waiting for them in every port they
visit. ◀

3 a traveller on the water: *I'm afraid I'm not a very good
sailor.* (=I get sick when I travel on the water) **4** a person who regularly goes SAILING (2) **5 all the nice girls
love a sailor** the title of an old popular song, sometimes
mentioned by people who are praising sailors **6 home
is the sailor, home from sea** *quote* a phrase from a poem
by Robert Louis Stevenson, sometimes used humorously

sailor suit /ˈ·· ·/ *n* a usu. blue and white suit, esp. for a
child, copied from a sailor's uniform, and worn esp.
formerly

sail·plane /ˈseɪlpleɪn/ *n* a GLIDER (=plane with no engine)
for long flights which rises in upward movements of air

Sains·bu·ry's /ˈseɪnzbəriz||-beriz/ one of a group of British
SUPERMARKETs selling mainly food and drink but also
other goods. Sainsbury's has a MIDDLE-CLASS image and
most of its shops are in the richer SE of England and
in the Midlands.

Sainsbury Wing /ˈ··· ˌ·/ [*the*] the new part of the National
Gallery in Trafalgar Square

saint /seɪnt/ *n* **1** a person who is officially recognized after
death by (a branch of) the Christian church as being specially holy and worthy of formal honour in the church:
Joan of Arc was made a saint in 1920. | *You need the* **pa-
tience of a saint** *for this job.* (=you need to be very patient) **2** *infml* a very good and completely unselfish person: *I don't know how she puts up with that terrible
husband of hers; she's a real saint.* — ~**hood** *n* [U]

Saint /sənt; *strong* seɪnt/ *n* [A] (*written abbrev.* **St**) (used as
a title before a saint's name)

Saint Albans see ST ALBANS

Saint An·drew /ˈ· ˈ··/ (first century AD) a fisherman who
became a follower of Jesus, the national SAINT of Scotland. **St Andrew's Day**, 30th November, is celebrated as
the Scottish national day.

Saint Andrews see ST ANDREWS

Saint Andrew's Cross /ˈ· ˌ·· ˈ·/ *n* the national flag of Scotland, which is blue with two DIAGONAL white bands

Saint Au·gus·tine /sənt ɔːˈɡʌstɪn ‖ seɪnt ˈɔːɡəstiːn/ also
Saint Augustine of Hippo— (354–430) an early Christian thinker and writer whose works, esp. *Confessions*
and *The City of God*, have had a great influence in the
development of Christianity

Saint Ber·na·dette /sənt ˌbɜːnəˈdet‖seɪnt ˌbɜːr-/ also **St Bernadette of Lourdes** /ˈ· ˌ··· · ˈ·/— (1844–79) a girl who
claimed to have seen the Virgin Mary at Lourdes, which
made Lourdes become a place of PILGRIMAGE, esp. for the
sick.

Saint Bernard see ST BERNARD

Saint Chris·to·pher /sənt ˈkrɪstəfəʳ‖seɪnt-/ (died ?250) a man
supposed to have carried the young Christ across the
river, and so a special saint (=PATRON SAINT) of travellers.
Some people wear a small metal picture of Saint
Christopher on a chain round their necks or have one
in their cars to protect them when they are travelling:
He wore a Saint Christopher.

Saint Clair, Lindi see Lindi ST CLAIR

Saint Da·vid /ˈ· ˈ··/ (died ?601) a Welsh BISHOP and the
national SAINT of Wales. **St David's Day**, 1st March, is
celebrated as the Welsh national day.

saint·ed /ˈseɪntɪd/ *adj* **1** made a SAINT (1); CANONIZED **2**
[A] *old-fash* (of a dead person) like a SAINT; holy **3 my
sainted aunt** *old-fash infml, esp. BrE* (used for expressing surprise)

Saint Fran·cis of As·si·si /sənt ˌfrɑːnsɨs əv əˈsiːsiː‖ seɪnt ˌfræn-/ (1182–1226) an Italian MONK who began the Franciscan ORDER¹ (9). He is remembered for his lack of pride and love of animals, esp. birds.

Saint Francis of Assisi

Saint Fran·cis Xa·vi·er /sənt ˌfrɑːnsɨs ˈzeɪviər‖ seɪnt ˌfræn-/ (1506–52) a Spanish Jesuit MISSIONARY who went abroad to teach the Christian religion and helped found the Society of Jesus. He spent the last 11 years of his life in India, South East Asia and Japan.

Saint George /· ˈ·/ (fourth century AD?) the national SAINT of England, a soldier in the Roman army who was martyred (MARTYR) in Asia Minor. He is said to have saved the life of a woman by killing a DRAGON (=an imaginary dangerous animal). **St George's Day**, 23rd April, is celebrated as the English national day.

Saint George's Cross /· ·ˈ· ˈ·/ [the] the national flag of England, which is white with a red cross

Saint Hel·ens see ST HELENS

Saint Ives see ST IVES

Saint James's see ST JAMES'S

Saint Joan of Arc

Saint Joan of Arc /sənt ˌdʒəʊn əv ˈɑːk‖ seɪnt-, -ˈɑːrk/ (1412–31) a French military leader and national HEROINE who heard voices telling her to fight the English who were in her country. Dressed as a man, she led an army which defeated the English, but she was caught and burnt after being found guilty of WITCHCRAFT and HERESY. She was made a SAINT in 1920.

Saint John /· ˈ·/ (first century AD) a follower of Jesus Christ and a member of the early Christian church. He is thought to have written several of the books of the New Testament in the Bible: the Gospel according to St John, the three Epistles, and Revelation. He was the brother of Saint James and is sometimes called **St John the Evangelist** and **St John the Divine**.

Saint John's Am·bu·lance see ST JOHN AMBULANCE

Saint John the Bap·tist /· ˌ· ·ˈ··/ (about 12 BC–28 AD) a religious teacher in the New Testament of the Bible who baptized (BAPTIZE) Jesus in the river Jordan

Saint John the Baptist

Saint Jo·seph of Ar·i·ma·thae·a /sənt ˌdʒəʊzɨf əv ˌærɨməˈθiːə‖ seɪnt-/ (1st century AD) a rich Jewish supporter of Jesus in the New Testament who buried Jesus's body in his own TOMB. He is believed to have brought the Holy Grail to England and built the first Christian church in Britain, at Glastonbury.

Saint Jude /sənt ˈdʒuːd ‖ seɪnt-/ (1st century AD) a writer in the New Testament, believed to be the brother of Jesus

Saint Kath·a·rine's Dock see ST KATHARINE'S DOCK

Saint Kilda see ST KILDA

Saint Kitts-Ne·vis see ST KITTS-NEVIS

Saint Lau·rent /sæn lɒˈrɒŋ‖-ləʊˈrɑːn/, **Yves** /iːv/ (1936–) French clothes DESIGNER known for efforts to bring fashionable clothes to ordinary people on a large scale

Saint Law·rence see ST LAWRENCE

Saint Leger see ST LEGER

Saint Lou·is see ST LOUIS

Saint Lu·cia see ST LUCIA

Saint Luke /sənt ˈluːk‖ seɪnt-/ (first century AD) a member of the early Christian church. He is thought to have been a doctor and to have written the Gospel according to St Luke, the third book of the New Testament of the Bible, which describes the life and teaching of Jesus Christ.

saint·ly /ˈseɪntli/ adj of, like, or suitable to a SAINT; very holy: a saintly man/life —**liness** n [U]

Saint Mark /· ·ˈ·/ (first century AD) one of the followers of Jesus Christ and a member of the early Christian church. He is thought to have written the Gospel according to St Mark, the second book of the New Testament of the Bible, which describes the life and teaching of Christ.

Saint Mar·tha and Saint Ma·ry /sənt ˌmɑːθə ənd sənt ˈmeəri‖ seɪnt ˌmɑːrθə ənd seɪnt-/ (first century AD) in the Bible, two sisters whom Jesus visited. Mary sat and listened to his teachings, but Martha was more concerned to bring him food and drink. They are regarded as representing active Christians, who do good works, and CONTEMPLATIVE Christians, who think deeply about religion.

Saint Martin-in-the-Fields see ST MARTIN IN THE FIELDS

Saint Ma·ry Mag·da·lene /sənt ˌmeəri mægdəˈliːni‖ seɪnt-/ (first century AD) according to the Bible, a woman whom Jesus Christ cured. She saw the CRUCIFIXION and was the first person to see him after he rose from the dead. Although the Bible does not say so, some people think she is the same woman as the PROSTITUTE who washed Jesus's feet.

Saint Mat·thew /sənt ˈmæθjuː‖ seɪnt-/ (first century AD) a follower of Jesus Christ and a member of the early Christian church. He is thought to have been a tax collector and to have written the Gospel according to St Matthew, the first book of the New Testament of the Bible, which describes the life and teaching of Christ.

Saint Michael see ST MICHAEL

Saint Mo·ritz see ST MORITZ

Saint Nich·o·las /· ·ˈ··/ (fourth century AD) the SAINT who is supposed to look after Russia, children, sailors, and traders. He was a BISHOP who began the custom of giving gifts to children on the night before his special day (December 6th) which is still kept in some countries such as Holland, but in others has been moved to CHRISTMAS DAY.

Saint Pan·cras see ST PANCRAS

Saint Pat·rick /sənt ˈpætrɪk‖ seɪnt-/ (389?–461) the national SAINT of Ireland. **St Patrick's Day**, 17th March, is celebrated in Ireland and the US, where people often wear green clothes, to honour St Patrick.

Saint Patrick's Ca·the·dral /· ·ˈ· ·ˈ··/ the largest Roman Catholic church in the US. It is in New York City on Fifth Avenue and was built between 1858 and 1879

Saint Paul¹ /sənt ˈpɔːl‖ seɪnt-/ (c. AD3 to c. 64 or 67) born Saul of Tarsus. He was asked as a young man to try to bring Christianity to Damascus to an end, but on his way there a light blinded him and he heard Jesus ask "Why do you PERSECUTE me?" When he got his sight back he became a Christian and spent the rest of his life teaching people about Jesus. Many of the letters of the New Testament in the Bible were written by Saint Paul.

Saint Paul² the capital city of Minnesota in the US. It is a river port on the Mississippi next to the city of Minneapolis and is an important industrial and business centre. —see colour map on pages 1374–5

Saint Paul's Ca·the·dral /· ·ˈ· ·ˈ··/ also **St Paul's**— infml n [the] a fine CATHEDRAL in central London built (1675–1710) by Sir Christopher Wren; one of London's best-known LANDMARKS —see picture at Sir Christopher WREN and see colour map on page 817

Saint Pe·ter /· ·ˈ··/ (died 64?) the leader of the 12 followers (DISCIPLES) of Jesus Christ, who became the leader of the early Christians. Roman Catholics regard him as the first Pope. He is sometimes known as **Simon Peter**.

Saint Peter's the largest church in the world, in the Vatican City, Rome. It is visited by many tourists.

Saint Petersburg see ST PETERSBURG

Saint Peter's Square /· ˌ·· ˈ·/ the large square outside St Peter's, Rome, where many people gather to hear the POPE's Christmas message

Saint-Saëns /ˌsæn ˈsɒns‖ˌsæn ˈsɑːns/, **Ca·mille** /kæˈmiːl/ (1835–1921) a French COMPOSER best known for his OPERA *Samson and Delilah* and the popular *Carnival of Animals*

saint's day /ˈ· ·/ n the day each year on which the Christian church honours a particular SAINT: *St David's Day (1st March)* —compare NAME DAY

Saint Swith·in's Day /sənt ˈswɪðɪnz deɪ‖seɪnt-/ 15th July. According to an old story, if it rains on that day it will rain for 40 days following.

Saint Thomas see ST THOMAS

Saint Trinian's see ST TRINIAN'S

Saint Tropez see ST TROPEZ

Saint Val·en·tine's Day /· ˈ··· ˌ·/ also **Valentine's Day**— n February 14th, on which a greeting card (VALENTINE) is sent to someone one loves, but usu. without giving the name of the sender. Sometimes presents are exchanged or red roses given, as a sign of love.

Saint Vincent see ST VINCENT

Saint Vi·tus's Dance /sənt ˈvaɪtəsˌz ˌdɑːns‖seɪnt, -ˌdæns/ n [U] a nervous disorder that makes limbs and face suddenly move

saith /seθ/ *old use or bibl* says

sake[1] /seɪk/ n **1** **for the sake of: a** in order to help, improve, or bring advantage: *He's going to live by the coast for the sake of his health. | I'm only doing it for your sake; I don't care about it myself. | For both our sakes, please do as I ask.* **b** for the purpose of: *I'm not talking just for talking's sake; this is important! | Let's assume,* **for the sake of argument**, *that what you say is true.* **2 for Christ's/God's/goodness/heaven's/pity('s) sake** *infml* **a** (used when asking strongly for something): *For goodness sake don't tell him!* **b** (used as an expression of annoyance): *What's the matter now, for God's sake?* —see also **for old times' sake** (OLD (9))

▷ USAGE **For Christ's sake** is the strongest expression of those above. Both this expression and **for God's sake** may offend some people, and should be used with care. The gentlest expression of those above is **for goodness sake.**◁

sa·ke[2] /ˈsɑːki/ n [U] a Japanese alcoholic drink made from rice and usu. served warm in small cups

Sak·ha·rov /ˈsækərɒf‖-rɔːf/, **An·drei** /ˈɑːndreɪ/ (1921–89) a Russian PHYSICIST and DISSIDENT (=protestor) who was sent away from Moscow for his views. His EXILE was ended by Gorbachev and he won the Nobel Peace Prize in 1975.

Sa·ki /ˈsɑːki/ the name used by British short story writer H H Munro (1870–1916)

saks /sæks/ a fashionable and expensive New York department store, known esp. for its clothes

sa·laam /səˈlɑːm/ v [I] to perform a deep bending of the body while putting the inside of the right hand on the forehead, used as a respectful greeting in parts of the East —salaam n

sa·la·ble , saleable /ˈseɪləbəl/ adj that can be sold; fit for sale or easy to sell: *a salable commodity* —**bility** /ˌseɪlə-ˈbɪl‹ti/ n [U]

sa·la·cious /səˈleɪʃəs/ adj fml expressing or causing strong sexual feelings, usu. in an unpleasant or shocking way: *The story of the rape was treated in a disgustingly salacious manner by some of the newspapers.* — ~**ly** adv — ~**ness, -city** /səˈlæsˌti/ n [U]

sal·ad /ˈsæləd/ n [C;U] **1** a mixture of usu. raw vegetables served cold either with a main dish or, esp. with other foods added, as a main dish on its own: *I'll have a steak and a green salad (=*LETTUCE *and other green vegetables) | cheese/egg/ham salad | to mix/toss a salad | a salad bowl* **2** raw or cold cooked food cut into pieces and usu. mixed with a thick sharp-tasting liquid: *potato salad* — see also FRUIT SALAD

salad cream /ˈ·· ·/ n [U] esp. BrE a thick cream-coloured liquid, similar to MAYONNAISE but usu. sweeter, for putting on salads —compare SALAD DRESSING

salad days /ˈ·· ·/ n [P] old-fash infml one's time of youth and inexperience

salad dress·ing /ˈ·· ˌ··/ n [C;U] a liquid mixture, esp. one containing oil and VINEGAR, for putting on salads — compare SALAD CREAM

sal·a·man·der /ˈsæləmændər/ n a small animal that is like a LIZARD but with soft skin and lives partly on land and partly in water

sa·la·mi /səˈlɑːmi/ n [U] a large SAUSAGE with a strong salty taste, usu. thinly cut and eaten cold

sal·a·ried /ˈsælərid/ adj having or receiving a salary, usu. as opposed to wages: *salaried workers/jobs*

sal·a·ry /ˈsæləri/ n [C;U] money, usu. paid directly into one's bank account once a month, that one receives as payment from the company or organization one works for: *He's on a very good salary now. | a salary of sixteen thousand (=£16,000) a year* —compare EMOLUMENT, WAGES; see PAY[2] (USAGE)

sale /seɪl/ n **1** [C;U] (an) exchange of property or goods for money; act of selling: *I told her how marvellous the new product was, and I soon made a sale.* (=she bought it) | *The law forbids the sale of alcohol to people under 18.* **2** [C] a special offering of goods in a shop at lower prices than usual. Sales in Britain are usu. held in January and in the summer: *This shirt was a bargain — only £10 in a sale. | Have the January sales started yet? | a clearance sale | usual price £3, sale price £1.49* —see also JUMBLE SALE **3** [C] a selling of articles to whoever offers the highest price; AUCTION: *a sale of fine old paintings* **4** [S] also **sales** pl. — the total amount sold: *We're hoping for a large sale/large sales for our new product.* **5 for sale** offered to be sold, esp. by a private owner: *"How much is that picture?" "It's only on display; it's not for sale." | There's a "For Sale" sign outside their house. | They've put their house up for sale.* **6 on sale: a** offered to be sold, esp. in a shop: *The latest model of this video recorder is now on sale in your shops.* **b** AmE at or in a SALE (2): *I got this hat on sale; it was very cheap.* **7 (on) sale or return** supplied to a seller in such a way that the seller pays only for what he or she sells, and can send the rest back: *The newspapers are supplied to the shop on a sale or return basis.* —see also SALES, BILL OF SALE

sale·a·ble /ˈseɪləbəl/ adj SALABLE

Sa·lem /ˈseɪləm/ a town in Massachusetts, in the US, famous in history for its trying and hanging of WITCHes in 1692 (called the **Salem Witch Trials**). People sometimes use the words **witch hunt** to describe what happened at Salem and also what has happened in other situations in which innocent people have been punished for things they did not do, esp. the situation in the US during the HUAC hearings on COMMUNISM.

sale of work /ˌ· · ˈ·/ n BrE an event at which people sell things they have made, e.g. cakes or toys, in order to collect money for CHARITY

sale·room /ˈseɪlrʊm, -ruːm/ esp. BrE ‖ **sales·room** /ˈseɪlzrʊm, -ruːm/esp. AmE— n a place where AUCTION sales are held

sales /seɪlz/ adj [A] of or for selling: *this year's sales figures/forecast | our company's new sales director | We're having a special sales drive.* (=trying hard to sell more products)

sales·clerk /ˈseɪlzklɑːk‖-klɜːrk/ n AmE for SHOP ASSISTANT

sales·girl /ˈseɪlzgɜːl‖-gɜːrl/ n a usu. young female SHOP ASSISTANT

sales·man /ˈseɪlzmən/ n **-men** /mən/ a male salesperson.
►CULTURAL NOTE Many people do not altogether trust what a salesman tells them (his PATTER), because they know he is trying to sell something.◄

sales·man·ship /ˈseɪlzmənʃɪp/ n [U] skill in selling: *It's not good salesmanship to bully a customer into buying a product. | (fig.) It took some clever salesmanship to get our plan accepted by the chairman.*

sales·per·son /ˈseɪlzpɜːsən‖-pɜːr-/ n **-people** /piːpəl/ **1** a sales representative **2** (used esp. in job advertisements, etc.) a SHOP ASSISTANT

sales pitch /ˈ· ·/ n infml a salesperson's special way of talking about the goods he/she is trying to sell

sales rep·re·sen·ta·tive /ˈ· ···ˌ····/ n a person who goes from place to place, usu. within a particular area, selling and taking orders for their firm's goods

sales re·sist·ance /ˈ· ·ˌ··/ n [U] unwillingness to buy something; ability to keep oneself from being persuaded by a skilful salesperson

sales slip /ˈ· ·/ n AmE a RECEIPT (=record of things bought) given in a shop

sales talk /ˈ· ·/ n [U] talking intended to persuade or sell, esp. by praising what is for sale

sales tax /ˈ· ·/ n [C;U] (an amount or rate of) money charged as tax in addition to the ordinary price of an article or service. In the US sales tax is collected by city, COUNTY, and state governments, so it varies a lot from place to place, between 0 and 10 per cent: *Most states in the US have sales taxes.* —compare PURCHASE TAX, VAT

sales·wo·man /ˈseɪlzˌwʊmən/ n -women /ˌwɪmɪn/ a female SALESPERSON

Sal·ford /ˈsɔːlfəd‖-fərd/ a city within Greater Manchester, NW England, known for its university, CATHEDRAL, docks (DOCK[1]) and engineering and chemical industries

sa·li·ent[1] /ˈseɪliənt/ adj fml standing out most noticeably or importantly: *The salient features/points of his plan are summed up in this report.*

salient[2] n tech an angle pointing outwards, esp. in the wall of a fort or in a line of holes dug in a battlefield for defence

sa·line /ˈseɪlaɪn/ adj tech of or containing salt: *a saline solution* —-linity /səˈlɪnɨti/ n [U] : *to test the salinity of the water*

Sal·in·ger /ˈsælɪndʒər/, **J. D.** (1919–) an American writer whose most famous book is *Catcher in the Rye*

Salis·bu·ry /ˈsɔːlzbəri‖-beri/ a city in S England famous for its large CATHEDRAL, which attracts many tourists

Salisbury Plain /ˌ··· ˈ·/ a large piece of open country in the S of England, used by the army as a training area. Stonehenge, a structure of stone circles from 2500–1500 BC, is on Salisbury Plain.

Salisbury steak /ˌ··· ˈ·/ n AmE a dish made of BEEF finely cut and formed into a flat shape, then cooked in GRAVY

sa·li·va /səˈlaɪvə/ n [U] the natural watery liquid produced in the mouth

sa·li·va·ry /səˈlaɪvəri‖ˈsælɨveri/ adj [A] of saliva or the organs (**salivary glands**) producing it

sal·i·vate /ˈsælɨveɪt/ v [I] tech or humor to produce (an increased amount of) saliva in the mouth: *I was salivating at the thought of the cream cakes.* —-vation /ˌsælɨˈveɪʃən/ n [U]

Salk /sɔːk, sɔːlk/, **Jo·nas** /ˈdʒəʊnəs/ (1914–) an American scientist who produced a protection against POLIO (the **Salk vaccine**)

sal·low[1] /ˈsæləʊ/ adj (of the skin) rather yellow and unhealthy-looking: *a sallow complexion* —~ness n [U]

sallow[2] n a tree of the WILLOW family

sal·ly[1] /ˈsæli/ n 1 a quick attack and return to a position of defence; SORTIE 2 fml a clever or sharply humorous remark: *Her witty sallies made him angry.*

sally[2] v

sally forth/out phr v [I] old use or humor to go or come out, esp. from a safe place to meet some difficulty: *She opened the door and sallied forth to face the waiting crowd of journalists.*

Sally Ar·my /ˌ··· ˈ··/ BrE infml for SALVATION ARMY

salm·on /ˈsæmən/ n salmon or salmons 1 [C;U] a large fish of the northern oceans with silvery skin and pink flesh that swims up rivers to lay its eggs. It is thought of as being expensive and only for special occasions: *to go fishing for salmon* | *tinned salmon* | **smoked salmon sandwiches** 2 [U] also **salmon pink** /ˌ·· ˈ·◂/– yellowish-pink —see also ROCK SALMON

sal·mo·nel·la /ˌsælməˈnelə◂/ n [U] a bacterium that causes food poisoning, stomach pains, etc. Salmonella is often found in incorrectly cooked chicken and sometimes present in uncooked eggs.

salmon trout /ˈ··· ·/ n [C;U] a large TROUT with pink flesh

Sa·lo·me /səˈləʊmi/ in the Bible, the STEPDAUGHTER of Herod whose dancing pleased him so much that he offered her anything she wanted. She asked for the head of John the Baptist.

sal·on /ˈsælɒn‖səˈlɑːn/ n 1 a stylish or fashionable small shop, esp. where services rather than goods are sold: *a hairdressing salon* | *a beauty salon* 2 (esp. in France in

the 18th century) a regularly-held fashionable gathering, esp. of writers, painters, musicians, etc., at the home of a well-known person

sa·loon /səˈluːn/ n 1 also **saloon car** /·ˈ· ·/BrE‖ **sedan** AmE– a car for four to six passengers, with a roof, two or four doors, and a separate enclosed space for cases, bags, boxes, etc. (boot BrE‖trunk AmE) —compare ESTATE CAR, HATCHBACK, SPORTS CAR 2 a saloon bar 3 a large public drinking place, esp. in an American town in the WILD WEST 4 a grandly furnished room for the social use of a ship's passengers

saloon bar /·ˈ· ·/ also **lounge bar**– n BrE a comfortably furnished room in a PUB, where drinks usu. cost a little more than in the PUBLIC BAR. Women, or men and women together, usu. sit in a saloon bar. —see also PUB

Sal·op /ˈsæləp/ an old name for Shropshire

sal·sa /ˈsælsə‖ˈsɑːl-/ n [U] 1 a hot SAUCE made of TOMATOes, onions, CHILLIs, etc. usu. eaten with Mexican or Spanish food: *Do you want salsa on your taco?* 2 a type of popular music based on Latin American dance music. Singers and musicians often dance at the same time as they are singing and playing.

sal·si·fy /ˈsælsɨfi/ n [U] a plant with purple flowers whose long fleshy root is eaten as a vegetable (but not commonly)

salt[1] /sɔːlt/ n 1 [U] also **common salt**, tech **sodium chloride**– a very common colourless or white solid substance found in the earth and in seawater which has many uses including preserving food and giving it more taste: *The vegetables need more salt.* | *cooking table salt* | *Please pass the salt.* —see also ROCK SALT 2 [C] tech any of a class of chemical substances which may be formed by the combining of an acid and a BASE[1] (5) or metal — see also EPSOM SALTS, SMELLING SALTS 3 **the salt of the earth** a person or people regarded as good hearted and dependable 4 **take something with a grain/pinch of salt** to remain doubtful about something; not necessarily believe all of: *You should take what he says with a pinch of salt; he doesn't exactly tell lies, but he sometimes stretches the truth.* —see also **rub salt into the/someone's wounds** (RUB[1]), **worth one's salt** (WORTH)

salt[2] v [T] 1 to add salt to; put salt on: *Have you salted the vegetables?* | *I just love salted peanuts.* 2 [(down)] to preserve with salt: *They salted down most of the meat for later use.* 3 to put salt or other substances on (roads) to reduce the danger from ice

salt sthg. ↔ **away** phr v [T] infml to save (esp. money) for the future, perhaps dishonestly or illegally: *There were allegations that the military rulers had salted away millions of dollars in Swiss bank accounts.*

salt[3] adj 1 [A] formed by salty water: *a salt lake* 2 [A] preserved with salt: *salt pork* 3 containing, full of, or tasting of salt; salty: *salt tears/water* —~ness n [U] tech

SALT /sɔːlt/ see STRATEGIC ARMS LIMITATION TALKS

salt·cel·lar /ˈsɔːltˌselər/ BrE‖**salt shaker** AmE– n a container for salt at meals, esp. a small pot with usu. one hole in the top for shaking salt out —compare PEPPER POT

Salt Lake Cit·y /ˌ·· ˈ··/ a city in W central US, the capital of Utah, best known as the centre of the MORMON religion —see colour map on pages 1374–5

salt·lick /ˈsɔːltˌlɪk/ n 1 a large block of a salty substance for sheep and cows to LICK (=move their tongues over) 2 a naturally salty piece of ground where animals get salt in this way

salt·pan /ˈsɔːltpæn/ n a natural or artificial hollow place from which salt water dries up leaving a surface of salt

salt·pe·tre BrE‖ **-ter** AmE /ˌsɔːltˈpiːtər/ n [U] a salty-tasting powdery substance (**potassium nitrate**) used in making GUNPOWDER and matches, and in preserving meat

salt shak·er /ˈ· ˌ··/ n AmE for SALTCELLAR

salt truck /ˈ· ·/ n AmE for GRITTER

salt·wa·ter /ˈsɔːltˌwɔːtər‖-ˌwɔː-, -ˌwɑː-/ adj [A] of or living in salty water or the sea: *saltwater plants* —opposite **freshwater**

salt·y /ˈsɔːlti/ adj 1 of, containing, or tasting of salt: *This soup's too salty.* 2 old-fash (of talk, stories, etc.) slightly improper in an amusing or exciting way; RACY: *salty humour* —~iness n [U]

sa·lu·bri·ous /səˈluːbriəs/ adj 1 socially desirable or RESPECTABLE: *They live in a very salubrious area.* 2 fml *or lit* favourable to good health: *salubrious living conditions* − ~**ness** *n* [U]

sal·u·ta·ry /ˈsæljᵿtəri‖-teri/ *adj* causing or likely to cause an improvement in character, future behaviour, health, etc.: *The accident was a salutary lesson/experience; I'll never drink and drive again.*

sal·u·ta·tion /ˌsæljᵿˈteɪʃən/ *n fml* **1** [C;U] (an) expression of greeting by words or action **2** [C] a word or phrase such as "Ladies and Gentlemen", "Dear Sir", "Dear Miss Jones", etc., at the beginning of a speech or letter

sa·lute¹ /səˈluːt/ *v* **1** [I;T] to make a SALUTE² (1a) (to): *Always salute when you pass an officer!* **2** [T] *fml* to honour and praise, esp. in a formal or ceremonial way: *On this very special evening we salute the splendid work of the local police.* **3** [T] *fml* to greet, esp. with polite words or with a sign: *He saluted his friend with a wave of the hand.*

salute² *n* **1** [C] a military sign of recognition, such as **a** a raising of the right hand to the forehead: *He gave a smart salute.* **b** a ceremonial firing of guns or lowering of flags in honour of a person of very high rank: *a 21-gun salute* **2** [C;U] *fml* (a) greeting; salutation: *He raised his arm in salute.* **3 take the salute** (of a person of high rank) to stand while being saluted by soldiers marching past

sal·vage¹ /ˈsælvɪdʒ/ *n* [U] **1** the act or process of saving something from destruction, esp. saving a wrecked ship or its goods from the sea: *to mount a salvage operation* **2** goods or property that are saved from being destroyed: *a sale of salvage from the wreck*

salvage² *v* [T (**from**)] to save (goods or property) from loss or damage: *We were unable to salvage anything when the factory burnt down.* | (fig.) *After it was revealed that he'd also stolen from his employers, there was little he could do to salvage his battered reputation.* − ~**able** *adj*

sal·va·tion /sælˈveɪʃən/ *n* [U] **1** something that saves or preserves from danger, loss, ruin, or failure: *After so much dry weather, this rain has been the farmers' salvation.* **2** *tech* (esp. in the Christian religion) the state of being saved from the power and effect of evil: *the salvation of souls*

Salvation Ar·my /·ˌ·· ˈ··/ also **Sally Army** *infml*− [the] a Christian organization that has military uniforms and ranks, holds simple religious services with music, and is best known for its help to poor people −compare **Church Army**

sal·va·tion·ist /sælˈveɪʃənᵻst/ *n* (*often cap.*) a member of the Salvation Army

salve¹ /sælv, sɑːv‖sæv/ *n* [C;U] (an) oily substance for putting on a cut, wound, sore place, etc., to help the forming of new skin; OINTMENT: *lip salve*

salve² *v* [T] *fml* to make (esp. uncomfortable feelings) less painful: *He felt guilty, so he tried to salve his conscience by bringing her a bunch of flowers.*

sal·ver /ˈsælvər/ *n* a large metal plate for serving food, drink, etc., esp. at a formal meal: *a silver salver*

sal·vo /ˈsælvəʊ/ *n* -**vos** *or* -**voes** [(**of**)] **1** a firing of several guns at once, in a ceremony or battle: *a salvo of gunfire* **2** a sudden burst: *a salvo of boos greeted the announcement.* −compare VOLLEY¹ (1)

sal vo·lat·i·le /ˌsæl vəˈlætᵻli/ *n* [U] a form of SMELLING SALTS

Sal·zburg /ˈsæltsbɜːg‖ˈsɔːlzbɜːrg/ *n* a city in Austria famous for its yearly music FESTIVAL and for being where Mozart was born

Sa·mar·i·tan /səˈmærᵻtən/ *n* in Britain, a member of **the Samaritans**, an organization helping people who are experiencing great suffering of mind or thinking of killing themselves, and have no one to share their feelings with. The Samaritans usu. talk to people on the telephone rather than in person and the service is free. −see also GOOD SAMARITAN

sam·ba /ˈsæmbə/ *n* (a piece of music for) a quick dance of Brazilian origin

Sam·bo /ˈsæmbəʊ/ *n AmE taboo derog sl* a black man (from a story about a little black boy called Sambo who ate a lot of PANCAKEs)

same¹ /seɪm/ *adj* **1** [*the, this, that, these, those*+A] not changed or different; not another or other: *"Is he still going out with the same girl?" "No, he's got a new girlfriend."* | *My father sits in the same chair every evening.* | *The broadcast was heard all over the whole country at the*

same time. | *I know it was wrong, but I would do the same thing again in the same situation.* | *You've made the same mistake as last time/the same mistake that you made last time.* | *He was promoted on the same day that she was.* | *They met early in 1970 and got married later that same year.* | *Those same people who support lower taxes complain when the Government cuts services.* **2** [*the*+A] alike in (almost) every way: *Men and women should get the same pay for doing the same jobs.* | *At the party she saw another woman wearing the same dress.* | *"Do you use butter or margarine?" "It doesn't matter; it all* **amounts to/comes to the same thing."** (=has the same result) **3 at the same time: a** together **b** in spite of this; yet: *He can be very rude but at the same time you can't help liking him.* **4 by the same token** in the same way: *I agree that he hasn't given us many new ideas, but by the same token neither have we given him any.* **5 in the same boat** in the same unpleasant situation; facing the same dangers: *If you lose your job I'll lose mine, so we're both in the same boat.* **6 just/all the same** in spite of this; NEVERTHELESS: *I realize she can be very annoying, but all the same I think you should apologize for losing your temper with her.* **7 same difference** *AmE infml* no difference; the result is the same: *"But if you don't go out with Bill, Linda will." "Same difference," she shrugged.* (either way, she won't be with Bill). **8 the same old story** *infml* the usual excuse or difficulty

▷ USAGE Compare **same** and **similar**. **Same** suggests things that are completely unchanged or exactly alike: *I've still got the same car as I had before.* | *These two banknotes look exactly the same, though one of them is counterfeit.* **Similar** suggests things that are alike in most ways, but not in every detail: *The birds are similar in appearance, but the male is more brightly coloured.*◁

same² *pron* **1** (used with **the**) the same thing, person, condition, etc.: *They may look the same, but they're really quite different.* | *Thanks for helping me; I'll do the same for you sometime.* | *"Is your wife any better?" "About the same, thanks."* (=no more or less ill than before) | *Things haven't been/It's not been the same since he left.* (=life has not been so good) | *"Has he put any new ideas in the report?" "No, it's just more of the same."* (=the same ideas as before) **2** *old-fash or humor* (used without **the**) the things mentioned: *He was good at spending money but not so good at earning same.* **3 (And the) same to** ˈ**you!** *infml* (used as a reply to a greeting or as an angry reply to a rude remark): *"Happy Christmas!" "Same to you!"* | *"Go to Hell!" "And the same to you!"* **4 (the) same again, please** *infml* (an order for another drink of the same kind) −see also **all the same to** (ALL²), **one and the same** (ONE¹)

same³ *adv* **1 the same (as)** in the same way (as): *These two words are pronounced differently but they're spelt the same (as each other).* **2 same as** *infml* just like: *I have my pride, same as anyone else.*

same·ness /ˈseɪmnᵻs/ *n* [U] **1** the state of being the same; very close likeness; SIMILARITY **2** *derog* lack of variety: *Don't you ever get tired of the sameness of the work in this office?*

same·y /ˈseɪmi/ *adj BrE infml* dull because lacking variety: *His novels tend to be very samey.*

sam·iz·dat /ˈsæmɪzdæt‖ˈsɑːmiːzˌdɑːt/ *n* [U] a system in the former USSR by which books, magazines, etc., that were forbidden by the state were secretly printed

Sa·mo·a /səˈməʊə/ a group of islands in the S Pacific, esp. Savai'i and Upolu, officially called **Western Samoa**; capital Apia; population 169,000 (1989) −**Samoan** *n, adj*

sa·mo·sa /sæˈməʊsə/ *n* an Indian small three-sided pastry case filled with cut-up meat, vegetables, etc., and cooked in hot fat

sam·o·var /ˈsæməvɑːʳ/ *n* a large metal container used esp. in Russia to boil water for making tea

sam·pan /ˈsæmpæn/ *n* a light flat-bottomed boat used along the coasts and rivers in China and Southeast Asia

sam·ple¹ /ˈsɑːmpəl‖ˈsæm-/ *n* [(**of**)] **1** a small part representing the whole; typical quantity, thing, event, etc.: *The nurse took a sample of my blood/a blood sample.* | *I'd like to see some samples of your work.* | *Here are some sample questions from last year's exam.* | *Bring a sample* (=of URINE) *when you come to see the doctor.* **2** a small amount of a product that allows one to find out what it is like: *They're giving away* free samples/*sample bottles of this new kind of cooking oil.*

sample² *v* [T] **1** to take and examine a SAMPLE¹ (1) of; test: *I sampled the wine before giving it to the others.* **2** to get to know about by experience; TRY out: *Once you've sampled the pleasures of country life, you won't want to live in the city.*

sam·pler /ˈsɑːmplər‖ˈsæm-/ *n* **1** a decorative piece of cloth with the alphabet, family names and dates, a picture, etc., stitched on it with thread, done to show one's skill at sewing **2** a music computer which can record a sound from outside itself and then produce it at any given PITCH

Sam·son /ˈsæmsən/ a man in a Bible story who was very strong until a woman named Delilah tricked him into having his hair cut off, from which came his strength. He was then made a prisoner and blinded. His strength returned as his hair grew and he pulled down a TEMPLE upon himself and his enemies: *Edberg wouldn't allow me to cut his hₐir until after Wimbledon. He told me it gave him the strength of Samson.*

sam·u·rai /ˈsæmuraɪ/ *n* **-rai** *or* **-rais** a member of a military class of high rank in Japan in former times

San An·dre·as fault /ˌsæn ændreɪəs ˈfɔːlt/ [*the*] a crack between two of the plates of the Earth's surface which forms a line from the N to the S of California. Movement of these plates causes EARTHQUAKES.

San An·to·ni·o /ˌsæn ænˈtəʊniəʊ/ a city in S Texas known for its large numbers of Mexican-Americans and for the ALAMO, where Texans were defeated by much larger numbers of Mexicans in 1836

san·a·to·ri·um /ˌsænəˈtɔːriəm/ ‖ *also* **sanitarium** *AmE*– *n* **-iums** *or* **-ia** /riə/ a kind of hospital for sick people who are getting better and need treatment, rest, etc., esp. over a long period of time

San·cho Pan·za /ˌsæntʃəʊ ˈpænzə‖ˌsɑːntʃəʊ ˈpɑːn-/ the friend and companion of Don Quixote in the story by Miguel de Cervantes

sanc·ti·fy /ˈsæŋktɪfaɪ/ *v* [T] *fml* **1** to make holy: *This is sanctified ground, and we may not tread upon it.* **2** [*usu. pass.*] to SANCTION² (2) **--fication** /ˌsæŋktɪfɪˈkeɪʃən/ *n* [U]

sanc·ti·mo·ni·ous /ˌsæŋktɪˈməʊniəs◂/ *adj fml derog* disapproving of others because one thinks one is good, right, etc., and they are not; SELF-RIGHTEOUS – ~**ly** *adv* – ~**ness** *n* [U]

sanc·tion¹ /ˈsæŋkʃən/ *n* **1** [U] *fml* formal or official permission, approval, or acceptance: *The minister can only act in this matter with the sanction of Parliament.* **2** [C] *fml* a formal action or punishment (to be) ordered when a law or rule is broken: *The ultimate sanction is to suspend troublemakers from the debate.* **3** [C *usu. pl.*] an action, such as the stopping of trade, taken by one or more countries against a country which is breaking international law: *Western nations took economic sanctions against/imposed tough sanctions on the rebel regime.* | *Many firms were accused of sanctions-busting.* (=doing business with a country with which trade had been forbidden) **4** [C] *fml or tech* something that forces the keeping of a rule or standard: *In certain societies shame was the only sanction against wrongdoing.*

sanction² *v* [T] *fml* **1** to accept, approve, or permit, esp. officially; AUTHORIZE: *The church would not sanction the king's second marriage.* **2** to make acceptable: *It was a foolish custom, but one sanctioned by long usage.*

sanc·ti·ty /ˈsæŋktɪti/ *n* [U] **1** holiness; sacredness (SACRED): *There was an air of sanctity in the old church.* | *You should respect the sanctity of marriage.* (=esp. by not having sex outside marriage) **2** holiness of life: *a woman of great sanctity*

sanc·tu·a·ry /ˈsæŋktʃuəri,-tʃəri‖-tʃueri/ *n* **1** [C] an area for birds or animals where they cannot be hunted and their animal enemies are controlled: *a bird sanctuary* **2** [C;U] (a place of) protection or safety from harm, esp. for a person escaping from officers of the law: *The outlaw was granted sanctuary in the church.* **3** [C] the part of a religious building considered most holy, esp. the area in front of the ALTAR in a Christian church

sanc·tum /ˈsæŋktəm/ *n* **1** a holy place inside a temple **2** *infml* a private place or room where one can be quiet and alone: *Don't disturb him when he's in his* **inner sanctum.**

Sanc·tus /ˈsæŋktəs/ [*the*] the fourth part of the religious service of the MASS, esp. when performed with music

sand¹ /sænd/ *n* [U] loose material of very small fine grains, found in wide masses along seacoasts and in deserts, and used for making cement and glass and for rubbing away roughness: *The children were playing in the sand* (=in a pile of sand)/*on the sand.* (=by the seashore) –see also SANDS, SANDY

sand² *v* [T] **1** [(DOWN)] to make smoother by rubbing with a rough surface, esp. SANDPAPER: *Sand the walls down before you paint them.* **2** to put sand on, esp. to prevent slipping

Sand /sɒnd‖sɑːnd/, **George** /ʒɔːʒ‖ʒɔːrʒ/ (1804–76) a French female writer whose real name was Amandine Dupin. Her novels (NOVEL) *Indiana* and *Lélia* express her FEMINIST beliefs.

san·dal /ˈsændl/ *n* a light shoe made of a flat bottom with usu. leather bands to hold it on the foot, worn esp. in warm weather –see PAIR (USAGE), and see picture at SHOE

▶CULTURAL NOTE Sandals are connected in some people's minds with people who have LIBERAL opinions and with JESUS FREAKS. ◀

san·dal·wood /ˈsændlwʊd/ *n* [U] a hard yellowish sweet-smelling south Asian wood used in making small boxes, figures, etc. Its oil is used in making soap.

sand·bag¹ /ˈsændbæg/ *n* a bag filled with sand or earth, esp. as used for piling up to form a wall or protection against explosions, rising water, etc.

sandbag² *v* **-gg-** [T] **1** to put sandbags on: *Workers were sandbagging the riverbanks to prevent flooding.* **2** [(**into**)] *AmE infml* to force (someone) roughly to do something

sand·bank /ˈsændbæŋk/ *n* a bank of sand in a river, HARBOUR, etc.

sand·bar /ˈsændbɑːʳ/ *n* a stretch of sand formed by moving currents, esp. across the mouth of a river

sand·blast /ˈsændblɑːst‖-blæst/ *v* [T] to clean or cut metal, glass, etc., with a machine that sends out a high-speed stream of sand

sand·box /ˈsændbɒks‖-bɑːks/ *n AmE* a low box holding sand for children to play in –compare SANDPIT

Sand·burg /ˈsændbɜːg‖-bɜːrg/, **Carl** /kɑːl‖kɑːrl/ (1878–1967) an American writer and poet who won PULITZER PRIZES for his book about Abraham Lincoln and for his poetry, which included strong statements about cities and industry

sand·cas·tle /ˈsænd͵kɑːsəl‖-͵kæ-/ *n* a small model, esp. of a castle, built of sand by children when playing on a BEACH

sand dol·lar /ˈ· ͵··/ *n AmE* a flat SEA URCHIN (an animal which lives in the ocean) which when it dies leaves behind a flat, round shell with a flower-like centre: *The children were collecting sand dollars at the water's edge.*

sand dune /ˈ· ·/ *n* a DUNE

sand·er /ˈsændəʳ/ *also* **sanding ma·chine** /ˈ··· ·͵·/– *n* a machine with a fast-moving rough surface like SAND-PAPER, for making surfaces smoother

Sanders, Colonel see COLONEL SANDERS

sand fly /ˈ· ·/ *n* a small biting fly common on seashores

Sand·hurst /ˈsændhɜːst‖-hɜːrst/ the Royal Military Academy in the village of Sandhurst in S England. It has the image of providing the best and most respected training for future British army officers among the MIDDLE-CLASS and UPPER-CLASS people: *I dined at Sandhurst among scarlet-coated officers and much silver.* | *The senior officers were mostly Sandhurst men.* –compare WEST POINT

San Di·e·go /sæn diˈeɪgəʊ/ a city in S California best known as a port and naval centre, for its ZOO, and for its excellent year round weather –see colour map on pages 1374–5

San·di·nis·ta /ˌsændɪˈniːstə◂/ *n* a member of a LEFT-WING political group in Nicaragua which overthrew (OVERTHROW) the DICTATOR Somoza in 1979 and took over the government, but who were later defeated in elections in the late 1980s. Because the Sandinistas were partly supported by COMMUNIST governments in the USSR and Cuba, the US wanted them out of power and gave money to a group of GUERRILLA fighters called CONTRAS in an attempt to make the government fall.

S & L /ˌes ənd ˈel/ n AmE SAVINGS AND LOAN ASSOCIATION

sand·man /ˈsændmæn/ **-men** /men/ n [the] the man who makes children sleepy, according to their parents and FOLKTALES: *I'll tuck you in and soon the sandman will come and you'll have nice dreams.*

San·down Park /ˌsændaʊn ˈpɑːk‖-ˈpɑːrk/ a horse-racing course in England

sand·pail /ˈsændpeɪl/ n AmE a small bucket used by children when playing in sand, esp. when building sandcastles at the seaside

sand paint·ing /ˈ·ˌ·/ n AmE a painting made by Native Americans, esp. in the southwest, in which they use coloured sand rather than paint

sand·pa·per[1] /ˈsændˌpeɪpəʳ/ n [U] paper covered on one side with fine sand or a similar substance, used for rubbing over surfaces to make them smoother

sandpaper[2] v [T] to rub with sandpaper

sand·pip·er /ˈsændˌpaɪpəʳ/ n a small bird with long legs and a long beak, found esp. around muddy and sandy shores

sand·pit /ˈsændˌpɪt/ n esp. BrE a hollow place in the ground or an enclosed space containing sand for children to play in —compare SANDBOX

San·dring·ham /ˈsændrɪŋəm/ also **Sandringham House** /ˌ··· ˈ·/— a large country house in the E of England where the British king or queen lives for part of the year around Christmas

sands /sændz/ n [P] **1** a stretch of sand: *across the burning sands of the desert* | *golden sands* **2** *fml or lit* moments in time, as if measured by sand in an HOURGLASS, considered as passing quickly: *The sands of his life are fast running out.* (=he will soon die)

sand·shoe /ˈsændʃuː/ n BrE a light cloth shoe such as a PLIMSOLL

sand·stone /ˈsændstəʊn/ n [U] soft rock formed by sand fixed in a natural cement

sand·storm /ˈsændstɔːm‖-ɔːrm/ n a windstorm in which sand from a desert is blown about

sand trap /ˈ· ·/ n AmE for BUNKER (3) —see picture at GOLF

sand·wich[1] /ˈsænwɪdʒ‖ˈsændwɪtʃ, ˈsænwɪtʃ/ n **1** two pieces of bread, usu. spread with butter, and with some other usu. cold food between them. Many people have sandwiches for their midday meal and there are often **sandwich bars** in city centres: *a cheese/jam sandwich* —see also CLUB SANDWICH, OPEN SANDWICH **2** BrE a cake of two flat parts with JAM or cream between them

sandwich[2] v [T ı obj+adv/prep, esp. **between**] to fit or place tightly or with difficulty between two other things: *Our car was sandwiched between two big trucks, almost touching them.* | *I'm very busy but I'll try to sandwich that job in between visitors.*

sandwich board /ˈ··· ·/ n a pair of large advertising signs for hanging at the front and back over the shoulders of a person (**sandwich man**) who walks about in public. Sandwich boards are sometimes seen which say "the end of the world is NIGH" (=coming soon). These are carried by religious people trying to warn others that they should believe in God because the world will soon end.

sandwich course /ˈ··· ·/ n BrE a course of study in an industrial or professional subject at a college or university which includes periods of usu. three or six months spent working for a company

sand·y /ˈsændi/ adj **1** consisting of sand or having sand on the surface: *a sandy beach* | *My towel's all sandy!* **2** (esp. of hair) yellowish-brown —**-iness** n [U]

sane /seɪn/ adj **1** healthy in mind; not mad: *He's been certified sane.* —opposite **insane 2** apprec based on or showing good reasonable thinking; sensible: *a very sane solution to a delicate problem* —see also SANITY — **~ly** adv

San·fo·rized /ˈsænfəraɪzd/ adj AmE tdmk (of cloth) treated with a process that prevents SHRINKAGE (=growing smaller) after washing: *Is this cotton Sanforized?* | *I only buy Sanforized shirts.*

San Fran·cis·co /ˌsæn frənˈsɪskəʊ/ a city and port in W California known for its beautiful setting and the great EARTHQUAKE and fire of 1906 which almost destroyed it. It is a financial centre and has many institutions of education and CULTURE. —see colour map on pages 1374–5

sang /sæŋ/ past tense of SING

sang·froid /ˌsɒŋˈfrwɑː ‖ ˌsɔːŋ-/ n [U] Fr calm courage; great self-control during danger or difficulty

a cable car in San Francisco

san·gri·a /sæŋˈgriːə, sæn-, ˈsæŋgriə/ n [U] a Spanish cold drink made from red wine, fruit juice, and water

san·gui·na·ry /ˈsæŋgwɪnəri‖ -neri/ adj lit marked by, fond of, much wounding and killing

san·guine /ˈsæŋgwɪn/ adj fml quietly hopeful; expecting the best — **~ly** adv

san·i·ta·ry /ˈsænɪtəri‖-teri/ adj **1** [A] of or for health, esp. the treatment or removal of human waste substances, dirt, or infection: *sanitary fittings, such as lavatories and bidets* | *The local* **sanitary inspector** *will check that the restaurant's kitchens are clean.* **2** clean; free from danger to health: *It's not sanitary to let flies come near food.* —see also INSANITARY

sanitary tow·el /ˈ····· ˌ··/ also **pad, sanitary napkin** AmE— n a soft pad worn between a woman's legs during her PERIOD (4) to take up the flow of MENSTRUAL blood —compare TAMPON

san·i·ta·tion /ˌsænɪˈteɪʃən/ n [U] the use of means for protecting public health, esp. by the removing and treatment of waste

sanitation work·er /ˌ···ˈ·· ˌ··/ n AmE for DUSTMAN

san·i·tize also **-tise** BrE /ˈsænɪtaɪz/ v [T] **1** usu. derog to make less unpleasant, dangerous, strongly expressed, etc., in order not to offend people: *to sanitize a report* **2** to clean thoroughly; to make SANITARY

san·i·ta·ri·um /ˌsænɪˈteəriəm/ n **-iums** or **-ia** /-riə/ AmE for SANATORIUM

san·i·ty /ˈsænɪti/ n [U] the quality of being SANE: *to question someone's sanity* —opposite **insanity**

sank /sæŋk/ past tense of SINK

San Ma·ri·no /ˌsæn məˈriːnəʊ/ a small country in Italy, in the Apennines, near Rimini; capital San Marino; population 23,000 (1989)

San Quent·in /ˌsæn ˈkwentɪn/ (a town in California where there is) a large prison: *He's doing 10–20 in San Quentin.*

San·skrit /ˈsænskrɪt/ adj, n [U] (of or in) an ancient language of India from which many modern Indian languages are descended

sans ser·if /ˌsæn ˈserɪf, ˌsænz-/ n [U] (in printing) letters without SERIFS and with all strokes of equal thickness

San·ta Claus /ˈsæntə klɔːz‖ˈsænti klɔːz, ˈsæntə/ also **Santa** infml, **Father Christmas** BrE— (a person dressed as) an imaginary old man in red clothes and a long white beard who is believed by children to come down the CHIMNEY at Christmas to bring their presents

Santa Claus

► CULTURAL NOTE Before Christmas children write letters to Santa Claus telling him what they would like for Christmas. On Christmas Eve they often leave out something for him to eat or drink. He is supposed to fly about the sky in a SLEIGH (an animal-drawn vehicle which slides along snow on two metal blades) pulled by REINDEER. Santa Claus is thought to live at the North Pole where he spends most of the year in his workshop making toys for children with the help of elves (ELF). People think of him as a happy man who says "Ho, ho, ho": *Does your daughter still believe in Santa Claus?* —see also extra information on page 215 and colour picture on page 1212◄

San·ta Fe /ˌsæntə ˈfeɪ/ the small capital city of New Mexico, known for its long association with Mexicans and Native Americans. It is a government and tourist centre.

Santa Fe Trail /ˌ··· ·/ [the] an important road in the West of the US, used by 19th-century American settlers, starting in Missouri and ending in Santa Fe

Santa Ma·ri·a /ˌsæntə məˈriːə/ one of the three ships which sailed to America with Christopher Columbus in 1492 – see also NINA, PINTA

Santa's Grot·to /ˌ·· ˈ··/ n (in Britain) a place prepared at Christmas usu. in a big shop where children pay to go in and see a man dressed as Santa Claus who listens to their requests for presents and usu. gives them a little present himself

San·ti·a·go /ˌsæntiˈɑːgəʊ/ the capital and largest city of Chile, in S America

San·to Do·min·go /ˌsæntəʊ dəˈmɪŋgəʊ/ a former COLONY of Spain on the island of Hispaniola

São Pau·lo /saʊm ˈpaʊləʊ/ a city in SE Brazil, the largest city in S America and Brazil's financial and industrial centre

São To·mé /saʊn təˈmeɪ/ an island off W Africa in the Gulf of Guinea; a former Portuguese colony; capital São Tomé; population 116,000 (1989)

sap¹ /sæp/ n **1** [U] the watery juice carrying food, chemical products, etc., through a plant **2** [C] infml, esp. AmE a stupid person likely to be tricked or treated unfairly: *Didn't you know I was joking, you sap?* **3** [C] AmE a COSH

sap² v -pp- [T] **1** to weaken or destroy, esp. during a long time: *Her long illness gradually sapped her strength.* **2** to hit with a sap (3)

sa·pi·ent /ˈseɪpiənt/ adj lit wise and full of deep knowledge – ~ly adv —ence n [U]

sap·ling /ˈsæplɪŋ/ n a young tree

sap·per /ˈsæpəʳ/ n BrE a soldier whose job is doing digging and building work

sap·phire /ˈsæfaɪəʳ/ n [C;U] a precious stone of a transparent bright blue colour

Sap·pho /ˈsæfəʊ/ an ancient Greek poet remembered for poems about love. She is esp. admired today by LESBIANS. —**Sapphic** adj

sap·py /ˈsæpi/ adj **1** full of SAP¹ (1) **2** AmE infml silly; foolish

sap·wood /ˈsæpwʊd/ n [U] the younger outer wood in a tree, which is lighter and softer than the HEARTWOOD

sar·a·band , -bande /ˈsærəbænd/ n (a piece of music for) a court dance of the 17th–18th centuries

Sar·a·cen /ˈsærəsən/ n a name for a Muslim in former times, esp. the time of the CRUSADES

Sar·a·je·vo /ˌsærəˈjeɪvəʊ/ a city in Bosnia-Hercegovina, known esp. because the murder there of Archduke Franz Ferdinand started the First World War in 1914. It is now the capital city of Bosnia.

Sa·ra Lee /ˌseərə ˈliː/ tdmk an American maker of PROCESSED FOODS, best known for its frozen sweet foods

Sa·ran Wrap /səˈræn ræp/ n [U] tdmk AmE for CLINGFILM

Sa·ra·wak /səˈrɑːwək/ a state of Malaysia in NW Borneo, which used to be a British PROTECTORATE

sar·cas·m /ˈsɑːkæzəm‖ˈsɑːr-/ n [U] speaking or writing using expressions which clearly mean the opposite to what is felt, esp. in order to be unkind or offensive in an amusing way: *She was an hour late. "Good of you to come," he said with heavy/withering sarcasm.* —compare IRONY

sar·cas·tic /sɑːˈkæstɪk‖sɑːr-/ adj using or marked by sarcasm – ~ally /kli/ adv : *"How kind of you," she said sarcastically when he let the door slam in her face.*

sar·coph·a·gus /sɑːˈkɒfəgəs‖sɑːrˈkɑː-/ n -gi /gaɪ/ or -guses a usu. decorated stone box for a dead body, as used in ancient times

sar·dine /sɑːˈdiːn◂‖ˌsɑːr-/ n **1** a young small fish, esp. the PILCHARD, cooked fresh or preserved in oil and packed in flat tins **2 like sardines** infml packed or crowded very tightly together: *The commuters were packed into the train like sardines (in a can).*

Sar·din·i·a /sɑːˈdɪniə‖sɑːr-/ an island in the Mediterranean Sea, south of Corsica and west of Italy. It is an area of Italy with some self-government.

sar·don·ic /sɑːˈdɒnɪk‖sɑːrˈdɑːnɪk/ adj seeming to regard oneself as too important to consider a matter, person, etc., seriously; full of SCORN: *a sardonic smile* – ~ally /kli/ adv

sarge /sɑːdʒ‖sɑːrdʒ/ n infml for SERGEANT: *Come over here, sarge!*

Sar·gent /ˈsɑːdʒənt‖ˈsɑːr-/, **John Singer** (1856–1925) an American artist who is remembered esp. for his paintings of people

Sargent, Sir Malcolm (1895–1967) an English musician who directed the playing of several British ORCHESTRAS

sa·ri , saree /ˈsɑːri/ n a dress consisting of a length of light cloth wrapped gracefully round the body, worn esp. by Hindu women

Sark /sɑːk‖sɑːrk/ one of the Channel Islands between England and France, politically part of Britain

sar·ky /ˈsɑːki‖ˈsɑːr-/ adj BrE infml for SARCASTIC

sar·nie /ˈsɑːni‖ˈsɑːr-/ n BrE infml for SANDWICH

sa·rong /səˈrɒŋ‖səˈrɔːŋ, səˈrɑːŋ/ n a loose skirt consisting of a length of cloth wrapped round the waist, as worn by Malayan women and men

sarsa·pa·ril·la /ˌsɑːspəˈrɪlə, ˌsɑːsəpə-‖ˌsæspə-, ˌsɑːrspə-/ n [U] a drink flavoured with SASSAFRAS

sar·to·ri·al /sɑːˈtɔːriəl‖sɑːr-/ adj [A] fml or humor concerning (the making of) men's clothes: *a man of great sartorial elegance* (=neatly and stylishly dressed) – ~ly adv

Sar·tre /ˈsɑːtrə‖ˈsɑːrtrə/, **Jean-Paul** /ʒɒn pɔːl‖ʒɑːn-/ (1905–80) French PHILOSOPHER and writer of books and plays. He is best known for his writings on EXISTENTIALISM.

SAS /ˌes eɪ ˈes/ [the + sing./pl. v] Special Air Service; a small unit in the British Army which is specially trained to work against people carrying out military attacks on those in power in a country

SASE /ˌes eɪ es ˈiː/ AmE self-addressed, stamped envelope; an envelope on which one writes one's own address and stamps for it to be posted to one: *Send $5 and a large SASE to receive our hamburger recipe book.* —compare S.A.E.

sash¹ /sæʃ/ n a beltlike length of cloth worn round the waist as part of a garment, or (in ceremonial dress and usu. as a mark of some honour) over one shoulder

sash² n a frame into which sheets of glass are fixed to form part of a window, door, etc.

sa·shay /sæˈʃeɪ/ v [I+adv/prep] AmE infml often humor (of a person) to move or go, esp. smoothly or easily

sash win·dow /ˈ· ˌ··/ n a window of two sashes which opens by sliding one up or down behind or in front of the other. The sashes are connected to weights inside the frame by a **sash cord** so that they do not fall down; this type of window is not used in modern buildings. – compare CASEMENT WINDOW

Sas·katch·e·wan /səˈskætʃəwən/ a PROVINCE in Canada, bordering the US on the south

sass¹ /sæs/ n, v AmE infml for SAUCE¹ (2)

sass² v AmE to show disrespect through speech to (a parent, teacher, etc.): *Don't you sass me, young lady!*

sas·sa·fras /ˈsæsəfræs/ n [C;U] the dried outer covering of the root of) a small Asian and N American tree

Sas·se·nach /ˈsæsənæk/ n ScotE usu. derog an English person: *Did you hear that some Sassenachs have bought that house down the road?*

sas·sy /ˈsæsi/ adj AmE **1** (of a child) disrespectful to someone in authority **2** apprec (of a woman) lively and bold; SAUCY

sat /sæt/ past tense & participle of SIT

Sat. written abbrev. for: Saturday

SAT /ˌes eɪ ˈtiː/ the Scholastic Aptitude Test; a two-part examination which must be taken by all students who wish to attend US universities. The PSATs, (the first tests) are usually taken during a student's JUNIOR year in HIGH SCHOOL; these results are made available to colleges and universities. Students in their SENIOR year take the SATs, and have the results sent to the colleges they hope to attend. Universities consider the results of the test (**SAT scores** or **SATs**) to help them decide which students will be offered a place. A perfect result is 1600, or 800 for the VERBAL test., 800 for the math (MATHEMATICS) test. —see also PSAT and see extra information on page 408

Sa·tan /ˈseɪtn/ esp. fml or tech **1** the Devil, esp. considered as the chief evil power or as God's opponent **2 Get thee behind me, Satan** phrase from the Bible do not encourage me to do something wrong

sa·tan·ic /sə'tænɪk/ *adj* **1** *esp. lit* extremely cruel or evil **2** of satanism: *satanic rites* —see also DARK SATANIC MILLS − − **ally** /kli/ *adv*

sat·an·is·m /'seɪtənɪzəm/ *n* [U] (*often cap.*) the worship of the Devil −−**ist** *adj, n*

satch·el /'sætʃəl/ *n old-fash* a small bag of strong cloth or leather, usu. with a band for carrying over the shoulder: *He carried his books in his school satchel.*

sate /seɪt/ *v* [T (**with**) *usu. pass.*] *fml* to satisfy with more than enough of something, esp. something bad: *Still not sated with killing, the invaders murdered thousands more of the inhabitants.*

sa·teen /sə'tiːn/sæ-/ *n* [U] shiny cotton cloth made to look like SATIN

sat·el·lite /'sætₔlaɪt/ *n* **1** a body in space that moves round a larger one, esp. a PLANET: *The moon is a satellite of the Earth.* **2** a man-made object intended to move around the Earth, moon, etc., for some purpose: *the launch of a communications and weather satellite* | *The broadcast came from America by/via satellite.* **3** something, esp. a country, that is controlled by or depends on something else −compare CLIENT STATE

satellite dish /'··· ¸·/ also **dish** − *n* an object like a dish which is fixed to the outside of a house where people wish to receive satellite television

satellite earth sta·tion /¸··· '· ¸··/ *n* a station on the ground that receives radio or television signals from a station above the earth and sends them out to the local area

satellite television /¸··· '····, ¸··· ·'··/ also **satellite TV** /¸··· ¸· '·/− *n* [U] the broadcasting of television programmes over a wide area by the use of a satellite in space. *Satellite Television in Britain has five stations of which BSkyB is the largest.* −see also CABLE TELEVISION, DBS

sa·ti·ate /'seɪʃieɪt/ *v* [T *usu. pass.*] *fml* to satisfy (esp. physical needs) fully, esp. too fully: *We sat back, satiated after our huge meal.*

sa·ti·e·ty /sə'taɪəti/ *n* [U] *fml* the state of being (too much) filled or satisfied

sat·in /'sætₔn/ *n* [U] a very fine smooth cloth mainly of silk, which is shiny on the front and dull on the back: *satin slippers* −see also SATINY

sat·in·wood /'sætₔnwʊd/ *n* [C;U] (the very hard smooth wood of) an East Indian tree, used esp. in making beautiful furniture

sat·in·y /'sætₔni/ *adj* very pleasantly smooth, shiny, and soft: *satiny skin*

sat·ire /'sætaɪə⁻/ *n* [C (**on**);U] (a work of) literature, theatre, etc., intended to show the foolishness or evil of some person, organization, or practice in an amusing way: *His new play is a satire on the fashion industry.* −compare PARODY¹ (1)

sa·tir·i·cal /sə'tɪrɪkəl/ also **sa·tir·ic** /sə'tɪrɪk/− *adj* using or being satire: *satirical remarks* − − **ly** /kli/ *adv*

sat·ir·ize also **-ise** *BrE* /'sætₔraɪz/ *v* [T] to use satire against: *a play satirizing the fashion industry*

sat·is·fac·tion /¸sætₔs'fækʃən/ *n* **1** [C;U (**at, with**)] (something that gives) a feeling of happiness or pleasure: *Being able to work with children is one of the greatest satisfactions of this job.* | *We can look back with satisfaction on a job well done.* −opposite **dissatisfaction** **2** [U (**of**)] *fml* fulfilment of a need, desire, etc.: *the satisfaction of public demand* **3** [U] *fml* the condition of being completely persuaded; certainty: *It has been proved* **to my satisfaction** (=I am now certain) *that you are telling the truth.* **4** [U] *fml* **a** something that makes a person feel that damage done to his/her honour has been removed: *I got the satisfaction of finally being credited with the ideas he said were his.* **b** the chance to defend one's honour, esp. (in former times) by fighting a DUEL: *I demand satisfaction!*

sat·is·fac·to·ry /¸sætₔs'fæktəri◂/ *adj* good enough to be pleasing, or for a particular purpose, rule, standard, etc.: *He could not provide a satisfactory excuse for his absence.*| *Of all the pens he tried, only one was satisfactory.* | *Sales are up 20% from last year; that's very satisfactory.* − opposite **unsatisfactory** −−**rily** *adv*

sat·is·fy /'sætₔsfaɪ/ *v* [T *not in progressive forms*] **1** to please (someone), esp. by giving them enough: *We offered them £100, then £150, then £200, but they still weren't satisfied.* | *Some people are very hard to satisfy.* | *OK, I've done everything you asked; now are you satisfied?* | *They asked for champagne, but I think they'd* **be satisfied with sparkling wine.** (=would accept it as being good enough) | *a satisfied smile* −opposite **dissatisfy** **2** to be or give enough for; fulfil (a need, desire, etc.) of (someone): *Just to satisfy my curiosity, how much did you pay for your car?* | *He satisfied the examiner.* (=he passed his examination) **3** *fml* to be correct or good enough for (a demand, rule, standard, etc.); meet: *You can't vote until you have satisfied all the formal conditions.* | *x=2 satisfies the equation x²=4.* **4** [(**of**) *often pass.*] to persuade completely; cause to no longer feel doubt: *I was unable to satisfy them of the truth of my story.* [+*obj*+(*that*)] *The police are satisfied that their witness is telling the truth.* −see also SELF-SATISFIED

sat·is·fy·ing /'sætₔsfaɪ-ɪŋ/ *adj* giving satisfaction: *a satisfying meal* (=with enough food) | *It's a very satisfying feeling when you've done a good job.* − − **ly** *adv*

sat·su·ma /sæt'suːmə/ *n esp. BrE* a small seedless orange-like fruit

sat·u·rate /'sætʃəreɪt/ *v* [T (**with**) *often pass.*] **1** to put as much liquid as possible into; make completely wet: *His shirt was saturated with/in blood.* **2c** to fill completely so that no more can be held: *They saturated the area with police to prevent any trouble.* | *The market for houses is saturated.* (=there are too many houses for sale, and not enough buyers) **3** *tech* to put as much of a solid substance as possible into (a chemical SOLUTION)

saturated fat /¸sætʃəreɪtₔd 'fæt/ *n* a fat with a particular kind of chemical structure. Saturated fats are usu. solid at room temperature, such as those found in meats, milk, cream, butter, and cheese. It is thought that eating a lot of these fats can lead to a high CHOLESTEROL level in the blood. −compare POLYUNSATURATED

sat·u·ra·tion /¸sætʃə'reɪʃən/ *n* [U] **1** the act of saturating or state of being saturated **2** extremely heavy military force used against an enemy: *The airforce commander ordered* **saturation bombing** *of the area.* **3** *tech* (of a colour) freedom from mixture with white

saturation point /···'·· ·/ *n* [S;U] a point beyond which further things cannot be accepted, added, contained, etc.: *The number of summer tourists in the area had reached saturation point.*

Sat·ur·day /'sætədi‖ ər /(*written abbrev.* **Sat.**) *n* [C;U] the SIXTH day of the week, between Friday and Sunday.

▶ CULTURAL NOTE Although some people work on Saturdays most office workers do not and use Saturday for shopping and other necessary jobs in the house or outside. Some people also play or watch sport on Saturday and a lot of people go out to the cinema or for a meal, etc. on Saturday night: *I always visit my Mum on Saturdays/on a Saturday because I'm working during the week.* | *Many sports matches are played on Saturdays.* | *He'll arrive on Saturday.* | *(BrE infml & AmE) He'll arrive Saturday.* | *It happened on Saturday morning.* | *She left last Saturday.* | *We play tennis on Saturdays.* | *My birthday is on a Saturday this year.* −see DAY (CULTURAL NOTE)◀

Saturday girl /'··· ¸·/ *n BrE* a girl or young woman who works in a shop only on a Saturday when the shop is busy

Saturday Night Fe·ver /¸··· · '··/ a film made in 1977 with John Travolta. The music and clothing in the film are now often considered to be typical of the 1970s. −see colour picture on page 685

Saturday Night Live /¸sætədi naɪt 'laɪv ‖ -tər-/ a US television programme which began in the 1970s and became known for its COMEDY and unusual performances. Many well-known entertainers started their professional lives on this programme.

Saturday night spe·cial /¸··· · '··/ *n AmE* a HANDGUN of a kind easily available in the US, and often used in crimes

Sat·urn /'sætən‖-ərn/ **1** the PLANET sixth in order from the sun, and surrounded by large rings of matter floating in space −see picture at SOLAR SYSTEM **2** in Roman MYTHOLOGY, the father of Zeus and god of AGRICULTURE

sat·ur·na·li·a /¸sætə'neɪliə‖-tər-/ *n* **-lias** *or* **-lia** /liə/ *lit* an occasion on which people enjoy themselves in a wild exciting way; ORGY

sat·ur·nine /'sætənaɪn‖-ər-/ *adj esp. lit* sad and solemn, often in a threatening way

sat·yr /'sætə⁻/ *n* **1** (in ancient Greek literature) a god usu.

represented as half human and half goat —compare FAUN
2 *lit* a man with very strong sexual desires

sauce¹ /sɔːs/ n **1** [C;U] a quite thick usu. cooked liquid put on or eaten with food: *The prawns were served in a delicious sauce.* | *I love ice cream with chocolate sauce.* | *tomato|apple sauce* —see also TARTAR SAUCE, WHITE SAUCE, WORCESTER SAUCE **2** [S;U] *BrE*‖**sass** *AmE infml*— rude, but often harmless, disrespectful talk, for example to a parent, teacher, etc.; CHEEK: *None of your sauce, my girl!* | *He told me I was old enough to be his mother. What a sauce!* —see also SAUCY **3 what's sauce for the goose (is sauce for the gander)** *BrE*‖**what's good for the goose is good for the gander** *AmE*— if one person (esp. female) is allowed to behave in a certain way, then so is the other person (esp. male)

sauce² *v BrE*‖**sass** *AmE*— [T] *infml* to speak rudely to (a parent, teacher, etc.)

sauce boat /'· ·/ n see BOAT¹ (3)

sauce·pan /'sɔːspæn, -pən/ n a deep usu. round metal cooking pot with a handle and usu. a lid —see picture at PAN

sau·cer /'sɔːsər/ n a small plate with edges curving upwards, for putting a cup on —see also FLYING SAUCER

sauc·y /'sɔːsi/ adj infml **1** *BrE*‖**sassy** *AmE*— harmlessly, and perhaps amusingly, disrespectful **2** producing sexual interest in an amusing way; RISQUE: *saucy postcards* (=with pictures containing jokes about sex) **—ily** adv **—iness** n [U]

Sau·di /'saʊdi/ n a person who comes from or whose parents come from Saudi Arabia —**Saudi** adj

Saudi A·ra·bi·a /ˌ·· ·'····/ an oil producing country in SW Asia, occupying most of the Arabian PENINSULA; capital Riyadh; population 14,435,000 (1989) —**Saudi Arabian** /ˌ·· ·'····ˑ/ adj

sau·er·kraut /'saʊəkraʊt‖-ər-/ n [U] a German dish made from cut-up CABBAGE allowed to become sour by keeping it in salt

sau·na /'saʊnə, 'sɔːnə‖'saʊnə/ also **sauna bath** /'·· ·/— n (a period of sitting or lying in) a room that is specially heated to high temperatures, esp. by steam from burning wood. It is thought to be good for one's health. — compare TURKISH BATH

Saun·ders /'sɔːndəz‖-dərz/, **Er·nest** /'ɜːnɪst‖'ɜːr-/ (1935–) a wealthy British businessman who was put in prison for THEFT (=stealing) and other charges in 1990, but was let out before finishing his sentence because he appeared to be suffering from a mental illness —see also GUINNESS AFFAIR

Saunders, Jen·ni·fer /'dʒenɪfər/ (1957–) a British actress and COMEDIENNE probably best known for her appearances with another comedienne, Dawn French, esp. in the television show *French and Saunders*

saun·ter /'sɔːntər/ v [I+adv/prep] to walk in an unhurried way, and esp. in a CONFIDENT manner —**saunter** n [S]

saus·age /'sɒsɪdʒ‖'sɔː-/ n [C;U] a mixture of fresh or preserved meat with SPICES, and sometimes bread-like materials, in a tube of thin animal skin, for cooking and serving whole or for eating as cut-off pieces: *pork sausages* | *A kilo of garlic sausage, please.* | *He stuffed the chicken with sausage meat.* —see also LIVER SAUSAGE

sausage dog /'·· ·/ n BrE infml for DACHSHUND

sausage roll /ˌ·· '·/ n BrE a small piece of sausage meat in a tubelike covering of pastry

sau·té¹ /'saʊteɪ‖saʊ'teɪ/ v **-téed** or **-téd** /'teɪd/ [T] to cook quickly in a little hot oil or fat: *Sauté the onions for five minutes.*

sauté² adj [A] sautéed: *sauté potatoes*

Sau·ternes esp. *BrE* ‖ **-terne** *AmE* /saʊ'tɜːn‖-ɜːrn/ n [U] a sweet gold-coloured French wine

sav·age¹ /'sævɪdʒ/ adj **1** forcefully cruel or violent; fierce; FEROCIOUS: *a savage dog* | *savage anger* | *Today's newspapers made a savage attack on the unions for their refusal to negotiate.* **2** [A] *old-fash or derog* uncivilized; PRIMITIVE: *savage tribes* — **~ly** adv — **~ness** n [U]

savage² v [T] (esp. of an animal) to attack and bite fiercely: *She was savaged by a mad dog.*

savage³ n old-fash or derog a member of an uncivilized or undeveloped tribe or group: *These civilizations flourished while Europeans were still savages living in caves.*

sav·ag·e·ry /'sævɪdʒəri/ n [C usu. pl.;U] (an act of) savage

behaviour; cruelty: *He beat his wife with great savagery.* | *the savageries of war*

sa·van·na, **-nah** /sə'vænə/ n [C;U] (an open flat area of) grassy land in a warm part of the world

sav·ant /'sævənt‖sə'vɑːnt, sæ-/ n lit a person having great knowledge of some subject

save¹ /seɪv/ v **1** [T (**from**)] to make safe from danger, harm, or destruction: *"He's fallen into the water!" "Don't worry; I'll save him."* | *He saved his friend from drowning.* | *The surgeons fought to save her life.* | *The sudden fall in interest rates saved the company from bankruptcy.* | *They hoped to save their marriage* (=prevent it from failing) *by having another baby.* | (fig.) *You saved my life* (=helped me when I was in a very difficult situation) *by lending me that £1000.* **2** [I (UP, **for**)] to keep and add to an amount of money for later use: *Children should learn to save.* | *We're saving (up) for a new car.* —see also SAVER, SAVINGS **3** [T] **a** to prevent or avoid the waste of (money, time, work, etc.): *It will save time if we go by car instead of walking.* | *You can save fuel if you drive at a regular speed.* | *energy-saving modern building methods* [+obj(i)+obj(d)] *If you buy the family-size box it will save you £1.* **b** [(**for**)] to keep for future use or enjoyment later: *He saved his strength for the end of the race.* | *If there is any food left over, save it for later.* [+obj(i)+obj(d)] *Will you save me a seat on the bus?* | (fig.) *You can save your apologies; I don't want them!* **4** [T (**from**)] to make unnecessary (for): *A brush with a long handle will save you from having to bend down to clean the floor.* [+obj(i)+obj(d)] *Will you go to the shop for me? It'll save me a trip.* [(+obj)+v-ing] *If you lend me a pound, it will save (me) having to go to the bank.* | *a labour-saving gadget* **5** [T] (esp. of a GOALKEEPER) to stop (a shot or a ball) from going into the net —see also SAVE² **6 save one's skin|neck|bacon** *infml* to escape from a serious danger: *He lied in court to save his skin.* (=otherwise he might have been sent to prison, or punished by death) **7 save the day** to bring success when failure had seemed certain: *We thought we'd have to abandon the talks, but Sir Alfred saved the day by suggesting a compromise acceptable to both sides.* **8 to save one's life** (*usu. in negatives*) *infml* even with the greatest effort; at all: *I couldn't play the piano to save my life.* —see also FACE-SAVING

save on sthg. phr v [T] to avoid wasting: *We use a wood fire, to save on electricity.*

save² n (in football, HOCKEY, etc.) a quick action by the GOALKEEPER which prevents the opponents from making a point: *"Oh, good save!"* —see also SAVE¹ (5)

save³ also **saving**— prep fml or old use **1** except (for): *She answered all the questions save one.* | *I agree with you, save that you have got one or two facts wrong.* **2 saving your presence** without meaning any offence to you: *Saving your presence, I don't think the suggestion is very sensible.* —see BUT (USAGE)

sav·er /'seɪvər/ n **1** (*often in comb.*) something that prevents loss or waste: *Our new washing machine is a real time- and money-saver.* **2** esp. *BrE* a person who saves money, e.g. with a bank or BUILDING SOCIETY

Save the Chil·dren Fund /ˌ·· '·· ˌ·/ [the] a large international organization (a CHARITY) for the care of children, esp. in poor countries

Sav·ile /'sævɪl/, **Sir Jimmy** (1926–) a British television personality and presenter, originally of popular music. He was given his KNIGHTHOOD for raising very large amounts of money for CHARITY and had a well-known television programme called *Jim'll Fix It*.

Savile Row /ˌsævɪl 'raʊ◄/ a street in London, known as the centre of the fashionable men's clothing industry, esp. high quality suits

saving grace /ˌ·· '·/ n the one good thing that makes something acceptable: *It was an awful film — its saving grace was the beautiful photography.*

sav·ings /'seɪvɪŋz/ n [P] money saved, esp. in a bank

savings ac·count /'·· ·ˌ·/ n a bank account which earns INTEREST¹ (5) —compare DEPOSIT ACCOUNT

savings and loan as·so·ci·a·tion /ˌ·· · '· ···ˌ·/ also **S & L, thrift** n AmE for BUILDING SOCIETY —see also **S & L crisis**

savings bank /'·· ·/ n **1** a bank which offers accounts which earn INTEREST¹ (5) (esp. formerly) **2** a bank: *Trustee Savings Bank*

savings bond /'·· ·/ n a BOND¹ (3) sold by the US

government which can be exchanged after a fixed period of time for its cost with interest; they are often given as gifts, esp. to children

sa·viour *BrE* ‖ **-vior** *AmE* /ˈseɪvjəʳ/ *n* **1** [C] a person or thing that saves from danger or loss: *the saviour of his people* **2** [(the)] (*usu. cap.*) (in the Christian religion) Jesus Christ

sav·oir-faire /ˌsævwɑː ˈfeəʳ‖-ˈwɑːr-/ *n* [U] *Fr, apprec* the ability to do and say the proper and polite thing on every social occasion

sa·vo·ry /ˈseɪvəri/ *n* **1** [U] a plant used in cooking to add taste to meat, beans, etc. **2** [C] *AmE for* SAVOURY

sa·vour¹ *BrE* ‖ **-vor** *AmE* /ˈseɪvəʳ/ *v* [T] to enjoy slowly and purposefully: *She drank the wine slowly, savouring every drop.*

    savour of sth. *phr v* [T *no pass.*] to have a (slight) quality of; suggest: *They were suspicious of any law that savoured of more government control.*

savour² *BrE* ‖ **-vor** *AmE*– *n* [S;U] *rather fml* **1** [(of)] a taste or smell **2** (power to excite) interest: *Life seems to have lost most of its savour for him.*

sa·vour·y¹ *BrE* ‖ **-vory** *AmE* /ˈseɪvəri/ *adj* **1** pleasant or attractive in taste **2** [*usu. in negatives*] *fml* morally attractive or good; WHOLESOME: *This place doesn't have a very savoury reputation.* –opposite **unsavoury** **3** *BrE* (of a dish) having the taste of meat, cheese, vegetables, salt, etc., without sugar –opposite **sweet**

savoury² *BrE* ‖ **-vory** *AmE*– *n* a small salty dish, sometimes served at the end of a formal meal

sa·voy /səˈvɔɪ/ *n* a type of CABBAGE with curled leaves

Savoy [*the*] an expensive and fashionable hotel in London

sav·vy /ˈsævi/ *n* [U] *apprec sl* practical knowledge and ability; KNOW-HOW

saw¹ /sɔː/ *past tense of* SEE

saw² *n* a hand-driven or power-driven tool for cutting hard materials, having a thin flat blade with a row of V-shaped teeth on the edge –see picture at TOOL

saw³ *v* **sawed, sawn** /sɔːn/*esp. BrE* ‖ **sawed** *esp. AmE* [I;T] to cut with a saw: *That dead branch ought to be sawn off.* | *He sawed through a power cable by accident.* | *I sawed the logs up into little pieces.* | *She was busy sawing logs.* (=sawing a long piece of wood into logs) | (fig.) *He sawed at the loaf with a blunt bread knife.* (=pressing the knife backwards and forwards)

saw⁴ *n* a short well known saying (esp. in the phrase **old saw**)

saw·bones /ˈsɔːbəʊnz/ *n* **sawbones** *humor, esp. AmE* a doctor or SURGEON

saw·buck /ˈsɔːbʌk/ *n* *AmE infml* a $10 bill

saw·dust /ˈsɔːdʌst/ *n* [U] dust or very small pieces of wood made by a saw in cutting

saw·horse /ˈsɔːhɔːs‖-hɔːrs/ *n* a wooden frame to hold up something being sawn (SAW³)

saw·mill /ˈsɔːˌmɪl/ *n* a factory where logs are cut into boards by a power-driven saw

sawn-off shot·gun /ˌ· · ˈ··/ *BrE* ‖ **sawed-off shotgun** *AmE*– *n* a SHOTGUN with a short barrel, often carried as a weapon by criminals

Saw·yer /ˈsɔːjəʳ/, **Tom** the main character in *The Adventures of Tom Sawyer* by Mark Twain, who is a clever and daring boy but often in trouble. In one story Tom is given the job of whitewashing (WHITEWASH) a fence; he persuades his friends to do the work by making them think that he is having more fun than they are. His best friend is Huckleberry Finn. –see colour picture on page 1145

sax·i·frage /ˈsæksɪfreɪdʒ/ *n* [U] a small plant with bright flowers, growing esp. in rocky places

Sax·on /ˈsæksən/ *n* a member of the German group which came to live in England in the 5th century –**Saxon** *adj*

sax·o·phone /ˈsæksəfəʊn/ *also* **sax** /sæks/*infml*– *n* a metal musical instrument of the WOODWIND family, with a single REED, used mostly in JAZZ, military, and dance music –**phonist** /sækˈsɒfənɪst‖ˈsæksəfəʊnɪst/ *n*

say¹ /seɪ/ *v* **said** /sed/, *3rd person sing. present tense* **says** /sez/ **1** [T (**to**)] **a** to pronounce (a sound, word, etc.): *"What did you say?" "I said, 'You're standing on my toe!'"* | *She stood on my foot and didn't even say sorry!* | *You children must learn to say "please" and "thank you".* |

(fig.) *So I said to myself* (=thought) *"I wonder what she means".* **b** to pronounce (a formal set of words) aloud: *Have you said your prayers?* **2** [I *only in negatives and questions*;T] to express (a thought, intention, opinion, question, etc.) in words: *Don't believe anything he says.* | *"Why did she leave?" "I don't know – she didn't say."* [+(*that*)] *He says he's thirsty.* | *He said (that) he would like another drink.* | *It says in the instructions that you should mix it carefully first.* [+*obj*-] *Did she say how she got here? He's "Do you think it will rain?" "I should say so|not."* (=I think it will/will not.) | *"What's he going to do now?" "I'd rather not say."* (=I don't want to tell anyone.)| *"Who can say?"* (=I don't know.) **3** [T *often pass.*] to give as a general opinion; claim: *Well, you know what they say – blood's thicker than water.* (=this is a common saying or PROVERB) [+(*that*)] *They say* (=it is many people's opinion that) *there's going to be an election soon.* | *It's said that he's the richest man in the world.* [+*obj+to-v; pass.*] *He's said to be the richest man in the world.* **4** [T] to show; INDICATE: *What does your watch say?* | *The fact that she gave the money back says a lot about her honesty.* (=proves she is honest) [+(*that*)] *She was smiling but her eyes said she was unhappy.* **5** [T *usu. imperative*] to suppose; suggest; ASSUME: *Would you take an offer of, say* (=for example), *£500 for your car?* | *Can you come to dinner? Say, 7.30?* [+(*that*)] *(Let's) say (that) your plan fails; then what do we do?* **6** [T+*to-v; obj*; *not in progressive forms*] *infml* to direct or instruct someone: *She said to meet her at the station.* | *It says on the bottle to take a spoonful every four hours.* **7 do as I say, not as I do** a phrase used in criticizing people who order others to act in a particular way, but do not themselves act in this way: *The boss is so strict about us all keeping to the correct working hours, but he always leaves half an hour early–it's do as I say, not as I do.* **8 go without saying** to be clear; not need stating: *It goes without saying that our plans depend on the weather.* **9 having said that** in spite of what has just been said; NEVERTHELESS: *She didn't do a very good job, but having said that, I don't think I could have done any better.* **10 I say** *BrE infml* **a** (used for calling someone's attention): *I say, can you see anything up there?* **b** *old-fash* (a rather weak expression of interest, anger, etc.): *"My husband is ill today." "I say! I'm sorry to hear that."* **11 not to say** and almost; or perhaps even: *He sounded annoyed, not to say furious.* | *It would be foolish, not to say mad, to sell your car.* **12 say fairer (than that)** *BrE infml* to make a more generous statement or offer: *I'll give you £20 for it; I can't say fairer than that.* **13 say for oneself/for something** to offer as an excuse or as something in favour or defence: *You're late again! What have you got to say for yourself?* | *It was a strange idea, with very little to be said for it.* **14 Say no more!** *infml* Your/The meaning is very clear!: *"I saw him leaving her flat at 6.30 in the morning." "Say no more!"* **15 say no (to)** *infml* to refuse an offer (of): *I wouldn't say no to another drink.* (=I'd like one) **16 say someone nay** *lit or old use* to forbid someone: *If he wants to smoke in his own house, who can say him nay?* **17 say the word** *infml* to give one's approval or a signal for something to be done or started **18 say what you like** *infml* even though you may not agree: *Say what you like, I thought it was a marvellous film.* **19 say ˈwhen** (*usu. imperative*) *infml* to tell someone when to stop, esp. when they are pouring a drink

▷ USAGE The answer to "say when" is "When," but it is also acceptable to say "Stop", "That's enough, thank you," etc.◁

20 that is to say: a *also* **i.e.** *abbrev.*– expressed another (more exact) way: *Let's go back to the original plan, that is to say you go ahead by plane and I'll follow by car with the equipment.* **b** or at least: *He's coming; that's to say he promised to.* **21 to say nothing of** without even considering; not to mention (MENTION¹) (4): *Three people were badly hurt, to say nothing of the damage to the building.* **22 What do you say?** *infml* You'll agree, won't you?: *Let's go into business together; what do you say?* | *What do you say we go into business|to going into business together?* **23 when all is said and done** it must be remembered that: *When all's said and done, he's only a little kid still; don't expect too much too soon.* **24 you can say ˈthat again** *infml* (used for expressing strong agreement): *"It's hot today." "You can say that again!"* (=yes, it's extremely hot) **25 You don't say (so)!** *infml* (an expression of slight surprise, often used in a SARCASTIC way) **26 You said it!** *infml* **a** I did not want to say that, but I agree with you: *"It's wrong again, but then I was never any good at maths." "You said it!"* **b** *esp. AmE* You're right; I agree: *"Let's go home." "You said it! I'm tired."* —see also **can't say boo to a goose** (BOO¹), **say uncle** (UNCLE)

▷ USAGE Compare **say, tell,** and **inform. Say** is nearly always transitive and cannot have a person as its object: *He said, "I'm tired".* | *He said that he was tired.* | *He said a few words then sat down.* **Tell** is nearly always transitive and can have one object: *He told a funny story.* | *He told us about his adventures.* or two objects, one of which must be a person: *He told us a funny story.* **Inform** (*fml*) is always transitive and its object is always a person: *He informed us that he was tired.* Of these words, only **say** can be used with the actual words spoken: *He said, "Open the door",* and only **tell** can be used with commands: *He told me to open the door.* —see also SPEAK (USAGE), TALK (USAGE)◁

say² *n* [S;U (**in**)] **1** (a) power or right of (sharing in) acting or deciding: *The workpeople had no say in how their factory was run.* | *Haven't I got any say in where I sleep tonight?* **2 have/say one's say** *infml* to have/use the chance to say something, esp. to express one's opinion in a determined way: *He always has to have his say, even if he knows nothing about the subject.*

say³ *interj AmE infml* (used for expressing surprise or a sudden idea): *Say, haven't I seen you before somewhere?*

Say·ers /ˈseɪəz‖-ərz/, **Dor·o·thy** /ˈdɒrəθi‖ˈdɔː-/ **L** (1893–1957) English writer very well-known for her DE-TECTIVE stories which include the character Lord Peter Wimsey

say·ing /ˈseɪ-ɪŋ/ *n* a well-known wise statement: *"There's no smoke without fire",* **as the saying goes.** (=that is what people often say)

Sayle /seɪl/, **A·lex·ei** /əˈleksi/ (1952–) an actor, writer and COMEDIAN from Liverpool who appeared in the British television programme *The Young Ones* among other things

say-so /ˈ· ·/ *n* [(**on**) S (**of**)] *infml* **1** a personal statement without proof: *Why should I believe it just on your say-so?* (=because you have said it) **2** permission: *I was allowed to come home from hospital on the doctor's say-so.*

S-bend /ˈes bend/ *BrE‖***S-curve** *AmE— n* **1** a turn in the road in the shape of an "S", considered dangerous to drivers **2** a piece of waste pipe in the shape of an "S" which keeps bad smells out of a building

SC *written abbrev. for:* SOUTH CAROLINA

scab /skæb/ *n* **1** [C] a hard mass mainly of dried blood which forms on the skin over a cut or wound while it is getting better **2** [U] **a** any of various diseases causing hard spots on plants **b** scabies in animals **3** [C] *derog sl* a worker who works while others in the same workplace are on STRIKE² (1); BLACKLEG —compare STRIKEBREAKER

scab·bard /ˈskæbəd‖-ərd/ *n* a usu. leather or metal tube, for hanging from a belt, enclosing the blade of a sword, knife, etc.; SHEATH

scab·by /ˈskæbi/ *adj* **1** covered with scabs or diseased with scab or scabies **2** (esp. children's *sl* (of a person) nasty, unpleasant

sca·bies /ˈskeɪbiz/ *n* [U] a skin disease marked by scabs and an unpleasant itching (ITCH¹) sensation

sca·bi·ous /ˈskeɪbiəs/ *n* [U] a European plant with usu. light purple flowers

sca·brous /ˈskeɪbrəs/ *adj lit derog* unpleasant by association with improper or shocking subjects; RISQUE

scads /skædz/ *n* [P (**of**)] *AmE infml* large numbers or amounts: *There were scads of people at the concert.*

Sca·fell Pike /ˌskɔːfel ˈpaɪk/ a mountain in the Lake District, NW England, the highest in England

scaf·fold /ˈskæfəld, -fəʊld/ *n* **1** a structure built up from usu. metal poles and boards, esp. round a building being built, painted, or repaired, for workmen to stand on **2** (esp. in former times) a raised stage for the killing of criminals by hanging or by cutting off their heads: *to mount the scaffold* **3** *AmE for* CRADLE¹ (4)

scaf·fold·ing /ˈskæfəldɪŋ/ *n* [U] poles and boards (to be) built into a system of scaffolds

scag /skæg/ *n* [U] *sl for* HEROIN

sca·lar /ˈskeɪləʳ/ *adj, n tech* (of) a quantity that has size but no direction and is represented as a point on a SCALE¹ (1) —compare VECTOR (1)

scal·a·wag /ˈskæləwæg/ *n esp. AmE for* SCALLYWAG

scald¹ /skɔːld/ *v* [T] **1** to burn (skin) with hot liquid: *He scalded his tongue on/with the hot coffee.* | *They were scalded by steam from the burst pipe.* **2** *tech* to heat (esp. milk) until it is almost boiling

scald² *n* a skin burn from hot liquid or steam

scald·ing /ˈskɔːldɪŋ/ *adj* extremely hot: **scalding hot** *water* | (fig.) *The report was subjected to scalding criticism in the papers.*

scale¹ /skeɪl/ *n* **1** [C] a set of numbers or standards for measuring or comparing: *The force of the wind is measured on a standard scale of 0–12.* | *Where do secretaries come on the company's pay scale?* | *On a scale of one to ten, how do you rate his performance?* | *a long way down the scale* —see also SLIDING SCALE **2** [C] a set of marks, esp. numbers, on an instrument at exactly fixed distances apart, esp. for measuring: *a ruler with a metric scale* | *the scale on a barometer* **b** a piece of wood, plastic, etc., with such marks along the edge **3** [C;U] a rule or set of numbers comparing measurements on a map or model with actual measurements: *a scale of 1 inch to the mile* | *a scale of 1:25,000* | *The plans of the building were drawn precisely* **to scale.** (=showing all the parts in the same relationship to each other as the parts of the actual building) | *He built a* **scale model** *of the aircraft carrier.* (=exactly the same in all details, but much smaller) **4** [C;U] size or level in relation to other things or to what is usual: *a large-scale business operation* | *We are now seeing unemployment on an unprecedented scale.* | *Many companies are now expanding to benefit from* **economies of scale.** (=being able to produce things more cheaply by doing so in large quantities) **5** [C] a set of musical notes in order, upward or downward, and at fixed separations: *a scale in the key of A* (=with the note A for its base) | *A pianist must keep practising his scales.* **6** [C] *esp. AmE* SCALES —see also FULL-SCALE

scale² *n* **1** [C] any of the many small flat stiff pieces forming (part of) the outer body covering of some animals, esp. fish, snakes, etc. **2** [U] greyish material forming around the inside of hot water pipes, a pot in which water is boiled, etc.; FUR¹ (3) **3 the scales fell from my eyes** *lit or fml* I was suddenly able to see what had always been clear to others —see also SCALY

scale³ *v* [T] to remove the SCALES² (1) from: *Scale the fish before cooking them.* —see also DESCALE

scale⁴ *v* [T] **1** to climb up (something steep), esp. using equipment to help one: *The commandos scaled the cliff.* **2** [+*obj*+UP/DOWN] to increase or reduce, esp. by a fixed rate: *The company has begun to scale down its operations in Africa.*

scale⁵ *v* [L+*n*] *BrE infml* (esp. of a BOXER) to weigh (the stated amount)

sca·lene /ˈskeɪliːn/ *adj* [A] *tech* (of a TRIANGLE) having no sides equal in length —compare EQUILATERAL, ISOSCELES

scales /skeɪlz/ also **scale** *esp. AmE— n* [P] **1** a pair of pans for weighing an object by comparing it with a known weight; BALANCE: *Put it on/in the scales.* —see PAIR (USAGE) **2** a weighing machine: *bathroom scales* —see also **tip the scales** (TIP³), and see picture at KITCHEN

Scales, Dame Pru·nel·la /pruːˈnelə/ (1932–) an English actress known for her work on radio, television, and in theatre. She played John Cleese's wife, Sybil, in the British television SERIES *Fawlty Towers.*

scales of jus·tice /ˌ· · ˈ··/ [*the*+P] a pair of SCALES (1) used to represent JUSTICE —see colour picture on page 751

scal·lion /ˈskæljən/ *n AmE for* SPRING ONION

scal·lop¹, **scol-** /ˈskɒləp‖ˈskɑː-/ *n* **1** a sea animal (a MOLLUSC) that is used for food and lives inside a pair of large wavy-edged shells that can be used as little dishes **2** (any of) a row of small curves forming an edge or pattern: *a dress with scallops round the neck*

scallop², **scol-** *v* [T] **1** to cut or make scallops in (an edge or line): *a dress with a scalloped neck* **2** *AmE* to bake in a cheesy or creamy liquid: *scalloped potatoes*

scal·ly·wag /ˈskæliwæg/ *esp. BrE* ‖ usu. **scalawag** *AmE— n usu. humor* a trouble-making or dishonest person, esp. a child

scalp[1] /skælp/ n **1** the skin on the top of the human head, where hair grows **2** *infml* a clear mark of victory over the stated person: *He's out for the minister's scalp.* (=wants him to admit defeat and leave his job)

scalp[2] v [T] **1** (esp. of a Native American in former times) to cut off the scalp of (a dead enemy) as a mark of victory **2** *AmE infml* to buy and then resell at very high prices for profit: *He'd been scalping theatre tickets.*

scal·pel /'skælpəl/ n a small sharp knife used by doctors in operations, for fine work on models, by some kinds of artist

scalp·er /'skælpər/ n *AmE for* TOUT[2]

scal·y /'skeɪli/ adj covered with SCALES[2] (1) or SCALE[2] (2) —**iness** n [U]

scam /skæm/ n sl a clever and dishonest plan or course of action

scamp /skæmp/ n *infml* a trouble-making but usu. playful child: *Come back here with my hat, you young scamp!*

scam·per /'skæmpər/ v [I+adv|prep] to run quickly taking short steps, usu. playfully or (esp. of a small animal) when frightened: *Giggling, the children scampered back into the house.*

scam·pi /'skæmpi/ n [U] (a dish made from) large PRAWNS

scan[1] /skæn/ v -nn- **1** [T (for)] to examine closely using a regular plan or fixed method, esp. making a search for something: *We scanned|The radar scanned the sky for enemy planes.* **2** [T] to look at quickly without careful reading, often looking for a particular thing: *I scanned the newspaper while I waited for the train.* | *She scanned the list of names to see if hers was on it.* **3** [I;T] *tech* **a** (of poetry) to have a regular pattern of repeated beats according to fixed rules **b** to find or show such a pattern in (a poem or line of poetry) —see also SCANSION **4** [T] *tech* (of a beam of ELECTRONS) to be directed to (a surface) so as to cover it with lines which are close together, as in the making of a television picture —see also SCANNER

scan[2] n an act of scanning: *The doctors gave him an ultrasonic brain scan.* | *to conduct a scan of the adult population*

scan·dal /'skændl/ n **1** [C] (something that causes) a public feeling that something is improper or shocking: *The minister is at the centre of a recent scandal over revelations about his financial interests.* | *the Westminster sex scandal that broke* (=became public knowledge) *in the mid-1980s* | (fig.) *The price of petrol is a scandal!* (=is much too high) **2** [U (**about**)] true or false talk which brings harm, shame, or disrespect to someone: *I'm not interested in scandal about the neighbours!* —see also SCANDALOUS

scan·dal·ize also **-ise** *BrE* /'skændəl-aɪz/ v [T *usu. pass.*] to offend (someone's) feelings of what is right or proper: *I was absolutely scandalized to hear that the council has demolished that lovely old building.*

scan·dal·mon·ger /'skændəl‚mʌŋgər‖-‚mɑ:ŋ-, -‚mʌŋ-/ n *derog* a person who spreads scandal

scan·dal·ous /'skændələs/ adj offensive to feelings of what is right or proper: *It's scandalous that you still haven't been paid.* — ~**ly** adv

Scan·di·na·vi·a /‚skændɪ'neɪviə/ **1** an area of N Europe consisting of Norway, Sweden, Denmark, and usu. Finland and Iceland **2** the piece of land in N Europe consisting of Norway and Sweden

Scan·di·na·vi·an /‚skændɪ'neɪviən◂/ n a person who comes from, or whose parents come from Scandinavia — **Scandinavian** adj

scan·ner /'skænər/ n an instrument for scanning (SCAN[1] (1,4)): *Using a scanner, we can look at the unborn foetus in the womb.*

scan·sion /'skænʃən/ n [U] (the act of showing) the way a line of a poem SCANS[1] (3a)

scant /skænt/ adj hardly enough: *He paid scant attention to what was said.*

scant·y /'skænti/ adj hardly (big) enough in size or quantity; almost too small, few, etc.; MEAGRE: *a scanty breakfast* —**ily** adv : *photos of* **scantily-clad** *girls* (=with hardly any clothes on) —**iness** n [U]

Sca·pa Flow /‚skɑ:pə 'fləʊ/ an area of sea between two of the Orkney Islands in N Scotland. It was an important naval base during the First World War and 71 German warships which had surrendered (SURRENDER) were sunk here.

scape·goat /'skeɪpgəʊt/ n a person or thing taking the blame for the fault of others, often unwillingly —compare WHIPPING BOY

scap·u·la /'skæpjʊlə/ n *med for* SHOULDER BLADE —see picture at SKELETON

scar[1] /skɑ:r/ n a mark remaining on the skin or on an organ from a wound, cut, etc.: *That cut will leave a nasty scar.* | *Scar tissue began to form over the wound.* | (fig.) *The country still bears the scars of the recent war.*

scar[2] v -**rr**- [T] to mark with a scar: (fig.) *The terrible experience had scarred him for life.* (=had a deep and long-lasting effect on him)

scar·ab /'skærəb/ n **1** also **scarab bee·tle** /'··‚··/— a large black BEETLE **2** a representation of this, often in a small stone, used in ancient Egypt for decoration and as a sign of life after death

Scar·bor·ough /'skɑ:bərə‖'skɑ:rbɜ:rəʊ/ a town on the NE coast of England which is a popular place for people from Yorkshire, esp. WORKING-CLASS people, to go for the day or for their holidays

scarce[1] /skeəs‖skeərs/ adj **1** not much or many compared with what is wanted; hard to find; not common: *Good fruit is scarce in winter, and costs a lot.* —compare COMMON[1] (1) **2** **make oneself scarce** *infml* to go away or keep away, esp. in order to avoid trouble —see RARE (USAGE)

scarce[2] adv lit hardly; scarcely: *I could scarce believe my eyes.*

scarce·ly /'skeəsli‖'skeər-/ adv **1** hardly; almost not: *Scarcely had he arrived when he had to leave again.* | *She spoke scarcely a word of English|scarcely spoke a word of English.* **2** (almost) certainly not: *"You should have gone in." "Well, I could scarcely have gone in there while they were undressing, could I!"* —see HARDLY (USAGE)

scar·ci·ty /'skeəsɪti‖'skeər-/ n [C;U (**of**)] a state of being scarce; lack: *the present scarcity of labour*

scare[1] /skeər/ v **1** [T] to cause sudden fear to; frighten: *Don't let the noise scare you; it's only the wind.* **2** [T+obj+adv|prep] to cause to go or do something by frightening: *If you make a noise you'll scare off the animals.* | *The high price is scaring away possible buyers.* | *The announcement scared many politicians into voting for the change in the law.* **3** [I] to be frightened: *I don't scare easily, you know!* **4** **scare the hell/shit out of** *taboo* to frighten extremely —see also SCARED, SCARY

scare sthg. **up** phr v [T (**from**)] *infml, esp. AmE* to make from things that are hard to find or not easy to use: *I'll see if I can scare up a meal from the scraps of food in the kitchen.*

scare[2] n **1** [S] a sudden feeling of fear: *What a scare you gave me, appearing suddenly in the dark!* **2** [C] a usu. mistaken or unreasonable public fear: *There's been quite a scare about the possible side effects of this new drug.* | *a recent series of bomb scares*

scare[3] adj [A] intended to cause fear: *The newspapers have been printing scare stories about a possible war.*

scare·crow /'skeəkrəʊ‖'skeər-/ n **1** an object (often old clothes hung on sticks) in the shape of a person, set up in a field to keep birds away from crops **2** *infml, usu. humor derog* a very (thin and) untidy-looking person

scarecrow

scared /skeəd‖skeərd/ adj **1** [(**of**)] full of fear; frightened: *their scared faces* | *I'm scared of snakes.* | *"Why won't you come on the trip? Are you scared?"* [+to-v(that)] *I'm scared to fly in a plane|scared that it might crash.* **2** **to be scared stiff/silly/(half) to death/out of one's wits** to be extremely frightened —see FRIGHTENED (USAGE)

scared·y cat /'skeədi kæt‖'skeər-/ n *infml derog* (used esp. by children) a scared person

scare·mon·ger /'skeə‚mʌŋgər‖'skear‚mɑ:ŋ-, -‚mʌŋ-/ n *derog* a person who spreads reports intended to cause a public SCARE; ALARMIST

scare sto·ry /'·‚··/ n a story in the newspapers or which people are telling others which makes people worried about something which is not really worrying: *All this stuff in the papers about the dangers of eating eggs, they're just scare stories, aren't they?*

scare·y /ˈskeəri/ adj SCARY

scarf¹ /skɑːf‖skɑːrf/ n **scarfs** or **scarves** /skɑːvz‖skɑːrvz/ a piece of cloth, usu. long and narrow or sometimes (esp. for women) square, for wearing round the neck, head, or shoulders for warmth or decoration

scarf² vt [I (up/down)] AmE infml eat eagerly; SCOFF³: *We scarfed down three pizzas after the movie.*

Scar·gill /ˈskɑːgɪl‖ˈskɑːr-/, **Arthur** (1938–) the president of the British National Union of Mineworkers, often in disagreement with the Conservative government for his strong defence of miners' rights, esp. during the STRIKE² (1) of 1984–1985

scar·i·fy /ˈskeərˌfaɪ, ˈskærˌfaɪ/ v [T] **1** to break up and loosen the surface of (a road or field) with a pointed tool **2** med to make small cuts on (an area of skin) with a sharp knife **3** lit to attack fiercely in words —**·fication** /ˌskeərˌfɪˈkeɪʃən, ˌskær-/ n [U]

Scar·lat·ti /skɑːˈlæti‖skɑːr-/, **Do·men·i·co** /dɒˈmenɪkəʊ‖ dəʊ-/ (1685–1757) an Italian writer of music, mainly for the HARPSICHORD, for which he wrote over 500 pieces

scar·let /ˈskɑːlɪt‖-ɑːr-/ adj having a very bright red colour: *His face was scarlet with embarrassment.* —**scarlet** n [U]

scarlet fe·ver /ˌ··ˈ··/ also **scar·la·ti·na** /ˌskɑːləˈtiːnə‖ -ɑːr-/— n [U] a serious and easily-spread disease, esp. of children, marked by a painful throat and red spots on the skin

Scarlet Let·ter /ˌ··ˈ··/, **The** a book by Nathaniel Hawthorne in which the main female character must wear a large red letter A for being an ADULTERESS

scarlet pim·per·nel /ˌ·· ˈ···/ n a PIMPERNEL with bright red flowers

Scarlet Pimpernel, The a book by Baroness Orczy about an Englishman who, using a number of DISGUISEs, helped people from noble families escape from France during the REVOLUTION. He took a flower, the scarlet pimpernel, as his sign and was therefore called The Scarlet Pimpernel. —see also **they seek him here** (SEEK)

scarlet wom·an /ˌ·· ˈ··/ n old-fash, euph or humor a woman who has sexual relations with many different partners, esp. a PROSTITUTE

Scar·man /ˈskɑːmən‖ˈskɑːr-/, **Lord Les·lie George** /ˈlezli dʒɔːdʒ‖-dʒɔːrdʒ/ (1911–) an English BARRISTER and judge. He is known esp. for being head of the inquiry into the Brixton RIOTs in 1981 and for producing the **Scarman Report** which discussed the causes of the riots

Scarman Re·port [the] a report by Lord Justice Scarman on the Toxteth Riots which said that two of the causes of them were the disadvantages suffered by some racial groups and the attitude of the police

scarp /skɑːp‖skɑːrp/ n tech a line of natural cliffs

scar·per /ˈskɑːpəʳ‖-ɑːr-/ v [I] BrE sl to run away: *Here come the police; we'd better scarper.*

scarves /skɑːvz‖skɑːrvz/ pl. of SCARF

scar·y /ˈskeəri/ adj infml causing or marked by fear: *a scary dark street* | *the scariest story I ever heard*

scat¹ /skæt/ v [I usu. imperative] infml to go away fast: *Come on, you kids, scat!*

scat² n [U] a style of JAZZ singing without real words, when the voice is used to sound like a musical instrument

scath·ing /ˈskeɪðɪŋ/ adj (of speech or writing) bitterly cruel in judgment: *scathing criticism* —see also UNSCATHED — **~ly** adv

sca·tol·o·gy /skæˈtɒlədʒi‖-ˈtɑː-/ n [U] (writing marked by) a nasty or dirty interest in sex or EXCREMENT —**·gical** /ˌskætəˈlɒdʒɪkəl◂‖-ˈlɑː-/ adj

scat·ter¹ /ˈskætəʳ/ v **1** [I;T] to separate or cause (a group) to separate widely: *The searchers scattered all over the countryside looking for her.* | *The birds scattered at the sound of the gun.* | *The gunshot scattered the birds.* **2** [T] to spread widely in all directions (on) (as if) by throwing: [+obj+**on, over**] *The farmers were scattering seed on the fields.* [+obj+**with**] *They scattered the fields with seed.* | (fig.) *He scatters money about as if he were rich.* **3** **scatter (something) to the four winds** to (cause to) be thrown or sent violently in all directions —compare SPRINKLE¹ (1)

scatter² also **scat·ter·ing** /ˈskætərɪŋ/— n [S (of)] a small number or amount separated widely (as if) by scattering: *a scatter(ing) of telephone calls during the day*

scat·ter·brain /ˈskætəbreɪn‖-ər-/ n infml a likeable but careless, forgetful, or unthinking person — **~ed** adj : *He's so scatterbrained I sometimes think he'd forget his own name!*

scat·tered /ˈskætəd‖-ərd/ adj small and far apart; widely and irregularly separated: *villages scattered among the hills* | *The weather forecast says we'll have scattered showers today.*

scat·ty /ˈskæti/ adj BrE infml slightly mad or scatterbrained —**·tiness** n [U]

scav·enge /ˈskævˌndʒ/ v [I;T] **1** [(on)] (of an animal) to feed on (waste or decaying flesh): *homeless dogs scavenging (on) kitchen waste* **2** [(for)] to search for or find (food, usable objects, etc.) at no cost, esp. among waste or unwanted things: *old men scavenging (for food) in dustbins* | *We might be able to scavenge a few useful bits and pieces from that wrecked car.*

scav·eng·er /ˈskævˌndʒəʳ/ n **1** a creature, such as the VULTURE or JACKAL, that SCAVENGES (1) **2** a person who SCAVENGES (2)

SCE /ˌes siː ˈiː/ Scottish Certificate of Education; the examination board of the Scottish Education Department which sets three levels of examination in a range of subjects taken in Scottish schools, regarded as important by universities and employers. SCE **'O' Grades** are taken at 15 or 16, SCE **Highers** are taken a year later, and Sixth Year Studies are taken a year later in the last year at school. —see also extra information on page 408

sce·na·ri·o /sɪˈnɑːriəʊ‖-ˈnæ-, -ˈne-/ n **-rios 1** a written description of the action to take place in a film, play, etc. **2** a description of a possible course of action or events: *He outlined several convincing scenarios for the outbreak of a nuclear war.* —see also NIGHTMARE SCENARIO, WORST CASE SCENARIO

scene /siːn/ n **1** [C] **a** (in a play) any of the divisions, often within an act, during which there is no change of place or time: *Hamlet, Act 5, Scene ii* **b** (in a film, broadcast, etc.) a single piece of action in one place: *a love scene* | *And now the scene shifts to the warehouse, where the murderer is lying in wait.* | (fig.) *I'm getting bored with this job; I could do with a change of scene.* **2** [C] an event or course of action regarded as like something in a play or film: *Angry scenes in Parliament followed the minister's statement.* **3** [C] a place seen (as if) in a picture: *a peaceful country scene* | *a painter of street scenes* **4 a** [the+S (of)] a place where an event or action happens: *These objects were found at the scene of the crime.* | *Our reporter was the first person on the scene.* **b** [C (of)] such a place marked by the stated quality: *After the train crash, the station was a scene of absolute panic.* **5** [C] derog a show of anger or feelings, esp. between two people in public: *I'm ashamed of you,* **making a scene** *in the restaurant like that!* **6** [S] **a** infml an area of the stated activity: *What's new on the pop scene?* | *to dominate the political scene* **b** AmE situation: *We walked into a really bad scene.* **7** [S] old-fash sl the sort of thing a person likes: *Classical music isn't really my scene.* **8 behind the scenes** out of sight; secretly: *Such decisions are made behind the scenes, without public knowledge.* **9 (come) on the scene** infml (to become) present: *He came on the scene just when his country needed a great man to lead them.* **10 set the scene** to provide a base for (future talk or happenings): *The unjust peace agreement set the scene for another war.* —see also **steal the scene** (STEAL¹); see SCENERY (USAGE)

sce·ne·ry /ˈsiːnəri/ n [U] **1** natural surroundings, esp. in beautiful and open country —see also SCENIC **2** the set of painted backgrounds and other articles used on a theatre stage

▷ USAGE Compare **scenery, landscape, view,** and **scene. Scenery** [U] is the general appearance of part of the country, considered from the point of view of beauty: *We passed through some beautiful scenery on our journey through the Lake District.* A **landscape** [C] is any combination of hills, valleys, fields, etc., seen in a particular area: *The landscape was typical of the Lake District, with high mountains, lakes, and deep valleys.* **View** [C] is used to talk about what you see at a distance from a particular place, considered from the point of view of how much you are able to see: *You'll* *get a fine* **view** *of the town from the top of the hill.* (=you will be able to see a lot of the town) A **scene** [C] is what you see both close up and at a distance, and may include people and movement: *a happy* **scene** *of children playing in the park.*◁

scene·shift·er /ˈsiːnˌʃɪftəʳ/ *n* a worker who moves stage scenery in a theatre

sce·nic /ˈsiːnɪk/ *adj* of or showing (attractive) natural scenery: *Let's take the* **scenic route,** *along the coast.* | *a scenic poster* — ~**ally** /kli/ *adv*

scent[1] /sent/ *n* **1** [C] a smell, esp. **a** a particular usu. pleasant smell: *the scent of roses* **b** as left by an animal and followed by hunting dogs: *The hounds followed the stag's scent.* | (fig.) *He managed to throw his pursuers off his scent.* (=escaped from them) **2** [U] *esp. BrE for* PERFUME[1] **3** [(the) S] a way to discover something; TRACK: *This scientist thinks he's* **on the scent** *of a cure for heart disease, although others think he's following* **a false scent.** — ~**less** *adj*

scent[2] *v* [T] **1** (esp. of an animal) to smell, esp. to tell the presence of by smelling: *The dogs had scented a fox.* **2** to get a feeling or belief of the presence or fact of (esp. something bad); SUSPECT: *She scented danger.* [+(that)] *I scented that all was not well.* **3** (**with**) *usu. pass.*] to fill with a SCENT[1] (1a,2): *The air was scented with spring flowers.*

Scep·ter'd isle /ˌseptəd ˈaɪl‖-tərd-/ *n* **this scepter'd isle** *quote* Great Britain (from the play *Richard II* by William Shakespeare): *Perhaps the only permanent solution is to desert this scepter'd isle for warmer climes.*

scep·tic *BrE* ‖ **skep-** *AmE* /ˈskeptɪk/ *n* a person who is sceptical, esp. about the claims made by a religion

scep·ti·cal *BrE* ‖ **skep-** *AmE* /ˈskeptɪkəl/ *adj* [(**of, about**)] unwilling to believe a claim or promise; doubting; distrustful: *Everyone says our team will win, but I'm sceptical (of/about it).* — ~**ly** /kli/ *adv*

scep·ti·cis·m *BrE* ‖ **skep-** *AmE* /ˈskeptᵻsɪzəm/ *n* [U] a doubting state or habit of mind; dislike of believing without certainty; doubt: *Their claim is being treated with some scepticism in Washington.*

scep·tre *BrE* ‖ **-ter** *AmE* /ˈseptəʳ/ *n* a short rod carried by a king or queen on ceremonial occasions as a sign of power —compare MACE[1]

sched·ule[1] /ˈʃedjuːl‖ˈskedʒʊl, -dʒəl/ *n* **1** a planned list or order of things to be done, dealt with, etc.: *to draw up a factory production schedule* | *an exhausting/a very full schedule* | *to stick to/keep one's schedule* **2** [(of)] a formal list, such as **a** a list of prices: *a schedule of postal charges* **b** *esp. AmE* a timetable of trains, buses, etc. **c** *fml* a list of details related to some other matter in writing: *a schedule of repairs attached to a builder's estimate* **3 ahead of/on/behind schedule** before/at/after the planned or expected time: *We finished the project ahead of schedule.*

schedule[2] *v* [T] **1** [(**for**) *usu. pass.*] to plan for a certain future time: *The meeting is scheduled for Thursday.* [+obj+to-v] *It is scheduled to take place on Thursday.* **2** to put (a flight, train, etc.) into a timetable; make a regular service: *We're trying to schedule another early morning train to London.*

scheduled flight /ˌ·· ˈ·/ *n* an AEROPLANE service which is part of a timetable and flies at the same time every day or every week: *We're going by scheduled flight because we're fed up with charter flights being delayed.* —compare CHARTER FLIGHT

Sche·her·a·za·de /ʃəˌherəˈzɑːdə, -ˈzɑːd/ *see* SHEHERAZADE

sche·ma /ˈskiːmə/ *n* **-mata** /mətə/ *fml or tech* a representation of an arrangement or plan; DIAGRAM

sche·mat·ic /skiːˈmætɪk, skɪ-/ *adj* of or like a schema or SCHEME[1] (2): *A schematic drawing shows the main outlines but leaves out many details.* — ~**ally** /kli/ *adv*

sche·ma·tize *also* **-tise** *BrE* /ˈskiːmətaɪz/ *v* [T] to express or show in a very simple, formal, (too) neat way

scheme[1] /skiːm/ *n* **1** *esp. BrE* a formal, official, or business plan: *to propose a new health insurance scheme* **2** a system; an ordered arrangement: *It's hard to see any scheme in what this writer has written: it's very confused.* —see also COLOUR SCHEME **3** a clever dishonest plan: [+to-v] *a scheme to escape taxes* **4 the scheme of things** the way things are, regarded as an ordered system

scheme[2] *v* [I (**for, against**)] to make clever dishonest

plans; PLOT[2] (1): *I've never trusted that scheming bastard.* [+to-v] *They've been scheming to get me dismissed from my job.* —**schemer** *n*

scher·zo /ˈskeətsəʊ‖ˈskeər-/ *n* **-zos** /səʊz/ a quick playful piece of music for instruments, usu. part of a longer piece

Schick·e·le /ˈʃɪkəli/, **Peter** (1935–) an American musician who treats CLASSICAL music in a joking way and who, under the name of P.D.Q. Bach, has written such works as *Concerto for Piano vs. Orchestra* and *Pervertimento for Bagpipes*

Schil·ler /ˈʃɪləʳ/, **Frie·drich von** /ˈfriːdrɪk, -ɪx vɒn‖-vɑːn/ (1759–1805) a German writer of plays and poetry, and PROFESSOR of history, best known for his *Ode to Joy*, set to music as part of Beethoven's Choral Symphony, No. 9

schis·m /ˈsɪzəm, ˈskɪzəm/ *n tech* [C;U (**in, between**)] (a) separation between parts originally of the same group, esp. in the Christian church

schis·mat·ic /sɪzˈmætɪk, skɪz-/ *n, adj tech, usu. derog* (a person) supporting schism

schist /ʃɪst/ *n* [U] a rock that naturally breaks apart into thin flat pieces

schiz·oid /ˈskɪtsɔɪd/ *adj tech* (typical) of or like schizophrenia or a SPLIT PERSONALITY

schiz·o·phre·ni·a /ˌskɪtsəʊˈfriːniə, -sə-/ *n* [U] *tech* a disorder of the mind marked by a separation of a person's mind and feelings, causing at last a drawing away from other people into a life in the imagination only —compare SPLIT PERSONALITY

schiz·o·phren·ic /ˌskɪtsəʊˈfrenɪk◂, -sə-/ *adj, n tech* (typical of) a person with schizophrenia — ~**ally** /kli/ *adv*

schlep , schlepp /ʃlep/ *v* -**pp-** *AmE infml* **1** [T] to carry or drag (esp. something heavy which makes one tired): *I schlepped all these books home with me.* **2** [I (AROUND)] to spend a lot of time and effort in getting from one place to another: *I've been schlepping around for an hour trying to get here.*

Schlitz /ʃlɪts/ *n* [C;U] *tdmk* a type of beer made by an American company

schlock /ʃlɒk‖ʃlɑːk/ *n, adj* [U] *AmE* (a thing, esp. a work of art) of low quality or value: *Most of the paintings in his show were just schlock.*

schmaltz , schmalz /ʃmɔːlts, ʃmælts‖ʃmɔːlts, ʃmɑːlts/ *n* [U] *infml derog* art or esp. music which brings out feelings in a too easy, not serious or delicate, way — ~**y** *adj*

Schmidt /ʃmɪt/, **Hel·mut** /ˈhelmuːt/ (1918–) a West German politician, member of the Social Democratic party, and Chancellor from 1974 to 1983. He helped to introduce yearly talks on ECONOMICS with other European and world countries.

schmooze /ʃmuːz/ *v* [I] *AmE infml, usu. derog* to talk about unimportant things; make SMALL TALK: *A cocktail party full of people schmoozing.*

schmuck /ʃmʌk/ *n AmE infml* a fool

Schna·bel /ˈʃnɑːbəl/, **Ar·tur** /ˈɑːtʊəʳ‖ˈɑːr-/ (1882–1951) an American pianist known for his fine playing of Beethoven

schnapps /ʃnæps/ *n* [U] a strong alcoholic drink rather like GIN

schnit·zel /ˈʃnɪtsəl/ *n* [C;U] a small piece of VEAL covered with bits of bread for quick cooking in oil

schnook /ʃnʊk/ *n AmE infml* a stupid person: *Don't be such a schnook.*

schnoz·zle /ˈʃnɒzəl‖ˈʃnɑː-/ *n AmE humor* nose: *Jimmy "Schnozzle" Durante was an American Jewish comedian famous for his big nose.*

schol·ar /ˈskɒləʳ‖ˈskɑː-/ *n* **1** [(of)] a person with great knowledge of, and skill in studying, a subject, esp. a non-science subject: *a Greek scholar* (=one with great knowledge of esp. ancient Greek) | *Islamic scholars* **2** [*usu. in negatives*] *infml* a clever and educated person: *I'm afraid I've never been much of a scholar.* **3** the holder of a SCHOLARSHIP (1) **4** *lit or BrE old use* a child in school —see STUDENT (USAGE)

schol·ar·ly /ˈskɒləli‖ˈskɑːlərli/ *adj* **1** concerned with serious detailed study: *a scholarly journal* **2** *usu. apprec* of or like a SCHOLAR (1)

schol·ar·ship /ˈskɒləʃɪp‖ˈskɑːlər-/ *n* **1** [C (**to**)] a sum of money or other prize given to a student by an official

body, esp. to pay (partly) for a course of study: *She won a scholarship to Oxford.* | *a state scholarship* (=given by a US state for study in one of its universities) **2** [U] the knowledge, work, or method of scholars; exact and serious study: *Her book is a fine piece of scholarship.*

scho·las·tic /skəˈlæstɪk/ *adj* [A] *fml* **1** of schools and/or teaching **2** of scholasticism

scho·las·ti·cis·m /skəˈlæstɬsɪzəm/ *n* [U] a method for the study of thought, esp. religious thought, based on ancient writings and practised in Europe from the 9th to the 17th centuries

school¹ /skuːl/ *n* **1** [C] a place of education for children: *Which school do your children go to?* | *a primary/secondary school* | *village schools* | *school uniform* | (fig.) *He had learned everything in the school of experience.* —see also APPROVED SCHOOL, CHURCH SCHOOL, COMPREHENSIVE², CONVENT SCHOOL, ELEMENTARY SCHOOL, GRAMMAR SCHOOL, HIGH SCHOOL, JUNIOR HIGH SCHOOL, MIDDLE SCHOOL, PREPARATORY SCHOOL, PRIMARY SCHOOL, PRIVATE SCHOOL, PUBLIC SCHOOL, SCHOOL OF HARD KNOCKS, SPECIAL SCHOOL, SUNDAY SCHOOL **2** [U] **a** attendance or study at a school: *He began school at the age of 5.* | *Is your child of school age?* (=old enough to go to school) | *Jimmy has always found school difficult.* **b** the day's work at a school: *School begins at 8.30.* | *I walk home after school.* **3** [C+*sing./pl. v*] the body of students (and teachers) at such a place: *The whole school was/were down at the sports field.* **4** [C;U] an establishment for teaching a particular subject, skill, etc.: *a driving school* | *She goes to (an) art school at night.* —see also FINISHING SCHOOL **5** [C;U] (in certain universities) a department concerned with a particular subject: *the School of Law* | *He went to medical school for three years.* **6** [C] a group of people with the same methods, opinions, style, etc.: *Rembrandt and his school* —see also SCHOOL OF THOUGHT **7** [C;U] *AmE* a university —see also OLD SCHOOL

school² *v* [T (in)] *fml* to teach, train, or bring under control: *a dog well schooled in obedience* [+obj+to-v] *He schooled himself to listen to others because he knew he talked too much.*

school³ *n* [(of)] a large group of one kind of fish or certain other sea animals swimming together: *a school of whales*

school board /ˌ· ˈ·/ *n AmE* the group of people who govern a school or school district. They are usu. elected and some of them are the parents of children in the school(s) concerned.

School Cer·tif·i·cate /ˌ· ·ˈ···/ *n* an examination in any of a range of subjects taken in British schools between 1917 and 1951. This was replaced by the O-level examination.

school·child /ˈskuːltʃaɪld/, **school·boy** /-bɔɪ/ *masc.*, **school·girl** /-gɜːl‖-gɜːrl/ *fem.*, **school·kid** /-kɪd/ *infml* — *n* **-children** /tʃɪldrən/ a child attending school, esp. regarded as one who is not yet grown up: *schoolboy humour* (=silly childish jokes)

schoolboy

school·day /ˈskuːldeɪ/ *n* a day of the week (in Britain and the US, usu. Monday to Friday) when children usu. attend school: *I'd forgotten today was Sunday—I thought it was a schoolday!*

school·days /ˈskuːldeɪz/ *n* [P] the time of one's life when one attended school

school din·ner /ˌ· ˈ···/ also **school lunch**— *n* the meal given to children at school in the middle of the day. People in Britain often make jokes about school dinners, esp. the PUDDINGs, which people remember as being heavy, filling, and sticky.

school dis·trict /ˈ· ˌ···/ *n AmE* an area within one state that includes a number of PRIMARY and SECONDARY schools which are governed together. In country areas a school district may include several towns; a large city may contain more than one school district. —compare LOCAL EDUCATION AUTHORITY

school·fel·low /ˈskuːlˌfeləʊ/ *n BrE* a SCHOOLMATE

school gov·ern·or /ˌ· ˈ···/ *n BrE* a member of the mainly non-teaching body at a school who take decisions on how it should be run, who should be employed, etc.

school·house /ˈskuːlhaʊs/ *n* **-houses** /ˌhaʊzɬz/ a school building, esp. for a small village school

school·ing /ˈskuːlɪŋ/ *n* [U] education or attendance at school: *He had only five years of schooling.*

school·leav·er /ˈ· ˌ··/ *n BrE* a student who has just left or is about to leave school after completing a course of study: *jobs for school-leavers*

▷ USAGE In American English, to talk of leaving school suggests that one has left without finishing, or dropped out. The closest *AmE* terms to the *BrE* **school-leaver** are **highschool graduate** or **graduating senior**.◁

school·marm /ˈskuːlmɑːm‖-mɑːrm/ *n infml humor* **1** *derog* an old-fashioned, exact, and easily shocked woman who likes giving orders **2** *esp. AmE old-fash* a woman teacher at a school

school·mas·ter /ˈskuːlˌmɑːstəʳ‖-ˌmæ-/**school·mis·tress** /-ˌmɪstrɬs/ *fem.*— *n esp. BrE* **1** a teacher at a PUBLIC SCHOOL **2** *old use* a schoolteacher

school·mate /ˈskuːlmeɪt/ also **schoolfellow**— *n* a child at the same school: *We were schoolmates twenty years ago.*

school of hard knocks /ˌ· · ˌ· ˈ·/ [*the*] *infml* life's experiences, esp. unlucky ones: *I was educated in the school of hard knocks.*

school of thought /ˌ· · ˈ·/ *n* **schools of thought** a group of people with the same way of thinking, opinion, etc.: *There are different schools of thought on the best method of growing tomatoes.*

school·room /ˈskuːlruːm, -rʊm/ *n* **1** a room used for teaching in a school **2** a one-room school in a small village, now very rare

school run /ˈ· ˌ·/ *n BrE* the driving of children to and from school: *She finds she is kept very busy with school runs, after-school activities, etc.*

school·teach·er /ˈskuːlˌtiːtʃəʳ/ *n* a teacher at a school

school tie /ˌ· ˈ·/ *n* a tie worn as part of a school uniform by boys and girls in Britain

school·work /ˈskuːlwɜːk‖-wɜːrk/ *n* [U] study for or during school classes

school year /ˌ· ˈ·/ *n* the period of a year during which pupils stay in the same class at school, usu. beginning in the autumn and ending the following summer

schoo·ner /ˈskuːnəʳ/ *n* **1** a fast sailing ship with usu. two MASTs (=upright poles supporting the sails) and sails set along the length of the ship rather than across it **2** a large tall drinking glass, esp. (*BrE*) for SHERRY or (*AmE* & *AustrE*) for beer

Schu·bert /ˈʃuːbət‖-bərt/, **Franz** /fræns/ (1797–1828) an Austrian writer of music best known for his songs and symphonies (SYMPHONY)

Schu·mann /ˈʃuːmən‖-mɑːn/, **Rob·ert** /ˈrɒbət‖ˈrɑːbərt/ (1810–56) a German writer of music best known for his piano works, who also wrote songs and ORCHESTRAL works

schwa /ʃwɑː/ *n tech* a vowel sounded typically in word parts spoken without STRESS (=special force) and shown in this dictionary as /ə/ or /ˌə/: *The "a" in "about" is a schwa.*

Schwar·zen·eg·ger /ˈʃwɔːtsənegəʳ‖ˈʃwɔːr-/, **Arnold** (1947–) an American actor born in Austria, whose BODY BUILDING appearance won him the titles of Mr Germany and Mr Universe. He is best known for his part in the film *Terminator* in which he plays the HERO. —see colour picture on page 685

Schwarz·kopf /ˈʃvɑːtskɒpf‖ˈʃwɔːrtskɑːpf/, **Elisabeth** (1915–) a German singer who sang several different types of work but was esp. known for LIEDER

Schwarz·kopf /ˈʃwɔːtskɒpf‖ˈʃwɔːrtskɑːpf/, **Norman** (1934–) an American army general who was head of their successful forces during the GULF WAR with Iraq in 1990 to 1991. He was given the NICKNAME **Stormin' Norman**, perhaps from OPERATION DESERT STORM.

Schweit·zer /ˈʃwaɪtsəʳ/, **Albert** (1875–1965) a German medical doctor known for his MISSIONARY work in Africa. He was also a musician and thinker, and was given the Nobel Peace prize in 1952.

sci·at·ic /saɪˈætɪk/ *adj med* of the HIPS: *the sciatic nerve* (=along the back of the upper legs)

sci·at·i·ca /saɪˈætɪkə/ *n* [U] *not tech* pain in the area of the lower back, HIPS, and legs

sci·ence /ˈsaɪəns/ n **1** [U] (the study of) knowledge which can be made into a system and which usu. depends on seeing and testing facts and stating general natural laws: *Science has taught us how atoms are made up.* | *The computer is one of the marvels of modern science.* | *a science teacher* | *developments in science and technology* **2** [C;U] a branch of such knowledge, esp. **a** any of the branches usu. studied at universities, such as BIOLOGY, CHEMISTRY, PHYSICS, ENGINEERING, and sometimes MATHEMATICS: *government support for the sciences* —compare ARTS; see also NATURAL SCIENCE **b** anything which may be studied exactly: *military science* | *Do you think cooking is an art or a science?* —see also SOCIAL SCIENCE, **blind with science** (BLIND²)

science fic·tion /ˌ·· ˈ··/ also **sci-fi** /ˌsaɪ ˈfaɪ/ *infml—* n [U] stories about imaginary future developments in science and their effect on life, often concerned with space travel —compare FANTASY

Science Mu·se·um /ˈ·· ·,··/ [*the*] the building in W London where most important scientific items are put or kept on show

science park /ˈ·· ·/ n an area where there are a lot of companies that are concerned esp. with new TECHNOLOGY and scientific study

sci·en·tif·ic /ˌsaɪən ˈtɪfɪk◄/ adj **1** [*no comp.*] of or being science or its principles or rules: *scientific equipment* | *scientific research* | *scientific proof* **2** needing or showing exact knowledge, skill, or use of a system; SYSTEMATIC: *scientific baby care* | *We do keep accounts for the business, but we are not very scientific about it.* —opposite **unscientific** (for 2) — ~**ally** /kli/ adv

Scientific A·mer·i·can /ˌ···· ·ˈ···/ a monthly magazine with articles about new discoveries and developments in all the sciences, written for educated readers

scientific meth·od /ˌ···· ˈ··/ n [C;U] a way of trying to prove the truth or falsity of an idea by setting up a test (EXPERIMENT) in which known things are controlled so that unknown things may be determined, and so that others doing the same test will get the same results

sci·en·tist /ˈsaɪəntˌɪst/ n a person who works in a science, esp. PHYSICS, CHEMISTRY, or BIOLOGY

sci·en·tol·o·gy /ˌsaɪənˈtɒlədʒi/—ˈtɑːl-/ n [U] (*sometimes cap.*) a religion started in the US by L Ron Hubbard, which says that Christ was only one of several important teachers. Its methods of raising money and treatment of people who have left the religion have been the subject of several legal cases.

Scil·ly Isles /ˈsɪli ˌaɪlz/ n [P] a group of about 140 islands off SW England, five of which are lived on; capital Hugh Town on the island of St Mary's. The Scilly Isles are popular with tourists.

scim·i·tar /ˈsɪmˌɪtər/ n a sword with a curved blade that is sharp on the outer edge, formerly used in the Middle East —see picture at SWORD

scin·til·la /sɪnˈtɪlə/ n [S (of) usu. in questions and negatives] *fml* the slightest bit: *There's not a scintilla of truth in what he says.*

scin·til·late /ˈsɪntˌɪleɪt/ v [I (with)] **1** usu. *lit* to throw out quick flashes of light or SPARKs **2** *apprec* to be full of life and cleverness: *scintillating conversation* —**-lation** /ˌsɪntˌɪˈleɪʃ ən/ n [U]

sci·on /ˈsaɪən/ n **1** a living part of a plant, usu. a young SHOOT, that is cut off, esp. for fixing onto another plant as a GRAFT **2** [(of)] *lit* a young or most recent member of a usu. noble or famous family

scis·sors /ˈsɪzəz/—ərz/ n **1** [P] two sharp blades having handles at one end with holes for the fingers, fastened at the centre so that they open in the shape of the letter X and cut when they close: *I need scissors/some scissors/a pair of scissors for this job.* | *These scissors are very sharp.* —compare SHEARS; see PAIR (USAGE) **2** [S] a movement of the body in certain sports, esp. **a** (in wrestling (WRESTLE)) a hold in which a person locks their legs round their opponent **b** (in the HIGH JUMP) a way of jumping in which the person faces the bar as he or she goes over it

scissors-and-paste /ˌ··· ·ˈ·/ adj [A] *infml* (of printed matter) stuck together from cut-up pieces: (fig.) *There's nothing new in the book; it's just a scissors-and-paste job.* (=put together from other writings)

scle·ro·sis /sklˌɪˈrəusˌɪs/ n **-ses** /siːz/ [C;U (**of**)] *med* (a)

hardening of some usu. soft organ or part of the body — see also MULTIPLE SCLEROSIS —**-tic** /sklˌɪˈrɒtɪk||-ˈrɑː-/ adj

scoff¹ /skɒf||skɔːf, skɑːf/ v [I (**at**)] to speak or act disrespectfully; laugh (at): *A hundred years ago people scoffed at the idea that man would ever fly.* — ~**er** n [usu. pl.]

scoff² n [usu. pl.] an expression of laughing disrespect: *He ignored the scoffs of the critics.*

scoff³ v [T (UP)] *infml, esp. BrE* to eat (esp. all of something) eagerly and fast: *Who's scoffed all the cake?*

scoff·law /ˈskɒflɔː||ˈskɔːf-, ˈskɑːf-/ n *AmE* someone who disregards (usu. less important) laws: *parking scofflaw*

scold¹ /skəʊld/ v [T] *old-fash* to speak angrily and complainingly to (someone who has done something wrong): *He was severely scolded by his mother.* — ~**ing** n [C;U] : *I'm in for* (=going to get) *a scolding when I get home.*

scold² n [usu. sing.] *old use* a woman who is always complaining or quarrelling

scol·lop /ˈskɒləp||ˈskɑː-/ n, v SCALLOP

sconce /skɒns||skɑːns/ n a usu. decorative holder which may be fixed to a wall, for one or more candles or electric lights; used esp. in a church

scone /skɒn, skəʊn||skəʊn, skɑːn/ [*also* **biscuit** *AmE*— n a soft usu. round breadlike cake of a size for one person, sometimes containing dried fruit

Scone, stone of see STONE OF SCONE

scoop¹ /skuːp/ n **1** any of various containers or tools for holding and moving liquids or loose materials, such as **a** a small deep SHOVEL-shaped tool held in the hand for digging out corn, flour, etc.: *a kitchen scoop* | *a measuring scoop* **b** a deep round spoon for digging out soft food: *an ice-cream scoop* **c** the bucket on an earth-moving machine **2** [(of)] *also* **scoop·ful** /-fʊl/— the amount held by any of these: *Two scoops of ice cream, please.* **3** a usu. exciting news report printed, broadcast, etc., before one's competitors can do so —compare EXCLUSIVE² **4 What's the scoop?** *esp. AmE infml* (asked of someone expected to provide needed information)

scoop² v [T] **1** [+obj+adv/prep] to take up or out (as if) with a SCOOP¹: *She scooped some ice cream out of the tub.* | *He scooped his books up off the floor.* **2** (of a newspaper) to make an important news report before (another newspaper): *The "News" scooped the other newspapers by revealing the prince's marriage plans.* **3** *infml* to get ahead of or defeat, esp. by being faster: *We scooped the other companies by making the best offer for the contract.*

scoot /skuːt/ v [I] *infml* to go quickly and suddenly: *There's the bus; you'll have to scoot if you want to catch it!*

scoot·er /ˈskuːtər/ n **1** a child's vehicle with two small wheels, an upright handle fixed to the front wheel, and a narrow board for one foot, pushed by the other foot touching the ground **2** a MOTOR SCOOTER —see BICYCLE (USAGE), DRIVE (USAGE), TRANSPORT (USAGE)

scope¹ /skəʊp/ n [U] **1** [(**of**)] the area within the limits of a question, subject, action, etc.; RANGE: *The politics of a country would be outside the scope of a book for tourists.* | *to broaden/widen the scope of the report* | *very narrow in scope* **2** [(**for**)] space or chance for action or thought; OPPORTUNITY: *There's considerable/not much scope for initiative in this job.*

scope²

    scope *sbdy./sthg.* **out** *phr v AmE infml* find and examine: *It's getting late, should we scope out a restaurant?*

Scopes tri·al /ˈskəʊps ˌtraɪəl/ *also* **Monkey trial**— [*the*] the 1925 American court case of biology teacher **John Scopes** who was prosecuted (PROSECUTE) for teaching Darwin's THEORY of EVOLUTION in a State which was against this because it preferred to teach the story of the Creation given in the Bible. It raised questions about the separation of religion and government (or church and state). —see also Clarence DARROW

scorch¹ /skɔːtʃ||skɔːrtʃ/ v **1** [I;T] to burn slightly so as to change or be changed in colour, taste, etc.: *The iron was too hot and he scorched his shirt .* | *The meat was black and scorched on the outside but still raw inside.* | *Heat it gently so that it doesn't scorch.* **2** [T] to dry up and take the life out of (plants) with a strong dry heat: *The fields had been scorched by the hot summer sun.* | *scorching heat* **3** [I+adv/prep] *BrE infml* to travel very fast: *The car scorched down the road at 90 miles an hour.*

scorch² n **1** [C] a scorched place; mark made by burning on a surface **2** [U] the appearance of scorching produced by some plant diseases

scorched earth pol·i·cy /ₜˈ ˈˌ ˌ···/ *n* the destruction by an army of all useful things, esp. crops, in an area before leaving it to an advancing enemy

scorch·er /ˈskɔːtʃəʳ‖-ɔːr-/ *n infml* **1** a very hot day **2** something very exciting, angry, fast, powerful, etc.

score¹ /skɔːʳ/ *n* **1** [C] the number of points, runs, marks, GOALs (2), etc., made in a game, competition, sport, etc.: *The score stood at|was one-nil* (=1-0) *with a minute left in the game.* | *Is anybody* **keeping (the) score** (=recording it) *in this game?* | *a record score* **2** [C *usu. sing.*] an act of gaining points, etc., in a game, etc.: *What a brilliant score!* **3** [C] **a** a written copy of a piece of music, esp. for a large group of performers: *a full score* (=showing all the parts in separate lines on the page) | *a vocal score* (=showing only the singers' parts) **b** the music for a film or play: *Who wrote the film score?* **4** [C *usu. sing.*] a reason: *We have enough money; don't worry* **on that score.** **5** [C] an old disagreement or hurt kept in mind; GRUDGE²: *I've got* **a score to settle** *with him.* (=I want to make sure he is punished.) **6** [*the*+S] *infml* the true, often unfavourable, facts of a situation: *What's the score?* | *John will explain what's happened − he knows the score.* **7** [C] also **score mark** /ˈ· ·/− a line made or cut on a surface with a sharp instrument: *deep scores on the floor* −see also SCORES

score² *v* **1** [I;T] to gain (one or more points, GOALs (2), etc.) in a sport, game, competition, etc.: *Arsenal scored in the final minute of the game.* | *All the contestants scored well|highly in the quiz.* | *Which batsman has scored most runs this season?* **2** [T] to give a (certain number of points) to (someone) in a sport, game, or competition: [+*obj(i)*+*obj(d)*] *The Canadian judge scored her 15.* | *In darts, a bullseye scores (you) 50 points.* **3** [I] to record the score of a sports match as it is played: *Will you score for us?* **4** [I;T] to gain or win (a success, victory, prize, etc.): *Archer has scored again with another popular book.* | *The bomb scored a hit on the bridge.* **5** [T (**for**)] to write or arrange (music), esp. for a particular combination of instruments: *This piece is scored for strings and percussion.* **6** [I+*prep*; T+*obj*+*prep*] to make (a clever and successful point), esp. in an argument against someone: *I hate conversations where people try to* **score (points) off** *each other.* **7** [T] to mark or cut one or more lines on (as if) with a sharp instrument: *Score the paper to make it easy to fold.* **8** [I (**with**)] *sl* to gain a sexual success: *Did you score (with her) last night?* **9** [I;T] *sl* to obtain a supply of (a usu. illegal drug)

score sthg. ↔ out/through *phr v* [T] *fml* to draw a line through (one or more written words) to show that they should not be read; CROSS **out**

score³ *determiner, n* **score** or **scores** *esp. old use or bibl* (*often in comb.*) (a group of) 20: *According to the Bible, we can expect to live for three score|threescore years and ten.* (=70 years) −see also SCORES

score·board /ˈskɔːbɔːd‖ˈskɔːrbɔːrd/ *n* a large board on which the score of a game is recorded as it is played

score·card /ˈskɔːkaːd‖ˈskɔːrkɑːrd/ *n* a printed card used by someone watching a sports match, race, etc., to record what happens in it

scor·er /ˈskɔːrəʳ/ also **score·keep·er** /ˈskɔːˌkiːpəʳ ‖ ˈskɔːr-/ *n* **1** a person who keeps the official record of a sports match and its score as it is played **2** a player who scores points, GOALs, etc.

scores /skɔːz‖skɔːrz/ *n* [P (**of**)] a lot: *There were scores of people there, maybe eighty or more.*

scorn¹ /skɔːn‖skɔːrn/ *n* [U (**for**)] strong and sometimes angry disrespect towards a person or thing that is regarded as worthless; CONTEMPT: *He* **poured scorn on** *my suggestion.* (=expressed scorn for it) − ~ **ful** *adj* : *a scornful laugh* | *his scornful dismissal of the democratic process* − ~ **fully** *adv*

scorn² *v* [T] *usu. lit* to refuse to accept or consider, esp. because of scorn or pride: *She scorned all our offers of help.* [+*to-v*] *He scorned to hide away like a coward.*

Scor·pi·o /ˈskɔːpiəʊ‖-ɔːr-/ *n* **1** [U] the eighth sign of the ZODIAC, represented by a scorpion **2** [C] a person born between October 23 and November 21 −see ZODIAC (USAGE) and see picture at ZODIAC

scor·pi·on /ˈskɔːpiən‖-ɔːr-/ *n* a tropical insect-like creature

with a long body and a curving tail which stings poisonously

Scor·se·se /skɔːˈseɪzi‖skɔːr-/, **Martin** (1942−) an American film director whose works include *Taxi Driver* and *The Last Temptation of Christ*

Scot /skɒt‖skɑːt/ also **Scotsman, Scots·wom·an** /ˈskɒtswʊmən ‖ ˈskɑː-/*fem.* − *n* a person who comes from or whose parents come from Scotland

scotch /skɒtʃ‖skɑːtʃ/ *v* [T] *fml* to take strong action to stop; put an end to: *You can scotch the rumour by explaining the true facts immediately.* | *We soon scotched that idea.*

Scotch¹ also **Scotch whis·ky** *fml*− *n* [C;U] (a glass of) a strong alcoholic drink (WHISKY) made in Scotland: *"Scotch on the rocks,* (=with ice) *please."*

Scotch² *adj* SCOTTISH −see USAGE there

Scotch broth /ₜˈ ˈ·/ *n* [U] thick soup made from vegetables, meat, and BARLEY

Scotch egg /ₜˈ ˈ·/ *n BrE* a boiled egg cooked inside a covering of SAUSAGE meat

Scotch mist /ₜˈ ˈ·/ *n* [C;U] a thick mist mixed with light rain

Scotch tape /ₜˈ ˈ·, ˈ· ·/ *n, v AmE tdmk for* SELLOTAPE

Scotch whis·ky /ₜˈ ˈ···/ *n* [C;U] SCOTCH

scot-free /ₜˈ ˈ·/ *adj* [F] *infml* without harm, or esp. punishment that one deserves: *The murderer* **got off scot-free.**

Scot·land /ˈskɒtlənd‖ˈskɑːt-/ a country in the United Kingdom north of England; capital Edinburgh. Scotland has many LOCHs (=lakes) and islands, and in parts it is very mountainous. The Gaelic language is still spoken in some parts of the west Highlands and Outer Hebrides. Most political decisions about Scotland are made in London which some groups, like the Scottish National Party (SNP) think is wrong and are trying to change. The national SYMBOL of Scotland is the THISTLE and its PATRON SAINT is Saint Andrew. −see also DEVOLUTION, SAINT ANDREW'S CROSS and see colour map on page 816

Scot·land Yard /ₜˈ·· ˈ·/ also **New Scotland Yard**− (the main office of) the division of the London police dealing with serious crimes −see also CID

Scots /skɒts‖skɑːts/ *adj* SCOTTISH −see USAGE there

Scots Greys /ₜˈ ˈ·/ [*the*] a Scottish REGIMENT (=a large division of men) in the British army

Scots Guards /ₜˈ ˈ·/ [*the*] a Scottish REGIMENT (=a large division of men) in the British army

Scots law /ₜˈ ˈ·/ *n* [U] see SCOTTISH LEGAL SYSTEM

Scots·man /ˈskɒtsmən ‖ ˈskɑːts-/ [*the*] one of the main Scottish newspapers, read esp. in the east around Edinburgh −see also extra information on page 893

Scott, Dred see DRED SCOTT CASE

Scott, George C (1926−) an American actor best known for his film parts, esp. strong-willed characters such as soldiers. He was the first actor to refuse an OSCAR.

Scott, Sir Peter (1909−89) a British ORNITHOLOGIST (=person who studies birds) and artist and writer of many books on birds. He also supported or led various bodies who work for the protection of nature.

Scott, Robert Falcon (1868−1912) an officer in the British navy who led two journeys to the Antarctic, and died while returning from the South Pole during the second one; he is often called **Scott of the Antarctic**

Scott, Ron·nie /ˈrɒni ‖ ˈrɑː-/ (1927−) a British SAXOPHONE player who runs Britain's best known JAZZ club, "Ronnie Scott's" in London, attracting musicians of international standard

Scott, Sir Wal·ter /ˈwɔːltəʳ/ (1771−1832) a Scottish writer and poet, esp. famous for his stories of Scottish life, including several based on historical characters, e.g. *The Heart of Midlothian* and *Ivanhoe*

Scot·tish /ˈskɒtɪʃ‖ˈskɑːtɪʃ/ also **Scots, Scotch**− *adj* of Scotland

▷ USAGE **Scottish** and **Scots** are the usual forms of the adjective. **Scots** is usually used only of people: *a* **Scottish** *plant* | *a* **Scots/Scottish** *lawyer.* **Scotch** is often considered derogatory, ignorant, or old-fashioned except when used of the products of Scotland: **Scotch** *whisky* | **Scotch** *beef.*◁

Scottish Bal·let /ₜˈ·· ˈ···‖ₜ·· ·ˈ·/ the main BALLET company in Scotland

Scottish Ed·u·ca·tion De·part·ment /ˌ·· ··ˈ·· ·ˌ··/ [the] see SED

Scottish E·pis·co·pal Church /ˌ·· ·ˌ··· ˈ·/ [the] the ANGLICAN church in Scotland

Scottish High·lands /ˌ·· ˈ··/ [the +P] the mountainous area in the northern half of Scotland —see colour map on page 818

Scottish Le·gal System /ˌ·· ˈ·· ˌ··/ [the] also **Scots Law**— the system of law in Scotland based on CIVIL LAW (2). This is different to the English system although the final court of APPEAL for Scotland as well as England is the House of Lords. Acts of Parliament do not necessarily operate in Scotland because the law is different.

Scottish Na·tion·al Par·ty /ˌ·· ˈ··· ˌ··/ see SNP

Scottish Of·fice /ˈ·· ˌ··/ [the] a British government office responsible for carrying out the government's policies (POLICY) in Scotland

Scottish Op·e·ra /ˌ·· ˈ···/ the main OPERA company of Scotland

Scot·ty /ˈskɒti‖ˈskɑː-/ also **Mr Scott**— a character in the television programme *Star Trek*, known esp. for the phrase said to him "Beam me up, Scotty" —see also **Beam me up, Scotty** (BEAM)

scoun·drel /ˈskaʊndrəl/ n esp. fml or old-fash a wicked, selfish, or dishonest man: *an utter scoundrel*

scour¹ /skaʊəʳ/ v [T (**for**)] to go through every part of (an area) thoroughly in search of someone or something: *The police are scouring the countryside for the escaped prisoners.*

scour² v [T] **1** to clean or remove by hard rubbing with a rough material: *to scour dirty pots and pans* **2** [(OUT)] (of a stream of water) to form by wearing or washing away: *Water had scoured out a passage in the soft rock.*

scour³ n [S] an act of scouring

scour·er /ˈskaʊərəʳ/ n a tool, esp. a small ball of plastic wire or net, for cleaning cooking pots and pans

scourge¹ /skɜːdʒ‖skɜːrdʒ/ n **1** a cause of great harm or suffering: *the scourge of war* (=war causes great suffering) **2** a whip used formerly for punishment: (fig.) *Jack Evans, the self-appointed scourge of the political left*

scourge² v [T] **1** to beat with a whip **2** to cause great harm or suffering to; AFFLICT: *a country scourged by disease and war*

scouse /skaʊs/ n BrE infml, sometimes derog **1** [C] also **scous·er** /ˈskaʊsəʳ/— someone who comes from the area round Liverpool in northwest England **2** [U] the way of speaking of someone from this area **3** [U] a type of STEW² (1) —**scouse** adj

scout¹ /skaʊt/ n **1** [C] (often cap.) **a** also **boy scout**— a member of an association (the **Scouts** or the **Boy Scouts of America**) for training boys in various useful skills such as lighting a fire, and for developing their character. Scouts traditionally carry a PENKNIFE and their MOTTO is "Be Prepared." **b** also **girl scout**— AmE for GUIDE¹ —see also SCOUT'S HONOUR (5) **2** [C] a soldier sent out to search the land ahead of an army, esp. for information about the enemy **3** [S (AROUND, ROUND)] infml an act of scouting: *Take a scout round to see what you can find.* **4** [C] also **talent scout**— a person who is employed to find and hire young people of special ability, esp. for a sports team or for a place of entertainment

scout² v **1** [I+adv/prep] to go looking for something: *We scouted around for a shop that was open late.* **2** [T (OUT, for)] to go through or look carefully at (a place) to get information about it: *The commander sent a party to scout (out) the area for water.*

scout·ing /ˈskaʊtɪŋ/ n [U] (often cap.) the activities of SCOUTS¹ (1)

scout·mas·ter /ˈskaʊtˌmɑːstəʳ‖-ˌmæ-/ n an adult leader of a group of scouts¹ (1)

Scout's hon·our /ˌ·· ˈ··/ phrase often humor (said when one is trying to persuade another of one's honesty, esp. when the other may think one is lying): *Scout's honour! There were five cookies left when I went to bed.*

scowl¹ /skaʊl/ n a threatening expression of the face showing anger or strong disapproval; angry FROWN

scowl² v [I (**at**)] to make a scowl; FROWN angrily: *He scowled heavily.*

scrab·ble /ˈskræbəl/ v [I (ABOUT)] infml to move (one's fingers) wildly and quickly (as if) looking for something: *She scrabbled about on the floor picking up the coins she'd dropped.*

Scrabble tdmk a board game in which players try to make words out of the letters they have drawn from a pile

scrag¹ /skræg/ v -gg- [T] infml to attack roughly and angrily

scrag² also **scrag end** /ˌ·· ˈ·/— n [U] BrE the bony part of a sheep's neck, used usu. for boiling to make STEW or soup; one of the cheaper types of meat

scrag·gly /ˈskrægəli/ adj AmE infml (esp. of things that grow) poor and uneven-looking; badly grown

scrag·gy /ˈskrægi/ adj infml derog, often humor thin and bony: *You don't expect that scraggy old horse to win, do you?*

scram /skræm/ v -mm- [I often imperative] infml to get away fast; run away: *You're not wanted here, so scram!* | *Let's scram!*

scram·ble¹ /ˈskræmbəl/ v **1** [I+adv/prep] to move or climb quickly, esp. over a rough or steep surface: *I scrambled up the cliff/over the rocks for a better look at the sea.* **2** [I+adv/prep, esp. **for**] to struggle or compete with others eagerly or against difficulty: *People were scrambling madly for shelter/scrambling to get out of the way.* **3** [T] to change the order of the signals in (a radio or telephone message) with a machine (a **scrambler**) so that it cannot be understood without being received on a special instrument **4** [T (UP)] to mix (esp. words or things on a flat surface) together without order; JUMBLE **5** [I] (of a military aircraft) to take off quickly, e.g. because of a sudden enemy attack

scramble² n **1** [S] an act of moving or climbing, esp. over a rough surface: *It's quite a scramble to get to the top of the hill!* **2** [S (**for**)] an eager and disorderly struggle: *a mad scramble for the best seats/jobs* **3** [C] a motorcycle race over very rough ground

scrambled egg /ˌ·· ˈ·/ also **scrambled eggs**— n [U] eggs prepared by mixing the white and the yellow parts together before cooking

scrap¹ /skræp/ n **1** [C (**of**)] a small piece; bit: *a scrap of paper* | *scraps of news* | (fig.) *There's not a scrap of truth in what he says.* —see picture at PIECE **2** [U] material which cannot be used for its original purpose but which may have some value: *He sold his car for scrap/for its scrap value.* (=as metal to be used again) | *a scrap-metal dealer* —see also SCRAPS, SCRAP PAPER, SCRAPPY¹

scrap² v -pp- [T] **1** to get rid of as no longer useful or wanted: *The government has scrapped its plans for earnings-related pensions.* **2** to make into SCRAP¹ (2): *The navy's biggest aircraft carrier is being scrapped.*

scrap³ n infml a usu. sudden, short, noisy but not serious fight or quarrel between a few people: *The boys are always getting into scraps.* —see also SCRAPPY²

scrap⁴ v -pp- [I] infml to fight or quarrel: *dogs scrapping over a bone*

scrap·book /ˈskræpbʊk/ n a book of empty pages in which a collection of photographs, newspaper articles, etc., is fastened. They are often made up by children or people with a special interest and may follow a particular subject e.g. one's favourite singer/sport etc. or simply be a collection of things one has seen or read and liked.

scrape¹ /skreɪp/ v **1** [T+obj+adv/prep] to remove (unwanted material) from a surface by pulling or pushing an edge firmly across it repeatedly: *I scraped the mud from my boots.* | *I scraped the skin off the potatoes.* **2** [T (DOWN)] to clean or make (a surface) smooth in this way: *She scraped the door (down) before painting it again.* | *He scraped his boots clean before coming into the house.* **3** [I+adv/prep;T (**on**, **against**)] to (cause to) rub roughly against a surface: *The old car drove off, with its exhaust pipe scraping along the ground.* | *He scraped his chair against the wall.* | *She scraped her fingernail down the wallpaper to see if it would tear.* **4** [T] to hurt or damage in this way: *He scraped his knee when he fell/scraped his car when he drove through the narrow gate.* **5** [T (OUT)] to make (a hole or hollow place) by scraping **6** [I+adv/prep] **a** to live, keep a business, etc., with no more than the necessary money: *We don't earn much, but we manage to scrape by/along somehow.* **b** to succeed by doing work of the lowest acceptable quality: *She just scraped through the exam.* (=passed it by one or two marks) **7 scrape a living** to get just enough food or money to stay alive **8 scrape the (bottom of the) barrel** *infml* to take, use, suggest, etc., something of the lowest quality: *Is he the best speaker they could get for the meeting? They're really scraping the bottom of the barrel!* —see also **bow and scrape** (BOW¹)

scrape sthg. ↔ **up/together** also **scratch up/ together** *AmE phr v* [T] to gather (a total, esp. of money) with difficulty by putting small amounts together: *We scraped up enough to pay the deposit.*

scrape² n **1** an act or sound of scraping **2** a mark or wound made by scraping: *They just suffered a few cuts and scrapes, nothing serious.* **3** *infml* an unpleasant, but not very serious, situation or difficulty: *She gets into these silly scrapes because she doesn't think before she acts.*

scrap·er /'skreɪpə\ʳ/ n a tool for scraping: *a paint scraper*

scrap heap /'··/ n **1** [C] a pile of waste material, esp. metal **2** [*the*] *infml* a place for unwanted things, people, or ideas: *Suddenly I lost my job; it was a great shock to be on the scrapheap at 50.* | *We can now put this whole affair on the scrapheap of history.* (=we can forget about it)

scra·pie /'skreɪpi/ n [U] a disease of sheep and goats, caused by a VIRUS, that usu. kills them

scrap·ings /'skreɪpɪŋz/ n [P] things (to be) scraped from a surface: *scrapings taken from the paint for chemical tests*

scrap pa·per /'· ··/ *esp. BrE* ‖ usu. **scratch paper** *AmE*— n [U] paper, esp. in single sheets already used on one side, which may be used instead of more expensive paper for unimportant notes, shopping lists, etc.

scrap·ple /'skræpəl/ n [U] *AmE* a dish made from meat and CORNMEAL

scrap·py¹ /'skræpi/ adj derog made of disconnected pieces; not well arranged or planned: *a scrappy, badly-written report*

scrappy² adj AmE infml **1** liking to fight **2** determined; GUTSY

scraps /skræps/ n [P] pieces of food not eaten at a meal, and thrown away: *We feed the kitchen scraps to the pigs.* — compare LEFTOVERS

scratch¹ /skrætʃ/ v **1** [I;T] to make a mark on (a surface) or a small wound in (a person's skin) by rubbing with something pointed or rough: *Be careful the cat doesn't scratch you!* | *The dog's scratching at the door to be* (=because it wants to be) *let in.* | *I scratched the side of the car as I was driving through the gate.* | *I scratched my hand on a rose thorn.* | *The record is very badly scratched.* **2** [T+obj+adv/prep] to put or remove by doing this: *He scratched his name on the wall with a knife.* | *The dog has scratched some of the paint off the door.* **3** [I;T] to rub (a part of the body) lightly and repeatedly, esp. to stop an ITCH² (1): *Don't keep scratching your nose/those insect bites.* **4** [I;T] **a** to remove (oneself, a horse, etc.) from a race or competition before it starts: *The horse was scratched on the day before the race.* **b** to remove from consideration; ABANDON: *I guess we can scratch that idea.* | *They scratched their plans for the weekend.* **5 scratch the surface** [usu. in negatives] to deal with only the beginning of a matter or only a few of many cases: *This report is very superficial; it doesn't even scratch the surface of the problem.*

scratch sthg. **up/together** *phr v AmE* **scrape together** (SCRAPE¹)

scratch² n **1** [C] a mark or small wound made by scratching: *There were some nasty scratches on the beautiful mahogany table.* | *I don't need a bandage; it's only a scratch.* | *She came out of the accident **without a scratch.*** (=unhurt) **2** [C] a sound made (as if) by scratching: *You couldn't hear the music because of all the hisses and scratches on the record.* **3** [S] an act of scratching a part of the body: *The dog was* **having a scratch.** (=scratching itself) **4** [U] a type of music produced by stopping a record while it is playing and moving it by hand to make a scratching sound **5** [C] (of a player in GOLF) having a HANDICAP¹ (2) of zero **6 from scratch** *infml* starting from the beginning or with nothing: *It's completely ruined, so we'll have to do it all again/start from scratch.* | *Did you make that cake from scratch or did you use a cake*

mix? **7 up to scratch** *infml* in(to) good condition or at/to an acceptable standard: *The pianist was not feeling well and her performance wasn't up to scratch.* —see also SCRATCHY

scratch³ adj [A *no comp.*] made or put together in a hurry using whatever could be found: *Many of our best players were injured, so we could only put out a scratch side.*

scratch·ings /'skrætʃɪŋz/ n [P] *BrE* small pieces of cooked PORK skin usu. eaten cold; often sold in bags in PUBS — compare CRACKLING

scratch·pad /'skrætʃpæd/ n esp. AmE a small pile of loosely-joined sheets of paper for writing informal notes

scratch pa·per /'· ··/ n [U] AmE for SCRAP PAPER

scratch test /'· ·/ n a test made by scratching (SCRATCH¹ (1)) the skin with a substance then waiting for a reaction in order to see if one has an ALLERGY to the substance

scratch·y /'skrætʃi/ adj **1** (of a recording or its sound) spoiled by scratches **2** (of clothes) hot, rough, and uncomfortable: *a scratchy woollen shirt* **3** made as if by scratching paper with a pen: *What's her name? I can't read this scratchy signature.* —**iness** n [U]

scrawl¹ /skrɔːl/ v [T] to write in a careless, hurried, awkward, or unskilful way; SCRIBBLE: *to scrawl a few hurried lines*

scrawl² n infml **1** [C usu. sing.] something written awkwardly, or fast and carelessly: *She just sent us a scrawl on a card to say she was having a good time.* **2** [S] an awkward or irregular way of writing: *This letter must be from Frank; I recognize his scrawl.*

scraw·ny /'skrɔːni/ adj infml derog (of a person, animal, or part of the body) without much flesh on the bones; thin: *his scrawny neck*

scream¹ /skriːm/ v [I;T] (OUT) to cry out loudly on a high note, esp. in fear, pain, great excitement, or anger, or sometimes laughter: *I screamed for help.* | *She was screaming hysterically.* | *We screamed with laughter at her joke.* | *He screamed out a warning not to touch the electric wire.* | *The crowd screamed its approval.* | *a screaming baby* | (fig.) *The wind screamed down the chimney.* [+to-v] (fig.) *These injustices simply scream to be remedied.* (=it is extremely clear that they must be)

scream² n **1** [C] a sudden loud cry expressing anger, pain, fear, or sometimes laughter: *Her loud screams could be heard all over the house.* | *a scream of anguish* | (fig.) *The scream of the jets overhead drowned our conversation.* **2** [S] *infml* an extremely funny person, thing, joke, etc.: *She thought it was an absolute scream when I fell off my chair.*

scream·ing /'skriːmɪŋ/ adj **1** attracting a lot of attention: *a screaming tabloid exposé* **2** very funny: *a screaming new comedy* **~ly** adv

scree /skriː/ n [U] a mass of small loose broken rocks on the side of a mountain —see picture at MOUNTAIN

screech¹ /skriːtʃ/ v **1** [I;T] (OUT) to make an unpleasant high sharp sound, esp. because of terror or pain; SHRIEK: *A man was peering in at her. She screeched in fright and drew the curtains.* | *"Leave me alone!" she screeched.* **2** [I] (of a machine, esp. of a TYRE or BRAKES) to make a noise like this: *The lorry came to a screeching halt.* (=stopped suddenly) | (fig.) *The project screeched to a halt/standstill when the government withdrew all funding.*

screech² n a screeching sound: *a screech of brakes*

screed /skriːd/ also **screeds** pl.— n BrE infml derog a long and usu. dull speech or piece of writing: *He'd written screeds and screeds, but none of it was of any interest.*

screen¹ /skriːn/ n **1** an upright frame, sometimes made of folding parts, which is used as a small usu. movable wall for dividing a room or for protecting people from view, from cold air, from fires, etc.: *They put a screen round his bed so the doctor could examine him.* | *Always put a screen in front of the fire if children are playing nearby.* **2** [(for)] something that protects, shelters, or hides: *We planted a screen of trees to keep out the wind.* | *His used-car firm was just a screen for illicit drug trading.* **3** a surface on which a cinema film is shown: *We sat at the front, very close to the screen.* | *She first appeared on the screen* (=acted in her first film) *ten years ago.* | *The play was adapted for the screen* (=rewritten to be made into a film) *by its original author.* —see also SMALL SCREEN **4** the front glass surface of an electrical instrument, esp. a television, on which pictures or information appear: *Using a VDU, you can change the text* **on screen.** | *This popular show will be back on your screens* (=broadcast on television) *again next year.* —see picture at COMPUTER **5** a frame holding a net or a surface with holes in it, used for separating large things, which do not pass through the holes, from small things, which do: *We'd better get the screens up on the windows; bugs are starting to get in.*

screen

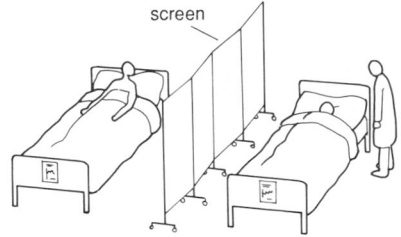
screen

screen² *v* [T] **1** [(**from**)] to shelter or protect from light, wind, etc.: *He screened his eyes with his hand.* **2** [(OFF, **from**)] to hide from view (as if) with a screen: *A floppy hat screened her face.* | *Part of the room was screened off as a reception area.* **3** [(**from**)] to protect from harm or punishment: *He admitted the crime in order to screen his wife, who was the real criminal.* **4** [(OUT) *often pass.*] to test in order to find out ability, health, suitability, loyalty, etc., and so be able to remove those that do not reach the proper standard: *A hundred carefully screened people were invited to dinner with the President.* | *Unsuitable candidates were screened out.* (=were got rid of after being tested) **5** [*usu. pass.*] to show or broadcast (a film or television show): *The big match is being screened live.*
screen sthg. ↔ **out** *phr v* [T] to prevent from coming through by a covering or SCREEN¹ (1,2): *The curtains screen out the sunlight.*

Screen Ac·tors' Guild /ˈ· ·· ˌ·/ see SAG

screen door /ˈ· ˌ·/ *n* a door outside the main door at the front or back of a house that lets air in but keeps insects out. They are common all over the US but rare in Britain.

screen·ing /ˈskriːnɪŋ/ *n* **1** [C;U] (a) showing of a film: *The new film gets its first London screening next week.* **2** [U] the process of screening (SCREEN² (4)) people or things: *more efficient breast cancer screening*

screen·play /ˈskriːnpleɪ/ *n* a story written for a film or television

screen print·ing /ˈ· ˌ·/ *n* [U] SILK SCREEN

screen test /ˈ· ˌ·/ *n* a test of someone's ability to act in films

screen·writ·er /ˈskriːnraɪtəʳ/ *n* a person who writes the words for actors in films, often using the words in a book which is being made into a film as his or her starting point

screw¹ /skruː/ *n* **1** [C] a type of fastener that is like a nail but has a raised edge winding round it (THREAD¹ (4)) and a special cut in its top to hold a tool, usu. a SCREWDRIVER, for turning and pressing it into the material to be fastened —see also CORKSCREW **2** [C] *tech* a PROPELLER, esp. on a ship **3** [C (**of**)] *BrE old-fash* a small twisted paper packet: *a screw of tobacco* **4** [C] *sl* (used by prisoners) a prison guard **5** [C] *taboo sl* **a** an act of having sex with: *a good screw* **b** someone considered as a person to have sex with: *a good screw* **6** [S] *BrE sl* pay; wages **7** **have a** ¹**screw loose** *humor* to be slightly mad **8** **put/tighten the screws on** *infml* to force (someone) to do as one wishes, esp. by increasing pressure and threats

screw² *v* **1** [T+obj+adv|prep] to fasten with one or more screws: *The table legs are screwed to the floor.* **2** [I+adv| prep;T+obj+adv|prep] **a** to turn or tighten (a screw or something that moves in the same way): *Screw the two pipes together end to end.* | *Screw the lid on tightly.* **b** (of such a thing) to turn or tighten: *The two pieces screw together.* —see also UNSCREW **3** [T+obj+adv|prep] to twist (paper or cloth) carelessly or so as to make a ball: *She screwed the letter up angrily|screwed the letter into a ball and threw it away.* **4** [T+obj+adv|prep, esp. **out of**] *infml* to get by forcing or twisting or by great effort or threats:

We eventually managed to screw a promise out of them. **5** [I;T] *taboo sl* to have sex (with) **6** [T(for); I(out of)] to treat badly, esp. by taking an unfair advantage of: *I really got screwed on this new sander.* | *They screwed us for $5 on the price of the room.* | *You'll get screwed out of your last dollar in that place.* **7** [T *usu. imperative*] *taboo sl* (used for showing extreme annoyance with the stated person or thing): *"No, I won't lend you the money." "Well, screw you!"* —see also **have one's head screwed on** (HEAD)

screws

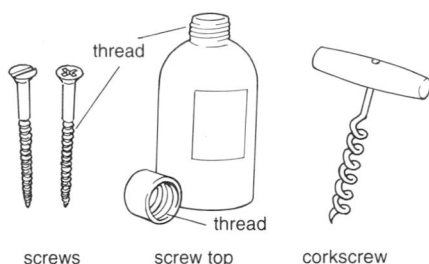
thread   thread
screws   screw top   corkscrew

screw sthg. ↔ **up** *phr v* [T] **1** to twist (one's face) or make (one's eyes) narrower, esp. during effort or to show disapproval or uncertainty: *She screwed up her eyes in the bright light.* **2** *infml* to ruin; cause to fail: *It was such a simple plan; how could you have screwed it up?* **3** [(**about**) *usu. pass.*] *infml* to cause to become confused, anxious, unhappy, etc.: *He's divorced, and he's really screwed up about his relationships with women.* **4 screw up one's courage** to stop oneself from being afraid

screw·ball /ˈskruːbɔːl/ *n* **1** *infml, esp. AmE* a person whose ideas or actions seem wild or mad, usu. in a harmless way **2** *AmE infml* (in BASEBALL) a ball which is thrown to a BATTER³ and spins in the opposite direction to a curve

screw·driv·er /ˈskruːˌdraɪvəʳ/ *n* **1** a tool with a narrow blade at one end which fits into the hole cut in the top of a screw for turning it into and out of its place —see picture at TOOL **2** an alcoholic drink made from VODKA and orange juice

screw top /ˌ· ˈ·◂/ *n* a cover which is made to be twisted tightly onto the top of a bottle or other container —see picture at SCREW

screw·y /ˈskruːi/ *adj infml* strange or slightly mad: *Something has gone screwy in my calculation; this can't be the right answer.* | *He has lots of mad ideas, each one screwier than the last!*

scrib·ble¹ /ˈskrɪbəl/ *v* **1** [I] to write meaningless marks: *She can't write yet, but she loves to scribble with a pencil.* **2** [T] to write (usu. something that is hard to read) carelessly or in a hurry: *She scribbled a note to the milkman.*

scribble² *n* **1** [C] also **scribbles** *pl.*— a meaningless written marking **2** [S;U] (a way of) writing which is careless and hard to read: *His handwriting is nothing but (a) scribble.*

scrib·bler /ˈskrɪbləʳ/ *n derog or humor* a writer

scribe /skraɪb/ *n* a person employed to copy things in writing, esp. in times before the invention of printing

scrim·mage /ˈskrɪmɪdʒ/ *n* **1** [C] *infml* a disorderly fight between two or usu. more people **2** [C] (in AMERICAN FOOTBALL) the time that one team has possession of the ball from receiving a kick until they lose it **3** [U] a practice game (of football, BASKETBALL, etc.) often among members of the same team —see also LINE OF SCRIMMAGE —**scrimmage** *v* [I]

scrimp /skrɪmp/ *v* [I] to save money slowly and with difficulty, esp. by living less well than usual: *She had to* **scrimp and save** *to pay for her holiday.*

scrim·shaw /ˈskrɪmʃɔː/ *n* [U] *AmE* WHALE bones or IVORY that has been made into decorative shapes

scrip /skrɪp/ *n* [U] *tech* an official paper which allows the holder to get something, esp. paper printed for use as money in certain shops, at certain times, etc.

script /skrɪpt/ *n* **1** [C] a written form of a speech, play, film, or broadcast: *to depart from the script* **2** [C;U] the set of letters used in writing a language; ALPHABET: *Anyone learning Arabic must learn Arabic script.* **3** [S;U] *fml* writing done by hand, esp. as in English with the letters of words joined: *He wrote with a flowing script.* | *copperplate script* **4** [C *usu. pl.*] *BrE* a piece of writing done by a student in an examination, to be read and given a mark by a teacher

script·ed /'skrɪptɪd/ *adj* (esp. of a speech or broadcast) having a SCRIPT (1) or read from a script —opposite **unscripted**

scrip·tur·al /'skrɪptʃ ərəl/ *adj* (*sometimes cap.*) of, found in, or according to a holy writing, esp. the Bible

scrip·ture /'skrɪptʃəʳ/ *n* [U] **1** also **the scriptures** *pl.—* (*usu. cap.*) (used by Christians) the Bible **2** also **scriptures** *pl.—* the holy books of the stated religion: *Buddhist scriptures*

script·writ·er /'skrɪptˌraɪtəʳ/ *n* a writer of scripts for films, broadcasts, etc.

scrof·u·la /'skrɒfjʊlə‖'skrɔː-ˌ'skrɑː-/ *n* [U] a disease in which organs in the neck become swollen —**lous** *adj*

scroll[1] /skrəʊl/ *n* **1** a piece of paper or other writing material, with usu. official writing on it, that is or can be rolled up: *At the ceremony he was presented with a scroll commemorating his achievements.* | *parchment scrolls with ancient writings on them* **2** a decoration or shape like a rolled-up piece of paper —see also DEAD SEA SCROLLS

scroll[2] *v* [T;I(up/down)] *tech* to move (information) on a SCREEN[1] (4) connected to a computer, in a continuous movement from bottom to top: *How do you stop this thing scrolling?* | *Scroll down* (=towards the end of a FILE) *to see what the last line is.* | *Do I have to scroll up to the top before I close the file?*

scroll·work /'skrəʊlwɜːk‖-wɜːrk/ *n* [U] decoration in a pattern of SCROLLS[1] (2)

scrooge /skruːdʒ/ *n infml derog* (*usu. cap.*) an extremely ungenerous person who keeps all their money for themselves (from the character of Ebenezer Scrooge in the story *A Christmas Carol* by Charles Dickens, who is very mean and thinks that Christmas is a waste of time and money): *Campaigners have hit out at scrooge companies for failing to help them financially.* | *My landlord makes Scrooge look extravagant.* | *a heartless Scrooge*

Scrooge

scro·tum /'skrəʊtəm/ *n* **-ta** /tə/ *or* **-tums** *tech* the bag of flesh holding the TESTICLES of male animals

scrounge /skraʊndʒ/ *v* [I;T (off)] *infml, often derog* to get (something) without work or payment or by persuading others: *He's always scrounging off his friends.* (=esp. getting money from them) | *Can I scrounge a cigarette off you?* —**scrounger** *n* : *The government plans to clamp down on social security scroungers.*

scrub[1] /skrʌb/ *v* **-bb-** **1** [I (at);T] to rub hard at (something) in order to clean, e.g. with a stiff brush: *You'll have to scrub hard to get that stain out/to scrub hard at that stain to get it out.* | *He scrubbed the floor (clean).* **2** [T] *infml* to remove from consideration or from a list; no longer do or have; CANCEL: *We've had to scrub our plans to go abroad this year; we've got no money.* —see CLEAN (USAGE)

scrub up *phr v* [I] (of a doctor) to wash one's hands and arms before doing an operation

scrub[2] *n* [S] an act of scrubbing: *Give that dirt/that floor a good hard scrub.*

scrub[3] *n* [U] low-growing plants including bushes and short trees growing in poor soil and usu. forming a thick covering over the ground —see also SCRUBBY

scrub·ber[1] /'skrʌbəʳ/ *n AmE* a hand-held plastic or wire mass used for cleaning pots and pans

scrubber[2] *n BrE derog sl* **1** a woman who has sex with many partners **2** a female PROSTITUTE

scrubbing brush /'··· ·/ *esp. BrE* ‖ *usu.* **scrub brush** /'· ·/ *AmE— n* a stiff brush for heavy cleaning jobs, like scrubbing floors —see picture at BRUSH

scrub·by /'skrʌbi/ *adj* **1** covered by, made of, or like SCRUB[3] **2** *infml derog* of small size or importance

Scrubs /skrʌbs/, **The** see WORMWOOD SCRUBS

scruff[1] /skrʌf/ *n* **the scruff of the neck** the flesh at the back of the neck: *He caught/grabbed/took him by the scruff of the neck and threw him out.*

scruff[2] *n BrE infml* a dirty and untidy person

scruf·fy /'skrʌfi/ *adj* dirty and untidy: *The hotel looked rather scruffy so we decided not to stay there.* | *What a scruffy little boy!*

scrum /skrʌm/ *also* **scrummage** *fml— n* **1** (in RUGBY) a group formed by the front players of both teams pushing against each other with their heads down and shoulders together, to try to get the ball which is thrown onto the ground between them —see picture at RUGBY **2** *BrE infml* (the forming of) a disorderly struggling crowd: *There was the usual scrum for tickets when the box office opened.*

scrum·half /ˌskrʌm'hɑːf‖-'hæf/ *n* (in RUGBY) a player whose job is to put the ball into the scrum

scrum·mage /'skrʌmɪdʒ/ *v, n* [I] (in RUGBY) (to take part in) a scrum

scrump /skrʌmp/ *v* [T] *BrE infml* to steal fruit (esp. apples) from the trees it is growing on

scrump·tious /'skrʌmpʃəs/ *adj infml* (esp. of food) extremely good; DELICIOUS

scrum·py /'skrʌmpi/ *n* [U] a strong kind of CIDER (=an alcoholic apple drink) of South West England

scrunch /skrʌntʃ/ *v infml* **1** [T (UP)] to press and twist into a ball in the hand; CRUMPLE: *He scrunched up the envelope and threw it away.* **2** [I] to make the sound of being crushed together: *The gravel scrunched under our feet as we walked up the path.*

scru·ple[1] /'skruːpəl/ *n* **1** [C *usu. pl.*] a moral principle which keeps one from doing something; a doubt about the rightness of an action: *He has absolutely no scruples; he'll do anything to get what he wants.* **2** [U *usu. in negatives*] the desire to do what is right; conscience: *If it was the only way to get my son set free, I would act completely without scruple.* (=willingly do something bad or immoral)

scruple[2] *v* [I+*to-v*;*usu. in negatives*] to be unwilling to do something because one thinks it is wrong: *He wouldn't scruple to charge you double its value if he thought you'd pay.*

scru·pu·lous /'skruːpjʊləs/ *adj* **1** *fml* correct even in the smallest detail; exact: *You must take the most scrupulous care to keep the wound free from dirt.* **2** *apprec* carefully doing only what is right; exactly honest: *A less scrupulous man wouldn't have given me the money back.* —opposite **unscrupulous** (for 2) — ~ **ly** *adv* : *scrupulously clean/fair* — ~ **ness** *n* [U]

scru·ti·neer /ˌskruːtɪ'nɪəʳ/ *n BrE* an official examiner or counter of votes in an election

scru·ti·nize *also* **-nise** *BrE* /'skruːtɪnaɪz/ *v* [T] to examine very closely and carefully: *The customs officer scrutinized his face for any signs of nervousness.*

scru·ti·ny /'skruːtɪni/ *n* [U] a close study or look; careful and thorough examination: *A minister's actions come under/are subjected to minute/continuous scrutiny in the press.*

scu·ba /'skuːbə/ *n* an instrument used for breathing while swimming under water, consisting of a container of air fastened to the back and connected by a rubber pipe to the mouth: *scuba diving*

scud /skʌd/ *v* **-dd-** [I+*adv/prep*] *lit* (esp. of clouds and ships) to move along quickly

Scud *n* a Soviet-developed surface-to-surface MISSILE (= flying weapon) fired from a movable or immovable base and carrying either a regular WARHEAD or NUCLEAR WARHEAD

scuff[1] /skʌf/ *v* [U(UP)] **1** [T] to make a rough mark or marks on the smooth surface of (shoes, furniture, a floor, etc.): *The floor was badly scuffed (up) where they had been dancing.* **2** [I] (of shoes, floors, etc.) to be damaged in this way

scuff[2] *also* **scuff·mark** /'skʌfmɑːk‖-mɑːrk/— *n* a mark made by scuffing

scuf·fle /'skʌfəl/ *n* a disorderly fight among a few people, usu. not serious or long: *A few isolated scuffles broke out* *when police tried to move the demonstrators.* —**scuffle** v [I (**with**)]

scull /skʌl/ n [I;T] to row (a small light boat, esp. for one person) — **-er** n

scul·le·ry /ˈskʌləri/ n a room next to the kitchen, esp. in a large or old house, for rough cleaning jobs such as washing dishes and pots

scul·lion /ˈskʌljən/ n old use a boy doing cleaning work in a kitchen

sculp·tor /ˈskʌlptər/ n someone who makes sculptures

sculp·tur·al /ˈskʌlptʃərəl/ adj of or looking like sculpture

sculp·ture[1] /ˈskʌlptʃər/ n **1** [U] the art of shaping solid representations of people, animals, or objects out of stone, wood, clay, metal, etc.: *She studied sculpture at art school.* | *the sculpture class* **2** [C;U] (a piece of) work produced by this art: *There are some interesting abstract sculptures in this gallery.* —compare STATUE

sculpture[2] also **sculpt** /skʌlpt/— v [T] **1** to make by shaping: *sculptured pillars* | (fig.) *The water had sculptured the rocks into strange shapes.* **2** to make a figure of (a person or thing) in sculpture: *a Greek god sculptured in marble* —compare CARVE[1] (1)

scum /skʌm/ n **1** [S;U] a covering of usu. unpleasant material that forms on the surface of liquid: *When the meat is boiling, remove the scum.* **2** [P] derog worthless immoral people: *These scum who fight at football matches must be severely dealt with!* | *They are* **the scum of the earth.** (=the worst people in the world) **3** derog (used when speaking to a worthless immoral person) — ~**my** adj

scup·per[1] /ˈskʌpər/ v [T] BrE **1** to sink (one's own ship) intentionally **2** [usu. pass.] infml to wreck or ruin (a plan, chance, etc.)

scupper[2] n [usu. pl.] an opening in the side of a ship at the level of the DECK (=upper floor) to allow water to run off it into the sea

scurf /skɜːf/ n [U] small dry loose bits of dead skin, esp. in the hair — ~**y** adj

scur·ril·i·ty /skəˈrɪləti, skʌ-/ n [U] fml scurrilousness or scurrilous language

scur·ri·lous /ˈskʌrələs/ adj fml making or containing very rude, improper, or evil and usu. untrue statements: *He has been the target of some scurrilous attacks in the newspapers.* — ~**ly** adv — ~**ness** n [U]

scur·ry[1] /ˈskʌri/ v [I+adv/prep] to move hastily, esp. with short quick steps; hurry: *The mouse scurried into its hole when the cat appeared.*

scurry[2] n [S;U] a movement or esp. sound of scurrying: *I heard the scurry of feet in the hall.*

scur·vy[1] /ˈskɜːvi/ n [U] a disease marked by bleeding and caused by not eating fruit and vegetables with VITAMIN C: *In former times, sailors often suffered from scurvy.*

scurvy[2] adj [A] old-fash dishonourable; deserving no respect; DESPICABLE: *What a scurvy trick to let your friend take the blame for your mistake!* —**·vily** adv

scut·tle[1] /ˈskʌtl/ v [I+adv/prep] to rush with short quick steps, esp. in order to escape: *The children scuttled off/away when they saw the policeman.*

scuttle[2] v [T] to sink (a ship, esp. one's own) by making holes in the bottom

scuttle[3] n a COALSCUTTLE

scut·tle·butt /ˈskʌtlbʌt/ n [U] AmE infml interesting but possibly untrue story; GOSSIP

scuz·zy /ˈskʌzi/ adj AmE sl unpleasant and dirty

Scyl·la and Cha·ryb·dis /ˌsɪlə ənd kəˈrɪbdəs/ **between Scylla and Charybdis** between two things which are equally dangerous (from the ancient stories of a MONSTER and a WHIRLPOOL which threatened sailors in the sea between Italy and Sicily)

scythe[1] /saɪð/ n a tool that has a long curving blade fixed to a long wooden pole and is worked with a swinging movement to cut grain or long grass —compare SICKLE

scythe[2] v [I;T (DOWN, **through**)] to cut down (as if) with a scythe: *The motorbike scythed (a path) through the crowd.*

SD written abbrev. for SOUTH DAKOTA

SDI /ˌes diː ˈaɪ/ Strategic Defence Initiative; a US government plan for the use of special weapons to destroy enemy MISSILEs in space —see also STAR WARS

SDLP /ˌes diː el ˈpiː/ [the] Social Democrat and Labour Party; a party formed in N Ireland in 1970 with mainly CATHOLIC supporters and whose aim is to unite N Ireland and the Republic of Ireland

SDP /ˌes diː ˈpiː/ n abbrev. for: SOCIAL DEMOCRATIC PARTY

SE written abbrev. for: southeast(ern)

sea

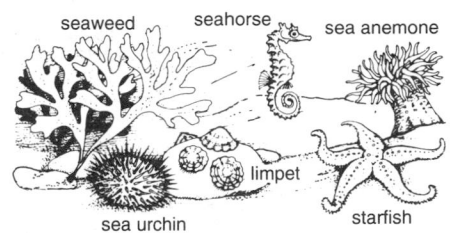

seaweed   seahorse   sea anemone

limpet

sea urchin   starfish

sea /siː/ n **1** [(the) U] esp. BrE ‖ **ocean** esp. AmE—the great body of salty water that covers much of the Earth's surface; ocean: *I enjoy swimming in the sea (esp.BrE)/in the ocean (esp. AmE).* | *boats sailing on the sea* | *Two thirds of the Earth is covered by sea.* | *The sea is calm today.* (=with not many big waves) | *A gale is forecast, so we can expect rough/heavy/stormy seas.* (=with big waves) | *She lives in a little cottage by the sea.* (=on the coast) | *He travelled by air, but sent his heavy luggage* **by sea.** (=on a ship) | *We've now been* **at sea** *three days.* (=our ship's voyage has lasted three days) | *He was buried at sea.* (=his dead body was dropped into the sea from a boat) | *We shall* **put to sea** (=start our voyage) *on the next high tide.* | *When he was 15 he ran away* **to sea.** (=to become a sailor) | *a sea voyage* —see also HIGH SEAS **2** [C] (often cap., esp. as part of a name) a large body of salty water smaller than an ocean, either **a** a part of the ocean: *the North Sea (northeast of Britain)* **b** a body of water (mostly) enclosed by land: *the Dead Sea* | *the Mediterranean Sea* **3** [S (**of**)] a large mass or quantity spread out in front of one: *The actor looked out from the stage onto a sea of faces.* **4** [C] (usu. cap. as part of a name) any of a number of broad plains on the moon: *the Sea of Tranquillity* **5 at sea** infml as if lost; not understanding: *I'm afraid I'm all/completely at sea with this maths problem.* **6 go down to the sea in ships** phrase from the Bible a slightly changed phrase from the Book of Psalms, used as a formal or poetic way of saying "go to sea" —see also DEAD SEA, SEA LEGS

sea air /ˌ· ˈ·/ n [U] the fresh air at the seaside, said by many people to be good for one: *Let's go for a walk on the beach and take in some sea air.*

sea a·nem·o·ne /ˈ· ·ˌ·····/ also **anemone**— n a simple sea animal with a jelly-like body and brightly-coloured flower-like parts that can often sting —see picture at SEA

sea·bed /ˈsiːbed/ [the] the land at the bottom of the sea

Sea·bee /ˈsiːˌbiː/ n a member of the US Navy division that builds structures needed in areas where there is fighting

sea·bird /ˈsiːbɜːd/ n any of the birds living near the sea or finding food in it

sea·board /ˈsiːbɔːd/ n the part of a country along a seacoast: *the eastern seaboard of the US*

sea·borne /ˈsiːbɔːn/ n carried or brought in ships: *a seaborne attack* | *seaborne trade*

sea breeze /ˈ· ·/ n a cool light wind blowing from the sea onto the land

sea cap·tain /ˈ· ˌ··/ n not tech a person in command of a ship, esp. one carrying goods for trade

sea change /ˈ· ·/ n a complete change in the character or nature of something: *His public image underwent a drmatic sea change.*

sea dog /ˈ· ·/ n lit or humor a sailor with long experience

sea·far·ing /ˈsiːˌfeərɪŋ/ adj [A] esp. lit **1** of, about, or doing the job of a sailor: *a seafaring man* | *a story from my seafaring days* **2** having strong connections with the sea and sailing: *Britain is a seafaring nation.*

sea·food /ˈsiːfuːd/ n [U] fish and fishlike animals from the sea, esp. SHELLFISH, which can be eaten

sea·front /ˈsiːfrʌnt/ n [C;the] the part of a coastal town that is on the edge of the sea, often with a broad path along it for holiday visitors: *a seafront hotel*

sea·girt /ˈsiːgɜːt‖-gɜːrt/ n poet surrounded by the sea

sea·go·ing /ˈsiːˌgəʊɪŋ/ adj [A] OCEANGOING

sea·gull /ˈsiːgʌl/ n a GULL¹ —see picture at WATER BIRD

sea·horse /ˈsiːhɔːs‖-hɔːrs/ n a very small fish with a neck and head that look like those of a horse —see picture at SEA

sea is·land cot·ton /ˌ· ·· ˈ···/ n [U] cotton of a kind grown in the US and West Indies having long soft threads and making a fine cloth

Sea King /ˈ· ˌ·/ tdmk a make of HELICOPTER

seal

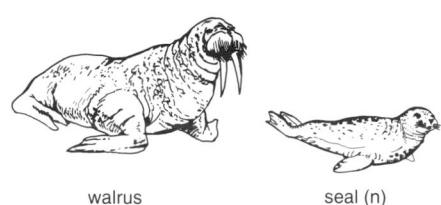

walrus   seal (n)

seal¹ /siːl/ n seals or seal a large fish-eating animal living mostly on cool seacoasts and floating ice, with FLIPPERS (=broad flat limbs) suitable for swimming

seal² n **1** the official mark of a government, company, etc., often made by pressing a pattern into red WAX or making an unremovable mark on paper, which is fixed to certain formal and official writings: *This document carries the royal seal.* | (fig.) *The scheme has the chairman's seal of approval.* (=he thinks it is very good) | *The Great Seal of the United States* **2** a small piece of paper, WAX, or wire fastened across an opening **a** to stop people from opening it without permission **b** to protect it from esp. air or water: *The seal on this bottle is broken.* **3** [usu. sing.] a tight connection on a machine, for keeping gas or liquid in or out: *The seal has worn and the machine is losing oil.* **4 set the seal on** lit to bring to an end in a suitable way; formally end: *This international award has set the seal on a long and distinguished career.*

seal³ v [T] **1** to fix a SEAL² (1) onto: *an official document, signed and sealed* **2** [(UP, DOWN)] to fasten or close (as if) with a SEAL² (2) or a tight cover or band of something: *The envelope was firmly sealed.* | *She sealed the parcel with sticky tape.* | *These birds seal (up) the holes and cracks in their nests with mud.* | *The platoon was sent out under sealed orders.* (=secret orders not to be read until a particular time or place) | (fig.) *I'm sorry, I can't tell you; my lips are sealed.* (=I have promised not to tell) **3** [(by, with)] to settle; make (more) certain, formal, or solemn: *They sealed their agreement by shaking hands.* **4 seal someone's fate/doom** infml to make someone's death, punishment, or ruin certain: *The bank's refusal to lend any more money sealed the company's fate.*

seal sthg./sbdy. ↔ **in** phr v [T] to keep inside or contained without a chance to escape

seal sthg. ↔ **off** phr v [T] to close tightly so as not to allow entrance or escape: *Police sealed off the area where the murderer was known to be hiding.*

sea lane /ˈ· ·/ n see LANE (4)

sea legs /ˈ· ·/ n [P] infml the ability to walk, feel comfortable, and not be sick on a moving ship: *He found his sea legs* (=got used to being on a boat) *after a couple of days.*

seal·er¹ /ˈsiːlə^r/ also **seal·ant** /ˈsiːlənt/— n [C;U] a thing or material which SEALS³ (2), esp. (a covering of) paint, polish, etc., on a surface to keep other liquids from going into or through it

sealer² n a person or ship that hunts SEALS¹

sea lev·el /ˈ· ˌ··/ n [U] the average height of the sea, used as a standard for measuring heights on land: *Mount Everest is 29,028 feet above sea level.* | *Death Valley in California is 280 feet below sea level.*

seal·ing /ˈsiːlɪŋ/ n [U] the hunting or catching of SEALS¹

sealing wax /ˈ·· ·/ n [U] a solid substance, often red and

sold in small bars, which melts and then hardens quickly, and is used for SEALS² (1,2)

Sea·link Sten·a Line /ˌsiːlɪŋk ˈstenə ˌlaɪn/ a private company which takes people and goods by sea from England to France, Ireland, and the islands to the south of England

sea li·on /ˈ· ˌ··/ n sea lions or sea lion a large SEAL¹ of the Pacific Ocean, often used to perform tricks in the CIRCUS

seal·skin /ˈsiːlˌskɪn/ n [U] the skin or fur of certain kinds of SEALS¹, esp. as used in clothing or made into leather. It is far less popular than formerly and to some people unacceptable after films were seen showing the violence of the CULL (=killing) and the large number of seals being killed including babies whose fur was esp. desirable.

Sea·ly·ham /ˈsiːliəm‖ˈsiːlihæm/ n a small dog with short legs and white fur; so-called because they were originally from the village of Sealyham in Wales

seam /siːm/ n **1** a line of stitches joining two pieces of cloth, leather, etc.: *to tack a seam* | (fig.) *The little hall was practically* **bursting at the seams.** (=it was completely full of people) —see picture at SHOE **2** the crack, line, or raised mark where two edges meet: *They used to fill the seams of wooden boats* (=the cracks between the pieces of wood) *with tar to stop the water getting in.* **3** a narrow band of one kind of mineral, esp. coal, between masses of other rocks: *a coal seam* —compare VEIN **4 come apart at the seams a** (of clothing or cloth) to be separating at the seams usu. because the stitching is old or poor: *Those trousers are coming apart at the seams.* **b** (an expression) to fail completely; to be ruined: *First I had the flu and now I've broken my arm — I think I'm coming apart at the seams!* | *Our plans for a holiday this year are coming apart at the seams.* — **~less** adj : *seamless stockings*

sea·man /ˈsiːmən/ n **-men** /mən/ **1** a sailor on a ship, other than an officer **2** a member of a navy in any of the lowest group of ranks, below PETTY OFFICER **3** a man skilled in handling ships at sea —see also ABLE SEAMAN

sea·man·like /ˈsiːmənlaɪk/ adj apprec typical of a good and skilful seaman

sea·man·ship /ˈsiːmənʃɪp/ n [U] the skill of handling a ship and directing its course

seam bowl·er /ˈ· ˌ··/ n (in cricket) a BOWLER who makes the ball BOUNCE on its SEAM and so turn away from a straight line

sea mile /ˈ· ·/ n a NAUTICAL MILE

sea mist /ˈ· ·/ n [C;U] (a) mist on land coming in from the sea or caused by a warm wind from the sea

seam·stress /ˈsiːmstrɪs/ n a woman whose job is sewing

seam·y /ˈsiːmi/ adj (not of a person) unpleasant, esp. in being rough and immoral; SORDID: *The novel gives a vivid description of* **the seamy side** *of city life.* —**·iness** n [U]

sé·ance /ˈseɪɑːns, -ɒns‖ˈseɪɑːns/ n a meeting where people try to talk to or receive messages from the spirits of dead people

► CULTURAL NOTE A typical séance takes place in a darkened room with people sitting around a table holding hands with each other. There is a MEDIUM present who goes into a TRANCE and who then becomes the instrument through which the spirits answer the questions of the people present who are usu. trying to contact dead friends or relatives. Sometimes a OUIJA board is used. Everyone puts a finger on e.g. an upturned glass in the middle of the board and a question is asked. The glass then moves around the board without pressure from the people and spells out the answers. There are many people who believe these happenings are tricks and the established Church does not approve of séances. ◄

Sea of Mar·ma·ra /ˌsiː əv ˈmɑːmərə‖-ˈmɑːr-/ [the] an INLAND (=surrounded by land) sea in NW Turkey, between the Bosphorus and the Dardanelles

sea·plane /ˈsiːpleɪn/ n an aircraft which can take off from and come down on water

sea·port /ˈsiːpɔːt‖-pɔːrt/ n a large town on a coast or connected to a coast by water, with a HARBOUR used by large ships

sea pow·er /ˈ· ˌ··/ n **1** [U] the strength of a country's navy **2** [C] a country with a powerful navy

sear¹ /sɪə^r/ v [T] **1** to burn with sudden powerful heat:

(fig.) *The terrible experience is seared on/into my memory.* (=so that I shall never be able to forget it) **2** to cook the outside of (a piece of meat) quickly, usu. to keep its juice in **3** to dry up (a plant); cause to WITHER —see also SEARING

sear² *adj* SERE

search¹ /sɜːtʃ‖sɜːrtʃ/ *v* **1** [I (**through**);T (**for**)] to look at, through, into, etc., or examine (a place or person) carefully and thoroughly to try to find something: *I've been searching high and low/everywhere but I can't find it.* | *He searched through his pockets for a cigarette.* | *Scientists are still searching for a cure to the common cold.* | *She searched desperately for some reason to stay.* | *We searched the house from top to bottom.* | *The police searched the suspect but found no weapon on him.* | *They searched the woods for the little boy.* | *a computer program that searches text for spelling errors* | *She searched his face for some indication of how he felt.* | (Fig.) *I've* **searched my conscience** (=thought hard about whether I acted correctly) *and I still think I did the right thing.* | (*fml*) *to search after truth* **2 Search ¹me!** *infml* I don't know!: *"What's the time?" "Search me; I haven't got a watch."* — **~er** *n*
search sthg./sbdy. ↔ **out** *phr v* [T] to find (out) or uncover by searching: *With clever questioning the lawyer searched out the weaknesses in the witness's statement.*

search² *n* [(**for**)] **1** an act of searching: *The police conducted a long search for the lost child.* | *We did a computer search for all the hyphenated words.* | *I went off* **in search of** (=to try to find) *a garage where I could buy some petrol.* | *birds flying south in search of winter sun* **2 search and rescue** an act of searching, esp. in the mountains, sea, forest, etc., for people who are lost and may need medical help when found. This is often done by people who are specially trained: *a search and rescue operation for the lost boy*

search·ing /ˈsɜːtʃɪŋ‖ˈsɜːr-/ *adj* sharp and thorough; anxious to discover the truth; PENETRATING: *She gave me a searching look, as if doubting what I told her.* | *a searching review of police procedures* — **~ly** *adv*

search·light /ˈsɜːtʃlaɪt‖ˈsɜːr-/ *n* a large light with a powerful beam which can be turned in any direction, used for looking for aircraft in the sky at night, for lighting up prison walls so that prisoners cannot escape in the dark, etc.

search par·ty /ˈ· ˌ·· / *n* [C+*sing./pl. v*] a group of people searching, esp. for a lost person: *After the climbers had been missing for six hours, search parties were sent out.*

search war·rant /ˈ· ˌ·· / *n* a written order given by a court to police to allow them to search a place, e.g. to look for stolen goods. Police may not enter a building and search it without either the owner's permission or a search warrant: *to issue a search warrant*

sear·ing /ˈsɪərɪŋ/ *adj* **1** burning; unpleasantly hot: *A searing pain shot through her leg.* | *the searing heat of the desert* **2** *infml* causing or describing very strong feelings, esp. of a sexual kind: *a searing novel of love and passion*

Sears /sɪəz‖sɪərz/ also **Sears Roe·buck & Co.** /ˌ· ˈ··· ·ˌ·/ *n* a large national American store which sells tools, clothing, and almost everything for the family through its many branch stores and also through its MAIL-ORDER CATALOGUE

seas /siːz/ *n* [(*the*)U] the great body of salty water that covers much of the Earth's surface; ocean —see also HIGH SEAS, SEA

sea·scape /ˈsiːskeɪp/ *n* a picture of a scene at sea —compare LANDSCAPE¹ (2)

sea scout /ˈ· ·/ *n* (*often caps.*) a member of a group of usu. young people who specialize in sea and water activities —see also SCOUT

sea ser·pent /ˈ· ˌ··/ *n* an imaginary large snake-like animal once believed to live in the sea: *Old maps often picture sea serpents swimming in the oceans.*

sea·shell /ˈsiːʃel/ also **shell**— *n* a shell of a sea animal, such as a COCKLE, WINKLE, etc., esp. as found on the seashore. When people find large seashells they often hold them to their ears because it is said that if you do this you will hear the sound of the sea coming from the shell.

sea·shore /ˈsiːʃɔːʳ/ *n* [(*the*) U] land along the edge of the sea, usu. sand or rocks

sea·sick /ˈsiːˌsɪk/ *adj* sick because of the movement of a ship — **~ness** *n* [U]

seaside

sea·side /ˈsiːsaɪd/ [*the*] **1** the edge of the sea, esp. as a holiday place: *We spent two weeks at/by the seaside in the summer.* | *seaside resorts* **2 I do like to be beside the seaside** the first line of a popular old British song now used in other ways: *Britons no longer like to be beside the seaside: the era of the bucket and spade holiday seems to be over.* —see SHORE (USAGE), compare BEACH, COAST —see also extra information on page 630

▶ CULTURAL NOTE A lot of British people go to the seaside for their summer holidays, and the STEREOTYPE is of them sitting on the beach with a picnic even if the weather is cold and windy. The parents sit in DECKCHAIRS and try to get a TAN as soon as the sun comes out. The children build SANDCASTLES with buckets and spades, go for DONKEY rides, and eat ROCK² (4) or ICECREAM. When they are tired of the beach they may go for a walk along the PROMENADE or PIER. ◄

sea·son¹ /ˈsiːzən/ *n* **1** spring, summer, autumn, or winter **2** a period of time each year marked by a weather: *the rainy season* **b** greater or less activity: *After Christmas is the quiet season for business.* **c** a sporting activity: *(The) football season begins next week.* **d** a particular farming activity: *the planting season* **e** a particular animal activity: *the mating season* **f** hunting, fishing, etc.: *the coarse fishing season* **3** *infml for* SEASON TICKET **4 in season: a** (of fresh foods) at the time when they are usually ready for eating: *Fruit is cheapest in season.* **b** (esp. of holiday business) at the busiest time of year: *Hotels cost more in season.* **c** (of certain female animals) on HEAT² (4) **d** (of an animal) permitted to be hunted at the time: *Are grouse in season now?* **5 out of season** not in SEASON¹ (4a, b) **6 Season's Greetings!** (a greeting on a card sent during the Christmas SEASON (2g)) esp. in the US, this greeting is often sent to people who are not Christians and to whom it might be unsuitable to say "Merry Christmas" **7 season of goodwill** a way of describing Christmas, suggesting that it is a time when people should behave in a kind, friendly way to each other **8 season of mists and mellow fruitfulness** *quote* the first line of the poem *To Autumn* by John Keats, remembered and reused by many people: *Does the season of mists and mellow fruitfulness send you scurrying to the shops to get your Christmas shopping done?* —see also CLOSE SEASON, HIGH SEASON, LOW SEASON, OPEN SEASON, SILLY SEASON

season² *v* [T] **1** [(**with**)] to give special taste to (a food) by adding salt, pepper, a SPICE, etc. —see also SEASONING **2** to make (wood) hard and fit for use by gradual drying

sea·so·na·ble /ˈsiːzənəbəl/ *adj fml* **1** suitable or useful for the time of year: *seasonable weather.* **2** coming at a good or proper time: *seasonable advice* —compare SEASONAL —**bly** *adv*

sea·son·al /ˈsiːzənəl/ *adj* depending on the seasons, esp. happening or active only at a particular time of the year: *seasonal employment at a holiday camp* —compare SEASONABLE

seasonally ad·just·ed fig·ures /ˌ··· ·ˌ·· ˈ··/ *n* [P] the number of people with no job which increases at certain times of the year, e.g. in February which is a low period for farmers and in July when young people leave school: *The seasonally-adjusted figure has risen by 70,000.*

sea·soned /ˈsiːzənd/ *adj apprec* having much experience in the stated activity: *a seasoned traveller/journalist*

sea·son·ing /ˈsiːzənɪŋ/ *n* [C;U] something that seasons food

season tick·et /ˈ·· ˌ··‖ˌ·· ˈ··/ also **season** *infml*— *n* a ticket for a number of journeys, performances, etc. during a particular period, sold at a lower price than you would have to pay altogether if you paid for each journey, etc. separately —compare COMMUTATION TICKET

seat¹ /siːt/ n **1** a place for sitting: *What can we use for seats? | He sat down on|in the nearest available seat. | She got into|sat in the front|back seat of the car. | We reserved seats on the train. | Have you booked our theatre seats? | The show is about to start, ladies and gentlemen, so please take your seats.* (=sit down) | *Please come in and have|take a seat. | a 150-seat airliner* **2** [*usu. sing.*] the part on which one sits: *He had grass stains on the seat of his trousers. | Don't put your feet on the seat of the chair.| My seat's rather sore from horse riding!* **3** a place as a member of an official or controlling body: *She won a seat|lost her seat in Parliament at the election. | Her ambition is a seat on the company's main board. | a safe Labour seat* **4** [(*of*)] *fml* a place where a particular activity happens; CENTRE: *Oxford and Cambridge are England's most famous seats of learning. | London is the British* **seat of government.** **5** *tech* a way of sitting on a horse: *She's got a good seat.* (=rides well) **6 by the seat of one's pants** *infml* guided by one's experience rather than by machines, help from others, a formal plan, etc.: *With all her navigational equipment broken, she was flying by the seat of her pants.* **7 in the ¹driving seat** (*BrE*) ‖ **in the driver's seat** (*AmE*) in control **8 -seater** /siːtəʳ/ something with the stated number of seats or places to sit: *My little car's just a two-seater. | a three-seater sofa* —see also BACK SEAT, HOT SEAT

seat² v [T] **1** [*often pass.*] to cause or help to sit: *I glanced at the man seated next to me.* (=the man who was sitting next to me). | (*fml*) *Please* **be seated.** (=sit down) **2** [*not in progressive forms*] (of a room, table, etc.) to have room for seats for (a certain number of people): *The hall seats|will seat 200.* —see also SEATING **3** to fit (esp. a machine part) into a hole or close fitting place: *Make sure the washer is firmly seated before tightening the pipe.* —see also UNSEAT; see SIT (USAGE)

seat belt /'· ·/ also **safety belt—** n a belt fastened round a seated person in a car, plane, etc., to protect them from sudden movement. Seat belts must be worn at all times in Britain by drivers and front seat passengers and by back seat passengers in cars which have them fitted. In the US, seat belt laws vary from state to state —see picture at CAR

seat·ing /'siːtɪŋ/ n [U] (a way of arranging) seats: *a seating plan for the dinner guests | the seating capacity of the hall* (=the number of people who can sit in it)

SEATO /'siːtəʊ/ Southeast Asia Treaty Organization; an organization formed by Australia, Britain, France, New Zealand, the Philippines, Thailand, and the US for giving military help to each other in Southeast Asia and the Southwest Pacific area

Se·at·tle /sɪ'ætl/ a city and port in W Washington state, in the US; a business and industrial centre —see colour map on pages 1374–5

seat·work /'siːtwɜːk ‖ -wɜːrk/ n [U] *AmE* work, esp. written work, done by children at their desks at school without help from their teacher

sea ur·chin /'· ,··/ n a small ball-shaped sea animal that has a hard shell with many sharp points —see picture at SEA

sea·wall /ˌsiː'wɔːl ‖ 'siːwɔːl/ n a wall built along the edge of the sea to keep it from flowing over an area of land

sea·ward /'siːwəd ‖ -wərd/ adj **1** facing or directed towards the sea **2** coming in off the sea: *a seaward wind*

sea·wards /'siːwədz ‖ -wərdz/ also **seaward** – adv towards the sea

sea·way /'siːweɪ/ n **1** a course commonly followed by ships on the sea **2** a river or similar stretch of deep water, allowing ocean ships to travel far inside land

sea·weed /'siːwiːd/ n [U] a plant that grows in the sea; some seaweed is used for food —see also LAVER and see picture at SEA

sea·wor·thy /'siːwɜːði ‖ -ɜːr-/ adj (of a ship) in proper and safe condition; fit for a sea voyage —**-thiness** n [U]

se·bum /'siːbəm/ n fatty matter which comes out from under the skin to oil the hair and skin

SEC /ˌes iː 'siː/ abbrev. for: SECURITIES AND EXCHANGE COMMISSION

sec¹ /sek/ n infml for SECOND² (3): *Just hang on|wait a sec, will you?*

sec² abbrev. for: SECRETARY (3)

sec·a·teurs /'sekətɜːz ‖ ˌsekə'tɜːrz/ ns [P] *BrE* strong scissors for cutting bits off garden plants —see PAIR (USAGE), and see picture at GARDEN

se·cede /sɪ'siːd/ v [I (from)] *fml* to formally leave a group or organization, esp. because of disagreement: *One of the states has seceded from the federation.*

se·ces·sion /sɪ'seʃən/ n [U] formal separation from a group or organization: *The secession of some southern states from the USA in the 1860s led to a civil war.* — ~ **ist** n

se·clude /sɪ'kluːd/ v [T (in)] *fml* to keep (esp. oneself) away from other people

se·clud·ed /sɪ'kluːdɪd/ adj very quiet and private: *a secluded country house | a secluded life*

se·clu·sion /sɪ'kluːʒən/ n [U] **1** the state of being secluded; quietness and privateness: *He lives in almost total seclusion these days.* **2** [(*of*)] the act of secluding: *In some countries the seclusion of women* (=keeping them away from men) *is still the custom.*

Se·combe /'siːkəm/, **Sir Harry** (1921–) a Welsh singer and COMEDIAN. He is popular performer on radio, television, stage, and cinema and is esp. remembered for his part in the GOON SHOW.

sec·ond¹ /'sekənd/ determiner, adv, pron 2nd: *That's the second time you've asked me that. | the Second World War | They're rich enough to own a second car.* (=they have 2 cars) *| a second-year student at university | Bill only finished second|in second place in the race. | He was|came a poor second.* (=a long way behind the first person) *| They hold elections* **every second year.** (=one year out of every two) *| I hear she's had another baby. Is that her second or her third? | the second of a series of programmes on Russia | First, what happened? Second, why? | the second-largest car manufacturer in the country | As car manufacturers they are* **second only to** *Nissan in size.| As a footballer he is* **second to none.** (=the best) *| He was the second oldest child.* (=there was only one older than him) —see TABLE 1; see FIRSTLY (USAGE)

second² n **1** a length of time equal to 1/60 of a minute: *His time for the 100 metre sprint was 10.2 seconds. | The seconds ticked by.* **2** *tech* a measure of an angle equal to 1/3600 of a degree, or 1/60 of a MINUTE¹ (3) **3** [*usu. sing.*] a moment: *I'll be back in a second. | Have you got a second?* (=I want to talk to you) —see also SPLIT SECOND

second³ n **1** a person who helps someone who is fighting in a BOXING match or DUEL **2** [*usu. pl.*] *infml* a damaged or imperfect article for sale at a lower price: *If you want to buy dishes cheaply, you ought to get factory seconds.* **3** [(**in**)] the next-to-highest class of British university degree: *a second in history* —see also TWO-ONE, TWO-TWO; see DEGREE (CULTURAL NOTE)

second⁴ v [T] to support formally (a formal suggestion made at a meeting), so that argument or voting can follow: *"Will anyone second this motion?" "I second it, Mr Chairman."* — ~ **er** n : *Is there a seconder for that motion?*

se·cond⁵ /sɪ'kɒnd ‖ sɪ'kɑːnd/ v [T (from, to)] *usu. pass.*] *BrE fml* to move (someone) from their usual duties to a special duty, usu. for a limited time: *I've been seconded to the accounts department while they're short of staff.* — ~ **ment** n [C;U] : *She is* **on secondment** *to the accounts department at the moment.*

Second Ad·vent /ˌ·· '··/ n SECOND COMING

sec·ond·a·ry /'sekəndəri ‖ -deri/ adj **1** (of education, a teacher, etc.) for children from the age of 11 or 12 up to the age of 16 or 18 —compare PRIMARY¹ (2) **2** [(**to**)] not so important, valuable, etc., as the main one(s): *In addition to the main question, there are various secondary matters to talk about. | All other considerations are secondary to his safety.* **3** *tech* later than, developing from, taken from, etc., something earlier or original: *a secondary infection brought on by a cold* —**-rily** /'sekəndərˌli ‖ ˌsekən-'derˌli/ adv

secondary col·our /ˌ···· '··/ n a colour made by mixing two PRIMARY COLOURS (=red, yellow, or blue)

secondary mod·ern /ˌ···· '··/ also **secondary modern school** /ˌ···· '·· ,·/— n (in Britain, esp. formerly) a school for children over the age of 11 who are not expected to go on to higher study later. Although most children go to COMPREHENSIVE² schools now, there are still some secondary modern schools. —compare COMPREHENSIVE², GRAMMAR SCHOOL (1)

secondary school /ˌ···· ˌ·/ n a school for children between the ages of 11 and 16 or 18, above the level of PRIMARY education —compare PRIMARY SCHOOL, COMPREHENSIVE², GRAMMAR SCHOOL, SECONDARY MODERN; see also extra information on page 407

secondary stress /ˌ····· �··/ also **secondary ac·cent** /ˌ····· �··/— n [C;U] tech the next-to-strongest STRESS (=force) given in speech to part of a word or compound, and shown in this dictionary by the mark ˌ

second base /ˌ·· ·/ n 1 the base in BASEBALL which must be touched second by a BATTER trying to make a RUN² (10b) 2 also **second baseman**— the person who defends the area around the second base

second best /ˌ·· ·◄/ adj not as good as the best: my second-best trousers | The shop didn't have quite what we wanted so we had to settle for second best. | England **came off second best** (=were defeated) in the big football match.

second child·hood /ˌ·· ·◄/ n [S] euph the period when an old person's mind becomes weak and childish; DOTAGE

second class /ˌ·· ·/ n 1 [U] a class of mail a (in Britain) in which letters and parcels are delivered less quickly than by FIRST CLASS: I sent it second class. b (in the US and Canada) for newspapers and magazines 2 [U] the travelling conditions which are cheaper than FIRST CLASS, esp. on a train: We're travelling second class. 3 [C] fml for SECOND³ (3)

second-class /ˌ·· ·◄/ adj 1 below the highest standard; INFERIOR: Why should women be treated as second-class citizens? 2 [A] of, for, or being second class: a second-class stamp/ticket

Second Com·ing /ˌ·· ·◄/ [the] the future coming of Christ to Earth from heaven to judge the world on the last day, as believed by Christians

second cous·in /ˌ·· ·◄/ n the child of one's parent's COUSIN (1)

second-de·gree /ˌ··· ·◄/ adj [A] (of a burn) of the next-to-highest level of seriousness; less serious than THIRD-DEGREE

second-guess /ˌ·· ·◄/ v [T] AmE infml 1 to make a judgment about (someone or something) only afterwards, when an event has already taken place 2 to try to say in advance what (someone) will do, how (something) will happen, etc.

second-hand¹ /ˌ·· ·◄/ adj, adv 1 owned or used by someone else before; not new: a second-hand car | I got this book second-hand. 2 (learnt) from someone or something other than the point of origin: It was a second-hand report, based on what his friends had told him . —compare FIRSTHAND

second-hand² adj [A] dealing in second-hand goods. u second-hand shop

second hand /ˌ·· ·/ n the pointer that shows seconds on a clock or watch

second-in-com·mand /ˌ···· ···◄/ n a person, esp. a military officer, next in rank below the commander or director

second lan·guage /ˌ·· ···/ n a language which a person speaks in addition to the one they learned as a child, esp. when used frequently and well: She was born in Greece and came to Britain when she was 12, so English is her second language.

second lieu·ten·ant /ˌ·· ·◄/ n a military rank —see TABLE 3

sec·ond·ly /ˈsekəndli/ adv as the second of a set of facts, reasons, etc.; SECOND: First I need your name and address. Secondly, what's your date of birth?

second na·ture /ˌ·· ···/ n [U] a very firmly fixed habit: It's second nature for me to get up early, (=I always do it) even though I'm retired now.

second per·son /ˌ·· ···/ n [the+S] a form of a verb or PRONOUN that is used to show the person spoken to: "You" is a second person pronoun. | "You are" is the second person singular and plural of "to be". —compare FIRST PERSON, THIRD PERSON

second-rate /ˌ·· ·◄/ adj of low quality; INFERIOR: a second-rate film —compare FIRST-RATE

second read·ing /ˌ·· ···/ n the second reading out of a

suggested new law in parliament – see BILL¹ (2) (CULTURAL NOTE)

sec·onds /ˈsekəndz/ n [P] infml an additional serving of food at a meal; a second HELPING: He asked for seconds.

second sight /ˌ·· ·/ n [U] the ability to see or know about future or far-away things

second-string /ˌ·· ·◄/ adj [A] being one who sometimes comes in to take the place of another in a team, group, etc., rather than being a regular member —compare FIRST-STRING

second thought /ˌ·· ·/ n [C;U] a thought that a usu. past decision or opinion may not be right: I said I wouldn't do it, but **on second thoughts** (BrE) ‖ **on second thought** (AmE) I think I will. | We'd decided to sell our house, but then we began to have second thoughts. | He'd betray his own mother without a second thought.

second wind /ˌsekənd ˈwɪnd/ n [S] the return of one's strength during hard physical activity, when it seemed that one had become too tired to continue: (fig.) She was struggling with the new job at first, but now she's got her second wind she's doing very well.

Second World War /ˌ·· · ·/ also **World War II**— [the] (1939–45) a war involving every major power in the world. On one side were the Allied forces (chiefly Great Britain, France, Poland, and after 1941 the US, and the USSR) and on the other side the Axis forces (Germany, Japan, and Italy). The main reason for the war was the rise of governments which exercised complete control over everyone and were prepared to use armed force to achieve their aims. The war ended when Germany surrendered (SURRENDER) and the American army dropped ATOMIC BOMBS on Hiroshima and Nagasaki forcing Japan to surrender. A large number of people were killed or wounded.

▶ CULTURAL NOTE Although many British people lost their lives during the Second World War, many people in Britain, esp. those who did not live in cities that were bombed, look back to the war with pride and even fondness. The soldiers who fought in the war, esp. the pilots, are thought of as HEROs. Many people who remained in Britain during the war did special jobs which they enjoyed, e.g. working on the land or being involved with the Home Guard (a group of volunteers who trained together to defend the country from attack). People remember the feelings of togetherness which the war brought to people, and they often remember with humour the hardships of the war years, e.g. the lack of certain fresh foods. People also remember many wartime songs with fondness, esp. those sung by Vera Lynn. —compare FIRST WORLD WAR. In the US ordinary people were not affected by the war as much as were people in Britain. The only attack on the US directly was by the Japanese at Pearl Harbor in Hawaii, which led the US to enter the war. —see also BATTLE OF BRITAIN, BLITZ, Winston CHURCHILL, D-DAY, DUNKIRK, HATION ◄

se·cre·cy /ˈsiːkrəsi/ n [U] 1 the practice of keeping secrets: Secrecy is important to our plans. | I have been **sworn to secrecy** (=made to promise that I will not tell anyone) about this. 2 the state of being secret: The plan was shrouded in secrecy. (=kept very secret)

se·cret¹ /ˈsiːkrət/ adj 1 [(from)] that other people are prevented from knowing about: These plans must be kept secret (from our competitors). | We discovered a secret passage behind the wall. | a secret rendezvous —see also TOP-SECRET 2 [A] (of a person) not known by others to be the stated thing: John is a secret admirer of Helen, though he has never spoken to her. 3 [F (about)] careful in keeping secrets; SECRETIVE — ~ly adv : They were secretly married last week.

secret² n 1 [C] something kept hidden or known only to a few people: Our plan must remain a secret. | He has no secrets from me; he tells me everything. | Can you **keep** (=not tell) **a secret?** | closely-guarded/dark secrets —see also OPEN SECRET 2 [C] something unexplained; mystery: the secret of how life on earth began 3 [S] a single or most important means of gaining a good result: What's the secret of baking perfect bread? (=How do you do it?) 4 **in secret** in a private way or place; unknown to (most) others: They met in secret to discuss the arrangements.

secret a·gent /ˌ·· ···/ n a person gathering information secretly or doing secret jobs, esp. for a foreign government; SPY

sec·re·tar·i·al /ˌsekrɪˈteəriəl◂/ *adj* of or for (the work of) a secretary: *a secretarial college* (=teaching people to be secretaries)

sec·re·tar·i·at /ˌsekrɪˈteəriət/ *n* [C+*sing.*/*pl. v*] an official office or department with a SECRETARY (2) or esp. secretary-general as its head: *the United Nations Secretariat in New York*

Secretariat a horse which won many American horse races

sec·re·ta·ry /ˈsekrɪtəri‖-teri/ *n* **1** a person with the job of typing letters, keeping records, arranging meetings, etc., for someone: *She got a job as personal secretary to the company chairman.* | *His secretary says he's still out at lunch.* | *a good/efficient secretary*

▶ CULTURAL NOTE In Britain, the STEREOTYPE of a secretary is of a young, attractive woman who is very concerned about her appearance, and who spends a lot of time talking on the telephone to her friends, and filing (FILE (2)) her nails. In the US this image of a secretary is not as strong, but people do make jokes about bosses having AFFAIRS with their secretaries. —compare PA; see also COMPANY SECRETARY ◀

2 a government official, such as **a** (in Britain) a minister (**Secretary of State**), or a high non-elected official (the **Permanent Secretary**) in a department: *the Home/Foreign Secretary* | *the Secretary of State for Home/Foreign Affairs* **b** (in the US) a non-elected head of a large department: *the Secretary of the Treasury* | *the Secretary of State* (=dealing with foreign affairs) **c** a government representative below the rank of AMBASSADOR: *the First/Second/Third Secretary at the British Embassy* **3** an official of an organization who keeps records, writes official letters, etc.: *the Honorary Secretary of the Golf Club* | *the General Secretary of the Trades Union Congress*

secretary-gen·e·ral /ˌ… ˈ…/ *n* (*sometimes cap.*) the chief official in charge of running a large organization, esp. an international organization or a political party: *the Secretary-General of the United Nations*

Secretary of State /ˌ…·· · ˈ·/ [*the*] **1** a politician who is head of a certain government department e.g. Northern Ireland, Scotland, or Wales, or the Environment, Education and Science, etc. **2** *AmE* a politician who is in charge of affairs abroad —compare FOREIGN SECRETARY

secret drink·er /ˌ·· ˈ··/ *n* a person who often drinks alcohol, but does not want other people to know this

se·crete¹ /sɪˈkriːt/ *v* [T] *tech* (esp. of an animal or plant organ) to produce (a usu. liquid substance): *Tears are secreted by an organ under the upper eyelid.* —compare EXCRETE

secrete² *v* [T] *fml* to put (something) where it cannot be seen or found; hide

se·cre·tion /sɪˈkriːʃən/ *n* **1** [C;U] *tech* **a** a usu. liquid material produced by part of a plant or animal **b** the production of such material **2** [U] *fml* the act of hiding something

se·cre·tive /ˈsiːkrɪtɪv, sɪˈkriːtɪv/ *adj* [(about)] *often derog* liking to keep one's thoughts, intentions, or actions hidden from other people — ~ **ly** *adv* — ~ **ness** *n* [U]

secret po·lice /ˌ·· ·ˈ·/ *n* [(the) +*sing.*/*pl. v*] a government-controlled police force that acts in secret, esp. against political enemies of the government. They usu. operate in countries which are not DEMOCRATIC.

secret ser·vice /ˌ·· ˈ··/ *n* **1** *BrE, not tech* a government organization which tries to get secret information about other countries. The British MI5 and the American CIA are secret services. **2** *AmE* a government department dealing with special kinds of police work, esp. protecting high government officials

secret so·ci·ety /ˌ·· ·ˈ···/ *n* a group of people who have come together for some common purpose (e.g. religious, magical, social, or political) which uses special secret words and signs and makes special promises and keeps its activities secret. One of these societies in Britain and the US is the FREEMASONS.

sect /sekt/ *n often derog* a small group of people with their own particular set of beliefs and practices, usu. within or separated from a larger esp. religious group: *a breakaway sect*

sec·tar·i·an /sekˈteəriən/ *adj usu. derog* of or between one or more sects, esp. as shown in great strength and narrowness of beliefs: *sectarian conflict/violence in Northern Ireland* — ~ **ism** *n* [U]

sec·tion¹ /ˈsekʃən/ *n* **1** [C (**of**)] a separate part of a larger object, place, group, etc.: *the business section of a city* | *Few politicians are liked by all sections of the community.* (=everyone) | *She plays in the orchestra's brass section.* (=those who play brass instruments) | *a bookcase which comes apart into sections* | *Signals control each section of the railway track.* | *the aircraft's tail section* | *My section of the office deals with record-keeping.* **2** [C] any of the equal parts into which some fruits, such as the orange, are naturally divided; SEGMENT **3** [C;U] a representation on paper of something as if it were cut either **a** from top to bottom and looked at from the side or **b** from one side to the other and looked at from the top: *The architect drew the house* in section. —compare ELEVATION (3), PLAN¹ (3); see also CROSS-SECTION **4** [C;U] *tech* (a) cutting by a doctor in an operation: *First the surgeon performed the section of the blood vessel.* (=cut it) **5** [C] (in MATHEMATICS) the figure formed by the points where a solid body is cut by a flat surface: *conic sections* **6** [C] a very thin flat piece cut from skin, a plant, etc., to be looked at under a microscope

section² *v* [T] *tech* **1** to cut or show a SECTION¹ (3,6) from **2** (of a doctor) to cut (a part of the body) in an operation

sec·tion·al /ˈsekʃənəl/ *adj* **1** [*no comp.*] made up of sections that can be put together or taken apart: *sectional furniture* **2** *often derog* limited to one particular group or area: *sectional interests that have a divisive effect within the party* (=small groups of people who try and get what they want rather than being loyal to the party as a whole) **3** [*no comp.*] of or based on a SECTION¹ (3): *a sectional view of the bands of rock in the earth*

sec·tion·al·is·m /ˈsekʃənəlɪzəm/ *n* [U] *often derog* (too) great loyalty within only one section of a group

Section Eight /ˌ·· ˈ·/ *n AmE* a dismissal from the US army for having an unsuitable character or being unfit for military work

sec·tor /ˈsektəʳ/ *n* **1** a part of a field of activity, esp. of business, trade, etc.: *employment in the public and private sectors* (=those controlled by the government, and by private business) | *the banking sector* | *the electronics sector* (=the companies that produce ELECTRONIC goods) **2** any of the parts into which an area is divided for the purpose of esp. military control: *the British sector in Berlin* **3** *tech* an area in a circle enclosed by two straight lines drawn from the centre to the edge —compare SEGMENT

sec·u·lar /ˈsekjʊləʳ/ *adj* **1** not connected with or controlled by a church; not religious: *secular music/education* **2** encouraging or practising secularism: *our modern secular society* **3** (of a priest) living among ordinary people (rather than as a MONK) —compare REGULAR¹ (11)

sec·u·lar·is·m /ˈsekjʊlərɪzəm/ *n* [U] a system of social organization which keeps out all forms of religion

sec·u·lar·ize also **-ise** *BrE* /ˈsekjʊləraɪz/ *v* [T] to make (more) secular, esp. by removing from the control or influence of the church

se·cure¹ /sɪˈkjʊəʳ/ *adj* **1** [(**from, against**)] safe; protected against danger or risk: *a secure stronghold* | *secure from attack* **2** closed, firm, or tight enough for safety: *Make the windows secure before leaving the house.* **3** sure to be won or not to be lost; certain: *His place in history is now secure.* | *Why do you want to be an actor? Why not get a secure job in the civil service?* **4** having no doubt, fear, or anxiety: *a secure family background* | *It may be some years before the new company can gain a secure foothold in the market.* | *He acted in the secure belief that he was right.* | *The little boy felt secure near his parents.* —opposite **insecure** (except 2) — ~ **ly** *adv* : *securely locked and bolted*

secure² *v* [T] **1** to hold or close tightly: *They secured the windows when the storm began.* **2** [(**from, against**)] to make safe: *Extra men are needed to secure the camp against attack.* | *new investment to secure the company's future* **3** [(**for**)] *fml* to get, esp. as the result of effort: *He's managed to secure the release of the hostages.* **4** to give a legal promise that (something) will be paid back: *a secured loan*

Se·cu·ri·cor /sɪˈkjʊərɪkɔːʳ/ a British company which takes money from shops, etc. in guarded vehicles to banks

Se·cu·ri·ta·te /sɪˌkjʊərɪˈtaːteɪ/ [*the*] the Romanian secret police under Nicolae Ceaucescu

Securities and Ex·change Com·mis·sion /·ˌ··· · ·ˈ· ·ˌ··/ also **SEC**— [the] an American government organization which makes sure that people and companies obey the laws about the sale of STOCKS¹ (3) and BONDS¹ (3)

Securities and In·vest·ments Board /·ˌ··· · ·ˈ·· ˌ·/ also **SIB**— [the] a British organization responsible for controlling INVESTMENT businesses to prevent deceitful or dishonest behaviour

se·cu·ri·ty /sɪˈkjʊərᵻti/ n **1** [U] the state of being secure: *Once the jewels were safely locked up in the bank he had no more anxieties about their security.* | *the security of a good home and loving family* **2** [U] a protection against lawbreaking, violence, enemy acts, escape from prison, etc.: *For security reasons the passengers have to be searched.* | *Strict security measures were in force during the President's visit.* | *The terrorists somehow slipped through the tight security net.* | *a* **maximum security** *prison* | *The* **security forces/services** (=police and army) *were unable to keep order in the streets.* | **Security guards** (=people employed to protect) *stood around the president.* | *in the interests of state/national security* | *an airport security check* **b** [+sing./pl. v] a department concerned with this: *I'll have to inform Security about this.* **3** [U (**from**, **against**)] something which protects or makes secure: *The money I've saved is my security against bad times in the future.* **4** [U] valuable property promised to a lender in case repayment is not made or other conditions are not met: *He got a big loan from the bank, but he had to put up his house as security.* — compare GUARANTEE¹ (3) **5** [C *usu. pl.*] an official piece of writing, esp. a BOND or piece of STOCK¹ (3), giving the owner the right to certain property: *There has been heavy trading in government securities.* — see also SOCIAL SECURITY

security blan·ket /·ˈ··· ˌ··/ n esp. AmE **1** a BLANKET, soft toy, etc. which a small child likes to hold, often while sucking his thumb, and without which he will cry **2** anything which is treated like a security blanket: *That pipe is my father's security blanket.* | *She carries that calculator everywhere, like a security blanket.*

security clear·ance /·ˈ··· ˌ··/ n CLEARANCE (3)

Security Coun·cil /·ˈ··· ˌ··/ [the] a body within the United Nations whose member countries are concerned with peacekeeping

security guard /·ˈ··· ·/ n someone, usu. at the entrance to or inside a building, who looks out for people who might be trying to do something harmful or wrong, often checking people's bags as they arrive

security risk /·ˈ··· ˌ·/ n a person whose loyalty or ability to keep secrets is doubtful and who cannot be given certain government jobs

security ser·vice /·ˈ··· ˌ··/ n a government organization which protects a country's secrets against enemy countries or protects the ruling group against attempts to remove it. MI5 in Britain and the CIA in the US are security services.

SED /ˌes iː ˈdiː/ [the] Scottish Education Department; a British government department responsible for education in Scotland —compare DEPARTMENT OF EDUCATION AND SCIENCE

se·dan /sɪˈdæn/ n AmE & AustrE for SALOON (1)

sedan chair /·ˌ· ·ˈ·/ n an enclosed seat carried on poles by two people, one in front and one behind, used in former times for carrying a person through the streets

se·date¹ /sɪˈdeɪt/ adj never showing hurry or excitement: *a sedate seaside town where a lot of old people live* | *to proceed at a sedate pace* — **~ly** adv — **~ness** n [U]

sedate² v [T *often pass.*] to cause (esp. a person) to become sleepy or calm, esp. with a sedative

se·da·tion /sɪˈdeɪʃən/ n [U] (the causing of) a sleepy or calm state, esp. with a sedative: *She's been put under sedation and is resting quietly in bed.*

sed·a·tive /ˈsedətɪv/ n, adj tech (a drug) that lessens nervousness, excitement, or pain and often causes sleep: *Give the patient a sedative to help him sleep.* | *medicine with sedative effects*

sed·en·ta·ry /ˈsedəntəri‖-teri/ adj **1** fml done while sitting down, and not giving one the chance to move about much: *a sedentary job* **2** tech not moving from one place to another; settled: *a sedentary population*

sedge /sedʒ/ n [U] a grasslike plant with three-sided stems growing usu. in groups on low-lying wet ground — **sedgy** adj

sed·i·ment /ˈsedᵻmənt/ n [S;U] solid material that settles at the bottom of a liquid: (*a*) *brownish sediment in the bottom of the wine bottle* | *a pipe blocked by sediment* — compare SLUDGE

sed·i·men·ta·ry /ˌsedᵻˈmentəri◂/ adj made of material from the earth that has been moved around and then left in a place by water or ice: *sedimentary rock*

sed·i·men·ta·tion /ˌsedᵻmenˈteɪʃən, -mən-/ n [U] the natural process by which bits of rock, earth, etc., are gathered, moved around, and then left in a place by water or ice

se·di·tion /sɪˈdɪʃən/ n [U] esp. law speaking, writing, or action intended to encourage people to disobey the government. In DEMOCRATIC countries where freedom of speech operates, this law is rarely used against people.

se·di·tious /sɪˈdɪʃəs/ adj esp. law causing or likely to cause sedition: *a seditious speech/speaker* — **~ly** adv

se·duce /sɪˈdjuːs‖-ˈduːs/ v [T] **1** to persuade (usu. someone younger and with less sexual experience) to have sex with one **2** [+obj+adv/prep] to cause or persuade (someone) to do something, esp. something unwise or rather bad; ENTICE: *He was seduced into leaving the company by the offer of higher pay elsewhere.* | *The warm weather seduced me away from my studies.* —**ducer** n

se·duc·tion /sɪˈdʌkʃən/ n **1** [C;U] (an act of) seducing: *the seduction scene in Act Two of the opera* **2** [C *usu. pl.*] a thing or quality that attracts by its charm

se·duc·tive /sɪˈdʌktɪv/ adj very desirable or attractive; hard to refuse, esp. sexually: *her seductive voice* | *a seductive offer of higher pay* — **~ly** adv — **~ness** n [U]

sed·u·lous /ˈsedjʊləs‖ˈsedʒə-/ adj fml apprec showing careful attention, effort, and determination; ASSIDUOUS: *a sedulous worker* — **~ly** adv

see¹ /siː/ v saw /sɔː/, seen /siːn/ **1** [I *not in progressive forms*] to use the eyes; have or use the power of sight: *He doesn't see very well with/in his right eye.* | *It was so dark I could hardly see (to do my work).* | (fig.) *She claims to* **see into the future.** (=know what is going to happen) **2** [T *not in progressive forms*] to get sight of; notice, examine, or recognize by looking: *I looked for her, but I couldn't see her in the crowd.* | *Can you see what's going on over there?* | *Let me see your ticket, please.* | *For more information, see* (=look at) *page 153.* [+wh-] *I could see that they'd been crying.* [+wh-] *Can you see where I put my glasses?* [+obj+to-v/v-ing] *I saw him leave the house/saw him leaving the house.* [+obj+to-v; pass.] (fml) *The dark-haired man was seen to leave the house.* | *It's not enough to make promises — they must be seen to be doing something about the problem.* [+obj+v-ed] *He saw his own brother murdered by the terrorists.* | *I'll have to change my clothes before we go out — I don't want to be seen like this!* **3** [T *not in progressive forms*] to have experience of; UNDERGO: *You and I have seen some good times together.* | *This old house has* **seen better days.** (=is in bad condition) | *During the war he saw service in the Far East.* **4** [T *not in progressive forms*] to understand or learn by looking, through experience, etc.; come to know: *It took me a while to see the truth of her remarks.* | *Seeing his confusion, I offered to help.* [+that] *I'm glad to see that you're enjoying your work.* | *I see in the paper (that) the government have done badly in the local elections.* [+wh-] *It'll be interesting to see how he reacts to this.* | *"I'm afraid I'm a bit late." "So I see."* **5** [I;T *not in progressive forms*] to recognize the meaning, purpose, or importance of; understand: *"Do you see what I mean?" "Yes; now I see."* | *She laughed politely even though she didn't* **see the joke.** | *I can't* **see the point** *of learning Latin if you're never going to use it.* | *She thinks it's too risky, and I must admit I can* **see her point.** (=I understand why she thinks that) | *I've tried to explain that we haven't got the money to do it, but he just won't* **see reason.** (=accept that what I say is right) [+wh-] *I can't* **see** *why she's so against the idea.* [+(that)] *The recipe says use cream, but I can't see that it matters.* (=I don't think it does matter) **6** [T+obj+adv/prep; *not in progressive forms*] to regard or consider in a particular way: *She sees this incident as further proof of his incompetence.* (=thinks that it is further proof of this) | *As I see it* (=according to my view of the situation), *the blame lies with the driver.* | *How do you see the current situation in the Middle East?* (=what is your judgment of it?) | *He sees things differently now that he's joined the management.* | *You must do whatever you* **see fit.** (=consider right or sensible)` **7** [T (**as**) *not in progressive forms*] to form a picture of (something or someone) in the mind; imagine; VISUALIZE: *I can't see her as* (=don't think it probable that she will become) *a ballet dancer.* | *I see little hope of any improvement.* | *I can see a great future for you in music.* | *He kept telling me how useful his new invention would be, but I couldn't see it myself.* (=it did not seem to me that it would be useful) [+*obj+v-ing*] *I can't see her lending me any money.* (=I am sure she will not) **8** [I;T+*wh-;obj*] to (try to) find out: *I'm not sure if I can lend you that much money: I'll have to see.* (=I'll decide later) | *"Can we go to the zoo, dad?" "We'll see."* (=perhaps, but perhaps not) | *I'll see what I can do/see what the trouble is.* | *If you can hang on for a moment, I'll see if she's in.* | *Let's see if we can* (=let's try to) *do it a bit better this time.* **9** [T+(*that*);*obj;not in progressive forms*] to make sure; take care: *See you're ready at 8 o'clock.* | *I promise to see that the job is done on time.* **10** [T] to visit, meet, or receive as a visitor: *The doctor can't see you yet: he's seeing someone else at the moment.* | *We're going to see grandma in hospital tomorrow.* | **"See you later, Pete."** *"Yes,* **see you/be seeing you."** (=goodbye) **11** [T+*obj+adv/prep*] to go with; ACCOMPANY: *Someone ought to see the children safely home.* | *I'll see you to the door.* **12** [T] (of a place or period) to have (an event or set of events) happen in or during it: *The fifth century saw the end of the Roman Empire in the West.* (=that was when it ended) | *This year has seen a big increase in road accidents.* **13** [T] (in the card game of POKER) to answer (an opponent) by risking an equal amount of money **14 let me see** (used to express a pause for thought): *"Do you recognize this music?" "Let me see ... Yes, now I do."* **15 not see beyond the end of one's nose** *infml* to think that one's own affairs are the only ones that matter **16 not see someone for dust** *BrE infml* to be unable to see someone because they have left in a great hurry: *If he hears there's work to be done, you won't see him for dust!* **17 not see the wood** *BrE*‖**forest** *AmE* **for the trees** *infml* to fail to understand something clearly or completely because of giving too much attention to small details **18 see eye to eye (with)** to agree completely (with); have the same opinion (as): *He and his brother always see eye to eye.* **19 Seeing is believing** *infml* (used for expressing disbelief in something that cannot be believed until one has actually seen it) **20 see one's way (clear) to** *esp. BrE* to be able or willing to (esp. lend money): *I was wondering if you could see your way to lending me £50.* **21 see red** to become very angry **22 see someone right** *old-fash infml* to make sure that someone is properly rewarded **23 see stars** to see flashes of light, esp. as the result of being hit on the head **24 see the back/last of** *infml* to have no further association with (something or someone), esp. because it has finished or because they have gone: *I haven't enjoyed dealing with this company and I'll be glad to see the back of them!* **25 see the colour of someone's money** *infml* to be shown proof that someone is willing or able to pay **26 see the light: a** to understand or accept an idea or the truth of something **b** to have a religious experience which changes one's belief **c** *infml* to come into existence: *This suggestion first* **saw the light (of day)** *as early as 1935.* **27 see things** *infml* to think that one sees something when there is nothing there: *I must be seeing things* (=I cannot believe what I have seen)*; they can't have bought another new car!* —see also **hear things** (HEAR) **28 you see: a** (used in explanations) *"Why are you so late?" "Well, you see, the bus broke down."* **b** (used for softening a following statement): *You see; there's another side to what you've been saying* ...

▷ USAGE 1 Compare **see, look at,** and **watch. To see** is to experience with the eyes, and it does not depend on what you want to do. In this meaning, you say *Can you* **see** *anything?* but not *Are you* **seeing** *anything?* When you use your eyes on purpose and with attention you **look at** something: *Stop looking at me like that!* To **watch** is to look for some time at something that may move: you **watch** television or a football match. 2 Compare *I* **saw** *him cross the road* (=I saw the whole journey from one side to the other) and *I* **saw** *him crossing the road* (=I saw him at a moment when he was in the middle). **Feel, hear,** and **watch** can also be used in these two ways. —see also CAN (USAGE)◁

see about sthg. *phr v* [T] **1** to make arrangements for; deal with: [+*obj/v-ing*] *It's time for me to see about dinner/to see about cooking dinner.* **2** to consider further: *"Dad, will you take us to the football match tomorrow?" "Well, I'll (have to) see about that."* (=perhaps I will take you) **3 We'll (soon) see about 'that!** *infml* I will prevent that from happening or continuing!

see sthg. **in** sbdy./sthg. *phr v* [T *usu. in questions and negatives*] to find attractive in: *I don't know why she married that awful man; I can't think what she sees in him.*

see sthg. **of** sbdy. *phr v* [T] to see or be with (someone) to the stated degree: *Where's Dave? I've seen nothing of him* (=have not seen him) *all week.* | *They're good friends and see a lot of each other.* (=are together a lot)

see sbdy./sthg. ↔ **off** *phr v* [T] **1 (at)** to go to an airport, station, etc., with (someone who is beginning a journey): *He saw his friend off at the bus station.* **2 a** to chase away: *Her dog saw off the two thieves.* **b** to remain firm and undefeated until (something or someone dangerous) stops being active: *Our troops saw off three enemy attacks within three days.*

see sbdy./sthg. **out** *phr v* [T] **1** to last until the end of: *Will our supplies see the winter out?* **2** to go to the door with (someone who is leaving): *Don't worry; I'll see myself out.* (=so you need not do so)

see round/over sthg. *phr v* [T] to visit and examine: *Would you like to see round the old castle?*

see through *phr v* [T] **1** (**see through** sthg./sbdy.) to recognize the truth about (an excuse, false statement, deceiving person, etc.); not be deceived by: *She knew him well enough to see through his laughter and realize he was upset about what had happened.* **2** (**see** sbdy. **through** (sthg.)) to provide things for, support, or help until the end of (a time or difficulty): *He had just enough money to see him through (a year abroad).*

see to sthg./sbdy. *phr v* [T] to deal with or take care of: *You ought to have your eyes seen to by a doctor.* | *Will you* **see to** *the children?* | *Will you* **see to it that** (=make sure that) *this letter gets posted today?*

see² *n* the area governed by a BISHOP; DIOCESE —see also HOLY SEE

seed¹ /siːd/ *n* **1** [C;U] a usu. small hard object produced by most plants, from which a new plant of the same kind can grow, and which is used for planting: *poppy seeds* | *a large bag of grass seed* | *a seedpod* | (fig.) *The government's repressive policies are* **sowing the seeds of** (=may lead to) *rebellion.* | (fig.) *His reaction planted the seeds of doubt in her mind.* —see picture at FRUIT **2** [C] *AmE for* PIP¹ **3** [C] a seeded (SEED² (5)) player in a competition: *the top seed at Wimbledon* **4** [U] *bibl* everyone who is descended from a particular person, esp. considered as forming a particular race: *According to the Bible we are all the seed of Adam.* **5 go/run to seed: a** (of a plant) to produce seed, having passed the time when flowers are produced **b** *infml* (of a person) to become unattractive and unhealthy-looking, esp. by becoming lazy, careless, or old — ~ **less** *adj* : *a seedless orange*

seed² *v* **1** [I] (of a plant) to produce seeds **2** [T (**with**) *often pass.*] to plant seeds in (a piece of ground) **3** [T] to remove seeds from (fruit) **4** [T (**with**)] to cause to be filled or scattered with something that develops or produces a result: *We seeded the clouds with chemicals to make them produce rain.* —see also CLOUD SEEDING **5** [T *usu. pass.*] to place (esp. a tennis player at the start of a competition) in order of likelihood to win: *seeded players* | *She was seeded fourth at Wimbledon.* (=was officially considered the fourth best player) —see also UNSEEDED

seed³ *adj* [A] kept for planting: *seed potatoes/corn*

seed-bed /ˈsiːdbed/ *n* **1** an area of ground, esp. specially prepared, where seeds are planted **2** [(**of**)] a place or condition favourable for development, esp. of something bad: *the city's slums were a seedbed of rebellion*

seed-corn /ˈsiːdkɔːn‖-kɔːrn/ *n* [U] **1** corn of good quality that is used for planting **2** something that is of great value because it can be used for future developments

seed-ling /ˈsiːdlɪŋ/ *n* a young plant grown from a seed and not from a part cut off another plant

seed pearl /ˈ·ˌ·/ *n* a very small and often imperfect PEARL —see also PEARL

seeds-man /ˈsiːdzmən/ *n* **-men** /mən/ a grower and seller of seeds, esp. for flowers and vegetables

seed·y /ˈsiːdi/ *adj infml* **1** *derog* having a poor, dirty, uncared for, worn-out appearance: *a rather seedy and unpleasant part of town* **2** *old-fash infml* slightly unwell and/or in low spirits: *I've been feeling a bit seedy for the last couple of days.* —**iness** *n* [U]

See·ger /ˈsiːgəʳ/, **Pete** /piːt/ (1919–) American singer and writer of FOLK² songs (= songs about ordinary people) and a person with special knowledge of on BANJO and GUITAR who made folk music popular again in the 1950s

see·ing /ˈsiːɪŋ/ also **seeing that** /ˈ·· ·/, **seeing as** *infml*, **seeing as how** /ˈ··· ·,·/ *nonstandard*— *conj* as it is true that; considering the fact that; SINCE³ (2): *Seeing (that) she's legally old enough to get married, I don't see how you can stop her.*

seeing eye dog /ˌ·· ˈ· ˌ·/ *AmE for* GUIDE DOG

seek /siːk/ *v* **sought** /sɔːt/ **1** [I (**after, for**);T (OUT)] *fml or lit* to make a search (for); try to find or get (something): *We are earnestly seeking after the truth.* | *The travellers sought shelter from the rain.* | *Will the president seek re-election at the end of his term of office?* | *He sought out his friend in the crowd.* **2** [T] *fml* to ask for; go to request: *You should seek advice from your lawyer on this matter.* **3** [T+*to-v;obj*] *fml or lit* to try; make an attempt: *The company is seeking to improve its profitability.* **4** [T] to move naturally towards: *Water seeks its own level.* | *The compass pointer always seeks the north.* **5 seek one's fortune/seek fame and fortune** *esp. lit* to try to find success in the world: *He left home to seek his fortune.* | *He majored in political science before seeking fame and fortune in New York.* **6 they seek him here, they seek him there** *quote* the first words of a short poem about the Scarlet Pimpernel, a character in a book of the same name who helped people escape from the French Revolution, and who the French government tried unsuccessfully to catch **7 seek, and ye shall find** *saying from the Bible* people who look for something long or thoroughly enough will find it —see also HIDE-AND-SEEK, SELF-SEEKING, SOUGHT-AFTER, ~**er** *n*

seem /siːm/ *v* [L *not in progressive forms*] to give the idea or effect of being; be in appearance; appear: *The strong wind makes the temperature seem lower than it really is.* | *She didn't seem convinced by the argument.* | *There seems (to be) every reason to believe that business will get better.* | *Things are not always what they seem (to be).* | *You must do whatever seems best to you.* | *It seems like years since I last saw you.* | *"It seems (as if) there will be an election soon." "So it seems."* [+*to-v*] *I seem to have lost my keys.* [+(*that*)] *It seems/(fml) It would seem that there is no way out of our difficulty.*

seem·ing /ˈsiːmɪŋ/ *adj* [A] *fml* that seems to be so, usu. as opposed to what is; APPARENT: *For all his seeming calmness, he was really very nervous.* | *an explanation of the seeming contradictions*

seem·ing·ly /ˈsiːmɪŋli/ *adv* **1** judging by the facts as one knows them: *There is seemingly nothing we can do to stop the plan going ahead.* **2** according to outward appearance, usu. as opposed to what is actually the case: *seemingly endless problems*

seem·ly /ˈsiːmli/ *adj old-fash or lit* (esp. of behaviour) pleasing by being suitable to an occasion or to social standards —**liness** *n* [U]

seen /siːn/ *past participle of* SEE¹

seep /siːp/ *v* [I+*adv/prep*] (of a liquid or gas) to make its way gradually through small openings in a material: *Water had seeped into the house through cracks in the roof.* | *Blood seeped through the bandage.*

seep·age /ˈsiːpɪdʒ/ *n* [S;U] (a) gradual flow of a liquid by seeping: *flooding caused by seepage from the drains*

seer /sɪəʳ/ *n lit & old use* someone who can see into the future and tell what will happen; PROPHET. Seers were thought of as wise men.

seer·suck·er /ˈsɪəˌsʌkəʳ/ˈsɪər-/ *n* [U] a light usu. cotton cloth with flat bands between slightly raised bands

see·saw¹ /ˈsiːsɔː/ ‖ also **teeter-totter** *AmE*— *n* a board which is balanced in the middle and on which children sit at opposite ends, so that when one end goes up the other goes down

seesaw² *v* [I] to move backwards and forwards, up and down, or between opponents or opposite sides: *The fight seesawed to and fro, with first one boxer and then the other being on top.* | *seesawing prices*

seethe /siːð/ *v* [I] **1** [(**with**)] to be in a state of anger,

unrest, or excited movement: *The country was seething with political unrest.* | *a seething mass of people* | *I was absolutely seething, I can tell you.* (=extremely angry) **2** (of a liquid) to move about wildly and roughly, as if boiling: *The sea was seething around the rocks.*

see-through /ˈ· ·/ *adj* [A] (esp. of a garment) that can be (partly) seen through; transparent: *a see-through blouse*

SEGA /ˈseɪgə/ a Japanese company making computer games

seg·ment¹ /ˈsegmənt/ *n* **1** any of the parts into which something can be cut or divided: *a dish of orange segments* | *The company dominates this segment of the market.* —see pictures at FRUIT and PIECE **2** *tech* an area inside a circle between its edge and a CHORD (=a straight line across it) —compare SECTOR **3** *tech* the part of a line between two points on the line

seg·ment² /segˈment/ *v* [I;T] to divide or be divided into segments

seg·men·ta·tion /ˌsegmenˈteɪʃən, -mən-/ *n* [S;U] division into segments

seg·re·gate /ˈsegrɪgeɪt/ *v* [T *usu. pass.*] to separate or set apart, esp. from a different social group: *Boys and girls are segregated in this school.*

seg·re·gat·ed /ˈsegrɪgeɪtɪd/ *adj* for the use of only one group, esp. a racial group

seg·re·ga·tion /ˌsegrɪˈgeɪʃən/ *n* [U] the separation of a social or racial group from others, esp. by the laws in some US states between 1896 and 1954, which prevented black people from using the same schools, hotels, restaurants, seats in buses and in theatres and parks, etc., as white people

▷ USAGE The opposite of segregation is **integration**; however, **desegregation** is usu. used when someone is referring to **reversing** (=getting rid of) a system of segregation already in place, as in the US after 1954. —compare APARTHEID; see also BROWN vs BOARD, CIVIL RIGHTS MOVEMENT, PLESSY vs FERGUSON◁

sei·gneur /seˈnjɜːʳ‖seɪ-/ *n* (in a FEUDAL system) a nobleman or landowner; lord

Seiko /ˈseɪkəʊ/ *tdmk* a product, esp. a watch, made by the Japanese company Seiko

seine /seɪn/ also **seine net** /ˈ· ·/— *n* a fishing net with weights along one edge causing it to hang straight down and enclose fish when the ends are drawn together

Seine *n* [*the*] a river, 780 km (480 miles) long, in N France. It flows through Paris and Rouen and into the English Channel coast near Le Havre.

seis·mic /ˈsaɪzmɪk/ *adj tech* of or caused by EARTHQUAKEs

seismic wave /ˌ·· ˈ·/ *n* a movement in the earth, caused by an EARTHQUAKE, a very large explosion, or a very large object hitting the earth from space

seis·mo·graph /ˈsaɪzməgrɑːf‖-græf/ *n* an instrument for recording and measuring the shaking of the ground in an EARTHQUAKE

seis·mol·o·gy /saɪzˈmɒlədʒi‖-ˈmɑː-/ *n* [U] *tech* the scientific study of shaking movements in the surface of the earth —**gist** *n*

seize /siːz/ *v* [T] **1** to take possession of **a** by official order: *The weapons found in the house were seized by the police.* **b** by force: *The army seized power in a coup.* **2** to take hold of eagerly, quickly, or forcefully; GRAB: *He seized my hand, shook it, and said how glad he was to see me.* | (fig.) *If you get the opportunity to work abroad, you should seize it with both hands.* **3** [*often pass.* (**with**)] (of feelings or thoughts) to attack or take control of (someone's body or mind): *He was seized with sudden chest pains/with a desire for revenge.* **4 seize the day** to not delay in doing something, esp. something enjoyable. The phrase comes from the Latin *carpe diem*, mentioned in a poem by Horace.

seize on/upon sthg. *phr v* [T] to take and use suddenly or eagerly: *She had always wanted to go to London, so she seized on the offer of a free trip.*

seize up *phr v* [I] (of (part of) a machine) to become stuck and fail to move or work; JAM² (5): *The engine seized up.* | (fig.) *The snowstorm was so heavy that the city's whole transport system seized up.*

sei·zure /ˈsiːʒəʳ/ *n* **1** [U (**of**)] the act of seizing: *The courts ordered the seizure of all her property.* **2** [C] a sudden attack of an illness: *He died of a heart seizure.* | (fig.) (*humor*) *Your mother will have a seizure if you dye your hair pink!*

Selassie see HAILE SELASSIE

sel·dom /'seldəm/ *adv* not often; rarely: *He very seldom* (=hardly ever) *eats breakfast.* | *She seldom, if ever, reads a book.* (=She reads rarely, or perhaps not at all.) —see NEVER (USAGE), RARELY (USAGE)

se·lect[1] /sɪ'lekt/ *v* [T (**for, from**)] *rather fml* to take as best, most suitable, etc., from a group; choose: *She selected a diamond ring from the collection.* | *These oranges have been carefully selected.* [+obj+to-v] *He was selected to play for England.*

select[2] *adj fml apprec* **1** carefully chosen and limited to a small number of the highest quality: *A select group were invited to the wedding reception.* **2** limited to the use of people of high social class or great wealth; EXCLUSIVE: *This is a very select area; you have to be rich to live here.*

select com·mit·tee /·,· ·'··/ *n* [+*sing.*|*pl. v*] **1** a committee of the British parliament that is appointed for a certain length of time to consider a particular matter, such as defence, trade, employment, etc. **2** a committee of the US Congress which is established to examine one subject or suggested new law only for a limited time: *Both the Senate and the House created select committees to examine the Iran-Contra affair.* —compare STANDING COMMITTEE

se·lec·tion /sɪ'lekʃən/ *n* **1** [U] the act of selecting or the fact of being selected: *His selection as a presidential candidate was quite unexpected.* **2** [C (**from**)] something or someone selected: *The orchestra played selections from Gilbert and Sullivan.* **3** [C (**of**) *usu. sing.*] a collection of things of one kind, such as goods for sale; range: *The shop has a fine selection of cheeses.* —see also NATURAL SELECTION

se·lec·tive /sɪ'lektɪv/ *adj* **1** careful in choosing: *He's always very selective when he buys his suits.* **2** having an effect only on certain things; not general: *You need a selective weed killer that won't damage your garden flowers.* | *selective strike action* — *~ly adv* : *They quoted from the report selectively in order to support their argument.* — *~ness n* [U] —**tivity** /sɪ,lek'tɪvəti/,

se·lec·tor /sɪ'lektər/ *n* a person or instrument that selects, esp. a member of a committee choosing a sports team

se·le·ni·um /sɪ'li:niəm/ *n* [U] a poisonous ELEMENT (=a simple substance) that is not a metal and is used esp. in light-sensitive electrical instruments and as a colouring material

self /self/ *n* **selves** /selvz/ **1** [C;U] the whole being of a person, taking into account their nature, character, abilities, etc.: *He put his whole self into the job, working night and day.* | *Knowledge of self increases as one gets older.* **2** [C] a particular or typical part of one's nature: *I'm feeling better but I'm still not quite my old self.* (=as I was before my illness) | *Under a stressful cross-examination they began to reveal their true selves.* | *her better self* (=the best part of her nature) **3** [U] one's own advantage or profit: *She always thinks of others, never of self.* | *It's always the same with him—self, self, self.* (=he is SELFISH) **4** [U] (used in esp. business writing) himself/herself; oneself

self- see WORD FORMATION

self-ab·ne·ga·tion /,· ··'··/ *n* [U] ABNEGATION

self-ab·sorbed /,· ·'·◄/ *adj* paying all one's attention to oneself and one's own affairs —**sorption** *n* [U]

self-act·ing /,· '··◄/ *adj* working by itself; AUTOMATIC

self-ad·dressed /,· ·'·◄/ *adj* addressed for return to the sender: *Please enclose a self-addressed envelope with your order.* —see also S.A.E.

self-ad·he·sive /,· ·'··◄/ *adj* (of e.g. an envelope) having a sticky surface so that it does not need liquid or glue to fix it closed or fix it to something else

self-ap·point·ed /,· ·'··◄/ *adj usu. derog* chosen by oneself for a job or position, unasked and usu. unwanted: *Why should this self-appointed guardian of public morals say what we can and cannot watch on television?*

self-as·sem·bly /,· ·'··◄/ *adj* (that can be) put together by oneself from parts bought in a shop: *self-assembly furniture*

self-as·ser·tive /,· ·'··◄/ *adj* forceful in making others take notice of oneself or in claiming things for oneself — *~ness, -tion— n* [U]

self-as·sured /,· ·'·◄/ *adj* sure of one's own abilities; confident —**surance** *n* [U]

self-ca·ter·ing /,· '··/ *adj esp. BrE* (of a holiday or holiday lodging) in which one cooks one's own meals

self-cen·tred /,· '··◄/ *adj* interested only in oneself; SELFISH — *~ness n* [U]

self-col·lect·ed /,· ·'··◄/ *adj* SELF-POSSESSED

self-com·mand /,· ·'·/ *n* [U] *fml for* SELF-CONTROL

self-com·posed /,· ·'·◄/ *adj* having one's emotions under control; calm

self-con·fessed /,· ·'·◄/ *adj* [A] admitted by oneself to be the stated usu. bad kind of person: *a self-confessed liar* —see also CONFESSED

self-con·fi·dent /,· '··/ *adj usu. apprec* sure of one's own power to succeed: *You couldn't help admiring the self-confident way she stood up to speak to the big crowd.* — *~ly adv* —**dence** *n* [U]

self-con·grat·u·la·tion /,· ···'··/ *n* [U] *usu derog* giving oneself (too) much recognition for one's good fortune or achievements: *an orgy of self-congratulation* **self-congratulatory** *adj* : *a smug, self-congratulatory smile*

self-con·scious /,· '··/ *adj* **1** nervous and uncomfortable about oneself as seen by others: *I could never be an actor; I'm too self-conscious.* | *The young girl felt very self-conscious about the large spot on her chin.* **2** having or expressing knowledge or understanding about oneself or itself; CONSCIOUS: *I found the film's artistic camerawork rather too self-conscious.* (=it did not seem natural or effortless) — *~ly adv* — *~ness n* [U]

self-con·tained /,· ·'·◄/ *adj* **1** complete in itself; independent: *a self-contained flat with its own entrance, kitchen, bathroom, etc.* **2** (of a person) habitually not showing feelings or depending on others' friendship

self-con·tra·dic·to·ry /,· ··'··/ *adj* containing two opposite parts or statements which cannot both be true

self-con·trol /,· ·'·/ *n* [U] control over one's feelings; power to hold back the expression of strong feelings: *I must admit I nearly lost my self-control and hit him.* —**trolled** *adj*

self-de·cep·tion /,· ·'··/ *n* the act of deceiving oneself; the state of being deceived by oneself (e.g. about one's reasons or character) **self-deceptive** *adj*

self-de·feat·ing /,· ·'··◄/ *adj* having the effect of preventing its own success: *Their attempt to prevent opposition by closing down the newspapers was self-defeating—the opposition only increased.*

self-de·fence /,· ·'·/ *n* [U] the act or skill of defending oneself, one's actions, one's rights, etc. Self-defence classes for women have become popular in recent years because of the number of attacks on women: *the art of self-defence* (=BOXING, JUDO, etc.) | *He shot the man in self-defence.* (=only to protect himself)

self-de·ni·al /,· ·'··/ *n* [U] *fml* the act or habit of holding oneself back from doing enjoyable things or of not satisfying one's own desires, usu. done for religious or moral reasons —**nying** *adj*

self-des·truct /,self dɪ'strʌkt/ *v* [I] *esp. AmE* to destroy itself: *If the missile malfunctions, it will self-destruct.* —**self-destruct** *adj* [A] : *a self-destruct mechanism*

self-des·truc·tion /,· ·'··/ *n* [U] destroying oneself or itself —**tive** *adj* : *a self-destructive tendency to see herself as a failure*

self-de·ter·mi·na·tion /,· ···'··/ *n* [U] the right of the people who live in a country to make a free decision about the form of their government, esp. whether or not to be independent of another country

self-dis·ci·pline /,· '··/ *n* [U] the training of oneself to control one's habits, actions, and desires: *You'll need plenty of self-discipline if you're going to work from home.* —**plined** *adj*

self-doubt /,· '·/ *n* [U] lack of belief in oneself and one's abilities

self-drive /,· '·◄/ *adj BrE* (of a vehicle) that can be or has been hired to be driven by oneself

self-ed·u·cat·ed /,· '····◄/ *adj* educated by one's own efforts, esp. by reading books, and not formally in school

self-ef·fac·ing /,· ·'··◄/ *adj* keeping oneself from attracting attention, esp. because one lacks confidence: *a shy self-effacing man* —**facement** *n* [U]

self-em·ployed /,· ·'·◄/ *adj* earning money from one's own business rather than being paid by an employer: [also *n, the*+P] *a special pension scheme for the self-employed* —**ployment** *n* [U]

self-es·teem /ˌ· ·'·/ *n* [U] one's good opinion of one's own worth: *The critical newspaper reviews damaged/were a blow to his self-esteem.*

self-ev·i·dent /ˌ· '···◂/ *adj* plainly true without need of proof; clear from the statement itself: *It's self-evident she won't pass, so why are they entering her for the exam?* — ~**ly** *adv*

self-ex·am·in·a·tion /ˌ· ···'··/ *n* [U] consideration of one's own actions and reasons for action, esp. to judge them according to some standards, religious beliefs, etc.

self-ex·plan·a·to·ry /ˌ· ·'·····/ *adj* (esp. of speaking or writing) explaining itself; easily understood and needing no further explanation: *I think the printed instructions are fairly self-explanatory, so I'll let you get on with it.*

self-ex·pres·sion /ˌ· ·'··/ *n* [U] the expression of one's own character e.g. in artistic form, through one's behaviour —**self-expressive** *adj*

self-ful·fill·ing proph·e·cy /ˌ· ·ˌ·· '···/ *n* a statement about what may happen in the future which comes true because it has been made: *The vice-president made a self-fulfilling prophecy when he said the company would soon go bankrupt — now all the investors are withdrawing their money.*

self-gov·ern·ment /ˌ· '···/ also **self-rule**— *n* [U] government of a country by its own people, free from outside control or influence; independence

self-gov·ern·ing /ˌ· '···◂/ *adj* (of a country or organization) free from outside control; independent: *Instead of being controlled by a Regional Health Authority, each hospital should be a* **self-governing trust**.

self-help /ˌ· '·/ *n* [U] the action of providing help or support for oneself without depending on others: *self-help groups* (=in which you give and get help, and help yourself) *for drug addicts/dieters*

self·hood /'selfhʊd/ *n* '5[U] the knowledge of oneself as an independent person; the sense of one's INDIVIDUALITY

self-im·age /ˌ· '··/ the idea one has of one's own personality, looks, or mental ability: *Children who are bullies often have a poor self-image and try to make themselves feel better by punishing other children.*

self-im·port·ance /ˌ· ·'··/ *n* [U] too high an opinion of one's own importance —**ant** *adj* : *a self-important little man who enjoys telling other people what to do* —**antly** *adv*

self-im·posed /ˌ· ·'·◂/ *adj* that one has forced oneself to accept, without it being suggested or demanded by anyone else: *a self-imposed limit of three cigarettes a day | self-imposed exile*

self-in·dul·gence /ˌ· ·'··/ *n* [U] the tendency to allow oneself pleasure or comfort too easily **gent** *adj* : *I know it's very self-indulgent of me, but I'm going to have another piece of cake. | a self-indulgent film* (=in which the director has concerned himself too much with his own particular feelings or interests) —**gently** *adv*

self-in·terest /ˌ· '··/ *n* [U] concern for what is best for oneself or is most to one's own advantage: *Self-interest, rather than compassion, prompted his large donation to the charity, which he knew would be reported in the press.* — ~**ed** *adj*

self·ish /'selfɪʃ/ *adj* concerned with or directed towards one's own advantage without care for others: *What a selfish boy you are; let the other children share your toys. | She acted from purely selfish motives.* —opposite **unselfish** — ~**ly** *adv* — ~**ness** *n* [U]

self-knowl·edge /ˌ· '··/ *n* [U] knowledge of one's own nature and character, the reasons why one does things, etc.

self·less /'selfləs/ *adj apprec* caring only for others and not for oneself; completely unselfish: *selfless devotion to duty* — ~**ly** *adv* — ~**ness** *n* [U]

self-lock·ing /ˌ· '··◂/ *adj* (esp. of a door) locking by its own action when closed

self-made /ˌ· '·◂/ *adj* having gained success and esp. wealth by one's own efforts alone, starting without money or social position: *He's very proud of being a* **self-made man**.

self-pit·y /ˌ· '··/ *n* [U] too much pity for one's own sorrows or troubles: *Instead of* **wallowing in self-pity** *they*

---

should do something positive to improve their situation. — ~**ing** *adj*

self-por·trait /ˌ· '··/ *n* **1** an artist's work of him/herself **2** a spoken or written description of one's own character

self-pos·sessed /ˌ· ·'·◂/ *adj* showing self-possession; calm and confident — ~**ly** /ˌ· ·'···/ *adv*

self-pos·ses·sion /ˌ· ·'··/ *n* [U] firm control over one's own feelings and actions, esp. in difficult or unexpected situations

self-pres·er·va·tion /ˌ· ··'··/ *n* [U] the keeping of oneself safe from harm or death, esp. as an action done naturally by living things: *Animals have an instinct for self-preservation.*

self-pro·claimed /ˌ· ·'·◂/ *adj* called by oneself and usu. unsupported by others: *self-proclaimed leader/hero*

self-rais·ing flour /ˌ· ·· '·/ *BrE* ‖ **self-rising flour** *AmE*— *n* [U] flour that contains BAKING POWDER —compare PLAIN FLOUR

self-re·li·ant /ˌ· ·'·◂/ *adj* able to act without depending on the help of others: *Even though she's in her nineties, the old lady is still very self-reliant.* —**ance** *n* [U]

self-re·spect /ˌ· ·'·/ *n* [U] proper respect for, or pride in, oneself; DIGNITY: *She's got too much self-respect to beg her boyfriend to stay.*

self-re·spect·ing /ˌ· ·'··◂/ *adj* [A *usu. in negatives*] **1** having self-respect: *No self-respecting actor would appear in a pornographic film.* **2** *infml* properly so-called; real; true: *No self-respecting town would be without its cinema in those days.*

self-re·straint /ˌ· ·'·/ *n* [U] the ability to keep the expression of one's feelings, or one's desires under control: *Why can't you exercise some self-restraint?*

Sel·fri·dges /'selfrɪdʒɪz/ [+*sing./pl. v*] a large department store in Oxford Street, London, famous esp. for its food department: *Has/Have Selfridges got a furniture department?*

self-right·eous /ˌ· '··◂/ *adj derog* proudly sure of one's own rightness or goodness, esp. in opposition to the beliefs and actions of others — ~**ly** *adv* — ~**ness** *n* [U]

self-ris·ing flour /ˌ· ·· '·/ *n* *AmE for* SELF-RAISING FLOUR

self-rule /ˌ· '·/ *n* [U] SELF-GOVERNMENT

self-sac·ri·fice /ˌ· '···/ *n* [U] the giving up of things that one cares deeply about in order to help others or for some good or important purpose —**ficing** *adj*

self·same /'selfseɪm/ *adj* [*the, this, that, these, those*+A] *lit* exactly the same: *two great victories on the self-same day*

self-sat·is·fied /ˌ· '···/ *adj* too pleased with oneself; COMPLACENT: *a smug self-satisfied smirk.* —**faction** /ˌ· ··'··/ *n* [U]

self-seek·er /ˌ· '··/ *n* someone who is concerned only with their own advantage

self-seek·ing /ˌ· '···◂/ *adj* doing things only for one's own advantage: *a dishonourable self-seeking politician* —**self-seeking** *n* [U]

self-serv·ice /ˌ· '··◂/ *adj* using a system by which buyers collect what they want and then pay at a special desk: *a self-service cafeteria/petrol station* —**self-service** *n* [U]

self-start·er /ˌ· '··/ *n* **1** (a button which one presses to start) a usu. electric apparatus for starting a car engine **2** *infml* an active and effective person who is able to work on their own: *PA wanted for busy office. Must be self-starter.*

self-styled /ˈ·· ·/ *adj* [A] *usu. derog* given the stated title by oneself, usu. without any right to it: *The self-styled saviour of his people is in fact a dictator.*

self-suf·fi·cient /ˌ· ·'··◂/ *adj* [(in)] able to provide what one needs without outside help, esp. (of a country) without buying goods and services from abroad: *Britain is now self-sufficient in oil.* —**ciency** *n* [U]

self-sup·port·ing /ˌ· ·'··◂/ *adj* earning enough money to pay its/one's costs without getting into debt or needing money from outside: *We're hoping that this business will become self-supporting in one or two years.*

self-will /ˌ· '·/ *n* [U] strong unreasonable determination to follow one's own wishes, esp. in opposition to others —**willed** /ˌ· '·◂/ *adj*

self-wind·ing /ˌself 'waɪndɪŋ/ *adj* (of a wristwatch) winding itself as a result of the natural movement of the human arm

Sel·kirk·shire /ˈselkɜːkʃər‖-ɜːr-/ a former COUNTY of SE Scotland, now part of the Borders REGION

sell¹ /sel/ v **sold** /səʊld/ **1** [I;T **(for, to)**] to give or pass (property or goods) to someone else in exchange for money: *I'd like to buy your house if you're willing to sell.* | *I'm thinking of selling my car.* | (fig.) *These unprincipled voters are willing to sell their votes.* (=vote for whoever will pay or give them most) [+obj(i)+obj(d)] *I sold him the painting*|*sold the painting to him for £5,000.* | *The painting was sold to an American buyer.* —compare BUY **2** [T] to help or cause (something) to be bought: *Bad news sells newspapers.* | *The famous author's name on the cover is enough to sell the book.* **3** [T] to offer (goods) for sale: *My job is selling insurance.* | *Do you sell cigarettes in this shop?* **4** [I **(at, for)**] to be bought; get a buyer or buyers: *This magazine sells for*|*at £1.50.* | *The concert tickets cost too much and sold badly*|*didn't sell.* **5** [T] to gain a sale of; be bought in (the stated quantity): *This record has sold over a million copies.* **6** [T **(to, on)**] *infml* to make (something) acceptable, believable, or desirable to (someone) by persuading: *Will they be able to sell their ideas to the voters?* [+obj(i)+obj(d)] *Can you sell the boss your plan?* | *You've sold me on joining the squash league.* | *I'm completely sold on the idea; I think it's a brilliant suggestion.* **7** [T *usu. pass.*] *infml rare* to trick; cheat; deceive: *We've been sold!* **8 sell oneself: a** to make oneself or one's ideas seem attractive to others: *I'm no good at job interviews — I just don't know how to sell myself.* **b** to give up one's principles in exchange for money or other gain **9 sell one's soul (to the devil)** to act dishonourably in exchange for money, power, fame, etc. **10 sell someone a pup** *BrE old-fash infml* to trick someone into buying something worthless **11 sell someone down the river** to put someone in great trouble by being disloyal to them; BETRAY someone **12 sell something/someone short** to value something or someone too low: *When you say John is inefficient, I think you're selling him short.*

sell sthg. ↔ **off** *phr v* [T] to get rid of (goods) by selling, usu. cheaply: *We're selling off these tins of fruit at reduced prices because they're slightly damaged.*

sell out *phr v* **1 a** [I (of);T (=sell sthg. out) *pass.*] to sell all of (what was for sale): *I'm afraid we have completely sold out (of shirts in your size), sir.* | *Sorry, the tickets are sold out.* | *The match was completely sold out.* (=there were no tickets left) **b** [I] (of something for sale) to be all bought: *The shirts were cheap and sold out fast.* **2** [I **(to)**] to sell one's (share in a) business: *I was getting too old to run my pub, so I sold out to a large brewery and retired to the country.* **3** [I **(to, on)**] to be disloyal or unfaithful to one's principles or friends, esp. for money: *He was a good writer, but he sold out and now just writes for money.* —see also SELL-OUT

sell (sthg. ↔) **up** *phr v* [I;T] *esp. BrE* to sell (everything one owns, esp. a business): *He sold up (his business) and emigrated to Australia.*

sell² *n* [S] *BrE infml* a deception: *These chocolates are hollow in the middle—what a sell!* —see also HARD SELL, SOFT SELL

Sel·la·field /ˈseləfiːld/ a NUCLEAR power station in Cumbria, N England, formerly called Windscale, where nuclear FUEL is reprocessed (REPROCESS) (=treated so that it can be used again)

sell-by date /ˈ··· ˌ·/ *n* a date stamped onto a product which decays, e.g. milk, after which it must no longer be offered for sale in a shop

sell·er /ˈselər/ *n* **1** a person who sells things —compare BUYER **2** (*sometimes in comb.*) a product with the stated type or amount of sales: *He hopes his new book will be a bigger seller than the last.* —see also BEST-SELLER

Sel·lers /ˈseləz‖-lərz/, **Peter** (1925–1980) an English actor well-known for the funny characters he played esp. Dr Strangelove and Inspector Clouseau, and his funny radio show *The Goon Show*

seller's mar·ket /ˌ·· ˈ··/ *n* [S] a state of affairs in which there are not many goods for sale, buyers have little choice, and prices tend to be high —compare BUYER'S MARKET

selling point /ˈ··· ·/ *n* a fact or quality which can be strongly mentioned in favour of a product in order to persuade people to buy it: *The computer's two main selling points are that it's cheap and portable.*

selling price /ˈ··· ·/ *n* the price at which something is sold, esp. to the final customer or user

sel·lo·tape¹ /ˈseləteɪp, ˈseləʊ-/ *BrE* ‖ **Scotch tape** *tdmk*, **tape** *AmE*— *n* [U] *tdmk (often cap.)* sticky thin clear material in long narrow lengths which is used for sticking paper, mending light objects, etc.: *a roll of sellotape*

sellotape² *BrE* ‖ **Scotch tape** *tdmk*, **tape** *AmE*— *v* [T] *tdmk* to put together or mend with sellotape

sell-out /ˈ·· ·/ *n* [*usu. sing.*] **1** a performance, sports match, etc., for which all tickets are sold **2** *infml* an act of disloyalty or unfaithfulness to one's principles or friends; BETRAYAL —see also SELL **out**

sel·vage , **-vedge** /ˈselvɪdʒ/ *n* the edge of a piece of cloth that is strengthened on both sides to prevent threads from coming out

selves /selvz/ *pl. of* SELF

se·man·tic /sɪˈmæntɪk/ *adj* of meaning in language — **~ally** /kli/ *adv* : *"Purchase" and "buy" are semantically the same.* (=have the same meaning)

se·man·tics /sɪˈmæntɪks/ *n* [U] the study of the meaning of words and other parts of language

sem·a·phore /ˈseməfɔːr/ *n* [U] a system of sending messages using two flags held one in each hand in various positions to represent letters and numbers

sem·blance /ˈsembləns/ *n* [S **(of)**] *fml* an appearance; outward form or seeming likeness: *We had to call in the troops to bring a*|*some semblance of* (=at least some) *order to the riot-torn city.*

se·men /ˈsiːmən/ *n* [U] a liquid produced by the male sex organs which carries SPERM and is passed into the female during the sexual act

se·mes·ter /sɪ̩ˈmestər/ *n* either of the two periods into which a year at high schools and universities, esp. in the US, is divided —compare TERM¹ (2)

sem·i /ˈsemi/ *n* **semis** *BrE infml* **1** a SEMIDETACHED house **2** *infml* a SEMIFINAL **3** *AmE* an articulated (ARTICULATE² (3)) lorry

semi- see WORD FORMATION

sem·i·au·to·mat·ic /ˌsemiɔːtəˈmætɪk◄/ *adj* (of a gun) that loads each new bullet by itself but has to have its TRIGGER pulled to fire each shot

sem·i·breve /ˈsemibriːv/ *BrE* ‖ **whole note** *AmE*— *n* a musical note with a time value equal to two MINIMs —see picture at NOTATION

sem·i·cir·cle /ˈsemi̩sɜːkəl‖-ɜːr-/ *n* **1** half a circle **2** a group arranged as if along the outside curve of this: *The teacher asked the pupils to sit in a semicircle to listen to the story.* —**cular** /ˌsemiˈsɜːkjʊlər◄‖-ˈsɜːr-/ *adj*

sem·i·co·lon /ˌsemiˈkəʊlən‖ˈsemi̩kəʊlən/ *n* a mark (;) used in writing and printing to separate independent parts of a sentence and different things in a list —compare COLON² and see picture at PUNCTUATION MARK

sem·i·con·duc·tor /ˌsemikənˈdʌktər/ *n* a substance, such as SILICON, which allows the passing of an electric current more easily than an INSULATOR, but not as well as a CONDUCTOR. Semiconductors are used in making TRANSISTORs.

sem·i·de·tached /ˌsemidɪˈtætʃt◄/ *n, adj* **1** *BrE* ‖ **duplex** *AmE*— (a house) that is one of a pair of joined houses — compare DETACHED (1), TOWN HOUSE; and see picture at HOUSE and see colour picture on page 162 **2** following accepted customs and standards without thinking

sem·i·fi·nal /ˌsemiˈfaɪnl◄/ *n* either of a pair of matches whose winners then compete against one another to decide the winner of the whole competition — **~ist** *n*

sem·i·nal /ˈseminəl/ *adj* **1** *fml apprec* influencing future development in a new way: *Stravinsky's "Rite of Spring" was a seminal work.* **2** [A *no comp.*] of, producing, or being SEMEN: *seminal fluid*

sem·i·nar /ˈseminɑːr/ *n* a small group, esp. a class of advanced students with a teacher, meeting to study or talk about a subject

sem·i·na·ry /ˈseminəri‖-neri/ *n* **1** a college for training esp. ROMAN CATHOLIC priests **2** *old-fash fml* a school: *a young ladies' seminary*

Sem·i·nole /ˈseminəʊl/ *n* [C; *the*+P] (a member of) a Native American people which lived in Florida. The Seminoles made peace with the US government, but were then forced to move to special areas in Oklahoma. —see NATIVE AMERICAN (CULTURAL NOTE)

sem·i·ot·ics /ˌsemiˈɒtɪks‖-ˈɑːtɪks/ also **sem·i·ol·o·gy** /ˌsemiˈɒlədʒi‖-ˈɑːl-/— n [U] tech the study of signs and their meaning in the exchange of information, esp. in language —**ician** /ˌsɪmiɒˈtɪʃən/, **semiologist** /ˌsemiˈɒlədʒɪst‖-ˈɑːl-/ n

sem·i·pre·cious /ˌsemiˈpreʃəs◂/ adj (of a jewel, stone, etc.) of lower value than a PRECIOUS STONE

sem·i·pro·fes·sion·al /ˌsemiprəˈfeʃənəl◂/ adj taking part in an activity for pay but not as a full-time job: *a semiprofessional footballer/musician*

sem·i·qua·ver /ˈsemiˌkweɪvəʳ/ BrE ‖ **sixteenth note** AmE— n a short musical note, with a time value half as long as a QUAVER — see picture at NOTATION

semi-skimmed /ˌ·· ˈ·◂/ BrE‖**two percent (milk)** AmE— adj (of milk) having had about half of the fat removed

Se·mit·ic /sɪˈmɪtɪk/ adj **1 a** of a race of people (the **Se·mites**) including Jews and Arabs and, in ancient times, Babylonians, Assyrians, etc. **b** of any of the languages of these people **2** Jewish —see also ANTI-SEMITISM

sem·i·tone /ˈsemɪtəʊn/ BrE ‖ **half step** AmE— n a difference in PITCH³ (7) (=highness of a musical note) equal to that between two notes which are next to each other on a piano

sem·i·trop·i·cal /ˌsemiˈtrɒpɪkəl◂‖-ˈtrɑː-/ adj SUBTROPICAL

sem·i·vow·el /ˈsemiˌvaʊəl/ n tech a speech sound, such as /w/ or /j/, between a vowel and a consonant

sem·i·week·ly /ˌsemiˈwiːkli◂/ adj, adv appearing or happening twice a week —compare BIWEEKLY

sem·o·li·na /ˌseməˈliːnə◂/ n [U] grains of crushed wheat used esp. in making PASTA and smooth cooked milky dishes: *semolina pudding*

Sem·tex /ˈsemteks/ n [U] tdmk the name of a plastic explosive produced in Czechoslovakia and sometimes used by the IRA

SEN /ˌes iː ˈen/ n abbrev. for: STATE ENROLLED NURSE

sen·ate /ˈsenɪt/ n (usu. cap.) **1** [(the) C+sing./pl. v] the smaller and more important of the two parts of the central law-making body in such countries as Australia, France, and the US: *The Senate has voted to support the President's defence plans.* —see also extra information on page 568

▶ CULTURAL NOTE The US Senate has 100 senators, two from each state, who are elected by the people in that state. A senator serves for six years. —compare CONGRESS (1), HOUSE OF REPRESENTATIVES ◀

2 [the+S+sing./pl. v] the highest council of state in ancient Rome **3** [(the) C+sing./pl. v] the governing council at some universities **4** [(the) C + sing./pl.v] **state senate** the governing council in US states

sen·a·tor /ˈsenətəʳ/ n (often cap.) a member of a SENATE (1,2): *Senator Kennedy* —see also extra information on page 568

sen·a·to·ri·al /ˌsenəˈtɔːriəl◂/ adj [A] fml of a senate or senator

send /send/ v sent /sent/ **1** [T (to)] to cause to go or be taken to a place, in a particular direction, etc., without going oneself: *It will get there quicker if you send it by airmail.* | *Did you send a birthday card to Susan?* (=by post) [+obj(i)+obj(d)] *Did you send Susan a birthday card?* | *The spacecraft sent pictures back to Earth.* | *We are sending our luggage ahead by sea.* | *I had some coffee sent up to my room.* [+obj+to-v] *I'll have to send my passport to be renewed.* **2** [T] **a** to direct or order (someone) to go: *"I've come to collect the films." "Who sent you?"* | *The allies agreed to send reinforcements.* | *to send a criminal to prison* | *The doctor sent me to bed.* | *The general sent his men into battle.* [+obj+to-v] *She sent her daughter to buy some milk.* | *We'll send someone round to repair your TV.* **b** [+obj+adv/prep] to arrange or make it possible for (someone) to go: *Are you going to send your children to private schools?* | *The company are sending me on a management course.* **3** [T+obj+v-ing] to cause to move quickly and uncontrollably: *The explosion sent glass flying everywhere.* | *The punch in the chest sent me reeling.* **4** [T+obj+adj/adv/prep] to cause to have a particular feeling or be in a particular state: *This noise is sending me mad!* | *The explosion sent the whole place into total confusion.* | *His boring speeches always send me to sleep.* **5** [T+obj+adv/prep, esp. OUT, FORTH] esp. lit to produce from

itself: *The crowd sent out a roar of approval.* | *The branches are sending forth buds.* **6** [I (for);T (to)] to cause (a message, request, or order) to be made known; give (a command, request, etc.): *The King sent and had the man brought to him.* | *We may have to send to Japan for the spare parts.* | *Send for help/a doctor!* | *Mother sends her love and says she hopes to see you soon.* [+to-v] *He sent to tell us he couldn't come.* [+obj(i)+obj(d)] *Send them my best wishes when you see them.* **7 send someone packing** infml to tell someone unwanted to leave at once **8 send word** to send a message

send away/off phr v **1** [T] (**send** sbdy./sthg. ↔ **away**) to send to another place: *He sent his son away/off to school in Germany.* **2** [I (for)] to order goods to be sent by post: *She sent away/off for a set of bed linen she saw advertised in a magazine.*

send down phr v **1** [T] (**send** sthg./sbdy. ↔ **down**) to cause to go down: *Reports of the company's bad trading figures sent its share prices down.* **2** [I (to)] to send a message, order, etc., to a lower place: *I'll send down to the kitchen for some more coffee.* **3** [T usu. pass.] (**send** sbdy. ↔ **down**) BrE to dismiss (a student) from a university because of bad behaviour **4** [T] (**send** sbdy. ↔ **down**) BrE infml to send to prison: *He was sent down for ten years for robbing a bank.*

send sthg. ↔ **in** phr v [T] to send (something for official consideration, such as a form) to a place where it will be dealt with: *Listeners sent in their suggestions to the radio station.*

send off phr v **1** [T] (**send** sthg. ↔ **off**) to post (a letter, parcel, message, etc.) **2** [T] (**send** sbdy. ↔ **off**) BrE (in sport) to order (a player) to leave the field because of a serious breaking of the rules **3** [I (for);T (=**send** sbdy./sthg. ↔ **off**)] to SEND **away** —compare SEND-OFF

send sthg. ↔ **on** phr v [T] **1** to send (a letter) to the address to which the receiver has since moved: *When he moved he left instructions for his letters to be sent on to his new address.* **2** to send (belongings) in advance to a point on a journey

send out phr v **1** [T] (**send** sthg./sbdy. ↔ **out**) to send from a central point: *Make sure you send out the invitations in good time.* | *The satellite is sending out radio signals.* | *The order was/The goods were sent out from the warehouse yesterday.* **2** [I (for, to)] (to try) to obtain something from somewhere else: *The coffee in the office vending machine is so bad that we prefer to send out (for it) to a local restaurant.*

send sbdy./sthg. ↔ **up** phr v [T] **1** to cause to go up: *Good news sent prices up on the market.* **2** BrE infml to copy the funny or silly qualities, actions, etc., of (a subject, person, etc.) to amuse others; make fun of —see also SEND-UP **3** AmE infml to send to prison

send·er /ˈsendəʳ/ n a person who sends esp. a letter, parcel, message, etc.

send-off /ˈ· ·/ n infml a usu. planned show of good wishes at the start of a journey, a new business, etc.: *We were given a wonderful send-off at the airport.* —see also SEND **off**

send-up /ˈ· ·/ BrE ‖ **takeoff** AmE— n [(of)] infml a copying of the funny or silly qualities, actions, etc., of something or someone in order to make people laugh; PARODY: *The comedian did a send-up of the prime minister.* —see also SEND **up** (2)

Sen·e·ca /ˈsenɪkə/ (about 4 BC–65 AD) a Roman thinker, politician, and writer of plays who was a noted speaker and NERO's teacher, practically ruling during Nero's first years as EMPEROR. He killed himself when he was ordered to, after it was said that he was working against Nero.

Seneca a Native American nation in western New York and eastern Ohio, which is a republic with four RESERVATIONS (=special areas) and about 4000 people —see NATIVE AMERICAN (CULTURAL NOTE)

Sen·e·gal /ˌsenɪˈɡɔːl/ a country in W Africa bordered by the Atlantic Ocean in W; capital Dakar; population 7,172,000 (1989) — ~ **ese** /ˌsenɪɡɔːˈliːz◂/ n, adj

se·nes·cent /sɪˈnesənt/ adj fml or med growing old; showing signs of old age —**cence** n [U]

se·nile /ˈsiːnaɪl/ adj of or caused by old age; showing the weakness of body or esp. of mind connected with old age: *The poor old lady's getting senile. She keeps hiding things and then says we've stolen them.* | *He's suffering from*

senile dementia. (=the medical condition of weakness of the mind in old age)

se·nil·i·ty /sɪˈnɪlɨti/ n [U] the weakness of mind or body connected with old age

se·ni·or /ˈsiːniəʳ/ n, adj [(to)] **1** (someone who is) older: *He's my senior* (=is older than me) *by two years.* | *Senior pupils have certain privileges.* —compare JUNIOR (1) **2** (someone) of high or higher rank: *a very senior officer/ minister* | *He is senior to me, though he's younger.* — compare JUNIOR (2) **3** AmE (a student) of the last year in a HIGH SCHOOL or university course —compare FRESHMAN (2), SOPHOMORE, JUNIOR (4); see MAJOR (USAGE)

Senior adj (abbrev. is **Sr** or **Snr** BrE) [after n] esp. AmE the older (esp. of two men in the same family who have exactly the same name): *The letter was addressed to John Smith Snr.* —compare JUNIOR¹

senior cit·i·zen /ˌ··· ˈ···/ n euph an old person, esp. a person over the age of 60 or 65 —compare OAP

se·ni·or·i·ty /ˌsiːniˈɒrɨti‖-ˈɔːr-, -ˈɑːr-/ n [U] **1** the condition of being higher in rank or older: *The officers were listed in order of seniority.* **2** official advantage coming from the length of one's service in an organization: *I sacrificed two years' seniority by taking the overseas posting.*

sen·na /ˈsenə/ n [U] a tropical plant. It has leaves, and fruit, known as SENNA PODS, which are dried and used as a LAXATIVE (=a medicine to help the action of the bowels). People sometimes make jokes about the effect of senna pods.

Se·ñor /seˈnjɔːʳ‖seɪˈnjɔːr/ n (used as a title for a Spanish-speaking man): *Señor Gomez* | *Good morning, Señor.*

Se·ño·ra /seˈnjɔːrə‖seɪˈnjɔːrə/ n (used as a title for a Spanish-speaking woman, esp. a married woman)

Se·ño·ri·ta /ˌsenjɔːˈriːtə/ n (used as a title for an unmarried Spanish-speaking girl): *Will the Señorita require anything more?*

sen·sa·tion /senˈseɪʃən/ n **1** [C;U] (a) direct feeling, such as of heat or pain, coming from one of the five natural senses, esp. the sense of touch: *After the accident he could feel no sensation/there was no sensation in his arm.* | *a drug that produces a tingling sensation in the skin* **2** [C] a general feeling in the mind or body that one cannot describe exactly: [+that] *I knew the train had stopped, but I had the sensation that it was still moving.* **3** [C] (a cause of) a state of excited interest: *The new discovery was/ caused a great sensation.* | *The scandal has created a sensation in Paris.*

sen·sa·tion·al /senˈseɪʃənəl/ adj **1** infml apprec wonderful; very good or exciting: *Your team won? That's sensational!* | *You look sensational in that black dress!* **2** often derog causing, or intended to cause, excited interest, attention, or shock: *a sensational murder trial* | *sensational headlines* — ~**ly** adv

sen·sa·tion·al·is·m /senˈseɪʃənəlɪzəm/ n [U] derog the intentional producing of excitement or shock, esp. by newspapers, magazines, etc.: *The paper was accused of sensationalism in its reporting of the murder trial.* —**ist** n

sense¹ /sens/ n **1** [U] good and esp. practical understanding and judgment: *He had the (good) sense to go by train rather than drive after hearing the forecast of icy conditions.* | *You should have had enough sense to turn off the electricity supply before disconnecting the wires.* | *There's* **no sense in** *getting angry about it.* (=getting angry will have no good effect) | *Where's the sense in going by boat when the plane costs no more and is quicker?* | (infml) *"I think he's a useless player." "Talk sense* (=speak reasonably); *he's brilliant!"* —see also COMMON SENSE, HORSE SENSE **2** [C (**of**)] any of the five natural powers of sight, hearing, feeling, tasting, and smelling which give a person or animal information about the outside world: *I lost my sense of smell/taste.* | *a keen sense of smell* (=a powerful ability to smell things) —see also SIXTH SENSE **3** [C;U (**of**)] (an) ability to understand or make judgments about the stated thing: *I'm afraid I haven't got a very good sense of direction, so I easily get lost.* | *She's got (a) good business sense, so the company should do well in her hands.* | *The comedian put his success largely down to a good sense of timing.* **4** [S+**of**/that] a feeling, esp. one that is hard to describe exactly: *The incident left me with a sense of helplessness.* | *a new sense of urgency at the arms-control talks* | *I don't know why, but I had this sense that someone was in the room with me.* **5** [C] a meaning: *I'm using "man" in its broadest sense, including both men and*

women. | *The different senses of a word in this dictionary are marked by the numbers 1, 2, etc.* | *He's in every sense* (=in all meanings of the word) *a gentleman.* **6** [U] fml an opinion shared by most people present, esp. as suggested by what they have said: *"I won't take a vote," said the chairman, "but the sense of the meeting seems to be that we approve of the plan."* **7 in a sense** when considered from only one point of view; partly: *You are right in a sense, but you don't know all the facts.* **8 make sense: a** to have a clear meaning: *No matter how I tried to read it, the sentence didn't make (any) sense (to me).* **b** to be a wise course of action: *It makes sense to take care of your health.* **9 make sense (out) of** to understand: *Can you make (any) sense of what this writer is saying?* —see also SENSES

sense² v [T] **1** to have a feeling that (something) exists or is there, without having direct proof: *The horse sensed danger and stopped.* | *I could sense her growing irritation, so I got up and left.* [+(that)] *I sensed that there was someone in the room with me.* [+wh-] *I could sense how unhappy she was feeling.* **2** (esp. of a machine) to discover and record; DETECT: *a device to sense the presence of poisonous gases*

Sense and Sen·si·bil·i·ty /ˌ·· ˌ··ˈ···/ a NOVEL by Jane Austen about the difficulties young women meet in their search for husbands

sense·less /ˈsensləs/ adj **1** showing a lack of meaning, thought, or purpose; foolish; POINTLESS: *senseless violence* **2** unconscious: *The box fell on his head and knocked him senseless.* | (fig.) *He was bored senseless* (=extremely) *by the discussion, and found it hard to keep his eyes open.* — compare INSENSIBLE (1) — ~**ly** adv — ~**ness** n [U]

sense of hu·mour /ˌ·· ˈ··/ n [S] the ability to understand and enjoy sthg. or sbdy. that is funny, or to make people laugh: *She's got a good/no sense of humour.*

sense of oc·ca·sion /ˌ·· ··ˈ··/ n [S] **1** a natural feeling that tells one how one should behave at a particular social event **2** suitable feeling produced in someone by an important event

sense or·gan /ˈ· ˌ··/ n a part of the body, such as the eye, nose, tongue, or ear, by which the brain receives messages from the outside world

sens·es /ˈsensɨz/ n [P] one's ability to think (reasonably): *You must have* **taken leave of your senses** (=be mad) *to have done such a thing.* | *Nobody* **in their right senses** *would pay that much for a painting!* *She felt faint in the hot room, but going out into the fresh air she quickly* **regained her senses.** (=stopped feeling faint) | *When will she* **come to her senses** *and see that he is a totally unsuitable man to marry?* | *He refuses to pay, but perhaps you can* **bring him to his senses.** (=make him behave sensibly)

sen·si·bil·i·ty /ˌsensɨˈbɪlɨti/ also **sensibilities** pl.— n [U] **1** fml delicate feeling about style or what is correct, esp. in art or behaviour: *Only a person of the greatest sensibility would appreciate all the subtle nuances of this painting.* | *It somewhat wounded her sensibilities to be addressed in that vulgar manner.* **2** [(**to**)] sensitiveness or awareness (AWARE): *sensibility to pain/the delicate nature of the situation*

▷ USAGE Compare **sensibility** and **sensible, sensitivity** and **sensitive. Sensibility** is not related to **sensible** in its meaning of "reasonable and practical" but is closer to **sensible of** (="conscious of "). If people have delicate feelings and are quick to enjoy or suffer you can say that they have great **sensibility/sensitivity** or that they are **sensitive. Sensitive/sensitivity** can also be used to suggest that someone is very conscious of other people's opinions and can easily be hurt: *Be careful not to criticize him too much. He's very* **sensitive.**◁

sen·si·ble /ˈsensɨbəl/ adj **1** reasonable; having or showing good sense: *a sensible suggestion* | *It was very sensible of you to bring your umbrella.* | *She's very sensible about money.* | *We'll be doing a lot of walking, so you'd better bring some sensible* (=comfortable and strong) *shoes with you.* | *Surely it would be sensible to get a second opinion before taking any further action.* **2** fml noticeable: *a sensible increase in temperature* **3** [F+**of**] old-fash fml knowing; recognizing; conscious: *He was sensible of the trouble he had caused.* —see INSENSIBLE (USAGE), SENSIBILITY (USAGE), WISE (USAGE) —**bly** adv

sen·si·mil·i·an /ˌsensɪˈmɪliən/ n, adj [U] AmE a type of CANNABIS (an illegal drug) which is of HAWAIIAN origin and is extremely strong

sen·si·tive /ˈsensɪtɪv/ adj **1** [(to)] strongly or easily influenced or changed by something: *sensitive to cold/pain* | *light-sensitive photographic paper* **2** [(about)] *sometimes derog* having feelings that are easily hurt; easily offended: *Don't be so sensitive – I wasn't criticizing you.* | *Don't mention that she's put on weight – she's very sensitive about it.* –compare HYPERSENSITIVE **3** showing delicate feelings or judgment in art, music, taste, etc.: *a sensitive performance/actor* –opposite **insensitive** **4** [(to)] knowing or being conscious of the feelings and opinions of others: *He's very sensitive to his pupils' need for encouragement and knows when to praise them.* –opposite **insensitive** **5** (of an apparatus) measuring exactly: *a more sensitive thermometer* **6** containing highly secret information: *sensitive official papers* **7** needing to be dealt with carefully so as not to cause trouble or offence; delicate: *This is such a sensitive issue that perhaps the press should not be told.* | *a price-sensitive market* (=one in which a product will be bought only if the price is exactly right) –see SENSIBILITY (USAGE) – **~ly** adv –**tivity** /ˌsensɪˈtɪvɪti/ also – **ness** /ˈsensɪtɪvnɪs/ n (U)

sen·si·tize also -ise BrE /ˈsensɪtaɪz/ v [T (to)] to make sensitive: *sensitized photographic film* | *His illness had sensitized him to bright light.* –compare DESENSITIZE

sen·sor /ˈsensəʳ/ n tech an apparatus used for discovering the presence of a particular quality or effect, such as light, heat, sound, etc., esp. in small quantities

sen·so·ry /ˈsensəri/ adj fml of or by the bodily senses or their use: *sensory stimuli* –see also ESP

sen·su·al /ˈsenʃuəl/ adj **1** of the feelings of the body rather than the mind: *purely sensual pleasures* **2** interested in or making one think of physical, esp. sexual, pleasure: *sensual curves/lips* | *a sensual woman* – **~ity** /ˌsenʃuˈælɪti/ n [U]

▷ USAGE Compare **sensual** and **sensuous**. A **sensual** person is usually one who wants physical and especially sexual pleasure; something that is **sensual** suggests or gives pleasure. **Sensuous** is used of something that gives pleasure to the senses, or that suggests pleasure found in the senses and in the body: *She uses beautiful* **sensuous** *lines in her drawings.*◁

sen·su·al·ist /ˈsenʃuəlɪst/ n derog a person very interested in sensual pleasure

sen·su·ous /ˈsenʃuəs/ adj **1** apprec giving pleasure to the senses: *The cat stretched itself with sensuous ease in the warm sun.* | *the sensuous feeling of soft velvet on the skin* **2** full of powerful images or sounds suggesting esp. bodily pleasure: *sensuous music* **3** SENSUAL (2) –see SENSUAL (USAGE) – **~ly** adv – **~ness** n [U]

sent /sent/ past tense & participle of SEND

sen·tence¹ /ˈsentəns/ n **1** (in grammar) a group of words that forms a statement, command, EXCLAMATION, or question, usu. contains a subject and a verb, and (in written English) begins with a capital letter and ends with any of the marks .!? The following are all sentences: "Sing the song again." "Birds sing." "How well he sings!" "Who sang at the concert last night?" –compare CLAUSE (1), PHRASE¹ (1) **2** (an order given by a judge which fixes) a punishment for a criminal declared to be guilty in court: *a six-year (prison) sentence* | *He received a heavy/light* (=long/short) *sentence.* | *The sentence was two years (in prison) and a fine of £10,000.* | *When the jury has given its verdict, the judge will* **pass/pronounce sentence (on** him). | *The* **death sentence** (=being killed) *has been abolished in Britain, and now you get a* **life sentence** (=being put in prison for a very long time) *for murder.* | *While he was* **under sentence of death** (=waiting to be officially killed) *he was not allowed to speak to other prisoners.*

sentence² v [T (to) often pass.] (of a judge or court) to give a punishment to: *He was sentenced to three years in prison.*

sen·ten·tious /senˈtenʃəs/ adj fml derog full of supposedly wise remarks about proper behaviour or morality – **~ly** adv

sen·tient /ˈsenʃənt/ adj fml or tech having feelings and some kind of consciousness: *Man is a sentient being*

sen·ti·ment /ˈsentɪmənt/ n **1** [U] *sometimes derog* tender feelings of pity, love, sadness, etc., or remembrance of such feelings in the past: *There's no place for sentiment in business affairs!* | *It's not a beautiful watch, but I wear it for sentiment because it was my father's.* **2** [C;U] fml (a) thought or judgment caused or influenced by feeling: *The prime minister has condemned this act of terrorism, and the other party leaders have expressed similar sentiments.* | *There is strong public sentiment on the question of unemployment.* **3** [C] also **sentiments** pl.– fml or pomp an opinion about a matter: *I share your sentiments.* | *(Those are) my sentiments exactly.* (=I totally agree.) **4** [C] fml or pomp a phrase expressing a wish or feeling: *A birthday card usually has a suitable sentiment like "Happy Birthday" on it.*

sen·ti·ment·al /ˌsentɪˈmentl◁/ adj **1** showing or based on tender feelings rather than reasonable or practical judgments: *The old clock was a present from my father and has* **sentimental value.** | *She kept all the old photographs for* **sentimental reasons.** **2** derog showing too much of such feelings, esp. of a weak or insincere kind: *sentimental love stories* – **~ly** adv

sen·ti·ment·al·is·m /ˌsentɪˈmentəl-ɪzəm/ n [U] fondness for sentimentality – **~ist** n

sen·ti·men·tal·i·ty /ˌsentɪmenˈtælɪti/ n [U] usu. derog the quality of being SENTIMENTAL (esp. 2)

sen·ti·ment·al·ize also -ise BrE /ˌsentɪˈmentəlaɪz/ v derog **1** [T] to treat or consider in a sentimental way: *It's a sentimentalized description of what was really a terrible time to live in.* **2** [I (over, about)] to speak, write, etc., sentimentally: *sentimentalizing about his childhood*

sen·ti·nel /ˈsentɪnəl/ n lit or old use a guard; sentry

sen·try /ˈsentri/ n a soldier standing as a guard outside a building, entrance, etc.

sentry box /ˈ··· ·/ n a narrow shelter for a sentry to stand in while on duty

Seoul /səʊl/ the capital city of South Korea, a business, industrial, and CULTURAL centre

se·pal /ˈsepəl/ n tech any of the small leaves directly under a flower –see picture at FLOWER

sep·a·ra·ble /ˈsepərəbəl/ adj [(from)] fml that can be separated –opposite **inseparable** – **~bly** adv – **~bility** /ˌsepərəˈbɪlɪti/ [U]

sep·a·rate¹ /ˈsepəreɪt/ v **1** [I;T (from)] to move apart; (cause to) become disconnected physically or in the mind: *Once the spacecraft was in orbit, the satellite separated from its launcher.* | *The two friends separated at the crossroads.* | *He found the two boys fighting and stepped in to separate them.* | *They were great friends and couldn't be separated.* (=were always together) | *As we joined the big crowd I got separated from my friends.* | *They were once very close* (=good friends), *but their opposing political views have separated them.* | *In any discussion of the matter, the two issues must be clearly separated.* (=recognized as different) **2** [T (OFF) often pass.] to keep apart; mark a division between: *The two parts of the town were separated by a river.* | *A partition separated the rooms.* **3** [I;T (UP, into, from)] to break or divide up into the parts forming the whole: *An orange separates (up) into ten or twelve pieces.* | *War separated the family.* | *The teacher separated the children into two groups.* | *Break the eggs and separate the whites from the yolks.* **4** [I] to stop living together as husband and wife, esp. by a formal agreement **5** [I;T (OUT, from)] to (cause to) leave a mixture and form a mass by itself: *If you heat the sauce too much, the butter will separate out.*

sep·a·rate² /ˈsepərɪt/ adj **1** not the same; different: *This word has three separate meanings.* | *The restaurant and the bar in this establishment are under separate management.* | *She's been warned on three separate occasions that the standard of her work is not good enough.* **2** [A] not shared with another; INDIVIDUAL: *We have separate rooms.* | *We* **went our separate ways** (=went in different directions) *after the party.* **3** [F (from)] apart: *Keep the onions separate from the bread or they'll make it smell.* – **~ly** adv : *They arrived together but left separately.* | *Each problem should be assessed separately.* | *The American hostages were held separately from the rest.*

separate but e·qual /ˌ··· · ˈ··/ adj describing the practice of separating black people and white people and giving them (supposedly) equal services, such as schools, houses, hotels, seats on buses and trains, and restaurants. This was legal in the US from 1896 until 1954, when the Supreme Court decided that blacks could not be forced to go to separate schools from whites. —see also BROWN VS. BOARD OF EDUCATION OF TOPEKA, CIVIL RIGHTS, PLESSEY VS. FERGUSON, SEGREGATION

sep·a·rates /ˈsepərɨts/ also **coordinates**— n [P] separate women's garments that can be worn together in various combinations, such as a shirt and skirt or a coat and trousers

sep·a·ra·tion /ˌsepəˈreɪʃən/ n 1 [U (**of**)] the act of separating or the fact of being separated: *arrangements for the separation of rival supporters at a football match* | *the separation of church and state* 2 [C;U (**from**)] (a time of) being or living apart: *Lengthy separation of the boy from his mother could lead to psychological problems.* 3 [C] *law* a formal agreement by a husband and wife to live apart, —compare DIVORCE¹, see also TRIAL SEPARATION

separation of church and state /···,··· ,·· ˈ·/ n [U] the belief or law that the church should not be involved in governing a country, and that the state should not be allowed to govern religion. This belief is strong in the US, where, for example, prayer is generally not allowed in public schools.

separation of pow·ers /···,··· ˈ·/ also **balance of powers, checks and balance system**— n [U] the practice (from a political idea by MONTESQUIEU) of controlling a government's power by dividing it into three branches: the power to make laws (the LEGISLATIVE branch), the power to judge (the JUDICIARY branch), and the power to give orders (the EXECUTIVE branch). The American CONSTITUTION and government are based on this idea.

sep·a·rat·is·m /ˈsepərətɪzəm/ n [U] the belief that a particular political or religious group or unit should be separate, and not part of a larger whole —**ist** n : *Sikh separatists in India, who want to form an independent state*

sep·a·ra·tor /ˈsepəreɪtər/ n a machine for separating esp. liquids from solids or cream from milk

se·pi·a /ˈsiːpiə/ n [U] 1 a reddish-brown paint or ink made from liquid produced by CUTTLEFISH: *a sepia drawing* (=one made with this) 2 the colour of this: *an old-fashioned sepia photograph*

sep·sis /ˈsepsɨs/ n [U] *med* a poisoning of part of the body by disease bacteria, often producing PUS (=a poisonous yellowish substance) there

Sep·tem·ber /sepˈtembər/ (*written abbrev. is* **Sept.**) n [C;U] 1 the ninth month of the year, between August and October.

▶CULTURAL NOTE In Britain and in the US, September is the end of the summer and the beginning of autumn, when the days are getting shorter. In Britain, the days are often misty and sunny. It is the time that people think of as HARVEST time (= the time when the crops are gathered), and it is the start of the new school year after the long summer holiday: *It happened on September the eleventh/the eleventh of September/(AmE) September eleventh.* | *This office opened in September 1991.* | *She started work here last September/the September before last.* ◀

2 thirty days hath September an old poem which people use to remind themselves of how many days the different months have:
> *Thirty days hath September,*
> *April, June, and November,*
> *And all the rest have thirty-one,*
> *Excepting February alone,*
> *Which hath but twenty-eight days clear,*
> *and twenty-nine in each leap year.*

sep·tet /sepˈtet/ n 1 [+*sing./pl. v*] a group of seven singers or musicians performing together 2 a piece of music for seven performers —compare OCTET, SEXTET

sep·tic /ˈseptɪk/ adj esp. BrE infected with disease bacteria: *a septic finger*

sep·ti·cae·mi·a esp. BrE ‖ **-cemia** AmE /ˌseptɨˈsiːmiə/ n [U] *tech for* BLOOD POISONING

septic tank /ˈ··· ·/ n a large container, esp. near buildings in country areas, into which body waste matter is carried by pipes to be treated chemically

sep·tu·a·ge·nar·i·an /ˌseptʃuədʒɨˈneəriən/ n a person who is between 70 and 79 years old

Sep·tu·a·ges·i·ma /ˌseptʃuəˈdʒesɨmə/ the third Sunday before LENT

se·pul·chral /sɨˈpʌlkrəl/ adj 1 *fml or lit* like or suitable for a grave: *the sepulchral gloom of the crypt* | (fig.) *a sepulchral voice* (=deep and frightening) 2 *tech* of the burial of the dead

sep·ul·chre BrE ‖ **-cher** AmE /ˈsepəlkər/ n *old use or bibl* a small building or room in which dead people are placed; TOMB. This word is known to most people only as used for the place where Christ was buried. —see also WHITED SEPULCHRE

se·quel /ˈsiːkwəl/ n [(**to**)] 1 a book, film, etc., which continues the course of action of, or has the same characters as, an earlier one 2 something that follows something else, esp. as a result: *In/As an unexpected sequel to the leaders' meeting, new trade agreements between the two countries have been announced.*

se·quence /ˈsiːkwəns/ n 1 [C (**of**)] a group of things that are arranged in or happen in an order, esp. following one another in time: *a sequence of historical plays by Shakespeare* | *A sequence of bad accidents has prompted the council to put up warning signs.* 2 [U] the order in which things or events follow one another; SUCCESSION: *Please keep the numbered cards in sequence; don't mix them up.* | *The sequence of events on the night of the murder still isn't known.* 3 [C] a part of a story, esp. in a film, dealing with a single subject or action; scene: *In the next sequence we see the hero rescuing the girl.*

se·quenc·ing /ˈsiːkwənsɪŋ/ n [U (**of**)] *fml* arrangement in an order, esp. in time: *In a busy railway station the sequencing of trains is a difficult job.*

se·quen·tial /sɨˈkwenʃəl/ adj fml of, forming, or following in (a) sequence — **~ ly** adv : *They are numbered sequentially, from 1 to 100.*

se·ques·tered /sɨˈkwestəd‖-ərd/ adj lit quiet and hidden away from other people: *a sequestered spot by the river bank*

se·ques·trate /sɨˈkwestreɪt, ˈsiːkwɨ-/ also **se·ques·ter** /sɨˈkwestər/— v [T *usu. pass.*] *law* to take control of (the property of a debtor, of someone who has disobeyed a court, etc.) by legal order until the debts are paid or the court's order is obeyed —**tration** /ˌsiːkwɨˈstreɪʃən/ n [C;U] : *The judge ordered the sequestration of the union's funds.*

se·quin /ˈsiːkwɨn/ n a very small flat round shiny piece of metal or plastic sewn onto a garment for decoration: *Her ballgown is decorated with thousands of sequins.* —**quined** adj

se·quoi·a /sɨˈkwɔɪə/ n 1 REDWOOD 2 *tech* the group (GENUS) of trees which include REDWOOD trees

Se·quoy·ah /sɨˈkwɔɪə/ (1760?–1843) a Native American of the Cherokee TRIBE who invented a system of writing for the Cherokee language so that he could record his tribe's way of life

se·ra·glio /sɨˈrɑːljəʊ/ n **-glios** a HAREM (1)

ser·aph /ˈserəf/ n **-aphs** *or* **-aphim** /rəfɪm/ any of the six-winged ANGELS of the highest rank guarding the seat of God according to the Bible —compare CHERUB (3)

se·raph·ic /sɨˈræfɪk/ adj lit like or typical of a seraph, esp. in beauty or purity; SUBLIME: *a seraphic smile/child*

Serb /sɜːb‖sɜːrb/ n 1 a member of a people from Serbia and nearby areas 2 [U] their language; Serbian (2) — **Serb** adj : *the Serb nation*

Serb·i·a /ˈsɜːbiə‖ˈsɜːr-/ part of the former Yugoslavia; capital Belgrade; population 9,760,000 (1988)

Serb·i·an /ˈsɜːbiən‖ˈsɜːr-/ n 1 a Serb (1) 2 [U] the Serbo-Croatian language as spoken in Serbia or its written form using the CYRILLIC ALPHABET —compare CROATIA — **Serbian** adj

Serb·o-Cro·a·tian /ˌsɜːbəʊ krəʊˈeɪʃən◂ ‖ˌsɜːr-/ also **Serbo-Cro·at** /ˌ·· ˈ···◂/— n [U] the language of the Serbs and the CROATS. The Serbian form is written in the CYRILLIC ALPHABET and the CROATIAN form in the Roman alphabet. —**Serbo-Croatian** adj

sere , sear /sɪər/ adj lit dried up: *the sere and withered leaves of autumn*

ser·e·nade¹ /ˌserɨˈneɪd/ n 1 a song or other piece of music sung or played in the open air at night, esp. to a woman by a lover 2 a piece of gentle tuneful music, usu. in several parts, played by a small group of instruments

serenade² v [T] to sing or play a SERENADE to

ser·en·dip·i·ty /ˌserən'dɪpˌti/ n [U] *lit or humor* the natural ability to make interesting or valuable discoveries by accident

se·rene /sɪ'riːn/ adj **1** completely calm and peaceful; free from trouble, anxiety, or sudden activity: *a serene summer night | a serene smile | She just says what she thinks, with serene indifference to whether it may offend people.* **2** [A] (part of a royal title in some countries): *His Serene Highness* — ~ **ly** adv —**renity** /sɪ'renɪti/ n [U]

serf /sɜːf‖sɜːrf/ n a farm worker, esp. in former times in a FEUDAL system, who had to work for a particular master —compare SLAVE

serf·dom /'sɜːfdəm‖'sɜːr-/ n [U] the state or fact of being a serf

serge /sɜːdʒ‖sɜːrdʒ/ n [U] a strong usu. woollen cloth used esp. for suits

ser·geant /'sɑːdʒənt‖'sɑːr-/ n **1** a military rank. British sergeants usu. have three V-shaped marks on the upper arm of the uniform. —see TABLE 3 **2** a police officer of next to the lowest rank, typically also having such uniform marks —see also FLIGHT SERGEANT; see FATHER (USAGE)

sergeant-at-arms /ˌ… ·'·/ n a SERJEANT-AT-ARMS

sergeant ma·jor /ˌ… '··◂/ n a military rank —see TABLE 3

se·ri·al[1] /'sɪəriəl/ n a written or broadcast story appearing in parts at fixed times: *"The Archers" is a British radio serial that has been heard every day for many years. | Several magazines have bid for the serial rights of my novel.*

serial[2] adj of, happening in, or arranged in a SERIES or row of things one after the other in their right order: *placed in serial order | serial processing on a computer* —compare PARALLEL[1] (3) — ~ **ly** adv

se·ri·al·ize also **-ise** BrE /'sɪəriəlaɪz/ v [T *often pass.*] to print or broadcast (a story already written) as a serial: *"Oliver Twist" was serialized on television.* —**ization** /ˌsɪəriəlaɪ'zeɪʃən‖-lə-/ n [C;U (**of**)]

serial kil·ler /'… ˌ··/ n one who MURDERs a number of people at different times and in different places

serial num·ber /'… ˌ··/ n a number given to and usu. printed on each of a large number of similar things in order to be able to tell them apart: *The police know the serial numbers of the stolen banknotes.*

se·ries /'sɪəriːz/ n series **1** [(**of**)] a group of things of the same kind or related in some way, coming one after another or in order: *The Philharmonic Society is putting on a series of twelve concerts this winter. | This is the latest in a series of proposals on arms limitation. | They carried out a series of experiments to test the new drug.* **2** a group of books with related subjects, in a similar style, etc., printed by one company and often under a single name: *We're publishing a new series on ethnic music next year.* **3** (in cricket and BASEBALL) a group of specially important games played one after another: *a Test series between England and Australia* **4** one of a group of programmes on television or radio which are shown regularly over a period of weeks **5 in series** *tech* (of a number of electrical apparatuses) connected in such a way that the same electricity passes through each part one after the other —compare **in parallel** (PARALLEL[2])

ser·if /'serɪf/ n a short line at the upper or lower end of the stroke of some sorts of printed letters —see also SANS SERIF

se·ri·o·com·ic /ˌsɪəriəʊ'kɒmɪk◂‖-'kɑː-/ adj fml both serious and funny: *a seriocomic novel*

se·ri·ous /'sɪəriəs/ adj **1** not easy to deal with; causing worry and needing attention; not slight: *The storm caused serious damage. | The company is in serious financial difficulties. | There are serious objections to these proposals. | serious crime | a serious injury/situation* **2** as if thinking deeply about important or worrying matters: *You look very serious; is anything the matter? | a serious manner/expression* **3** not joking or funny; (intended) to be considered as sincere: *Do you think he's serious about leaving* (=really intends to leave) *his wife? | He's not a serious contender for the job.* (=he is very unlikely to get it) | *"Management have decided to give us an extra day's holiday as a special bonus." "You can't be serious!"* **4** of an important kind; needing or having great skill or thought: *This subject has never been paid any serious*

attention. | *a serious article* (=intended to make one think rather than to amuse) | *serious music* | (fig., *humor*) *We'll be doing some serious drinking* (=we'll drink a lot of alcohol) *over Christmas.* — ~ **ness** [U]

serious crime squad /ˌ… '· ˌ·/ n a British police department established in certain areas specifically to be responsible for serious crime

Serious Fraud Of·fice /ˌ… '· ˌ··/ [*the*] a British government department whose work is to find out whether people or companies have behaved deceitfully and illegally in order to make money

se·ri·ous·ly /'sɪəriəsli/ adv **1** in a serious way: *She was seriously injured in the accident. | He's so frivolous; he never takes anything seriously.* (=treats anything as being serious) **2** *infml* (used at the beginning of a sentence to turn attention away from a joke or towards a serious statement or subject): *Seriously though, you ought to take more care of your health.*

ser·jeant-at-arms , **sergeant-** /ˌsɑːdʒənt ət 'ɑːmz‖ ˌsɑːrdʒənt ət 'ɑːrmz/ n **serjeants-at-arms** (in Britain) an officer of a law court, parliament, etc., with the duty of keeping order during meetings

ser·mon /'sɜːmən‖'sɜːr-/ n [(**on**)] **1** a religious talk given as part of a Christian church service, usu. based on a sentence from the Bible: *The minister preached a sermon on the importance of brotherly love.* **2** *infml derog* a long and solemn warning or piece of advice

ser·mon·ize also **-ise** BrE /'sɜːmənaɪz‖'sɜːr-/ v [I] *derog* to give moral advice, esp. in too long and solemn a way

Sermon on the Mount /ˌ… · · '·/ [*the*] (in the Bible) a talk given by Jesus teaching about moral behaviour

ser·pent /'sɜːpənt‖'sɜːr-/ n **1** *lit and bibl* a snake, esp. a large one.

▶ CULTURAL NOTE In the Bible a serpent in the Garden of Eden encourages Adam and Eve, the first man and woman, to disobey God and eat the fruit from the Tree of Knowledge. —see also FALL, SNAKE[1] (CULTURAL NOTE)◀

2 *esp. bibl* a wicked person who leads people to do wrong or harms those who are kind to him **3** *usu. cap.* the DEVIL

ser·pen·tine /'sɜːpəntaɪn‖'sɜːrpəntiːn/ adj *lit* twisting like a snake; following a course with many curves; winding: *the serpentine course of the river*

Serpentine [*the*] a lake in Hyde Park in London. It is a custom for some people to swim in it on Christmas Day.

SERPS /sɜːps‖sɜːrps/ State Earnings-Related Pension Scheme; a British government system which pays a regular income to those who have reached the age to stop work, based on the earnings of their working life

ser·rat·ed /sɪ'reɪtɪd, se-/ adj having (an edge with) a row of connected V-shapes like teeth: *A knife for cutting bread has a serrated edge. | a serrated leaf* —**serration** /-'reɪʃən/ n [C;U]

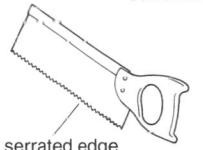
serrated

serrated edge

ser·ried /'serɪd/ adj [A *no comp.*] *lit* pressed closely together; CROWDED: *The serried ranks* (=large numbers close together) *of his supporters filled the square.*

se·rum /'sɪərəm/ n **-rums** or **-ra** /rə/ **1** [C;U] (a) liquid prepared from animal blood containing disease-fighting substances used for putting into a sick person's blood: *antisnakebite serum* —compare VACCINE **2** [U] *tech* the watery part of an animal or plant liquid, esp. blood

ser·vant /'sɜːvənt‖'sɜːr-/ n **1** a person who is paid to do personal services for someone, such as cleaning or cooking, esp. in their house: *In the last century many people used to employ servants.* **2** [(**of**)] *fml* a person who serves someone, rather than controlling their activities: *A politician should be a servant of the people.* —see also CIVIL SERVANT

serve[1] /sɜːv‖sɜːrv/ v **1** [I (**in, on, under**);T (**as**)] to do work (for); give service (to): *He served in the army/on the committee. | to serve as a member of parliament | He has served the company for fifty years, first as office boy and eventually as managing director. | Membership is restricted to serving officers in the armed forces.* | (fig.) *If my* **memory serves** (me) (=if I remember correctly), *it happened on*

a Tuesday. **2** [T (**with**) *often pass.*] to provide with something necessary or useful: *A single pipeline serves all the houses with water.* | *The outlying islands are served by a ferry which calls twice a week.* **3** [I;T (UP, OUT)] to offer (food, drinks, a meal, etc.) for eating or drinking: *Could you all come to the table—we're ready to serve.* | *What time is breakfast served in this hotel?* | *We're not allowed to serve alcohol in this club.* | *How can you dare to serve up such a terrible meal?* | *This dish serves six.* (=there is enough of it for six people to eat) [+*obj(i)*+*obj(d)*] *She served us tea and toast.* [+*obj*+**to**] *She served tea and toast to us.* [+*obj*+**with**] *She served us with tea and toast.* [+*obj*+*adj*] *Make sure you serve the coffee hot.* **4** [T *usu. pass.*] (esp. of a person employed in a shop) to attend to (a customer), e.g. by showing or esp. selling goods to them: *Are you being served?* (=Is someone else already attending to you?) | *They refused to serve him in the cocktail bar because he wasn't wearing a tie.* **5** [T (**as, for, in**)] to pass and complete (a period of time): *She served two years (in prison) for theft.* | *He has served his sentence/his time and should be freed.* | *Reagan served two terms as President.* **6** [I (**for, as**);T] *fml* to be good enough or suitable for (a purpose): *One room had to serve as/for both bedroom and living room.* | *I haven't got a hammer, but this stone should serve (my purpose).* | *This incident serves as a reminder of how dangerous these weapons really are.* [+*to-v*] *This polythene sheet should serve to keep out the rain for a while.* | *Her remarks served only to worsen the situation.* (=had the effect of making it worse) **7** [I;T] (in tennis, VOLLEYBALL, etc.) to begin play by hitting (the ball) to the opponent: *It's your turn to serve.* | *to serve an ace* **8** [T] *law* to deliver (an official order to appear in court): *Has the summons been served yet?* [+*obj*+**on**] *The bailiff served a summons on him.* [+*obj*+**with**] *He served him with a summons.* **9 serve someone right** *infml* to be a suitable punishment for someone: *After all you've eaten it serves you right if you feel ill.*

serve sthg. ↔ **out** *phr v* [T] to work until the end of (a period of time fixed for a duty, esp. one already begun)

serve² *n* an act or manner of serving (SERVE¹ (7)), esp. in tennis

serv·er /ˈsɜːvəʳ‖ˈsɜːr-/ *n* **1** something used in serving food, esp. a specially shaped tool for putting a particular kind of food onto a plate: *salad servers* **2** a player who SERVEs¹ (7), esp. in tennis **3** a person who helps a priest during the EUCHARIST

serv·e·ry /ˈsɜːvəri‖ˈsɜːr-/ *n esp. BrE* the part of an informal eating place where people get food to take back to their tables

serv·ice¹ /ˈsɜːvɪs‖ˈsɜːr-/ *n* **1** [U] attention to customers in a shop or esp. to guests in a hotel, restaurant, etc.: *The service in this place is slow/bad; sometimes you have to wait ten minutes for service.* | *This computer supplier provides very good after-sales service.* (=gives the customer help and advice after the sale) —see also ROOM SERVICE, SELF-SERVICE **2 a** [C;U] (the operation of) a business or organization doing useful work or supplying a need: *Is there any railway service here on Sundays?* | *A good postal service* | *motorway services* (=a place for users of a MOTORWAY which has restaurants, petrol stations, shops, and TOILETS) **b** [C *usu. pl.*] a useful business or job that does not produce goods: *The value of a country's* **goods and services** *is its GNP.* | **service occupations** *such as education, hairdressing, architecture, and the legal profession* —see also NATIONAL HEALTH SERVICE, SOCIAL SERVICE **3** [U] a work or duty done for someone: *He died* **in the service of** (=serving) *his country.* **b** active use: *This old coat has* **seen** *a lot of* **service**/*has* **given good service.** (=been used for a long time) | *This type of aircraft has been in service since the early 1970s.* **4** [C *usu. pl.*] *fml* an act or job done for someone: *You may need the services of a lawyer in this affair.* | *He was rewarded for his services to the government.* | *Thank you very much; you've* **done** *me a* **great service.** (=helped me very much) **5** [C *often pl.*;U] (duty in) any of the ARMED FORCES: *She joined the* **services.** (=joined the army, navy, etc.) | *The Royal Navy is sometimes called the* **Senior Service.** | *He spent many years overseas on* **active service.** (=fighting or ready to fight) —see also NATIONAL SERVICE, SECRET SERVICE **6** [C] a fixed form of public worship; a religious ceremony

▶ CULTURAL NOTE In a Christian service there are usu. prayers, readings from the Bible, HYMNs (= religious songs), and a SERMON (= talk by a priest). In the Christian

church, the main services are on Sundays. There are special services for weddings and funerals, and for Christmas: *Our church has three services each Sunday.* | *a marriage/funeral/memorial service* ◀

7 [(*the*) C *usu. sing.*] *esp. BrE* a particular government department: *She works in the diplomatic/the foreign service.* —see also CIVIL SERVICE **8** [C;U] an examination of a machine to keep it in good condition: *I'm taking my car in for its 5000-mile service.* | *a typewriter service centre* **9** [C] an act or manner of serving (SERVE¹ (7)), esp. in tennis: *He has a good fast service.* | *It's your service.* (=your turn to serve) **10** [C] the dishes, tools, etc., needed to serve a stated meal: *a silver tea service* **11** [U (**of**)] *law* the delivering of an order to appear in court: *the service of a writ* **12** [U] *old-fash* employment as a servant in someone's home: *She was* **in service** *all her life.* **13 at your service** *polite or pomp* willing to help: *If you need any help, I and my car are at your service.* **14 of service** useful; helpful: *(polite) Can I be of (any) service to you?* —see also LIP SERVICE

service² *v* [T] **1** to examine (a machine) and make any necessary repairs: *I'm having my car serviced.* | *Regular servicing will prolong the life of the machine.* **2** *tech* to pay the interest on (a debt): *Some of these countries are no longer able to service their massive loans.*

service³ *adj* [A] for the use of people working in a place, rather than the public: *a service entrance* | *service stairs*

ser·vi·cea·ble /ˈsɜːvɪ̮səbəl/ *adj* that can be used; fit for (long or hard) use: *a serviceable pair of shoes* **—bly** *adv* **—bility** /ˌsɜːvɪ̮səˈbɪlɪ̮ti‖ˌsɜːr-/ *n* [U]

service charge /ˈ·· ·/ *n* **1** an amount of money added to a restaurant bill by the restaurant to reward the waiters for their work —compare TIP **2** an amount of money paid to the LANDLORD of a block of flats for common services e.g. cleaning the stairs

service club /ˈ·· ·/ *n AmE* an organization, often for men only, that has local branches in which members work together in ways to support the COMMUNITY: *Rotary, Lions, Kiwanis, and other service clubs*

service flat /ˈ·· ·/ *n BrE* a flat whose rent includes a charge for certain services, such as cleaning, providing sheets, etc.

service in·dus·try /ˈ·· ·,···/ *n* [C;U] (any particular group of) businesses which are considered to provide a service rather than a product, such as accounting, insurance, or advertising

ser·vice·man /ˈsɜːvɪ̮smən‖ˈsɜːr-/ **ser·vice·wom·an** /-ˌwʊmən/ *fem.*— *n* **-men** /mən/ a member of the army, navy, etc.

service road /ˈ·· ·/ *n* a small road along one side of a main road for the use of local traffic

service sta·tion /ˈ·· ·,·/ *n* a GARAGE¹ (2)

ser·vi·ette /ˌsɜːviˈet‖ˌsɜːr-/ *BrE*‖**napkin** *AmE*— *n* a table NAPKIN (1) —see picture at PLACE SETTING

ser·vile /ˈsɜːvaɪl‖ˈsɜːrvəl, -vaɪl/ *adj derog* behaving like a slave; allowing oneself to be controlled completely by another: *servile obedience* **— ~ly** /ˈsɜːvaɪl-li‖ˈsɜːrvəl-li, -vaɪl-li/ *adv* **—vility** /sɜːˈvɪlɪ̮ti‖sɜːr-/ *n* [U]

serv·ing /ˈsɜːvɪŋ‖ˈsɜːr-/ *n* [(**of**)] an amount of food for one person; HELPING: *a large serving of potatoes*

ser·vi·tor /ˈsɜːvɪ̮təʳ‖ˈsɜːr-/ *n old use* a male servant

ser·vi·tude /ˈsɜːvɪ̮tjuːd‖ˈsɜːrvɪ̮tuːd/ *n* [U] *lit* the condition of a slave or one who is forced to obey another: *They spent their lives in servitude (to the enemy conquerors).*

ser·vo /ˈsɜːvəʊ‖ˈsɜːr-/ *n* **servos** a servomotor or servomechanism —see picture at ENGINE

ser·vo·mech·a·nis·m /ˈsɜːvəʊˌmekənɪzəm‖ˈsɜːr-/ *n* an apparatus that supplies power to (part of) a machine and controls its operation

ser·vo·mo·tor /ˈsɜːvəʊˌməʊtəʳ‖ˈsɜːr-/ *n* a machine which allows a heavy operation to be done with only a slight effort by the user

ses·a·me /ˈsesəmi/ *n* [U] a tropical plant grown for its seeds and their oil, used esp. in cooking —see also OPEN SESAME

Sesame Street /ˈ·· ·,·/ *n* an American television programme for young children which teaches numbers, letters, and other lessons, with characters such as Big Bird, Kermit the Frog, Oscar, and the Cookie Monster

ses·sion /ˈseʃən/ *n* **1** a formal meeting or group of meetings of an organization, esp. a law-making body or court: *The next session of Parliament will begin in November.* | *Be seated! This court is now in session.* (=it has now formally begun) **2** a meeting or period of time used esp. by a group for a particular purpose: *a recording session* | *a jazz session* | *a drinking session* | *a question-and-answer session* **3** *ScotE* any of the parts of the year when teaching is given at a university —see also QUARTER SESSIONS

ses·sions /ˈseʃənz/ *n* [P] **1** PETTY SESSIONS **2** QUARTER SESSIONS

set¹ /set/ *v* **set,** *present participle* **setting** ■ to put something into a particular place or position **1** [T+*obj*+*adv/prep*] to put (something) in the stated place or position, esp. so that it remains there: *The hotel porter took her suitcases from the taxi and set them down at the reception desk.* | *The waiter set a plate of food down in front of me.* | *to set a ladder against a wall* | *to set pen to paper* (=begin to write) | *That man's not my brother—I've never* **set eyes on** (=seen) *him before!* —see also SET² (1), CLOSE-SET **2** [T+*obj*+*adv/prep*; *usu. pass.*] to show the action of (a story, play, etc.) as happening in the stated place and time; give a SETTING (3b) to: *The book is set in 17th-century Spain.* ■ to put someone or something into a particular state or activity **3** [T+*obj*+*adj/adv/prep*] to cause to be in a stated condition: *I opened the cage and set the bird free.* | *This mistake must be set right.* | *She set the papers on fire./set them alight* | *to set the accounts in order* | *The discovery of oil set the country on the road to modernization.* | *We have the government's approval, so we are now ready to* **set things in motion/set the ball rolling.** (=begin a planned course of action) | *The children are safe so you can* **set your mind at rest.** (=stop worrying) — see FIRE (USAGE) **4** [T+*obj*+*v-ing*] to cause to start: *Your remarks have set me thinking.* | *He set the machine going with a push.* ■ to prepare or arrange something for use **5** [T (**for**)] to put into correct condition for use: *I set the camera for a long-distance shot.* | *She set the alarm for 7.30 a.m.* (=fixed it so that it would ring then) | *He set the table* (=put the plates, glasses, etc., on it) *for dinner.* | *The stage is set for the next part of the play.* | *His activities are so regular you could set your watch* (=make it show the right time) *by him.* —see CLOCK (USAGE) **6** [T (**UP**)] to arrange for printing: *Today most books are set (up) by machine.* —see also TYPESETTER ■ to establish something or fix it into position **7** [T] to fix or establish (a rule, time, standard, number, etc.): *The price was set at £1000.* | *Have you set a date for your wedding yet?* | *The government has set strict limits on pay increases.* | *By allowing them to go unpunished we are setting a dangerous precedent.* | *He set a new land speed record.* | *The preliminary discussion between them* **set the tone** (=established suitable conditions) *for a succession of fruitful meetings.* [+*obj(i)*+*obj(d)*] *Her behaviour sets us all a good example.* **8** [T] to fix (a precious stone) into (a piece of jewellery): [+*obj*+**in**] *He had the diamond set in a ring.* [+*obj*+**with**] *The ring is set with three diamonds.* | (fig., *fml*) *The dark sky was set with bright stars.* **9** [I;T] **a** (of a broken bone) to mend in a fixed position **b** to put (a broken bone) into a fixed position so that it will mend **10** [T] to arrange (hair) when wet so that it will be in a particular style when dry **11** [T] **a** [+*adv/prep*, esp. DOWN] to place (esp. oneself) in or on a seat; sit: *They bought some drinks at the bar then set themselves down at a table.* **b** to fix (a part of the body) firmly, esp. to show strong feelings, determination, etc.: *He set his jaw and refused to agree to anything I said.* | *She has* **set her face against** (=she firmly opposes) *her daughter's marriage.* | *The child has* **set his heart** *on that toy.* (=wants it very much) | *I've* **set my mind** *on this plan and I won't give it up.* ■ other meanings **12** [T] to give (a piece of work) for (someone) to do: *Who set (the questions for) the exam?* | *Which books have been set for this year's English exam?* [+*obj(i)*+*obj(d)*] *The teacher set the class various exercises.* | *The fall in oil prices has set the government a difficult problem.* | *We set them to work clearing up all the rubbish.* —see also SET² (3) **13** [T] to write or provide music for (a poem or other words to be sung): *Housman's poems were* **set to music** *by Vaughan Williams.* **14** [I;T] **a** to cause (a liquid, soft material, etc.) to become solid: *Set the jelly by putting it in a cold place.* | (fig.) *set-in-concrete ideas* **b** (of such materials) to harden or become solid: *It will take two or three days for the concrete to set.* **15** [I] (of the sun, the moon, a star, etc.) to pass downwards out of sight below the horizon: *In the winter the sun sets early.* —opposite

rise **16** [I] *tech* (of a plant) to form and develop seed or fruit: *Our apple trees set well last year even though there was a water shortage.* **17** [I;T] *tech* (of a dog) to point out the position of (an animal or bird) with its nose while keeping still
■ **phrasal verbs**

set about sbdy./sthg. *phr v* [T] **1 a** to begin to do or deal with; start: *The sooner we set about it the sooner we'll finish.* [+*v-ing*] *We set about clearing up the mess.* | *I wouldn't even know how to set about mending a watch.* **b** to deal with; do: *He set about this job in completely the wrong way.* **2** *infml* to attack: *Our dog set about the postman.*

set sbdy./sthg. **against** sbdy./sthg. *phr v* [T] **1** [(OFF)] to lessen the bad effect of (something) by treating it as not open to (something else bad) or by comparing it with (something good): *Certain business losses can be set (off) against taxes.* | *He has many virtues to set against his faults.* —compare OFFSET **2** to cause to oppose: *Religious wars set family against family.*

set sthg./sbdy. ↔ **apart** *phr v* [T (**from**)] to show to be clearly different and usu. better: *His mastery of colour sets him apart from other painters of his era.*

set sthg. ↔ **aside** *phr v* [T] **1** also **set by**— to save for a special purpose: *She set aside a little money each week.* | *Try to set aside some time to visit him.* **2** to leave out of consideration: *Setting aside my wishes in the matter, what would you really like to do?* **3** *law* to declare to be of no effect: *The judge set aside the decision of the lower court.*

set back *phr v* [T] **1** (**set** sthg. ↔ **back**) to place at esp. the stated distance behind something: *The house is set 15 feet back from the road.* **2** (**set** sthg. ↔ **back**) to delay the advance or development of, esp. by the stated period; make late by a certain amount: *The bad weather will set back our building plans (by three weeks).* —see also SET-BACK **3** (**set** sbdy. **back**) *infml* to cost (someone) a large amount of money: *That's a nice suit; it must have set you back a bit/a few pounds.*

set sbdy./sthg. ↔ **down** *phr v* [T] **1** *BrE* (of a vehicle or its driver) to stop and let (a passenger) get out: *The bus sets the children down just outside the school gate.* **2** [*usu. pass.*] to establish as what must be done: *It's clearly set down that you're not allowed to vote twice.* **3** *old-fash* to make a written record of: *I have set down everything that happened, exactly as I remember it.*

set in *phr v* [I] (of a disease, bad weather, etc.) to begin and probably continue: *Winter sets in early in the north.* | *The sky looks as if a storm may be setting in.* | *Fortunately the wound was treated before infection could set in.*

set off *phr v* **1** [I] also **set forth** esp. *lit*, **set out**— to begin a journey: *It's getting late — time to set off.* | *They set off in search of the lost child.* **2** [T] (**set** sthg. ↔ **off**) to cause to explode: *The bomb could be set off by the slightest vibration.* | *They set off the fireworks as soon as it got dark.* **3** [T] (=**set** sthg. ↔ **off**) to cause (sudden activity): *The relaxation of the licensing laws set off a sudden boom in the liquor industry.* | *The President's remarks set off a frantic round of activity in the White House.* **4** [T] (**set** sbdy. ↔ **off**) *infml* to cause sudden activity in: *The slightest bit of dust sets me off/sets me off sneezing.* **5** [T] (**set** sthg. ↔ **off**) to make (something) more noticeable or pleasing to look at by putting it near something different: *The sapphire necklace set off her eyes beautifully.*

set on *phr v* [T] **1** (**set** sbdy./sthg. **on** sbdy.) to cause to attack or chase: *If you dare to come to my house again, I'll set the dog/the police on you!* **2** (**set on** sbdy.) also **set upon**— *old-fash* (esp. of a group) to attack: *He was set on by robbers who took all his money.*

set out *phr v* **1** [T] (**set** sthg. ↔ **out**) to arrange or spread out in order: *Set out the chairs for the meeting in rows of ten.* | *The meal was set out on a long table.* | *The gardens have been beautifully set out.* **2** [I] to SET OFF (1) **3** [I] to begin a usu. long or difficult course of action with a clear purpose: *He obviously set out with the intention of overthrowing the régime.* [+*to-v*] *I think you're deliberately setting out to annoy me.* **4** [T] (**set** sthg. ↔ **out**) also **set forth** *fml*— to explain (facts, reasons, etc.) in order, esp. in writing: *The reasons for my decision are set out in my report.*

set to *phr v* [I] *old-fash infml* to begin eagerly or with determination: *If we all set to, we can finish cleaning the house in an hour.* —compare SET-TO

set sbdy./sthg. ↔ **up** *phr v* [T] **1** to put into position: *Roadblocks were set up by the police to catch the escaped*

prisoner. **2** to establish or arrange (an organization, business, plan, etc.): *The council set up a committee to look into unemployment.* | *He set up a trust fund for his niece.* | *As part of the selection procedure, the board set up a situation to test the candidates' ability to make decisions.* **3** to produce; cause: *The high winds set up dangerous driving conditions.* | *Electrical interference set up a high-pitched hum in the radio.* **4** to prepare (an instrument, machine, etc.) for use: *The production team arrived early to set up the cameras and recording equipment.* **5** [+obj +adv/prep; often pass.] to provide with what is necessary or useful: *That inheritance has set him up for life.* | *We're well set up with emergency medical supplies.* **6** [(for) often pass.] BrE infml to cause to seem guilty; INCRIMINATE: *The criminals claimed that they had been set up (by the police).* —see also SET-UP **7 set up house/home** to begin to live in a place: *They got married and set up house together.*

set (sbdy.) **up as** sthg. *phr v* [T] **1** to establish (oneself) in business as: *He set (himself) up as a painter and decorator and soon had plenty of work.* **2** [no pass.; not in progressive forms] to claim (oneself) to be: *He sets himself up as* (=claims that he is) *an authority on French painting, but he really knows very little about it.*

set² *adj* **1** having the stated position; placed: *a city set on a hill* | *He had very deep-set eyes.* | *The house is set back from the road/set in beautiful grounds.* —see also SET¹ (1) **2** fixed; that cannot be changed: *I have to study at set hours each day.* | *a set time/wage* **3** [A] which must be studied: *The teacher gave us a list of* **set books** *for the course.* —see also SET¹ (12) **4** [A] BrE (of a restaurant meal) with a single fixed dish for each course and at a fixed price: *I'll have the set lunch, please.* **5** [F+on, upon, against]* having a fixed intention; determined: *He's very set on going, and I can't make him see that it's a bad idea.* | *The government's* **dead set** *against* (=very opposed to) *the plan.* **6** [F (for)] infml ready; prepared: *I'm all set, so we can go now.* | *The starter of a race often says: "On your marks – get set – go!"* | *Are you all set for the journey?* [+to-v] *I was (all) set to leave the house when the telephone rang.* **7** usu. derog (of part of the body, manner, state of mind, etc.) fixed in position; unmoving: *She greeted her guests with a set smile.* (=a probably insincere smile) | *She's a woman of set opinions and won't change her mind now.* | *He's about 80 now, and very* **set in his ways.** (=has very fixed habits) **8** [F+to-v] likely: *The temperature is set to* (=will probably) *drop very low tonight.* | *This issue seems set to cause serious embarrassment to the government.*

set³ *n* **1** [C (of)] a group of connected things; group forming a whole: *a set of gardening tools* | *a set of fingerprints* | *a set of stairs* | *a 21-piece tea set* (=cups, plates, teapot, etc.) | *a chess set* (=all the pieces for playing the game) | *We are now facing a whole new set of problems.* | *a peculiar set of circumstances* **2** [C] an apparatus for receiving and showing television signals (or for receiving radio signals): *a colour television set* | *Is your set* (=television) *working?* —see also CRYSTAL SET **3** [C] **a** the scenery, furniture, etc., placed on a stage to represent the scene of (part of) the action of a play: *a set designer* **b** a place where a film is acted: *Everyone must be on the set ready to begin filming at eight o'clock.* **4** [C] a part of a tennis match which is won by winning at least six games, and beating one's opponent by at least two games or winning a TIEBREAKER: *Becker won the second set 6-4.* —see TENNIS (USAGE) **5** [C] a part of a concert or group of musical acts, esp. of popular music or JAZZ: *The group played a very impressive set.* **6** [S] an act or result of setting one's hair (SET¹ (10)): *I'd like a* **shampoo and set,** *please.* **7** [(the) S+sing./pl. v] a group of people of a particular social type: *He goes around with a rather wild set.* —see also JET SET **8** [S] the hardening of a liquid, soft solid, etc.: *You'll get a better set if you use gelatine.* **9** [(the) S (of)] the position in which one holds part of one's body: *From the set of her shoulders it was clear that she was tired.* **10** [C] tech (in MATHEMATICS) a collection of numbers, points, etc.: *The set {x,y} has two members.* —see also NULL SET **11** [C] a small brown round root planted in order to grow onions: *onion sets* **12** [(the) U (of)] poet the going down of esp. the sun towards and below the horizon —see also SUNSET

set·back /'setbæk/ *n* something that delays or prevents successful progress: *a major setback to our hopes of reaching an agreement* —see also SET **back**

set book /ˌ· '·/ *n* (in Britain) a book chosen by an examining board to be studied by schoolchildren or students for a literature examination

set piece /ˌ· '·◂/ *n* an especially effective scene in a play, work of art, etc., carefully planned using a well-known formal pattern or style: *The trial scene at the end of the play is an impressive set piece.*

set·square /'setskweəʳ/ *BrE* ‖ **triangle** *AmE*– *n* a flat three-sided usu. plastic plate having one right angle and used for drawing or testing angles —see picture at MATHEMATICS

set·tee /se'tiː/ *esp. BrE* also **sofa, couch** ‖ usu. **sofa, couch** *AmE*– *n* a long seat with a back and usu. arms for seating more than one person —see picture at LIVING ROOM

set·ter /'setəʳ/ *n* **1** a long-haired dog often trained to point out the positions of animals or birds for shooting —see also SET¹ (17) **2** (*often in comb.*) a person or thing that sets: *a setter of traps/of fashions* —see also TRENDSETTER, TYPESETTER

set the·o·ry /ˈ· ˌ···/ *n* [U] the branch of MATHEMATICS that deals with SETS³ (10)

set·ting /'setɪŋ/ *n* **1** [the+S+of] the action of a person or thing that sets: *the setting of the sun* **2** [C] the way or position in which something, esp. an instrument, is set: *This machine has two settings, fast and slow.* **3** [C usu. sing.] **a** a background; set of surroundings: *What a beautiful setting the hotel is in, with these high mountains all around.* **b** the time and place where the action of a book, film, etc., is shown as happening: *Our story has its setting in ancient Rome.* **4** [C] a piece of metal holding a stone in a piece of jewellery: *a diamond in a gold setting* —see also PLACE SETTING

set·tle¹ /'setl/ *v* **1** [I+adv/prep;T+obj+adv/prep] to place (someone or oneself) so as to be comfortable: *He settled back in his chair and closed his eyes.* | *She settled the child on the sofa.* **2** [I (on, over, upon);T] to come or bring to rest, esp. from above, from flight, etc.: *A bird settled on the branch.* | *Dust had settled on the tables and chairs.* | *Stand the bottle upright for a few days to settle the sediment.* | (fig.) *An eerie stillness had settled on/over the town.* **3** [I (DOWN, to);T] to make or become quiet, calm, still, etc.: *We won't know what's really happened until the noise and excitement have settled down.* | *This medicine should settle your nerves/your stomach.* | *Settle down, children; stop running about!* | *Something was worrying me, and I couldn't settle (down) to my work.* —see also SETTLE **down** **4** [T] to decide on; fix; make the last arrangements about: *That's settled; we'll go tomorrow.* | *"The car won't start." "Well,* **that settles it** (=that has decided the matter); *we can't go out tonight."* [+(that)/wh-] *We've settled that we'll go to Wales, but we still haven't settled when we're going.* —see also SETTLE **on** (1) **5** [I (with);T] to end (an argument, esp. in law); bring (a matter) to an agreement: *They settled their quarrel/differences in a friendly way.* | *The two companies* **settled** *(their dispute)* **out of court.** (=came to an agreement about it between themselves rather than letting a court of law decide about it) **6** [T often pass.] (of people) to go and live in (a place): *The American West was hardly settled until the 19th century.* | *the settled coastal areas of Australia* **7** [I+adv/prep] to start to live in a place: *They got married and settled near Manchester.* **8** [I] to sink slowly to a lower level; SUBSIDE: *The crack in the wall is caused by the building/the ground settling.* **9** [T] to pay (a bill or money claimed): *The insurance company settled the claim quickly.* | *Please settle your account within seven days.* **10 settle one's affairs** to put all one's business matters into order, esp. for the last time because one thinks one may be going to die —see also **when the dust has settled** (DUST¹)

settle down *phr v* **1** [I;T (=settle sbdy. down)] to (cause to) sit comfortably: *She settled (herself) down in a chair with a book and a cup of tea.* **2** [I] to establish a home and live a quiet life: *I hate all this travel; I want to get married and settle down.* **3** [I] to become used to a way of life, job, etc.: *He soon settled down in his new school.* **4** [I (to)] to start giving one's serious or whole attention to a job, activity, etc.: *I must settle down and do my homework.* —see also SETTLE¹ (3)

settle for sthg. *phr v* [T *no pass.*] to accept or agree to (something less than the best, or less than one hoped for): *I want £900 for my car and I won't settle for less.* | *She had to settle for an unskilled job because there was no work for people with her qualifications.*

settle (sbdy.) **in** *phr v* [I;T] to (help to) move comfortably into or get used to a new home, job, etc.: *She quickly settled in at her new job.*

settle into sthg. *phr v* [T] to get used to (new surroundings, a new job, etc.): *It didn't take me long to settle into a new routine.*

settle on/upon *phr v* [T]   **1** (**settle on** sthg./sbdy.) to decide or agree on; choose: *She wanted blue and I wanted yellow, so we settled on green.*   **2** (**settle** sthg. **on** sbdy.) *BrE, fml* to give (money, property, etc.) to (a person) formally in law: *She settled a small yearly sum on each of her children.*

settle up *phr v* [I (**with**)]   **1** to pay what is owed on an account or bill: *As soon as we'd finished our meal we settled up and left. | I can't take your money, sir; please settle up with the lady at the cash desk.*   **2** (of two or more people) to pay and receive what is owed: *You bought the tickets and I paid for the meal. Shall we settle up now?*

settle² *n* a long wooden seat with a high solid back, and a bottom part which is a chest with a lid one can sit on. The settle is a typically 17th-century piece of furniture.

set·tled /ˈsetld/ *adj* unlikely to change; fixed: *settled weather/habits* —opposite **unsettled**

set·tle·ment /ˈsetlmənt/ *n*   **1** [C;U (**of**)] an agreement or decision ending an argument, question, etc.: *The whole country is hoping for the settlement of this strike. | The management have **reached a settlement** with the union over the pay dispute. | a pay settlement | a divorce settlement*   **2** [C] a usu. recently built small village in an area with few people; a newly settled place: *a small settlement on the edge of the desert*   **3** [U (**of**)] the movement of a new population into a place to live there: *the settlement of the American West*   **4** [C;U] a payment of money claimed: *We are sending you a cheque for £400 in settlement of your claim.*   **5** [C (**on, upon**)] a formal gift or giving of money or property: *He made a settlement on his daughter when she married.*   **6** [U] the slow sinking of a building, the earth under it, etc.; SUBSIDENCE

set·tler /ˈsetləʳ/ *n* a member of a new population, esp. in an area with few people: *early settlers in Australia*

set-to /ˈ· ·/ *n* [S (**with**)] *infml* a short fight or quarrel — compare SET **to**

set-up /ˈ· ·/ *n* [*usu. sing.*]   **1** an arrangement or organization: *He's new to the office and doesn't know the set-up yet. | He and his wife live in different houses — it's a very strange set-up.*   **2** *infml* an arrangement made secretly in advance in order to trick someone: *When the photographer suddenly walked in just as he was getting into bed with the girl, he realized it was a set-up.* —see also SET **up** (6)

Seu·rat /ˈsɜːrɑː‖suˈrɑː/, **Georges** /ʒɔːʒ‖ʒɔːrʒ/ (1859–91) a French painter who developed the method of POINTILLISM (=painting with small dots of pure colour)

Seuss /zjuːs/, **Dr** (1904–   ) an American writer whose funny stories, poems, and pictures are very popular with young children, and include *The Cat in the Hat, Horton Hears a Who*, and *How the Grinch Stole Christmas*

sev·en /ˈsevən/ *determiner, n, pron* (the number) 7 —see TABLE 1; see also **at sixes and sevens** (SIX) —**-enth** *determiner, n, pron, adv*

seven ag·es of man /ˌ·· ˌ·· · ·/ *n* [*the*+P] seven different stages of a person's life from being a baby to being an old person. This idea is known from Shakespeare's play *As You Like It.*

Seven Dead·ly Sins /ˌ·· ˌ·· ·/ [*the*+P] according to the Christian church in the Middle Ages, the seven ways of behaving very badly. The sins are pride, LECHERY (=continual searching for sexual pleasure), ENVY (=the feeling one has towards someone who has possessions one would like to have), anger, COVETOUSNESS (=wanting things one does not possess), GLUTTONY (=eating too much), and SLOTH (=being lazy).

Seven Dwarfs /ˌ·· ·/ *n* [*the*+P] the band of small men in the story *Snow White.* In the Walt Disney film of the story their names were Doc, Grumpy, Sleepy, Bashful, Happy, Sneezy, and Dopey.

7-E·le·ven /ˌsevən ɪˈlevən/ (any branch of) a chain of American shops that sell food, drinks, magazines, and common things used in the home. They are slightly more expensive than other shops but are open long hours, sometimes 24 hours a day, and are usu. found in busy areas where they are convenient for many people. There are a few in Britain.

747 /ˌsevən fɔː ˈsevən‖-fɔːr-/ *n* a large plane, a JUMBO JET

seven-league boots /ˌ·· · ˈ·/ *n* [P] a pair of boots belonging to an OGRE in a fairy story, which could travel a great distance at each step

seven seas /ˌ·· ˈ·/ [*the*+P] all the seas and oceans of the world: *He **sailed the seven seas** looking for adventure.*

sev·en·teen /ˌsevənˈtiːn◂/ *determiner, n, pron* (the number) 17 —see TABLE 1, —**-teenth** *determiner, n, pron, adv*

seventh day /ˌ·· ˈ·◂/ [*the*] the day which, according to the Bible, God set aside as a day of rest; the SABBATH

Seventh-Day Ad·vent·ist /ˌ·· · ˈ···/ *n* a person belonging to branch of PROTESTANTISM whose members believe that Christ will return to Earth in the near future, and who take Saturday rather than Sunday as their religious day of rest

seventh heav·en /ˌ·· ˈ··/ *n* [(**in**) U] *infml humor* a state in which one is completely happy; BLISS: *He's in the/his seventh heaven when he's watching football.*

737 /ˌsevən ˈθriː/ *n* a passenger plane made by the Boeing Corporation

sev·en·ties /ˈsevəntiz/ *n*   **1** [*the*] also **'70s**— the 1970s (=the years from 1970 to 1979): *the admission of China to the UN in the early seventies*   **2** in his/her/their **seventies** aged from 70 to 79: *She was still mountain-climbing in her seventies.*   **3** [*the*] the numbers from 70 to 79, esp. when used to measure temperature: *a lovely sunny day with temperatures in the seventies*

sev·en·ty /ˈsevənti/ *determiner, n, pron* (the number) 70 — see TABLE 1, —**-tieth** *determiner, n, pron, adv*

seventy-eight, 78 /ˌ·· · ·/ *n* a record, now old-fashioned, that is played by being turned round 78 times every minute —compare FORTY-FIVE (2)

7-Up /ˌsevən ˈʌp/ *n* [C;U] *tdmk* (a bottle, can, or glass of) a popular non-alcoholic CARBONATED drink which tastes of LEMON and LIME

Seven Won·ders of the World /ˌ·· · ˌ·· · · ˈ·/ [*the*+P] the seven structures which were considered by MEDIEVAL and ancient writers to be the most interesting in the ancient world. The structures were the PYRAMIDS of Egypt, the Hanging Gardens of Babylon, the STATUE of Zeus at Olympia, the temple of Artemis at Ephesus, the MAUSOLEUM (burial-place) at Halicarnassus, the Colossus (a very large statue) at Rhodes, and the Pharos (a LIGHT-HOUSE) at Alexandria.

seven-year itch /ˌ·· · ·ˈ·/ *n* [(*the*) S] *infml* a feeling of dissatisfaction with one's marriage that is said to develop after about seven years

Seven Years' War /ˌ·· · ˈ·/ [*the*] a war fought in Europe, N America, and India between 1756 and 1763. The war was about French and English colonies (COLONY), and also Austria and Prussia wanting to control Europe. As a result of the war, France lost most of its land in India and N America to Britain, and Prussia became a leading European power under Frederick II.

sev·er /ˈsevəʳ/ *v fml*   **1** [T] **a** to divide into usu. two parts, esp. by cutting: *a severed artery* **b** [(**from**)] to separate, esp. by violent cutting: *His arm was severed from his body in the accident.*   **2** [T] to bring to an end (a relationship, etc.); break off: *We have severed all diplomatic relations with that country. | The new director wants to sever all ties with our sister company.*   **3** [I] to break: *The rope severed and he fell.* — **~ance** *n* [C;U (**of**)] : *The border incidents led to (a) severance of relations between the two countries.* —see also SEVERANCE PAY

sev·er·al¹ /ˈsevərəl/ *determiner, pron* more than a few but not very many; some: *I go there several times each year. | Several newspapers published the story. | The damage will cost several thousand pounds to repair. | Several of the prisoners said they had been badly treated.*

several² *adj* [A no comp.] *lit or fml* separate; different; RESPECTIVE: *They shook hands and went their several ways.* — **~ly** *adv* : *Shall we consider these questions severally, or all together?*

severance pay /ˈ··· ·/ *n* [U] money paid by a company to one of their workers losing their job through no fault of their own, esp. when the job is no longer necessary because of reorganization in the company

se·vere /sɪˈvɪəʳ/ *adj*   **1** causing serious harm, pain, worry, or discomfort: *She received severe head injuries in the accident. | She was in severe pain. | (the severest (=coldest)*

winter for ten years | *The bad harvests led to severe food shortages.* | *This is a severe setback for the government.* | *The rejection came as a severe blow to his pride.* **2** not kind or gentle in treatment; not allowing failure or change in rules, standards, etc.; STERN; STRICT: *She had a severe look on her face.* | *severe discipline* | *a severe judge* | *Don't be too severe on him — he couldn't help it.* — compare MILD **3** likely to cause failure or show up weakness; difficult: *Competition for the job is very severe.* | *The underwater trials will provide the severest test yet of the engine's capabilities.* **4** expressing a strongly unfavourable judgment: *severe criticism* **5** completely plain and without decoration; AUSTERE: *the severe beauty of a simple church building* — **~ly** *adv* : *severely disabled* —**verity** /sɪˈverɪti/ *n* [C;U] : *At first we didn't realize the severity of her wounds.* | *"Of course you can't leave the room," he said with some severity.*

Sev·ern /ˈsevən‖-vərn/ [the] a river of S Wales and SW England, flowing from the Welsh mountains to the Bristol Channel

Severn Bore /ˌ‥ ˈ‥/ [the] a large, moving wave of water which appears from time to time in the River Severn and moves away from the sea

Severn Bridge /ˌ‥ ˈ‥/ [the] a SUSPENSION BRIDGE, opened in 1966, which carries the M4 MOTORWAY over the River Severn, joining SW England with S Wales

Severn Trent /ˌ‥ ˈ‥/ a water company in central England that deals with the supply of water to people and businesses, and the removal and treatment of SEWAGE

Se·ville /səˈvɪl/ a city in SW Spain, said to be one of the most beautiful cities in the world, and famous for its historical buildings, esp. the alcazar (castle) built by the MOORS who held Seville between 712 and 1248

Seville or·ange /ˌ‥· ˈ‥·/ *n* a bitter variety of orange which is used for making MARMALADE

sew /səʊ/ *v* **sewed, sewn** /səʊn/ also **sewed** *AmE* [I;T+*obj* +*adv/prep*] to join or fasten (esp. cloth) by stitches made with thread; make or mend (esp. pieces of clothing) with needle and thread: *They learnt to sew at school.* | *Would you sew on this button/sew this button onto my shirt?*
  sew sthg. ↔ **up** *phr v* [T] **1** to close or repair by sewing: *Will you sew up this hole in my trousers?* **2** *infml* to settle satisfactorily: *We should have the whole deal sewn up by the end of the week.* **3** *infml* to put into one's control; make sure of winning or gaining: *With such a big lead in the opinion polls, they've really got the election sewn up.*

sew·age /ˈsjuːɪdʒ, ˈsuː-‖ˈsuː-/ *n* [U] the waste material and water carried in sewers: *The city needs a new* **sewage disposal** *system.* | *a* **sewage farm** (=a place where sewage is treated ready to be got rid of)

Sew·ard /ˈsjuːəd‖-ərd/, **William Henry** (1801–72) an American government leader who served under President Lincoln and President Johnson, and is most remembered for the buying of Alaska, which at the time was called **Seward's folly**

Sew·ell /ˈsjuːəl‖ˈsuː-/, **An·na** /ˈænə/ (1820–78) an English writer known for her children's book *Black Beauty*, about a horse

sew·er /ˈsjuːəʳ, ˈsuːəʳ‖ˈsuːər/ *n* an artificial passage or large pipe under the ground for carrying away water and waste material from the human body to a place where they can be got rid of

sew·er·age /ˈsjuːərɪdʒ, ˈsuː-‖ˈsuː-/ *n* [U] the (system of) removing and dealing with waste matter and water through sewers: *Our town has a modern sewerage system.*

sew·ing /ˈsəʊɪŋ/ *n* [U] work that has been or is to be sewn: *She put her sewing away in the basket.*

sewing ma·chine /ˈ‥ ‥ˌ‥/ *n* a machine for stitching material, worked by hand or by electricity

sex¹ /seks/ *n* **1** [U] the condition of being either male or female: *What sex is this fish?* | *In the space marked "sex", put an "M" for male or an "F" for female.* **2** [C] the set of all male or female people: *the male sex* | *the opposite sex* | *There are members of both sexes in the class.* | *a single-sex club* **3** [U] SEXUAL INTERCOURSE: *Do you think sex outside marriage is always wrong?* | *The couple went for therapy because they hadn't* **had sex** (**with one another**) *for years.*
  ▶CULTURAL NOTE Sex is seen as an accepted part of

being married. In the past sex between people who were not married was seen as wrong. Sex before or outside marriage is now very common, although some people, esp. people who are religious, still think it is wrong.◀

4 [U] activity connected with (and including) this act: *There's a lot of sex and violence in this film.* | **sex education** *in schools* **5 -sexed** /sekst/having the stated amount of sexual desire: *highly-sexed* | *over-sexed* —see also FAIR SEX, GENTLE SEX

sex² *v* [T] *esp. tech* to find out whether (esp. an animal) is male or female: *His job is sexing day-old chickens.*

sex·a·ge·nar·i·an /ˌseksədʒɪˈneəriən/ *n* a person who is between 60 and 69 years old

Sex·a·ges·i·ma /ˌseksəˈdʒesɪmə/ the second Sunday before LENT

sex ap·peal /ˈ‥ ‥ˌ‥/ *n* [U] the power of being sexually exciting to other people; attractiveness to someone of the opposite sex: *She's got a lot of sex appeal.*

sex change /ˈ‥ ‥/ *n* a medical treatment or operation which changes a person's body so that they look like a person of the opposite sex: *John has had a sex change and has taken the name Janine.*

Sex Dis·crim·i·na·tion Act /ˌ‥ ‥‥ˌ‥ ‥/ [the] a British law passed in 1975 to prevent **sex discrimination** (=unfair treatment of a person because they are of a particular sex) esp. in matters of employment and education. Sexual discrimination is usu. against women.

sex ed·u·ca·tion /ˈ‥ ‥ˌ‥‥/ *n* [U] education in the physical processes and emotions involved in sex between humans. In Britain and the US this is taught to children in school.

sex·is·m /ˈseksɪzəm/ *n* [U] the belief that one sex is not as good, clever, etc., as the other, esp. when this results in unfair treatment of women by men —compare CLASSISM

sex·ist /ˈseksɪst/ *adj, n derog* (someone, esp. a man) showing sexism: *I'm tired of his sexist remarks about women drivers!* | *a sexist film*

sex·less /ˈsekslɪs/ *adj* **1** *derog* sexually uninteresting; not SEXY **2** not male or female; NEUTER¹ (2)

sex life /ˈ‥ ‥/ *n* the sexual activities of a person: *He's been too busy with his work to have much of a sex life.* | *I wonder how her sex life's going?*

sex-linked /ˈ‥ ‥/ *adj* connected with the sex GENES of only one sex, and so passed on to children only by parents of that sex: *a sex-linked hereditary disease* | *Is baldness sex-linked?*

sex ob·ject /ˈ‥ ‥ˌ‥/ *n* a person admired only because they are sexually attractive, and not for other qualities they may have

sex of·fend·er /ˈ‥ ‥ˌ‥/ *n* a person who is guilty of a crime related to sex: *rapists and other sex offenders* | *Attacks on sex offenders in prison are on the increase.*

sex·ol·o·gy /sekˈsɒlədʒi‖-ˈsɑː-/ *n* [U] the study of sexual behaviour, esp. among human beings —**gist** *n*

sex or·gan /ˈ‥ ‥ˌ‥/ *n* a part of the body concerned with the producing of children, such as the PENIS, VAGINA, or WOMB

Sex Pis·tols /ˈ‥ ‥ˌ‥/ a British popular music group who played PUNK ROCK. Although they existed for only a short time (1975–78), they became famous for swearing and deliberately failing to appear at concerts, as well as for their loud music with its offensive words. The best-known members of the group were Johnny Rotten and Sid Vicious.

sex·ploi·ta·tion /ˌseksplɔɪˈteɪʃən/ *n* [U] *infml derog* the use of sex or sexual activity to make money, esp. in films, magazines, etc.: *a sexploitation movie*

sex·pot /ˈsekspɒt‖-pɑːt/ *n infml humor* (often considered offensive by women) a sexy woman

sex shop /ˈ‥ ‥/ *esp. BrE‖usu.* **adult bookstore** *AmE*— *n* a shop selling goods (such as PORNOGRAPHY) related to sex and sexual practices

sex sym·bol /ˈ‥ ‥ˌ‥/ *n* a person who represents the idea of sex to the public: *sex symbols such as Marilyn Monroe or Madonna*

sex·tant /ˈsekstənt/ *n* an instrument for measuring angles between stars so that one can calculate the position of one's ship or aircraft

sex·tet /seks'tet/ *n* **1** [+*sing./pl. v*] a group of six singers or musicians performing together **2** a piece of music for six performers —compare QUINTET, SEPTET

sex·ton /'sekstən/ *n* a person with the job of taking care of a church building and sometimes of ringing the church bell and digging graves

sex·tu·plet /sek'stju:plət||-'stʌ-/ *n* any of six people born at one birth

sex·u·al /'seksuəl/ *adj* **1** of, connected with, or including SEXUAL INTERCOURSE or the urge for this: *sexual desires* | *a sexual relationship* | *a disease passed on by sexual contact* **2** [*no comp.*] of, between, or needing male and female: *sexual conflict* | *sexual reproduction* —see EROTIC (USAGE) — ~ **ly** *adv* : *sexually immature* | *sexually arousing* | *a sexually explicit film*

sexual a·buse /ˌseksuəl ə'bju:s/ *n* [U] the action of forcing people, esp. children, to take part in sexual practices: *alleged sexual abuse of children in care/of prisoners* —see ABUSE²

sexual di·scrim·i·na·tion /ˌ··· ·ˌ··'··/ [U] the unfair treatment of people because of their sex, usu. the unfair treatment of women. Sexual discrimination is illegal in Britain and the US, and people and companies can be taken to court if it is thought that they are guilty of sexual discrimination. —see also SEX DISCRIMINATION ACT

sexual har·ass·ment /ˌ··· '···, ˌ··· ·'··/ *n* [U] the act of annoying somebody, esp. a woman, by making remarks about sex or acting in a way which suggests a desire for sex in a situation where this is not suitable or welcome behaviour, esp. at work: *sexual harassment of woman at work*

sexual in·ter·course /ˌ··· '···/ also **intercourse**— *n* [U] *fml* the bodily act between two humans in which the sex organs are brought together, either to make a baby, or for pleasure

sex·u·al·i·ty /ˌseksʃu'æli̥ti/ *n* [U] interest in, the expression of, or the ability to take part in sexual activity

sexually trans·mit·ted dis·ease /ˌ····· ·ˌ··· ·'·/ also **STD**— *n* a disease which is passed through sexual intercourse, such as AIDS, HERPES, or GONORRHEA and SYPHILIS, often called VENEREAL DISEASES. Some STDs are treatable if found early enough: *an STD clinic*

sex·y /'seksi/ *adj infml apprec* **1** sexually exciting: *sexy girls/pictures/underwear* —see EROTIC (USAGE) **2** up to date and attracting a lot of interest: *Robotics seems to be a sexy subject at the moment.* —**ily** *adv* —**iness** *n* [U]

Sey·chelles /sei'felz/ [*the*+P] a country (official name, the Republic of Seychelles) made up of around 85 islands in the Indian Ocean, to the E of Kenya; capital Victoria; population 67,000 (1989) —**Seychellois** /ˌseifel'wɑ:◂/ *adj*

SF /ˌes 'ef/ *abbrev. for*: SCIENCE FICTION

S4C /ˌes fɔ: 'si:||-fɔ:r-/ a Welsh language television CHANNEL

Sgt *written abbrev. for*: SERGEANT

sh, shh /ʃ/ *interj* (used for demanding silence or less noise): *Sh! You'll wake the baby!* —see also SHUSH

shab·by /'ʃæbi/ *adj derog* **1** untidy and of low quality because of long use or lack of care: *a shabby old hat* | *a shabby bed-sitter* **2** (of a person) wearing shabby clothes: *a shabby old tramp* **3** ungenerous, dishonourable; unfair: *What a shabby trick, driving off and leaving me to walk home!* | *shabby treatment* —**bily** *adv* —**biness** *n* [U]

Sha·bu·oth /ʃə'vu:rəs||-əut, -əuθ/ also **Feast of Weeks**— a Jewish holiday to remember the occasion when the Ten Commandments were made known to Moses on Mount Sinai

shack¹ /ʃæk/ *n* a small roughly built house or hut

shack² *v*
   shack up *phr v* [I (with, TOGETHER)] *infml, esp. derog* (of a person, or man and woman) to live together while unmarried: *She's shacking up with her boyfriend.*

shack·le /'ʃækəl/ *n* something, esp. joined metal rings, for fastening the arms or legs to each other or to something else, so as to prevent movement: *The prisoners were kept in shackles.* | (fig.) *Our people must throw off the shackles of slavery and seize their independence.*

shackle² *v* [T *usu. pass.*] *esp. lit* to tie up (as if) with shackles: *His hands were shackled together.* | *We are shackled by old customs.*

shad /ʃæd/ *n* shad a north Atlantic fish used for food

shade¹ /ʃeɪd/ *n* **1** [(*the*) U] slight darkness or shelter from direct light, esp. from sunlight outdoors, made by something blocking it: *I'm too hot in the sun; let's get into the shade.* | *They were sitting in the shade of a tree/a wall.* | *There was no shade to be found in the desert.* | *The temperature was 32° in the shade.* (=outdoors but not measured in direct sunlight) —see USAGE **2** [C] (*often in comb.*) something that keeps out light or its full brightness: *a green eyeshade* | *a lampshade* **3** [U] representation of shadow or darkness in a picture, painting, etc.: *This artist uses light and shade to good effect.* **4** [C] a degree or variety of colour: *It was painted in various shades of blue.* **5** [C+of] a slight difference in degree; NUANCE: *This word has several shades of meaning.* | *There are different shades of opinion within the party.* **6** [S] (often before adjectives or adverbs) a little bit: *That music is just a shade too loud.* | *I was a shade embarrassed by their personal questions.* **7** [C] *lit* the spirit of a dead person; GHOST **8 put in(to) the shade** *infml* to cause to seem much less important by comparison: *Their splendid present really put my poor little contribution in the shade.* **9 made in the shade** *AmE infml* (an expression used when someone/something is sure to succeed, or is already very successful): *We* **have it made in the shade!** | *Made in the shade — we'll definitely win!* | *My brother's* **got it made in the shade***; he was just accepted into law school!* —see also SHADES
   ▷ USAGE **Shade** is any place sheltered from the sun. The dark shape made by the **shade** of something is a **shadow**.◁

shade² *v* **1** [T (from)] to shelter from direct light or heat: *She raised her hand to shade her eyes from the sun.* **2** [T (IN)] to represent the effect of shade or shadow on (an object in a picture): *The shaded-in background adds depth to the drawing.* **3** [I+*adv/prep*] to change slowly, gradually, or by slight degrees: *This is a question where right and wrong shade into one another.* (=are so close that it is hard to tell them apart) | *Its colour was a sort of blue shading off into grey.*

shades /ʃeɪdz/ *n* [P] **1** *infml for* SUNGLASSES **2** *lit* darkness: *The shades of evening were falling fast.* (=it was getting dark in the evening) **3** *AmE for* ROLLER BLIND **4 shades of** *old-fash infml* this reminds me of (something in the past): *Shades of my old father! He would have agreed with all you've said.*

shad·ing /'ʃeɪdɪŋ/ *n* [U] the process or result of filling in an area in a picture to represent darkness or less brightness

shad·ow¹ /'ʃædəu/ *n* **1** [U] also **shadows** *pl.*— darkness caused by the blocking of direct light, esp. sunlight: *The small window threw a patch of sunlight onto the floor, but the rest of the room was in shadow.* | *He walked along in the shadows hoping no one would recognize him.* **2** [C] a dark shape made on a surface by something between the surface and direct light: *As the sun set, the shadows lengthened.* | *The tree* **cast its shadow** (=produced the dark shape of a tree) *on the wall.* | (fig.) *The coming war* **cast a shadow** (=a feeling of future trouble) *over Europe.* | *He's such a timid chap; he's* **afraid of his own shadow.** | (fig.) *She had to live in her father's shadow.* (=her father's power or fame were so great that people did not notice her) —see SHADE¹ (USAGE) **3** [C] a dark area like a shadow: *The shadows under her eyes were caused by lack of sleep.* **4** [C] *infml* a form without substance or from which the real substance has gone: *After his illness he was only* **a shadow of his former self.** (=not nearly so strong, active, etc., as he used to be) | *She* **wore** *herself* **to a shadow** *by working too hard and not eating properly.* **5** [C] a person or thing who follows another closely: *The dog was his master's shadow.* **6** [S (of)] *usu. in questions and negatives*] a slightest bit: *He's guilty; there's not a/the shadow of a doubt about it.* (=it is completely certain) — see also FIVE O'CLOCK SHADOW, **afraid of one's own shadow** (AFRAID)

shadow² *v* [T] **1** to follow and watch closely, esp. secretly: *He felt he was being shadowed, but he couldn't see anyone behind him.* | *Our planes shadowed the Soviet fighters until they left our airspace.* **2** *lit* to make a shadow on; darken (as if) with a shadow: *Trees shadowed the pool.*

shadow³ *adj* [A] (in Britain) belonging to the Shadow Cabinet: *the shadow foreign secretary*

shad·ow-box /ˈʃædəʊbɒks‖-bɑːks/ v [I] to fight with an imaginary opponent, esp. as training for BOXING – – ~ **ing** n [U] : (fig.) *Let's stop this shadow-boxing* (=testing each other's opinions or intentions) *and get down to discussing the main point of dispute between us.*

Shadow Cab·i·net /ˌ··ˈ···/ [the+sing.|pl.v] a group of politicians in the opposition party in the British Parliament who each study and speak about the work of a particular minister in the government —compare CABINET (2)

Shadows /ˈʃædəʊz/, **The** a British popular music group who were the BACKING group for the singer Cliff Richard in the 1960s, and were also successful on their own

shad·ow·y /ˈʃædəʊi/ adj **1** hard to see or know about clearly: *Attila the Hun is a shadowy and little-known historical figure.* **2** full of shade; in shadow: *the shadowy depths of the forest*

shad·y /ˈʃeɪdi/ adj **1** in or producing shade: *a shady part of the garden* | *a shady tree* **2** infml derog probably dishonest: *a shady politician* | *He's known to have been involved in several shady business deals.*

Shaf·fer /ˈʃæfəʳ/, **Peter** (1926–) an English writer of plays, best known for *The Royal Hunt of the Sun*, *Equus*, and *Amadeus*

shaft¹ /ʃɑːft‖ʃæft/ n **1** [C] a long or thin pole to which the sharp end of a spear, ARROW, or similar weapon is fixed **2** [C] the long handle of a hammer, AXE, GOLF CLUB, or similar tool **3** [C] a bar which turns, or around which a belt or wheel turns, to pass on power or movement, esp. from an engine to something driven by the engine: *a propeller shaft* | *the crankshaft in a car engine* **4** [C] a long passage, usu. in an up-and-down or sloping direction: *a mine shaft* | *a ventilator shaft* | *a lift shaft* **5** [C] either of the pair of poles between which an animal is fastened to pull a vehicle **6** [C (of)] a beam of light coming through an opening: *A shaft of sunlight pierced the gloom.* **7** [C (of)] lit a sharply funny or hurtful remark: *No one is safe from his shafts of wit.* **8** [the+S] AmE sl severe and unfair treatment: *It's always me that gets the shaft.* | *She gave her boyfriend the shaft* (=stopped going out with him)

shaft² v [T often pass.] AmE sl to treat unfairly and very severely: *We got shafted on that sale: they tricked us into paying too much.*

Shaftes·bu·ry Av·e·nue /ˌʃɑːftsbəri ˈævˌnjuː‖ˌʃæftsberi ˈævˌnuː/ a street in central London leading NE from Piccadilly Circus. There are many West End theatres on and near Shaftesbury Avenue

shag¹ /ʃæg/ n **1** [U] rough strong tobacco cut into small thin pieces **2** [C] a large black seabird **3** [C] BrE taboo sl an act of having sex

shag² v **-gg-** [T] BrE taboo sl to have sex with; a word usu. used by men

shagged out /ˌ·ˈ·/ adj [F] BrE sl very tired; an expression usu. used by men

shag·gy /ˈʃægi/ adj **1** being or covered with long, uneven, and untidy hair: *a shaggy beard|dog* **2** (of hair, material, etc.) having a rough untidy surface: *a shaggy coat|mat* —**-giness** n [U]

shaggy-dog sto·ry /ˌ·· ·· ˌ··/ n a long joke which has an ending that is purposely weak or meaningless

shah /ʃɑː/ n the title held by the non-elected leaders of some Middle Eastern countries, esp. formerly in Iran —see also Mohammed Reza PAHLAVI

shake¹ /ʃeɪk/ v **shook** /ʃʊk/, **shaken** /ˈʃeɪkən/ **1** [I;T] to (cause to) move up and down or from side to side with quick short movements: *The house shook when the earthquake started.* | *She was shaking with laughter|anger|fear.* | *Her voice shook with emotion.* | *She must have had a very bad fright; she was* **shaking like a leaf.** | (fig.) *He was* **shaking in his shoes** (=very nervous) *at the thought of making a speech in public.* | *The medicine must be well shaken before use.* | *The angry crowd* **shook their fists** *at the police.* | *He shook salt onto his food.* | *She shook the sand out of her shoes.* | *The dog shook himself dry.* | *The little boy shook himself free of his mother's grasp.* **2** [T (UP); often pass.] to trouble the mind or feelings of; cause to lose confidence or self-control; upset: *She was badly shaken (up) by the accident|by the bad news.* **3** [T] to make less certain; weaken; UNDERMINE: *Nothing can shake my belief in her honesty.* —see also UNSHAKEABLE **4 more than one can shake a stick**

at infml or humor a very large number (of): *She's won more races than you can shake a stick at.* **5 shake a leg** infml usu. imperative] to act fast; hurry: *You'd better shake a leg if you want to catch that train!* **6 shake hands** to take and hold someone's right hand in one's own for a moment, often moving it up and down, as a sign of greeting, goodbye, agreement, or pleasure: *The two men shook hands (with each other)|shook each other's hands|shook each other* **by the hand.** **7 shake one's head** to move one's head from side to side in order to answer "no" or show disapproval —compare NOD¹ (1) **8 shaken, not stirred** an instruction for making a COCKTAIL (=mixed alcoholic drink), famous as a phrase said by James Bond in the stories by Ian Fleming: *a vodka Martini, shaken, not stirred* **9 shake on it** infml to shake hands with someone as a sign of agreement: *Let's shake on it.*

shake down phr v infml **1** [T] (**shake** sthg. ↔ **down**) BrE to take on a SHAKEDOWN (1) voyage **2** [T] (**shake** sbdy. ↔ **down**) infml, esp. AmE to get money from by a trick or threats **3** [T] (**shake** sbdy. ↔ **down**) AmE infml to search thoroughly —see also SHAKEDOWN (3) **4** [I+adv/prep] BrE to use unusual sleeping arrangements, such as not sleeping in a bed, or sleeping in a bed with someone who is not one's usual sleeping partner: *Don't give up your bed for me; I can shake down on the floor.* —see also SHAKEDOWN (4) **5** [I] BrE old-fash to become familiar with and able to deal with a new situation: *He's new in the office but he'll soon shake down.*

shake sbdy./sthg. ↔ **off** phr v [T] to get rid of; free oneself from; escape from: *We managed to shake off our pursuers in the crowd.* | *I've had a cold for two weeks now – I just can't shake it off.*

shake sthg. ↔ **out** phr v [T] to clean (something) by opening it out and shaking it: *He took the dirty mat outside and shook it out.* —compare SHAKEOUT

shake sthg. ↔ **up** phr v [T] **1** infml to make big changes in (an organization), esp. so as to make it more effective: *The new chairman will shake up the company.* —see also SHAKE-UP **2** to mix by shaking

shake² n **1** [C usu. sing.] an act of shaking: *She answered "no" with a shake of the head.* **2** [C] AmE infml for MILK SHAKE **3** [S] AmE infml treatment of the stated type: *He's a dealer who'll give you a fair shake.* **4 in two shakes (of a lamb's tail)** infml very soon —see also SHAKES

shake-down /ˈʃeɪkdaʊn/ n infml **1** a last test operation of a new ship or aircraft before it is put into general use: *a shakedown voyage|flight* **2** AmE an act of getting money dishonestly, esp. by threats **3** AmE a thorough search **4** a place prepared as a bed —see also SHAKE down

shake-out' /ˈʃeɪkaʊt/ n **1** a situation in which, because of a sudden drop in general industrial or business activity, weaker firms tend to go out of business **2** a SHAKE-UP — compare SHAKE out

shak·er /ˈʃeɪkəʳ/ n a container or instrument used in shaking or shaking out esp. the stated thing: *He mixed us a drink in the cocktail shaker.* | *a salt shaker* —compare SIFTER

Shaker a member of a religious group, **the Shakers**, which separated from the Quakers of England in 1747 and went to the US in 1774. They were known for shaking with emotion while worshipping. Their numbers decreased after the mid-1800s, largely because the true Shakers believed in being CELIBATE (=not having sex) and therefore had no children. Today, the Shakers are remembered esp. for their simple and attractive furniture-making.

shakes /ʃeɪks/ n infml **1** [the +P] nervous shaking of the body from disease, fear, habitual drinking of alcohol, etc.: *I began to get the shakes just thinking about the examination.* **2 no great shakes (as/at)** not very good, skilful, effective, etc.: *He's no great shakes as a piano player, but he can sing well.*

William Shakespeare

Shakes·peare /ˈʃeɪkspɪəʳ/, **William** (1564–1616) an English writer of plays, one of the most famous ever, born in Stratford-upon-Avon in England. Among the most famous of his plays are the tragedies (TRAGEDY) of *Romeo and Juliet*, *Julius Caesar*, *Hamlet*, *Othello*, *King Lear*, and *Macbeth*, the comedies (COMEDY) of *A Midsummer Night's Dream*, *The Merchant of Venice*, and *Twelfth Night*, and the HISTORICAL plays *Richard III* and *Henry V*. Many well-known expressions come from Shakespeare, and his work is famous for its sensitive view of human nature and for the richness of its language. Shakespeare also wrote some very good poetry, esp. the *Sonnets*, and worked as an actor at the Globe Theatre in London. He married Anne Hathaway in 1582 and they had three children. He is buried at Stratford-on-Avon, and houses connected with him and his family can be visited there, as well as the **Royal Shakespeare Theatre** where his plays are regularly performed. —see colour picture on page 1146 **–Shakespearean** /ʃeɪkˈspɪəriən/ *adj* : *a Shakespearean actor*

shake-up /ˈ· ·/ also **shakeout** — *n infml* a rearrangement of an organization: *There's been a government shake-up, with ministers losing their jobs.* —see also SHAKE **up** (1)

shak·y /ˈʃeɪki/ *adj infml* **1** shaking or unsteady, esp. from nervousness, weakness, or old age: *I'm still a bit shaky after that bout of flu.* **2** not solid or firm; weak and easily shaken; undependable: *This ladder's rather shaky.* | *The team got off to a pretty shaky start this season, losing their first three matches.* | *The book puts forward such shaky arguments that they're impossible to take seriously.* **––ily** *adv* **––iness** *n* [U]

Sha·la·la /ʃəˈleɪ₁lə/, **Donna** /ˈdɒnə/ (1941–) a former university official who became Secretary of Health and Human Services under President Bill Clinton in 1993

shale /ʃeɪl/ *n* [U] soft rock made of hardened mud or clay which divides naturally into thin sheets

shall /ʃəl; *strong* ʃæl/ *v 3rd person sing.* **shall**, *negative short form* **shan't** [*modal+to-v*] **1** (sometimes used with I and **we** to express the future tense): *We shall be away next week.* (compare *They will be away next week.*) | *I shall have completed my report by Friday.* **2** (used esp. with I and **we**, in questions or offers that ask the hearer to decide): *I'll tell her we'll come, shall I?* (=is that agreed?) | *What shall I do about it?* | *Shall I* (=do you want me to) *open the window?* **3** *fml* (used esp. in official writing to show a promise, command, or law): *Payment shall be made by cheque.* —see also SHALT, SHOULD; see NOT (USAGE) and LANGUAGE NOTE: Modals

▷ USAGE In ordinary modern speech **will**, or the short form **'ll**, is used more often than **shall** in the first meaning.◁

shal·lot /ʃəˈlɒt‖ʃəˈlɑːt/ *n* a vegetable like a small onion

shal·low¹ /ˈʃæləʊ/ *adj* **1** not deep; not far from top to bottom: *a shallow river/dish/grave* | *He got in at the shallow end of the swimming pool.* **2** *derog* lacking deep or serious thinking; SUPERFICIAL: *shallow arguments* | *a shallow thinker whose opinions aren't worth much* **3** (of breathing) not coming from or reaching very low in the chest —compare DEEP¹ (3) **––ly** *adv* **––ness** *n* [U]

shallow² *v* [I] *fml* to become SHALLOW¹ (1): *The river shallows at this point.*

shal·lows /ˈʃæləʊz/ *n* [*(the)* P] a shallow area in a body of water: *the shallows near the mouth of the river*

sha·lom /ʃæˈlɒm‖ʃæˈləʊm/ *interj* (a Jewish greeting or goodbye)

shalt /ʃəlt; *strong* ʃælt/ *v* **thou shalt** *old use or bibl* you shall

sham¹ /ʃæm/ *n* **1** [S] something that is not what it appears, pretends, or is claimed to be; piece of deceit: *The agreement was a sham; neither side intended to keep to it.* **2** [U] falseness; PRETENCE: *I'm a blunt straightforward man; I hate sham.*

sham² *adj* [A] not what it appears, pretends, or is claimed to be; IMITATION: *sham jewellery/compassion*

sham³ *v* **-mm-** [I;T] to put on the false appearance of (a disease, condition, feeling, etc.): *He isn't really ill; he's only shamming.*

sha·man /ˈʃɑːmən/ *n* someone who (it is believed) works in the world of spirits while in a TRANCE (=dreamlike state) for the purpose of curing the sick and gaining important knowledge, and who often has a knowledge of how to use plants, etc., for medicine —compare MEDICINE MAN, WITCH DOCTOR

sha·man·is·m /ˈʃɑːmənɪzəm/ *n* any system of belief in shamans and the world of spirits —see also SHAMAN **––ist** *n* **––istic** /₁ʃɑːməˈnɪstɪk◂/ *adj*

sham·a·teur /ˈʃæmətəʳ, -tʃʊəʳ, -tʃəʳ, ʃæmˈtɜːʳ/ *n BrE infml derog* a sports player who officially plays for no money but in fact receives payment **– –ism** *n* [U]

sham·ble /ˈʃæmbəl/ *v* [I+*adv/prep*] *usu. derog* to walk awkwardly or carelessly, dragging the feet: *The old tramp shambled wearily up the path.* | *He walked with a* **shambling gait.**

sham·bles /ˈʃæmbəlz/ *n* [S] *infml* (a place or scene of) great disorder, (as if) the result of destruction; MESS (1): *After the noisy party the house was (in) a shambles.* | *She* **made a (complete) shambles** *of the accounts.*

sham·bol·ic /ʃæmˈbɒlɪk‖-ˈbɑː-/ *adj BrE infml* completely disordered or confused

shame¹ /ʃeɪm/ *n* **1** [U] a feeling of deep moral discomfort or loss of self-respect caused by consciousness of guilt, immoral behaviour, inability, or failure: *She was full of shame at her bad behaviour.* | *You may well hang your heads in shame; it was a terrible thing to do.* **2** [U *usu. in questions and negatives*] the ability to feel this: *He had no (sense of) shame and never felt guilty.* | *You mean they actually dance around on stage with no clothes on! Have they no shame?* **3** [U] loss of honour; DISGRACE: *Your bad behaviour brings shame on the whole school.* | *There's no shame in being poor.* **4** [S] an unfortunate state of affairs; something one is sorry about: *What a shame that it rained on the day of your garden party!* | *You should practise more often — it's a shame to waste such talent.* **5** (a shout used to show disapproval of a speaker): *The minister's speech brought cries of "Shame!"* **6** **put someone/something to shame** to SHAME² (2) someone or something: *Your beautiful garden puts my few little flowers to shame.* **7 Shame on you!** You ought to be ashamed! —see also **Nice... , shame about the...** (PITY)

shame² *v* [T] **1** to bring dishonour to; DISGRACE: *Such an act of cowardice by an officer shames his whole regiment.* **2** to show to be lacking in quality, ability, etc., by comparison: *They have a record of industrial peace which shames other companies.* **3** to cause to feel shame: *It shames me to say it, but I told a lie.* **4** [+*obj*+**into, out of**] to force or urge by causing feelings of shame: *I tried to shame her into voting in the election, but she has no sense of public duty.*

shame·faced /₁ʃeɪmˈfeɪst◂/ *n* showing suitable shame or knowledge that one has acted wrongly: *a shamefaced apology* | *He had the grace to look shamefaced about it.* **– –ly** /-ˈfeɪs₁dli/ *adv*

shame·ful /ˈʃeɪmfəl/ *adj* deserving blame; which one ought to be ashamed of: *a shameful lack of knowledge about current affairs* | *their shameful treatment of political prisoners* | *the football team's shameful performance in the cup final* **– –ly** *adv* : *Her education had been shamefully neglected.* **– –ness** *n* [U]

shame·less /ˈʃeɪmləs/ *adj* **1** (of a person) unable to feel suitably ashamed, esp. in matters of sex or morals: *a shameless woman/liar* **2** done without shame; greatly and openly immoral: *shameless deception/disloyalty* | *a shameless distortion of the truth* **– –ly** *adv* **– –ness** *n* [U]

Sha·mir /ʃæˈmɪəʳ/, **Yitz·hak** /ˈjɪtsɑːk/ (1915–) a PRIME MINISTER of Israel (1983–84 and 1986–92)

sham·my /ˈʃæmi/ *n* [C;U] CHAMOIS²

sham·poo¹ /ʃæmˈpuː/ *n* **-poos** **1** [C;U] a usu. liquid soaplike product used for washing the hair, CARPETS, etc.: *a medicated shampoo for dandruff* **2** [C] an act of shampooing: *Give it another shampoo.*

shampoo² *v* **-pooed**, *present participle* **-pooing** [T] to wash with shampoo

sham·rock /ˈʃæmrɒk ‖ -rɑːk/ *n* [U] a plant, esp. a type of CLOVER, that has three leaves on each stem and is used as the national sign of Ireland

shamrock

sha·mus /ˈʃɑːməs/ *n AmE sl old-fash* PRIVATE DETECTIVE

shan·dy /ˈʃændi/ *n* [C;U] *BrE* a drink made from a mixture of beer and GINGER BEER or LEMONADE (1)

shang·hai /ˌʃæŋˈhaɪ/ v [T (**into**)] **1** infml to trick or force into doing something unwillingly: We were shanghaied into agreeing to their demands. **2** (esp. in former times) to make (someone) unconscious by hitting them or by alcoholic drink and then put them on a ship to serve as a sailor

Shang·hai a city in E China, in Jiangsu PROVINCE but independent of it. Shanghai is a port and an industrial centre.

Shan·gri-La /ˌʃæŋgri ˈlɑː/ a distant beautiful imaginary place where everything is pleasant: I found the island idyllic, and on my return to New York felt that I had turned down Shangri-La.

shank /ʃæŋk/ n **1** [C] esp. tech a straight long or narrow usu. central or connecting part of something, such as **a** the smooth part of a SCREW **b** the smooth end of a DRILL where it is held to be turned **c** the long straight central part of an ANCHOR¹ **2** [C] a part which sticks out at the back of a metal or leather button, by which it can be sewn onto a garment **3** [C;U] (a piece of) meat cut from the leg of an animal **4** [C usu. pl.] old use the part of the leg between the knee and ankle —see picture at HORSE

Shan·khill Road /ˌʃæŋkɪl ˈrəʊd/ [the] a road in Belfast, known because of the violent acts which have taken place there

shanks's po·ny /ˌʃæŋksɨz ˈpəʊni/ n [U] old-fash BrE infml, usu. humor one's own legs as a method of going from place to place; walking

Shan·non /ˈʃænən/ [the] a river in the Republic of Ireland, flowing into the Atlantic at Limerick

Shannon Air·port /ˌ·· ˈ·/ an airport for TRANSATLANTIC (2) flights, near **Ennis** in COUNTY Clare in the Republic of Ireland

shan't /ʃɑːnt‖ʃænt/ v esp. BrE short for: shall not: Shall I go, or shan't I?

shan·tung /ʃænˈtʌŋ/ n [U] a silk cloth with a slightly rough surface

shan·ty¹ /ˈʃænti/ n a small roughly built usu. wooden or metal house

shanty² n a song formerly sung by sailors as they did their work

shan·ty·town /ˈʃæntiˌtaʊn/ n (a part of) a town made up of roughly built houses of thin metal, wood, etc., where poor people live —compare SLUM

shape¹ /ʃeɪp/ n **1** [C;U] the outer form of something, by which it can be seen (or felt) to be different from something else: The sign was triangular in shape. | a cake in the shape of a heart (=heart-shaped) | We saw a vague shape through the mist but we couldn't see who it was. | Houses come (=are built) in all shapes and sizes. **2** [(the) S (of)] the general character, form, or nature of something; COMPLEXION: Who was responsible for the final shape of the report? | These events have changed the whole shape of British politics/society. | It looks as though this interactive form of advertising is **the shape of things to come**. (=the way things will be in the future) **3** [S] a particular form or way of appearing; GUISE: I'm not looking for trouble **in any shape or form**. (=of any kind) | I hadn't enough money to pay for my ticket, but rescue came **in the shape of** (=and it was) my neighbour, who lent me £5. **4** infml **in/into/out of shape**: **a** in/into/out of (proper) condition, health, effectiveness, etc.: Our garden is in good shape after all the rain. | Let's try and get this room into shape before mother gets home. | She's been working too hard and she's in pretty bad shape. (=unwell, unfit, etc.) **b** esp. AmE having/not having a healthy body: I used to be in much better shape and could run five miles. | I must get into shape before bikini season! **5 knock/lick into shape** infml to bring to the proper or desired standard of skill, performance, etc.: There are a lot of new players in the team, but we'll soon lick them into shape. **6 take shape** to develop towards completion: An idea slowly took shape in his mind. — ~ **less** adj: a shapeless old sweater — ~ **lessly** adv — ~ **lessness** n [U]

shape² v [T] **1** to make or form, esp. to give a particular shape or form to: You'll have to shape the clay before it dries out. [+obj+**from**] The bird shaped its nest from mud and sticks. [+obj+**into**] The bird shaped the mud and sticks into a nest. **2** to influence and fix the course or form of: Childhood experiences that shape a person's character. | moral dilemmas which shaped his philosophy

3 [usu. pass.] to make (a piece of clothing) fit the body closely: This dress is shaped at the waist and doesn't need a belt.

shape up phr v [I] **1** to develop well or in the stated way: The new students seem to be shaping up quite nicely. **2** (usu. used threateningly or angrily) to begin to perform more effectively, behave better, etc.: You'd better shape up, young man, if you want to get anywhere in this job!

SHAPE /ʃeɪp/ Supreme Headquarters Allied Powers Europe; the place in Belgium where the Supreme Allied Commander Europe, one of the military commanders of NATO, is based

shaped /ʃeɪpt/ adj (often in comb.) having the stated shape: a cloud shaped like a dragon | a heart-shaped cake

shape·ly /ˈʃeɪpli/ adj fml apprec (esp. of a woman's body or legs) having an attractive shape; WELL-PROPORTIONED —**shapeliness** n [U]

shard /ʃɑːd‖ʃɑːrd/ also **sherd**— n a broken piece of a glass or clay bowl, cup, etc.

share¹ /ʃeəʳ/ n **1** [S (**in, of**)] the part belonging to, owed to, or done by a particular person: my share of the cake/bill | If you want a share in/of the pay, you'll have to do **your fair share** of the work. | We still have the largest market share, but the competition is growing fast. | I had no share in (=was not one of the people who made) this decision. | The prime minister has **come in for her (full) share of** (=has rightly received much) criticism over the question of unemployment. | I've had more than my fair share (=a lot) of troubles in my time. | Don't you **pay for all this** — let's **go shares**. (=divide the cost between us) —see also TIMESHARE **2** [C (**in**)] any of the equal parts into which the ownership of a company can be divided, which are offered for sale to the public: He told his stockbroker to sell his shares in Allied Chemicals. | She's got all her money in **stocks and shares**. | This year the company paid a dividend of 50p per share. | Share prices rose in heavy trading. —compare STOCK¹ (3); see also ORDINARY SHARE, PREFERENCE SHARE

share² v **1** [I (**in**);T (**with, among, between**)] to have, use, pay, or take part in (something) with others or among a group, rather than singly: We haven't enough books for everyone; some of you will have to share. (=use one book for two or more people) | Children should be taught to share their toys. (=allow other children to use them) | I have to share the bathroom with the other tenants. | We shared the cost of the meal. | We all share (in) the responsibility for these terrible events. | I think we all share your concern about this matter. (=we are all worried about it) | Don't keep them all to yourselves; we must **share and share alike**. (=share things between us equally) | It's always better to share (=tell others about) your worries and problems. | a shared experience | shared ownership **2** [T (OUT, **among, between**)] to divide and give out in shares: At his death his property was shared (out) between his children. —see also SHARE-OUT —**sharer** n

share³ n old-fash a PLOUGHSHARE

share·crop·per /ˈʃeəˌkrɒpəʳ‖ˈʃeərˌkrɑː-/ n esp. AmE (esp. formerly in the southern US) a farmer who farms someone else's land (a TENANT farmer), and pays the landowner usu. half of the crop. The farmer also owes the land-owner for a home, food, seeds, and tools, and so usu. receives very little of the crop and is very poor.

share·hold·er /ˈʃeəˌhəʊldəʳ‖ˈʃeər-/ esp. BrE ‖ **stockholder** esp. AmE— n an owner of SHARES¹ (2) in a business

share-out /ˈ·· ·/ n [S (**of**)] an act of giving out shares of something: a share-out of the stolen goods

sha·ri·a , sheria /ʃəˈriːə/ n [U] a system of laws followed by Muslims

Sha·rif /ʃəˈriːf/, **O·mar** /ˈəʊmɑːʳ/ (1932–) an Egyptian-born film actor who appeared in films such as Dr Zhivago and Lawrence of Arabia

shark¹ /ʃɑːk‖ʃɑːrk/ n shark or sharks a large usu. grey fish that lives esp. in warm seas, has several rows of sharp teeth, and is often dangerous to people —see also JAWS

shark² n infml a person clever at getting money from others in dishonest or unpleasant ways, esp. by lending money at high rates of interest: a loan shark

Shar·on and Tra·cey /ˌʃærən ənd ˈtreɪsi/ BrE derog two female names that are used to suggest that their owners, usu. young women, are rather stupid and lazy, speak poorly, and are impolite in their way of treating other

Spring
In Britain spring is a season which lasts from March to May. In the US March, April and May are also considered spring months, but spring may be longer or shorter than this in different parts of the country. When British people think of spring they think of flowers (especially daffodils), baby lambs, new leaves on the trees and a feeling of cheerfulness and new life. In many parts of the US people associate spring with the spring thaw, when all the snow melts and the weather becomes warmer. There are many poems about spring and it is a time associated with love. Easter takes place during spring.

Easter egg

Easter bunny

Fall
In the US the fall (autumn BrE) is a long and beautiful season from September to November. American people often go to the countryside to admire the colours of the leaves, especially in New England. There are many poems about the fall and it is a time of year associated with a feeling of gentle sadness because summer has ended and winter is coming. In the fall people celebrate Halloween (in both Britain and the US), Thanksgiving (in the US only) and Bonfire Night (in Britain only).

fireworks

bonfire

witch

jack o'lantern

At Christmas people decorate their homes and usually have a Christmas tree with coloured balls or lights on it. They often put their presents under the tree and do not open them until Christmas Day. There is a tradition that children should put a long sock, called a Christmas stocking, at the end of their bed or by the chimney so that Santa Claus will fill it with presents. Santa Claus is supposed to visit each house on Christmas Eve by climbing down the chimney. He travels on a sleigh pulled by reindeer that can fly, including one called Rudolph who has a red nose and is the subject of a Christmas song.

skiing

ice-skating

snowman

shark

people (a phrase esp. made popular by the JOURNALIST **Keith Waterhouse** in the *Daily Mail*, writing about two girls who work in a shop): *Service with a smile is making a comeback, but Sharon and Tracey still lurk behind some shop counters.*

sharp[1] /ʃɑːp‖ʃɑːrp/ *adj* **1** having or being a thin edge or point with which it is easy to cut things or make a hole in them: *a sharp knife* | *I cut my foot on a sharp stone.* | *a sharp-pointed needle* —opposite **blunt** **2** not rounded; marked by hard lines and narrow angles: *a sharp nose* **3** having a quick change in direction; sudden: *You make a sharp right turn at the crossroads.* | *a sharp rise[fall in prices* **4** clear in shape or detail; DISTINCT: *a sharp photographic image* | *He looked rather quiet and dull, in sharp contrast to his wife, who was smartly dressed and very talkative.* **5** quick and sensitive in attention, thinking, seeing, hearing, etc.: *a sharp mind* | *sharp eyes* | *sharp questioning* | *It was very sharp of you to have noticed that.* | *The teacher kept a sharp watch on the children when they visited the zoo.* **6** causing a sensation like that of cutting, biting, or stinging: *a sharp wind[frost* | *The wine has a sharp taste; I think it's gone off.* | *The branch broke with a sharp crack.* **7** (of a pain) severe and sudden —opposite **dull** **8** quick and strong, (as if) showing urgency: *I heard a sharp knocking at the door.* **9** [(with)] intending or intended to hurt; angry; severe: *He was rather sharp with his secretary when she got back late from lunch.* | *That woman has a very* **sharp tongue.**| *sharp criticism* **10** [F] (in music) higher than the correct note —compare FLAT[2] (7) **11** [after *n*] (of a note in music) higher than the stated note by a SEMITONE: *a symphony in the key of G sharp* —compare FLAT[2] (8), NATURAL[1] (6) **12** *infml, sometimes derog* fashionably fine: *He's a very sharp dresser.* —see also SHORT SHARP SHOCK – – **ly** *adv* : *He replied very sharply when I criticized him.* | *Opinions are sharply divided.* | *Prices have risen sharply.* – – **ness** *n* [U]

sharp[2] *adv* **1** exactly at the stated time: *The meeting starts at 3 o'clock sharp; don't be late!* **2** sharply, esp. suddenly and quickly: *You turn sharp right at the crossroads.* **3** (in music) higher than the correct note: *You're singing sharp.* —compare FLAT[3] (2); see also **look sharp** (LOOK[1] (16))

sharp[3] *n* (in music) **1** a SHARP[1] (11) note **2** the sign # for this —compare FLAT[1] (5), NATURAL[2] (2)

Sharp a Japanese company making electronic equipment such as MICROWAVES and computers

Sharp, Ce·cil /ˈseʃl/ (1859–1924) an English FOLK musician. He started the English Folk Dance Society in 1911 and is famous for having saved a great deal of folk music from being forgotten.

sharp·en /ˈʃɑːpən‖ˈʃɑːr-/ *v* [I;T] to become or make sharp or sharper: *He sharpened his pencil with a knife.* | *Her voice sharpened as she became impatient.*

sharp end /ˌ· ·/ *n* [the+S (of)] *infml* the part of a job, organization, etc., where the most severe problems are experienced

sharp·en·er /ˈʃɑːpənər, ˈʃɑːpnər‖ˈʃɑːr-/ *n* a machine or tool for sharpening knives, pencils, etc.

Sharpe·ville /ˈʃɑːpvɪl‖ˈʃɑːrp-/ a town near Johannesburg, South Africa, where on 21 March 1960 police shot dead 69 black people who were protesting against Apartheid

Sharpe·ville Six /ˌ· ·· ˈ·/ [the] a group of black South Africans who were going to be hanged for causing the death of a Sharpeville COUNCILLOR in 1984. They were saved

from hanging in 1988, in a decision that had been widely discussed around the world.

sharp-eyed /ˌ· ˈ· ◂/ *adj* having good sight in the eyes, and being quick to use it: *You'd have to be very sharp-eyed to find any mistakes in her spelling.*

sharp·ish /ˈʃɑːpɪʃ‖ˈʃɑːr-/ *adv BrE infml* quickly: *We'd better get moving pretty sharpish if we want to catch that bus.*

Shar·ples /ˈʃɑːpəlz‖ˈʃɑːr-/, **E·na** /ˈiːnə/ a character in the British television SOAP OPERA *Coronation Street*, played by Violet Carson (1905–83) —see also CORONATION STREET

sharp prac·tice /ˌ· ˈ··/ *n* [U] behaviour or a trick in business that is dishonest but not quite illegal

sharp-shoot·er /ˈʃɑːpˌʃuːtər‖ˈʃɑːrp-/ *n* a person skilful in shooting, esp. one with the job of firing exactly aimed single shots at an enemy

shat /ʃæt/ *past tense & participle of* SHIT[1]

Shat·ner /ˈʃætnər/, **William** (1931–) a Canadian actor known esp. for playing the part of Captain Kirk in the television SERIES *Star Trek*

Shatt-al-Ar·ab /ˌʃæt æl ˈærəb/ [the] a river ESTUARY in SE Iraq, formed by the rivers Tigris and Euphrates, and flowing SE to the Persian Gulf

shat·ter /ˈʃætər/ *v* **1** [I;T] to break suddenly into very small pieces, usu. as a result of force or violence: *I dropped the mirror on the floor and it shattered.* | *A stone shattered the window.* | (fig.) *Hopes of reaching an agreement were shattered today.* —compare SPLINTER[2] (1) **2** [T *usu. pass.*] *infml* to shock; have a strong effect on the feelings of: *We were shattered to hear of her sudden death.* | *shattering news* **3** [T *usu. pass.*] *infml, esp. BrE* to cause to be very tired and weak: *I feel completely shattered after that run up the hill.*

shat·ter·proof /ˈʃætəpruːf‖-ər-/ *adj* made so as not to shatter: *a shatterproof glass windscreen*

shave[1] /ʃeɪv/ *v* **1** [I;T (OFF)] to cut off (a beard or face hair) close to the skin with a RAZOR or shaver: *I cut myself while I was shaving.* | *I've decided to shave off my beard.* **2** [T] to cut off hair from the face of: *The barber shaved him.* **3** [I+*adv/prep*;T] to cut all the hair from (a part of the body): *She shaves her legs and under her arms.* **4** [T (OFF)] to cut off (very thin pieces) from (a surface): *I shaved (a few millimetres from) the bottom of the door to make it close properly.* | (fig.) *The production costs are very high – can't you shave anything off the price?* | *She shaved a few milliseconds off her previous lap record.* **5** [T] *infml* to come close to or touch in passing: *The car just shaved the wall while it was cornering.*

shave[2] *n* [usu. sing.] an act or result of shaving: *I'm just going to have a shave.* | *You can't get a good* **close shave** (=that cuts the hair close to the surface of the skin) *with an electric shaver.* | *a* **wet shave** (=with shaving cream, etc.) —see also CLOSE SHAVE

shav·en /ˈʃeɪvən/ *adj* with all the hair shaved off: *his shaven head* —see also CLEAN-SHAVEN, UNSHAVEN

shav·er /ˈʃeɪvər/ *n* a tool for shaving, esp. an electric-powered instrument for shaving hair from the face and body —compare RAZOR and see picture at RAZOR

shav·ing /ˈʃeɪvɪŋ/ *n* [usu. pl.] a very thin piece cut from a surface with a sharp blade: *a pile of wood shavings on the floor*

shaving cream /ˈ·· ·/ *n* [U] a mixture made mostly of soap for putting on the face, usu. with a **shaving brush,** to keep the face hair soft and wet while shaving (SHAVE[1])

shaving foam /ˈ·· ·/ *n* [U] SHAVING CREAM, usu. from an AEROSOL

Sha·vu·ot /ʃəˈvuːəs‖-əot, -əʊθ/ *n* [U] see PENTECOST (1)

Shaw /ʃɔː/, **Ar·tie** /ˈɑːti‖ˈɑːr-/ (1910–) an American JAZZ musician, CLARINET player, and bandleader whose bands were among the most popular in the late 1930s and 1940s

Shaw, George Ber·nard /dʒɔːdʒ ˈbɜːnəd‖dʒɔːrdʒ ˈbɜːrnərd/ (1856–1950) an Irish writer and CRITIC, famous for his writings on Socialism and for his clever plays which point out faults in moral attitudes and in society. His best-known play is *Pygmalion.*

shawl /ʃɔːl/ *n* a piece of usu. soft decorated cloth that can be square, TRIANGULAR, or long and narrow, for wearing over a woman's head or shoulders or wrapping round a baby

Shaw·nee /ˌʃɔːˈniː/ *n* **Shawnee** *or* **Shawnees** [C; *the* +P] (a member of) a Native American people which lived in the central Ohio valley as hunters and farmers, until the US government moved them to Oklahoma, where they now number about 2000 —see NATIVE AMERICAN (CULTURAL NOTE)

she[1] /ʃi; *strong* ʃiː/ *pron* (used as the subject of a sentence) **1** that female person or animal: *She's certainly a pretty girl. Who is she?* **2** (used for something thought of as female, esp. a country or a ship or other vehicle): *The liner docked yesterday, and she will spend two months being refitted.* —see HE (USAGE) **3 Who's "she"—the cat's mother?** *BrE* (a phrase to remind someone that it is considered rather impolite in Britain to talk about someone who is with you as "she" (or "he"), and that the person's name should be used instead): *"She didn't hear you." "Who's "she"—the cat's mother?" "Sorry; Carole didn't hear you."*

she[2] /ʃiː/ *n* [S] *infml* a female: *Is the new baby a he or a she?*

she- see WORD FORMATION

s/he *pron* (used in writing as the subject of a sentence when one wishes to include both men and women) he or she: *If any student wishes to speak to the head of department s/he should first make an appointment.*

sheaf /ʃiːf/ *n* **sheaves** /ʃiːvz/ [(of)] **1** a bunch of grain plants tied together, esp. as left standing in a field to dry after gathering: *sheaves of corn* **2** a collection of long or thin things held or tied together; BUNDLE: *The speaker came into the hall carrying a sheaf of notes.*

shear /ʃɪəʳ/ *v* **sheared, sheared** *or* **shorn** /ʃɔːn‖ʃɔːrn/ **1** [T] to cut off wool from (sheep) **2** [T] *esp. lit* to cut off (hair): *the day when her baby curls were shorn* **3** [I;T (OFF)] *tech* to break or cause (esp. a thin rod, pin, etc.) to break in half because of a sideways or twisting force: *The bolts had sheared, allowing the door to fly open.* **4 be shorn of something** *esp. lit* to have something completely removed from one: *Shorn of all real power by the new laws, the office of deputy president soon became obsolete.*

shears /ʃɪəz‖ʃɪərz/ *n* [P] **1** large scissors **2** a heavy cutting tool which works like scissors: *pruning shears* —see PAIR (USAGE), and see picture at GARDEN

sheath /ʃiːθ/ *n* **sheaths** /ʃiːðz/ **1** a close-fitting case for a knife or sword blade or the sharp part of a tool **2** *BrE* a CONDOM **3** a long close-fitting part of a plant or of an animal organ that acts as a covering **4** a sheathing

sheathe /ʃiːð/ *v* [T] **1** to put away in a SHEATH (1): *He sheathed his sword.* **2** [(with, in)] to enclose in a protective outer cover: *The nuclear reactor is sheathed with lead.*

sheath·ing /ˈʃiːðɪŋ/ *n* [C;U] a protective outer cover, e.g. for a building, ship, etc.

sheath knife /ˈ· ·/ *n* a knife with a fixed (not folding) blade for carrying in a sheath

She·ba /ˈʃiːbə/, **Queen of** a wealthy ruler who visited King Solomon in a Bible story

she·bang /ʃəˈbæŋ/ *n* [S] *infml, esp. AmE* affair; business; thing (esp. in the phrase **the whole shebang**)

she·been /ʃəˈbiːn/ *n esp. IrE* a place where alcoholic drink is illegally sold

she·chi·ta /ʃeˈhiːtɑː/ *n* [U] the process of killing an animal for food according to Jewish law

shed[1] /ʃed/ *n* (*often in comb.*) a lightly built single-floored building, often wooden, used esp. for storing things: *a toolshed/cattle shed/garden shed* —compare HUT

shed[2] *v* **shed**; *present participle* **shedding** [T] **1** *esp. lit* to cause to flow out; pour out: *It's too late to change your mind now, so there's no point in shedding tears* (=crying or worrying) *over it.* | *These clues* **shed** *new* **light on** *the mystery.* (=make it clearer) | *The army brought down the government, but without* **shedding any blood.** (=without causing any killing or wounding) —see also BLOODSHED **2** (of a plant or animal) to have (its skin, leaves, hair, etc.) come off or fall out naturally: *Most trees shed their leaves in autumn.* | *Some snakes shed their skin each year.* **3** to get rid of (something not wanted or needed): *I'd like to shed a few pounds* (=become thinner) *before the summer.* | *The factory is planning to shed about a quarter of its workforce.* | *to shed one's inhibitions* **4** *BrE* (of a vehicle) to drop (a load of goods) by accident: *The road was blocked where a large lorry had shed its load.* **5** (of a

surface) to keep (a liquid) from entering; REPEL: *A duck's back sheds water.*

she'd /ʃid; *strong* ʃiːd/ *short for:* **1** she would **2** she had

sheen /ʃiːn/ *n* [S;U] smooth brightness or shininess of a surface; LUSTRE: *Her hair had a beautiful sheen.*

Sheen, Martin an American film actor

sheep /ʃiːp/ *n* **sheep** **1** a grass-eating animal that is farmed for its wool and its meat: *a flock* (=group) *of sheep grazing in a field* | *sheep farming in Australia*

sheep

▶CULTURAL NOTE Sheep are thought of as rather silly animals that are easily led and will follow each other without thinking about it. —see also BAA, EWE, LAMB, RAM; see MEAT (USAGE)◀

2 [*often pl.*] *derog* someone who is very easily persuaded into doing things, who obeys orders without thinking, or who acts in a particular way because others are doing so **3 the sheep from the goats** *esp. BrE* those who are good, able, successful, etc., from those who are not: *This difficult exam should* **separate/sort out the sheep from the goats.** —see also BLACK SHEEP, **count sheep** (COUNT[1] (8)), **one may as well be hanged for a sheep as a lamb** (HANG[1] (14))

sheep·dip /ˈʃiːpˌdɪp/ *n* [C;U] a chemical (used in a) bath for sheep to kill harmful insects in their wool

sheep·dog /ˈʃiːpdɒg‖-dɔːg/ *n* a dog trained to control sheep, often a COLLIE —see also OLD ENGLISH SHEEPDOG

sheep·ish /ˈʃiːpɪʃ/ *adj* uncomfortable because one knows one has done something wrong or foolish; EMBARRASSED: *a sheepish smile* — **~ly** *adv* — **~ness** *n* [U]

sheep's eyes /ˈ· ˌ·/ *n* [P] *infml* a silly look suggesting that one is in love: *He was* **making sheep's eyes at** *her.*

sheep·skin /ˈʃiːpˌskɪn/ *n* [C;U] the skin of a sheep with the wool still on, made into leather: *a sheepskin coat/rug*

sheer[1] /ʃɪəʳ/ *adj* **1** [A] pure; unmixed with anything else; nothing but: *He won by sheer luck/determination.* | *The sheer size of the country* (=the simple fact that it is so big) *causes tremendous communications problems.* | *It would be sheer folly to buy such a large car — we wouldn't be able to afford to run it.* **2** very steep; (almost) straight up and down; PERPENDICULAR: *a sheer cliff* **3** very thin, fine, light in weight, and almost transparent: *ladies' sheer stockings*

sheer[2] *adv* straight up or down: *The mountain rises sheer from the plain.*

sheer[3] *v* [I+*adv/prep*, esp. OFF, AWAY] to turn (as if) to avoid hitting something; change direction quickly: *The boat came close to the rocks and then sheered away.*

sheet[1] /ʃiːt/ *n* **1** a large four-sided piece of usu. cotton or nylon cloth used in a pair on a bed, one above and one below a person lying in it: *We change the sheets* (=put clean ones on the bed) *every week.* **2** [(of)] a broad regularly shaped piece of a thin or flat material, such as paper, glass, or metal: *a sheet of glass* | *They wrapped his fish and chips in a sheet of newspaper.* | *sheet metal* (=metal in sheets) **3** [(of)] a broad stretch or surface of something thin: *A sheet of ice covered the lake.* **4** [(of) *often pl.*] a moving or powerful wide mass: *The rain was coming down in sheets.* | *A sheet of flame blocked his way out of the burning house.* —see also BALANCE SHEET, SPREADSHEET, **white as a sheet** (WHITE[1])

sheet[2] *n tech* a rope or chain controlling the angle between a sail and the wind

sheet an·chor /ˈ· ˌ··/ *n* **1** a ship's largest ANCHOR, used only in time of danger **2** a person or thing that is a main or only support in time of trouble

sheet·ing /ˈʃiːtɪŋ/ *n* [U] (cloth or other material for making) sheets: *cotton sheeting* | *metal sheeting*

sheet light·ning /ˌ· ˈ··, ˌ· ˈ··/ *n* [U] lightning in the form of a sudden flash of brightness that covers the whole sky —compare FORKED LIGHTNING, HEAT LIGHTNING

sheet mu·sic /ˈ· ˌ··, ˌ· ˈ··/ *n* [U] music printed on single sheets and not bound in book form

Shef·field /ˈʃefiːld/ an industrial city in S Yorkshire, in the N of England, famous for the making of tools, special steels, and (esp. formerly) CUTLERY. Sheffield has a university, and two football teams. —see also HILLS-BOROUGH and see colour map on page 818

She·her·a·za·de, Scheherazade /ʃə,herə'zɑːdə, -'zɑːd/ the woman in the *Arabian Nights* who tells her husband Shahriyar the thousand and one stories collected in that book, to prevent him from carrying out the threat he had made to kill her —see also ARABIAN NIGHTS

sheikh , sheik /ʃeɪk‖ʃiːk/ *n* **1** an Arab chief or prince **2** a Muslim religious leader or teacher

sheikh·dom , sheikdom /'ʃeɪkdəm‖'ʃiːk-/ *n* a place under the government of a SHEIKH (1)

shei·la /'ʃiːlə/ *n sl, esp. AustrE* a girl

shek·el /'ʃekəl/ *n* the standard unit of money in Israel

shek·els /'ʃekəlz/ *n* [P] *humor* money

shel·duck /'ʃeldʌk/ **shel·drake** /'ʃeldreɪk/*masc.*– *n* a large brightly-coloured European duck

shelf /ʃelf/ *n* **shelves** /ʃelvz/ **1** a flat usu. long and narrow board fixed against a wall or in a frame, for putting or storing things on: *I'm putting up some new kitchen shelves.* | *a bookshelf* | *supermarket shelves* | *a product that sold so badly that it wasn't worth the shelf space given to it in the shop* **2** a natural formation shaped like a shelf, esp. a narrow surface (LEDGE) of rock underwater —see also CONTINENTAL SHELF **3 off the shelf** that can be bought at once, without being specially ordered: *off-the-shelf computer software packages* —compare **off the peg** (PEG¹) **4 on the shelf** *infml* **a** (esp. of a woman) not likely to marry, esp. because too old **b** put aside or not used because no one wants it —see also SHELVE

shelf life /'· ·/ *n* [usu. sing.] the length of time a product (esp. food, chemicals, etc.) will last without any reduction in quality, esp. while being kept in a shop

shell¹ /ʃel/ *n* **1** [C;U] (*often in comb.*) a hard outer covering of a nut, egg, or seed, or of certain types of animal: *a snail/oyster shell* | *an ornament made of shells* (=SEASHELLs) —see also EGGSHELL, NUTSHELL, SEASHELL, SHELLFISH, and see pictures at NUT, SLUG and TORTOISE **2** [C] an explosive shaped like a very large bullet, for firing from a large gun: *Shells were bursting all around.* —compare BULLET **3** [C] the outside structure or outer surface of something, esp. something whose contents are missing or have been destroyed: *All that remained of the building after the fire was an empty shell.* | *His grief had left him a mere shell of a man.* **4 come out of one's shell** *infml* to stop being nervous or quiet in a social situation and begin to be friendly, willing to talk, etc.

shell² *v* [T] **1** to remove from a shell or similar natural outer covering, esp. a POD: *shelled prawns* | *He was shelling peas.* **2** to fire SHELLs¹ (2) at: *Our artillery shelled the enemy positions.*
    shell (sthg. ↔) **out** *phr v* [I;T] *infml* to pay (money), esp. unwillingly: *I've had to shell out (more money) to repair the car again.*

Shell *n* a very large international oil company

she'll /ʃil; *strong* ʃiːl/ *short for*: she will: *She'll come if she can.*

shel·lac /ʃə'læk/ *n* [U] a thick orange-coloured or transparent alcohol-based liquid used like paint as a shiny protective covering

shel·lack·ing /ʃə'lækɪŋ/ *n* [usu. sing.] *AmE infml* a severe defeat

Shel·ley /'ʃeli/, **Ma·ry Woll·stone·craft** /'meəri 'wʊlstənkrɑːft‖-kræft/ (1797–1851) an English writer, and the wife of Percy Bysshe Shelley. Her most famous book is the HORROR STORY *Frankenstein*.

Shelley, Per·cy Bysshe /'pɜːsi bɪʃ‖'pɜːr-/ (1792–1822) an English poet. His most famous works were written after 1818 when he settled in Italy with his second wife, Mary Wollstonecraft Shelley, and include *Adonais* (in memory of John Keats), *Prometheus Unbound*, and the short poem *To a Skylark*.

shell·fire /'ʃelfaɪəʳ/ *n* [U] the firing or shooting of explosive shells: *The town came under heavy shellfire.*

shell·fish /'ʃel,fɪʃ/ *n* **shellfish** **1** [C] an animal without a BACKBONE that lives in water and has a shell: *Lobsters and oysters are shellfish.* **2** [U] such animals as food: *Do you like shellfish?*

shell game /'· ·/ *n AmE* **1** a game meant to deceive the person who is watching it. In the game a small object is

placed under one of three cups and then the cups are moved quickly into different positions. The person watching must then say which of the cups the object is under. **2** something meant to deceive, esp. in order to gain money through cheating: *These door-to-door insurance salesmen are playing a shell game to get your hard-earned cash.*

shell-like /'· ·/ *n* a word in your shell-like *BrE infml humor* a word in your ear; a phrase used when you want to talk to someone privately

shell-shock /'ʃelʃɒk‖-ʃɑːk/ *n* [U] *old-fash for* COMBAT FATIGUE

shell-shocked /'ʃelʃɒkt‖-ʃɑːkt/ *adj* **1** mentally ill because of the STRESS of war: *shellshocked soldiers* **2** *infml* having an unsteady, confused feeling in the head: *She's only just finished writing her dissertation, so she's a bit shellshocked.*

shell suit /'· ·/ *n* a loose-fitting, brightly coloured informal suit made of thin shiny material such as NYLON, with similar material covering the inner surface, fitting tightly at the ends of the arms and legs. They became popular in the early 1990s for adults and children.

shel·ter¹ /'ʃeltəʳ/ *n* **1** [C] a building or roofed enclosure that gives cover or protection: *a wooden shelter in a public garden* | *an air-raid shelter* | *a bus shelter* (=a roofed enclosure at a bus stop) | *a nuclear fallout shelter* | *a shelter for the homeless* (=a house or other building where they can live) **2** [U] cover and protection: *In the storm I took shelter under a tree.* | *Everyone ran for shelter when the bombing started.* | *The mosque provided shelter for hundreds of families whose homes had been flooded.* | *The refugees' immediate need is for food, clothing, and shelter.* —see also TAX SHELTER

shelter

bus shelter

shelter² *v* **1** [T (**from**)] to protect from harm; give shelter to: *These plants must be sheltered from direct sunlight.* | *sheltering the homeless* | *a sheltered valley* (=protected from extreme weather conditions) **2** [I+adv/prep] to take shelter; find protection: *In the storm people were sheltering (from the rain) in the doorways of shops.*

Shelter a British organization (CHARITY), begun in 1966, which works to help homeless people

shel·tered /'ʃeltəd‖-ərd/ *adj* **1** *often derog* kept away from harm, risk, or unpleasant realities, esp. to an unhealthy degree: *He's led a sheltered life.* **2** [A *no comp.*] providing a place to live where people are employed to look after those who live there: *sheltered housing/accommodation for the elderly*

shelve /ʃelv/ *v* **1** [T] *fml* (esp. of books) to put on a shelf; arrange on shelves: *Oversize books are shelved in the East Library.* **2** [T] to put aside until a later time: *We've had to shelve our holiday plans because I've just lost my job.* **3** [I (DOWN, UP)] (of land) to slope gradually: *The land shelves towards the sea.*

shelves /ʃelvz/ *pl. of* SHELF

shelv·ing /'ʃelvɪŋ/ *n* [U] (material for) shelves

Shen·an·do·ah /,ʃenən'dəʊə/ in the US, a river and a valley between the Allegheny and Blue Ridge Mountains in NW Virginia. **Shenandoah National Park**, in the Blue Ridge Mountains, covers about 300 sqare miles, and includes woods and **Skyline Drive**, from which the Shenandoah Valley can be seen.

she·nan·i·gans /ʃɪ'nænɪgənz/ *n* [P] *infml* **1** rather dishonest practices or tricks **2** slightly annoying playfulness or fun; MISCHIEF

Shep·ard /'ʃepəd‖-ərd/, **Sam** /sæm/ (1943–) an American writer and actor. His plays include *The Tooth of Crime* and *Fool for Love*

shep·herd¹ /'ʃepəd‖-ərd/ *n* **1** a person who takes care of sheep in the fields or open country **2** [(**of**)] (esp. in religious situations) someone who takes care of people: *new church organization which will increase every minister's effectiveness as the shepherd of his flock* —see also GOOD SHEPHERD, LORD IS MY SHEPHERD

shepherd² *v* [T+*obj*+*adv*/*prep*] to lead, guide, or take care of like sheep: *The teacher was shepherding the group of children into the bus.*

shep·herd·ess /ˈʃepədes‖-ərdǰs/ *n* (esp. in poetry and art) a woman or girl who takes care of sheep in the field or open country

Shepherds Mar·ket /ˌ··ˈ··/ a once-fashionable area of London now known esp. for PROSTITUTION

shepherd's pie /ˌ··ˈ·/ also **cottage pie**– *n* [U] a baked dish made of cut-up cooked meat covered with cooked potato

Sher·a·ton¹ /ˈʃerətən/ [*the*] one of a group of large expensive hotels

Sheraton² *adj* the graceful style (of a piece of furniture) made in Britain around 1800 by **Thomas Sheraton**: *a Sheraton card table*

sher·bet /ˈʃɜːbət‖ˈʃɜːr-/ *n* 1 [U] *BrE* a powder eaten as a sweet or added to water to make a cool drink, esp. for children 2 [C] *esp. AmE for* SORBET (1)

sherd /ʃɜːd‖ʃɜːrd/ *n* (esp. in ARCHAEOLOGY) a SHARD –see also POTSHERD

she·ri·a /ʃəˈriːə/ *n* [U] SHARIA

Sher·i·dan /ˈʃerǰdən/, **Rich·ard Brins·ley** /ˈrɪtʃəd ˈbrɪnzli‖ -tʃərd-/ (1751–1816) an English politician and writer of plays, born in Dublin. He is famous for his comedies (COMEDY) *The Rivals* and *The School for Scandal*, which gently criticize the society of his time.

sher·iff /ˈʃerǰf/ *n* 1 (in the US) an elected officer in a local area with duties including carrying out the orders of courts and preserving public order. In the past, the sheriff wore a metal BADGE in the shape of a star. 2 [(of)] (in Britain) a HIGH SHERIFF 3 the chief judge of a county or district in Scotland, who hears cases in a sheriff court –see also extra information on page 742

sheriff court /ˈ·· ˌ·/ *n* the main lower court of law in Scotland, dealing with both CIVIL and criminal cases –see also extra information on page 742

Sheriff of Not·ting·ham /ˌ··· ˈ···/ [*the*] according to old stories, the main enemy of Robin Hood –see also ROBIN HOOD and see colour picture on page 620

Sherlock Holmes see Sherlock HOLMES

Sherman Tank /ˌʃɜːmən ˈtæŋk‖ˌʃɜːr-/ *n* the most-used TANK (2) of the US armed forces in the Second World War: (fig.) *You can't come barging in here like a Sherman Tank expecting us to drop what we're doing!*

Sher·pa /ˈʃɜːpə‖ˈʃɜːr-/ *n* a member of a Himalayan people who are very good at climbing mountains, and are often employed to guide other mountain climbers

sher·ry /ˈʃeri/ *n* [U] a pale or dark brown strong wine (of a kind originally) from Spain –see picture at GLASS

Sher·wood For·est /ˌʃɜːwʊd ˈforǰst‖ˌʃɜːrwʊd ˈfɔː-, ˌfɑː-/ an area of ancient forest in central England, mainly in Nottinghamshire, which was formerly a royal huntingground. Sherwood Forest is famous as the place where Robin Hood is supposed to have lived.

she's /ʃiz; *strong* ʃiːz/ *short for:* 1 she is: *She's working in an office.* 2 she has: *She's got a new job.*

She Stoops to Con·quer /ˌ· ˌ· · ˈ···/ a humorous play by Oliver Goldsmith, written in 1773

Shet·land Is·lands /ˌʃetlənd ˈaɪləndz/ [*the*+P] also **Shetland, the Shetlands**– a group of about 100 islands off the N coast of Scotland, further N than the Orkneys. The capital is Lerwick, on Mainland, the largest island. The main industries of the islands are fishing, farming, producing wool clothes, and, more recently, handling the oil which is taken from nearby areas of the North Sea. –see colour map on page 818

Shetland po·ny /ˌ··· ˈ···/ *n* a rough-haired strong very small horse

Shet·lands /ˈʃetləndz/ [*the*+P] the SHETLAND ISLANDS

Shetland sheep·dog /ˌ··· ˈ···/ *n* a breed of SHEEPDOG which originally came from the Shetland Islands and which looks like, but is smaller than, the COLLIE

shew /ʃəʊ/ *v* **shewed** /ʃəʊd/, **shewn** /ʃəʊn/ [I;T] *old use* to show

shh /ʃ/ *interj* 1 (used for demanding silence or less noise): *"Shh! You sound like a herd of elephants!"* 2 **shh/schh, you know who**... an advertising SLOGAN used for many years for Schweppes drinks

Shi·a, Shiah /ˈʃiːə/ *n* [*the*+P] 1 the Shiite branch of the Muslim religion 2 [C] a Shiite

shi·a·tsu /ʃiˈɑːtsuː/ *n* [U] an ancient Japanese form of treatment which uses pressure on many different places on the body to prevent illness and to treat disorders such as headaches, backaches, and emotional problems. In the West it is considered a form of ALTERNATIVE MEDICINE – compare ACUPRESSURE, ACUPUNCTURE

shib·bo·leth /ˈʃɪbəleθ‖ˈʃɪbəlǰθ/ *n* a once-important or widely accepted custom or principle which no longer has much meaning

shield¹ /ʃiːld/ *n* 1 a broad piece of metal, wood, or strong plastic that is carried (e.g. by soldiers in former times, or by policemen) as a protection against being hit: *The police were equipped with riot shields.* 2 a representation of a shield, usu. wide at the top and curving to a point at the bottom, used for a COAT OF ARMS, a BADGE, a prize in sport, etc. 3 a protective cover, esp. on a machine – see also HEAT SHIELD, WINDSHIELD

shield² *v* [T (**from**)] to protect or hide from harm or danger through action to defend oneself: *She lied to the police to shield her friend.* | *He raised his arm to shield himself from the blow.*

shift¹ /ʃɪft/ *v* 1 [I;T] to change in position or direction; move from one place to another: *He shifted impatiently in his seat during the long speech.* | *There were four of us trying to lift the heavy box, but we couldn't shift it.* | *The wind shifted and blew the mist away.* | (fig.) *Don't try to shift the blame onto me!* | (fig.) *The recent hijacking has shifted attention away from internal problems.* 2 [T] *esp. BrE* to get rid of or remove: *a new washing powder that will shift any stain* | *The thieves couldn't shift* (=sell) *any of those stolen colour televisions.* 3 [I] *BrE infml* to move very fast: *That motorbike was really shifting!* 4 [I;T] *esp. AmE* to CHANGE¹ (7) (GEAR in a vehicle): *I shifted into top gear.* 5 **shift for oneself** *old-fash* to take care of oneself; live as well as one can by one's own efforts: *He's had to shift for himself since his mother died.*

▷ USAGE **Shift** is rather informal in the meaning of "move or remove something". Compare *Will you* **shift** "move or remove something". Compare *Will you* **shift** *that car?* and *Could you possibly* **move** *your car, please?*◁

shift² *n* 1 [(in)] a change in position, direction, or character: *There's been a shift in the wind/in political opinion.* | *the gradual shift of workers away from manufacturing and towards the service industries* 2 a [+*sing./pl. v*] a group of workers which takes turns with one or more other groups: *The night shift arrives/arrive at six o'clock.* b the period of time worked by such a group: *I'm on day shift this week.* | *shift workers* 3 a a loosefitting straight simple woman's dress b *old use* a woman's dresslike undergarment 4 [*usu. pl.*] *old-fash* a trick or method used in a time of difficulty; EXPEDIENT 5 **make shift (with)** *old-fash* to use what can be found because one lacks anything better –see also GEAR LEVER, MAKESHIFT, STICK SHIFT

shift key /ˈ·· ·/ *n* the KEY¹ (3) on a KEYBOARD (e.g. of a TYPEWRITER) which is pressed in order to print a capital letter –see picture at TYPEWRITER

shift·less /ˈʃɪftləs/ *adj* lazy and lacking the desire to succeed – ~**ly** *adv* – ~**ness** *n* [U]

shift stick /ˈ·· ·/ *n AmE for* GEAR LEVER –see also STICK SHIFT and see picture at BICYCLE

shift·y /ˈʃɪfti/ *adj infml* looking evil/dishonest; not to be trusted; FURTIVE: *shifty eyes* | *a shifty little man* ––**ily** *adv* ––**iness** *n* [U]

Shi·ite /ˈʃiː-aɪt/ *n, adj* (a member) of the second-largest branch of the Muslim religion, which is based on the teachings and acts of Muhammad's COUSIN Ali and of the teachers who came after him –compare SUNNI

Shi·ko·ku /ˈʃiːkəʊkuː/ the smallest of Japan's four main islands

shil·ling /ˈʃɪlɪŋ/ *n* 1 (a silver-coloured coin worth) an amount of money in use in Britain until 1971, equal to 12 old pence and ¹/₂₀ of £1 2 a unit of money in Kenya, Uganda, Tanzania, and Somalia, equal to 100 cents 3 **look as though one has lost a shilling and found sixpence** *BrE infml* to look rather unhappy

shil·le·lagh /ʃiˈleɪli/ *n* an Irish weapon like a thick, heavy stick, often referred to as being something typically Irish

shil·ly-shal·ly /ˈʃɪli ˌʃæli/ *v* [I] *infml derog* to waste time without reaching a decision or taking action

shim·mer /'ʃɪmə^r/ v [I] to shine with a soft trembling light: *The water shimmered in the moonlight.* —**shimmer** n [U]: *the shimmer of the desert air in the midday heat*

shin[1] /ʃɪn/ n the bony front part of the leg between the knee and ankle

shin[2] *BrE*‖**shinny** *AmE*— v -nn- [I+adv/prep] to climb up or down a tree, pole, etc., esp. quickly and easily, using the hands and legs: *She shinned up a tree to get a better view.* | *to shin down a drainpipe*

shin·bone /'ʃɪnbəʊn/ also **tibia** *med*— n the front bone in the leg below the knee —see picture at SKELETON

shin·dig /'ʃɪndɪɡ/ n *old-fash infml* **1** a noisy party, dance, etc. **2** a noisy quarrel or disagreement

shine[1] /ʃaɪn/ v **shone** /ʃɒn‖ʃəʊn/ **1** [I] to produce light: *It was a fine morning with the sun shining (down).* | *They must be at home — there's a light shining in the bedroom.* | (fig.) *His honesty shines through.* (=He is very clearly honest.) **2** [I] to REFLECT (=throw back) light; be bright: *The polished surface shone in the sun.* | *She brushed her hair till it shone.* | (fig.) *eyes shining with happiness* **3** [T+obj+adv/prep] to direct (a lamp, beam of light, etc.): *He shone a light in my eyes/shone a torch into the cave.* **4** [T] (*past tense & participle* **shined**) to polish; make bright by rubbing: *Shine your shoes before going out.* **5** [I *not in progressive forms*] to be clearly excellent (at a skill, school subject, etc.): *He's a pretty good student, but sports are where he really shines.*

shine[2] n [S] **1** brightness, esp. caused by REFLECTION; shining quality: *The wooden surface had a beautiful shine.* **2** an act of polishing, esp. of shoes: *These shoes need a shine.* **3** **take a shine to someone** *infml* to start to like someone as soon as one has met them, esp. without any clear reason —see also **(come) rain or shine** (RAIN[1])

shin·gle[1] /'ʃɪŋɡəl/ n [U] small unevenly rounded pieces of stone, larger than GRAVEL, covering large areas of seashore —**gly** adj : *a shingly beach*

shingle[2] n **1** a small thin piece of building material, esp. wood, laid in rows to cover a roof or wall **2 hang out one's shingle** *AmE* to start a business for oneself: *When I get my law degree I'm going to hang out my shingle in my old home town.*

shin·gles /'ʃɪŋɡəlz/ n [U] a disease caused by an infection of certain nerves and producing usu. painful red spots, often in a band round the waist

shin·ing /'ʃaɪnɪŋ/ adj [A] noticeably excellent: *a shining example of courage*

shin·ny /'ʃɪni/ v [I] *AmE for* SHIN[2]

Shin·to /'ʃɪntəʊ/ also **Shin·to·is·m** /'ʃɪntəʊɪzəm/— the ancient religion of Japan, including the worship of gods that represent various parts of nature, and of people who died in the past

shin·ty /'ʃɪnti/ n [U] a game played in Scotland, similar to HOCKEY

shin·y /'ʃaɪni/ adj (esp. of a smooth surface) giving off light, as if polished; bright: *a shiny new 10p coin* | *shiny shoes/hair* —**iness** n [U]

ship[1] /ʃɪp/ n **1** a large boat for carrying people or goods on the sea: *It's much slower to cross the Atlantic by ship.* | *a naval/merchant/cruise ship* | *a ship-to-shore radio link* —see BOAT (USAGE), TRANSPORT (USAGE), VESSEL (USAGE), and see picture at SAIL **2** *old-fash infml* a large aircraft or esp. spacecraft **3 I see no ships** *quote* a phrase believed to have been used by Lord Nelson before the battle of Copenhagen. He had received orders to leave the area because Danish ships were approaching. He put his telescope to his blind eye and said, "I see no ships." His ships stayed where they were, and won the battle that followed. **4 ships that pass in the night** people who meet by chance and who are unlikely to meet again (from a poem by H W Longfellow): *She's a woman I met briefly at a conference; we were just ships that pass in the night, though.* **5 when one's 'ship comes in/home** *infml* when one becomes rich

ship[2] v -pp- [T] **1** to send or carry by ship: *I'm flying to America but my car is being shipped.* **2** to send (esp. a large article) to a distant place by post or other means: *We ship our products anywhere within Great Britain.* **3** [+obj+adv/prep, esp. OFF] *infml* to order to go somewhere; send; DISPATCH: *As soon as the doctor saw her he shipped her off to hospital.* **4** (of a boat) to take in (water) over

the side: *The boat began to ship water and we thought it would sink.* **5** to hold (one's OARS) to the side of the boat without rowing

ship bis·cuit /'· ˌ··/ also **ship's biscuit, hard tack**— n [U] a hard-baked bread eaten esp. formerly by sailors at sea

ship·board /'ʃɪpbɔːd‖-bɔːrd/ n **on shipboard** on board ship; on a ship: *goods stored on shipboard* | *a shipboard romance*

ship·build·er /'ʃɪpˌbɪldə^r/ n a person or company that plans and makes ships —**ing** n [U]

ship·mate /'ʃɪpmeɪt/ n a fellow sailor on the same ship

ship·ment /'ʃɪpmənt/ n **1** [C (**of**)] a load of goods sent together by sea, road, or air: *A large shipment of grain has just arrived.* **2** [C;U] the action of sending, carrying, and delivering goods: *The goods were ready for shipment/lost in shipment.*

ship·per /'ʃɪpə^r/ n someone who makes shipments of goods: *wine shippers*

ship·ping /'ʃɪpɪŋ/ n [U] **1 a** ships considered as a group: *The canal has been closed to shipping.* **b** all the ships belonging to a particular country: *British shipping has decreased in recent years.* **2** the sending and delivery of goods: *There's a shipping charge of £5 added to the price.*

shipping fore·cast /'·· ˌ··/ n a radio broadcast saying what the weather will be like at sea

ship's chand·ler /ˌ· '··/ n someone who trades in supplies for ships

ship·shape /'ʃɪpʃeɪp/ adj [F] made clean and neat; in good order. In Britain, this word is sometimes used in the old-fashioned phrase **(all) shipshape and 'Bristol fashion**, which means the same.

ship·wreck[1] /'ʃɪp-rek/ also **wreck**— n [C;U] (a) destruction of a ship, usu. accidental as a result of hitting rocks or sinking

shipwreck[2] v [T *usu. pass.*] to cause (esp. a person) to suffer shipwreck: *The shipwrecked sailors were rescued by helicopter.*

ship·wright /'ʃɪp-raɪt/ n a person who works on building and repairing ships

ship·yard /'ʃɪp-jɑːd‖-jɑːrd/ n a place where ships are built or repaired

shire /ʃaɪə^r/ n *old use for* a COUNTY[1] —see also SHIRES

shire horse /'· ·/ n a large powerful English horse used for pulling loads

shires /ʃaɪəz‖ʃaɪərz/ [*the*+P] (*usu. cap.*) the country areas of England away from the big cities, esp. in the centre of England: *The government gets a lot of its support from the Shires.* | *the shire counties*

▶ CULTURAL NOTE The Shires are famous for hunting, esp. fox hunting, and are thought by many to contain a large number of rich country people with RIGHT-WING political views.◀

shirk /ʃɜːk‖ʃɜːrk/ v [I;T] *derog* to avoid (unpleasant work or responsibilities) because of laziness, lack of determination, etc. — ~ **er** n

Shir·ley Tem·ple /ˌʃɜːli 'tempəl‖ˌʃɜːr-/ n ROY ROGERS

shirt /ʃɜːt‖ʃɜːrt/ n **1** a piece of clothing for the upper part of the body that is usu. of light cloth with a collar and SLEEVES, is fastened in front with buttons, and is typically worn by a man —see also HAIR SHIRT, NIGHTSHIRT, SWEATSHIRT, T-SHIRT, UNDERSHIRT **2 have the shirt off someone's back** *infml* to take everything from someone, usu. because one is owed it, but in an unnecessarily MEAN[1] way **3 put one's shirt on** *infml* to risk all one's money on; BET heavily on: *That horse is bound to win; put your shirt on it.* —see also STUFFED SHIRT, **keep one's shirt on** (KEEP[1])

shirt·front /'ʃɜːtfrʌnt‖'ʃɜːrt-/ n the part of a shirt covering the chest, esp. the stiff front part of a formal white shirt

shirt·sleeve /'ʃɜːtˌsliːv‖'ʃɜːrt-/ adj [A] *infml* not wearing JACKETs, esp. because of hot weather or informality: *There was a large shirtsleeve crowd to watch the cricket match.* | *shirtsleeve* (=informal and direct) *diplomacy*

shirt·sleeves /'ʃɜːtsliːvz‖'ʃɜːrt-/ n **in (one's) shirtsleeves** wearing nothing over one's shirt: *On hot days the men in the office work in their shirtsleeves.*

shirt·tail /'ʃɜːt-teɪl‖'ʃɜːrt-/ n the part of a shirt below the wearer's waist

shirt·waist·er /ˈʃɜːtˌweɪstəʳ‖ˈʃɜːrt-/ *BrE*‖ **shirt·waist** /ˈʃɜːtˌweɪst‖ˈʃɜːrt-/*AmE*— *n* a woman's dress in the style of a man's shirt

shirt·y /ˈʃɜːti‖ˈʃɜːr-/ *adj infml, esp. BrE* bad-tempered; angry and rude: *He gets a bit shirty if you contradict him.*

shish ke·bab /ˈʃɪʃ kɪˌbæb‖-baːb/ *n* a KEBAB cooked on a SKEWER

shit¹ /ʃɪt/ *v* **shit** or **shitted** or **shat** /ʃæt/; *present participle* **shitting** *taboo* **1** [I] to pass solid waste from the bowels; DEFECATE **2** [T] to make (something) dirty by passing solid waste from the bowels into it **3 shit oneself: a** to pass solid waste from the bowels accidentally **b** *infml* to be very afraid

shit² *n taboo* **1** [U] solid waste from the bowels; EXCRE-MENT: *dog shit* **2** [S] an act of passing this waste from the body: *to have a shit* **3** [U] stupid talk; NONSENSE: *That's a load of shit.* **4** [C] a worthless or unpleasant person: *He's a complete shit.* **5 in the shit** in trouble **6 not give/care a shit** not to care even a small amount: *I don't give a shit what you think.* **7 the shit (is going to/will) hit the fan** *infml* there (will be or) was a lot of trouble, esp. from someone in authority: *When I didn't come home until three in the morning, the shit really hit the fan — my parents and the police were all shouting at me at once.* | *If the press hear about this, the shit's going to hit the fan.* —see also BULLSHIT; **scare the shit out of** (SCARE¹)

shit³ *interj taboo* (expressing anger or annoyance)

shit·house /ˈʃɪthaʊs/ *n AmE taboo sl* **1** an outdoor TOILET **2 built like a brick shithouse** (of a man or woman) having a very broad, strong looking body

shits /ʃɪts/ *n* [*the*+P] *taboo for* DIARRHOEA

shit·ty /ˈʃɪti/ *adj taboo* unpleasant; nasty

shiv·er¹ /ˈʃɪvəʳ/ *v* **1** [I (**with**)] to shake slightly, esp. because of cold or fear; tremble: *The little dog was shivering with cold.* | *shivering with terror* **2 Shiver me timbers!** a phrase said by old sailors, PIRATEs, etc., in stories, to express surprise or annoyance

shiv·er² *n* a feeling or act of shivering: *A sudden scream sent shivers (up and) down my spine.* (=frightened me)

shiv·er³ *n* [*usu. pl.*] *esp. lit* any of the very small pieces into which something is broken when it is hit or dropped

shiv·ers /ˈʃɪvəz‖-ərz/ *n* [*the*+P] *infml* **1** tremblings typical of a fever **2** feelings of strong unreasonable dislike or fear: *Snakes give me the shivers.*

shiv·er·y /ˈʃɪvəri/ *adj* (of a person) trembling from cold, fear, or fever

shoal¹ /ʃəʊl/ *n* an underwater bank of sand not far below the surface of the water, making it dangerous to boats

shoal² *n* [C+*sing./pl. v.*] **1** a large group of fish swimming together **2** [(**of**)] also **shoals** *pl.*— *infml, often derog* lots, esp. in large groups: *Shoals of tourists visit the palace in summer.*

shock¹ /ʃɒk‖ʃaːk/ *n* **1** [C;U] (the state or feeling caused by) a sudden, unexpected, and usu. very unpleasant event or situation that severely upsets the mind and feelings: *His death came as/was a great shock to us all.* | *speechless from shock* | (*infml*) *I got a bit of a shock* (=was unpleasantly surprised) *when I saw the size of the bill.* **2** [C;U] (a) violent force from a hard blow, crash, explosion, etc.: *The shock of the explosion was felt far away; the* **shock waves** *spread for miles.* | (fig.) *His resignation has sent* **shock waves** *through Parliament.* **3** [C] an ELECTRIC SHOCK **4** [U] *med* the weakened state of the body with reduced activity of the heart, lungs, etc., esp. following damage to the body: *Several of those who survived the accident have been taken to hospital in a state of shock/suffering from shock.*

shock² *v* [T] **1** to cause usu. unpleasant or angry surprise to: *The violence and bad language in the programme shocked many of the viewers.* | *It shocked me to see/I was shocked to see how my neighbours treated their children.* | *We were shocked at/by his sudden death.* | *The explicit advertising campaign sets out to shock people into driving more carefully.* **2** [*usu. pass.*] to give an ELECTRIC SHOCK to: *Anyone touching that wire could get badly shocked.*

shock³ *adj* [A] (esp. in newspapers) that shocks one; very surprising: *England's football team suffered a shock defeat at the hands of Luxembourg.* | *shock tactics*

shock⁴ *n* [(**of**)] a thick bushy mass, esp. of hair

shock ab·sorb·er /ˈ· ·ˌ··/ *n* an apparatus made usu. of a rod moving in and out of a tube of liquid, fixed near each wheel of a vehicle to lessen the effect of rough roads, or on an aircraft to make a smoother landing

shocked /ʃɒkt‖ʃaːkt/ *adj* [A] caused by a sudden unpleasant surprise: *A shocked silence greeted the announcement.*

shock·er /ˈʃɒkəʳ‖ˈʃaː-/ *n usu. humor* a person or thing that shocks one as being improper, wild, or immoral

shock hor·ror /ˌ· ˈ··◂/ *adj* [A] *infml, esp. BrE* very worrying or shocking; a phrase used by or thought to be typical of HEADLINES in low-quality newspapers: *Shock horror crime surge probe!* (=a worrying study about an increase in crime)

shock·ing /ˈʃɒkɪŋ‖ˈʃaː-/ *adj* **1** causing shock; very offensive, wrong, or upsetting: *a shocking accident* | *The play was considered too shocking* (=immoral) *to be staged at the time it was written.* **2** *BrE infml* very bad (though not evil): *What a shocking waste of time!* | *I've got a shocking cold.* — **~ly** *adv*: *shockingly rude behaviour* | *shockingly bad grammar*

shocking pink /ˌ·· ˈ·◂/ *adj, n* [U] (having a) very bright strong pink colour

shock·proof /ˈʃɒkpruːf‖ˈʃaːk-/ *adj* (esp. of a watch) not easily damaged by being dropped, hit, shaken, etc.

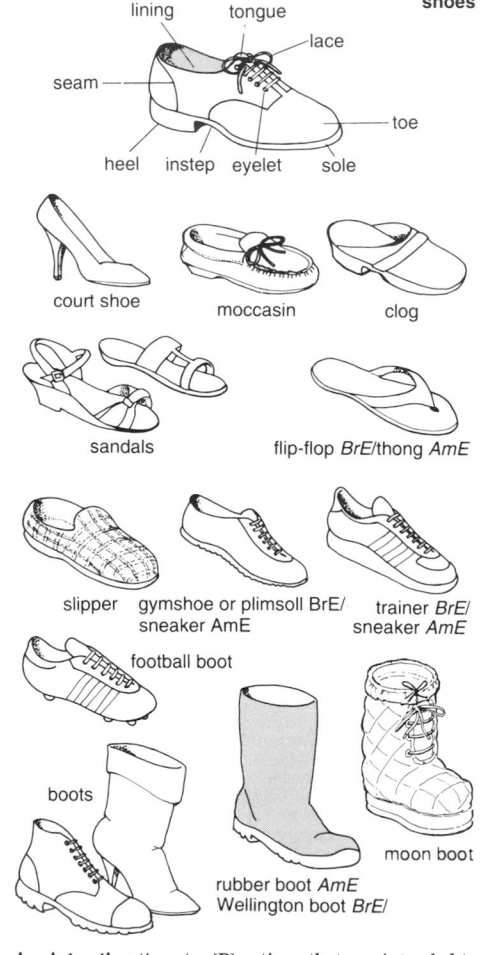

shoes

lining tongue lace

seam

toe

heel instep eyelet sole

court shoe

moccasin

clog

sandals

flip-flop *BrE*/thong *AmE*

slipper gymshoe or plimsoll *BrE*/ sneaker *AmE*

trainer *BrE*/ sneaker *AmE*

football boot

boots

moon boot

rubber boot *AmE*/ Wellington boot *BrE*/

shock tac·tics /ˈ· ˌ··/ *n* [P] actions that are intended to achieve their result by using surprise and force: *If she won't be persuaded nicely, we'll have to use shock tactics.*

shock treat·ment /ˈ· ˌ··/ also **shock ther·a·py** /ˈ· ˌ···/— *n* [U] *med* treatment of some disorders of the mind by using powerful electric shocks or drugs —see also ELECTRIC SHOCK THERAPY

shock troops /ˈ· ·/ n [P] soldiers chosen and trained for use in sudden forceful attacking

shod[1] /ʃɒd‖ʃɑːd/ *past tense & participle of* SHOE[2]

shod[2] *adj usu. lit* wearing or provided with shoes of the stated kind: *poor badly-shod children* | *expensively-shod ladies*

shod·dy /ˈʃɒdi‖ˈʃɑːdi/ *adj* **1** made or done cheaply and badly: *shoddy goods|workmanship* **2** ungenerous or dishonourable: *a shoddy trick* —**·dily** *adv* —**·diness** *n* [U]

shoe[1] /ʃuː/ n **1** an outer covering for the human foot, typically of leather and having a hard base (SOLE) and a support (HEEL) under the heel of the foot: *She put on|laced up|took off her shoes.* | *leather shoes with rubber soles* | *a pair of canvas tennis shoes* | *high-heeled shoes* | *dancing shoes* | *shoe shops* —compare BOOT[1] (1), SANDAL, SLIPPER; see PAIR (USAGE) **2** a HORSESHOE **3 in someone's shoes** in someone's situation; experiencing what someone else has to experience: *I'm glad I'm not in his shoes just now, with all those debts to pay!* | *If I were in your shoes I'd refuse.* **4 step into|fill someone's shoes** to take the place and do the job of someone: *Will anyone be able to fill her shoes now that she's left the company?* **5 if the shoe fits, wear it** *AmE*‖**if the cap fits, wear it** *BrE saying* if a remark about someone is true or suggests something true, that person should accept it: *"Are you saying I'm a fool?" "If the shoe fits…"* —see also BRAKE SHOE

shoe[2] *v* **shod** /ʃɒd‖ʃɑːd/ *or* **shoed**, *present participle* **shoeing** [T] to fix a HORSESHOE on: *A man who shoes horses is called a farrier.*

shoe·horn[1] /ˈʃuːhɔːn‖-hɔːrn/ n a curved piece of metal or plastic for putting inside the back of a shoe when putting the shoe on, to help the heel go in easily

shoehorn[2] *v* [T] *infml* to force into a limited space: *They managed to shoehorn two more passengers into the crowded bus.* | *a tiny new house shoehorned in between two others*

shoe·lace /ˈʃuːleɪs/ *also* **lace**— n a thin cord passed through holes on both sides of the front opening of a shoe and tied to fasten the shoe on: *Do up your shoelaces.* —see PAIR (USAGE)

shoe·mak·er /ˈʃuːmeɪkəʳ/ n COBBLER

Shoemaker, Willie (1931–) an American JOCKEY (=a person who rides horses in races)

shoe·shine /ˈʃuːʃaɪn/ n an act of polishing the shoes

shoe·string[1] /ˈʃuːˌstrɪŋ/ n **1** *esp. AmE for* SHOELACE **2 on a shoestring** *infml* with a very small amount of money: *He started his business on a shoestring and built it up.*

shoestring[2] *adj* |A| *infml* operating on, done with, or being a small amount of money: *The whole company runs on a shoestring budget.* | *a shoestring enterprise*

shoe·tree /ˈʃuːtriː/ n a piece of wood or plastic and metal put inside a shoe to keep it in the right shape when it is not being worn

Sho·gun /ˈʃəʊɡʌn/ n one of the military governors who ruled Japan before the REVOLUTION of 1867–68

shone /ʃɒn‖ʃəʊn/ *past tense & participle of* SHINE

shoo[1] /ʃuː/ *interj* (said, usu. not angrily, to animals or small children) Go away!

shoo[2] *v* [T] *infml* to drive away (as if) by saying "shoo": *She shooed the birds off the bushes.* | *He shooed the children out of the kitchen.*

shoo-in /ˈ· ·/ n *AmE infml* a person expected to win a race, election, etc. easily: *Clinton is a shoo-in for the Democratic nomination.*

shook /ʃʊk/ *past tense of* SHAKE

shoot[1] /ʃuːt/ *v* **shot** /ʃɒt‖ʃɑːt/ **1** [I;T (**at**)] (of a person) to fire (a gun): *I'm coming out with my hands up: don't shoot!* | *He shot at the bird, but missed it.* (compare *He shot the bird and killed it.*) | *A dangerous murderer has escaped and the police have orders to* **shoot on sight** (=as soon as they see him)/**shoot to kill.** | *She learnt how to shoot a rifle when she was only 10.* [+obj+adv|prep] *He shot his way out of prison.* (=escaped by shooting at people) **2** [T] (of a person or weapon) to send out (bullets, ARROWS, etc.) with force: *I shot an arrow at the target.* | *It's just a toy; you can't shoot real bullets with it.* | *This gun shoots .38 bullets.* **3** [T] to hit, wound, or kill with a bullet, etc.: *He shot a bird.* | *We heard on the news that the President*

had been shot. | *He was shot three times in the arm.* | *I accidentally shot myself in the foot.* | *The postmaster was shot dead by the robbers.* **4** [I;T] to hunt or kill (birds or animals) as a sport: *They go to Scotland every autumn to shoot (grouse).* **5** [T (**at**)] to send out as if from a gun: *Everyone shot questions at the chairman.* [+obj(i)+obj(d)] *She shot him an indignant glance.* **6** [I+adv|prep] to move very quickly or suddenly: *He shot past me on the motorway at about 110 miles an hour* | *The pain shot up my arm.* | *The snake's tongue shot out.* | *They shot out through the back door when they saw the police coming.* | *I get these* **shooting pains** *in my back.* (=sudden sharp pains that travel through the body) **7** [T] to pass quickly by or along: *The robbers' car shot the traffic lights.* (=went past them when they were signalling cars to stop) | *We shot the rapids in our canoe.* **8** [T] to move (a BOLT[1] (2)) across so as to be in a locked or unlocked position **9** [I;T] to make (a photograph or film) (of): *We'll be ready to shoot as soon as all the cameras are loaded.* | *This film was shot on location in California|was shot in colour.* | *He had the idea of shooting them against a completely plain white background* **10** [I] (of a plant) to put out SHOOTS[2] (1) **11** [I] to kick, throw, etc., a ball so as to make a point in a game: *Our striker got into a good position to shoot, but then missed his kick.* **12** [T] *infml* (in GOLF) to make (the stated number of strokes) in playing a complete game: *Miller shot a 69 today.* **13** [T] *AmE* to play (a game of esp. BILLIARDS, CRAPS, POOL[2] (3), or MARBLES): *Let's shoot some|a game of pool.* **14** [T] *sl* to take (a drug) directly into the blood using a needle: *She'd been shooting heroin.* **15 have shot one's bolt** (*BrE*)/**one's wad** (*AmE*) *infml* to have used up all one's strength, arguments, etc., and have nothing left **16 shoot a line** *BrE infml for* BOAST[1] (1) **17 shoot it out (with)** *infml* to have a SHOOT-OUT (with) **18 shoot one's mouth off** *infml* to talk loudly and foolishly about what one does not know about or should not talk about **19 shoot the bull/the breeze** *AmE infml*, *also* **shoot the shit** *taboo AmE—* to have an informal, not very serious, conversation: *They sat around shooting the bull until late at night.* —see also SHOT **20 shoot the moon** to MOON[2] **21 - shooter** a person or weapon that shoots the stated thing: *a rifleshooter* | *a peashooter*

shoot sbdy./sthg. ↔ **down** *phr v* [T] **1** to bring down and destroy (a flying aircraft) by shooting **2** *also* **shoot down in flames**— *a infml* to say "no" firmly to; REJECT: *So there's another of my bright ideas shot down by the chairman!* **b** to show or claim to be wrong or mistaken: *It's my view – and shoot me down if you like – that he's the most talented of modern painters.*

shoot for/at sthg. *phr v* [T] *infml, esp. AmE* to try to reach; aim at: *We're shooting this year for a 50% increase in sales.*

shoot through *phr v* [I] *infml, esp. AustrE* **1** to leave, esp. in a hurry **2** to die

shoot up *phr v* **1** [I] to go upwards, increase, or grow quickly: *Flames shot up into the air.* | *Prices/Costs have shot up lately.* | *Little Jimmy's certainly shooting up.* (=getting taller quickly) **2** [T] (**shoot** sthg./sbdy. ↔ **up**) *infml* to damage or wound by shooting: *His plane had been badly shot up by enemy fighters.* **3** [I;T (=**shoot up** sthg.)] *sl* to take (a drug) directly into the blood using a needle

shoot[2] n **1** a new growth from (a part of) a plant, esp. a young stem and leaves **2** an occasion for shooting, esp. of animals: *He invited us to his country estate for a weekend shoot.* **3** an area of land where animals are shot for sport

shoot·er /ˈʃuːtəʳ/ n *sl, esp. BrE* a gun; a word typically used in GANGSTER films

shoot·ing /ˈʃuːtɪŋ/ n **1** [C] a usu. criminal act of wounding by firing a gun: *politically-motivated shootings* **2** [U] the sport of shooting animals and birds: *the shooting season* | *a* —see HUNT (USAGE)

shooting gal·le·ry /ˈ·· ˌ···/ n an enclosed place, esp. at a FAIR[3], where people shoot guns at fixed or moving objects to win prizes, for practice, etc.

shooting i·ron /ˈ·· ˌ·/ n *old-fash infml* a gun, esp. a REVOLVER; a word which is supposed to be used by COWBOYS: *OK, pardner, grab your shooting irons and get out of town!*

shooting match /ˈ·· ·/ n **the whole shooting match** *infml* the whole thing or affair

shooting star /ˌ·· ˈ·/ also **falling star**— n not tech a small piece of material from space which burns brightly as it passes through the Earth's air; METEOR

▶ CULTURAL NOTE There is an old belief that when someone sees a shooting star, they are supposed to be able to make a wish for something they want to happen. ◀

shooting stick /ˈ·· ·/ n a pointed walking stick with a top which opens out to form a seat, used for sitting outdoors, esp. by UPPER-CLASS country gentlemen

shoot-out /ˈ· ·/ n infml a battle or exchange of shots between gunfighters, usu. to decide which will be victorious or to settle a quarrel —see also **shoot it out** (SHOOT¹ (17))

shop¹ /ʃɒp‖ʃɑːp/ n **1** [C] esp. BrE ‖usu. **store** AmE— (often in comb.) a room or building where goods are regularly kept and sold, or services are sold: The shops in town close at 5.30. | a bookshop | a sweetshop | a betting shop | a shop window | I'm just going out to the shops to get some food. —see also BUCKET SHOP, COFFEE SHOP **2** [C] a place where things are made or repaired; WORKSHOP: When the cars have been assembled they go to the factory's paint shop to be painted. | a repair shop —see also SHOP FLOOR, SHOP STEWARD **3** [U] AmE a subject taught in school which shows students how to use tools and machinery to make things out of wood or metal; INDUSTRIAL ART: shop class | I'm taking shop this year. | I made it in wood/metal shop. **4** [U] infml business; activity: He's **set up shop** (=started a business) as a lawyer in town. | The whole country **shuts up shop** (=stops doing business) on Christmas Day. **5** [U] infml subjects connected with one's work: Let's not **talk shop** outside office hours. **6 all over the shop** BrE infml scattered in disorder: There were clothes and books lying around all over the shop. —see also CLOSED SHOP, OPEN SHOP

shop² v -pp- **1** [I (for)] to visit one or more shops in order to buy things: I went shopping today in town. | I was shopping for a new dress, but I couldn't find anything I liked. —see also WINDOW-SHOP; see CUSTOMER (USAGE) **2** [T] BrE derog sl to tell the police about (a criminal): The murderer was shopped by his girlfriend. — –**per** n

shop around phr v [I] to compare prices or values in different shops before buying: We shopped around before deciding which car to buy.

shop as·sis·tant /ˈ· ·ˌ··/ BrE ‖ **salesclerk** AmE— n a person who serves customers in a shop —see ATTEND (USAGE), OFFICER (USAGE)

shop-fit·ting /ˈʃɒpfɪtɪŋ‖ˈʃɑːp-/ n [U] BrE the activity or profession of selling and putting in equipment in shops, such as shelves, COUNTERS¹ (1), DISPLAY cases, etc.

shop floor /ˌ· ˈ·/ n [the+S] **1** the area, e.g. in a factory, where the ordinary workers do their work: The chairman started his working life on the shop floor **2** [+sing./pl. v] the people who work on the shop floor, as opposed to the MANAGERS: How will the shop floor react to these proposals?

shop·keep·er /ˈʃɒpˌkiːpəʳ‖ˈʃɑːp-/ esp. BrE ‖ usu. **storekeeper** AmE— n a person, usu. the owner, in charge of a small shop

shop·lift /ˈʃɒpˌlɪft‖ˈʃɑːp-/ v [I] to take goods from a shop without paying: She was fined for shoplifting. — –**er** n : The notice said "We always prosecute shoplifters."

shop·lift·ing /ˈʃɒplɪftɪŋ‖ˈʃɑːp-/ n [U] the act of taking goods from a shop without paying for them

shop·per /ˈʃɒpəʳ‖ˈʃɑːpəʳ/ n a person who buys things from a shop: streets crowded with Christmas shoppers —see CUSTOMER (USAGE)

shop·ping /ˈʃɒpɪŋ‖ˈʃɑː-/ n [U] **1** the goods bought in one visit to a shop or shops: Let me carry your shopping. | Put the shopping in this basket. **2** an act or occasion of visiting the shops to buy things: I normally do all my shopping on Saturdays. | Don't forget—there are only **17 shopping days till Christmas!** (=only 17 days on which it is possible to go to the shops)

shopping cen·tre /ˈ·· ˌ··/ n a group of shops of different kinds planned and built together in one area, often enclosed under one roof

shopping pre·cinct /ˈ·· ˌ··/ n an area in a town where there are a lot of shops, and where cars are not allowed to drive

shop·soiled /ˈʃɒpsɔɪld‖ˈʃɑːp-/ BrE ‖ **shop·worn** /-wɔːn ‖-wɔːrn/ AmE— adj slightly damaged, dirty, or imperfect as a result of being handled or kept on view in a shop for a long time: (fig., derog.) He brought out the same old shop-soiled arguments as before.

shop stew·ard /ˌ· ˈ··/ n a TRADE UNION officer who is elected by the members of his or her union in a particular place of work to represent them. Some people, esp. those with RIGHT-WING political views, think that shop stewards have too much power and are likely to persuade workers to go on strike for unimportant reasons

shop·walk·er /ˈʃɒpwɔːkəʳ‖ˈʃɑːp-/ esp. BrE ‖ **floorwalker** esp. AmE— n a person employed in a large shop to help the customers and to watch the SHOP ASSISTANTS to see that they are working properly —compare STORE DETECTIVE

shore¹ /ʃɔːʳ/ n **1** [C;U] also **shores** pl.— the land along the edge of a large area of water, such as an ocean or lake: We could see a boat about a mile from the shore/off the shore. | It was wonderful to see the shores of England again after so long at sea. | Many of these birds migrate to our shores (=to this country) during the summer. **2** [U] land rather than the sea: The sailors were warned not to get into trouble while they were on shore. (=away from their ship) —see also ASHORE, OFFSHORE, ONSHORE

▷ USAGE The place where the land meets the water can be the **bank, shore, coast, seaside,** or **beach.** The edges of a river are its **banks.** The usual word for the edge of a sea is **shore.** However, we use **coast** when we are thinking of places on maps, of weather, or of naval defence: It is difficult to walk on such a rocky shore. | a holiday on the north coast of Spain. The **seaside** BrE‖**coast** AmE, or the **beach** is the area by the sea considered as a place of enjoyment: digging in the sand at the **seaside.** A **beach** is part of the shore that is smooth, without cliffs or rocks. The only words that can be used of lakes are **shore** and (of a large lake) **beach.**◁

shore² v [T (UP)] to support (something that is in danger of falling) e.g. with a large piece of wood: We had to shore up the damaged wall. | (fig.) They tried to shore up the failing economy by means of tax increases.

shore leave /ˈ· ˌ·/ n [U] time allowed for sailors to leave their ships and go on shore

shorn /ʃɔːn‖ʃɔːrn/ past participle of SHEAR

short¹ /ʃɔːt‖ʃɔːrt/ adj **1** measuring a small or smaller than average amount from one end to the other; little in distance or length (opposite **long**) or in height (opposite **tall**): It's only a short way/distance from here. | She had her hair cut short. | A straight line is the shortest distance between two points. | He's rather a short man, shorter than his wife. **2** [F+for] a shorter (and often more usual) form of, or way of saying: The word "pub" is short for "public house". —see also SHORT³ (4) **3** lasting only a little time, or less time than usual or expected: a short visit of only half an hour | She was here a short while ago. | I have such a short memory; I can't remember what you told me yesterday. | His speech was short and to the point. | The signal for the fire alarm is three short rings followed by one long ring. | Because of the emergency, a meeting had to be arranged **at short notice.** (=not a long time in advance) —opposite **long 4** [(of)] not having or providing what is needed; failing to reach an acceptable level or standard: "I'm short of money this week; can you lend me some?" "Sorry: I'm rather short myself." | The shopkeeper was found guilty of using short weights/measures. | These goods are **in short supply** so the price will be high. [after n] I need £1 but I'm 5p short: I've only got 95p. | Our car broke down only two miles short of the town. —see LACK (USAGE) **5** [F+on] infml without very much or enough of (esp. a desirable quality): He's a nice boy but short on brains. (=not clever) —opposite **long on 6** [(with)] rudely impatient; CURT: I'm sorry I was a bit short with you on the phone this morning — I was rather busy. —see also SHORT-TEMPERED **7** (of a speech sound) pronounced quickly or without force: /æ/, as in "cat", is a short vowel, but /ɑː/, as in "cart", is long. **8** (of pastry) falling easily into pieces; CRUMBLY **9 make short work of** infml to deal with or defeat quickly and easily: The children made short work of the meal. **10 nothing short of** (used to add force to a statement) nothing less than: The closure of the factory will be nothing short of a disaster/of disastrous for the people in the area. **11 short and sweet** infml or humor not wasting time or words; short and direct in expression: The chairman's speech was short and sweet. **12 short of: a** not quite reaching; up to but not including: *We'd tried everything to get our money short of actually suing them.* **b** except for; without: *Short of calling a protest meeting I don't know how we can show our opposition.* —see also SHORTLY **13 short sharp shock** a sudden, unpleasant experience, esp. one intended as a punishment. The phrase originally comes from W S Gilbert's OPERA *The Mikado* (1885), and was later used by British Conservative politicians to describe a system of short but firm punishments for young criminals. — ~ **ness** *n* [U]

short² *adv* **1** suddenly; in an ABRUPT way: *The driver stopped short when the child ran into the street.* | *I'm afraid I must stop you short there, minister, as we're running out of time on the programme.* —see also **stop short of** (STOP¹) **2 be taken/caught short** *BrE infml* to have a sudden and strong need, esp. to go to the TOILET **3 go short (of)** to be without enough (of): *I'm giving my dinner to the children; they mustn't go short (of food).* **4 run short (of): a** to use almost all one has (of); not have enough left: *We've run short of oil.* **b** to become less than enough: *The supply of oil is running short.* —see also **cut something short** (CUT¹), **fall short** (FALL¹), **sell something/someone short** (SELL¹)

short³ *n* **1** *infml* a short film shown before the main film at a cinema **2** *BrE infml* a drink of strong alcohol, such as WHISKY or GIN **3** *infml for* SHORT CIRCUIT **4 for short** as a shorter way of saying it: *My name is David, or Dave for short.* —see also SHORT¹ (2) **5 in short** to put it into as few words as possible; all I mean is: *This is our most disastrous and embarrassing defeat ever; in short, a fiasco.* —see also SHORTS

short⁴ *v* [I;T] *infml for* SHORT-CIRCUIT (1)

short·age /ˈʃɔːtɪdʒ‖ˈʃɔːr-/ *n* [C;U (of)] a condition of having less than is needed; an amount lacking: *There were severe food shortages during the war.* | *There's no shortage of skilled workers but there aren't enough jobs for them.*

short back and sides /ˌ· ·ˌ· · ˈ·/ *n* [S] *BrE* a man's haircut in which the hair round the ears and at the back of the neck is cut very short. Men in the armed forces usually have haircuts like this.

short·bread /ˈʃɔːtbred‖ˈʃɔːrt-/ *n* [U] a hard sweet BISCUIT made with a lot of butter

short·cake /ˈʃɔːtkeɪk‖ˈʃɔːrt-/ *n* [U] **1** *BrE* thick shortbread **2** *AmE* cake, usu. of a kind like SCONES, over which sweetened fruit is poured: *strawberry shortcake*

short·change /ˌ· ˈ·/ *v* [T] **1** to give back less than enough money to (a buyer who has paid for something with more than the exact money) **2** *infml* to cheat or fail to reward fairly: *When the band only played for 15 minutes the fans felt they had been shortchanged.*

short·cir·cuit /ˌ· ˈ··/ *v* **1** [I;T] to (cause to) have a SHORT CIRCUIT **2** [T] to get something done without going through; BYPASS: *I short-circuited the usual procedures by a simple telephone call.*

short circuit *n* a faulty electrical connection that makes the current flow along the wrong path and so usu. puts the power supply out of operation

short·com·ing /ˈʃɔːtˌkʌmɪŋ‖ˈʃɔːrt-/ *n* [usu. pl.] a fault; failing; DEFECT: *In spite of all her shortcomings I still think she's one of the best teachers in the school.* | *The inspection revealed serious shortcomings in our safety procedures.*

short·crust pas·try /ˌʃɔːtkrʌst ˈpeɪstri‖ˌʃɔːrt-/ *n* a pastry used for PIES, FLANS, etc., made with half as much fat as flour

short cut /ˌ· ˈ·, ˈ· ·‖ˈ· ·/ *n* [(to)] a quicker more direct way than the usual way: *We were late for school, so we took a short cut across the fields.* | (fig.) *There aren't really any short cuts to learning English.*

short·en /ˈʃɔːtn‖ˈʃɔːrtn/ *v* [I;T] to make or become shorter: *to shorten a skirt/a report* —opposite **lengthen**

short·en·ing /ˈʃɔːtnɪŋ‖ˈʃɔːrt-/ *n* [U] fat for combining with flour in pastry mixtures

short·fall /ˈʃɔːtfɔːl‖ˈʃɔːrt-/ *n* [(of, in)] an amount by which something fails to reach the amount that is needed, expected, or hoped for: *We now expect a shortfall of about £1 million in the company's profits because of the sudden rise in the cost of materials.*

short·hand /ˈʃɔːthænd‖ˈʃɔːrt-/ *n* [U] **1** also **stenography** *AmE*— fast writing in a system using signs or shorter forms for letters, words, phrases, etc.: *The secretary made notes in shorthand/made shorthand notes.* —compare LONGHAND **2** [(for)] a shorter and often purposely less clear way of expressing something: *He's been "relocated", which is government shorthand for "given a worse job a long way away".*

short·hand·ed /ˌʃɔːtˈhændɪd◄‖ˌʃɔːrt-/ *adj* lacking the necessary number of helpers or workers: *A lot of people are on holiday this month, so we're a bit shorthanded.*

shorthand typ·ist /ˌ·· ˈ··/ *esp. BrE* ‖ also **stenographer** *esp. AmE*— *n* a person who uses shorthand to write down what someone is saying, and then types (TYPE²) a copy of it

short·haul /ˈ· ·/ *adj* [A] (of an aircraft flight) covering a fairly short distance —compare LONG-HAUL

short·ie /ˈʃɔːti‖ˈʃɔːrti/ *n* humor derog SHORTY

short·list /ˈ· ·/ *v* [T (for) usu. pass.] *BrE* to put on a SHORT LIST: *He's been short-listed for the director's job.*

short list *n BrE* a list of the few most suitable people for a job, chosen from all the people who were considered at first: *She was on the short list for the position of director.* | *to draw up a short list*

short·lived /ˌ· ˈ·◄/ *adj* (esp. of a feeling or condition) lasting only for a short period: *Their opposition to the plan was short-lived.*

short·ly /ˈʃɔːtli‖ˈʃɔːrt-/ *adv* **1** soon; (in) a little time: *Ms Jones will be back shortly.* | *The President returned to work shortly after his operation.* **2** impatiently; not politely; in a SHORT¹ (6) way: *She answered me rather shortly.* **3** in a few words

short·or·der cook /ˈ·· ·· ˌ·/ *n AmE* a cook in a restaurant such as a COFFEE SHOP who cooks foods that do not need a lot of preparation and which cook quickly, such as HAMBURGERS

short·range /ˌ· ˈ·◄/ *adj* [A] of or covering a short distance or a short time: *short-range weather forecasts* | *a short-range missile*

shorts /ʃɔːts‖ʃɔːrts/ *n* [P] **1** short trousers ending at or above the knees, as worn in playing games, in hot weather, or by children. Shorts are usually worn in rather informal situations. **2** *esp. AmE* men's short UNDERPANTS —see PAIR (USAGE)

short·sheet /ˈ· ·/ *v* [T] *AmE infml* to rearrange the sheet on someone's bed, so that the sheet that would usually cover someone's feet is too short (usu. done as a joke, esp. at SUMMER CAMPs in the US) —compare APPLE-PIE BED

short shrift /ˌʃɔːt ˈʃrɪft‖ˌʃɔːrt-/ *n* [U] unfairly quick or unsympathetic treatment, giving little attention: *My suggestion was given short shrift.* | *The armed forces are well funded but education is getting short shrift.*

short·sight·ed /ˌʃɔːtˈsaɪtɪd◄‖ˌʃɔːrt-/ *adj* **1** *esp. BrE* ‖ **nearsighted** *esp. AmE*— unable to see objects clearly if they are not close to the eyes —opposite **longsighted** **2** *derog* not considering the likely future effects of present action; lacking FORESIGHT: *It's very shortsighted (of you) not to spend money on repairing your house.* —opposite **farsighted** — ~ **ly** *adv* — ~ **ness** *n* [U]

short·staffed /ˌ· ˈ·◄/ *adj* without enough workers: *If you're looking for a job, I hear they're very short-staffed at the biscuit factory.*

short·stop /ˈʃɔːtstɒp‖ˈʃɔːrtstɑːp/ *n* (in BASEBALL) the player who plays in the area between second and third BASE¹ (6) and tries to stop any balls that are hit into that area —see picture at BASEBALL

short sto·ry /ˌ· ˈ··/ *n* a short invented written story, shorter than a NOVEL, usu. containing only a few characters and often dealing with feelings rather than events

short·tem·pered /ˌ· ˈ··◄/ *adj* **1** getting angry early: *He's rather short-tempered these days.* **2** showing impatience and anger: *a short-tempered reply*

short·term , short term /ˌ· ˈ·◄/ *adj, n [the+S]* (concerning) a short period of time; (in or for) the near future: *short-term planning/borrowing* | *This is only a short-term solution to our problems.* | *Profits will fall in the short term, but should start to rise next year.* —opposite **long-term**

short time /ˌ· ˈ·◄/ *n* [U] *BrE* work at a factory, office, etc., for a shorter than usual period each day or week: *Workers were put on short time because raw materials were scarce.*

short wave /₁·ˈ·◂/ *n* [U] radio broadcasting or receiving on waves of less than 60 metres in length, which can be sent around the world —compare LONG WAVE, MEDIUM WAVE

short·y , shortie /ˈʃɔːti‖ˈʃɔːrti/ *n humor derog* (used when speaking to or about a short person)

Sho·sho·ne /ʃəʊˈʃəʊni/ *n* a Native American group of tribes which lived between southeast California and West Wyoming, hunting BUFFALO. Later, the Comanche tribes separated from the group and moved to what is now Texas, and today there are about 8000 Shoshone on RESERVATIONS (3) —see NATIVE AMERICAN (CULTURAL NOTE)

Shos·ta·ko·vich /₁ʃɒstəˈkəʊvɪtʃ‖₁ʃɑːs-/, **Di·mi·tri** /dɪˈmiːtri/ (1906–75) a Russian COMPOSER. His most famous works include an OPERA *The Lady Macbeth of the Mtensk* (1934), the *Ninth Symphony* (1945), and the *Tenth Symphony* (1953).

shot¹ /ʃɒt‖ʃɑːt/ *n* **1** [C] the action of shooting a weapon or the sound that it makes: *She fired three shots.* | (fig.) *With this speech he has* **fired the opening shots** (=taken the first action) *in the election campaign.* | *I heard a shot.* **2** [C] a kick, hit, throw, etc., of a ball in an attempt to make a point in a game: *His shot went wide of‖to the right of the goal.* | *Watson won the golf match by two shots.* | *Good shot!* **3** [C] a person who shoots with the stated degree of skill: *She's a good‖crack* (=very good)‖*poor shot.* **4** [C (**at**) *usu. sing.*] *infml* a chance or attempt to do something; GO² (2): *It's a difficult job but I'd like (to have) a shot at it.* **5** [U] nonexplosive metal in the form of balls for shooting from SHOTGUNs or from CANNONs in former times —see also BUCKSHOT, GRAPESHOT **6** [C] the heavy metal ball used in the SHOT PUT **7** [C] *infml* a photograph: *I got some good shots of the carnival.* **8** [C] a single part of a cinema film made by one camera without interruption: *an action shot* **9** [C] *infml* a taking of a drug or VACCINE into the bloodstream through a needle; INJECTION: *a shot of penicillin* **10** [C] *infml* a sending up of a spacecraft or ROCKET: *a moon shot* (=for a journey to the moon) **11** [C] *infml* a chance with the stated degree of risk: *The horse is an 8 to 5 shot to win the race.* —see also LONG SHOT **12** [C (**of**) *esp. AmE*] a small alcoholic drink for swallowing at once: *a shot of vodka* | *a shot glass* **13 like a shot** *infml* without any delay and esp. eagerly: *When he offered me the job, I accepted like a shot.* **14 not by a** ˈ**long shot** *esp. AmE* not at all; not by any means: *The problem isn't solved yet, not by a long shot.* **15 shot across the bows** something done or said as a warning to someone not to carry out a plan **16 shot in the arm** *infml* something that has the effect of producing a better, more active and more confident condition: *Everyone agrees that the economy needs a shot in the arm from a consumer spending spree.* **17 shot in the dark** *infml* a guess unsupported by arguments —see also BIG SHOT, PARTING SHOT, **call the shots** (CALL¹) **18 cheap shot** *AmE infml derog* a nasty INSULT (=a rude of offensive remark): *That was a cheap shot, saying she was fat and stupid!*

shot² *adj* **1** [F+**of**] *BrE infml* rid of; finished with: *I was glad to be*‖*get shot of that nasty cold.* **2** [(**with**)] woven in two different colours, one along and one across the material, giving a changing effect of colour: *a dress of shot silk.* **3** [F] *infml* destroyed or worn out because of hard treatment: *My nerves are shot; I need a holiday.* **4 shot through with** *esp. lit* having a lot of (a particular quality) in a mixture; full of: *His stories are shot through with a gentle sadness.*

shot³ *past tense & participle of* SHOOT

shot·gun /ˈʃɒtɡʌn‖ˈʃɑːt-/ *n* a gun fired from the shoulder, usu. having two barrels and firing SHOT¹ (5), esp. to kill birds —see also SAWN-OFF SHOTGUN

shotgun wed·ding /₁·· ˈ··/ *n often humor* a wedding that has to take place, usu. because the woman is going to have a baby and her parents want her and the baby to be publicly respectable. In CARTOONs the man and woman are often shown with the woman's father holding a shotgun to force the man to marry his daughter.

shot put /ˈ· ·/ *n* [*the*+S] a sporting competition to throw a heavy metal ball (SHOT¹ (6)) the furthest distance —see

colour picture on page 883 — ~ **ter** *n* : *an Olympic shot putter*

should /ʃəd; *strong* ʃʊd/ *v 3rd person sing.* **should**, *negative short form* **shouldn't** [*modal+to-v*] **1 a** (expressing duty or what is necessary or desirable) ought to: *If you see anything unusual you should call the police.* | *He shouldn't have*‖*oughtn't to have said that.* (=he said it but it was bad to do so) | *You shouldn't be so impatient with him.* | *They should be made to repay the money they stole.* | (showing annoyance) *Why shouldn't I buy a new coat — I haven't bought one for five years!* **b** (expressing likelihood, esp. of a desirable event or result) will probably: *The photos should be ready (by) tomorrow morning.* | *It should be fairly easy to get her to agree.* | *There shouldn't be any difficulty about getting you a visa.* **2** (used after **that** in certain expressions of feeling or opinion): *It's odd that you should mention him.* (=The fact that you have mentioned him is odd.) | *I was anxious that our plan should not fail.* | *I suggest that John should go*‖(*AmE* also) *that John go.* | *They demanded that there should be an official inquiry.* **3** *fml* (used in conditional sentences about what is possible in the future): *I don't think it will happen, but if it should, what shall we do?* | *Should you be interested* (=if you are), *I have a book on the subject you might like to see.* **4** (used for turning direct statements into questions, usu. for expressing amusement or surprise): *As I left the house, who should come to meet me but my old friend Sam!* (=my old friend Sam came to meet me) | *At that point, what should happen but (that) the car wouldn't start.* **5** *fml or old-fash, esp. BrE* **a** (used instead of **shall** in conditional sentences with **I** and **we** as the subject and a past tense verb): *I should be surprised if he came.* | *I should* (=you ought to) *stay in bed if I were you.* **b** (in reported speech) shall: *I promised I should be back before nightfall.* (=I said "I shall be back before nightfall".) **6** *infml humor* (expressing the opposite meaning) ought not to; needn't: *With all his money, he should worry about a little thing like £5!* **7 I should have thought** *fml, esp. BrE* (in remarks expressing surprise or sometimes annoyance): *Twenty degrees? I should have thought it was colder than that.* **8 I should like** *fml or polite, esp. BrE* I want: *I should like to ask the minister a question.* | *I should like a bath.* —see LIKE¹ (USAGE) **9 I should think** I believe or expect: *"Can you come?" "Yes, I should think so."* | *I shouldn't think this will cause any problems.* **10 I should think so!**‖**not!** of course!‖of course not!: *"We all went to a disco, but Granny didn't join us." "I should think not, at her age!"* —see OUGHT (USAGE) and LANGUAGE NOTE: Modals

▷ USAGE In meanings **5, 7,** and **8, should** is rather formal in modern English, and **would** is more common. In all the other meanings **should** is the ordinary word to use. —see also BETTER (USAGE), MUST (USAGE), NOT (USAGE), OUGHT (USAGE)◁

shoul·der¹ /ˈʃəʊldəʳ/ *n* **1** [C] the part of the body at each side of the neck where the arm of a person, or the FORELEG of an animal, is connected: *He had a parrot on his right shoulder.* | *Put this coat over your shoulders in case you get cold.* | *With the heavy pack on her shoulders* (=the shoulders and upper part of the back) *she couldn't run very fast.* | *He just* **shrugged his shoulders** (=raised them) *and said he didn't care what she thought.* —see picture at HORSE **2** [C] the part of a garment that covers this part of the body: *a jacket with wide shoulders* **3** [C] something shaped like a shoulder or pair of shoulders, such as **a** a slope near the top of a mountain **b** the outward curve of a bottle below the neck —see picture at MOUNTAIN **4** [C;U] the upper part of the front leg of an animal, used as meat: *a shoulder of lamb* **5 a shoulder to cry on** (someone from whom one gets) sympathy: *After my divorce I needed a shoulder to cry on.* **6 put one's shoulder to the wheel** to start to work with great effort and determination **7 shoulder to shoulder** side by side; close together: (fig.) *We stand shoulder to shoulder on this issue.* (=have the same opinions, intentions, etc.) —see also COLD SHOULDER, HARD SHOULDER, **have a chip on one's shoulder** (CHIP¹), **head and shoulders above** (HEAD¹), **rub shoulders with** (RUB¹), **straight from the shoulder** (STRAIGHT²)

shoulder² *v* [T] **1 a** to place (a load) on one's shoulder(s) **b** to accept (a heavy responsibility, duty, etc.): *The local residents are being asked to shoulder the costs of the repairs.* **2** [+*obj+adv*‖*prep*] to push with the shoulders: *He shouldered his way to the front, shouldering others* *aside.* **3 shoulder arms** [*usu. imperative*] (of a soldier) to hold a weapon upright so that it touches or rests on one shoulder

shoulder bag /ˈ·· ·/ *n* a bag that hangs from the shoulder on a band of leather

shoulder blade /ˈ·· ·/ also **scapula** *med*– *n* either of the two flat bones on each side of the upper back –see picture at SKELETON

shoulder-high /ˌ·ˌ· ˈ·◂/ *adj* as high as one's shoulder: *I've got a shoulder-high filing cabinet I want to sell.*

shoulder-length /ˌ·· ˈ·◂/ *adj* (of hair) reaching one's shoulders: *shoulder-length brown hair*

shoulder pad /ˈ·· ·/ *n* a fairly thick flat piece of material or FOAM RUBBER which is fixed under the shoulders of a woman's piece of clothing. As well as for style, shoulder pads are thought to be worn by women to express power or authority: *female executives wearing suits with shoulder pads* –see POWER DRESSING

shoulder strap /ˈ·· ·/ *n* **1** a narrow band of material on a dress, etc., that goes over the shoulder and holds it up **2** a wide band of material which is fixed to an object to make it easy to carry, by hanging it from the shoulder: *My suitcase has a shoulder strap. | a briefcase with a leather shoulder strap*

should·n't /ˈʃʊdnt/ *short for:* should not –see OUGHT (USAGE)

shouldst /ʃədst; *strong* ʃʊdst/ **thou shouldst** *old use or bibl* you should

shout¹ /ʃaʊt/ *v* [I;T (OUT)] **1** to make a loud sound with the voice; speak or say very loudly: *I can hear you all right; there's no need to shout. | He shouted for help. | I wish you'd stop shouting* (=speaking loudly and angrily) *at the children. | The crowd shouted slogans and threw stones at the police. | She shouted out a warning. | "Help!" he shouted. | I shouted to him to stop.* [+obj+adj] *He shouted himself hoarse.* (=made his voice rough and weak by shouting so much) **2 all over bar the shouting** *BrE infml* almost finished, so that the result is no longer in doubt: *England were leading 6–1 at half time, so it was all over bar the shouting.* **3 shout something from the rooftops** to let everyone know about something. **shout** sbdy. ↔ **down** *phr v* [T] to prevent from being heard, by shouting: *The crowd shouted down the unpopular speaker.*

shout² *n* **1** [C] a loud cry or call: *a warning shout | shouts of delight from the football crowd* **2** [S] *BrE or AustrE infml* a particular person's turn to buy drinks for others: *It's my shout; would you like another beer?*

shove¹ /ʃʌv/ *v* **1** [I; T] to push, esp. in a rough or careless way: *There was a lot of pushing and shoving to get on the bus. | They shoved me aside to get at the food.* **2** [T+obj+adv/prep] to put (something) carelessly: *Just shove it in the cupboard. | He quickly shoved the papers into his pocket/under the desk.* **3** [I+adv/prep] *infml, esp. BrE* to move oneself: *Shove over, mate, and make some room for me to sit down.* **shove** sbdy. **around** *phr v* [T] *infml* to push rudely and/or give orders to: *Don't let him shove you around.* **shove off** *phr v* [I] **1** (of a boat or the person in it) to leave the shore **2** [*usu. imperative*] *infml, not polite* to go away; leave: *Shove off! I'm busy.*

shove² *n* [*usu. sing.*] a strong push: *We gave the car a good shove and moved it out of the mud.*

shove-half·penny /ˌ· ˈ···/ *n* [U] (in Britain) a game, usu. played in PUBS, in which coins are pushed across a board with a sharp TAP⁴ from one's hand

shov·el¹ /ˈʃʌvəl/ *n* **1** a tool with a broad usu. square or rounded blade fixed to a handle, used for lifting and moving loose material –compare SPADE¹ **2** a part like this on a digging or earth-moving machine

shovel² *v* **-ll-** *BrE* ‖ **-l-** *AmE* [I;T] to take up, move, make, or work (as if) with a shovel: *He shovelled away the snow. | She shovelled the food greedily into her mouth.*

show¹ /ʃəʊ/ *v* **showed, shown** /ʃəʊn/ *or* **showed 1** [T (**to**)] to offer for seeing; allow or cause to be seen: *He showed his ticket at the door. | She never shows her feelings. | The news report showed harrowing pictures of the famine victims. | She's beginning to show her age.* (=seem as old as she really is) *| The patient is showing signs of improvement.* (=seems to be improving) *| I showed my*

driving licence to the policeman.* [+obj(i)+obj(d)] *She showed me the picture she'd painted.* [+obj+v-ing] *The photograph showed the baby laughing.* **2** [I] to appear or be noticeable; be able to be seen: *Don't worry about that tiny stain; it won't show. | He was very upset but he didn't let it show.| The lights showed faintly through the mist. | His happiness showed in his smile. | She did very little work on this report, and it shows!* (=it is very clear to see) **3** [T+obj+wh-] to point out to: *He showed me where he lived.| Show me which book you bought.* **4** [T] to have as a mark or number; INDICATE *or* REGISTER: *The clock showed 20 minutes past 2. | The latest results show a 15% rise in our profits.* **5** [T+obj+adv/prep] to go with and guide or direct: *May I show you to your seat? | Show the gentleman in/out, please.* –see also SHOW **around**, SHOW **over 6** [T] to explain; make clear to (someone) by words or esp. actions: *Don't just tell me how to do it; show me.* [+obj+wh-] *The introduction shows you how to use the dictionary.* **7** [T] to prove; allow the truth of to be seen: *This excellent piece of work shows/just goes to show what is possible if you try hard.* [+(that)] *The report shows that the police are still popular with the majority of the public. | His remarks showed he didn't understand what we were talking about.* [(+obj)+wh-] *Only six people passed the exam, which shows (you) how difficult it was.* [+obj+n, adj] *The results show her to be cleverer than we thought.| He showed himself a brave man in battle. | The report showed the accident to have been the driver's fault.* **8** [T *not in progressive forms*] (esp. of a material) to allow to be easily seen: *This light-coloured dress will show the dirt.* **9** [I;T] to offer or be offered as a performance, esp. at a cinema: *"What's showing at the cinema?" "They're showing a Marx Brothers film."* **10** [T] to put on view, esp. to be judged at a SHOW² (2); EXHIBIT: *His paintings are being shown at the local art gallery.* **11** [T] to cause to be felt or noticed in one's actions: *The government has shown very little understanding of this problem. | You should show a bit more respect to your teachers.* [+obj(i)+obj(d)] *They showed their enemies no mercy.* **12** [I] *sl for* SHOW **up** (4): *I came to meet my friend, but he never showed.* **13 show a clean pair of heels** *BrE old-fash infml* to run away fast **14 show a leg** [*usu. imperative*] *BrE infml* to get out of bed **15 show one's face** to make an appearance in a place that people expected me to avoid: *I'm surprised he dares to show his face here after the way he behaved last week.* **16 show one's hand** to make one's power or intentions clear, esp. after keeping them secret for a time **17 show one's teeth: a** to act threateningly **b** to make one's power clear **18 show someone** *infml* to prove to someone that one is better, more effective, etc., than they are, or than they think one is: *Well, he really showed her!* (=he proved he was correct/better/etc.) *| My Dad says I'm too little to ride a horse all by myself, but I'll show him!* (=I'll prove that I'm not) **19 show someone the door** to make it clear that someone is not welcome and should leave **20 show someone who's boss** *infml* to prove to someone who is threatening one's authority that one is more powerful than them: *That jumped-up little clerk! I'll soon show him who's boss!* **21 show the way** to set an example for others' future work: *With its low-cost home computers the company has shown the way (into this very profitable market).* **22 to show for** [*usu. in questions or negatives*] as a profit or reward from: *He had nothing to show for his life's work except a lot of memories.*

show sbdy. **around/round** (sthg.) *phr v* [T] to be a guide to (someone) on a first visit to (a place): *Before you start work, I'll show you around (the building) so that you can meet everyone.*

show off *phr v* **1** [I] *derog* to behave so as to try to get attention and admiration for oneself, one's abilities, etc.: *I wish you'd stop showing off – we all know how clever you are!* –see also SHOW-OFF **2** [T] (**show** sthg./sbdy. ↔ **off**) to show proudly or to the best effect: *He couldn't wait to show off his new car to his friends. | The white dress showed off her dark skin.*

show sbdy. **over** sthg. *phr v* [T] *esp. BrE* to guide through (esp. an interesting building or a house for sale): *The director showed the Prime Minister over the new production plant.*

show up *phr v* **1** [I;T (=**show** sthg. ↔ **up**)] to (cause to) be easily and clearly seen: *The cracks in the wall show up in the sunlight; the sunlight shows them up. | The unexpected riots showed up the deficiencies in police training.* **2** [T] (**show** sbdy./sthg. ↔ **up**) to make clear the unpleasant truth about: *I intend to show up this decep-tion|show up this man for the liar he is.* **3** [T] (**show sbdy.** ↔ **up**) to cause to feel shame; EMBARRASS: *When we go to parties my husband always shows me up by telling rude jokes.* **4** [I] *infml* to arrive as expected or arranged: *Did everyone you invited show up?*

show² *n* **1** [C] a performance, esp. in a theatre or NIGHT-CLUB or on radio or television: *a popular comedy show on TV | Let's go out and see a show, or perhaps a film.* —see also CHAT SHOW, FLOOR SHOW, GAME SHOW **2** [C] a public showing; collection of things for the public to look at; EX-HIBITION: *a cat|flower|car show | They're holding a one-woman show of her paintings at the gallery.* **3** [S+of] a showing of some quality; DISPLAY: *a little show of bad tem-per | The occupying army staged a big military parade as* **a show of strength.** —see also OF HANDS **4** [S (of)] an outward appearance, esp. as opposed to what is really true; PRETENCE: *I made a show of interest|of being interested, but I really couldn't have cared less.* **5** [U] *usu. derog* grandness; splendid appearance or ceremony; OS-TENTATION: *All this ceremony is just empty show|is just done for show; it doesn't mean a thing.* **6** [S] *infml* an or-ganization, field of activity, etc.: *She's the boss, in charge of the whole show. | Who's running this show?* **7** [S] *infml* an effort of the stated kind; attempt: *Our team* **put up a poor show** (=performed badly) *in the final and lost heav-ily.* **8 get this show on the road** *infml* to start to work or start a trip or journey **9 on show** being shown to the public: *All the items will be on show until the day of the sale.* **10 the show must go on** *saying* nothing must be allowed to stop a performance, event, etc.; life must con-tinue in spite of difficulties —see also **Good show** (GOOD¹), **steal the show** (STEAL¹)

show³ *adj* [A] complete with furniture, decorations, etc., so as to give possible buyers a good idea of what other similar houses, flats, etc., for sale will be like: *a show house|flat*

show and tell /ˌ· · ˈ·/ *n* [U] *AmE* an activity for young chil-dren in school in which they bring an object and tell the class about it: *Ramona brought in a fossil for show and tell.*

show busi·ness /ˈ· ˌ··/ also **show·biz** /ˈʃəʊbɪz/ *infml— n* [U] **1** the entertainment business; the job of people who work in television, films, the theatre, etc.: *She's in show busi-ness. | a well-known show business personality* **2 That's show business!** (an expression used to suggest that one should not be too disappointed, unhappy, etc., because life is just hard sometimes) **3 There's no business like show business** the first line of an old popular song

show·case /ˈʃəʊkeɪs/ *n* a glass-sided box in which objects are placed for looking at in a shop or MUSEUM: *The thieves smashed the showcase and stole the vase.* | (fig.) *Her new one-woman programme is a good showcase for her talents.* (=allows them to be seen in the best possible way)

show·down /ˈʃəʊdaʊn/ *n* [*usu. sing.*] *infml* a settlement of a quarrel or matter of disagreement in an open direct way: *He and I are heading for a showdown over this problem.*

show·er¹ /ˈʃaʊəʳ/ *n* **1** [C] a fall of rain (or snow) lasting a short time: *Scattered showers are expected this after-noon. | Snow showers are forecast for later.* —see also SHOWERY; see RAIN (USAGE) **2** [C (**of**)] a fall or sudden rush of many small things or drops of liquid: *a shower of water|sparks|confetti* **3** [C] **a** an act of washing the body by standing under running water: *She's having|tak-ing a shower.* —see also COLD SHOWER **b** an apparatus for this, from which water flows out through many small holes and which is usu. in an enclosure in a bathroom **4** [S+*sing.|pl. v*] *BrE infml derog* a group of unpleasant, worthless, lazy, etc., people **5** [C] *AmE* a party given on a special occasion by a woman's friends at which they give her suitable gifts: *a wedding shower | a baby shower* (=for a new mother)

shower² *v* **1** [I] to rain or pour down in showers: *It's started to shower; you'd better take your umbrella. | Nuts showered down when we shook the tree.* **2** [T] to scatter heavily (on); pour: [+*obj*+**with**] *The pipe burst, shower-ing us with oil.* | [+*obj*+**on**] *It showered oil on us.* | (fig.) *She was showered with compliments|gifts.* | (fig.) *Honours were showered on him.* **3** [I] to have a SHOWER¹ (3a)

shower gel /ˈ··· ·/ *n* a kind of LIQUID soap used to wash your-self in the shower

shower head /ˈ··· ·/ *n* the top part of a SHOWER¹ (3b) out of which the water comes

show·er·proof /ˈʃaʊəpruːf‖ˈʃaʊər-/ *adj* (of a piece of cloth-ing, etc.) not allowing much or any rain to pass through: *This raincoat is useless and they said it was showerproof.*

shower tray /ˈ··· ·/ *n* the bottom part of a SHOWER¹ (3b) in which you stand while having a shower

show·er·y /ˈʃaʊəri/ *adj* (of weather) bringing rain from time to time but not for long: *a showery day*

show·girl /ˈʃəʊgɜːl‖-gɜːrl/ *n* a girl in a group of singers or dancers, usu. in very fancy dress, in a musical show

show·ing /ˈʃəʊɪŋ/ *n* **1** [S] a record of success or quality; performance: *After its poor showing in last night's game, the team is unlikely to reach the finals.* | *On its current showing* (=according to the way it is performing now) *the party should do well in the forthcoming election.* **2** [C] an act of putting on view: *We're going to a showing of his latest paintings.* | *a special showing of the movie "King Kong"*

show jump·ing /ˈ· ˌ··/ *n* [U] *BrE* a form of horseriding com-petition judged on ability and often speed in jumping a course of fences —**·er** *n*

show·man /ˈʃəʊmən/ *n* **-men** /mən/ **1** a person whose bus-iness is producing plays, musical shows, public enter-tainments, etc.: *a fairground showman* **2** a person who is good at gaining public attention: *In local politics it helps to be a bit of a showman.* — ~**ship** *n* [U]

shown /ʃəʊn/ *past participle of* SHOW¹

show-off /ˈ· ·/ *n* *infml derog* a person who SHOWS **off** (1): *He's such a show-off!*

show of hands /ˌ· · ˈ·/ *n* [S] a vote taken by counting the raised hands of voters: *The chairman took a show of hands.*

show·piece /ˈʃəʊpiːs/ *n* a fine example fit to be admired by everyone: *This Ming vase is the showpiece of my collec-tion.* | *a showpiece factory*

show·place /ˈʃəʊpleɪs/ *n* a place which is open to or visited by the public because of its beauty, historical interest, etc.: *Visit Warwick Castle, showplace of the Midlands.*

show·room /ˈʃəʊrʊm, -ruːm/ *n* a large room where exam-ples of goods for sale can be looked at: *a car|furniture showroom*

show·stop·ping /ˈʃəʊstɒpɪŋ‖-stɑː-/ *adj apprec* so good that the watchers' expressions of approval interrupt the per-formance: *a showstopping song-and-dance act* —**·per** *n*

Show·time /ˈʃəʊtaɪm/ *a* CABLE television CHANNEL in the US which shows films and other programmes

show trial /ˈ· ˌ·/ *n* *usu. derog.* a trial set up by a govern-ment mainly to produce an effect on public opinion, rather than to find out if someone is guilty. Show trials are used usually by TOTALITARIAN governments: *A series of show trials were staged after the rebellion.*

show·y /ˈʃəʊi/ *adj usu. derog* very colourful, bright, atten-tion-getting, etc., but usu. without much real beauty, skill, etc.: *a showy person|dress* —**·ily** *adv* —**·iness** *n* [U]

shrank /ʃræŋk/ *past tense of* SHRINK

shrap·nel /ˈʃræpnəl/ *n* [U] metal scattered in small pieces from an exploding bomb or SHELL¹ (2): *He suffers from an old shrapnel wound.*

shred¹ /ʃred/ *n* [(**of**)] **1** [C *often pl.*] a small narrow piece torn or roughly cut off: *a shred of tobacco|cloth | My scarf was* **in shreds** (=completely torn up) *after the dog had chewed it up.* | (fig.) *He came out of the meeting with his reputation in shreds.* (=completely ruined) —see also **tear something to shreds** (TEAR²) **2** [S *usu. in negatives*] a smallest piece; bit: *There's not a shred of truth* (=no truth at all) *in his statement.* —see picture at PIECE

shred² *v* **-dd-** [T] **1** to cut or tear into shreds: *Coleslaw is made with shredded cabbage.* **2** to put through a SHRED-DER (2): *Shred these documents before anyone sees them.*

Shredded Wheat /ˌ··· ˈ·/ *n* [U] a type of breakfast CEREAL (2). A well-known advertisement in Britain challenges (CHALLENGE) people to eat three Shredded Wheat, and suggests that anyone who can will be successful at any physical activity they do.

shred·der /ˈʃredəʳ/ *n* **1** a kitchen tool for shredding food **2** a machine which tears paper into very small pieces that cannot be read: *Put the secret documents in|through the shredder.*

shrew /ʃruː/ n **1** a very small mouselike animal with a long pointed nose **2** lit a bad-tempered woman

shrewd /ʃruːd/ adj **1** showing good practical judgment, esp. of what is to one's own advantage: a shrewd judge of other people's ability | a shrewd lawyer/businesswoman **2** well-reasoned and likely to be right: a shrewd guess − ~ly adv − ~ness n [U]

shrew·ish /ˈʃruːɪʃ/ adj lit being or typical of a bad-tempered woman − ~ly adv − ~ness n [U]

Shrews·bu·ry /ˈʃrəʊzbəri‖ˈʃruːzberi/ a town in England close to the border with Wales where the local government for Shropshire is based

shriek /ʃriːk/ v [I;T] to make or say with a wild high cry, usu. resulting from anger, excitement, or fear: "Help!" she shrieked. | They were all shrieking with laughter. − **shriek** n : He gave a shriek of terror.

shrift n see SHORT SHRIFT

shrike /ʃraɪk/ n a type of greyish bird with a hooked beak, which feeds on insects and other small creatures

shrill /ʃrɪl/ adj **1** (of a sound) high and sounding sharp or even painful to the ear; PIERCING: a shrill whistle **2** (of words or people) marked by continuous expressions of angry disapproval; STRIDENT: The newspapers became even shriller in their attacks. − ~ness n [U] −**shrilly** /ˈʃrɪl-li, ˈʃrɪli/ adv

shrimp /ʃrɪmp/ n **1** a small CRUSTACEAN (=sea creature with an outer shell) with ten legs and a FAN-shaped tail −compare PRAWN **2** AmE a PRAWN **3** derog, usu. humor a small person

shrimp cock·tail /ˌ· ˈ··/ n [C;U] an American dish served before the main course of a meal consisting of PRAWNS with a hot-tasting tomato sauce

shrine /ʃraɪn/ n **1** a place for religious worship which is considered holy: an ancient shrine | to go on a pilgrimage to the Shrine of St James **2** a container holding the remains of a holy person's body **3** a place held in respect because of its connections with a famous person or event: Stratford, the shrine of Shakespeare

Shrin·er /ˈʃraɪnər/ n (in the US) a member of a secret organization that admits Masons of high rank. They are known to Americans mostly for their CHARITY work for children, and for their travelling CIRCUS.

shrink¹ /ʃrɪŋk/ v **shrank** /ʃræŋk/or **shrunk** /ʃrʌŋk/, **shrunk 1** [I; T] to (cause to) become smaller (as if) from the effect of heat or water: Washing wool in hot water will shrink it/make it shrink. | Meat shrinks by losing some of its fat in cooking. | The number of students has shrunk (from 120 to 75). | shrinking profits | the shrinking pound (=becoming lower and lower in value) −see also PRESHRUNK, SHRUNKEN **2** [I+adv/prep] esp. lit to move back and away, esp. because of fear: Fearing a beating, the dog shrank into a corner.

shrink from sthg. phr v [T+obj/v-ing] to avoid or be unwilling to do (something difficult or unpleasant): He shrank from the thought of having to kill anyone.

shrink² n humor, infml a PSYCHOANALYST or PSYCHIATRIST

shrink·age /ˈʃrɪŋkɪdʒ/ n [U] the act or amount of shrinking; loss in size: As a result of shrinkage, the shirt is now too small to wear. | a further shrinkage in the size of the work force

shrinking vi·o·let /ˌ·· ˈ···/ n humor, infml someone who lacks self-confidence; a SHY person

shrink-wrap /ˈ· ·/ v -pp- [T] to enclose (a product) in clear plastic film which is then shrunk, usu. by heating, to make a tight fit: I don't like markets that shrink-wrap the vegetables. − ~ped adj

shriv·el /ˈʃrɪvəl/ v -ll- BrE ‖ -l- AmE [I;T (UP)] to (cause to) dry out and become smaller, twisting into small folds: The crops had (been) shrivelled up in the dry heat. | (fig.) a shrivelled old man

Shrop·shire /ˈʃrɒpʃər‖ˈʃrɑːp-/ a COUNTY in W England near the border with Wales. Its local government is based at Shrewsbury.

shroud¹ /ʃraʊd/ n **1** also **winding sheet**− a cloth for covering a dead body for burial −see also TURIN SHROUD **2** something that covers and hides: A shroud of secrecy hangs over/surrounds the plan.

shroud² v [T (in)] usu. pass.] to cover and hide: The hills were shrouded in mist. | The whole affair was shrouded in mystery.

Shrove Tues·day /ˌʃrəʊv ˈtjuːzdi‖-ˈtuː-/ [C;U] the day before Ash Wednesday, which is the first day of the solemn period of Lent when Christians FAST and eat only certain foods. In Britain many people make PANCAKES on Shrove Tuesday, so it is also informally called Pancake Day − see also ASH WEDNESDAY, LENT, MARDI GRAS

shrub /ʃrʌb/ n a low bush with several woody stems: The azalea is an attractive shrub. | shrub roses | ornamental shrubs

shrub·be·ry /ˈʃrʌbəri/ n [C;U] (a part of a garden planted with) shrubs forming a mass or group

shrug¹ /ʃrʌg/ v -gg- [I;T] to raise (one's shoulders), usu. as an expression of doubt or lack of interest, or because one does not know about something: She just shrugged (her shoulders), saying she didn't know and didn't care.

shrug sthg. ↔ **off** phr v [T] to treat as unimportant or easily dealt with: She just shrugs off the pain and gets on with the job. | to shrug off criticism | This is a serious problem and it can't just be shrugged off as if it didn't exist.

shrug² n an act of shrugging: She answered with a shrug (of her shoulders). | He just gave a shrug.

shrunk /ʃrʌŋk/ past tense & participle of SHRINK¹

shrunk·en /ˈʃrʌŋkən/ adj [A] fml or lit having been shrunk (SHRINK¹): They kept the shrunken heads of their enemies as war trophies. | a further decline in our already shrunken motor industry

shtick /ʃtɪk/ n AmE infml a piece of acting, usu. meant to be amusing, which always follows the same sort of pattern: The movie goes from comic shtick to problem-drama shtick, and fuses them.

shuck¹ /ʃʌk/ n esp. AmE an outer covering, esp. of a plant −see also SHUCKS

shuck² v [T] esp. AmE to remove (esp. a vegetable) from an outer covering: He was shucking peas.

shucks /ʃʌks/ interj AmE infml (an inoffensive expression of annoyance or disappointment): "I'm not going." "Aw, shucks. I was hoping you would."

shud·der¹ /ˈʃʌdər/ v [I (at)] to shake uncontrollably for a moment, esp. from fear, cold, or strong dislike; tremble: I shuddered at the sight of the dead body. | She slammed on the brakes and the car shuddered to a halt. [+to-v] (fig.) I **shudder to think** how big the bill will be! (=I am afraid it will be very high)

shudder² n an act of shuddering: The dramatic announcement sent a shudder (of excitement) through the audience.

shuf·fle¹ /ˈʃʌfəl/ v **1** [I;T] to mix up (CARDS) so as to produce a chance order ready for a game to begin: She shuffled the cards expertly. **2** [T] to move or push about or to different positions: He tried to look busy shuffling papers from one pile to another on his desk. −see also RESHUFFLE **3** [I+adv/prep;T] to walk by dragging (one's feet) slowly along: The old lady shuffled across the room. | He walked along shuffling his feet. **4 shuffle off this mortal coil** BrE euph, usu. humor to die −−**fler** n

shuffle² n **1** [C] an act of shuffling cards: Give the pack a good shuffle first. | It's your shuffle. (=your turn to shuffle) **2** [S] a slow dragging walk

shuf·fle·board /ˈʃʌfəlbɔːd‖-bɔːrd/ n [U] a game, sometimes played on ships, in which round flat wooden pieces are pushed along a smooth surface to try to make them come to rest on numbered areas. It is popular with older people.

shuf·ti /ˈʃʊfti/ n [S (at)] BrE old-fash sl a quick view or look: Come and have/take a shufti at this!

shun /ʃʌn/ v -nn- [T] to avoid with determination; keep away from: He was a shy man who shunned all publicity. | Since the scandal she's been shunned by her neighbours.

'shun /ʃʌn/ interj ATTENTION²

shunt¹ /ʃʌnt/ v [T often pass.] **1** BrE ‖ **sidetrack** AmE− to move (a railway train or carriage) from one track to another, esp. to a SIDING **2** [+obj+adv/prep] infml to move to one side or away from a centre of activity: Smith has been shunted (off) to one of the company's smaller offices. − ~er n

shunt² n [usu. sing.] **1** an act of shunting **2** a tube put in the body by a doctor to move blood or other liquid from one place to another **3** BrE sl a car crash; COLLISION

shush /ʃʊʃ/ v infml **1** [I usu. imperative] to become quiet:

Shush; somebody might hear us! **2** [T] to tell to be quiet, esp. by saying "sh": *She shushed him.* —compare HUSH[1]

shut /ʃʌt/ *v* **shut**, *present participle* **shutting** **1** [I;T] to go or put into a covered, blocked, or folded-together position; close: *The wood has swollen and the door won't shut.* | *Shut the gate so that the dog can't get out.* | *He shut his eyes and tried to sleep.* | *Keep the windows shut until the rain stops.* | *I shut the book and put it away.* | *You'd better* **keep your mouth shut** *and not tell anyone about this.* **2** [T+obj+adv/prep] to hold or keep from leaving, entering, or moving, e.g. by closing a door or window: *He shut himself in his room to think.* | *Can't we do anything to shut that dreadful noise out?* | *She accidentally shut her skirt in the door and tore it.* | *to shut out unwelcome thoughts from one's mind* —see also SHUT-IN **3** [I;T] *esp. BrE||usu.* **close** *AmE–* to (cause to) stop operating: *The shops shut at 5.30.* | *He lost his job when they shut the factory.* —compare SHUT **down**, SHUT **up** (3); see OPEN (USAGE)

shut sbdy. ↔ **away** *phr v* [T] to put or keep in a place away from everyone else; ISOLATE: *She shut herself away in a cottage in the country for a year to write her novel.*

shut down *phr v* [I;T (=**shut** sthg. ↔ **down**)] to (cause to) stop operating, esp. for a long time or forever: *The whole company shuts down for three weeks' summer holiday.* | *The company has threatened to shut down the mine if the strike is not resolved.* —compare SHUT (3), SHUT **up** (3); see also SHUTDOWN

shut off *phr v* **1** [I;T (=**shut** sthg. ↔ **off**)] to stop the flow or operation (of), e.g. by turning a handle or pressing a button: *The machine shuts off automatically if a certain temperature is reached.* | *They shut off the gas and electricity before they went on holiday.* **2** [T (**from**) *often pass.*] (**shut** sthg./sbdy. ↔ **off**) to keep separate or away: *The valley is shut off by mountains from the rest of the world.* | *It's nice to be shut off from day-to-day problems while on holiday.*

shut out *phr v* [T] (**shut** sbdy./sthg. ↔ **out**) *AmE* **1** to prevent from taking part; EXCLUDE **2** to beat (an opponent who makes no points): *The Chicago Bears shut out the Denver Broncos.* —see also SHUTOUT

shut up *phr v* **1** [I *usu. imperative*; T (=**shut** sbdy. **up**)] *infml, not polite* to (cause to) stop talking; be or make quiet: *Shut up! I'm trying to think.* | *Can't you shut that dog up?* | *He was going to tell the newspapers, so we offered him £1000 to shut him up.* **2** [T] (**shut** sbdy./sthg. ↔ **up**) to keep enclosed; CONFINE: *He shut himself up in his room and refused to come out.* **3** [I;T (=**shut** sthg. ↔ **up**)] to make (a place, esp. a shop at the end of a business day) safe before leaving by locking doors, etc.; close: *Business was slow so we shut up (the shop) early for the day.* —compare SHUT (3), SHUT **down**; see also SHOP[1]

shut·down /ˈʃʌtdaʊn/ *n* a stopping of work or operation because of a labour quarrel, holiday, repairs, lack of demand, damage, etc.: *The manager ordered a complete shutdown of the nuclear reactor, as there was a danger of an explosion.* —see also SHUT **down**

Shute /ʃuːt/, **Nev·il** /ˈnevəl/ (1899–1960) an English writer, whose many popular adventure NOVELs include *A Town Like Alice* and *On the Beach*

shut·eye /ˈ·· ·/ *n* [U] *infml* sleep: *It's time to get a bit of shut-eye.*

shut·in /ˈ·· ·/ *n, adj AmE* (of or being) a person who cannot or does not wish to come out of their house: *medical care for shut-ins*

shut·out /ˈʃʌtaʊt/ *n AmE* a game in which only one side makes points

shut·ter[1] /ˈʃʌtər/ *n* **1** a part of a camera which opens for an exact *usu.* very short time to let light fall on the film: *Press the shutter.* | *a shutter speed of 1/250 second* —see picture at CAMERA **2** either of a pair of wood or metal covers that can be unfolded in front of the outside of a window to block the view or keep out the light **3 put up the shutters** *infml* to close a business at the end of the day or for ever

shutter[2] *v* [T *usu. pass.*] to close (as if) with SHUTTERS (2): *The deserted town was a sad sight, with all the shops shuttered and the people gone.*

shut·tle[1] /ˈʃʌtl/ *n* **1** (a vehicle used for) a regular journey from one place to another and back by air, railway, bus, etc., usu. over a short distance: *the London to Paris air shuttle* **2** a spacecraft that can be used more than

once **3** a pointed instrument used in weaving to pass the thread across and between the threads that form the length of the cloth **4** *infml* a shuttlecock

shuttle[2] *v* [T+obj+adv/prep] to move by a SHUTTLE[1] (1): *We shuttled the passengers to the city centre by helicopter.*

shut·tle·cock /ˈʃʌtlkɒk||-kɑːk/ *esp. BrE* || *usu.* **birdie** *AmE– n* a small light feathered object with a round base, for hitting across the net in the game of BADMINTON

shuttle di·plo·ma·cy /ˈ·· ·,··/ *n* [U] international talks, e.g. to try to make peace, carried out by someone who travels between the countries concerned taking messages and suggesting answers to problems

shuttlecock

shuttle ser·vice /ˈ·· ,··/ *n* a frequent air, bus, or train service between two places fairly near to each other: *There's a shuttle service between the town centre and the station.*

shy[1] /ʃaɪ/ *adj* **1** [(**of**)] nervous in the company of others; lacking self-confidence: *When the children met the queen, they were too shy to speak.* | *He's shy of women.* | *a shy smile* **2** (of an animal) unwilling to come near people; TIMID **3** [(**of**)] *esp. AmE* lacking; short: [after *n*] *We're still three votes shy (of the number we need to win).* **4 Once bitten, twice shy** *saying* A person who has had a bad experience will be more careful in the future **5 -shy** afraid of; not liking: *She's camera-shy and hates being photographed.* —see also GUNSHY, WORKSHY, **fight shy of** (FIGHT[1]) – **~ly** *adv* – **~ness** *n* [U]

shy[2] *v* [I (**at**)] (esp. of a horse) to make a sudden sideways or backward movement, esp. from fear: *The horse shied at the loud noise and threw its rider.*

shy away from sthg. *phr v* [I+obj/v-ing] to avoid because of fear, dislike, or lack of self-confidence: *She tends to shy away from (accepting) responsibility.*

shy[3] *v* [T] *old-fash infml* to throw with a quick movement

shy[4] *n BrE infml* **1** a throw **2** [(**at**)] an attack in words: *He took a few good-natured shies at his opponents.* —see also COCONUT SHY

Shy·lock /ˈʃaɪlɒk||-lɑːk/ *n* **1** a HEARTLESS Jewish MONEY-LENDER in Shakespeare's play *The Merchant of Venice.* Shylock lends a sum of money to another character, Antonio, but when Antonio is unable to pay the money back, Shylock claims to have the right to cut a pound of flesh from Antonio's body. —see also MERCHANT OF VENICE, **one's pound of flesh** (POUND) **2** someone who is very mean and demands too high a price for something: *How much do you want, you little Shylock?*

shys·ter /ˈʃaɪstər/ *n AmE infml* a dishonest person, esp. a lawyer or politician

si /siː/ *n* [C;U] TI

Si·ad Barre /ˌsiːæd ˈbɑːʳ/, **Mo·ham·ed** /məʊˈhæmɪd/ (1921–) an army general who took power and became president of Somalia in 1969. He was forced to leave his country in 1991 after a CIVIL WAR had begun.

Si·am /ˌsaɪˈæm/ the name of Thailand until 1939

Si·a·mese cat /ˌsaɪəmiːz ˈkæt/ *n* a type of blue-eyed short-haired cat with pale grey or light brown fur and darker ears, feet, tail, and face

Siamese twin /ˌ··· ˈ·/ *n* either of a pair of people joined together from birth at some part of their bodies

SIB /ˌes aɪ ˈbiː/ *abbrev. for:* SECURITIES AND INVESTMENTS BOARD

Si·be·li·us /sɪˈbeɪliəs/, **Jean** /ʒæn/ (1865–1957) a Finnish COMPOSER of highly personal music which is also thought to express Finnish CULTURE

Si·be·ri·a /saɪˈbɪəriə/ a very large area in the former Soviet Union, rich in minerals but low in population. It is known for being extremely cold, and for being the place where Soviet governments used to send anyone who disagreed with them to prison. **––rian** *adj*

sib·i·lant[1] /ˈsɪbɪlənt/ *adj fml* making or being a sound like that of *s* or *sh*: *a sibilant whistling sound*

sibilant[2] *n tech* a sibilant sound, such as /s, z, ʃ, ʒ/ in English

sib·ling /ˈsɪblɪŋ/ also **sib** /sɪb/ *infml– n fml* a brother or sister: *sibling rivalry*

sib·yl /ˈsɪbɪl, -bəl/ n any of several women in the ancient world who were thought to know the future

sic¹ /sɪk/ adv Lat (used after a word in writing to show that it has been printed or quoted (QUOTE¹) intentionally, even though it is a mistake): *The foreign student wrote about "many informations" (sic) in his English essay.*

sic² also **sick** v **sicced, siccing** [T] AmE **1** (of dogs or animals) to cause to attack; set on: *He sicced his dog on me.* **2 Sic 'em!** (said to a dog) Attack them!

Si·ci·ly /ˈsɪsᵻli/ an island in the Mediterranean sea which is part of Italy; capital Palermo. Sicily is often spoken of in connection with the Mafia. —**lian** /sᵻˈsɪliən/ n, adj

sick¹ /sɪk/ adj **1** not well; ill; having a disease: *The President is a very sick man.* | *She's visiting her sick uncle in hospital.* | *The cow looks pretty sick; you should call in the vet.* | *Jim's not at work — he's off sick today.* | *Many of the soldiers reported sick with food poisoning.* | *Did Mary call in sick today? I haven't seen her.* —see ILL (USAGE) **2** [F] BrE ‖ **sick to one's stomach** AmE— upset in the stomach so that one wants to throw up what is in it; feeling NAUSEA; QUEASY: *We began to feel sick as soon as the ship started to move.* —see also **be sick 3** [A] causing or typical of this feeling: *a sick smell/feeling* **4** [F] so influenced by unpleasant feelings that one (almost) feels ill: *He was sick with fear.* | *Why didn't you say you were going to be late? I've been worried sick.* (=extremely worried) | *(lit) feeling sick at heart* (=very unhappy) **5** [F+of] also **sick and tired** infml— feeling annoyance, dislike, and impatience from too much of something: *I'm sick of (listening to) your complaints; be quiet!* **6** unnaturally or unhealthily cruel; MORBID: *a sick joke/mind* **7 be sick** esp. BrE to throw up what is in the stomach; VOMIT: *He suddenly felt sick, and was sick twice before he could even get to the bathroom.* | *The cat's been sick on the carpet.* **8 look sick** infml, esp. AmE to look worthless by comparison: *She's such a good swimmer she makes me look sick.* **9 make someone sick** infml to be strongly displeasing to someone: *It makes me sick, the way they exploit their workers!* **10 on the 'sick list** infml (absent because of being) ill **11 sick as a parrot** BrE extremely disappointed; a phrase often thought of in connection with football players describing how they feel when they have lost a match **12 take sick** old-fash to become ill: *He took sick and died a week later.* —see also AIRSICK, CAR-SICK, HOMESICK, SEASICK, TRAVELSICK

▷ USAGE 1 In British English to be/feel sick is to VOMIT or feel that one is going to VOMIT. It is therefore confusing to say *I was sick yesterday* meaning "I was ill", but it is all right to use **sick** in this meaning before a noun: *a sick child.* 2 A **sick** person has a disease, not for example a wound or a broken leg, although one may be on **sick leave** or receive **sick pay** for these reasons. —see also ILL (USAGE)◁

sick² n **1** [the+P] people who are ill: *The sick and wounded were allowed to go free.* **12** [U] BrE infml for VOMIT²

sick³ v AmE SIC²

sick sthg. ↔ **up** phr v [T] BrE infml for VOMIT¹

sick·bay /ˈsɪkbeɪ/ n a room on a ship, in a school, etc., with beds for people who are ill

sick·bed /ˈsɪkbed/ n esp. lit the bed where a person lies ill: *We visited him in his sickbed.*

sick build·ing syn·drome /ˌ· ˈ·· ˌ··/ n [U] a pattern of illness typically suffered by workers in buildings which have AIR CONDITIONING but whose windows do not open: *The doctor said his flu was the result of sick building syndrome.*

sick call /ˈ· ·/ n [U] AmE for SICK PARADE

sick·en /ˈsɪkən/ v **1** [T] to cause to feel strong (almost) sick feelings of dislike or anger; NAUSEATE: *Their hypocrisy sickens me.* **2** [I] to become ill; show signs of a disease: *The animal began to sicken and soon died.* | *(BrE) She's got a temperature; maybe she's sickening for something.* (=is about to become ill)
sicken for sthg. phr v [T no pass.] esp. lit to lose one's desire for or interest in: *At last he sickened of endlessly drinking and gambling.*

sick·en·ing /ˈsɪkənɪŋ, ˈsɪknɪŋ/ adj extremely displeasing or unpleasant; disgusting (DISGUST): *It's sickening to see such cruelty.* | *He fell and hit his head on the floor with a sickening thud.* — ~ **ly** adv

sick head·ache /ˌ· ˈ··/ n infml a bad headache, esp. a MIGRAINE or a headache with SICKNESS (2)

sick·le /ˈsɪkəl/ n a tool with a hook-shaped blade, held in the hand, used for cutting grain or long grass —compare SCYTHE¹

sick leave /ˈ· ·/ n [(on) U] time spent away from a job during illness

sickle-cell a·nae·mi·a /ˌ··· ·ˈ····/ n [U] a HEREDITARY condition, found esp. in black people, in which the red blood cells have a curved shape, causing general weakness and illness

sick·ly /ˈsɪkli/ adj **1** often ill; weak and unhealthy: *a sickly child* | *a sickly-looking plant* **2** unpleasantly weak, pale, or silly: *His face was a sickly yellow.* | *a sickly smile* **3** causing a sick feeling: *a sickly smell*

sick·ness /ˈsɪknᵻs/ n **1** [C;U] (a) condition of being ill; illness or disease: *There have been a lot of people off work this week owing to sickness.* | *(fig.) the nation's economic sickness* **2** [U] the condition of feeling sick; NAUSEA: *A wave of sickness came over me.* **3 in sickness and in health** a phrase from the Christian marriage service related to promises by the man and woman to love and care for each other in both good and bad health —see also MARRIAGE —see also MORNING SICKNESS, MOTION SICKNESS, SLEEPING SICKNESS

sickness ben·e·fit /ˈ·· ˌ···/ n [U] BrE money paid, esp. by the government, to someone who is too ill to work — compare UNEMPLOYMENT BENEFIT

sick note /ˈ· ·/ n a note written by someone's doctor, mother, etc., to explain officially that someone is ill

sick·o /ˈsɪkəʊ/ n AmE infml a person who is mentally either ill or not like people usu. are

sick-out /ˈ· ·/ n AmE a STRIKE² in which all the workers at a company say that they are ill at the same time

sick pa·rade /ˈ· ·ˌ·/ BrE ‖ **sick call** AmE— n [(on) U] the daily time or place for soldiers to report themselves as ill

sick pay /ˈ· ·/ n [U] money paid by an employer to a worker for time spent away from a job during illness

sick·room /ˈsɪk-rʊm, -ruːm/ n a room where someone lies ill in bed

sic tran·sit glo·ri·a mun·di /ˌsɪk ˌtrænzɪt ˌɡlɔːriə ˈmʊndi/ phrase Lat so passes the glory of the world; used esp. when speaking of the short time for which things, esp. power and fame, last on Earth

side¹ /saɪd/ n **1** [C] (sometimes in comb.) a surface of something that is not its top, bottom, front, or back: *The front door is locked; we'll have to go round to the side (of the building).* | *They threw the box over the side of the ship into the sea.* | *The sides of the bowl were beautifully painted.* | *The display case had glass sides.* | *The house was halfway up the side of the hill/up the hillside.* **2** [C] any of the flat surfaces of something: *A cube has six sides.* | *Which side of the box do you put the label on?* **3** [C] (often in comb.) an edge or border: *A square has four equal sides.* | *I sat at the side of the road/at the roadside.* | *a ringside seat* (=at the edge of the RING¹ (5)) *for the boxing match* —see also SEASIDE **4** [C] either of the two surfaces of a thin flat object: *Write on only one side of the paper.* | *This coin has the queen's head on one side and a lion on the other.* | *Fold the cloth with the right sides facing.* —see also FLIP SIDE **5** [C] a part, place, or division according to a real or imaginary centre or central line: *I live on the other side of town.* | *He had a scar on the right side of his face.* | *Cars drive on the left side of the road in Britain.* | *I saw her on the far side of the room.* | *The enemy were attacking on every side/on all sides.* **6** [C usu. sing.] the place or area directly next to someone or something: *On one side of the window was a mirror, and on the other a painting.* | *On either side of the front gates stood a tall tree.* | *His daughter walked at/by his side.* (=beside him) | *During her illness he never left her side.* (=was always with her) **7** [C] the part of the body from the shoulder to the top of the leg: *a pain in my side/my left side* **8** [C] a part or quality to be considered, usu. in opposition to another; ASPECT: *Try to look at all sides/both sides of the question before deciding.* | *His kindness was a side of his character that few people knew about.* | *Try to stress the positive side of the government's record.* | *We've kept our side of the agreement, so now it's up to you to keep your side.* **9** [C] (a group which holds) a position in a quarrel, war, etc.: *In most wars, neither side wins.* | *Whose side*

are you on (=who do you support) – *mine or hers?* | *I never* **take sides.** (=support one side against the other) **10** [C+*sing.*/*pl. v*] *esp. BrE* a sports team: *Our side is/are winning.* **11** [C] the family line of the stated parent: *He's Scottish on his mother's side.* **12** [S] *BrE infml* a television station; CHANNEL: *This programme's pretty boring; what's on the other side?* **13** [C] a page of writing; one side of a sheet of paper: *How many sides have we got to write for this essay?* **14** [C+*of*] either half of an animal's body cut along the BACKBONE, when considered as food: *a side of beef/bacon* **15** [U] *BrE* the spinning of a SNOOKER ball caused by hitting it on the side rather than in the middle **16 get on the right/wrong side of someone** *infml* to win/lose someone's favour **17 let one's/the side down** *esp. BrE infml* to behave in a way that causes trouble, shame, or failure for one's family, team, etc. **18 on one's side** giving one an advantage and increasing one's chances of success: *The champion is a more experienced fighter, but the challenger has got youth on his side.* (=has the advantage of being younger) **19 on the side: a** as or from a sometimes dishonest additional activity: *He's a teacher, but he makes a little money on the side by repairing cars in his free time.* –see also SIDELINE[1] **b** *AmE* (of food) in addition, but not on/in the same dish: *waffles with sausage on the side* **20 on the ... side** *infml* rather; too: *I like the house but I think the price is a bit on the high side* (=rather high). **21 on the right/wrong side of** younger/older than (a stated age): *She's still on the right side of 40.* **22 on the right/wrong side of the law** not breaking/breaking the law **23 on/to one side: a** out of consideration for the present; for possible use later: *Let's leave that question on one side.* | *I try to put a few pounds to one side each week.* **b** away from other people for a private talk: *I can't let her go on like this; I must take her to one side and give her some advice.* **24 side by side** next to (one) another: *The two bottles stood side by side on the table.* **25 this side of** *infml* without going as far as: *At that restaurant you get the best Chinese food this side of Peking.* **26 -sided** /saɪdᵻd/having the stated number or kind of sides: *a three-sided field* | *a steep-sided mountain* –see also ALONGSIDE, ASIDE, BACKSIDE, INSIDE, ONE-SIDED, OUTSIDE, **look on the bright side** (LOOK[1]), **on the safe side** (SAFE[1]), **split one's sides** (SPLIT[1])

side² *adj* [A] at, from, towards, etc., the side: *a side door* | *a side view of an object*

side³ *v* [I+**with/against**] to support one person or group in a quarrel, fight, etc., against another: *Frank sided with David in the argument.*

side-arm /ˈsaɪd-ɑːm‖-ɑːrm/ *n* [*usu. pl.*] a weapon carried or worn at one's side, such as a sword or PISTOL

side-board /ˈsaɪdbɔːd‖-bɔːrd/ *n* a piece of DINING ROOM furniture like a long table with a cupboard below to hold dishes, glasses, etc.

side-burns /ˈsaɪdbɜːnz‖-bɜːrnz/ also **side-boards** /ˈsaɪdbɔːdz ‖ -bɔːrdz/ *BrE– n* [P] hair grown down the sides of a man's face in front of the ears

side-car /ˈsaɪdkɑːʳ/ *n* a usu. one-wheeled enclosed seat fastened to the side of a motorcycle to hold a passenger

side dish /ˈ· ·/ *n* a dish one eats with and in addition to a main dish: *a side dish of salad*

side ef-fect /ˈ· ·ˌ·/ *n* an effect, often one that is unexpected or unwanted, happening in addition to the one that is intended: *The new drug was withdrawn when it was found to have harmful side effects.* | *The tourist industry is worried about the possible side effects of these strict immigration controls.*

side is-sue /ˈ· ˌ··/ *n* a question or subject apart from the main one; something of not much importance which may take one's attention away from the main matter: *We mustn't let the meeting get bogged down in side issues.*

side-kick /ˈsaɪdˌkɪk/ *n infml, humor, esp. AmE* a (less important) helper or companion

side-light /ˈsaɪdlaɪt/ *n* [*often pl.*] **1** [C] *BrE* ‖ **parking light** *AmE–* either of a pair of lamps fixed usu. on the front of a vehicle at or near the sides –compare HEADLIGHT, and see picture at CAR **2** [(on)] a piece of additional perhaps not very important information: *The study of uniforms can give some interesting sidelights on military history.*

side-line¹ /ˈsaɪdlaɪn/ *n* **1** an activity in addition to one's regular job or business: *Jane's a doctor, but she does a*

bit of writing as a sideline. | *We're a computer company but we have a profitable sideline producing calculators.* –see also **on the side** (SIDE¹ (19)) **2** a line marking the limit of play at the side of a football field, tennis court, etc. –see picture at TENNIS **3** also **sidelines** *pl.*– the area just outside this line and out of the area of play: *The coach stood on the sideline(s) shouting to his players.* | (fig.) *Her injury put her* **on the sidelines** (=prevented her from taking part) *for the rest of the season.*

sideline² *v* [T *usu. pass.*] *AmE* to put (a person, esp. a player) out of action from the main activity

side-long /ˈsaɪdlɒŋ‖-lɔːŋ/ *adj* [A] directed sideways: *He threw a sidelong glance in her direction.*

side-on /ˌ· ˈ·◂/ *adj, adv* from one side rather than from in front: *a side-on crash*

side or-der /ˈ· ˌ··/ *n* a restaurant order for a separate dish to be eaten together with the main dish: *I'll have the chef's special with a side order of french fries.* –see also **on the side** (SIDE¹)

si-der-e-al /saɪˈdɪəriəl/ *adj* [A] *tech* of or calculated by the stars. Sidereal measurements of time are based on the **sidereal day**, equal to 23 hours 56 minutes 4.09 seconds.

side-sad-dle¹ /ˈsaɪdˌsædl/ *adv* on a sidesaddle: *She rode sidesaddle.*

sidesaddle² *n* a woman's SADDLE (=seat for putting on a horse) on which both legs are placed on the same side of the horse's back

side-show /ˈsaɪdʃəʊ/ *n* **1** a separate small show at a fair or CIRCUS, usu. offering a game or amusement in addition to the main entertainment **2** a less interesting or less serious activity compared with a more serious main one: *This brief conflict was a mere sideshow compared with the world war that followed.*

side-slip /ˈsaɪdˌslɪp/ *v* -**pp**- [I] to slip, slide, or SKID² sideways, esp. in a car or on SKIs –**sideslip** *n*

side-split-ting /ˈsaɪdˌsplɪtɪŋ/ *adj* causing uncontrollable laughter; extremely funny: *a sidesplitting joke*

side-step /ˈsaɪdstep/ *v* -**pp**- [I;T] **1** to take a step to the side to avoid (something, esp. a blow): *The champion sidestepped the challenger's punch.* **2** to avoid (an unwelcome question, problem, etc., esp. dishonestly; EVADE): *Politicians are good at neatly sidestepping reporters' questions.* –**sidestep** *n*

side street /ˈ· ·/ *n* a narrow less important street, esp. one that meets a main street –compare BACK STREET

side-stroke /ˈsaɪdstrəʊk/ *n* [S;U] a way of swimming by lying on one side moving the arms one by one and kicking the legs like scissors: *to do a fast sidestroke*

side-swipe¹ /ˈsaɪdswaɪp/ *n* [(at)] *infml* an attacking remark made in the course of making other statements about something completely different: *In her article on the state of the theatre she took a few sideswipes at the government's policy towards the arts.*

sideswipe² *v* [T] *AmE* to strike with a blow directed along the side: *to sideswipe a parked car*

side-track¹ /ˈsaɪdtræk/ *v* [T *usu. pass.*] **1** to cause to leave one subject or activity and follow another usu. less important one; DIVERT: *I was looking up Russian history in the encyclopedia when I got sidetracked by a fascinating article on chess.* | *We were supposed to be discussing the building plans but we got sidetracked into talking about politics.* | *Some corrupt officials tried to sidetrack our investigation.* **2** *AmE for* SHUNT¹ (1)

sidetrack² *n* an unimportant line of thinking followed instead of keeping on a more important one

side-walk /ˈsaɪdwɔːk/ *esp. AmE* ‖ usu. **pavement** *BrE– n* a hard surface or path at the side of a street for people to walk on: *He stepped off the sidewalk* | *a sidewalk café* –see picture at HOUSE

sidewalk art-ist /ˈ·· ˌ··/ *n AmE for* PAVEMENT ARTIST

sidewalk caf-e /ˈ·· ˌ·‖ ˈ·· ˌ·/ *AmE for* PAVEMENT CAFE

side-ways /ˈsaɪdweɪz/ *adj, adv* **1** [(ON)] with one side (and not the front or back) forward or up: *He was so fat that he could only get through the door sideways (on).* **2** to or towards one side: *She stepped sideways/took a sideways step.*

side-wheel-er /ˈ· ˌ··/ *n AmE for* PADDLE STEAMER

side-wind-er /ˈsaɪdwaɪndəʳ/ *n* **1** a N American snake **2** a MISSILE that is fired in the air towards something that is also in the air, which it finds because of its heat

sid·ing /ˈsaɪdɪŋ/ n a short railway track connected to a main track, used for loading and unloading, for carriages not in use, etc.

si·dle /ˈsaɪdl/ v [I+adv/prep, esp. UP, to] to move uncertainly or secretively, as if ready to turn and go the other way: *He sidled up to the stranger in the street and tried to sell him the stolen ring.* | *She sidled out of the crowded room.*

SIDS /ˌes aɪ diː ˈes/ n Sudden Infant Death Syndrome; a formal name for COT DEATH

siege /siːdʒ/ n 1 [C;U] an operation by an army surrounding a defended place and repeatedly attacking it, blocking its supplies, etc., in order to force the defenders to accept defeat: *a state of siege* | *the siege of Troy* | *The Greeks laid siege to* (=started a siege of) *Troy.* | *After many weeks the siege was raised.* (=came to an end) | (fig.) *Newspapermen laid siege to the flat where the murdered girl's mother was staying.* —see also BESIEGE   2 [C] a situation in which an armed criminal keeps people as prisoners in a building: *After an 18-hour siege, the police stormed the house and captured the gunman.*

Sieg·fried Line /ˈsiːgfriːd ˌlaɪn/ 1 the name given by the Germans to the line of defence that their armies were spread along in September 1918   2 a name given by the British to an area of the Western Front in the Second World War. There is a famous song that was sung by British soldiers in this war which begins "We're going to hang out our washing on the Siegfried Line..."

si·en·na /siˈenə/ n [U] earthy material which is brownish yellow (in the form of **raw sienna**), and reddish brown when burned (**burnt sienna**), used as colouring matter for paint

si·er·ra /siˈerə/ n [often pl.] a row, range, or area of sharply-pointed mountains: *hiking in the high sierras*

Si·er·ra Club /·ˈ·· ·ˌ·/ an American group that is concerned about the environment and which tries to influence Congress about environmental subjects. It is also a social club for people who like to walk in the mountains.

Sierra Le·one /siˌerə liˈəʊn/ a country in W Africa; capital Freetown; population 4,047,000 (1989) — **~ an** /-liˈəʊniən/ n, adj

Sierra Ma·dre /siˌerə ˈmɑːdreɪ/ a system of mountain ranges in Mexico

Sierra Ne·va·da /·ˌ··· ·ˈ·/ 1 also **Sierras**— a mountain range in California in the US —see colour map on pages 1374/5   2 a mountain range in S Spain

si·es·ta /siˈestə/ n a short sleep after the midday meal, as is the custom in many warm countries: *I think I'll have/take a short siesta.* —compare NAP[1]

sieve[1] /sɪv/ n a tool or container, made of a wire or plastic net on a frame, or of a solid sheet with holes, used for separating large and small solid bits, or solid things from liquid: *Put the soup through a sieve.* | (infml) *I'm afraid I've got a memory/mind like a sieve.* (=I easily forget things.)

sieve[2] v [T] 1 to put through a sieve: *Sieve the sauce to get the lumps out.*   2 [+obj+adv/prep, esp. OUT] to separate with a sieve: *You'll need to sieve out the stones from the soil.*

sift /sɪft/ v 1 [T] to put (something non-liquid) through a sieve, sifter, or net: *Sift the flour first.*   2 [I (**through**);T] to make a close and thorough examination of (things in a mass or group): *She sifted through her papers to find the lost letter.* | *We must sift the evidence very carefully before we come to any conclusions.*   3 [T+obj+adv/prep, esp. OUT, **from**] to separate, esp. by carefully examining: *It's hard to sift (out) the truth from the lies in this case.*

sift·er /ˈsɪftər/ n (often in comb.) a container with many small holes in the top, for scattering or cleaning powdery foods: *a flour sifter* —compare SHAKER

sigh[1] /saɪ/ v [I] 1 to let out a deep breath slowly and with a sound, usu. expressing sadness, tiredness, or satisfaction: *She sighed with relief/with despair.* | *He thought of all the opportunities he had missed, and sighed.*   2 (esp. of the wind) to make a sound like this   3 [(**for**)] lit to feel a mixture of sadness and fond desire, esp. about something past, far away, etc.; grieve: *sighing for her lost youth*

sigh[2] n an act or sound of sighing: *We all heaved/let out* (=made) **a sigh of relief** *when we heard that they were safe.*

sight[1] /saɪt/ n 1 [U] the power of seeing; EYESIGHT; VISION: *He lost his sight* (=was blinded) *in an accident.* | *He's got good sight for a man of his age.* | *Her sight is failing.* —see also SECOND SIGHT   2 [S;U(of)] the seeing of something: *The crowd waited for a sight of the Queen passing by.* | *The house is hidden from sight behind trees.* (=you cannot see it) | *I always faint at the sight of* (=when I see) *blood.* | *I caught sight of* (=saw for a moment) *my old friend in town today.* | *I saw her for a moment but then lost sight of her* (=could no longer see her) *in the crowd.* | (fig.) *I can't bear/stand the sight of her.* (=I dislike her very much) | **At first sight** (=when seen or considered for the first time) *it looked like a simple accident, but later the police became suspicious.*   3 [C] something that is seen: *What a beautiful sight those roses make!* | *the familiar sight of the postman going along the street*   4 [U] presence in one's view; the range of what can be seen: *She's too careful with her children — she never lets them out of her sight.* | *The boat was within sight of land.* | *The train came round the bend into sight.* | *Keep out of sight!* (=make sure no one sees you) | (fig.) *Peace is now in sight.* (=likely to come soon) | (fig.) *The strike has now lasted six months, and there is still no end in sight.* —see also LINE OF SIGHT   5 [C usu. pl.] something worth seeing, esp. a place visited by tourists: *to see the sights of London* —see also SIGHTSEEING   6 [C often pl.] a part of an instrument or weapon which guides the eye in aiming: *To aim, line up the front and rear sights on the gun.* | *I had the deer in my sights, but it moved before I could fire.* —see picture at GUN   7 [S] infml something which looks very bad or makes people laugh: *What a sight you are, with paint all over your clothes!* | *This room looks a sight. It's the untidiest place I've ever seen!*   8 [S] infml a lot; a great deal: *This car is costing me a darn sight more to run than I expected.* | *It's a jolly sight wetter this summer than last.*   9 **at/on sight** as soon as seen or shown, without delay: *The guard had orders to shoot on sight.* (=without finding out who was there)   10 **by sight** by recognition, not by personal knowledge of someone: *I only know her by sight.*   11 **in the sight of** lit in the judgment or opinion of: *We are all equal in the sight of God.*   12 **out of sight** esp. AmE extremely good: *That curry you made was really out of sight.*   13 **out of sight, out of mind** something that is not seen is soon forgotten: *If you don't want Billy to break that toy, put it away; out of sight, out of mind.*   14 **set one's sights (on)** aim (at); direct one's efforts (towards): *"She's set her sights on becoming a secretary." "I would have thought she could have set her sights a bit higher than that."*   15 **sight for sore eyes** infml a person or thing that one is glad to see at last; a welcome sight   16 **sight unseen** without a chance of seeing or examining: *I bought the antique books sight unseen.* —see also **lose sight of** (LOSE)

sight[2] v [T] to get a view of, esp. after a time of looking; see for the first time: *The sailors gave a shout when they sighted land.* | *Several rare birds have been sighted in this area.*

sight·ed /ˈsaɪtɪd/ adj (of a person) able to see; not blind —see also CLEAR-SIGHTED, FARSIGHTED, LONGSIGHTED, SHORTSIGHTED

sight·ing /ˈsaɪtɪŋ/ n a case of someone or something being sighted: *There have been several sightings of these rare birds/of the escaped murderer in this area.*

sight·less /ˈsaɪtləs/ adj lit or tech unable to see; blind

sight-read /ˈsaɪt riːd/ v **sight-read** /ˈsaɪt red/ [I;T] to play or sing (written music) when one looks at it for the first time, without practice — **~ er** /ˈsaɪt ˌriːdər/ n — **~ ing** n [U]

sight screen /ˈ· ·/ n (in cricket) a large, usu. white, movable SCREEN placed at the edge of a cricket field behind the BOWLER and used to help the BATSMAN see the ball more clearly

sight·see·ing /ˈsaɪtˌsiːɪŋ/ n [U] the visiting of famous or interesting places, esp. by tourists: *Some people like to lie on the beach, but I prefer (to go) sightseeing.* | *a sightseeing holiday* —see also SIGHT[1] (5)

sight·se·er /ˈsaɪtˌsiːər/ n a person who goes sightseeing

sign[1] /saɪn/ n 1 [C(of)] a standard mark; something which is seen and represents a generally-known meaning; SYMBOL: *Crowns, stars, and stripes are signs of military rank.* | *The number –5 begins with the sign –, the* **minus sign.** | *Written music uses lots of signs, like mf, mt, and ms.*   2 [C] a movement of the body intended to express a particular meaning or command; signal: *Don't ring the bell yet; wait until I give the sign.* [+*to-v*|*that*] *She put her finger to her lips as a sign to be quiet*|*a sign that we should be quiet.* **3** [C] a notice giving information, warning, directions, etc.: *Pay attention to the traffic*|*road signs.* | *Can't you read that sign? It says "No Smoking".* **4** [(of)] something that shows or points to the presence or likely future existence of a particular condition, fact or quality: *Swollen ankles can be a sign of heart disease.* | *The new tough laws are being interpreted as a sign of the government's determination to tackle this problem.* | *The economy is* **showing signs of** *improvement*|**showing every sign of** *improvement.* | [+(*that*)] *There are signs that the economy is improving.* | *Her irritable behaviour is* **a sure sign** *that she's worried about something.* | *I looked all over the place, but there was* **no sign of** (=I could not see) *him anywhere.* | *I could see* **no sign of life** *in the deserted town.* | **Signs are** (=we expect) *that he'll be back this evening.* **5** [C] a STAR SIGN any of the 12 divisions of the year represented by groups of stars: *Which sign (of the zodiac) were you born under?* – see ZODIAC (USAGE), and see picture at ZODIAC **6** [C] *esp. bibl* a wonderful act of God; MIRACLE **7** [U] *AmE infml* for SIGN LANGUAGE: *Do you know sign?* **8 a sign of the times** *usu. derog* something that is typical of the (bad) way things are just now: *Beer at £2 a pint! Ah well, I suppose it's a sign of the times.* **9 the sign of the cross** a hand movement down and across the chest in the shape of the CROSS[1] (3), done e.g. as a sign of respect in front of the ALTAR, or to guard oneself against evil (CROSS[1])

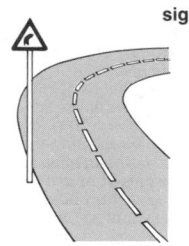

sign

sign² *v* [I;T] **1** to write (one's name) on (a written paper), esp. for official purposes, to show one's agreement, show that one is the writer, etc.: *Sign here, please.* | *The documents are ready to be signed.* | *He signed (his name on) the cheque.* | *Britain has just signed a new trade agreement with Japan.* (=has reached an agreement and made it formally complete by signing a paper) **2** *esp. BrE* to start to employ or be employed, esp. in football, by signing a contract: *The local football team has signed a new goalkeeper; he has* **signed for**/**with** *the local team.* | *The record companies are looking for new groups to sign.* **3** *esp. AmE* to use SIGN LANGUAGE: *Is the governor's speech going to be signed?* | *I can't sign fast enough to keep up with him.* **4 sign on the dotted line** *infml* to agree to something quickly and unconditionally – ~ **er** *n*

sign sthg. ↔ **away** *phr v* [T] to give up (ownership, a claim, a right, etc.) formally, esp. by signing a paper: *She signed away her share in the property.*

sign for sthg. *phr v* [T] to sign one's name to show that one has received (something): *Certain kinds of mail have to be signed for when they are delivered.*

sign in *phr v* [I] to record one's name when arriving: *Visitors to the club should sign in at the entrance.* – opposite **sign out**

sign off *phr v* [I] **1** (of a radio or television station) to stop broadcasting, esp. at the end of the day **2** to end an informal letter, esp. with a signature: *"I'd better sign off now. Love, John."*

sign on *phr v* **1** [I;T (=**sign** sbdy. ↔ **on**)] to (cause to) join a working force, by signing a paper: *He signed on as a sailor.* **2** [I] *BrE* to give notice officially to the government that one has become unemployed, or that one is still unemployed, so that one is allowed to receive BENEFIT: *She's been signing on for the last six months.*

sign out *phr v* [I] **1** to record one's name when leaving – opposite **sign in** **2** [T] (**sign** sthg. ↔ **out**) to record the removal or borrowing of: *to sign out a book from the library*

sign sthg. ↔ **over** *phr v* [T (**to**)] to give (one's rights, ownership, etc.) formally to someone else esp. by signing a paper: *Grandmother has signed the farm over to my brother.*

sign to sbdy. *phr v* [T] to make a movement as a sign to: [+*obj*+*to-v*] *I signed to the waiter to bring us the bill.*

sign up *phr v* [I;T (=**sign** sbdy. ↔ **up**) (**for**)] to (cause to) sign an agreement to take part in something, or to take a job; ENLIST: *There was an attempt to sign up more* men for the police force, but not many signed up. [+*to-v*] *I've signed up to take a course at the local college.*

sig·nal¹ /ˈsɪɡnəl/ *n* **1** something intended to warn, command, or give a message, such as a special sound or action: *A red lamp is often used as a danger signal.* | *She made a signal with her arm for a left turn.* | (fig.) *This opinion poll is a clear signal to the President that the voters do not support his foreign policy.* – see also SMOKE SIGNAL **2** [(for)] an action which causes something else to happen: *Don't start yet – wait for the signal.* [+*to-v*] *When I look at my watch, it's a signal (for us) to leave.* **3** a railway apparatus next to the track, usu. of green, yellow, and red lights, to tell train drivers whether they can go ahead or must stop: *The train must stop when the signal's (on) red.* **4** a sound, image, or message sent by waves, as in radio or television: *We live too far from the city to get a strong television signal.* | *The navy has picked up a radar signal from the missing boat.*

signal² *v* **-ll-** *BrE* ‖ **-l-** *AmE* **1** [I (**to, for**)] to give a signal: *She was signalling wildly, waving her arms.* | *The general signalled to his officers for the attack to begin.* **2** [T] to express, warn, or tell (as if) by a signal or signals: *Both sides have signalled their willingness to start negotiations.* [+*obj*+*to-v*] *The policeman signalled the traffic to move forward slowly.* [+(*obj*+) *that*] *The thief signalled (his friend) that the police were coming.* **3** [T] to be a clear sign or proof of; MARK: *The defeat of 1066 signalled the end of Saxon rule in England.*

signal³ *adj* [A] *fml* very noticeable; not ordinary; CONSPICUOUS: *a signal achievement* | *the minister's signal failure to deal with this matter.* – – **ly** *adv* : *The minister has signally failed to deal with this matter.*

signal box /ˈ··· ·/ *BrE* ‖ **signal tow·er** /ˈ··· ˌ··/*AmE* – *n* a small raised building near a railway from which the signals and POINTS (1) are controlled

sig·nal·ize also **-ise** *BrE* /ˈsɪɡnəlaɪz/ *v* [T *usu. pass.*] *fml* to make noticeable or different; DISTINGUISH: *Her work is signalized by great attention to detail.*

sig·nal·man /ˈsɪɡnəlmən/ *n* **-men** /mən/ **1** *esp. BrE* someone who controls railway traffic and signals **2** also **sig·nal·ler** /ˈsɪɡnələ^r/– a member of the army or navy trained in signalling

sig·na·to·ry /ˈsɪɡnətəri‖-tɔːri/ *n* [(**to, of**)] any of the signers of an agreement, esp. among nations: *Most western nations are signatories to*|*of this treaty.*

sig·na·ture /ˈsɪɡnətʃə^r/ *n* **1** a person's name written by himself/herself, e.g. at the end of a letter, or on a cheque or official paper as a mark that the document is AUTHENTIC: *They returned her cheque because she hadn't put her signature on it.* –compare AUTOGRAPH[1] **2** the act of signing one's name: *Will you witness my signature?* –see also KEY SIGNATURE, TIME SIGNATURE

signature tune /ˈ··· ·/ *n* a short piece of music used regularly in broadcasting to begin and end a particular show or as the special mark of a radio station –compare THEME SONG

sign·board /ˈsaɪnbɔːd‖-bɔːrd/ *n* a board with a sign or notice on it esp. giving details of a future event or advertising a product

sig·net /ˈsɪɡnɪt/ *n* an object used for printing a small pattern in WAX as an official or private SEAL² (1), and often fixed to or part of a finger ring (a **signet ring**)

sig·nif·i·cance /sɪɡˈnɪfɪkəns/ *n* [S;U] *rather fml* the quality of being significant; importance, meaning, or value: *This new discovery of oil is of great significance to the country's economy.* | *Could you explain to me the significance of this part of the contract?* | *The peace talks have taken on a new significance now that there has been a change of leadership.* –opposite **insignificance**

sig·nif·i·cant /sɪɡˈnɪfɪkənt/ *adj* **1** of noticeable importance, effect, or influence: *There has been a significant improvement in the company's safety record.* | *This is one of the most significant studies of the subject.* | *significant changes in the employment laws* | *There has been no significant rainfall for weeks.* –opposite **insignificant** **2** having a special meaning, indirectly expressed: *a significant smile* | *It is significant that the government has not actually denied these rumours.* – – **ly** *adv* : *The police released him but, significantly, they didn't give him back his passport.*

significant oth·er /·ˌ··· ˈ··/ *n AmE infml or humor* one's husband, wife, or lover; a person that one has a marriage-like relationship with

sig·nif·i·ca·tion /ˌsɪgnɪfʌˈkeɪʃən/ n *fml or pomp* the intended meaning of a word; SENSE¹ (5)

sig·ni·fy /ˈsɪgnʌfaɪ/ v **1** [T] *fml* to be a sign of; represent; mean; DENOTE: *What does this strange mark signify?* | *His latest speech may signify a shift in his foreign policy.* [+*that*] *A fever usually signifies that there is something wrong with the body.* **2** [I;T] *fml* to make known (esp. an opinion) by an action: *Will those in favour of the suggestion please signify (their agreement) by raising their hands?* **3** [I;T *usu. in questions and negatives*] to matter; have importance (for): *What does it signify if you're rich or poor, as long as you're happy?* | *Never mind that mistake; it doesn't signify.*

sign·ing /ˈsaɪnɪŋ/ n *BrE* someone who has just signed a contract to play or perform, esp. in football: *McGregor, our latest signing, will play his first game next Saturday.*

sign lan·guage /ˈ· ˌ··/ n [U] a system of hand movements for expressing meanings, esp. as used by DEAF people

▶CULTURAL NOTE Though the US and Britain share a spoken language, the sign languages used by deaf people in the two countries are not the same.◀

Si·gnor /siːˈnjɔːʳ, ˈsiːnjɔːʳ/ n (used as a title for an Italian-speaking man): *Signor Francatelli*

Si·gno·ra /siːˈnjɔːrə/ n (used as a title for a (married) Italian-speaking woman)

Si·gno·ri·na /ˌsiːnjɔːˈriːnə‖-njə-/ n (used as a title for an unmarried Italian-speaking girl)

sign·post¹ /ˈsaɪnpəʊst/ n a sign showing directions and distances, esp. at a place where roads meet: *follow the signposts* | *The signpost said "Bedford 2 miles".*

signpost

signpost² v [T] *esp. BrE* **1** [*usu. pass.*] to provide with signposts to guide the driver: *These country roads aren't very well signposted.* **2** to show clearly and unmistakably: *They have signposted their conclusions in the report.*

Si·ha·nouk /ˈsiːənuːk/, **Prince Nor·o·dom** /ˌnɒrəˈdɒm‖ˌnɔːrəˈdɑːm/ (1922–) the ruler of Cambodia during many of the years from 1941, under titles including king, PRIME MINISTER, and head of state. Starting in 1982 he led the government in EXILE of Cambodia. He returned to his country in 1991.

Sikes /saɪks/, **Bill** a violent thief who murders his girlfriend in Charles Dickens' book *Oliver Twist*

Sikh /siːk / n a member of a religion (**Sikhism**) that developed from Hinduism in the 16th century to become a completely separate religion which is important in modern India. Male Sikhs usu. have beards and wear TURBANS.

si·lage /ˈsaɪlɪdʒ/ n [U] grass or other plants cut and stored in a SILO away from air for preservation as winter food for cattle

Sil·bu·ry Hill /ˌsɪlbəri ˈhɪl‖-beri/ a MOUND of late NEOLITHIC times near Avebury in S England

si·lence¹ /ˈsaɪləns/ n **1** [U] absence of sound; complete quiet: *There was nothing but silence in the empty house.* | *The silence was broken by a loud cry.* **2** [U] the state of not speaking or making a noise: *She received the bad news* **in silence.** | *Her forceful arguments* **reduced** *her opponents* **to silence.** (=they could not reply) **3** [U (**on**)] failure to mention a particular thing, esp. when unexpected or difficult to explain: *I can't understand the government's silence on such an important matter.* **4** [U] failure to write a letter, to telephone, etc.: *After two years' silence he suddenly got in touch with us again.* **5** [C] a moment or period of any of these conditions: *We observed a one-minute silence in memory of the war dead.* | *His offensive remarks were followed by an embarrassed silence.* | *There were long unexplained silences between her letters.* **6 silence is golden** *saying* it is good to be completely quiet –see also CONSPIRACY OF SILENCE

silence² v [T] **1** to cause or force to stop making a noise:

He silenced the noisy children with a fierce look. | *The enemy's guns were silenced* (=prevented from firing) *by repeated bombings.* **2** to force to stop expressing opinions, making opposing statements, etc.: *The president silenced his opponents by having them put in prison.*

si·lenc·er /ˈsaɪlənsəʳ/ n an apparatus for reducing noise, such as **a** a part for fitting round the end of the barrel of a small gun **b** *BrE* ‖ **muffler** *AmE*– a part of a petrol engine which fits onto the EXHAUST pipe (=where burnt gases come out)

si·lent /ˈsaɪlənt/ adj **1** free from noise; quiet: *the silent hours of the night* | *The old house was quite silent.* | *When it is operating, this dishwasher is almost silent.* **2** not speaking or using spoken expression: *a silent prayer* | *silent reading* **3** [(**on**)] making no statement; failing or refusing to express an opinion, decision, etc.: *The law is silent on this difficult point.* | *If you are arrested you have a right to remain silent.* **4** (of a letter in a word) not having a sound; not pronounced: *The "w" in "wreck" is silent.* **5 silent as the grave** completely silent, perhaps suggesting mystery – ~ **ly** adv

silent film /ˌ·· ˈ·/ n also **silent** *BrE infml* ‖ **silent mov·ie** /ˌ·· ˈ··/ *esp. AmE*– a film with no sound, esp. a black and white film made before 1927 and starring (STAR') people such as Charlie Chaplin, Buster Keaton, and Rudolph Valentino. People's movements in them appear sudden and not at all smooth. A few words appeared on the screen to help people follow the story, and a piano was usu. played in the cinema when they were shown. – compare TALKIE

silent ma·jor·i·ty /ˌ··· ·ˈ···/ n [*the*] *esp. AmE* most of the people in a country, thought of as quietly accepting and supporting the actions of the government

Silent Night /ˌ··· ˈ·/ the title of and first words of a popular Christmas song (CAROL), originally written in German and now sung in many languages

silent part·ner /ˌ··· ˈ··/ n *AmE for* SLEEPING PARTNER

sil·hou·ette¹ /ˌsɪluˈet/ n a dark image, shadow, or shape, seen against a light background: *When she switched on the light her silhouette appeared on the curtain.* | *I saw the silhouette of the tower against the dawn sky.*

silhouette

silhouette² v [T (**against, on**)] *usu. pass.*] to cause to appear as a silhouette: *The birds were silhouetted against the bright sky.*

sil·i·ca /ˈsɪlɪkə/ n [U] a chemical compound that is found naturally as sand, QUARTZ, and FLINT and is used in making glass

sil·i·cate /ˈsɪlɪkeɪt, -kʌt/ n [C;U] *tech* any of a large group of very common solid mineral substances

sil·i·con /ˈsɪlɪkən/ n [U] a simple substance (ELEMENT) that is not metal and is found in combined forms in nature in great quantities

silicon chip /ˌ··· ˈ·/ n a CHIP¹ (6) in a computer or other ELECTRONIC machinery

Silicon Val·ley /ˌ··· ˈ··/ a part of California, largely around San Francisco and San Jose, famous for the invention and production of computers and SILICON CHIPS

sil·i·cone /ˈsɪlʌkəʊn/ n [U] any of a group of chemicals that are unchanged by heat and cold, and are used in making types of rubber, oil, and RESIN (2)

silicone im·plant /ˌ··· ·ˈ··/ n a piece of silicone that is put into the body, esp. during COSMETIC SURGERY. The most common type of silicone implant is one put into a woman's breast to make it appear larger. There has recently been some disagreement among doctors as to whether these implants may have a harmful effect on the body.

sil·i·co·sis /ˌsɪlʌˈkəʊsʌs/ n [U] a lung disease, esp. among miners, stonecutters, etc., caused by breathing of SILICA dust over long periods –compare BLACK LUNG, PNEUMOCONIOSIS

silk /sɪlk/ n **1** [U] (smooth soft cloth made from) fine thread which is produced by a silkworm: *a dress made of the finest silk* | *artificial silk* | *a silk blouse/kimono*

▶CULTURAL NOTE Silk is an expensive material, and clothes or other objects made of silk are considered to be beautiful and to suggest that the owner is rich.◀

2 [C] *BrE tech* a KC or QC **3 take silk** *BrE tech* to become a K.C. or Q.C. —see also SILKS **4 you can't make a silk purse from/out of a sow's ear** nothing good can be made from material that is bad, or of poor quality

silk·en /ˈsɪlkən/ *adj lit* **1** soft, smooth, and shiny like silk; silky: *silken hair* **2** made of silk: *silken garments*

Silk Road /ˈ· ˌ·/ [*the*] an ancient ROUTE along which silk was carried from China through Asia to the Eastern Mediterranean and Europe

silks /sɪlks/ *n* [U;P] the coloured shirts worn by JOCKEYs

silk screen /ˈ· ˈ·◂/ *n* [U] a way of printing on a surface by forcing paint or ink onto it through a specially prepared stretched piece of cloth

silk·worm /ˈsɪlkwɜːm‖-wɜːrm/ *n* a CATERPILLAR (=type of young insect) which produces a COCOON (=a covering for its body) of silk

silk·y /ˈsɪlki/ *adj* like silk; soft, smooth and shiny; fine: *the cat's fine silky fur* | *silky hair* | (fig.) *a silky voice* —**ily** *adv* —**iness** *n* [U]

sill /sɪl/ *n* the flat piece at the base of an opening or frame, esp. a window —see also WINDOWSILL

sil·la·bub /ˈsɪləbʌb/ *n* SYLLABUB

Sills /sɪlz/, **Bev·er·ly** /ˈbevəli ‖ -ər-/ (1929–   ) an American OPERA singer and actress

sil·ly[1] /ˈsɪli/ *adj* **1** having or showing a lack of good sense and judgment; foolish; not serious or sensible: *It's silly to go out in the rain if you don't have to.* | *How silly of me! I've left my key at home.* | *He's called Algernon? What a silly name!* | *a silly-looking hat* | *That's the silliest idea I've ever heard!* **2** [F] *infml* unable to think or feel clearly; senseless: *I took a swing at him and knocked him silly.* | *After-dinner speeches bore me silly.* (=very much) **3** (of a fielding (FIELD[2] (1)) position in cricket) in front of and dangerously near the BATSMAN: *silly mid-off* —**liness** *n* [U]

silly[2] also **silly bil·ly** /ˈ·· ˌ··/— *n infml* a silly person; a word used especially when talking to children: *No, silly, I didn't mean that!*

silly sea·son /ˈ·· ˌ··/ [*the*] *infml, esp. BrE* a period in the summer when there is less political news than usual, and so newspapers print silly stories about unimportant things: *The silly season must be upon us when a letter from Professor Anthony Field is devoted to hamburgers in Hampstead.*

si·lo /ˈsaɪləʊ/ *n* **-los** **1** a round tower-like enclosure on a farm for storing winter food for cattle **2** a large underground enclosure used **a** as a base from which a large MISSILE can be fired **b** for storing e.g. winter food or FUEL

silt[1] /sɪlt/ *n* [U] loose sand, mud, soil, etc., carried in running water and then dropped, e.g. at the entrance to a harbour, by a bend in a river, etc.

silt[2] *v*
    silt up *phr v* [I;T] (=**silt** sthg. ↔ **up**)] to fill or become filled with silt: *The old harbour silted up years ago; it's now all silted up.*

sil·van /ˈsɪlvən/ *adj esp. lit* SYLVAN

sil·ver[1] /ˈsɪlvəʳ/ *n* **1** [U] a soft whitish precious metal that is a simple substance (ELEMENT), carries electricity very well, can be brightly polished, and is used in jewellery, coins, and knives, forks, etc.: *hallmarked silver* **2** [U] coins made of silver or a similar metal, and not of copper: *All I've got is a £5 note and about a pound in silver.* **3** [U] spoons, forks, dishes, etc., for the table, made of silver or a similar metal: *to polish the silver* **4** [C] a SILVER MEDAL **5 sell off the family silver** to sell a valuable ASSET (=piece of property), which ought to be kept for future use, for less than its real value in order to get money quickly and easily. The phrase was used a lot in the 1980s in speaking of the government's PRIVATIZATION of companies formerly owned by the state. **6 thirty pieces of silver** (in the Bible) the payment that Judas received for betraying (BETRAY) Jesus. The expression is sometimes used to describe money that someone receives for a disloyal action.

silver[2] *adj* **1** made of silver: *polished silver forks* | *Is your ring silver?* —see also SILVER SPOON **2** of the colour of silver: *a silver-haired old man*

silver[3] *v* [T] *tech* to cover with a thin shiny silver-coloured surface so as to make a mirror

Silver[1] the name of the Lone Ranger's horse. The Lone Ranger used to cry out "Hi ho Silver away!" before galloping (GALLOP) away on him. —see also LONE RANGER

Silver[2], **Long John** see LONG JOHN SILVER

silver an·ni·ver·sa·ry /ˌ·· ··ˈ···/ *n AmE* SILVER WEDDING

silver birch /ˌ·· ˈ·/ *n* the common BIRCH tree, which has a silvery-white trunk and branches

silver cer·tif·i·cate /ˈ·· ·ˌ···/ *n* the former official name of US paper money, when there was a quantity of silver held by the government worth the value represented

silver dol·lar /ˌ·· ˈ··/ *n* a former US one dollar coin, now collected and valuable because of its high silver content

sil·ver·fish /ˈsɪlvəfɪʃ‖-ər-/ *n* **-fish** *or* **-fishes** a small silver-coloured wingless insect which is found in houses and which sometimes damages paper and cloth

silver ju·bi·lee /ˌ·· ˈ···/ *n* the date that is exactly 25 years after the date of a particular important event: *to celebrate the Queen's Silver Jubilee* —compare DIAMOND JUBILEE, GOLDEN JUBILEE

silver lin·ing /ˌ·· ˈ···/ *n* an unexpected good side or good result of a bad or unfortunate happening (from a phrase **every cloud has a silver lining**): *However much gloom and doom might appear the order of the day in the current business world, there is invariably a silver lining somewhere doing its best to break through the depression.*

silver med·al /ˌ·· ˈ··/ also **silver-** *n* a MEDAL of silver given to the person who comes second in a race or competition —see also BRONZE MEDAL, GOLD MEDAL

silver pa·per /ˌ·· ˈ··◂/ also **silver foil** /ˌ·· ˈ·◂/— *n* [U] paper with one bright metallic surface, used e.g. in packets for cigarettes or food

silver plate /ˌ·· ˈ·◂/ *n* [U] metal with a thin outer surface of silver — **-plated** /ˌ·· ˈ··◂/ *adj* : *a silver-plated spoon*

Sil·vers /ˈsɪlvəz‖-vərz/, **Phil** /fɪl/ (1912–85) an American actor and COMEDIAN best remembered for playing the part of Sergeant Bilko —see also Sergeant BILKO

silver screen /ˌ·· ·ˈ·/ *n* [*the*] the film industry: *Chaplin and other stars of the silver screen*

sil·ver·smith /ˈsɪlvəˌsmɪθ‖-ər-/ *n* a person who makes things out of silver

silver spoon /ˌ·· ·ˈ·/ *n* **born with a silver spoon in one's mouth** to be born into a very wealthy family: *She was born with a silver spoon in her mouth, so she has no idea how most people live.*

Sil·ver·stone /ˈsɪlvəstəʊn‖-vər-/ a motor racing CIRCUIT (1) in Northamptonshire in England

silver-tongued /ˌ·· ·ˈ·◂/ *adj esp. lit* able to give fine persuading speeches; ELOQUENT

sil·ver·ware /ˈsɪlvəweəʳ‖-vər-/ *n* [U] **1** things made of silver, esp. knives, spoons, dishes, etc. **2** *AmE* CUTLERY made of any metal

silver wed·ding /ˌ·· ˈ···/— also **silver wed·ding an·ni·versa·ry** *BrE* /ˌ·· ··ˈ···,····‖ **silver anniversary** *esp. AmE*— *n* the date that is exactly 25 years after the date of a wedding and on which people usually celebrate. It is customary to give people who have been married for 25 years presents made of silver. —compare DIAMOND WEDDING, GOLDEN WEDDING

sil·ver·y /ˈsɪlvəri/ *adj* **1** like silver in shine and colour **2** *esp. lit* having a pleasant metallic or musical sound: *silvery bells* | *peals of silvery laughter*

Sim /sɪm/, **Al·as·tair** /ˈæləsteəʳ/ (1900–76) a Scottish stage and film actor

Si·me·non /ˈsiːmənɒn‖ˌsiːməˈnɔːn/, **Georges** /ʒɔːʒ‖ʒɔːrʒ/ (1903–89) a French writer esp. of DETECTIVE stories. His most famous character is the detective Inspector Maigret —see also MAIGRET

sim·i·an /ˈsɪmiən/ *adj, n tech* (of or like) a monkey or APE

sim·i·lar /ˈsɪmələʳ, ˈsɪmɪləʳ/ *adj* **1** [(to)] like or alike; of the same kind; almost but not exactly the same in nature or appearance: *He was advised not to eat bread, cake, and other similar foods.* | *We have similar opinions; my opinions are similar to hers.* | *These two signatures are very similar; can you tell them apart?* | *My train was 20 minutes late in the morning and there was a similar delay in the evening.* **2** [no comp.] *tech* exactly the same in shape but not size: *Similar triangles have equal angles.* —see also SIMILARLY; see SAME (USAGE)

sim·i·lar·i·ty /ˌsɪmɪˈlærɪti/ *n* [(**between**)] **1** [U] the quality of being alike or like something else; RESEMBLANCE: *How much similarity is there between the two religions?* | *What strikes me about his poetry is its similarity to Wordsworth's.* **2** [C] a point or quality in which things are similar: *The police say there are some similarities between this murder and one that happened last year.*

sim·i·lar·ly /ˈsɪmɪ̱ləli‖-ərli/ *adv* **1** in a similar way: *They were similarly dressed.* **2** as is similar: *Men must wear a jacket and tie; similarly, women must wear a skirt or dress, not trousers.*

sim·i·le /ˈsɪmɪli/ *n* [C;U] (the use of) an expression which describes one thing by directly comparing it with another (as in *as white as snow*), using the words **as** or **like** —compare METAPHOR

sim·mer¹ /ˈsɪməʳ/ *v* [I;T] to (cause to) cook gently in liquid at or just below boiling point: *The soup was left to simmer.* | (fig.) *The crowd was* **simmering with** *excitement* (=could hardly control its excitement) *as the two fighters stepped into the rɪng.* —see COOK (USAGE)
  simmer down *phr v* [I *often imperative*] *infml* to become calmer; control one's excitement: *Simmer down, Mary; it won't help to lose your temper.*

simmer² *n* [S] a heat just below boiling; condition of simmering: *Bring the vegetables to a simmer.*

sim·nel cake /ˈsɪmnəl ˌkeɪk/ *n* a rich cake formerly eaten on certain religious days esp. in Lancashire, NW England

Si·mon /ˈsaɪmən/, **Neil** /niːl/ (1927–) a US writer of COMIC plays and musical shows

Simon and Gar·fun·kel /ˌsaɪmən ənd gɑːˈfʌŋkəl‖-gɑːr-/ two American popular music singers, Paul Simon (1941–) and Art Garfunkel, who appeared together for many years. They separated in 1970 at the height of their success and have both been successful on their own. One of their best-known songs is *Bridge Over Troubled Water*.

Si·mone /sɪˈməʊn/, **Ni·na** /ˈniːnə/ (1933–) an American JAZZ singer and piano player known for her support of the CIVIL RIGHTS MOVEMENT in the US in the 1960s

Simon Says /ˌ·· ˈ·/ *n* [U] a game played usu. by children in which players do not perform the action suggested by the leader except when he/she says the words "Simon says" first: *"Simon says touch your nose."*

si·mo·ny /ˈsɪməni, ˈsaɪ-/ *n* [U] *derog* (in former times) the buying and selling of appointments in the Christian church

sim·pat·i·co /sɪmˈpætɪkəʊ/ *adj AmE infml* **1** (of a person) likable **2** in agreement: *He and I are simpatico about a lot of things.*

sim·per /ˈsɪmpəʳ/ *v* [I] to smile in a silly unnatural way; used especially of girls —**simper** *n* – ~**ingly** *adv*

sim·ple /ˈsɪmpəl/ *adj* **1** without decoration; plain; not ELABORATE: *a simple dress* | *simple but well-prepared food* | *Their buildings are constructed in a plain and simple style.* **2** easy to understand or do; not difficult: *a simple explanation* | *The plan sounds simple enough but it won't be so simple to put it into action.* | *a simple but effective solution to the problem* | *I wish we could offer you more money, but I'm afraid it's not as simple as that.* **3** consisting of only one thing or part, rather than a number of parts combined: *Bacteria are simple forms of life.* | *A knife is a simple tool.* | *A* **simple sentence** *has only one verb.* —compare COMPLEX¹ (3), COMPOUND² (2) **4** (of something non-physical) without anything added or mixed; pure: *She did it for the simple reason that she had no choice.* | *His motive was simple greed, nothing else.* | *The simple truth is, I don't know.* **5** making no claim to special qualities, abilities, or importance; natural or sincere: *I'm just a simple farmer.* | *a woman of simple tastes* | *simple faith* **6** easily tricked; foolish: *You may be joking but she's simple enough to believe you.* **7** [F] *euph, old use* weak-minded: *I'm afraid old Jack is a bit simple.* —see also SIMPLY

simple frac·ture /ˌ·· ˈ··/ *n med* a broken or cracked bone which does not cut through the surrounding flesh —compare COMPOUND FRACTURE

simple in·terest /ˌ·· ˈ··/ *n* [U] interest calculated on an original sum of money without adding in the interest

already earned —compare COMPOUND INTEREST

simple life /ˌ·· ˈ·/ *n* [*the*+S] *infml apprec* life without the problems of having many possessions, using modern machines, etc.

simple ma·chine /ˌ·· ·ˈ·/ *n tech* any of the several machine parts, such as the wheel, LEVER, screw, etc., of which all machinery is made

simple-mind·ed /ˌ·· ˈ··◂/ *adj* having little ability to think or understand, or little experience of the world: *The instructions are so easy I should think even the most simpleminded person could follow them.*

Simple Si·mon /ˌ·· ˈ··/ a foolish person who believes anything and everything (from the name of a foolish young man in a NURSERY RHYME)

sim·ple·ton /ˈsɪmpəltən/ *n old-fash* a weak-minded trusting person

sim·pli·ci·ty /sɪmˈplɪsɪti/ *n* [U] the quality of being simple: *She writes with a beautiful simplicity of style.* | *He believes everything with childlike simplicity.* | *For the sake of simplicity* (=to make it easy to understand) *the tax form is divided into three sections.* | *The plan was* **simplicity itself** (=very simple); *how could it fail?*

sim·pli·fy /ˈsɪmplɪ̱faɪ/ *v* [T] to make plainer, easier, or less full of detail: *Try to simplify your explanation for the children.* | *an attempt to simplify the tax laws* —compare COMPLICATE (1); see also OVERSIMPLIFY —**fication** /ˌsɪmplɪ̱fɪˈkeɪʃən/ *n* [C;U]

sim·plis·tic /sɪmˈplɪstɪk/ *adj derog* treating difficult matters as if they were simple; tending to OVERSIMPLIFY: *This is a very complex problem, and we won't get anywhere with such simplistic solutions.* – ~**ally** /kli/ *adv*

sim·ply /ˈsɪmpli/ *adv* **1** in a simple way; easily, plainly, clearly, or naturally: *On her small income they live very simply.* | *To put it simply* (=to explain it in a simple way), *the new proposals mean that the average worker will be about 10% better paid.* **2** just; only: *I don't like driving; I do it simply because I have to get to work each day.* | *I'm afraid I simply don't know.* **3** *infml* really; very (much): *What a simply gorgeous day it is today!*

Simply Red /ˌ·· ˈ·/ a British band which plays popular music. Their main singer is **Mick Hucknall**.

Simp·son¹ /ˈsɪmpsən/, **Bart** /bɑːt‖bɑːrt/ the boy from the CARTOON family the Simpsons. He is a TROUBLEMAKER who often rides a SKATEBOARD and has various phrases which he typically uses, e.g. "Eat my shorts". —see also SIMPSONS

Simpson², O J (1947–) an American FOOTBALL (2) player who later became an actor

Simp·son³ /ˈsɪmpsən/, **Wal·lis** /ˈwɒlɪ̱s‖ˈwɑː-/ (1896–1986) the American-born woman, generally known as **Mrs Simpson**, who married Edward, Duke of Windsor (formerly Edward VIII). When they married she became the Duchess of Windsor —see also ABDICATION

Simp·sons /ˈsɪmpsənz/, **the** an American CARTOON family, Homer, Marge, Bart, Lisa, and baby Maggie. They are yellow with bulging (BULGE²) eyes, and the children have SPIKY heads. They are a fun-loving family with an attitude that many people, esp. older people, find rather offensive.

sim·u·la·crum /ˌsɪmjʊˈleɪkrəm/ *n* -**crums** or -**cra** /krə/ [(**of**)] *lit or fml* a likeness or representation

sim·u·late /ˈsɪmjʊ̱leɪt/ *v* **1** [T] *fml or tech* to give the effect or appearance of; IMITATE: *A sheet of metal was shaken to simulate the noise of thunder.* **2** to make a working model or representation of (a situation or process)

sim·u·lat·ed /ˈsɪmjʊ̱leɪtɪ̱d/ *adj fml or tech* made to look, feel, etc., like the real thing: *This coat is made of simulated fur; it's not real mink.* | *a simulated nuclear explosion*

sim·u·la·tion /ˌsɪmjʊ̱ˈleɪʃən/ *n* [C;U (**of**)] **1** *fml or tech* (a) representation; IMITATION **2** a model or representation of a course of events in business, science, etc., esp. by computer calculation to study the effects of possible future changes or decisions

sim·u·la·tor /ˈsɪmjʊ̱leɪtəʳ/ *n* an apparatus which allows a person in training to feel what real conditions are like, for example in traffic or in an aircraft, spacecraft, etc.: *a flight simulator*

sim·ul·cast /ˈsɪmʊlkɑːst‖ˈsaɪmʊlkæst/ *v* **simulcast** [T *usu. passive*] *AmE* to broadcast (a programme) on television and radio at the same time, so as to take advantage of the better sound quality on radio: *The concert is being simulcast live on Channel 11 and WFMT.* —**simulcast** *n*

sim·ul·ta·ne·ous /ˌsɪməl'teɪnɪəs◁‖ˌsaɪ-/ *adj* happening or done at exactly the same time: *There was a flash of lightning and a simultaneous crash of thunder.* | *a simultaneous broadcast of the concert on TV and radio* — ~ **ly** *adv*: *Two books on the same subject appeared simultaneously.* — ~ **ness, -ity** /ˌsɪməltə'niːʒti‖ˌsaɪ-/*fml*— *n* [U]

sin¹ /sɪn/ *n* **1** [C] an offence against God or a religious law: *The Bible says adultery is a sin.* | *the sin of pride* | *to commit a sin* —compare CRIME **2** [U] *fml* disobedience to God: *Which of us is without sin?* **3** [C] *infml, esp. humor* something that is regarded as wrong or shameful: *I think it's a sin, all this money they're wasting on the new leisure centre.* **4 for one's sins** *humor* (used for suggesting jokingly that something is rather like a punishment): *I'm the local party organizer, for my sins.* **5 the sins of the father** bad actions done by someone in the past, which cause trouble for someone else in the present **6 live in sin** *old-fash euph or humor* (of two unmarried people) to live together as if married —see also SEVEN DEADLY SINS **7 your sins will find you out** *saying* your bad actions will be discovered, and you will be punished for them. This phrase is often used humorously: *Haven't you answered his letter yet? You bad 'un, your sins will find you out!* — ~ **less** *adj*

sin² *v* **-nn-** [I (**against**)] to break God's laws; do wrong: *"We have sinned against you and against our fellow men."* (prayer) —see also SINNER

sin³ *abbrev. for:* SINE

Si·nai¹ /'saɪnaɪ/ the part of Egypt between the Gulf of Aqaba and the Gulf of Suez and the Suez Canal

Sinai², Mount the mountain in the Middle East on which, according to the Bible, Moses received the Ten Commandments from God

Si·na·tra /sɪ'nɑːtrə/, **Frank** (1915–) an American popular music singer and film actor. He first became successful as a singer with big bands in the 1940s. One of his most famous songs is *My Way*. He is one of the best-known and most successful popular singers of the 20th century, and is sometimes called **"Old Blue Eyes"** by people who like him very much. People sometimes joke that someone has "retired (RETIRE) more times than Frank Sinatra", because Sinatra has said that he is retiring several times but has always returned to making public performances. —see colour picture on page 554

Sin·bad /'sɪnbæd/ see SINDBAD

since¹ /sɪns/ *adv* (used with the present perfect or past perfect tenses) **1** at a time between then and now: *Her husband died ten years ago but she has since remarried.* | *I saw him on Wednesday, but I haven't spoken to him since.* | *The 1948 election was unlike any other election, before or since.* **2** from then until now: *He came to England three years ago and has lived here* **ever since.** **3** before now; ago: *I've* **long since** *forgotten what our quarrel was about.*

since² *prep* **1** (used with the present perfect or past perfect tenses) from (a point in past time) until now; during the period after: *I haven't seen her since last week/since her illness.* | *Until last week I hadn't seen her since 1973.* | *The book has sold over a million copies since its publication.* | *It's a long time since breakfast.* —compare FOR¹ (7) **2 since when** *AmE infml* (used in questions to express surprise and disapproval): *Since when do you eat with your elbows on the table?* | *Since when am I supposed to keep track of her every time she leaves the house?*

since³ *conj* **1** (used with the present perfect or past perfect tenses) **a** after the past time when: *It's been years since I enjoyed myself so much as last night.* | *When I met him last week, it was the first time we had seen each other since we were at school.* | *Since leaving Paris, we've visited Brussels and Amsterdam.* **b** continuously (and up to the present time) from the time when: *We've been friends* **(ever) since** *we met at school.* **2** as; as it is a fact that; because: *Since you can't answer the question, perhaps we'd better ask someone else.* | *He must have shut the door since he was the last one to leave.*

sin·cere /sɪn'sɪər/ *adj* (of a person, feelings, or behaviour) without any deceit or falseness; real, true, or honest; GENUINE: *a sincere apology* | *He has a sincere admiration for his opponent's qualities.* | *I don't think she was*

completely sincere in what she said. —opposite **insincere**

sin·cere·ly /sɪn'sɪəli‖-'sɪər-/ *adv* **1** in a sincere way; truly: *I sincerely hope your father will be well again soon.* | *a sincerely held belief* **2 Yours sincerely/Sincerely yours** (the usual polite way of ending a formal letter when addressing someone by their actual name) —see YOURS (USAGE)

sin·cer·i·ty /sɪn'serᶾti/ *n* [U] the quality of being sincere; honesty and lack of deceit: *I don't doubt her sincerity.* | *I may say* **in all sincerity** *that your support has been very valuable.* —opposite **insincerity**

Sin·clair¹ /'sɪŋkleər/, **Sir Clive** /klaɪv/ (1940–) an English inventor of electronic equipment, e.g. the first pocket television —see also SINCLAIR C5

Sinclair², Up·ton /'ʌptən/ (1878–1968) an American writer whose NOVELs, esp. *The Jungle*, about the meat industry, brought attention to injustices and wrongs in many areas of society

Sinclair C5 /ˌsɪŋkleə siː 'faɪv‖-kleər-/ *n tdmk* a small car for one person invented by Sir Clive Sinclair in 1985. It used a BATTERY and PEDALs, and never became very popular.

Sind·bad , Sinbad /'sɪnbæd/ also **Sindbad the Sail·or** /ˌ··
· '··/— the main character in a story from the *Arabian Nights*, who has many adventures at sea —see also ARABIAN NIGHTS, ROC, OLD MAN OF THE SEA

Sin·dy /'sɪndi/ also **Sindy doll** /'·· ˌ·/— *tdmk* (in Britain) a small toy DOLL in the shape of an attractive young woman which is very popular among young girls. She can be dressed in many different sets of clothes — compare BARBIE DOLL

sine /saɪn/ *n tech* the FRACTION (1) calculated for an angle by dividing the length of the side opposite it in a RIGHT-ANGLED TRIANGLE by the length of the side opposite the right angle —compare COSINE, TANGENT

si·ne·cure /'saɪnɪkjʊər, 'sɪn-/ *n often derog* a paid job with few or no duties

si·ne di·e /ˌsaɪni 'daɪ-iː, ˌsɪni 'diːeɪ/ *adv Lat tech* without fixing a date for a next meeting: *The meeting was adjourned sine die.*

sin·e qua non /ˌsɪni kwɑː 'nəʊn‖-'nɑːn/ *n* [(**for, of**)] *Lat fml* a necessary condition; what must exist or be had in order for something else to be possible: *A good knowledge of Italian is a sine qua non for the job in our Rome office.*

sin·ew /'sɪnjuː/ *n* [C;U] **1** *not tech* a strong cord in the body connecting a muscle to a bone; TENDON **2** also **sinews** *pl.— lit* means of strength or support: *the sinew(s) of our national defence*

sin·ew·y /'sɪnjuːi/ *adj* **1** (of meat) containing sinew; not easy to cut or eat **2** having strong muscles

sin·ful /'sɪnfəl/ *adj* **1** *esp. lit or bibl* being or guilty of sin; wicked: *a sinful deed/man* **2** *infml* seriously wrong or bad; REGRETTABLE: *a sinful waste of time and money* — ~ **ly** *adv* — ~ **ness** *n* [U]

sing¹ /sɪŋ/ *v* **sang** /sæŋ/, **sung** /sʌŋ/ **1** [I;T] to produce (music, musical sounds, songs, etc.) with the voice: *Birds sing loudest in the early morning.* | *We enjoy singing carols at Christmas.* [+*obj*(*i*)+*obj*(*d*)] *Sing us a song.* | *She sang her baby to sleep.* (=sang to make it go to sleep) **2** [I] to make or be filled with a high ringing sound: *My ears are still singing from the loud noise.* | *An enemy bullet sang past my ear.* **3** [I (**of**);T] *lit* to speak, tell about, or praise in poetry: *Poets sang the king's praises* (=praised him); *they sang of his brave deeds.*
  sing along *phr v* [I] to sing with someone: *Sing along if you know the words.*
  sing (sthg. ↔) **out** *phr v* [I;T] *infml* to shout or sing loudly: *Sing out if you think you know the answer.*

sing² *n AmE* an occasion of many people or CHOIRs singing together: *There will be an all-fraternity sing next Friday night.* —see also SING SING

sing. *written abbrev. for:* singular

Sing·a·pore /ˌsɪŋə'pɔː◁‖'sɪŋəpɔːr/ a country in SE Asia, well known as a business and COMMERCIAL centre; capital Singapore City; population 2,685,000 (1989)

Sing a song of six·pence /ˌ· · ˌ· · '··/ a well-known NURSERY RHYME (=old poem for children) which begins:
*Sing a song of sixpence, A pocket full of rye,
Four-and-twenty blackbirds, Baked in a pie.
When the pie was opened, The birds began to sing,
Now wasn't that a dainty dish, To set before the king?*

singe[1] /sɪndʒ/ v [T] to burn lightly on the surface or edge: *I'm afraid I've singed your shirt with the hot iron.* | *He got too near the fire and singed his beard.*

singe[2] n a slight burn; an act or mark of singeing

sing·er /'sɪŋər/ n a person who sings, esp. as a way of making money: *Placido Domingo, the famous opera singer* | *a pop singer* | *She's a good singer.*

Singer, I·saac Ba·shev·is /'aɪzək baː'ʃevɪs/ (1904–91) an American Jewish writer who won the Nobel Prize for Literature. He is best known for his short stories. He wrote in Yiddish but his work was translated into English and many other languages.

singer-song·writ·er /ˌsɪŋə 'sɒŋraɪtər‖ˌsɪŋər 'sɔːŋ-/ n a person who both sings and writes songs: *a concert by singer-songwriter Paul Simon*

Singh /sɪŋ/, **Vish·wa·nath Pra·tap** /'vɪʃwənaːt prə'taːp/ (1931–) an Indian politician, Prime Minister from 1989 after forming the **Janata Dal**, an opposition party

Sing·ha·lese /ˌsɪŋgə'liːz◂/ n SINHALESE

Sing·in' in the Rain /ˌsɪŋɪn ɪn ðə 'reɪn/ an American musical film made in 1952 with Gene Kelly. The film contains the famous song also called *Singin' in the Rain*. —see picture on page 685

sin·gle[1] /'sɪŋgəl/ adj **1** [A] being (the) only one: *The letter was written on a single sheet of paper.* | *A single tree gave shade from the sun.* | *His single aim was to make money.* | *Not a single one of her neighbours gave her any help.* **2** having only one part, quality, etc.; not double or MULTIPLE[1]: *For a strong sewing job use double, not single, thread.* | *A single flower has only one set of petals.* | *a single-sex school* (=for boys or girls only, not both) — compare DOUBLE[1] (1) **3** [A] separate; considered by itself; INDIVIDUAL: *Cigarette smoking is the single most important cause of lung cancer.* | *There's no need to write down every single word I say.* | *the highest price ever paid for a single work of art* | *It has cost us every single penny we've got.* (=all our money) —see also SINGLE PARENT **4** unmarried: *He's still single.* | *a single woman* —compare MARRIED **5** for the use of only one person: *a single bed* | *a single room in a hotel* (=with a bed for only one person) —compare DOUBLE[1] and see picture at BED (2) **6** BrE ‖ **one-way** AmE— (of a ticket or its cost) for a trip from one place to another but not back again —compare RETURN[3]; see also SINGLY

single[2] n **1** BrE a SINGLE[1] (6) ticket: *A second class single to London, please.* —compare RETURN[2] (5) **2** a record with only one short song on each side: *The group's latest single comes out on Friday.* | *a 12" single* —compare LP **3** [usu. pl.] an unmarried person: *a singles bar* (=where unmarried people can meet) **4 a** (in cricket) a single RUN[2] (10) **b** (in BASEBALL) a hit that allows the BATTER to reach first BASE[1] (6) **5** AmE a one dollar BILL: *Anybody got five singles?* —see also SINGLES

single[3] v
single sbdy./sthg. ↔ **out** phr v [T (for)] to separate or choose from a group, esp. for special treatment or attention: *They were all to blame; why single him out for punishment?*

single-breast·ed /ˌ··'··◂/ adj (of a coat or JACKET) fastened in the centre at the front with only one row of buttons —compare DOUBLE-BREASTED

single cream /ˌ··'·/ n [U] (in Britain) a cream that is thinner and lighter than DOUBLE CREAM and is suitable for pouring —compare DOUBLE CREAM

single cur·ren·cy /ˌ··'···/ n a CURRENCY (=type of money) that is shared by several or many, different countries. In Britain this is thought of in connection with the plans of some politicians in Europe to have only one type of money in the European Community: *paving the way for monetary union and a single currency*

single-deck·er /ˌ··'·◂/ n a bus with only one level – compare DOUBLE-DECKER

Single Eu·ro·pe·an Act /ˌ··ˌ···ˌ·'·/ [the] an agreement in 1986 between the heads of government of the countries of the European Community to allow free movement of people, goods, and services within the European Community

Single Eu·ro·pe·an Mar·ket /ˌ··ˌ···· '··/ also **single market**— [the] the free movement of goods and services between the countries of the European Community, beginning in 1992

single fig·ures /ˌ·· '··/ n [P] the numbers from 0 to 9: *Interest rates should drop to single figures in the New Year.*

single file /ˌ·· '·/ also **Indian file** old-fash— adv, n [U] (moving in) a line of people, vehicles, etc., one behind another: *We walked single file|in single file along the narrow passage.*

single-hand·ed /ˌ·· '··◂/ adj, adv [A] done by one person; working alone; without help from others: *a single-handed voyage across the Atlantic* | *He rebuilt his house single-handed.* ~**ly** adv

single hon·ours /ˌ·· '··/ n [U] BrE a degree course in which only one main subject is studied —compare JOINT HONOURS

single mar·ket /ˌ·· '··/ [the] see SINGLE EUROPEAN MARKET

single-mind·ed /ˌ·· '··◂/ adj having one clear aim or purpose: *She worked with single-minded determination, letting nothing distract her.* | *He's very single-minded about his work.* — ~**ly** adv — ~**ness** n [U]

sin·gle·ness /'sɪŋgəlnɪs/ n [U] fml the directing of all one's thoughts, efforts, etc., to a particular aim; CONCENTRATION: *He worked with great* **singleness of purpose** (=determination) *for his friend's election.*

single pa·rent /ˌ·· '··◂/ n a woman who no longer lives with the father of her children, or a man who no longer lives with the mother of his children, or a woman who has chosen to have a child on her own: *a single parent family*

sin·gles /'sɪŋgəlz/ n singles a match, esp. of tennis, played by one player against one other person —compare DOUBLES

singles bar /'·· ˌ·/ n a bar used esp. as a meeting place esp. for young, single people

sin·glet /'sɪŋglɪt/ n BrE a man's garment without SLEEVES worn as a VEST, or as an outer shirt when playing some sports

sin·gle·ton /'sɪŋgəltən/ n tech (in card games) a card that is the only one of its SUIT[1] (2) held by a player

Sin·gle·ton, Val·e·rie /'væləri/ (1937–) an English television and radio PRESENTER

single track road /ˌ··· '·/ n (in Britain) a road in some country areas such as the Scottish Highlands which is only wide enough for one car. A single track road usu. has passing places to allow cars going in opposite directions to pass each other and fast cars to get past slow cars going in the same direction.

single yel·low line /ˌ·· ˌ·· '·/ n (in Britain) a mark along the side of a road in a town which means that you can wait there for a short time but that you cannot park there —compare DOUBLE YELLOW LINES

sin·gly /'sɪŋgli/ adv separately; by itself or themselves; one by one: *Some guests came singly, others in groups.*

Sing Sing /'· ·/ a prison in New York, once widely known for its severe DISCIPLINE

sing·song /'sɪŋsɒŋ‖-sɔːŋ/ n **1** [S] a repeated rising and falling of the voice in speaking: *She talked in a strange singsong (voice).* **2** [C] BrE an informal gathering or party for singing songs

sin·gu·lar[1] /'sɪŋgjʊlər/ adj **1** of or being a word or form representing exactly one: *The noun "mouse" is singular; it is the singular form of "mice".* | *Collective nouns can be used with a singular or plural verb.* —compare PLURAL **2** fml very noticeable; unusually great: *a woman of singular beauty* | *He showed a singular lack of tact in the way he handled the situation.* **3** old-fash fml very unusual or strange; out of the ordinary —see also SINGULARLY

singular[2] n (a word in) a form representing only one: *"Trousers" has no singular; it can't be expressed in the singular.*

sin·gu·lar·i·ty /ˌsɪŋgjʊ'lærɪti/ n **1** [U] old-fash fml strangeness **2** [C] tech for BLACK HOLE **3** [C] a set of events which do not obey known laws of nature, such as those supposed to have happened at the BIG BANG, or inside a BLACK HOLE

sin·gu·lar·ly /'sɪŋgjʊləli‖-lərli/ adv fml **1** particularly; very (much): *a singularly beautiful woman* | *a singularly unsuccessful attempt to gain publicity* **2** old-fash strangely; in an unusual way

Sin·ha·lese /ˌsɪnhə'liːz◂/ also **Singhalese** – n **1** one of the peoples of Sri Lanka **2** a language of Sri Lanka – **Sinhalese** adj

sin·is·ter /ˈsɪnᵻstə⁰/ adj threatening, intending, or suggesting evil or unpleasantness: *In the shadows we could make out a sinister figure in a black cloak.* | *a sinister plot* | *(infml) There's a sinister-looking crack in the roof.*

sink¹ /sɪŋk/ v sank /sæŋk/or sunk /sʌŋk/, sunk 1 [I;T] a to go down below a surface, out of sight, or to the bottom (of water): *This rubber ball won't sink; it floats.* | *The ship hit a rock and sank with the loss of a hundred lives.* | *The moon sank below the hills.* | (fig.) *That actress you used to like seems to have* **sunk without trace.** (=disappeared completely from public notice) b to cause (esp. a ship) to sink: *The ship was sunk by an enemy torpedo.* | (fig., infml) *This lack of money could sink our plans* (=make them fail); *if we can't get some more investment we're sunk.* 2 [I] to fall to a lower level or position: *It was several days before the flood waters sank and life returned to normal.* 3 [I (to)] to get smaller; go down in number, value, strength, etc.: *The population of the island has sunk from a hundred to twenty.* | *The Bank of England took action to prevent the pound from sinking* (=losing value) *any further.* | *His voice sank to a whisper.* | (fig.) *How could you sink to (doing) this?* (=to such bad or dishonourable behaviour) 4 [I+adv/prep] to fall or pass uncontrollably into another state, esp. because of tiredness or lack of strength: *She fainted and sank to the ground.* | *He sank into the chair and fell asleep at once.* | *She sank into a deep sleep/into unconsciousness.* 5 [I] a to become weaker; fail; DETERIORATE: *The patient is* **sinking fast** *and may not live through the night.* b to lose confidence or hope: *My* **heart/spirits sank** *when I realized how much work I still had to do.* —see also SINKING FEELING 6 [I+adv/prep] to pass gradually into a worse condition; DECLINE: *a neglected inner-city area that has sunk further into poverty and decay* | *He sank into a deep depression.* | *Our hearts sank when we heard the news.* 7 [T] to make by digging into the earth: *We sank a well to try and find water.* | *to* **sink a mine shaft** 8 [T] to stop considering, esp. because of a more important aim; forget: *We've got to sink our differences/disagreements and fight our common enemy.* 9 [T (**in, into**)] to put (money, labour, etc.) into; INVEST: *I've sunk all my money into this business, so it had better succeed.* 10 [T] infml (in games like GOLF and SNOOKER) to cause (a ball) to go into a hole 11 **sink or swim** to fail or succeed without help from others: *He was left by his family to sink or swim by himself.* —see also SUNKEN, **rats deserting a sinking ship** (RAT¹) – – **able** adj

sink in phr v [I] 1 to enter a solid through the surface: *If the ink sinks in it'll be hard to remove the mark from the cloth.* 2 to become fully understood; get a firm place in the mind: *The news was such a shock, it still hasn't really sunk in yet.*

sink (sthg.) **into** sthg. phr v to put, force, or go below or into: *The dog sank its teeth into my leg.*

sink² n 1 a a large open container esp. in a kitchen, for washing pans, vegetables, etc., fixed to a wall and usu. with pipes to supply and carry away water: *The dirty dishes are in the sink.* —compare WASHBASIN, and see picture at KITCHEN b esp. AmE a WASHBASIN 2 [+of] esp. lit an evil place; DEN: *a sink of corruption* —see also **everything but the kitchen sink** (KITCHEN)

sink·er /ˈsɪŋkə⁰/ n a weight fixed to a fishing line or net to keep the end down under water —see also **hook, line, and sinker** (HOOK)

sinking feel·ing /ˈ·· ˌ··/ n [S] infml an uncomfortable feeling in the stomach caused by hunger or by fear or helplessness, esp. because something bad is about to happen —see also SINK¹ (5b)

sinking fund /ˈ·· ·/ n a sum of money saved by a government, company, etc., and added to regularly, for paying a debt at a future time

sin·ner /ˈsɪnə⁰/ n esp. lit or bibl a person who SINS; someone who has disobeyed God

Sinn Fein /ˌʃɪn ˈfeɪn/ an Irish political organization that wishes Northern Ireland to become part of the Republic of Ireland and supports the use of force against British rule there —see IRA

Sino- see WORD FORMATION

si·nol·o·gy /saɪˈnɒlədʒi‖-ˈnɑː-/ n [U] fml the study of Chinese language, history, literature, etc. **—gist** n

sin·u·ous /ˈsɪnjuəs/ adj twisting like a snake; full of curves; winding: *The river wound its sinuous way across the plain.* | *a dancer's sinuous grace* **—osity** /ˌsɪnjuˈɒsᵻti‖-ˈɑː-/ n [C;U] – – **ly** adv

si·nus /ˈsaɪnəs/ n any of the air-filled spaces in the bones of the face that have an opening into the nose: *I always get sinus trouble* (=a sinus infection) *in cold weather.*

Sioux /suː/ also **Dakota** n [C;the+P] (a member of) a Native American people of the area of the US that is now Minnesota and North and South Dakota —see NATIVE AMERICAN (CULTURAL NOTE)

sip¹ /sɪp/ v **-pp-** [I (**at**);T] to drink, taking only a little at a time into the front of the mouth: *I sipped at it suspiciously, not knowing what it was going to taste like.* | *She sipped her tea delicately.*

sip² n [(**of**)] a very small amount of a drink: *She took another sip of her tea.*

si·phon¹ , sy- /ˈsaɪfən/ n 1 a tube that is bent so that a liquid can be drawn upwards and then downwards through it to a lower level 2 a kind of bottle for holding SODA WATER and forcing it out by gas pressure: *a soda-siphon*

siphon² , sy- v [T (OFF, OUT)] to draw off or remove by means of a siphon: *The thieves had siphoned petrol out of my tank.* | (fig.) *We need a new road to siphon off some of the traffic from the town centre.*

sir /sə⁰; strong sɜː⁰/ n 1 (used respectfully when speaking to an older man or one of higher rank, e.g. to an officer by a soldier, to a male customer in a shop, or (BrE) to a male teacher by a school child): *"Report back to me in an hour, sergeant." "Yes, sir."* | *Are you being served, sir?* | (BrE) *Sir, can we go home now please?* —compare MADAM 2 **no sir!** AmE infml certainly not!: *I won't have any of that cheap plastic, no sir!*

Sir n 1 (a title used before the first name of a KNIGHT¹ (2) or BARONET): *Sir James Wilson* | *Sir James* (but not *Sir Wilson*) —see also ARISE, DUB 2 (used at the beginning of a formal letter, in such phrases as **Dear Sir(s)** or **My dear Sir**) —compare MADAM 3 BrE infml one's male teacher: *Look out – Sir's coming back!* —compare MISS³ (2)

sire¹ /saɪə⁰/ n 1 the father of a four-legged animal, esp. a horse —compare DAM³ 2 old use (used when speaking to a king): *The people await you, sire.*

sire² v [T] (esp. of a horse) to be the father of: *This horse has sired several race winners.*

si·ren /ˈsaɪərən/ n 1 an apparatus for making a loud long warning sound, as used on ships, police cars, and fire engines and for air-attack warnings: *factory/police sirens* —compare HORN¹ 2 a (in ancient Greek literature) any of a group of woman-like creatures whose sweet singing caused sailors to sail towards them and caused the wreck of their ships b a dangerous beautiful woman; used esp. in newspapers: *screen/Hollywood sirens like Marilyn Monroe* | *a sultry blonde sex siren*

Sir·han Sir·han /sɜːˌhɑːn sɜːˈhɑːn‖sɜːrˌhæn sɜːrˈhæn/ (1944–) the man who murdered Robert Kennedy

sir·loin /ˈsɜːlɔɪn‖ˈsɜːr-/ also **sirloin steak** /ˌ·· ˈ·/– n [C;U] (a piece of) BEEF cut from the best part of the lower back. Sirloin is usually expensive and therefore considered by some people as a special meal.

si·roc·co /sᵻˈrɒkəʊ‖-ˈrɑː-/ n **-cos** a hot wind blowing from the desert of N Africa across to southern Europe

sir·rah /ˈsɪrə/ n old use (an angry disrespectful way of addressing a man)

Sir Win·ston Chur·chill /sə ˌwɪnstən ˈtʃɜːtʃᵻl‖sər-, -ˈtʃɜːr-/ [the] a British sailing ship that is used to train esp. young people in TEAMWORK, and help their personal development

sis /sɪs/ n infml, esp. AmE (used when speaking to one's sister)

si·sal /ˈsaɪsəl, -zəl/ n [U] (a tropical plant whose leaves produce) a strong white thread-like substance used in making cord, rope, and mats

Sis·sing·hurst /ˈsɪsɪŋhɜːst‖-hɜːrst/ a castle in Kent, England, which has world-famous gardens

sis·sy¹ also **cissy** BrE /ˈsɪsi/ n infml derog a boy who looks or acts like a girl in some way; one who lacks qualities believed to be typical of men or boys, e.g. one who cries

sissy² also **sis·si·fied** /ˈsɪsɪfaɪd/, also **cissy** BrE— adj infml derog typical of a sissy; girlish

sis·ter /ˈsɪstə⁰/ n 1 a female relative with the same parents: *Joan and Mary are sisters.* | *Joan is Mary's younger* *sister.* | *Peter has an older sister.* **2** a female member of the same group (used esp. by supporters of the WOMEN'S MOVEMENT) **3** something, such as a company or organization, that belongs to the same group as something else and is closely connected to it: *The company owns the Daily Express and its sister newspaper the Daily Star.* **4** *BrE (often cap.)* (a title for) a nurse (usu. a female) in charge of a department (WARD) of a hospital: *Sister Brown* | *the night sister* —compare CHARGE NURSE **5** *(often cap.)* (a title for) a woman member of a religious group, esp. a NUN: *Sister Mary* | *a Christian sister* **6** *AmE sl* (used when speaking to a woman): *All right, sister, drop that gun!*

sis·ter·hood /ˈsɪstəhʊd‖-ər-/ *n* **1** [C+*sing./pl. v*] a society of women living a religious life **2** [U] a sisterly relationship, esp. as claimed among women supporting the WOMEN'S MOVEMENT

sister-in-law /ˈ··· ͵·/ *n* sisters-in-law, sister-in-laws **1** the sister of one's husband or wife **2** the wife of one's brother **3** the wife of the brother of one's husband or wife

sis·ter·ly /ˈsɪstəli‖-ər-/ *adj* of or like a sister; typical of a loving sister: *sisterly affection* —**-liness** *n* [U]

Sis·tine chap·el /͵sɪstiːn ˈtʃæpəl/ *[the]* a CHAPEL in the Vatican, Rome, famous for its ceiling painted by Michelangelo

Si·su·lu /sɪˈsuːluː/, **Wal·ter** /ˈwɔːltəʳ/ (1912–) a South African CIVIL RIGHTS worker and the first full-time Secretary General of the African National Congress. He was in prison for 25 years for his opposition to APARTHEID.

Sis·y·phus /ˈsɪsɪfəs/ in CLASSICAL MYTHOLOGY, a king whose punishment after death was to roll a large BOULDER (=very big stone) to the top of a steep hill. Whenever it got near the top, it rolled down again and he had to start again. —**Sisyphean** /͵sɪsɪˈfiːən◂/ *adj*

sit /sɪt/ *v* **sat** /sæt/; *present participle* **sitting 1** [I+*adv/prep*] to rest on a chair or other seat or on the ground, in a position with the upper body upright and bent at the waist: *He sat at his desk working.* | *They were all sitting round the fire.* | *She usually sits at the back of the class.* | *Don't just sit there watching — come and help me!* —see USAGE **2** [I+*adv/prep*;T+*obj*+*adv/prep*] to (cause to) go into this position; (cause to) take a seat: *Sit down, please.* | *Come and sit over here.* | *She sat the baby (down) on the grass.* | *He came over and sat beside me/sat in the chair next to mine.* —see also SIT **down 3** [I] (of an animal or bird) to be in or go into a position with the tail end of the body resting on a surface: *He's trained his dog to sit at the word of command.* | *a bird sitting on the wall* **4** [I+*adv/prep*, esp. **on, with**] a to lie; rest; be in a place or position and not move: *The books sat unread on the shelf for years.* | *a village sitting on the side of a hill* | *There were some family photos sitting on the mantelpiece.* | *The coat doesn't sit well on you.* (=fits badly) **b** to be accepted pleasantly: *I don't think his dinner/our suggestions sat very well with him.* **5** [I+*adv/prep*, esp. **on**] to have a position in an official body: *She sits on several committees.* | *He used to represent the Democrats but he now sits (on the council) as an Independent.* —see also SITTING² **6** [I] (of an official body) to have one or more meetings: *The court sat until all the arguments for both sides had been heard.* —see also SITTING¹ (4) **7** [I (**for**)] to (take up a position to) be painted or photographed: *I'm sitting for my portrait next week.* **8** [T] *esp. BrE* to take (a written examination): *I'm sitting my A-levels in the summer.* —see also SIT **for 9** [I] (of a hen) to cover eggs to bring young birds to life **10** [I (**for**)] to BABY-SIT **11 are you sitting comfortably? Then I'll begin** a phrase said at the beginning of *Listen with Mother*, a former children's radio programme, and now often used humorously: *Right, here's what we've got to do this week. Are you sitting comfortably? Then I'll begin.* **12 be sitting pretty** *infml* to be in a very favourable position: *With profits up 125% the company is sitting pretty.* **13 sit at the feet of** *lit or pomp* to receive instruction from; be the pupil of (esp. a famous teacher) **14 sit in judgment (on)** to give a judgment, opinion, or decision (about), sometimes when one has no right to do so **15 sit on someone's tail** to drive close behind someone for some distance, sometimes because the driver is waiting for a suitable chance to pass: *That guy's been sitting on my tail for about ten miles. I wish he'd pass me.* **16 sit tight** *infml* to keep in the same position; not move: *If your car breaks down, just sit tight*

and wait for the police to come along. | *(fig.) If he tries to persuade you, just sit tight.* (=don't change your mind) —see also SITTER, SITTING¹

▷ USAGE 1 You **sit** *at* a table or desk, *on* a chair, a branch etc., and *in* a tree or an armchair. 2 Compare **sit, be seated,** and **seat. Be seated** *(fml)* means to be in a sitting position or to find a **seat:** *He* **was seated.** (=He was in a sitting position.) | *Is everyone* **seated?** (=Has everyone found a seat?) To **seat** usually means "to provide **seats** for": *This hall will* **seat** *100 people.*◁

sit about/around *phr v* [I] *infml* to sit doing nothing, esp. while waiting or while others are active

sit back *phr v* [I] **1** to rest one's back in a comfortable chair **2** to rest and take no active part, esp. after hard effort or when action is needed: *You can't just sit back and watch while they ruin our country.* | *We've paid for this holiday, we might as well* **sit back and enjoy it.**

sit by *phr v* [I] to fail to take proper or necessary action: *I can't sit by and see these dreadful atrocities committed.*

sit down *phr v* [I *usu. in progressive forms*] to be seated; sit: *Everyone was sitting down when I came in, so I told them to stand up.* | *He gave his speech sitting down.* —see also SIT (2), SIT-DOWN

sit for sthg. *phr v* [T] *BrE* to (prepare to) take an examination for: *She sat for a scholarship but failed to win it.* —see also SIT (7,8,10)

sit in *phr v* [I] **1** [(**for, as**)] to take someone else's usual place, esp. in a regular meeting or office job: *The president is ill so the secretary will be sitting in for her (as chairman at the meeting).* **2** [(**on**)] to attend without taking an active part: *Members of the public are allowed to sit in on some Town Council meetings.* **3** to take part in a SIT-IN

sit on sthg./sbdy. *phr v* [T] **1** *infml* to delay taking action on: *He's been sitting on my letter for months; why doesn't he answer it?* | *The government are sitting on this controversial report.* (=refusing to make it public) **2** *infml* to force rudely into silence or inactivity: *She's always been sat on by her elder brothers.* **3 sit on one's hands** *infml* to take no action when action is needed — see also SIT (4, 5)

sit sthg. ↔ **out** *phr v* [T] **1** to remain seated during (a dance): *I don't feel like dancing; let's sit this one out.* **2** also **sit through**— to remain seated or inactive until the end of (esp. something unpleasant): *Although we were bored to death by the play, we sat it out in silence.* | *to sit out the crisis/the war/the storm*

sit up *phr v* **1** [I;T (=**sit** sbdy. **up**)] to (cause or help to) rise to a sitting position from a lying position: *Sit up and take your medicine.* | *She sat the old man up in bed.* —see also SIT (2) **2** [I] to sit properly upright in a chair: *Sit up straight; don't slouch over the table!* **3** [I (**for**)] to stay up late; not go to bed: *We sat up to watch the midnight movie.* | *Don't sit up/ōr me if I'm late.* **4** [I (**at, to**)] to take one's seat at a table: *Dinner's ready! Come and sit up (at/to the table).* **5** [I] *infml* to show sudden interest, surprise, or fear: *These new crime statistics should make people* **sit up and take notice.** —see also SIT-UP

si·tar /ˈsɪtɑːʳ, sɪˈtɑːʳ/ *n* a North Indian musical instrument with a long neck and a number of metal strings

sit·com /ˈsɪtkɒm‖-kɑːm/ *n* [C;U] a SITUATION COMEDY

sit-down¹ /ˈ· ·/ *n* **1** also **sit-down strike** /͵· · ˈ·/— a stopping of work by workers in an office, factory, etc., who refuse to leave until their demands are met **2** *BrE infml* an act or period of being seated: *After all that running about I could do with a sit-down.* —see also SIT **down**

sit-down² *adj* [A] (of a meal) at which people are served while seated at a table: *a sit-down dinner for twenty people*

site¹ /saɪt/ *n* **1** [(**of**)] a place where something of special interest existed or happened: *The site of the battle of Waterloo is in Belgium.* | *an archaeological site* **2** a piece of ground for building on: *a building construction site* | *the site of a proposed missile base* | *Protective helmets must be worn* **on site.**

site² *v* [T+*obj*+*adv/prep*; *usu. pass.*] to put or build in a particular position: *The company is trying to decide where to site the new factory.* | *The house is beautifully sited to give superb views over the valley.*

sit-in /ˈ· ·/ *n* a method of expressing dissatisfaction and anger in which a group of people enter a public place, stop its usual business, and refuse to leave: *They are*

staging a sit-in at the local hospital because the government is threatening to close it. —see also SIT **in** (3)

sit·ter /ˈsɪtəʳ/ n **1** a person whose picture is (being) taken or painted **2** a BABY-SITTER —see also SIT (7, 10) **3** *infml* an easy shot at GOAL in football

sit·ting¹ /ˈsɪtɪŋ/ n **1** a serving of a meal for a number of people at one time: *There will be two sittings for dinner, one at 7 o'clock and one at 8.30.* **2** an act or period of having one's picture taken or painted **3** a period of time spent seated in a chair: *I read the book in/at a single sitting.* **4** a meeting of an official body; SESSION —see also SIT (6,7)

sitting² *adj* [A] *BrE* (of a person) that is now a member of an official body, such as a parliament: *The sitting member will be hard to defeat in the election.* —see also SIT (5)

Sitting Bull /ˌ·· ˈ·/ (1834–90) a Native American chief. He and his Sioux followers defeated Custer's US army in a famous battle at Little Bighorn. He later appeared in Buffalo Bill's Wild West Show.

sitting duck /ˌ·· ˈ·/ n *infml* someone or something that is easy to attack or cheat

sitting room /ˈ·· ·/ n *esp. BrE for* LIVING ROOM

sitting tar·get /ˌ·· ˈ·/ n [(for)] *infml* someone or something that is in a defenceless position and is easy to attack: *The company's bad performance made it a sitting target for a takeover bid from its main rival.*

sitting ten·ant /ˌ·· ˈ··/ n *BrE* someone who lives in a rented house or flat

sit·u·ate /ˈsɪtʃueɪt/ v [T+obj+adv/prep] *fml* to put in a particular place or position; LOCATE: *The council are trying to decide where to situate the new hospital.*

sit·u·at·ed /ˈsɪtʃueɪtɪd/ adj [F+adv/prep] **1** in the stated place or position: *The house is situated in charming surroundings/is conveniently situated for the shops.* **2** in the stated situation: *The government is rather awkwardly situated.* | *How are you situated for money?* (=have you got enough?) | *They're well situated to exploit this new market.*

sit·u·a·tion /ˌsɪtʃuˈeɪʃən/ n **1** a position or state at a particular time; set of conditions, facts, and events having an effect on a person, society, etc.: *With no rain for the last three years, the country is in a desperate situation.* | *What is your assessment of the current political situation?* | *the serious international debt situation* —see CONDITIONS (USAGE) **2** *old-fash or tech* a job; position in work: *She managed to get a situation as a parlour maid.* **3** *fml* a position with regard to surroundings: *The house is in a charming situation, on a wooded hillside.*

situation com·e·dy /ˌ···· ˈ···/ also **sitcom**— n [C;U] a popular (form of) humorous television or radio show typically having a number of standard characters who appear in different stories each week

Situations Va·cant /ˌ···· ˈ··/ also **Sits Vac** *written abbrev.—* [the] *BrE* the name sometimes given to the part of a newspaper where jobs are advertised: *Have you looked in the Situations Vacant columns?*

sit-up /ˈ· ·/ n a muscle-training movement in which someone sits up from a lying position, keeping their legs straight and on the floor

six /sɪks/ determiner, n, pron **1** (the number) 6 —see TABLE 1 **2** (in) cricket a hit worth six RUNs² (10), in which the ball crosses the edge of the playing area before touching the ground: *That's easily a six.* **3 at sixes and sevens** *BrE infml* confused or undecided; in disorder: *I'm at sixes and sevens about what to do.* **4 six of one and half a dozen of the other** *infml* (a situation that is) good and bad to an equal degree **5 six of the best** *BrE infml* a beating, esp. six blows with a stick given to a schoolchild as a punishment —see also **knock someone for six** (KNOCK¹ (5))

six-foot·er /ˌ· ˈ···/ n *infml* a tall person, more than six feet (1.83 metres) tall

six-pack /ˈ· ·/ n a set of six bottles or CANs² (2) of a drink sold in a paper or plastic case for carrying: *He was carrying a six-pack (of beer).*

six·pence /ˈsɪkspəns/ n [C;U] (in Britain until 1971) (a small silver-coloured coin worth) the sum of six pennies (PENNY); 6d

six-shoot·er /ˈ· ˌ··/ also **six-gun** /ˈsɪksgʌn/— n *AmE* a REVOLVER (small gun) holding six bullets

six·teen /ˌsɪkˈstiːn◄/ determiner, n, pron (the number) 16 —see TABLE 1 —see also AGE OF CONSENT — ~ **th** determiner, n, pron, adv

sixteenth note /·ˈ· ·/ n *AmE for* SEMIQUAVER —see picture at NOTATION

sixth /sɪksθ/ determiner, n, pron, adv 6th —see TABLE 1

sixth form /ˈ· ·/ n [C+sing./pl. v] the highest level in a British SECONDARY (1) school. Students usu. go into the sixth form at the age of about 16 and stay there for two years, preparing to take their A LEVELs. Sixth-form students usu. have more freedom in what they wear, in their choice of activities, etc., than students lower down the school —see also LOWER SIXTH, UPPER SIXTH —**sixth-former** n : *I'll be a sixth-former next year*

sixth-form col·lege /ˌ·· ˈ ···/ n a British STATE SCHOOL for students over the age of 16. Some young people prefer to go to a sixth-form college because they feel it gives them more freedom than an ordinary school. —see also extra information on page 408

sixth sense /ˌ· ˈ·/ n [S] an ability to know things without using any of the five ordinary senses: *A sixth sense told me that I was being followed.*

six·ties /ˈsɪkstiz/ n [P] **1** [the] also **'60s**— the 1960s (=the years from 1960 to 1969)

▶CULTURAL NOTE The sixties are remembered as a time of great social change, when young people in many Western countries started to reject the ways of behaving and the ideas of their parents. There were many changes in the type of clothes young people wore, and in the music they listened to, and some young people took drugs and enjoyed more sexual freedom than in the past. Because of these developments, the sixties are sometimes called the **swinging sixties**. The sixties were also the time of the HIPPIES and of political protests, esp. in the US against the Vietnam War and of NUCLEAR weapons. —see also PERMISSIVE SOCIETY◀

2 in his/her/their sixties aged from 60 to 69: *"How old is she?" "I guess she's (somewhere) in her sixties."* **3** [the] the numbers from 60 to 69, esp. when used to measure temperature: *a cool summer day with the temperature in the low sixties* | *the upper sixties*

six·ty /ˈsɪksti/ determiner, n, pron (the number) 60 —see TABLE 1 —**tieth** determiner, n, pron, adv

sixty-four-thou·sand-dol·lar ques·tion, $64,000 question /ˌ··· ˌ··· ˌ·· ˈ··/ also [the] *infml* the most important and difficult question, for which the answer may not yet be known; question on whose answer a very great deal depends: *"Are you taking Pam out tonight?" "Ah, that's the sixty-four-thousand dollar question!"*

▶CULTURAL NOTE This expression came into use because of a television game show which used those words before asking the last question. In the US, the programme was called *The $64,000 Challenge*, and in 1959 it was found that some of the people who played the game had been given the questions in advance so that the game was not played fairly. This caused a SCANDAL.◀

Sixty Min·utes /ˌ·· ˈ··/ an American television news programme which examines several subjects on each show. It has been on since 1968.

sixty-nine /ˌ·· ˈ·/ n [U] a sexual position in which each partner can touch the other's sex organs with the lips at the same time

size¹ /saɪz/ n **1** [C;U] (a degree of) bigness or smallness: *What's the size of your patio?* (=how big is it?) | *Houses come* (=are built) *in all* **shapes and sizes.** | *They are trying to estimate the size of this potential market for their new product.* | *Their army is about half the size of ours.* | *The amount of interest you pay depends on the size of the loan.* **2** [U] bigness: *The company is able to keep its prices down simply because of its size.* | *None of the jewels were of any size.* (=they were quite small) | *You should see the size of their dog!* (=it's very big) **3** [C] any of a set of standard measures according to which goods are produced: *We stock dresses in women's and children's sizes.* | *I take a size 8 shoe.* | *What size bottle would you like? The small size is 55p and the large size is 85p.* **4 size isn't important** a phrase people sometimes use jokingly, thinking of a well-known piece of advice to men who are worried about the size of their PENIS. Or they may also say something like **you know what they say about size**... **5 that's about the size of it** *infml* that's a fair statement of the matter **6 -sized** /saızd/also **-size**— of the stated size or number: *a medium-sized car | bite-size chunks | a good-sized* (=large) *crowd* —see also **cut someone down to size** (CUT down), **try something for size** (TRY¹)

size² *v* **1** to make (an object) a certain size **2** to SORT things out according to their size **3** to establish the size of: *Those apples have not been sized yet.*
   size sthg./sbdy. ↔ **up** *phr v* [T] to consider and form an opinion or judgment about: *He sized the situation up at a glance and took immediate action.*

size³ *n* [U] a thick liquid mixture made from glue, flour and other materials, used for giving stiffness and a hard shiny surface to paper, cloth, etc.

size⁴ *v* [T] to cover or treat with SIZE³

size·a·ble, sizable /ˈsaızəbəl/ *adj* rather large; CONSIDER·ABLE: *a sizeable income*

Size·well /ˈsaızwəl/ a NUCLEAR power station in Suffolk, England

siz·zle /ˈsɪzəl/ *v* [I] to make a sound like water falling on hot metal or food cooking in hot fat: *The meat was sizzling in the pan.* —**sizzle** *n* [U]

siz·zler /ˈsɪzələʳ/ *n infml* a very hot day: *Yesterday was a real sizzler!*

SJ *abbrev. for:* (after the name of a Jesuit) Society of Jesus: *Francis Xavier, SJ*

ska /skɑː/ *n* [U] a kind of popular music from the West Indies, similar to REGGAE

skag, scag /skæg/ *n* [U] *sl for* HEROIN

skate¹ /skeıt/ *n* **1** also **ice skate**— either of a pair of boots with metal blades fitted to the bottom, allowing the wearer to move quickly on ice **2** a ROLLER SKATE —see picture at ROLL **3** **get/put one's skates on** *infml* to move, act, or work quickly; hurry

skate² *v* [I] **1** to move on skates: *We skated across the frozen lake. | I'm going skating.* **2** **(skate) on thin ice** *infml* (to be) doing something risky — ~**er** *n*
   skate over/round sthg. *phr v* [T] to avoid treating seriously; fail to give necessary attention to: *Instead of trying to solve the problems, the committee skated over them.*
   skate through (sthg.) *phr v* [I;T] *infml* to gain easy success (in): *She skated through her English exam.*

skate³ *n* **skate** *or* **skates** a large flat sea fish that can be eaten

skate·board /ˈskeıtbɔːd‖-bɔːrd/ *n* a short board with two small wheels at each end, for standing on and riding — compare ROLLER SKATE — ~**er** *n* — ~**ing** *n* [U]

ske·dad·dle /skɪˈdædl/ *v* [I] *infml humor* to run away

skeet shoo·ting /ˈskiːt ˌʃuːtıŋ/ *n* [U] the sport of shooting at clay objects thrown into the air to give the effect of flying birds

Skeg·ness /ˌskegˈnes◂/ also **Skeg·gy** /ˈskegi/ *infml*— a town on the E coast of England which is a popular place esp. for WORKING-CLASS people from central England to go for the day or for their holidays

skein /skeın/ *n* [(of)] **1** a loosely wound length of thread or YARN **2** a large group of wild GEESE in the sky

skel·e·tal /ˈskelɪtəl/ *adj* of or like a skeleton: *the skeletal bodies of the starving people* | (fig.) *a skeletal report* (=giving only the main points, and not providing details)

skel·e·ton¹ /ˈskelɪtən/ *n* **1** the structure consisting of all the bones in a human or animal body **2** a set of these bones (or models of them) held in their positions, e.g. for use by medical students **3** [(of)] something forming a structure on which more is built or added: *the steel skeleton of a new skyscraper | I've written the skeleton of my report, but I have to fill in the details.* **4** an extremely thin person or animal: *The poor old man was just a skeleton.* **5** *infml* an unpleasant often shocking event or fact from the past that a person or family keeps secret (esp. in the phrase **skeleton in the closet/cupboard** (BrE))

skeleton² *adj* [A] enough to keep an operation or organization going, and no more: *During the strike British Rail is providing only a skeleton service, with five trains a day.* | *a skeleton staff*

skeleton key /ˈ··· ·/ *n* **1** BrE ‖ **master key** AmE—a key made to open a number of different locks **2** AmE an old-fashioned key

skep·tic /ˈskeptık/ *n* AmE for SCEPTIC — ~**al** *adj* — ~**ally** /kli/ *adv* —**ism** /ˈskeptɪsɪzəm/ *n* [U]

---

sketch¹ /sketʃ/ *n* **1** a simple, quickly-made, and not detailed drawing: *Rembrandt's sketches for his paintings | a pencil/charcoal sketch* **2** a short written or spoken description: *On the back of the book there is a brief biographical sketch of the author.* **3** a short humorous scene on stage, television, etc., that is part of a larger show: *The next sketch features a man going into a pet shop to complain about his dead parrot.*

the human skeleton

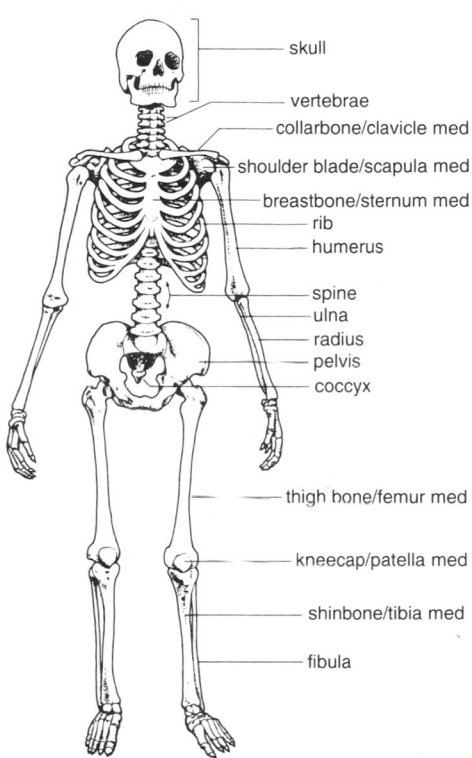

skull

vertebrae

collarbone/clavicle med

shoulder blade/scapula med

breastbone/sternum med

rib

humerus

spine

ulna

radius

pelvis

coccyx

thigh bone/femur med

kneecap/patella med

shinbone/tibia med

fibula

sketch² *v* **1** [I;T] to draw a sketch (of) **2** [T (IN, OUT)] to describe roughly with few details: *Let me just sketch in/out the main points of our plan.* — ~**er** *n*

sketch·book /ˈsketʃbʊk/ *n* a book containing quick drawings or plain paper for making quick drawings: *Shall I show you what I did in my sketchbook today?*

sketch·pad /ˈsketʃpæd/ also **sketchbook**— *n* a number of sheets of paper fastened together for drawing on

sketch·y /ˈsketʃi/ *adj often derog* not thorough or complete; lacking details: *My memory of what happened is rather sketchy.* | *rather sketchy coverage of an important news story* —**ily** *adv* —**iness** *n* [U]

skew¹ /skjuː/ *v* [T] to cause to be not straight or exact; twist; DISTORT: *A few inaccurate figures could skew the results of the survey.*

skew² *n* **on the skew** not straight; sloping or twisted; ASKEW

skew·bald /ˈskjuːbɔːld/ *n, adj* (a horse) coloured with large white and esp. brown shapes —compare PIEBALD

skew·er¹ /ˈskjuːəʳ/ *n* a long metal or wooden pin for putting through (pieces of) meat while cooking, used e.g. to make KEBABS

skewer² *v* [T] to fasten or make a hole through (as if) with a skewer: *Skewer the chicken before you cook it.*

skew-whiff /ˌ·ˈ·◂/ *adj* [F] BrE *infml, usu. humor* not straight; skewed: *She came in out of the wind with her hat rather skew-whiff.*

ski¹ /skiː/ *n* **skis** **1** either of a pair of long thin narrow pieces of wood, plastic, or metal curving up in front, that are fastened to boots and used for travelling on snow **2** a RUNNER (3) shaped like a ski on a small motor vehicle, skibob, or SKI PLANE

ski² *v* **skied** /skiːd/, *present participle* **skiing** [I] to go on skis for sport or as a means of travel: *I'm learning to ski.* | *We skied down the hill.* | *They always* **go skiing** *in January.* —see also SKIER, SKI LIFT, SKI POLE, SKI RUN, WATER SKIING and see colour picture on page 1212

▶CULTURAL NOTE Skiing holidays are now very popular in Britain, esp. among young people. There are three main areas in Scotland where British people ski —the Cairngorms, Glencoe, and Glenshee. Otherwise, they go abroad, esp. to France, Austria, or Switzerland. The US has several well-known ski areas, e.g. in the Rocky Mountains, Vermont, and the Grand Tetons.◀

ski·bob /ˈskiːbɒb‖-bɑːb/ *n* a bicycle-like vehicle with skis instead of wheels

ski boot /ˈ· ·/ *n* a specially made boot fastened to the foot and locked into position on a ski —see PAIR (USAGE) and see picture at SHOE

skid¹ /skɪd/ *v* **-dd-** [I] (of a vehicle or wheel) to slip or slide sideways, esp. uncontrollably: *If the road's icy it's easy to skid.* | *He came skidding round the corner on his motorbike.*

skid² *n* **1** [*usu. sing.*] an act or path of skidding: *I put the brakes on and the car* **went into a skid.** (=started skidding) | *There were skid marks on the road where the van had crashed.* **2** a bladelike part which in some aircraft is used in addition to wheels for landing on: *helicopter skids* **3** [*usu. pl.*] also **pallet** *AmE*— a piece of usu. wood placed under a heavy object to raise it off the floor or to move it **4 on the skids** *infml* certain to fail or come to an end: *I hear their marriage is on the skids.* **5 put the skids under** *infml* to cause to fail

skid·pan /ˈskɪdpæn/ *n BrE* a prepared slippery surface where drivers practise controlling skidding vehicles

skid row /ˌskɪd ˈrəʊ/ *n* [(**on**) U] *AmE infml* a poor dirty part of a town where unemployed and drunk people gather: *He's headed for skid row, for sure.*

ski·er /ˈskiːəʳ/ *n* **1** a person who SKIS²: *downhill skiers in the Olympics* | *She's a good skier.* **2** *infml* a person who WATER SKIS

skiff /skɪf/ *n* a small light boat for rowing or sailing by one person

skif·fle /ˈskɪfəl/ *n* [U] *esp. BrE* music popular in the late 1950s, based on American FOLK² music and played partly on instruments made by the performers

ski in·struct·or /ˈ· ·ˌ··/ *n* a person who teaches people to SKI.

▶CULTURAL NOTE The STEREOTYPE of a ski instructor is of a tall, good-looking man with an attractive SUNTAN who enjoys a lot of sexual attention from the women he teaches.◀

ski jump /ˈ· ·/ *n* (a competition for jumping on SKIS at high speed from) a steep downward slope ending in a cliff

skil·ful usu. **skillful** *AmE* /ˈskɪlfəl/ *adj* having or showing skill; ADEPT: *a skilful pianist|negotiator* | *her skilful handling of a delicate situation* — **~ly** *adv*

ski lift /ˈ· ·/ *n* a power-driven endless wire rope with seats for carrying people to the top of a slope to SKI

skill /skɪl/ *n* [C;U] (a) special ability to do something well, esp. as gained by learning and practice: *Reading and writing are two different skills.* | *a course that teaches basic computer skills|management skills* | *He handled the negotiations with great skill.* | *a painter of great skill*

skill·cen·tre /ˈskɪlsentəʳ/ *n* a government training centre for young people in Britain, to help them find jobs

skilled /skɪld/ *adj* [(**in, at**)] having or needing skill: *We need skilled workers|workers skilled in welding for this job; it's a highly skilled job.* —opposite **unskilled**

skil·let /ˈskɪlɪt/ *n AmE for* FRYING PAN —see picture at PAN

skim /skɪm/ *v* **-mm-** **1** [T (OFF, **from**)] to remove (floating fat or solids) from the surface of a liquid: *She skimmed (off) the cream from the milk.* | (fig.) *Does private education skim off all the best students from the state system?* **2** [I (**through, over**);T] to read quickly to get the main ideas: *I've skimmed (through) the report but I haven't had time to look at it in detail.* **3** [I+adv|prep;T] to (cause to) move quickly along a course near or touching (a surface):

Birds skimmed (over) the waves looking for food. | *The plane skimmed the treetops.* | *He was idly skimming flat stones across the surface of the pond.* — **~mer** *n*

skimmed milk /ˌ· ˈ·/ also **skim milk**— *n* [U] milk from which the cream has been removed

▶CULTURAL NOTE Many more people buy skimmed milk or semi-skimmed milk now than in the past because full cream milk contains more fat, which is supposed not to be very good for one's health.◀

skimp /skɪmp/ *v* [I (**on**);T] to spend, provide, or use less of (something) than is really needed: *When you make this dish, don't skimp (on) the cream.* (=use lots of it)

skimp·y /ˈskɪmpi/ *adj* that has been skimped on; not enough; SCANTY: *It was a skimpy meal, with hardly enough for everyone.* | *a skimpy dress* (=very short and/or tight) | *skimpy evidence* —**ily** *adv* —**iness** *n* [U]

skin¹ /skɪn/ *n* **1** [U] **a** the natural outer covering of an animal or human body, from which hair may grow: *Babies have soft skin.* | *a skin disease* | *I was out in the thunderstorm, and I got absolutely* **soaked to the skin.** (=extremely wet) | (fig.) *He won't worry about the criticism; he's got a pretty* **thick skin.** (=is not easily upset) **b** the skin on one's face: *My skin's very bad at the moment.* (=my face is very dry or esp. very SPOTTY) | *skin problems* —see also SKINCARE, THIN-SKINNED **2** [C;U] (*sometimes in comb.*) the skin of an animal for use as leather, fur, etc.: *It takes a lot of skins to make a fur coat.* | *a sheepskin jacket* **3** [C] **a** a natural outer covering of some fruits and vegetables: *banana skins* | *onion skins* —see picture at FRUIT **b** the outer covering of a SAUSAGE **4** [C;U] the solid surface that forms over a liquid when it gets cool or is left in the air: *Do you like skin on your rice pudding?* **5** [C] *tech* an outer surface built over a structure: *Aircraft wings have metal or cloth skins.* **6 by the skin of one's teeth** *infml* only just; with very little additional time or space: *We had to run for the train, and caught it by the skin of our teeth.* **7 get under someone's skin** *infml* to annoy or excite someone deeply **8 no skin off someone's nose** *infml* not something that upsets or causes disadvantage to someone: *If she won't accept my help that's her problem — it's no skin off my nose.* **9 skin and bone(s)** *infml* very thin: *The poor little dog was all skin and bone.* **10 under the skin** beneath the outside appearance; at heart: *We may be of different races but we're sisters under the skin.* **11 -skinned** /skɪnd/having or showing the stated type or colour of skin: *smooth-skinned* | *fair-skinned* —see also THICK-SKINNED, THIN-SKINNED, **save one's skin** (SAVE¹)

skin² *v* **-nn-** [T] **1** to remove the skin from: *to skin a deer|an onion* | (fig., *infml*) *He'll* **skin you alive** (=punish you very severely) *if he finds out what you've done.* **2** to hurt by rubbing off some skin: *I skinned my knee when I fell.* —see also **keep one's eyes skinned** (EYE¹) **1 there's more than one way to skin a cat** *infml* there are more ways or methods of getting something done. This phrase, often changed, is usu. used to suggest that there is a different, possibly illegal, way of doing something when the usual method is not possible: *He won't move out of the house, and the lawyers can't help, but there's more than one way of skinning a cat!*

skin·care /ˈskɪnkeəʳ/ *adj, n* [U] (the act of) looking after one's skin, esp. the skin of a woman's face: *our new range of skincare products*

skin-deep /ˌ· ˈ·◂/ *adj* [F] not going deep; only on the surface; SUPERFICIAL: *Their differences of opinion are only skin-deep; they basically share the same beliefs.*

skin-dive /ˈ· ·/ *v* [I] to swim under water without heavy breathing apparatus and not wearing a protective suit: *We're going skin-diving to look at the coral reef.* —**skin diver** *n* —**skin diving** *n* [U]

skin flick /ˈ· ·/ *n sl* a film showing a lot of sex

skin·flint /ˈskɪnˌflɪnt/ *n derog* someone who dislikes spending or giving money; MISER

skin·ful /ˈskɪnfʊl/ *n* [S] *BrE infml* an amount of alcohol to make one drunk: *He must have had a skinful; he can hardly walk in a straight line!*

skin graft /ˈ· ·/ *n* an operation to repair a burn, wound, etc., by taking a piece of healthy skin to put in place of the damaged skin

skin·head /ˈskɪnhed/ *n* (esp. in Britain) a young person, usu. male, with hair that is shaved off (SHAVE¹) or cut very short, esp. one of a group that sometimes behaves violently. Male skinheads often wear heavy boots such as Doc Martens, BRACES, and an EARRING in one ear: *A gang of skinheads terrorized the holidaymakers.*

skin·less /ˈskɪnləs/ *adj* not having a skin, esp. a SKIN¹ (3)

Skin·ner /ˈskɪnəʳ/, **Bur·rhus Fred·e·ric** /ˈbʌrəs ˈfredərɪk ‖ˈbɜː-/ (1904–90) a US PSYCHOLOGIST whose work developed the ideas of BEHAVIOURISM. His books include *Beyond Freedom* and *Dignity.*

skin·ny /ˈskɪni/ *adj infml, often derog* very thin, esp. in a way that is unattractive —see THIN (USAGE)

skinny-dip·ping /ˈ·· ˌ··/ *n* [U] *esp. AmE* swimming with no clothes on. This is chiefly enjoyed by young people, esp. when done at night or in secret. —**dipper** *n*

skint /skɪnt/ *adj* [F] *BrE infml* completely without money; BROKE

skin-tight /ˌ· ˈ·◄/ *adj* (of clothes) fitting tightly against the body: *skin-tight jeans | a skin-tight sweater*

skip¹ /skɪp/ *v* **-pp-** **1** [I] to move in a light dancing way, with quick steps and jumps: *The little girl skipped along at her mother's side.* **2** [I+*adv/prep*] to move in no fixed order: *The speaker kept skipping from one subject to another.* | *Let's skip to the last item on the agenda, and we'll deal with these other matters later.* **3** [I (**over**);T] to pass over or leave out; not do or deal with (the next thing): *Every time the record comes to that part of the music, the needle skips.* | *His heart skipped a beat when he saw how high up he was.* | *She skipped (over) the boring bits of text and just looked at the pictures.* **4** [T] *infml* to fail to attend or take part in (an activity); intentionally miss: *I'm going to skip lunch today.* **5** [I] *BrE* ‖ **jump rope** *AmE*– to jump over a rope passed repeatedly beneath one's feet, as a game or for exercise —see also SKIPPING ROPE **6** [I (OFF, OUT); T] *infml* to leave hastily and secretly, esp. to avoid being punished or paying money: *She skipped off/out without paying her bill.* | *The thieves have skipped the country.*

skip² *n* a light quick stepping and jumping movement: *With a hop and a skip she was gone.*

skip³ *BrE*‖**dumpster** *AmE*– *n* a large container for carrying heavy materials, esp. GARBAGE or old bricks, wood, etc., to be taken away

ski pants /ˈ· ·/ *n* [P] **1** special warm trousers with no opening around the ANKLES, worn for winter sports **2** fashionable tight trousers worn by women

ski plane /ˈ· ·/ *n* an aircraft with SKIS (2) instead of wheels, for landing on snow

ski pole /ˈ· ·/ also **ski stick** *BrE*– *n* either of a pair of pointed short poles held for balance and for pushing against the snow when wearing SKIS

skip·per¹ /ˈskɪpəʳ/ *n infml* a captain of a ship or a sports team: *Tell the skipper.* | *"What next, skipper?"*

skipper² *v* [T] *infml* to be the skipper of; lead

skipping rope /ˈ·· ·/ *BrE*‖**jump rope** *AmE*– *n* a piece of rope several metres long, usu. with handles, over which people SKIP¹(5). It is used esp. by young girls and by people doing exercises to keep fit.

skirl /skɜːl‖skɜːrl/ *n* [(*the*) S (**of**)] *esp. lit* a loud high sound as made by BAGPIPES

skir·mish¹ /ˈskɜːmɪʃ‖-ɜːr-/ *n* **1** a fight between small groups of soldiers, ships, etc., at a distance from the main forces and not part of a large battle **2** a short or unplanned exchange of arguments between opponents — compare PITCHED BATTLE

skirmish² *v* [I (**with**)] to fight in a skirmish — **~er** *n*

skirt¹ /skɜːt‖skɜːrt/ *n* **1** [C] a woman's outer garment that hangs down freely from the waist: *Skirts were worn* (=came down to) *just below the knee at that time.* | *a pleated skirt* —compare DRESS² (1) **2** [C] also **skirts** *pl.*– a circular guarding or covering part of a vehicle or machine: *a hovercraft's rubber skirts* **3** [U] *old-fash sl* girls or women considered as sexual objects: *a nice bit of skirt* (=woman)

skirt² *v* [I+**round, around**;T] **1** to be or go round the outside of; go around: *The old footpath skirts the village.* | *We decided to skirt (round) the town centre.* **2** to avoid (a difficult question or subject that ought to be dealt with): *The speech was most disappointing; it skirted round all the main questions.*

skirting board /ˈ··· ·/ *BrE* ‖ **baseboard** *AmE*– *n* [C;U] (a) board fixed along the base of a wall where it meets the floor of a room —see picture at LIVING ROOM

ski run /ˈ· ·/ *n* a track marked out on a slope for skiing (SKI) on

skit /skɪt/ *n* [(**on**)] a short usu. humorous acted-out scene, often copying and making fun of something: *They did* (=performed) *a skit on beauty contests — it was hilarious.*

skit·ter /ˈskɪtəʳ/ *v* [I] (of a small creature) to run quickly and lightly

skit·tish /ˈskɪtɪʃ/ *adj* **1** not serious or responsible; silly and changeable in mind; FRIVOLOUS: *a charming but skittish young woman* **2** (esp. of a horse or cat) easily excited and made afraid — **~ly** *adv* — **~ness** *n* [U]

skit·tle /ˈskɪtl/ *n* **1** a bottle-shaped object used in the game of skittles **2** *BrE infml for* a PIN¹ (5)

skit·tles /ˈskɪtlz/ *n* [U] a British game in which a player tries to knock down skittles by throwing or rolling a ball or other object at them —see also **not all beer and skittles** (BEER)

skive /skaɪv/ *v* [I (OFF)] *BrE infml* to avoid work or duty or leave it early without permission —**skiver** *n*

skiv·vies /ˈskɪviz/ *n* [P] *AmE infml* a man's undergarments, esp. a VEST¹ (1) and UNDERPANTS

skiv·vy¹ /ˈskɪvi/ *n BrE derog* a servant, esp. a girl, who does only the dirty unpleasant jobs in a house

skivvy² *v* [I] *BrE infml* (esp. of a woman) to do the dirty unpleasant jobs in a house: *I don't see why I should spend my time skivvying for you.*

Sko·da /ˈskəʊdə/ *tdmk* a Czechoslovak company that makes a particular small car that is quite cheap

Skol /skɒl‖skəʊl/ *tdmk* a type of LAGER made by a Danish company: *A pint of Skol, please.*

sku·a /ˈskjuːə/ *n* a large North Atlantic seabird

skul·dug·ge·ry, **skullduggery** /ˌskʌlˈdʌgəri/ *n* [U] *infml, esp. humor* secretly dishonest or unfair action: *Some skulduggery no doubt went on during the election.*

skulk /skʌlk/ *v* [I+*adv/prep*] to hide or move about secretly, trying not to be noticed, usu. through fear or for some bad purpose: *I found him skulking in the cupboard, and he couldn't explain why he was there.*

skull /skʌl/ *n* the bone of the head, which encloses the brain: (fig., *infml*) *Can't you get it into your thick skull* (=understand) *that we can't afford it?* —see picture at SKELETON

skull and cross·bones /ˌskʌl ənd ˈkrɒsbəʊnz‖-ˈkrɔːs-/ *n* [(*the*) S] a sign for death or danger consisting of a picture of a skull with two long bones crossed below it, used esp. **a** on bottles containing poison **b** on PIRATES' flags in former times

skull·cap /ˈskʌlkæp/ *n* a simple closefitting cap for the top of the head, as worn sometimes by some priests, and Jewish men, esp. when they are in the holy places of their religion

skunk /skʌŋk/ *n* **1** a small black and white N American animal which gives out a powerful bad-smelling liquid as a defence when attacked **2** *infml, usu. humor* a person who is bad, unfair, unkind, etc.

sky¹ /skaɪ/ *n* **1** [(*the*) S;U] also **skies** *pl.*– the upper air; the space above the Earth where clouds and the sun, moon, and stars appear: *The sky turned dark as the storm came near.* | *There's a bit of blue sky between the clouds.* | *The skies were grey when we arrived in London.* | *The rocket shot up into the sky.* —compare HEAVEN **2 Red sky at night, shepherd's/sailor's delight** *quote* the first line of an old poem for children, meaning that the weather will be good the next day if the sky is red at night. The poem finishes **Red sky in the morning, shepherd's warning/sailors take warning**, meaning that the weather will be very bad after a red sky in the morning. **3 the sky's the limit** *infml* there is no upper limit, esp. to the amount of money that can be spent —see also **gone to the great … in the sky** (GREAT), **pie in the sky** (PIE), **praise someone/something to the skies** (PRAISE¹)

sky² *v* [T] (in cricket) to hit (a ball) high into the air

Sky see SKY TV

sky-blue /ˌ· ˈ·◄/ *adj* of the pleasant bright blue colour of a clear sunny sky —**sky blue** *n* [U]

sky·cap /ˈskaɪkæp/ n AmE a person who carries passengers' cases at an airport

sky·div·ing /ˈskaɪˌdaɪvɪŋ/ n [U] the sport of jumping from an aircraft and making movements while falling before opening a PARACHUTE —**diver** n

Skye /skaɪ/ an island off the NW coast of Scotland. It is the largest island of the INNER HEBRIDES, and is famous esp. because of an old popular song *Over the sea to Skye*. It is mainly mountainous and is regarded as a very beautiful and ROMANTIC place. —see colour map on page 818

sky·er /ˈskaɪər/ n (in cricket) a ball hit high into the air

sky-high /ˌ· ˈ·◂/ adv, adj infml very high, esp. unacceptably high; at or to a very high level: *Prices have gone sky-high.* | *sky-high interest rates* —see also **blow something sky-high** (BLOW[1] (18))

sky·jack /ˈskaɪdʒæk/ v [T] to HIJACK (an aircraft) — **~er** n — **~ing** n [C;U]

Sky·lab /ˈskaɪlæb/ the first American space station, in 1973. ASTRONAUTS were sent up to do scientific tests and other work in space. The space station burnt up in 1979 when it came back into the Earth's ATMOSPHERE.

sky·lark[1] /ˈskaɪlɑːk‖-lɑːrk/ n a small bird (LARK) that sings while flying upwards

skylark[2] v [I (ABOUT)] old-fash infml to play rather wildly; have fun; LARK **about**

sky·light /ˈskaɪlaɪt/ n a glass-covered opening in a roof to let in light —see picture at HOUSE

sky·line /ˈskaɪlaɪn/ n a shape or view made by scenery, esp. tall city buildings, against the background of the sky: *the dramatic New York skyline*

sky·rock·et[1] /ˈskaɪˌrɒkɪt‖-ˌrɑː-/ v [I] infml (esp. of a price, amount, etc.) to go up suddenly and steeply

sky·rock·et[2] n a ROCKET[1] (3)

sky·scrap·er /ˈskaɪˌskreɪpər/ n a very tall modern city building

Sky TV /ˌskaɪ tiː ˈviː/ also **Sky Tel·e·vi·sion** /ˌ· ···ˈ··/ (in Britain) a number of television CHANNELS broadcast from Europe and received at one's house by a SATELLITE DISH. For example, there is a news channel, a sport channel, and a MOVIE channel. Sky TV began in 1989 and in November 1990 joined with British Satellite Broadcasting (BSB) to form British Sky Broadcasting (BSkyB).

Sky·walk·er /ˈskaɪwɔːlkər/, **Luke** the HERO (=the main good character) in the Star Wars films, who fought against and defeated the evil Darth Vader —see also DARTH VADER, STAR WARS and see colour picture on page 685

sky·writ·ing /ˈskaɪraɪtɪŋ/ n [U] the act of using special smoke released from an aircraft to write words in the sky: *Skywriting is often used by advertisers to reach people at the beaches during the summer.*

slab /slæb/ n 1 [C (of)] a thick flat usu. four-sided piece (of stone, metal, wood, food, etc.): *The patio was made of stone slabs.* | *a slab of cake* —see picture at PIECE 2 [the+S] infml the table top, often made of stone, on which a dead body is laid in a hospital or MORTUARY

slack[1] /slæk/ adj 1 (of a rope, wire, etc.) not pulled tight —opposite **taut** 2 not firm in keeping control; LAX: *slack discipline/supervision* 3 not busy or active; SLUGGISH: *Winter is the slack season at most hotels.* | *Business is slack just now.* 4 not taking proper care or effort; NEGLIGENT: *You've been very slack in your work recently.* — **~ly** adv — **~ness** n [U]

slack[2] v [I] derog to be lazy; not work well or quickly enough: *Stop slacking and get on with your work.* — **~er** n **slack off/up** phr v [I] to reduce speed, effort, or tightness; slacken: *It's natural to slack off towards the end of a hard day's work.*

slack[3] n [U] the part of a rope, wire, etc., that hangs loose: *The sailors pulled at the rope to* **take up the slack.** (=make it tighter)

slack[4] n [U] coal in very small pieces

slack·en /ˈslækən/ v [I;T (OFF)] to make or become slack; reduce in activity, force, etc., or in tightness: *The train slackened speed/Our speed slackened as we approached the station.* | *The demand for coal begins to slacken (off) in the spring.* | *Slacken the tent ropes before it rains.* —compare TIGHTEN

slacks /slæks/ n [P] 1 infml, esp. AmE trousers: *a shirt and slacks* | *dress/corduroy slacks* —see PAIR (USAGE)

▷ USAGE **Slacks** is used in American English, esp. in speech, where British people usu. use **trousers**. For most American speakers the difference between **jeans** and **slacks** is that **jeans** have the back pockets sewn on, and **slacks** have back pockets on the inside. **Slacks** are suitable for more formal occasions than **jeans**.◁ 2 BrE old-fash a woman's trousers for informal wear

slag[1] /slæg/ n 1 [U] lighter glasslike waste material left when metal is separated from its natural rock 2 [C] BrE derog sl a woman or girl whose sexual behaviour is regarded as unacceptable, e.g. because she has had sexual relationships with too many men, or with a man whom she hardly knew

slag[2] v -gg-
slag sbdy./sthg. ↔ **off** phr v [T] BrE sl to make extremely unfavourable remarks about; CRITICIZE: *He claims to like her, but he's always slagging her off behind her back.*

slag·heap /ˈslæghiːp/ n esp. BrE a pile of slag at a mine, factory, etc.

slain /sleɪn/ past participle of SLAY

slake /sleɪk/ v [T] lit to satisfy (thirst) with a drink; QUENCH

sla·lom /ˈslɑːləm/ n a race for people on SKIS or in CANOES down a winding course marked out by flags

slam[1] /slæm/ v -mm- 1 [I;T] to shut loudly and with force: *He stormed out, and the door slammed (shut) behind him.* | *Please don't slam the door.* 2 [T+obj+adv/prep] infml to push, move, place, etc., hurriedly and with great force: *She slammed on the brakes* (=worked them very quickly and strongly) *and the car came to a stop.* | *He slammed the papers down on my desk and angrily walked out.* 3 [T] (used in newspapers) to attack with words: *The paper's headline was "Minister slams Local Government spending".* 4 **slam the door (in someone's face/on someone)** to refuse rudely to meet someone, accept an offer, etc.: *We offered to negotiate, but they slammed the door in our face(s).*

slam[2] n [S] the act or loud noise of a door closing violently —see also GRAND SLAM

slam dunk /ˈ· ·/ v [I;T] (in BASKETBALL) to DUNK (3) (throw) a ball through the basket using a lot of force: *And Abdul-Jabbar runs down the floor and slam dunks!* —**slam dunk** n : *a pass to Jordan for a slam dunk*

slam·mer /ˈslæmər/ n sl a prison: *He was thrown in the slammer.*

slan·der[1] /ˈslɑːndər‖ˈslæn-/ n 1 [C] an intentional false spoken report, story, etc., which unfairly damages the good opinion held about a person by others 2 [U] the making of such a statement, esp. as an offence in law: *The company is suing her for slander because of her remarks about their safety record.* —compare LIBEL

slander[2] v [T] to speak slander against; harm by making a false statement: *He claims he was slandered at the meeting.* — **~er** n

slan·der·ous /ˈslɑːndərəs‖ˈslæn-/ adj being or containing slander: *a slanderous allegation* — **~ly** adv

slang[1] /slæŋ/ n [U] very informal language that includes new and sometimes not polite words and meanings, is often used among particular groups of people, and is usu. not used in serious speech or writing. Slang words and phrases are marked sl in this dictionary: *schoolboy/prison slang* | *"Slag off" is British slang for/is a slang expression for "criticize".* —see also RHYMING SLANG — **~y** adj derog : *Don't use such slangy expressions in your essays.*

slang[2] v [T] BrE infml to attack with rude angry words: *After the accident the two drivers started slanging each other/started a* **slanging match** *in the middle of the road.*

slant[1] /slɑːnt‖slænt/ v 1 [I;T] to be or put at an angle, instead of being straight up and down or HORIZONTAL; (cause to) slope: *slanting handwriting* | *a slanting roof* | *The sunlight slanted through the trees.* 2 [T usu. pass.] usu. derog to express or describe (facts, events, etc.) in a way favourable to a particular opinion: *The newspaper report was slanted towards/in favour of the unions.* — **~ingly** adv

slant[2] n 1 [S] a slanting direction or position: *a steep slant* | *The lines are drawn at/on a slant.* 2 [C (on)] sometimes derog a particular way of looking at or expressing facts or a situation: *Reading the reports in foreign newspapers gives you an interesting new slant on the* *election.* | *The editorial had an anti-union slant.*

slant·wise /ˈslɑːnt-waɪz‖ˈslænt-/ *adj, adv* at a slant; in a slanting direction

slap¹ /slæp/ *n* **1** a quick hit with the flat part of the hand: *He gave her a slap on the cheek.* **2 slap in the face** *infml* an action that seems to be aimed directly and intentionally against someone else; REBUFF: *It was a slap in the face for her parents when she ignored their advice and gave up her job.* **3 slap on the back** *infml* an expression of praise or thanks for something done; CONGRATULATIONS **4 slap on the wrist** *infml* a gentle (perhaps too gentle) punishment or warning: *The law ought to be tougher; we shouldn't just give criminals a slap on the wrist!*

slap² *v* **-pp-** **1** [T] to hit quickly with the flat part of the hand: *She slapped her little boy for being rude.* | *If you touch me again I'll slap your face!* **2** [I+prep;T] to move against (a surface) with a sound like a slap: *The small waves slapped against the jetty.* **3** [T+obj+adv|prep, esp. on] to place or put quickly, roughly, or carelessly: *He slapped the document down on the desk.* | *She slapped the paint thickly on the wall.* | *The council has slapped a demolition order on the old building.*

▷ USAGE Compare **slap**, **smack**, and **punch**. **Slap** and **smack** are both used about hitting someone with an open hand. **Slap** is usually used about hitting someone across the face: *She slapped his face.* **Smack** is used especially about hitting children: *Be quiet or I'll smack you!* | *I'll smack your bottom if you don't behave.* **Punch** is used about hitting someone or something with a closed hand: *A boxer tries to punch his opponent.* It is generally believed that women tend to **slap** and men tend to **punch**.◁

slap sbdy./sthg. ↔ **down** *phr v* [T] *infml* to force into silence or inactivity, esp. rudely or unfairly, because of disapproval, annoyance, etc.: *When I try to make intelligent contributions at meetings, the chairman always slaps me down.*

slap³ also **slap-bang** /ˌ·ˈ·/— *adv* [+prep] *infml* directly; right; SMACK³ (2): *The car ran slap into a tree.* | *The crisis blew up slap-bang in the middle of my holiday, and I had to return home.*

slap and tick·le /ˌ·ˈ·ˈ··/ *n* [U] *BrE old-fash infml, humor* playful lovemaking: *We were having a bit of slap and tickle in the back row of the cinema.*

slap·dash /ˈslæpdæʃ/ *adj* done, made, etc., in a hasty careless way: *very slapdash workmanship* | *She's very slapdash with her work.*

slap·hap·py /ˈslæpˌhæpi/ *adj infml* cheerfully slapdash or irresponsible

slap·stick /ˈslæpˌstɪk/ *n* [U] humorous acting (COMEDY) that depends on rather violent fast action and simple jokes. A typical slapstick scene might include someone being hit in the face with a CUSTARD PIE or people accidentally running into one another or hitting one another

slap-up /ˈ·-·/ *adj* [A] *BrE infml* (esp. of food) excellent and in large quantities: *He promised us a slap-up meal at the best restaurant in town.*

slash¹ /slæʃ/ *v* **1** [I (at);T] to cut with long sweeping violent strokes, using a sword, knife, or sharp tool: *She slashed at the bushes with a stick.* | *He tried to commit suicide by slashing his wrists.* | *Some vandals had slashed the seat covers on the train.* | *We slashed our way through the dense vegetation.* | (fig.) *The paper has made a slashing* (=very fierce) *attack on the government.* **2** [T *usu. pass.*] *infml* to reduce (an amount, price, etc.) very greatly: *"This week only: prices slashed!"* (shop advertisement) | *The new president slashed the defence budget by almost 30%.* **3** [I+adv|prep] (esp. of rain) to come hard down and across: *The rain slashed against the window.* **4** [T (with) *usu. pass.*] to cut (a piece of clothing) in order to sew in or show a different colour in the opening

slash² *n* **1** [C] a long sweeping cut or blow **2** [C] a straight cut making an opening in a piece of clothing **3** [S] *BrE infml, not polite* an act of passing water from the body; used mostly by men: *I'm just going to have a slash.* **4** [C] also **slash mark** /ˈ·-·/— an OBLIQUE²: *"7|2" can be read as "seven slash two".*

slash and burn /ˌ·-·ˈ·/ *adj* characterized by the cutting down and burning of trees and bushes to make land available for crops: *slash and burn agriculture*

slat /slæt/ *n* a thin narrow flat piece of wood, plastic, etc.,

esp. in furniture or VENETIAN BLINDs — ~ted *adj* : *a slatted bench*

slate¹ /sleɪt/ *n* **1** [U] a heavy usu. dark grey rock that can easily be split into flat thin pieces **2** [C] a small piece of slate or other material used for laying in rows to cover a roof: *Several slates blew off during the storm.* **3** [C] a small board made of slate or wood, used esp. formerly for writing on with chalk **4** [*the*+S] *infml BrE* a record of things bought but not yet paid for: *Two whiskies, please; and could you put them* **on the slate?** (=I will pay for them at a later date) **5** [C] an imaginary record of the past, esp. of mistakes, faults, disagreements, etc.: *Let's* **wipe the slate clean** *and forget our past quarrels.* | *You're all beginning here* **with clean slates** (=having done no wrong); *make sure you keep it that way.* **6** [C] *AmE* a list of people, esp. those of the same party, who are CANDIDATEs in an election

slate² *v* [T] **1** to cover (a roof) with slates **2** [+*obj*+**for**|*to-v usu. pass.*] *esp. AmE* **a** to choose for a position or job: *She's slated to be the next chairman.* **b** to expect or plan to happen: *The meeting is slated to take place|slated for next week.*

slate³ *v* [T] *BrE infml* to attack in words; severely CRITICIZE: *His latest play has been really slated by the critics.*

slat·tern /ˈslætən‖-ərn/ *n old-fash derog* a dirty untidy woman — ~ly *adj*

slat·y /ˈsleɪti/ *adj* like or containing slate: *a slaty grey colour*

slaugh·ter¹ /ˈslɔːtəʳ/ *n* [U] **1** the killing of many people or animals, esp. cruelly, wrongly, or in a battle; MASSACRE: *The battlefield was a scene of terrible slaughter.* **2** the killing of animals for meat: *The pigs are fattened until they're ready for slaughter.*

slaughter² *v* [T] **1** to kill (esp. many people) cruelly or wrongly; MASSACRE: *Thousands of people are needlessly slaughtered each year in road accidents.* **2** to kill (an animal) for food **3** *infml* to defeat severely in a game — see KILL (USAGE)

slaugh·ter·house /ˈslɔːtəhaʊs‖-ər-/ also **abattoir** *BrE— n* **-houses** /ˌhaʊzɪz/ a building where animals are killed for meat

Slav /slɑːv‖slɑːv, slæv/ *n, adj* (a member) of any of the East European peoples speaking Slavic languages

slave¹ /sleɪv/ *n* **1** a person who is legally owned by someone else; servant without personal freedom who is treated as a piece of property: *brutal and inhumane treatment of slaves* | *He treats his wife like a slave.* —compare SERF; see also ENSLAVE, WAGE SLAVE; see SLAVERY (CULTURAL NOTE) **2** [(of, to)] a person completely in the control of another person or thing: *We're all the slaves of habit.* | *He's a slave to drink.* **3 What did your last slave die of?** *infml humor* (used to someone who has just asked you to do something that you think they should do themselves)

slave² *v* [I (AWAY)] to work like a slave; work hard with little rest: *I slaved* (*away*) *all day over a hot stove to produce this meal, and now they've hardly eaten any of it.*

slave driv·er /ˈ·ˌ·ˈ··/ *n infml derog* someone who makes people work very hard: *The boss is a real slave driver.*

slave la·bour /ˌ·ˈ··/ *n* [U] **1** slaves used for work: *The pyramids were largely built by slave labour.* **2** *humor* hard work done for little or no pay, or because one is forced to do it

slav·er¹ /ˈslævəʳ/ *v* [I] **1** to let liquid (SALIVA) come out of the mouth uncontrollably, because of excitement, hunger, etc.: *The dog was slavering.* **2** [(over)] *esp. infml, usu. derog* to be eager or excited, esp. in an offensively unpleasant way: *The papers pretend to disapprove of this scandal, while at the same time slavering over every salacious detail.*

slav·er² /ˈsleɪvəʳ/ *n old use* **1** a ship that carried slaves **2** a person in the business of selling slaves

sla·ve·ry /ˈsleɪvəri/ *n* [U] **1** the system of having slaves: *the abolition of slavery* **2** the condition of being a slave: *The prisoners were sold into slavery.* —see also WHITE SLAVERY

▶CULTURAL NOTE The main associations of slavery for British and American people are with the SLAVE TRADE from the 17th to the 19th centuries and with the suffering of black slaves in the South of the US. Slavery was one of the causes of the American Civil War in 1861 and was finally officially ended at the end of the Civil War with the victory of the northern states —see also ABOLITIONIST, AFRICAN-AMERICAN, CIVIL WAR, EMANCIPATION PROCLAMATION, Abraham LINCOLN; see also SLAVE TRADE (CULTURAL NOTE)◀

slave state /'· ·/ *n* any of the US states where slavery was permitted and practised before 1865 —see also SLAVERY (CULTURAL NOTE)

slave trade /'· ·/ also **slave traf·fic** /'· ˌ··/— [*the*] the business of buying and selling slaves, which is forbidden by law in all countries

▶CULTURAL NOTE In Britain and the US this is thought of in connection with the forced carrying away of Africans as slaves in the 17th to 19th centuries. They were mostly taken to the colonies (COLONY) of European countries, and to America, esp. the South, where they worked on large farms. By the mid-nineteenth century the slave trade was no longer legal in many countries, but continued in the southern states of the US. —see also SLAVERY (CULTURAL NOTE)◀

Sla·vic /'slɑːvɪk, 'slæ-/ also **Sla·von·ic** /slə'vɒnɪk‖-'vɑː-/— *adj* of the East European people (Slavs) including Russians, Czechs, Slovaks, Poles, Yugoslavs, etc., or their languages

slav·ish /'sleɪvɪʃ/ *adj derog* **1** showing complete obedience to, dependence on, and willingness to work for others; slavelike: *Her slavish devotion to duty is unhealthy.* **2** copying or copied very closely or exactly from something else; not fresh or original: *It's a slavish translation, very faithful to the original but hardly understandable in English.* —~**ly** *adv* —~**ness** *n* [U]

slaw /slɔː/ *n AmE* COLESLAW

slay /sleɪ/ *v* **slew** /sluː/, **slain** /sleɪn/ [T] *lit or AmE* to kill violently; (*AmE*) *"Top businessman slain by terrorists"* (title of newspaper story) —see KILL (USAGE) —~**er** *n*

SLD /ˌes el 'diː/ [*the* + *sing./pl. v*] SOCIAL AND LIBERAL DEMOCRATS

sleaze /sliːz/ *n* [C;U] *AmE infml* (a thing or person having) the quality of being sleazy: *I like her but her brother's a real sleaze.* | *There's lots of sleaze moving into this neighbourhood now.*

slea·zy /'sliːzi/ *adj derog* cheap, dirty, poor-looking, and often suggesting immorality; DISREPUTABLE: *They took me to a sleazy back-street hotel that could easily have been a brothel.* —**ziness** *n* [U]

sled /sled/ *v* **-dd-** [I] *AmE* SLEDGE² —**sled** *n*

sledge¹ /sledʒ/ *n BrE‖***sled** *AmE—* **1** a vehicle made for carrying people or goods over snow, having two long metal blades and sometimes pulled by dogs **2** a light frame or board, sometimes on metal blades, used for sliding over snow, esp. for sport —compare SLEIGH

sledge² *BrE‖***sled, coast** *AmE—* *v* [I] to go or race down slopes on a sledge: *When it snows we* **go sledging.**

sledge·ham·mer /'sledʒˌhæməʳ/ *n* a large heavy hammer for swinging with both hands to drive in posts, break stones, etc.

sleek¹ /sliːk/ *adj* **1** (esp. of hair or fur) smooth and shining (as if) from good health and care: *a sleek Siamese cat* **2** attractively neat in appearance, and without unnecessary decoration: *The new car's sleek lines* (=attractive shape) *should make it very popular* —~**ly** *adv* —~**ness** *n* [U]

sleek² *v* [T+*obj*+*adv/prep*] to cause (hair or fur) to be smooth and shining: *He sleeked down/back his hair with water before going out.*

sleep¹ /sliːp/ *n* **1** [U] the natural resting state of unconsciousness of the body: *Try to get eight hours' sleep a night.* | *I haven't had enough sleep lately.* | (fig.) *He says there might be trouble, but I'm not going to* **lose any sleep** (=become anxious) *over it.* **2** [S] an act or period of sleeping: *I had a short sleep after lunch.* | *She fell into a deep sleep.* **3 get to sleep** [*usu. in negatives*] to succeed in sleeping: *I couldn't get to sleep last night; I was too excited.* **4 go to sleep: a** to begin to sleep; fall asleep **b** *infml* (of an arm, leg, etc.) to become unable to feel, or begin to feel PINS AND NEEDLES **5 put to sleep** *euph* **a** to kill (a suffering animal) without cruelty **b** *infml* to make (a person) unconscious, esp. for an operation —see also ASLEEP, BEAUTY SLEEP

sleep² *v* **slept** /slept/ **1** [I] to rest in sleep: *He likes to sleep for an hour in the afternoon.* | *I didn't sleep very well last*

night. | *I usually* **sleep late** *on Sundays.* | *As he'd missed his train, we invited him to* **sleep the night** *with us.* (=sleep in our house for that night) **2** [T] to provide beds or places for sleep for (a number of people): *The back seat of the car folds down to sleep two.* **3 sleep like a log** *infml* to sleep deeply, esp. without moving **4 sleep rough** to sleep in uncomfortable conditions, esp. out of doors **5 to sleep: perchance to dream** *quote* a phrase from Shakespeare's play *Hamlet*, sometimes used by people speaking about what may happen after death

sleep around *phr v* [I] *infml derog* to have sex with a lot of different people; be PROMISCUOUS

sleep in *phr v* [I] **1** to intentionally sleep later than usual in the morning; LIE in (1): *I often sleep in on Sundays.* —compare OVERSLEEP **2** *BrE* to sleep at one's place of work; LIVE **in** —opposite **sleep out**

sleep sthg. ↔ **off** *phr v* [T] **1** to get rid of (a feeling or effect of something) by sleeping: *He went to bed to sleep off his enormous lunch.* **2 sleep it off** *infml* to sleep until one is no longer drunk

sleep on sthg. *phr v* [T] to delay deciding on (a problem) until the next day; spend a night considering: *Look, there's no need to make a decision now; why don't you go home and sleep on it?*

sleep out *phr v* [I] **1** to sleep away from home or outdoors **2** *BrE* to sleep away from one's place of work —opposite **sleep in**

sleep through sthg. *phr v* [T] to fail to wake up during; be asleep and miss hearing, seeing, etc.: *I don't know how you could have slept through that dreadful noise/thrilling performance.*

sleep together *phr v* [I] (of two people who are not married) to have sex

sleep with sbdy. *phr v* [T] to have sex with (someone one is not married to)

Sleep, Wayne (1948–) a popular English male BALLET dancer, who often appears on British television

sleep·er /'sliːpəʳ/ *n* **1** a person sleeping **2** a person who sleeps in the stated way: *I didn't hear the explosion — I'm a heavy/sound sleeper.* | *a light sleeper* **3** *esp. BrE* ‖ usu. **tie** *AmE—* any of the row of heavy pieces of wood, metal, etc., supporting a railway track **4** a train with beds for sleeping through the night **5** *BrE* a small ring worn in the ear, so as to keep open a hole made there for an EARRING **6** *esp. AmE* something, such as a book, play, record, etc., that has a delayed or unexpected success

sleeping bag /'·· ·/ *n* a large warm bag filled with soft material for sleeping in when camping

Sleeping Beauty

Sleeping Beau·ty /ˌ·· '··/ *n* someone who appears to be sleeping peacefully (from the story of the Sleeping Beauty, in which a princess falls asleep for a hundred years until a prince's kiss breaks the SPELL (3) and wakes her): *Just look at our Sleeping Beauty.*

sleeping car /'·· ·/ *n* a railway carriage with beds for passengers —compare COUCHETTE

sleeping dogs /'·· ˌ·/ *n* [P] **let sleeping dogs lie** not to make trouble for oneself by continuing to remember old arguments and problems one had with someone else

sleeping part·ner /ˌ·· '··/ *BrE* ‖ **silent partner** *AmE— n* a partner in a business who takes no active part in its operation

sleeping pill /'·· ·/ also **sleeping tab·let** /'·· ˌ··/— *n* a PILL which helps a person to sleep

▶CULTURAL NOTE One can normally only get sleeping pills in Britain with a doctor's PRESCRIPTION. In the US several kinds are available, both prescription and non-prescription: *She died from an overdose of sleeping pills.* ◀

sleeping po·lice·man /ˌ·· ·ˈ··/ *esp. BrE* ‖ **speed bump** *AmE*— *n* a narrow raised part placed across a road to force traffic to move slowly

sleeping sick·ness /ˈ·· ˌ··/ *n* [U] a serious African disease carried by the TSETSE FLY, that causes loss of weight, fever, and great tiredness

sleep·less /ˈsliːpləs/ *adj* **1** not providing sleep: *I've spent many sleepless nights worrying about what I should do.* **2** *lit* not sleeping or able to sleep: *He lay sleepless on his bed.* — ~ **ly** *adv* — ~ **ness** *n* [U]

sleep·walk·er /ˈsliːpˌwɔːkəʳ/ *n* a person who gets up and walks about while asleep. It is believed by many people that you should not wake someone when they are sleepwalking. —**walking** *n* [U] —**sleepwalk** *v* [I]

sleep·y /ˈsliːpi/ *adj* **1** tired and ready for sleep; DROWSY **2** quiet; inactive or slow-moving: *a sleepy country town* —**ily** *adv* : *"What time is it?" she said sleepily* —**iness** *n* [U]

sleep·y·head /ˈsliːpihed/ *n infml* a sleepy person, esp. a child: *Wake up, sleepyhead!*

sleet¹ /sliːt/ *n* [U] partly frozen rain; ice falling in fine bits mixed with water: *The rain/snow turned to sleet.* —see RAIN (USAGE) — ~ **y** *adj*

sleet² *v* [it+I] (of sleet) to fall: *It's started sleeting.*

sleeve /sliːv/ *n* **1** a part of a garment for covering (part of) an arm: *a dress with short/long sleeves* | *He rolled up his sleeves and started to dig.* **2** *esp. BrE* ‖ usu. **jacket** *AmE*— a stiff envelope for keeping a RECORD² (4) in **3** a tube with two open ends for enclosing something, esp. a machine part **4 have/keep something up one's sleeve** *infml* to keep something secret for use at the right time in the future: *I've got a few ideas up my sleeve if this method doesn't work.* **5** -**sleeved** /sliːvd/having sleeves of the stated length or shape: *a short-sleeved shirt* —see also **laugh up one's sleeve** (LAUGH¹), **wear one's heart on one's sleeve** (WEAR¹) — ~ **less** *adj*

sleeve notes /ˈ· ˌ·/ *BrE*‖**liner notes** *AmE*— *n* [P] printed information on a SLEEVE (2) about the contents of the RECORD² (4) inside

sleigh /sleɪ/ *n* a large usu, horse drawn vehicle which slides along on snow on two metal blades – compare SLEDGE¹ —see colour picture on page 1212

sleight of hand /ˌslaɪt əv ˈhænd/ *n* [U] skill and quickness of the hands in doing tricks: *He made the coin disappear by sleight of hand.* | (fig.) *It was a remarkable piece of political sleight of hand to get such an unpopular policy accepted.*

slen·der /ˈslendəʳ/ *n* **1** *apprec* delicately or gracefully thin in the body; not fat: *a slender woman/figure* —see THIN (USAGE) **2** (pleasingly) thin compared to length or height; not wide or thick: *The spider hung suspended on its slender thread.* **3** slight, small and hardly enough; MEAGRE: *(euph) a person of slender means/resources* (=without much money) | *They won the election, but only with a very slender majority.* — ~ **ness** *n* [U]

slen·der·ize /ˈslendəraɪz/ *v* [I;T] *AmE old-fash* to make (oneself) thinner by eating less, playing sports, etc.

slept /slept/ *past tense & participle of* SLEEP

sleuth /sluːθ/ *n humor for* DETECTIVE (2)

S lev·el /ˈes levəl/ *n* an examination at a very high standard in the British GCE, higher than an A level, usu. taken at the age of 18

slew¹ /sluː/ *past tense of* SLAY

slew² ‖ also **slue** *AmE*— *v* [I;T (ROUND, AROUND)] to (cause to) turn or swing violently: *I lost control of the car and it slewed round.*

slew³ *n* [(of) *usu. sing.*] *infml* a large number; lot: *We've got a whole slew of difficulties.*

slewed /sluːd/ *adj* [F] *BrE old-fash sl* drunk

slice¹ /slaɪs/ *n* **1** [(of)] a thin flat piece cut from something: *a slice of bread/cake* | (fig.) *They wanted to make sure they got a slice of the profits/of the market.* —see CHUNK (USAGE), and see picture at PIECE **2** a kitchen tool with a broad blade for lifting and serving pieces of food —see also FISH SLICE **3** (in sports like GOLF and tennis) (a stroke causing) a flight of a ball towards one side, rather than straight ahead **4 a slice of the cake**

(BrE) ‖ **pie** *(AmE)* a share in something, esp. a sum of money: *Cities like Birmingham are hoping to get a bigger slice of the grant cake this year.*

slice² *v* **1** [T (UP)] to cut into slices: *Slice the cucumber, please.* | *She sliced up the cake.* **2** [T+*obj*+*adv/prep*] to cut off as a slice: *He sliced off a thick piece from the loaf.* **3** [I+*adv/prep*;T] to cut with a knife: *He sliced (into/through) his fingers by accident when cutting vegetables.* **4** [I;T] to hit (a ball) in a SLICE¹ (3) **5 any way you slice it** *AmE infml* however you consider it

sliced bread /ˌ· ˈ·/ *n* [U] **1** bread that is sold already cut into slices. **2 (think something is) the best/greatest thing since sliced bread** *infml* (to think, possibly foolishly, very highly of) something new which appears to be wonderful: *He thinks his new word processor is the best thing since sliced bread.*

slice of life /ˌ·· ·ˈ·/ *n* [S] a representation or experience of life as it really is: *one of those modern dramas that tries to give you a slice of life rather than just entertain you*

slick¹ /slɪk/ *adj* **1** skilful and effective, so as to seem easy: *The dancers gave a very slick performance.* **2** clever, effective, or able to persuade but often not honest: *a slick salesman/advertising campaign* | *slick sales talk* **3** (esp. of roads or tyres) smooth and slippery **4** *AmE approv* very good: *a slick new car* | *These new programs are really slick.* — ~ **ly** *adv* — ~ **ness** *n* [U]

slick² *n* **1** *infml* an OIL SLICK **2** *AmE for* GLOSSY MAGAZINE

slick³ *v*

slick sthg.↔**down** *phr v* [T] to make (esp. hair) smooth and shiny with water, oil, etc.

slick·er /ˈslɪkəʳ/ *n* **1** *infml, usu. humor* a well-dressed, self-confident, but probably untrustworthy person —see also CITY SLICKER) **2** *AmE* a coat made to keep out the rain

slide¹ /slaɪd/ *v* **slid** /slɪd/ **1** [I;T] to (cause to) go smoothly over a surface, remaining continually in CONTACT with it: *She slid along the ice.* | *He slid his glass across the table top.* | *Slide the drawer out carefully.* —compare GLIDE **2** [I+*adv/prep*] to pass or move quietly and unnoticed; slip: *She slid out of the room when no one was looking.* | *He slid over/around the question without answering it.* | *She slid the gun out of sight/into her pocket.* **3** [I] to go down to a lower level: *Will the government take action to support the sliding pound?* —see also BACKSLIDE **4 let something slide** *infml* to let a situation or condition continue, esp. getting worse, without taking action or trying to stop it, usu. because of laziness

slide² *n* **1** a slipping movement over a surface: *The car went into a slide on the ice.* **2** a downward movement, esp. of prices, amounts, etc.; fall: *How can we halt the slide in living standards?* **3** an apparatus for sliding down: *a children's playground slide* **4** a small piece of film in a frame for passing strong light through to show a picture on a surface: *They showed us some colour slides of their holiday.* | *a slide show/projector* **5** a small piece of thin glass to put an object on for looking at under a microscope: *He mounted the specimen on a slide* **6** (*usu. in comb.*) a sudden fall of material down a hill: *a snowslide/rockslide/mudslide* —see also LANDSLIDE **7** a HAIR SLIDE **8** a sliding machine part, such as the U-shaped tube on a TROMBONE —see picture at BRASS

slide rule /ˈ· ˌ·/ *n* an instrument for calculating numbers, usu. made of a ruler marked with LOGARITHMs, with a middle part that slides along its length

sliding door /ˌ· ˈ·/ *n* a door that slides across an opening rather than swinging from one side of it

sliding scale /ˌ·· ˈ·/ *n* a system of pay, taxes, etc., calculated by rates which may vary according to changing conditions

slight¹ /slaɪt/ *adj* **1** small in degree; not considerable, noticeable, or serious: *a slight pain* | *a slight improvement* | *There's been a slight change in the plans.* | *I haven't the slightest idea* (=I have no idea) *what you're talking about.* **2** *esp. lit* not strong-looking; thin and delicate: *Her slight frame was shaken by bouts of coughing.* **3 in the slightest** (*usu. in negatives*) at all: *"Do you mind if I open the window?" "Not in the slightest; please do."* — ~ **ness** *n* [U]

slight² *v* [T] to treat (a person or group) rudely, without respect, or as if unimportant — ~ **ingly** *adv*

slight³ *n* [(**on, to**)] a slighting act; INSULT: *I'm afraid he took your remark as a slight on/to his work.*

slight·ly /'slaɪtli/ adv **1** to a slight degree; a bit; rather: *This one's slightly better than that, but not much.* | *I feel slightly ill.* **2** in a slight way: *a small slightly-built man*

Sli·go /'slaɪgəʊ/ a COUNTY in the W of the Republic of Ireland

sli·ly /'slaɪli/ adv see SLY

slim[1] /slɪm/ adj **-mm-** apprec **1** (esp. of a person) attractively thin; not fat

▶CULTURAL NOTE It is thought attractive and desirable by many people to be slim: *a slim elegant girl* | *slim hips* | *to keep slim by taking regular exercise* —see THIN (USAGE)◀

2 (of hope, probability, etc.) very small; slight: *Our chances of winning are slim.* — ~**ly** adv — ~**ness** n [U]

slim[2] v **-mm-** **1** [I] BrE to (try to) make oneself thinner by eating less, taking a lot of exercise, etc.: *I don't want any cake; I'm slimming|trying to slim|on a slimming diet.* — see also DIET **2** [T (DOWN)] to reduce in size or number: *attempts to slim (down) the company's workforce* — ~**mer** n — ~**ming** n [U]

Slim also **Slim dis·ease** /'· ·₁·/— n [U] EAfr Eng for AIDS

slime /slaɪm/ n [U] an unpleasant partly-liquid substance, such as the thick sticky liquid produced by the skin of various fish and SNAILS: *The snails left a trail of slime.* | *a pond covered in green slime*

slim·y /'slaɪmi/ adj **1** like, covered with, or being slime; unpleasantly slippery, esp. to touch: *a slimy mess of squashed fruit* **2** derog trying to please in order to gain advantage, for oneself; insincerely HUMBLE: *a slimy manner* —**iness** n [U]

sling[1] /slɪŋ/ v **slung** /slʌŋ/ [T] **1** [+obj+adv/prep] to cause to hang or be loosely supported: *She slung her coat over her shoulder.* | *A line of flags was slung between the trees.* **2** infml to throw, esp. roughly or with effort: [+obj+adv/prep] *He slung it into the wastepaper basket.* | (fig.) *If you don't attend all the lectures you'll get slung off|slung out of the course.* [+obj(i)+obj(d)] *Sling me the keys.* **3 sling mud at** to say unfair and damaging things about (esp. a political opponent) **4 sling one's hook** BrE sl to go away

sling[2] n **1** a piece of cloth for hanging from the neck to support a damaged arm or hand: *She had her arm in a sling.* **2** an apparatus of ropes, bands, etc., for holding heavy objects to be lifted or carried **3** a length of cord with a piece of leather in the middle, held at the ends and swung round, used in former times for throwing stones with force **4** a cloth band on a weapon for carrying it upright behind the shoulder or across the back **5 the slings and arrows (of outrageous fortune)** quote all the difficulties and opposition people have to face in their lives (a phrase from Shakespeare's play *Hamlet*)

sling·shot /'slɪŋʃɒt‖-ʃɑːt/ n AmE for CATAPULT[1] (1)

slink /slɪŋk/ v **slunk** /slʌŋk/ [I+adv/prep] to move quietly and secretly (esp. away from something), as if in fear or shame: *The defeated army slunk back to its strongholds in the mountains.*

slink·y /'slɪŋki/ adj infml apprec (esp. of a garment) smooth and rather tight, so as to show off the lines of the body: *her slinky black dress* —**ily** adv —**iness** n [U]

slip[1] /slɪp/ v **-pp-** **1** [I] to slide a short distance out of place quickly and unexpectedly, or fall by sliding: *My foot slipped and I nearly fell.* | *It was icy, and people were slipping and sliding all along the street.* | *The soap slipped out of my hand.* —see also SLIPPERY **2** [I+adv/prep] to move smoothly, secretly, or unnoticed: *She slipped into|out of the room when no one was looking.* | *I'm just going to slip down to the shops.* | *As the years slipped by|past, I thought less about her.* | (fig.) *I'm sorry I told them your secret — it just slipped out.* | (fig.) *The terrorists managed to slip through the airport's security net.* | (fig.) *You're not going to let a wonderful chance like that slip through your fingers, are you?* **3** [T] to put or give smoothly, secretly, or unnoticed: [+obj+adv/prep] *I slipped a note into her hand under the table.* | *He slipped his arm round her.* [+obj(i)+obj(d)] *He slipped the waiter £5 to get them a good table.* **4** [I+into/out of; T+obj +ON/OFF] to put on or take off (a garment) quickly: *He slipped out of his jacket.* | *She slipped her swimsuit on.* — see also SLIP-ON. **5** [T] to get free from (a fastening): *The dog slipped his collar and ran away.* | *The boat slipped its moorings.* **6** [T] to escape from (one's attention, memory, etc.); be forgotten or unnoticed by: *I'm sorry I*

forgot his birthday; the date completely slipped my mind. **7** [I (UP)] to make a slight mistake: *The office slipped up and the letter was never sent.* —see also SLIP-UP **8** [I] to fall from a standard; get worse or lower: *I'm afraid the National Theatre Company is slipping; this year's productions have been very poor.* | *Profits have slipped slightly this year.* **9 let slip: a** to fail to follow (a chance, offer, etc.) **b** to say without intending; make known accidentally: *She let slip that she was intending to leave the company.* **10 slip a disc** to get a SLIPPED DISC **11 slip something over on** infml, esp. AmE to trick (someone) cleverly

slip[2] n **1** [C] an act of slipping or sliding **2** [C] a usu. slight mistake: *If you make a slip, rub it out neatly.* | *"Jim" was a slip of the tongue; I meant to say "John".* —see also FREUDIAN SLIP **3** [C] a woman's undergarment which hangs from the shoulders or waist: *Your slip's showing.* **4** (in cricket) a fielding (FIELD[2] (1)) position close to the BATSMAN and just behind him on the off (OFF[4]) side: *Gower was caught at slip.* **5 give someone the slip** infml to escape from someone, esp. someone who is chasing one —see also PILLOWCASE **6 there's many a slip 'twixt the cup and the lip** a plan or intention may easily go wrong before it is fully carried out or when it seemed to be about to succeed

slip[3] n **1** [(of)] a usu. small or narrow piece of paper: *She marked her place in the book with a slip of paper.* | *Write your name and address on this pink slip.* **2** tech a small branch cut for planting; CUTTING **3** [+of; usu. sing.] old-fash infml a small thin young person: *She's only a slip of a girl.* **4** a place next to a PIER or in a HARBOUR to keep a boat in the water

slip·case /'slɪp₁keɪs/ n a usu. cardboard protective cover with one open end, for keeping a book in

slip·cov·er /'slɪpkʌvəʳ/ n AmE **1** a DUST JACKET **2** a loose cloth cover for furniture which is easily removed for cleaning

slip·knot /'slɪpnɒt‖-nɑːt/ n a knot that can be tightened round something by pulling one of its ends

slip-on /'· ·/ adj [A] (of shoes) able to be put on without fastenings: *slip-on shoes* —**slip-on** n : *a pair of slip-ons*

slip·page /'slɪpɪdʒ/ n [C;U] (the amount of) slipping: *a steep slippage in the peso* | *a general slippage in management discipline*

slipped disc /₁· '·/ n [S] a painful movement out of place of one of the DISCs (=connecting parts) between vertebrae (VERTEBRA) in the human back —see also **slip a disc** (SLIP[1] (10))

slip·per /'slɪpəʳ/ n also **carpet slipper** old use— n a light shoe with the top made from soft material, usu. worn indoors —see also GLASS SLIPPER; see PAIR (USAGE), and see picture at SHOE

slip·per·y /'slɪpəri/ adj **1** difficult to hold or to stand on, drive on, etc., without slipping: *Drive very carefully; the roads are wet and slippery.* | *a slippery fish* **2** infml not to be trusted; SHIFTY: *Don't lend any money to him—he's a slippery customer.* (=an untrustworthy person) —**iness** n [U]

slippery slope /₁··· '·/ n BrE a situation in which it is difficult to change your mind or go back: *Once they've tried soft drugs they're really on the slippery slope to addiction.*

slip·py /'slɪpi/ adj infml **1** slippery **2 look slippy** [usu. imperative] BrE to hurry up; be quick

slip road /'· ·/ BrE‖**ramp** AmE— n a road for driving onto or off a MOTORWAY

slip·shod /'slɪpʃɒd‖-ʃɑːd/ adj careless; not exact or thorough: *a slipshod piece of work* | *slipshod reasoning*

slip·stream[1] /'slɪpstriːm/ n **1** an area of low air pressure just behind a fast-moving vehicle, e.g. a racing car, which helps a following driver to keep up his or her speed easily **2** a stream of air driven backwards by an aircraft engine

slipstream[2] v [I] to drive in the slipstream of the vehicle in front

slip-up /'· ·/ n a usu. slight unintentional mistake —see also SLIP[1] (7)

slip·way /'slɪpweɪ/ n a track sloping down into the water for moving ships into or out of water

slit[1] /slɪt/ n a long narrow cut or opening: *Light shone* *through a slit under the door.* —compare SLOT[1]

slit[2] *v* **slit**; *present participle* **-tt-** [T] to make a slit in; cut, esp. carefully or intentionally: *Her long dress was slit up to the knee in Chinese style.* | *They slit his throat.* | *She slit the envelope open with a knife.*

slith·er /ˈslɪðər/ *v* [I+*adv*/*prep*] **1** to move (one's body) in a slipping or twisting way: *a snake slithering through the long grass* **2** to slide or slip (while trying to walk): *People were slithering about on the icy pavement.*

slith·er·y /ˈslɪðəri/ *adj* slippery in appearance or feeling

sliv·er /ˈslɪvər/ *n* [(of)] a small thin pointed and often sharp piece cut or torn off: *a sliver of glass from the broken window* —see picture at PIECE

sliv·o·vitz /ˈslɪvəvɪts, ˈsliː-/ *n* [U] a strong alcoholic drink made in SE Europe from PLUMs

Sloane Rang·er /ˌsləʊn ˈreɪndʒər/ also **Sloane** *infml*— *n derog* (in Britain) a STEREOTYPE of a young person, esp. a woman, who comes from an upper MIDDLE-CLASS family, esp. from the country areas in the south of England, and a particular set of CONSERVATIVE values. Sloane Rangers typically wear DESIGNER clothes and spend a lot of time on their social lives, esp. in fashionable places such as Chelsea. People often joke about them driving Range Rovers, wearing Barbour jackets and GREEN WELLIES, and saying "OK yah" and calling their parents "Mummy and Daddy" past the usual age for using these terms. Their lifestyle is thought to be very SHALLOW[1] (2): *The '90s have brought a new, more broad-minded and thoughtful breed of thirtysomething Sloanes.* —compare COUNTY[2], see also HOORAY HENRY —**Sloane, Sloaney** *adj*

Sloane Square /ˌ· ˈ·/ a fashionable, expensive place to live in London

slob /slɒb‖slɑːb/ *n infml* a rude, lazy, dirty, or carelessly dressed person: *When are you going to get out of bed, you fat slob?*

slob·ber /ˈslɒbər‖ˈslɑː-/ *v* [I] *derog* **1** to have SALIVA (=the liquid produced by the mouth) running from one's mouth: *I hate having dogs slobbering all over my hand.* **2** [(over)] to express feelings of admiration too openly and without careful judgment: *This is the worst sort of poetry, slobbering over the beauties of nature.* —compare DROOL

sloe /sləʊ/ *n* a small bitter kind of PLUM

sloe gin /ˌ· ˈ·/ *n* [U] an alcoholic drink made with sloes, GIN, and sugar

slog[1] /slɒg/ *v* **-gg-** **1** [I+*adv*/*prep*] *infml esp. BrE* to do hard dull work without stopping; make one's way by continuous effort: *That maths homework was really difficult; I slogged away at it for hours!* | *We slogged up the hill through the mud.* **2** [I;T] *infml esp. BrE* (esp. in cricket) to hit (the ball) hard and wildly — ~**ger** *n*

slog[2] *n* **1** [S;U] *BrE* (a period of) hard dull work without stopping. *It was a real slog addressing all those envelopes.* | *the long hard slog ahead* **2** [C] *BrE* (esp. in cricket) a wild hard hit **3** [C] a period of difficult walking: *a long slog up the mountain*

slo·gan /ˈsləʊgən/ *n* a short phrase expressing a usu. political or advertising message: *"Small is beautiful" was his slogan.* | *demonstrators chanting anti-nuclear slogans* | *to daub slogans on walls* —compare MOTTO (1)

sloop /sluːp/ *n* **1** a small sailing ship with one central MAST (=pole) and sails along its length **2** a small armed ship such as a CUTTER (1b)

slop[1] /slɒp‖slɑːp/ *v* **-pp-** **1** [T] to cause (a liquid) to go over the side of a container; SPILL: *He stirred in the sugar vigorously, slopping tea into the saucer as he did so.* **2** [I+*adv*/*prep*] (of a liquid) to do this: *Some of the soup slopped over the edge of the bowl.* —compare SLOSH **3** [T] *AmE* to feed (pigs)
slop about/around *phr v* [I] *infml* **1** *derog* to move about in a lazy purposeless way **2** to play in or move about in anything wet or dirty
slop out *phr v* [I] *BrE* (of a prisoner) to empty SLOPS[2] (4) from a CHAMBER POT

slop[2] also **slops** *pl.*— *n* [U] **1** *derog* tasteless liquid food **2** liquid waste from food or drinks: *slops from the tea and coffee cups* **3** food waste, esp. for feeding to animals **4** *BrE* dirty water or URINE

slope[1] /sləʊp/ *v* [I] to lie or move in a direction neither completely upright nor completely flat; be or go at an angle:

The mountains slope down to the sea. | *The floor slopes badly here.* | *sloping handwriting*
slope off *phr v* [I] *BrE infml* to go away secretly, esp. so as to escape or avoid work: *As soon as the boss left I sloped off home.*

slope[2] *n* **1** a surface that slopes; a piece of ground going up or down: *to climb a steep slope* | *a gentle slope* | *a ski slope* | (fig.) *The party is on the slippery slope to ruin.* **2** a degree of sloping; a measure of an angle from a level direction: *a slope of 30 degrees*

slop·py /ˈslɒpi‖ˈslɑːpi/ *adj* **1** not careful or thorough enough: *This is a very sloppy piece of work.* **2** *infml* (esp. of clothes) loose, informal, and careless-looking or dirty-looking: *a sloppy old sweater* **3** *infml* silly in showing feelings: *sloppy sentimentalism* —**pily** *adv* —**piness** *n* [U]

sloppy joe /ˌslɒpi ˈdʒəʊ‖ˌslɑː-/ *n AmE* a dish made from BEEF with SPICEs added served on a BUN

slosh /slɒʃ‖slɑːʃ/ *v infml* **1** [I;T] to move or cause (a liquid) to move about (as if) against the sides of a container: *Water sloshed about in the bottom of the boat.* | *She sloshed the wine around in her glass* —compare SLOP[1] **2** [I+*adv*/*prep*] to walk through water or mud noisily: *We sloshed along in our rubber boots.* **3** [T] *BrE* to hit; PUNCH

sloshed /slɒʃt‖slɑːʃt/ *adj* [F] *infml* drunk

slot[1] /slɒt‖slɑːt/ *n* **1** a long straight narrow opening or hollow place, esp. in a machine or tool: *Put a coin in the slot.* | *a slot in the top of a screw* —compare SLIT[1] **2** *infml* a place or position in a list, system, organization, etc.: *He's been given a regular ten-minute slot on the radio.* | *to fill advertising slots*

slot[2] *v* **-tt-** **1** [I+*adv*/*prep*; T+*adv*/*prep*, esp. IN, **into**] to put or be put into a SLOT[1] (1): *You buy this bookcase in sections and slot them together.* | *"This box has a removable lid which slots back in like this", he said, slotting it into the box.* **2** *infml, esp. BrE* to fit into a SLOT[1] (2); find a place for or be found a place: *This new car slots in between the economy model and the executive model in our range.* | *I've got some urgent business to discuss. Can you slot me in after lunch?*

sloth /sləʊθ/ *n* **1** [C] a slow-moving animal of central and S America that lives in trees and hangs by all four legs from branches **2** [U] *esp. lit* unwillingness to work; laziness. Sloth is one of the Seven Deadly Sins. —see also SEVEN DEADLY SINS

sloth·ful /ˈsləʊθfəl/ *adj esp. lit* unwilling to work or be active; lazy — ~**ly** *adv* — ~**ness** *n* [U]

slot ma·chine /ˈ· ·ˌ·/ *n* **1** *BrE* a VENDING MACHINE **2** *AmE* for ONE-ARMED BANDIT

slot·ted /ˈslɒtɪd‖ˈslɑː-/ *adj* having a SLOT[1] (1) cut into it: *a slotted screw*

slotted spat·u·la /ˌ·· ˈ···/ *n AmE for* FISH SLICE —see picture at KITCHEN

slouch[1] /slaʊtʃ/ *n* **1** [S] a tired-looking round-shouldered way of sitting, standing, or walking **2** [C *usu. in negatives*] *infml* a lazy, slow, or useless person: *He's no slouch when it comes to writing books.* (=he writes them quickly and often)

slouch[2] *v* [I] to sit, stand, or walk with a slouch: *She slouches around the house all day, doing nothing.* — ~**ingly** *adv*

slouch hat /ˌ· ˈ·/ *n* a man's soft hat with a BRIM that can be pulled down

slough[1] /slʌf/ *v*
slough sth. ↔ **off** *phr v* [T] **1** (esp. of a snake) to throw off (dead outer skin) **2** *esp. lit* to get rid of as something worn out or unwanted
slough over *phr v* [T] *AmE* to treat as unimportant, esp. in order to hide a problem or difficulty: *He sloughed over all the details about how much it would cost and said we could drive it home tonight.*

slough[2] /slaʊ‖sluː, slaʊ/ *n* **1** a place of deep mud or MARSH **2** [(of)] *lit* a bad condition from which one cannot easily get free: *a slough of self-pity*

Slough /slaʊ/ a modern, industrial town in Berkshire, S England

Slough of Des·pond /ˌslaʊ əv dɪ ˈspɒnd‖ˌsluː- əv dɪ ˈspɑːnd, slaʊ-/ [*the*] *lit or pomp* a situation full of doubts and fears (from the name of a place in John Bunyan's *The Pilgrim's Progress*)

Slo·va·ki·a /sləʊˈvɑːkiə/ one of the main parts of Czechoslovakia, which controls its own local affairs

Slo·ve·ni·a /sləʊˈviːniə/ a country in SE Europe bordered by Austria, Italy, and Croatia, formerly part of Yugoslavia; capital Ljubljana; population 1,940,000 (1988) —**nian** *n, adj*

slov·en·ly /ˈslʌvənli/ *adj* **1** (of habits, etc.) not clean, neat, or orderly; untidy: *How can you bear to live in such slovenly conditions?* **2** very carelessly done: *a slovenly piece of work* —**liness** *n* [U]

slow[1] /sləʊ/ *adj* **1** not moving, acting, or happening quickly; having less than a usual or average speed: *a slow train* | *slow music* | *the slow erosion of rock by wind and rain* **2** a taking a long time or a longer time than usual: *Heavy traffic made our journey very/painfully slow.* | *a restaurant with slow service* | *a long slow process* **b** taking too long, esp. because of unwillingness; not PROMPT: *a slow response to our request for help* [F+*to*-*v*] *The public has been rather slow to recognize/grasp the implications of the new law.* **3** [F; after *n*] (of a clock) showing a time that is earlier than the true time, often by a stated amount: *The station clocks are (two minutes) slow.* —see CLOCK (USAGE) **4** [A] not intended for quick movement: *the slow lane of a motorway* **5** not very active; dull: *Business is slow just now.* **6** not good or quick in understanding; dull in mind: *our slowest pupils* | *I'm sorry I'm so slow today; I didn't get much sleep last night.* | *He's so* **slow off the mark/slow on the uptake** (=slow in understanding) *that you have to repeat the simplest instructions.* **7 slow and steady wins the race** success is gained by steady continuous effort (from the story of the Tortoise and the Hare in Aesop, in which the TORTOISE, moving slowly but steadily, wins a race) — ~ **ly** *adv* : *The time passed slowly.* | *The project is slowly gathering momentum.* | *We are slowly groping towards an understanding of these things.* — ~ **ness** *n* [U]

slow[2] *v* [I;T] (UP, DOWN)] to make or become slower: *The train slowed as it went around the bend.* | *Business slows up/down at this time of year.* | *She slowed the car to a crawl.* | *His bad leg slows him down a lot.* —see also SLOWDOWN

slow[3] *adv* slowly —see also GO-SLOW

▷ USAGE **Slowly** is the usual adverb. **Slow** (*adv*) is rarely used except in combination with other words: **slow**-*moving traffic.* But the comparative and superlative forms **slower** and **slowest** are just as common as *more* **slowly** and *most* **slowly**: *John ran* **slower**/*more* **slowly** *than the others and missed the train.*◁

slow·coach /ˈsləʊkəʊtʃ/ *BrE*‖**slowpoke** *AmE n* a person who thinks, moves, or acts slowly: *Hurry up, slowcoach!*

slow·down /ˈsləʊdaʊn/ *n* **1** a lessening of speed or activity; slowing down: *a slowdown in economic growth* **2** *AmE for* GO-SLOW

slow hand·clap /ˌ·ˈ···/ *n* a slow clapping (CLAP[1]) action of the hands, showing annoyance or impatience: *The audience were impatient for the show to begin, and started a slow handclap.*

slow mo·tion /ˌ·ˈ···◁/ *n* [U] action which takes place at a much slower speed than in real life, esp. as shown for special effect in films: *a replay of the athlete's performance in slow motion*

slow move·ment /ˈ·ˌ··/ *n* the slow part of a piece of music such as a CONCERTO or SYMPHONY. The slow movement is often the second of four MOVEMENTS (4).

slow pitch /ˈ·ˌ·/ *n* [U] a game like SOFTBALL played by teams of men and women together in which the ball is thrown so that it goes high in the air before it enters the area where the hitter is: *Slow pitch leagues are a popular way to socialize.*

slow·poke /ˈsləʊpəʊk/ *n AmE for* SLOWCOACH

slow-wit·ted /ˌ·ˈ··◁/ *adj* slow at understanding things

slow·worm /ˈsləʊwɜːm‖-wɜːrm/ *n* a small harmless European LIZARD with very small eyes and no legs, that moves like a snake

SLR /ˌes el ˈɑːʳ/ *n* single lens reflex; a camera that allows the user to view the subject through the same LENS through which the picture is taken

sludge /slʌdʒ/ *n* [U] **1** soft mud or other dirty matter which settles at the bottom of a liquid: *to clear sludge from the*

drains —compare SEDIMENT **2** the mudlike product of SEWAGE treatment **3** dirty waste oil in an engine — **sludgy** *adj*

slue /sluː/ *v* [I;T] *AmE for* SLEW[2]

slug[1] /slʌg/ *n* **1** a small soft limbless plant-eating creature, related to the SNAIL but with no shell, that often damages garden plants **2 slugs and snails and puppy dogs' tails** a phrase from a NURSERY RHYME (=an old song or poem for children) saying what little boys are made of

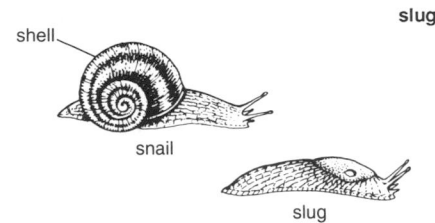

slug

shell

snail

slug

slug[2] *n* **1** a lump or piece of metal, esp. **a** *infml, esp. AmE* a bullet **b** *AmE* a coin-shaped object illegally put into a machine in place of a coin **2** [(of)] *infml, esp. AmE* an amount of strong alcoholic drink taken at one swallow: *a slug of whiskey*

slug[3] *v* **-gg**- [T] *infml* **1** *esp. AmE* to strike with a heavy blow, esp. with the closed hand and so as to make unconscious **2 slug it out** to fight fiercely to the end

slug·gard /ˈslʌgəd‖-ərd/ *n lit* a habitually lazy person

slug·ger /ˈslʌgəʳ/ *n AmE infml* (in BASEBALL) a person who hits the ball very hard

slug·gish /ˈslʌgɪʃ/ *adj* slow-moving; not very active or quick: *a sluggish stream/car engine* | *This humid heat makes you feel rather sluggish.* | *Trading on the stock exchange has been sluggish today.* — ~ **ly** *adv* — ~ **ness** *n* [U]

sluice[1] /sluːs/ *n* a passage for water with an opening (a **sluice gate** or **sluice valve**) through which the flow can be controlled or stopped

sluice[2] *v* **1** [T (OUT, DOWN)] to wash with floods or streams of water (as if) from a sluice: *We sluiced out the cowshed.* **2** [I+*adv/prep*] (of water) to come (as if) from a sluice; come in streams

slum[1] /slʌm/ *n* **1** also **slums** *pl.*— a city area of poor living conditions and old unrepaired buildings, esp. in the centre of a city: *living in the slums of London* | *derelict slum property* —compare GHETTO, SHANTYTOWN **2** *infml derog* a very untidy place — ~ **my** *adj*

slum[2] *v* **-mm**- *infml* **1** [I *usu. in progressive forms*] to visit a place on a much lower social level than one's own, esp. for interest or amusement **2 slum it** *old-fash* to accept or choose a lower standard of living than one is used to: *We'll have to slum it in the kitchen while the dining room is being painted.*

slum·ber[1] /ˈslʌmbəʳ/ *v* [I] *lit* to lie asleep; sleep peacefully — ~ **er** *n*

slumber[2] also **slumbers** *pl.*— *n* [S;U] *lit* a state of sleep: *He woke the princess from her slumber.*

slum·ber·ous /ˈslʌmbərəs/ also **slum·brous** /ˈslʌmbrəs/— *adj lit* sleepy; wanting or suggesting sleep

slum·lord /ˈslʌmlɔːd ‖ -lɔːrd/ *n AmE* a LANDLORD (person who owns property to let) in a poor part of a city

slump[1] /slʌmp/ *v* [I] **1** [+*adv/prep*] to drop down suddenly and heavily: *He was sitting slumped over his typewriter, with a knife in his back.* **2** to go down suddenly or severely in number or strength: *Sales have slumped badly in the last month.* **3** [I;T] to sit, stand, or walk with one's shoulders rounded or bent forward

slump[2] *n* **1** a period of seriously bad business conditions and unemployment; DEPRESSION (2): *the economic slump of the 1930s* **2** a sudden fall in value, trade, etc.: *a slump in prices/demand* **3** *esp. AmE* a period of time when a player or team does not play well

slung /slʌŋ/ *past tense & participle of* SLING

slunk /slʌŋk/ *past tense & participle of* SLINK

slur[1] /slɜːʳ/ *v* **-rr**- [T] **1** to pronounce (a sound in a word) unclearly or not at all: *You could tell from his slurred speech that he was drunk.* **2** *tech* to sing or play (notes) in a smooth and connected manner

slur² *n* **1** [S] a slurring way of speaking **2** [C] *tech* a curved line, ⌢ or ⌣, written over or under musical notes to show that they must be played smoothly without separation

slur³ *v* **-rr-** [T] to make unfair damaging remarks, suggesting dishonesty, etc. **—slur** *n* [(on)] : *He felt the remarks cast a slur on his reputation.*

slurp /slɜːp‖slɜːrp/ *v* [I;T] *infml* to move or drink with the sound of noisy sucking: *The oil slurped into the barrels.* | *Don't slurp your soup, children.*

slur·pee /ˈslɜːpi ‖ -ɜːr-/ *n tdmk, AmE* a drink made with crushed ice and a sweet liquid, usu. tasting of fruit

slur·ry /ˈslʌri‖ˈslɜːri/ *n* [U] a watery mixture, esp. of clay, mud, LIME, or MANURE

slush /slʌʃ/ *n* [U] **1** partly melted snow; watery snow **2** [U] *infml derog* literature, books, films, etc., concerned with silly love stories **3** [C;U] *AmE* (a glass of) a drink made with crushed ice and a sweet liquid: *a cherry slush* **— ~ y** *adj*

slush fund /ˈ· ·/ *n esp. AmE* a sum of money (**slush money**) secretly kept for dishonest use, such as by a politician in an election

slut /slʌt/ *n derog* **1** a sexually immoral woman **2** an untidy lazy woman **— ~ tish** *adj*

sly /slaɪ/ *adj* **1** not telling others one's intentions or thoughts; having or showing a secretive nature: *You're a sly one! Why didn't you tell us you were going to get married?* | *a sly smile* **2** clever in deceiving; dishonestly tricky: *a sly old fox* **3 on the sly** *infml* secretly and usu. dishonestly or illegally: *I think she's making expensive personal telephone calls from work on the sly.* **—slyly, slily** *adv* **— ~ ness** *n* [U]

smack¹ /smæk/ *v* [T] **1** to strike quickly and forcefully, esp. with the flat part of the hands making a loud noise: *If you children don't behave, I'll smack your bottoms!* —compare SPANK¹; see SLAP² (USAGE) **2** to open and close (one's lips) noisily, esp. as a sign of eagerness to eat **3** [+obj+adv/prep] to put firmly, making a quick loud noise: *He smacked down a £5 note and said "Keep the change!"*

smack² *n* **1** a quick loud noise: *The book hit the floor with a smack.* **2** [(on)] *infml* a loud kiss: *She gave him a smack on the cheek.* **3** [(on, in)] *infml* a quick loud forceful blow: *a smack on the jaw* **4** [(at)] *infml* an attempt: *I'm willing to have a smack at it.*

smack³ *adv* [+adv/prep] *infml* **1** with force: *The car ran smack into a wall.* **2** also **smack-dab, smack-bang** /ˌ· ˈ·/ *esp. AmE* directly; exactly; right: *There it was, smack in the middle of the room.*

smack⁴ *n* a small sailing boat used for fishing

smack⁵ *v*
smack of sthg. *phr v* [T] to have a taste or suggestion of (something negative or unwanted): *His remarks smack of disloyalty.* | *The government's change of heart smacks of expediency.*

smack⁶ also **scag, skag—** *n* [U] *sl for* HEROIN

smack·er /ˈsmækə^r/ *n infml* **1** [usu. pl.] also **smack·er·oo** /ˌsmækəˈruː/— a pound or dollar **2** a loud kiss

small¹ /smɔːl/ *adj* **1** of less than usual or average size, weight, amount, force, importance, etc.; not large: *He's a small man, only five feet tall.* | *My daughter is small for her age.* | *The mouse is a very small animal.* | *a small number of people* | *He has a small family.* | *She'd managed to save a small amount of money.* | *You made one or two small mistakes, but otherwise your work was good.* | *These shoes are too small for me.* —opposite **large 2** [A] young: *This is a story for small children.* **3** [A] doing only a limited amount of a business or activity: *He's in business in a small way.* | *a small farmer/shopkeeper* | *She's a very small eater.* (=does not eat a lot) **4** [A] very little; slight: *It's small consolation to know that he lost as much on the deal as I did.* | *You've been eating far too much* **— small wonder** (=it is not surprising) *you're getting fat!* **5** (of a letter) LOWER CASE: *"Church" is sometimes written with a capital C and sometimes with a small c.* | (fig.) *I'm a democrat, with a small "d".* (=I believe in principles of freedom, but do not belong to the Democratic Party.) **6 feel/look small** to feel/look ashamed or unimportant **7**

small is beautiful a phrase meaning that small things can be better than large things, esp. institutions, businesses, and governments (from the book by **E.F. Schumacher** *Small is Beautiful*): *Small is no longer beautiful for fabric patterns.* | *Liechtenstein proves that small can be profitable as well as beautiful.* —see LITTLE (USAGE) **— ~ ness** *n* [U]

small² *adv* in a small manner: *He writes so small I can't read it.*

small³ *n* [the+S+of] the small narrow part of something, esp. the middle part of the back where it curves in: *a pain in the small of the back* —see also SMALLS

small ad /ˈ· ·/ *n BrE for* CLASSIFIED AD

small arms /ˈ· ·‖ˌ· ˈ·/ *n* [P] guns made to be held in one or both hands for firing

small beer /ˌ· ˈ·/ *BrE* ‖ **small potatoes** *AmE— n* [U] *infml derog* a person or thing of little importance: *He thinks he's a mainstay of the company, but he's really rather small beer.*

small busi·ness /ˌ· ˈ···/ *n* a business which usu. employs fewer than 50 people and has a quite small financial TURNOVER

small busi·ness·man /ˌ· ˈ···/ *n* someone who owns a SMALL BUSINESS: *good news for all small businessmen*

small change /ˌ· ˈ·/ *n* [U] money in coins of small value: (fig.) *With a turnover of £150 million, £20,000 is small change to them.*

small claims court /ˌ· ˈ· ˌ·/ *n* a court where people can bring cases to get back money under a certain (quite low) amount from other people or from businesses

small farm·er /ˌ· ˈ···/ *n* someone who owns a small farm

smallest room /ˌ· ˈ·/ [the] *BrE euph* the TOILET

small for·tune /ˌ· ˈ···/ *n* [usu. sing.] *infml* a lot of money: *That new car must have cost you a small fortune!*

small fry /ˈ· ·/ *n* **small fry** [usu. pl.] *infml* a young or unimportant person

small·hold·er /ˈsmɔːlˌhəʊldə^r/ *n BrE* a person who owns or rents a smallholding

small·hold·ing /ˈsmɔːlˌhəʊldɪŋ/ *n BrE* a piece of land farmed by one person, smaller than an ordinary farm

small hours /ˈ· ·/ *BrE*‖**wee hours** *ScotE and AmE— n* [the+P] the early morning hours just after midnight: *He came rolling home from the party in the small hours.*

small in·tes·tine /ˌ· ·ˈ··/ *n* the long narrow twisting tube in the body, into which food first passes from the stomach and where most of its chemical change takes place —compare LARGE INTESTINE

small-mind·ed /ˌ· ˈ···◄/ *adj* having or showing a mind that is very limited and ungenerous; PETTY: *She made you pay for a sprig of parsley? How small-minded can you get?* —compare NARROW-MINDED **— ~ ness** *n* [U]

small po·ta·toes /ˌ· ·ˈ··/ *n* [P] *AmE for* SMALL BEER

small·pox /ˈsmɔːlpɒks‖-pɑːks/ *n* [U] a serious infectious disease that caused spots which left marks on the skin. By 1980 there were no cases of this disease anywhere in the world because of the effectiveness of the smallpox VACCINE.

small print /ˈ· ˌ·/ also **fine print—** *n* [(the)U] something that is purposely made difficult to understand or is easy not to notice, such as part of an agreement or CONTRACT: *It says in the small print that we're responsible for all repairs.*

smalls /smɔːlz/ *n* [P] *BrE old-fash infml* small articles of underclothing, handkerchiefs, etc.

small-scale /ˌ· ˈ·◄/ *adj* small in size and operation: *a small-scale undertaking*

small screen /ˈ· ˌ·/ *n* [the+S] television: *a film made for the small screen*

small talk /ˈ· ·/ *n* [U] light conversation on unimportant or non-serious subjects: *people making small talk at a cocktail party*

small-time /ˌ· ˈ·◄/ *adj* limited in activity, profits, wealth, ability, etc.; unimportant: *a small-time criminal* —compare BIG TIME **—-timer** *n*

small town /ˌ· ˈ·/ *n AmE* a town of a size up to about 10,000 people
▶CULTURAL NOTE The word **village** in American English

has associations with the Old World or the Third World, and is usu. not used of small settlements in the US: *I grew up in a small town.* | *There are a lot of small towns in this area.* ◀

—**small-town** /ˌ·ˈ·◀/ *adj*: *her small-town background*

small town val·ues /ˌ·ˈ·ˈ··/ *n* [P] *AmE* behaviour and ideas connected with people from small towns, including honesty, friendliness, politeness, PATRIOTISM, and MODESTY, but sometimes also suggesting narrow-mindedness (NARROW-MINDED)

smarm·y /ˈsmɑːmi‖-ɑːr-/ *adj* unpleasantly and falsely polite; UNCTUOUS

smart[1] /smɑːt‖smɑːrt/ *adj* **1** *esp. BrE* neat and stylish in appearance: *You look very smart in that new shirt.* | *a smart new car* —see also SMARTEN **2** *esp. AmE* **a** good or quick in thinking; clever: *If he's as smart as he says, why did the cops catch him?* —see CLEVER (USAGE) **b** disrespectful, esp. towards someone older such as one's teachers or parents; IMPUDENT: *Don't get smart with me, young man!* **3** *BrE* quick and forceful: *a smart blow on the head* | *a smart rise/fall in prices* **4** being or used by very fashionable people: *London's smartest restaurant* — ~**ly** *adv*: *She was very smartly dressed.* — ~**ness** *n* [U]

smart[2] *v* [I] **1** to cause or feel a painful stinging sensation, usu. in one part of the body and not lasting long: *The place where he had cut his knee was smarting.* | *The smoke made my eyes smart.* **2** to be hurt in one's feelings; suffer in mind: *She was still smarting from/over his unkind words.*

smart[3] *n* **1** a smarting pain **2** something that hurts the feelings or pride: *He felt the smart of their insult for many days.*

smart al·eck /ˈsmɑːt ˌælɪk‖-ɑːr-/ also **smart-arse** /ˈ··/ *BrE sl*‖**smart-ass** *AmE sl*— *n infml* a person who annoys others by claiming to know everything and trying to sound clever — ~**y** *adj*

smart card /ˈ· ˌ·/ *n* a CREDIT or DEBIT card with a memory CHIP[1] (6). It records and remembers any business one does with it.

smart·en /ˈsmɑːtn‖-ɑːr-/ *v*
smarten up *phr v* [I;T (=**smarten** sbdy./sthg. ↔ **up**)] **1** to improve in appearance; (cause to) become neat or stylish: *We smartened the office up with a fresh coat of paint.* | *Smarten yourself up before you go in to the interview.* **2 smarten up one's act** *infml* to try harder and become more effective

Smar·tie /ˈsmɑːti‖ˈsmɑːr-/ *tdmk* (in Britain) a small chocolate sweet with a coloured sugar covering

smart set /ˈ· ˌ·/ [*the+sing./pl.v*] the very fashionable members of society, considered as a group

smart·y-pants /ˈsmɑːti pænts‖ˈsmɑːr-/ *n* **smarty-pants** *infml* a SMART ALECK

smash[1] /smæʃ/ *v* **1** [I;T (UP)] to (cause to) break into pieces violently and noisily: *I dropped the plate on the floor and it smashed/it smashed to smithereens.* | *Jimmy smashed up his car on the motorway.* (=completely wrecked it in a crash) —see also SMASH-UP; see BREAK (USAGE) **2** [I+*adv/prep*; T+*obj*+*adv/prep*] to go, drive, throw, or hit forcefully, as against something solid; crash: *She lost control of the car and smashed into a lamppost.* | *He smashed his fist down on the table and demanded immediate service.* **3** [T] to defeat, destroy, or put an end to: *The army smashed the rebellion.* | *The police claim to have smashed this drugs-ring.* | *His performance smashes all previous records.* **4** [T] (in games like tennis) to hit (the ball) with a SMASH[2] (3)

smash[2] *n* **1** (the sound of) a violent breaking; crash: *the smash of glasses breaking on the floor* **2** a powerful blow: *a smash that sent his opponent to the floor* **3** a hard downward attacking shot in tennis and similar games: *to play a smash* **4** a SMASH HIT **5** a SMASH-UP: *They were killed in a smash on the motorway.*

smash-and-grab /ˌ··ˈ·/ *adj* [A] *esp. BrE* (of a robbery) done by quickly breaking a shop window, taking the valuable things behind it, and running away

smashed /smæʃt/ *adj* [F] *infml* drunk

smash·er /ˈsmæʃər/ *n infml* **1** something that is very fine or that one admires **2** a very attractive person

smash hit /ˌ·ˈ·/ *n* a very successful new play, book, film, etc.: *I predict this play will be the smash hit of the season.*

Smash Hits /ˌ·ˈ·/ a magazine for young people with articles on POP[3] and ROCK music

smash·ing /ˈsmæʃɪŋ/ *adj infml, esp. BrE*, becoming old-fashioned very fine; wonderful; excellent: *We had a smashing holiday.*

smash-up /ˈ· ·/ *n* a serious road or railway accident: *a smash-up involving five cars*

smat·ter·ing /ˈsmætərɪŋ/ *n* [(**of**)] **1** a small scattered number or amount **2** limited knowledge: *I picked up a smattering of German during my stay.*

smear[1] /smɪər/ *n* **1** a mark or spot made by smearing: *paint smears* **2** *esp. med* (an act of taking) a small amount of cells from the body prepared for examining under a microscope: *Women are advised to have a cervical smear every five years.* **3** an unproved charge made intentionally to try to turn public feelings against someone: *The Democrats have come up with several new smears about the Republican candidate.*

smear[2] *v* **1** a [T] to cause (a sticky or oily material) to spread on or go across (a surface): *Be careful: if you touch the wall you'll smear the fresh paint.* [+*obj*+**on, over**] *She smeared sun tan lotion all over herself.*[+*obj*+**with**] *The sides of the child's mouth were smeared with chocolate.* **b** [I] (of such material) to do this: *Be careful; the paint may smear.* —compare SMUDGE; see SPREAD (USAGE) **2** [I;T] to (cause to) lose clearness by smearing or rubbing: *Several words had/were smeared and I couldn't read them.* **3** [T] to make a SMEAR[1] (3) against; charge unfairly

smear cam·paign /ˈ· ·ˌ·/ *n* a deliberate attempt (e.g. through newspapers or television) to damage people's good opinion of someone

smear test /ˈ· ·/ ‖ also **pap smear** *AmE*— *n* a medical test made by examining a SMEAR[1] (2), esp. of cells from a woman's CERVIX for discovering CANCER

smell[1] /smel/ *v* **smelled** *or* **smelt** /smelt/ [*not in progressive forms*] **1** [I] to have or use the sense of the nose: *I've got a cold and I can't smell.* **2** [T] to notice, examine, discover, or recognize by this sense: *Smell these flowers — they've got a lovely scent.* | *I think I smell gas!* [+*v-ing*] *I can smell burning.* [+(*that*)] *I could smell that the milk wasn't fresh.* [+*wh-*] *My horse can always smell when rain is coming.* [+*obj*+*v-ing*] (fig.) *I could smell trouble/danger coming, so I left.* —compare SNIFF[1]; see CAN (USAGE 4) **3** [I+*adv/prep*, esp. **of, like**; L+*adj*] to have an effect on the nose; have a particular smell: *The room smelt of stale beer/smelt as if it had not been cleaned recently.* | *a sweet-smelling flower* | *This book smells old.* **4** [I (**of**)] to have an unpleasant smell: *His breath smells.* | *The meat had been left out for days and had started to smell.* —compare STINK[1] **5** [I] to seem or appear: *Her explanation of the events didn't smell right to me.* **6 smell a rat** *infml* to guess that something wrong or dishonest is happening **7 smell fishy** (of an event, etc.) to seem false; cause one to think that there is more information than one has: *He can't be working late again! It smells very fishy to me.*

▷ USAGE **Smelt** is more common in British English than **smelled**, but **smelled** is more common in American English. —see also CAN (USAGE 4)◁

smell sbdy./sthg. ↔ **out** *phr v* [T] **1** to discover or find (as if) by smelling: *The hounds smelt out a fox.* | *A good reporter must be able to smell out a news story.* **2** *BrE*‖**smell** sbdy/sthg ↔ **up** *AmE* to cause (a place) to be unpleasant because of a bad smell: *That fish is smelling the kitchen out.*

smell[2] *n* **1** [U] the power of using the nose to discover the presence of substances in the air: *A mole tracks its food by smell alone.* | *These dogs have a marvellous sense of smell.* **2** [C (**of**)] a quality that has an effect on the nose: *Some flowers have stronger smells than others.* | *There was a smell of burning.* | *a musty smell* **3** [C] an unpleasant smell; ODOUR: *This new air freshener gets rid of smells fast.* —compare STINK[2]; see also SMELLY **4** [C *usu. sing.*] an act of smelling something: *Have a smell of this wine; does it seem all right?*

smelling salts /ˈ··· ·/ *n* [P] a strong-smelling chemical, esp. AMMONIA, formerly often carried in a small bottle, for curing faintness

smell·y /ˈsmeli/ *adj* unpleasant-smelling: *smelly socks* —**·iness** *n* [U]

smelt[1] /smelt/ *past tense & participle of* SMELL[1] —see SMELL[1] (USAGE)

smelt² v [T] to melt (ORE) for separating and removing the metal

smelt³ n smelts or smelt a small fish of lakes and coasts

smid·gin, smidgen /ˈsmɪdʒɪn/ n [S] infml a small amount; bit: *"More cheese?" "Just a smidgin, please."*

smile¹ /smaɪl/ n **1** an expression of the face with the mouth turned up at the ends and the eyes bright, that usu. expresses amusement, pleasure, approval, or sometimes bitter feelings: *She had a proud/lovely smile on her face.|He was wearing/his face creased into a broad smile.| a smile of welcome* **2 all smiles** infml very happy-looking: *The winner was all smiles as he heard the results of the voting.*

▷ USAGE A **smile** is an expression of the face showing amusement or happiness. A **grin** is a very wide smile which usually shows the teeth. A **leer** is an unpleasant smile suggesting cruelty, thoughts of sex, etc., and a **smirk** is a silly, satisfied smile. −see also LAUGH (USAGE)◁

smile² v **1** [I (at); T] to have or make (a smile): *the children's happy smiling faces | It's rare to see him smile. | She smiled at me in a friendly fashion.* [+to-v] *When I look back at my youth, I smile* (=am amused) *to think how foolish I was. | She smiled a cheerful smile.* −compare GRIN **2** [T] to express with a smile: *She smiled a greeting.* **3** [I (on)] esp. lit to act or look favourably: *The weather smiled on us.* (=it was a fine day) −**smilingly** adv

smirch /smɜːtʃ/ v [T] fml to bring dishonour on

smirk /smɜːk/ v [I] derog to smile in a silly self-satisfied way, often at someone else's misfortune −see SMILE (USAGE) −**smirk** n : *a triumphant smirk*

Smir·noff /ˈsmɜːnɒf/ n [U] tdmk a type of VODKA

smirr /smɪər/, **smurr** n ScotE a fine misty rain −**smirr** v [I]

smite /smaɪt/ v smote /sməʊt/, **smitten** /ˈsmɪtn/ [T (DOWN)] **1** old use & lit to strike hard **2** esp. bibl & lit to destroy, attack, or punish as if by a blow **3** [(by, with)] usu. pass.] to have a powerful sudden effect on: *He was smitten by/with grief. | She's been smitten down* (=has become ill) *with flu.* −compare SMITTEN

smith /smɪθ/ n (usu. in comb.) a worker in metal, esp. a BLACKSMITH −see also GOLDSMITH, SILVERSMITH

Smith¹ a very common name in Britain and the US, often used **a** by someone wanting a name to use as an example e.g. on a form to be filled in **b** by someone who does not want their real name to be known: *They checked in to the hotel as Mr and Mrs John Smith.*

Smith², Adam (1723–90) a Scottish ECONOMIST who established a school of thought in ECONOMICS and is best known for a work known as *The Wealth of Nations*

Smith³, Bes·sie /ˈbesi/ (1900–1937) an American BLUES singer known as "the Empress of the Blues", whose style influenced many other singers

Smith⁴, Cy·ril /ˈsɪrɪl/ (1928–) an English politician, well-known for saying exactly what he thinks and for being an extremely large man

Smith⁵, De·li·a /ˈdiːliə/ a English writer of cookery books who has also had a cookery SERIES on British television

Smith⁶, Harvey 1 (1938–) an English sportsman who rides horses in SHOW JUMPING competitions **2 do a Harvey Smith** BrE to do a V-SIGN (2) (from an occasion when Harvey Smith did a V-sign towards the judges in a show jumping competition)

Smith⁷, I·an /ˈiːən/ (1919–) the PRIME MINISTER of Rhodesia from 1964 to 1978 −see also ZIMBABWE

Smith⁸, John (1938–) a Scottish politician who became leader of the British Labour Party in 1992

Smith⁹, Joseph (1805–44) the American religious teacher who started the Church of Jesus Christ of Latter-Day Saints, usu. known as the Mormon Church −see also MORMON

Smith¹⁰, Dame Maggie (1934–) an English actress who has won two Oscars

Smith¹¹ also **Smith's−, W H** one of a group of shops selling books, newspapers, cards, etc. They can be found in many towns in Britain and in a few places in the US.

Smith and Wes·son /ˈsmɪθ ən ˈwesən/ n tdmk a make of gun: *I always keep my Smith and Wesson under my pillow at night.*

smith·e·reens /ˌsmɪðəˈriːnz/ n (in)to smithereens infml into extremely small bits; to complete destruction: *The windscreen of the car was smashed to smithereens in the collision.*

Smith·field /ˈsmɪθfiːld/ the name of the main meat market in London

Smith·so·ni·an In·sti·tu·tion /smɪθˌsəʊniən ˌɪnstɪˈtjuːʃən‖ -ˈtuːʃən/ [the] a large group of different MUSEUMS, scientific buildings, and collections in Washington, DC, established in 1846 using money left by James Smithson, an English scientist

Smith Square /ˌ· ˈ·/ the place in London where the Conservative Party's Central Office is, and where the other main British political parties used to have their head offices

smith·y /ˈsmɪði‖ -θi, -ði/ n a BLACKSMITH'S place of work

smit·ten /ˈsmɪtn/ adj esp. humor in love, esp. suddenly fond of a person −compare SMITE (3)

smock /smɒk‖smɑːk/ n **1** a piece of clothing like a long loose shirt, esp. as worn by women, or to protect the clothes in former times by farm workers and painters **2** a piece of clothing worn by a woman who is PREGNANT

smock·ing /ˈsmɒkɪŋ‖ ˈsmɑː-/ n [U] decoration, esp. on children's dresses, made by gathering cloth into small regular folds held tightly with fancy stitching

smog /smɒg‖smɑːg, smɔːg/ n [U] a thick dark unpleasant mist that is sometimes present in certain large cities because of all the smoke and waste gases

smoke¹ /sməʊk/ n **1** [U] the usu. white, grey, or black gas produced by things burning: *Clouds of smoke belched from the burning building. | A pillar of smoke rose high into the air. | I love the smell of bonfire smoke. | The room was full of cigarette smoke. | a puff/wisp of smoke* **2** [S] an act of smoking tobacco: *There's a ten-minute break; time to have a cup of coffee and a smoke.* **3** [C] infml something, esp. a cigarette, that is smoked **4** [the+S] infml, esp. AmE the big city, as opposed to the country. **5 go up in smoke** infml to have no result; come to nothing: *They withdrew their financial support, so the whole scheme went up in smoke.* **6 There's no smoke without fire** also **Where there's smoke there's fire** If unfavourable things are being said about someone or something, they are probably at least partly true. − **∼less** adj : *Coke is a smokeless fuel.*

smoke² v **1** [I;T] to suck or breathe in smoke from burning tobacco, i.e. cigarettes, a pipe, etc.: *I don't smoke. | I used to smoke twenty (cigarettes) a day.*

▶CULTURAL NOTE Fewer people in Britain and the US smoke now because they realize it is bad for their health, although it is very common for young people to try cigarettes for a while. The government prints warnings about the dangers of smoking, e.g. lung CANCER, on cigarette packets. −see also CHAIN-SMOKE, SMOKER, SMOKING◀

2 [T] to breathe in smoke from burning an illegal drug: *students smoking pot in the sixties* **3** [I] to give off smoke: *smoking chimneys in the town's industrial area* **4** [I] to give off too much smoke, esp. because it cannot escape into the air: *a smoking fireplace* **5** [T] to preserve and give a special taste to (meat, fish, etc.) by hanging it in smoke: *smoked salmon/sausage* **6** [T] to darken with smoke, esp. by allowing smoke to settle on and cover a surface: *The sun should only be looked at through smoked glass.*

smoke sbdy./sthg.↔**out** phr v [T] to fill a place with smoke in order to force (a person, animal, etc.) to come out from hiding −compare FUMIGATE

smoke a·larm /ˈ· ·ˌ·/ also **smoke de·tec·tor** /ˈ· ·ˌ··/− n an electronic apparatus which, when fixed in a room, will make a loud warning sound (ALARM) when smoke is present. People are encouraged to have one in their homes, and the law in many US areas demands that one be used in every place where someone lives: *The smoke alarm suddenly went off.*

smoke-filled room /ˌ· · ˈ·/ n AmE becoming old fash a room full of powerful men who are thought to be making important decisions, without asking other people who they consider to be less important, but who may care very much about what decisions are made

smokeless zone /ˌ·· ˈ·/ n (in Britain), an area esp. a big city, where no smoke is allowed, so that only substances which produce no smoke (**smokeless fuels**) can be burned

smok·er /ˈsməʊkəʳ/ n 1 a person who smokes: *He's a heavy smoker.* (=smokes a lot of cigarettes) 2 a railway carriage where smoking is allowed —opposite **non-smoker**

smoke-screen /ˈsməʊkskriːn/ n 1 a cloud of smoke produced for hiding a place or activity from enemy sight 2 something that hides one's real intentions: *to throw up a smokescreen*

smoke sig·nal /ˈ· ˌ··/ n a signal to people some distance away made, esp. by Native Americans in former times, by repeatedly covering a smoking fire for particular periods of time and then allowing the trapped smoke to rise into the air

smoke·stack /ˈsməʊkstæk/ n 1 the tall chimney of a factory or ship 2 *AmE for* a FUNNEL (2)

smokestack in·dus·try /ˈ·· ˌ···/ n [usu. pl.] *esp. AmE* a branch of industry that produces heavy goods or industrial materials, such as cars, ships, or steel

Smo·key the Bear /ˌsməʊki ðə ˈbeəʳ/ (in the US) an imaginary bear with many human features who represents the US Forest Service in its attempts to prevent forest fires. He is often shown wearing a hat and blue JEANS, and saying "Only *you* can prevent forest fires."

Smokey the Bear

Only you can prevent forest fires

smok·ing /ˈsməʊkɪŋ/ n [U] the practice or habit of sucking in tobacco smoke from cigarettes, a pipe, etc.: *The sign says "no smoking".* (=one is not allowed to smoke) | *There are a few smoking compartments* (=where one can smoke) *on this train.* —see also PASSIVE SMOKING; see SMOKE² (CULTURAL NOTE)

smok·ing gun /ˌ·· ˈ·/ n *AmE* an object that suggests or shows that something bad (i.e. a crime) has happened in the place where it is found

smok·y /ˈsməʊki/ adj 1 filled with or producing (too much) smoke: *a smoky room/fire* 2 with the taste or appearance of smoke: *a smoky kiss* | *smoky grey eyes* —**iness** n [U]

Smoky Mountains see GREAT SMOKY MOUNTAINS

smol·der /ˈsməʊldəʳ/ v [I] *AmE for* SMOULDER

smooch /smuːtʃ/ v [I (**with**)] *infml* to kiss and hold someone or each other lovingly, esp. without concern for other people around: *They were smooching in the back row of the cinema.*

smooth¹ /smuːð/ adj 1 having an even surface without sharply raised or lowered places, points, lumps, etc.; not rough: *a smooth road* | *as smooth as silk* | *The tyres were old and had been worn smooth.* | *Feel this; it's as smooth as a baby's bottom!* —opposite **rough** 2 (of a liquid mixture) without lumps; evenly thick: *Beat until smooth.* —opposite **lumpy** 3 even in movement without sudden changes or breaks: *Bring the car to a smooth stop.* | *I hope you'll have a smooth flight.* —opposite **bumpy** 4 free from problems or difficulties: *a smooth journey* | *Her progress from local manageress to company director had not been smooth.* 5 not bitter or sour; pleasant in the mouth: *This sherry is very smooth.* —opposite **harsh, rough** 6 *usu. derog* (too) pleasant, polite, or untroubled in manner; avoiding or not showing difficulties; SUAVE: *I never trust these smooth salesmen.* —see also **take the rough with the smooth** (ROUGH²) — ~ **ly** adv — ~ **ness** n [U]

smooth² v [T] 1 [(OUT, DOWN)] to make smooth or smoother: *She smoothed out the tablecloth/smoothed the wrinkles out of the tablecloth.* | *He smoothed down his hair.* | (fig.) *This agreement will smooth the way to peace.* 2 [+obj+adv/prep] to rub (a liquid, cream, etc.) gently over or into a surface: *She smoothed suntan lotion over her legs.* 3 [(AWAY)] to remove (roughness) from a surface: *This face cream claims to smooth away wrinkles.* | *There are a few problems to be smoothed away before we complete the project.*

  smooth sthg.↔**over** phr v [T] to make (difficulties) seem small or unimportant: *He managed to smooth over the bad feelings between his wife and daughter.*

smooth·ie, smoothy /ˈsmuːði/ n *infml, derog or humor* a SMOOTH¹ (6) person

smooth-talk·ing /ˈ· ˌ··/ adj *usu. derog* too pleasant and able to persuade in speech **smooth-talker** /ˌ·ˈ··/ n : *He's a real smooth-talker.*

smor·gas·bord /ˈsmɔːɡəsbɔːd‖ˈsmɔːrɡəsbɔːrd/ n 1 [C;U] (a restaurant meal in which people serve themselves from) a large number of different dishes, esp. Scandinavian dishes 2 [C (**of**)] a variety: *From the mid-1080s, American viewers turned increasingly away from network television to the smorgasbord of choice offered by the cable television and VCRs.*

smote /sməʊt/ *past tense of* SMITE

smoth·er¹ /ˈsmʌðəʳ/ v [T] 1 [(**with, in**)] to cover thickly or heavily: *The back window of their car was smothered in little stickers.* | *He smothered her with kisses.* 2 to keep from developing, growing, or getting out; STIFLE: *I just managed to smother a yawn.* | *They smothered all opposition.* | (fig.) *a child smothered with too much love* 3 to kill from lack of air: *He smothered his victim with a pillow.* 4 to put out or keep down (a fire) by keeping out air

smoul·der *BrE* ‖ **smol-** *AmE* /ˈsməʊldəʳ/ v [I] 1 to burn slowly with little or no flame 2 [(**with**)] to have, show, or be violent feelings that are kept from being expressed: *The workforce were smouldering with discontent.* | *smouldering anger/passion* | *smouldering eyes*

SMSA /ˌes em es ˈeɪ/ n Standard Metropolitan Statistical Area; any of a number of city areas in the US that are chosen for the purpose of gathering and comparing information about their populations, quality of life, etc. An SMSA is sometimes made up of several cities that have spread into one another.

smudge¹ /smʌdʒ/ n a dirty mark with unclear edges made esp. by rubbing: (fig.) *The incident in the brothel is a smudge on his character.* —**smudgy** adj

smudge² v [I;T] to make or become dirty with a smudge: *The signature was smudged and I couldn't read it.* | *The ink has smudged.* | *He smudged the paper with his dirty hands.* —compare SMEAR²

smug /smʌɡ/ adj -**gg**- *derog* too pleased with oneself; showing too much satisfaction with one's own qualities, position, etc.; COMPLACENT: *a smug smile* | *unbearably smug* — ~ **ly** adv — ~ **ness** n [U]

smug·gle /ˈsmʌɡəl/ v [T] 1 to take (esp. goods) illegally from one country to another, esp. to avoid paying the necessary tax: *to smuggle watches/cigarettes into France* | *She smuggled her notes into the examination.* | *He managed to smuggle a message out of prison to his friends.* — ~ **gler** n : *The Customs men caught the smuggler.* —**gling** n [U] : *a large drug-smuggling operation*

smurr /smɜːʳ/ n [U] SMIRR

smut /smʌt/ n 1 [C;U] (a small piece of) material like dirt or SOOT that blackens or makes dark marks 2 [U] *infml* morally offensive books, stories, talk, etc. 3 [U] a FUNGUS disease of grasses and grains that turns plant parts into black dust

smut·ty /ˈsmʌti/ adj *infml* slightly morally offensive because of being concerned with TOILETS or esp. sex: *Little boys telling each other smutty jokes behind the bike sheds* | *a smutty magazine* —**tily** adv —**tiness** n [U]

snack¹ /snæk/ n an amount of food smaller than a meal that is eaten informally between meals. A snack might be anything, from a chicken leg or a HOT DOG to a bar of chocolate: *I only had time for a quick snack.* | *I'm having a snack attack.* (=have a strong desire for a snack.)

snack² v [I] to eat a snack: *Don't snack between meals.* | *snacking on potato chips*

snack bar /ˈ· ·/ n an informal public eating place that serves snacks

snack food /ˈ· ·/ n [C;U] [usu. pl.] a food that is intended to be eaten as a snack, e.g. CRISPS, PEANUTS, POPCORN, etc. Such foods are usu. regarded as having very little benefit to one's health.

snaf·fle¹ /ˈsnæfəl/ v [T] *BrE infml* to get, esp. by deceitful means or stealing: *She snaffled some pens and paper from the office.*

snaffle² also **snaffle bit** /ˈ·· ·/— n a BIT² (1) made of two short joined bars, for putting in a horse's mouth

sna·fu /snæˈfuː/ n *AmE infml* a state of being wrong or unworkable

snag¹ /snæɡ/ n 1 a difficulty, esp. a hidden or unexpected one: *Its the perfect car for me, only snag is, I can't afford it!* **2** a rough or sharp part of something that may catch and hold or cut things passing against it **3** a tear made (as if) by catching on a snag

snag² *v* **-gg-** [T] **1** to catch on a SNAG¹ (2): *She snagged her tights on the rough edge of the chair.* **2** *AmE infml* to catch or get, esp. by quick action: *I'll try to snag the waiter next time he walks by.*

snail /sneɪl/ *n* a small plant-eating creature with a soft body, no limbs, and usu. a hard shell on its back, which moves very slowly —see picture at SLUG

snail's pace /ˈ·ˌ·/ *n* [S] *infml* a very slow speed or rate of activity

snake¹ /sneɪk/ *n* **1** an animal with a long thin limbless body, large mouth, and FORKED tongue, that usu. feeds on other animals and often has a poisonous bite: *The snake slithered/wriggled away.*

▶CULTURAL NOTE Many people in Britain and the US have a fear of snakes, even though they may never have seen a real one. In the Bible, the snake (also called a **serpent**) is the creature that persuades Eve, the first woman,

snake

cobra

to take a bite of an apple that God has forbidden Adam and Eve to eat, and so is the cause of them having to leave the perfect world of the Garden of Eden. Because of the snake's evil action, God punishes it by making it CRAWL on its BELLY for ever. This is why in Christianity the snake has a strong association with evil.◀

2 *derog* a deceitful person **3** *tech* a system in which the values of certain countries' money are allowed to vary against each other within narrow limits **4 snake in the grass** *derog, often humor* a false friend —compare SERPENT (2)

snake² *v* [I+adv/prep; T+obj+adv/prep] to move in a twisting way; wind (one's way or body) in moving: *The train snaked (its way) through the mountains.*

snake-bite /ˈsneɪkbaɪt/ *n* [U] the result or condition of being bitten by a poisonous snake

snake charm-er /ˈ·ˌ··/ *n* a person who controls snakes, usu. by playing music, as a public entertainment. In pictures, Indian snake charmers are often shown playing a pipe, making a snake rise out of a basket.

snake oil /ˈ·ˌ·/ *n* [U] *AmE* any substance sold as a medicine which is in fact worthless or harmful

snake pit /ˈ·ˌ·/ *n AmE* an uncomfortable place full of danger or trouble

snakes and lad-ders /ˌ·· ˈ··/ *n* [U] (*sometimes cap. S and L*) a board game in which players move pieces according to the throw of a DICE and may move upwards and forwards along pictures of ladders but are forced downwards and backwards along pictures of snakes. Sometimes the successes and failures of life are compared to a game of snakes and ladders.

snak-y /ˈsneɪki/ *adj* like a snake, esp. in winding or twisting: *a snaky road*

snap¹ /snæp/ *v* **-pp-** **1** [I;T] (usu. of something thin and stiff) to (cause to) break suddenly and sharply off or in two parts: *The branch snapped under the weight of the snow.* | *I snapped the stick in half.* | *She snapped off a piece of chocolate.* | (fig.) *My nerves finally snapped under the pressure of work.* **2** [I+adv/prep; T+obj+adv/prep] to move so as to cause a sharp sound like something suddenly breaking: *The lid snapped shut.* **3** [I (at);T] to speak or say quickly, usu. in an annoyed way: *He tends to snap at people when he's got a headache.* | *"You're late!" she snapped.* | *He snapped out an order.* **4** [I (at)] to close the jaws quickly: *The dog was snapping at my ankles.* (=trying to bite them) **5** [T] *infml* to photograph **6 snap one's fingers** to attract attention by making a noise by moving the second finger quickly along the thumb: (fig.) *He comes running to help her whenever she snaps her fingers.* (=whenever she demands it) **7 snap one's fingers at** *BrE* to show no respect for: *As an artist she's always snapped her fingers at convention.* **8 snap out**

of it *infml* [*usu. imperative*] to free oneself quickly from an unhappy or unhealthy state of mind **9 snap someone's head off** *infml* to answer someone in a sharp angry way: *I just asked a simple question; there's no need to snap my head off!* **10 snap to it** ‖ also **snap it up** *AmE*— to hurry up: *Come on, snap to it!*

snap sthg. ↔ **up** *phr v* [T] to take or buy quickly and eagerly: *It's a real bargain; you should snap it up!*

snap² *n* **1** [C] an act or sound of snapping: *The branch broke with a snap.* | *He summoned the waiter with a snap of his fingers.* **2** [C] also **snapshot**— an informal photograph taken with a hand-held camera **3** [C] (*in comb.*) a thin dry sweet BISCUIT: *ginger snaps* **4** [U] a card game in which players lay down cards one after the other and try to be the first to notice and call out "snap" when two similar cards are laid down together **5** [U] *infml* eager effort; ZIP: *Come on, put some snap in it!* **6** [S] *AmE infml* something that is very easy to do **7** *AmE for* PRESS-STUD **8 snap, crackle, and pop** a phrase from an advertisement for a breakfast CEREAL, referring to (REFER) the noise it makes when milk is poured on it —see also COLD SNAP

snap³ *adj* [A] done quickly and without warning or long consideration: *The prime minister called a snap election to take place in four weeks' time.* | *It's risky to make snap judgments.*

snap⁴ *interj BrE* **1** *infml* (said when one notices two similar things together): *Snap! You're wearing the same hat as me!* **2** (said in the game of SNAP (4) when one notices that two similar cards have been laid down)

snap-drag-on /ˈsnæpˌdrægən/ also **antirrhinum**— *n* a garden plant with white, red, or yellow flowers

snap fas-ten-er /ˈ· ˌ··/ also **snap but-ton** /ˈ· ˌ··/— *n AmE for* PRESS STUD —see picture at FASTENER

snap-per /ˈsnæpər/ *n* a fish found in warm seas, often used as food

snap-pish /ˈsnæpɪʃ/ *adj* speaking habitually in a rude annoyed way; bad-tempered — ~**ly** *adv* — ~**ness** *n* [U]

snap-py /ˈsnæpi/ *adj infml* **1** stylish; fashionable: *a snappy dresser* (=someone who wears stylish clothes) **2 make it snappy** also **look snappy** *BrE*— (*usu. imperative*) to hurry up —**pily** *adv* —**piness** *n* [U]

snap-shot /ˈsnæpʃɒt‖-ʃɑːt/ *n* a SNAP² (2)

snare¹ /sneər/ *n* **1** a trap for catching an animal, esp. an apparatus with a rope or wire which catches the animal's foot: *a rabbit snare* **2** also **snares** *pl.*— a situation or course of action that may lead to one being trapped or deceived

snare² *v* [T] **1** to catch (as if) in a snare **2** *infml* to get by skilful action: *You've snared a good job there!*

snare drum /ˈ· ·/ *n* a small flat military kind of drum used also in bands, having metal springs stretched across the bottom to allow a continuous sound

snarl¹ /snɑːl‖snɑːrl/ *v* **1** [I (at)] (of an animal) to make a low angry sound while showing the teeth: *The dog snarled at me.* **2** [I(at);T] to speak or say in an angry bad-tempered way: *"Shut up!" he snarled.*

snarl² *n* an act or sound of snarling; angry GROWL: *He gave a vicious snarl.*

snarl³ *v* [T (UP) *usu. pass.*] to twist or mix together so as to make movement difficult: *Traffic was badly snarled (up) near the accident.*

snarl-up /ˈ· ·/ *n* a confused state, esp. of traffic

snatch¹ /snætʃ/ *v* **1** [I;T] to take hold of (something) with a sudden quick often violent movement; GRAB: *Don't snatch, children; ask for it nicely.* | *The thief snatched her handbag and ran.* | *The boy was snatched from his home by two armed men.* **2** [T] to take quickly as chance allows, sometimes wrongfully or without permission: *I snatched a look at the answers while the teacher was out of the room.* | *He managed to snatch an hour's sleep on the train.* —~**er** *n*: *There's a gang of bag snatchers* (=people who snatch HANDBAGS) *working the park.*

snatch at sthg. *phr v* [T] **1** to try to snatch: *He snatched at the ball but dropped it.* | *She snatched wildly at the branches as she fell.* **2** to accept or try to get eagerly: *She was always ready to snatch at any opportunity for advancement.*

snatch² *n* **1** [(at)] an act of snatching (at) something: *He made a snatch at the piece of paper, but too late — it had*

blown away. **2** [*usu. pl.*] a short period of time or activity: *I slept in snatches* (=waking up often) *during the night.* **3** [(**of**)] a short and incomplete part of something that is seen or heard: *to overhear a snatch of conversation*

snatch squad /ˈ··/ *n* a group of policemen who go into a crowd of people and ARREST someone quickly and suddenly

snaz·zy /ˈsnæzi/ *adj infml* good-looking or attractive in a neat stylish or showy way: *a snazzy suit* —**zily** *adv*: *snazzily dressed*

sneak¹ /sniːk/ *v* **snuck** /snʌk/*AmE* **1** [I+*adv*/*prep*] to go quietly and secretly, so as not to be seen: *I managed to sneak past the guard.* | *We sneaked round to the back door.* **2** [T] *infml* to steal secretly or cleverly: *The boy was caught sneaking an apple from a shop.* | (fig.) *I managed to sneak a look at the report on her desk.* **3** [I (**on**)] *BrE derog sl* (used by schoolchildren) to give information, esp. to a teacher, about the wrongdoings of others

  sneak up *phr v* [I (**on, behind**)] to come near silently, keeping out of sight until the last moment: *Don't sneak up on me like that! You gave me quite a shock!*

sneak² *n* **1** *BrE derog sl* a person who SNEAKS¹ (3) **2** *AmE* a person who SNEAKS¹ (1) or sneaks up

sneak³ *adj* coming quickly or unexpectedly: *a sneak attack*

sneak·er /ˈsniːkər/ *n AmE* an informal shoe with a rubber SOLE¹ (2) and leather or strong cloth around the foot — see PAIR (USAGE) and see picture at SHOE

sneak·ing /ˈsniːkɪŋ/ *adj* [A] **1** secret; not openly expressed: *I don't like her at all, but I can't help having a sneaking admiration for what she's done.* **2** (of a feeling or belief) not proved but probably right: *I had a sneaking suspicion the plan wouldn't work.*

sneak pre·view /ˌ· ˈ··/ *n* [(**of**)] a chance to look at something new, esp. a film, before anyone else or any member of the public has seen it

sneak thief /ˈ· ·/ *n* a thief who steals things quietly and quickly and without using force, esp. from public places

sneak·y /ˈsniːki/ *adj derog* acting or done secretly and deceitfully, esp. in a clever way —**ily** *adv* —**iness** *n* [U]

sneer¹ /snɪər/ *v* [I] **1** to smile or laugh with a curl of the lips; to express proud dislike and disrespect **2** [(**at**)] to speak or behave as if something is not worthy of serious attention: *Don't sneer at their religion.* — ~**ingly** *adv*

sneer² *n* a sneering look or remark

sneeze¹ /sniːz/ *v* [I] **1** to have a sudden uncontrolled burst of air out of the nose, usu. caused by discomfort in the nose: *The dust made him sneeze.* | *The baby keeps sneezing* — *she must be getting a cold.* | *a fit of sneezing*

▶ CULTURAL NOTE When a person sneezes, someone in the room might say "Bless you!" or "Gesundheit!", and the person might reply "Thank you." ◀

2 not to be sneezed at *infml, often humor* worthy of consideration; not to be considered unfavourably: *An offer of £1000 tax-free is not to be sneezed at.*

sneeze² *n* an act, sound, etc., of sneezing. The sound made by a sneeze is expressed in writing by the word "Atishoo!", or sometimes "Achoo!"

snick /snɪk/ *v* [T] *BrE* **1** to make a small cut or mark on; NICK **2** (in cricket) to hit (the ball) off the edge of the BAT —**snick** *n*

snick·er /ˈsnɪkər/ *v, n esp. AmE for* SNIGGER —see LAUGH (USAGE)

Snick·ers /ˈsnɪkəz‖-ərz/ *n tdmk* a chocolate bar with PEANUTS and CARAMEL inside

snide /snaɪd/ *adj* expressing an unfavourable opinion in a way that is usu. indirect but unpleasant and hurts people's feelings: *He was always making snide remarks about her cooking.* — ~**ly** *adv* — ~**ness** *n* [U]

sniff¹ /snɪf/ *v* **1** [I] to draw air into the nose with a sound, esp. in short repeated actions. Many British people consider it rude to sniff in public: *His mother told him to stop sniffing and blow his nose.* **2** [I(**at**);T] to do this in order to discover a smell in or on: *He sniffed the crisp morning air.* | *The dog sniffed at the lamppost.* —compare SMELL¹ **3** [T] to say in a proud complaining way: *"I expected something rather nicer," she sniffed.* —see also SNIFFY **4** [T] also **snort**— to take (a harmful drug) through the nose: *sniffing cocaine* —see also GLUE SNIFFING — ~**er** *n*

  sniff at sthg. *phr v* [T] to dislike or refuse proudly: *Such a good offer is not to be sniffed at.*

sniff out sthg. *phr v* [T] *infml* to discover or find out (as if) by smelling: *Police sent dogs into the crowd to sniff out drugs.* | (fig.) *trying to sniff out the cause of the problem*

sniff² *n* an act or sound of sniffing: *He gave a loud sniff.* '*Is this milk OK? Here, have a sniff.*

sniffer dog /ˈ··· ·/ *n* a dog that has been trained by the police to find drugs and explosives by smelling them

snif·fle¹ /ˈsnɪfəl/ *v* [I] to sniff repeatedly in order to keep liquid from running out of the nose, esp. when one is crying or has a cold: *For goodness sake, stop sniffling!* —**fler** *n*

sniffle² *n* **1** an act or sound of sniffling **2** also **sniffles** *pl.*— *infml* the signs of a cold in the nose; liquid blocking or running from the nose: *It's not a real cold, only a sniffle.* | *Little Sharon's got the sniffles again.*

sniff·y /ˈsnɪfi/ *adj infml* **1** unpleasantly proud by habit **2** showing signs of dislike or disapproval; DISDAINFUL: *She was rather sniffy about my suggestion, so I didn't pursue it.*

snif·ter /ˈsnɪftər/ *n* **1** *old-fash infml, esp. BrE* a small amount of an alcoholic drink **2** *AmE* a bowl-like glass that grows narrower at the top, on a short STEM¹, for drinking BRANDY —see picture at GLASS

snig·ger¹ /ˈsnɪgər/ *esp. BrE* ‖ **snicker** *esp. AmE*— *v* [I (**at**)] *usu. derog* to laugh quietly or secretly in a disrespectful way: *The children sniggered at the old lady's strange hat.* —see LAUGH (USAGE)

snigger² *esp. BrE* ‖ **snicker** *esp. AmE*— *n usu. derog* an act or sound of sniggering

snip¹ /snɪp/ *n* **1** [C] a short quick cut with scissors: *Make a snip in the cloth here.* **2** [S] *BrE infml* an article for sale at a surprisingly cheap price; BARGAIN: *At £20 for a dozen, they're a snip.* **3 have the snip** *BrE infml* to have a VASECTOMY —see also SNIPS

snip² *v* **-pp-** [T (**OFF**)] to cut (as if) with scissors, esp. in short quick strokes: *She snipped the string and untied the parcel.* | *He snipped off the corner of the packet.*

snipe¹ /snaɪp/ *v* [I (**at**)] **1** to shoot from a hidden position at unprotected people, such as an enemy not in battle **2** to say nasty things; make an unpleasant attack in words —**sniper** *n* : *The army patrol was picked off by snipers.*

snipe² *n* **snipe** *or* **snipes** **1** a bird with a very long thin beak that lives in wet places and is often shot for sport **2** *AmE derog* a strongly disliked person

snip·pet /ˈsnɪpɪt/ *n* [(**of**)] *infml* a small bit of something, esp. a short piece from something spoken or written: *I managed to overhear a few interesting snippets of information.*

snip·py /ˈsnɪpi/ *adj AmE infml* quick to show anger, offence, or disobedience

snips /snɪps/ *BrE*‖**tin shears** *AmE*— *n* [P] heavy scissors for cutting metal sheets —see PAIR (USAGE)

snit /snɪt/ *n* [S] *AmE infml* an angry state of mind, esp. one which the speaker thinks is unnecessary: *She's been* **in a snit** *since I took the car without telling her.*

snitch¹ /snɪtʃ/ *v infml* **1** [I (**on**)] *derog* to tell about the wrongdoings of a friend **2** [T] to steal (esp. something unimportant and of small value) by taking quickly

snitch² *n BrE infml, usu. humor* nose

sniv·el /ˈsnɪvəl/ *v* **-ll-** *BrE* ‖ **-l-** *AmE* [I] to act or speak in a weak complaining crying way: *I've warned you. If you fail, don't come snivelling back to me.* | *a snivelling coward* — ~**ler** *BrE* ‖ ~**er** *AmE n*

snob /snɒb‖snɑːb/ *n derog* **1** a person who pays too much attention to social class, and dislikes or keeps away from people of a lower class **2** a person who is too proud of having special knowledge or judgment in the stated subject, and thinks that something liked by many people is no good: *a musical snob who only likes Mozart* | *It's not really a very good make of car, but it does have a certain* **snob value/snob appeal.** (=it is greatly admired by a particular set of people)

snob·be·ry /ˈsnɒbəri‖ˈsnɑːb-/ *n* [U] the attitude and behaviour of snobs

snob·bish /ˈsnɒbɪʃ‖ˈsnɑː-/ also **snob·by** /ˈsnɒbi‖ˈsnɑːbi/— *adj* typical of a snob, esp. in being too proud about one's social position: *a snobbish attitude* | *Don't be so snobbish!* — ~**ly** *adv* — ~**ness** *n* [U]

snog /snɒg‖snɑːg/ *v* **-gg-** [I] *BrE infml* to hold and kiss each other, esp. for a period of time; a word used by young people —**snug** n

snook /snuːk‖snʊk, snuːk/ n see **cock a snook (at)** (COCK²)

snoo·ker¹ /ˈsnuːkəʳ‖ˈsnʊ-/ n [U] a game played on a table covered in green cloth with 15 red balls, six balls of other colours, and a white ball. One hits the white ball with a CUE (=a long stick) onto the coloured balls, in a particular order, so that they fall into any of six POCKETS (=holes) round the table in order to make points. It is played esp. by men and is very popular in Britain — compare BILLIARDS, POOL² (3) —see REFEREE (USAGE)

snooker² v [T often pass.] BrE infml to put into a situation in which one can no longer take action: *The council has turned down our application, so now we're really snookered.*

snoop¹ /snuːp/ v [I (ABOUT, AROUND)] infml derog to search, look into, or concern oneself with other people's property or affairs without permission; PRY: *I caught him snooping around in my office.* — ~**er** n

snoop² n infml an act of snooping

Snoop·y /ˈsnuːpi/ a CARTOON dog in a COMIC STRIP called *Peanuts*

Snoopy

Snoopy © 1958

snoot·y /ˈsnuːti/ adj infml proudly rude; HAUGHTY: *He's too snooty to associate with his old friends now he's rich.* —**·ily** adv —**·iness** n [U]

snooze /snuːz/ v [I] infml to have a short sleep; DOZE — **snooze** n

snore¹ /snɔːʳ/ v [I] to breathe noisily through the nose and mouth while asleep: *He was snoring heavily.* —**snorer** n

snore² n a noisy way of breathing when asleep; a noise of snoring: *deafening snores*

snor·kel /ˈsnɔːkəl‖-ɔːr-/ n a tube **a** with a MOUTHPIECE, used for allowing a swimmer under water to breathe **b** for carrying air to a SUBMARINE —**snorkel** v [I] : *to go snorkeling*

snorkel

snorkel—

snort¹ /snɔːt‖snɔːrt/ v 1 [I] to make a rough noise by forcing air down the nose: *The horse snorted and stamped its hoof impatiently.* 2 [I;T] to express impatience or anger, or sometimes amusement) (as if) by this sound: *"Certainly not," he snorted. | She snorted contemptuously with derision.* 3 [T] sl for SNIFF¹ (4): *She'd been snorting cocaine.*

snort² n 1 an act or sound of snorting: *He gave a snort of derision/laughter.* 2 old-fash infml a drink of strong alcohol taken with one act of swallowing

snort·er /ˈsnɔːtəʳ‖-ɔːr-/ n [usu. sing.] BrE old-fash infml something that is unusually fine or esp. violent, powerful, difficult, etc.

snot /snɒt‖snɑːt/ n infml, not polite 1 [U] the thick MUCUS (=fluid) produced in the nose 2 [C] a SNOTTY (1) person

snot·ty /ˈsnɒti‖ˈsnɑːti/ adj infml derog 1 also **snotty-nosed** /ˈ·· ·/— (esp. of a young person) trying to act as if one is important; rude: *I'm not going to be told what to do by some snotty-nosed little clerk!* 2 wet and dirty with MUCUS: *a snotty nose*

snout /snaʊt/ n the long nose of any of various animals, such as a pig —see picture at HEDGEHOG

snow¹ /snəʊ/ n 1 [U] water in the air which has frozen and falls in the form of soft white FLAKES (=pieces) in cold weather, often covering the ground thickly: *Some mountains are covered in snow all year round. | The kids were playing in the snow. | Many roads were blocked by deep snow. | crisp/mushy snow*

▶ CULTURAL NOTE Snow is thought of in connection with winter and esp. Christmas. —compare SLUSH; see RAIN

(USAGE) and see colour picture on page 1212◄

2 [C] a fall of snow: *one of the heaviest snows this winter* 3 [U] sl COCAINE in powder form

snow² v 1 [it+I] (of snow) to fall: *Look! It's snowing.* 2 [T] AmE infml to persuade or win the respect of (someone), esp. by making oneself sound important: *I was really snowed by his smooth manners and polite talk.*

snow sbdy./sthg.↔**in/up** phr v [T usu. pass.] (of snow) to pile up on the ground, roads, etc., so as to prevent travel to or from (a place) or by (a person): *We were snowed in for three days last winter. | The village was snowed up twice last year.*

snow sbdy.↔**under** phr v [T (**with**) usu. pass.] to cause to have more of something than one can deal with: *I'm completely snowed under with work at the moment.*

snow·ball¹ /ˈsnəʊbɔːl/ n 1 a ball pressed or rolled together from snow, as thrown at each other by children: *to have a snowball fight* 2 **a snowball's chance in hell** [usu. in negatives] infml any chance at all (of succeeding, lasting, etc.): *He doesn't have a snowball's chance in hell of getting that job.*

snowball² v [I] (of a plan, problem, etc.) to grow bigger at a faster and faster rate

snow blind·ness /ˈ· ˌ··/ n [U] eye pain and (near) blindness for a time, caused by continuously looking at snow in bright sunlight —**snow-blind** adj

snow·bound /ˈsnəʊbaʊnd/ adj blocked or kept indoors by heavy snow: *snowbound traffic*

snow-capped /ˈ· ·/ adj lit (of a mountain) covered in snow at the top

Snow·don /ˈsnəʊdn/ a mountain in Wales. It is the highest point in England and Wales. —see colour map on page 818

Snowdon, Lord also the **Earl of Snowdon** fml— (1930–) an English photographer who was married to Princess Margaret, the sister of the British Queen. They divorced (DIVORCE) in 1978.

Snow·do·ni·a /snəʊˈdəʊniə/ a mountainous area in N Wales which is a National Park

snow·drift /ˈsnəʊˌdrɪft/ n a deep bank or mass of snow piled up by the wind: *The car was buried in a snowdrift.*

snow·drop /ˈsnəʊdrɒp‖-drɑːp/ n a European plant with a small white flower which appears in the early spring, often when snow is still on the ground —see picture at FLOWER

snow·fall /ˈsnəʊfɔːl/ n 1 [C] a fall of snow 2 [S;U] the amount of snow that falls: *This area has an average snowfall of eight centimetres per year.*

snow·field /ˈsnəʊfiːld/ n a wide stretch of ground always covered in snow

snow·flake /ˈsnəʊfleɪk/ n 1 a small flat six-sided bit of frozen water that falls as snow 2 a small falling mass of snowflakes

snow job /ˈ· ·/ n AmE sl an act of deceiving someone, esp. by giving them lots of misinformation

snow·line /ˈsnəʊlaɪn/ [the] the level beyond which snow never melts

snow·man /ˈsnəʊmæn/ n -**men** /men/ a figure of a person made out of large balls of snow, esp. by children. A snowman will often have pieces of coal, etc., for its eyes, mouth, and buttons, and a CARROT for a nose. In pictures it is often shown wearing a hat and SCARF. —see also ABOMINABLE SNOWMAN and see colour picture on page 1212

snow·mo·bile /ˈsnəʊməbiːl‖-məʊ-/ n a small vehicle with a motor that moves over snow or ice on an endless metal track instead of wheels —**·biling** n : *We're going snowmobiling this weekend.*

snow pea /ˈ· ·/ n AmE for MANGETOUT

snow·plough BrE ‖ **-plow** AmE /ˈsnəʊplaʊ/ n an apparatus or vehicle for pushing snow off roads or railways

snow route /ˈ· ·/ n AmE an important route in a town or city from which cars must be removed when it snows, so that the road can be cleared for traffic: *I got a ticket for leaving the car on a snow route.*

snow·shoe /ˈsnəʊʃuː/ n either of a pair of light flat frames with narrow bands of leather stretched across it, worn on the foot to allow a person to walk on snow without sinking in

snow·storm /ˈsnəʊstɔːm‖-ɔːrm/ n a very heavy fall of snow, esp. blown by strong winds

snow·suit /ˈsnəʊsuːt, -sjuːt ‖ -suːt/ n AmE a usu. one-piece warm piece of clothing worn by children, esp. when playing in the snow

snow tire /ˈ· ·/ n AmE a special car tyre with deep TREAD² (2) (=pattern of lines) or with STUDS¹ (2) (=pointed hard lumps that stick out) used when driving on snow or ice in order to grip the road better

snow-white /ˌ·ˈ·◂/ adj as white as snow; pure white

Snow White

Snow White the main character in an old FAIRYTALE (=story for children). Snow White is a beautiful princess who has a jealous STEPMOTHER. The stepmother owns a magic mirror which when asked "Mirror, mirror, on the wall, who is the fairest of us all?" always answers that she is the most beautiful, until one day it says "Snow White". The stepmother is very angry and sends Snow White into the forest to be killed. Snow White does not die, but finds and lives with seven DWARFS. Her stepmother tries to kill her with a poisoned apple, but instead of dying she goes to sleep until a prince kisses her and wakes her, and they live happily ever after: *Charlie wore a dainty little green suit that made him look like one of Snow White's dwarfs.* —see also SEVEN DWARFS

snow·y /ˈsnəʊi/ adj 1 full of snow or snowing: *Today will be snowy in many areas.* 2 esp. lit pure (white): *snowy (white) hair* —-**iness** n [U]

SNP /ˌes en ˈpiː/ also **Scottish National Party, Scot Nats** infml— [the] a Scottish political party which wants Scotland to be independent from England

Snr written abbrev. for: SENIOR: *James Taylor, Snr*

snub¹ /snʌb/ v -bb- [T] to treat (someone) rudely, esp. by intentionally paying no attention to them: *I tried to make a suggestion but she snubbed me.*

snub² n an act of snubbing someone

snub³ adj [A] (of a nose) flat and short; STUBBY

snub-nosed /ˌ·ˈ·◂/ adj having a snub nose

snuck /snʌk/ AmE past tense & past participle of SNEAK¹

snuff¹ /snʌf/ n [U] 1 tobacco made into powder for breathing into the nose: *a pinch of snuff* 2 **up to snuff** old-fash infml having the necessary ability or quality

snuff² v [T (OUT)] 1 to put out (a candle or candle flame) by pressing the burning part with one's fingers or with a snuffer 2 **snuff it** BrE infml to die
snuff sthg.↔**out** phr v [T] to put a sudden end to: *It was tragic to think of a young life so needlessly snuffed out.*

snuff³ v [I;T] (esp. of an animal) to draw (air or a smell) into the nose with a sound; SNIFF

snuff·er /ˈsnʌfəʳ/ n a tool with a small bell-shaped end on a handle, for putting out candles

snuf·fle /ˈsnʌfəl/ v to make repeated small noises through the nose: *The pigs were snuffling round the trough.*

snug¹ /snʌg/ -gg- adj 1 apprec giving or enjoying warmth, comfort, peace, protection, etc.; COSY: *He showed us into a snug little sitting room with a fire burning.* | *The children were tucked up snug and warm in bed.* 2 (of clothes) **a** fitting closely and comfortably: *This jacket is a nice snug fit.* **b** fitting too closely: *The dress was a bit snug under the arms.* 3 **as snug as a bug in a rug** infml very comfortable: *You'll be as snug as a bug in a rug in your new sleeping bag.* — –**ly** adv — ~**ness** n [U]

snug² n BrE a small room or enclosed place for sitting privately, esp. in a PUB

snug·gle /ˈsnʌgəl/ v [I+adv/prep] infml to settle into a warm comfortable position: *Snuggle up to me and I'll keep you warm.* | *The children had snuggled down in bed.*

so¹ /səʊ/ adv 1 to such a (great) degree: *Don't be so silly!* | *He was so fat (that) he couldn't get through the door.* | *He couldn't get through the door, he was so fat.* | *I ate so much food (that) I was almost sick.* | *He saw so many new things he couldn't remember them all.* | *I've never been so poor as not to be able to afford a meal.* | *Stop telling me to hurry up! I can only go so fast.* | *(fml) I've never seen so beautiful a child.* (=such a beautiful child) | *You mustn't worry so.* —see SUCH (USAGE) 2 (used in place of something stated already, esp. after a verb marked [+(that)]): *He hopes he'll win and I hope so too.* | *If you're going to go out you'd better do so quickly.* | *Are you married? If so* (=if you are)*, give your wife's name.* | *If you say so I'll have to believe it.* | *Martha's got a job, or so she tells me.* | *"Is it interesting?" "Yes, more so* (=more interesting) *than I'd expected."* | *He was angry and quite rightly so.* (=he was right to be angry) | *"Have we missed the start of the film?" "I'm afraid so."* —compare NOT (2) 3 (usu. followed by **be, have, do,** or a verb like **will, can,** or **should** and then its subject) in the same way; also; LIKEWISE: *I'd like another drink, and so would John.* (=John would like another drink too) | *"Ann can play the piano." "So can I!"* (compare *"Ann can't play the piano." "Nor/Neither can I."* (=I, also, can't play the piano.) | *(Just) as the French like their wine, so the English like their beer.* 4 in this way; in that way: *First, you turn the engine on, so.* | *"I've known him since he was so high" she said, holding out her arm to indicate a height of a few feet.* | *(infml) Cut up the apples like so.* 5 (followed by **there** or a PRONOUN subject and then **be, have, do,** or a verb like **will, can,** or **should**) certainly; yes; it is true: *"There's a fly in your coffee." "So there is!"* | *"Look, your wife has just come in." "So she has."* 6 esp. polite very: *We're so glad you could come!* | *Thank you; you've been so (very) kind.* | *(infml) She's **ever** so nice!* 7 fml therefore: *These applications are past the expiry date, and so void.* 8 AmE or dial BrE (used esp. by children, for answering a negative charge or statement): *"I didn't do it." "You did so! You did so do it!"* 9 **so ... as** (usu. in questions or negatives) as ... as: *He's not so foolish as I thought.* —see also **as/so far as** (FAR¹)*,* **as/so long as** (LONG²)*;* see AS (USAGE) 10 **so as to: a** in order to: *The desks are kept some distance apart, so as to prevent cheating.* **b** in such a way as to: *The day was dark, so as to make a good photograph hard to get.* 11 **so long!** infml goodbye! 12 **so many/much: a** a certain number/amount (not stated exactly): *We make a charge of so much per day.* **b** an amount equal to; all: *All these silly books are just so much waste paper!* —see also **and so on/forth** (AND), **even so** (EVEN¹), **so much for** (MUCH²), **just so** (JUST¹), **or so** (OR)

so² conj 1 with the result that: *It was dark, so I couldn't see what was happening.* | *She wrote a famous book, and so won a place in history.* 2 therefore: *I had a headache, so I went to bed.* | *I'm busy today, so can you come back tomorrow?* 3 with the purpose (that): *I packed him a little food so (that) he wouldn't get hungry.* 4 (used at the beginning of a sentence) **a** (with weak meaning): *So here we are again.* **b** (to express discovery): *So that's what you've been up to while I've been away!* **c** what if?; what does it matter that?: *So, I made a mistake. It's not the end of the world!* 5 **so what?** infml why is that important?; why should I care?: *"He says he doesn't like you." "So what?"*

so³ adj [F] 1 in accordance with actual facts; true: *You know very well that just isn't so.* | *Is that really so?* 2 (used in place of an adjective already stated): *Of all the careless people in the office no one is more so than Bill.* | *He's clever — probably too much so for his own good.* 3 arranged exactly and tidily: *If everything isn't **just/ exactly** so, he gets angry.* —see also SO-SO

so⁴, soh, sol n [S;U] the fifth note in the SOL-FA musical SCALE

soak¹ /səʊk/ v 1 [I;T (in)] to (cause to) remain in or be completely covered by a liquid, esp. so as to become soft or completely wet: *Leave the dirty clothes to soak.* | *First, soak the beans in water for two hours.* | *a rag soaked in petrol* —see also SOAKED 2 [I+adv/prep; T usu. pass.] (of a liquid) to enter (a solid) through the small openings of a surface: *The ink had soaked through the thin paper onto the picture beneath.* | *a rain-soaked field* 3 [T+obj+adv/

prep, esp. OUT] to remove by soaking: *to soak out a stain* | *to soak a label off a jar* **4** [T] *infml derog* to charge a very high amount of money to: *They really soak the tourists in that restaurant.*

soak sthg.↔**up** *phr v* [T] to draw in (a liquid) through a surface: *He got out his handkerchief to soak up the blood.* | *The ground soaked up the rain.* | (fig.) *We sat on the beach soaking up the sun.* | (fig.) *to soak up information*

soak² *n* **1** an act or state of soaking: *I enjoy a good long soak in the bath after a hard day's work.* **2** *BrE humor derog* a person who is often or usually drunk (esp. in the phrase **old soak**)

soaked /səʊkt/ *adj* [F] **1** thoroughly wet, esp. from rain; SODDEN: *You poor thing, you're soaked to the skin!* | *Your clothes are soaked through!* **2 soaked in/with** full of; steeped (STEEP²) in: *a place soaked in history*

soak·ing /ˈsəʊkɪŋ/ *adv, adj* very wet

soaking so·lu·tion /ˈ··· ·ˌ··/ *n* [C;U] a liquid into which one puts CONTACT LENSes when one is not wearing them

so-and-so /ˈ·· ˌ·/ *n* **so-and-sos 1** [U] someone or something; a certain one not named: *Meetings are always like that, with so-and-so saying it's a splendid idea, so-and-so saying it'll never work, etc.* —compare SUCH AND SUCH **2** [C] *euph* (used instead of a stronger word like BASTARD) an unpleasant, annoying, etc., person: *John's usually nice enough but he can be a (right) so-and-so at times.*

soap¹ /səʊp/ *n* **1** [U] a usu. solid substance that produces a LATHER (=soft white mass) when rubbed with water and is used for cleaning, esp. the body: *I never use soap on my face – it makes my skin too dry.* | *a bar/cake/tablet of soap in the soap dish* | *toilet soap* (=with a pleasant smell, for washing the face and hands) | *a box of* **soap flakes** *for washing clothes* —compare DETERGENT; see also SOFT SOAP **2** [C] *infml for* SOAP OPERA

soap² *v* [T] to rub soap on or over: *Will you soap my back for me?* —see also SOFT-SOAP

Soap, Joe see JOE BLOGGS

soap·box /ˈsəʊpbɒks‖-bɑːks/ *n* **on/off one's soapbox** *infml* stating/no longer stating one's strongly-held opinions loudly and forcefully: *Whenever anyone mentions the subject of meat he gets on his soapbox and says how wicked and unhealthy meat-eating is.*

soap bub·ble /ˈ· ˌ··/ *n* a ball of air enclosed by a thin skin of soap

soap dish /ˈ· ·/ *n* a small dish or container, put on a WASH-BASIN, into which soap is placed

soap·flakes /ˈsəʊpfleɪks/ *n* [P] small thin pieces of soap used for washing delicate clothes

soap-on-a-rope /ˌ··· ˈ·/ *n* a piece of soap on a bit of string which one can hang up conveniently while having a SHOWER¹ (3a)

soap op·e·ra /ˈ· ˌ···/ also **soap** *infml*– *n* a television or radio programme about the continuing daily life and troubles of characters in it, which is broadcast regularly, e.g. two or three times a week, or sometimes every day. In both the US and Britain there are soap operas that have been running for 20 years or more. Most people either like or strongly dislike soap operas. —compare HORSE OPERA; see also CORONATION STREET, DALLAS, EASTENDERS, NEIGHBOURS

soap·stone /ˈsəʊpstəʊn/ *n* [U] a soft stone that feels like soap, from which TALCUM POWDER is made

soap·suds /ˈsəʊpsʌdz/ *n* [P] SUDS

soap·y /ˈsəʊpi/ *adj* **1** containing or full of soap: *Wash it well in soapy water.* **2** like soap: *This cheese has a rather soapy taste.* **3** *infml derog* falsely or too pleasant; SLIMY —**iness** *n* [U]

soar /sɔːʳ/ *v* [I] **1 a** to fly, esp. at a great height without moving the wings: *The eagles soared high above the valleys.* **b** (of a GLIDER) to fly on rising currents of warm air **2** to rise rapidly or to a very high level: *The rocket soared into the sky.* | *The temperature soared to 80°.* | *soaring prices* **3** [*not in progressive forms*] to be very high, esp. so as to give one a feeling of splendid power: *The cliffs soar 500 feet into the air.*

sob¹ /sɒb‖sɑːb/ *v* **-bb- 1** [I;T+*obj*+*adv/prep*] to cry while making short bursts of sound as one breathes in, because of sadness or fear: *A little girl was sitting sobbing in the corner.* | *She sobbed herself to sleep.* (=sobbed until she

fell asleep) | (*infml*) *to sob one's heart out* (=very strongly) **2** [T (OUT)] to say or tell while sobbing: *He sobbed out the whole sad story.* – ~**bingly** *adv*

sob² *n* an act or sound of sobbing: *to let out a heavy protracted sob*

S.O.B. /ˌes əʊ ˈbiː/ *n taboo* SON-OF-A-BITCH

so·ber¹ /ˈsəʊbəʳ/ *adj* **1** not under the influence of alcohol; not drunk: *I've never seen him sober.* —compare DRUNK² **2** *rather fml* thoughtful, serious, or solemn; not silly: *On more sober reflection, I resolved to turn down the offer.* **3** *fml* not decorative or brightly-coloured – ~**ly** *adv*

sober² *v* [I;T (DOWN)] to make or become serious or thoughtful: *She's sobered down a lot as she's got older.* | *a sobering thought/reminder*
    sober up *phr v* [I;T (=**sober** sbdy. ↔ **up**)] to make or become sober; get or be rid of the effect of alcohol: *I hope this coffee will sober me up.* | *He sobered up enough to drive home.*

So·bers /ˈsəʊbəz‖-bərz/, **Gar·y** /ˈgæri/ (1936–) a West Indian cricketer considered to be one of the best of all time

so·bri·e·ty /səˈbraɪəti/ *n* [U] *fml* the state of being sober

so·bri·quet /ˈsəʊbrɪkeɪ/ also **soubriquet**– *n lit* an unofficial name or title; NICKNAME

sob sto·ry /ˈ· ˌ··/ *n infml derog* a story intended to make the hearer or reader cry, feel pity, or feel sorry

Soc. *n written abbrev. for* SOCIETY

so·ca /ˈsəʊkə/ *n* [U] a style of popular music which combines SOUL MUSIC and CALYPSO

so-called /ˌ· ˈ·◂/ *adj* [A] *often derog* commonly called or named so, but often improperly or undeservedly: *The so-called expert on international affairs turned out to be a young research student.* | *so-called Christians who show no love to anyone*

soc·cer /ˈsɒkəʳ‖ˈsɑː-/ *n* [U] FOOTBALL (1)

so·cia·ble¹ /ˈsəʊʃəbəl/ *adj* fond of being with others; enjoying social life; friendly: *a pleasant, sociable couple* —opposite **unsociable** —**bly** *adv* —**bility** /ˌsəʊʃəˈbɪləti/ *n* [U]

▷ USAGE It is better to use **sociable**, rather than **social**, to mean "cheerful and friendly": *to spend a* **sociable** *evening drinking.* Use **social** to mean **a** "connected with society": **social** *history*, or **b** "connected with living in a group and meeting people": *her busy* **social** *life.*◁

sociable² *n AmE for* SOCIAL²

so·cial¹ /ˈsəʊʃəl/ *adj* **1** of human society, its organization, or quality of life: *We talked about various social questions, such as unemployment and education.* | *social inequalities* | *social trends* –see SOCIETAL (USAGE) **2** based on rank in society (sometimes different from wealth or political power): *friends of his own social level* ooo *also* so-CIAL CLASS, SOCIAL MOBILITY **3 a** helping to form good relationship with friends **b** of good relationships with friends: *A little social drinking does no harm, but beware of drinking alone.* | *poor social skills* (=poor ability to form relationships) –see also SOCIAL LIFE **4** [A] intended for friendly or non-business meetings: *Our firm has a good social club.* **5** forming groups or living together by nature: *Ants are social insects.* **6** *infml* fond of being with others; sociable: *I'm not feeling very social this evening.* –see also ANTISOCIAL, UNSOCIAL; see SOCIABLE (USAGE) – ~**ly** *adv* : *drinking within socially acceptable limits*

social² ‖ also **sociable** *AmE*– *n old-fash* a planned informal friendly gathering of members of a group, club, or church

Social and Lib·e·ral Dem·o·crats /ˌ···· ˌ··· ˈ···/ [*the*+P] the formal title of the Liberal Democrats –see LIBERAL DEMOCRATS

Social Chap·ter /ˌ·· ˈ··/ also **European Social Chapter** – [*the*] a document produced by the EUROPEAN COMMUNITY and agreed upon by all member states except the United Kingdom (and therefore not legally in force) which contains details of the most important employment and social rights that should be available in member countries. The document covers areas such as freedom of movement, employment and payment, health and safety, living and working conditions, equal treatment between men and women, protection of children and young people and a number of other things.

British society is considered to be divided into three main groups of classes – the UPPER CLASS, the MIDDLE CLASS, and the LOWER or WORKING CLASS. This is known as the CLASS SYSTEM and it is important to know something about it if you want to understand British people and society. Most British people grow up with a deep knowledge and understanding of the class system even if they are not very conscious of it. Most people know which class they belong to and are able to tell which class another person comes from by the way they speak, their clothes, their interests or even the type of food they eat.

Social class is not only about behaviour and attitudes. For example, although many upper class people are rich and may own a lot of land, having a lot of money does not make a person upper class. It is also important to come from a particular kind of family, have friends who are considered suitable, have been to a certain type of PRIVATE SCHOOL and speak with the right kind of ACCENT. There are people who are poor but who do not think of themselves as working class because their family background, education, political opinions, etc. are different to those of most working-class people. Many people do not like the class system but it is impossible to pretend that these differences do not exist or that British people do not sometimes form opinions in this way.

Many kinds of foods, activities, and aspects of lifestyle are associated with one particular class. These are often referred to, e.g. in jokes and stories, in order to convey information about a person's social class. For example, if a man is described as enjoying a few beers and a game of darts in the pub on a Saturday night, British speakers would guess that the man is working class. These tables should help you to understand the kinds of words which can be used to convey information about social class.

Food

upper class	middle class	working class
Cordon Bleu		bangers & mash
champagne → → → → → → → →		fish & chips
caviar		pie & chips
smoked salmon		beer
	health foods	
	e.g. wholemeal bread	
	foreign food	tomato ketchup
	e.g. avocado, pasta → → → → → →	
	restaurants	junk food
		meat & 2 veg
		Chinese & Indian food
		especially takeaways

Education

upper class	middle class	working class
Eton, Harrow	grammar school	comprehensive
public school ← ← ← ← state school → → → →		
prep school		
finishing school		technical college
	Oxford	
	Cambridge	
	← ← ← ← university → → → →	
	polytechnic	

Work/Jobs

upper class	middle class	working class
←professional & white-collar jobs → → → → → →		blue-collar & manual jobs
judge	teacher → → → → → →	miner
stockbroker	accountant	mechanic
company director	bank manager	factory worker
MP → → → → → → →	doctor	shop assistant
a job in the City → → → → → → →		lorry driver
no job because the person is very rich, 'the idle rich'		

Housing

upper class	middle class	working class
own several homes	own their own home	council house or council flat
own a stately home	have a second home	(owned or rented) inner city areas
large landowner	semi-detached	
live in Mayfair and Knightsbridge (rich areas of central London)	or detached house in suburbs	

Leisure

upper class	middle class	working class
ballet	theatre	
opera	cinema → → → → → → →	
	television → → → → → → → → →	
	radio → → → → → → → → →	
← ← ← ← ← ← ← art galleries		
	museums	
	radio 4	
	BBC 2	ITV
	Channel 4	soap operas e.g. Coronation St
	← ← ← ← ← ← ← pubs	
	wine bars → → →	working men's clubs

Sports and games

upper class	middle class	working class
polo		football
any sport involving horses		darts
horse racing		horse racing
		bingo
		snooker
← ← ← ← ← ← ← ski-ing		
← ← ← ← ← ← ← sailing		racing pigeons (in the north)
← ← ← ← ← ← ← tennis → → → → → → →		
← ← ← ← ← ← ← rugby → → → → → → →		
← ← ← ← ← ← ← cricket → → → → → → →		
← ← ← ← ← ← ← golf		
fox hunting		
hunting, shooting and fishing		

Politics

upper class	middle class	working class
Conservative	Conservative	Conservative
	← ← ← ← ← Labour → → → → → →	
	SDP	
	Liberals	
	Green Party	

Holidays

upper class	middle class	working class
	walking holidays	package
	Lake District	tours
Mustique	Devon	Benidorm
Gstaad	Cornwall	Costa del Sol
The Caribbean	France	Ibiza
	Tuscany	Blackpool
cruises → → → → →		British seaside
	camping	caravans
Orient Express	villas	holiday camps
	gites	
	holiday cottages	
	←←←←← B & B → → → → →	

social class /ˌ··ˈ·/ *n* a group of people who have the same economic and social position in society: *legislation that will affect every social class, from manual workers to peers of the realm* —see also MIDDLE CLASS, UPPER CLASS, WORKING CLASS and see extra information on page 1258

social climb·er /ˌ··ˈ··/ *n derog* a person who spends money or tries to make friends in order to be accepted by a group of people of a higher class

social con·science /ˌ··ˈ··/ *n* [S] concern for poorer people and their quality of life: *She has a highly-developed social conscience, and does a lot of voluntary work to help the less well-off.*

social con·tract /ˌ··ˈ··/ *n* an agreement between a group in society and a government that explains and limits the rights and duties of each of them (from a book by the French thinker Jean Jacques Rousseau, *The Social Contract*, 1762)

social de·moc·ra·cy /ˌ··ˈ·ˌ··/ *n* [C;U] (a political and economic system based on) the ideas of equality and public ownership of the means of production, achieved through government of the people by their elected representatives: *Social democracy gives You a voice.* | *Britain has never been a social democracy.*

social dem·o·crat /ˌ··ˈ··/ *n* someone who supports the system of social democracy

Social Dem·o·crat and La·bour Par·ty /ˌ··ˌ···· ·ˈ·· ˌ··/ see SDLP

Social Dem·o·cratic Party /ˌ··ˈ·ˈ·· ˌ··/ also **Social Democrats** /ˌ··ˈ····/, **SDP** [*the+sing./pl. v*] a British political party formed in 1981 and sharing many of the opinions of the Liberal Party. It was led for most of its existence by David Owen. In 1988 most of its members joined with the Liberal Party to form the Social and Liberal Democrats, although the Social Democratic Party still officially existed for several years —see also SOCIAL AND LIBERAL DEMOCRATS

social dis·ease /ˈ·· ·ˌ·/ *n euph for* VENEREAL DISEASE

social drink·er /ˈ·· ˌ··/ *n* a person who drinks alcohol when they are with friends, but not when alone

social fund /ˈ·· ˌ·/ [*the*] (in Britain) a sum of money set aside by the government from which certain poor people who need money for a particular purpose can be given it

social grac·es /ˌ··ˈ··/ *n* [P] attractive qualities with regard to manners, appearance, speech, and behaviour: *His professor is certainly lacking in the social graces!*

so·cial·is·m /ˈsəʊʃəl-ɪzəm/ *n* [U] (*sometimes cap.*) any of various beliefs or systems (sometimes considered to include Communism) aiming at public ownership of the means of production and the establishment of a society in which every person is truly equal —compare CAPITALISM, COMMUNISM

▶CULTURAL NOTE In the US, socialism is generally unpopular and not respected and politicians often accuse their opponents of supporting it.◀

so·cial·ist¹ /ˈsəʊʃəl-ɪst/ *n* **1** a believer in socialism **2** (*usu. cap.*) a member of a socialist political party

▶CULTURAL NOTE In Britain, people sometimes informally call the Labour Party **the socialists.**◀

3 We are all Socialists now *quote* a phrase used by a 19th century Liberal politician, **Sir William Harcourt,** which people sometimes ADAPT

socialist² *adj* **1** of or supporting socialism: *socialist principles/ideals/tendencies* **2** (*usu. cap.*) of, supporting, or agreeing with any of various esp. Western European parties who support greater equality of wealth and more government ownership of business: *the Socialist manifesto*

Socialist Work·er /ˌ··· ˈ··/ a British newspaper produced by a strongly LEFT-WING political group, whose members give it out to people in public places

so·cia·lite /ˈsəʊʃəl-aɪt/ *n* a person well known for going to many fashionable parties

so·cial·ize also **-ise** *BrE* /ˈsəʊʃəl-aɪz/ *v* **1** [I (**with**)] to spend time with others in a friendly way: *I enjoy socializing with my students after class.* —compare FRATERNIZE (1) **2** [T] *tech* to make fit or train for life in a society. —**ization** /ˌsəʊʃəl-aɪˈzeɪʃən/-ʃələ-/ *n* [U] : *new programmes for the socialization of young offenders* (=criminals)

socialized medi·cine /ˌ···· ·ˈ·· ‖ ˌ··· ·ˈ··/ *n* [U] *AmE* medical care provided by a government and paid for by taxes —see NATIONAL HEALTH SERVICE

social life /ˈ·· ·ˌ/ *n* [C;U] the activities one does with one's friends, e.g. going to a party, out for dinner, or for a drink: *She may not be able to come. She has a very busy social life.*

social mo·bil·i·ty /ˌ··· ·ˈ···ˌ/ *n* [U] the ability to move into a different social class, esp. up into the higher one: *He swears by the old school tie, the ultimate aid to social mobility.*

social sci·ence /ˌ··· ·ˈ·‖ˈ·· ˌ·/ *n* **1** [U] also **social studies**— the study of people in society, usu. including history, politics, ECONOMICS, SOCIOLOGY, and ANTHROPOLOGY **2** [C] any of these: *the social sciences* —compare NATURAL SCIENCE —**entist** *n*

social se·cu·ri·ty /ˌ··· ·ˈ···/ *n* [U] **1** *BrE* ‖ **welfare** *AmE* – government money paid to people who are unemployed, old, ill, etc.

▶CULTURAL NOTE Some people think that the social security system is too complicated and the payments too low. Other people get annoyed by some people receiving social security because they appear not to be trying to find work and make a lot of claims for money which taxpayers provide: *He's on social security.* (= receiving government money) | *claimants attending the social security office* | *social security benefit*◀

2 *AmE* (*often cap.*) the system of government payments, esp. to RETIRED people —see also DEPARTMENT OF SOCIAL SECURITY

Social Security Num·ber /ˌ··· ·ˈ··· ˌ··/ *abbrev.* **SSN**— *n* a number of the form 000-00-0000 which the US government gives to all working people in order to bring them into the WELFARE system —see also FICA, SOCIAL SECURITY (1)

social serv·ice /ˌ··· ·ˈ··‖·· ˌ··/ *n* a service that is necessary for society to work properly and is provided by a government or supported by government money: *Should the railways make a profit or should they be regarded as a social service?*

social serv·ices /ˌ··· ·ˈ···/ *n* [*the*+P] *esp. BrE* the special services provided by a government or local council to help people, such as education, health care, etc.: *Her children were being abused and have been taken into the care of the social services.*

social stud·ies /ˈ·· ·ˌ··/ *n* [P] SOCIAL SCIENCE

social work /ˈ·· ·ˌ/ *n* [U] work done by government or private organizations to improve bad social conditions and help people in need

social work·er /ˈ·· ˌ··/ *n* a person who is employed in SOCIAL WORK: *The police have called social workers in to help the dead man's family.*

so·ci·e·tal /səˈsaɪətl/ *adj* [A] of society: *societal attitudes/ resources*

▷ USAGE **Societal** is much more limited in its use than **social**. It is used about a particular society, not human society generally, and is esp. used by students of SOCIAL SCIENCE.◁

so·ci·e·ty /səˈsaɪ⅟ti/ *n* **1** [U] people in general, considered with regard to the structure of laws, organizations, etc., that makes it possible for them to live together: *Society has a right to expect people to obey the law.* | *He is a danger to society, and ought to be locked up.* **2** [C;U] a particular broad group of people who share laws, organizations, customs, etc.: *Such behaviour is unacceptable in a civilized society.* | *Britain is a multi-racial society.* | *Drug abuse is one of the problems confronting modern Western society.* | *He thinks greed is a product of the consumer society.* | *Shopaholics are a new problem, born of the affluent society.* **3** [C] an organization or club of people with similar aims, interests, etc.: *She joined the university film society.* | *a member of the Law Society* **4** [U] the fashionable group of people of the upper classes in a place: *At the age of 21 a girl was introduced into* (**high**) **society.** | *a well-known society hostess* | *a society wedding* **5** [U] *fml* the companionship or presence of (other people): *He shunned the society of others, preferring to be alone.* —see also BUILDING SOCIETY, FRIENDLY SOCIETY

▷ USAGE Compare **society** [U] and **community** [C]. *The* **community** is a general expression for the people as a whole in a particular village, town, city or area: *Keep the streets clean for the good of the* **community.**

Society is a more general word for people considered in relation to each other, perhaps in one country, or even in many countries: *the problems of modern society.* —see also FOLK¹ (USAGE), RACE³ (USAGE)◁

Society of Friends /·ₙ··· ·ₙ·/ [*the*] the formal name of the QUAKERS

Society of Je·sus /·ₙ··· ·ₙ·/ [*the*] the formal name of the JESUITS

socio- see WORD FORMATION

so·ci·o·bi·ol·ogy /ₙsəʊsiəʊbaɪˈɒlədʒi, ₙsəʊʃiəʊ-‖-ˈɑːl-/ n [U] the study of social behaviour in animals including its change over long periods of time and its usefulness for making sure that the different kinds of animals continue to exist

so·ci·o·ec·o·nom·ic /ₙsəʊsiəʊekəˈnɒmɪk, ₙsəʊʃiəʊ-, -iːkə-‖ -ˈnɑː-/ *adj* based on a combination of social and money conditions: *The different classes in society are known technically as socioeconomic groups.* — ~ally /kli/ *adv*

so·ci·ol·o·gy /ₙsəʊsiˈɒlədʒi, ₙsəʊʃi-‖-ˈɑːlə-/ n [U] the scientific study of societies and human behaviour in groups —compare ANTHROPOLOGY, ETHNOLOGY, SOCIAL SCIENCE —gist n —gical /ₙsəʊsiəˈlɒdʒɪkəl◂, ₙsəʊʃiə-‖-ˈlɑː-/ *adj* —gically /kli/ *adv*

so·ci·o·path /ˈsəʊsiəpæθ, ˈsəʊʃiə-/ n **1** *tech* a person whose habitual behaviour with and towards others is considered unacceptable, unbalanced, and possibly dangerous —compare PSYCHOPATH **2** *not tech* a PSYCHOPATH — ~ic /ₙsəʊsiəˈpæθɪk◂, səʊʃiə-/ *adj*

sock¹ /sɒk‖sɑːk/ n **1** a covering of soft material for the foot and usu. part of the lower leg, usu. worn inside a shoe: *My socks keep falling down.* | *He's wearing odd socks.* (=they do not match) | *knee-length socks* | *ankle socks* — compare STOCKING; see PAIR (USAGE) **2 pull one's socks up** *BrE infml* to make an effort to improve oneself, one's work, etc. **3 put a sock in it** *humor, esp. BrE* to keep quiet; stop talking

sock² v [T(on)] *infml* **1** to strike hard: *He socked his opponent on the jaw.* **2 sock it to someone** *old-fash* to express oneself or behave forcefully: *It was a great performance; you really socked it to them!*

sock³ n [(on) usu. sing.] *infml* a forceful blow, esp. with the closed hand: *a hefty sock on the jaw*

sock·et /ˈsɒkₓt‖ˈsɑː-/ n **1** a piece of plastic or other material with holes in it, which is fixed into a wall or on to the end of a wire, and to which electrical equipment can be connected for the electricity supply: *Plug the iron into that socket, will you?* **2** an opening or hollow place into which something fits: *He was so astonished that his eyes nearly fell out of their sockets!*

sock·ing /ˈsɒkɪŋ‖ˈsɑː-/ *adv infml, esp. BrE* extremely (big): *It had grown into a **socking great** tree.*

Sock Shop /ˈ· ·/ [*the*] one of a group of shops which sells socks, TIGHTS, etc.

Soc·ra·tes /ˈsɒkrətiːz‖ˈsɑːk-/ (about 470–399 BC) a famous Greek thinker, and teacher of Plato. He is known for encouraging people always to question everything. He upset the leaders of Greek society, who made him kill himself by drinking poisonous HEMLOCK.—**-tic** /səˈkrætɪk/ *adj* : *Socratic methods*

sod¹ /sɒd‖sɑːd/ n *BrE taboo sl* **1** a stupid or annoying person, esp. a man: *My boss can be an absolute sod at times.* | *You sod! That was the last cake!.* **2** something that causes a lot of trouble or difficulty: *a sod of a job* **3 not give/care a sod** not to care at all

sod² v -dd- [T usu. imperative] *BrE taboo sl* (used for expressing annoyance or displeasure at the stated thing or person): *Sod this radio! Why won't it work?* | *Oh sod it, I've missed my train!*

sod off *phr v* [I usu. imperative] *BrE taboo sl* to go away: *He got angry and told me to sod off.*

sod³ n [U] *esp. fml or lit in BrE* a piece of earth with grass and roots growing in it; TURF¹ (1)

sod farm /ˈ· ·/ n *AmE* a business which grows and sells SOD³

so·da /ˈsəʊdə/ n **1** [C;U] (a drink of) SODA WATER: *Could you put more soda in my campari, please?* | *Two whisky and sodas, please.* | *a soda siphon* **2** [U] also **soda pop**— *esp. AmE for* POP² (2): *a bottle of orange soda* **3** [C] an ICE-CREAM SODA: *A chocolate soda, please.* **4** [U] *not tech* SODIUM (in such phrases as **bicarbonate of soda**)

soda crack·er /ˈ·· ₙ··/ also **cracker**— n *AmE* a small thin unsweetened BISCUIT, often eaten with cheese

soda foun·tain /ˈ·· ₙ··/ n *AmE, becoming old-fash* a place in a shop at which fruit drinks, ice cream, etc., are served

soda wa·ter /ˈ·· ₙ··/ also **soda** ‖ also **club soda** *AmE*— n [U] water filled under pressure with gas (CARBON DIOXIDE) which gives it a more pleasant and fresher taste

sod·den /ˈsɒdn‖ˈsɑːdn/ *adj* heavy with wetness; SOAKED: *We trudged across the sodden ground.*

sod·ding /ˈsɒdɪŋ‖ˈsɑː-/ *adj* [A] *BrE taboo sl* (used for giving force to an expression, esp. showing annoyance): *Why won't this sodding car start?*

so·di·um /ˈsəʊdiəm/ n [U] a silver-white metal that is a simple substance (ELEMENT), found in nature only in combination with other substances

sodium bi·car·bo·nate /ₙ··· ·ₙ···/ n [U] *tech* BICARBONATE

sodium chlo·ride /ₙ··· ·ₙ·/ n [U] *tech for* SALT

Sod·om and Go·mor·rah /ₙsɒdəm ənd gəˈmɒrə‖ₙsɑː-, -ˈmɔː-/ any place or places considered particularly evil or wicked, esp. regarding sexual behaviour (from the story in the Bible of the towns of Sodom and Gomorrah which were destroyed by God for their wickedness): *Some people have a biblical attitude towards Aids. It's like Sodom and Gomorrah to them — the plagues have descended.* | *Newspapermen arrived in droves after the town was dubbed the new Sodom by a local priest.*

sod·o·mite /ˈsɒdəmaɪt‖ˈsɑː-/ n *old-fash* a person practising sodomy

sod·o·my /ˈsɒdəmi‖ˈsɑː-/ n [U] *fml or law* any of various sexual acts other than the usual sexual act between a man and a woman, esp. the putting of the male sex organ into the ANUS of esp. another male

sod's law /ₙ· ˈ·/ *BrE* ‖ also **Murphy's law** *esp. AmE*— *humor* (*often cap.* S) the natural tendency for things to go wrong if it is possible for them to go wrong: *According to Sod's law, if you drop a piece of bread and butter, it will land butter-side down.*

so·fa /ˈsəʊfə/ n a comfortable seat with raised arms and a back, wide enough for usu. two or three people; SETTEE: *Sit on the sofa.* —see picture at LIVING ROOM

sofa bed /ˈ·· ·/ n a sofa which can be changed into a bed

So·fi·a /ˈsəʊfiə/ the capital city of Bulgaria

soft /sɒft‖sɔːft/ *adj* **1** not firm against pressure; not hard or stiff: *His foot sank slightly into the soft ground.* | *a soft chair/bed* **2** less hard than average: *Lead is one of the softer metals.* | *soft cheese* **3** pleasantly smooth and delicate to the touch; not rough: *a baby's soft skin* **4** quiet; not making much noise; not loud: *a whisper so soft I could hardly hear* **5** restful and pleasant to the senses, esp. the eyes: *Soft lights and sweet music create a romantic atmosphere.* | *The room was decorated in soft pastel colours.* —opposite **harsh** **6** with little force; light; gentle: *Give it a soft tap with the hammer.* | *a soft breeze* **7** *infml, often derog* not needing hard work; easy: *He's got a pretty soft job in the ministry.* —see also SOFT OPTION **8** [(with)] too kind; not severe enough: *I think the courts are too soft with these young offenders.* | *You big soft thing! Why did you agree to help them when you know you can't afford the time?* —opposite **hard (on)** —see also SOFTY **9** [(on)] not showing (enough) firmness in opposing or dealing with something: *The government was accused of* **taking a soft line** (=not being firm enough) *with the unions.* | *His political enemies said he was soft on Communism.* **10** not in good bodily condition; weak; FLABBY: *He'd got soft after all those years in a desk job.* **11** *infml* dealing with opinions, ideas, etc., rather than numbers and facts: *Psychology would be regarded as one of the soft sciences.* **12** [A] not of the worst, most harmful, etc., kind: *soft porn* | *Cannabis is a* **soft drug.** —opposite **hard** **13** *not tech* (in English pronunciation) **a** (of the letter *c*) having the sound /s/ and not /k/: *The c in acid is soft.* **b** (of the letter *g*) having the sound /dʒ/ and not /g/: *The g in age is soft.* —opposite **hard** —see also WATER SOFTENER **14** (of water) free from certain minerals; allowing soap to LATHER (=form a white mass) easily: *We're lucky that the local water is quite soft.* —opposite **hard** **15** *infml, esp. NEngE* foolish **16 be soft on someone** *infml* to be very attracted to someone sexually —see also SOFT SPOT **17 soft in the head** *infml* foolish; mad — ~ly *adv* : *Music played softly in the background. She stroked his hair softly.* | *A breeze blew softly across the lake.* — ~ness n [U]

soft·ball /ˈsɒftbɔːl‖ˈsɔːft-/ n [U] a game similar to BASEBALL but played on a smaller field with a slightly larger and softer ball, usu. by girls or women or by groups of men and woman together

soft-boiled /ˌ· ˈ·◄/ adj (of an egg) boiled not long enough for the YOLK to become solid, i.e. for between about three and five minutes: He likes his eggs soft-boiled. —compare HARD-BOILED

soft cop·y /ˈ· ˌ·/ n [U] tech information stored in a computer's memory or shown on a SCREEN, rather than in printed form —compare HARD COPY

soft cov·er /ˈ· ˌ·/ n [U] AmE PAPERBACK

soft drink /ˈ· ·/ n a drink which contains no alcohol and is served cold

soft·en /ˈsɒfən‖ˈsɔː-/ v [I;T (UP)] to (cause to) become soft(er), gentle, less stiff, or less severe: The ice cream softened and began to melt. | His voice softened sympathetically. | The government's attitude on this question has softened recently. | a cream for softening dry skin | He told her the bad news very gently, trying to **soften the blow**. —opposite **harden**

    soften sbdy./sthg.↔**up** phr v [T] **1** to weaken (an enemy's defences) before an attack, e.g. by bombing **2** infml to break down the opposition of; prepare for PERSUASION: You'll have to soften her up before you ask for a pay rise!

soft·e·ner /ˈsɒfənəʳ‖ˈsɔː-/ n **1** something that breaks down someone's possible opposition to an idea or request before they are told about it **2** infml for a WATER SOFTENER

soft fo·cus /ˌ· ˈ··/ n [U] an arrangement of the LENS in usu. a camera so that the lines of the object to be photographed are not clear. It is thought that photographs taken in this way make things look more ROMANTIC: All these photos of brides have been taken in soft focus.

soft fruit /ˌ· ˈ·/ n [C;U] esp. BrE a small eatable fruit that has no hard skin or hard inside seed: Strawberries and raspberries are soft fruit(s).

soft fur·nish·ings /ˌ· ˈ···/ n [P] esp. BrE (the materials used to make) curtains, mats, seat covers, etc., used in decorating a room

soft-head·ed /ˌ· ˈ··◄/ adj stupid; silly **soft-head** /ˈ· ·/ n

soft-heart·ed /ˌsɒftˈhɑːtᵻd◄‖ˌsɔːftˈhɑːr-/ adj having tender feelings; easily moved to pity; quick to forgive — ~ **ness** n [U]

soft·ie /ˈsɒfti‖ˈsɔːf-/ n infml a SOFTY

soft land·ing /ˌ· ˈ··/ n a slow coming down of a spacecraft to Earth, the moon, etc., without damage

soft·ly-soft·ly /ˌ· ˈ··/ adj slow and careful: He's very nervous so we'll have to try a softly-softly approach.

soft mar·ga·rine /ˌ· ··ˈ· ‖ ˌ· ˈ···/ n [U] a food tasting rather like butter, but made mainly from vegetable fats. It always stays soft, even when it is cold.

soft op·tion /ˌ· ˈ··/ n often derog an easier thing; a course of action that will give one less trouble: Faced with such strong opposition, he **took the soft option** and gave in to most of their demands. | Don't imagine that computer studies is a soft option; it's quite a tough course.

soft pal·ate /ˌ· ˈ··/ n the soft back part of the top of the mouth —compare HARD PALATE

soft-ped·al /ˌ· ˈ··‖ˈ· ·◄/ v [T] -ll- BrE ‖ -l- AmE [T] infml to make (a subject, fact, suggestion, etc.) seem unimportant; PLAY **down**: The council are soft-pedalling their housing policy until the local elections.

soft porn /ˌ· ˈ·/ n [U] magazines, pictures, etc., that are considered to be only slightly PORNOGRAPHIC. They are therefore generally regarded as TASTELESS but harmless by many British and US people, although an increasing number of people do not like women being shown in this way —compare HARD PORN

soft sell /ˌ· ˈ·◄/ n (the) S] selling by suggestion or gentle persuading of buyers —opposite **hard sell**

soft-soap /ˈ· ·/ v [T (into)] infml to persuade or make calmer, less angry, etc., by saying nice things: She soft-soaped him into agreeing to help her.

soft soap /ˌ· ˈ·/ n [U] infml saying nice things about people, esp. as a way of getting something one wants from them; FLATTERY

soft-spok·en /ˌ· ˈ··◄/ adj apprec having a gentle quiet voice

soft spot /ˈ· ·/ n [(for)] infml a feeling of special kindness or liking; fondness: He's a bit of a rogue, but I've got quite a soft spot for him.

soft touch /ˌ· ˈ·/ n infml someone from whom it is easy to get what one wants, esp. money or help, because they are kind, easily deceived, etc.

soft·ware /ˈsɒftweəʳ‖ˈsɔːft-/ n [U] tech the set of systems (in the form of PROGRAMs rather than machine parts) which is stored on MAGNETIC TAPE or DISK and controls the operation of a computer: Can you load the new software for me? | a software package | word processing/spreadsheet software —compare FIRMWARE, HARDWARE

soft·wood /ˈsɒftwʊd‖ˈsɔːft-/ n **1** [U] wood from EVERGREEN trees, such as PINE and FIR, that is cheap and easy to cut **2** [C] a tree that has wood of this type —compare HARDWOOD

soft·y , softie /ˈsɒfti‖ˈsɔːfti/ n infml **1** a person who is easily moved to pity or who is SENTIMENTAL **2** a weak or very easily persuaded person

SOGAT /ˈsəʊgæt/ (in Britain) the Society of Graphical and Allied Trades; an important TRADE UNION for printing workers

sog·gy /ˈsɒgi‖ˈsɑːgi/ adj completely wet; heavy and usu. unpleasant with wetness: The ground was soggy after the heavy rain. | They served up some rather soggy tomato sandwiches. —-**gily** adv —-**giness** n [U]

soh /səʊ/ n [S;U] SO⁴

So·ho /ˈsəʊhəʊ/ an area in central London famous for its theatres, NIGHTCLUBS, SEX SHOPS, and restaurants, esp. of Chinese food

SoHo an area of Manhattan, New York City, south of Houston Street, known for fashionable shops and restaurants —see colour map on page 1376

soi·gné , -gnée fem. /ˈswɑːnjeɪ‖swɑːnˈjeɪ/ adj fml dressed or arranged fashionably and with care in detail

soil¹ /sɔɪl/ n **1** [U] the top covering of the earth in which plants grow; ground: an area of rich/sandy soil **2** [the+S] usu. pomp where a farmer works; the life or land of a farm: She makes her living from the soil. | a man of the soil **3** [U] usu. pomp a place or country: This is my native soil. —see also NIGHT SOIL; see LAND (USAGE)

soil² v [T] fml to make dirty, esp. slightly or on the surface or with bodily waste matter: Put all soiled sheets into this basket. | children who soil themselves after the age of three | (fig.) I wouldn't soil my hands on/with such a dishonest scheme.

soi·ree , -rée /ˈswɑːreɪ‖swɑːˈreɪ/ n esp. pomp an evening party, often including an artistic performance, e.g. of music or poetry

soj·ourn¹ /ˈsɒdʒɜːn‖ˈsəʊdʒɜːrn/ n esp. lit a stay in a place other than one's home for a time

sojourn² v [I+adv/prep] lit to live for a time in a place: Jesus sojourned many days in the desert. — ~ **er** n

sol /sɒl‖səʊl/ n [S;U] SO⁴

sol·ace¹ /ˈsɒlᵻs‖ˈsɑː-/ n **1** [U] comfort in grief or anxiety; lessening of trouble in the mind: I'm afraid he took his solace in drink. (=drank alcohol to comfort himself) **2** [C (to)] fml something that provides this: Her daughter was a great solace to her in her bereavement.

solace² v [T] lit to give comfort in mind to or for; CONSOLE

so·lar /ˈsəʊləʳ/ adj **1** of or from the sun: solar time **2** using the power of the sun's light and heat: a solar heating system | the production of solar energy

solar cell /ˌ··· ˈ·/ n an apparatus for producing electric power from sunlight

so·lar·i·um /səʊˈleəriəm/ n -ia /riə/ or -iums a room, usu. enclosed by glass, where one can sit in bright sunlight

solar pan·el /ˌ··· ˈ··/ n a number of SOLAR CELLs working together: They have a solar panel on their roof that powers their central heating. —see picture at SPACE STATION

solar plex·us /ˌsəʊlə ˈpleksəs/ n [the+S] **1** med the system of nerves between the stomach and the BACKBONE **2** not tech the front part of the body below the chest: I punched him in the solar plexus.

solar sys·tem /ˈ··· ˌ··/ n **1** [(the)] (often caps.) the sun together with the PLANETs going round it **2** [C] such a system round another star

solar year /ˌ··· ˈ·/ n tech the length of time in which the

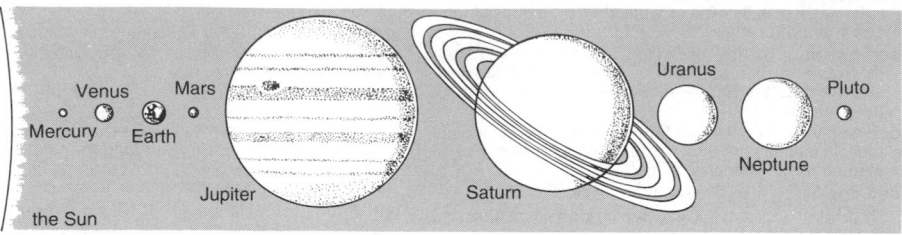

Venus Mars Mercury Earth Jupiter Saturn Uranus Pluto Neptune the Sun

Earth goes once round the sun, equal to 365 days 5 hours 49 minutes

sold /səʊld/ *past tense & participle of* SELL¹

sol·der¹ /ˈsɒldər, ˈsəʊl-‖ˈsɑːdər/ *n* [U] soft metal, usu. a mixture of lead and tin, used when melted for joining other metal surfaces

solder² *v* [T] to join or repair with solder: *That electrical connection should be soldered.* —compare WELD

soldering i·ron /ˈ··· ¡··/ *n* a tool which is heated, usu. by electricity, for melting and putting on solder

sol·dier¹ /ˈsəʊldʒər/ *n* **1** someone who serves in the military forces of a country; a member of an army, esp. one who is not an officer: *The soldier saluted.* | *Stand to attention, soldier!* **2** **old soldiers never die (they simply just fade away)** a phrase from a humorous British army song of the First World War —compare SAILOR; see also MILITARY SERVICE, SOLDIERS, UNKNOWN SOLDIER

soldier² *v*
soldier on *phr v* [I] *esp. BrE* to continue working; work steadily, esp. in spite of difficulties: *He doesn't like the job but he'll soldier on until they can find a replacement for him.*

sol·dier·ing /ˈsəʊldʒərɪŋ/ *n* [U] the life or job of a soldier

sol·dier·ly /ˈsəʊldʒəli‖-ərli/ *adj lit apprec* typical or worthy of a good soldier: *He had an upright soldierly bearing.*

soldier of for·tune /¡··· · ¹··/ *n lit or euph* a person who travels in search of military action, for adventure or pay; a MERCENARY

sol·diers /ˈsəʊldʒəz‖-ərz/ *n* [P] *BrE* long narrow pieces of bread or TOAST, often given to small children e.g. to dip into a SOFT-BOILED egg

sol·dier·y /ˈsəʊldʒəri/ *n* [(the) U+sing.|pl. v] *lit* a body of soldiers, esp. of the stated (often bad) type

sole¹ /səʊl/ *n* **1** the bottom surface of the foot, esp. the part on which one walks or stands —see picture at FOOT **2** the part of a piece of footwear covering this, esp. the flat bottom part of a shoe not including the heel —see picture at SHOE **3** -soled /səʊld/having soles of the stated type: *thick-soled shoes*

sole² *v* [T *usu. pass.*] to put a new sole on (a shoe): *I'm having my shoes soled and heeled.*

sole³ *n* **sole** *or* **soles** [C;U] a flat fish that is often used for food —see also LEMON SOLE

sole⁴ *adj* [A] **1** being the only one; only: *The sole survivor of the crash was a little baby.* **2** belonging or allowed to one person or group only; not shared: *a sales representative with sole responsibility for sales in the North East* —see also SOLELY

so·le·cis·m /ˈsɒlɨsɪzəm‖ˈsɑː-/ *n tech or pomp* a breaking of rules about what is proper, esp. in grammar or social politeness

sole·ly /ˈsəʊl-li/ *adv* not including anything else or any others; only: *I am concerned solely for your welfare.* | *I hold you solely responsible.*

sol·emn /ˈsɒləm‖ˈsɑː-/ *adj* **1** [A] (of a promise) made with great seriousness and no intention of breaking it: *Do you give me your solemn word|pledge that you won't go there?* **2** serious; without humour or lightness; GRAVE: *The judge looked solemn as he was about to pass sentence.* | *The signing of this treaty is a solemn moment in our nation's history.* **3** of the grandest and most formal kind: *The new ambassador was received with solemn ceremonies.* — ~ **ly** *adv* — ~ **ness** *n* [U]

so·lem·ni·ty /səˈlemnɨti/ *n* **1** [U] the quality of being solemn; formality or seriousness: *He took up the gavel, with mock solemnity.* **2** [C *usu. pl.*] a formal act or quality proper for a grand or solemn event: *All the solemnities of the occasion were observed.*

sol·em·nize also **-nise** *BrE* /ˈsɒləmnaɪz‖ˈsɑː-/ *v* [T] *fml or tech* to perform (esp. a marriage) with formal religious ceremony —**nization** /¡sɒləmnaɪˈzeɪʃən‖¡sɑːləmnə-/ *n* [U]

So·lent /ˈsəʊlənt/ [the] the narrow piece of sea between the Isle of Wight and the S coast of England

sol-fa /¡sɒl ˈfɑː‖¡səʊl-/ *n* [U] the system which represents the notes of the musical SCALE¹ (5) by any of seven short words (DO⁴, RE¹, MI, FA, SO⁴, LA, and TI), esp. for singing

so·li·cit /səˈlɪsɨt/ *v* **1** [I;T (for)] *fml* to ask for (money, help, a favour, etc.) from (a person): *May I solicit your advice on a matter of some importance?* **2** [I] *esp. law* (esp. of a woman) to offer oneself for sex in return for pay; advertise oneself as a PROSTITUTE: *The police arrested her for soliciting.* **3** [T] *AmE* to sell by taking orders for a product or service, esp. by going to people's houses or places of business — ~ **ation** /sə¡lɪsɨˈteɪʃən/ *n* [C;U]

so·lic·i·tor /səˈlɪsɨtər/ *n* **1** (esp. in England) a lawyer who gives advice, does the necessary work when property is bought and sold (CONVEYANCING), and speaks esp. in the lower courts of law. In 1992 it was decided that solicitors could also argue cases in the higher courts, which formerly only BARRISTERS were able to do. —compare ADVOCATE, BARRISTER; see LAWYER (CULTURAL NOTE) **2** *AmE* a person whose job it is to SOLICIT (3) **3 No Solicitors** *AmE* (a sign to show that) people selling things are not welcome

so·lic·i·tor gen·e·ral /·,··· ¹···/ *n* **solicitors general 1** (in Britain) a law officer next in rank below the ATTORNEY GENERAL in a government. The solicitor general is usu. a member of the House of Commons and a BARRISTER, not a solicitor. **2** (in the US) a state law officer who deals with cases involving the rights of the state and cases involving the interests of the public. They are next in rank below the state attorney generals.

so·lic·i·tous /səˈlɪsɨtəs/ *adj* [(about, of, for)] *fml* **1** giving eager, kind, or helpful care: *a solicitous employer* **2** anxious; carefully interested: *He seemed most solicitous for your welfare.* — ~ **ly** *adv* — ~ **ness** *n* [U]

so·lic·i·tude /səˈlɪsɨtjuːd‖-tuːd/ *n* [U] *fml* anxious, kind, or eager care

sol·id¹ /ˈsɒlɨd‖ˈsɑː-/ *adj* **1** not needing a container to hold its shape; not liquid or gas: *The milk in the bottles had frozen solid.* **2** having an inside that is filled up; not hollow: *Children's bicycles sometimes have solid rubber tyres.* **3** made of close and tightly packed material; COMPACT¹: *They dug down until they hit solid rock.* **4** firm and well made: *a very solid wall* | *This report you've written is a very solid piece of work.* | *There are solid reasons|grounds for believing that this is possible.* **5** [A] completely of the stated substance, esp. a metal or colour, and not mixed with others: *This watch is solid gold.* **6** *tech* of or having length, width, and height; THREE-DIMENSIONAL: *A sphere is a solid figure.* | *Solid geometry is the study of lines, figures, angles, etc., in space.* **7** that may be depended on; SECURE: *a solid supporter of the government* | *a solid base from which to attack the American market* **8** [(for, against)] *BrE* in or showing complete agreement: *The strike was 100 per cent solid.* (=all the workers took part) | *The members were solid against the idea.* —see also SOLIDARITY **9** *infml* without spaces or breaks; continuous: *I waited for three solid hours and then went home.* | *a solid line of people|cars* — ~ **ly** *adv*: *We're solidly behind* *you; you have our complete support.* — ~**ness** *n* [U]

solid² *n* **1** a solid object; something that does not flow: *Water becomes a solid when it freezes.* **2** [*usu. pl.*] an article of non-liquid food: *He's still too ill to take solids.* **3** [*usu. pl.*] the part of a liquid which has the qualities of a solid when separated from the SOLVENT: *milk solids* **4** *tech* (esp. in GEOMETRY) an object that takes up space, having length, width, and height: *A cube is a solid with six faces.*

sol·i·dar·i·ty /ˌsɒlɪˈdærɪti‖ˌsɑː-/ *n* [U (**with**)] loyal agreement of interests, aims, or principles among a group: *The union leaders appealed for workers' solidarity.*

Solidarity a Polish TRADE UNION formed in 1980 and led by Lech Walesa. Solidarity arranged STRIKES as a way of making the Communist government of Poland agree to political and economic changes, and many of its leaders were put in prison. By 1989 Solidarity had become so powerful that the government was forced to accept it as a political party and later that year **Tadeusz Mazowiecki**, one of its leaders, became PRIME MINISTER —see also GDANSK, Lech WALESA

solid fuel /ˌ··ˈ·‖ˌ··ˈ··/ *n* a substance that is burnt to produce heat or power that is solid, rather than a liquid or gas, e.g. coal

so·lid·i·fy /səˈlɪdɪfaɪ/ *v* [I;T] to (cause to) become solid, hard, or firm: *If you leave it in a cool place, the jelly will solidify.* | *This new law has had the effect of solidifying opposition to the government.* —**fication** /səˌlɪdɪfɪˈkeɪʃən/ *n* [U]

so·lid·i·ty /səˈlɪdɪti/ *n* [U] *usu. apprec* the quality or state of being firm, not hollow, well made, dependable, or in agreement: *The Victorians built their furniture with great solidity.* | *Any doubts about the solidity of the pound will almost automatically decrease its value.*

solid-state /ˌ··ˈ·◂/ *adj tech* of, being, or having electrical parts, esp. TRANSISTORS, that run without heating or moving parts: *a solid-state stereo system*

sol·i·dus /ˈsɒlɪdəs‖ˈsɑː-/ *n* -**di** /daɪ/ an OBLIQUE²

Sol·i·hull /ˌsəʊliˈhʌl/ a town in central England, SE of Birmingham

so·lil·o·quize also -**quise** *BrE* /səˈlɪləkwaɪz/ *v* [I] to speak in soliloquy

so·lil·o·quy /səˈlɪləkwi/ *n* [C;U] (an act of) talking to oneself alone, esp. a speech in a play in which a character's private thoughts are spoken to those watching the play —compare MONOLOGUE

sol·ip·sis·m /ˈsɒlɪpsɪzəm‖ˈsəʊ-, ˈsɑː-/ *n* [U] *tech* a system of thought that admits only the self as something existing or knowable —**tic** /ˌsɒlɪpˈsɪstɪk◂‖ˌsəʊ-, ˌsɑː-/ *adj*

sol·i·taire /ˌsɒlɪˈteəʳ‖ˌsɑː-/ *n* **1** [C] (a piece of jewellery having) a single jewel, esp. a large and expensive diamond **2** [U] a game played by one person with small pieces of wood or plastic or balls on a board **3** [U] *AmE for* PATIENCE (3)

sol·i·ta·ry¹ /ˈsɒlɪtəri‖ˈsɑːlɪteri/ *adj* **1** habitually alone, esp. by choice: *He's a solitary sort of fellow.* | *a solitary life* **2** [A] *esp. lit* alone without companions: *a solitary bird on the lonely shore* —see ALONE (USAGE) **3** in a lonely place; REMOTE: *a solitary inn at the edge of the moors* **4** [A *usu. in questions and negatives*] single: *Can you give me one solitary piece of proof for what you say?* —**ily** /ˈsɒlɪtərɪli‖ˈsɑːlɪtərˌli/ *adv*

solitary² *n* **1** [U] *sl for* SOLITARY CONFINEMENT **2** [C] *lit* a person who lives completely alone; HERMIT

solitary con·fine·ment /ˌ····· ·ˈ··/ *n* [in U] the keeping of a person in a closed place, esp. inside a prison, without any chance of seeing or talking to others, usu. as a form of additional punishment: *sentenced to three months' solitary confinement*

sol·i·tude /ˈsɒlɪtjuːd‖ˈsɑːlɪtuːd/ *n* [U] *fml* the state of being alone away from companionship

so·lo¹ /ˈsəʊləʊ/ *n* -**los** **1** [C] a piece of music for one performer —compare DUET **2** [C] a job or performance, esp. an aircraft flight, done by one person alone **3** [U] a card game like WHIST but in which each player plays against the others in turn without a partner

solo² *adj, adv* **1** without a companion or esp. instructor: *When did you first fly solo?* **2** of, for, or played as a musical solo: *There's a fine solo passage for the oboe here.* | *This passage is to be played solo by the piano.*

so·lo·ist /ˈsəʊləʊɪst/ *n* a performer of a musical solo

Sol·o·mon /ˈsɒləmən‖ˈsɑː-/ (died about 922 BC) a king of Israel, the son of king David. He is said to have been extremely wise. The most famous example of this wisdom is a story in the Bible about two women who each claimed to be the mother of a particular baby. Solomon told them that, since they could not agree, the baby would have to be cut in two. One of the women immediately gave up her right to the child. Solomon knew that this woman must be its mother and it was returned to her: *The person the President chooses to advise him on foreign policy these days needs the wisdom of Solomon.* —see also SONG OF SOLOMON

Solomon Is·lands /ˈ··· ˌ··/ [*the*+P] a nation formed of several islands in the SW Pacific to the E of Papua, New Guinea; capital Honiara; population 317,000 (1989)

sol·stice /ˈsɒlstɪs‖ˈsɑː-/ *n* the time of either the longest day in the year (about June 22) or the shortest day in the year (about December 22) —compare EQUINOX; see also MIDSUMMER DAY, SUMMER SOLSTICE, WINTER SOLSTICE

Sol·ti /ˈʃɒlti‖ˈʃəʊl-/, **Sir Georg** /dʒɔːdʒ‖dʒɔːrdʒ/ (1912–　) a British CONDUCTOR, born in Hungary, who has been musical director of many important ORCHESTRAS

sol·u·ble /ˈsɒljʊbəl‖ˈsɑː-/ *adj* **1** [(**in**)] that can be dissolved (DISSOLVE) in a liquid: *These tablets are soluble in water.* **2** *fml* that can be solved: *Is the problem soluble?* —opposite **insoluble** —**bility** /ˌsɒljʊˈbɪlɪti‖ˌsɑː-/ *n* [U]

so·lu·tion /səˈluːʃən/ *n* **1** [C (**to**)] an answer to a difficulty or problem: *We bought a second car; it was the solution to all our problems.* | *There are no simple solutions to the unemployment problem.* | *He finally came up with[found a solution.* —see also FINAL SOLUTION, SOLVE **2** [C;U] (a) liquid containing a solid or gas mixed into it, usu. without chemical change: *Prepare a weak sugar solution.* (=with little sugar in the water) —compare COLLOID **3** [(**in**)U] *tech* the state or action of being mixed into liquid like this: *sugar in solution in water*

solve /sɒlv‖sɑːlv, sɔːlv/ *v* [T] to find a solution to, an explanation of, or a way of dealing with (something): *Can you solve this riddle[crossword clue?* | *Sherlock Holmes solved many murder cases.* —**solvable** *adj* —**solver** *n*

sol·vent¹ /ˈsɒlvənt‖ˈsɑː-, ˈsɔːl-/ *adj* having enough to pay all money owed; not in debt: *When I get my pay cheque I'll be solvent again.* —opposite **insolvent** —**vency** *n* [U]

solvent² *n* [C;U] (a) liquid able to turn a solid substance into liquid: *Alcohol and petrol are useful solvents for grease stains that will not come off in water.*

solvent a·buse /ˈ·· ·ˌ·/ *n* [U] *fml for* GLUE-SNIFFING

Sol·zhe·nit·syn /ˌsɒlʒəˈnɪtsən‖ˌsəʊl-/, **Al·ex·an·der** /ˌælɪgˈzɑːndəʳ‖-ˈzæn-/ (1918–　) a Russian writer who spent many years in prison because of his criticism of Stalinism and the system of government in the Soviet Union. He was forced to leave the Soviet Union in 1974 and went to live in the US. His books include *One Day in the Life of Ivan Denisovich, Cancer Ward,* and *The Gulag Archipelago.* He was given the Nobel Prize for literature in 1970.

So·ma·li /səˈmɑːli/ *n* **1** [C] a person who comes from or whose parents come from Somalia **2** [U] the main language of Somalia —**Somali** *adj*

So·ma·li·a /səˈmɑːliə/ *adj* a country in E Africa bordering on Ethiopia, Kenya, and Djibouti; capital Mogadishu; population 7,339,000 (1989)

som·bre *BrE* ‖ **-ber** *AmE* /ˈsɒmbəʳ‖ˈsɑːm-/ *adj* **1** sadly serious; GRAVE²: *A funeral is a sombre occasion.* **2** (of a colour or sight) like or full of shadows; dark: *the sombre November skies* — ~**ly** *adv* — ~**ness** *n* [U]

som·bre·ro /sɒmˈbreərəʊ‖sɑːm-/ *n* -**ros** a man's tall hat with a very wide flat BRIM, worn esp. in Mexico

some¹ /səm; *strong* sʌm/ *determiner* a little, a few, or a certain or small number or amount of: *I bought some sugar and some apples.* | *They own some land in London.* | *I saw some people I knew.* | *May I offer you some tea (or a cup of tea)?* —see MORE (USAGE), and LANGUAGE NOTE: Articles

some² /sʌm/ *determiner* **1** a certain amount or number (of), but not all: *Some parts of the country are quite mountainous.* | *Some days you win, and some days you lose.* **2** a(n); an unknown or unstated (one): *"Can you give me some idea of the cost?" "No, I'm afraid I haven't any*

idea." | Go away! Come back some other time. | There must be some reason for what he's done. **3** quite a large number, part, or amount of: *This generous donation should go some way* (=quite a long way) *towards paying our costs.| The fire went on for quite some time* (=several hours) *before it was brought under control.* **4** *infml* (used before a noun at the beginning of a sentence) no kind of; no ... at all: *Some help that is! We're no further on than we were before! | Some friend you are! You won't even lend me £1! | "Surely you'll finish the work by tonight?" "Some hope!"* **5** *infml* a fine or important; quite a: *That was some speech you made! | It was (quite) some party!* **6** **some ... or (an)other** (*sometimes in comb.*) one or several which the speaker cannot or does not care to state exactly: *He's staying with some friends or other in the country. | I'm not making this story up; I must have heard it somewhere or other.*

▷ USAGE 1 In negative sentences, **any** and **no** are used instead of **some**: *I haven't any/I have no socks.* 2 In questions **any, anyone,** etc., are usually used. *Have you got any money? | Can you see any cars in the street? | Have you talked to* **anyone** *about your problem? If* **some, someone,** etc., are used in questions, it means that the answer "yes" is expected. Compare *Is there* **something** *to eat?* (=I can smell food!) *| Is there* **anything** *to eat?* (=I'm hungry!) This kind of question is often used in offers and invitations: *Would you like* **some** *more cake? | Shall I bring* **some** *food to the party?*◁

some³ *pron* **1** a little, a few, or a certain or small amount: *He asked for money and I gave him some.* (compare *but I didn't give him any*) *| "Do you sell cream cakes?" "Yes, there are some in the window."* **2** [(of)] certain ones or a certain part but not all: *Some of his stories were quite amusing. | Some* (=some people) *say it was an accident, but I'm not sure.* **3 and ¹then some** *infml, esp. AmE* a lot more: *"They say he earns $40,000." "And then some!"*

some⁴ *adv* **1** (used usu. before a number) about: *There were some 40 or 50 people there.* **2** *AmE* rather; a little: *"Are you feeling better today?" "Some, I guess."* **3 some little/few** quite a lot of: *I hope this is the last we see of him for some little time!* **4 some more** an additional amount or quantity (of): *Would you like some more cake/apples?*

some·bod·y¹ /ˈsʌmbɒdi, -bədi‖-baːdi/ *pron* someone; some but no particular or known person: *There's somebody on the phone for you. | Somebody has parked their/his car right in front of mine.* —see also SOMEONE; see EVERYONE (USAGE), SOME (USAGE), SOMETHING (USAGE)

somebody² *n* [U] someone who is well known, has a high position, etc.; an important person: *Now that he's been promoted he thinks he's really somebody.*

some·day /ˈsʌmdeɪ/ *adv* at some uncertain future time: *Perhaps someday I'll be rich.*

some·how /ˈsʌmhaʊ/ *adv* **1** by some means; in some way not yet known or stated: *Don't worry; we'll get the lost money back somehow.* **2** for some reason that is not clear: *Somehow I seem to have two knives and no fork! | I think she's right but somehow I'm not completely sure.*

some·one /ˈsʌmwʌn/ *pron* **1** a person; some but no particular or known person; somebody: *There's someone on the phone for you. | If you don't know the answer, ask someone (else).* (=another person) *| Someone has parked their/his car right in front of mine.* **2 or someone** or a person of that sort: *This job needs a repairman or a builder or someone.* **3 someone/somebody up there (likes you)** *infml* God (likes you): *Wow! What a lucky shot! I think somebody up there likes you...* —see EVERYONE (USAGE), SOME (USAGE), SOMETHING (USAGE)

some·place /ˈsʌmpleɪs/ *adv esp. AmE for* SOMEWHERE

som·er·sault /ˈsʌməsɔːlt‖-ər-/ *n* a jump or rolling backward or forward (not sideways) movement in which the feet go over the head before the body returns upright: *He did a triple somersault. | to* **turn a somersault** *in mid-air* —compare CARTWHEEL —**somersault** *v* [I] : *He somersaulted through the window.*

Som·er·set /ˈsʌməset‖-mər-/ a COUNTY in SW England, known for producing very good CIDER. Its local government is based in Taunton.

Somerset House /ˌ... ˈ·/ a building in the Strand in London where documents were kept containing information about British people such as their names, when they were born, etc. The office dealing with these documents

is now at St Catherine's House in **Kingsway** in London, but people still often call it Somerset House.

Somerset Maugham, W. see W. Somerset MAUGHAM

some·thing /ˈsʌmθɪŋ/ *pron* **1** some unstated or unknown thing: *I've got something in my eye. | I was looking for something a little cheaper. | If there's no bread, we'll eat something else.* (=some other thing) *| We'll get something to eat at that snack bar. | I've got* **a little something** *for you.* (=a small present) —compare SOME² (2); see SOME (USAGE) **2** a thing of some value: *At least we didn't lose any money. That's something! | You can't get something for nothing.* (=a profit without any risk or effort) *| There's something in* (=some truth in) *what you say; I'll take your advice. | It's* **quite something** *to have sailed across the Atlantic on your own.* (=it is a brave/clever thing to have done) **3 or something** *infml* (used when the speaker is not sure): *He said he was going shopping or something.| The train gets in at 3.17 or something (like that).* **4 something like:** a rather like: *The building looked something like a church.* **b** *infml* about; approximately (APPROXIMATE): *There were something like 1000 people present.* **5 something of a/an** *infml* rather a/an; a fairly good: *He's something of an expert on growing vegetables.* **6 something old, something new, something borrowed, something blue** a phrase describing what a woman should wear at her wedding, according to TRADITION **7 something over/under** rather more/less than: *It cost something over £500.* **8 something to do with** (having) a connection with: *His job has/is something to do with oil.* **9 -something** *sometimes humor* (used after a number, esp. one showing someone's age, to show that one does not know or need to give it exactly): *There are more fiftysomething Europeans than ever before.*

▷ USAGE Notice the position of the adjective after words like **something, someone, anything, anywhere, nobody, nowhere:** *I'm looking for* **something** *different.| Have you got* **anything** *new? No,* **nothing** *special. | Let's go* **somewhere** *warm.*◁

some·time¹ /ˈsʌmtaɪm/ *adv* at some uncertain or unstated time **a** in the future: *We'll take our holiday sometime in August, I think.* **b** in the past: *Our house was built sometime around 1905.*

sometime² *adj* [A] *fml* having been once but now no longer; former: *Sir Richard Marsh, (the) sometime chairman of British Rail*

some·times /ˈsʌmtaɪmz/ *adv* on some occasions but not all: *Sometimes I come by train, but usually I come by car.* —see NEVER (USAGE)

some·way /ˈsʌmweɪ/ *adv AmE infml for* SOMEHOW (1)

some·what /ˈsʌmwɒt‖-wɑːt/ *adv* **1** by some degree or amount; a little; rather: *The price was somewhat higher than I'd expected. | They were suffering somewhat from the heat.* **2 more than somewhat** *BrE pomp* to quite a large degree: *His behaviour displeased me more than somewhat.* **3 somewhat of** *pomp* a kind of; rather: *The cake we made was somewhat of a failure.*

some·where /ˈsʌmweəʳ/ ‖ also **someplace** *esp. AmE*— *adv* **1** (in, at, or to) some place: *He's somewhere in the garden.| I don't like this restaurant — let's go* **somewhere else.** (=to some other place) *| They're looking for somewhere to stay. | He's finally told us the price — now we're getting somewhere!* (=some result) **2** some number or amount: *somewhere between 40 and 60 students | somewhere in the region of £1 million* **3 or somewhere** or in/at/to some other place: *I'd like to go away, perhaps to Greece or somewhere.* —see SOME (USAGE), SOMETHING (USAGE)

Somme /sɒm‖saːm/ [*the*] an area in N France where many battles were fought during the First World War. Very many soldiers died there, both from the fighting itself and from the terrible conditions on the battlefield. —see FIRST WORLD WAR (CULTURAL NOTE)

som·nam·bu·lis·m /sɒmˈnæmbjʊ̆lɪzəm‖saːm-/ *n* [U] *fml or tech* the action or habit of walking about while asleep —**list** *n*

som·no·lent /ˈsɒmnələnt‖ˈsɑːm-/ *adj fml or lit* **1** nearly falling asleep; DROWSY **2** causing or suggesting sleep: *a somnolent summer's afternoon* —**~ly** *adv*

So·mo·za /səˈməʊzə/, **An·as·ta·si·o** /ˌænəˈstɑːsiəʊ/ (1896–1956) the president of Nicaragua for many years who ruled as a DICTATOR until he was killed. His second son, Anastasio Somoza Debayle was also president until he was forced to leave the country by the Sandinistas in 1979. —see also SANDINISTA

son /sʌn/ n **1** [C] someone's male child: *Mr and Mrs Jones have three sons.* | *Their eldest son is a teacher.* | *the king's* **son and heir** | (fig.) *sons of Britain who fell in battle* **2** [C *usu. pl.*] a male descendant: *The sons of the first discoverers are still on the islands after centuries.* **3** [*the*] (*usu. cap.*) (in the Christian religion) the second person of the TRINITY; Christ **4 a** (used as an informal form of address by an older man or woman to a much younger man or boy): *What's your name, son?* **b** (used by a Roman Catholic priest to a man who has come to admit his SINS): *Are you willing to do penance for your sins, my son?*

so·nar /ˈsəʊnɑːr, -nər/ n [U] an apparatus using sound waves for finding the position of underwater objects, such as MINES³ (3) or SUBMARINES

so·na·ta /səˈnɑːtə/ n a piece of music for one or two instruments, one of which is usu. a piano, made up of usu. three or four short parts of varying speeds: *the slow movement of Beethoven's fifth piano sonata*

Sond·heim /ˈsɒndhaɪm‖ˈsɑː-/, **Ste·phen** /ˈstiːvən/ (1930–) an American popular music songwriter known for the clever and amusing words to his songs. He wrote the words for the musical show *West Side Story* and both words and music for many other shows, including *A Little Night Music.*

son et lu·mi·ere /ˌsɒn eɪ ˈluːmieər‖ˌsɑːn-/ n [U] *esp. BrE* a performance which uses recorded sounds and coloured lights to tell the story of a historical place or event – compare ILLUMINATIONS

song /sɒŋ‖sɔːŋ/ n **1** [C] (*often in comb.*) a usu. short piece of music with words for singing: *Sing us a song.* | *a lovesong* | *songs with intelligent lyrics* | *a famous songwriter* **2** [U] the act or art of singing: *She suddenly* **burst into song. 3** [C;U] the music-like sound of a bird or birds: *the song of the lark* | *birdsong* **4 (going) for a song** *infml* (being offered for sale) very cheaply **5 on song** *BrE* performing at one's best: *The team was really on song this afternoon, and won easily.* —see also SWANSONG

song and dance /ˌ· · ˈ·/ n [S;U] *infml* **1** *esp. BrE* an unnecessary or useless show of confusion, anger, excitement, etc.; FUSS: *There's no need to make such a song and dance about a tiny scratch on the car.* **2** *AmE* a complicated or misleading explanation: *She gave us a song and dance about where she'd been all day.*

song·bird /ˈsɒŋbɜːd‖ˈsɔːŋbɜːrd/ n a bird that can produce musical sounds: *Thrushes and nightingales are songbirds.*

song·book /ˈsɒŋbʊk‖ˈsɔːŋ-/ n a book of songs with music for singing

Song of Sol·o·mon /ˌ· · ˈ···/ also **Song of Songs** /ˌ· · ˈ·/, **Canticles**— n a book in the Bible supposed to have been written by Solomon. It contains love poems which represent the love of God for his people.

Songs of Praise /ˌ· · ˈ·/ (in Britain) a well-known Sunday evening television programme in which HYMNS are sung by people in different churches around Britain

song·ster /ˈsɒŋstər‖ˈsɔːŋ-/ n *lit* **1** also **song·stress** /-strɪs/ *fem.*— a skilled singer **2** a songbird

son·ic /ˈsɒnɪk‖ˈsɑː-/ *adj tech* **1** of or at the speed of sound in air, about 340 metres per second (741 miles per hour) —see also SUBSONIC, SUPERSONIC **2** [A] of sound waves

sonic boom /ˌ·· ˈ·/ also **sonic bang** *BrE*— n an explosive sound produced by the shock wave from an aircraft travelling faster than the speed of sound

son-in-law /ˈ· · ˌ·/ n **sons-in-law, son-in-laws** the husband of one's daughter —compare DAUGHTER-IN-LAW

son·net /ˈsɒnɪt‖ˈsɑː-/ n a 14-line poem with any of several fixed formal RHYME patterns. The most famous sonnets in the English language are those written by Shakespeare.

son·ny /ˈsʌni/ n *old-fash* (used in speaking to a young boy): *Better go home to your mother, sonny.*

son-of-a-bitch /ˌ·· · ˈ·/ n **sons-of-bitches, son-of-a-bitches** *taboo* someone one strongly dislikes; BASTARD (2): *That son-of-a-bitch stole my car!*

son-of-a-gun /ˌ·· · ˈ·/ n **sons-of-guns** *infml apprec* (used esp. by a man to a close male friend) a man who wins the

social approval of his group by having the qualities typical of a man and being daring, humorous, etc.

son of God /ˌ· · ˈ·/ also **son of Man**— [*the*] (*often cap.* S) the MESSIAH in the Christian and Jewish religions

so·nor·ous /ˈsɒnərəs, səˈnɔːrəs‖səˈnɔːrəs, ˈsɑːnərəs/ *adj* having a pleasantly full loud sound: *a sonorous bell/voice* – ~**ly** *adv* – ~**ness, -ity** /səˈnɒrɬti‖səˈnɔː-/ n [U]

Sons and Lov·ers /ˌ· · ˈ··/ a NOVEL by D H Lawrence about the son of an English coal miner, considered to be one of his best works —see also D H LAWRENCE

Sons of Lib·er·ty /ˌ· · ˈ···/ [*the*] secret groups formed in the US before the American Revolution which wanted the American colonies (COLONY) to be independent of Britain

Son·tag /ˈsɒntæg‖ˈsɑːn-/, **Su·san** /ˈsuːzən/ (1933–) an American writer, well-known for her descriptions of modern life. Her writings include *Against Interpretation* and *Under the Sign of Saturn.*

So·ny /ˈsəʊni/ a well known Japanese company that makes electronic goods esp. in the area of entertainment, e.g. TVs and PERSONAL STEREOS —see also WALKMAN

Soo·chow /ˌsuːˈtʃaʊ/ see SUZHOU

soon /suːn/ *adv* **1** before long; within a short time: *I must be going soon, so I won't have another drink.* | *We soon saw that we'd made a mistake.* [+*adv*/*prep*] *It happened soon after breakfast.* | (used in making threats) *I'll soon show her who's the boss here!* **2** quickly; early: *Please get that report done as soon as possible* – **the sooner the better.** | *I can't come until tomorrow, at the soonest.* | *He got married as soon as* (=at once after) *he left university.* | *I'd confidently predicted they'd win, but I spoke too soon* – *they were beaten in the final race.* | *The fire brigade arrived at last, not a moment too soon.* (=they almost arrived too late) **3** (in phrases expressing comparisons) readily; willingly: *I'd sooner die than marry you!* | *"Would you like to dance?" "I'd just as soon not* (=no), *if you don't mind."* **4 no sooner ... than** when ... at once: *No sooner had we sat down than we found it was time to go.* | *No sooner said than done!* (=it will be/has been done very fast) —see HARDLY (USAGE) **5 sooner or later** certainly, although one cannot be sure when: *If you cheat, you'll be found out sooner or later.*

soot /sʊt/ n [U] black powder produced by burning: *The inside of a chimney soon gets covered in soot.* see also SOOTY

soothe /suːð/ v [T] **1** [(DOWN)] to make less angry, excited, or anxious; comfort or calm: *He'd got very annoyed about it, and it took all her tact to soothe him down.* | *to make soothing noises* **2** to make less painful: *This medicine should soothe your sore throat.* | *soothing lotions* – **soothingly** *adv*

sooth·say·er /ˈsuːθˌseɪər/ n *old use* a person who was believed to be able to tell the future. Soothsayers were usually very old and very wise.

sooty /ˈsʊti/ *adj* covered in, or consisting of, soot: *sooty paws/pawprints*

Soot·y n a hand GLOVE PUPPET in the form of a little bear, who appears on children's television programmes in Britain. He does not speak and is very NAUGHTY. —see also SWEEP

sop¹ /sɒp‖sɑːp/ n [(**to**)] *derog* something (usu. of little real value) that is offered to gain someone's favour or stop them complaining: *The company agreed to make regular inspections of the river, as a sop to the environmental lobby.*

sop² v **-pp-**
sop sthg.↔up *phr v* [T] to take (a liquid) into a solid so as to leave a dry surface: *He sopped up all the spilt milk with a sponge.* —see also SOPPING

soph·is·m /ˈsɒfɪzəm‖ˈsɑː-/ n *fml derog* **1** [C] an argument which looks correct but is false, esp. one intended to deceive **2** [U] SOPHISTRY (1) —**-ist** n

so·phis·ti·cate /səˈfɪstɪkeɪt/ n *fml* a sophisticated person

so·phis·ti·cat·ed /səˈfɪstɪkeɪtɪd/ *adj* **1** experienced in and understanding the ways of society, esp. showing signs of this by good taste, clever conversation, wearing fashionable clothes, etc.: *a sophisticated audience who appreciated the subtlety of the play* | *a sophisticated writer* | *The fashion magazines show what the sophisticated woman is wearing this year.* | *He thinks it's sophisticated to smoke with a cigarette holder.* **2** produced or developed with a high level of skill and knowledge: *sophisticated machinery/arguments | highly sophisticated filming techniques* —**·ion** /sə₁fɪstɪ'keɪʃən/ *n* [U]: *Your son's essays show great maturity and sophistication.*

soph·ist·ry /'sɒfₔstri‖'saː-/ *n fml derog* **1** [U] the use of false arguments that deceive **2** [C *usu. pl.*] a SOPHISM (1)

Soph·o·cles /'sɒfəkliːz‖'saːf-/ (about 496 BC–about 406 BC) a Greek poet. He wrote the famous TRAGIC play *Oedipus Rex.*

soph·o·more /'sɒfəmɔːʳ‖'saː-/ *n AmE* a student in the second year of study in a college or HIGH SCHOOL —compare FRESHMAN, JUNIOR, SENIOR

sop·o·rif·ic /₁sɒpə'rɪfɪk◀‖₁saː-/ *adj* causing one to fall asleep: *a soporific drug/speech* — **~ally** /kli/ *adv*

sop·ping /'sɒpɪŋ‖'saː-/ *adv, adj infml* very wet: *Her clothes were sopping (wet).*

sop·py /'sɒpi‖'saːpi/ *adj BrE infml* **1** too full of expressions of tender feelings like sorrow, love, etc.: *a soppy love story* **2** [F+about] having a very great fondness (for): *She's just soppy about animals.* **3** foolish

so·pra·no /sə'praːnəʊ‖-'præ-/ *n* **-nos 1** (a woman or child with, or a musical part for) a high singing voice, above ALTO (2) **2** a musical instrument which plays notes in this highest range —**soprano** *adj, adv : a soprano voice | to sing soprano*

sor·bet /'sɔːbeɪ‖'sɔːrbₔt/ *n* [C;U] **1** also **sherbet** *AmE—* WATER ICE with the addition of the white of an egg, milk, etc.: *a spoonful of blackcurrant sorbet* **2** *AmE for* WATER ICE

Sor·bonne /sɔː'bɒn‖sɔːr'baːn/ [*the*] a very old part of the University of Paris

sor·cer·er /'sɔːsərəʳ‖'sɔːr-/ **sor·cer·ess** /-rₔs/ *fem.— n* a person who is believed to be magic because of their use of the power of evil spirits. The popular image of a sorcerer in books, stories etc., is of an old man in a pointed hat and a long CLOAK which often has pictures of the moon and stars on it. —compare WITCH, WIZARD

sorcerer's ap·pren·tice /₁·⋯ ·'··/ a piece of music by the French COMPOSER **Paul Dukas** (1865–1935), based on a poem by Goethe about a boy who works for a sorcerer and lazily tries to do his work using magic, but everything goes wrong

sor·cer·y /'sɔːsəri‖'sɔːr-/ *n* [U] the art and practice of a sorcerer

sor·did /'sɔːdₔd‖'sɔːr-/ *adj* **1** wicked and dishonourable; not noble: *Gradually the whole sordid story of how he had cheated and lied to his friends came out.* **2** dirty or in bad condition (as if) from lack of money and care; SQUALID: *He lived in a sordid little bed-sit.* — **~ly** *adv* — **~ness** *n* [U]

sore¹ /sɔːʳ/ *adj* **1** painful or aching from a wound, infection, or (of a muscle) hard use: *I've got a cold and a sore throat. | I'm sore/My legs are sore from all that running yesterday. | I have a sore finger.* **2** [A] *infml* likely to cause offence: *Don't joke about his weight: it's a rather sore point with him.* **3** [F at] *infml, esp. AmE* angry, esp. from feeling unjustly treated: *Don't get sore (at me); I didn't mean it!* —see also **sight for sore eyes** (SIGHT), SORELY — **~ness** *n* [U]: *some soreness and swelling in the infected area*

sore² *n* a painful usu. infected place on the body: *The poor animal was covered with sores.* —see also COLD SORE

sore·head /'sɔːhed‖'sɔːr-/ *n AmE infml* an unpleasant person, esp. one who does or says cruel things: *Don't be such a sorehead! I only asked if you'd had a good game.*

sore·ly /'sɔːli‖'sɔːrli/ also **sore** *old use— adv fml* very much; greatly: *These improvements are sorely needed.*

sor·ghum /'sɔːgəm‖'sɔːr-/ *n* [U] a type of corn grown in tropical areas —see picture at CEREAL

so·ror·i·ty /sə'rɒrₔti‖sə'rɔː-/ *n* (at some American universities) a club of women students usu. living in the same house (a **sorority house**)

▶ CULTURAL NOTE Students who are in sororities often enjoy them very much, developing many friendships with their **sorority sisters**, and sometimes doing work for CHARITY together, but students who are not in a sorority sometimes see sorority sisters as more interested in fashion, clothes, and having fun than in studying. The names of sororities and fraternities (FRATERNITY) are Greek letters, such as Sigma Nu, so people in these clubs are sometimes called Greeks. —compare FRATERNITY (2); see also RUSH² (6)◀

sor·rel /'sɒrəl‖'sɔː-, 'saː-/ *n* [U] a plant with sour-tasting leaves used in cooking

Sor·ren·to /sə'rentəʊ/ a town on the SW coast of Italy near Naples, where many people, esp. British people, go on holiday

sor·row¹ /'sɒrəʊ‖'saː-, 'sɔː-/ *n* [C *often pl.*; U (**over, at, for**)] **1** (a cause of) unhappiness over loss or wrongdoing; sadness; grief: *We all share your sorrow over this sad loss.| Life has many joys and sorrows. | the conventional expressions of sorrow and sympathy* —see also **drown one's sorrows** (DROWN); see SORRY (USAGE) **2 more in sorrow than in anger** (to say or do something) in a way which shows that one is sad or disappointed, rather than angry, about the situation mentioned: *"Unless you can tackle your drink problem, I'm going to have to let you go", said the boss, more in sorrow than in anger.* — **~ful** *adj* — **~fully** *adv* — **~fulness** *n* [U]

sorrow² *v* [I (**over, at, for**)] *esp. lit* to feel or express sorrow; grieve: *a sorrowing heart*

sor·ry¹ /'sɒri‖'saːri, 'sɔːri/ *adj* **1** [F (**for, about**)] feeling sadness, pity, or sympathy, esp. for another person's misfortune; grieved: *He was/felt sorry for her and tried to cheer her up. | I feel sorry for whoever marries her! | I came in looking very sorry for himself, and I could tell he'd had a bad day. | "You're my cat?" "It died." "I'm sorry (about that)."* [+to-v] *I was sorry to hear that your cat had died. | I'm sorry to say* (=I must tell you, but it makes me sad) *that our efforts have failed.* [+(that)] *I'm sorry you didn't pass your exam.* **2** [F (**for, about**)] having a sincere feeling of shame or unhappiness at one's past actions, and expressing a wish that one had not done them: *If you say you're sorry (for what you did), I'm sure she'll forgive you.* [+(that)] *I'm sorry I lost my temper. | I can't tell you how sorry I am.* (=I am extremely sorry) *| I'm sorry I ever came here; I wish I'd stayed at home!* **3** [F] (used for expressing polite refusal or disagreement, or excusing oneself, etc.): *I'm sorry but I won't be able to come/but I can't agree with that.* **4** [A] causing pity mixed with disapproval: *He was a sorry sight in his dirty and torn old clothes. | You've made a sorry mess of this piece of work. | It's a **sorry state of affairs** (=unsatisfactory) when you have to wait an hour to be served.*

▷ USAGE Compare **sorry** and **sorrowful**. You say *"(I'm) sorry"* if you step on someone's toe, etc., and *I'm **very sorry** (to hear that)* when you hear about another person's troubles. If you *feel **sorry** for* someone you feel pity for them. **Sorrowful** would not be used for either of these meanings of **sorry**, and would not be used about yourself. It is a much stronger and rather literary word meaning "looking, sounding or feeling very unhappy": *I could see how unhappy she was from her **sorrowful** face.* —see also EXCUSE¹ (USAGE)◁

sorry² *interj* **1** (used for expressing polite refusal, disagreement, excusing oneself, etc.): *"That's my coffee, I think." "Sorry". | Sorry, but you can't come in. | Sorry, did I step on your toe?* **2** *esp. BrE* (used for asking someone to repeat something one has not heard properly): *"I'm cold." "Sorry?" "I said I was cold."*

sort¹ /sɔːt‖sɔːrt/ *n* **1** [(**of**)] a group of people, things, etc., all sharing certain qualities; type; kind: *They sell many different sorts of wine here. | What sort of music do you like best? | There were all sorts of colours/colours of all sorts* (=many different colours) *to choose from. | What sort of (a) man is he?* (=What is he like?) *| I don't like that sort of book/those sorts of book/(infml) those sorts of books.* —see KIND (USAGE) **2** [*usu. sing.*] *infml* a person of the stated type: *That was nice of her; she's not such a bad sort* (=quite a nice person) *after all.* **3 a sort of (a)** a faint, unexplained, or unusual kind of: *I had a sort of (a) feeling you'd say that. | After the soup we had a sort of stew — I'm not sure what was in it.* **4 it takes all sorts (to make a world)** any society consists of people who vary greatly in their habits, characters, opinions, etc. **5 of sorts/a sort** of a poor or doubtful kind: *It's a painting of sorts, but hard to describe.* **6 sort of** *infml* in some way or degree; rather: *It was sort of odd that he didn't come.| I was feeling sort of ... well ... ill, really.* —see KIND (USAGE) **7 out of sorts** *infml* feeling unwell or annoyed **8 what sort of** *infml* (used for asking angry questions): *What sort of an excuse is that?* (=I do not think it is a good one) | *What sort of time do you call this to come in?* (=I think it is very late)

sort² *v* **1** [I (**through**); T (**out**)] to put (things) in order; place according to kind, rank, etc.; arrange: *I've been sorting (through) these old papers to see what can be thrown away.* | *She got a job sorting letters in the Post Office.* | *They sorted the apples according to size|into large ones and small ones.* **2** [T] *esp. ScotE* to mend; repair: *We need to get the washing machine sorted.* — ~**er** *n*

sort sbdy./sthg. ↔ **out** *phr v* [T] **1** [(**from**)] to separate from a mass or group: *Sort out the papers to be thrown away, and put the rest back.* | *a preliminary audition to sort out the talented performers from the rest* **2** *BrE* to deal with; make clear: *It was just a silly quarrel that's now been sorted out.* | *Have you sorted out how to get there yet?* —see also SORT-OUT **3** to make (a person) less confused or unsettled: *She was depressed when I went round, but I sorted her out.* | *Take these pills — they'll sort you out.* (=make you better) **4** *BrE infml* to attack and punish: *Let me get my hands on them! I'll sort them out!*

sor·tie /'sɔːtiǁ'sɔːrti/ *n* **1** a short attack made by an army from a position of defence **2** a flight to bomb an enemy base, city, etc. **3** *infml* a short trip into an unfamiliar or unfriendly place: (fig.) *His first sortie into the world of film-making wasn't very successful.*

sorting of·fice /'·· ˌ··/ *n* a part of a POST OFFICE where letters are separated into different groups according to where they are being sent to

sort-out /'· ·/ *n* [*usu. sing.*] *BrE infml* an act of putting things in order: *This room's very untidy; it needs a good sort-out.* —see also SORT **out**

SOS /ˌes əʊ 'es/ *n* **1** the letters *SOS* used as an international signal calling for help, esp. by ships in trouble. The letters SOS were chosen because they are easy to do in MORSE CODE, they do not have another meaning: *He tapped out an SOS on the pipes he was chained to.* **2** an urgent message from someone in trouble: *The radio often broadcasts SOSs|SOS messages to find the relatives of someone who is very ill.* —compare MAYDAY

so-so /'· ·/ *adj, adv infml* neither very bad(ly) nor very good/well: *Business is only so-so at the moment.* | *"How's the work going?" "So-so."*

sot /sɒtǁsɑːt/ *n esp. lit* a person who is habitually drunk and unable to think clearly

Soth·e·by's /'sʌðəbiz/ a famous AUCTION HOUSE which arranges the sale of rare and valuable things such as paintings, furniture, etc.—compare CHRISTIE'S

sot·tish /'sɒtɪʃǁ'sɑː-/ *adj esp. lit* stupid, like a sot — ~**ness** *n* [U]

sot·to vo·ce /ˌsɒtəʊ 'vəʊtʃiǁˌsɑː-/ *adj, adv fml* in a soft voice so that other people cannot hear: *They were passing sotto voce remarks while he gave his talk.*

sou /suː/ *n* [S *usu. in negatives*] *BrE infml* the smallest amount of money: *I had to pay £10 for the taxi and it left me without a sou.*

sou·bri·quet /'suːbrɪkeɪ/ *n* a SOBRIQUET

souf·flé /'suːfleɪǁsuː'fleɪ/ *n* [C;U] a light airy dish made from eggs, flour, milk, and usu. cheese, fruit, or some other food to give taste, baked to be eaten at once

sough /sʌf, saʊ/ *v, n* [I] *lit* (to make) the sound of the wind in trees

sought /sɔːt/ *past tense & participle of* SEEK

sought-af·ter /'· ˌ··/ *adj* wanted or popular because of rarity or high quality: *He's one of the world's most sought-after singers.*

souk /suːk/ *n* a market in a Muslim country

soul¹ /səʊl/ *n* **1** [C] the part of a person that is not the body and is thought not to die; the central or most important part of a person; the quality that makes a person human: *They say that hardship is good for the soul.* (=makes you a better person) —compare SPIRIT¹ (1)

▶CULTURAL NOTE In the Christian religion people believe that when you die your soul goes to Heaven if you believe in Christ or to Hell if you have been wicked and do not believe in Christ —see also HEAVEN, HELL◀

2 [U] the attractive quality produced by honesty or true deep feeling: *It was a stylish performance but lacking in soul.* | *You don't care if they cut down that beautiful old tree. You've got no soul!* —see also SOULFUL, SOULLESS **3**

[C] *esp. lit or old-fash* a person: *You mustn't call a (living) soul.* | *She's a dear old soul.* | *He's had a lot of troubles to put up with, (the) poor soul!* **4** [C (**of**)] a central, most important or most active part: *He tells such good jokes, he's the life and soul of any party.* (=makes any party full of fun) **5** [*the*+S+**of**] the perfect example: *Your secret's safe with him; he's the soul of discretion.* **6** [U] SOUL MUSIC: *the sound of soul* | *a soul group* **7** **upon my soul!** *old-fash* (used for expressing great surprise or shock) —see also **keep body and soul together** (BODY), **heart and soul** (HEART), **sell one's soul** (SELL)

soul² *adj* [A] *AmE* of or for black people: *soul food* | *soul music*

soul broth·er /'· ˌ··/ **soul sis·ter** *fem.— n AmE* (used esp. among young black people) a black person

soul-des·troy·ing /'· ˌ··/ *adj derog* (esp. of a job) very uninteresting: *It's soul-destroying work.*

soul food /'· ·/ *n* [U] *AmE* food that is popular with black people in the Southern US

▶CULTURAL NOTE This is usu. southern-style country cooking and includes a variety of meat and vegetables, such as CHITTERLINGS (= pig stomach, etc.), ham HOCKS, and COLLARD GREENS —compare CAJUN◀

soul·ful /'səʊlfəl/ *adj* full of feeling; expressing deep feeling: *a soulful look|song* — ~**ly** *adv* — ~**ness** *n* [U]

soul·less /'səʊl-ləs/ *adj derog* having or showing no attractive or tender human qualities: *a big soulless office building* — ~**ly** *adv* — ~**ness** *n* [U]

soul mate /'· ·/ *n* a person with whom one feels one shares a very close feeling or interest: *We'd only known each other for a few hours, but I felt we were soul mates.*

soul mu·sic /'· ˌ··/ *n* [U] popular music usu. performed by black singers and showing feelings strongly and directly. It began in America and is closely related to RHYTHM AND BLUES. There have been many famous singers in soul music, but the most famous is probably James Brown who is known as 'the godfather of soul' —see also James BROWN, MOTOWN

soul-search·ing /'· ˌ··/ *n* [U] a deep examination of one's mind and conscience: *After many hours of soul-searching he decided to admit his guilt.*

sound¹ /saʊnd/ *n* **1** [C;U] what is or may be heard; (something that causes) a sensation in the ear: *Strange sounds came from the next room.* | *I could hear the sound of voices|laughter|footsteps.* | *Don't make a sound, any of you.* (=keep quiet) | *There are over twenty different consonant sounds in English.* | *Sound travels|Sound waves travel at 340 metres per second in air.* | *a muffled|clear sound* | *a wailing sound* —see NOISE (USAGE) **2** [(*the*)S(**of**)] an idea produced by something read or heard: *From the sound of it, I'd say the matter was serious.* | *I don't like the sound of this; how long has she been missing?* **3** [U] a thing broadcast or played from a recording machine for listening to rather than for seeing: *There is interference on vision, and for the moment we are continuing our programme on sound only.* | *a sound recording* **b** loudness of a television, film, etc.: *I can't hear what they're saying; turn the sound up.* **4 a sound mind in a sound body** the state of somebody who is physically and mentally healthy (from the Latin phrase *mens sana in corpore sano*) **5 full of sound and fury, signifying nothing** *quote* a phrase from Shakespeare's play *Macbeth*, used by people in criticizing something which sounds impressive or threatening, but which has little meaning or is not important: *Jim sometimes flies off the handle and has these tantrums — full of sound and fury, signifying nothing!* — ~**less** *adj* — ~**lessly** *adv* : *He crept soundlessly into the room.*

sound² *v* **1** [L] to seem when heard: *Your cough sounds better.* | *Does this sentence sound right?* | *He had a very odd-sounding name.* | *From the way you describe him he sounds a real idiot.* | **It sounds as if/as though** *the government doesn't know what to do.* | *That* **sounds like** (=seems) *a good idea!* [+to-v] (*nonstandard*) *She sounds to be a very strange woman.* **2** [I] to make a sound; produce an effect that can be heard: *The bell sounded for dinner at eight o'clock.* | *The trumpets sounded as the champion entered.* **3** [T] to cause (esp. a musical instrument) to make a sound: *A bell is sounded at eight o'clock.* | *Sound your horn to warn the other driver.* **4** [T] to signal by making sounds: *They sounded the "all clear" after the air raid.* | *Sound the alarm!* **5** [T *usu. pass.*] *tech* to express as a sound; pronounce: *The "s" in "island" is not sounded: it's silent.* **6** [T] *tech* to measure the depth of (a body of water), esp. by using a line with a weight on it (**sounding line**) or a machine (**echo sounder**) that sends out sounds which come back off the bottom —see also SOUNDINGS (1)

sound off *phr v* [I (**about**)] **1** *infml, usu. derog* to express an opinion freely and forcefully, esp. in a complaining manner: *He's always sounding off about the poor pay of teachers in this country.* **2** *AmE* to call out (usu. one's name or number in an order) loudly

sound ↔ **out** *phr v* [T (**on, about**)] to try to find out the opinion or intention of: *I wrote to him to sound out his views on the new project.* —see also SOUNDINGS (2)

sound³ *adj* **1** in good condition; without disease or damage: *The surveyor reported that all the walls were completely sound.* | *(law) The doctor certified that she was* **of sound mind.** (=not mad) —opposite **unsound** **2** showing good sense or good judgment: *That's very sound advice; you should take it.* | *She's a very sound woman to have on the committee.* | *politically sound* | *a man of sound judgment* | *a sound investment that is sure to bring good profits* —opposite **unsound** **3** thorough; complete: *to give employees a sound training* **4** [A] severe; hard: *a sound beating* **5** (of sleep) deep and untroubled **6 as sound as a bell: a** (of a person) without disease **b** (of a thing) in perfect condition — ~**ly** *adv*: *She slept soundly throughout the night.* | *We were soundly* (=severely and completely) *beaten by our opponents.* — ~**ness** *n* [U]

sound⁴ *adv* **sound asleep** deeply asleep

sound⁵ *n* **1** a fairly broad stretch of sea water mostly surrounded by coast **2** a water passage connecting two larger bodies of water and wider than a STRAIT

sound bar·ri·er /ˈ· ˌ···/ *n* [*the*+S] the sudden increase in the force opposing an object in flight as it gets near the speed of sound: *A jet plane was the first to* **break the sound barrier.** (=go faster than sound)

sound bite /ˈ· ·/ *n* a short part of a speech or a statement, esp. one made by a politician, which is broadcast on radio or television, e.g. as part of a news programme. A sound bite is often only one sentence long.

sound check /ˈ· ·/ *n* the process of checking that all the equipment such as MICROPHONES, SPEAKERS, etc. is working well before a concert, and that the sound produced is of the desired quality

sound ef·fects /ˈ· ·ˌ·/ *n* [P] sounds produced by people or machines to give the effect of natural sounds needed in a radio or television broadcast or a film, for example, putting COCONUT shells down repeatedly on a hard surface to give the sound of a horse's hooves (HOOF)

sounding board /ˈ·· ·/ *n* **1** a board fixed over and behind a stage, PULPIT, etc., to allow a speaker or performer to be heard more loudly and clearly **2** [(**for**)] a means used for testing thoughts, opinions, etc.: *As the professor's assistant, my function was often simply to be a sounding board for his latest ideas.*

sound·ings /ˈsaʊndɪŋz/ *n* [P] **1** measurements made by sounding (SOUND²(6)) water **2** carefully quiet or secret enquiries: *I've asked her to take soundings to find out if Sir John would be willing to accept the chairmanship.*

Sound of Mu·sic /ˌ· · ˈ··/, **The** a very successful musical film made in the US in 1965 with Julie Andrews. In the film Julie Andrews sings the song *The Hills are Alive (with the sound of music).* —see colour picture on page 685

sound·proof¹ /ˈsaʊndpruːf/ *adj* that sound cannot get through or into: *soundproof walls* | *a soundproof room*

soundproof² *v* [T] to make soundproof

sound·track /ˈsaʊndtræk/ *n* **1** the recorded music from a film **2** the band near the edge of a piece of film where sound is recorded

sound wave /ˈ· ·/ *n* the form which sound takes when it travels

soup¹ /suːp/ *n* [C;U] **1** (any of many kinds of) liquid cooked food often containing small pieces of meat, fish, or vegetables: *tomato soup* | *a bowl of soup* | *a good selection of packet soups* **2 from soup to nuts** *AmE infml* from beginning to end, completely and in detail **3 in the soup** *infml* in trouble

soup² *v*
  soup sthg. ↔ **up** *phr v* [T] **1** to increase the power of

(an engine) or the size of the engine of (a car), esp. with a SUPERCHARGER **2** *infml, often derog* to make bigger, more exciting, more attractive, etc.: *His second book is just a souped-up version of his first one.*

soup·çon /ˈsuːpsɒn‖-sɑːn/ *n* [S (**of**)] *Fr, fml or humor* a little bit: *It just needs a soupçon more salt.*

soup kitch·en /ˈ· ˌ··/ *n* a place where people with no money and often no homes can get free food. Soup kitchens are run by organizations such as churches or charities (CHARITY) and they provide tea and coffee and simple food (not necessarily soup).

soup spoon /ˈ· ·/ *n* a rounded spoon about the size of a DESSERTSPOON, used for eating soup —see pictures at SPOON and PLACE SETTING

sour¹ /saʊəʳ/ *adj* **1** having the taste that is not bitter, salty, or sweet, and is produced esp. by acids: *Lemons are sour.* | *sour green apples* —compare BITTER¹ (1), SWEET¹ (1) **2** having the taste of fermentation (FERMENT) (=chemical action by bacteria): *This milk has gone sour; it has a sour taste* **3** having or expressing a bad temper; unfriendly; SULLEN: *He gave me a sour look.* **4** [F] *infml* bad or wrong; disappointing: *The project* **turned sour/went sour** *on us when we found no oil and our backers pulled out their money.* — ~**ly** *adv* — ~**ness** *n* [U]

sour² *v* [I;T] to (cause to) become sour: *The milk has soured overnight.* | *Various unhappy experiences have soured her view of life.*

sour³ *n esp. AmE* a drink made with LEMON juice, sugar, and the stated strong alcohol: *a whiskey sour*

source¹ /sɔːs‖sɔːrs/ *n* [(**of**)] **1** a place from which something comes; means of supply: *We'll have to find a new source of income.* | *I haven't been able to track down the source of the rumour/to locate the source of the contamination.* **2** a cause: *This faulty connection is the source of the engine trouble.* **3** the place where a stream of water starts: *We followed the river back to discover its source.* —compare SPRING² (2) **4** a person or thing that supplies information: *When writing an academic article, always list your sources.* | *source material* | *I've heard from a reliable source that the company is doing very badly.*

source² *v* [T] to find a SOURCE¹ (1) of: *A team of eager, resourceful buyers who monitored the fashion scene was dispatched to the Far East to source cheap copies.*

source code /ˈ· ·/ *n* [U] *tech* a computer PROGRAM in a form readable by a person who knows the language it is written in —compare MACHINE CODE

sour cream /ˌ· ˈ·/ also **soured cream** *BrE*— *n* [U] cream made sour by adding a kind of bacteria, and used in various foods

sour·dough /ˈsaʊədəʊ‖ˈsaʊər-/ *n* [U] uncooked bread mixture (DOUGH) which is kept for a period of time and then used in cooking bread, cakes, etc. to help them to rise

sour grapes /ˌ· ˈ·/ *n* [U] the fact of pretending to dislike what one really desires, because it is unobtainable: *Since losing the election, John says he never really wanted to be a politician anyway, but I think it's just sour grapes.*

sour·puss /ˈsaʊəpʊs‖-ər-/ *n humor derog* a person with no sense of humour, who always complains and is never satisfied

Sou·sa /ˈsuːzə/, **John Philip** (1854–1932) an American musician who wrote music and led bands. His **Sousa marches** (music written to walk to), esp. *The Stars and Stripes Forever*, are very popular in the US.

sou·sa·phone /ˈsuːzəfəʊn/ *n* a very large brass musical instrument used esp. in bands and usu. fitted round the player's left shoulder

souse /saʊs/ *v* [T] **1** to dip in water or pour water over; make completely wet **2** to preserve (esp. fish) by placing it in water with salt in it, VINEGAR, etc.: *soused herrings*

soused /saʊst/ *adj* [F] *infml* drunk

south¹ /saʊθ/ *written abbrev.* **S** *n* (*often cap.*) **1** [*the*+S;U] the direction which is down from the centre line of the Earth (EQUATOR); the direction which is on the right of a person facing the rising sun: *I'm lost; which direction is South?* | *A strange light appeared in the south.* | *The airport is a few kilometres to the south of London.* **2** [*the*] the southern part of a country —see NORTH (USAGE)

south² *adj* [A] **1** (*sometimes cap.*) in the south or facing the south: *The south side of the building gets a lot of sun.* |

She lives in South America. **2** (of a wind) coming from the south: *a gentle south wind* —see NORTH (USAGE)

south³ *adv* **1** (*often cap.*) towards the south: *The room faces south, so we get a lot of sun.* | *The birds fly south in winter.* | *Lisbon is (a long way) south of Oporto.* **2 down south** *infml* to or in the south of the country: *We're planning to move down south.*

South [*the*] **1** the SE states of the US, esp. in talking about politics or history

▶ CULTURAL NOTE The South has played an important part in American history. Before the Civil War many black people were brought from Africa to states in the South to work in cotton fields (PLANTATIONS) as slaves. The Civil War (1861 – 65) was fought partly over slavery. After the war, in which the South was defeated by the North, the slaves were freed, but most Southern states created laws which kept black people and white people separate. During the 1950s and 60s, when black people demanded CIVIL RIGHTS (equal rights as citizens), many white people in the South refused to accept changes and there was often violence, esp. by members of the Ku Klux Klan. The South is now seen as a place where family, good manners, and religious values are stronger, and it is sometimes called the **Bible Belt** because there are many Christian FUNDAMENTALIST churches there. Southerners are considered to be CONSERVATIVE (= not wanting change) politically but the Democratic Party is also strong in the South. Most people from the South have strong, slow accents (DRAWLS) which are slightly different in each state. —see also DEEP SOUTH ◀

2 the Southern part of England

▶ CULTURAL NOTE The South of England is seen by British people as being richer than the rest of Britain. People from other parts of the country often think that people from the South are unfriendly and too concerned with making money. They also think that people in the South, esp. London, are not interested in what is happening in the North or in Scotland, Wales, and Ireland. —see also SOUTHEAST ◀

3 the poorer countries of esp. southern parts of the world, such as Africa and South America; THIRD WORLD

South Af·ri·ca /· ¹···/ a country in Southern Africa, bordered by Botswana and Zimbabwe; capital Johannesburg; population 34,492,000 (1989). Very many people all over the world did not approve of South Africa's former political plan of keeping white and black people separate (called APARTHEID), or of the system of government where a MINORITY of people has the power. Some governments would not trade with South Africa or meet its politicians. There are many people inside South Africa who are working to change the political situation and it is beginning to change as black people are gaining more political power. —see also ANC, Steve BIKO, Nelson MANDELA

South Af·ri·can /· ¹···/ *n* a person who comes from or whose parents come from lives in South Africa —**South African** *adj*

South·all /¹saʊθɔːl/ an area of W London near Heathrow Airport, where many Asians live

South A·mer·i·ca /· · ¹···/ a CONTINENT to the SE of North America, lying between the Atlantic and Pacific Oceans, mainly S of the EQUATOR —**South American** *adj,n*

South·amp·ton /saʊθˈhæmptən, saʊˈθæmp-/ a city and important port in S England which has a university

South Aus·tra·li·a /· · ·¹···/ a state in central S Australia whose capital is Adelaide

South Bank /¹· ¸·/ [*the*] a part of London, in Lambeth on the S bank of the river Thames, which is one of the most important CULTURAL centres in the capital. The National Theatre, the National Film Theatre, the Royal Festival Hall (used for concerts), the Museum of the Moving Image, and the Hayward Gallery (an art GALLERY) are all there. —see colour map on page 817

south·bound /¹saʊθbaʊnd/ *adj* travelling or leading towards the south: *southbound ships* | *the southbound side of the motorway*

South Car·o·li·na /¸saʊθ kærəˈlaɪnə/ *written abbrev.* **SC** a state in the SE of the US. It was one of the 13 original British colonies (COLONY) —see colour map on pages 1374–5

South Cir·cu·lar /¸· ¹···/ [*the*] a road in London which goes through many of the areas south of the River Thames

South Da·ko·ta /¸saʊθ dəˈkəʊtə/ *written abbrev.* **SD** a state

in the central part of the US —see colour map on pages 1374–5

South Downs /¸· ¹·/ [*the*] a range of hills in S England — compare NORTH DOWNS

south-east¹ /¸saʊθˈiːst◂/ *written abbrev.* **SE** *n* (*often cap.*) **1** [*the*+S;U] the direction which is half-way between south and east: *The wind's in* (=is coming from) *the southeast.* **2** [*the*+S] the SOUTHEASTERN part of a country

southeast² *adj* [A] (of a wind) coming from the southeast —**southeast** *adv* : *to sail southeast* | *Madagascar is southeast of Tanzania.*

South East /¸· ¹·/ [*the*] the SE part of England, including London, with a high population and many industries, esp. service industries (SERVICE INDUSTRY)

▶ CULTURAL NOTE People in Britain think if the South East as being richer than other parts of Britain, and as not having the social and economic problems that exist in other parts of the country, e.g. unemployment, crime, homelessness, etc.: *They moved down to the affluent South East.* | *It seems that even the South East may be affected by this recession.* ◀

Southeast A·sia /¸·· ¹··/ a part of the world between India, China, and the Pacific Ocean which includes the nations of Brunei, Myanmar, Indonesia, Cambodia, Laos, Malaysia, the Philippines, Singapore, Thailand, and Vietnam

south-east·er /¸saʊθˈiːstər/ *n* a strong wind or storm coming from the southeast

south-east·er·ly /¸saʊθˈiːstəli‖-ər-/ *adj* **1** towards or in the southeast: *Rain will spread to southeasterly regions by tomorrow morning.* **2** (of a wind) coming from the southeast

south-east·ern /¸saʊθˈiːstən‖-ərn/ *adj* (*often cap.*) of the southeast part, esp. of a country

south-east·ward /¸saʊθˈiːstwəd‖-wərd/ *adj* going towards the southeast: *in a southeastward direction* —**southeastwards, southeastward** *adv* : *sailing southeastwards*

South·end on Sea /¸saʊθend ɒn ¹siː‖-ɑːn-/ a town on the SE coast of England, near London, which is a popular place for people from London, esp. WORKING-CLASS people, to go for the day or for their holidays

south·er·ly /¹sʌðəli‖-ər-/ *adj* **1** towards or in the south: *We set off in a southerly direction.* **2** (of a wind) coming from the south: *gentle southerly breezes*

south·ern /¹sʌðən‖-ərn/ *adj* [*no comp.*] (*often cap.*) of or belonging to the south part of the world or of a country: *She lives in southern Italy.* | *in the southern hemisphere* —see NORTH (USAGE) and see picture at GLOBE

Southern Alps /¸·· ¹·/ [*the*+P] mountain ranges on the South Island of New Zealand. Their highest point is Mount Cook, which is the highest point in New Zealand.

Southern Bap·tist /¸·· ¹··/ *n* a member of a church that is part of the Baptist Church, formed in the Southern US in 1845. It is known for its FUNDAMENTALIST beliefs.

Southern belle /¸·· ¹·/ *n AmE* (esp. formerly) a woman from the South with beauty, good manners, and high social standing

Southern Com·fort /¸·· ¹··/ *n* [U] *tdmk* a strong, sweet alcoholic drink which is made in the American south

South·ern·er /¹sʌðənər‖-ðər-/ *n* a person who lives in or comes from the southern part of a country —see SOUTH¹ (2)

Southern Ire·land /¸·· ¹··/ see REPUBLIC OF IRELAND

southern lights /¸·· ¹·/ *n* [*the*+P] (*usu. caps.*) see AURORA

south·ern·most /¹sʌðənməʊst‖-ərn-/ *adj* [*no comp.*] furthest south: *the southernmost tip of the mainland*

Southern States /¸·· ¹·/ [*the*] the states of the US that lie south of the Mason-Dixon Line, between Pennsylvania and West Virginia

Southern Wa·ter /¸·· ¹··/ a water company in S England that deals with the supply of water to people and businesses and the removal and treatment of SEWAGE

Sou·they /¹saʊði/, **Rob·ert** /¹rɒbət‖ ¹rɑːbərt/ (1774–1843) an English writer and poet who became POET LAUREATE in 1813 and now is remembered esp. for his book *Life of Nelson* and for short poems such as *The Battle of Blenheim*

South·fork /¹saʊθfɔːk‖-fɔːrk/ the name of the home of the Ewing family in the American television programme *Dallas* —see DALLAS

South Geor·gia /ˌ·ˈ··/ an island in the S Atlantic, E of Cape Horn, which is under British control. Nobody lives there except British soldiers and a few scientists. Both Britain and Argentina think the island should belong to them. —see also FALKLANDS WAR

South Gla·mor·gan /ˌ·ˈ··/ a COUNTY in S Wales. Cardiff, the capital of Wales, is in South Glamorgan.

South Is·land /ˈ· ˌ··/ [(the)] one of the two main islands of New Zealand, whose main towns are Christchurch and Dunedin. It is important for sheep farming and the growing of WHEAT.

South Ken·sing·ton /ˌ·ˈ··/ also **South Ken** /ˌ·ˈ·/ infml — a part of London which contains the Science Museum and the Natural History Museum, and is a fashionable and expensive place to live

South Ko·re·a /ˌ·ˈ··/ a country in NE Asia bordering on the Sea of Japan and the Yellow Sea; capital Seoul; population 42,380,000 (1989) —see also KOREA

South of France /ˌ·ˈ·/ [the] the part of France along the coast between Marseilles and the border with Monaco, which is also called the French Riviera.

▶ CULTURAL NOTE This area is a very popular place to go on holiday. In the past only very rich people went there, and places like Cannes and Cap d'Antibes are still seen as places where rich, famous, and fashionable people go, but now many ordinary people from many countries also go on holiday there. —see also RIVIERA ◀

South Pa·cif·ic /ˌ·ˈ··/ a very popular old musical play and film

south·paw /ˈsaʊθpɔː/ n **1** BrE a left-handed BOXER (1) **2** AmE infml a left-handed person, esp. a left-handed PITCH·ER² (in BASEBALL)

South Pole /ˌ·ˈ·/ n [the] (the lands around) the most southern point on the surface of the Earth —see also MAGNETIC POLE, NORTH POLE; and see picture at GLOBE

South Sea Bub·ble /ˌ·· · ˈ··/ [the] the name given in Britain to a period of financial SPECULATION at the beginning of the 18th century. Many people invested (INVEST) money with the **South Sea Company**, a company which made money from trade with other countries. There was much dishonest dealing in the company and in the end the company failed, causing many people to lose the money that they had invested.

South Seas /ˌ·ˈ·/ [the] the oceans of the southern HEMISPHERE (=half of the world), esp. the S Pacific —**South Sea** /ˈ· ·/ adj [A] : the South Sea islands

South Wales /ˌ·ˈ·/ the southern part of Wales, that contains many of the coal areas and large industries of Wales —see also WALES

south·ward /ˈsaʊθwəd‖-wərd/ adj going towards the south: a southward journey

south·wards /ˈsaʊθwədz‖-wərdz/ also **southward**— adv towards the south: We sailed southwards. | It's farther southward than you might think. —see also SOUTH³

South·wark /ˈsʌθək‖-ərk/ a BOROUGH of London on the S side of the river Thames which has a famous CATHEDRAL

south·west¹ /ˌsaʊθˈwest◄/ written abbrev. **SW** n (often cap.) **1** [the+S;U] the direction which is half-way between south and west: The wind's in (=is coming from) the southwest. **2** [the+S] the southwestern part of a country **3** [the+S] the southwestern part of the US, including the states of Arizona and New Mexico, and parts of Texas, Utah, and Colorado. It is known esp. for its style of buildings, decorations, and furniture, which is influenced by Native American and Mexican styles and is connected in people's minds with ADOBE, colours such as brown and dark orange, and patterns based on Native American art: Her interior decoration is done in southwest style.

southwest² adj [A] (of a wind) coming from the southwest —**southwest** adv : to sail southwest | Spain is southwest of France.

south·west·er /ˌsaʊθˈwestər/ also **sou'wester**— n a strong wind or storm from the southwest

south·west·er·ly /ˌsaʊθˈwestəli‖-ərli/ adj **1** towards or in the southwest **2** (of a wind) coming from the southwest

south·west·ern /ˌsaʊθˈwestən‖-ərn/ adj (often cap.) of the southwest part, esp. of a country

south·west·ward /ˌsaʊθˈwestwəd‖-wərd/ adj going towards the southwest: in a southwestward direction —

southwestwards, southwestward— adv : sailing southwestwards

Southwest Wa·ter /ˌ·· ˈ··/ a water company in SW England that deals with the supply of water to people and businesses and the removal and treatment of SEWAGE

South York·shire /ˌ·ˈ··/ a COUNTY in the N of England

sou·ve·nir /ˌsuːvəˈnɪər, ˈsuːvənɪər/ n [(of)] an object (to be) kept as a reminder of an event, trip, place, etc.: He bought a little model of the Eiffel Tower as a souvenir of his holiday in Paris.

sou'west·er /saʊˈwestər/ n **1** a hat of shiny material worn to keep off the rain with a wide band coming far down over the neck, typically worn by fishermen **2** a SOUTHWESTER

sove·reign¹ /ˈsɒvrɪn‖ˈsaːv-/ n **1** fml a king or queen; the person with the highest power in a country: loyal subjects of our sovereign **2** a former British gold coin worth £1

sovereign² adj in control of a country; ruling: Sovereign power must lie with the people.

So·vi·et /ˈsəʊviət, ˈsɒ-‖ˈsəʊ-, ˈsaː-/ adj of the USSR (the Soviet Union /ˌ·ˈ··/) or its people: the Soviet armed forces

Soviet bloc /ˌ·ˈ· ˈ·/ [the] a popular name for the former USSR and its allies (ALLY), including countries of E Europe as well as COMMUNIST countries such as China, North Korea, Vietnam, Cuba, etc.

Soviet U·nion /ˌ·ˈ··/ see USSR

sow¹ /səʊ/ v sowed, sown /səʊn/ or sowed [I;T (with)] to plant or scatter (seeds) on (a piece of ground): These seeds should be sown in April; that's the best time to sow. | Sow your carrots early. | We're sowing the field with grass. | (fig.) His words had sowed the seeds of suspicion in their minds. — ~er n

sow² /saʊ/ n a fully grown female pig —compare BOAR (1), HOG¹ (1,2)

So·wet·o /səˈwetəʊ/ the name for a group of towns where only black people live near Johannesburg in South Africa. In 1976 a student protest against the use of the Afrikaans language instead of English in schools became a RIOT and many people were killed. Soweto is seen as a centre for people who oppose the South African government's policy of APARTHEID.

sox /sɒks‖saːks/ n [P] infml esp. AmE socks

soy /sɔɪ/ also **soy·a** /ˈsɔɪə/— n [U] soya beans: soya flour

soya bean /ˈ·· ·/ also **soy·bean** /ˈsɔɪbiːn/— n (the bean of) an Asian plant grown for its seeds which produce oil and are rich in PROTEIN

So·yin·ka /sɔɪˈjɪŋkə/, **Wo·le** /ˈwəʊleɪ/ (1934–) a Nigerian writer of plays, poems, and NOVELs who won the Nobel Prize in 1986

soy sauce /ˌ·ˈ·‖ˈ· ·/ n [U] dark brown liquid made from soya beans used esp. in Chinese and Japanese cooking

soz·zled /ˈsɒzəld‖ˈsaː-/ adj [F] BrE humor drunk

spa /spaː/ also **watering place**— n **1** a place with a spring of mineral water where people come for cures of various diseases.

▶ CULTURAL NOTE Spas used to be very fashionable places in Britain, esp. in the 18th and 19th centuries, but now they are no longer popular with British people. ◀

2 AmE JACUZZI **3** ‖ also **health spa** AmE— a GYMNASIUM which people usu. pay to use in order to keep fit, and which may include a swimming pool, exercise machines, etc.: I've just joined the spa.

space¹ /speɪs/ n **1** [U] something measurable in length, width, or depth; distance, area, or VOLUME that can be used or filled by a physical object; room: There's not enough space in the cupboard for all my clothes. | We'll have to clear some space to make room for the new sofa. | Keep some space between you and the car ahead. | In the space of ten miles the road rises 1000 feet. **2** [C;U] a quantity or bit of this for an often stated purpose: I couldn't find a parking space. | You need permission to fly in that country's air space. | Where the book had been there was just an empty space. | Please save a space (=an empty place) for me in the queue. **3** [U] that which surrounds all objects and continues outwards in all directions: I don't think he saw me; he was just staring into space. **4** [U] what is outside the Earth's air; where the stars and

PLANETs are: *The satellite has been in* **(outer) space** *for a year.* | *space travel* **5** [C;U] also **spaces** *pl.*— (an area of) land not built on. *the vast empty spaces of the prairies* | *This new town was planned to have some* **open space** *near the centre.* | *They hiked for miles across wide open spaces.* **6** [C;U] a period of time: *There's been a 100% increase in sales* **within/in/during the space of** *only two years.* **7** [C] **a** an area or distance left between written or printed words, lines, etc.: *Write your answers in the blank spaces/in the spaces provided.* **b** the width of a typed (TYPE) letter: *The word "the" takes three spaces.* —see also BREATHING SPACE

space[2] *v* [T+*obj*+*adv*/*prep*; usu. pass.] to place apart; arrange with spaces between: *The pictures in the gallery were well spaced out.* | *Space the desks two metres apart so that the pupils can't cheat.* | *We spaced our family out over five years.* (=left even periods of time between having babies during those years)

space-age /ˈ· ·/ *adj infml, usu. apprec* very modern

space bar /ˈ· ·/ *n* the part of a TYPEWRITER below the lowest row of keys that is pressed to make a space —see picture at TYPEWRITER

space cap·sule /ˈ· ˌ··/ *n* a vehicle which may carry people or animals, and travels into space to obtain information and then comes back to Earth

space·craft /ˈspeɪs-krɑːft‖-kræft/ *n* **spacecraft** a vehicle able to travel in SPACE[1] (4): *a manned spacecraft*

spaced out /ˌ· ˈ◂/ *adj infml* not fully conscious of what is happening around one, e.g. because of the effect of drugs

space heat·er /ˈ· ˌ··/ *n* an electric or FUEL-burning machine for heating an enclosed area or room

Space In·vad·ers /ˈ· ·ˌ··/ *n* [U] *tdmk* a computer game often found in public places, in which the player tries to destroy attacking SPACESHIPS

Spa·cek /ˈspeɪsek/, **Sissy** (1949–) an American film actress known esp. for her part in the films *Carrie* and *Coal Miner's Daughter*

space·man /ˈspeɪsmæn/ **space·wom·an** /-ˌwʊmən/ *fem.*— **-men** /men/ **1** *infml for* ASTRONAUT **2** (esp. in stories) a being that visits the Earth from another world

space probe /ˈ· ·/ *n* a PROBE[1]

spaceship

space·ship /ˈspeɪsˌʃɪp/ *n* (esp. in stories) a spacecraft for carrying people through space, often imagined as looking like a FLYING SAUCER

space shut·tle /ˈ· ˌ··/ *n* a vehicle for **a** carrying people and supplies between the Earth and a space station **b** carrying people into space to do scientific EXPERIMENTs, put SATELLITEs into space, etc.

space sta·tion /ˈ· ˌ··/ *n* a large spacecraft intended to stay above the Earth and act as a base for scientific tests, for flying further out into space, etc.

space·suit /ˈspeɪs-suːt, -sjuːt‖-suːt/ *n* a protective suit for wearing in SPACE[1] (4), covering the whole body and provided with an air supply: *a leak in her spacesuit* —see picture at SUIT

space-time /ˌ· ˈ·/ *n* [U] *tech* a system which has length, depth, height, and time

spac·ey /ˈspeɪsi/ *adj, adv AmE infml* not fully conscious of what is happening around one; behaving strangely, as if one were taking drugs: *He acts kind of spacey but he's really a nice guy.* | *The lady next door is pretty spacey; I'd never let her take care of the kids.*

spac·ing /ˈspeɪsɪŋ/ *n* [U] placement or arrangement apart, esp. of typed (TYPE) or printed lines: *Type this letter*

with/in **single/double/triple spacing.** (=lines with no/one/two empty lines between them)

space station

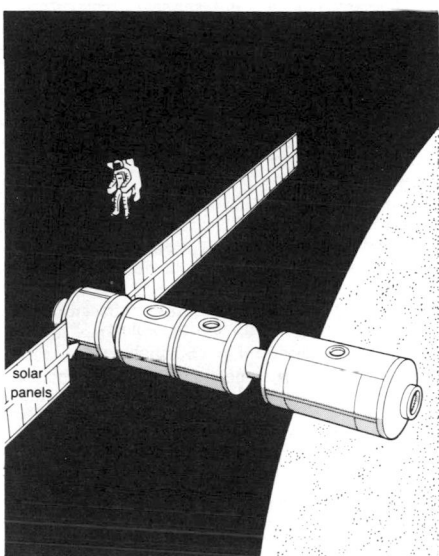

solar panels

spa·cious /ˈspeɪʃəs/ *adj apprec* having a lot of room; ROOMY: *a spacious office* – – **ly** *adv* – – **ness** *n* [U]

spade[1] /speɪd/ *n* **1** a tool for digging earth, sand, etc., with a handle and a broad usu. metal blade for pushing into the ground with the foot: *a child's bucket and spade* —compare SHOVEL[1] (1), and see picture at GARDEN **2** [(of)] also **spade·ful** /-fʊl/— the amount carried by this —see also **call a spade a spade** (CALL)

spade[2] *n* **1 a** a black figure shaped like a pointed leaf printed on a playing card **b** a card belonging to the SUIT (=set) of cards that have one or more of these figures printed on them: *the four/queen of spades* | *I only have two spades in my hand.* —see CARDS (USAGE) and see picture at CARDS **2** *old-fash derog sl* a black person (considered extremely offensive)

spade·work /ˈspeɪd-wɜːk ‖ -wɜːrk/ *n* [U] hard work done in preparation for an event or course of action: *I did all the spadework, then she came and finished it off and got all the credit.*

spa·ghet·ti /spəˈgeti/ *n* [U] Italian PASTA (=food made from flour mixed with water) in the shape of long strings, cooked in boiling water —compare MACARONI, TAGLIATELLE, VERMICELLI

Spaghetti Junc·tion /·ˌ·· ˈ··/ *n* **1** *AmE* a place where a lot of roads cross over each other **2** a place in Birmingham in central England where a lot of roads meet and cross over each other

spaghetti west·ern /·ˌ·· ˈ··/ *n* a film about American COW-BOYs in the Wild West esp. by an Italian director and made in Europe

Spain /speɪn/ a country in SW Europe, on the Iberian PENINSULA, which includes the Balearic and Canary islands; capital Madrid; population 38,811,000 (1989). Spain is a member of the EC and has a king, Juan Carlos, as well as a PRIME MINISTER. Spain is a very popular place for British people to go on holiday or even to live, and holidays to Spain are often very cheap, particularly those in special holiday towns like Benidorm. —see also BENIDORM, ETA[2], FRANCO, GIBRALTAR, SPANISH, SPANISH CIVIL WAR

spake /speɪk/ *old use or poet, past tense of* SPEAK

Spam /spæm/ *n* [U] *tdmk* a kind of inexpensive tinned meat, usu. eaten cold, made mainly of PORK (=pig meat) and pink in colour. Spam was popular in Britain esp. during and after the Second World War, but is not eaten so much now. It is still quite popular in the US.

span[1] /spæn/ *past tense of* SPIN

span² n **1** a stretch between two limits, esp. in time; period: *Over a span of three years a surprising amount has been achieved.* **2** a length of time over which the stated thing continues or works well: *a short attention/ life/memory span | an unbroken span of concentration* **3** a (part of a) bridge, arch, etc., between supports: *The bridge crosses the river in a single span. | the central span of the aqueduct* —compare SPREAD² (2); see also WINGSPAN

span³ v **-nn-** [T] **1** to form an arch or bridge over: *A bridge spanned the stream.* **2** to include in space or time; go from one end to the other end of: *His interests spanned a wide range of subjects. | The game has a history spanning three centuries.*

span⁴ adj see SPICK-AND-SPAN

Span·dau /ˈspændaʊ/ a prison in W Berlin, Germany, where Rudolf Hess, the Nazi war criminal, was kept

span·gle¹ /ˈspæŋɡəl/ n a small piece of shiny metal or plastic sewn in large numbers esp. on dresses, to give a shining effect; SEQUIN

spangle² v [T (**with**)] to give a shining effect to (as if) with spangles; decorate with shining objects

Span·iard /ˈspænjəd‖-ərd/ n a Spanish person

span·iel /ˈspænjəl/ n a small or middle-sized short-legged dog with long ears and long wavy hair —see picture at DOG

Span·ish¹ /ˈspænɪʃ/ adj of Spain or its language

Spanish² n [U] the language spoken in Spain and also in some parts of South America

Spanish-A·mer·i·can War /ˌ··· ·,··· ˈ·/ [the] (1898) a war between the US and Spain in which the US demanded Cuba's independence from Spain. The war began soon after the explosion of the American battleship **Maine** near Havana, Cuba. The US was successful in freeing Cuba, and gained the islands of the Philippines, Guam, and Puerto Rico, and thus became a world power. Theodore Roosevelt (a later president) first became famous through his military success in the Spanish-American War, when he led a group of volunteers (=unpaid workers) called the **Rough Riders.**

Spanish Civ·il War /ˌ··· ,·· ˈ·/ [the] a war which was fought in Spain from 1936 to 1939 between the RIGHT-WING Nationalists and the LEFT-WING Loyalists. Many people from other countries joined the International Brigades to fight for the Loyalists, and for many young people of the 1930s saving Spain from the Nationalists was an important IDEAL. Many writers and poets wrote about the war or went to fight, including the American writer Ernest Hemingway. The Nationalists won the war and from the end of the war until 1975 Spain was ruled by the RIGHT-WING leader General Franco. —see also FRANCO

Spanish fly /ˌ··· ˈ·/ n [U] AmE a substance made from dried insects which is supposed to be an APHRODISIAC (=drug causing sexual excitement). It is talked about more often than it is seen or used.

Spanish in·flu·en·za /ˌ··· ··ˈ···/ also **Spanish flu** /ˌ··· ˈ·/— n an illness which killed many people all over the world in 1917 and 1918

Spanish Main /ˌ··· ˈ·/ [the] a part of the coast of NW South America, from which Spanish ships carried gold back to Spain, esp. during the 16th and 17th centuries. Many of these ships were attacked by PIRATES, and there are many stories and films about the exciting adventures of the people who sailed round the Spanish Main.

Spanish ome·lette /ˌ··· ˈ···/ n a thick OMELETTE made with cooked vegetables such as potatoes, onions, and peppers

spank¹ /spæŋk/ v [T] to strike (esp. a child) with quick force (as if) with the open hand, esp. on the BUTTOCKS —compare SMACK¹ (1) —**spank** n — **ing** n [C;U] : *If you don't stop that noise, you'll get a spanking.*

spank² v [I+adv/prep, esp. ALONG] to go or esp. sail quickly

spank·ing¹ /ˈspæŋkɪŋ/ adj [A] apprec quickly moving; BRISK: *to move at a spanking pace*

spanking² adv infml (used before adjectives like **new, clean, fine,** etc.) very; completely: *a spanking new car*

span·ner /ˈspænər/ BrE ‖ **wrench** AmE— n **1** a metal tool with jaws or a hollow end, for fitting over and twisting NUTS (2) —see also RING SPANNER, and see picture at TOOL **2 spanner in the works** BrE infml a cause of confusion or ruin to a plan or operation: *A sudden thunderstorm*

put/threw a spanner in the works and we had to abandon our plans for a day out.

spar¹ /spɑːr/ n a thick pole, esp. one used on a ship to support sails or ropes —compare MAST (1)

spar² v **-rr-** [I (**with**)] **1** to BOX³ without hitting hard, esp. in practice (between **sparring partners**) or in testing an opponent's defence **2** to exchange words as if fighting or competing: *The two MPs were sparring with each other across the floor of the House.*

spare¹ /speər/ v [T] **1** [(**for**)] to give up (someone or something that is not being used or is not needed); afford to give: *We're so busy that no one in the office can be spared for any other work. | Can you spare £5?* (=please give me £5) (+obj(i)+obj(d)] *Can you spare me five minutes?* (=so that I can talk to you for a short time) | *"Have you got enough?" "Yes; we've got enough and to spare."* (=more than enough) **2** [usu. in questions and negatives] to keep from using, spending, etc.: *No trouble was spared to make sure the guests enjoyed themselves.* | **No expense was spared** *in providing the food and wine.* (=a lot of money was spent) **3** [+obj(i)+obj(d)] to not give (someone) (something unwelcome): *It was a horrible accident – I'll spare you the details.* **4** [+obj(i)+obj(d)] to save (someone) (need or trouble): *Use the telephone and spare yourself a visit.* **5** esp. lit to keep from punishing, harming, attacking, or killing: *Take my money but spare my life! | We give thanks to God that our leader was spared.* (=did not die) **6 spare someone's blushes** infml to avoid making someone feel silly and awkward, esp. by praising them too much **7 spare the rod and spoil the child** an old saying popular esp. in the 19th century in Britain, meaning that children need to be punished by being hit in order to grow into well-behaved adults **8 to spare** left over; not used or needed for use: *We have just enough money to buy it, with 11 pence to spare. | I've got a few moments to spare if you want to talk to me.* —see also UNSPARING

spare² adj **1** not in use but kept for use if needed: *a spare tyre/bedroom* **2** not needed for use; free: *What do you like doing in your **spare time?*** (=when you are not working or busy) | *Have you got a spare moment? There's something I'd like to discuss.* **3** rather thin; LEAN **4 go spare** BrE infml to become very anxious and/or angry

spare³ n **1** a second object of the same kind that is kept for possible use **2** a SPARE TYRE (1) **3** [often pl.] BrE for SPARE PART

spare part /ˌ· ˈ·◂/ n a new part of a vehicle or other machine to take the place of a part that is damaged, broken, or worn

spare-part sur·ge·ry /ˌ· · ˈ···/ n [U] infml the putting of an artificial organ or an organ from a dead person into the body of a living person, to take the place of an organ that is diseased or damaged

Spare Rib /ˌ· ˈ·/ a magazine produced in Britain by a group of women working together. It has articles on political subjects as well as stories by women and information on subjects of interest to women, esp. RACISM and FEMINISM, and is read mainly by FEMINISTS.

spare·ribs /ˈspeəˌrɪbz/ n [P] (a dish of cooked) pig's RIBS with the meat which sticks to them

spare room /ˌ· ˈ·/ n a bedroom in a house, which the family does not need or use and which is usu. kept for guests

spare tyre /ˌ· ˈ·/ n **1** also **spare wheel, spare**— an additional tyre carried in a vehicle for use if one of the tyres on the wheels is damaged **2** humor a noticeably fat waist

spar·ing /ˈspeərɪŋ/ adj [(**with, in, of**)] using or giving little; FRUGAL: *Whisky's expensive, so be sparing with it. | He was rather sparing in giving praise.* — —**ly** adv : *There's not much left, so use it sparingly.*

spark¹ /spɑːk‖spɑːrk/ n **1** a small bit of burning material thrown out by a fire or by the striking together of two hard objects: *Sparks flew into the air as the burning building collapsed.* | (fig.) *They've always hated each other, and whenever they meet* **the sparks fly.** (=there is angry quarrelling) | (fig.) *The murder of the ambassador was the spark that set off the war.* **2** a flash of light produced by electricity passing across a space **3** [(**of**)] a very small but important bit, esp. of a quality; TRACE: *If you had a spark of consideration for your family you wouldn't take so many stupid risks. | We couldn't even raise a spark of interest/enthusiasm for our plan.* —see also SPARKS, BRIGHT SPARK

spark² v **1** [I] to produce a SPARK (1,2) **2** [T (OFF)] to be the cause of (esp. something violent or unpleasant); lead to: *This accidental killing sparked (off) major riots in the cities.* **3** [T] *esp. AmE* to encourage; STIMULATE into greater activity: *It was this incident that sparked her interest in politics.* **4** [I] *AmE infml old-fash* to pay attention to a man or woman one likes and perhaps hopes to marry; FLIRT: *They were sparking by the gate when her father called her to come in.*

Spark, Mu·ri·el /'mjʊəriəl/ (1918–) a Scottish writer known esp. for her book *The Prime of Miss Jean Brodie*

spar·kle¹ /'spɑːkəl‖'spɑːr-/ v [I] to shine in small flashes: *Her diamonds sparkled in the sunlight.* | (fig.) *His eyes sparkled with merriment* –see also SPARKLING

sparkle² n [C;U] an act or the quality of sparkling: *the sparkle of a diamond* | (fig.) *The new play didn't have much sparkle to it.* (=was rather dull)

spar·kler /'spɑːklər‖'spɑːr-/ n **1** a hand-held FIREWORK, usu. held by children, in the form of a stick with chemicals stuck to it that give off harmless bright sparks of fire as it burns down. In Britain, sparklers are sold only in the weeks before Guy Fawkes Night and only to people over the age of 16. In the US, they are only sold before the Fourth of July but in some areas they are illegal. **2** *sl* a diamond

spark·ling /'spɑːklɪŋ‖'spɑːr-/ adj apprec full of life and brightness: *She gave a sparkling performance of the sonata.* | *sparkling wit*

sparkling wine /ˌ·· '·/ n [U] a type of wine which gives off BUBBLES of gas. Wine like this made in the Champagne area of France is called Champagne. No other sparkling wine can be called Champagne.

spark plug /'· ·/ also **sparking plug** /'·· ˌ·/ *BrE* – n a part that screws into a petrol engine and makes an electric SPARK¹ (2) to explode the petrol mixture –see picture at ENGINE

sparks /spɑːks‖spɑːrks/ n old-fash sl an electrician or radio OPERATOR

spar·row /'spærəʊ/ n a small brownish bird very common in many parts of the world –see also HEDGE SPARROW, HOUSE SPARROW, and see picture at BIRD

sparse /spɑːs‖spɑːrs/ adj with only a few scattered examples in a large area; not growing or existing in large amounts or quantities: *The sparse vegetation will only feed a small population of animals.* | *Our information on the events is still rather sparse.* – –ly adv : *The room was very sparsely furnished, with just a bed and a chair.* | *a sparsely populated area* – –ness n [U]

Spar·ta /'spɑːtə‖'spɑːr-/ a city of ancient Greece which became a centre for soldiers and the military arts

Spar·ta·cus /'spɑːtəkəs‖'spɑːr-/ (?–71 BC) a Roman GLADIATOR who was the leader of a REVOLT by 90,000 slaves which was defeated in 72 BC

spar·tan /'spɑːtn‖-ɑːr-/ adj simple, severe, and without attention to comfort: *spartan living conditions* | *a spartan attitude to life*

spas·m /'spæzəm/ n **1** a sudden uncontrolled tightening of muscles: *a muscle spasm* | *If breathing is not restored, the patient may go into spasm.* **2** [(of)] a sudden violent effort, feeling, or act: *spasms of grief|laughter|coughing*

spas·mod·ic /spæz'mɒdɪk‖-'mɑː-/ adj **1** not continuous; showing short periods of activity; irregular: *His interest in his school work is rather spasmodic.* | *spasmodic bursts of energy* –compare PERIODIC **2** of or like a spasm: *a spasmodic jerk* – –ally /kli/ adv

spas·tic /'spæstɪk/ n, adj **1** (a person) suffering from a condition (**spastic paralysis**) in which some parts of the body will not move because the muscles stay tightened **2** *derog sl* (used esp. by children) (a person who is) foolish, lacking in skill, etc.

spat¹ /spæt/ past tense & participle of SPIT¹

spat² n [usu. pl.] a cloth covering for the ankle worn, esp. formerly, by men above a shoe, fastened by side buttons and a band under the shoe

spat³ n infml a short unimportant quarrel

spate /speɪt/ n [S+of] **1** esp. BrE a large number or amount, esp. of events of the same kind, coming together in time: *There's been a spate of accidents on this stretch*

of road recently. | *the recent spate of terrorist activity* **2** *esp. AmE* a large amount of words, feelings, etc. being expressed at once: *a spate of foul language* **3 in spate** flooding; full of rushing water: *a river in full spate*

spa·tial /'speɪʃəl/ adj tech or fml of or connected with SPACE¹ (1): *This part of the brain judges the spatial relationships between objects.* – –ly adv

spat·ter¹ /'spætər/ v **1** [T] to scatter (drops of a liquid) on (a surface): [+obj+prep] *As the car raced past, it spattered mud on my clothes|in my face|all over my suit.* [+obj+**with**] *The car spattered me|my clothes with mud.* | *a blood-spattered wall* **2** [I (on)] (of a liquid) to fall or be thrown off in drops onto a surface: *A little of the hot cooking oil spattered on the wall.*

spatter² n **1** a spattered drop or spot **2** [usu. sing.] a small amount: *a spatter of rain*

spat·u·la /'spætjʊlə‖-tʃələ/ n **1** any of various tools with a wide flat not very sharp blade, used esp. in the kitchen for spreading, mixing, or lifting soft substances –see picture at KITCHEN **2** *BrE* a small tool with a flat blade used by doctors to flatten the tongue when examining the throat –compare TONGUE DEPRESSOR

spawn¹ /spɔːn/ v **1** [I;T] (of water animals like fishes and FROGS) to lay (eggs) in large quantities together **2** [T] *infml* to bring into existence, esp. in large numbers: *The computer industry has spawned a lot of new companies.*

spawn² n [U] the eggs of water animals like fishes and FROGS, laid together in a soft mass –see also FROGSPAWN

spay /speɪ/ v [T] to remove (part of) the sex organs of (a female animal): *Have you had your cat spayed?*

SPCK /ˌes piː siː 'keɪ/ Society for Promoting Christian Knowledge; an organization which uses literature to try to spread the message of Christianity around the world

speak /spiːk/ v **spoke** /spəʊk/, **spoken** /'spəʊkən/ **1** [I (**to**, **with**, **about**)] to express thoughts aloud, using the voice; talk: *I was so shocked I couldn't speak.* | *They sat down opposite each other, but it was some moments before they spoke.* (=had a conversation) | *I'd like to speak to|with you about my idea.* | *Is that the man you spoke of?* (=told me about) | *After their quarrel they're still not speaking (to each other)|not* **on speaking terms.** (=willing to talk and be polite to each other) | *Speaking (in my capacity) as chairman, I am in favour of this idea.* –see USAGE **2** [T] to express or say: *Do you think he was speaking the truth?* | *Not a word was spoken about the embarrassing affair.* | *I'd like to meet his daughter; everyone* **speaks very well/highly of** *her.* (=praises her) | *You mustn't* **speak ill of** (=say unkind things about) *the dead.* **3** [T] to be able to talk in (a language): *Do you speak English?* | *English is spoken here.* | *We need a French-speaking secretary.* **4** [I (**to**, **about**, **on**)] to make a speech: *I've invited her to speak to the club on|about her experiences in Central America.* | *He spoke in favour of|against the motion.* –see also SPEAKER **5** [I (**of**)] to express thoughts, ideas, etc., in some other way than by talking: *Actions speak louder than words.* | *Everything at the party spoke of* (=showed that there probably had been) *careful planning.* **6** [I+adv] (only in the present participle) to express one's meaning from the stated point of view: *Generally speaking, I think you're right.* | *The show may make big profits, but artistically speaking* (=from an artistic point of view) *it's terrible.* **7 speak now, or forever hold your peace** *quote* a slightly changed phrase from the Christian marriage service, now often used humorously to say that if someone objects to something they should say so immediately or not at all **8 so to speak** *infml* (used when one uses an unusual or METAPHORICAL expression) as one might say; rather: *That baker knows which side his bread is buttered* (=knows what will be of most advantage to himself), *so to speak!* **9 speak in tongues** to say words or sounds that cannot be understood, esp. when in a state of great excitement during a Christian religious ceremony: *We sometimes speak in tongues during the service.* **10 speak one's mind** to express one's thoughts (too) directly: *I'm furious about it, and I intend to speak my mind to the company chairman.* **11 speak out of turn** to speak at the wrong time or in an unwise or impolite way **12 speak volumes (for)** *infml* to show or express (something) very clearly or fully: *He refused to answer their accusations, but his silence spoke volumes.* (=strongly suggested his guilt) **13 to speak of** [usu. negative] worth mentioning; of much value: *We've had*

no rain to speak of, only a few drops. —see also **in a manner of speaking** (MANNER)

▷ USAGE 1 To **speak of** *something* is rather more formal than to **speak about** *it.* 2 In British English it is more usual to **speak to** *someone* than to **speak with** *someone,* which suggests a long, formal talk. But in American English, **speak with** is used more generally. —see also SAY (USAGE), TALK (USAGE)◁

speak for sbdy./sthg. *phr v* [T] **1** to express the thoughts, opinions, etc., of: *That lawyer is speaking for the defence|the prosecution.* | *"Tom and I aren't very good at maths." "Speak for yourself!" said Tom.* (="I'm good at maths, even if you aren't!") | *I'm ready to decide, but I can't speak for my colleagues.* **2** [*usu. pass.*] to get the right to (something) in advance; RESERVE: *The first 300 cars in the new model have already been spoken for.* **3** to be a witness of; give an idea of: *Their manners speak well for their upbringing.* (=show it was good) **4 speak for itself|themselves** to be very clear and need no further explanation or proof: *The company has had a very successful year: the figures speak for themselves.* —see also SPOKEN FOR

speak out *phr v* [I (**against**)] to speak bravely and openly, esp. after remaining silent for a time: *Will no one speak out against the tyranny of this government?*

speak to sbdy./sthg. *phr v* [T] *infml euph* to speak severely to: *He was late again today; it's time you spoke to him|time he was spoken to!*

speak up *phr v* [I] **1** to speak more loudly: *Speak up, please; I can't hear you.* **2** [(**for**)] to give one's opinion freely and clearly: *It's about time someone spoke up for* (=supported openly) *these basic truths.*

-speak see WORD FORMATION

speak·eas·y /ˈspiːkˌiːzi/ *n* (esp. in the US in the 1920s and 1930s) a place for going to buy and drink alcohol illegally. Speakeasies were often connected with GANGSTERS and seen as exciting, wicked places. —see also PROHIBITION

speak·er /ˈspiːkəʳ/ *n* **1** a person making a speech, or who makes speeches in a stated way: *Our first speaker tonight is Mr Postlethwaite.* | *an entertaining after-dinner speaker* **2** [(**of**)] a person who speaks a particular language: *a speaker of English|an English speaker* **3** that part of a radio or record player from which sound comes out: *a pair of speakers* —see picture at LIVING ROOM

Speaker *n* a British parliamentary official who is elected by Members of Parliament and whose job is to keep order during discussions in the House of Commons. The Speaker must not give any advantages to a particular political party: *the Speaker of the House of Commons* | *I'd like to propose a motion, Mr Speaker.*

Speaker of the House /ˌ··· ˈ·/ *n* the person who controls the course of business in the US House of Representatives. He is suggested for the position by the party which holds the most seats and is voted on by all members of the House.

Speaker's Cor·ner /ˌ·· ˈ··/ a part of Hyde Park in London where people go when they want to tell other people about their political opinions. Anyone can go there and make a speech about any subject they like and other people will listen to them and sometimes argue with them.

speaking clock /ˌ··· ˈ·/ *n* a telephone service in Britain which continuously tells the time

speaking tube /ˈ··· ·/ *n* a pipe through which people in different rooms in a house, on a ship, etc., may speak to one another

spear¹ /spɪəʳ/ *n* **1** a pole with a sharp point at one end used esp. formerly by soldiers and hunters as a weapon: *to hurl a spear* **2** a young thin pointed leaf or stem growing directly from the ground: *asparagus spears*

spear² *v* [T] to make a hole in or catch (as if) with the point of a spear: *He reached out and speared a piece of her meat with his fork.* | *The hunters were spearing fish in the stream.*

spear·head¹ /ˈspɪəhed‖ˈspɪər-/ *n* [(**of**) *usu. sing.*] a person or group that begins and leads an attack or course of action forcefully

spearhead² *v* [T] to lead forcefully: *Which of the opposition parties is going to spearhead the attack on the government?*

spear·mint /ˈspɪəˌmɪnt‖ˈspɪər-/ *n* [U] a common MINT¹ (1) plant widely grown and used for its fresh taste: *spearmint*

chewing gum | *spearmint(-flavoured) toothpaste*

spec /spek/ *n* **on spec** *BrE infml* as a risk or SPECULATION (2): *I bought some oil shares on spec.* | *We haven't booked a hotel in advance, we're going on spec.*

spe·cial¹ /ˈspeʃəl/ *adj* **1** of a particular kind; not ordinary, regular, or usual: *This is a special case, deserving special treatment.* | *They've put on a special train to take the supporters to the match.* | *children with special educational needs* | *Why should you get more than anyone else? What's so special about you?* | *I only wear this suit on special occasions.* **2** also **especial** *fml* particularly great; to an unusually great degree: *She's a special friend of mine.* | *Take special care tonight because the roads are icy.* —see also SPECIALLY

spe·cial² *n* **1** something that is not of the regular or ordinary kind: *Are you going to the match on the football special or the ordinary train?* | a two-hour television special on the African famine **2** *AmE infml* an advertised reduced price in a shop: *They're having a special on ice cream this week.* | *Ice cream is on special this week only!*

special a·gent /ˌ·· ˈ··/ also **FBI agent**— *n AmE* a person who works for the FBI

Special Branch /ˈ·· ˌ·/ [(*the*)] a department of the British police force concerned with crimes or other activities against the state or the political system

special con·sta·ble /ˌ·· ˈ···/ *n* (in Britain) a person who has another job but who is employed as a POLICEMAN or POLICEWOMAN when more help is needed

special de·liv·e·ry /ˌ·· ·ˈ···/ *n* a letter or parcel for which additional money is paid so that it will arrive later or earlier in the day than the usual time —**special delivery** *adv* : *I sent it special delivery.*

special ef·fect /ˌ·· ·ˈ·/ *n* an image or sound in a film or television programme that was made by a person or a machine: *The special effects in Star Wars broke new ground in the film industry.*

special forc·es /ˌ·· ˈ··/ *n* [P] soldiers who have special training in fighting against GUERRILLA or TERRORIST attackers

special in·terest group /ˌ·· ˈ·· ˌ·/ *n* [C +*sing.|pl. v*] a group of people that share an INTEREST, esp. an organization that attempts to influence government action; a PRESSURE GROUP

spe·cial·ism /ˈspeʃəlɪzəm/ *n* **1** [C] an activity in which someone specializes; SPECIALITY (1) **2** [U] limiting one's activities to particular things or subjects

spe·cial·ist /ˈspeʃəlɪst/ *n* [(**in**)] **1** a person who has special interests or skills in a limited field of work or study: *a specialist in African history* **2** a doctor who gives treatment in a particular way or to certain kinds of people or diseases: *Her local doctor couldn't tell what was wrong, so he sent her to see a specialist.* | *a heart specialist*

spe·cial·i·ty /ˌspeʃiˈælˌti/ ‖ *usu.* **spe·cial·ty** /ˈspeʃəlti/ *AmE*— *n* **1** a special field of work or study: *Her speciality is ancient Greek poetry.* **2** [(**of**)] a particularly fine or excellent product: *I can recommend the vegetable pie — it's the* **speciality of the house.** (=restaurant)

spe·cial·ize also **-ise** *BrE* /ˈspeʃəlaɪz/ *v* [I (**in**)] to limit all or most of one's study, business, etc., to a particular activity or subject: *After she qualified as a lawyer, she decided to specialize in contract law.* | *a company that specializes in (producing) home computers* —**ization** /ˌspeʃəlaɪˈzeɪʃ*ə*n‖-lə-/ *n* [C;U] : *There is too much specialization of subjects too early in our schools.*

spe·cial·ized also **-ised** *BrE* /ˈspeʃəlaɪzd/ *adj* suitable or developed for one particular use: *Don't try doing it yourself; it requires specialized knowledge|highly specialized equipment.*

special li·cence /ˌ·· ˈ··/ *n law* an official permission given by the Church of England for a marriage at a time or place not usu. allowed

spe·cial·ly /ˈspeʃəli/ *adv* ESPECIALLY

special needs /ˌ·· ·ˈ·/ *n* [P] needs that a person has because they have particular mental or physical problems: *a school for children with special needs*

Special O·lym·pics /ˌ·· ·ˈ··/ [*the* +P] a number of sports events and games arranged for children and adults who have mental or physical problems: *A boy with Down's Syndrome won a gold medal in swimming in the Special Olympics.*

special plead·ing /ˌ·· ˈ·· / n [U] argument that unfairly fails to mention things that are unfavourable to a case

special re·la·tion·ship /ˌ·· ·ˈ··/ n the special close relationship between Britain and the US

special school /ˈ·· ˌ·/ n tech a school for children who have a disability of mind or body, where they are given special help

spe·cies /ˈspiːʃiːz/ n -cies **1** tech a division of animals or plants below a GENUS, which are alike in all important ways, and which can breed together to produce young of the same kind: *This rare bird has become an* **endangered species**. (=is in danger of becoming EXTINCT) **2** [(of)] infml a type; sort: *a strange species of car*

spe·cif·ic¹ /spɪˈsɪfɪk/ adj **1** detailed and exact; clear in meaning or explanation: *You say your factory is in England; can you be a bit more specific?* | *She gave us very specific instructions.* **2** [A] particular; fixed, determined, or named: *There's a specific tool for each job.* **3** [F+to] limited to; found only in: *This disease is specific to horses.* — ~**ity** /ˌspesɪˈfɪsəti/ n [U] fml

specific² n [(for)] tech a drug that has an effect on a particular disease —see also SPECIFICS

spe·cif·ic·al·ly /spɪˈsɪfɪkli/ adv **1** of the stated kind and no other; particularly: *The book was written specifically for children.* | *It is not a specifically Christian idea but is found in many religions.* **2** exactly and clearly: *The police specifically told you to avoid the main road, so why are you on it?* **3** speaking more exactly; NAMELY: *Several countries, specifically the US, Britain, and France, have signed the agreement.*

spe·ci·fi·ca·tion /ˌspesɪfɪˈkeɪʃən/ n **1** [C] also **specifications** pl.— a detailed plan or set of descriptions or directions: *The new missile has been built according to strict government specifications.* | *The designer drew up his specifications for the new car.* **2** [U (of)] the act of specifying

specific grav·i·ty /ˌ·,·· ˈ··/ n tech the weight of a substance divided by the weight of the amount of water that would fill the same space; DENSITY (2) compared with water

spe·cif·ics /spɪˈsɪfɪks/ n [P] matters to be decided exactly; details: *Now that we've agreed on the general principles, let's get down to specifics and formulate a plan.*

spe·ci·fy /ˈspesɪfaɪ/ v [T] to state exactly; describe fully so as to choose or name: *I specified blue for the bedroom walls, but the decorators have painted them white.* [+wh-] *Did you specify where the new office furniture was to be put?* [+that] *The rules clearly specify that competitors are not allowed to accept payment.*

spe·ci·men /ˈspesɪmɪn/ n **1** [(of)] a single typical thing or example: *This is a very fine specimen of the oak.* (=is a very fine OAK tree) **2** [(of)] a piece or amount of something for being shown, tested, etc.; SAMPLE: *The doctor will need a specimen of your blood.* | *The botanist mounted his specimens* (=pieces of plants) *on slides and examined them under a microscope.* **3** infml derog a person of the stated usu. undesirable kind: *Who's that revolting specimen your daughter's going out with?*

spe·cious /ˈspiːʃəs/ adj fml derog seeming right or correct but not so in fact: *a specious argument* | *specious logic* — compare SPURIOUS — ~**ly** adv — ~**ness** n [U]

speck /spek/ n [(of)] a very small piece, spot, or coloured mark: *I've got a speck of dirt on my shirt|a speck of dust in my eye.* | (fig.) *The car accelerated away and was soon just a speck on the horizon.* —see picture at PIECE

speck·le /ˈspekəl/ n a small irregular mark; coloured speck, esp. in a large number covering a surface —**led** adj : *speckled eggs*

spec·ta·cle /ˈspektəkəl/ n **1** a grand public show or scene: *The great military parade was a magnificent spectacle.* **2** [(of)] any unusual thing or situation to be seen and noticed: *We are now witnessing the curious spectacle of a government being attacked by its own supporters.* **3** an object of laughter, disrespect, or pity: *Take that ridiculous hat off and stop* **making a spectacle of** **yourself**.

spec·ta·cles /ˈspektəkəlz/ also **specs** /speks/ infml— n [P] rather fml GLASSES to help people to see: *I must get a new pair of spectacles|some new spectacles.* —see also **rose-coloured spectacles** (ROSE-COLOURED); see picture at GLASSES

spec·tac·u·lar¹ /spekˈtækjʊlərʳ/ adj unusually interesting or grand; attracting excited notice; very IMPRESSIVE: *There was a spectacular explosion when the firework factory blew up.* | *The new play was a spectacular success.* | *a spectacular waterfall* — ~**ly** adv

spectacular² n a spectacular entertainment: *a television spectacular with lots of famous stars*

spec·tate /spekˈteɪt‖ˈspekteɪt/ v [I (at)] to be present as a spectator; watch

spec·ta·tor /spekˈteɪtəʳ‖ˈspekteɪtər/ n a person who watches esp. an event or sport without taking part: *The big match attracted 25,000 spectators.* | *Football is our most popular* **spectator sport**. (=sport that people go and watch) —see ATTEND (USAGE)

Spectator [the] a magazine with high-quality WRITING about politics, CURRENT AFFAIRS, and the ARTS. It was started in 1711 by Joseph Addison and Sir Richard Steele. Different VERSIONS of it are sold in Britain and the US.

Spec·tor /ˈspektəʳ/, **Phil** /fɪl/ (1940–) an American popular music RECORD PRODUCER and songwriter

spec·tral /ˈspektrəl/ adj **1** of or like a spectre: *spectral writing|fingers* **2** [no comp.] tech of or made by a SPECTRUM (1,2)

spec·tre BrE ‖ **-ter** AmE /ˈspektəʳ/ n fml or lit **1** a spirit without a body; GHOST **2** [(of)] something that is seen in the imagination and causes fear: *The spectre of unemployment haunted|stalked the land.*

spec·tro·scope /ˈspektrəskəʊp/ n an apparatus for forming and looking at spectra (SPECTRUM (1)) —**scopic** /ˌspektrə-ˈskɒpɪk‖-ˈskɑː-/ adj

spec·tros·cop·y /spekˈtrɒskəpi‖-ˈtrɑː-/ n [U] the use of a spectroscope

spectrum

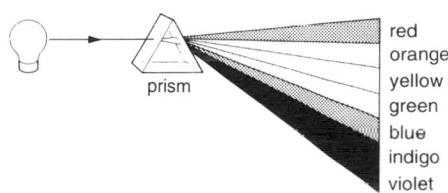

prism — red / orange / yellow / green / blue / indigo / violet

spec·trum /ˈspektrəm/ n -tra /trə/ **1** a set of bands of coloured light in the order of their WAVELENGTHs, into which a beam of light may be separated, e.g. by a PRISM (2): *Red and violet are at opposite ends of the spectrum.* **2** a range of any of various kinds of waves: *a radio|sound spectrum* **3** a broad and continuous range: *There's a wide spectrum of opinion(s) on this question.* | *Our speakers tonight come from both ends of the political spectrum.*

spec·u·late /ˈspekjʊleɪt/ v **1** [I (about, on); T+that; obj] to think about or talk about a matter without having the necessary facts; make guesses: *We don't know all the circumstances, so it would be pointless to speculate (on what happened).* | *The police are speculating that this incident may be linked to a similar attack two weeks ago.* **2** [I (in)] to buy or deal in goods, SHARES¹ (2), etc., whose future price is still uncertain, in the hope of a large profit: *He'd been speculating in gold shares, and lost a lot of money.* —**lator** n : *property speculators*

spec·u·la·tion /ˌspekjʊˈleɪʃən/ n [C;U] **1** (an example of) the act of speculating: *His remarks have led to intense speculation about the possibility of tax cuts.* | *She has dismissed the rumours of her resignation as pure speculation.* | *It's not a matter for speculation.* | [+that] *There's some speculation that the Prime Minister already knew of the scandal.* **2** (a case of) buying and selling in the hope of profit from price rises rather than from actual business earnings: *property speculation*

spec·u·la·tive /ˈspekjʊlətɪv‖-leɪtɪv/ adj **1** of or based on speculation: *a speculative guess|purchase* **2** [A no comp.] based on reason alone and not facts about the world: *speculative philosophy* — ~**ly** adv

sped /sped/ past tense & participle of SPEED

speech /spiːtʃ/ n **1** [U] the act or power of speaking; spoken language: *Only human beings are capable of speech.* | *She had a* **speech impediment.** (=could not speak properly) **2** [U] the way of speaking of a person or group: *I think young people are sometimes disrespectful|sloppy in their speech.* **3** [C (**to**)] an act of speaking formally to a group of listeners: *I had to* **give/make/deliver a speech** *to the Press Club.* | *The (text of the) minister's speech was sent to the newspapers in advance.* **4** [C] a usu. long set of lines for an actor to say in a play —see also DIRECT SPEECH, FIGURE OF SPEECH, INDIRECT SPEECH, PART OF SPEECH

speech day /ˈ· ·/ n a day once a year at a British school when parents come, speeches are made, and prizes are given out to children who have done well in their studies

spee·chi·fy /ˈspiːtʃɪfaɪ/ v [I] *infml derog* to make a speech or speeches, esp. in a proud self-important way

speech·less /ˈspiːtʃləs/ adj [(**with**)] unable for the moment to speak because of strong feeling, shock, etc.: *I was speechless with anger.* – – **ly** adv – **ness** n [U]

speech syn·the·siz·er /ˈ· ˌ····/ n a computer system that can produce sounds similar to those of human speech

speech ther·a·py /ˌ· ˈ···, ˌ· ˈ···/ n [U] treatment for helping people with various kinds of difficulties in speaking properly —**pist** n

speed[1] /spiːd/ n **1** [C;U] a (rate of movement) calculated by dividing the distance travelled by the time taken: *We were driving along at a slow but steady speed of about 30 mph.* | *This plane can reach speeds in excess of 2000 kilometres an hour.* | *We can't go any faster – we're already at top|full speed.* | *running|driving at* **breakneck speed** (=extremely fast) | *to travel at the speed of light|sound* **2** [U] quickness of movement or action: *When we're travelling* **at speed** (=fast) *the passing countryside just seems a blur.* | *Work is progressing* **at full|top speed.** (=as fast as possible) | *The train pulled out of the station and began to* **pick up|gather speed.** | *Everyone was surprised by the speed with which the dispute was settled.* | *The police are advising motorists to reduce speed because of the fog.* | *a course in speed-reading* (=fast reading) **3** [C] the degree to which photographic film is sensitive to light: *The speed of this film is too low for such dim light.* **4** [C] a GEAR[1] (1) on a car, bicycle, etc. (esp. in such phrases as **three/four/five-speed**): *a five-speed gearbox* **5** [U] *drug-users' sl for* AMPHETAMINE —see also HIGH-SPEED

speed[2] v **speeded** or **sped** /sped/ **1** [I+*adv/prep*; T+*obj+adv/prep*] to go, pass, or take quickly: *The holidays simply sped by.* | *We saw the thieves speeding off in their getaway car.* | *Security guards sped her to a waiting helicopter.* **2** [I usu. in progressive forms] to go or drive too fast; break the speed limit: *Was I really speeding, officer?* **3 speed someone on their way** to be present at the start of someone's journey to say goodbye
    speed up phr v [I;T(=**speed** sthg.↔**up**)] to (cause to) move, go, or happen faster: *We'd better speed up if we want to get there in time.* | *Production of the new model must be speeded up.* | *The new system will speed up the process of applying for a passport.* —**speed-up** /ˈ· ·/ n

speed·boat /ˈspiːdbəʊt/ n a small power-driven boat built for high speed

speed bump /ˈ· ˌ·/ n *AmE for* SLEEPING POLICEMAN

speed·ing /ˈspiːdɪŋ/ n the offence of driving faster than the legal limit: *She was found guilty of speeding and fined £50.*

speed lim·it /ˈ· ˌ··/ n the fastest speed allowed by law on a particular stretch of road
    ▶ CULTURAL NOTE In Britain the speed limit for driving on MOTORWAYS is 70 mph (= miles per hour) and the speed limit for driving in towns is 30 mph unless there is a traffic sign showing a different speed. In the US the speed limit on FREEWAYS is 55 mph, some HIGHWAYS have a speed limit of 65 mph, and the speed limit for driving on most city streets is usu. 35 mph. *You must keep within/not exceed the speed limit.* | *The police imposed a speed limit of 30 mph.* ◀

speed of light /ˌ· · ˈ·/ [*the*] the speed at which light travels through space, which is 186,000 miles or 300,000 km per second

speed of sound /ˌ· · ˈ·/ n [*the*] the speed at which sound travels, which varies according to what it is travelling

through. It travels through the air at sea level, when the temperature is 0°C, at a rate of 1,088 feet or 331.6 metres per second.

speed·om·e·ter /spɪˈdɒmɪtər, spiː-‖-ˈdɑː-/ also **spee·do** /ˈspiːdəʊ/*BrE infml*— n an instrument in a vehicle for showing how fast it is going —see picture at CAR

speed trap /ˈ· ·/ n a stretch of road watched by hidden policemen to catch drivers going too fast

speed·way /ˈspiːdweɪ/ n [C;U] (the sport of racing motorcycles or cars on) a closed racing track

speed·well /ˈspiːdwel/ n [U] a small European wild plant with light blue or white flowers

speed·y /ˈspiːdi/ adj going, working, or happening quickly or without delay: *a speedy little car.* | *The accusations brought a speedy denial.* | *We sent him a card that said "Best wishes for a speedy recovery".* —**ily** adv —**iness** n [U]

spe·le·ol·o·gy /ˌspiːliˈɒlədʒi‖-ˈɑːlə-/ n [U] **1** the scientific study of CAVES **2** *fml* the sport of walking and climbing in CAVES —**gist** n —**gical** /ˌspiːliəˈlɒdʒɪkəl‖-ˈlɑː-/ adj

spell[1] /spel/ v **spelt** /spelt/ *esp. BrE* ‖ **spelled** *esp. AmE* **1** [I;T] to form (a word or words) by writing or naming letters in the correct order: *children learning to spell* | *The Americans spell some words differently from the British.* | *"How do you spell your name?" "I spell it S-M-Y-T-H."* **2** [T *no pass.*] (of letters in order) to form (a word): *B-O-O-K spells "book".* **3** [T] *infml* to add up to (a usu. unpleasant result); mean: *This development could spell disaster for the steel industry.* — **er** n : *I've always been a bad speller.*
    spell sthg. **out** phr v [T] **1** to write or say (a word) letter by letter: *He spelt his name out for me.* **2** to explain in the clearest or most detailed way: *a report that spells out the government's plans for housing* | *I should have thought it was obvious, but if you want me to spell it out for you – I'm leaving you.* **3** *AmE* to write a whole word and not shorten it: *There are few occasions when Mr. or Jr. should be spelled out instead of abbreviated.*

spell[2] n **1** an unbroken period of time, esp. taken up with the stated activity, events, etc.: *There will be spells of sunshine|sunny spells this afternoon.* | *I had|did a spell in the army before I became a policeman.* | *After a short spell in hospital she was soon back at work.* **2** a usu. quickly-passing period of illness of the stated kind: *a coughing spell* | *a dizzy spell* **3** (in cricket) a period of bowling (BOWL[2] (16)) by a particular bowler: *Botham had a good spell after lunch.*

spell[3] n **1** [S] a condition caused by magical power; ENCHANTMENT: *The witch put the princess under a spell, and she fell asleep for ten years.* | (fig.) *The audience was hostile at first, but soon fell under the spell of her charming personality.* **2** [C] the magic words producing this condition: *to cast a spell over someone*

spell[4] v **spelled** [T] *esp. AustrE & AmE* to take the turn of; allow (someone else) to rest by taking over their work: *Let me spell you on duty so that you can have your coffee break.*

spell·bind /ˈspelbaɪnd/ v **-bound** /baʊnd/ [T] to hold the complete attention of; FASCINATE: *The children watched spellbound as the magician produced rabbits and pigeons from his hat.* | *a spellbinding performance* – **er** n

spel·ler /ˈspelər/ also **spelling book** /ˈ·· ·/ – n *AmE* a book which helps teach children to spell words correctly

spell·ing /ˈspelɪŋ/ n **1** [U] the action of forming words correctly from letters, or the ability to do this: *Her spelling has improved.* **2** [C] an ordered set of letters forming a word: *The British and American spellings of "colour" are different.*

spelling bee /ˈ·· ˌ·/ n *AmE* a competition in which the winner is the person or group which correctly spells aloud the most words

spelt /spelt/ *past tense & participle of* SPELL

spe·lunk /spɪˈlʌŋk/ v [I] *AmE* to go into rooms and passages under the ground (CAVES) as a sport —**ing** n : *He goes spelunking on weekends.* —**er** n

Spence /spens/, **Sir Basil** (1907–76) a Scottish ARCHITECT best known as the architect of Coventry Cathedral

spend /spend/ v **spent** /spent/ **1** [I;T (**on**)] to give out (money or something used instead of money) in payment for goods or services: *I'm good at spending but not at* saving. | *There will have to be big cuts in government spending.* | *They spend a lot of money on advertising.* | *He spent all his winnings on a slap-up meal.* | *Would you spend £200 on a new coat?* | *The repairs cost quite a lot, but it was* **money well spent.** (=a sensible way of spending money) **2** [T+*obj*+*v-ing*/*adv*/*prep*] to pass or use (time): *We spent a pleasant hour or two talking with our friends.* | *He's spent half his life writing this book.* | *Where shall we spend our holidays?* | *He spent three years in prison.* **3** [T] *esp. lit* to wear out or use completely: *The storm soon spent itself/its force.* **4 spend a penny** *BrE euph for* URINATE

spend·a·hol·ic /ˌspendəˈhɒlɪk‖-ˈhɔː-/ also **compulsive shopper**– *n AmE* a person who is unable to stop spending money and buying more and more things

spend·er /ˈspendər/ *n* a person who spends money in the stated amounts or ways: *This is a shop for* **big spenders.** (=is an expensive shop)

Spender, Sir Ste·phen /ˈstiːvən/ (1909–) an English poet and CRITIC whose books of poetry include *The Still Centre* and *The Generous Days*

spending mon·ey /ˈ··· ˌ·/ *n* [U] POCKET MONEY

spend·thrift /ˈspendˌθrɪft/ *n derog* a person who spends money wastefully; EXTRAVAGANT person

Spen·ser /ˈspensər/, **Ed·mund** /ˈedmənd/ (?1552–99) an English poet famous esp. for his EPIC poem *The Faerie Queene* which he never finished

spent¹ /spent/ *past tense & participle of* SPEND

spent² *adj* **1** already used; no longer for use: *spent cartridges* | *spent fuel rods from a nuclear-power plant* | (fig.) *Do you think Scottish nationalism is now a* **spent force?** (=no longer has power or influence) **2** [F] *lit* worn out; extremely tired

sperm /spɜːm‖spɜːrm/ *n* **sperm** *or* **sperms** **1** [C] a cell produced by the sex organs of a male animal, which usu. swims in a liquid and is able to unite with the female egg to produce new life **2** [U] the liquid from the male sex organs in which these swim; SEMEN

sper·ma·cet·i /ˌspɜːməˈseti‖-ɜːr-/ *n* [U] a solid oily substance found in the head of the sperm whale and used in making skin creams, candles, etc.

sper·ma·to·zo·a /ˌspɜːmətəˈzəʊə‖-ɜːr-/ *n* **-zoon** /ˈzəʊən/ *sing.* [P] *tech* sperms

sperm bank /ˈ· ˌ·/ *n* a place in which SEMEN is kept to be used in medical operations to help women to become PREGNANT

sper·mi·cide /ˈspɜːmɪˌsaɪd‖ˈspɜːr-/ *n* [C;U] a substance that kills sperms, used as a cream or liquid during the sex act for stopping women from becoming PREGNANT

sperm whale /ˈ· ·/ *n* a large WHALE which is hunted for the oil in its very large head, for fat, and for spermaceti

Sper·ry /ˈsperi/, **El·mer Am·brose** /ˈelmər ˈæmbrəʊz/ (1860–1930) an American engineer and inventor who developed several ways to help ships to stay on course, such as the Sperry AUTOPILOT

spew /spjuː/ *v* **1** [I+*adv*/*prep*;T ˌ*obj*+*adv*/*prep*] to (cause to) come out in a rush or flood: *Lava spewed forth from the volcano.* | *The burst pipe was spewing out dirty water.* | *a factory spewing toxic fumes into the atmosphere* **2** [I; T (UP)] *BrE sl for* VOMIT

SPF /ˌes piː ˈef/ Sun Protection Factor; a number which is written on a bottle of SUNTAN cream to show how much protection it gives from the sun. For example, SPF 15 gives high protection and SPF 3 gives low protection.

sphag·num /ˈsfægnəm/ *n* [C;U] any of a large group of MOSSes *growing in wet areas which can go to make up* PEAT and which are used by gardeners for packing plants

sphere /sfɪər/ *n* **1** a round shape in space; ball-shaped mass; solid figure all points of which are equally distant from a centre: *The Earth is not a perfect sphere.* **2** an area or range of interest or activity: *a well-known personality in the sphere of broadcasting* | *Government is extending its* **sphere of influence** *to cover all parts of our lives.* **3** *old use or lit* any of the transparent shells containing stars, PLANETs, etc., that were formerly thought to turn around the Earth

-sphere see WORD FORMATION

spher·i·cal /ˈsferɪkəl/ *adj* having the shape of a sphere; ball-shaped

sphe·roid /ˈsfɪərɔɪd/ *n tech* a shape which is not quite a sphere, esp. one that is slightly longer in one direction and has two endpoints

sphinc·ter /ˈsfɪŋktər/ *n med* a muscle which surrounds and can tighten to close a passage in the body: *the anal sphincter*

sphinx /sfɪŋks/ *n* an ancient Egyptian image of a lion, lying down, with a human head

Sphinx [*the*] **1** a very large and ancient sphinx at Al Jizah in Egypt which many people go to see **2** in GREEK MYTHOLOGY, a creature with the head of a woman and the body of a lion. She lay outside Thebes and killed people who could not answer her RIDDLE (=very difficult question). Oedipus answered the riddle, and the Sphinx killed herself.

spic, spik /spɪk/ *n AmE derog sl* a Spanish-speaking American, esp. a Puerto Rican (considered extremely offensive)

spice¹ /spaɪs/ *n* **1** [C;U] any of various vegetable products used, esp. in powder form, for giving a taste to other foods: *Pepper and nutmeg are spices.* | *a spice rack* **2** [S;U] interest or excitement, esp. as added to something else: *He put in a few risqué stories to add spice to the speech.* | *They say* **variety is the spice of life.** (=makes life more interesting)

spice² *v* [T (UP, with)] to add spice to

spick-and-span /ˌspɪk ən ˈspæn/ *adj* (of a room, house, etc.) completely clean and tidy again

Spiderman

spic·y /ˈspaɪsi/ *adj* **1** having or producing a pleasantly strong taste and smell; containing or tasting like SPICE (1): *hot spicy food* **2** exciting, esp. from being slightly shocking or rude: *spicy stories* —**·ily** *adv* —**·iness** *n* [U]

spi·der /ˈspaɪdər/ *n* a small eight-legged creature which makes silk threads, usu. into COBWEBS for catching insects to eat

Spi·der·man /ˈspaɪdəmæn‖-dər/ an imaginary HERO of COMIC STRIPS and films who is able to climb very high walls like a SPIDER and catch criminals in a WEB which he throws over them —compare SUPERMAN

spider

spi·der·web /ˈspaɪdəweb‖-dər-/ *n AmE for* COBWEB

spi·der·y /ˈspaɪdəri/ *adj* long and thin like a spider's legs: *the old lady's spidery writing*

spiel /ʃpiːl, spiːl/ *n* [C;U] *sl, usu. derog* fast talk, esp. intended to persuade: *the salesman's spiel*

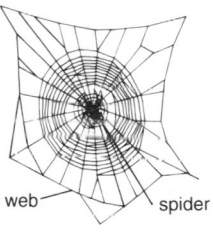
web   spider

Spiel·berg /ˈspiːlbɜːg‖-bɜːrg/, **Ste·ven** /ˈstiːvən/ (1946–) an American film DIRECTOR who has made many very popular films, including *Jaws, ET, Raiders of the Lost Ark,* and *Empire of the Sun.* His films are well-known for being very fast-moving and full of exciting action.

spig·ot /ˈspɪgət/ *n* **1** an apparatus for turning on and off a flow of liquid from a container, esp. a barrel **2** *esp. AmE* an outdoor TAP

spik /spɪk/ *n a* SPIC

spike¹ /spaɪk/ *n* **1** something long and thin with a sharp point, esp. a pointed piece of metal: *spikes along the top of a fence* **2** any of the metal points fixed in the bottom of a shoe for holding the ground, esp. in sports **3** *tech* (on a GRAPH) a sharp, esp. upward, point describing a change **4** the head of a grain-producing plant such as corn or wheat

spike² *v* [T] **1** to drive a spike or spikes into **2** [(with)] to add a strong alcoholic drink to (a weak or nonalcoholic one) **3** to stop (esp. an article in a newspaper) from being printed or spread: *The editor spiked the story.* | *The government spiked the rumour.* **4 spike someone's guns** *BrE infml* to prevent someone from attacking; take away an opponent's power

spik·y /'spaɪki/ *adj* **1** having long sharp points: *a spiky cactus* **2** *BrE infml* easily offended or annoyed

spill¹ /spɪl/ *v* **spilt** /spɪlt/ *esp. BrE* ‖ **spilled** *esp. AmE* — **1** [I;T] to (cause to) pour out accidentally, esp. over the edge of a container: *She slipped and the wine spilt all over her skirt.* | *I'm afraid I've spilt some coffee on the rug.* **2** [I+*adv/prep*, esp. OVER] to spread beyond limits: *The crowd spilt over from the church into the streets.* | *There is a danger that the conflict will spill over into the neighbouring towns.* —see also OVERSPILL **3** [T *often pass.*] *esp. lit* to cause (blood) to flow by wounding or killing: *A lot of blood was spilled in that battle.* **4 spill the beans** *infml* to tell a secret too soon or to the wrong person — see also **cry over spilt milk** (CRY)

spill² *n* **1** also **spill·age** /'spɪlɪdʒ/— an act or amount of spilling: *oil spills* **2** *infml* a fall from a horse, bicycle, etc.: *She had a nasty spill when her horse shied.*

spill³ *n* a thin piece of wood or twisted paper for lighting lamps, pipes, etc.

spill·way /'spɪlweɪ/ *n* a passage for water over or around a DAM (=wall for holding back water)

spin¹ /spɪn/ *v* **span** /spæn/ *BrE or* **spun** /spʌn/, **spun**; *present participle* **spinning 1** [I;T] to (cause to) turn round and round fast: *The wheel was spinning on its axle.* | *The teacher spun round to see who had spoken.* | *The steam spins a turbine to produce electricity.* | *The washing machine's spinning at the moment.* (=the part which contains the clothes is turning round fast to remove the water) | *We span the coin to see who would have first turn.* | (fig.) *I'd drunk so much my head was spinning.* (=I felt ill and faint) **2** [I;T] to make (thread) by twisting (cotton, wool, etc.): *Before weaving we spin the thread/spin the wool into thread.* | *a spinning mill* | (fig.) *The old sea captain sat by the fire* **spinning yarns.** (=telling stories) —see also SPINNING WHEEL **3** [T] to produce in a thread-like form: *This machine spins fibreglass.* | *The spider spins a web to catch flies.* | *spun gold/nylon* **4** [I+*adv/prep*] *infml* to move fast on wheels: *We were spinning along at 80 miles per hour.*

spin sthg↔**off** *phr v* [T] **1** to produce as a SPIN-OFF **2** *esp. AmE* to form (a separate, partly-independent company) from parts of an existing company

spin sthg. ↔ **out** *phr v* [T (**over**)] **1** *derog* to make (something) last an unnecessarily long time: *He span out his farewells so much that I thought he was never going.* | *She tried to spin the job out over two days.* **2** to cause to last as long as possible: *I've only got £10, and we've got to spin it out over the whole week.*

spin² *n* **1** [C] an act of spinning: *Try your luck on a spin of the wheel!* (=at a game of ROULETTE) **2** [S;U] fast turning movement: *a spin of ten turns per second* | *to put a lot of spin on a tennis ball when hitting it* | *I'll just give the washing a quick spin* (i.e. remove the water by putting it in a washing machine and causing it to turn round very fast) **3** [C] *infml* a short trip for pleasure, esp. in a car: *Let's go for a spin in my new car.* **4** [C] also **tailspin** *AmE* a steep circular fall by an aircraft: *The plane went into/came out of a spin.* **5** [S] *infml* a steep drop: *The bad news sent stock-market prices into a spin.* **6** [S] *BrE infml* a state of confused anxiety; PANIC: *He's really got himself into a spin over his driving test.* —see also FLAT SPIN **7** [S] *AmE infml* a way of providing information which makes it seem favourable to a particular person or political party: *They're trying to put a positive spin on the latest unemployment figures.* **8** [S] a property of an ELEMENTARY PARTICLE which influences its behaviour with other particles

spi·na bif·i·da /ˌspaɪnə 'bɪfɪdə/ *n* [U] *med* a serious condition in which the SPINE (1) is split down the middle from birth, leaving the spinal cord unprotected

spin·ach /'spɪnɪdʒ, -ɪtʃ‖-ɪtʃ/ *n* [U] a vegetable whose soft loose green leaves can be eaten and which contains a lot of IRON.

▶CULTURAL NOTE Children are sometimes told to eat spinach even if they do not like the taste because it is believed to be very good for their health. In a well-known CARTOON, the character Popeye eats spinach to make him strong. —see also POPEYE◀

spin·al /'spaɪnl/ *adj* of or for the SPINE (1): *spinal disease*

spinal col·umn /ˈ··· ˌ··/ *n* SPINE

spinal cord /ˌ··· ˈ·/ *n* the thick cord of nerves enclosed in

the SPINE (1) by which messages are carried to and from the brain

spin·dle /'spɪndl/ *n* **1** a machine part round which something turns **2** a round pointed rod used for twisting the thread in spinning

spin·dly /'spɪndli/ *adj* (esp. of a leg) long, thin, and weak-looking: *The young horse was standing unsteadily on its spindly legs.* | *spindly rose bushes*

spin doc·tor /ˈ· ˌ··/ *n esp. AmE infml* a person who makes information or events seem favourable to someone, esp. to a politician: *The White House spin doctors are hard at work explaining the President's about-face on taxes.*

spin-dry /ˌ· ˈ·/ *v* [T] *esp. BrE* to remove most of the water from (washed clothes) in a special machine (**spin-dryer** /ˌ· ˈ··/) that spins round and round very fast

spine /spaɪn/ *n* **1** also **backbone, spinal col·umn** /ˌ··· ˈ··/ *fml* — the row of bones in the centre of the back of human beings and certain animals that supports the body and protects the SPINAL CORD —see picture at SKELETON **2** a stiff sharp-pointed plant or animal part; PRICKLE: *a hedgehog's/cactus's spines* —see also SPINY, and see picture at HEDGEHOG **3** the part of a book where the pages are fastened and the title is usu. printed

spine-chil·ling /ˈ· ˌ··/ *adj* very frightening but in a way that people enjoy: *a spine-chilling ghost story/horror movie*

spine·less /'spaɪnləs/ *adj* **1** *derog* without moral strength or courage: *I was too spineless to stand up to the boss, so I ended up working all weekend.* **2** (of an animal) having no SPINE (1) — ~ **ly** *adv* — ~ **ness** *n* [U]

spi·net /spɪ'net‖'spɪnət/ *n* a small HARPSICHORD

spin·na·ker /'spɪnəkər/ *n* a large three-sided sail that has a rounded shape when blown out by the wind, carried on some racing boats for going with the force of the wind —see picture at YACHT

spin·ner /'spɪnər/ *n* **1** a person who SPINs thread for cloth **2 a** a cricket ball thrown with a spinning action **b** a BOWLER of such balls **3** a BAIT for catching fish that goes round and round when pulled through the water **4** (in some games) a movable pointer which is spun and stops at a point showing the number, kind, etc., of moves to be made —see also MONEY-SPINNER

spin·ney /'spɪni/ *n BrE* a small area full of trees and low-growing plants; COPSE

spinning jen·ny /ˈ··· ˌ··/ *n* an industrial machine of former times allowing one person to spin a number of threads at once

spinning wheel /ˈ··· ·/ *n* a small machine used esp. formerly at home to SPIN thread, in which a foot-driven wheel moves a SPINDLE

spin-off /ˈ· ·/ *n* **1** a usu. useful product or result of a process other than the main one; BY-PRODUCT —see also SPIN **off** **2** *AmE* a television programme involving characters which were originally in another programme: *The spin-off from "The Cosby Show" about the daughter at college wasn't on for very long.*

spin·ster /'spɪnstər/ *n sometimes derog* an unmarried woman, usu. one who is no longer young and/or seems unlikely to marry —compare BACHELOR — ~ **hood** *n* [U]

spin the bot·tle /ˌ· · ˈ··/ *n* [U] a game in which one person of a group sitting in a circle spins a bottle in the middle and receives a kiss from the person of the opposite sex at whom the bottle points when it stops spinning

spin·y /'spaɪni/ *adj* like or full of SPINEs (2): *a fish's spiny fins*

spi·ral¹ /'spaɪərəl/ *adj* in the form of a curve winding round and round a central point and continually moving closer towards it or further away from it: *a spiral watch-spring* | *a spiral nebula*

spiral² *n* **1** a spiral curve **2** a process of continuous upward or downward movement: *We are in danger of getting into an* **inflationary spiral.**

spirals

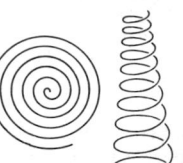

spiral³ *v* **-ll-** *BrE* ‖ **-l-** *AmE* [I] **1** [+*adv/prep*] to move in a spiral course; rise or fall in a winding way: *The stairs spiralled round the central* pillar. | *The damaged plane spiralled to earth.* **2** to fall or esp. rise continuously: *the spiralling cost of legal services*

spiral stair·case /ˌ··ˈ···/ *n* a set of stairs in the form of a spiral, built around a central COLUMN. They are found esp. in castles, churches, or large houses.

spire /spaɪə^r/ *n* a roof rising steeply to a point on top of a tower, esp. on a church; (the top of a) STEEPLE —see also DREAMING SPIRES

spir·it¹ /ˈspɪrɪt/ *n* **1** [C] the part of a person's mind that is able to think and is **a** talked about as clearly opposed to the body: *He was tortured by the secret police; but they could not break his spirit.* | (fig.) *I can't come to your wedding, but I'll be there* **in spirit**. (=I'll be thinking about you at the time when it happens) **b** thought of as remaining alive, esp. without appearing in physical form: *He is dead, but his spirit lives on.* | *She was possessed by evil spirits.* —compare SOUL¹ (1); see also HOLY SPIRIT; see also **the spirit is willing but the flesh is weak** (FLESH) **2** [S (**of**)] the central quality or force of something: *He came to the party, but didn't really* **enter into the spirit** *of it.* (=did not try to enjoy it) | *You should try to obey* **the spirit of the law** (=the law's real intention) *even if you don't always follow its letter.* (=what it actually says) **3** [S] an intention or feeling in the mind; ATTITUDE: *I hope you will take my remarks in the spirit in which they were intended, and not be offended.* | *They came to the meeting in a spirit of genuine reconciliation.* **4** [U] *apprec* a quality of lively determination or brave effort: *She played the sonata with great spirit.* | *He fell over several times but, with considerable spirit, got up and finished the race.* **5** [U] strongly-felt loyalty to the stated group of which one is a member: *team/community spirit* —see also PUBLIC SPIRIT **6** [C] a person thought of because of a particular quality or activity: *one of the leading spirits of the party* **7** also **spirits** *pl.* — [C] a strong alcoholic drink produced by distillation (DISTIL): *Whisky is a spirit, and so is brandy.* | *I never drink spirits.* **8** also **spirits** *pl.*— [U] any of various liquids, such as alcohol, used esp. for breaking down solids or as FUELs —see also METHYLATED SPIRITS, WHITE SPIRIT **9** **-spirited** /ˈspɪrɪtɪd/ having the stated feelings or SPIRITS: *mean-spirited* | *public-spirited* | *high-spirited* —see also LOW-SPIRITED, SPIRITS

spirit² *v* [T+*obj*+*adv/prep*] to take in a secret or mysterious way: *The actress was spirited off/away in a car before the reporters could get to her.*

spir·it·ed /ˈspɪrɪtɪd/ *adj apprec* full of SPIRIT¹ (4); forceful: *a spirited quarrel* | *a spirited defence of his policies* | *a spirited horse*

spir·it·less /ˈspɪrɪtləs/ *adj* **1** weak or lazy; without SPIRIT¹ (4) **2** sad; not cheerful; in low SPIRITS — **~ness** *n* [U]

spirit lev·el /ˈ···ˌ···/ ‖ also **level** *AmE*— *n* a tool for testing whether a surface is level, made of a bar containing a short glass tube of liquid with a BUBBLE which will be in the centre if the surface is level

Spirit of St. Lou·is /ˌspɪrɪt əv sənt ˈluːi‖-seɪnt ˈluːəs/, **The** the aircraft in which Charles Lindbergh made the first flight by one person across the Atlantic Ocean

spir·its /ˈspɪrɪts/ *n* [P] the cheerful or sad state of one's mind: *Their letters of support raised my spirits.* | *He was* **in high/low spirits**. (=cheerful/not cheerful)

spir·i·tu·al¹ /ˈspɪrɪtʃuəl/ *adj* **1** of the spirit rather than the body: *one's spiritual nature* | *The priest is responsible for your spiritual welfare.* **2** religious: *an adviser in spiritual matters* **3** [A] related or close in spirit; connected by qualities or interests of a deep kind: *She's English, but India is her* **spiritual home**. **4** [after *n*] *fml* of the church: **the lords spiritual** (=BISHOPS) *sit in Parliament.* —compare TEMPORAL (1) — **~ly** *adv*

spiritual² *n* a religious song of the type sung originally by the black people of the US

spir·i·tual·is·m /ˈspɪrɪtʃuəlɪzəm/ *n* [U] the belief that the dead may send messages to living people usu. through a MEDIUM (=person with special powers) —**ist** *n*: *a spiritualist seance* —**istic** /ˌspɪrɪtʃuˈlɪstɪk◂/ *adj*

spir·i·tu·al·i·ty /ˌspɪrɪtʃuˈælɪti/ *n* [U] the quality of being interested in spiritual or religious matters, worship, prayer, etc.; DEVOTION

spir·i·tu·ous /ˈspɪrɪtʃuəs/ *adj* [A] *fml or tech* being or containing alcohol: *spirituous liquors*

spit¹ /spɪt/ *v* **spat** /spæt/ also **spit** *AmE*; *present participle*

---

spitting 1 [I(**at, on**); T (**OUT**)] to throw out (liquid or other contents) from the mouth with force: *He spat at his opponent contemptuously.* | *I didn't want to eat the pips so I spat them out.* | *He's very ill and spitting blood.* **2** [T (**OUT**)] to say or express sharply or angrily, as if spitting: *She spat out her reply.* **3** [*it*+I (**with**)] *esp. BrE* to rain very lightly: *We can't go out yet; it's still spitting (with rain).* **4** [I] (esp. of a fire or something cooking) to make small explosions; SPUTTER: *The sausages were spitting in the pan.* **5 spit it out** [*usu. imperative*] *infml* to say openly and without delay what one is thinking or worrying about

spit² *n* **1** [U] the liquid in the mouth; SALIVA **2** [*the*+**of**] the exact likeness: *That boy is the spit of his father.* —see also SPITTING IMAGE

spit³ *n* **1** a thin pointed rod for sticking meat onto and turning, for cooking over a fire: *A huge side of beef was slowly roasting on the spit.* **2** a small usu. sandy point of land running out into a stretch of water

Spit·al·fields /ˈspɪtlfiːldz/ *a* part of E London, where there was a market for fruit, vegetables, and meat. The old market has been closed and is being moved to another place.

spit and pol·ish /ˌ· · ˈ··/ *n* [U] *infml* great attention to a clean and shiny appearance, esp. in the army, navy, etc.

spit and saw·dust /ˌ· · ˈ··/ *adj* [A] *BrE infml* (of PUBS) simple, rough, and dirty

spit·ball /ˈspɪtbɔːl/ *n AmE* **1** a small piece of paper which has been shaped into a ball and made wet with SALIVA: *The boys were throwing spitballs when the teacher came back to the classroom.* **2** a BASEBALL which has been made wet with SALIVA so that it moves in an unusual way: *The rules of baseball do not allow a pitcher to throw spitballs.*

spite¹ /spaɪt/ *n* [U] **1** an unpleasant desire to annoy or harm another person, esp. in some small way: *I'm sure he took my parking space just* **out of/from spite**. —see also SPITEFUL **2 in spite of** taking no notice of, or not prevented by; DESPITE: *I went out in spite of the rain.* | *In spite of a slight improvement in sales, the company is still making a loss.*

spite² *v* [T] to annoy or harm (someone) intentionally, esp. in some small way: *I'm sure he took my parking space just to spite me.*

spite·ful /ˈspaɪtfəl/ *adj* showing spite or full of spite: *a nasty spiteful little boy* | *It was very spiteful of her to do that.* — **~ly** *adv* — **~ness** *n* [U]

spit·fire /ˈspɪtfaɪə^r/ *n infml* a person, esp. a woman, with a fierce temper

Spitfire *n* an aircraft flown by the British in the Second World War

spitting im·age /ˌ·· ˈ··/ *n* [*the*+**of**] an exact likeness: *It's incredible; she's the spitting image of her mother!*

Spitting Image a British television programme in which rubber models of well-known people act out recent news or political events in a humorous way

Spitting Image

spit·tle /ˈspɪtl/ *n* [U] SPIT² (1)

spit·toon /spɪˈtuːn/ ‖ also **cus·pidor** *AmE*— *n* a container set on the floor in a public room, esp. formerly, for spitting (SPIT¹) into. In Britain and North America, spittoons are rarely found now as it is considered rude to spit.

Spitz /spɪts/, **Mark** (1950–) an American swimmer who won seven gold MEDALs at the Olympic Games in Munich in 1972

spiv /spɪv/ *n BrE infml derog* a man who lives by cheating society, making money in small rather dishonest ways

splash¹ /splæʃ/ *v* **1** [I+*adv/prep*;T+*obj*+*adv/prep*] **a** (of a liquid) to fall, hit, or move noisily, in drops, waves, etc.: *The rain splashed on/against the window.* **b** to cause (a liquid) to do this: *She splashed cologne all over her body.|I'm afraid I've splashed a bit of coffee on the carpet.* **2** [T (**with**)] to throw or scatter a liquid against (something): *He splashed his face with cold water to try to wake himself up.* **3** [I] to move noisily in a liquid, making it fly about: *The children were splashing about in the* *bath.* | *to walk along, splashing through the puddles* **4** [T] *infml* to give a lot of space to (a news story); report as if very important: *The paper splashed the story on page one.* | *Her name was splashed across the front page.* **5** [I;T (OUT, on)] *infml, esp. BrE* to spend (a lot of money) on nice but unnecessary things: *I splashed out (£300) on a new television.* | *She doesn't mind splashing her money about.*

splash down *phr v* [I] (esp. of a spacecraft) to land in the sea —see also SPLASHDOWN

splash² *n* **1** a splashing act, movement, or noise: *They dived into the water with a splash.* **2** a mark made by splashing: *There's a splash of paint on the floor.* | *These flowers bring a* **splash of colour** *into the room.* **3** *infml* a forceful, favourable, and noticeable effect: *His first novel* **made (quite) a splash.** | *a splash of publicity* **4** *esp. BrE* a small added amount of liquid, esp. to a drink: *Just a splash of soda, please.*

splash³ *adv* [+*prep*] *infml* with a splash: *It fell splash into the lake.*

splash-down /ˈsplæʃdaʊn/ *n* [C;U] (a) landing by a spacecraft in the sea: *Apollo 16 has made a successful splashdown in the Pacific.* —see also SPLASH **down**

splash guard /ˈ·ˌ·/ *n AmE for* MUDFLAP —see picture at CAR

splash·y /ˈsplæʃi/ *adj esp. AmE* big, bright, and very noticeable; FLASHY

splat¹ /splæt/ *n* [S] *infml* a noise like something wet hitting a surface and being flattened

splat² *v* -**tt**- [I;T (**against**)] *infml* to (cause to) make a splat: *The tomatoes splatted against the windscreen.*

splat·ter /ˈsplætəʳ/ *v* [I;T] to SPLASH with small drops of liquid; SPATTER

splatter mov·ie /ˈ·· ˌ·/ *n AmE* a film in which there are many frightening murders or accidents which are very bloody

splay /spleɪ/ *v* [I;T (OUT)] to spread out, esp. in an unnatural and awkward way: *The table suddenly collapsed, its four legs splaying out.* | *She splayed out her fingers.*

splay·foot·ed /ˈspleɪfʊtɪd/ *adj* having very flat spread-out feet

spleen /spliːn/ *n* **1** [C] a small organ near the upper end of the stomach that controls the quality of the blood supply and produces certain blood cells **2** [U] *lit or fml* violent anger, esp. expressed suddenly: *When I get so frustrated and angry, I have to* **vent my spleen on** (=let my anger out towards) *someone.*

splen·did /ˈsplendɪd/ *adj* **1** grand in appearance or style; causing admiration; IMPRESSIVE: *The walls were hung with splendid silks and tapestries.* | *Their wedding was a splendid affair.* **2** very fine; excellent: *We had a splendid holiday.* – – **ly** *adv* : *Joe and my father are getting along splendidly.*

splen·dif·er·ous /splenˈdɪfərəs/ *adj BrE infml humor* splendid

splen·dour *BrE* ‖ -**dor** *AmE* /ˈsplendəʳ/ *also* **splendours** *pl.*– *n* [U] excellent or grand beauty: *We admired the splendour of the mountain scenery.* | *the faded splendours of the old Majestic Hotel*

sple·net·ic /splɪˈnetɪk/ *adj lit* bad-tempered; habitually angry or unpleasant

splice¹ /splaɪs/ *v* [T] **1** [(**to, onto, TOGETHER**)] to join (two things) together end to end to make one continuous length, e.g. by weaving (ropes), sticking (pieces of film), etc.: *The tape in this cassette is broken; can you splice the ends together?* **2** [*usu. pass.*] *BrE infml* to join in marriage: *It's twelve years now since we got spliced.*

splice² *n* an act or place of joining end to end

splic·er /ˈsplaɪsəʳ/ *n* an apparatus for joining pieces of film or recording TAPE together neatly

splint /splɪnt/ *n* a flat piece of wood, metal, etc., used for keeping a broken bone in position while it mends

splin·ter¹ /ˈsplɪntəʳ/ *n* [(**of**)] a small sharp-pointed piece, esp. of wood, broken off something: *I got a splinter in my finger while I was sawing the wood.* | *Some splinters of glass had got into his eye.* —see also picture at PIECE

splinter² *v* **1** [I;T] to (cause to) break into small, sharp-pointed pieces —compare SHATTER **2** [I (OFF)] to separate from a larger organization or become divided into separate parts or groups

splinter group /ˈ·· ˌ·/ *n* a group of people that has separated from a larger body: *After the leader's controversial speech, several splinter groups left the movement in protest.*

split¹ /splɪt/ *v* **split**; *present participle* **splitting** **1** [I;T] to (cause to) divide along a length, esp. with force or by a blow or tear: *This soft wood splits easily.* | *His coat had split down the back.* | *I was out in the back yard splitting logs.* **2** [I;T (UP, into)] to divide into separate parts: *Rutherford discovered how to split the atom by fission.* | *The river splits into three smaller streams at this point.* | *I think the article would be easier to read if you split it up (into sections).* **3** [T (between)] to divide among people; share: *Let's split the cost three ways/between the three of us.* **4** [I;T (UP, into)] to separate into opposing groups or parties: *Now, children, you must split up into two groups for this game.* | *This quarrel threatens to split the Republicans (into two opposing groups).* | *The government is deeply split on this issue.* | *The committee was* **split right down the middle** *on this proposal.* (=into two opposing groups of exactly equal size) **5** [I (UP, with)] to end a friendship, marriage, etc.: *He's split with his girlfriend.* | *Have you heard that John and Anne have split up?* **6** [I (on)] *BrE infml* (esp. among children) to tell secret information about someone: *If I tell you where I'm going, promise you won't split on me?* **7** [I] *old-fash sl* to leave quickly: *I'm getting tired of this place; let's split!* **8** **split hairs** to concern oneself with small unimportant differences, esp. in arguments: *"It's not 1000 jobs lost; it's only 967." "It's still far too many – stop splitting hairs!"* —see also HAIR-SPLITTING **9** **split one's sides** *infml* to become weak with uncontrollable laughter —see also SIDE-SPLITTING **10** **split the difference** *infml* to agree on an amount halfway between: *You say £12 and I say £10, so let's split the difference and call it £11.* —see also SPLITTING

split² *n* **1** [(**in**)] a cut or break made by splitting: *Can this split in the tabletop be mended?* **2** [(**in**)] a division or separation, esp. within a usu. undivided group: *Arguments over policy led to a split in the party.* **3** a division and sharing out: *a three-way split* (=between three people) **4** a dish made from fruit, esp. a banana, cut into two pieces with ice cream on top —see also SPLITS

split end /ˈ· ˈ·/ *n* [*usu. pl.*] the end of a human hair that has split into several parts, esp. because the hair has not been treated gently enough

split in·fin·i·tive /ˌ· ·ˈ···/ *n* a phrase in which an adverb or other word is put between "to" and an INFINITIVE, as in "to easily win". It is better to avoid split infinitives because many people regard them as bad English. —see also **to boldly go where no man has gone before** (BOLDLY)

split-lev·el /ˌ· ˈ···/ *adj* (of a building or room) having floors at different heights in different parts: *a split-level flat/dining room*

split pea /ˌ· ˈ·/ *n* a dried PEA separated into its two natural halves

split per·son·al·i·ty /ˌ· ···ˈ···/ *n not tech* a condition in which a person has two very different ways of behaving – compare SCHIZOPHRENIA

split ring /ˌ· ˈ·/ *also* **key ring**– *n* a metal ring of two turns pressed flat together, used for holding keys in such a way that they can be slipped on and off

splits /splɪts/ *n* [*the*+S] a movement in which a person's legs are spread wide apart and touch the floor along their whole length: *Can you do the splits?*

split sec·ond /ˌ· ˈ···/ *n* an extremely short period of time; moment: *I don't know how he escaped – I only took my eyes off him for a split second!* –**split-second** *adj* : *I had to make a split-second decision.*

splits·ville /ˈsplɪtsvɪl/ *adj* [F] *AmE sl* separated from something or someone: *They've been splitsville since we found out about his affair with the waitress.*

split tick·et /ˌ· ˈ··/ *n* (in elections in the US) a vote in which the voter has voted for some CANDIDATES of one party and some CANDIDATES of the other party —compare STRAIGHT TICKET

split·ting /ˈsplɪtɪŋ/ *adj* (of a headache) very severe

splodge /splɒdʒ‖splɑːdʒ/ *BrE* ‖ **splotch** /splɒtʃ‖splɑːtʃ/ *esp. AmE*– *n* [(**of**)] *infml* an irregular coloured or dirty mark or spot; BLOTCH: *There were some splodges of paint on the carpet.* –**splodgy** *adj*

splosh /splɒʃ‖splɑːʃ/ *v* [I] *infml* to make or move with a loud

SPLASH: *The little boy was sploshing about in his bath.* —**splosh** *n*

splurge /splɜːdʒǁsplɜːrdʒ/ *v* [I;T (**on**)] *infml* to spend more (money) than one can usually afford: *He splurged all his winnings on an expensive new camera.* —**splurge** *n* : *She went out on a splurge when she got her first wage packet.*

splut·ter¹ /ˈsplʌtəʳ/ *n* a wet spitting (SPIT¹) noise: *The fire went out with a few splutters as the rain began to fall.*

splutter² *v* **1** [I;T] to talk or say quickly and as if confused: *"But ... but ..." she spluttered.* | *He was spluttering with rage.* **2** [I] to make a wet spitting (SPIT¹) noise: *The candle spluttered and went out.*

Spock¹ /spɒkǁspɑːk/, **Dr Ben·ja·min** /ˈbendʒəmɪ̱n/ (1903–) an American doctor who wrote books giving advice on how parents should look after their children, including the *Common Sense Book of Baby and Child Care*, which suggested that parents should allow their children more freedom than was fashionable at the time. Dr Spock is also remembered in the US for protesting against the Vietnam War in the 1960s.

Spock², **Mr** a character from the SCIENCE FICTION television programme *Star Trek*. Mr Spock is a man from the PLANET Vulcan who has large pointed ears and special powers which humans do not have. He is also very LOGICAL and does not have human emotions. He finds it difficult to understand why humans cannot control their feelings.

Mr Spock

Spode /spəʊd/ *n* [U] fine, expensive CHINA or PORCELAIN made at the factory started by Josiah Spode at Stoke-on-Trent in 1764 and still made today

spoil¹ /spɔɪl/ *v* **spoiled** *or* **spoilt** *BrE* /spɔɪlt/ **1** [T] to destroy the value, quality or pleasure of; ruin: *We've had a wonderful day out; let's not spoil it now by having a quarrel.* | *The cook had spoilt the soup by putting too much salt in it.* | *The big orange sign on the front has spoiled the character of the old building.* **2** [I] to lose goodness; decay: *The food will spoil if you don't keep it cool.* **3** [T] to make (esp. a child) selfish by too much generosity or giving too much attention or praise: *His grandmother spoils him.* | *Her husband behaves just like a spoilt child.* **4** [T] to treat very or too well; INDULGE: *"I shouldn't have another chocolate ... " "Go on, spoil yourself!"* | *There are so many lovely things I could wear tonight, I'm spoilt for choice.* (=it is very difficult to decide) **5** [I] *tech* to fill in (a voting paper) wrongly so that it can no longer be officially counted **6** [I] **be spoiling for a fight** to be very eager to fight or quarrel: *It was obvious from his attitude that he was spoiling for a fight.*

▷ USAGE In Britain, **spoilt** is the usual form of the past participle in meanings 3 and 4, especially when it is used as an adjective: *a spoilt child* | *I feel spoilt by all the kindness you've shown me.* In the US, **spoiled** is used for these meanings.◁

spoil² also **spoils** *pl.* — *n* [U] *fml or lit* things taken, esp. by an army from a defeated enemy or by thieves: *The robbers divided up their spoils.* | *the spoils of victory/war*

spoil·age /ˈspɔɪlɪdʒ/ *n* [U] *fml or tech* waste resulting from something being spoiled: *We lost several tons of grain through spoilage.*

spoil·er /ˈspɔɪləʳ/ *n* **1** a person or thing that spoils **2** a surface on an aircraft, car, etc., intended to interrupt the smooth flow of air: *A racing car needs a spoiler to stop it lifting off the road at high speeds.* **3** *AmE* (in sports) a person or a team that spoils another's winning record: *The Bears have won all seven of their games thus far, but the Vikings look to be the spoilers this time around.*

spoil·sport /ˈspɔɪlspɔːt‖-ɔːrt/ *n infml derog* a person who puts an end to other people's fun

spoils sys·tem /ˈ· ͵··/ *n AmE* a system in which politicians give public jobs to people who supported them before they were elected. This system was common in the US until the late 1800s.

spoilt /spɔɪlt/ *past tense & participle of* SPOIL¹ —see SPOIL (USAGE)

spoke¹ /spəʊk/ *past tense of* SPEAK

spoke² *n* **1** any of the bars which connect the outer ring of a wheel to the centre, e.g. on a bicycle: *a bent spoke* —see picture at BICYCLE **2 put a spoke in someone's wheel** *infml* to prevent someone from going ahead with plans; THWART

spok·en /ˈspəʊkən/ *past participle of* SPEAK

-spoken see WORD FORMATION

spoken for /ˈ··· ·/ *adj* [F] *infml* **1** (of a thing) being kept aside for someone: *I'm afraid that particular model is already spoken for.* **2** (of a person) closely connected with a person of the opposite sex: *You'd better stop flirting with Jim – he's spoken for.* —see also SPEAK for

spokes·per·son /ˈspəʊks͵pɜːsən‖-ɜːr-/ also **spokes·man** /-mən/ *masc.*, **spokes·wom·an** /-͵wʊmən/ *fem.* — *n* - **peo·ple** /-͵piːpəl/ a person chosen to speak officially for a group: *A government spokesperson said today that there would be an official inquiry.* | *a spokesman for the miners' union* —see PERSON (USAGE)

spo·li·a·tion /͵spəʊliˈeɪʃən/ *n* [U] *fml* the action of violent or intentional spoiling or destruction: *the spoliation of the environment*

spon·dee /ˈspɒndiːǁˈspɑːndiː/ *n tech* a measure of poetry consisting of two strong (or long) beats —**daic** /spɒnˈdeɪ-ɪkǁspɑːn-/ *adj*

sponge¹ /spʌndʒ/ *n* **1** [C] a type of simple sea creature that does not move but grows a spreading rubber-like frame full of small holes **2** [C;U] a piece of a sponge, or of a similar artificial substance made from rubber, which can suck up and hold water and is usu. used for washing: *to squeeze out a sponge* **3** [C] a person who SPONGES² (3) on other people **4** [C;U] *BrE* a sponge cake —see also **throw in the sponge** (THROW in)

sponge² *v* **1** [T (DOWN, OFF, OUT)] to clean by rubbing with a wet cloth or SPONGE¹ (2): *We sponged down the walls to get the worst of the dirt off.* **2** [T (UP)] to remove (liquid) with a cloth, SPONGE¹ (2), etc.: *The nurse sponged (up) the blood from the wound.* **3** [I;T (**off, on, from**)] *derog* to live or get (money, meals, etc.) free by taking advantage of other people's generosity or weakness: *It's ridiculous to accuse people who need state benefits of sponging off the state.*

sponge bag /ˈ· ·/ *n BrE* a small usu. plastic bag for carrying one's soap, toothbrush, etc.

sponge cake /ˈ· ·/ *n* [C;U] (a) light cake made from eggs, sugar, and flour but usu. no fat

spon·ger /ˈspʌndʒəʳ/ *n derog* a person who SPONGES² (3) on other people

spong·y /ˈspʌndʒi/ *adj* like a SPONGE; soft, full of air, and sometimes rather wet; not firm: *a spongy texture* | *spongy bread/ground* —**-iness** *n* [U]

spon·sor¹ /ˈspɒnsəʳ‖ˈspɑːn-/ *n* **1** a person who takes responsibility for a person or thing: *If I'm going to go and live in the US, I must get an American sponsor.* | *the sponsor of a new bill being debated in Parliament* **2** a business which pays for a show, broadcast, sports event, etc., usu. in return for advertising: *The opera house could not survive without commercial sponsors.* **3** a person who agrees to pay someone money, usu. for CHARITY, if they complete (part of) an activity

spon·sor² *v* [T] to act as a sponsor for: *The baseball match is being sponsored by a cigarette company.* | *a government-sponsored research programme*

sponsored walk /͵··· ˈ·/ *n* a walk done to collect money for CHARITY, in which people offer money for each mile that the walkers walk

spon·sor·ship /ˈspɒnsəʃɪp‖ˈspɑːnsər-/ *n* [U] **1** an act of supporting and paying for (part of) an activity: : *The expedition is seeking sponsorship from one of the major banks.* | *government sponsorship* **2** money obtained from SPONSORS (2): *They've had to raise large amounts of sponsorship.*

spon·ta·ne·i·ty /͵spɒntəˈniːɪ̱ti, -ˈneɪɪ̱tiǁ͵spɑːn-/ also **spon·ta·ne·ous·ness** /spɒnˈteɪniəsnəs‖spɑːn-/— *n* [U] *fml* the quality of being spontaneous: *His enthusiasm was somewhat lacking in spontaneity, I thought.*

spon·ta·ne·ous /spɒnˈteɪniəsǁspɑːn-/ *adj* happening as a result of natural feelings or causes, without outside force or influence, or without being planned: *Her successful jump brought a spontaneous cheer from the crowd.* | *His offer of help was quite spontaneous; he hadn't been told to make it.* | *They think it caught fire because a chemical reaction caused* **spontaneous combustion**. – ~ **ly** *adv* : *These medical conditions can often cure themselves spontaneously, without medical intervention*

spoof /spuːf/ *n* [(of, on)] *infml* a funny untrue copy or description; PARODY: *The show is a spoof of|on university life.* –**spoof** *v* [T] *AmE infml* : *He spoofed the President's habit of falling down.*

spook[1] /spuːk/ *n infml for* GHOST[1] (1)

spook[2] *v infml, esp. AmE* [T] to cause to be suddenly afraid: *Something spooked the horses and they ran away.*

spook·y /ˈspuːki/ *adj infml* causing fear in a strange way; EERIE: *a spooky old house*

spool /spuːl/ *n* **1** a wheel-like object for winding a length of electric wire, recording TAPE, camera film, etc., round **2** *AmE for* REEL[1]: *a spool of thread*

spoons

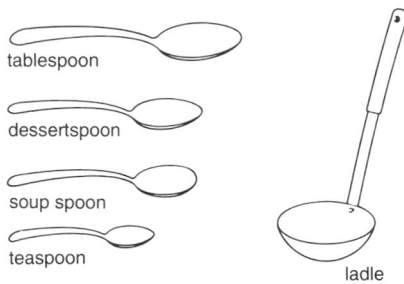

tablespoon

dessertspoon

soup spoon

teaspoon

ladle

spoon[1] /spuːn/ *n* **1** (*often in comb.*) a tool for mixing, serving, and eating food, consisting of a small bowl-shaped part with a handle: *a silver|plastic spoon* | *a soup spoon* **2** [(of)] a spoonful: *Two spoons of sugar, please.* –see also DESSERTSPOON, GREASY SPOON, SOUP SPOON, TABLESPOON, TEASPOON, WOODEN SPOON, **born with a silver spoon in one's mouth** (SILVER)

spoon[2] *v* **1** [T+*obj*+*adv*|*prep*] to pick up or move with a spoon: *Spoon the mixture into glasses.* | *to spoon up soup* **2** [I] *AmE sl* to kiss and hold a person of the opposite sex: *They were spooning on the front porch.*

spoo·ner·is·m /ˈspuːnərɪzəm/ *n* an expression in which the first sounds of two words have changed places, usu. with a funny result (as in *sew you to a sheet* for *show you to a seat*)

spoon-feed /ˈ· ·/ *v* -**fed** [T] **1** to feed (esp. a baby) with a spoon **2** *usu. derog* to present (information or opinions) to someone in a very easy form that needs no thinking: *It's wrong to spoon-feed your students.* [+*obj*+to] *He spoon-fed political theory to his students.* [+*obj*+with] *He spoon-fed his students with political theory.*

spoon·ful /ˈspuːnfʊl/ *n* **spoonfuls** *or* **spoonsful** /ˈspuːnzfʊl/ [(of)] (*often in comb.*) the amount that a spoon will hold: *Two spoonfuls of sugar, please.*

spoor /spɔːʳ, spʊəʳ/ *n* a (single example from a) track of footmarks or waste droppings left by a wild animal

spo·rad·ic /spəˈrædɪk/ *adj* happening irregularly; INTERMITTENT: *There were reports of sporadic fighting in the streets.* | *sporadic outbursts of the disease|of violence* – ~ **ally** /kli/ *adv*

spore /spɔːʳ/ *n* a very small seedlike usu. single cell produced by some plants and simple animals and able to develop into a new plant or animal: *a mushroom's spores carried on the wind*

spor·ran /ˈspɒrən‖ˈspɔː-, ˈspɑː-/ *n* a fur-covered bag worn, esp. in Scottish national dress, in front of a KILT

sport[1] /spɔːt‖spɔːrt/ *n* **1** [C;U] an outdoor or indoor game, competition, or activity needing physical effort and skill and usu. carried on according to rules: *Football is my favourite sport.* | *What other sports do you like?* | *I've never really been keen on sport.* | *Parachuting is an exciting| strenuous|dangerous sport.* | *winter sports* –see

RECREATION (USAGE) and see colour picture on page 884 **2** [C] *infml* a person with a generous nature, esp. one who accepts defeat or trouble in a cheerful uncomplaining way: *Be a sport and let me borrow your bike.* | *She's a real sport|a good sport* **3** *AustrE infml* (used as a friendly form of address, esp. when speaking to a man): *Good on you, sport!* **4** *AmE infml* (used as a friendly form of address, esp. when speaking to a boy): *"What do you say, Sport? Want to go to the game?"* **5** [C] *tech* a plant or animal that is different in some important way from its usual type: *This insect's a sport; it has seven legs.* **6** [U] *fml* joking fun: *The remarks were only made* **in sport**. **7** **the sport of kings** *pomp* horse racing –see also SPORTS, BLOOD SPORT

sport[2] *v* **1** [T] to wear or show publicly and sometimes proudly; SHOW **off**: *She came in today sporting a new fur coat.* **2** [I] *usu. lit* to act or move playfully; FROLIC: *Lambs were sporting in the field.*

sport·ing /ˈspɔːtɪŋ‖ˈspɔːr-/ *adj* **1** fair-minded and generous, esp. in sports: *It was very sporting of him to admit that his shot was out.* –opposite **unsporting** **2** offering the kind of fair chance to compete that is usual in a game: *She gave me a sporting chance of winning by letting me start first.* **3** [A no comp.] **a** of, for, or taking part in sports: *sporting goods* | *All sporting nations wish to take part in the Olympic Games.* **b** of or fond of country sports like hunting or horse racing: *a painter of sporting scenes* – ~ **ly** *adv*

Sporting Life /ˌ·· ˈ·/ a British daily newspaper which deals mainly with horse racing

spor·tive /ˈspɔːtɪv‖ˈspɔːr-/ *adj esp. lit* playful – ~ **ly** *adv* – ~ **ness** *n* [U]

sports[1] /spɔːts‖spɔːrts/ *n* [P] *BrE* a meeting at which people compete in running, jumping, throwing, etc. (ATHLETICS): *The school sports are next week.*

sports[2] *adj* [A no comp.] **1** of, for, or connected with sport: *the sports page of the newspaper* | *a sports commentator* **2** ‖ also **sport** *AmE*– (esp. of clothes) informal in style: *Do I have to wear a suit to the dinner, or will a sports jacket be good enough?*

sports car /ˈ· ·/ ‖ also **sport car** *AmE*– *n* a low fast car, usu. having a roof which can be folded back or removed –compare ESTATE CAR, HATCHBACK, SALOON (1)

sports cen·tre /ˈ· ˌ··/ *n* a building where many different types of indoor sports can be played, e.g. football, swimming, and keep fit activities

sports day /ˈ· ·/ *n* (esp. in Britain) a day when the pupils at a school has sports competitions: *It's our sports day next Friday.*

Sports Il·lus·trat·ed /ˌ· ˈ····/ a weekly American magazine read mostly by men, with articles about different sports, teams, professional players, etc.

sports jac·ket /ˈ· ˌ··/ ‖ also **sport coat** /ˈ· ·/, **sports coat** *AmE*– *n* a man's JACKET, esp. one made of TWEED or a similar material, worn on INFORMAL occasions

sports·man /ˈspɔːtsmən‖ˈspɔːr-/ **sports·wom·an** /-ˌwʊmən/ *fem.*– *n* -**men** /mən/ **1** someone who plays or enjoys usu. several different sports, esp. outdoor sports: *a fine|talented sportsman* **2** someone who plays sports in a fair and generous spirit

sports·man·like /ˈspɔːtsmənlaɪk‖ˈspɔːr-/ *adj* showing sportsmanship

sports·man·ship /ˈspɔːtsmənʃɪp‖ˈspɔːr-/ *n* [U] a spirit of honest fair play, esp. in sports

sport shirt /ˈ· ·/ *n* a shirt for men which can be worn outside the trousers

sports schol·ar·ship /ˈ· ˌ····/ *n* money given to a college student to pay for his/her education because it is expected that he/she will be very good at sports, esp. football. Sports scholarships are connected in people's minds with colleges that are better known for their sports teams than their ACADEMIC standards: *He went to Alabama on a sports scholarship.*

sports·wear /ˈspɔːtsweəʳ‖-ɔːr-/ *n* [U] clothes worn esp. when playing sport: *our new range of sportswear*

sport·y /ˈspɔːti‖ˈspɔːrti/ *adj infml* **1** *esp. BrE* good at and/or fond of sport: *I'm not very sporty.* **2** (esp. of clothes) good-looking in a bright informal way: *sporty new trousers* –**iness** *n* [U]

spot[1] /spɒt‖spɑːt/ *n* **1** [C (of)] a usu. round part or area that is different from the main surface, in colour or some other way: *a white dress with blue spots* | *There was a sticky spot on the floor.* | *He wiped a spot of black paint off the door handle.* **2** [C] a small round raised diseased mark on the skin: *Did you know you had a spot on your nose?* | *With measles you get spots all over your skin.* **3** [C] a particular place: *a nice spot for a picnic* | *This is our favourite holiday spot.* | *On this map X marks the spot where the treasure is buried.* | *He stood* **rooted to the spot** (=unable to move) *in fear.* | *War journalists have to travel to the world's* **trouble spots.** | *Can you show me the exact spot where it hurts?* | (fig.) *It's been a terrible week at the office, but there was one* **bright spot**: *the new assistant is very good.* –see also BEAUTY SPOT, BLACK SPOT, BLIND SPOT, HIGH SPOT, HOT SPOT **4** [S] an area of mind or feelings: *I'm afraid you touched a rather tender spot when you mentioned his former wife.* –see also SOFT SPOT **5** [S (of)] *BrE infml* a little bit; small amount: *Let's have a spot of lunch* | *I'm afraid there's been* **a spot of bother.** (=a bit of trouble) **6** [C] *infml* a difficult position or situation; FIX² (1): *Now we're really in a spot!* **7** [C] a place in a broadcast; SLOT: *He got a guest spot on a well-known variety show.* **8** [C] *infml* a position in an organization, system of ranks, etc.: *She finished in the top spot/the number-one spot in the world tennis rankings.* **9** [C] *infml for* SPOTLIGHT¹ (1) **10** [S] *AmE infml* a piece of paper money (BILL¹(3)) of the amount stated: *a ten-spot* (=a ten-dollar bill) **11** **hit the spot** *AmE infml* to satisfy one's hunger, esp. with something that tastes good: *That pie really hit the spot, Mildred.* **12** **on the spot: a** at once: *Anyone breaking the rules will be asked to leave on the spot.* **b** at the place of the action: *When the fighting started police and reporters were soon on the spot.* **c** without moving away from where one is: *The gym teacher made us do running on the spot.* **d** in a position of having to make the right answer or decision: *His direct question* **put me on the spot**; *I couldn't make an excuse or lie.* **13 Out, damned spot!** *quote* a phrase from Shakespeare's play *Macbeth*, said by Lady Macbeth when trying to remove spots of blood from her hands after she has killed Duncan

spot² *v* **-tt-** **1** [T] to pick out with the eye; see or recognize, esp. with effort or difficulty: *He's a very tall man, easy to spot in a crowd.* | *She spotted a bad mistake in the accounts.* | *They were spotted by the police as they were entering the bank.* [+obj+v-ing] *He was spotted leaving the building soon afterwards.* **2** [T (with)] *usu. pass.*] to mark with (coloured) spots: *I chose a white cloth spotted with green.* | *a spotted dog* **3** [T (with)] *usu. pass.*] to place or scatter one by one on a surface, in an area, etc.: *The yellow fields were spotted with red poppies.* **4** [it+I] *BrE* (of rain) to fall lightly and irregularly: *It's spotting (with rain) again.* **5** [T+obj(i)+obj(d)] *AmE* to allow as an advantage in a game: *He spotted his opponent three points and still won.* **6** [T] to help by preventing a fall in a sport, e.g. GYMNASTICS: *The coach spotted her on the dismount.*

spot³ *adj* [A] *tech* for buying or paying at once, not at some future time: *They won't give credit; they want* **spot cash.**| *What's the* **spot price** *for oil?* | *spot wheat*

spot⁴ *adv* [+prep] *BrE infml* exactly: *She arrived spot on time.* –see also SPOT-ON

spot check /ˌ· ˈ·‖ˈ· ˌ·/ *n* [(on, for)] an examination of some members of a group that are chosen, usu. by chance, as being typical of the whole group: *The police didn't search everyone for drugs; they just made spot checks.* –**spot check** *v* [T (for)]

spot·less /ˈspɒtləs‖ˈspɑːt-/ *adj* completely clean: *a spotless white shirt* | (fig.) *a spotless reputation* – ~**ly** *adv* – ~**ness** *n* [U]

spot·light¹ /ˈspɒtlaɪt‖ˈspɑːt-/ *n* **1** [C] (a bright round area of light made by) a lamp with a narrow beam which can be directed at a particular object: *The spotlight followed her round the stage.* –see picture at LIGHT **2** [*the*] public attention: *Throughout his political career he's always been* **in the spotlight.**

spotlight² *v* [T] **-lighted** *or* **-lit** /lɪt/ to direct attention to: *The article spotlights the difficulties of the unemployed.*

spot-on /ˌ· ˈ·◂/ *adj, adv BrE infml* exactly right: *Your judgment/guess turned out to be spot-on.* –see also SPOT⁴

spotted dick /ˌ· ˈ·/ *n* [C;U] a heavy sweet boiled British PUDDING with CURRANTS in it. It is thought of as typical old-fashioned British food.

spot·ter¹ /ˈspɒtə⁰‖ˈspɑː-/ *n esp. BrE* a person who looks for or watches the stated thing: *a bird spotter* | *a keen train spotter*

spotter² *adj* [A] used for keeping watch on an enemy's actions: *a spotter plane*

spot·ty /ˈspɒti‖ˈspɑːti/ *adj usu. derog* **1** *BrE infml* having spots on the face: *spotty youths* **2** *AmE* with some parts different from others, esp. in quality; PATCHY: *a rather spotty performance*

Spotty Dog /ˌ· ˈ·/ a character in *The Woodentops*, a British television programme for children in the 1960s. It was a small wooden dog which walked with its legs stiff and not bending.

spouse /spaʊs, spaʊz/ *n usu. fml or law* a husband or wife

spout¹ /spaʊt/ *v* **1** [I;T (OUT)] to come out or throw out in a forceful stream; GUSH: *Water was spouting out from the pipe.* | *The well spouted oil.* **2** [T] *infml derog* to pour out in a stream of words: *He's always spouting poetry at people.* | *to spout platitudes* **3** [I] (of a WHALE) to throw out a tall stream of water from a hole in the head – – ~**er** *n*

spout² *n* **1** an opening from which liquid comes out, such as a tube, pipe, or small U- or V-shaped lip for pouring liquid from a container: *the spout of a teapot* **2** a forceful esp. rising stream of liquid –see also WATERSPOUT **3** **up the spout** *BrE infml* **a** in a hopeless state or position **b** PREGNANT (1)

sprain¹ /spreɪn/ *v* [T] to damage (a joint in the body) by sudden twisting: *I've sprained my ankle.* | *a sprained wrist*

sprain² *n* an act or result of spraining a joint: *That's a bad/nasty sprain.* –compare STRAIN² (4)

sprang /spræŋ/ *past tense of* SPRING¹

sprat /spræt/ *n* a small European HERRING

Sprat, Jack see JACK SPRAT

spraun·cy /ˈsprɔːnsi/ *adj BrE infml* **1** lively **2** stylish

sprawl¹ /sprɔːl/ *v* **1** [I+adv/prep; T+obj+adv/prep; usu. pass.] to stretch one's body out wide or awkwardly in lying or sitting: *He found her sprawled out in a comfortable chair asleep.* **2** [I+adv/prep] to spread out ungracefully over a wide area: *The city sprawls for miles in each direction.* | *a sprawling refugee camp*

sprawl² *n* [*usu. sing.*] **1** a sprawling position of the body **2** an irregular ungraceful spreading mass: *This area is a classic example of* **urban sprawl.** (=of city buildings spreading in an unplanned and unattractive way)

spray¹ /spreɪ/ *v* **1** [I+adv/prep] (of liquid) to be scattered or forced out in very small drops under pressure: *There was a hole in the hose, and water sprayed out all over me.* **2** [T] to throw or force out (liquid) in very small drops on (a surface, person, field of crops, etc.): *We spray the crops to prevent disease.* [+obj+**on**, **over**] *He sprayed paint on/over the wall.* [+obj+**with**] *He sprayed the wall with paint.* | (fig.) *The gangsters sprayed the car with machine-gun bullets.*

spray² *n* **1** [U] water in very small drops blown from the sea, a waterfall, a wet road surface, etc.: *We parked the car by the sea and it got covered with spray.* **2** [C;U] (a can or other container holding) liquid to be sprayed out under pressure: *a quick-drying spray paint* | *Did you bring along any insect spray?* (=to kill insects) | *a can of hair spray* (=to keep hair in place)

spray³ *n* (an arrangement of flowers, jewels, etc., in the shape of) a small branch with its leaves and flowers

spray·er /ˈspreɪəʳ/ *n* a person or apparatus that sprays out a liquid: *Use a paint sprayer for such a big wall.* | *A crop sprayer flew low over the field.*

spray gun /ˈ· ·/ *n* an apparatus held like a gun for pumping out liquid in very small drops

spread¹ /spred/ *v* **spread** **1** [I;T (OUT)] to (cause to) open, reach, or stretch out, so as to cover or include a greater area; (cause to) be longer, broader, wider, etc.: *In the last five years the city has spread out rapidly in all directions.* | *A frown spread across his face.* | *The bird spread its wings ready for flight.* | *Spread the map out on the floor.* | *The line of police spread out to search the fields.* **2** [I+adv/prep; not in progressive forms] to cover a large area or period of time: *The city now spreads as far as the coast.* | *a university course that spreads over a wide range of subjects* **3** [I;T] to (cause to) have effect or influence over a wider area: *The fire soon spread to the adjoining buildings.* | *Infectious diseases are very easily spread.* | *The threat of a shutdown spread alarm and despondency among the workforce.* **4** [I;T (AROUND)] to make or become (more) widely known: *The news of the gold discovery* **spread like wildfire.** (=spread extremely rapidly) | *Who's been spreading malicious rumours about me?* **5 a** [T] to put (a covering) on (a surface): [+obj+on] *Spread butter on the bread.* [+obj+with] *Spread the bread with butter.* **b** [I+adv] to be able to be used for covering a surface: *Butter doesn't spread well when it's cold.* **6** [T (over, among)] to scatter, share, or divide over an area, period of time, etc.; DISTRIBUTE: *We plan to spread the cost over three years.* | *They invested in several different companies in order to spread the risks.* **7** [T] *old-fash* to prepare (a table or meal) before eating: *The table was spread for tea.* **8 spread one's wings** to begin to take part in new activities or start a new life – – ~**able** *adj*

▷ USAGE Note the patterns in these sentences: *She* **spreads** *her toast with butter.* | *She* **spreads** *butter on/over her toast.* Several other verbs (**sprinkle, strew,** etc.) can have the same patterns. Any verb in this dictionary which is followed by the note "see SPREAD (USAGE)" has these patterns.◁

spread² *n* **1** [(*the*) S (**of**)] the act or action of spreading: *The rapid spread of the disease is alarming the medical authorities.* | *efforts to halt the spread of nuclear weapons* **2** [C *usu. sing.*] a range or area over which something spreads: *This tree has a spread of 100 feet.* | *The various dealers' prices show a wide spread.* (=there is a large difference between the highest and lowest) – compare SPAN² **3** [C] a newspaper or magazine article or advertisement usu. covering one or more pages and with pictures: *The paper is running a double-page spread featuring photos of the wedding.* **4** [U] a soft food for spreading on bread: *a tube of cheese spread* **5** [C] *infml* a large or grand meal: *magnificent spread* **6** [C] *esp. AmE* a large farm or esp. RANCH: *He has a 1000-acre spread in Texas.* –see also BEDSPREAD, MIDDLE-AGED SPREAD

spread-ea·gle /ˌ· ˈ··‖ˈ· ˌ··/ *v* [T *usu. pass.*] to put (someone, esp. oneself) into a position with arms and legs spread out: *He lay spread-eagled on the bed.*

spread·sheet /ˈspredʃiːt/ *n* a type of computer PROGRAM that allows figures (e.g. about sales, taxes, and profits) to be shown in groups on a SCREEN¹ (4) so that quick calculations can be made

spree /spriː/ *n* a period of wild irresponsible fun, spending, drinking, etc.: *When I got my prize money we all went out on a spree.* | *a shopping/spending spree*

sprig /sprɪg/ *n* [(**of**)] a small end of a stem or branch with leaves: *He decorated the chicken with sprigs of parsley.* | *a sprig of mistletoe/holly*

spright·ly /ˈspraɪtli/ *adj* cheerful and active; LIVELY: *a sprightly dance/old man* —**liness** *n* [U]

spring¹ /sprɪŋ/ *v* **sprang** /spræŋ/ also **sprung** /sprʌŋ/ *AmE,* **sprung** **1** [I+adv/prep] to move quickly and suddenly upwards or forwards as if by jumping: *He sprang to his feet/sprang to the door/sprang over the wall.* | *The soldiers sprang to attention.* | (fig.) *She sprang to the president's defence when his policies were criticized.* **2** [I+adv/prep] to appear or come into being or action quickly or from nothing: *A wind suddenly sprang up.* | *Towns had sprung up in what had been a dry desert.* | *I turned the key and the engine sprang into life.* | *Tears sprang to her eyes.* | (*infml*) *Where did you spring from? I thought you were in America.* **3** [L+adj;T] to open or close quickly (as if) by

the force of a spring: *The box sprang open when I touched the button.* | *to spring a trap* **4** [T (**on**)] to make happen or make known suddenly and unexpectedly: *We sprang a surprise party on them.* | *He sprang the news of his marriage on his parents.* **5** [T] *infml* to arrange for (someone) to escape from prison **6 spring a leak** (of a ship, container, etc.) to begin to let liquid through a crack, hole, etc.

spring from sthg. *phr v* [T] to be a product or result of; have as its origin: *His fear of dogs springs from a bad experience as a child.*

spring² *n* **1** [C;U] the season between winter and summer; the part of the year when leaves and flowers appear: *I go on holiday in (the) spring.* | *a wet spring* | *last spring* | *spring flowers* –see colour picture on page 1211 **2** [C] also **springs** *pl.* – a place where water comes up naturally from the ground: *a bubbling spring* | *hot springs* – compare SOURCE (3) **3** [C] an object, usu. a length of metal wound round, which can be forced together or pressed down, and will return to its original shape when let go: *the springs of a mattress* | *a watch spring* | *What an uncomfortable chair! It needs new springs.* **4** [U] the quality of this object: *There's not much spring in this old bed.* **5** [S;U] an active healthy quality: *There was a letter from him at last, and she walked to work that morning with* **a spring in her step.** **6** [C] an act of springing: *The cat made a sudden spring at the mouse.*

Spring Bank Hol·i·day /ˌ· ˈ· ˌ···/ also **Spring Holiday** /ˌ· ˈ···/ *n* [C;U] the last MONDAY in MAY which is a public holiday in England, Wales, and N Ireland

spring·board /ˈsprɪŋbɔːd‖-bɔːrd/ *n* **1** a strong bendable board for jumping off to give height to a DIVE or jump – compare DIVING BOARD **2** [(**to, for**)] a starting point where power is built up for future action: *They are hoping that their successes in the local elections will be a springboard to victory in next year's national election.*

spring·bok /ˈsprɪŋbɒk‖-bɑːk/ *n* -**boks** or -**bok** **1** a fast-running graceful South African GAZELLE (=small deer) **2** a SPORTSMAN or SPORTSWOMAN playing for South Africa, esp. at RUGBY or cricket, in an international match or tour abroad

spring break /ˌ· ˈ·/ *n AmE* a usu. two-week long springtime holiday from college or university. Some students travel to sunny places such as Florida for their spring break and enjoy themselves by having a lot of alcohol.

spring chick·en /ˌ· ˈ··/ *n* **1** *esp. AmE* a young chicken suitable for cooking **2** [*usu. in negatives*] *infml* a young person: *She's no spring chicken.* (= she's old)

spring-clean¹ /ˌ· ˈ·/ *v* [I;T] *esp. BrE* to clean (a place) thoroughly, as people often clean houses in the spring

spring-clean² /ˈ· ·/ *BrE* ‖ **spring-clean·ing** /ˈ· ˌ··/ *AmE*– *n* [S] a thorough cleaning, esp. of a house

spring fe·ver /ˌ· ˈ··/ *n* [U] *AmE* a feeling of wanting to do something new, different, and exciting: *He's got spring fever and is finding it hard to study.*

spring on·ion /ˌ· ˈ··/ *BrE* ‖ **scallion, green onion** *AmE*– *n* an onion with a small white round part (BULB) and long green stem, usu. eaten raw

spring roll /ˌ· ˈ·‖ˈ· ·/ also **pancake roll** *BrE* ‖ **egg roll** *AmE*– *n* a Chinese food consisting of a thin case of egg pastry filled with bits of vegetable and often meat and usu. cooked in oil

Spring·steen /ˈsprɪŋstiːn/, **Bruce** /bruːs/ (1949–) an American popular music singer and songwriter who first became successful in the 1970s, known esp. for his live performances in concert

spring tide /ˌ· ˈ·/ *n* a large rise and fall of the sea at the times of the new and full moon –compare NEAP TIDE

spring·time /ˈsprɪŋtaɪm/ *n* [(*the*) U] the season of spring; time of spring weather

spring train·ing /ˌ· ˈ··/ *n* [U] *AmE* the period during which a BASEBALL team gets ready for competition

spring·y /ˈsprɪŋi/ *adj* having SPRING² (4); able to come back to its original shape; RESILIENT: *a light springy sword* | *springy turf*

sprin·kle¹ /ˈsprɪŋkəl/ *v* **1** [T] to scatter (small drops of liquid or small bits of solid matter) on or over (a surface or area): [+obj+prep] *He sprinkled vinegar on his fish and chips.* | *She sprinkled sand along the icy path.* [+obj+with] *She sprinkled the path with sand.* | (fig.) *His* *sermon was liberally sprinkled with quotations from the Bible.* —compare SCATTER[1]; see SPREAD (USAGE)   **2** [*it+I*] to rain lightly

sprinkle[2] *n* [*usu. sing.*]   **1** a light rain   **2** a sprinkling

sprin·kler /'sprɪŋklər/ *n*   **1** an apparatus for sprinkling water: *a garden sprinkler* —see picture at GARDEN   **2** a system of fire protection inside a building with pipes for sprinkling water which are turned on by high heat

sprin·kling /'sprɪŋklɪŋ/ *n* [(of) *usu. sing.*] a small scattered group or amount: *We've only had a sprinkling of snow.| There was a sprinkling of new faces at the meeting.*

sprint[1] /sprɪnt/ *v* [I] to run at one's fastest speed, esp. for a short distance: *The runners sprinted down the finishing straight.* —see RUN (USAGE)   **— er** *n*

sprint[2] *n*   **1** [S] an act of sprinting: *He put on/made a sprint to catch the bus.*   **2** [C *usu. sing.*] a short race for runners: *the 100-yard sprint*

Sprint·er /'sprɪntər/ *n* the name of a fast train on British local railways

sprite /spraɪt/ *n*   **1** a fairy, esp. a playful graceful one: *a water sprite*   **2** an image produced on a SCREEN[1] (4) by a computer, of a special type that can be drawn in LAYERS to give a real life effect to a picture

Sprite *n tdmk* a sweet FIZZY non-alcoholic drink that has no colour and tastes of LEMON and LIME

sprit·zer /'sprɪtsər/ *n* [C;U] (a glass of) a drink made with a little SODA WATER: *A white wine spritzer, please.*

sprock·et /'sprɒkɪt‖'sprɑː-/ *n*   **1** also **sprocket wheel** /'·· ·/— a wheel with a row of teeth for fitting into and turning a bicycle chain, a photographic film with holes, etc.   **2** a single one of these teeth

sprog /sprɒg‖sprɑːg/ *n BrE sl* a child

sprout[1] /spraʊt/ *v*   **1** [I;T (**from, up**)] to (cause to) grow, appear, or develop: *Leaves are beginning to sprout from the trees. | You've sprouted a beard since I last saw you! | a forest of chimneys sprouting from the rooftops*   **2** [I] to send out new growths: *These old potatoes have begun to sprout.*

sprout[2] *n*   **1** a new growth on a plant; SHOOT[2] (1)   **2** *BrE* a BRUSSELS SPROUT —see picture at VEGETABLE   **3** *AmE* an ALFALFA sprout —see also BEANSPROUT

spruce[1] /spruːs/ *n* [C;U] (the wood of) a tree that grows in northern countries and has short needle-shaped leaves that remain in winter

spruce[2] *adj* neat and clean in appearance; SMART: *looking very spruce in his new suit* **— ly** *adv* **— ness** *n* [U]

spruce[3] *v* **spruce** (sbdy./sthg. ↔) **up** *phr v* [I;T] *infml* to make (esp. oneself) spruce: *I must go and spruce (myself) up|get spruced up before dinner.*

sprung[1] /sprʌŋ/ *past participle & (AmE) past tense of* SPRING

sprung[2] *adj* supported or kept in shape by springs: *a sprung mattress*

spry /spraɪ/ *adj* (esp. of older people) active and quick in movement: *He's 75 and still spry as a kitten.* **— ness** *n* [U]

spud /spʌd/ *n infml* a potato

spume /spjuːm/ *n* [U] *esp. lit* a light, white air-filled mass on the top of a liquid, esp. on the sea; FOAM

spun /spʌn/ *past tense & participle of* SPIN

spunk /spʌŋk/ *n* [U]   **1** *infml* courage; spirit   **2** *BrE taboo* for SEMEN **— y** *adj*

spur[1] /spɜːr/ *n*   **1** a U-shaped object with a point or toothed wheel that is worn round the heel of a rider's boot and used to direct a horse or urge it to go faster: *He dug in his spurs.*   **2** [(**to**)] an event or influence that encourages action; INCENTIVE: *We hope these criticisms will act as a spur to increased effort.*   **3** a length of high ground coming out from a range of higher mountains   **4** a railway track or road that goes away from a main line or road   **5** a stiff sharp growth on the back of some birds' legs   **6** **on the spur of the moment** without preparation or planning —see also SPUR-OF-THE-MOMENT

spur[2] *v* **-rr-** [T (**ON**)]   **1** to use spurs to make (a horse) go faster   **2** to urge or encourage forcefully to work harder, perform better, etc.: *She spurred her team on to greater efforts.*

spu·ri·ous /'spjʊəriəs/ *adj fml*   **1** based on wrong or

incorrect reasoning: *spurious arguments/logic* —compare SPECIOUS   **2** false or pretended; not GENUINE: *spurious sympathy*   **3** *tech* not really the product of the time, writer, etc., shown or claimed: *There are some spurious lines in this ancient poem, which were added later.* **— ly** *adv* **— ness** *n* [U]

spurn /spɜːn‖spɜːrn/ *v* [T] *esp. fml or lit* to refuse or send away with angry pride; REJECT: *She spurned all offers of help. | a spurned lover*

spur-of-the-mo·ment /ˌ· · · '···◂/ *adj* [A] *infml* done, made, or happening without preparation or planning: *a spur-of-the-moment decision*

Spurs /spɜːz‖spɜːrz/ see TOTTENHAM HOTSPUR

spurt[1] /spɜːt‖spɜːrt/ *v*   **1** [I;T] to (cause to) flow out suddenly or violently: *Water spurted from the broken pipe. | The broken pipe was spurting water.*   **2** [I (**for**)] to make a short sudden effort or increase of activity or speed: *The runner spurted for the line.*

spurt[2] *n*   **1** a short sudden increase of activity, effort, or speed: *He does his work in erratic spurts. | She put on a sudden spurt and overtook all the other runners.*   **2** [(**of**)] a sudden usu. short pouring out of liquid or gas: *The boiler gave off a spurt of steam.*

Sput·nik /'spʊtnɪk/ *n* any of a number of SATELLITEs put into space by the Soviet Union, esp. **Sputnik I** which was the first man-made satellite to go around the Earth

sput·ter /'spʌtər/ *v*   **1** [I] to make repeated soft explosive sounds: *The car's engine started, sputtered for a moment, and died again.*   **2** [I;T] to speak or say in confusion — **sputter** *n* : *the sputter of hot fat in the pan*

spu·tum /'spjuːtəm/ *n* [U] *med* liquid from the mouth, esp. as coughed up from the lungs in some diseases

spy

spy[1] /spaɪ/ *n* a person employed to find out secret information, esp. from an enemy or a competitor in business: *The security police have uncovered/exposed/captured a foreign spy.*

▶CULTURAL NOTE The popular image of a spy is of a brave, attractive man like James Bond or a mysterious man or woman in dark GLASSES. —compare DOUBLE AGENT, MOLE[1] (2)◀

spy[2] *v*   **1** [I (**on, upon**)] to work as a spy, trying to find out secret information: *He was expelled from the country for spying on their naval bases. | She has been charged with spying for an enemy power.* —compare DOUBLE AGENT   **2** [I (**into, on**)] to watch or search secretly: *From behind her curtain she could spy on her neighbours. | It's wrong to spy into other people's affairs. | We think we can do business with them, but we've sent a representative to* **spy out the land** (=collect some more information about them) *before we decide.*   **3** [T] *esp. lit* to catch sight of; discover after some looking: *She suddenly spied her friend in the crowd.* [+*obj+v-ing*] *I spied him hiding behind the door.*

Spy·catch·er /'spaɪkætʃər/ *a* book written by a former British spy, Peter Wright, which shocked the public in 1987 because it revealed (REVEAL) secrets about the government and about government spies. Many members of the government, especially the PRIME MINISTER, Mrs Thatcher, opposed the book and as a result it was banned (BAN) in Britain.

spy·glass /'spaɪɡlɑːs‖-ɡlæs/ *n* a small TELESCOPE, used esp. in former times

Spy Who Came in from the Cold /ˌ· · · '· · · '·/, **The** a book by John Le Carré written in 1963, about a British spy in East Germany who wanted to go back to the West

sq *written abbrev. for:* square: *6 sq metres*

squab /skwɒb‖skwɑːb/ n a young PIGEON (=kind of bird), esp. as food

squab·ble /'skwɒbəl‖'skwɑː-/ v [I (**about, over**)] to take part in a continuing quarrel, esp. over something unimportant: *What are you children squabbling about now?* —**squabble** n

squad /skwɒd‖skwɑːd/ n [C+*sing.*|*pl. v*] **1** a group of people, usu. highly trained, working as a team: *a bomb squad* | *a fire-fighting squad* | *The final England football team will be chosen from their squad of 14.* **2** a small group of soldiers, often together for a particular duty: *a drill squad* —see also DEATH SQUAD, FIRING SQUAD, FLYING SQUAD

squad car /'· ·/ n esp. AmE a car used by police on duty; PATROL CAR

squad·dy /'skwɒdi‖'skwɑː-/ n esp. BrE infml a soldier, esp. one who is not an officer

squad·ron /'skwɒdrən‖'skwɑː-/ n [C+*sing.*|*pl. v*] a military or naval unit, esp. a middle-sized airforce unit with between 10 and 18 aircraft: *a squadron of bombers/warships*

squadron lead·er /'·· ,··/ n an officer in the British airforce below a WING COMMANDER —see TABLE 3

squal·id /'skwɒlɪd‖'skwɑː-/ adj **1** very dirty and unpleasant, esp. as a result of lack of care or lack of money: *How can they live in such squalid conditions?* | *squalid slums* **2** having or concerning low moral standards; SORDID: *a squalid story of sex and violence* — ~**ly** adv

squall¹ /skwɔːl/ n a sudden strong wind often bringing rain or snow: (fig.) *domestic squalls* (=short but noisy arguments) — ~**y** adj : *squally showers*

squall² v [I] to cry (out) noisily: *Can't you stop that baby squalling?* —**squall** n

squal·or /'skwɒlər‖'skwɑː-/ n [U] the condition of being SQUALID (1): *ten people living in squalor in a single room*

squan·der /'skwɒndər‖'skwɑːn-/ v [T (**on**)] to spend foolishly; use up wastefully: *The council has been squandering the ratepayers' money.* | *to squander a valuable opportunity* — ~**er** n

Squan·to /'skwɒntəʊ ‖ 'skwɑːn-/ (1585?–1622) a Native American who helped the Pilgrims survive their first years in North America by showing them where to hunt and fish and how to plant corn

square¹ /skweər/ n **1** a shape with four straight equal sides forming four right angles —compare OBLONG, RECTANGLE; see picture at QUADRILATERAL **2** a piece of material in this shape: *a square of cloth* —see picture at PIECE **3** (the buildings surrounding) a broad open area in a town, usu. in the form of a square: *The market is held in the town square.* | *The American embassy in London is in Grosvenor Square.* **4** [(**of**)] the number obtained when another number is multiplied by itself: *16 is the square of 4.* —see also SQUARE³ (3), SQUARE ROOT **5** a space on a game board: *He moved his queen two squares forward.* **6** old-fash sl a person who does not know or follow the latest ideas, styles, etc. **7** a straight-edged often L-shaped tool for drawing and measuring right angles —see also SET SQUARE, T-SQUARE **8 on the square** old-fash infml honestly; fairly

square² adj **1** [no comp.] having four equal sides and four right angles; being a square: *A handkerchief is usually square.* | *a square tower/box* **2** forming a right angle: *a square corner* | *square shoulders* **3** [A no comp.] being a measurement of area equal to that of a square with sides of the stated length: *10,000 square centimetres equals 1 square metre.* | *The forest covers an area of 1500 square miles.* **4** [after n; no comp.] being the stated length from a corner in both directions: *The room is six metres square.* **5** [F (**with**)] level: *That shelf isn't quite square (with the other one); can you straighten it?* **6** fair and honest: *a square deal* —see also **fair and square** (FAIR²) **7** [F] equal in points: *The teams are all square at one goal each.* **8** [F] having no debts to one another that are still to be settled: *I've paid what I owe them so we are all square now.* **9** old-fash sl of or like a SQUARE¹ (6); old-fashioned **10** (in cricket) in a position at (about) right angles to the hitter **11 a square peg in a round hole** infml someone who is not suited to the job they hold, the group they belong to, etc.; MISFIT —see also SQUARELY — ~**ness** n [U]

square³ v **1** [T (OFF, UP)] to put into a shape with straight lines and right angles: *He squared off the end of the piece*

of wood. | *"I won't be threatened," she said, squaring her shoulders defiantly.* **2** [T (OFF)] to divide into squares or mark with squares: *squared paper* **3** [T usu. pass.] to multiply (a number) by itself once: *2 squared equals 4.* (written 2²=4) —see also SQUARE¹ (4), SQUARE ROOT **4** [I;T (**with**)] to (cause to) match known or accepted facts, standards, aims, etc.; be in agreement or bring into agreement: *His statement doesn't square with* (=fit) *the facts.* | *They've tried to persuade me to do it, but I can't square it with my conscience.* | *I haven't got time to ask the boss if it's all right — would you square it with her for me?* **5** [T] to cause (totals of points or games won) to be equal: *Britain won the second match to square the series at one each.* **6** [T] infml to pay or pay for; settle: *I've squared my account at the store.* **7** [T] infml to pay or settle dishonestly, esp. by a BRIBE: *There are government officials who will have to be squared if we're to get this scheme approved.* **8 square the circle** to attempt something impossible

square (sthg.) away phr v [T; usu. pass.] AmE infml **1** to finish, esp. the last details: *I have to get this report squared away before I leave tonight.* **2** to tidy (a place): *As soon as the station wagon is squared away* (=things are put in the right places in the car), *we can go.*

square up phr v [I] **1** infml to pay what is owed; settle a bill: *Let's square up; how much do I owe you?* **2** [(**to**)] also **square off**— to take up or get ready to begin fighting

square up to sthg./sbdy. phr v [T] to face (an opponent or a difficult situation) with determination: *I admire the way she squared up to the problem.*

square-bash·ing /'· ,··/ n [U] BrE infml practice, esp. in marching, by soldiers

square brack·et /ˌ· '··/ n [usu. pl.] esp. BrE a BRACKET¹ (2a)

square dance /'· ·/ n a type of country dance in which four pairs of dancers face each other to form a square

▶CULTURAL NOTE In the US, square dancing is often associated with the West of the country, but it is done all over the US and many children learn square dances in school. There is usually a **caller** who tells the dancers which steps to do, and he often talks very fast and uses special names for the steps.◀

square knot /'· ·/ n AmE for REEF KNOT

square leg /ˌ· '·/ n (in cricket) a fielding (FIELD² (1)) position

square·ly /'skweəli‖'skweər-/ also **square**— adv **1** in a fair and honest way **2** [+prep] directly: *He looked her squarely in the eye.* | *The report puts the blame for the accident squarely on the driver of the train.*

square meal /ˌ· '·/ n infml a good satisfying and healthy meal: *You need to eat three square meals a day.*

Square Mile /ˌ· '·/ [the] the part of London, to the E of the centre, where most of the important banks and financial and business institutions, such as the Stock Exchange, are found

square one /ˌ· '·/ n [U] the starting point: *The committee rejected all our plans, so now we're* **back to square one.**

square-rigged /ˌ· '··◂/ adj (of a ship) having sails set across rather than along the length of the ship —compare FORE AND AFT

square root /ˌ· '·/ n the number which when multiplied by itself equals a particular number: *If 3 is the square root of 9* (written √9), *then 3 x 3=9.*

squash¹ /skwɒʃ‖skwɑːʃ, skwɔːʃ/ v **1** [T] to force into a flat shape; crush: *I sat on my hat/the box/the tomato and squashed it.* | *The car was squashed flat by the lorry.* | *The flowers I was carrying got squashed in the crowded train.* **2** [I+adv|prep;T+obj+adv|prep] to push or fit into a small space, esp. with difficulty; SQUEEZE: *They all squashed into the tiny compartment.* | *I squashed a few more clothes into my case and forced it shut.* **3** [T] to force into silence or inactivity: *I squashed him with a sarcastic remark.* | *to squash dissent/rumours*

squash² n **1** [S] the condition of being squashed: *Five people in this car is a bit of a squash, but we'll manage.* **2** [U] also **squash rack·ets** /'· ··/ fml— a game played in a four-walled court by usu. two people with RACKETS¹ (smaller than for tennis) and a small rather soft rubber ball —compare RACQUETBALL **3** [U] BrE a sweet drink made by adding water to the juice of a CITRUS fruit: *a glass of orange/lemon squash* —compare CRUSH² (2)

squash

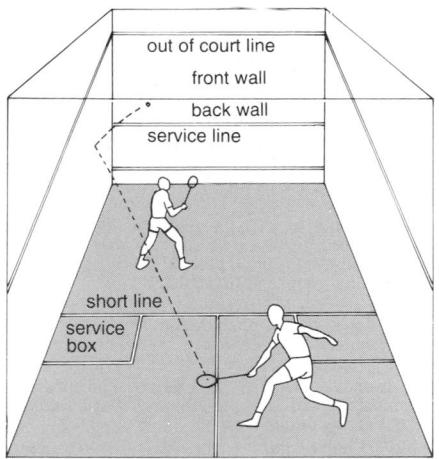

out of court line
front wall
back wall
service line

short line
service box

see also picture at **racquetball**

squash³ *n* [C;U] *esp. AmE* any of a group of large vegetables with hard skins, including MARROWs, GOURDs, and PUMPKINS

squash·y /ˈskwɒʃi‖ˈskwɑːʃi, ˈskwɔːʃi/ *adj infml* soft and easy to press or crush: *squashy overripe tomatoes* —**iness** *n* [U]

squat¹ /skwɒt‖skwɑːt/ *v* -tt- [I] 1 [(DOWN, on)] to sit on a surface with the knees bent and the legs drawn fully up under the body, esp. balancing on the front of the feet: *He squatted down beside the footprints and examined them closely.* | *to squat on one's haunches.* 2 [(in, on)] to live in an empty building without owning it, paying rent, or getting permission —see also SQUATTER 3 [(on)] *AmE* to settle on public or government-owned land in the hope of owning it some day. This was esp. formerly when people were first settling in the western part of the US: *He and his family squatted on some land near a lake.*

squat² *n* 1 [S] a squatting position 2 [C] *BrE* an empty building for squatting in

squat³ *adj* -tt- ungracefully short or low and thick: *an ugly squat tower*

squat·ter /ˈskwɒtəʳ‖ˈskwɑː-/ *n* 1 *BrE* a person who lives in an empty building without permission or payment of rent

▶CULTURAL NOTE In Britain, some people, esp. young people, move into and live in empty houses and flats in this way esp. in cities. If the building is owned by a local authority, they sometimes allow squatters to stay there if, for example, there is a plan to pull the building down. If the property is privately-owned, the owner may take legal action to get squatters out.◄

2 a settler on unowned land who does not pay rent but has legal rights over it (**squatter's rights**) and may sometimes become its owner

squaw /skwɔː/ *n* a Native American Indian wife, esp. in former times

squawk¹ /skwɔːk/ *v* [I] 1 (esp. of certain types of bird) to make a loud sharp cry: *His parrot squawks all day long.* 2 *infml* to complain loudly: *They're always the first to squawk when their rights are infringed.* — ~ **er** *n*

squawk² *n* an act or noise of squawking: *the squawks of seagulls/of taxpayers*

squeak¹ /skwiːk/ *v* [I] 1 to make a short very high, but not loud, sound: *The mouse squeaked.* | *These old bedsprings squeak whenever I move.* | *a squeaking door* 2 [+adv/prep] *infml* to succeed, pass, or win narrowly, only just avoiding failure: *Only eight could go on to the next round, and I squeaked through in eighth place.* — ~ **er** *n*

squeak² *n* a short very high soft sound: *the squeak of a mouse* | *(infml) I don't want to hear another squeak out*

of you! (=keep quiet) —see also BUBBLE AND SQUEAK, NARROW SQUEAK

squeak·y /ˈskwiːki/ *adj* 1 that squeaks: *a squeaky door/voice* 2 **squeaky clean** *infml, esp. AmE* **a** very clean **b** *humor* morally pure: *her squeaky clean public image*

squeal¹ /skwiːl/ *v* [I] 1 to make a long very high sound or cry: *The children squealed with delight.* 2 [(on)] *sl* to give secret information about one's criminal friends to the police — ~ **er** *n*

squeal² *n* a long very high sound or cry: *There was a squeal of tyres/brakes as the car stopped suddenly.* | *Squeals of delight/protest came from the children.*

squeam·ish /ˈskwiːmɪʃ/ *adj* easily shocked, upset, or made to feel sick by unpleasant things: *I could never be a nurse; I'm too squeamish.* | *It's a violent film, so don't go if you're squeamish.* — ~ **ly** *adv* — ~ **ness** *n* [U]

squee·gee /ˈskwiːdʒiː/ *n* a tool with a straight-edged rubber blade and short handle, for removing or spreading liquid on a surface: *She cleaned the windows with a squeegee.* —**squeegee** *v* [T]

squeeze¹ /skwiːz/ *v* 1 [T] to press firmly together, esp. from opposite sides: *She squeezed the tube hard and the last of the toothpaste came out.* | *He squeezed her arm sympathetically.* | *Would you squeeze some oranges and make me a glass of juice?* | *He squeezed out the wet sponge.* 2 [T+obj+adv/prep] to get or force out by squeezing: *She squeezed the water out of the sponge/squeezed some toothpaste onto her brush.* | *(fig.) He managed to squeeze ten pages of text out of one small incident.* | *(fig.) The company is being squeezed out of this market by very aggressive competition.* 3 [I+adv/prep;T+obj+adv/prep] to fit by forcing, pressing, or crowding: *Is the car full or can I squeeze in?* | *He was so fat that he could only just squeeze through the door.* | *(fig.) It was a close game, but we managed to squeeze home* (=win narrowly) *by two points.* | *She tries to squeeze her feet into shoes that are too small.* 4 [T+obj+adv/prep] to provide with a place/or space, esp. with difficulty; find space or time for: *You'll find the shop squeezed between two big office buildings.* | *How can you squeeze so many things into a day?* | *I know the doctor is extremely busy, but do you think he could squeeze me in* (=see me) *for two minutes?* 5 [T] to cause money difficulties to, esp. by means of tight controls or severe demands: *Many businesses are being squeezed by high costs and reduced sales.* | *The latest cuts will result in the education budget being squeezed still further.*

squeeze² *n* 1 [C] an act of pressing in from opposite sides or around: *He gave her hand a gentle squeeze.* 2 [C (of)] a small amount pressed out: *I like my tea with a squeeze of lemon.* —see picture at PIECE 3 [S] *infml* a crowded state; SQUASH: *There's room for one more, but it'll be a (tight) squeeze.* 4 [C *usu. sing.*] (esp. in business) a difficult situation caused by short supplies, tight controls, or high costs: *a credit squeeze* 5 **put the squeeze on** *infml* to put pressure on: *They're putting the squeeze on him to sign that agreement.*

squeeze-box /ˈskwiːzbɒks‖-bɑːks/ *n infml for* ACCORDION

squeez·er /ˈskwiːzəʳ/ *n* an apparatus that presses the juice from fruit, esp. oranges and LEMONs

squelch /skweltʃ/ *v* 1 [I] to make, or move while making, a sound of a partly liquid substance being pressed down and drawn up, for example when stepping through mud: *We squelched up the muddy lane to the farm.* 2 [T] *AmE* to make (someone) be silent or feel unimportant, esp. by saying something cruel: *He squelched her showing off by making a sarcastic remark about her clothes.* —**squelch** *n* [*usu. sing.*] : *the squelch of swamp water in their boots* — ~ **y** *adj* : *squelchy ground*

squib /skwɪb/ *n* 1 a small toy explosive 2 a short not usu. serious piece of writing, esp. attacking a politician or political party —see also DAMP SQUIB

squid /skwɪd/ *n* **squid** *or* **squids** a sea creature with ten arms at one end of a long soft body that is strengthened by a thin flat structure inside —see picture at OCTOPUS

squidg·y /ˈskwɪdʒi/ *adj BrE infml* soft and wet, e.g. like thick mud

squiff·y /ˈskwɪfi/ *adj old-fash BrE infml* slightly drunk

squig·gle /ˈskwɪgəl/ *n infml* a short wavy or twisting line, esp. written or printed: *What do these squiggles on the map mean?* —**gly** *adj* : *squiggly lines*

squint¹ /skwɪnt/ v [I] **1** to look with almost closed eyes: *The sun was so bright I had to squint.* | *He took careful aim, squinting down the rifle barrel.* **2** [*not in progressive forms*] to have a SQUINT² (1)

squint² n **1** a disorder of the eye muscles causing the eyes to look in two different directions: *He's got a bad squint.* **2** [(at)] an act of looking hard through nearly closed eyes **3** [(at)] *AmE infml* a quick look; GLANCE: *Take a squint at these figures.*

squire¹ /skwaɪəʳ/ n **1** (in former times) the main land-owner in an English village or country place —compare LAIRD **2** (in former times) a KNIGHT's armour-carrier **3** *BrE infml* (used esp. by a man as a friendly way of speaking to another man whose name is not known, and who may be of a higher social class)

squire² v [T] *AmE* to travel with (someone) as their companion to various social events: *He squired her around town.*

squire·ar·chy , **squirarchy** /'skwaɪərɑːkɪ‖-ɑːr-/ n [C+*sing.*|*pl. v*] the class of country landowners holding political power, esp. in England until 1832

squirm /skwɜːm‖skɜːrm/ v [I] to twist the body about, esp. from discomfort, shame, or nervousness: *The eels squirmed in the fisherman's net.* | *She was squirming with embarrassment.* | (fig.) *The film was so sentimental that it made me squirm.* —**squirm** n

squir·rel /'skwɪrəl‖'skwɜːrəl/ n a small animal with a long furry tail that climbs trees and eats nuts which it also stores for the winter: *a red*|*grey squirrel* —see picture at RODENT

squirt¹ /skwɜːt‖skwɜːrt/ v **1** [I;T] to force or be forced out in a thin fast stream: *Water squirted from the punctured hose.* | *Squirt oil into the lock.* **2** [T (with)] to hit or cover with such a stream of liquid: *The children squirted their father with water from a plastic bottle.* —**-er** n

squirt² n **1** [(of)] a quick thin stream of liquid: *Give the lock a couple of squirts of oil.* —see picture at PIECE **2** *old-fash derog* a young or small person, esp. a male, who is rude or acts too importantly

squirt gun /'· ·/ n *AmE for* WATER PISTOL

squish /skwɪʃ/ v *infml* **1** [I+*adv*|*prep*] to press down gently on a substance, such as mud, which is soft and wet, so that one makes a soft noise **2** [T] *infml* to SQUASH or SQUEEZE: *Careful, don't squish the tomatoes.* —**squish** n [*usu. sing.*] — **~y** *adj*

Sr *written abbrev. for:* **1** [after n] (added to the name of a man, when he and his son have the same name) SENIOR: *Douglas Fairbanks Sr* **2** [A] SEÑOR: *Sr Lopez*

Sri Lan·ka /sri: 'læŋkə/ an island in S Asia, in the Indian Ocean, SE of India, formerly called Ceylon; capital city, Colombo; population 16,806,000 (1989). It was ruled by the British from 1798 to 1948. —**Sri Lankan** n,adj

SRN /ˌes ɑːr 'en/ n abbrev. for: STATE REGISTERED NURSE

SRO /ˌes ɑːr 'əʊ/ n STANDING ROOM only

SS /'es es/ [A] n abbrev. for: STEAMSHIP

SS /ˌes 'es◂/ [*the*] the special soldiers of the NAZIs in Germany who protected Adolf Hitler and, from 1929, were commanded by Heinrich Himmler. They controlled the secret police, the Gestapo, and the CONCENTRATION CAMPS where millions of people died in the 1930s and 1940s. They were also known as the Blackshirts.

ssh /ʃ/ ‖ **shh** *AmE—* interj (used for asking for silence or less noise)

SSI /ˌes es 'aɪ/ n [U] Supplemental Security Income for the Aged, Blind, and Disabled; in the US, money given to poor people over 65 or who are blind or who have a disability

SSN /ˌes es 'en/ n *AmE abbrev. for:* SOCIAL SECURITY NUMBER

SST /ˌes es 'ti:/ n supersonic transport; an aircraft that can travel faster than the speed of sound

St *written abbrev. for:* **1** [A] SAINT: *St Luke's Gospel* **2** [after n or adj] Street: *Oxford St* | *Church St* | *Main St*

stab¹ /stæb/ v **-bb-** [I (**at**);T(**in**)] **1** to strike forcefully (into) with the point of something sharp, esp. a knife, rather than with its edge: *Caesar was stabbed to death.* | *She stabbed him in the leg with a knife.* **2** to make forceful pushing movements with (something pointed); JAB: *He stabbed his finger at her*|*at the page angrily.* **3 stab someone in the back** to do harm to someone by whom

one is liked or trusted; BETRAY someone — **~ber** n

stab² n **1** [(at)] an act of stabbing or trying to stab someone: *He made a vicious stab at me with a broken bottle.* | *She was taken to hospital with severe stab wounds.* **2** [(of)] a sudden sharp painful feeling: *I felt a stab of pain*|*fear*|*remorse.* **3** [(at)] *infml* a try: *I don't think I'd be much good, but I'm willing to have*|*make a stab at it.* **4 stab in the back** an attack from someone supposed to be a friend; BETRAYAL

stab·bing¹ /'stæbɪŋ/ adj (esp. of pain) as if made by a knife; sharp and sudden: *a stabbing sensation*|*pain in his foot*

stabbing² n a crime in which a person is stabbed: *There was a stabbing near the university last night.*

sta·bil·i·ty /stə'bɪlɪti/ n [U] the quality or state of being stable: *His constant absences threaten the stability of his marriage.* | *the stability of the pound* | *a long period of political stability* —opposite **instability**

sta·bil·ize also **-ise** *BrE* /'steɪbɪlaɪz/ v [I;T] to (cause to) become firm, steady, or unchanging: *The price of coffee has been rising and falling sharply, but has now (been) stabilized.* —**-ization** /ˌsteɪbɪlaɪ'zeɪʃən‖-lə-/ n [U]

sta·bil·iz·er also **-iser** *BrE* /'steɪbɪlaɪzəʳ/ n an apparatus or chemical that stabilizes something: *The ship's stabilizers keep it steady in bad weather.*

sta·ble¹ /'steɪbəl/ adj **1** not easily moved, upset, or changed; firm; steady: *The ladder isn't very stable.* | *a stable marriage*|*government*|*rate of exchange* | *a politically stable country* **2** unlikely to behave unreasonably; dependable: *He's a bit neurotic, but his wife's a very stable person.* **3** *tech* (of a substance) tending to keep the same chemical or atomic state; not breaking down naturally —opposite **unstable** —**-bly** adv

stable² n **1** also **stables** pl.— *BrE* a (part of a) building for keeping and feeding horses in: *a stable door* **2** *AmE* a (part of a) building for keeping and feeding horses, cattle, etc., in **3** [(of)] a group of racing horses with one owner or trainer: *She's built up an impressive stable of steeplechasers over the years.* | (fig.) *The new British boxing champion is from Terry Dixon's stable of fighters.*

stable³ v [T] to put or keep (a horse) in a stable

stable boy /'·· ·/ also **stable lad** *BrE* ‖ **sta·ble·boy** /'steɪbəlbɔɪ/, **stable·man** /-mən, -mæn/ *AmE—* n a man or boy who works in a stable and looks after horses

sta·bling /'steɪblɪŋ/ n [U] space in STABLES² (1): *There's stabling here for five horses.*

stac·cat·o /stə'kɑːtəʊ/ adj, adv (of music) (having notes) cut short in playing; disconnected(ly): (fig.) *He spoke in a high-pitched, staccato manner.* —compare LEGATO

stack¹ /stæk/ n **1** [(of)] an orderly pile of things one above another: *a stack of papers*|*dishes*|*coins* —see PILE (USAGE) and see picture at PILE **2** a large pile of grain, grass, etc., stored outdoors —see also HAYSTACK **3** [(of)] also **stacks** pl.— esp. *BrE infml* a large amount or number: *I've got stacks of work*|*a stack of work to do.* **4** also **stacks** pl.— a part of a library where books are stored close together —see also CHIMNEYSTACK, SMOKESTACK, **blow one's stack** (BLOW)

stack² v **1** [I;T (UP)] to form or make into a neat pile: *They are specially packaged so that they stack easily.* | *Stack the books up against the wall.* **2** [T (with)] *usu. pass.*] to put piles of things on or in (a place): *The floor was stacked with boxes.* **3** [T (against)] *infml* to arrange (esp. playing cards) dishonestly so as to give oneself an unfair advantage: *He accused his opponent of stacking the cards.* | (fig.) *I don't think we'll win; the cards*|*odds are stacked against us.* (=everything is to our disadvantage) **4** [T (UP)] to make (an aircraft) fly in a pattern with others waiting for a turn to land at an airport
   stack up phr v [I (**against**)] *infml, esp. AmE* to compare; match: *How does their product stack up against those of their commercial rivals?*

stacked /stækt/ adj *AmE infml* (of a woman) having large breasts and an attractive body; women find this word offensive

sta·di·um /'steɪdiəm/ n **-diums** or **-dia** /diə/ (a sports field surrounded by) a large sometimes unroofed building with rows of seats: *a football*|*baseball stadium* —see colour picture on page 883

staff¹ /stɑːf‖stæf/ n **1** [C+*sing.*|*pl. v*] the group of workers who carry on a job or do the work of an organization, esp.

of a teaching or business organization: *The school's staff is/are excellent.* | *I have a staff of 15.* | *It's good to have you* **on** (=as a member of) **our/the staff** —compare WORKFORCE; see also GENERAL STAFF, GROUND STAFF **2** [P] *BrE* members of such a group: *She's in charge of about 20 staff.| complaints by (members of) staff about working conditions.* | *a special car park for the senior staff* | *The reorganization may lead to staff reductions.* **3** [C] *(pl* **staves**) a long thick stick of the kind that is **a** carried when walking or **b** used as a mark of office **4** [C] a pole for flying a flag on; FLAGPOLE **5** [C] (in music) a STAVE¹ (1)

staff² *v* [T **(with)** *usu. pass.*] to provide the workers for: *The refugee centre is staffed mainly by/with volunteers.* —see also OVERSTAFFED, UNDERSTAFFED

staff nurse /ˈ· ˌ·/ *n* a British hospital nurse next in rank below a SISTER (4)

staff of·fi·cer /ˈ· ˌ···/ *n* an officer who helps a military commander of high rank rather than commanding soldiers himself

staff of life /ˌ· · ˈ·/ *[the]* *lit* bread, thought of as the most important kind of food

Stafford /ˈstæfəd‖-fərd/ a town in W central England, where the local government for Staffordshire is based

Staf·ford·shire /ˈstæfədʃəʳ‖-fərd-/ *written abbrev.* **Staffs**— a COUNTY in W central England famous esp. for its factories making CHINA (=plates, cups, etc.)

staff ser·geant /ˈ· ˌ···/ *n* a military rank —see TABLE 3

stag /stæg/ *n* **1** *(pl.* **stags** *or* **stag**) a fully grown male deer **2** *BrE* a person who buys shares in a new company hoping to sell them quickly at a profit **3 go stag** *AmE infml* (of a man) to go to a social event without a female companion: *He went stag to the prom.* —see also STAG NIGHT, STAG PARTY

stage¹ /steɪdʒ/ *n* **1** the raised floor on which plays are performed in a theatre: *a stage set for an indoor scene* | *The actor was* **on stage** *for most of the play.* | *He'd always wanted to go* **on the stage.** (=become an actor) | *Her servant enters/exits* **stage left/right.** (=from the left/right side of the stage as one looks out towards the theatre seats) | *a well-known novel that has been adapted for the stage* (=for performance as a play) | (fig.) *He's very vain; he always wants to be at the centre of the stage.* —see picture at THEATRE **2** a particular point or period in the course of a process or set of events; state reached at a particular time: *The plan is still in its early stages/at an early stage.* | *The calculations are rechecked at every stage of the construction.* | *At this stage of the negotiations, it would be unwise to comment on their chances of success.| Don't worry about your daughter's odd behaviour; it's just* **a stage she's going through.** | *the stages of development of the frog* | *The proposed new law is currently at the committee stage.* —compare PHASE¹ (1), STEP¹ (6); see also COMMITTEE STAGE **3 a** a part of a journey: *We travelled by (easy) stages, often stopping along the way.* **b** a fixed division of a race that takes place over several days: *That cyclist won the second stage of the Tour de France.* **4** a single complete driving part of a ROCKET¹ (1): *a three-stage rocket* **5** a STAGECOACH **6 Don't put your daughter on the stage, Mrs Worthington** the title of an old humorous popular song which warned parents that life in the theatre encouraged immorality in young people **7 All the world's a stage** *quote* a phrase from Shakespeare's play *As You Like It.* It is the first line of a long speech comparing the world to a stage and the different parts of a person's life to different characters that the person plays **8 set the stage for** to prepare for or make possible: *The unjust peace treaty merely set the stage for another war.* —see also LANDING STAGE

stage² *v* [T] **1** to perform or arrange for public show; put on: *to stage a play/an art show/a charity football game* **2** to cause to happen, esp. for public effect: *The union staged a one-day strike.* | *The pop star staged a row with his manager in a restaurant to get maximum publicity.*

stage·coach /ˈsteɪdʒkəʊtʃ/ *also* **stage**— *n* (in former times) a horse-drawn closed vehicle carrying passengers on regular services between fixed places

stage di·rec·tion /ˈ· ·ˌ··/ *n* a written description of something an actor must do on stage in performing a play: *Here the stage direction says "Goes and looks out of the window".*

stage door /ˌ· ˈ·◂/ *n* the side or back door in a theatre, used by actors and stage workers

stage fright /ˈ· ·/ *n* [U] nervousness felt by someone performing or esp. about to perform in public

stage·hand /ˈsteɪdʒhænd/ *n* someone who works on a theatre stage, moving scenery, painting scenery, etc.

stage-man·age /ˈ· ˌ··/ *v* [T] *infml* to arrange or prepare for public effect, esp. so that a desired result will happen in a way that will appear natural: *The press conference was cleverly stage-managed so that the President would not have to answer any embarrassing questions.*

stage man·ag·er /ˈ· ˌ···/ *n* the person in charge of a theatre stage during a performance

stage name /ˈ· ˌ·/ *n* a name used professionally by an actor instead of his or her real name

stage-struck /ˈsteɪdʒstrʌk/ *adj* in love with the theatre and esp. with the idea of being an actor

stage whis·per /ˌ· ˈ··/ *n* **1** an actor's loud whisper supposedly not heard by other actors on the stage **2** a loud whisper intended to be heard by everyone

stag·ey /ˈsteɪdʒi/ *adj* STAGY

stag·fla·tion /stægˈfleɪʃən/ *n* [U] an economic condition in which there is INFLATION (=continuing rise in prices) but the ECONOMY is not growing, so many people do not have jobs and businesses are not doing well: *economic stagflation during a recession*

stag·ger¹ /ˈstægəʳ/ *v* **1** [I+adv/prep] to walk or move unsteadily and with great difficulty, almost falling: *The drunken man staggered towards us/away.* | *He staggered to the door, bleeding from his wounds.* | *(infml) I finally staggered into bed at 3 o'clock in the morning.* —compare TOTTER **2** [T] to cause to feel shocked disbelief; seem almost unbelievable to: *Her incredible story staggers the imagination.* | *I was staggered by his outrageous suggestion.* **3** [T] to arrange (esp. working hours, holidays, etc.) not to begin and end at the same time **4** [T] to start (a race on a track with a bend) with each runner starting at a different place so that in the end everyone runs the same distance, e.g. in a 400 metres race

stagger² *n* an unsteady movement of a person having trouble walking or standing

stag·ger·ing /ˈstægərɪŋ/ *adj* almost unbelievable; very surprising and shocking: *It cost a staggering £30,000!* – – **ly** *adv*

stag·ing /ˈsteɪdʒɪŋ/ *n* **1** [C;U] the action or art of performing a play: *an imaginative modern-dress staging of "Hamlet"* **2** [U] movable boards and frames for standing on; SCAFFOLDING

staging post /ˈ··· ·/ *n* a place at which regular stops are made on long journeys: *Bahrain is a staging post on the flight from Britain to Australia* —compare STOPOVER

stag·nant /ˈstægnənt/ *adj* **1** (esp. of water) not flowing or moving, and often bad-smelling: *a stagnant pond covered with scum* **2** not developing or growing; inactive; STATIC: *Due to low investment, our industrial output has remained stagnant.* – – **ly** *adv* —**nancy** *n* [U]

stag·nate /stægˈneɪt‖ˈstægneɪt/ *v* [I] to become stagnant; stop moving or developing: *a stagnating economy* | *She didn't want to stagnate in her dull office job until she retired.* —**nation** /stægˈneɪʃən/ *n* [U]: *economic stagnation*

stag night /ˈ· ·/ *n* the night before a man's wedding, which he spends with his male friends only, usu. having a party or (in Britain) a few drinks in a pub

stag par·ty /ˈ· ˌ··/ *n* a party for men only esp. on the night before a man's wedding: *He had a hangover after drinking too much at his stag party.* —compare HEN PARTY

stag·y, stagey /ˈsteɪdʒi/ *adj derog* as if acting or acted on stage; not natural: *a very stagy manner* —**ily** *adv* —**iness** *n* [U]

staid /steɪd/ *adj* having a serious and dull nature; unadventurous: *a staid old bachelor* | *staid attitudes* – – **ly** *adv* – – **ness** *n* [U]

stain¹ /steɪn/ *v* **1** [I;T] to mark or discolour in a way that is lasting or difficult to remove: *This carpet stains easily, so try not to spill anything on it.* | *His teeth were stained with nicotine from years of smoking.* **2** [T] to change in colour, esp. by darkening with a DYE or chemical substance: *I'm going to stain the chairs (brown) with wood*

dye to match the table. | *(tech) to stain a specimen for microscopic analysis*

stain² *n* **1** [C] *(often in comb.)* a stained place or spot: *The police found blood stains on the suspect's clothes.* | *I washed the tablecloth several times but couldn't get the gravy stains out.* | *(fig.) He was released without a stain on his character.* (=with no suggestion at all that he was guilty or bad) **2** [C;U] a chemical for darkening esp. wood or for putting on things under a microscope so as to make them easier to see

stained glass /ˌ·ˈ·◂/ *n* [U] glass of different colours used for making pictures and patterns in windows, esp. in church windows

stain·less /ˈsteɪnləs/ *adj* **1** of a kind not easily marked or stained, esp. by RUST: *a set of* **stainless steel** *cutlery* **2** *lit* without a mark of guilt or shame

stair /steəʳ/ *n* **1** *esp. lit* stairs: *We climbed down the steep winding stair.* | *The stair carpet was held down by stair rods.* **2** any of the steps in a set of stairs: *She sat on the bottom stair.*

stair·case /ˈsteəkeɪs‖ˈsteər-/ also **stair·way** /-weɪ/— *n* a set of stairs with its supports and side parts for holding on to —see also ESCALATOR

stair rods /ˈ·ˌ·/ *n* [P] *BrE infml* **raining stair rods** raining very hard

stairs /steəz‖steərz/ *n* [P] **1** a fixed length of steps built for going from one level to another, esp. inside a building: *He ran up|down the stairs.* | *She was standing at the top|bottom|foot of the stairs with her hand on the banister.* | *The attic is up five* **flights of stairs.** (=is on the fifth floor) —see also DOWNSTAIRS, UPSTAIRS **2 above|below stairs** (in former times) in the masters'/servants' part of the house

stair·way /ˈsteəweɪ‖ˈsteər-/ *n* a staircase

stair·well /ˈsteəwel‖ˈsteər-/ *n* the space, going up through all the floors of a building, where the stairs are

stake¹ /steɪk/ *n* **1** a pointed piece of wood, metal, etc., for driving into the ground as a mark, for holding a rope, etc. **2** (in former times) a post to which a person was tied for being killed, esp. by burning: *Heretics were often* **burnt at the stake.** | *(fig.) It's a fairly important principle, but I wouldn't* **go to the stake for** *it.* (=take great risks to defend it) **3** [(**in**)] a share in something, esp. in a business, that gives one an interest in whether it succeeds or fails: *We must give young people the feeling that they have a stake in the country's future.* | *The company is selling off its 15% stake in the Commercial Bank.* **4** money risked on the result of something; esp. a horse race; BET¹ (2) **5 at stake** at risk; dependent on what happens: *The company is on the verge of bankruptcy, and hundreds of jobs are at stake.* —see also STAKES **6 pull up stakes** *AmE infml* to leave one's job or home: *I'm going to pull up stakes and move to Montana.*

stake² *v* [T] **1** [(**on**)] **a** to risk (money) on the result of a race or competition **b** to risk the loss of (something valuable, such as one's life or public position) on a result, esp. because one is confident of success: *The prime minister is staking his reputation|credibility on a successful outcome to the arms talks.* | *I've staked all my hopes on you.* **2** [(UP)] to fasten or strengthen with STAKES¹ (1): *to stake a young tree* **3** [(OFF, OUT)] to mark or enclose (an area of ground) with STAKES¹ (1): *The muddiest corner of the field has been staked off.* **4 stake (out) a|one's claim (to)** to make a claim; state that one has a right to have something: *He staked a claim to the land where he'd found the gold.* | *(fig.) With her latest novel she stakes her claim to greatness.*

stake sthg. ↔ out *phr v* [T] *infml, esp. AmE* (esp. of the police) to watch (a place) continuously in secret — **stakeout** /ˈsteɪk-aʊt/ *n*

stake sbdy. to sthg. *phr v* [T] *AmE* to provide (someone) with the money needed to pay for (something): *My father's promised to stake me to a new car when I'm 18.*

stake·hold·er /ˈsteɪkˌhəʊldəʳ/ *n* **1** a person chosen to hold the money given by opponents in a race, BET, etc., and give it all to the winner **2** *law* a person, usu. a lawyer, who takes charge of property during the time of a quarrel or sale

stakes /steɪks/ *n* **1** [P] the prize or reward (at risk) in a competition or activity: *We're playing for very high stakes.* **2** [S+*sing.|pl. v*] a horse race in which the prize

money is made up equally by the owners of the horses: *The Acorn Stakes is|are being run at 3.00.*

stal·ac·tite /ˈstæləktaɪt‖stəˈlæktaɪt/ *n* a sharp downward-pointing part of a CAVE roof, like an ICICLE, formed over a long time by mineral-containing water dropping from the roof

stal·ag /ˈstælæg‖ˈstɑːlɑːg/ *n* a German camp for prisoners of war during the Second World War

stal·ag·mite /ˈstæləgmaɪt‖stəˈlægmaɪt/ *n* an upward-pointing part of a CAVE floor formed by drops from a stalactite and often joining it to form a solid connection between roof and floor

St Al·bans /sənt ˈɔːlbənz‖seɪnt-/ a city in S England, just N of London. It is known esp. for its CATHEDRAL and its Roman ruins.

stale¹ /steɪl/ *adj* **1** no longer fresh; no longer good to eat, smell, etc.: *stale bread* | *stale air* **2** no longer interesting; not new or exciting: *He told the same stale old jokes I've heard fifty times before.* | *stale news* **3** (of a person) without interest, liveliness, or new ideas, esp. as a result of doing the same thing for too long: *I'm getting stale in this job — I need a change.* — ~ness *n* [U]

stale² *v* [I] to become stale

stale·mate¹ /ˈsteɪlmeɪt/ *n* [C;U] **1** (in CHESS) a position in which one of the players does not have his king in CHECK¹ (8), but has no allowable move, which means that neither player wins **2** a situation in which neither side in a quarrel can get an advantage; DEADLOCK: *The discussions with the miners' union ended in (a) stalemate.* — compare CHECKMATE¹

stalemate² *v* [T] to bring to a stalemate

Sta·lin /ˈstɑːlɪn/, *Joseph* (1879–1953) a leader of the USSR from 1924 to 1953, born in Georgia, who was responsible for developing the farming and industry of the USSR. He also led the USSR in the war against Germany (1941–45) and reached agreements after the war which brought much of Eastern Europe under Soviet control. He is now remembered esp. for his cruelty, as he killed or imprisoned his political opponents and used his secret police to terrorize ordinary people. He was severely criticized by Khrushchev in 1956 and later by Gorbachev. —see picture on page 752

Sta·lin·grad /ˈstɑːlɪngræd/ the old name for the city of Volgograd in the former USSR on the river Volga. The city was almost destroyed in the Battle of Stalingrad in 1942–43.

Sta·lin·is·m /ˈstɑːlɪnɪzəm/ *n* [U] the political, social, and economic principles and practice of COMMUNISM developed by Stalin which had centralized planning, the total power of the leader of the state, and the widespread use of terror —**Stalinist** *n*

stalk¹ /stɔːk/ *n* **1** a long narrow part of a plant supporting one or more leaves, fruits, or flowers; stem: *cabbage stalks* | *broken stalks of wheat* —see pictures at FLOWER and FRUIT **2** a thin upright object: *A crab's eyes are on stalks.*

stalk² *v* **1** [T (**to**)] to hunt by following closely and quietly and staying hidden: *We stalked the wounded tiger to its lair.* **2** [I+*adv|prep*] to walk stiffly, proudly, or with long steps: *When his request was refused, he stalked out.* **3** [I;T] *esp. lit* (of GHOSTS and evils regarded as living things) to move silently (through) in a threatening manner: *Disease stalked (through) the city.* — ~ er *n*

Stalk·er /ˈstɔːkəʳ/, *John* a British police officer of very high rank who went to Northern Ireland in 1984 to lead an inquiry into the actions of the RUC (the police force of Northern Ireland) following claims that the RUC were using a shoot-to-kill policy against the IRA. In June 1986, he was removed from the inquiry. Stalker claimed that he was removed from the shoot-to-kill inquiry for political reasons, and the **Stalker affair** was given much attention in the newspapers and on television and caused discussion and concern.

stalking horse /ˈ··ˌ·/ *n* something or someone that hides a true purpose, esp. a CANDIDATE for political office put forward to hide or draw attention away from the real candidate: *John Taylor's name has been suggested for the election of a new president but I think he is just a stalking horse.*

stall¹ /stɔːl/ *n* **1** *esp. BrE* (*often in comb.*) a table or small open-fronted shop in a public place: *a market stall* | *a* *fruitstall* | *a bookstall*　**2** an indoor enclosure for an animal: *The cattle are in their stalls.*　**3** any of a row of fixed usu. roofed seats along the sides in the central part of some large churches: *the choir stulls*　**4** a small enclosure inside a room: *a separate shower stall in the bathroom*　**5** a FINGERSTALL —see also STALLS

stall² *v*　**1** [I;T] **a** (of an engine or vehicle) to stop because there is not enough power or speed to keep going: *The engine/car stalled on the hill.* **b** to cause (an engine or vehicle) to do this: *An inexperienced pilot can easily stall his plane.*　**2** [I] *infml* to delay in order to gain time, avoid taking a decision, etc.; intentionally take no action: *Stop stalling and answer my question!*　**3** [T] *infml* to deal with by delaying; put off: *Perhaps we can stall the sale until we are sure of having enough money.* | *The boss is coming! Stall him for a moment.*

stall³ *n* an act or example of stalling a machine: *The plane went into a stall.*

stall·hold·er /ˈstɔːlˌhəʊldəʳ/ *n BrE* a person who rents and keeps a market stall

stal·lion /ˈstæljən/ *n* a fully-grown male horse kept for breeding —compare MARE

Stal·lone /stəˈləʊn/, **Syl·ves·ter** /sɪlˈvestəʳ/ (1946–) an American film actor, best-known for playing the part of Rambo in the films of that name —see picture at RAMBO and colour picture on page 685

stalls /stɔːlz/ *n* [(*the*)P] *BrE* the seats on the main level of a theatre or cinema: *a good seat in the front of the stalls* – see picture at THEATRE

stal·wart¹ /ˈstɔːlwət‖-wərt/ *adj* strong and firm in body, mind, determination, etc.; STAUNCH: *a stalwart supporter/fighter* | *stalwart support* – ~**ly** *adv* – ~**ness** *n* [U]

stalwart² *n* a firm dependable follower, esp. of a political party

sta·men /ˈsteɪmən/ *n tech* the male POLLEN-producing part of a flower —see picture at FLOWER

Stam·ford Bridge /ˌstæmfəd ˈbrɪdʒ‖-fərd-/　**1** a village in N England where King Harold won a battle shortly before he was killed at the Battle of Hastings in 1066　**2** the football ground of Chelsea Football Club in W London

stam·i·na /ˈstæmɪnə/ *n* [U] the strength of body or mind to fight tiredness, discouragement, or illness: *You need great stamina to run the 10,000 metres.*

stam·mer¹ /ˈstæməʳ/ *v* [I;T (OUT)] to speak or say with pauses and repeated sounds, either habitually or because of excitement, fear, etc.: *She stammers when she feels nervous.* | *He stammered out his thanks.* | *"Th-th-thank you,"* *he stammered.* – compare STUTTER¹ (1) – ~**er** *n* – ~**ingly** *adv*

stammer² *n* [*usu. sing.*] the habit of stammering in speech: *He's got a bad stammer.*

stamp¹ /stæmp/ *v*　**1** [I+*adv/prep*] to bring the foot or feet down hard; step with force: *He was stamping about in the snow trying to keep his feet warm.* | *She stamped on the insect and killed it.* | *stamping around the house in a furious temper* | (fig.) *Any opposition or disagreement was quickly stamped on.* (=stopped)　**2** [T] to strike downwards (with the foot): *She stamped her feet in anger.*　**3** [T] to mark (a pattern, sign, letters, etc.) on (an object or surface) by pressing: *The immigration officer stamped my passport.* [+*obj*+*on*] *The office stamps the date on all incoming letters.* [+*obj*+*with*] *They stamp all incoming letters with the date.* | (fig.) *His years in the army had stamped him with an air of brisk authority.*　**4** [T] to stick a stamp onto: *Did you remember to stamp that letter?* | *Enclose a stamped addressed envelope.*　**5** [T (**as**)] to put into a class or type; CHARACTERIZE: *The newspapers had unfairly stamped him as* (=said he was) *a liar.*

stamp sthg. ↔ **out** *phr v* [T]　**1** to put an end to (usu. something bad) completely: *Do you think this new law will stamp out the illegal drugs trade?*　**2** to form or produce by means of heavy pressure from a shaped tool or machine: *a large machine that stamps out car bodies*

stamp² *n*　**1** also **postage stamp**– *fml*– a small usu. foursided piece of paper sold by post offices in various values for sticking on a letter, parcel, etc., to be posted: *a 20-cent stamp* | *a stamp collector*　**2** *BrE* a piece of paper like this for sticking to certain official papers to show that tax (**stamp duty**) has been paid　**3** *AmE* a mark or pattern pressed or printed onto a paper to show that it is official or that tax has been paid　**4** an instrument or tool for

pressing or printing onto a surface: *a date-stamp*　**5** a mark or pattern made by this: *The stamp in your library book shows it must be returned tomorrow.* | (fig., *fml*) *Her remarks bear* **the stamp of** *truth.* (=seem true) | (fig.) *The traumatic events* **left their stamp on** (=had a lasting effect on) *his mind.*　**6** an act of stamping, esp. with the foot　**7** a TRADING STAMP　**8** *fml or pomp* a kind; sort: *I wouldn't trust a man of his stamp.* —see also FOOD STAMP, RUBBER STAMP

Stamp Act /ˈ· ·/ [*the*] a tax which the British government put on the American colonies (COLONY) in 1765 which said that various documents would have to carry a stamp which had to be paid for. The people in the colonies protested that they were being taxed but had no one in Parliament to speak for them (**"taxation without representation"**). The tax was removed in 1766, but was still one of the events that led to the American Revolutionary War.

stamp du·ty /ˈ· ˌ··/ *n* [U] a tax payable in Britain on certain legal documents which have to be officially checked

stam·pede¹ /stæmˈpiːd/ *n*　**1** a sudden rush of frightened animals　**2** a sudden mad rush or mass movement: *There's been a stampede to buy gold before the price goes up.*　**3** *AmE & CanE* a RODEO, usu. also with competitions, shows, dancing, etc.: *The Calgary Stampede*

stampede² *v* [I;T (**into**)] to (cause to) go in a stampede or unreasonable rush: *a herd of stampeding cattle* | *Rumours of a shortage stampeded people into buying up food.*

stamping ground /ˈ··· ·/ *n infml* a favourite very familiar place: *This part of town is one of Jack's old stamping grounds.*

stance /stɑːns‖stæns/ *n* [*usu. sing.*]　**1** a way of standing, esp. when getting ready to hit the ball in various sports: *First take up the correct stance.*　**2** [(**on**)] a way of thinking, esp. a publicly-stated position regarding a particular situation; ATTITUDE: *What's your government's stance on nuclear disarmament?* | *The President has adopted a tough stance on terrorism.* —compare POSTURE¹

stanch /stɑːntʃ‖stɔːntʃ, stɑːntʃ/ *v* [T] *AmE for* STAUNCH²

stan·chion /ˈstɑːntʃən‖ˈstæn-/ *n* a strong bar standing straight up as a support

stand¹ /stænd/ *v* **stood** /stʊd/ ■ to be in, get into, or put into an upright position　**1** [I] to support oneself on the feet in an upright position: *I couldn't get a seat on the bus, so I had to stand.* | *Don't just stand there; help me!* | *Stand still while I do up your buttons.* —see also STAND **up** (1)　**2** [I;T (UP)] to (cause to) rise to an upright position: *The children all stood* (up) *when the head teacher entered the hall.* | *He stood the little girl on the wall so that she could see.*　**3** [I+*adv/prep*] to perform a particular action or take a particular position while standing: *We stood in a rough circle as she explained her plan.* | *The soldiers stood to* **attention.** | **Stand back** (=step backwards) *and let the doctor through.* | **Stand clear** *of the elevator doors, please.* ■ to be in, stay in, or get into a particular place or position　**4** [I;T+*obj*+*adv/prep*] to (cause to) rest in a position, esp. upright or on a base: *Few houses were left standing after the bombing raid.* | *The table stood in the corner.* | *He stood the clock on the shelf.* | (fig.) *These new findings* **stand** *the accepted scientific theory* **on its head.** (=show it to be completely untrue)　**5** [I;L+*adj*] to remain unmoving or unused: *The car stood in the garage for weeks with no one to drive it.* | *Some of the machinery is* **standing idle.** (=not being used) | *houses standing empty*　**6** [I] (of a liquid) to be still; not flow or be moved: *The water lay in standing pools.* | *Leave the mixture to stand overnight.*　**7** [L+*n*] to put oneself in a particular position: *The dog* **stood guard** *over his master's belongings.* | *The police released him when his father* **stood bail/surety** *for him.*　**8** [I] *AmE* (of a vehicle) to park for a short time for waiting, loading, etc. (used esp. on signs in the phrase **no standing**) ■ to be in, stay in, or get into a particular state or situation　**9** [I+*adv/prep*] to be in, stay in, or get into a particular position or state: *Stand fast/firm* (=be determined) – *don't let them tell you what to do.* | *If we all* **stand together** (=remain united) *we'll get what we want.* | *My assistant isn't very good; I have to* **stand over him** (=watch him closely) *all the time to make sure he does the work.* | (fig.) *I didn't want to* **stand in her way** (=spoil her chances), *so I withdrew my application for the job.* | *Everyone in the company* **stands in awe of** *her.* (=admires and/or fears her) [L+*v-ed*] *The company stands condemned at the bar of public opinion.* | *He* **stands accused of** (=is charged with) *plotting to overthrow the government.* **10** [I+*adv/prep*] to be in a particular situation or have a particular character: *How do things stand between you two at the moment?* | *As things stand at the moment* (=in the present situation) *I doubt if the company can agree to this request.* | *Where does the party stand on the issue of immigration?* (=what is its policy?) **11** [I+*adv/prep*] **a** to show a particular level or amount: *Inflation currently stands at nine per cent.* | *Your bank balance stands at £460.* **b** to have a rank or position in a range of values: *I know your son stands high in his opinion.* | *How does England's team stand in comparison to the other teams in Europe?* **12** [I+*to-v*] to be in a position to gain or lose: *If this new law is passed, we stand to lose our tax advantage.* **13** [I *not in progressive forms*] to remain true or in force; remain VALID: *Don't forget; my offer of help still stands.* | *The court of appeal ruled that the conviction should be allowed to stand.* ■ other meanings **14** [I+*adv/prep*; L+*n*] to be in height: *He stands 5 feet 10 inches.* | *The building stands over 200 feet high.* **15** [T *usu. in questions and negatives; not in progressive forms*] to accept successfully or without undesirable results; bear: *I can't stand whisky.* | *This work will hardly stand close examination.* | *Do you think she can stand the pace (of work) here?* | *I think the Prime Minister's decision will* **stand the test of time.** (=still be thought correct by people after some years) | *He wants to marry me but I can't* **stand the sight of** *him.* (=dislike him extremely) [+*v-ing*] *I can't stand seeing children smoking.* [+*obj+v-ing*] *I never could stand people telling me what to do.* | *(humor) I could stand another of those cream cakes!* —see also STAND **for** (2); see BEAR (USAGE) **16** [T+*obj(i)+obj(d)*] to pay the cost of (something) for (someone else); give as a TREAT² (2): *Let me stand you a drink/meal.* **17** [I (**for**)] *BrE* ‖ **run** *esp. AmE*— to compete for an office in an election; be a CANDIDATE: *She intends to stand for Parliament/for club president.* ■ fixed phrases **18 If you can't stand the heat, get out of the kitchen** if you are not able to deal with the problems and pressures of your job, you should change your job; a phrase first used by the US president Harry S. Truman **19 know how/where one stands (with someone)** to know how someone feels about one: *She always says what she thinks, so you always know where you stand with her.* **20 stand a chance/hope** to have a chance/hope: *She stands a good chance of winning.* | *You don't stand a hope of getting the job!* **21 Stand and deliver!** (said in former times by armed robbers to travellers in carriages) Stop and give me your valuable possessions! **22 stand corrected** to admit that one's statements, opinions, etc., have been wrong: *You're quite right, it was Monday, not Tuesday; I stand corrected.* **23 standing on one's head** *infml* very easily; without any trouble or effort: *A genius like you can solve that problem standing on your head!* **24 stand on ceremony** to follow the formal rules of behaviour: *Do take your jacket off; we don't stand on ceremony in this house.* **25 stand one's ground: a** to refuse to be forced backwards **b** to refuse to accept defeat in an argument, claim, etc. **26 stand on one's dignity** *sometimes derog* to demand to be treated with proper respect **27 stand on one's hands/head** to support oneself on the hands/head and hands, with the feet in the air **28 stand on one's own (two) feet** *infml* to be able to live and provide what one needs without help from others **29 stand or fall by** to depend on completely for one's success: *This theatre gets no subsidies, so it stands or falls by the quality of its productions.* **30 stand pat** *AmE infml* to refuse to change: *She's standing pat on her decision not to allow flexible working hours.* **31 stand someone in good stead** to be of good use to someone when needed: *The experience you have gained here will stand you in good stead in later life.* **32 stand to reason** to be clear to all sensible people: *It stands to reason that she won't accept the job if we don't offer her a reasonable salary* **33 stand trial** to be tried in court: *He stood trial for murder.* —see also **make someone's hair stand on end** (HAIR), **leave someone standing** (LEAVE), **not have a leg to stand on** (LEG) ■ phrasal verbs

stand by *phr v* **1** [T] (**stand by** sbdy.) to remain loyal to, esp. in a difficult situation; support and not desert: *His parents were upset when he was arrested but stood by him.* **2** [T] (**stand by** sthg.) to remain faithful to (a promise, agreement, etc.); keep to: *I'll stand by my* promise. | *I stand by what I said earlier.* **3** [I] to remain inactive when action is needed: *We couldn't stand idly by while people starved.* | *How can you stand by and watch/and do nothing when she needs help?* **4** [I (**for**)] to wait and be ready for action if needed: *Stand by for trouble!* [+*to-v*] *A helicopter was standing by to get the president out if any trouble developed.* | *Stand by to receive a message.* —see also BYSTANDER, STANDBY

stand down *phr v* **1** [I] to give up one's position or chance of election: *I'm prepared to stand down in favour of a younger man.* —see also STEP **down 2** [I] to leave the witness box in court: *Thank you, Mr Frost. You may stand down.* **3** [I;T (=**stand** sbdy. ↔ **down**)] *esp. BrE* (of a soldier) to go off duty **b** to send (a soldier) off after a period of being on duty

stand for sthg. *phr v* [T] **1** to be a sign or short form of; represent; mean: *"His name's James B Clarke." "What does the B stand for?"* **2** [*usu. in questions and negatives*] to allow to continue; accept without complaining: *I wouldn't stand for that sort of treatment if I were you.* [+*v-ing*] *I won't stand for being treated like a child.* —see also STAND¹ (15) **3** to have as a set of aims or principles; support: *Before we vote for him, we want to know what he stands for.*

stand in *phr v* [I (**for**)] to take the place of the usual person for a time: *I'm standing in for the regular man while he's on holiday.* —see also STAND-IN

stand out *phr v* [I] **1** to have an easily-seen shape, colour, etc.; be very noticeable: *The new road sign is easy to read; the words stand out well.* | (fig.) *Didn't you realize she was interested in you? I should have thought it* **stood out a mile!** (=was very clear) **2** [(**from, among**)] to be much better or the best: *Among mystery writers, Agatha Christie stands out as a real master.* —see also OUTSTANDING **3** [(**against**)] to be firm in opposition: *I'm standing out against his idea.*

stand to *phr v* [I;T (=**stand** sbdy. **to**)] *tech, esp. BrE* **a** (of a soldier) to take up a position ready for action **b** to order (a soldier) to stand to

stand up *phr v* **1** [I *usu. in progressive forms*] to STAND¹ (1): *I've been standing up all day; it'll be a relief to sit down.* | *Stand up straight, boy; don't slouch!* —see also STAND¹ (2) **2** [I+*adv/prep*] to stay in good condition after testing or hard use; wear or last well: *It's a robust little car that will stand up (well) to a lot of rough handling.* **3** [I] to be accepted as true or proven: *The charges you've made would never stand up in court.* **4** [T] (**stand** sbdy. ↔ **up**) *infml* to fail to meet (someone, esp. of the opposite sex) as arranged: *Where is my boyfriend? If he's stood me up I'll never speak to him again!* **5** *infml* **stand up and be counted** to make one's opinions known, esp. when it is dangerous or not to one's advantage to do so —see also STAND-UP

stand up for sbdy./sthg. *phr v* [T] to defend against attack; support: *She stood up for me/my proposals during the discussion.* | *You must stand up for your rights!*

stand up to sbdy. *phr v* [T] to refuse to accept unjust unfavourable treatment of oneself by (someone): *Don't let her say things like that about your work — you should stand up to her a bit more.*

stand² *n* **1** a small often outdoor shop or place for showing things; STALL¹ (1): *an ice-cream stand* | *Come and find out more about the new car at our company's stand at the exhibition.* —see also NEWSSTAND **2** (*often in comb.*) a frame, desk, base, or other piece of furniture for putting something on: *a hatstand* | *an umbrella stand* **3** also **stands** *pl*— an open-fronted building at a sports ground with rows of seats or standing spaces rising behind each other —see also GRANDSTAND **4** a strong effort of defence or opposition: *In February 1916 the French Army made a stand at Verdun.* | *The local people mounted a determined stand against the closure of the school.* **5** (in cricket) a period of two batsmen (BATSMAN) being in together, esp. one that lasts a long time in which there are many runs **6** [(**on**)] a firm publicly-stated position or opinion: *If he wants my vote he'll have to* **take a stand** *on the question of East-West relations.* **7** a place where taxis wait to be hired **8** *AmE for* WITNESS BOX: *Will the next witness please* **take the stand**? —see also ONE-NIGHT STAND

stan·dard¹ /ˈstændəd‖-ərd/ *n* **1** [*often pl.*] **a** a level or degree of quality that is considered proper or acceptable: *We work to a high standard of precision.* | *This teacher sets high standards for his pupils.* | *Your recent work has been*

below standard/*hasn't been* **up to standard.** (=has been below an acceptable level) | *the airline's rigorous safety standards* | *The hotel offers the highest standards of comfort and service.* | *I don't think all this bad language on TV should be allowed; there are certain standards* (=of morals) *that should be kept up.* **b** an accepted measure or level used for purposes of comparison: *In India this is a high salary, though by European standards it is quite low.* **2** something fixed as a rule for measuring weight, value, purity, etc.: *The government has an official standard for the purity of silver.* —see also GOLD STANDARD **3** a ceremonial flag: *the royal standard* **4** a pole with an image or shape at the top formerly carried at the front of an army: *the standard of the Roman legions* **5 a** something that is established, familiar, or widely used: *This business computer has become a standard.* **b** a popular song that has become well established and is sung by many singers

standard² *adj* **1** of the usual or regularly used kind; not rare or special: *These nails come in three standard sizes.* | *Searching handluggage at airports is now standard practice|procedure.* | *the standard rate of income tax* (=the rate paid by most people) **2** [A] generally recognized as correct or acceptable: *It's one of the standard books on the subject.* | *standard spelling|pronunciation* | *standard English* (=as used by educated speakers) —see also NONSTANDARD, SUBSTANDARD

Standard see EVENING STANDARD

standard-bear·er /ˈ··ˌ··/ *n* **1** (in former times) a soldier who carried the STANDARD¹ (4) at the front of an army **2** an important leader in a moral argument or movement: *one of the standard-bearers of the anti-nuclear movement*

stan·dard·i·za·tion /ˌstændədaɪˈzeɪʃən‖-dərdə-/ *n* [U] **1** the making of standard parts which can be used in many different machines, operations, etc. **2** the setting of levels of quality for articles, as done by the BSI

stan·dard·ize also **-ise** *BrE* /ˈstændədaɪz‖-ər-/ *v* [T] to cause to fit a single standard; make to be alike in every case: *Efforts to standardize English spellings have not been completely successful.* | *All their cars are produced using standardized parts.*

standard lamp /ˈ·· ·/ *BrE* ‖ **floor lamp** *AmE—* *n* a lamp on a tall base which stands on the floor of a room —see pictures at LIGHT and at LIVING ROOM

standard of liv·ing /ˌ··· ˈ··/ also **living standard** — *n* the degree of wealth and comfort in everyday life that a person, group, country, etc. has: *This nation has a low|enjoys a high standard of living.* —compare COST OF LIVING

Standard Oil /ˌ··· ˈ·/ a large American oil company begun in the 19th century by John D. Rockefeller. It was broken up into smaller companies in 1911 when it was found to be controlling the oil industry in the US. Some of these smaller companies are still called Standard Oil.

standard time /ˌ·· ˈ·/ *n* [U] the time to which all clocks in a particular area of the world are set

stand·by /ˈstændbaɪ/ *n* **-bys** **1** a person or thing that is kept ready to be used: *Powdered milk is a good standby in an emergency.* | *If the electricity fails, the hospital has a standby generator.* **2 on standby: a** ready to be called into action at any time: *A special team of police were kept on standby during the crisis period.* **b** ready to travel, esp. on a plane, only if there is a seat that no one else wants: *passengers on standby* | *a standby ticket* —see also STAND by

stand-in /ˈ·· ·/ *n* **1** a person who takes the part of an actor at certain unimportant or dangerous moments in a film —see also STUNT MAN **2** a person who takes the place or job of someone else for a time —see also STAND in

stand·ing¹ /ˈstændɪŋ/ *adj* [A] **1** continuing in use or in force; PERMANENT: *I've got a standing order for two pints of milk a day.* | *We have a standing invitation; we can visit them whenever we like.* | *His meanness has become something of a standing joke.* | *Before the days of standing armies there were only small local forces in peacetime.* —see also STANDING ORDER **2** done from a standing position: *The runners set off from a standing start.* | *The audience loved her and gave her a standing ovation at the end of the performance.*

standing² *n* [U] **1** rank or position, esp. based on the opinion of other people; position in a system, organization, or list: *a lawyer of high standing* | *He's a man of some standing* (=much respected and of high rank) *in the community.* | *The scandal has damaged the company's standing in the eyes of the public.* **2** time during which something has remained in existence; DURATION: *an agreement of several years' standing* | *Her opposition to the plan is of long standing.* (=She has been against the plan for a long time.) —see also LONG-STANDING

standing com·mit·tee /ˈ··· ·ˌ··/ *n* **1** a committee of members of the British parliament which considers possible changes to a BILL¹ (2) (=suggested new law) after its SECOND READING in the House of Commons **2** a committee in the US Congress which has responsibility for examining BILLs: *Ways and Means is a standing committee concerned with issues of tax, budgets, etc.* —compare SELECT COMMITTEE

standing joke /ˌ··· ˈ·/ *n* a joke or humorous subject that is so well-known to a group of people that they laugh whenever it is mentioned: *My spelling mistakes are a standing joke in our office.*

standing or·der /ˌ··· ˈ··/ also **banker's order**— *n* [C;U] *BrE* an order to a bank to pay a fixed amount from an account to a named person or organization at a regular time each month, year, etc.: *I pay my insurance premiums by standing order.* —compare DIRECT DEBIT

standing room /ˈ·· ·/ *n* [U] space for standing in a theatre, sports ground, etc., usu. sold after all seats have been filled: *I'm afraid there's standing room only.*

standing stone /ˌ··· ˈ·/ *n* a large stone which is set upright in the ground, often as part of a pattern such as a circle or a line.

▶CULTURAL NOTE The most famous standing stones are those at Stonehenge in England and Carnac in France. People do not know why these stones were set upright and arranged in patterns or exactly when it was done, but some people think the arrangements may have once been used to study the sun and moon or for religious purposes.◀

stand·off half /ˈstændɒf ˌhɑːf ‖ -ɔːf ˌhæf/ *n* a FLY HALF

stand·off·ish /stændˈɒfɪʃ‖-ˈɔːfɪʃ/ *adj infml* rather unfriendly; coldly formal — ~ **ly** *adv* — ~ **ness** *n* [U]

stand·pipe /ˈstændpaɪp/ *n* a pipe connected directly to a water supply and providing water to a central or public place

stand·point /ˈstændpɔɪnt/ *n* a position from which things are seen and opinions are formed; POINT OF VIEW: *Let's look at this from an historical standpoint|from the standpoint of the ordinary voter.*

St An·drews /sənt ˈændruːz‖seɪnt-/ a city in E Scotland known esp. for its university and its GOLF courses

stand·still /ˈstændˌstɪl/ *n* [S] a condition of no movement or activity; stop: *She brought the car to a standstill.* | *Work was at a standstill.*

stand-up /ˈ·· ·/ *adj* [A] **1** done or for use by people standing up: *a stand-up meal* **2** (of COMEDY or its performer) depending on telling jokes rather than on acting: *a stand-up comedian* **3** (of a collar) made to stand stiffly up without folding

Stan·ford /ˈstænfəd‖-fərd/ an American university in California, S of San Francisco

▶CULTURAL NOTE Stanford is a highly respected LIBERAL university. In the 1980s and 90s it began teaching literature by women, minorities (MINORITY), and by people from other cultures in its literature courses. This upset some people, who worried that important works of Western civilization, such as those by Plato and Shakespeare, would not be taught in order to find time to teach these other works.◀

Stan·i·slav·sky /ˌstænɪˈslævski‖-ˈslɑːv-/, **Con·stan·tin** /ˈkɒnstəntiːn‖ˈkɑːn-/ (1863–1938) a Russian actor and theatre director known esp. for his METHOD of training actors to draw upon their inner emotions which was later developed in the US

stank /stæŋk/ *past tense of* STINK

Stanley, Port see PORT STANLEY

Stan·ley /ˈstænli/, **Sir Henry Morton** (1841–1904) a Welsh EXPLORER and newspaper reporter. In 1871, he was sent by an American newspaper to find David Livingstone in Africa where he delivered his famous greeting, "Dr. Livingstone, I presume?"

Stanley Cup /ˌ··· ˈ·/ [*the*] a prize given to the winner of the National Hockey League, which is made up of ICE HOCKEY teams from Canada and the US

Stan·sted /ˈstænsted/ an airport which is 30 miles NE of London, in Essex

stan·za /ˈstænzə/ n a group of lines in a repeating pattern forming a division of a poem: *the third stanza*

staph·y·lo·coc·cus /ˌstæfɨləʊˈkɒkəs‖-ˈkɑːk-/ n -ci /kaɪ/ a bacterium that causes infection of wounds, esp. in hospitals

sta·ple¹ /ˈsteɪpəl/ n 1 a small piece of thin wire with two square corners which is driven into sheets of paper, etc., and bent over on the other side to hold them together — see also STAPLER 2 a small U-shaped piece of strong wire with pointed ends which is hammered in to hold something in place

staple² v [T] to fasten with staples: *He stapled the papers together.*

staple³ adj [A] 1 forming the main part; BASIC: *Oil is Nigeria's staple export.* | *These people live on a staple diet of rice and vegetables.* | (fig.) *television's staple diet of soap operas and quiz shows* 2 used all the time; usual: *He came out with his staple excuse, which was that he was too busy.*

staple⁴ n [usu. pl.] 1 a food that is used and needed in the house all the time: *Don't forget staples like sugar and salt when you go to the shops.* 2 tech a main product that is produced or sold: *Bananas and sugar are the staples of Jamaica.*

sta·pler /ˈsteɪplər/ n a usu. small hand tool for driving staples into paper

star¹ /stɑːr/ n 1 [C] a very large mass of burning gas in space, esp. one that can be seen as a small bright point of light in a clear sky at night: *When it is dark, the stars come out.* (=can be seen) | *a science-fiction film about travelling to distant stars* | *Our sun is a star.* | *stars twinkling in the heavens* —see also FALLING STAR, FIXED STAR, SHOOTING STAR, STARRY 2 [C] a a shape with five or more points that is supposed to represent a star b a piece of metal in this shape for wearing as a mark of office, rank, honour, etc.: *a four-star general* c a sign in this shape used with numbers usu. from one to five in various systems, to judge standards or quality. In Britain, stars are given to good hotels, from one star, which is the cheapest, up to five stars, which is the most comfortable and most expensive: *The guidebook awards this hotel three stars.* d an ASTERISK 3 [C] a a famous or very skilful performer: *She wanted to be a Hollywood (film) star.* | *a young actress with star quality* | *a football star* b the main performer in a film, play, etc. —see also ALL-STAR, CO-STAR, SUPERSTAR 4 [C usu. pl.] a PLANET or sign of the ZODIAC regarded as deciding one's fate: *She was born under an unlucky star.* | *He always reads the "What Your Stars Foretell" column in the daily paper.* 5 [S] fml or lit a person's fame or chance of getting it: *Her star seems very much in the ascendant.* (=she is becoming successful) | *His star has set/is on the wane and people have begun to forget him.* —see also STARRY-EYED, **reach for the stars** (REACH), **see stars** (SEE¹), **thank one's lucky stars** (THANK) 6 **star in the East** the star which, according to the Bible, appeared in the sky when Jesus was born, to show the way to the place of his birth — —**less** adj

star² v -rr- 1 [T] to have as a main performer; FEATURE: *Tonight we're showing the film "Limelight", starring Charlie Chaplin.* 2 [I (in)] to appear as a main performer: *Humphrey Bogart starred in a lot of very good films.* | *She has a starring role in a new TV show.* 3 [T] to mark with one or more stars (ASTERISKs): *In the list the starred questions are the most difficult.*

star·board /ˈstɑːbəd‖ˈstɑːrbərd/ n [U] the right side of a ship or aircraft as one faces forward —compare PORT²

starch¹ /stɑːtʃ‖stɑːrtʃ/ n 1 [U] a white tasteless substance forming an important part of foods such as grain, rice, beans, and potatoes 2 [C;U] (a) food containing this: *You're getting too fat; you should avoid sugars and starches.* 3 [U] a product made from this, usu. in powder form, for stiffening cloth

starch² v [T] to stiffen with STARCH¹ (3): *starched tablecloths/collars*

star cham·ber /ˌ· ˈ··/ n sometimes derog (often caps.) 1 a court or similar body that deals with cases in secret and gives severe judgments 2 (in Britain) a group of ministers who decide how much money a government department will be allowed to spend if that department cannot reach agreement with the Treasury

starch·y /ˈstɑːtʃi‖ˈstɑːr-/ adj 1 like or full of starch: *starchy foods* 2 infml stiffly correct and formal in one's manner; STUFFY (2) —**ily** adv

star-crossed lov·ers /ˌ· · ˈ··/ n [P] lit unlucky lovers who are unable to be together because of particular events or situations. The most famous star-crossed lovers are Romeo and Juliet. —see ROMEO AND JULIET

star·dom /ˈstɑːdəm‖ˈstɑːr-/ n [U] the state of being a very famous performer: *After her amazing performance in the film she shot to stardom.*

star·dust /ˈstɑːdʌst‖ˈstɑːr-/ n [U] lit an imaginary substance consisting of shiny dust that has magical qualities

stare¹ /steər/ v [I] 1 [(at)] to look steadily for a long time, e.g. in great surprise or shock: *He sat staring into space, thinking deeply.* | *She stared at the letter in disbelief.* 2 [+adv/prep] to be very plain to see: *The lies in the report were so obvious; they stared out at us from every paragraph.* 3 **stare someone in the face: a** to be very easily seen; be too clear to miss: *I'd spent ages looking for the key, and there it was staring me in the face all the time.* | (fig.) *The solution is staring us in the face* (=is very clear); *we must borrow from the bank.* **b** (of something bad) to be about to happen to someone: *At 2-0 down with a minute to go, defeat was staring us in the face.* —see GAZE (USAGE)

stare sbdy. ↔ **out** BrE ‖ **stare** sbdy. ↔ **down** AmE— phr v [T] to force to look away under the power of a long steady look

stare² n an act or way of staring; long steady look: *a beautiful girl who always gets admiring stares from men* | *a disbelieving/incredulous stare*

star·fish /ˈstɑːˌfɪʃ‖ˈstɑːr-/ n -fish or -fishes a flat sea animal with five arms forming a star shape and a mouth and rows of tube feet on the lower surface —see picture at SEA

star·gaz·er /ˈstɑːˌɡeɪzər‖ˈstɑːr-/ n 1 often humor a someone who practises ASTRONOMY b an ASTROLOGER 2 someone who spends time thinking about impractical ideas instead of giving attention to their present activities —**ing** n [U]

stark¹ /stɑːk‖stɑːrk/ adj 1 hard, bare, or severe in appearance, without any pleasant or decorative additions: *The stark jagged rocks were silhouetted against the sky.* | (fig.) *The film shows the stark realities of life for the poor and hungry.* 2 [A] complete; UTTER: *The dead man's eyes were wide open with a look of stark terror.* | *His actions were in stark contrast to his words.* — —**ly** adv

stark² adv 1 **stark naked** infml without any clothes; completely NAKED 2 **stark raving/staring mad** humor completely mad

Stark, Dame Frey·a /ˈfreɪə/ (1893–1993) an English traveller and writer known for her books about her travels in the Middle East

stark·ers /ˈstɑːkəz‖ˈstɑːrkərz/ adj [F] BrE humor sl NAKED (1)

star·let /ˈstɑːlɨt‖ˈstɑːr-/ n a young actress who plays small parts in films, hoping to become famous

star·light /ˈstɑːlaɪt‖ˈstɑːr-/ n [U] the light given by the stars, often considered to be ROMANTIC: *a walk in the starlight*

star·ling /ˈstɑːlɪŋ‖ˈstɑːr-/ n a very common usu. greenish-black European bird

star·lit /ˈstɑːˌlɪt‖ˈstɑːr-/ adj esp. lit lighted by the stars; bright with many stars: *a starlit night*

Star of Beth·le·hem /ˌ· · ˈ··/ [the] the star which, in the Bible, appeared in the sky when Jesus was born, to show the way to the place of his birth

Star of Da·vid /ˌ· · ˈ··/ [the] a star with six points which represents Judaism and the state of Israel. In Nazi Germany, Jews were forced to wear this sign so that everyone could see that they were Jews.

Starr /stɑːr/, **Rin·go** /ˈrɪŋɡəʊ/ (1940–) an English musician who was the drummer in the popular British rock group, the BEATLES, during the 1960s until they split up in 1970

star·ry /ˈstɑːri/ adj filled with stars: *a starry winter sky*

starry-eyed /ˌ·· ˈ·◄/ adj infml (appearing very happy because) full of unreasonable or silly hopes: *a starry-eyed optimist*

Stars and Bars /ˌ· · ˈ·/ [the] AmE the CONFEDERATE¹ flag

Stars and Stripes /ˌ· · ˈ·/ [the] AmE the flag of the US — see picture at FLAG

Star·ship En·ter·prise /ˌstaːʃɪp ˈentəpraɪz‖ˌstaːr-, -tər-/ [the] the space ship in the SCIENCE FICTION television programme *Star Trek* —see STAR TREK

star sign /ˈ· ·/ *n* any of the 12 divisions of the year represented by groups of stars: *What is your star sign?*

Star·sky and Hutch /ˌstaːski ənd ˈhʌtʃ‖ˌstaːr-/ an American television programme of the 1970s, also shown in Britain, about two policemen, played by David Soul and Paul Michael Glaser

Star-Span·gled Ban·ner /ˌ· ·· ˈ··/ [the] **1** the NATIONAL ANTHEM (=national song) of the US **2** *AmE pomp* the flag of the US

star-stud·ded /ˈ· ˌ··/ *adj infml* filled with famous performers: *a star-studded cast*

start¹ /staːt‖staːrt/ *v* **1** [I;T (OFF, **with**)] to (cause to) go into a state of (movement, operation, or activity); begin: *Has the meeting started yet?* | *We'll start (the meal) (off) with onion soup.* | *I started my journey at dawn.* | *We start work at 8.30 every morning.* | *Let's start (the meeting) by electing a chairman.* | *All our machinery was lost in the fire so we had to start from scratch.* (=start again from the beginning) [+to-v|v ing] *It's started to rain/started raining.* | *I started to learn French/started learning French when I was ten.* [+obj+v-ing] *The slightest bit of dust starts me (off) sneezing.* **2** [I;T (UP)] to (cause to) come into existence: *How did the trouble start?* | *Who started that rumour?* | *I'm trying to start up a swimming club.* | *We're thinking of starting a family.* (=having our first baby) **3** [I (UP);T] to (cause to) begin operation: *The car won't start.* (=its engine cannot be made to work) | *The clock keeps stopping and starting; I wonder what's wrong with it.* | *I can't get the fire started.* (=it cannot be made to burn) **4** [I (IN, on)] to begin doing a job or a piece of work: *In this office we start at 9.00 in the morning.* | *You're hired; when can you start?* | *Will I have time to start (in) on digging the garden tonight?* **5** [I (OFF, OUT, for)] to begin a journey: *It's a long trip; we'll have to start (out/off) early and start back for home in the afternoon.* **6** [I+adv|prep, esp. **at, from**] to go from a particular point; have a beginning or lower limit: *Prices start at £5.* | *The train starts from London.* | *Starting from next week, all employees will receive a 10% pay increase.* **7** [T] to begin using: *We finished this bottle of wine; shall we start a new one?* | *Start each page on the second line.* **8** [L (OFF, OUT)] to begin one's life, a course of action, etc., by being: *He started out poor/a poor office boy, and now he's a millionaire!* | *If you want to be a champion swimmer you've got to start young.* **9** [I] to take part in a match or competition from the beginning: *The horse went lame and was unable to start.* **10** [I] *infml* to begin to be annoying, by arguing, asking for things, etc.: *Oh, don't you start again!* **11** [I (at)] to make a quick uncontrolled movement, esp. from sudden surprise: *She started at the noise* | *The touch on his shoulder made him start.* **12** [I+adv|prep] *esp. lit* to move suddenly and violently from rest: *He started angrily to his feet.* | *Blood started from the wound.* **13 start (all) over again** also **start over** *esp. AmE*— to begin again as before or as at the beginning **14 start something** *infml* to make trouble; start a fight: *Are you trying to start something?* **15 to start with: a** at the beginning: *I was a bit nervous to start with, but I soon got used to it.* **b** also **for a start**— (used before the first in a list of facts, reasons, etc.): *It won't work: to start with, it would take too long, and secondly it would cost too much.*

▷ USAGE **1** You can **start/begin** *to do* something or you can **start/begin** *doing* something, but the "doing" form is less common with **begin.** You cannot use the "doing" form when the first verb is in the *-ing* form: *I'm* **beginning/starting** *to cook the dinner,* or when the second verb deals with feelings or the mind: *She* **started/began** *to understand.* **2 Begin** cannot be used instead of **start** before **off, up, out, back,** or in the meanings **a** (of a machine) to (cause to) start working: *The car won't* **start, b** to start in a match or competition, **c** to make a surprised or sudden movement. **3 Commence** is used like **begin,** not **start,** and is very formal.◁

start² *n* **1** [C] a beginning of activity or development: *The start of the race must be delayed.* | *The play* **got off to a bad start** *when one of the actors forgot his opening lines.* | *a good education that gave her the best possible* **start in life** | *It's getting late; we'd better* **make a start on** *the cooking.* (=begin to do it) | *The whole holiday was* really enjoyable, **from start to finish.** **2** [*the*+S] the first part or moments: *The start of the film was rather dull.* **3** [C] a place of starting: *The runners lined up at the start.* **4** [C;U (**on, over**)] the amount by which one person is ahead of another: *The thieves have a three hour start on us so their track will be hard to follow.* **5** [C *usu. sing.*] a sudden uncontrolled movement, esp. of surprise: *I woke up from the bad dream with a start.* **6 for a start** see START¹ (15b) —see also FALSE START, FLYING START, HEAD START

START /staːt‖staːrt/ see STRATEGIC ARMS REDUCTION TALKS

start·er /ˈstaːtəʳ‖ˈstaːr-/ *n* **1** a person, horse, car, etc., in a race or match at the start: *Of eight starters, only three finished the race.* **2** a person who gives the signal for a race to begin: *The starter fired his starting gun.* | *The horses are now* **under starter's orders.** (=will soon begin to race) **3** an instrument for starting a machine, esp. an electric motor (**starter motor**) for starting a petrol engine —see picture at ENGINE **4** *infml, esp. BrE* the first part of a meal: *Would you like soup or melon as a starter?* **5 for starters** *infml* first of all; as a beginning —compare BEGINNER; see also NONSTARTER, SELF-STARTER

starter home /ˈ··· ·/ *n BrE* a small house or flat which does not cost very much to buy and is usu. bought by a young person or man and woman buying their first home: *We need to develop more low cost starter homes to help the younger generation gain a footing on the property ladder.*

▶CULTURAL NOTE In Britain, more than half the population own their homes and it is common for people to buy and sell several homes in their lifetime.◀

starting block /ˈ·· ·/ *n* either of a pair of blocks fixed to the ground against which a runner's feet push off at the start of a race

starting gate /ˈ·· ·/ *n* a gate or set of gates which opens to start a horse, dog, or SKI race

starting price /ˈ·· ·/ *n* the last PRICE¹ (2) (=return for money risked) offered just before a horse or dog race begins

star·tle /ˈstaːtl‖ˈstaːrtl/ *v* [T] to cause (someone) to be suddenly surprised, sometimes making them jump; give an unexpected slight shock to: *You startled me! I didn't hear you come in.* | *a startling revelation/piece of news* | *She gave a startled jump.* | *We were startled by the news/startled to hear they were getting divorced.* **—lingly** *adv* : *startlingly pale*

Start·rite /ˈstaːtraɪt ‖ ˈstaːr-/ a British company which makes good quality shoes, esp. for children

Star Trek /ˈ· ˌ·/ a popular American SCIENCE FICTION television programme of the 1960s about the adventures of a space vehicle, the **Starship Enterprise**, and the characters on the space vehicle. There are also several Star Trek films. —see also Captain Jim KIRK, SCOTTY, Mr SPOCK, TREKKIE; see also **beam me up, Scotty** (BEAM³), **to boldly go where no man has gone before** (BOLDLY)

start-up /ˈ· ·/ *adj AmE* of the money needed to begin a new business: *high start-up costs*

starv·a·tion /staːˈveɪʃən‖staːr-/ *n* [U] suffering or death from lack of food: *dying of starvation* | *(infml) I'm on a starvation diet.* (=eating very little food in order to become thinner)

starvation wag·es /·ˈ··· ˌ··/ *n* [P] wages that are not enough to pay for the things necessary for life

starve /staːv‖staːrv/ *v* [I;T] **1** to (cause to) suffer or die from great hunger: *Thousands of people could starve if the crops fail again.* | *They got lost in the desert and starved to death.* | *I'd rather starve than work for that company!* | *starving children in the famine area* | *(infml) What's for lunch? I'm starving! (BrE)/I'm starved! (AmE)* (=very hungry) **2** [(of)] to (cause to) suffer from not having some stated thing: *The teachers said the schools were being starved of resources.* | *neglected children who are starved of affection*

starve·ling /ˈstaːvlɪŋ‖ˈstaːr-/ *n lit* a person or animal that is thin and unhealthy from lack of food

star wars /ˈ· ˌ·/ *n* [U] *infml* see STRATEGIC DEFENCE INITIATIVE

Star Wars a popular SCIENCE FICTION film of the 1970s about the battle between the HERO, Luke Skywalker, and Darth Vader, an evil person who wears a black MASK over his face and comes from an evil EMPIRE. The film was directed by Steven Spielberg and is remembered for its many new and exciting SPECIAL EFFECTS. —see colour picture on page 685

stash¹ /stæʃ/ v [T+obj+adv|prep] infml to store secretly; hide: *He keeps his money stashed (away) under the bed.*

stash² n [(of)] infml a secret store: *a stash of drugs*

Sta·si /'staːzi/ [the] the popular name for the State Security Police in East Germany until 1989. They were known for secretly watching people and telling the government what ordinary citizens were doing.

state¹ /steɪt/ n 1 [C (of)] a condition in which a person or thing is; a particular way of being, feeling, or thinking considered with regard to its most important or noticeable quality: *Water can exist in three states: a liquid state, a gaseous state (=steam), and a solid one. (=ice) | I'm very concerned about the state of her health. | The survivors of the fire are still in a state of shock. | He seems to be in a rather confused* **state of mind.** *| A state of war now exists between the two countries. | The house we're buying is in a very good* **state of repair.** *| the deteriorating state of the country's roads | an embarrassing* **state of affairs** (=situation) **2** [(the) U] (often cap.) the government or political organization of a country: *Should industry be controlled by the state? | The ministers were discussing important* **matters of state.** *| What is the proper relationship between Church and State? | state-owned railways | state secrets* —see also POLICE STATE, WELFARE STATE **3** [C] a country considered as a political organization: *Most former colonies have now become self-governing states. | France is one of the member states of the EEC.* —see RACE (USAGE) **4** [C] (often cap.) any of the smaller partly self-governing areas making up certain nations: *the 50 states of the US | Queensland is one of the states of Australia. | the state elections in California* **5** [U] the grandness and ceremony connected with governments and rulers: *The Queen drove to the palace in state. | The President paid a* **state visit** *to Britain. | The opening of Parliament is one of the great* **state occasions.** —see also **lie in state** (LIE¹); **6** [C usu. sing.] infml a very nervous, anxious, or excited condition: *She let herself get* **in/into a state** *before the exams.*

state² v [T] **1** to say, express, or put into words, esp. formally: *State your name and address. | This book states the case for women's rights very clearly.* [+(that)] *The witness stated that he had not seen the woman before.* [+wh-] *Please state whether you are married or single.* **2** to mention exactly, esp. before or in advance; SPECIFY: *Theatre tickets must be used on the stated date.*

state at·tor·ney /ˌ· ·'··/ n see STATE'S ATTORNEY

state ben·e·fits /ˌ· '···/ n [P] (in Britain) money given by the government to people who are poor, without a job, ill, etc. —see also CHILD BENEFIT, HOUSING BENEFIT, SICKNESS BENEFIT, UNEMPLOYMENT BENEFIT

state court /ˈ· ˌ·/ n a court in the US which hears cases that have to do with state laws or a state's CONSTITUTION —see also extra information on page 742

state·craft /'steɪtkrɑːft‖-kræft/ n [U] the art of government; the skill of being a STATESMAN

State De·part·ment /ˈ· ·ˌ··/ [the] the American government department which deals with foreign affairs —compare FCO

State En·rolled Nurse /ˌ· ·ˌ· '·/ (abbrev. **SEN**) n a nurse who has passed a certain examination of the General Nursing Council of England and Wales or of Scotland — see also STATE REGISTERED NURSE

state·hood /'steɪthʊd/ n [U] the condition of being **a** an independent nation **b** any of the states making up a nation such as the US

state·house /'steɪthaʊs/ [the] the CAPITOL building of a US state

state·less /'steɪtləs/ adj having no citizenship; not officially belonging to any country: *stateless refugees* — ~ ness n [U]

state·ly /'steɪtli/ adj **1** formal; ceremonious: *The procession moved at a slow and stately speed.* **2** grand in style or size; NOBLE¹ (2): *a row of tall stately columns* —**liness** n [U]

stately home /ˌ··· '·/ n (in Britain) a large country house, usu. of historical interest and containing fine works of art, esp. one which people pay to visit —compare COUNTRY HOUSE, PALACE (2)

state·ment /'steɪtmənt/ n **1** [C] something that is stated; a written or spoken declaration, esp. of a formal kind: *The police took down the witness's statement. | a signed/sworn statement | The punishment for making false statements to the tax authorities can be severe.* [+that] *His statement that he had nothing to do with the affair was greeted with some scepticism. | The police have issued a statement urging the public to cooperate in this inquiry.* **2** [C] a list showing amounts of money paid, received, owing, etc., and their total: *I get a* **bank statement** *every month.* **3** [U] fml expression in words: *The details of the agreement need more exact statement.*

Stat·en Is·land /ˈstætn ˌaɪlənd/ an island in the US which is one of the five BOROUGHs of New York City. A boat called the **Staten Island ferry** takes passengers between Manhattan and Staten Island.

state of e·mer·gen·cy /ˌ· ·· ·'···/ n a state declared officially by a government in the event of a dangerous situation, e.g. caused by a natural happening such as a severe storm or flood or by political protests. Once a state of emergency has been declared, a government can act quickly and sometimes in a way which would not usu. be allowed: *After the hurricane, the President declared a state of emergency.*

state-of-the-art /ˌ· ·· '·◁/ adj using the most modern and recently-developed methods, materials, or knowledge: *state-of-the-art technology*

State of the U·nion ad·dress /ˌ· ·· '·· ·ˌ·/ [the] a speech given in January each year by the President of the US to Congress and the nation, which gives his view of the economic condition of the US and his plans for the future

State O·pen·ing of Par·lia·ment /ˌ· ·ˌ··· '···/ [the] the occasion each year when the Queen officially opens the British parliament after its summer break and makes a speech saying what the government plans to do —see colour picture on page 950

state park /ˌ· '·/ n a usu. large park owned by a US state, often in a beautiful area

State Re·gis·tered Nurse /ˌ· ·ˌ··· '·/ (abbrev. **SRN**) n (in Britain) a nurse who is fully qualified (QUALIFY) —see also STATE ENROLLED NURSE, REGISTERED GENERAL NURSE

state·room /'steɪtrʊm, -ruːm/ n a passenger's private room, esp. a large and comfortable one, on a ship

States /steɪts/ [the] infml the US

state's at·tor·ney /ˌ· ·'··/ also **state attorney**— n AmE the lawyer who represents the state in court cases: *He spent three years as assistant state's attorney for Cook County.*

state school /ˈ· ˌ·/ n a British school which receives money from the government and provides free education

▶CULTURAL NOTE Most British children attend state schools at all levels from the age of 5 to the age of 16 or 18. These are usu. called PRIMARY SCHOOL (often divided into INFANT and JUNIOR) and SECONDARY SCHOOL. There are also some state NURSERY SCHOOLS for children under 5. — compare PUBLIC SCHOOL◀

state's ev·i·dence /ˌ· '···/ n AmE for QUEEN'S EVIDENCE

state·side /'steɪtsaɪd/ adj, adv AmE infml of, in, or towards the US

states·man /'steɪtsmən/ n -men /mən/ usu. apprec a political or government leader, esp. one who is respected as being wise, honourable, and fair-minded —see also ELDER STATESMAN — ~ **like** adj — ~ **ship** n [U]

states' rights /ˈ· ˌ·/ n [P] a principle based on the tenth AMENDMENT to the CONSTITUTION of the US which says that if a particular power is not given to a particular state or forbidden to a state by the constitution, that power belongs to the particular state and not to the US government. There have been many disagreements about this in US history. It was used as an argument in support of Southern states which allowed SLAVERY before the CIVIL WAR and in the 20th century by Southern opponents of the US government's CIVIL RIGHTS programmes.

state su·preme court /ˌ· ·ˌ· '·/ n (in the US) the highest, most important court in a state —see also extra information on page 742

state tax /ˈ· ·/ n (in the US) an amount of money which must be paid to the state

state troop·er /ˌ· '··/ n AmE a member of a police force which operates everywhere in a state

state u·ni·ver·si·ty /ˈ· ··ˌ··/ n AmE a university which receives money from a state to help pay its costs: *The state universities in California are well-respected.*

stat·ic[1] /'stætɪk/ *adj* **1** not moving, changing, or developing, esp. in a way that is undesirable. *Prices on the stock market are rather static at the moment.* | *The characters in his novels seem rather static.* —compare DYNAMIC (1) **2** [A *no comp.*] *tech* of or being electricity not flowing in a current, but collecting on the surface of objects: *Some people get static electricity in their hair.*

static[2] *n* [U] noise or other effects caused by electricity in the air and blocking or spoiling regular radio or TV signals

stat·ics /'stætɪks/ *n* [U] the science dealing with the forces that produce balance in objects that are not moving — compare DYNAMICS

sta·tion[1] /'steɪʃən/ *n* **1** [C] **a** (the building or buildings at) a place where the stated public vehicles regularly stop so that passengers can get on and off, goods can be loaded etc.: *a bus/coach station* | *a tube/subway station* | *(AmE) a train station* **b** *esp. BrE* also **railway station** *fml*— a place like this where trains regularly stop: *I drove her to the station and saw her off in the train.* | *We left from Victoria Station.* | *The station waiting room* **2** [C] a building that is a centre for the usu. stated kind of service or activity: *a biological research station* | *a lifeboat station* | *I'd like you to come down to the station* (=police station) *and answer a few questions please, sir.* | *a petrol station* | *a polling station* (=where people vote in an election) **3** [C] an organization that broadcasts on television or radio: *I can't get/pick up* (=hear) *many foreign stations on this little radio.* | *This programme's boring — what's on the other station?* **4** [C] a usu. small military establishment: *a naval station* **5** [C] a large sheep or cattle farm in Australia or New Zealand **6** [C] *old-fash* one's position in life; social rank: *She married* **beneath her station.** (=married someone of a lower social class) **7** [U] *tech* (esp. of a warship) position in relation to others in a group —see also ACTION STATIONS, COMFORT STATION, SPACE STATION

station[2] *v* [T+*obj*+*adv/prep*; *often pass.*] to put (esp. a person) into a certain place for esp. military duty: *Guards were stationed round the prison.* | *During most of my time in the army I was stationed in Germany.* | *Police officers had stationed themselves at all the entrances to the building.*

sta·tion·a·ry /'steɪʃənəri‖-neri/ *adj* standing still; not moving: *A stationary target is easiest to aim at.* | *How did you manage to drive into a stationary vehicle?*

station break /'·· ·/ *n AmE* a pause during a radio or television broadcast for local stations to give their names

sta·tion·er /'steɪʃənər/ *n* a person in charge of a shop that sells stationery: *I bought some pencils at the stationer's (shop).*

sta·tion·er·y /'steɪʃənəri‖-neri/ *n* [U] **1** materials for writing; paper, pens, pencils, etc. **2** paper for writing letters, usu. with matching envelopes: *a letter on hotel stationery*

sta·tion house /'·· ·/ *n AmE for* POLICE STATION

sta·tion·mas·ter /'steɪʃənˌmɑːstər‖-ˌmæs-/ *n* the person in charge of a railway station

stations of the Cross /ˌ··· '·/ [*the*+P] (*often cap. S*) a set of 14 pictures showing events during Christ's last sufferings and death, usu. put up in order round the walls inside a Roman Catholic church

station wag·on /'·· ˌ··/ *n AmE for* ESTATE CAR

sta·tis·tic /stə'tɪstɪk/ *n* a single number in a collection of STATISTICS

stat·is·ti·cian /ˌstætɪ'stɪʃən/ *n* a person who works with statistics: *Government statisticians predict a fall in unemployment by 1995.*

sta·tis·tics /stə'tɪstɪks/ *n* **1** [P] a collection of numbers which represent facts or measurements: *These statistics show that there are 57 deaths per 1000 children born.* | *He backed up his assertions by quoting the latest statistics.* | *There are no reliable statistics for the population in this period.* —see also VITAL STATISTICS

▶CULTURAL NOTE People often suggest that they are doubtful about the value of particular statistics by saying "you can prove anything with statistics" and people sometimes mention a famous remark made by Mark Twain: "There are three kinds of lies: lies, damned lies, and statistics."◀

2 [U] the science of dealing with and explaining such numbers: *Statistics is a branch of mathematics.* —**·tical** *adj* : *There is no statistical evidence for his claim that women are worse drivers than men.* —**·tically** /kli/ *adv* : *The variation is not statistically significant.*

statue

sta·tive /'steɪtɪv/ *adj tech* (in grammar) being a verb that describes a state rather than an action or event, such as *belong* in *This book belongs to me* or *contain* in *This drink contains alcohol.* Stative verbs are not usu. used in PROGRESSIVE[1] (4) forms. —compare DYNAMIC (3)

pedestal

stat·u·a·ry /'stætʃuəri‖-tʃueri/ *n* [U] *fml or tech* statues: *a fine collection of Greek statuary*

stat·ue /'stætʃuː/ *n* a usu. large likeness, of a person, animal, etc., made in solid material such as stone or metal: *to put up/erect a statue* | *a bronze statue of Queen Victoria* —compare SCULPTURE[1] (2)

the Statue of Liberty

Statue of Lib·er·ty /ˌ··· · '···/ [*the*] a statue of a woman on Liberty Island, in New York Harbour, given to the US by France in 1884 to celebrate the American and French REVOLUTIONS. The woman is holding up a TORCH in her right hand and represents freedom. —see colour map on page 1376. The words written at the base of the statue are famous and well-known to most Americans. These words are:

Give me your tired, your poor,
Your huddled masses yearning to breathe free,
The wretched refuse of your teeming shore.
Send these, the homeless tempest-tossed to me!
I lift my lamp beside the golden door.

stat·u·esque /ˌstætʃu'esk◂/ *n* like a statue in grace, formal beauty, grandness, etc.: *a tall statuesque woman*

stat·u·ette /ˌstætʃu'et/ *n* a very small statue for putting on a table or shelf —compare BUST[1] (1)

stat·ure /'stætʃər/ *n* [C;U] *fml* **1** the degree to which someone is admired or regarded as important and influential, based on their proved worth: *a politician of (considerable) stature, who is widely respected by people of all parties* **2** a person's natural height: *She had not yet grown to (her) full stature.* | *diminutive stature*

sta·tus /'steɪtəs‖'steɪtəs, 'stæ-/ *n* **1** [C;U] one's legal position, or condition: *Please state your name, age, and* **marital status.** (=whether you are married or not) | *What's your status in this country? Are you a citizen or an alien?* **2** [U] **a** one's social or professional rank or position, considered in relation to other people: *What's her status in the organization?* **b** high social position; recognition and respect by others **3** [C] a state or situation at a particular time: *What's the status of the talks between the government and the unions?* (=what stage have they reached, are they being successful, etc.)

status sym·bol /'·· ˌ··/ *n usu. derog* something which a person owns only to make an impression on other people and show his or her high social position, e.g. an expensive car or fashionable clothing

status quo /ˌsteɪtəs 'kwəʊ‖ˌsteɪ-, ˌstæ-/ [*the*] the state of things as they are; existing state of affairs: *They are opposed to changes in the tax laws: they want to maintain/preserve the status quo.*

stat·ute /'stætʃuːt/ *n* a law passed by a lawmaking body, e.g. Parliament, and formally written down. British courts, unlike those of the US, cannot question a statute's effect: *Protection for the consumer is laid down by statute.*

statute book /'·· ·/ *n* [*the*] *not tech* a real or imaginary written collection of the laws in existence: *The government would like to see this new law* **on the statute book** (=in operation) *as soon as possible*.

statute law /'··· ·/ ‖ also **statutory law** /'····· ‚·/ *AmE*— *n* [U] the body of written laws established by a parliament or similar body —compare COMMON LAW

statute of lim·i·ta·tions /‚··· · ···'··/ *n AmE tech* a law which lists the amount of time during which action may be taken on a legal question or crime: *The statue of limitations on murder is very long.* (=action can be taken against a murderer for a very long time after the crime)

stat·u·to·ry /'stætʃʊtəri‖-tʃətɔːri/ *adj* fixed or controlled by law: *This guarantee does not affect your statutory rights.* | *statutory control of wages* | *a statutory age limit*

statutory rape /‚····· '·/ *n AmE tech* SEXUAL INTERCOURSE with a person who is a MINOR (=below the age at which they are responsible in law for their actions)

statutory sick pay /‚····· '· ·/ *n* [U] money which, according to law, must be paid by an employer to a worker who is too ill to work: *You are entitled to statutory sick pay, except for the first three days of your absence.*

staunch¹ /stɔːntʃ‖stɔːntʃ, stɑːntʃ/ *adj apprec* dependably loyal; STEADFAST: *a staunch friend and ally* | *a staunch supporter of the Democratic party* — ~**ly** *adv* — ~**ness** *n* [U]

staunch² ‖ also **stanch** *AmE*— *v* [T] to stop the flow of (esp. blood) from (a wound): *The nurse staunched (the blood from) the wound.*

stave¹ /steɪv/ *n* **1** also **staff**— the set of five lines on which music is written **2** any of the thin curved pieces of wood fitted edge to edge to form the sides of a barrel

stave² *v*

stave in *phr v* **staved** *or* **stove** /stəʊv/ [I;T (=**stave** sthg. ↔ **in**)] to break or be broken inwards: *The ship's side was stove in by the crash.*

stave sthg. ↔ **off** *phr v* **staved** [T] to keep away for a time; hold at a distance: *We had just enough food to stave off hunger.* | *He managed to stave off some of the more embarrassing questions.*

staves /steɪvz/ *pl. of* STAFF¹ (3)

stay¹ /steɪ/ *v* **1** [I] to stop and remain rather than go on or leave: *I've got to go to a meeting later, so I can't stay.* | *I stayed late at the party last night.* | *Can you stay for/to dinner?* **2** [I+adv/prep; L] to continue to be in a particular place, position, or state; remain; keep or be kept: *Don't turn off here; stay on this road.* | *Stay away from my daughter!* | *Get out and stay out!* | *My children stayed out late/stayed in* (=stayed out of/in the house) *last night.* | *The price has gone down, but I doubt whether it will stay down.* | *The men stayed out (on strike) for a week.* | *I stayed up* (=did not go to bed) *until 2.00 in the morning.* | *Please stay where you are.* | *I don't know whether to stay in teaching* (=to remain a teacher) *or to try to get another job.* [+adj] *The weather has stayed warm all week.* [+n] *He never got promoted, and stayed a private during all his time in the army.* **3** [I (**at, with**)] to live in a place for a while as a visitor or guest: *My mother is staying (with us) this week.* | *We're staying at a hotel.* | *I stayed the night at a friend's house.* (=stayed from one day to the next) **4** [I *usu. imperative*] *old use* to stop; wait a moment: *But stay! What is this?* **5** [T] *fml* to reduce the strength of: ALLAY: *stay their fears* **6 be here to stay/have come to stay** to become generally accepted: *Do you think coloured hair is here to stay, or will the fashion change again?* **7 stay after school** *euph* to be given a DETENTION (2) **8 stay put** *infml* to remain in one place; not move: *Just stay put for a minute while I look for him.* **9 stay the course** to last successfully until the end of something; not give up in spite of difficulties

▷ USAGE 1 You **stay** *at* a hotel, but *with* friends (=in their house). 2 **Remain** is more formal than **stay**, and cannot be used in meanings 3, 4, 5, 6, 7 and 8 above. —see also LIVE (USAGE)◁

stay on *phr v* [I (**as**)] to remain after the usual or expected time for leaving: *Are you going to stay on at school after you're sixteen?*

stay² *n* **1** [C *usu. sing.*] a usu. limited time of living in a place: *a short stay in hospital* | *long-stay patients* **2** [C;U] *law* a stopping or delay by order of a judge: *The prisoner was granted (a)* **stay of execution** (=the punishment was not carried out) *because new facts in his case had come to light.*

stay³ *n* **1** a strong wire or rope used for supporting a ship's MAST —see also STAYS **2** a short piece of plastic or wire used for keeping the COLLAR of a man's shirt stiff

stay-at-home /'·· ‚·/ *n infml derog* someone who habitually stays at home and has an unadventurous life

stay·er /'steɪəʳ/ *n usu. apprec* a horse or person who can keep going to the end of a long race, course, etc.

staying pow·er /'·· ‚··/ *n* [U] the power to keep going to the end; ENDURANCE; STAMINA

stays /steɪz/ *n* [P] a lady's old-fashioned undergarment stiffened by pieces of bone and worn tight around the waist

St Ber·nard /sənt 'bɜːnəd‖‚seɪnt bərˈnɑːrd/ *n* a large strong Swiss dog used esp. formerly for helping lost mountain travellers. Pictures of St Bernards often show them carrying a wooden container of BRANDY tied round their necks.

St Clair /sənt 'kleəʳ‖seɪnt-/, **Lin·di** /'lɪndi/ a British woman who used to be a PROSTITUTE and has now formed a political party to put pressure on the government to change the laws on PROSTITUTION, to protect prostitutes and make it easier for them to work. She is sometimes referred to as a "Miss Whiplash".

std *written abbrev. for:* standard

STD /‚es tiː 'diː/ *n* [U] **1** subscriber trunk dialling; the telephone system in Britain allowing people to connect their own long-distance calls by use of a special number (the **STD code**) for each different telephone exchange **2** *abbrev. for:* SEXUALLY TRANSMITTED DISEASE

stead /'sted/ *n* **in someone's stead** *fml* in someone's place; instead of someone: *While the chairman is away, another director will act in his stead.* —see also INSTEAD, **stand someone in good stead** (STAND¹)

stead·fast /'stedfɑːst‖-fæst/ *adj fml or lit* **1** *apprec* faithful; steadily loyal: *a steadfast friend* **2** steady; not moving or movable: *a steadfast gaze* — ~**ly** *adv* — ~**ness** *n* [U]

stead·y¹ /'stedi/ *adj* **1** firm or fixed in position, movement, or state; well controlled; not shaking: *Hold that candle steady.* | *Take steady aim, then fire.* | *Don't worry; the ladder's* **steady as a rock.** (=completely firm) | *It's a delicate job needing* **a steady hand/steady nerves.** — opposite **unsteady** **2** moving or developing in an even, continuous way; regular: *a steady speed* | *a long period of steady economic growth* | *a steady east wind* **3** not changing; STABLE: *My son's finally found himself* **a steady job.** **4** *apprec* dependable and serious-minded: *She needs to marry someone steady.* —**ily** *adv* : *His condition has got steadily worse.* —**iness** *n*

steady² *v* [I;T (DOWN)] to become or make steady: *The pound has steadied after early losses on the money markets.* | *He steadied his trembling hand with an effort.* | *A glass of whisky will steady your nerves.*

steady³ *adv AmE* **go steady** (of a boy and a girl) to have a firm relationship and to go out together regularly.

▶CULTURAL NOTE In the US it is quite usual for boys and girls of HIGH SCHOOL age (14 – 17) to go steady, and often exchange small gifts, typically rings.◀

steady⁴ also **steady on** /‚·· '·/— *interj BrE infml* be careful; watch what you're doing: *Steady (on)! You nearly knocked my glass out of my hand!*

steady⁵ *n AmE* the boy or girl one is going steady with: *Jill is Ray's steady.*

steady state theo·ry /‚·· '· ‚··/ *n* [the] *tech* the idea that things in space have always existed and have always been going further apart as new atoms come into being —compare BIG BANG THEORY

steak /steɪk/ *n* **1** [C;U] a thick flat piece of meat from cattle (or from a stated animal or large fish), cut from the fleshy part and of good quality: *"How would you like your steak done, sir?" "Rare/Medium rare/Well-done, please."* | *a fillet steak* | *Two gammon steaks, please.* | *a salmon steak* —see also MINUTE STEAK **2** [U] *BrE* such cattle meat of a less good quality, usu. used in small pieces in dishes with vegetables or pastry

steak and kid·ney pie /‚·· ··· '·/ *n* [C;U] a dish containing steak and KIDNEY with a PASTRY top. It is thought of as a typical British dish.

steak and kidney pud·ding /‚··· ··· '··/ *n* [C;U] a dish containing steak, KIDNEY, and SUET, that is cooked in steam for a long time

steak·house /ˈsteɪkhaʊs/ n a restaurant that serves esp. steak

steak tar·tare /ˌ·ˈ·/ n [U] minced (MINCE) steak eaten raw, usu. with a raw egg

steal¹ /stiːl/ v stole /stəʊl/, stolen /ˈstəʊlən/ 1 [I;T (from)] to take (what belongs to someone else) without any right to it: *He was sent to prison for stealing.* | *My bicycle was stolen while I was in the shop.* | *They've had their car stolen.* (=someone has stolen it) | *There's a risk that rival companies will steal our ideas.* 2 [T (from)] to take or get quickly, secretly, or without permission: *I stole a kiss from her.* | *He stole a glance at the pretty girl across the table.* 3 [I+adv/prep] to move secretly or quietly: *He stole out of the house without anyone seeing him.* | (lit) *The evening shadows began to steal across the lawn.* 4 [T] (in BASEBALL) to move to (the next BASE¹ (6)) before another player has hit the ball: *Henderson has twelve stolen bases to his credit this season.* 5 **steal a march on** to secretly or unexpectedly gain an advantage over (someone) by taking quick action 6 **steal someone's heart** to cause someone to fall in love, usu. not intentionally: *He stole my heart as soon as he smiled and said my name.* 7 **steal someone's thunder** infml to gain for oneself the success or recognition that should have gone to someone else, by doing oneself what they had intended to do 8 **steal the scene/show** to get all the attention and praise expected by someone else at a show or other event

▷ USAGE One **steals** things. One **robs** people (of things): *I've been robbed!* | *He robbed me of my watch!* | *He stole my watch!*◁

steal² n [S] infml, esp. AmE something for sale very cheaply: *At 20 bucks this camera was a steal!*

stealth /stelθ/ n [U] fml the action of moving or acting secretly or unseen: *He removed the keys from the cloakroom by stealth.*

stealth bomb·er /ˈ· ˌ··/ n an American BOMBER aircraft which cannot be discovered by RADAR instruments

stealth·y /ˈstelθi/ adj quiet and secret; (trying to remain) unseen: *a stealthy glance at her watch* —**ily** adv

steam¹ /stiːm/ n [U] 1 water in the state of a gas produced by boiling: *clouds of steam* 2 power or effort produced by steam under pressure, and used for making things work or move: *The engines are driven by steam.* | *steam-powered machinery* | *Up on the bridge, the captain ordered full steam ahead.* (=the ship to go forward with the fastest speed) | (fig.) *We've got government approval, so now we can* **go full steam ahead** *with our plans.* | (fig.) *He started off with great enthusiasm, but now he's beginning to* **run out of steam.** | (fig.) *There wasn't room for me in their car, so I had to get there* **under my own steam.** (=without help from anyone else) 3 the mist formed by water becoming cool: *Steam formed on the inside of the kitchen windows.* 4 railway operation by steam engines: *the age of steam* 5 infml strong feelings or active strength considered as trapped by self-control: *I was so angry I* **let off steam** (=tried to lose my anger) *by shouting at the dog.* | *The children are* **letting off steam** (=running about and playing) *in the garden.* | *By the end of the meeting she had really built up a* **head of steam.** (=she was very angry)

steam² v 1 [I] to give off steam, esp. when very hot: *a mug of steaming hot coffee* 2 [I+adv/prep] to travel by steam power: *The ship steamed into the harbour.* 3 [T] to cook by heating with steam: *a steamed pudding* | *steamed rice* —see COOK (USAGE) 4 [T+obj+adj/adv/prep] to use steam on, esp. for unsticking or softening: *He steamed the letter open.* | *She steamed the stamp off the envelope.*
steam up phr v [I; T(=**steam** sthg. ↔ **up**)] to cover or be covered with steam: *His glasses (got) steamed up when he came into the warm room.* —see also STEAMED-UP

steam³ adj [A no comp.] 1 powered by steam under pressure: *a STEAM ENGINE/train* 2 BrE humor old-fashioned: *a steam radio*

steam·boat /ˈstiːmbəʊt/ n a steam-powered boat made for going on rivers and along coasts

steam·ed-up /ˌ· ˈ·/ adj [F] infml excited and angry: *Don't get so steamed-up about it — it's really not important.*

steam en·gine /ˈ· ˌ··/ n an engine powered by steam esp. in a train

▶CULTURAL NOTE The steam engine was first developed in Britain by James Watt in 1769. It brought great improvements in the making and movement of goods and played an important part in the INDUSTRIAL REVOLUTION. ◀

steam·er /ˈstiːmər/ n 1 a STEAMSHIP —see also PADDLE STEAMER 2 a container in which one cooks food with steam 3 a person taking part in the action of STEAMING

steam·ing /ˈstiːmɪŋ/ n [U] AmE sl the criminal activity of running with a group of others through a crowded street, shop, or train and stealing money and valuable things from the people there

steam i·ron /ˈ· ··/ n an electric iron that holds water and makes steam which goes into the clothes for easier pressing

steam·roll /ˈstiːmrəʊl/ AmE for STEAMROLLER²

steam·roll·er¹ /ˈstiːmˌrəʊlər/ n 1 a heavy steam-powered machine with very wide wheels for driving over and flattening road surfaces 2 infml a force that crushes all opposition

steamroller² ‖ also **steamroll** AmE— v [T] infml to crush or force using very great power or pressure: *He steamrollered his bill through Parliament against fierce opposition.*

steamship

steamship /ˈstiːmˌʃɪp/ n a large non-military ship driven by steam power

steam shov·el /ˈ· ˌ··/ n AmE for EXCAVATOR (2)

steed /stiːd/ n usu. poet a horse, esp. for riding: *his trusty steed*

Steed a character from the British television SERIES *The Avengers.* Steed is a well-dressed wealthy English gentleman who, with his young female companion Emma Peel, fights against crime and criminals.

steel¹ /stiːl/ n [U] 1 a metal consisting of iron in a hard strong form containing some CARBON and sometimes other metals, and used in building materials, cutting tools, machines, etc.: *a steel sword blade* | *a set of* **stainless steel** *knives and forks* | *the steel industry* (=industry making steel) | (fig.) *You must have* **nerves of steel** (=very strong nerves) *to be able to climb up that tall chimney.* 2 lit fighting weapons: *Let's give the enemy a taste of our steel.* —see also COLD STEEL

steel² v [T] to make (esp. oneself) hard, unfeeling, or determined: [+obj+to-v] *He steeled himself to tell her about her father's death.*

Steel, Sir David (1938–) a British politician born in Scotland who was leader of the Liberal Party from 1976 to 1988. In 1988, the Liberal Party joined with the Social Democratic Party to form a new party called the Social and Liberal Democrats, of which David Steel was joint leader for a short time.

steel band /ˈ· ·/ n [C+sing./pl. v] a band of a type originally heard in the West Indies, playing drums cut from metal oil barrels to sound particular notes

Steele¹ /ˈstiːl/, **Sir Richard** (1672–1729) an Irish writer who established the magazine the Tatler, for which his friend Joseph Addison wrote

Steele², **Tommy** (1936–) an English actor and popular music singer who has appeared in several successful stage MUSICAL, in films, and on television

steel gui·tar /ˌ· ·ˈ·/ also **pedal steel guitar**— n a musical instrument with 10 strings that is played using a steel bar and a PEDAL (=foot-operated bar) to produce different notes. It is very commonly heard in country and western music.

steel wool /ˌ· ˈ·/ n [U] material that is a mass of fine sharp-edged steel threads used for rubbing a surface smooth, removing paint, etc.—compare WIRE WOOL

steel·works /ˈstiːlwɜːks‖-wɜːrks/ n **steelworks** [C+*sing.*|*pl. v*] a factory where steel is made —**steelworker** n : *The steelworkers have voted against strike action.*

steel·y /ˈstiːli/ adj like steel; hard, cold, strong, or bright: *He fixed her with a steely glare.* | *steely blue eyes* | *steely determination*

steep[1] /stiːp/ adj **1** rising or falling quickly or at a large angle: *This hill's too steep to ride up on a bicycle.* | *a steep rise in prices|fall in living standards* **2** *infml* (of a demand or esp. a price) unreasonable; too much: *He's asking £500 for his old car, which I think is a bit steep!* — ~ly adv : *The rocks rose steeply out of the river.* — ~ness n [U]

steep[2] v [I;T (**in**)] **1** to (let) stay in a liquid, for softening, cleaning, bringing out a taste, etc.; SOAK: *Steep the stained cloth in bleach overnight.* | *The shirts are steeping.* **2 steeped in** thoroughly filled or familiar with: *a very ancient building that is steeped in history* | *The daily lives of the tribe were steeped in custom and tradition.*

steep·en /ˈstiːpən/ v [I;T] to become or make steeper: *The slope steepened as we went higher.*

stee·ple /ˈstiːpəl/ n a church tower with a top part (SPIRE) rising to a high sharp point

stee·ple·chase /ˈstiːpəltʃeɪs/ n **1** a horse race over a course of more than two miles with various jumps to be made —compare FLAT RACING **2** a running race with jumps, esp. a 3000-metre race with 35 jumps to be made during the run

stee·ple·jack /ˈstiːpəldʒæk/ n a person who works on towers, tall chimneys, steeples, etc., repairing them, painting them, etc.

steer[1] /stɪər/ v **1** [I;T] to make (esp. a boat or road vehicle) go in a particular direction: *She steered with one hand while trying to adjust the rear-view mirror with the other.*| *He steered the boat carefully between the rocks.* | (fig.) *I steered the visitors towards the garden.* | (fig.) *She tried to steer the conversation away from such dangerous topics.*| (fig.) *steering a bill through Parliament* **2** [I+adv|prep; T+obj+adv|prep] to follow or change to (a particular course), esp. in a boat: *We turned about and steered (a course) for Port-of-Spain.* | *to steer a middle course between two extremes* **3** [I+adv|prep] (of a boat or vehicle) to act when one turns its steering wheel: *How does your car steer? Does it take the corners well?* **4 steer clear (of)** *infml* to keep away (from); avoid: *I should steer clear of the fish stew; it's not very nice!*

▷ USAGE You can **steer** *ships, cars, lorries,* etc., and also such things as *cycles* and *sledges,* but not *aircraft;* for these, the usual verbs are **fly** and **pilot.** —see also BOAT (USAGE), CAR (USAGE), DRIVE (USAGE)◁

steer[2] n a young male animal of the cattle family with its sex organs removed, kept for meat —compare BULLOCK, HEIFER, OX

steer·age /ˈstɪərɪdʒ/ n [U] (esp. in former times) the part of a passenger ship for those with the cheapest tickets: *We travelled (in the) steerage.* | *steerage passengers*

steering com·mit·tee /ˈ·· ·,··/ n [C+*sing.*|*pl. v*] a committee that guides or directs a particular piece of activity

steering wheel /ˈ·· ·/ n a wheel which one turns to make a vehicle or ship turn left or right —see picture at CAR

steers·man /ˈstɪəzmən‖ˈstɪərz-/ n -**men** /mən/ esp. *lit* a person who steers a ship or boat; HELMSMAN

Stef·fens /ˈstefənz/, **Lincoln** (1866–1936) an American writer, known esp. for the many magazine articles that he wrote about the crime and dishonesty in city governments, including those collected in *The Shame of the Cities*

stein /staɪn/ n **1** a tall thick cup for beer, often decorated and having a lid **2** *AmE for* TANKARD

Stein, Ger·trude /ˈgɜːtruːd‖ˈgɜːr-/ (1874–1946) an American writer whose works include *The Autobiography of Alice B. Toklas*

Stein·beck /ˈstaɪnbek/, **John** (1902–68) an American writer best-known for his NOVELs which show great feeling and concern for poor people and their problems. His best known works are *The Grapes of Wrath, Cannery Row, East of Eden* and *Of Mice and Men.* He won the Nobel Prize for literature in 1962.

Stei·nem /ˈstaɪnəm/, **Glo·ri·a** /ˈglɔːriə/ (1934–) an American writer who established the magazine *Ms.* and is known for her FEMINIST views and work

Stei·ner /ˈstaɪnər/, **Ru·dolf** /ˈruːdɒlf‖-aːlf/ (1861–1925) an Austrian thinker who developed a system to try to explain the world by giving importance to the human spirit. There are still some private schools around the world which are based on his teachings. They are often called **Steiner Schools** or **Waldorf Schools.**

Stein·way /ˈstaɪnweɪ/ tdmk a company that makes good quality pianos, established in New York by **Henry Steinway** (1797–1871): *They've just bought a new Steinway.*

Stel·la Ar·tois /ˌstelər aːˈtwaː‖-aːr-/ n tdmk a kind of LAGER

stel·lar /ˈstelər/ adj [A] tech of the stars: *a stellar map* —see also INTERSTELLAR

stem[1] /stem/ n **1 a** the central part of a plant above the ground, from which branches grow **b** a plant part which supports a leaf or flower; STALK **2** a narrow upright part which supports another: *the stem of a wine glass* —see picture at GLASS **3** the narrow tube of a tobacco pipe **4** the part of a word whose spelling remains the same when different endings are added on to it: *From the stem "driv-", we get "drives", "driven", and "driving".* —compare ROOT[1] (5) **5 from stem to stern** all the way from the front to the back, esp. of a ship **6 -stemmed** /stemd/ having the stated type or number of stems: *long-stemmed roses|wine glasses*

stem[2] v -**mm**- [T] *fml* to stop (the flow of): *How can we stem the bleeding|the flow of blood?* | (fig.) *A radical change of policy is necessary if the government is to* **stem the tide** *of public opinion against it.*
  stem from sthg. *phr v* [T] to exist or happen as a result of; have as an origin or cause: *The present difficulties stem from our failure to deal with the problem when it first arose.*

stench /stentʃ/ n [usu. sing.] *fml* a very strong bad smell: *the stench of rotting meat|* (fig.) *of official corruption*

sten·cil[1] /ˈstensəl/ n **1** a piece of material, esp. card or metal, in which patterns or letters have been cut **2** the pattern or letters made by putting paint or ink through the spaces in this onto paper, etc.

stencil[2] v -**ll**- *BrE* ‖ -**l**- *AmE* [T] to make (a copy of) by using a stencil

Sten·dhal /ˈstɒndaːl‖sten'daːl/ (1783–1842) a French writer whose best-known books are *Le Rouge et le Noir* and *La Chartreuse de Parme*

Sten gun /ˈsten ˌɡʌn/ n a small British SUBMACHINE GUN

ste·nog·ra·pher /stəˈnɒɡrəfər‖-ˈnɑː-/ also **sten·o** /ˈstenəʊ/— n esp. old use or AmE for SHORTHAND TYPIST

ste·nog·ra·phy /stəˈnɒɡrəfi‖-ˈnɑː-/ also **sten·o** /ˈstenəʊ/ AmE for SHORTHAND (1)

sten·to·ri·an /stenˈtɔːriən/ adj fml or lit (of the voice) very loud; powerful: *"Get out," he roared, in stentorian tones.*

step[1] /step/ n **1** an act of moving by raising one foot and bringing it down somewhere else: *With every step I took the load seemed to get heavier.* | *Take two steps forward and two steps back.* | (lit) *The sun was setting as he directed|bent his steps* (=walked) *towards home.* **2** the sound this makes: *I heard a step in the corridor.* —compare FOOTSTEP **3 a** the distance covered in one step: *a tobacconist, and just a few steps further on a newsagent* **b** [S] a short distance: *It's just a step from my house to his.* —compare PACE[1] (2) **4** a flat narrow surface, esp. one in a set of surfaces each higher than the one before, on which the foot is placed for climbing up and down; stair, RUNG of a ladder, etc.: *Mind the step outside the door.* — see also DOORSTEP, STEPS **5** an act, esp. one of a set of actions, which should produce a certain result: *Our first step must be a change in working hours; then we must decide how to improve conditions.* | *We must* **take steps** (=take action) *to help the families of those who were hurt.*| *It's only a short step from this proposal to selling off all our assets.* | *These new arrangements may not be the final answer to our problems, but at least they're a* **step in the right direction.** | *The new therapy is seen as a major step in the treatment of|towards the cure of nervous disorders.* **6** a degree on a scale, or a stage in a process: *For every year you've worked here you go up another step on the salary scale.* | *He supported her every step of the way* (=completely) | *I hear she's been promoted to sales manager; that's quite a step up for someone so young.* | *A teacher should always be at least* **one step ahead** *of his pupils.* (=should know more than them and be prepared for their questions, needs, etc.) —compare STAGE[1] (2) **7**

a particular movement of the feet in dancing: *I'm trying to learn a new step.* —see also QUICKSTEP **8** *esp. AmE* (in music) a TONE¹ (6) **9 in step/out of step: a** (esp. of soldiers) marching in such a way that each person's right foot and left foot move forward at the same time/a different time as other people's **b** (of a person or behaviour) in/not in accordance or agreement with others: *He is out of step with modern life.* | *to keep in step with fashion* **10 one small step for a man, one giant leap for mankind** *quote* the first words said by the ASTRONAUT Neil Armstrong when he became the first man to walk on the moon in 1969 —see picture on page 752 **11 step by step** gradually: *He learnt the rules step by step.* | *step-by-step instructions* —see also **watch one's step** (WATCH¹)

step² *v* **-pp-** [I+*adv/prep*] **1** to raise one foot and put it down, usu. in front of the other, in order to move along: *I stepped forward to receive my prize.* | *The conductor stepped down from the podium.* | *She stepped carefully around the puddle.* | *He stepped aside to allow the hurrying nurses to pass.* | (fig.) *The police have appealed for witnesses to step forward.* (=to offer to help the police) **2** *fml* to go a short distance on foot: *Step into the house/inside while you're waiting.* | *Kindly step this way.* (=come where I have shown you) **3** [esp. **on**] to bring the foot down; TREAD: *She stepped on a loose stone and twisted her ankle.* **4 step on it/on the gas** *infml* to go faster **5 step out of line** *derog* to act differently from others or from what is expected —see also SIDESTEP

step down/aside *phr v* [I (**as, in favour of**)] to leave one's job, official position, etc.: *The chairman feels it is time he stepped down (in favour of a younger man).*

step in *phr v* [I] to enter an argument or begin to take action in an affair; INTERVENE: *If the dispute gets any worse the government will have to step in.*

step out *phr v* **1** [I] *BrE old-fash* to start walking fast: *Come on! If we step out we'll be there in half an hour.* **2** [I] *esp. AmE* to go outside or go somewhere: *Molly stepped out but she'll be back soon.* **3** [T] **step out on** *AmE infml* to be unfaithful to (one's husband or wife)

step sthg.↔**up** *phr v* [T] to increase (an amount of something) in size or speed: *We're trying to step up production to meet the increased demand.*

step- see WORD FORMATION

step·broth·er /ˈstepbrʌðəʳ/ *n* a male person whose father or mother has married one's mother or father

step·child /ˈsteptʃaɪld/ *n* **-chil·dren** /tʃɪldrən/ a child that one's husband/wife has as a result of an earlier marriage and for whom one has no legal responsibility; a **step-son** or **stepdaughter**

step·daugh·ter /ˈstepdɔːtəʳ/ *n* a female stepchild

step·fa·ther /ˈstepfɑːðəʳ/ *n* a man one's mother has married who is not one's natural father

Step·ford Wives /ˌstepfəd ˈwaɪvz‖-fərd-/, **The** a book by Ira Levin, also made into a successful film, about a group of married women in a village, who are made to act in a very PASSIVE way by the men of the village. The women are only interested in cooking, cleaning their houses, and pleasing their husbands in every way.

Steph·an·o·pou·los /ˌstefən ˈɒpələs/, **George** (1961–) US President Bill Clinton's Director of Communications

Ste·phen·son¹ /ˈstiːvənsən/, **George** (1781–1848) an English engineer who built the first train with a steam engine in 1814 and the first public railway in 1825. He is remembered esp. for his steam train "The Rocket".

Stephenson², **Rob·ert** /ˈrɒbət‖ˈrɑːbərt/ (1803–1859) an English engineer, the son of George Stephenson. He continued his father's work on the development of the steam-powered train, but is best-remembered as a builder of bridges, including that over the Menai Straits.

step·lad·der /ˈstepˌlædəʳ/ *n* a sloping framework of two parts, one of which is like a ladder, which is used in the house for reaching high places and can be folded together for storing

step·moth·er /ˈstepmʌðəʳ/ *n* a woman one's father has married who is not one's natural mother

▶CULTURAL NOTE In children's stories a stepmother is often shown as being a wicked, cruel person who does not love her stepchildren (STEPCHILD), and is sometimes also shown as a WITCH.◀

step·par·ent /ˈstepˌpeərənt/ *n* a stepmother or STEPFATHER

steppes /steps/ *n* [*the*+P] (*often cap.*) a large area of land without trees, esp. that in Russia and parts of Asia and southeast Europe

stepping stones

stepping-stone /ˈ··· ·/ *n* **1** any of a row of large stones with a level top, which one walks on to cross a river or stream **2** [(**to**)] a way of improvement or gaining success: *Are good exam results a stepping-stone to a well-paid career?*

steps /steps/ *n* [P] **1** a number or set of STEPS¹ (4), usu. outside and made of stone: *She climbed the* **flight of steps** *to the door.* | *He took a photograph of her on the church steps.* —compare STAIRS, STAIRCASE **2** *BrE for* STEPLADDER —see PAIR (USAGE)

step·sis·ter /ˈstepsɪstəʳ/ *n* a female person whose father or mother has married one's mother or father

step·son /ˈstepsʌn/ *n* a male STEPCHILD

Step·toe and Son /ˈsteptəʊ ənd ˌsʌn/ a very popular British television COMEDY programme about Albert and Harold Steptoe, a father and son who work as RAG-AND-BONE men in London. First shown in the 1960s, it is considered one of the best British television comedies.

ster·e·o¹ /ˈsteriəʊ, ˈstɪər-/ *n* **-os 1** [C] a record player which gives out sound from two places by means of two SPEAKERS —see picture at LIVING ROOM **2** [U] stereo sound: *This programme is being broadcast* **in stereo.**

stereo² also **ster·e·o·phon·ic** /ˌsteriəˈfɒnɪk◂, ˌstɪər-‖-ˈfɑː-/ *fml—* *adj* using a system of sound recording, broadcasting, or receiving in which the sound comes from two different places, to give an effect of greater reality: *a stereo recording* | *a stereo record player* —compare MONO, QUADRAPHONIC

ster·e·o·scop·ic /ˌsteriəˈskɒpɪk◂‖-ˈskɑː-/ *adj* seen or seeing (as if) with depth and distance, rather than as a flat picture: *stereoscopic vision*

stereo sys·tem /ˈ··· ˌ·/ *n* *AmE for* MUSIC CENTRE

ster·e·o·type¹ /ˈsteriətaɪp/ *n* [(**of**)] *usu. derog* (someone or something that represents) a fixed set of ideas about what a particular type of person or thing is like, which is (wrongly) believed to be true in all cases: *She believes that she is not a good mother because she does not fit the stereotype of a woman who spends all her time with her children.* | *The characters in the film are just stereotypes, with no individuality.* | *racial stereotypes* —**typical** /ˌsteriəʊˈtɪpɪkəl◂/ *adj*

stereotype² *v* [T] *derog* to have, show, or encourage a fixed and usu. incorrect idea of what (someone or something) is like; regard as an example of a general type: *It's wrong to stereotype people, as if they were all alike.* | *a stereotyped view of teachers* | *stereotyped answers*

ster·ile /ˈsteraɪl‖-rəl/ *adj* **1** [*no comp.*] (of a living thing) unable to produce young: *Because of exposure to dangerous radiation, the woman had become sterile.* —compare FERTILE **2** free from all harmful bacteria and similar extremely small living things: *An operating theatre should be a sterile environment.* **3** (of land) unable to produce crops **4** *derog* (of ideas or speech) lacking new thought, imagination, etc. —**ility** /stəˈrɪlɪti/ *n* [U]

ster·il·ize also **-ise** *BrE* /ˈsterɪlaɪz/ *v* [T] to make STERILE (1,2): *to have the cat sterilized* | *Have these instruments been sterilized, nurse?* | *sterilized milk* —**izer** *n* —**ization** /ˌsterɪlaɪˈzeɪʃən‖-lə-/ *n* [U]

ster·ling¹ /ˈstɜːlɪŋ‖-ɜːr-/ *n* [U] *tech* the type of money used in Britain, based on the pound (£): *The value/strength of sterling has risen.* | *sterling travellers cheques.* [after *n*] *the* **pound sterling** (=the British pound)

sterling² *adj* [A] **1** [*no comp.*] *tech* (of gold and esp. silver) of a fixed standard of pureness **2** *fml* of the highest standard, esp. in being loyal, dependable, and brave: *We all admire her sterling qualities.* | *a sterling effort*

stern¹ /stɜːn‖stɜːrn/ *adj* **1** showing firmness and severity: *a stern teacher* | *stern discipline* **2** showing displeasure or disapproval: *a stern look/rebuke* – **~ly** *adv* – **~ness** *n* [U]

stern² *n* the back part of a ship –compare BOW⁵, and see picture at YACHT

Stern, Isaac (1920–) an American VIOLIN player, born in Russia

Sterne /stɜːn‖stɜːrn/, **Laur·ence** /ˈlɒrəns‖ˈlɔː-/ (1713–68) an English writer of NOVELS, born in Ireland, best-known for his humorous work *Tristram Shandy*

Ster·no /ˈstɜːnəʊ ‖ -ɜːr-/ *n* [U] *tdmk* a soft quite solid substance which burns steadily, kept in a small can and often used as a small movable cooker, e.g. when camping

ster·num /ˈstɜːnəm‖-ɜːr-/ *n* **-nums** *or* **-na** /nə/ *med for* BREASTBONE –see picture at SKELETON

ste·roid /ˈstɪərɔɪd, ˈste-/ *n* any of various chemical compounds, including many HORMONEs, that have a strong effect on the workings of the body.

▶ CULTURAL NOTE Steroids are sometimes used by sports people to strengthen the body and improve performance although their use is illegal in most national and international sports competitions.◀

ster·to·rous /ˈstɜːtərəs‖-ɜːr-/ *adj* *lit or humor* making a noisy sound while breathing: *a stertorous sleeper* – **~ly** *adv*

stet /stet/ *interj* (used as a note for asking a printer not to remove or change writing which has been crossed out)

steth·o·scope /ˈsteθəskəʊp/ *n* a medical instrument with two pipelike parts that fit into a doctor's ears and a cuplike part that is put on someone's chest, so that the doctor can hear the sound of the heartbeat

stet·son /ˈstetsən/ *n tdmk* (*often cap.*) a man's tall hat with a wide edge (BRIM) standing out round the head, worn esp. in the American West by COWBOYS –see picture at HAT

ste·ve·dore /ˈstiːvↄdↄːʳ/ *n esp. old fash AmE* a person whose job is loading and unloading ships; DOCKER

Ste·ven·age /ˈstiːvənɪdʒ/ a town in Hertfordshire, England, which was developed as a NEW TOWN in 1946

Ste·vens¹ /ˈstiːvənz/, **Cat** (1947–) a British popular music singer, songwriter, and GUITAR player successful in the 1960s and 1970s

Stevens², **Thad·de·us** /ˈθædiəs/ (1792–1868) an American politician and member of the House of Representatives who was a leader of the Republicans' Reconstruction programme after the Civil War

Stevens³, **Wallace** (1879–1955) an American poet whose collections of poems include *Harmonium* and *The Man with the Blue Guitar*

Ste·ven·son¹ /ˈstiːvənsən/, **Ad·lai** /ˈædlaɪ/ **E** (1900–65) an American politician in the Democratic Party who was governor of Illinois from 1949 to 1953. He ran for president in 1952 and 1956, but was defeated on both occasions by Eisenhower. He is remembered as an internationalist and a thoughtful politician who supported suggestions for change.

Stevenson², **Rob·ert Lou·is** /ˈrɒbət ˈluːiː ‖ ˈrɑːbərt/ (1850–94) a Scottish writer whose books *Treasure Island* and *Kidnapped* are among the best-known adventure stories in English. He also wrote the famous book, *The Strange Case of Dr Jekyll and Mr Hyde*.

stew¹ /stjuː‖stuː/ *v* [I;T] **1** to cook or be cooked slowly and gently in liquid: *stewed apples* –see COOK (USAGE) **2 stew in one's (own) juice** *infml* to (be left to) suffer as a result of one's own actions

stew² *n* **1** [C;U] a dish consisting usu. of meat and vegetables cooked together in liquid: *a vegetable/fish/beef stew* –see also IRISH STEW; see COOK (USAGE) **2** [S] **a** *infml* a confused anxious state of mind: *There's no need to get in a stew; everything will be all right.* **b** a difficult situation; MESS: *the government's attempts to get out of the stew it has got itself into*

stew·ard /ˈstjuːəd‖ˈstuːərd/ *n* **1 stew·ard·ess** /-dↄs/ *fem.*– a person who serves passengers on a ship, plane, train, etc.: *the chief steward* | *an air stewardess* (=on a plane) **2** *BrE* a man who arranges and is in charge of a public amusement, such as a horse race, a meeting, etc.: *The winning jockey may not have ridden fairly, so there will*

have to be a **stewards' enquiry.** **3** a man who arranges the supply and serving of food in a place such as a club or college **4** *esp. old use* a man who is employed to look after a house and lands, such as a farm –see also SHOP STEWARD

stew·ard·ship /ˈstjuːədʃɪp‖ˈstuːərd-/ *n* [U (**of**)] *fml or pomp* the responsibilities connected with something: *He has faithfully exercised the stewardship of his post.*

Stew·art /ˈstjuːət‖ˈstuːərt/, **Jackie** (1939–) a Scottish racing driver who won 27 Grand Prix races and won the world CHAMPIONSHIP three times

Stewart, James (1908–) an American film actor known for his easily recognizable slow way of speaking. His many films include *Mr Smith Goes to Washington*, *The Philadelphia Story* and *Shenandoah*.

Stewart, Rod (1945–) a British popular music singer and songwriter, born in London and successful esp. in the 1970s and 1980s. He is known for his pride in his Scottish family background and his love of football. His songs include *Sailing* and *Tonight's the Night*.

stewed /stjuːd‖stuːd/ *adj* **1** *BrE* (of tea) kept too long before pouring, and so tasting too strong and bitter **2** cooked in liquid: *stewed prunes/tomatoes* **3** [F] *infml* drunk

stewing steak /ˈ··· ·/ *n* [U] BEEF(=meat from a cow) that is not tender enough to eat if it is not cooked slowly in liquid for a long time, or made into a STEW

St Hel·ens /sↄnt ˈhelənz‖seɪnt-/ an industrial town in Merseyside, NW England, E of Liverpool

St Helens, Mount a mountain in the S of Washington State, US, a VOLCANO which erupted (ERUPT) in 1980 after a quiet period of over a hundred years

Stich /ʃtɪk, ʃtɪx/, **Mi·chael** /ˈmaɪkəl/ (1968–) a German tennis player who won at Wimbledon in 1991

sticks

lacrosse stick

batons

walking stick

chopsticks

crook

hockey stick

stick¹ /stɪk/ *n* **1** [C] a small thin branch or part of a branch that has fallen or been cut from a tree: *We gathered some sticks to build a fire.* –see also TWIG **2** [C] a thin rod of wood or metal used to support the body when walking; WALKING STICK: *Since the accident she has had to walk with a stick.* –see also CANE¹ (4) **3** [C] a long thin piece of wood used **a** for hitting: *I'll take a stick to (=hit) that dog if it doesn't keep quiet.* –see also BIG STICK **b** for playing certain sports: *a lacrosse/hockey stick* **4** [C (**of**)] a thin rod of any material: *a stick of rock* (=a hard kind of sweet) | *a stick of chalk/celery/dynamite/butter/gum* | *incense sticks* **5** [U] *BrE infml* severe treatment: *She really gave him (the)* **stick** *about the way he made a mess of the contract negotiations.* | *Those workmen will get some stick from me if they don't finish their job properly.* **6** [C] *old-fash infml, esp. BrE* a person of the stated type: *He's a dull/dry* **old stick.** | *She's quite a nice old stick when you get to know her.* **7** [C] also **stick of furniture**– *infml* a piece of furniture, esp. of little value or importance: *After the terrible fire we were left with hardly a stick (of furniture).* –see also STICKS, **get (hold of) the wrong end**

of the stick (WRONG¹), **more than one can shake a stick at** (SHAKE¹)

stick² *v* **stuck** /stʌk/ **1** [T+*obj*+*adv*/*prep*] to push (esp. a pointed object) into or through something: *Don't stick pins into the chair!* | *She stuck her fork into the meat.* **2** [I;T] to (cause to) be fixed (as if) with a sticky substance: *What's wrong with this stamp? It won't stick.* | *The paint was still wet and the door handle stuck to my hand.* | *"The handle's broken off." "Stick it with glue."* | *He stuck down the flap of the envelope.* | *He stuck the picture on the wall.* **3** [I] to become fixed in position; not move: *He tried to poke his head through the tiny opening, but it stuck.* | *I can't get this door to open — it keeps sticking.* | (fig.) *a chance remark which stuck in their mind* (=which she (frequently) remembered) —see also STUCK² **4** [T+*obj*+*adv*/*prep*] *infml* to put: *Stick your coat down over there.* | *She stuck the flowers in a vase of water.* **5** [T *usu. in questions and negatives; not in progressive forms*] *infml, esp. BrE* to like or accept; bear: *I can't stick her husband.* | *I can't stick this dull job any longer.* [+*v-ing*] *I can't stick waiting around like this.* **6** [I] *infml* to remain in effect, esp. by being able to be proved: *The police won't bring the case to court because they don't think they can make the charges stick.* **7** [T] *sl* to keep (something unwanted): *If that's all you're prepared to pay, you can stick your job.* (=because I certainly do not want it) **8 stick in one's throat** *infml* to be hard to accept: *Having to pay out £50 for such a small repair really sticks in my throat.* **9 stick it to someone** *AmE infml* treat someone very badly, esp. by charging too much money: *They really stuck it to us when they saw we were driving a Cadillac.*

stick about/around *phr v* [I] *infml* to not go away; stay or wait in a place, esp. in the hope of some advantage

stick at sthg. *phr v* [T] **1** to continue to work hard at: *If we stick at it, we should finish the job by midnight.* **2** to be unwilling to do (esp. something wrong) (usu. in the phrase **stick at nothing**): *He'll stick at nothing, not even breaking the law, to get his own way.*

stick by sthg./sbdy. *phr v* [T] *infml* to continue to support: *I still stick by what I said in the first place: I don't believe her.* | *I'll always stick by my friends.*

stick out *phr v* **1** [I;T (=**stick** sthg.↔**out**)] to (cause to) come outwards from a surface or main part; (cause to) PROJECT: *Her ears stick out.* | *I stuck my tongue out at him.* (=esp. as a rude sign of dislike) | *She stuck out her foot and tripped him over.* **2** [I] *infml* to be very clearly seen: *He's guilty and it sticks out a mile.* (=is very clear) | *When I turned up at the formal dinner wearing jeans and a sweatshirt I stuck out like a sore thumb.* (clearly looked very unsuitable) **3** [T] (**stick** sthg. ↔ **out**) to continue to the end of (something difficult): *I don't know if I'll be able to stick out the evening.* | *I don't like this course, but I'll stick it out somehow.* **4 stick one's neck out** *infml* to take a risk; say or do something that may fail, be wrong, or harm one: *A politician supporting an unpopular law is sticking his neck out; he may lose the next election.*

stick out for sthg. *phr v* [T] to refuse to accept less than (what one asked for): *In spite of the boss's refusal, the staff are sticking out for higher pay.*

stick to sthg. *phr v* [T] **1** to act according to or keep to (something); not give up: *I've made my decision and I'm going to stick to it.* | *We haven't got much time, so please stick to the point.* (=don't talk about anything other than the subject we are supposed to be talking about) | *I didn't like that China tea; I'll stick to Indian tea in future.* —see also STICK-TO-ITIVENESS **2 stick to one's guns** *infml* to continue to express one's beliefs or carry on a course of action in spite of attacks

stick together *phr v* [I] *infml* (of two or more people) to stay loyal to each other

stick up *phr v* [T] *infml* **1** (**stick up** sthg./sbdy.) to rob or threaten with a gun: *to stick up a bank* **2** [*usu. imperative*] (**stick up** sthg.↔**up**) to raise (the hands) when threatened with a gun: *He stuck a gun into my back and said "Stick 'em up."* —see also STICK-UP

stick up for sbdy. *phr v* [T] to support and defend by words or actions: *When they hit you, you should stick up for yourself instead of crying.* | *When everyone else was criticizing him she was the only one who stuck up for him.*

stick with sbdy./sthg. *phr v* [T] *infml* **1** to stay close to or loyal to: *I know you're new in this job, but stick with me and you'll be all right.* **2** *infml* to remain in the memory of: *One thing he said really stuck with me...* **3**

stick with it to continue, esp. in spite of difficulties; PERSIST

stick³ *adj AmE infml* (of a car) having a MANUAL TRANSMISSION: *Is your car stick or automatic?*

stick·ball /ˈstɪkbɔːl/ *n* [U] a game similar to BASEBALL played by children in the US with any small ball and a stick (usu. a BROOMSTICK)

stick·er /ˈstɪkəʳ/ *n* **1** a small piece of paper or other material (LABEL) with a picture or message on the front, which can be stuck on to things: *The back window of his car is covered with stickers with the names of the places he's visited.* —see also BUMPER STICKER **2** *infml apprec* a determined person

stick fig·ure /ˈ· ˌ··/ *n* a very simple drawing of a person, using lines for the limbs and a circle for the head

sticking plas·ter /ˈ··· ˌ··/ *n BrE fml for* PLASTER¹ (2)

sticking point /ˈ··· ˌ·/ *n* something that prevents an agreement: *In the strike talks, the question of compulsory redundancy could prove a sticking point.*

stick in·sect /ˈ· ˌ··/ *BrE* ‖ **walkingstick** *AmE*— *n* a usu. wingless insect with a long thin body like a stick

stick-in-the-mud /ˈ· · · ˌ·/ *n infml derog* a person who will not change or accept new things: *He's stubborn and conservative; in fact he's a real old stick-in-the-mud!*

stick·le·back /ˈstɪkəlbæk/ *n* a small fish with several sharp points on its back

stick·ler /ˈstɪkləʳ/ *n* [(**for**)] *infml* a person who considers a particular quality, sort of behaviour, etc. to be very important, and demands that people should act in accordance with this: *The sergeant major's a stickler for discipline.*

stick-on /ˈ· ·/ *adj* [A] which has a sticky substance on the back by which it can be fixed: *a stick-on price label*

stick·pin /ˈstɪkˌpɪn/ *n AmE* a decorative pin, esp. one worn on a tie

sticks /stɪks/ *n* [*the*+P] *infml, often derog* a country area far from modern life: *They live out in the sticks.*

stick shift /ˈ· ·/ *n AmE* **1** a GEAR LEVER **2** a car that uses a GEAR LEVER

stick-to-it·ive·ness /stɪk ˈtuː ɪtɪvnɪs/ *n* [U] *AmE infml* the ability to continue with effort, esp. in the face of difficulties

stick-up /ˈ· ·/ *n infml* a robbery carried out by threatening with a gun —see also STICK UP

stick·y /ˈstɪki/ *adj* **1** made of, containing, or covered with a substance, esp. a thick liquid, which stays fixed to anything it touches, and is used for fastening things firmly together: *sticky sweets* | *His fingers are sticky with jam.* | *sticky labels* **2** *infml* (of a situation) difficult; awkward: *He put me in rather a sticky position by telling me that secret; they're sure to ask me about it.* **3** [F (**about**)] *infml* not willing to help, be generous, etc.: *I asked him to lend me some money, but he was rather sticky about it.* **4 have sticky fingers** *AmE infml* to be likely to steal something: *That boy has sticky fingers. Keep an eye on him while he's in the store.* —**iness** *n* [U]

sticky end /ˌ·· ˈ·/ *n* [*usu. sing.*] *BrE infml* bad or dishonourable ruin, destruction, etc., esp. an unpleasant death: *He'll come to/meet a sticky end if he goes on driving so crazily.*

sticky wick·et /ˌ·· ˈ··/ *n* [(**on**) S] *BrE infml* a situation that is or may become difficult

Stieg·litz /ˈstiːɡlɪts/, **Al·fred** /ˈælfrəd/ (1864–1946) an American photographer who helped to establish photography as a form of art

stiff¹ /stɪf/ *adj* **1** not easily bent or changed in shape; RIGID: *stiff paper* | *Shoes are often stiff when they're new.* | *Beat the egg whites until stiff.* **2** (esp. of joints or muscles of the body) not bending or moving easily, and often painful: *I can't play the piano like I used to — my fingers have gone stiff from lack of practice.* | *a stiff back* | *I feel very stiff the day after his first weight-training class.* | *I had difficulty turning the key — the lock's very stiff.* **3** *formal;*

not friendly: *a stiff smile* | *Her rather stiff manner puts people off.* **4** [A] *infml* strong, esp. in alcohol: *I need a stiff whisky.* | *a stiff dose of medicine* **5** not showing any willingness to be kind; severe: *The judge gave him a stiff sentence.* **6** difficult to do or to deal with: *They gave me a very stiff assignment.* | *There's stiff competition for this job.* (=a lot of people are trying to get it) | *a stiff climb/examination* **7** full of determination: *The army encountered stiff resistance from rebels in the hills.* **8** *infml* unacceptable, esp. unacceptably expensive: *a stiff price to pay* — ~**ly** *adv* — ~**ness** *n* [U]

stiff² *adv* extremely: *I was* **frozen/bored/scared stiff.**

stiff³ *n sl* **1** a dead body **2** a formal unfriendly person **3** *AmE* an ordinary working person

stiff·en /ˈstɪfən/ *v* **1** [I;T] to make or become firm: *The dress is made of a very light material, but it's stiffened with a thicker material underneath.* | (fig.) *He took a glass of brandy to stiffen his resolve.* **2** [I] to become suddenly anxious or less friendly, esp. when afraid or offended: *He stiffened at her rude remarks.*

stiff·en·er /ˈstɪfənəʳ/ *n* a thing which stiffens something: *a pair of collar stiffeners*

stiff-necked /ˌ·ˈ·◄/ *adj fml* refusing to change or obey; proudly OBSTINATE

stiff up·per lip /ˌ·ˌ·· ˈ·/ *n* [S] the ability to accept bad luck or unpleasant events without appearing upset. This is thought to be typical of British people, esp. UPPER-CLASS British people: *British men are taught to* **keep a stiff upper lip** *and show no emotion.*

sti·fle /ˈstaɪfəl/ *v* **1** [I;T] to (cause to) be unable to breathe comfortably, esp. because of heat and lack of fresh air: *I'm stifling in here; open a window, someone!* | *It was a* **stifling (hot)** *day.* | *stifled to death by the fumes* **2** [T] to prevent from happening or developing: *I was so sleepy I could scarcely stifle a yawn.* | *to stifle opposition/a revolt* | *stifled growth*

stig·ma /ˈstɪgmə/ *n* **1** a feeling of shame or dishonour: *There should be no stigma attached to being poor.* **2** the top of the centre part of a flower which receives the POLLEN which allows it to form new seeds —see picture at FLOWER

stig·ma·ta /ˈstɪgmətə, stɪgˈmɑːtə/ *n* [P] (marks similar to) the marks on Christ's body caused by nails, said to have been produced in the same form on the bodies of certain very holy people

stig·ma·tize also **-tise** *BrE* /ˈstɪgmətaɪz/ *v* [T (**as**)] to describe (someone or something) in a very disapproving way: *a country that has been stigmatized as the least creditworthy of the debtor nations* | *People with handicaps shouldn't be stigmatized.*

stiles

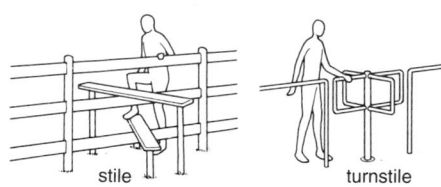

stile   turnstile

stile /staɪl/ *n* an arrangement of usu. two high steps which must be climbed to cross a fence or wall outdoors, esp. between fields

sti·let·to /stɪˈletəʊ/ *n* **-tos** a knife used as a weapon, with a very narrow pointed blade; small DAGGER

stiletto heel /·ˌ·· ˈ·/ *n* a high thin heel of a woman's shoe

still¹ /stɪl/ *adv* **1** (even) up to now and at this moment/up to then and at that moment: *Are you still here? You should have gone home hours ago.* | *When I came back at midnight she still hadn't finished.* | *Are you on page one still?* | *Do you still play tennis?* **2** even so; in spite of that: *I know he's admitted putting the money back, but that still doesn't explain how it came to be missing in the first place.* | *It's raining; still, we must go out.* **3** (used for making comparisons stronger) even: *It's cold now, but it'll be still colder tonight.* | *The first question is difficult, the second one is more difficult, and the third is still more difficult/*

more difficult still. **4** *esp. fml or lit* besides; yet: *He gave still another reason/another reason still.*

▷ USAGE Compare **still, already,** and **yet. Still** suggests surprise that something has continued later than someone might expect: *The coffee's* **still** *hot.* **Already** is used to express surprise that something has happened earlier than expected: *This coffee's cold* **already. Yet** is used in negatives and questions to talk about things that (although expected) have not happened or may not have happened: *I haven't had breakfast* **yet.** | *Has Bill arrived* **yet?** It is also used formally instead of **still** in sentences like these: *I have* **still/yet** *to hear the truth.* (=I have not yet been told the truth) | *We may* **still/even yet** *have problems.* (=our problems are not over yet) | *I walked* **still/yet** (=even) *more slowly.*◁

still² *adj* **1** [F] not moving: *Keep still while I fasten your shoe.* **2** without wind: *It was a hot still airless day.* **3** [F] quiet; silent; calm: *It was so still you could have heard a pin drop.* **4** [A] (of a drink) not containing gas: *still orange (juice)* **5** **still waters run deep** a person who is quiet may have very strong feelings, deep knowledge, etc. — ~**ness** *n* [U]

still³ *v* [T] *esp. fml or lit* **1** to make quiet, calm, or still: *The food stilled the baby's cries.* **2** to put an end to (fears, worries, etc.)

still⁴ *n* **1** [C] a photograph of a scene from a (cinema) film **2** [*the*+of] *esp. lit* quietness; calm: *In the still of the evening the animals come down to the pool to drink.*

still⁵ *n* an apparatus for making alcohol: *They were arrested for running an illegal still.*

still·birth /ˈstɪlbɜːθ, ˌstɪlˈbɜːθ‖-ɜːrθ/ *n* a birth in which the baby is born dead —compare ABORTION, MISCARRIAGE

still·born /ˈstɪlbɔːn, ˌstɪlˈbɔːn‖-ɔːrn/ *adj* born dead: *The child was stillborn.* | (fig.) *a stillborn idea/scheme* (=never started or acted upon)

still life /ˌ· ˈ·◄/ *n* **still lifes** [C;U] a picture of an arrangement of objects, esp. (a) painting of flowers and fruit

still·ly /ˈstɪli/ *adj poet* quiet; calm

stilt /stɪlt/ *n* [usu. pl.] **1** either of a pair of poles, with supporting pieces for the feet, which allow the user to walk raised above the ground: *The clown walked along on stilts.* **2** any of a set of poles supporting a building above ground or water level: *houses on stilts*

stilt·ed /ˈstɪltɪd/ *adj derog* (of a style of writing or speaking) very formal and unnatural — ~**ly** *adv*

Stil·ton /ˈstɪltən/ *n* [U] a strong-tasting English cheese which is white with grey-blue marks in it

stim·u·lant /ˈstɪmjʊlənt/ *n* **1** something, esp. a drug, which increases one's power to be active for a time: *Caffeine is a stimulant.* **2** [(**to**)] something which encourages further or greater activity; stimulus: *The lowering of interest rates will act as a stimulant to economic growth.*

stim·u·late /ˈstɪmjʊleɪt/ *v* [T] *fml* **1** [(**to**)] to cause to become more active, grow faster, etc.: *Light stimulates plants/plant growth.* | *I hoped my warning would stimulate her to greater efforts.* | *The intention of lowering interest rates is to stimulate the economy.* **2** [+*obj*+*to-v*] to encourage by exciting the mind or interest: *An inspiring conductor can stimulate the singers to excel.* —**lation** /ˌstɪmjʊˈleɪʃən/ *n* [U]

stim·u·lat·ing /ˈstɪmjʊleɪtɪŋ/ *adj* **1** that makes one feel active and healthy: *I find swimming the most stimulating form of exercise.* **2** pleasant because suggesting or encouraging new ideas or ways of thinking: *We had a most stimulating conversation.*

stim·u·lus /ˈstɪmjʊləs/ *n* **-li** /laɪ/ [(**to**)] something that causes activity: *Light is a stimulus to growth in plants.* | *The finding of oil has provided a great stimulus to their economy.*

sting¹ /stɪŋ/ *v* **stung** /stʌŋ/ **1** [T] to wound or hurt with a STING² (1): *She was stung on the arm by a bee.* **2** [I] to have or use a STING² (1,2): *Some insects sting.* **3** [T] to cause sharp pain to: *The whip stung him.* | *The smoke is stinging my eyes.* | (fig.) *He was stung by the criticism.* | (fig.) *The severity of their condemnation stung her into action.* | (fig.) *a stinging retort* **4** [I] to feel a sharp pain: *My eyes are stinging from the smoke.* **5** [T (**for**)] *sl* to take too much money from: *They stung him for $1000.* — ~**er** *n*

sting² *n* **1** a sharp often poisonous organ used as a weapon by some animals, esp. insects: *Does a bee die when it loses* *its sting?* **2** a pain-producing substance contained in hairs on a plant's surface: *Many nettles have a sting.* **3** a sharp pain, wound, or mark caused (as if) by a plant or animal: *Rub ointment on to the wasp sting.* | *the sting of salt rubbed into a wound* | *Winning the doubles championship* took the sting out of *losing the match to a younger man.* **4** an act of deceiving someone to gain advantage, esp. carried out by police to trap criminals: *Acting on this tip-off, the FBI launched a sting operation.* **5** **'sting in its/the tail** a part, esp. of a story or suggestion, which is unexpectedly harmful or unpleasant, esp. to the hearer: *The plan has a sting in its tail: it means we lose one day's holiday.*

Sting (1951–) the stage name of a popular music singer who used to sing with the British group **Police**. His real name is **Gordon Sumner**.

stinging net·tle /ˈ·· ¡··/ *n* a NETTLE plant with leaves that sting if you touch them

sting·ray /ˈstɪŋreɪ/ *n* a large seafish with several sharp points on its back at the base of its tail

stin·gy /ˈstɪndʒi/ *adj* [(with)] *infml* having or showing unwillingness to give esp. money; mean: *He's too stingy to give money to charity.* | *a stingy meal* (=a small one of rather bad quality) | *He's stingy with his money.* —**gily** *adv* —**giness** *n* [U]

stink¹ /stɪŋk/ *v* **stank** /stæŋk/ *or* **stunk** /stʌŋk/, **stunk** [I] **1** [(of)] to give a strong bad smell: *The place stank of decayed fish.* **2** *infml* to have an unpleasant, offensive, or immoral quality: *Frankly, your plan stinks!* (=is very bad) | *This whole affair really stinks.* | *His name stinks.* (=everyone dislikes him)
   stink sbdy./sthg. ↔ **out** *phr v* [T] *infml* **1** *BrE* ‖ **stink up** *AmE*– to fill with a bad smell: *The burning pan has stunk the house out.* **2** (of something which smells bad) to drive away: *The smell of his cooking stank us all out of the house!*

stink² *n* **1** [C] a strong unpleasant smell: *There's a stink of cats in here.* **2** [S (about)] *infml* an act of noisy complaining: *If something isn't done soon to put this right I'm going to* **kick up/raise a stink.** (=complain very strongly) | *The scandal caused quite a stink.*

stink-bomb /ˈ· ·/ *n* a small container which gives off an extremely bad smell when it is broken

stink·er /ˈstɪŋkəʳ/ *n BrE old-fash infml* something or someone very unpleasant or bad: *This cold I've got is a real stinker!*

stink·ing¹ /ˈstɪŋkɪŋ/ *adj* [A] **1** having a very bad smell **2** *infml* very unpleasant or bad: *I've got an absolutely stinking cold.* | *I wish I'd never come to live in this stinking country.* **3** *infml* (used for giving force to an expression, esp. showing annoyance): *You can keep your lousy stinking money; I don't want it!*

stinking² *adv infml derog* very (in the phrase **stinking rich**)

stint¹ /stɪnt/ *v* [I (on);T (of)] *usu. in negatives]* to give too small an amount (of): *Don't stint yourself (of anything); take all you want.* | *When you make this recipe, don't stint (on) the butter.* (=use lots)

stint² *n* **1** a limited or fixed amount or period of work, esp. shared work: *He did a two-year stint in the army when he left school.* | *Make sure you do your stint; don't leave it all to the others.* **2 without stint** *fml* without limits and esp. very generously: *She gave of her time and money without stint.*

sti·pend /ˈstaɪpend/ *n* money paid regularly for professional duties, esp. to a priest, or to someone on a low income: *a government/student stipend*

sti·pen·di·a·ry¹ /staɪˈpendiəri‖-dieri/ *adj* receiving a stipend

stipendiary² *also* **stipendary ma·gi·strate** /·,···· ·····/— *n BrE* a MAGISTRATE paid by the state

stip·ple /ˈstɪpəl/ *v* [T] to draw or paint (a picture, pattern, etc.) with short strokes or dots instead of lines to make areas of colour, darkness, etc. —**pling** *n* [U]

stip·u·late /ˈstɪpjʊleɪt/ *v* [T] to state as a necessary condition, esp. of an agreement or offer: *He stipulated payment in advance.* | *I stipulated green, so why have you painted it red?* [+(that)] *She stipulated that all her expenses would have to be refunded.*

stip·u·la·tion /ˌstɪpjʊˈleɪʃən/ *n* [C;U] a stating or statement of conditions: *Exact stipulation of your requirements* would have made it easier to fulfil your order satisfactorily. [+that] *She agreed, but with several stipulations/ with the stipulation that she be allowed a share in the profits.*

stir¹ /stɜːʳ/ *v* **-rr-** **1** [T] to move (esp. something mainly liquid) around and mix something into it with a spoon or similar object: *I've put sugar in your coffee but I haven't stirred it.* **2** [T+obj+adv/prep] to put or mix by stirring: *She stirred the sugar into her tea.* **3** [I;T] *often lit* to make or cause a slight movement (in): *She stirred in her sleep.* | *A light breeze stirred the surface of the lake.* | (fig.) *Interest began to stir among the listeners.* (=they began to be interested) **4** [I (from);T] to cause (oneself) to move or wake: *She doesn't stir* (=wake or get up) *before nine o'clock.* | *It's too cold to stir from the fire*|*the house.* | *If you don't stir yourselves* (=hurry up) *you'll be late!* **5** [T (to)] to produce (strong feelings) in (someone): *The story stirred her sympathy.* | *His speech stirred us to action.* — see also STIRRING **6** [I] *infml* to cause trouble between others, esp. by spreading false stories: *He enjoys stirring.* —see also STIRRER **7 stir one's stumps** *BrE infml* to hurry up; act quickly: *If we don't stir our stumps we'll miss that plane.* **8 stir the blood** *esp. lit* to produce strong feelings, esp. of pleasant excitement
   stir up *phr v* [T] *derog* **1** (**stir sthg. ↔ up**) to cause (trouble): *Don't stir up trouble unnecessarily.* | *He was accused of stirring things up*|*stirring up the dispute.* —see also STIR¹ (6) **2** (**stir sbdy. ↔ up**) to upset: *The news really stirred her up.* | *What's he all stirred up about?*

stir² *n* **1** [C] an act of stirring: *Give the paint a stir before using it.* **2** [C (of) *usu. sing.*] a slight movement: *There was a stir of excitement/interest as she entered.* **3** [S] (public) excitement: *His resignation caused/created quite a stir.*

stir³ *n* [(in) U] *old-fash sl* prison

stir-fry /ˈ· ·/ *v* [T] to cook by mixing around in very hot oil for a short time: *The Chinese often stir-fry their vegetables.*

Stir·ling¹ /ˈstɜːlɪŋ‖ˈstɜːr-/ a town in central Scotland where the Scottish kings once lived. It has a castle and a university.

Stirling², James (1926–) a British ARCHITECT whose buildings at the universities of Leicester, Oxford, and Cambridge caused discussion and disagreement

Stir·ling·shire /ˈstɜːlɪŋʃəʳ‖ˈstɜːr-/ a former COUNTY of central Scotland, now a local government DISTRICT (=area) within the Central REGION

stir·rer /ˈstɜːrəʳ/ *n infml, esp. BrE* a person who likes to cause trouble between others; TROUBLEMAKER

stir·ring /ˈstɜːrɪŋ/ *adj apprec* which produces strong feelings, esp. of excitement; ROUSING: *stirring music* | *a stirring speech* — ~**ly** *adv*

stir·rup /ˈstɪrəp‖ˈstɜː-/ *n* a D-shaped metal piece for a rider's foot to go in, hanging from the side of a horse's SADDLE —see picture at HORSE

stirrup cup /ˈ··· ·/ *n BrE* a cupful of strong drink given to someone setting out on a journey, esp. a rider about to start a FOXHUNT

stirrup pump /ˈ·· ¡·/ *n* a small hand-operated water pump with a D-shaped part that one puts one's foot through to hold it to the ground

stitch¹ /stɪtʃ/ *n* **1** [C] (in sewing) a movement of a needle and thread into cloth at one point and out at another: *I'll just put a couple of stitches in that tear and it'll be as good as new.* **2** [C] a turn of the wool round the needle in knitting (KNIT): *I've* **dropped a stitch.** (=because the wool has come off the needle) **3** [C] the piece of thread or wool seen in place after the completion of such a movement **4** [C;U] a particular style of sewing or knitting: *Purl and plain are the two main stitches in knitting.* | *an embroidery stitch* —see also CHAIN STITCH, CROSS-STITCH **5** [C *usu. pl.*] a piece of thread which sews the edges of a wound together: *The cut needed 15 stitches.* | *When are you having your stitches out?* **6** [S] a sharp pain in the side of one's body, esp. caused by running **7** [S *usu. in negatives*] *infml* clothes: *The maid walked in without knocking, and he* **hadn't got a stitch on.** (=was completely NAKED) **8 in stitches** laughing uncontrollably: *Her jokes had us all in stitches.* **9 a stitch in time (saves nine)** it is better to sort out problems early and quickly, when it is still easy to do so, than to wait until they get worse and become much harder to deal with

stitch² *v* [I;T (UP)] to sew; put stitches on to fasten together or for decorative effect: *Will you stitch (up) this hole for me?* | *She stitched the button on the shirt.* | *Stitch the front and back of the dress together.*
stitch sthg. ↔ **up** *phr v* [T] *infml* to complete (something) satisfactorily, esp. so that it cannot be changed: *We've got the whole deal stitched up.*

St Ives /sənt ˈaɪvz‖seɪnt-/ a small town on the coast of Cornwall in SW England, popular with tourists and a centre for water sports and painters

St James's /sənt ˈdʒeɪmzɪz‖seɪnt-/ an expensive area of central London known esp. for its gentlemen's clubs

St James's Pal·ace /·ˌ··ˈ··/ a royal palace in London

St James's Park /·ˌ··ˈ·/ a small royal park near Buckingham Palace in London —see colour map on page 817

St John Am·bu·lance /·ˌ·ˈ···/ also **St John's Ambulance**— a British organization whose unpaid members are trained to give FIRST AID to anyone who is hurt or becomes ill. They often attend sports and other public events.

St Kath·a·rine's Dock /sənt ˌkæθərɪnz ˈdɒk‖seɪnt-, -ˈdɑːk/ a place in London where ships used to be unloaded, now a centre for sailing boats and an area attractive to tourists

St Kil·da /sənt ˈkɪldə‖seɪnt-/ a rocky island W of Scotland, famous for its sheep. No one lives there now.

St Kitts-Ne·vis /sənt ˌkɪts ˈniːvɪs‖seɪnt-/ (officially called **St Christopher-Nevis**) an island state in the West Indies in the E Caribbean Sea, consisting of three islands: St Kitts, Nevis, and Anguilla; capital Basseterre; population 50,000 (1989)

St Law·rence Riv·er /·ˌ··ˈ··/ [*the*] a N American river which flows from Lake Ontario to the Gulf of St Lawrence and forms part of the border between the US and Canada —see colour map on pages 1374-5

St Lawrence Sea·way /·ˌ··ˈ·/ [*the*] a waterway in N America through the St Lawrence River and all the Great Lakes which can be used by large ships. It was built by the US and Canada and first opened in 1959.

St Le·ger /sənt ˈledʒəʳ‖seɪnt-/ [*the*] a well-known British horse race run in September at Doncaster. It is for three-year-old horses and was established in 1776.

St Lou·is /sənt ˈluːi, -ˈluːɪs‖seɪnt ˈluːɪs/ a city in the S of the US, a port and centre for many industries and also known for its JAZZ and BLUES music —see colour map on pages 1374-5

St Lu·cia /sənt ˈluːʃə‖seɪnt-/ an island nation in the West Indies, one of the Windward Islands, S of Martinique; capital Castries; population 148,000 (1989)

St Mar·tin-in-the-Fields /·ˌ···-··ˈ·/ a church in London famous for its small ORCHESTRA

St Mi·chael /sənt ˈmaɪkəl‖seɪnt-/ *tdmk* the name used by Marks and Spencer to label their products: *the St Michael brand name*

St Mo·ritz /ˌsæn məˈrɪts‖-məʊ-/ a town in SE Switzerland which is a fashionable and expensive winter sports centre

stoat /stəʊt/ *n* a small brown furry European animal that looks rather like a WEASEL and eats other animals — compare ERMINE

stock¹ /stɒk‖stɑːk/ *n* **1** [C (**of**)] also **stocks** *pl.*— a supply of something for use: *We've laid in (=provided ourselves with) stocks of food in case there are shortages later.* | *How long will coal stocks last?* | (fig.) *He became well known for his stock of good jokes.* **2** [C;U] (a supply of) goods for sale, esp. in a shop: *Have you any of the blue shirts in stock?* | *We haven't much stock left after the Christmas rush.* **3** [C;U] **a** money lent to a government or company, on which interest is paid **b** the ownership of a public company, usu. divided into shares: *She put all her money into government stock(s).* | *He invested his savings in stocks and bonds.* **4** [C;U] a liquid made by boiling meat, bones, etc., and used in cooking **5** [U] the degree to which people think about someone or something favourably; popularity: *After it made huge tax cuts, the government's stock rose very high.* **6** [U] farm animals, esp. cattle; LIVESTOCK **7** [C] **a** a plant from which CUTTINGs are grown **b** a stem onto which another plant is grafted (GRAFT) **8** [C;U] the people from whom someone is descended: *She came of (a) peasant/noble stock.* **9** [C]

a piece of wood used as a support or handle, esp. for a gun —see picture at GUN **10** [C] a garden flower with a sweet smell **11 take stock (of)** to consider a situation carefully so as to take a decision: *Before rushing into something irrevocable, let's sit back and* **take stock of the situation.** —see also STOCKTAKING, STOCKS, FILM STOCK, LAUGHINGSTOCK, **lock, stock, and barrel** (LOCK¹)

stock² *v* [T] **1** to keep supplies of, esp. for sale: *That shop stocks all types of shoes.* **2** [(UP, with)] to provide with a supply: *We make sure we're always well stocked (up) with candles, just in case.* | *an excellently stocked library*
stock up *phr v* [I (**on, with**)] to provide oneself with a full store of goods: *We've got plenty of fruit and vegetables, but we must stock up on meat.* | *to stock up with food for the holiday*

stock³ *adj* [A] **1** *usu. derog* commonly used, esp. without much meaning: *They came out with the stock excuse: "operating difficulties".* **2** kept in STOCK¹ (2), esp. because it is of a standard or average type: *shoes in all the stock sizes*

stock·ade¹ /stɒˈkeɪd‖stɑː-/ *n* a wall or fence of upright pieces of wood (STAKES) built for defence

stockade² *v* [T] to put a stockade round for defence

stock·breed·er /ˈstɒkˌbriːdəʳ‖ˈstɑːk-/ *n* a farmer who breeds cattle

stock·brok·er /ˈstɒkˌbrəʊkəʳ‖ˈstɑːk-/ *n* someone whose job is buying and selling STOCKS¹ (3), BONDS¹ (3), and SHARES¹ (2) for other people —**ing** *n* [U] : *a career in stockbroking* | *a stockbroking firm*

stockbroker belt /ˈ···ˌˌ·/ *n BrE infml* an area at the edge of a city where rich people live in large houses and from which they travel to their work

stock·car /ˈstɒk-kɑːʳ‖ˈstɑːk-/ *n* **1** an ordinary car changed so that it can be used in a special type of rough car race (**stockcar racing**) —compare HOT ROD **2** *AmE* a railway carriage for carrying cattle

stock cube /ˈ· ·/ *n* a solid lump of dried material which when mixed with water forms a STOCK¹ (4)

stock ex·change /ˈ· ·ˌ·/ also **stock market**— *n* (*often caps.*) **1** [C] a place where STOCKS¹ (3), BONDS¹ (3), and SHARES¹ (2) are bought and sold: *The news caused a flurry of activity on the London Stock Exchange.* **2** [*the*] the business of doing this: *She made a tidy profit with some shrewd investments on the Stock Exchange.*

stock·hold·er /ˈstɒkˌhəʊldəʳ‖ˈstɑːk-/ *n AmE for* SHAREHOLDER

Stock·holm /ˈstɒkhəʊm‖ˈstɑːk-/ the capital city of Sweden which is a port and also an important centre of business, art, and education

stock·i·net , -nette /ˌstɒkɪˈnet‖ˌstɑː-/ *n* [U] a soft elastic material, used esp. for BANDAGEs

stock·ing /ˈstɒkɪŋ‖ˈstɑː-/ *n* **1** a closely fitting garment for a woman's leg and foot which is usu. made from a thin light material, esp. nylon —compare NYLONS, SOCK, TIGHTS **2** *old-fash or fml* a man's sock **3 in one's stocking/stockinged feet** wearing no shoes: *He was six feet tall in his stocking feet.* (=without shoes to increase his height) —see also BODY STOCKING, CHRISTMAS STOCKING; see PAIR (USAGE) and see colour picture on page 1212

stocking cap /ˈ··· ˌ·/ *n AmE* a woollen hat that fits closely over the head and ears to keep them warm —see picture at HAT

stocking-fill·er /ˈ··· ˌ··/ also **stocking-stuffer** *AmE*— *n* a small inexpensive Christmas present put into a CHRISTMAS STOCKING

stock-in-trade /ˌ·· · ·ˈ·/ *n* [U] **1** something habitually used, esp. a skill or quality important to a person's job: *A pleasant manner is part of a politician's stock-in-trade.* **2** things used in carrying on a business

stock·ist /ˈstɒkɪst‖ˈstɑː-/ *n BrE* a person or firm that keeps a particular sort of goods for sale: *Our chain of shops are stockists for "Woofo" dog food.*

stock·job·ber /ˈstɒkˌdʒɒbəʳ‖ˈstɑːkˌdʒɑː-/ *n derog in AmE* (in Britain until 1986) a person who buys and sells for a STOCKBROKER; a JOBBER

stock·man /ˈstɒkmən‖ˈstɑːk-/ *n* **-men** /mən/ a man employed to look after farm animals

stock mar·ket /ˈ· ˌ··/ *n* STOCK EXCHANGE

stock mar·ket crash /ˈ· ˌ·· ˌ·/ *n* a sudden failure of the business of buying and selling on the stock market, which may be caused by loss of confidence, sudden political changes, or other unexpected events: *He lost a lot of money in the recent stock market crash.*

stock·pile[1] /'stɒkpaɪl||'staːk-/ *n* 1(**of**) a large store of goods, weapons, etc. for future use, esp. ones which may become difficult to obtain

stock·pile[2] *v* [T] to keep adding to a store of (goods, weapons, etc.) esp. in case of future need: *The two superpowers have been stockpiling nuclear weapons.*

stock·pot /'stɒkpɒt||'staːkpaːt/ *n* a container used in cooking for the continuous making of STOCK[1] (4)

Stock·port /'stɒkpɔːt||'staːkpɔːrt/ a town and area in Greater Manchester, NW England

stock·room /'stɒkrʊm, -ruːm||'staːk-/ *n* a store room, esp. for goods in a shop: *Many of the less often used library books are kept not on the shelves, but in the stockroom.*

stocks /stɒks||staːks/ *n* [*the*+P] 1 (in former times) a wooden frame in which criminals were imprisoned by the feet and sometimes hands in public view —compare PILLORY[1] 2 [(**on**)] a framework in which a ship is held while being built 3 **on the stocks** *BrE* being prepared but not yet ready

stock-still /ˌ·ˈ·/ *adv BrE* not moving at all; completely still: *He stood stock-still and listened.*

stock·tak·ing /'stɒkˌteɪkɪŋ||'staːk-/ *n* [U] 1 *BrE* ‖ **inventory** *AmE*— the making of a list of all the goods that one has a supply of at a particular time, esp. in a shop 2 a careful consideration of the state of one's life, what one wants to do in the future, etc.: *He felt his fortieth birthday was a time for stocktaking.*

Stock·ton /'stɒktən||'staːk-/, **Earl of** —see Harold MACMILLAN

Stockton-on-Tees /ˌ··· · ˈ·/ also **Stockton**— a town in Cleveland, England, near the mouth of the River Tees

stock·y /'stɒki||'staː-/ *adj* (esp. of a person or animal) thick, short, and strong; STURDY —**ily** *adv* : *He was stockily built.* (=was stocky) —**iness** *n* [U]

stock·yard /'stɒkjɑːd||'staːkjɑːrd/ *n* a place where cattle, sheep, etc. are kept before being taken away, e.g. to a market

stodge /stɒdʒ||staːdʒ/ *n* [U] *BrE infml* 1 food that is heavy and uninteresting and makes one's stomach feel uncomfortably full 2 dull unimaginative writing

stodg·y /'stɒdʒi||'staː-/ *adj infml* 1 (of food) heavy, filling, and sticky: *stodgy puddings* 2 uninteresting and difficult: (of a person) dull and rather formal in manner —**iness** *n* [U]

sto·ic /'stəʊɪk/ *n* someone who shows no feelings of dislike, worry, etc., and does not complain when something unpleasant happens to them —compare EPICUREAN

sto·ic·al /'stəʊɪkəl/ also **stoic**— *adj* patient when suffering; like a stoic —~**ally** /kli/ *adv* : *He accepted his defeat stoically.*

sto·i·cis·m /'stəʊɪsɪzəm/ *n* [U] the behaviour of a stoic; patience and courage when suffering

stoke /stəʊk/ *v* [T (UP, **with**)] to fill (an enclosed fire) with coal or other FUEL: *He stoked the fire/the furnace (with coal).*
     stoke up *phr v* [I (**with, on**)] to stoke a fire, FURNACE, etc.: *Don't forget to stoke up before going to bed.* | (fig.) *Before going out into the cold, we stoked up on* (=filled our stomachs with) *porridge and bacon and eggs.*

stoke·hold /'stəʊkhəʊld/ also **stoke·hole** /-həʊl/— *n* a room in a ship where heat and power are produced from FURNACES

Stoke Man·de·ville /ˌstəʊk ˈmændəvɪl/ a hospital in Buckinghamshire, S England, which treats people who have severe injuries (INJURY) to the SPINE

Stoke-on-Trent /ˌ·· · ˈ·/ a city in Staffordshire, England on the River Trent. It is the centre of the area known as the Potteries, famous for making pots and dishes since the late 18th century.

stok·er /'stəʊkər/ *n* a person who puts FUEL into a FURNACE

Stoker, Bram /bræm/ (1847–1912) an Irish writer remembered esp. for his book *Dracula* —see also DRACULA

Sto·kow·ski /stə'kɒfski||-'kɔː-/, **Le·o·pold** /'liːəpəʊld/ (1887–1977) an American CONDUCTOR, born in London,

who helped to introduce modern music to the US. He appeared in films, and directed the music for the Disney film *Fantasia.*

STOL /stɒl||staːl/ *adj* [A] short takeoff and landing; working by means of a system which makes it possible for an aircraft to take off and land by running only a short distance along the ground, on a RUNWAY —compare VTOL

stole[1] /stəʊl/ *past tense of* STEAL

stole[2] *n* a long straight piece of material worn on the shoulders, esp. worn by women with fine clothes for a social occasion: *a fur/silk stole*

sto·len /'stəʊlən/ *past participle of* STEAL: *a stolen car*

stol·id /'stɒlɪd||'staː-/ *adj often derog* showing no excitement when strong feelings might be expected; IMPASSIVE —~**ly** *adv* —~**ness**, ~**ity** /stɒ'lɪdɪti/ *n* [U]

stom·ach[1] /'stʌmək/ *n* 1 [C] a baglike organ in the body where food is broken down for use by the body (by the process of DIGESTION) after being eaten: *a pain in the stomach* | *Don't go out to work* **on an empty stomach**. (=without eating) | *The smell of frying onions really* **turns my stomach**. (=makes me feel sick) | (fig.) *a gory film, unsuitable for those with* **delicate stomachs** (=who feel sick easily) 2 [C] the front part of the body below the chest; ABDOMEN: *He sat with his hands folded across his stomach.* | *She was lying on her stomach.* (=face downwards) | *a flat stomach* | *a punch in the stomach* 3 [U+**for**; *usu. in negatives*] a desire to eat; APPETITE: *I've no stomach for this heavy food.* **b** liking or desire, esp. for something unpleasant: *He hasn't the stomach/He's got no stomach for a fight.* (=is afraid of fighting) —see also **have butterflies in one's stomach** (BUTTERFLY)

stom·ach[2] *v* [T *usu. in questions and negatives*] 1 to accept without displeasure; bear; ENDURE: *I can't stomach his jokes.* 2 to eat without dislike or illness: *I can't stomach heavy food.*

stom·ach·ache /'stʌmək-eɪk/ *n* [C;U] (a) continuing pain in the (area of the) stomach, esp. because of food passing through the body —see ACHE (USAGE)

stomach pump /'··· ·/ *n* an apparatus with a tube for drawing out the contents of the stomach, esp. after someone has swallowed poison

stomp /stɒmp||staːmp, stɔːmp/ *v* [I+*adv/prep*] *infml* to walk or dance with a heavy step: *He stomped angrily up the stairs.*

stone[1] /stəʊn/ *n* 1 [C] a piece of rock, esp. not very large, either of natural shape or cut out specially for building: *He threw a stone at the dog.* | *The aircraft's engine failed and it dropped like a stone.* (=fell straight down) 2 [U] (*often in comb.*) solid mineral material; (a type of) rock: *The wall was of concrete, faced with stone.* | *stone steps* | (fig.) *He had a heart of stone.* (=was very cruel or unsympathetic) —see also LIMESTONE, SANDSTONE, SOAPSTONE 3 [C] (*pl.* **stone** or **stones**) *BrE* a measure of weight: *He weighs 13 stone(s).* | *a 20-stone man* —see TABLE 2 4 [C] ‖ also **pit** *AmE*— a single hard seed inside some fruits, such as the CHERRY, PLUM, and PEACH —compare PIP[1], and see picture at FRUIT 5 [C] a single PRECIOUS STONE; GEM: *These stones should be worth at least £5000.* 6 [C] a piece of hard material formed in an organ of the body, esp. the BLADDER or KIDNEY —see also GALLSTONE 7 (**let he who is without blame**) **cast the first stone** *phrase from the Bible* it is unfair for people to criticize or blame someone because they have probably done the same thing wrong themselves: *"Are you prepared to cast the first stone?" Suchet demanded of the jury.* 8 **stone walls do not a prison make** *quote* a phrase from a poem by Richard Lovelace meaning that one can still feel free even when in prison —see also GRAVESTONE, GRINDSTONE, HAILSTONE, HEADSTONE, KEYSTONE, LODESTONE, MILLSTONE, PAVING STONE, ROLLING STONE, STEPPING-STONE, **get blood from a stone** (BLOOD[1]), **kill two birds with one stone** (KILL[1])

stone[2] *v* [T] 1 to throw stones at (someone or something), esp. as a punishment: *The criminal was stoned to death.* | *The rioters stoned my car.* 2 also **pit** *AmE*— to take the seeds out of (4) out of (usu. dried fruit): *stoned raisins* 3 **Stone the crows!** also **Stone 'me!** — *BrE old-fash infml* (used for expressing surprise, disbelief, etc.)

Stone Age /'· ·/ *n* [*the*] the earliest known time in human history, when only stone was used for making tools, weapons, etc. —compare BRONZE AGE, IRON AGE

stone-cold /ˌ·ˈ·◂/ adj extremely cold; as cold as possible: *The body's stone-cold; he must have been dead for hours.* | (fig.) *I haven't had a single drink; I'm* **stone-cold sober.** (=completely sober)

stoned /stəʊnd/ adj [F] sl **1** under the influence of drugs **2** very drunk

stone-dead /ˌ·ˈ·◂/ adj completely dead

stone-deaf /ˌ·ˈ·◂/ adj completely unable to hear

stone fruit /ˈ· ·/ n [C;U] BrE (a) fruit of the types which have a STONE¹ (4)

stone-ground /ˈ· ·/ adj (of flour) made by crushing between MILLSTONES

Stone·henge /ˌstəʊnˈhendʒ◂‖ˈstəʊnhendʒ/ a group of very large, tall stones arranged in circles which stand on Salisbury Plain in Wiltshire, S England. They were put there in pre-historic times (about 2500–1500 BC), perhaps as a religious sign or perhaps as a way to study the sun, moon, and stars. They are also thought to have been used for religious ceremonies by Druids, although this is not generally accepted by scientists. Stonehenge is a popular tourist attraction. In the 1980s it also began to attract large groups of people who now come every year on Midsummer Day to celebrate the SUMMER SOLSTICE. The occasion sometimes causes problems between the police and the many people, including hippies (HIPPY) and NEW AGE TRAVELLERS, who come at this time. —see colour map on page 818

stone·less /ˈstəʊnləs/ BrE ‖ **pitted** AmE— adj (of fruit) without STONES¹ (4) or having had the stones removed

stone·ma·son /ˈstəʊnˌmeɪsən/ also **mason**— n a person whose job is cutting stone into shape for building

Stone of Scone /ˌstəʊn əv ˈskuːn/ [the] the stone seat once used in ceremonies declaring new kings of Scotland. The stone is kept in Westminster Abbey, London, but has been removed several times by Scottish Nationalists who believe that it should be returned to Scotland.

stone's throw /ˈ· ·/ n [S (AWAY, **from**)] a short distance: *Our house is only a stone's throw from the station.*

stone·wall /ˌstəʊnˈwɔːl/ v [I] **1** to intentionally delay or block movement or development in a discussion or argument, esp. by unnecessary talk, or by refusing to answer questions **2** to refuse to obey an order, esp. from the police or other authority **3** (of a BATSMAN in cricket) to play slowly and carefully — **~er** n

Stonewall a British organization which tries to end DISCRIMINATION against HOMOSEXUAL men and women by lobbying (LOBBY²) MPs to change the laws that affect homosexuals. —compare OUTRAGE

stone·ware /ˈstəʊnweəʳ/ n [U] pots and other containers made from a special hard clay that contains FLINT (=a hard stone)

stone-washed /ˌ·ˈ·◂/ adj (usu. of DENIM garments) washed by beating with stones, which has the effect of softening the material

stone·work /ˈstəʊnwɜːk‖-wɜːrk/ n [U] the parts of a building made of stone, esp. those decorated with special shapes

stonk·ered /ˈstɒŋkəd‖ˈstɑːŋkərd/ adj AustrE or NZE infml very tired

stonk·ing /ˈstɒŋkɪŋ‖ˈstɑːnk-/ adj BrE sl amazingly good: *He scored a stonking goal.*

ston·y /ˈstəʊni/ adj **1** containing or covered with stones: *stony soil* **2** cruel; showing no pity or feeling: *a stony stare* | *a stony heart* | *Their pleas were heard in stony silence.* **3 fall on/upon stony ground** (of a request, joke, piece of advice, etc.) to be ignored or get an unfavourable reaction: *I put the new ideas to my boss, but I'm afraid they fell upon stony ground.* —**ily** adv

stony broke /ˌ·· ˈ·/ adj [F] BrE infml having no money at all

stood /stʊd/ past tense & participle of STAND

stooge /stuːdʒ/ n **1** the partner in a stage COMEDY act whose purpose is to appear foolish, esp. by being made fun of by the other partner **2** infml derog a person who habitually does what another person wants

stool /stuːl/ n **1** a seat without a supporting part for the back or arms: *a bar stool* | *a piano stool* —see picture at KITCHEN **2** fml or tech a piece of solid waste matter (FAECES) passed from the body —see also FOOTSTOOL, **fall between two stools** (FALL¹ (15))

stool·pi·geon /ˈstuːlˌpɪdʒən/ ‖ also **stool·lie** /ˈstuːli/AmE— n sl usu. derog a person, e.g. a criminal, who helps the police to trap another; INFORMER

stoop¹ /stuːp/ v [I] **1** [(DOWN)] to bend the upper body forwards and down: *I had to stoop (down) to go through the low doorway.* **2** [I] to stand habitually with the back and shoulders bent forwards: *He used to stoop, but he did exercises to make his shoulders straight.*
stoop to sthg. phr v [T] to fall to a low standard of behaviour by allowing oneself to do (something): *She'd stoop to anything to get her own way.* [+v-ing] *I know you'd never stoop to lying.*

stoop² n [S] a habitual position with the shoulders bent forwards or rounded: *He's developed a stoop in his old age.*

stoop³ n AmE dial a raised area at the door of a house, esp. one big enough for people to sit on; PORCH

stooped /stuːpt/ adj having a stoop: *a stooped old man*

stoop·ing /ˈstuːpɪŋ/ adj (esp. of the shoulders or upper back) rounded or bent forwards

stop¹ /stɒp‖stɑːp/ v -pp- **1** [I;T] to (cause to) no longer move or no longer continue an action or activity: *Don't jump off the train before it stops.* | *Do the buses stop (=so that people can get on/off) at the market?* | **Stop, thief!** (=stop running) | *I think my watch has stopped.* (=is no longer working) | *They* **stopped dead in their tracks** (=very suddenly) *when they saw the bull charging towards them.* | *He put his hand out to stop the bus.* | *How do you stop the machine?* | *Apply pressure on the wound to stop the bleeding.* | *The dispute has stopped production of the newspaper.* [+v-ing] *We stopped working at teatime.* | *Stop making such a noise!* **2** [T (**from**)] to prevent: *I'm going, and you can't stop me.* [+obj+v-ing] *Her parents are trying to stop me seeing her.* | *You must stop her (from) telling them.* **3** [I;T] to (cause to) end: *The rain has stopped.* | *The referee stopped the fight.* **4** [I] to pause; interrupt a journey, activity, etc. before continuing: *I stopped at the first word I didn't recognize.* | *We stopped for tea at a village café.* | *He stopped for a moment to tie up his shoelace.* **5** [I] esp. BrE to remain; stay: *I've such a lot of work to do — I'll have to stop in tonight.* (=not go out) | *We stopped up* (=did not go to bed) *until three o'clock.* | *We invited him to tea and he stopped for supper!* | *I won't take my coat off — I'm not stopping.* **6** [T (UP)] to block: *There's something inside stopping (up) the pipe.* | (fig.) *a bribe large enough to stop his mouth* (=persuade him not to tell secrets) —compare UNSTOP **7** [T] to prevent from being given or paid: *The bank stopped his cheque because he had no money in his account.* **8** [T] (in music) to put the fingers on (holes or strings) in order to change the note played by an instrument **9 stop at nothing (to do something)** to be ready to take any risk (in order to do something) **10 stop short of (doing)/short at something** to decide against doing (a wrong, dangerous, or serious action); not do: *She wouldn't stop short of stealing* (=she would steal) *if she thought it would help her children.* — **~pable** adj

▷ USAGE Note the patterns in *He* **stopped** *to listen* (=he paused in order to listen), *He* **stopped** *listening* (=he didn't listen any more), and *He* **stopped** *me (from) listening* (=he didn't allow me to listen).◁

stop around phr v [I] infml, esp. AmE to make a short visit, esp. to someone's home
stop by (sthg.) phr v [I;T] to make a short visit to (esp. someone's house): *Why don't you stop by (my house) on your way home?*
stop sthg. ↔ **down** phr v [T] to make (the opening of a camera LENS) smaller so that less light gets in when one takes a photograph
stop in phr v [I (**at**)] infml to make a short visit, esp. to someone's home
stop off phr v [I] infml to interrupt a journey to make a short visit to another place, to rest, to visit friends, etc.: *On our way to Scotland we stopped off in York to do some sightseeing.* | *Let's stop off for a drink.*
stop over phr v [I] to make a short stay before continuing a journey: *We stopped over in Dubai on our way to India.* —see also STOPOVER

stop² n **1** an act of stopping or the state of being stopped: *We went straight there; we didn't make any stops on the way.* | *Work on the project has* **come to a stop.** (=has stopped) **2** a place beside a road where public vehicles stop for passengers, esp. a BUS STOP: *I'm getting off at the next stop.* | *This is your stop.* (=where you need to get off)

3 esp. BrE a dot as a mark of PUNCTUATION, esp. a FULL STOP **4** the part of a camera which moves to control the amount of light entering **5** a set of pipes on an ORGAN (4) which provide notes with a particular type of sound quality **6** also **plosive** —tech a consonant sound, such as /p/or /k/, made by stopping the flow of air completely and then suddenly letting it out of the mouth. **7 pull out all the stops** to make the greatest possible effort: He pulled out all the stops to complete the work in time. **8 put a stop to** to stop (esp. an undesirable activity): The new law put a stop to all the tax evasion that had been going on. —see also DOORSTOP

stop·cock /ˈstɒpkɒk‖ˈstɑːrpkɑːk/ also **turncock** BrE— n a VALVE which can be opened or closed to control the flow of water in a pipe

Stopes /stəʊps/, **Ma·rie** /ˈmɑːri‖məˈriː/ (1880–1958) an English scientist who established the first British birth-control CLINIC in London in 1921 and introduced sex education in her books Married Love and Wise Parenthood. At the time, her work was strongly criticized and opposed by the medical establishment and by the Catholic Church.

stop-gap /ˈstɒpgæp‖ˈstɑːp-/ n something or someone that fills a need for a time, until a better one can be found: They've lent us an old TV as a stopgap until our new one's delivered. | a stopgap measure | a stopgap secretary

stop-go /ˌ· ˈ·◂/ adj [A] BrE infml derog of or being a time in which periods of activity and inactivity quickly follow each other, esp. in the operation of a country's money supply, industry, etc.: the government's stop-go policy of alternate inflation and deflation

stop-light /ˈstɒplaɪt‖ˈstɑːp-/ n AmE for TRAFFIC LIGHT

stop·o·ver /ˈstɒpˌəʊvə‖ˈstɑːp-/ n a short stay between parts of a journey, e.g. on a long plane journey: On the London-Singapore flight there is a stopover at Bombay. —compare STAGING POST; see also STOP **over**

stop·page /ˈstɒpɪdʒ‖ˈstɑː-/ n **1** [C] (a) stopping, esp. of work: All these stoppages (=esp. strikes) are costing the company a fortune. **2** [C;U] esp. BrE an amount officially subtracted from one's pay, esp. before one gets it: After all stoppages he takes home £120 a week. **3** [C;U] a blocked place or condition: a stoppage of air | a stoppage in the pipe/artery

Stop·pard /ˈstɒpɑːd‖ˈstɑːpɑːrd/, **Dr Mir·i·am** /ˈmɪriəm/ (1937–) a British doctor and well-known writer and broadcaster on health and child care

Stoppard, Tom (1937–) a British writer of plays, born in Czechoslovakia, whose plays include Rosencrantz and Guildenstern are Dead, Jumpers, Travesties and The Real Thing

stop·per /ˈstɒpər‖ˈstɑː-/ n an object which fits in and closes the opening of esp. a bottle or JAR —**stopper** v [T (UP)]

stop-ping /ˈstɒpɪŋ‖ˈstɑː-/ BrE ‖ **local** AmE adj [A] (of a train) that stops at all stations

stop press /ˌ· ˈ·◂/ [the] late news added to a newspaper after the main part has been printed

stop·watch /ˈstɒpwɒtʃ‖ˈstɑːpwɑːtʃ, -wɔːtʃ/ n a watch which can be stopped and started at any time, so that the time taken by an event or action can be measured exactly: We timed the race with a stopwatch.

stor·age /ˈstɔːrɪdʒ/ n [U] **1** the act of storing: storage of perishable produce | storage space | Check and follow storage instructions. **2** a place for storing goods: His furniture is **in storage** while he finds a new house. **3** the price paid for having things, e.g. furniture, stored —see also COLD STORAGE

store¹ /stɔːr/ v [T] **1** [(UP)] to make and keep a supply of (something) for future use: The squirrels are busy storing (up) nuts so they will have food in the winter. | (fig.) You're storing up trouble for yourself by not admitting the truth straightaway. | (fig.) Why don't you tell him instead of storing up grudges against him? **2** [(AWAY)] to put or keep in a special place while not in use: While she was abroad she stored her furniture in a warehouse. | A mass of data is stored in the computer. **3** [(with)] to fill with supplies: The ship was stored with provisions.

store² n **1** [(of)] a supply for future use: This animal makes a store of nuts for the winter. | a vast store of statistical data | adding some items to my food store **2** a large building in which articles are stored; WAREHOUSE: a

---

grain store **3** a large shop: a furniture store —see also CHAIN STORE, DEPARTMENT STORE **4** esp. AmE a shop: the local village store | a liquor/bargain/variety store **5** [(of)] a large number or amount: That's just one from his store of silly jokes. **6 in store: a** BrE being stored: My furniture's in store while I'm abroad. **b** about to happen: There's a shock in store for him. | We have a few surprises in store. **7 set … store by** to consider that (something) is of the stated amount of importance: He sets great/little store by his sister's advice. —see also STORES

store brand /ˈ· ·/ n AmE OWN LABEL

store de·tec·tive /ˈ· ·ˌ··/ n a person employed in a large shop to watch customers and stop them stealing goods —compare SHOPWALKER

store·front /ˈstɔːfrʌnt‖ˈstɔːr-/ n AmE (a building having) the front of a store facing a street: storefronts for rent | a party set up in an empty storefront

storefront church /ˌ··· ˈ·/ n AmE a church operating in a storefront. Storefront churches are typically EVANGEL-ICAL churches in poor parts of towns and cities and usu. have fairly loud and unusual religious services

store·house /ˈstɔːhaʊs‖ˈstɔːr-/ n -**houses** /ˌhaʊzɪz/ **1** [(of)] apprec a place or person full of information: The library is a storehouse of knowledge. | He is a storehouse of useful ideas. **2** a STORE² (2)

store·keep·er /ˈstɔːˌkiːpər‖ˈstɔːr-/ n AmE for a SHOPKEEPER

store·room /ˈstɔːrʊm, -ruːm/ n a room where goods are kept until needed

stores /stɔːz‖stɔːrz/ n **stores 1** [P] supplies of things in continuous military use, such as clothing, food, and EQUIPMENT: ship's stores | The quartermaster is in charge of stores. **2** [the+S+sing./pl. v] the building, room, etc. in an army camp, ship, etc. where these are kept: He works in the quartermaster's stores. **3** [C+sing./pl. v] BrE a shop in which many different types of goods are sold: There's a small general stores in the village where you can get anything from stamps to potatoes.

sto·rey BrE ‖ **story** AmE /ˈstɔːri/ n **1** any of the levels on which a building is built: There are three storeys including the ground floor. **2** -**storey** also -**storeyed** BrE ‖ -**storied** /stɔːrɪd/ AmE— having the stated number of storeys: a five-storey(ed) office building

Storey, David (1933–) an English writer of plays and NOVELS. His first successful novel was This Sporting Life in 1960, and his many plays include Home and The Changing Room.

sto·ried /ˈstɔːrid/ adj [A no comp.] lit being the subject of many stories; famous

stork /stɔːk‖stɔːrk/ n a large white bird with a long beak, neck, and legs.

▶ CULTURAL NOTE In former times, young children were told that new babies were brought by a stork. —see picture at WATER BIRD◀

Stork n [U] BrE tdmk a type of MARGARINE, known esp. for its television advertisements which tested people on whether they could taste the difference between Stork and butter

storm¹ /stɔːm‖stɔːrm/ n **1 a** a violent weather condition with strong wind, rain, and often lightning; RAINSTORM: crops damaged by heavy storms | winds of storm force **b** (in comb.) a violent weather condition with strong wind and the stated thing: a snowstorm/thunderstorm/sand-storm **2** [(of)] a sudden violent show of feeling: The shocking revelations caused quite a storm. | a storm of tears/protest **3** [+of] a loud angry expression: The deci-sion was greeted with a storm of abuse/booing. **4 storm in a teacup** BrE infml a lot of worry and nervous annoy-ance over something unimportant **5 take by storm: a** to defeat by a sudden violent attack: The soldiers took the city by storm. **b** (of a performer or performance) to gain the great approval of: Her singing took New York/the theatre by storm.

▷ USAGE **Storm** is the general word for rough, and es-pecially windy weather conditions. A large, violent storm with a circular wind is called a **cyclone** in the tropics, a **typhoon** in the western Pacific, and a **hur-ricane** in the western Atlantic Ocean. A smaller storm of this kind is called a **whirlwind**. A storm of this kind with a narrow path is called a **tornado** or **twister** if it goes over land and a **waterspout** if it goes over water. —see also RAIN (USAGE), WIND (USAGE)◁

storm² v **1** [T] to attack with sudden violence: *Our armies stormed the city.* **2** [I+adv/prep] to go with violent anger: *She stormed out of the room.*

storm·bound /ˈstɔːmbaʊnd‖-ɔːr-/ adj prevented from travelling by stormy weather

storm cloud /ˈ· ·/ n a dark cloud which may bring rain: (fig.) *The storm clouds (of war) are gathering over Europe.* (=there is a threat of war)

Stor·min' Nor·man /ˌstɔːmɪn ˈnɔːmən ‖ ˌstɔːrmɪn ˈnɔːr-/ a NICKNAME for the American General Norman Schwarzkopf, who led the soldiers of the West in the Gulf War

Stor·mont /ˈstɔːmənt‖ˈstɔːr-/ a castle in Belfast which was the Parliament House of Northern Ireland. An independent Parliament for Northern Ireland was established there in 1921 but following violence in 1969, it was ended by the British government, who re-introduced direct rule from London in 1972. In the 1970s and 1980s there were a few attempts to re-establish a parliament at Stormont but these failed.

storm troop·er /ˈ· ˌ··/ n (esp. in Germany before and during World War 2) a soldier in a private political army that habitually used cruel and violent methods: *using storm trooper tactics*

storm window /ˈ· ˌ··/ n AmE a window fitted to the outside of an existing window to provide additional protection from severe weather. Storm windows are usu. used in winter, and replaced with SCREENs in the summer: *We'd better put up the storm windows this weekend.*

storm·y /ˈstɔːmi‖-ɔːr-/ adj **1** having a storm or storms: *stormy weather | a stormy day | a stormy sky* (=suggesting that there will be a storm) **2** full of noisy expressions of usu. angry feeling; TEMPESTUOUS: *It was a stormy meeting which could easily have ended in a fight. | a stormy love affair* —**ily** adv

stormy pet·rel /ˌ·· ˈ··/ also **storm petrel** /ˈ· ˌ··/— n a small black and white seabird of the north Atlantic Ocean and the Mediterranean Sea

Stor·no·way /ˈstɔːnəweɪ‖ˈstɔːr-/ a town on the E coast of the island of Lewis on the Outer Hebrides, Scotland

sto·ry¹ /ˈstɔːri/ n **1** [(about)] an account of events, real or imagined: *She wrote a story about space exploration. | a true-life love story | the story of Snow White and the Seven Dwarfs | He promised to tell the children a story as soon as they'd got into bed. | Before we decide who was responsible, we want to hear his* **side of the story.** (=how he, as opposed to the other person, describes what happened) | *Well, that's my story,* (=that's what I say happened) *and I'm sticking to it. | the remarkable* **success story** *of how a woman gave up her ten-year addiction to drugs and alcohol. | There's no need to be frightened; it's only a story.* (=it's only about imaginary events) | *... And then there's the question of what happened to him afterwards. But* **that's another story.** (=which I shall not describe now) | (fig.) *Crime is increasing in the US, and* **it's the same story** *in Britain.* (=it's increasing there too) | (fig.) *It's* **the same old story** (=the usual undesirable situation)*; mounting debts and not enough money to pay them with.* **2** what people are saying; RUMOUR: *The* **story goes** (=people are saying) *that he's run off with his secretary, but I can't believe it, can you?* **3** [(on)] an article in a newspaper, magazine, etc.: *I'm afraid we can't print your story on the fraud scandal; it might be libellous. | What's this week's* **cover story?** (=the story which is concerned with the picture on the cover of a magazine) **4** *infml euph* (used by and to children) a lie: *The teacher told him off for* **telling stories.** —see also SHORT STORY, TALL STORY, **the same old story** (SAME); see HISTORY (USAGE)

story² n AmE for STOREY

sto·ry·book /ˈstɔːrɪbʊk/ adj [A] as perfectly happy as in an imaginary story for children: *a storybook romance/ending*

story line /ˈ·· ·/ n the events in a film, book, or play; PLOT¹ (1)

sto·ry·tell·er /ˈstɔːriˌtelər/ n **1** a person who is telling a story, esp. to children **2** *infml euph* a person, esp. a child, who tells lies

stoup /stuːp/ n **1** a container used in former times for drinking from: *a stoup of wine* **2** a container for holy water (=blessed by a priest) inside the entrance to a church

stout¹ /staʊt/ adj **1** *often euph* rather fat and heavy: *She became stout as she grew older.* —see FAT (USAGE) **2** *esp. lit or pomp* strong; thick; too solid to break: *He cut a stout stick to help him walk.* **3** [A] brave; determined; RESOLUTE: *a stout supporter of the team* —**~ly** adv : *He defended himself stoutly against their accusations.* —**~ness** n [U]

stout² n [U] a strong dark beer

stout·heart·ed /ˌstaʊtˈhaːtɪd◄‖-aːr-/ adj esp. lit brave and determined

stove¹ /stəʊv/ n **1** an enclosed apparatus for cooking or heating which works by burning wood, coal, oil, gas, etc., or by electricity —compare COOKER, FIRE¹ (3), HEATER, OVEN, and see picture at KITCHEN **2** AmE the top of a cooker: *The eggs are frying on the stove.*

stove² past tense and participle of STAVE

stove·pipe hat /ˌstəʊvpaɪp ˈhæt/ n infml, esp. AmE a man's tall silk hat

stow /stəʊ/ v [T (AWAY)] to put or pack away, esp. tidily or so as not to be in the way: *The ship's cargo is stowed in the hold. | You can stow your bags (away) under the desk for the time being.* | (fig.) *They must have been hungry; they certainly stowed away* (=ate) *a huge supper.*

stow away phr v [I] to hide on a ship or plane in order to make a free journey or escape unseen: *He stowed away on a cargo ship bound for Boston.* —see also STOWAWAY

stow·age /ˈstəʊɪdʒ/ n [U] **1** the act of stowing **2** the space allowed for keeping goods, esp. on a ship: *There's not enough stowage.*

stow·a·way /ˈstəʊəweɪ/ n a person who hides on a ship or plane to get a free journey or escape —see also STOW away

Stowe /stəʊ/, **Har·ri·et Beech·er** /ˈhæriət ˈbiːtʃər/ (1811–1896) an American writer most famous for her book *Uncle Tom's Cabin* which was highly influential in encouraging anti-slavery feelings in the North before the Civil War. In the 20th century the book has been criticized for the way it represents relations between black and white people and "Uncle Tom" has become an expression of disapproval —see also UNCLE TOM

St Pan·cras /sənt ˈpæŋkrəs‖seɪnt-/ one of the main-line stations in London

St Pe·ters·burg /sənt ˈpiːtəzbɜːg‖seɪnt ˈpiːtərzbɜːrg/ a Russian city on the Baltic, known as Petrograd and then Leningrad when Russia was part of the USSR

Stra·chey /ˈstreɪtʃi/, **Lyt·ton** /ˈlɪtn/ (1880–1932) an English writer known esp. for his short, humorous and CRITICAL accounts of well-known 19th century personalities in *Eminent Victorians*

strad·dle /ˈstrædl/ v [T] **1** to have one's legs on either side of: *He sat straddling the fence. | to straddle a horse* **2** to be or happen on either side of (something), rather than in the middle or on just one side: *The village straddles the frontier.*

Strad·i·va·ri·us /ˌstrædɪ'veəriəs, -'vaːr-/ also **Strad** /stræd/ infml— n a high-quality VIOLIN made by the Italian maker Antonio Stradivari (1644–1737)

strafe /straːf‖streɪf/ v [T] to attack with heavy gunfire from a low-flying aircraft

strag·gle /ˈstrægəl/ v [I+adv/prep] usu. derog **1** to move, grow, or spread loosely and untidily, without ordered shape: *straggling branches | Houses straggled across the countryside.* **2** to move singly or in small groups away from a main group: *The last few marathon runners straggled in four hours after the winners had arrived.* —**gler** n : *We'll have to wait for the stragglers to catch up.*

strag·gly /ˈstrægəli/ adj growing or lying in a loosely spread out, untidy way: *straggly hair | straggly branches*

straight¹ /streɪt/ adj **1** not bent or curved: *A straight line is the shortest distance between two points. | Blond hair is more often straight than curly. | a chair with a straight back* **2** level or upright: *Put the mirror straight. | Stand up straight. | Is my tie straight?* **3** [F] tidy; neat; in order: *Put your hair straight. | I'm trying to get the house straight before the visitors arrive.* **4** [(with)] honest, open, and truthful: *Are you being straight with me? | I couldn't get a straight answer to a straight question.* —compare LEVEL **5** [F] correct: *Just to* **put the record straight,** *this is what really happened. | Let me* **set you straight about** *that.* (=make sure that you understand the true facts) **6** [A] simple and with nothing added; concerning only two things or people: *The workers were given a straight choice between taking a pay cut and losing their jobs.* | *a straight swap* —see also STRAIGHT FIGHT **7** [A; after *n*] in regular or unbroken order; CONSECUTIVE: *After 15 straight wins our team finally lost.* | *a two-hour straight live concert* **8** also **neat**— (of alcohol) without added water: *a straight whisky* | *I drink my whisky straight.* **9** [A] serious; of the usual kind; CONVENTIONAL: *the straight theatre* | *I prefer straight plays to comedies or musicals.* | *He's wild but his sister is really straight.*| *The whole business was straight; nothing bizarre happened.* **10** (of the face) not laughing; with a serious expression: *We couldn't keep our faces straight when he fell over the dog.* **11** [F] *infml* in a satisfactory situation, esp. because not owing any money **12** *sl* HETEROSEXUAL **13** not a drug-user — ~ **ness** *n* [U]

straight² *adv* **1** [+*adv/prep*] in a straight line: *The book you're looking for is straight in front of you.* **2** [+*adv/prep*] directly and esp. without delay: *Go straight to school without stopping.* | *He went/got straight to the point.* (=said what he thought at once) | *We'll meet in the hall straight after breakfast.* **3** clearly: *I've had too much to drink; I can't see straight.* | *I'm too tired to think straight.* | (*infml*) *So I told him straight,* (=using plain language) *if you don't shut up, I'll punch you on the nose.* **4 go straight** to stop being a criminal **5 straight from the shoulder** *infml* expressed plainly and directly without trying to avoid unpleasantness **6 straight off** *infml* at once; without delay **7 straight out** *infml* without trying to hide one's meaning; clearly: *I told him straight out what I thought of him.* —see also STRAIGHT-OUT **8 straight up** *BrE infml* (used esp. in statements or questions about whether something is true): *"That car cost me £900." "Straight up?"* (=Is that true?) *"Straight up!"* (=Yes.)

straight³ *n* **1** [*usu. sing.*] BrE ‖ **straightaway** *AmE*— a straight part or place, esp. on a race track: *The runners came up the finishing straight.* **2** *sl* **a** a HETEROSEXUAL **b** a person who is not a drug-user

straight and nar·row /ˌ· · ˈ··/ [*the*] *euph or humor* an honest life, not that of a criminal (esp. in the phrases **keep to/stray from the straight and narrow**)

straight-arm /ˈ· ·/ *v* [T] *AmE* (esp. in American football) to protect oneself from (an opponent or attack) by holding the arm straight out: *We straight-armed our way through the crowd.*

straight·a·way¹ /ˌstreɪtəˈweɪ/ *adv* at once; without delay; IMMEDIATELY: *I'll do it straightaway if you're in a hurry.* | *"Can you order me a taxi, please?" "Straightaway, sir."*

straightaway² *n AmE for* STRAIGHT³ (1)

straight·edge /ˈstreɪt-edʒ/ *n* a measure or ruler which is also used for testing whether things are level or completely flat

straight·en /ˈstreɪtn/ *v* [I;T (OUT, UP)] to (cause to) become straight or level: *There's a series of bends, then the road straightens out.* | *Straighten your hat.*

straighten sthg./sbdy. ↔ **out** *phr v* [T] **1** to settle (something) by removing the confusions or difficulties in it; put right: *His business affairs are in a terrible mess; they'll take ages to straighten out.* | *to straighten out a misunderstanding* **2** *infml* to remove difficulties, esp. bad behaviour or worries, in the life of: *Perhaps a talk with the priest will help to straighten Jack out.*

straighten up *phr v* **1** [I] to get up from a bent-over position **2** [T] (**straighten** sthg.↔**up**) to make tidy: *Straighten your room up.* **3** straighten out

straight-faced /ˌ· ˈ·◄/ *adj* showing no sign of amusement on the face — ~ **ly** /-ˈfeɪstli, -ˈfeɪsᵻdli/ *adv*

straight fight /ˌ· ˈ·/ *n* a competition, esp. in an election, between only two people or parties

straight·for·ward /ˌstreɪtˈfɔːwəd◄‖-ˈfɔːrwərd-/ *adj* **1** (of a person or their behaviour) honest and open; not hiding anything: *At least he was quite straightforward about it; you can't say he was trying to deceive you.* **2** not difficult to understand or explain; simple: *The question's quite straightforward; why can't you answer it?* **3** [A] not limited or lessened by any conditions; complete: *a straightforward refusal* — ~ **ly** *adv*

straight·jack·et /ˈstreɪtˌdʒækᵻt/ *n* a STRAITJACKET

straight man /ˈ· ·/ *n* a performer whose job is to set up situations that allow his companion(s) to make jokes

straight-out /ˌ· ˈ·◄/ *adj* [A] *esp. AmE* direct in speech; not trying to: *I gave him a straight-out answer.* —see also **straight out** (STRAIGHT²)

straight shoot·er /ˌ· ˈ··/ *n AmE infml apprec* a person who goes after what he wants in a very direct way

straight tick·et /ˌ· ˈ··/ *n* (in elections in the US) a vote in which the voter has voted for all the CANDIDATES of one party: *I vote the straight democratic ticket.* —compare SPLIT TICKET

straight·way /ˈstreɪt-weɪ/ *adv old use or bibl* at once; without delay

strain¹ /streɪn/ *v* **1** [T] to damage or weaken (oneself or a part of the body) through too much effort or pressure: *You'll strain yourself/strain a muscle trying to lift that heavy weight.* | *Don't strain your eyes trying to read in this dim light.* **2** [T] to separate (a liquid and solid) by pouring them into a container with very small holes, esp. a strainer: *Strain the vegetables and serve immediately.* | *Has this tea been strained?* **3** [T] to make (something) go beyond acceptable limits: *I think it's rather straining the truth to say he's handsome.* | *My patience has been strained to the limit(s).* **4** [T] to use to the greatest possible degree: [+*obj*+*to-v*] *I strained my ears to try and hear what they were saying.* **5** [I] to make (too) great efforts: *a writer straining after effect* (=trying too hard to gain an effect) [+*to-v*] *There was so much noise that I had to strain to hear what he was saying.* | *The singer had to strain to reach the high notes.* **6** [I (**against**)] *esp. lit* to press oneself closely: *He strained against the prison bars/against the ropes which tied him.* **7 strain every nerve** *esp. lit* to try as hard as possible

strain at sthg. *phr v* [T] **1** to stretch or pull tightly: *The boats were straining at their moorings.* **2 straining at the leash** eager to be free, esp. so that one can do what one wants —compare **champing at the bit** (BIT²)

strain² *n* [C;U] **1 a** a condition of being tightly pulled or stretched: *The rope broke under the strain.* **b** the force causing this: *The strain on these massive cables supporting the bridge is enormous; scientists use a* **strain gauge** *to measure it.* **2** a state in which one is greatly troubled by anxieties and difficulties: *The additional work put a great strain on him.* | *She's under a lot of strain at the moment; her daughter's very ill.* | *the stresses and strains of business life* **3** a state of difficulty, distrust, opposition, etc. between people or groups; TENSION: *the current strain in relations between the two countries* **4** damage to a part of the body caused by too great effort and often stretching of muscles: *back strain* —compare SPRAIN

strain³ *n* **1** [C (**of**)] a breed or type of plant or animal: *This strain (of wheat) can grow even during a cold spring.* **2** [S (**of**)] also **strains** *pl.*— *esp. lit* a tune; notes of music: *a pleasant strain* | *We heard* **the strains of** *the violin/a well-known song.* **3** [S (**of**)] a particular quality which tends to develop, esp. one passed from parents to children: *There's a strain of madness in her family.* **4** [S] *fml* the meaning of what one says or writes or the way in which it is expressed: *He had appeared to be most sympathetic, but his comments in private were in a very different strain.*

strained /streɪnd/ *adj* **1** not natural in behaviour; unfriendly; TENSE: *His manner was strained.* | *a strained smile* | *Relations between them are rather strained.* **2** showing the effects of worry or tiring work: *You're looking a bit strained.*

strain·er /ˈstreɪnəʳ/ *n* an instrument of netlike material in the shape of a small bowl which keeps back solids when a liquid is poured through it

strait¹ /streɪt/ also **straits** *pl.*— *n* (*often cap. as part of a name*) a narrow passage of water between two areas of land, usu. connecting two seas: *the Straits of Dover* —see also STRAITS

strait² *adj esp. bibl* narrow and therefore usu. difficult to pass through

strait·ened /ˈstreɪtnd/ *adj fml, usu. euph* difficult because lacking money: *They lost most of their money and now live* **in straitened circumstances**.

strait·jack·et, **straight·jack·et** /ˈstreɪtˌdʒækᵻt/ *n* **1** a garment which holds the arms close into the body, preventing the wearer, esp. a mad person, from making violent movements **2** *derog* something which prevents free development: *the straitjacket of censorship*

strait·laced /ˌstreɪtˈleɪst◂/ adj derog having severe, rather old-fashioned ideas about morals: She's too straightlaced to laugh at rude jokes.

straits /streɪts/ n [P] an extremely difficult situation, such as illness or lack of money: Now that father's lost his job, we're **in dire/desperate straits.**

strand¹ /strænd/ n [(**of**)] a single thin thread, wire, string, piece of hair, etc.: Many strands are twisted together to form a rope. | a strand of cotton | (fig.) strands of an argument | (fig.) At the end of the story the writer brings together all the strands of the plot.

strand² n esp. poet a shore or BEACH beside a sea, lake, or river

Strand [the] a famous street and small area in central London. The Savoy Hotel is here, and also many theatres.

strand·ed /ˈstrændɪd/ adj in a very unfavourable position or situation, esp. alone among dangers and unable to get away: The tide had gone out, leaving the boat stranded on the rocks. | There I was, (left) stranded in a foreign country with no passport or money.

strange /streɪndʒ/ adj 1 difficult to explain or understand; unusual or surprising: He's always here; it's strange you've never met him. | He's got a strange habit of stroking his nose when he's trying to think. | They put her strange behaviour down to severe emotional pressure. | a strange noise/smell/situation | One of Dali's strangest paintings. | She found it strange to think of her son getting married. | It's funny you should mention it; strange to say, I was wondering the same thing myself. 2 [(to)] not known or experienced before; unfamiliar: all alone in a strange place/country | The street he stood in was strange to him. | Tell your children not to talk to strange men. 3 [F+to] fml lacking knowledge or experience (in); not used to: She was strange to their customs, and found everything very confusing. – – **ly** adv : He's often here, but strangely (enough), I've never met him. – – **ness** n [U]

strange bed·fel·lows /ˌ· ˈ···/ n [P] people working together who would not usu. be expected to be friendly to each other, used esp. in the phrase, "Politics makes strange bedfellows"

strang·er /ˈstreɪndʒəʳ/ n 1 a person who is unfamiliar: They never talk to strangers. | "Have you met each other before?" "No, we're strangers." | A complete/perfect stranger waved to me in the street. | (lit) She is **no stranger to** (=very familiar with) misfortune. 2 a person in a new or unfamiliar place: "Can you tell me the way to the station?" "I'm sorry, I'm a stranger here myself." 3 **Hello, stranger!** infml (a greeting used to someone one has not seen for a long time)

Strangers' Gal·le·ry /ˈ·· ˌ···/ [the] (in Britain) the part of the House of Commons and the House of Lords open to the public

Strange·ways /ˈstreɪndʒweɪz/ a prison in Manchester where prisoners took control and did much damage in 1990, as a protest against poor conditions in British prisons

stran·gle /ˈstræŋɡəl/ v [T] to kill by pressing on the throat with the hands, a rope, etc. to stop breathing: He strangled his victim with a nylon stocking. | (fig.) This government's policies are slowly strangling the economy. –**gler** n

stran·gle·hold /ˈstræŋɡəlhəʊld/ n 1 a strong hold round the neck, so as to stop someone breathing 2 [(**on**)] derog a strong control or influence which prevents free movement, development, etc.: A few large firms have a stranglehold on the production of this essential commodity.

stran·gu·late /ˈstræŋɡjʊleɪt/ v [I;T] med to (cause to) become tightly pressed so as to stop the flow of blood: a strangulated hernia

stran·gu·la·tion /ˌstræŋɡjʊˈleɪʃən/ n [U] the act of strangling or state of being strangled: The cause of death was strangulation.

strap¹ /stræp/ n 1 [C] a narrow band of strong material, such as leather, used as a fastening or support: a watch strap | Fasten the straps round the case. –see also CHINSTRAP, SHOULDER STRAP 2 [the+S] BrE the giving of punishment by hitting with a thick narrow piece of leather

strap² v -pp- [T] 1 [+obj+adv/prep] to fasten in place with

one or more straps: She strapped the bag onto her back. | Make sure you're firmly strapped in (=with a SEAT BELT) before the plane takes off. 2 [(UP) often pass.] BrE ‖ tape AmE– to tie BANDAGEs firmly round (a part of the body that has been hurt, esp. a limb)

strap·hang·ing /ˈstræpˌhæŋɪŋ/ n [U] BrE infml 1 supporting oneself while standing in a moving bus, underground train, etc., by holding on to a strap which hangs from the roof 2 derog commuting (COMMUTE¹ (1)) –**er** n

strap·less /ˈstræpləs/ adj (of a dress, etc.) leaving the shoulders completely bare: a strapless evening gown

strapped /stræpt/ adj [F (**for**)] infml having little or no money: I can't pay you; I'm rather strapped (for cash).

strap·ping /ˈstræpɪŋ/ adj infml big and strong: a fine, strapping man

Stras·berg /ˈstræzbɜːɡ‖-bɜːrɡ/, **Lee** (1901–82) an American acting teacher and director who introduced the acting ideas of Stanislavsky to the US. From 1948, he was head of the Actors' Studio in New York City.

Stras·bourg /ˈstræzbɜːɡ‖ˈstrɑːsbɜːrɡ/ a city in NE France which is the meeting place of the European Parliament. Its historic buildings include the CATHEDRAL and university.

stra·ta /ˈstrɑːtə‖ˈstreɪtə/ n 1 pl. of STRATUM 2 (pl. **stratas**) nonstandard for STRATUM (3)

strat·a·gem /ˈstrætədʒəm/ n fml a trick or plan to deceive an enemy or to gain an advantage

stra·te·gic /strəˈtiːdʒɪk/ also **stra·te·gi·cal** /-kəl/– adj 1 (done) for reasons of strategy; being part of a plan, esp. in war: a strategic decision | We made a strategic withdrawal, so that we could build up our forces for a renewed attack. | strategic bombing 2 useful or right for fulfilling a particular purpose: Policemen were stationed at strategic points round the football ground in case of crowd trouble. | A package ideal for those who want to go for long-term strategic investment rather than short-term profits. 3 used in fighting wars: secret purchases of strategic materials – – **ally** /kli/ adv : The trap was strategically placed just at the point where the mouse always came out.

Strategic Arms Lim·i·ta·tion Talks /·ˌ·· · ··ˈ·· ˌ·/ also **SALT**– [the + P] talks between the USSR and the US to limit the number of weapons kept by each country. Two agreements were reached in 1974 (SALT I) and in 1979 (SALT II). In 1980, the US refused to accept the agreement because the USSR's army entered Afghanistan by force.

Strategic Arms Re·duc·tion Talks /·ˌ·· · ·ˈ·· ˌ·/ also **START**– n [the + P] talks between the USSR and the US to reduce the number of NUCLEAR weapons kept by each country. The talks started in 1982, and in 1987 the US President Reagan and Soviet leader Gorbachev signed an agreement to destroy all intermediate-range nuclear warheads.

Strategic De·fense I·ni·tia·tive /·ˌ·· ·ˈ· ·ˌ···/ also **SDI, star wars**– an American government plan which aims to destroy enemy MISSILES in space introduced by President Reagan in 1983 –see also STAR WARS

strat·e·gist /ˈstrætɪdʒɪst/ n a person skilled in planning, esp. of military movements

strat·e·gy /ˈstrætɪdʒi/ n 1 [U] **a** the art of planning in advance the movements of armies or forces in war: a master of strategy **b** skilful planning generally 2 [C] a particular plan for gaining success in a particular activity, e.g. in a war, a game, or a competition, or for personal advantage: [+for/to-v] I think we have worked out a strategy for dealing with/to deal with this situation. | Our strategy was to play defensively for most of the game, with sudden attacking bursts. | marketing strategies

Strat·ford-on-A·von /ˌstrætfəd ˈɒpən ˈeɪvən‖-fərd əpɑːn-/ a town in Warwickshire, central England, on the River Avon. It is famous as the birthplace of William Shakespeare and very popular with tourists. Places of interest include the Royal Shakespeare Theatre and the house where Shakespeare lived with his wife, Anne Hathaway. –see colour map on page 818

Strath·clyde /stræθˈklaɪd/ a REGION in central Scotland whose centre is the city of Glasgow

strat·i·fi·ca·tion /ˌstrætɪfɪˈkeɪʃən/ n 1 [U] the act of stratifying or state of being stratified 2 [C;U] a arrangement in strata (STRATUM) **b** the positioning of different strata in relation to one another

strat·i·fy /ˈstrætɪˌfaɪ/ v [T usu. pass.] to arrange in separate levels or strata (STRATUM): *a stratified society* | *stratified rock*

strat·os·phere /ˈstrætəsfɪəʳ/ n [the+S] the outer part of the air which surrounds the Earth, starting at about ten kilometres (six miles) above the Earth

stra·tum /ˈstrɑːtəm‖ˈstreɪ-/ n **-ta** /tə/ **1** a band of rock of a certain kind, esp. with other types above and below it in the ground **2** a level of earth, such as one where remains of an ancient civilization are found by digging **3** [(of)] a level of people in society; social class: *Such inequalities are found in every stratum|in all strata of society.*

Strauss /straʊs/, **Jo·hann** /ˈjəʊhæn‖-hɑːn/ (1825–99) an Austrian COMPOSER who wrote more than 400 waltzes (WALTZ) including the very popular *Blue Danube* and *Tales from the Vienna Woods*

Strauss, Richard (1864–1949) a German COMPOSER and CONDUCTOR known esp. for his OPERAs, e.g. *Der Rosenkavalier*

Stra·vin·sky /strəˈvɪnski/, **I·gor** /ˈiːgɔːʳ/ (1882 1971) an American musician, born in Russia, remembered esp. for his BALLET music including *The Firebird, Petrouchka* and *The Rite of Spring*. His work is known for being modern and very original.

straw /strɔː/ n **1** [U] dried stems of grain plants, such as wheat, used for animals to sleep on, and for making articles such as baskets and mats, etc.: *a straw hat* **2** [C] a single dried stem of wheat, rice, etc. **3** [C] a thin tube of paper or plastic for sucking up liquid: *drinking fruit juice through a straw* **4** [S usu. in questions and negatives] something of the smallest value: *I don't care/give a straw for* (=don't care at all about) *your opinion.* **5 straw in the wind** a sign of what may happen: *These stories of arms build-up along the border are straws in the wind.* **6 the straw that breaks the camel's back** a small problem or unpleasant event which, when added to existing troubles, is too much to bear – see also LAST STRAW, MAN OF STRAW, **make bricks without straw** (BRICK), **clutch at straws** (CLUTCH)

straw·ber·ry /ˈstrɔːbəri‖-beri, -bəri/ n **1** [C] (a plant which grows near the ground and has) a soft red juicy fruit with small pale seeds on its surface: *strawberries and cream* | *strawberry jam* – see picture at BERRY **2** [U] a dark pink colour

strawberry blonde /ˌ··· ˈ·/ n (a woman with hair of) a light reddish yellow colour

straw boat·er /ˌ· ˈ··/ also **boater**– n BrE a stiff hat made of straw usu. worn in summer.

▶CULTURAL NOTE In Britain, straw boaters are usu. connected with the upper classes and with boating on rivers, esp. in a PUNT. They are worn by boys at some PUBLIC SCHOOLs. – see picture at HAT◀

straw boss /ˈ· ·/ n AmE a person who manages a few other workers and also does the same job as them

strawberry mark /ˈ··· ·/ n a reddish area of skin present from birth; BIRTHMARK

straw-col·oured /ˈ· ˌ··/ adj light yellow

straw man /ˌ· ˈ·/ n a MAN OF STRAW (2)

straw poll /ˌ· ˈ·/ also **straw vote**– n an unofficial test of opinions before an election, to see what the result is likely to be

stray[1] /streɪ/ v [I (from)] to wander away, esp. from the right or proper path or place: *Some of the sheep have strayed (from the flock|into the neighbouring fields).* | *a warship that had strayed into the enemy's territorial waters* | (fig.) *Her thoughts strayed from the subject.*

stray[2] n **1** an animal lost from its home or having no home: *She always wanted a cat so she has adopted a stray.* **2** a child without a home (in the phrase **waifs and strays**) **3** infml someone or something which has got separated from others of the same kind

stray[3] adj [A] **1** wandering; lost: *stray cats* **2** separated from others; met by chance: *He was hit by a stray bullet.* | *You may find a few stray examples of it, but it's not very common.* | *a few stray clouds/hairs*

streak[1] /striːk/ n **1** [(of)] a thin line or band, different from what surrounds it: *Streaks of grey began to appear in her*

black hair. | *a streak of lightning* **2** [(of)] a quality of someone's character which is different from their other or usual qualities, usu. in a bad way: *She's got a mean|stubborn streak.* **3** a limited period during which one has repeated experiences of the same kind, esp. success or failure: *I'd hit a|I was on a* **winning/losing streak**, *and kept winning|losing a lot of money betting on horses.* | *a gambler's* **lucky streak 4** like **a streak of lightning** infml very quickly: *He disappeared round the corner like a streak of lightning.*

streak[2] v **1** [I+adv/prep] to move very fast: *The cat streaked across the road with the dog behind it.* **2** [T] to cover with streaks: *His face was streaked with dirt/tears.* **3** [I] to run in a public place as a streaker

streak·er /ˈstriːkəʳ/ n a person who runs across a public place with no clothes on as a way of attracting attention

streak·y /ˈstriːki/ adj marked with streaks: *The dye hadn't worked well, and had left her hair rather streaky.* | **Streaky bacon** (BrE) has lines of fat among the meat.

stream[1] /striːm/ n **1** a natural flow of water moving across country between banks, narrower than a river: *a mountain stream* **2** [(of)] something flowing or moving forwards continuously: *A steady stream of visitors came to the house.* | *a stream of traffic* | (fig.) *a stream of abuse* –see also BLOODSTREAM, MAINSTREAM **3** [usu. sing.] (the direction of) a current of water: *We were just floating along with the stream.* | (fig.) *He hasn't the courage to go against the stream (of public opinion).* –see also DOWNSTREAM, UPSTREAM **4** esp. BrE (in schools) a level of ability within a group of pupils of the same age: *She's in the top stream|the A stream.* **5 on stream** tech in(to) production: *The supply of oil from the North Sea has now come on stream.*

stream[2] v **1** [I+adv/prep] to flow fast and strongly; pour out: *The pipe broke and water streamed onto the floor.* –compare TRICKLE **2** [I+adv/prep] to move in a continuous flowing mass: *The crowd streamed out of the football ground.* **3** [I+adv/prep] to be blown so as to stretch out at full length: *The wind caught her scarf/hair, and it streamed out behind her.* **4** [I (with)] to give out a continuous flow: *Her eyes were streaming with tears.* | *I've got a* **streaming cold.** (=with liquid flowing from the nose) **5** [T] BrE‖**track** AmE to group (schoolchildren) in STREAMs[1] (4)

stream·er /ˈstriːməʳ/ n **1** a long narrow piece of coloured paper, used esp. for decoration at parties **2** a long narrow flag

stream·line /ˈstriːmlaɪn/ v [T] **1** to form into a smooth shape which moves easily through water or air: *a streamlined racing car* **2** to make (a business, organization, etc.) more simple and therefore more effective in working: *How can we streamline our production processes?*

stream of con·scious·ness /ˌ· · ˈ···/ n [(the)] U] (esp. in literature) (the expression of) thoughts and feelings exactly as they pass through the mind, rather than giving them the ordered structure usual in books, etc.

Streep /striːp/, **Mer·yl** /ˈmerɪl/ (1949–) an American film actress whose many successful films include *Kramer vs. Kramer, The French Lieutenant's Woman,* and *Out of Africa* –see colour picture on page 228

street /striːt/ n **1** (written abbrev. **St** BrE‖**St.** AmE) a road with houses or other town buildings on one or both sides: *101 Oxford Street, London* | *a street map of Brighton* (=showing the names and positions of all the roads) | *street musicians* (=performing out of doors in towns) – see also HIGH STREET **2 be on/walk the streets: a** to be homeless **b** euph to be a PROSTITUTE **3 not in the same street (as)** infml not of the same good standard (as) **4** **streets ahead (of)** infml much better (than) **5** **up/down one's street/alley** in one's area of interest or activity: *You ought to tell John about that new book – it'll be right up his street.* –see also BACK STREET, EASY STREET, SIDE STREET, **man in the street** (MAN[1] (17))

▷USAGE 1 A **street** is in the middle of a town, and usually has shops and other buildings. A **road** can be in the town or the country, and usually leads to another town, or to another part of a town. 2 British speakers often say *in a* **street/road** where American speakers say *on a* **street/road**: *the shops in the High Street* (BrE) | *the stores on Main Street* (AmE) | *a house in Bristol Road* (BrE) | *a house on Boston Road* (AmE) – see also WAY (USAGE)◁

street·car /ˈstriːtkɑːʳ/ n AmE for TRAM

Streetcar Named De·sire /ˌ·· ˌ· ·ˈ·/, **A** a play by Tennessee Williams made into a film with Marlon Brando and Vivien Leigh in 1951

street-cred·i·bil·i·ty /ˌ· ··ˈ···/ also **street-cred** /ˈ· ·/infml— n [U] popular acceptance and approval among young people: *Sooty was declared non-sexist today – he's now a bear with street-cred and a New Man approach.* —**ble** /ˈ· ˌ···/ adj

Street-Por·ter /ˌ· ˈ··/, **Jan·et** /ˈdʒænɪt/ (1946–) an English television broadcaster and producer known esp. for her Cockney ACCENT, her appearance, and her programmes for young people

street val·ue /ˈ· ˌ··/ n [C;U] the price for which something, esp. an illegal drug, can be sold informally in the street, in a PUB, etc., rather than in a shop: *This heroin has a street value of £500.*

street·walk·er /ˈstriːtˌwɔːkəʳ/ n old-fash a PROSTITUTE who stands or walks about in the street to attract customers

street·wise /ˈstriːtwaɪz/ adj infml clever and knowledgeable enough to manage in the hard, sometimes dangerous, world of the city streets: *She is too young and not streetwise enough to live in London on her own.*

Strei·sand /ˈstraɪsænd/, **Bar·bra** /ˈbɑːbrə‖ˈbɑːr-/ (1942–) an American singer and actress who has performed on stage and in many successful film musicals including *Hello Dolly*, *The Way We Were*, and *A Star is Born*

strength /streŋθ, streŋθ/ n **1** [C;U] the quality or degree of being strong or powerful: *He does weight-training to build up his (physical) strength.* | *She succeeded by strength of will alone.* | *Our financial independence enables us to argue from a position of strength.* | *The enemy withdrew after we made a show of strength.* | *Her strength as a novelist lies in her perceptiveness and compassion.* | *the current strength of the dollar* | *You can get this drug in various strengths.* **2** [C (**of**)] something providing force or power: *The great strength of my plan is that it's so cheap compared to the others.* | *the strengths and weaknesses of her argument* **3** [U] force, esp. measured in numbers: *His supporters came* **in strength** (=many came) *to see the fight.* | *The police force is 400 men* **below strength**, (=less than the number of members it should have) *but next year it should be* **at full strength. 4 from strength to strength** with continuing and growing success: *Our new company is going from strength to strength.* **5 on the strength** BrE infml being a member of an organization, company, armed force, etc.: *"Are you on the strength here?" "No, I'm just helping out for a week."* **6 on the strength of** because of; persuaded or influenced by: *I bought it on the strength of his advice.* —compare WEAKNESS

strength·en /ˈstreŋθən, ˈstrenθən/ v [I;T] to become or make strong or stronger: *They strengthened the wall with metal supports.* | *The wind strengthened during the night.* | *If we could find some eyewitnesses it would greatly strengthen your case.* | *The dollar has strengthened against other currencies.* (=increased in value) | *Their opposition only strengthened her resolve.*

stren·u·ous /ˈstrenjuəs/ adj **1** taking or needing great effort or strength: *a strenuous climb* | *strenuous exercise* | *He made strenuous attempts to stop her.* **2** very active: *a strenuous supporter/opponent of women's rights* — ~**ly** adv : *She strenuously denied their allegations.* — ~**ness** n [U]

strep throat /ˌstrep ˈθrəʊt/ n [C;U] AmE infml an infected, very painful throat condition caused by streptococcus

strep·to·coc·cus /ˌstreptəˈkɒkəs‖-ˈkɑː-/ n **-ci** /kaɪ/ a bacterium growing in chains that causes various infections, esp. in the throat (**strep throat**) —**cal** adj

strep·to·my·cin /ˌstreptəʊˈmaɪsɪn, -tə-/ n [U] a strong drug used in medicine for killing harmful bacteria

stress¹ /stres/ n **1** [C;U] (a state of worry resulting from) pressure caused by the problems of living, too much work, etc.: *the* **stresses and strains** *of a busy business executive's life* | *stress-related diseases such as heart disease* | *He's* **under** *a lot of* **stress** *because his wife is very ill.* | *I think her headaches are caused by stress.* **2** [C;U (**on**)] force of weight caused by pressure: *The vehicles passing over put stress on the old bridge.* | *This instrument measures the stresses in an aircraft's wing.* **3** [U (**on**)] a sense of special importance; EMPHASIS: *The teacher laid*

particular **stress** *on the need for accuracy.* **4** [C;U (**on**)] the degree of force put on a part of a word when it is spoken, or a note in music, making it seem stronger than other parts or notes: *In "under", the main stress is on "un".* —compare INTONATION; see also PRIMARY STRESS, SECONDARY STRESS

stress² v [T] **1** to give particular importance to; mention strongly; EMPHASIZE: *He stressed the need for careful spending if they were not to find themselves without enough money.* **2** to give force to (a word or word-part) when speaking: *The word "machine" is stressed on its second syllable.*

stressed out /ˌ· ˈ·/ adj infml suffering greatly from STRESS¹ (1): *He's really stressed out because he has so many financial problems.*

stress·ful /ˈstresfəl/ adj full of problems that cause great worry: *a stressful week*

stress man·age·ment /ˈ· ˌ···/ n [U] any system of recognizing, controlling, and reducing one's reactions to the stresses of everyday life, esp. those connected with the business world. Such a system usu. includes various methods of relaxation.

stress mark /ˈ· ·/ n a mark (' or ˌ) showing that STRESS¹ (4) comes on a certain part of a word

stretch¹ /stretʃ/ v **1** [I;T] to (cause to) become wider or longer: *I tried stretching the shoes, but still my feet wouldn't fit into them.* | *The sleeves of my jersey have stretched so much that they cover my hands.* **2** [T (**OUT**)] to cause to reach full length or width: *He stretched out his arm to try and reach the apple.* | *She stretched the rope between two poles.* | *The painter stretched the canvas on a frame.* | (fig.) *I'm not stretched enough* (=made to use all my abilities) *by my work.* | (fig.) *You're stretching my patience to the limit.* **3** [I+adv/prep] to spread out in space or time: *The forest stretched for miles.* | *The desert stretched away into the distance/as far as the eye could see.* | *The project should have been finished last year, but now it looks as though it will stretch (on) into next year.* | (fig.) *I'm afraid our financial resources don't stretch to* (=we can't afford) *a second car.* **4** [I not in progressive forms] to be elastic: *Don't worry if this sweater seems small, the material stretches.* **5** [I (**OUT**)] to straighten the limbs or body to full length: *She got out of bed and stretched.* | *The cat stretched out in front of the fire.* **6** [T] infml to cause to go beyond natural or proper limits: *Just this once I'll stretch the rules and let you leave work early.* | *The work's going to be a little late, but fortunately they're prepared to stretch the deadline.* | *I think to call her beautiful is stretching it a bit, don't you?* (=claiming too much, because she is not very beautiful) | *His story of his part in the rescue stretched their credulity.* (=they could hardly believe it) **7 stretch a point** to allow a rule to be broken in a small way, a usual practice to be slightly changed, etc.: *We'll stretch a point and let the baby travel free, though you should have bought him a ticket.* **8 stretch one's legs** infml to have a walk, esp. after sitting for a time — ~**able** adj

stretch² n **1** [C usu. sing.] an act of stretching, esp. of the body: *I got out of bed and had a good stretch.* **2** [U] the (degree of) ability to increase in length or width; elasticity: *For tracksuits you need material with plenty of stretch.* | *stretch fabrics* | *stretch socks* **3** [C (**of**)] a level area or SECTION of land or water: *They built their holiday home on a very pleasant stretch of coastline.* | *You get a lot of accidents on this stretch of road.* **4** [C usu. sing.] (a part of a race track considered as) a particular stage of a race: *The runners are now coming into* **the final/finishing/homestretch. 5** [C (**of**)] a continuous period of time: *She did a stretch of ten years service abroad.* | *They had to remain standing for hours* **at a stretch.** (=without stopping) **6** [C usu. sing.] sl a period of time in prison: *a five-year stretch for robbery* **7 at full stretch** using or having to use all one's abilities: *Hospital services are at full stretch to cope with the emergency.* **8 by a stretch of the imagination** (usu. in negatives) even if one tried very hard to believe it: *That couldn't be true, by any stretch of the imagination.*

stretch cov·er·alls /ˌ· ˈ···/ n AmE for BABYGRO

stretch·er /ˈstretʃəʳ/ n a covered frame on which a sick or wounded person can be carried by two people

stretcher-bear·er /ˈ·· ˌ··/ n a person, esp. a soldier, who carries one end of a stretcher

stretcher par·ty /ˈ·· ˌ··/ *n* [C+*sing./pl. v*] a group of stretcher-bearers, esp. on a battlefield

stretch lim·o /ˈstretʃ ˌlɪməʊ/ also **stretch lim·ou·sine** /ˈ· ˌ···, ˌ· ··ˌ·/ *fml n* a very large comfortable car (LIMOUSINE) that has been made even longer to give passengers in the back seat lots of room

stretch·mark /ˈstretʃmɑːk‖-mɑːrk/ *n* [*usu. pl.*] a line or other mark left on a woman's stomach after she has given birth to a child

stretch·y /ˈstretʃi/ *adj* (of a material) elastic; able to stretch: *stretchy cotton* — **-iness** *n* [U]

strew /struː/ *v* **strewed, strewn** /struːn/ *or* **strewed** [T] *esp. lit* **1** to scatter irregularly: [+*obj*+**over**/**on**] *There were papers strewn all over the floor*/*strewn on the bed.* | [+*obj*+**with**] (fig.) *conversation liberally strewn with* (=full of) *swear words* **2** *lit* to lie scattered over; BESTREW (1): *Flowers strewed the path.* | *the rubbish-strewn streets* —see SPREAD (USAGE)

strewth /struːθ/ *interj BrE old-fash sl* (an expression of surprise, annoyance, etc.)

stri·at·ed /straɪˈeɪtʃd‖ˈstraɪeɪtʃd/ *adj tech* having narrow lines, bands of colour, etc.; STRIPED

stri·a·tion /straɪˈeɪʃən/ *n tech* **1** [C *usu. pl.*] a STRIPE (1) or line **2** [U] the condition of being marked with STRIPES or lines

strick·en /ˈstrɪkən/ *adj rather fml* (*often in comb.*) showing the effect of trouble, anxiety, illness, etc.: *Supplies of food and medicine were rushed to the stricken city.* | *stricken with polio* | *stricken by doubts* | *grief-stricken* —see also PANIC-STRICKEN

strict /strɪkt/ *adj* **1 a** [(**with**)] severe and demanding obedience, esp. in rules of behaviour: *a strict teacher* | *They are very strict with their children.* —compare SEVERE (2) **b** which must be obeyed: *He had strict instructions not to tell anyone.* **2 a** exact, perhaps too narrow; exact: *a strict interpretation of the facts* **b** complete: *a strict teetotaller* | *He told me about it* **in strict secrecy**/**in the strictest confidence.** —**ly** *adv* : **Strictly (speaking),** *spiders aren't really insects, although many people think they are.* | *Strictly between ourselves* (=no one else must know), *I hear he's resigning.* —**ness** *n* [U]

stric·ture /ˈstrɪktʃə‖-ər/ *n* [(**on**)] *fml* **1** [*often pl.*] an expression of blame: *The judge was severe in his strictures on their behaviour.* **2** something that strictly limits, morally or physically: *Because of our religion, there are certain strictures on our behaviour.*

stride¹ /straɪd/ *v* **strode** /strəʊd/, **stridden** /ˈstrɪdn/ [I+*adv*/*prep*] to walk with long steps or cross with one long step: *She strode purposefully up to the door and knocked loudly.* | *He strode across the stream.*

stride² *n* **1** a long step in walking **2** an advance or development: *The firm has made great*/*considerable* **strides** *since it was taken over by the larger company.* **3 get into one's stride** to begin to work or do something effectively and well as a result of experience, interest, etc. **4 take something in one's stride** to accept and deal with an unpleasant or unfamiliar situation without difficulty or loss of control: *Some people would have been shocked and unable to work, but he takes everything in his stride.* —see also STRIDES

stri·dent /ˈstraɪdənt/ *adj derog* with a hard sharp usu. loud sound or voice, esp. containing a high unpleasant note: *a strident voice*/*speaker* | (fig.) *The unions are getting more strident in their demands.* — **ly** *adv* —**dency** *n* [U]

strides /straɪdz/ *n* [P] *infml, esp. AustrE* trousers

strid·u·late /ˈstrɪdjʊleɪt‖-dʒe-/ *v* [I] *tech* (of certain insects) to make a rough high sound by rubbing parts of the body together — **-lation** /ˌstrɪdjʊˈleɪʃən‖-dʒə-/ *n* [U]

strife /straɪf/ *n* [U] *rather fml* trouble between people; CONFLICT: *family strife* | *a time of political strife* | *bombing and looting in the strife-torn city*

strike¹ /straɪk/ *v* **struck** /strʌk/ **1** [T] *rather fml* to hit sharply or forcefully: *She struck him with her hand.* | *The mountaineer was struck on the head by a falling stone.* | *The ship struck a rock and started to sink.* | *The tower was struck by lightning.* | *A tornado struck the farm.* | [+*obj*(i)+*obj*(d)] *He struck his opponent a tremendous blow on the jaw.* | (fig.) *to strike a blow for freedom* **2** [I (OUT)] to make an attack, esp. with sudden force: *He leapt back as the animal struck.* | *He struck out at his attackers.* |

Lightning struck in several places but no one was hurt. | (fig.) *We were sailing along without a care in the world when suddenly disaster struck; we hit an iceberg.* | (fig.) *a wage agreement which* **strikes at the heart of** (=severely damages) *the government's economic policy* **3** [T+*obj*+*adj*; *usu. pass.*] to cause to suddenly or unexpectedly become: *They were struck dumb with amazement.* **4** [T+*obj*+*adv*/*prep*] to cause a sudden feeling of (fear, worry, etc.): *The prospect struck terror into their hearts.* **5** [T] to light by hitting against a hard surface: *She struck a match.* **6** [I;T] **a** to make known (the time), esp. by the hitting of a bell: *The clock has just struck.* | *The clock struck five* (*o'clock*). **b** (of time) to be made known in such a way: *Five o'clock has just struck.* **7** [I (**for**)] to stop working because of disagreement: *workers striking for better working conditions* | *the right to strike* | *striking miners* **8** [T+*obj*+*adv*/*prep*] *esp. fml or tech* to remove (something written or printed), esp. officially: *His name was struck off*/*from the list of candidates.* —see also STRIKE **off, STRIKE out** (1) **9** [T] to find (a material, place, etc.), esp. suddenly: *They struck oil.* | *After tramping for miles through the forest, we finally struck the road.* | *After months of successful work we struck some difficulties.* — see also STRIKE **on 10** [T] to produce or reach (agreement, equality, etc.): *It's hard to* **strike a balance** *between caution and boldness.* | *I'll* **strike a bargain** *with you: you go and buy the book and I'll cook it.* **11** [T (**as**)] to have a particular (strong) effect on; IMPRESS: *How does the room strike you?* | *He was struck by her air of confidence.* | *It struck me as rather odd that he refused to give his name.* **12** [T *not in progressive forms*] to come suddenly to the mind of; OCCUR **to**: *It struck me that you might like some coffee, so I've brought some up.* | *A terrible thought struck me — had I locked the door?* **13** [T] to stand, sit, etc. with one's body in (a particular position): *He struck the customary pose of a well-known politician, and everyone laughed.* | (fig.) *Both sides were more interested in* **striking attitudes** (=drawing attention to their perhaps insincere views) *than in having a meaningful discussion.* **14** [T] *tech* to produce (a coin or similar object): *A commemorative medal has been struck for the occasion.* **15** [T] *tech* to lower (sails or a flag) **16 strike a chord** to remind someone of something, esp. because of similarity **17 strike a note of** to express (a need for): *His new book strikes a warning note*/*a note of warning against government overspending.* | *I should like to strike a note of caution.* **18 strike camp** to take down tents when leaving a camping place **19 strike it rich** *infml* to become suddenly rich **20 strike while the iron's hot** [*usu. imperative*] to make use of a favourable occasion as soon as it comes, without losing valuable time **21 within** **'striking distance (of)** very near (to) —see also STRICKEN

▷ USAGE **Strike** meaning "to hit" is more formal than **hit**, and **hit** is more common in conversation: *Go on! Hit him!* | *The police report stated that the man had been* **struck** *by a car.*◁

strike sbdy. **↔ down** *phr v* [T *often pass.*] to cause to suddenly die or become seriously ill: *It's tragic that such a talented young artist was* **struck down in his prime.** | *He was struck down by multiple sclerosis.*

strike sbdy./sthg. **↔ off** (sthg.) *phr v* [T *often pass.*] to remove (someone or their name) from (an official list): *The doctor was struck off (the medical register)* (=he was no longer allowed to practise as a doctor) *for professional misconduct.*

strike on/**upon** sthg. *phr v* [T] to discover; HIT **on**: *I've struck on a plan.*

strike out *phr v* **1** [T] (**strike** sthg. **↔ out**) also **strike through** — *fml* to remove (unwanted writing) by drawing a line through it; CROSS **out**: *Mr, Mrs, Miss, Ms ... (Strike out whichever does not apply.)* **2** [I+*adv*/*prep*] to go determinedly in the stated direction, esp. by swimming: *He struck out towards the ship.* | *The hikers struck out across country.* **3** [I] to start an independent life or a new activity: *She left the family business and* **struck out on her own.** **4** [T] (**strike** sbdy. **↔ out**) in BASEBALL to put (a player) out as a result of throwing three STRIKES² (4) **5** [I] to end one's turn at BAT by swinging at the ball three times without a successful hit: *He struck out in the second inning.* **6** [I] *AmE sl* to be unsuccessful at something, esp. at winning sexual favour from someone

strike up (sthg.) *phr v* **1** [I;T] to begin playing or singing: *The band struck up (a march) and the parade begin.* **2** [T (**with**)] to start to make (a friendship or conversation): *They struck up an acquaintance (with each other) on the plane.*

strike² *n* **1** a time when no work is done because of disagreement, e.g. over pay or working conditions: *The whole workforce is/has gone* (**out**) **on strike**. | *an unofficial strike* | *a strike ballot* | *The union has voted to take strike action.* —compare LOCKOUT; see also GENERAL STRIKE, HUNGER STRIKE **2** an attack, esp. by aircraft whose bombs hit the place attacked: *retaliatory strikes on/against enemy bases* —see also FIRST STRIKE **3** success in finding esp. a mineral in the earth: *an oil strike* | *a lucky strike* **4** (in BASEBALL) a swing at the ball that does not result in a successful hit, either from missing or from the ball going outside the play area **5** (in BOWLING) the knocking down of all the PINS¹ (6) (=bottle-shaped objects) on the first of two allowed rolls of the ball

strike·bound /ˈstraɪkbaʊnd/ *adj* unable to move, act, or travel because of a STRIKE² (1): *Britain's strikebound coal industry*

strike·break·er /ˈstraɪkˌbreɪkəʳ/ *n* a person who takes the job of someone else who is on STRIKE² (1) —compare BLACKLEG, SCAB (3) —**breaking** *n* [U]

strike·out /ˈstraɪkaʊt/ *n* (in BASEBALL) an act of putting a player out as a result of throwing three STRIKES² (4): *In tonight's game Hershiser threw twelve strikeouts.*

strike pay /ˈ· ·/ *n* [U] money paid to workers on STRIKE² (1) from their trade union's **strike fund(s)**

strik·er /ˈstraɪkəʳ/ *n* **1** a person on STRIKE² (1) **2** an attacking player in a football team

strik·ing /ˈstraɪkɪŋ/ *adj* which draws the attention, esp. because noticeable or unusual: *a very striking woman* (=esp. beautiful in an unusual way) | *a striking idea* | *There were some striking similarities between the two books.* — —**ly** *adv* : *The two books were strikingly similar.*

striking dis·tance /ˈ·· ˌ·/ *n* **within striking distance (of)** very close (to): *The two sides are within striking distance of an agreement.*

strim /strɪm/ *v* to cut with a Strimmer

Strim·mer /ˈstrɪməʳ/ *n BrE tdmk* also **Weed Whacker** *AmE tdmk* a machine for cutting grass, which is held in the hand and moved around just above the ground. It has a piece of strong plastic string instead of a metal blade.

string¹ /strɪŋ/ *n* **1** [C;U] (a) narrow cord made of threads twisted together and used to tie, fasten, etc.: *Puppets are worked by strings.* | *She tied the parcel up with string.* | *a piece of string* | *a ball of string* —compare ROPE¹ (1) **2** [C] a thin metal wire or piece of CATGUT, usu. one of several, stretched across a musical instrument to give sound when hit, pulled suddenly, etc. **3** [C (**of**)] of a set of objects connected together on a thread: *a string of onions/pearls* **4** [C (**of**)] a set of things, events, etc. following each other closely: *We've had a whole string of complaints about the programme.* | *She's appeared in a string of successful films.* **5 have someone on a string** *infml* to be able to make someone act as one wishes: *The little boy's got his mother on a string.* **6 no strings attached** (esp. of an agreement) with no limiting conditions: *He'd promised me £1000 for the job without any strings attached, but now he's said I have to finish it by the end of the month.* **7 pull strings** to use secret influence: *He had to pull a few strings to get that job.* **8 two strings/a second string/another string to one's bow** *infml* an additional interest, ability, or idea which can be used, as well as the main one: *He had two strings to his bow, so when he lost his job as a toolmaker he was able to take up gardening professionally.* —see also STRINGS, FIRST-STRING, G-STRING, HAMSTRING, PURSE STRINGS, SECOND-STRING

string² *v* **strung** /strʌŋ/ [T] **1** to put together or with others onto a thread, so as to form a STRING¹ (3): *The beads were strung on very fine nylon.* | (fig.) *an illiterate who can hardly string a sentence together* **2** to put one or more STRINGS¹ (2) on (a musical instrument) —see also HIGHLY-STRUNG **3** to remove the strings from (beans)
string along *phr v infml* **1** [T] (**string sbdy. ↔ along**) to encourage the hopes of deceitfully: *He'll never be paid the money they promised him; they're just stringing him along.* **2** [I (**with**)] to go (with someone else) for a time, esp. for convenience: *If you're going into town I'll string along with you.*

string sthg. **↔ out** *phr v* [T] to spread out in a line: *She strung out twelve pairs of socks along the washing line.* | *The cars were strung out along the motorway.* —see also STRUNG-OUT
string sthg./sbdy. **↔ up** *phr v* [T] **1** to hang high: *They strung up lights in the garden.* **2** *infml* to put to death by hanging, as a punishment —see also STRUNG-UP

string³ *adj* [A] **1** made of string, esp. woven into a net: *a string bag/vest* **2** for or made up of players with stringed instruments: *a string quartet* | *a string orchestra*

string bean /ˌ· ˈ·/ *n AmE* **1** a climbing bean with long, pencil-shaped green PODs which are used as food **2** *sl* a very tall, thin person

stringed in·stru·ment /ˌ· ˈ···/ *n* a musical instrument with one or more STRINGS¹ (2): *A violin is a stringed instrument.* —see also STRINGS

strin·gent /ˈstrɪndʒənt/ *adj* **1** (esp. of rules, limits, etc.) severe; making difficult demands: *stringent laws/restrictions* | *stringent measures to deal with street crime* **2** marked by severe lack of money or by firm controls on the supply of money: *stringent economic conditions* — –**ly** *adv* —**gency** *n* [U]

string·er /ˈstrɪŋəʳ/ *n* a reporter, often self-employed, who works in a usu. far away place and sends in news stories to a newspaper or television station when there is something worth reporting

string quar·tet /ˌ· ·ˈ·/ *n* a group of four performers on stringed instruments, usually consisting of two VIOLINS, a VIOLA, and a CELLO

strings /strɪŋz/ *n* [(*the*) P] the set of (players with) STRINGED INSTRUMENTS in an ORCHESTRA

string tie /ˈ· ·/ *n* a BOLO TIE

string·y /ˈstrɪŋi/ *adj usu.-derog* **1** full of threadlike parts (FIBRES): *some stringy old beans* **2** thin, so that the muscles show: *stringy arms* —**iness** *n* [U]

strip¹ /strɪp/ *v* **-pp-** **1** [T (OFF, **off**, **from**, **of**)] **a** to remove parts of or the covering from (something), esp. by pulling or tearing: *The locusts had completely stripped the trees (of leaves).* **b** to remove (parts of something or the covering from something): *Locusts had stripped the leaves off | from the trees.* | *Before decorating the room they stripped the paint/the wallpaper from the walls.* **2** [I (OFF);T] to undress, usu. completely: *She stripped to* (=took off all her clothes except) *her bathing suit.* | *They stripped off and jumped into the pool.* | *The customs men stripped him and searched him.* **3** [T (DOWN)] to take (esp. an engine) apart; DISMANTLE: *We'll have to strip the engine (down) to find the fault.* —see also STRIPPED-DOWN **4** [T] to tear the THREAD (=raised twisting part) violently from (a GEAR¹ or SCREW¹ (1)): *If you try and put the car into reverse while you're going forward you'll strip the gears.* —see also STRIPPER
strip sbdy./sthg. **of** sthg. *phr v* [T] to take away (something of value) from: *The robbers stripped the house of all valuable articles.* | *The court martial found him guilty, and he was stripped of his rank.* | *preserving processes which strip food of its natural goodness*

strip² *n* **1** [(**of**)] a narrow piece: *a strip of land/paper* **2** an occasion or performance of taking one's clothes off, esp. as in STRIPTEASE: *The dancer did a strip.* **3** *BrE* the clothes of a particular colour worn by a football team: *Everton have a blue and white strip.* —see also COMIC STRIP, LANDING STRIP, **tear someone off a strip** (TEAR)

strip³ [*the*] *AmE* an area of mixed businesses along a road or HIGHWAY, often outside or at the edge of a town or city: *a restaurant out on the strip*

The Strip

Strip [*the*] a long road in Las Vegas famous for its many CASINOs *and large hotels which are brightly lit at night*

strip car·toon /ˌ· ·ˈ·/ *n BrE for* COMIC STRIP

strip club /ˈ· ·/ *n BrE* a small theatre where STRIPPERs (1) perform

stripe /straɪp/ *n* **1** a band of colour, among one or more other colours: *Tigers' coats are tawny with black stripes.* | *a shirt with blue and white stripes* **2** a usu. V-shaped band worn on the arm of a uniform as a sign of rank: *A sergeant has three stripes.* **3** [S] kind or type: *antiwar demonstrators and people of that stripe* **4 earn one's stripes** to do something to deserve a rank or position: *Yeltsin may yet earn his stripes over the Kurile Islands.* **–stripy, stripey** *adj* : *a stripy pattern/coat*

striped /straɪpt/ *adj* having stripes of colour: *striped silk* | *a blue and white striped shirt*

strip light·ing /ˈ· ˌ··, ˌ· ˈ··/ *n* [U] lighting provided by long FLUORESCENT tubes; usu. used in public places rather than in people's homes

strip·ling /ˈstrɪplɪŋ/ *n esp. lit* a young man

strip mall /ˈ· ˌ·/ also **mini-mall**– *n AmE* a small SHOPPING CENTRE, often found on a STRIP³, that consists of a single row of shops with parking spaces in front of them

strip min·ing /ˈ· ˌ··/ *n esp. AmE* mining using OPENCAST methods —compare OPENCAST

stripped-down /ˈ· ·/ *adj* reduced to simple form by the removal of additional parts: *a stripped-down old car*

strip·per /ˈstrɪpəʳ/ *n* **1** [C] *infml* a striptease performer **2** [C;U] a tool or usu. liquid substance for removing something from a surface: *a bottle of paint stripper*

strip·po·gram , strippagram /ˈstrɪpəgræm/ *n* someone who is paid by another person to remove some or all of their clothes in public, usu. at a social event, as a way of playing a PRACTICAL JOKE on a third person. People sometimes send strippograms to friends on their birthdays – compare KISSOGRAM

strip po·ker /ˌ· ˈ··/ *n* a game of POKER² in which players pay their losses by removing articles of clothing

strip·tease /ˈstrɪptiːz, ˌstrɪpˈtiːz/ *n* [C;U] a performance, esp. by a woman, in which the performer takes off her or his clothes in a sexually exciting way

strive /straɪv/ *v* **strove** /strəʊv/, **striven** /ˈstrɪvən/ [I (**for, against, after**)] *fml or lit* to struggle hard; make a great effort, esp. to gain something: *He strove for recognition as an artist.* | *striving after perfection/against injustice* [+to-*v*] *striving to improve their public image*

strobe light /ˈstrəʊb ˌlaɪt/ also **strobe**– *n* a light which goes on and off very quickly, often used in DISCOs

stro·bo·scope /ˈstrəʊbəskəʊp/ *n* an instrument that allows one to study and measure movement by giving repeated very short views of the moving object, e.g. by shining a light on and off

strode /strəʊd/ *past tense of* STRIDE

strog·a·noff /ˈstrɒɡənɒf‖ˈstrɔːɡənɔːf/ *adj* [*after n*] (of meat) cooked with onions, SOUR CREAM, and usu. MUSHROOMS: *beef stroganoff with noodles*

stroke¹ /strəʊk/ *v* [T] **1** to pass the hand over gently, esp. for pleasure: *The cat likes being stroked.* | *He stroked his beard reflectively.* **2** *esp. AmE* to treat very kindly in order to bring about good relations or some desired result: *You'll have to stroke her a little if you want the job done on time.*

stroke² *n* **1** [C] a hit, esp. with (the edge of) a weapon: *He was sentenced to fifty strokes of the whip.* | *He split the log with one stroke of the axe.* | *a stroke of lightning* **2** [C] an act of stroking: *He gave the dog a stroke.* **3** [C] an occasion when a blood tube in the brain suddenly bursts or is blocked, which damages the brain and can cause loss of the ability to move some part of the body: *He's had a stroke.* **4** [C] an act of hitting the ball in sport; SHOT: *The batsman played some beautiful strokes.* | *She won the golf match by two strokes.* (=needed to play two fewer strokes than her opponent) —see also GROUND STROKE **5** [C] a line made by a single movement of a pen or brush in writing or painting: *She drew in his face with a few strokes.* | *a brushstroke* | (fig.) *He signed away all their rights* **with a stroke of the pen. 6** [C] (a single movement or set of movements that is repeated in) a method of swimming or rowing: *She can't swim yet but she's made*

a few strokes with her arms. | *Butterfly is his strongest stroke.* | *They rowed a fast stroke.* —see also BACKSTROKE, BREASTSTROKE, SIDESTROKE **7** [S+**of**] an unexpected piece (of luck): *What a* **stroke of luck** *you were still here when I got back!* **8** [S (**of**)] a sudden act showing esp. the stated quality: *It was a* **stroke of genius** (=very clever) *to suggest this short cut.* | *It was an inspired stroke to make them bring their own food.* **9** [C] the sound made by a clock in giving the time: *She arrived* **on the stroke of** *12.* (=at 12 o'clock exactly) | *At the third stroke* (=on the telephone clock) *it will be 10.38 precisely.* **10** [C] *BrE*‖**slash** *AmE* an OBLIQUE²: *The serial number is seventeen stroke one.* (=17/1) **11** [S (**of**)] *infml* a single piece (of work); any work: *He just sits there all day and never does a stroke (of work).* **12** [C] a rower who sets the speed for others rowing with him or her: *He was (the) stroke/rowed stroke in the winning boat.* **13 at a stroke** with a single firm act; at once: *If any politician promises to improve things at a stroke, don't believe him.* **14 off one's stroke** not performing at one's best —see also HEATSTROKE, SUNSTROKE

stroll /strəʊl/ *v* [I] to walk a short distance slowly or lazily, esp. for pleasure: *We strolled in/around the park for an hour or so.* | *The manageress was furious when the new trainee strolled into work two hours late.* —**stroll** *n* : *Let's go for a stroll.*

stroll·er /ˈstrəʊləʳ/ *n* **1** a person who strolls or is strolling **2 a** *BrE* a light PUSHCHAIR that can be folded up **b** *AmE for* PUSHCHAIR —see picture at PRAM

stroll·ing /ˈstrəʊlɪŋ/ *adj* [A] (of an entertainer) travelling around the country giving informal performances on the way: *strolling players/musicians*

Strom·bo·li /ˈstrɒmbəli‖ˈstraːm-/ *a* VOLCANIC island in the Tyrrhenian Sea N of Sicily

strong /strɒŋ‖strɔːŋ/ *adj* **1 a** physically powerful; able to use great force, make great effort, etc.: *strong arms* | *He must be very strong to be able to lift that car.* **b** having or able to use great power or influence: *America is one of the strongest nations in the world.* | *a strong personality* | *strong leadership* **2 a** (of a thing) not easily broken, spoilt, changed, or destroyed: *strong shoes* | *strong furniture* | *a strong will* | *strong beliefs* | *a strong economy* **b** (of a person, body, etc.) not easily becoming ill; healthy; ROBUST: *a strong baby* | *The old lady has a strong constitution/heart.* | *You need a* **strong stomach** *to watch these violent films.* (=you should not watch them if you are easily upset) **3** moving with great force: *a strong wind/current* **4** having a powerful effect on the mind or senses: *a strong smell/taste* | *strong feelings* | *a strong impression/resemblance* **5** having the expected, necessary, or typical qualities to a high degree: *strong* (=persuasive) *evidence* | *The film has a strong cast.* (=has many good and/or famous actors) | *a novel with a strong story line* | *strong suspicions* | *I told him in the strongest possible terms* (=very forcefully) *that I disagreed with him.* **6** (of a drink, drug, etc.) having a lot of the material which gives taste, produces effects, etc.: *The tea is too strong.* | *a strong curry* | *strong painkilling drugs* | *Avoid strong drink.* (=alcoholic drinks) —compare WEAK (3) **7** showing a high likelihood of success, victory, etc.: *a strong possibility that England will win* | *Their chances are not very strong.* | *She's a strong contender for the party leadership.* **8** [after *n*] having the stated number, esp. of members: *Our club is 50 strong.* | *a 6000-strong workforce* **9** [F+**on**] **a** good at doing: *They're very strong on desserts in this restaurant.* **b** eager and active in dealing with: *The customs people are very strong on drug smugglers at this airport.* **10** [F] *esp. BrE infml* unacceptable: *It's a bit strong to punish them for such a small thing.* **11** [*no comp.*] (of a verb) which does not add a regular ending in the past tense, but may change a vowel: *"Speak" is a strong verb; its past tense is "spoke".* —compare WEAK (6) **12 (still) going strong** active and powerful, esp. after a long period or when old: *Grandfather's clock is still going strong.* **13 the strong, silent type** a type of man, often shown in old adventure films, who is very strong physically and does not talk or laugh very much —see also STRENGTH – **~ly** *adv* : *I strongly recommend that you refuse.* | *a strongly-built table*

strong·arm /ˈstrɒŋɑːm‖ˈstrɔːŋɑːrm/ *adj* [A] *infml, usu. derog* using (unnecessary) force: *The police had used strongarm methods/tactics to make him admit his guilt.* **strongarm** *v* [T] : *The kidnappers strongarmed him into the back of their car.*

strong·box /'strɒŋbɒks‖'strɔːŋbɑːks/ *n* a strongly-made lockable usu. metal box for keeping valuable things in, such as jewels

strong force /'· ˌ·/ *n* [*the*] the strongest of the four FUNDAMENTAL FORCES. It holds together the very small PARTICLES inside the NUCLEUS of an atom.

strong·hold /'strɒŋhəʊld‖'strɔːŋ-/ *n* **1** a strongly defended place or position: *a guerrilla stronghold* **2** [+of] a place where a particular activity or way of life is common or general: *The old London clubs are among the last strongholds of male privilege.*

strong lan·guage /ˌ·ˈ···/ *n* [U] *euph* swearing; curses

strong-mind·ed /ˌ·ˈ···◂/ *adj* firm in beliefs, wishes, etc.; determined: *He is very persuasive, and you need to be pretty strong-minded to say "no" to him.* — ~**ly** *adv* — ~**ness** *n* [U]

strong point /'· ·/ *n* a skill, quality, etc., which one has a lot of: *Spelling isn't her strong point.* (=she is not good at it)

strong room /'· ·/ *n* a room in a bank, etc., with a special thick door and walls, where valuable objects can be kept

strong suit /'· ˌ·/ *n AmE infml* something one is very good at doing: *He's writing a play now but detective stories are really his strong suit.*

strong-willed /ˌ·ˈ·◂/ *adj* having strength of will; determined

stron·ti·um /'strɒntiəm‖'strɑːntʃiəm, -tiəm/ *n* [U] a soft metal that is a simple substance (ELEMENT)

strontium 90 /ˌstrɒntiəm 'naɪntɪ‖ˌstrɑːntʃiəm-, -tiəm-/ *n* [U] a form of strontium which is given off by atomic explosions and has harmful effects on people and animals

strop /strɒp‖strɑːp/ *n* a narrow piece of leather used for sharpening RAZORS

stro·phe /'strəʊfi/ *n tech* **1** (esp. in ancient Greek plays) a song by a group of actors, answered by another group in the same way **2** a group of lines in a poem — **·phic** *adj*

strop·py /'strɒpi‖'strɑːpi/ *adj BrE infml* bad-tempered, unwilling to help, and tending to argue

strove /strəʊv/ *past tense of* STRIVE

struck /strʌk/ *past tense & participle of* STRIKE

struc·tur·al /'strʌktʃərəl/ *adj* of a structure, esp. of the main part of a building: *The storm caused no structural damage.* | *structural unemployment* (=caused by changes in the structure of society) — ~**ly** *adv*

structural en·gi·neer /ˌ··· ··ˈ·/ *n* an engineer skilled in planning the building of large structures, e.g. bridges

struc·tu·ral en·gi·neer·ing /ˌ··· ··ˈ···/ *n* a branch of engineering that deals with building large structures, e.g. bridges

struc·tur·al·is·m /'strʌktʃərəlɪzəm/ *n* [U] a method of study, esp. in the social sciences and LINGUISTICS, which places particular importance on the relationships and patterns of organization that lie below the surface — **·ist** *adj, n*

struc·ture¹ /'strʌktʃəʳ/ *n* **1** [U (of)] an arrangement or organization; the way in which parts are formed into a whole: *the structure of the brain* | *cell structure* | *the structure of a sentence* | *the financial structure of the organization* | *a company's price structure/pricing structure* (=the range of prices it charges) **2** [C] something formed of many parts, esp. a building: *a six-storey brick structure*

structure² *v* [T] to arrange (esp. ideas) into a whole form, in which each part is related to others: *You need to structure your arguments more carefully.* | *a well structured report*

stru·del /'struːdl/ *n* [C;U] a sort of cake of Austrian origin, made of light pastry with fruit inside: *apple strudel*

strug·gle¹ /'strʌgəl/ *v* [I (**with**)] **1** to make violent movements, esp. when fighting against a stronger person or thing: *It's hard to rescue drowning people because they struggle so much.* | *He struggled with his assailants and eventually drove them off.* | *She struggled out of the net which had trapped her.* [+to-v] *They were struggling to get out of the burning car.* | (fig.) *At 3-0 down with five minutes to go, we were really struggling.* (=likely to lose) **2** to make great efforts, esp. when trying to deal with a difficult problem or situation: *I was struggling with the accounts.* | *She struggled* (=walked with difficulty) *up the stairs with her heavy bags.* [+to-v] *He struggled to control his temper.* | *young writers who have to struggle for recognition* | *struggling young writers*

struggle² *n* a hard fight or bodily effort; great or determined effort: *Three people were hurt in the struggle.* | *Despite his terrible injuries, he wouldn't give up the struggle for life.* | (*euph*) *We shall continue our* **armed struggle** (=war) *until the government is defeated.* | *With a struggle, he controlled his feelings.* | *It was/I had a struggle to make myself heard in all the noise.* | *the struggle for survival* | *a struggle for independence* | *Which of the contenders will come out on top in the power struggle?* — see also CLASS STRUGGLE

strum /strʌm/ *v* -**mm**- [I (**on**);T] to play (a tune) carelessly or informally on (a musical instrument) by brushing one's fingers over its strings, esp. without skill: *She was strumming (on) her guitar/strumming a tune on her guitar.*

strum·pet /'strʌmpɪt/ *n old use derog for* a female PROSTITUTE

strung /strʌŋ/ *past tense & participle of* STRING

strung-out /ˌ· ˈ·◂/ *adj* [F (**on**)] *infml* **1** strongly influenced by or unable to stop taking drugs: *strung-out on heroin* **2** extremely tired

strung-up /ˌ· ˈ·◂/ *adj infml, esp. BrE* very nervous, worried, or excited

strut¹ /strʌt/ *v* -**tt**- [I] *usu. derog* to walk proudly and stiffly, esp. with the chest pushed forwards and trying to look important: *The male bird strutted in front of the female.*

strut² *n* **1** a usu. long thin piece of wood or metal supporting a part of a building, aircraft, etc. **2** [*usu. sing.*] a strutting way of walking

strych·nine /'strɪkniːn‖-naɪn, -niːn/ *n* [U] a poisonous drug used as a medicine in very small amounts

St Thom·as /· ˈ··/ an island in the US Virgin Islands in the West Indies

St Trinian's

St Trin·i·an's /sənt ˈtrɪniənz ‖ seɪnt-/ the name of a British private, girl's school in a humorous CARTOON of the 1950s and later in a number of humorous films. The school is shown as being very badly run, and the girls as being badly behaved and always involved in activities which are more or less illegal.

St Tro·pez /ˌsæn trəˈpeɪ/ a fashionable holiday town on the S coast of France, which used to be very popular with the rich and famous but is now popular with many ordinary people. It is connected in some people's minds with women going onto the BEACH with bare breasts, as this was one of the first holiday towns where this happened.

Stu·art /'stjuːət‖'stuːərt/ the name of the royal family that ruled Scotland from 1371 to 1603 and Britain from 1603 to 1649 and from 1660 to 1714 —see also MARY, QUEEN OF SCOTS

Stuart, Charles Edward (1720–88) also known as **The Young Pretender** and **Bonnie Prince Charlie**, the son of James Edward Stuart. He believed he had a right to be the King of Britain and led the Jacobite Rebellion in 1745–46, but was defeated. He is the HERO of many Scottish ROMANTIC stories. —see also Flora MACDONALD

Stuart, Gil·bert /'gɪlbət‖-bərt/ (1755–1828) an American painter famous esp. for his picture of George Washington

Stuart, James Edward (1688–1766) also called **The Old Pretender**, the son of King James II (James VII of

Scotland) who believed he had a right to be King of Britain, but whose attempts to become king failed

Stuart, Mary see MARY, QUEEN OF SCOTS

stub¹ /stʌb/ n **1** a short end of something, esp. a cigarette or pencil, left when the rest has been used **2** a piece of a cheque or ticket left in a book of these as a record after the main part has been torn out **3** the part of a ticket returned to the owner after it has been torn, as proof of payment

stub² v -bb- [T] to hurt (one's toe) by hitting it against something
    stub sthg. ↔ **out** phr v [T] to stop (a cigarette) burning by pressing the end against something

stub·ble /'stʌbəl/ n [U] short stiff pieces of something which grows, esp. a short beard or the remains of wheat after being cut: *Farmers often burn the stubble after they've cut the corn.* | *Ever since designer stubble became fashionable, he's been very lazy about shaving.* —**bly** adv : *a stubbly growth of beard*

stub·born /'stʌbən∥-ərn/ adj **1** determined, esp. to an unreasonable degree; with a strong will: (derog) *He's a stubborn child who won't obey his mother.* | (apprec) *The defenders put up stubborn resistance but were eventually defeated.* **2** difficult to move, change, etc.: *This lock's rather stubborn; it needs oiling.* | *stubborn stains* – ~ **ly** adv – ~ **ness** n [U]

Stubbs /stʌbs/, **George** (1724–1806) an English artist known esp. for his paintings of horses and other animals

stub·by /'stʌbi/ adj infml, often derog short and thick: *stubby little fingers*

stuc·co /'stʌkəʊ/ n [U] a covering of PLASTER on the walls of buildings, often formed into decorative shapes – ~ **ed** /'stʌkəʊd/ adj

stuck¹ /stʌk/ past tense & participle of STICK: *The paper's stuck to my finger.*

stuck² adj [F] **1** fixed in position; impossible to move: *The door's stuck; we'll have to get out through the window.* | *He got his finger stuck/His finger got stuck in the hole.* **2** infml unable to go further or do anything further, esp. because of difficulties: *I'm stuck; can you give me some help with this sum, Dad?* | *If the bank won't lend us the money we'll really be stuck.* | *She was stuck at home looking after the children.* **3** [+with] infml having to do, have, or deal with, esp. unwillingly: *We were stuck with relatives who came to stay unexpectedly.* **4** [+on] infml having a great liking for; fond of (esp. someone): *Jane's really stuck on her new teacher.* **5** **get stuck in(to)** BrE infml to start work or an activity eagerly or forcefully: *Here's your dinner; get stuck in!* | *He got completely stuck into that book you gave him; we could hardly get him to say a word!* –see also STICK²

stuck³ n [in+U] BrE sl trouble: *You'll be in dead stuck if the boss finds out what you've done!*

stuck-up /ˌ·ˈ·◂/ adj infml derog proud and thinking oneself to be important: *She's too stuck-up to speak to her old friends.*

stud¹ /stʌd/ n **1** a fastener used instead of a button and button hole, esp. a COLLAR STUD or PRESS-STUD **2** a pointed or lumplike part that sticks out from the bottom of a shoe, a tyre, etc., to prevent slipping: *The ground's wet – you'll need football boots with long studs.* **3** a small nearly flat piece of metal fixed with others into a road surface to mark off areas **4** a large nail with a large head, used for decoration: *The great oak door had iron studs in it.*

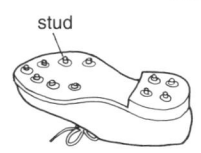

stud

stud² v -dd- [T (with)] to cover with STUDs¹: *He wore a belt studded with brass nails.* | (fig.) *The sky was studded with stars.* –see also STAR-STUDDED

stud³ n **1** a number of horses or other animals kept for breeding: *This horse has been retired from racing and has now been put out to stud.* (=being used for breeding) | *a stud farm* **2** derog or humor a man who has sex a lot and who thinks he is very good at it: *He reckons he's a real stud.*

stud·book /'stʌdbʊk/ n a list of names of animals, esp. race

horses, from which other animals have been bred

stu·dent /'stjuːdənt∥'stuː-/ n **1** a person who is studying, esp. at a place of education or training: *a history student* (=studying history) | *a student of* (=taught by) *Yehudi Menuhin*
▶ CULTURAL NOTE In Britain, the STEREOTYPE of a student is of someone who does not spend very much time studying, but spends a lot of time drinking and enjoying themselves. In the US, students are generally understood to work hard and **play hard** (= enjoy themselves).◀
2 [+of] a person with the stated interest: *a student of human nature*
▷ USAGE Compare **student, pupil,** and **scholar.** Anyone studying at a college or university is a **student.** In the US, this word is also used for younger people in schools, but in Britain these are usually **pupils.** A **pupil** can also be a grown-up person studying under a famous musician, etc. A **scholar** is either a **a** pupil (British English, old use), **b** someone whose education is being paid for because they have done very well, or **c** someone (perhaps an old person) who has studied a difficult subject for a long time and knows a lot about it.◁

student loans /ˌ·· ˈ·/ n a method of paying for education in which students at universities and colleges borrow money from banks and repay it when they begin work after completing their studies
▶ CULTURAL NOTE Many countries including the US already have student loans. In Britain, student loans are slowly being introduced; they are very unpopular with many people who believe that they will prevent poorer students from receiving higher education.◀

students' u·nion /ˌ·· ˈ··/ also **student union**– n **1** [+sing./pl. v] an association of students, esp. one in a particular British college or university, or one for students from many places of education –compare NATIONAL UNION OF STUDENTS **2** (a part of) a building where students go to meet socially

student teach·er /ˌ·· ˈ··/ n a person who is training to become a teacher and is doing some teaching as part of their training

student teach·ing /ˌ·· ˈ··/ n [U] AmE for TEACHING PRACTICE

stud·ied /'stʌdid/ adj often derog carefully thought about or considered, esp. before being expressed, and perhaps therefore not sincere: *a studied remark* | *She spoke with studied politeness.*

stu·di·o /'stjuːdiəʊ∥'stuː-/ n -os **1** a room from which broadcasts are made or in which recordings are made: *a television studio* **2** a also **studios** pl.– a place where cinema films are made: *Pinewood Studios* **b** a film-making company: *Some of Hollywood's leading studios are interested in signing her.* **3** a a workroom for a painter, photographer, etc.: *one of London's leading design studios* **b** a company producing artistic or photographic work **4** a room or other place where dancing or dancelike exercise can be practised or taught **5** also **studio flat** /ˈ··· ·/ BrE ‖ **studio a·part·ment** /ˈ··· ·ˌ··/ esp. AmE– a one-room flat; BED-SITTER

studio au·di·ence /ˌ·· ˈ··/ n people who watch (or may be involved in) a television or radio programme while it is being made: *Thank-you to our studio audience and to all our listeners/viewers at home.*

studio couch /ˈ··· ·/ n a piece of furniture for more than one person to sit on, which can be made into a bed

stu·di·ous /'stjuːdiəs∥'stuː-/ adj **1** fond of studying: *a serious and studious young man* **2** [A] fml careful: *He always pays studious attention to detail.* – ~ **ly** adv – ~ **ness** n [U]

stud·y¹ /'stʌdi/ n **1** [U] also **studies** pl.– fml the act of studying one or more subjects: *He spent the entire afternoon in study.* | *You must give more time to your studies.* | *How are your medical studies progressing?* **2** [C (of)] a thorough enquiry into a particular subject, esp. including a piece of writing on it: *the university's department of social studies* | *She's made a study of the language of Shakespeare's plays.* | *The government has ordered a* **feasibility study** *in connection with the proposed new airport.* | *a study group working on aspects of the company's financial policy* **3** [C] a room used for private work or study or as an office: *the headmaster's study* **4** [C (of)] a drawing or painting of a detail, esp. for combining later into a larger picture: *a study of a flower*

5 [C] a piece of music for practice: *Chopin's piano studies*
6 in a brown study *BrE infml* deep in thought —see also CASE STUDY

study² *v* **1** [I;T] to spend time in learning (one or more subjects), esp. as part of an educational course: *He studies French.* | *She is studying to be a doctor.* | *a violinist who studied under* (=was taught by) *Yehudi Menuhin* **2** [T] to examine carefully; SCRUTINIZE: *She studied the report/the map.* | *He studied her face.*

study hall /'·· ͵·/ *n* [U] *AmE* (in American schools) a period of time during a school day in which a student does not have a class and usu. goes somewhere to study: *I've got study hall from two to three today.*

stuff¹ /stʌf/ *n* [U] **1** *infml* matter; material: *What's this sticky stuff on the floor?* | *This beer's been very popular; we've sold gallons of the stuff.* (=of the beer) | *Would you like some more beer, or would you prefer a drop of the* **hard stuff**? (=strong alcohol) | *This meat's good stuff!* | *There are one or two good articles in the magazine but otherwise it's all pretty boring stuff.* **2** *infml* things in a mass, esp. one's possessions or the things needed to do something: *I can't carry all my stuff alone!* | *Have you brought your swimming stuff?* **3** *lit or pomp* inner quality: *Such experiences are the* **(very) stuff of** *life.* (=are what life is made of) | *You're not giving up? I thought you were* **made of sterner stuff** *than that.* (=were more determined) **4** *old use* cloth **5 do one's stuff** *infml* to do what is necessary in a particular situation, esp. when one is the only person present who can do it **6 Stuff and nonsense!** /͵·· '··/ *That's untrue/a stupid idea!* **7 'That's the stuff!** *infml* That's the right thing to do/say! —see also HOT STUFF, **know one's stuff** (KNOW¹)

stuff² *v* **1** [T (**with**)] to fill with a substance: *Don't stuff the pillow too tight.* | *He stuffed the shoe with newspaper.* | *His pocket was stuffed full of dirty handkerchiefs.* **2** [T+*adv/prep*, esp. **into**] to push, esp. as filling material: *Don't stuff anything else in, or the bag will burst.* | *He stuffed the handkerchief into his pocket.* **3** [T] to fill the skin of (a dead animal), to make it look real: *a stuffed elephant* **4** [T] to put STUFFING (2) inside: *Has the chicken been stuffed?* | *cheese-stuffed potatoes* **5** [I;T] *infml* to cause (oneself) to eat as much as possible: *The children have been stuffing themselves (with cakes) all morning.* **6 get stuffed** *sl* (used for expressing very strong dislike, anger, etc.): *He only offered me £2 for it, so I told him to get stuffed.* (=I refused the offer angrily)

stuff sthg. ↔ **up** *phr v* [T *often pass.*] to block completely: *Stuff up that hole with some newspaper.* | *I'm all stuffed up/have got a stuffed-up nose* (=have my nose blocked because of a cold) *today.*

stuffed an·i·mal /͵· '···/ *n* *AmE* for SOFT TOY

stuffed shirt /͵· '·, '· ·/ *n derog* someone who acts as if they were grand and important; POMPOUS person

stuff·ing /'stʌfɪŋ/ *n* [U] **1** material used as a filling for something: *Use feathers as stuffing.* | (fig.) *I'm afraid that long illness has really* **knocked the stuffing out of** *him.* (=made him weak and powerless) **2** ‖ also **dressing** *AmE* finely cut-up food (e.g. a mixture of bread, egg, onion, and HERBs) placed inside a bird or piece of meat before cooking: *sage-and-onion stuffing*

stuff·y /'stʌfi/ *adj derog* **1** (having air) which is not fresh: *a stuffy room/atmosphere* **2** (of ideas, manners, etc.) formal and old-fashioned; PRIM: *Don't be so stuffy — of course they can use the same bedroom.* —**ily** *adv* —**iness** *n* [U]

stul·ti·fy /'stʌltɪͺfaɪ/ *v* [T] *fml* to make stupid or dull in mind: *the stultifying effect of uninteresting work* —**fication** /͵stʌltɪfɪ'keɪʃən/ *n* [U]

stum·ble¹ /'stʌmbəl/ *v* [I] **1** [(**on, over**)] to hit one's foot against something while moving along and start to fall: *He stumbled and fell.* | *She stumbled on a stone/over a branch.* **2** [+*adv/prep*, esp. **along**] to walk unsteadily: *I stumbled upstairs and dropped into bed.* **3** [(**at, over**)] to stop and/or make mistakes in speaking or reading aloud: *He stumbled at/over the long word.* | *Somehow he stumbled through his speech and sat down with great relief.*

stumble across/on/upon sbdy./sthg. *phr v* [T] to meet or discover by chance: *While I was doing my research, I stumbled on some fascinating new data.*

stumble² *n* an act of stumbling

stumbling block /'·· ·/ *n* [(**to**)] something which prevents action, advance, or development; OBSTACLE: *The question of overtime pay proved to be an insurmountable stumbling block to agreement.*

stump¹ /stʌmp/ *n* **1** the base of a tree left after the rest has been cut down **2** (in cricket) any of the three upright pieces of wood at which the ball is thrown —see picture at CRICKET **3** the useless end of something long which has been worn down, such as a tooth, pencil, etc.; STUB **4** the remaining part of a limb which has been cut off —see also **stir one's stumps** (STIR)

stump² *v* **1** [I+*adv/prep*] to move, esp. heavily or awkwardly: *He stumped angrily up the stairs.* **2** [T] *infml* to leave (someone) unable to reply; BAFFLE¹: *You've/That question's got me stumped; I don't know the answer.* **3** [T] (in cricket) to end the turn to hit of (a BATSMAN) who has moved outside the hitting area, by touching the STUMPS¹ (2) with the ball **4** [I;T] *AmE* to travel in or around (an area) making appearances to gain political support: *The candidates are stumping Vermont.* | *He'll be stumping hard for the next three months.*

stump up (sthg.) *phr v* [I;T] *infml, esp. BrE* to pay (money), esp. unwillingly: *He eventually stumped up £5 for the charity, but only after we'd asked him several times.*

stump·y /'stʌmpi/ *adj infml, usu. derog* (esp. of the body or part of the body) short and thick: *stumpy little fingers*

stun /stʌn/ *v* -**nn**- [T] **1** to make unconscious by hitting on the head: *I was momentarily stunned by the fall.* **2** to shock or surprise very greatly: *He seemed completely stunned by the jury's verdict of guilty.* | *a stunned silence*

stung /stʌŋ/ *past tense & participle of* STING

stun gun /'· ·/ *n* a weapon like a long stick which gives out a very strong electric current and can be used to make people unconscious. In some countries stun guns are used by the police to control RIOTS.

stunk /stʌŋk/ *past tense & participle of* STINK

stun·ner /'stʌnər/ *n old-fash infml* someone or something very attractive, esp. a woman: *She's a real stunner.*

stun·ning /'stʌnɪŋ/ *adj* **1** extremely attractive or beautiful: *stunning scenery* | *She looks absolutely stunning in that dress.* **2** very surprising or shocking: *stunning news* — ~**ly** *adv* : *stunningly* (=extremely) *obvious*

stunt¹ /stʌnt/ *v* [T] to prevent the full growth of: *Lack of the right food may stunt growth.* | *He had a small stunted body.*

stunt² *n* **1** an often dangerous act of skill: *In the film he had to drive a car into the sea, and other hair-raising stunts.* | *The plane flew upside down, turned over twice, and did a few more stunts before landing.* | *stunt flying* | (fig.) *If you go on* **pulling stupid stunts** (=doing silly things) *like that, you'll lose us all our money.* **2** an action which gains attention, esp. in advertising: *They had girls going round dressed up as chickens as a* **publicity stunt** *for their new chickenburgers.*

stunt man /'· ·/ **stunt wom·an** /'· ͵··/ *fem.*— *n* a person who takes over from an actor when something dangerous has to be done in a film so that the actor does not have to take risks

stu·pe·fy /'stjuːpͺfaɪ‖'stuː-/ *v* [T *often pass.*] *fml* **1** to surprise greatly and usu. annoy; AMAZE: *stupefying inefficiency* **2** to make unable to think or feel: *He was in a stupefied state after all the drugs they'd given him.* —**faction** /͵stjuːpͺ'fækʃən‖͵stuː-/ *n* [U]

stu·pen·dous /stjuː'pendəs‖stuː-/ *adj* surprisingly great or good: *a stupendous effort/discovery* | *We had a stupendous time at the party.* — ~**ly** *adv*

stu·pid /'stjuːpͺd‖'stuː-/ *adj* **1** silly or foolish, either generally or in particular: *a stupid person/idea* | *It was stupid of you to turn it upside down without closing the lid.* | *I think you were stupid not to accept his offer.* **2** [A] *infml* (of a thing) annoying: *This stupid drawer won't open.* — ~**ly** *adv*

stu·pid·i·ty /stjuː'pɪdͺti‖stuː-/ *n* **1** [U] the quality of being stupid **2** [C *usu. pl.*; U] (an example or act of) stupid behaviour

stu·por /'stjuːpər‖'stuː-/ *n* [C;U] a state in which one cannot think or use one's senses: *a drunken stupor*

stur·dy /'stɜːdi‖-ɜːr-/ *adj apprec* **1** strong and firm, esp. in body; not likely to break or fall, esp. because of thickness: *With his sturdy legs he could keep running for hours.* | *Make sure that fence you're putting up is good and* *sturdy.* | *a sturdy oak tree* **2** unwilling to be defeated; determined: *They kept up a sturdy opposition to the plan.* —**ily** *adv* : *She sturdily denied her guilt.* —**iness** *n* [U]

stur·geon /ˈstɜːdʒən‖-ɜːr-/ *n* a large fish which can be eaten and from which CAVIAR is obtained

stut·ter¹ /ˈstʌtəʳ/ *v* **1** [I; T] to speak or say with difficulty in producing sounds, esp. habitually repeating the first consonant: *"I c-c-can't help it", he stuttered.* —compare STAMMER **2** [I] to work or move unevenly or jumpily: *I pressed the starter and the old engine stuttered into life.* — **~er** *n* — **~ingly** *adv*

stutter² *n* the habit of stuttering in speech: *He has a nervous stutter|speaks with a stutter.*

Stutt·gart /ˈʃtʊtɡɑːt‖-ɡɑːrt/ an industrial city in SW Germany, the capital of Baden-Württemberg state

STV /ˌes tiː ˈviː/ Scottish Television; one of the British television companies controlled by the ITC, transmitting programmes to E Anglia

St Vin·cent /sənt ˈvɪnsənt‖seɪnt-/ an island nation in the West Indies consisting of the main island, St Vincent, and the small islands, the Grenadines in the Windward Islands; capital Kingstown; population 110,000 (1989)

sty¹ /staɪ/ *n* a PIGSTY

sty² **stye** /staɪ/ *n* an infected place on the edge of the eyelid, usu. red and swollen

Sty·gi·an /ˈstɪdʒiən/ *adj lit* unpleasantly dark: *We groped our way through the Stygian gloom.*

style¹ /staɪl/ *n* **1** [C;U] a general manner of doing something which is typical or representative of a person or group, a time in history, etc.: *the modern style of architecture* | *a painting in the style of Picasso* | *Some people have criticized the Prime Minister's style of leadership.* **2** [C;U] **a** the particular choice of words or manner of expression used by or typical of a writer or speaker: *The letter is written in a formal style.* | *He is supposed to be a great writer, but I don't like his style.* **b** a habitual way of spelling, of using PUNCTUATION, of using capital letters, etc.: *Our house style* (=in our company) *is to use* -ize *rather than* -ise. **3** [C] a type or sort, esp. of goods: *They sell every style of mirror.* | *a new style garlic press* **4** [U] *apprec* high quality, skill, or grace in performance, manner, social behaviour, or appearance: *He has great style: he wears hand-made clothes, drives a beautiful car, gives the best parties.* | *He performed the violin solo with a beautiful sense of style.* **5** [C;U] fashion, esp. in clothes: *70s styles look very odd today.* | *jackets in the latest style* | *Long hair is definitely* **out of style** *at the moment.* **6** [S] *infml* someone's characteristic way of behaving; what someone would do: *I wouldn't tell lies to you; that's not my style.* **7** [C] *tech* a correct title: *The eldest son of an earl takes the style "Lord".* **8** the centre part of a flower below the STIGMA —see picture at FLOWER **9 in style** so as to cause admiration by being fashionable and spending a lot of money: *When they got married they decided to do it in style, and gave a big party.* **10** -**style: a** in the manner of the stated person, place, etc.: *He wears his hair long, hippie-style.* | *I like my hamburgers served American-style.* **b** like the stated thing in appearance only: *a leather-style briefcase* (=not made of real leather)—see also HAIRSTYLE, LIFESTYLE, **cramp someone's style** (CRAMP) — **~less** *adj*

style² *v* [T] **1** to arrange or form in a certain (good) pattern, shape, etc.; DESIGN: *This sofa was styled in Italy.* | *The dress is carefully styled for maximum comfort.* | *She's having her hair styled by a famous hairdresser.* **2** [+obj+n] to give (a title) to: *He styles himself "Lord".* —see also SELF-STYLED

styling brush /ˈ·· ˌ·/ *n* a heated brush used, esp. by women, to give shape to the hair

styling mousse /ˈ·· ˌ·/ *n* a light substance, like FOAM (1), used on the hair to help it keep its style

styl·ish /ˈstaɪlɪʃ/ *adj apprec* fashionable; ELEGANT: *He's a stylish dresser.* — **~ly** *adv* — **~ness** *n* [U]

styl·ist /ˈstaɪlɪ̩st/ *n* **1** (*often in comb.*) a person who develops or arranges styles of appearance: *a hair stylist* (=who cuts and arranges people's hair) **2** a person who carefully develops a good style of writing

styl·is·tic /staɪˈlɪstɪk/ *adj* of style, esp. in writing or art: *Note the stylistic differences between the genuine painting and the forgery.* — **~ally** /kli/ *adv*

styl·is·tics /staɪˈlɪstɪks/ *n* [U] the study of style in written or spoken language

styl·ize also -**ise** *BrE* /ˈstaɪlaɪz/ *v* [T] (in art or description) to treat or present (something) in a fixed often less detailed style, rather than exactly as it is in real life: *Playing cards are marked with stylized (representations of) hearts, diamonds, etc.*

sty·lus /ˈstaɪləs/ *n* **1** a needle-like instrument, with a diamond or other hard jewel on the end, that picks up the sound signals from a record in a RECORD PLAYER **2** a pointed instrument used in ancient times for writing on WAX

sty·mie /ˈstaɪmi/ *v* [T] *infml* to prevent from taking action or being put into action; stop; THWART: *His plan for improving the business was stymied by a lack of funds.*

styp·tic /ˈstɪptɪk/ *n, adj tech* (a substance) which stops bleeding

sty·ro·foam /ˈstaɪərəˌfəʊm/ *n* [U] *AmE tdmk for* POLYSTYRENE

Sty·ron /ˈstaɪərən/, **William** (1925–) an American writer, known esp. for his powerful, often poetic NOVELS, e.g. *Sophie's Choice*

Styx /stɪks/ [*the*] in CLASSICAL MYTHOLOGY a river in Hades across which the souls of dead people were carried in a boat by Charon

suave /swɑːv/ *adj sometimes derog* having or showing very good smooth manners, esp. in an insincere way — **~ly** *adv* —**suavity**, **~ness**— *n* [U]

sub¹ /sʌb/ *n infml* **1** a SUBMARINE² **2** (esp. in sport) a SUBSTITUTE¹: *England brought on their sub in the second half.* **3** *BrE for* SUBSCRIPTION **4** *BrE* an amount of money paid to someone from their wages before the usual day of payment **5** a SUBEDITOR **6** *AmE* a SUBMARINE SANDWICH: *I usually just get a sub for lunch.* | *a sub shop*

sub² *v* -**bb**- *infml* **1** [I (**for**)] to act as a SUBSTITUTE¹ **2** [T] *BrE* to give a SUB¹ (4) to **3** [T] to SUBEDIT

sub- see WORD FORMATION

sub·al·tern /ˈsʌbəltən‖səˈbɔːltərn/ *n BrE* an army officer lower in rank than a captain

sub·aq·ua /sʌb ˈækwə/ *adj* [A] *BrE* for underwater sports, such as skin diving (SKIN-DIVE): *a sub-aqua club*

Su·ba·ru /ˈsuːbəruː/ *tdmk* a car made by the Japanese company Subaru

sub·a·tom·ic /ˌsʌbəˈtɒmɪk◂ ‖ -ˈtɑː-/ *adj tech* smaller than an atom: *subatomic particles*

sub·com·mit·tee /ˈsʌbkəˌmɪti/ *n* [C+*sing.|pl.v*] a smaller group formed from a larger committee to deal with a certain matter in more detail

sub·com·pact /ˌsʌbˈkɒmpækt ‖ -ˈkɑːm-/ *n AmE* a car that is smaller than a COMPACT

sub·con·scious¹ /ˌsʌbˈkɒnʃəs‖-ˈkɑːn-/ *adj* [*no comp.*] (of thoughts, feelings, etc.) not fully known or understood by the conscious mind; present at a hidden level of the mind — **~ly** *adv*

subconscious² also **unconscious**— [*the*] the level at which one's mind works without one being conscious of it, having thoughts and feelings that one does not actively know about —see CONSCIOUS (USAGE)

sub·con·ti·nent /ˌsʌbˈkɒntɪ̩nənt‖-ˈkɑːn-/ *n* a large mass of land not quite large enough to be called a CONTINENT: *the Indian subcontinent* (=includes India, Sri Lanka, Pakistan, and Bangladesh)

sub·con·ti·nen·tal /ˌsʌbkɒntɪˈnentl◂ ‖ -kɑːn-/ *n, adj AmE* (a person) of a subcontinent, esp. the Indian subcontinent

▷ USAGE American English uses **subcontinental** when referring to people from the Indian subcontinent, and **Asian** or **Oriental** for people from East or Southeast Asia. British English generally uses **Asian** for all of these.◁

sub·con·tract /ˌsʌbkənˈtrækt‖-ˈkɑːntrækt/ *v* [T (**to**)] to hire someone else to do (work which one has agreed to do): *Our building firm is very busy at the moment, so we're subcontracting the roofing to another company.*

sub·con·trac·tor /ˌsʌbkənˈtræktəʳ‖-ˈkɑːntræk-/ *n* a person or firm that has had work subcontracted to it

sub·cul·ture /ˈsʌbˌkʌltʃəʳ/ *n* (the behaviour, beliefs, and customs of) a particular group of people within a society, often a group whose behaviour is disapproved of by most people: *the drug subculture of the big cities*

sub·cu·ta·ne·ous /ˌsʌbkjuːˈteɪniəs◂/ *adj tech* beneath the skin: *subcutaneous fat* — ~**ly** *adv*

sub·di·vide /ˌsʌbdɪˈvaɪd/ *v* [T (**into**)] to divide (something that is already divided) into smaller parts: *The house is being subdivided into flats.*

sub·di·vi·sion /ˈsʌbdɪˌvɪʒən/ *n* [C;U] (a part which results from) the act of subdividing **2** [C??]?? *AmE* an area of land that has been subdivided for building houses on

sub·due /səbˈdjuː‖-ˈduː/ *v* [T] to gain control of, esp. by defeating: *She tried to subdue her anger.* | *Napoleon subdued much of Europe.*

sub·dued /səbˈdjuːd‖-ˈduːd/ *adj* **1** below usual brightness, loudness, etc.; gentle: *subdued lighting* | *a subdued voice* **2** unnaturally or unusually quiet in behaviour: *You seem very subdued tonight: is anything worrying you?*

sub·ed·it /ˌsʌbˈedɪt/ also **sub** *infml*— *v* [T] to examine and put right (others' writing) as a subeditor

sub·ed·i·tor /ˌsʌbˈedɪtər/ also **sub** *infml*— *n* a person whose job is to examine and improve or put right something written by another person, such as a newspaper article

sub·group /ˈsʌbgruːp/ *n* a separate, smaller, and sometimes less important part of a group

sub·head·ing /ˈsʌbˌhedɪŋ/ *n* a short title phrase at the beginning of any of the parts of a piece of writing

sub·hu·man /sʌbˈhjuːmən‖-ˈhjuː-, -ˈjuː-/ *adj usu. derog* of less than human qualities: *Anyone who could commit such terrible atrocities must be subhuman.* | *subhuman intelligence* —compare INHUMAN

Su·bic Bay /ˌsuːbɪk ˈbeɪ/ a very large American military base in the Philippines

sub·ject¹ /ˈsʌbdʒɪkt/ *n* **1** [(**of**)] the thing that is dealt with or represented in a piece of writing, work of art, etc.: *The subject of her book is sailing.* | *She wrote a book* **on the subject of** *sailing.* | *The subject of the painting is the Battle of Waterloo.* **2** something being talked about or considered: *He was clearly embarrassed to talk about his private life, and tried to* **change the subject.** | *And while we're* **on the subject of** (=while we're talking about) *money, what about that £10 I lent you?* | *The budget has been the subject of much debate/criticism.* **3** a branch of knowledge studied, esp. in a system of education: *History is my favourite subject/my best subject at school.* | *She's taking three subjects in her exams.* **4** *tech* (in grammar) a noun, noun phrase, or PRONOUN that usu. comes before a main verb and represents the person or thing that performs the action of the verb or about which something is stated, such as *she* in *She hit John* or *elephants* in *Elephants are big* —compare OBJECT¹ (4) **5** a person who lives in the land of, is protected by, and owes loyalty to a certain state or esp. royal ruler: *all the Queen's subjects* | *a subject of the United Kingdom* | *a British subject* — compare ALIEN² (2), CITIZEN (2), NATIONAL² **6** [(**of, for**)] *fml* a cause: *His strange clothes were the subject of* (=caused) *great amusement/were a subject for amusement.* **7** a person or animal to whom something is done in an EXPERIMENT: *an experiment to study the effects of smoking, with mice as the subjects*

subject² *adj* **1** [F+**to**] tending or likely (to have): *He's subject to ill health.* (=often becomes ill) | *The arrangements are subject to change* (=may be changed) *at short notice.* **2** [F+**to**] governed (by) or dependent (on): *All such gatherings are subject to the laws on political meetings.* | *The plans are subject to ministerial approval.* (=the minister has to agree to them, and he may not) **3** [A *no comp.*] *fml* or *lit* governed by someone else; not independent: *a subject race* **4 subject to** depending on: *Subject to your approval* (=if you approve), *we'll go ahead.*

sub·ject³ /səbˈdʒekt/ *v* [T] *fml* or *lit* to bring under firm control; not allow to have free expression: *The Aztecs subjected the neighbouring tribes (to their rule).*

subject sbdy./sthg. **to** sthg. *phr v* [T *often pass.*] to cause to experience or suffer: *We were subjected to a good deal of ill-mannered abuse.* | *He was subjected to torture.* | *The scientists subjected the products to a number of rigorous tests.* | *No one would willingly subject himself to such indignities.*

sub·jec·tion /səbˈdʒekʃən/ *n* [U] *fml* **1** [(**of**)] the act of subjecting: *an ambitious and ruthless country intent on the subjection of the surrounding states* **2** [(**to**)] a state of dependence, esp. in which one cannot do anything except

if someone else allows it: *The children lived in complete subjection while their father was alive.*

sub·jec·tive /səbˈdʒektɪv/ *adj* **1** *often derog* influenced by personal feelings and therefore perhaps unfair: *This is a very subjective judgment of her abilities.* —opposite **objective 2** [*no comp.*] existing only in the mind; imaginary: *The ghostly presence was just a subjective sensation/impression.* **3** (in grammar) of the subject — ~**ly** *adv* —**tivity** /ˌsʌbdʒekˈtɪvɪti/ *n* [U]

subject mat·ter /ˈ·· ˌ··/ *n* [U] what is being talked about in speech or writing or represented in art: *His speech was clever and witty, although the subject matter wasn't interesting in itself.* | *I'm afraid the style doesn't match the subject matter.*

sub·join /ˌsʌbˈdʒɔɪn/ *v* [T (**to**)] *fml* or *pomp* to add (a sentence or phrase) at the end: *My comments on the report are here subjoined.*

sub ju·di·ce /ˌsʌb ˈdʒuːdɪsi‖ˌsʊb ˈjuːdɪkeɪ/ *adj* [F] *law, Lat* (of a legal case) now being considered in court, and therefore not allowed to be publicly mentioned, e.g. in a newspaper

sub·ju·gate /ˈsʌbdʒʊgeɪt/ *v* [T] to defeat and make obedient: *a subjugated people* —**gation** /ˌsʌbdʒʊˈgeɪʃən/ *n* [U]

sub·junc·tive /səbˈdʒʌŋktɪv/ *n* (in grammar) a verb form, or a set of verb forms (a MOOD²), used in some languages to express doubt, wishes, situations that do not actually exist, etc.: *In "if I were you" the verb "were" is in the subjunctive/is a subjunctive.* —compare IMPERATIVE² (1), INDICATIVE² —**subjunctive** *adj*

sub·lease¹ /ˈsʌb-liːs‖ˌsʌbˈliːs/ *n* an agreement by which someone who rents property from its owner then rents (part of) that property to someone else —see also LEASE

sub·lease² /sʌbˈliːs/ *v* [I;T] to sublet

sub·let /sʌbˈlet/ *v* -**tt**- [I;T] to rent (a property one rents from its owner) to someone else: *He rents the house and sublets a room to a friend.* —see also LET, SUBTENANT

sub·lieu·ten·ant /ˌsʌb-ləˈtenənt, -lef-‖-luː-/ *n* a naval rank —see TABLE 3 —see picture at RANK

sub·li·mate /ˈsʌblɪmeɪt/ *v* [T] *fml* or *tech* **1** to replace (natural urges, esp. sexual ones) with socially acceptable activities **2** (in chemistry) to change (a solid substance) to a gas by heating it and then change it back to a solid, in order to make it pure —**mation** /ˌsʌblɪˈmeɪʃən/ *n* [U]

sub·li·mate² /ˈsʌblɪmɪt/ *n tech* (in chemistry) a solid after it has been sublimated

sub·lime /səˈblaɪm/ *adj* **1** causing deep feelings of wonder, joy, etc.: *sublime music* | (*infml*) *What a sublime* (=very good) *meal that was!* **2** [A] *infml derog* complete and usu. careless, unknowing, or unintentional: *With a sublime disregard for the rules he parked his car right in front of the main entrance.* | *sublime ignorance* **3 from the sublime to the ridiculous** (when comparing two things, occasions, etc.) starting with something wonderful, but followed by something silly — ~**ly** *adv* : *sublimely unaware of the risk she was taking* — ~**ness, -limity** /səˈblɪmɪti/ — *n* [U]

sub·lim·i·nal /sʌbˈlɪmɪnəl/ *adj* (shown) at a level of the mind which the senses are not conscious of: *Subliminal advertising on television* (=that is shown for too short a time for one to be conscious of it) *has been banned.*

sub·ma·chine gun /ˌsʌbməˈʃiːn gʌn/ *n* a light MACHINEGUN

sub·ma·rine¹ /ˈsʌbməriːn, ˌsʌbməˈriːn/ *adj tech* growing or used under or in the sea: *submarine plant life* | *a submarine cable*

submarine² also **sub** *infml*— *n* a ship, esp. a warship, which can stay under water: *a nuclear submarine*

sub·mar·i·ner /sʌbˈmærɪnər‖ˈsʌbməriːnər/ *n* a sailor working and living in a submarine

submarine sand·wich /ˈ··· ˌ··/ also **sub**— *n AmE* a long bread roll split open and filled with meat, cheese, etc.

sub·merge /səbˈmɜːdʒ‖-ɜːr-/ *v* [(**in**)] **1** [I;T] to (cause to) go under the surface of water: *At the first sign of danger the submarine will submerge.* | *You have to submerge the photographic plates in the fluid.* | *dangerous submerged rocks* **2** [T] to cover or completely hide: *Her happiness at seeing him submerged her former worries.* | *the submerged two-thirds of the population* (=those who are not noticed, and esp. have fewer advantages than the rest) |

(fig.) *I'm absolutely submerged in work.* (=have a very large amount to do)

sub·mer·si·ble /səb'mɜːsɪbəl‖-'ɜːr-/ *n, adj tech* (a boat) which can go under water

sub·mer·sion /səb'mɜːʃən‖-'mɜːrʒən/ also **sub·mer·gence** /səb'mɜːdʒəns‖-'ɜːr-/— *n* [U (**in**)] the act of submerging or state of being submerged

sub·mis·sion /səb'mɪʃən/ *n* **1** [C; U] **a** (an act of) submitting or being submitted: *He battered his opponent into submission.* | *June the third is the last date for submission of entries for the competition.* **b** [C] something submitted: *The magazine welcomes submissions from its readers.* **2** [U] *fml* what one thinks and wishes to state; opinion: **In my submission** (=I think) *these proposals are completely unworkable.* **3** [U (**to**)] *fml* obedience: *I shall give up my claim, in submission to your wishes.* **4** [C] *law* something offered for consideration, esp. a request or suggestion: *The court has received submissions from both parties to the dispute.* [+*that*] *The lawyer made a submission that her client be allowed full costs.*

sub·mis·sive /səb'mɪsɪv/ *adj* gentle and (too) willing to obey orders: *He expects his wife to be meek and submissive.* — **~ly** *adv* — **~ness** *n* [U]

sub·mit /səb'mɪt/ *v* **-tt-** **1** [I (**to**)] to admit defeat: *He was losing the fight but he would not submit.* **2** [T (**to**)] to offer for consideration: *We are submitting the proposal to the committee for their approval.* | *They submitted a tender for the contract.* **3** [T+(*that*); *obj*] *fml or law* to suggest or say: *My lord, I respectfully submit that the prosecution has failed to prove its case.* **4** [T (**to**)] *fml* to allow (one-self) to agree to obey: *We will submit ourselves to the court's judgment.*

sub·nor·mal /ˌsʌb'nɔːməl‖-ɔːr-/ *adj* less than is usual, average, etc., esp. in the abilities of the mind: *He was born subnormal and will never learn to read.* | *subnormal temperatures*

sub·or·bit·al /sʌb'ɔːbɪtl‖-'ɔːr-/ *adj tech* of or being less than one complete ORBIT (=journey round the Earth or a similar body in space): *a suborbital space flight*

sub·or·di·nate[1] /sə'bɔːdɪnət‖-ɔːr-/ *adj* [(**to**)] of a lower rank or position; less important: *All other considerations are subordinate to our need for steady profits.*

subordinate[2] *n* someone who is of lower rank in a job, and takes orders from his or her SUPERIOR (=the person higher in rank): *He treats his subordinates very badly.* — compare INFERIOR[2]

sub·or·din·ate[3] /sə'bɔːdɪneɪt‖-ɔːr-/ *v* [T (**to**)] to put in a position of less importance: *He subordinated his wishes to the general good of the group.* —**-ation** /sə₁bɔːdɪ'neɪʃən‖-ɔːr-/ *n* [U]

subordinate clause /ˌ···'·‖'·/ *n* a DEPENDENT CLAUSE

sub·orn /sə'bɔːn‖-ɔːrn/ *v* [T] *fml* to persuade (someone) to do wrong, esp. to tell lies in a court of law, usu. for payment: *The penalties for attempting to suborn witnesses are heavy.* — **~ation** /ˌsʌbɔː'neɪʃən‖-ɔːr-/ *n* [U]

sub·plot /'sʌbplɒt‖-plɑːt/ *n* a PLOT (=set of events) that is of less importance than and separate from the main plot of a play, story, etc.

sub·poe·na[1] /sə'piːnə, səb-/ *n law* a written order to attend a court of law

subpoena[2] *v* **-naed** [T] *law* to order to attend a court by means of a subpoena: *The defence has subpoenaed three witnesses.*

sub-post·mas·ter /ˌ·'···/ **sub-postmistress** *fem. n* in Britain, a person who runs a sub-post office

sub-post of·fice /ˌ·'·· ,··/ *n* a post office in Britain that is not wholly owned by the government and that offers fewer services than a main post office. Sub-post offices are often part of a larger shop and they are usu. found in small villages or in areas of large towns far away from the main post office.

sub·rou·tine /ˌsʌbruː'tiːn/ *n tech* a part of a computer PROGRAM containing a set of instructions for performing a particular operation, which can be used repeatedly in the program

sub·scribe /səb'skraɪb/ *v* [(**to**)] **1** [I] *esp. BrE* to pay money regularly (in support of some good aim): *We subscribe to an animal protection society.* **2** [T] *esp. BrE* to give (money): *Everyone in the office subscribed a couple of pounds towards his wedding present.* **3** [I] to pay regu-

larly in order to receive a magazine, newspaper, etc.: *I subscribe to "Time" magazine.* **4** [T] *fml* to sign (one's name): *I subscribed my name to the document.* [+*obj+n*] *I subscribed myself F. Smith.*

  subscribe for sthg. *phr v* [T] *fml* to agree to pay or buy: *I've subscribed for £1000 (worth of shares).*

  subscribe to sthg. *phr v* [T *often in questions and negatives*] to agree with; approve of: *I've never subscribed to the theory that people are more important than animals.*

sub·scrib·er /səb'skraɪbər/ *n* **1** someone who subscribes or has subscribed: *a special Christmas offer to the magazine's subscribers* **2** someone who receives the use of a service over a period of time, for which they pay: *a telephone subscriber*

sub·scrip·tion /səb'skrɪpʃən/ *n* **1** also **sub** *BrE infml*— an amount of money given, esp. regularly, for membership of a society, in order to receive a magazine, etc.: *Have you paid your annual subscription yet?* | *a cable television service financed by subscriptions* **2** an agreement to pay regularly for something: *a subscription concert* (=only for people who pay to go regularly)

sub·sec·tion /'sʌbsekʃən/ *n* a part of a SECTION

sub·se·quent /'sʌbsɪkwənt/ *adj* coming after or following something else: *We made plans for a visit, but subsequent difficulties with the car prevented it.* [F+**to**] *The events I'm speaking of were subsequent to* (=after) *the war.* — **~ly** *adv*: *He said he was a wealthy aristocrat, but it subsequently* (=afterwards) *emerged that he was an impostor.* —compare CONSEQUENT

sub·ser·vi·ent /səb'sɜːviənt‖-ɜːr-/ *adj* [(**to**)] **1** *derog* habitually willing to do what others want; tending to obey others' wishes: *a subservient waiter/manner* **2** *fml* less important; SUBORDINATE: *All other considerations are subservient to the need for quick profit.* — **~ly** *adv* —**-ence** *n* [U]

sub·set /'sʌbset/ *n* a set that is part of a larger set esp. in MATHEMATICS

sub·side /səb'saɪd/ *v* [I] **1** (of a building) to sink gradually further into the ground **2** (of land) to have its surface fall suddenly to a lower level because of lack of support: *After the heavy rains part of the road subsided.* | (fig.) *She subsided wearily into a chair.* **3** (of bad weather or other violent or unusual conditions) to return to its usual level; become less: *The floods subsided.* (=went down) | *The wind subsided.* (=became less strong and gradually stopped) | *His anger quickly subsided.* | *The high demand for housing in the area is expected to subside.*

sub·si·dence /səb'saɪdəns, 'sʌbsɪdəns/ *n* [C;U] (an act of) subsiding or the state of having subsided; sinking of land or buildings: *Is your house insured against subsidence?*

sub·sid·i·a·ri·ty /səb₁sɪdi'ærɪti/ *n* [U] a political POLICY in which more power, e.g. to make decisions, is given to smaller groups of people, esp. more power is taken away from the European Community and given the countries who belong to the Community so that they can make their own decisions

sub·sid·i·a·ry[1] /səb'sɪdiəri‖-dieri/ *adj* [(**to**)] connected with but of less importance than the main plan, work, company, etc.: *Can I ask a subsidiary question?* (=one that is connected with and follows on from my first one) | *subsidiary details*

subsidiary[2] *n* a company of which more than 50 per cent is owned by the parent company or whose board of directors is controlled by the parent company: *James Capel is a subsidiary of Hong Kong Bank.*

sub·si·dize also **-dise** *BrE* /'sʌbsɪdaɪz/ *v* [T] (of someone other than the buyer) to pay part of the cost of (something) for (someone), usu. to keep cost to the buyer low or to help a service, organization, etc., which has not got enough money: *subsidized school meals* | *Farming is partly subsidized by the government.* | *The local authority is subsidizing the transport service.* —**-dizer** *n* —**-dization** /ˌsʌbsɪdaɪ'zeɪʃən‖-də-/ *n* [U]

sub·si·dy /'sʌbsɪdi/ *n* money paid, esp. by the government or an organization, to make prices lower, make it cheaper to produce goods, etc.: *This industry depends for its survival on government subsidies.* | *trade subsidies*

sub·sist /səb'sɪst/ *v* [I (**on**)] *fml* to keep alive, esp. when having only small amounts of money or food: *They subsisted on bread and water/on £25 a week.*

sub·sis·tence /səb'sɪstəns/ *n* [U] **1** the ability to live, esp.

with little money or food: *Subsistence is not possible in such conditions.* **2** living with the smallest amount (of food or money) necessary: *a subsistence allowance | subsistence farmers* (=who produce just enough food to live on)

subsistence crop /·ˈ··· ·/ *n* a crop grown for use by the grower rather than for sale —compare CASH CROP

subsistence lev·el /·ˈ··· ˌ··/ *n* [S] a very poor standard of living, which only provides those things which are absolutely necessary and nothing more: *Many of the poorer farmers live at subsistence level.*

sub·soil /ˈsʌbsɔɪl/ *n* [U] the lower level of soil, with larger grains than that on the surface, but above the hard rock

sub·son·ic /ˌsʌbˈsɒnɪk◂ ‖ -ˈsɑː-/ *adj* below the speed of sound: *subsonic flight | a subsonic airliner* —compare SUPERSONIC

sub·stance /ˈsʌbstəns/ *n* **1** [C] a material; type of matter: *a sticky substance | radioactive substances | manufacturers of diethylene glycol, a substance used in antifreeze for car engines | Heroin is an illegal substance.* **2** [U] *fml* truth: *There is no substance in the rumours that the princess is pregnant. | The rumours are completely without substance.* **3** [(the) U (of)] *fml* the real meaning, without the unimportant details; ESSENCE: *His speech meandered on for half an hour, but the substance of what he said was/what he said in substance was that too many people have too little money.* **4** [U] *fml* importance, esp. in relation to real life: *Instead of endlessly debating points of procedure, why aren't we discussing matters of substance? | It was an amusing speech, but without much substance.* (=without important or serious ideas, etc.) **5** [U] *fml or lit* wealth: *a man of substance*

sub·stan·dard /ˌsʌbˈstændəd◂ ‖ -ərd/ *adj* not as good as the average; not of an acceptable sort: *substandard work/materials* —compare NONSTANDARD (1), STANDARD

sub·stan·tial /səbˈstænʃəl/ *adj* **1** solid; strongly made: *a substantial mahogany desk* **2** large enough to be satisfactory: *a substantial meal/salary* **3** large enough to be noticeable or to have an important effect: *They made substantial changes to the arrangements.* **4** [A] concerning the important part or meaning: *Though they disagreed on details, they were in substantial agreement over the plan.* **5** *fml* wealthy: *a very substantial family in the wool trade*

sub·stan·tial·ly /səbˈstænʃəli/ *adv* **1** mainly; in the important part: *There are one or two minor differences, but they're substantially the same.* **2** quite a lot: *Your contribution helped us substantially.*

sub·stan·ti·ate /səbˈstænʃieɪt/ *v* [T] *fml* to prove the truth of (something said, claimed, etc.): *Can you substantiate your claim in a court of law?* —**·ation** /səbˌstænʃiˈeɪʃən/ *n* [U] : *evidence produced in substantiation of her allegations*

sub·stan·tive¹ /ˈsʌbstəntɪv/ *n tech* a noun —**·tival** /ˌsʌbstənˈtaɪvəl◂/ *adj*

sub·stan·tive² /səbˈstæntɪv, ˈsʌbstəntɪv/ *adj fml or tech* **1** having reality, actuality, or importance; firm: *substantive discussions* (=in which subjects of importance are discussed and progress is made) *| It was a lengthy speech but he made few substantive points.* **2** (in grammar) expressing existence: *The substantive verb is "to be".* **3** [A] real and continuing, rather than lasting for only a limited time: *the substantive rank of colonel* — —**ly** *adv*

sub·sta·tion /ˈsʌbˌsteɪʃən/ *n* a place where electricity is passed on from a generating (GENERATE) station into the general system

sub·sti·tute¹ /ˈsʌbstɪtjuːt‖-tuːt/ *n* [(for)] a person or thing acting or used in place of another: *The leading singer couldn't appear, and her substitute clearly didn't know the role very well. | The recipe calls for butter, but you can use margarine as a substitute. | England brought on their substitute (player) when one of their players got injured.| This is the only genuine sort; accept no substitutes. |* **There's no substitute for** *sensible eating and exercise* (=they are the best things) *if you want to keep fit. | a substitute teacher | sugar or a sugar substitute, such as saccharin*

substitute² *v* [(for)] **1** [T] to put (something or someone) in place of another: *We substituted red balls for blue, to see if the baby would notice. | Those on slimming diets should substitute the sugar with saccharin/substitute sac-*

charin *for the sugar.* **2** [I] to act as a substitute; be used instead: *He substituted for the worker who was ill.* —see REPLACE (USAGE) —**·tution** /ˌsʌbstɪˈtjuːʃən‖-ˈtuː-/ *n* [C;U (for)] : *The England manager made two substitutions in the second half. | The substitution of wine for water would improve the taste of the stew.*

sub·stra·tum /ˈsʌbˌstrɑːtəm‖-ˌstreɪ-/ *n* **-ta** /tə/ a level (STRATUM) lying beneath another, esp. in the earth: *a substratum of rock | (fig.) a substratum* (=hidden quality) *of truth in the argument*

sub·struc·ture /ˈsʌbˌstrʌktʃər/ *n* a solid base underground which supports something above ground

sub·sume /səbˈsjuːm‖-ˈsuːm/ *v* [T (under)] *fml* to include as a member of a group or type: *For purposes of the survey, typists are subsumed under office workers.*

sub·ten·ant /ˌsʌbˈtenənt/ *n* a person to whom a place is SUBLET by the TENANT; person who pays rent to the original renter

sub·tend /səbˈtend/ *v* [T] *tech* (in GEOMETRY) to have (the stated angle or ARC) opposite to it: *This side of the triangle subtends an angle of 30 degrees.*

sub·ter·fuge /ˈsʌbtəfjuːdʒ‖-ər-/ *n* [C;U] *fml* (deceit by) a secret trick or slightly dishonest way of doing something: *We had to resort to a little harmless subterfuge to organize her birthday treat without her finding out about it.*

sub·ter·ra·ne·an /ˌsʌbtəˈreɪniən◂/ *adj* beneath the surface of the Earth; underground: *subterranean rivers*

sub·ti·tle /ˈsʌbˌtaɪtl/ *n* a less important title printed beneath the main title of a book

sub·ti·tled /ˈsʌbˌtaɪtld/ *adj* having subtitles or the stated subtitle: *He wrote "My Years on the Bench", subtitled "Autobiography of a Judge".*

sub·ti·tles /ˈsʌbˌtaɪtlz/ *n* [P] words printed over a film in a foreign language to translate what is being said: *a French film with English subtitles*

sub·tle /ˈsʌtl/ *adj* **1** delicate; not easy to notice, understand, or explain: *a subtle taste | subtle differences in meaning | His attempt to offer us a bribe was not exactly subtle.* (=he did not hide his intentions well) **2** clever in arrangement, esp. so as to deceive people: *a subtle plan* **3** very clever in noticing and understanding: *a subtle mind* —**·tly** *adv* : *subtly different*

sub·tle·ty /ˈsʌtlti/ *n* **1** [U] the quality of being subtle: *He argued his case with considerable subtlety.* **2** [C often *pl.*] a subtle idea, thought, or detail: *I think the translator missed some of the subtleties of the original.*

sub·to·tal /ˈsʌbˌtəʊtl/ *n* the total of a single set of figures, esp. on a bill, which will be added to others to form a whole total

sub·tract /səbˈtrækt/ *v* [T (**from**)] to take (a number, amount, etc.) from something larger: *If you subtract 10 from 30 you get 20.* —compare ADD (2), DEDUCT

sub·trac·tion /səbˈtrækʃən/ *n* [U] the act of subtracting or state of being subtracted —compare ADDITION

sub·trop·i·cal /ˌsʌbˈtrɒpɪkəl◂ ‖-ˈtrɑː-/ also **semitropical**— *adj* of or suited to an area near the tropics: *a subtropical climate | subtropical vegetation*

sub·urb /ˈsʌbɜːb‖-ɜːrb/ *n* [(**of**)] an outer area of a town or city, where people live: *Blackheath is a suburb of London.* —see also SUBURBS

sub·ur·ban /səˈbɜːbən‖-ɜːr-/ *adj often derog* of, for, or in the suburbs, esp. as considered dull or unimaginative: *a suburban railway | suburban streets with houses all the same | suburban life | suburban attitudes* —see colour picture on page 0000

sub·ur·ban·ite /səˈbɜːbənaɪt‖-ɜːr-/ *n infml, often derog* a person who lives in the suburbs

sub·ur·bi·a /səˈbɜːbiə‖-ɜːr-/ *n* [U] *often derog* (the behaviour, opinions, and ways of living typical of people who live in) the suburbs

sub·urbs /ˈsʌbɜːbz‖-ɜːr-/ ‖ also **burbs** *AmE infml*— [*the*+P] the area on the edge of a city, where most people live, as opposed to the shopping and business centre.

▶ CULTURAL NOTE In Britain and the US, the suburbs are generally thought of as an area where middle-class families live. They are also thought of as being dull and unimaginative: *a semi-detached house in the suburbs of Manchester*◀

sub·ven·tion /səb'venʃən/ n fml a SUBSIDY or gift of money for a special use

sub·ver·sive[1] /səb'vɜːsɪv‖-ɜːr-/ adj (dangerous because) trying or likely to destroy established ideas and take power away from those at present in control, esp. secretly: *The government is trying to ban this magazine because it prints subversive ideas.* | *a subversive influence* – ~ ly adv – ~ness n [U]

subversive[2] n a subversive person

sub·vert /səb'vɜːt‖-ɜːrt/ v [T] fml to try to destroy the power and influence of (a government, an established system, etc.) – -version /səb'vɜːʃən‖-'vɜːrʒən/ n [U]

sub·way /'sʌbweɪ/ n 1 BrE ‖ underpass AmE– a path under a road or railway by which it can be safely crossed 2 AmE for UNDERGROUND railway –compare METRO, TUBE (4)

suc·ceed /sək'siːd/ v 1 [I (in)] to do what one has tried or wanted to do: *If you try hard you'll succeed.* | *Police have finally succeeded in solving the mystery.* | *The first time she took the exam she failed, but the second time she succeeded (in passing).* | (fig., humor) *I tried to pick all the bottles up together, but succeeded only in dropping* (=failed and dropped) *all of them.* scc COULD (USAGE) 2 [I] to be done or completed as one had wished, with a favourable result: *I don't think his later novels succeed as well as his earlier ones.* | *Our plan succeeded, and soon we were in complete control.* 3 [I] to do well in life, esp. in gaining high position or popularity: *She's the type of person who succeeds anywhere.* 4 [I (to);T (as)] to be the next to take a position or rank (after): *When the duke dies, his eldest son will succeed to the title.* | *Lord Davis succeeded Sir Hugh as chairman of the commission.* 5 [T] fml to follow; come after: *A silence succeeded his words.* | *The company are developing a new generation of computers to succeed their existing range.* 6 **If at first you don't succeed, try, try, and try again** an old saying

suc·cess /sək'ses/ n 1 [U (in)] a degree of succeeding; a good result: *Did you have any success* (=did you succeed) *in persuading her to change her mind?* | *His career has been a real success story; from office boy to millionaire in five years.* | *We tried to get them to agree, but without much success.* | *a low success rate* 2 [C] a person or thing that succeeds or has succeeded: *His new book/play was a great success/an overnight success.* | *She's just started up a new company; I hope she makes a success of it.* | *In spite of our doubts, the new secretary has proved a great success.*

suc·cess·ful /sək'sesfəl/ adj 1 [(in)] having done what one has tried to do: *Were you successful* (=did you succeed) *in persuading him to change his mind?* | *I'm afraid my attempt to make a cake wasn't very successful.* | *a very successful performance* | *successful peace talks* 2 having gained a high position in life, one's job, etc.: *They're advertising luxury apartments ideal for the successful young executive.* –opposite **unsuccessful** – ~ ly adv

suc·ces·sion /sək'seʃən/ n 1 [U] the act of following one after the other: *The days followed each other in quick/close succession and still no news came.* | *It happened four times in succession.* (=successively) 2 [S (of)+sing./pl. v] a number of people or things following each other closely: *A succession of visitors came to the door.* 3 [U (to)] the act of succeeding (SUCCEED (4)) to an office or position: *In the event of the heir's death, the succession passes to his brother.* | *her succession to the throne* –compare ACCESSION

suc·ces·sive /sək'sesɪv/ adj following each other closely: *It happened on two successive days.* | *successive waves of invaders* – ~ ly adv

suc·ces·sor /sək'sesər/ n 1 [(as, to)] a person who takes an office or position formerly held by someone else: *My successor as chairman takes over next week.* 2 fml a person or thing that comes after another: *The transistor seemed astounding enough when it was introduced, but its successor, the microchip, is immeasurably more powerful.* –compare PREDECESSOR

success sto·ry /·'·· ·, ··/ n (an account of) a person's development from being poor and unknown to being rich, famous, and successful

suc·cinct /sək'sɪŋkt/ adj apprec clearly expressed in few words: *a very succinct explanation/style* – ~ ly adv – ~ness n [U]

suc·co·tash /'sʌkətæʃ/ n [U] AmE a dish made from CORN and LIMA BEANS cooked together

suc·cour[1] BrE ‖ **-cor** AmE /'sʌkər/ n [U] fml or lit help given to someone in difficulty

succour[2] BrE ‖ **-cor** AmE– v [T] fml or lit to help (someone in difficulty): *succouring the needy*

suc·cu·bus /'sʌkjʊbəs/ n -bi /baɪ/ a female devil supposed to have sex with a sleeping man –compare INCUBUS

suc·cu·lent[1] /'sʌkjʊlənt/ adj 1 apprec juicy: *a succulent steak* 2 tech (of a plant) having thick soft leaves or stems that can hold a lot of liquid –**-lence** n [U]

succulent[2] n tech a SUCCULENT[1] (2) plant, such as a CACTUS

suc·cumb /sə'kʌm/ v [I (to)] fml 1 to stop opposing; give in (to greater strength or force, a desire, etc.): *After an artillery bombardment lasting several days the town finally succumbed.* | *They held out for some hours in the face of our persuasive offers, but eventually they succumbed.* | *to succumb to temptation/blackmail* 2 to die (because of): *He finally succumbed to the illness.*

such[1] /sʌtʃ/ predeterminer, determiner 1 (sometimes with as) of that kind; of the same kind; like that: *People such as him/Such people as him shouldn't be allowed in here.* | *The regulations apply to all such hospitals.* (=all hospitals of the type described) | *We've planted lots of different flowers, such as* (=for example) *roses, carnations, and poppies.* | *He said "Get out!" or* **some such** *rude remark.* | *"Can I speak to Alice Smith?" "No such person* (=no one called Alice Smith) *lives here."* 2 (sometimes with **as** or **that**) so great; so good, bad, or unusual: *He's such a kind man.* (=he is very kind) | *She tells such funny jokes.* | *It was such a lovely day we decided to go for a picnic.* | *It wasn't such a hard exam after all.* | (fml) *The force of the explosion was such that it blew out all the windows/was such as to blow out all the windows.* | *The explosion blew out all the windows, such was its force.* 3 **such** ... **as** fml any that: *Such accommodation as she could find was expensive.* 4 **such as it is/they are** although it/they may not be worth much: *You can borrow my exam notes, such as they are.* (=they are not very good) –compare **for what it's worth** (WORTH[1])

▷ USAGE In general, **such** comes before nouns, or before adjectives followed by nouns. **So** comes before adjectives alone, or before *much, many, few.* Compare **such** and **so** in these examples: **a** *It was* **such** *an interesting meeting.* | *The meeting was* **so** *interesting.* **b** *There were* **such** *a lot of people.* | *There were* **so** *many people.* **c** *It was* **such** *a shock.* | *It was* **so** *shocking.* But note also these patterns: *His courage was* **such** *that* ... | *His courage was* **so** *great that* ... **such** *a nice man;* also **so** *nice a man* (fml).◁

such[2] pron 1 fml that thing, fact, or action: *We had predicted a Welsh victory, and such indeed was the result.* 2 **and such** fml and SUCHLIKE[2] 3 **as such** properly so named; in the exact meaning of the stated thing: *It's not an agreement as such, but it will have virtually the same effect as one.* 4 **such as** fml any people or things that; those that: *Such (of you) as wish to leave may do so.*

such and such /'·· ·, ·/ predeterminer infml a certain (time, amount, etc.) not named: *If they tell you to come on such and such a day, don't agree if it's not convenient.*

such·like[1] /'sʌtʃlaɪk/ adj [A] of that kind; similar: *tennis and cricket and suchlike summer sports*

suchlike[2] pron infml things of that kind: *Do you enjoy plays, films, and suchlike?*

Su·chou /ˌsuː'tʃaʊ/ see SUZHOU

suck[1] /sʌk/ v 1 [I;T] to draw (liquid) into the mouth by using the tongue, lips, and muscles at the side of the mouth, with the lips tightened into a small hole: *a baby sucking at its mother's breast* | *She was sucking milk through a straw.* 2 [I (AWAY, at); T] to hold (something) in the mouth and move one's tongue against it, esp. so as to melt and eat it: *He was sucking (away at) a sweet.* | *The baby was sucking its thumb.* 3 [T+obj+adv/prep] to draw powerfully: *They fell overboard into the sea, and the powerful currents sucked them under.* | (fig.) *Britain's high interest rates are sucking in a lot of foreign money.* | (fig.) *Gullible people can easily get sucked into dishonest schemes by unscrupulous tricksters.* 4 [I] AmE sl not polite to be extremely disagreeable or unacceptable: *This film really sucks.*

suck up phr v [I (to)] BrE infml derog to try to make

oneself liked, esp. by unnaturally nice behaviour to someone: *She's always sucking up to her teacher.*

suck² *n* an act of sucking: *He had a suck of his ice lolly.*

suck·er /'sʌkəʳ/ *n* **1** a person or thing that sucks **2** an organ by which an animal can hold on to a surface: *This fly has suckers on its feet.* **3** a flat piece of soft material, e.g. rubber, which sticks to a surface by SUCTION: *You stick this hook to the wall with a sucker, then hang something from it.* **4** a piece of new plant growth coming out through the ground from the root or lower stem of a plant **5** [(for)] *infml* **a** a person who is easily deceived or tricked: *You're a sucker to believe his stories!* **b** someone who likes the stated thing so much that they cannot refuse it: *I'm a sucker for ice cream.* | *He's a sucker for beautiful women.* (=is so attracted by them that they can easily take advantage of his fondness) **6** *AmE for* LOLLIPOP

sucking pig /'·· ·/ also **suckling pig—** *n* [C;U] (a) young pig still taking milk from its mother, esp. as cooked and eaten on special occasions

suck·le /'sʌkəl/ *v* [I;T] **a** to feed (a baby or young animal) with milk from the breast: *a sheep suckling her lamb* **b** (of a baby or young animal) to suck milk from the breast (of) —compare BREAST-FEED, NURSE² (3)

suck·ling /'sʌklɪŋ/ *n lit or old use* a young human or animal still taking milk from the mother

su·crose /'suːkrəʊz, 'sjuː-/ *n* [U] *tech* the common form of sugar

suc·tion /'sʌkʃən/ *n* [U] the act of removing air or liquid from a container or from between two surfaces so that either **a** another gas or liquid enters or **b** the two surfaces stick together because of the pressure of the air outside: *Dirt and dust are drawn into a vacuum cleaner by suction.* | *It's stuck to the wall with a suction cap BrE‖cup AmE.* (=a small usu. round piece of rubber or plastic that works by suction)

suction pump /'··· ·/ *n* a pump which works by removing air to make a VACUUM, so that the material to be pumped is sucked in

Su·dan /suˈdæn, -ˈdɑːn/ [*the*] a country in NE Africa, the largest country in Africa; capital Khartoum; population 24,485,000 (1989)

Su·dan·ese /ˌsuːdəˈniːz◂/ *n* [*the* +P] people from the Sudan —**Sudanese** *adj*

sud·den /'sʌdn/ *adj* **1** happening, coming, or done quickly and unexpectedly: *a sudden illness* | *a sudden change of plan* | *a sudden sharp increase in the cost of oil* | *This marriage is very sudden — they've only known each other a few weeks.* **2 all of a sudden** *infml* suddenly **— —ly** *adv* : *I suddenly remembered that I hadn't locked the door.* | *We were talking on the phone when, suddenly, the line went dead.* **— ~ness** *n* [U]

sudden death /ˌ·· ·/ *n* [U] an additional period of play in a sport to decide which player or team is the winner. The sudden death ends as soon as one player or team gains the lead: *Nick Faldo won the Open golf championship after a sudden death play-off.*

Sudden In·fant Death Syn·drome /ˌ·· ˌ·· ·· ˌ··/ also **SIDS—** *n* [U] *tech* a formal name for COT DEATH

Su·de·ten·land /suːˈdeɪtənlænd/ [*the*] an area in N Czechoslovakia which was taken over by Germany under Hitler in 1938, just before the Second World War

suds /sʌdz/ also **soapsuds—** *n* [P] the mass of small balls of air (BUBBLEs) formed on the top of soapy water —**sudsy** *adj*

sue /sjuː‖suː/ *v* [I;T (for)] to make a legal claim (against), esp. for an amount of money, because of some loss or damage that one has suffered: *If you don't return our property, we'll sue.* | *He was sued for* (=because of) *libel|malpractice|breach of contract.* | *I'll sue them for* (=in order to get) *every penny they've got.*

▶CULTURAL NOTE Suing is esp. common in the US. One may sue a doctor who has not given proper treatment. Employees may sue their employers for **workmen's compensation** if they have an accident at work. One may sue a driver who has caused a traffic accident. Even a homeowner can be sued if a visitor falls and gets hurt due to the owner's carelessness. ◀

sue for sthg. *phr v* [I] *fml* to beg or ask for: *The other side realize they are beaten, and are suing for peace.*

suede , suède /sweɪd/ *n* [U] soft leather with a rough surface: *suede shoes*

Sue El·len /ˌsuː ˈelən/ a character in the American television SERIES *Dallas*, the wife of JR Ewing, known for drinking and crying a lot

su·et /'suːɪt, 'sjuːɪt‖'suː-/ *n* [U] hard fat from round an animal's KIDNEYs, used in cooking **— ~y** *adj*

suet pud·ding /ˌ·· ˈ··/ *n* a sweet dish made with fruit and suet and usu. steamed, considered to be a TRADITIONAL British dish and now thought by many people to be too heavy and filling

Su·ez /'suːɪz‖ˌsuːˈez◂/ a port in NE Egypt, at the S end of the Suez Canal

Suez Ca·nal /ˌ·· ·ˈ·/ [*the*] a CANAL in NE Egypt which joins the Mediterranean Sea with the Gulf of Suez and the Red Sea. It is an important path for the shipping trade.

Suez Cri·sis /ˌ·· ˌ··‖ˌ·ˈ·· ˌ··/ [*the*] an event in 1956 in which Britain and France sent ships and soldiers to the area around the Suez Canal after Egypt had declared that it was going to NATIONALIZE the canal. The United Nations and many countries in the world opposed Britain's action, and the ships and soldiers left later in the year. It was seen by many British people as a serious defeat for Britain and a sign that Britain was no longer an important world power.

suf·fer /'sʌfəʳ/ *v* **1** [I (for)] to experience pain, difficulty, or loss: *He died very quickly; he didn't suffer much.* | *She was very generous to him but she suffered for it when he ran away with all her money.* | *If the factory closes, the other local businesses are bound to suffer too.* **2** [T] to experience or have to deal with (something painful or unpleasant): *If you break the law, you must be prepared to suffer the consequences.* | *The army suffered heavy losses* (=many soldiers were killed) *in the battle.* | *She suffered multiple injuries in the car accident.* | *He suffered the humiliation of being forced to resign.* | *to suffer a defeat|a setback* —see also SUFFER **from 3** [I] to become gradually worse; lessen in quality, esp. through lack of care and attention: *He started drinking a lot and his work suffered.* **4** [T] *fml* to accept without dislike or complaint; TOLERATE: *He doesn't* **suffer fools (gladly).** **5** [T+obj+to-v] *old use* to allow —see also LONGSUFFERING

suffer from sthg. *phr v* [T] to experience (something unpleasant, such as an illness), esp. over a long period of time or habitually: *She suffers from headaches.* | *Our business has suffered from lack of investment.*

suf·fer·ance /'sʌfərəns/ *n* **on sufferance** *fml* with permission, though not welcomed: *He's here on sufferance.*

suf·fer·er /'sʌfərəʳ/ *n* a person who suffers, esp. from the stated illness: *headache sufferers*

suf·fer·ing /'sʌfərɪŋ/ *n* [C;U] (an experience of) pain and difficulty generally: *the suffering of innocent people caused by war* | *She bore her sufferings bravely.*

suf·fice /səˈfaɪs/ *v* [*not in progressive forms*] *fml* **1** [I (for)] to be enough; provide what is needed: *Her income suffices for her needs.* **2** [T] (esp. of food) to be enough for; satisfy: *Some bread and soup will suffice me.* **3 suffice it to say (that)** *rather pomp* (used for suggesting that the short statement which follows is enough to express one's meaning): *I could mention other examples of your bad work, but suffice it to say that your performance has been unsatisfactory.*

suf·fi·cien·cy /səˈfɪʃənsi/ *n fml* **1** [U] the state of being or having enough **2** [S (of)] a supply which is enough

suf·fi·cient /səˈfɪʃənt/ *adj* [(for)] *rather fml* enough; as much as is needed for a purpose: *There was sufficient food for everybody.* [+to-v] *There were sufficient supplies to feed everybody.* | *There wasn't much food but it was sufficient for our needs.* | *We haven't got sufficient information from which to draw a conclusion.* —opposite **insufficient**; see ADEQUATE (USAGE), ENOUGH (USAGE)

suf·fix /'sʌfɪks/ *n* an AFFIX² added to the end of a word (as in kind*ness*, quick*ly*) —compare PREFIX¹ (1)

suf·fo·cate /'sʌfəkeɪt/ *v* [I;T] to (cause to) die because of lack of air: *The baby suffocated under its pillow.* | (fig.) *Open a window; I'm suffocating in here!* (=because there is not enough fresh air) | (fig.) *the suffocating effect of so many rules and regulations* **—cation** /ˌsʌfəˈkeɪʃən/ *n* [U]

Suf·folk /'sʌfək/ a COUNTY on the E coast of SE England

suf·fra·gan /'sʌfrəgən/ *adj* [A; after *n*] (of a BISHOP) helping a bishop of higher rank in his work: *the suffragan bishop of Colchester | the bishop suffragan*

suf·frage /ˈsʌfrɪdʒ/ n [U] the right to vote in national elections.

▶ CULTURAL NOTE In Britain, women were first given the right to vote in 1918. In the US, black people were given the right to vote in 1868 by the **14th Amendment** to the CONSTITUTION. Women were given suffrage in 1920 by the **19th Amendment**: *When was* **universal suffrage** (= the right of everyone to vote) *introduced in your country?*◀

suf·fra·gette /ˌsʌfrəˈdʒet/ n (in Britain and the US in the early 20th century) a woman who was a member of a group that tried to obtain for women the right to vote, esp. by acts which brought public attention to their demands. In Britain, the suffragettes are remembered esp. for tying themselves to fences outside official buildings in London as a means of protest. —see also Emmeline PANKHURST

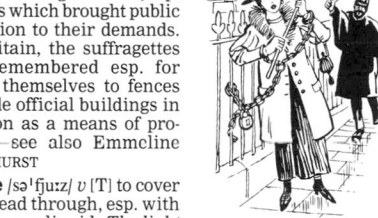
suffragette

suf·fuse /səˈfjuːz/ v [T] to cover or spread through, esp. with a colour or liquid: *The light of the setting sun suffused the clouds.* —**fusion** /səˈfjuːʒən/ n [U]

sug·ar¹ /ˈʃʊgəʳ/ n 1 [U] a sweet white or brown substance which is obtained from plants, esp. SUGARCANE and BEET, and used in food and drinks: *Do you take sugar in your coffee?* 2 [C] *tech* any of several sweet substances formed in plants —compare GLUCOSE 3 *infml, esp. AmE* (used when speaking to someone you like, usu. by a man to a woman) 4 **sugar and spice and everything nice** a phrase from a NURSERY RHYME (=an old song or poem for children) saying what little girls are made of

sugar² v [T] 1 to put sugar in; sweeten: *Did you sugar my tea?* 2 **sugar the pill** to make something seem less unpleasant

sugar beet /ˈ·· ·/ n [U] BEET (1)

sug·ar·cane /ˈʃʊgəkeɪn‖-ər-/ n [U] a tall upright tropical plant from whose stems sugar (**cane sugar**) is obtained

sugar-coat·ed /ˌ·· ˈ··◂/ adj covered with sugar

sugar dad·dy /ˈ·· ·‚·/ n *infml, usu. derog* an older man who provides a young woman with money and presents in return for sex or companionship

sugared al·mond /ˌ·· ˈ··/ n a sweet made of a whole ALMOND (=type of nut) covered with hard (coloured) sugar

Sug·ar·loaf Moun·tain /ˌʃʊgələʊf ˈmaʊntᵻn‖-gər-/ a mountain in Rio de Janeiro in SE Brazil

sugar lump /ˈ·· ·/ n a square piece of solid sugar

sugar ma·ple /ˈ·· ‚·/ n a kind of MAPLE tree that grows in the NE of the US. Liquid (SAP) taken from the tree is used as MAPLE SYRUP.

sug·ar·y /ˈʃʊgəri/ adj 1 containing sugar or tasting of sugar 2 *derog* too sweet, nice, kind, etc., in an insincere way: *poems full of sugary sentiments about love*

sug·gest /səˈdʒest‖səgˈdʒest/ v [T] 1 to mention as a possibility; state as an idea for consideration; PROPOSE: *I'd like to suggest an alternative plan.* [+v-ing|(that)] *I suggest leaving now|that we leave now.* [+wh-] *Can you suggest how we should do it?* 2 to give signs (of); make clear, perhaps indirectly; INDICATE: *Her expression suggested anger.* | *The disorganized meeting suggested a lack of proper planning.* [+that] *The latest figures suggest that business is improving.* 3 to cause (a new idea) to appear or form in the mind: *The sight of the vultures suggested the idea for his new horror film.*

sug·ges·ti·ble /səˈdʒestᵻbəl‖səg-/ adj (of people) easily influenced: *a suggestible child* | *She's at a suggestible age.*

sug·ges·tion /səˈdʒestʃən‖səg-/ n 1 [C] something suggested: *Your suggestions are unworkable.* | *I'd like to make|offer a suggestion.* [+that] *He rejected my suggestion that we should appoint Roger.* —see REFUSE (USAGE) 2 [U] the act of suggesting: **At your suggestion** (=as you suggested) *I planted the tree over there.* 3 [S+of] a slight

sign; TRACE: *I detected a suggestion of malice in his remarks.* 4 [S+of|that; *usu. in questions and negatives*] even an unlikely possibility: *There's never been any suggestion of his being allowed|that he will be allowed out of prison.* 5 [U] (in PSYCHOLOGY) an indirect way of causing an idea to be accepted by the mind, e.g. by HYPNOTISM

sug·ges·tive /səˈdʒestɪv‖səg-/ adj 1 which shows or seems to show thoughts of sex: *suggestive remarks* 2 [F+of] *fml* which leads the mind into a particular way of thinking: *It's an abstract painting suggestive of a desert landscape.* —**ly** adv: *"Do you want to come upstairs?" she said suggestively.*

Su·har·to /suːˈhɑːtəʊ‖-ɑːr-/, **T N J** (1921–) an army general who became president of Indonesia in 1967

su·i·cid·al /ˌsuːᵻˈsaɪdl◂, ˌsjuː-‖ˌsuː-/ adj 1 [*no comp.*] of or with a tendency to suicide: *a hospital ward for suicidal patients* 2 wishing to kill oneself: *I was feeling positively suicidal.* 3 likely to lead to death or destruction: *They made a suicidal attempt to climb the mountain in terrible weather.* | *suicidal driving* — **ly** adv

su·i·cide /ˈsuːᵻsaɪd, ˈsjuː-‖ˈsuː-/ n 1 [C;U] the act of killing oneself: *She tried to* **commit suicide**. | *The doctors pumped out her stomach after her attempted suicide.*

▶ CULTURAL NOTE In Britain and most American states it is not against the law to kill yourself, or to attempt suicide, but it is a crime to encourage or help someone else to do so, even if they want to do it and ask for your help.◀

2 [C] *law* a person who does this 3 [U] a course of action that destroys one's position: *It would be political suicide to hold an election now.*

suicide pact /ˈ··· ‚·/ n an arrangement between two or more people to commit suicide at the same time

suits

single-breasted suit   double-breasted suit

suit¹ /suːt, sjuːt‖suːt/ n 1 a a set of clothes made of the same material, usu. including a short coat (JACKET) with trousers or a skirt: *a dark|tweed suit* b (*usu. in comb.*) a garment or set of garments for a special purpose: *a swim suit* | *a spacesuit* (=for travelling through space) | *the knight's* **suit of armour** —see also WETSUIT 2 any of the four sets of cards used in games —see also MAJOR SUIT; see CARDS (USAGE) 3 a LAWSUIT 4 *old use* the act of asking a woman to marry (esp. in the phrases **plead/press one's suit**) 5 (**not**) **one's strong(est) suit** (not) one's best quality or what one is good at: *Politeness is not his strong suit.* —see also LONG SUIT, **in one's birthday suit** (BIRTHDAY), **follow suit** (FOLLOW)

suit² v [T] 1 to satisfy or please; be acceptable or convenient for: *"Will it suit you if I come around at three?" "Yes, that'll suit me fine."* | *He can be very charming when it suits him.* (=when it is to his advantage) 2 [*no pass.*] to match or look good on (someone): *That colour doesn't suit her.* 3 to have the right qualities or be of the right kind for; be APPROPRIATE for: *That song doesn't suit her voice.* | *These clothes aren't really suited to a tropical climate.* | *Jane and Steve are ideally suited (to each other).* 4 **suit oneself** *infml* to do what one likes, esp. when that is different from what other people are doing: *"I don't really feel like going out tonight." "Suit yourself."* 5 **suit someone down to the ground** to be very pleasing or very suitable for someone: *Mary's new job suits her down to the ground.* 6 **suit someone's book** *BrE infml* to suit someone's plans

suit sthg. to sthg. *phr v* [T] *fml* to make something suitable for; ADAPT to: *to suit the punishment to the crime*

sui·ta·bil·i·ty /ˌsuːtəˈbɪlᵻti, ˌsjuː-‖ˌsuː-/ n [U (**for**)] the fact or degree of being suitable: *There's no doubt about her suitability for the job.*

sui·ta·ble /ˈsuːtəbəl, ˈsjuː-‖ˈsuː-/ adj [(**for, to**)] of the right type or quality for (a particular person, purpose, etc.): *Is she suitable for the job?* | *a suitable school for the children* | *(fml) a residence suitable to his important position* [+to-v] *Is this a suitable moment to break for a cup of coffee?* —opposite **unsuitable** — ~**ness** n [U] —**bly** adv : *I pointed it out to her, and she looked suitably ashamed of herself.*

suit·case /ˈsuːtkeɪs, ˈsjuːt-‖ˈsuːt-/ also **case**— n a large container for carrying clothes and possessions when travelling, often in the form of a flat box: *Remember to label your suitcase before you go to the airport.*

suite /swiːt/ n **1** a set of matching furniture for a room: *a* **three-piece suite** (=a SETTEE and two chairs) | *a suite of dining-room furniture* | *a pink bathroom suite* (=a bath, TOILET, and WASHBASIN) **2** [(**of**)] a set of expensive rooms in a hotel: *She always has a suite at the Ritz when she comes to town.* **3** a piece of music with several loosely connected parts **4** [+sing./pl. v] the people who work for, advise, or help an important person: *the President and his suite* —see also RETINUE **5** [(**of**)] a group of related computer PROGRAMS which make up a set: *a full suite of business software including a word processing program and a spreadsheet*

suit·ing /ˈsuːtɪŋ, ˈsjuː-‖ˈsuː-/ n [U] tech material, esp. woven wool, for (men's) clothing

sui·tor /ˈsuːtəʳ, ˈsjuː-‖ˈsuː-/ n esp. old use a man wishing to marry a particular woman

su·ki·ya·ki /ˌsuːki ˈjɑːki/ n [U] a Japanese dish consisting of thin slices (SLICE) of meat, vegetables, etc. cooked in SOY SAUCE with sugar and Japanese rice wine (SAKE)

Suk·koth /ˈsʊkəʊt, -kəʊθ/ also **Feast of Tabernacles**— a Jewish FESTIVAL which celebrates the gathering of the crops, and remembers the time in Jewish history when small shelters (**sukkahs**) were made by the Jews when they were in the WILDERNESS

Sul·ei·man I /ˌsʊliˌmɑːn əʊ ˈfɜːst‖-ˈfɜːrst/ (?1494–1566) a Turkish ruler, also known as **Suleiman the Magnificent**, who greatly improved the Ottoman Empire in its government and CULTURE

sul·fa drug /ˈsʌlfə drʌg/ AmE for SULPHA DRUG

sul·fate /ˈsʌlfeɪt/ AmE for SULPHATE

sul·fide /ˈsʌlfaɪd/ AmE for SULPHIDE

sul·fur /ˈsʌlfəʳ/ AmE for SULPHUR

sulk /sʌlk/ v [I] (esp. of children) to be silently bad-tempered, esp. for an unimportant reason: *The little boy sulked because he couldn't go to the circus.*

sulks /sʌlks/ n [the+P] BrE a state of silent bad temper (esp. in the phrases **have/be in a fit of the sulks**)

sulk·y /ˈsʌlki/ adj **1** showing that one is sulking: *a sulky frown* **2** tending to sulk: *a sulky child* —**ily** adv —**iness** n [U]

sul·len /ˈsʌlən/ adj **1** silently showing dislike or bad temper: *a look of sullen resentment* | *She's rather sullen.* **2** esp. lit (of the sky or weather) dark and unpleasant; GLOOMY — ~**ly** adv — ~**ness** n [U]

Sul·li·van /ˈsʌlɪvən/, **Sir Arthur** (1842–1900) an English COMPOSER known esp. for working with WS Gilbert to write COMIC OPERAS such as *The Gondoliers* and *HMS Pinafore*

Sullivan, Ed /ed/ (1902–74) an American entertainer who ran the *Ed Sullivan Show*, which started on television in 1948 and continued until the 1960s. The show was esp. popular with older people. Sullivan brought many MUSICIANS and COMEDIANS onto his show and it helped many of them to become famous. Many older Americans first saw the Beatles and the Rolling Stones on his show and this helped them to become popular in the US.

Sullivan, Louis Henry (1856–1924) an American ARCHITECT who worked in Chicago, building SKYSCRAPERS such as the Wainwright Building

Sul·lom Voe /ˌsʌləm ˈvəʊ/ the name of the largest oil TERMINAL in the Shetland islands in the north of Scotland

sul·ly /ˈsʌli/ v [T] fml or lit to spoil or reduce the (high) value or perfection of: *a scandal that sullied his reputation*

sul·pha drug BrE‖-fa- AmE /ˈsʌlfə drʌg/ also **sul·phon·a·mide** BrE‖-fon- AmE /sʌlˈfɒnəmaɪd‖-ˈfɑː-/ n any of a group of drugs used against diseases caused by bacteria

sul·phate BrE ‖ -fate AmE /ˈsʌlfeɪt/ n [C;U] a SALT¹ (2) formed from sulphuric acid: *copper sulphate*

sul·phide BrE ‖ -fide AmE /ˈsʌlfaɪd/ n [C;U] a mixture of sulphur with another substance: *sulphide of arsenic*

sul·phur BrE ‖ -fur AmE /ˈsʌlfəʳ/ n [U] a simple substance (ELEMENT) that is found in different forms, esp. as a light yellow powder

sulphur di·ox·ide /ˌ··· ·ˈ··/ n [U] a heavy poisonous gas that is a cause of air POLLUTION in industrial areas

sul·phu·ric ac·id BrE‖-fu- AmE /sʌlˌfjʊərɪk ˈæsɨd/ n [U] a powerful acid —see also VITRIOL

sul·phu·rous BrE ‖ -fu- AmE /ˈsʌlfərəs/ adj of, like, or with sulphur

sul·tan /ˈsʌltən/ n (often cap.) a ruler in some Muslim countries, esp. in former times

sul·ta·na /sʌlˈtɑːnə‖-ˈtænə/ n **1** a small seedless kind of RAISIN (=dried fruit) used in cakes, etc. **2** (often cap.) the wife, mother, or daughter of a sultan

sul·tan·ate /ˈsʌltəneɪt, -nɨt/ n **1** a country ruled by a sultan: *the sultanate of Oman* **2** the position of a sultan or the period of a sultan's rule

sul·try /ˈsʌltri/ adj **1** (of weather) hot, airless, and uncomfortable **2** (esp. of a woman or her appearance) causing or showing strong sexual attraction or desire: *a sultry look/smile* —**triness** n [U]

sum¹ /sʌm/ n **1** [C (**of**)] an amount (of money): *I had to spend a large sum/large sums of money to get it back.* | *The company was sold for an undisclosed sum.* | *(humor) It cost me* **the princely sum of £2.** (=It only cost me £2.) —see also LUMP SUM **2** [C] esp. BrE a simple calculation, by adding, multiplying, dividing, etc.: *learning to do sums at school* **3** [the+S (**of**)] the total produced when numbers, amounts, etc., are added together: *The sum of 6 and 4 is 10.* **4** [the+S (**of**)] SUM TOTAL **5 do one's sums** to calculate whether one has enough money for something: *Well, I've done my sums, and I think I can manage a holiday this year.* **6 in sum** fml in simple words; in a short phrase: *It was, in sum, a complete failure.*

sum² v

sum up phr v **-mm-** **1** [I;T (=**sum** sthg.↔**up**)] to give a statement of the main points of (a report, a speech, a trial, etc.); SUMMARIZE: *The last section sums up all the arguments on either side.* | *So,* **to sum up** (=this is a statement of the main points), *we've got to pay more attention to profitability and cost control.* | *At the end of the trial, the judge summed up.* —see also SUMMING-UP **2** [T] (**sum** sbdy./sthg.↔**up**) to consider and form a judgment of: *She summed up the situation at a glance.*

Su·ma·tra /sʊˈmɑːtrə/ the second largest island of Indonesia, formerly a Dutch COLONY —**Sumatran** adj,n

Su·mer /ˈsuːməʳ/ the southern part of ancient Mesopotamia, where one of the world's oldest civilizations lived. The people are believed to have invented CUNEIFORM writing and vehicles with wheels.

Su·me·ri·an /sʊˈmɪəriən‖-ˈmeər-/ adj of the people, language, art, etc. of Sumer —**Sumerian** n

sum·ma cum lau·de /ˌsʌmə kʌm ˈlɔːdi, -ˈlaʊdeɪ‖ˌsʊmə kʊm ˈlaʊdi/ adj, adv AmE the highest HONOURS (2) given to American university or college students when they finish their studies —see also DEGREE (CULTURAL NOTE) compare CUM LAUDE

sum·mar·ize also **-ise** BrE /ˈsʌməraɪz/ v [I;T] to make a short general statement of the main points of (something longer or more detailed): *She summarized the aims of the new party in a couple of sentences.*

sum·ma·ry¹ /ˈsʌməri/ n [(**of**)] a short account giving the main points: *Write me a one-page summary of this report.* | *a news summary*

summary² adj fml done at once without attention to formal rules or details, or, in the case of punishments, without considering forgiveness: *summary justice* —**rily** /ˈsʌmərɨli‖sʌˈme-/ adv : *He was summarily dismissed.*

sum·mat /ˈsʌmət/ pron BrE dial something: *Summat's up.* (=something is wrong; there is a problem)

sum·ma·tion /sʌˈmeɪʃən/ n fml **1** a summary; SUMMING-UP **2** a total

sum·mer¹ /ˈsʌməʳ/ n **1** [C;U] the season between spring and autumn; the part of the year when the sun is hottest and the days are longest: *I go on holiday in summer/in* **high summer.** (=the warmest time) | *a hot summer* | *last* summer | the summer of 1940 | summer dresses   **2** [C usu. pl.] old use or lit a year of one's age: He looked younger than his 70 summers. —see also INDIAN SUMMER

summer² v [I+adv/prep] rare to spend the summer

Summer, Don·na /ˈdɒnə‖ˈdɑː-/ (1948–) an American popular music singer

Summer Bank Hol·i·day /ˌ··· · ˈ···/ [the] (in England and Wales) a bank holiday on a Monday at the end of August

summer camp /ˈ·· ˌ·/ n [C;U] (in the US) a place where children can stay for a short time in tents or huts during the summer holidays and learn outdoor skills such as swimming, boating, and how to make a fire

summer hol·i·days /ˌ·· ˈ···/ n [P] a holiday taken during the summer. British people usu. take their main holiday in the summer, esp. in August, and many people go away for one or two weeks, often to a place by the sea, either in Britain or abroad.

sum·mer·house /ˈsʌməhaʊs‖-ər-/ n **-houses** /ˌhaʊzˌz/ a small building in a garden, with seats in the shade

summer of dis·con·tent /ˌ··· · ˌ·ˈ·/ [the] the summer of 1989 when there were a lot of STRIKES² (1) in Britain at the same time —see also WINTER OF DISCONTENT

summer pud·ding /ˌ·· ˈ··/ n [C,U] a TRADITIONAL British sweet dish made from pieces of bread and summer fruits such as berries, which are left to mix together in a bowl before serving, and then turned out in the shape of the bowl

summer school /ˈ·· ·/ n [C;U] a course of lessons, talks, etc., arranged in addition to the year's work in a university, college, or school after the start of the summer holiday

summer sol·stice /ˌ·· ˈ··/ [the] the day, usu. around June 22nd, when the sun is above the TROPIC OF CANCER and as far to the North as possible, so that places in the N HEMISPHERE, like Britain, have the longest day of the year and places in the S hemisphere have the shortest day of the year. The summer solstice is not usu. celebrated in Britain or the US, but in Britain a few people, esp. Druids, do celebrate it by watching the sun rise on that day at Stonehenge. —compare EQUINOX, WINTER SOLSTICE

sum·mer·time /ˈsʌmətaɪm‖-ər-/ n [(the) U] the season of summer; the time of hot weather

sum·mer·y /ˈsʌməri/ adj of, like, or suitable for summer: girls in light summery dresses

summing-up /ˌ·· ˈ·/ n **summings-up** a SUMMARY, esp. one given by the judge at the end of a trial —see also SUM **up**

sum·mit /ˈsʌmˌt/ n **1** [C (of)] the top of a mountain: The climbers reached the summit of Mount Everest yesterday morning. —compare PEAK¹ (1) and see picture at MOUNTAIN **2** [the+S (of)] fml the highest point, degree, etc.: the summit of scientific achievement **3** [C] a meeting between heads of government: the recent Geneva summit | a summit meeting

sum·mon /ˈsʌmən/ v [T] fml **1** to order officially to come: He was summoned to the palace/summoned into the presence of the Queen. [+obj+to-v] He was summoned to appear before the revolutionary court. **2** to tell or request people to come to; CONVENE: to summon a meeting

summon sthg. ↔ **up** phr v [T] to bring (a quality) out of oneself, esp. with an effort: She had to summon up all her strength to lift the rock.

sum·mons¹ /ˈsʌmənz/ n **-monses** an order to appear in a court of law: They **served a summons on** him. (=ordered him to appear in court)

summons² v [T usu. pass.] to give a summons to; order to appear in court: The witness was summonsed.

su·mo /ˈsuːməʊ/ also **sumo wrest·ling** /ˌ·· ˈ··/— n [U] a Japanese form of wrestling (WRESTLE), involving special ceremonies as well as entertainment, in which two men try to force each other to the ground or out of a ring marked on the floor. The men (**sumo wrestlers**) are known for their great size and strength, and the sport is taken very seriously in Japan.

sump /sʌmp/ n **1** BrE, ‖ **oil pan** AmE— a part of an engine that holds the supply of oil **2** the lowest point of a DRAINAGE system where liquids or wastes collect

sump·tu·ous /ˈsʌmptʃuəs/ adj expensive and grand: sumptuous furnishings — ~ **ly** adv — ~ **ness** n [U]

sum to·tal /ˌ·· ˈ··/ n [the+S (of)] the whole, esp. when less

than expected or needed: The sum total of her experience is one year working abroad.

sun¹ /sʌn/ n **1** [the] the burning star in the sky around which the Earth moves and from which it receives light and heat —see picture at SOLAR SYSTEM **2** [(the)+S;U] light and heat from the sun: She was sitting in the sun reading a book | a watery sun | I've had too much sun; I don't feel very well. **3** [C] any star round which PLANETS may turn **4 under the sun** (used for giving force to an expression) at all: She was the last person under the sun I expected to see there. —see also **place in the sun** (PLACE¹ (18))

sun² v **-nn-** [T] to cause (oneself) to sit or lie in sunlight: She was sunning herself in the garden.

Sun [the] a British TABLOID daily newspaper. It generally supports the ideas of the Conservative party and is considered to be very RIGHT-WING. It is also known for often having a picture of a woman with bare breasts on page three of the newspaper. —see also PAGE THREE GIRL, SUN READER, TABLOID and see also extra information on page 896

Sun. written abbrev. for: Sunday

sun·baked /ˈsʌnbeɪkt/ adj (usu. of a place) hardened by or having a lot of hot sunshine: the sunbaked earth | the sunbaked shores of the Caribbean

sun·bathe /ˈsʌnbeɪð/ v [I] to sit or lie in strong sunlight, esp. with very few clothes on, in order to make the body brown: We've been sunbathing on the beach. —**-bather** n

▶CULTURAL NOTE Sunbathing is very popular in Britain and the US, as it is fashionable to have a SUNTAN (= browning of the skin caused by the sun). Many people now think that too much sunbathing is dangerous, as it can cause skin CANCER. ◀

sun·beam /ˈsʌnbiːm/ n a small quantity or beam of sunlight (esp. as seen indoors)

sun·bed /ˈsʌnbed/ n a bedlike frame on which one lies in the sun, or when using a SUNLAMP

Sun·belt /ˈsʌnbelt/ [the] the southern and esp. southwestern parts of the US, from Virginia to S California

sun·bon·net /ˈsʌnbɒnˌt‖-bɑː-/ n an old-fashioned woman's hat used as protection from the sun's heat

sun·burn /ˈsʌnbɜːn‖-bɜːrn/ n [U] (the condition of having) sore skin caused by spending too much time in strong sunlight —compare SUNTAN —**-burnt, -burned** adj

sun·dae /ˈsʌndeɪ‖-di/ n a dish made from ice cream with fruit, sweet-tasting juice, nuts, etc.: a strawberry/chocolate sundae

Sun·day /ˈsʌndi/ (written abbrev. **Sun.**) n [C;U] the last day of the week, between Saturday and Monday: He'll arrive on Sunday. | (BrE infml & AmE) He'll arrive Sunday. | It happened on Sunday morning. | She left last Sunday. | My birthday is on a Sunday this year. | Christians go to church on Sundays. —see also **in a month of Sundays** (MONTH) and DAY (CULTURAL NOTE)

Sunday best /ˌ·· ˈ·/ n [U] old-fash one's best clothes, which are only worn on special occasions, for example to church on Sundays: She came in her Sunday best, but found everyone else in jeans and T-shirts.

Sunday driv·er /ˌ·· ˈ··/ n derog a person who does not drive very often, typically an old person who takes their car out on Sundays and drives very slowly and carefully, annoying other drivers

Sunday Ex·press /ˌ·· · ·ˈ·/ [the] a British newspaper which is printed and sold every Sunday —see also extra information on page 896

Sunday joint /ˌ·· ˈ·/ also **Sunday roast**— n BrE a large piece of cooked meat, eaten as part of a TRADITIONAL Sunday lunch

Sunday lunch /ˌ·· ˈ··/ also **Sunday din·ner** /ˌ·· ˈ··/— n [U] a meal usu. eaten at about one o'clock on Sundays, with the whole family together

▶CULTURAL NOTE In Britain, Sunday lunch is an important meal for many families, as it may be the only meal eaten by the whole family together. The TRADITIONAL Sunday lunch consists of roast beef served with YORKSHIRE PUDDING, GRAVY, roast potatoes, and other vegetables, followed by a sweet dish. ◀

Sunday Mir·ror /ˌ·· ˈ··/ [the] a British newspaper which is printed and sold every Sunday —see also extra information on page 896

Sunday pa·per /ˌ·· ˈ···/ n any of the newspapers which are printed and sold on Sundays. They usually have more pages than daily newspapers and may be divided into different parts or SUPPLEMENTs on subjects such as sport, holidays, business, jobs, etc.: *It takes me all day to read the Sunday papers* | *We never get a Sunday paper.* —see also extra information on page 896

Sunday Post /ˌ·· ˈ·/ also **Post**— [the] a Scottish Sunday newspaper which supports TRADITIONAL values and has many stories about ordinary people. It is very popular in Scotland and is also read by Scottish people in many other parts of the world.

Sunday roast /ˌ·· ˈ·/ n a SUNDAY JOINT

Sunday school /ˈ·· ·/ n [C;U] (a place where Christian children receive) religious teaching on a Sunday

Sunday Sport /ˌ·· ˈ·/ [the] a British TABLOID newspaper which is printed and sold every Sunday —see also extra information on page 896

Sunday Tel·e·graph /ˌ·· ˈ···/ [the] a serious British newspaper which is printed and sold every Sunday. It is known for its generally RIGHT-WING political opinions. —see also DAILY TELEGRAPH —see also extra information on page 896

Sunday Times /ˌ·· ˈ·/ [the] a serious British newspaper which is printed and sold every Sunday —see also extra information on page 896

Sunday trad·ing /ˌ·· ˈ···/ BrE ‖ **Sunday o·pen·ing** /ˌ·· ˈ···/ AmE— n [U] the opening of shops for business on Sundays

▶ CULTURAL NOTE There are laws in England which allow only certain kinds of shops to open on a Sunday. Some British people would like all shops to open on Sundays, but others think that Sunday should be kept as a special day for going to church and spending time with one's family. ◀

sun·deck /ˈsʌndek/ n a part of a ship where people sit in the sun

sun·der /ˈsʌndəʳ/ v [T] lit to break into parts, esp. violently —see also ASUNDER

Sun·der·land /ˈsʌndələnd‖-dər-/ a port and industrial town in NE England, on the river Wear

sun·dial /ˈsʌndaɪəl/ n an apparatus, used esp. in former times, which shows the time according to where the shadow of a pointer falls

sun·down /ˈsʌndaʊn/ n [U] sunset

sun·down·er /ˈsʌnˌdaʊnəʳ/ n infml, esp. BrE an alcoholic drink taken in the evening

sun·drenched /ˈsʌndrentʃt/ adj (of a place) having a lot of hot sunshine: *a sundrenched tropical island*

sun·dries /ˈsʌndriz/ n [P] small articles of various types, not important enough to be named separately: *Items such as envelopes, paper, and stamps were lumped together in the bill as sundries.*

sun·dry /ˈsʌndri/ adj [A] fml various: *books, pens, and sundry other articles* —see also **all and sundry** (ALL³)

sun·flow·er /ˈsʌnˌflaʊəʳ/ n a garden plant which grows very tall, with a large yellow flower and seeds which can be eaten or used for making cooking oil

sung /sʌŋ/ past participle of SING

sun·glass·es /ˈsʌnˌɡlɑːsɪz‖-ˌɡlæ-/ also **dark glasses**— n [P] dark glasses used esp. to protect the eyes from bright sunlight

sun god /ˈ· ·/ n a god in some ancient religions who was considered to represent and/or have power over the sun

sun·hat /ˈsʌnhæt/ n a hat with a wide surround to protect the face, head, and neck from the sun

sunk /sʌŋk/ past tense & participle of SINK

sunk·en /ˈsʌŋkən/ adj 1 [A] which has (been) sunk: *a sunken ship* | *sunken treasure* 2 (of a part of the body) having fallen inwards, esp. because of tiredness, old age, or illness; hollow: *sunken eyes/cheeks* 3 [A] built below the surrounding level: *a sunken garden/sunken bath*

sun·lamp /ˈsʌnlæmp/ also **sunray lamp** /ˈ·· ·/— n a lamp which gives out ULTRAVIOLET light and is used esp. for making the skin brown because this is considered attractive

sun·less /ˈsʌnləs/ adj lit lacking natural light: *in the sunless depths of the forest*

sun·light /ˈsʌnlaɪt/ n [U] natural light from the sun: *bright/pale sunlight* | *a patch of sunlight* | *Our garden gets a lot of sunlight.*

sun·lit /ˈsʌnlɪt/ adj brightly lit by the sun

sun lounge /ˈ· ·/ BrE ‖ **sun porch**, **sun par·lor** /ˈ· ˌ··/ AmE— n a room with large windows which let in a lot of bright sunlight

Sun·na, Sunnah /ˈsʊnə, ˈsʌ-/ [the] the body of ancient Muslim law based on the words and acts of Muhammed

Sun·ni /ˈsʊni/ adj, n -**nis** (of or being) a Muslim who follows the branch of the Muslim religion based only on the teachings and acts of Muhammed —compare SHIITE

sun·ny /ˈsʌni/ adj 1 having bright sunlight: *a sunny room/day* 2 cheerful: *a sunny smile* —**niness** n [U]

sunny-side up /ˌ··· ˈ·/ adj [F] AmE (of an egg) cooked in hot fat on one side only, not turned over in the pan

sun·ray /ˈsʌnreɪ/ adj [A] using ULTRAVIOLET light: *sunray treatment* —see also SUNLAMP

Sun read·er /ˈ· ˌ···/ n BrE derog a person who has RIGHT-WING political opinions and is not very well educated, thought to be the sort of person who reads the Sun newspaper

sun·rise /ˈsʌnraɪz/ also **sun-up** infml— n [C;U] the time when the sun appears in the morning: *We got up at sunrise.* | *watching the sunrise* | *a beautiful sunrise*

sunrise in·dus·try /ˈ·· ˌ···/ n an industry, such as ELECTRONICS or the making of computers, that uses modern processes and is taking the place of older industries that use heavy machinery

sun·roof /ˈsʌnruːf/ n 1 a flat roof of a building where one can enjoy the sun 2 a car roof with a part which can be moved back to let in air and light —see picture at CAR

sun screen /ˈ· ˌ·/ n [U] an oil or liquid that is rubbed into the skin to protect it from the sun's harmful RAYS

sun·set /ˈsʌnset/ n [C;U] 1 the time when the sun disappears as night begins: *They stopped work at sunset.* | *He sat watching the sunset.* | *You get beautiful sunsets in the tropics.* 2 drive/ride/sail off into the sunset humor to drive, ride, or sail away in a way that suggests a happy ending of an old Hollywood ROMANTIC film

Sunset Boule·vard /ˌ·· ˈ···/ also **Sunset Strip** /ˌ·· ˈ·/— a famous street that runs through Hollywood, California. It is connected with the film industry and rich film stars, mostly because of a well-known film named after the street.

sunset law /ˈ·· ˌ·/ n a law in most US states which says that some state programmes must be examined regularly to see if they are still useful

sun·shade /ˈsʌnʃeɪd/ also **parasol**— n a light folding circular frame, similar to an UMBRELLA but usu. covered with colourful material and held over the head for protection from the sun

sun·shine /ˈsʌnʃaɪn/ n [(the)] U] strong sunlight: *I was sitting in the garden enjoying the sunshine.* | *She has brought some sunshine into my life.* (=made me happy)

sunshine law /ˈ·· ˌ·/ n a type of law in the US which says that many government organizations (city, state, and national) must allow the public to attend their meetings

sun·spot /ˈsʌnspɒt‖-spɑːt/ n a small dark cooler area on the sun's surface, as seen through a TELESCOPE

sun·stroke /ˈsʌnstrəʊk/ n [U] fever, weakness, headache, etc., caused by too much strong sunlight, esp. on the head —compare HEATSTROKE

sun·tan /ˈsʌntæn/ also **tan**— n the browning of the skin caused by being in strong sunlight —compare SUNBURN; see also SUNBATHE (CULTURAL NOTE) —**tanned** adj

suntan cream /ˈ·· ˌ·/ also **suntan oil**— n [U] a cream or oil that is rubbed into the skin to prevent the skin from burning in hot sun, and to encourage it to turn brown

sun·trap /ˈsʌntræp/ n a sheltered place that gets a lot of sunshine: *The back garden is a real suntrap.*

sun-up /ˈ· ·/ n [U] infml SUNRISE

sun vi·sor /ˈ· ˌ··/ n a movable flat piece fitted to the top of a car window to protect the driver's eyes from bright sunshine

Sun Yat-sen /ˌsʊn ˌjæt ˈsen/ (1867–1925) a Chinese nationalist politician whose real name was **Sun Zhong-shan**, who became president of China in 1912 after helping to remove the ruling EMPEROR

sup¹ /sʌp/ v -pp- [I (UP);T] ScotE & N EngE to drink (esp. beer) in small mouthfuls —**sup** n

sup² v -pp- [I (**on, off**)] old use to eat (as) supper: They supped on bread and cheese.

su·per¹ /ˈsuːpəʳ, ˈsjuː-‖ˈsuː-/ adj infml, becoming old-fash wonderful; extremely good: It's a super place for a holiday. | What a super idea! | That sounds super.

super² n BrE infml **1** BrE a SUPERINTENDENT, esp. in the police **2** AmE SUPERINTENDENT (3)

super- see WORD FORMATION

su·per·a·bun·dant /ˌsuːpərəˈbʌndənt◂,ˌsjuː-‖ˌsuː-/ adj fml or pomp more than enough —**-dance** n [S (**of**)] : She has a superabundance of energy.

su·per·an·nu·at·ed /ˌsuːpərˈænjueɪtɪd, ˌsjuː-‖ˌsuː-/ adj fml or tech **1** too old for work **2** old-fashioned; OBSOLETE: superannuated ideas

su·per·an·nu·a·tion /ˌsuːpərænjuˈeɪʃən, ˌsjuː-‖ˌsuː-/ n [U] fml or tech money paid as a PENSION, esp. from one's former place of work

superannuation scheme /ˌ···ˈ·· ˌ·/ n BrE a kind of PENSION PLAN which is controlled by and contributed to by one's employer: The company has an excellent superannuation scheme.

su·perb /sjuːˈpɜːb, suː-‖suːˈpɜːrb/ adj excellent; of the highest quality: The food was superb. | a superb performance —**~ly** adv

Super Bowl /ˈ·· ·/ [the] the game played each year in late January on a Sunday (**Super Bowl Sunday**) that decides which team is the overall winner (CHAMPION) in American professional football. It was first played in 1967 and a ROMAN NUMERAL is used to show the number of each year's game: Super Bowl XXVI —see also FOOTBALL (2) and see extra information on page 501

su·per·charge /ˈsuːpətʃɑːdʒ, ˈsjuː-‖ˈsuːpərtʃɑːrdʒ/ v [T often pass.] **1** to increase the power of (an engine) with a supercharger **2** to fill with (too much) power, strong feeling, etc.: an atmosphere supercharged with emotion

su·per·charg·er /ˈsuːpəˌtʃɑːdʒəʳ, ˈsjuː-‖ˈsuːpərˌtʃɑːr-/ n an apparatus for producing more power from an engine by forcing air into the place where FUEL, such as petrol, burns —see also TURBOCHARGER

su·per·cil·i·ous /ˌsuːpəˈsɪliəs◂, ˌsjuː-‖ˌsuːpər-/ adj derog (as if) thinking that others are of little importance; HAUGHTY: a supercilious wave of the hand | a supercilious manner —~ly adv : He smiled superciliously when I described my modest collection. —~ness n [U]

su·per·con·duc·tiv·i·ty /ˌsuːpəkɒndəkˈtɪvₔti, ₓsjuː-‖ₓsuːpər-/ n [U] the ability of certain metals to allow electricity to pass freely (without RESISTANCE) when at the lowest temperatures possible

su·per·con·duc·tor /ˌsuːpəkənˈdʌktəʳ, ₓsjuː-‖ₓsuːpər-/ n a substance that possesses the quality of superconductivity

Su·per·drug /ˈsuːpədrʌg, ˈsjuː-‖ˈsuːpər-/ (in Britain) one of a group of shops selling medical items and TOILETRIES, usu. at low prices

su·per·du·per /ₓsuːpəˈduːpəʳ, ₓsjuː-◂‖ₓsuːpər-/ adj infml, becoming old-fash wonderful; SUPER

su·per·e·go /ₓsuːpərˈiːgəʊ, -ˈegəʊ, ₓsjuː-‖ₓsuː-/ n -gos tech (in Freudian PSYCHOLOGY) the moral self or conscience; the one of the three parts of the mind that is partly conscious and that rewards and punishes us by our feelings of guilt or rightness, according to our respect for the rules of society —compare EGO (2), ID

su·per·fi·cial /ₓsuːpəˈfɪʃəl◂, ₓsjuː-‖ₓsuːpər-/ adj **1** [no comp.] on the surface; not deep: a superficial wound | a superficial resemblance between two people **2** not thorough or complete: She has a superficial knowledge of the language. | a superficial inspection **3** derog showing a lack of deep feelings or serious thinking; SHALLOW¹ (2): He's so superficial. | a very superficial analysis of the situation —~ly adv —~ity /ₓsuːpəfɪʃiˈælₔti, ₓsjuː-‖ ₓsuːpər-/ n [U]

su·per·flu·i·ty /ₓsuːpəˈfluːₔti, ˈsjuː-‖ₓsuːpər-/ n [S (**of**)] fml or pomp a larger amount than is needed

su·per·flu·ous /suːˈpɜːfluəs, sjuː-‖suːˈpɜːr-/ adj fml more than is necessary; not needed or wanted: He had already

been told, so our comments were superfluous. | superfluous energy —~ly adv —~ness n [U]

Su·per·glue /ˈsuːpəgluː, ˈsjuː-‖ˈsuːpər-/ n [U] tdmk a very strong kind of glue which sticks very quickly and is difficult to remove **superglue** v [T]

su·per·grass /ˈsuːpəgrɑːs, ˈsjuː-‖ˈsuːpərgræs/ n BrE a person, esp. a criminal, who supplies the police with a lot of information about the activities of other criminals in order to reduce his/her own punishment

su·per·gun /ˈsuːpəgʌn, ˈsjuː-‖ˈsuːpər-/ n a very large gun, esp. the one that Iraq was trying to build in 1990, made up of steel tubes sent secretly into the country: There have been more questions in the British parliament about the Iraqi supergun affair.

su·per·he·ro /ˈsuːpəˌhɪərəʊ, ˈsjuː-‖ˈsuːpər-/ n a character in stories who has special qualities such as great strength, the ability to fly, and special senses, and uses these to help people and to save the world from evil —see also SUPERMAN

su·per·high·way /ˈsuːpəˌhaɪweɪ, ˈsjuː-‖ˈsuːpər-/ n AmE a very large MOTORWAY —see EXPRESSWAY (USAGE)

su·per·hu·man /ₓsuːpəˈhjuːmən◂, ₓsjuː-‖ₓsuːpərˈhjuː-, -ˈjuː-/ adj seeming beyond human powers: It will require a superhuman effort to get the job finished on time.

su·per·im·pose /ₓsuːpərɪmˈpəʊz, ₓsjuː-‖ₓsuː-/ v [T (**on**)] to put (something) over something else, esp. so that both can be (partly) seen: Using two projectors, we can superimpose one film image on the other.

su·per·in·tend /ₓsuːpərɪnˈtend, ₓsjuː-‖ₓsuː-/ v [T] to be in charge of and direct (official work)

su·per·in·tend·ent /ₓsuːpərɪnˈtendənt, ₓsjuː-‖ₓsuː-/ n **1** a person who is officially in charge of an activity, a place, etc.: superintendent of schools **2** a British police officer of middle rank **3** AmE also **super** a person who manages an APARTMENT BUILDING

su·pe·ri·or¹ /suːˈpɪəriəʳ, sjuː-‖sʊ-/ adj **1** [(**to**)] of higher rank or class: I'll report you to your superior officer! **2** [(**to**)] better in quality or value: Of the two books, I think this one is superior (to that). **3** of high quality: This is a very superior make of car, sir. | superior craftsmanship **4** derog (as if) thinking oneself better than others: He smiled a superior smile as he drove past in his expensive new car. **5** [A] tech higher in position; upper: the superior limbs (=the arms) **6** [after n] (usu. cap.) (a title for) the head of a religious group: Mother/Father Superior —compare INFERIOR¹; see MAJOR (USAGE) —~ity /sʊˌpɪəriˈɒrₔti, sjuː-‖sʊˌpɪəriˈɔːr-, -ˈɑːr-/ n [U (**over**)] : their obvious superiority over the other team

superior² n [often pl.] a person of higher rank, esp. in a job: He always does what his superiors tell him. —compare INFERIOR¹

Superior, Lake the largest of the Great Lakes on the border between Canada and the US; the largest freshwater lake in the world —see colour map on pages 1374–5

superior court /·ˈ··· ˌ·/ n a STATE COURT which hears many different types of cases, esp. serious cases

superiority com·plex /·ˌ··ˈ··· ˌ··/ n infml a condition of the mind in which someone believes that they are much better, more important, clever, etc., than other people —compare INFERIORITY COMPLEX

su·per·la·tive¹ /suːˈpɜːlətɪv, sjuː-‖sʊˈpɜːr-/ adj **1** [no comp.] (in grammar) of the form of an adjective or adverb expressing the highest degree of comparison: "Biggest" is the superlative form of "big". | "Worst" is the superlative form of "bad". —compare COMPARATIVE¹ (1), POSITIVE¹ (5) **2** best; of the highest quality: of superlative quality | a superlative performance

superlative² n **1** [the+S] the superlative form of an adjective or adverb: "Biggest" is the superlative of "big". **2** [C] a word in this form, esp. when expressing great praise or admiration: She described the place with a string of superlatives. (=several superlative adjectives)

su·per·la·tive·ly /suːˈpɜːlətɪvli, sjuː-‖sʊˈpɜːr-/ adv (esp. of something good) very; to a very high degree: superlatively happy

Super League /ˈ·· ˌ·/ n a football LEAGUE¹ formed from the best football teams in Britain

su·per·man /ˈsuːpəmæn, ˈsjuː-‖ˈsuːpər-/ **superwoman** fem.— n -men /men/ a person of very great or SUPERHUMAN ability or strength

Superman

Superman an American HERO of COMIC STRIPS and films who fights for truth and justice, using his special powers, such as being able to fly and having great strength. Most of the time he leads the life of an ordinary man, Clark Kent, but whenever he is needed he quickly changes into a special COSTUME, and becomes Superman. —compare BATMAN, SPIDERMAN; see also Clark KENT, KRYPTON

su·per·mar·ket /'su:pəˌmɑːkɪt, 'sju:-‖'su:pərˌmɑːr-/ ‖ also **grocery store** AmE– n a large shop where customers serve themselves with food and other goods needed in the home. The customers use large TROLLEYs and often buy enough food to last for a week or even a month. Goods usu. cost less in supermarkets than they do in smaller shops: *Small corner shops simply cannot compete with the supermarkets on prices.*

su·per·nat·u·ral¹ /ˌsu:pə'nætʃərəl◂, ˌsju:-‖ˌsu:pər-/ adj impossible to explain by natural laws; of or caused by the powers of spirits, gods, and magic: *supernatural forces* – ~ly adv

supernatural² n [the+S] matters and experiences connected with unknown forces and spirits: *belief in the supernatural*

su·per·no·va /ˌsu:pə'nəʊvə, ˌsju:-‖ˌsu:pər-/ n a very large exploding star seen in the sky as a bright mass —compare NOVA

su·per·nu·me·ra·ry /ˌsu:pə'nju:mərəri, ˌsju:-‖ˌsu:pər'nu:məreri/ n, adj fml (a person or thing) additional to the usual or necessary number

su·per·pow·er /'su:pəˌpaʊəʳ, 'sju:-‖'su:pər-/ n a nation that has very great military and political power: *Britain is no longer a superpower.*

su·per·sede /ˌsu:pə'si:d, ˌsju:-‖ˌsu:pər-/ v [T often pass.] to take the place of (usu. something older), esp. as an improvement: *The cinema has been superseded by television as the most popular form of entertainment.*

su·per·son·ic /ˌsu:pə'sɒnɪk◂, ˌsju:-‖ˌsu:pər'sɑː-/ adj (flying) faster than the speed of sound: *a supersonic aircraft | supersonic flight* —compare SUBSONIC

su·per·star /'su:pəstɑːʳ, 'sju:-‖'su:pər-/ n an extremely famous performer, esp. a popular musician or film actor

su·per·sti·tion /ˌsu:pə'stɪʃən, ˌsju:-‖ˌsu:pər-/ n [C;U] a belief which is not based on reason or fact but on old ideas about luck, magic, etc.

► CULTURAL NOTE Some common superstitions are mentioned below. It is thought to be unlucky to walk under ladders, or to break a mirror. If someone spills salt they should pick a little up and throw it over their left shoulder into the face of the devil. A black cat crossing one's path is thought by some to be lucky. In the theatre, rather than saying "Good Luck" one should say "Break a leg". Also in the theatre, Shakespeare's play *Macbeth* should be spoken of as "the Scottish Play" and not by name. —see also LUCKY, UNLUCKY◄

su·per·sti·tious /ˌsu:pə'stɪʃəs◂, ˌsju:-‖ˌsu:pər-/ adj strongly influenced by superstition – ~ly adv

su·per·store /'su:pəstɔːʳ, 'sju:-‖'su:pər-/ n BrE a very large shop, often on the edge of a town, with its own car park, selling food, clothing, electrical goods, or furniture, usually fairly cheaply and with a good choice —compare DISCOUNT STORE

su·per·struc·ture /'su:pəˌstrʌktʃəʳ, 'sju:-‖'su:pər-/ n **1** a structure that is built up on top of a base, such as the upper parts of a ship or the part of a building above the ground **2** an arrangement, system, etc., which has

grown from a simpler base: *a superstructure of religion based on nature worship*

su·per·tank·er /'su:pəˌtæŋkəʳ, 'sju:-‖'su:pər-/ n an extremely large ship (TANKER) which can carry large quantities of gas or liquid, esp. oil

su·per·tax /'su:pətæks, 'sju:-‖'su:pər-/ n [U] (formerly in Britain), additional income tax paid only by people with very high incomes

Super Tues·day /ˌ·· '··/ AmE the second Tuesday in March of a presidential election year, on which many states, esp. in the South, hold a PRIMARY election (an election which helps decide who will run for president from each political party)

su·per·vene /ˌsu:pə'vi:n, ˌsju:-‖ˌsu:pər-/ v [I] fml to happen unexpectedly, esp. in a way that stops or interrupts an event or situation

su·per·vise /'su:pəvaɪz, 'sju:-‖'su:pər-/ v [I;T] to keep watch over (a job or activity, or the people doing it) as the person in charge –-visor n –-visory adj : *She works there in a supervisory capacity.*

su·per·vi·sion /ˌsu:pə'vɪʒən, ˌsju:-‖ˌsu:pər-/ n [U] the act or fact of supervising: *The work was done under my supervision.* (=I supervised it)

su·per·wom·an /'su:pəwʊmən, 'sju:-‖'su:pər-/ n -women /ˌwɪmɪn/ (sometimes cap.) **1** a female SUPERMAN **2** a woman who has a CAREER at the same time as running a home and bringing up children, and makes it seem easy

su·pine /'su:paɪn, 'sju:-‖su:'paɪn/ adj fml **1** lying on one's back, looking upwards —compare PRONE (2) **2** inactive and ineffective, and perhaps too ready to allow others to take control: *a supine acceptance of their decision* – ~ly adv

sup·per /'sʌpəʳ/ n [C;U] a meal taken in the evening: *What time do you have supper? | It happened at/during supper. | We had fish for supper. | It's supper time!* —see DINNER (USAGE)

sup·plant /sə'plɑːnt‖sə'plænt/ v [T] to take the place of (sometimes unfairly or improperly): *She's been supplanted in her aunt's affections by her brother.* (=her aunt now likes him more) | *a new system to supplant outdated working methods*

sup·ple /'sʌpəl/ adj bending or moving easily and gracefully, esp. in the joints of the body: *She exercises every day to keep herself supple.* – ~ness n [U]

sup·ple·ment¹ /'sʌplɪmənt/ n **1** an additional amount that makes something complete or supplies something else that is needed: *a dietary supplement* **2** an additional part at the end of a book or as a separate part of a newspaper, magazine, etc.: *Do you read the Sunday colour supplements?* —see also extra information on page 896

sup·ple·ment² /'sʌplɪment/ v [T (by, with)] to add to; provide a supplement to: *She supplements her regular income by doing a bit of teaching in the evenings.*

sup·ple·men·ta·ry /ˌsʌplɪ'mentəri◂/ adj l(to) **1** additional: *There is a supplementary water supply in case the main supply fails.* **2** tech (of angles or an angle) making up 180° together, or with the other angle: *An angle of 120° is supplementary to an angle of 60°; they are* **supplementary angles.** —compare COMPLEMENTARY (2)

supplementary ben·e·fit /ˌ···· '···/ n [U] (formerly in Britain) money given by the state to those (e.g. old or unemployed people) whose income does not reach a level officially regarded as being enough to live on, now called INCOME SUPPORT —compare WELFARE (3)

sup·pli·ant /'sʌpliənt/ n, adj fml or lit (a person) begging, praying, or requesting

sup·pli·cant /'sʌplɪkənt/ n fml or lit a person begging for something, esp. from someone in power or from God

sup·pli·cate /'sʌplɪkeɪt/ v [I;T] fml or lit to beg (God or someone in a position of power), esp. for help –-cation /ˌsʌplɪ'keɪʃən/ n [C;U]

sup·pli·er /sə'plaɪəʳ/ also **suppliers** pl.– n a firm that supplies something, esp. goods: *If the typewriters are faulty, return them to the suppliers. | a leading supplier of aircraft parts*

sup·plies /sə'plaɪz/ n [P] food or other necessary materials for daily life, esp. for a group of people over a period of time: *The army was trapped in the pass for several days, and began to run short of supplies. | I need to get* *some school supplies.* (=paper, pens, pencils, etc.)

sup·ply¹ /sə'plaɪ/ v [T] **1** [(to)] to provide (something that is needed): *The factory supplied a uniform to each of its workers.* **2** [(with)] to provide things to (a person) for use: *The firm that used to supply us has gone out of business.* | *An informer supplied the police with the names of those involved in the crime.* | *The new recruits were supplied with uniforms.* | *Our allies kept us supplied with weapons.* **3** *fml* to satisfy (a need): *The new bridge supplies a long-felt need.*

supply² *n* **1** [C (of)] *usu. sing.*] an amount for use: *Bring a large supply of food with you.* −see also SUPPLIES, SUPPLY AND DEMAND **2** [U (of)] (a system for) the supplying of something needed: *The supply of electricity/The electricity supply has been threatened by recent strikes.* **3 in short supply** difficult to obtain because of shortage; SCARCE: *Potatoes are in short supply because of the bad harvest.* −see also MONEY SUPPLY

supply³ *adj* [A] used for bringing or storing supplies: *a supply train* | *a supply dump*

supply and de·mand /ˌ·, · · ·ˌ·/ *n* [U] the balance between the amount of goods for sale and the amount that people actually want to buy, esp. as this influences prices: *The reason they're so expensive is that they're very scarce and everyone wants them; it's all a matter of supply and demand.*

supply-side /ˌ·'· ·/ *adj* [A] *tech* (of economic ideas and models) favouring the producers of goods, e.g. by low taxes, so that they will find it easy to increase supplies: *supply-side economics/arguments* −compare DEMAND-SIDE −**supply-sider** *n*

supply teach·er /ˌ·'· ·ˌ·/ *BrE* ǁ **substitute teacher** *AmE* — *n* a teacher who takes the place of regular teachers for short periods while they are away

sup·port¹ /sə'pɔːt‖-ɔːrt/ v [T] **1** to bear the weight of, esp. so as to keep in place or prevent from falling; hold up: *The middle part of the bridge is supported by two huge towers.* | *Do you think those shelves can support so many books?* | (fig.) *The Federal Reserve Bank intervened to support the falling dollar.* **2 a** to provide esp. money for (a person) to live on: *Her father supported her until she got married.* | *She needs a high income to support such a large family.* **b** to provide the necessities of life (for people or animals): *This dry land won't support many cattle.* **3** to pay the cost of (a habit, activity, etc.): *He must need a fortune to support his drinking habits/extravagant tastes.* **4** to approve of and encourage: *Do you support their demands for independence?* | *The proposal was supported by a large majority in the Senate.* **5** to be loyal to, esp. by attending matches or performances: *Which football team do you support?* **6** to (seem to) show the truth or correctness of; SUBSTANTIATE: *The results support my original theory.* | *fresh evidence to support her allegations* **7** *fml* (with *can/cannot*) to bear; ENDURE: *I cannot support this heat.* −see also INSUPPORTABLE

support² *n* **1** [U] the state of being supported so as not to fall: *The roof may need extra support.* **2** [C] something that bears the weight of something else: *the supports of a bridge* **3** [U] active approval aimed at helping the success of something: *The local people have given us a lot of support in our campaign.* | *This proposal has my full support.* | *They signed a petition in support of the workers' demands.* | *We'll soon drum up support for the proposal.* (=get many people's approval) **4** [U] sympathetic encouragement and help: *Your support has meant a lot to me during this difficult time.* **5** [U] money to live on: *The judge ordered him to be kept in custody as he had no (visible) means of support.* (=had no money or job) −see also CHILD SUPPORT **6** [C] an apparatus which is worn to hold in place a weak or displaced part of the body

sup·por·ta·ble /sə'pɔːtəbəl‖-ɔːr-/ *adj* [*usu. in negatives*] *fml* bearable −opposite **insupportable**

sup·port·er /sə'pɔːtəʳ‖-ɔːr-/ *n* a person who supports a particular activity or team, defends a particular principle, etc.: *I'm a strong supporter of women's rights.* | *Several of the English football supporters were arrested after the match.*

support group /·'· ·/ *n* a group of people who meet to help each other with a particular problem, e.g. alcoholism

supporting part /·,·· '·/ also **supporting role**— *n* a small part in a play or film

supporting pro·gramme /·,·· '··/ *BrE* ǁ **opening number, opening show** *AmE*— *n* the film or films shown in addition to the main film in a performance, or the performers in a show who appear in addition to the main star

sup·por·tive /sə'pɔːtɪv‖-ɔːr-/ *adj apprec* giving (additional) encouragement, help, etc., esp. to someone who is in a difficult position: *Mary was so supportive when my husband died.*

sup·pose¹ /sə'pəʊz/ v [T *not usu. in progressive forms*] **1** [+(*that*);*obj*] to consider to be probable; ASSUME: *As she's not here, I suppose she must have gone home.* | *There's no reason to suppose that his new book will be any better than his last one.* | *"He must have missed the train, then." "Yes, I suppose so."* | *I don't suppose she'll agree.* | (in polite requests) *I don't suppose you could give me a lift to the station, could you?* **2** [+*obj*+*to-v*|*adj*;*usu. pass.*] *fml* to believe; have as an opinion: *He was generally supposed to have left the country.* | *She was commonly supposed (to be) extremely rich.* **3** *fml* to have as a condition; PRESUPPOSE: *The company's plan supposes a steady increase in orders.* **4 be supposed to: a** to have a duty or responsibility to do something: *Everyone is supposed to bring a bottle to the party.* | *You're not supposed to smoke in here.* (=you are not allowed to) **b** to be intended to: *This law is supposed to help the poor.* **c** to be generally considered to be; have the REPUTATION of being: *I haven't seen it myself, but it's supposed to be a very good film.*

suppose² also **sup·pos·ing** /sə'pəʊzɪŋ/— *conj* **1** what would/will happen if: *Suppose it rains, what shall we do?* | *It's a good idea, but suppose your mother were to find out?* **2** (used for making a suggestion): *Suppose we wait a while.*

sup·posed /sə'pəʊzd, sə'pəʊzɪd/ *adj* [A] *often derog* believed to be (so), though without much proof: *Her supposed wealth is in fact a very small sum.* | *supposed experts*

sup·pos·ed·ly /sə'pəʊzɪdli/ *adv* as is believed, perhaps wrongly; as it appears: *Supposedly, she's a rich woman.* | *this supposedly unbiased report*

sup·po·si·tion /ˌsʌpə'zɪʃən/ *n* **1** [U] the act of supposing or guessing: *His version of the events is pure supposition.* (=is based only on guessing) **2** [S (+*that*)] an idea which is a result of this; a guess: *The police are acting on the supposition that she took the money.*

sup·pos·i·to·ry /sə'pɒzɪtəri‖sə'pɑːzɪtɔːri/ *n* a small piece of easily meltable medicine that can be placed inside a lower opening of the body (the RECTUM or the VAGINA) −compare PESSARY (1)

sup·press /sə'pres/ v [T] **1** to destroy or bring to an end by force: *Opposition to the government was quickly suppressed.* **2** to prevent from being shown: *She could hardly suppress a smile.* | *You shouldn't try to suppress your feelings of anger* **3** to prevent from being printed or made public: *The government used their emergency powers to suppress the magazine/to suppress the truth about the accident.* − ~ **ion** /sə'preʃən/ *n* [U (of)] : *The suppression of the revolt took a mere two days.*

sup·pres·sor /sə'presəʳ/ *n* **1** a person or thing that suppresses **2** *BrE* a small apparatus which prevents an electrical machine from causing INTERFERENCE (=bad quality sound or a bad picture) on a television or radio

sup·pu·rate /'sʌpjʊreɪt/ v [I] (of a wound) to form or give out PUS (=infected matter) −**ration** /ˌsʌpjʊ'reɪʃən/ *n* [U]

su·pra·na·tion·al /ˌsuːprə'næʃənəl◂, ˌsjuː-‖-ˌsuː-/ *adj* concerning more than one country; going beyond national powers, interests, borders, etc.: *a supranational organization*

su·prem·a·cist /sə'preməsəst/ *n* a person who believes in the supremacy of the stated group: *a white supremacist* (=someone who believes in the supremacy of white people)

su·prem·a·cy /sə'preməsi/ *n* [U] the state of being supreme: *Germany planned to challenge Britain's naval supremacy.* | *their unchallenged supremacy in the field of electronics*

su·preme /suː'priːm, sjuː-, sə-‖suː-, suː-/ *adj* **1** having the highest position, with regard to power, importance, or influence: *An American general was appointed* **Supreme Allied Commander** *in Europe.* **2** highest in degree: *supreme happiness/courage* | *It required* **a supreme effort of will** *to stop myself from laughing.* | *Soldiers who*

die for their country are said to have made **the supreme sacrifice.** —see also SUPREMELY

su·prême /suːˈpriːm, -ˈprem, sjʊ-‖suː-, suː-/ *adj* [F] *Fr* (of a food) served with a thick rich liquid made with cream and eggs: *chicken suprême*

Supreme Be·ing /ˌ·ˈ··/ [*the*] *lit* God

Supreme Court /ˌ·ˌ· ˈ·/ [*the*] **1** the most court of law in certain countries **2** a court in England and Wales consisting of the High Court, the Court of Appeal, and the Crown Court **3** the highest court and final court of APPEAL in the US FEDERAL system and for some cases in the state courts: *The full US Senate will decide today whether to confirm Judge Thomas's appointment to the Supreme Court.* —see colour picture on page 751

▶CULTURAL NOTE The US Supreme Court has nine judges, called **justices**, who are on the court for as long as they wish to serve. The president suggests suitable judges for the court when a position becomes open, and the Senate must approve of his choice. The Supreme Court decides which cases it wants to hear, and these cases often attract a lot of public attention. Cases which come before the Supreme Court often concern the US Constitution, such as the right to free speech. —see also extra information on page 742◀

Supreme Court Justice /ˌ·ˌ· ˈ··/ *n* any of the nine judges who serves on the US Supreme Court. They serve for life, after being appointed by the president and approved by Congress. One of them is called the **chief justice**.

su·preme·ly /suːˈpriːmli, sjuː-, sə-‖suː-, suː-/ *adv* as much as possible; extremely: *supremely happy|confident*

Su·premes /suːˈpriːmz, sjuː-, sə-‖suː-, suː-/, **The** a female American popular music group formed in 1959, which was one of the most successful MOTOWN groups in the 1960s. Diana Ross was a member of the group until 1969.

Supreme So·vi·et /ˌ·ˌ· ˈ···/ [*the*] the highest lawmaking body of the Soviet Union

su·prem·o /suːˈpriːməʊ, sjuː-‖suː-, suː-/ *n* **-mos** *BrE infml* a ruler or director with unlimited powers: *England's soccer supremo*

Supt. *written abbrev. for:* SUPERINTENDENT

sur·charge¹ /ˈsɜːtʃɑːdʒ‖ˈsɜːrtʃɑːrdʒ/ *v* [T (**on**)] to make an additional charge to or for, after an original payment has been made: *He was surcharged on the parcel.*

surcharge² *n* an amount charged in addition to the usual amount or the amount already paid, e.g. for a letter with too few stamps on it: *We had to pay a* **fuel surcharge** *on our airline tickets because of the sudden increase in the cost of oil.* | *an import surcharge*

sur·coat /ˈsɜːkəʊt‖ˈsɜːr-/ *n* an armless garment worn over armour in former times

surd /sɜːd‖sɜːrd/ *n tech* a quantity which cannot be shown in whole numbers: *The square root of two is a surd.*

sure¹ /ʃʊəʳ/ *adj* **1** [F] having no doubt; confident in one's knowledge of something: *I think so, but I'm not sure.* [+(*that*)] *I'm sure he'll come.* [+*wh-*] *I'm not sure whether to go.* | *I wasn't sure about|of the way, so I asked someone.* | *I* **feel sure** *I've met her before somewhere.* | *He's confident that they'll win, but I'm* **not so sure. 2** [F+*to-v*] certain (to happen): *It's a really good film — you're sure to like it.* | *It's sure to rain.* **3** [F+*of*] certain (of having or gaining something): *I've never felt surer of success.* **4** certain to be true or exact: *One thing is sure; he can't have gone far.* | *Those black clouds are* **a sure sign** *(that) it's going to rain.* **5 be sure to** don't forget to: *Be sure to turn everything off before you go to bed.* **6 make sure of something|that: a** to find out if something is certainly true: *I think I locked the door, but I'll just go back and make sure (of it|that I did).* **b** to take action so that something will certainly happen: *Make sure (that) you get here before midnight.* | *They made sure of winning by scoring two goals in the last five minutes.* **7 sure of oneself** *sometimes derog* believing (too) strongly in one's own abilities, actions, etc.; very confident: *She's very sure of herself.* —see also SELF-ASSURED **8 to be sure, for sure** it must be accepted (that); ADMITTEDLY: *Some people may disagree, to be sure, but that doesn't mean I'm wrong.* —see also SURELY — ~ **ness** *n* [U]

▷ USAGE **Sure** can be used in the same way as **certain** in sentences about events like this: *He's* **sure/certain** *to come tomorrow* | *I'm not* **sure/certain** *(whether) I'll*

be able to come. But it cannot be used in sentences like this: *It is* **certain** (not **sure**) *that he'll come tomorrow.*◁

sure² *adv* **1** *infml, esp. AmE* certainly: *Sure I will.* | *"Are you all right?" "Sure."* | (*AmE*) *He sure is tall.* —see SURELY (USAGE) **2 for sure** *infml* certainly so: *She won't lend you any money, and that's for sure.* **3 sure enough** exactly as was expected: *They all said it would fall down and* **sure enough** *it did.* | *"Are you coming tomorrow?" "Sure enough!"*

sure·fire /ˈʃʊəfaɪəʳ‖ˈʃʊər-/ *adj* [A] *infml* certain to happen or succeed: *a surefire winner|cure*

sure·foot·ed /ˌʃʊəˈfʊt̬d◂‖ˌʃʊər-/ *adj* **1** able to walk firmly without slipping or falling in difficult places **2** able to make exact judgments, even in a difficult situation — ~ **ly** *adv* — ~ **ness** *n* [U]

sure·ly /ˈʃʊəli‖ˈʃʊərli/ *adv* **1** I believe, hope, or expect: *Surely you remember him?* | *You know him, surely?* | *It should surely be possible for them to reach an agreement.* —see USAGE **2** in a sure way: *We made our way up the mountain* **slowly but surely.** (=safely) | *The violinist played the difficult passage skilfully and surely.* (=confidently) **3** *AmE old fash* yes: *"Would you hand me that book over there?" "Surely"*

▷ USAGE **Surely** does not usually have the same meaning as **certainly**. Compare *He* **surely** *doesn't expect me to pay him immediately.* (=I hope he doesn't expect this and I don't think he ought to) and *He* **certainly** *doesn't expect me to pay him immediately.* (=I know he doesn't expect the money now.) But, especially in American English, **surely** (often shortened to **sure**) can be used, like **certainly** and **of course** in answer to requests, to show willingness to help: *"Can I borrow this book?" "Yes,* **certainly|of course|surely|sure."** —see also CERTAINLY (USAGE), COURSE (USAGE)◁

sure thing /ˌ·ˈ·/ *interj infml, esp. AmE* (used for expressing agreement with a statement or request): *"Buy a paper on the way home, will you." "Sure thing!"*

sur·e·ty /ˈʃʊərᵻti/ *n* [C;U] **1** a person who takes responsibility for the behaviour of another, esp. to be responsible if the other person fails to pay a debt, appear in court, etc.: *Are you willing to* **stand surety** *for your brother?* **2** money given to make sure that a person will appear in court —see also BAIL¹ (1)

surf¹ /sɜːf‖sɜːrf/ *n* [U] the FOAM (=white air-filled water) formed by waves on the sea when they come in towards rocks, a shore, etc.

surf² *v* [I] to ride as a sport over waves coming in towards the shore, on a SURFBOARD. This sport is connected with California or Australia, and the Beach Boys, who recorded popular songs about surfing. It is considered a GLAMOROUS or fashionable activity because it suggests a sunny CLIMATE and the lifestyle that goes with it: *If the waves are big enough, we'll* **go surfing.** —see also WINDSURFING — ~ **er** *n*

sur·face¹ /ˈsɜːfᵻs‖ˈsɜːr-/ *n* **1** [C] the outer part of an object, esp. when considered with regard to its roughness or smoothness: *the surface of the moon* | *the smooth surface of a polished table* | *How is the coal brought to the surface?* | *a flat working surface* | *He had to drive slowly over the uneven surface of the road.* **2** [C] the top of a body of liquid: *The surface of the lake was quite still.* | *The stone sank below the surface of the pond.* | *The* **surface tension** *of a body of liquid ensures that its surface covers the smallest possible area.* **3** [(*the*)] the part that is easily seen, not the main (hidden) part: *He seems rather shy* **on the surface,** *but he's quite different when you get to know him.* | *Beneath that apparently calm surface is a man of fierce temper.* | *These measures hardly* **scratch the surface** *of the problem.* (=deal only with its easily seen parts, not the more important parts)

surface² *v* **1** [I] to come to the surface of water: *Fish were surfacing to catch insects.* | (fig.) *Old rivalries have begun to surface again.* **2** [T] to give a surface to; cover (esp. a road) with hard material **3** [I] *infml, often humor* to wake up or get out of bed and make one's first appearance of the day: *He doesn't usually surface until 10 o'clock.*

surface³ *adj* [A] **1** being or working on the surface of the earth or sea, rather than beneath it: **Surface workers** *are paid less than their colleagues who work down the mines.* | *The Americans are strengthening their* **surface fleet.** (=not including SUBMARINES) **2** (of post) travelling by land and sea: *Surface mail takes much longer than air-mail.* **3** having no importance or depth; SUPERFICIAL: *surface difficulties/friendliness*

surface-to-air /ˌ··· ˈ·◂/ *adj* [A] (of a weapon) fired from the Earth towards aircraft: *surface-to-air missiles*

surface-to-surface /ˌ··· ˈ···◂/ *adj* [A] (of a weapon) fired from land or sea at a TARGET that is also on the Earth's surface: *a suface-to-surface missile*

surf-board /ˈsɜːfbɔːd‖ˈsɜːrfbɔːrd/ *n* a long narrow piece of plastic, wood, etc., for riding on waves as they come in towards the shore

sur-feit[1] /ˈsɜːfɪt‖ˈsɜːr-/ *n* [S (**of**)] *rather fml* too large an amount or supply; more than is needed or reasonable: *a surfeit of food/television*

surfeit[2] *v* [T (**with**)] *fml* to cause (esp. oneself) to have too much of something; SATIATE

surge[1] /sɜːdʒ‖sɜːrdʒ/ *n* [(**of**) *usu. sing.*] a sudden powerful forward movement, or of or like a wave: *A surge of demonstrators broke through the fence.* | (fig.) *He felt a surge of anger at the sight.* | (fig.) *a surge of support/enthusiasm for the plan* | *a sudden surge in sales*

surge[2] *v* [I+*adv/prep*] **1** to move, esp. forward, in or like powerful waves: *The crowd surged past him/surged through the gates.* **2** [esp. UP] (of a feeling) to appear quickly and powerfully: *Anger surged (up) within him.*

sur-geon /ˈsɜːdʒən‖ˈsɜːr-/ *n* a doctor whose job is to perform medical operations —see also DENTAL SURGEON

Surgeon Gen-e-ral /ˌ··· ˈ···/ *n* **Surgeons General** (in the US) the chief medical officer in the army, navy, or esp. the government. The Surgeon General is responsible for matters that have an effect on public health, e.g. the warnings on cigarette packets.

sur-ge-ry /ˈsɜːdʒəri‖ˈsɜːr-/ *n* **1** [U] the performing of medical operations, usu. including the cutting open of the skin: *Your condition is serious and requires surgery.* (=you will need an operation) —see also PLASTIC SURGERY —see also extra information on page 829 **2** [C;U] *BrE* ‖ **clinic** *AmE*— (the hours of opening of) a place where one or a group of doctors or DENTISTs give people advice on their health and medicines to treat illnesses: *Their surgery is in James Street.* | *What time does surgery finish?* —compare CLINIC[1] **3** [C] *BrE* a period of time during which people can come and see a member of parliament, lawyer, etc., and ask their advice: *Our local MP holds a surgery on Saturday mornings.*

sur-gi-cal /ˈsɜːdʒɪkəl‖ˈsɜːr-/ *adj* **1** of or used for surgery: *a surgical knife* —compare MEDICAL **2** [A] (of a garment) made and worn as a treatment for a particular physical condition: *surgical stockings* — ~ **ly** /kli/ *adv*

surgical spir-it /ˌ··· ˈ··/ *BrE* ‖ **rubbing alcohol** *AmE*— *n* [U] a type of alcohol used for cleaning wounds or skin in hospital

surgical strike /ˌ··· ˈ·/ *n* an attack which bombs a particular building or place: *surgical strikes on missile sites*

Su-ri-nam , Suriname /ˌsʊərɪˈnæm‖-ˈnɑːm/ a country in NE South America between Guyana and French Guiana, formerly known as **Dutch Guiana**; capital Paramaribo; population 398,000 (1989) — ~ **ese** /ˌsʊərɪnəˈmiːz◂/ *n, adj*

sur-ly /ˈsɜːli‖ˈsɜːrli/ *adj* bad-tempered and bad-mannered, esp. habitually: *a surly look/refusal* | *She's always so surly; she never smiles at anyone.*

sur-mise[1] /səˈmaɪz‖sər-/ *v* [T+*obj*/(*that*)] *fml* to suppose as a reasonable guess, though without clear proof: *From his letter I surmised that he was unhappy.*

sur-mise[2] /səˈmaɪz, ˈsɜːmaɪz‖sər-, ˈsɜːr-/ *n* [C;U] *fml* (an) opinion not based on clear proof; guess: *His remarks were pure surmise.* | *a series of wild surmises*

sur-mount /səˈmaʊnt‖sər-/ *v* [T] *fml* **1** to succeed in dealing with (esp. a difficulty); OVERCOME: *I think most of these obstacles can be surmounted.* —see also INSURMOUNTABLE **2** [*usu. pass.*] to be above or on top of: *The house was surmounted by a tall chimney.* — ~ **able** *adj*

sur-name /ˈsɜːneɪm‖ˈsɜːr-/ also **family name** ‖ *usu* **last name** *AmE*— *n* the name a person shares with all members of their family. In English the surname is usu. said last, e.g. in the name George Henry Smith the surname is Smith: *"What's Alan's surname?" "Johnson."* —compare FIRST NAME

sur-pass /səˈpɑːs‖sərˈpæs/ *v* [T] *fml* to go beyond in amount,

quality, or degree; EXCEED: *The results surpassed all our expectations.*

sur-pass-ing /səˈpɑːsɪŋ‖sərˈpæs-/ *adj* [A] *lit* to a degree above anything else: *her surpassing beauty*

sur-plice /ˈsɜːplɪs‖ˈsɜːr-/ *n* a garment made of white material worn over a darker garment during religious services by some Christian priests and church singers

sur-plus /ˈsɜːpləs‖ˈsɜːr-/ *n, adj* (an amount) additional to what is needed or used: *Mexico has a large surplus of oil/a large oil surplus.* | *These chairs are* **surplus to requirements;** *send them back.* | *We're giving away all our surplus apples.* | *Japan's big* **trade surplus** *with the rest of the world* (=gained by selling more goods to other countries than are bought from other countries)

sur-prise[1] /səˈpraɪz‖sər-/ *n* **1** [U] the feeling caused by something unexpected: *You can imagine my surprise when she told me she'd got married last year.* | **Much to my surprise** (=I did not expect this to happen), *they offered me the job.* **2** [C] an unexpected event: *It was a pleasant surprise to see them again.* | *News of the company's financial difficulties came as an unpleasant surprise to the shareholders.* | *We're holding a* **surprise party** *for her retirement.* | *a* **surprise attack** (=made without warning) **3 take someone by surprise** to happen unexpectedly and cause surprise to, esp. in a way that leaves one unprepared: *The sudden cold weather took us all by surprise.*

surprise[2] *v* [T] **1** to cause surprise or shock to: *Her refusal surprised us all.* | *It surprised me to see so many people there.* **2** to find, catch, or attack when unprepared: *They surprised the burglars in the act of opening the safe.*

sur-prised /səˈpraɪzd‖sər-/ *adj* [(**at**)] feeling or showing surprise or shock: *a surprised expression on her face* | *I was surprised at/by her reaction.* [F+*to-v*/(*that*)] *We were surprised to learn that he was French.* | *I'm surprised (that) she didn't sack you on the spot.* | *I* **wouldn't be surprised** *if he changed his mind.* (=he probably will change his mind)

sur-pris-ing /səˈpraɪzɪŋ‖sər-/ *adj* unusual or unexpected; causing surprise: *It's surprising how big they are.* | *He reacted with surprising speed.* | *It's* **hardly surprising** *that she was annoyed.* (=this is exactly what one would expect) — ~ **ly** *adv* : *It was surprisingly easy.*

sur-real /səˈrɪəl/ *adj* having a strange dreamlike unreal quality

sur-real-is-m /səˈrɪəlɪzəm/ *n* [U] a modern type of art and literature in which the painter, writer, etc., connects unrelated images and objects in a strange dreamlike way; famous surrealist painters include Marc Chagall and Salvador Dali

sur-real-ist /səˈrɪəlɪst/ *n, adj* (a painter, writer, or other person) concerned with surrealism. *the surrealist movement active in the 1930s*

sur-real-is-tic /səˌrɪəˈlɪstɪk◂/ *adj* **1** of or concerned with surrealism: *a surrealistic painting* **2** surreal

sur-ren-der[1] /səˈrendə[r]/ *v* **1** [I;T (**to**)] to give up or give in to the power (esp. of an enemy), as a sign of defeat: *After three days, the hijackers surrendered (themselves) to the police.* | (fig.) *The government has surrendered to the pressure of big business and lowered interest rates.* **2** [T] *fml* to give up possession or control of, completely or for a short time: *I hereby surrender all claim to the money.* | *You'll have to surrender your passport at the hotel desk.*

surrender[2] *n* [C;U] the act of surrendering: *They were forced to make an* **unconditional surrender.** | *We will fight on to the end; there will be no surrender.*

sur-rep-ti-tious /ˌsʌrəpˈtɪʃəs◂/ *adj* done, gained, etc., secretly, usu. for dishonest reasons: *When no one was looking he took a surreptitious puff on his cigarette.* — ~ **ly** *adv* — ~ **ness** *n* [U]

sur-rey /ˈsʌri ‖ ˈsɜː-/ *n AmE* a light horse-drawn carriage with four wheels and two seats

Surrey a COUNTY in SE England

sur-ro-ga-cy /ˈsʌrəgəsi‖ˈsɜːr-/ *n* [U] **1** the state of being a surrogate **2** the act of becoming a SURROGATE MOTHER

sur-ro-gate /ˈsʌrəgeɪt, -gↄt‖ˈsɜːr-/ *n, adj fml* (a person or thing) acting or used in place of another; SUBSTITUTE

surrogate moth-er /ˌ··· ˈ··/ *n* a woman who has a baby for another woman who cannot have one herself, using either an egg or SPERM from the two people who will be the baby's parents. There is some disagreement about the ETHICS of this, esp. when the surrogate mother decides that she wants to keep the baby after it is born. In Britain and the US it is now against the law to pay a surrogate mother, but she can agree to become one as a favour for a friend or relative. $- \sim$ **hood** n

sur·round[1] /sə'raʊnd/ v [T] **1** to be all around on every side: *A high wall surrounds the prison camp.* | *She was sitting on the floor surrounded by books.* | (fig.) *The whole affair is surrounded by controversy.* | (fig.) *a beautiful woman surrounded by* (=having many) *admirers* **2** to go around and take up position on every side, esp. in order to prevent escape: *The police surrounded the house.*

surround[2] n a usu. decorative edge or border: *This old fireplace has a very attractive surround.*

sur·round·ing /sə'raʊndɪŋ/ *adj* [A] around and nearby: *in the surrounding area*

sur·round·ings /sə'raʊndɪŋz/ n [P] everything that surrounds a place or person, esp. as it influences the quality of life: *The house is situated in very pleasant surroundings.* | *She grew up in comfortable surroundings.* —compare ENVIRONMENT

sur·veil·lance /sɔː'veɪləns‖sɜːr-/ n [U] a close watch kept on someone, esp. someone who is believed to have criminal intentions: *The police have been keeping her under surveillance.* | *strict surveillance of all incoming flights*

sur·vey[1] /sə'veɪ‖sər-/ v [T] **1** to look at, examine, or consider (a person, place, or condition) as a whole: *We surveyed the view from the top of the hill.* | *If you survey the current state of British industry, it's pretty discouraging.* **2** to examine the condition of (a building), esp. professionally: *Have the house surveyed before you buy it.* —see also SURVEYOR **3** *tech* to measure and record on a map the details of (an area of land): *to survey the east coast* **4** [*often pass.*] to question when making a SURVEY[2] (1a): *Almost 60% of those surveyed said they supported the President's action.*

sur·vey[2] /'sɜːveɪ‖'sɜːr-/ n **1 a** a general examination or study (of conditions, opinions, etc.), esp. carried out by asking people questions: *to do/make/carry out a survey of public attitudes* | *The latest survey shows a majority in support of government policy.* **b** a general (usu. written) description (of a situation, set of ideas, etc.): *She has written a survey of modern English literature.* **2** a professional examination of a house, esp. for someone who may buy it: *Make sure you get a proper survey.*

sur·vey·or /sə'veɪə‖sər-/ n a person whose job is to SURVEY[1] (2,3) buildings or land —see also QUANTITY SURVEYOR

sur·viv·al /sə'vaɪvəl‖sər-/ n **1** [U] the fact or likelihood of surviving: *Hopes are fading for the survival of the missing climbers.* | (fig.) *fighting for his political survival* **2** [C] *esp. BrE* something which has continued to exist from an earlier time, esp. when similar ones have disappeared; RELIC: *That fashion is a survival from the 1970s.*

survival kit /·'·· ·/ n a packet containing the few articles needed to keep one alive when one is lost or hurt beyond the range of help

survival of the fit·test /·,··· · '··/ n [U] **1** (a quote from *Principles of Biology* by the English PHILOSOPHER Herbert Spencer (1820–1903); NATURAL SELECTION **2** any situation in which unsuccessful competitors are quickly destroyed or defeated. The phrase is sometimes used humorously in other ways: *Remarkable survival of the quickest.*

sur·vive /sə'vaɪv‖sər-/ v **1** [I (on)] to continue to live or exist, esp. after coming close to death: *Her parents died in the accident, but she survived.* | *He survived in the desert for a week on biscuits and water.* | *Very few of these old coins survive.* (=are still in existence now) | (fig.) *"How can you cope with this huge amount of work?" "Don't worry; I'll survive."* **2** [T] to continue to live or exist after: *Few buildings survived the fire.* | *She survived her sons.* | *The government is unlikely to survive the next election.* —**vivable** *adj* : *Is nuclear war survivable?*

sur·vi·vor /sə'vaɪvə‖sər-/ n a person or living thing who has continued to live, esp. in spite of coming close to death: *There was only one survivor from/of the plane crash.* | (fig.) *Don't worry about him; he's a survivor.* (=he always manages to continue in spite of difficulties)

Su·sann /suː'zæn/, **Jac·que·line** /'dʒækəliːn/ (1926–74) an American writer of popular NOVELs, e.g. *Valley of the Dolls*

sus·cep·ti·ble /sə'septᵻbəl/ *adj* **1** [(to)] easily influenced (by): *He is very susceptible to persuasion.* **2** [F+to] likely to suffer from: *She's rather susceptible to colds.* **3** tending to experience strong feelings easily; IMPRESSIONABLE: *He's a very susceptible boy.* **4** [F+of] *law or fml* able to have or be changed by: *This agreement is not susceptible of alteration.* —**bility** /sə,septᵻ'bɪlᵻti/ n [U (to)] : *This policy has no regard for the susceptibilities* (=strong feelings) *of the minority groups.*

su·shi /'suːʃi/ n [U] Japanese food consisting of pieces of raw fish on top of cooked rice: *a sushi bar* (=a place where this is served)

sus laws /'sʌs lɔːz/ n [P] *BrE, sl* (formerly) laws which allowed the police to stop and ARREST a person thought to be about to COMMIT a crime, esp. a street crime, without needing formal EVIDENCE. These laws caused a great deal of bad feeling against the police, who were believed by some, esp. young black people, to treat them in particular with SUSPICION.

sus·pect[1] /sə'spekt/ v [T *not in progressive forms*] **1** to believe (esp. something bad) to be true or likely: *She was found dead in her apartment, and the police suspect murder.* | *They said the problem was in the engine, which was just what I had suspected.* [+(that)] *We suspected (that) he was the murderer even before we were told.* **2** [(of)] to believe (someone) to be guilty: *They suspect him of murder/of giving false evidence.* | *Who do you suspect?* | *She was suspected of being a spy.* | *police surveillance of suspected terrorists* **3** to doubt the truth or value of; distrust: *I suspect his motives.* **4** [+(that);obj] *infml* to suppose or guess: *I suspect you may be right.*

sus·pect[2] /'sʌspekt/ n a person who is suspected of guilt, esp. in a crime: *The police have arrested two suspects.*

suspect[3] *adj* of uncertain truth, quality, legality, etc.: *The customs authorities have impounded some suspect crates and ordered them to be opened.* | *His fitness is suspect, so we can't risk including him in the team.*

sus·pend /sə'spend/ v [T] **1** to stop or cause to be inactive or ineffective for a period of time: *Parliament has been suspended because of the civil unrest.* | *Sales of this drug have been suspended until more tests have been performed.* | *I'd like to suspend judgment on this until I've heard more of the facts.* **2** [(from)] to prevent from taking part in a team, belonging to a group, etc., for a time, usu. because of misbehaviour or breaking rules: *She has been suspended from the team.* **3** [+obj+adv/prep, prep, from] *fml* to hang from above: *They suspended a rope from a branch.* **4** [*usu. pass.*] *fml* to hold still in liquid or air: *They could see the dust suspended in the beam of light.*

suspended an·i·ma·tion /·,··· ·'··/ n [U] **1** temporary suspension of life in the body, as in a person who has almost drowned **2** (esp. in SCIENCE FICTION stories) such a state, which someone is held in or trapped in, to be brought back to normal life later

suspended sen·tence /·,·· '··/ n a punishment given by a court of a period in prison which the offender only has to serve if he or she COMMITs another crime in that period of time. This type of sentence can be given for a crime where the punishment is up to two years in prison, and is given for two main reasons; first, to reduce the prison population, and secondly, because the court believes that the threat of prison will be enough to stop the person re-offending. —compare CONDITIONAL DISCHARGE

sus·pend·er /sə'spendər/ *BrE* ‖ **garter** *AmE*— n a fastener hanging down from an UNDERGARMENT (a **suspender belt/garter belt**) to hold a woman's STOCKINGs up. These are now less common, as many women prefer to wear TIGHTS instead, but stockings are considered more sexy and may be worn for this reason.

sus·pend·ers /sə'spendəz‖-ərz/ n [P] *AmE for* BRACES —see PAIR (USAGE)

sus·pense /sə'spens/ n [U] a state of uncertainty about something that is undecided or not yet known, causing either anxiety or sometimes pleasant excitement: *The competitors in the beauty contest were kept in suspense waiting for the result.* | *The suspense was unbearable.* | *The children waited in suspense to hear the end of the story.*

sus·pen·sion /sə'spenʃən/ n **1** [U] the act of suspending or the fact of being suspended: *The government has* ordered the immediate suspension of exports to that country. | I thought her suspension from the team was a very harsh punishment. **2** [C] a liquid mixture with very small pieces of solid material contained but not combined in the liquid —compare COLLOID see SUSPEND (4) **3** [C] the apparatus fixed to the wheels of a car, motorcycle, etc., to lessen the effects of rough road surfaces

suspension bridge /·'··· ·/ n a bridge hung from CABLES (=strong steel ropes) fixed to towers

sus·pi·cion /sə'spɪʃən/ n **1** [C;U] **a** (a) belief that someone is or may be guilty; a case of suspecting or being suspected (SUSPECT¹ (2)): She's been arrested on suspicion of spying. | I'm not sure who took it, but I have my suspicions. **b** lack of trust: She always treated us with suspicion. **2** [C] a feeling of suspecting (SUSPECT¹) the truth or existence of something bad or unpleasant: The boy's pale face and lack of appetite aroused the teacher's suspicions. [+(that)] I have a suspicion (that) you're right. **3** [S (of)] a slight amount (of something seen, heard, tasted, etc.): just a suspicion of garlic in the soup

sus·pi·cious /sə'spɪʃəs/ adj **1** [(of , about)] suspecting (SUSPECT¹) guilt or wrongdoing; not trusting: suspicious of her intentions | I'm a bit suspicious about that package that's been left in the corridor. | His strange behaviour made the police suspicious. **2** causing one to suspect (SUSPECT¹) guilt, wrongdoing, etc.; SUSPECT³: suspicious behaviour | That package in the corridor looks a bit suspicious. | If you see anything suspicious, inform the police at once. | a suspicious-looking character − ~ly adv : She looked at me suspiciously. | He was arrested for acting suspiciously. | (humor) That pen you're using looks suspiciously like the one I lost last week.

suss /sʌs/ v [T+(that);obj] BrE sl to discover the fact that; REALIZE: I soon sussed that he wasn't telling the truth. **suss** sthg. ↔ **out** phr v [T] BrE sl to find out details about quietly or secretly: They must have sussed out the layout of the office before planning the robbery.

Sus·sex /'sʌsɪ̯ks/ a former COUNTY in S England, divided since 1974 into East Sussex and West Sussex

sus·tain /sə'steɪn/ v [T] **1** to keep up the strength, spirits, or determination of: A light meal won't sustain us through the day. | She ate a good sustaining breakfast before she went out. | The knowledge that a rescue team would be searching for them sustained the trapped miners. **2** to keep in existence over a long period; MAINTAIN: He couldn't sustain his interest in it. | She owes her success to sustained hard work. | three years of sustained economic growth **3** fml to suffer (harm or loss): The car sustained severe damage in the accident. **4** fml to hold up (the weight of something): I don't think this floor will sustain the weight of a grand piano. **5** law to accept as being in accordance with the law or justice: The judge sustained the lawyer's objection.

sus·tain·able /sə'steɪnəbəl/ adj (of a policy, process, etc.) able to continue or last for a long time: sustainable economic development | a sustainable rate of growth

sus·te·nance /'sʌstənəns/ n [U] fml **1** the ability of food to keep people strong and healthy: You won't get much sustenance out of one bar of chocolate. **2** food which does this; NOURISHMENT: The children were thin and badly in need of sustenance.

Sut·cliff /'sʌtklɪf/, **Rosemary** (1920–92) an English writer of books, for adults and children, set in the past, e.g. The Eagle of the Ninth

Sut·cliffe /'sʌtklɪf/, **Peter** (1946–) the name of the famous murderer known as the Yorkshire Ripper

Suth·er·land¹ /'sʌðələnd‖-ðər-/ a former COUNTY in NW Scotland, now part of the Highland REGION

Sutherland², Don·ald /'dɒnəld‖'dɑː-/ (1934–) a Canadian film actor known for his films such as Don't Look Now and Ordinary People

Sutherland³, Graham (1903–80) an English painter and artist, known mainly for his picture of Winston Churchill which was later burned on the instructions of Lady Churchill

Sutherland⁴, Dame Joan /dʒəʊn/ (1926–) an Australian SOPRANO singer, who came to England in 1951 and later sang in The Magic Flute and Don Giovanni

su·tra /'suːtrə/ n (a piece of) Hindu holy writing

sut·tee /'sʌtiː/ n [U] the ancient custom in the Hindu religion of a wife being burnt with her dead husband. This is forbidden in India now, but is still carried out in spite of this and the woman is believed to go to the Hindu PARADISE as a reward.

Sut·ton Hoo /ˌsʌtn 'huː/ a place in Suffolk, E England, where people digging in 1939 found a SAXON ship with weapons, jewellery, and other things believed to have been buried with a king in the seventh century

su·ture¹ /'suːtʃər/ n (a stitch or stitches used in) the sewing together of a wound

suture² v [T] to sew up with sutures: The doctor sutured the wound.

Su·va /'suːvə/ the capital of Fiji, on the island of Viti Levu

Su·wan·nee /sə'wɒni‖-'wɑː-/ also **Swanee**– a river in the S of the US, flowing through Georgia and Florida to the Gulf of Mexico made famous by the song "Swanee River" by Stephen Foster

su·ze·rain /'suːzəreɪn‖-rən, -reɪn/ n fml, becoming rare **1** a state which controls the foreign affairs of another state **2** (in former times) a ruling lord

su·ze·rain·ty /'suːzərənti/ n [U] fml, becoming rare the fact or state of being a suzerain

Su·zhou /ˌsuː'dʒəʊ/ also **Su·chou, Soochow**– a city in E China, also known as **Wuxian** or **Wu-hsein**, known for its PAGODAs and making of silk

Suz·man /'sʊzmən/, **Hel·en** /'helən/ (1917–) a South African politician and worker for human rights, esp. for racial equality within her country

Su·zu·ki /sə'zuːki/ n a motorcycle made by the Japanese company Suzuki

Suzuki meth·od /·'··· ˌ··/ n [the] tdmk a system of teaching young children to play the VIOLIN, by making them copy and repeat the music teacher

svelte /svelt/ adj apprec (esp. of a woman) thin, graceful, and well-shaped; SLIM

Sven·ga·li /sven'ɡɑːli/ n a person with a strange power to make other people act in a certain, esp. bad, way (from a character in the NOVEL Trilby by George du Maurier): He still continues to exert a Svengali-like hold over her career. | The judge branded him a Svengali who sapped his wife's self-esteem.

Sverd·lovsk /ˌsveəd'lɒfsk‖ˌsveərd'lɔːfsk/ a city in the Ural mountains in Russia; an industrial and CULTURAL centre

SW written abbrev. for: southwest(ern)

swab¹ /swɒb‖swɑːb/ n **1** a small piece of material used for holding liquid to be tested for infection, for cleaning wounds, etc. **2** a test using such a piece of material: Take a swab of his throat, nurse. **3** a cleaning cloth, esp. as used on the floors of a ship

swab² v -bb- [T] **1** [(DOWN)] to clean (esp. the floors (DECKs) of a ship): The young sailor had to swab down the decks every morning. **2** [(OUT)] to clean (a wound) with a swab

swad·dle /'swɒdl‖'swɑːdl/ v [T] to wrap (a baby) tightly in many coverings

swaddling clothes /'·· ·/ n [P] esp. bibl the pieces of cloth wound round swaddled babies

swag /swæɡ/ n [U] **1** sl the goods obtained in a robbery. In British CARTOONs thieves often have a bag marked "swag". —compare LOOT **2** AustrE a set of clothes and belongings wrapped in a cloth, as carried by travellers and wanderers

swag·ger¹ /'swæɡər/ v [I] to walk with a swinging movement, in a way that shows too much self-confidence or self-satisfaction: He swaggered down the street after winning the fight. − − **er** n − ~ingly adv

swagger² n [S;U] an over-confident and self-satisfied manner, esp. of walking: He walked down the street with a swagger.

Swag·gert /'swæɡət‖-ərt/, **Jimmy** (1935–) an American PREACHER (=religious leader) and television EVANGELIST. In 1988 Swaggert was forced to admit that he had visited a PROSTITUTE (=a woman who exchanges sex for money).

Swa·hi·li /swɑː'hiːli, swə-/ n **1** [U] a BANTU language spoken in eastern and central Africa, and used as a LINGUA FRANCA **2** [C] **Swahili** or **-lis** a member of the Bantu people of Zanzibar who originally spoke this language −**Swahilian** adj

swain /sweɪn/ *n lit or poet* a young man in a country village, esp. a lover or admirer of a girl

SWALK /swɔːlk, swælk‖swɔːlk/ *phrase* sealed with a loving kiss (written on the back of an envelope to express the feelings of the sender)

swal·low¹ /ˈswɒləʊ‖ˈswɑː-/ *v* **1** [T] to move (food or drink) down the throat from the mouth and towards the stomach: *to swallow a mouthful of bread/soup | Swallow your medicine!* **2** [I] to make this movement of the throat, esp. as a sign of nervousness: *He swallowed hard, and walked into the interview room.* **3** [T] *infml* to accept patiently or without question: *They can't treat me like that; I'm not going to swallow it. | Her excuse was obviously a lie, but he* **swallowed it whole**. *| I find that a bit hard to swallow.* **4** [T] to hold back (uncomfortable feelings, tears, etc.); not to show or express: *When he lost his job he had to* **swallow his pride** *and ask for money from his sister.* **5 swallow one's words** to admit that something one said is wrong

  swallow sbdy./sthg. ↔ **up** *phr v* [T] to take in or use up completely; cause to disappear: *The increase in travel costs swallowed up our pay increase. | She was swallowed up by the crowd and we lost sight of her. | a small company that was swallowed up by one of the multinationals*

swallow² *n* an act of swallowing or an amount swallowed

swallow³ *n* **1** a small bird with pointed wings and a double-pointed tail, which comes to northern countries in summer —see picture at BIRD **2 one swallow does not make a summer** do not think that the troubles of life are over because you have sorted out one difficulty

swallow dive /ˈ··· ·/ *BrE* ‖ **swan dive** /ˈ· ·/*AmE— n* a DIVE² into water, starting with the arms stretched out from the sides of the body

Swallows and Am·a·zons /ˌ··· · ˈ···/ a book for children by Arthur Ransome, written in 1930, about the adventures of a group of children playing in boats

swam /swæm/ *past tense of* SWIM

swa·mi /ˈswɑːmi/ *n* a Hindu religious teacher

swamp¹ /swɒmp‖swɑːmp, swɔːmp/ *n* [C;U] (an area of) land which is always full of or covered with water —compare MARSH — **~y** *adj* : *swampy ground*

swamp² *v* [T] **1** [*usu. pass.*] to cause to have a large amount, e.g. of work or problems, to deal with; INUNDATE: *We were swamped with phone calls after our advertisement in the paper.* **2** to make completely wet; flood

swan¹ /swɒn‖swɑːn/ *n* a large white bird, similar to a duck but bigger and with a long neck, which lives on rivers and lakes —see picture at WATER BIRD

swan² *v* **-nn-** [I+*adv/prep*] *infml* to go or travel purposelessly or irresponsibly: *She spent the summer* **swanning around** *Europe. | What makes you think you can* **swan off** *to the cinema when you should be at work?*

Swa·nee /ˈswɒni‖ˈswɑː-/ see SUWANNEE

swank¹ /swæŋk/ *v* [I] *infml* to behave or speak in a very self-confident way, esp. to get attention and admiration: *Stop swanking; you're not the only person who's got a fast car.*

swank² *n infml* **1** [U] proud self-confident talk or behaviour, intended to attract admiration: *Don't pay any attention to all his talk about fast cars; it's just a lot of swank.* **2** [C] a person who swanks

swank·y /ˈswæŋki/ ‖ also **swank** *AmE adj infml* **1** very fashionable or expensive; POSH: *It was a really swanky party.* **2** *derog* tending to swank

Swan Lake /ˌ· ˈ·/ (the name of) a famous BALLET with music by Tchaikovsky, written in 1895 and first performed in Russia

Swann /swɒn‖swɑːn/, **Don·ald** /ˈdɒnəld‖ˈdɑː-/ (1923–) a Welsh songwriter and performer, esp. with Michael Flanders

Swan·sea /ˈswɒnzi‖ˈswɑːnsi/ a city in Wales with a university; once an industrial port used for coal, now attractive to tourists for the nearby GOWER PENINSULA and the mountains of the BRECON BEACONS —see colour map on page 818

Swan·son /ˈswɒnsən‖ˈswɑː-/, **Glo·ri·a** /ˈɡlɔːriə/ (1897–1983) an American actress known for appearances in silent films

swan·song /ˈswɒnsɒŋ‖ˈswɑːnsɔːŋ/ *n* the last piece of work or performance of a poet, painter, etc.: *Shakespeare's*

"Henry VIII" turned out to be his **swansong**.

swan-up·per /ˌ· ˈ··/ *n BrE* a person whose job is to catch and mark CYGNETS (=young SWANS) to show who owns them

swan-up·ping /ˌ· ˈ··/ *n* [U] *BrE* the practice of catching CYGNETS and marking their beaks to show who owns them, esp. the custom of doing this every year on the river Thames

swap¹, **swop** /swɒp‖swɑːp/ *v* **-pp-** [I;T (ROUND, OVER, **for**, **with**)] *infml* to exchange (goods or positions), usu. so that each person gets what they want: *I swapped three of my foreign stamps for three of hers. | I liked her coat and she liked mine, so we swapped/I swapped coats with her. | I want to sit where you're sitting: shall we* **swap round/swap over/swap places**? [+*obj(i)+obj(d)+***for**] (*infml*) *I'll swap you three of mine for one of yours.*

swap², **swop** *n infml* **1** [*usu. sing.*] an exchange: *Let's* **do a swap**. **2** a thing that has been or may be exchanged

swap meet /ˈ· ˌ·/ *n AmE* a gathering where people buy and sell or exchange used goods

SWAPO /ˈswɑːpəʊ/ the South-West Africa People's Organization; a Namibian independence movement

sward /swɔːd‖swɔːrd/ *n old use or lit* a stretch of grassy land; GREENSWARD

swarf /swɔːf‖swɔːrf/ *n* [U] small bits of metal, plastic, etc., produced by a cutting tool in operation

Swar·fe·ga /swɔːˈfiːɡə‖swɔːr-/ *n* [U] *tdmk, BrE* a green substance like JELLY which is used for cleaning oil, paint, etc. off the skin

swarm¹ /swɔːm‖swɔːrm/ *n* [C+*sing./pl. v*] **1** a large group of insects moving in a mass, esp. bees with a QUEEN¹ (3) **2** [(**of**)] also **swarms** *pl.—* a moving crowd of people or mass of animals: *Swarms of tourists jostled through the square.*

swarm² *v* [I] **1** [+*adv/prep*] to move in a crowd or mass: *As the fire spread, people came swarming out of the building. | The photographers swarmed round her.* **2** (of bees) to leave a HIVE (=place where bees live) in a swarm to find another home

  swarm with sbdy./sthg. *phr v* [T *no pass.*] to be full of (a moving crowd of people or animals): *The place was swarming with tourists.*

swarm³ *v* [I+*adv/prep*] *rare* to climb using the hands and feet: *He swarmed up the tree. | She swarmed down the rope.*

swar·thy /ˈswɔːði‖-ɔːr-/ *adj* (of a person or their skin) rather dark-coloured

swash·buck·ling /ˈswɒʃˌbʌkəlɪŋ‖ˈswɑːʃ-, ˈswɔːʃ-/ *adj* like or about daring men who are fond of adventures, sword fighting, etc.: *a swashbuckling pirate film starring Errol Flynn*

swas·ti·ka /ˈswɒstɪkə‖ˈswɑː-/ *n* an ancient sign consisting of a cross with each arm bent at a right **angle**, used in the 20th century **as** a sign for the Nazi Party

swastika

swat¹ /swɒt‖swɑːt/ *v* **-tt-** [T] to hit (an insect) with a flat object or hand, esp. to kill it

swat² *n* **1** an act of swatting **2** a flat object with a handle for killing flies; FLYSWATTER

SWAT /swɒt‖swɑːt/ Special Weapons and Tactics; a group within the American police which is specially trained to use weapons and deal with dangerous criminals who have weapons

swatch /swɒtʃ‖swɑːtʃ/ *n* a piece (of cloth) as an example of a type or quality of material; SAMPLE

Swatch *n tdmk* a watch from Switzerland, made from plastic and often in bright colours

swath /swɒθ‖swɑːθ/ also **swathe**— *n* **1** a line or area of grass or crops that has been cut by a machine or a SCYTHE (=a grass-cutting tool) **2** any large area of a particular type: *Acid rain is now affecting great swaths of Western Europe.* —see also **cut a swath through** (CUT¹)

swathe /sweɪð‖swɑːð, swɔːð, sweɪð/ *v*
  swathe sthg./sbdy. **in** sthg. *phr v* [T *usu. pass.*] *esp. lit or fml* to wrap round in cloth: *His head was swathed in bandages. |* (fig.) *hills swathed in mist*

swat·ter /ˈswɒtəʳ‖ˈswɑː-/ n an instrument for killing flies; SWAT² (2)

sway¹ /sweɪ/ v **1** [I;T] to (cause to) swing from side to side: *The trees were swaying gently in the wind.* | *She swayed her body in time with the music.* | (fig.) *I'm swaying between two opinions.* **2** [T *often pass.*] to influence (someone), esp. so that they change their opinion: *When you're choosing a career don't be swayed just by promises of future high earnings.* | *He's very easily swayed.*

sway² n **1** swaying movement: *The sway of the ship made him fall over.* **2** *old use or lit* power to rule; control: *In medieval times the Church* **held sway over** *many countries.*

Swa·zi /ˈswɑːzi/ n zi or zis **1** [C] a member of the BANTU people of Swaziland **2** [U] the language spoken by the people of Swaziland —**Swazi** adj

Swa·zi·land /ˈswɑːzilænd/ a country in SE Africa bordered by South Africa and Mozambique; capital Mbabane; population 763,000 (1989)

swear /sweəʳ/ v **swore** /swɔːʳ/, **sworn** /swɔːn‖swɔːrn/ **1** [I (at)] to use offensive words that are socially unacceptable; curse: *Stop swearing in front of the children.* | *He tripped over the dog and swore at it.* | *She banged her thumb with the hammer and swore softly, under her breath.* **2** [T] to promise or declare formally or by OATH: *The soldiers swore allegiance to the constitution of the United States.* [+to-v/(that)] *The witness swore to tell the truth/swore that she would tell the truth.* | *a sworn statement* **3** [I;T (on)] to declare (an OATH), esp. in a court of law: *Before giving evidence you have to swear an oath/swear on the Bible.* **4** [T+(that);obj;not in progressive forms] *infml* to state firmly: *He said he was there all the time, but I swear I never saw him.*

  swear by sthg. *phr* v [T *not in progressive forms*] *infml* to have great confidence in the value of: *He swears by vitamin C pills, and says he hasn't had a cold since he started taking them.*

  swear sbdy. ↔ **in** *phr* v [T *often pass.*] **1** to cause to take an OATH of loyalty: *The new President was sworn in.* | *a swearing-in ceremony* **2** to cause (a witness) to take the OATH in a court of law

  swear to *phr* v [T] **1** (**swear** sbdy. **to** sthg.) to cause to make a solemn promise of: *You must swear him to silence.* | *sworn to secrecy* **2** [*no pass.;usu. in negatives*] (**swear to** sthg.) to declare the truth of with certainty: *I think it was him I saw, but I couldn't/wouldn't swear to it.* [+v-ing] *I couldn't swear to having seen him.*

swear box /ˈ· ·/ *BrE* ‖ **cuss box** *AmE—* n a box which some people keep and which they ask people to put money in when they swear, usu. to try to stop people swearing

swear·word /ˈsweəwɜːd‖ˈsweərwɜːrd/ n a word considered offensive or shocking by most people

▶ CULTURAL NOTE Some swearwords, often called **four-letter words** and marked taboo in this dictionary, such as **fuck**, are considered very shocking, and would not be used on a television programme or in conversation unless with the intention of causing offence. These words are often removed from films on television, although they may be allowed in the cinema because the film will be given an **X-certificate**, or rated X in the US, which means that only adults can see it. Some people may use these words in the company of their friends but would not use them in front of their parents or their children. There is also an old-fashioned belief that it is wrong to swear when there are women in the room. Other swearwords, such as **damn**, **hell**, or **bloody**, are less strong, and are more acceptable, especially in a situation where someone hurts themselves or does something stupid, but even these words will give offence to some, esp. older people or religious people, and care should always be taken before using any swearword. It is also considered bad to swear in front of children. ◀

sweat¹ /swet/ v **1** [I] also **perspire** *euph or tech—* to have sweat coming out through the skin: *He was sweating after his run/sweating with fear.* **2** [I] to show liquid on the surface, coming from inside: *The cheese is sweating.* **3** [I] *infml* to be in a state of great anxiety or nervous impatience: *We were really sweating as we waited for them to announce the results.* | *Don't tell them yet; make them sweat a bit.* **4** [T] *BrE* to cook gently in melted fat: *Sweat the vegetables until the juices run out.* **5 sweat blood** *infml* to work unusually hard: *I've sweated blood over this report.* **6 sweat one's guts out** *infml* to work very hard

on something, esp. in a physical way: *I've sweated my guts out trying to get this shed built in time*

  sweat sthg. ↔ **out** *phr* v [T] **1** to get rid of (an illness) by causing oneself to sweat **2 sweat it out** *infml* **a** to take hard exercise: *They were sweating it out in the gym.* **b** to suffer an unpleasant situation until it ends: *The young medical student hated watching his first operation, but he had to sweat it out.*

sweat² n **1** [U] also **perspiration** *fml or euph—* liquid which comes out from the body through the skin to cool it: *I was covered in sweat/dripping with sweat after playing football.* **2** [S] *infml* an anxious state: *It's really quite a simple task; there's no need to get in a sweat about it.* **3** [S] *infml* hard and usu. uninteresting work: *This job's quite a sweat; I'm exhausted already.* **4** [C] *old-fash infml* a person of great experience, esp. a soldier (esp. in the phrase **old sweat**) **5 no sweat** *infml* (used for saying that something will not cause any difficulty): *"Are you sure you can do it in time?" "No sweat."* —see also COLD SWEAT

sweat·band /ˈswetbænd/ n a narrow piece of material **a** sewn or stuck round the inside of a hat to prevent damage by sweat **b** worn round the wrist or forehead to prevent sweat running down, esp. during sport

sweat·ed /ˈswetɪd/ adj [A] *derog* done by workers forced to work long hours for little money: *sweated labour*

sweat·er /ˈswetəʳ/ n a knitted (KNIT) usu. woollen GARMENT for the top of the body, usu. without buttons or other fastenings and pulled on over the head —compare CARDIGAN and see also JERSEY, JUMPER, PULLOVER

sweat gland /ˈ· ·/ n any of the many small organs under the skin from which liquid comes out to cool the skin

sweat pants /ˈ· ·/ n *AmE* thick cotton trousers worn during sports, usu. having string to hold them at the waist (a DRAWSTRING) and elastic at the ankles.

sweat·shirt /ˈswet-ʃɜːt‖-ʃɜːrt/ n a thick cotton GARMENT with long SLEEVES worn on the upper part of the body

sweat·shop /ˈswet-ʃɒp‖-ʃɑːp/ n *derog* a factory or workroom where workers are employed for long hours and low pay often in bad conditions

sweat·y /ˈsweti/ adj **1** covered in or containing sweat: *I shook his sweaty hand.* **2** smelly with sweat: *sweaty socks* **3** unpleasantly hot; causing one to sweat: *a sweaty day/job* —**iness** n [U]

swede /swiːd/ *BrE* ‖ **rutabaga** *AmE—* n [C;U] a round yellow vegetable like a large TURNIP

Swede n a person who comes from or whose parents come from Sweden

Swe·den /ˈswiːdn/ a kingdom in Scandinavia, N Europe; capital Stockholm; population 8,493,000 (1989). It is known for its high standard of living and system of WELFARE, paid for by taxes.

Swe·dish /ˈswiːdɪʃ/ n **1** [U] the North Germanic language spoken in Sweden **2** [*the*+P] the people of Sweden —**Swedish** adj

Swee·ney¹ /ˈswiːni/ [*the*] *BrE sl* FLYING SQUAD

Swee·ney², The a British television programme of the 1970s, with John Thaw and Dennis Waterman as members of the Flying Squad. It was fairly violent, concerned with street crime and had plenty of action.

Sweeney Todd /ˌ·· ˈ·/ a character in an old play who was a man's hairdresser (BARBER) who murdered his customers and had them made into meat pies

sweep¹ /swiːp/ v **swept** /swept/ **1** [T] to clean (a floor or similar surface) using a brush: *He swept the room/the path.* | *She swept the floor clean.* —see USAGE **2** [T+ obj+adv/prep] **a** to remove by brushing: *She swept all the dead leaves off the patio.* **b** to remove or move with a brushing or swinging movement: *The wind swept the leaves away.* | *He swept the papers into a drawer.* **3** [I+adv/prep;T] to move quickly and powerfully (all over): *The crowd swept through the gates.* | *Thunderstorms swept the whole country.* | *A wave of panic swept over her.* | (fig.) *The new dance craze swept the country.* (=was soon popular everywhere) **4** [T+obj+adv/prep] to carry along quickly and powerfully: *They were swept into power on a wave of anti-union feeling.* | *We were swept along by the crowd.* **5** [I+adv/prep] (of a person) to move quickly in a proud or determined way: *She swept angrily out of the room.* | *He swept past the journalists without stopping to*

talk to any of them. | (fig.) *He swept to victory in the elections.* (=he won easily)   **6** [I+*adv/prep*] to be or lie in a curve across land; STRETCH: *The railway line sweeps round the bend in the valley.* | *The hills sweep down to the sea.*   **7** [T] to move across while watching or giving a view of: *The old man's eyes swept the horizon.*   **8 sweep the board** to win (easily) everything that can be won: *I swept the board at the casino last night.*   **9 sweep someone off their feet: a** to cause someone to fall suddenly in love with one **b** to persuade someone completely and suddenly: *The people were swept off their feet by the force of the speaker's arguments.*   **10 sweep something under the carpet** (*BrE*)/**under the rug** (*AmE*) to keep (something bad or shocking) secret

▷ USAGE Compare **brush** and **sweep.** You can **brush** any surface (a shelf, a coat, your teeth, the floor, etc.) using especially a brush with a short handle, held in one hand. You **sweep** a floor, a yard, etc., using a brush with a long handle, held in two hands. —see also CLEAN (USAGE)◁

sweep sthg. ↔ **aside** *phr v* [T] to refuse to pay any attention to: *All our objections were swept aside.*

sweep sthg. ↔ **away** *phr v* [T] to remove or destroy completely: *All these ancient privileges will be swept away when the revolution comes.* | (fig.) *I was swept away* (=completely persuaded) *by her enthusiasm.*

sweep up *phr v*   **1** [I;T (=**sweep** sthg. ↔ **up**)] to clean a place, esp. by sweeping (waste from) the floor: *After all the guests had left, I swept up (all the mess).*   **2** [T] (**sweep** sbdy. ↔ **up**) to pick up in one quick powerful flowing movement: *She swept the child up in her arms and ran off.*

sweep² *n*   **1** an act of sweeping: *This floor needs a good sweep.*   **2** a long swinging movement of the arm with a weapon, etc.: *With a sweep of his sword he cut through the rope.*   **3** [*usu. sing.*] a long curved line or area of country: *The long sweep of the distant hills could just be seen.*| (fig.) *I was most impressed with the* **broad sweep of** her **argument.** (=covering all parts of the subject)   **4** an act of moving out over a broad area to search, attack, etc.: *The rescue services did one last sweep to try and find the missing yachtsman.*   **5** *infml for* SWEEPSTAKE: *I won £2 in the office sweep.*   **6** *infml for* CHIMNEYSWEEP —see also CLEAN SWEEP

Sweep a hand PUPPET in the form of a black and white dog, who appears on children's television in Britain. He is a friend of Sooty. —see also SOOTY

sweep·er /ˈswiːpəʳ/ *n*   **1** a person or thing that sweeps: *a road sweeper*   **2** *BrE* (in football) a player who defends from behind other defending players

sweep·ing /ˈswiːpɪŋ/ *adj*   **1** including or having an effect on many things; EXTENSIVE: *sweeping plans/changes*   **2** showing a lack of consideration of facts or details; too general: *a sweeping statement/generalization* — ~ **ly** *adv*

sweep·ings /ˈswiːpɪŋz/ *n* [P] dirt, dust, etc., which is left to be swept up

sweep·stake /ˈswiːpsteɪk/ also **sweep** *infml*— *n* a form of betting (BET²), usu. on a horserace, in which those who hold tickets for the winners win all the money paid by those who bought tickets

sweet¹ /swiːt/ *adj*   **1** having a taste like that of sugar: *a sweet apple* | *This tea is too sweet.* (=contains too much sugar) | *Do you like sweet or dry wine?* —compare BITTER¹ (1), SOUR¹ (1)   **2** pleasing to the senses: *sweet music* | (fig.) *the* **sweet smell of success**   **3** (esp. of small or young things) charming; lovable: *Your little boy looks very sweet in his new coat.*   **4** gentle, kind, or attractive in manner: *a sweet temper/smile* | *How sweet of you to remember my birthday.*   **5** [F+on] *old-fash infml* in love with — ~ **ly** *adv* — ~ **ness** *n* [U]

sweet² *n*   **1** [C] *BrE* || usu **candy** *AmE*— a small piece of sweet food made of sugar or chocolate, etc.: *Eating sweets is bad for your teeth.*   **2** [C;U] *BrE* || **dessert** *AmE* sweet food served at the end of a meal: *Are we having any sweet?* | *Ice cream is my favourite sweet.* —see DESSERT (USAGE)   **3** *becoming rare* (used when speaking to a loved one): *Don't cry, my sweet.*

sweet-and-sour /ˌ·ˈ··ˈ·◂/ *adj* [A] (of a SAUCE or a food prepared with it, esp. in Chinese cooking) having both sweet and sour tastes together: *sweet-and-sour pork*

sweet·bread /ˈswiːtbred/ *n* an organ (the PANCREAS or THYMUS) from a sheep or young cow, used as food

sweet corn /ˈ· ·/ *BrE* || **corn** *esp. AmE*— *n* [U] (the tender young seed of) a sweet type of MAIZE

sweet·en /ˈswiːtn/ *n*   **1** [I;T] to make or become sweeter: *Shall I sweeten your coffee?* (=by adding sugar to it)   **2** [T] to make kinder, gentler, etc.; soften: *A good meal sweetened his temper.*   **3** [T (UP)] *infml* to give money or presents to in order to persuade: *They'll have to be sweetened (up) if we want them to award us the contract.*

sweetened con·densed milk /ˌ··· ·ˈ· ·/ *n* [U] *AmE for* CONDENSED MILK

sweet·ener /ˈswiːtnəʳ/ *n*   **1** a (piece of a) substance used to sweeten food and drink, esp. instead of sugar: *She usually uses honey as a sweetener rather than sugar.* | *a packet of artificial sweeteners*   **2** *infml* something given or offered in order to persuade someone, esp. in a way that is not open and honest: *These tax cuts are just a pre-election sweetener.*

sweet FA /ˌswiːt ef ˈeɪ/ also **sweet Fan·ny Ad·ams** /ˌ· ·· ˈ··/— *n* [U] *BrE, euph* nothing at all: *"How much did they pay you for that job?" "Sweet FA."* (*euph* for **sweet fuck-all**, *taboo*)

sweet gum /ˌ· ˈ·/ *n* a common North American tree with fairly large five-pointed leaves, hard wood, and seeds like prickly balls

sweet·heart /ˈswiːthɑːt‖-hɑːrt/ *n*   **1** a person whom one loves: *They were sweethearts for ten years before they married.* —see also CHILDHOOD SWEETHEART   **2 a** (used when speaking to someone you love or to a member of your family): *Don't cry, sweetheart.* **b** (used informally as a friendly form of address, esp. by or to a woman): *What can I get you, sweetheart?* (=said e.g. by a person working in a shop or a restaurant) —see DARLING¹ (1) (CULTURAL NOTE)

sweet·ie /ˈswiːti/ *n*   **1** *BrE infml* (used esp. by and to children) a SWEET² (1)   **2** *infml* an attractive lovable little person or thing: *Look at that little dog; isn't he a sweetie!* —see DARLING¹ (CULTURAL NOTE)   **3** *AmE* sweetheart

sweetie pie /ˈ··· ·/ *n AmE* sweetheart

sweet·meat /ˈswiːtmiːt/ *n old use* a sweet or any food made of or preserved in sugar

sweetness and light /ˌ··· ·ˈ·/ *n* [U] friendliness; pleasantness, esp. when not a usual part of someone's character: *She's all sweetness and light when she's talking to her mother-in-law.*

sweet noth·ings /ˌ··· ˈ··/ *n* [P] *humor* things said by lovers to each other: *He spent the whole evening whispering sweet nothings in her ear.*

sweet pea /ˌ·· ˈ·‖ˈ·· ·/ *n* a climbing plant with sweet-smelling flowers

sweet pep·per /ˌ·· ˈ··/ || also **Bell pepper** *AmE*— *n* a GREEN PEPPER or one of the less strong forms of RED PEPPER —see also PEPPER¹ (2)

sweet po·ta·to /ˌ·· ·ˈ···, ·ˈ·ˌ··/ || also **yam** *AmE*— *n* a vegetable which looks similar to a potato but has bright orange flesh, and is the root of a tropical climbing plant; often eaten at THANKSGIVING in the US

sweet roll /ˌ· ˈ·/ *n AmE for* DANISH PASTRY

sweet talk /ˈ· ˌ·/ *n* [U] *infml* insincere talk intended to please or persuade; FLATTERY

sweet-talk /ˈ· ·/ *v* [T] *infml* to (try to) persuade by charming insincere talk or FLATTERY

sweet tooth /ˌ· ˈ·, ˈ· ·/ *n* [S] *infml* a liking for things that are sweet and sugary

swell¹ /swel/ *v* **swelled, swollen** /ˈswəʊlən/ *or* **swelled**   **1** [I (UP)] to gradually increase in fullness and roundness to beyond the usual or original size: *Her ankle swelled (up)* (=became swollen) *after the fall.* | (fig.) *His heart* **swelled with pride** *as he watched his daughter win the race.*   **2** [T] to increase the size or amount of: *We asked them to come to the meeting to* **swell the numbers.** | *The newly-arrived refugees* **swelled the ranks of** (=added to the number of) *the unemployed in the big city.*   **3** [I;T (OUT)] to fill or be filled, giving a full round shape: *The wind swelled (out) the sails.* | *The sails swelled (out) in the wind.*

swell² *n*   **1** [S] the rolling movement of large stretches of the sea up and down, without separate waves: *There's a very heavy swell today, so we're not going sailing.*   **2** [S] an increase of musical sound; CRESCENDO   **3** [S] roundness and fullness: *the firm swell of her breasts* **4** [C] *old-fash infml* a fashionable or important person

swell³ *adj AmE old-fash infml* very good; excellent: *What a swell idea!*

swell·ing /'swelɪŋ/ *n* **1** [C] a swollen place on the body: *I had a nasty swelling on my foot.* **2** [U] the condition of being swollen: *Their bites can cause swelling.*

swel·ter /'sweltəʳ/ *v* [I] (of a person) to experience the effects of great heat: *We had to sit and swelter in the classroom while our friends were down at the beach.*

swel·ter·ing /'sweltərɪŋ/ *adj* unpleasantly hot: *Open a window; it's sweltering in here!*

swept /swept/ *past tense & participle of* SWEEP

swept-back /ˌ· '·◄/ *adj* having the front edge pointing backwards at an angle from the main part: *swept-back hair* | *an aircraft with swept-back wings*

swerve¹ /swɜːv‖swɜːrv/ *v* [I] **1** to turn suddenly to one side (when moving along): *The car swerved to the right.* | *A dog ran in front of the car and we swerved to avoid it.* **2** [(from)] *usu. in negatives*] to change from an idea or purpose: *I will never swerve from my declared policy on this matter.*

swerve² *n* a swerving movement: *a sudden swerve to the left*

swift¹ /swɪft/ *adj* **1** *esp. lit* moving or able to move at great speed, esp. without effort; fast: *a swift runner* **2** ready or quick in action; PROMPT: *a swift reply* | *The president promised swift and effective retribution against the terrorists.* [F+to-*v*] *They have been swift to deny these rumours.* – **~ly** *adv* – **~ness** *n* [U]

swift² *n* a small brown fast-flying bird with pointed wings, similar to a SWALLOW³

Swift, Jon·a·than /ˈdʒɒnəθən‖ˈdʒɑː-/ (1667–1745) an Irish SATIRICAL writer and CLERIC, who wrote *Gulliver's Travels* as well as many shorter works attacking CORRUPTION in religion and education

swig /swɪg/ *v* -**gg**- [T] *infml* to drink, esp. quickly in large mouthfuls: *They just sat there swigging beer all night.* – **swig** *n* : *He took a swig of beer.*

swill¹ /swɪl/ *v* **1** [T (OUT, DOWN)] to wash (an area) by pouring large amounts of water; FLUSH: *Get a bucket and swill the yard (down).* **2** [I;T] *derog* to drink, esp. carelessly and in large amounts: *They just sat in the pub swilling (beer) all night.*

swill² *n* **1** [U] pig food, mostly uneaten human food in partly liquid form **2** [S] an act of washing a place with large amounts of water

swim¹ /swɪm/ *v* **swam** /swæm/, **swum** /swʌm/; *present participle* **swimming** **1** [I] to move oneself through water by using the arms and legs, a tail, FINS, etc.: *We're all going swimming* | *She's teaching the children to swim.* | *They watched the fish swimming in the aquarium.* | *Some snakes can swim.* –see also BACKSTROKE, BREASTSTROKE, BUTTERFLY, CRAWL² (2), DIVE, DOG PADDLE, and SIDESTROKE **2** [T] to cross or complete (a distance) by doing this: *to swim a river/100 metres* **3** [T] to use (a particular stroke) in swimming: *She can swim breaststroke, backstroke, and crawl.* **4** [I (with, in)] to be full of or surrounded with liquid: *The soup was swimming with fat.* | *meat swimming in gravy* **5** [I] to cause one to feel DIZZY; seem to spin round and round: *He was hot and tired and his head was swimming.* **6 swim with/against the tide** to follow/not follow the behaviour of other people around one –see also **sink or swim** (SINK¹) – – **mer** *n* : *She's a strong swimmer.*

swim² *n* **1** [S] an act or occasion of swimming: *Let's go for a swim!* **2 in the swim** *infml* knowing about and concerned in what is going on in modern life

swim·ming /'swɪmɪŋ/ *n* [U] the act or sport of one who swims: *Swimming is a good form of exercise.* | *a swimming club* | *wearing a swimming cap* –see REFEREE (USAGE)

swimming bath /'·· ·/ also **swimming baths** *pl.*– *n BrE* a public SWIMMING POOL, usu. indoors –see also BATHS; see BATH (USAGE)

swimming cos·tume /'·· ˌ··/ *BrE* ‖ **bathing suit, swim suit** *AmE*– *n* a single piece of clothing worn by women for swimming –compare BIKINI, SWIMMING TRUNKS

swim·ming·ly /'swɪmɪŋli/ *adv old-fash infml* easily and successfully: *Everything's going swimmingly.*

swimming pool /'·· ·/ also **pool**– *n* a large usu. outdoor container filled with water, and used for swimming

swimming trunks /'·· ·/ also **bathing suit, swim suit**– *n* [P] a piece of clothing, like very short or legless trousers, worn by men for swimming –compare SWIMMING COSTUME; see PAIR (USAGE)

swimsuit /'··/ *n* a piece of clothing worn for swimming, either by a man or a woman; SWIMMING TRUNKS, a SWIMMING COSTUME, or a BIKINI

swim·wear /'swɪmweəʳ/ *n* [U] clothing suitable for swimming: *Swimwear sale now on!* (sign in a shop)

Swin·burne /'swɪnbɜːn‖-bɜːrn/, **Al·ger·non Charles** /'ældʒənən tʃɑːlz‖-dʒɜːr-, tʃɑːrlz/ (1837–1909) an English poet known for his Greek-style TRAGEDY *Atalanta in Calydon*

swin·dle¹ /'swɪndl/ *v* [T (**out of**)] to cheat (someone), esp. so as to get money illegally: *She swindled him out of his life savings.* (=took them by cheating) –**dler** *n*

swindle² *n* an example of swindling: *a big tax swindle*

Swin·don /'swɪndən/ a town in Wiltshire, S England

swine /swaɪn/ *n* **1** (*pl.* **swine**) *old use or tech* a pig: *swine fever* **2** (*pl.* **swine** *or* **swines**) *sl* an extremely unpleasant person: *Leave her alone, you (filthy) swine!*

swine·herd /'swaɪnhɜːd‖-hɜːrd/ *n lit or old use* a man or boy who looks after pigs

swing¹ /swɪŋ/ *v* **swung** /swʌŋ/ **1** [I;T] to (cause to) move backwards and forwards or round and round from a fixed point above: *The sign was swinging in the wind.* | *The children were swinging on a rope.* | *The soldiers marched along, swinging their arms.* **2** [I+adv/prep;T+obj/prep] to (cause to) move in a smooth curve: *A large black car swung into the drive.* | *She swung the car through the gates.* | *The heavy gate swung shut.* **3** [I+adv/prep;T+obj +adv/prep] to (cause to) move from one point to another by a movement through the air: *They swung (themselves) down from the top of the wall.* | *The cranes swung the big crates onto the ship.* **4** [I+adv/prep;T+obj+adv/prep] to (cause to) turn quickly round: *He swung round and said "Why are you following me?"* | (fig.) *This will swing public opinion against the government.* **5** [I+adv/prep] to walk rapidly and actively with light steps: *He went swinging down/along the street whistling a little tune.* **6** [I] *infml* to play with a pleasant exciting beat: *That music/band really swings.* **7** [T] *infml* to arrange or complete successfully, often by slightly dishonest means: *I'll see if I can swing it for my wife to come with me on that business trip.* | *to swing a business deal* **8** [I (**for**)] *old-fash infml* to be killed by hanging by the neck, as a punishment: *He'll swing for this!* **9 swing the lead** /led/ *BrE infml derog* to avoid doing one's work or duty, esp. by pretending to be ill

swing² *n* **1** [C] a swinging movement: *He took a swing at the tree with his axe.* **2** [C] (in GOLF) the swinging movement of the arms and body used when DRIVING (=hitting the ball): *I spent months correcting my swing.* **3** [C] (a ride on) a seat, esp. for children, which is fixed from above by ropes or chains and on which one can swing backwards and forwards: *The children are playing on the swings in the park.* **4** [C] a noticeable change, esp. from one opinion to another: *There has been a big swing in public opinion.* | *a swing of five per cent to/against the Socialists* **5** [S] (in music) a strong regular beat: *I like music that goes with a swing.* | (fig.) *The party was really going with a swing.* (=was enjoyable, lively, and successful) **6** [U] JAZZ music of the 1930s and 1940s with a strong regular beat, usu. played by a big band **7 get into the swing of (smthg)** to get used to doing something and get good at doing it or enjoy doing it: *It's difficult work, but once you get into the swing of it, you'll find you can do it quickly.* **8 in full swing** having reached a very active stage: *The party was in full swing when the police burst in.* **9 what you lose on the swings you gain on the roundabouts** (often shortened to **swings and roundabouts**) *infml, BrE* the disadvantages of a particular situation or course of action are balanced by the advantages: *It's a bit of a swings and roundabouts situation.*

swing door /ˌ· '·/ *n* a door which can be pushed open from inside or out and which swings backwards and forwards after use

swinge·ing /'swɪndʒɪŋ/ *adj BrE* (esp. of arrangements

concerning money) very severe in force, degree, etc.: *The government has announced* **swingeing cuts** (=reductions) *in public spending.*

swing·er /'swɪŋəʳ/ *n infml, becoming old-fash* **1** a lively fashionable person who leads an active social life, esp. going to a lot of parties, NIGHTCLUBS, etc. **2** someone who behaves in a sexually free way

swing·ing /'swɪŋɪŋ/ *adj infml* **1** full of life and fun: *a swinging party* **2** fashionably free and modern, esp. in sex life: *the swinging sixties*

swinging six·ties /ˌ·· '··/ [*the*+P] the years 1960–69 in Britain and the US, esp. in the sense of the freedom young people felt to have sex, wear unusual clothes, and discuss new ideas

Swing Low, Sweet Char·i·ot /ˌ· ˌ· · '···/ an American religious song (SPIRITUAL) that used to be sung by people working in the fields

swing·om·e·ter /swɪŋ'ɒmɪtəʳ‖-'ɑːm-/ *n BrE infml* a DEVICE made from a pointer and a DIAL, which is used on television during elections to show the changing support for a political party: *The swingometer shows a ten per cent swing to the Liberal Democrats.*

swing set /'· ˌ·/ *n* a large frame which holds several SWINGS² (2) and sometimes a SLIDE, often built on children's playgrounds, and sometimes in a family garden

swing-wing /ˌ· '·◂/ *adj* [A] (of an aircraft) having wings that can be swung forwards for low speeds and backwards for high speeds

swin·ish /'swaɪnɪʃ/ *adj* extremely unpleasant or difficult to deal with: *a swinish person/problem* | *swinish behaviour* – –**ly** *adv* – –**ness** *n* [U]

swipe¹ /swaɪp/ *n* **1** a forceful sweeping stroke or blow: *She made a swipe at the mosquito.* **2** an attack in words: *In her latest article, she* **takes a swipe at** *the fashionable critics.* —compare SIDESWIPE

swipe² *v* **1** [I (at);T] to (try to) hit hard, esp. with an uncontrolled swing of the arm: *She swiped at his head, but he got out of the way.* **2** [T] *infml* to steal: *Who's swiped my pen?*

swirl¹ /swɜːl‖swɜːrl/ *v* [I+*adv/prep*;T+*obj*+*adv/prep*] to move quickly with twisting turns: *The water swirled about his feet/swirled down the plughole.* | *The leaves were swirled away on the wind.*

swirl² *n* **1** a swirling movement: *She danced with a swirl of her skirt.* **2** [(of)] a twisting mass (of water, dust, etc.); EDDY: *Swirls of smoke rose through the trees.*

swish¹ /swɪʃ/ *v* **1** [I+*adv/prep*;T] to (cause to) move quickly through the air making a sharp whistling noise: *The whip swished through the air.* | *The cow swished its tail.* **2** [I] (esp. of clothes) to make a soft sound in movement: *Her silk dress swished as she passed.* –**swish** *n* : *The horse gave a swish of its tail.*

swish² *adj infml* fashionable and expensive: *a very swish restaurant*

Swiss /swɪs/ *adj* of or from Switzerland

Swiss ar·my knife /ˌ· '·· ˌ·/ *n* a small knife with usu. two blades and several other tools which fold into the handle, such as a can opener, a bottle opener, etc. —compare PEN KNIFE

Swiss army knife

Swiss chard /ˌ· '·/ *n* [C;U] CHARD

Swiss cheese /ˌ· '·/ *n* [U] any hard pale yellow or white cheese with holes, such as Emmentaler or Gruyère

Swiss Fam·i·ly Rob·in·son /ˌ· ··· '···/, **The** a book for children written in 1813 by the Swiss writer Johann Wyss about a family on a desert island

Swiss Guard /ˌ· '·/ [*the*+P] the group of men who work as bodyguards in the Vatican

swiss roll /ˌ· '·/ *also* **jelly roll** *AmE*– *n* [C;U] a cake baked in a thin piece and then rolled up with a sweet substance (JAM or cream) inside

swiss steak /ˌ· '·/ *n AmE* a piece of BEEF cooked in tomatoes (TOMATO)

switch¹ /swɪtʃ/ *n* **1** an apparatus for stopping or starting the flow of an electric current, esp. one which is moved

up or down with the hand: *a light switch* **2** a complete, esp. unexpected, change: *There's been a switch in our plans.* **3** a small thin stick: *a hazel switch*

switch² *v* **1** [I+*adv/prep*;T] to change or exchange, esp. completely or unexpectedly: *The wind has switched round from north to east.* | *He got tired of teaching and switched to writing stories.* | *Let's switch positions.* | *Wait until the lights have switched to green.* | *to switch one's allegiance* [T+*obj*+*adv/prep*] to change or move by a switch: *Switch the freezer to the extra cold setting.* – –**able** *adj*

switch off *phr v* **1** [I;T (=**switch** sthg. ↔ **off**)] to turn (an electric light or apparatus) off by means of a switch: *Switch off when you've finished using the electric typewriter.* | *Switch the television off.* –see OPEN (USAGE) **2** [I] *infml* to stop listening or paying attention: *He just switches off when you try to talk to him.*

switch on *phr v* [I;T (=**switch** sthg. ↔ **on**)] to turn (an electric light or apparatus) on by means of a switch: *"It doesn't work." "Have you switched (it) on?"* –see also SWITCHED-ON; see OPEN (USAGE)

switch over *phr v* **1** [I+*prep*] to change completely: *She switched over from supporting the Republicans to supporting the Democrats.* **2** [I;T (=**switch** sthg. ↔ **over**)] *esp. BrE* to change from one radio or television station to another: *I'm tired of this programme; switch (it) over to the other channel.*

Switch *n* [U] (in Britain) a system which means that people can pay for goods with a plastic card instead of using a cheque book, and the money is taken out of their bank account: *"Do you take Switch?"* | *a Switch card* –see also DEBIT CARD

switch·back /'swɪtʃbæk/ *n* a road or track going up and down steep slopes and round sharp bends, such as a mountain road or a railway for amusement at a FAIR³ (1)

switch·blade /'swɪtʃbleɪd/ *n AmE for* FLICK KNIFE

switch·board /'swɪtʃbɔːd‖-bɔːrd/ *n* (the people who control) a central apparatus at which telephone lines are connected and disconnected, for example in an office building: *If you want an outside line, you'll have to ask the switchboard.* | *Angry callers* **jammed the switchboard** *at the White House.* (=because so many people were telephoning at the same time) —compare TELEPHONE EXCHANGE

switched-on /ˌ· '·◂/ *adj infml, becoming old-fash* quick to notice or become conscious of new ideas, opinions, fashions, etc.

switch·es /'swɪtʃɪz/ *n* [P] *AmE for* POINTS (1)

switch·gear /'swɪtʃɡɪəʳ/ *n* [U] equipment for making electrical connections in a system

Swith·in, **Swithun** /'swɪðɪn/, **Saint** see SAINT SWITHIN'S DAY

Swit·zer·land /'swɪtsələnd‖-sər-/ a country in W Europe; capital Bern; population 6,647,000 (1989). It is known for having remained NEUTRAL in the two world wars, and being the base of international groups such as the Red Cross. It is also a world centre for banking and the management of money and famous for its chocolate and its cheese, and for making clocks and watches.

swiv·el¹ /'swɪvəl/ *v* -**ll**- *BrE* ‖ -**l**- *AmE* [I;T (ROUND)] to turn (quickly) round (as if) on a central point: *She swivelled round in her chair as I came in.*

swivel² *n* an apparatus joining two parts in such a way that they can turn independently: *a swivel chair* (=a chair that turns) –see picture at CHAIR

swiz, **swizz** /swɪz/ *n* [S] *BrE infml* something that makes one feel cheated or disappointed

swiz·zle stick /'swɪzəl ˌstɪk/ *n* a stick or glass rod for mixing drinks

swol·len¹ /'swəʊlən/ *past participle of* SWELL¹

swollen² *adj* increased beyond the usual size, often because of the presence of water or air inside, which is not usually present: *Her foot was very swollen after her accident.* | *The swollen river burst its banks.*

swollen head /ˌ·· '·/ *BrE* | **big head** *AmE*– *n* [S] too great a sense of one's own importance: *If you keep telling him how clever he is, he'll get a swollen head.* – –**ed** /ˌ·· '··◂/ *adj*

swoon¹ /swuːn/ *v* [I] **1** *lit or humor* to experience deep effects of joy, desire, etc., as if fainting (FAINT²) usu. said of women: *The young girls swooned when they saw their favourite pop singer.* **2** *esp. old use* to lose consciousness; FAINT[2]

swoon[2] *n esp. old use* a FAINT[3]: *He fell down in a swoon from sheer hunger.*

swoop[1] /swuːp/ *v* [I] **1** to move down suddenly and steeply, esp. to attack: *The hawk swooped (down) and seized the rabbit.* **2** [(on)] *infml* to make a sudden surprise attack: *The police swooped as the gang came out of the bank.*

swoop[2] *n* a swooping action or movement: *"Police arrest five in dawn drugs swoop."* (title of newspaper story) —see also **at one fell swoop** (FELL[4])

swoosh /swuːʃ/ *v, n* SWISH[1] (1)

swop /swɒp‖swɑːp/ *v, n* SWAP

sword /sɔːd‖sɔːrd/ *n* **1** a weapon with a long sharp metal blade and a handle, used in former times **2 put to the sword** *old use or lit* to kill with a sword: *All the villagers were mercilessly put to the sword.* **3 they that live by the sword shall perish by the sword** *saying from the Bible* people who use violence to achieve things will be defeated finally by violence

sword dance /ˈ··/ *n* a Scottish dance which includes jumping over swords laid on the ground —**sword dancer** *n*

sword·fish /ˈsɔːdfɪʃ‖-ɔːr-/ *n* swordfish *or* swordfishes a large fish with a long pointed upper jaw like a sword

sword in the stone /ˌ··· ˈ·/ [*the*] according to old stories, the sword called Excalibur which was stuck in a stone and which would make the person who pulled it out King of England —see also ARTHURIAN LEGEND

sword of Dam·o·cles /ˌsɔːd əv ˈdæməkliːz‖ˌsɔːrd-/ *n* swords of Damocles something bad that may happen at any time (from an ancient Greek story in which a king seats Damocles under a sword that hangs from a single hair to show him that rulers have their fears and worries as well as their power and happiness): *The possibility of another illness hung over his happiness like a sword of Damocles.*

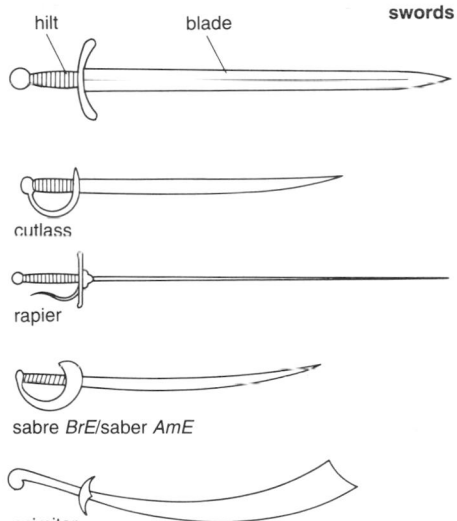

swords

hilt   blade

cutlass

rapier

sabre *BrE*/saber *AmE*

scimitar

sword·play /ˈsɔːdpleɪ‖-ɔːr-/ *n* [U] the movement and skill used in fighting with swords

swords·man /ˈsɔːdzmən‖-ɔːr-/ *n* **-men** /mən/ a (skilled) fighter with a sword

swords·man·ship /ˈsɔːdzmənʃɪp‖-ɔːr-/ *n* [U] skill in fighting with a sword

swore /swɔːʳ/ *past tense of* SWEAR

sworn[1] /swɔːn‖swɔːrn/ *past participle of* SWEAR

sworn[2] *adj* [A] complete and with no possibility of changing: *They are* **sworn enemies.**

swot[1] /swɒt‖swɑːt/ *BrE* ‖ **grind** *AmE*— *n infml derog* someone who works (too) hard at their studies, esp. when trying to get good examination results, and seems to have no other interests

swot[2] *v BrE* ‖ **cram** *AmE*— **-tt-** [I] *infml* to study hard
swot sthg. ↔ **up** *phr v* [T] *BrE infml* to work hard in order to learn (a subject one is studying), usu. before an examination: *She's swotting up her French irregular verbs.*

swum /swʌm/ *past participle of* SWIM[1]

swung /swʌŋ/ *past tense & participle of* SWING[1]

syb·a·rite /ˈsɪbəraɪt/ *n fml or lit* a person who lives a life of pleasure in extremely comfortable surroundings

syb·a·rit·ic /ˌsɪbəˈrɪtɪk◄/ *adj fml or lit* of or like a sybarite: *She found happiness, and a sybaritic new life in the sun.*

syc·a·more /ˈsɪkəmɔːʳ/ *n* **1** a European tree with fairly large five-pointed leaves and seeds that float to the ground on wing-like parts **2** an American PLANE TREE

syc·o·phant /ˈsɪkəfənt/ *n fml derog* a person who FLATTERs (=praises insincerely) those in positions of power in order to gain personal advantage: *The President surrounded himself with sycophants.* —**ic** /ˌsɪkəˈfæntɪk◄/ *adj* : *"Of course, you're absolutely right", he said with a sycophantic smile.*

Syd·ney /ˈsɪdni/ the largest city in Australia, known for its bridge and OPERA house

Syd·ow /ˈsɪdəʊ/, **Max von** /mæks vɒn‖-vɑːn/ (1929–) a Swedish actor who often worked with the director Ingmar Bergman. His films include *The Exorcist* and *Hannah and her Sisters.*

Sykes /saɪks/, **Er·ic** /ˈerɪk/ (1923–) an English actor known for his funny films and television work, esp. with Hattie Jacques

syl·lab·ic /sɪˈlæbɪk/ *adj tech* having or forming one or more syllables. *"N" is a syllabic consonant in "button".*

syl·la·ble /ˈsɪləbəl/ *n* a word or part of a word which contains a vowel sound or a consonant acting as a vowel: *There are two syllables in "window": "win-" and "-dow".*

syl·la·bub sil- /ˈsɪləbʌb/ *n* [C;U] a dish made of sweetened cream or milk mixed with wine and usu. egg whites

syl·la·bus /ˈsɪləbəs/ *n* **-buses** *or* **-bi** /baɪ/ an arrangement of subjects for study over a period of time, esp. a course of studies leading to an examination: *I see "Hamlet" is on this year's syllabus for the English literature exam.* —compare CURRICULUM

syl·lo·gis·m /ˈsɪlədʒɪzəm/ *n tech* (in LOGIC) a reasoned argument in which there are two statements which must lead to a third statement (as in "all men will one day die; Socrates is a man; therefore one day Socrates will die") —**gistic** /ˌsɪləˈdʒɪstɪk◄/ *adj*

sylph /sɪlf/ *n* **1** a graceful SLENDER woman or girl **2** according to old stories, a spirit of the air —compare NYMPH

sylph·like /ˈsɪlf-laɪk/ *adj esp. lit or humor* (of a woman or her body) attractively thin and graceful: *her sylphlike figure*

syl·van , sil- /ˈsɪlvən/ *adj* [A] *lit or poet* of or in woods and the country: *a sylvan glade*

sym·bi·o·sis /ˌsɪmbiˈəʊsɪs‖-baɪ-, -bi-/ *n* [U] *fml or tech* the condition of two different living things which depend on each other for certain advantages, often with one living on the other's body: *This bird lives in symbiosis with cattle; it picks insects from their skin to eat.* —**otic** /-ˈɒtɪk◄‖-ˈɑːtɪk◄/ *adj* : *a symbiotic relationship*

symbol

washable   hand wash   can be dry cleaned

do not wash   cool iron   do not iron

some washing symbols

sym·bol /ˈsɪmbəl/ *n* **1** [(of)] something which represents or suggests something else, such as an idea or quality: *In the picture the tree is the symbol of life and the snake the symbol of evil.* | *The flag of the occupying army was regarded by the people as a symbol of oppression.* | *The dove is a symbol of peace.* —compare EMBLEM **2** [(for)] a letter, sign, or figure which expresses a sound, operation, number, chemical substance, etc.: *"H_2O" is the symbol for water.* | *According to the symbol on the label, this sweater should be washed by hand.* | *We use phonetic symbols as a guide to pronunciation in this dictionary.*

sym·bol·ic /sɪmˈbɒlɪk‖-ˈbɑː-/ also **sym·bol·i·cal** /-ɪkəl/— *adj* [(of)] of, being, or using a symbol: *a symbolic painting* | *The snake is symbolic of evil.* − − **ally** /kli/ *adv*

sym·bol·is·m /ˈsɪmbəlɪzəm/ *n* [U] the use of symbols, esp. in literature, painting, films, etc.: *a novel full of religious symbolism*

sym·bol·ize also **-ise** *BrE* /ˈsɪmbəlaɪz/ *v* [T] **1** to be a symbol of: *A wedding ring symbolizes the union of husband and wife.* **2** to represent by one or more symbols —**ization** /ˌsɪmbəlaɪˈzeɪʃən‖-bələ-/ *n* [U]

sym·met·ri·cal /sɪˈmetrɪkəl/ also **sym·met·ric** /sɪˈmetrɪk/— *adj* having both sides exactly alike: *The human face is more or less symmetrical.* —opposite **asymmetric** − − **ly** /kli/ *adv*

sym·me·try /ˈsɪm̩tri/ *n* [U] **1** exact likeness in size, shape, form, etc., between the opposite sides of something − opposite **asymmetry** **2** an effect of pleasing balance: *We admired the symmetry of the building's design/of the painting.*

sym·pa·thet·ic /ˌsɪmpəˈθetɪk◂/ *adj* **1** feeling or showing sympathy: *She was very sympathetic when my mother died.* **2** [F (to, towards)] showing (a willingness to give) agreement or approval: *They were quite sympathetic to our proposals.* | *They promised to give our suggestions a sympathetic hearing.* **3** pleasant; similar to what one likes or wants; CONGENIAL: *a sympathetic atmosphere at the party* − − **ally** /kli/ *adv*

sympathetic ma·gic /ˌ···· ˈ··/ *n* [U] magic in which an action performed in one place is thought to cause or influence a similar event in another place

sym·pa·thies /ˈsɪmpəθiz/ *n* [P] **1** feelings of support or loyalty: *Although I pity him, my sympathies lie/are with his family.* | *No one's quite certain where her political sympathies lie.* **2** a message of comfort in grief: *She sent her sympathies on the death of her friend's husband.*

sym·pa·thize also **-thise** *BrE* /ˈsɪmpəθaɪz/ *v* [I (**with**)] to feel or show sympathy or approval: *I know you feel angry, and I sympathize.* | *It's hard to sympathize with her political opinions.*

sym·pa·thiz·er /ˈsɪmpəθaɪzəʳ/ *n* often derog someone who shows sympathy with a person or a cause, esp. a political point of view: *He was suspected of being a Communist Party sympathizer.* | *a sympathizer of the women's rights movement*

sym·pa·thy /ˈsɪmpəθi/ *n* [U] **1** sensitivity to and understanding of the sufferings of other people, often expressed in a willingness to give help: *She squeezed his hand in sympathy.* | *I didn't get much sympathy from the doctor when I told him about my pains.* | *The documentary aroused public sympathy for victims of the disaster.* | *The president sent a message of sympathy/expressed his sympathy.* **2** agreement with or understanding of the feelings or thoughts of other people: *I have a lot of sympathy for what they're trying to do.* | *I am in sympathy with her aims, but I don't like the way she goes about achieving them.* **3** active support of other workers: *The dock workers have come out in sympathy (with the miners)* (=stopped work as a sign of support for them); *it's a sympathy strike.* —compare EMPATHY; see also **tea and sympathy** (TEA (7))

sympathy card /ˈ··· ˌ·/ *n* a card expressing sympathy, sent to someone a member of whose family has just died

sym·pho·ny /ˈsɪmfəni/ *n* a piece of music for an ORCHESTRA (=a large group of instruments), usu. having four main parts (=MOVEMENTS) —**nic** /ˌsɪmˈfɒnɪk‖-ˈfɑːn-/ *adj*

symphony or·ches·tra /ˈ··· ˌ···/ *n* a large ORCHESTRA (=large group of musical instruments) which performs symphonies and other similar musical works

sym·po·si·um /sɪmˈpəʊziəm/ *n* **-siums** or **-sia** /ziə/ *fml* a meeting between scientists or other people experienced

in a particular subject, in order to talk about a certain area of interest

symp·tom /ˈsɪmptəm/ *n* [(of)] **1** an outward or noticeable sign of disease: *The symptoms don't appear until a few days after you're infected.* | *Yellow skin is a symptom of jaundice.* **2** an outward sign of a usu. bad or undesirable condition or event: *The lower production levels are a symptom of widespread dissatisfaction among the workforce.* | *He recognizes the symptoms, but refuses to admit that he has marital problems.* —see also WITHDRAWAL SYMPTOMS

symp·to·mat·ic /ˌsɪmptəˈmætɪk◂/ *adj* [(of)] being a sign of a particular esp. bad condition: *Their refusal to take part in the inquiry is symptomatic of their distrust of the police.* − − **ally** /kli/ *adv*

syn·a·gogue /ˈsɪnəgɒg‖-gɑːg/ *n* a building where Jews meet for religious worship

sync, synch /sɪŋk/ *n* [U] *infml* a correct working arrangement; synchronization: *The film and its soundtrack are out of sync.* (=not going properly together)

syn·chro·mesh /ˈsɪŋkrəʊmeʃ/ *n* [U] a part of the GEARs in a car which allows them to change smoothly

syn·chro·ni·ci·ty /ˌsɪŋkrəˈnɪsɪti/ *n* (an example of) the happening at the same place, time, or period of time, of two or more events which are similar or related

▷ USAGE Unlike COINCIDENCE, SYNCHRONICITY is only used when the speaker believes that there is or may be some connection between the two events besides chance, such as God, FATE, or some other PSYCHIC force (=which cannot be explained by science): *Some people study the synchronicities between planetary changes and major changes in the world's problems.* | *the synchronicity of changes in animal behaviour before earthquakes*◁

syn·chro·nize ‖ also **-nise** *BrE* /ˈsɪŋkrənaɪz/ *v fml* **1** [I;T (**with**)] to (cause to) happen at the same time or the same speed: *You have to synchronize the soundtrack with the film.* (=make the sound fit the pictures) | *The soundtrack and the film don't synchronize.* **2** [T] to set (clocks and watches) so that all show exactly the same time: *Let's synchronize watches.* —**nization** /ˌsɪŋkrənaɪˈzeɪʃən‖-krənə-/ *n* [U]

synchronized swim·ming /ˌ··· ˈ··/ *n* [U] a form of swimming, usually performed by women, which is like a dance in the water while music is playing. The swimmers make patterns with their bodies but do not move fast or over long distances.

syn·chro·nous /ˈsɪŋkrənəs/ *adj* tech of or being a method of sending information over telephone lines at a fixed speed which is synchronized by the equipment used. It is faster than ASYNCHRONOUS because it does not use BITs to show the beginning and end of each character.

syn·co·pate /ˈsɪŋkəpeɪt/ *v* [T] tech to change (the beat of music) by giving force to the beats that are usu. less forceful: *a syncopated rhythm* —**pation** /ˌsɪŋkəˈpeɪʃən/ *n* [U]

syn·co·pe /ˈsɪŋkəpi/ *n* [U] tech the loss of consciousness in fainting (FAINT²)

syn·di·cal·is·m /ˈsɪndɪkəlɪzəm/ *n* [U] a political system or belief whose aim is control of industry by the workers —**ist** *adj, n*

syn·di·cate¹ /ˈsɪndɪ̩kət/ *n* [C+*sing./pl. v*] a group of people or companies combined together for a particular purpose, usu. business: *Our companies formed a syndicate to bid for the big new contract.* | *A syndicate of local businessmen is/are bidding for the contract.*

syn·di·cate² /ˈsɪndɪ̩keɪt/ *v* **1** [T] to arrange for (written work, photographs, etc.) to be sold to a number of different newspapers, magazines, etc.: *His column is syndicated throughout America.* **2** [I;T] to form into a syndicate —**cation** /ˌsɪndɪ̩ˈkeɪʃən/ *n* [U]

syn·drome /ˈsɪndrəʊm/ *n* **1** tech a set of medical SYMPTOMs which represent a physical or MENTAL disorder —see also DOWN'S SYNDROME **2** *infml* a pattern of qualities, events, etc., typical of a general condition: *Their lifestyle is typical of the bored middle-aged housewife syndrome.*

Synge /sɪŋ/, **J M** (1871–1909) an Irish writer famous for his plays such as *The Playboy of the Western World*

syn·od /ˈsɪnəd/ *n* an important meeting of church members to make decisions on church matters (esp. in the Christian church)

syn·o·nym /ˈsɪnənɪm/ n a word with the same meaning or nearly the same meaning as another word in the same language: *"Sad" and "unhappy" are synonyms.* — compare ANTONYM

sy·non·y·mous /sɪˈnɒnɪməs‖-ˈnɑː-/ adj [(with)] having the same meaning or nearly the same meaning (as): *"Sad" and "unhappy" are synonymous.* | *"Sad" is synonymous with "unhappy".* | (fig.) *She seems to think that being poor is synonymous with being lazy.* — ~ly adv

sy·nop·sis /sɪˈnɒpsɪs‖-ˈnɑːp-/ n -ses /siːz/ [(of)] a short account of something longer, such as the story of a film, play, or book; SUMMARY

sy·nop·tic gos·pels /sɪˌnɒptɪk ˈgɒspəlz‖-ˌnɑːptɪk ˈgɑː-/ n [the+P] (usu. cap.) the accounts of Christ's life written by Matthew, Mark, and Luke (but not John), which all tell the same story in a similar way

syn·tac·tic /sɪnˈtæktɪk/ adj concerning or obeying the rules of syntax — ~ally /kli/ adv : *"Be" and "become" are often used in the same way syntactically.*

syn·tax /ˈsɪntæks/ n [U] 1 the rules of grammar which are used for ordering and connecting words to form phrases or sentences 2 the rules which describe how words and phrases are used in a computer language —compare MORPHOLOGY

syn·the·sis /ˈsɪnθəsɪs/ n -ses /siːz/ [(of)] 1 [U] the combining of separate things, ideas, etc., into a complete whole: *the synthesis of rubber from petroleum* —compare ANALYSIS 2 [C] something, such as a substance or an idea, made by combining various parts: *Their beliefs are a synthesis of Eastern and Western religions.*

syn·the·size also -sise BrE /ˈsɪnθəsaɪz/ v [T] to make up or produce by combining parts, esp. to make (something similar to a natural product) by combining chemicals: *to synthesize a drug* —compare ANALYSE

syn·the·siz·er also -siser BrE /ˈsɪnθəsaɪzəʳ/ n an electrical instrument that can produce many different sorts of sound, such as those of various musical instruments, which is usu. played with a KEYBOARD, like a piano, and is used esp. in popular music —see also SPEECH SYNTHESIZER

syn·thet·ic /sɪnˈθetɪk/ adj produced by synthesizing; not naturally produced; artificial: *synthetic rubber* | *synthetic fibres* — ~ally /kli/ adv

syph·i·lis /ˈsɪfəlɪs/ n [U] a very serious disease, passed on during sexual activity or from parent to child. This disease, like any VENEREAL disease is considered very embarrassing, and someone who had it would be ashamed to tell anyone; but in both Britain and the US there are special CLINICs where it can be treated —compare GONORRHEA, SEXUALLY TRANSMITTED DISEASE

syph·i·lit·ic /ˌsɪfəˈlɪtɪk◄/ n, adj (a person) suffering the effects of syphilis

sy·phon /ˈsaɪfən/ n, v SIPHON

Sy·ra·cuse /ˈsaɪrəkjuːz/ a port on the east coast of Sicily, in Italy, a centre of Greek life in the eighth century BC

Syr·i·a /ˈsɪriə/ a country in the Middle East bordering on Turkey, Iraq, Jordan, Israel, and Lebanon; population 11,719,000 (1989) —**Syrian** adj,n

sy·ringe¹ /sɪˈrɪndʒ/ n an instrument used esp. in science and medicine, which consists of a hollow tube into which liquid can be sucked and from which it can be pushed out, esp. through a needle, to put drugs into the body — see also HYPODERMIC

syringe² v [T] to clean with a syringe: *She had to have her ears syringed.*

syr·up /ˈsɪrəp‖ˈsɜː-, ˈsɪ-/ n [U] 1 sweet liquid, esp. sugar and water: *tinned peaches in syrup* 2 a very thick sticky pale liquid made from sugar: *golden syrup* | *maple syrup* —see also CORN SYRUP 3 medicine in the form of a thick sweet liquid: *cough syrup* | *syrup of figs*

syr·up·y /ˈsɪrəpi‖ˈsɜː-, ˈsɪ-/ adj 1 like or containing syrup 2 derog too sweet, nice, kind, etc.: *a syrupy romantic novel*

sys·tem /ˈsɪstəm/ n 1 [C] a group of related parts which work together forming a whole: *A strike disrupted the postal system.* | *a heating/air-conditioning system* | *the solar system* | *a computer system* | *the digestive system* | *the nervous system* 2 [C (of, for)] an ordered set of ideas, methods, or ways of working: *What are the differences between the American and British systems of government?* | *She has a special system for winning money on horse races.* 3 [U] the use of orderly methods: *You need some system in your work if you want to succeed.* 4 [C] the body, thought of as a set of working parts: *All this idleness and overeating must be bad for the system/your system.* 5 [C] the workings of a computer or set of computers: *a fault in the system* | *systems design* —see also OPERATING SYSTEM 6 [the+S] infml the impersonal official forces that seem to govern one's life and limit one's freedom: *She just blames it all on the system.*

sys·te·mat·ic /ˌsɪstəˈmætɪk◄/ adj often apprec based on orderly methods and careful organization; thorough: *The way he works isn't very systematic.* | *The police made a systematic search of the building.* — ~ally /kli/ adv

sys·te·ma·tize ‖ also -tise BrE /ˈsɪstəmətaɪz/ v [T] to arrange in a system or by a set method —**-tization** /ˌsɪstəmətaɪˈzeɪʃən‖-mətə-/ n [U]

sys·te·mic /sɪsˈtemɪk, -ˈtiːmɪk‖sɪsˈtemɪk/ adj tech having an effect on the whole of something, esp. a living thing: *systemic drugs* | *Systemic insecticides spread all through a plant and kill any insects that feed on it.*

systems a·nal·y·sis /ˌ··· ·ˈ···/ n [U] the process of examining a system or activity to see whether it can be improved or carried out more effectively, esp. using computers to do this

systems an·a·lyst /ˈ··· ˌ···/ n someone who studies activities, such as business or industrial operations, and uses computers to plan ways of carrying them out, improving them, etc.

T

T, **t** /tiː/ **T's, t's** *or* **Ts, ts** **1** the 20th letter of the English alphabet **2 to a T** *infml* exactly; perfectly: *That dress fits Jean to a T.* —see also T-BONE, T-SHIRT, **cross one's "t's" and dot one's "i's"** (CROSS²)

't /t/ *old use or poet* it (in the words **'tis, 'twas, 'twere, 'twill, 'twould**): *'Twas* (=it was) *a chill winter's day.*

ta /taː/ *interj BrE sl* thank you

TA /ˌtiː ˈeɪ/ [*the*] TERRITORIAL ARMY

tab /tæb/ *n* **1** a small piece or narrow length of cloth, paper, etc., fixed to something to help in opening or handling it, or to show what it is, who owns it, etc.: *You open the can by pulling the metal tab.* **2** *infml* a bill, esp. for a meal or drinks; the whole cost of something: *Don't expect me always to* **pick up the tab.** (=pay the bill) **3 keep tabs/a tab on** *infml* to watch closely (esp. someone who is believed to have bad or criminal intentions): *The police have been keeping tabs on him.*

ta·bas·co /təˈbæskəʊ/ also **tabasco sauce** /ˌ·ˌ·· ˈ·/— *n* [U] *tdmk* a very hot-tasting red SAUCE made from peppers, used for giving a special taste to food

tab·bou·leh /tæˈbuːleɪ‖tɑˈbuːlə/ *n* [U] a SALAD dish from the Middle East, made from cracked wheat, vegetables, oil, and HERBS

tab·by /ˈtæbi/ *n* **1** a cat with usu. dark bands and marks on its grey or brown fur, or orange bands on light fur: *grey tabby* | *orange tabby* **2** *rare* a female cat —compare TOMCAT

tab·er·nac·le /ˈtæbənækəl‖-bər-/ *n* **1** a movable tent-like structure used in worship by the Jews in ancient times **2** a building of worship in certain Christian churches: *the Baptist Tabernacle* **3** a small decorated box in which the holy bread and wine are kept in Roman Catholic churches

ta·ble¹ /ˈteɪbəl/ *n* **1** [C] a piece of furniture with a flat top supported by one or more upright legs: *a kitchen table* | *a card table* (=for playing cards on) | *a table lamp* (=made to be placed on a table) | *a table knife* (=for eating with) | *I've booked a table for two at the restaurant.* | *new efforts to get them back to the* **negotiating table** (=where opponents can talk about their disagreements) —see also COFFEE TABLE, HIGH TABLE **2** [C+*sing.*/*pl. v*] the people sitting at a table: *John's clever stories kept the whole table amused.* **3** [S] *esp. old-fash or pomp* the stated kind or quality of food served at a meal: *Cyril keeps an excellent table.* (=serves very good meals) | *I always choose something from the* **cold table** *in restaurants.* (=from the cold meat or vegetable dishes) **4** [C] a printed or written set of figures, facts, or information arranged in orderly rows across and down the page: *There is a table of contents at the front of this dictionary.* **5** [C] also **multiplication table**— a list which young children repeat to learn what number results when a number from 1 to 12 is multiplied by any of these numbers: *The three times table starts: once three is three, two threes are six, three threes are nine.* (1×3=3, 2×3=6, 3×3=9) **6 at table** *BrE fml or pomp* during a meal; having a meal: *It's bad manners to blow your nose at table.* **7 on the table: a** having been suggested or offered for consideration: *The management has put a reasonable wage offer on the table, so it is up to the unions to decide whether to accept it.* **b** *AmE* remaining to be talked about at a later time: *The proposal is still on the table.* **8 under the table** *infml* (of money) given in order to influence someone dishonestly: *They offered me £500 under the table if I would vote against the government's plans.* —see also **drink someone under the table** (DRINK¹) **9 turn the tables (on someone)** to suddenly take a position of strength or advantage that was formerly held by someone else, and change from being weaker to being stronger: *She played badly in the first set, but then she turned the tables on her opponent and won the match.*

table² *v* [T] **1** *BrE* to suggest (a subject, report, etc.) for consideration by a committee, parliament, etc.: *The opposition has tabled an amendment to the bill.* **2** *esp. AmE* to leave (a subject, report, etc.) until a later date for consideration

tab·leau /ˈtæbləʊ‖ˈtæbləʊ, tæˈbləʊ/ *n* **-leaux** /ləʊz/ *or* **-leaus** a lifelike representation, on a stage, of a famous scene or historical event by a group of people who do not move or speak

ta·ble·cloth /ˈteɪbəlklɒθ‖-klɔːθ/ *n* a cloth for covering a table, esp. during a meal

ta·ble d'hôte /ˌtɑːbəl ˈdəʊt/ [*the*] *Fr* a complete meal of several dishes served at a fixed price in a hotel or restaurant: *I'll have the table d'hôte (dinner).* —compare A LA CARTE

ta·ble·land /ˈteɪbəl-lænd/ also **tablelands** *pl.*— *n* a large area of high flat land; a PLATEAU

table lin·en /ˈ·· ˌ·/ *n* [U] tablecloths and NAPKINS

table man·ners /ˈ·· ˌ·/ *n* [P] the way someone follows the customary rules and correct social behaviour when attending and eating a meal: *His table manners were atrocious.*

ta·ble·mat /ˈteɪbəlmæt/ *n* a small mat made of material that will not let heat pass, placed under hot dishes to protect a table's surface

ta·ble·spoon /ˈteɪbəlspuːn/ *n* **1** ‖*usu.* **serving spoon** *AmE*— a large spoon used for serving food —see picture at SPOON **2** *AmE* (a spoon which holds) a unit of measurement equal to 1/128 of a US pint of liquid **3** (of)] also **ta·ble·spoon·ful** /ˈteɪbəlˌspuːnfʊl/ (*pl.* **-spoonfuls, -spoonful**)— the amount held by these

tab·let /ˈtæblət/ **1** a small round solid piece of medicine; a PILL: *The doctor told me to take two tablets before every meal.* | *sleeping tablets* —see picture at PILL **2** a small block (of soap) **3** a shaped flat piece of stone or metal with words cut into it: *Her memorial is carved on that stone tablet on the wall.* —see also TABLETS OF STONE

table ten·nis /ˈ·· ˌ·/ also **ping-pong** *infml*— *n* [U] an indoor game played on a table by two or four players who use small BATS to hit a small hollow plastic ball to each other across a net

tablets of stone /ˌ·· · ˈ·/ *n* [P] **written in tablets of stone** stated or written in a very firm, definite way and not able to be changed

ta·ble·ware /ˈteɪbəlweəʳ/ *n* [U] the plates, glasses, knives, forks, spoons, etc., used when eating a meal

table wine /ˈ·· ˌ·/ *n* [U] wine intended for drinking with a meal, esp. wine that is not very expensive

tab·loid /ˈtæblɔɪd/ *n* a newspaper of which two pages make up one printing PLATE¹ (7), and which contains many pictures, and short accounts of the main points of the news: *I never read the tabloids. The story is being dismissed as the irresponsible gossip of the tabloid press.* —compare QUALITY PAPER; see also extra information on page 896 —**tabloid** *adj*

ta·boo¹ /təˈbuː, tæˈbuː/ *adj* **1** strongly forbidden by social custom, esp. because offensive or likely to cause social discomfort: *There are certain rude words that are taboo in ordinary conversation.* | *Don't talk to her about her divorce — it's a* **taboo subject.** **2** [*no comp.*] *tech* too holy or evil to be touched, named, or used: *This land is the burial place of tribal chiefs and is therefore taboo.*

taboo² *n* **-boos** [C;U] (a) strong social or religious custom forbidding a particular act or word: *Is there a taboo against sex before marriage in your society?*

tab·u·lar /ˈtæbjʊləʳ/ *adj* arranged in the form of a TABLE¹ (4): *The information is shown in tabular form.*

tab·u·la ra·sa /ˌtæbjʊlə ˈrɑːzə/ *n* **tabulae rasae** /-liː ˈrɑːziː/ *Lat* something, esp. the mind, existing in its original state, before anything has been added to change it

tab·u·late /ˈtæbjʊleɪt/ *v* [T] to arrange (facts, figures, etc.) in the form of a TABLE¹ (4) —**lation** /ˌtæbjʊˈleɪʃən/ *n* [C;U]

tach·o·graph /ˈtækəɡrɑːf‖-græf/ *n* an apparatus for recording the speed of a vehicle, esp. a TRUCK, and the distance it has travelled

ta·chom·e·ter /tæˈkɒmɪtəʳ‖-ˈkɑː-/ *n* (esp. in vehicles) an instrument used to measure speed, esp. the rate at which an engine turns

ta·cit /ˈtæsɪt/ *adj* [A *no comp.*] *fml* accepted or understood without actually being written down or openly expressed: *It is believed the management and the unions have reached a* **tacit agreement** *on the matter.* | *The deal had the tacit approval/backing of the President.* — —**ly** *adv*

ta·ci·turn /ˈtæsɪˌtɜːn‖-ɜːrn/ adj fml tending to speak very little; not liking to say a lot – ~ **ly** adv – ~ **ity** /ˌtæsɪˈtɜːnᵻti‖ -ɜːr-/ n [U]

tack¹ /tæk/ n **1** [C] a small nail with a sharp point and flat head: He hammered a tack into the wall and hung a small picture from it. **2** ‖ also **thumbtack** AmE– infml for DRAWING PIN **3** [C;U] the direction of a sailing ship as shown by the position of its sails: Ships on starboard tack (=with the wind coming from their right) have right of way. **4** [C] a course of action or thought, esp. one that is completely different from a previous one: The speaker suddenly changed tack/started off on a different tack and left us all rather confused. **5** [C] a long loose stitch used for fastening pieces of cloth together before sewing them properly –see also BRASS TACKS, HARD TACK, THUMBTACK

tack² v **1** [T] to fasten with a tack: She tacked a notice to the board. | He tacked down the lid of the box. **2** [I] to change the course of a sailing ship so that the wind blows against its sails from the opposite direction **3** [T] also **baste**– to fasten or join (cloth) with long loose stitches: Tack the sleeves on, then sew them up.
 tack sthg. ↔ **on** phr v [T (to)] infml to add (esp. something that was not originally planned) to the end of a speech, book, etc.: The bit about help for poorer countries had obviously just been tacked on as an afterthought.

tack·le /ˈtækəl/ v **1** [T] to take action in order to deal with: What's the best way to tackle this problem? | new measures aimed at tackling unemployment **2** [I;T] (in football or HOCKEY) to (try to) take the ball away, from (an opponent) **3** [I;T] (in RUGBY or American football) to force (the player with the ball) to the ground to prevent him from passing it or running with it: (fig.) The robber tried to get away but a man ran and tackled him. **4** [T] to speak to directly and fearlessly so as to deal with a problem: If she keeps missing school like this you'll have to tackle her parents about it.

tackle² n **1** [C] (in football or HOCKEY) an act of trying to take the ball from an opponent: a strong/hard tackle **2** [C] (in RUGBY or American football) an act of stopping the opponent carrying the ball by taking hold of him and bringing him down **3** (in American football) a player whose job is to tackle an opponent **4** [U] the equipment used in certain sports: Don't forget to bring your **fishing tackle**. (=rod, line, hooks, etc.) **5** [C;U] (a system of) ropes and wheels (PULLEYS) for working a ship's sails, lifting heavy weights, etc.

tack·y /ˈtæki/ adj **1** sticky: The paint on the door is still tacky. **2** infml, esp. AmE **a** of bad taste **b** cheap and with too much decoration; GAUDY **c** low-class –**ily** adv –**iness** n [U]

tac·o /ˈtækəʊ‖ˈtɑː-/ n -**cos** a type of Mexican food made from a TORTILLA (=flat bread made usu. of MAIZE or flour) folded in two to hold a filling, usu. of BEEF or chicken

Taco Bell /ˈ . ˌ . / n a FAST-FOOD restaurant in the US which serves Mexican food

tact /tækt/ n [U] the ability to do or say the right thing at the right time; skill in dealing with people without causing offence or upsetting them: It's a rather delicate situation and you'll need a lot of tact to handle it. – ~ **less** adj : What a tactless remark! – ~ **lessly** adv – ~ **lessness** n [U]

tact·ful /ˈtæktfəl/ adj showing tact; careful not to cause offence or upset people: It was very tactful of you to leave when you did. – ~ **ly** adv : I tactfully refrained from mentioning his argument with the boss.

tac·tic /ˈtæktɪk/ n [often pl.] a plan or method that is intended to gain a desired result: The general planned his tactics for the following day's battle. | In order to avoid taking immediate action, they used/adopted the classic delaying tactic of setting up a committee of inquiry. – see also TACTICS

tac·tic·al /ˈtæktɪkəl/ adj **1** [no comp.] of tactics: a general of great tactical skill **2** done in order to get a desired result in the end: This is purely a tactical withdrawal; when we have strengthened our forces we will attack again. **3** (of weapons) for use only over short distances, close to the base of operations: tactical nuclear missiles – ~ **ly** /kli/ adv

tactical vot·ing /ˌ . ‥ ˈ ‥/ n [U] the practice of voting for a person or party (in an election) that one does not favour, in order to prevent the election of an even less favoured person who would otherwise win

tac·ti·cian /tækˈtɪʃən/ n a person skilled in tactics

tac·tics /ˈtæktɪks/ n [U+sing./pl. v] the art of arranging military forces for battle and moving them during battle: An army commander must be skilled in tactics.

tac·tile /ˈtæktaɪl‖ˈtæktl/ adj tech of or able to be felt by the sense of touch: the tactile organs | a tactile sensation

tad·pole /ˈtædpəʊl/ n a small black creature with a long tail and round head that lives in water and grows into a FROG or TOAD

Ta·dzhi·ki·stan, Tajikistan /tɑːˌdʒiːkɪˈstɑːn/ one of the republics of the former USSR

tae kwon do /ˌtaɪ kwɒn ˈdəʊ‖-kwɑːn-/ n [U] an Oriental system of SELF defence, which is like KARATE, using kicking and punching (PUNCH¹ (1))

taf·fe·ta /ˈtæfᵻtə/ n [U] thin shiny smooth stiff cloth made from silk, nylon, etc.

taf·fy /ˈtæfi/ n esp. AmE a soft sweet made by boiling usu. brown sugar and then pulling it until it is light in colour; **taffy pulls** used to be popular events in the "olden days", and **salt water taffy** is still popular in the US today, and comes in many light colours and FLAVOURS

Taffy n BrE sl, sometimes derog a Welshman

Taft /tæft/, **Lo·ra·do** /ləˈreɪdəʊ/ (1860–1936) an American SCULPTOR known for his FOUNTAINS

Taft, William Howard (1857–1930) an American Republican, president of the US from 1909 to 1913

tag¹ /tæg/ n **1** a small piece of paper, material, etc., fixed to something to show what it is, who owns it, what it costs, etc.: a name tag | an identification tag | (fig.) a car with a $20,000 price tag (=that costs $20,000) **2** a metal or plastic point at the end of a cord, SHOELACE, etc. **3** a well known phrase or sentence, esp. one in a foreign language: His writing is always full of Latin tags. **4** also **question tag**– a phrase such as "isn't it?", "won't it?", "does she?", etc., added to the end of a sentence to make it a question or ask for agreement

tag² v -**gg**- [T] **1** to fasten a tag to: Tag the bottles now or we'll forget which one is which. **2** [+obj+as/n] to regard or describe (someone) in a particular way: Ever since she failed her exam she's been tagged as stupid/tagged a failure.
 tag along phr v [I] infml to go with someone by following closely behind: The baby elephant was tagging along behind its mother. | Whenever we go out she always tags along, although no one ever invites her.
 tag sthg. ↔ **on** phr v [T] to fix or add to something; TACK on: He decided to tag on an extra paragraph at the end summarizing what he'd said.

tag³ n [U] a children's game in which one player chases and tries to touch the others

Ta·ga·log /təˈɡɑːlɒɡ‖-ləɡ/ n **1** [C] a member of a people living in the Philippines **2** [U] the language spoken by these people

ta·glia·tel·le /ˌtæljəˈteli ‖ ˌtɑː-/ n [U] Italian PASTA (=food made from flour mixed with water) in the shape of long thin flat pieces, cooked in boiling water –compare MACARONI, SPAGHETTI, VERMICELLI

Ta·gore /təˈɡɔːʳ/, **Ra·bin·dra·nath** /rəˈbɪndrənɑːθ/ (1861–1941) a Bengali Indian writer, one of the most influential Indian writers of the 20th century, known for Gitanjali, and Chitra, a play which he translated into English

ta·hi·ni /təˈhiːni/ also -**tahina** /-nə/– n [U] a thick substance made from ground (GRIND) SESAME seeds, used in Middle Eastern cookery, and esp. for making HUMMUS

Ta·hi·ti /təˈhiːti/ an island in French Polynesia, in the Pacific Ocean

Ta·hi·tian /təˈhiːʃən/ n **1** [C] someone who comes from or whose parents come from Tahiti **2** [U] the language spoken in Tahiti –**Tahitian** adj

tai chi, tai ji, t'ai chi /ˌtaɪ ˈtʃiː, -ˈdʒiː/ also **tai chi chuan** /ˌtaɪ tʃiː ˈtʃwɑːn, -ˌdʒiː-/– (sometimes caps.) n [U] a Chinese form of physical exercise which involves moving the body very slowly, to train the body and mind in balance and control. It is esp. suitable for older people, and is practised in large groups in Chinese parks.

tail¹ /teɪl/ n **1** the movable long growth at the back or end of a creature's body: a bird's tail | a fish's tail | The dog wagged his tail. –see pictures at BIRD and HORSE

2 something like this in appearance, shape, or position: *a comet's tail* | *He wore a coat with tails.* (=a TAILCOAT) | *We saw the tail* (=back end) *of the procession disappearing round the bend.* | *I prefer to sit towards the tail of the plane.* | *(infml) I hate it when the driver behind* sits on my tail. (=follows my car too closely) —see picture at AIR-CRAFT **3** *infml* a person employed to watch and follow someone, esp. a criminal: *The police have* put a tail on me, *so they know my every move.* **4 (a case of) the tail wagging the dog** (a case of) something unimportant causing important decisions to be made **5 with one's tail between one's legs** in a state of complete defeat **6 turn tail** to turn round defeated (and run away): *They fought for a few moments, then turned tail and fled.* **7** -tailed /teɪld/ *having a tail of the stated sort: a curly-tailed pig* —see also TAILS, **not be able to make head or tail of** (HEAD[1]) — ~less *adj*

tail[2] *v* [T] *infml* to follow closely behind (someone) in order to watch what they do, where they go, etc.: *The police have been tailing me — they know I'm here.*

tail back *phr v* [I] *esp. BrE* to form a tailback: *The traffic was tailing back all the way to the city centre.*

tail off *phr v* [I] to lessen in quantity, strength, or quality: *The volume of traffic has begun to tail off.*

tail·back /ˈteɪlbæk/ *esp. BrE*‖usu. **back-up** *AmE— n esp. BrE* a still or slow-moving line of vehicles covering a certain distance on the road from where the traffic has been stopped, e.g. by an accident, road repairs, etc.: *A lorry has overturned on the M1, causing a three-mile tailback for southbound travellers.*

tail·board /ˈteɪlbɔːd‖-bɔːrd/ *also* **tailgate** *esp. AmE— n* the board at the back of a cart or large vehicle that can be let down or removed to make loading and unloading easier

tail·coat /teɪlˈkəʊt, ˈteɪlkəʊt/ *also* **cutaway—** *n* a man's coat with a long back divided into two below the waist and a front part that does not come below the waist —see also TAILS

tail end /ˌ· ˈ·/ *n* [(of) usu. sing.] the very last part: *We just got there in time to see the tail end of the film.*

tail end·er /ˌteɪl ˈendər/ *n* (in cricket) a relatively poor BATS-MAN who comes in near the end of the team's INNINGS

tail·gate[1] /ˈteɪlɡeɪt/ *n* **1** a TAILBOARD **2** the door at the back of a HATCHBACK car

tailgate *v* [I;T] *AmE infml* to drive (too) closely behind (a vehicle)

tail·light /ˈteɪl-laɪt/ *n* a red light at the back of a vehicle so that it can be seen in the dark —see picture at CAR

tai·lor[1] /ˈteɪlər/ *n* a person who makes clothes, esp. outer garments for men such as coats and suits —compare DRESSMAKER

tailor[2] *v* [T+*obj*+*adv*/*prep*] to make (an outer garment) by cutting and sewing cloth, esp. to fit a particular person: *a beautifully tailored suit* | (fig.) *We can tailor the insurance policy to/according to your special needs.*

tailor-made /ˌ··ˈ·◂/ *adj* [(for)] exactly suited to a special need, a particular person, etc.: *This job's tailor-made for John.*

tail·piece /ˈteɪlpiːs/ *n* a part added at the end; APPENDAGE: *He added a tailpiece describing what happened after the end of the war.*

tail pipe /ˈ· ·/ *n* *AmE for* EXHAUST[2] (1)

tails /teɪlz/ *n* **1** [U] the side of a coin which does not have the head of a king, queen, president, etc., on it: *I'll toss you for it —* **heads or tails?** —compare HEADS **2** [P] a formal evening TAILCOAT, usu. black and worn with a white BOW TIE: *For a formal occasion at the palace you must wear tails.* —compare DINNER JACKET, and see picture at EVENING DRESS

tail·spin /ˈteɪlˌspɪn/ *n* an uncontrolled spinning fall by a plane, in which the tail spins in a wider circle than the front

tail·wind /ˈteɪlˌwɪnd/ *n* a wind coming from behind

taint[1] /teɪnt/ *v* [T] **1** to cause to seem impure or undesirable, esp. by bringing into CONTACT with something bad or unpleasant: *His political reputation is tainted by his connection with an unpopular government.* **2** *esp. AmE* to make (food) unfit for use, esp. because of decay: *tainted meat*

taint[2] *n* [S (of)] a slight touch of decay, infection, or bad

or immoral influence: *Can we be sure they are free from any taint of disloyalty?*

Tai·pei /ˌtaɪ ˈpeɪ/ the capital city of Taiwan

Tai·wan /ˌtaɪˈwɑːn/ an island off the SE coast of China; capital Taipei; population 19,900,000 (1988)

Tai·wan·ese /ˌtaɪwəˈniːz◂/ *n* [*the* +P] people from Taiwan —**Taiwanese** *adj*

Ta·ji·ki·stan /tɑːˌdʒiːkɪˈstɑːn/ a country in central Asia bordered by Uzbekistan, Kirghizia, China, and Afghanistan; capital Dushanbe; population 5,112,000 (1989)

Taj Ma·hal /ˌtɑːdʒ məˈhɑːl/ [*the*] a beautiful white building in Agra, N India, built as a burial place for the wife of the EMPEROR Shah Jehan

take[1] /teɪk/ *v* **took** /tʊk/, **taken** /ˈteɪkən/ ■ to move something from one place to another **1** [T] to move or carry from one place or position to another: *I often forget to take my umbrella.* | *Don't forget to take your bag when you go.* [+*obj*+*adv*/*prep*] *We usually take the children to school in the car.* | *Take your feet off the table.* | *The arrested man was taken away in a police car.* | *That notice has been up for weeks — it's time it was taken down.* | *She's gone to the dentist to have a tooth taken out.* | *I don't want this chair — take it away.* | *The drug was found to be dangerous, and was taken off the market.* (=so that it could no longer be sold) | *What do you get if you take* (=subtract) *four from nine?* [+*obj*(*i*)+*obj*(*d*)] *Take your mother a cup of tea.* —see BRING (USAGE) **2** [T] to remove or use without permission or by mistake: *Someone's taken my pen.* | *The last bit of her book is taken straight from my article on the subject.* ■ to get something into one's possession **3** [T] to get possession or control of; seize; CAPTURE: *Enemy forces have taken the airport.* | *500 prisoners were taken in the battle.* | *The general swore to take back the fort whatever the cost.* | *She took my bishop and I took her queen.* (=in CHESS) **4** [T] to get for oneself: *Take a seat.* | *She took second prize.* | *Why should he take all the credit when things go well?* | *to take control of the situation* | *We usually take* (=rent) *a cottage in the country in the summer.* | *She made a slow start in the race, but eventually* **took the lead.** (=got into the leading position) **5** [T] to get hold of (something) with the hands; GRASP: *She took my arm/took me by the arm and led me across the road.* | *He took her in his arms and kissed her.* | *Let me take your jacket.* | *She took a spade and planted the potatoes.* ■ to accept **6** [T *not in progressive forms*] to be willing to accept: *The shop will take it back if it doesn't fit.* | *Do they take traveller's cheques?* | *I don't see why I should take the blame for this.* | *That's my last offer — you can* **take it or leave it.** **7** [T *not in progressive forms*] to accept as true or worthy of attention: *If you take my advice you'll sell that at once.* | *I can't take I'm right — you'll just have to* **take my word for it.** | *What you've said doesn't change my position, but* **I take your point.** (=understand or accept your argument) **8** [T *not in progressive forms*] to accept or suffer as unavoidable: *The president has taken a lot of criticism over this.* | *The staff reluctantly agreed to take a cut in wages.* **9** [T *not in progressive forms*] to be able to hold or contain: *The tank will take about 12 gallons.* | *The bus takes up to 55 passengers.* | *I don't think this shelf will take any more books.* **10** [T *not in progressive forms*] to (be willing to) bear; ENDURE: *I can't take much more of his nagging.* | *I find her self-righteous manner rather* **hard to take.** ■ to need for a purpose **11** [T] to need (a stated amount of time): *The journey takes two hours.* (=you need two hours to make it) [+*obj*(*i*)+*obj*(*d*)] *The flight took us ten hours.* | *It took her all afternoon to finish it.* **12** [T] to need in order to work properly; accept: *The machine only takes 5-pence coins.* (=only works if you put 5-PENCE coins in it) | *The verb "kill" takes a direct object.* | *What sort of batteries does it take?* **13** [T] to need in order to gain a particular result: *That takes some believing.* (=is hard to believe) | *It took ten men to break the door down.* | *It takes a lot of nerve/courage to do a thing like that.* — see also **have what it takes** (TAKE[1] (29)), TAKE **up** ■ used without strong meaning with certain nouns, to show an action or feeling **14** [T] to perform the actions connected with: *I'm going to take* (=have) *a walk/a bath/a break.* | *Before giving evidence, you have to take* (=swear) *the oath.* | *When are you taking your driving test?* | *She's taking* (=studying) *history at university.* | *You have to be prepared to take risks in this job.* | *We will have to take steps to see that the rules are obeyed.* | *She didn't even take the trouble to phone me.* —see HAVE[3] (USAGE) **15** [T] to have or experience (a certain feeling): *Why do you always take offence when I make suggestions?* | *He doesn't take much interest in his work.* | *They took pity on the refugees and allowed them to stay.* | *I'm inclined to take a more optimistic view* ■ other meanings　**16** [T (IN, UP)] to introduce into the body by swallowing, eating, drinking, breathing, etc.: *The doctor gave me some medicine to take for my cold.* | *I opened the window and took a breath of fresh air.* | *Do you take sugar in your tea?* | *Plants take up water through their roots.*　**17** [T] to use as a way of getting from one place to another: *My sister goes to work on the bus but takes the train coming home.* | *Take the second turning on the left.*　**18** [T] to test or measure: *Nurse, take this man's temperature, please.* | *They're taking a sample of public opinion.*　**19** [T] to make by photography: *I had my picture taken this morning.*　**20** [T (DOWN)] to write down: *The policeman took (down) my name and address.* | *Will you take notes on the meeting, please?*　**21** [T+obj+adv/prep;not in progressive forms] to have the stated feelings as to; consider: *I always take your suggestions seriously.* | *I took your nod as a sign of approval/to mean that you approved.* | *Of course I didn't tell her your secret — what do you take me for?* (=what sort of person do you think I am?) | **I take it** (=I suppose) *you'll be making a complaint about her behaviour.*　**22** [T+obj+adv/prep] to separate into pieces: *He took the watch to bits/to pieces to mend it.* —see also TAKE **apart**　**23** [T] to (attempt to) get over or round (something that prevents one's advance); NEGOTIATE (3): *The horse took that last fence well.* | *We took the bend at 90 miles an hour.*　**24** [I] to have the intended effect; work successfully: *The colour took and her white dress is now red.* | *Did the vaccination take?*　**25** [T often pass.] to attract; delight: *The little house took my fancy.* | *The child was really taken by the little dog.* | *I was quite taken with that young man.*　**26** [I;T] (of a fish) to bite (the hook of a fisherman): *The fish don't seem to be taking today.* | (fig.) *He took the bait and fell into the swindler's trap.*　**27** [T] *esp. lit* (of a male) to have sex with ■ fixed phrases　**28 be taken sick/ill** to become ill, esp. suddenly　**29 have what it takes** *infml* to have the qualities needed for success: *That girl's got what it takes to be a star.*　**30 it takes all sorts (to make a world)** (a phrase said when one thinks someone is behaving rather strangely)　**31 take it from 'me** believe me when I say: *You can take it from me that there won't be an election this year.* —see also **take place** (PLACE[1])　**32 you can't take it with you (when you go)** you will have no use for material possessions when you die ■ phrasal verbs

take after sbdy. *phr v* [T *not in progressive forms*] to look or behave like (an older relative): *Mary really takes after her mother; she has the same eyes, nose, and hair.*

take apart *phr v* [T]　**1 (take** sthg.↔**apart)** to separate (a small machine, clock, etc.) into pieces; DISMANTLE: *Take the watch apart and see if you can see what's wrong with it.* —compare TAKE **down**; see also TAKE[1] (22)　**2 (take** sbdy. **apart)** *infml* a to defeat very severely in a sport or game: *England were really taken apart by Italy in last night's match.* **b** to find serious fault with; speak angrily to or CRITICIZE severely

take away from sthg. *phr v* [T] to lessen the effect or value of (something good or desirable); DETRACT **from**: *His refusal to accept the prize does not take away from his success in winning it.*

take back *phr v* [T]　**1 (take** sthg. ↔ **back)** to admit that one was wrong in (what one said): *I'm sorry I was rude; I take back everything I said.*　**2 (take** sbdy. **back)** to cause to remember or think about a past time: *Seeing that old film really took me back!* —see also TAKE[1] (1,3,6)

take sthg. ↔ **down** *phr v* [T]　**1** to separate (a large machine or article) into pieces, esp. in order to repair it or move it: *We'll have to take the engine down to get to the gearbox.* —compare TAKE **apart**　**2** to lower (a garment worn below the waist) without actually removing it: *to take down one's trousers* —see also TAKE[1] (1,20)

take sbdy./sthg.↔**in** *phr v* [T]　**1** to receive into one's home; provide lodgings for (a person): *He had nowhere to sleep so we offered to take him in.*　**2** to include: *This is the total cost of the holiday, taking everything in.* | *When I go to New York for meetings, I usually take in a movie.* (=include it in the day's activities)　**3** to make (clothes) narrower: *My dress is a bit loose round the waist — could you take it in for me?* —compare LET **out** (3)　**4** to understand fully; GRASP: *It took me a long time to take in what you were saying.*　**5** to deceive: *Don't be taken in by his promises.* —see also TAKE[1] (16)

take off *phr v*　**1** [T] **(take** sthg. ↔**off)** to remove (esp. clothes): *Take your coat off.* —opposite **put on**　**2** [I] (of a plane, SPACECRAFT, etc.) to rise into the air at the beginning of a flight　**3** [T] **(take** sbdy.↔**off)** *infml* to copy the speech or manners of (someone), esp. for amusement; MIMIC: *The actor made everyone laugh by taking off the members of the royal family.*　**4** [T] **(take** sthg. **off)** to have a holiday from work on (the stated day) or for (the stated period): *I'm taking Thursday off because I'm moving house.* | *Take a few days off, Michael.*　**5** [I] begin to become successful, popular, or well-known: *It was at this point that her acting career really took off.*　**6** [I] *infml* to go away, esp. on a journey: *She just took off without saying goodbye to anyone.* —see also TAKE[1] (1), TAKEOFF

take on *phr v*　**1** [T] **(take** sbdy.↔**on)** to start to employ: *We've decided to take on a new clerk in the accounts department.*　**2** [T] **(take on** sthg.) to begin to have (a quality or appearance); ASSUME (3): *These insects can take on the colour of their surroundings.* | *His face took on a worried expression.*　**3** [T] **(take** sbdy.↔**on)** to start a quarrel or fight with: *Why don't you take on someone your own size?* | *The trade union made the mistake of trying to take on the government.*　**4** [T] **(take** sthg.↔**on)** to accept (work, responsibility, etc.): *My doctor says I'm too tired and has advised me not to take any more work on.*　**5** [I] *old-fash infml* to be excited and worried: *Don't take on so; there's nothing to worry about.*

take sbdy./sthg.↔**out** *phr v* [T]　**1** to go somewhere with (a person) as a social activity: *I'm taking the children out to the theatre tonight.* | *He keeps asking if he can take me out, but I don't really find him attractive.*　**2** to obtain officially: *Have you taken out insurance on your house yet?*　**3** *euph or tech* to destroy, kill, or cause to be ineffective: *We took the factory out by bombing it.*　**4 take someone out of himself/herself** to amuse or interest someone who is feeling unhappy or unwell　**5 take it out of someone** *infml* to use all someone's strength: *The long journey seems to have taken it out of her.* —see also TAKE[1] (1)

take sthg. **out on** sbdy. *phr v* [T] to express (one's feelings) by making (someone else) suffer: *It's not my fault you've had a bad day; don't take it out on me.*

take (sthg. ↔**) over** *phr v* [I;T] to gain control over and responsibility for (something): *Who do you think will take over now that the governor has been dismissed?* | *I'm feeling too tired to drive any more; will you take over?* —compare OVERTAKE; see also TAKEOVER

take to sbdy./sthg. *phr v* [T]　**1** to feel a liking for, esp. at once: *I took to Paul as soon as we met.* | *I'm not sure if he'll take to the idea.*　**2** to begin as a practice, habit, etc.: *All this gloomy news is enough to make you take to drink.* [+v-ing] *Just lately he's taken to hiding his socks under the carpet.*　**3** to go for rest, hiding, escape, etc.: *Father's ill, so he's taken to his bed.* | *The criminals took to the hills to escape from the police.*

take sbdy./sthg. ↔ **up** *phr v* [T]　**1** to begin to spend time doing; interest oneself in: *John took up acting while he was at college.* [+v-ing] *Alfred's just taken up playing the guitar.*　**2** to ask about or take further action about: *I'll take this matter up with my lawyers.* | *No one took up my suggestion.*　**3** (of things or events) to fill or use (space or time), esp. in a way that is undesirable: *The job took up most of Sunday.* | *These boxes of yours are taking up too much space.*　**4** *AmE* ‖ **cut down** *BrE*— (of trousers, skirts, etc.) to reduce in length by putting in a new HEM (=folding and sewing the bottom of the garment); to HEM　**5** [(on)] to accept the offer of: *Can I take you up on your offer of a meal?*　**6** to continue: *I'll take up the story where I finished yesterday.* —see also TAKE[1] (11,16), TAKEUP

take up with sbdy. *phr v* [T]　**1** to become friendly with (esp. someone undesirable): *She's taken up with a rather wild crowd.*　**2 taken up with** very busy with: *He can't help; he's too taken up with his own problems.*

take² *n*　**1** the filming of a scene for a cinema film: *We had to do six takes before the director was satisfied.*　**2** [*usu. sing.*] *infml* the amount of money taken, esp. by a business: *Our take was up* (=we received more money) *this week.* —see also DOUBLE TAKE　**3** [(**on**)] *AmE* a way of experiencing or understanding something: *What's your take on this situation?* | *He has a different take on reality than most people.*

take·a·way /ˈteɪkəweɪ/ *BrE* ‖ **carryout, takeout** *AmE*— *n* (a meal bought from) a shop from which cooked meals can be taken away to be eaten somewhere else: *Let's get*

a takeaway — I can't be bothered to cook. | *There's a Chinese takeaway in the town centre.* —compare **to go** (GO¹ (31))

take-home pay /ˌ· · ˌ·/ n [U] wages left after all taxes, PENSION payments, etc., have been paid

take-off /ˈteɪk-ɒf‖-ɔːf/ n **1** [C;U] the beginning of a flight, when a plane, spacecraft, etc., rises from the ground: *We had a smooth takeoff.* | *You're not allowed to smoke until after takeoff.* **2** [C] the act of leaving the ground in making a jump: *A long-jumper needs to get his takeoff exactly right.* **3** [C (**of**)] *infml* an amusing copy of someone's typical behaviour: *She does a marvellous takeoff of the Queen.* —see also TAKE off

take-out /ˈteɪkaʊt/ n *AmE for* TAKEAWAY

take-o-ver /ˈteɪkˌəʊvəʳ/ n an act of gaining control, esp. of a business company by buying most of the shares —see also TAKE over

takeover bid /ˈ··· ˌ·/ n a BID² to gain control of a company by buying most of the SHARES¹ (2)

ta-ker /ˈteɪkəʳ/ n [*usu. pl.*] *infml* someone who is willing to accept an offer: *I advertised my car for sale at £250, but there were no takers.*

take-up /ˈteɪkʌp/ n the rate at which people buy or accept something offered by a company, government, etc.: *Despite the advertising campaign, there hasn't been a very big takeup of shares so far.* —see also TAKE up

tak-ing /ˈteɪkɪŋ/ adj old-fash attractive; FETCHING

tak-ings /ˈteɪkɪŋz/ n [P] money received, esp. by a shop: *After we closed, we count the day's takings.*

Talbot see PEUGEOT

talc /tælk/ n [U] **1** a soft smooth greenish-grey mineral that feels like soap and is used in making paints, plastics, and various body powders **2** *infml* talcum powder

tal-cum pow-der /ˈtælkəm ˌpaʊdəʳ/ n [U] a very fine powder of crushed talc, which is put on the body to dry it or make it smell pleasant

tale /teɪl/ n **1** a story of imaginary events, esp. of an exciting kind: *tales of adventure* —see also TALL STORY **2** a report or description, perhaps not completely true, of an event or situation: *We listened to their tales about life in the prisoner-of-war camp.* **3** a false or unkind account: *Children shouldn't tell tales.* (=tell lies about each other) —see also TELLTALE² **4 and thereby hangs a tale** *quote* a phrase from several plays by William Shakespeare. People use this phrase when something is mentioned about which there is a lot more to tell. **5 a tale told by an idiot** *quote* a phrase from Shakespeare's play *Macbeth*, used when saying that something has no meaning **6 old wives' tale** a foolish old-fashioned belief, once thought to be true

tale-bear-er /ˈteɪlˌbeərəʳ/ n *old use* a person who intentionally spreads false or unkind pieces of news around

tal-ent /ˈtælənt/ n **1** [S (**for**);U] (a) special natural ability or skill: *He has a talent for drawing.* | *She has great musical/artistic talent.* —see GENIUS (USAGE) **2** [U+*sing./pl. v*] people who have (a) talent: *There was a lack of local talent, so the drama group hired an actor from London.* | *a competition to encourage young talent.* **3** [U+*sing./pl. v*] *BrE sl* sexually attractive people: *We stood on the corner eyeing up the talent.*

tal-ent-ed /ˈtælənt‖d/ adj having or showing talent: *a very talented actor*

talent scout /ˈ··· ·/ n a SCOUT¹ (4)

Tale of Two Cit-ies /ˌ· ··· ˈ··/, A a book by Charles Dickens, written in 1859, set in Paris and London at the time of the French Revolution

tal-is-man /ˈtæl‖zmən/ n -s an object which is believed to have magic powers of protection

talk¹ /tɔːk/ v **1** [I (**to, with, about**)] to use or produce words; speak: *Human beings can talk; animals can't.* | *Come here; I want to talk to you.* | *Union leaders have been talking with the president about the proposed new law.* | *They were all talking at once.* | *I don't know what you're talking about!* (=I don't understand what you mean) **2** [I] to express thoughts as if by speech: *People who cannot speak or hear can talk by using signs.* **3** [I] to copy human speech: *Have you taught your parrot to talk?* **4** [I] *infml* to give information, usu. unwillingly: *In spite of the police interrogation, the suspect refused to talk.* **5**

[I] to speak about other people's actions and private lives; GOSSIP: *Don't park your car outside my house; you know how people talk!* **6** [T] to express in words: *Don't talk such nonsense!* **7** [T] to speak about; DISCUSS: *Now the meal's over it's time to talk business.* **8 now you're talking** *infml* (used for expressing very eager agreement or acceptance): *"Instead of Blackpool, why don't we go to the South of France for our holidays this year?" "Now you're talking!"* **9 You can talk!/You're a fine one to talk!, Look who's talking!** *infml* (used to suggest, often humorously, that someone should not find fault because they are just as bad): *"Don't play your radio so loud." "You're a fine one to talk!"* (=you play your own radio even louder) **10 talk a blue streak** *AmE* to talk very quickly without stopping: *He can talk a blue streak if he's given the chance.* **11 talk back** *AmE for* **answer back** (ANSWER²) **12 talk of the devil** (used when someone who has just been mentioned actually arrives): *John said he'd be coming — and talk of the devil, here he is now.* **13 talk through one's hat** to say something stupid; talk about something one knows nothing about: *He says he understands economic theory, but he's talking through his hat!* **14 talk tough** to say in a very determined way that you will do something, esp. something to control someone else: *The Home Secretary talked tough and wheeled out two new measures against the joyriders.* **15 talk turkey** *infml, esp. AmE* to talk seriously and openly, esp. about business matters **16 We have ways of making you talk** a phrase used as a threat in old British films by German soldiers questioning prisoners, now often used humorously

▷ USAGE 1 **Speak** and **talk** are very close in meaning, but **talk** usually gives the idea of a conversation, rather than of a single person making statements: *We* **talked** *for hours about politics.* | *The director* **spoke** *to us about the company's plans.* 2 **Speak** and **talk** are sometimes transitive, but can never have a person as their object: *Do you* **speak** *French?* | *You're* **talking** *nonsense!* —see also SAY (USAGE), SPEAK (USAGE)◁

talk sbdy./sthg.↔**down** *phr v* [T] **1** to guide (a plane or its PILOT) safely to the ground, esp. when it is impossible to see well, by giving instructions by radio **2** *AmE infml* to persuade to be more calm: *At one point she threatened to fine us all but we talked her down.* | *The police are trying to talk down that guy about to jump off the bridge.*

talk down to sbdy. *phr v* [T] to speak to as if one were more important, more clever, etc.; PATRONIZE

talk sbdy. **into** sthg. *phr v* [T] to persuade (someone) to do (something): *He refused at first, but I managed to talk him into it.* [+v-ing] *She talked me into buying a new car.* —compare TALK out of

talk sthg.↔**out** *phr v* [T] **1** to settle by talking: *Unions and employers usually try to talk out their differences before taking action against each other.* **2** *BrE* to prevent (a law) from being accepted by talking in Parliament until there is no time left for voting

talk sbdy. **out of** sthg. *phr v* [T] **1** to persuade (someone) not to do (something): *See if you can talk her out of it.* [+v-ing] *The policeman talked the man out of jumping from the top of the building.* —compare TALK into **2 talk one's way out of** to escape from (trouble) by talking: *She could talk her way out of anything!*

talk sthg.↔**over** *phr v* [T (**with**)] to speak about thoroughly and seriously, esp. in order to settle a problem or reach a decision: *If you're worried about this change of career, why don't you talk it over with your family?*

talk round *phr v* [T] **1 (talk** sbdy. **round)** to persuade (someone) to change their mind: *She resisted at first, but we were finally able to talk her round (to our point of view).* **2 (talk round** sthg.**)** to avoid speaking directly about (a matter)

talk² n **1** [S (**with, about**)] a conversation: *I met Mr Jones in the street and had a long talk with him about his operation.* **2** [C (**on, about**)] an informal speech or LECTURE: *She gave a talk on Mozart to the college Music Society.* **3** [U] a particular way of speech or conversation: *baby talk* | *his slick sales talk* | *That's fighting talk!* (=a brave or threatening way of talking) —see also SMALL TALK, SWEET TALK **4** [U] empty or meaningless speech: *His threats are just talk. Don't worry!* **5** [*the*+S+**of**] a subject much talked about by everyone in a particular place:

Her sudden marriage is the talk of the street. —see also
TALKS

talk·a·tive /ˈtɔːkətɪv/ *adj* liking to talk a lot — ~**ness** *n* [U]

talk·er /ˈtɔːkəʳ/ *n* **1** a person who talks, esp. one who talks
a lot or in a persuasive way: *What a talker that man is —
no one else can get a word in!* | *She's a good talker.* **2**
a bird that can copy human speech

talk·ie /ˈtɔːki/ *n old use infml* a cinema film with sounds
and words —compare SILENT FILM

talking book /ˌ·· ˈ·/ a book recorded onto TAPE or COMPACT
DISC for blind people to listen to

Talking Heads /ˌ·· ˈ·/ an American NEW WAVE music group
begun in 1974 by David Byrne. Their songs include *Psycho Killer* and *Road to Nowhere.*

talking point /ˈ·· ·/ *n* a subject of argument or conversation

talking-to /ˈ·· ·/ *n infml* an angry talk in order to blame or
CRITICIZE; scolding (SCOLD): *I'm going to give that boy a
good talking-to!*

talks /tɔːks/ *n* [P] a formal exchange of opinions and views:
The two presidents met for talks. | *peace talks*

talk show /ˈ· ·/ *n AmE for* CHAT SHOW

tall /tɔːl/ *adj* **1** having a greater than average height: *a tall
man/building/tree* **2** [after *n*] having the stated height:
He is six feet tall. **3** **tall, dark, and handsome** (of a man)
very attractive —see HIGH (USAGE) — ~**ish** *adj* — ~**ness**
n [U]

Tal·la·has·see /ˌtæləˈhæsi/ the state capital of Florida in
the US —see colour map on pages 1374–5

tall·boy /ˈtɔːlbɔɪ/ *BrE* || **highboy** *AmE*— *n* a tall piece of
wooden furniture containing several drawers

Tal·ley·rand /ˈtælirænd/, **Charles Mau·rice** /ʃɑːl mɔːˈriːs‖
ʃɑːrl-/ (1754–1838) a French politician who was foreign
minister under Napoleon and represented France at the
CONGRESS of Vienna in 1814–15

Tal·linn , **-Talin** /ˈtælɪn‖ˈtɑː/ the capital city of Estonia

tall or·der /ˌ· ˈ··/ *n* [S] *infml* a request or piece of work that
is unreasonably difficult to perform

tal·low /ˈtæləʊ/ *n* [U] hard animal fat used for making
candles

tall pop·py /ˌ· ˈ··/ *n AustrE* a rich or famous person who
acts in a way that shows that they think they are
important

tall ship /ˌ· ˈ·/ *n* a ship with sails set across rather than
along the length of the ship; *a SQUARE-RIGGED ship*

tall sto·ry /ˌ· ˈ··/ *BrE* || *usu.* **tall tale** /ˌ· ˈ·/ *AmE*— *n* a story
that EXAGGERATES (=makes events and things seem
larger, better, or worse than they actually were)

tal·ly¹ /ˈtæli/ *n* **1** a record of things done, points made in
a game, etc.: *Don't forget to keep a careful tally of what
you spend.* | *England's tally at the moment is 15 points,
against Scotland's 11.* **2** (in former times) a stick with
NOTCHes cut in it to show an amount of money owed, a
quantity of goods delivered, etc.

tally² *v* **1** [I **(with)**] to be exactly equal or in agreement;
match: *Your figures don't tally with mine.* | *Our figures
don't tally.* **2** [T **(UP)**] to calculate (points won, a total,
an account, etc.); count

tal·ly-ho /ˌtæliˈhəʊ/ *interj, BrE* (an expression shouted by
a fox hunter when he or she sees the fox)

Tal·mud /ˈtælmʊd/ [*the*] the body of Jewish law concerned
with religious and non-religious life

tal·on /ˈtælən/ *n* a sharp powerful curved nail on the feet
of some hunting birds, used for catching animals for food

tam·a·rind /ˈtæmərɪnd/ *n* (the fruit of) a tropical tree

Tam·bo /ˈtæmbəʊ/, **Ol·i·ver** /ˈɒlɪvəʳ‖ˈɑː-/ (1917–) a South
African nationalist politician, who was president of the
AFRICAN NATIONAL CONGRESS from 1977 to 1990. He left
South Africa in 1960 when the ANC was banned (BAN).

tam·bour /ˈtæmbʊəʳ/ *n* a small circular frame made from
two circles of wood, one of which fits inside the other to
hold cloth firmly in place while patterns are being sewn
on it

tam·bou·rine /ˌtæmbəˈriːn/ *n* a small hand-held DRUM made
from a circular frame with a skin stretched over and
small metal plates fastened round the edge —see picture
at PERCUSSION

tame¹ /teɪm/ *adj* **1** not fierce or wild; trained to live with

people: *a tame animal* **2** *infml* dull; unexciting and
uninteresting: *The football match was so tame that we left
early.* — ~**ly** *adv* — ~**ness** *n* [U]

tame² *v* [T] to train (a wild, uncontrollable, or fierce
animal) to be gentle and often also to obey commands:
(fig.) *One day man will tame nature.* —compare DOMES-
TICATE (1) —**tamable** *or* **tameable** *adj* —**tamer** *n*

Tam·il /ˈtæmᵻl/ *n* **1** [C] a member of a people of S India
and Sri Lanka **2** [U] the language spoken by these people —**Tamil** *adj*

Tamil Na·du /ˌtæmᵻl nɑːˈduː/ a state in SE India, formerly
called **Madras**

Tamil Ti·gers /ˌ·· ˈ··/ [*the*] a group of GUERRILLAs who support a separate state for the Tamil Hindu people of Sri
Lanka

Taming of the Shrew /ˌ·· · · ˈ·/, **The** a humorous play by
William Shakespeare. The main character is Kate, a rich
and unfriendly woman who is eventually persuaded by
her lover to marry him.

tam-o'-shan·ter /ˌtæm ə ˈʃæntəʳ/ *n* a Scottish cap, usu.
woollen, with a POMPOM in the centre, worn pulled down
on one side —see picture at HAT

tamp /tæmp/ *v* [T+*obj*+*adv*/*prep*] *rare* to pack tightly or
force down by repeated light blows

Tam·pa /ˈtæmpə/ a city in W Florida in the US —see colour
map on pages 1374–5

Tam·pax /ˈtæmpæks/ *n tdmk* a popular make of TAMPON

tam·per /ˈtæmpəʳ/ *v*
   tamper with sth*g. phr v* [T] to touch or make changes
   in (something) without permission, esp. so as to cause
   damage: *After the accident it was found that the car had
   been tampered with.*

tamper-ev·i·dent /ˌ·· ˌ···/ *adj* (of a JAR or packet) made to
show whether someone has opened it before it is sold in
the shops: *tamper-evident packaging* | *Baby-food jars are
now tamper-evident.* —see also CONSUMER TERRORISM

tamper-proof /ˈ·· ·/ *adj* (of a JAR or packet) made in a way
that prevents someone opening it before it is sold, for example to add poison or to damage it in some way —see
also CONSUMER TERRORISM

tam·pon /ˈtæmpɒn‖-pɑːn/ *n* a tube-shaped mass of cotton
or similar material fitted into a woman's VAGINA to AB-
SORB the monthly bleeding —compare SANITARY TOWEL

tan¹ /tæn/ *v* -**nn**- **1** [T] to change (animal skin) into leather
by treating with TANNIN **2** [I;T] to (cause to) become
brown, esp. by sunlight: *Janet tanned quickly in the hot
sun.* | *This special chemical liquid will tan you as you
sleep.* **3** **tan someone's hide** also **tan the hide off
someone**— *infml* to beat someone severely

tan² *n* **1** [U] a light yellowish brown colour: *tan shoes* **2**
[C] a SUNTAN: *All the people who went abroad for their
holidays came back with nice tans.*

tan³ *abbrev. for:* TANGENT (2)

tan·dem /ˈtændəm/ *n* **1** a bicycle built for two riders sitting one behind the other **2 in tandem** with both working closely together: *The two computers operate in
tandem.*

tan·doo·ri /tænˈdʊəri/ *n* [U] (meat, bread, etc., cooked by)
a northern Indian method of cooking in a large closed
clay pot: *tandoori chicken*

tang /tæŋ/ *n* [S] a strong sharp taste or smell: *the salty tang
of the sea air* — ~**y** *adj* : *tangy oranges*

Tang *n* [U] *tdmk* a powder which when mixed with water
makes a drink that tastes rather like oranges. Tang was
developed for the US space programme for the AS-
TRONAUTS.

Tan·gan·yi·ka /ˌtæŋgənˈjiːkə/ see TANZANIA

Tanganyika, Lake a large lake between Zaïre and
Tanzania

tan·gent /ˈtændʒənt/ *n* **1** a straight line touching the edge
of a curve but not cutting across it **2** *tech* the FRACTION
calculated for an angle by dividing the length of the side
opposite it in a RIGHT-ANGLED TRIANGLE by the length of
the side next to it —compare COSINE, SINE **3 go/fly off at
a tangent** *infml* to change suddenly from one subject,
course of thought, etc., to another: *It's impossible to have
a logical discussion with him — he keeps going off at a
tangent.*

tan·gen·tial /tænˈdʒenʃəl/ adj 1 fml having only an indirect connection or importance; PERIPHERAL: tangential comments 2 fml moving or going out in different directions; showing DIVERGENCE 3 [(to)] tech (having the nature) of a TANGENT (1) — ~ ly adv

tan·ge·rine /ˌtændʒəˈriːn‖ˈtændʒəriːn/ n 1 [C] a small sweet orange with a loose skin that comes off easily 2 [U] a dark or reddish orange colour

tan·gi·ble /ˈtændʒɪbəl/ adj 1 clear and certain; real; not imaginary: The police need tangible proof of his guilt before they charge him. | The policy has not yet brought any tangible benefits. —opposite **intangible** 2 fml that can be felt by touch: Sculpture is a tangible art form. —**bly** adv —**bility** /ˌtændʒɪˈbɪlɪti/ n [U]

Tan·giers /tænˈdʒɪəz‖-ˈdʒɪərz/ also **Tangier** a port in Morocco

tan·gle¹ /ˈtæŋɡəl/ v [I;T (UP)] 1 to (cause to) become a confused mass of disordered and twisted threads: This fine thread tangles easily. | The wind tangled her hair. | My scarf got tangled up in the barbed wire fence. | (fig.) the complex, tangled politics of this region —see also ENTANGLE 2 O what a tangled web we weave, When first we practise to deceive! quote a phrase from Marmion by Sir Walter Scott. People use the phrase when someone is not telling the truth and getting themselves into more difficulties.
    tangle with sbdy. phr v [T] infml to quarrel, argue, or fight with

tangle² n 1 [(of)] a confused disordered mass: We had to cut our way through a tangle of branches. 2 a confused disordered state: The wool was in such a tangle that it was useless. | He got into an awful tangle with his homework, and had to ask me to help. 3 [(with)] infml a quarrel, fight, or disagreement

tan·go¹ /ˈtæŋɡəʊ/ n -gos (a piece of music for) a lively dance of Spanish American origin

tango² v [I] 1 to dance the tango 2 **it takes two to tango** both people are responsible for what they have done: She says he led her astray, but it takes two to tango.

tan·gram /ˈtæŋɡræm/ n a Chinese PUZZLE which uses a large square which is cut into TRIANGLEs and other shapes, to make different figures

tank /tæŋk/ n 1 a large container for storing liquid or gas: The tank in my car holds 40 litres of petrol. | a fish tank 2 an enclosed heavily armed and armoured vehicle that moves on two endless metal belts (CATERPILLARs) 3 esp. IndE & PakE a large artificial pool for storing water —see also THINK TANK

tan·kard /ˈtæŋkəd‖-ərd/BrE ‖ **stein** AmE— n a large usu. metal drinking cup, usu. with a handle and lid, used for drinking beer

tanked up /ˌ· ˈ·/ adj [F] BrE sl drunk, esp. from drinking beer

tank·er /ˈtæŋkər/ n a ship, plane, or railway or road vehicle specially built to carry large quantities of gas or liquid, esp. oil —see also OIL TANKER

tank top /ˈ· ·/ n 1 BrE a usu. woollen, tightfitting top without SLEEVEs, worn over a BLOUSE or shirt and popular esp. in the 1970s 2 AmE a top without SLEEVEs which is made of very light material such as cotton, for wearing in very hot weather

tan·ner¹ /ˈtænər/ n a person whose job is making animal skin into leather by tanning (TAN¹)

tanner² n BrE old sl for SIXPENCE

tan·ne·ry /ˈtænəri/ n a place where animal skin is made into leather by tanning (TAN¹)

tan·nin /ˈtænɪn/ also **tan·nic ac·id** /ˌtænɪk ˈæsɪd/— n [U] a reddish acid made from the BARK (=the outer covering) of certain trees, esp. the OAK, used in preparing leather, making ink, etc. It is also found naturally in tea leaves, GRAPE skins, etc.

Tan·noy /ˈtænɔɪ/ n [(the)] S] tdmk, esp. BrE a system of giving out information to the public by means of LOUDSPEAKERs: We heard the flight announcement over the Tannoy at the airport.

tan·ta·lize also **-lise** BrE /ˈtæntəl-aɪz/ v [T] to make (someone) want something even more strongly by keeping it just out of reach: While we were shut up in the classroom, the tantalizing smell of cooking wafted up from down-

stairs. —**lizingly** adv: We were tantalizingly close to finding the solution.

tan·ta·lus /ˈtæntəl-əs/ n a case in which bottles of alcoholic drink can be locked up in such a way that they can be seen

tan·ta·mount /ˈtæntəmaʊnt/ adj [F+to] having the same value, force, or effect as (esp. something bad or unwanted): This invasion is tantamount to a declaration of war. | They have now abandoned their former policy, which is tantamount to admitting that it was wrong.

tan·trum /ˈtæntrəm/ n a sudden attack of childish bad temper or anger: That spoilt child always flies into a tantrum/throws a tantrum when he's contradicted.

Tan·za·ni·a /ˌtænzəˈniːə/ a country in East Africa formed by the union of Tanganyika and Zanzibar; capital Dodoma; population 24,802,000 (1989) —**nian** n,adj

Tao /taʊ, daʊ/ also **Dao**— n [U] 1 (in Taoism) the universal force producing agreement in nature 2 (in Taoism) the best way of living, in agreement with nature and the universe

Taoi·seach /ˈtiːʃək, -ʃəx/ [the] the title of the PRIME MINISTER of the Republic of Ireland

Tao·is·m /ˈtaʊɪzəm, ˈdaʊ-/ n [U] a religion developed in ancient China teaching a simple way of life and the principle of not trying to change the natural course of events, also in later times concerned with magic and good fortune —**ist** adj, n

tap¹ /tæp/ n 1 ‖ also **faucet** AmE— an apparatus for controlling the flow of liquid or gas from a pipe or container, esp. one for water: I turned on the tap and hot water came out. | He left the taps running and the bath overflowed. | bathroom taps | a gas tap —see picture at KITCHEN and at LABORATORY 2 an act or example of tapping (TAP² (2)) someone's telephone —see also WIRETAP 3 a specially shaped object made to fit and close the opening in a barrel 4 **on tap: a** (of beer) from a barrel **b** infml ready for use when needed; AVAILABLE: We've got a lot of experts on tap to advise us.

tap² v -pp- [T] 1 to use or take what is needed from: We have enormous reserves of oil still waiting to be tapped. 2 to listen secretly or illegally to (a person, telephone conversation, etc.) by making a connection to (the telephone, a telephone wire, etc.): The secret agent suspects that his phone is being tapped. 3 to open (a barrel) so as to draw off (liquid) 4 to get liquid from (the trunk of a tree) by making a hole in it: to tap maple/rubber trees 5 [(for)] BrE infml to get money from: He tapped me for a fiver.
    tap into sthg. phr v [T] to TAP² (1): to tap into our currency reserves/recent developments in technology

tap³ v -pp- [I;T (on)] 1 to hit (the hand, foot, etc.) lightly against something: The teacher tapped her fingers on the desk impatiently. | She tapped her feet in time to the music. | He was tapping away on his typewriter until late into the night. 2 to hit (something) lightly with a quick short blow, esp. to attract attention: I tapped (on) the window to let them know I'd arrived. —compare KNOCK¹ (1)

tap⁴ n [(on)] a short light blow: I heard a tap on the window.

tap·a /ˈtæpə/ n [usu. P] a small dish of food eaten as part of the first course of a meal in Spain or in Spanish RESTAURANTs. Tapas may be fish, vegetable, or meat dishes.

tap dance /ˈ· ˌ·/ n a stage dance in which musical time is beaten on the floor by the feet of the dancer, who wears special shoes with pieces of metal on the bottom —**tap dancer** n —**tap dancing** n [U]

tape¹ /teɪp/ n 1 [C;U] (a long thin piece of) narrow material used for various purposes such as tying up parcels, marking out areas of ground, etc.: to put insulating tape on electric wires | adhesive tape 2 also **adhesive tape, sticky tape, Sellotape** tdmk ‖ **Scotch tape** AmE tdmk— (a piece of) narrow material which is sticky on one or both sides, used to stick things, esp. paper products, together —see also MASKING TAPE 3 [C;U] **a** (a length of) narrow plastic material covered with a special MAGNETIC substance on which sound can be recorded and played back on a TAPE RECORDER **b** a CASSETTE **c** a VIDEOTAPE¹ 4 [C (of)] also **tape re·cord·ing** /ˈ· ·ˌ·/— a length of this on which a performance, piece of music, speech, etc., has been recorded: We listened to some tapes of her songs. 5 [the+S] a string stretched across the finishing line in a race and broken by the winner **6** [C] a TAPE MEASURE — see also RED TAPE, TICKERTAPE

tape² *v* **1** [I;T] *a* also **tape-re-cord** /ˈ·· ·ˌ·/, **record**— to record (sound) on TAPE¹ (3) with a TAPE RECORDER *b* to VIDEOTAPE²: *We've taped the rock concert/the interview.* **2** [T (UP)] to fasten or tie (a parcel, packet, etc.) with TAPE¹ (1) **3** *AmE* to stick something onto something else using tape¹ (2) **4** [T (UP) *often pass.*] *AmE for* STRAP² (2): *The doctors have taped up his swollen ankle.* **5** *BrE* **have someone/something taped** *infml* to understand thoroughly or have learnt how to deal with someone/something: *The arrangements are rather complicated, but I think I've got it all taped.* | *You can't fool her — she's got you taped.*

tape deck /ˈ· ·/ *n* the apparatus in a TAPE RECORDER that winds the TAPE¹ (2) and records and plays back sound, esp. one that is connected to a separate system

tape mea·sure /ˈ· ˌ··/ *n* a long band of narrow cloth or bendable steel, marked with divisions of length, used for measuring —compare RULER (2)

ta·per¹ /ˈteɪpəʳ/ *v* [I;T (OFF)] **1** to (cause to) become gradually narrower towards one end: *The animal's tail tapered off to a point.* | *She had long tapering fingers.* **2** to slow down or decrease gradually: *Interest in the scandal seems to be tapering off.*

taper² *n* **1** [*usu. sing.*] a gradual decrease in the width of a long object **2** a very thin candle **3** a length of string covered in WAX, used esp. in former times for lighting candles, lamps, etc.

tape re·cord·er /ˈ· ·ˌ··/ *n* an electrical apparatus which can record sound on TAPE¹ (2) and play it back

tap·es·try /ˈtæpᵻstri/ *n* [C;U] (a usu. large piece of) heavy cloth on which coloured threads are woven to produce a picture, pattern, etc.: *The walls of the banqueting hall were hung with tapestries.* | (fig., pomp) *Such strange events are all part of* **life's rich tapestry.** —**tried** *adj*

tape·worm /ˈteɪpwɜːm‖-wɜːrm/ *n* a long flat worm that when fully-grown lives in the bowels of human beings and other animals

tap·i·o·ca /ˌtæpiˈəʊkə ◂/ *n* [U] small hard white grains made from the crushed dried roots of CASSAVA, esp. used for making sweet dishes

ta·pir /ˈteɪpəʳ/ *n* tapir *or* tapirs a piglike animal of tropical America and Southeast Asia, with thick legs, a short tail, and a long nose

tap·pet /ˈtæpᵻt/ *n* a machine part that passes on movement, esp. a part in an engine that passes on movement from a CAM to a VALVE or a part that turns an apparatus on and off at set times

tap·root /ˈtæpruːt/ *n* the main root of a plant, which grows straight down and produces smaller side roots

taps /tæps/ *n* [U] a song or a tune played on the BUGLE last thing at night in an army camp or SUMMER CAMP, or at military funerals or services. In the US, a particular tune is associated with taps, and the words: *Day is done./ Gone the sun,/ from the lakes, to the hills, to the skies./ All is well./ Safely rest./ God is nigh.*

tar¹ /tɑːʳ/ *n* **1** [U] a black substance, thick and sticky when hot and hard when cold, used for making road surfaces, preserving wood, etc. —see also COAL TAR **2** [C] *becoming rare* a JACK TAR

tar² *v* **-rr-** [T] **1** to cover with tar: *They're tarring the road.* **2 tar and feather** to put tar on (someone) and then cover them with feathers as a punishment **3 tarred with the same brush** having, or (often unfairly) believed to have, the same faults

ta·ra·ma·sa·la·ta /ˌtærəməsəˈlɑːtə/ *n* [U] a Greek food consisting of a pink mixture made from the eggs of certain fish

tar·an·tel·la /ˌtærənˈtelə/ *n* (a piece of music for) a fast Italian dance

ta·ran·tu·la /təˈræntjᵿlə‖-tʃələ/ *n* a large hairy slightly poisonous SPIDER from Southern Europe and tropical America, believed by most people to be much more poisonous than it really is

tar ba·by /ˈ· ˌ··/ *n* something which sticks to or weighs down a person and is very difficult to remove (from the DOLL covered in tar in one of the stories about Brer Rabbit by J C Harris)

Tar·buck /ˈtɑːbʌk‖ˈtɑːr-/, **Jimmy** (1940–) an English television presenter and COMEDIAN

Tar·dis /ˈtɑːdɪs‖ˈtɑːr-/ [*the*] the machine in which Doctor Who and his friends travel through time. It looks like an old police telephone box, and is much larger inside than it is outside. —see DR WHO

tar·dy /ˈtɑːdi‖ˈtɑːrdi/ *adj esp. fml or lit* **1** delayed beyond the proper or expected time; late: *We apologize for our tardy response to your letter.* | *a tardy arrival* **2** acting or moving slowly; SLUGGISH: —**dily** *adv* —**diness** *n* [U]

tare¹ /teəʳ/ *n* [*usu. sing.*] *tech* **1** the weight of wrapping material in which goods are packed **2** the weight of an unloaded goods vehicle **3** this amount subtracted when weighing a loaded goods vehicle, in order to calculate the actual weight of the goods

tare² *n* [*usu. pl.*] *bibl* an unwanted plant growing among corn; WEED

target

tar·get¹ /ˈtɑːgᵻt‖ˈtɑːr-/ *n* **1 a** something fired at in shooting practice, esp. a round card or board with circles on it: *He fired and hit/but missed the target.* | *The soldiers were doing their* **target practice.** *b* any object or place at which an attack is directed: *The enemy's main target is our oil refinery.* **2 a** a total or amount/object which one aims to reach; GOAL: *I've set myself a target of saving £5 a week.* | *We have failed to meet* (=reach) *this year's production target of 25,000 cars.* | *I'm on a diet, and my target weight is 70 kilos.* | *The government's house-building programme is* **(bang) on target.** (=they have built the (exact) number that they aimed to build) *b* a limited group, area, etc., at which something is specially directed: *What's the target readership of this paper?* (= What sort of people are expected to read it?) **3** [(*of*)] a person or thing that is made the object of unfavourable remarks, jokes, etc.: *This plan will be the target of a great deal of criticism.*

target² *v* [T (**on, at**)] **1** to aim at a target: *The enemy's missiles are targeted on our cities.* **2** to cause to have an effect on a particular, intentionally limited group: *Welfare spending is being cut, so it should be targeted on the people who need it most.*

tar·iff /ˈtærᵻf/ *n* **1** a tax collected by a government on goods coming into or going out of a country —see TAX (USAGE) **2** *esp. BrE* a list of fixed prices, such as the cost of meals or rooms, charged by a hotel, restaurant, etc.

Tar·ka the Ot·ter /ˌtɑːkə ðɪ ˈɒtəʳ‖ˌtɑːrkə ðɪ ˈɑː-/ a book written for children by Henry Williamson in 1927

tar·mac¹ /ˈtɑːmæk‖ˈtɑːr-/ *n* **1** [U] also **tar·ma·cad·am** /ˌtɑːməˈkædəm‖ˌtɑːr-/ *usu.* **asphalt** *AmE*— a mixture of TAR and very small stones, used for making the surface of roads **2** [*the*+S] an area covered with tarmac, esp. one used for landing aircraft on: *The plane had to wait half an hour on the tarmac because of fog.*

tarmac² *v* **-macked, -macking** [T] to cover (a road's surface) with tarmac

tarn /tɑːn‖tɑːrn/ *n* (*often cap. as part of a name*) a small mountain lake or pool, esp. in the north of England

tar·nish¹ /ˈtɑːnɪʃ‖ˈtɑːr-/ *v* [I;T] to make or become dull, discoloured, or less bright: *Silver, copper, and brass need to be polished frequently to prevent them from tarnishing.* | (fig.) *a tarnished reputation*

tarnish² *n* [S;U] dullness; loss of brightness or polish

ta·ro /ˈtɑːrəʊ/ *n* taros a tropical plant grown for its thick root which is boiled and eaten as food

tar·ot /ˈtærəʊ/ [*the*] [*the*] a set of 78 cards, sometimes used for telling the future. 22 of the cards have symbolic pictures on them.

tar·pau·lin /tɑːˈpɔːlᵻn‖tɑːr-/ *n* [C;U] (a sheet or cover of) heavy cloth specially treated so that water will not pass through it: *The load on the trailer had a (sheet of) tarpaulin strapped over it.*

tar·ra·gon /ˈtærəgən/ *n* [U] **1** (a small European plant grown for its) strong-smelling leaves that give a special taste to food

tar·ry¹ /ˈtæri/ *v* [I] *old use or lit* **1** to stay in a place, esp. when one should leave; LINGER **2** to delay or be slow in starting, going, coming, etc.: *Do not tarry on the way.*

tar·ry² /ˈtɑːri/ *adj* covered with TAR

tar·sus /ˈtɑːsəs‖ˈtɑːr-/ *n* **-si** /saɪ/ *med* (the seven small bones in) the ankle —**-sal** *adj*

tart¹ /tɑːt‖tɑːrt/ *n* **1** [C;U] *BrE* a usu. open pastry case containing fruit or JAM —see PIE (USAGE) **2** [C] *infml derog* **a** a girl or woman who is, or appears to be, sexually immoral **b** a PROSTITUTE

tart² *adj* **1** sharp to the taste; acid-tasting; sour: *a tart apple* **2** having a bitter and unkind quality; SARCASTIC: *Her tart reply upset me.* — —**ly** *adv* — —**ness** *n* [U]

tart³ *v*

tart sbdy./sthg.↔**up** *phr v* [T] *BrE infml, usu. derog* to make noticeably attractive or decorative by painting in bright colours, putting on cheap jewellery or colourful clothes, etc.: *I wish she wouldn't tart herself up when she goes dancing.* | *They've tarted up that old cottage so much you wouldn't recognize it.*

tar·tan /ˈtɑːtn‖ˈtɑːrtn/ *n* **1** [U] woollen cloth woven with bands of different colours and widths crossing each other at right angles, of a kind worn originally by Scottish Highlanders: *a tartan skirt/kilt* **2** [C] a special pattern on this cloth worn by a particular Scottish CLAN, and known by the clan's name: *the Macdonald tartan*

tar·tar¹ /ˈtɑːtəʳ‖ˈtɑːr-/ *n* [U] **1** a hard chalklike substance that forms on the teeth —compare PLAQUE (2) **2** a reddish-brown substance that forms on the insides of wine barrels **3** also **cream of tartar** /ˌ·· ˈ··/— a white powder made by treating this or from chemicals, used in baking and in medicine

tar·tar² *n infml* (*often cap.*) a fierce person with a violent temper (from the **Tartars** or **Tatars** of the USSR, because of their fierce fighters esp. in the 14th and 15th centuries)

tar·tar·ic ac·id /tɑːˌtærɪk ˈæsd‖tɑːr-/ *n* [U] a strong acid of plant origin used in preparing certain foods and medicines

tar·tar sauce , **tartare sauce** /ˌ·· ˈ·/ *n* [U] a white egg-based SAUCE that includes very small pieces of strong-tasting vegetables and is eaten esp. with fish

Tar·zan /ˈtɑːzæn‖ˈtɑːr-/ **1** the main character in the Tarzan stories by Edgar Rice Burroughs, about a boy cared for and raised by APES. He swings from tree to tree, is very strong, and is friendly with the animals. He meets a woman called Jane who becomes his companion in one of the stories. The phrase "Me Tarzan. You Jane" comes from this relationship. Films were later made of Burroughs' stories and of some written by other people: *He was wearing only a Tarzan-style loincloth.* **2**

Johnny Weismuller as Tarzan

a NICKNAME for Michael Heseltine, British politician, because of his long, flowing hair, similar to Tarzan's in the stories and films

Tash·kent /tæʃˈkent/ a city and capital of Uzbekistan

task /tɑːsk‖tæsk/ *n* **1** *fml* a piece of work (that must be) done, esp. if hard or unpleasant; duty: *I was set/given the thankless task of reorganizing the office filing system.* | *The new government's prime* (=main) *task is to reduce the level of inflation.* | *He quickly performed the tasks he had been set.* **2 take someone to task** to speak severely to someone for a fault or failure; REPRIMAND: *He's been taken to task for his habitual lack of punctuality.*

task force /ˈ· ·/ *n* [C+*sing./pl. v*] **1** a military force under one commander sent to a place for a special purpose: *A*

combined naval and army task force was sent to recapture the island. **2** any group formed for a short time to deal with a particular problem: *The government set up a task force to clear up the area following the earthquake.*

task·mas·ter /ˈtɑːskˌmɑːstəʳ‖ˈtæskˌmæstər/ **task·mis·tress** /-ˌmɪstrəs/ *fem.*— *n* someone who makes people work very hard, esp. at unpleasant jobs: *Our teacher's a very hard taskmaster, but he certainly gets good results from his students.*

Tas·ma·ni·a /tæzˈmeɪniə/ a large island forming a state of Australia, off its SE coast

Tas·man Sea /ˌtæzmən ˈsiː/ a part of the South Pacific Ocean between Australia and New Zealand

Tass , **TASS** /tæs/ the official national news organization of the former Soviet Union

tas·sel /ˈtæsəl/ *n* **1** a bunch of threads tied together into a round ball at one end and hung as a decoration on clothes, flags, curtains, etc. **2** the flower-like part that grows out of the top of some plants, esp. MAIZE —see also DETASSEL —**-selled** *BrE* ‖ **-seled** *AmE* /ˈtæsəld/ *adj*

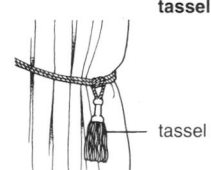
tassel

tassel

taste¹ /teɪst/ *n* **1** [U] the special sense by which a person or animal knows one food from another: *I've got a cold, so I've lost my sense of taste.* **2** [S;U] the sensation that is produced when a particular food or drink is put in the mouth and that makes it different from other foods or drinks by its saltiness, sweetness, bitterness, etc: *Sugar has a sweet taste.* | *This cake has no taste/very little taste.* | *This milk has got a funny taste — I think it may have gone sour.* | (fig.) *an unpleasant experience that left a bad taste in her mouth* (=made her feel angry, upset, etc.) **3** [C (of) *usu. sing.*] a small quantity of food or drink that is tasted: *I had a taste of the soup to see if it needed more salt.* | (fig.) *Once you've had a taste* (=a short experience) *of life in our country you won't want to return home.* **4** [U] the ability to make good or suitable judgments in matters such as beauty, style, fashion, music, or social behaviour; DISCERNMENT: *His jokes about the President's illness were in* **(very) bad/poor taste.** | *The furnishings and paintings had been chosen with impeccable taste.* **5** [C;U (**for, in**)] a personal liking for something: *What are your tastes in music?* (=What kind of music do you like?) | *I've always had a taste for 19th century literature.* | *She has expensive taste in clothes.* | *Their house has not been decorated to* **my taste** (=in a way that I like), *but it's very luxurious.* | *Their trip to America gave them a taste for western consumer goods.* **6 to taste** (used in instructions for cooking) in the quantity desired: *Add salt and pepper to taste.* —see also ACQUIRED TASTE, AFTERTASTE

taste² *v* **1** [T] to test the taste of (food or drink) by taking a little into the mouth: *I always taste food before adding salt.* | *This cake is delicious — would you like to taste it?* **2** [T *not in progressive forms*] to experience the taste of: *I've got a cold so I can't taste what I'm eating.* **3** [T *not in progressive forms*] to eat or drink: *The escaped prisoner had not tasted food for three days.* | *I've never tasted such delicious beef!* | (fig.) *Since tasting* (=experiencing) *the excitement of big city life, she never wants to live in the country again.* **4** [I+*adv/prep*, esp. **of, like**;L+*adj*; *not in progressive forms*] to have a particular taste: *These oranges taste nice.* | *This meat's been overcooked and doesn't taste of anything.* | *This soup tastes of chicken.* | *I've never eaten kiwi fruit — what does it taste like?* | *a sweet-tasting berry* —see CAN (USAGE)

taste bud /ˈ· ·/ *n* a group of cells on the tongue which can tell the difference between foods according to their taste

taste·ful /ˈteɪstfəl/ *adj* having or showing good TASTE¹ (4): *a tasteful arrangement of flowers* —compare TASTY (1) — **~ly** *adv* — **~ness** *n* [U]

taste·less /ˈteɪstləs/ *adj* **1** having no taste; not tasting of anything: *tasteless soup* **2** having or showing bad TASTE¹ (4): *a tasteless remark* — **~ly** *adv* : *a tastelessly furnished room* — **~ness** *n* [U]

▷ USAGE Compare **tasteless** and **distasteful**. When **tasteless** is used of food, it means "having no **taste**". When it is used of people, furniture, clothes, etc., it means "having or showing bad **taste**": *The potatoes were* **tasteless** *without salt.* | *a* **tasteless,** *over-*

furnished room. **Distasteful** is not used in either of these meanings, but only of unpleasant things that must be done: *It is my* **distasteful** *duty to warn you ...*◁

tast·er /ˈteɪstəʳ/ *n* **1** a person whose job is testing the quality of foods, teas, wines, etc., by tasting them: *a wine taster* **2** [(of)] a small example of something so that one can see if one will like it: *Here's just a taster of the novel, to whet your appetites.*

tast·y /ˈteɪsti/ *adj* **1** (not usu. of sweet food) having a pleasant noticeable taste; full of FLAVOUR: *a tasty meal* — compare TASTEFUL **2** *infml* (esp. of news) interesting, esp. when concerned with sex or improper behaviour: *a tasty piece of gossip about our neighbour* **3** *infml, esp. BrE* (used esp. by men of a woman) attractive (usu. considered offensive to women) —**iness** *n* [U]

tat¹ /tæt/ *n* [U] *BrE infml derog* something of very low quality

tat² *n* see TIT FOR TAT

ta-ta /tæˈtɑː/ *interj infml, BrE* goodbye

Ta·tar /ˈtɑːtəʳ/ see TARTAR²

Tate /teɪt/**, Jef·frey** /ˈdʒefri/ (1943–) an English CONDUCTOR who has worked at the Royal Opera House in Covent Garden and with the English Chamber Orchestra, as well as in Paris and New York

Tate and Lyle /ˌteɪt ənd ˈlaɪl/ *tdmk* a British company that makes sugar and sugar products

Tate Gal·le·ry /ˌ· ˈ····/ , also **Tate** *infml*— [the] an ART GALLERY in SW London known esp. its encouragement of modern art

ta·ter /ˈteɪtəʳ/ *n AmE, sl for* POTATO

Ta·ti /tæˈtiː/**, Jacques** /ʒækˈʒɑːk/ (1908–82) a French actor in COMEDY films of the 1940s and 1950s, best known for *Monsieur Hulot's Holiday*

Tatler /ˈtætləʳ/**, The 1** a famous magazine published in London in the early eighteenth century, started by Sir Richard Steele, containing poetry, stories, news, etc. **2** a British monthly magazine which reports on the social events and lives of rich and fashionable people

tat·tered /ˈtætəd‖-ərd/ *adj* **1** (esp. of clothes) old and torn: *a tattered shirt/banner* **2** (of a person) dressed in old torn clothes

tat·ters /ˈtætəz‖-ərz/ *n* [P] **1** old torn or worn-out clothing or bits of cloth **2 in tatters** (of clothes) old and torn: (fig.) *His reputation is in tatters.* (=ruined)

tat·tle /ˈtætl/ *v infml, derog* **1** [I] *infml, usu. derog* to talk about small unimportant things, or other people's private affairs; GOSSIP —see also TITTLE-TATTLE **2** *also* **tell on**— (usu. said by children) to tell (a parent, teacher, or other adult) that another child has done something bad, usu. in order to get the other child into trouble (=have them punished): *Don't tattle on me!* —**tler** *n*

tat·tle·tale /ˈtætlteɪl/ *n* (said of children) someone who tattles: *We're not playing with you any more, because you're a tattletale!*

tat·too¹ /təˈtuː, tæˈtuː/ *n* **-toos** a pattern, picture, or message put on the skin by tattooing: *The sailor had a tattoo saying "I love Anne" on his chest.*

tattoo² *v* [T] **1** to make (a pattern, picture, message, etc.) on the skin by pricking (PRICK) with a needle and then pouring coloured DYEs in: *He had the words "I love Anne" tattooed on his chest.* **2** to mark by doing this: *a tattooed arm/chest*

tattoo³ *n* **-toos 1** an outdoor military show with music, usu. at night: *the Edinburgh tattoo* **2** a rapid continuous beating of drums, esp. played as a military signal

tat·too·ist /təˈtuːɪst, tæ-/ *n* a person whose job is tattooing

tat·ty /ˈtæti/ *adj infml derog, esp. BrE* untidy or in bad condition; SHABBY: *tatty clothes* | *a few tatty old chairs* —**tily** *adv* —**tiness** *n* [U]

Ta·tum /ˈteɪtəm/**, Art** (1910–56) an American JAZZ piano player, almost blind from birth, thought of by many people as one of the greatest jazz pianists

taught /tɔːt/ *past tense & participle of* TEACH

taunt¹ /tɔːnt/ *v* [T **(with, for)**] to try to make (someone) angry or upset by making unkind remarks, laughing at faults or failures, etc.: *They taunted her with her inability to swim.* | *He was taunted by the other schoolchildren for being fat.* —**~ingly** *adv*

taunt² *n* [*often pl.*] a remark or joke intended to hurt someone's feelings or make them angry: *cruel taunts about her ill health*

Taun·ton /ˈtɔːntən/ a town in Somerset in SW England, where the local government for that COUNTY is based. It is known for its farming and farm machinery, and for CIDER making.

Tau·rus /ˈtɔːrəs/ *n* **1** [U] the second sign of the ZODIAC, represented by a BULL **2** [C] a person born between April 21 and May 22 —see ZODIAC (USAGE) and see picture at ZODIAC **3** an electronic trading system on the British Stock Exchange

taut /tɔːt/ *adj* **1** tightly drawn; stretched tight: *Pull the string taut!* | *taut muscles* —opposite **slack 2** showing signs of worry or anxiety; TENSE: *a taut expression on her face* —**~ly** *adv* —**~ness** *n* [U]

taut·en /ˈtɔːtn/ *v* [I;T] to make or become taut

tau·tol·o·gy /tɔːˈtɒlədʒi‖tɔːˈtɑː-/ *n* [C;U] (an) unnecessary repeating of the same idea in different words, as in the sentence *He sat alone by himself.* —**gical** /ˌtɔːtəˈlɒdʒɪkəl‖-ˈlɑː-/ *adj* —**gically** /kli/ *adv*

tav·ern /ˈtævən‖-ərn/ *n old use* a PUB

taw·dry /ˈtɔːdri/ *adj* cheaply showy in appearance and quality; lacking good TASTE¹ (4): *tawdry jewellery* —**drily** *adv* —**driness** *n* [U]

taw·ny /ˈtɔːni/ *adj* having a brownish yellow colour: *a lion's tawny fur*

tax¹ /tæks/ *n* **1** [C;U **(on)**] (an amount of) money which must be paid to the government according to income, property, goods bought, etc.: *In Britain, the Inland Revenue collects taxes.* | *The government plans to increase taxes by five per cent over the next year.* | *If you sell the painting you'll have to pay capital gains tax (on it).* | *Half of my wages go in tax.* | *a plan to impose a tax on betting* | *They are promising big tax cuts.* | *The payments were spread over a long period for tax purposes.* (=in order to pay less tax on them) —see also CORPORATION TAX, DIRECT TAX, INCOME TAX, POLL TAX, PURCHASE TAX, VAT **2** [S+on] a heavy demand; STRAIN: *The long journey would be too much of a tax on my father's strength.* **3 before/after tax** before/after paying the tax on money received: *What does he earn before tax?*

▷ USAGE Compare **tax, tariff, duty,** and **dues. Tax** is the most general word when talking about money collected by a government. A **tariff** is a tax set by a government on general types of goods entering or leaving the country: *a tariff on electronic goods.* **Duty** (often **duties**) is used about particular sums of money paid as tax in connection with particular goods or events: *I had to pay customs duty on the stereo system I had brought from Japan.* | *death duties* (=a tax on property paid when the owner dies). **Dues** (*pl.*) is used about sums of money paid officially (but not directly to a government) for the use of something or for advantages given: *harbour dues* | *trade union dues.*◁

tax² *v* [T] **1** to charge a tax on: *Tobacco and alcoholic drinks are taxed heavily in Britain.* **2** to make heavy demands on; STRAIN: *I found they were taxing my patience by asking such stupid questions.* —see also TAXING —**~able** *adj* : *taxable income/profit*

tax sbdy. with sthg. *phr v* [T+obj/v-ing] *fml* to charge with or blame for (something bad): *He was taxed with neglecting the safety regulations.*

tax·a·tion /tækˈseɪʃən/ *n* [U] **1** the act of taxing: *The government obtains revenue through* **direct taxation** (=the taxing of income) *and* **indirect taxation.** (=the taxing of goods) **2** money raised from taxes: *We must increase taxation if we are to spend more on education.* **3 taxation without representation** —see BOSTON TEA PARTY

tax a·void·ance /ˈ· ·ˌ··/ *n* [U] any legal way of reducing the amount of tax one has to pay —compare TAX EVASION

tax break /ˈ· ·/ *n AmE* a reduction in taxes that can be had by taking advantage of government rules that may change from time to time: *The government is offering tax breaks to companies that are environment friendly.* | *a tax break for insulating your home*

tax-de·duc·ti·ble /ˌ· ·ˈ····/ *adj* that may legally be subtracted from one's total income before it is taxed: *My travelling expenses are tax-deductible.*

tax-de-ferred /ˌ··ˈ·◂/ adj AmE not taxed until a later time: *tax-deferred income/savings*

tax disc /ˈ··/ n (in Britain) a small round piece of paper which car drivers must stick on their WINDSCREEN to show that they have paid their road tax —see picture at CAR

tax e-va-sion /ˈ··ˌ··/ n [U] illegally paying less tax than one should e.g. by not declaring certain income —compare TAX AVOIDANCE

tax ex-ile /ˈ··ˌ··/ n a person who leaves a country to avoid paying high taxes, and goes to live in another country. Such people are usu. POP STARS, film stars, or other people who earn large amounts of money.

tax-free /ˌ··ˈ·◂/ adj, adv free from taxation: *She earns £16,000 a year tax-free in her job overseas.* | *a tax-free salary*

tax ha-ven /ˈ··ˌ··/ n a place where many people, esp. rich people **(tax exiles)**, choose to live because it has very low rates of tax

taxis

a New York cab

tax-i¹ /ˈtæksi/ also **tax-i-cab** /ˈtæksikæb/ *fml*, **cab**— n a car with a driver that can be hired for a charge that is based on the length and time of the journey: *I came out of the station and* **hailed a taxi.** (=waved at one to make it stop) | *It's quicker by taxi.* —see TRANSPORT (USAGE)

a London taxi

taxi² v [I] (of a plane) to move slowly along the ground before taking off or after landing: *The plane taxied along the runway.*

tax-i-der-mist /ˈtæksɪˌdɜːmɪst‖ -ɜːr-/ n a person whose job is taxidermy

tax-i-der-my /ˈtæksɪˌdɜːmi‖-ɜːr-/ n [U] the art of specially cleaning, preparing, and preserving the skins of fish, birds, and animals, and filling them with special

a British taxi

material so that they look like living creatures

tax-i-me-ter /ˈtæksiˌmiːtər/ n a small machine fitted in taxis to calculate the charge for each journey

tax-ing /ˈtæksɪŋ/ adj needing great effort; DEMANDING: *Such a long rough journey would be very taxing for an old man.*

tax in-spect-or /ˈ··ˌ··/ n a government official whose job it is to decide how much a person, company, etc. must pay in taxes

taxi rank /ˈ·· ·/ also **taxi stand** ‖ **cabstand** esp. AmE— n a place where taxis wait to be hired

tax-man /ˈtæksmæn/ n -men /men/ **1** [C] a tax collector or tax inspector **2** [the] esp. BrE the government department that collects taxes: *George loves to hate the taxman*

tax-on-o-my /tækˈsɒnəmi‖-ˈsɑː-/ n [U] fml or tech the system or process of putting things, esp. plants and animals, into various classes according to their natural relationships

tax-pay-er /ˈtæks-peɪər/ n any person or organization that has a legal duty to pay tax: *The opposition parties have condemned the new airport as a waste of taxpayers' money.*

tax re-lief /ˈ··ˌ·/ n [U] not having to pay a tax esp. the IN-COME TAX one usu. pays on a certain amount of the money

one earns: *I get tax relief on the first two thousand pounds of my income.*

tax shel-ter /ˈ·· ˌ··/ n a plan or method which allows one legally to avoid paying tax

tax thresh-old /ˈ·· ˌ··/ n the level of income at which one starts to pay tax

tax write-off /ˈ·· ·ˌ·/ n AmE, infml something that is TAX DEDUCTIBLE, such as a gift to CHARITY, or a loss taken in a financial deal

tax year /ˈ·· ˌ·/ n a year at the end of which one's taxable income is calculated. In Britain the tax year begins on April 6th. In the US it begins on January 1st.

Tay /teɪ/ [the] a river in E Central Scotland which enters the sea at Dundee and flows through Tayside

Tay Bridge /ˌ·· ˈ·/ [the] a bridge over the river Tay at Dundee

Tay-lor /ˈteɪlər/, A J P (1906–90) an English HISTORIAN, who became popularly known through his appearances on television

Taylor, Elizabeth also **Liz** /lɪz/ infml— (1932–) an American film ACTRESS, born in London. She began making films at the age of ten, but is perhaps at least as well known for her marriages, of which there have been eight (two to Richard Burton). —see colour picture on page 228

Taylor, James (1948–) an American singer of popular music known for his many love songs

Taylor, Zach-a-ry /ˈzækəri/ (1784–1850) an American soldier and politician. He was president of the US (1849–50) and was against SLAVERY.

Tay-side /ˈteɪsaɪd/ a REGION in E Scotland whose main city is Dundee

TB /ˌtiː ˈbiː/ BrE‖**Tb** AmE— abbrev. for: TUBERCULOSIS

T-ball , **Tee-ball** /ˈtiː bɔːl/ n tdmk a game like BASEBALL played in the US by young children who hit the ball off a stick (TEE)

T-bill /ˈtiː bɪl/ AmE abbrev. for TREASURY BILL

T-bone /ˈtiː bəʊn/ also **T-bone steak** /ˌ·· ·ˈ·/— n a thinly cut piece of BEEF with a T-shaped bone in it

tbs also **T, tbsp**— n abbrev. for TABLESPOON (3)

TBS /ˌtiː biː ˈes/ AmE the TURNER BROADCASTING SYSTEM

TCCB /ˌtiː siː siː ˈbiː/ n [the] the TEST AND COUNTY CRICKET BOARD

TCP /ˌtiː siː ˈpiː/ n [U] tdmk a liquid ANTISEPTIC

Tchai-kov-sky /tʃaɪˈkɒfski‖-ˈkɔːf-/, **Pe-ter Il-yich** /ˈpiːtər ˈɪlɪtʃ/ (1840–93) a Russian COMPOSER who wrote symphonies (SYMPHONY), BALLETS, and OPERAs. His music is rich, emotional, and often rather sad.

tea /tiː/ n **1** [U] a hot brown drink made by pouring boiling water onto leaves of a special kind. It is thought of as a typically British drink: *a cup of tea* | *Do you take milk and sugar in your tea?* **2** [U] the specially treated, dried, and finely cut leaves of an Asian bush used for making tea: *China tea* | *Ceylon tea* **3** [C usu. pl.] a cup of tea: *Three teas and a coffee please.* **4** [C;U] BrE a small meal served in the afternoon with a cup of tea: *We have tea at four o'clock.* | *She made sandwiches and a cake for tea.* | *It's teatime!* —see also CREAM TEA, HIGH TEA; see DINNER (USAGE) **5** [U] a drink made by putting leaves or roots of the stated plant in boiling water, sometimes drunk for medicinal purposes: *mint tea* | *camomile tea* —see also BEEF TEA, GREEN TEA **6 not for all the tea in China** infml (used when making a refusal): *I wouldn't go back to that job for all the tea in China.* **7 tea and sympathy** a lot of attention and kindness which is not completely sincere and is not followed by practical help: *Mr Major is serious in his concern for lesbians and gay men and wants to demonstrate that his meeting with Sir Ian McKellen was more than public relations, tea and sympathy, he should announce the repeal of Clause 28 immediately.* —see also **one's cup of tea** (CUP¹)

tea-bag /ˈtiːbæg/ n a small paper bag with tea leaves inside which makes enough tea for one person

tea break /ˈ·· ·/ also **coffee break**— n a short pause from work in the middle of the morning or afternoon for a drink, a rest, something light to eat, etc.

tea cad-dy /ˈ·· ˌ··/ also **caddy**— n a small box, tin, etc., in which (esp. loose leaf) tea is kept

tea-cake /ˈtiːkeɪk/ n BrE a small round cake made of a

sweetened breadlike mixture with dried fruit (CURRANTS, RAISINS, etc.) in it, cut in two, and eaten hot or cold with butter

teach /tiːtʃ/ v **taught** /tɔːt/ 1 [I;T **(to)**] to give (someone) training or lessons in (a particular subject, how to do something, etc.); pass on knowledge or skill (to): *I teach (chemistry) at the local junior school.* | *She prefers teaching older pupils.* | *I want to learn to drive; will you teach me?* | *She teaches English to foreign students.* [+obj(i)+obj(d)] *My mother taught me this song.* [+obj+wh-] *Didn't your parents teach you how to behave in this sort of situation?* [+obj+to-v] *Who taught you to play the piano?* —compare LEARN (1) 2 [T] to (try to) make known and accepted: *Christianity teaches humility.* [+obj(i)+obj(d)] *Experience teaches us our limitations.* 3 [T+obj+to-v] *infml* to show (someone) the bad results of doing something, so that they will not do it again: *"I got wet through." "That'll teach you to go out without an umbrella."* | (in threats) *I'll teach you to be rude to me!* 4 **He who can, does. He who cannot, teaches** *quote* a phrase from *Maxims for Revolutionists* by George Bernard Shaw 5 **teach one's grandmother to suck eggs** *BrE infml* to give advice to someone who knows all about the matter already 5 **teach someone a lesson** to show someone the bad results of doing something, so that they will not do it again — **~able** *adj*

▷ USAGE Compare **teach, instruct, train,** and **coach. Teach** is the general word for helping a person or group of people to learn something. If you **instruct** (rather formal) a person or group of people you pass on knowledge to them, but you cannot be sure that they have learned anything: *He* **instructed** *us in Latin, but some of us made little progress.* You can **train** a person or group of people up to a necessary level in a particular skill or profession, and you can even **train** an animal: *It takes several years to* **train** *a doctor.* | *to* **train** *a dog to do tricks.* You can **coach** a person or group of people, often outside the ordinary educational system, such as in sports, and often for a particular examination which they find difficult and which they must pass: *Because he failed the chemistry examination at school, he had to be* **coached** *in chemistry at a private educational institution.*◁

teacher

teach·er /ˈtiːtʃəʳ/ n a person who teaches, esp. as a profession: *My husband's a history teacher at the local school.* | *the University Teachers' Association*

teacher's pet /ˌ··ˈ·/ n *infml, usu. derog* (usu. said by children about one child in the class) the teacher's favourite, or believed favourite, student, often the subject of jealousy amongst the other students

teacher train·ing /ˈ··ˌ··/ n [U] the process of training people how to teach in schools: *a teacher training course* | *a teacher training college*

tea chest /ˈ· ·/ n a large wooden box in which tea is packed, often used afterwards for storing things

teach-in /ˈ· ·/ n an exchange of opinions about a subject of interest, held e.g. in a college by students, teachers, guest speakers, etc.

teach·ing /ˈtiːtʃɪŋ/ n [U] 1 the work or profession of a teacher: *She's planning to go into teaching.* (=become a teacher) 2 also **teachings** *pl.*— that which is taught, esp. the moral, political, or religious beliefs taught by a person of historical importance: *Christians try to follow Christ's teaching/teachings.* | *the teachings of Freud*

teaching hos·pi·tal /ˈ·· ˌ···/ n a hospital where medical students can practise medicine under the guidance of experienced doctors

teaching prac·tice /ˈ·· ˌ··/ *BrE‖***student teaching** *AmE—* n [U] a period of teaching children in a school, done by a person who is training to be a teacher

teach your·self book /ˌ· ·ˈ· ·/ n a book that teaches a particular subject or skill: *Teach yourself typing/Japanese*

tea cloth /ˈ· ·/ n 1 *BrE* a small cloth for spreading over a small table from which tea is to be served 2 a TEA TOWEL

tea co·sy /ˈ· ˌ··/ n a thick covering put over a teapot to keep the contents hot

tea·cup /ˈtiːkʌp/ n a cup in which tea is served —see also **storm in a teacup** (STORM)

tea·gar·den /ˈtiːˌɡɑːdn‖-ɑːr-/ n 1 an outdoor restaurant where drinks and light meals are served 2 a large area of land on which tea is grown; tea PLANTATION

tea·house /ˈtiːhaʊs/ n **-houses** /ˌhaʊzᵻz/ a special house in China or Japan where tea is served, often with great ceremony

teak /tiːk/ n [C;U] (a large tree from India, Burma, and Malaysia that gives) a very hard yellowish brown wood that does not decay and is used for making esp. ships and good quality furniture

teal /tiːl/ n teal a small wild duck

teal blue /ˌ· ˈ·◂/ n a dark greenish blue

tea·leaf /ˈtiːliːf/ n **-leaves** /liːvz/ 1 any of the very finely cut pieces of leaf used for making tea, esp. as left in a teapot or teacup after tea has been drunk 2 *BrE humor sl* a thief

team[1] /tiːm/ n [C+*sing./pl. v*] 1 a group of people who work, act, or esp. play together: *John's in the school hockey team.* | *Our team is/are winning.* | *a team of researchers* | *The government is led by an able team of experienced ministers.* | *Cricket is a* **team game.** | *I didn't do it on my own; it was a* **team effort.** 2 two or more animals pulling the same vehicle: *The carriage was drawn by a team of four white horses.* | *a team of oxen* —see also PAIR[1] (4)

team[2] *v*

team up *phr v* [I **(with)**] to work together for a shared purpose: *I teamed up with June to do the job.*

team-mate /ˈ· ·/ n someone who plays in the same team as oneself

team spir·it /ˌ· ˈ··/ n [U] willingness to work with other people as part of a team: *Come on John, show some team spirit.*

team·ster /ˈtiːmstəʳ/ n *AmE* a person who drives a TRUCK (=a large road vehicle)

Team·sters /ˈtiːmstəz‖-ərz/ also **Teamsters' U·nion** /ˌ·· ˈ···/— [*the*] the largest TRADE UNION in the US, with almost two million members. It was at the centre of a well-known political and financial SCANDAL in the 1950s, and again in 1988.

team·work /ˈtiːmwɜːk‖-wɜːrk/ n [U] the ability of a group of people to work together effectively; (work done through) combined effort

tea par·ty /ˈ· ˌ··/ n a social gathering (usu. made up of women) in the afternoon, at which tea is drunk —see also BOSTON TEA PARTY

tea·pot /ˈtiːpɒt‖-pɑːt/ n a container with a handle and a SPOUT (=bent pouring pipe), in which tea is made and served —see picture at POT

tear[1] /tɪəʳ/ n 1 a drop of salty liquid that flows from the eye, esp. because of pain or sadness: *I burst into tears* (=suddenly started crying) *when I heard the bad news.* | *Few of us shed any tears when he left.* (=we were not sorry) | *He reduced me to tears.* (=made me cry) | *Tears rolled down her cheeks/There were tears in her eyes as she waved goodbye.* | *tears of joy/gratitude/laughter* 2 **in tears** crying: *The little girl was in tears because she'd lost her mother.* —see also CROCODILE TEARS

tear[2] /teəʳ/ v **tore** /tɔːʳ/, **torn** /tɔːn‖tɔːrn/ 1 [T] to pull apart or into pieces by force, intentionally or unintentionally, esp. so as to leave irregular edges: *I tore my sleeve on a thorn.* | *an old torn dress* | *She tore his letter into little pieces.* | *I had to tear the photo out of the newspaper because I couldn't find the scissors.* | *She tore a hole in her dress* (=made a hole by tearing) *when she climbed over*

the wall. —see BREAK (USAGE) **2** [I] to become torn: *This material tears easily, so be careful when you wear it.* **3** [T+obj+adv/prep] to remove by sudden force: *Several trees were torn up* (=from the ground) *in last night's storm.* | *Our roof was torn off by the hurricane.* | *He tore off his clothes and dived in to save the drowning child.* | (fig.) *unhappy children torn from their parents* **4** [T (APART, **between**) *usu. pass.*] to divide by the pull of opposing forces; destroy the peace of: *a country torn apart by war* | *I'm torn between loyalty to my family and my love for Susan.* (=I can't decide which to obey) **5** [I+adv/prep] *infml* to move excitedly with great speed: *The excited children tore noisily down the street.* | *He tore out of the house when he realized how late he was.* | *I'm in a tearing hurry.* (=a great hurry) **6 tear someone limb from limb** *lit or humor* to beat or attack (someone) very severely **7 tear one's hair (out)** to be very excited or anxious: *sitting in a traffic jam on the way to the airport, tearing my hair out* **8 tear oneself away** to leave unwillingly: *He had to tear himself away from the party to catch the last bus home.* **9 tear someone off a strip/tear a strip off someone** *BrE infml* to express severe disapproval of someone; REPRIMAND **10 tear someone's heart out** to fill someone with sadness **11 tear something to shreds/pieces** *infml* to find many faults in something; judge extremely severely: *The critics tore his new novel to shreds.* **12 That's torn it!** *BrE infml* That has ruined everything! That is very unfortunate!: *That's torn it! I've shut my key in the car.*

tear sthg.↔**down** *phr v* [T] (esp. of a building) to pull down, esp. violently; destroy: *These beautiful old Georgian houses are being torn down to make way for a new road.*

tear into sbdy./sthg. *phr v* [T *no pass.*] *infml* to attack violently with blows or words; LAY **into**

tear sthg.↔**off** *phr v* [T] *infml* to write or produce rapidly: *The secretary tore off two letters in five minutes.*

tear sthg. ↔ **up** *phr v* [T] to destroy completely by tearing: *The magician tore up a £5 note and then made it whole again.* | (fig.) *I believe the government intends to tear up its agreement with the unions.*

tear³ /teər/ *n* a torn place in cloth, paper, etc. —see also WEAR AND TEAR

tear·a·way /ˈteərəweɪ/ *n BrE infml* a young person who behaves in a wild and uncontrolled way (mainly used by older people and with some fondness): *The young tearaway's in trouble with the police again.*

tear·drop /ˈtɪədrɒp‖ˈtɪərdrɑːp/ *n* a single tear: *A teardrop ran down her cheek.*

tear·ful /ˈtɪəfəl‖ˈtɪər-/ *adj* **1** full of tears; crying: *The mother was trying to comfort the tearful little girl.* | *a tearful farewell* **2** likely to cry: *These sad love stories always make me feel a bit tearful.* — ~**ly** *adv* — ~**ness** *n* [U]

tear gas /ˈtɪə gæs‖ˈtɪər-/ *also* **CS gas**— *n* [U] a stinging chemical gas that causes blindness for a short time by making the eyes produce tears. It is used by police to control crowds: *The police used tear gas to disperse the crowd.* **tear-gas** *v* [T] **-ss-**

tear·jerk·er /ˈtɪədʒɜːkəʳ‖ˈtɪərdʒɜːr-/ *n infml* a very sad book, film, play, etc., intended to make people cry

tea·room /ˈtiːruːm, -rʊm/ *n* a restaurant where tea and light meals are served

tease¹ /tiːz/ *v* **1** [I;T] to make jokes about or laugh at unkindly or playfully: *At school the other children always teased me because I was fat.* | *Don't take it seriously — he was only teasing.* **2** [T] to annoy (an animal or person) on purpose: *Stop teasing the cat!* **3** [T] *esp. AmE for* BACKCOMB

tease sthg.↔**out** *phr v* [T] to remove, straighten, or loosen carefully and patiently with the fingers: *She teased out the knots in her hair.*

tease² *n infml* **1** someone who teases a lot or likes teasing: *He's a terrible tease.* **2** someone who excites another esp. sexually, with no intention of satisfying them

tea·sel , **-zel**, **-zle** /ˈtiːzəl/ *n* **1** a plant with prickly leaves and flowers **2** a dried flower from this plant, used in former times for brushing cloth so as to give it a soft surface

teas·er /ˈtiːzəʳ/ *n* **1** *infml* a difficult question **2** a TEASE² (2)

tea ser·vice /ˈ·ˌ··/ *also* **tea set** /ˈ·ˌ·/— *n* a matching set of

cups, plates, teapot, etc., used in serving tea

tea shop /ˈ·ˌ·/ *n* a TEAROOM

tea·spoon /ˈtiːspuːn/ *n* **1** a small spoon used for mixing sugar into tea, coffee, etc. **2** [(of)] *also* **tea·spoon·ful** /-fʊl/ (*pl.* **-spoonfuls**, **-spoonsful**)— the amount held by a teaspoon —see picture at SPOON

teat /tiːt/ *n* **1** *BrE* ‖ **nipple** *AmE*— a specially shaped rubber object with a hole in it, fixed to the end of a bottle so that a baby can suck from it **2** an animal's NIPPLE

tea tow·el /ˈ·ˌ··/ *BrE*‖**dish towel** *AmE*— *n* a cloth for drying cups, plates, etc., after they have been washed —see picture at KITCHEN

tea trol·ley /ˈ·ˌ··/ *esp. BrE* ‖ **tea wag·on** *esp. AmE*— *n* a small table on wheels, from which food and/or drinks are served —see picture at TROLLEY

Teb·bit /ˈtebɪt/, **Lord Norman** (1931–) a British Conservative politician who was CHAIRMAN of the party (1985–87). He was hurt in a bomb attack on the Grand Hotel in Brighton in 1985. He is associated with the phrase "get on your bike" after saying in a speech that people with no jobs should go out (on their bicycles) and look for work.

TEC /tek/ *n* Training and Enterprise Council; an organization paid for by the government whose aim is to help people to TRAIN for new jobs (esp. people without a job) or to start or run their own business

tech /tek/ *n infml for* TECHNICAL COLLEGE

tech·ni·cal /ˈteknɪkəl/ *adj* **1** [*no comp.*] having or giving special and usu. practical knowledge, esp. of an industrial or scientific subject: *technical experts* | *technical training* —compare ACADEMIC¹ (2) **2 a** of or related to such a subject. Technical words or phrases are marked *tech* in this dictionary: *The flight was delayed owing to technical reasons.* (=a fault in the engine or other machinery) | *"Precipitation" is a technical term used by weather scientists for "rain".* **b** needing special knowledge in order to be understood: *This book is too technical for me.* **3** [*no comp.*] according to an (unreasonably) exact acceptance of the rules: *The result was a technical defeat for the government, but otherwise of limited importance.* | *a technical infringement of the rules* —see also TECHNICALITY **4** of or related to TECHNIQUE: *the pianist's technical brilliance* — ~**ly** /kli/ *adv* : *Technically, you could be prosecuted for this, but I don't suppose you will be.* | *a technically brilliant pianist.*

technical col·lege /ˈ···ˌ··/ *also* **tech** *infml*— *n* (esp. in Britain) a college providing courses (usu. not to degree level) in practical subjects, art, social studies, etc., for students who have left school —compare POLYTECHNIC, UNIVERSITY

tech·ni·cal·i·ty /ˌteknɪˈkælɪti/ *n* a small detail or rule, esp. one that needs special knowledge in order to be understood or that may seem unnecessary: *The general explained the military technicalities of the matter to the newspaper reporters.* | *He lost the race on a technicality.* (=he should have won, but he broke a particular rule, and so lost)

technical knock·out /ˌ··· ˈ·/ *also* **TKO**— *n* the ending of a BOXING match because one of the fighters cannot continue, e.g. because he is too badly hurt

tech·ni·cian /tekˈnɪʃən/ *n* **1** a highly skilled scientific or industrial worker: *a laboratory technician* **2** someone who has a good technique

Tech·ni·col·or /ˈteknɪkʌləʳ/ *n* [U] *tdmk* a colour film process used for the cinema in which the three PRIMARY COLOURs are recorded on separate films and then mixed together: *filmed in Technicolor*

tech·nique /tekˈniːk/ *n* [C;U] (a) method of doing something that needs skill, esp. in art, music, literature, etc.: *If you want to learn to paint, I suggest you study Raphael's technique.* | *new techniques for producing special effects in films* | *sophisticated modern printing techniques* | (humor) *He has no trouble getting lots of girlfriends; I wonder what his technique is.*

tech·no·crat /ˈteknəkræt/ *n often derog* a highly skilled scientific specialist in charge of the organization of a country, industry, etc.

tech·no·fear /ˈteknəʊ ˌfɪəʳ/ *n* [U] *infml* fear of things which are very technical and complicated, e.g. computers: *At one time or another all of us feel threatened by techno-fear.*

tech·no·log·i·cal /ˌteknəˈlɒdʒɪkəl◄‖-ˈlɑː-/ *adj* related to technology: *The development of the steam engine was the greatest technological advance of the 19th century.* | *the rapid pace of technological change* – ~**ly** /kli/ *adv* : *technologically backward countries*

tech·nol·o·gist /tek'nɒlədʒ₃st‖-'nɑː-/ *n* a specialist in technology

tech·nol·o·gy /tek'nɒlədʒi‖-'nɑː-/ *n* **1** [C;U] (a branch of) knowledge dealing with scientific and industrial methods and their practical use in industry; practical science: *a high level of technology* | *agricultural|nuclear technology* | *The system uses advanced computer and satellite technologies.* **2** [U] machinery, methods, etc., based on this knowledge: *The printing plant uses the very latest technology.* | *We already have the technology to do this.* –see also INFORMATION TECHNOLOGY, NEW TECHNOLOGY

technology trans·fer /·'··· ,··/ *n* [U] the giving or selling of modern equipment such as computers, or the knowledge necessary to operate the equipment, by Western countries to developing countries

tec·ton·ic plate /tek,tɒnɪk 'pleɪt‖-,tɑː-/ *n* any of the large, solid plates that make up the solid surface of the Earth, and which support the land

Te·cum·seh /tɪ'kʌmsə/ (1765?–1813) a Native American man, of the Shawnee TRIBE. who led a group of tribes to defend their lands against white settlers and the US army, who were trying to take over the land – see also NATIVE AMERICAN (CULTURAL NOTE)

teddy bear

ted·dy bear /'tedi beə^r/ also **teddy**– *n* a toy bear filled with soft material, which is a very common British and American child's toy

Teddy Bears' Pic·nic /,·· · '··/, The a popular song for children in the 1950s

teddy boys

teddy boy /'tedi bɔɪ/ also **ted** /ted/– *n* (in Britain, esp. in the 1950s) a young man who dressed in a style similar to that of the early 20th century, usu. wearing a long loose JACKET, narrow trousers, and thick soft shoes

te·di·ous /'tiːdiəs/ *adj* long, tiring, and uninteresting; BORING: *a tedious book|speaker|lecture* – ~**ly** *adv* – ~**ness** *n* [U]

te·di·um /'tiːdiəm/ *n* [U] tediousness

tee¹ /tiː/ *n* (in GOLF) (the area surrounding) a small pile of sand or a specially-shaped plastic or wooden object from which the ball is first driven at the beginning of each hole –see picture at GOLF

tee² *v*
   tee off *phr v* [I] (in GOLF) to drive the ball from a tee
   tee (sthg.↔) **up** *phr v* [I;T] (in GOLF) to prepare to hit (the ball) by placing it on a tee –see picture at GOLF

Tee-ball /'tiː bɔːl/ *n* T-BALL

teed off /,tiːd 'ɒf‖-'ɔːf/ *adj AmE, sl* angry or annoyed

teem /tiːm/ *v* [I (DOWN, with)] *infml* (of liquid) to flow or pour very heavily: *The rain teemed down for hours.* [*it*+I] *It's absolutely teeming (with rain).*
   teem with sthg. *phr v* [T *no pass.*] (of a place) to be full of (esp. a certain type of creature): *This river teems with all kinds of fish in summer.*

teem·ing /'tiːmɪŋ/ *adj* [A] *esp. lit* **1** (of a place) full of

creatures: *the teeming jungle* **2 teeming shore** *quote* a phrase taken from the words written on the Statue of Liberty in New York Harbor –see STATUE OF LIBERTY

teen /tiːn/ *n, adj sl* TEENAGER

teen·age /'tiːneɪdʒ/ also **teen·aged** /'tiːneɪdʒd/– *adj* [A] of, for, or being a teenager: *teenage fashions* | *their teenage daughter*

Teenage Mu·tant He·ro Tur·tles /,·· ,·· ,·· '··/ *n* [P] the HEROes of an extremely popular but short-lived collection of books, films and CARTOONS for children in the early 1990s. They had their origin in the US as the **Teenage Mutant Ninja Turtles**, a group of green TURTLEs known for fighting violently, and gave rise to a very successful industry of Turtle clothing, toys, food, and many other things.

teen·ag·er /'tiːneɪdʒə^r/ *n* a young person of between 13 and 19 years old –see CHILD (USAGE)

teens /tiːnz/ *n* [P] the period of one's life between and including the ages of 13 and 19: *She's in her teens.* | *He's in his late teens.* (=about 16-19 years old)

tee·ny /'tiːni/ *adj infml* very small; TINY

tee·ny·bop·per /'tiːni,bɒpə^r‖-,bɑː-/ *n infml, becoming old-fash* a young person between the ages of about 9 and 14, esp. a girl, who is very interested in popular music and the bands who play it, the latest fashions, etc.

tee·ny wee·ny /,tiːni 'wiːni◂/ also **teen·sy ween·sy** /,tiːnzi 'wiːnzi◂/, **teeny**, **teensy**– *adj infml* (used esp. by or to children) very small

tee·pee /'tiːpiː/ *n* a TEPEE –see colour picture on page 358

Tees /tiːz/ [*the*] a river in NE England which passes through the heavily industrial area known as Teeside

tee shirt /'· ,·/ *n* a T-SHIRT

Tee·side , **Teesside** /'tiːzsaɪd/ a large, heavily industrial area in NE England

tee·ter /'tiːtə^r/ *v* [I (**on**)] to stand or move unsteadily, as if about to fall: *She teetered along in her high-heeled shoes.* | (fig.) *The government is teetering on the brink of defeat* (=is close to being defeated) *over its latest plans.*

teeter-tot·ter /'·· ,··/ *n AmE for* SEESAW

teeth

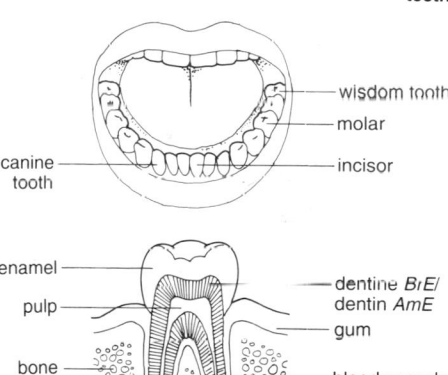

a cross-section of a tooth

teeth /tiːθ/ *n* [P] **1** *pl. of* TOOTH **2** *infml* effective force or power: *When will the police be given the necessary teeth to deal with young criminals?* **3 get one's teeth into** *infml* to do (a job) very actively, purposefully, and with interest **4 in the teeth of** against the strength of; in spite of opposition from: *The government persisted in introducing the new measures in the teeth of public opinion.* **5 set someone's 'teeth on edge** to give someone the unpleasant sensation caused by certain acid tastes or high sounds: *The noise of the chalk scraping on the blackboard sets my teeth on edge.* –see also **armed to the teeth** (ARMED), **take the bit between one's teeth** (BIT²), **cut one's teeth on** (CUT¹), **kick in the teeth** (KICK¹), **lie in one's teeth** (LIE³), **show one's teeth** (SHOW¹), **by the skin of one's teeth** (SKIN¹)

teethe /tiːð/ *v* [I *usu. in progressive forms*] (esp. of a baby) to grow teeth

Diagram labels (teeth): wisdom tooth, molar, incisor, canine tooth. Cross-section labels: enamel, pulp, bone, nerve, dentine *BrE*/dentin *AmE*, gum, blood vessels.

teething troub·les /ˈ··ˌ··/ n [P] problems happening during the early stages of an activity or operation: *We're having a few teething troubles with the new computer.*

tee·to·tal /ˌtiːˈtəʊtl◄/ *adj* never drinking alcohol, or opposed to the drinking of it

tee·to·tal·ler *BrE* ‖ **-taler** *esp. AmE* /tiːˈtəʊtələr/ *n* a person who never drinks alcohol

TEFL /ˈtefəl/ *n* [U] Teaching English as a Foreign Language; the teaching of English to people whose first language is not English —compare EFL, ESL, ESOL, TESL, TESOL

Tef·lon /ˈteflɒn‖-lɑːn/ *n* [U] *tdmk* a plastic which things do not easily stick to, and which is often used in making cooking pans, so that they can be easily cleaned

▶CULTURAL NOTE People sometimes use the word Teflon to describe someone who does something wrong but cannot be proved to have done it, or to describe someone whom people still like or respect even when that person has done something wrong or silly. For example, in the US some people called President Reagan the Teflon president because he was still popular even when the country's debts were growing and when the Iran-Contra affair was becoming known: *Teflon Don John Gotti turns to Velcro as he is convicted of murder, racketeering, and other charges.*◄

Tehe·ran , Tehran /ˌteəˈrɑːn‖teˈrɑːn/ the capital and largest city of Iran, and the industrial centre of the country

Tel A·viv /ˌtel əˈviːv/ the second largest city of Israel which was at one time also the capital

tele- see WORD FORMATION

tel·e·cast /ˈtelikɑːst‖-kæst/ *n* a broadcast on television

tel·e·com·mu·ni·ca·tions /ˌtelikəmjuːnɪˌkeɪʃənz/ *n* [P] the process or business of receiving or sending messages by telephone, radio, television, or telegraph: *great improvements in telecommunications* | *the telecommunications industry* | *a telecommunications satellite*

Tel·e·com Tow·er /ˌtelɪˌkɒm ˈtaʊər‖-kɑːm-/ [*the*] a tall building in London which used to be called the **Post Office Tower** and on which are several TRANSMITTERS. British Telecom has an office there —see colour map on page 817

tel·e·gram /ˈtelɪɡræm/ ‖ also **wire** *AmE*— *n* (a piece of paper with) a message sent by telegraph: *We informed them by telegram that we would be arriving early.*

▶CULTURAL NOTE In Britain, when a person is one hundred years old they receive a telegram from the Queen congratulating (CONGRATULATE) them. During the First World War and the Second World War people also received a telegram if their son or husband had been killed.◄

tel·e·graph¹ /ˈtelɪɡrɑːf‖-ɡræf/ *n* 1 [U] a method of sending messages either by using radio signals or (esp. formerly) electrical signals along wire: *The news came by telegraph.* 2 [C] an apparatus that receives or sends messages in this way —see also BUSH TELEGRAPH —**graphic** /ˌtelɪˈɡræfɪk◄/ *adj* : *a telegraphic message* —**graphically** /kli/ *adv*

telegraph² *v* 1 [I;T (**to**)] to send (a message) or inform (a person) by telegraph: *The news was telegraphed across the Atlantic.* [+obj(i)+obj(d)] *We telegraphed her the bad news.* 2 [T] to make (what one is going to do) very easy to see or discover: *He telegraphs his punches.*

Telegraph [*the*] the DAILY TELEGRAPH

te·leg·ra·pher /tɪˈleɡrəfər/ also **te·leg·ra·phist** /tɪˈleɡrəfɪst/— *n* a person employed to send and receive messages by telegraph

tel·e·graph·ese /ˌtelɪɡrəˈfiːz‖-ɡræfˈiːz/ *n* [U] a style of writing used in telegrams, in which unnecessary words are not included (as in *Arriving Wednesday* for *I am arriving on Wednesday.*)

telegraph pole /ˈ··· ·/ also **telegraph post** *BrE*‖**telephone pole** *AmE*— *n* a tall wooden pole for supporting telephone wires —compare UTILITY POLE

telegraph wire /ˈ··· ·/ *n* a wire for carrying telegraphic messages

te·leg·ra·phy /tɪˈleɡrəfi/ *n* [U] *tech* the sending of messages by electrical signals

tel·e·ki·ne·sis /ˌtelikɪˈniːsɪs, -kaɪ-/ *n* [U] *tech* the moving of solid objects by the power of the mind alone

tel·e·mar·ket·ing /ˈteliˌmɑːkɪtɪŋ‖-ˌmɑːr-/ *n* [U] the practice of telephoning people to find out if they would be interested in buying something —compare TELESALES

tel·e·mes·sage /ˈtelimesɪdʒ/ *n* *tdmk* a form of TELEGRAM, sent by telephone or TELEX through the Post Office

te·lem·e·try /tɪˈlemɪtri/ *n* [U] *tech* the collection of information by a special instrument (a **telemeter**) that measures quantities and sends the results by radio to a distant place

tel·e·ol·o·gy /ˌteliˈɒlədʒi‖-ˈɑː-/ *n* [U] *tech* the belief that all things and events were specially planned to fulfil a purpose —**gist** *n* —**gical** /ˌteliəˈlɒdʒɪkəl◄‖-ˈlɑː-/ *adj* —**gically** /kli/ *adv*

tel·e·path·ic /ˌtelɪˈpæθɪk◄/ *adj* 1 *infml* able to practise telepathy: *How did you know I was going to say that? You must be telepathic!* 2 of, sent by, or like telepathy: *telepathic messages* — ~ **ally** /kli/ *adv*

te·lep·a·thy /tɪˈlepəθi/ *n* [U] the sending of thoughts, messages, etc., from one person's mind to another's without the ordinary use of the senses

tel·e·phone¹ /ˈtelɪfəʊn/ also **phone**— *n* 1 an apparatus or system for sending or receiving sound, esp. speech, over long distances by electrical means: *If the telephone rings, can you answer it?* | *Your mother was on the telephone earlier.* (=she called by telephone) | *I spoke to him* **by telephone/on the telephone.** | *Are you* **on the telephone?** (=have you got one?) | *What's your telephone number?* | *a threatening telephone call* | *I'm sure my telephone's being tapped.* 2 the part of a telephone into which one speaks; RECEIVER: *I was so angry with him I slammed down the telephone.*

▷USAGE **Telephone** can be used as a noun or a verb, and so can the short form **phone**. If you want to **telephone** your mother (or **call** her, **ring** her (**up**), **give** her **a ring**), you **dial** her (**phone**) **number**, which can be found in the **phone book** or **directory**. If it is a long-distance call, you may have to ask the **operator** to connect you. The phone will **ring**, and if your mother is at home she will **answer** by picking up the **receiver**. If she is busy she may ask you to **call back** later. If she doesn't want to speak to you, she may **hang up** (=replace the receiver). If she is already **on the phone** when you call her, her number is **engaged** (*BrE*) ‖ **busy** (*AmE*). A telephone in a public place is a **phone box** or **call box** *BrE* ‖ **phone booth** *AmE*.◁

telephone² also **phone**— *v* [I;T] 1 to speak to (someone) by telephone or send (a message) by telephone: *He telephoned to say he'd been delayed.* | *If you telephone your order to the shop they'll deliver it.* 2 to (try to) become connected with (a place or person) by telephone: *I've been telephoning all morning, but I haven't been able to speak to the doctor.* | *You can't telephone Glasgow directly from here; you have to go through the operator.*

telephone box /ˈ··· ˌ·/ also **call box, phone box** *BrE* ‖ **phone booth, telephone booth** *esp. AmE*— *n* *BrE* a small hut or enclosure containing a telephone for use by the public

telephone call /ˈ··· ·/ also **phone call, call** *n* a call made on a telephone: *a threatening telephone call.* | *My answering machine showed that I'd had three phone calls while I was out.*

telephone di·rec·to·ry /ˈ··· ·ˌ···/ *n* *fml for* PHONE BOOK

telephone ex·change /ˈ··· ·ˌ·/ *n* a central place, usu. a building, where . telephone connections are made — compare SWITCHBOARD

telephone number /ˈ··· ˌ··/ *n* 1 the number you have to DIAL to connect with a particular telephone: *What's your telephone number?* 2 **telephone numbers** *infml* a very large amount of money. *I don't know how much he earns, but we're certainly* **talking telephone numbers.**

te·leph·o·nist /tɪˈlefənɪst/ *n* *BrE* a person who makes telephone connections at a telephone exchange or SWITCHBOARD

te·le·pho·to lens /ˌtelɪˌfəʊtəʊ ˈlenz/ *n* a special camera LENS that makes it possible to take pictures of distant things as if they were close

tel·e·print·er /ˈtelɪˌprɪntər/ also **tel·e·type·writ·er** /ˌtelɪˈtaɪpraɪtər/ *esp. AmE*— *n* a machine with a KEYBOARD for typing TELEX messages and a printer for printing messages received

Tel·e·prompt·er /ˈtelɪprɒmptər‖-prɑːmp-/ *n* *tdmk* a machine that unrolls lines of enlarged writing, placed in front of someone appearing on television so that they can read it yet appear to be speaking naturally

tel·e·sales /ˈteliseɪlz/ also **teleselling**— *n* [U] the practice of telephoning people in order to sell them things: *I think* *she works in telesales.* —compare TELEMARKETING

tel·e·scope¹ /ˈteləˌskəʊp/ *n* a tubelike scientific instrument that makes distant objects look nearer and larger —see also RADIO TELESCOPE; compare BINOCULARS, MICROSCOPE

telescope² *v* 1 [I;T] to (cause to) become shorter in length or time: *The two buses telescoped together in the collision.* | *For the purposes of the film, three months' action is telescoped into two hours.* 2 [T] to become shorter by one part sliding over another: *This instrument will telescope small enough to fit into this box.* /

tel·e·scop·ic /ˌteləˈskɒpɪk◄||-ˈskɑː-/ *adj* 1 made of parts that slide one over another so that the whole can be made shorter: *The tripod has telescopic legs.* 2 of or like a telescope: *a telescopic lens* 3 seen or obtained by means of a telescope: *a telescopic picture of the moon*

tel·e·sell·ing /ˈteliselɪŋ/ *n* [U] TELESALES

Tel·e·tex /ˈteliteks/ *n tdmk* 1 [U] an internationally standardized system for sending messages between computers and related equipment over telephone lines. It is faster and has more features than TELEX, which it may one day replace. 2 [C] a message received or sent in this way —compare FAX²

tel·e·text /ˈtelitekst/ *n* [U] (*sometimes cap.*) a system of broadcasting written information (e.g. news) on television — see also CEEFAX, ORACLE

tel·e·van·ge·lis·m /ˌteliˈvændʒəlɪzəm/ *n* [U] the use of television programmes to persuade people to become Christians common in the US

► CULTURAL NOTE For many people, televangelism has associations with emotional language and attempts to obtain money from those watching, not always for honest purposes.◄

tel·e·van·ge·list /ˌteliˈvændʒəlɪst/ also **tv evangelist, television e·van·ge·list** /ˌ···· ·ˈ···/— *n* someone, usu. a Protestant Christian, who talks about religion on television in an EVANGELICAL way. Common in the US, some have raised very large amounts of money for their churches in this way, though not all ask for money. Recently, some televangelists have been found guilty of using the money they raised for non-religious purposes, and of behaving in non-religious ways.

tel·e·vise /ˈteləvaɪz/ *v* [T] to broadcast by television: *The President's news conference was televised.*

tel·e·vi·sion /ˈteləˌvɪʒən, ˌteləˈvɪʒən◄/ also **TV, telly** *BrE infml*— *n* 1 [C] also **television set** /·ˈ·· ·, ˌ···· ·/ *fml*— a boxlike apparatus with a SCREEN that receives broadcast signals and turns them into pictures and sound: *a colour/black-and-white television* —see picture at LIVING ROOM 2 [U] (the watching of) the shows received by a television: *The children watch far too much television.* | *the television news* 3 [U] **a** the method of broadcasting pictures and sound by means of electrical waves: *Who invented television?* **b** the business of making and broadcasting shows on a television: *Jean works in television as a reporter.* | *a television producer* 4 **on (the) television** broadcast or broadcasting by television: *What's on television tonight?* | *The President spoke to the nation on television.*

television li·cence /ˌ···· ˌ··, ··ˈ·· ˌ··/ *n* (in Britain) an official paper from the government giving permission to use a television in one's home

► CULTURAL NOTE In Britain it is illegal to use a television in your home without paying for a yearly licence. Money from licences helps the government to pay for BBC programmes. In the US no licence is necessary; there, advertisements on television pay for the television companies.◄

tel·ex¹ /ˈteleks/ *n* 1 [U] the system of sending messages from one TELEPRINTER to another by telephone line, SATELLITE, etc.: *We'll give you our reply by telex.* 2 [C] a message received or sent in this way: *A telex has just arrived from Hong Kong.* —compare FAX², TELETEX (2)

telex² *v* [I;T (to)] to send (a message, information, news, etc.) to (a person, place, company, etc.) by telex: [+obj+that] *Telex Australia that prices are to be increased by 10%.* [+obj+obj(d)] *Telex them the news urgently.*

Tel·ford /ˈtelfəd||-fərd/, **Thomas** (1757–1834) a Scottish ARCHITECT and engineer known for his work on bridges, roads, and CANALS; some of his hundreds of bridges are still in use today

tell /tel/ *v* **told** /təʊld/ 1 [T (**about, of, to**)] to make (some-

thing) known in words to (someone); express in words: *If you knew you were going to be late, why didn't you tell me?* | *He's good at telling jokes.* | *Do you always tell the truth?* | *Tell me all about your new job.* | *The boss will have to be told about this.* | *He told us of his wonderful adventures in foreign lands.* [+obj(i)+obj(d)] *I always tell the children a story* | *tell a story to the children before they go to bed.* [+obj+(that)] *John told us he'd seen you in town.* [+obj+wh-] *Could you tell me when it will be ready/how much it will cost?* | *I can't tell you how pleased I am* (=I'm very pleased) *to hear your good news.* | **Don't tell me** *you've forgotten your keys again!* (=I am disappointed or annoyed that you have done this) | *I'm right,* **I tell you!** (=you can be certain that I am right) | (*infml*) **I'll tell you what** (=here is a suggestion) — *let's go out for a drink.* —see also TELL of 2 [T] to cause (someone) to know what they must do; order; direct: *That child has got to learn to do what/as he's told.* [+obj+wh-] *Don't try to tell me how to behave!* [+obj+to-v] *I told you to get here early, so why are you late?* —see ORDER² (USAGE) 3 [T+obj+that/wh-] to show; make known; INDICATE: *This red light tells you that the machine is ready to use/tells you whether the machine is on or off.* 4 [I;T] to know for certain; recognize or be sure: [+(that)]: *It was so dark I couldn't tell it was you.* | *I can tell that it's a camel by the fact that it has a hump.* [+wh-] *It's difficult to tell when it will be finished/how long it will take, because we've never done this sort of job before.* [+obj+from/APART] *I can't tell Jane from Sarah/tell Jane and Sarah apart — they look so alike.* | *"Do you think he's going to win?" "Who can tell?"* 5 [T+obj; usu. in past tense] to warn or advise: [+(that)] *I told you he was a fool, but you wouldn't listen to me.* [+obj+to-v] *I told you not to print that story, and now look what's happened!* | *I won't say* **"I told you so",** *but I did!* 6 [I (**on**)] *fml* to be noticeable; have an effect: *Eventually the tennis champion's greater experience began to tell, and he won easily in the end.* | *All those late nights are beginning to tell on your work.* (=have a bad effect on it) —see also TELLING 7 [I (**on**)] *infml* to speak someone's secret to someone else; inform against: *You won't tell on me, will you — otherwise I'll be in trouble!* 8 **all told** altogether; when everyone or everything has been counted 9 **tell me another** *infml, esp. humor* I don't believe you; I think you're joking or lying 10 **tell tales (out of school)** to talk about things that should remain secret —see also TALE (3), TELLTALE 11 **tell the time** to read the time from a clock or watch or by other means 12 **there is no telling** it is impossible to know: *There's no telling what will happen if she meets him while she's in this bad temper.* 13 **to tell (you) the truth** (used to introduce a personal opinion, to admit something, etc.): *To tell the truth, I don't really like her.* 14 **you can never tell** also **you never can tell** — one can never be sure about something: *"Do you think we'll be lucky this time?" "You never can tell."* (=perhaps) 15 **you're telling me** *infml* (used for showing very strong agreement): *"This is a steep hill." "You're telling me! I need a rest."* —see SAY (USAGE)

tell against sbdy. *phr v* [T *no pass.*] to count in judgment against, and so prevent the success of: *His prison record told against him when he tried to get a job.*

tell of sthg./sbdy. *phr v* [T] *esp. lit* to mention; describe: *This ancient poem tells of the deeds of a famous warrior.*

tell sbdy. **↔ off** *phr v* [T] 1 *infml* (esp. of a teacher, parent, manager, etc.) to talk angrily to (someone who has done something wrong); REPRIMAND: *The teacher told him off for not doing his homework.* —see also TELLING-OFF 2 *fml* to separate (a group) from the whole body for special work or to do something: [+obj+to-v/for] *Ten soldiers were told off to dig ditches/for guard duty.*

Tell, William a famous character in Swiss stories who was forced to use his great skill with a CROSSBOW to shoot an apple off his son's head. He later killed the powerful man who made him do this, beginning the movement which resulted in an independent Switzerland. See picture on page 1362

tell·er /ˈteləʳ/ *n* 1 *esp. AmE* a person employed to receive and pay out money in a bank 2 a person who counts votes

tell·ing /ˈtelɪŋ/ *adj* having a great or important effect; SIGNIFICANT: *The most telling factor in their defeat was their lack of reliable supplies.* | *a telling argument* —see also TELL (6) — **~ly** *adv*

telling-off /ˌ··· ˈ·/ *n* severe or angry words spoken to someone because they have done something wrong;

William Tell

REPRIMAND: *The child was given a good telling-off for stealing apples.* –see also TELL **off**

tell·tale[1] /'telteɪl/ *adj* [A] that makes a fact known, esp. an unpleasant fact: *The murderer was given away by a few telltale bloodstains on his car seat.* | *telltale signs of a slow-down in business activity*

telltale[2] *n infml derog* a person who informs about other people's secrets, wrong actions, etc. (mainly used by or of children)

tel·ly /'teli/ *n* [C;U] *BrE infml* (a) television

te·me·ri·ty /tɪˈmerəti/ *n* [U] *fml* foolish confidence; rashness (RASH[1]): *She had the temerity to ask for a pay increase after only three days' work.*

temp[1] /temp/ *n infml* a person, esp. a secretary, employed to work in an office for a short or limited period of time while someone is absent, while there is a great deal of work, etc.

temp[2] *v* [I] *infml, esp. BrE* to work as a temp: *She's temping during the university vacation.*

temp agency /'· ,···/ see TEMPING AGENCY

tem·per[1] /'tempər/ *n* **1** [C] a person's present or habitual state of mind, esp. with regard to whether they are angry or easily become angry: *Jean's in a bad temper* (=angry) *because she missed the bus and had to walk to work.* | *He has a naturally even/sweet temper.* (=is calm and pleasant by nature) | *He was behaving so stupidly that I found it hard to keep my temper/that I nearly lost my temper.* (=became angry) | *Tempers were becoming rather frayed* (=people were getting angry), *so the chairman brought the meeting to an end.* | *When tempers have cooled* (=when everyone has become calm again) *we will decide what to do.* **2** [C;U] *infml* an angry, impatient, or bad state of mind: *Be careful what you say to her – she's got quite a temper.* (=she easily becomes angry) | *a fit of temper* | *John's in a temper today, so try not to annoy him.* | *She flies into a temper if you contradict her.* **3** [U] *tech* the degree to which a substance, esp. a metal, has been hardened or strengthened by tempering (TEMPER[2]) **4 out of temper** *old-fash fml* angry **5 -tempered** /tempəd‖-ərd/having a temper of the stated kind: *a bad-tempered old man* –see also HOT-TEMPERED, ILL-TEMPERED

temper[2] *v* [T] **1** to bring (metal, clay, etc.) to the desired degree of hardness or firmness by special treatment: *Steel is tempered by heating it and then putting it into cold water.* **2** [(**with**)] *fml or lit* to make less severe by adding something else: *Let justice be tempered with mercy.*

tem·pe·ra /'tempərə/ *n* [U] *tech* a method of painting in which the colouring material is mixed with a thick liquid, such as egg

tem·pe·ra·ment /'tempərəmənt/ *n* [C;U] a person's nature, esp. as it influences how they think or behave; DISPOSITION: *Actors often have excitable temperaments.* | *Whether a person likes a routine office job or not depends largely on temperament.*

tem·pe·ra·men·tal /ˌtempərəˈmentl◄/ *adj* **1** *usu. derog* having frequent changes of temper; easily excited or made angry; UNPREDICTABLE: *The actress was so temperamental that many people refused to work with her.* | (fig.) *I'm afraid my old car is a bit temperamental and doesn't always start.* **2** caused by one's temperament: *I have a temperamental dislike of sports.* – **-ly** *adv* : *He's temperamentally unsuited to office work.*

tem·pe·rance /'tempərəns/ *n* [U] **1** total avoidance of alcoholic drinks: *a temperance society* **2** *fml* self-control in speech, behaviour, or esp. the drinking of alcohol

temperance move·ment /'··· ,··/ *n* an effort by an organization to persuade people not to drink alcohol. Such movements began in the US, Britain, and N Europe in the 19th century because of the increase in alcoholism. –see also PROHIBITION

tem·pe·rate /'tempərət/ *adj* **1** (of parts of the world, CLIMATE, etc.) free from very high or very low temperatures: *The temperate zones of the world are found to the north and south of the tropics.* | *temperate plants* (=that live in a temperate climate) **2** *fml* practising or showing self-control: *temperate habits/behaviour* –see also INTEMPERATE

tem·pe·ra·ture /'tempərətʃər/ *n* **1** [C] the degree of heat or coldness of a place, object, etc.: *What's the average temperature in London on a summer's day?* | *a sudden rise/fall/change in temperature* | *high temperatures* | *These divers work in sub-zero temperatures.* | *The nurse took my temperature* (=measured the heat of my body) *with a thermometer.* –see CELSIUS, FAHRENHEIT **2** [S] a bodily temperature higher than the correct one; a fever: *If you have got/are running a temperature you should stay in bed.*

tem·pest /'tempɪst/ *n esp. lit* a violent storm

Tempest, The a play by William Shakespeare, a TRAGICOMEDY about a MAGICIAN, Prospero, who is exiled (EXILE) on an island with his daughter, Miranda, and Caliban, a witch's son

tem·pes·tu·ous /temˈpestʃuəs/ *adj lit* very rough; stormy; violent: *the tempestuous sea/wind* | (fig.) *a tempestuous meeting of the city council* – **-ly** *adv* – **-ness** *n* [U]

temping a·gen·cy /'·· ,··/ ‖ also **temp agency** *AmE*– *n* a business that makes its money by supplying people (esp. secretaries) to work in an office for a short or limited period of time while someone is absent or while there is a great deal of work, etc.

tem·plate, templet /'templeɪt, -plət/ *n* a thin board or plate cut into a special shape or pattern, used as a guide for cutting metal, wood, clay, etc.

tem·ple[1] /'templ/ *n* a building or place for the worship of a god or gods, esp. in the Hindu, Buddhist, Sikh, Mormon, or modern Jewish religions: *the Temple of Heavenly Peace in Peking* | *an ancient Greek/Roman temple*

temple[2] *n [usu. pl.]* **1** either of the flattish areas on each side of the forehead –see picture at HEAD **2** *AmE* either of the parts of a pair of glasses that hooks over the ear

Temple[1] a part of the City of London consisting of two of the Inns of Court; the Inner Temple and the Middle Temple. Many lawyers and BARRISTERS work there.

Temple[2], **Shir·ley** /'ʃɜːli‖ 'ʃɜːr-/ (1928–) an American film ACTRESS who was the child star of over 20 films in the 1930s, and in later life, as **Shirley Temple Black**, became a US AMBASSADOR. She was very popular when her films first appeared because of her style of singing, dancing and acting and her curly golden hair.

Shirley Temple

tem·po /'tempəʊ/ *n* **-pos** or (tech) **-pi** /piː/ **1** the speed at which music is or should be played: *at a fast tempo* **2** the rate or pattern of movement, work, or activity; PACE: *the busy tempo of city life*

tem·po·ral /'tempərəl/ *adj* **1** *fml* related to practical material affairs as opposed to religious affairs: *The Church has no temporal power in the modern state.* –compare SPIRITUAL[1] (4) **2** *tech* of or limited by time: *"When" and "while" are temporal conjunctions.*

tem·po·ra·ry /'tempərəri, -pəri‖-pəreri/ *adj* lasting only for a limited time: *Students often find temporary jobs during their summer holidays.* | *We apologize for the temporary inconvenience caused by these building works.* | *a temporary setback* –compare PERMANENT, PROVISIONAL – **-rily** /'tempərərəli‖ˌtempəˈrerəli/ *adv* : *The daily flight to Dallas has been temporarily suspended.* – **-riness** /'tempərərinəs‖-pəreri-/ *n* [U]

temporary re·strain·ing or·der /ˌ····· ·'·· ,··/ also **TRO**– *n*

AmE law a court order (INJUNCTION) to make someone do or not do something immediately. It is usu. given by a judge in a situation where it is thought that action must be taken immediately, before there is time for a full hearing in court.

tem·po·rize also **-rise** *BrE* /ˈtempəraɪz/ *v* [I] *fml* to delay or avoid making a decision in order to gain time

tempt /tempt/ *v* [T (**into, to**)] **1** to persuade or attract (someone) to do something that seems pleasant or advantageous but may be unwise or immoral; make (someone) want to do something: *The Devil tempted Christ by offering him power over all the world.* | *A rival company is trying to tempt her away from her present job with an offer of more money.* | *a tempting offer* | *I think these enticing displays of goods in shops only tempt people into stealing.* (=encourage them to steal) [+obj+to-v] *The fine weather tempted us to go outside.* | *It's a very attractive offer, and I'm tempted to accept.* (=I would like to accept but am not sure if I should) | *Can I tempt you to another cream bun?* **2 tempt fate/providence** to risk failure by depending too much on luck − ~**er** *n* − ~**ingly** *adv*

temp·ta·tion /tempˈteɪʃən/ *n* **1** [U] the act of tempting or the state of being tempted **2** [C] something very attractive; a thing or situation that tempts one: *the temptations of a big city* [+to-v] *I tried to resist/overcome the temptation to laugh.*

temp·tress /ˈtemptrɪs/ *n lit or humor* a woman who tempts men to sexual immorality

tem·pus fu·git /ˌtempəs ˈfjuːdʒɪt/ *phrase Lat quote* time flies or passes very quickly (a phrase from Virgil's *Georgics*)

ten /ten/ *determiner, n, pron* **1** (the number) 10 −see TABLE 1 **2 be ten a penny** *infml* to be very common or of little value **3 ten to one** *infml* very likely: *Ten to one the train will be late.* −**tenth** *determiner, n, pron, adv*

ten·a·ble /ˈtenəbəl/ *adj* **1** (esp. of a belief, argument, etc.) that can be successfully defended; reasonable: *To say that the government can't afford it is not a tenable argument.* −opposite **untenable 2** [F (**for**)] (of an office, job, etc.) that can be held by someone for a usu. stated period of time: *How long is the post tenable (for)?*

te·na·cious /tɪˈneɪʃəs/ *adj* holding firm to a course of action, esp. in a courageous way; not easily letting go or accepting defeat; PERSISTENT: *He held on to my arm with a tenacious grip.* | *She has proved a very tenacious opponent of the new road scheme.* − ~**ly** *adv* − ~**ness** *or* **-city** /tɪˈnæsɪti/ *n* [U]

ten·an·cy /ˈtenənsi/ *n* **1** [C] the length of time during which someone uses a room, land, building, etc., for which they have paid rent: *a six-month tenancy* **2** [U] the possession and use of a room, land, building, etc., for which rent is paid: *rights of tenancy* | *a tenancy agreement*

ten·ant /ˈtenənt/ *n* a person who pays rent for the use of a room, building, land, etc.: *Do you own your house or are you a tenant?* | *a council tenant* −compare OWNER-OCCUPIER; see also SITTING TENANT

tenant farm·er /ˌ·· ˈ··/ *n* a person who farms land rented from someone else −see also SHARECROPPER

ten·ant·ry /ˈtenəntri/ *n* [*the*+S+*sing./pl. v*] all the tenant farmers renting land from one person in one place

tench /tentʃ/ *n* **tench** *or* **tenches** a European fish that lives in lakes and rivers

Ten Com·mand·ments /ˌ· ·ˈ··/ also **Decalogue** *fml*− *n* [*the* + P] according to the Bible, God's laws as given to Moses on Mount Sinai. They say how we should live our lives, treat other people, etc. They appear in the Christian, Jewish and Islamic religions. "Thou shalt not kill" is one of the Ten Commandments.

tend¹ /tend/ *v* [I] **1** to have a tendency; be likely (to do or be) something; do or be often or usually: [+*to-v*] *Janet tends to get* (=usually gets) *very angry if you disagree with her.* | *It tends to rain here a lot in the spring.* [+*adv/prep*], esp. **to, towards**] *The sort of music they play varies, but tends towards jazz.* −see APT (USAGE) **2** [+*adv/prep*] to move or develop one's course in a certain direction: *Interest rates are tending upwards.*

tend² *v* [T] *old-fash* **1** to take care of (a living thing); look after: *She tended her husband lovingly during his long illness.* | *The nurse skilfully tended the soldiers' wounds.* | *a farmer tending his sheep* **2** *AmE* to serve customers in (a store, bar, etc.): *a bartender*

tend to sthg./sbdy. *phr v* [T] to TEND² (1): *The nurse tended to the soldier's wounds.*

Ten Days That Shook the World /ˌ· ·· ˌ· · ˈ·/ a book by John Reed about the 1917 Russian Revolution

ten·den·cy /ˈtendənsi/ *n* **1** [(**to, towards**)] a natural likelihood of developing, thinking, or behaving in a particular way; PROPENSITY: *She has artistic tendencies.* | *He's always had a tendency to/towards frivolity.* [+*to-v*] *his tendency to view world affairs purely in terms of the East-West conflict* **2** [(**to, towards**)] a general movement or development in a certain direction or towards a certain condition; TREND: *an increasing tendency towards the use of firearms by criminals* [+*to-v*] *There is a growing tendency for people to work at home instead of in offices.* **3** [+*sing./pl. v*] *BrE* a group within a political party that supports ideas different from and usu. more extreme than those of the main party −see also MILITANT TENDENCY

ten·den·tious /tenˈdenʃəs/ *adj fml derog* (of a speech, remark, book, etc.) expressing a particular opinion; intended to influence the reader or hearer in a particular direction, esp. on a subject causing strong feelings or argument − ~**ly** *adv* − ~**ness** *n* [U]

ten·der¹ /ˈtendər/ *adj* **1** painful; sore; sensitive to the touch: *The wound is still very tender.* | (fig.) *Don't mention his divorce − it's a very tender subject.* (=a subject which could upset him) **2** easy to bite through; soft: *beautifully tender meat* −opposite **tough 3** gentle and loving; sympathetic; kind: *a tender heart* | *tender loving care* **4** [A] *lit or humor* young; inexperienced: *a child of tender years* | *He was sent to boarding school at the tender age of eight.* − ~**ly** *adv* − ~**ness** *n* [U]

tender² *n* **1** a vehicle carrying coal and/or water, pulled behind a railway engine **2** a small boat for carrying passengers, supplies, etc., between the shore and a larger boat **3** (*often in comb.*) a person who takes care of something: *a bartender*

tender³ *n* a statement of the price one would charge for providing goods or services or for doing a job: *to submit a tender* −see also LEGAL TENDER

tender⁴ *v* **1** [I (**for**)] to make a formal offer to do something at a particular price: *Several firms have tendered for the new road-building contract.* **2** [T (**to**)] *fml* to present for acceptance: *The minister tendered his resignation to the Queen, but was asked to reconsider his decision.* **3** [T] *fml* to offer in payment: *"Passengers should tender the exact fare. Change will not be given on this bus."* (notice)

ten·der·foot /ˈtendəfʊt‖-ər-/ *n* **-foots** *or* **-feet** /fiːt/ **1** *AmE infml* a person who has recently arrived in a rough place, such as formerly the western US, where life is hard **2** an inexperienced beginner: *a political tenderfoot*

ten·der·heart·ed /ˌtendəˈhɑːtɪd‖-dərˈhɑːr-/ *adj* easily made to have feelings of love, pity, or sorrow: *She was too tenderhearted to refuse.* − ~**ly** *adv* − ~**ness** *n* [U]

Tender is the Night /ˌ··· · ˈ·/ a book by F Scott Fitzgerald written in 1934, based on his own life, about an alcoholic doctor and his mad wife on the French Riviera

ten·der·ize also **-ise** *BrE* /ˈtendəraɪz/ *v* [T] to make (meat) tender by special preparation

ten·der·loin /ˈtendəlɔɪn‖-ər-/ *n* [U] tender meat taken from each side of the backbone of cows or pigs: *pork/beef tenderloin*

ten·don /ˈtendən/ *n* a thick strong cord that connects a muscle to a bone

ten·dril /ˈtendrɪl/ *n* a thin leafless curling stem by which a climbing plant fastens itself to a support

ten·e·ment /ˈtenəmənt/ *n* a large building divided into flats, esp. in the poorer areas of a city

Ten·e·rife /ˌtenəˈriːf/ one of the Canary Islands off the NW coast of Africa, a very popular holiday place with British and other (mainly European) tourists

ten·et /ˈtenɪt/ *n fml* a principle or belief held by a person, religious group, etc., esp. one that forms part of a larger system of beliefs: *socialist tenets*

ten-gal·lon hat /ˌ· ·· ·· ˈ·/ *n* a tall hat made of soft material with a very wide BRIM, of a kind worn by COWBOYS in the US

Ten Green Bot·tles /ˌ· ·· ˈ··/ a song about ten green bottles hanging on a wall and becoming fewer and fewer as they fall off the wall

ten·ner /ˈtenəʳ/ n BrE infml £10 or a ten-pound note: It costs a tenner. | I've only got tenners.

Ten·nes·see /ˌtenəˈsiː◂/ written abbrev. **TN**– a state in the S central US, with an ECONOMY based on industry and farming, and whose cities include Memphis, Nashville, Chattanooga, and Knoxville –see colour map on pages 1374–5

Ten·ni·el /ˈteniəl/, **Sir John** (1820–1914) an English artist who drew the pictures for Alice's Adventures in Wonderland and Through the Looking-Glass. He drew CARTOONs for the magazine Punch for over 50 years.

tennis

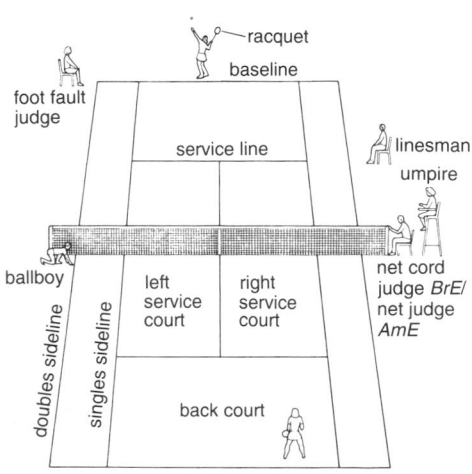

a tennis court

ten·nis /ˈtenɪs/ n [U] **1** a game for two people or two pairs of people who use RACKETs to hit a small soft ball backwards and forwards across a low net dividing a specially marked level court: Do you play tennis? | a tennis player/racket/ball/court –see also DECK TENNIS, LAWN TENNIS, WIMBLEDON **2 anyone for tennis?** a phrase from plays of the 1920s and 1930s and usu. said by UPPER-CLASS people when inviting others to play tennis. It is used humorously by other people.

▷ USAGE In an important **tennis match** the person in charge is called the **umpire**; the winner of such a match is the one who wins the larger number of **sets** (=groups of **games**).◁

tennis el·bow /ˌ·· ˈ·· / n [U] a painful condition of the elbow caused esp. by too much repeated twisting of the hand

tennis shoe /ˈ·· ˌ· / n AmE for TRAINER

Ten·ny·son /ˈtenɪsən/, **Al·fred** /ˈælfrɪd/, **Lord** (1809–92) an English poet who was made POET LAUREATE, and whose works include The Charge of the Light Brigade

ten·on /ˈtenən/ n a specially cut end of a piece of wood made to fit exactly into a shaped opening (MORTISE) in another piece of wood and so form a joint

ten·or /ˈtenəʳ/ n **1** [C] (usu. a man with) a high male singing voice, lower than ALTO (1) and higher than BARITONE **2** [C] a musical instrument with the same range of notes as this: a tenor saxophone **3** [(the) S (of)] fml the general direction, course, or character: It seemed nothing could disturb the even tenor of our existence in those happy prewar days. **4** [(the) S (of)] fml the general meaning (of something written or spoken): I understood the tenor of his speech but not the details.

ten·pin /ˈtenˌpɪn/ n any of the ten bottle-shaped wooden objects that one tries to knock down in BOWLING

tenpin bowl·ing /ˌ·· ˈ·· / BrE ‖ **ten·pins** /ˈtenˌpɪnz/ AmE– n [U] BOWLING

tense¹ /tens/ adj **1** having, showing, or causing nervous anxiety: I was so tense the night before my exams that I couldn't sleep. | a tense situation/atmosphere **2** stretched tight; stiff; TAUT: tense muscles –see also TENSION – ~ly adv – ~ness n [U]

tense² v [I;T (UP)] to (cause to) become tense

tense³ n [C;U] any of the forms of a verb that show the time and continuance or completion of the action or state expressed by the verb: "I am" is in the present tense, "I was" is past tense, and "I will be" is future tense.

tensed up /ˌ· ˈ·/ adj [F] nervously anxious: John seems very tensed up; do you know what's worrying him?

ten·sile /ˈtensaɪl‖ˈtensəl/ adj tech **1** [A no comp.] related to TENSION (1, 2): The **tensile strength** of a rope is the amount of weight it can hold without breaking. **2** that can be stretched: tensile rubber

ten·sion /ˈtenʃən/ n **1** [U] (a feeling of) nervous anxiety, worry, or pressure: The doctor said I was suffering from nervous tension. | **Tension mounted** (=increased) as we waited for the exam results to be published. **2** [C usu. pl.;U] an anxious, untrusting, and perhaps dangerous condition in the relationship between people, countries, etc.: the racial tensions of a big American city | The signing of this agreement will help to reduce/defuse international tension. | The border dispute has been a continuing source of tension. **3** [U] the degree of tightness or stiffness of a wire, rope, the body, etc.: When he tightened the guitar string, it snapped under the tension. | muscle tension **4** [U] the amount of a force stretching something: This wire will take 50 pounds tension before breaking. **5** [U] tech electric power: "Danger. High tension wires. Keep clear!" (notice)

1066 /ˌten sɪksti ˈsɪks/ the year 1066, the year of the Battle of Hastings and the Norman Conquest of Britain. For some reason it is one of the few dates in British history which most British people know.

1066 And All That /ˌten sɪksti ˈsɪks ənd ɔːl ˌðæt/ a humorous book about British history written by Sellars and Yeatman

tent /tent/ n **1** a movable shelter made esp. of cloth or plastic material supported by a structure of poles and ropes, used esp. by campers: a row of tents | a tent peg –see picture at PEG **2** a similar covered frame used for giving support or protection, esp. in the treatment of illness: Put a tent over his legs to stop them being rubbed by the sheets. –see also OXYGEN TENT

ten·ta·cle /ˈtentɪkəl/ n a long snakelike boneless jointless limb on certain creatures, used for moving, feeling, seizing, touching, etc. –see picture at OCTOPUS

ten·ta·tive /ˈtentətɪv/ adj **1** not certain or fully developed; not firm or complete: We've made tentative plans for a holiday but haven't decided anything certain yet. | a tentative arrangement/agreement **2** done without confidence; HESITANT: a tentative smile – ~ly adv – ~ness n [U] : the tentativeness of his reply

ten·ter·hooks /ˈtentəhʊks‖-əʳ-/ n **on tenterhooks** in a worried, anxious, or nervous state of mind; in a state of anxious expectation

tenth /tenθ/ determiner, n, pron, adv 10th –see TABLE 1

ten·u·ous /ˈtenjuəs/ adj **1** (of something non-physical) having little meaning or strength; slight; INSIGNIFICANT: The connection between the film and the book it's supposed to be based on is fairly tenuous. | tenuous evidence **2** fml or lit very thin: The spider hung from a tenuous silky thread. – ~ly adv – ~ness n [U]

ten·ure /ˈtenjəʳ, -jʊəʳ/ n [U] fml **1** the act, right, or period of holding land or a job: He remained popular throughout his tenure of the office of president. | One of the conditions of tenure is that you must keep the land under cultivation. **2** esp. AmE the right to stay in a job, esp. as a university teacher, without needing to have a new contract of employment, usu. given after a fixed number of years: Has she got tenure? | a tenure-tracked position (=one which will lead to tenure) at Harvard

Ten·zing /ˈtensɪŋ/, **Sherpa** (1914–86) a Nepalese mountain climber and guide whose correct name was **Tenzing Norgay**. He and Sir Edmund Hillary were the first men to reach the top of Mt. Everest.

te·pee, teepee, tipi /ˈtiːpiː/ n a round tent of the type used by some Native Americans, esp. those living on the PLAINS –see colour picture on page 358

tep·id /ˈtepɪd/ adj (esp. of liquid) only slightly warm; LUKEWARM: tepid water | (fig.) The critics' reaction to the new film was rather tepid. (=showed only slight approval) – ~ly adv – ~ness or – ~ity /teˈpɪdɪti/ fml– n [U]

te·qui·la /tɪˈkiːlə/ n [U] a strong alcoholic drink made in Mexico

tequila sun·rise /ˌ·ˌ ˈ··/ n a COCKTAIL (1) made from tequila, orange juice, and GRENADINE

ter·cen·te·na·ry /ˌtɜːsenˈtiːnəri‖ˌtɜːrsenˈtenəri, tɜːrˈsentəneri/ also **ter·cen·ten·ni·al** /ˌtɜːsenˈteniəl‖ˌtɜːr-/— n the day or year exactly 300 years after a particular event

Teresa, Mother see MOTHER TERESA

Ter·kel /ˈtɜːkəl‖ˈtɜːr-/, **Studs** /stʌdz/ (1912–) an American writer and radio personality whose books, including *Working* and *The Good War*, are based on experiences and memories of ordinary American people

term[1] /tɜːm‖tɜːrm/ n **1** a fixed or limited period of time: *The President is elected for a four-year term (of office).* | *her second term as Prime Minister* | *a term of imprisonment* | *When does his term expire?* **2 a** *BrE* any of three periods of time into which the teaching year is divided at schools, universities, etc. **b** ‖ also **semester** *AmE*– any of two periods of time into which this teaching year is divided in the US: *the summer term* | *Are there any exams at the end of term/any end-of-term exams?* –compare SEMESTER; see also HALF TERM, MIDTERM **3** a period of time during which a court, parliament, etc., meets **4** [*usu. sing.*] *tech* the end of a period of time during which something lasts: *Since our contract is getting near its term we must negotiate a new one.* | *The doctor said my wife was too near her term* (=the day on which she is to give birth to a child) *to travel by air.* **5** [*often pl.*] a word or expression that has a particular meaning or is used in a particular activity, job, profession, etc.: *a medical term* | *a term used in the building trade* | *The word "moron" is a term of abuse.* (=a word used when speaking nastily or unkindly to someone) | *She spoke in glowing terms* (=very approvingly) *about your work.* | *I told him in no uncertain terms* (=in plain and direct language) *to mind his own business.* **6** each of the various parts in an expression in MATHEMATICS **7 in the long/medium/short term** over a long/middle-sized/short period of time: *In the short term we expect to lose money on this book, but in the long term we hope to make large profits.* | *the government's medium-term financial strategy* –see also TERMS, LONG-TERM, SHORT-TERM

term[2] v [T+obj (+as)+n/adj] to name, call, or describe; DESIGNATE: *The chairman of this parliament is termed "the Speaker".* | *a pay offer which the union termed as absurd*

ter·ma·gant /ˈtɜːməgənt‖ˈtɜːr-/ n, adj [A] *esp. lit* (a woman who is) noisy and quarrelsome

ter·mi·nal[1] /ˈtɜːmɪnl̩‖ˈtɜːr-/ adj **1** of or being an illness that will cause death: *terminal cancer* | *the terminal wards of a hospital* **2** *esp. tech* of or at the end or limit of something – **~ly** adv : *terminally ill*

terminal[2] n **1 a** a place or set of buildings for the use of passengers joining or leaving a bus, ship, etc., at the beginning or end of its journey: *the Ocean Terminal at Southampton* **b** an AIR TERMINAL –compare TERMINUS **2** a point at which connections can be made to an electric system (CIRCUIT) **3** an apparatus, usu. consisting of a KEYBOARD and a SCREEN, by which a user can give instructions to and get information from a computer, esp. a large computer to which many users are connected

ter·mi·nate /ˈtɜːmɪneɪt‖ˈtɜːr-/ v [I+adv/prep;T] *fml* to come or bring to an end: *The next train terminates here.* (=it goes no further) | *Your contract has been terminated.* | *to terminate a pregnancy*

ter·mi·na·tion /ˌtɜːmɪˈneɪʃən‖ˌtɜːr-/ n **1** [C;U (of)] (an) act of terminating **2** [C] *BrE euph or tech for* ABORTION **3** [C] *tech* the last part or letter of a word

Ter·min·a·tor /ˈtɜːmɪneɪtər‖ˈtɜːr-/, **The** a film with Arnold Schwarzenegger set in Los Angeles in the near future in which a lot of people are killed. This film was followed by *Terminator II.* –see colour picture on page 685

ter·mi·nol·o·gy /ˌtɜːmɪˈnɒlədʒi‖ˌtɜːrmɪˈnɑː-/ n [C;U] (a system of) specialized words and expressions used in a particular science, profession, activity, etc.: *medical terminology* —**ogical** /ˌtɜːmɪnəˈlɒdʒɪkəl◂‖ˌtɜːrmɪnəˈlɑː-/ adj —**ogically** /kli/ adv

ter·mi·nus /ˈtɜːmɪnəs‖ˈtɜːr-/ n **-ni** /naɪ/ or **-nuses** a stop or station at the end of a railway or bus line –compare TERMINAL[2] (1)

ter·mite /ˈtɜːmaɪt‖ˈtɜːr-/ also **white ant**– n an antlike insect that lives in very large groups in tropical areas, eats and destroys wood, and builds large hills of hard earth –see picture at INSECT

term·ly /ˈtɜːmli‖ˈtɜːr-/ adj esp. *BrE* happening each TERM[1] (2): *termly exams*

terms /tɜːmz‖tɜːrmz/ n [P] **1** the conditions of an agreement, contract, etc.: *a contract specifying the terms of employment* | *According to/Under the terms of the agreement, British ships will be allowed to take a limited quantity of fish each year.* | *If I agree to do it, it will be on my own terms.* (=I will name the conditions) **2** [(at, on)] the stated conditions concerning payment, prices, etc.: *We sell furniture at very reasonable terms.* | *to negotiate a loan on favourable terms* | *He bought the car on easy terms.* (=paying for it gradually, not all at once) **3** [(on)] a relationship of the stated quality: *I'm not on very good terms with her* (=we are not friendly) *at the moment.* | *After their argument they weren't on speaking terms.* (=refused to speak to each other) | *We met on equal terms.* (=as equals) **4 come to terms with** to accept (something one does not want to accept): *It's hard to come to terms with going blind.* **5 in terms of ... /in ... terms** with regard to; from the point of view of: *The book has been well reviewed, but in terms of actual sales/in sales terms it hasn't been very successful.* | *In business terms the project is not really viable, but it would add to the prestige of the company.* | *We're thinking in terms of* (=considering) *moving to the South, as there are so few jobs in the North.* | *The recent increase in inflation means that our income has been reduced in real terms.* (=after taking account of price rises) | *It sounds like a good suggestion, but I wonder what it will mean in practical terms.* (=in actual fact)

terms of ref·er·ence /ˌ·· ˈ···/ n [P] the subject(s) to which an inquiry, report, etc., has been limited: *This problem is outside the committee's terms of reference.*

tern /tɜːn‖tɜːrn/ n a long-winged black and white fork-tailed seabird

terp·si·cho·re·an /ˌtɜːpsɪkəˈriːən◂‖ˌtɜːr-/ adj *lit or pomp* of dancing

ter·race /ˈterəs/ n **1** *esp. BrE* a row of houses joined to each other –compare TOWN HOUSE **2** *AmE* a BALCONY or PORCH **3** [*usu. pl.*] *esp. BrE* any of a number of wide steps on which watchers stand at a football match **4 a** *BrE*‖*usu.* **patio** *AmE* a flat area next to a house usu. with a stone floor, used as an outdoor living area **b** a flat roof used as an outdoor living area –see also PATIO **5** a flat level area cut from a slope, usu. one of a number rising one behind and above the other, used esp. for growing crops

terraced house /ˌ··· ˈ·/ *BrE* ‖ **row house** *AmE*– n a house which is part of a TERRACE (1) –see picture at HOUSE and see colour picture on page 162

ter·ra·cot·ta /ˌterəˈkɒtə◂‖-ˈkɑː-/ n [U] hard reddish brown baked clay: *a terracotta vase*

ter·ra fir·ma /ˌterə ˈfɜːmə‖-ˈfɜːr-/ n [U] *pomp or humor* dry land: *After such a rough voyage we were glad to reach terra firma again.*

ter·rain /teˈreɪn, tɪ-/ n [C;U] an area of land, esp. when considered with regard to whether it is rough, smooth, easy or difficult to cross, etc.: *rocky terrain*

ter·ra·pin /ˈterəpɪn/ n **terrapin** or **terrapins** a small TURTLE that lives in rivers and lakes in warm areas, sometimes kept as a pet

Ter·rence Hig·gins Trust /ˌterəns ˈhɪgɪnz ˌtrʌst/ [the] a British CHARITY organization which was started in 1983 and gives help and advice to people suffering from or worried about AIDS and HIV INFECTION

ter·res·tri·al /tɪˈrestriəl/ adj **1** of the Earth (rather than the moon, space, etc.) –see also EXTRATERRESTRIAL **2** of, living on, or being land (rather than water): *terrestrial animals* – **~ly** adv

ter·ri·ble /ˈterɪbəl/ adj **1** extremely severe; causing suffering, destruction, etc.: *a terrible war/accident/winter* **2** causing great dislike, shock, or fear: *Suddenly there was a terrible noise, and the train came off the rails.* | *It was a terrible sight.* **3** *infml* extremely bad; AWFUL: *We had a terrible time on holiday.* | *What a terrible meal!*

terrible twos /ˌ··· ˈ·/ [the +P] the condition of being a small child, around two years old, whose behaviour is often rather difficult: *"How old is little Johnny now?" "He's just approaching the terrible twos!"*

ter·ri·bly /ˈterᵻbli/ *adv* **1** *infml* very; extremely: *I've been terribly worried about you all day.* | *We were terribly lucky to find you here.* | *I'm terribly sorry to have kept you waiting.* **2** very badly, severely, etc.: *He played that piece of music terribly.*

ter·ri·er /ˈteriəʳ/ *n* a small active dog of a type originally used for hunting

ter·rif·ic /təˈrɪfɪk/ *adj infml* **1** very good and esp. enjoyable; excellent: *We had a terrific time at the disco.* | *What a terrific party!* **2** very great in size or degree: *She drove at a terrific speed*

ter·rif·i·cally /təˈrɪfɪkli/ *adv infml* very; extremely: *It's terrifically cold again today.*

ter·ri·fied /ˈterᵻfaɪd/ *adj* [(of, at)] very much afraid; badly frightened: *a terrified child* | *I'm terrified of snakes.* | *He was terrified at the thought of parachuting.* [F+(*that*)] *We were terrified (that) the bridge would collapse.* —see FRIGHTENED (USAGE)

ter·ri·fy /ˈterᵻfaɪ/ *v* [T] to fill with terror or fear: *Heights terrify me!* | *a terrifying ordeal*

ter·ri·to·ri·al¹ /ˌterᵻˈtɔːriəl◄/ *adj fml* **1** [*no comp.*] of or being land or territory: *Most of Britain's former territorial possessions are now independent.* | *The two countries had a territorial dispute over which one owned the island.* **2** (of animals, birds, etc.) showing a tendency to guard one's own TERRITORY (2)

territorial² *n* (*often cap.*) a member of the British Territorial Army

Territorial Ar·my /ˌ···· ˈ··/ also **TA, Territorials**— [*the*] a military force of people who are trained in their free time to be able to defend Britain —compare HOME GUARD, NATIONAL GUARD

territorial wa·ters /ˌ···· ˈ··/ *n* [P] the sea near a country's coast, over which that country has legal control and in which foreigners are not allowed to catch fish

ter·ri·to·ry /ˈterᵻtəri‖-tɔːri/ *n* [C;U] **1 A** (an area of) land, esp. considered with regard to the government that owns or controls it: *The explorers claimed the land as British territory.* | *The guerillas were operating inside South African territory.* | *We travelled through unknown territory.* | (fig.) *The company is moving into unfamiliar/virgin territory with this new range of computer software.* | (fig.) *You're (treading) on rather dangerous territory if you mention that incident; it upsets him.* **b** US **territories**, such as the Virgin Islands and Guam; most US states were once US territories **2** (an) area regarded by a person or esp. an animal as belonging to it alone and defended against others entering it: *The blackbird sang to warn other birds off its territory.* **3** (an) area for which one person or branch of an organization is responsible: *As the company's northern sales manager I'm responsible for quite a large territory.* **4** *infml* an area of interest or knowledge: *I'm afraid I can't tell you the answer to that — esoteric religions are a bit outside my territory.*

ter·ror /ˈterəʳ/ *n* **1** [S (of);U] extreme fear: *The people ran from the enemy in terror.* | *a look of sheer terror on his face* | *I have a terror of insects.* **2** [(*the*) S (of)] someone or something that causes extreme fear: *The criminal was the terror of the neighbourhood.* **3** [U] violent action for political purposes; terrorism: *The resistance movement started a campaign of terror/a terror campaign against the colonial rulers.* **4** [C] *infml* an annoying person, esp. a child: *Your son's a real terror! Can't you control him?* —see also REIGN OF TERROR

ter·ror·is·m /ˈterərɪzəm/ *n* [U] the use of violence or the threat of violence to obtain political demands: *The government is determined to combat* (=oppose) *international terrorism.*

ter·ror·ist /ˈterərᵻst/ *n* someone who uses violence to obtain political demands: *Terrorists have claimed responsibility for the bomb blast which killed 20 people.* | *terrorist attacks* —compare GUERRILLA, PARTISAN²; see also CONSUMER TERRORIST

ter·ror·ize also **-ise** *BrE* /ˈterəraɪz/ *v* [T] **1** to fill with terror or force into obedience by threats or acts of violence: *Bandits have been terrorizing the border regions.* (=the people who live there) | *the terrorizing of innocent people* **2** [(*into*)] to force by the use of threats of violence: *The postmaster was terrorized into handing over the money.*

terror-strick·en /ˈ··· ˌ··/ also **terror-struck** /ˈ··· ·/— *adj* filled with great terror

ter·ry·cloth /ˈterɪklɒθ‖-klɔːθ/ also **ter·ry** /ˈteri/— *n* [U] a thick usu. cotton material with uncut threads on both sides, used esp. for making TOWELs, bath mats, nappies (NAPPY), etc.

terse /tɜːs‖tɜːrs/ *adj* (of a speaker or style of speaking) using as few words as possible, sometimes in a way that seems rude; CONCISE: *His terse reply ended the conversation.* – **~ly** *adv* – **~ness** *n* [U]

ter·tia·ry /ˈtɜːʃəri‖ˈtɜːrʃieri, -ʃəri/ *adj fml or tech* third in place, degree, order, or rank

tertiary ed·u·ca·tion /ˌ···· ··ˈ··/ *n* [U] HIGHER EDUCATION

Te·ry·lene /ˈterᵻliːn/ *n* [U] *tdmk, BrE* an inexpensive man-made cloth similar to nylon

Tes·co /ˈteskəʊ/ also **Tesco's**— [+ *sing./pl. v*] one of a group of SUPERMARKETs, selling mainly food but also many other products for the house, found in most large British towns and cities: *Tesco's has a lot of special offers at the moment.*

TESL /ˈtesl/ *n* [U] Teaching English as a Second Language; English as it is taught to people living in an English-speaking country and whose first language is not English —compare EFL, ELT, ESL, ESOL, TEFL

TESOL /ˈtesɒl‖-sɑːl/ *n* [U] *esp. AmE* teaching English to speakers of other languages; the principles and practice of teaching English to speakers of other languages – compare EFL, ELT, ESL, ESOL, TEFL

TESSA /ˈtesə/ *n* (in Britain) a Tax-Exempt Special Savings Account; an account with a bank or BUILDING SOCIETY which earns interest on which no tax is payable if the capital is left untouched for at least five years

tes·sel·la·ted /ˈtesᵻleɪtᵻd/ *adj tech* made of small flat pieces of variously coloured stones that form a pattern: *a tessellated pavement*

Tess of the D'Ur·ber·villes /ˌtes əv ðə ˈdɜːbəvɪlz‖-ˈdɜːrbər-/ a book by Thomas Hardy, written in 1891. Like Hardy's other books it is set in the ancient kingdom of Wessex (now SW England) and describes country life as well as the sad story of a young woman, Tess.

test¹ /test/ *n* **1** a number of questions, exercises, jobs, etc., for measuring someone's skill, cleverness, or knowledge of a particular subject; short examination: *a history test* | *an intelligence/aptitude test* | *You can't drive a car unaccompanied by an experienced driver until you've passed your driving test.* **2** a short medical examination: *an eye test* | *a blood test* **3** an occasion of using something, such as a machine or weapon, to see if it works properly: *nuclear weapons tests* | *This new aircraft is undergoing safety tests.* | *Tests have shown that these new tyres are significantly safer.* **4** any situation or condition in which the qualities of something are clearly shown: *The difficulties she faced were a real test of character.* | *This round-the-world voyage will really put his sailing experience to* **the test.** | *This old song has* **stood the test of time.** (=is still popular, or still seems good, even after a long time has passed) **5** something used as a standard when judging or examining something else: *Employers will use this agreement as a test in dealing with future wage claims.* —see also TEST CASE **6** (usu. *cap.*) a TEST MATCH: *Botham will not be playing tomorrow, the last day of the Third Test.* —see also ACID TEST, BREATH TEST

test² *v* **1** [T] to study or examine by means of a test: *to have one's eyes tested* | *The teacher is testing the students on their French.* | *a new agreement that bans the testing of nuclear weapons* | (fig.) *I think he made these proposals mainly to test public opinion.* **2** [T] to provide difficult conditions for; TAX² (2): *These wet roads really test a car's tyres.* | *These are* **testing times** (=a difficult period) *for our country.* | *Listening to his continuous stream of empty chatter really tested my patience.* **3** [I;T (for)] to search by means of tests: *The company is testing (the ground) for oil.* **4 test the water** check people's reaction to something before carrying out a plan: *We should test the water before we introduce a smoking ban in the staffroom.* – **~er** *n*

Test Act /ˈ· ·/ [*the*] an ACT² (2) passed in 1673 in Britain to stop Catholics taking public office or becoming members of Parliament. The act was repealed (REPEAL) in 1828.

tes·ta·ment /ˈtestəmənt/ *n fml* **1** a person's WILL² (5): *Her solicitor drew up her* **last will and testament.** **2** [(to)] something that shows or proves something else very clearly: *This aircraft's safety record is an impressive testament to its designers' skill.* —see also NEW TESTAMENT, OLD TESTAMENT

tes·ta·men·ta·ry /ˌtestəˈmentəri◂/ *adj law* of or done according to a WILL² (5)

Test and Coun·ty Crick·et Board /ˌ· · ˌ·· ˈ·· ˌ·/ [*the*] the governing body of the sport of professional cricket in Britain

tes·tate /ˈtesteɪt, -tɪt/ *adj law* (of a person) having made a legal WILL² (5) before dying —opposite **intestate**

tes·ta·tor /teˈsteɪtəʳ‖ˈtesteɪ-, teˈsteɪ-/ **tes·ta·trix** /tesˈteɪtrɪks/ *fem.— n law* the maker of a WILL² (5)

test ban /ˈ· ·/ *n* an agreement between states to stop testing atomic weapons: *a test-ban treaty*

test card /ˈ· ·/ *n* ‖ **test pattern** *AmE* a pattern or picture broadcast on televisionso that the picture produced on a television set can be tested and changed

test card

test case /ˈ· ·/ *n* a case in a court of law which establishes a particular principle and is then used as a standard against which other such cases can be judged

test drive /ˈ· ·/ *n* an occasion of driving something, usu. a car, to see if it works properly: *To arrange a test drive, contact your local Volvo dealer.* —**test-drive** *v* [T]

tes·ti·cle /ˈtestɪkəl/ *n* either of the two round SPERM-producing organs in the male, enclosed in a bag of skin (the SCROTUM) behind and below the PENIS

tes·ti·fy /ˈtestɪfaɪ/ *v* [I (**against, for, to**);T+*that*;*obj*] **1** to make a solemn statement of what is true, esp. in a court of law: *A married woman is not allowed to testify against her husband in court.* | *He agreed to testify on behalf of/for the accused.* | *The witness testified (under oath) that he'd seen the defendant run out of the bank after it had been robbed.* **2** *fml* to be proof; allow to be clearly seen: *Her nervous behaviour testified to her guilt/that she was guilty.* **3** *AmE* (esp. in an EVANGELICAL or FUNDAMENTALIST church service) to stand up and tell other people about how God has helped you in your life: *Who would like to testify?*

tes·ti·mo·ni·al /ˌtestɪˈməʊniəl/ *n* **1** a formal written statement concerning a person's character, ability, willingness to work, etc. —see REFERENCE (USAGE) **2** something given or done to show thanks, praise, or admiration to someone, e.g. for loyal service

tes·ti·mo·ny /ˈtestɪməni‖-məʊni/ *n* [C;U] **1** a formal statement that something is true, as made by a witness in a court of law: *His testimony is crucial to the prosecution's case.* | *She was accused of false testimony.* **2** [(**of, to**)] any fact or situation that shows or proves something very clearly: *These fine new towns are (a) testimony of/to the government's farsighted policies.*

tes·tis /ˈtestɪs/ *n* **-tes** /tiːz/ *tech for* TESTICLE

test match /ˈ· ·/ *also* **test—** *n* a cricket or RUGBY match played between teams of different countries —see also CRICKET

tes·tos·ter·one /teˈstɒstərəʊn‖-ˈtɑː-/ *n* [U] the bodily substance (HORMONE) that causes male animals to have male parts or qualities

test pi·lot /ˈ· ˌ··/ *n* a pilot who flies new aircraft in order to test them

test tube /ˈ· ·/ *n* a small tube of thin glass, closed at one end, used in scientific tests —see picture at LABORATORY and at TUBE

test-tube ba·by /ˈ· · ˌ··/ *n* **1** a baby born as the result of ARTIFICIAL INSEMINATION **2** a baby started outside the body and then planted inside a female to develop naturally

tes·ty /ˈtesti/ *adj* impatient and bad-tempered; IRRITABLE: *a testy old man* | *testy remarks* —**tily** *adv* —**tiness** *n* [U]

tet·a·nus /ˈtetənəs/ *also* **lockjaw** *infml— n* [U] a serious disease caused by bacteria that enter the body through cuts and wounds and stiffen the muscles, esp. of the jaw. If a person is badly cut, he or she can get a course of INJECTIONS to prevent tetanus.

tetch·y /ˈtetʃi/ *adj* sensitive in a bad-tempered way; easily offended: *She's so tetchy; she flares up at the least little criticism.* —**ily** *adv* —**iness** *n* [U]

tête-à-tête¹ /ˌteɪt ɑː ˈteɪt, ˌteɪt ə ˈteɪt/ *n* a private conversation between two people. The word is sometimes used instead of, e.g., CHAT by people who want to show their wide command of language: *a cosy tête-à-tête*

tête-à-tête² *adv fml or pomp* (of two people) together in private (used in the same way as the noun): *We dined tête-à-tête.*

teth·er¹ /ˈteðəʳ/ *n* **1** a rope or chain to which an animal is tied so that it is free to move within a limited area **2 the end of one's tether** the condition of having used up all one's patience, strength, etc., and of being able to bear nothing more: *After a difficult day at work, she just about reached the end of her tether when her car broke down on the way home.*

tether² *v* [T] to fasten (an animal) with a tether

Tet·ley /ˈtetli/ *tdmk* a company which produces a make of tea sold in Britain and the US

Teu·ton·ic /tjuːˈtɒnɪk‖tuːˈtɑː-/ *adj* **1** of or being the ancient German peoples of northwestern Europe **2** *humor* (of qualities) of a kind that is sometimes thought to be typical of German people: *Teutonic thoroughness/lack of humour/efficiency*

Tex·a·co /ˈteksəkəʊ/ *tdmk* a large OIL and PETROL company: *Texaco are likely to announce price rises tomorrow.* | *a Texaco garage*

Tex·as¹ /ˈteksəs/ *written abbrev.* **TX—** a large state in the American South which is an important centre of the oil and gas industries, and also of cattle and crop farming. Its cities include Houston, Dallas, Fort Worth, San Antonio, Austin, and El Paso. Texas is associated with COW-BOYS, or, more recently, with oil. It is sometimes thought of as the place where everything is bigger than anywhere else. —see colour map on pages 1374-5

Texas², *also* **Texas Home·care** /ˌteksəs ˈhəʊmkeəʳ/— (in Britain) (any branch of) a chain of large shops selling things with which to decorate, improve or repair one's house, garden furniture, plants, etc.

Texas Long·horn /ˌ·· ˈ··/ LONGHORN

Texas Rang·ers /ˌ·· ˈ··/ [*the*] a special group of policemen in the American state of Texas, known esp. for fighting criminals in the 1800s and for defending Texas

text /tekst/ *n* **1** [U] the main body of writing, esp. in a book, as opposed to notes, pictures, etc.: *Children won't like this book because there is too much text and too few pictures.* | *This disk can store the equivalent of 500 pages of text.* **2** [*the*+S (**of**)] the exact original words of a speech, article, etc.: *Our newspaper is printing the full text of the President's speech.* **3** [C (**of**)] any of the various forms in which a book, article, etc., exists; copy: *the original text of "War and Peace"* **4** [C] a sentence from the Bible that is read and talked about by a priest in church: *The text for my sermon today comes from Matthew 1:4.* **5** [C] a textbook: *"Hamlet" is a* **set text** (=one of the books that must be studied) *for this year's English exam.*

text·book¹ /ˈtekstbʊk/ *n* a book containing information for the study of a particular subject, esp. one that is used by students because it is generally regarded as providing information that can be trusted —see also COURSE BOOK

textbook² *adj* [A] **1** as good as everyone thinks it ought to be; IDEAL: *She'd tried her best to be a textbook mum.* | *That shot of Becker's was superb — textbook stuff.* **2** typical: *This is an absolutely textbook example of what I've been talking about.*

tex·tile /ˈtekstaɪl/ *n* a material made by weaving: *Their main exports are textiles, especially silk and cotton.* | *a textile factory*

tex·tu·al /ˈtekstʃuəl/ *adj* of the text: *There are significant textual differences between the two editions of this book.* | *textual criticism*

tex·ture /ˈtekstʃəʳ/ *n* [C;U] **1** the degree of roughness or smoothness, coarseness (COARSE) or fineness, of a surface, substance, or material, esp. as felt by touch: *the delicate texture of her skin* | *the smooth texture of silk* | *a soil with a loose sandy texture* | (fig.) *the rich texture of Shakespeare's English* **2** **-textured** /ˈtekstʃəd‖-əʳd/having a texture of the stated kind: *coarse-textured cloth* —**tural** *adj* —**turally** *adv*

textured vege·ta·ble pro·tein /ˌ··· ,··· '··/ also **TVP**– n [U] a substance made from beans that is used in place of meat

TGIF /ˌtiː dʒiː aɪ 'ef/ interj abbrev. for Thank God it's Friday; a phrase used by people at the end of a working week when they are looking forward to two days of rest at the weekend

TGWU /ˌtiː dʒiː dʌbəlju: 'juː/ [the] the Transport and General Workers' Union; one of the main TRADE UNIONS in Britain

Thack·e·ray /'θækəreɪ/, **Wil·liam Make·peace** /'wɪljəm 'meɪkpiːs/ (1811–63) an English writer born in India whose books include Vanity Fair

Thai /taɪ/ n **1** the people from Thailand **2** the language of Thailand —**Thai** adj

Thai·land /'taɪlænd, -lənd/ a country in SE Asia on the Gulf of Thailand; capital Bangkok; population 55,448,000 (1989); its former name was **Siam**

tha·lid·o·mide /θə'lɪdəmaɪd/ n [U] (sometimes cap.) tdmk a drug formerly frequently used for making people calm or sleepy, until it was discovered in the early 1960s that it caused unborn babies to develop wrongly, esp. without arms or legs: a thalidomide victim

Thames /temz/ [the] **1** the main river flowing through London, and England's most important river: She lives south of the Thames | The Thames Valley —see also ISIS and see picture at ESTUARY and colour maps on pages 817 and 818 **2** set the **'Thames on fire** [usu. in negatives] BrE infml to do anything unusually successful: Jim's a nice boy, but he'll never set the Thames on fire.

Thames Flood Bar·ri·er /ˌ· '· ,···/ also **Thames Barrier**– [the] a structure built at Woolwich in London to control very high TIDES to protect the city from floods

Thames·link /'temzlɪŋk/ a British Rail train service that allows passengers to travel through London across the Thames without changing stations

Thames Tel·e·vi·sion /ˌ· '····, ˌ· ··'··/ one of the British television companies controlled by the ITC, transmitting programmes to London and SE England

Thames Wa·ter /ˌ· '··/ a water company in SE England that deals with the supply of water to people and businesses and the removal and treatment of SEWAGE

than¹ /ðən; strong ðæn/ conj **1** (used for introducing the second part of an unequal comparison): I know him better than you (do). (=you may know him well, but I know him better) | Jean runs faster than John. | Paul is taller than I am. | Profits are higher than they were last year. | Don't tell them any more than they need to know. | Nothing is more unpleasant than finding/than to find insects in your bath. | They work better together than if they're alone. **2** (used for introducing the less acceptable choice in statements of what one wants to do): I'd rather play football than go swimming. | She said she'd rather leave her job than be forced to work for such an unpleasant man. **3** fml except; OTHER than: You leave me with no option than to resign. **4** (used esp. after **hardly, scarcely,** and **no sooner**) when; as soon as: Scarcely had I started to speak than he began to argue with me.

than² prep **1** in comparison with: Paul is taller than me. | They arrived earlier than usual. | They favour gradual rather than radical change. | I was more annoyed than worried when they didn't come home. (=annoyed but not really very worried) **2** (used in comparing measures or amounts): She drove at more than 100 miles per hour. | There were fewer than 50 people at the meeting. | Offenders are liable to a fine of not more than £100.

thane /θeɪn/ n **1** also **thegn**– (in early English history) a man belonging to a class of a rank between nobles and ordinary men, who held land from the king in return for military service **2** (in early Scottish history) a low-ranking member of the noble class

thank /θæŋk/ v [T (for)] **1** to express one's gratefulness to (someone); give thanks to: The old lady thanked me for helping her across the road. | You've been so helpful – how can we ever thank you? –see also THANK YOU **2** to regard (someone) as responsible for something bad; blame: You can thank the government for this latest rise in oil prices. (=they are to blame) | He's only got himself to thank that she's left him – he treated her very badly. **3** **I'll thank you** (used when requesting something forcefully or rudely): I'll thank you to keep quiet while I'm speaking/to mind your own business. **4** **thank God/good**-

ness/heaven (an expression of great thankfulness): "Your son's alive." "Thank God!" **5** **thank one's lucky stars** infml to be grateful, esp. for a lucky escape: We can thank our lucky stars that the rope didn't break.

thank·ful /'θæŋkfəl/ adj **1** glad that something good has happened: [F+(that)|to-v] After the long boring lecture I was thankful that I was/thankful to be out in the fresh air again. **2** [(for)] grateful: I expected a bigger payment, but I suppose you have to be **thankful for small mercies.** (=grateful to receive anything, however small) – – **~ness** n [U]

thank·ful·ly /'θæŋkfəli/ adv **1** in a thankful way; with thankful feelings **2** I am thankful that: Those things are very popular in America, but thankfully they haven't come over here yet.

thank·less /'θæŋkləs/ adj **1** not likely to be rewarded with thanks or success: She has the **thankless task** of trying to rehabilitate these young criminals. **2** rare not feeling or showing thanks; ungrateful – – **~ly** adv – – **~ness** n [U]

thanks¹ /θæŋks/ n [P] **1** (words expressing) gratefulness: She did the work without expecting any thanks. | His good leadership has earned the thanks of a grateful nation **2** **thanks to** because of: The company has had a successful year, thanks mainly to the improvement in export sales. | It was thanks to your stupidity that we lost the game. | It was **no thanks to** you that we won. (=we won in spite of you) —see also VOTE OF THANKS

thanks² interj THANK YOU

thanks·giv·ing /ˌθæŋks'gɪvɪŋ◂/ n [C;U] (an) expression of gratefulness, esp. to God

Thanksgiving also **Thanks·giving Day** /ˈ··· ,·/– n [C;U] the fourth Thursday in November, which in the US is a public holiday

▶CULTURAL NOTE A day of feasting and prayer, it celebrates the thanksgiving to God in 1621 by the second group of English settlers in what became the US. After losing many men through hunger during their first winter in Plymouth, Massachusetts, the settlers were taught how to grow MAIZE and other crops by the NATIVE AMERICANS. When they gathered (HARVESTed) those crops that autumn they knew they had enough to live on through the second winter, and so they had a feast of thanksgiving with the Native Americans. Today, more Americans travel to see their families on this than on any other day of the year. The Thanksgiving dinner is traditionally TURKEY and STUFFING, SWEET POTATOES, many and various vegetables, and PUMPKIN PIE. ◀

Thanksgiving

thank·you /'θæŋkjuː/ n, adj [A] (an act of) expressing thanks: We owe Mrs Jones a special thankyou for all her help. | a thankyou card

thank you /'· ·/ also **thanks**– interj **1** [(for)] (used politely to mean) I am grateful to you: Thank you for the nice present you sent me. | Thank you very much for helping me with my homework. | "Here's what you asked for." "Thanks/Many thanks/Thanks a lot." **2** (used in certain phrases to show that a situation is very satisfactory and that change is not wanted): Under the present system these lawyers are **doing very nicely thank you,** and they won't welcome any changes. **3** **no, thank you** (used when refusing an offer politely): "Would you like a cup of tea?" "No, thank you; I've just had one."

▷ USAGE If you are offered something that you do not want, you reply "No, **thank you".** If you say only **"Thank you"** it means that you want it: "Have a drink!" "Thank you. Beer, please."◁

that¹ /ðæt/ determiner those /ðəuz/ **1** being the person, thing, idea, etc., which is understood or has just been mentioned: Who was that man I saw you talking to? | Those sweets you gave me were very nice. | The clock struck 12, and at that moment she came in through the door. | Later that same day (=the day that is presently being talked about), the President called a meeting of his advisers. **2** being the one of two or more people or things that is further away in time, place, thought, etc.: This room (we're in) is a lot warmer than that one (across the *passage).* | *Do you want to sit in this chair (here) or that one (over there)?*

that² /ðæt/ *pron* **those** **1** the person, thing, idea, etc., which is understood or has just been mentioned: *Who told you that?* | *Who gave you those?* | *Who was that I saw you with last night?* | *So that's why you don't like him.* | *Come at 6 o'clock – that seems early enough.* | *First we went to the butcher's, and after that* (=then) *we went to the greengrocer's.* | *If you carry on behaving like that* (=as you have been doing) *you'll go straight to bed without any supper.* | *She slammed the book down on the table, and with that* (=after doing that) *ran angrily out of the room.* **2** (used with **be**) the thing or person that is far or further away in place, time, thought, etc.: *That's your coat on the hook. This one's mine.* | *"Who's that?"* (=the person there) *"It's me."* **3** *fml* the one or kind: *The finest wines are those from France.* | *The cost of the air fare is higher than that of the rail fare.* **4** such a thing or things: *"He cheated me out of all my money and then left me." "Ah well,* **that's** *life, I suppose!"* (=such things happen and must be accepted) | *He makes big promises and never does anything about it.* **That's men for you!** (=that is typical of men) **5 and all that** also **and that** *BrE nonstandard*– and so on; and all such things: *I used to take drugs and all that when I was young.* **6 that is** in other words: *The fare is reduced for children, that is, anyone under 15 years old.* **7 that's a** (used when telling or persuading a child or animal to do something): *Don't cry, that's a good boy!* **8 that's that** (esp. expressing determination) that is the end of the matter; that settles the matter: *I'm not going to do it and that's that.*

that³ /ðət; *strong* ðæt/ *conj* **1** (used for introducing various kinds of CLAUSE) **a** (used after verbs, nouns, or adjectives marked [+(*that*)] in this dictionary): *She said (that) she would come early.* | *The rules state quite clearly that smoking is not allowed.* | *Is it true (that) you're getting married?* | *I'm afraid that I can't help you.* | *I'll give it to you on condition (that) you don't break it.* | *The fact that you don't like her has nothing to do with the matter.* **b** (used as if) in answering a question beginning with **what**: *"What was his reason for not coming to the meeting?" "The reason was that he forgot."* | *The problem is that we didn't bring enough money.* **c** (used esp. after **so** or **such** to express purpose or result): *He was so rude that|He spoke in such a rude manner that she refused to reply.* | *Bring it closer so (that) I can see it better.* | *(fml) Bring it closer so (that) I may see it better.* **d** (used for expressing reason): *We rejoice that you are safe.* **2** (used as a RELATIVE PRONOUN) **a** (as the subject of a CLAUSE) which/who: *Did you see the letter that came today?* | *He's the greatest man that's ever lived.* **b** (as the object of the verb in a CLAUSE) which/whom: *Did you get the books (that) I sent you?* | *There are lots of things (that) I need to do before I leave tonight.* **c** (as the object of a PREPOSITION in a CLAUSE) which/whom: *There's the man (that) I was telling you about.* | *They've found the gun that she was shot with.* **d** (introducing a CLAUSE) in, on, for, or at which: *The day that he came I was out.* | *The speed (that) she drives, I'm surprised she hasn't killed herself!* **e** according to; as far as: *He's never been here that I know of.* **3** *lit* (used for introducing an expression of desire): *Oh that I could fly!* (=I wish I could fly!) | *Would (that) he had never come!* (=I wish he had never come!)

▷ USAGE 1 In ordinary speech **that** can often be left out before a noun clause, especially after common verbs of saying or thinking: *She said (that) it wasn't time.* | *I think (that) it's fine.* | *He told me (that) he agreed.* | *I'm glad (that) you passed your exam.* | *I knew (that) he had arrived.* It is not usually left out in formal English or after more formal verbs of saying: *She stated* **that** *the report was incomplete.* 2 **That** can only be used instead of **who** or **which** when they limit the meaning of a noun more narrowly: *Which of my brothers did you meet? The one* **who/that** *lives in Glasgow, or the one* **who/that** *lives in Leeds?* It cannot be used to introduce additional information in sentences like: *This is my father,* **who** (NOT **that**) *lives in Leeds.* (=I am introducing my father and telling you where he lives)◁

that⁴ /ðæt/ *adv* [*usu. in questions and negatives*] *infml* so; to such a degree: *It wasn't that good, actually.* (=it was quite good but not very good) | *We haven't seen* **all that** *much of her recently.* | *(BrE dial) I was that hungry I could have eaten a horse!*

thatch¹ /θætʃ/ *v* [T] to cover (a roof) or the roof of (a building) with thatch: *Our house has a thatched roof.* – ~ **er** *n*

thatch² *n* **1** [U] roof covering of STRAW, REEDS, etc. **2** [C] *humor* a mass of thick or untidy hair on the head

thatched cot·tage /ˌ· '··/ *n* a house in the country with a thatched roof. Thatched cottages are considered to be very attractive and old-fashioned. –see colour picture on page 162

Thatch·er¹ /'θætʃəʳ/, **De·nis** /'denɪs/ (1915–) the husband of Margaret Thatcher. He was a director of a large oil company when they married in 1951. The image of Denis Thatcher that British people have is mostly from SATIRICAL television programmes and articles in the press, which say jokingly, with no proof at all, that he is a TIPPLER, and enjoys playing GOLF.

Thatch·er², **Mar·ga·ret Hil·da** /ˈmɑːɡərət ˈhɪldə ‖ ˈmɑːr-/, also **Mrs Thatcher, Maggie** *infml*– (1925–) the first woman PRIME MINISTER of Britain (1979–90) now officially called **Lady Thatcher**. She was born Margaret Roberts, the daughter of a GROCER in Grantham, in central England. She studied chemistry at Oxford University and, later the law. In 1951 she married Denis Thatcher. As leader of the Conservative Party from 1975 she strongly influenced its political

Margaret Thatcher

PHILOSOPHY, which during this period came to be known as **Thatcherism**. The Conservatives were returned to power three times under her leadership. During their government there was a move towards PRIVATIZATION; taxes were lowered and INFLATION fell, but unemployment rose. Mrs Thatcher became noted for her determination and was given the NICKNAME "the Iron Lady". She also made a famous speech in which she said "the Lady's not for turning", meaning that she would not change her policies (POLICY) because of criticism. Mrs Thatcher enjoyed increased popularity during the Falklands War, but in the late 1980s her position became more uncertain and then suddenly in November 1990 she lost an important vote within her party and became an ordinary BACKBENCH member of parliament –see also IRON LADY, MONETARISM, THATCHERISM, THATCHERITE – ~ **ist** *adj*

Thatch·er·is·m /'θætʃərɪzəm/ *n* [U] the political and economic policies (POLICY) connected with Margaret Thatcher, including MONETARISM, firm control of public spending, and the importance of FREE MARKET CAPITALISM and FREE ENTERPRISE

Thatch·er·ite /'θætʃəraɪt/ *n* someone in the British Conservative Party who followed Mrs Thatcher and agreed with all her views and policies (POLICY) –**Thatcherite** *adj*

That's Life /ˌ· '·/ a BBC television programme about ordinary people's problems and rights, famous for showing unusual and amusing things, e.g. dogs that sing and strangely shaped vegetables. It is introduced by Esther Rantzen who has also given publicity to serious health and social questions.

thaw¹ /θɔː/ *v* **1** [I;T (OUT)] to change from a solid frozen state to become liquid, soft, or bendable, as a result of an increase in temperature to above freezing point: *The snow is thawing.* | *Make sure the frozen chicken is properly thawed before you cook it.* | (fig.) *Come and thaw out in front of the fire.* (=get warm) –compare MELT **2** [*it*+I] (of the weather) to become warm enough for snow and ice to melt: *It often doesn't thaw until June in Siberia.* **3** [I] to become friendlier, less severe or formal, etc.: *After their third meeting she began to thaw.*

thaw² *n* **1** a period of warm weather during which snow and ice melt **2** an improvement in relations after a period of unfriendliness, esp. between countries

Thaw, John (1942–) an English actor known esp. for playing the parts of two policemen, *The Sweeney* and *Inspector Morse*, on British television

the¹ /ðə; *before vowels* ðɪ; *strong* ðiː/ *definite article, determiner* **1** (used for mentioning a particular thing, either because you already know which one is being talked about or because only one exists): *We have a cat and two* *dogs; the cat* (=our cat) *is black and the dogs* (=our dogs) *are white.* | *Please take these letters to the post office.* (=it is understood that you know which post office and where it is) (compare *You can pay your phone bill at a post office.* (=any post office)) | *The sun* (=there is only one sun) *is shining.* | *The sky is blue.* | *the Queen of Denmark* (=Denmark has only one queen) | *Another meeting will be held later in the year.* | *Who do you think will win the election?* | *It's the tallest building in the world.* | *I spoke to her on the telephone.* | *For our holidays we went to the South of France.* | *She sailed across the Atlantic in a small boat.* **2** one's: *She hit him on the* (=his) *ear.* | *How's the* (=your) *arm today?* | *The* (=my) *car broke down again today.* | (*infml*) *Have you met the* (=my) *wife?* **3** (used before an adjective to make it into a noun): *How can we help the old and the poor?* (=old people and poor people) | *The English* (=English people) *drink a lot of beer.* | *You're asking me to do the impossible.* (=something that is impossible) | *The accused was/were brought into the court.* **4** (used before a singular noun to make it general): *The lion is a wild animal.* (=lions are wild animals) | *The computer has revolutionized office work.* **5** (used before words for human activities, esp. musical, but usu. not including sports): *He's studying the law.* | *I'm learning the piano.* (=learning to play pianos) | *She plays the violin.* (compare *She plays tennis.*) **6** (used, often with strong pronunciation, for showing that the following noun is best, best-known, most approved, most important, most wanted, etc.): *This is the life for me.* (=this is what I enjoy doing most) | *You can't be the Paul McCartney!* **7** (used before names of measures): *This cloth is sold by the metre.* (=is measured in metres to calculate its price) | *We're paid by the hour.* | (*esp. BrE*) *These apples are 90p the dozen.* (=you get 12 for 90p) **8** (used before a noun that stands for the activity connected with it): *He took to the bottle.* (=began drinking a lot of alcohol) | *a campaign to bring back the electric chair* (=the system of punishing people by death in an electric chair) **9** (used before the plural of 20, 30, 40, etc., to show a period of ten years): *In the 30s* (=from 1930 to 1939) *there was a lot of unemployment.* **10** (used before a noun, esp. in negatives, to show an amount or degree needed for a purpose) enough: *I haven't the time to talk to you just now.* | *He didn't have the common sense to send for a doctor.* **11** (used when describing someone or something in expressions of strong feeling): *He's stolen my parking space, the bastard!* | *This screw won't go in properly, the stupid thing!* | *"He's won a holiday in Hawaii." "The lucky devil!"* **12** (used after **how**, **what**, **where**, **who**, and **why** in expressions of strong feeling): *What the hell are you doing here?*

▷ USAGE 1 **The** is not used with certain words, except when there is something else before or after the noun that tells us which one or what kind is meant. This is true of the following: **a** abstract nouns, such as *music, history, time, beauty, work.* Compare *Life is difficult* and **The** *life of a writer is difficult.* **b** names of substances and materials, such as *wine, silk, coal, gold, sugar: She gave us beer and cheese; I drank* **the** *beer but I didn't eat* **the** *cheese.* **c** names of times after *at, by, on: at sunset* | *by night* | *on Monday* (Compare *during* **the** *night* | *on* **the** *Monday after Christmas.*) **d** names of meals after *at, before, during, for,* and the verb *have: after/at/before/during breakfast* | *coffee for breakfast* | *When do you have breakfast?* (Compare **The** *breakfast she gave us was good.*) **2 The** is not used **a** with most names of diseases: *He's got smallpox.* **b** in many fixed expressions such as: *by car, at school, in bed, in prison, arm in arm, face to face, husband and wife, from beginning to end* **c** after [T+*obj*+*n*] verbs describing a change of state: *They made him President.* | *They crowned him king.* | *They appointed her captain.* **d** when someone is directly addressed: *Come quickly, doctor!* 3 Names and titles either include **the** as part of the name, or they do not. These must be learnt. But note **a** Some ordinary words can be used like names. Compare **the** *father of a family* and *I'll ask Father!* **b** Names can be used like ordinary words. Compare *London is a big city* and **the** *London of the 1890s* (=London during this period).◁

the² *adv* **1** (used in comparisons, to show that two things happen together): *The more he eats, the fatter he gets.* | *"When do you want this done?" "The sooner the better."* **2** (used in comparisons, to show that someone or something is more, less, etc., than before): *He's had a holiday, and looks (all) the better for it.* | *She tried to explain it to*

me, but I was **none the wiser.** (=I still did not understand) **3** (used for showing that someone or something is more than any other): *He likes you the best.* | *I had the greatest* (=extreme) *difficulty understanding her.*

thea·tre *BrE*‖**theater** *AmE* /ˈθɪətəʳ/ *n* **1** [C;*the*] (a special building or place for) the performance of plays. Going to the theatre is very expensive in London, less so in other areas, and is thought by some people to be an activity for clever people, except if one goes to see a musical. In the US it is also thought very expensive, esp. in New York, and Americans visiting Britain often go to the theatre because they find it cheaper than in the US: *London's theatres* | *an evening at the theatre* | *an open-air theatre* | *Do you enjoy the theatre?* **2** [(*the*) U] the work or activity of people who write or act in plays: *modern Russian theatre* | *She's been in the theatre all her life.* –compare DRAMA **3** [C] ‖ *usu.* **auditorium** *AmE*– a room with rows of seats one above the other, where people can watch or listen to the stated activity: *a lecture theatre* **4** [C] a scene of important military events: *the Pacific theatre of World War II* **5** [C] *BrE* ‖ **operating room**, **OR** *AmE*– an OPERATING THEATRE: *a theatre nurse* **6** [C] *esp. AustrE & AmE* a CINEMA

theatre

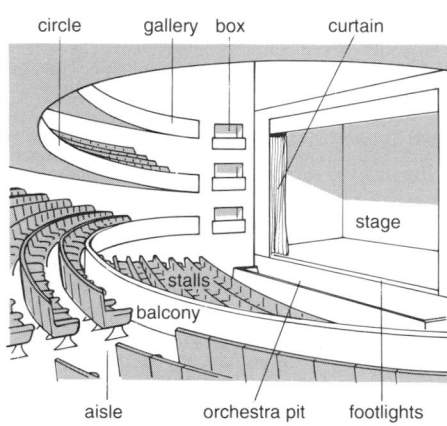

thea·tre·go·er /ˈθɪətəˌgəʊəʳ/‖-tər-/ *n* a person who regularly goes to the theatre

theatre in the round /ˌ·· ··· ˈ·/ *n* a theatre with the stage in the middle and the people sitting on (almost) all sides

the·at·ri·cal /θiˈætrɪkəl/ *adj* **1** of or for the theatre: *a theatrical company* **2** *usu. derog* (of a person or their behaviour) showy and unnatural; HISTRIONIC – ~ **ly** /kli/ *adv*

the·at·ri·cals /θiˈætrɪkəlz/ *n* [P] stage performances: *amateur theatricals*

Thebes /θiːbz/ an ancient city in S Egypt, where the TOMB (=grave) of Tutankhamen is to be found

thee /ðiː/ *pron old use* (object form of **thou**) you

theft /θeft/ *n* [C;U] (an example of) the crime of taking someone else's property from a place; stealing: *The building has been insured against fire and theft.*

thegn /θeɪn/ *n* a THANE (1)

their /ðəʳ; *strong* ðeəʳ/ *determiner* (*possessive form of* **they**) **1** of or belonging to them: *They washed their faces.* | *He was surprised by their interest.* | *They spend all their time together.* | *Has anyone here lost their watch?* **2** (with general meaning): *Everyone wants what is theirs by right.* –compare HIS¹ (2); see EVERYONE (USAGE)

theirs /ðeəz‖ðeərz/ *pron* (*possessive form of* **they**) **1** of those people, animals, or things already mentioned: *I do my work, and they do theirs.* (=their work) | *Our dog is a male, theirs is a female/theirs are females.* | *She's a friend of theirs.* **2** (with general meaning): *Everyone wants what is theirs by right.* –compare HIS² (2)

the·is·m /ˈθiːɪzəm/ *n* [U] the belief that a personal God exists and that he has made his existence known through the Bible, church, dreams, etc. –compare DEISM –**ist** *n* –**istic** /θiːˈɪstɪk/ *adj* –**istically** /kli/ *adv*

them¹ /ðəm; *strong* ðem/ *pron* (*object form of* **they**): *Where* *are my shoes? I can't find them.* | *He bought them drinks.* | *He bought drinks for them.* —see ME (USAGE)

them² /ðem/ *determiner nonstandard* those: *Did you see them shoes she was wearing?*

theme¹ /θiːm/ *n* **1** the subject of a talk, piece of writing, etc.: *His stories are linked by the theme of self-discovery.* | *The theme of this year's journalism conference is the question of censorship.* **2** a short simple tune on which a piece of music is based **3** *AmE* a short piece of writing, esp. done for school: *Your homework tonight is to write a two-page theme on the subject of pollution.*

theme² *v* [T] to make (things) appear to be similar or all on one theme: *a set of themed attractions, all based on aspects of the Wild West*

theme park /ˈ· ·/ *n* an outdoor area containing amusements, such as games of skill and big machines to ride on, which are sometimes all based on a single subject (e.g. space travel) —see also ALTON TOWERS, DISNEYLAND

theme song /ˈ· ·/ also **theme tune**— *n* a song or tune often repeated during a musical play, cinema picture, etc. — compare SIGNATURE TUNE

them·selves /ðəmˈselvz/ *pron* **1** (*reflexive form of* **they**): *They're enjoying themselves.* | *They bought themselves a new car.* | *They're pleased with themselves.* | *I hope nobody will hurt themselves* **2** (*strong form of* **they**): *They built the house themselves.* **3** *infml* (in) their usual state of mind or body: *They soon came to themselves.* (=regained consciousness) | *They don't seem to be feeling themselves this morning.* (=feeling as they usually do) **4** (all) by themselves alone; without help: *They did it all by themselves.* **5** in themselves without considering the rest: *things that are unimportant in themselves* **6** to themselves for their private use; not shared: *a whole house to themselves* —see YOURSELF (USAGE)

then¹ /ðen/ *adv* **1** at that time: *We lived in the country then.* | *I was still unmarried then.* | *He met the princess, or Lady Diana Spencer as she then was, in 1975.* | *Will we still be alive then?* | *I hope we'll have finished by/before then.* | *When you see her, then you'll understand.* | **From then on** (=starting at that time), *he worked harder.* **2** next; afterwards: *Let's go for a drink and then go home.* | *Dinner was followed by coffee and then came the speeches.* | *First Jane and then the others started clapping.* **3** in that case: *If you want to go home, then go.* | *What shall we do, then? Swim?* **4** as a result; therefore: *If x=5 and y=3, then xy=15.* | *Go out by the back door, then no one will see you.* **5** besides; also: *You must ask John to the party, and then there's Paul — don't forget him.* **6** (used when expressing a general opinion about something that has gone before or something one has just heard): *The result of all this activity, then, was that the government became very unpopular.* | *That must have been a surprise, then!* **7** but then (again) however: *I like watching television but then (again) I wouldn't miss it if I didn't have one.* — see also **now and then** (NOW¹), **there and then** (THERE¹)

then² *adj* [A] being so at the time: *The matter was reported to the then head of the secret service.*

thence /ðens/ *adv fml* **1** from that place; after leaving that place: *We made our way to the coast and thence by sea to France.* **2** *fml rare* therefore; for that reason: *Just because he has remained silent, may we thence deduce that he has some guilty secret?*

thence·forth /ðensˈfɔːθ‖ˈðensfɔːrθ/ also **thence·for·ward** /ðensˈfɔːwəd‖-ˈfɔːrwərd/— *adv fml* from that time

theo- see WORD FORMATION

the·od·o·lite /θiˈɒdəlaɪt‖θiˈɑː-/ *n* an instrument used by SURVEYORS for measuring angles

the·o·lo·gian /ˌθiːəˈləʊdʒən/ *n* a person who has studied theology

theological sem·i·na·ry /ˌ····· ····/ also **seminary**— *n esp. AmE* a college for the study of theology, esp. for the training of MINISTERS or priests

the·ol·o·gy /θiˈɒlədʒi‖θiˈɑː-/ *n* **1** [U] the study of religion and religious ideas and beliefs: *He read/studied theology at university.* **2** [C;U] a particular body of beliefs about religion: *According to Muslim theology there is only one God.* —**-ogical** /ˌθiːəˈlɒdʒɪkəl◂‖-ˈlɑː-/ *adj*: *Priests are trained at theological colleges.* —**-ogically** /kli/ *adv*

theo·rem /ˈθɪərəm/ *n tech* (esp. in MATHEMATICS) a statement that can be shown to be true by reasoning

theo·ret·i·cal /θɪəˈretɪkəl/ also **the·o·ret·ic** /θɪəˈretɪk/— *adj* **1** based on or concerning theory, not practical experience: *theoretical physics* **2** existing only in theory, not in practice; HYPOTHETICAL: *the theoretical ancestors of modern man* | *It's a theoretical possibility, but I don't suppose it will happen.*

theo·ret·i·cally /θɪəˈretɪkli/ *adv* **1** in a theoretical way; not practically: *First I'll explain how it works theoretically, then I'll give you a practical demonstration.* **2** according to theory but not really: *Theoretically he's in charge, but in fact his secretary takes all the decisions.*

theo·rist /ˈθɪərɪst/ also **the·o·re·ti·cian** /ˌθɪərəˈtɪʃən/— *n* a person who forms or studies the theory of a subject: *a leading political theorist*

theo·rize also **-rise** *BrE* /ˈθɪəraɪz/ *v* [I (**about, on**);T+*that;obj*] to form a theory or theories; SPECULATE: *It's easy to theorize about the reasons for the crisis, but we don't have the facts.*

theo·ry /ˈθɪəri/ *n* **1** [C] a reasonable or scientifically acceptable explanation for a fact or event, which has not been proved to be true: *According to Darwin's theories, human beings and monkeys are descended from the same ancient animal.* | *to disprove a theory* [+*that*] *The detective's theory is that the murderer was well known to the victim.* **2** [U] (the part of a science or art that deals with) general principles and knowledge as opposed to practical methods or skills; set of rules or principles for the study of a subject: *musical theory* | *We have two chemistry exams, one on theory and one practical.* | *political theory* | (fig.) **In theory** *the train should arrive at 9.15* (=this is the official time of arrival), *but* **in practice** *it is quite often late.* —compare PRACTICE **3** [U] (in MATHEMATICS) a body of principles, theorems, etc., belonging to one part of the subject: *Set theory deals with the behaviour of groups of mathematical elements.*

theory of e·vo·lu·tion /ˌ··· ···ˈ···/ [*the*] the theory that all beings developed from one original type of being, most famously supported by Charles Darwin, who also suggested that only the fittest (FIT²(2)) types live on, while the rest die

theory of rel·a·tiv·i·ty /ˌ··· · ···ˈ····/ [*the*] *tech* one of two theories expressed by Albert Einstein about the relationship between time, size, and mass

the·os·o·phy /θiˈɒsəfi‖-ˈɑː-/ *n* [U] **1** teaching about God and the world, esp. involving direct experience of, or understanding of God **2** (*often cap.*) the teachings of an American movement which follows Buddhist and Hindu ideas about EVOLUTION and REINCARNATION —**theosophist** *n* —**theosophical** /ˌθiːəˈsɒfɪkəl◂‖-ˈsɑː-/ *adj* —**theosophically** /-kli/ *adv*

ther·a·peu·tic /ˌθerəˈpjuːtɪk◂/ *adj* **1** of or for the treating or curing of disease: *therapeutic exercises/diets* **2** *infml* having a good effect on one's health or state of mind: *I find swimming/sewing very therapeutic.* —**~ally** /kli/ *adv*

ther·a·peu·tics /ˌθerəˈpjuːtɪks/ *n* [U] the branch of medicine concerned with the treatment and cure of disease

ther·a·pist /ˈθerəpɪst/ *n* **1** a specialist in a particular branch of therapy: *a speech therapist* **2** *AmE* a PSYCHOANALYST

ther·a·py /ˈθerəpi/ *n* [C;U] the treatment of illnesses of the mind or body, esp. without drugs or operations: *He's having therapy for his arthritis.* | *She's been* **in therapy** *for years* (she has been having PSYCHOANALYSIS for years). — see also GROUP THERAPY, OCCUPATIONAL THERAPY, PHYSIOTHERAPY, PSYCHOTHERAPY, RADIOTHERAPY, SPEECH THERAPY

Ther·a·va·da /ˌθerəˈvɑːdə/ *adj* of the form of Buddhism practised in Kampuchea, Laos, Myanmar, Sri Lanka, and Thailand. It is based on the teachings of the Buddha as recorded in the Pali Canon —compare MAHAYANA

there¹ /ðeər/ *adv* **1** to, at, or in that place: *I liked living there.* | *Go and stand over there.* (compare *Come and stand over here.*) | *It's cold out there.* | *I like Scotland; the people there are very friendly.* **2** at that point: *He brought his historical account up to the 18th century and stopped there.* | *There I disagree with you.* **3** (used for drawing attention to someone or something, usu. followed by the verb if the subject is not a pronoun): *There goes John.* | *There he goes.* | *Hello there!* **4** *infml* (usu. used after a noun) being present in that place: *Can you pass me that book there?* | (*nonstandard*) *When are you going to get that there hole mended?* **5 all there** *infml* [*usu. in negatives*]

healthy in the mind: *I don't think she's all there.* (=I think she's mad.) **6 because it is there** the answer given by a mountain climber called George Mallory when asked why he wanted to climb a certain mountain **7 get there** *infml* to succeed in reaching an aim, completing a job, etc.: *You'll get there in the end if you work hard!* **8 there and back** to a place and back again: *It's 50 miles there and back.* **9 there and then** also **then and there**— at that time and place, esp. without any delay: *She offered him the job and he accepted there and then.* **10 there's a** (used when telling or persuading a child or animal to do something): *Don't speak with your mouth full, there's a good boy!* **11 there you are: a** here is what you wanted: *There you are! A nice cup of tea.* **b** I told you so: *There you are. I knew I was right.* **12 there you go** *infml* **a** you are doing again what you usually do: *There you go, talking about people behind their backs again.* **b** (used for expressing sad acceptance of an unfortunate event): *He lost all his money; well, there you go.*

there² /ðeəʳ, ðəʳ/ *pron* (used for showing that something or someone exists or happens, usu. as the subject of **be**, **seem**, or **appear**): *There's a fly in my soup.* | *There's someone at the door to see you.* | *Is there anything you want to tell me?* | *There aren't any cakes left.* | *There appears to have been a nasty accident.* | *There don't seem to be any missing.* | *I don't want there to be any doubt about this.* | *Everything was silent, and then there came a strange knocking at the door.* | (*fml*) *At no stage has there been any consultation with the director about this.*

▷ USAGE 1 **There** tells us that someone or something that has not been mentioned before exists, happens, etc. It is more natural to say **There's** *a man at the door* than *A man is at the door.* 2 If the person or thing has already been mentioned or thought of, **there** cannot be used. Compare *"Is there anyone outside?" "Yes,* **there's** *someone waiting"* and *"Who's that man outside?" "It's Harry."* (=we already know that someone is outside). 3 Do not confuse **there** (usually /ðəʳ/) in these sentences with **there** (/ðeəʳ/) the adverb of place. Compare the pronunciation of **there** in **there's** (=I am mentioning for the first time) *a man waiting to see you* and *Look!* **There's** (=in that place) *that man I was telling you about!* In American English, both of these usages are usu. pronounced in the same way.◁

there³ /ðeəʳ/ *interj* (used for expressing victory, satisfaction, encouragement, sympathy, etc.): *There! Do you feel better now?* | **There, there.** *Stop crying.* | *There. I told you I was right!* | *It only lasted a week, but there! What can you expect for £5?*

there·a·bouts /ˌðeərəˈbaʊts/ also **there·a·bout** /-ˈbaʊt/ *AmE*— *adv* near that place, time, number, etc.: *I'll see you at 9 o'clock or thereabouts.*

there·af·ter /ðeəʳˈɑːftəʳ‖-ˈæf-/ *adv fml* after that in time or order; afterwards: *Thereafter we had no further communication with them.* —compare HEREAFTER¹

there·by /ðeəˈbaɪ, ˈðeəbaɪ‖-ər-/ *adv fml or law* by that means; by doing or saying that: *He became a British citizen, thereby gaining the right to vote.* —compare HEREBY

there·fore /ˈðeəfɔːʳ‖ˈðeər-/ *adv rather fml* **1** as a result; for that reason; so: *The item you requested is no longer available and therefore we are|and we are therefore returning your cheque.* | *These birds are very rare and therefore protected by law.* **2** (used in reasoning) as this proves; it follows that: *I think, therefore I exist.*

there·in /ðeəʳˈɪn/ *adv* **1** *fml or law* in that (place or piece of writing): *... and everything therein contained* —compare HEREIN **2** *fml* in that particular matter: *She would never agree to marry him and therein lay the cause of his unhappiness.*

there·in·af·ter /ˌðeərɪnˈɑːftəʳ‖-ˈæf-/ *adv law* later in the same official paper, statement, etc.

There is a green hill far a·way /· ˌ· ˌ· ˌ· ˌ· ·ˈ·/ a well-known HYMN (=religious song) sung at Easter

there·of /ðeəʳˈɒv‖-ˈɑːv/ *adv fml or law* of or belonging to that or it: *All citizens of the United States are ruled by the laws thereof.* —compare HEREOF

there·on /ðeəʳˈɒn‖-ˈɔːn, -ˈɑːn/ *adv fml* **1** on that or it: *I read the report and wrote some remarks thereon.* **2** THEREUPON (1)

there·to /ðeəˈtuː‖ðeəʳˈtuː/ *adv fml or law* to that (agreement or piece of writing): *... any conditions attaching thereto ...*

there·un·der /ðeəʳˈʌndəʳ/ *adv fml or law* **1** under that, it, or them: *the land, with any minerals found thereunder ...* **2** below, following, or in accordance with (something written): *the items listed thereunder*

there·up·on /ˌðeərəˈpɒn, ˈðeərəpɒn‖-pɔːn, -pɑːn/ *adv fml* **1** as a result of that; about that matter: *... if all are agreed thereupon ...* **2** without delay after that; then: *Thereupon she asked me to marry her.* —compare HEREUPON

therm /θɜːm‖θɜːrm/ *n* (a measurement of heat equal to) 100,000 British Thermal Units, used in Britain for measuring the amount of gas used by each user

therm- see WORD FORMATION

ther·mal¹ /ˈθɜːməl‖ˈθɜːr-/ *adj* **1** [A] of, using, producing, or caused by heat: *thermal insulation designed to prevent the loss of body heat* **2** naturally warm or hot: *thermal springs*

thermal² *n* a rising current of warm air, esp. as used by GLIDER pilots to gain height

ther·mi·on·ics /ˌθɜːmiˈɒnɪks‖ˌθɜːrmiˈɑː-/ *n* [U] *tech* the branch of science that deals with the outward flow of ELECTRONs from heated metal —**ic** *adj*

thermionic valve /ˌ·ˈ·· ˈ·/ *BrE* ‖ **thermionic tube** *AmE*— *n tech* a system of ELECTRODEs arranged in an airless glass or metal container, esp. used to control the flow of current in radios and televisions

ther·mo·dy·nam·ics /ˌθɜːməʊdaɪˈnæmɪks‖ˌθɜːr-/ *n* [U] the branch of science that deals with the relationship between heat and the power that works and drives machines, and the making of one into the other

ther·mom·e·ter /θəˈmɒmɪtəʳ‖θərˈmɑː-/ *n* an instrument for measuring and showing temperature, esp. a thin glass tube containing a special liquid, usu. MERCURY, that rises and falls as the temperature rises and falls; usu. used under the tongue or ARMPIT or in the RECTUM —see also CLINICAL THERMOMETER; see INSTRUMENT (USAGE)

ther·mo·nu·cle·ar /ˌθɜːməʊˈnjuːkliəʳ‖ˌθɜːrməʊˈnuː-/ *adj* of, using, or caused by the very high temperatures that result when the central parts of atoms are joined together: *a thermonuclear device* (=bomb) | *thermonuclear war* (=using such bombs)

ther·mo·plas·tic /ˌθɜːməʊˈplæstɪk◂‖ˌθɜːrmə-/ *n* [C;U] *tech* a plastic that is soft and bendable when heated — **thermoplastic** *adj*

ther·mos /ˈθɜːməs‖ˈθɜːr-/ *n tdmk for* FLASK (3)

ther·mo·set·ting /ˈθɜːməʊˌsetɪŋ‖ˈθɜːr-/ *adj tech* (of plastic) that becomes hard and unbendable after having been once heated and shaped

thermos flask /ˈ·· ·/ *n* a FLASK (3) —see picture at FLASK

ther·mo·stat /ˈθɜːməstæt‖ˈθɜːr-/ *n* an apparatus that can be set to keep a room, machine, etc., at an even temperature by disconnecting and reconnecting a supply of heat when necessary —see picture at ENGINE

THES /ˌtiː eɪtʃ iː ˈes/ *abbrev. for* TIMES HIGHER EDUCATION SUPPLEMENT

the·sau·rus /θɪˈsɔːrəs/ *n* a book of words that are put in groups together according to connections between their meanings rather than in an alphabetical list —compare DICTIONARY

these /ðiːz/ *plural of* THIS —see ONE (USAGE)

The·se·us /ˈθiːsiəs/ in CLASSICAL MYTHOLOGY, a brave man of Athens who killed the Minotaur and married the queen of the Amazons

the·sis /ˈθiːsɪ̣s/ *n* **-ses** /siːz/ **1** a long piece of writing on a particular subject, based on original work and written for a higher (POSTGRADUATE) university degree, esp. the degree of PHD: *a doctoral thesis* | *I'm writing my thesis on Shakespeare's use of metaphor.* —compare DISSERTATION **2** *fml* an opinion or statement put forward and supported by reasoned argument: *Their main thesis is that inflation is caused by increases in the money supply.*

thes·pi·an /ˈθespiən/ *adj, n pomp or humor* (often *cap.*) (of) an actor, esp. in the theatre: *the thespian art*

thews /θjuːz‖θuːz/ *n* [P] *lit* **1** muscles **2** physical strength

they /ðeɪ/ *pron* (used as the subject of a sentence) **1** those people, animals, or things: *My brother and sister are here. They visit every week.* | *Take these books; they might be useful.* **2** people in general: *They say prices are going to*

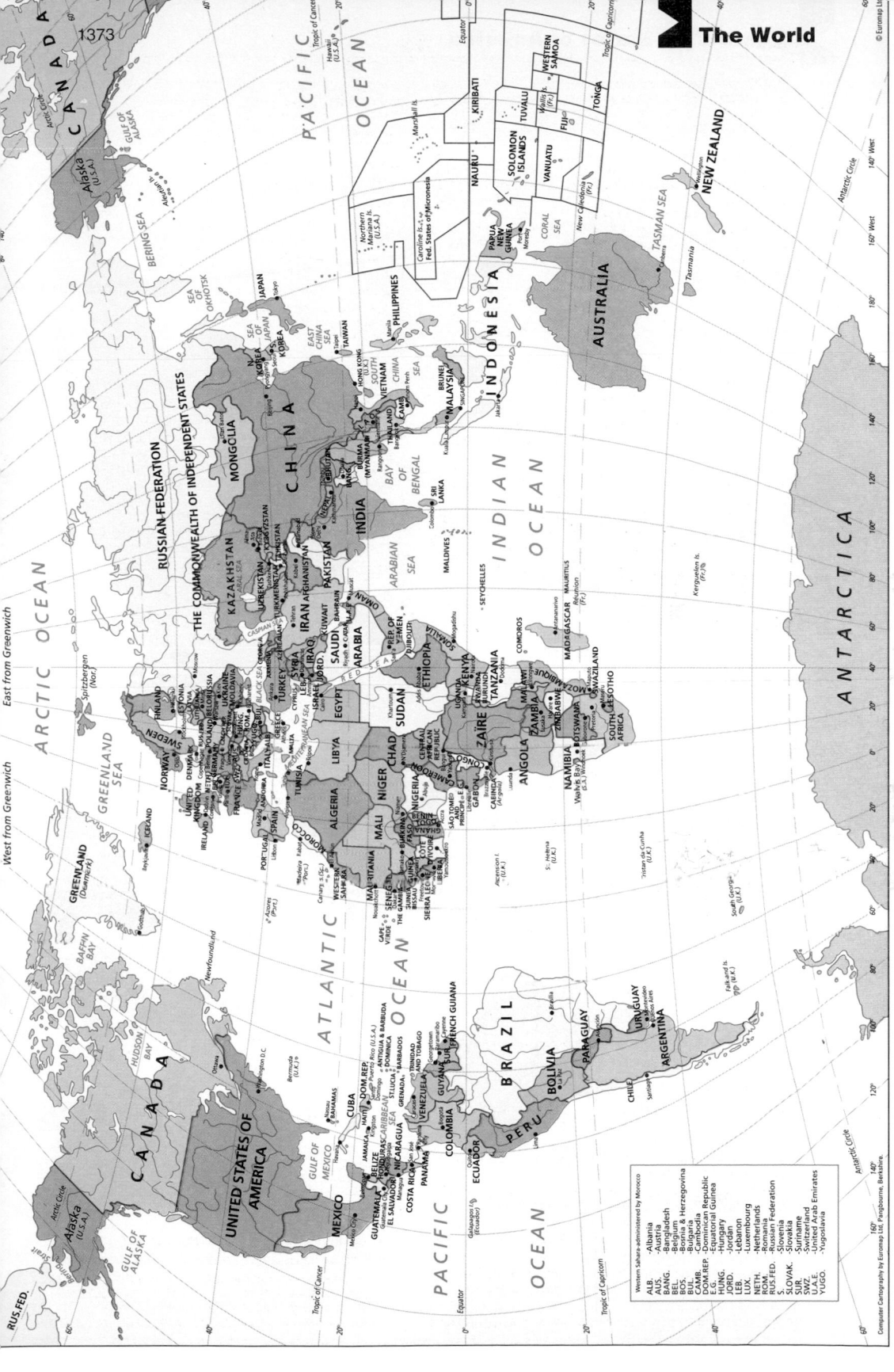

The World

N

CANADA

Seattle

Washington

Rocky Mountains

Montana

North Dakot

Oregon

Idaho

Wyoming

South Da

PACIFIC OCEAN

California

Nevada

Great Salt Lake

Nebr

Sierra Nevada

Salt Lake City

Denver

Utah

Colorado River

Colorado

San Francisco

Golden Gate Bridge

Las Vegas

HOLLYWOOD

Hoover Dam

Grand Canyon

New Mexico

Los Angeles

Disneyland

San Diego

Phoenix

Rio Grande

El Paso

Arizona

Honolulu

Hawaii

MEXICO

1375

The United States of America is a very large country which is divided into 50 separate states. There are many different types of weather and land, with desert in the south west near Mexico and snowy mountains in Alaska (the most northern part). New York is the biggest city in the US, but the capital city, where the President lives, is Washington D.C. Native Americans lived in America for a long time before large numbers of people came from Europe to live there.

The United States is the world's richest and most industrial country. Most of the industries are in the north eastern part of the country, particularly in the area around the Great Lakes.

Maine

New England

The Great Lakes

Lake Superior

Minnesota

Lake Michigan

Lake Huron

New Hampshire

Vermont

Lake Ontario

St. Paul

New York

Boston

Minneapolis

Wisconsin

Michigan

Niagara Falls

Rhode Island

Massachusetts

Connecticut

Detroit

New York City

Milwaukee

Pennsylvania

Philadelphia

Long Island

Iowa

Chicago

Cleveland

New Jersey

Lake Erie

Baltimore

Indiana

Ohio

Delaware

Illinois

Cincinnati

Pittsburgh

Maryland

Missouri

Washington D.C.

Indianapolis

West Virginia

ansas City

St Louis

sas

Missouri River

Kentucky

Virginia

The White House

Statue of Liberty

Appalachian Mountains

Nashville

North Carolina

ATLANTIC OCEAN

homa

Tennessee

Arkansas

Memphis

South Carolina

lahoma City

Birmingham

Charleston

Mississippi

Dallas

Atlanta

Mississippi River

Alabama

Georgia

Fort Worth

Texas

Tallahassee

Florida

in

Houston

New Orleans

Orlando

Louisiana

Cape Canaveral

Tampa

Fort Lauderdale

Corpus Christi

GULF OF MEXICO

600 km.

Miami

Florida Keys

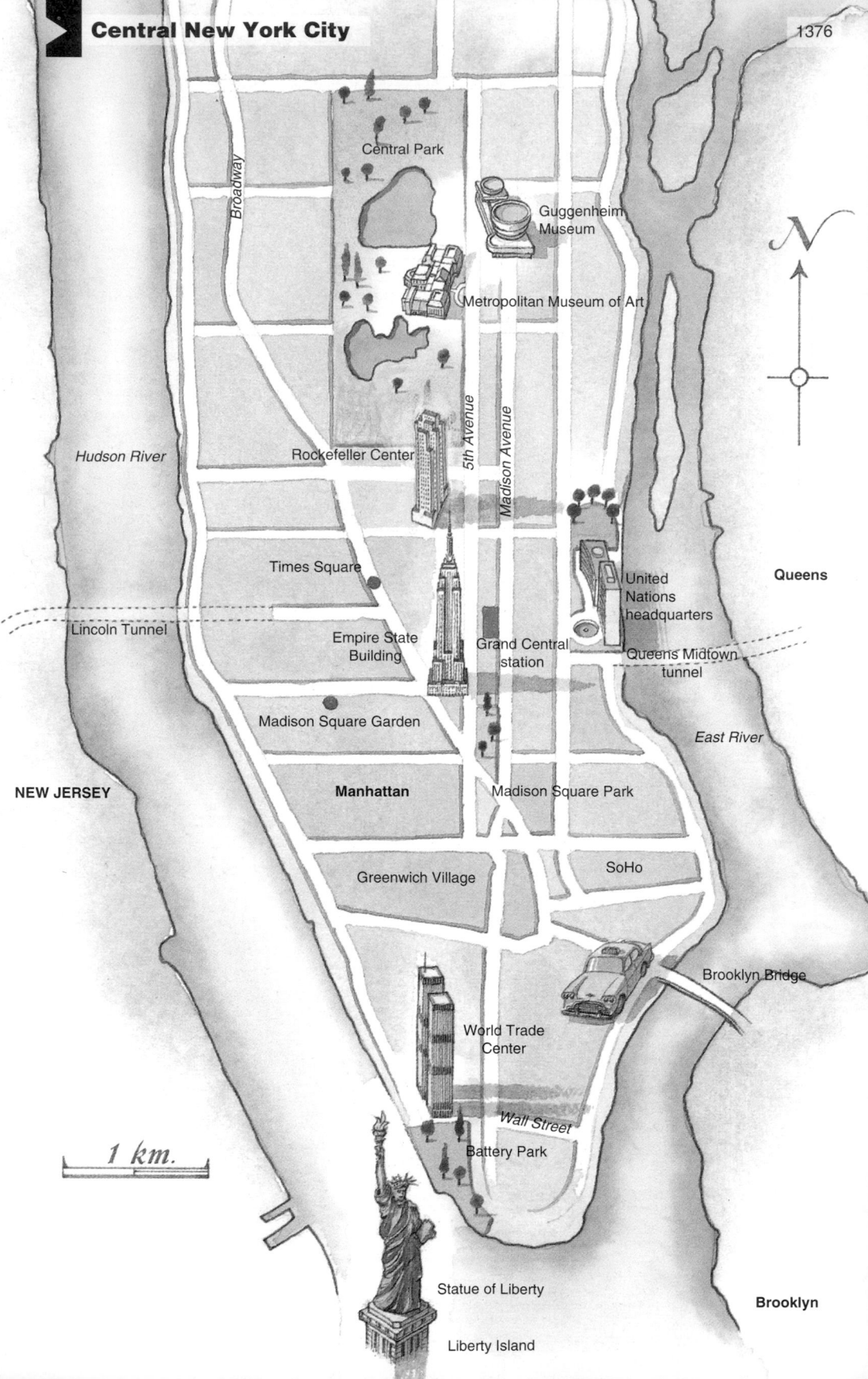

Central Park

Guggenheim Museum

Metropolitan Museum of Art

Broadway

Hudson River

5th Avenue

Madison Avenue

Rockefeller Center

Times Square

United Nations headquarters

Queens

Lincoln Tunnel

Empire State Building

Grand Central station

Queens Midtown tunnel

Madison Square Garden

East River

NEW JERSEY

Manhattan

Madison Square Park

Greenwich Village

SoHo

Brooklyn Bridge

World Trade Center

1 km.

Wall Street

Battery Park

Statue of Liberty

Liberty Island

Brooklyn

increase again. (=that is the general opinion) | (*infml*) *John's as clever as they come.* (=very clever) **3** the government, local council, or other unknown people who control one's life: *I see they're putting up taxes again|digging up the road again.* **4** (used in order to avoid saying **he** or **she** after a singular noun or pronoun when one wants to include people of either sex): *If anyone has any information on this subject, will they please let me know afterwards.* —see EVERYONE (USAGE), HE (USAGE)

they'd /ðeɪd/ *short for* (in compound tenses): **1** they had: *If only they'd been there.* **2** they would: *They'd never believe you.*

they'll /ðeɪl/ *short for:* they will: *They'll arrive tomorrow.*

they're /ðəʳ; *strong* ðeəʳ, ðeɪəʳ/ *short for:* they are: *They're the best you can buy.*

they've /ðeɪv/ *short for* (esp. in compound tenses): they have: *They've lost again.* | (*esp. BrE*) *They've a wonderful new house.*

thi·a·mine /ˈθaɪəmiːn/ also **vitamin B₁, aneurin**— *n* [U] a natural chemical substance found in some foods which is necessary to prevent some illnesses: *People who do not receive enough thiamine in their diets should take a vitamin supplement.*

thick¹ /θɪk/ *adj* **1 a** having a large or larger than average distance between opposite surfaces; not thin: *a thick book* | *thick walls* | *a thick layer of snow* **b** (of a round object) wide in relation to length: *thick wire* **2** [after *n*] measuring in depth, width, or from side to side: *The castle walls are two metres thick.* **3** (of liquid) not watery; not flowing easily: *thick soup* **4** difficult to see through; DENSE: *thick mist* | *thick clouds of smoke coming out of the factory chimneys* **5** [F+**with**] full of or covered with (esp. something unpleasant): *The air was thick with smoke.* | *furniture thick with dust* | *The whole area was thick with policemen.* **6** closely packed; made of many objects set close together: *a thick forest* | *long thick hair* **7 a** (of an ACCENT¹) very noticeable: *a thick Liverpool accent* **b** (of speech or the voice) not clear: *He spoke in a voice thick with emotion.* **8** *BrE infml* aching and/or unable to think clearly: *My head's rather thick this morning after all that beer I drank last night.* **9** *infml* (of a person) stupid; slow to understand **10** [F] *infml, esp. BrE* beyond what is reasonable or satisfactory: *It's **a bit thick** to expect me to work until midnight!* **11** [F (**with**)] *infml* very friendly: *Jean and John seem very thick (with each other).* **12 as thick as two (short) planks** *BrE sl* very stupid **13 as thick as thieves** *infml* very friendly **14 get/give a thick ear** *BrE* to receive or give a blow on the ear causing it to swell as a punishment (esp. used in threats): *I'll give you a thick ear if you pull the dog's tail again!* **15 thick on the ground** *infml, esp. BrE* plentiful: *Grants for the arts are not too thick on the ground these days.* **16 the thick end of** *BrE infml* almost as much as (an amount): *The car cost me the thick end of £10,000.* —see also THICKNESS — —**ly** *adv*

thick² *adv* **1** so as to be thick; thickly: *The flowers grew thickest near the wall.* **2 lay it on thick** *AmE infml* to praise very much but perhaps not very sincerely; FLATTER: *He laid it on pretty thick about her beautiful singing voice.* **3 thick and fast** *infml* quickly and in large numbers: *The election results are coming in thick and fast.*

thick³ *n* **1** [(*the*) S (**of**)] the part, place, time, etc., of greatest activity: *in the thick of the battle|the rush hour traffic* **2 through thick and thin** through both good and bad times; faithfully: *She stuck by* (=remained with) *her husband through thick and thin.*

thick·en /ˈθɪkən/ *v* [I;T] to make or become thick: *The mist is thickening.* | *I always thicken my soups by adding flour.* —see also **the plot thickens** (PLOT)

thick·en·er /ˈθɪkənəʳ, ˈθɪknəʳ/ also **thick·en·ing** /ˈθɪkənɪŋ, ˈθɪknɪŋ/— *n* [C;U] a substance used for thickening a liquid: *gravy thickener*

thick·et /ˈθɪkɪt/ *n* a thick growth of bushes and small trees: *The fox hid in the thicket where the dogs could not reach it.*

thick·head·ed /ˌθɪkˈhedɪd◂/ also **thick·wit·ted** /ˌθɪkˈwɪtɪd◂/— *adj infml* extremely stupid: *He's so thickheaded he can't understand the simplest instructions.*

thick·ness /ˈθɪknɪs/ *n* **1** [C;U] the quality or degree of being thick: *The beam has a thickness of 4 inches.* | *The length of nails you need depends on the thickness of the planks.* **2** [C (**of**)] a LAYER¹ (1): *I wrapped the ice cream*

in three thicknesses of newspaper to keep it cool.

thick·set /ˌθɪkˈset◂/ *adj* having a broad strong body; STOCKY: *The boxing champion was short and thickset.*

thick-skinned /ˌ·ˈ·◂/ *adj sometimes derog* insensitive, esp. to blame, disapproval, etc.; not easily offended

thief /θiːf/ *n* **thieves** /θiːvz/ a person who steals, esp. without using violence: *a car thief* —compare BURGLAR, ROBBER

thieve /θiːv/ *v* **1** [I] *infml or lit* to steal things; rob people; act as a thief: *Those thieving children keep stealing our apples.* **2** [T] *nonstandard* to steal

thiev·ing /ˈθiːvɪŋ/ also **thiev·e·ry** /ˈθiːvəri/ *fml or lit*— *n* [U] stealing; THEFT

thiev·ish /ˈθiːvɪʃ/ *adj lit* of or like a thief: *thievish habits* — —**ly** *adv* — —**ness** *n* [U]

thigh /θaɪ/ *n* the top part of the human leg, between the knee and the HIP —see picture at SKELETON

thim·ble /ˈθɪmbəl/ *n* a small protective metal or plastic cap put over the finger that pushes the needle during sewing

thim·ble·ful /ˈθɪmbəlfʊl/ *n* [(**of**)] *infml* a very small quantity (of liquid)

thin¹ /θɪn/ *adj* -**nn**- **1 a** having a smaller than average distance between opposite surfaces; not thick: *a thin board* | *thin ice* | *thin summer clothes* | *Keep your voice down or they'll hear you in the next room — the walls are* **paper-thin. b** (of a round object) narrow in relation to length; fine: *thin string|wire* **2** having little fat on the body; not fat: *She looked thin after her illness.* —see USAGE **3** *often derog* (of a liquid) watery; flowing easily; weak: *thin beer* | *This sauce is too thin.* **4** not closely packed; made of few objects widely separated; SPARSE: *Your hair's getting very thin.* | *a thin audience* | *A thin rain began to fall.* **5** easy to see through; not DENSE: *thin mist* | *The air on top of the mountain was very thin.* **6** (of a sound or note) lacking in strength and fullness: *a thin high voice* **7** *derog* (esp. of something said or written) not having the necessary qualities to gain the intended result; unsatisfactory: *a thin excuse* | *It was quite an entertaining speech, but rather thin in terms of content.* | *His jokes are beginning to* **wear thin** (=become less funny) *because he's told them so often.* **8 have a thin time** *BrE infml* to have an unpleasant, uncomfortable, or esp. unsuccessful time: *He's been having rather a thin time (of it) since his wife left him.* **9 thin end of the wedge** *esp. BrE* something which seems unimportant but will open the way for more serious things of a similar kind: *You're letting one or two employees take days off here and there — this is just the thin end of the wedge.* **10 thin on the ground** *infml, esp. BrE* not plentiful: *Taxis seem very thin on the ground tonight — we'll have to walk.* **11 thin on top** *infml euph* becoming BALD (=hairless) — —**ly** *adv*: *Spread the butter thinly.* | *a thinly-veiled|thinly-disguised threat* (=clearly a threat, but not expressed in threatening language) — —**ness** *n* [U]

▷ USAGE **1 Thin** is a general word to describe people who have little or no fat on their bodies. If someone is **thin** in a pleasant way, we say they are **slim** or (less common) **slender**: *I wish I were as* **slim/slender** *as you.* We could also say **lean** (=thin in a strong and healthy way): *a lean, muscular body.* If they are too thin they are **skinny** (*infml*), **underweight**, or (worst of all) **emaciated**: *He looks very* **thin/skinny/underweight** *after his illness.* | *The prisoners were* **emaciated.** 2 **Thin** can be used for things: *a thin pole*, but not usually for flat surfaces (especially surfaces where a person might go) or for openings. Instead we say **narrow**: *a* **narrow** *road* | *a* **narrow** *bed* | *a* **narrow** *gap.* 3 **Fine** is used to describe things that are **thin** when you are giving the idea of careful, sensitive work: *She drew with a* **fine** *pen.* | **fine** *silk thread* —see also FAT (USAGE).◁

thin² *adv* so as to be thin; thinly: *Don't cut the bread so thin.*

thin³ *v* -**nn**- **1** [I;T (OUT)] to make or become thinner, fewer, or less closely packed: *We should wait until the mist thins before we start our journey.* | *Thin the paint by adding turpentine.* | *The crowd began to thin out.* | *His hair is thinning.* **2** [T (OUT)] to pull up the weaker ones from (a mass of young plants) so that the stronger ones have room to grow freely —see also THINNER

thin air /ˌ·ˈ·/ *n* [U] *infml* a state of not being seen or not existing: *I can't find that book anywhere — it's disappeared*

into thin air! | *We can't just produce another £1000 out of thin air.*

thine¹ /ðaɪn/ *pron old use, bibl, or poet* (*possessive form of* **thou**) yours: *"For thine is the kingdom, the power, and the glory ..."* (prayer)

thine² *determiner old use, bibl, or poet* (before a vowel or *h*) THY: *"Drink to me only with thine eyes."* (Ben Jonson)

thing /θɪŋ/ *n* **1** [C] a material object; an object that need not or cannot be named: *What's that thing you've got on your head?* | *What do you use this thing for?* | *"You can't leave that thing there,"* shouted the policeman. | *I opened the door and the first thing I saw was a cloud of smoke.* | *Have you seen my pen? I can't find the thing|the wretched|stupid|damned thing* (=it) *anywhere.* (shows annoyance) | *My son likes making things out of wood.* **2** [C] a separate but non-physical object that can be thought about or talked about, such as a quality, idea, or statement: *What a nasty thing to say to your sister!* | *I just said the first thing that came into my head.* | *One of the things I like about her is that she's very honest.* | *He seems to be more interested in things of the mind than things of the body.* | *One thing is certain – I'm not lending him any money again.* | *She talked very fast and I couldn't understand a thing she said.* | *The job has got a lot of things going for it.* (=several advantages) | *There's* **no such thing as** *a cure for all ills.* (=such a thing does not exist) **3** [C] that which has been or will be done; an action, activity, or event: *What's the next thing we have to do?* | *I hope I'm doing the right thing in accepting this job.* | *We're expecting great things from our new manager.* | *The first thing is for you to talk to your teacher.* (=that is what you should do first) | *If you do that she might resign, which is the last thing we want.* (=we do not want this to happen at all) | *A funny thing happened at work today.* | *You couldn't help getting ill – it's* **just one of those things.** (=an event that cannot be avoided) **4** [C] a subject; matter: *There's one more thing I wanted to say.* | *There are one or two things I'd like to discuss with you.* | *Let's just forget the whole thing.* **5** [C] a person or animal: *He's been very ill, poor thing.* | *There wasn't a living thing in the woods.* **6** [C] a garment; piece of clothing: *I haven't got a thing to wear!* | *Did you bring your swimming things?* **7** [*the*] that which is necessary or desirable: *I think I've got* **just the thing** *you need.* | *Cold beer's just the thing on a hot day!* **8** [*the* (**in**)] the fashion or custom: *She was wearing the latest thing in shoes.* | *It's not* **the (done) thing** *to eat off your knife.* **9** [S] *sl* an activity very satisfying to one personally: *Everyone should be free to* **do their (own) thing.** **10 a thing of the past** something which no longer exists: *Good manners seem to have become a thing of the past.* **11 for** '**one thing** (used for introducing a reason): *For one thing we can't afford it, and for another it's ugly.* **12 have a thing about** *infml* to have unusually strong feelings, usu. of like or dislike, about: *He's got a thing about planes – he just won't go on them.* **13 make a thing of** *infml* to give too much importance to: *I disagree with you, but don't let's make a thing of it!* **14 taking one thing with another** considering everything that needs to be considered – see also THINGS, CLOSE THING, NEAR THING, SURE THING, **first thing** (FIRST¹) **good thing** (GOOD²)

▷ USAGE **The thing is** can be used in informal conversation when you give a reason for something you have said, or introduce something which you think is the main point: *I've got a bit of a problem.* **The thing is,** *all the banks are closed. So could you lend me some money until tomorrow?* | *"Why won't you marry me, Mary?" "I'm sorry, John.* **The thing is,** *I don't want to marry anyone."*◁

thing·a·ma·jig , **thingumajig, thingummyjig** /ˈθɪŋəmə̱dʒɪg/ *also* **thing·a·ma·bob** /ˈθɪŋəmə̱bɒb‖-bɑːb/, **thing·um·my** /ˈθɪŋəmi/, **thing·ie** /ˈθɪŋi/— *n infml* a person or thing, esp. one whose name one has forgotten or does not know: *Have you got the thingamajig for opening bottles?*

things /θɪŋz/ *n* [P] **1** personal possessions; belongings: *Pack your things. We're going to leave.* **2** the general state of affairs at a particular time; situation: *The car ran out of petrol, and to make things worse I didn't have any money on me.* | *The way things stand at the moment, we can't possibly afford a holiday.* | *Cheer up – things aren't as bad as they seem.* **3** the dishes, cups, knives, etc., used for the stated meal: *We must clear away the breakfast*

things. **4 all things to all men** pleasing to everyone or useful for everything: *You should stop trying to be all things to all men.* **5 of 'all things** (used for expressing surprise): *She ordered frogs' legs, of all things!* –see also **hear things** (HEAR), **see things** (SEE¹)

think¹ /θɪŋk/ *v* **thought** /θɔːt/ **1** [I (**about**);T] to use the power of reason; make judgments or careful considerations; use the mind to form ideas and opinions: *She thought long and hard before coming to a decision.* | *My headache was so bad I could hardly think straight.* | *You look very thoughtful; what are you thinking about?* | *thinking great thoughts* | *teaching children to* **think for themselves** (=to form their own opinions) | *I thought to myself* (=I had the thought), *"He's behaving very oddly."* –see also THINK **about 2** [T] to believe; consider; have an opinion: [+(*that*)] *The police think that the bomb was planted by terrorists.* | *I think she's wrong, don't you?* | *"Do you think it will rain?" "Yes, I think so."* | *Who do you think murdered the old lady?* (=in your opinion, who murdered her?) | *I don't think she'll come.* (=I think she will not come.) | *I don't think she'll come; I know she'll come.* (=Not only do I think she'll come, but I know she'll come.) | *From the way he behaves, you'd think he owned the company.* (=he behaves in a way that suggests this, though it is not true) [+*obj*+*n*|*adj*] (*fml*) *He thinks himself a great poet.* | *I thought her rather clever.* [+*obj*+*to-v;pass.*] *The government is thought to be planning an election in June.* (=this is what most people think) –see also THINK **of** (2) **3** [T+*wh-;obj*] (used after **cannot** and **could not**) to imagine; understand: *I can't think why you did it.* | *He's a most unpleasant man – I can't think why she married him.* **4** [T+*wh-;obj*] to reason about; bring to mind; remember: *Think how big and varied the world is.* | *Try and think where you last saw him.* **5** [T+(*that*);*obj*] to have as a half-formed intention or plan: *I think I'm going to make some tea – would you like a cup?* | *We thought we'd go swimming tomorrow.* | *"You'll go swimming tomorrow, will you?" "Yes, I thought so."* (=that is my intention) [+*to-v*] (*old use*) *They thought to deceive me, but I was too clever for them.* –see also THINK of (1) **6** [T+(*that*);*obj*] to expect: *She said she'd kill him, but I never thought she'd actually do it.* | *We didn't think we'd be this late.* | *Who would have thought that she'd end up as prime minister?* (shows surprise) | *"He's in trouble with the police again." "I* **thought as much."** (=That's just what I expected.) **7** [T+*to-v;obj;usu. in negatives*] to be sensitive or thoughtful enough (to do something): *I didn't think to ask her if she had passed her exam.* **8** [T+(*that*);*obj*] (used in requests): *Do you think you could help me with this box?* **9 think aloud** to speak one's thoughts as they come **10 think big** *infml* to plan to do things on a large scale rather than carefully or in a limited way **11 think on one's feet** to think and make decisions quickly **12 think twice** to think very carefully about something: *I should think twice before accepting that offer; it sounds rather suspicious.* **13 I think, therefore I am** *quote* a phrase used by the French PHILOSOPHER René Descartes –see also **see/think fit to** (FIT²) – **~ er** *n* : *Bertrand Russell, one of the great thinkers of our age*

▷ USAGE **1** To make this word stronger, say *I* **thought** *hard.* | *I* **thought** *deeply.* **2** In negative sentences, the negative normally goes with **think**, not with the next verb: *I don't* **think** *she'll come.* | *They didn't* **think** *he was good enough.*◁

think about sthg. *phr v* [T] **1** to consider seriously before making a decision: *"Dad, will you buy me a new bike?" "I don't know; I'll have to think about it."* **2** to THINK **of** (1,2)

think of sbdy./sthg. *phr v* [T] **1** to have formed a possible but not firmly settled plan for: *I'd thought of blue for this room.* [+*v-ing*] *We're thinking of going to France for our holidays, but we haven't decided for certain yet.* –see also THINK¹ (5) **2** to have as an opinion about: *What do you think of|about the government's latest offer to the teachers?* –see also THINK¹ (2) **3** to take into account; consider: *Do be careful – think of the risks you're taking.* | *It's a nice idea, but think of the cost!* **4** (used after **cannot** and **could not** and in the infinitive after **try, want,** etc.) to remember: *I can't think of his name.* | *I tried to think of her phone number, but I just couldn't remember it.* **5 not think much of** to have a low opinion of: *I don't think much of these so-called improvements to the town centre.* **6 not think of** *infml* not consider or not be able to: *I wouldn't think of letting you walk home on a night like this.* **7 think better of something** to change one's opinion about something; decide wisely against something: *I was going to ask him to help, but thought better of (doing) it.* **8 think highly/well/little/poorly/etc. of** to have a good/bad/etc. opinion of (someone or something): *We all think very highly of her.* —see also WELL-THOUGHT-OF **9 think nothing of** to regard as usual or easy: *He thinks nothing of walking four miles to work and back every day.* **10 think nothing** '**of it** (a reply to thanks or an APOLOGY) I'm very glad to have helped you **11 think the world of** to care about very much: *He may get angry sometimes, but really he thinks the world of you.*

   think sthg. ↔ **out/through** *phr v* [T] to consider carefully and in detail, esp. so that all the possible results of an action are understood in advance; reach a decision about (something) after much careful thought: *I don't think the government has really thought out/thought through all the consequences of this decision.* —see also THOUGHT-OUT

   think sthg. ↔ **over** *phr v* [T] to consider seriously: *Your offer is very attractive, but I need to think it over before I can let you know my decision.*

   think sthg. ↔ **up** *phr v* [T] to invent (esp. an idea): *The prisoners tried to think up a plan for escape.*

think² *n* [S (**about**)] *infml* an act of thinking, esp. about a difficulty or question: *I'll have to* **have a think** *about this before I give you an answer.* | *If you think I'm going to lend you a pound you've* **got another think coming.** (=you'll have to think of someone else to ask, because I certainly won't lend you a pound)

Think·er /ˈθɪŋkəʳ/, **The** a SCULPTURE by Rodin of a man deep in thought —see picture at RODIN

think·ing¹ /ˈθɪŋkɪŋ/ *n* [U] **1** the act of using one's mind to produce thoughts and ideas: *I've been doing some thinking and I've decided to change my job.* **2** a way of thinking about something; opinion; judgment: *What's the Administration's thinking on this matter?* | **To my way of thinking** (=in my opinion), *they are making a serious mistake.* **3 put on one's** '**thinking cap** *infml* to think seriously about something —see also WISHFUL THINKING

thinking² *adj* [A] *apprec* thoughtful; able to think, esp. clearly and seriously: *All thinking people agree that something must be done about world hunger.* | *plans to develop a thinking computer*

think tank /ˈ· ·/ *n* [C+*sing./pl. v*] a committee of people experienced in a particular subject, established by an organization, government, etc., to develop ideas and advise on matters related to that subject

thin·ner /ˈθɪnəʳ/ *n* [U] a liquid, such as TURPENTINE, added to paint to make it spread more easily

thin-skinned /ˌ· ˈ·◄/ *adj sometimes derog* sensitive; (too) easily offended; TOUCHY

third /θɜːd‖θɜːrd/ *determiner, adv, n, pron* **1** 3rd —see TABLE 1 **2** [C (**in**)] the third and usu. lowest class of British university degree: *He got a third in Chemistry.* —see DEGREE (CULTURAL NOTE)

third base /ˌ· ˈ·/ *n* (in BASEBALL) the third of the four BASES which a player must touch before gaining a point (RUN)

third class /ˌ· ˈ·◄/ *n* [C] *fml for* THIRD (2)

third de·gree /ˌ· ·ˈ·◄/ *n* [*the*+S] *infml* hard questioning and/or rough treatment of a person in order to obtain information or a statement of guilt: *The police gave the suspect the third degree.*

third-degree /ˈ· ·ˌ·/ *adj* [A] (of a burn) of the highest level of seriousness

Third Man /ˌ· ˈ·/, **The** a NOVEL about spies (SPY) by Graham Greene set in Vienna at the end of the Second World War, later made into a very successful film with Orson Welles

third par·ty /ˌ· ˈ·◄/ *n tech or law* **1** a person other than the two main people concerned in an agreement, contract, law case, etc. **2** a person not named in an insurance agreement, but who will be protected by the insurance if an accident happens

third per·son /ˌ· ˈ·◄/ *n* [*the*+S] **1** a form of a verb or PRONOUN that is used for showing the person or thing that is being spoken about: *"He", "she", "it", and "they" are third person pronouns.* | *"They are" is the third person plural of "to be".* **2** a way of telling a story in which the teller uses the third person: *The story was written in*

the third person; it began "He was born in . . .". —compare FIRST PERSON, SECOND PERSON

third-rate /ˌ· ˈ·◄/ *adj* of very poor quality; INFERIOR

Third Read·ing /ˌθɜːd ˈriːdɪŋ‖ˌθɜːrd-/ *n* the third and final reading out of a suggested new law in parliament — see BILL¹ (2) (CULTURAL NOTE)

Third Reich /ˌ· ˈ·/ [*the*] the German DICTATORSHIP between 1933 and 1945, including Germany and all the countries that Hitler intended it should take over

Third World /ˌ· ˈ·◄/ [*the*] the industrially less developed countries of the world considered as a group

thirst¹ /θɜːst‖θɜːrst/ *n* **1** [S;U] a sensation of dryness in the mouth caused by the need to drink; desire for drink: *After running five miles we had quite a thirst.* | *He* **quenched** (=satisfied) **his thirst** *with a large glass of beer.* | *A long, thirst-quenching drink.* **2** [U] lack of drink, esp. for a long period: *The soldiers died of thirst in the desert.* **3** [(*the*) S+**for**] a strong desire; CRAVING: *the thirst for excitement/knowledge*

thirst²

   thirst for/after sthg. *phr v* [T] *lit* to have a strong desire for: *Our people thirst for independence.*

thirst·y /ˈθɜːsti‖ˈθɜːr-/ *adj* **1** feeling thirst: *Salty food makes you thirsty.* | (fig.) *The fields are thirsty for rain.* **2** [A] causing thirst: *Chopping logs is* **thirsty work.** **3** [F+**for**] having a strong desire for: *She was thirsty for power.* —**ily** *adv*

thir·teen /ˌθɜːˈtiːn◄‖ˌθɜːr-/ *determiner, n, pron* (the number) 13. This number is thought to be unlucky by many people. —see TABLE 1 —**teenth** *determiner, n, pron, adv*

thir·ties /ˈθɜːtiz‖ˈθɜːr-/ *n* [P] **1** [*the*] also '**30s**— the 1930s (=the years from 1930 to 1939): *The film is set in the thirties during the Depression.* **2 in his/her/their thirties** aged from 30 to 39: *Most of my colleagues are in their thirties.* **3** [*the*] the numbers from 30 to 39

thir·ty /ˈθɜːti‖ˈθɜːrti/ *determiner, n, pron* (the number) 30. For many young people, thirty is the age at which they think one begins to grow old. —see TABLE 1 —see also **thirty pieces of silver** (SILVER) —**tieth** *determiner, n, pron, adv*

Thirty-nine Ar·ti·cles /ˌ··· ˈ···/ [*the* + P] a set of basic teachings and beliefs of the Church of England, written in 1571, which the Church still asks its ministers to agree to in principle before appointment

thirty some·thing /ˈ··· ˌ··/ *n* **1** the age range of 30–39 **2** a person of this age, esp. one who is seen as being successful in their profession, having a young family, middle-class, well-educated, and perhaps a YUPPIE: *a party for thirty somethings*

Thirty Years' War /ˌ··· ˈ·/ [*the*] a European war fought mainly in Germany between 1618 and 1648. It led to the Habsburgs and the Holy Roman Empire losing power in Europe.

this¹ /ðɪs/ *determiner* **these** /ðiːz/ being the person, thing, idea, etc., which is understood or (about to be) mentioned: *I saw Mrs Jones this morning.* | *Wait until you've heard this story!* | *These latest revelations will severely damage the President's reputation.* | *Who's this Mr Black we keep hearing about?* | *There will be another meeting later this week.* | *Come here* **this minute!** (=at once) | *They should have arrived by this time.* (=by now) | *If we keep losing money at this rate we may have to close the factory.* **2** being the one of two or more people or things that is nearer in time, place, thought, etc.: *You look in this box (here) and I'll look in that one (over there).* | *I'm surprised you like that picture; I prefer this one.* | *Is the meeting this Friday or next Friday?* **3** *infml* a certain: *This man came up to me in the street and started making rude suggestions ...* | *There were these two Irishmen called Pat and Mike ...*

this² *pron* **these** **1** the thing, action, etc., which is understood or (about to be) mentioned: *Who told you this?* | *Wait until you've heard this!* | *What's this?* | *This is what you must do.* | *Do it like this.* (=in the way shown) | *This has been the best year in the company's history.* | *We're getting some new machines next month, and this* (=this fact) *will help us to increase production.* **2** (used with **be**) the thing or person that is near or nearer in place, time, thought, etc.: *This is your book, isn't it?* | *"This is my sister." "How do you do?"* | *This is more comfortable than that one over there.* | (on the telephone)

to: *I wouldn't think of letting you walk home on a night like this.* **7 think better of something** to change one's opinion about something; decide wisely against something: *I was going to ask him to help, but thought better of (doing) it.* **8 think highly/well/little/poorly/etc. of** to have a good/bad/etc. opinion of (someone or something): *We all think very highly of her.* —see also WELL-THOUGHT-OF **9 think nothing of** to regard as usual or easy: *He thinks nothing of walking four miles to work and back every day.* **10 think nothing of it** (a reply to thanks or an APOLOGY) I'm very glad to have helped you **11 think the world of** to care about very much: *He may get angry sometimes, but really he thinks the world of you.*

think sthg. ↔ **out/through** *phr v* [T] to consider carefully and in detail, esp. so that all the possible results of an action are understood or decided in advance; reach a decision about (something) after much careful thought: *I don't think the government has really thought out/thought through all the consequences of this decision.* —see also THOUGHT-OUT

think sthg. ↔ **over** *phr v* [T] to consider seriously: *Your offer is very attractive, but I need to think it over before I can let you know my decision.*

think sthg. ↔ **up** *phr v* [T] to invent (esp. an idea): *The prisoners tried to think up a plan for escape.*

think² *n* [S (about)] *infml* an act of thinking, esp. about a difficulty or question: *I'll have to have a think about this before I give you an answer.* | *If you think I'm going to lend you a pound you've got another think coming.* (=you'll have to think of someone else to ask, because I certainly won't lend you a pound)

Think·er /'θɪŋkəʳ/, **The** a SCULPTURE by Rodin of a man deep in thought —see picture at RODIN

think·ing¹ /'θɪŋkɪŋ/ *n* [U] **1** the act of using one's mind to produce thoughts and ideas: *I've been doing some thinking and I've decided to change my job.* **2** a way of thinking about something; opinion; judgment: *What's the Administration's thinking on this matter?* | **To my way of thinking** (=in my opinion), *they are making a serious mistake.* **3 put on one's 'thinking cap** *infml* to think seriously about something —see also WISHFUL THINKING

thinking² *adj* [A] *apprec* thoughtful; able to think, esp. clearly and seriously: *All thinking people agree that something must be done about world hunger.* | *plans to develop a thinking computer*

think tank /'· ·/ *n* [C+*sing.*/*pl. v*] a committee of people experienced in a particular subject, established by an organization, government, etc., to develop ideas and advise on matters related to that subject

thin·ner /'θɪnəʳ/ *n* [U] a liquid, such as TURPENTINE, added to paint to make it spread more easily

thin-skinned /ˌ· '·◄/ *adj* *sometimes derog* sensitive; (too) easily offended; TOUCHY

third /θɜːd‖θɜːrd/ *determiner, adv, n, pron* **1** 3rd —see TABLE 1 **2** [C (**in**)] the third and usu. lowest class of British university degree: *He got a third in Chemistry.* —see DEGREE (CULTURAL NOTE)

third base /ˌ· '·/ *n* (in BASEBALL) the third of the four BASES which a player must touch before gaining a point (RUN)

third class /ˌ· '·◄/ *n* [C] *fml for* THIRD (2)

third de·gree /ˌ· ·'·◄/ *n* [*the*+S] *infml* hard questioning and/or rough treatment of a person in order to obtain information or a statement of guilt: *The police gave the suspect the third degree.*

third-degree /'· ··/ *adj* [A] (of a burn) of the highest level of seriousness

Third Man /ˌ· '·/, **The** a NOVEL about spies (SPY) by Graham Greene set in Vienna at the end of the Second World War, later made into a very successful film with Orson Welles

third par·ty /ˌ· '··◄/ *n tech or law* **1** a person other than the two main people concerned in an agreement, contract, law case, etc. **2** a person not named in an insurance agreement, but who will be protected by the insurance if an accident happens

third per·son /ˌ· '··◄/ *n* [*the*+S] **1** a form of a verb or PRONOUN that is used for showing the person or thing that is being spoken about: *"He", "she", "it", and "they" are third person pronouns.* | *"They are" is the third person plural of "to be".* **2** a way of telling a story in which the teller uses the third person: *The story was written in*

the third person; it began "He was born in ...". —compare FIRST PERSON, SECOND PERSON

third-rate /ˌ· '·◄/ *adj* of very poor quality; INFERIOR

Third Read·ing /ˌθɜːd 'riːdɪŋ‖ˌθɜːrd-/ *n* the third and final reading out of a suggested new law in parliament —see BILL¹ (2) (CULTURAL NOTE)

Third Reich /ˌ· '·/ [*the*] the German DICTATORSHIP between 1933 and 1945, including Germany and all the countries that Hitler intended it should take over

Third World /ˌ· '·◄/ [*the*] the industrially less developed countries of the world considered as a group

thirst¹ /θɜːst‖θɜːrst/ *n* **1** [S;U] a sensation of dryness in the mouth caused by the need to drink; desire for drink: *After running five miles we had quite a thirst.* | *He quenched* (=satisfied) **his thirst** *with a large glass of beer.* | *A long, thirst-quenching drink.* **2** [U] lack of drink, esp. for a long period: *The soldiers died of thirst in the desert.* **3** [(*the*) S+**for**] a strong desire; CRAVING: *the thirst for excitement/knowledge*

thirst²
thirst for/after sthg. *phr v* [T] *lit* to have a strong desire for: *Our people thirst for independence.*

thirst·y /'θɜːsti‖'θɜːr-/ *adj* **1** feeling thirst: *Salty food makes you thirsty.* | (fig.) *The fields are thirsty for rain.* **2** [A] causing thirst: *Chopping logs is* **thirsty work.** **3** [F+**for**] having a strong desire for: *She was thirsty for power.* —**ily** *adv*

thir·teen /ˌθɜː'tiːn◄‖ˌθɜːr-/ *determiner, n, pron* (the number) 13. This number is thought to be unlucky by many people. —see TABLE 1 —**teenth** *determiner, n, pron, adv*

thir·ties /'θɜːtiz‖'θɜːr-/ *n* [P] **1** [*the*] also **'30s**— the 1930s (=the years from 1930 to 1939): *The film is set in the thirties during the Depression.* **2 in his/her/their thirties** aged from 30 to 39: *Most of my colleagues are in their thirties.* **3** [*the*] the numbers from 30 to 39

thir·ty /'θɜːti‖'θɜːrti/ *determiner, n, pron* (the number) 30. For many young people, thirty is the age at which they think one begins to grow old. —see TABLE 1 —see also **thirty pieces of silver** (SILVER) —**tieth** *determiner, n, pron, adv*

Thirty-nine Ar·ti·cles /ˌ··· '···/ [*the* + P] a set of basic teachings and beliefs of the Church of England, written in 1571, which the Church still asks its ministers to agree to in principle before appointment

thirty some·thing /'·· ˌ··/ *n* **1** the age range of 30–39 **2** a person of this age, esp. one who is seen as being successful in their profession, having a young family, middle-class, well-educated, and perhaps a YUPPIE: *a party for thirty somethings*

Thirty Years' War /ˌ··· '·/ [*the*] a European war fought mainly in Germany between 1618 and 1648. It led to the Habsburgs and the Holy Roman Empire losing power in Europe.

this¹ /ðɪs/ *determiner* **these** /ðiːz/ being the person, thing, idea, etc., which is understood or (about to be) mentioned: *I saw Mrs Jones this morning.* (=before midday today) | *Wait until you've heard this story!* | *These latest revelations will severely damage the President's reputation.* | *Who's this Mr Black we keep hearing about?* | *There will be another meeting later this week.* | *Come here* **this minute!** (=at once) | *They should have arrived by this time.* (=by now) | *If we keep losing money at this rate we may have to close the factory.* **2** being the one of two or more people or things that is nearer in time, place, thought, etc.: *You look in this box (here) and I'll look in that one (over there).* | *I'm surprised you like that picture; I prefer this one.* | *Is the meeting this Friday or next Friday?* **3** *infml* a certain: *This man came up to me in the street and started making rude suggestions ...* | *There were these two Irishmen called Pat and Mike ...*

this² *pron* **these 1** the thing, idea, action, etc., which is understood or (about to be) mentioned: *Who told you this?* | *Wait until you've heard this!* | *What's this?* | *This is what you must do.* | *Do it like this.* (=in the way shown) | *This has been the best year in the company's history.* | *We're getting some new machines next month, and this* (=this fact) *will help us to increase production.* **2** (used with **be**) the thing or person that is near or nearer in place, time, thought, etc.: *This is your book, isn't it?* | *"This is my sister." "How do you do?"* | *This is more comfortable than that one over there.* | (on the telephone)

Hullo! This is Jane Robinson speaking ... **3** this time or place; now or here: *I thought he'd have got back before this.* **4 this, that, and the other** also **this and that—** *infml* various things; all sorts of things: *We were sitting there talking about this, that, and the other.* **5 What's all 'this?** What is the trouble, matter, etc., here?

this³ *adv infml* to this degree: *I've never been out this late before.* | *Cut off about this much thread.*

This·be /ˈθɪzbi/ the female lover of Pyramus —see PYRAMUS AND THISBE

This is Your Life /ˌ·· ··· ˈ·/ a British and American television programme in which a famous person's life story ͵is told. All their friends and relations are brought to meet them, and the whole thing is a complete surprise to the person concerned.

this·tle /ˈθɪsəl/ *n* a wild plant with prickly leaves and yellow, white, or esp. purple flowers. The thistle is the national sign of Scotland.

this·tle·down /ˈθɪsəldaʊn/ *n* [U] the soft feathery substance fastened to the seeds of the thistle, by means of which they float through the air

thith·er /ˈðɪðəʳ‖ˈθɪðər/ *adv old use* to that place; in that direction —see also **hither and thither** (HITHER)

Thom·as /ˈtɒməs‖ˈtɑː-/, **Clar·ence** /ˈklærəns/ (1948–) a judge on the US Supreme Court since 1991. When Thomas was being questioned by members of Congress for his position on the Supreme Court, a woman who had once worked with him said that he made sexual advances towards her. This case was widely reported in the news. Congress did, however, approve Thomas for this position.

Thomas, Dy·lan /ˈdɪlən/ (1914–53) a Welsh poet best known for his play for radio, *Under Milk Wood*

Thomas, I·si·ah /aɪˈzaɪə/ (1961–) an American BASKETBALL player

Thomas, Ron·ald Stu·art /ˈrɒnəld ˈstjuːət‖ˈrɑːnəld ˈstuːərt/ (1913–) a Welsh poet who wrote about old Welsh values in poems such as *Song at the Year's Turning*

Thomas Cook /ˌ·· ˈ·/ a well-known TRAVEL AGENCY and holiday company in Britain —see also Thomas COOK

Thomas the Tank En·gine /ˌ··· ˈ· ͵··/ (a set of books, television programmes and films about) a little steam railway engine and his friends, very popular with British children in the 1950s, and again in the 80s and 90s

Thomp·son /ˈtɒmpsən‖ˈtɑː-/, **Da·ley** /ˈdeɪli/ (1958–) an English ATHLETE who won GOLD MEDALS in the DECATHLON at the 1980 and 1984 Olympic Games

Thom·son Di·rec·to·ry /ˈtɒmsən daɪˌrektəri, dɪ-‖ˈtɑːm-/ [*the*] a book in which local businesses advertise, giving their addresses and telephone numbers, and which is sent free of charge to every private house and business in Britain —compare YELLOW PAGES

thong /θɒŋ‖θɔːŋ/ *n* a narrow length of leather used as a fastening, whip, etc.

thongs /θɒŋz‖θɔːŋz/ *n* [P] *AmE & AustrE* a type of open shoe (SANDAL) which is held on by the toes and loose at the back —see PAIR (USAGE), and see picture at SHOE

Thor /θɔːʳ/ in NORSE MYTHOLOGY, the god of THUNDER usu. pictured with a HAMMER

tho·rax /ˈθɔːræks/ *n* **-races** /rəsiːz/ *or* **-raxes** *tech* **1** the part of the human body between the neck and ABDOMEN **2** a part like this in other animals **3** the part of an insect's body that carries the legs and wings —see picture at INSECT

Tho·reau /ˈθɔːrəʊ‖θəˈrəʊ/, **Henry David** (1817–62) an American writer best known for *Walden* and *Civil Disobedience*, a short piece of writing on refusing to obey unfair laws which influenced Gandhi and Martin Luther King, Jr. —see also WALDEN POND

thorn /θɔːn‖θɔːrn/ *n* **1** [C] a small sharp pointed growth on the stem of a plant: *the thorns on a rose bush* **2** [C;U] (*usu. in comb.*) a bush, tree, or other plant having such growths —see also HAWTHORN **3 a thorn in one's flesh/side** a continual cause of problems or annoyance —see also CROWN OF THORNS

thorn·y /ˈθɔːni‖ˈθɔːrni/ *adj* **1** prickly; having thorns **2** difficult to deal with; causing worry or trouble: *a thorny problem* —**iness** *n* [U]

thor·ough /ˈθʌrə‖ˈθʌrəʊ, ˈθʌrə/ *adj* **1** complete in every way: *a thorough search* | *They have promised a thorough inquiry into the plane crash.* **2** [A] being fully or completely (the stated thing): *This has been a thorough waste of time.* **3** (of a person) careful with regard to detail; METICULOUS: *She's very thorough.* — **~ly** *adv* : *After a hard day's work I feel thoroughly tired.* | *We thoroughly enjoyed your party.* — **~ness** *n* [U]

thor·ough·bred /ˈθʌrəbred‖ˈθʌrəʊ-, ˈθʌrə-/ *n, adj* (an animal, esp. a horse) descended from parents of one very good breed; the type of horse used in racing —compare PUREBLOODED, PUREBRED

thor·ough·fare /ˈθʌrəfeəʳ‖ˈθʌrəʊ-, ˈθʌrə-/ *n fml* **1** a road for public traffic, esp. a busy main road: *Nevskii Prospekt is Leningrad's busiest thoroughfare.* **2 No thoroughfare** (written on signs) not open to the public; no way through; no entrance

thor·ough·go·ing /ˌθʌrəˈgəʊɪŋ◂/ *adj* **1** very thorough; complete in every way: *a thoroughgoing search* **2** [A] complete; UTTER: *a thoroughgoing fool*

Thorpe /θɔːp‖θɔːrp/, **Jer·e·my** /ˈdʒerəmi/ (1929–) a British politician who was leader of the Liberal Party from 1967–76. He gave up the leadership of the party in 1976, when it was suggested that he had had a HOMOSEXUAL relationship several years earlier.

Thorpe, Jim /dʒɪm/ (1888–1953) an American ATHLETE who won GOLD MEDALS in the Olympics in 1912 and later played American FOOTBALL. Thorpe's Olympic medals were taken away from him when it was learned that he had once received money for playing BASEBALL, but many years after his death it was decided that he had won the medals fairly and they were returned to his family.

those /ðəʊz/ *pl. of* THAT¹,²: *Will those* (=the people) *who want to join the club please sign here?* —see ONE² (USAGE)

thou /ðaʊ/ *pron old use or bibl* **1** (used as the subject of a sentence with special old forms of verbs such as **art, canst, didst,** etc.) you: *"Thou hast spoken wisely."* (The Bible) —see also HOLIER-THAN-THOU **2 thou shalt not** the first words of most of the Ten Commandments in the Bible, e.g. *"Thou shalt not steal"*, now sometimes used humorously when giving a rule or warning: *"Thou shalt not covet thy neighbour's automobile!" I warned him.* | *Thou shalt not borrow my toothbrush.*

though¹ /ðəʊ/ *conj* **1** in spite of the fact that; even if: *Though/Even though it's hard work, I enjoy it.* | *Offenders were dealt with firmly though fairly.* | *Hardworking though he was, there was never enough money to pay the bills.* | *a competent, though hardly exciting, piece of work* **2 as though** as if: *He sounds as though he's got a sore throat.* —see also ALTHOUGH

though² *adv* (not used at the beginning of a CLAUSE) in spite of the fact; NEVERTHELESS: *It's hard work; I enjoy it though.* | *He's a bad manager. There's no reason, though, to dismiss him.*

thought¹ /θɔːt/ *past tense & participle of* THINK

thought² *n* **1** [U] the action of thinking; REFLECTION: *He sat there, deep in thought.* **2** [U] serious consideration: *Give her offer plenty of thought before you accept it.* **3** [C (**about, on, of**)] something that is thought; a product of thinking; idea, opinion, etc.: *Let me have your thoughts on the subject.* | *With his piercing gaze I almost imagined he could read my thoughts.* | *"Why don't we go by train?" "Yes, that's a thought."* (=a good idea) | *I've just had a thought — what will happen if she forgets to come?* | *"Do you think she's going to leave?" "The thought had crossed my mind."* (=I had already considered this possibility.) **4** [U (**of**) *usu. in questions and negatives*] intention: *I had no thought of annoying you.* | *You must give up all thought of John.* (=must not think about him or hope to be with him) **5** [U] the particular way of thinking of a social group, person, period, country, etc.: *ancient Greek thought* **6** [C;U (**for**)] (an example of) attention or consideration: *With no thought for her own safety she jumped into the river to save the drowning child.* | *"I'm sorry to disturb you." "That's all right; don't give it a thought."* —see also SCHOOL OF THOUGHT, SECOND THOUGHT

thought·ful /ˈθɔːtfəl/ adj **1** (showing that one is) thinking deeply; PENSIVE: *The girl looked thoughtful for a moment and then answered.* | *a thoughtful frown* | *You look thoughtful; is anything wrong?* **2** apprec paying attention to the wishes, feelings, needs, etc., of other people; CONSIDERATE: *It was very thoughtful of you to stop and give me a lift.* | *a thoughtful person* – ~ly adv – ~ness n [U]

thought·less /ˈθɔːtləs/ adj not thinking; showing a selfish or careless lack of thought: *It was thoughtless of you to forget your sister's birthday.* – ~ly adv – ~ness n [U]

thought-out /ˌ· ˈ·◂/ adj produced or developed after consideration: *a well|badly thought-out scheme* –see also THINK out

Thought Po·lice /ˈ· ·ˌ·/ [the] a type of police force, in George Orwell's NOVEL *Nineteen Eighty-Four*, who try to control and restrict people's thoughts. The expression is sometimes used to describe people who try to tell other people what opinions they should have and what words they should use: *The left-wing feminist thought police tell us that we can no longer use the word "mankind".* –see also NINETEEN EIGHTY-FOUR

Thoughts of Chair·man Mao /ˌ· ·ˌ·· ˈ·/, The a book containing the teachings of Mao Zedong, first produced in China in 1964, and also known as the **little red book**

thou·sand /ˈθaʊzənd/ determiner, n, pron thousand or thousands (the number) 1000: *There were thousands* (=a very large number) *of people there.* –see TABLE 1

Thousand and One Nights /ˌ·· · ˌ· ˈ·/, The see ARABIAN NIGHTS

thou·sandth /ˈθaʊzənθ/ determiner, n, pron, adv 1000th – see TABLE 1

thral·dom BrE ‖ **thralldom** AmE /ˈθrɔːldəm/ n [U] lit slavery

thrall /θrɔːl/ n [(to)] lit **1** [C] a slave; SERF **2** [U] slavery: (fig.) *Her beauty held him in thrall.*

thrash /θræʃ/ v **1** [T] to hit hard (as if) with a whip or stick, as a punishment **2** [T] infml to defeat thoroughly, esp. in a game **3** [I+adv/prep, esp. ABOUT] to move wildly or violently about: *The fishes thrashed about in the net.*

thrash sthg. ↔ **out** phr v [T] **1** to talk about thoroughly in order to find an answer: *We thrashed out our differences round the conference table.* **2** to produce by much talk and consideration: *After a whole night of argument we thrashed out a plan|an agreement.*

thread

— thread —

thread¹ /θred/ n **1** [C;U] (a line of) very thin cord made by spinning cotton, wool, silk, etc., used in sewing or weaving: (*a piece of*) *cotton|nylon thread* **2** [C (of)] something with the fineness or thinness of this: *a thread of light* **3** [C (of)] a line of reasoning connecting the parts of an argument or story: *I'm afraid I've lost the thread of your argument.* **b** a repeated pattern or idea: *There is a consistent thread running through all these policies.* **4** [C] a raised line that winds round the outside of a screw or the inside of a NUT (2), BOLT¹ (1), etc.: *The thread's gone.* (=broken)–see also **hang by a thread** (HANG¹) –see picture at SCREW

thread² v [T] **1** to pass a thread through: *to thread a needle* (=put one end of a thread through the EYE (=the hole) of a needle) | *a scarf threaded with gold* **2** [(onto)] to put (a film or TAPE¹ (2)) in place on an apparatus **3** [(TOGETHER)] to connect by running a thread through: *The little girl threaded the shells together and wore them round her neck.* **4** to cut a THREAD¹ (4) on (a screw, NUT (2), BOLT¹ (1), etc.) **5 thread one's way through** to make one's way carefully through (streets, crowds, forests, etc.)

thread·bare /ˈθredbeəʳ/ adj **1** (of material, clothes, etc.) very thin because of a lot of use; very worn **2** having been so much used as to be no longer interesting or effective: *threadbare excuses*

Threadneedle Street see OLD LADY OF THREADNEEDLE STREET

threat /θret/ n **1** [C;U] an expression of an intention to hurt, punish, cause pain, etc., esp. if one's instructions or demands are not obeyed: *Those children do not take their father's threats very seriously.* | *They used the threat of strike action to enforce their demands.* | *They said they would invade us, but it's just an* **empty threat** – *they have no army.* [+to-v] *They carried out their threat to kill her.* | *I obeyed his orders, but only* **under threat of** punishment. **2** [C (to) usu. sing.] a person, thing, or idea regarded as a possible danger: *While the killer goes free he is a threat to everyone in the town.* | *The existence of these weapons poses a grave threat to the future of the world.* | *Some people see computers as a threat to their jobs.* **3** [C (of) usu. sing.] a sign, warning, or possibility of coming danger: *The clouds brought a threat of rain.* | *The threat of bankruptcy hung over the company.*

threat·en /ˈθretn/ v **1** [T (with)] **a** to express a threat against (someone): *The strikers were threatened with dismissal if they did not return to work.* | *a threatening letter* **b** to express (a threat) against someone: *He threatened a terrible vengeance.* [+to-v] *The terrorists threatened to blow up the plane if their demands were not met.* **2** [T] to give warning of (something bad): *The black clouds threatened rain.* | *a threatening sky* **3** [I] (of something bad) to seem likely to happen: *While danger threatens we must all be on our guard.* **4** [T] to be a danger or threat to; seem likely to (harm, spoil, ruin, etc.): *Noisy traffic threatens the peace of the village.* | *He's very unhappy about her promotion; he seems to feel that his own job is threatened.* (=that he may lose it) [+to-v] *The incident threatens to ruin his chances in the election.* – ~**ingly** adv

three /θriː/ determiner, n, pron **1** (the number) 3 –see also **two's company, three's a crowd** (TWO); see TABLE 1 –see also PACKET OF THREE **2** (**yes, sir, yes sir**) **three bags full** a phrase from the NURSERY RHYME (=an old song or poem for children) *Baa, baa, black sheep.* The phrase is often used humorously when saying that someone is giving you a lot of orders and expects you to obey them all without asking any questions

Three Blind Mice /ˌ· · ˈ·/ a NURSERY RHYME (=an old song or poem for children), about three blind mice who have their tails cut off by a farmer's wife: *Three blind mice! See how they run!*

three-cor·nered /ˌ· ˈ··◂/ adj **1** having three corners **2** having three competitors, parties, etc.: *The election was a three-cornered fight.*

three-D , 3-D /ˌ· ˈθriː ˈdiː·◂/ n [U] a THREE-DIMENSIONAL (1) form or appearance: *They watched a horror film in 3D.*

three-day e·vent /ˌ· · ·ˈ·/ n esp. BrE a horse-riding competition which lasts three days and includes DRESSAGE, CROSS-COUNTRY riding, and SHOW JUMPING

three-day week /ˌ· · ˈ·/ n a working week of three days instead of the usual five, caused by lack of work or other bad economic conditions

three-di·men·sion·al /ˌ· ·ˈ···◂/ adj **1** having or seeming to have length, depth, and height **2** described or shown in great depth or detail, so as to seem alive; LIFELIKE: *The characters in his novels are always three-dimensional.*

three-half·pence /ˌ· ˈ··/ also **penny-halfpenny**– n [U] BrE 1½d; (the value of) one and a half old pennies (PENNY)

Three Kings /ˌ· ˈ·/ [the + P] see MAGI

three-leg·ged race /ˌ· ˈ··· ·/ n a race run by competitors in pairs, each pair having their inside legs tied together. These races are mainly run at young school children's sports days.

three-line whip /ˌ· · ˈ·/ n (in Britain) an order given by party leaders to Members of Parliament belonging to their party, telling them that they must vote in a particular way or be considered disloyal to their party

Three Lit·tle Pigs /ˌ· ·· ˈ·/, The a children's story in which three little pigs build houses of different materials which a BIG BAD WOLF tries to blow down

3M /θriː ˈem/ Minnesota Mining and Manufacturing; an American company that makes many different industrial products and goods used in the home

Three Men in a Boat /ˌ· ˌ· ·· ˈ·/ a humorous book written in 1889 by Jerome K. Jerome, about three men and a dog who row up the Thames on holiday

Three Mile Is·land /ˌ· · '··/ the place in Pennsylvannia in the US where, in 1979, a NUCLEAR power plant went wrong, causing fears of a terrible accident. This led to changes in the way some of these plants are made and stopped the building of others.

Three Mus·ket·eers /ˌ· ··'·/ tdmk (in the US) a CANDY BAR (=bar-shaped sweet) that has chocolate on the outside and inside

Three Musketeers, The a NOVEL by Alexandre Dumas, set in 17th century France, about three sword fighters who guard Louis XIII, the king of France. They are remembered for saying "All for one, and one for all!", meaning that they would always support and protect one another.

three·pence /'θrepəns, 'θrʌ-/ n BrE [U] 3d; (the value of) three old pennies (PENNY): It cost threepence.

three·pen·ny bit /ˌθrepəni 'bɪt, ˌθrʌ-/ a small round silver coin or a small 12-sided copper coin formerly used in Britain with a value of three old pennies (PENNY)

Threepenny Op·e·ra /ˌ·· '···/, **The** a retelling of The Beggars Opera, by Bertold Brecht and Kurt Weill

three·piece /'· ·/ adj [A] consisting of or made in three matching parts: a three-piece suit (=matching trousers, JACKET, and WAISTCOAT) | a three-piece suite (=two matching chairs and a SOFA)

three·ply /'· ·/ adj (of wool, wood, etc.) having three LAYERS, STRANDS, etc. to make one stronger piece of material

three·point turn /ˌ· · '·/ n an operation for turning a vehicle in the opposite direction in a small space by going forwards, then backwards, then forwards again. The ability to perform this is part of the British driving test and some US state driving tests.

3.2 beer /ˌθriː tuː 'biəʳ/ n [U] beer which is 3.2 per cent alcohol; sold in some US states to people under the legal drinking age, and sometimes made available to soldiers

three·quar·ter /ˌ· '···•/ adj [A] consisting of three fourths (¾) of the whole: a three-quarter length coat

three·ring cir·cus /ˌ· · '··/ n a CIRCUS which has three areas of entertainment going on at the same time 2 AmE a very busy, confusing place: It was like a three-ring circus in there.

three R's /ˌθriː 'ɑːz‖-'ɑːrz/ [the+P] reading, writing, and ARITHMETIC (=working with numbers) considered as forming the base of children's education. The expression comes from the sound at the beginning of the words "reading", "writing", and "(a)rithmetic".

three·score /'θriːskɔːʳ/ determiner, n, pron lit or poet 1 60 2 threescore years and ten phrase from the Bible 70 years, viewed as the average length of time a person is likely to live

three·some /'θriːsəm/ n [usu. sing.] infml a group of three people or things, often as sexual partners

three·star /'· ·/ adj [A] of a good quality or standard (on a scale which has one-star as the lowest quality and five-star as the highest): a three-star hotel

Three Stoog·es /ˌ· '··/ [the] three American COMEDIANS, named Curly, Larry, and Moe, who appeared in a television show in the 1950s. The Three Stooges did silly things, often blamed each other for mistakes, and often hit each other with different objects, such as FRYING PANS.

three·wheel·er /ˌ· '··•/ n a car with three wheels

Three Wise Men /ˌ· · '·/ [the + P] see MAGI

Three Wise Mon·keys /ˌ· · '··/ [the+P] a representation of three MONKEYS sitting in a row, one with its hands covering its ears, another with its hands covering its eyes and the third with its hands covering its mouth. They are supposed to represent "see no evil, hear no evil, speak no evil".

thren·o·dy /'θrenədi/ n lit a funeral song for the dead

thresh /θreʃ/ v [I;T] to separate the grain from (corn, wheat, or other grain-bearing plants) by beating it with a special tool or with a **threshing machine** - - **er** n

thresh·old /'θreʃhəʊld, -ʃəʊld/ n 1 (a piece of wood or stone fixed beneath) a doorway forming an entrance to a building. It is an old custom for a newly married woman to be carried across the threshold of her new house by her husband. 2 [usu. sing.] the place or point of beginning, esp. of an important event or new development. Scientists are now **on the threshold of** a better understanding of how the human brain works. | Its opponents say the new missile will lower the **nuclear threshold.** (=the point at which NUCLEAR weapons begin to be used in a war) 3 esp. tech the lowest level at which something begins to operate, happen, produce an effect, etc.: She has a very low threshold of pain|a low pain threshold. (=She feels pain easily.) | a 15% increase in tax thresholds

threw /θruː/ past tense of THROW

thrice /θraɪs/ adv old use three times

thrift /θrɪft/ n 1 [U] fml wise and careful use of money and goods; avoidance of waste 2 [C] also **thrift in·sti·tu·tion** /'· ··,··‖-·/— AmE for SAVINGS BANK or SAVINGS AND LOAN ASSOCIATION

thrift·shop /'θrɪftʃɒp‖-ʃɑːp/ n AmE a shop which sells used goods, such as clothing or things to be used in the house, often to raise money for CHARITY

thrift·y /'θrɪfti/ adj using money and goods carefully and wisely; showing or practising thrift: a thrifty housewife|meal —ily adv —iness n [U] —see also SPENDTHRIFT

thrill¹ /θrɪl/ n (an event or situation that produces) a sudden very strong feeling of excitement, joy, or sometimes fear, that seems to flow round the body like a wave: Meeting the famous footballer was a great thrill for the children. | I felt a thrill of terror as the door began to creak open.

thrill² v [I (at, to);T] to (cause to) feel a thrill or thrills: We thrilled to (=when we heard) his tales of South Sea adventure. | What a thrilling game; the winner was in doubt until the last minute. | (fig.) We were thrilled (=very pleased) to hear about your new job. - **-ingly** adv

thrill·er /'θrɪləʳ/ n a book, play, or film that tells a very exciting story, esp. of crime and violence

thrive /θraɪv/ v **thrived** or **throve** /θrəʊv/, **thrived** [I] to develop well and be healthy, strong, or successful; FLOURISH: Few plants or animals thrive in the desert. | the thriving computer industry | a thriving business | How are your children? Thriving, I hope!

thrive on phr v [T] to enjoy and do well as a result of, perhaps unexpectedly: Most people wouldn't like to have so much responsibility, but she seems to thrive on it.

throat /θrəʊt/ n 1 the passage from the back of the mouth down inside the neck that divides into two passages, one taking air to the lungs, the other taking food to the stomach: I've got a fish bone stuck in my throat. | She's off work because of a sore throat. 2 the front of the neck: The murderer cut the old man's throat. —see picture at HEAD 3 **at each other's throats** fighting, arguing, disagreeing, etc., bitterly and violently 4 **cut one's own throat** to behave in a way, esp. through pride or anger, which will only bring harm to oneself: We'll only be cutting our own throats if we try to undercut them. 5 **force/thrust/ram something down someone's throat** to force someone to accept or listen to something, esp. one's ideas or opinions, unwillingly 6 **-throated** /θrəʊtɪd/ having a throat of the stated kind: a red-throated bird —see also CUTTHROAT, DEEP THROAT, **jump down someone's throat** (JUMP¹ (11)), **stick in one's throat** (STICK²)

throat·y /'θrəʊti/ adj infml (of a person) having a low rough voice: a throaty singer | You sound throaty today. Have you got a cold? —ily adv —iness n [U]

throb¹ /θrɒb‖θrɑːb/ v -bb- [I] (of the heart, a machine, etc.) to beat heavily and regularly: My pulse was throbbing with excitement. | Her leg was throbbing with pain. | throbbing drums

throb² n a strong low continuous beat: the throb of machinery —see also HEARTTHROB

throes /θrəʊz/ n [P] 1 esp. lit violent sudden pains, esp. caused by dying (esp. in the phrase **death throes**) 2 **in the throes of** struggling with (some difficulty): a country in the throes of war | We're just in the throes of moving to a new house.

throm·bo·sis /θrɒm'bəʊsɪs‖θrɑːm-/ n -ses /siːz/ [C;U] the medical condition of having a CLOT (=a thickened or solid mass of blood) in a blood tube or the heart —see also CORONARY²

throne /θrəʊn/ n 1 [C] the ceremonial chair of a king, queen, BISHOP, etc. 2 [the+S] the rank or office of a king or queen: He was only 15 when he **came to the throne/ascended the throne.** (=became king) —see also **power behind the throne** (POWER¹ (12)) 3 [the] humor *sl* a TOILET (1): *Sorry, you can't see him just now – he's on the throne.*

throng[1] /θrɒŋ‖θrɔːŋ/ *n* [C (**of**)+*sing.|pl. v*] a large crowd (of people or things): *Throngs of visitors crowded through the art gallery.*

throng[2] *v* [I+*adv|prep*;T] to go (as if) in a crowd, filling a place or building: *People thronged to see the new play. | Passengers thronged the station waiting for their trains. | streets thronged with Christmas shoppers*

throt·tle[1] /ˈθrɒtl‖ˈθrɑːtl/ *v* [T] to seize (someone) tightly by the throat to stop them breathing; STRANGLE: *She nearly throttled me when she tied my tie for me. | (fig.) These government restrictions are going to throttle our trade.*

throttle (sthg. ↔) **down** *phr v* [I;T] to reduce the flow of petrol, oil, etc., to (an engine) so as to reduce speed

throttle[2] *n* a VALVE (=a doorlike part) in a pipe that opens and closes to control the flow of liquid, gas, oil, etc., into an engine

through[1] /θruː/ *prep* **1** in at one side, end, or surface of (something) and out at the other: *The train went through a tunnel. | I threw it through the window. | Water flows through this pipe. | He pushed his way through the crowd to the door. | We couldn't see through the mist. | Is it quicker to drive round the town, or straight through the centre? | (fig.) He drove straight through (=did not stop at) a red traffic light.* **2** by means of: *I got this job through an employment agency. | It was through John that they found out.* **3** as a result of; because of: *The war was lost through bad organization. | How many working days were lost through sickness?* **4** a from the beginning to the end of: *He is very weak and is not expected to live through the night. | I read right through|half way through the article but found it uninteresting. | The company is going through a difficult period.* **b** into and out of a process or operation that has a beginning and end: *The new law has completed its passage through Congress. | We went through the security check and boarded the plane.* **5** over the surface of or within the limits of: *We travelled through France and Belgium on our holidays.* **6** among or between the parts or single members of: *The monkeys swung through the trees. | I searched through my papers for the missing document.* **7** having finished, or so as to finish, successfully: *Did you get through your exams? | Her encouragement helped him through the crisis.* **8** AmE (esp. in expressions of time) up to and including: *Wednesday through Saturday* –see INCLUSIVE (USAGE) **9** against and in spite of (a noise): *The politician struggled to speak through the shouts of the crowd.* –see also THRU

through[2] *adv* **1** in at one side, end, or surface, and out at the other: *The guard at the entrance wouldn't let us through.* **2** [(**to**)] all the way; along the whole distance: *Does this train go* **right through** *to London?* **3** from the beginning to the end; to completion: *Have you read the letter (right) through?* **4** to a favourable or successful state: *"How did you do in your examinations?" "I got* **through** *with good marks."* **5** [(**to**)] *esp. BrE* (when telephoning) in a state of being connected to a person or place: *"Can you* **put** *me* **through** *to Mr Jones?" "You're through now."* **6** in every part; thoroughly: *I got* **wet through** *in the rain. | Have you really thought this matter through?* **7 through and through** completely; in every way

▷ USAGE When you telephone in Britain, the operator might ask *Are you* **through?** meaning "Are you connected to the other speaker?". In the US, this question could mean "Have you finished?".◁

through[3] *adj* **1** [A] a allowing a continuous journey: *Is this a through train or do I have to change? | The sign says "No Through Road", so we'll have to go another way.* **b** coming from and going to somewhere outside a local area: *through traffic* **2** [F (**with**)] *infml* finished; done: *I'm not through just yet; I should be finished in an hour.* **3** [F (**with**)] *infml* having no further relationship: *Jane and I are through. | I'm through with men|alcohol|you.*

through·out[1] /θruːˈaʊt/ *prep* in, to, through, or during every part of: *It rained throughout the night. | The disease spread throughout the country.*

throughout[2] *adv* (usu. at the end of a sentence) right through; in, to, through, or during every part: *The house has been repainted throughout. | The army remained loyal throughout.*

through·put /ˈθruːpʊt/ *n* the amount of work, materials,

etc., dealt with in a given time, e.g. by a computer

Through the Look·ing-Glass /ˌ· · ˈ·· ·/ a children's book by Lewis Carroll, in which Alice visits a strange world –see also ALICE IN WONDERLAND, TWEEDLEDUM AND TWEEDLEDEE

through·way /ˈθruːweɪ/ *n* a THRUWAY

throve /θrəʊv/ *past tense of* THRIVE

throw[1] /θrəʊ/ *v* **threw** /θruː/, **thrown** /θrəʊn/ **1** [I;T (**at, to**)] to cause (something) to move rapidly through the air by a sudden movement or straightening of the arm: *It's my turn to throw. | He threw the ball 100 metres. | Someone threw a stone at me. | Throw the ball to me. | [+obj(i)+obj(d)] Throw me the ball. | (fig.) She threw me an angry look.* (=looked angrily at me) | *(fig.) We can't solve this problem simply by* **throwing money at it.** (=by no other method except spending a lot of money) **2** [T+*obj*+*adv|prep*] to move or put suddenly or forcefully into a particular position or state: *If you keep breaking the club rules you'll get thrown out.* (=you'll be forced to leave) | *The general threw a ring of soldiers around the area to prevent the riots from spreading. | She threw herself down on the bed. | This new system has thrown us all into confusion. | The unexpected attack momentarily threw her off balance but she quickly regained control.* **3** [T+*obj*+*adv|prep*, esp. OFF, ON] to put on or take off (a garment) hastily: *She threw off her clothes and jumped into the water. | She threw a shawl over her shoulders.* **4** [T] to move (a SWITCH, handle, etc.) in order to connect or disconnect parts of a machine, apparatus, etc. **5** [T] to send out or direct: *The sun threw shadows on the grass. | The single light bulb threw a dim light.* | (fig.) *I wonder if this new clue will* **throw** *any further* **light on** *the mystery.* | (fig.) *This new evidence* **throws doubt on** *his explanation.* (=suggests that it is not true) **6** [T] to hit (someone) with (a blow, stroke, etc.): *He was disqualified for throwing an illegal punch.* **7** [T] to roll (a DICE) **8** [T] to get (a particular number) by rolling a DICE: *I threw a six.* **9** [T] to cause to fall to the ground: *His horse threw him.* **10** [T] *infml* to arrange or give (a party, dinner, etc.) **11** [T] *infml* to confuse; shock: *His unexpected answer threw me for a moment.* **12** [T] to shape (an object) on a POTTER'S WHEEL **13** [T] to make (one's voice) appear to be coming from somewhere other than its actual place of origin: *Ventriloquists have to be able to throw their voice.* **14** [T] *infml* to lose (a fight or match) on purpose **15** [T] *infml* to have a sudden attack of (usu. violent feelings): *I can't tell my parents – they'd* **throw** *a fit! | The little girl* **threw** *a* **tantrum|scene** *when she was told to stay behind.*

16 throw something (back) in someone's face *infml* to mention to someone in a blaming way something that they have done; REPROACH someone with something: *But all that happened years ago; why do you throw it (back) in my face now?* **17 throw caution to the winds** to behave intentionally in a way that shows no concern for the possible (bad) results of one's actions; take risks on purpose **18 throw cold water on** to speak discouragingly about (a plan, suggestion, etc.) **19 throw good money after bad** to waste money by spending it on something that has already failed or is certain to bring no good result **20 throw oneself at: a** to rush violently towards (someone) **b** to attempt forcefully to win the love of (someone) **21 throw oneself into** to do or take part in eagerly and actively **22 throw one's hat into the ring** to (declare one's intention to) join in and compete **23 throw one's weight about/around** *derog* to give orders to others, because one thinks one is important **24 throw the book at** *infml* (esp. of the police or a judge) to make all possible charges against (someone) – ~ **er** *n*

throw sthg. ↔ **away** *phr v* [T] **1** to get rid of (something not wanted or needed); DISCARD: *You should throw away all those old clothes you never wear.* **2** to lose by foolishness; waste: *This could be the best chance you'll ever have; don't throw it away.* –see also THROWAWAY

throw sbdy./sthg. **back on** *phr v* [T *usu. pass.*] to cause to have to depend on (something) after something else has failed: *Her friends had deserted her, and she was thrown back on her own resources.*

throw sthg. ↔ **in** *phr v* [T] *infml* **1** to supply in addition to something else without increasing the price: *When I bought the house, I got the carpets and curtains thrown in.* **2** AmE to add to a discussion, plan, etc.: *I threw in an idea that would shorten the production process.* **3 throw in the sponge/towel** *infml* to admit defeat

throw sbdy./sthg. ↔ **off** phr v [T] **1** to free oneself from (something bad); recover from: *It took me a week to throw off my cold.* **2** to escape from (someone or something chasing one): *We'll throw them off at the bridge.* **3** to cause (someone) to lose their way, direction, etc.: *The criminal dived into the river to* **throw** *the police dogs* **off the track.** —see also THROW¹ (2)

throw sthg. **open** phr v [T (to)] **1** to allow the general public to enter (a place): *The queen has thrown open her castle for the summer.* **2** to make open: *The competition was thrown open to sportsmen from all countries.*

throw sbdy./sthg. ↔ **out** phr v [T] **1** to get rid of; DISCARD or force to leave: *You really should throw out that filthy old sofa and get a new one.* **2** to refuse to accept; REJECT: *The committee threw out my suggestions.* **3** to say carelessly or without considering the result: *The teacher threw out a few ideas* (=offered some suggestions) *and asked the students to write an essay.* **4** BrE to confuse or worry: *Her sudden resignation completely threw me out.*

throw sbdy. ↔ **over** phr v [T] infml to end a relationship with

throw sthg./sbdy. ↔ **together** phr v [T often pass.] **1** sometimes derog to build or make hastily: *I just threw the meal together so I hope it's all right.* **2** to bring together, esp. into a relationship: *Chance threw us together at a party.*

throw up phr v **1** [T] (**throw** sthg. ↔ **up**) infml to stop doing: *I hear you've thrown up your job.* **2** [I] infml for VOMIT¹ **3** [T] (**throw** sbdy./sthg. ↔ **up**) to produce; bring into existence: *The discussion has thrown up a lot of interesting ideas.*

throw² n **1** an act of throwing **2** the distance to which something is thrown: *a throw of 100 metres | a record throw* **3** the result of throwing in DARTS, DICE, etc. —see also STONE'S THROW

throw·a·way /ˈθrəʊəweɪ/ adj [A] **1** (of a remark) said with false carelessness, seeming to have no regard for the effect: *The comedy script is full of throwaway lines.* **2** intended to be thrown away after use: *a throwaway paper cup* —see also THROW AWAY

throw·back /ˈθrəʊbæk/ n [(to)] (an example of) a return to something in the past: *These modern fashions are a throwback to the 1950s.*

throw·in /ˈ· ·/ n (in football) an act of throwing the ball back on from the side of the field after it has gone out of play

thru /θruː/ adj, adv, prep AmE infml through

thrum /θrʌm/ v -mm- [I (on);T] rare to STRUM

thrush¹ /θrʌʃ/ n a singing bird with a brownish back and spotted breast —see picture at BIRD

thrush² n [U] an infectious disease of the mouth and throat, esp. in children, and of the VAGINA in adult women, caused by the FUNGUS Candida Albicans

thrust¹ /θrʌst/ v thrust **1** [T+obj+adv/prep] to push forcefully and suddenly: *The thieves thrust him into the back room and tied him up. | He thrust the gun into his pocket.|* (fig.) *The actress said she had been perfectly happy until fame was* **thrust upon** *her.* (=she became famous without wanting to be) **2** [I (at)] to make a sudden forward stroke with a sword, knife, etc.

thrust² n **1** [C] a forceful forward movement or push: *The invading army made a sudden thrust to the north. |* (fig.) *The company is planning a big new thrust into the Japanese market.* **2** [U] tech the force pushing an object, esp. a plane, forward; forward-moving power of an engine: *This rocket engine develops several thousand pounds of thrust.* **3** [U (of)] the main meaning or central point: *The thrust of her argument was that all state interference in industry was wrong.* —see also CUT AND THRUST

thrust·er /ˈθrʌstər/ n a small ROCKET, esp. for controlling the height or direction of a spacecraft

thru·way , throughway /ˈθruːweɪ/ n AmE a very wide road for high-speed traffic which one must usu. pay to use

thud¹ /θʌd/ n a dull sound as caused by a heavy object falling to the ground: *The encyclopedia fell to the floor with a thud.*

thud² v -dd- [I+adv/prep] to move, fall, or hit something so as to make a thud: *The arrow thudded into the target.*

thug /θʌg/ n a violent man, esp. a criminal

thumb¹ /θʌm/ n **1** the short thick finger that is set apart from the other four —see picture at HAND **2** the part of

a GLOVE that fits over this **3** all **thumbs** infml very awkward with the hands: *I seem to be all thumbs today.* **4** **thumbs down** (an expression of dissatisfaction or disapproval shown by holding the thumb downwards): *Our plan got the thumbs down.* (=was not accepted) **5** **thumbs up** (an expression of satisfaction, victory, or approval shown by holding the thumb upwards): *The chairman has given our plan the thumbs up.* (=approved it) **6** **under someone's thumb** infml under the control, power, or influence of someone —see also GREEN THUMB, TOM THUMB, RULE OF THUMB, OPPOSABLE THUMB, **twiddle one's thumbs** (TWIDDLE¹)

thumb² v [T] **1** infml to ask passing motorists for (a free ride) by holding out one's hand with the thumb raised: *I thumbed a lift to London.* —compare HITCH¹ (2) **2** **thumb one's nose at** infml to refuse to accept or consider, esp. in an offensive way: *Young people in the 1960s thumbed their noses at traditional sexual morality.*

thumb through (sthg.) phr v [I;T] to look through (a book) quickly

thumb·nail¹ /ˈθʌmneɪl/ n the nail on the upper outer end of the thumb

thumbnail² adj [A] (of something written) quite short: *a thumbnail sketch/description*

thumb·screw /ˈθʌmskruː/ n an instrument used in former times to cause great pain by crushing the thumbs

thumb·tack /ˈθʌmtæk/ n AmE for DRAWING PIN —see picture at PIN

thump¹ /θʌmp/ v **1** [I+adv/prep;T] to hit with a heavy blow: *The boxer's fist thumped into the punchbag. | The little boy threatened to thump his brother. |* (fig.) *He thumped out a tune on the old piano.* **2** [I] to produce a repeated dull sound by beating, falling, walking heavily, etc.: *The excitement made her heart thump. |* (fig.) *I've got a thumping headache.*

thump² n (the dull sound of) a heavy blow

thump·ing /ˈθʌmpɪŋ/ adj, adv [A] esp. BrE infml very (big): *a thumping great house | The government was returned to power with a thumping majority.*

thun·der¹ /ˈθʌndər/ n [U] **1** the loud explosive noise that usu. follows a flash of lightning: *There's thunder in the air.* (=thunder seems likely) | (fig.) *We could hear the thunder of distant guns. |* (fig.) *He came in with a face* **like/as black as thunder.** (=showing great anger) **2** in **thunder** old-fash (used for giving force to an angry question): *What in thunder do you think you're doing?* —see also BLOOD-AND-THUNDER, **steal someone's thunder** (STEAL¹)

▷ USAGE Note the fixed phrase **thunder and lightning.**◁

thunder² v **1** [it+I] to produce thunder: *The dog always hides under the bed when it thunders.* **2** [I+adv/prep] **a** to produce loud deep sounds like this: *The guns thundered in the distance.* **b** to move making such sounds: *The huge aircraft thundered along the runway.* **3** [T (OUT)] to shout loudly: *"Get out!" he thundered.* — **~er** n

Thun·der·birds /ˈθʌndəbɜːdz‖-dərbɜːrdz/ a popular British television programme for children in which the characters are PUPPETS. It is about a family of brothers who save people in danger using special aircraft and other vehicles, called **Thunderbird 1, Thunderbird 2,** etc. The programmes used to begin with the words "Thunderbirds are go!" —see colour picture on page 686

thun·der·bolt /ˈθʌndəbəʊlt‖-dər-/ n **1** a flash of lightning and crash of thunder together **2** an imaginary weapon thrown by the god Jupiter, causing thunder and lightning **3** a sudden event which causes great shock, anxiety, etc.: *The news of his death was a real thunderbolt.*

thun·der·clap /ˈθʌndəklæp‖-ər-/ n a single loud crash of thunder

thun·der·cloud /ˈθʌndəklaʊd‖-ər-/ n a large dark cloud producing thunder and lightning

Thun·der·er /ˈθʌndərər/, **The** an informal name for *The Times* newspaper

thun·der·head /ˈθʌndəhed ‖ -ʳr-/ n a large cloud which appears very tall and which will produce thunder

thun·der·ing /ˈθʌndərɪŋ/ adj, adv [A] BrE old-fash infml very (great, bad, severe, etc.): *That's a thundering (great) lie!*

thun·der·ous /ˈθʌndərəs/ adj extremely loud: *thunderous applause* – ~**ly** adv

thun·der·storm /ˈθʌndəstɔːm‖-dərstɔːrm/ n a storm of very heavy rain and thunder and lightning

thun·der·struck /ˈθʌndəstrʌk‖-ər-/ adj [F] extremely surprised; shocked

thun·der·y /ˈθʌndəri/ adj (of the weather) giving signs that thunder is likely

Thur·ber /ˈθɜːbəʳ‖ˈθɜːr-/, James (1894–1961) an American humorous writer and CARTOONIST (=person who makes humorous drawings). His work appeared often in *New Yorker* magazine.

Thurs·day /ˈθɜːzdi‖ˈθɜːr-/ (written abbrev. **Thur.** or **Thurs.**) n [C;U] the fourth day of the week, between Wednesday and Friday: *He'll arrive on Thursday.* | (*BrE infml & AmE*) *He'll arrive Thursday.* | *It happened on Thursday afternoon.* | *She left last Thursday.* | *We do all our shopping on Thursdays.* | *My birthday is on a Thursday this year.* –see DAY (CULTURAL NOTE)

thus /ðʌs/ adv fml **1** in this manner; in the way stated: *The police tapped the terrorists' phone, and the information thus collected was used at their trial.* | (*old use*) *Thus said the Lord...* **2** by this means or with this result; HENCE: *The new machines will work twice as fast, thus greatly reducing costs.* **3 thus far** until now; to this point

thwack /θwæk/ n, v WHACK

thwart¹ /θwɔːt‖θwɔːrt/ v [T] to prevent from happening or succeeding: *Our plans for a picnic were thwarted by the rain.*

thwart² n tech a seat across a rowing boat, for the rower

thy /ðaɪ/ determiner old use (*possessive form of* **thou**) your: *We praise thy name, o Lord.*

thyme /taɪm/ n [U] a small plant grown for its leaves, which are used for giving a special taste to food

thy·mus /ˈθaɪməs/ also **thymus gland** /ˈ·· ˌ·/ — n an organ in the chest or neck of most animals with backbones, which helps develop the body's ability to fight disease, and is most active in the young

thy·roid /ˈθaɪrɔɪd/ also **thyroid gland** /ˈ·· ˌ·/ — n an organ in the neck that has an important effect on the development of the mind and body –see picture at RESPIRATORY

thy·self /ðaɪˈself/ pron old use **1** (*reflexive form of* **thou**) **2** (*strong form of* **thou**) –see YOURSELF (USAGE)

ti /tiː/ also **si**– n [S;U] the seventh note in the SOL-FA musical scale

Ti·a Ma·ri·a /ˌtiːə məˈriːə/ n [C,U] tdmk a strong alcoholic drink made in the West Indies, usu. drunk from a small glass after a meal

Tian·an·men Square /ˌtjen-ænmən ˈskweəʳ/ a very large public square in Peking, which in 1989 was the scene of violent fighting between mainly unarmed Chinese students and the army, ending in defeat for the students, with an unknown number of deaths

ti·a·ra /tiˈɑːrə/ n **1** a piece of jewellery that looks like a small crown, worn on the head by women at formal dances, dinners, etc. **2** the crown worn by the POPE

Ti·bet /tɪˈbet/ a self-governing REGION of SW China, consisting mainly of very high country and mountains; capital Lhasa

Ti·bet·an /tɪˈbetn/ n **1** [C] a person from Tibet **2** [U] the language of Tibet –**Tibetan** adj : *a Tibetan monk*

tib·i·a /ˈtɪbiə/ n -**iae** /i-iː/ or -**ias** med for SHINBONE –see picture at SKELETON

tic /tɪk/ n a sudden uncontrolled movement of the muscles, esp. in the face, usu. because of a nervous illness: *He has a nervous tic.* –compare TWITCH²

tick¹ /tɪk/ n **1** a short sudden regularly repeated sound made by a clock or watch **2** *BrE* ‖ **check** *AmE*– mark (✓) put against an answer, name on a list, etc., to show that it is correct, that the person is present, etc. **3** infml, esp. *BrE* a short time; moment: *I'll be down in a tick.* | *I'm going to the shops but I'll only be a couple of ticks.*

tick² v **1** [I] (of a clock, watch, etc.) to make a regularly repeated short sudden sound **2** [T (OFF)] *BrE* ‖ **check** *AmE*– to mark (an answer, name, etc.) with a TICK¹ (2) to show that it is correct **3 make someone/something tick** infml to provide a person/thing with reasons for behaving, working, etc., in a particular way: *He's a strange*

character; *I've never been able to work out what makes him tick.*

tick away phr v **1** [T] (**tick** sthg.↔**away**) (of a clock, watch, etc.) to show the passing of (minutes, seconds, etc.) by ticking: *The old grandfather clock ticked away the hours.* **2** [I] (of time) to go by: *As the hours ticked away, we waited anxiously for news.*

tick sbdy. ↔ **off** phr v [T] **1** *BrE infml* ‖ **tell** sbdy. **off** *AmE* to speak sharply to, expressing disapproval or annoyance –see also TICKING OFF **2** *AmE infml* to make angry or to annoy: *He ticks me off by the way he's always taking charge.*

tick over phr v [I] esp. *BrE* **1** (of a motor engine) to continue working at the slowest possible speed but without moving the vehicle **2** to continue to operate, but usu. at a low level of activity: *During the summer months the company just ticks over.* | *an increase in government spending to keep the economy ticking over*

tick³ n a very small insect-like animal that buries itself in the skin of animals and sucks their blood

tick⁴ n [(on)] U] *BrE infml for* CREDIT¹ (1), esp. with a small shop: *Will you let me have these things on tick until I get paid tomorrow?*

tick·er /ˈtɪkəʳ/ n esp. *BrE sl* the heart: *She's got a weak ticker.*

tick·er·tape /ˈtɪkəteɪp‖-ər-/ n [U] very long narrow lengths of paper on which information is printed by a special machine. Tickertape is sometimes thrown from high buildings in the US to greet famous people who are visiting a town: *The astronauts were given a tickertape welcome in New York.* | *A* **tickertape parade** *was held for the returning soldiers.*

tick·et¹ /ˈtɪkɪt/ n **1** [C] a printed piece of paper or card given to someone to show that they have paid for a service such as a journey on a bus, entrance into a cinema, etc.: *a bus/train/cinema ticket* | *a ticket collector at a railway station* | *Entrance to the theatre is* **by ticket** *only.* –see also SEASON TICKET **2** [C] a piece of card or paper that shows the price, size, etc., of an object for sale in a shop **3** [C] a printed notice of an offence against the driving laws, which means that the offender must pay money as a punishment: *If you leave your car there you might get a* **(parking) ticket.** **4** [C] esp. *AmE* a list of people supported by one political party in an election: *on the Democratic ticket* **5** [the+S] infml the thing needed: *That cup of coffee was just the ticket.*

ticket² v [T (for)] **1** to intend (something) for a certain use or purpose: *These cars have been ticketed for sale abroad.* **2** esp. *AmE* to give a TICKET¹ (3) to: *She was ticketed for illegal parking.* **3** to put a TAG or LABEL on

tick·ing /ˈtɪkɪŋ/ n [U] the thick strong usu. cotton cloth used for making MATTRESS and PILLOW covers

ticking off /ˌ·· ˈ·/ *BrE* ‖ **telling off** esp *AmE*– n **tickings off** a usu. spoken expression of annoyance or disapproval: *I got a ticking off from the teacher for being late.* –see also TICK **off**

tick·le¹ /ˈtɪkəl/ v **1** [T] to touch (someone, part of their body, etc.) lightly with the fingers, a feather, etc., to produce laughter or a feeling of nervous excitement. **2** [I] to feel or give a sensation of being tickled in part of the body: *I don't like these rough sheets; they tickle.* | *My foot tickles/is tickling.* **3** [T] to delight or amuse: *I was tickled by her description of the wedding.* **4 tickled pink/to death** infml very pleased or amused: *He's tickled pink with his new stereo system.* **5 tickle the ivories** humor to play the piano

tickle² n an act or feeling of tickling: *I've got a slight tickle in my throat and it's making me cough.* –see also SLAP AND TICKLE

tick·lish /ˈtɪklɪʃ/ adj **1** (of a person or part of their body) sensitive to being tickled **2** (of a problem, situation, etc.) difficult; needing special care and attention – ~**ly** adv – ~**ness** n [U]

tick-tack-toe, tic-tac-toe /ˌtɪk tæk ˈtəʊ / n [U] *AmE for* NOUGHTS AND CROSSES

tid·al /ˈtaɪdl/ adj [no comp.] of or having a TIDE: *tidal currents* | *The river is tidal up to this bridge.*

tidal wave /ˈ·· ·/ also **tsunami** fml– n a very large dangerous ocean wave caused by an underwater explosion, EARTHQUAKE, etc.: (fig.) *There was a tidal wave of public disapproval against the government's plans.*

tid·bit /ˈtɪdˌbɪt/ n AmE for TITBIT

tid·dler /ˈtɪdlə^r/ n BrE infml **1** a very small fish **2** a small child **3** something small and unimportant: Compared with some of its commercial rivals, the company is just a tiddler.

tid·dly , -dley /ˈtɪdli/ adj BrE infml euph **1** slightly drunk **2** very small

tid·dly·winks /ˈtɪdliwɪŋks/ also **tid·dle·dy·winks** /ˈtɪdl-diwɪŋks/ AmE— n [U] a game, played mainly by children, in which the players try to make small round pieces of plastic jump into a cup by pressing their edges down hard with a larger piece of plastic

tide¹ /taɪd/ n **1** [(the) C] the regular rise and fall of the sea caused by the pull of the moon and sun: The sea comes right up to the cliffs when the tide is in. (=has risen to its highest point) | The tide is rising/falling. | The tide is beginning to turn. (=has reached its highest/lowest point and is changing direction) —see also HIGH TIDE, LOW TIDE **2** [C] a current of water caused by this: Strong tides make swimming dangerous. **3** [C usu. sing.] a feeling or tendency that moves or changes like the tide: The tide of public opinion seems to be turning against the government. | The head teacher called a meeting in an attempt to **stem** (=hold back) **the (rising) tide** of protest against his methods. | It's easier to **swim with the tide** than to oppose the views of the majority. | The victory at Midway began the **turn of the tide** in the battle for the Pacific (it marked a change in the luck of those fighting). **4** [U] old use (usu. in comb.) time of the day or year: Christians rejoice at Christmastide. | The shadows of eventide (=evening) began to fall.

tide² v

tide sbdy. **over** (sthg.) phr v [T] to help through (a difficult period): Can you lend me £10 to tide me over (the next few days)?

tide·mark /ˈtaɪdmɑːk‖-mɑːrk/ n **1** a mark left by the tide at its lowest or highest point **2** infml a mark round the inside of an emptied bath that shows the level to which the bath had been filled **3** humor a dirty mark on the skin left by incomplete washing, often by children

tide·wa·ter /ˈtaɪdˌwɔːtə^r‖-ˌwɔː-, -ˌwɑː-/ n [U] **1** water that flows onto the land when the tide is very high **2** the water in the TIDAL parts of rivers and streams

tide·way /ˈtaɪdweɪ/ n **1** a narrow stretch of water through which the tide flows **2** a strong current running through a tideway

tid·ings /ˈtaɪdɪŋz/ n [P (of)] old use news: The messenger brought tidings of the battle. | glad tidings. (=good news)

ti·dy¹ /ˈtaɪdi/ adj **1** neat and orderly in appearance or habits: a tidy room | a tidy person | (fig.) a tidy mind **2** [A] infml (of amounts) quite large; SUBSTANTIAL: That must have cost you a tidy sum. | a tidy profit —**dily** adv —**diness** n [U]

tidy² v [I;T (UP)] to make neat; put in order: When are you going to tidy your room up? | We'll have to tidy away these papers before we have dinner.

tie¹ /taɪ/ n **1** also **necktie** esp. AmE— a band of cloth worn round the neck inside a shirt collar and tied in a knot at the front —compare CRAVAT and see also BLACK-TIE, BOW TIE, OLD SCHOOL TIE, WHITE-TIE **2** a cord, string, etc., used for fastening something: She closed the freezer bag with a plastic tie. **3** [usu. pl.] something that unites; BOND: family ties | ties of friendship **4** [usu. sing.] something that takes one's attention and limits one's freedom: Young children can be a tie. **5** (the result of) a game, election, etc., in which each competitor gains an exactly equal number of points, votes, etc.; DRAW: The election ended in a tie. —see also CUP TIE **6** AmE for SLEEPER (3)

tie² v tied; present participle tying **1** [T+obj+adv/prep] to fasten with a cord, rope, etc.: Make sure the parcel is securely tied up before you post it. | Tie this label onto your suitcase. | She tied her horse to the post. | The robbers tied him up and locked him in the cupboard. | (fig.) I've been tied to (=too busy to leave) my desk/to the house for the last few weeks. | I'd like to help you but I'm afraid **my hands are tied**. (=I am not free to act as I wish) **2** [T] to fasten by drawing together and knotting: Can you tie your own shoe laces yet? | She tied a scarf over her head. | to tie a knot (=form one in this way) **3** [I] to be fastened by string, LACEs, etc., that are drawn together and knotted: My dress ties at the back. **4** [T (to)] usu. pass.] to cause

to be connected or dependent in some way: The rise in welfare payments is tied to the retail price index. **5** [I (with, for)] to be equal to an opponent in a competition: I tied with my friend for second place in the exams. **6** [T usu. pass.] to finish (a match, competition, etc.) with equal points **7 tie one on** AmE sl to get drunk: He really tied one on at the office Christmas party. **8 tie the knot** pomp to get married **9 tie someone (up) in knots** infml to confuse someone completely, esp. with difficult questions

tie sbdy. **down** phr v [T] **1** to limit the freedom of; RESTRICT: Having an old sick relative to look after really ties you down. **2** [(on, to)] to force to take a particular course of action, accept particular conditions, etc.: He seemed very vague about it, but eventually I managed to tie him down to the Saturday.

tie in phr v [I (with)] to have a close connection (to); CORRESPOND (with): This witness's information doesn't tie in with the facts. | We've planned this broadcast to tie in with (=happen at the same time as) the anniversary celebrations. —see also TIE-IN

tie sthg. ↔ **up** phr v [T often pass.] **1** [(in)] to place (money) in an account, business, etc., where free use is limited: All his money is tied up in stocks and shares. **2** to limit the free use of (money, property, etc.) by legal conditions: Under the terms of the trust the money was tied up until her 21st birthday. **3** [(with)] to connect; LINK: The police are trying to tie up his escape from prison with the murder. **4** delay or limit the free movement of: The accident tied up the traffic for hours. | I can't come out tonight – I'm a bit **tied up** at work. (=very busy) —see also TIE-UP

tie·break·er /ˈtaɪˌbreɪkə^r/ also **tie·break** /ˈtaɪbreɪk/— n **1** (in tennis) a number of quickly-played points (not part of a standard game), played to decide the winner of a SET³ (4) in which each side has won six games **2** (in a game or QUIZ where more than one competitor has gained the same number of correct answers) a final question to decide who wins

tied cot·tage /ˌ· ˈ··/ n a house owned by a farmer and rented to one of his workers for as long as the worker continues to be employed by the farmer

tied house /ˌ· ˈ·/ n BrE a PUB that is controlled by a particular beer-making firm, and must sell the beer that the firm makes —compare FREE HOUSE

tie-dye /ˈ· ·/ v [T] to tie (a garment) in knots and colour it with DYE so that some parts take more dye than others

tie-in /ˈ· ··/ n **1** [(between, with)] a TIE-UP (1) **2** a product, such as a record, book, toy, etc., that is connected in some way with a new film, TV show, sporting event, etc. —see also TIE **in**

tie-on /ˈ· ·/ adj [A] (of a LABEL, TAG, etc.) fastened to an object by tying

tie·pin /ˈtaɪˌpɪn/ n a small decorative CLIP¹ (1), often of silver or gold, for holding a TIE¹ (1) in place —see picture at PIN

tier /tɪə^r/ n **1** any of a number of rows or levels, esp. of seats, shelves, etc., rising one behind or above another: Her wedding cake had three tiers. | (fig.) The Health Service in Britain has three tiers (=levels) of management. **2** -**tiered** /tɪəd‖tɪərd/ having the stated number of tiers

Ti·er·ra del Fue·go /tɪˌerə del ˈfweɪgəʊ/ a group of islands off the S coast of S America, owned by Chile and Argentina

tie-up /ˈ· ··/ n **1** [(between, with)] a close connection, esp. of cause and effect; LINK: Doctors have established a tie-up between cigarette smoking and lung cancer. **2** a partnership; MERGER **3** AmE a short interruption in work because of an accident, industrial trouble, etc. —see also TIE **up**

tiff /tɪf/ n a slight quarrel: a lovers' tiff

Tif·fa·ny glass /ˈtɪfəni glɑːs‖-glæs/ n [U] a shiny coloured glass which cannot be clearly seen through, often used to make decorative objects such as VASES and LAMP SHADES

tif·fin /ˈtɪfɪn/ n [U] IndE & PakE or old-fash BrE a light meal taken at midday or in the middle of the morning

ti·ger /ˈtaɪgə^r/ **tigress** fem.— n **1** (pl. tigers or tiger) a very large fierce Asian wild cat that has yellowish fur with black bands. A poem about a tiger by William Blake begins with the words:

Tiger! Tiger! burning bright
In the forests of the night. —see picture at BIG CATS **2**
a person like a tiger in fierceness, courage, etc. —see also
PAPER TIGER

tiger lil·y /ˈ··ˌ··/ *n* a LILY (= type of plant) grown esp. for
its black-spotted, hanging, orange flowers

tight¹ /taɪt/ *adj* **1** closely fastened, held, knotted, etc.;
firmly fixed in place: *This drawer is so tight I can't open
it.* **2** pulled out as far as possible; fully stretched; TAUT:
Pull the thread tight. | *The cover of the drum has to be
stretched until it's really tight.* **3** fitting part of the body
(too) closely: *tight shoes* | *These trousers are* **a tight fit.**
—see also SKIN-TIGHT **4** well ordered or firmly controlled:
marching in tight formation | *There was tight security at
the airport when the President's plane landed.* | (*infml*)
The jazz group is very tight. (=playing exactly together) |
Spending is kept within tight limits. | *The captain* **runs
a tight ship. 5** leaving no free room or time; fully
packed: *I've got a very tight schedule today so I can't see
you until tomorrow.* | *Pack the cases as tight as possible.*
6 forming a small angle: *The aircraft had to do a tight
turn to avoid the mountain.* **7** producing an uncomfortable feeling of closeness in part of the body: *a tight feeling in the chest* **8** marked by close competition: *It was
a very tight finish; we scored the winning goal in the last
minute.* **9** (of money) difficult to obtain, except at high
rate of interest **10** *infml derog* ungenerous with money
11 [F] *infml* (rather) drunk **12** **in a tight corner/spot**
infml in a difficult situation —see also AIRTIGHT, WATER-
TIGHT — ~ **ly** *adv* — ~ **ness** *n* [U]

tight² *adv* **1** closely; firmly; tightly: *She held him tight in
her arms.* | *The door was shut tight.* **2** *infml* thoroughly;
well: *Sleep tight!* —see also **sit tight** (SIT)
▷ USAGE Although **tight** is often used as an adverb,
some people like the forms **tightly**/*more* **tightly**/*most*
tightly better.◁

tight·en /ˈtaɪtn/ *v* [I;T (UP)] **1** to (cause to) become tight or
tighter: *We must tighten these screws/ropes.* | *to tighten
borrowing limits* —compare SLACKEN **2** **tighten one's
belt** *infml* to try to live on less money: *She's lost her job
so she had to tighten her belt.*
     tighten (sthg.↔) **up** *phr v* **I** (**on**);T] to (cause to) be-
come firmer or more severe: *The government is tighten-
ing up (on) the driving laws.*

tight·fist·ed /ˌtaɪtˈfɪstɪd◄/ *adj infml* very ungenerous, esp.
with money; STINGY: *a tightfisted old skinflint* — ~ **ness**
n [U]

tight·knit /ˌtaɪtˈnɪt◄/ *adj AmE* well arranged: *a tightknit
plan*

tight·lipped /ˌ··ˈ·◄/ *adj* **1** having the lips pressed together,
esp. in determination or anger **2** unwilling to talk; silent: *He remained tight-lipped when questioned about his
resignation.*

tightrope

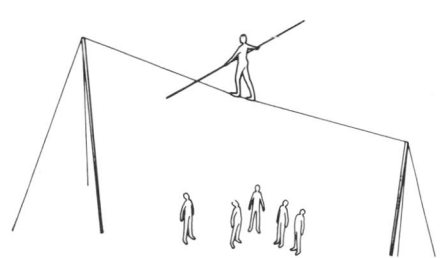

tight·rope /ˈtaɪt-rəʊp/ *n* a tightly stretched rope or wire,
high above the ground, on which tightrope walkers perform: (fig.) *The government is walking a tightrope between being too tough and not wanting to seem too weak.*

tightrope walk·er /ˈ·· ˌ··/ *n* a person skilled in walking or
doing tricks on a tightrope

tights /taɪts/ *n* [P] **1** *BrE* ‖ **panty hose** *AmE*— a very close
fitting garment made of thin material which one can see
through and covering the legs and lower part of the body,
as worn by girls and women **2** a similar garment which
is usu. coloured and cannot be seen through **3** *esp. BrE*

‖ usu. **leotard** *AmE* — a similar garment covering the
legs and body, worn by ACROBATS, BALLET dancers, etc. —
see PAIR (USAGE); compare NYLONS, SOCK, STOCKING

tight·wad /ˈtaɪtwɒd‖-wɑːd/ *n AmE, infml derog* a person
who does not spend or give money easily: *His dad's a real
tightwad who won't give him a dime.*

ti·gress /ˈtaɪgrɪs/ *n* a female tiger

Ti·gris /ˈtaɪgrɪs/ [*the*] a river in SW Asia, flowing through
Turkey and Iraq, with the SITEs of several ancient cities
on its banks

til /tɪl/ also **'til** *prep, conj AmE nonstandard* TILL¹

til·de /ˈtɪldə/ *n* a mark (~) placed over the letter *n* in Spanish as a sign that it is to be pronounced /nj/

tile¹ /taɪl/ *n* **1** a thin shaped piece of baked clay used for
covering roofs, walls, floors, etc. **2** an object like this
made from plastic, rubber, etc., and used for covering
floors and walls: *cork tiles* **3** a marked playing piece
used in certain games: *Scrabble*®tiles **4 (out) on the
tiles** *BrE infml* enjoying oneself in a wild manner: *a
night on the tiles*

tile² *v* [T] to cover (a roof, floor, wall, etc.) with tiles: *a tiled
floor* — **tiler** *n*

till¹ /tɪl, tl/ *prep, conj* until: *I'll keep it for you till Monday/till
you come back.* —see TO (USAGE)

till² /tɪl/ *n* a drawer where money is kept in a shop —see also
have/with one's fingers in the till (FINGER¹)

till³ /tɪl/ *v* [T] *old use* to cultivate (the ground) — ~ **er** *n*

till·age /ˈtɪlɪdʒ/ *n* [U] *old use* the act or practice of cultivat-
ing land

til·ler /ˈtɪləʳ/ *n* a long handle fastened to a small boat's RUD-
DER so that it can be turned easily —see picture at YACHT

tilt¹ /tɪlt/ *v* [I;T] to (cause to) slope (as if) by raising one end:
*The table top suddenly tilted and all the plates and glasses
crashed onto the floor.* | (*fig.*) *This piece of evidence may
tilt the balance of opinion against the defendant.*
     tilt at sbdy. *phr v* [T] **1** to attack in speech or writing
2 (in former times) to charge at with a LANCE **3 tilt at
windmills** to fight imaginary enemies

tilt² *n* **1** [C;U] a slope: *She wore her hat at a tilt over her
left eye.* **2** [C] an act of tilting; tilting movement **3** [C
(at)] an attack in speech or writing: *In his newspaper
column this week he has one of his regular tilts at modern
fashions.* **4 (at) full tilt** *infml* at full speed; with full
force: *They rode down the hill at full tilt.*

tim·ber¹ /ˈtɪmbəʳ/ *n* **1** [U] *BrE* ‖ usu. **lumber** *AmE*— wood
for building **2** [U] growing trees, esp. considered as a
supply of wood for building **3** [C] a wooden beam, esp.
forming part of a structure, such as a ship or a roof —see
also HALF-TIMBERED

tim·ber² /ˌtɪmˈbɜːʳ/ *interj* (a warning shouted when a cut
tree is about to fall down)

tim·ber·line /ˈtɪmbəlaɪn‖-ər-/ *n* [*the*+S] the TREELINE

tim·bre /ˈtæmbəʳ, ˈtɪm-/ *n* [C;U] *tech* the quality in a sound
which allows one to tell the difference between sounds
of the same level and loudness when made by different
musical instruments or voices

tim·brel /ˈtɪmbrəl/ *n old use for* TAMBOURINE

Tim·buk·tu /ˌtɪmbʌkˈtuː/ a city in Mali, W Africa, a centre
of the salt industry. People sometimes mention Timbuktu as an example of a place that is very far away:
enough cars to stretch from here to Timbuktu

time¹ /taɪm/ *n* **1** [U] a continuous measurable quantity
from the past, through the present, and into the future:
The universe exists in space and time. **2** [U] the passing
of the days, months, and years, considered as a whole:
*Time goes by/passes quickly when you're enjoying your-
self.* | *In ten years' time* (=10 years from now) *the children
will all have grown up.* | *Only* **time will tell** *if you're
right.* (=in the future we will find out if you were right) |
They'll have to change their decision; it's **only a matter/
question of time.** (=it must happen, but we do not yet
know when) **3** [U] a particular system of measuring
time: *British Summer Time* | *Eastern Standard Time* **4**
[S;U] a limited period, e.g. the period that passes between
two events, or the period needed or allowed for the completion of an action: *It will take you a long time to learn
French properly.* | *Take more time and care over your
work.* | *That all happened some time ago.* | *I don't get
much time to watch television.* (=periods when I have

nothing else to do, and therefore can watch television) | *I'd love to stop and talk but I'm afraid I haven't* **got (the) time.** (=I am too busy doing other things) | *The traffic was light, so we* **made good time.** (=went more quickly than expected) | *What do you do in your* **spare time/free time?** (=when you are not working, studying, etc.) | *I can't decide yet — I need more time to think.* **5** [C] an occasion: *Every time I go there I seem to get sick.* | *"How many times did you try to phone her?" "I called seven times." | Next time you're in London come and visit us.* | **Nine times out of ten** (=nearly always) *the train is late.* **6** [C] also **times** *pl.*— a period or occasion and the particular experience connected with it: *We had a good time at the party.* | *We had* **the time of our lives.** (=we enjoyed ourselves greatly) | *The 1930s were hard times for many people.* | *I hear they gave him a pretty hard time at the interview.* (=asked him difficult questions, etc.) | *If you join the navy, don't expect to* **have an easy time (of it).** (=have an easy comfortable life) **7** [C] also **times** *pl.*— a period in history: *in ancient times* | *in Queen Victoria's time* **8** [(*the*) S] a particular point in the day stated in hours, minutes, seconds, etc.: *"What's the time?" "It's half past ten." | "What time does that programme start?" "10 o'clock."* **9** [C;U] (*sometimes in comb.*) a particular point in the day, year, etc.: *We both arrived at the same time.* | *By the time you receive this letter I will be on my way home.* | *It's quite warm for this time of year.* (=warmer than it usually is at this time) | *This time last year* (=at the same date a year ago) *I didn't have a job.*| *in summertime* **10** [C;U] (*sometimes in comb.*) a moment or period that is intended or suitable for a particular activity or event: [+*to-v*] *He's in a good mood, so now's the time to ask him about that loan.* | *Come on children, it's time for bed/it's bedtime.* [+(*that*)] *It's time you were in bed.* | *question time in the House of Commons* | *If you are thinking of buying a house,* **there's no time like the present.** (=now is the best time to do it) **11** [U] the point at which something is expected or arranged to happen: *to die before one's time* | *The plane arrived* **(dead) on time.** (=at exactly the right time) | *The work was completed* **ahead of time.** (=earlier than expected) | *"The train is just coming." "And* **about time** too/not before time!" (=it is later than expected) **12** [U] the moment at which something starts or esp. stops: *At 10.30 the landlord calls "Time!" and we all have to finish our drinks and leave.* | **Time's up!** *Put your pencils down and pass forward your test papers.* –see also FULL TIME, OPENING TIME **13** [C] the period in which an action is completed, esp. a performance in a race: *His time for the mile was just under four minutes.* **14** [U] *tech* the rate of speed of a piece of music: *You* **beat time** *and I'll play.* –see also **keep time** (TIME¹ (35b)) **15** [U] a period of imprisonment *infml* or of employment with the military: *He's* **done time/served time** *for burglary.* | *He served his time in the army and then went to college.* **16 about time** *infml* (used for suggesting that something should be done now or should have been done earlier): *It's about time you had your hair cut!* **17 against time** in an effort to do something within a certain limited period: *working against time to get the job finished* **18 ahead of one's time** –see TIME¹ (25b) **19 all the time** continuously: *Why must you keep complaining all the time?* **20 at a time** in a group of the stated number: *Please come in one at a time* (=singly), *not all together.* **21 a time to be born, and a time to die** phrase from the Bible a phrase from the Book of Ecclesiastes, part of a longer passage which begins: *For everything there is a season, and a time for every matter under heaven,* and which is sometimes used by people saying that there is a proper time for any action **22 at one time** formerly: *At one time they used to mine coal in these valleys.* **23 at the time** at the moment when something happened: *It seemed like a good idea at the time.* **24 at times** sometimes: *At times I wonder if it's all worthwhile.* **25 before one's time: a** before one was born or came to a place:*I don't remember her — she must have been before my time.* **b** also **ahead of one's time**— too modern or original for the period one lives in: *As a painter, he was before his time.* **26 behind the times** old-fashioned **27 for a time** for a short period: *For a time the police thought she might be guilty, but before long they eliminated her from their list of suspects.* **28 for the time being** for a limited period at present: *Can you share a room for the time being? We'll let you have one on your own next week.* **29 from time out of mind** *lit or pomp* for a very long time **30 from time to time** sometimes; not

very often: *They come to see us from time to time.* **31 have a lot of time for** *infml* to like and respect (esp. a person) **32 have no time for** *infml* to dislike; be unwilling to waste one's time with: *I have no time for people who mistreat animals.* **33 in no time (at all)** very quickly: *We'll have that leak fixed in no time.* **34 in time: a** after a certain amount of time has passed: *In time you'll forget him.* **b** early or soon enough: *Will you be home in time to see the children before they go to bed?* **c** at the correct rate or speed: *to sing/march/play in time* **35 keep time: a** (of a clock, watch, etc.) to work correctly **b** to follow the correct TIME¹ (14) **36 keep up/move/march with the times** to change one's own ideas, methods, etc., at the same rate as changing fashions, scientific developments, or social customs **37 many a time** *lit or old use* often; frequently **38 not give someone the time of day** to refuse to speak to or spend time with someone, esp. because one considers them unimportant **39 take one's time (over): a** to use as much time as is necessary (to do); not hurry: *There's no hurry; take your time!* **b** to take more time than is reasonable (to do): *The workmen seem to be taking their time over repairing this road!* **40 take time to smell the roses** not to spend one's whole life rushing and working, but to spend some time enjoying oneself **41 time after time** also **time and (time) again**— repeatedly: *I've told you time after time not to park there!* **42 time and a half** payment of a worker at one and a half times the usual rate: *We get time and a half for working on Sundays.* **43 time heals all wounds** *saying* grief and other kinds of emotional pain become less difficult to bear over a period of time **44 time is money** *saying* one should not waste time when one could be working and earning money **45 time is of the essence** it is important that we hurry and do not delay —see also TIMES, BIG TIME, DOUBLE TIME, FULL-TIME, HALF TIME, HIGH TIME, LEAD TIME, LOCAL TIME, PART-TIME, SHORT TIME, **beat time** (BEAT¹), **bide one's time** (BIDE), **in good time** (GOOD¹), **in one's own good time** (GOOD¹), **kill time** (KILL¹), **mark time** (MARK²), **move with the times** (MOVE¹), **in the nick of time** (N ICK¹), **for old times' sake** (OLD), **once upon a time** (ONCE¹ (8)), **play for time** (PLAY²), **at the same time** (SAME¹), **sign of the times** (SIGN¹)

▷ **USAGE 1** If you use time sensibly or on things that are neither good nor bad, you **spend** time: *You should* **spend** *an hour every day practising the piano.* | *I* **spend** *a lot of (my) time wondering about Tom.* If you use time badly you **waste** time: *I* **wasted** *a whole hour trying to find a garage.* If you are trying to keep to a certain timetable you may also **lose** time: *I drove quickly, trying to make up for* **lost** time. | *We* **lost** *quite a lot of time on the journey because of a breakdown.* | If you have too much time which you try to fill you may **pass** the time: *Listening to the radio helps her to* **pass** the time. Or even (if you are waiting for something) **kill** time: *I'm just standing here,* **killing** *time until the shop opens.* **2** At 11.45, it is *a quarter of/to 12* in American English but *a quarter to 12* in British English. At 12.15 *it is a quarter after/past 12* in American English but *a quarter past 12* in British English. —see also CLOCK (USAGE), O'CLOCK (USAGE), TO (USAGE)◁

time² *v* [T] **1** [*usu. pass.*] to arrange or set the time at which (something) happens or is to happen: *You timed your arrival well; we were just going to have dinner.* [+*obj+to-v*] *The train is timed to arrive at six o'clock.* **2** [(*at*)] to measure the speed or the time taken by: *We timed our journey; it took us two hours.* | *Jenkins was timed at 3 minutes 53 seconds for the 1500 metres.* **3** to hit (a ball) or make (a shot) at just the right moment: *a perfectly timed shot* —see also ILL-TIMED, MISTIME, WELL-TIMED

Time *n* an American weekly news magazine that is sold in the US and around the world

time-and-mo·tion /ˌ· · '··/ *adj* [A] concerning the measurement and study of the effectiveness of work, esp. in industry: *a time-and-motion study*

time bomb /'· ·/ *n* **1** a bomb that can be set to explode at a particular time **2** a situation, esp. in politics, that is likely to become very dangerous or difficult to handle: *The high level of youth unemployment is a time bomb that could one day have disastrous social consequences.*

time capsule /'· ˌ··/ *n* a container that is filled with objects representative of its time and then buried, so that it can be dug up and examined in a future age

time card /'· ·/ *n AmE for* TIME SHEET

time clock /'· ·/ n a special clock which records the hour and minute one arrives at and leaves work: *He has to* **punch a time clock.**

time-con·sum·ing /'· ·ˌ··/ adj using or taking a long time or too much time: *Keeping the house clean can be a very time-consuming job.*

time ex·po·sure /'· ·ˌ··/ n [C;U] (a picture taken by) EX-POSURE of film to the light for more than a second when taking a photograph

time-hon·oured /'· ˌ··/ adj fml or pomp respected because of age or long use: *a time-honoured custom*

time im·me·mo·ri·al /ˌ· ··'···/ n from/since time im-memorial *lit or pomp* since long ago in the past: *From time immemorial the tribe have buried their dead on this island.*

time·keep·er /'taɪmˌkiːpəʳ/ n **1** a person who records the time of competitors in a race, workers in a factory, etc. **2** a clock or watch considered for its ability to tell the right time: *This old watch of mine's a good timekeeper.*—-keeping n [U]

time lag /'· ·/ also **lag**— n a period of time between the first and second of two closely connected events

time-lapse /'· ··/ adj [A] *tech* of or being a method of film-ing very slow actions (such as flowers growing) using many single pictures taken some time apart, which when run at the ordinary speed of a film show the action much faster

time·less /'taɪmləs/ adj **1** lasting for ever; independent of time; unending: *the timeless universe* **2** *apprec* not changed by time: *the timeless beauty of Venice* – ~ **ly** adv – ~ **ness** n [U]

time lim·it /'· ˌ··/ n [(on)] a period of time within which something must be done

time·ly /'taɪmli/ adj fml happening at just the right time; OPPORTUNE: *Your timely warning saved our lives.* —-liness n [U]

time ma·chine /'· ··ˌ·/ n an imaginary machine which can move a person backwards or forwards in time

time-out /'· ·/ n [C;U] **1** a short break during a sporting match, used for rest, instructions from the manager who calls for it, etc.: *The German requested a three-minute time-out to receive treatment.* **2** *infml* any short period of rest from an activity which involves a lot of effort

Time Out /ˌ· '·/ a weekly London magazine giving details of all the events and LEISURE activities available in the city, esp. for young adults

time·piece /'taɪmpiːs/ n tech or old use a clock or watch

tim·er /'taɪməʳ/ n a person or machine that measures or records time: *Don't forget to set the timer on the oven/video recorder.* —see also EGG TIMER

times¹ /taɪmz/ n (used to show an amount that is calculated by multiplying something the stated number of times): *Their house is at least three times as big as ours/three times bigger than ours.*

times² prep multiplied by: *Three times three equals nine.* (3 × 3=9)

Times, The 1 a national daily newspaper in Britain: *an article in The Times | Can I look at your Times?* —see also extra information on page 896 **2** the LOS ANGELES TIMES **3** the NEW YORK TIMES

time-sav·ing /'taɪmˌseɪvɪŋ/ adj reducing the time usually taken to do something, e.g. by being more effective: *a timesaving device* —**timesaver** n

time·scale /'taɪmskeɪl/ n the period of time within which something is completed or is expected to be completed: *The timescale for this job is approximately two years.*

Times Ed·u·ca·tion Sup·ple·ment /ˌ· ··'·· ˌ···/ also **TES**—[the] a British weekly newspaper on educational matters produced by *The Times*

time-serv·er /'taɪmˌsɜːvəʳ‖-ɜːr-/ n derog someone who shapes their opinions and behaviour to please those in power at the time, in the hope of gaining advantage —**serving** n, adj [U]

time-share /'taɪmʃeəʳ/ n, adj (of the arrangement by which one buys or sells) a house, flat, etc. in which people buy the right to spend one or more weeks a year on holiday —see also extra information on page 632

time-shar·ing /'· ·ˌ··/ n [U] **1** the handling by a computer

of more than one PROGRAM at the same time **2** the buy-ing of a timeshare

time sheet /'· ·/ ‖ also **time card** *AmE*— n a sheet on which the hours worked by a person are recorded

Times High·er Ed·u·ca·tion Sup·ple·ment /ˌ· ··' ·· ˌ···/ also **THES**— n [the] a British weekly newspaper on educational matters in the universities and other insti-tutions of higher education, produced by *The Times*

time sig·nal /'· ˌ··/ n a signal, esp. one broadcast on radio, showing an exact moment in time, so that clocks, watches, etc., may be set right

time sig·na·ture /'· ˌ···/ n tech a mark, usu. in the form of two numbers one above the other, used when writing music, to show the RHYTHM of the music

Times Lit·e·ra·ry Sup·ple·ment /ˌ· '···· ˌ···/ also **TLS**— [the] a British weekly newspaper which contains articles and information about literature, esp. about new books, produced by *The Times*

Times Square

Times Square /ˌ· '·/ a place in New York City near many theatres. Each year there is a large New Year's Eve celebration in Times Square and at midnight, a large red ball is lowered down a building to show that the New Year has begun. —see colour map on page 1376

time switch /'· ·/ n an electrical SWITCH that can be set to start a machine or operation at a particular time

time·ta·ble¹ /'taɪmˌteɪbəl/ n esp. *BrE* ‖ **schedule** *AmE*— **1** a list of the times at which buses, trains, planes, etc., ar-rive and leave **2** a list of the times of classes in a school, college, etc. —compare CURRICULUM **3** a plan having a list of the times at which stated events are to happen: *the government's timetable for this session of Parliament | our timetable for the week/visit/meeting*

timetable² v [T usu. pass.] esp. *BrE* ‖ **schedule** *AmE*— **1** [(for)] to plan for a particular future time: *The meeting is timetabled for 2 o'clock.* [+obj+to-v] *It is timetabled to begin at 2 o'clock.* **2** to arrange according to a timeta-ble: *Timetabling is the responsibility of the deputy headmaster.*

time-worn /'taɪmwɔːn‖-wɔːrn/ adj showing signs of damage and decay through age: (fig.) *timeworn clichés/excuses* (=used too often to have value)

time zone /'· ·/ n any of the 24 parts, each about 15° wide, into which the Earth is divided for the purpose of keep-ing time. Each time zone is usu. one hour different from those on either side.

tim·id /'tɪmɪd/ adj afraid; lacking courage or confidence: *a timid deer/young girl* – ~ **ly** adv – ~ **ity** /tɪˈmɪdɪti/ n [U]

tim·ing /'taɪmɪŋ/ n [U] the choosing of exactly the right mo-ment to do something so as to get the best effect: *I don't think much of their timing – introducing a new brand of suntan oil in November. | The batsman's/dancer's timing is perfect.*

tim·o·rous /'tɪmərəs/ adj fml easily frightened; nervous and lacking confidence – ~ **ly** adv – ~ **ness** n [U]

tim·pa·ni /'tɪmpəni/ n [(the) U+sing./pl. v] a set of KETTLEDRUMS

tim·pa·nist /'tɪmpənɪst/ n a person who plays a KETTLEDRUM

tin¹ /tɪn/ n **1** [U] a soft whitish metal that is a simple sub-stance (ELEMENT), is easily shaped, and is used to cover metal objects with a protective shiny surface: *a tin box* **2** [C (of)] *BrE* ‖ **can** esp. *AmE*— a small closed metal con-tainer in which food or drink is sold: *a tin of beans | a sardine tin* **3** [C] a metal container in which food is a stored: *a biscuit tin* **b** cooked (*esp. BrE* ‖ **pan** *esp. AmE*): *a bread tin* | *a roasting tin* —see picture at TRAY

tin² *BrE* ‖ **can** *esp. AmE—* *v* **-nn-** [T] to preserve (esp. food) by packing it in tins: *tinned fruit/meat*

tinc·ture /ˈtɪŋktʃəʳ/ *n* [C;U (**of**)] *tech* a medical substance mixed with alcohol: *tincture of iodine*

tin·der /ˈtɪndəʳ/ *n* [U] material that burns easily, used esp. for lighting fires: *The plants are as dry as tinder/are* **tinder-dry** *after the long hot summer.*

tin·der·box /ˈtɪndəbɒks‖-dərbɑːks/ *n* **1** a box containing tinder, a FLINT, and steel, used in former times instead of matches for providing a flame **2** a very dangerous uncontrollable place or situation: *Racial tension was high, and the southern states were a real tinderbox.*

tine /taɪn/ *n tech* a point or narrow pointed part of a fork, a deer's ANTLERs, etc.

tin ear /ˌ· ˈ·/ *n* [S] *AmE infml* a lack of ability to tell the difference between different musical notes: *He tries to play the piano but he's got a tin ear.*

tin·foil /ˈtɪnfɔɪl/ ‖ also **aluminum foil** *AmE—* *n* [U] a very thin bendable sheet of shiny metal, used as a protective wrapping, esp. for covering food before cooking it

ting /tɪŋ/ *v* [I;T] to (cause to) make a high clear ringing sound —**ting** *n* : *The glass went "ting" as I tapped it with my knife.*

ting·a·ling /ˌtɪŋəˈlɪŋ/ *n infml* a high clear ringing sound, esp. as made by a small bell

tinge¹ /tɪndʒ/ *v* [T (**with**) *usu. pass.*] **1** to give a slight degree of a colour to (an object or colour): *black hair tinged with grey* **2** to give a slight degree of a quality to: *Her admiration for him was tinged with jealousy.*

tinge² *n* [S (**of**)] a slight degree (of a colour or quality): *There was a tinge of sadness in her voice.*

tin·gle /ˈtɪŋgəl/ *v* [I (**with**)] to feel a slight, not unpleasant, stinging sensation: *My cheeks tingled with the cold.* — **tingle** *n* [S] : *I felt a tingle of excitement.* —**gly** *adj*

tin god /ˌ· ˈ·/ *n infml derog* someone not very important who behaves, or is admired, as though they were more important than they really are

tin hat /ˌ· ˈ·/ *n infml* a metal hat worn by modern soldiers for protection; HELMET

tin·ker¹ /ˈtɪŋkəʳ/ *n* **1** [C] a person who travels from place to place mending metal pots, pans, etc. **2** [S (**with**)] an act of tinkering **3** [C] *BrE infml* a disobedient or annoying young child **4 tinker, tailor, soldier, sailor** the first words of a children's RHYME which is said in order to find out what job one will have when one grows up or what the job of one's husband will be

tinker² *v* [I+*adv/prep*, esp. **with**] to work without a fixed plan or useful results, making small changes, esp. when trying to repair or improve something: *He's been tinkering with that engine for hours, but it still won't go.* | *She spent the afternoon tinkering about in the garden shed.* | *It's no use just tinkering with the problem; we've got to make some fundamental changes.*

Tin·ker·bell /ˈtɪŋkəbel ‖ -ər-/ a FAIRY (=an imaginary small person with wings) who helps Peter Pan in the story by J.M. Barrie. Tinkerbell talks to Peter Pan by making bell-like sounds. —see also PETER PAN and see colour picture on page 619

Tin·ker·toys /ˈtɪŋkətɔɪz ‖ -ər-/ *n* [P] *AmE tdmk* a children's toy consisting of wooden rods of different colours and lengths which are joined together with wheel-like wooden blocks to build models of buildings, cars, animals, etc.

tin·kle /ˈtɪŋkəl/ *v* [I;T] **1** to (cause to) make light metallic sounds: *little tinkling bells* | *The drops of water tinkled into the metal fountain.* **2** *euph infml* to URINATE (used of or by children): *Do you need to tinkle, dear?*

tinkle² *n* [*usu. sing.*] **1** a tinkling sound **2** *BrE infml* a telephone call: *I'll give you a tinkle tomorrow.* **3** *euph infml* an act of urinating (URINATE); used of or by children

Tin Man /ˌ· ˈ·/ [*the*] a character from the book and film *The Wizard of Oz.* He is made of metal and does not have a heart, but in the story he goes to see the Wizard of Oz to ask him to give him a heart. —see colour picture on page 685

tin·ni·tus /ˈtɪnɪtəs/ *n* [U] *med* an illness in which one hears noises, such as ringing, that are not there

tin·ny /ˈtɪni/ *adj* **1** of, like, or containing tin **2** having a thin metallic sound: *a cheap stereo that gives a tinny sound* **3** *infml* (esp. of something metal) cheaply and badly made —**niness** *n* [U]

tin o·pen·er /ˈ· ˌ···/ *BrE* ‖ **can opener** *esp. AmE—* *n* a tool for opening tins —see picture at KITCHEN

tin pan al·ley /ˌ· ˈ··/ (*often caps.*) esp. formerly, writers, players, and producers of popular music

tin·plate /ˈtɪnpleɪt/ *n* [U] very thin sheets of iron or steel covered with tin

tin·pot /ˈ· ·/ *adj* [A] *infml* worthless and unimportant, but perhaps thinking oneself to be important: *a tin-pot dictator*

tin·sel /ˈtɪnsəl/ *n* [U] **1** very thin sheets, lengths, or threads of shiny material used for decorations, esp. at Christmas **2** something showy that is really cheap or worthless: *the tinsel and glamour of Hollywood* – –~**ly** *adj*

Tin·sel·town /ˈtɪnsəltaʊn/ *infml, humor* HOLLYWOOD

tin shears /ˈ· ˌ·/ *n* [P] *AmE for* SNIPS

tint¹ /tɪnt/ *n* *esp. lit or tech* a pale or delicate shade of a colour; slight degree of a colour: *The painting glowed with beautiful autumn tints.* | *She has had red tints put in her hair.*

tint² *v* [T] to give a slight or delicate colour to: *a sports car with tinted glass in all the windows* | *She has had her hair tinted (blue).*

tin·tack /ˈtɪntæk/ *n* a short nail made of iron covered with tin

Tin·ta·gel /tɪnˈtædʒəl/ a ruined castle on the N coast of Cornwall. According to old stories, King Arthur held his court there.

Tin·tin /ˈtɪntɪn/ the main character in the *Tintin* picture stories by G R Hergé. Tintin is a young man with a dog called Snowy. The stories have been very popular since the 1920s, and some of them were made into CARTOON films.

Tintin

tin·tin·nab·u·la·tion /ˌtɪntɪ-næbjʊˈleɪʃən/ *n* [C;U] *tech or pomp* the sound or ringing of bells

© HERGÉ

Tin·to·ret·to /ˌtɪntəˈretəʊ/ (1518–94) an Italian artist born in Venice, best known for his religious paintings

tin·type /ˈtɪntaɪp/ *n* a photograph made by an old process which used tin instead of paper as a substance on which to develop the picture

ti·ny /ˈtaɪni/ *adj* extremely small: *a tiny baby/room/profit*

tip¹ /tɪp/ *n* [(**of**)] **1** the usu. pointed end of something: *Using the tip of the brush, paint in some very fine lines.* | *a town at the southern tip of India* | *(fig.) He's an artist to the* **tips of his fingers.** (=completely) —see also FINGERTIP **2** a small piece or part acting as an end, cap, or point: *the tip of a billiard cue* —see also FILTER TIP **3 on the tip of one's tongue** not quite able to be remembered: *Now what's her name? It's on the tip of my tongue.* **4 the tip of the iceberg** a small sign of a much larger situation, problem, etc.: *The official statistics on drug addiction are only the tip of the iceberg; the real figure may well be much higher.*

tip² *v* **-pp-** [T] **1** to supply a TIP¹ to (something): *tipped cigarettes* **2** [(**with**)] to cover the end or point of: *The arrows had been tipped with poison.*

tip³ *v* **-pp-** **1** [T+*obj+adv/prep*] *esp. BrE* to pour (a substance) from one container into another, onto a surface, etc.: *I weighed the flour and tipped it into the bowl.* | *The truck tipped a load of sand onto the road.* **2** [I;T (OVER, UP)] to (cause to) fall over unintentionally: *Who knocked the bottle over? It couldn't have tipped over by itself.* **3** [I;T] to (cause to) lean at an angle: *The children tipped the table and the glasses fell off.* **4 tip the balance/scales** to influence the result of an event in one particular way when several results are possible: *Your support tipped the balance in our favour.* | *The American declaration of war in 1917 tipped the scales against Germany.* **5 tip the scales at** *infml* to weigh (the stated weight)

tip⁴ *n* **1** *esp. BrE* ‖ **dump** *esp. AmE—* a large place where unwanted waste is taken and left: *a rubbish tip* **2** *BrE infml* an extremely untidy and dirty place: *Your room's a real tip; when are you going to clean it out?*

tip⁵ *n* a small amount of money given as a gift, usu. in addition to the official price, for a small service performed: *Shall I leave a tip for the waiter?* | *a tip of 10%*

tip⁶ *v* **-pp-** [I;T] to give a TIP⁵ to: *Did you remember to tip the driver?* [+*obj(i)*+*obj(d)*] *I tipped the hairdresser £1 for doing such a good job.* —**tipper** *n* : *She's not a very good tipper.* (=does not give large tips)

tip⁷ *n* [(on)] a helpful piece of advice: *The manual is full of useful tips.* | **Take my tip** *and keep well away from that place.*

tip⁸ *v* **-pp-** [T (**as, for**)] to mention or regard as one who is likely to do something: *Smith is being widely tipped as* (=most people expect Smith will be) *the next chairman.* [+*obj*+*to-v*] *Which horse are you tipping to win the next race?*

　　tip sbdy. ↔ **off** *phr v* [T] to give a warning or a piece of secret information to: *Thanks for tipping me off about those shares; I made a tidy profit out of them.* [+*obj*+*that*] *The police were tipped off that a bank robbery was being planned.*

ti·pi /ˈtiːpiː/ *n* TEPEE

tip-off /ˈ· ·/ *n infml* a warning or piece of secret information: *The police received a tip-off about the robber's plans.*

Tip·pe·ca·noe /ˌtɪpɪkəˈnuː/ a battle won by US soldiers led by William Henry Harrison over Native Americans in Indiana. After the battle Harrison was often called "Tippecanoe".

Tip·pe·ra·ry /ˌtɪpəˈreəri/ a town and COUNTY in the S Republic of Ireland. There is a well-known song from the First World War called *Its a Long Way to Tipperary.*

Tip·pett /ˈtɪpət/, **Sir Mi·chael** /ˈmaɪkəl/ (1905–) an English COMPOSER of music for voices and instruments, also known for his OPERAS. His works include *A Child of Our Time.*

Tipp-Ex /ˈtɪpeks/ *BrE* ‖ **Liquid Paper** *tdmk*, **white out** *AmE*— *n* [U] *tdmk* a (usu. white) liquid used to paint out mistakes in writing, typing, etc.; often wrongly spelled **Tippex**

Tip-pex /ˈtɪpeks/ *BrE* ‖ **white (out)** *AmE* *v* [T(**out**)] to paint out a mistake in writing, typing, etc. using Tipp-Ex® or a similar product

tip-ple /ˈtɪpəl/ *n* [*usu. sing.*] *infml* an alcoholic drink: *What's your favourite tipple?*

tip-pler /ˈtɪpləʳ/ *n infml* or *euph* someone who drinks (too much) alcohol habitually

tip-ster /ˈtɪpstəʳ/ *n* a person who gives information and advice about the likely winners of horse and dog races, esp. in return for money or as in a job

tip-sy /ˈtɪpsi/ *adj infml* slightly drunk —**sily** *adv* —**siness** *n* [U]

tip-toe¹ /ˈtɪptəʊ/ *n* **on tiptoe** on one's toes with the rest of the feet raised above the ground: *He stood on tiptoe and tried to see over the wall.*

tiptoe² *v* [I] to walk on tiptoe: *She tiptoed quietly out of the room so as not to wake him up.*

tip-top /ˌ· ·/ *adj infml* of the highest quality; excellent: *in tip-top condition*

ti-rade /taɪˈreɪd, tɪ-‖ˈtaɪreɪd, tɪˈreɪd/ *n* a long very angry disapproving speech; DIATRIBE: *He delivered a tirade against drug dealers.*

tire¹ /taɪəʳ/ *v* [I (**of**);T] to (cause to) become tired: *After walking for two hours I began to tire.* | *Jean never tires of talking about her work.* | *a very tiring day looking after the children*

　　tire sbdy. ↔ **out** *phr v* [T] to cause to become completely tired; EXHAUST: *The children have really tired me out.* | *I'm tired out; I think I'll go to bed.*

tire² *n AmE for* TYRE —see pictures at BICYCLE and at CAR

tired /taɪəd‖taɪərd/ *adj* **1** feeling weak and lacking power in the body or mind, esp. as a result of long activity; needing rest or sleep: *I'm so tired I could sleep for a week.* | *resting their tired legs after a long walk* **2** [F (**of**)] having lost interest or patience: *I'm tired of watching television; let's go for a walk.* | *I'm tired of your lame excuses.* **3** *derog* showing lack of imagination or new ideas: *The same tired old subjects come up year after year.* **4 tired**

and emotional *BrE humor euph* drunk — ~**ly** *adv* — ~**ness** *n* [U]

tire-less /ˈtaɪələs‖ˈtaɪər-/ *adj apprec* never or rarely getting tired: *a tireless fighter against injustice* — ~**ly** *adv*

Ti·re·si·as /taɪˈriːsiæs/ in ancient Greek and Roman stories, the blind PROPHET who told of the crimes of Oedipus

tire-some /ˈtaɪəsəm‖ˈtaɪər-/ *adj pomp or fml* causing annoyance or impatience: *Do as you're told, you tiresome child.* | *I've missed the train; how tiresome!* | *tiresome repetitions* — ~**ly** *adv*

ti-ro /ˈtaɪərəʊ/ *n* a TYRO

Ti-rol , Tyrol /tɪˈrəʊl/ a mountainous area in Austria, popular with tourists and having many places to SKI

'tis /tɪz/ *Lit* it is

tis-sue /ˈtɪʃuː, -sjuː‖-ʃuː/ *n* **1** [U] (the material formed by) animal or plant cells, esp. those that are similar in form and purpose and make up the stated organ: *lung tissue* | *leaf tissue* **2** [U] also **tissue pa·per** /ˈ·· ˌ··/— light thin paper used for wrapping, packing, etc. **3** [C] also **Klee-nex** *tdmk*— a piece of soft paper, esp. used for blowing the nose on; paper handkerchief: *a box of tissues* **4** [C (**of**)] *fml* something formed as if by weaving threads together; network: *Her story was a tissue of lies.* (=completely untrue)

tit¹ /tɪt/ *n infml, not polite* **1** also **titty**— **a** a woman's breast **b** a NIPPLE **2** *BrE* a stupid worthless person **3 get on someone's tits** *BrE* to annoy someone greatly

tit² also **titmouse** *fml*— *n* a small European bird

ti-tan /ˈtaɪtn/ *n esp. lit (sometimes cap.)* a person of great strength, importance, size, cleverness, etc.: *Douglas Fairbanks Sr., a titan of the screen* | *The debate is being seen as a clash of the political Titans.* —see also TITANS

Ti·ta·ni·a /tɪˈtɑːniə‖-ˈteɪ-/ the queen of the fairies (FAIRY (1)) and wife of Oberon in Shakespeare's play *A Midsummer Night's Dream*

ti·tan·ic /taɪˈtænɪk/ *adj* of great size, strength, power, importance, etc.: *a titanic struggle*

Titanic [*the*] a British passenger ship, thought of as impossible to sink, which on her first trip in 1912 hit an ICE-BERG and sank, causing over 1500 deaths

ti·ta·ni·um /taɪˈteɪniəm/ *n* [U] a silvery grey light strong metal that is a simple substance (ELEMENT), used esp. for making compounds with other metals

Ti·tans /ˈtaɪtnz/ [*the*] in CLASSICAL MYTHOLOGY, the gods who ruled the universe until Zeus became the most powerful god

tit-bit /ˈtɪtˌbɪt/ *esp. BrE* ‖ **tidbit** *AmE*— *n* **1** a small piece of particularly nice food **2** [(**of**)] *infml* a small but interesting piece: *a few titbits of gossip*

titch·y /ˈtɪtʃi/ *adj BrE infml, often derog* extremely small

tit-fer /ˈtɪtfəʳ/ *n BrE old-fash sl* a hat

tit for tat /ˌ· · ˈ·/ *n* [U] *infml* something unpleasant done in return for something unpleasant one has suffered: *I didn't invite her to my party because she didn't invite me to hers. It was just tit for tat.*

tithe /taɪð/ *n* a tax of one tenth of one's yearly profit or income paid, esp. in former times, for the support of the priest of the local church

Ti-tian /ˈtɪʃən/ (1490–1576) an Italian painter from Venice, greatly admired for his use of striking colours

Tit·i·ca·ca /ˌtɪtɪˈkɑːkə/ the largest fresh water lake in S America, and the highest in the world, in the Andes mountains

tit-il·late /ˈtɪtɪleɪt/ *v* [T] to excite pleasantly, esp. sexually —**lation** /ˌtɪtɪˈleɪʃən/ *n* [U]

tit-i·vate , titti- /ˈtɪtɪveɪt/ *v* [I;T] *infml, often humor* to make (esp. oneself) pretty or tidy

ti-tle /ˈtaɪtl/ *n* **1** [C] a name given to a book, painting, play, etc.: *The title of this play is "Othello".* **b** a particular book: *This novel was one of last year's best-selling titles.* **2** [C] a word or name, such as "Mr", "Lord", "Lady", "Doctor", "General", etc., given to someone to be used before their name as a sign of rank, profession, etc. **3** [S;U (**to**)] *tech* the legal right to ownership or possession: *Has he any title to this land?* **4** [C] the position of unbeaten winner in certain sports competitions; CHAM-PIONSHIP (2): *They're fighting for the world title tonight.* | *a title fight* —see also ENTITLE, SUBTITLES

ti·tled /'taɪtld/ *adj* having a noble title, such as "Lord"

title deed /'·· ·/ *n* a piece of paper giving legal proof of a person's right of ownership of property

ti·tle-hold·er /'taɪtl,həʊldəʳ/ *n* **1** a person or team who is at present the unbeaten winner of a sports competition **2** the holder of a title deed

title page /'·· ·/ *n* the page at the front of a book giving the title, writer's name, etc.

title role /'·· ·/ *n* the chief part in a play, after which the play is named: *He played the title role in "Hamlet"*. (=he played the part of Hamlet)

tit·mouse /'tɪtmaʊs/ *n* **-mice** /maɪs/ *fml for* TIT²

Ti·to /'tiːtəʊ/, **Marshal** (1892–1980) a PRIME MINISTER and president (1953–80) of Yugoslavia who kept his country apart from the influence of the USSR

tit·ter /'tɪtəʳ/ *v* [I] *often derog* to laugh quietly in a nervous or silly way —see LAUGH (USAGE) —**titter** *n* : *She gave a nervous titter.*

tit·tle /'tɪtl/ *n* [S *usu. in questions and negatives*] *old-fash infml BrE* a very small amount; bit: *There is **not one jot or tittle** of truth in these allegations.* (=no truth at all)

tittle-tat·tle /'tɪtl ,tætl/ *n* [U] *infml, usu. derog* talk about other people's lives, activities, etc.; GOSSIP —**tittle-tattle** *v* [I]

tit·ty /'tɪti/ *n infml* a TIT¹ (1)

tit·u·lar /'tɪtʃʊləʳ/ *adj* holding a title but not having the duties, responsibilities, or power of office: *He is the titular head of government, but his chief minister holds all the real power.*

Ti·tus Groan /,taɪtəs 'grəʊn/ a book written in 1946 by Mervyn Peake. It is a Gothic FANTASY about the life of Titus, 77th EARL of Groan, in his castle, Gormenghast.

tiz·zy /'tɪzi/ also **tizz** /tɪz/ *esp. BrE* — *n* [*usu. sing.*] *infml* a state of excited worried confusion: *Don't get in a tizzy.*

T-junc·tion /'tiː ,dʒʌŋkʃən/ *n BrE* a place where two roads, pipes, etc., join and form the shape of a letter T

TKO /,tiː keɪ 'əʊ/ *abbrev. for* TECHNICAL KNOCK-OUT

TLC /,tiː el 'siː/ *infml* tender loving care; kindness and caring towards a loved one: *A little TLC and he'll soon be on his feet again.*

Tlin·git /'tlɪŋgɪt/ *n* (a member of) a group of Native Americans who live in Alaska, many of whom earn their livings by TRADITIONAL methods of fishing and weaving — see also NATIVE AMERICAN (CULTURAL NOTE)

TM /,tiː 'em/ *abbrev. for:* TRANSCENDENTAL MEDITATION

TN *written abbrev for:* TENNESSEE

TNT /,tiː en 'tiː/ *n* [U] trinitrotoluene; a powerful explosive

to¹ /tə; *before vowels* tʊ; *strong* tuː/ *prep* **1 a** in a direction towards: *the road to London* | *She stood up and walked to the window.* | *a journey to China* | *She threw the ball to me.* (=for me to catch. Compare *She threw the stone at me.*=to hurt me) **b** in a direction continuing from: *The town lies (about 20 miles) to the north of New York.* **2** so as to be in: *We're hoping to go to London for our holidays this year.* | *The robber was sent to prison for five years.* **3** reaching as far as: *The water came (right up) to our necks.* **4** so as to be (in a state of): *She sang the baby to sleep.* | *The mob stoned her to death.* | *Wait until the lights change to green.* | *After two difficult years the company is now on the road to recovery.* **5** in a touching position with: *The two lovers danced cheek to cheek.* | *The paper stuck firmly to the wall.* **6** facing or in front of: *They stood face to face|back to back.* | *I sat with my back to the engine.* **7** until and including: *Count (from 10) to 20.* | *I read the book from beginning to end.* | *They stayed from Friday night to|until Sunday morning.* | *It's 10 miles (from here) to London.* | *a nine-to-five job* | *I'm soaked to the skin.* | *They were killed* **to a man/to the last man.** (=they were all killed) —see INCLUSIVE (USAGE) **8** for the attention or possession of: *Have you told all your news to John?* | *I want a present to give to my wife.* | *This is a letter to Mildred from George.* | *You have no right to this land.* | *Will they give you an office to yourself?* (=for your own use, not shared with anyone else) **9** in connection with: *What's your answer to that?* | *She's always kind to animals.* | *a danger to one's health* | *What have you done to the radio? It's not working.* | *There's always an element of risk to starting up a new business.* **10** for; of: *Have you got the key to this lock?* | *He got a job as secretary to a*

doctor. **11** in relation with; in comparison with: *I know he's successful but he's nothing to what he could have been.* | *England beat Scotland by two goals to one.* **12** as far as concerns: *That sounds rather suspicious to me.* | *It costs £10, and to some people that's a lot of money.* | *She has not,* **to my knowledge** (=as far as I know), *written any books since that one.* **13** (with words about addition) as well as; and: *Add two to four.* (compare *Subtract two from four.*) | *In addition to John, there are the girls.* **14** forming; making up: *There are 100 pence to every pound.* | *There are 11 francs to the pound.* **15** in accordance with: *Your dress isn't really to my liking.* | *You will hear of something to your advantage.* **16** so as to cause (esp. a feeling): *He broke it, (greatly) to my annoyance.* | *To my great surprise, we won!* **17** (of time) before: *It's five (minutes) to four."* *"No, it's only ten to four."* | *How long is it to dinner?* | *only two weeks to Christmas* **18** per: *This car does 30 miles to the gallon.* **19** in honour of: *Let's drink to the health of our respected foreign guests.* | *a monument to the war dead* **20 (a number) to (a number): a** between (a number) and (a number): *He drowned in 10 to 12 feet of water.* | *She's 40 to 45.* **b** compared with: *It's 100 to 1 he'll lose.* (=100 times as likely)

▷ USAGE Compare **to** and **till/until** in expressions of time. **To** is used **a** when speaking of the clock: *It's five* **to** *four,* **b** when a time is moved forward: *They've brought the date of the meeting forward* **to** *Wednesday* (but *They've postponed the meeting* **till** *Wednesday),* **c** in certain expressions like **to** *the last,* **to** *this day,* **to** *date.* **To** or **till/until** can be used **a** in considering the length of time before an event: *It's an hour* **to/till** *dinner,* **b** with **from**: *We stayed* **from** *June* **to/till** *September.* —see also INCLUSIVE (USAGE). Otherwise use **till/until**: *We stayed* **until** *seven. I didn't see him* **till** *last week.* —see also O'CLOCK (USAGE), TIME (USAGE)◁

to² /tuː/ *adv* **1** into a shut position: *The wind blew the door to.* **2** into consciousness: *John didn't come to for half an hour after he'd fallen and hit his head.* —see also TO-AND-FRO, **close to** (CLOSE³)

to³ /tə; *before vowels* tʊ; *strong* tuː/ (used before a verb to show it is the INFINITIVE, but not before **can**, **could**, **may**, **might**, **will**, **would**, **shall**, **should**, **must**, or **ought**; it is left out after verbs that have the patterns [+*to-v*] or [+*obj+to-v*]; the verb that should follow **to** is sometimes left out if it can be understood. Note the following patterns: **a** (after verbs): [I+*to-v*] *He lived to be 90.* | *I used to live in New York.* [T+*to-v*] *He wants to leave.* | *He can leave if he wants to.* [T +*obj+to-v*] *They allowed us to go.* (compare [+*obj+to-v*] *They let us go.* | (with reported commands) *He told them to shoot.* (=He said "Shoot!") | *He told them (not) to.* **b** (after **how**, **where**, **who**, **whom**, **whose**, **which**, **when**, **what**, or **whether**): [T+*wh-*] *I know where to go but I don't know how to get there.* | *She wondered whether or not to go|wondered whether to or not.* [T+*obj+wh-*] *Would you tell me when to leave?* **c** (after nouns): [C+*to-v*] *an attem pt to land* [P+*to-v*] *the qualifications to drive* [U+*to-v*] *some reason to leave* **d** (after adjectives): [+*to-v*] *an easy thing to do* [F+*to-v*] *I'm glad|sorry|happy to say...* **e** (when speaking about the verb, as in grammar): *"To find" takes a direct object.* | *To wear boots would be safest.* | *It would be safest to wear boots.* | *What they really should have done was to accept.* **f** (used to show purpose) in order to: *They left early to catch the train.* | *I want some scissors to cut my nails (with).* **g** in the pattern **too**+*adj+to-v*: *It's too cold to go out.* **h** (in the pattern *adj*+**enough**+*to-v*): *It's cold enough to snow.* **i** (in the pattern *to-v* at the beginning of a statement): *To be honest* (=speaking honestly), *I don't know anything about it.* | *To put it another way, do you like him?* | *To begin with, let's...* **j** (in the pattern **There is**+*n+to-v*): *There were plenty of things to eat.* | *There's also the cost to consider.* (=we must consider it)

▷ USAGE It is often considered bad English to put any other word between **to** and the verb that follows it, making a "split infinitive": *He was wrong* **to** *suddenly say that.* But sometimes there is nowhere else to put the word: *Your job is* **to** *really understand these children.* | *He likes to half close his eyes.*◁

toad /təʊd/ *n* an animal like a large FROG, that usu. lives on land, but goes into water for breeding

Toad also **Toad of Toad Hall** /, · · ,· '·/— one of the main characters in the children's story *The Wind in the Willows* by Kenneth Grahame

toad-in-the-hole /ˌ··· ˈ·/ n [U] a British dish of SAUSAGES baked in BATTER (=a mixture of eggs, milk, and flour)

toad-stool /ˈtəʊdstuːl/ n a usu. poisonous or uneatable type of FUNGUS

toad-y¹ /ˈtəʊdi/ n derog someone who is too nice to people of higher rank, esp. for personal advantage; SYCOPHANT

toady² v [I (**to**)] derog to be too nice to someone of higher rank, esp. for personal advantage: *Johnson's promotion is the result of toadying to the boss.*

to-and-fro¹ /ˌ··· ˈ·/ adj (of a repeated journey or movement) forwards and backwards or from one side to the other: *a to-and-fro movement* **—to and fro** adv : *The teacher walked to and fro in front of the class as he spoke.* | *The pendulum swung to and fro.*

to-and-fro² n [(*the*) S (**of**)] infml activity in which people or things move from place to place, pass in opposite directions, etc.: *the busy to-and-fro of passengers in the airport* —see also TO-ING AND FRO-ING

toast¹ /təʊst/ n **1** [U] bread made brown by being placed close to heat, usu. eaten hot with butter: *I like toast for breakfast.* | *a slice of toast* **2** [C (**to**)] an act of drinking esp. wine in a ceremonial way in order to show respect or admiration for someone or something or to express good wishes to someone: *Ladies and gentlemen, I'd like to* **propose a toast** *to the bride and groom.* | *They* **drank a toast** *to the Queen.* **3** [*the*+S] the person or thing in whose honour this is done **4** [*the*+S+**of**] someone or something extremely popular in the stated place or with the stated people: *After the success of her show she was the toast of Broadway/of singers everywhere*

toast² v [T] **1** to make (bread, cheese, etc.) brown by placing it close to heat —see COOK (USAGE) **2** infml to warm thoroughly: *He was toasting his feet by the fire.* **3** to drink a TOAST¹ (1)

toast·er /ˈtəʊstəʳ/ n an electrical apparatus for making TOAST¹ (1) —see picture at KITCHEN

toast·ie /ˈtəʊsti/ n a toasted SANDWICH: *a cheese and ham toastie*

toasting fork /ˈ··· ·/ n a long-handled fork for holding bread in front of an open fire to make TOAST¹ (1)

toast·mas·ter /ˈtəʊstˌmɑːstəʳ‖-ˌmæ-/ n a person who says what the TOASTs¹ (2) are and introduces speakers at a formal dinner

toast·y /ˈtəʊsti/ adj AmE infml warm, dry, and comfortable: *The bed felt toasty and I didn't want to get up.*

to·bac·co /təˈbækəʊ/ n -**cos** **1** [U] the dried leaves of a type of plant as prepared for smoking in cigarettes, pipes, etc., or for chewing (CHEW) or SNUFF: *a report on the harmful effects of tobacco* | *pipe tobacco* **2** [C] a particular type of tobacco: *a mild/strong tobacco*

to·bac·co·nist /təˈbækənɪst/ n a person in charge of a shop that sells tobacco, cigarettes, etc.

to·bog·gan /təˈbɒɡən‖-ˈbɑː-/ n a light frame or board, sometimes on metal blades, used for sliding over snow, esp. down slopes for sport; SLEDGE¹ (2) **—toboggan** v [I] : *The children love to go tobogganing when it snows.*

to·by jug /ˈtəʊbi dʒʌɡ/ n (in Britain) a small container for drinking from, in the form of a fat old man wearing a three-cornered hat. People sometimes collect toby jugs because some are worth a lot of money.

toc·ca·ta /təˈkɑːtə/ n a piece of music, esp. for the ORGAN, piano, or similar instrument, in a free style with difficult passages that show the player's skill

Tocque·ville /ˈtɒkvɪl‖ˈtəʊk-/, **A·lex·is de** /əˈleksɪs də/ (1805–59) a French writer and politician who travelled in the US and then wrote a book called *Democracy in America* which examined the strengths and weaknesses of the American system of government

toc·sin /ˈtɒksɪn‖ˈtɑːk-/ n esp. lit (a bell rung as) a warning signal

tod /tɒd‖tɑːd/ **on one's tod** BrE infml alone; by oneself

to·day¹ /təˈdeɪ/ adv **1** during or on the present day: *Are we going shopping today?* | *He was released from prison early today.* | (*BrE*) *I'm starting my new job a week today/today week.* (=a week from today) **2** during or at the present time; NOWADAYS: *We export more cars today than we've ever done before.* | *Young people today have no manners.* **3** here today and gone tomorrow present or fashionable for only a very short time: *another of those*

pop singers who are here today and gone tomorrow

today² n [U] **1** this present day: *Today's my birthday!* | *Have you seen today's paper?* **2** this present time, period, etc.: *The computers of today/today's computers are far more powerful than those of five years ago.*

Today a popular national daily newspaper in Britain. It is a TABLOID

Todd /tɒd‖tɑːd/, **Sweeney** see SWEENEY TODD

tod·dle /ˈtɒdl‖ˈtɑːdl/ v [I] **1** to walk with short unsteady steps, as a small child does **2** [+adv/prep] infml to walk; go: *I'm just toddling over to Mary's. Why don't you come?*

tod·dler /ˈtɒdləʳ‖ˈtɑːd-/ n a small child who has just learnt to walk —see CHILD (USAGE)

tod·dy /ˈtɒdi‖ˈtɑːdi/ n [C;U] a sweetened mixture of WHISKY and hot water: *A* **hot toddy** *is just the thing for your cold.*

to-do /təˈduː/ n **to-dos** infml **1** [usu. sing.] a state of excited confusion or annoyance; FUSS: *What a to-do about nothing!* **2** AmE rare for DO³ (1)

toe¹ /təʊ/ n **1** any of the five small movable parts at the end of each foot —see picture at FOOT **2** the part of a sock, shoe, etc., that covers the toes: *sandals with open toes* —see picture at SHOE **3 on one's toes** watchful and ready for action; ALERT —compare FINGER; see also **from top to toe** (TOP¹), **tread on someone's toes** (TREAD¹)

toe² v **toe the line** to obey orders or rules; act in accordance with what is usual or expected

toe cap /ˈ· ·/ n a strong covering over the toe of a shoe or boot

toe·hold /ˈtəʊhəʊld/ n a very small place on a rock, etc. just big enough to take part of the foot and thus give support to a climber

toe·nail /ˈtəʊneɪl/ n the nail on the upper end of a toe —see picture at FOOT

toff /tɒf‖tɑːf/ n old-fash infml, esp. BrE a rich and/or well-dressed person of high social class

tof·fee, **toffy** /ˈtɒfi‖ˈtɑːfi/ n [C;U] **1** (a piece of) a hard sticky sweet brown substance made by boiling sugar and butter with water **2 for toffee** also **for nuts**— BrE infml (esp. after **can't**) at all: *He can't sing for toffee!*

toffee ap·ple /ˈ·· ˌ··/ ‖ also **candy apple**, **taffy apple** AmE— n an apple covered with toffee, held on a small stick. Toffee apples are usu. bought by children, esp. at the SEASIDE, at FAIRs, or at Halloween.

toffee-nosed /ˈ··· ·/ adj BrE infml thinking oneself important because of one's social position; SNOBBISH

to·fu /ˈtəʊfuː/ n [U] a soft, cheeselike food much used in Japanese, VEGETARIAN etc. cooking, which is made from the milk of the SOYA BEAN

tog /tɒɡ‖tɑːɡ, tɔːɡ/ n -**gg-**
    tog obdy. **up/out** phr v [T (**in**)] infml to dress (esp. oneself) in specially fine or formal clothes —see also TOGS

to·ga /ˈtəʊɡə/ n a long loose flowing outer garment worn by the citizens of ancient Rome

to·geth·er¹ /təˈɡeðəʳ/ adv **1** so as to form a single group, body, or object; so as to be joined: *Tie these two pieces of string together.* | *Add these numbers together.* | *It's broken, but I can stick it together (again) with glue.* | *We hope these new proposals will bring the two sides in the dispute together.* (=into a state of agreement) | *Your argument does not hold together well.* **2** in or into one place: *People came together from all over the country to attend his funeral.* **3** with each other: *We went to the dance together, but got separated soon after we arrived.* | *Charles and I were at school together.* (=we went to the same school) | *The strings and the brass weren't quite together* (=did not play their notes exactly with each other) *in that passage.* | *She and her ex-husband are getting back together.* —see also GO **together**, LIVE **together**, SLEEP **together 4** to each other: *His eyes are too* **close together**. **5** at the same time: *Why do all the bills always come together?* **6** considered as a whole: *Taken together, these measures should create a lot of new jobs.* —see also PUT **together 7** working or acting in united agreement; combined: *We stand together in our determination to defend our rights.* **8** old-fash without interruption: *It rained for four days together.* **9 together with** as well as; in addition to: *He sent her some roses, together with a nice letter.* —see also ALTOGETHER

together² adj infml apprec **1** very much in control of one's life, feelings, etc.; very well organized (ORGANIZE): *I admire Jane; she's a really together person.* **2 get it together** to have things under control

to·geth·er·ness /təˈgeðənɨs‖-ðər-/ *n* [U] a feeling of being united with other people in a friendly relationship

tog·gle /ˈtɒgəl‖ˈtɑː-/ *n* a short shaped bar of wood used as a button —see picture at FASTENER

To·go /ˈtəʊgəʊ/ a country in W Africa bordered by the Gulf of Guinea, Ghana, and Benin; capital Lomé; population 3,349,000 (1989) —**Togolese** /ˌtəʊgəˈliːz◂/ *n, adj*

togs /tɒgz‖tɑːgz, tɔːgz/ *n* [P] *infml* clothes, esp. for a particular activity

toil¹ /tɔɪl/ *n* [U] *esp. fml or lit* **1** hard or continuous work —see also TOILS; see WORK (USAGE) **2 Double, double, toil and trouble; Fire burn and cauldron bubble.** *quote* a rhyme used by the three witches (WITCH) in Shakespeare's play *Macbeth* —see colour picture on page 1146

toil² *v* [I+*adv/prep*] *esp. fml or lit* **1** to work for a long time and with great effort **2** to move slowly with great effort or pain: *The slaves toiled up the hill pulling the heavy blocks.*

toi·let /ˈtɔɪlɨt/ *n* **1** [C] an apparatus, usu. a seatlike bowl, fixed to the floor and connected to a pipe (DRAIN), used for getting rid of the body's waste matter **2** [C] *esp. BrE* a room containing a toilet —see USAGE **3** [U] *old-fash fml* the act of washing and dressing oneself: *Madam does not wish to be interrupted while she is at her toilet.*

▷ USAGE In British English **toilet** is a generally acceptable, but **lavatory** and **WC** (becoming old-fashioned except when talking about the plans of houses) are also used. **Loo** is a fairly common informal word. **Public conveniences** is the formal expression for specially built buildings containing toilets used by the public, and these are often called **the gents** (for men's toilets) and **the ladies** (for women's toilets). In American English **bathroom, restroom,** and **washroom** are commonly used for **toilet,** and **john** is a common informal word. Public toilets are usu. called **the men's room** and the **women's room**: *Excuse me. Can you tell me where the* **toilet**/*the* **loo**/*the* **gents**/*the* **ladies**/*the* **bathroom** (*AmE*)/*the* **restroom** (*AmE*) *is?*◁

toilet bag /ˈ·· ·/ *n* a bag for holding toiletries

toilet pa·per /ˈ·· ˌ··/ also **toilet tissue, lavatory paper**— *n* [U] thin paper, in a continuous length or single pieces, for cleaning oneself after passing waste matter from the body

toi·let·ries /ˈtɔɪlɨtriz/ *n* [P] articles or substances used in washing, making oneself tidy, etc.: *toothpaste, shaving foam, cologne, and other men's toiletries*

toilet roll /ˈ·· ·/ *n esp. BrE* a rolled-up continuous length of TOILET PAPER

toilet-trained /ˈ·· ·/ *adj* POTTY-TRAINED

toilet train·ing /ˈ·· ˌ··/ *n* [U] the teaching of a young child when and how to use the toilet

toilet wa·ter /ˈ·· ˌ··/ *n* [U] a pleasant-smelling but not very strong PERFUME¹ (2)

toils /tɔɪlz/ *n* [P] *esp. lit* something in which one becomes firmly trapped

to·ing and fro·ing /ˌtuːɪŋ ən ˈfrəʊɪŋ/ also **to-ings and fro-ings** *pl.*— *n* [U] *infml* busy unproductive activity: *After a lot of to-ing and fro-ing they reached a decision.*

To·kay /təʊˈkeɪ/ a sweet, heavy wine made in Tokay in Hungary

to·ken¹ /ˈtəʊkən/ *n* **1** [(**of**)] an outward sign; something that represents a fact, event, feeling, etc.: *All the family wore black as a token of their grief.* | *Please accept this small gift as* **a token of our gratitude.** | *They waved a white flag* **in token of** (=to show) *surrender.* **2** [(**of**)] something that acts as a reminder; KEEPSAKE; SOUVENIR: *My husband gave me a ring as a token of our first meeting.* **3** *BrE* ‖ **gift certificate** *AmE*— a sort of special ticket, usu. fixed to a greetings card, which one can exchange for the stated thing in a shop: *a £10 record token* | *a book token* | *a gift token* (=that one can exchange for anything in a particular shop) **4** a piece of metal used instead of coins for a particular purpose —see also **by the same token** (SAME¹)

token² *adj* [A] **1** done or given as a small sign representing something greater: *a token payment* **2** usu. derog

done or given so as to seem acceptable: *They made a token effort.* | *a token gesture of support* | *It seemed to us she'd been invited onto the committee as the token woman.*

to·ken·ism /ˈtəʊkənɪzəm/ *n* [U] *derog* the practice of giving official favour to representatives of special groups in society only to produce an appearance of fairness

To Kill a Mock·ing·bird /· ˌ· ·· ˈ··ː/ an American NOVEL by Harper Lee, which was later made into a film. The story takes place in Alabama during the Depression and concerns children learning about racial PREJUDICE.

To·ky·o /ˈtəʊkiəʊ/ the capital and largest city of Japan, and its main financial,business and ADMINISTRATIVE centre; population 8,348,000 (1987). Tokyo is one of the largest and busiest cities in the world.

told /təʊld/ *past tense & participle of* TELL

tol·e·ra·ble /ˈtɒlərəbəl‖ˈtɑː-/ *adj* fairly good or acceptable; that can be tolerated —see also INTOLERABLE

tol·e·ra·bly /ˈtɒlərəbli‖ˈtɑː-/ *adv fml or pomp* to a limited degree; fairly: *I feel tolerably well today.*

tol·e·rance /ˈtɒlərəns‖ˈtɑː-/ *n* **1** [U (**for, of, towards**)] also **toleration**— *apprec* willingness to accept or allow behaviour, beliefs, customs, etc., which one does not like or agree with, without opposition: *Try and show some tolerance.* | *a country with a reputation for tolerance towards religious minorities* | *the government's tolerance of political dissent* **2** [C;U (**of, to**)] the ability to suffer pain, hardship, etc., without being harmed or damaged: *Many old people have a very limited tolerance to cold.* **3** [C;U] *tech* the amount by which the measure of a value can vary from the amount intended, without causing difficulties: *This machine part was built* **to a tolerance of** *0.01 millimetres.* (=if it is bigger or smaller by more than this amount it will not fit or work properly) **4** [C;U (**to, of**)] *tech* the degree to which a cell, animal, plant, etc., can successfully oppose the effect of a poison, drug, etc.

tol·e·rant /ˈtɒlərənt‖ˈtɑː-/ *adj* [(**of, towards**)] showing or practising tolerance: *a tolerant father* —see also INTOLERANT —~**ly** *adv*

tol·e·rate /ˈtɒləreɪt‖ˈtɑː-/ *v* [T] **1** to allow (something one does not agree with) to be practised or done freely without opposition; permit **2** to suffer (someone or something) without complaining or becoming annoyed: *I won't tolerate your bad manners any longer.* | *He never could tolerate bores.* —see BEAR (USAGE)

tol·e·ra·tion /ˌtɒləˈreɪʃən‖ˌtɑː-/ *n* [U] TOLERANCE (1), esp. of religious beliefs or practices that are different from those recognized by the state: *religious toleration*

to let /· ˈ·· / *BrE*‖**for rent** *AmE*— *adj* (of a house, flat or other building) available to be rented: *a "To Let" sign*

Tol·kien /ˈtɒlkiːn‖ˈtɑːl-/, **J R R** (1892–1973) an English writer and university teacher best known for his FANTASY books *The Hobbit* and *The Lord of the Rings*

toll¹ /təʊl/ *n* **1** a tax paid for the right to use a road, HARBOUR, etc. **2** [*usu. sing.*] the cost in health, life, etc., of an illness, an accident, etc.: *the usual heavy death toll on the roads at Christmas* | *Years of hardship and neglect had* **taken their toll** (*on his health*). (=harmed it)

toll² *v* **1** [I;T] **a** to ring (a bell) slowly and repeatedly **b** (of a bell) to be rung slowly and repeatedly **2** [T] (of a bell) to tell or make known by doing this: *The church bell tolled the hour.*

toll³ *n* [(*the*) S] the sound of a tolling bell

toll·booth /ˈtəʊlbuːθ/ *n* a place where TOLLS¹ (1) are or were collected

toll-free /ˌ· ˈ·◂/ *adj AmE* (of a telephone call) paid for by the organization receiving it rather than the person making it —compare FREEFONE —**toll-free** *adv*

toll·gate /ˈtəʊlgeɪt/ *n* a gate across a road at which a TOLL¹ (1) must be paid

toll·house cook·ie /ˌtəʊlhaʊs ˈkʊki/ also **chocolate-chip cookie** *n AmE* a small, heavy cake (BISCUIT) which has small pieces of chocolate in it

toll road /ˈ· ·/ *n* a road on which a TOLL¹(1) must be paid

toll·way /ˈtəʊlweɪ/ *n AmE* a MOTORWAY, often running a long distance, which the motorist must pay to use: *the Illinois Tollway* —see EXPRESSWAY (USAGE)

Tol·pud·dle Mar·tyrs /ˌtɒlpʌdl ˈmɑːtəz‖ˌtɑːlpʌdl ˈmɑːrtərz/ [*the*+P] a group of English farm workers at Tolpuddle in

Dorset who formed a TRADE UNION in 1833. They were put in prison and then sent to Australia as CONVICTs because of this, but later freed after great public protest.

Tol·stoy /ˈtɒlstɔɪ‖ˈtəʊl-/, **Count Leo** (1828–1910) a Russian writer best known for his long NOVELs *War and Peace* and *Anna Karenina*

tom·a·hawk /ˈtɒməhɔːk‖ˈtɑː-/ *n* a light AXE formerly used by Native Americans in war and hunting —see picture at AXE

Tom and Jer·ry /ˌtɒm ənd ˈdʒeri‖ˌtɑːm-/ a television CARTOON cat and mouse. Tom is always chasing Jerry, but Jerry is more clever than Tom and usu. finds ways of escaping.

to·ma·to /təˈmɑːtəʊ‖-ˈmeɪ-/ *n* **-toes** [C;U] a soft fleshy juicy red fruit eaten raw or cooked as a vegetable: *a pound of tomatoes | a tomato salad* —see picture at VEGETABLE

tomb /tuːm/ *n* a grave, esp. a large decorative one built to have a large space inside where the dead person is placed

Tomb of the Un·known Sol·dier /ˌ· · · ˌ·· ˈ··/ [*the*] see UNKNOWN SOLDIER

tom·bo·la /tɒmˈbəʊlə‖tɑːm-/ *n* [U] *esp.* BrE a game in which tickets are chosen by chance to win prizes

tom·boy /ˈtɒmbɔɪ‖ˈtɑːm-/ *n* a spirited young girl who enjoys rough and noisy activities — ~**ish** *adj*

Tom Brown's School·days /ˌ· ˌ· ˈ··/ an 1857 book which described life in a 19th century English boy's private school. The book describes much bullying (BULLY) of younger boys by older boys. —see also FLASHMAN

tomb·stone /ˈtuːmstəʊn/ *n* a GRAVESTONE

Tombstone a city in Arizona in the US, SITE of the OK Corral, where one of the Wild West's most famous gun fights took place

tom·cat /ˈtɒmkæt‖ˈtɑːm-/ also **tom** /tɒm‖tɑːm/*infml*— *n* a male cat —compare TABBY (2)

Tom Col·lins, tom collins /ˌ· ˈ··/ *n* AmE a drink made with alcohol, usu. GIN, the juice of a LEMON or LIME, and sugar

Tom, Dick and Har·ry /ˌ· ˌ· ˈ··/ *n* [S] *derog* anybody, no matter who he or she may be: *You don't think I'd tell any Tom, Dick and Harry, do you?*

tome /təʊm/ *n esp. lit or humor* a large heavy book

tom·fool·er·y /tɒmˈfuːləri‖tɑːm-/ *n fml* **1** [U] foolish behaviour **2** [C *usu. pl.*] a foolish act

Tom Jones /ˌ· ˈ·/ the title of a NOVEL by Henry Fielding, concerning the (esp. sexual) adventures of an ORPHAN in his young adult years

Tom·lin /ˈtɒmlɪn‖ˈtɑːm-/, **Lily** (1939?–) an American actress and COMEDIENNE

Tom·my /ˈtɒmi‖ˈtɑː-/ *n infml, old-fash* a British soldier of the lowest rank

tom·my gun /ˈtɒmi ɡʌn‖ˈtɑː-/ *n infml* a light MACHINEGUN

tom·my·rot /ˈtɒmirɒt‖ˈtɑːmirɑːt/ *n* [U] *old-fash.* complete nonsense

to·mor·row[1] /təˈmɒrəʊ‖-ˈmɔː-, -ˈmɑː-/ *adv* during or on the day following today: *I hope it will be sunny tomorrow. | I'll be back tomorrow night. | (BrE) I'm starting my new job a week tomorrow/tomorrow week.* (=a week from tomorrow)

tomorrow[2] *n* **1** [U] the day following today: *Tomorrow will be my birthday! | I'll see you at tomorrow's meeting.| Will it be ready in time for tomorrow?* —see DAY (USAGE) **2** [S;U] the future: *a brighter tomorrow | tomorrow's world/The computers of tomorrow will be even more powerful than the ones we use now.* **3 never put off till tomorrow what you can do today** *saying* necessary jobs should always be done immediately, for if they are left till later they may be forgotten and never get done **4 tomorrow and tomorrow and tomorrow** *quote* a well-known line from a speech by Macbeth in Shakespeare's play *Macbeth*

Tom Sawyer see Tom SAWYER

Tom Thumb /ˌ· ˈ·/ a child in a fairy story who was only as big as a thumb: *rows of Tom Thumb-sized cars and lorries*

tom-tom /ˈ·· ·/ *n* a long narrow drum usu. played by being beaten with the hands

ton /tʌn/ *n* **1** [C] (*pl.* **tons** or **ton**) a measure of weight — see TABLE 2 **2** [C (**of**)] also **tons** *pl.*— *infml* a very large quantity: *I bought tons of fruit while it was cheap.* **3** [S]

infml a heavy weight: *This book* **weighs a ton.** (=is very heavy) **4** [(*the*) S] *old-fash infml* 100 miles per hour: *The motorcyclist must have been* **doing a ton** *as he passed me.* —see also TON-UP **5 come down on someone like a ton of bricks** *infml* to turn the full force of one's anger against someone, usu. as a punishment —see also TONS; compare TONNE

ton·al /ˈtəʊnl/ *adj* of tonality or tone or having tonality — see also ATONAL

ton·al·i·ty /təʊˈnælɪti/ *n tech* **1** [C;U] the character of a tune depending on the musical KEY in which it is played **2** [C] a musical KEY

tone[1] /təʊn/ *n* **1** [C] the quality or character of the sound produced by a particular instrument or singing voice: *That piano has a beautiful tone.* **2** [C] also **tones** *pl.*— a particular quality of the voice regarded as expressing a particular feeling or meaning; manner of expression: *The speaker urged us in ringing tones to support his cause.| I don't like your tone (of voice); don't take that tone with me.* (=I am annoyed or displeased by the way you are talking to me) **3** [S;U] **a** the general quality or nature of something: *the optimistic tone of the report | Her friendly opening speech* **set the tone for** *the whole conference.* **b** high quality of character: *These dreadful people* **bring down/lower the tone of** *the neighbourhood.* **4** [C] a variety or shade of a colour, different from other varieties because of more light or darkness, the addition of a slight quantity of another colour, etc.: *a picture painted in various tones of blue* —see also TWO-TONE **5** AmE for NOTE[1] (5) **6** [C] ‖ also **step** *esp. AmE— tech* a difference in the highness of a musical note equal to that between two notes which are two notes apart on a piano: *There is a tone between B and C sharp; B and C are half a tone apart.* —see also SEMITONE **7** the sound made by various electronic instruments, esp. push-button telephones or telephone answering machines: *Please leave a message after the tone.* **8** [U] *tech* the healthy and proper state of firmness of the organs, muscles, etc., of the body: *Exercise improves muscle tone.* **9 -toned** /təʊnd/ having the stated TONE[1] (1) —see also DIALLING TONE

tone[2] *v*

tone sthg. ↔ **down** *phr v* [T] to reduce the violence or forcefulness of; MODERATE: *In his public statement he toned down the criticisms he had made in private. | That orange paint's rather garish for the bedroom; I'd tone it down a bit!*

tone in *phr v* [I (**with**)] to match; HARMONIZE: *I think black shoes would tone in better with your coat than red ones.*

tone sbdy./sthg. ↔ **up** *phr v* [T] to make stronger, healthier, or more lively: *Swimming is the best way to tone up your body.*

tone-deaf /ˌ· ˈ·◂/ *adj* unable to tell the difference between different musical notes

tone lan·guage /ˈ· ˌ··/ *n tech* a language, such as Chinese or Yoruba, in which highness or lowness of sound are used for expressing the difference in meaning between words that otherwise sound the same

tone·less /ˈtəʊnləs/ *adj* lacking colour, spirit, etc.; lifeless; dull: *a toneless voice/reply* — ~**ly** *adv*

tone po·em /ˈ· ˌ··/ *n* a piece of music written to represent a poetic idea, scene, etc., musically

Tong·a /ˈtɒŋə‖ˈtɑː-/ a country (**Kingdom of Tonga**) consisting of about 170 islands in the SW Pacific ocean, an independent member of the British Commonwealth since 1970; capital Nuku'alofa; population 119,000 (1989) —**Tongan** *n, adj*

tongs /tɒŋz‖tɑːŋz, tɔːŋz/ *n* [P] an instrument consisting of two movable arms joined at one end, used for holding or lifting various objects: *She used (a pair of) tongs to put some more coal on the fire. | sugar tongs for picking up lumps of sugar* —see pictures at FIREPLACE and LABORATORY

tongue /tʌŋ/ *n* **1** [C] the movable fleshy organ in the mouth, used for tasting, moving food around, and, in human beings, for producing speech **2** [U] the tongue of an animal such as the cow, cooked as food: *ham and tongue sandwiches* **3** [C] any of various objects like a tongue in shape, such as the piece of hanging metal in the middle of a bell or the piece of material under the LACEs in a shoe: *Tongues of flame shot out from the*

burning hut. | *a tongue of land* —see picture at SHOE   4 [C] *fml or lit* a spoken language: *This dictionary is specially intended for people whose native tongue is not English.*   5 [*(the)* S] (in certain phrases) the tongue considered as the organ of speech: *She has rather a sharp tongue.* (=severe or unkind way of speaking) | *Hold your tongue!* (=Keep quiet!) | *I meant to say Friday, not Monday: it was a* **slip of the tongue.**   6 **get one's tongue (a)round** *infml* to pronounce (a difficult word, name, etc.) correctly: *I find it hard to get my tongue round these Polish names.*   7 **give/get a tongue-lashing** *AmE infml* to give or receive a spoken expression of annoyance or disapproval: *He got a tongue-lashing from his mother for tracking mud all over the living-room carpet.*   8 **set tongues wagging** to cause much interest and talk; make people GOSSIP   9 **speak with a forked tongue** *AmE humor* (a phrase used by Native Americans in old films or people copying them) to lie: *White man speaks with forked tongue.*   10 **(with) (one's) tongue in (one's) cheek** *infml* without seriously meaning what one says: *He described me as a brilliant singer, but he said it tongue in cheek/with his tongue in his cheek.* | *a tongue-in-cheek remark*   11 **-tongued** /tʌŋd/a having a tongue of the stated kind: *a fork-tongued snake* **b** (habitually) speaking in the stated manner: *a sharp-tongued critic* —see also MOTHER TONGUE, **bite one's tongue** (BITE¹), **the rough side of one's tongue** (ROUGH¹), **on the tip of one's tongue** (TIP¹)

tongue de·press·or /ˈ· ·ˌ·ˌ·/ *n AmE* a thin, flat piece of wood rounded at both ends used by a doctor to hold down the tongue while examining the throat —compare SPATULA (2)

tongues /tʌŋz/ **speak in tongues** to speak as if in a TRANCE, as part of a religious experience, using words of no known language

tongue-tied /ˈ· ·/ *adj* unable to speak freely, esp. because of awkwardness in the presence of others

tongue twist·er /ˈ· ˌ·/ *n* a word or phrase that is difficult to speak quickly or correctly

ton·ic¹ /ˈtɒnɪk‖ˈtɑː-/ *adj* **1** *tech* (in music) of or based on the TONIC² (3)   2 *fml* healthy and strengthening: *Sea air has a tonic quality.*

tonic² *n* **1** [C (for) *usu. sing.*] something that increases health, strength, or confidence: *Country air is the best tonic for someone who lives in the city.* | *When I was depressed I found her advice a real tonic.*   2 [C] a medicine intended to give the body more strength, esp. when tired: *You look run-down; you need a tonic.* | *tonic wine*   3 [*(the)* S] *tech* the first note of a musical scale of eight notes —compare DOMINANT²

tonic sol-fa /ˌ··· ˈ·/ *n* [U] a method of showing musical notes by the first letters of the words in the SOL-FA system

tonic wa·ter /ˈ·· ˌ··/ also **tonic** ‖ *usu.* **quinine water** *AmE—* *n* [U] gassy water made bitter by the addition of QUININE, often added to strong alcoholic drinks: *a gin and tonic*

to·night¹ /təˈnaɪt/ *adv* on or during the night of today: *I've been really tired today so I think I'll go to bed early tonight.* | *at 9 o'clock tonight*

tonight² *n* [U] the night of today: *Tonight is a very special occasion.* | *Did you hear tonight's radio news?*

Tonight Show /ˈ·· ˌ·/, **The** an American television programme shown late at night which consists of conversations with famous people and music. The HOST (=person who runs the show) of the *Tonight Show* for many years was Johnny Carson, and most people know that he was always introduced with the words, "Here's Johnny!" Carson always began the show with a humorous MONOLOGUE (=a speech by one person) about current events and always finished it by making a movement like someone hitting a GOLF ball. When Carson left in 1992 he was replaced by Jay Leno.

ton·nage /ˈtʌnɪdʒ/ *n* [C;U] **1** the size of a ship or the amount of goods it can carry, expressed in TONs   2 all the ships of a nation, esp. those that carry goods: *There were heavy losses in Britain's merchant tonnage during the Battle of the Atlantic.*

tonne /tʌn/ *n* **tonnes** *or* **tonne** a measure of weight — compare TON; see TABLE 2

tons /tʌnz/ *adv infml* very much: *I feel tons better after that drink!*

ton·sil /ˈtɒnsəl‖ˈtɑːn-/ *n* either of two small roundish organs of flesh at the sides of the throat near the back of the tongue which were once commonly removed in childhood by operation: *She had to have her tonsils out.* —see picture at RESPIRATORY

ton·sil·li·tis , tonsilitis /ˌtɒnsɟˈlaɪtɟs‖ˌtɑːn-/ *n* [U] a painful soreness of the tonsils

ton·so·ri·al /tɒnˈsɔːriəl‖tɑːn-/ *adj usu. humor* of a men's HAIRDRESSER or his work

ton·sure /ˈtɒnʃəʳ‖ˈtɑːn-/ *n* **1** [U] the religious act of removing all the hair from the top part of the head as a sign one is a MONK   2 [C] the part of the head that has had the hair removed in this way

Ton·to /ˈtɒntəʊ‖ˈtɑːn-/ a Native American character in the American television programme *The Lone Ranger*, who was the Lone Ranger's friend and companion —see LONE RANGER

ton-up /ˈ· ·/ *adj* [A] *BrE old-fash infml* (of a driver) liking to travel at high speeds, esp. over 100 miles per hour

to·ny /ˈtəʊni/ *adj AmE infml* fashionable, with style, and expensive: *a tony restaurant uptown*

Tony A·ward /ˈ·· ·ˌ·/ also **Tony**— *n* a prize given to the best theatre actor, best actress, best play, etc., shown in New York in a particular year

too /tuː/ *adv* **1** (before adjectives and adverbs) more than enough; to a higher degree than is necessary, right, or good: *You're going (much) too fast, slow down!* | *This dress is (a bit) too small for me.* | *We got there too late and missed the plane. There's been (far) too little rain lately and the crops are suffering.* [+to-v] *It's too cold to go swimming.*| *It's too early for us to go yet.* | *It was too good an opportunity to miss.* (not *a too good opportunity*) | *He's too much of a coward* (=too cowardly) *to fight.*   2 Very: *Thanks for all your help — you're too kind!* | *I haven't been too well lately.* (=I've been rather ill) | *She won't be too pleased when she hears about this.* | *We were* **only too** *pleased* (=very pleased) *to be able to help.*   3 (not at the beginning of a CLAUSE) also; in addition; as well: *I can dance and sing too.* | *I can dance. I can sing too.* (compare *I can't dance. I can't sing either.*) | *"I enjoyed that film." "Yes, I liked it too."* | *It snowed yesterday; in October too!* (=this is surprising) —compare EITHER⁴; see ALSO (USAGE)   4 *infml, esp. AmE* in fact: *"I won't do it." "You will too!"* (=you must)

▷ USAGE 1 You can say *The day is* **too** *hot* or *It's* **too** *hot a day.* (Notice the word order.) **Too** cannot be used before ordinary adjectives in the pattern **too** + adjective + noun; you can say *The coffee is* **too** *sweet* but not *the* **too** *sweet coffee.* 2 *He's* **too** *much of a coward to shoot* means either **a** "for him to shoot others" or **b** "for others to shoot him".◁

took /tʊk/ *past tense of* TAKE

tool¹ /tuːl/ *n* **1** a simple instrument that is held in the hands and used for doing special jobs, such as a hammer, spade, or SCREWDRIVER: *a set of tools* —see also MACHINE TOOL; see MACHINE (USAGE)   2 something necessary or useful for doing one's job: *Words are the tools of his trade.* | *This computer program gives managers a valuable planning tool.*   3 [(of)] a person unfairly or dishonestly used by another for the other person's own purposes: *The king was just the tool of the military government.*   4 *taboo sl for* PENIS —see also **down tools** (DOWN⁵)

tool² *v* **1** [T] to shape or make with a tool: *The artist tooled a pattern onto the cover of the book with a hot needle.* | *hand-tooled leather boots*   2 [I+adv/prep] *infml* to ride or drive: *We were tooling along (the road) at 50 miles per hour.*

tool (sthg. ↔) **up** *phr v* [I;T] to prepare (a factory) for production by providing the necessary tools and machinery

tool box /ˈ· ·/ *n* a box for tools

tool kit /ˈ· ·/ *n* a number of different tools for doing most jobs

tool·shed /ˈtuːlʃed/ *n* a small wooden building in a private garden where garden or other tools are kept

toot /tuːt/ *v* [I;T] **1** to (cause to) make a short warning or greeting sound with a horn, whistle, etc.: *The drivers were tooting their horns.*   2 *AmE sl* to take (the drug COCAINE) up through the nose —**toot** *n* : *to give a toot on one's horn*

tools

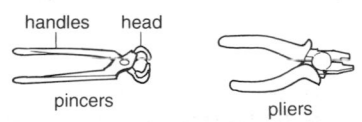

handles   head

pincers   pliers

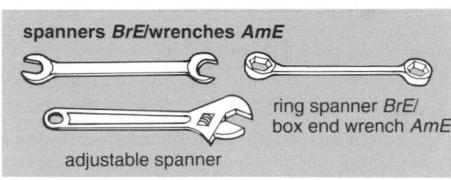

spanners *BrE*/wrenches *AmE*

ring spanner *BrE*/
box end wrench *AmE*

adjustable spanner

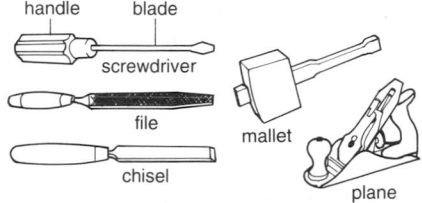

handle   blade

screwdriver

file

mallet

chisel

plane

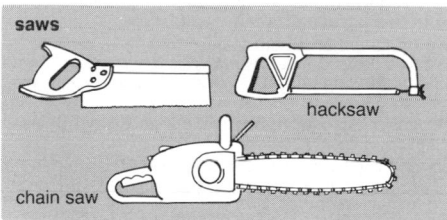

saws

hacksaw

chain saw

see also pictures at **axe,** drill and hammer

tooth /tuːθ/ *n* **teeth** /tiːθ/ **1** any of the small hard bony objects growing in the upper and lower parts of the mouth of most animals, used for biting and chewing (CHEW) food: *Brush your teeth twice a day.* | *I'm going to the dentist to have a tooth out.* —see picture at TEETH **2** any of the narrow pointed parts that stand out from a comb, SAW, COG, etc. **3 tooth and nail** with great violence or determination: *We* **fought tooth and nail** *to get our plans accepted.* **4 -toothed** /tuːθt/having teeth of the stated kind or number —see also TEETH. SWEET TOOTH. **long in the tooth** (LONG¹ (8)) – **~ less** *adj*

tooth·ache /ˈtuːθ-eɪk/ *n* [C;U] (a) pain in a tooth —see ACHE (USAGE)

tooth·brush /ˈtuːθbrʌʃ/ *n* a small brush used for cleaning one's teeth —see picture at BRUSH

tooth·comb /ˈtuːθkəʊm/ *n* see FINE-TOOTH COMB

tooth fai·ry /ˈ· ˌ··/ *n* an imaginary small person who some parents tell their children will leave them a coin in return for a tooth which has fallen out, if they leave the tooth under their PILLOW at night

tooth·less /ˈtuːθləs/ *adj* having no teeth: *a toothless smile*

tooth·paste /ˈtuːθpeɪst/ *n* [U] a specially prepared substance for cleaning one's teeth

tooth·pick /ˈtuːθ-pɪk/ *n* a short thin pointed piece of wood, plastic, etc., used for removing food stuck between one's teeth

tooth pow·der /ˈ· ˌ··/ *n* [U] a specially prepared powder for cleaning one's teeth

tooth·some /ˈtuːθsəm/ *adj fml* or *humor* (esp. of food) pleasant: *toothsome delicacies*

tooth·y /ˈtuːθi/ *adj infml* having or showing many or big teeth: *a toothy grin*

toot·le /ˈtuːtl/ *v infml* **1** [I+*adv*/*prep*] *BrE* to go or drive in an unhurried manner: *I must just tootle down to the shops for some flour.* **2** [I;T] to TOOT continuously and quietly: *He was tootling (on) his trumpet.* —**tootle** *n*

toots /tʊts/ also **tootsie** *n AmE infml old fash* (used as a friendly form of address to a woman, which some women find offensive): *Hi toots! How are you doing?*

toot·sie , **tootsy** /ˈtʊtsi/ *n* **1** (used by or to a child) a foot **2** *AmE infml* TOOTS

top¹ /tɒp‖tɑːp/ *n* **1** [C (**of**)] the highest or upper part: *the top of the hill* | *The mountain tops were hidden in mist.* | *Her name was at the top of the list/page.* | *the top* (=upper surface) *of my desk* | *the table top* | *He wore a woolly hat with a little red bobble* **on top. 2** [(*the*) S (**of**)] the best, most important or most successful part or place: *She is always at the top of the class.* (=always gets the highest marks) | *He started life at the bottom and worked his way up to the top.* | *The workers in this industry have always been at the top of the wages league.* | *The company will have to expand if it wants to stay* **on top. 3** [C] a cover, esp. for a small container: *I can't unscrew the top of this bottle.* | *He left the top off the toothpaste.* —compare CAP, LID; see picture **4** [C] a garment worn on the upper part of the body: *a skirt with a matching top* **5** [(**in**) U] the highest GEAR¹ (3) of a motor vehicle **6** [C *usu. pl.*] the highest part(s) of a plant, usu. leaves: *birds flying through the treetops* | *turnip tops* **7** the first half of an INNING: *the top of the ninth* **8 at the top of one's voice** (shouting or singing) as loudly as possible **9 at top speed** very fast **10 from top to bottom** (of a place or organization) all through; completely: *This company needs reorganizing from top to bottom.* **11 from top to toe** (of a person) completely: *She was dressed in green from top to toe.* **12 from the top** *infml* from the beginning: *Play the song through again from the top.* **13 get on top of** *infml* to be too much or too difficult for: *This work is getting on top of me.* **14 off the top of one's head** at once, without careful thought: *I'm not sure of the answer, but off the top of my head I'd say there were about 30.* **15 on top of: a** in addition to: *He lost his job and on top of that his wife left him.* **b** in complete control of: *a competent teacher who's really on top of his job* **16 on top of the world** very happy **17 over the top** *infml, esp. BrE* more than is reasonable, sensible, or proper: *His jokes are always in such bad taste; he can't be funny without going over the top.* **18 the top of the tree** *infml* the highest position in a profession **19 top whack** *BrE infml* at most; at the highest: *The rate's about £7 an hour, or maybe £8 top whack.* —compare BOTTOM¹; see also TOPS, BIG TOP, SCREW TOP, **blow one's top** (BLOW¹), **thin on top** (THIN¹ (11))

top² *adj* of or at the top, highest, best, most important, etc.: *the top floor of a building* | *Our team's on top form* (=playing very well) *this month.* | *one of this country's top businessmen* | *Bob* **came (out) top** *in the exam.* | *He got top marks.* | *They agreed to give the matter top priority.*

top³ *v* **-pp-** [T] **1** to be higher, better, or more than: *Our profits have topped £1,000,000 this year.* | *I can top your story with an even funnier one.* | *A rival company has topped our offer with a bid of $25 million.* **2** [(**with**)] to provide or form a top for: *The cake was topped with cream.* **3** (in sport) to hit (a ball) above the centre **4 top the bill** to be the chief actor or actress in a show or play

top sthg. ↔ **off** *phr v* [T] *esp. AmE* **1** to complete successfully by a last action: *Let's top off the evening with a drink.* **2** to TOP out (2)

top out *phr v* **1** [I] to reach a highest point (and stop rising): *Do you think interest rates have topped out now?* **2** [T] (**top** sthg. ↔ **out**) *esp. BrE* to complete the building of (a large building), esp. with a special ceremony

top sthg./sbdy. ↔ **up** *phr v* [T] *esp. BrE* **1** [(**with**)] **a** to fill (a partly empty container) with liquid: *to top up the petrol tank* **b** *infml* to put more drink into (a person's) glass: *Your glass is nearly empty; let me top you up!* **2** to complete or bring to an acceptable level by adding something: *The director's salary is topped up by a share in the company's profits.*

top⁴ *n* **1** a child's toy that is made to spin and balance on its point by twisting it sharply **2 like a top** (sleeping) deeply and well

to·paz /ˈtəʊpæz/ *n* [C;U] (a precious stone cut from) a transparent yellowish mineral

top brass /ˌ· ˈ·/ *n* [(*the*) U+*sing./pl. v*] *infml* people in positions of high rank, esp. the armed forces

top·coat /ˈtɒpkəʊt‖ˈtɑːp-/ *n* **1** [C;U] the last covering of paint to be put on a surface —compare UNDERCOAT **2** [C] an OVERCOAT

top dog /ˌ· ˈ·/ *n infml* the person in the highest or most important position, esp. after a struggle or effort

top-down /ˌ· ˈ·/ *adj* beginning with the general principles of a situation and working from there to specific details

top drawer /ˌ· ˈ·◂/ *n* [the+S] *old-fash infml* the highest social class: *She's not quite* **out of the top drawer** *you know, my dear.* —**top-drawer** *adj*

top·dress·ing /ˌtɒpˈdresɪŋ‖ˈtɑːpˌdresɪŋ/ *n* [C;U] a covering of LIME, sand, MANURE, etc., spread over land but not dug into it

to·pee , topi /ˈtəʊpiː‖təʊˈpiː/ *n* a hard hat for protecting the head in tropical sunshine

top-flight /ˌ· ˈ·◂/ *adj infml* of highest position or quality: *top-flight scientists/executives*

top gear /ˌ· ˈ·/ *n* [U] **1** the highest GEAR¹ (3) of a motor vehicle: *The car will cruise at 80 miles per hour in top gear.* **2** a state of great or highest activity: *With just two weeks to go till the election, the party's electoral campaign is in top gear.*

top hat /ˌ· ˈ·/ *n* a man's tall black or grey silk hat, now worn only on formal occasions —see picture at HAT

top-heav·y /ˌ· ˈ·◂/ *adj* not properly balanced because of too much weight at the top; too heavy at the top in relation to the bottom: (fig.) *With so many high-ranking executives, this organization's getting top-heavy.*

to·pi·a·ry /ˈtəʊpiəri‖-pieri/ *n* [U] **1** the art of cutting trees and bushes into decorative shapes **2** (a garden containing) trees and bushes so cut

top·ic /ˈtɒpɪk‖ˈtɑː-/ *n* a subject for conversation, talk, writing, etc.: *Politics or religion are always interesting topics of conversation.*

top·ic·al /ˈtɒpɪkəl‖ˈtɑː-/ *adj* of, dealing with, or being a subject of interest at the present time: *topical issues | The recent events in China have made this film very topical.* – –**ly** /kli/ *adv* – –**ity** /ˌtɒpˈkælᵻti‖ˌtɑː-/ *n* [U]
▷ USAGE **Topical** has the same connection with time as **local** has with place: *of great* **topical** *interest* (=interesting now but not always) | *of great* **local** *interest* (=interesting here but not everywhere).◁

top·knot /ˈtɒpnɒt‖ˈtɑːpnɑːt/ *n* a knot or bunch of hair, RIB-BONS, etc., worn on the top of the head

top·less /ˈtɒpləs‖ˈtɑːp-/ *adj, adv* **1** (of a woman) with the upper part of the body, including the breasts, bare: *a beach where women go topless | topless waitresses* **2** (of a garment) leaving the upper part of a woman's body, including the breasts, uncovered: *a topless swimsuit*

top-lev·el /ˈ· ·◂/ *adj* [A] very high or highest in level of authority, importance, or quality: *top-level management | Top-level talks are to be held between the heads of state.*

top·most /ˈtɒpməʊst‖ˈtɑːp-/ *adj* [A] highest; right at the top

top-notch /ˌ· ˈ·◂/ *adj infml* of highest rank or quality; being one of the best possible

Top of the Pops /ˌ· · · ˈ·/ a British television programme in which POP³ groups play their latest music

to·pog·raph·er /təˈpɒɡrəfəʳ‖-ˈpɑː-/ *n* a person skilled in topography

to·pog·ra·phy /təˈpɒɡrəfi‖-ˈpɑː-/ *n* [U] (the science of describing or mapping) the character of an area, esp. as regards the shape and height of the land —**phical** /ˌtɒpəˈɡræfɪkəl‖ˌtɑː-, ˌtəʊ-/ *adj* —**phically** /kli/ *adv*

top·per /ˈtɒpəʳ‖ˈtɑː-/ *n infml for* TOP HAT

top·ping¹ /ˈtɒpɪŋ‖ˈtɑː-/ *n* [C;U] something put on top of food to make it look nicer, taste better, etc.

topping² *adj old-fash infml, esp. BrE* excellent

topping-out /ˌ· · ˈ·/ *n* [U] *tech, esp. BrE* the act of finishing the roof of a new building, often marked by a ceremony in which a small tree is nailed to a high point on the roof: *a topping-out ceremony*

top·ple /ˈtɒpəl‖ˈtɑː-/ *v* [I;T] (OVER)) to (cause to) become unsteady and fall down: *The pile of bricks toppled over.* | (fig.) *This scandal could topple the government.*

top-rank·ing /ˈ· ·◂/ *adj infml* of the highest skill or quality: *a top-ranking car/company/executive*

tops /tɒps‖tɑːps/ *n* [the+S] *old-fash infml* the very best: *She's the tops at tennis/in her field.*

TOPS /tɒps‖tɑːps/ the name of a course introduced by the British government to help people at work to train for better jobs

top-se·cret /ˌ· ˈ···◂/ *adj* that must be kept completely secret, usu. because of military value: *top-secret documents/ information*

top-shelf /ˌ· ˈ·◂/ *adj* [A] (of a magazine) of a sexually exciting nature: *She had spent five years modelling for top-shelf magazines in a strange variety of underwear.*
► CULTURAL NOTE Such magazines are usually kept on the top shelf in a shop, so that children cannot reach them.◄

top·side /ˈtɒpsaɪd‖ˈtɑːp-/ *n* [U] *BrE* high quality BEEF cut from the upper leg of the animal

top·soil /ˈtɒpsɔɪl‖ˈtɑːp-/ *n* [U] (soil from) the upper level of soil, in which most plants have their roots

top·spin /ˈtɒpˌspɪn‖ˈtɑːp-/ *n* [U] turning movement given to a ball in such a way that it spins forward in the air

Top·sy /ˈtɒpsi‖ˈtɑːp-/ a character in the NOVEL *Uncle Tom's Cabin* by Harriet Beecher Stowe. Topsy is a small black girl who, when asked if she knew who made her (i.e. whether she had heard of God), replies "I expect I just growed". The name Topsy is often used in speaking about things whose real origin is not known: *The constitution just grew, like Topsy.*

top·sy-tur·vy /ˌtɒpsi ˈtɜːvi◂‖ˌtɑːpsi ˈtɜːrvi◂/ *adj, adv* in a state of complete disorder and confusion: *He left his room all topsy-turvy.* | *The whole world's going topsy-turvy.*

top ta·ble /ˌ· ˈ··/ *BrE* ‖ **head table** *AmE*— *n* a table at a formal meal where the most important people or those people giving speeches sit, e.g. at a wedding

Top Ten /ˌ· ˈ·/ *[the]* the ten best-selling records brought out in a particular week

top-up /ˈ· ·/ *n* an amount added to sthg. to raise or keep it to a desired level: *Would you like a top-up?* (=more drink in your glass) | *I think the car needs a top-up* (=more water or petrol).

tor /tɔːʳ/ *n esp. BrE* (the top of) a high rocky hill, esp. in Devon and Cornwall

Tor·ah /ˈtɔːrə/ *[the]* **a** the first five books of the Jewish Bible **b** all the writings and teachings concerned with the practice of Judaism

torch /tɔːtʃ‖tɔːrtʃ/ *n* **1** *BrE* ‖ **flashlight** *AmE*— a small electric light carried in the hand: *The burglar shone his torch into the dark room.* **2** a mass of burning material tied to a stick and carried by hand to give light: *The Olympic torch is carried by runners to the place where the Games are being held.* | (fig., *fml*) *to pass on the torch of knowledge to future generations* **3** *AmE for* BLOW LAMP —see also **carry a torch for** (CARRY¹ (17))

torch·light /ˈtɔːtʃlaɪt‖ˈtɔːr-/ *n* [U] light produced by TORCHes (1, 2): *They held a torchlight procession to celebrate the festival.*

torch sing·er /ˈ· ˌ··/ *n* a person who sings a torch song

torch song /ˈ· ˌ·/ *n* a song, usu. about love or unhappiness, sung with much emotion

tore /tɔːʳ/ *past tense of* TEAR

to·re·a·dor /ˈtɒriədɔːʳ‖ˈtɔː-, ˈtɑː-/ *n* a man who takes part in a Spanish BULLFIGHT, esp. one riding on a horse

tor·ment¹ /ˈtɔːment‖ˈtɔːr-/ *n* **1** [C *usu. pl.*;U] (a) very great pain or suffering in mind or body: *She was in torment with her toothache.* **2** [C (to)] something or someone that causes this

tor·ment² /tɔːˈment‖tɔːr-/ *v* [T] **1** to cause to suffer great pain in mind or body: *The knowledge of his guilt tormented him.* | *tormented by hunger* **2** to annoy, esp. cruelly: *The little boy tormented his younger sister.* – –**or** *n*

torn /tɔːn‖tɔːrn/ *past participle of* TEAR: *My dress got torn.* | *a torn dress*

tor·na·do /tɔːˈneɪdəʊ‖tɔːr-/ also **twister** *AmE infml*— *n* -does *or* -dos a very violent wind in the form of a very tall wide pipe of air that spins at great speed. Tornadoes are common in the American Midwest in spring and autumn, and often do great damage. Authorities broadcast a **tornado warning** when one is expected in an area. —see STORM (USAGE)

Tornado *n* a British fighter-bomber aircraft, used by the RAF, which uses SMART WEAPON TECHNOLOGY such as LASERS to find TARGETS

To·ron·to /təˈrɒntəʊ‖-ˈrɑːn-/ a city and port on Lake Ontario, Canada. Toronto is the capital of Ontario PROVINCE and the second largest city in Canada.

tor·pe·do¹ /tɔːˈpiːdəʊ‖tɔːr-/ *n* **-does** a long narrow explosive apparatus that is driven along under the surface of the sea by its own motors and aimed at ships in order to destroy them

torpedo² *v* [T] to attack or destroy (a ship) with a torpedo: (fig.) *The opposition parties united to torpedo the government's plan in Parliament.* (=attack it and make it ineffective)

tor·pid /ˈtɔːpɪd‖ˈtɔːr-/ *adj* **1** *fml* lazy or inactive; moving or thinking slowly: *a torpid mind* | *The heat and humidity made us (feel) torpid.* **2** *tech* (esp. of an animal that sleeps through the winter) having lost the power of feeling or moving — **~ly** *adv*

tor·por /ˈtɔːpəʳ‖ˈtɔːr-/ also **tor·pid·i·ty** /tɔːˈpɪdɪ̩ti‖tɔːr-/— *n* [S;U] *fml or tech* a condition of (lazy) inactivity; the state of being torpid: *This heat induces torpor.*

torque /tɔːk‖tɔːrk/ *n* [U] *tech* twisting force; power that produces ROTATION: *A car engine delivers torque to the propeller shaft.*

Tor·que·ma·da /ˌtɔːkwɪˈmɑːdə‖ˌtɔːrkə-/, **Tom·ás de** /ˈtɒməs də ‖ təʊˈmɑːs-/ (1420–98) a Spanish DOMINICAN who set up the INQUISITION in Spain. He is known for the cruel methods which he ordered the Inquisition to use against religious opponents.

Tor·re·mo·li·nos /ˌtɒrɪ̩məˈliːnɒs‖ˌtɔːrəməˈliːnəʊs/ a holiday town in Spain popular with young British tourists

tor·rent /ˈtɒrənt‖ˈtɔː-, ˈtɑː-/ *n* [(of)] **1** a violently rushing stream, esp. of water: *The rain fell* **in torrents.** | *A torrent of water swept down the valley.* | (fig.) *a torrent of abuse*

tor·ren·tial /təˈrenʃəl‖tɔː-/ *adj* caused by or like a torrent: *torrential rain*

Tor·rey Can·yon /ˌtɒri ˈkænjən‖ˌtɔː-/ [the] an oil TANKER which went on the rocks on the coast of Cornwall in 1967, causing great damage to the area from the oil

tor·rid /ˈtɒrɪ̩d‖ˈtɒ-, ˈtɑː-/ *adj* **1** *lit or tech* (esp. of weather) very hot: *the torrid desert sun* **2** full of strong feelings and uncontrolled activity, esp. sexual: *a torrid story of sex and violence* | *a torrid love affair* — **~ly** *adv*

tor·sion /ˈtɔːʃən‖ˈtɔːr-/ *n* [U] *tech* **1** the act of twisting or turning **2** the state of being twisted or turned **3** the force that moves a rod, wire, etc., back into the correct shape after it has been twisted out of shape

tor·so /ˈtɔːsəʊ‖ˈtɔːr-/ *n* **-sos** **1** the human body without the head and limbs **2** a representation of this in stone, metal, etc.

tort /tɔːt‖tɔːrt/ *n law* a wrongful but not criminal act, that can be dealt with in a CIVIL court of law

tor·til·la /tɔːˈtiːjə‖tɔːr-/ *n* a type of thin round flat bread made from MAIZE or WHEAT flour, eaten esp. in Mexico

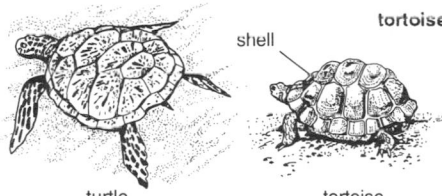
tortoise
shell

turtle   tortoise

tor·toise /ˈtɔːtəs‖ˈtɔːr-/ *n* a slow-moving land animal that has its body covered by a hard rounded shell into which it can pull its legs, tail, and head for protection —compare TURTLE

Tortoise and the Hare /ˌ··· ··· ˈ·-/, **The** an old story (FABLE) by Aesop in which a TORTOISE and a HARE have a race which the tortoise wins by moving slowly but steadily while the hare, knowing he is faster, stops halfway and falls asleep. The moral of the story is "Slow and steady wins the race".

tor·toise·shell /ˈtɔːtəʃel, ˈtɔːtəʃel‖ˈtɔːr-/ *n, adj* [U] (made of or looking like) the hard shell of the tortoise or TURTLE, which is brown with yellowish marks, and is sometimes polished and used for making combs, small decorative boxes, etc.

tor·tu·ous /ˈtɔːtʃuəs‖ˈtɔːr-/ *adj* **1** twisted; winding; full of bends: *a tortuous mountain road* **2** not direct; confusingly COMPLICATED: *a tortuous explanation* — **~ly** *adv* — **~ness** *n* [U]

tor·ture¹ /ˈtɔːtʃəʳ‖ˈtɔːr-/ *n* **1** [U] the act of causing someone severe physical pain, done e.g. out of cruelty, as a punishment, or to force someone to give information: *instruments of torture, such as the rack and thumbscrew* | *The military government's systematic use of torture against political prisoners* **2** [C;U] (a) severe pain or suffering caused in the mind or body: *the tortures of jealousy* | *It was sheer torture to hear him play the violin so badly.*

torture² *v* [T] to cause great pain or suffering to; practise torture on: *The police tortured him to make him confess to the crime.* | (fig.) *She was tortured with/by guilt.* **–turer** *n*

Tor·vill and Dean /ˌtɔːvɪl ənd ˈdiːn‖ˌtɔːr-/ Jayne Torvill (1957–) and Christopher Dean (1958–), a successful pair of English dancers on ice

To·ry /ˈtɔːri/ *n, adj* (a member) of the British Conservative Party: *a lifelong Tory* | *Tory principles* — **~ism** *n* [U]

Tory Par·ty /ˈ·· ̩·· / also **the Tories**— *n* [the; + sing./pl. v] the British Conservative Party

Tos·ca·ni·ni /ˌtɒskəˈniːni‖ˌtɑːs-/, **Ar·tu·ro** /ɑːˈtuərəʊ ‖ ɑːr-/ (1817–1957) an Italian CONDUCTOR who became musical director at La Scala before moving to the US and leading several important ORCHESTRAS

To·shi·ba /tɒˈʃiːbə ‖ tɑː-/ *n* a Japanese company making televisions, computers, and other electronic equipment

toss¹ /tɒs‖tɔːs/ *v* **1** [T (to)] to throw esp. in a careless or aimless way: *They tossed their hats in the air.* | *The children tossed the ball to each other.* [+obj(i)+obj(d)] *I tossed him a cigarette.* **2** [I;T (ABOUT)] to (cause to) move about continuously in an aimless or violent way: *My husband was tossing about/tossing and turning all night. He couldn't get to sleep.* | *The boat was tossed this way and that in the stormy sea.* **3** [I;T (UP, for)] to throw or FLIP (a coin) in the air in order to decide something, according to which side lands face upwards: *The two captains tossed (up)/tossed a coin before the match.* (=to decide which team would play first, etc.) | *There's only one cake left — I'll toss you for it.* (=compete with you for it by tossing a coin) —see also TOSS-UP **4** [T] to throw (a PANCAKE) into the air from a FRYING PAN so that it turns over in the air and lands back in the pan **5** [T (in, with)] to mix or shake lightly: *Toss the cooked vegetables in butter.* **6** [T] to move or lift (part of the body) rapidly: *The horse tossed its head back and smelt the wind.* | *She tossed her head angrily.*

    toss off *phr v* **1** [T] (**toss** sthg. ↔ **off**) to produce quickly with little effort: *The painter tossed off a couple of sketches before lunch.* **2** [T] (**toss** sthg. ↔ **off**) to drink quickly: *Jack tossed off several pints of beer in quick succession.* **3** [I;T (=**toss** sbdy. ↔ **off**)] *BrE taboo sl* to MASTURBATE

toss² *n* **1** [C] an act of tossing: *with a toss of her head* **2** [the+S] an act of tossing a coin to decide something: *Our team won the toss so we play first.* **3** [C] *old-fash* a fall, esp. as a result of being thrown from a horse **4** [S *usu. in negatives*] *BrE sl* the least amount; anything: *I couldn't* **give a toss** (=I don't care at all) *what he thinks.* —see also **argue the toss** (ARGUE (5))

toss-up /ˈ·· ·/ *n* **1** [S] *infml* an even chance; an uncertainty: *It's a toss-up between the two of them as to who will get the job.* (=either of them might equally well do so) | *It's a toss-up whether we'll manage to finish this job in time.* **2** [C *usu. sing.*] an act of tossing a coin to decide something

tos·ta·da /tɒˈstɑːdə‖təʊ-/ *n* a type of Mexican food made with a fried (FRY) TORTILLA with meat or beans and often LETTUCE and TOMATO on top

tot¹ /tɒt‖tɑːt/ *n* **1** *infml* a very small child: *a picture book for* **tiny tots** **2** [(of)] a small amount of a strong alcoholic drink: *a tot of rum/whisky*

tot² *v* **-tt-**

    tot sthg.↔**up** *phr v* [T] *infml* to add up (numbers, money, etc.)

to·tal¹ /ˈtəʊtl/ *adj* [no comp.] **1** complete; ABSOLUTE: *We sat in total silence.* | *He stayed away, in total disregard of my instructions.* | *I'm afraid the performance wasn't exactly a total success.* **2** [A] being a total; considered as a complete amount: *the total number of cars produced this month* — **~ly** *adv* : *I totally agree with you.* | *She's totally committed to the cause.* | *Their personalities are totally*

different: Gradable and Non-gradable Adjectives, Intensifying Adjectives

total² n **1** a number or quantity obtained as the result of addition; complete amount: *Add these numbers together and tell me the total.* | *A total of 20,000 people visited the castle on the first day it was open to the public.* **2 in total** when all have been added up: *These products, in total, account for about 80% of all our sales.* —see also SUM TOTAL

total³ v **-ll-** *BrE* ‖ **-l-** *AmE* **1** [L+n] to be when added up: *They have debts totalling £100,000.* **2** [T (UP)] to find the total of; add up **3** [T] *AmE* to damage (a car) so badly that it cannot be repaired: *Her car got totalled but she wasn't hurt.*

Total a British company dealing in oil: *a Total petrol station*

total e·clipse /ˌ·· ·'·/ n an ECLIPSE in which all the light of the sun or moon, viewed from the Earth, seems to disappear

to·tal·i·tar·i·an /təʊˌtælɪ̩'teəriən/ adj of or based on a political system in which every citizen is subject to the power of the state, which exercises complete control over all areas of life: *a totalitarian state*

to·tal·i·tar·i·an·is·m /təʊˌtælɪ̩'teəriənɪzəm/ n [U] the practices and principles of a totalitarian state

to·tal·i·ty /təʊˈtælɪ̩ti/ n [U] *fml* **1** the state of being whole; completeness: *to look at the problem in its totality* **2** a total amount; sum

to·tal·i·za·tor also **-isator** *BrE* /'təʊtəl-aɪˌzeɪtəʳ‖-lə-/ n *fml* a tote

tote¹ /təʊt/ v [T (AROUND)] *infml, esp. AmE* to carry esp. in one's arms or near one's body: *She came in toting the baby in her arms and a diaper bag over her shoulder.* | *gun-toting cowboys*

tote² n **1** ‖ also **parimutuel machine** *AmE*— a machine that shows the number of BETs placed on each horse or dog in a race and the amount to be paid to the people who risked money on the winners **2** [the] (+cap.) *BrE* a short name for the Horserace Totalisator Board, an organization that operates a betting (BET²) system and owns over 100 betting shops

tote bag /'· ̩·/ n esp. AmE a large bag for carrying things in

to·tem /'təʊtəm/ n **1** (a representation, esp. on wood, of) an animal, plant, or object that is thought by certain societies, esp. Native Americans, to have a close relationship with the tribal group and is used as a sign of that tribe **2** *often derog* something that is thought of as especially worthy of respect in a society — ~**ic** /təʊˈtemɪk/ adj

totem pole /'·· ·/ n **1** a tall wooden pole with one or more totems cut or painted on it, put up by the Native Americans of northwest N America **2 top man on the totem pole** *AmE infml* the most important person in an organization

toto see IN TOTO

To·to /'təʊtəʊ/ the dog belonging to Dorothy in *The Wizard of Oz* —see WIZARD OF OZ

Tot·ten·ham Court Road /ˌtɒtn-əm kɔːt ˈrəʊd‖ˌtɑːtn-əm kɔːrt-/ n [(the)] a street in central London, noted for its shops selling radio, television, VIDEO, and computer equipment

Tottenham Hot·spur /ˌtɒtn-əm ˈhɒtspɜːʳ‖ˌtɑːtn-əm ˈhɑːt-/ an English football team based in N London. They are also known as **Spurs**.

Tottenham Three /ˌtɒtn-əm ˈθriː ‖ ˌtɑːt-/ n [the+P] three people who were sent to prison in Britain in 1985 for killing a police officer during a RIOT in N London. They were all found not guilty in 1991, and it was suggested that the police had acted wrongly to make them seem guilty. Along with other cases, this case has raised questions in Britain about police questioning of people they have caught for a crime, and about the way mistakes in justice are put right —compare BIRMINGHAM SIX, GUILDFORD FOUR, MAGUIRE SEVEN; see also BROADWATER FARM ESTATE

tot·ter /'tɒtəʳ‖'tɑː-/ v [I] **1** to shake or move unsteadily from side to side as if about to fall: *The pile of books tottered then fell.* | (fig.) *The empire is tottering (on the edge of ruin).* **2** [+adv/prep] to walk with weak unsteady steps: *The old lady tottered down the stairs.* —compare STAGGER¹ (1)

tot·ter·y /'tɒtəri‖'tɑː-/ adj unsteady; shaky

totting-up /ˌ·· '·/ n [U] the former British legal practice of forbidding people from driving if they had been guilty of more than a certain number of traffic offences: *He would have been disqualified under the totting-up method*

tou·can /'tuːkən, -kæn/ n a tropical American bird with bright feathers and a very large beak

touch¹ /tʌtʃ/ v **1** [I;T] to be separated (from) by no space at all; be in CONTACT (with): *They stood close together with their shoulders touching.* | *The branches hung down and touched the water.* | (fig.) *The speedometer needle touched* (=reached) *90 mph.* **2** [I;T] to feel, strike lightly, or make connection (with), esp. with the hands or fingers: *Don't touch!* | *Visitors are requested not to touch the paintings.* | *If I stand on a chair I can touch the ceiling with a stick.* **3** [T usu. in negatives] to handle: *Don't touch anything until the police arrive.* | *"Who's broken my pen?" "Not me — I never touched it!"* | (fig.) *He swore he'd never touch a drink* (=drink alcohol) *again.* | (fig.) *You've hardly touched your food — I hope you're not ill.* | (fig.) *Those cars are very low quality; I wouldn't touch them.* (=I would never buy one) —see also BARGE POLE **4** [T usu. in negatives] to compare with; be equal to: *Your work will never touch the standard set by Robert.* | *When it comes to making speeches, there's no one to touch him.* (=no one else is as good) **5** [T] to have an effect on the feelings of; cause to feel pity, sympathy, etc.: *His sad story so touched us that we nearly cried.* —see also TOUCHED, TOUCHING **6** [T (IN)] to mark with light strokes; put in with a pencil or brush: *He drew her head, and quickly touched in the eyes, nose, and mouth.* —see also TOUCH UP **7** [T] *fml* to concern: *a serious matter that touches your future* **8 touch bottom: a** to reach the bottom: *The boat almost touched bottom in the shallow channel.* **b** to reach the lowest level: *After weeks of uncertainty, morale in the company has touched bottom.* **9 touch wood** esp. *BrE* ‖ **knock on wood** *AmE*— (used as if to keep away bad luck, so that something good may continue): *I've never been without a job, touch wood!* — ~ **able** adj

touch down phr v [I] **1** (of a plane or spacecraft) to land **2** (in RUGBY) to press the ball to the ground behind one's opponent's GOAL in order to win a TRY

touch sbdy. **for** sthg. phr v [T] *infml* to persuade to give one (money): *He tried to touch me for £10.*

touch sthg. ↔ **off** phr v [T] **1** to cause to explode **2** to start or cause (esp. violent activity): *The government's actions touched off a storm of protest.*

touch on/upon sthg. phr v [T] to talk about shortly, and perhaps without enough detail: *In her speech she touched on the need for further economies.* | *The major problems have hardly been touched on in this debate.*

touch sthg./sbdy. ↔ **up** phr v [T] **1** to improve by making small changes or additions: *The car's paintwork needs touching up.* **2** *BrE infml* to touch someone in a sexually improper way

touch² n **1** [U] the sense of feeling by which an object is known to be hard, smooth, rough, etc., by being brought into connection with a part of the body, esp. the fingers **2** [S] the effect caused by touching something; way something feels: *the silky touch of soft velvet* **3** [C usu. sing.] an act of touching: *He felt the touch of her hand on his shoulder.* | *With this new typewriter you can correct mistakes* **at the touch of a button.** **4** [U] connection, esp. so as to receive information; CONTACT: *I'm trying to get* **in touch with** *my brother; he emigrated to Australia, and I* **lost touch with** *him/we* **lost touch** *(with each other).* | *I haven't really* **kept in touch with** *people I knew at school.* | *Goodbye for now; I'll* **be in touch.** | *I'd like to go back to teaching, but I'm* **out of touch with** *my subject now.* | (fig., derog) *So many of these politicians are* **out** *of touch.* (=do not know about the realities of ordinary modern life) **5** [S] a particular way of doing things: *This delicate work needs a woman's touch.* | *At this restaurant you get service with a personal touch.* (=each customer is looked after in a careful friendly way) **6** [C] a small addition or detail that improves or completes something: *That little windmill in the corner of the painting is a nice touch.* | *I'm just* **putting the finishing touches to** *the cake.* **7** [S] a special ability to do something needing skill, esp. artistic work: *Your recent work's been bad; I hope you're not* **losing your touch.** **8** [S (of)] a slight attack, esp. of an illness: *She was off work with a touch of flu.* | *I think I've had* **a touch of the sun.** (=slight SUN-STROKE) **9** [S (of)] a slight amount: *This soup could do* with a touch more salt. | There was a touch of frost in the night. | That seemed a touch (=slightly) unfair to me. **10** [U] (in SOCCER or RUGBY) the area of ground outside the field of play: He kicked the ball into touch. **11 to the touch** when felt: A cat's fur is soft to the touch. —see also SOFT TOUCH

touch-and-go /ˌ·· ˈ·/ adj risky; of uncertain result: a touch-and-go situation | It was touch-and-go whether the doctor would get there in time.

touch-down /ˈtʌtʃdaʊn/ n **1** the landing of a plane or spacecraft **2** (in RUGBY) an act of touching down (TOUCH **down** (2)) **3** (in American football) an act of moving the ball across the opposing team's GOAL LINE

tou·ché /ˈtuːʃeɪ‖tuːˈʃeɪ/ interj (an expression used when admitting the rightness or force of a person's argument, reply, etc., meaning) "That is a good point against me!"

touched /tʌtʃt/ adj [F] **1** feeling grateful: I was deeply touched by their present. [+(that)/to-v] I'm touched that you remembered me|touched to be remembered. —see also TOUCH¹ (5) **2** infml slightly mad

touch foot·ball /ˈ· ˌ··/ n [U] AmE a game of American football in which touching the person with the ball stops play

touch·ing¹ /ˈtʌtʃɪŋ/ adj causing a feeling of pity, sympathy, etc.: The two lovers parting at the station — what a touching scene it made. —see also TOUCH¹ (5) – ~ly adv

touching² prep lit or old use about; concerning

touch·line /ˈtʌtʃlaɪn/ n a line along each of the two longer sides of a sports field, esp. in football

touch·pa·per /ˈtʌtʃˌpeɪpəʳ/ n **1** a piece of slow-burning paper fitted into a FIREWORK, which one lights in order to start the firework burning **2 light the blue touch-paper and retire immediately** BrE a written instruction on a FIREWORK, sometimes used humorously to mean that something noisy and violent, such as an angry quarrel, is just about to start and people should stay away

touch·stone /ˈtʌtʃstəʊn/ n [(of)] something used as a test or standard; CRITERION

touch-tone phone /ˈ· · ˌ·/ n tdmk a telephone that produces different sounds when its different numbered buttons are pushed. Touch-tone phones are widely used in the US to operate pre-recorded telephone information services.

touch-type /ˈ· ·/ v [I] to type without having to look at the letters on the TYPEWRITER; read and type what one is reading at the same time

touch·y /ˈtʌtʃi/ adj **1** derog easily offended or annoyed; too sensitive: She's in a very touchy mood today. **2** needing skilful or delicate handling: a touchy situation in Northern Ireland —**ily** adv —**iness** n [U]

tough¹ /tʌf/ adj **1** strong; not easily weakened or broken; able to suffer difficult or severe conditions: Only tough breeds of sheep can live in the mountains. | a tough vehicle designed for use on all kinds of road **2** derog difficult to cut or eat: tough meat —opposite **tender 3** showing strong determination; UNCOMPROMISING: We won the contract, but only through a lot of tough negotiating. | The President's tough stance on terrorism. **4** difficult to do or deal with; not easy; needing effort: a tough job/problem | She's a pretty **tough customer/tough nut.** (=a strong, difficult person) | The company faces tough competition. **5** rough; without kind or sympathetic feelings or manners: This is a tough neighbourhood. | The government has threatened to **get tough with** people who try to avoid paying taxes. **6** [(on)] infml unfortunate: Tough luck! | It's very tough on her that she should lose her job because of someone else's mistake. | "I'm getting wet!" "Tough!" (said unsympathetically) You should have brought your umbrella. —see also HARD LUCK – ~ly adv – ~ness n [U]

tough² n old-fash infml a rough violent person, esp. a criminal

tough³ v
    tough sthg. ↔ **out** phr v [T] infml to get through and defeat (a difficult situation) by having a strong will: A lot of people would have resigned in the face of such accusations, but he stayed and **toughed it out.**

tough·en /ˈtʌfən/ v [I;T (UP)] to become or make tough: toughened glass | Three years in the army toughened him up.

tough luck /ˌ· ˈ·/ interj, n HARD LUCK

Tou·louse-Lau·trec /tuːˌluːz ləʊˈtrek/, **Hen·ri de** /ˈɒnri dəˈɑːnˈriː-/ (1864–1901) a French painter, well known for his brightly-coloured POSTERs, esp. those advertising performances by famous entertainers of his time

tou·pee /ˈtuːpeɪ‖tuːˈpeɪ/ n a small artificial piece of hair specially shaped to fit exactly over a place on a man's head where the hair no longer grows

tour¹ /tʊəʳ/ n **1** [(round, around)] a journey for pleasure, during which several places of interest are visited: a tour round Europe | a walking/cycling tour | a leading tour operator (=company that arranges holidays) —see also PACKAGE TOUR **2** [(round)] a short trip to or through a place, to see it: We went on a guided tour round the castle. | a city sightseeing tour **3** (in) a period of duty at a single place or job, esp. abroad: a two-year tour (of duty) in Germany **4** [(of)] a planned journey from place to place as made e.g. by a theatre company or a sports team, in order to perform, play, or appear in several places: the England cricketers' tour of India | The National Youth Theatre is **on tour** in the North at present. | The Queen was in Sydney today on the first leg (=stage) of her Australian tour.

tour² v [I (round);T] to visit on a tour: We're touring (round) Italy for our holidays this year. | a touring holiday

tour de force /ˌtʊə də ˈfɔːs‖ˌtʊər də ˈfɔːrs/ n [S] lit or fml, apprec a show of great skill: Her speech to the Democratic Party convention was a tour de force.

Tour de France /ˌ· · ˈ·/ [the] a famous bicycle race that takes place in France each year. The Tour de France goes all the way round the country and takes several days to complete.

tour·is·m /ˈtʊərɪzəm/ n [U] **1** the practice of travelling for pleasure, esp. on holidays **2** the business of providing holidays, tours, hotels, etc., for tourists: The country depends on tourism for much of its income.

tour·ist /ˈtʊərɪst/ n **1** a person travelling for pleasure: Oxford is full of tourists in the summer. | a tourist hotel **2** a sportsman on TOUR¹ (4)

tourist at·trac·tion /ˈ·· ·ˌ··/ n a place or event which attracts large numbers of tourists: Stratford-upon-Avon is a major tourist attraction

tourist class /ˈ·· ·/ n [U] (on a ship or aircraft) the standard travelling conditions which are fairly cheap and suitable for ordinary travellers: I always travel tourist class. | a tourist class ticket —compare BUSINESS CLASS, CABIN CLASS

tourist in·dus·try /ˈ·· ˌ···/ n all the businesses, hotels, MUSEUMS, etc. that make most of their money from tourists: a good year for the tourist industry

tourist of·fice /ˈ·· ˌ··/ also **tourist in·for·ma·tion of·fice** /ˌ··· ···ˈ·· ˌ··/— n an office giving information to tourists about things to see, places to stay, and means of travel in a particular place: Is there a tourist office in this town?

tour·ist·y /ˈtʊərɪsti/ adj usu. derog full of or suitable for tourists: The village is beautiful, but it's become a bit too touristy.

tour·na·ment /ˈtʊənəmənt, ˈtɔː-‖ˈtɜːr-, ˈtʊər-/ n **1** an event in which a number of games are played, the winner being the player who wins the greatest number of games: a tennis/chess tournament **2** (in former times) a competition of courage and fighting skill between noble soldiers

tour·ney /ˈtʊəni, ˈtɔː-‖ˈtɜːr-, ˈtʊər-/ n old use or pomp a tournament

tour·ni·quet /ˈtʊənɪkeɪ, ˈtɔː-‖ˈtɜːrnɪkət, ˌtʊər-/ n something, esp. a band of cloth, that is twisted tightly round an arm or leg to stop bleeding: *We had to apply a tourniquet to his leg.*

tour of du·ty /ˌ· · ˈ··/ n TOUR¹(3)

tour op·e·rat·or /ˈ· ˌ····/ n BrE a company which arranges tours, esp. PACKAGE TOURS: *a small tour operator running three coaches* | *Tour operators are reporting a sharp fall in bookings as a result of the war.*

tou·sle /ˈtaʊzəl/ v [T usu. pass.] to disarrange (esp. the hair); make untidy

tout¹ /taʊt/ v 1 [I (for);T] derog to try repeatedly to persuade people to buy (one's goods), use (one's services), etc.: *At one time, solicitors were not allowed to advertise; it was regarded as* **touting for business.** | *Our company does not tout its wares on television.* 2 [T (as)] often derog to praise greatly, esp. as a form of advertising: *This show is being widely touted in the press as the greatest ever on Broadway.* 3 AmE to give information on a horse in a race in return for money

tout² BrE ‖ **scalper** AmE– n derog a person who offers tickets illegally and in short supply for sale at a price higher than usual: *A* **ticket tout** *offered me a £5 Cup Final ticket for £60.*

tow¹ /təʊ/ v [T] to pull (esp. a vehicle) along by a rope or chain: *We towed the car to the nearest garage/towed the boat into the harbour.*

tow² n 1 [C] an act of towing: *My car's broken down; will you give me a tow?* 2 [U] the state of being towed: *We* **took** *the boat* **in tow.** | *The van is* **on tow.** 3 **in tow** infml following closely behind: *She arrived with all her children in tow.*

to·wards /təˈwɔːdz‖tɔːrdz/ esp. BrE ‖ **to·ward** /təˈwɔːd‖tɔːrd/esp. AmE– prep 1 in the direction of, without necessarily reaching: *She was walking towards town when I met her.* | *They have taken the first step towards reaching an agreement.* | *We've made great strides towards sexual equality.* 2 in a position facing: *He stood with his back towards me.* | *The house faces towards the river.* 3 near; just before in time: *Towards the end of the afternoon it began to rain.* 4 in relation to: *What is their policy/attitude towards America?* 5 for the purpose of; for part payment or fulfilment of: *We save £10 towards our holidays each week.*

tow·a·way /ˈtəʊəweɪ/ n AmE a vehicle which is standing where it is not allowed and which may be taken away by the police –**towaway** adj : *a towaway zone* (an area in which vehicles may be taken away by the police)

tow·el¹ /ˈtaʊəl/ n (often in comb.) a piece of cloth or paper used for rubbing or drying wet skin, dishes, etc.: *a bath towel* | *a hand towel* –see also SANITARY TOWEL, TEA TOWEL, **throw in the towel** (THROW in) and see picture at ROLL

towel² v -ll- BrE ‖ -l- AmE [T (DOWN)] to rub or dry with a towel

tow·el·ette /ˌtaʊəˈlet/ n AmE a small, wet, soft piece of paper used to clean a part of one's body: *a package of towelettes* | *a box of towelettes made especially for babies*

tow·el·ling BrE ‖ **toweling** AmE /ˈtaʊəlɪŋ/ n [U] thickish cloth, used esp. for making towels

towel rail /ˈ·· ·/ also **towel rack**– n a bar or frame on which towels can be hung, esp. in a bathroom: *The bathroom fittings include a heated towel rail.*

tow·er¹ /ˈtaʊər/ n 1 a tall building standing alone or forming part of a castle, church, etc.: *a bell tower* | *the Tower of London* –see picture at CHURCH 2 a tall structure, often made of metal, used for signalling, broadcasting, etc.: *the Eiffel Tower* | *an air traffic control tower* –see also CLOCK TOWER

tower² v [I (above, over)] to be very tall, esp. in relation to the height of the surroundings: *The high mountains towered over the little town.* | (fig.) *a giant company that towers over its rivals*

Tower [the] the TOWER OF LONDON: *In the old days people could be sent to the Tower for insulting the monarch like that.*

tower block /ˈ·· ·/ n BrE a tall block of flats or offices –see colour picture on page 162

Tower Bridge /ˌ·· ˈ·/ a bridge which crosses the River Thames in London, just to the E of the Tower of London. The part of the bridge which carries the road is in two pieces which can be lifted to make room for ships passing under the bridge –see colour map on page 817

Tower Ham·lets /ˌ·· ˈ··/ a BOROUGH of London, on the N side of the River Thames which includes the Docklands area

tow·er·ing /ˈtaʊərɪŋ/ adj [A] 1 very tall: *towering trees/skyscrapers* 2 of great importance; OUTSTANDING: *one of the towering intellects of our time* 3 very great; INTENSE: *She was in a towering rage.* (=extremely angry)

Tower of Babel /ˌ·· · ˈ··/ n [the] a tower in a story in the Bible whose builders intended it to reach to HEAVEN. They made God angry so that he made them all speak different languages. They could not understand each other, and were unable to finish building the tower. People sometimes mention the Tower of Babel when describing a scene of confusion, disorder and the noise of many voices. –see also BABEL

Tower of Lon·don /ˌ·· · ˈ··/ also **Tower**– [the] an ancient FORTRESS to the E of the City of London, on the N side of the River Thames, formerly a place where the king and queen lived, and a prison for important people. It is now a MUSEUM, and the place where the CROWN JEWELS are kept. The Tower of London is ceremonially guarded by the Yeomen of the Guard or "Beefeaters" –see colour map on page 817

tower of strength /ˌ·· · ˈ·/ n apprec someone who can always be depended on to give help, sympathy, and support in times of trouble

tow·head /ˈtaʊhed/ n a person with very light-coloured hair – –ed adj : *a towheaded little boy*

town /taʊn/ n 1 [C] a large area with houses and other buildings where people live and work, usu. smaller than a city and larger than a village 2 [C+sing./pl. v] all the people who live in such a place: *The whole town is/are furious about the council's education policy.* 3 [(the) U] the business or shopping centre of a town: *We went to (the) town to do some shopping today.* | *She's* **out of town** *on business at the moment.* 4 [U] the chief city of an area (in England, usu. London): *I was in town on business last week.* 5 [the+S] (life in) towns and cities in general: *I prefer the town to the country.* 6 **go to town** infml a to behave wildly, esp. by spending a lot of money: *He's really gone to town this time and bought a Rolls Royce.* b to do something with great thoroughness and keenness: *The newspapers have* **gone to town on** *this scandal about the minister and his mistress.* (=printed many shocking stories about it) 7 **(out) on the town** infml enjoying oneself wildly, esp. at night, in places of entertainment –see also GHOST TOWN, MAN-ABOUT-TOWN, MARKET TOWN, NEW TOWN, **blow town** (BLOW¹), **paint the town red** (PAINT²)

town and gown /ˌ·· · ˈ·/ n [U] the ordinary people of a town or city, and its university or college students, between whom there are often thought to be differences of background and attitude which prevent a happy relationship –**town-and-gown** adj : *a real town-and-gown atmosphere*

town clerk /ˌ· ˈ·/ n an official who keeps records, advises on legal matters, and acts as secretary of a town

town cen·tre /ˌ· ˈ··/ BrE ‖ **downtown** AmE– n the area in the centre of a town, often the oldest part of the town and the place where official buildings are: *Few people live in the town centre – it is mostly made up of shops and offices.*

town coun·cil /ˌ· ˈ··/ esp. BrE ‖ **city council** AmE– n a group of people responsible for arranging public services such as roads, the collection of waste, public parks, and (in Britain) council housing in a town: *She has served on the town council for 15 years.*

town cri·er /ˌ· ˈ··/ n (esp. in former times) a person employed to walk about the streets shouting out news, warnings, etc. Town criers used to ring a bell and shout "Oyez! Oyez!" to get people's attention.

town·ee /taʊˈniː/ BrE ‖ **townie, towny** AmE– n infml, often derog someone who lives in a town, esp. one whose experience is limited to town life: *I found a couple of townees having a picnic in the bull field yesterday*

town hall /ˌ· ˈ·/ n a public building used for a town's local government –compare CITY HALL

town house /'· ·/ *n* **1** a house in a town or city, esp. a fashionable one in a central area **2** a house in a town belonging to someone who also owns a house in the country **3** *AmE* a house in a group of houses which share one or more walls and often have no gardens —compare SEMIDETACHED, TERRACE (1)

town meet·ing /ₗ· '··/ *n AmE* a meeting held by people in a town to decide and discuss questions that are important to the town. Town meetings are commonly held in New England states.

Town Mouse and the Coun·try Mouse, The /ₗ· ₗ· · · · '·· ₗ·/ an old story about a town mouse who invites a poor country mouse to visit him in the town. By the end of the story, both mice decide that they prefer their own way of life to that of the other mouse.

town plan·ning /ₗ· '··/ ‖ usu. **urban planning** *AmE*— *n* [U] the study of the way towns work, including traffic, where people live, services, etc., and the planning of the way they are built to make them as effective as possible —**ner** *n*

town·scape /'taʊnₗskeɪp/ *n* (a painting of) a view of a town

Towns·hend /'taʊnzend/, **Peter** (1945–) an English ROCK³ musician who formerly played with the group **The Who**

town·ship /'taʊnʃɪp/ *n* **1** (in Canada and the US) a town, or town and the area around it, that has certain powers of local government **2** (in South Africa) a town where black citizens live

township vi·o·lence /ₗ·· '··/ *n* [U] cases of violence in South African townships between township people and the police, or esp. between groups of blacks, e.g. supporters of the African National Congress and of the Inkatha Freedom Party

towns·man /'taʊnzmən/ **towns·wom·an** /-ₗwʊmən/ *fem.*— *n* **-men** /mən/ *esp. lit or old use* a person who lives in a town

towns·peo·ple /'taʊnzₗpiːpəl/ also **towns·folk** /-fəʊk/— *n* **1** [*the*+P] the people who live in a particular town considered as a group **2** [P] people who live in towns as opposed to the country

tow·path /'təʊpɑːθ‖-pæθ/ *n* a path along the bank of a CANAL or river, used esp. formerly by horses pulling boats

tow·rope /'təʊrəʊp/ *n* a rope, chain, etc., by which something is towed (TOW¹)

tow truck /'· ·/ *n AmE* a strong vehicle which can pull cars behind or on the back of it: *Call a tow truck to take the car to the mechanic's.*

tox·ae·mi·a, **toxemia** /tɒk'siːmiə‖tɑːk-/ *n* [U] *med* a medical condition in which the blood contains poisons

tox·ic /'tɒksɪk‖'tɑːk-/ *adj* poisonous or caused by poisonous substances: *a toxic drug* | *The factory had been sending out toxic waste/fumes.* — ~**ity** /tɒk'sɪsₗti‖tɑːk-/ *n* [U]

tox·i·col·o·gy /ₗtɒksɪ'kɒlədʒi‖ₗtɑːksɪ'kɑː-/ *n* [U] the scientific and medical study of poisons, their nature and effects, and the treatment of poisoning —**gist** *n*

toxic shock syn·drome /ₗ·· '· ₗ··/ *n* [U] a serious illness esp. of young women, involving a high temperature and a sudden drop in blood pressure, which is thought to be connected with the use of TAMPONS

toxic waste /ₗ·· '·/ *n* [C;U] waste products from industry which are harmful to the environment, people, or animals. Many people are concerned with the dangers of toxic waste and the safety of places that are supposed to get rid of it: *a toxic waste dump*

tox·in /'tɒksₗɪn‖'tɑːk-/ *n* a poisonous substance, esp. one produced by bacteria in a living or dead plant or animal body and usu. causing a particular disease

Tox·teth /'tɒkstəθ‖'tɑːk-/ *n* an area of central Liverpool with many black and unemployed people, which was the scene of violent RIOTs in 1981

toy¹ /tɔɪ/ *n* an object for children to play with: *Don't play with that gun; it's not a toy!* | *a toy soldier* | *a toy shop*

toy² *adj* [A] being a small breed of dog kept as a pet: *a toy poodle*

toy³ *v*

  toy with sthg. *phr v* [T] **1** to consider (an idea) not very seriously: *He toyed with the idea of becoming an actor.* **2** to handle or play with purposelessly: *While he was talking to me, he toyed with a pencil.*

toy boy /'· ·/ *n BrE infml* a young man taken as a lover or companion by an older woman

Toy·o·ta /tɔɪ'əʊtə/ a car or other motor vehicle made by the Japanese company Toyota

trace¹ /treɪs/ *v* [T] **1** [(to)] to find (a thing or person) by following their course: *Government scientists have been unable to trace the source of the epidemic.* | *I can't trace that letter you sent me.* | *The criminal was traced to London.* (=was discovered to be in London by searching) **2** [(BACK, to)] to find the origins of by finding proof or by going back in time: *His family can trace its history back to the 10th century.* | *The whole rumour was traced (back) to someone who had a grudge against him.* **3** to follow the course, development, or history of: *His new book traces the beginnings of the Labour movement.* **4** to copy (a drawing, map, etc.) by drawing its lines on transparent paper placed on top of it — —**able** *adj*

trace² *n* [(of)] **1** [C;U *often in questions and negatives*] a mark or sign showing the former presence or passing of some person, vehicle, or event: *Did the police find any trace of the murderer?* | *We've lost all trace of our daughter.* (=we no longer know where she is) | *They have disappeared without (a) trace in the jungle.* **2** [C] a very small amount of something: *They found traces of poison in the dead man's blood.*

trace³ *n* either of the ropes, chains, or lengths of leather by which a cart, carriage, etc., is fastened to an animal that is pulling it —see also **kick over the traces** (KICK)

trace el·e·ment /'· ₗ··/ *n tech* a simple chemical substance that is necessary for healthy growth and development, found in plants and animals in very small quantities

trac·er /'treɪsəʳ/ *n* a bullet that leaves a line of smoke or flame behind it so that its course can be seen

trac·e·ry /'treɪsəri/ *n* [U] decorative patterns with branching and crossing lines, as in the upper parts of many church windows

Tracey¹ see SHARON AND TRACEY

Tra·cey² /'treɪsi/, **Stan** /stæn/ (1926–) a British JAZZ musician who plays piano, is a band leader, and writes music

tra·che·a /trə'kiːə‖'treɪkiə/ *n med for* WINDPIPE —see picture at RESPIRATORY

tra·cho·ma /trə'kəʊmə/ *n* [U] *tech* a painful illness that attacks the transparent covering over the eye and the inner surface of the eyelids

trac·ing /'treɪsɪŋ/ *n* a copy of a map, drawing, etc., made by tracing (TRACE¹ (4))

tracing pa·per /'·· ₗ··/ *n* [U] strong transparent paper used for tracing (TRACE¹ (4))

track¹ /træk/ *n* **1** also **tracks** *pl.*— a line or set of marks left by a person, animal, vehicle, etc., that has passed before: *The dog followed the fox's tracks into the woods.* | *tyre tracks in the mud* | *He's escaped from prison, but the police are on his track.* (=following him, esp. by looking for his tracks) | (fig.) *A good spy must know how to* **cover his tracks** *well.* (=keep his movements or activities secret) —see also TRAIL **2** a narrow path or road, esp. a rough one: *a cycle track* | *a mountain track* —see WAY (USAGE) **3** also **tracks** *pl.*— a railway line **4** *AmE* **a** (a) sport that involves COMPETITIVE running **b** (a) sport that involves both running and/or jumping (both TRACK EVENTS and FIELD EVENTS): *Carl Lewis is a famous track star.* | *She went out for track in the spring* (she joined the school's track team). —see colour picture on page 883 **5** the course or line taken by something as it moves or travels: *These new weather satellites can follow the track of storms.* | (fig.) *That's one approach to the problem, I suppose, but personally I think you're* **on the wrong track.** (=are mistaken) **6** a course specially prepared for racing: *a racetrack* **7** an endless belt used over the wheels of some very heavy vehicles to make movement over rough ground easier: *tank tracks* **8** any of the pieces of music on an LP or TAPE¹ (3): *I like the last track on this side.* **9** any of the bands on which material can be recorded on a TAPE¹ (2) **10 in one's tracks** *infml* where one is at that moment; suddenly: *The criminal stopped dead in his tracks when the door opened behind him.* **11 keep/lose track (of)** to keep/fail to keep oneself informed about a person, situation, etc.: *It's difficult to keep track of all the new ideas and developments in education.* | *I lose all track of time when I listen to this music.* **12 make**

tracks *infml* to leave, esp. in a hurry **13 off the track** *AmE infml* not a part of the subject or purpose being dealt with: *We must not get off the track, we are discussing the budget now, not the sales figures.* —see also ONE-TRACK MIND, **off the beaten track** (BEATEN), **on the wrong side of the tracks** (WRONG[1])

track[2] *v* **1** [T (**to**)] to follow the track of (an animal, plane, ship, person, etc.): *They tracked the wolf to its lair/criminal to his hiding-place.* | *a space tracking station/system* (=for following the course of spacecraft) **2** [I] *tech* (of a moving part of a recording machine) to be in the correct position or along or ALIGNMENT; follow the correct course: *Adjust the tracking control.* **3** [I+*adv/prep*] (of a television or film camera) to move round while taking a distant picture: *a tracking shot* **4** [T] *AmE* to leave tracks (marks of feet): *The boy tracked mud all over the newly washed kitchen floor.* **5** *AmE for* STREAM[2] (5) — –**er** *n* : *Police tracker dogs are searching for the missing child.*

  track sbdy./sthg. ↔ down *phr v* [T] to find by searching or following tracks: *We tracked down the animal by following the trail of bloodstains which it had left.* | (fig.) *I finally tracked down the sort of ribbon I needed in a little shop near the station.*

track and field /ˌ· · ˈ·/ *n* [U] *AmE* ATHLETICS

track e·vent /ˈ· ·ˌ·/ *n* a COMPETITIVE sports event that is a running race —compare FIELD EVENT

tracking sta·tion /ˈ·· ˌ··/ *n* a station from which objects esp. SATELLITES and SPACESHIPS can be recognized and followed through space

track·lay·er /ˈtræk₁leɪəʳ/ *n* *AmE for* PLATELAYER

track·less /ˈtrækləs/ *adj lit* without paths, roads, etc.: *a trackless forest*

track meet /ˈ· ·/ *n AmE* a sports competition consisting of TRACK EVENTs and FIELD EVENTs held at one place

track rec·ord /ˈ· ˌ··/ *n* the degree to which someone or something has performed well or badly up to now: *The company has a good track record in the export trade.*

track·suit /ˈtræksuːt, -sjuːt‖-suːt/ *n* a warm loose-fitting suit worn by sportsmen or sportswomen when training but usu. not when playing, racing, etc. —see picture at SUIT — –**ed** *adj* : *tracksuited runners*

tract[1] /trækt/ *n fml* a short piece or writing, esp. one dealing with a religious or moral subject

tract[2] *n* **1** [(**of**)] a wide stretch of land: *vast tracts of desert in Australia* **2** *med* a system of related organs in an animal, with one particular purpose: *the digestive tract*

trac·ta·ble /ˈtræktəbəl/ *adj fml or tech* easily controlled, worked, or persuaded —see also INTRACTABLE — –**tability** /₁træktəˈbɪlₔti/ *n* [U]

trac·tion /ˈtrækʃən/ *n* [U] *esp. tech* **1** the act of drawing or pulling a heavy load over a surface **2** the form or type of power used for this: *steam traction* **3** the force that prevents a wheel from slipping over the surface on which it runs: *Wet or muddy surfaces can cause a loss of traction.* **4** the process of being pulled by a special medical apparatus in order to cure a broken bone or similar INJURY: *Her leg's in traction.*

traction en·gine /ˈ·· ˌ··/ *n* a large vehicle, usu. worked by steam power, used for pulling heavy loads along roads

trac·tor /ˈtræktəʳ/ *n* a powerful motor vehicle with large wheels and thick tyres used for pulling farm machinery (PLOUGHs, DRILLs[3] (1), etc.) or other heavy objects

Tra·cy /ˈtreɪsi/, **Spen·cer** /ˈspensəʳ/ (1900–67) an American actor popular esp. for the films he made with Katharine Hepburn, such as *Adam's Rib* —see picture at Katherine HEPBURN

trad[1] /træd/ also **trad jazz**— *n* [U] a style of JAZZ originally played in New Orleans about 1920, marked by free expression within a set instrumental structure —see also DIXIELAND

trad[2] *adj infml, esp. BrE for* TRADITIONAL

trade[1] /treɪd/ *n* **1** [U] the process of buying, selling, or exchanging goods, within a country or between countries: *The fall in the value of the pound may help to stimulate international trade.* | *a new trade agreement between England and France* **2** [*the*+S] a particular business or industry: *He works in the cotton trade/tourist trade.* **3** [C] a job, esp. one needing special skill with the hands: *Being a printer is a trade; being a lawyer is a profession.* | *He's a printer by trade.* —see JOB (USAGE) **4** [S (**in**)] the

stated level of business activity, esp. in selling: *Outside the castle he was doing a good/roaring trade* (=very good) *in souvenirs.* **5** [(*the*) U+*sing./pl. v*] the people who work in a particular business or industry: *a specialist magazine intended for the trade* | *trade journals* —see also TRADES, FREE TRADE, STOCK-IN-TRADE

trade[2] *v* **1** [I (**with**)] to buy and sell goods: *Britain built up her wealth by trading with other countries.* | *The US is one of our major* **trading partners**. (=we do a lot of trade with them) **2** [T (**for**)] to exchange (a product, goods, etc.): *I traded my radio for a typewriter.* | *The early settlers traded copper for corn.* | (fig.) *They were standing in the middle of the yard trading insults.* (=shouting INSULTs at each other) **3** [I (**at, with**)] *AmE* to shop regularly

  trade sthg. ↔ **in** *phr v* [T (**for**)] to give in part payment when buying something new: *He traded his old car in for a new one.* —**trade-in** /ˈ· ·/ *n, adj* : *trade-in price/value*

  trade sthg. ↔ **off** *phr v* [T (**against**)] to balance (one situation or quality) against another, with the aim of producing an acceptable or desirable result: *The government hopes to retain its popularity by trading off rising unemployment against the fall in inflation.* —see also TRADE-OFF

  trade on/upon sthg. *phr v* [T] to take unfair advantage of (someone's good nature, sympathy, etc.)

  trade up *phr v* [I] to trade in something (e.g. a car) for a similar thing which is more expensive or valuable: *He's sold his Ford Escort and traded up to a Sierra.*

trade def·i·cit /ˈ· ˌ···/ *n* TRADE GAP

Trade De·scrip·tions Act /ˌ· ·ˈ·· ˌ·/ [*the*] a law passed in Britain in 1968 according to which goods and services must be correctly and honestly described, and not said to be better than they are for the purposes of advertising

trade dis·count /ˈ· ˌ··/ *n* a reduction made in the price of goods sold to shopkeepers, etc. who are going to sell the goods to the general public

trade fair /ˈ· ˌ·/ *n* a usu. large gathering of companies in order to show their products or services and increase their business by taking orders

trade gap /ˈ· ·/ also **trade deficit**— *n* the difference between the value of what a country buys from other countries and what it sells abroad when the former is the larger figure

trade-in /ˈ· ·/ *n AmE* a used item, usu. a car, given to reduce the price of a new item: *They gave us $3000 off the price of the new car when we used our old one as a trade-in.*

trade·mark /ˈtreɪdmɑːk‖-mɑːrk/ *n* **1** a special name, sign, word, etc., which is marked on a product to show that it is made by a particular producer, and which may legally only be used by that producer **2** a particular sign, way of acting, etc., by which a person or thing may habitually be recognized: *Appearing briefly in his own films was a trademark of Alfred Hitchcock.*

trade name /ˈ· ·/ also **brand name**— *n* a name given by a producer to a particular product, by which it may be recognized from among similar products made by other producers —compare OWN LABEL

trade-off /ˈ· ·/ *n* a balance between two (opposing) situations or qualities, intended to produce an acceptable or desirable result: *In order to keep prices low, there has to be a trade-off between quality and quantity.* —see also TRADE **off**

trade price /ˈ· ·/ *n* the price at which goods are sold by producers to shops

trad·er /ˈtreɪdəʳ/ *n* a person who buys and sells goods

trade route /ˈ· ·/ *n* a way across land or sea habitually used by traders or their vehicles and ships

trades /treɪdz/ *n* [*the*+P] the TRADE WINDs

trade school /ˈ· ˌ·/ *n AmE* a school one may attend to learn a TRADE

trade se·cret /ˌ· ˈ··/ *n* a secret concerning a certain trade and known only to those working within the business: *Can you tell me how to make this or is it a trade secret?*

trades·man /ˈtreɪdzmən/ *n* -**men** /mən/ **1** *esp. BrE* a person who buys and sells goods, esp. a shopkeeper **2** *esp. BrE* a person who comes to private houses to deliver goods (esp. in the phrase **tradesman's entrance**) **3** *AmE* a man who works at a TRADE[1] (3)

trades·peo·ple /ˈtreɪdzˌpiːpəl/ n [P] esp. BrE people who buy and sell goods, esp. shopkeepers

Trades U·nion Con·gress /ˌ··· ·· ·ˈ··/ n see TUC

trade un·ion /ˌ·· ˈ··/ also **trades union** BrE ‖ usu. **union, labor union** AmE— n an organization of workers, esp. in a particular trade or profession, formed to represent their interests and deal as a group with employers. In Britain the trade unions are thought to have a strong LINK with the Labour Party, although this is not now as strong as it used to be. — ~ism n [U] — ~ist n

trade wind /ˈ· ·/ n a tropical wind that blows almost continually towards the EQUATOR (=the imaginary line running round the middle of the Earth) from either the northeast or the southeast

trading es·tate /ˈ·· ·ˌ·/ n an INDUSTRIAL ESTATE

trading post /ˈ·· ·/ n a small place for carrying on trade in a distant lonely area, started by settlers esp. to exchange goods for local products

trading stamp /ˈ·· ·/ also **stamp**— n a type of stamp given by a shop to a customer each time the customer spends a certain amount, for sticking in a book and later exchanging for goods or money

tra·di·tion /trəˈdɪʃən/ n **1** [U] the passing down of the beliefs, practices, and customs from the past to the present: *The British are said to be lovers of tradition.* **2** [C] a customary way of thinking or behaving that has been passed down in this way and continuously followed for a long time: *This newspaper has a long tradition of attacking corruption and mismanagement.* | *He intends to continue the family tradition and seek a career in politics.* **3** [U] the body of principles, beliefs, practices, experience, etc., passed down from the past to the present: *In the West, women* **by tradition** *wear white dresses when they get married.* | *This decision represents a complete* **break with tradition.** (=is different from what has ever been done before) | *According to tradition, this house was visited by Henry VIII.*

tra·di·tion·al /trəˈdɪʃənəl/ adj of or in accordance with tradition: *The traditional English breakfast includes bacon and eggs.* — ~**ly** adv : *Traditionally, women in the West are married in long white dresses.*

tra·di·tion·al·is·m /trəˈdɪʃənəlɪzəm/ n [U] a very great respect for tradition —**ist** n

trad jazz /ˌ· ˈ·/ n [U] TRAD¹

tra·duce /trəˈdjuːs‖-ˈduːs/ v [T] fml to speak falsely of (someone, their character, etc.), esp in order to make other people think badly of them —**ducer** n

Tra·fal·gar /trəˈfælgəʳ/ , **Cape** the most south-westerly point of Spain. In the sea near the cape, British ships under Nelson won an important sea battle against the French and Spanish in 1805.

Trafalgar Square /·ˌ·· ˈ·/ a square in central London, where Pall Mall, the Strand, and Charing Cross Road meet. Trafalgar Square is where Nelson's Column stands, and is also known for the large numbers of PIGEONs which come there and are fed by tourists —see colour map on page 817

traf·fic¹ /ˈtræfɪk/ n [U] **1** the movement of people or vehicles along roads or streets, of ships in the sea, planes in the sky, etc.: *The traffic's very heavy this morning.* (=there are lots of cars on the road) | *The job of an* **air traffic controller** *is to make sure aircraft can fly safely without getting too close to each other.* **2** the people, vehicles, etc., in this movement: *The cyclist weaved his way through the busy traffic.* **3** business done by a railway, ship or air travel company, etc., in carrying goods or passengers: *passenger traffic* **4** [(in)] trade, esp. in illegal goods: *the traffic in drugs/drug traffic*

traffic² v -ck-

traffic in sthg. phr v [T] to carry on trade, esp. of an illegal or improper kind, in (a particular type of goods): *trafficking in stolen goods*

traf·fi·ca·tor /ˈtræfɪkeɪtəʳ/ n BrE, becoming rare an INDICATOR (=flashing light on a car that shows a driver's intention of turning left or right)

traffic calm·ing /ˈ·· ·ˌ·/ n [U] the use of methods such as building SLEEPING POLICEMEN across a road, or making the road narrower, to prevent vehicles from passing too quickly through an area

traffic cir·cle /ˈ·· ·ˌ·/ n AmE for ROUNDABOUT¹ (1)

traffic cone /ˈ·· ·ˌ·/ n a CONE-shaped marker used on a road esp. for showing where repairs are being done

traffic cop /ˈ·· ˌ·/ n AmE infml **1** a police officer who directs traffic by standing in the road and waving his arms **2** a police officer who stops drivers who break the law and writes them a TICKET (3) (=written notice of an offence against the driving laws)

traffic is·land /ˈ·· ˌ··/ n an ISLAND (2)

traffic jam /ˈ·· ˌ·/ n a situation in which there is so much traffic on a road that it moves only very slowly (or not at all)

traf·fick·er /ˈtræfɪkəʳ/ n [(in)] a person who carries on trade, esp. in illegal goods: *drug traffickers*

traffic light /ˈ·· ·/ also **traffic sig·nal** /ˈ·· ˌ··/— n [usu. pl.] any of a set of coloured lights used for controlling and directing traffic, esp. where one road crosses another

traffic of·fence /ˈ·· ·ˌ·/ n an illegal act connected with driving a motor vehicle, esp. speeding (driving too fast) or illegal parking

traffic war·den /ˈ·· ˌ··/ n BrE an official responsible for controlling the parking of vehicles on city streets

tra·ge·di·an /trəˈdʒiːdiən/ n fml an actor or writer of TRAGEDY (2)

tra·ge·di·enne /trəˌdʒiːdiˈen/ n old-fash or pomp an actress of TRAGEDY (2)

tra·ge·dy /ˈtrædʒədi/ n **1** [C] a serious play that ends sadly, esp. with the main character's death, and is often intended to teach a moral lesson: *"Hamlet" is one of Shakespeare's best known tragedies.* **2** [U] plays like this considered as a branch of literature **3** [C;U] a terrible, unhappy, or unfortunate event: *Their holiday ended in tragedy when their hotel caught fire.* | *It was a great tragedy that she died so young.*

tra·gic /ˈtrædʒɪk/ adj **1** very sad, unfortunate, etc.: *a tragic accident* **2** [A no comp.] of TRAGEDY (2): *a tragic actress* —compare COMIC — ~**ally** /kli/ adv

tra·gi·com·e·dy /ˌtrædʒɪˈkɒmədi‖-ˈkɑː-/ n [C;U] a (type of) play or story that combines tragic and amusing parts —**comic** adj

trail¹ /treɪl/ v **1** [T] to drag or allow to drag behind, esp. without making any effort: *He sat on the side of the boat and trailed his feet in the water.* **2** [I (ALONG, behind)] to be dragged along behind: *Her long skirt was trailing along in the mud behind her.* **3** [T (to)] to follow the trail of; TRACK² (1): *The police trailed the criminal to his hiding-place.* **4** [I+adv/prep] to walk slowly and tiredly: *The defeated army trailed along the road/trailed back to camp.* **5** [I] (of a plant) to grow over or along the ground: *trailing ivy* **6** [I;T] to fall behind (a competitor): *At half-time our team was trailing by two goals to one.* | *According to the latest polls, the Republicans trail the Democrats by 10%.* **7** [T] to advertise in advance by means of a TRAILER (2)

trail off phr v [I] (esp. of a voice) to become gradually weaker and reduce to nothing

trail² n **1** the track or smell of a person or animal, esp. as followed by a hunter: *The hunters followed the tiger's trail.* | *The bank robbers rode off, with the sheriff's men* (**hard/hot**) **on their trail.** (=following (closely) behind them) **2** a path across rough country made by the passing of people or animals: *The trail led over Boulder Pass and then descended to a lake.* **3** [(of)] a stream of dust, smoke, people, vehicles, etc., behind something moving: *The car raced past, leaving a trail of dust.* | (fig.) *He left a trail of broken hearts/unpaid bills behind him.* —see also **blaze a/the trail** (BLAZE²)

trail·blaz·er /ˈtreɪlbleɪzəʳ/ n someone who begins or discovers something that has not been done before: *a trailblazer in the field of medicine*

trail·er /ˈtreɪləʳ/ n **1** a vehicle pulled by another vehicle: *He transports his boat by putting it on a trailer behind his car.* **2** an advertisement for a new film or TV show, usu. consisting of small pieces taken from it **3** AmE for CARAVAN (1)

trailer house /ˈ·· ·/ n a MOBILE HOME

trailer park /ˈ·· ·/ also **trailer court**— n AmE an area where many trailers stand and are used as houses: *The hurricane destroyed a trailer park on the edge of town.*

Trail of Tears /ˌ· · ˈ·/ [the] the way travelled by several TRIBES (groups) of Native Americans who were forced by

In Britain people get married either in church or in a REGISTRY OFFICE. In the US people often get married in a house, a garden, a park, a hotel, or in a WEDDING CHAPEL as well as in church. Most people, when they think of a wedding, think of people getting married in church and the many customs that go with this type of wedding, called a WHITE WEDDING. Even people who are not religious often want to have a TRADITIONAL white wedding in a church.

The main people at the wedding

There are special names for some of the people in the wedding ceremony. The woman who is getting married is called the BRIDE and the man is called the BRIDEGROOM or GROOM. The man has a male friend with him called the BEST MAN and the bride has some female friends called the BRIDESMAIDS. It is traditional for the bride to wear a long white dress and a white VEIL and to carry flowers in a BOUQUET. She is also supposed to wear '**something old, something new, something borrowed and something blue**' because this will bring her luck. The groom wears a suit or sometimes a TUXEDO (in the US) or MORNING SUIT (in Britain). Everyone else wears their best clothes and the women often buy hats specially.

a British bride and bridegroom after the wedding ceremony

be your wedded husband/wife?'. The bride and bridegroom each say '*I will*'. At the end of the ceremony, the priest or minister says: '*I pronounce you man and wife*' which means that they are officially married. The bride and bridegroom then sign the REGISTER (=a special book which is the official record of their marriage).

a US garden wedding

Before the ceremony

The bridegroom is not supposed to see the bride on the day of the wedding until they meet in church as this is considered to be bad luck.

The bridegroom arrives at the church first and waits inside, near the ALTAR (=part at the front of the church), with the best man.

The families of the bride and bridegroom, and the wedding guests, sit in rows in the church.

Just before the wedding ceremony begins, the bride arrives at the church in a car with her father. The car is usually an expensive car, such as a Rolls Royce or a limousine, hired for the occasion and decorated with RIBBONS. There are often jokes made about the bride arriving late at the church.

The ceremony

It is the custom for the bride's father to '**give her away**' (=officially to 'give' her to the bridegroom). The bride and her father walk slowly up the AISLE (=central passage) of the church, with the bridesmaids. People sometimes talk about '**walking up the aisle**' when they mean 'getting married'. When the bride and bridegroom are together at the altar the priest or minister begins the wedding service. The words that are said during the wedding service are very well known to most people. During the service, the bridegroom gives the bride a WEDDING RING (=a plain gold ring) and says '*With this ring I thee wed*' (='With this ring I marry you'). Sometimes the bride also gives a ring to the bridegroom. The priest or minister asks the bride and bridegroom in turn: '*Will you have this man/woman to*

After the ceremony

Outside the church, the friends of the bride and bridegroom throw CONFETTI (=small pieces of coloured paper) or rice over them. Photographs are usually taken of the bride and bridegroom and their families and friends.

The reception

After the photographs everyone usually goes to a hotel for the wedding RECEPTION, which is a special meal (wedding breakfast) and party to celebrate the wedding. During the meal the bride and bridegroom cut the WEDDING CAKE and give it to their guests. At the end of the meal there are speeches, usually made by the bride's father, the bridegroom and the best man. It is traditional for the best man to make a speech in which he talks about funny and embarrassing (EMBARRASS) things that have happened to the bridegroom in the past.

Before the reception ends the bride and bridegroom usually

a US wedding chapel

cutting the cake

drive away to another hotel to spend their wedding night before beginning their HONEYMOON (=a holiday taken by people who have just got married). People often make rude jokes about the wedding night because in the past it was usually the first time the couple had sex. The car the couple drive away in has usually been decorated by their friends. There is often a sign saying '**just married**' and sometimes tin cans are tied to the back of the car. Before she leaves the bride throws her bouquet to her friends to catch. According to custom, the woman who catches it will be the next one to get married.

the US government to move from their homes to RESERVATIONS west of the Mississippi River from the 1820s to the 1840s. Many people died of illness and bad treatment. —see also NATIVE AMERICAN (CULTURAL NOTE)

train[1] /treɪn/ n **1** a line of connected railway carriages pulled by an engine: *to catch/miss the train* | *I prefer travelling* **by train.** | *There is no train service* (=trains do not run) *between here and Wales.* —see also BOAT TRAIN **2** a long line of moving people, animals, and vehicles: *a camel train* **3** a part of a long dress (e.g. one worn for a wedding) that spreads over the ground behind the wearer **4** [+of] a chain of related events, thoughts, actions, etc.: *The telephone rang and interrupted my* **train of thought.** **5** *old use* a group of servants or officers attending a person of high rank

▷ USAGE You can travel **by** train, or **on** a particular train. At the beginning of your journey you **get on(to)** the train and at the end of your journey you **get off** (it), **get out** (of it), or **alight** *fml* (from it). —see also DRIVE (USAGE), TRANSPORT (USAGE)◁

train[2] v **1** [I;T (**as, in**)] to give or be given a course of instruction or practice, esp. in a profession or skill: *She trained as a singer under a famous professor of music.* [+obj+to-v] *These dogs are trained to detect explosives.* [+to-v] *He's training to be a doctor.* | *a well trained dog/voice* **2** [I;T (**for**)] to prepare for a test of physical skill, esp. by exercising: *Every morning John spends two hours training for the race.* **3** [T] to direct the growth of (a plant) by bending, cutting, tying, etc. **4** [T (**on**)] to aim (a gun, camera, etc.) at something or someone: *The firemen trained their hoses on the burning building.* —see TEACH (USAGE) – – **able** *adj*

train·bear·er /ˈtreɪnˌbeərəʳ/ n an attendant who holds up the TRAIN[1] (3) of a dress, esp. at a wedding

train·ee /ˌtreɪˈniː◂/ n a person who is being trained: *a trainee reporter*

train·er /ˈtreɪnəʳ/ n **1** a person who trains people or animals for sports, work, etc. **2** *BrE* ‖ **sneaker, tennis shoe** *AmE*— a strong shoe for sports; thick PLIMSOLL —see PAIR (USAGE), and see picture at SHOE

train·ing /ˈtreɪnɪŋ/ n **1** [S;U (**in**)] the process of training or being trained; instruction: *On the course she received (a) thorough training in every aspect of the job.* | *a training programme* **2** [U (**for**)] a course of special exercises, practice, food, etc., to keep sportsmen or animals healthy and fit: *The champion has* **gone into training/is in training** *for his next fight.* **3 in/out of training** in/not in a good healthy condition for a sport, test of skill, etc.

training col·lege /ˈ··· ˌ··/ n [C;U] *BrE* a college, usu. for adults, that gives specialized instruction: *a teacher training college* | *a training college for pilots*

Training and En·ter·prise Coun·cil /ˌ··· ˈ··· ˌ··/ see TEC

training shoe /ˈ·· ˌ·/ n *BrE* a TRAINER (2)

train set /ˈ· ·/ n a toy train together with the railway lines and other equipment that goes with it

train spot·ter /ˈ· ˌ··/ n *BrE* a person who collects the numbers of railway engines and information about them as a HOBBY. People often make jokes about train spotters because they are considered to be boring people who are only interested in small details and boring facts and always wear ANORAKS. —**train spotting** n [U]

train spotter

traipse /treɪps/ v [I+adv/prep] *infml* to walk tiredly or wander: *I've been traipsing round the shops all morning.*

trait /treɪ, treɪt‖treɪt/ n *fml* a particular quality, esp. of a person; CHARACTERISTIC: *Anne's generosity is one of her most pleasing traits.*

trai·tor /ˈtreɪtəʳ/ n *derog* someone who is disloyal, esp. to their country: *He was hanged as a traitor.* | *a traitor to the cause of women's rights*

trai·tor·ous /ˈtreɪtərəs/ *adj derog, esp. lit* of or like a traitor; TREACHEROUS – – **ly** *adv*

tra·jec·to·ry /trəˈdʒektəri/ n *tech* the curved path of an object fired or thrown through the air: *the trajectory of a bullet* —compare ELEVATION (4)

tram /træm/ *also* **tram·car** /ˈtræmkɑːʳ‖*esp. BrE* ‖ usu. **streetcar, trolley** *AmE*— n a sort of bus used in cities that is driven by electricity and runs along metal tracks set in the road

tram·lines /ˈtræmlaɪnz/ n [P] *BrE* **1** the metal tracks, set in the road, along which a tram runs **2** *infml* either of the pairs of lines on the edges of a tennis court, marking additional space used only when four people are playing

tram·mels /ˈtræməlz/ n [P] *fml or lit* something that limits or prevents free movement, activity, or development: *the trammels of material wealth* —see also UNTRAMMELLED

tramp[1] /træmp/ v [I+adv/prep;T] to walk (through or over) with firm heavy steps: *Who's been tramping all over this carpet in muddy shoes?* | *The children tramped the woods looking for berries.* | *I've tramped the streets/tramped all round town looking for work.*

tramp[2] n **1** [C] *often derog* a person with no home or job, who wanders from place to place and usu. begs for food or money **2** [C] *also* **tramp steam·er** /ˈ· ˌ··/— a ship that does not make regular trips but takes goods to any port **3** [C] *derog, esp. AmE* an immoral woman **4** [C] a long walk: *We went for a tramp through the woods.* **5** [(the) S] the sound of heavy walking: *the steady tramp of soldiers' feet on the road*

tram·ple /ˈtræmpəl/ v [I+adv/prep;T (DOWN)] to step heavily with the feet (on); crush under the feet: *The hunter was trampled to death by a wild elephant.* | (fig.) *You can't just trample on her feelings like that.*

tram·po·line /ˈtræmpəliːn‖ˌtræmpəˈliːn/ n an apparatus on which ACROBATS and GYMNASTS jump up and down to perform exercises, consisting of a sheet of material tightly stretched and held to a metal frame by strong springs

trance /trɑːns‖træns/ n a sleeplike condition of the mind in which one does not notice the things around one: *a hypnotic trance* | *He didn't answer when I spoke — he seemed to be* **in a trance.**

tran·ny /ˈtræni/ n *BrE old-fash infml for* TRANSISTOR (2)

tran·quil /ˈtræŋkwɪl/ *adj* pleasantly calm, quiet, or peaceful; free from anxiety, worry, etc.: *a tranquil life in the country* | *a tranquil lake* | *a tranquil smile* – – **ly** *adv* – – **lity** *BrE* ‖ – **ity** *AmE* /træŋˈkwɪlɪti/ n [U]

tran·quil·lize *also* **-lise** *BrE* /ˈtræŋkwɪlaɪz/ v [T] to make (esp. an animal) calm or peaceful, usu. by means of a drug

tran·quil·lizer *also* **-liser** *BrE* /ˈtræŋkwɪlaɪzəʳ/ n a drug used for reducing nervous anxiety and making a person calm and peaceful: *She's been on tranquillizers since the accident.*

trans- see WORD FORMATION

trans·act /trænˈzækt/ v [T] *fml* to carry out (esp. a piece of business or trade)

trans·ac·tion /trænˈzækʃən/ n *fml* **1** [C] something transacted; a piece of business: *The bank charges a fixed rate for each transaction.* **2** [U(of)] the act of transacting: *the transaction of business*

Trans-Am Cham·pi·on·ship /ˌ· ˈ· ˌ·····/ [the] a number of sports car races held in the US and Canada

trans·at·lan·tic /ˌtrænzətˈlæntɪk◂/ *adj* **1** on the other side of the Atlantic ocean: *one of America's transatlantic military bases* **2** crossing the Atlantic ocean: *transatlantic flights* **3** concerning countries on both sides of the Atlantic ocean: *a transatlantic agreement*

trans·cei·ver /trænˈsiːvəʳ/ n a radio set which can both send and receive messages

trans·cend /trænˈsend/ v [T] *fml or lit, usu. apprec* **1** to go or be above or beyond the limits of: *The desire for peace transcended political differences.* | *The size of the universe transcends human understanding.* **2** to go beyond in size, strength, quality, etc.; SURPASS: *His latest symphony transcends anything he has ever written before.*

tran·scen·dent /trænˈsendənt/ *adj fml or lit, usu. apprec* going far beyond ordinary limits: *the transcendent genius of Mozart* – – **ly** *adv* – **dence, -dency** n [U]

tran·scen·den·tal /ˌtrænsenˈdentl◂/ *adj* going beyond human knowledge, understanding, and experience; impossible to discover or understand by practical experience or reason – – **ly** *adv*

tran·scen·den·tal·is·m /ˌtrænsenˈdentəl-ɪzəm/ n [U] *fml or tech* the belief that knowledge and the principles of reality can be obtained by studying thought and not necessarily by practical experience —**ist** n

transcendental med·i·ta·tion /ˌ····· ··ˈ···/ *also* **TM**— n [U] a method of becoming calm and untroubled by repeating in one's mind special religious words, esp. a Hindu MANTRA. Transcendental meditation was esp. popular in the 1960s and 1970s.

trans·con·ti·nen·tal /ˌtrænzkɒntɪˈnentl, ˌtræns-ǁ-kɑːn-/ adj crossing a CONTINENT: *a transcontinental railway*

tran·scribe /trænˈskraɪb/ v [T] *fml* **1** [(into)] to write an exact copy of: *to transcribe an ancient manuscript* **2** to write down fully; turn into a written form: *A secretary transcribed the witnesses' statements|the taped recordings.* **3** to represent (speech sounds) by means of special (PHONETIC) letters **4** [(into)] to write in the alphabet of another language **5** [(for)] to arrange (a piece of music) for a different instrument or voice than the original **6** [(onto)] to TRANSFER[1] (3)

tran·script /ˈtrænskrɪpt/ n [(of)] **1** an exact written or printed copy; something transcribed: *A transcript of the tapes was presented as evidence in court.* **2** AmE an official document of a college or university which lists a student's classes and the GRADES received: *Students can pick up copies of their transcripts at the registrar's office in Murphy Hall.*

tran·scrip·tion /trænˈskrɪpʃən/ n **1** [U] the act or process of transcribing: *The pronunciations of words are shown by a system of phonetic transcription.* **2** [C (of)] a transcript

tran·sept /ˈtrænsept/ n the part of a cross-shaped church that crosses the main body of the church at RIGHT ANGLES

trans·fer[1] /trænsˈfɜːʳ/ v **-rr-** [(from, to)] **1** [I;T] to move from one place, job, position, etc., to another: *The management decided to transfer production of the newspaper to its new plant in Scotland.* | *That football player is hoping to transfer|be transferred to another team soon.* | *I've transferred my allegiance to this new brand.* **2** [I;T] to (cause to) move or change from one vehicle to another in the course of a journey: *At London we transferred from the train to a bus.* **3** [T] to copy (recorded material): *Callas's original recording has been transferred to compact disc.* **4** [T] *law* to give the ownership of (property) to another person — **~able** adj

trans·fer[2] /ˈtrænsfɜːʳ/ n **1** [C;U] an act or process of transferring: *She's hoping for a transfer to another part of the company.* | *the electronic transfer of money* **2** [C] someone or something that has transferred **3** [C] *esp. BrE* ǁ **decal** *esp. AmE*— a drawing, pattern, etc., for sticking or printing onto a surface: *He had a transfer of Mickey Mouse on the back of his shirt.* **4** [C] *esp. AmE* a ticket allowing a passenger to change from one bus, train, etc., to another without paying more money

trans·fer·ence /ˈtrænsfərəns|trænsˈfɜːr-/ n [U] *fml* **1** the act of transferring or state of being transferred **2** *med* the redirecting of feelings and wishes, esp. ones that have been unconsciously kept since childhood, to a new object, esp. a doctor who is treating one's mind

transfer fee /ˈ·· ˌ·/ n *BrE* the sum of money paid by one professional football club to another for the transfer of a player

transfer pas·sen·ger /ˈ·· ˌ···/ n a passenger, esp. one travelling by air, who will be continuing his or her journey beyond a place, e.g. an airport, where he or she is at present: *Transfer passengers should report to the transfer desk in the air terminal.*

trans·fig·ure /trænsˈfɪɡəʳǁ-ɡjər/ v [T] *fml or lit* to change (someone or something) in outward form or appearance, esp. in order to make beautiful or perfect: *a face transfigured with joy* —**uration** /ˌtrænsfɪɡjˈʊreɪʃən/ n [C;U]

trans·fix /trænsˈfɪks/ v [T (with)] *fml* **1** to force a hole through (as if) with a sharp pointed weapon: *an animal transfixed with a spear* —compare IMPALE **2** [*usu. pass.*] to cause to be unable to move or think because of terror, shock, etc.: *He stood transfixed when I told him the terrible news.*

trans·form /trænsˈfɔːmǁ-ˈfɔːrm/ v [T (into)] to change completely in form, appearance, or nature: *A steam engine transforms heat into power.* | *In only 20 years the country has been transformed into an advanced industrial power.* |

Getting that new job has completely transformed her! (=changed her behaviour, appearance, etc.) — **~able** adj — **~ation** /ˌtrænsfəˈmeɪʃənǁ-fər-/ n [C;U (into)] : *the transformation of heat into power* | *In recent years his ideas have undergone a complete transformation.* | *You've painted the room blue all over; what a transformation!*

trans·form·er /trænsˈfɔːməʳǁ-ɔːr-/ n an apparatus for changing electrical force, usu. from one VOLTAGE to another

trans·fu·sion /trænsˈfjuːʒən/ n [C;U] *fml* (an act of) putting the blood of one person into the body of another: *The driver lost a lot of blood as a result of the accident so he was rushed to hospital for a (blood) transfusion.*

trans·gress /trænzˈgresǁtræns-/ v *fml* **1** [T] to go beyond (a proper or legal limit): *His behaviour transgressed the unwritten rules of social conduct.* **2** [I] to do wrong; offend against a moral principle — **~ion** /ˈgreʃən/ n [C;U] — **~or** /ˈgresəʳ/ n

tran·si·ent[1] /ˈtrænzɪəntǁˈtrænʃənt/ *also* **transitory**— adj *fml* **1** lasting for only a short time; quickly passing: *transient happiness* **2** (usu. of a person) passing quickly through a place or staying for only a short time: *a transient population* —**ence**, -**ency** n [U]

transient[2] n *AmE* a person who has no home and moves from place to place: *transients sleeping in the park*

tran·sis·tor /trænˈzɪstəʳ, -ˈsɪstəʳ/ n **1** a small electrical apparatus, esp. used in radios, televisions, etc., for controlling the flow of an electrical current —compare VALVE (2) **2** *also* **transistor ra·di·o** /·ˌ·· ˈ···/ *fml*— a usu. small radio that has transistors instead of VALVES

tran·sis·tor·ize *also* **-ise** *BrE* /trænˈzɪstəraɪz, -ˈsɪs-/ v [T] to provide with transistors: *a transistorized circuit*

tran·sit /ˈtrænsʌt, -zʌt/ n **1** [U] the going or moving of people or goods from one place to another: *The goods were damaged|lost in transit.* | *a transit lounge in the airport* (=for passengers who are changing planes) **2** [C;U] *tech* (a) movement of a PLANET or moon across the face of a larger body in space, esp. the sun

Transit n *tdmk* a well-known model of VAN or light LORRY made by the Ford Motor Company in Britain

transit camp /ˈ·· ˌ·/ n a camp in which esp. REFUGEES live temporarily before moving on to the place where they will settle permanently: *There is a transit camp in Vienna for Jews who leave the Soviet Union to settle in Israel.*

tran·si·tion /trænˈzɪʃən, -ˈsɪ-/ n [C;U (from, to)] *fml* (an example of) the act of changing or passing from one form, state, subject, or place to another: *a peaceful transition from colonial rule to self-government* | *a period of transition* — **~al** adj — **~ally** adv

tran·si·tive /ˈtrænsʌtɪv, -zʌ-/ adj *tech* (of a verb) that must take an object or a phrase acting like an object. Transitive verbs are marked [T] in this dictionary: *"Break" is intransitive in the sentence "The cup fell and broke" but transitive in "I broke the cup".* —compare DITRANSITIVE, INTRANSITIVE —**transitive** n

tran·si·to·ry /ˈtrænzʌtəriǁ-tɔːri/ n TRANSIENT

Trans·kei /trænsˈkaɪ/ [*the*] a HOMELAND in SE South Africa, bordering on Lesotho to the N and the Indian Ocean to the SE. Transkei has been independent of South Africa since 1976 but is not recognized internationally as a separate country and is ECONOMIC*ally* dependent on South Africa.

trans·late /trænsˈleɪt, trænz-/ v **1** [I;T (from, into)] to change (speech or writing) from one language into another: *She translated the book from French into English.* —compare INTERPRET (3) **2** [I] to be changed from one language into another: *Poetry doesn't always translate easily.* **3** [T (into)] to change from one form to another: *If we get elected we will be able to translate our ideas into action.* —**latable** adj

trans·la·tion /trænsˈleɪʃən, trænz-/ n [C;U] the act of translating or something that has been translated, esp. from one language to another: *She's doing an English translation of "Faust".* | *I've only read Tolstoy in translation.* (=in English, not in Russian)

trans·la·tor /trænsˈleɪtəʳ, trænz-/ n a person who translates from one language to another, esp. in writing as a profession —compare INTERPRETER (1)

trans·lit·e·rate /trænzˈlɪtəreɪtǁtræns-/ v [T (from, into, as)] *fml or tech* to write (a word, name, sentence, etc.) in the alphabet of a different language or writing system —**ation** /ˌtrænzlɪtəˈreɪʃənǁ ˌtræns-/ n [C;U]

trans·lu·cent /trænz'luːsənt‖træns-/ adj not transparent but clear enough to allow light to pass through: *translucent glass in a bathroom window* —**cence, -cency** n [U]

trans·mi·gra·tion /ˌtrænzmaɪ'greɪʃən‖ˌtræns-/ n [U] the passing of the soul at death into another body

trans·mis·sion /trænz'mɪʃən‖træns-/ n **1** [U (**of**)] the act of transmitting or state of being transmitted: *the transmission of disease* **2** [C] something broadcast on television, radio, etc.: *We interrupt our normal transmissions to bring you a special news flash.* **3** [C] the parts of a vehicle that carry power from the engine to the wheels

trans·mit /trænz'mɪt‖træns-/ v **-tt- 1** [I;T (**to**)] to send out (electric signals, messages, news, etc.) by radio, etc.; broadcast: *The survivors of the shipwreck transmitted a distress signal every hour.* **2** [T (**to**)] to send or pass from one person, place, or thing to another: *This infection is transmitted by mosquitoes.* | *The information is transmitted from one computer to another through a telephone line.* **3** [T] to allow to travel through or along itself: *Glass transmits light but not sound.*

trans·mit·ter /trænz'mɪtər‖træns-/ n someone or something that transmits, esp. an apparatus that sends out radio or television signals

trans·mog·ri·fy /trænz'mɒɡrɪfaɪ‖træns'mɑː-/ v [T] *usu. humor* to change completely (as if) by magic —**fication** /trænzˌmɒɡrɪfɪ'keɪʃən‖træns mɑː-/ n [C;U]

trans·mute /trænz'mjuːt‖træns-/ v [T (**into**)] *fml or tech* to change from one form, nature, substance, etc., into another, esp. of a better kind: *Medieval alchemists attempted to transmute base metals into gold.* —**mutable** adj —**mutation** /ˌtrænzmjuː'teɪʃən‖ˌtræns-/ n [C;U]

tran·som /'trænsəm/ n **1** a bar of wood above a door or separating a door from a window above; LINTEL **2** a horizontal bar of wood or stone fitted across a window to divide it in two **3** a flat surface which forms the back part of a square-ended boat **4** also **transom win·dow** /'·· ˌ··/—*AmE for* FANLIGHT —see also OVER-THE-TRANSOM

trans·par·en·cy /træn'spærənsi, -'speər-/ n **1** [U] the quality of being transparent **2** [C] a piece of photographic film, usu. in a square holder, by means of which a picture can be seen when light is passed through it; SLIDE[2] (4)

trans·par·ent /træn'spærənt, 'speər-/ adj **1** allowing light to pass through so that objects behind can be clearly seen; *Plain glass is transparent.* **2** thin or fine enough to be seen through: *a transparent silk blouse* **3 a** easy to understand; clear: *The meaning of this passage seems quite transparent.* **b** *often derog.* about which there is no doubt; OBVIOUS: *a transparent lie* —compare OPAQUE — **ly** adv

tran·spi·ra·tion /ˌtrænspɪ'reɪʃən/ n [U] *tech* the act of transpiring (TRANSPIRE (3))

tran·spire /træn'spaɪər/ v **1** [it+I+(*that*)] (of a fact, secret, etc.) to become known: *It later transpired that he hadn't been telling the truth.* **2** [I] *infml* to happen: *Let's wait and see what transpires.* **3** [I;T] *tech* (of the body, a plant, etc.) to give off (esp. watery waste matter) through the surface of the body, leaves, etc.

trans·plant[1] /træns'plɑːnt‖-'plænt/ v [T (**from, to**)] **1** to move (a plant) from one place and plant it in another **2** to move (an organ, piece of skin, hair, etc.) from one part of the body to another or from one person or animal to another: *to transplant a heart* **3** to move from one place and settle or establish elsewhere: *Under the Tudors many English people were transplanted to Ireland.* | *The entire business — factory, offices, and warehouse — was transplanted to Texas.* — ~**ation** /ˌtrænsplɑːn'teɪʃən‖-plæn-/ n [U]

trans·plant[2] /'trænsplɑːnt‖-plænt/ n **1** an act or operation of transplanting an organ, piece of skin, hair, etc.: *This surgeon has done several heart/kidney transplants.* | *transplant surgery* **2** the thing transplanted in such an operation: *The transplant has taken/has been rejected.* | *a skin transplant* —compare IMPLANT

trans·po·lar /ˌtrænz'pəʊlər‖træns-/ adj *fml* across the North or South Pole or POLAR area

trans·pond·er /træn'spɒndər‖-'spɑː-/ n a radio or RADAR apparatus that sends out a particular signal when it receives a signal telling it to do so

trans·port[1] /'trænspɔːt‖-ɔːrt/ n **1** [U (**of**)] ‖ also **transportation** *esp. AmE*— the act of transporting or state of being

transported: *The transport of goods by air is very expensive.* **2** [U] **a** ‖ also **transportation** *esp. AmE*— a means or system of carrying passengers or goods from one place to another: *Moscow's public transport system is among the finest in the world.* | *The Department of Transport is responsible for the country's roads and railways.* **b** *infml* a method of being transported: *I'd like to go to the concert, but I haven't any transport.* (=no car, bicycle, etc., to take me there) **3** [C] a ship or aircraft for carrying soldiers or supplies: *a troop transport* **4 in a transport/transports of** *lit* filled with (a very strong feeling of joy, delight, etc.)

▷ USAGE 1 for most methods of transport, use **by** when you are talking about how someone gets to a place: *He came* **by** *taxi/bus/plane/etc.* But for walking use **on foot**: *He came* **on foot.** 2 When talking about events that happen while using a particular form of transport, use either **on**: *I banged my knee while I was* **on** *my bike.* | *I met an old friend* **on** *the train/on the bus/on the boat*, or **in**: *We sat next to each other* **in** *the car/in(or* **on**) *the plane.* —see also BICYCLE (USAGE), BOAT (USAGE), BUS (USAGE), CAR (USAGE), DRIVE (USAGE), PLANE (USAGE), STEER (USAGE), TRAIN (USAGE)◁

trans·port[2] /træn'spɔːt‖-ɔːrt/ v [T] **1** (**from, to**)) to carry (goods, people, etc.) from one place to another; CONVEY: *Trains transport the coal to the ports.* **2** [(**to**)] (in former times) to send a criminal to a distant land as a punishment **3** [*usu. pass.*] *lit* to fill with delight, joy, or any strong feeling — ~**able** adj

Transport and Gen·e·ral Work·ers' U·nion /ˌ··· ˌ····· ˈ·· ˌ··/ [*the*] see TGWU

trans·por·ta·tion /ˌtrænspɔː'teɪʃən‖-spər-/ n [U] **1** *esp. AmE for* TRANSPORT[1] (1,2a) **2** (in former times) the sending of a criminal to a distant land as a punishment

transport caf·e /'·· ˌ··‖'·· ·ˌ·/ *BrE* ‖ **truck stop** *AmE*— n a cheap eating place on a main road, used mainly by long-distance heavy-vehicle drivers

trans·port·er /træn'spɔːtər‖-ɔːr-/ n a long vehicle on which one or more cars or other vehicles can be carried: *a tank/car transporter*

Transport Min·is·ter /'·· ˌ···/ n the minister in the British government who is responsible for the spending of government money on roads, railways, and other state-run transport systems, and for making laws concerning transport

transport plane /'·· ˌ·/ n an aircraft which is used for carrying goods or people, esp. military equipment or soldiers: *a Lockheed "Hercules" transport plane*

transport ship /'·· ˌ·/ n a ship used esp. for carrying soldiers

trans·pose /træn'spəʊz/ v [T] *fml* **1** to REVERSE the order or position of (usu. two things): *If you transpose the letters of "at" it reads "ta".* **2** to write or perform (a piece of music) in a musical KEY[1] (4) different from the original one —**position** /ˌtrænspə'zɪʃən/ n [C;U]

trans·put·er /trænz'pjuːtər‖træns-/ n a specially powerful computer MICROCHIP that can handle extremely large amounts of information very fast

trans·sex·u·al /træn'sekʃuəl‖træns'sek-/ adj, n (of or being) a person who is physically of one sex but has an urge to be or look like a person of the opposite sex, esp. by means of a medical operation

Trans-Si·be·ri·an Rail·way /ˌ·· ·ˌ···· '··/ [*the*] a railway connecting Moscow and Vladivostok, built between 1891 and 1905

tran·sub·stan·ti·a·tion /ˌtrænsəbstænʃi'eɪʃən/ n [U] *tech* the belief that the bread and wine offered by the priest at the MASS (=a Christian religious service) becomes the body and blood of Christ —compare CONSUBSTANTIATION

Trans·vaal /'trænzvɑːl‖ˌtræns'vɑːl/ [*the*] a PROVINCE in the NE of South Africa. The Transvaal was first settled in the mid-1830s by Boer farmers, and became a centre of Afrikaner CULTURE and of the opposition to British rule which led to the Boer War.

trans·verse /trænz'vɜːs‖træns'vɜːrs/ adj [no comp.] *fml or tech* lying or placed across: *a transverse beam* — ~**ly** adv

trans·ves·tite /trænz'vestaɪt‖træns-/ n a person who wears or gets sexual pleasure from wearing the clothes of the opposite sex —**tism** n [U]

Tran·syl·va·ni·a /ˌtrænsɪl'veɪniə/ a REGION of central and W

Romania, now a centre of the Romanian steel and chemical industries. Transylvania is most famous for being the place where with Count Dracula is supposed to have lived. —see also DRACULA

trap¹ /træp/ n **1** an apparatus for catching and holding animals: *a mouse caught in a trap* **2 a** a difficult or dangerous position in which one is caught by deception or carelessness and from which one cannot escape: *He fell into the trap of underestimating his opponent.* **b** a plan for deceiving and tricking a person: *The police* **set a trap** *to catch the thief.* **3** *sl* a mouth: *Shut your trap!* (= Be quiet!) | *You can rely on him to* **keep his trap shut.** (=he won't tell the secret) **4** a light two-wheeled vehicle pulled by a horse: *a pony and trap* **5** a U or S shaped part of a pipe, that holds water and prevents the escape of smelly gas from waste pipes **6** an apparatus from which a dog is set free at the beginning of a GREYHOUND race **7** also **sandtrap**— *AmE for* BUNKER (3) —see also DEATH TRAP, POVERTY TRAP, SPEED TRAP

trap² v **-pp-** [T] **1** to place or hold firmly with no possibility of escape: *Twenty miners were trapped underground after the fire.* **2** [(into)] to trick; deceive: *By clever questioning they trapped him into (making) a confession.* **3** to catch (an animal) in a trap, esp. for food or fur or as a business **4** to hold back; block: *Sand and leaves trapped the water in the stream.*

trap·door /ˈtræpdɔːʳ/ n a small door covering an opening in a roof or floor

tra·peze /trəˈpiːz/ n a short bar hanging high above the ground from two ropes used by GYMNASTs and ACROBATS: *trapeze artists*

tra·pe·zi·um /trəˈpiːziəm/ *BrE* ‖ **trapezoid** *AmE*— *n* **-iums** *or* **-ia** /iə/ *tech* (in MATHEMATICS) a four-sided shape in which only one pair of sides is parallel —see picture at QUADRILATERAL

trap·e·zoid /ˈtræpɪzɔɪd/ *BrE* ‖ **trapezium** *AmE*— *n tech* (in MATHEMATICS) a four-sided shape in which no sides are parallel —see picture at QUADRILATERAL

trap·per /ˈtræpəʳ/ n a person who traps wild animals, esp. for their fur

trap·pings /ˈtræpɪŋz/ n [P] *often derog* articles of dress or decoration, esp. as an outward sign of rank: (fig.) *the trappings of power, such as titles and privileges*

Trap·pist /ˈtræpɪst/ n a member of a Roman Catholic ORDER (=religious society) whose members never speak, and live according to very severe rules

trap·shoot·ing /ˈtræpˌʃuːtɪŋ/ n [U] the sport of shooting at clay plates or balls fired into the air by a powerful spring

trash¹ /træʃ/ n [U] **1** something of extremely low quality or value: *His new film is absolute trash.* | *What you're saying is absolute trash.* (=nonsense) **2** ‖ also **garbage**— *AmE* waste material to be thrown away; RUBBISH **3** [+*sing.*|*pl. v*] *esp. AmE* a worthless person or worthless people

trash² v [T] *sl* to destroy, damage, or make dirty

trash·can /ˈtræʃkæn/ n *AmE* a DUSTBIN or a public LITTER BIN

trash com·pac·tor /ˈ· ·ˌ·-/ n *AmE* a machine which presses rubbish together into a very small packet, used in some kitchens in the US

trash·men /ˈtræʃmen/ n [P] *AmE* the people who collect the rubbish from most private homes and businesses and who are usu. paid by the local government

trash·y /ˈtræʃi/ adj of extremely low quality or value, esp. of low artistic quality: *trashy novels* —**iness** n [U]

trat·to·ri·a /ˌtrætəˈriːə‖ˌtrɑː-/ n an Italian name often given to Italian restaurants: *the Trattoria Gambini*

trau·ma /ˈtrɔːmə, ˈtraʊmə/ also **trau·mat·is·m** /ˈtrɔːmətɪzəm, ˈtraʊ-/— n **1** damage to the mind caused by a sudden shock or terrible experience **2** *med* a wound

trau·mat·ic /trɔːˈmætɪk/ adj (of an experience) deeply and unforgettably shocking: *the traumatic events of his childhood, when both his parents had been killed* — ~**ally** /kli/ adv

trau·ma·tize also **-tise** *BrE* /ˈtrɔːmətaɪz/ v [T] **1** to shock deeply and unforgettably **2** *med* to wound

trav·ail² /ˈtræveɪl/ n [U] *old use* **1** also **travails** *pl.*— very hard work **2** the pains of giving birth to a child: *a woman in travail*

travail² v [I] *old use* to work very hard

trav·el¹ /ˈtrævəl/ v **-ll-** *BrE* ‖ **-l-** *AmE* **1** [I] to go from one place to another, esp. to a distant place; make a journey: *If I had a lot of money, I'd travel.* | *He travelled across Spain on a donkey.* | *He has travelled widely.* (=to many places) | (fig.) *Her mind travelled back to* (=she remembered) *her childhood.* **2** [T] to go through or over: *I've travelled* (=been to all parts of) *the world during my time in the navy.* **3** [T] to move (a stated distance) on a journey: *We travelled 100 miles on our first day.* **4** [I+*adv*/*prep*] to pass, go, move, be sent, etc.: *At what speed does light travel?* | *Some wines travel badly.* (=the taste is spoiled when they are moved long distances) | *The news travelled fast.* **5** [I+*adv*/*prep*] to go from place to place in order to sell and take orders for one's firm's goods: *My husband travels for a London firm.* | *He travels in* (=sells) *cosmetics.* —see also TRAVELLER (2) **6** [I] *infml* to go very quickly: *That motorbike was really travelling; it must have been doing 100 miles an hour.* **7** (in BASKETBALL) to run with the ball without bouncing (BOUNCE) it **8 have gun/typewriter/guitar etc., will travel** a phrase used by someone who is willing to travel anywhere to do their job **9 travel light** to travel without many bags and cases

travel² n [U] travelling: *They say travel broadens the mind.* (=teaches you things) | *Snow and high winds have disrupted travel in many parts of Britain.* —see also TRAVELS

▷ USAGE Compare **travel(s), journey, voyage,** and **trip.** The general activity of moving from place to place is **travel**: *He came home after years of foreign travel.* If a person moves from place to place over a period of time we speak of their **travels**: *Did you go to Rome during your travels?* A **journey** (usu. **trip** *AmE*) is the time spent and the distance covered in going from one particular place to another: *a long journey by train from Paris to Moscow* | *Persepolis was ten days' journey across the desert.* A **voyage** has the same meaning but is only by sea: *The voyage from England to Australia used to take several months.* A **trip** is a short journey, or one on which you spend only a short time in another place, then come back. *We'll have time for a trip to France next weekend.*◁

travel a·gen·cy /ˈ·· ˌ···/ also **travel agent's, travel bu·reau** /ˈ·· ˌ···/— n a business that arranges travel, e.g. by buying tickets, finding hotel rooms, etc.: *He went into the travel agent's on impulse and booked a week in France.*

travel a·gent /ˈ·· ˌ··/ n a person who owns or works in a travel agency

trav·el·a·tor /ˈtrævəleɪtəʳ/ n a TRAVOLATOR

Trav·el·card /ˈtrævəlkɑːd‖-kɑːrd/ n a special travel ticket at a reduced price for travel in Greater London on trains, buses, and the Underground

travel ex·pens·es /ˈ·· ·ˌ··/ n *AmE for* TRAVELLING EXPENSES

trav·elled *BrE* ‖ **traveled** *AmE* /ˈtrævəld/ adj **1** (of a person) experienced in travel to the stated degree: *a much/widely travelled writer* **2** (of a road, area, etc.) used by travellers (to the stated degree): *a well travelled road*

trav·el·ler *BrE* ‖ **traveler** *AmE* /ˈtrævələʳ/ n **1** a person on a journey: *She joined her fellow travellers.* **2** [(in)] *BrE* a SALES REPRESENTATIVE —see also COMMERCIAL TRAVELLER **3** *BrE for* GIPSY

traveller's cheque /ˈ··· ·/ n a cheque bought from a bank or travel agency that can be exchanged for the money of the country one is in, used by travellers abroad: *to cash one's traveller's cheques*

trav·el·ling *BrE* ‖ **traveling** *AmE* /ˈtrævəlɪŋ/ adj [A] **1** that travels: *a travelling theatre company* **2** carried by or used by a traveller: *a travelling alarm clock* | *a travelling rug* —see picture at CLOCK **3** of or connected with travel

travelling ex·pens·es /ˈ··· ·ˌ··/ *BrE* ‖ **travel expenses** *AmE*— n [P] money paid back to one usu. by an employer to replace the cost of journeys made for that employer

travelling peo·ple /ˈ··· ˌ··/ also **travellers, travelling folk** /ˈ··· ˌ·/ n [P] *BrE* gipsies (GIPSY) or similar people who have no fixed home and travel around the country

travelling sales·man /ˌ··· ˈ··/ n a SALES REPRESENTATIVE

trav·el·ogue also **-og** *AmE* /ˈtrævəlɒg‖-lɔːg, -lɑːg/ n a film or talk describing travel in a particular country, a person's travels, etc.

trav·els /ˈtrævəlz/ n [P] travelling; journeys, esp. abroad: *He described some of the things he'd seen on/during his travels.* —see TRAVEL² (USAGE)

trav·el·sick /ˈtrævəlˌsɪk/ adj sick because of the movement of a vehicle — ~**ness** n [U]

tra·verse¹ /ˈtrævɜːrs‖trəˈvɜːrs/ v 1 [T] fml to pass across, over, or through: *The lights traversed the sky searching for enemy planes.* 2 [I] tech to make a traverse

tra·verse² /ˈtrævɜːrs‖-ɜːrs/ n tech a movement to the side across the face of a very steep slope of rock or ice, to a place where climbing is easier

trav·es·ty /ˈtrævɪˌsti/ n [(of)] a copy or example of something that completely misrepresents the true or intended nature of the real thing: *So much information had been given in advance to the newspapers that the politician's trial was a **travesty of justice**.* (=was very unjust)

trav·o·la·tor, travelator /ˈtrævəleɪtəʳ/ BrE ‖ **moving sidewalk** AmE— n an endless moving band set into a floor for moving people, saving them the effort of walking, esp. in airports and shopping centres

Tra·vol·ta /trəˈvəʊltə/ n, **John** (1954–) an American popular music singer, dancer, and actor, best known for appearing in the films *Saturday Night Fever* and *Grease* — see colour picture on page 685

trawl¹ /trɔːl/ v [I;T (**for**)] to fish with a trawl: *The boats were out trawling the bay for herring.*

trawl² n 1 a large fishing net with a wide mouth that is drawn along the sea bottom 2 also **trawl line** /ˈ·ˌ·/AmE— a long fishing line to which many smaller fishing lines are fastened

trawl·er /ˈtrɔːləʳ/ n a fishing boat that uses a trawl

trawl·er·man /ˈtrɔːləmən‖-lər-/ n -**men** /mən/ a man who works on a trawler

trays

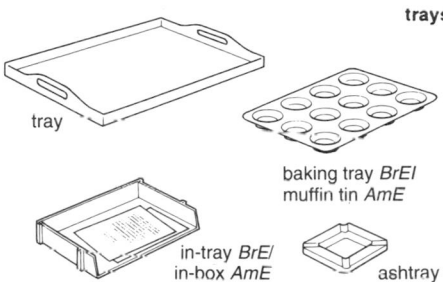

tray

baking tray *BrE*/
muffin tin *AmE*

in-tray *BrE*/
in-box *AmE*   ashtray

tray /treɪ/ n a flat piece of plastic, metal, wood, etc., with raised edges used for carrying small articles, esp. cups, plates, food, etc.: *He put the toast on the breakfast tray.* | *a silver tray* | *a tray of glasses* (=holding a lot of glasses) | (*BrE*) *His secretary put his mail in his **in tray** and took the documents he had dealt with from his **out tray**.*

treach·e·rous /ˈtretʃərəs/ adj 1 showing great disloyalty and deceit: *a treacherous plot to poison the king* 2 full of hidden dangers: *treacherous currents* | *treacherous weather conditions for drivers* — ~**ly** adv

treach·e·ry /ˈtretʃəri/ n 1 [U] great disloyalty and deceit; unfaithfulness —compare TREASON 2 [C *usu. pl.*] a disloyal or deceitful action

trea·cle /ˈtriːkəl/ BrE ‖ **molasses** AmE— n [U] a very thick sticky dark liquid made from sugar

trea·cly /ˈtriːkli/ adj BrE 1 thick and sticky; like treacle: *treacly black mud* 2 (of a drink or liquid food) too thick and sweet: (fig.) *a story full of treacly sentiment*

tread¹ /tred/ v **trod** /trɒd‖trɑːd/, **trodden** /ˈtrɒdn‖ˈtrɑːdn/ 1 [I+adv/prep, esp. **on**] to put one's foot when walking; step: *Don't tread on the flowers!* | *She trod on some glass and cut her foot.* | (fig.) *You'll have to tread carefully when you discuss that subject with him; he's rather sensitive about it.* 2 [T] to press firmly or crush with the feet: *In some parts of the world they still tread grapes to make wine.* | *Don't tread mud into the carpet.* 3 [T] esp. lit to walk along; follow: *Every day he trod the same path through the woods.* 4 [T] to make (a path) by walking 5 **tread a measure** BrE old use to dance 6 **tread on someone's**

heels to follow very closely behind someone 7 **tread on someone's toes/corns** to offend someone, esp. by insensitive remarks or behaviour 8 **tread water** to stay upright in deep water with the head above the surface by moving the feet up and down as if one is riding a bicycle

▷ USAGE **Tread** is understood but considered formal by most American speakers. They are often more likely to use **step**: *Don't step on the flowers.* For sense 2, **track** is more common: *Don't track mud on the carpet.* **Tread grapes** and **tread water** are both used in American English.◁

tread² n 1 [S] the act, manner, or sound of walking: *We heard our father's heavy tread on the staircase.* 2 [C;U] the pattern of raised lines on a tyre 3 [C] the part of a step or stair on which the foot is placed

trea·dle /ˈtredl/ n an apparatus worked by the feet to drive a machine: *the treadle of an old sewing machine*

tread·mill /ˈtredˌmɪl/ n a MILL worked by people treading on steps fixed to the edge of a large wheel or by animals treading an endless belt: (fig.) *She was glad to escape from the treadmill of office life.* (=its repeated uninteresting work)

trea·son /ˈtriːzən/ n [U] (the crime of) great disloyalty to one's country, esp. by helping its enemies or by violent opposition to those in power: *to commit treason* — compare TREACHERY; see also HIGH TREASON

trea·so·na·ble /ˈtriːzənəbəl/ also **trea·son·ous** /ˈtriːzənəs/— adj law of or being treason: *Plotting to kill the king is a treasonable offence.* —**bly** adv

trea·sure¹ /ˈtreʒəʳ/ n 1 [U] wealth in the form of gold, silver, jewels, etc.: *buried treasure* 2 [C] a very valuable object: *The library has many art treasures.* 3 [C] infml a person considered very precious: *My secretary's a real treasure.*

treasure² v [T] to keep or consider as precious; CHERISH: *treasured memories/possessions*

treasure hunt /ˈ·· ˌ·/ n a game in which each player or team tries, with the help of CLUES, to be the first to find whatever has been hidden

Treasure Is·land /ˌ·· ˈ··/ an adventure story by Robert Louis Stevenson about PIRATES looking for buried TREASURE. The best-known character is a pirate called Long John Silver, who only has one leg.

trea·sur·er /ˈtreʒərəʳ/ n a person in charge of the money belonging to a club, organization, political party, etc.: *to elect/appoint a new treasurer*

treasure trove /ˌtreʒə ˈtrəʊv‖-ʒər-/ n 1 [U] esp. law money, gold, jewels, or other valuable objects found hidden usu. in the ground, and claimed by no one. In Britain, such things are taken as belonging to the king or queen, but the finder may be allowed to keep them. In the US the finder is usu. allowed to keep them. 2 [C *usu. sing.*] a collection of valuable things found unexpectedly

trea·su·ry /ˈtreʒəri/ n 1 [*the*+S+*sing.*/*pl. v*] (*usu. cap.*) the government department that is responsible for managing the money system of a country and for carrying out government plans in relation to taxes and public spending: *The Treasury exercises tight control over public spending.* —compare EXCHEQUER 2 [C] (esp. in former times) the place where the money of a government is kept

Treasury Bench /ˈ··· ˌ·/ [*the*] the first row of seats to the right of the Speaker in the House of Commons, used by the most important government ministers

Treasury bill /ˈ··· ˌ·/ also **T-bill** infml— n an American government BOND. Treasury bills are sold to raise money for the government and usu. bought by large financial institutions around the world. —see also GILT-EDGED

treat¹ /triːt/ v 1 [T+obj+adv/prep, esp. **like**] to act or behave towards in the stated way: *This firm has always treated its workers well.* | *She treats us like children.* (=as if we were children) | *Try to treat all your students the same.* 2 [T+obj+adv/prep] to deal with or handle in the stated way: *This delicate glass must be treated with care.* | *The newspapers treated the story in a sensational way.* | *They are claiming that their request has been unfairly treated.* 3 [T+obj+adv/prep, esp. **as**] to regard or consider in the stated way: *Our employer treated our suggestions as a joke.* 4 [T (**for**)] to try to cure by medical means: *My sister is being treated for a heart condition.* —compare CURE¹ 5 [T (**to**)] to buy or give (someone) something special, as a friendly act: *No, no, put your money*

away; let me treat you! | *I'm going to treat myself to a holiday in the Seychelles next year.* **6** [T] to put (something) through a chemical or industrial process in order to change it: *This car has been specially treated against rust.* **7** [I (**with**)] *fml* (esp. of opposing groups) to talk in order to reach an agreement, end a war, etc. **8 treat someone like dirt** *infml* to treat someone as if they were worthless — ~**able** *adj*

▷ USAGE A doctor can **treat** (=try to **cure**) a person who is ill, or give **treatment** in the form of medicine, special food, exercise, etc. But we do not say that a doctor has **cured** someone until that person is completely well again.◁

treat of sthg. *phr v* [T] *fml* to be about; deal with (a subject): *a poem treating of love*

treat² *n* **1** something that gives great pleasure or delight, esp. when unexpected: *I took my son to the zoo as a birthday treat.* **2** something that the stated person will pay for, for other people: *This meal is my treat, so put your money away.* —see also DUTCH TREAT

trea·tise /ˈtriːtᵻs, -tᵻz/ *n* [(**on**)] a serious book or article that examines a particular subject

treat·ment /ˈtriːtmənt/ *n* **1** [U] the act or manner of treating someone or something: *the newspapers' sensational treatment of the story* | *The prisoners complained of ill treatment by their guards.* | *These minority groups were given preferential treatment* | *The foreign VIPs were given* **the full treatment** (=were entertained and looked after in a very special way) *during their tour of the island.* **2** [C;U (**for**)] (a substance or method used in) the treating of illness by medical means: *a new treatment for asthma* | *He's receiving/undergoing treatment for cancer* | *Her illness is not* **responding to** (=being cured by) **treatment.** —see TREAT (USAGE)

treat·y /ˈtriːti/ *n* **1** [C] (*sometimes cap.*) an agreement made between countries, esp. after a war, and formally signed by their representatives: *The conference drew up the terms of the peace treaty.* | *to ratify a treaty* | *the Treaty of Versailles* —compare CONVENTION (3), PACT **2** [U] *tech* agreement between people: *We sold the house by private treaty.*

Treaty of Brest-Li·tovsk /ˌtriːti əv ˌbrest lᵻˈtɒfsk‖-ˈtɔːfsk/ [*the*] a peace agreement made on March 3rd 1918 between Germany and its allies (ALLY) and Soviet Russia

Treaty of Rome /ˌ·· ˈ·/ [*the*] an agreement made in 1958 between Belgium, France, West Germany, Italy, Luxembourg, and the Netherlands, which established the Common Market

Treaty of Ver·sailles /ˌ··· ˈ·/ *n* [*the*] an agreement made in June 1919 between the ALLIES and Germany, which ended the First World War, punished Germany for the war and formed the League of Nations

treb·le¹ /ˈtrebəl/ *predeterminer* three times as big, as much, or as many as; multiplied by three: *They sold the house for treble the amount they paid for it.*

treble² *v* [I;T] to make or become three times as great in number, size, or amount: *Their profits have trebled in the last two years.*

treble³ *n* **1** [C] a boy with a high singing voice **2** [U] the upper half of the whole range of musical notes —compare BASS¹ (2) —**treble** *adj, adv* : *a treble recorder* | *to sing treble*

treble chance /ˌ·· ˈ·/ *n* [*the*+S] (in Britain) a method of competing in the football POOLS by guessing whether matches will be home wins, away wins, or DRAWS

treble clef /ˌ·· ˈ·/ *n tech* a sign (𝄞) on a musical STAVE showing that a note written on the bottom line of the stave is the E above MIDDLE C —compare BASS CLEF

tree /triː/ *n* **1** a tall plant with a wooden trunk and branches, that lives for many years: *She sat in the shade of the apple tree.* | *to climb a tree* | *to plant a tree* | *to cut down/chop down a tree* **2** a bush or other plant with a treelike form: *a banana tree* **3** a drawing with a branching form, esp. as used for showing family relationships —see also CHRISTMAS TREE, FAMILY TREE, TREE OF KNOWLEDGE, **bark up the wrong tree** (BARK¹), **grow on trees** (GROW), **up a gum tree** (GUM TREE), **the top of the tree** (TOP¹) — ~**less** *adj*

tree fern /ˈ· ·/ *n* a large tropical FERN that grows to the size of a tree

tree·line /ˈtriːlaɪn/ also **timberline** — *n* [*the*+S] **1** the

---

trees

maple   willow

horse chestnut   conker *BrE*/   oak   acorn
                 chestnut *AmE*

pinecone   fircone
pine   fir

height above sea level beyond which trees will not grow **2** the northern or southern limit in the world beyond which trees will not grow

tree-lined /ˈ· ·/ *adj* having a line of trees: *a tree-lined avenue/road*

Tree of Know·ledge /ˌ·· ˈ··/ [*the*] (in the Bible) the tree in the Garden of Eden whose fruit Adam and Eve were forbidden by God to eat. When they ate the fruit and learned about the difference between good and evil, they were made to leave the Garden of Eden —see also FALL

tree sur·ge·ry /ˈ· ˌ···/ *n* [U] treatment of damaged trees and other work, e.g. pruning (PRUNE¹), carried out as part of the professional care of trees grown for shade or for decoration —**tree surgeon** *n*

tre·foil /ˈtriːfɔɪl, ˈtrefɔɪl/ *n* **1** any of several small plants that has leaves divided into three little leaves **2** a decorative shape like the leaf of one of these plants, used esp. in patterns on stone

trek /trek/ *v* -**kk**- [I+*adv/prep*] to make a long difficult journey, esp. on foot: *We went trekking in the mountains for our holiday.* —**trek** *n* : *to go on/for a trek* | (fig.) *It's a real trek* (=a long journey) *to get to the shops from where we live.* —compare HIKE; see also PONY TREKKING

Trek·kie /ˈtreki/ *n* a keen follower of the American SCIENCE FICTION television programme *Star Trek*, esp. someone who goes to CONVENTIONS (=gatherings) with other followers of the programme —see also STAR TREK

trel·lis /ˈtrelᵻs/ *n* [C;U] (a) light upright frame of long narrow pieces of wood, esp. used as a support for climbing plants: *roses growing on a trellis* —compare LATTICE

trem·ble¹ /ˈtrembəl/ *v* [I] **1** to shake uncontrollably with quick short movements, usu. from fear, excitement, or weakness: *He was trembling with rage.* | *The whole house trembled as the train went by.* | *a voice trembling with emotion* **2** [(**at, for**)] to feel great fear and anxiety about something: *We all trembled at the prospect of an enemy invasion.* [+*to-v*] *I tremble to think what's going to happen.* — ~**blingly** *adv*

tremble² *n* [S] an act of trembling

tre·men·dous /trɪˈmendəs/ *adj* **1** very great in size, amount, or degree: *This rocket travels at a tremendous speed.* | *We heard a tremendous explosion.* | *We've had a tremendous amount of rain recently.* | (*infml*) *She's a tremendous tulker.* (=talks a lot) **2** *infml* wonderful: *We went to a tremendous party last night* – – **ly** *adv*

trem·o·lo /ˈtremələʊ/ *n* **-los** *tech* a special slightly shaking effect produced by rapidly varying the sound of a musical note, esp. when played on a stringed instrument, or when sung

trem·or /ˈtremərˡ/ *n* **1** a shaking movement of the ground: *an earth tremor* (=a small EARTHQUAKE) **2** a shaking or trembling movement caused by fear, nervousness, illness, weakness, etc.: *The story was so frightening that it sent tremors down my spine.* | *There was a slight tremor in his voice as he said hello to her.* | *a tremor of excitement*

trem·u·lous /ˈtremjʊləs/ *adj fml* slightly shaking, esp. because of nervousness: *a tremulous voice* – – **ly** *adv* – **~ness** *n* [U]

trench /trentʃ/ *n* **1** a long narrow hole cut in the ground; ditch: *To grow roses, first dig a trench and fill it with manure.* **2** [*often pl.*] a deep ditch dug in the ground as a protection for soldiers: *In the First World War the soldiers fought in trenches.* –compare DUGOUT (2) **3** *tech* a long narrow deep valley in the sea bed

tren·chant /ˈtrentʃənt/ *adj* (of language) forceful, effective and direct; not minding about giving offence: *a hard hitting speech with some trenchant comments about the government's failures* | *trenchant criticism* – – **ly** *adv* –**-chancy** *n* [U]

trench coat /ˈ· ·/ *n* a loose-fitting raincoat with a belt and pockets, esp. made in a military style. Trench coats are often thought of in connection with PRIVATE DETECTIVEs because many of them wear coats like this in books and films.

trench·er /ˈtrentʃərˡ/ *n* a large wooden plate used, esp. in former times, for serving food

trench·er·man /ˈtrentʃəmən‖-ʃərˡ-/ *n* **-men** /mən/ *BrE* lit or *humor* a person who eats a lot

trench war·fare /ˈ· ˈ··/ *n* [U] a way of fighting a war, in which opposing armies are placed in sets of TRENCHes facing each other: *The stalemate of trench warfare was broken by the invention of the tank.*

trend /trend/ *n* **1** a general tendency or direction in the way a situation is changing or developing: *There has been a recent trend among judges towards giving more severe punishments.* | *The rise in violent crime is a disturbing new trend.* | *The stock market had a good day, but the underlying trend of the market is downward.* **2** a fashion or style: *to set a new trend*

trend·set·ter /ˈtrendˌsetərˡ/ *n infml* a person who starts or popularizes the latest fashion –**-ting** *adj*

trend·y¹ /ˈtrendi/ *adj esp. BrE infml, sometimes derog* very fashionable; very influenced by the latest fashions: *a trendy dress|restaurant|girl* | *These ideas are typical of the trendy middle-class liberals.* –**-ily** *adv* –**-iness** *n* [U]

trendy² *n BrE infml derog* a trendy person: *a restaurant full of young trendies*

Trent /trent/ [*the*] a river in the Midlands of England, flowing NE into the Humber

Trent Bridge /ˈ· ˈ·/ a cricket ground in Nottingham, England

tre·pan /trɪˈpæn/ *v* **-nn-** [T] to cut a round piece of bone out of (the SKULL) as part of a medical operation

tre·phine¹ /trɪˈfiːn‖-ˈfaɪn/ *v* [T] *tech* to trepan

trephine² *n tech* a special medical instrument with a sharp fine-toothed circular cutting edge used in trephining

trep·i·da·tion /ˌtrepɪˈdeɪʃən/ *n* [U] *fml* a state of anxiety about something bad that might happen; APPREHENSION: *I waited for the results in a state of some trepidation.*

tres·pass¹ /ˈtrespəs, -pæs/ *v* [I] **1** [(on)] to enter privately owned property or land without permission **2** *old use or bibl* to do wrong; SIN – – **er** *n* : *Trespassers will be prosecuted.* (written on a notice)
  trespass on/upon sthg. *phr v* [T] *fml* to take an unfair advantage of; make too much use of: *It would be trespassing on their generosity to accept any more from them.*

trespass² *n* **1** [C;U] (an act or offence of) trespassing: *the laws relating to trespass* **2** [C] *old use or bibl* a wicked or wrong action; SIN **3 Forgive us our trespasses** a phrase from the LORD'S PRAYER

tress·es /ˈtresᵻz/ *n* [P] *lit* a woman's long hair

tres·tle /ˈtresəl/ ‖ usu. **sawhorse** *AmE*– *n* a wooden beam fixed at each end to a pair of spreading legs, used, usu. in pairs, as a removable support for a table (**trestle table**) or other flat surface

Tre·vith·ick /trᵻˈvɪθɪk/, **Richard** (1771–1833) an English engineer who invented the high-pressure steam engine, which was used in the first steam railway engine in 1804

trews /truːz/ *n* [P] *rare* trousers, esp. TARTAN trousers –see PAIR (USAGE)

trey /treɪ/ *n AmE dial* a playing card with three marks on it: *I've got two pair, treys and sevens.*

tri·ad /ˈtraɪæd/ *n* **1** a group of three closely related people or things **2** (*often cap.*) a Chinese criminal secret society

tri·al /ˈtraɪəl/ *n* **1** [C;U] (an act of) hearing and judging a person, case, or point of law in a court: *The murder trial lasted six weeks.* | *He is in detention awaiting trial.* | *The case was sent for trial at the crown court.* | *He is* (**going**) **on trial** (=being tried in court) *for armed robbery.* –see also SHOW TRIAL, **stand trial** (STAND¹) and see also extra information on page 742 **2** [C;U] (an act or period of) testing to ensure quality, usefulness, safety, etc.: *The new aircraft has performed very well in its initial trials.* | *I've appointed a secretary for a trial period to see how well she does the job.* | *a new drug that is undergoing clinical trials* | *I took the car on trial|on a two weeks' trial, but I didn't like it so I took it back.* | *a* **trial marriage** (=when two people live together without being married, to see if they would be suitable partners) –see also TRIAL BALLOON **3** [C (**to**)] an annoying thing or person; cause of worry or trouble: *That child is a trial to his parents.* | *After many* **trials and tribulations**, *we finally reached our destination.*

trial and er·ror /ˌ··· ·ˈ··/ *n* [U] a way of getting satisfactory results by trying several methods and learning from one's mistakes: *We established our present working methods by a process of trial and error.*

trial bal·loon /ˌ·· ·ˌ·/ *n AmE* information about a plan or intention made known in order to test opinion, esp. of the public: *The White House sent up a trial balloon by warning congress it might veto the new welfare bill.*

trial by ju·ry /ˌ·· ·ˈ··/ *n* the type of trial used in the British and US legal systems, in which a JURY hears the details of a case in a court of law and makes a decision about it

trial run /ˌ·· ·ˈ·/ *n* an act of testing something new to see if it works properly: *Give the car a trial run and see what you think of it.*

trial sep·a·ra·tion /ˌ··· ···ˈ··/ *n* a period during which a husband and wife agree to live apart for a time while they decide whether to remain married or get a DIVORCE¹(1)

triangles

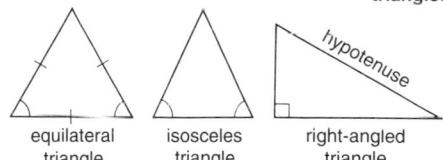

equilateral   isosceles   right-angled
triangle   triangle   triangle

tri·an·gle /ˈtraɪæŋɡəl/ *n* **1** a flat shape with three straight sides and three angles –see picture at MATHEMATICS **2** a three-cornered or three-sided figure, object, or piece: *a triangle of land* **3** a small three-sided musical instrument made of a bent steel rod, played by being struck with another steel rod –see picture at PERCUSSION **4** *AmE for* SETSQUARE –see also BERMUDA TRIANGLE, ETERNAL TRIANGLE

tri·an·gu·lar /traɪˈæŋɡjʊlərˡ/ *adj* **1** of or shaped like a triangle **2** *fml* having or concerning three people or groups: *a triangular sporting competition*

tri·an·gu·la·tion /traɪˌæŋɡjʊˈleɪʃən/ *n* [U] a method of finding one's position by measuring the angles and lines of a triangle on a map

triangulation sta·tion /··ˈ··ˌ·· ˈ··/ *BrE* ‖ **bench mark** *AmE*– *n* a point used in triangulation when a map is being made, often marked by a square-sided block of stone on top of a hill

tri·ath·lon /traɪˈæθlən/ *n* a sporting competition in which competitors take part in three events, esp. long-distance running, swimming, and cycling

trib·al /ˈtraɪbəl/ adj of a tribe or tribes: *a tribal dance* | *a tribal chief* | *tribal warfare/divisions*

trib·al·is·m /ˈtraɪbəl-ɪzəm/ n [U] **1** the organization of a social group into a tribe **2** *sometimes derog* tribal loyalty, esp. as it influences people's behaviour and ideas

tribe /traɪb/ n [C+*sing./pl. v*] **1** a social group made up of people of the same race, beliefs, customs, language, etc., living in a particular area often under the leadership of a chief: *the tribes living in the Amazonian jungle* | *a member of the Zulu tribe* —see RACE (USAGE) **2** a named group within a tribal society that descends from one family: *the tribes of Somalia* | *the Beni Mtir tribe of Berbers* **3** a group of related plants or animals: *the cat tribe*

tribes·man /ˈtraɪbzmən/ **tribes·wom·an** /-ˌwʊmən/ *fem.*— n -men /mən/ a member of a tribe, esp. formerly

trib·u·la·tion /ˌtrɪbjʉˈleɪʃən/ n [C;U] (a cause of) trouble, grief, worry, suffering, etc.: *After many* **trials and tribulations,** *we finally reached our destination.*

tri·bu·nal /traɪˈbjuːnl/ n [C+*sing./pl. v*] a court of people officially appointed to deal with special matters: *The rent tribunal reduced my rent.* | *He took his case of unfair dismissal to the industrial relations tribunal.*

trib·une /ˈtrɪbjuːn/ n **1** an official of ancient Rome elected by the ordinary people to protect their interests **2** (*usu. cap.*) a common name for a newspaper, esp. in the US: *the Chicago Tribune* | *the Herald-Tribune*

Tribune Group /ˈ·· ˌ·/ [*the*] (in Britain) a group of left-wing Labour Members of Parliament, established in 1966

trib·u·ta·ry[1] /ˈtrɪbjʉtəri‖-teri/ n a stream or river that flows into a larger stream or river: *the tributaries of the Rhine*

tributary[2] adj [(to)] *fml* (of a person, country, etc.) having a duty to pay TRIBUTE (3) to another: *tributary states*

trib·ute /ˈtrɪbjuːt/ n **1** [C;U] something done, said, or given to show respect or admiration for someone: *I'd like to* **pay tribute to** (=praise and thank) *the office staff for all the hard work they've put in on this project.* | *Everyone in the office gave money towards a* **floral tribute** (=special flowers) *for his funeral.* **2** [S+to] something that clearly shows the effect or influence of a particular good quality or action: *The new engine's performance is a tribute to the skill of its designers.* **3** [C;U] (a) payment made by one ruler, government, or country to another as the price of peace, protection, etc.

trice /traɪs/ n **in a trice** *esp. BrE infml* in a moment; in the shortest possible time

tri·ceps /ˈtraɪseps/ n **triceps** or **tricepses** the large muscle that runs along the back of the upper arm

trich·i·no·sis /ˌtrɪkɪˈnəʊsɪs/ n [U] *med* a serious disease which can be caused by eating PORK which has not been thoroughly cooked

tri·chlo·ro·e·thane /ˌtraɪklɔːrəʊˈiːθeɪn/ n [U] a poisonous liquid chemical compound, used as a SOLVENT

tri·chol·o·gy /trɪˈkɒlədʒi‖-ˈkɑː-/ n [U] *tech* the study and treatment of disorders of hair growth —**gist** n

trick[1] /trɪk/ n **1** a clever set of actions done to entertain people, esp. by using skill to confuse them: *He performed some clever magic tricks.* | *No one could work out how I did the card tricks.* —compare JOKE[1] (1) **2** a clever act or plan meant to deceive or cheat someone: *He got the money by a trick.* | (fig.) *I thought I saw a ghost, but perhaps it was only* **a trick of the light.** (=a deceiving appearance) —see also DIRTY TRICK **3** a troublesome but playful act; PRANK: *The children loved playing tricks on their teacher.* —compare PRACTICAL JOKE **4** a quick or clever way to do something or get a desired result; special skill or KNACK: *John taught me the trick of pouring wine without spilling any.* | *There's a trick to opening this lock.* | (*infml*) *Don't make fun of your grandfather just because he's old; he could* **teach you a trick or two.** (=he knows more than you do) | *If you want to start your own car business you should ask his advice — he knows all the* **tricks of the trade.** | *She used* **every trick in the book** *to pull off the deal.* **5** the cards played or won in one ROUND of a game of cards —see CARDS (USAGE) **6** [(of)] a strange or typical habit: *He has a trick of pulling at his earlobe when he speaks to you.* **7** *AmE sl* **a** sex with a PROSTITUTE **b** a one-time sexual partner, esp. of a PROSTITUTE **8 do the trick** *infml* to fulfil one's purpose or

intention; do what is needed: *This medicine ought to do the trick.* (=cure the illness) **9 How's tricks?** *infml* (used as a greeting) How are you? **10 not/never miss a trick** *infml* to know exactly what is happening, and never fail to take advantage of a favourable situation —see also CONFIDENCE TRICK, HAT TRICK

trick[2] adj [A] **1** made for playing tricks: *a trick spoon that melts in hot liquid* **2** full of intentionally hidden and unexpected difficulties: *That's not fair; it was a* **trick question!** **3** *AmE* weak and likely to give way unexpectedly: *a trick knee*

trick[3] v **1** [T (into)] to deceive: *The police tricked him into making a confession.* **2** [I (with)] *AmE sl* to find a sexual partner

trick sbdy./sthg. ↔ **out/up** *phr v* [T+obj+adv/prep, esp. in] *fml or lit* to dress in bright or decorative things: *tricked out in ribbons/in a gaudy outfit*

trick·e·ry /ˈtrɪkəri/ n [U] the use of tricks to deceive or cheat

trick·le[1] /ˈtrɪkəl/ v [I+adv/prep] to flow in drops or in a thin stream: *Blood/a tear trickled slowly down his cheek.* | (fig.) *The children trickled into the classroom.* —compare STREAM

trickle down *phr v* [I (to)] (usu. of money) to slowly reach people at the bottom of a HIERARCHY after being put in at the top: *Their intention is that the tax cuts for the rich will trickle down to the poor.* —see also TRICKLE-DOWN EFFECT

trickle[2] n [S (of)] a thin slow flow or movement: *The number of refugees from the area has now slowed to a trickle.*

trickle charg·er /ˈ·· ˌ··/ n *BrE* an apparatus for charging a BATTERY, esp. one on a motor vehicle, at a steady slow rate

trickle-down ef·fect /ˌ· ˈ· ·ˌ·/ n the process by which some ECONOMISTS believe that additional money or other capital in the hands of a few people at the top of an organization will later reach people at the bottom: *The improved economy should have a* **trickle-down effect** *on the unemployed.*

trick or treat /ˌ· · ˈ·/ n, interj (in the US) a children's practice of going to people's houses on HALLOWE'EN and asking for TREATs under threat of playing TRICKs on people who refuse —**trick-or-treat** v [I] : *to go trick-or-treating*

trick·ster /ˈtrɪkstər/ n a person who deceives or cheats people

trick·y /ˈtrɪki/ adj **1** (of a situation, piece of work, etc.) difficult to handle or deal with; full of hidden or unexpected difficulties: *I'm in a rather tricky position; can you help me out?* | *a tricky question* | *This problem may prove rather tricky for the government.* **2** deceitful; clever in cheating; CRAFTY: *Be careful how you deal with him; he's a* **tricky customer.** (=person) —**iness** n [U]

tri·col·our *BrE* ‖ **-or** *AmE* /ˈtrɪkələr‖ˈtraɪˌkʌlər/ n **1** [*the*] (*usu. cap.*) the national flag of France **2** [C] a flag with three equal bands of different colours

tri·cy·cle /ˈtraɪsɪkəl/ n a bicycle with three wheels, two at the back and one at the front, used esp. by small children

tri·dent /ˈtraɪdənt/ n a forklike instrument or ancient weapon with three points

Trident a type of American MISSILE which is fired from a SUBMARINE. Each Trident can send several explosive charges to different places. There has been considerable argument in Britain as to whether the country should buy Tridents.

tried[1] /traɪd/ past tense & participle of TRY[1]

tried[2] adj [no comp.] found to be good or trustworthy by experience or testing: *a tried and tested method* | *He's a* **tried and true** *friend.*

tri·en·ni·al /traɪˈeniəl/ adj done or happening every three years

tri·er /ˈtraɪər/ n apprec a person who tries hard; someone who always does their best, even if they do not often succeed

trif·fid /ˈtrɪfɪd/ n an imaginary plant which grows to a great size, moves about, and attacks people (from the NOVEL *The Day of the Triffids* by John Wyndham)

tri·fle[1] /ˈtraɪfəl/ n **1** [C;U] a British dish of plain cakes set in fruit and jelly covered with cream and/or CUSTARD **2** [C] *fml* an article or thing of little value or slight importance; matter of slight importance: *I don't* *know why you waste your money/time on such trifles.* **3** **a trifle** *fml* to some degree; rather: *I'm a trifle annoyed about it.*

trifle² *v*
　trifle with sbdy./sthg. *phr v* [T] *fml* to treat without the necessary seriousness or respect: *The boss is not a person to be trifled with.*

tri·fling /ˈtraɪflɪŋ/ *adj fml* of slight importance or little value; INSIGNIFICANT: *It only cost a trifling sum.* | *a trifling matter*

trig·ger¹ /ˈtrɪɡəʳ/ *n* a small piece of metal pressed by the finger to fire a gun: *to pull the trigger* —see also HAIR TRIGGER, and see picture at GUN

trigger² *v* [T (OFF)] to start or cause (esp. a number of events, often of an undesirable kind, that happen one after the other): *Large price increases could trigger demands for even larger wage increases.* | *The successful hijacking triggered a spate of terrorist activity.*

trigger-hap·py /ˈ·· ˌ··/ *adj* **1** too ready to shoot; ready to shoot for the slightest reason **2** not responsible enough, esp. in matters which could lead to war; too ready to use violent methods: *a trigger-happy government that ordered the shooting of anyone who entered their territory*

trig·o·nom·e·try /ˌtrɪɡəˈnɒmɪtri‖-ˈnɑː-/ *n* [U] the branch of MATHEMATICS that deals with the relationship between the sides and angles of TRIANGLES

trig point /ˈtrɪɡ pɔɪnt/ *n infml for* TRIANGULATION STATION

trike /traɪk/ *n infml for* TRICYCLE

tril·by /ˈtrɪlbi/ also **trilby hat** /ˌ·· ˈ·/ — *n esp. BrE* a man's soft FELT hat with a fold in the top

tri·lin·gual /ˌtraɪˈlɪŋɡwəl◂/ *adj* of, using, or able to speak three languages: *a trilingual secretary* — *~ly adv*

trill¹ /trɪl/ *n* **1** *tech* the rapid repeating of two musical notes a TONE apart in turn **2** a sound or number of repeated sounds like this, esp. as made by a bird **3** *tech* a speech sound like this, such as that produced by the point of the tongue against the part of the mouth just behind the upper front teeth

trill² *v* [I;T] to sing, play, or pronounce with a trill: *The birds were trilling in the treetops.*

tril·lion /ˈtrɪljən/ *determiner, n, pron* **trillion** *or* **trillions** **1** (the number) one million million; 1,000,000,000,000; 10¹² **2** [(of)] also **trillions** *pl.* — *infml* a very large number; lots — *~th determiner, n, pron, adv*

tri·lo·bite /ˈtraɪləbaɪt/ *n* a small sea creature of very long ago, whose remains are found in large numbers in some areas

tril·o·gy /ˈtrɪlədʒi/ *n* a group of three related books, plays, etc., connected by a shared subject but each complete in itself: *It's the second part of/the second play in a trilogy.*

trim¹ /trɪm/ *v* **-mm-** [T] **1** [(OFF)] to make neat, even, or tidy by cutting or removing unwanted parts: *I'm having my hair trimmed tomorrow.* | *Trim off the loose threads.* | *a neatly-trimmed beard* **2** [(with)] to decorate, esp. round the edges: *a jacket trimmed with fur* **3** to reduce, esp. by removing what is unnecessary: *You must trim your costs if you want to increase your profits.* **4** to move (a sail) into the correct position so that the boat will sail well **5 trim one's sails** to spend less money, because one can afford less — *~mer n* : *a hedge trimmer*

trim² *n* **1** [S] an act of cutting: *My beard needs a trim.* **2** [U] *infml* proper condition; readiness or fitness: *The team was in (good) trim for the match.* **3** [U] *tech* the degree to which an aircraft or spacecraft is level in relation to a fixed point, such as the horizon **4** [S;U] additional decoration, esp. on a car: *Her new sports car was dark blue with a white trim.*

trim³ *adj* **-mm-** tidy; in good order; pleasingly neat in appearance: *trim gardens* | *a trim figure* — *~ly adv*

tri·ma·ran /ˈtraɪməræn/ *n* a small sailing boat, used for pleasure or racing, that is made of three separate but connected boatlike parts (HULLS) side by side

tri·mes·ter /trɪˈmestəʳ‖traɪ-/ *n AmE* **1** any of three equal TERMs at a school or college **2** a period of three or about three months, esp. of a woman's PREGNANCY: *a first-trimester miscarriage*

trim·ming /ˈtrɪmɪŋ/ *n* [*usu. pl.*] **1** a decoration or pleasant addition: *We had roast duck with all the trimmings.* (=vegetables, potatoes, SAUCE, etc.) **2** a piece cut off from a larger piece: *hedge trimmings*

Trin·i·dad and To·ba·go /ˌtrɪnɪˌdæd ənd təˈbeɪɡəʊ/ a country in the West Indies, N of Venezuela, made up of the islands of Trinidad and Tobago; capital Port of Spain; population 1,263,000 (1989)

tri·ni·tro·tol·u·ene /ˌtraɪnaɪtrəʊˈtɒlju·iːn‖-ˈtɑː-/ *n* [U] see TNT

trin·i·ty /ˈtrɪnɪti/ *n fml or lit* a group of three

Trinity [*the*] (in the Christian religion) the union of the three forms of God (the Father, Son, and Holy Spirit) as one God

Trinity House /ˌ··· ˈ·/ a British authority responsible for providing LIGHTHOUSEs and LIGHTSHIPs around the coast of Britain, and also for licensing (LICENSE) pilots (=people who guide ships into ports etc.)

Trinity term /ˈ··· ˌ·/ *n* [C;U] (in Britain) the summer TERM at some schools and universities

trin·ket /ˈtrɪŋkɪt/ *n* a piece of jewellery or other small decorative article of fairly low value

tri·o /ˈtriːəʊ/ *n* **-os** **1** [+*sing./pl. v*] a group of three people or things: *The committee is headed by a trio of ministers.* **2** [+*sing./pl. v*] three singers or musicians performing together: *a jazz trio* **3** a piece of music for three performers —compare DUET, QUARTET

trip¹ /trɪp/ *v* **-pp-** **1** [I (**over**);T (UP)] **a** to catch one's foot (in or on something) and lose one's balance: *The fisherman tripped over a root and fell into the river.* **b** to cause (someone) to do this: *The boy put his foot out to trip the teacher up.* **2** [I;T (UP)] to (cause to) make a mistake: *This lawyer always tries to trip witnesses up by asking confusing questions.* —compare CATCH out **3** [I+adv/prep] *esp. lit* to move or dance with quick light steps: *The little girl tripped down the path.* | (fig.) *It's an interesting poem, but it hardly trips off the tongue.* (=it is difficult to say aloud) —see also TRIPPINGLY **4** [T] to cause (a SWITCH, spring, etc.) to operate: *A thief climbing in tripped the wire and set the alarm ringing.* **5** [I (OUT)] *sl* to be under the influence of a mind-changing drug such as LSD **6 trip the light fantastic** *pomp or humor* to dance

trip² *n* **1** [(to)] a journey, esp. a short one for pleasure or for a particular purpose: *We went on a bus trip/a boat trip.* | *I forgot to buy milk so I had to make another trip to the shops.* | *I think I'll take a trip to see him.* | *a business trip to Japan* | *a day trip to France* —see also DAY TRIP, ROUND TRIP, TRIPPER; see TRAVEL² (USAGE) **2** a fall; act of tripping **3** *sl* a period under the influence of a mind-changing drug such as LSD: *a bad trip* | (fig., *derog*) *He's on a real power trip now that he's in charge.* (=he is enjoying his power very much) —see also EGO TRIP **4** *rare* a mistake: *a trip of the tongue*

tri·par·tite /traɪˈpɑːtaɪt‖-ˈpaɪr-/ *adj fml* **1** having three parts: *a tripartite leaf* **2** shared by three people, organizations, etc.: *a tripartite agreement* —compare BIPARTITE

tripe /traɪp/ *n* [U] **1** the rubbery wall of the stomach of the cow eaten as food: *boiled tripe and onions* **2** *infml* worthless or stupid talk, ideas, writing, etc.: *Why do you read such tripe?*

trip·le¹ /ˈtrɪpəl/ *v* [I;T] **1** to (cause to) grow to three times the amount or number: *The firm tripled its profits last year.* **2** (in BASEBALL) to hit a TRIPLE³

triple² *adj* **1** having three parts or members **2** three times repeated: *He was convicted of a triple murder.* (=of killing three people at the same time)

triple³ *n* (in BASEBALL) a hit that allows the BATTER to reach THIRD BASE safely

triple A /ˌ·· ˈ·/ *n AmE* the spoken form of AAA, the American Automobile Association: *"Call triple A!"*

Triple Crown /ˌ··· ˈ·/ [*the*] a title for winning all three of a set of important events in various sports, esp. winning **a** (in British horse-racing) the St Leger, the Derby, and the Two Thousand Guineas **b** (in American horse-racing) the Preakness, the Belmont Stakes, and the Kentucky Derby or **c** (in Rugby Union) beating all three of the other home countries

triple jump /ˈ··· ·/ *n* [*the*+S] an ATHLETICS event in which the competitors take off and land on one foot, follow it by jumping on one foot and landing on the other, and finish with a jump from both feet

trip·let /ˈtrɪplɪt/ *n* **1** [*usu. pl.*] any of three children born of the same mother at the same time **2** a group of three lines in a poem —compare COUPLET

trip·lex[1] /'tripleks‖'trɪ-, 'traɪ-/ n [U] (often cap.) BrE tdmk a special safety glass made of a sheet of transparent plastic between two sheets of glass, esp. used in car windows

triplex[2] n, adj AmE (a unit, esp. a flat) having rooms on three floors of a building: a triplex apartment —compare DUPLEX

trip·li·cate[1] /'trɪplɪkᵻt/ adj consisting of or existing in three parts that are exactly alike: triplicate copies of the contract

triplicate[2] n in triplicate in three copies, one of which is the original: All our forms have to be filled out in triplicate.

tri·pod /'traɪpɒd‖-pɑːd/ n a three-legged support, e.g. for a camera: to set up a tripod —see picture at LABORATORY

Trip·o·li /'trɪpəli/ a city and port in NW Libya, the capital of Libya and its largest industrial centre

tri·pos /'traɪpɒs‖-pɑːs/ n (a course of study for) the set of examinations for the BA degree at Cambridge University

trip·per /'trɪpəʳ/ n esp. BrE, often derog a person on a pleasure trip, esp. one lasting only one day: In summer, the seaside towns are full of **day trippers**.

trip·ping·ly /'trɪpɪŋli/ adv esp. lit lightly and easily

trip·tych /'trɪptɪk/ n tech a picture made in three parts so that the side ones can be folded inwards over the middle one —compare DIPTYCH

trip·wire /'trɪp,waɪəʳ/ n a wire stretched across the ground, that causes a trap, explosive, etc., to work if a person or animal catches it with their foot

tri·reme /'traɪriːm/ n an ancient warship with three rows of OARS on each side

tri·sect /traɪ'sekt/ v [T] tech (in MATHEMATICS) to divide into three esp. equal parts

Tris·tan da Cun·ha /,trɪstən də 'kuːnə, -njə/ a group of islands in the Atlantic Ocean, between South Africa and South America. The people living there had to be taken away when a VOLCANO erupted (ERUPT) in 1961, but were able to return two years later.

Tris·tram and I·sol·de /,trɪstrəm ənd ɪ'zɒldə‖-ɪ'səʊld/ also **Tris·tan and I·seult** /,trɪstən ənd ɪ'suːlt/ the characters, Tristram (a man) and Isolde (a woman) in an old love story, written around AD 1185

Tris·tram Shan·dy /,trɪstrəm 'ʃændi/ a character in a book by Laurence Sterne, considered to be one of the earliest NOVELS written in English. The book describes the humorous adventures of a group of amusing characters including Tristram Shandy himself.

trite /traɪt/ adj derog (of a remark, idea, etc.) used or said too often to be interesting or meaningful; unoriginal and insincere: All the messages of condolence in these cards sound really trite. | At the risk of sounding trite, I wish you were here. — **~ly** adv — **~ness** n [U]

tri·umph[1] /'traɪəmf/ n 1 [C (over)] a complete victory or success: His new film is an absolute triumph. | The story of her triumph over cancer is very moving. | They held a party to celebrate their election triumph. 2 [U] the joy or satisfaction caused by this: shouts of triumph | The victorious army returned in triumph. 3 [C] (in ancient Rome) a procession in honour of a victorious general

triumph[2] v [I (over)] to gain victory or success, esp. in dealing with a very difficult situation or opponent; PREVAIL: to triumph over adversity/over a disabling illness

Triumph n 1 a former English type of motor cycle, famous for its speed 2 a former English type of car, which was quite expensive and considered to be of good quality

tri·um·phal /traɪ'ʌmfəl/ adj of or marking a triumph: a triumphal arch/procession

tri·um·phant /traɪ'ʌmfənt/ adj 1 victorious or successful: a triumphant army 2 taking great pride and joy in one's success or victory: The victorious general made a triumphant return. — **~ly** adv: "I've done it!" he exclaimed triumphantly.

tri·um·vir·ate /traɪ'ʌmvᵻrᵻt/ n [C+sing./pl. v] 1 a group of three people together governing a country, esp. in ancient Rome 2 fml a group of three, esp. one regarded by others as threatening

triv·et /'trɪvᵻt/ n 1 a three-legged stand for holding a pot over a fire 2 a metal stand, usu. with short legs, placed under a hot pot or dish to protect a surface

triv·i·a /'trɪviə/ n [P] 1 unimportant or useless matters or details; TRIFLES[1] (2) 2 detailed facts connected with current or past events, famous people, etc.: sports trivia | Here's a good trivia question for you: Who played Mrs Danvers in "Rebecca"?

triv·i·al /'trɪviəl/ adj 1 usu. derog of little worth or importance; INSIGNIFICANT: Why do you get angry over such trivial matters? | It cost a trivial sum. (=a small amount) 2 ordinary: trivial everyday duties — **~ly** adv

triv·i·al·i·ty /,trɪvi'ælᵻti/ n usu. derog 1 [C] something trivial 2 [U] the state of being trivial

triv·i·al·ize also **-ise** BrE /'trɪviəlaɪz/ v [T] to treat (something) as if it is trivial; reduce to unimportance: These newspapers' sensational treatment of the news trivializes it. — **-ization** /,trɪviəlaɪ'zeɪʃən ‖ -lə-/ n

Trivial Pur·suit /,··· ·ˈ·/ tdmk a game in which players have to answer questions on different subjects, such as music and sport. This game was very fashionable in the mid-1980s.

TRO /,tiː ɑːr 'əʊ/ n abbrev. for: TEMPORARY RESTRAINING ORDER

Troc·a·de·ro /,trɒkə'dɪərəʊ‖,trɑːkə'de-/ [the] a place in London, near Piccadilly Circus, with many shops, EXHIBITIONS, and other forms of entertainment

tro·chee /'trəʊkiː/ n tech a measure of poetry consisting of one strong (or long) beat followed by one weak (or short) beat, as in "father" —compare IAMB — **-chaic** adj

trod /trɒd‖trɑːd/ past tense & participle of TREAD

trod·den /'trɒdn‖'trɑːdn/ past participle of TREAD

trog·lo·dyte /'trɒglədaɪt‖'trɑːg-/ n a person who lives in a CAVE, esp. in PREHISTORIC (=very ancient) times

troi·ka /'trɔɪkə/ n 1 a Russian carriage drawn by a team of three horses side by side 2 a group of three people working together, esp. in government; TRIUMVIRATE

Troi·lus and Cres·si·da /,trɔɪləs ənd 'kresᵻdə/ a play by William Shakespeare about the Trojan War

Tro·jan[1] /'trəʊdʒən/ n 1 a person living in the ancient city of Troy 2 **work like a Trojan** apprec to work very hard: We worked like Trojans to get the job finished on time.

Trojan[2] n AmE tdmk a type of CONDOM

Trojan horse /,·· ·ˈ·/ also **Wooden Horse of Troy**— n something or someone that attacks or weakens something secretly from within. The expression comes from the wooden horse with Greek soldiers hiding inside, used in the Trojan War. —see colour picture on page 423

Trojan War /,·· ·ˈ·/ n [the] a war which is said to have been fought between the Greeks and the Trojans because the Trojan prince Paris had carried off Helen, wife of Menelaus, a Greek king. The war was won by a trick in which Greek soldiers, hidden inside a wooden model of a horse, were taken into Troy by the Trojans who thought that the horse was a gift. Homer describes the Trojan War in his book the Iliad.

troll[1] /trəʊl/ n (in ancient Scandinavian stories) any of a race of beings with special powers, variously described as friendly or evil, as very small or very large, and as living in CAVES or hills

troll[2] /trɒl‖trəʊl/ v [I (for)] rare to try to catch fish by pulling a line through the water behind a slow-moving boat

trol·ley /'trɒli‖'trɑːli/ n 1 esp. BrE ‖ **cart** AmE— a low two-wheeled or four-wheeled cart or vehicle, esp. one pushed by hand: a shopping trolley 2 BrE ‖ **cart** AmE— a small table on very small wheels, from which food and drinks are served: a tea trolley 3 a trolleybus 4 AmE for TRAM —see picture at SAN FRANCISCO 5 **off one's trolley** infml, often humor mad

trol·ley·bus /'trɒlibʌs‖'trɑː-/ n a bus that draws power from a pair of electric wires running above it

trol·lop /'trɒləp‖'trɑː-/ n old-fash derog 1 a very untidy woman or girl 2 a sexually immoral woman or girl

Trol·lope /'trɒləp‖'trɑː-/, Anthony (1815–82) an English writer whose NOVELS, such as Barchester Towers, are famous for their description of VICTORIAN England

trom·bone /trɒm'bəʊn‖trɑːm-/ n a large brass musical instrument with a long sliding tube that is made longer or shorter to vary the note —see picture at BRASS

trom·bon·ist /trɒm'bəʊnᵻst‖trɑːm-/ n a person who plays a trombone

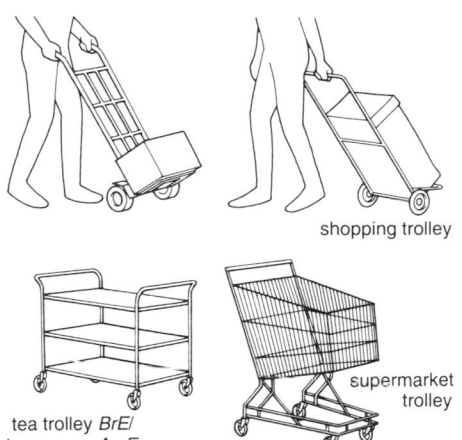

shopping trolley

supermarket trolley

tea trolley *BrE*/
tea wagon *AmE*

troop[1] /truːp/ *n* [C +sing./pl. v] **1** a group of people or wild animals, esp. when moving: *a troop of monkeys/children* **2** a group of soldiers, esp. CAVALRY (=soldiers who fight on horses) or soldiers in armoured vehicles. Two or more troops make up a SQUADRON. **3** a group of SCOUTS under the guidance of an adult leader —compare TROUPE, see also TROOPS

troop[2] *v* **1** [I+adv/prep] to move together in a group: *We all trooped into the meeting.* **2 troop the colour** *BrE* to carry an army flag ceremonially in front of a group of soldiers —see also TROOPING THE COLOUR

troop car·ri·er /'· ˌ···/ *n* a ship, aircraft, or vehicle used for carrying large numbers of soldiers

troop·er /'truːpəʳ/ *n* **1** a soldier of the lowest rank in the CAVALRY or in a part of the army that uses armoured vehicles: *He was swearing like a trooper.* (=using a lot of offensive language) **2** *AmE* a member of a STATE[1] (4) police force

Trooping the Col·our /ˌ··· '··/ [*the*] a ceremony held on the British Queen's official birthday in June, when many horse and foot soldiers march across Horse Guards Parade in London carrying their flags and the Queen her self takes the SALUTE[2] (3)

troops /truːps/ *n* [P] soldiers: *If the police can't keep order we must send in the troops.* —**troop** *adj* [A]: *monitoring troop movements*

troop·ship /'truːpˌʃɪp/ *n* a ship carrying a large number of soldiers

trope /trəʊp/ *n tech* (a word or phrase used as) a FIGURE OF SPEECH

tro·phy /'trəʊfi/ *n* **1** a prize given for winning a race, competition, or test of skill, esp. a CUP[1] (4) or PLAQUE: *She presented/awarded the trophy to the winning team.* | *swimming/boxing trophies* **2** something taken or gained after much effort, esp. in war or hunting: *He hung the lion's head on the wall as a trophy.*

trop·ic /'trɒpɪk‖'trɑː-/ *n* either of the two imaginary lines drawn round the world at about 23½° north (**the tropic of Cancer**) and south (**the tropic of Capricorn**) of the EQUATOR —see also TROPICS, and see picture at GLOBE

trop·i·cal /'trɒpɪkəl‖'trɑː-/ *adj* **1** of or found in the tropics: *tropical flowers* | *a tropical climate* | *tropical medicine* (=the study of diseases of the tropics) **2** very hot: *tropical weather* — **~ly** /kli/ *adv*

trop·ics /'trɒpɪks‖'trɑː-/ *n* [*the*+P] the hot area of the world between the two tropics: *living in the tropics*

Tros·sachs /'trɒsəks, -æks‖'trɑː-/ [*the*] a valley in central Scotland, between Loch Achray and Loch Katrine. The name is also given to a larger area stretching N from Aberfoyle and Loch Ard to Lochs Katrine, Achray, and Venachar.

trot[1] /trɒt‖trɑːt/ *n* **1** [S] the fairly quick movement of a horse in which a front foot and the opposite back foot move as a pair; movement between a walk and a CANTER: *We set off at a trot.* **2** [C] a ride at this speed: *I'm going for a trot down the lane.* **3** [S] a fairly fast human speed between a walk and a run; a slow run or quick walk **4** [C] *AmE for* CRIB[1] (4b) **5 have the trots** *infml, usu. humor* to have DIARRHOEA **6 on the trot** *infml* **a** one after another: *She won three races on the trot.* **b** in a state of continuous activity: *I've been on the trot all day at work.*

trot[2] *v* **-tt-** **1** [I;T] to (cause to) move at the speed of a trot: *The horse/The riders came trotting down the lane.* —compare CANTER[2], GALLOP[2] **2** [I+adv/prep] *infml* (of a person) to move fairly quickly; hurry: *I must be trotting along now or I'll miss the bus.*

trot sthg.↔**out** *phr v* [T] *infml* to say or write (something already said or heard) in an uninteresting unchanged way: *He trotted out the same old excuses.*

Trot *n infml derog* a Trotskyite

troth /trəʊθ‖trɔːθ, trɑːθ, trəʊθ/ *n old use* **1 by my troth** (used as an expression of strong feeling) **2 in troth** truly; INDEED —see also **plight one's troth** (PLIGHT[2])

Trot·sky /'trɒtski‖'trɑː-/ , **Le·on** /'liːɒn‖-ɑːn/ (1879–1940) a Russian leader who took an important part in the REVOLUTION (1) of 1917 which gave birth to the USSR. He wrote a great deal on Communism, and opposed Stalin for power after Lenin's death, but was forced to leave, and after living in several countries, settled in Mexico City where he was later murdered.

Trot·sky·ist /'trɒtskiɪ̆st‖'trɑːt-/ also **Trot·sky·ite** /-skiaɪt/ *derog*, **Trot** *derog sl*— *adj, n* (of or being) a person who favours the political principles of Leon Trotsky, esp. his belief in the need for a working class seizure of state power all over the world if SOCIALISM is to be firmly established

trot·ter /'trɒtəʳ‖'trɑː-/ *n* **1** an animal that trots **2** a pig's foot used as food

trou·ba·dour /'truːbədɔːʳ, -dʊəʳ/ *n* a singer and poet who travelled round the noble courts of Italy and Southern France in the 12th and 13th centuries

trou·ble[1] /'trʌbəl/ *n* **1** [C;U (with)] (something that causes) difficulty, worry, annoyance, or suffering: *By not dealing with the problem now they are just storing up trouble for the future.* | *Paying the rent is the least of my troubles at present.* (=I have other more serious problems to worry about) | *We're having a bit of trouble with the baby — he won't sleep at night.* [+v-ing] *I never have any trouble getting the car started.* | **The trouble with** *this job* (=the thing that is unsatisfactory about it) *is that the pay is too low.* | *I have to pay this bill by Tuesday, but* **the trouble is** (=the problem I face is the fact that) *I don't get my salary until Friday.* **2** [U] a difficult or dangerous position or situation: *The little boy was in trouble so I swam out to save him.* | *If you play with dangerous chemicals like that you're just* **asking for trouble.** (=taking a great risk) | *The new company did well at first, but then* **ran into trouble.** (=got into difficulties) **3** [U (with)] a position in which one is blamed for doing wrong or thought to have done wrong: *My son's always* **getting into trouble** *with the police.* | *She told a lie rather than get her friend into trouble.* **4** [S;U] (something that causes) more than usual work or effort; inconvenience: *I hope we haven't* **put you to any trouble.** | *"We must thank you for* **taking the trouble** *to cook"* (=giving yourself the work of cooking) *us a meal." "It was no trouble at all."* | *You could use a computer to do the calculations, but it might be* **more trouble than it's worth.** (=getting the results may need more effort than they are worth) **5** [U] also **troubles** *pl.*— (an occasion of) political or social disorder: *There's been a lot of trouble in that country in the past year.* | *The trouble started when the police tried to break up the demonstration.* —see also TROUBLES **6** [U (with)] failure to work properly: *There seems to be some trouble with the central heating system.* | *The car's got some sort of engine trouble again.* | *I've got heart trouble* (=pain or illness), *but it's nothing serious.* **7** [C (with)] a fault; a bad or annoying quality: *The trouble with you is that you don't listen!* | *The trouble with your idea is that it creates as many problems as it solves.* **8 get a woman into trouble** *old-fash euph* to make a woman PREGNANT —see also TEETHING TROUBLES

trouble² v **1** [T] *rather fml* to make (someone) anxious, nervous, worried, etc.: *You look troubled; is anything worrying you?* | *troubling news* | (fig.) *a troubled company* (=one which is in financial difficulties) **2** [T(**for**)] (esp. in polite requests) to cause inconvenience to (someone): *I'm sorry to trouble you, but can you tell me the way to the station?* | *May I trouble you for the salt?* (=please pass it to me) [+*obj*+*to*- v] *Can I trouble you to close the door?* (=please close it) **3** [I (**about**) *usu. in questions and negatives*] to cause inconvenience to oneself: *Don't trouble about the door; I'll close it.* [+*to*-v] *Don't trouble to write when I'm away.* **4** [T] to cause (someone) pain or suffering: *He's been troubled by a bad back since he was a child.* **5** [T] *esp. lit* to force into irregular or violent movement; AGITATE: *The wind troubled the surface of the lake.* —see also **fish in troubled waters** (FISH² (5))

trouble and strife /ˌ·· · ·ˈ·/ n BrE dial (RHYMING SLANG for) wife: *Where's your trouble and stife tonight then?*

trouble-free /ˌ·· ˈ·◂/ adj causing no difficulty, worry, or suffering: *She leads a trouble-free existence.* | *We've had two years of trouble-free motoring with that car.*

troub·le·mak·er /ˈtrʌbəlˌmeɪkəʳ/ n derog a person who habitually causes trouble, esp. by making others feel discontented

Troub·les /ˈtrʌbəlz/ n [*the*+P] a name used esp. by people in Northern Ireland for the political disorder and violence there —see also NORTHERN IRELAND

troub·le·shoot·er /ˈtrʌbəlˌʃuːtəʳ/ n **1** a person employed to discover and remove causes of trouble in machines, organizations, etc. **2** *esp. AmE* a guide, often in the form of a printed table, that lists common problems found in a product or activity and ways to deal with them

troub·le·some /ˈtrʌbəlsəm/ adj causing trouble or anxiety; worrying or annoying: *a troublesome child/cough*

trouble spot /ˈ·· ˌ·/ n a place where esp. political trouble often happens: *a journalist covering the world's trouble spots*

trough /trɒf‖trɔːf/ n **1** a long narrow open container, esp. for holding water or food for animals: *a pig's trough* **2** a long narrow hollow area between two waves of the sea: (fig.) *The business cycle is a series of **peaks and troughs**.* (=periods of great activity followed by periods of little activity) **3** *tech* (in METEOROLOGY) a long area of fairly low pressure between two areas of high pressure

trounce /traʊns/ v [T] to defeat completely: *We were thoroughly trounced by the opposing team.*

troupe /truːp/ n [C (**of**)+*sing.*/*pl.* v] a company (of singers, actors, dancers, etc.) —compare TROOP¹

troup·er /ˈtruːpəʳ/ n infml apprec someone who has worked at the same thing for a long time, esp. in the entertainment business: *a veteran Hollywood trouper*

trou·ser /ˈtraʊzəʳ/ adj [A] of trousers: *There's a tear in your trouser leg.* | *a trouser pocket*

trouser press /ˈ·· ·/ n an apparatus in which trousers can be kept when they are not being worn, in such a way that the cloth will be kept smooth

trou·sers /ˈtraʊzəz‖-ərz/ ‖ usu. **pants**, **slacks** *AmE*— n [P] an outer garment covering the body from the waist to the ankles, or sometimes to the knees, with a separate part fitting over each leg: *He bought himself some trousers/a pair of trousers.* —compare JEANS, SHORTS; see also **wear the trousers** (WEAR¹); see PAIR (USAGE), SLACKS (USAGE)

trouser suit /ˈ·· ·/ BrE ‖ **pantsuit** *AmE*— n a woman's suit consisting of a JACKET and matching trousers, fashionable in the 1970s

trous·seau /ˈtruːsəʊ, truːˈsəʊ/ n -seaux /səʊz/ *or* -seaus the personal possessions, including clothes and articles for the home, that a woman brings with her when she marries

trout /traʊt/ n **1** [C;U] (*pl.* **trout** *or* **trouts**) a river (or sometimes sea) fish, used for food **2** [C] (*pl.* **trouts**) BrE infml derog an unattractive or annoying old person (esp. in the phrase **old trout**)

trove n see TREASURE TROVE

Trow·bridge /ˈtrəʊbrɪdʒ/ a town in SW England where the local government for Wiltshire is based

trow·el /ˈtraʊəl/ n **1** a tool with a flat blade for spreading cement, PLASTER, etc. **2** a garden tool like a small spade

with a curved blade, for digging small holes, lifting up plants, etc. —see picture at GARDEN

Troy /trɔɪ/ an ancient city in NW Turkey, said to be the place where the Trojan War was fought

troy weight /ˈ· ·/ n [U] *tech* a British system, now rarely used, of measuring the weight of gold, silver, and jewels: *It weighs two ounces troy.* —compare AVOIRDUPOIS

tru·an·cy /ˈtruːənsi/ also **tru·ant·ing** BrE /ˈtruːəntɪŋ/— n [U] the act of purposely staying away from school without permission: *a rise in truancy figures*

tru·ant /ˈtruːənt/ n **1** a pupil who purposely stays away from school without permission **2 play truant** ‖ also **play hookey** *AmE infml*— to stay away from school on purpose, without permission

truce /truːs/ n (an agreement between enemies or opponents for) the stopping of fighting or arguing, usu. for a short time: *to declare/call a truce* —compare ARMISTICE, CEASE-FIRE

Tru·cial States /ˌtruːʃəl ˈsteɪts/ [*the*+P] a former name for the UNITED ARAB EMIRATES

trucks

articulated lorry *BrE*/semi *AmE*

forklift truck

breakdown truck *BrE*
tow truck *AmE*

see also picture at **van**

truck¹ /trʌk/ n **1** also **lorry** *BrE*— a large motor vehicle for carrying goods in large quantities: *to load a truck* —compare VAN **2** *BrE* ‖ **car** *AmE*— an open railway vehicle for carrying goods: *coal trucks* **3** a simple vehicle for carrying goods, pulled or pushed by hand

truck² n [U] **1** *AmE* vegetables or fruit grown for sale; PRODUCE² **2 have no truck with** to intentionally avoid dealing with, esp. having any business or social connections with

truck³ v [T+*obj*+*adv*/*prep*] *esp. AmE* **1** to carry by truck **2** *infml* move or go, esp. without difficulty: *trucking along at 70 miles an hour* | *It's late, we'd better get trucking.* (=leave)

truck·er /ˈtrʌkəʳ/ also **truck·man** /ˈtrʌkmən/— n *AmE* a truck driver

truck farm /ˈ· ·/ n *AmE for* MARKET GARDEN

truck·ing /ˈtrʌkɪŋ/ n [U] *AmE* the business of carrying goods on motor vehicles

truck·le /ˈtrʌkəl/ v **truckle to** sbdy./sthg. *phr v* [T *no pass.*] *old-fash derog* to be weakly obedient towards

truckle bed /ˈ·· ˌ·/ BrE ‖ **trundle bed** *AmE*— n a low bed, usu. on small wheels, that can be slid under a larger bed

truck·load /ˈtrʌkləʊd/ n [(**of**)] the amount that fills a truck

truck stop /ˈ· ·/ n *AmE for* TRANSPORT CAFE

truc·u·lent /ˈtrʌkjʉlənt/ adj always willing to quarrel or attack; bad-tempered — ~ **ly** adv —**lence** n [U]

Tru·deau /ˈtruːdəʊ ‖ truːˈdəʊ/, **Pi·erre** /piˈeəʳ/ (1919–) a Canadian politician who was elected leader of the Canadian Liberal party in 1968 and was PRIME MINISTER twice (1968–79 and 1980–84)

trudge¹ /trʌdʒ/ v [I+adv/prep] to walk with heavy steps, slowly and with effort: *The old man trudged home through the deep snow.*

trudge² n a long tiring walk

true¹ /truː/ adj **1** in accordance with fact or reality: *a true story* | *Is it true you're going away?* | *"That singer's beautiful." "True, but she can't sing."* | *She told me about her amazing new job – it sounded almost too good to be true.* | *His excuse was rather unusual, but it rang true* (=sounded true) *and I accepted it.* | *It is true that the project involves a certain amount of risk, but I still think we should go ahead.* | *The story is very true to life.* (=like real life) **2** [A] actual, as opposed to what is thought or claimed: *I didn't realize the true seriousness of the country's problems until I went there myself.* | *Her true motives only emerged later.* **3** real; not false; GENUINE: *True love should last for ever.* **4** [(to)] faithful; loyal: *a true friend* | *John always stays true to his principles.* **5** in accordance with an original or standard; proper, correct, or exact: *I think the painter has produced a very true likeness.* | *He's religious in the truest sense of the word.* **6** [A] *tech* having all the particular qualities typical of its class: *The whale is a true mammal, even though it may look like a fish.* **7** [F] correctly fitted, placed, or formed: *If the door's not exactly true it won't close properly.* **8 come true** to happen just as was wished, expected, or dreamt: *When I won all that money it was as if all my dreams had come true.* **9 true to form/type** behaving or acting (esp. badly) just as one would expect —see also TRULY, TRUTH

true² adv **1** without going to one side or the other; exactly: *The arrow flew straight and true into its target.* **2** *tech* without varying from type: *These sheep will breed true.* **3** *old use* in a true manner; truthfully

true³ n **out of true** not having the exact position or correct shape or balance

true-blue /ˌ·ˈ·◂/ adj infml **1** completely loyal **2** BrE completely faithful to the principles of the CONSERVATIVES: *a true-blue Tory*

true-born /ˌtruːˈbɔːn‖-bɔːrn◂/ adj lit apprec actually so by birth: *a trueborn Scot*

True Con·fes·sions /ˌ·-·ˈ·-·/ a magazine full of supposedly true stories about people's problems in love, marriage, and relationships, often told in a rather sensational manner. It is thought to be typical of a number of magazines of its kind: *Her private life is right out of "True Confessions".*

true-heart·ed /ˌtruːˈhɑːtɪd◂‖-ˈhɑːr-/ adj lit apprec faithful; loyal

true-life /ˌ·ˈ·◂/ adj [A] based on fact: *a true-life adventure story*

true-love /ˈtruːlʌv/ n lit or poet the person one loves; SWEETHEART

true north /ˌ·ˈ·/ n [U] north as it appears on maps, calculated in relation to the AXIS (centre line) of the Earth rather than the north MAGNETIC POLE

Truf·faut /ˈtruːfəʊ‖truːˈfoʊ/, **Fran·çois** /ˈfrɒnswɑː‖frɑːnˈswɑː/ (1932–84) a French film director whose films include *Jules et Jim* and *Day for Night*

truf·fle /ˈtrʌfəl/ n **1** a fleshy blackish or light brown FUNGUS that grows underground and is a rare and expensive food **2** a rich soft creamy sweet made with chocolate: *a rum truffle*

trug /trʌg/ n BrE rare a broad flattish basket used in gardens to carry flowers, tools, etc.

tru·is·m /ˈtruːɪzəm/ n a statement that is clearly true, esp. one that is too plain to need mentioning

tru·ly /ˈtruːli/ adv **1** exactly; in accordance with the truth: *A spider cannot truly be described as an insect.* **2** really: *There was a truly beautiful view from the window.* **3** fml sincerely: *I am truly grateful for all your help.* | *He is truly sorry.* **4 Yours truly** esp. AmE (used at the end of a business letter, just before the signature) —see YOURS (USAGE) —see also **well and truly** (WELL¹)

Tru·man /ˈtruːmən/, **Harry S** (1884–1972) an American Democratic politician who was the 33rd President of the US (1945–53). He gave the authority for the dropping of atomic bombs on Japan in 1945, set up the Marshall Plan, and took the US into the Korean War. Truman is also remembered for having a sign on his desk saying "The Buck Stops Here" (=the final responsibility for making a decision is mine).

trump¹ /trʌmp/ n **1** (in card games) any card of a SUIT chosen to be of higher rank than the other three suits: *I had to play a trump to win the trick.* **2 no trump** (in the game of BRIDGE³) an offer or attempt to play without any particular SUIT¹ (2) as TRUMPS **3** AmE for TRUMPS

trump² v [T] to beat (a card) or win (a TRICK¹ (5)) by playing a trump

trump sthg. ↔ **up** phr v [T] to invent (a false reason, charge, etc.) in order to harm someone: *He was sent to prison on a trumped-up charge.*

Trump, Don·ald /ˈdɒnəld‖ˈdɑː-/ (1946–) a wealthy American businessman who owns **Trump Tower**, a large office building

trump card /ˈ·ˌ·/ also **master card**— n a trump: (fig.) *The government has/holds a trump card in the negotiations,* (=a clear and unquestionable advantage that will help it to win) *since it controls the finances.* | (fig.) *Then the defence played its trump card and called a surprise witness who had seen the prisoner somewhere else at the time of the robbery.*

trump·e·ry /ˈtrʌmpəri/ adj [A] old-fash lit **1** (of an object) decorative or attractive but of very little value **2** (of an idea, opinion, action, etc.) worthless

trum·pet¹ /ˈtrʌmpɪt/ n **1** a brass musical instrument consisting of a long metal tube curved round once or twice and widening out at the end, played by blowing —see picture at BRASS **2** the loud cry of an elephant —see also EAR TRUMPET, **blow one's own trumpet** (BLOW¹)

trumpet² v **1** [I] (of an elephant) to make a loud sound **2** [T] often derog to declare or make known loudly: *She's always trumpeting the cleverness of her son.* | *the government's much-trumpeted farm subsidy programme*

trum·pet·er /ˈtrʌmpɪtər/ n a trumpet player

trumps /trʌmps/ n [P] **1** ‖ also **trump** AmE— (in card games) a SUIT chosen to be of higher value than the other three suits: *Hearts are trumps.* **2 turn/come up trumps** infml to do the right or necessary thing, esp. unexpectedly at the last moment: *The dress rehearsal was dreadful, but they turned up trumps on the night and gave an excellent performance.*

trun·cate /trʌŋˈkeɪt‖ˈtrʌŋkeɪt/ v [T] fml or tech to shorten (as if) by cutting off the top or end: *a severely truncated debate* —**-cation** /trʌŋˈkeɪʃən/ n [U]

trun·cheon /ˈtrʌnʃən/ n ‖ also **nightstick** AmE— n a short thick stick carried as a weapon by policemen

trun·dle /ˈtrʌndl/ v [I+adv/prep;T+obj+adv/prep] to (cause to) move heavily or awkwardly on wheels: *The fruit seller trundled his cart along the street.*

trundle bed /ˈ·· ˌ·/ n AmE for TRUCKLE BED

trunk /trʌŋk/ n **1** the thick wooden main stem of a tree **2** a large heavy case or box in which clothes or belongings are stored or packed for travel **3** the very long round nose of an elephant **4** tech the human body apart from the head and limbs **5** AmE for BOOT¹ (2) —see also TRUNKS and see picture at CAR

trunk call /ˈ·ˌ·/ n BrE old-fash a long-distance telephone call

trunk road /ˈ·ˌ·/ n BrE a main road for long-distance travel

trunk route /ˈ·ˌ·/ n BrE a main road or railway line for long-distance travel

trunks /trʌŋks/ n [P] SHORTS worn by men for swimming —see PAIR (USAGE)

Tru·ro /ˈtrʊərəʊ/ a town in the SW of England, where the local government for Cornwall is based

truss¹ /trʌs/ v [T (UP)] **1** to tie up firmly and roughly with cord, rope, etc.: *The robbers trussed up their victim and left him for dead.* **2** to prepare (a chicken, duck, etc.) for cooking by tying the legs and wings in place

truss² n **1** a special belt worn to support a HERNIA and to prevent it growing or spreading **2** a frame or structure built to support a roof, bridge, etc.

trust¹ /trʌst/ n **1** [U (in)] firm belief in the honesty, goodness, worth, etc., of someone or something; confidence; faith: *I don't place any trust in the government's promises.* | *Don't worry about a thing; put your trust in me.* | *an agreement made on a basis of mutual trust* **2** [C;U] (an arrangement for) the holding and controlling of a property or money for the advantage of someone else: *a charitable trust* | *The money will be held in trust for you until you're 21.* **b** care or responsibility: *The children have*

been placed in my trust. | *Our national heritage has been left to us in trust* (=to protect and pass on) *by earlier generations.* | *She's not yet old enough to be employed in* **a position of trust.** (=an important position with serious responsibilities) **3** [C] a group of firms that have combined to reduce competition and control prices to their own advantage —see also ANTITRUST LAW **4 take something on trust** to accept something without proof or close examination: *"How do I know you're telling the truth?" "You'll just have to take it on trust."* —see also UNIT TRUST

trust² *v* [T] **1** to believe in the honesty and worth of (someone or something); have confidence in: *"Why did you lend him all that money?" "I trusted him."* | *You can't trust these car salesmen; they'll say anything to sell their cars.* | *I don't trust his judgment.* [+obj+to-v] *Can they be trusted to look after the house while we're away?* | *a trusted adviser* | **a tried and trusted** remedy **2** to depend on; be sure about: *You can't trust the English weather.* [+obj+to-v] *You can't trust the trains to run on time.* | (fig., humor) *Trust you to say something embarrassing!* (=you always do) **3** [+(that);obj] fml to hope, esp. confidently: *I trust you enjoyed yourself.* | *Everything went all right, I trust.*
  trust in sbdy./sthg. *phr v* [T] fml to have faith in; believe in: *We trust in God.*
  trust to sthg. *phr v* [T] to depend on: *You trust too much to luck/your memory.*

trust·ee /ˌtrʌsˈtiː◂/ *n* **1** a person or firm that holds and controls property or money for the advantage of someone else **2** a member of a group appointed to control the affairs of a company, college, or other organization: *a trustee of the National Theatre*

Trustee Sav·ings Bank /ˌ·· ˈ·· ·/ also **TSB**— [the] one of the main British banks, formed from a number of locally managed SAVINGS BANKs in 1986, branches of which are found in many cities and towns in Britain

trust·ee·ship /trʌsˈtiːʃɪp/ *n* **1** [C;U] the position of trustee **2** [U] government of an area by a country or countries appointed by the United Nations **3** [C] also **trust ter·ri·to·ry** /ˈ· ˌ····/— an area under this form of government

trust·ful /ˈtrʌstfəl/ also **trust·ing** /ˈtrʌstɪŋ/— *adj* (too) ready to trust others: *the trustful nature of a small child* — ~**ly** *adv* — ~**ness** *n* [U]

trust fund /ˈ· ·/ *n* money belonging to someone but held and controlled for their advantage by a TRUSTEE (1)

trust fund ba·by /ˈ· · ˌ··/ *n* AmE sl a person born wealthy because of money from parents or other relatives

trust·wor·thy /ˈtrʌstˌwɜːði‖-ˌ3ːr-/ *adj apprec* worthy of trust; dependable —**thiness** *n* [U]

trust·y¹ /ˈtrʌsti/ *adj* [A] old use or humor that can be trusted; dependable; faithful: *my trusty sword* | *My trusty old car will get us home safely.*

trusty² *n* a prisoner given special rights because of good behaviour in prison

truth /truːθ/ *n* **truths** /truːðz, truːθs/ **1** [the+U] that which is true; the true facts: *You must always* **tell the truth.** | *He said he stayed away because he was ill, but the truth of the matter is that he didn't want to see you.* **2** [U] the state or quality of being true: *I don't doubt the truth of what you say.* | *Do you think there's any truth in these rumours?* | *There wasn't* **a grain of truth** (=any truth at all) *in what she said.* **3** [U] sincerity; honesty: *There was no truth in his expressions of friendship.* **4** [C] a fact or principle accepted as true or for which proof exists: *the truths of science* | *an indisputable truth* **5** **in truth** fml in fact; really **6** **the truth, the whole truth, and nothing** **but the truth** part of the formal speech that people make before they give EVIDENCE in a court of law: *I swear by almighty God that the evidence I shall give will be the truth, the whole truth, and nothing but the truth* **7 truth is stranger than fiction** *saying* things that happen in real life are often more surprising or strange than things that happen in stories **8 truth will out** *saying* the truth about something that has happened will be discovered in the end —see also HALF-TRUTH, HOME TRUTH, MOMENT OF TRUTH, **to tell (you) the truth** (TELL)

Truth, Soj·our·ner /ˈsɒdʒənəʳ ‖ ˈsəʊdʒ3ːrnər/ (about 1797–1883) a freed American slave with deep religious beliefs who became an ABOLITIONIST and often spoke in public against slavery

truth drug /ˈ· ˌ·/ BrE ‖ **truth se·rum** /ˈ· ˌ··/ AmE— *n* any of various drugs which are supposed to make a person, esp. somebody being questioned about a crime, likely to tell the truth or speak freely

truth·ful /ˈtruːθfəl/ *adj* **1** (of a statement, account, etc.) true: *a truthful account of what happened* **2** (of a person) who habitually tells the truth: *a truthful boy* — ~**ly** *adv* — ~**ness** *n* [U]

try¹ /traɪ/ *v* **1** [I;T+to-v;obj] to make an effort or attempt (to do something): *I don't think I can do it, but I'll try.* | *If you don't succeed the first time, try again.* | *Don't criticize him so much; he's* **trying his best/his hardest.** | *He tried to stand on his head, but he couldn't.* | *The two sides are still trying to reach an agreement.* | *Try to get there on time.* | *I tried hard not to laugh when I saw his new haircut.* **2** [T+v-ing] to attempt and do (something) as a possible way of gaining a desired result: *If the car won't start, try pushing it.* —see USAGE **3** [T (OUT)] to test (something) by use, action, and experience, in order to find out about its quality, worth, effect, usefulness, etc.: *Have you tried this new soap?* | *The idea sounds fine, but we need to try it out in practice.* | *Have you ever tried mountain-climbing?* [+v-ing] *We tried growing all our own vegetables, but found it was impossible to grow enough for the family.* —see also TRY-OUT **4** [T] to attempt to open (a door, window, etc.): *I tried the door's locked, but I'll try it just in case.* **5** [T (for)] to examine and judge (a legal case or a person who is thought to be guilty of a crime) in a court of law; put on TRIAL: *They're going to try him for murder.* | *His case will be tried in the High Court.* **6** [T] to put (someone or their nerves, patience, etc.) to a severe test; cause to suffer, esp. with continual small annoyances: *His constant questioning is enough to* **try the patience of a saint!** —see also TRYING **7 try and** infml (not used with the verb forms **tried** or **trying**) to try to: *You must try and come to the party.* | *I'll try and telephone you tomorrow.* **8 try one's hand (at)** to make a first attempt (at): *I tried my hand at rollerskating for the first time yesterday.* **9 try something (on/out) for** size infml to do or use something for a time to see if it is useful, if one likes it, etc.

▷ USAGE 1 You can make this verb stronger by using *hard*: *He* **tried** *hard/very hard/very hard indeed.* 2 Note the difference between *He* **tried** *to open the door* (=but he couldn't) and *He* **tried** *opening the door* (=he opened it, to see what would happen).◁
  try for sthg. BrE ‖ **try out for** sthg. AmE— *phr v* [T] to make an attempt to get or win; compete for, e.g. by taking part in a test: *She's trying for a scholarship to the university.* | *I'm going to try out for football* (=attempt to get a place in a school team) *next year.* —see also TRY-OUT
  try sthg. ↔ **on** *phr v* [T] **1** to put on (a garment, hat, shoes, etc.) to test the fit, examine the appearance, etc. **2 try it on** BrE infml to behave in a deceiving or disobedient manner, esp. to discover how much of this behaviour will be allowed —see also TRY-ON

try² *n* **1** [(at)] an attempt to do something: *Let me have a try (at it).* | *She didn't manage to break the record, but it was a good try.* | *This may not work, but it's* **worth a try.** **2** (in RUGBY) four points won by touching the ball on the ground behind the opposing team's GOAL LINE, giving one the right to try to kick a GOAL

try·ing /ˈtraɪ-ɪŋ/ *adj* difficult, worrying, or annoying: *We've had a lot of problems in the office recently, it's been (a) very trying (time) for all of us.* —see also TRY¹ (6)

try-on /ˈ· ·/ *n* [S] BrE infml an attempt to deceive, esp. to see if someone will believe something false: *Ignore his constant references to not having any money; it's just a try-on.* —see also **try it on** (TRY on)

try-out BrE ‖ **tryout** AmE /ˈ· ·/ *n* [S] infml a trial or test of fitness for some purpose: *Cheerleading tryouts will be held on Friday afternoon.*

tryp·an·o·some /ˈtrɪpənəsəʊm/ *n* a microscopic creature which lives in the blood of various animals, including humans, and causes illnesses, e.g. SLEEPING SICKNESS

try square /ˈ· ·/ *n* an instrument shaped like a letter L, used for marking out RIGHT ANGLES and testing whether work, esp. woodwork, is square

tryst /trɪst, traɪst/ *n* old use or humor **1** an arrangement between lovers to meet at a secret place or time **2** the meeting or meeting place arranged by lovers

tsar, czar, tzar /zɑːᵊ, tsɑːᵊ/ n (until 1917) the male ruler of Russia

tsa·ri·na , czarina, tzarina /zɑːˈriːnə, tsɑː-/ n (until 1917) **1** the female ruler of Russia **2** the wife of the tsar

tsar·is·m , czarism, tzarism /ˈzɑːrɪzəm, ˈtsɑː-/ n [U] a system of government under a tsar esp. the system in Russia before 1917 **tsarist, czarist** adj, n

TSB /ˌtiː es ˈbiː/ abbrev. for: TRUSTEE SAVINGS BANK

tset·se fly, tzetze fly /ˈtetsi flaɪ, ˈtsetsi-, ˈsetsi-/ also **tsetse—** n a blood-sucking African fly that causes SLEEPING SICK- NESS and other serious diseases

T-shirt , tee shirt /ˈtiː ʃɜːt‖-ʃɜːrt/ n a collarless garment of light stretchy material for the upper body for informal wear: *She was wearing jeans and a T-shirt.*

tsp written abbrev. for: TEASPOON: *one tsp of salt*

T-square /ˈtiː skweəᵊ/ n a large ruler shaped like a letter T, used esp. in drawing parallel lines

tsu·na·mi /tsʊˈnɑːmi/ n fml TIDAL WAVE

TSW /ˌtiː es ˈdʌbəljuː/ Television South West; one of the British television companies controlled by the ITC, send- ing out programmes to the south west of England

TT /ˌtiː ˈtiː/ [the] Tourist Trophy; a set of British motor- cycle races, held every year on the Isle of Man

TU /ˌtiː ˈjuː/ abbrev. for TRADE UNION

Tu·a·mo·tu Ar·chi·pel·a·go /tuːəˌməʊtuː ɑːkɪˈpeləɡəʊ‖-ɑːrk-/ [the] a group of about 80 CORAL islands in the S Pacific, in French Polynesia

tub /tʌb/ n **1 a** a large round open container for washing, storing, etc.: *an old wooden washing tub* | *He grows roses in tubs on the terrace.* **b** a small often round container for food, etc., usu. made of plastic or paper: *a tub of marga- rine* **2** infml a BATHTUB **3** infml an awkward slow boat: *Is this old tub going to make it to port?* **4** AmE infml a short, fat person: *Their children are all tubs.*

tu·ba /ˈtjuːbə‖ˈtuːbə/ n a large brass musical instrument that produces low notes —see picture at BRASS

tu·bal preg·nan·cy /ˌtjuːbəl ˈpregnənsi‖ˌtuː-/ also **ectopic pregnancy** med— n a PREGNANCY in which the fertilized (FERTILIZE) egg begins to grow in the FALLOPIAN TUBE in- stead of the WOMB. Usually a woman with a tubal preg- nancy must have a medical operation to save her life.

tub·by /ˈtʌbi/ adj infml rather short and fat —see FAT (USAGE)

tubes

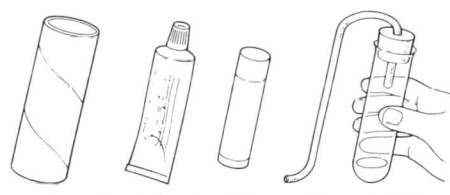

a cardboard   a tube of   a tube   rubber   a test
tube   toothpaste of glue tubing   tube

tube /tjuːb‖tuːb/ n **1** [C] a hollow round pipe of metal, glass, rubber, etc., used esp. for carrying or holding liquids — see also INNER TUBE, TEST TUBE, TUBING **2** [C (of)] a small soft metal or plastic container, closed at one end and fit- ted with a cap at the other, for holding a soft wet mix- ture, such as TOOTHPASTE, paint, etc., which is pushed out of the tube by tightly pressing it: *a tube of glue/tooth- paste* **3** [C] a hollow pipe or organ in the body: *the bron- chial tubes* **4** [(the) S] (sometimes cap.) BrE infml for UN- DERGROUND³: *a tube station/train* | *She goes to work on the tube/by tube.* —compare SUBWAY **5** [C] a CATHODE RAY TUBE **6** [the] AmE infml for TELEVISION **7** [C (of)] infml, esp. AmE a tin of beer **8 go down the tubes** infml, esp. AmE to be ruined or brought to a sudden un- wanted end: *These welfare programs could go down the tubes if the Administration has its way.*

tube·less /ˈtjuːbləs‖ˈtuːb-/ adj having no INNER TUBES: *tubeless tyres*

tu·ber /ˈtjuːbəᵊ‖ˈtuː-/ n a fleshy swollen underground stem, such as the potato, from which new plants grow — ~**ous** adj

tu·ber·cu·lar /tjuːˈbɜːkjʊləᵊ‖tuːˈbɜːr-/ also **tu·ber·cu·lous** /tjuːˈbɜːkjʊləs‖tuːˈbɜːr-/— adj of, suffering from, or caus- ing tuberculosis

tu·ber·cu·lo·sis /tjuːˌbɜːkjʊˈləʊsɪs‖tuːˌbɜːr-/ also **TB**— n [U] a serious infectious disease that attacks many parts of the body, esp. the lungs

tub·ing /ˈtjuːbɪŋ‖ˈtuː-/ n [U] tubes: *ten metres of copper tub- ing* | *rubber tubing* —see picture at LABORATORY and TUBE

Tub·man /ˈtʌbmən/, **Har·riet** /ˈhæriət/ (about 1820–1913) an escaped slave in the US who became an ABOLITIONIST, working in the UNDERGROUND RAILROAD to free other slaves. She also served in the American Civil War.

tub-thump·er /ˈ· ˌ··/ n BrE infml a public speaker who tries to persuade or interest listeners by exciting strong or vio- lent feelings —**ing** adj, n [A;U] : *a tub-thumping speech*

tu·bu·lar /ˈtjuːbjʊləᵊ‖ˈtuː-/ adj made of or in the form of a tube or tubes: *tubular metal furniture* | *tubular bells*

TUC /ˌtiː juː ˈsiː/ n [the] Trades Union Congress; the associ- ation of British trade unions

tuck¹ /tʌk/ v [T+obj+adv/prep] **1** to take the edge or end of (a garment, piece of material, etc.) and put or push it into a desired or convenient position, usu. a narrow space: *Tuck your shirt into your trousers.* **2** to put (esp. something flat) into a convenient narrow space for pro- tection, safety, etc.: *He had a book tucked under his arm.* | *Tuck that money into the top of your sock for safekeeping.* **3** to place (esp. a building) in a private and/or almost hid- den place: *Our house is tucked away among the trees.* | *The post office is tucked behind the grocery store.* —see also nip and tuck

tuck sthg. ↔ **away** phr v [T] infml **1** to store in a safe place: *She's got a lot of money tucked away.* **2** to eat (a lot of food)

tuck in phr v **1** [I (to)] infml, esp. BrE to eat eagerly: *Come along, children, tuck in!* | *I was just tucking into my dinner when the phone rang.* —see also TUCK-IN **2** [T] AmE for TUCK up

tuck sbdy. ↔ **up** phr v [T (in)] to make (esp. a child) comfortable in bed by pulling the sheets tight: *He tucked the children up in bed and said goodnight.*

tuck² n **1** [C] a narrow flat fold of material sewn into a garment for decoration or to give a special shape: *Her new dress was a bit too big, so her mother took a tuck in it.* **2** [U] BrE old-fash food, esp. cakes, sweets, etc , as eaten by schoolchildren

Tuck, Friar see FRIAR TUCK

tuck·er¹ /ˈtʌkəᵊ/ n [U] AustrE & NZE infml food: *He packed his lunch in his tucker bag.* —see also **one's best bib and tucker** (BIB)

tuck·er² v [T (OUT)] usu. pass.] infml, esp. AmE to tire greatly: *The children were tuckered out after the picnic.*

tuck-in /ˈ· ·/ n [usu. sing.] BrE infml a big meal —see also TUCK in (1)

tuck shop /ˈ· ·/ n BrE, old-fash a place in a school where sweets, drinks, etc. are sold to pupils

Tu·dor /ˈtjuːdəᵊ‖ˈtuː-/ adj **1** of the English royal family that ruled from 1485 to 1603: *Henry VIII was a Tudor king.* **2** of, or typical of the Tudor period. The Tudor style of house building often used HALF-TIMBERED walls (=with the black wood of the frame showing in the white outer walls): *Tudor houses/furniture* —see colour picture on page 227

Tudor, Henry HENRY VII

Tu·dors /ˈtjuːdəz‖ˈtuːdərz/ [the+P] the members of the Tudor family: *After the Tudors, James I came to the throne.*

Tues·day /ˈtjuːzdi‖ˈtuːz-/ (written abbrev. **Tue.** or **Tues.**) n [C;U] the second day of the week, between Monday and Wednesday: *He'll arrive on Tuesday.* | (BrE infml & AmE) *He'll arrive Tuesday.* | *It happened on Tuesday morning.* | *She left last Tuesday.* | *She works at home on Tuesdays.* | *My birthday is on a Tuesday this year.* —see DAY (CUL- TURAL NOTE)

tuft /tʌft/ n [(of)] a bunch of (hair, feathers, grass, etc.) growing or held closely together at the base — ~**ed** adj

tug¹ /tʌɡ/ v **-gg-** [I (at);T] to pull hard with force or much effort: *The small child tugged at her sleeve to try and get her attention.* | *We tugged the boat out of the water.*

tug² n a sudden strong pull: *He gave the rope a sharp/ gentle tug to free it.*

tug³ also **tug·boat** /ˈtʌgbəʊt/— n a small powerful boat used for pulling and/or guiding ships into a port, up a river, etc.

tug-of-love /ˌ·· ·ˈ◄/ n BrE infml (esp. in newspapers) a situation in which a child's parent tries to get the child back from someone else who is looking after him/her, such as the child's other parent or an ADOPTIVE parent: *"Tug-of-love Mum in dramatic chase"*(title of newspaper story)

tug-of-war /ˌ·· ·ˈ·/ n a test of strength in which two teams pull against each other on a rope, each trying to pull the other over the winning line

Tuil·e·ries /ˈtwiːləri/ [the] a large public garden in central Paris, near the Louvre

tu·i·tion /tjuːˈɪʃən‖tuː-/ n [U] **1** fml instruction or teaching, esp. of people in small groups: *Students' grants cover their* **tuition** *fees.* | *He's having extra tuition in physics.* **2** esp. AmE the price of or payment for instruction: *He's already paid a year's tuition.*

tu·lip /ˈtjuːlɪp‖ˈtuː-/ n a garden plant that grows from a BULB and has large colourful cup-shaped flowers on top of tall stems in the spring. There is a well-known song called *Tiptoe throough the Tulips* —see picture at FLOWER

Tull /tʌl/ , **Jeth·ro** /ˈdʒeθrəʊ/ (1674–1741) an English AGRICULTURALIST who introduced new methods of farming and invented a machine for sowing (SOW¹) seeds

tulle /tjuːl‖tuːl/ n [U] a thin soft silk or nylon netlike material used for making dresses, VEILs, etc.

Tul·sa /ˈtʌlsə/ a city in NE Oklahoma in the US. It is an important centre of the US oil industry.

tum·ble¹ /ˈtʌmbəl/ v **1** [I+adv/prep] to fall suddenly or helplessly; roll over or down quickly or violently: *The little boy tripped and tumbled down the stairs.* | (fig.) *Stock market prices tumbled* (=fell sharply) *after rumours of a rise in interest rates.* **2** [I (DOWN)] to fall to pieces; fall down; COLLAPSE: *The hut we built is already tumbling down.* —see also TUMBLEDOWN **3** [I+adv/prep] to move or go in confusion or disorder: *The children tumbled off the bus into the park.* **4** [T+obj+adv/prep] to throw about in a confused mass **5** [I (**to**)] sl, esp. BrE to understand suddenly; REALIZE: *It was a long time before she tumbled (to what I meant).* **6** [I] AmE to perform TUMBLING acts

tumble² n a fall, esp. one from a height: *He's taken a few nasty tumbles recently.* —see also ROUGH-AND-TUMBLE

tum·ble·down /ˈtʌmbəldaʊn/ adj [A] in a condition of near ruin: *a tumbledown old house* —see also TUMBLE¹ (2)

tum·ble-dry·er, -drier /ˌ·· ˌ··/ n a heated container in which washed clothes are spun gently round and round to dry them —**tumble-dry** v [T]

tum·bler /ˈtʌmbləʳ/ n **1** a flat-bottomed drinking glass with no handle or stem: *a set of six tumblers* **2** the part in a lock that must be turned by a key before the lock will open **3 a** old-fash for ACROBAT **b** AmE someone who practises tumbling

tum·ble·weed /ˈtʌmbəlwiːd/ n [U] a plant growing in the desert areas of N America which breaks off its root in autumn and is blown about by the wind

tum·bling /ˈtʌmblɪŋ/ n [U] AmE a sport similar to GYMNASTICS, but with all exercises performed on a mat or floor, without equipment

tum·brel , -bril /ˈtʌmbrəl/ n a simple cart used for taking prisoners to the GUILLOTINE in the French Revolution

tu·mes·cent /tjuːˈmesənt‖tuː-/ adj tech swollen or swelling —**-cence** n [U]

tu·mid /ˈtjuːmɪd‖ˈtuː-/ adj tech (of a part of the body) swollen —**-ity** /tjuːˈmɪdɪti‖tuː-/ n [U]

tum·my /ˈtʌmi/ n infml the stomach; used mainly by children: *a tummy ache*

tu·mour BrE ‖ **-mor** AmE /ˈtjuːməʳ‖ˈtuː-/ n a mass of diseased cells in the body which have divided and increased too quickly, causing swelling and illness: *a brain tumour* | *a benign/malignant tumour* —compare GROWTH (4)

tu·mult /ˈtjuːmʌlt‖ˈtuː-/ n [C;U] fml the confused noise and excitement of a big crowd, fighting, etc.; state of confusion and excitement; UPROAR: *His announcement was drowned in the tumult.*

tu·mul·tu·ous /tjuːˈmʌltʃuəs‖tuː-/ adj very noisy and disorderly; full of tumult: *a tumultuous welcome* | *tumultuous applause* —**~ly** adv

tu·mu·lus /ˈtjuːmjɵləs‖ˈtuː-/ also **barrow**— n -luses or -li /laɪ/ a large pile of earth put over a grave by people in very ancient times

tu·na /ˈtjuːnə‖ˈtuːnə/ n tuna or tunas **1** [C] also **tunny** BrE— a large sea fish caught for food **2** [U] also **tuna fish** /ˈ·· ·/— the flesh of this fish, usu. sold ready cooked in tins

tuna melt /ˈ·· ˌ·/ n AmE a dish consisting of bread and tuna with melted cheese on top, usu. eaten for LUNCH

Tun·bridge Wells /ˌtʌnbrɪdʒ ˈwelz/ a town in SW Kent, SE England, which was an important SPA in the 17th and 18th centuries. Tunbridge Wells is often thought of as a place with many older, right-wing people who are strongly opposed to social change and are easily shocked. People sometimes make jokes about letters to newspapers signed "Disgusted of Tunbridge Wells".

tun·dra /ˈtʌndrə/ n [(the)] U] a cold treeless plain in the far north of Europe, Asia, and N America, which is frozen hard in winter

tune¹ /tjuːn‖tuːn/ n **1** a number of musical notes, played or sung one after the other, that form a pleasing pattern of sound; arrangement of musical sounds: *He strolled along humming/whistling a tune.* **2** in/out of tune: a at/not at the correct PITCH (=musical level): *The piano is out of tune.* b in/not in agreement or sympathy: *His ideas were in tune with the period in which he lived.* **3** to the tune of infml to the amount of: *in debt to the tune of £5000* —see also call the tune (CALL¹), carry a tune (CARRY¹ (18)), change one's tune (CHANGE¹), dance to someone's tune (DANCE¹)

tune² v [T (UP)] **1** to set (a musical instrument) at the proper PITCH (=musical level): *The musicians/orchestra tuned their instruments (up) before the concert began.* —see also TUNE **up**, TUNING FORK **2** to put (an engine) in good working order for top speed and best performance: *The engine needs some fine tuning.* —see also TUNE-UP **3** [I+IN, to;T (to)] to set (a radio or television) to receive broadcasts from a particular station: *We always tune in (to Radio 4) to hear the 10 o'clock news.* | *Stay tuned (to this channel) for the latest news from Washington.* | *I tuned the radio to the BBC World Service.* **4 tuned in (to)** in touch with what is happening or with what people are thinking or saying: *an astute politician who's tuned in to popular feeling on this issue*

tune sbdy./sthg. **out** phr v [T;I] AmE to ignore or stop listening (to someone): *She tuned out after I said no extra money was involved.* | *You have to just tune him out when he gets angry.*

tune up phr v [I] to set a musical instrument at the proper PITCH (=musical level): *The orchestra is tuning up ready to begin.* —see also TUNE² (1)

tune·ful /ˈtjuːnfəl‖ˈtuːn-/ adj having a pleasing tune; pleasant to listen to —**~ly** adv —**~ness** n [U]

tune·less /ˈtjuːnləs‖ˈtuːn-/ adj unmusical; unpleasant to listen to: *a tuneless hum* —**~ly** adv

tun·er /ˈtjuːnəʳ‖ˈtuː-/ n **1** the part of a radio or television that receives the signals and changes them into sound and/or pictures **2** a person who tunes musical instruments: *a piano tuner*

tune-up /ˈ· ·/ n an act of tuning (TUNE² (2)) an engine

tung·sten /ˈtʌŋstən/ also **wolfram**— n [U] a hard metal that is a simple substance (ELEMENT), used esp. in the production of steel

tu·nic /ˈtjuːnɪk‖ˈtuː-/ n **1** a loose-fitting garment, usu. without SLEEVEs, which reaches to the knees and is usu. worn with a belt around the waist, esp. of a kind worn in former times **2** a specially shaped short coat worn by soldiers, police officers, etc., as part of a uniform

tuning fork /ˈ·· ·/ n a small steel instrument, consisting of a stem that divides into two and producing a pure musical note of fixed PITCH (=musical level) when struck, used in tuning musical instruments

tuning peg /ˈ·· ·/ n a PEG¹ (3) —see picture at PEG

Tu·nis /ˈtjuːnɪs‖ˈtuː-/ the capital city of Tunisia, in the NE of the country

Tu·nis·i·a /tjuːˈnɪziə‖tuːˈniːʒə/ a country and republic in NW Africa, bordered by Algeria, Libya, and the Mediterranean Sea; capital Tunis; population 7,990,000 (1989) —**Tunisian** n, adj

tun·nel¹ /ˈtʌnl/ n a usu. man-made underground passage:

The train went through a tunnel. | *The prisoners dug a tunnel to try to escape, but it caved in.* —see also WIND TUNNEL, **light at the end of the tunnel** (LIGHT[1] (15))

tunnel[2] *v* -ll- *BrE* || -l- *AmE* **1** [I;T] to make a tunnel under or through (a hill, river, etc.): *Engineers are tunnelling (under) the river.* | *The prisoners tunnelled their way to freedom.* **2** [T] to make or form as or like a tunnel: *They tunnelled a passage under the perimeter fence.* — —**ler**, ~**er** *n*

tunnel vi·sion /'·· ,··/ *n* [U] **1** a condition in which one's eyes are damaged so that one can only see straight ahead, not to the sides **2** *derog* a tendency to consider only part of a question or hold only one opinion, without even trying to examine others

tun·ny /'tʌni/ *n* tunny *or* tunnies *BrE* a TUNA

tup·pence /'tʌpəns/ *n* [C;U] *BrE* TWOPENCE

tup·penny /'tʌpni/ *adj* [A] *BrE* TWOPENNY

Tup·per·ware /'tʌpəweəʳ‖-pər-/ *n* [U] *tdmk* a type of plastic goods, esp. containers, sold not in shops but by people who ask friends round for **Tupperware parties**, social gatherings where the goods are offered for sale and the seller receives part of any money collected

tur·ban /'tɜːbən‖'tɜːr-/ *n* **1** a head covering of Muslim origin, worn by men in parts of North Africa and southern Asia, consisting of a long length of cloth wound tightly round the head **2** a small tight-fitting hat worn by women —-**baned** *adj*

tur·bid /'tɜːbɪd‖'tɜːr-/ *adj fml or tech* **1** (of a liquid) not clear or transparent; muddy; thick: *the turbid waters of the river* **2** (of smoke, clouds, etc.) heavy and dark; DENSE **3** confused: *the turbid images of a dream* — ~**ness**, ~**ity** /tɜː'bɪdəti‖tɜːr-/ *n* [U]

tur·bine /'tɜːbaɪn‖'tɜːrbən, -baɪn/ *n* an engine or motor in which the pressure of a liquid or gas, usu. at very high temperatures, drives a special wheel, producing a circular movement: —see also GAS TURBINE, WIND TURBINE and see picture at WINDMILL

tur·bo·charg·er /'tɜːbəʊˌtʃɑːdʒəʳ ‖ 'tɜːrbəʊˌtʃɑːr-/ also **turbo** /'tɜːbəʊ‖'tɜːr-/infml— *n* an apparatus, worked by a turbine driven by a vehicle's waste gases, that sends the air-petrol mixture into an engine at higher than usual pressure, making it more powerful —**turbocharge** *v* [T]

tur·bo·jet /'tɜːbəʊdʒet‖'tɜːr-/ *n* **1** a powerful engine that produces forward movement by forcing out a stream of hot air and gases behind itself, used esp. in aircraft **2** an aircraft getting power from this type of engine

tur·bo·prop /'tɜːbəʊprɒp‖'tɜːrbəʊprɑːp/ *n* **1** a turbine engine that drives a PROPELLER **2** an aircraft getting power from this type of engine

tur·bot /'tɜːbət, -bət‖'tɜːrbəʊ/ *n* **turbot** *or* **turbots** [C;U] a large European fish with a flat diamond-shaped body, used as food

tur·bu·lence /'tɜːbjʊləns‖'tɜːr-/ also **tur·bu·len·cy** /-lənsi/— *n* [U] **1** the state of being turbulent: *political turbulence* **2** irregular and violent movement of the air: *The flight was very uncomfortable because of turbulence.*

tur·bu·lent /'tɜːbjʊlənt‖'tɜːr-/ *adj* **1** violent and disorderly; having a restless or uncontrolled quality: *turbulent weather|winds* | *a turbulent period of history* | *a turbulent crowd* **2 Will no one rid me of this turbulent priest?** *quote* a phrase that is supposed to have been said by Henry II of England, which led to the murder of the priest Thomas Becket at Canterbury Cathedral — ~**ly** *adv*

turd /tɜːd‖tɜːrd/ *n* **1** *taboo* a piece of solid waste material passed from the body **2** *taboo sl* an offensive person

tu·reen /tjʊ'riːn‖tə'riːn/ *n* a large deep dish with a lid, from which soup is served at a table

turf[1] /tɜːf‖tɜːrf/ *n* **turfs** *or* **turves** /tɜːvz‖tɜːrvz/ **1** [U] a surface made up of earth and a thick covering of grass: *the smooth turf of a bowling green* **2** [C] *AmE usu.* **sod** a piece of this: *She bought some turves to repair her lawn.* **3** [*the*+S] the sport or world of horseracing **4** [U] *sl, esp. AmE* an area claimed by a group as its own; this word is used esp. by young GANG members

turf[2] *v* [T] to cover (a piece of land) with turf
turf sbdy./sthg. ↔ **out** *phr v* [T (**of**)] *infml, esp. BrE* to throw out; get rid of: *He's been turfed out of the club for not paying his bill.*

turf ac·coun·tant /'· ·,··/ *n BrE fml for* BOOKMAKER

Tur·ge·nev /tʊəˈɡeɪnjef‖tʊər-/, **I·van** /'aɪvən/ (1818–83) a Russian writer of books, short stories, and plays, best known for his play *A Month in the Country* and his book *Fathers and Sons*

tur·gid /'tɜːdʒɪd‖'tɜːr-/ *adj* **1** *fml derog* (of language or style) too solemn and self-important **2** *tech* swollen, e.g. by a liquid or inner pressure — ~**ly** *adv* — ~**ity** /tɜː'dʒɪdəti‖tɜːr-/ *n* [U]

Tu·rin /tjʊəˈrɪn‖tʊ-/ a city on the River Po in NW Italy, the capital of Piedmont REGION and a centre of the Italian car industry. The Italian name is **Torin**.

Tu·ring /'tjʊərɪŋ‖'tʊ-/, **A·lan** /'ælən/ (1912–54) an English MATHEMATICIAN and computer scientist who, before computers had been invented, imagined the possibility of a machine which could perform processes similar to human thought

Turin Shroud /,·· '·/ the cloth believed by some people to have covered the dead body of Jesus Christ after he had been crucified (CRUCIFY) and to be marked with the face of Jesus. It is now kept in Turin.

Turk /tɜːk‖tɜːrk/ *n* a person who comes from or whose parents come from Turkey —see also YOUNG TURK

tur·key /'tɜːki‖'tɜːrki/ *n* **1** [C] a large bird, rather like a large chicken, kept on farms for its meat which is eaten, esp. at Christmas and (in the US) at Thanksgiving **2** [U] the flesh of this bird as food: *slices of roast turkey* **3** [C] *AmE infml* **a** a failure: *The movie we saw last night was a real turkey.* **b** a useless or silly person —see also COLD TURKEY, **talk turkey** (TALK[1] (15))

turkey

Turkey a country in W Asia and SW Europe, between the Mediterranean and Black Seas; capital Ankara; population 56,741,000 (1989). Turkey has been a republic since 1923, and was the centre of the OTTOMAN EMPIRE.

Turkish /'tɜːkɪʃ ‖ 'tɜːr-/ *adj* of Turkey

Turkish bath /,·· '·/ *n* a health treatment for the body in which one sits in a very hot steamy room, often followed by a cold SHOWER[1] (3) and a MASSAGE — compare SAUNA

Turkish cof·fee /,·· '··/ *n* [C;U] a strong finely-ground (GRIND) coffee which is drunk black and with sugar, usu. from small cups

Turkish de·light /,·· ·'·/ *n* [U] a very sweet pink, white, or green jelly-like substance covered in powder sugar or chocolate, eaten in lumps as a sweet

Turk·men·i·stan /,tɜːkmenə'stɑːn‖,tɜːrkmenə'stæn/ a country in central Asia bordered by Uzbekistan, Iran, Afghanistan, and the Caspian Sea; capital Ashkhabad; population 3,534,000 (1989)

Turks and Cai·cos Is·lands /,tɜːks ənd 'keɪkəs ,aɪləndz‖,tɜːrks-/ [*the*+P] a group of 30 islands in the British West Indies, SE of the Bahamas; capital Grand Turk

tur·me·ric /'tɜːmərɪk‖'tɜːr-/ *n* [U] (an Asian plant with a yellowish root crushed to) a fine powder that is used for giving a special taste and colour to food, esp. CURRY

tur·moil /'tɜːmɔɪl‖'tɜːr-/ *n* [S;U] a state of confusion, excitement, and trouble: *She couldn't think; her mind was in (a) complete turmoil.* | *His assassination threw the country into turmoil.*

turn[1] /tɜːn‖tɜːrn/ *v* **1** [I;T] to (cause to) move round a central or fixed point: *The big wheel turned slowly.* | *She turned the key in the lock.* | *I turned the screw a few more times to tighten it.* **2** [I;T (OVER)] to (cause to) move so that a different side faces upwards or outwards: *She turned over and went to sleep.* | *He was* **tossing and turning** *all night, unable to sleep.* | *Fry the steak for five minutes then turn it and fry the other side.* | *He turned the pages of the book.* | *She turned back the sheets.* | *She turned down the corner of the page to keep her place.* | *He turned the jacket inside out|turned the glass upside down.* **3** [I+*adv/prep*;T+*adv/prep*] to (cause to) change position or direction so as to face or move in a particular direction: *Turn right at the end of the street.* | *She turned away and began to cry.* | *We turned onto the motorway at Royston.* | *(fig.) As his debts grew bigger, he turned to* crime. (=became a criminal) | (fig.) *Can you help me? I'm desperate; I* **don't know which way to turn.** (=who to ask for help) | (fig.) *Our luck has turned.* (=become better) | *The tide is turning.* | *The bus turned into the hotel entrance.* | *Angrily, he* **turned on his heel(s)** (=turned suddenly) *and walked out.* | *She turned her car round and drove off in the opposite direction.* —see also TURN **back**, TURN **off** (3)   **4** [I (ROUND, AROUND)] to bend round or look round: *He turned (round) and waved.* | *She turned to me and smiled.*   **5** [T] to go round: *The car turned the corner.* | (fig.) *Exports have been low this year, but recently the figures have been improving; we seem to have* **turned the corner.**   **6** [T+*obj*+*adv*/*prep*, esp. **on**] to aim or point; set or direct in a particular direction: *The firemen turned their hoses on the blazing building.* | *She turned the aerial towards the transmitter.* | *He turned his back on her.* | (fig.) *How can you* **turn your back on** (=not help) *people in need?* | (fig.) *We should now turn our attention to other aspects of the problem.*   **7** [T] to do or perform by moving round a fixed point: *The skater turned a neat circle on the ice.*   **8** [L;T+*obj*+*adj*] to change so as to become (esp. something bad): *She suddenly turned pale when she heard the bad news.* | *He turns nasty if you laugh at him.* | *His hair turned grey* | *In autumn the leaves turn brown.* | *The milk will turn sour if you don't put it in the fridge.* | *The King's trusted minister* **turned traitor** *and poisoned him.* | *One of the gang* **turned informer** *and gave the police the details of the robbery.* | *The Congressman is a former football player* **turned politician.** (=a football player who has now become a politician) | *This hot sun will turn the grass brown.* —see BECOME (USAGE)   **9** [I+*adv*/*prep*;T+*obj*+*adv*/*prep*, esp. **from, into**] to change in form or nature: *Water turns into ice when it freezes.* | *In fifty years this place has turned from a little village into a large town.* | *Their amusement turned to horror when they realized what had happened.* | *The witch turned the prince into a frog.* | *The President's unfortunate remark turned the incident from a trivial matter into a serious controversy.*   **10** [T *not usu. in progressive forms*] to reach or pass (a certain age, time, amount, etc.): *It's just turned 3 o'clock.* (=It is just after 3 o'clock.) | *"I wonder how old he is." "He must be turned 40."* (=older than 40)   **11** [I;T] to (cause to) feel uncomfortable, sick, etc.: *Fatty food* **turns my stomach.** | *Don't tell me any more of the gory details* — *you're* **making my stomach turn.**   **12** [T] to shape (wood or metal); form: *These craftsmen turn wood on lathes.*   **13** [I;T] to (cause to) become sour: *The heat has turned the milk.* | (fig.) *The terrible tragedy had quite* **turned her brain.** (=made her slightly mad)   **14** [T] *old-fash or AmE* to hurt (one's ankle) by twisting it   **15 turn a phrase** to say a clever thing neatly   **16 turn somewhere upside down** to search everywhere in a place, esp. untidily or roughly: *The police turned his flat upside down looking for drugs.* —see also **turn one's back on** (BACK¹), **turn a blind eye (to)** (BLIND¹), **turn the other cheek** (CHEEK¹), **turn a deaf ear to** (DEAF), **turn in one's grave** (GRAVE¹), **not turn a hair** (HAIR), **turn one's hand to** (HAND¹), **turn someone's head** (HEAD¹), **turn over a new leaf** (LEAF¹), **turn one's nose up (at)** (NOSE¹), **turn the tables (on someone)** (TABLE¹), **turn tail** (TAIL¹), **turn up trumps** (TRUMPS), **turn turtle** (TURTLE)

turn (sbdy.) **against** sbdy./sthg. *phr v* [T] to (cause to) become opposed to or an enemy of: *The minister has turned against his former colleagues.* | *He claims that his ex-wife has turned the children against him.*

turn sbdy. ↔ **away** *phr v* [T]   **1** to refuse to let in: *The hall was full, and hundreds of fans had to be turned away.*   **2** to refuse to give one's sympathy, help, or support to

turn (sbdy.) ↔ **back** *phr v*   **1** [I] to go in the opposite direction: *We turned back when it started snowing.*   **2** [T] to stop from going forward: *They were turned back at the border by the security police.*   **3** [(on)] **turn back the clock** return to an earlier state or condition: *legislation that turns back the clock on human rights*

turn sbdy./sthg. ↔ **down** *phr v* [T]   **1** to reduce the force, speed, loudness, etc., of (something) by using controls: *Turn that radio down at once!* | *to turn down the heating* —opposite **turn up**   **2** to refuse (a request or offer or the person that makes it; REJECT): *Thank you, but I'll have to turn down your offer.* | *He proposed to her, but she turned him down.* (=refused to marry him) —see REFUSE (USAGE)

turn (sbdy./sthg. ↔) **in** *phr v* [T]   **1** to give back to the proper or original owner; return: *You must turn in your*

gun when you leave the army.*   **2** [T] **a** to gain or produce as a result of work: *The company has turned in record profits this year.* *AmE* to hand in (work that one has done): *This is a poor piece of work you've turned in.*   **3** [T] to deliver to the police: *The wanted man turned himself in.*   **4** [I] *infml* to go to bed

turn off *phr v*   **1** [T] (**turn** sthg. ↔ **off**) to stop the flow of (water, gas, etc., in a pipe) by screwing a TAP tighter: *He turned the gas off/turned off the hot water.*   **2** [T] (**turn** sthg. ↔ **off**) to stop the operation of (a radio, light, etc.), esp. by using a button or SWITCH: *She turned the TV off.* | *Turn off the light.* —see OPEN² (USAGE)   **3** [I;T (=**turn off** sthg.)] to leave (one road, esp. a main road) and take another: *We turned off (the freeway) at Detroit.* —see also TURN-OFF (1)   **4** [I;T (=**turn** sbdy. ↔ **off**)] *infml* to (cause to) lose interest: *I turned off when they started talking about computers.*   **5** [T] (**turn** sbdy. ↔ **off**) *infml* to cause a feeling of dislike in (someone) or fail to interest them sexually: *It really turns me off to see you biting your toenails.* —see also TURN-OFF

turn on *phr v*   **1** [T] (**turn** sthg. ↔ **on**) to cause (water, gas, etc., in a pipe) to flow by unscrewing a TAP: *She turned the water on.*   **2** [T] (**turn** sthg. ↔ **on**) to cause (a radio, light, etc.) to operate, esp. by using a button or SWITCH: *He turned on the TV.* | (fig.) *She turns on her charm whenever she wants anything.* —see OPEN² (USAGE)   **3** [T] (**turn on** sthg.) to depend on: [+*v-ing*] *The success of the negotiations turns on getting the agreement of the Italian delegation.*   **4** [T] (**turn on** sbdy.) also **turn upon** sbdy.— to attack suddenly and without warning   **5** [T] (**turn** sbdy. ↔ **on**) *infml* to excite or interest strongly, and often sexually —see also TURN-ON   **6** [I;T (=**turn** sbdy. ↔ **on**)] **a** *sl* to (cause to) take an illegal drug, esp. for the first time: *He turned her on to cocaine.* **b** to (cause to) find (something useful or interesting): *My uncle turned me on to these new plant holders.*

turn out *phr v*   **1** [T] (**turn** sthg. ↔ **out**) to stop the operation of (a light) by turning a SWITCH: *Turn the light out.*   **2** [T] (**turn** sbdy. ↔ **out**) to force to leave; send away: *Her father turned her out (of the house) when she became pregnant.*   **3** [I] to come out or gather (as if) for a meeting, public event, etc.: *Enormous crowds turned out for the procession.* —see also TURNOUT   **4** [T] (**turn** sthg. ↔ **out**) *infml* to produce; make: *This factory can turn out 100 cars a day.*   **5** [T] (**turn** sthg. ↔ **out**) to clear or empty the contents of (a cupboard, drawer, etc.): *The policeman told him to turn out his pockets.*   **6** [L] to happen to be, or be found to be, in the end: *It's turned out nice and sunny again.* | *The party turned out a success.* (=although we thought it might not be) [+*to-v*] *To our surprise the stranger turned out to be* (=we discovered that he was) *an old friend of my mother's.* | *His statement turned out to be false./It turned out that his statement was false.*   **7** *esp. BrE* **turned out** well/badly dressed —see also TURNOUT (2)

turn (sbdy./sthg. ↔) **over** *phr v*   **1** [T] to think about carefully; consider in various ways: *She turned the problem over in her mind.*   **2** [T (**to**)] to deliver into the possession or control of someone else, esp. the police: *They turned the wanted man over to the authorities.* | *The confidential report has been turned over to the President.* | *He turned the business over to his two children.*   **3** [T] to do business or sell goods worth (the stated amount): *The store is currently turning over £1000 a week.* —see also TURNOVER (2)   **4** [I;T] to run or cause (an engine) to run at lowest speed —see also TURN¹ (2)

turn sthg. **round** *BrE* ∥ **around** *AmE*— *phr v* [T] to complete the processing of: *our company can turn round a batch of 50 pressings inside two hours*

turn to *phr v*   **1** [T] (**turn to** sbdy./sthg.) to go to for help, advice, sympathy, comfort, etc.: *I can't tell my parents about it; I don't know who to turn to.* | *In his desperation, he turned to drink.* (=alcohol)   **2** [T] (**turn to** sthg.) to look at (the stated page) in a book   **3** [I] *old-fash* to begin work; work hard: *The committee turned to and soon produced a plan.*

turn (sbdy./sthg. ↔) **up** *phr v*   **1** [T] to increase the force, speed, loudness, etc., of (something) by using controls: *Turn the radio up; I can't hear it.* —opposite **turn down**   **2** [I] to be found after being lost, esp. without being searched for: *The missing bag turned up, completely empty, in the lake.* —see also TURN-UP   **3** [I] to arrive; make one's appearance: *She turns up late for everything.*   **4** [I] to happen, esp. unexpectedly and fortunately: *Don't worry, something's sure to turn up.*   **5** [T] to find by thoroughly searching; UNEARTH: *The police have turned up a lot of new information about the wanted man.* **6** [T] ‖ usu. **take up** *AmE* to shorten (a garment) by folding up the bottom

turn upon sbdy. *phr v* [T] to TURN **on** (4)

turn² *n* **1** [C] an act of turning; single movement completely round a fixed point: *Don't pull the handle; give it a turn.* **2** [C] a change of direction: *a turn in the river* | *Make a left turn after the bank.* —see also TURNING **3** [C] a place or appointed time in a fixed order, that gives one the chance or duty to do something: *You've missed your turn so you'll have to wait.* | *He asked each of us in turn.* [+to-v] *It's my turn to drive next.* | *You can't all do it together; you'll have to* **take turns/take it in turns.** (=do it one after the other) **4** [*the*+S **(of**)] a point of change in time: *He was born at the turn of the century.* (e.g., in about 1899 or 1900) **5** [S] a change from an existing situation or condition; new development: *I'm afraid she's* **taken a turn for the worse.** (=has become more ill) | *There's been an unusual* **turn of events.** (=something unusual has happened) **6** [S] a particular style, habit, or tendency: *He was of a melancholy* **turn of mind.** (=was sad by nature) | *She has a witty* **turn of phrase.** (=can express things in a clever funny way) **7** [S] *infml* a sudden shock: *You gave me quite a turn when you shouted out like that.* **8** [C] *infml* a sudden attack of illness: *She's had one of her funny turns again.* **9 a good/bad turn** an action that has a good or helpful/bad or unhelpful effect on someone: *She* **did me a good turn** *by lending me that money.* **10 at every turn** in every place or at every moment; continually: *The committee of inquiry was frustrated at every turn, and was unable to discover the truth.* **11 by turns** also **turn and turn about**— one after another; in order **12 cooked/done to a turn** (of food) perfectly cooked: *The steak was done to a turn.* **13 in turn** afterwards in the correct or expected order: *I told Frank and he in (his) turn told Sheila.* **14 one good turn deserves another** *saying* one should express one's gratefulness for a kind or helpful act by doing a similar one in return **15 on the turn: a** about to turn or change: *The tide is on the turn.* | *Public opinion on this issue seems to be on the turn.* **b** (of milk) on the point of becoming sour **16 out of turn** at an unsuitable time or in an unsuitable way: *I hope I haven't* **spoken out of turn**; *I didn't know it was supposed to be secret.*

turn·a·bout /ˈtɜːnəbaʊt‖ˈtɜːrn-/ *n* **1** also **turnaround**— an act of turning in a different or opposite direction: (fig.) *The government's sudden turnabout on unemployment has caused some confusion.* **2 turnabout is fair play** *AmE saying* one deserves a chance to do or try what one has seen another person do (usu. said when someone has expressed surprise at one's actions)

turn·a·round /ˈtɜːnəraʊnd‖ˈtɜːrn-/ *n esp. AmE* **1** *for* TURN-ROUND and TURNABOUT **2** a place for a vehicle to turn around, esp. at the end of a street

turn·coat /ˈtɜːnkəʊt‖ˈtɜːrn-/ *n derog* someone who changes their party, moral principles, or loyalty

turn·cock /ˈtɜːnkɒk‖ˈtɜːrnkɑːk/ *n* a STOPCOCK

turn·er /ˈtɜːnəʳ‖ˈtɜːr-/ *n* a person who shapes wood or metal on a LATHE —see also TURN¹ (12)

Turner , Jo·seph Mal·lord Wil·liam /ˈdʒəʊzɪf ˈmæləd ˈwɪljəm‖-ˈmælərd-/ (1775–1851) an English LANDSCAPE painter who used large areas of light and colour to express the effects of the forces of nature, as in his famous painting *The Fighting Téméraire*

Turner, Nat /næt/ (1800–31) an American slave who led a successful REBELLION by slaves against their masters and was hanged for his part in this

Turner, Tina /ˈtiːnə/ (1938–) an American popular music singer who first became successful with her husband Ike. They separated in 1974 and 10 years later that she became successful again, esp. in live concerts. —see colour picture on page 554

Turner Broad·cast·ing Sys·tem /ˌ·· ˈ··· ˌ··/ [*the*] also **TBS**— an American television company based in Atlanta, Georgia, whose programmes are shown mostly on CABLE and SATELLITE television

turn·ing /ˈtɜːnɪŋ‖ˈtɜːr-/ *BrE* ‖ **turn** *AmE*— *n* a place where one road branches off from another: *Go down the road, and take the first turning on the right.*

turning cir·cle /ˈ·· ˌ··/ *n* the smallest circle round which

a motor vehicle can be driven: *Although it's a big car it has a surprisingly small turning circle.*

turning point /ˈ·· ·/ *n* a point in time at which a very important change takes place: *a turning point in our country's industrial development*

tur·nip /ˈtɜːnɪp‖ˈtɜːr-/ *n* [C;U] (a plant producing) a large round yellowish or white root which is used as a vegetable

turn·key¹ /ˈtɜːnkiː‖ˈtɜːrn-/ *n old use for* JAILER

turnkey² *adj* [A] constructed and/or delivered ready to operate: *a turnkey project for a nuclear plant* | *turnkey computer systems*

turn-off /ˈ·· ·/ *n* **1** a smaller road branching off from a main road —see also TURN **off** (3) **2** *infml* something that causes one to feel dislike or lose interest, esp. sexually —see also TURN **off** (4,5)

Turn of the Screw /ˌ· ··· ˈ·/, **The** a GHOST story by Henry James in which a woman believes that evil dead people are influencing two children she is caring for

turn-on /ˈ· ·/ *n infml* something that excites or interests one strongly, esp. sexually —see also TURN **on** (5)

turn·out /ˈtɜːnaʊt‖ˈtɜːrn-/ *n* **1 a** the number of people who attend a gathering; ATTENDANCE **b** the number of people who actually vote at an election: *Intense interest in the election ensured a* **high turnout.** —see also TURN **out** (3) **2** [*usu. sing.*] *infml* the manner or style in which a person is dressed: *a colourful turnout* —see also TURN **out** (7) **3** *AmE* a wide place in a narrow road where cars can pass or park

turn·o·ver /ˈtɜːnˌəʊvəʳ‖ˈtɜːrn-/ *n* **1** [S] the rate at which a particular kind of article is sold: *These new products have had a quick turnover.* (=many have been sold in a short time) **2** [S] the amount of business done in a particular period, measured in money: *The shop has a turnover of £5000 a week.* —see also TURN **over** (3) **3** [S] the rate at which workers leave a company or organization and new workers are employed to take their places: *They have a very high turnover of staff because their working conditions are so bad.* **4** [C] a small fruit PIE: *an apple turnover* —compare POPOVER **5** *AmE* an act of a team's losing possession of the ball (in football or BASKETBALL) because of breaking the rules

turn·pike /ˈtɜːnpaɪk‖ˈtɜːrn-/ *also* **pike, turnpike road** /ˌ·· ˈ·/— *n* **1** *AmE* a main road for the use of fast-travelling traffic, esp. one which drivers must pay to use **2** (formerly in Britain) a road which travellers had to pay to use —see EXPRESSWAY (USAGE)

turn·round /ˈtɜːnraʊnd‖ˈtɜːrn-/ *BrE* ‖ **turnaround** *esp. AmE*— *n* **1** (the time taken for) receiving and dealing with something and sending it back, esp. the arrival, unloading, reloading, and leaving of a plane, ship, etc. —see also TURN **round 2** [*usu. sing.*] a change to an opposite and usu. better situation: *The turnround in the football club's fortunes dates from the day they got their new manager.*

turn·stile /ˈtɜːnstaɪl‖ˈtɜːrn-/ *n* a small gate with arms spinning round on a central post, set in an entrance to let people in one at a time, usu. after payment —see picture at STILE

turn·stone /ˈtɜːnstəʊn‖ˈtɜːrn-/ *n* a small bird which lives by the sea and turns over stones, looking for small animals to eat

turn·ta·ble /ˈtɜːnˌteɪbəl‖ˈtɜːrn-/ *n* **1** the round spinning surface on which a record is placed to be played **2** a large flat round surface, sunk into the ground, onto which railway engines run to be turned round

turn-up /ˈ· ·/ *n* **1** [C] *BrE* ‖ **cuff** *AmE*— a narrow band of cloth turned upwards at the bottom of a trouser leg **2** [S] also **turn-up for the book** /ˌ· ···· ˈ·/— *BrE infml* an unexpected and surprising event

tur·pen·tine /ˈtɜːpəntaɪn‖ˈtɜːr-/ *also* **turps** /tɜːps‖tɜːrps/ *BrE infml*— *n* [U] a thin oil made from the wood of certain trees, used for removing unwanted paint from clothes, brushes, etc., for mixing with paint to make it thinner, and in medicine

Tur·pin /ˈtɜːpɪn‖ˈtɜːr-/ , **Dick** (1706–39) an English HIGH-WAYMAN who was hanged at York, but who later came to be seen as a popular HERO

tur·pi·tude /ˈtɜːpɪˌtjuːd ‖ ˈtɜːrpɪˌtuːd/ *n* [U] *fml or pomp* shameful wickedness: *gross moral turpitude*

tur·quoise¹ /ˈtɜːkwɔɪz, -kwɑːz‖ˈtɜːrkwɔɪz/ n [C;U] (a shaped piece of) a precious greenish-blue mineral. Turquoise is often used in Native American jewellery.

turquoise² adj of the colour of turquoise

tur·ret /ˈtʌrət‖-/ n 1 a small tower, usu. at a corner of a larger building and usu. either decorative or for defence —see picture at CASTLE 2 a low heavily armoured metal DOME on a TANK (2), plane, warship, etc., that spins round to allow its guns to be aimed in any direction − ~ed adj

tur·tle /ˈtɜːtl‖ˈtɜːrtl/ n turtles or turtle 1 an animal that lives esp. in water and has a soft body covered by a hard bony shell into which the head, legs, and tail can be pulled for protection —compare TORTOISE; see also MOCK TURTLE SOUP, and see picture at TORTOISE 2 turn turtle (of a ship) to turn over; CAPSIZE

tur·tle·dove /ˈtɜːtldʌv‖ˈtɜːr-/ n a bird with a pleasant soft cry, whose males and females are supposed to love each other very much

tur·tle·neck /ˈtɜːtlnek‖ˈtɜːr-/ n esp. AmE (a garment with) a POLO NECK

turves /tɜːvz‖tɜːrvz/ n pl. of TURF¹

Tus·ca·ny /ˈtʌskəni/ a REGION in N central Italy; capital Florence. Tuscany is famous for its Chianti wine and is a popular place for middle-class British people to go for a holiday

tush¹ /tʌʃ/ interj old use (an expression of dissatisfaction usu. mixed with blame)

tush² n AmE sl for BOTTOM¹ (3)

tusk /tʌsk/ n a very long pointed tooth, usu. one of a pair, that comes out beyond the mouth in certain animals, esp. the elephant

Tus·ke·gee In·sti·tute /tʌsˈkiːgi ˌɪnstɪ̩tjuːt‖-tuːt/ [the] one of the first colleges for black people in the US. It was started by Booker T WASHINGTON in 1881 in Tuskegee, Alabama

tusk·er /ˈtʌskər/ n infml an elephant

Tus·saud /təˈsɔːd‖tuˈsou/, **Ma·rie** /ˈmɑːri‖məˈriː/ (1760–1850) a Swiss woman who made models of people in WAX, including famous people guillotined (GUILLOTINE) in the French Revolution. In 1802 she established Madame Tussaud's in London. —see also MADAME TUSSAUD'S

tus·sle¹ /ˈtʌsəl/ v [I (with)] infml to fight roughly without weapons; struggle roughly

tussle² n infml a rough struggle or fight: After quite a tussle we beat them by one point.

tus·sock /ˈtʌsək/ n a small thick mass of grass

tut interj (the sound like a /t/ made by sucking rather than forcing air out, and often read as /tʌt/, used for expressing slight disapproval or annoyance): Tut (tut)! I've got some chalk on my coat.

Tu·tan·kha·men, Tutankha- **Tutankhamen**
mon /ˌtuːtənˈkɑːmən/ (14th century BC) an Egyptian PHARAOH (=ruler) whose burial place and the valuable things in it were discovered in 1922. Many of these things can now be seen in London.

tu·te·lage /ˈtjuːtɪlɪdʒ‖ˈtuː-/ n [U] fml 1 instruction; teaching: He made good progress under her tutelage. 2 the state or period of being under someone's care and protection 3 responsibility for someone, their education, property, actions, etc.; protection

tu·te·la·ry /ˈtjuːtɪləri‖ˈtuːtɪleri/ adj [A] fml or tech providing protection; acting as a GUARDIAN: tutelary deities

tu·tor¹ /ˈtjuːtər‖ˈtuː-/ n 1 a teacher who gives private instruction to a single pupil or to a very small class and who sometimes lives with the family of his or her pupil: a maths/French tutor | a piano tutor 2 (in British universities and colleges) a teacher who directs the studies of a number of students and/or is responsible for giving them advice about personal matters

tutor² v [T (in)] fml to act as a tutor to; give instruction to —see TEACH (USAGE)

tu·to·ri·al¹ /tjuːˈtɔːriəl‖tuː-/ n (esp. in British universities

and colleges) a period of instruction given by a TUTOR¹ (2): I've got a tutorial at 2.00.

tutorial² adj fml of a tutor or his/her duties

tut·ti frut·ti /ˌtuːti ˈfruːti/ n, adj [U] (ice cream) with very small pieces of mixed fruit and crushed nuts mixed in

tut-tut¹ /ˌ· ˈ·/ interj TUT

tut-tut² /ˌtʌt ˈtʌt/ v -tt- [I] infml to express impatience, annoyance, disapproval, etc., by saying tut-tut

tu·tu /ˈtuːtuː/ n a short skirt made of many folds of stiffened material worn by women BALLET dancers

Tutu, Des·mond /ˈdezmənd/ (1931–) a South African ARCHBISHOP and a strong opponent of APARTHEID. Archbishop Tutu received the Nobel Prize for peace in 1984.

Tu·va·lu /tuːˈvɑːluː/ a nation in the S Pacific Ocean, E of the Solomon Islands, made up of nine low CORAL islands; capital Fongafale on Funafuti; population 9,000 (1989). Tuvalu was formerly called the **Ellice Islands**.

tu-whit tu-whoo /tə ˌwɪt tə ˈwuː/ interj the sound made by an OWL

tux·e·do /tʌkˈsiːdəʊ/ also **tux** /tʌks/infml— n -dos AmE a man's jacket, usu. black, worn on formal occasions, e.g. weddings; a DINNER JACKET —see picture at EVENING DRESS

TV /ˌtiː ˈviː◂/ n [C;U] (a) television: What's on TV tonight? | This film was made for TV. | a TV presenter

TV-AM /ˌtiː viː eɪ ˈem/ a British independent television company which made BREAKFAST TELEVISION programmes

TV din·ner /ˌ· ˈ··/ n a complete dinner conveniently frozen in a packet, that only needs to be heated for a short time before eating

tv e·van·ge·list /ˌ· · · ˈ···/ see TELEVANGELIST

TV Guide /ˌ· ˈ·/ n a US weekly magazine which gives details and times of television programmes

TVP /ˌtiː viː ˈpiː/ n [U] TEXTURED VEGETABLE PROTEIN

TV Times /ˌ· · ˈ·/ n a British weekly magazine which gives details and times of television programmes as well as articles about television stars and programmes

twad·dle /ˈtwɒdl‖ˈtwɑːdl/ n [U] fml foolish talk or writing; nonsense

twain /tweɪn/ n [(the) U] old use or poet (a set of) two; pair: "East is East, and West is West, and never the twain shall meet." (Rudyard Kipling)

Twain , Mark (1835–1910) an American writer and HUMORIST, best known for his NOVELs The Adventures of Tom Sawyer and The Adventures of Huckleberry Finn, and for his descriptions of life on the Mississippi River. His real name was Samuel Longhorne Clemens.

twang¹ /twæŋ/ n 1 a quick ringing such as the sound made by pulling, then suddenly freeing, a very tight string or wire 2 [usu. sing.] a quality of sound of human speech produced by pronouncing the words at the back of the mouth or through the nose: He spoke with a nasal twang.

twang² v [I;T] to (cause to) make a twang: to twang a ruler/a guitar string

'twas /twɒz‖twɑːz/ short for: (old use or poet) it was

twat /twɒt, twæt‖twɑːt/ n taboo sl 1 old-fash the female sex organ 2 BrE an unpleasant or foolish person

tweak /twiːk/ v [T] infml 1 to take hold of, pull, and twist (esp. the ear or nose) with a sudden movement 2 to make small changes to (something such as a car engine or computer PROGRAM) in order to improve its performance —tweak n : He gave her ear a friendly little tweak.

twee /twiː/ adj BrE infml too delicate or pretty; unpleasantly DAINTY: That painting of little cottages with lace curtains is rather twee.

tweed /twiːd/ n [U] a rough woollen cloth woven from threads of several different colours used mostly to make JACKETs, suits, and coats: a tweed suit —see also HARRIS TWEED

Tweed [the] a river in S Scotland and NE England, rising in the Borders REGION of Scotland and flowing to the North Sea at Berwick-upon-Tweed

Twee·dle·dum and Twee·dle·dee /ˌtwiːdlˌdʌm ənd twiːdlˈdiː/ two characters in Lewis Carroll's Through the Looking-Glass, who are fat, always quarrelling, and look exactly like each other. Their names are often used to describe two people or groups who are almost exactly the same as one another, esp. when one seems to be as bad as the other: *There seems to be little to choose between the Tweedledum of one party and the Tweedledee of the other.*

tweeds /twi:dz/ *n* [P] (a suit of) tweed clothes, associated esp. with upper class people who live in the country

tweed·y /ˈtwi:di/ *adj* **1** of or like tweed **2** *BrE often rather derog* dressed frequently in tweeds, or seeming to show a liking for healthy outdoor activities in the country: *tweedy ladies with thick leather walking shoes*

'tween /twi:n/ *prep poet* between

tweet /twi:t/ *v* [I] to make the short weak high noise of a small bird; CHIRP —**tweet** *n*

tweet·er /ˈtwi:tər/ *n* a LOUDSPEAKER that gives out high sounds —compare WOOFER

twee·zers /ˈtwi:zəz/ *n* [P] a small tool made from two narrow pieces of metal joined at one end, used for picking up, pulling out, and handling very small objects: *He pulled out the splinter with tweezers.* —see PAIR (USAGE)

twelfth /twelfθ/ *determiner, adv, n, pron* 12th —see TABLE 1; see also GLORIOUS TWELFTH

twelfth man /ˌ· ˈ·/ *n* [(the)] the member of a cricket team who plays if any other member of the team is hurt or cannot play

Twelfth Night /ˌ· ˈ·/ **1** the evening before EPIPHANY, formerly a time of great celebrations to mark the end of the CHRISTMAS period **2** a humorous play by William Shakespeare

twelve /twelv/ *determiner, n, pron* **1** (the number) 12 —see TABLE 1; see also DOZEN **2 twelve good men and true** a phrase used to describe the twelve people on a JURY

twelve·month /ˈtwelvmʌnθ/ *n* [S] *old-fash* a year

12-step pro·gram /ˌtwelv step ˈprəʊgræm/ *n AmE* RECOVERY PROGRAM

twen·ties /ˈtwentiz/ [P] *n* **1** [the] also **'20's**— the 1920s (—the years from 1920 to 1929): *Fitzgerald wrote about the lifestyle of wealthy Americans in the twenties.* **2 in his/her/their twenties** aged from 20 to 29: *She has three sons, all in their twenties.* **3** [the] the numbers from 20 to 29

20th Cen·tu·ry-Fox /ˌtwentiəθ sentʃəri ˈfɒks‖-ˈfɑːks/ *n* an American film production company

twen·ty /ˈtwenti/ *determiner, n, pron* (the number) 20 —see TABLE 1 —**tieth** *determiner, n, pron, adv*

twenty-first /ˌ·· ˈ·◂/ *n BrE infml* a person's twenty-first birthday, often celebrated as a special occasion, e.g. with a party, because, in the past, people were given the legal rights of adults only when they were 21. In Britain cards sent to people for their 21st birthday often show a picture of a key, standing for the "key of the door" i.e. the right to act independently of one's parents. —see also ADULT (CULTURAL NOTE)

24 hour clock /ˌtwenti fɔːr aʊə ˈklɒk ‖ -aʊər ˈklɑːk/ *n* a clock, or a system of telling the time, according to which, for example, one O'CLOCK in the afternoon is called 1300 hours (pronounced "13 hundred hours"): *The trains run according to the 24 hour clock.*

twenty-one /ˌ·· ˈ·◂/ *n* [U] *AmE for* BLACKJACK (1)

20 Ques·tions /ˌtwenti ˈkwestʃənz/ also **Animal, Vegetable, or Mineral** *AmE*— a game in which one person thinks of an object and others have to guess what it is by asking questions about which can be answered with yes or no

Twenty-Third Psalm , 23rd Psalm /ˌ·· ˈ·/ [the] a well-known PSALM in the Bible that begins with the words "The Lord is my Shepherd"

twenty-twenty vi·sion , 20/20 vision /ˌ··· ·· ˈ··/ *n* [U] perfect ability to see: *To be a pilot you must have twenty-twenty vision.*

twenty-two, ·22 /ˌtu: ˈtu/ *n AmE* a gun that takes a small bullet, used for hunting small animals

twerp, twirp /twɜːp‖twɜːrp/ *n infml* an annoying or silly person; fool

twice /twais/ *predeterminer, adv* two times: *I've read the book twice.* | *He was shot twice in the chest.* (=with two bullets) | *I work twice as hard as him.* | *He eats twice what you eat.* | *twice the amount that you eat.* | *Take the medicine twice a day.* | *performances twice daily* | *Since his holiday*

he's been twice the man he was. (=he's been a lot healthier, more able, etc.) —see also **once or twice** (ONCE[1]), **think twice** (THINK[1])

twice-told /ˌ· ˈ·◂/ *adj* [A] *lit or old-fash* already told before; well known: *a twice told tale*

Twick·en·ham /ˈtwɪkənəm/ an area in London famous as the place where the English Rugby Football Union ground is. RUGBY matches between England and Wales, Scotland, Ireland, and France take place there.

twid·dle[1] /ˈtwɪdl/ *v* **1** [I (**with**);T] to play with (something) with the hands, usu. purposelessly: *She irritated him by constantly twiddling (with) her pencil.* | *She twiddled the dial on the radio to see what stations she could pick up.* **2 twiddle one's thumbs** *infml* to do nothing useful or helpful; waste time

twiddle[2] *n infml* a small twist or turn, esp. a decorative or unnecessary one —**twiddly** *adj*

twig[1] /twɪg/ *n* a small very thin woody stem branching off from a branch on a tree or bush: *The bird built a nest from twigs.* —see also STICK[1] (1)

twig[2] *v* **-gg-** [I;T] *infml* to (suddenly) understand (a situation): *I dropped some hints, but he hasn't twigged yet.*

Twig·gy /ˈtwɪgi/ (1949–) an English model (Twiggy Lawson) who was popular esp. in the 1960s. She was known esp. for being very thin, and her appearance helped to spread the idea that thin women were very attractive. She is also an actress, and her films include *The Boyfriend.*

Twiggy

twi·light /ˈtwaɪlaɪt/ *n* [U] **1** the time when day is about to become night: (fig.) *old ladies in the twilight of their lives* | (fig.) *These secret agents occupy a* **twilight zone** *between legality and illegality.* **2** the faint darkish light in the sky during this time —compare DUSK —**-lit** /-lɪt/ *adj*

Twilight Zone /ˈ·· ˌ·/ an American television programme, shown from 1959 to 1963, which told a different story every week, usu. a FANTASY or SCIENCE FICTION one

twill /twɪl/ *n* [U] strong cloth woven to have parallel sloping lines across its surface

twin[1] /twɪn/ *n* **1** either of two children born of the same mother at the same time: *My brother and I look so alike that people often think we are twins.* | *Jean and John are twins.* —see also IDENTICAL TWIN, SIAMESE TWIN **2** either of two people or things closely related or connected, or very like each other —**twin** *adj* [A]: *a twin-engined plane* | *a policy to combat the* **twin** *problems of poverty and unemployment*

twin[2] *v* **-nn-** [T (**with**)] *esp. BrE* to join (a town) closely with another town in another country to encourage friendly relations: *Harlow in England is twinned with Stavanger in Norway.*

twin bed /ˌ· ˈ·/ *n* **1** [*usu. pl.*] either of a pair of single beds in a room for two people —see picture at BED **2** *AmE* a single bed —**twin-bedded** /ˌ· ˈ·◂/ *adj* : *a twin-bedded room*

Twin Cit·ies /ˌ· ˈ··/ [the+P] the American cities of Minneapolis and Saint Paul, in Minnesota

twine[1] /twaɪn/ *n* [U] strong cord or string made by twisting together two or more threads or strings: *a ball of twine*

twine[2] *v* [I+*adv/prep*;T] to twist or wind: *The stems of ivy twined round the tree trunk.* | *You make a rope by twining strings together.*

twinge /twɪndʒ/ *n* [(**of**)] a sudden sharp attack (of pain): *a twinge of toothache*|(fig.) *conscience*

Twi·nings /ˈtwaɪnɪŋz/ *tdmk* a British company that sells tea

Twin·kie /'twɪŋki/ n AmE tdmk a sweet, sticky, yellow cake filled with a white sugary substance, eaten as a SNACK

Twinkies

▶CULTURAL NOTE In a law case in the 1980s, a man who had shot and killed two public officials in San Francisco was defended in court on the grounds that his judgment was affected by eating too much sweet food. He won his case, and from it came the idea of the **Twinkie defence**, which people now use to describe a legal defence which uses strange and FAR-FETCHED arguments.◀

twin·kle¹ /'twɪŋkəl/ v [I] **1** to shine through darkness with a soft light that rapidly changes from bright to faint: *twinkling stars* **2** [(with)] (of the eyes) to be bright with cheerfulness, pleasure, amusement, etc.

twinkle² n [(the) S] **1** a repeated momentary bright shining of light **2** a brightness in the eyes from cheerfulness, pleasure, amusement, etc.: *"I'm only teasing you," he said with a twinkle in his eye.* **3 when you were just a twinkle in your father's eye** *infml humor* at a time before you were born

Twinkle, twinkle, lit·tle star /ˌ·· ˌ·· ˌ·· '·/ a NURSERY RHYME (=an old song or poem for children):
Twinkle, twinkle, little star,
How I wonder what you are.
Up above the world so high,
Like a diamond in the sky.

twin·kling /'twɪŋklɪŋ/ n **1** [S] *infml* a moment; very short period of time: *I'll be back in a twinkling.* **2 in the twinkling of an eye** in a very short time

twin·ning /'twɪnɪŋ/ n BrE the action or result of joining a town closely with another town in another country to encourage friendly relations: *She works for the Council and is responsible for twinning.* | *a very successful twinning, with frequent exchanges between the two towns' schools*

twin set /'· ·/ n BrE a woman's JUMPER (2) and CARDIGAN made to be worn together. Twin sets, often with a string of PEARLS, are associated with older, fairly upper-class, British women who support the Conservative party.

twin town /ˌ· '·/ n a town which has been twinned (TWIN²) with another: *Oxford's twin town Bonn*

twin-tub /'· ·/ n a type of washing machine with two parts, one for washing and the other for spin-drying: *I'm going to buy a twin-tub this time.*

twirl¹ /twɜːl‖twɜːrl/ v [I;T] to (cause to) turn round and round quickly; (cause to) spin or wind round: *twirling round the dance floor* | *He twirled the keys round his fingers.* — ~er n

twirl² n a sudden quick spin or circular movement —**twirly** adj

twirp /twɜːp‖twɜːrp/ n a TWERP

twist¹ /twɪst/ v **1** [I;T] to (cause to) change shape by bending, curling, or turning: *He twisted and turned, trying to free himself from the ropes.* | *Her face was twisted with pain.* | *The little girl twisted the wire into the shape of a star.* **2** [T+obj+adv/prep, esp. **round**, TOGETHER] to wind: *She twisted her hair round her fingers to make it curl.* | *Twist the two ends of the wire together.* (=join them by winding them round each other) **3** [I] to move in a winding course: *a twisting mountain road* **4** [T] to turn, esp. with a movement of the hand: *Twist that knob to the right and the box will open.* | *He twisted the cap off the bottle.* | *She twisted her head round to try and see what was happening.* **5** [T] to hurt (a joint or limb) by pulling and turning it sharply: *He's twisted his ankle.* **6** [T] *derog* to change the true or intended meaning of (a statement, words, etc.): *The newspapers deliberately twisted her words to make her look guilty.* **7 twist someone round one's little finger** *infml* to get someone to do whatever one wants; be able to persuade or influence someone to do anything **8 twist someone's arm: a** to bend someone's arm up and behind their back to cause pain **b** to persuade someone to do what one wants, by threats or by making a very forceful request

twist² n **1** [C] an act of twisting **2** [C] a bend: *a road with a lot of twists and turns in it* **3** [C] an unexpected change or development: *By a strange twist of fate they both died*

of the same disease. | *There's an unusual twist at the end of the book — the detective is murdered.* **4** [C] something made by twisting two or more lengths together: *a twist of tobacco* (=a roll of tobacco leaves twisted together) **5** [the+S] a dance, popular in the 1960s, in which the dancers twist their bodies in time with fast noisy music **6** [C] a small piece of LEMON or LIME put in an alcoholic drink **7 round the twist** BrE infml mad —see also **get one's knickers in a twist** (KNICKERS¹) —**twisty** adj : a twisty road

Twist , Ol·i·ver /ˈɒlɪvəʳ‖-ˈɑːr-/ the main character in Charles Dickens' NOVEL *Oliver Twist*. Oliver is a poor boy who lives in a WORKHOUSE. The most famous scene in the book is when he holds out his bowl and asks for more food. —see also OLIVER TWIST

twist·ed /'twɪstɟd/ adj having unnatural and wicked feelings or desires: *a twisted mind/personality*

twist·er /'twɪstəʳ/ n infml **1** a dishonest person who cheats other people **2** AmE for TORNADO or WHIRLWIND —see also TONGUE TWISTER

twist-tie /'· ·/ n a short piece of thin wire, covered in paper or plastic, which is twisted around the open end of a plastic bag to close it

twit¹ /twɪt/ n infml a stupid fool

twit² v -tt- [T (**about, on, with**)] BrE old-fash to make fun of (someone) because of their foolish behaviour, a mistake, a fault, etc.; RIDICULE

twitch¹ /twɪtʃ/ v **1** [I;T] to (cause to) make a quick short sudden movement, usu. without conscious control: *Your eye is twitching.* | *The horse twitched its ears.* | *His face twitched with pain.* **2** [T] to give a sudden quick pull to (something); JERK

twitch² n an act of twitching, esp. a repeated short sudden movement of a muscle, done without conscious control: *a nervous twitch* —compare TIC

twitch·y /'twɪtʃi/ adj anxious about something and so behaving in a nervous way: *What are you so twitchy about?* | *I get twitchy for a cigarette if I don't have one for a couple of hours.*

twit·ter¹ /'twɪtəʳ/ v [I] **1** (of a bird) to make a number of short rapid sounds **2** [(**on, about**)] infml derog (of a person) to talk rapidly (as if) from nervous excitement: *He's always twittering on about unimportant things.*

twitter² n **1** [(the) S;U] short high rapid sounds made by birds **2** [S] infml a state of nervous excitement: *She's been all of a twitter since her daughter announced her engagement to the prince.* —**tery** adj

Twit·ty /'twɪti/, **Con·way** /'kɒnweɪ‖'kɑːn-/ (1933–93) an American COUNTRY AND WESTERN singer

twixt /twɪkst/ prep pomp or poet between

two /tuː/ determiner, n, pron **1** (the number) 2: *I've got one brother and two sisters.* | *twenty-two* (=22) | *two-thirds* (=⅔) | *a two-year jail sentence* | *He couldn't decide which violin to buy as he liked the two of them equally well.* | *Let's divide/break it* in two. (=into two parts) —see TABLE 1 **2 put two and two together (and make four/five)** infml to guess the meaning of what one sees or hears (and come to the correct/wrong answer): *"How did you know I was going abroad?" "I saw you had a travel book about Spain, and put two and two together."* **3 That makes two of us** I am in the same position as you: *"I think I'm getting a cold." "That makes two of us."* **4 Two can play at 'that game** (used as a threat) You are not the only one who can get advantages by behaving like that; I can too! **5 two's company, three's a crowd** saying a third person is not wanted by two people who are happy together: *I won't come to the cinema with you and Sharon; two's company, three's a crowd.* **6 Two wrongs don't make a right** saying an evil act is not put right or made good by doing another evil act —see also **one or two** (ONE¹), **be two/ten a penny** (PENNY)

two-bit /'· ·/ adj [A] **1** AmE infml derog of small importance; INSIGNIFICANT **2 two-bit piece** old-fash a quarter; 25c

two-by-four, 2 × 4 /ˌ· · '·/ n a piece of wood of any length that is about two inches thick and four inches wide. It is the standard size of wood for housebuilding in the US.

two cents /ˌ· '·/ n AmE **1** a very small amount of money: *I wouldn't give you two cents for that old beater.* **2 two cents worth** one's (unwelcome) opinion about a subject being discussed: *Here comes Robert, I suppose we'll have to hear his two cents worth.*

2CV /ˌtuː siː ˈviː/ n see DEUX-CHEVAUX

two-edged /ˌ· ˈ·◁/ adj 1 having two cutting edges: *a two-edged sword* 2 having two possible meanings or results, one favourable and one unfavourable: *a two-edged argument*

two-faced /ˌtuː ˈfeɪst◁/ adj derog deceitful or insincere

two-hand·ed /ˌ· ˈ···◁/ adj 1 used with or using both hands: *a heavy two-handed sword* | *the tennis player's two-handed backhand* 2 (esp. of a tool) worked by or needing two people: *a two-handed saw*

two-line whip /ˌ· ˈ· ˈ·/ n an order given to Members of the British Parliament which is less urgent than a THREE-LINE WHIP

two-min·ute si·lence /ˌ· ··· ˈ···/ n a period of two minutes at 11 o'clock on Remembrance Sunday, in which people in Britain remain silent to remember the people who died in the two World Wars

two-one /ˌ· ˈ·/ n (in Britain) the higher of the two levels of a second-class university degree: *He got a two-one.* — see DEGREE (CULTURAL NOTE)

two·pence also **tuppence** BrE /ˈtʌpəns‖ˈtʌpəns, ˈtuːpens/ n 1 [U] two pence (old or new) 2 [C] a British coin worth two pence: the twopence is a silver coin, now used only as MAUNDY MONEY 3 **not care/give twopence** BrE infml not to care at all 4 **not give someone twopence for** BrE infml not to be interested in having

two·pen·ny also **tuppenny** BrE infml /ˈtʌpəni‖ˈtʌpəni, ˈtuːpeni/ adj [A] 1 costing two pence 2 also **twopenny-half·pen·ny** /ˌ··· ˈ···/— BrE infml almost worthless; of very little value

two-per·cent milk /ˌ· ··· ˈ·/ n [U] AmE for SEMI-SKIMMED MILK

two-piece /ˌ· ˈ·◁/ adj [A] consisting of two matching parts: *a two-piece suit* (=with JACKET and trousers)

two-ply /ˌ· ˈ·/ adj consisting of two sets of thread or two thicknesses: *two-ply tissues*

Two Ron·nies /ˌtuː ˈrɒniz‖-ˈrɑː-/, **The** a popular British television COMEDY programme of the 1970s, which had Ronnie Corbett and Ronnie Barker as the main performers

two·some /ˈtuːsəm/ n [usu. sing.] infml two people or things; pair: *John and Helen make a nice twosome, don't you think?*

two-star /ˈ· ·/ adj [A] of a fairly good standard or quality: *a two-star restaurant*

two-step /ˈ· ·/ n (a piece of music for) a dance with long sliding steps

two-stroke /ˈ· ·/ adj, n (of, being, or powered by) an INTERNAL-COMBUSTION ENGINE in which all the events happening inside the engine are completed in one up-and-down movement of a PISTON —compare FOUR-STROKE

Two Thou·sand Guin·eas, **2000 Guineas** /ˌ· ··· ˈ···/ [the] a famous British horse race run at Newmarket

two-time /ˈ· ·/ v [T] infml to be unfaithful to (a girlfriend or boyfriend) by having a secret relationship with someone else —**two-timer** n

two-tone /ˈ· ·/ adj [A] coloured in two colours or in two varieties of one colour: *two-tone shoes*

two-two /ˌ· ˈ·/ n (in Britain) the lower of the two levels of a second-class university degree: *He only got a two-two.* —see DEGREE (CULTURAL NOTE)

two-way /ˌ· ˈ·◁/ adj 1 moving or allowing movement in both directions: *a two-way street* | *two-way traffic* 2 (of radio equipment) for sending and receiving signals

two-way mir·ror /ˌ· · ˈ···/ n a mirror that can be seen through when looked at from the back, used for watching people secretly

TX written abbrev. for: TEXAS

ty·coon /taɪˈkuːn/ n a businessman or industrialist with great wealth and power: *a business tycoon*

ty·ing /ˈtaɪ-ɪŋ/ present participle of TIE

Ty·le·nol /ˈtaɪlənɒl‖-nɔːl/ n tdmk a medicine that reduces pain and fever; it does not contain ASPIRIN

Ty·ler /ˈtaɪləʳ/, **John** (1790–1862) the president of the US from 1841 to 1845

Tyler, **Wat** /wɒt‖wɑːt/ (died 1381) an English REBEL who led the PEASANTS' REVOLT

tym·pa·num /ˈtɪmpənəm/ n -na /nə/ or -nums med for EARDRUM

Tyn·dale /ˈtɪndəl/, **William** (1492–1536) an English translator of the Bible

Tyne /taɪn/ [the] a river in NE England, flowing through Newcastle-upon-Tyne to the North Sea —see colour map on page 818

Tyne and Wear /ˌtaɪn ənd ˈwɪəʳ/ a METROPOLITAN COUNTY in NE England, made up of parts of Northumberland and Durham, and including Newcastle-upon-Tyne

Tyne·side /ˈtaɪnsaɪd/ the built-up area on the banks of the Tyne from Newcastle-upon-Tyne to the E coast. Tyneside is noted for its failing industries, such as building ships and digging for coal, and for unemployment.

Tyne-Tees /ˈ· ˌ·/ one of the British television companies controlled by the ITC, sending out programmes to NE England

Tyn·wald /ˈtɪnwəld/ [the] the parliament of the Isle of Man

type[1] /taɪp/ n 1 [C (**of**)] a particular kind, class, or group; group or class of people or things that share certain qualities and are different from those outside the group or class: *a new/common type of camera* | *Macaroni is a type of pasta.* | *What type of plant is this?* | *She's the type of person I admire.* | *I like Italian-type ice cream.* | *The store sells most types of wine.* | *There have been several incidents of this type in recent weeks.* —see also TYPICAL 2 [C;U] (any of the) small blocks of metal or wood with raised letters on them, used in printing 3 [U] printed letters: *italic type* 4 [C] a person of the stated kind: *She's an odd type.* | *a sporty type* | *He's not really my type.* (=the sort of person that attracts me) 5 fml a person or thing that has all the features of a particular group or class; standard example —see also **bad type** (BAD[1] (9)), **true to type** (TRUE[1])

type[2] v 1 [I;T] to write with a typewriter or using a WORD PROCESSOR: *He types with only two fingers.* —see also TYPIST 2 [T] tech to find out the type of (something): *The doctor was unable to type the rare disease.*

type·cast /ˈtaɪpkɑːst‖-kæst/ v [T] to repeatedly give (an actor) the same kind of part: *He's been typecast as a murderer because he looks rather sinister.*

type·face /ˈtaɪpfeɪs/ also **face**— n a group of letters, numbers, and other characters of the same size and style used in printing

type·script /ˈtaɪpˌskrɪpt/ n a typewritten copy of something, esp. as prepared for being printed

type·set·ter /ˈtaɪpˌsetəʳ/ n a person or machine that arranges or sets type for printing

type·set·ting /ˈtaɪpsetɪŋ/ n [U] the activity or profession of arranging type for printing. *She works in typesetting.* | *How much will the typesetting for this cost?*

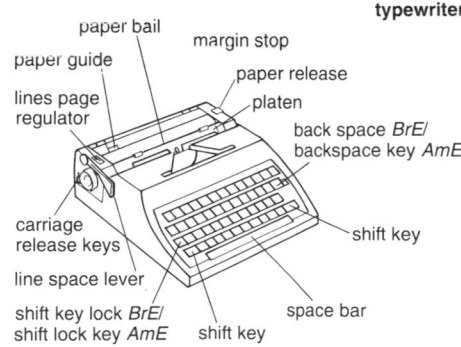

typewriter

paper bail
margin stop
paper guide
paper release
lines page regulator
platen
back space BrE/
backspace key AmE
carriage release keys
shift key
line space lever
shift key lock BrE/
shift lock key AmE
shift key
space bar

type·writ·er /ˈtaɪpˌraɪtəʳ/ n a machine that prints letters by means of keys which when struck by the fingers press onto paper through a long narrow piece of ink-filled material (RIBBON): *an electric/portable typewriter*

type·writ·ten /ˈtaɪpˌrɪtn/ adj written using a typewriter

ty·phoid /ˈtaɪfɔɪd/ also **typhoid fe·ver** /ˌ· ··· ˈ···/ fml— n [U]

a serious infectious disease that attacks the bowel, causing fever, severe discomfort, and often death, produced by bacteria that get into the body by means of food or drink

Typhoid Ma·ry /ˌ⋯ ˈ⋯/ (died 1938) an Irishwoman in the US who was found to be a carrier of typhoid, and thought to have infected many people with it. The name is sometimes used to describe a person who is expected to cause widespread trouble and is therefore avoided.

Ty·phoo /taɪˈfuː/ n tdmk [U] a well-known kind of tea sold in Britain

ty·phoon /taɪˈfuːn/ n a very violent tropical storm with a circular wind in the western Pacific —compare CYCLONE, HURRICANE; see STORM (USAGE)

ty·phus /ˈtaɪfəs/ n [U] an infectious disease, carried by lice (LOUSE) and FLEAS, that causes severe fever, very bad headaches, red spots over the body, and nervous sickness

typ·i·cal /ˈtɪpɪkəl/ adj [(of)] **1** showing the main signs or qualities of a particular kind, group, or class; representative of its type: *a typical British summer* | *a typical 18th century church* | *This painting is fairly typical of his early work.* **2** showing the usual behaviour or manner; CHARACTERISTIC: *It was typical of him to be so rude.* | *(infml) "I'm afraid I forgot your book again." "Typical!"*

typ·i·cally /ˈtɪpɪkli/ adv **1** in a typical manner: *He's typically American.* **2** in a typical case or in typical conditions: *Typically, he would come in late and then say he had to go early.* | *The disease typically takes several weeks to appear.*

typ·i·fy /ˈtɪpɪfaɪ/ v [T] **1** [not in progressive forms] to be a typical mark or sign of: *the high quality that typifies all his work* **2** [not in progressive forms] to be a typical example of: *The shoe-shine boy who becomes a millionaire typifies the American Dream.* **3** fml to represent in a typical manner, e.g. by an image, model, or likeness: *In this book we have tried to typify the main classes of verbs.*

typing pool /ˈ⋯ ⋅/ n a group of typists in a large office who type letters for any members of the office

typ·ist /ˈtaɪpɪst/ n **1** a secretary employed mainly for typing (TYPE²) letters —see also SHORTHAND TYPIST **2** a person who uses a TYPEWRITER: *He's a good typist/a slow typist.*

ty·po /ˈtaɪpəʊ/ n infml a typographic mistake

ty·pog·ra·pher /taɪˈpɒɡrəfəʳ‖-ˈpɑː-/ n **1** a printer **2** a TYPESETTER; COMPOSITOR **3** a person who DESIGNS TYPEFACES

ty·po·graph·ic /ˌtaɪpəˈɡræfɪk◂/ also **ty·po·graph·ic·al** /-kəl/— adj of typography: *It shouldn't say "Englihs"; that's a typographic error.* — ~**ally** /kli/ adv

ty·pog·ra·phy /taɪˈpɒɡrəfi‖-ˈpɑː-/ n [U] **1** the work of preparing and setting material for printing **2** the arrangement, style, and appearance of printed matter

ty·ran·ni·cal /tɪˈrænɪkəl/ also **tyr·an·nous** /ˈtɪrənəs/— adj severely and unjustly cruel, esp. in exercising power: *his tyrannical rule* | *her tyrannical father* —see also TYRANT —**cally** /kli/ adv

tyr·an·nize also **-nise** BrE /ˈtɪrənaɪz/ v [T] to use power over (a person, country, etc.) with unjust cruelty

ty·ran·no·sau·rus /tɪˌrænəˈsɔːrəs/ also **tyrannosaurus rex** /⋯ˌ⋯ ˈ⋅/— n a large fierce flesh-eating DINOSAUR

tyr·an·ny /ˈtɪrəni/ n **1** [U] the use of power cruelly and/or unjustly to rule a person or country: *the tyranny of a police state* **2** [C often pl.] a cruel or unjust act, esp. by a person in power **3** [U] government by a ruler with complete power, usu. gained by unjust means: *(fig.) the tyranny of the clock, which makes us get up when we don't want to*

ty·rant /ˈtaɪərənt/ n a ruler with complete power, usu. gained unjustly and by force, who rules cruelly and unjustly —see also TYRANNICAL

tyre BrE ‖ **tire** AmE /taɪəʳ/ n **1** a thick band of rubber, either solid or filled with air, that fits round the outside edge of a wheel, esp. on a motor vehicle or bicycle, as a running surface and to soften shocks: *a punctured/burst tyre* | *There's no tread on this tyre* (=the surface has become smooth) — *you should put on/fit a new one.* | *to blow up/inflate a tyre* (=put air into it) —see also SPARE TYRE, and see pictures at BICYCLE and CAR **2** a protective metal band fitted round a wooden wheel

tyre pres·sure /ˈ⋯ ⋅/ n the pressure of air inside a particular tyre: *The current tyre pressure for this car is 40 pounds per square inch.* | *Check the tyre pressures with a tyre pressure gauge.*

ty·ro, tiro /ˈtaɪərəʊ/ n BrE old-fash fml a beginner; person with little experience

Ty·rol /tɪˈrəʊl/ [the] see TIROL

Ty·rone /tɪˈrəʊn/ a former COUNTY of W Northern Ireland, bordered to the W by County Donegal

Tyson /ˈtaɪsən/, **Mike** (1966–   ) an American BOXER who was the World HEAVYWEIGHT CHAMPION from 1986–1990. In 1992 he was sent to prison for RAPE (=forcing a woman to have sex).

tzar /zɑːʳ, tsɑːʳ/ n a TSAR

tza·ri·na /zɑːˈriːnə, tsɑː-/ n a TSARINA

tze·tze fly /ˈtetsi flaɪ, ˈtsetsi-, ˈsetsi-/ n a TSETSE FLY

U

U¹, u /juː/ **U's, u's** or **Us, us** the 21st letter of the English alphabet

U² adj BrE old-fash infml or humor of a word or action/used by or typical of the UPPER CLASS; correct or socially proper: *It isn't U to call the midday meal "dinner".* — opposite **non-U**

U³ n, adj (in Britain) (a film) that has been officially accepted as suitable for all age groups —compare PG; see also G

U2 /ˌjuː ˈtuː/ an Irish popular music group from Dublin, successful in the 1980s and known esp. for their political songs

UAE /ˌjuː eɪ ˈiː/ abbrev. for UNITED ARAB EMIRATES

UB40 /ˌjuː biː ˈfɔːti ‖ -ˈfɔːr-/ n (in Britain) an official card which shows that a person, named on the card, is receiving UNEMPLOYMENT BENEFIT: *reduced entry fee for UB40 holders*

u·biq·ui·tous /juːˈbɪkwɪ̩təs/ adj fml (esp. of something that is not liked or approved of) appearing, happening, or existing everywhere: *We were plagued throughout our travels by the ubiquitous mosquito.* — ~**ly** adv — ~**ness** n [U]

U-boat /ˈjuː bəʊt/ n a German SUBMARINE, esp. as used in the Second World War

UCCA /ˈʌkə/ the Universities Central Council on Admissions; an official body in Britain which receives and deals with people's requests to study for degrees at universities —see also CLEARING (2)

UCCA Hand·book /ˌ·· ˈ···/ [the] the book, produced by UCCA, which lists the courses available at British universities and the levels at which one usually needs to pass examinations to gain entrance to them

UCLA /ˌjuː siː el ˈeɪ/ the University of California at Los Angeles; one of the branches of the state-supported University of California, known esp. for its sports teams

UDA /ˌjuː diː ˈeɪ/ [the] the Ulster Defence Association; an illegal Protestant PARAMILITARY organization in Northern Ireland, which takes violent action in opposition to the actions of the IRA

ud·der /ˈʌdəʳ/ n a baglike organ of a cow, female goat, etc., from which milk is produced

UDI /ˌjuː diː ˈaɪ/ esp. BrE Unilateral Declaration of Independence; a declaration of independence made by a state without the agreement of another state which is protecting it: *Rhodesia declared UDI in 1965.*

UDM /ˌjuː diː ˈem/ [the] the Union of Democratic Mineworkers; a British TRADE UNION formed by a group of mineworkers who disagreed with the action and views of the NUM during the miners' STRIKE² (1) of 1984–85

UDR /ˌjuː diː ˈɑːʳ/ [the] the Ulster Defence Regiment; a PARAMILITARY force set up by the British government in 1969 to work with the Royal Ulster Constabulary (RUC). The UDR has become closely connected with the British Army, and members of the UDR, which is made up of Northern Irish people, have often been attacked by the IRA. In 1992 the UDR joined with the Royal Irish Rangers to become the Royal Irish Regiment.

UFO

UFO /ˈjuːfəʊ, ˌjuː ef ˈəʊ/ n **UFO's** or **UFOs** an Unidentified Flying Object; a strange object in the sky, often thought to be a spacecraft piloted by creatures from another world. Not many people believe that UFOs really exist, but they often appear in SCIENCE FICTION stories and films: *UFO sightings*

U·gan·da /juːˈɡændə/ a country in E central Africa bordered by Tanzania, Rwanda, and Sudan; capital Kampala; population 17,804,000 (1989) — **dan** n,adj

ugh /ʊx, ʌɡ/ interj (an expression of strong dislike): *Ugh! This medicine tastes awful!*

ug·ly /ˈʌɡli/ adj **1** unpleasant to look at; extremely unattractive: *his ugly face | ugly houses/furniture/surroundings* **2** very unpleasant or threatening: *An ugly scene developed when some people in the crowd started fighting. | an ugly wound | Those clouds look ugly; we may have rain. | We were having quite a friendly discussion until politics reared its ugly head.* (=began to be talked about, with unpleasant results) **3 ugly as sin** very ugly —**liness** n [U]

Ugly A·mer·i·can /ˌ··· ·ˈ···/ n [(the)] an American abroad who behaves offensively, esp. in a way that attracts attention

ugly duck·ling /ˌ·· ˈ··/ n infml a person less attractive, skilful, etc., than others in early life but developing beyond them later (from a story in which a baby bird, thought to be an ugly DUCKLING, grows up to be a beautiful SWAN): *I've been an ugly duckling for too long to believe my transformation into a swan will last.*

Ugly Sis·ters /ˌ·· ˈ··/ n [(the)+P] the sisters of Cinderella. The Ugly Sisters are typical PANTOMIME characters, usu. played by male actors —see also CINDERELLA and see colour picture on page 357

UHF /ˌjuː eɪtʃ ˈef/ n [U] ultrahigh frequency; (the sending out of radio waves at) the rate of 300,000,000 to 3,000,000,000 HERTZ, producing excellent sound quality: *a UHF television set* —compare VHF

uh-huh /ˈʌ hʌ‖ʌ ˈhʌ/ interj infml yes

UHT milk /ˌjuː eɪtʃ tiː ˈmɪlk/ n [U] (in Britain) milk which has been heated to a very high temperature to kill bacteria which would otherwise cause it to turn sour, and therefore can be kept for longer than ordinary milk

UK /ˌjuː ˈkeɪ/ n [the] the United Kingdom (of Great Britain and Northern Ireland)

▷ USAGE The full formal title of the country is **the United Kingdom of Great Britain and Northern Ireland**, usually shortened to **the United Kingdom**. **The United Kingdom** includes **Great Britain** and **Northern Ireland**. **Great Britain** includes **England**, **Scotland**, and **Wales**, but not any part of **Ireland**. In less formal language, **Great Britain** is sometimes used to mean the same as **the United Kingdom**. In ordinary language, the expressions most often used are **Britain** and **the UK**. For **Great Britain, Ireland,** and all the other islands round about, **the British Isles** can be used.◁

UKAEA /ˌjuː keɪ eɪ iː ˈeɪ/ [the] the United Kingdom Atomic Energy Authority; a British government authority which controls the study of atomic ENERGY

UK Ni·rex /ˌjuː keɪ ˈnaɪreks/ a British organization responsible for storing RADIOACTIVE waste

U·kraine /juːˈkreɪn/ [the] a member of the Commonwealth of Independent States in E Europe bordered by Poland and Slovakia in W, by Belorussia and Russia in N and E, and by Romania and Moldavia in S; formerly part of the USSR. Capital Kiev; population 51,704,000 (1989). The Ukraine contains some of the best farming land in E Europe; produces coal, and is a centre of heavy industry. —**Ukranian** n,adj

u·ku·le·le , ukelele /ˌjuːkəˈleɪli/ n a musical instrument with four strings, like a small GUITAR, used in playing Hawaiian music and sometimes by COMIC performers

UL /ˌjuː ˈel/ see UNDERWRITERS' LABORATORIES

ul·cer /ˈʌlsəʳ/ n a sore place appearing on the skin inside or outside the body which may bleed or produce poisonous matter: *a stomach ulcer | mouth ulcers* — ~**ous** adj

ul·cer·ate /ˈʌlsəreɪt/ v [I;T] to (cause to) turn into or become covered with one or more ulcers —**ation** /ˌʌlsəˈreɪʃən/ n [U]

ul·lage /ˈʌlɪdʒ/ n [U] tech the amount by which the liquid, esp. wine, in an unopened bottle does not come up to the top; amount of air in a bottle

Ulls·wa·ter /ˈʌlzwɔːtəʳ‖-wɔː-, -wɑː-/ one of the lakes in the LAKE DISTRICT, NW England, to the E of Keswick

ul·na /ˈʌlnə/ n med the inner bone of the lower arm, on the side opposite to the thumb —see picture at SKELETON

Ul·ster /ˈʌlstəʳ/ 1 another name for Northern Ireland, used esp. in newspapers and broadcasting: the troubles in Ulster 2 an area in the N of Ireland, consisting of the six counties (COUNTY) of Northern Ireland and the Ulster PROVINCE of the Republic of Ireland (County Cavan, County Monaghan, and County Donegal)

Ulster De·fence As·so·ci·a·tion /ˌ··ˈ··ˌ···ˌ·/ [the] see UDA

Ulster Defence Re·gi·ment /ˌ··ˈ·ˌ··/ [the] see UDR

Ulster Dem·o·crat·ic U·nion·ist Par·ty /ˌ··ˌ···ˈ···ˌ·/ [the] a Northern Ireland Protestant political party formed in 1969 and led by the Reverend Ian Paisley, often seen as attracting the support of those holding extreme views

Ulster Free·dom Fight·ers /ˌ··ˈ··ˌ·/ [the+P] a PARAMILITARY group in Northern Ireland which is the armed branch of the UDA

Ulster U·nion·ists /ˌ··ˈ··ˌ/ [P] a group of three PROTESTANT political parties in Northern Ireland, who want Northern Ireland to remain part of the UK. The three Ulster Unionist parties are: the official Unionist Party, connected with the British Conservative Party, the Ulster Popular Unionist Party, and the Ulster Democratic Unionist Party, led by the Reverend Ian Paisley.

Ulster Vol·un·teer Force /ˌ··ˈ··ˌ·/ (also UVF) [the] a Protestant TERRORIST organization in Ireland which has been illegal since 1966

Ulster Vol·un·teers /ˌ··ˈ··ˌ/ [the+P] a private army set up in 1913 to prevent Irish Home Rule

ult /ʌlt/ BrE fml, becoming rare (used after a date in business letters) of last month: the meeting held on the 24th ult

ul·te·ri·or /ʌlˈtɪərɪəʳ/ adj intentionally hidden or kept secret, esp. because bad: I suspect he may have had ulterior motives for being so generous.

ul·ti·mate¹ /ˈʌltᵻmᵻt/ adj [A] 1 being or happening at the end of a process or course of action; FINAL: They're going to London first, but their ultimate destination is Rome. | Their ultimate objective is the removal of all nuclear weapons. 2 considered as an origin or base; FUNDAMENTAL: The sun is the ultimate source of energy. | The ultimate responsibility lies with the president. 3 infml greatest; better or worse than any other: To look for the gas leak with a lighted match really was the ultimate stupidity. | With a top speed of 200 miles per hour, this is the ultimate sports car.

ultimate² n [the+S (in)] the ULTIMATE ¹ (3) thing; the highest point: the ultimate in stupidity/in luxury

ul·ti·mate·ly /ˈʌltᵻmᵻtli/ adv in the end; after everything or everyone else has been taken into account: Ultimately, the success of the product depends on good marketing. | Many experts gave their opinions, but ultimately the decision lay with the president.

ul·ti·ma·tum /ˌʌltᵻˈmeɪtəm/ n -tums or -ta /tə/ a last statement of conditions that must be met, esp. under threat of force: He gave his daughter an ultimatum: unless she stopped taking drugs he would throw her out of the house. | to deliver/issue an ultimatum

ultra- see WORD FORMATION

ul·tra·high fre·quen·cy /ˌʌltrəhaɪ ˈfriːkwənsi/ n [U] see UHF

ul·tra·ma·rine /ˌʌltrəməˈriːn◂/ adj having a very bright blue colour —ultramarine n [U]

ul·tra·son·ic /ˌʌltrəˈsɒnɪk◂‖-ˈsɑː-/ adj (of a sound wave) beyond the range of human hearing

ultra·sound /ˈʌltrəsaʊnd/ n [U] sound that is too high for human beings to hear: They examined the baby in her womb using an ultrasound scanner.

ul·tra·vi·o·let /ˌʌltrəˈvaɪələt◂/ adj 1 (of light that is) beyond the purple end of the range of colours (SPECTRUM) that can be seen by human beings: ultraviolet rays —compare INFRARED 2 [A] using this light to cure certain skin diseases, examine old writing, etc.: an ultraviolet lamp

U·lu·ru /ˈuːluruː/ the Australian Aboriginal name for Ayers Rock

U·lys·ses /juːˈlɪsiːz/ 1 the Latin name for Odysseus 2 a NOVEL by James Joyce, regarded by many as one of the

greatest works of literature of the 20th century

um /ʌm, əm/ interj (used when one cannot decide what to say next): And then he ... um ... just seemed to ... um ... disappear!

um·ber /ˈʌmbəʳ/ adj having a brown earthlike colour, esp. as used in painting —umber n [U]

um·bil·i·cal cord /ʌmˌbɪlɪkəl ˈkɔːd‖-ˈkɔːrd/ n the long narrow tube of flesh which before birth joins the young to the organ which feeds it inside the mother: The nurse cut the baby's umbilical cord.

um·brage /ˈʌmbrɪdʒ/ n fml take umbrage (at) to show that one's feelings have been hurt (by); take offence

um·brel·la /ʌmˈbrelə/ n 1 an arrangement of cloth over a folding frame with a handle, used for keeping rain off the head: It began to rain so she put up/opened her umbrella. | an umbrella stand —compare SUNSHADE 2 a protecting power or influence; protection: The new country was formed under the political umbrella of the United Nations. 3 something which covers or includes a wide range of different parts: The Association of Councils is just an umbrella organization; it has no real power of its own.

UMIST /ˈjuːmɪst/ University of Manchester Institute of Science and Technology; a branch of the University of Manchester which teaches science and technical subjects like CHEMICAL ENGINEERING

um·laut /ˈumlaut/ n a sign (··) placed over a German vowel letter to show how it is pronounced —compare DIAERESIS

um·pire¹ /ˈʌmpaɪəʳ/ also ump /ʌmp/ AmE infml n a judge in charge of a game —see REFEREE (USAGE), and see pictures at BASEBALL, at CRICKET, and at TENNIS

umpire² ‖ also ump AmE infml— v [I;T] to act as an umpire for (a game or competition)

ump·teen /ˌʌmpˈtiːn◂/ determiner, pron infml a large number (of): I've seen that film umpteen times. —-teenth n, determiner : For the umpteenth time, don't do that!

'un /ən/ pron infml or nonstandard one: He's a bad 'un. (=a wicked immoral person) | I'll take those apples; they look like good 'uns.

un- see WORD FORMATION

UN /ˌjuː ˈen/ [the] United Nations (Organization); an international organization to which nearly all the countries in the world belong. Its head offices are in New York City. The UN tries to make sure there is peace in the world and that all countries work together to deal with international problems. —see also UN SECURITY COUNCIL and colour map on pages 1376

un·a·bashed /ˌʌnəˈbæʃt◂/ adj not ashamed or discouraged, esp. when something unusual or embarrassing (EMBARRASS) happens: His trousers fell down but he appeared quite unabashed. | an unabashed stare

un·a·bat·ed /ˌʌnəˈbeɪtᵻd◂/ adj fml (of a wind, a person's strength, etc.) without losing force: The storm continued unabated/with unabated violence.

un·a·ble /ʌnˈeɪbəl/ adj [F+to-v] rather fml not able: He seems unable to understand the simplest instructions. | I'd like to go, but I'm unable to. —see also INABILITY

un·a·bridged /ˌʌnəˈbrɪdʒd◂/ adj (esp. of something written, a speech, etc.) given in its full form; not shortened: complete and unabridged

un·ac·cep·ta·ble /ˌʌnəkˈseptəbəl◂/ adj not good enough to be accepted or approved: unacceptable behaviour | Mass unemployment is the unacceptable face of (=something bad which comes with) modern technology. | Violent crime has reached an unacceptable level.

un·ac·com·pa·nied /ˌʌnəˈkʌmpənid◂/ adj 1 [(by)] without someone or something else going too: Children unaccompanied by an adult/Unaccompanied children will not be admitted. 2 without music as ACCOMPANIMENT (2): an unaccompanied song

un·ac·coun·ta·ble /ˌʌnəˈkaʊntəbəl◂/ adj fml very surprising; not easily explained: His disappearance was quite unaccountable. —compare ACCOUNTABLE; see also ACCOUNT for (1) —-bly adv: He was unaccountably delayed.

unaccounted for /ˌ·ˈ··· ·/ adj not explained, found, or understood: Five men are still unaccounted for after yesterday's mining accident. | an unaccounted for change in the weather

un·ac·cus·tomed /ˌʌnəˈkʌstəmd◂/ adj 1 [A] not usual: his unaccustomed silence 2 [F+to] not used to (something).

People who are making a speech sometimes begin, as a joke, with the words "Unaccustomed as I am to public speaking..."

un·a·dopt·ed /ˌʌnəˈdɒptɬd◂‖-ˈdɑːp-/ *adj BrE* (of a road surface) not to be repaired by the town council, but the responsibility of those who live on the road

un·a·dul·te·rat·ed /ˌʌnəˈdʌltəreɪtɬd◂/ *adj* **1** (esp. of food) not mixed with impure or less pure substances **2** [A] complete; UTTER: *unadulterated nonsense*

un·ad·vised /ˌʌnədˈvaɪzd◂/ *adj fml* not sensible; done without thinking or taking advice: *an unadvised haste* — ~**ly** /ˌʌnədˈvaɪzɬdli/ *adv*

un·af·fect·ed /ˌʌnəˈfektɬd◂/ *adj* **1** [(by)] not affected (AFFECT[1]): *People in the south of the country were unaffected by the drought.* **2** *apprec* natural in behaviour or character: *the unaffected delight of a child* — ~**ly** *adv*

un·aid·ed /ʌnˈeɪdɬd/ *adv* without help: *It was the first time she had walked unaided since the accident.*

un·al·loyed /ˌʌnəˈlɔɪd◂/ *adj esp. lit* not mixed, esp. with unpleasant feelings: *unalloyed happiness*

un·am·big·u·ous /ˌʌnæmˈbɪgjuəs◂/ *adj* clear; that cannot be misunderstood: *unambiguous remarks*

un·A·mer·i·can /ˌ·ˈ··◂/ *adj* (esp. of political activity and loyalty) unfavourable or opposed to the US; thought to be against American customs and ways: *He was accused of un-American activities.* —see also HUAC

u·na·nim·i·ty /ˌjuːnəˈnɪmɬti/ *n* [U] *fml* the state or fact of being unanimous

u·nan·i·mous /juːˈnænɬməs/ *adj* **1** (of people) all agreeing completely: *Politicians from all parties were (completely) unanimous in condemning his action.* [+that] *The committee were unanimous that the application should be turned down.* **2** (of a decision, statement, etc.) supported or agreed by everyone: *The vote for the motion was unanimous.* | *He was elected Club President by a unanimous decision.* — ~**ly** *adv*

un·an·nounced /ˌʌnəˈnaʊnst◂/ *adj* having given no sign of arriving or being present; appearing unexpectedly: *He burst into the doctor's room quite unannounced and started shouting at her.*

un·an·swe·ra·ble /ʌnˈɑːnsərəbəl‖ʌnˈæn-/ *adj* **1** which cannot be argued against or opposed, esp. (of a charge) because clearly true or right: *an unanswerable case in law* **2** (of a question) having no answer

un·ap·pe·ti·zing /ʌnˈæpɬtaɪzɪŋ/ *adj* (of food) not looking or smelling good: *an unappetizing smell/meal* | (fig) *a rather unappetizing project/prospect*

un·ap·proach·a·ble /ˌʌnəˈprəʊtʃəbəl◂/ *adj* (of a person) hard to talk to; not seeming to encourage friendliness: *a cold, aloof, unapproachable man*

un·armed /ʌnˈɑːmd◂‖-ˈɑːr-/ *adj* **1** not carrying a weapon **2** [A] using no weapons: *unarmed combat*

unarmed com·bat /ˌ·· ˈ··/ *n* [U] fighting without weapons: *The Royal Marines are as skilled in unarmed combat as they are in weapon-handling.*

un·asked /ʌnˈɑːskt‖-ˈæskt/ *adv* without being asked: *I love it when he does the washing-up unasked.*

un·as·sum·ing /ˌʌnəˈsjuːmɪŋ◂, -ˈsuː-‖-ˈsuː-/ *adj apprec* not showing a wish to be noticed or given special treatment; modest: *the champion's unassuming manner* — ~**ly** *adv*

un·at·tached /ˌʌnəˈtætʃt◂/ *adj* **1** not married or ENGAGED (1) **2** [(to)] not connected: *unattached buildings*

un·at·tend·ed /ˌʌnəˈtendɬd◂/ *adj* alone, without people present or in charge: *Your car may get damaged here if you leave it unattended.* | *unattended luggage*

un·au·thor·ized /ʌnˈɔːθəraɪzd/ *adj* without the approval or support of the person, body, etc. involved: *an unauthorized biography*

un·a·vail·ing /ˌʌnəˈveɪlɪŋ◂/ *adj esp. lit* not having any effect; FUTILE: *an unavailing attempt to save her*

un·a·void·a·ble /ˌʌnəˈvɔɪdəbəl◂/ *adj* that cannot be avoided; impossible to escape: *The latest consignment was subject to unavoidable delays.* —**ably** *adv*: *I'm sorry I'm late; I was unavoidably detained.*

un·a·ware /ˌʌnəˈweər/ *adj* [F (of)] not having knowledge or consciousness (of something): *He seemed to be unaware of the trouble he was causing.* [+that] *He was completely unaware that he was being watched.*

un·a·wares /ˌʌnəˈweəz‖-ˈweərz/ *adv* **1** unexpectedly or without warning: *I think I must have taken/caught her unawares* (=surprised her by my presence), *because she looked round guiltily when I called her name.* **2** *fml or lit* unintentionally or without noticing: *He dropped it unawares.*

un·bal·ance /ʌnˈbæləns/ *v* [T] to make slightly mad: *His terrible experience unbalanced him/his mind.* | *an unbalanced person/character* —compare BALANCED

un·bar /ʌnˈbɑːr/ *v* -**rr**- [T] **1** to remove a locking bar from (a door or gate) **2** *fml* to make open: *These concessions could unbar the way to peace.*

un·bear·a·ble /ʌnˈbeərəbəl/ *adj* too bad or too unpleasant to be accepted; INTOLERABLE: *He's unbearable when he's in a bad temper.* | *unbearable heat* | *unbearable pain* —**bly** *adv*: *It was an unbearably hot day.*

un·beat·a·ble /ʌnˈbiːtəbəl/ *adj* that cannot be defeated: *The White Sox are unbeatable this year.*

un·beat·en /ʌnˈbiːtn/ *adj* not defeated: *unbeaten in the last five games*

un·be·known /ˌʌnbɪˈnəʊn/ also **un·be·knownst** /ˌʌnbɪˈnəʊnst/— *adj, adv* [F (to)] without the stated person knowing: *Unbeknown to his parents, he had not been to school for a week.*

un·be·lief /ˌʌnbɬˈliːf/ *n* [U] *fml* lack of belief or refusal to believe in matters of religious faith —compare DISBELIEF

un·be·lie·va·ble /ˌʌnbɬˈliːvəbəl/ *adj* **1** too improbable to be believed: *Her excuse was frankly unbelievable.* **2** very surprising: *She's got an unbelievable number of cats!* | *He showed unbelievable stupidity.* —**bly** *adv*: *Her singing voice is unbelievably good.*

un·be·liev·er /ˌʌnbɬˈliːvər/ *n* a person who has no faith, esp. religious faith

un·bend /ʌnˈbend/ *v* -**bent** /ˈbent/ **1** [I;T] to (cause to) become straight **2** [I] to behave in a less formal and severe manner; RELAX: *She finds it hard to unbend, even at parties.* —compare UNWIND

un·bend·ing /ʌnˈbendɪŋ/ *adj* unable or unwilling to change one's opinions, decisions, etc.: *an unbending will* | *a stern unbending man*

un·bid·den /ʌnˈbɪdn/ *adj esp. lit* not asked for or expected; uninvited

un·bind /ʌnˈbaɪnd/ *v* -**bound** /ˈbaʊnd/ [T] to loosen the fastenings of; free from something that ties or wraps

un·bleached /ʌnˈbliːtʃt◂/ *n* not treated with a chemical BLEACH. The demand for unbleached products has grown because they are thought to be better for the environment: *an unbleached cotton T-shirt* | *unbleached tea bags*

un·blem·ished /ʌnˈblemɬʃt/ *adj* not spoiled, esp. by a fault or bad action: *an unblemished reputation*

un·blink·ing /ʌnˈblɪŋkɪn/ *adj* not showing emotion or uncertainty

un·born /ʌnˈbɔːn◂‖-ˈɔːrn◂/ *adj* not yet born or existing: *the rights of the unborn child* | *generations yet unborn*

un·bos·om /ʌnˈbʊzəm/ *v* [T (to)] *fml or lit* to tell the secret feelings, esp. troubles and worries, of (oneself)

un·bound·ed /ʌnˈbaʊndɬd/ *adj esp. lit* limitless; far-reaching: *unbounded joy*

un·bowed /ʌnˈbaʊd◂/ *adj esp. lit* not defeated: *They left the battlefield, bloody but unbowed.* (=wounded but not beaten)

un·bri·dled /ʌnˈbraɪdld/ *adj esp. lit* not controlled and too active or violent: *His unbridled tongue* (=speech) *has often got him into trouble.* | *unbridled lust*

un·buck·le /ʌnˈbʌkəl/ *v* [T] to undo by loosening a BUCKLE: *He unbuckled his belt.*

un·bur·den /ʌnˈbɜːdn‖-ɜːr-/ *v* [T (of)] *fml* **1** to take away a load or worry from: *A servant hurried to unburden him of his bags.* **2** to free (oneself, one's mind, etc.) by talking about a secret trouble: *She unburdened herself of her terrible secret.*

un·cal·cu·lat·ed /ʌnˈkælkjɬleɪtɬd/ *adj* not planned in advance; SPONTANEOUS

un·called-for /ʌnˈkɔːld fɔːr/ *adj* not deserved, necessary, or right: *His rudeness was quite uncalled-for.* | *an uncalled-for intrusion*

un·can·ny /ʌnˈkæni/ *adj* very strange or mysterious; not natural or usual: *He bore an uncanny resemblance to my*

dead brother. | *She's got an uncanny knack of anticipating what you're going to tell her.* —**nily** *adv*

un·ce·re·mo·ni·ous /ˌʌnserəˈməʊniəs/ *adj* **1** not done politely; rudely quick: *She finished the meal with unceremonious haste.* | *He made an unceremonious exit.* **2** informal; without ceremony — ~ **ly** *adv* : *He was kicked out unceremoniously into the street.* — ~ **ness** *n* [U]

un·cer·tain /ʌnˈsɜːtn‖-ɜːr-/ *adj* **1** [F (of)] not certain; doubtful: *I'm uncertain of his intentions.* [+wh-] *I'm uncertain how to get there.* **2** [F] undecided or unable to decide: *Our holiday plans are still uncertain.* **3** likely to change: *uncertain weather* **4 in no uncertain terms** very clearly, and perhaps rudely: *I told him in no uncertain terms what I thought of him.* — ~ **ly** *adv* : *He felt his way uncertainly down the dark passage.* — ~ **ty**, ~ **ness** *n* [C;U]: *the uncertainties of life* | *I believe there's some uncertainty (about) whether she's coming.*

uncertainty prin·ci·ple /·ˈ··· ˌ···/ [the] the scientific law explaining that it is impossible to know both the speed and position of an ELEMENTARY PARTICLE. The more exactly that one is determined, the less exactly the other can be.

un·char·i·ta·ble /ʌnˈtʃærɪtəbəl/ *adj* not kind, helpful, or fair in judging others; too severe: *It was rather uncharitable of you to comment on her large nose.* | *an uncharitable refusal* —**bly** *adv*

un·char·ted /ʌnˈtʃɑːtɪd‖-ɑːr-/ *adj esp. lit* (of a place) not known well enough for records, esp. maps, to be made: *sailing into uncharted waters* | *the uncharted forests of Brazil* —see also CHART[2]

un·checked /ˌʌnˈtʃekt◂/ *adj* **1** not prevented from moving, developing, etc.: *an unchecked flow of blood* | *The disease spread unchecked.* —see also CHECK[2] (3) **2** not tested for quality, correctness, etc.: *The goods should not have left the factory unchecked.* —see also CHECK[2] (1)

un·chris·tian /ʌnˈkrɪstʃən,-tiən/ *adj fml* not kind, helpful, generous, etc. Many people would avoid using this word when speaking of somebody who is not a Christian: *unchristian behaviour* | *That's a rather unchristian thing to say, isn't it?*

un·civ·il /ʌnˈsɪvəl/ *n* rude; bad-mannered: *uncivil remarks/behaviour*

un·clas·si·fied /ʌnˈklæsɪfaɪd/ *adj* **1** not arranged in any particular order: *unclassified football results* **2** (of information) not secret or sensitive: *not on the SECURITY list*

un·cle /ˈʌŋkəl/ *n* **1** (*often cap.*) the brother of one's father or mother, or the husband of one's aunt: *He's my uncle.* | *Take me swimming, Uncle (Jack)!* —see USAGE **2** a man whose brother or sister has a child: *My sister had a little boy yesterday, so I'm now an uncle!* **3** a man who is a friend or neighbour of a small child or its parents —see AUNT (CULTURAL NOTE) **4 say uncle** *AmE infml* to admit defeat; give up —see also DUTCH UNCLE

▷ USAGE We can use **uncle**, **auntie/aunty**, and (less commonly) **aunt** when addressing the people directly: *How are you,* **uncle/auntie?** We can also add the person's first name with **uncle**, **aunt**, and (less commonly) **auntie/aunty**: *Good morning,* **Uncle** *John/* **Aunt** *Margaret.* —see also FATHER (USAGE)◁

un·clean /ˌʌnˈkliːn◂/ *adj* **1** not pure, esp. according to religious belief, often because of a condition of the body which may infect others: *In ancient times lepers were thought unclean.* **2** *bibl* (esp. in the Jewish religion) (of an animal) that must not be eaten — ~ **ness** *n* [U]

un·clear /ˌʌnˈklɪəʳ◂/ *adj* not clear or plain; difficult to see, understand, etc.: *an unclear picture/explanation* | *I'm rather unclear about what I'm doing here.*

Uncle Re·mus /ˌʌŋkəl ˈriːməs/ a name used by the American wroter Joel Chandler Harris (1848–1908), the writer of the "Brer Rabbit" stories for children

Uncle Sam /ˌʌŋkəl ˈsæm/ *infml lit* the US, esp. the US government: *Uncle Sam comes to help of needy refugees.* | *film stars from the land of Uncle Sam*

▶CULTURAL NOTE Uncle Sam first appeared in the

Uncle Sam

1800s, esp. on POSTERS asking people to join the armed forces, pointing his finger and saying "Uncle Sam needs you!" His TOP HAT and clothes are always decorated with the **Stars and Stripes** of the American flag, and he is a SYMBOL of the US.◀

Uncle Tom /ˌʌŋkəl ˈtɒm‖-ˈtɑːm/ *n* **1** the main character of Harriet Beecher Stowe's NOVEL *Uncle Tom's Cabin*, a kindly black slave who is ill-treated by his owner, Simon Legree **2** *derog* a black person who is too respectful to white people

Uncle Tom Cobbleigh see Uncle Tom COBBLEIGH

un·com·for·ta·ble /ʌnˈkʌmftəbəl, -ˈkʌmfət-‖-ˈkʌmfərt-, -ˈkʌmft-/ *adj* **1** not comfortable: *an uncomfortable chair* | *I'm uncomfortable in this chair.* **2** troubled by one's situation, esp. one's position in relation to others; embarrassed (EMBARRASS); ILL AT EASE: *He felt uncomfortable when his parents started arguing in front of him.* —**bly** *adv*

un·com·mit·ted /ˌʌnkəˈmɪtɪd◂/ *adj* [(to)] not having firmly decided or promised to support a particular group, political belief, course of action, etc.

un·com·mon /ʌnˈkɒmən‖-ˈkɑː-/ *adj* unusual

un·com·mon·ly /ʌnˈkɒmənli‖-ˈkɑː-/ *adv fml* very; unusually: *That's uncommonly kind of you.*

un·com·mu·ni·ca·tive /ˌʌnkəˈmjuːnɪkətɪv‖-keɪt-/ *adj* not willing to talk much or give information

un·com·pro·mis·ing /ʌnˈkɒmprəmaɪzɪŋ‖-ˈkɑːm-/ *adj* refusing to change one's ideas or decisions; not prepared to COMPROMISE: *uncompromising attitudes/beliefs* — ~ **ly** *adv*

un·con·cerned /ˌʌnkənˈsɜːnd‖-ɜːr-/ *adj* **1** [(about)] not worried or anxious, esp. when one perhaps should be: *She seemed quite unconcerned about the risks she was taking.* **2** [F (with)] not interested or taking part: *She is unconcerned with school affairs.* — ~ **ly** /ˌʌnkənˈsɜːndli‖-ɜːr-/ *adv*

un·con·di·tion·al /ˌʌnkənˈdɪʃənəl/ *adj* not limited by any conditions: *The victorious army demanded* **unconditional surrender.** — ~ **ly** *adv*

un·con·firmed /ˌʌnkənˈfɜːmd‖-ɜːr-/ *adj* without official support: *We've received unconfirmed reports of an explosion in Central London.*

un·con·scion·a·ble /ʌnˈkɒnʃənəbəl‖-ˈkɑːn-/ *adj fml* unreasonable in degree or amount: *He was absent an unconscionable time.* (=too long) —**bly** *adv*

un·con·scious[1] /ʌnˈkɒnʃəs‖-ˈkɑːn-/ *adj* **1** having lost consciousness: *She hit her head and was unconscious for several minutes.* | *He was knocked unconscious by a falling rock.* **2** [F+of] not knowing about something; UNAWARE: *He was quite unconscious of having offended them.* **3** not intentional: *unconscious neglect of a serious problem* —see CONSCIOUS (USAGE) — ~ **ly** *adv* — ~ **ness** *n* [U]: *in a state of unconsciousness*

unconscious[2] *n* [the+S] the SUBCONSCIOUS

un·con·sid·ered /ˌʌnkənˈsɪdəd◂‖-ərd◂/ *adj* **1** not carefully thought out: *an unconsidered action* **2** *fml* disregarded; unnoticed: *a few unconsidered objects left lying about*

un·con·sti·tu·tion·al /ˌʌnkɒnstɪˈtjuːʃənəl‖-kɑːnstɪˈtuː-/ *adj* not in agreement with the principles of a CONSTITUTION, esp. that of the US: *The Supreme Court ruled that the decision of the lower court was unconstitutional.* —see CONSTITUTIONALITY (CULTURAL NOTE) — ~ **ity** /ˌʌnkɒnstɪˌtjuːʃəˈnælɪti ‖ -kɑːnstɪˌtuː-/ *n* [U]

un·con·vinc·ing /ˌʌnkənˈvɪnsɪŋ◂/ *adj* not easy to believe or accept: *an unconvincing excuse* | *I found his argument unconvincing.* — ~ **ly** *adv*

un·co·or·di·na·ted /ˌʌnkəʊˈɔːdɪneɪtɪd‖-ˈɔːr-/ *adj* having no working relationship between two or more parts (e.g. of the body, a business, etc.): *I'm too uncoordinated to play the piano.* | *The time scale of this plan is totally uncoordinated.*

un·cork /ʌnˈkɔːk‖-ɔːrk/ *v* [T] to open (esp. a bottle or barrel) by removing the CORK[1] (2)

un·count·a·ble /ʌnˈkaʊntəbəl/ *adj* that cannot be counted. Uncountable nouns are marked [U] in this dictionary: *"Is 'furniture' countable or uncountable?" "It's uncountable; you can't say 'two furnitures'!"* —compare COUNT NOUN

un·coup·le /ʌnˈkʌpəl/ *v* [T] to separate (esp. joined railway carriages); free from a fastening

un·couth /ʌnˈkuːθ/ *adj* not having good manners; awkward or impolite in speech and behaviour: *an uncouth young man* −~**ly** *adv* −~**ness** *n* [U]

un·cov·er /ʌnˈkʌvəʳ/ *v* [T] **1** to remove a covering from: *In spring we uncover the swimming pool.* **2** to find out (something unknown or kept secret); discover: *The police have uncovered a plot to rob this bank.*

un·crit·i·cal /ʌnˈkrɪtɪkəl/ *adj* [(of)] not making or showing any judgments; (unwisely) accepting, without deciding if good or bad: *She is quite uncritical of his behaviour.* | *He has rather an uncritical eye for paintings.* −−**cally** /kli/ *adv*

un·crowned king /ˌʌnkraʊnd ˈkɪŋ/ **uncrowned queen** *fem.*− *n* [*the*+S **(of)**] the person generally considered to be the best, most famous, etc., in a particular activity: *Martina Navratilova, the uncrowned queen of women's tennis in the 1980s*

un·crush·a·ble /ʌnˈkrʌʃəbəl/ *adj* **1** (of materials and cloth) staying smooth and not forming unwanted folds **2** *esp. lit* (of a person, a person's will, etc.) that will not admit defeat: *her uncrushable spirit*

unc·tu·ous /ˈʌŋktʃuəs/ *adj fml* full of unpleasantly insincere kindness, interest, etc.: *unctuous praise* − ~**ly** *adv* − ~**ness** *n* [U]

un·cut /ʌnˈkʌt◂/ *adj* **1** (of a film or story) not made shorter, e.g. by having violent or sexually improper scenes removed: *the uncut version of "Lady Chatterly's Lover"* **2** (of a diamond or other precious stone) not shaped and formed for wearing, use in jewellery, etc.

un·daunt·ed /ʌnˈdɔːntɪd/ *adj* [(by)] not at all discouraged or frightened by danger or difficulty −see also DAUNT

un·de·ceive /ˌʌndɪˈsiːv/ *v* [T] *fml* to inform (someone) of the truth, esp. when they are mistaken: *She thought he was a famous film director, but I had to undeceive her.*

un·de·cid·ed /ˌʌndɪˈsaɪdɪd/ *adj* **1** [F (**about, as to**)] having not made a firm decision; in doubt: *About a third of the voters are still undecided as to how they will vote.* [+*wh-*] *I'm undecided whether to go to France or Italy for my holidays.* **2** without a result; not settled: *The match was left undecided.* − ~**ly** *adv* − ~**ness** *n* [U]

un·de·mon·stra·tive /ˌʌndɪˈmɒnstrətɪv◂/ *adj* not showing one's feelings: *an undemonstrative father/audience* − ~**ly** *adv*

un·de·ni·a·ble /ˌʌndɪˈnaɪəbəl◂/ *adj* clear and certain: *His ability is undeniable.* | *It's undeniable that she is the best person for the job.* −−**bly** *adv*

un·der¹ /ˈʌndəʳ/ *prep* **1** in or to a lower place than; directly below; covered by: *The box is under the table.* | *Can you breathe under water?* | *We sheltered under the tree.* (=covered by its branches) | *The insect crept under the door.* | *a village under* (=at the base of) *the hill* | *What are you wearing under your coat?* **2** less than: *It costs under £5.* | *a temperature (of) under 30°* | *Children under* (=younger than) *14 cannot see this film.* −opposite **over**; compare BELOW² **3** working for; controlled by: *She has three secretaries under her.* −opposite **over 4** during the rule of: *Spain under Franco* **5** in the class of: *Iron is listed under "Metals" in the index.* | *I think this problem comes under the heading of industrial diseases.* **6** according to: *Under the terms of the agreement, you have to pay a weekly rent.* | *He was detained under the Prevention of Terrorism Act.* **7** experiencing the effects of: *The hospital is under threat of closure.* (=is threatened with being closed) | *They took this decision under pressure from the unions.* | *We had to work under great difficulties.* | *I was under the impression* (=I believed, perhaps wrongly) *that the exams started on Monday.* **8** in or into a state of: *At last we brought the fire under control.* | *The patient is under an anaesthetic.* **9** in the process of: *The matter is still under review/under discussion.* **10 under way a** moving: *You can't use the toilets till the train is under way.* **b** happening now; in PROGRESS: *Plans are under way for a big celebration.*

▷ USAGE Compare **under, beneath, underneath,** and **below. 1** Under is the most common word when one thing is directly under another thing, or covered by it: **under** *the bed* | **under** *the blanket.* **Beneath** can also be used in this way, but may suggest that the two objects are not close to each other: *The submarine waited, far* **beneath** *the ship.* **Beneath** is also used in poetic or literary writing: *They strolled together* **beneath** *the summer moon.* **2 Under** (opposite **over**) is used when

there is movement from one side to another: *The boy crawled* **under** *the fence.* **Underneath** is used instead of **under, a** to give more force to the idea of covering, touching, or hiding: *The letter had been pushed* **underneath** *the carpet by accident.* | *The old mine goes right* **underneath** *the city,* **b** at the end of a sentence: *She wore a red coat with a blue dress* **underneath. 3 Below** (opposite **above**) suggests only that one thing is in a lower position than an other: *There is a lake* **below** *the village, further down the valley.* −see also ABOVE (USAGE)◁

under² *adv* **1** in or to a lower place; directly below −see also **down under** (DOWN¹ (19)) **2** less or younger than stated: *Children of nine or under must be accompanied by an adult.*

under- see WORD FORMATION

un·der·a·chieve /ˌʌndərəˈtʃiːv/ *v* [I] *euph* to perform less well than one could, esp. at one's school work −−**chiever** *n*

un·der·act /ˌʌndərˈækt/ *v* [I;T] *sometimes apprec* to act (a part in a play) with very little force −opposite **overact**

un·der·age /ˌʌndərˈeɪdʒ◂/ *adj* too young for some purpose, esp. to vote, buy alcohol, or hold a driving LICENCE − opposite **overage**

un·der·arm¹ /ˈʌndərɑːm/ also **underhand**− *adj, adv* (in sport) with the arm not moving above the shoulder: *He bowled underarm.* | *an underarm throw* −opposite **overarm**

underarm² *adj* [A] *euph* of or for the ARMPIT: *underarm deodorants*

un·der·bel·ly /ˈʌndəˌbeli/−ər-/ *n* [(*the*) S (**of**)] *esp. lit or pomp* the weak or undefended part of a place, a plan, etc.

un·der·brush /ˈʌndəbrʌʃ/−ər-/ *n* [U] *esp. AmE* thick UNDERGROWTH in a forest

un·der·cap·i·tal·ize also **-ise** *BrE* /ˌʌndəˈkæpɪtl-aɪz/−dər-/ *v* [T *often pass.*] to supply (a business) with too little money for it to operate profitably

un·der·car·riage /ˈʌndəˌkærɪdʒ/−ər-/ *n* an aircraft's wheels and wheel supports −see picture at AIRCRAFT

un·der·charge /ˌʌndəˈtʃɑːdʒ/ˌʌndərˈtʃɑːdʒ/ *v* [I (**for**);T (**by**)] to charge (someone) too little or less than the correct price: *They undercharged me by 60 pence.* −opposite **overcharge**

un·der·class /ˈʌndəklɑːs/−dərklæs/ *n* a social class of people seen as being outside the society in which they live, esp. because they have little chance of training or employment, little money, or no regular way of living

un·der·clas·sman /ˈʌndəklɑːsmən/−dərklæs-/ **-wom·an** /ˌwʊmən/ *fem*− *n* **-men** /mɛn/ *AmE* a student in the first two years of a school or college, i.e. a FRESHMAN or SOPHOMORE: *Underclassmen are not allowed locker privileges at the gym.* −compare UPPERCLASSMAN

un·der·clothes /ˈʌndəkləʊðz, -kləʊz/−dər-/ also **un·der·cloth·ing** /ˈʌndəˌkləʊðɪŋ/−dər-/− *n* [P] *rather fml for* UNDERWEAR

un·der·coat /ˈʌndəkəʊt/−dər-/ *n* [C;U] a covering of paint put onto a surface as a base for a top covering of paint − compare TOPCOAT

un·der·cov·er /ˌʌndəˈkʌvəʳ◂/−dər-/ *adj* acting or done secretly, not publicly, esp. as a SPY or for gain: *an undercover agent* | *undercover payments*

un·der·cur·rent /ˈʌndəˌkʌrənt/−dərˌkɜːr-/ *n* **1** a hidden current of water beneath the surface **2** [(**of**)] a hidden tendency in feelings, opinions, etc., esp. when this is different from what appears to be happening: *an undercurrent of discontent*

un·der·cut /ˌʌndəˈkʌt/−ər-/ *v* **-cut**; *present participle* **-cutting** [T] to sell goods or services more cheaply than (a competitor)

un·der·de·vel·oped coun·try /ˌʌndədɪveləpt ˈkʌntri/−dər-/ *n* a country that needs to develop its industries and improve living conditions; a DEVELOPING COUNTRY

un·der·dog /ˈʌndədɒg/ˈʌndərdɔːg/ *n* **1** a weaker person, country, etc., that is always treated badly by others **2** a person, team, etc., that is expected to lose in a competition with another. British people are often thought to support the underdog in a competition and to want them to win: *In their football match with Brazil, Switzerland are the underdogs.*

un·der·done /ˌʌndə'dʌn◀‖-ər-/ adj not completely cooked, esp. (of meat) still red —opposite **overdone**

un·der·dressed /ˌʌndə'drest◀‖-dər-/ adj wearing clothes which are less formal than what is considered correct for a particular occasion: I felt underdressed at Bill's leaving party, standing there in my jeans and rugby shirt in a roomful of men wearing suits and ties.

un·der·es·ti·mate¹ /ˌʌndər'estɪ̣meɪt/ v 1 [I;T] to guess too low a value for (an amount): We underestimated the cost of materials, and ended up taking a loss. 2 [T] to have too low an opinion of: Don't underestimate him/his abilities. —opposite **overestimate**

un·der·es·ti·mate² /ˌʌndər'estɪ̣mɪ̣t/ n an ESTIMATE which is too small

un·der·ex·pose /ˌʌndərɪk'spəʊz/ v [T] to give too little light to (a film or photograph) —opposite **overexpose**

un·der·felt /'ʌndəfelt‖-ər-/ BrE‖**rug pad** AmE— n [U] soft rough material placed between a CARPET and the floor

un·der·floor /ˌʌndə'flɔː.ʳ◀‖-ər-/ adj (esp. of heating systems) laid beneath the surface of the floor: underfloor heating

un·der·foot /ˌʌndə'fʊt‖-ər-/ adv 1 below one's feet; for walking on: The ground was stony underfoot. 2 under the foot, esp. against the ground: Some of the children got trampled underfoot as the crowd fled in panic. 3 in the way, so as to be annoying: The children are always getting underfoot.

un·der·fund /ˌʌndə'fʌnd‖-ər-/ v [T] to supply less than enough money for: The childcare programme has been continuously underfunded. — —ing n [U]

un·der·gar·ment /'ʌndəˌɡɑːmənt‖'ʌndərˌɡɑːr-/ n fml or old-fash a piece of UNDERWEAR

un·der·go /ˌʌndə'ɡəʊ‖-dər-/ v -went /'went/, -gone /'ɡɒn‖ 'ɡɔːn/ [T] to experience (esp. something unpleasant, unwelcome, or difficult): She's undergoing treatment at the hospital. | The company has undergone some major changes in the last five years.

un·der·grad·u·ate /ˌʌndə'ɡrædʒuɪ̣t‖-ər-/ also **un·der·grad** /'ʌndəɡræd‖-ər-/ infml— n a student who is doing a university course for a BACHELOR'S DEGREE —compare GRADUATE¹ (1)

un·der·ground¹ /ˌʌndə'ɡraʊnd‖-ər-/ adv 1 under the earth's surface: The nuclear waste was buried deep underground. 2 in secret; in or into a secret place, hidden from public view: The news has been passed on underground, but hasn't appeared in the newspapers. | The terrorists have had to **go underground** (=leave ordinary life for a time)

un·der·ground² /'ʌndəɡraʊnd‖-ər-/ adj 1 below the surface of the earth: an underground passage 2 a representing a view which is not generally accepted, esp. in art, literature, etc.: underground newspapers b operating secretly and often illegally, esp. in opposition to an established political system: an underground group of anti-government guerillas

underground³ n 1 [(the) S] also **tube** BrE ‖ **subway** AmE— (often cap.) a railway system in which the trains run in tubes underground, esp. (in Britain) the one in London: We went on the Underground/by underground. —compare METRO 2 [the+S+ sing./pl. v] a (esp. in the 1960s and 1970s) a loose group of people in society opposed to accepted ideas in art, politics, etc. b a group working in secret to fight or oppose the rulers of a country

the symbol for the London Underground

Underground Rail·road /ˌ··· '··/ [the] a loosely arranged system in America before the Civil War to help escaping slaves

un·der·growth /'ʌndəɡrəʊθ‖-dər-/ n [U] bushes, small trees, and other plants growing around and under trees: I could hear an animal scuttling about in the undergrowth.

un·der·hand¹ /ˌʌndə'hænd◀‖-ər-/ adj, adv UNDERARM¹

underhand² also **un·der·hand·ed** /ˌʌndə'hændɪ̣d◀‖-ər-/— adj dishonest, esp. secretly: He acquired the money in a most underhand manner/by underhand methods. —**handedly** adv —**handedness** n [U]

un·der·lay /'ʌndəleɪ‖-ər-/ n [C;U] (a piece of) material laid under a CARPET, esp. to preserve the quality of the carpet and to keep heat in: foam underlay

un·der·lie /ˌʌndə'laɪ‖-ər-/ v -lay /'leɪ/, -lain /'leɪn/ [T] to be a hidden cause or meaning of: I think a lack of confidence underlies his aggressive manner. | The underlying message of the report was quite optimistic.

un·der·line /ˌʌndə'laɪn‖-ər-/ also **underscore**— v [T] 1 to draw a line under (a word), esp. to show its importance or draw attention to it 2 to give force to (an idea, feeling, etc., which has been expressed or shown); EMPHASIZE: She underlined her disapproval of the proceedings by walking out.

un·der·ling /'ʌndəlɪŋ‖-ər-/ n derog a person of low rank or position in relation to another; SUBORDINATE: The chairman did not attend the meeting; he sent one of his underlings.

un·der·manned /ˌʌndə'mænd◀‖-ər-/ adj (e.g. of a factory or ship) not having enough workers; UNDERSTAFFED — opposite **overmanned**

un·der·men·tioned /ˌʌndə'menʃənd◀‖-dər-/ adj [A] BrE fml which is/are mentioned later in the same piece of writing: Please supply me with the undermentioned goods ... [also n, the+P] The undermentioned will report for duty ... —compare ABOVE-MENTIONED

Under Milk Wood /ˌ··· ·. '··/ a play by Dylan Thomas, originally performed on the radio, which is set in an imaginary Welsh village and full of humour and sensitive descriptions of people

un·der·mine /ˌʌndə'maɪn‖-ər-/ v [T] 1 to wear away the earth beneath, removing support: The house is unsafe since the foundations were undermined by floods. 2 to weaken or destroy gradually: Criticism undermines his confidence. | These incidents could seriously undermine support for the police.

un·der·neath¹ /ˌʌndə'niːθ‖-ər-/ prep, adv under; below: The letter was pushed underneath the door. | Underneath his rather severe manner, he is really very kind-hearted. | She wore a fur coat with nothing underneath. —see UNDER (USAGE)

underneath² n [(the) S] BrE infml the lower part of something; bottom surface; UNDERSIDE: There's a crack on the underneath of the bowl.

un·der·nour·ished /ˌʌndə'nʌrɪʃt‖ˌʌndər'nɜː-, -'nʌ-/ adj having eaten too little food, or food of too low quality, and suffering lack of growth and development: This child is seriously undernourished. —**ishment** n [U]

un·der·pants /'ʌndəpænts‖-ər-/ n [P] underclothes covering the lower part of the body and sometimes the top part of the legs —compare KNICKERS; see PAIR (USAGE)

un·der·pass /'ʌndəpɑːs‖'ʌndərpæs/ n a passage, path, or road built beneath a road or railway line

un·der·pay /ˌʌndə'peɪ‖-ər-/ v -paid /'peɪd/ [T] to pay (someone) too little for their work: We're overworked and underpaid! —opposite **overpay**

n·der·pin /ˌʌndə'pɪn‖-ər-/ v -nn- [T] 1 to support (esp. a wall) from below, e.g. by means of a solid piece of material 2 to give strength or support to (esp. an argument): A solid basis of evidence underpins her theory.

un·der·play /ˌʌndə'pleɪ‖-ər-/ v [T] 1 to make (something) appear less important than it really is; PLAY **down** 2 to UNDERACT 3 **underplay one's hand** to take careful action, showing less of one's plans, intentions, or strength than one could

un·der·priv·i·leged /ˌʌndə'prɪvɪ̣lɪdʒd◀‖-dər-/ adj euph (of a person) not having the advantages of an average person's life; poor, living in bad housing, having low-quality education, etc.: underprivileged children [also n, the+P] special help for the underprivileged

un·der·rate /ˌʌndə'reɪt/ v [T] to have too low an opinion of the quality of; UNDERESTIMATE: It would be dangerous to underrate his ability. | a much underrated film —opposite **overrate**

un·der·re·source /ˌʌndərɪ'zɔːs, -'sɔːs‖-ɔːrs/ v [T] to provide too little money, equipment, etc. for: The project will never be a success if it continues to be underresourced.

un·der·score /ˌʌndə'skɔː.ʳ‖-ər-/ v [T] to UNDERLINE

un·der·seal /'ʌndəsiːl‖-dər-/ v [T] to put a coat of a thick paint, usu. containing rubber, on the UNDERSIDE of (a motor vehicle) to help prevent RUST from forming

un·der·sec·re·ta·ry /ˌʌndəˈsekrɪtəri‖ˌʌndərˈsekrɪteri/ *n* (*often cap.*) **1** (in Britain) a person who is in charge of the daily work of a government department, either a member of parliament of the governing party (**parliamentary undersecretary**) or a CIVIL SERVANT (**permanent undersecretary**), and who helps and advises a minister **2** *AmE* (in other countries) a very high official in a government department

un·der·sell /ˌʌndəˈsel‖-ər-/ *v* **-sold** /ˈsəʊld/ [T] **1** to sell goods at a lower price than (a business competitor) **2** to put too low a value on the good qualities of (a person or thing), esp. when persuading or selling: *I think he undersold himself at the job interview.*

un·der·sexed /ˌʌndəˈsekst◂‖-ər-/ *adj* having unusually little sexual desire —opposite **oversexed**

un·der·shirt /ˈʌndəʃɜːt‖ˈʌndərʃɜːrt/ *n AmE for* VEST (1)

un·der·side /ˈʌndəsaɪd‖-ər-/ *n* [(*the*) S] the part below; lower side or surface: *The underside of the rock was covered with seaweed.*

un·der·signed /ˈʌndəsaɪnd‖-ər-/ *adj* [A] *fml* whose signature appears beneath this writing: [also *n*, *the*+P] *We, the undersigned, wish to be considered for election: John Smith, Joe Brown, Mary White.*

un·der·sized /ˌʌndəˈsaɪzd◂‖-ər-/ also **un·der·size** /-ˈsaɪz◂/— *adj* smaller than usual; too small

un·der·staffed /ˌʌndəˈstɑːft◂‖ˌʌndərˈstæft◂/ *adj* having too few workers, or fewer than usual; UNDERMANNED: *The office is understaffed since the last secretary left.* —opposite **overstaffed**

un·der·stand /ˌʌndəˈstænd‖-ər-/ *v* **-stood** /ˈstʊd/ [*not in progressive forms*] **1** [I;T] to know or recognize the meaning of (something) or the words spoken by (someone): *Do you understand this notice?* | *I can't understand modern art.* | *She spoke so fast I couldn't understand her.* | *Don't you ever do that again, do you understand?* (=a threat) | *I found I could easily* **make myself understood** (=make my meaning clear) *by using sign language.* **2** [T] to know well the character of and have a sympathetic feeling towards (a person, their behaviour, etc.): *If he really loves her he'll understand.* | *A good teacher needs to understand children.* | *I can't understand him when he behaves so badly.* [+wh-] *I can understand why you're annoyed/how you feel.* | *Now we* **understand one another**/ **each other** (=each knows what the other wants and an agreement has been reached), *we can proceed.* **3** [I (**about**);T] to know about and be able to explain the nature of (something), esp. through learning or experience: *I've never really understood the political situation in the Lebanon.* [+wh-] *You don't need to understand how computers work in order to use them.* | *He doesn't really understand about money.* (=doesn't know how to deal with it wisely) **4** [T] *often fml or polite* to have been informed; have found out (a fact): [+(*that*)] *I understand you're coming to work for us.* | *"She's coming to work for us." "So I understand." | I understood he was married, but apparently he isn't.* | **Am I to understand** (=are you telling me) *that you do not intend to pay this bill?* | *He* **gave me to understand** (=told me) *that he would not be returning.* [+obj+to-v] *The ex-president is understood to have secretly left the country.* (=it is thought he has left) **5** [T] to take or judge (as the meaning); INTERPRET: *As I understand it* (=according to my judgment of the situation), *our real problem is lack of time not lack of money.* | *He made a few encouraging comments, and I understood this as meaning he approved.* [+(*that*)] *By "children" it's understood (that) they mean people under 14.* [+obj+to-v] *We understood them to mean that they would wait for us.* **6** [T *often pass.*] to add in the mind (something not stated or expressed, esp. a word) to make a meaning complete: *When I say "Come and help", the object "me" is understood.*

un·der·stand·a·ble /ˌʌndəˈstændəbəl‖ˌʌndər-/ *adj* **1** that can be understood; COMPREHENSIBLE: *The loudspeaker announcement was barely understandable.* **2** as might have been expected; reasonable: *It was quite understandable that he was annoyed.* **-bly** *adv* : *He was understandably annoyed.*

un·der·stand·ing¹ /ˌʌndəˈstændɪŋ‖-ər-/ *n* **1** [U] ability to know and learn; INTELLIGENCE: *beyond a child's understanding* **2** [S;U (**of**)] knowledge of the nature of something, based esp. on learning or experience: *I have little understanding/only a limited understanding of economics/*

computers/American politics. **3** [C *usu. sing.*] a private, not formal, agreement: *We have* **come to an understanding.** (=reached an agreement) [+that] *I lent him money* **on the understanding** *that* (=on condition that) *he paid it back the next month.* **4** [U (**of**)] the way in which one judges the meaning of something; INTERPRETATION: *According to my understanding of the letter, it means something quite different.* **5** [S;U] a sympathetic relationship based on knowing the true character of someone: *There is (a) deep understanding between them.* | *It is hoped that these talks will improve international understanding.*

understanding² *adj apprec* sympathetic and therefore not often blaming or getting annoyed: *Luckily, I have a very understanding boss.*

un·der·state /ˌʌndəˈsteɪt‖-ər-/ *v* [T] **1** to cause (something) to seem less important than it really is: *They understated the seriousness of the crime.* —opposite **overstate 2** to express without full force or show, holding back feelings: *In an understated speech he made clear his views.* | *an understated evening dress* (=not showy)

un·der·state·ment /ˌʌndəˈsteɪtmənt‖-dər-/ *n* [C;U] (a) statement which is not strong enough to express the full or true facts or feelings: *To say the film was bad is an understatement.* | *You call him rich? That's the* **understatement of the year**; *he owns more than any man in Britain!*

un·der·stud·y¹ /ˈʌndəˌstʌdi‖-ər-/ *n* an actor who learns a part in a play so as to be able if necessary to take the place of the actor who usually plays that part

understudy² *v* [T] to be an understudy for (an actor or actress) in (a part): *She understudied (Maggie Smith as) Desdemona.*

un·der·take /ˌʌndəˈteɪk‖-ər-/ *v* **-took** /ˈtʊk/, **-taken** /ˈteɪkən/ [T] *fml* **1** to take up or accept (a duty or piece of work, esp. one that is difficult or needs effort): *She undertook responsibility for the changes.* | *The Channel Tunnel is one of the biggest engineering projects ever undertaken.* **2** [*obj*] to promise or agree: [+to-v] *He undertook to pay the money back within six months.* [+that] *He undertook that he would pay it back.*

un·der·tak·er /ˈʌndəteɪkəʳ‖-dər-/ *n* a person whose job is to arrange funerals

un·der·tak·ing¹ /ˌʌndəˈteɪkɪŋ‖ˈʌndərteɪ-/ *n* **1** [*usu. sing.*] something undertaken; a job, piece of work, or anything needing effort: *Starting a new business can be quite a risky undertaking.* **2** *fml* a promise; PLEDGE: [+to-v/that] *We have had a personal undertaking from the Prime Minister to deal with the matter/that he will deal with the matter.*

un·der·tak·ing² /ˈʌndəˌteɪkɪŋ‖-ər-/ *n* [U] the business of an undertaker

under-the-coun·ter /ˌ··· · ˈ···◂/ *adj infml* (bought or sold) secretly, often illegally: *under-the-counter sales/payments* —see also COUNTER¹ (3)

un·der·tone /ˈʌndətəʊn‖-dər-/ *n* **1** a quiet voice: *He spoke in an undertone.* **2** [(**of**)] a feeling or quality that is not openly expressed but can still be recognized: *There was an undertone of sadness in her letter.* —compare OVERTONES

un·der·tow /ˈʌndətəʊ‖-dər-/ *n* [S] the current beneath the surface which pulls back towards the sea as a wave breaks on the shore

un·der·used /ˌʌndəˈjuːzd◂‖-dər-/ *adj* (esp. of public buildings etc.) not used as much as it/they could be: *The municipal sports centre is underused and losing money.*

un·der·val·ue /ˌʌndəˈvæljuː‖-ər-/ *v* [T] to have too low an opinion of the value or importance of: *She felt that the company undervalued her/her work.*

un·der·wa·ter /ˌʌndəˈwɔːtəʳ◂‖ˌʌndərˈwɔːtər, -ˈwɑː-/ *adj, adv* (used, done, etc.) below the surface of a stretch of water: *underwater swimming* | *underwater cameras* | *The ship was underwater when they reached her.* | *They swam underwater.*

un·der·wear /ˈʌndəweəʳ‖-dər-/ also **underclothes, underclothing** *rather fml*— *n* [U] the clothes worn next to the body under other clothes, such as UNDERPANTS, BRAS, etc.

un·der·weight /ˌʌndəˈweɪt◂‖-ər-/ *adj* weighing less than is expected or usual: *The potatoes are underweight by a kilo.* [after *n*] *He's several pounds underweight.* —opposite **overweight**; see THIN (USAGE)

un·der·went /ˌʌndə'went‖-ər-/ *past tense of* UNDERGO

un·der·whelm /ˌʌndə'welm‖-ər-/ *v* [T] *often humor* to impress very little, or less than was intended or expected: *He underwhelmed us with his recitation of nursery rhymes in Latin.* | *an underwhelming new film*

un·der·world /'ʌndəwɜːld‖'ʌndərwɜːrld/ *n* [*the*+S] **1** (*usu. cap.*) (esp. in ancient Greek stories) the place where the spirits of the dead live **2** the criminal world; criminals considered as a social group

un·der·write /ˌʌndə'raɪt/ *v* **-wrote** /'rəʊt/, **-written** /'rɪtn/ [T] **1** *fml* to support with money and esp. take responsibility for possible failure: *The government has agreed to underwrite the new project with a grant of £5 million.* **2** *tech* to take responsibility for fulfilling (an insurance agreement)

un·der·writ·er /'ʌndəˌraɪtər‖-dər-/ *n* a person who makes insurance contracts

Underwriters' La·bor·a·tories /'···· ·ˌ···‖'···· ˌ····/ *also* **UL–** an American organization which tests the safety of electrical equipment and puts its mark on that which it approves: *This television is approved by Underwriters' Laboratories.* | *a UL-listed lamp*

un·de·served /ˌʌndɪ'zɜːvd◂‖-ɜːr-/ *adj* which has not been earned: *undeserved attention/criticism*

un·de·si·ra·ble¹ /ˌʌndɪ'zaɪərəbəl◂/ *adj fml* unpleasant and unwanted: *Long delays are undesirable, but sometimes unavoidable.* | *efforts to rid the football clubs of undesirable elements* | *The incident could have undesirable consequences for the government.* —compare DESIRABLE (1) **—bly** *adv* **—bility** /ˌʌndɪzaɪərə'bɪlᵻti/ *n* [U]

undesirable² *n fml derog* an undesirable person, esp. someone regarded as immoral, criminal, or socially unacceptable

un·de·vel·oped /ˌʌndɪ'veləpt◂/ *adj* (usu. of a place) in its natural state, esp. not having industry, mines, building, modern farming, etc. —see also DEVELOP (3), UNDERDEVELOPED COUNTRY

un·dies /'ʌndiːz/ *n* [P] *infml or humor* articles of esp. women's UNDERWEAR

un·dig·ni·fied /ʌn'dɪgnᵻfaɪd/ *adj* lacking in seriousness or formality; appearing foolish: *an undignified exit* | *undignified behaviour*

un·dis·charged /ˌʌndɪs'tʃɑːdʒd◂‖-ɑːr-/ *adj tech* **1** (of an account or debt) not paid —see also DISCHARGE¹ (4) **2** (of a person who owes money) not yet allowed by the court to stop repayments; still legally in debt: *an undischarged bankrupt*

un·di·vid·ed /ˌʌndɪ'vaɪdᵻd◂/ *adj* complete: *Give me your undivided attention.*

un·do /ʌn'duː/ *v* **-did** /'dɪd/, **-done** /'dʌn/ [T] **1** to unfasten (something tied or wrapped): *Undo the string round the parcel.* | *I undid the parcel.* —see also UNDONE, DO **up** (1); see OPEN² (USAGE) **2** to remove the effects of: *The disastrous fire undid months of hard work.* **3** [*usu. pass.*] *old use* to ruin the position or hopes of: *I am undone! My secret has been discovered!* **4** [usu. pass.] to upset very seriously: *She was undone by the news of the accident.*

un·do·ing /ʌn'duːɪŋ/ *n* [S] the cause of someone's ruin, shame, failure, etc.; DOWNFALL: *In the end his ambition was his undoing.* (=caused him to fail) —compare MAKING (2)

un·done /ˌʌn'dʌn◂/ *adj* [F] unfastened or loose: *One of your buttons is undone/has come undone.*

un·doubt·ed /ʌn'daʊtᵻd/ *adj* known for certain to be (so); UNQUESTIONABLE: *his undoubted talent* —see DOUBT² (USAGE) **— ~ ly** *adv* : *That is undoubtedly true.*

un·dreamed-of /ʌn'driːmd ɒv ‖ -ɑːv/ *also* **un·dreamt-of** /ʌn'dremt-/— *adj* beyond, and esp. better or more than, what can be imagined: *undreamed-of happiness/ wealth* | *These technical advances were undreamed-of even 20 years ago.*

un·dress¹ /ʌn'dres/ *v* **1** [I] to take one's clothes off **2** [T] to take the clothes off (someone): *I undressed the baby and put him in his bath.*

undress² *n* [U] **1** *fml* lack of clothes: *The little boy ran out of the house, still in a **state of undress**.* **2** *tech* military uniform not for ceremonial occasions

un·dressed /ˌʌn'drest◂/ *adj* **1** [F] not wearing any clothes: *The doctor told me to **get undressed**.* (=take my clothes

off) **2** (of a wound) not treated with drugs and covered —see also DRESS¹ (5) **3** (of an animal skin) not yet fully treated or preserved as leather

un·due /ˌʌn'djuː◂‖-duː-◂/ *adj* [A] *fml* more than is reasonable, suitable, or necessary; EXCESSIVE: *It would be wise not to give undue importance to his criticisms.* | *with undue haste* —see also UNDULY

un·du·late /'ʌndjᵿleɪt‖-dʒə-/ *v* [I] *rather fml* to move or lie like waves rising and falling: *undulating hills* **—lation** /ˌʌndjᵿ'leɪʃən‖-dʒə-/ *n* [C;U]: *the gentle undulations of the English landscape*

un·du·ly /ʌn'djuːli‖-'duː-/ *adv fml* in an undue way; too much (so): *We're not unduly worried/not worried unduly.*

un·dy·ing /ʌn'daɪ-ɪŋ/ *adj* [A] which will never end; ETERNAL: *our undying love* | *undying fame*

un·earned /ʌn'ɜːnd◂‖-'ɜːrnd◂/ *adj* **1** not obtained by working: *unearned income/wealth* **2** not deserved: *unearned praise*

un·earth /ʌn'ɜːθ‖-'ɜːrθ/ *v* [T] **1** to dig up: *The police unearthed a skeleton in his garden.* **2** to discover by careful searching: *The reporter had unearthed some interesting secrets about her.*

un·earth·ly /ʌn'ɜːθli‖-'ɜːr-/ *adj* **1** very strange and unnatural; GHOSTLY: *I felt an unearthly presence in the room.* **2** [A] *infml* (of time) very inconvenient, esp. because too early or late: *What an unearthly time of night to call!* **—liness** *n* [U]

un·ease /ʌn'iːz/ *n* [U] *esp. lit* anxiety; worry

un·eas·y /ʌn'iːzi/ *adj* **1** feeling anxious, uncertain, and uncomfortable in the mind: *I'm uneasy about this decision.* **2** causing uneasy feelings; not settled; likely to end without warning: *The nuclear deterrent has maintained an uneasy peace since World War II.* **3** not comfortable or at rest: *uneasy sleep* **—ily** *adv* **—iness** *n* [U]
▷ USAGE **Uneasy** does not mean "difficult".◁

un·e·co·nom·ic /ˌʌniːkə'nɒmɪk◂, ˌʌnekə-‖-'nɑː-/ *adj* **1** resulting in loss of money or not producing (enough) profit: *The factory is uneconomic and will have to be closed down.* —opposite **economic 2** *also* **un·e·co·nom·i·cal** /-kəl/— wasteful: *an uneconomic use of time* —compare ECONOMICAL **— ~ ally** /kli/ *adv*

un·ed·i·fy·ing /ʌn'edᵻfaɪ-ɪŋ/ *adj* unpleasant or offensive to the moral sense: *The film treated us to the unedifying spectacle of a woman having her eyes cut out.*

un·ed·u·cat·ed /ʌn'edjᵿkeɪtᵻd‖-dʒə-/ *adj* showing a lack of (good) education: *uneducated speech*

un·em·ployed /ˌʌnɪm'plɔɪd◂/ *adj* **1** not having a job: *He's unemployed at present.* [also *n, (the)* P] *The number of unemployed is rising all the time.* **2** *fml* not being used profitably: *unemployed wealth*

un·em·ploy·ment /ˌʌnɪm'plɔɪmənt/ *n* [U] **1** the number of people without work in a group or society, in relation to the number of people wanting work: *In this period, unemployment reached record levels.* **2** the state of being unemployed: *These closures will mean unemployment for about 500 workers.* **3** *AmE infml for* UNEMPLOYMENT BENEFIT: *He's been collecting unemployment for six weeks.* | *Do I qualify for unemployment?* —compare FULL EMPLOYMENT

unemployment ben·e·fit /··'·· ˌ···/ ‖ *also* **unemployment com·pen·sa·tion** /··'·· ··ˌ··/ *AmE— n* [U] a sum of money paid regularly by the state to an unemployed worker, esp. the money paid in Britain to unemployed workers who have made a certain number of NATIONAL INSURANCE payments: *He's been living off unemployment benefit for three months, and still has no job.*

un·end·ing /ʌn'endɪŋ/ *adj* (esp. of something unpleasant) continuing (or seeming to be) without end: *an unending struggle to survive*

un·en·light·ened /ˌʌnɪn'laɪtənd◂/ *adj* **1** without knowledge or understanding: *After his complicated explanation I'm afraid I was still completely unenlightened.* **2** having wrong beliefs because of lack of knowledge; SUPERSTITIOUS —see also ENLIGHTENED

un·en·vi·a·ble /ʌn'enviəbəl/ *adj* difficult and unpleasant; not to be wished for: *The policeman had the unenviable job of telling her that her husband had been killed.*

un·e·qual /ʌn'iːkwəl/ *adj* **1** [(to)] not of equal size, value, etc.: *unequal amounts* **2** not balanced or fair; ONE-SIDED: *an unequal contest* **3** [F+to] *fml* (of a person) not having enough strength, ability, etc.; INADEQUATE: *He proved to be unequal to the job.* (=could not do it) — ~ **ly** *adv* — ~ **ness** *n* [U]

un·e·qualled *BrE* ‖ **unequaled** *AmE* /ʌnˈiːkwəld/ *adj fml* greater or esp. better than any other: *unequalled courage* | *The school's success rate is unequalled.* —see also EQUAL³ (2)

un·e·quiv·o·cal /ˌʌnɪˈkwɪvəkəl◂/ *adj fml* completely clear; allowing no possibility of doubt: *an unequivocal refusal* —**cally** /kli/ *adv*

un·er·ring /ʌnˈɜːrɪŋ/ *adj* habitually making no mistakes, esp. in hitting something or reaching the right point: *With unerring judgment|aim he repeatedly hit the centre of the target.* — ~ **ly** *adv*

UNESCO /juːˈneskəʊ/ United Nations Educational, Scientific, and Cultural Organization; an organization through which richer nations help poorer ones

un·e·ven /ʌnˈiːvən/ *adj* **1** not smooth, flat, or level: *The road surface is very uneven here.* | *Her hair has been badly cut and the ends are uneven.* **2** irregular: *His heart beat at an uneven rate.* —compare EVEN² (4) **3** varying in quality or in type; INCONSISTENT: *His work has been rather uneven this year.* (=has often been bad) **4** not equal or balanced equally: *an uneven contest* **5** (of a number) ODD — ~ **ly** *adv* : *The two teams are unevenly matched.* (=not equal in size or ability) — ~ **ness** *n* [U]

un·e·vent·ful /ˌʌnɪˈventfəl◂/ *adj* with nothing unusual or exciting happening: *an uneventful life|day|journey* — ~ **ly** *adv* — ~ **ness** *n* [U]

un·ex·am·pled /ˌʌnɪɡˈzɑːmpəld◂‖-ˈzæm-/ *adj fml* greater or better than anything else of the same type has ever been; EXCEPTIONAL: *unexampled bravery*

un·ex·cep·tio·na·ble /ˌʌnɪkˈsepʃənəbəl◂/ *adj fml* that cannot be disapproved of; quite satisfactory: *unexceptionable behaviour* —**bly** *adv*

un·ex·cep·tion·al /ˌʌnɪkˈsepʃənəl/ *adj fml* not at all unusual; ordinary

un·ex·pur·gat·ed /ʌnˈekspəɡeɪtɪd‖-pər-/ *adj* (of a book, play, etc.) with nothing that is considered improper taken out; complete

un·fail·ing /ʌnˈfeɪlɪŋ/ *adj* (esp. of something good) always present; never lost; continuous: *with unfailing interest|good humour* —see also FAIL¹ (5,6) — ~ **ly** *adv*

un·fair /ˌʌnˈfeəʳ◂/ *adj* not just, reasonable, or honest: *It's very unfair that the whole class should be punished because of one person's mistake.* | *Her friendship with the director gave her an unfair advantage at the interview.* — ~ **ly** *adv* : *He claims he was unfairly dismissed.*

unfair dis·mis·sal /ˌ··· ·ˈ··/ *n* [U] a situation in employment law in which a person has been unjustly dismissed from a job which he/she has held for two years or more: *You can claim unfair dismissal, and may be able to get your job back.*

un·faith·ful /ʌnˈfeɪθfəl/ *adj* [(to)] **1** having a sexual experience or relationship with someone other than one's husband or wife: *She was unfaithful (to her husband) for years before he found out.* —see also ADULTERY (CULTURAL NOTE) **2** *rare* not faithful or loyal — ~ **ly** *adv* — ~ **ness** *n* [U]

un·fal·ter·ing /ʌnˈfɔːltərɪŋ/ *adj fml, usu. apprec* firm; not changing or hesitating (HESITATE): *her unfaltering sense of duty* —see also FALTER — ~ **ly** *adv*

un·fath·om·a·ble /ʌnˈfæðəməbəl/ *adj esp. lit* too strange or mysterious to understand: *an unfathomable mystery* —**bly** *adv*

un·fa·vou·ra·ble *BrE* ‖ **-vorable** *AmE* /ʌnˈfeɪvərəbəl/ *adj* [(for, to)] opposite to what is wanted or needed; not favourable: *The new play received unfavourable reviews.* (=which disapproved of it) | *an unfavourable situation for starting a new business* —**bly** *adv*

un·feel·ing /ʌnˈfiːlɪŋ/ *adj* cruel; not sensitive or sympathetic towards others: *It was unfeeling of them not to grant him leave to go and see his sick wife.* — ~ **ly** *adv*

un·fet·tered /ʌnˈfetəd‖-ərd/ *adj esp. fml or lit* free from control; not tied by severe rules: *The new city developed quickly, unfettered by the usual planning regulations.*

un·fit /ˌʌnˈfɪt◂/ *adj* **1** not in good health or good physical condition: *She was unfit and couldn't play in the big match.* **2** [(for)] not having the right qualities or skills:

an unfit mother | *She is unfit for motherhood.* [F+*to-v*] *He is unfit to hold public office.* — ~ **ness** *n* [U]

un·flag·ging /ʌnˈflæɡɪŋ/ *adj* without becoming tired or weak; TIRELESS: *unflagging interest|enthusiasm* — ~ **ly** *adv*

un·flap·pa·ble /ʌnˈflæpəbəl/ *adj infml apprec* never losing one's calmness, even in difficult situations: *My secretary's quite unflappable and would keep working even if the office was burning down!* —**bly** *adv*

un·flinch·ing /ʌnˈflɪntʃɪŋ/ *adj apprec, esp. lit* firm and fearless: *unflinching eyes* | *unflinching courage* — ~ **ly** *adv*

un·fold /ʌnˈfəʊld/ *v* [I;T] **1** to open from a folded position: *She unfolded the map and spread it on the table.* **2** to (cause to) become clear, more fully known, etc.: *The story unfolds as the film goes on.* | *It was a strange tale he unfolded.*

un·fore·seen /ˌʌnfɔːˈsiːn◂‖-fɔːr-/ *adj* unexpected: *unforeseen delays* | *Due to unforeseen circumstances the opening has been postponed.*

un·for·get·ta·ble /ˌʌnfəˈɡetəbəl◂‖-fər-/ *adj usu. apprec* (of an experience) too strong in effect to be forgotten: *The colours of Africa|England in the spring are unforgettable.* | *an unforgettable holiday* —**bly** *adv*

un·for·tu·nate¹ /ʌnˈfɔːtʃənɪt‖-ˈfɔːr-/ *adj* **1** having, showing, or bringing bad luck, esp. undeserved bad luck: *an unfortunate accident* | *These unfortunate people have been thrown out of their homes.* **2** that makes one sorry; REGRETTABLE: *It is most unfortunate that I was not informed about this earlier.* (=it would have been better if I had been) **3** *euph* rather rude or tactless (TACT): *an unfortunate remark which had clearly caused offence* | *He has a rather unfortunate manner.*

unfortunate² *n euph, esp. fml or lit* an unlucky person, esp. who has no social advantages, no home or job, etc.

un·for·tu·nate·ly /ʌnˈfɔːtʃənətli‖-ˈfɔːr-/ *adv* it is|was a bad thing that …; I am afraid that … : *Unfortunately, they were out when we called.*

un·found·ed /ʌnˈfaʊndɪd/ *adj* not supported by facts; baseless: *unfounded rumours|accusations* | *The suggestion that I wanted her to leave is quite unfounded.*

un·fre·quent·ed /ˌʌnfrɪˈkwentɪd◂/ *adj fml* not often visited by many people: *an unfrequented spot*

un·frock /ʌnˈfrɒk‖ʌnˈfrɑːk/ *v* [T] to DEFROCK

un·furl /ʌnˈfɜːl‖-ɜːrl/ *v* [T] to unroll and open (a flag, sail, etc.)

un·gain·ly /ʌnˈɡeɪnli/ *adj* not graceful; awkward in movement: *a tall ungainly youth* —**liness** *n* [U]

un·glued /ʌnˈɡluːd/ *adj* [F] *AmE infml* upset: *He came unglued when I told him about the fire.*

un·god·ly /ʌnˈɡɒdli‖-ˈɡɑːd-/ *adj* **1** *lit derog* showing lack of respect for God and religion; WICKED **2** [A] *infml* unreasonable: *I had to get up at an ungodly hour this morning.* (=very early)

un·gov·er·na·ble /ʌnˈɡʌvənəbəl‖-vər-/ *adj fml* uncontrollable: *an ungovernable temper*

un·grate·ful /ʌnˈɡreɪtfəl/ *adj* **1** not expressing thanks, esp. when thanks are deserved; not grateful: *an ungrateful child* | *Don't be so ungrateful!* **2** *fml or lit* (of work or action) unpleasant and bringing no reward or result; THANKLESS — ~ **ly** *adv* — ~ **ness** *n* [U]

un·grudg·ing /ʌnˈɡrʌdʒɪŋ/ *adj* willing; without holding back: *ungrudging support*

un·guard·ed /ʌnˈɡɑːdɪd‖-ɑːr-/ *adj* unwisely careless, esp. in speech: *I agreed to do it in an unguarded moment, and I've regretted it ever since.* | *an unguarded remark*

un·guent /ˈʌŋɡwənt/ *n lit* a thick oily substance used on the skin; OINTMENT

un·hand /ʌnˈhænd/ *v* [T *usu. imperative*] *old use* to take one's hands off (someone); stop holding

un·hap·pi·ly /ʌnˈhæpɪli/ *adv* **1** in an unhappy way **2** unfortunately: *Unhappily, she was not able to complete the course.*

un·hap·py /ʌnˈhæpi/ *adj* **1** not happy; sad: *an unhappy face|childhood* **2** [(about, at)] not satisfied or comfortable in the mind; UNEASY: *We are unhappy about|at the way the press has treated this incident.* **3** *fml* unsuitable: *an unhappy remark|choice of colours* **4** unlucky: *an unhappy coincidence* —**piness** *n* [U]

un·health·y /ʌn'helθi/ adj **1** not usually in good health: *unhealthy children who don't get good food and fresh air* **2** not likely to give good health: *unhealthy living conditions* | *an unhealthy environment* **3** showing illness or bad health: *an unhealthy pale skin* **4** derog unnatural; MORBID: *an unhealthy interest in torture and pain* —**ily** adv —**iness** n [U]

un·heard /ʌn'hɜːd ◁ ‖-'ɜːrd ◁/ adj [F] not listened to: *Her complaints went* (=were) *unheard.*

unheard-of /·'· ·/ adj very unusual; never having happened in the past; UNPRECEDENTED: *It's unheard-of for anyone to pass the exam so young.*

un·hinge /ʌn'hɪndʒ/ v [T] to make mad: *The terrible experience has unhinged him/his mind.*

un·hitch /ʌn'hɪtʃ/ v [T] **1** unfasten; free from being connected **2 get unhitched** AmE infml DIVORCE

un·ho·ly /ʌn'həʊli/ adj **1** [A] infml terrible; unreasonable: *They made an unholy din.* **2** not holy or not respecting what is holy

unholy al·li·ance /·,·· ·'··/ n a grouping of people or esp. organizations that are usu. separate or opposed but have come together for a bad purpose

un·hoped-for /ʌn'həʊpt fɔːʳ/ adj too good to be expected: *unhoped-for success*

un·horse /ʌn'hɔːs‖-'ɔːrs/ v [T usu. pass.] esp. lit to cause to fall from a horse

uni- see WORD FORMATION

UNICEF /'juːnɪˌsef/ United Nations International Children's Fund; an organization that helps children in the world suffering from disease, hunger, etc.

u·ni·corn /'juːnɪˌkɔːn‖-kɔːrn/ n in ancient stories, an imaginary horselike animal with one long straight horn growing out of the front of its head

u·ni·cy·cle /'juːnɪsaɪkl/ n a vehicle moved by PEDALS, like a bicycle, but with only one wheel

un·i·den·ti·fied /ˌʌnaɪ'dentɪfaɪd ◁/ adj whose name, nature, or origin is unknown: *An unidentified man was seen near the scene of the murder.* —see also UFO

u·ni·fi·ca·tion /ˌjuːnɪfɪˈkeɪʃən/ n [U] the act or result of unifying; uniting: *The unification of Italy resulted in a single country instead of several kingdoms.*

Unification Church /ˌ···'·· ˌ·/ [the] the official name for the MOONIES

u·ni·form¹ /'juːnɪfɔːm‖-fɔːrm/ n [C;U] a certain type of clothing which is worn by all the members of a group or organization, e.g. in the army, a school, or the police: *Policemen and postmen wear blue uniforms.* | *school uniform* | *He was* **in uniform** (=in the army, navy, etc.) *for three years.*

uniform² adj the same all over; not different or varying in any way; regular: *The air-conditioning system maintains a uniform temperature throughout the building.* | *rows of dull uniform houses* — **~ly** adv : *The sky was uniformly* (=completely) *grey.* | *These cakes are uniformly* (=all) *disgusting.* — **~ity** /ˌjuːnɪˈfɔːmɪti‖-ɔːr-/ n [U]: *the drab uniformity of the houses in this area*

uniform busi·ness rate /ˌ··· '·· ˌ·/ n (in Britain) a standard charge payable by businesses for local government services, introduced at the time of the Community Charge

u·ni·formed /'juːnɪˌfɔːmd‖-ɔːr-/ adj wearing uniform: *Two policemen came to the door; one was uniformed and the other was in plain clothes.*

u·ni·fy /'juːnɪfaɪ/ v [T] **1** to combine parts of (something) to form a single whole: *Spain was unified in the 16th century.* **2** to make all the same; make uniform

u·ni·lat·e·ral /ˌjuːnɪˈlætərəl ◁/ adj done by or having an effect on only one side, esp. one of the political groups in an agreement: *a unilateral declaration of independence by a member country* | **unilateral** *nuclear* **disarmament** —compare BILATERAL, MULTILATERAL — **~ly** adv : *The government imposed the new pay deal unilaterally.*

U·ni·le·ver /'juːnɪˌliːvəʳ/ a British company dealing in food products, DETERGENTs, etc.

un·im·peach·a·ble /ˌʌnɪm'piːtʃəbəl ◁/ adj fml apprec that cannot be doubted or questioned: *an unimpeachable character/witness* | *I heard the rumour from an unimpeachable source.* —**bly** adv

un·im·proved /ˌʌnɪmˈpruːvd ◁/ adj esp. AmE (of land) not built upon, farmed, or connected to services such as water, SEWER, electricity, etc.: *a sale of unimproved lots*

un·in·formed /ˌʌnɪn'fɔːmd ◁‖-ɔːr-/ adj showing a lack of knowledge or enough information: *an uninformed guess* | *uninformed opinions* —see also INFORMED

un·in·hab·i·ta·ble /ˌʌnɪn'hæbɪtəbəl ◁/ adj unfit to be lived in: *The planet Jupiter is uninhabitable.* —opposite **habitable**; see also INHABIT

un·in·hib·it·ed /ˌʌnɪn'hɪbɪtɪd ◁/ adj free in behaviour and feelings, esp. doing and saying what one likes without worrying about what other people think; having no INHIBITIONS: *an uninhibited person* | *uninhibited laughter* — **~ly** adv

un·i·ni·ti·at·ed /ˌʌnɪ'nɪʃieɪtɪd/ n [the+P] fml or humor people who are not among those who have special knowledge or experience

un·in·spired /ˌʌnɪn'spaɪəd ◁‖-ərd ◁/ adj dull; not showing imagination: *an uninspired performance*

un·in·spir·ing /ˌʌnɪn'spaɪərɪŋ ◁/ adj not encouraging the imagination or interest: *an uninspiring lecture/piece of architecture*

un·in·terest·ed /ʌn'ɪntrɪstɪd/ adj [(in)] not interested —see DISINTERESTED (USAGE)

un·in·ter·rupt·ed /ˌʌnɪntə'rʌptɪd ◁/ adj continuous — **~ly** adv

u·nion /'juːnjən/ n **1** [C+sing./pl. v] (often cap.) (esp. in names and titles) a club or society, esp. a TRADE UNION: *Do you belong to a union?* | *the Students' Union* **2** [C] (often cap.) a group of countries or states joined together: *the Soviet Union* | *the US president's State of the Union address* **3** [S;U] the act of joining or state of being joined into one: *This artist's work shows a perfect union of craftsmanship with/and imagination.* **4** [C;U] lit or pomp marriage: *Their union was blessed by children.* (=They had children.) **5** (often cap.) the northern states during the US Civil War: *the Union army*

Union Car·bide /ˌjuːnjən 'kɑːbaɪd‖-'kɑːr-/ an American chemicals company whose factory in Bhopal, India leaked (LEAK¹(1)) poisonous substances in 1984, causing deaths and illness on a large scale among its workers and the surrounding population

u·nion·is·m /'juːnjənɪzəm/ n [U] trade unionism (TRADE UNION) —**ist** n

Unionism n [U] the principles of a political party (**Ulster Unionists**) that wishes Northern Ireland to remain part of the United Kingdom —**ist** n, adj

u·nion·ize also **-ise** BrE /'juːnjənaɪz/ v [I;T] to (cause to) become a member of a TRADE UNION: *unionized labour* | *This factory has recently unionized/been unionized.* —**ization** /ˌjuːnjənaɪ'zeɪʃən‖ˌjuːnjənə-/ n [U]

Union Jack /ˌ·· '·/ also **Union Flag** /'·· ·/ tech— [the] the national flag of Great Britain, made up of three flags (the crosses of Saints George, Andrew, and Patrick) representing England, Scotland, and Northern Ireland. Union Jacks are waved or flown on PATRIOTIC occasions. —see picture at FLAG

Union of South Af·ri·ca /ˌ··· ·· '···/ [the] the official name of SOUTH AFRICA

Union of So·vi·et So·cia·list Re·pub·lics /ˌ··· ·,··· ,··· ·'··/ also **USSR, Soviet Union**— [the] until 1991, the largest country in the world, bordering on the Arctic and Pacific Oceans, and the Baltic and Black Seas, and made up of 15 republics. The USSR was formed after the Russian Revolution in 1917 as a COMMUNIST state, under the leadership of Lenin. The country was for a long time one of the two SUPERPOWERs (the other being the USA), but it broke apart when most of its republics failed to support the president Mikhail Gorbachev. Eleven of the newly independent states grouped together to form the Commonwealth of Independent States (CIS), but some, such as Latvia, became completely independent states —see also COLD WAR, GLASNOST, PERESTROIKA, STALIN

Union Sta·tion /ˌ·· '··/ the name of the main passenger train station in many US cities: *Chicago Union Station*

union suit /'·· ˌ·/ n AmE for COMBINATIONS

u·nique /juː'niːk/ adj **1** [no comp.] being the only one of its type: *Each person's fingerprints are unique.* (=different from anyone else's) **2** infml unusual: *The town is fairly unique in the wide range of leisure facilities it offers.* **3**

greater or esp. better than any other: *a unique knowledge of ancient Roman coins* — **~ly** *adv* — **~ness** *n* [U]

▷ USAGE Many people think it is incorrect to use expressions like "almost unique", "fairly unique", etc., since they suggest that **unique** does not mean "the only one".◁

u·ni·sex /ˈjuːnɪˌseks/ *adj* of one type which can be used by both male and female: *unisex clothes* | *a unisex hairdresser*

u·ni·son /ˈjuːnɪsən, -zən/ *n* [(**in**) U] **1** the doing of something by everyone in agreement or at the same time: *The governments acted in unison to combat terrorism.* **2** musical performance in which everyone plays or sings the same note

u·nit /ˈjuːnɪt/ *n* **1** [+*sing./pl. v*] a group of things or people forming a complete whole but usu. part of a larger group: *The commander sent a unit of cavalry out to investigate.* | *The family is the smallest social unit.* | *She works in the X-ray unit at the hospital.* **2** [(**of**)] an amount or quantity used as a standard of measurement: *The pound is the standard unit of currency in Britain.* | *Give him two units of morphia.* **3 a** (*usu. in comb.*) a piece, esp. of furniture, storage equipment, etc., esp. one which can be fitted with others of the same type: *a kitchen unit* | *a sink unit* **b** any of the usu. numbered divisions of a TEXTBOOK **4** *esp. tech* a single complete thing: *The car factory's output is now up to 15,000 units* (=cars) *per month.* **5** *tech* **a** the smallest whole number; the number 1 **b** any whole number less than ten: *hundreds, tens, and units*

U·ni·tar·i·an /ˌjuːnɪˈteəriən◂/ *n, adj* (a member) of a branch of the Christian church which believes in religious freedom

u·nite /juːˈnaɪt/ *v* [I;T] **1** to make or form a single complete whole; make or become one; join: *The priest united them in marriage.* | *The two colours/rivers mixed and united.* | *The two companies plan to unite.* **2** [(**in, for, against**)] to come or bring together into one group for a shared action or purpose: *They united in condemning this terrorist outrage.* [+*to-v*] *The two governments have united to combat terrorism.* | *The threat of war united the various political groups in the country.*

u·nit·ed /juːˈnaɪtɪd/ *adj* **1** firmly joined in a state of love, agreement, etc.: *They are a very united family.* **2** with everyone concerned having the same aim: *a united effort* | *We are united in our determination to eradicate famine.* **3** [A] (*cap. in names*) politically joined — **~ly** *adv*

United *n* (used in the names of British football clubs): *Manchester United*

United Ar·ab Em·ir·ates /·ˌ·· ˌ·· ˈ···/ [*the* + P] (abbrev. **UAE**) a country in NE Arabia, between Qatar and Oman, made up of seven EMIRATES (Abu Dhabi, Ajman, Dubai, Ras al Khayma, Sharjah, and Umm al Qaywayn); capital Abu Dhabi; population 1,546,000 (1989). The land is mainly desert, but the country sells a great deal of oil.

United Ar·tists /·ˌ·· ˈ··/ a film company (STUDIO (2)) in Hollywood, California

United Farm Work·ers /·ˌ·· ˈ· ˌ··/ (*abbrev.* **UFW**) [*the*] and American TRADE UNION that represents mostly poor MIGRANT people who move around picking fruit and vegetables to earn a living

United King·dom /·ˌ·· ˈ··/ [*the*] a country in W Europe, officially called the United Kingdom of Great Britain and Northern Ireland, made up of England, Wales, Scotland, and Northern Ireland; capital London; population 57,205,000 (1989) —compare ENGLAND and see UK (USAGE)

United Na·tions /·ˌ·· ˈ··/ see UN

United Ne·gro Col·lege Fund /·ˌ·· ˌ·· ˈ·· ˌ·/ [*the*] an American CHARITY that supports black students and black universities

United Re·formed Church /·ˌ·· ·ˈ· ˌ·/ [*the*] a branch of the Christian church formed in 1972 when the Presbyterian Church of England joined with the Congregational Church of England and Wales

United States of A·mer·i·ca /·ˌ·· ˌ· ··ˈ···/ also **United States** /·ˌ·· ˈ·/, **USA, US, America**— [*the*+P] a country in North America, made up of 50 states and the District of Columbia, where the capital is; capital Washington D.C.; population 248,762,000 (1989). The land was colonized (COLONIZE) mainly by the British and the French in the 17th century, but growing disagreement

between Britain and the colonies (COLONY) led to the American Revolution and the Declaration of Independence in 1776. Further lands were added to the nation over the following century. Differences between the North and the South led to the Civil War. The United States is the chief industrial nation in the world, and is noted for its high standard of living, as well as for its large need for ENERGY and raw materials.

United Way /·ˌ·· ˈ·/ [*the*] an American CHARITY that collects money mostly from working people and divides it among several other charities

unit trust /·ˌ· ˈ·/ *BrE* ‖ **mutual fund** *AmE*— *n* a company through which one can buy SHAREs in many different businesses

u·ni·ty /ˈjuːnɪti/ *n* **1** [S;U] the state of being united, joined, or in agreement together: *church unity* | *Her speech was an appeal for party unity.* | *a new unity of purpose* **2** [C] a single whole thing made from related parts **3** [U] *tech* the number one: *A number less than unity is zero or a minus number.*

u·ni·ver·sal /ˌjuːnɪˈvɜːsəl◂‖-ɜːr-/ *adj* **1** concerning or shared by all members of a group: *There was universal agreement as to who should become chairman.* (=everyone agreed) | *universal rejoicing* **2** of or for everyone or everything; widespread; general: *a subject of universal interest* | *universal primary education* (=for all the children in a country) — **~ity** /ˌjuːnɪvɜːˈsælɪti‖ -ɜːr-/ *n* [U]

Universal a film company (STUDIO (2)) in Hollywood, California

Universal Dec·la·ra·tion of Hu·man Rights /·ˌ····· ··ˌ·· · ˌ·· ˈ·/ [*the*] a 1948 statement by the United Nations about the rights which all people in the world should have

universal joint /·ˌ···· ˈ·/ *n* a JOINT, e.g. in a machine, which can turn in all directions

u·ni·ver·sal·ly /ˌjuːnɪˈvɜːsəli‖-ɜːr-/ *adv* **1** by everyone: *universally accepted/disliked* **2** everywhere: *universally present*

u·ni·verse /ˈjuːnɪˌvɜːs‖-ɜːrs/ *n* [*the*+S] (*often cap.*) all space and everything that exists in it: *Stars are found in every part of the known universe.*

u·ni·ver·si·ty /ˌjuːnɪˈvɜːsɪti◂‖-ɜːr-/ *n* [C;U] a place of education at the highest level, where degrees are given: *Did you go to university?* (=study at a university) | *a university professor/campus* —see also extra information on page 408

University Chal·lenge /·ˌ····· ˈ··/ a very difficult QUIZ show on British television, played by students from universities and colleges and presented by Bamber Gascoigne. People remember it esp. for the CATCHPHRASE "Your starter for ten..." (=your first question for ten points).

University of Chi·ca·go /·ˌ·· ··· ·ˈ·/ [*the*] a private university on the south side of Chicago, known for its RESEARCH, PUBLICATIONS, and teaching of high standard in law, business, medicine, and other fields

University of Lon·don /·ˌ··· · ˈ··/ [*the*] a university based in London, originally formed out of University College and King's College in 1836. It is the oldest university in England after the universities of Oxford and Cambridge.

UNIX /ˈjuːnɪks/ *n* [U] *tdmk* a computer OPERATING SYSTEM that runs on computers of all different sizes and kinds

un·just /ˌʌnˈdʒʌst◂/ *adj* not right or fair; not JUST[2]: *an unjust judge/decision*

un·kempt /ˌʌnˈkempt◂/ *adj* **1** having untidy clothes and hair **2** (of the hair) untidy

un·kind /ˌʌnˈkaɪnd◂/ *adj* not kind; cruel or thoughtless: *an unkind remark* | (fig.) *unkind weather* — **~ly** *adv* : *She spoke unkindly.* | *She didn't mean it unkindly.* — **~ness** *n* [C;U] —see also **the unkindest cut** (CUT[2] (12))

un·know·ing /ʌnˈnəʊɪŋ/ *adj esp. lit* not knowing or understanding; UNAWARE: *By buying the stolen jewels she became an unknowing accomplice to the robbery.* — **~ly** *adv*

un·known[1] /ˌʌnˈnəʊn◂/ *adj* [(**to**)] whose name, nature, or origin is not known: *a previously unknown* (=not famous) *painter*

unknown[2] *n* an unknown person or thing: *The director cast her in a leading part when she was a young unknown of 18.* | *The space voyagers set off on their journey into the unknown.*

unknown quan·ti·ty /ˌ·· '···/ n **1** a person or thing whose qualities and abilities are not yet known **2** (in MATHEMATICS) a number represented by the letter x

Unknown Sol·dier /·ˌ·· '···/ n a soldier whose name is not known, whose body is buried within a national MONU-MENT (usu. called the **Tomb of the Unknown Soldier**) as a representative of all the people in the same nation who died in a war, esp. in the First or Second World Wars

un·law·ful /ʌn'lɔːfəl/ adj esp. tech against the law; illegal: unlawful assembly —**ly** adv : unlawfully killed

un·lead·ed /ˌʌn'ledᵻd/ adj (of petrol) not containing compounds of lead. Unleaded petrol was introduced in Britain in the late 1980s, largely because of public anxiety about the harmful effects of lead in the environment. It has been used in the US since the 1970s.

un·learn /ˌʌn'lɜːn‖-ɜːrn/ v [T] to forget intentionally (something learnt, such as a fact or belief): We've had to unlearn the old system of teaching mathematics.

un·leash /ʌn'liːʃ/ v [T (on, upon)] to set (feelings, forces, etc.) free from control and allow them to act with full force: All his anger was unleashed upon us. | The enemy bombers unleashed a terrible attack on the city.

un·leav·ened /ʌn'levənd/ adj (of bread) made without YEAST, and therefore rather flat and solid

un·less /ʌn'les, ən-/ conj if ... not; except on the condition that: Do not leave the building unless instructed to do so.| Unless the government agrees to give extra money, the theatre will have to close.

▷ USAGE Compare **unless** and **if...not**. 1 **Unless** is not used of imaginary events. We cannot use **unless** in these sentences: She would have died (=an imaginary event) **if** the doctors had **not** saved her. | If he weren't so stupid (=an imaginary situation) he would understand. 2 **Unless** can only be used instead of **if ... not** when there is an idea of ending an intention or situation that already exists (not of starting a new one): I'll stay at home **unless** I'm invited/**if** I'm **not** invited to the party (=an invitation would end my present intention to stay at home). **Unless** is very unlikely in the following sentence: I'll be angry **if** I'm **not** invited to the party (=not being invited would make me angry, but I am not angry at present).◁

un·let·tered /ʌn'letəd‖-ərd/ adj fml or lit **1** not well educated **2** not able to read; ILLITERATE

un·like¹ /ˌʌn'laɪk◄/ prep **1** different from: She's very unlike her mother. | Unlike their commercial rivals, the company has made big profits this year. **2** not typical of: It's unlike him to be late: he's usually on time.

unlike² adj [F] fml or lit not alike; different

un·like·ly /ʌn'laɪkli/ adj **1** [F] not expected; improbable: He may come, but it's very unlikely. | It's unlikely that the thieves will ever be caught. [+to-v] They're unlikely to marry. —opposite **likely 2** not likely to be true: an unlikely story|explanation —**liness, -lihood** n [U]

un·list·ed /ʌn'lɪstᵻd/ adj **1** not listed on an official STOCK EXCHANGE list: unlisted securities —see also USM **2** AmE for EX-DIRECTORY: Her phone number is unlisted.

un·load /ʌn'ləʊd/ v **1** [T] to remove (a load) from (something): Have you unloaded the car/the parcels from the car? **2** [I;T] to have (a load) removed: The ship is unloading (its cargo) in the harbour. **3** [I;T] to remove the bullets, etc., from (a gun) or film from (a camera) **4** [T (on)] infml to get rid of (something unwanted): They've bought up thousands of cheap videos which they want to unload on the British market. —compare OFF-LOAD — ~**er** n

un·lock /ʌn'lɒk‖-lɑːk/ v [T] to unfasten the lock of: She unlocked the door and then opened it. | (fig.) Scientists have unlocked the secrets of the atom.

un·looked-for /ʌn'lʊkt fɔːʳ/ adj esp. lit unexpected

un·loose /ʌn'luːs/ v [T] to UNLEASH: He unloosed a stream of abuse.

un·loos·en /ʌn'luːsən/ v [T] to make loose(r) or unfasten; loosen: He sat down and unloosened his belt.

un·luck·y /ʌn'lʌki/ adj not lucky; having or bringing bad luck: We've been very unlucky with that car — it's always breaking down. | She was unlucky enough to break her leg on the first day of her holiday. —**ily** adv

▶CULTURAL NOTE Some things which are considered unlucky are: Friday when it is the 13th day of a month, walk-ing under a ladder, breaking a mirror, and, in Britain, seeing just one MAGPIE. Few people really believe that these things bring bad luck, but unlucky things are still sometimes mentioned —see also SUPERSTITION (CULTURAL NOTE)◀

un·made /ˌʌn'meɪd◄/ adj **1** (of a bed) not having the sheets, etc., put in order ready for sleeping **2** BrE ‖ **un-paved** AmE— (of a road) without a finished level surface

un·manned /ˌʌn'mænd◄/ adj (of a machine, esp. a spacecraft) having no people on board or in control: an unmanned mission to Mars | an unmanned level crossing

un·man·ner·ly /ʌn'mænəli‖-ər-/ adj fml derog impolite; ILL-MANNERED: unmannerly behaviour

un·mar·ried /ˌʌn'mærɪd◄/ adj not married; SINGLE: unmarried mothers

un·mask /ʌn'mɑːsk‖-mæsk/ v [T] to show the hidden truth about: The thief was unmasked. (=we found out who it was)

un·matched /ˌʌn'mætʃt◄/ adj with no like it; greater or better than any other; MATCHLESS: unmatched courage | He remains unmatched as a writer of satire.

un·men·tio·na·ble /ʌn'menʃənəbəl/ adj too shocking to be spoken about

un·men·tio·na·bles /ʌn'menʃənəbəlz/ n [P] old euph or humor for UNDERCLOTHES

un·mind·ful /ʌn'maɪndfəl/ adj [F+of] fml forgetting or not taking into account: Unmindful of the consequences, she allowed them to do as they wished.

un·mis·ta·ka·ble /ˌʌnmᵻ'steɪkəbəl/ adj clearly recognizable; too clear to be mistaken for anything else: the unmistakable sound of breaking glass | That must be Jim — his walk's unmistakable. —**bly** adv

un·mit·i·gat·ed /ʌn'mɪtᵻgeɪtᵻd/ adj [A] (of something bad) complete; not lessened or excused in any way: unmitigated rudeness | The conference was an unmitigated disaster.

un·moved /ʌn'muːvd/ adj [F] **1** showing no pity or sympathy: He remained unmoved by her appeals. —compare MOVE¹ (5) **2** not worried; calm

un·nat·u·ral /ʌn'nætʃərəl/ adj **1** not natural; different from what is usual or expected: a pearl of unnatural size and beauty | It's not unnatural that she should feel annoyed. **2** derog against ordinary and generally accepted ways of behaving: unnatural sexual practices **3** not sincere: an unnatural laugh|manner — —**ly** adv : an unnaturally large head | He had expected, not unnaturally, that she would be there to meet him.

un·ne·ces·sa·ry /ʌn'nesəsəri‖-seri/ adj not necessary or wanted; additional to what is needed or expected: Don't bring any unnecessary luggage. | That was an unnecessary remark; it would have been better not to mention her ex-husband. —**rily** /ʌn'nesəsərəli‖ˌʌn-nesə'serəli/ adv : an unnecessarily severe punishment

un·nerve /ˌʌn'nɜːv‖-ɜːrv/ v [T] to take away (someone's) courage or confidence: an unnerving experience | The experience completely unnerved me.

un·num·bered /ˌʌn'nʌmbəd‖-ərd◄/ adj **1** not having a number marked: an unnumbered Swiss bank account **2** esp. lit too many to be counted

UNO /ˈjuːnəʊ/ abbrev for United Nations Organization — see UN

un·ob·tru·sive /ˌʌnəb'truːsɪv◄/ adj usu. apprec not very noticeable or easily seen: He's a quiet unobtrusive student, but he always does well in exams. — ~**ly** adv : The new office block blends unobtrusively with its surroundings. — ~**ness** n [U]

un·of·fi·cial /ˌʌnə'fɪʃəl◄/ adj not official: an unofficial meeting | It's unofficial (=has not yet been officially stated), but I know he's got the job. — ~**ly** adv

unofficial strike /ˌ···· '··/ n a STRIKE²(1) which has not been approved in advance by the TRADE UNION involved

un·or·tho·dox /ʌn'ɔːθədɒks‖ʌn'ɔːrθədɑːks/ adj different from usual or ordinary beliefs, methods, etc.: He's got a very unorthodox style of playing tennis, but he usually wins. | unorthodox opinions | an unorthodox form of medical treatment —compare HETERODOX

un·pack /ʌn'pæk/ v **1** [I;T] to remove (possessions) from (a container): Have you unpacked (your clothes/your suit-case) yet? **2** [T] tech to change (information stored in a computer) into a form that takes up more space but is easier to understand **3** [T] *infml* to make (a word or statement) more clear by showing or telling parts of it that are not understood: *Could you unpack that remark about my sister's boyfriend?*

un·paid /ˌʌnˈpeɪd◂/ *adj* **1** which has not been paid: *I'm just the unpaid maid in this house!* | *an unpaid bill* **2** (used of work, etc.) done without receiving payment: *unpaid voluntary work*

un·pal·at·a·ble /ʌnˈpælətəbəl/ *adj fml* unpleasant and difficult for the mind to accept: *Sometimes the truth is unpalatable.*

un·par·al·leled /ʌnˈpærəleld/ *adj fml* too great to be equalled: *an unparalleled success* | *a period of unparalleled economic prosperity*

un·par·lia·men·ta·ry /ˌʌnpɑːləˈmentəri‖-pɑːr-/ *adj tech* (of an action or remark in a parliament) not in accordance with the accepted rules of behaviour in parliament — compare PARLIAMENTARY

un·pick /ʌnˈpɪk/ *v* [T] to take out (the stitches) from (something): *First unpick the old stitches/the seams.*

un·placed /ˌʌnˈpleɪst◂/ *adj BrE* not one of the first three to finish in a race or competition

un·play·a·ble /ʌnˈpleɪəbəl/ *adj* **1** (of music) too difficult to be played **2** (of a ball in sports) too well thrown, hit, etc., to be hit back; too difficult to hit **3** (of a piece of ground used for sports) not suitable for playing on

un·pleas·ant /ʌnˈplezənt/ *adj* causing dislike, annoyance, or displeasure; not pleasant or enjoyable; DISAGREEABLE: *unpleasant smells/weather* | *an unpleasant experience/job* | *The bad sales figures came as an unpleasant surprise.* | *He was very unpleasant to me* (=rude or unkind) *when I asked him for his advice.* — ~ly *adv* — ~ness *n* [C;U] : *Don't let the recent unpleasantness spoil our friendship!*

un·plug /ʌnˈplʌg/ *v* [T] **1** to disconnect (an electrical apparatus) from an electric CIRCUIT by removing a PLUG: *I've unplugged the TV set.* **2** to remove (e.g. an electric PLUG) from its SOCKET: *Unplug the cable from the back of the computer.*

un·plumbed /ˌʌnˈplʌmd◂/ *adj* not known about because of not having been examined or explored (EXPLORE): *exploring the unplumbed depths of personality*

un·pre·ce·dent·ed /ʌnˈpresᵻdentᵻd/ *adj* never having happened before: *unprecedented rainfall/price increases* —see also PRECEDENT — ~ly *adv*

un·pre·dict·a·ble /ˌʌnprɪˈdɪktəbəl◂/ *adj* **1** that cannot be predicted (PREDICT): *the unpredictable consequences of a major war* **2** (of a person) tending to show sudden unexpected changes, in behaviour, ideas, etc.; not dependable or STABLE

un·pre·pos·ses·sing /ˌʌnpriːpəˈzesɪŋ/ *adj* not immediately noticeable; ordinary: *an unprepossessing man/building*

un·pre·ten·tious /ˌʌnprɪˈtenʃəs◂/ *adj apprec* not attempting to seem special, important, wealthy, etc.; without PRETENSION: *It's an unpretentious little house but very elegantly furnished.* — ~ly *adv* — ~ness *n* [U]

un·prin·ci·pled /ʌnˈprɪnsᵻpəld/ *adj fml* (done) without regard to moral values, standards of honourable behaviour, etc.; UNSCRUPULOUS: *unprincipled behaviour* | *an unprincipled scoundrel* —see also PRINCIPLE

un·prin·ta·ble /ʌnˈprɪntəbəl/ *adj* (of words) too offensive to be printed, esp. in a newspaper: *Her reply was unprintable.*

un·pro·fes·sion·al /ˌʌnprəˈfeʃənəl◂/ *adj derog* not typical of the standard which is expected in a particular profession or activity: *unprofessional conduct* | *It was unprofessional of you not to check the facts before issuing the statement.* | *a very unprofessional piece of work* — ~ly *adv*

un·prompt·ed /ʌnˈprɒmptᵻd/ /ʌnˈprɑːmp-/ *adj fml, often apprec* done or produced without being asked for, suggested, etc.; SPONTANEOUS: *her unprompted generosity*

un·pro·voked /ˌʌnprəˈvəʊkt◂/ *adj* (esp. of a bad action) not caused or forced by another action; without PROVOCATION: *an unprovoked attack*

un·pun·ished /ʌnˈpʌnɪʃt/ *adj* [F] not given any punishment: *Their behaviour cannot be allowed to* **go unpunished.**

un·qual·i·fied /ʌnˈkwɒlᵻfaɪd‖-ˈkwɑː-/ *adj* **1** [(for)] not having suitable knowledge or QUALIFICATIONS: *unqualified*

school-leavers [F+*to-v*] *I am quite unqualified to talk on this subject.* **2** not limited; complete: *It was an unqualified success.*

un·ques·tio·na·ble /ʌnˈkwestʃənəbəl/ *adj* which cannot be doubted; certain; INDISPUTABLE: *His keenness is unquestionable, but he may not be experienced enough.* — compare QUESTIONABLE — **-bly** *adv* : *unquestionably the best tennis player in the country*

un·ques·tion·ing /ʌnˈkwestʃənɪŋ/ *adj* without any doubt, delay, or argument: *an unquestioning trust in God* | *unquestioning obedience*

un·qui·et /ʌnˈkwaɪət/ *adj esp. lit* not calm or at rest: *an unquiet stillness hung over the countryside as the thunderclouds gathered.*

un·quote /ˌʌnˈkwəʊt/ *adv* (a word used in speech for showing that one has come to the end of a QUOTATION (2)): *The figures given are (quote) "not to be trusted" (unquote), according to this writer.*

un·rav·el /ʌnˈrævəl/ *v* -ll- *BrE* ‖ -l- *AmE* **1** [I;T] to become or cause (threads, cloth, etc.) to become separated or unwoven: *This sweater has started to unravel.* **2** [T] to make clear (a mystery)

un·rea·da·ble /ʌnˈriːdəbəl/ *adj* **1** *derog* too dull to be read; not worth reading **2** ILLEGIBLE — **-bly** *adv*

un·real /ˌʌnˈrɪəl◂/ *adj* (of an experience) seeming imaginary or unlike reality — **~ity** /ˌʌnriˈælᵻti/ *n* [U]

un·rea·so·na·ble /ʌnˈriːzənəbəl/ *adj* **1** going beyond what is fair, acceptable, or sensible: *I think she is making quite unreasonable demands on us.* | *It's unreasonable to expect me to work all night.* **2** (of prices, costs, etc.) too great —opposite **reasonable** — **-bly** *adv* — **~ness** *n* [U]

un·rea·son·ing /ʌnˈriːzənɪŋ/ *adj fml* not using or influenced by the power of reason: *unreasoning anger*

un·re·gen·e·rate /ˌʌnrɪˈdʒenərᵻt◂/ *adj fml derog* making no attempt to change one's bad practices: *an unregenerate liar*

un·re·lent·ing /ˌʌnrɪˈlentɪŋ◂/ *adj* continuous, without decreasing in power or effort: *a week of unrelenting activity* —see also RELENT, RELENTLESS — ~ly *adv*

un·re·lieved /ˌʌnrɪˈliːvd◂/ *adj* (of something bad) not varied in any way; continuous or complete: *unrelieved anxiety/gloom/hardship* —see also RELIEVE — ~ly /ˌʌnrɪˈliːvᵻdli/ *adv* : *unrelievedly dull*

un·re·mit·ting /ˌʌnrɪˈmɪtɪŋ◂/ *adj fml* (of something difficult) never stopping; continuous: *an unremitting struggle* — ~ly *adv*

un·re·quit·ed /ˌʌnrɪˈkwaɪtᵻd◂/ *adj fml* not given in return (esp. in the phrase **unrequited love**)

un·re·served /ˌʌnrɪˈzɜːvd◂‖-ɜːr-/ *adj* **1** *fml* without limits; complete: *They have my unreserved support.* **2** (of seats) not reserved (RESERVE¹) — ~ly /ˌʌnrɪˈzɜːvᵻdli‖-ɜːr-/ *adv* : *She apologized unreservedly.*

UN res·o·lu·tion /ˌ· · ··ˈ·◂·/ *n* a formal statement made by the United Nations expressing its decision on a particular matter and instructing its members on what they should do

un·rest /ʌnˈrest/ *n* [U] a state of troubled or dissatisfied confusion, often with fighting: *widespread social unrest in the big cities* | *a period of industrial unrest with continual strikes*

un·re·strained /ˌʌnrɪˈstreɪnd◂/ *adj* not held back or controlled: *unrestrained anger/violence* | *the unrestrained use of force* — ~ly /ˌʌnrɪˈstreɪnᵻdli/ *adv* — ~ness *n* [U]

un·ri·valled *BrE* ‖ **-valed** *AmE* /ʌnˈraɪvəld/ *adj fml* better than any other; extremely good: *an unrivalled knowledge of Chinese art* | *As a war photographer he is unrivalled.* —see also RIVAL²

un·roll /ʌnˈrəʊl/ *v* [I;T] to open from a rolled position: *She unrolled the map/the carpet.*

un·ruf·fled /ʌnˈrʌfəld/ *adj apprec* calm; not worried: *He appeared quite unruffled by these questions.*

un·ru·ly /ʌnˈruːli/ *adj* **1** wild in behaviour; difficult to control: *unruly children* **2** not easily kept in place: *unruly hair* — **-liness** *n* [U]

un·sad·dle /ʌnˈsædl/ *v* [T] **1** to remove the SADDLE from (a horse) **2** to UNSEAT (1)

un·safe sex /ˌʌnseɪf ˈseks/ *n* [U] sexual activities, esp. having sex without using a CONDOM, which put one or both partners at risk of infection, esp. from AIDS

un·said /ʌnˈsed/ *adj* [F] (thought of but) not spoken: *a tactless remark that would have been* **better left unsaid**

un·sat·u·rat·ed fat /ˌʌnˌsætʃəreɪtᵻd ˈfæt/ *n* a fat with a particular kind of chemical structure. There are two kinds: **monounsaturated fats**, found in olive oil, peanuts, and avocados, and **polyunsaturated fats**, found in sunflower oil, soybean oil, and corn oil. Unsaturated fats are believed to be better for health than SATURATED FATS. — compare SATURATED FAT

un·sa·vour·y *BrE* ‖ **-vory** *AmE* /ʌnˈseɪvəri/ *adj* unpleasant, esp. in being morally unacceptable: *an unsavoury character* (=person)/*reputation* | *his unsavoury business activities*

un·scathed /ʌnˈskeɪðd/ *adj* [F] not harmed: *He walked away from the accident completely unscathed.*

un·scram·ble /ʌnˈskræmbəl/ *v* [T] to put (esp. a message in CODE) back into order so that it can be understood

un·screw /ʌnˈskruː/ *v* [T] **1** to remove the screws from: *We had to unscrew the hinges to take down the door.* **2** to undo by twisting: *I can't unscrew the top of this bottle.*

un·script·ed /ˌʌnˈskrɪptᵻd◂/ *adj* (esp. of a broadcast talk or conversation) not written or planned before; not based on a SCRIPT: *an unscripted interview*

un·scru·pu·lous /ʌnˈskruːpjᵿləs/ *adj* not caring about honesty and fairness in getting what one wants; completely without principles: *unscrupulous business methods* | *an unscrupulous salesman* — ~ **ly** *adv* — ~ **ness** *n* [U]

un·sea·so·na·ble /ʌnˈsiːzənəbəl/ *adj* (of weather) unusual for the time of year, esp. bad —**bly** *adv* — ~ **ness** *n* [U]

un·seat /ʌnˈsiːt/ *v* [T] **1** also **unsaddle**— (of a horse) to throw off (a rider) **2** to remove from a position of political power

UN Se·cu·ri·ty Coun·cil /ˌ· ·ˈ··· ˌ··/ [the] a branch of the United Nations with 15 members, including the US, Russia, China, France, and Britain. The UN Security Council can use economic or military force to settle international disagreements which seem likely to threaten world peace.

un·seed·ed /ˌʌnˈsiːdᵻd◂/ *adj* not chosen as a SEED¹ (3), esp. in a tennis competition

un·see·ing /ˌʌnˈsiːɪŋ◂/ *adj esp. lit* not noticing anything; (as if) blind: *She stared out of the window with unseeing eyes.* — ~ **ly** *adv*

un·seem·ly /ʌnˈsiːmli/ *adj fml* not proper or suitable (in behaviour); likely to attract disapproval: *They left with unseemly haste.* —**liness** *n* [U]

un·seen /ˌʌnˈsiːn/ *n esp. BrE* a piece of writing not previously seen which is to be translated into one's own language as part of an examination: *a French unseen* —see also **sight unseen** (SIGHT (16))

Un·ser /ˈʌnsəʳ/, **Al** /æl/, **Sr.** (1939–   ) an American racing car driver

un·set·tle /ʌnˈsetl/ *v* [T] to make less calm, more anxious, dissatisfied, etc.: *The sudden changes unsettled her.* | *a rather unsettling film* —see also SETTLE¹ (3)

un·set·tled /ʌnˈsetld/ *adj* **1** not yet settled: *The dispute remains unsettled.* **2** (of weather, a political situation, etc.) changeable, esp. likely to become worse **3** (of the stomach) slightly ill: *My stomach's a bit unsettled after all that rich food.*

un·sha·kea·ble, **-kable** /ʌnˈʃeɪkəbəl/ *adj* firm, esp. in belief or loyalty: *an unshakeable faith in God*

un·shav·en /ʌnˈʃeɪvən/ *adj* not having shaved (SHAVE¹ (1)) or been shaved: *His unshaven face made him look rather disreputable.* | *He decided to stay unshaven.*

un·sight·ly /ʌnˈsaɪtli/ *adj* not pleasant to look at; ugly: *an unsightly spot on his nose* | *an unsightly modern office block* —**liness** *n* [U]

un·skilled /ˌʌnˈskɪld◂/ *adj* **1** not having training for a particular type of job: *an unskilled worker* **2** not needing special skill: *an unskilled job* —compare SKILLED

un·so·cia·ble /ʌnˈsəʊʃəbəl/ *adj* not enjoying social activity; not fond of being with people

un·so·cial /ˌʌnˈsəʊʃəl◂/ *adj* not suitable for combining with family and social life: *As a policeman you often have to work* **unsocial hours.**

un·so·phis·ti·cat·ed /ˌʌnsəˈfɪstᵻkeɪtᵻd◂/ *adj* not SOPHISTICATED: *an unsophisticated young woman* | *unsophisticated machinery*

un·sound /ˌʌnˈsaʊnd◂/ *adj* **1** (esp. of a person or a building) not in a healthy or strong condition: *His heart is unsound.* | *The apartment block was declared structurally unsound.* **2 a** not firmly based: *Her argument is unsound.* (=not based on correct reasoning) | *The proposal was rejected because it was considered economically unsound.* (=likely to waste money) **b** not acceptable according to a particular set of principles: *His views on defence are regarded by some party members as ideologically unsound.* **3 of unsound mind** *law* mad, and therefore not responsible for one's actions

un·spar·ing /ʌnˈspeərɪŋ/ *adj* [(**in**)] holding nothing back, esp. money or help; very generous: *He was unsparing in his efforts to save the hospital from closure.* — ~ **ly** *adv*

un·spea·ka·ble /ʌnˈspiːkəbəl/ *adj* terrible; too bad to describe: *unspeakable pain* | *his unspeakable crimes* —**bly** *adv* : *unspeakably cruel*/*rude*

un·spoilt /ʌnˈspɔɪlt◂/ ‖ usu. **un·spoiled** /-spɔɪld/ *AmE*— *adj* **1** not damaged or harmed: *She is completely unspoilt by her success.* **2** (of a place) not having changed for a long time: *the unspoilt beauty of these islands*

un·sta·ble /ʌnˈsteɪbəl/ *adj* **1** lacking strength, firmness, and balance: *This bookcase is rather unstable.* **2** not firmly based and likely to change or fail: *an unstable government*/*marriage* **3** (of a person) lacking steadiness of mind; changeable and not dependable **4** (of a chemical compound) likely to break down into simpler chemicals

un·stint·ing /ʌnˈstɪntɪŋ/ *adj fml* very generous: *her unstinting efforts*/*devotion* | *She was unstinting in her praise.*

un·stop /ˌʌnˈstɒp‖ˌʌnˈstɑːp/ *v* **-pp-** [T] **1** to remove something that stops a flow in: *to unstop a blocked pipe* —compare STOP¹ (6) **2** to open (something closed by a STOPPER, esp. a bottle)

un·stuck /ʌnˈstʌk/ *adj* [F] **1** not fastened or stuck on: *The label has come unstuck.* —see also STICK² (2,3) **2 come unstuck** *BrE* to be unsuccessful; not gain the intended result: *You may come unstuck if you try to cheat the tax office.*

un·stud·ied /ˌʌnˈstʌdid◂/ *adj fml* natural; not resulting from practice or effort: *unstudied grace* —compare STUDIED

un·sung /ˌʌnˈsʌŋ◂/ *adj esp. lit* not praised or famous although deserving to be: *an* **unsung hero** | *His achievements went unsung.*

un·swerv·ing /ʌnˈswɜːvɪŋ‖-ɜːr-/ *adj* firm and unchanging: *unswerving loyalty* —see also SWERVE¹ (2)

un·tan·gle /ˌʌnˈtæŋgəl/ *v* [T] to remove TANGLES from; make smooth and free from twisted parts: *Can you untangle these wires?* | (fig.) *I'll never untangle all these complicated tax debts.*

un·tapped /ˌʌnˈtæpt◂/ *adj* (of something useful or valuable) not yet put to use: *There are still vast untapped reserves of oil under the sea.*

un·ten·a·ble /ˌʌnˈtenəbəl/ *adj* (of a position, esp. in an argument) impossible to defend or show to be reasonable: *The Prime Minister is now in a completely untenable position, and must resign.* | *an untenable proposition*

un·thin·ka·ble /ʌnˈθɪŋkəbəl/ *adj* not acceptable; too bad to think about or regard as possible: *It's quite unthinkable that he should be expected to pay the whole cost himself.* | *Defeat is unthinkable.*

un·think·ing /ʌnˈθɪŋkɪŋ/ *adj* careless; done or said without considering the effect; THOUGHTLESS: *an unthinking remark* — ~ **ly** *adv*

un·ti·dy /ʌnˈtaɪdi/ *adj* not neat; MESSY: *an untidy room*/*house*

un·tie /ʌnˈtaɪ/ *v* [T] to undo (a knot or something tied): *Untie the string.* | *Untie me from the chair.*

un·til /ʌnˈtɪl, ən-/ also **till**— *prep, conj* **1** up to (the time that): *I waited until 10 o'clock, but he still didn't come.* | *Wait until I call.* | *We won't start until Bob comes.* | *He stayed from Monday till Friday.* | *The problem has never really arisen until now.* | *Until when do the pubs stay open?* | (*infml*) *He was here* **up until** *last week.* **2** as far as; up to (a place): *Stay on the train until Birmingham.* —see TO¹ (USAGE)

un·time·ly /ʌnˈtaɪmli/ *adj fml* **1** happening too soon; PREMATURE: *her untimely death* **2** not suitable for the occasion; INOPPORTUNE: *an untimely remark* —**liness** *n* [U]

un·tir·ing /ʌnˈtaɪərɪŋ/ *adj apprec* never stopping or showing tiredness, esp. in spite of hard work: *an untiring worker* | *her untiring efforts* – –**ly** *adv*

un·to /ˈʌntu:/ *prep old use or bibl* to: *She spoke unto him.*

un·told /ˌʌnˈtəʊld◂/ *adj* **1** too great to be counted or measured; limitless: *untold wealth* | *She has done untold damage to our chances.* **2** not told or expressed: *Her story remains untold.*

un·tou·cha·ble /ʌnˈtʌtʃəbəl/ *adj, n* [no comp.] (a person) of the lowest social group, esp. in the Hindu CASTE system

un·to·ward /ˌʌntəˈwɔːd||ˌʌnˈtɔːrd/ *adj fml* unexpected and undesirable: *We completed our journey without anything untoward happening.* – –**ly** *adv* – –**ness** *n* [U]

un·tram·melled *BrE* || **-meled** *AmE* /ʌnˈtræməld/ *adj fml* allowed to act or develop with complete freedom

un·true /ʌnˈtruː/ *adj* false; not true

un·truth /ʌnˈtruːθ, ˈʌntruːθ/ *n fml euph* a lie

un·used /ˌʌnˈjuːzd◂/ *adj* **1** not in use or having been used: *unused space* **2 unused to** /ʌnˈjuːst tʊ/ having little or no experience of (something): *I'm unused to the heavy London traffic.* [+v-ing] *I'm unused to having so much responsibility.*

un·u·su·al /ʌnˈjuːʒuəl, -ʒəl/ *adj* **1** rare; not common: *Heavy rain is unusual in this part of the world.* | *It's unusual to see him up so early in the morning.* **2** interesting because different from others; DISTINCTIVE: *I like that painting; it's most unusual.*

un·u·su·al·ly /ʌnˈjuːʒuəli, -ʒəli/ *adv* **1** very; more than is usual: *It's unusually hot today.* **2** in an unusual way

un·ut·te·ra·ble /ʌnˈʌtərəbəl/ *adj* [A] *fml or pomp* of the greatest or worst kind; terrible: *in unutterable pain* | *an unutterable fool* —**bly** *adv*

un·var·nished /ʌnˈvɑːnɪʃt||-ɑːr-/ *adj* [A] plain; without additional description: *Just give me the plain unvarnished truth.*

un·veil /ˌʌnˈveɪl/ *v* [T] to remove a covering from: *The queen today unveiled a plaque to open the new hospital.* | (fig.) *The car company will be unveiling its latest models* (=showing them publicly for the first time) *at a press conference tomorrow.*

un·versed /ˌʌnˈvɜːst||-ɜːr-/ *adj* [F+**in**] *fml or lit* not experienced or informed: *unversed in the ways of city life/in the world of business*

un·voiced /ˌʌnˈvɔɪst◂/ *adj* not expressed in words: *unvoiced fears*

un·waged /ˌʌnˈweɪdʒd◂/ *adj euph, esp. BrE* having no job; unemployed. [also *n*, *the* | T] *reduced rates for the unwaged*

un·war·rant·ed /ʌnˈwɒrəntɪd||-ˈwɔː-, -ˈwɑː-/ also **un·war·rant·a·ble** /ʌnˈwɒrəntəbəl||-ˈwɔː-, -ˈwɑː-/ *adj fml* unwelcome and done without good reason: *an unwarranted intrusion into our private affairs*

un·well /ʌnˈwel/ *adj* [F] ill, esp. for a short time

un·wiel·dy /ʌnˈwiːldi/ *adj* **1** awkward to move or handle because it is large, heavy, a strange shape, etc.: *an unwieldy piece of furniture* **2** difficult to use, manage, or control: *an unwieldy argument/method* | *a large unwieldy bureaucracy* —**diness** *n* [U]

un·will·ing /ʌnˈwɪlɪŋ/ *adj* not wanting to do something, or doing something without really wanting to; RELUCTANT: *an unwilling helper* (=who helped, but without eagerness) | *an unwilling student* [F+*to-v*] *I'm unwilling to lend him any more money after what happened last time.* – –**ly** *adv* : *He unwillingly gave his consent.*

un·wind /ʌnˈwaɪnd/ *v* **-wound** /ʌnˈwaʊnd/ **1** [I;T] to come undone or undo (something that has been wound round): *She unwound the wool from the ball.* **2** [I] *infml* to stop being nervous; RELAX, esp. after a period of great effort and pressure: *She found it hard to unwind after a busy day at work.* —compare UNBEND

un·wit·ting /ʌnˈwɪtɪŋ/ *adj fml* not knowing or not intended: *She was their unwitting accomplice.* (=she did not know she was helping them) | *an unwitting insult* – –**ly** *adv*

un·wont·ed /ʌnˈwəʊntɪd/ *adj* [A] *fml* not usual or expected; UNACCUSTOMED: *He arrived with unwonted punctuality.*

un·world·ly /ʌnˈwɜːldli||-ɜːr-/ *adj* not concerned with or experienced in the ways of society

un·writ·ten law /ˌʌnrɪtn ˈlɔː/ also **unwritten rule**— *n* a custom followed as a rule, though not formally or officially stated: *the unwritten law that women and children are saved first from a sinking ship*

un·zip /ˌʌnˈzɪp/ *v* **-pp-** [T] to open by undoing a ZIP (fastener): *She unzipped her dress.*

up¹ /ʌp/ *adv* **1** from below towards a higher position; away from the floor, the ground, or the bottom: *My pen fell on the floor and I picked it up.* | *Can you lift that box up onto the shelf for me?* | *The boy climbed up to a higher branch on the tree.* | *We swam a long way under water and then came up for air.* | *Hang the picture up on the wall.* | *It gets hot quickly when the sun comes up.* (=appears above the horizon) | *Up you come!* **2** at or in a higher position; above: *John's up in his bedroom.* | *The plane was flying 30,000 feet up.* | *We stayed in a little town up in the mountains.* **3** into an upright or raised position: *Everyone stood up when the teacher came in.* | *He turned up his collar to keep his neck dry.* | *They're putting up* (=building) *a new factory.* **4** in or towards the north: *He's flying up to Scotland from London.* | *They live up North.* —compare DOWN¹ (5) **5** along; towards (and as far as): *He came right up (to me) and asked my name.* | *He walked up to her.* | *Let's go up the road for something to eat.* **6** so as to increase in loudness, strength, level of activity, etc.: *Could you turn the radio up a bit, please.* | *Speak up! I can't hear you.* | *Competition between these companies is really hotting up.* **7** (so as to be) completely finished: *The money's all used up.* | *The party ended up with a song.* | *He won't eat up his vegetables.* | *He bought up all the flowers in the shop.* **8** so as to be all in small pieces: *I tore up the newspaper.* | *They divided up the money.* | *The plane hit the mountainside and broke up on impact.* **9** firmly; tightly; so as to be closed, covered, or joined: *She tied up the parcel.* | *He nailed up the door so they couldn't open it.* **10** so as to be together: *Please add up/count up these figures.* | *We collected up the fallen apples.* **11** (so as to be) on top: *I turned the board right side up.* **12** into consideration; so as to receive attention: *I'd like to bring up the question of the exam timetable.* | *The report has thrown up a number of unexpected problems.* **13** above and including: *Power was lost from the tenth floor up.* | *Children of 12 and up can enter without a guardian.* **14 up and down: a** higher and lower: *She was jumping up and down.* | (fig.) *"How's your father?" "Rather up and down, you know."* (=sometimes well, sometimes ill) **b** backwards and forwards: *I could hear him in his bedroom walking up and down.* —see also UPS AND DOWNS **15 up to: a** as far as; to and including: *Up to ten people* (=any number between one and ten) *can sleep in this tent.* | *Everyone has his part to play, from the office boy up to the President* | (fig.) *He's up to his ears/eyes/neck* (=very deeply) *in debt.* **b** also **up till**— until: *He was here up to a moment ago.* **c** (*usu. in questions or negatives*) good, well, or clever enough for: *Michael's not really up to that job.* [+*v-ing*] *My German isn't up to translating that letter.* | *Do you feel up to going out, or have you still got a headache?* **d** the duty or responsibility of (someone): *"Shall we go out?" "It's up to you."* (=You must decide.) **e** *infml* doing (something bad): *The children are very quiet; I wonder what they're up to/getting up to!* **16 Up (with)**... *infml* We want or approve of: *Up the workers!* —compare DOWN (21)

up² *prep* **1** to or in a higher place in; upwards by way of: *He climbed up the hill/the stairs/the ladder.* | *The water got up my nose.* **2** to or at the top or far end of: *Her office is up those stairs.* | *They live just up the road.* (=further along the road from here) **3** against the direction of the current of: *sailing up the Seine* **4** *BrE nonstandard* to; up to: *I'm going up the West End tonight.* | *He's up the pub.* **5 up and down: a** higher and lower on: *I was up and down the stairs all day answering the door.* **b** backwards and forwards along: *His eyes moved up and down the rows of people, looking for his son's face.* **6 Up yours!** *taboo sl* (used for expressing great dislike for or annoyance at a person)

up³ *adj* [no comp.] **1** [A] directed or going up: *We caught the up train.* (=to London, etc.; compare *the down train*) | *the up escalator* **2** [F] (of a road) being repaired; with a broken surface: *"Road Up"* (on a sign) **3** [F] (of a computer system) in operation; working —opposite **down**

4 [F] being at a higher level, e.g. in price, level or quantity; from a smaller to a larger amount: *The price of stamps has gone up* (=increased) *again.* | *Inflation is up by 2%.* | *Profits are up on* (=compared with) *last year.* **5** out of bed: *He got up very late.* | *We stayed up until midnight.* | *Are you up yet?* **6** [F *usu. in questions and negatives*] (in tennis and similar games) (of a ball) having hit the ground only once before being hit back **7** [F] *infml* charged with an offence; in court: *He's up before the judge for stealing.* —see also HAVE **up 8 be (well) up in/on** *infml* to know a lot about **9 up against** having to face or deal with: *We've come up against a problem.* | *We're really* **up against it** (=in serious difficulty) *now.* **10 up and about** *infml* out of bed (again) and able to walk —compare **out and about** (OUT¹) **11 up for a** intended or being considered for: *The house is up for sale.* | *This subject will be up for discussion at the next meeting.* **b** able and willing to do or experience; in the MOOD for: *Are you up for a game of cards?* | *I don't think I'm up for his jokes tonight.* **12 What's up?** *infml* (of something bad or unwelcome) What's happening? What's the matter?: *What's up? Why are they crying?* | *I knew something was up when I saw the smoke.*

up⁴ *v* **-pp-** *infml* **1** [T] to raise; increase: *They've upped their offer by a further 5%.* **2** [I] (used followed by **and** for adding force to the account of a surprising action): *Without saying another word, he upped and left.*

up- see WORD FORMATION

up-and-com·ing /ˌ·ˈ···◂/ *adj* [A] *apprec* showing signs of likely future success or popularity: *an up-and-coming young opera singer* | *an up-and-coming neighbourhood* —compare UPCOMING

up-and-un·der /ˌ·ˈ··/ *n* (in RUGBY) a high kick forwards followed by a rush to the place where the ball lands

up-and-up /ˌ·ˈ·/ *n* **on the up-and-up** *infml* **a** *BrE* improving; succeeding **b** *AmE* honest

U·pan·ish·ad /uːˈpʌnɪʃəd, -ʃæd ‖ uːˈpɑːnɪʃɑːd/ any of a collection of holy books which form the base of Hindu religion and PHILOSOPHY, together called the **Up·anishads**

up·beat /ˈʌpbiːt/ *adj infml* cheerful and full of hope: *The film had a very upbeat ending.* —compare DOWNBEAT

up·braid /ˌʌpˈbreɪd/ *v* [T (**with**)] *fml* to speak angrily to (someone) because they have done something wrong

up·bring·ing /ˈʌpˌbrɪŋɪŋ/ *n* [S] the care, training, and education that someone receives, esp. from their parents, when they are growing up: *a strict upbringing* | *The children had an easy-going upbringing.* —see also BRING **up**

up·chuck /ˈʌptʃʌk/ *v* [T;I] *AmE infml for* VOMIT

up·com·ing /ˈʌpˌkʌmɪŋ/ *adj* [A] about to happen: *the upcoming elections* —compare UP-AND-COMING

up-coun·try /ˌ·ˈ···◂/ *adj, adv* **1** in or from the inner parts of a country, away from the coast **2** from an area with few people, towns, etc., and without the manners and qualities that are thought typical of city people

up·date /ˌʌpˈdeɪt/ *v* [T] **1** to make more modern or up-to-date: *an updated model of this popular car* **2** [(**on**)] to supply with the latest information: *The minister's advisers updated her on the situation.* —**update** /ˈʌpdeɪt/ *n* : *a computer file update*

Up·dike /ˈʌpdaɪk/, **John** (1932–) an American writer noted for his NOVELs about the worries and misfortunes of modern middle-class life, such as *Rabbit, Run, Couples,* and *Rabbit is Rich*

up·end /ʌpˈend/ *v* [T] **1** to cause to stand on end or on any part that does not usually stand on the floor **2** *infml* to knock down: *He upended his opponent with a single punch.*

up·front /ˌʌpˈfrʌnt/ *adj* [F] very direct and making no attempt to hide one's meaning: *He's very upfront about his political views.* —see also **up front** (FRONT¹)

up·grade /ˌʌpˈɡreɪd/ *v* **1** [T] to give a position of more importance to (an employed person or a job): *He's hoping to be upgraded/to get his job upgraded.* **2** [I;T] to improve (something), esp. in quality or effectiveness: *You can upgrade your 32K computer to 64K simply by adding an expansion chip.* | *The course centre is in the process of upgrading its facilities.* | *At weekends standard-class passengers can pay an extra £3 and upgrade to first-class seats.* —opposite **downgrade**

up·heav·al /ʌpˈhiːvəl/ *n* [C;U] (a) great change, esp. with much activity, confusion, and sometimes violence: *What an upheaval it was when we had to change offices/move house.* | *a major political upheaval*

up·hill /ˌʌpˈhɪl◂/ *adj, adv* **1** (sloping or going) towards the top of a hill: *walking uphill* | *an uphill climb* [after *n*] *the road uphill* **2** needing much effort; ARDUOUS: *It's an uphill struggle/task teaching them mathematics.*

up·hold /ˌʌpˈhəʊld/ *v* **-held** /ˌʌpˈheld/ [T] **1** to defend (esp. a right or principle) against attack; prevent from being weakened or taken away: *It's up to the government to uphold the rights of individual citizens.* **2** to declare to be right; CONFIRM: *The judge upheld the lower court's decision.* **— ~ er** *n*

up·hol·ster /ʌpˈhəʊlstəʳ/ *v* [T] to provide (furniture) with comfortable coverings and fillings **— ~ er** *n*

up·hol·ster·y /ʌpˈhəʊlstəri/ *n* [U] **1** material that makes a comfortable covering and filling for furniture **2** the trade of an upholsterer

UPI /ˌjuː piː ˈaɪ/ United Press International; a company that gathers news stories from around the world and sells them to newspapers and other MEDIA

up·keep /ˈʌpkiːp/ *n* [U (**of**)] (the cost of) keeping something in good condition and working order: *The upkeep of this car/house is terribly expensive.*

up·land /ˈʌplənd/ also **uplands** *pl.— n* [U] the higher land in an area: *broad sunlit uplands* | *the upland areas of the country* | *an upland species of bird*

up·lift¹ /ˌʌpˈlɪft/ *v* [T] **1** to encourage cheerful or spiritual feelings in: *uplifting words* **2** *fml or lit* to raise high: *Let your voices be uplifted in song.*

up·lift² /ˈʌplɪft/ *n* [U] **1** upward support: *This new bra gives you plenty of uplift.* **2** (something which gives) a sense of joy or moral improvement

up·light·er /ˈʌplaɪtəʳ/ *n* a light placed at a low level to direct light upwards —compare DOWNLIGHTER

up-mar·ket /ˌ·ˈ··◂/ ‖ also **upscale** *AmE— adj* being or using goods produced to meet the demand of the higher social groups: *an up-market area of town* | *the up-market model of the car, with a larger engine* —compare DOWN-MARKET

up·on /əˈpɒn‖əˈpɑːn/ *prep fml* on: *They sat upon the ground.* | *travelling upon foot* | *We acted upon your advice.* —see also ON¹ (1,2,3,4,6,7,13), **once upon a time** (ONCE¹ (8)), **upon my word** (WORD¹ (17))

up·per¹ /ˈʌpəʳ/ *adj* [A] **1** in a higher position (than something lower): *the upper arm* | *Passengers may smoke only on the upper deck of the bus.* | *a job in the upper echelons* (=of very high rank) *of the Civil Service* **2** farther from the sea: *the upper reaches* (=areas) *of the Nile* —opposite **lower**

upper² *n* **1** the top part of a shoe above the HEEL and SOLE **2** (*often pl.*) *sl* any illegal drug which produces a feeling of energy or happiness, esp. an AMPHETAMINE —compare DOWNER **3 on one's uppers** *BrE old-fash infml* extremely poor

upper case /ˌ·· ˈ·◂/ *n* [U] letters written or printed in a large form (such as *A, B, C*) rather than in the usual small (LOWER CASE) form (such as *a, b, c*) —**upper case** *adj*

upper class /ˌ·· ˈ·◂/ also **upper classes** *pl.— n* [*the*+S+*sing./pl. v*] the highest social class; a small social class whose members often have noble titles (in Britain and some other European countries), own a great deal of land, and are usu. thought of as being very rich: *She's a typical product of the upper class/classes.* —**upper-class** *adj sometimes derog* : *an upper-class accent* —compare LOWER CLASS, MIDDLE CLASS, WORKING CLASS; see WORKING CLASS (USAGE) and extra information on page 1258

up·per·class·man /ˈʌpəklɑːsmən‖-ərklæs-/ , **wom·an** /-wʊmən/ *fem n* **-men** /men/ *AmE* a student in the last two years of a school or college, i.e. a JUNIOR or SENIOR —compare UNDERCLASSMAN

upper crust /ˌ·· ˈ·◂/ *adj, n* [*the*+S+*sing./pl. v*] *infml, often humor* the upper class

up·per·cut /ˈʌpəkʌt‖-ər-/ *n* (in BOXING) a blow with the hand moving upward to the chin

upper hand /ˌ·· ˈ·/ *n* [*the*+S] a position of advantage; control: *After many hours fighting we began to* **gain/get the upper hand.** (=started to win the fight)

Upper House /ˌ·· ˈ·/ also **Upper Cham·ber** /ˌ·· ˈ··/— n [the] one of the two branches of a parliament, esp. the one that is grander but smaller, less representative, and less powerful: *The House of Lords is the British Upper House.*

upper mid·dle class /ˌ·· ˌ· ˈ·/ n [S + sing.|pl. v] a social class that is considered to be higher than the middle class but not as high as the upper class, and which in Britain is thought to include professional people such as SUR-GEONs, university teachers, company directors, and important CIVIL SERVANTs —**upper middle-class** adj

up·per·most /ˈʌpəməʊst‖-pər-/ also **up·most** /ˈʌpməʊst/— adj, adv in the highest or strongest position: *the question that is|comes uppermost in our minds* (=that we think of most)

upper school /ˈ·· ·/ n (in Britain) the classes of a SECONDARY SCHOOL or a PUBLIC SCHOOL which contain older, esp. 14 to 18-year-old, pupils. An upper school usu. includes the SIXTH FORM: *Tuesday is the upper school's sports afternoon.*

upper sixth /ˌ·· ˈ·/ n [C+sing|pl. v] (sometimes cap) the second and final year of the SIXTH FORM in British schools —compare LOWER SIXTH

Upper Vol·ta /ˌʌpə ˈvɒltə‖ˌʌpər ˈvəʊltə/ a former name for BURKINA FASO

up·pi·ty /ˈʌpɨti/ also **up·pish** /ˈʌpɪʃ/— adj infml derog behaving as if one were better than other people or more important than one really is

up·right¹ /ˈʌp-raɪt/ adj apprec **1** (sitting or standing) straight up, esp. habitually: *a tall upright old man* | *She sat bolt upright.* (=very straight) **2** honest, fair, responsible, etc.: *an upright citizen* — **-ly** adv — **-ness** n [U]

upright² adv straight up; not bent

upright³ n a supporting beam which stands straight up

upright pi·an·o /ˌ·· ·ˈ··/ also **upright**— n a piano with strings set in an up-and-down direction —compare GRAND PIANO

up·ris·ing /ˈʌpˌraɪzɪŋ/ n an act of the ordinary people suddenly and violently opposing those in power; REBELLION: *The rebel leaders seized power in an armed uprising.*

up·roar /ˈʌp-rɔːr/ n [S;U] confused noisy activity, esp. with shouting and angry words: *There was uproar in Parliament when the minister made his controversial statement.* | *The whole place was in an uproar (over his statement).*

up·roar·i·ous /ʌpˈrɔːriəs/ adj **1** very noisy, esp. with laughter **2** very amusing; causing loud laughter: *an uproarious joke* — **-ly** adv

up·root /ˌʌpˈruːt/ v [T] **1** to tear (a plant with its roots) out of the earth **2** to remove from one's home, habitual surroundings, etc.: *To take the new job she had to uproot her whole family and settle abroad.*

UPS /ˌjuː piː ˈes/ United Parcel Service; an American company that delivers boxes and packed goods: *I think I'll ship it UPS.* | *Will UPS take a box that big?*

ups-a-dai·sy /ˈʌps ə ˌdeɪzi/ interj OOPS-A-DAISY

ups and downs /ˌ· · ˈ·/ n [P] infml good and bad periods following one another in turn: *Life is full of ups and downs.*

up·scale /ˌʌpˈskeɪl/ adj, adv AmE for UP-MARKET

up·set¹ /ʌpˈset/ v -set, present participle -setting [T] **1** to cause to fall over, turn over, or overflow, usu. accidentally, causing damage, loss, etc.: *He upset the cup and the coffee went all over the floor.* **2** to put (something) out of its settled state or order, causing confusion: *Our plans were upset by the sudden change in the weather.* | *If they develop these new weapons, it will upset the balance of power.* **3** to cause to worry, be sad, be angry, not be calm, etc.; DISTRESS: *Do what he wants, or you'll upset him.* | *This is very upsetting news.* | *She's most upset* (=sad and disappointed) *that you can't come.* **4** to make ill, usu. in the stomach: *Eating fish sometimes upsets me|my stomach.* —see also **upset the apple cart** (APPLE CART)

up·set² /ˈʌpset/ n **1** [C;U] an act of upsetting or state of being upset: *a complete upset of our plans* **2** [C] a slight illness, usu. of the stomach: *a stomach upset* **3** [C] an unexpected result: *It was a major upset when our local team beat the big league side.*

upset price /ˌ·· ·/ n AmE for RESERVE² (6)

up·shot /ˈʌpʃɒt‖ˈʌpʃɑːt/ n [(the) S (of)] the result in the end; OUTCOME: *What was the upshot of all that talk?*

up·side /ˈʌpsaɪd/ adj (esp. in business) showing an expectation or likelihood of advantage or success —opposite **downside** —**upside** n [S]

up·side down /ˌ·· ˈ·/ adv **1** in a position with the top turned to the bottom: *You've got that picture upside down.* **2** in disorder: *The office is being decorated so everything's upside down.* —see also **turn somewhere upside down** (TURN¹ (16))

up·stage¹ /ˌʌpˈsteɪdʒ◂/ adj, adv towards or at the back of a theatrical stage: *The actress moved upstage.* —opposite **downstage**

up·stage² /ʌpˈsteɪdʒ/ v [T] to take attention away from (someone else, esp. someone more important) for oneself: *The star of the show was upstaged by a brilliant young comedian.*

up·stairs /ˌʌpˈsteəz◂‖-ˈsteərz◂/ adv on or to the upper floor(s) of a building: *He ran upstairs.* | *My room is upstairs.* —compare DOWNSTAIRS; see also **kick upstairs** (KICK) —**upstairs** adj [A]: *an upstairs lavatory* —**upstairs** n [(the) S] : *The upstairs of this house is all new.*

Upstairs, Down·stairs /ˌ·· ˈ··/ a British television SERIES of the 1970s about a wealthy family who live in their London home with their servants during the early 1900s

up·stand·ing /ˌʌpˈstændɪŋ/ adj fml apprec **1** honest and responsible: *a sober upstanding citizen* **2** (of a person) tall and strong: *a fine upstanding man*

up·start /ˈʌpstɑːt/ n derog someone who has risen suddenly or unexpectedly to a high position and takes advantage of the power they have gained: *She was beaten to the top job by an upstart who joined the firm barely a year ago.*

up·state /ˌʌpˈsteɪt◂/ n AmE the northern part of a state, esp. when most of the population lives in the south: *upstate New York*

up·stream /ˌʌpˈstriːm◂/ adj, adv (moving) against the current, towards the beginning of a river, stream, etc. —opposite **downstream**

up·surge /ˈʌpsɜːdʒ‖-ɜːr-/ n **1** [(in)] a sudden rise: *the recent upsurge in the number of people buying video recorders* **2** [(of)] a sudden appearance of strong feeling: *an upsurge of joy*

up·swing /ˈʌpˌswɪŋ/ n [(in)] an improvement or increase in an amount or level: *an upswing in the President's popularity rating*

up·take /ˈʌpteɪk/ n **1** [the+S] infml ability to understand esp. something new: *I tried to explain it to him, but he's rather **slow on the uptake**.* **2** [C;U (of)] esp. tech the rate at which something is accepted, taken in, etc.: *the uptake of food and oxygen into an organism*

up·tight /ˈʌptaɪt, ʌpˈtaɪt/ adj sl tending to be angry and unfriendly because worried, nervous, etc.

up-to-date /ˌ·· ·ˈ·◂/ adj **1** modern; based on or using the most recent knowledge, ideas, inventions, etc.: *This factory uses the most up-to-date methods.* **2** including or having all the latest information: *an up-to-date map* | *Bring me up-to-date on all the latest news.* (=tell me about it)

up-to-the-min·ute /ˌ·· · ˈ··◂/ adj **1** very modern **2** including all the latest information

up·town /ˌʌpˈtaʊn◂/ adj, adv AmE to, towards, or in the higher or northern areas of a city or town; often where people live, not the business centre: *We went uptown.* | *uptown schools* —compare DOWNTOWN

up·turn /ˈʌptɜːn‖-ɜːrn/ n [(in)] a favourable change, esp. an increase: *an upturn in business activity|in house prices* —opposite **downturn**

up·turned /ˌʌpˈtɜːnd◂‖-ɜːr-/ adj **1** turning upwards at the end: *an upturned nose* **2** having been turned upside down: *The crowd set fire to an upturned car.*

up·ward /ˈʌpwəd‖-wərd/ adj [A] going up: *an upward movement of prices|of the hand* —opposite **downward**

upwardly-mo·bile /ˌ··· ˈ··/ adj able or wishing to move into a higher social class and become more wealthy

up·wards /ˈʌpwədz‖-wərdz/ ‖ also **upward** AmE— adv **1** towards a higher level, position, or price: *He looked upwards at the sky.* | *Costs are moving upwards.* | *She lay on the bed, face upwards.* (=with her face pointing upwards) —opposite **downwards 2 upward(s) of** infml more than: *It cost upwards of £50.*

up·wind /ˌʌpˈwɪnd/ *adj, adv* in the direction from which the wind is blowing

Ur /ɜːr/ also **Ur of the Chal·dees** /ˌɜːr əv ðə kælˈdiːz‖ -kɔːl-/ an ancient city in what is now modern Iraq, which existed from about 3500 BC to around the sixth century BC

U·rals /ˈjʊərəlz/ also **Ural Moun·tains** /ˌ·· ˈ··/— [*the* + P] a mountain system stretching across the W of Russia from the Kara Sea in the N to the STEPPES N of the Aral Sea. The Urals are often considered to mark the border between Europe and Asia.

u·ra·ni·um /jʊˈreɪniəm/ *n* [U] a heavy white metal that is a simple substance (ELEMENT), is RADIOACTIVE, and is used in the production of NUCLEAR power and weapons

U·ra·nus /ˈjʊərənəs, jʊˈreɪnəs/ **1** the PLANET seventh in order from the sun —see picture at SOLAR SYSTEM **2** in ancient Greek stories, the heaven and first ruler of the universe

ur·ban /ˈɜːbən‖ˈɜːr-/ *adj* [A] of a town or city: *urban life* | *urban areas*

Urban De·vel·op·ment Cor·po·ra·tion /ˌ··· ·ˈ··· ··ˌ··/ *n* (in Britain) an organization set up by the government to work in INNER CITIES, planning new uses for DERELICT land, e.g. for housing, offices, or sports grounds. The first two Urban Development Corporations began in 1981, in London's Docklands and around Liverpool.

ur·bane /ɜːˈbeɪn‖ɜːr-/ *adj usu. apprec* having a smooth and confident social manner — ~**ly** *adv* —**banity** /ɜːˈbænˌti‖ɜːr-/ *n* [U]

urban guer·ril·la /ˌ··· ·ˈ··/ *n* a terrorist who operates mainly in towns and cities: *a bomb attack carried out by urban guerrillas*

urban myth /ˌ··· ˈ·/ *n* an often-repeated story, usu. taken to be true, of an unusual and sometimes terrible event that happens to an ordinary person

Urban Pro·gramme /ˌ·· ˈ··/ [*the*] a British government programme to improve inner cities

urban re·new·al /ˌ··· ·ˈ··/ *n* [U] the redevelopment of decayed city areas by building new houses, shops, business areas, etc.: *a Federal urban renewal program*

ur·chin /ˈɜːtʃɪn‖ˈɜːr-/ *n old-fash or humor* a small dirty untidy child, esp. a boy —see also SEA URCHIN

Ur·du /ˈʊəduː, ˈɜːduː‖ˈʊər-/ *n* [U] an official language of Pakistan which is also widely used in India, esp. by Muslims. Urdu is related to Hindi and is usu. written in Persian SCRIPT.

u·re·thra /jʊəˈriːθrə/ *n med* the tube which carries waste liquid from the BLADDER, and in male animals also carries SEMEN

urge[1] /ɜːdʒ‖ɜːrdʒ/ *v* [T] **1** [+*obj*+*to-v*] to try very hard to persuade: *They urged us to give our support.* **2** [(on)] to suggest very strongly; draw attention to the importance of or need for: *The speaker urged immediate action against the illegal regime.* | *They urged on us the need for cooperation.* **3** [+*obj*+*adv*/*prep*] to drive or force (forward): *He urged the horses on with a whip.* | *The captain urged his team to greater efforts.*

urge[2] *n* a strong wish or need: *powerful sexual urges* [+*to-v*] *I had a sudden urge to tell the boss what I thought of him.*

ur·gent /ˈɜːdʒənt‖ˈɜːr-/ *adj* **1** very important and needing to be dealt with quickly or first: *It's not urgent; it can wait until tomorrow.* | *a very urgent message* | *in urgent need of medical attention* **2** *fml* showing that something must be done or dealt with quickly; PERSISTENT: *He was urgent in his demands.* — ~**ly** *adv* —**gency** *n* [U]: *a matter of great urgency*

U·ri·ah Heep /juːˌraɪə ˈhiːp/ **1** a rock band of the 1970s **2** see **Uriah** HEEP

u·ric /ˈjʊərɪk/ *adj* [A] *tech* of or found in urine: *uric acid*

u·ri·nal /ˈjʊərˌnəl, jʊˈraɪ-‖ˈjʊərˌ-/ *n* **1** an apparatus fitted to a wall into which men may urinate **2** a building containing urinals

u·ri·na·ry /ˈjʊərˌnəri‖-neri/ *adj* of or being the organs and passages of the body used for collecting and passing out urine: *the urinary tract*

u·ri·nate /ˈjʊərˌneɪt/ *v* [I] to pass urine from the body —**nation** /ˌjʊərˌˈneɪʃən/ *n* [U]

u·rine /ˈjʊərˌn/ *n* [U] liquid waste passed from the body

urn /ɜːn‖ɜːrn/ *n* **1** a large often decorative container (VASE), esp. one in which the ashes of a burnt dead body are kept **2** a large metal container in which large quantities of tea or coffee may be heated and kept

Ur·sa Ma·jor /ˌɜːsə ˈmeɪdʒər‖ ˌɜːr-/ also **Great Bear**— a group of stars, the PLOUGH

Ursa Mi·nor /ˌ·· ˈ··/ also **Little Bear**‖**Little Dipper** *AmE*— a group of bright stars (CONSTELLATION), which includes the POLE STAR

U·ru·guay /ˈjʊərəgwaɪ/ a country in SE South America; capital Montevideo; population 3,077,000 (1989) — **Uruguayan** /ˌjʊərəˈgwaɪən◂/ *n, adj*

us /əs, s; *strong* ʌs/ *pron* **1** (*object form of* **we**): *Did he see us?* | *She bought us a drink.* | *That house is too small for us.* **2** *BrE nonstandard* (*used esp. as an* INDIRECT OBJECT) me: *"Lend us a pound, mister", he said.* —see ME (USAGE)

US /ˌjuː ˈes◂/ *abbrev. for:* **1** also **USA** /ˌjuː es ˈeɪ/— the United States (of America) **2** of the United States: *the US navy*

us·age /ˈjuːzɪdʒ, ˈjuːsɪdʒ/ *n* **1** [C;U] (a) generally accepted way of using a language: *"Do you have?" is a common American usage; British speakers would be more likely to say "Have you got?"* | *a book on modern English usage* **2** [U] the way of using or treating something: *a radio designed for rough usage* **3** [U (of)] USE[2] (1)

USA To·day /ˌ· · · · ·ˈ·/ *n* an American newspaper that is sold in every state —see also extra information on page 896

USDA /ˌjuː es diː ˈeɪ/ United States Department of Agriculture; the American government organization which helps farmers and makes sure they follow the laws concerning food production

use[1] /juːz/ *v* **used** /juːzd/ [T] **1** to employ for a purpose; put into action or service: *During the war the castle was used as a prison/used for keeping prisoners in.* | *The company uses a computer to do its accounts.* | *We used the money to buy a new car.* | *The crowd refused to move, so the police had to use tear gas.* | *I use the buses a lot.* | *What sort of film does this camera use?* | (*infml*) *I think he's using* (=taking) *drugs.* | (*infml*) **I could use** (=I would like) *a cold drink!* **2** to finish; CONSUME: *All the paper has been used.* | *The car's using too much petrol.* —see also USE **up 3** to take unfair advantage of (someone); EXPLOIT: *He's just using you for his own ends.* **4** [+*obj*+*adv*/*prep*] *fml* to treat in the stated manner: *He considered that he had been ill* (=badly) *used.* —**usable** *adj*

use sthg. ↔ **up** *phr v* [T] to finish completely: *Try not to use up all the flour.*

use[2] /juːs/ *n* **1** [S;U (of)] the act or way of using or fact of being used: *a wasteful use of valuable resources* | *The use of water is being restricted during the drought.* | *the increasing use of computers in education* | *She* **put** *her knowledge of German* **to good use.** (=used it in a profitable way) **2** [U (of)] the ability or right to use something: *I gave him the use of my car while I was away.* | *He lost the use of both his legs in the accident.* **3** [C;U] the purpose or reason for using something: *What use does this tool have/serve?* | *a machine with many uses* **4** [U] the usefulness or advantage given by something: *Is this book any use?* (=is it useful/good) | *I think you'll find this book* **of use** (=useful) *(to you).* | *What's the use of worrying?* | *It's no use (your) complaining; they won't do anything about it.* **5 have no use for** to think that (esp. someone) is of no value; dislike: *She has no use for modern art – she prefers Renaissance painting.* **6 in use** being used **7 make use of** to use; take advantage of: *He made good use of his time there by learning the language.* **8 out of use** no longer used: *That expression has gone out of use.*

use[3] /juːs/ *v* **used** /juːst/*negative short form* **usedn't, usen't** /ˈjuːsənt/ *old-fash BrE* [I+*to-v*] (used in the past tense for showing that something always or regularly happened): *I used to go to the cinema a lot, but I never get the time now.* | *He didn't use to/used not to like fish (but now he does).* | *It used to be thought that the Earth was flat.* | *She doesn't work here now, but she used to.* | *Didn't she use to live in Coventry?* | *I'm surprised to see you smoking; you didn't use to/you used not to.* | (*fml*) *Used there to be a hotel* on that corner? | (old-fash BrE) I use(d)n't to like wine, but I'm quite fond of it now.

▷ USAGE 1 **Used to** and **would** are both used of habits or states that existed in the past, but no longer exist. But **would** is not used at the beginning of a story: *We* **used** *to swim every day when we were children* — *we* **would** *run down to the lake and jump in.* 2 **Used to** has various negative forms. Some people think that *He* **used not to** is better than *He* **didn't used/use to,** but all are possible. *He* **never used to** expresses the same idea. The best question form is probably **Did/Didn't** *he* **use/used to?** but **Used/Usedn't** *he* **to?/Used** *he* **not to?** also exist.◁

use-by date /ˈjuːz baɪ ˌdeɪt/ n a date marked on a product, esp. on food, to show the day or month before which the product should be used so that it will be fresh: *This cooked meat is past its use-by date.* —compare SELL-BY DATE

used /juːzd/ adj **1** (usu. of goods) which has already had an owner; SECOND-HAND: *used cars* **2 used to** /ˈjuːst tə, -tu/ in the habit of; ACCUSTOMED to: *I'm used to the noise.* | *I'm not used to spicy food.* | *I never* **got used to** *going to bed so late.* —see also USE³

use-ful /ˈjuːsfəl/ adj **1** effective in use; bringing help or advantage: *a useful idea/tool/piece of advice* | *The minister said that an inquiry would serve no useful purpose.* [+to-v] *She's a useful person to know.* **2** BrE infml satisfactory: *The England cricket team scored quite a useful total.* — ~**ly** adv — ~**ness** n [U]: *This old radio has* **outlived** *its* **usefulness.** (=is no longer useful, no longer works well, etc.)

useful life /ˌ·· ˈ·/ n humor the period of time which a machine operates well: *I think this photocopier is reaching the end of its useful life.*

use-less /ˈjuːsləs/ adj **1** not of any use; bringing no help or advantage: *a few useless suggestions* | *It's useless to complain* | *It's useless complaining.* (=Complaining is useless.) **2** esp. BrE infml derog not able to do anything properly; INCOMPETENT: *You're useless! You've done it wrong again!* — ~**ly** adv — ~**ness** n [U]

us-er /ˈjuːzəʳ/ n a person or thing that uses: *The factory is one of the biggest users of oil in the country.* | *road users* —see also END USER

user-friend-ly /ˌ·· ˈ··◂/ adj (esp. of a computer system) easy to operate or understand; not needing special training: *a user-friendly computer/textbook*

user in-ter-face /ˌ·· ˈ···/ n the part of a computer programme or SOFTWARE package that contains the commands and functions available to the person using the computer

US Ge-o-lo-gi-cal Sur-vey /ˌ· · ··,··· ˈ··/ a branch of the Department of the Interior that finds minerals and makes detailed maps of the US —compare ORDNANCE SURVEY

ush-er¹ /ˈʌʃəʳ/ n **1** someone who shows people to their seats, on an important occasion, for example in church at weddings **2** BrE someone who keeps order in a law court **3** someone who shows people to their seats in a theatre or cinema

usher² v [T+obj+adv/prep, esp. IN] fml to bring, esp. by showing the way: *She ushered the visitor into the room.* | *I ushered him to a seat.* | (fig.) *The bombing of Hiroshima* **ushered in** *the nuclear age.*

ush-er-ette /ˌʌʃəˈret/ n esp. BrE a woman or girl who works in a cinema, taking tickets, selling ice cream, and showing people to their seats in the dark

USIA /ˌjuː es aɪ ˈeɪ/ [the] United States Information Agency; a government department which sends representatives abroad to provide information about the United States

USM /ˌjuː es ˈem/ [the] Unlisted Securities Market; a part of the London Stock Exchange for smaller companies which cannot be listed officially with the Stock Exchange —compare OVER-THE-COUNTER (1)

US Mas-ters Tour-na-ment /ˌ· · ˈ·· ˌ···/ [the] MASTERS TOURNAMENT

USMC /ˌjuː es em ˈsiː/ [the] United States Marine Corps; see MARINE CORPS

USO /ˌjuː es ˈəʊ/ United Service Organization; an American organization that helps people in the armed forces,

esp. when they are travelling or abroad: *The USO lounge at O'Hare Airport*

US O-pen /ˌ· · ˈ··/ [the] **1** an important GOLF competition, one of the MAJOR competitions —see also BRITISH OPEN, MASTERS TOURNAMENT **2** an important tennis competition

USS /ˌjuː es ˈes◂/ United States Ship; letters which go before the name of a ship to show that it belongs to the American government: *USS Arizona*

Us-sher, Usher /ˈʌʃəʳ/, **James** (1581–1656) an Irish Protestant BISHOP who attempted to put exact dates to events described in the Bible

USSR /ˌjuː es es ˈɑːʳ/ until 1991, the largest country in the world, bordering on the Arctic and Pacific Oceans, and the Baltic and Black Seas, and made up of 15 republics. The USSR was formed after the Russian Revolution in 1917 as a COMMUNIST state, under the leadership of Lenin. The country was for a long time one of the two SUPER-POWERS (the other being the USA), but it broke apart when most of its republics failed to support the president Mikhail Gorbachev. Eleven of the newly independent states grouped together to form the Commonwealth of Independent States (CIS), but some, such as Latvia, became completely independent states —see also COLD WAR, GLASNOST, PERESTROIKA, STALIN

Us-ti-nov /ˈjuːstᵻnɒf‖-nɔːf/, **Sir Peter** (1921–) an English actor, PLAYWRIGHT, and film director, famous as a teller of amusing stories

usu. written abbrev. for: usually

u-su-al /ˈjuːʒuəl, ˈjuːʒəl/ adj **1** customary; in accordance with what happens or is done in most cases: *We will meet at the usual time.* | *This work isn't up to your usual standard.* | *His speech to the staff was the usual mixture of praise and threats.* | *Is it usual for him to be so late?* | *(infml) Will you have your usual, George?* (=the drink you usually have) **2** **as usual** as is common or has happened before: *As usual, he arrived last.*

u-su-al-ly /ˈjuːʒuəli, ˈjuːʒəli/ adv in most cases; generally: *We're usually in bed by ten.* | *I'm not usually so late.* | *I'm not late, usually.* | *It's more than usually crowded today.*

u-sur-er /ˈjuːʒərəʳ/ n fml derog a person who lends money which must be paid back at an unfairly high rate of interest

u-su-ri-ous /juːˈzjuəriəs‖juːˈʒuər-/ adj fml derog (of a price or rate of interest) unreasonably high — ~**ness** n [U]

u-surp /juːˈzɜːp‖-ɜːrp/ v [T] fml to take (power or position) for oneself illegally or without having the right to do so: *Henry IV usurped the throne of England.* | *The Vice-President is trying to usurp the President's authority.* — ~**er** n — ~**ation** /ˌjuːzɜːˈpeɪʃən‖-ɜːr-/ n [U]

u-su-ry /ˈjuːʒəri/ n [U] fml derog the practice of lending money to be paid back at an unfairly high rate of interest

U-tah /ˈjuːtɑː‖-tɔː/ written abbrev. **UT** a state in the W of the US, whose capital, Salt Lake City, is a centre of the Mormon religion. Most of the people who live in Utah are Mormon. —see colour map on pages 1374–5

Ute /juːt/ n [C;the+P] (a member of) a Native American people living mainly in Colorado and Utah —see NATIVE AMERICAN (CULTURAL NOTE)

u-ten-sil /juːˈtensəl/ n fml or tech an object with a particular practical use, esp. a tool or container: *kitchen/cooking utensils*

u-te-rus /ˈjuːtərəs/ n -**ri** /raɪ/ or -**ruses** med for WOMB —**rine** /-raɪn/ adj

U-ther Pen-drag-on /ˌjuːθə penˈdrægən‖-θər-/ in ARTHURIAN LEGEND, the king of the Britons and Arthur's father

u-til-i-tar-i-an /juːˌtɪlᵻˈteəriən/ adj **1** fml, sometimes derog made to be useful rather than decorative: *utilitarian furniture* **2** believing in utilitarianism —compare MATERIALISTIC

u-til-i-tar-i-an-is-m /juːˌtɪlᵻˈteəriənɪzəm/ n [U] a belief that the more people a course of action helps, the better it is

u-til-i-ty /juːˈtɪlᵻti/ n **1** [U] fml the degree of usefulness: *a research project with limited practical utility* **2** [C often pl.] a useful service for the public, such as supplies of water to the home, the bus service, etc.

utility pole /·ˈ··· ˌ·/ n AmE a tall wooden pole for supporting telephone and electric wires, etc. —compare TELE-GRAPH POLE

utility room /·ˈ···ˌ·/ n a room, esp. in a private house, used for storage and for keeping large household equipment in, such as washing machines and FREEZERS

u·til·ize also **-ise** BrE /ˈjuːtɪˌlaɪz/ v [T] fml or pomp to make (good) use of; use: It is to be hoped that in her new job her talents will be better utilized than before. —**izable** adj —**ization** /ˌjuːtɪˌlaɪˈzeɪʃən‖-lə-/ n [U]

ut·most¹ /ˈʌtməʊst/ also **ut·ter·most** /ˈʌtəməʊst‖-tər-/ esp. lit— adj [A] fml of the greatest degree; very great: With the utmost respect, I think you're wrong. | a matter of the utmost concern

utmost² also **uttermost** esp. lit— n [(the) S] the most that can be done: I did my utmost to prevent it.

u·to·pi·a /juːˈtəʊpiə/ n [C;U] (often cap.) an imaginary perfect world where everyone is happy and no one suffers: The story describes a social and ecological utopia.

u·to·pi·an /juːˈtəʊpiən/ adj often derog of or based on ideas of esp. a perfect society which are not practical: Some people seem to have a utopian view of the distant past. — compare IDEALIST

ut·ter¹ /ˈʌtər/ adj [A] (esp. of something bad) complete; AB-SOLUTE: It was an utter waste of time. | What utter rubbish he talks! | an utter moron

utter² v [T] esp. fml or lit to make (a sound) or produce (words), sometimes with difficulty: The wounded man uttered a groan. | She didn't utter a word all night.

ut·ter·ance /ˈʌtərəns/ n esp. fml or tech **1** [U] the act of speaking: She has not yet given utterance to (=expressed) her opinion. **2** [C] something that is said: Politicians have to be very careful in their public utterances.

ut·ter·ly /ˈʌtəli‖-ər-/ adv completely: You're utterly crazy! | He was utterly charmed by her

U-turn /ˈjuː tɜːn‖-ɜːr-/ n **1** a turning movement in a car which takes one back in the direction one came from: "No U-turns" (on road sign) **2** infml, usu. derog a complete change, resulting in the opposite of what has gone before: The government has done a U-turn on economic policy.

UV /ˌjuː ˈviː/ ULTRAVIOLET; used esp. when discussing light which is harmful to the eyes or skin

UVF /ˌjuː viː ˈef/ [the] Ulster Volunteer Force; an illegal organization in Northern Ireland which uses violence against people who want Northern Ireland to leave the UK and become part of an Irish state

u·vu·la /ˈjuːvjʊlə/ n **-las** or **-lae** /liː/ a small soft piece of flesh which hangs down from the top of the mouth at the back

u·vu·lar /ˈjuːvjʊlər/ n, adj tech (a consonant) produced with the back of the tongue touching or nearly touching the uvula

Uz·bek·i·stan /ˌʊzbekɪˈstaːn ‖ ʊzˌbekɪˈstæn/ a member of the Commonwealth of Independent States in central Asia, formerly called the **Uzbek Soviet Socialist Republic** when it was a member of the Soviet Union, and bordered by Afghanistan, Turkmenistan, Kazakhstan, the Aral Sea, Kirghizstan and Tadzhikistan; capital Tashkent; population 19,906,000 (1989) —**Uzbekistani** n, adj

V, v /viː/ **V's, v's** or **Vs, vs** **1** the 22nd letter of the English alphabet **2** the ROMAN NUMERAL (number) for 5

v written abbrev. for: **1** verb **2** infml very

V n a thing or part shaped like the letter V: She cut the material out in a V. —see also V-NECK, V-SIGN

v. BrE ‖ **vs.** AmE— abbrev. for: (esp. in sport or law) VERSUS (against): a report on the England v. Australia cricket match | the Supreme Court decision in Roe vs. Wade

V-1 /ˌviː ˈwʌn/ also **doodlebug** n a flying bomb used by the Germans in World War II

V-2 /ˌviː ˈtuː/ n a flying weapon (a type of MISSILE) used by the Germans in World War II

V8 /ˌviːˈeɪt/ tdmk a kind of drink made from the juices of eight different vegetables: How about a glass of V8?

V-8 /viː ˈeɪt/ n (a vehicle with) an INTERNAL COMBUSTION ENGINE with two rows of four CYLINDERS each, arranged at an angle to each other like a letter V

VA¹ n written abbrev. for VIRGINIA

VA² /ˌviː ˈeɪ/ n abbrev. for VETERANS AFFAIRS

vac /væk/ n BrE infml a university VACATION¹ (1b)

va·can·cy /ˈveɪkənsi/ n **1** [C] an unfilled place, such as a hotel room that is not being used: "Vacancies"|"No Vacancies" (sign on hotel) **2** [C] an unfilled job in a factory, office, etc.: We still have vacancies for drivers but all the other positions have been filled. **3** [U] derog emptiness of mind; lack of thought or interest

va·cant /ˈveɪkənt/ adj **1** (of a place or space, esp. one that is usually filled or is intended to be filled) empty; not filled with anything: There's a vacant place over there where we can park. | a vacant house/room (=not lived in) | Is this seat vacant? **2** (of a job) not at present filled: The job was advertised in the "Situations Vacant" column in the newspaper. **3** showing lack of interest or active or serious thought: He stared into space with a vacant expression on his face. — **~ly** adv : He stared vacantly into space.

vacant lot /ˌ··· ˈ·/ n esp. AmE an unused piece of land, esp. in a city, with nothing built on it: dealing drugs from a vacant lot | a vacant lot between apartment buildings

vacant pos·ses·sion /ˌ··· ·ˈ··/ n [U] tech, BrE ownership of a home or other building whose previous owner or TENANT has left, and which the new owner can move into immediately: We will have vacant possession of the house.

va·cate /vəˈkeɪt, veɪ-‖ˈveɪkeɪt/ v [T] fml to stop using, having, or living in: Guests must vacate their rooms by 11 o'clock. | He is expected to vacate his job soon.

va·ca·tion¹ /vəˈkeɪʃən‖veɪ-/ n **1** [C] a esp. AmE a holiday: They're in Florida **on vacation**. —see HOLIDAY (USAGE) and see also extra information on page 630 **b** esp. BrE any of the periods of holiday when universities (or law courts) are closed —see also LONG VACATION **2** [U (of)] fml the act of vacating

vacation² v [I (at, in)] esp. AmE to have a holiday: vacationing in Europe

va·ca·tion·er /vəˈkeɪʃənər‖veɪ-/ also **va·ca·tion·ist** /-ʃənˌst/— n AmE for HOLIDAYMAKER

vac·cin·ate /ˈvæksˌneɪt/ v [T (against)] to put vaccine into the body of (someone), as a protection against a disease —compare IMMUNIZE, INOCULATE —**-ation** /ˌvæksˌˈneɪʃən/ n [C;U (against)]

vac·cine /ˈvæksiːn‖vækˈsiːn/ n [C;U] a poisonous substance (containing a VIRUS) used for protecting people against diseases: smallpox/polio vaccine —compare SERUM (1)

vac·il·late /ˈvæsˌleɪt/ v [I (between)] usu. derog to be continually changing from one opinion or feeling to another; be uncertain of what action to take: They vacillated for some while between the two courses of action. —**-lation** /ˌvæsˌˈleɪʃən/ n [C;U]

va·cu·i·ty /vəˈkjuːˌti, væ-‖væ-/ n [U] fml stupidity; vacuousness

vac·u·ous /ˈvækjuəs/ adj fml **1** showing no sign of ideas, thought, or feeling: a vacuous expression **2** without

purpose; meaningless; empty: the vacuous life of many rich people — **~ly** adv — **~ness** n [U]

vac·u·um¹ /ˈvækjuəm, -kjʊm/ n **1** [C] a space that is completely empty of all gas, esp. one from which all air has been taken away **2** [S] a feeling of emptiness or loss: Her death left a vacuum in his life.

vacuum² v [T (OUT)] infml to clean (a house, room, floor, etc.) with a vacuum cleaner

vacuum clean·er /ˈ··· ˌ··/ also **hoover** BrE tdmk ‖ also **vacuum** AmE— n an electric apparatus which cleans floors and floor coverings by sucking up the dirt from them —compare CARPET SWEEPER

vacuum flask /ˈ··· ·/ ‖ usu. **vacuum bot·tle** /ˈ··· ˌ··/ AmE— n a FLASK (3)

vacuum-packed /ˌ··· ·ˈ‖ˌ··· ˈ·/ adj (esp. of food offered for sale in shops) packed in a wrapping from which most of the air has been removed so that the food will remain fresh: vacuum-packed kippers/salami

vacuum pump /ˈ··· ·/ n a pump for removing air or gas from an enclosed space

vacuum tube /ˈ··· ˌ·/ n AmE VALVE (2)

vag·a·bond /ˈvægəbɒnd‖-bɑːnd/ n esp. lit a person who lives a wandering life, esp. one who is thought to be lazy or worthless —compare VAGRANT

va·ga·ry /ˈveɪɡəri/ n [often pl.] any of a set of unusual or unexpected events or changes that have an effect on one: the vagaries of love/of human nature

va·gi·na /vəˈdʒaɪnə/ n the passage which leads from the outer sex organs of women or female animals, to the organ (WOMB) in which young are formed —**-nal** adj

va·gran·cy /ˈveɪɡrənsi/ n [U] the state or offence of being a vagrant

va·grant /ˈveɪɡrənt/ n fml or law a person who has no home or regular work, esp. one who is poor and begs —compare VAGABOND

vague /veɪɡ/ adj **1** not clear in shape or form; INDISTINCT: On the hillside, we could see the vague shapes of sheep coming through the mist. **2** not clearly described, expressed, known, or established: Our holiday plans are still rather vague. | vague promises of support | vague rumours of an election | I haven't the vaguest idea (=I don't know at all) who she is. **3** unable to think or express oneself clearly: She's so vague that I can never understand what she's trying to say. — **~ly** adv — **~ness** n [U]

Vail /veɪl/ a town in Colorado in the US, which is popular and fashionable for skiing (SKI)

vain /veɪn/ adj **1** full of self-admiration; thinking too highly of one's appearance, abilities, etc.; CONCEITED **2** without result; unsuccessful: a vain attempt to make him change his mind **3** esp. old use or lit without meaning or value; empty: vain threats/promises **4 in vain** uselessly, without a successful result: We tried in vain to make him change his mind. —see also VANITY, **take someone's name in vain** (NAME¹) — **~ly** adv : We tried vainly to persuade her not to go.

vain·glo·ry /veɪnˈɡlɔːri‖ˈveɪnglɔːri/ n [U] lit or old use great and unreasonable pride in one's abilities; great VANITY —**-rious** /veɪnˈɡlɔːriəs/ adj —**riously** adv

val·ance /ˈvæləns/ n **1** a narrow length of cloth hanging as a border from the edge of a shelf, or from the frame of a bed to the floor —see picture at LIVING ROOM **2** AmE for PELMET

vale /veɪl/ n (esp. lit or as part of a place name) a broad low valley: the Vale of Evesham | (pomp, humor) this vale of tears (=life, with all its difficulties)

val·e·dic·tion /ˌvælˌˈdɪkʃən/ n [C;U] fml (an act of) saying goodbye, esp. on very important or formal occasions

val·e·dic·to·ri·an /ˌvælˌdɪkˈtɔːriən/ n (in the US) the student who has received the best marks overall in his or her years in HIGH SCHOOL, college, or university and who gives the FAREWELL speech at COMMENCEMENT

val·e·dic·to·ry /ˌvælˌˈdɪktəri·/ adj fml or lit used in saying goodbye: valedictory remarks

Va·len·ci·a /vəˈlensiə‖-tʃiə, -siə/ a port in E Spain, the capital of Valencia PROVINCE, a popular winter RESORT with several historical buildings

va·len·cy /ˈveɪlənsi/ esp. BrE ‖ **va·lence** /-ləns/ esp. AmE— n tech a measure of the power of atoms to combine together to form compounds

val·en·tine /'væləntaɪn/ *n* **1** also **valentine card**– a greeting card sent to arrive on Saint Valentine's Day (February 14th), declaring one's love for someone, but usu. without giving the name of the sender **2** the person to whom a valentine is sent: *Who is your valentine?*

a valentine card

Valentine's Day /ˈ··· ˌ·/ SAINT VALENTINE'S DAY

Val·en·ti·no /ˌvælən'tiːnəʊ/, **Ru·dolph** /'ruːdɒlf‖-daːlf/ (1895–1926) an American film actor famous for playing the part of a lover in silent films, esp. *The Sheik*. He is sometimes mentioned as a typical example of a good looking, ROMANTIC man.

val·et /'vælɪt, 'væleɪ/ *n* **1** also **gentleman's gentleman**– a man's personal male servant, who looks after his clothes, cooks his food, etc. **2** someone who cleans and presses the clothes of people staying in a hotel: *the hotel valet service*

Valetta /və'letə/ see VALLETTA

val·e·tu·di·nar·i·an /ˌvælɪˌtjuːdɪˈneəriən‖-tuːrdnˈeə-/ *n old-fash fml* someone who is always thinking about the state of their health, even when this is not really necessary

Val·hal·la /væl'hælə/ in Norse MYTHOLOGY, a place in Asgard, the Norse heaven, where only the souls of those who died very bravely rest

val·i·ant /'væliənt/ also **val·or·ous** /'vælərəs/– *adj esp. fml or lit* very brave, esp. in war; HEROIC: *valiant resistance* | *a valiant but unsuccessful attempt to break the record* – ~**ly** *adv*

val·id /'vælɪd/ *adj* **1** (of a reason, argument, etc.) firmly based on what is true or reasonable; that can be defended: *a valid excuse for arriving late at work* **2** that can legally be used for a stated period or in certain conditions: *a train ticket valid for three months* | *a valid passport* – opposite **invalid 3** *law* written or done in a proper manner so that a court of law would agree with it – – **ly** *adv* – – **ity** /və'lɪdɪti/ *n* [U (**of**)]: *I would question the validity of that assumption.*

val·i·date /'vælɪdeɪt/ *v* [T] *fml* to make valid, esp. legally: *In order to validate the agreement, both parties sign it.* –**dation** /ˌvælɪ'deɪʃən/ *n* [C;U]

va·lise /və'liːz‖və'liːs/ *n* a small bag used while travelling, esp. for carrying clothes

Val·i·um /'væliəm/ *n* [U] *tdmk* a drug for making people feel calmer, less anxious, etc. Using Valium can cause people to become dependent on it. Although it is only available from doctors, it is thought that it is often ABUSEd (=harmfully or carelessly used) esp. in the US.

Val·ky·rie /'vælkɪˌriː‖væl'kɪriː/ *n* in Norse MYTHOLOGY, one of the female messengers of Odin who led the souls of the soldiers killed in battle to Valhalla

Val·let·ta, Valetta /və'letə/ the capital of the island of Malta, a port

val·ley /'væli/ *n* **1** an area of land lying between two lines of hills or mountains, often with a river running through it –see also RIFT VALLEY, and see picture at MOUNTAIN **2 the valley of Death** *quote* a phrase from Tennyson's poem *The Charge of the Light Brigade:*

Half a league, half a league,
Half a league onward.
All in the valley of Death
Rode the six hundred.

3 the valley of the shadow of death *quote* a phrase from the Bible often used when talking about death

▷ USAGE A deep, narrow mountain **valley**, with steep sides, is a **ravine** or **gorge**. If it is very small and steep it is a **gully;** if it is very large it is a **canyon**.◁

Valley Forge /ˌ·· '·/ a place in Pennsylvania in the US where George Washington's soldiers spent a very hard winter in 1777–8 during the American Revolutionary War. Many men died because of the cold and lack of food.

val·our *BrE* ‖ **-or** *AmE* /'vælər/ *n* [U] *esp. fml or lit* great bravery, esp. in war –see also VALIANT

val·u·a·ble¹ /'væljuəbəl, -jǧbəl‖'væljǧbəl/ *adj* **1** worth a

lot of money: *a valuable painting/property* **2** [(**for, to**)] having great usefulness or value: *years of valuable service* | *valuable advice* | *a waste of my valuable time*

▷ USAGE Things of great value are **valuable** or (much stronger) **priceless:** *This ancient gold coin isn't just* **valuable,** *it's* **priceless. Invaluable** is not used to talk about prices or money. It means "very useful indeed": *Your assistance has been* **invaluable.** | *Their advice proved* **invaluable** *to us on our journey.* Things of little or no value are **worthless** or (less common) **valueless:** *The metal looked like gold, but in fact it was* **worthless/valueless.**◁

valuable² *n* [*usu. pl.*] something, esp. something small such as a piece of jewellery, that is worth a lot of money: *Guests may deposit their valuables in the hotel safe.*

val·u·a·tion /ˌvælju'eɪʃən/ *n* **1** [C;U (**of**)] the action or business of calculating how much money something is worth: *We asked an expert to make a valuation of the painting.* **2** [C (**of, on**)] a value or price decided on: *The valuation (put) on the house was £90,000.*

val·ue¹ /'væljuː/ *n* **1** [S;U] the usefulness, helpfulness, or importance of something, esp. in comparison with other things: *You'll find this map of great value in helping you to get around London.* | *The government sets a higher value on defence* (=considers it more important) *than on education.* | *Their research into ancient languages seems to have little practical value.* **2** [C;U] the worth of something in money or as compared with other goods for which it might be exchanged: *Because of continual price increases, the value of the pound has fallen in recent years.* | *land values* | *I paid him £50 for the painting, but its true value/its market value must be at least £500.* | *The thieves took some clothes and a few books, but nothing of any value/of great value.* **3** [U] worth compared with the amount paid: *We offer the best value in London: only £5 for a meal with wine and coffee!* | *You always get* **value for money** *at that shop.* (=the goods are always worth the price charged) **4** [C] *tech* (in MATHEMATICS) the quantity expressed by a letter of the alphabet or other sign: *Let "x" have the value 25.* **5** [C] *tech* the length of a musical note –see also VALUES, FACE VALUE, NUISANCE VALUE, STREET VALUE; see VALUABLE (USAGE) – ~ **less** *adj*

value² *v* [T] **1** [(**at**)] to calculate the value, price, or worth of: *If you want to sell your collection of stamps you ought to have it valued.* | *The house has been valued at £42,000.* **2** to consider to be of great worth; ESTEEM: *I've always valued your friendship/your advice.* | *a valued friend*

value-ad·ded tax /ˌ··· '·/ *n* see VAT

value judg·ment /'·· ·· ˌ·/ *n* a judgment about the quality of something, based on opinion rather than facts: *Try to assess her actions without making value judgments.*

val·u·er /'væljuər/ *n* a person whose work is to decide how much money things are worth

val·ues /'væljuːz/ *n* [P] standards or principles; ideas about the worth or importance of certain qualities, esp. those generally accepted by a particular group: *moral values*

valve /vælv/ *n* **1** a doorlike part of a pipe or tube which opens and shuts so as to control the flow of liquid, air, gas, etc., through it: *The valves of the heart and blood vessels allow the blood to pass in one direction only.* –see picture at BICYCLE **2** *BrE* ‖ **vacuum tube** *AmE*– a closed glass tube with no air in it, used esp. formerly for controlling a flow of electricity in a radio, television, etc. – compare TRANSISTOR (1) **3** the part of a BRASS musical instrument that changes the sound –see picture at BRASS –see also BIVALVE, SAFETY VALVE

va·moose /væ'muːs, və-/ *v* [I *often imperative*] *AmE old-fash sl* to go away quickly

vamp /væmp/ *n old-fash* (esp. in the 1920s and 1930s) a woman who intentionally uses her charm to make men do things for her or give her money –**vamp** *v* [I;T] : *She vamped him shamelessly.*

vam·pire /'væmpaɪər/ *n* an evil spirit which is believed to live in a dead body and suck the blood of people while they are asleep at night

▶ CULTURAL NOTE Although people do not really believe they exist, vampires have many associations: they are supposed to be unable to stand the light of day, to have no REFLECTION in a mirror, to dislike GARLIC, to be afraid of the CROSS¹ (4), to sleep in COFFINS (= the boxes people are buried in), and to be finally killed only by having a STAKE (= a thick pointed stick) driven through their heart or by being shot with a silver bullet. The best-known vampire is Dracula, from Bram Stoker's book *Dracula*. ◀

vampire bat /'··· ·/ also **vampire**– *n* a South American BAT (=animal like a flying mouse) which sucks the blood of other animals

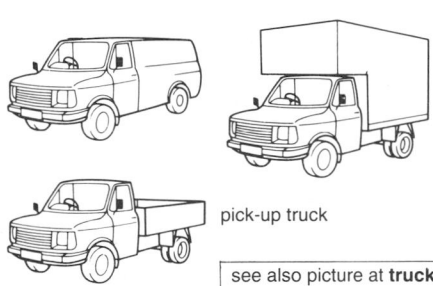

vans

pick-up truck

see also picture at **truck**

van¹ /væn/ *n* (*often in comb.*) **1** a road vehicle, usu. larger than a car but smaller than a TRUCK, having an enclosed box-shaped body and used for carrying goods and sometimes people: *a delivery van* | *a police van* | *a van driver* **2** *esp. BrE* a covered railway carriage for goods and sometimes people: *a luggage van* –see also GUARD'S VAN, REMOVAL VAN, MOVING VAN

van² *n* [*the*+S] *fml or lit for* VANGUARD (1,2) (esp. in the phrase **in the van**)

va·na·di·um /və'neɪdiəm/ *n* [U] a hard silvery metal used in making certain kinds of steel and DYES

Van·brugh /'vænbrə‖væn'bruː/, **Sir John** (1664–1726) an English PLAYWRIGHT and ARCHITECT, whose work on Blenheim Palace is considered to mark the highest stage of development of the Baroque style in England

Van Bur·en /væn 'bjuərən/, **Ab·i·gail** /'æbɟgeɪl/ see DEAR ABBY

Van Buren, Martin (1782–1862) the eighth president of the US (1837–41)

Van·cou·ver /væn'kuːvəʳ/ **1** a port in SW British Columbia, Canada, on the Pacific Ocean. Vancouver is Canada's third largest city and has a university. **2** an island off the SW coast of British Columbia, Canada, also called **Vancouver Island**

V & A /ˌviː ənd 'eɪ/ [*the*] *BrE infml for* VICTORIA AND ALBERT MUSEUM

van·dal /'vændl/ *n* a person who intentionally damages or destroys public property or things belonging to other people: *The seat-covers on the train had been ripped by vandals.*

van·dal·is·m /'vændəl-ɪzəm/ *n* [U] intentional and needless damage or destruction, esp. of public buildings and other public property

van·dal·ize also **-ise** *BrE* /'vændəl-aɪz/ *v* [T *often pass.*] to damage or destroy (esp. a piece of public property) intentionally: *We can't use any of the public telephones round here; they've all been vandalized.*

Van·der·bilt /'vændəbɪlt‖-ər-/ the name of a family of rich Americans who first made money in steamships and railways. The most well-known person in the family today is **Gloria Vanderbilt** (1924–), who CREATES fashionable clothes.

Van Dyck /væn 'daɪk/, **Sir Anthony** (1599–1641) a Flemish painter, known esp. for his PORTRAITS of Charles I and the royal family

van·dyke /væn'daɪk/ also **vandyke beard** /·ˌ· '·/– *n* a small, pointed beard which covers only the chin and over the top lip

vane /veɪn/ *n* a bladelike part of certain machines, which has a flat surface that makes it possible to use the force of wind or water as the driving power: *the vanes of a propeller* –see also WEATHER VANE

Van Gogh /væn 'gɒx, -'gɒf ‖ -'goʊ/, **Vin·cent** /'vɪnsənt/ (1853–90) a Dutch painter of the Post-Impressionist school, whose most famous work was done in the last

months of his life. His paintings are mainly in bright colours, with many small lines of paint in swirling (SWIRL) patterns. Van Gogh is also famous for cutting off his ear in a moment of near-madness. –see colour picture on page 1016

van·guard /'vængɑːd‖-gɑːrd/ *n* **1** [*the*+S] the leading position at the front of an army or group of ships moving into battle **2** [C+*sing.|pl. v*] the soldiers who take up this position: *The vanguard is|are under attack.* **3** [*the*+S] the leading or most advanced position in any course of development: *In the 19th century Britain was in the vanguard of industrial progress.* –compare REARGUARD

va·nil·la¹ /və'nɪlə/ *n* [U] a strong-smelling substance obtained from the beans of a tropical plant, used for improving the taste of certain sweet foods: *vanilla ice cream*

vanilla² *adj* **1** having the taste of vanilla **2** *sometimes derog* ordinary, uninteresting, and lacking excitement: *vanilla decor*

van·ish /'vænɪʃ/ *v* [I] **1** to disappear or go suddenly out of sight, esp. in an unexplained way: *With a wave of his hand, the magician made the rabbit vanish.* **2** to exist no longer; come to an end: *Many species of animal have now vanished (from the face of the earth).* | *My fears|hopes vanished.*

van·i·ty /'væn‚ti/ *n* [U] **1** the quality of being VAIN; unreasonable pride in oneself or one's appearance, abilities, etc.; CONCEIT: *"He's always looking at himself in the mirror." "What vanity!"* **2** *fml or lit* the quality of being without true lasting value: *the vanity of human wishes* **3** **vanity of vanities** *derog* a phrase used before mentioning something that shows great pride and stupidity: *He built a model castle in his front garden with, vanity of vanities, a procession of garden gnomes leading up to it.*

Vanity Fair /ˌ··· '·/ *fml derog* **1** the social life of a place or of the world, regarded as lacking seriousness and moral worth (from a place in the book *Pilgrim's Progress* by John Bunyan) **2** a NOVEL by William Thackeray, a SATIRE on upper-middle-class life in Victorian times **3** a magazine sold in the US and Britain that covers fashion and some current affairs

vanity plate /'··· ·/ *n AmE* a car NUMBERPLATE for which the owner has paid to have the combination of letters or numbers he or she wants: *She had vanity plates on her car which read WAVE2ME.*

vanity press /'··· ·/ *n AmE* a company to which writers can pay money to have their books printed. Books printed in this way may be sold by the writer but are not usu. sold in bookstores: *He had his poetry bound into a pretty little volume by a vanity press.*

vanity ta·ble /'··· ˌ··/ *n AmE* DRESSING TABLE

vanity u·nit /'··· ˌ··/ *n BrE* a furniture unit like a table with a WASHBASIN built into the top of it, usu. with a small cupboard below

van·quish /'væŋkwɪʃ/ *v* [T] *esp. lit* to defeat completely

van·tage-point *BrE* ‖ **vantage point** *AmE*– /'vɑːntɪdʒ pɔɪnt ‖ 'væn-/ *n* **1** a good position from which to attack, defend, or see something: *Security police took up vantagepoints overlooking the route of the procession.* **2** a point of view; PERSPECTIVE: *I quite agree that from your vantagepoint his action must have seemed unwise.*

Van·u·a·tu /ˌvænuˈɑːtuː/ a country in the SW Pacific Ocean, E of Australia, made up of a chain of VOLCANIC islands, formerly called the **New Hebrides**; capital Vila; population 136,000 (1989)

Van Winkle, Rip see RIP VAN WINKLE

vap·id /'væpɟd/ *adj fml* without liveliness, interest, or imagination; dull: *a vapid person|style of writing* – **~ly** *adv* – **~ness**, **~ity** /və'pɪd‚ti/ *n* [U]

va·por·ize ‖ also **-ise** *BrE* /'veɪpəraɪz/ *v* [I;T] to (cause to) change into vapour: *Water vaporizes when it boils.* –**ization** /ˌveɪpəraɪˈzeɪʃən‖-rə-/ *n* [U]

vapor trail /'··· ·/ *n AmE for* CONTRAIL

va·pour *BrE* ‖ **-por** *AmE* /'veɪpəʳ/ *n* **1** [C;U] a gaslike form of a liquid, such as mist or steam, often caused by a sudden change of temperature: *A cloud is a mass of vapour in the sky.* | *Strange vapours rose from the dark lake.* **2** [U] *tech* the gas to which the stated liquid or solid can be changed by the action of heat: *water vapour* –**vaporous** *adj* : *Vaporous clouds arose from the lake.*

va·pours *BrE* ‖ **-pors** *AmE* /'veɪpəz‖-ərz/ *n* [*the*+P] *old use*

or humor a state of feeling suddenly faint: *Arabella had the vapours if any indelicate subject was mentioned.*

var·i·a·ble¹ /ˈveəriəbəl/ *adj* **1** tending or likely to vary; not staying the same; not steady: *The winds today will be light and variable.* **2** that can be varied by the user: *The temperature inside the car is variable.* **3** *euph* varying in quality; sometimes good and sometimes bad; UNEVEN: *The team's performance this year has been very variable.* **—bly** *adv* **—bility** /ˌveəriəˈbɪlɨti/, **~ness** /ˈveəriəbəlnɨs/ *n* [U]

variable² *n esp. tech* something which can vary in quantity or size: *The time of the journey depends on a number of variables, such as the volume of traffic on the road.* | *There are too many variables to predict the result accurately.* —compare CONSTANT²

var·i·ance /ˈveəriəns/ *n* **at variance (with)** in opposition (to); not in agreement (with): *What he did was at variance with his earlier promises.*

var·i·ant¹ /ˈveəriənt/ *adj* [A *no comp.*] different; varying: *variant spellings* | *a variant form of a word*

variant² *n* [of] a (slightly) different form, e.g. of a word, phrase, or pronunciation: *"Favor" is the American variant of the British "favour".*

var·i·a·tion /ˌveəriˈeɪʃən/ *n* **1** [C;U (in)] (an example or degree of) the fact of varying: *The average price of new houses is about £50,000, but there are wide regional variations.* | *Because these clothes are handmade there may be some (slight) variations in colour.* **2** [C (on)] any of a set of short pieces of music, each based on the same simple tune but with different decorative changes or developments made to it: *Elgar's "Enigma Variations"*

var·i·cose veins /ˌværɨkəʊs ˈveɪnz/ *n* [P] a medical condition in which the blood tubes, esp. in the leg, have become very swollen

var·ied /ˈveərid/ *adj* **1** of different kinds; DIVERSE: *Varied opinions were expressed about the new play.* | *a singer with a very varied repertoire* **2** not staying the same; changing: *She's led a varied life.*

var·ie·gat·ed /ˈveərigeitɨd/ *adj* (esp. of a flower or leaf) marked irregularly in different coloured spots, lines, areas, etc.

var·ie·ga·tion /ˌveəriˈgeɪʃən/ *n* [U] irregular colour marking, esp. in plants

va·ri·e·ty /vəˈraɪəti/ *n* **1** [U] the fact of varying; difference in quality, type, or character: *She didn't like the work because it lacked variety; she was doing the same things all the time.* **2** [S (of)] a number or collection of different sorts of the same general type: *Everyone arrived late at the party, for a variety of (=many different) reasons.* | *The shirt is available in a (wide) variety of colours.* **3** [C (of)] a particular type that is different from others in a group to which it belongs; sort: *We're growing a new variety of wheat this year.* | *fast-growing varieties of fir tree* **4** [U] a form of entertainment for theatre or television in which a number of different types of short performance are given, such as singing, dancing, telling jokes, etc.: *a variety show/artiste* —compare MUSIC HALL, VAUDEVILLE **5 variety is the spice of life** *saying* the chance or the ability to do many different things, know many different people, etc., is what makes life enjoyable

Variety Club of Great Brit·ain /ˌ·ˈ··· ˌ· · · ˈ··/ [*the*] a CHARITY (1) organization whose members are in SHOW BUSINESS, which gives money, holidays, vehicles, etc. to poor or disabled children

variety meats /·ˈ··· ˌ·/ *n* [P] *AmE for* OFFAL

variety store /·ˈ··· ˌ·/ *n AmE* a shop which sells many different kinds of goods, often at low prices: *Variety stores such as K-Mart and Target sell everything from clothes to cameras to gardening equipment.*

var·i·ous /ˈveəriəs/ *adj* **1** different from each other; of (many) different kinds: *There has been snow today in various parts of the country.* | *For various reasons I'd prefer not to meet him.* | *The products we sell are* **many and various**. **2** [A *no comp.*] several; a number of: *Various people said they'd seen the accident.* —see DIFFERENT (USAGE)

var·i·ous·ly /ˈveəriəsli/ *adv fml* in various ways or at various times; differently: *The cost of the damage has been variously estimated at between £5000 and £25,000.*

var·let /ˈvɑːlɨt‖ˈvɑːr-/ *n old use* a wicked or worthless man; KNAVE

var·mint /ˈvɑːmɨnt‖ˈvɑːr-/ *n old-fash or dial, esp. AmE* a troublesome worthless person or animal, esp. a young male

var·nish¹ /ˈvɑːnɪʃ‖ˈvɑːr-/ *n* **1** [C;U] (a) liquid which, when brushed onto articles made esp. of wood and allowed to dry, gives a clear hard bright surface —see also NAIL VARNISH **2** [(*the*) S] the shiny appearance produced by using this substance: *Hot plates may spoil the varnish on a table.* —compare LACQUER

varnish² *v* [T] to cover with varnish or NAIL VARNISH: *a varnished table top* —see also UNVARNISHED

var·si·ty¹ /ˈvɑːsɨti‖ˈvɑːr-/ *n* [*the*+S] *BrE old-fash* university, esp. Oxford or Cambridge

varsity² *adj* [A] *AmE* being the chief group or team representing a university, college, or school, esp. in a sport: *the varsity football team*

var·y /ˈveəri/ *v* **1** [I (in)] to be different; have qualities that are not the same as each other: *Opinions on this matter vary.* | *The price varies according to the season.* | *Houses vary in size.* | *The quality of their products never varies; it is always excellent.* **2** [I (from);T] to (cause to) become different; change, esp. continually: *The weather varied from very cold to quite mild.* | *The security van that brings our wages always varies its route.* —see also VARIED

vas·cu·lar /ˈvæskjʊlərˈ/ *adj tech* of or containing tubes through which liquids move in the bodies of animals or plants: *a vascular system*

vase /vɑːz‖veɪs, veɪz/ *n* a decorative container, usu. shaped like a deep pot with a rather narrow opening at the top and usu. made of glass or baked clay, used for decoration or to put flowers in

vases

va·sec·to·my /vəˈsektəmi/ *n* [C;U] the medical operation of cutting the small tube that carries the male seeds (SPERM), done so that a man is unable to produce children

Vas·e·line /ˈvæsɨliːn/ *n* [U] *tdmk* a soft yellow or white jelly used for various medical and other purposes

vas·sal /ˈvæsəl/ *n* (during the Middle Ages) a person who promised to be loyal to a lord and to serve him or fight for him and who in return was given land by the lord

Vas·sar Col·lege /ˌvæsə ˈkɒlɪdʒ‖-sər ˈkɑː-/ *also* **Vassar**— an American college in New York State which originally was only for women students

vast /vɑːst‖væst/ *adj* very large and wide; great in amount or esp. in area: *The vast plains stretch for hundreds of miles.* | *The actors were brought from New York to London at vast expense.* **——ness** *n* [U]

vast·ly /ˈvɑːstli‖ˈvæstli/ *adv* very greatly: *This is vastly superior to his previous film.* | *a vastly overrated actress*

vast·ness·es /ˈvɑːstnɨsɨz‖ˈvæst-/ *n* [P] *esp. lit* a great empty area: *the vastnesses of space*

vat /væt/ *n* a very large barrel or other container for holding liquids, such as WHISKY, DYE, etc., esp. when they are being made

VAT /ˌviː eɪ ˈtiː, væt/ *n* [U] value-added tax; (in Britain and many other European countries) a tax added to the price of an article, and paid by the buyer to the seller, who then pays it to the government —compare SALES TAX

Vat·i·can /ˈvætɪkən/ [*the*] **1** the large palace in which the Pope (=head of the Roman Catholic Church) lives, in Rome: *At last, white smoke could be seen coming from the Vatican chimney.* **2** the government or office of the Pope: *The Vatican is taking a hard line on birth control.*

Vatican City /ˌ··· ˈ··/ the independent state within Italy which contains the Vatican and has its own PASSPORTS, money, etc. It also contains buildings which contain many of the world's greatest works of art.

Vatican Coun·cil /ˌ··· ˈ··/ [*the*] either of the two important councils of the Roman Catholic Church at which important church matters were discussed. The first (1869–70) discussed the Pope's INFALLIBILITY and the second (1962–65), known as Vatican II, discussed the place of the church in the modern world.

vau·de·ville /ˈvɔːdəvɪl, ˈvəʊ-/ *n* [U] *AmE* theatre, entertainment with songs, jokes, acts of skill, etc. Vaudeville shows were popular from the late 1800s until the 1950s.

Many famous COMEDIANs (=people who tell jokes) and actors began in vaudeville. —compare VARIETY

Vaughan Wil·liams /ˌvɔːn ˈwɪljəmz/, **Ralph** /reɪf/ (1872–1958) an English COMPOSER who is known for his arrangements using English FOLK music. His work includes *Norfolk Rhapsodies* and *Fantasia on a Theme by Thomas Tallis*.

vault[1] /vɔːlt/ n **1** also **vaults** pl.– a room with thick walls and a heavy door to protect it against fire and thieves, in which money, jewels, important papers, etc., are kept at a bank **2** also **vaults** pl.– an underground room a beneath the floor of a church, in which the bodies of the dead are placed b in which things are stored to keep them at the same cool temperature: *a wine vault* **3** a roof or CEILING made out of a number of arches, as in many churches

vault[2] v [I+adv/prep;T] to jump over (something) in one movement using the hands or a pole to gain more height: *The thief vaulted (over) the wall and ran away.* – ~ er n

vault[3] n a jump made by vaulting —see also POLE VAULT

vault·ed /ˈvɔːltɪd/ adj **1** in the form of a VAULT[1] (3): *a vaulted roof* **2** covered with a curved roof: *a vaulted passage*

vault·ing[1] /ˈvɔːltɪŋ/ n [U] arches in a roof

vaulting[2] adj [A] lit reaching or aiming for the highest point: *His vaulting ambition eventually caused his downfall.*

vaulting horse /ˈ··· ·/ also **horse**– n a wooden apparatus which people can jump over for exercise

vaunt[1] /vɔːnt/ v [T] esp. lit to praise (something) too much; BOAST about

vaunt[2] n lit an example of vaunting; BOAST

Vaux·hall /ˈvɒksɔːl‖ˈvɑːk-/ a British car maker now owned by General Motors of the US

VC /ˌviː ˈsiː/ n Victoria Cross; a special MEDAL given to members of the British armed forces who have performed acts of extreme bravery in war

VCR /ˌviː siː ˈɑːr/ n a video cassette recorder; a VIDEO[2] (2)

VD /ˌviː ˈdiː/ ‖ usu. **STD** AmE– n [U] venereal disease; disease passed from one person to another during sexual activity

VDU /ˌviː diː ˈjuː/ n visual display unit; an apparatus with a SCREEN which shows information, esp. from a computer or WORD PROCESSOR —see picture at COMPUTER

-'ve /v, əv/ short for: have: *We've finished.* | *If you've time, come and see me.*

veal /viːl/ n tech [U] meat from a CALF (=the young of a cow) —see MEAT (USAGE)

vec·tor /ˈvektər/ n tech **1** (in science) a quantity which has direction as well as size and which can be represented by an ARROW the length of which has a direct relationship with the size —compare SCALAR **2** an insect, such as a fly or MOSQUITO, which can carry a disease from one living thing to another **3** the course of an aircraft

Ve·da /ˈveɪdə/ n [P] the oldest writings of the Hindu religion

Ve·dan·ta /vɪˈdɑːntə, -ˈdæn-/ n the system of Hindu thought about religion

V-E Day /ˌviː ˈiː ˌdeɪ/ n Victory in Europe Day; May 8th 1945, the day on which victory in Europe in the Second World War was celebrated

veep /viːp/ n AmE infml for VICE PRESIDENT

veer /vɪər/ v [I] **1** [+adv/prep] to turn or change direction: *The car went out of control and veered across the road.* | (fig.) *We were talking about food, and then suddenly the conversation veered round to stomach diseases.* **2** tech (of the wind) to change direction, moving round in the order North–East–South–West —compare BACK[4] (5)

veg /vedʒ/ n veg [C;U] BrE infml (a) vegetable, usu. when cooked: *meat and two veg*

ve·gan /ˈviːgən‖ˈviːdʒən/ n a person who does not eat meat, fish, eggs, or cheese or drink milk. Many vegans will not wear or use animal products such as leather. —compare VEGETARIAN[1] —**vegan** adj

Ve·gas /ˈveɪgəs/ LAS VEGAS

ve·ge·bur·ger /ˈvedʒibɜːgər ‖ -ɜːr-/ n a BURGER made with vegetables, PULSEs, etc. but no meat

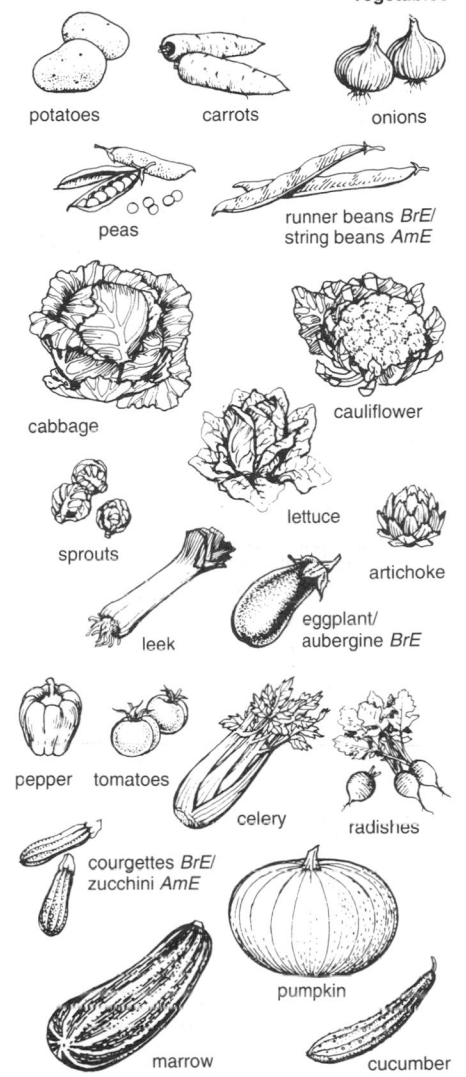

vegetables

potatoes   carrots   onions

peas   runner beans *BrE*/ string beans *AmE*

cabbage   cauliflower

sprouts   lettuce   artichoke

leek   eggplant/ aubergine *BrE*

pepper   tomatoes   celery   radishes

courgettes *BrE*/ zucchini *AmE*

pumpkin

marrow   cucumber

vege·ta·ble[1] /ˈvedʒtəbəl/ n **1** [C usu. pl.;U] a (part of a) plant that is grown for food to be eaten in the main part of a meal, rather than with sweet things; vegetables are often eaten together with a piece of meat or fish: *meat and vegetables* | *a packet of mixed vegetables* **2** [C] a type of this: *We grow a lot of different vegetables: potatoes, onions, beans, etc.* **3** [C] infml a human being who has little or no power of thought, or sometimes also movement: *Since she suffered brain damage in the accident she's just been a vegetable.*

vegetable[2] adj [A] of, growing like, or made or obtained from plants: *vegetable oils* | *the vegetable kingdom*

vegetable knife /ˈ··· ·/ n a small very sharp knife used for cutting up vegetables before they are cooked

vegetable mar·row /ˌ··· ˈ··/ n a MARROW (2)

vegetable oil /ˈ··· ·/ [U] oil used in cooking which is obtained from plants

ve·ge·tar·i·an /ˌvedʒɪˈteəriən◂/ n a person who does not eat meat or fish, but only vegetables, grains, fruit, eggs, etc., either for moral reasons or because it is thought to be healthier —compare VEGAN

vegetarian[2] adj **1** of or for vegetarians: *a vegetarian* *restaurant* **2** made up only of vegetables: *a vegetarian meal*

ve·ge·tar·i·an·is·m /ˌvedʒɪˈteəriənɪzəm/ n [U] the beliefs and practices of vegetarians

ve·ge·tate /ˈvedʒɪteɪt/ v [I] *derog* to have a dull inactive life without interests or social or physical activity: *Since he lost his job he's just been vegetating at home.*

ve·ge·ta·tion /ˌvedʒɪˈteɪʃən/ n [U] **1** plants in general **2** all the plants in a particular place: *the colourful vegetation of a tropical forest*

veg·gie /ˈvedʒi/ n *infml* **1** a vegetable **2** a vegetarian

ve·he·ment /ˈviːəmənt/ adj showing strong feelings; forceful: *She made a vehement attack on the government's policies.* | *a vehement denial* – –**ly** adv –**mence** n [U]

ve·hi·cle /ˈviːɪkəl‖ˈviːɪkəl, -hɪkəl/ n **1** *esp. fml or tech* something in or on which people or goods can be carried from one place to another, esp. something that moves on wheels, such as a bicycle, car, bus, TRUCK, etc.: *"Is this your vehicle* (=esp. car)*, sir?" asked the policeman.* | *a road vehicle* | *a heavy goods vehicle* | *a space vehicle* (=spacecraft) **2** [(for)] something by means of which something else can be passed on or spread; MEDIUM: *Television has become an important vehicle for spreading political ideas.* **3** [(for)] a means for showing off a certain person's abilities: *The writer wrote this big part in his play simply as a vehicle for the famous actress.*

vehicle e·mis·sions /ˌ··· ·ˈ··/ n [P] the substances given out from vehicle engines as EXHAUST[2](2), esp. with regard to the amounts of poisons contained in them and the levels which are allowed

ve·hic·u·lar /viːˈhɪkjʊlər/ adj *fml* of or being vehicles on roads: *vehicular traffic*

veil[1] /veɪl/ n **1** [C] a covering of thin material or net for the head or face, worn by women, often for religious reasons **2** [S (of)] something which covers or hides something else: *A veil of mist covered the trees.* | (fig.) *No one knew what the army was doing; there was a veil of secrecy over their activities.* **3 draw a veil over** to avoid speaking about or describing (something unpleasant) **4 take the veil** *lit or tech* (of a woman) to become a NUN

veil

veil[2] v [T (**in**)] to cover with a veil: (fig.) *The negotiations were veiled in secrecy.*

veiled /veɪld/ adj **1** wearing a veil **2** partly hidden or indirectly expressed: *veiled threats* | *a thinly veiled reference to the prime minister*

vein /veɪn/ n **1** [C] any of the tubes that carry blood from any part of the body to the heart –compare ARTERY **2** [C] any of the thin lines which run in a forked pattern through leaves and the wings of certain insects **3** [C (of)] a crack in rock, filled with useful or valuable metal or rock: *a vein of silver* –compare SEAM **4** [S+of] a noticeable amount (of a particular quality or tendency): *There's a vein of cruelty in his nature.* | *a rich vein of humour that runs through all her stories* **5** [in+S] a style or MOOD: *If I may speak in a serious vein* (=seriously) *for a moment...* | *a number of jokes all in the same vein*

veined /veɪnd/ adj having veins or veinlike markings: *a veined leaf* | *the many-veined wings of the bee* | *veined marble*

vein·ing /ˈveɪnɪŋ/ n [U] a pattern of VEINs (esp. 2)

ve·lar /ˈviːlər/ n, adj *tech* (a speech sound such as /k/ or /g/) made with the back of the tongue against or near the soft part of the top of the mouth

Ve·lás·quez /vəˈlæskwɪz, -wez‖-ˈlɑːskeɪs/, **Di·e·go Ro·drig·uez de Sil·va y** /diˈeɪgəʊ rɒˈdriːgez də ˈsɪlvə iː‖ -rɑːˈdriːz-/ (1599–1660) the most important painter of the Spanish school best known for his PORTRAITs of the Spanish court

vel·cro /ˈvelkrəʊ/ n [U] *tdmk (often cap.)* a material used for fastening things together, consisting of a surface covered with a large number of very small nylon points that can fasten tightly to another piece of velcro when the two pieces are pressed together

veld , veldt /velt/ n [*the*+S] the wild high flat mostly treeless grassland of South Africa

vel·lum /ˈveləm/ n [U] a material made from the skins of young cows, goats, or sheep, and used esp. for book covers and, in former times, for writing on

ve·loc·i·pede /vɪˈlɒsɪpiːd‖vɪˈlɒsˈlɑː-/ n *old use or humor* a bicycle

ve·loc·i·ty /vɪˈlɒsɪti‖vɪˈlɒsˈlɑː-/ n **1** [C] *tech* speed in a certain direction; rate of movement: *the velocity of light* **2** [S;U] *fml* high speed: *The car came round the corner at such a velocity that the driver was unable to keep it on the road.* –see also ESCAPE VELOCITY

vel·o·drome /ˈveladrəʊm/ n a track made for racing bicycles, often with seats at the side for people to watch the race

ve·lour , velours /vəˈlʊər/ n [U] a heavy material made from silk, cotton, etc., with a soft slightly furry surface

Vel·vee·ta /velˈviːtə/ n [U] *tdmk* (in the US) a kind of CHEESE

vel·vet /ˈvelvɪt/ n [U] a fine closely-woven material made of silk, nylon, cotton, etc., with a soft furry surface on one side only. Velvet is thought of in connection with LUXURY: *velvet curtains* | *a velvet jacket*

vel·ve·teen /ˌvelvɪˈtiːn/ n [U] a cheap material made of cotton but having the appearance of velvet

velvet rev·o·lu·tion /ˌ··· ··ˈ··/ n (*sometimes caps.*) a sudden great social or political change which takes place with little or no violence. The phrase is esp. used to describe events in some Communist countries of Europe in the early 1990s.

vel·vet·y /ˈvelvɪti/ adj *apprec* **1** (of a thing which is soft to the touch) looking or feeling like velvet: *the kitten's velvety fur* **2** (of a colour) having a soft deep look: *velvety brown* **3** (esp. of wine) very smooth to the taste; not acid

ve·nal /ˈviːnl/ adj *fml derog* **1** ready to behave in an unfair or dishonest way, esp. by using one's power or position to help other people in return for money or other reward: *venal judges* **2** (of an action, practice, or behaviour) done in order to gain money, rather than for the proper or honest reasons –compare VENIAL – –**ly** adv – –**ity** /viːˈnælɪti/ n [U]

vend /vend/ v [T] **1** *law* to sell (esp. land or other property) **2** *fml* to offer (small articles) for sale, usu. in public places

ven·det·ta /venˈdetə/ n **1** a long-lasting quarrel between families, in which the members of one family believe it to be their duty to kill those of the other family –compare FEUD[1] **2** a situation in which one person continually tries to harm another: *The politician claimed that the damaging stories were part of a press vendetta.* | *He said the papers were waging a vendetta against him.*

vending ma·chine /ˈ·· ·,·/ also **slot machine** BrE– n a machine in a public place from which articles such as packets of cigarettes, drinks, stamps, etc., can be obtained by putting a coin into it

vend·or , -er /ˈvendər/ n **1** a seller of small articles that can be carried about or pushed on a cart: *a fruit vendor* –see also NEWSVENDOR **2** *law* the seller of a house, land, etc.

ve·neer[1] /vɪˈnɪər/ n **1** [C;U] a thin covering of good quality wood, used for forming the outer surface of an article made of a cheaper material **2** [C (of) usu. sing.] outer appearance which hides the unpleasant reality: *Beneath that veneer of respectability there lurked a cunning and unscrupulous criminal.*

veneer[2] v [T (**with, in**)] to cover with a veneer

ven·e·ra·ble /ˈvenərəbəl/ adj **1** *fml apprec* (of an old person or thing) deserving great respect or honour, because of character, religious or historical importance, etc.: *the venerable walls of the cathedral* **2** [A no comp.] (*often cap.*) **a** (in the Church of England) (the title given to a priest) having the rank of ARCHDEACON: *the Venerable Percival Potter* **b** (in the Roman Catholic Church) (the title given to a dead person) who will in the future be declared a SAINT (=holy person) **3** *infml, esp. humor* old

ven·e·rate /ˈvenəreɪt/ v [T] *fml* to treat (a person or thing, esp. one that is old or connected with the past) with great respect and honour, and sometimes worship –**ration** /ˌvenəˈreɪʃən/ n [U]: *The Chinese people hold their ancestors in great veneration.*

ve·ne·re·al /vɪˈnɪəriəl/ adj *med* resulting from, connected with, or passed on by sexual activity: *venereal infections*

venereal dis·ease /·ˌ··· ·ˈ·/ also **VD**— n [C;U] a disease passed from one person to another during sexual activity: *Gonorrhea and syphilis are venereal diseases.*

Ve·ne·tian /vɪˈniːʃən/ n [C] a person who comes from VENICE —**Venetian** adj

ve·ne·tian blind /·ˌ·· ˈ·/ n a window covering made of long thin flat bars of metal, plastic, or wood fixed to strings in such a way that the bars can be raised or lowered, or turned in order to let in or shut out light —compare LOUVRE BLIND, ROLLER BLIND

Ven·e·zue·la /ˌvenɪˈzweɪlə/ a country in the N of South America which produces oil, coffee and other products; capital Caracas; population 19,246,000 (1989) —**lan** n,adj

ven·geance /ˈvendʒəns/ n **1** [U] punishment given to someone in return for harm they have done to oneself, one's family, etc.: *He swore to* **take vengeance on** *the people who had killed his sister.* —compare AVENGE, REVENGE **2 with a vengeance** infml to a high degree; with greater force than is usual: *The wind's blowing with a vengeance; it's almost impossible to walk against it.* **3 vengeance is mine (said the Lord)** *saying from the Bible* people should not try to take REVENGE themselves for wrongs which have been done to them, but should leave it to God to punish people

venge·ful /ˈvendʒfəl/ adj esp. lit showing a fierce desire to punish someone for the harm they have done to oneself —~**ly** adv —~**ness** n [U]

ve·ni /ˈveɪni/ Lat **veni, vidi, vici** /ˌveɪni ˌviːdi ˈviːki/ a phrase used by Julius Caesar. It is Latin for "I came, I saw, I conquered".

ve·ni·al /ˈviːniəl/ adj fml (of a fault, mistake, wrongdoing, etc.) of only slight importance and therefore forgivable: *a venial sin* —compare VENAL

Ven·ice /ˈvenɪs/ a city in north-east Italy rich in fine buildings and works of art and famous for its CANALs —see also DEATH IN VENICE

ven·i·son /ˈvenɪzən, -sən/ n [U] the flesh of a deer eaten as food. In Britain, venison is expensive and considered to be a rather special meat. In the US, only people who hunt deer as a sport usu. eat venison. —see MEAT (USAGE)

Venn di·a·gram /ˈven ˌdaɪəgræm/ n a way of showing relations among a number of things by the use of circles, each of which represents one thing and may OVERLAP to some degree with another circle: *This Venn diagram shows the percentages of speakers fluent in French, Arabic, and/or English.*

ven·om /ˈvenəm/ n [U] **1** liquid poison which certain snakes, insects, and other creatures use in biting or stinging **2** bitter anger or hatred; extreme bad feeling: *Her remarks about him were full of venom.*

ven·om·ous /ˈvenəməs/ adj **1** (of a snake, insect, etc.) having an organ that produces poison, able to attack with poison **2** full of bitter hatred, bad feeling, etc.; MALICIOUS: *a venomous look* —~**ly** adv

ve·nous /ˈviːnəs/ adj med **1** of the VEINs (=blood tubes) of the body —see also INTRAVENOUS **2** (of blood) that is returning to the heart —compare ARTERIAL (1)

vent[1] /vent/ v [T (**on**)] to give expression to (one's feelings), esp. unfairly: *He had had a bad day at work and vented his anger on his family.* (=directed it at them)

vent[2] n **1** a hole, opening, or pipe by which gases, smoke, air, or liquid can enter or escape from an enclosed space or a container: *an air vent* —see also VENTILATE, and see picture at CAR **2** tech the opening through which small animals, birds, fish, and snakes get rid of waste matter from their bodies **3** tech a long narrow straight opening at the bottom of a piece of clothing, at the sides or back **4 give vent to** to express (a strong feeling) freely: *He gave vent to his anger by kicking the chair.*

ven·ti·late /ˈventɪleɪt‖-tl-eɪt/ v [T] **1** to allow or cause fresh air to enter and move around inside (a room, building, etc.), thus driving out bad air, smoke, gas, etc.: *a well-ventilated room* **2** fml to permit or cause full public examination of (a subject or question) —**lation** /ˌventɪ-ˈleɪʃən‖-tl-eɪ-/ n [U]: *The workers complained about the factory's lack of ventilation.*

ven·ti·la·tor /ˈventɪleɪtər‖-tl-eɪ-/ n **1** an apparatus for ventilating a room, building, etc.: *a ventilator shaft* **2** an apparatus for pumping air into and out of the lungs of some-

one who cannot breathe properly: *The patient is on a ventilator.*

ven·tri·cle /ˈventrɪkəl/ n tech **1** either of the two spaces in the bottom of the heart that receive blood from the atria (ATRIUM) and push it out into the body **2** a small hollow place in an animal body or organ, esp. in the brain

ven·tril·o·quis·m /venˈtrɪləkwɪzəm/ n [U] the art of speaking or singing without moving one's lips or jaws, in such a way that the sound seems to come from someone else or from some distance away —**quist** n: *a ventriloquist's dummy*

ven·ture[1] /ˈventʃər/ n a course of action, esp. in business, of which the result is uncertain and there is a risk of loss or failure as well as a chance of gain or success: *a commercial|costly venture* | *The two companies have embarked on a* **joint venture** *to produce cars in America.*

venture[2] v fml **1** [I+adv/prep] to risk going somewhere or doing something (dangerous): *Today's the first time I've ventured out of doors since my illness.* **2** [T] to take the risk of saying (something that may be opposed or considered foolish); dare: *If I may* **venture an opinion**, *I'd say the plan needs closer examination.* [+to-v] *May I venture to suggest a few improvements?* **3** [T (**on**)] to take the risk of harming or losing: *He ventured his whole fortune on one throw of the dice.* **4 nothing ventured, nothing gained** *saying* one cannot obtain anything except by risking something or making an effort to obtain it **venture on/upon** sthg. phr v [T] to attempt (something dangerous or risky): *Now is not the time to venture on such an ambitious project.*

▷ USAGE **Venture**, which can be either a verb or a noun, carries the idea of risk to one's life or money: *a new business* **venture** | *Nobody* **ventured** (=dared) *to speak to the angry king.* An **adventure** (the more general word) suggests excitement, with or without some danger. In the plural it means the exciting life and activities of a character in a story: *This book is about the* **adventures** *of Sindbad the Sailor.*◁

venture cap·i·tal /ˈ··· ˌ···/ n [U] money lent to start up a new business company, esp. a risky one

ven·tur·er /ˈventʃərər/ n someone who takes great risks, esp. someone who risked their life, money, ships, etc., in distant places in former times: *merchant venturers*

Venture Scout /ˈ·· ˌ·/ n a member of the **Venture Scouts**, the branch of the Scout movement in Britain for boys and girls of 16 to 20 years old

ven·ture·some /ˈventʃəsəm‖-tʃər-/ adj esp. lit or AmE **1** (of a person) daring; ready to take risks **2** (of an action) risky —~**ness** n [U]

ven·ue /ˈvenjuː/ n the place where something is arranged to happen: *The Grand Hotel, venue of this week's talks, is packed out.* | *a change of venue*

Ve·nus /ˈviːnəs/ **1** the PLANET second in order from the sun, and next to the Earth —see picture at SOLAR SYSTEM **2** the Roman name of Aphrodite, goddess of beauty and love. A beautiful woman may sometimes be described as a Venus: *She rose like some Venus from the waves.*

Venus de Mi·lo /ˌviːnəs də ˈmiːləʊ, -ˈmaɪləʊ/ [the] a famous STATUE of Venus in the Louvre in Paris well known for having no arms

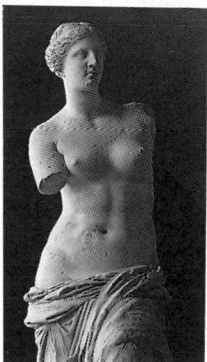

Venus de Milo

Venus fly·trap /ˌviːnəs ˈflaɪtræp/ n a plant which catches flies by quickly shutting together its leaves

ve·ra·cious /vəˈreɪʃəs/ adj rare truthful: *a veracious witness* —~**ly** adv

ve·rac·i·ty /vəˈræsɪti/ n [U] fml truthfulness

ve·ran·da, -dah /vəˈrændə/ ‖ also **porch** AmE— n an open area with a floor and a roof at the side of a house on the ground floor. Houses in hot countries sometimes have a veranda: *She sat in the shade on the veranda.* —compare PATIO

verb /vɜːb‖vɜːrb/ n a word or group of words that is used in describing an action, experience, or state (such as *wrote* in *She wrote a letter*, *put on* in *He put on his coat*, or *feels* in *She feels hungry*). In this dictionary the letter [I] shows that a verb is INTRANSITIVE and the letter [T] shows that a verb is TRANSITIVE: *the first person singular of the verb "to be"* | *to conjugate a verb* —see also AUXILIARY VERB, PHRASAL VERB

verb·al /ˈvɜːbəl‖ˈvɜːr-/ adj **1** spoken, not written: *a verbal description* —opposite **nonverbal** **2** connected with words and their use: *verbal skill* | *verbal abuse* —compare VERBOSE **3** of a verb —see also VERBAL NOUN

verb·al·ize also **-ise** BrE /ˈvɜːbəlaɪz‖ˈvɜːr-/ v [I;T] fml to express (something) in words: *He couldn't verbalize his fears.*

verb·al·ly /ˈvɜːbəli‖ˈvɜːr-/ adv in spoken words and not in writing

verbal noun /ˌ·· ˈ·/ also **gerund**— n a noun which describes an action or experience and has the form of a PRESENT PARTICIPLE: *"Building" is a verbal noun in "The building of the bridge was slow work", but simply a noun in "The bank was a tall building".* —compare PRESENT PARTICIPLE

ver·ba·tim /vɜːˈbeɪtəm‖vɜːr-/ adj, adv repeating the actual words exactly: *a verbatim account of the conversation* | *His memory was so good that he could repeat several of Shakespeare's plays verbatim.*

ver·bi·age /ˈvɜːbi-ɪdʒ‖ˈvɜːr-/ n [U] fml too many unnecessary words in speech or writing

ver·bose /vɜːˈbəus‖vɜːr-/ adj fml using or containing too many words: *a verbose sermon/explanation* —compare VERBAL, VOLUBLE – –**ly** adv – –**ness, -bosity** /ˈbɒsti‖ˈbɑː-/ n [U]

ver·bo·ten /fəˈbəutən‖fər-/ adj Ger not allowed; forbidden: *Being impolite to grown-ups was absolutely verboten in our household.*

ver·dant /ˈvɜːdənt‖ˈvɜːr-/ adj lit or poet (of land) covered with freshly growing green plants or grass: *the verdant landscape of spring* –**dancy** n [U]

Ver·di /ˈveədi‖ˈver-/, **Giu·sep·pe** /dʒuˈzepi/ (1813–1901) an Italian COMPOSER best known for his *Requiem* and for his OPERAs, including *La Traviata*, *Aida*, and *Rigoletto*

ver·dict /ˈvɜːdɪkt‖ˈvɜːr-/ n **1** the official decision a made by a JURY in a court of law at the end of a trial, esp. about whether the prisoner is guilty or not guilty: *The judge directed the jury to return a verdict of guilty.* | *to fail to reach a verdict* | *a majority verdict of 10 to 2* **b** made by an official or an official body, such as a TRIBUNAL: *The panel will be giving their verdict tomorrow.* | *the coroner's verdict* –see also OPEN VERDICT **2** [(on)] infml a statement of opinion; judgment or decision given on any matter: *What's your verdict on the film?*

ver·di·gris /ˈvɜːdɪgrɪː, -grɪːs‖ˈvɜːr-/ n [U] a greenish-blue substance which forms a thin covering on articles of copper or brass as a result of age or wet conditions

ver·dure /ˈvɜːdʒəʳ‖ˈvɜːr-/ n [U] lit or poet (the fresh green colour of) growing grass, plants, trees, etc.

verge¹ /vɜːdʒ‖vɜːrdʒ/ n **1** the edge or border, esp. of a road, path, etc.: *She walked along the grass verge, trying not to step into the road.* **2 on the verge of** very near to (the stated condition or action): *She was on the verge of tears.* (=nearly crying) | *scientists on the verge of a major breakthrough*

verge² v

verge on/upon sthg. phr v [T] to be near to (the stated quality or condition): *Her strange behaviour sometimes verges on madness.* | *very dark grey, verging on black*

ver·ger /ˈvɜːdʒəʳ‖ˈvɜːr-/ n esp. BrE a person who looks after the inside of a church, and performs small duties such as showing worshippers where they may sit

Ver·gil /ˈvɜːdʒɪl‖ˈvɜːr-/ VIRGIL

ver·i·fy /ˈverɪfaɪ/ v [T] to make certain that (a fact, statement, etc.) is correct or true; CONFIRM: *The prisoner's statement was verified by several witnesses.* | *These details are impossible to verify.* [+that] *Before the bank was willing to lend him money, it had to verify that he was the true owner of the house.* –**fiable** adj –**fication** /ˌverɪfɪˈkeɪʃən/ n [U]

ver·i·ly /ˈverɪli/ adv bibl or old use really; truly

ver·i·si·mil·i·tude /ˌverɪsɪˈmɪlɪtjuːd‖-tuːd/ n [U] fml the quality of seeming to be true; likeness to reality or real things

ver·i·ta·ble /ˈverɪtəbəl/ adj [A] fml (used to give force to an expression) that may truly be described as or compared to the stated thing; real: *Thank you for that lovely meal; it was a veritable feast!* –**bly** adv

ver·i·ty /ˈverɪti/ n [usu. pl.] fml or lit an accepted truth; general law or truth on which religious teachings, standards of right behaviour, etc., are based: *one of the eternal verities*

Ver·laine /vəˈleɪn‖vər-/, **Paul** (1844–96) a French poet, known esp. for works such as *Sagesse* and *Romances sans paroles*

Ver·meer /vəˈmɪəʳ‖vər-/, **Jan** /jæn/ or **Jo·han·nes** /jəuˈhænəs/ (1623–75) a Dutch painter famous for his use of colour and his scenes of the inside rooms of a house, often with the single figure of a woman in them

ver·mi·cel·li /ˌvɜːmɪˈseli, -ˈtʃeli‖ˌvɜːr-/ n [U] Italian PASTA (=food made from a mixture of flour and water) in the shape of very thin strings, cooked in boiling water — compare MACARONI, SPAGHETTI, TAGLIATELLE

ver·mic·u·lite /vɜːˈmɪkjʊlaɪt‖vɜːr-/ n [U] a type of MICA that is very light and is used for keeping heat inside buildings, growing seeds in, etc.

ver·mi·form ap·pen·dix /ˌvɜːmɪfɔːm əˈpendɪks ‖ ˌvɜːrmɪfɔːrm-/ n med for APPENDIX (1)

ver·mil·ion /vəˈmɪljən‖vər-/ adj, n [U] (having a) bright reddish-orange colour

ver·min /ˈvɜːmɪn‖ˈvɜːr-/ n [P] **1** small animals or birds that destroy crops, spoil food, or do other damage, and are difficult to control: *To a farmer, foxes are vermin because they steal and kill chickens.* –compare PEST **2** unpleasant biting insects, such as FLEAS, LICE, etc., that live on people's or animals' bodies, usu. by drinking their blood **3** useless unpleasant people who are a trouble to society: *He thinks all beggars are vermin.*

ver·min·ous /ˈvɜːmɪnəs‖ˈvɜːr-/ adj **1** full of VERMIN: *the tramp's verminous old coat* **2** derog (of a person) very unpleasant; nasty

Ver·mont /vəˈmɒnt‖vərˈmɑːnt/ written abbrev. **VT**– a state in the NE of the US. It produces many minerals, MAPLE SYRUP, and attracts many visitors for skiing (SKI), hunting, and fishing. –see colour map on pages 1374–5

ver·mouth /ˈvɜːməθ‖vərˈmuːθ/ n [U] a drink made from wine with the addition of bitter or strong-tasting substances from roots and HERBS. It is usu. drunk before a meal or in a COCKTAIL.

ver·nac·u·lar /vəˈnækjʊləʳl‖vər-/ n [C;the+S] the language spoken in a country or region, esp. as compared with the official language: *When he talked to the local people he lapsed into* (=went back to) *the vernacular.* – **vernacular** adj: *The Roman Catholic Church now uses vernacular services instead of Latin ones.*

ver·nal /ˈvɜːnl‖ˈvɜːrnl/ adj lit or tech [A] of, like, or appearing in the spring season

Verne /vɜːn‖vɜːrn/, **Jules** /dʒuːlz/ (1828–1905) a French writer who wrote SCIENCE FICTION. His most famous books are *Journey to the Centre of the Earth*, *Twenty Thousand Leagues Under the Sea*, and *Around the World in Eighty Days*.

ver·ru·ca /vəˈruːkə/ ‖ usu. **wart** AmE— n -cas or -cae /kiː/ a small hard often infectious growth on the skin, usu. on the bottom of the feet

ver·sa /ˈvɜːsə‖-ɜːr-/ see VICE VERSA

Ver·sailles /veəˈsaɪ‖ver-/ a city in N central France, where there is a beautiful palace and its gardens, built for King Louis XIV and now owned by the state. Several peace agreements were signed here, including the one which formally ended the First World War –see also TREATY OF VERSAILLES

ver·sa·tile /ˈvɜːsətaɪl‖ˈvɜːrsətl/ adj apprec **1** having many different kinds of skill or ability; easily able to change from one kind of activity to another: *a very versatile performer/campaign strategy* **2** having many different uses: *Nylon is a versatile material.* –**tility** /ˌvɜːsəˈtɪlɪti‖ˌvɜːr-/ n [U]

verse /vɜːs‖vɜːrs/ n **1** [U] writing arranged in regular lines, with a pattern of repeated beats as in music, and often with RHYMEs (=words of matching sound) at the end of some lines; language in the form of poetry —compare PROSE; see also BLANK VERSE, FREE VERSE **2** [C] **a** a set of lines of poetry which forms one part of a poem, and usu. has a pattern that is repeated in the other parts: *I learned three verses of the poem.* **b** a set of such lines forming the words to which the tune of a song is sung: *Let's sing the last verse.* —compare CHORUS¹ (1) **3** [C] any of the numbered (groups of) sentences that together form one numbered division (CHAPTER) of a holy book, esp. one of the books of the Bible —see also CHAPTER AND VERSE

versed /vɜːst‖vɜːrst/ *adj* [F+**in**] *fml* possessing a thorough knowledge of or skill in a subject, an art, etc.; experienced: *After ten years as an ambassador, she is* **well versed in** *the arts of diplomacy.*

ver·si·fi·ca·tion /ˌvɜːsɪfɪˈkeɪʃ*ə*n‖ˌvɜːr-/ *n* [U] *tech* the particular pattern or way in which a poem is written

ver·sion /ˈvɜːʃ*ə*n‖ˈvɜːrʒən/ *n* (**of**) **1** a slightly different form, copy, or style of an article: *This dress is a cheaper version of the one we saw in that shop.* **2** one person's account of an event, esp. as compared with that of another person: *The two newspapers gave different versions of what happened.* | *the accepted version of events* | *earlier/later versions* **3** a form of a written or musical work that exists in more than one form: *Did you read the whole book or only the abridged version?* | *an English version* (=translation), *of a German play* —see also AUTHORIZED VERSION, KING JAMES VERSION, REVISED STANDARD VERSION, REVISED VERSION

ver·so /ˈvɜːsəʊ‖ˈvɜːr-/ *adj, n* **-sos** [A;C] *tech* (being) a left-hand page of a book: *written on the verso (side)* —compare RECTO

ver·sus /ˈvɜːsəs‖ˈvɜːr-/ *prep* against; in opposition to: *The Finance Minister has to weigh up the benefits of tax cuts versus those of increased public spending.* | *It's going to be Mexico versus Holland in the final.*

ver·te·bra /ˈvɜːtɪbrə‖ˈvɜːr-/ *n* **-brae** /briː, breɪ/ any of the small hollow bones down the centre of the back which form the BACKBONE —see picture at SKELETON —**-bral** *adj*

ver·te·brate /ˈvɜːtɪbrət, -breɪt‖ˈvɜːr-/ *n tech* a living creature which has a BACKBONE: *Fish, birds, and human beings are vertebrates.* —compare INVERTEBRATE — **vertebrate** *adj*

ver·tex /ˈvɜːteks‖ˈvɜːr-/ *n* **-texes** *or* **-tices** /tɪsiːz/ [(**of**)] *tech* **1 a** the angle opposite the base of a figure such as a PYRAMID, CONE, TRIANGLE, etc. **b** the meeting point of the two lines of an angle **2** the highest point: *the vertex of an arch*

ver·ti·cal /ˈvɜːtɪkəl‖ˈvɜːr-/ *adj* forming an angle of 90 degrees with the level ground, or with a straight line in a figure; upright: *blue and green vertical stripes* | *a vertical line* | *The northern face of the mountain is almost vertical.* | *A* **vertical takeoff** *aircraft is one that can rise straight from the ground.* —compare HORIZONTAL — **~ly** /kli/ *adv*

vertical file /ˈ··· ˌ·/ *n* [usu. S] *AmE* a place in a library where printed materials are kept that do not form part of the regular collection: *We keep pamphlets and news releases in the vertical file.*

ver·tig·i·nous /vɜːˈtɪdʒɪnəs‖vɜːr-/ *adj fml* causing or suffering from vertigo, esp. by being at great height above the ground: *vertiginous heights*

ver·ti·go /ˈvɜːtɪgəʊ‖ˈvɜːr-/ *n* [U] a feeling of great unsteadiness, as though one's head were spinning round, often also with a sensation of sickness and faintness, and caused usu. by looking down from a great height: *He suffers from vertigo.*

verve /vɜːv‖vɜːrv/ *n* [U] *apprec* a strong feeling of life, force, and eager enjoyment, expressed through some activity or shown in some form of art: *He's a poor singer, but we had to admire the sheer verve of his performance.*

ve·ry¹ /ˈveri/ *adv* **1** (used for giving force to an expression) especially; to a great degree: *a very good cake* | *a very exciting book* | *It's very warm today.* | *I feel very tired after all that effort.* | *We must remember the very real problems of young people today.* | *The traffic is moving very slowly.* | *She was very nearly killed!* | *Thanks very much.* | *I feel very much better today.* | *His new book's very much the same as his last one.* | *I very much hope you'll be able to come.* | *That was very kind of you.* **2** (used for giving

force to superlative adjectives or to **own** or **same**) in the greatest possible degree: *The cake ought to be good — I used the very best ingredients.* | *This is the very last time I offer to help you.* | *He could have warned you he was coming, at the very least.* | *You're a lucky boy to have your very own boat.* | *two accidents in the very same place* **3** not very: **a** in no way; exactly the opposite of: *The teacher wasn't very pleased* (=was angry) *when he found a dead mouse on his desk.* **b** only slightly; to a small degree: *"Was the play interesting?" "Not very."* —see also **very good** (GOOD¹ (31), **very well** (WELL¹ (8)); see MOST (USAGE), QUITE (USAGE)

ve·ry² *adj* [A] (used for giving force to an expression) actual: *This is the very pen he used when he was writing the book. He used this very pen.* | *I'll go this very minute.* (=at once) | *They say he died in that very bed.* | *I found it at the very bottom* (=right at the bottom) *of the box.* | *She died at the very height of her fame.* | *The very thought of* (=even thinking about) *that terrible meal makes me feel sick.* | *Of course you can't go on your own.* **The very idea!** (=expresses surprise or shock) | *This little tool is* the **very thing** *for turning stiff taps.* (=it does it very well)

very high fre·quen·cy /ˌ··· · ˈ···/ *n* [U] (*often cap.*) see VHF

Ve·ry light /ˈvɪəri laɪt‖ˌveri ˈlaɪt, ˌvɪəri-/ *n* (a bright, sometimes coloured, light produced by) a special sort of burning bullet that is fired high into the air from a small gun (**Very pistol**), used esp. as a signal that someone is in danger and needs help

Very Rev·e·rend /ˌveri ˈrevərənd◂/ *n, adj* a title of respect for certain religious officials, namely a DEAN (1), a former MODERATOR (2), or a Scottish university PRINCIPAL² (1) who happens to be a church minister

ves·i·cle /ˈvesɪkəl/ *n med* a small hollow part in an organ or other bodily part, or a small swelling on the skin, usu. filled with liquid

ve·sic·u·lar /vɪˈsɪkjʊləʳ/ *adj med* of or marked by the formation of vesicles

ves·pers /ˈvespəz‖-ərz/ *n* [U | *sing./pl. v*] (*often cap.*) (in some branches of the Christian church) the evening service, esp. EVENSONG —compare COMPLINE, EVENSONG

Ves·puc·ci /veˈspuːtʃi/, **A·mer·i·go** /æˈmeriːgəʊ/ (1454–1512) an Italian sailor and EXPLORER, who travelled to the West Indies and South America and discovered the mouth of the Amazon river

ves·sel /ˈvesəl/ *n* **1** *fml* a ship or large boat, esp. of the stated kind: *a French naval vessel in the harbour.* | *a fishing vessel* | *a motor vessel* **2** *fml or old use* a usu. round container, such as a pot, cup, or barrel, used esp. for holding liquids: *a drinking vessel* **3** *tech* a tube, such as a VEIN, that carries blood or other liquid through the body, or plant juice (SAP) through a plant —see also BLOOD VESSEL

▷ USAGE **Vessel** meaning "ship" is formal or literary. The more ordinary words are **ship** or **boat**. —see also BOAT (USAGE)◁

vest¹ /vest/ *n* **1** *BrE* ‖ **undershirt** *AmE*— a short undergarment, usu. without coverings for the arms, worn on the upper part of the body: *a string vest* **2** a similar garment worn to protect the body: *The policeman survived because of his bulletproof vest.* **3** *AmE for* WAISTCOAT

vest² *v*
vest in *phr v* [T] *fml* **1** [*usu. pass.*] (**vest sthg. in** sbdy.) to give the official and legal right to possess or use (power, property, etc.) to: *In most countries the right to make new laws is vested in the people's representatives.* **2** [*no pass.*] (**vest in** sbdy./sthg.) (of power, property, etc.) to belong by right to: *In former times this power vested in the Church.*
vest sbdy. **with** sthg. *phr v* [T *usu. pass.*] *fml* to give (someone) the official and legal right to possess or use (power, property, etc.)

ves·tal vir·gin /ˌvestl ˈvɜːdʒɪn‖-ɜːr-/ *n* **1** any of the young unmarried women whose duty was to keep the holy fire always burning in the temple of Vesta, the Roman goddess of the house **2** *infml derog* a woman who will not have sex

vested in·terest /ˌ··· ˈ···/ *n* [(**in**)] *often derog* a share or right already held in something, that is of advantage to the holder: *It was difficult to end the system of slavery because many powerful people had a vested interest in keeping it.*

vested in·terests /ˌ·· '··/ n [P] usu. derog all the people having a vested interest in a particular business or situation, which they are unwilling to lose even for the good of the public: *It would be impossible to make a law forbidding smoking, because of the powerful vested interests who own the tobacco companies.*

ves·ti·bule /ˈvestɪbjuːl/ n **1** fml a wide passage or small room just inside the outer door of a (public) building through which all other rooms are reached; entrance hall **2** AmE an enclosed passage at each end of a railway carriage which connects it with the next carriage

ves·tige /ˈvestɪdʒ/ n [(of)] **1** a sign, mark, track, or other proof that someone or something formerly existed or was present: *These upright stones are the vestiges of some ancient religion.* | *The new act of parliament removed the last vestiges of royal power.* **2** fml (usu. in negatives) (of a quality, etc.) the smallest possible amount: *There's not a vestige of truth in the witness's statement.* (=it is completely untrue)

ves·ti·gi·al /veˈstɪdʒiəl, -dʒəl/ adj **1** fml that still remains, even though most has gone: *The Crown retains some vestigial power.* **2** tech being a limb or organ that either has never developed fully or has stopped being used and nearly disappeared: *Some snakes have vestigial legs.* —~ly adv

vest·ment /ˈvestmənt/ n [often pl.] fml a ceremonial garment, esp. as worn by priests for church services

ves·try /ˈvestri/ n **1** also **sacristy**— a small room in a church where holy cups and plates, official records, etc., are stored, and where the priest and church singers put on their ceremonial clothes **2** a room connected with a church building, used for prayer meetings, church business, etc.

ves·ture /ˈvestʃəʳ/ n [U] lit or poet clothing

Ve·su·vi·us /vɪˈsuːviəs/ also **Mount Vesuvius, Vesuvio** /-viəʊ/— an active VOLCANO in SE Italy. When Vesuvius erupted in AD 79, it buried the Roman city of Pompeii.

vet[1] /vet/ also **vet·e·ri·na·ry sur·geon** /ˌ····· '··/ BrE fml ‖ **veterinarian** /ˌvetərɪˈneəriən/AmE— n a person trained in the medical care and treatment of sick animals: *I took my dog to the vet/to the vet's.* (=the vet's SURGERY)

vet[2] v -tt- [T] infml, esp. BrE to examine carefully for correctness, past record, etc.: *The recruits were thoroughly vetted before they were allowed into the secret service.*

vet[3] n infml for VETERAN[2]: *a Vietnam vet*

vetch /vetʃ/ n a beanlike climbing plant

vet·e·ran[1] /ˈvetərən/ n, adj [C;A] **1** [(of)] someone who in the past has had experience in the stated form of activity, esp. in war: *My grandfather is a veteran of the Second World War.* —compare EX-SERVICEMAN **2** (a person) who has had long experience in some form of activity: *At the age of 12 the boy was already a veteran traveller, having flown all over the world with his father.* | *veteran politicians* **3** (a thing) that has grown old with long use: *Every year a race is held in England for veteran cars.* (=those made before 1905) | *This sewing machine is a real veteran.* —compare VINTAGE[2] (4)

veteran[2] also **vet** infml— n AmE someone, young or old, who has served in the armed forces, esp. during a war

Veterans Af·fairs /ˈ··· ·ˌ·/ also **VA, Veterans Ad·min·i·stra·tion** /ˈ··· ···ˌ··/— [the] an American government organization which deals with things concerning former members of the armed forces, such as health care, education, and PENSIONS (=money given to someone when they stop working)

Veterans Day /ˈ··· ·/ November 11th, when people in the US and Canada remember the end of fighting in the two World Wars —compare REMEMBRANCE DAY

Veterans of For·eign Wars /ˌ···· · ˌ·· ˈ·/ also **VFW**— an American organization whose members have fought in wars abroad and which sometimes acts as a PRESSURE GROUP on questions of American defence

vet·e·ri·nar·i·an /ˌvetərɪˈneəriən/ n AmE a VET[1]

vet·e·ri·na·ry /ˈvetərɪnəri‖-neri/ adj [A] tech connected with the medical care and treatment of sick animals, esp. farm animals and pets: *veterinary science* —see also VET[1]

ve·to[1] /ˈviːtəʊ/ n -toes [C (on);U] (a) refusal to give permission for something, or to allow something to be done; (act

of) forbidding something completely: *the threat of a presidential veto on this legislation* | *The French exercised their power of/right of veto in the Security Council to prevent the resolution being passed.* | *I've put a veto on football in the garden in case the children break any more windows.*

veto[2] v -toed; present participle -toing [T] to prevent or forbid (some action); refuse to allow (something): *The president last week vetoed a cereal price cut.*

vex /veks/ v [T] old-fash **1** to displease (someone); cause to feel angry or bad-tempered **2** [often pass.] to trouble (someone) continually; keep in discomfort or without rest

vex·a·tion /vekˈseɪʃən/ n **1** [U] fml the feeling, fact, or state of being vexed; displeasure **2** [C often pl.] old-fash something that vexes one

vex·a·tious /vekˈseɪʃəs/ adj old-fash vexing; displeasing; troublesome —~ly adv

vexed ques·tion /ˌ·· ˈ··/ n something that has caused much fierce argument and is difficult to decide; a troublesome matter or question: *the vexed question of how to deal with hunger-strikers*

V-for·ma·tion /ˈviː foːˌmeɪʃən ‖ -foːr-/ n the shape of a large number of birds flying together like the letter "V"

VFW /ˌviː ef ˈdʌbljuː/ n VETERANS OF FOREIGN WARS

VHF /ˌviː eɪtʃ ˈef/ n [U] very high frequency; (the sending out of radio waves at) the rate of 30,000,000 to 300,000,000 HERTZ, producing good sound quality: *This radio station broadcasts only on VHF.* | *a VHF radio* —compare UHF

vi·a /ˈvaɪə‖ˈviːə/ prep **1** travelling or sent through (a place) on the way: *We flew to Athens via Paris.* **2** by means of; using: *I sent a message to Mary via her sister.*

vi·a·ble /ˈvaɪəbəl/ adj **1** able to succeed in operation; FEASIBLE: *The scheme is not economically viable.* **2** tech able to continue to exist as or develop into a living thing: *viable births* —-bly adv —-bility /ˌvaɪəˈbɪlɪti/ n [U] : *commercial viability* | *the long-term financial viability of the company*

vi·a·duct /ˈvaɪədʌkt/ n a long high bridge which carries a road or railway line across a valley

vi·al /ˈvaɪəl/ n a PHIAL

vi·ands /ˈvaɪəndz/ n [P] old use food

vibes /vaɪbz/ n vibes infml **1** [C+sing./pl. v] a vibraphone **2** [P] VIBRATIONS (2): *good/bad/strange vibes*

vi·brant /ˈvaɪbrənt/ adj **1** (of colour or light) bright and strong **2** alive; forceful; powerful and exciting: *a city vibrant with life* | *a youthful vibrant voice* —~ly adv —-brancy n [U]

vi·bra·phone /ˈvaɪbrəfəʊn/ n a musical instrument consisting of a set of metal bars set in a frame, which are struck to produce notes that are made to vibrate

vi·brate /vaɪˈbreɪt‖ˈvaɪbreɪt/ v [I;T] to (cause to) shake continuously and very quickly with a fine slight movement that may often be felt or heard rather than seen: *Tom's heavy footsteps upstairs made the old house vibrate.* | *The air in the desert seemed to vibrate in the midday heat.* | *The hammers strike the piano strings and vibrate them.* | (fig.) *At night, the whole city vibrates with life.*

vi·bra·tion /vaɪˈbreɪʃən/ n **1** [C;U] (a) slight continuous shaky movement: *You can feel the vibrations when a plane flies over our house.* **2** [C usu. pl.] also **vibes**— sl an EMOTIONAL feeling or influence that can be felt as coming from a person or among a group; a word used esp. by younger people in the late 1960s and 1970s: *This disco's got fantastic vibes!*

vi·bra·to /vɪˈbrɑːtəʊ/ n -tos tech (in music) a slightly shaking effect given to the sound of the voice, or of stringed or wind instruments, for added expressiveness

vi·bra·tor /vaɪˈbreɪtəʳ ‖ˈvaɪbreɪtər/ n an instrument used for producing VIBRATIONS, esp. an electrical apparatus used on the body to produce pleasing (esp. sexual) sensations

vic·ar /ˈvɪkəʳ/ n **1** (in the Church of England) a priest in charge of an area (PARISH). In advertisements, television programmes, etc., vicars are often shown as polite, cheerful, and keen to be helpful, but also as UNWORLDLY (=not experienced in the ways of society) and easily shocked: *Good morning, vicar!* —compare RECTOR (1) **2** (in the Roman Catholic Church) a representative: *The Pope is known as the* **vicar of Christ**.

vic·ar·age /ˈvɪkərɪdʒ/ n the house of a VICAR (1)

vi·car·i·ous /vɪˈkeəriəs‖vaɪ-/ adj 1 experienced by the imagination through watching or reading about other people; indirect 2 fml experienced for other people: vicarious sufferings — ~ly adv — ~ness n [U]

vice¹ /vaɪs/ n 1 [C;U] (any particular kind of) evil behaviour or living, esp. in sexual practices, taking of harmful drugs, uncontrolled drinking habits, etc.: She was arrested by the police vice squad for prostitution. | The police have smashed a vice ring (=criminal group) in Chicago. 2 [C;U] (an example of) badness of character: the vice of greed|pride —opposite virtue 3 [C] infml, often humor a bad habit: "Would you like a whisky?" "No, thanks; alcohol isn't one of my vices!"

vice² esp. BrE ‖ vise AmE— n a tool with metal jaws that can be tightened, used for holding something firmly so that it can be worked on with both hands

vice- see WORD FORMATION

vice-chan·cel·lor /ˌ·ˈ·····‹/ n 1 (often cap. V and C) (in Britain) the officer who actually controls the affairs of a university; the real head of a university (since the CHANCELLOR (2) is appointed only as an honour) 2 (often cap. V and C) (in the US) the officer next in rank to the head (CHANCELLOR) of a university

vice·like /ˈvaɪs-laɪk/ adj very firm; giving no chance of movement or escape: He held me in a vicelike grip.

vice pres·i·dent /ˌ·ˈ····/ n 1 an officer next in rank to the president who usu. serves as president if the president becomes unable to serve, e.g. because of illness. In the US, the vice president is also responsible for acting as the president of the Senate: Vice president Dan Quayle 2 AmE a person responsible for a particular area of a company: our executive vice president for marketing

vice-re·gal /vaɪsˈriːɡəl/ adj of a viceroy

vice-reine /vaɪsˈreɪn‖ˈvaɪsreɪn/ n the wife of a viceroy

vice·roy /ˈvaɪsrɔɪ/ n a king's or queen's representative ruling for them in another country: When Britain ruled India, the British king was represented there by a viceroy.

Vice Squad /ˈ· ·/ [the] the division of the police force in either Britain or the US which deals with sexual and drug-related offences

vice ver·sa /ˌvaɪs ˈvɜːsə, ˌvaɪsi ‖ ɔːr / adv Lat in the opposite way from that just stated: When she wants to go out, he wants to stay in, and vice versa. (=when he wants to go out, she wants to stay in)

Vi·chy /ˈviːʃi/ a city in S central France where the government of France was during the Second World War. The authority of the **Vichy government** was not accepted by many French people because it followed the rules and laws given to it by the Germans who had taken control of France. When people discuss this period of France's history they sometimes call the country **Vichy France.** —see also FREE FRENCH, PETAIN

vi·cin·i·ty /vɪˈsɪnɪti/ n 1 [in+(the) U (of)] the surroundings; area very near to or around the stated place; neighbourhood: "Are there any shops in this vicinity?" (=near here) | All the ships in the vicinity of the crash joined in the search for survivors. 2 [U (of, to)] fml nearness: the house's vicinity to the station 3 in the vicinity of pomp about: His income is in the vicinity of £15,000 a year.

vi·cious /ˈvɪʃəs/ adj 1 cruel; having or showing hate and the desire to hurt: He gave the dog a vicious blow with his stick. | a vicious attack 2 dangerous; able or likely to cause severe hurt: a vicious-looking knife — ~ly adv — ~ness n [U]

vicious cir·cle /ˌ··· ˈ··/ n a set of events in which cause and effect follow each other until this results in a return to the first usu. undesirable or unpleasant position and the whole matter begins again: "Crime leads to prison, which leads to unemployment, which leads to crime. It's a vicious circle."

vi·cis·si·tudes /vɪˈsɪsɪtjuːdz‖-tuːdz/ n [P] fml continual changes, esp. from good to bad, in one's nature, condition of life, etc.: the vicissitudes of married life|of the oil industry

Vicks·burg /ˈvɪksbɜːɡ‖-bɜːrɡ/ a city in Mississippi, US, where an important battle was fought during the Civil War

vic·tim /ˈvɪktɪm/ n 1 [(of)] a person, animal, or thing that suffers pain, death, harm, destruction, etc., as a result of other people's actions, or of illness, bad luck, etc.: Four people were killed in the explosion, but police have not yet named the victims. | The murderer had cut his victim's throat. | That beautiful old building was knocked down last year, a victim of the council's desire for modern planning. | Thousands of trees have **fallen victim to** (=suffered from) this disease. 2 a person or animal killed and offered as a SACRIFICE (=gift) to a god: sacrificial victims

vic·tim·ize ‖ also -ise BrE /ˈvɪktɪmaɪz/ v [T] to cause (someone) to suffer unfairly: He claimed that in sacking him because of his political views, they'd victimized him. —-ization /ˌvɪktɪmaɪˈzeɪʃən‖-mə-/ n [U]: racial victimization

victimless crime /ˌ··· ˈ·/ n a crime in which no one suffers, usu. because the people involved have agreed to be involved: Prostitution is often called a victimless crime because both parties consent to the action taken.

vic·tor /ˈvɪktəʳ/ n esp. fml, lit, or pomp a winner in battle, or in a race, game, competition, or other kind of struggle —see also VICTORIOUS

Vic·to·ri·a¹ /vɪkˈtɔːriə/ 1 a large train station in central London: Trains to Brighton leave from Victoria. —see colour map on page 817 2 the capital city of the Canadian PROVINCE (1) of British Columbia, known for its reasonable winter weather and British influences 3 a state in SE Australia, which is very industrialized and has Melbourne as its capital city

Victoria², **Lake** the largest lake in Africa, on the borders of Uganda, Tanzania, and Kenya

Victoria³, **Queen** (1819–1901) queen of Great Britain and Ireland, EMPRESS of India and granddaughter of **George** III. Queen Victoria was the MONARCH who ruled for the longest period in English history, during which there was great industrial advancement, an EXPANSION in the **British Empire**, and an increase in the popularity of the MONARCHY. Victoria's husband **Prince Albert** was an important influence on her and the marriages of their nine children connected them with many royal families in Europe. Victoria is supposed to have said "We are not amused".

Queen Victoria

Victoria and Al·bert Mu·se·um /·,··· ,··· ·ˈ··/ also **V & A**— [the] a MUSEUM in London which includes valuable objects of all styles and periods, such as paintings, Indian works of art, glass, jewellery, and TEXTILES: an exhibition of Japanese prints at the V & A

Victoria Cross /·,··· ˈ·/ n see VC

Victoria Day /·ˈ··· ,·/ a public holiday held in May in Canada

Victoria Falls /·,··· ˈ·/ a WATERFALL on the Zambezi River between Zimbabwe and Zambia, which is a mile wide and falls four hundred feet

Vic·to·ri·an¹ /vɪkˈtɔːriən/ adj 1 [no comp.] of, made in, or living in the time when Queen Victoria ruled (1837–1901): Victorian women 2 describing the style of ARCHITECTURE of the time when Queen Victoria ruled Britain. Victorian buildings are typically built in red brick and are quite highly decorated. —see colour picture on page 227 3 usu. derog like the behaviour, moral standards, etc., of middle-class society in the time of Queen Victoria, esp. being or pretending to be very respectable, religious, pure, etc.: Victorian prudery | Victorian values

Victorian² n any English person living in the time when Queen Victoria ruled (1837–1901): Florence Nightingale and William Gladstone were famous Victorians.

Vic·to·ri·a·na /vɪkˌtɔːriˈɑːnə/ n [P] collectable things (e.g. DOLLS, lamps, spoons, etc.) from the Victorian age: I found an antique shop full of Victoriana.

victoria plum /·,··· ˈ·/ n a large, sweet, dark red PLUM

vic·to·ri·ous /vɪkˈtɔːriəs/ adj 1 [(in, over)] that has won: the victorious team 2 [A] of or showing victory: a victorious shout —see also VICTOR — ~ly adv

vic·to·ry /ˈvɪktəri/ n [C;U (in, over)] (an example of) the act of winning or state of having won, in war or in any kind of struggle: *Both sides were claiming victory last night.* | *The captain led his team to victory.* | *He only managed a narrow victory in the election; he won by 23 votes.* | *The early settlement of the strike was hailed as a victory for common sense.* | *to snatch victory from the jaws of defeat* (=to win when it seemed that one would lose) | *a resounding/overwhelming victory* | *to win an easy/decisive/clearcut victory* | *a sign ificant propaganda victory* | *to hold a victory rally* —opposite **defeat**; see also PYRRHIC VICTORY

Victory, The also **HMS Victory**— Admiral Nelson's own ship at the battle of Trafalgar in 1805, now preserved at Portsmouth in S England

victory gar·den /ˈ··· ˌ··/ n AmE a vegetable garden grown during the Second World War so that there would be more food available to send abroad

vict·ual /ˈvɪtl/ v -ll- BrE ‖ -l- AmE— tech **1** [T] to supply (usu. a large number of people) with food **2** [I] to take in and store supplies of food and drink —see also LICENSED VICTUALLER

vict·uals /ˈvɪtlz/ n [P] old use or dial (supplies of) food and drink

vi·cu·ña, -na /vɪˈkjuːnə‖vɪˈkuː-/ n **1** [C] a large South American animal, related to the LLAMA, from which soft wool of very good quality is obtained **2** [U] the cloth made from this wool: *a vicuña coat*

vi·de /ˈvaɪdi, ˈviːdi/ v [T only imperative] Lat fml (used for telling a reader where to find more about the subject) see; look at

vi·de·li·cet /vɪˈdiːlɪˌset, -ket‖-ˈde-/ adv Lat, fml for VIZ.

vid·e·o¹ /ˈvɪdiəʊ/ adj [A] **1** tech connected with or used in the showing of pictures by television: *video signals* —compare AUDIO and see picture at LIVING ROOM **2** using videotape: *a video recording*

video² n -os **1 a** [C;U] (a) videotape recording: *They showed a video of "Gone with the Wind".* | *I've got it on video.* | *a video shop* **b** [C] infml a videotape: *This video's full up; have we got any blank ones?* **2** [C] esp. BrE also **video cas·sette re·cor·der** /ˌ··· ·¹· ·ˌ··/, **vid·e·o·re·cor·der** /ˈvɪdiəʊriˌkɔːdə²‖-ɔːr-/, **vid·e·o·tape re·cor·der** /ˈ····· ·ˌ··/ fml a machine for making videotape recordings and playing them back: *Set the video to go on at 8.00.*

video³ esp. BrE ‖ **tape** esp. AmE— v -oed; present participle -oing [T] to videotape: *Could you video the documentary for me?*

video ar·cade /ˈ··· ·ˌ·/ n AmE a place where there are many video games which are started by putting money in them

vid·e·o·disc /ˈvɪdiəʊˌdɪsk/ n a round piece of plastic, like a record, from which recorded pictures can be played back in the same way as from a videotape

video game /ˈ··· ˌ·/ n a game played by pushing buttons which move parts of the pictures on the SCREEN of a video

vid·e·o nas·ty /ˌ··· ˈ··/ n BrE infml a video film including scenes of extremely unpleasant violence

vid·e·o·tape¹ /ˈvɪdiəʊteɪp/ also **video cas·sette** /ˌ··· ·¹·/, **tape** infml, **video** infml— n [C;U] (a container holding a long narrow band of) MAGNETIC material on which pictures, e.g. a television show, are recorded and from which they can be played back

videotape² also **tape** infml— v [T] to make a recording of (a television show) on videotape

vie /vaɪ/ v vied; present participle vying [I+adv/prep, esp. with, for] to compete (with someone) (for something): *They are vying for the lead.* [+to-v] *The shipping companies vied with each other to make the fastest Atlantic crossing.*

Vi·en·na /viˈenə/ the capital city of Austria, famous as a music and CULTURAL centre —see also CONGRESS OF VIENNA —**Viennese** /ˌviːəˈniːz◂/ n, adj

Viet Cong /ˌvjet ˈkɒŋ‖-ˈkɑːŋ/ also **Vietcong**— n (a member of) a group of GUERRILLAS (=unofficial soldiers) supported by the COMMUNIST government of North Vietnam during the Vietnam War

Viet·nam /ˌvjetˈnæm◂‖-ˈnɑːm/ a country in SE Asia, bordered by Cambodia, Laos, China, and the South China sea; capital Hanoi; population 65,682,000 (1989)

Viet·na·mese /ˌvjetnəˈmiːz◂/ n **1** [the + P] people from Vietnam **2** [U] the language of Vietnam —**Vietnamese** adj: *She's Vietnamese.* | *a Vietnamese restaurant*

Vietnam Vet·e·rans Me·mo·ri·al /ˌ·· ¹··· ·ˌ···/ also **Vietnam Memorial** /ˌ·· ·¹·ˌ··/— [the] a structure of polished black stone in the shape of a "V" which is sunk into the ground in the park area near the White House and the Capitol Building in Washington, DC. The names of all the soldiers killed in the Vietnam War are on the stone walls.

Vietnam War /ˌ·· ¹·/ also **Vietnam**— [the] (1954–75) a long CIVIL WAR in Vietnam between the North and the South. The government of the South, in SAIGON, was helped by the US and other countries to fight against the VIET CONG, GUERRILLAs (=unofficial soldiers) who were supported by the COMMUNIST government of the North. The South was unsuccessful even with US help.Many people in the West associate the war in Vietnam with the strong public protests against it. While half a million American soldiers were fighting in Vietnam, protest marches were common at home. **Protest songs** included the words, "hell no, we won't go!" and the saying, "make love, not war" became popular. Some young men refused to go to war for moral reasons. While some were allowed to become legal CONSCIENTIOUS OBJECTORs, others, called DRAFT DODGERs, either left the country or went to jail in protest. Many Americans protested when they saw horrific pictures of the war dead shown on television. Others objected that the soldiers who were DRAFTed (=made to go to war) were often poor or black, while wealthier whites could find ways to avoid the draft.When President Nixon finally brought the American forces home in 1973, they were not cheered in the streets for their courage, and they were sometimes treated badly by people who were against the war.Many more people now believe that the US should never have entered the war at all, for both moral and military reasons. Others still believe that the US could have helped the South to win. —see also BOAT PEOPLE, KENT STATE, MY LAI MASSACRE, VIETNAM VETERANS MEMORIAL

view¹ /vjuː/ n **1** [U] ability to see or be seen from a particular place; sight: *My view of the stage was blocked by the hat of the woman sitting in front of me.* | *The car turned the corner and was lost to our view/passed out of view.* (=could not be seen any more) | *The valley was hidden from view in the mist.* | *When we reached the top of the mountain, a wide plain came into view* (=could be seen)/*we came in view of* (=were able to see) *a wide plain below.* | *He fell off his horse in full view of all the television cameras.* (=seen clearly by all of them) | *There was no shelter within view.* (=that could be seen) | *The camera gave us a bird's eye view of the golf course.* (=showed it clearly from high above) **2** [C (of)] a something seen from a particular place, esp. a stretch of pleasant country; a scene: *The only view from my bedroom window is of some factory chimneys.* | *I'd like a room with a view* (=a good view), *please.* | *a marvellous/wonderful view* **b** a picture or photograph of scenery, a building, etc.: *a painter of sea views* —see SCENERY (USAGE) **3** [S (of)] a special chance to see or examine someone or something: *If we stand at this window, we'll get a better view (of the procession).* | (fig.) *The President will get an inside view of the problems involved when he visits a nuclear power plant tomorrow.* **4** [C (about, on)] a personal opinion, belief, idea, etc., about something: *What are your views on free university education?* | *He holds strong views about* (=feels strongly either for or against) *trade unions.* [+that] *He expressed/reiterated the view that he was a fool.* | *In my view, he's a fool.* | *We weren't very enthusiastic about it, but we agreed to fall in with his views.* (=do as he wished) | *She takes a dim/poor view of* (=thinks unfavourably of) *her son's recent behaviour.* | *He's got a rather limited world view.* (=he sees the world, life, etc., in a very narrow way) **5** [C (of) usu. sing.] an act or manner of seeing, considering, examining, etc.: *The book offers a rather sentimental view of literature in the 19th century.* [+that] *I take/share/strongly support the view that we should put less money into nuclear weapons.* | *a widely-held view which was confirmed by later events* | *the paper's rather jaundiced view of the government* | *the feminist view of this question* **6 in view** fml already planned or suggested: *He wants to find work, but he has nothing particular in view.* **7 in view of** considering; taking into consideration: *In view of his youth, the police have decided not to* press charges. **8 keep someone/something in view** to remember someone or something as a possibility or for future consideration if a favourable chance comes **9 on view** being shown to the public; offered to be seen and examined: *Her paintings are on view at the Hayward Gallery.* **10 take the 'long view (of something)** not to think only of the results which will follow at once from some action, but also of its effects in the more distant future **11 with a view to** *rather fml* with the intention of; in order to —see also POINT OF VIEW

view² v **1** [T+*obj+adv/prep*, esp. **as, with**] to consider; regard; think about: *I view his action as a breach of trust.| They viewed the future with some alarm. | The audience seemed to enjoy the show, but viewed from a theatrical standpoint, it was a disaster.* **2** [T] esp. tech to examine; look at thoroughly: *Several possible buyers have come to view the house.* **3** [I;T] tech to watch (esp. television): *The viewing figures for this programme have been poor.* (=not many people have watched it)

view·er /ˈvjuːəʳ/ n **1** a person who watches or is watching esp. television: *Angry viewers have written in to complain. | Regular viewers will remember that a few weeks ago... | This programme is for our younger viewers.* (=children) —compare LISTENER **2** an apparatus for looking at transparent colour photographs: *a slide viewer*

view·find·er /ˈvjuːˌfaɪndəʳ/ n an apparatus on a camera, which shows a small picture of what is to be photographed —see picture at CAMERA

view·point /ˈvjuːpɔɪnt/ n a POINT OF VIEW

vig·il /ˈvɪdʒɪl/ n [C;U] (an act of) remaining watchful for some purpose, esp. while staying awake during the night: *She kept an all-night vigil by the sick woman's bedside.| his lonely vigil*

vig·i·lance /ˈvɪdʒɪləns/ n [U] fml watchful care; continual attentiveness: *Thanks to their constant vigilance, a crisis was averted.*

vigilance com·mit·tee /ˈ··· ·ˌ··/ n [C+*sing./pl.* v] AmE a group of vigilantes

vig·i·lant /ˈvɪdʒɪlənt/ adj fml continually watchful or on guard; always prepared for possible danger: *The police said the public should remain vigilant.* — **~ly** adv

vig·i·lan·te /ˌvɪdʒɪˈlænti/ n sometimes derog a person, esp. a member of an unofficial organization, who tries by unofficial means to keep order and punish crime in an area where an official body either does not exist or does not work effectively: *vigilantes on the New York subway | a vigilante group* —see also VIGILANCE COMMITTEE

vi·gnette /vɪˈnjet/ n **1** a small drawing or pattern without a border, set into a book, esp. at the beginning or end of a CHAPTER **2** a short effective written description of a character or scene

vig·our BrE ‖ **-or** AmE /ˈvɪgəʳ/ n [U] usu. apprec active strength or force of mind or body; ENERGY: *For a man of seventy he still has surprising vigour. | Inspired by what she had said, he attacked the problem with renewed vigour.* —**vigorous** adj: *The minister made a vigorous defence of the government's policies. | These tomato plants are very vigorous.* (=growing strongly and healthily) — **vigorously** adv

Vikings

Vi·king /ˈvaɪkɪŋ/ n a man belonging to a race of Scandinavian people who attacked, and sometimes settled along, the coasts of northern and western Europe from the 8th to the 10th centuries. The Vikings are known for their skill in building ships and their sense of adventure. In pictures, Vikings are usu. shown wearing HELMETs with horns on them. —see picture at LONGSHIP —**Viking** adj: *Viking ships*

vile /vaɪl/ adj **1** fml shameful and evil; DESPICABLE: *a vile slander* **2** infml very bad, nasty, or unpleasant: *She has a vile temper. | This food is vile!* — **~ly** /ˈvaɪl-li/ adv — **~ness** n [U]

vil·i·fy /ˈvɪlɪfaɪ/ v [T] fml to say bad things about (someone or something) without good cause, esp. in order to influence others unfavourably —**-fication** /ˌvɪlɪfɪˈkeɪʃən/ n [C;U]

vil·la /ˈvɪlə/ n **1** a pleasant country house in its own garden, often used for only part of the year for holidays, esp. in southern Europe: *We're renting a villa in the south of France for the summer.* **2** (often cap. as part of the name of a house) BrE a large house on the edge of a town, usu. with a garden and usu. built before 1914: *South Villa | fine old 19th-century villas* **3** a large ancient Roman country house with the buildings and (farm)land belonging to it

Vil·la /ˈviːə/, **Pan·cho** /ˈpæntʃəʊ‖ˈpɑː-/ (about 1878–1923) a Mexican leader of a REVOLUTION against the Mexico government

vil·lage /ˈvɪlɪdʒ/ n **1** a collection of houses and other buildings, such as a church, school, PUB, and one or more shops, in a country area, smaller than a town: *the village pub | village life | in the tiny village of Debden in Essex* —compare CITY, TOWN; see also SMALL TOWN **2** [+*sing./pl.* v] all the people who live in such a place: *The whole village turned out to the baker's funeral.*

village green

village green /ˌ·· ˈ·/ n an area of grass in the centre of an English village for the use of all the people who live there. People often think of a game of cricket on the village green in the summer as being a very TRADITIONAL English scene.

village id·i·ot /ˌ·· ˈ···/ n a STEREOTYPE of a very stupid person, usu. a man, living in a village. He talks and behaves like a child, knows nothing of the modern world, and is generally treated kindly by the other people in the village. —compare YOKEL

vil·lag·er /ˈvɪlɪdʒəʳ/ n a person who lives in a village

Village Voice /ˈ·· ˌ·/, **The** a weekly US newspaper printed in Greenwich Village in New York, known esp. for news about ALTERNATIVE¹ (3) entertainment —see also extra information on page 896

vil·lain /ˈvɪlən/ n **1** (in old plays, films, and stories) a man who is the (or a) main bad character: *The villain carried off the young heroine and tied her to the railway line.* — opposite **hero 2** BrE infml, esp. humor a criminal: *Policemen don't spend all their time chasing villains, you know!* **3** infml a troublesome young person: *Stop eating all her sweets, you young villain!* **4 the 'villain of the piece** infml, often humor the person or thing to be blamed; the one that has caused all the trouble on some occasion

vil·lain·ous /ˈvɪlənəs/ adj esp. lit evil; threatening great harm: *He was brandishing a villainous-looking knife.*

vil·lain·y /ˈvɪləni/ n [U] esp. lit evil or wicked behaviour

vil·lein /ˈvɪlɪn, ˈvɪleɪn/ n a poor land worker in Europe in the Middle Ages who was given a small amount of land of his own in return for work on the land of a large landowner

vim /vɪm/ n [U] *old-fash infml* cheerful forcefulness; ENERGY: *Try and put a bit more* **vim (and vigour)** *into your performance!*

vin·ai·grette /ˌvɪnəˈgret, ˌvɪneɪ-/ n [U] a sharp-tasting mixture of oil, VINEGAR, salt, pepper, etc., used esp. on SALADs

Vinci see LEONARDO DA VINCI

vin·di·cate /ˈvɪndɪkeɪt/ v [T] 1 to show that charges made against (someone or something) are untrue; free from blame: *The report of the committee of enquiry completely vindicates him.* 2 to prove that (something) is true or right; JUSTIFY: *The success of your operation completely vindicates my faith in the doctor.* —**cation** /ˌvɪndɪˈkeɪʃən/ n [S;U (**of**)]

vin·dic·tive /vɪnˈdɪktɪv/ adj extremely unwilling to forgive; having or showing the desire to harm someone who has harmed you: *I don't like Kevin — he's got a nasty vindictive streak in him.* – –**ly** adv – –**ness** n [U]

vine /vaɪn/ n 1 also **grapevine**— a climbing plant with a woody stem that produces bunches of juicy green or purple fruit (GRAPEs) 2 *tech* any creeping or climbing plant with thin twisting stems, such as the IVY, the CUCUMBER, the MELON, etc.

vine fruit /ˈ·· ·/ n [C;U] fruit such as GRAPEs which are grown on vines

vin·e·gar /ˈvɪnɪɡər/ n [U] an acid-tasting liquid made usu. from MALT or sour wine, used in preparing and preserving vegetables, for putting on food, etc.

vin·e·gar·y /ˈvɪnɪɡəri/ adj 1 of or like vinegar; very sour: *This wine has a vinegary taste.* 2 unkind; bitter; sharptempered: *She has a vinegary tongue.* (=says unkind things)

vine·yard /ˈvɪnjəd‖-jərd/ n a piece of land planted with VINEs for wine production

vi·no /ˈviːnəʊ/ n [U] *infml for* wine

vi·nous /ˈvaɪnəs/ adj *fml, tech, or humor* of, like, caused by, or coloured like wine: *sounds of vinous laughter*

vin·tage¹ /ˈvɪntɪdʒ/ n 1 a particular year in which a wine is made: *This wine is of the 1961 vintage.* | *a very good vintage* 2 [usu. sing.] *tech* the yearly gathering of GRAPEs in an area and the making of new wine from them

vintage² adj [A] 1 (of wine) produced in a single year rather than being a mixture from different years: *vintage port* 2 of high quality and lasting value: *a vintage silent film* | *This has been a vintage year for the theatre in London; so many good plays have been produced.* 3 *infml* showing all the best qualities of the work of (the stated person): *This piece of music is vintage Beatles.* 4 *BrE* (of a car) made between 1919 and 1930. Some people like to have or collect vintage cars because of their interest and value —compare VETERAN¹ (3)

vint·ner /ˈvɪntnər/ n a person whose business is buying and selling wines

vi·nyl /ˈvaɪnl/ n [C;U] a firm bendable plastic used instead of leather, rubber, wood, etc., often used to cover the floor of a kitchen or bathroom: *vinyl wallpaper*

vi·ol /ˈvaɪəl/ n a stringed musical instrument of the 16th and 17th centuries, from which the modern VIOLIN was developed

vi·o·la /viˈəʊlə/ n a stringed musical instrument, like the VIOLIN but a little larger and producing a slightly deeper sound

vi·o·late /ˈvaɪəleɪt/ v [T] 1 to disregard or act against (something solemnly promised, accepted as right or legal, etc.): *A country isn't respected if it violates an international agreement.* 2 *fml* to break open, into, or through (something that ought to be respected or left untouched): *The thieves violated many graves in their search for the gold.* | (fig.) *The screech of jet planes violated the peace of the afternoon.* 3 *lit or euph* to have sex with (a woman) by force; RAPE – –**lator** n —**lation** /ˌvaɪəˈleɪʃən/ n [C;U (**of**)]: *brutal violations of human rights* | *a violation of Soviet air space* | *an action in violation of the club's regulations*

vi·o·lence /ˈvaɪələns/ n [U] 1 extreme force in action or feeling, esp. that causes damage, unrest, etc.: *The wind blew with great violence.* | *The violence of his words alarmed her.* 2 rough treatment; use of physical force on others, esp. to hurt or harm illegally: *Because of his frustration with the situation, he resorted to violence.* | *Many people say too much violence is shown on television.* | *sporadic outbreaks of violence in the crowd* | *robbery with violence* 3 **do violence to** *fml* to spoil; have a harmful effect on: *These modern boxlike buildings do violence to the beauty of the old city.*

vi·o·lent /ˈvaɪələnt/ adj 1 (of a person) uncontrollably fierce and usu. dangerous: *The madman was violent and had to be locked up.* 2 acting with or using great damaging physical force: *a violent storm* | *a violent kick* | *a violent attack* | *greater penalties for both violent and non-violent crimes* | *the scene of violent clashes between police and demonstrators* 3 forceful beyond what is usual or necessary: *She was in a violent temper and began throwing things about.* | *a violent quarrel* | *violent language* 4 produced by or being the effect of damaging physical force: *He died a violent death at the hands of his brother.* – –**ly** adv: *The cart lurched violently to the left.* | *He violently objects to the proposal.*

vi·o·let¹ /ˈvaɪələt/ n a small plant with sweet-smelling dark purplish-blue flowers —see also SHRINKING VIOLET

violet² adj having a purplish-blue colour

vi·o·lin /ˌvaɪəˈlɪn/ n a four-stringed wooden musical instrument, supported between the left shoulder and the chin and played by drawing a BOW³ (2) across the strings —see INSTRUMENT (USAGE) – –**ist** n

vi·o·lon·cel·lo /ˌvaɪələnˈtʃeləʊ/ n -los *fml for* CELLO

VIP /ˌviː aɪ ˈpiː/ n a very important person; person of great influence or fame: *They treated him like a VIP.* | *the VIP lounge at the airport*

vi·per /ˈvaɪpər/ n 1 a small poisonous snake 2 *esp. lit* a wicked or ungrateful person who does harm to others

vi·ra·go /vɪˈrɑːɡəʊ/ n -goes or -gos 1 *fml derog* a fierce-tempered complaining woman with a loud voice 2 *old use* a woman of great strength and courage

Virago a British company which publishes (PUBLISH) books, usu. in PAPERBACK, written by women: *feminist novels published by Virago*

vi·ral /ˈvaɪərəl/ adj of or caused by a VIRUS: *viral pneumonia*

Vir·gil, **Vergil** /ˈvɜːdʒl‖ˈvɜːr-/ (70–19 BC) a Roman poet best known for *The Aeneid*, which tells the story of Aeneas and the Trojans

vir·gin¹ /ˈvɜːdʒn‖ˈvɜːr-/ n a person, esp. a woman or girl, who has never had sex —see also VIRGINITY – –**al** adj: *virginal purity*

virgin² adj 1 [A] without sexual experience: *his virgin bride* 2 *esp. lit* fresh; unspoiled; unchanged by human activity: *no footmarks on the virgin snow* | (fig.) *America is virgin territory as far as our company is concerned.*

Virgin the name of several British companies started by Richard Branson, including the AIRLINE Virgin Atlantic and Virgin Records, a music recording company

vir·gin·als /ˈvɜːdʒnəlz‖ˈvɜːr-/ [P] a small square musical instrument like a piano, popular in the 16th and 17th centuries

virgin birth /ˌ·· ˈ·/ [the] (often caps.) the birth of Christ, which Christians believe to have been caused by God rather than by ordinary sexual union. Christians believe that Mary (the mother of Christ) was still a virgin when she gave birth to Christ.

Vir·gin·i·a /vəˈdʒɪniə‖vər-/ 1 *written abbrev.* **VA**— a state on the eastern coast of the US, considered to be a southern state. It was one of the 13 original British colonies (COLONY) —see colour map on pages 1374–5 2 n [U] a tobacco grown originally in the state of Virginia: *a Virginia cigarette*

virginia creep·er /ˌ··· ˈ···/ *esp. BrE* ‖ also **woodbine** *AmE*— n [U] a climbing garden plant often grown on walls, with large leaves that turn deep red in autumn

vir·gin·i·ty /vɜːˈdʒɪnɪti‖vɜːr-/ n [U] the state of being a virgin: *In many Western countries virginity is not as highly valued as it used to be.* | *She was 19 when she lost her virginity.* (=had sex with a man for the first time) —compare CHASTITY

Virgin Is·lands /ˈ·· ˌ··/ a group of about 100 small islands in the West Indies, owned by the US and Britain

Virgin Ma·ry /ˌ·· ˈ··/ *n* the mother of Jesus Christ, honoured esp. by the Catholic Church: *statues of the Virgin Mary*

Virgin Queen /ˌ·· ˈ·/ [*the*] Elizabeth I; because she never married and was thought to have never had sexual relations with a man

Virgin Mary

Vir·go /ˈvɜːgəʊ‖ˈvɜːr-/ *n* **-gos** **1** [U] the sixth sign of the ZODIAC, represented by a young girl **2** [C] a person born between August 23 and September 22 —see ZODIAC (USAGE) and see picture at ZODIAC

vir·ile /ˈvɪraɪl‖ˈvɪrəl/ *adj usu. apprec* **1** (of a man) having the full amount of strength and forceful qualities expected of a man, esp. in matters of sex: *She admired the virile young swimmer.* **2** *sometimes euph* forceful; manly; full of active strength: *His style of singing is very virile, but he doesn't have much feeling for the expressiveness of the words.*

vi·ril·i·ty /vɪˈrɪlɪti/ *n* [U] *usu. apprec* male sexual power; manly qualities

vi·rol·o·gy /vaɪəˈrɒlədʒi‖-ˈrɑː-/ *n* [U] the scientific study of (diseases caused by) viruses (VIRUS)

vir·tu·al /ˈvɜːtʃuəl‖ˈvɜːr-/ *adj* [A *no comp.*] almost what is stated; in fact though not officially: *The president was so much under the influence of his wife that she was the virtual ruler of the country.* | *a virtual certainty*

vir·tu·al·ly /ˈvɜːtʃuəli‖ˈvɜːr-/ *adv* almost; very nearly: *My book's virtually finished; I've only a few last-minute changes to make to it.* | *Virtually all the members were in agreement with the proposal*

virtual re·al·i·ty /ˌ··· ·ˈ···/ *n* an environment in which computers CREATE the effect of a world which seems almost completely real to the people in it

vir·tue /ˈvɜːtʃuː‖ˈvɜːr-/ *n* **1** [U] *fml* goodness, nobleness, and worth of character as shown in right behaviour: *a man of the highest virtue* —opposite **vice** **2** [C] a good quality of character or behaviour: *Among her many virtues are loyalty, courage, and truthfulness.* —opposite **vice** **3** [C;U] (an) advantage: *He said his plan had the virtue of being the easiest to implement.* | *a speech extolling the virtues of adult education* **4 by virtue of** also **in virtue of** *fml* as a result of; by means of: *Though she isn't British by birth, she's a British citizen by virtue of her marriage to an Englishman.* **5 make a virtue of necessity** to accept responsibility for or do cheerfully and with interest something that one cannot avoid —see also EASY VIRTUE, VIRTUOUS

vir·tu·os·i·ty /ˌvɜːtʃuˈɒsɪti‖ˌvɜːrtʃuˈɑː-/ *n* [U] *fml* a very high degree of skill in performing: *the violinist's incredible virtuosity*

vir·tu·o·so /ˌvɜːtʃuˈəʊzəʊ‖ˌvɜːrtʃuˈəʊsəʊ/ *n* **-sos** *or* **-si** /ziː‖si/ a person who has a very high degree of skill as a performer in one of the ARTS, esp. music: *a piano virtuoso* | *a virtuoso performance*

vir·tu·ous /ˈvɜːtʃuəs‖ˈvɜːr-/ *adj* **1** *fml* having or showing virtue **2** *derog* (too) satisfied with one's own good behaviour, and expressing this in one's manner towards those who have done wrong — **~ly** *adv*

vir·u·lent /ˈvɪrjʊlənt/ *adj* **1** (of a poison, a disease caused by bacteria, etc.) very powerful, quick-acting, and dangerous to life or health **2** *fml* (of a feeling or its expression) very bitter; full of hatred: *virulent abuse* — **~ly** *adv* **—lence, -lency** *n* [U]

vi·rus /ˈvaɪərəs/ *n* a living thing even smaller than bacteria which causes infectious disease in the body, in plants, etc.: *the common cold virus* | *the spread of virus infections* —compare MICROBE; see also COMPUTER VIRUS, VIRAL

vi·sa¹ /ˈviːzə/ *n* an official mark put onto a PASSPORT by a representative of a country, giving a foreigner permis-

sion to enter, pass through, or leave that country: *He has applied for an entry visa.* | *She was eventually granted an exit visa.* | *Their visas have run out/expired.*

visa² *v* **visaed** /-zəd/; *present participle* **visaing** [T] to provide a visa for (a PASSPORT): *You'll need to get your passport visaed if you want to go to America.*

Visa card /ˈ·· ·/ also **Visa—** *n tdmk* a plastic card used to obtain money, goods, and services which the user pays for later: *Do you take Visa?*

vis·age /ˈvɪzɪdʒ/ *n lit* **1** the face: *a smiling visage* **2 -visaged** /vɪzɪdʒd/ having the stated type of face: (fig.) *fair-visaged peace*

vis-à-vis /ˌviːz ɑː ˈviː, ˌviːz ə ˈviː/ *prep fml or pomp* with regard to; when compared to: *Where do we stand vis-à-vis last week's change in the law?*

vis·ce·ra /ˈvɪsərə/ *n* [(*the*) P] *med* the large inside organs of the body, such as the heart, lungs, stomach, etc. —**ral** *adj*

vis·count /ˈvaɪkaʊnt/ *n* (*often cap.*) a British nobleman below an EARL and above a BARON

vis·count·cy /ˈvaɪkaʊntsi/ *n* the rank or title of viscount

vis·count·ess /ˈvaɪkaʊntЅs/ *n* (*often cap.*) the wife of a viscount, or a woman with the rank of viscount in her own right

vis·cous /ˈvɪskəs/ also **vis·cid** /ˈvɪsЅd/ *tech*— *adj* (of a liquid) thick and sticky; that does not flow easily —**cosity** /vɪˈskɒsЅti‖-ˈskɑː-/ *n* [U]

vise /vaɪs/ *n AmE for* VICE²

Vish·nu /ˈvɪʃnuː/ a god in the Hindu religion

vis·i·bil·i·ty /ˌvɪzЅˈbɪlЅti/ *n* [U] **1** (esp. in official weather reports) the degree of clearness with which objects can be seen according to the condition of the air and the weather: *The fog is heavy, and visibility is down to 20 metres.* | *The search for survivors had to be abandoned due to poor visibility.* **2** ability to give a clear view: *Our car's large rear window gives excellent visibility.*

vis·i·ble /ˈvɪzЅbəl/ *adj* [(**to**)] **1** that can be seen; noticeable to the eye: *Signs of economic and social decay are clearly visible in the streets of the capital.* | *a dark, cloudy night with no stars visible (to the naked eye)* **2** that can be felt, experienced, heard, etc.; noticeable to the mind or senses: *What is this object? It seems to serve no visible purpose.* | *visible annoyance* **3** always appearing in public, on television, in the papers, etc.: *highly visible politicians*

vis·i·bly /ˈvɪzЅbli/ *adv* noticeably: *He was visibly shaken by her accusation.*

vi·sion /ˈvɪʒən/ *n* **1** [U] (the) ability to see: *I've had my eyes tested and the optician says that my vision is perfect.* —see also FIELD OF VISION, TWENTY-TWENTY VISION **2** [U] wise understanding of how the future will be; FORESIGHT: *We need a man of vision as leader of the party.* **3** [C+of] a picture seen in the mind; idea: *He conjured up a vision of the future.* | *There was so much traffic on the road that I had visions of missing* (=thought I would miss) *my plane.* **4** [C] something that is without bodily reality, seen (as if) in a dream, when in a sleeplike state, or as a religious experience: *She saw/had a vision in which God seemed to appear before her.* **5** [C *usu. sing.*] *esp. lit* a beautiful sight

vi·sion·a·ry¹ /ˈvɪʒənəri‖-neri/ *adj* **1** *apprec* having or showing VISION (2) **2** that exists only in the mind and probably cannot be fulfilled

visionary² *n* **1** a person whose aims for the future are noble or excellent but may lack reality or not be easy to put into practice **2** a (holy) person who has VISIONS (4)

vis·it¹ /ˈvɪzЅt/ *v* **1** [I;T] to go and spend time in (a place) or with (someone): *"Do you live in this town?" "No, we're only visiting."* | *While we're in Europe we ought to visit Holland.* | *When we were in London we visited the Tower twice.* | *Aunt Jane usually visits us for two or three weeks in the spring.* | (*AmE*) *Aunt Jane is visiting with us* (=staying with us) *this weekend.* —see also VISIT **with** **2** [T] to go to (a place) in order to make an official examination: *Schools have to be visited from time to time by education officers.* **3** [I+*adv*/*prep*] *AmE* to stay: *Anyone who's visiting in Edinburgh ought to go and see the castle.* **4** [I] *AmE* to talk socially with: *Mom and Aunt Jean would visit for hours.*

visit sthg. on sbdy./sthg. *phr v* [T] *esp. bibl* to direct (one's anger, a punishment, etc.) against: *God has visited his anger on us.*

visit with sbdy. *phr v* [T *no pass.*] *AmE* to talk socially with —see also VISIT¹ (1)

visit² *n* **1** [(**to, from**)] an act or time of visiting: *Their visits are usually quite short.* | *We came here on|for a visit, but we decided to stay.* | *We've just had a visit from the police.* | *I must* **pay a visit to** (=visit) *the doctor.* | *The Queen will make a* **state visit** (=not for personal reasons) *to the Far East next year.* | *an official visit* **2** *AmE* an act or time of talking socially with someone: *I dropped in on Barbara and we had a nice long visit.*

vis·i·ta·tion /ˌvɪzɪˈteɪʃən/ *n* **1** [(**by, of**)] *fml* a formal visit by someone in charge, esp. by a high official person to discover whether things are in good order, or by a priest **2** [(**of**)] *fml* an event believed to be an act of punishment, or sometimes of favour, from heaven: *The villagers thought that the storm was a visitation of God.* **3** [(**from**)] *infml, often humor* an unusually long social visit that is troublesome to the person visited

visiting card /'··· ·/ also **card—** *n* a small card with one's name and often address printed on it which one gives to people one visits. Visiting cards used to be commonly used in polite society when people visited each other at home, but this practice has largely stopped. —compare BUSINESS CARD

visiting hours /'··· ·/ *n* [P] the hours at which one is allowed to visit people in hospital: *What are the visiting hours at this hospital?*

vis·it·or /ˈvɪzɪtər/ *n* [(**to, from**)] **1** a person who visits or is visiting: *We only use our best china cups when we have visitors.* | *Visitors to the hospital are asked not to smoke.* | *The castle gets lots of visitors from America.* | *She received her distinguished visitors very graciously.* —see also PRISON VISITOR **2** *tech* a bird which spends only part of the year in a country

▷ USAGE Compare **visitor** and **guest**. If you are a **visitor**, you go and spend time with a person or in a place: *a visitor to London* | *I had an unwelcome visitor this morning – the Tax Inspector.* If you are a **guest**, you have been invited by a person, **a** to stay in the person's house, or **b** to have a meal, given or paid for by the person, or **c** to go to a concert, theatre, etc., paid for by the person. *We had several guests staying with us last weekend.* | *They asked me to spend the summer in Scotland as their guest.* | *Would you like to be my guest at the theatre tonight?* **Guest** is also used for people staying in a hotel: *Guests are requested to leave their room keys at the desk.*◁

visitors' book /'··· ·/ *n* a book in which visitors, esp. to a place of interest such as the house in which a famous person once lived, or staying in a hotel, write their names and addresses: *to sign the visitors' book*

vi·sor /ˈvaɪzər/ *n* **1** (in a suit of armour) a movable part of a HELMET which can be lowered to protect the face **2** an eye protector like the front part (PEAK) of a cap which keeps away the sunshine —see also SUN VISOR **3** *AmE for* PEAK¹ (4) **4** a flat, small, hard object which folds down from the roof inside a car over part of the front window to protect the driver's eyes from the sun

vis·ta /ˈvɪstə/ *n* [(**of**)] a distant view to which the eye is directed between narrow limits, e.g. by rows of trees: *a pleasant vista* | (fig.) *An endless vista of tedious days and nights stretched before us.*

vi·su·al /ˈvɪʒuəl/ *adj* of or gained by seeing: *a quick visual examination* | *a strong visual impact* | *The* **visual arts** *are painting, dancing, etc., as opposed to music and literature.* —see also VISUALLY

visual aid /ˌ··· '·/ *n* something that people can look at to help them understand, learn, remember, etc., such as a picture, map, photograph, or film. Visual aids are often used as materials in education.

visual arts /ˌ··· '·/ *n* art such as painting, SCULPTURE, etc. which makes its subject known by looking at it rather than reading or hearing it (as a book or music)

visual dis·play u·nit /ˌ··· ·'·· ˌ··/ *n* see VDU

vi·su·al·ize also **-ise** *BrE* /ˈvɪʒuəlaɪz/ *v* [T (**as**)] to form a picture of (something or someone) in the mind; imagine: *Though he described the place carefully, I couldn't visualize it because it was so different from what I'd known.* [+(*obj*)+v-*ing*] *Try to visualize (yourself) sailing through the sky on a cloud.* —**ization** /ˌvɪʒuəlaɪˈzeɪʃən‖-lə-/ *n* [U]

vi·su·al·ly /ˈvɪʒuəli/ *adv* **1** in appearance: *Visually the*

chair is very pleasing, but it's rather uncomfortable! **2** using VISUAL AIDS: *He explained the journey visually by the use of pictures and maps.*

vi·tal /ˈvaɪtl/ *adj* **1** [(**to, for**)] very necessary; of the greatest importance: *Your support is vital to|for the success of my plan.* | *It's vital that we (should) act at once.* | *issues of vital national importance* | *the vital ingredient* **2** [A] *tech* necessary in order to stay alive: *He was lucky that the bullet hadn't entered a* **vital organ.** (=any organ without which life cannot continue, such as the heart, brain, etc.) **3** *fml apprec* full of life and force: *Their leader's vital and cheerful manner filled his men with courage.* —see also VITALLY, VITALS

vi·tal·i·ty /vaɪˈtæləti/ *n* [U] *apprec* **1** spirit; cheerfulness; force: *I thought I detected a certain lack of vitality in her movements.* **2** ability to stay alive or working in an effective way: *This religious movement has shown surprising vitality, in spite of all that has been done to suppress it.* | *to sap the nation's vitality and spirit*

vi·tal·ly /ˈvaɪtl-i/ *adv* extremely: *Would it matter vitally if he failed?* | *vitally important*

vi·tals /ˈvaɪtlz/ *n* [(*the*) P] *esp. old use or humor* the main bodily organs (the lungs, heart, brain, and esp. the stomach and bowels) without which a person cannot continue to live

vital signs /ˌ·· '·/ *n* [P] *med* things that can be measured to see how well someone is, such as temperature, rate of heartbeat and breathing, etc.

vital sta·tis·tics /ˌ··· ·'··/ *n* [P] **1** *BrE infml, rather humor* the measurements, in INCHes of a woman's body round the chest, waist, and HIPs: *Jean's vital statistics are 38-24-38.* **2** certain facts, officially collected and arranged, about people's lives, esp. their births, marriages, deaths, and length of life

vit·a·min /ˈvɪtəmɪn, ˈvaɪ-‖ˈvaɪ-/ *n* **1** [C *usu. pl.*] any of several chemical substances which are found in very small quantities in certain foods, and are important for growth and good health: *This type of bread has added vitamins.* | *vitamin pills* **2** [U] any particular type of this, named by a letter of the alphabet (A, B, C, D, E, G, H, K, or P): *Oranges contain vitamin C.* | *vitamin B6*

vi·ti·ate /ˈvɪʃieɪt/ *v* [T *often pass.*] *fml* to weaken; spoil; harm the quality of: *The moral strength of his argument was vitiated by its impracticality.* —**ation** /ˌvɪʃiˈeɪʃən/ *n* [U (**of**)]

vit·i·cul·ture /ˈvɪtɪkʌltʃər/ *n* [U] *tech* (the study and science of) the growing of GRAPEs, esp. for making wine

Vi·ti Lev·u /ˌviːti ˈlevuː/ the largest and most important island of Fiji

vit·re·ous /ˈvɪtriəs/ *adj tech* of, made of, or like glass: *Vitreous rocks are especially hard and shiny.* | *vitreous enamel*

vit·ri·fy /ˈvɪtrɪfaɪ/ *v* [I;T] *tech* to (cause to) change into glass or a glasslike substance, by means of heat

vit·ri·ol /ˈvɪtriəl/ *n* [U] pure SULPHURIC ACID, which burns flesh deeply: (fig., *lit*) *the vitriol in his pen* (=cruel wounding quality in his writing)

vit·ri·ol·ic /ˌvɪtriˈɒlɪk◄‖-ˈɑːl-/ *adj fml* fiercely cruel in speech or judgment; causing sharp pain to the mind: *vitriolic criticism* —**~ally** /kli/ *adv*

vi·tro /ˈviːtrəʊ/ see IN VITRO

vi·tu·pe·ra·tion /vɪˌtjuːpəˈreɪʃən‖vaɪˌtuː-/ *n* [U] *fml* (the use of) angry speech and cursing

vi·tu·pe·ra·tive /vɪˈtjuːpərətɪv‖vaɪˈtuː-/ *adj fml* full of angry disapproval: *vituperative comments* —**~ly** *adv*

vi·va·ce /vɪˈvɑːtʃi, -tʃeɪ/ *adv, adj* (in music) played quickly and with spirit

vi·va·cious /vɪˈveɪʃəs/ *adj apprec* full of life and high spirits; LIVELY: *a vivacious girl* —**~ly** *adv* —**~ness**, **-city** /vɪˈvæsəti/— *n* [U]

Vi·val·di /vɪˈvældi‖-ˈɑːl-/, **An·to·ni·o** /ænˈtəʊniəʊ/ (about 1675–1741) an Italian COMPOSER who wrote CONCERTOS, OPERAS and SONATAS. He is best known for *The Four Seasons.*

vi·var·i·um /vaɪˈveəriəm/ *n tech* an enclosed place where animals are kept indoors in conditions as similar as possible to their natural surroundings

vi·va voc·e /ˌvaɪvə ˈvəʊsi, -ˈvəʊtʃi ‖ ˌvaɪvə ˈvəʊsi, ˌviːvə ˈvəʊtʃeɪ/ also **viva** *BrE infml— n* a spoken examination at a university

viv·id /ˈvɪvɪd/ adj **1** (of light or colour) bright and strong; producing a sharp sensation on the eye: *a vivid flash of lightning* | *vivid red hair* **2** that produces sharp clear pictures in the mind; lifelike: *a vivid description/dream* | *"I think he's married to two women." "Nonsense! You've got a vivid imagination!"* — ~ly adv — ~ness n [U]

viv·i·sec·tion /ˌvɪvɪˈsekʃən/ n [U] the performing of operations on animals not to cure sickness but as scientific EXPERIMENTS (=tests), esp. in order to increase medical knowledge of human diseases. Some people oppose vivisection because they think it is cruel to the animals. —see also ANIMAL RIGHTS GROUP

viv·i·sec·tion·ist /ˌvɪvɪˈsekʃənɪst/ n a person who practises or supports vivisection

vix·en /ˈvɪksən/ n **1** a female fox **2** *lit* a nasty bad-tempered woman

vix·en·ish /ˈvɪksənɪʃ/ adj *lit* (of a woman) fierce and bad-tempered

Viy·el·la /vaɪˈelə/ n [U] *tdmk* a soft material made of cotton and wool, that is made into shirts and other clothes

viz. /vɪz/ also **videlicet** *fml*— adv and it is/they are; that is to say: *On most English farms you'll find only three kinds of animal, viz. sheep, cattle, and pigs.*

▷ USAGE **1** Viz. is rather old-fashioned, and is less common than **namely** or **i.e. 2** Viz. may be read aloud as "namely". —see also NAMELY (USAGE)◁

Viz a British magazine for adults with COMIC STRIP stories full of rude jokes about sex and bodily processes

vi·zi·er /vɪˈzɪəʳ/ n (in former times) a minister in some Muslim countries

V-J Day /ˌviː ˈdʒeɪ ˌdeɪ/ Victory over Japan Day; August 15th 1945, the day on which victory over Japan in the Second World War was remembered

Vlad·i·vos·tok /ˌvlædɪ ˈvɒstɒk‖- ˈvɑːstɑːk/ a port and city on the eastern coast of Russia

V-neck /ˈviː nek/ n a neck opening of a dress, shirt, etc., with the front cut in the shape of a V **–V-necked** adj: *a V-necked sweater*

VoA /ˌviːəʊ ˈeɪ/ n [the] abbrev. for: VOICE OF AMERICA

vo·cab /ˈvəʊkæb/ n infml for VOCABULARY (2)

vo·cab·u·la·ry /vəˈkæbjʊləri, vəʊ-‖-leri/ n **1** [C;U] words known, learnt, used, etc.: *Our little boy's just starting to talk; he's got a vocabulary of* (=knows) *about ten words.* | *the average vocabulary of an intermediate student* | *to build up/extend one's vocabulary* | *to have a limited/extensive vocabulary* | *her musical vocabulary* | *The word "failure" is not in my vocabulary.* (=I will keep trying to do something, however difficult it is) —compare LEXIS **2** [C] a list of words, usu. in alphabetical order and with explanations of their meanings, less complete than a dictionary —see also GLOSSARY **3** [C,U] a list of the CODES or TERMS provided for use in a computer system

vo·cal¹ /ˈvəʊkəl/ adj **1** [A no comp.] of the voice; used in speaking: *The tongue is one of the vocal organs.* **2** [no comp.] produced by or for the voice; spoken, sung, or expressed aloud: *I like instrumental better than vocal music.* **3** infml expressing oneself freely and noisily in words; talking a great deal, usu. loudly: *He gave her very vocal support.* | *an increasingly vocal minority* — ~ly adv

vocal² n [often pl.] the sung part of a popular song, as opposed to the parts played on instruments: *a song by Wings, with Paul McCartney on vocals*

vocal cords /ˈ··· , ·ˌ· ˈ·/ n [P] thin bands of muscle inside the throat that produce sounds when air passes through them —see picture at RESPIRATORY

vo·cal·ist /ˈvəʊkəlɪst/ n a singer of popular songs, esp. one who sings with a band —compare INSTRUMENTALIST

vo·ca·tion /vəʊˈkeɪʃən/ n **1** [S (for)] particular fitness or ability for a certain kind of work, esp. of a worthy kind: *She's a good nurse because she has a real vocation for looking after the sick.* **2** [C] a job, esp. which one does because one has a special fitness or ability to give service to other people: *Teaching children ought to be a vocation as well as a way of earning money.* **3** [S] the belief that one has been chosen by God to lead a religious life: *He gave up being a priest when he lost his vocation.* —see JOB (USAGE)

vo·ca·tion·al /vəʊˈkeɪʃənəl/ adj of or preparing one for a

job: *vocational training* | *a vocational guidance counsellor* | *a vocational school*

vocational ed·u·ca·tion /·ˌ··· ··ˈ··/ n [U] education or training for specific jobs rather than for life in general or simply enjoyment

voc·a·tive /ˈvɒkətɪv‖ˈvɑː-/ n tech a particular form of a noun in certain languages, such as Latin, used when speaking or writing to someone or something **–vocative** adj

vo·cif·er·ate /vəˈsɪfəreɪt, vəʊ-‖vəʊ-/ v [I] fml to shout loudly and forcefully, esp. when complaining **––ation** /vəˌsɪfəˈreɪʃən, vəʊ-‖vəʊ-/ n [C;U] fml

vo·cif·er·ous /vəˈsɪfərəs, vəʊ-‖vəʊ-/ adj fml **1** noisy in expressing one's feelings: *a vociferous group of pickets* **2** expressed noisily in speech or by shouting: *vociferous demands* — ~ly adv — ~ness n [U]

vod·ka /ˈvɒdkə‖ˈvɑːdkə/ n [U] a strong, colourless, and almost tasteless alcoholic drink, made originally in Russia and the TRADITIONAL drink of this country

vogue¹ /vəʊg/ n [C (for);(the) U] the popular fashion or custom at a certain usu. not lasting time: *There seems to be a vogue for Chinese food at present.* | *Short skirts were in vogue/were all the vogue in the 1960s.*

vogue² adj [A] newly popular and much used, but likely soon to go out of favour: *vogue words*

Vogue a fashion magazine with articles and photographs dealing with clothes, beauty, and subjects of interest to women

voice¹ /vɔɪs/ n **1** [C;U] (the ability to make) the sound(s) produced in speaking and singing: *a high/low/deep voice* | *a hoarse/husky/rough voice* | *a gruff/kind/soft voice* | *I've got a bad cold and I've lost my voice.* | *We could hear the children's voices in the garden.* | *She's got a lovely voice.* | *My son's voice is breaking.* (=becoming lower like a man's) | *There was a growl in his voice.* | *He replied in an angry* **tone of voice.** | *a voice quivering with anger* | *She's in* **good voice** (=singing well) *today.* | *She* **lowered her voice**/*Her voice dropped as she told me the secret.* | *I had to* **raise my voice** (=speak louder) *to make myself heard.* | *Don't raise your voice* (=speak angrily) *to me!* | (fig.) *Not a voice was raised against the plan.* (=no one disagreed with it) | (fig.) *"I don't think you should get married." "Ah,* **the voice of experience!"** (=you are saying that because of your own (bad) experience) **2** [S;U (in)] the ability to express an opinion, to vote, or to influence other opinions, decisions, etc.: *I can't help you to get this job, as I have very little voice in the decision of the directors.* | *He added/lent his voice to the call for disarmament.* **3** [C usu. sing.] a a means of expression: *He became the recognized voice of the West Indian community in Britain.* | *The feminists have found their political voice at last.* | *the voice of reason/sanity* **b** an expressed wish or opinion: *The government should listen to the voice of the people/the majority.* **4** [C usu. sing.] tech the form of the verb which shows whether the subject of a sentence acts (**active voice**) or is acted on (**passive voice**) **5** give **voice to** fml to express (feelings, thoughts, etc.) aloud **6** with **one voice** lit all together; with everyone expressing the same opinion **7 -voiced** /vɔɪst/ having a voice of the stated quality: *loud-voiced* —see also **at the top of one's voice** (TOP¹); see NOISE (USAGE)

voice² v [T] **1** to express in words, esp. forcefully: *The chairman encouraged us all to voice our opinions.* **2** tech to produce (a sound, esp. a consonant) with a movement of the VOCAL CORDS as well as with the breath: /d/ *and* /g/ *are voiced consonants, but* /t/ *and* /k/ *are not.*

voice box /ˈ· ·/ n LARYNX

voice·less /ˈvɔɪsləs/ adj tech (of a speech sound, esp. a consonant) not voiced (VOICE²(2)): /f, k, t/ *are voiceless consonants.*

Voice of A·mer·i·ca /ˌ· · · ·ˈ···/ [the] an American radio station which broadcasts news and other programmes to other countries

voice-o·ver /ˈ· ··/ n the voice of an unseen person on a film or television show, who makes remarks or gives information about what is being shown

void¹ /vɔɪd/ adj **1** [F+of] fml empty (of); without; lacking; DEVOID: *That part of the town is completely void of interest for visitors.* **2** tech (esp. of an official agreement) having no legal force: *A contract signed by a child is void.* — see also NULL AND VOID

void² *n* **1** [*the*+S] *esp. lit* the space around the world which stretches out beyond the stars **2** [C *usu. sing.*] a deep empty space: *The ground began to shake and a sudden void opened under his feet.* **3** [C *usu. sing.*] a feeling of emptiness or loss: *Their son's death left a painful void in their lives.*

void³ *v* [T] **1** *fml or tech* to get rid of (the unwanted contents of something) by emptying or pouring out through a hole, tube, etc. **2** *law* to cause to be without effect; make void

voi·là , **voila** /vwɑːˈlɑː/ *interj Fr* (said when something or someone appears, perhaps in an unexpected or surprising way): *I just put everything inside, close the lid, push the button and...voilà! Vegetable purée!*

voile /vɔɪl/ *n* [U] a very fine, thin, almost transparent material of cotton, silk, or wool; it is used esp. to make women's summer clothing and curtains

vol /vɒl/ (*often cap.*) *abbrev for:* VOLUME (2)

vol·a·tile /ˈvɒlətaɪl‖ˈvɑːlətl/ *adj* **1** of a quickly changing, undependable nature, esp. easily becoming angry or dangerous: *a volatile character | The situation in the streets is highly volatile, and the army is being called in.* **2** (of a liquid or oil) easily changing into a gas: *Petrol is volatile.* —**·tility** /ˌvɒləˈtɪlɪti‖ˌvɑː-/ *n* [U]

vol-au-vent /ˌvɒl əʊ ˈvɒn‖ˌvɔːl əʊ ˈvɑːn/ *n* a very light small pastry case filled with meat, chicken, etc.

vol·can·ic /vɒlˈkænɪk‖vɑːl-/ *adj* **1** of, from, produced by, or caused by a volcano: *volcanic rocks | volcanic activity* **2** violently forceful: *a volcanic temper*

vol·ca·no /vɒlˈkeɪnəʊ‖vɑːl-/ *n* **-noes** or **-nos** a mountain with a CRATER (=large opening) at the top, and often others on the sides, through which LAVA (=melting rock), steam, gases, etc., sometimes escape with explosive force: *An active volcano may erupt at any time.* | *A dormant volcano is quiet at present.* | *An extinct volcano can no longer erupt.*

vole /vəʊl/ *n* (*often in comb.*) a small thick-bodied short-tailed animal of the rat and mouse family, which lives in fields, woods, banks of rivers, etc.

Vol·ga /ˈvɒlgə‖ˈvɑːl-/ a river in Russia which flows into the Caspian Sea. The Volga is the longest river in Europe.

vo·li·tion /vəˈlɪʃən‖vəʊ-, və-/ *n* [U] *fml* the act of using one's will; one's power to control, decide, or choose: *I didn't tell her to go; she went of her own volition.*

Volks·wag·en /ˈvɒlkswægən‖ˈvəʊks-/ *n tdmk* a German company that makes cars that are thought to be very RELIABLE —see also BEETLE

vol·ley¹ /ˈvɒli‖ˈvɑːli/ *n* **1** [of] a number of shots fired at the same time: *The soldiers fired a volley into the air as a warning to the rioters.* | (fig.) *a volley of curses* | (fig.) *a volley of blows* —compare SALVO **2** a kicking or hitting of a ball before it has hit the ground: *The tennis star played a fine forehand/backhand volley.* | *The footballer kicked the ball on the volley.* —see also HALF VOLLEY

volley² *v* **1** [I] (of guns) to be fired all together **2** [T+*obj*+*adv*/*prep*] to hit or kick (a ball) before it has hit the ground: *The footballer volleyed the ball into the back of the net.* **3** [I;T] (in tennis) to make a volley against (one's opponent)

vol·ley·ball /ˈvɒlibɔːl‖ˈvɑː-/ *n* [U] a team game in which a large ball is struck by hand backwards and forwards across a high net without being allowed to touch the ground —see REFEREE (USAGE)

volt /vəʊlt/ *n tech* the standard measure of the amount of electrical force needed to produce one AMP of electrical current where the RESISTANCE is one OHM

volt·age /ˈvəʊltɪdʒ/ *n* [C;U] electrical force measured in volts: *a high voltage fence* —compare RESISTANCE (3)

volte-face /ˌvɒlt ˈfɑːs‖ˌvɔːlt-/ *n* [*usu. sing.*] *esp. lit or fml* a change to a completely opposite opinion or course of action: *an extraordinary/surprising volte-face on the part of the government*

Vol·taire /vɒlˈteəʳ‖vəʊl-/, **Fran·çois Mar·ie Ar·ou·et de** /ˈfrɒnswɑː ˈmɑːri ˈæruːeɪ də‖ frɑːnˈswɑː məˈriː ɑːruːˈeɪ-/ (1699–1778) a French writer and PHILOSOPHER whose ideas had a great influence. His best-known works are *Candide* and the *Philosophical Dictionary.*

vol·u·ble /ˈvɒljŷbəl‖ˈvɑː-/ *adj fml, often derog* **1** (of a person) talking a lot **2** (of speech) expressed (esp. rather

fast) with many words: *voluble excuses* —compare VERBOSE —**·bly** *adv* —**·bility** /ˌvɒljŷˈbɪlɪti‖ˌvɑː-/ *n* [U]

vol·ume /ˈvɒljuːm‖ˈvɑːljəm/ *n* **1** [U] (degree of) loudness of sound: *The television's too loud; turn the volume down.* | *the volume control* **2** [U] the size of a solid thing or of a space, measured by multiplying the length by the width by the depth: *The volume of this container is 100,000 cubic metres.* —compare AREA (1) **3** [C;U] amount produced by some kind of activity: *The volume of passenger travel on the railways is decreasing.* | *Letters had poured in in large volumes.* **4** [C] any of a set of books of the same kind or together forming a whole: *We have a set of Dickens's works in 24 volumes.* | *You'll find the article in volume 9 of the encyclopedia.* **5** [C] *fml* a book, esp. a large one: *His library was full of rare old volumes.* —see also **speak volumes** (SPEAK)

vo·lu·mi·nous /vəˈluːmɪnəs, vəˈljuː-‖vəˈluː-/ *adj fml* **1** (of a garment) very loose and full; using much cloth: *a voluminous skirt* (of a container) very large; able to hold a lot: *a voluminous suitcase* **3** *often derog* producing or containing much writing: *a voluminous writer* | *a voluminous report* — ~**ly** *adv* — ~**ness** *n* [U]

vol·un·ta·ry¹ /ˈvɒləntəri‖ˈvɑːlənteri/ *adj* **1** (of a person or action) acting or done willingly, without being forced: *He made a voluntary statement to the police.* | *She took voluntary redundancy.* —compare COMPULSORY **2** [A] acting or done without payment; controlled or supported by people who give their money, services, etc., of their own free will: *Many social services are still provided by voluntary societies.* | *At election time the party needs a lot of voluntary helpers.* **3** *tech* under the control of the will: *the voluntary muscles* —opposite involuntary —**·tarily** /ˈvɒləntərŷli‖ˌvɑːlənˈteərŷli/ *adv* : *He made the promise quite voluntarily; I didn't force him to.*

voluntary² *n* a piece of music played in church before or after the service, usu. on an ORGAN

voluntary school /ˈ··· ˌ·/ *n* (in Britain) a school built by an independent, usu. religious, organization but which a local education authority is partly or completely financially responsible for. The two kinds of voluntary school are aided schools and controlled schools —see AIDED SCHOOL, CONTROLLED SCHOOL

Voluntary Ser·vice O·ver·seas /ˌ···· ˌ·· ··ˈ·/ see VSO

voluntary work /ˈ···· ˌ·/ *n* work which is done free by someone who wants to do it, usu. for an organization that helps people: *When he retired, he did a lot of voluntary work.*

vol·un·teer¹ /ˌvɒlənˈtɪəʳ‖ˌvɑː-/ *v* **1** [I (for);T] to offer (one's services or help) without payment or reward; make a willing offer, esp. when others are unwilling: *He volunteered for guard duty.* [+*to-v*] *Jenny volunteered to clear up afterwards.* **2** [I (for)] to offer to join the army, navy, or airforce of one's own free will, without being forced to —compare CONSCRIPT¹ **3** [T] to tell (something) without being asked: *He volunteered a statement to the police.* | *"It's not my car, it's my father's," she volunteered.*

volunteer² *n* [(for)] a person who has volunteered or is willing to volunteer: *This work costs us nothing; it's all done by volunteers.* | *Can I have a volunteer to collect the glasses?* —compare CONSCRIPT²

vo·lup·tu·a·ry /vəˈlʌptʃuəri‖-tʃueri/ *n lit, usu. derog* a person who gets great enjoyment from physical comfort, esp. sexual activity, and from having expensive things

vo·lup·tu·ous /vəˈlʌptʃuəs/ *adj* **1** *apprec* (esp. connected with women) of a kind that suggests or expresses sexual pleasure or enjoyment: *The dancer's movements were slow and voluptuous.* | *She had a full voluptuous mouth.* | *her voluptuous curves* **2** (of a woman) having a beautiful soft rounded body that excites sexual feeling **3** *a* giving a fine delight to the senses: *the voluptuous feeling of pure soft silk* **b** giving a satisfying feeling of rest and enjoyment: *voluptuous comfort* **4** *fml derog* too much concerned with the enjoyment of physical (esp. sexual) pleasures: *the voluptuous life of the Romans in ancient times* — ~**ly** *adv* — ~**ness** *n* [U]

Vol·vo /ˈvɒlvəʊ‖ˈvɑːl-/ *n tdmk* a Swedish company that makes cars that are considered safe and dependable

vom·it¹ /ˈvɒmŷt‖ˈvɑː-/ *v* [I;T] to throw up (the contents of the stomach) through the mouth; be sick: *The unpleasant smell made her feel so sick that she began to vomit.* | *He was vomiting blood.* | (fig.) *The volcano vomited out great* *black clouds of smoke.* (=sent them out with great force and in great quantity) —see SICK (USAGE)

vomit² *n* [U] food or other matter that has been vomited

Von·ne·gut /ˈvɒnᵻgʌt‖ˈvɑːn-/, **Kurt** /kɜːt‖kɜːrt/ (1922–) an American writer known for his BLACK HUMOUR and SCIENCE FICTION in books such as *Cat's Cradle* and *Slaughterhouse Five*

voo·doo /ˈvuːduː/ *n* [U] **1** (*often cap.*) a set of magical beliefs and practices used as a form of religion, particularly by the people of Haiti **2** magic; the practice of achieving something by means that are not usual or realistic: *"How do you think you're going to pass that test without studying? Voodoo?"* — ~**ism** *n* [U]

voodoo e·co·nom·ics /ˌ··· ·ˌ·/ *n* [U] *AmE* economic ideas which look attractive but will not work properly over time

vo·ra·cious /vəˈreɪʃəs, vɒ-‖vɔː-, və-/ *adj* **1** eating or wanting large quantities of food: *Pigs are voracious feeders.* | *a voracious appetite* **2** having or showing a limitless eagerness, like a hunger, for something: *She's a voracious reader of biographies.* — ~**ly** *adv* — ~**ness**, **-racity** /-ˈræsᵻti/ *n* [U]

vor·tex /ˈvɔːteks‖ˈvɔːr/ *n* **-texes** or **-tices** /tᵻsiːz/ **1** [C] a powerful circular moving mass of esp. water or wind that can draw objects into its hollow centre, as in a WHIRLPOOL or WHIRLWIND **2** [*the*+S (of)] *lit or pomp* a situation so powerful that one is helpless against it: *Against their will they were drawn into the vortex of war.*

vo·ta·ry /ˈvəʊtəri/ *n* [(of)] *fml or tech* a regular worshipper: *Roman soldiers were often votaries of Mars, the god of war.*

vote¹ /vəʊt/ *n* **1** [C (**on, about**)] an act of making a choice or decision on a matter by means of voting: *At the end of the meeting, a vote was taken on the motion.* | *We will have to put the matter to the vote.* | *to hold a free vote* (=in which one's party, etc., does not guide one's vote) | *a voice vote* —see also BLOCK VOTE **2** [C (**for, against**)] a (particular person's) choice or decision made by voting: *At the election I shall give my vote to/cast my vote for Tom Smith.* | *I know we can rely on your vote.* | *Announcing the tax cuts just before the election was the most blatant piece of vote-seeking I've ever seen.* | *vote-catching policies* | *an attempt to pull in votes* —see also CASTING VOTE **3** [S] a decision made by voting: *The vote yesterday went in his favour.* | *The vote was 215 to 84 against the motion, with 12 abstentions.* | *a very close vote* **4** [C] the piece of paper on which a choice is expressed: *Members were asked to place their votes in the ballot box.* | *He spoilt his vote* (=wrote on it or tore it, etc., so that it could not be officially counted) *in protest against the choice of candidates.* | *to count the votes* **5** [*the*+S] **a** the whole number of such choices: *The opposition vote seems to be growing.* (=more people are voting for them) **b** the opinion represented by such choices: *The women's vote will certainly be in favour of spending more on schools.* **6** [*the*+S] also **votes** *pl.*— the right to vote in political elections: *In Britain, young people are given the vote at the age of 18.* | *In the early part of the century they campaigned for votes for women.*

vote² *v* **1** [I (**for, against, on**)] to express one's choice officially from among the possibilities offered or suggested, usu. by marking a piece of paper (a BALLOT) secretly, or by calling out or raising one's hand at a meeting: *You're only 16; you're too young to vote.* (=to vote in an election to choose a parliament) | *They registered to vote.* | *I shall vote for Benn because I think he's the better man.* | *As we can't agree on this matter, let's vote on it.* | *Vote Cunningham* (=vote for Cunningham), *the man you can trust!* [+*to-v*] *We voted unanimously to refer the matter back to the committee.* [+*that*] *They voted that the meeting should be adjourned.* | *tactical voting* **2** [T+*obj*+*adv/prep*] to appoint or dismiss by means of a vote or election: *The government is afraid it will be voted out of office at the next election.* **3** [T] to agree, as the result of a vote, to provide (something): [+*obj*(*i*)+*obj*(*d*)] *Parliament has voted the town a large sum of money for a new road.* **4** [T+*obj*+*n*; *often pass.*] *infml* to state or agree as the general opinion: *The dinner was voted a great success.*

vote sbdy./sthg. ↔ **down** *phr v* [T] to defeat by voting

vote sthg. ↔ **through** *phr v* [T] to accept by voting

vote of cen·sure /ˌ·· · ˈ··/ *n* **votes of censure** a formal declaration of blame against someone, expressed by voting

vote of con·fi·dence /ˌ·· ˈ···/ *n* **votes of confidence** a formal declaration of support for the actions of someone, usu. expressed by voting: *The chairman was given a vote of confidence by the other members of the committee.*

vote of no con·fi·dence /ˌ·· ·ˌ· ˈ···/ *n* **votes of no confidence** a formal vote to express one's support or lack of it for the actions of a person or group of people, esp. the government: *The government face a vote of no confidence in the House of Commons this week.*

vote of thanks /ˌ·· ˈ·/ *n* **votes of thanks** [*usu. sing.*] a formal expression of thanks usu. made on a public occasion: *I'd like to propose a vote of thanks to Mrs Jarvis for all her hard work.*

vot·er /ˈvəʊtə\r/ *n* a person who votes or has the right to vote, esp. in a political election: *This policy will not appeal to the voters.* | *Labour voters* | *intimidation of voters* —see also FLOATING VOTER

voting booth /ˈ··· ·/ *n* POLLING BOOTH

voting ma·chine /ˈ··· ·ˌ·/ *n* a machine which records votes as they are made

vo·tive /ˈvəʊtɪv/ *adj* [A] *tech* given or done to fulfil a solemn promise made to God or a SAINT, usu. as thanks for a favour prayed for and received: *The church was full of votive candles.* | *a votive offering*

vouch /vaʊtʃ/ *v*

vouch for sbdy./sthg. *phr v* [T] **1** to declare one's firm belief in, from one's own personal experience or knowledge: *I've read this report carefully and I can vouch for its correctness.* **2** to take the responsibility for the future good behaviour of: *I'll vouch for my son, officer.*

vouch·er /ˈvaʊtʃə\r/ *n* **1** *BrE* a kind of ticket that may be used instead of money for a particular purpose: *a travel voucher* | *Some firms give their workers luncheon vouchers.* (=tickets with which they can buy a meal in certain restaurants) **2** *law* a RECEIPT or official declaration given to prove that accounts are correct or that money has already been paid

voucher sys·tem /ˈ·· ˌ··/ also **voucher plan** /ˈ·· ˌ·/— *n* (in the US) a system in which parents receive a voucher worth an amount of money which they can use to go to any public school or to help pay for a private school (a school one must pay for)

vouch·safe /vaʊtʃˈseɪf/ *v* [T] *lit or fml* to offer, give, say, or do (something) as an act of favour or kindness, esp. to someone lower in rank or position than oneself: *He did not vouchsafe a reply.* (=did not reply)

vow¹ /vaʊ/ *n* [(of)] a solemn promise or declaration of intention: *All the men took/made a vow of loyalty to their leader.* | *The members of this religious community are under a vow of silence.* (=have promised to God that they will not speak) [+*to-v*] *a vow to avenge their deaths*

vow² *v* [T] **1** [+*to-v/*(*that*);*obj*] to declare or swear solemnly. *He vowed to kill his wife's lover.* | *When young Phil was caught stealing he vowed he'd never do it again.* **2** [(**to**)] *fml* to promise to give by swearing solemnly, esp. to God: *Priests vow their lives to the service of the church.*

vow·el /ˈvaʊəl/ *n* **1** any of the human speech sounds in which the breath is let out without any closing of the air passage in the mouth or throat: *The simple vowel sounds of British English are represented in this dictionary by* /iː, ɪ, e, æ, ɑː, ɒ, ɔː, ʊ, ʌ, ɜː, ə/. **2** *not tech* a letter used for representing any of these: *The vowels in the English alphabet are* a, e, i, o, u, *and, sometimes,* y. —compare CONSONANT¹

vox pop /ˌvɒks ˈpɒp‖ˌvɑːks ˈpɑːp/ *n* *BrE infml* an inquiry carried out in the street by a television, radio, or newspaper reporter who tries to find out people's opinions on a matter of public interest

voy·age¹ /ˈvɔɪ-ɪdʒ/ *n* a journey, usu. long, made by boat or ship: *The voyage from England to India used to take six months.* | *When I give up work I shall go on/make/take a long sea voyage.* | *on the outward/homeward voyage* —see TRAVEL (USAGE)

voyage² *v* [I;T] *lit or fml* to make a long journey by (sea); travel over (the sea)

voy·ag·er /ˈvɔɪ-ɪdʒə\r/ *n* a person who travels by sea, esp. where risks or difficulties may be met

Voyager also **Voyager Pro·gram** /ˈ··· ˌ··/— *n* an American space programme which sent two spacecraft (PROBES) to travel past other PLANETS in this SOLAR SYSTEM

voy·eur /vwɑːˈjɜːʳ/ n **1** a person who obtains sexual excitement from watching the sexual activities of others, esp. in secret **2** a person who enjoys watching the private and esp. unpleasant activities of others — ~**ism** n [U] — ~**istic** /ˌvwɑːjəˈrɪstɪk◄/ adj — ~**istically** /kli/ adv

VP /ˌviː ˈpiː/ n abbrev. for: Vice President

vs. /ˈvɜːsəs‖ˈvɜːr-/ AmE for v.

V sign /ˈviː saɪn/ n **1** holding up the first two fingers of the hand in the shape of a V, with the back of the hand towards the body. It was used in the Second World War to show (a desire for) victory. The same sign was used in the 1960s and 1970s, but then called a **peace sign**, showing a desire for peace. **2** BrE a similar sign made with the back of the hand facing forwards, used for expressing great dislike or anger, and considered very offensive

VSO /ˌviː es ˈəʊ/ Voluntary Service Overseas; a British organization which sends people to developing countries for at least two years, to live and work there and to share their skills and knowledge with the local people

VT written abbrev. for VERMONT

VTOL /ˌviː tiː əʊ ˈel, ˈviːtɒl‖-tɑːl/ adj [A] (of an aircraft) vertical takeoff and landing; able to rise into the air and land without having to run for a certain distance along the ground, on a RUNWAY —compare STOL

Vul·can /ˈvʌlkən/ the Roman name for Hephaestus, god of fire and metalworking

vul·can·ize also **-ise** BrE /ˈvʌlkənaɪz/ v [T] to strengthen (rubber) by chemical treatment —**-ization** /ˌvʌlkənaɪˈzeɪʃən‖-nə-/ n [U]

vul·gar /ˈvʌlgəʳ/ adj **1** showing a lack of fine feeling or good judgment in the choice of what is suitable or beautiful: *The house was full of expensive but very vulgar furniture.* | *a vulgar display of wealth* **2** extremely rude or bad-mannered: *vulgar habits* — ~**ly** adv

vulgar frac·tion /ˌ··ˈ··/ ‖ also **common fraction** esp. AmE— n a FRACTION expressed by a number above and a number below a line, rather than as a DECIMAL: *¾ is a vulgar fraction.*

vul·gar·i·ty /vʌlˈgærɪ̩ti/ n **1** [U] the state or quality of being vulgar: *her appalling vulgarity* **2** [C often pl.] a particular example of vulgar speech or action

vul·gar·ize **-ise** BrE /ˈvʌlgəraɪz/ v [T] to spoil the quality of; lower the standard of (something that is good) —**-ization** /ˌvʌlgəraɪˈzeɪʃən‖-gərə-/ n [C;U]

Vulgar Lat·in /ˌ··ˈ··/ n [U] the form of Latin spoken in ancient Rome, esp. by the common people, as opposed to the written (CLASSICAL) language, and from which many modern languages, such as Italian, French, and Spanish, have developed

Vul·gate /ˈvʌlgeɪt, -gɪt/ [the] a special Latin translation of the Bible made in the 4th century, and commonly used in the Roman Catholic Church

vul·ne·ra·ble /ˈvʌlnərəbəl/ adj [(to)] **1** (of a place or thing) weak; not well protected; able to be easily attacked: *They were in a vulnerable position, with the enemy on the hill above them.* | *Your arguments are rather vulnerable to criticism.* **2** (of a person or their feelings) easily harmed, hurt, or wounded; sensitive: *a young and vulnerable girl* —**-bly** adv —**-bility** /ˌvʌlnərəˈbɪlɪ̩ti/ n [U (to)]

vul·ture /ˈvʌltʃəʳ/ n **1** a large ugly bird with an almost featherless head and neck, which feeds on dead animals. In jokes and humorous drawings, vultures often fly or sit above a person who is dying, esp. in a desert: *vultures circling overhead* **2** a person who uses people, esp. weak and helpless people, for his or her own advantage and gain: *He says moneylenders are the vultures of society.* — see also CULTURE VULTURE

vul·va /ˈvʌlvə/ n **-vae** /viː/ or **-vas** the place where the passage leading to the female sex organs has its opening on the body

VW /ˌviː ˈdʌbəljuː/ n abbrev. for VOLKSWAGEN

vy·ing /ˈvaɪ-ɪŋ/ present participle of VIE

W, w, w /ˈdʌbəljuː/ **W's, w's** or **Ws, ws** the 23rd letter of the English alphabet

W written abbrev. for: **1** west(ern) **2** a WATT

W-2 /ˌdʌbljuː ˈtuː/ also **W-2 form** /ˌ··· ˈ·ˌ·/— n (in the US) a form which employers prepare for their workers stating the amount the worker has earned that year and the amount of tax which has been taken out of their wages. The worker sends this form with his or her tax statement to the IRS.

WA written abbrev. for: WASHINGTON STATE

Wac /wæk/ n AmE infml a member of the US Women's Army Corps: Have you seen the new Wacs' uniforms?

WAC n [(the)] abbrev. for the Women's Army Corps of the US Army

wack·y /ˈwæki/ adj infml, esp. AmE silly; slightly mad —**iness** n [U]

wad /wɒd‖wɑːd/ n [(of)] **1** a thick collection of things, such as pieces of paper, folded, pressed, or fastened together: a wad of bank notes **2** a thick soft mass of material, esp. used for pressing into a hole or crack: She stuffed wads of cotton in her ears to keep out the noise. —see picture at PIECE

wad·ding /ˈwɒdɪŋ‖ˈwɑː-/ n [U] soft material, esp. cardboard as used for packing or LINT used in medicine

wad·dle /ˈwɒdl‖ˈwɑːdl/ v [I +adv/prep] to walk with short steps, swinging from one side to the other, like a duck: The fat man waddled up to her. —**waddle** n

wade /weɪd/ v **1** [I (across);T] to walk through (water): We waded across the stream. —compare PADDLE² (3) **2** [I] AmE for PADDLE² (3)

  wade in phr v [I] infml to interrupt esp. an argument forcefully and with determination: It wasn't his affair, but he waded in with his opinion.

  wade into sthg./sbdy. phr v [T] infml to begin (an attack on) forcefully and with determination: She waded into the task with more enthusiasm than skill. | I must have offended her somehow, because she really waded into me.

  wade through sthg. phr v [T] infml to go through or complete (something long, unpleasant, or uninteresting) with an effort: I've got all this correspondence to wade through before I can go home.

Wade, Virginia (1945–) an English tennis player who won at Wimbledon in 1977

wad·er /ˈweɪdər/ also **wading bird** /ˈ·· ·/— n a bird that walks about in water to find its food, and usu. has a long neck and long legs: Herons and curlews are waders.

wad·ers /ˈweɪdəz‖-dərz/ n [P] high rubber boots to protect the legs when one walks in water, e.g. while fishing

wadge /wɒdʒ‖wɑːdʒ/ n [(of)] BrE infml for WAD (1)

wad·i, wady /ˈwɒdi‖ˈwɑːdi/ n a usu. dry river bed in a desert, esp. in North Africa

wad·ing pool /ˈ·· ·/ n AmE for PADDLING POOL

Waf /wæf/ n AmE infml a woman serving in the US Air Force

wa·fer /ˈweɪfər/ n **1** a very thin BISCUIT eaten esp. with ice cream **2** a thin round piece of special bread used with wine in the Christian religious ceremony of COMMUNION

wafer-thin /ˌ··· ˈ·◂/ adj extremely thin

waf·fle¹ /ˈwɒfəl‖ˈwɑː-/ n a light sweet cake, usu. marked with raised squares, and often covered with a sweet liquid. It is cooked in a special pan called a **waffle iron**.

waffle² v [I (ON)] **1** BrE infml to talk or write meaninglessly and at great length: I tried to pin him down to a direct answer, but he just went waffling on. **2** AmE infml to be unable to decide which action to take; to WAVER or VACILLATE: As the President continues to waffle over his stance on tax hikes; Congress grows impatient. —**waffle** n [U]: His exam answer was just a lot of waffle.

waft /wɑːft, wɒft‖wɑːft, wæft/ v [I +adv/prep; T+obj+adv/prep] fml or lit to (cause to) move or go lightly (as if) on wind or waves: Cooking smells wafted along the hall. | A sudden gust of wind wafted the papers off her desk.

wag¹ /wæg/ v -gg- [I;T] (of a part of the body) to shake or be shaken quickly and repeatedly from side to side: The dog wagged its tail with pleasure. | The dog's tail wagged.| (fig.) You must stop visiting that woman; **tongues are beginning to wag**. (=people have noticed it and are talking about it)

wag² n [usu. sing.] an act of wagging; shake: The dog greeted its master with a wag of its tail.

wag³ n infml a clever and amusing talker, usu. male —see also WAGGISH

wage¹ /weɪdʒ/ n [S] wages: an average weekly wage of £110 | He gives most of his **wage packet** (=envelope containing) to his wife. | In our family both my husband and I are **wage earners**. (=have a job and earn money) | The government has introduced a **wage freeze**. (=has said that wages must not be increased) | The workers have asked for/demanded a **wage rise** of 10%. —see also WAGES, MINIMUM WAGE

wage² v [T] to begin and continue (a war): The government has pledged itself to wage (a) war against/on poverty and disease.(=to try to end them)

wa·ger¹ /ˈweɪdʒər/ n fml an amount of money risked on an uncertain result; BET: Would you care to have/place a small wager on that?

wager² v [T (on)] fml for BET²: [+(that)] I'll wager he's had enough of foreign travel, after that! [+obj(i)+obj(d)+(that)] She wagered me £5 that I would not do it.

wag·es /ˈweɪdʒɪz/ n [P] a payment made for work done, calculated by the hour, day, or week or by the amount produced, and usu. received daily or weekly: He gets/earns good wages. | low wages | to demand an increase in wages —compare SALARY; see also WAGE¹; see PAY (USAGE)

▶ CULTURAL NOTE In Britain and the US it is usu. BLUE-COLLAR workers or MANUAL workers who receive **wages**, which are usu. paid in CASH. WHITE COLLAR workers receive a **salary**, which is paid into their bank account every month.◀

wage slave /ˈ· ·/ n humor or derog someone who must work, esp. at a dull job, in order to earn money

wag·gish /ˈwæɡɪʃ/ adj infml of, like, or typical of a WAG³: waggish remarks —~**ly** adv —~**ness** n [U]

wag·gle /ˈwæɡəl/ v [I;T] infml to (cause to) move frequently from side to side: The car's broken aerial waggled in the breeze. | He can waggle his ears. —**waggle** n

Wag·ner /ˈvɑːɡnər/, **Richard** (1813–83) a German COMPOSER most famous for his long OPERAS including The Flying Dutchman and The Ring of the Nibelung

wagon

wag·on also **wag·gon** BrE /ˈwæɡən/ n **1** a strong four wheeled road vehicle, mainly for heavy loads, drawn esp. by horses: a covered wagon | The Indians attacked the pioneers' **wagon train**. (=a long line of wagons used in 19th-century America) —see colour picture on page 358 **2** BrE a railway goods vehicle, esp. one with an open top **3** esp. AmE a TROLLEY (2): a drinks wagon **4** AmE a small, four-wheeled vehicle with an open top and a handle at the front, often coloured red and used by children as a toy: Calvin sat down in his wagon and begged his dad to pull him along. **5 on the wagon** infml no longer willing to drink alcohol

wag·on-lit /ˌvæɡɒn ˈliː‖ˌvɑːɡən-/ n **wagons-lits** (same pronunciation) a SLEEPING CAR

wag·tail /ˈwæɡteɪl/ n a small European bird that moves its tail quickly up and down as it walks

waif /weɪf/ n esp. lit an uncared-for or homeless child or animal: a pitiful little waif | The old lady loved cats, and took any **waifs and strays** into her home.

Wai·ki·ki /waɪˈkiːki/ a BEACH in Hawaii near Honolulu

wail /weɪl/ v [I] often derog **1** to cry out with a long sound (as if) in grief or pain: Stop weeping and wailing and do something about it! | The wind wailed in the chimney all night. | "She's taken my apple, mummy," he wailed mournfully. **2 wailing and gnashing of teeth** humor the crying, pain, etc. that is believed to take place in HELL —**wail** n [(the) S] : the wail of the air-raid sirens

Wailing Wall /ˌ·· ·/ [the] a length of high stone wall in Jerusalem where Jews come to pray as an act of PILGRIMAGE

wain·scot /'weɪnskət, -skɒt‖-skət, -skɑːt/ also **wain·scot·ting** /'weɪnskətɪŋ, -skɒt-‖-skət-, -skɑːt-/ [U]— n **1** a SKIRTING BOARD **2** a wooden covering on esp. the lower half of the walls of a room in an old house — ~ted adj

waist /weɪst/ n **1** the narrow part of the human body below the chest: a 24-inch waist | wearing a belt round his waist **2** the part of a garment that goes round this part of the body: She took in the waist of her dress. **3** tech the narrow middle part of an apparatus, e.g. a stringed musical instrument **4** tech the middle part of a ship **5** -**waisted** /weɪstᵻd/a having a waist of the stated kind: trim-waisted girls **b** (of a garment) having a waist in the stated position relative to the wearer's waist: high-waisted trousers

waist·band /'weɪstbænd/ n the thickened or strengthened part of trousers, a skirt, etc., that fastens round the waist

waist·coat /'weɪskəʊt, 'weskət‖'weskət/ esp. BrE ‖ usu. **vest** AmE— n a close-fitting garment without arms that has buttons down the front and is usu. worn under a JACKET, esp. by men as part of a suit on formal occasions

waist·line /'weɪstlaɪn/ n (the length or position of) an imaginary line surrounding the waist at its narrowest part: No sugar for me, thanks; I'm watching my waistline. (=trying not to become fatter) | a dress with a high waistline

wait¹ /weɪt/ v **1** [I (**for, until,** ABOUT, AROUND)] to stay without doing anything until someone or something comes or something happens: Hurry up! I'm waiting. | Wait a minute! | Wait for me! | We waited and waited but no one came. | Don't **keep her waiting.** (=Don't make her wait.) | We waited (for) 20 minutes for the bus. | I'm waiting for them (to arrive). | She waited anxiously/ impatiently for him to make up his mind. | I can't wait until then; I'm going now. | I'm fed up with all this waiting around! [+to-v] Are you waiting to use the phone? | I **can't wait** to (=I am very eager to) tell them the good news! | Here, **wait a minute** (used for getting attention); isn't that my car? | The sign says "No Waiting". (=you are not allowed to park here) **2** [T] to delay acting until (the stated occasion): You can't have it yet; you'll have to **wait your turn.** | He was just waiting his chance to get his revenge. **3** [I (**until**)] to remain unspoken, unheard, or not dealt with: This news can't wait until tomorrow; I'll phone them now. | The business discussions can wait until after dinner. **4** [I (**for**) usu. in progressive forms] to be ready: Your supper's waiting (for you); don't let it get cold. **5** [T (**for**)] infml, esp. AmE to delay the beginning of (a meal): Don't wait dinner for me; I will be late. **6 wait and see: a** You will find out soon: "Where are we going, mummy?" "Wait and see!" **b** to wait until the future becomes clearer: I don't think my boss will let me, but I'll just have to wait and see. **7 wait at table** BrE fml ‖ **wait on table, wait tables** AmE— to serve meals, esp. as a regular job —see also WAIT ON (1)

▷ USAGE Compare **await, wait for,** and **expect.** If you **await** (fml) or **wait for** someone who will come or something that will happen, you arrange your timetable or actions so that you are ready, perhaps staying still and doing nothing else but wait: "Why are you standing there?" "I'm waiting for John (to come)." | "I'm waiting to use that machine." If you expect someone or something, you think the person will come or the event will happen, but you will probably not stay still because of this, and may not even make special arrangements: I'm expecting guests. | We're expecting a cold winter. | I expect to (=think I will) be here for another hour. | Mother expects me to (=has told me to and thinks I will) feed the baby. **Waiting** is a sort of activity, expecting is a state of mind.◁

wait on sbdy./sthg. phr v [T] **1** to serve food to, esp. in a restaurant **2** to wait for; to have not yet received: We're still waiting on the result of the 4.30 race. **3** also **wait upon**— old use to make a formal visit to (someone) **4 wait on someone hand and foot** to serve someone

with everything they want: Don't expect me to wait on you hand and foot; make your own breakfast!

wait up phr v [I (**for**)] infml **1** to delay going to bed: Don't wait up (for me); I'll be home very late. **2** AmE to stop while walking or running so that someone behind can come alongside: Hey, John! Wait up, will you.

wait² n [S (**for**)] an act or period of waiting: We had a long wait for the bus. | The murderer was **lying in wait** for (=hiding, waiting to attack) his victim.

Waite /weɪt/, **Ter·ry** /'teri/ (1939–   ) a British adviser to the Archbishop of Canterbury who went to the Middle East to try to obtain the freedom of some Western HOSTAGES. He was himself taken as a hostage and held for four years until he was released in 1991.

wait·er /'weɪtəʳ/ n a man who serves food at the tables in a restaurant: "Waiter! The menu, please." | a wine waiter —see FATHER (USAGE), and

Waiting for God·ot /ˌweɪtɪŋ fə 'gɒdəʊ‖-fər 'gɑː-/ an often-performed play by Samuel Beckett, about two men waiting for a third who never comes. People often use the phrase in situations of waiting for something they do not expect to come: I think waiting for this bus to turn up is like waiting for Godot.

waiting game /'·· ˌ·/ n [S] delaying to see what happens before taking action: The government is playing a waiting game with the unions that are on strike.

waiting list /'·· ·/ ‖ also **wait·list** /'weɪtlɪst/ AmE infml— n a list of people who have asked for something but cannot be given it at once: I'm afraid there are no vacancies at the moment, but I can put you on the waiting list.

waiting room /'·· ·/ n a room for people to wait in, e.g. for people waiting to see a doctor, in a station, etc.

wait·list·ed /'weɪtlɪstᵻd/ adj included on a waiting list, esp. for a seat on a plane: We're waitlisted for tomorrow's flight.

wait·ress /'weɪtrᵻs/ n a woman who serves food at the tables in a restaurant

Wait·rose /'weɪtrəʊz/ one of a group of SUPERMARKETS in Britain which sells GROCERIES

waive /weɪv/ v [T] esp. fml or tech to state officially that (a right, rule, etc.) is no longer in effect: We cannot waive this rule except in case of illness. | He has waived all claim to the money.

waiv·er /'weɪvəʳ/ n law (a written statement giving proof of) waiving a right, claim, etc.: Please sign this waiver.

wake¹ /weɪk/ v **woke** /wəʊk/ or **waked, woken** /'wəʊkən/ or **waked** [I;T (UP)] to (cause to) stop sleeping: She usually wakes (up) early. | I woke up with a start when the alarm rang. | Wake up, Jimmy, it's 7.00! | The children's shouts woke us out of/from our afternoon nap. | (fig.) The bad news finally woke the country to (=made it become conscious of) the danger of war. | (fig.) The argument woke old rivalries.

▷ USAGE Compare **wake (up), waken (up), awake** and **awaken.** The usual patterns are: I **woke (up)** [I], I **woke** him **(up)** [T], I **awoke** (I), I **wakened** him **up** [T] and I **awakened** him [T], but all of these verbs can be used in both intransitive and transitive patterns. The most common and least formal is probably **wake up/wake** someone **up.**◁

wake up phr v [I usu. imperative] infml to start to pay attention: Wake up at the back there!

wake² n **1** a track left by a ship in water —compare WASH² **2 in the wake of: a** close behind and in the same path of travel as: The car left clouds of dust in its wake. **b** as a result of: Hunger and disease followed in the wake of the war.

wake³ n a gathering to watch and grieve over a dead person on the night before the burial, sometimes with drink and special food, esp. in Ireland, northern parts of Britain, and in the US among Catholics

wake·ful /'weɪkfəl/ adj not sleeping or in which one cannot sleep; sleepless: a wakeful baby/night — ~ly adv — ~ness n [U]

wak·en /'weɪkən/ v [I;T (UP)] fml to (cause to) wake: We were wakened by a loud noise. —see WAKE (USAGE)

wakes week /'· ·/ a holiday week for factory and office workers in the N of England, when the whole business closed down for a period. The arrangement has largely been discontinued, but the times of these holidays, which varied from town to town, are often still called by this name.

wak·ey wak·ey /ˌweɪki 'weɪki/ *interj BrE infml humor* wake up!

wak·ing /'weɪkɪŋ/ *adj* [A] of the time when one is awake: *He spends all his* **waking** *hours working.* | *a waking dream*

Wal·den Pond /ˌwɔːldən 'pɒnd‖-'pɑːnd/ a small body of water (POND) in Massachusetts in the US near which Henry David Thoreau lived and after which he named his book *Walden, or Life in the Woods*

Wald·heim /'vɑːldhaɪm‖'wɔːld-/, **Kurt** /kɜːt‖kɜːrt/ (1918–) the secretary general of the UN from 1972 to 1981 and president of Austria since 1986. He has often been in the news because of CONTROVERSY in connection with his actions as a German army officer during the Second World War.

Wal·dorf-As·to·ri·a /ˌwɔːldɔːf æ'stɔːriə ‖ -dɔːrf-/ [*the*] a large, expensive hotel in New York City

Waldorf Sal·ad /ˌwɔːldɔːf 'sæləd ‖ -dɔːrf-/ *n* a dish made of apples, CELERY, nuts, and MAYONNAISE, eaten cold

Wales /weɪlz/ a country in the United Kingdom; capital Cardiff. Wales has high mountains, including Mount Snowdon. There is much AGRICULTURE in the N with the main industries, esp. COALMINING, being in the S. The Welsh language is spoken widely, esp. in the N, and is still the first language for many people. The national SYMBOLS of Wales are the LEEK, the DAFFODIL, and the red DRAGON. The PATRON SAINT of Wales is Saint David. –see colour map on page 818

Wales, Prince of the title of the HEIR to the British THRONE. The present Prince of Wales is Prince Charles.

Wa·les·a /vəˈwensə‖vəˈlensə, wɔ-/, **Lech** /lek, lex/ (1943–) the Polish leader of the TRADE UNION Solidarity. He won the Nobel Peace Prize in 1983 and became president of Poland after the Communist government failed.

walk¹ /wɔːk/ *v* **1** [I] to move along on foot in a natural way, in such a way that one foot is always touching the ground: *Walk, don't run!* | *When it's a nice day I walk to work, otherwise I go by bus.* | *We must have walked ten miles today.* | *Walking is a good form of exercise.* | *The old lady walked slowly round the garden.* | *He walked along the edge of the cliff.* | *I walked up to him and held out my hand.* **2** [T] to pass over, through, or along on foot: *She'd walked the streets all night looking for somewhere to stay.* | *He does a circus act, walking the tightrope.* | *How far is the station; can I walk it* (=is the distance short enough to walk) *or shall I call a taxi?* **3** [T+*obj+adv/prep*] to go on foot with (someone) to a stated place: *I'll walk you home/to the bus stop.* **4** [T] to take (an animal) for a walk; exercise: *He's walking the dog.* **5** [I] (of a spirit) to move about in a form that can be seen **6** [T+*obj+adv/prep*] to cause to move in a manner suggesting a walk: *Let's walk the heaviest ladder to the other end of the room.* **7** [I;T] (in BASEBALL) to be allowed to go to the first of four points (BASES¹ (6)) because the PITCHER² has thrown four balls outside the area he is aiming at: *The pitcher was taken out of the game after walking four batters in a row.* | *Garvey walked to first base.* **8 walk on air** *infml* to be extremely happy: *"Yes – he's walking on air!"* **9 walk someone off their feet/legs** *infml* to tire someone by making them walk too much **10 walk tall** *infml* to feel very confident; be justly proud of oneself **11 walk the plank** to be forced, esp. by PIRATEs in former times, to walk along a board laid over the side of a ship until one falls off into the sea

walk away from sbdy./sthg. *phr v* [T] **1** to come out of (an accident) unhurt or almost unhurt **2** *AmE infml* to run faster than or defeat without difficulty: *My horse just walked away from all the others in the race.* –see also WALKAWAY, WALK **off** with

walk into sthg. *phr v* [T] **1** to get caught by (something) through carelessness: *He walked right into our trap.* **2** to obtain (a job) very easily

walk off/away with sthg. *phr v* [T] *infml* **1** to steal and take away **2** to win easily: *He walked off with first prize.*

walk out *phr v* [I (**of**)] **1** to leave suddenly, esp. as an expression of disapproval **2** to go on STRIKE –see also WALKOUT

walk out on sbdy./sthg. *phr v* [T] *infml* to leave suddenly, esp. in a time of trouble; desert: *He just walked out on his wife and family without saying a word!*

walk over sbdy./sthg. *phr v* [T] *infml* **1** to treat badly: *Don't let your husband walk (all) over you like that; stand up to him!* **2** to win without difficulty against: *Our team just walked over the opposition.* –see also WALKOVER

walk sthg. **through** *phr v* [T] to practise (e.g. a part in a play) before the performance; REHEARSE (1): *Let's walk through this scene and see how long it takes.* | *I'd like to walk through this evacuation procedure with you before I do it on my own.* –see also WALK-THROUGH

walk up *phr v* [I *usu. imperative*] *infml* (used when inviting people to come in and see a performance, esp. outdoors, such as a CIRCUS) to enter: *Walk up, ladies and gentlemen!*

walk² *n* **1** [S] a natural way of moving on foot in which a person's feet are lifted one at a time, in such a way that one foot is always touching the ground: *He set off at a brisk walk.* **2** [S] the movement of creatures with four legs in which there are always at least two feet on the ground: *He slowed the horse into a walk.* **3** [C] a usu. short journey on foot, esp. for exercise or pleasure: *Let's go for/take a (short) walk.* | *She's taken the dog for a walk.* | *a ten-mile walk* | *a sponsored walk* | *a space walk* **4** [C] a place, path, or course for walking: *There are some beautiful walks in Sussex.* **5** [S] a distance to be walked: *The station's just a few miles' walk/a ten-minute walk from here.* **6** [S] the manner or style of walking: *His walk is just like his father's.* | *an odd walk* –see also WALK OF LIFE **7** [C] (in BASEBALL) the going to the first of four points (BASES¹ (6)) without having to hit the ball because the PITCHER² has thrown four balls outside the area he must aim at: *The pitcher threw four walks in a row before being removed from the game.*

walk·a·bout /'wɔːkəbaʊt/ *n* **1** a period spent, esp. by an Australian ABORIGINE, away from regular work travelling about on foot through the country **2** *infml, esp. BrE* a walk through crowds by an important person, mixing and talking informally with the people: *The Queen did her now-traditional walkabout in the main square.*

walk·a·way /'wɔːkəweɪ/ *n AmE infml* an easy victory: *That race was just a walkaway for my horse.* –see also WALK away from (2)

walk·er /'wɔːkər/ *n* **1** a person who walks, esp. for pleasure or exercise: *a fast walker* | *a keen hill-walker* **2** an apparatus for helping someone to walk, esp. a frame used by babies or people who cannot walk properly –compare ZIMMER

Walker, Al·ice /'ælɪs/ (1944–) a black American writer of stories and poetry. Her most famous NOVEL is *The Color Purple*, which won the Pulitzer Prize.

Walker Cup /'··ˌ·/ [*the*] a GOLF competition between two teams, one British and one American, of non-professional male golfers

walk·ies /'wɔːkiz/ *n* [P] *BrE infml* (used to dogs) a walk: *Come along, Spot; let's go walkies!* (=go for a walk)

walk·ie-talk·ie /ˌwɔːki 'tɔːki/ *n* a two-way radio that can be carried, allowing one to talk as well as listen

walk-in /'· ·/ *adj* [A] *esp. AmE* **1** large enough to be walked into: *a walk-in closet* **2** easy (esp. in the phrase **walk-in victory**)

walk·ing /'wɔːkɪŋ/ *adj* [A] **1** used in the process of moving on foot: *walking shoes* **2** consisting of or done by travelling on foot: *a walking holiday/tour* **3** *infml* human: *She knows so many words that she's a walking dictionary!*

walking pa·pers /'·· ˌ··/ *n* [P] *AmE infml for* MARCHING ORDERS

walking stick /'·· ·/ *n* **1** a stick used for supporting someone while walking –see picture at STICK **2** *AmE for* STICK INSECT

Walk·man /'wɔːkmən/ *n tdmk for* PERSONAL STEREO

walk of life /ˌ· · '·/ *n* a position in society, esp. either one's job or one's social rank: *The club's membership includes people from* **all walks of life/every walk of life**.

walk-on /'· ·/ *n* (someone who has) a small usu. nonspeaking part in a play: *a walk-on part*

walk·out /'wɔːk-aʊt/ *n* **1** the action of leaving a meeting or organization as an expression of disapproval: *a walkout by/of the Russian delegation* **2** a STRIKE² (1), esp. at its start: *The walkout was caused by a disagreement over pay and working conditions.* | *The union staged a* **walkout** *over the issue.* –see also WALK **out**

walk·o·ver /ˈwɔːkˌəʊvəʳ/ n infml 1 an easy victory 2 an advance from one part of a competition to the next without having to compete against anyone, because of the sickness or WITHDRAWAL of one's opponent —see also WALK over

walk-through /ˈ· ·/ n the actions of practising a part or PROCEDURE; a REHEARSAL —see also WALK through

walk-up /ˈ· ·/ n, adj [C;A] AmE infml 1 (a flat, office, etc.) in a tall block with no LIFT² (2): It's not easy living in a 6th-floor walk-up. 2 (a block of flats) that is tall but has no LIFT² (2)

walk·way /ˈwɔːkweɪ/ n a road or path, etc. built esp. for people to walk on: a pedestrian walkway | Let's cross over on the walkway.

wall¹ /wɔːl/ n 1 also walls pl.— an upright dividing surface, esp. of stone or brick, intended for defence or safety, or for enclosing something: The garden was surrounded by a high brick wall. | a garden/cellar wall | the ancient city walls of Cairo | (fig.) A wall of fire advanced through the dry forest. | (fig.) Our enquiries were met by a wall of silence. (=no one would tell us anything) —compare FENCE¹ (1); see also CHINESE WALL 2 the side of a building or room: He painted the walls blue. | Hang that picture on the wall. | a wall plaque 3 the covering or inner surface of something hollow: the walls of a blood vessel 4 to the wall BrE into a hopeless position: Unless the company gets some more investment soon it will go to the wall. (=be ruined) 5 up the wall infml in or into a state of great anger or near madness 6 Walls have ears infml Other people may hear us —see also OFF-THE-WALL, have one's back to the wall (BACK¹), bang one's head against a brick wall (HEAD¹), the writing is on the wall (WRITING)

wall² v [T] to provide, cover, or surround with a wall: an old walled town in Portugal

wall sthg. ↔ **off** phr v [T(from)] to separate or close off with one or more walls: This part of the house is walled off (from the rest of the house).

wall sbdy./sthg. ↔ **up** phr v [T] 1 to close (an opening) with a wall: The door had been walled up. 2 also **wall in**— to build a wall in order to keep (someone or something) in: The prisoner was walled up by his captors.

Wal·la·bies /ˈwɒləbiːz/∥ˈwɑː-/ n [P] Australia's international Rugby Union team

wal·la·by /ˈwɒləbi∥ˈwɑː-/ n a small Australian animal related to the KANGAROO

Wal·lace /ˈwɒlɪs ∥ ˈwɑː-/, **Ed·gar** /ˈedɡəʳ/ (1875–1932) a British writer, well known for his crime stories, many of which were filmed for television

Wallace, George (1919–) an American politician who has served several times as the governor of Alabama and has also run for president. Wallace is remembered for trying to prevent INTEGRATION (=mixing of black and white children) in Alabama schools because he believed the state laws should be followed rather than the national laws if the two laws were different. He is considered to be a supporter of STATE'S RIGHTS and is also often considered to be a RACIST. In 1972 he was shot and has had to move around in a WHEELCHAIR since then.

Wallace, Sir William (died 1305) a Scottish leader in the fight for independence from the English, who was hanged in London but is remembered as a popular HERO (1)

wal·lah, -la /ˈwɒlə∥ˈwɑːlə/ n IndE & PakE a person, usu. male, who has the stated type of work or does the stated duty or service: the book wallah

wall·chart /ˈwɔːltʃɑːt∥-ɑːrt/ n a large piece of paper with information on it, often in pictures, that is fastened to a wall, esp. in a classroom

Wal·ler /ˈwɒləʳ∥ˈwɑː-/, **Fats** /fæts/ (1904–43) an American JAZZ piano player, songwriter, and bandleader who influenced many other musicians and was known for his humorous performances

wal·let /ˈwɒlɪt∥ˈwɑː-/ n 1 ∥ also **billfold** AmE— a small flat leather case, for holding papers and paper money, carried esp. by a man: He opened/closed/folded his wallet. —compare PURSE¹ (1), and see picture at PURSE 2 AmE a PURSE 3 a long leather case for official papers

wall-eyed /ˌ· ˈ·◂/ adj AmE having an eye or both eyes which show too much white because the IRIS points to the side rather than straight ahead

wall-flow·er /ˈwɔːlˌflaʊəʳ/ n 1 a garden plant with sweet-smelling yellow or red flowers 2 infml a person who does not share (fully) in a social activity because of lack of CONFIDENCE or unpopularity, esp. a woman who has not been invited to dance

Wal·lis /ˈwɒlɪs ∥ ˈwɑː-/, **Sir Barnes** (1887–1979) an English aircraft engineer and inventor, remembered esp. for developing the BOUNCING BOMBS used against the Germans during the Second World War —see also BOUNCING BOMB, DAM BUSTERS

Wal·loon /wɒˈluːn ∥ wɑː-/ n 1 a French-speaking person of S and SE Belgium 2 [U] the French DIALECT of the Walloons —compare FLEMISH¹

wal·lop¹ /ˈwɒləp∥ˈwɑː-/ n infml a powerful blow: I gave him a real wallop.

wallop² v [T] infml 1 to hit hard 2 [(at)] to defeat thoroughly, esp. in a game: He walloped me at tennis.

wal·lop·ing /ˈwɒləpɪŋ∥ˈwɑː-/ adj [A] infml very big: a walloping (great) house in the country

wal·low¹ /ˈwɒləʊ∥ˈwɑː-/ v I (in) 1 to move, roll, or lie about happily in deep mud, dirt, water, etc., as some animals do: Pigs like wallowing in the mud. | (fig.) Don't just wallow in self-pity; do something about your problems! 2 (of a ship) to roll and struggle in a rough sea: The ship wallowed helplessly among the great waves.

wallow² n 1 [S (in)] an act of wallowing 2 [C] a place where animals come to wallow

wall paint·ing /ˈ· ˌ··/ n a picture actually painted on a wall, not just hung on one, esp. a FRESCO

wall·pa·per¹ /ˈwɔːlˌpeɪpəʳ/ n [C;U] (a particular) decorative paper (for) covering the walls of a room: We've put up/hung (a) plain/patterned wallpaper in the bedroom. | a roll of wallpaper

wallpaper² v [T] to cover the walls of (a room) with wallpaper

Wall's /wɔːlz/ also **Wall's ice cream** /ˌ· ˈ· ·/— n [U] tdmk a well-known British variety of ice cream

Wall Street /ˈ· ·/ (a street in New York City which is) the influential American centre for money matters and the buying and selling of business shares: a Wall Street stockbroker —compare CITY and see colour map on page 1376

Wall Street Crash /ˌ· · ˈ·/ [the] a sudden loss of confidence in the US STOCK MARKET after a period of rapidly increasing prices which leads to very low SHARE prices and general economic problems. The worst example of this was in 1929, which led to the Great Depression.

Wall Street Jour·nal /ˌ· · ˈ··/ [the] an American daily newspaper which prints articles on business, economics, and world news

wall-to-wall /ˌ· · ˈ·◂/ adj 1 (of a floor covering) over the whole floor: wall-to-wall carpeting 2 [A] infml, sometimes derog filling up all the possible space or time; continuous: Our stereo gives wall-to-wall sound. | wall-to-wall advertising on TV

wal·ly /ˈwɒli∥ˈwɑː-/ n BrE infml a foolish or useless person, esp. male

Wal-Mart /ˈwɔːl mɑːt∥-mɑːrt/ one of a group of US shops that sell many different kinds of goods at low prices

wal·nut /ˈwɔːlnʌt/ n 1 [C] (a tree that produces) an eatable nut shaped like a human brain: a coffee and walnut cake —see picture at NUT 2 [U] the wood of this tree, considered to be excellent for furniture: a walnut bureau

Wal·pole /ˈwɔːlpəʊl/, **Rob·ert** /ˈrɒbət∥ˈrɑːbərt/ (1676–1745) a British Whig politician who is usu. described as the first British PRIME MINISTER

wal·rus /ˈwɔːlrəs∥ˈwɔːl-, ˈwɑːl-/ n -ruses or -rus a large seaanimal, like a very large SEAL, with two long teeth (TUSKS) standing out from the face and pointing downwards —see picture at SEAL

walrus mous·tache /ˌ·· ·ˈ·∥ˌ·· ˈ··/ n a thick MOUSTACHE hanging down at both ends

Walt Disney see Walt DISNEY

Walt Dis·ney World /ˌwɔːlt ˈdɪzni ˌwɜːld ∥ -ˌwɜːrld/ tdmk the official name for DISNEYWORLD

Wal·ters /ˈwɔːltəz∥-ərz/, **Al·an** /ˈælən/ (1927–) a British ECONOMIST and adviser to Margaret Thatcher from 1981–89

Walters, Bar·ba·ra /ˈbɑːbərə∥ˈbɑːr-/ (1931–) an

American television personality best known for her IN-TERVIEWs (=recorded conversations) with famous people

Wal·ton /ˈwɔːltən/, **Bill** (1952–) an American BASKETBALL player

Walton, Sir William (1902–83) an English COMPOSER, best known for the ORATORIO *Belshazzar's Feast* and for the music for the film *Henry V*

Waltons /ˈwɔːltənz/, **The** a television programme about a family called the Waltons, living in the American state of Virginia in the early 1900s during the Great Depression. The family is very large, and the best-known character is **Johnboy**, who records his family's experiences in his DIARY. The stories and morals of **The Waltons** are old-fashioned, and many people find them too simple for today's world.

waltz¹ /wɔːls‖wɔːlts/ n **1** a rather slow formal dance for a man and a woman, performed esp. in a BALLROOM **2** music for this dance: *Strauss waltzes*

waltz² v **1** [I (**round**)] to dance a waltz **2** [I+adv/prep] *infml* to go easily, successfully, or confidently:*We can't just waltz up to a complete stranger and introduce ourselves.* | *He waltzed through the exam.* (=passed it easily) **3** [T+obj+adv/prep] *infml* to take suddenly or roughly: *The police waltzed him off to jail.*
waltz off with sthg. *phr v* [T] *infml* to WALK **off with**

Waltzing Matilda /ˌwɔːlsɪŋ məˈtɪldə‖ˌwɔːlts-/ an Australian song, often thought of as the national song of the country

Wal·worth Road /ˌwɔːlwəθ ˈrəʊd‖ˌwɔːlwərθ-/ the place in SE London where the Labour Party has its central office

wam·pum /ˈwɒmpəm‖ˈwɑːm-/ n [U] shells put into strings, belts, etc., and formerly used as money or decoration by Native Americans

wan /wɒn‖wɑːn/ adj esp. lit (appearing) ill, weak, and tired: *a wan smile* | *The child looked pale and wan.* – –**ly** adv – –**ness** n [U]

wand /wɒnd‖wɑːnd/ n a thin stick carried in the hand, esp. by a person who does magic tricks: *The conjurer waved his magic wand and pulled a rabbit out of the hat.*

wan·der /ˈwɒndər‖ˈwɑːn-/ v **1** [I (ABOUT, OFF);T] to move about or away from (an area), usu. on foot, without a fixed course, aim, or purpose: *Look at that little boy wandering about – perhaps he's lost his mother.* | *Johnny's wandered off somewhere.* | *Nomadic tribes wander these deserts.* | *the wandering tribes of the Sahara* | *a wandering minstrel* | (fig.) *The river wanders* (–follows a winding course) *through some very beautiful country.* **2** [I (**from**, **off**, OFF)] to move away from the main idea: *Don't wander off the point.* **3** [I] (of a person or thoughts) to be or become confused and unable to make or follow ordinary conversation: *I'm afraid my father's mind is wandering; he's 94, you know.* **4 I wandered lonely as a cloud** *quote* the first line of the poem *Daffodils* by William Wordsworth –see also DAFFODIL – –**er** n

wan·der·ings /ˈwɒndərɪŋz‖ˈwɑːn-/ n [P] movement from place to place, esp. away from the proper or usual course or place: *You must have seen a lot of strange things in your wanderings.*

wan·der·lust /ˈwɒndəlʌst‖ˈwɑːndər-/ n [S;U] a strong desire to travel to faraway places

Wands·worth /ˈwɒndzwəθ‖ˈwɑːndzwərθ/ **1** a BOROUGH in S London, known esp. for its prison **2** the prison at Wandsworth

wane¹ /weɪn/ v [I] to grow gradually smaller or less after being full or complete: *The moon waxes and wanes every month.* | *the waning power of the Roman Empire in the 5th century*

wane² n **on the wane** becoming smaller, weaker, or less: *By now the power of the Roman Empire was on the wane.*

wan·gle /ˈwæŋgəl/ v [T (**into**, **out of**)] *infml* **1** to obtain, persuade, etc., by cleverness or a trick: *I wangled an invitation (out of George).* | *I wangled George into giving me an invitation.* **2 wangle one's way into/out of** to get into (a good situation) or out of (a difficulty) by cleverness or a trick –**wangle** n

wank¹ /wæŋk/ v [I] *BrE taboo sl for* MASTURBATE

wank² n [S] *BrE taboo sl* an act of wanking

wank·er /ˈwæŋkər/ n *BrE taboo sl* a foolish or useless person

wan·na /ˈwɒnə‖ˈwɑː-/ **1** want to **2** want a

▷ USAGE **Want to** and **want a** are sometimes pronounced in this way. They may be written **wanna** in stories to show an informal, and especially American English, way of speaking: *I don't* **wanna** *go.* (=I don't want to go.) | **Wanna** *drink?* (=Do you want a drink?)◁

wan·na·be /ˈwɒnəbi‖ˈwɑː-/ n esp. AmE want to be; a person who wants to be like another person, esp. someone famous, and so wears similar clothes and tries to act like that person: *Madonna wannabes* –compare WOULD BE

want¹ /wɒnt‖wɔːnt, wɑːnt/ v [*not usu. in progressive forms*] **1** [T] to have a strong desire for: *I want a drink.* | *Ask him what he wants.* | *What do you want for your birthday?* (=What present would you like?) [+to-v] *Do you want to go now?* [+obj+to-v] *He wants you to wait here.* [+obj+adj/v-ed] *I want that letter ready/typed by tomorrow.* [+obj+v-ing; usu. in negatives] *I don't want people coming in and out all day.* (=I would not like it and will not allow it) | (*infml*) *She's been wanting to go to Japan for years.* **2** [T *often pass.*] to wish or demand the presence of: *Your mother wants you.* | *The second team will not be wanted this afternoon.* **3** [T (**for**) *often pass.*] (esp. of the police) to hunt or look for, esp. in order to catch: *He is wanted for murder/for questioning.* | *a wanted man* **4** [T] *infml* to need: *The house wants a new coat of paint.* [+v-ing] *This job wants doing at once.* **5** [T+to-v; *obj*] esp. BrE *infml* ought: *You want to see a doctor about your cough.* | *You don't want* (=ought not) *to work so hard.* | *The work wants to be done with great care.* **6** [I;T] *fml* to suffer from the lack (of): *In poorer countries many people still want food and shelter.* –see also WANT **for 7** [I+IN or OUT] AmE *infml or ScotE* to wish to come or go: *The cat wants in/out.* **8 want some doing** *infml* to need a great deal of effort

▷ USAGE **I want (to)** is rather a strong way of expressing a wish, and it may not seem polite to the person you are speaking to. **I'd like (to)** is often more suitable. – see also LIKE¹ (USAGE), WANNA (USAGE)◁
want for sthg. *phr v* [T *usu. in questions and negatives*] *fml* (of a person) to lack (esp. food, clothing, shelter, money, love, etc.): *The children have never wanted for anything.* (=have always had everything they needed)

want² n **1** [C;U (**of**)] (a) lack, absence, or need: *All his wants were satisfied/supplied.* (=He was given everything he needed.) | *The plants died for/from want of water.* | *I'll take this one for want of a better.* (=because there isn't a better one) **2** [U] *fml* severe lack of the things necessary to life: *They had lived all their lives in want.* **3 in want of** *fml* in need of: *The house is in want of repair.*

want ad /ˈ· ·/ n AmE for CLASSIFIED AD

want·ed /ˈwɒntɪd‖ˈwɔːn-, ˈwɑːn-/ adj being looked for by the police in connection with the one or more crimes: *He is wanted for the murder of a teenage girl.* | *France's most wanted criminal*

want·ing /ˈwɒntɪŋ‖ˈwɔːn-, ˈwɑːn-/ adj [F] **1** [+in] *fml* lacking: *wanting in gratitude* (=ungrateful) **2** [(in)] *fml* not good enough or strong enough: *The invention was tested and* **found wanting**. **3** *euph* weak-minded

wan·ton /ˈwɒntən‖ˈwɔːn-, ˈwɑːn-/ adj **1** (of something bad) having no just cause or no good reason: *wanton cruelty* | *a wanton waste of money* **2** *fml* (esp. of a woman) sexually improper; PROMISCUOUS: *wanton behaviour/glances* **3** *fml* uncontrolled: *wanton growth of plant life in the tropical rain forest* – –**ly** adv – –**ness** n [U]

wap·i·ti /ˈwɒpɪti‖ˈwɑː-/ n -**tis** or -**ti** a very large N American deer

Wap·ping /ˈwɒpɪŋ‖ˈwɑː-/ an area in E London where certain British national newspapers are produced

war /wɔːr/ n **1** [U] armed fighting between nations: *They went to war over the violation of their airspace.* | *The two countries have been* **at war** (*with each other*) *for years.* | *We must* **go to war against/declare war on** (=begin an armed struggle against) *our enemies.* | *The Allies* **waged war on/against** *Hitler.* **2** [C] an example or period of this. When British people talk about "the war", they usu. mean the Second World War: *He fought in both World Wars.* | *to provoke a war* | *the American War of Independence* | *a war of attrition* | *a war memorial* | *war graves* | *a war hero/veteran* | *war poets* (=writing during, and about, the war) | *a nuclear war* | *the war-torn city of Beirut* **3** [C;U] a struggle between opposing forces or for a particular purpose: *the war against disease* | *the oil-price war*

4 in the wars *infml* having been hurt or damaged − compare BATTLE¹ (1); see also CIVIL WAR, COLD WAR, PRISONER OF WAR, STAR WARS, WARRING

War and Peace /ₗ·ₗ· ·ₗ·/ a NOVEL by Leo Tolstoy, set during the Napoleonic Wars. It is sometimes used as an example of a very long book: *I was waiting so long I could have read "War and Peace".*

War Be·tween the States /ₗ· ·· · ·ₗ·/ *n [the]* the American Civil War. This expression is used mainly by people in the South of the US.

war·ble /'wɔːbəl‖'wɔːr-/ *v* [I] (esp. of a bird) to sing with a clear, continuous, yet varied note −**warble** *n* [S]

war·bler /'wɔːblə‖'wɔːr-/ *n* **1** any of various songbirds **2** *humor* an esp. female singer

war bon·net /'·ₗ··/ *n* a kind of hat with many feathers sewn onto it worn by some Native Americans either formerly or now in ceremonies

war bride /'· ₗ·/ *n* a woman who marries a foreign soldier (who is in her country because of war): *My father's American but my mother is English − she was a war bride.*

war cab·i·net /'· ₗ···/ *n* a group of very important British government ministers who meet to discuss the progress of a war

war chest /'· ·/ *n AmE infml* the money a government has which it can spend on a war

war clouds /'· ·/ *n* [P] signs that war is getting more likely: *War clouds were gathering over Europe in the summer of 1939.*

war crime /'· ·/ *n* an illegal and usu. cruel act during a war, such as the mistreatment of prisoners or the murder of many harmless people −**war criminal** /'· ₗ···/ *n*

war cry /'· ·/ also **battle cry**− *n* **1** a shout used by people fighting a war to show their courage and make the enemy afraid **2** a short statement, easy to remember, used for getting people to do something or oppose something, esp. in politics; SLOGAN: *"Equal Rights for Women!" was their war cry.*

War Cry, The the weekly newspaper of the Salvation Army

ward¹ /wɔːd‖wɔːrd/ *n* **1** a large room in a hospital, usu. for people needing similar treatment: *the maternity ward* | *the casualty ward* **2** a division of a city, esp. for political or management purposes: *Which ward does she represent on the local council?* −compare CONSTITUENCY **3** a person, esp. a child, who is under the protection of another person or of a law court: *Everyone was shocked when he married his young ward.* | *They are* **wards of court**/*of the state.* −compare GUARDIAN (2)

ward² *v*

ward sthg. ↔ **off** *phr v* [T] to prevent (something bad, such as danger, a blow, a cold, etc.); keep away or at a distance: *Brushing your teeth regularly helps to ward off tooth decay.* | *a necklace to ward off evil spirits*

war dance /'· ·/ *n* a dance performed esp. by tribes in preparation for battle or after a victory

war·den /'wɔːdn‖'wɔːrdn/ *n* **1** a person who looks after a place (and people): *the warden of an old people's home* **2** an official who helps to see that certain laws are obeyed: *an air-raid warden* −see also TRAFFIC WARDEN **3** *AmE* the head of a prison; GOVERNOR −see also CHURCHWARDEN

ward·er /'wɔːdə‖'wɔːr-/ *n BrE* a prison guard

war·drobe /'wɔːdrəub‖'wɔːr-/ *n* **1** *BrE* ‖ **closet** *AmE*− a large cupboard built in to a wall in which one hangs up clothes **2** a tall piece of furniture in which one hangs up clothes **3** a collection of clothes, esp. of one person or for one activity: *a summer wardrobe* **4** a collection of special clothes to be worn on stage: *The* **wardrobe mistress** *is in charge of the costumes.*

ward·room /'wɔːdrʊm, -ruːm‖'wɔːr-/ *n* the space in a warship where the officers live and eat, except for the captain

Ward's /wɔːdz‖wɔːrdz/ *infml for* MONTGOMERY WARD AND CO.

ware·house /'weəhaʊs‖'weər-/ *n* -**houses** /ₗhaʊzɪz/ a large building for storing things, esp. things that are to be sold

wares /weəz‖weərz/ *n* [P] *esp. lit* small articles for sale, usu. not in a shop: *a pedlar's wares*

war·fare /'wɔːfeə‖'wɔːr-/ *n* [U] military activity against an enemy; war: *to ban chemical warfare* | *guerrilla warfare* | (fig.) *economic warfare* −see also BIOLOGICAL WARFARE, GERM WARFARE, PSYCHOLOGICAL WARFARE

war game /'· ₗ·/ *n* **1** a pretended battle to test military plans **2** a game played with models of soldiers, horses, etc., by adults

war·head /'wɔːhed‖'wɔːr-/ *n* the explosive front end of a bomb or esp. MISSILE: *nuclear warheads trained on army bases*

War·hol /'wɔːhəʊl‖'wɔːr-/, **An·dy** /'ændi/ (1928−87) an American artist famous in the POP ART movement. He is most well-known for pictures of soup cans and of Marilyn Monroe.

Andy Warhol

war·horse /'wɔːhɔːs‖'wɔːr-hɔːrs/ *n* **1** (esp. in former times) a horse for use in war; CHARGER¹ **2** *infml* a soldier or a usu. male person in public life, such as a politician, who has seen a lot of action and is still eager for more **3** *infml, often derog* something frequently seen, heard, used, etc.: *Tchaikovsky's piano concerto, an old warhorse of the concert repertoire*

war·i·ly /'weərₗli/ *adv* in a very careful way, looking for danger: *"Do you like vodka?" "Yes. Why?" she said warily.* −**-iness** *n* [U]

war·like /'wɔːlaɪk‖'wɔːr-/ *adj* **1** liking or skilled in war: *a warlike nation* **2** ready for war or threatening war: *a warlike appearance*

war·lock /'wɔːlɒk‖'wɔːrlɑːk/ *n* (esp. in stories) a male WITCH (1)

war·lord /'wɔːlɔːd‖'wɔːrlɔːrd/ *n lit, sometimes derog* a high military leader

warm¹ /wɔːm‖wɔːrm/ *adj* **1** having or producing enough heat or pleasant heat: *warm milk* | *a warm bath* **2** having or giving a feeling of heat: *Are you warm enough?* | *The pillow was still warm.* | *It was warm work.* **3** able to keep in heat or keep out cold: *warm clothes* **4** showing or marked by strong feeling, esp. good feeling: *Please accept my warmest congratulations.* | *They gave her a* **warm welcome.** −compare HEATED **5** giving a pleasant feeling of cheerfulness or friendliness: *warm colours* | *a warm voice* **6** *AmE* slightly angry: *Warm words were exchanged.* (=angry things were said) **7** [F] (esp. in children's games) near to finding a hidden object, the answer, etc.: *You're getting warmer.* −compare COLD¹(4), HOT¹ (11) **8** (of a SCENT¹ (1b)) recently made; fresh: *The dogs were following a warm scent/trail.* −compare COOL¹; see also WARMTH; see COLD (USAGE) −−**ly** *adv*: *It's a cold day, so dress warmly.* | *They greeted each other warmly.* − **~ness** *n* [U]

warm² *v* **1** [T (UP)] to make warm: *They warmed their hands/themselves by the open fire.* | *A glass of rum will warm you up.* | *a warming fire/drink* **2** [I] (of a thing) to become warm: *The soup is warming in the pot.* −compare COOL²

warm sthg. ↔ **over** *phr v* [T] **1** *AmE for* WARM **up** (1) **2** *derog, esp. AmE* to use (an idea, argument, etc.) again

warm to sbdy./sthg. *phr v* [T] **1** also **warm towards**− to begin to like: *The students warmed to the new teacher at once.* **2** to become interested in; be full of ENTHUSIASM for: *The more he spoke, the more he warmed to his subject.*

warm (sbdy./sthg.↔) **up** *phr v* **1** [T] *esp. BrE* ‖ also **warm over** *AmE* −to reheat (cooked food) for eating **2** [I;T] to (cause to) become ready for action or performance by exercise or operation in advance: *The runners are warming up before the race.* | *Let's warm up the car engine a bit before we start.* | *He warmed up the audience by telling a few jokes before the show began.* **3** [I;T] *infml* to (cause to) become more excited or exciting: *Let's try and warm up this party!*

warm³ *n [the+S] esp. BrE* a warm place, state, or condition: *Come into the warm, out of the cold.*

warm-blood·ed /ₗ· '···◄/ *adj [no comp.]* having a body temperature that remains fairly high whether the temperature of the surroundings is hot or cold −compare COLD-BLOODED − **~ness** *n* [U]

war me·mo·ri·al /'· ·ₗ···/ *n* something, such as a STATUE or PILLAR, put up in memory of those killed in a war. War memorials are often found in small towns and villages as well as larger cities.

warm front /ˌ· '·/ n the advancing edge of a warm air mass; a technical world used when describing the weather — compare COLD FRONT

warm-heart·ed /ˌ· '···◁/ adj having good friendly feelings; kind: a warm-hearted offer of help —compare COLD-HEARTED — ~ly adv — ~ness n [U]

warming pan /'·· ·/ n a long-handled round covered copper container for hot coals, formerly used to warm a bed

war·mon·ger /'wɔːˌmʌŋgəʳ‖'wɔːrˌmɑːŋ-, -ˌmʌŋ-/ n derog a person who urges war or who tries to get a war started — ~ing n [U]

warmth /wɔːmθ‖wɔːrmθ/ n [U] the state or quality of being warm: the warmth of the fire|of his feelings

warm-up /'·· ·/ n a set of gentle exercises done to prepare oneself for an activity or sport: There'll be a warm up of about five minutes before the game begins. | The cars do a warm-up lap before the race.

warn /wɔːn‖wɔːrn/ v 1 [I;T (of, against)] to tell of something bad that may happen, or of how to prevent something bad: The message warned of possible danger. | He warned me against going there at night. [+obj+to-v] I warned her not to go near the dog, but she ignored me, and it bit her. [+obj+(that)] I warned them that there was a bull in the field. | A red warning light flashed on and off. 2 [T] to give knowledge to (someone) of some future need or action: If you warn the police when you go away on holiday, they will watch your house.
warn shdy. **off** (sthg.) phr v [T] to try to cause (someone) to go or stay away (from something) by warning or threats: The farmer warned us off (his fields).

War·ner /'wɔːnəʳ‖'wɔːr-/, **Jack** (1896–1981) an English actor best remembered for playing the part of a policeman, George Dixon in the long-running British television SERIES Dixon of Dock Green —see also DIXON OF DOCK GREEN

Warner, Glenn S. (Pop) (1871–1954) an American football trainer who invented several ways of placing players on the field to gain the most advantage

Warner Bros /'wɔːnə ˌbrʌðəz ‖ 'wɔːrnər ˌbrʌðərz/ n an American film company

warn·ing /'wɔːnɪŋ‖'wɔːr-/ n 1 [C;U (of)] telling in advance: The sirens sounded an air-raid warning. | They attacked without warning|without giving a warning. [+to-v] The terrorists gave the army a warning not to go near the building. | Before you can dismiss him, you must give him advance warning in writing. 2 [C (of)] something that warns: Let that be a warning to you.

War of 1812 /ˌwɔːr əv ˌeɪtiːn 'twelv/ [the] a war between the US and Britain, fought from 1812 to 1815 mainly over trade problems. During the war, British soldiers burned the White House and other buildings in Washington, D.C.

War of In·de·pen·dence /ˌ· · ···'··/ [the] esp. BrE for AMERICAN REVOLUTIONARY WAR

war of nerves /ˌ· · '·/ n an attempt to worry the enemy and destroy their courage by threats, PROPAGANDA, etc.

War of the Worlds /ˌ· · · '·/, **The** a book by H G Wells, one of the first great works of SCIENCE FICTION. In 1938 a US radio broadcast of a play based on the book frightened many people, who thought that the events described on the radio were real.

War on Want /ˌ· · '·/ a British organization (CHARITY) started in 1952 which collects money and goods and gives help to poor people in many countries of the world

warp¹ /wɔːp‖wɔːrp/ v [I;T] to (cause to) turn or twist out of shape: This wood warps easily in damp conditions. | (fig.) Her views of men had been warped by several bad experiences. | (fig.) If you really enjoy such unpleasant jokes you must have a warped mind.

warp² n 1 [S] a twist out of a true level or straight line 2 [the+S] tech threads running along the length of cloth —compare WEFT 3 [C] tech a rope or strong wire used for pulling a net along behind a fishing boat

war paint /'· ·/ n [U] 1 paint that members of some tribes put on their bodies before going to war, esp. in former times 2 humor for MAKE-UP (1)

war·path /'wɔːpɑːθ‖'wɔːrpæθ/ n on the warpath: a (esp.

formerly of Native Americans) preparing for battle b infml angry and looking for someone to fight or punish

war·rant¹ /'wɒrənt‖'wɔː-, 'wɑː-/ n 1 [C] a written order signed by an official of the law, esp. allowing the police to take certain action: You can't search my house without a warrant. (=a SEARCH WARRANT) | The magistrate issued a warrant for his arrest. —see also DEATH WARRANT 2 [U] fml proper reason for action; JUSTIFICATION —see also UNWARRANTED

warrant² v [T] 1 to cause to appear right or reasonable; JUSTIFY (2): This tiny crowd doesn't warrant such a large police presence. [+v-ing] Just because you like it, that doesn't warrant spending so much money on it. 2 fml to promise (that something is so); GUARANTEE: [+obj+adj] The grower warrants these plants (to be) free from disease. [+(that)] He warrants that they are free from disease. 3 [(+obj)+(that)] infml to declare as if certain: I'll warrant (you) we won't see him back here again.

warrant of·fic·er /'··· ···/ n a military rank —see TABLE 3

war·ran·ty /'wɒrənti‖'wɔː-, 'wɑː-/ n tech a written GUARANTEE: The manufacturers will have to repair the car without charge because it's still under warranty.

war·ren /'wɒrən‖'wɔː-, 'wɑː-/ n 1 a RABBIT WARREN 2 usu. derog a place in which too many people live, or in which one gets lost easily: a warren of narrow twisting old streets

Warren Re·port /ˌ· · ·ˌ·/ [the] the report of an American committee, led by Earl Warren, which studied the events surrounding the murder of US President John F. Kennedy. The committee (the **Warren Commission**) decided that Kennedy's killer had acted alone and was not part of a CONSPIRACY.

war·ring /'wɔːrɪŋ/ adj [A] at war; fighting each other: warring factions|families | (fig.) warring beliefs

war·ri·or /'wɒriəʳ‖'wɔː-, 'wɑː-/ n fml or lit a soldier or experienced fighting man, esp. in former times: a noble warrior | a Zulu warrior

War·saw /'wɔːsɔː‖'wɔːr-/ the capital city of Poland

Warsaw Ghet·to /ˌ·· '··/ [the] a group of around half a million Jews collected together in Warsaw by the Germans during the Second World War, most of whom died in CONCENTRATION CAMPS or in armed struggle

Warsaw Pact /ˌ·· '·/ also **Warsaw Trea·ty Or·gan·i·za·tion** /ˌ·· '· ···,·,·--/ [the] a defence agreement established in 1955 by Albania, Bulgaria, Czechoslovakia, E Germany, Hungary, Poland, Romania and the Soviet Union. It no longer exists now, since the end of COMMUNIST in much of E Europe.

war·ship /'wɔːˌʃɪp‖'wɔːr-/ n a naval ship used for war, esp. one armed with guns

Wars of the Ros·es /ˌ· · · '··/ n [the + P] the name given to the struggle (1455–85) between the noble family of Lancaster, represented by a red rose, and the noble family of York, represented by a white rose, to make their man king of England

wart /wɔːt‖wɔːrt/ n 1 a small hard lump on the skin, esp. of the face or hands 2 **warts and all** infml not failing to mention the bad parts: The documentary presented Elvis as a human being, warts and all. | a warts-and-all biography — ~y adj

wart·hog /'wɔːthɒg‖'wɔːrthɔːg, -hɑːg/ n an African wild pig with long front teeth that stick out of its mouth

war·time /'wɔːtaɪm‖'wɔːr-/ n [U] a time when a nation is at war: rationing in wartime | wartime newsreels | wartime France —opposite peacetime

War·wick /'wɒrɪk‖'wɔː-/ a town in central England, where the local government for Warwickshire is based

War·wick·shire /'wɒrɪkʃəʳ‖'wɔː-/ a COUNTY in W central England

war wid·ow /'· ˌ··/ n a woman whose husband has been killed in war, who receives a small regular payment from the state (a **war widow's pension**)

war·y /'weəri/ adj [(of)] careful; looking out for danger: wild animals wary of traps | a wary old politician who never says too much —see also WARILY

was /wəz; strong wɒz‖wəz; strong wɑːz/ 1st and 3rd person sing. past tense of BE: I was here yesterday. | That was John. —see NOT (USAGE)

wash¹ /wɒʃ‖wɔːʃ, wɑːʃ/ v 1 [T] to clean with liquid: She washed her hands in hot water|with soap and water. | This shirt needs washing. | Wash these marks off (the wall), will you? —see also WASHING **2** [I] also **wash up** AmE— to clean oneself or a part of one's body, esp. one's face and hands, with liquid: She washed and then went to bed. | You haven't washed behind your ears. **3** [I+adv/ prep] to be able to be cleaned with liquid without damage: This fabric doesn't wash well. **4** [T+obj+adv/prep, esp. AWAY] to carry by the force of moving water: farm animals and crops washed away by floods **5** [I (**against**, **over**);T] esp. lit to flow against or over (something) continually: The waves washed (against) the shore|washed over the deck. **6** [I (**with**) usu. in questions and negatives] infml to be able to be believed: His story just won't wash (with me). **7 wash one's dirty linen (in public)** to make unpleasant subjects public which ought to be kept private **8 wash one's hands of** infml to refuse to have anything more to do with or accept responsibility for: I've washed my hands of the whole affair. **9 wash your mouth out!** (a phrase said to someone who has just sworn or said something rude)

▷ USAGE Compare **wash** and **clean**. If you **wash** something you remove dirt from it using a liquid, usually water. If you **clean** something you remove dirt from it by any method – using a cloth, a brush, chemicals, water, etc. —see also CLEAN (USAGE)◁

wash sthg. ↔ **down** phr v [T] **1** to clean (something large) with a lot of water: She washed down the car|the walls|the yard. **2** [(**with**)] to swallow (food or medicine) with the help of liquid: We washed down our steak and chips with a glass of wine.

wash sthg. ↔ **out** phr v [T] **1** to cause to become free of an unwanted substance, such as dirt: Wash that cloth out for me. **2** to destroy or prevent by the action of water: The cricket match was washed out by rain. —see also WASHED-OUT, WASHOUT

wash out of sthg. phr v [T] AmE infml to fail or not be allowed to continue: He washed out of college after a year.

wash up phr v **1** [I] esp. BrE ‖ **do the dishes** AmE— to wash the dishes, plates, knives, forks, etc., after a meal —see also WASHING-UP **2** [I] AmE for WASH[1] (2) **3** [T] (**wash** sthg. ↔ **up**) (of waves) to bring in to the shore: The sea washed up the body of the drowned sailor. —see also WASHED-UP

wash[2] n **1** [S] an act of washing: Go upstairs and have a wash. | Give the car a good wash. **2** [C] a place where vehicles are washed: a car wash **3** [S;U] a movement of water caused by the passing of a boat —compare WAKE[2] **4** [(the) S] the flow, sound, or action of a mass of water: the wash of the waves against the rocks **5** [C;U] also **wash drawing**— (a) drawing made in water paint of one colour **6** AmE for WASHING **7** ‖ AmE also **dry wash**— a river bed that has no water most of the time **8 come out in the wash** infml **a** (of something shameful) to become known **b** to turn out all right in the end: Don't worry; it'll all come out in the wash! **9 in the wash** being washed: Your blue shirt is in the wash.

wash[3] adj [A] AmE infml washable: wash cotton

Wash [the] a wide BAY on the E coast of England between Norfolk and Lincolnshire

wash·a·ble /ˈwɒʃəbəl‖ˈwɔː-, ˈwɑː-/ adj that can be washed without damage: Is this cushion cover washable? —see picture at SYMBOL

wash-and-wear /ˌ· · ˈ·/ adj (of clothes) easily washed and dried, and not needing ironing

wash·ba·sin /ˈwɒʃˌbeɪsən‖ˈwɒʃ-, ˈwɑː-/ also **basin** BrE ‖ **sink**, **washbowl** /-ˌbəʊl/ AmE— n a large fixed container for water for washing the hands and face, esp. in a bathroom —compare SINK[2] (1a)

wash·board /ˈwɒʃbɔːd‖ˈwɔːʃbɔːrd, ˈwɑːʃ-/ n a board or piece of metal that is CORRUGATED (=has high and low places on the surface) and is used to rub clothes against while washing. Washboards are used as instruments in some kinds of American FOLK[2] music, such as SKIFFLE.

wash·cloth /ˈwɒʃklɒθ‖ˈwɔːʃklɔːθ, ˈwɑːʃ-/ n AmE for FACECLOTH

wash·day /ˈwɒʃdeɪ‖ˈwɔːʃ-, ˈwɑːʃ-/ also **washing day**— n [C;U] the day when clothes are washed: Monday is washday in our house.

wash draw·ing /ˈ· ˌ··/ n WASH[2] (5)

washed-out /ˌ· ˈ·◁/ adj **1** reduced in colour, as if from

too much washing: washed-out old curtains **2** very tired: She felt completely washed-out after working all night. —see also WASH OUT

washed-up /ˌ· ˈ·◁/ adj infml (esp. of a person) with no further possibilities of success: Let me tell you, friend, you're (all) washed-up in this town! —see also WASH **up**

wash·er /ˈwɒʃər‖ˈwɔː-, ˈwɑː-/ n **1** a ring of metal, plastic, rubber, etc., put over a BOLT[1] (1) or a screw to give a softer or larger pressing surface, or put between two pipes to make a better joint —see picture at BOLT **2** a person or machine that washes —see also DISHWASHER and see picture at KITCHEN **3** AmE for WASHING MACHINE

washer-dry·er, -drier /ˌ·· ˈ··/ n a machine which is both a washing machine and a TUMBLE-DRYER

wash·er·wom·an /ˈwɒʃəˌwʊmən‖ˈwɔːʃər-, ˈwɑː-/ n **-women** /ˌwɪmɪn/ (in former times) a woman whose job was to wash other people's clothes, often in her own home

wash·ing /ˈwɒʃɪŋ ‖ ˈwɔː-, ˈwɑː-/ ‖ also **wash** AmE— n [U] **1** the work of washing cloth or clothes: I must get the washing done tonight. —see picture at SYMBOL **2** cloth or clothes that need washing or have just been washed: a pile of dirty washing | Hang the washing out to dry.

washing day /ˈ·· ·/ n WASHDAY

washing line /ˈ·· ·/ esp. BrE ‖ n a piece of string stretched between two trees or poles in a garden on which wet clothes are hung to dry

washing ma·chine /ˈ·· ·ˌ·/ ‖ also **washer** AmE— n a machine for washing clothes: He loaded up the washing machine. —see picture at KITCHEN

washing pow·der /ˈ·· ˌ··/ BrE ‖ **clothes detergent, laundry detergent** AmE— n [U] a powdered soap which is used for washing clothes

Washington[1] see WASHINGTON, DC and WASHINGTON STATE

Washington[2] /ˈwɒʃɪŋtən‖ˈwɔː-, ˈwɑː-/, **Book·er T.** (1856–1915) an American teacher and ADMINISTRATOR who began the Tuskegee Institute, one of the first American colleges for black people. He also wrote an AUTOBIOGRAPHY called Up from Slavery.

George Washington

Washington[3], George (1732–99) the first president of the US

▶ CULTURAL NOTE Most Americans know historical facts about Washington, such as that he led the fight against the British during the American Revolutionary War, suffered a very cold winter with his men at Valley Forge, and was the first president. Most Americans also know that when Washington was a boy, he is supposed to have chopped down a CHERRY tree. The story says that when he was asked about the tree, Washington replied, "I cannot tell a lie. I did it with my little ax." Americans still think of Washington as an honest and honourable man. His home in Virginia, Mount Vernon, where he and his wife Martha lived, is a popular place for tourists to visit. A picture of Washington is on every one dollar BILL. He is often called "the father of his country". Washington's Birthday on February 22nd is celebrated as a public holiday on President's Day.◀

Washington, DC /ˌwɒʃɪŋtən diː ˈsiː ‖ ˌwɔː-, ˌwɑː-/ also **Washington, the District of Columbia, the District, DC** **1** the US capital city, on the EAST COAST. Washington's many government buildings include the WHITE HOUSE and the CAPITOL. It has no industry. **DC** stands for **District of Columbia**, meaning that Washington is a special DISTRICT not contained in any of the 50 states — compare WASHINGTON STATE and see colour map on pages 1374–5 **2** the American president and his advisers in the

White House: *Washington may slow the rapid with-drawal from the Kurdish "safe haven"*...

Washington Mon·u·ment /ˌ...
'.../ [*the*] a tall stone struc-ture in the park area near the White House and Capitol Building in Washington, DC, which honours President George Washington

The Washington Monument

Washington Post /ˌ... '·/ [*the*] a serious American news-paper printed in Washing-ton, DC —see extra informa-tion on page 896

Washington State /ˌ... '·/ also **Washington**— *written ab-brev*. **WA** a state in the northwest US, by the Pacific Ocean. Its capital is Olym-pia, and its largest cities are Seattle and Tacoma. Wash-ington (State) is known for its forests and its rainy, MILD¹ (2) weather —compare WASHINGTON, DC and see colour map on pages 1374–5

washing-up /ˌ... '·/ *n* [U] *BrE infml* **1** the washing of dishes, plates, etc., after a meal: *I'll do the washing-up*. **2** the dishes, plates, etc., that are waiting to be washed —see also WASH **up**

washing-up bowl /ˌ... '· ·/ *n BrE* a plastic bowl in a sink in which the washing-up is done

washing-up liq·uid /ˌ... '· ˌ··/ *BrE* ‖ **dishwashing liquid** *AmE*— *n* [U] a soap in liquid form put into hot water and used to wash dishes, knives, forks, spoons, etc.

wash·load /'wɒʃləʊd‖'wɔːʃ-, 'wɑːʃ-/ *n* the amount of cloth-ing one can put in a washing machine considered together: *I did one washload in the morning and another in the afternoon*

wash·out /'wɒʃ-aʊt‖'wɔːʃ-, 'wɑːʃ-/ *n infml* a failure: *That plan of yours was a complete washout.* —see also WASH **out**

wash·rag /'wɒʃræg‖'wɔːʃ-, 'wɑːʃ-/ *n AmE* FACECLOTH

wash·room /'wɒʃrʊm, -ruːm‖'wɔːʃ-, 'wɑːʃ-/ *n AmE euph for* TOILET (2) —see TOILET (USAGE)

wash·stand /'wɒʃstænd‖'wɔːʃ-, 'wɑːʃ-/ *n* a table in a bedroom, holding things needed for washing the face and hands, esp. in former times

was·n't /'wɒzənt‖'wɑː-/ *short for* was not: *It wasn't my fault!*

wasp

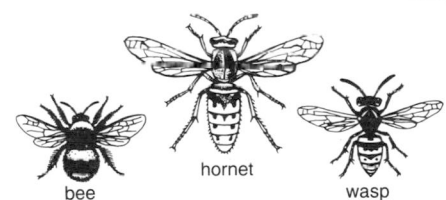

bee　　　hornet　　　wasp

wasp /wɒsp‖wɑːsp, wɔːsp/ *n* a fierce stinging yellow and black insect similar to the bee —see also HORNET

WASP, Wasp /wɒsp‖wɑːsp, wɔːsp/ *n esp. AmE* White Anglo-Saxon Protestant; an American whose family was origi-nally from northern Europe, esp. considered as a mem-ber of the class which has controlling influence or power in society —**Waspish** also **Waspy** *adj*

wasp·ish /'wɒspɪʃ‖'wɑː-, 'wɔː-/ *adj* sharply bad-tempered and cruel: *a nasty waspish remark* — ~ **ly** *adv* — ~ **ness** *n* [U]

wast /wəst; *strong* wɒst‖wəst; *strong* wɑːst/ *v* **thou wast** *old use or poet* (when talking to one person) you were

wast·age /'weɪstɪdʒ/ *n* [S;U] **1** loss or destruction of some-thing, esp. wasteful loss of something valuable **2** a reduction in numbers because of leaving, dying, etc.: *We expect to lose over 50 people from our work force every year by* **natural wastage**.

waste¹ /weɪst/ *n* **1** [S;U (**of**)] loss, wrong use, or lack of full use: *It's a waste of John's talents to use him for such an easy job.* | *Don't let all this good food* **go to waste!** (=be

wasted) | *It's* **a waste of time** (=useless) *trying to talk to her when she's in this mood.* | *I think betting is a com-plete waste of money.* **2** [U] used, damaged, or unwanted matter: *A lot of poisonous waste from the chemical works goes into the river.* | *Bodily waste is excreted in the form of faeces and urine.* —compare REFUSE²; see also NUCLEAR WASTE, WASTE DISPOSAL **3** [C] also **wastes** *pl.*— *esp. lit* an unused or useless stretch of land; a wide empty lonely stretch of water or land: *No crops will grow on these stony wastes.* | *the icy wastes of Antarctica* —see also WASTELAND

waste² *v* [T] **1** [(**on**)] to use wrongly, not use, or use too much of: *Don't waste your money on silly things; save it!* | *Don't waste electricity; turn off the lights when you go out.* **2** *fml* (esp. of a disease) to cause (the body) to lose flesh, muscle, strength, etc., gradually: *the poor wasted bodies of the concentration camp victims* | *a wasting disease such as tuberculosis* —see also WASTE **away 3** **waste one's breath** *infml* to have no effect with what one says: *Don't waste your breath trying to persuade them: they'll never listen.* **4** **waste not, want not** *saying* careful use of things one has, while one has them, will mean that one will never be hungry or in need (usu. said when the speaker is about to take or use something that another person has left behind or thrown away)

  waste away *phr v* [I] (esp. of a person or a part of the body) to gradually become thinner and weaker —see also WASTE² (2)

waste³ *adj* [A] **1** got rid of as worthless, damaged, or of no use: *waste material* **2** used for holding or carrying away what is worthless or no longer wanted: *waste pipes* **3** (esp. of an area of land) empty; ruined or destroyed —see also WASTE¹ (3), **lay waste** (LAY²)

waste·bas·ket /'weɪstˌbɑːskɪt‖-ˌbæ-/ *a* WASTEPAPER BASKET

wast·ed /'weɪstɪd/ *adj infml* very drunk

waste dis·pos·al /ˈ· ·ˌ··/ *n* **1** also **waste disposal unit** *BrE* ‖ **garbage disposal, garburetor** *tdmk AmE*— a machine connected to the waste pipe of a kitchen SINK² (1) which cuts solid waste into small pieces before it is carried away by the flow of water, thus avoiding blocking the pipes **2** [U] *esp. BrE* ‖ **disposal** *AmE*— the process of destroying or getting rid of used, damaged, or unwanted matter: *a waste disposal plant*

waste·ful /'weɪstfəl/ *adj* tending to waste things: *It's waste-ful to throw these away; we might be able to use them one day.* | *wasteful habits* — **ly** *adv* — ~ **ness** *n* [U]

waste·land /'weɪstlænd, -lənd/ *n* [C;U] (an area of) empty, unproductive, usu. ugly land: (fig.) *the industrial wastelands of northern England* (=with empty ruined old factories)

Waste Land /ˈ· ˌ·/, **The** a long poem by T S Eliot which has had a great influence on modern poetry since it ap-peared in 1922

waste pa·per /ˌ· '···/ *n* [U] paper got rid of because used, not necessary, or not fit for use

waste·pa·per bas·ket /ˌweɪstˈpeɪpə ˌbɑːskɪt, 'weɪstˌpeɪpə-‖ 'weɪstˌpeɪpər ˌbæ-/ ‖ also **waste·bas·ket** /'weɪstˌbɑːskɪt -ˌbæ-/ *esp. AmE*— *n* a small container, usu. indoors, into which one throws away unwanted paper, etc. —compare LITTER BIN

waste prod·uct /ˈ· ˌ··/ *n* something useless produced by the same action that produces something useful: *Urine is one of the body's waste products.*

wast·er /'weɪstəʳ/ *n* **1** (*often in comb.*) someone or some-thing that uses things wastefully, or causes or permits waste: *Washing clothes by hand is a real time-waster; you should get a washing machine.* **2** *derog* someone who uses their time and money foolishly, too quickly, etc., without thought for the future

was·trel /'weɪstrəl/ *n lit for* WASTER (2)

watch¹ /wɒtʃ‖wɑːtʃ, wɔːtʃ/ *v* **1** [I;T] to look (at) attentively: *Some of them were playing cards, and others were watch-ing.* (=looking at the people playing cards) | *I missed what was happening because I wasn't watching very closely.* | *She watched the train until it disappeared round the bend.* | *Do you watch a lot of television?* | *Watch me, and then try to copy what I do.* [+*wh-*] *Watch how I do it.* [+*obj +to-v*/*v-ing*] *We watched the sun set/setting behind the trees.* [+*to-v*] *She watched to see what he would do.* **2** [T] to be careful with or pay attention to: *You'd better watch Smith; I think he's a thief.* | *He watches his weight more as he grows older.* [+(*that*)] *Watch the milk doesn't boil*

over! [+*wh*-] *Watch how you use that knife; it's sharp!* **3 Watch it!** *infml* Be careful! **4 watch oneself** *AmE infml* **a** to be careful **b** to control one's habits: *I have to watch myself when it comes to chocolate* (=I try not to eat too much). **5 watch one's step** *infml* to act with great care **6 watch the clock** *infml* to be waiting for one's working day to end instead of thinking about one's work — see SEE (USAGE) — **-er** *n*

watch for *phr v* [T] to look for; expect and wait for: *She watched for her chance to speak.*

watch out *phr v* [I *usu. imperative*] *infml* to take care: *Watch out! There's a car coming!*

watch out for sthg./sbdy. *phr v* [T] **1** to keep on looking for: *Watch out for a tall man in a black hat.* **2** to be careful of: *Watch out for the dog/his temper!*

watch over sbdy./sthg. *phr v* [T] to guard and protect; take care of

watch² *n* **1** [C] a small clock to be worn, esp. on the wrist, or carried: *He wound up his watch.* —see CLOCK (USAGE) **2** [S;U] the act of watching carefully: *The sentry was keeping watch.* | *The police are* **keeping (a) close/careful watch on** *the activities of those men.* | *Be* **on the watch for** *thieves in this crowd.* **3** [S] a person or people ordered to watch a place or a person: *In spite of the watch set on the house, the thief escaped.* **4** [C+*sing./pl. v*;U] (sailors who have to be on duty during) a period of two or four hours at sea: *You'll take the first watch tonight.* | *Who's on watch now?* **5** [*the*+S+*sing./pl. v*] also **night watch**— a form of police force doing duty in towns at night in former times: *Call out the watch!* **6** [C *usu. pl.*] *esp. poet* a period (of the night) spent awake: *during the still watches of the night*

watchband /ˈwɒtʃbænd‖ˈwɑːtʃ-, ˈwɔːtʃ-/ *n AmE for* WATCHSTRAP

watch chain /ˈ· ˌ·/ *n* a chain fastened at one end to a watch and at the other to one's clothing

watch·dog /ˈwɒtʃdɒg‖ˈwɑːtʃdɔːg, ˈwɔːtʃ-/ *n* **1** a fierce dog kept to guard property **2** a person or organization that tries to guard against stealing, wasteful use of public money, undesirable practices, etc.: *a government watchdog on television advertising standards* | *the telecommunications watchdog OFTEL*

watch·ful /ˈwɒtʃfəl‖ˈwɑːtʃ-, ˈwɔːtʃ-/ *adj* [(for)] careful to notice things; VIGILANT: *She was watchful for any signs of activity in the empty house.* — **-ly** *adv* — **-ness** *n* [U]

watch·mak·er /ˈwɒtʃˌmeɪkəʳ‖ˈwɑːtʃ-, ˈwɔːtʃ-/ *n* a person who makes or repairs watches or clocks

watch·man /ˈwɒtʃmən‖ˈwɑːtʃ-, ˈwɔːtʃ-/ *n* **-men** /mən/ a guard, esp. of a building or an area with buildings on it —see also NIGHT WATCHMAN

watch night ser·vice /ˈ· · ˌ··/ *n* a church service which is held in Britain on 31st December to celebrate the New Year

watch·out /ˈwɒtʃaʊt‖ˈwɑːtʃ-, ˈwɔːtʃ-/ *n AmE* the act of watching for something; LOOKOUT (1): *Keep a watchout for errors like this one.*

watch·strap /ˈwɒtʃstræp‖ˈwɑːtʃ-, ˈwɔːtʃ-/ *BrE‖*also **watchband** *AmE*— *n* a band of leather, cloth, metal, etc., by which a wristwatch is kept fastened to the wrist

watch·tow·er /ˈwɒtʃˌtaʊəʳ‖ˈwɑːtʃ-, ˈwɔːtʃ-/ *n* a high tower from the top of which people can see what is coming a long way off, used esp. in former times

Watchtower, The a religious magazine of the Jehovah's Witnesses, which they often try to persuade people to read as they go from door to door

watch·word /ˈwɒtʃwɜːd‖ˈwɑːtʃwɜːrd, ˈwɔːtʃ-/ *n* a word or phrase that expresses a principle or guide to action of a person or group; SLOGAN: *Let constant vigilance be your watchword.*

wa·ter¹ /ˈwɔːtəʳ‖ˈwɔː-, ˈwɑː-/ *n* [U] **1** the most common liquid, without colour, taste, or smell, which falls from the sky as rain, forms rivers, lakes, and seas, and is drunk by people and animals: *The prisoner was given only bread and water.* | *The hotel has hot and cold running water* (=from TAPS) *in each room.* | *a glass of water* | *This reservoir supplies the whole city with water.* | *sea water* | *bathwater* (=water in a bath) **2** a mass or area of water, such as a lake, ocean, or river: *Help! He's fallen in the water.* | *She dived into the water and swam towards him.* | *After the flood most of the town was under water.* |

The goods came by water (=by boat), *not by air.* | *a wide stretch of open water*

▶ CULTURAL NOTE In the Bible, there is a story in which Jesus performed a MIRACLE by changing water into wine. There is also a story in the Bible in which Jesus walked on water. —see colour picture on page 424◀

3 the level of the sea (or of some rivers), at a particular time; TIDE: *The boat left* **at high/low water.** **4 above water** *infml* out of serious difficulty, esp. with regard to money: *The company has not had a very successful year but has managed to* **keep its head above water.** (=stay out of debt) **5 like water off a duck's back** *infml* (esp. of advice, warnings, or unpleasant experiences) having no effect on someone; not influencing someone's behaviour: *I must have told him a hundred times, and he always forgets — it's like water off a duck's back.* **6 water on the brain/knee/etc.,** liquid on the brain, knee, etc., as the result of disease **7 water under the bridge** past events which one can no longer change **8 water, water everywhere, but not a drop to drink** *quote* a slightly changed phrase from the poem *The Rime of the Ancient Mariner* by Samuel Taylor Coleridge —see also WATERS, HEAVY WATER, HOT WATER, SODA WATER, TOILET WATER, TONIC WATER, **in deep water** (DEEP¹), **of the first water** (FIRST¹), **hold water** (HOLD¹), **pour cold water on** (POUR)

wa·ter² *v* **1** [T] to pour water on (an area of land or a plant): *It's very dry; we must water the garden/the roses.* **2** [I] (esp. of the eyes or mouth) to form or let out water or watery liquid, esp. tears or SALIVA: *My eyes watered when I cut up the onions.* | *The delicious cooking smells make my mouth water.* —see also MOUTH-WATERING **3** [T] to supply (esp. an animal) with water to drink: *Have the horses been fed and watered?* **4** [T *often pass.*] *tech* (esp. of a river) to flow through (an area) and provide it with water: *Colombia is watered by the Magdalena, Atrato, San Juan, and other rivers.*

water sthg. ↔ **down** *phr v* [T *often pass.*] *often derog* **1** to weaken (a liquid) by adding water; DILUTE: *Waiter, this wine has been watered down!* **2** to make (a statement, report, etc.) weaker or less forceful, esp. by removing anything that might cause offence or opposition: *I've watered down the report's conclusions so as not to alarm the directors.* —see also WATERED-DOWN

Water Ba·bies /ˈ· ˌ··/, **The** a children's story by Charles Kingsley, which tells how a young boy called Tom falls into a river, becomes a water-baby, and learns all about good and evil from his water friends and enemies

wa·ter·bed /ˈwɔːtəbed‖ˈwɔːtər-, ˈwɑː-/ *n* a bed made out of RUBBER and filled with water. Waterbeds were esp. fashionable in the 1970s.

water bird /ˈ·· ·/ *n* any bird that swims or walks in the water

water bis·cuit /ˈ·· ˌ··/ *n* a rather hard BISCUIT made from flour and water

wa·ter·borne /ˈwɔːtəbɔːn‖ˈwɔːtərbɔːrn, ˈwɑː-/ *adj* carried by or travelling on water: *waterborne trade/diseases*

water bot·tle /ˈ·· ˌ··/ *n* a HOT-WATER BOTTLE

water buf·fa·lo /ˈ·· ˌ···/ *n* an Asian animal like a large cow that is often kept as a working animal

water butt /ˈ·· ·/ *esp. BrE* ‖ usu. **rain barrel** *AmE*— *n* a barrel for collecting rainwater

water can·non /ˈ·· ˌ··/ *n* **-non** *or* **-nons** an apparatus for forcing a stream of water under very high pressure against objects and esp. people: *Police drove off the demonstrators with water cannon.*

water chestnut /ˈ·· ˌ··/ *n* a white, nut-like fruit from a plant grown in water, often used in Chinese cooking

water clos·et /ˈ·· ˌ··/ *n* see WC

wa·ter·col·our *BrE* ‖ **watercolor** *AmE* /ˈwɔːtəˌkʌləʳ‖ˈwɔːtər-, ˈwɑː-/ *n* **1** [C *usu. pl.*;U] colours that are mixed with water, not oil, and used for painting pictures — compare OILS **2** [U] the art of painting such pictures **3** [C] a picture painted in this way —compare OIL PAINTING (2)

water cool·er /ˈ·· ˌ··/ *n AmE* an apparatus which cools drinking water from a large bottle, often found in offices

wa·ter·course /ˈwɔːtəkɔːs‖ˈwɔːtərkɔːrs, ˈwɑː-/ *n* **1** a natural or artificial passage through which water flows **2** a stream of water, such as a river or underground stream

water birds

gull

pelican

cormorant

swan

penguin

puffin

stork

flamingo

heron

wa·ter·cress /ˈwɔːtəkres‖ˈwɔːtər-, ˈwɑː-/ n [U] a strong-tasting plant with dark green leaves grown in water that is used as food, esp. in SALADS or soups

watered-down /ˌ‥ˈ‥◂/ adj usu. derog reduced in force; weakened: a watered-down version of the original —see also WATER **down**

watered silk /ˌ‥ˈ‥/ n [U] a special type of silk that has the appearance of being covered with shiny waves, like the surface of water

wa·ter·fall /ˈwɔːtəfɔːl‖ˈwɔːtər-, ˈwɑː-/ n water of a stream, river, etc., falling straight down over rocks, sometimes from a great height —see also FALLS

Wa·ter·ford crys·tal /ˌwɔːtəfəd ˈkrɪstl‖ˌwɔːtərfərd-, ˌwɑː-/ n [U] valuable glasses, VASES, etc. made from CRYSTAL (=a special kind of glass) in the town of Waterford in Ireland

water foun·tain /ˈ‥ ˌ‥/ n AmE for DRINKING FOUNTAIN

wa·ter·fowl /ˈwɔːtəfaʊl‖ˈwɔːtər-, ˈwɑː-/ n -fowl or -fowls [usu. pl.] any bird that swims, such as a duck or GOOSE, esp. one shot by hunters

wa·ter·front /ˈwɔːtəfrʌnt‖ˈwɔːtər-, ˈwɑː-/ n [usu. sing.] an area of land or a part of a town near a stretch of water, esp. when used as a port

Wa·ter·gate /ˈwɔːtəgeɪt‖ˈwɔːtər-, ˈwɑː-/ also the **Watergate Af·fair** /· ˈ‥‥ ·ˌ·/— the political SCANDAL in the early 1970s that led to US President Richard Nixon leaving office in 1974 to avoid being IMPEACHed (=charged with serious misbehaviour in office) by Congress. It was discovered that Nixon had known of and approved an attempt to obtain information about the Democratic CAMPAIGN for president by breaking into their offices in the Watergate Hotel building in Washington. Nixon also tried to prevent the Senate from receiving important information during their INVESTIGATION of the matter. The Senate investigation was shown on television, so the whole nation heard the TESTIMONY (=words said in a court by a witness) of politicians who worked for Nixon and said that he was involved and thus misused his power as president. The Senate also asked to hear the TAPES Nixon had made of conversations held in his office, but when they received them, parts of conversations seemed to have been deliberately removed from the tapes. Many details concerning the Watergate Affair were discovered by two *Washington Post* reporters, **Carl Bernstein** and **Bob Woodward**, who said that an important person in the government gave them information, and they called him **Deep Throat** to protect him. Watergate is often used as an example of the misuse of power.

wa·ter·hole /ˈwɔːtəhəʊl‖ˈwɔːtər-, ˈwɑː-/ n a small area of water in dry country, where wild animals go to drink

water ice /ˈ‥ ·/ esp. BrE ‖ **sorbet** AmE— n [C;U] a frozen sweet made of fruit juice or water with colour and taste added

watering can /ˈ‥‥ ·/ ‖ also **watering pot** AmE— n a container from which water can be poured through a long SPOUT onto garden plants —see picture at GARDEN

watering hole /ˈ‥‥ ˌ·/ n **1** a waterhole **2** humor a place where people go regularly to drink alcohol

watering place /ˈ‥‥ ·/ n **1** BrE a SPA **2** a waterhole

water jump /ˈ‥ ·/ n a stretch of water across which runners or horses must jump as part of a race or competition, esp. in a STEEPLECHASE or SHOW JUMPING

water lev·el /ˈ‥ ˌ‥/ n the height to which a mass of water has risen or sunk

water lil·y /ˈ‥ ˌ‥/ n a plant which grows in water, with large white, yellow, or pink flowers and flat leaves, often seen floating on the surface of a pool in gardens

wa·ter·line /ˈwɔːtəlaɪn‖ˈwɔːtər-, ˈwɑː-/ n [the+S] tech the position which the water reaches along the side of a ship

wa·ter·logged /ˈwɔːtəlɒgd‖ˈwɔːtərlɔːgd, ˈwɑː-, -lɑːgd/ adj so full of water as to be heavy, unusable, or unable to float: The football pitch was waterlogged so the match had to be cancelled.

Wa·ter·loo¹ /ˌwɔːtəˈluː◂‖ˌwɔːtər-, ˌwɑː-/ **1** a battle fought in 1815 near Brussels, Belgium in which Wellington led the British and Prussians and defeated Napoleon and the French **2** n a severe (and deserved) defeat after a time of unusual success: The British champion finally met his Waterloo (=was beaten) when he boxed for the world title. **3** one of the mainline railway stations in London just S of the Thames —see colour map on page 817

water main /ˈ‥ ·/ n a large underground pipe carrying a public supply of water

wa·ter·mark /ˈwɔːtəmɑːk‖ˈwɔːtərmɑːrk, ˈwɑː-/ n **1** a mark made on paper by the maker, seen only when it is held up to the light: The watermark on/in the banknote is to prevent forgery. **2** a mark showing the stated level reached by a river or the sea: This is the river's **high/low** watermark. | (fig.) The ancient culture had reached its high watermark. (=period of greatest success)

water mead·ow /ˈ‥ ˌ‥/ n a field, usu. near a river, which is often flooded

wa·ter·mel·on /ˈwɔːtəˌmelən‖ˈwɔːtər-, ˈwɑː-/ n [C;U] a large round fruit with green skin, juicy red flesh, and black seeds

wa·ter·mill /ˈwɔːtəˌmɪl‖ˈwɔːtər-, ˈwɑː-/ n a MILL that is driven by moving water, esp. in a river

water moc·ca·sin /ˈ‥ ˌ‥/ n a poisonous N American snake which lives in water

water pipe /ˈ‥ ˌ·/ n a HOOKAH

water pis·tol /ˈ‥ ˌ‥/ also **squirt gun**— n a toy gun which shoots water

water po·lo /ˈ‥ ˌ‥/ n [U] a game played by two teams of swimmers with a ball

wa·ter·pow·er /ˈwɔːtəˌpaʊəʳ‖ˈwɔːtər-, ˈwɑː-/ n [U] the power from moving water which can be used to produce electricity or to work machines; HYDROELECTRIC power

wa·ter·proof¹ /ˈwɔːtəpruːf‖ˈwɔːtər-, ˈwɑː-/ adj not allowing water, esp. rain, to go through —**waterproof** n BrE : waterproofs for hillwalking (=waterproof coats)

waterproof² v [T] to make waterproof, e.g. by putting rubber onto a material

water rat /ˈ‥ ·/ also **water vole**— n a small animal which lives in holes near a river and can swim

water rate /ˈ‥ ·/ n (in Britain) the charge made to each house-owner by the organization that supplies the public with water

water rights /ˈ‥ ˌ·/ n [P] the legal right to make use of water from a particular river, stream, lake, etc.

▶CULTURAL NOTE In the 1800s and early 1900s many landowners in the US argued over water rights. Today states argue over water rights, esp. over how much water each state can legally use. This question is esp. important in the south west US.◀

wa·ters /'wɔːtəz‖'wɔːtərz, 'wɑː-/ n [P] **1** sea near or belonging to the stated country: *fishing in Icelandic waters* **2** the water of the stated river, lake, etc.: *This is where the waters of the Amazon flow out into the sea.* **3** water containing minerals supposed to be good for the health, which comes up out of the ground from a spring and is drunk at a particular place: *He's taking* (=drinking) *the waters at Bath.* **4** *still waters run deep saying* a person who is quiet and says little often hides deep feelings or a lot of knowledge of a subject

Wa·ters, Muddy (1915–83) an American BLUES singer, songwriter, and GUITAR player, who greatly influenced many other singers of popular music

wa·ter·shed /'wɔːtəʃed‖'wɔːtər-, 'wɑː-/ n **1** the high land separating two river systems, from which each has its origin in many little streams **2** a time or event that marks a very important change, e.g. in a person's life or in a country's history: *Napoleon's retreat from Moscow was a watershed in his career/in European history.*

wa·ter·side /'wɔːtəsaɪd‖'wɔːtər-, 'wɑː-/ n [the+S] the edge of a river, lake, etc.: *waterside restaurants*

water ski·ing /'·· ,··/ n [U] a sport in which one travels over water on SKIs, pulled by a boat —**water ski** v [I] —**-er** n

water sof·ten·er /'·· ,··/ n a machine or chemical used for taking certain unwanted minerals, esp. chalk, out of water

water-sol·u·ble /'·· ,··/ adj that can be dissolved (DISSOLVE) in water

wa·ter·spout /'wɔːtəspaʊt‖'wɔːtər-, 'wɑː-/ n a wind condition (TORNADO) over the sea which carries water in a tall pipe-shaped turning mass —see STORM (USAGE)

water sup·ply /'·· ·,·/ n the flow of water provided for a building or area, and the system of lakes, pipes, etc., that provides it: *They turned off the water supply before installing the new heating system.*

water ta·ble /'·· ,··/ n the level at and below which water can be found in the ground

wa·ter·tight /'wɔːtətaɪt‖'wɔːtər-, 'wɑː-/ adj **1** through which no water can pass: *a watertight box* **2** produced with great care, so that there is no possibility of doubt, mistakes, or unintended results: *a watertight argument/plan/contract*

water tow·er /'·· ,··/ n a large container raised up in the air into which water is pumped, producing a steady pressure in order to supply water to buildings nearby

water va·pour /'·· ,··/ n [U] water in the form of gas in the air

water vole /'·· ·/ n a WATER RAT

wa·ter·way /'wɔːtəweɪ‖'wɔːtər-, 'wɑː-/ n a stretch of water, e.g. part of a river, which ships or boats can move on: *Canals and rivers form the inland waterways of a country.*

wa·ter·wheel /'wɔːtəwiːl‖'wɔːtər-, 'wɑː-/ n a wheel which is turned by moving water, esp. to give power to machines

wa·ter·wings /'wɔːtə,wɪŋz‖'wɔːtər-, 'wɑː-/ n [P] a joined pair of winglike plastic or rubber bags filled with air, worn under the arms to support a swimmer, esp. a child learning to swim

wa·ter·works /'wɔːtəwɜːks‖'wɔːtərwɜːrks, 'wɑː-/ n [P] **1** buildings, pipes, and supplies of water forming a public water system **2** *euph or humor, esp. BrE* the body's system and organs for removing URINE from the body: *I've been having a bit of trouble with the waterworks, doctor.* **3** *infml derog* crying: *Whenever she doesn't get what she wants, she turns on the waterworks.* (=starts to cry)

wa·ter·y /'wɔːtəri‖'wɔː-, 'wɑː-/ adj **1** *derog* containing too much water: *watery soup/coffee/potatoes* **2** very pale in colour: *a watery sun* **3** [A] *esp. lit* under the water: *The sailors came to a watery grave.* (=were drowned)

Wat·ford /'wɒtfəd ‖ 'wɑːtfərd/ a small town on the N edge of London —see also NORTH OF WATFORD

Wat·ling Street /'wɒtlɪŋ ,strɪːt‖'wɑː-/ a long Roman road stretching from Dover in the E to the river Severn in the W of England

Wat·ney's /'wɒtniz‖'wɑː-/ n tdmk a make of beer

WATS /wɒts‖wɑːts/ Wide Area Telephone Service; a telephone service which charges a fixed amount for a unlimited long-distance calls within a large area (such as the US) **b** a TOLL-FREE number —see also 800 NUMBER

Wat·son /'wɒtsən‖'wɑː-/, **Tom** /tɒm‖tɑːm/ (1949–) an American GOLF player who won many competitions in the 1970s and 1980s

Watson, Dr the ASSISTANT of Sherlock Holmes, a DETECTIVE in stories by Sir Arthur Conan Doyle. People often think of Sherlock Holmes using the phrase "Elementary, my dear Watson" when he is explaining to Dr Watson how easy it is to understand something.

watt /wɒt‖wɑːt/ n a measure of electrical power: *A kilowatt is 1000 watts.*

Watt, James (1736–1819) a Scottish inventor who was responsible for the development of the steam engine

watt·age /'wɒtɪdʒ‖'wɑː-/ n [S;U] power in watts: *an electric heater with a wattage of three kilowatts*

wat·tle /'wɒtl‖'wɑːtl/ n **1** [U] a mixture of thin sticks woven over thicker poles to form a fence or wall **2** [U] *AustrE* an Australian plant (ACACIA) with yellow flowers **3** [C] the red flesh growing from the head or throat of some birds, such as the TURKEY

wattle and daub /,··· '·/ n [U] a mixture of WATTLE with mud or clay, used esp. in former times to make the walls of houses

Waugh /wɔː/, **Eve·lyn** /'iːvl̩n/ (1903–66) an English writer of NOVELS, whose books include *Decline and Fall* and *Brideshead Revisited*

wave¹ /weɪv/ v **1** [I (at);T] to move (one's hand or something held in one's hand) as a signal, esp. in greeting: *The President waved at the crowd from the steps of the plane.* | *Wave to your father.* | *She waved her hand as she left.* | *The conjurer waved his magic wand.* **2** [T (to)] to express by waving the hand: *They waved goodbye.* [+obj(i)+obj(d)] *She waved us goodbye.* | (fig.) *You can wave goodbye to your chances of getting that job.* (=it is now impossible that you will get it) **3** [T+obj+adv/prep] to direct (a person) to move with a wave of the hand: *The policeman waved the traffic on.* | *She waved him away impatiently and went on with her work.* **4** [I] to move in the air, backwards and forwards, or up and down, without moving from one place: *The flag waved in the breeze.* **5** [I;T] to (cause to) lie or grow in regular curves: *Her hair waves naturally.*

wave² n **1** a raised moving part on the surface of a large body of water, esp. the sea, which is one of a number at even distances from each other: *The waves crashed/pounded against the rocks.* | *The little boat vanished beneath the waves.* (=sank) **2** a movement of the hand in waving: *With a wave of the hand he was gone.* | *Give your father a wave.* **3** [(of)] a particular feeling or pattern of behaviour or activity that suddenly begins to happen in an uncontrollable way, and is often passed on from person to person: *I felt a wave of nausea.* | *A wave of panic/indignation swept through the crowd.* | *The group was responsible for a wave of terrorist bombings.* | *a crime wave* —see also HEAT WAVE **4** a form in which some types of ENERGY (3), such as light and sound, move: *radio waves* —see also LONG WAVE, MEDIUM WAVE, SHORT WAVE **5** an evenly curved part of the hair: *a natural/permanent wave* —compare CURL¹ (1); see also MEXICAN WAVE
  wave sthg. aside phr v [T] to refuse to consider or treat as unimportant (esp. ideas, suggestions, etc.): *She waved his protests aside.*

Wave n AmE infml a woman serving in the US navy

wave band /'· ·/ n a set of sound waves of similar lengths, used esp. for broadcasting radio programmes

wave·length /'weɪvleŋθ/ n **1** the distance between one WAVE² (4) and another **2** a radio signal sent out on radio waves that are a particular distance apart **3** *(not) on the same wavelength* (dis)agreeing completely about all or the stated matters: *He and I are on the same wavelength concerning this development plan.* | *My mother-in-law and I are not on the same wavelength.*

wa·ver /'weɪvər/ v [I] to be uncertain or unsteady in movement or decision: *The flame wavered and then went out.* | *He wavered between accepting and refusing.* | *She never wavered in her loyalty to us.* —**-er** n —**-ingly** adv

wav·y /ˈweɪvi/ adj in the shape of waves; having regular curves: *wavy lines* —**iness** n [U]

wax¹ /wæks/ n [U] a solid material made of fats or oils which changes to a thick liquid when melted by heat: *candle wax* | *wax in the ears* (=a natural substance) see also BEESWAX

wax² v [T] to put wax on (e.g. a wooden floor), esp. as a polish

wax³ v **1** [I] (esp. of the moon) to grow gradually larger after being small or incomplete: *The moon* **waxes and wanes** *each month*. **2** [L+adj] *old use or humor* (of a person) to become: *The king waxed merry.* | *He waxed eloquent as he described his plans.*

waxed pa·per /ˌ· ˈ··/ also **wax paper**— n [U] esp. AmE paper which has a thin covering of wax to prevent it getting wet, used for wrapping food

wax·en /ˈwæksən/ adj **1** fml or lit very pale, as if ill: *a waxen face* **2** old use made of wax

wax·works /ˈwækswɜːks‖-wɜːrks/ n **waxworks** (a place where one can see) models of human beings made in wax. Madame Tussaud's in London is one of the most famous waxworks.

wax·y /ˈwæksi/ adj (pale) like wax —**iness** n [U]

way¹ /weɪ/ n **1** [C] the (right) road, path, etc., to follow in order to reach a place: *Is this the way out?* | *Can you tell me the way to the library?* | *If you* **lose your way**, *ask a policeman.* | *It's getting late; we must be* **on our way.** (=we must leave) | *The pilgrims were* **on the/their way to** (=travelling towards) *Canterbury.* | (fig.) *The new hospital is* **well on the way to** *being finished* (=is almost finished). | (fig.) *They claim to be* **leading the way** *in the fight against terrorism.* **2** [C] a direction: *Which way is the house from here?* | *Come this way.* (=in this direction) **3** [(the) S] also **ways** esp. AmE— the distance in space or time to be travelled in order to reach a place or point: *We were a long way from home.* | *A woman sat down beside me as we started, and she chattered nonstop the whole way.* | *Christmas is still a long way off.* | (fig.) *Prices vary* **all the way** *from £5 to £50.* | (fig.) *I'm with you* **all the way.** (=agree with and support you completely) **4** [C] a method or manner of doing something: *Do it this way.* | *These vegetables can be cooked in several different ways.* | *They are trying to find a way of settling the dispute.* | *We couldn't contact you — we had no way of knowing where you were.* | *We could have the car fixed here or get it towed home;* **either way** (=whichever course of action we choose) *it will be very expensive.* [+to-v] *What's the right way to say this in English?* | (infml) *She doesn't enjoy her job the way she used to.* (=as she used to) **5** [C] a particular manner or style of behaviour: *He has a pleasant way of speaking.* | *I don't like the way that* (=in which) *you laugh at her.* | *the American way of life* | *They eventually came round to our* **way of thinking.** (=began to share our opinion) **6** [C] a particular point or detail (of many possible): **In some ways** *it's quite a good idea, but the high cost makes it impossible.* | **In a way** *I can see what you mean, even though I don't share your point of view.* | *The result should* **in no way** *be seen as a defeat for the government.* **7** [S] (used esp. with verbs that do not express movement to describe an advance towards a particular result) one's path or course: *The acid bit its way through the metal.* | *She managed to talk her way out of a difficult situation.* | *He worked his way through college.* (=paid for his education by working at the same time) —see also **make one's way** (WAY¹ (21)) **8** [(the) S] the room or space needed for movement or activity: *I couldn't get through the door because there was a big box in the way.* | *Clear a way through the crowd.* | *Move out of my way so that I can get to the kitchen.* | (fig.) *Her social life* **got in the way** *of her studies.* (=prevented her from having the time she needed for studying) | (fig.) *The success of these talks will* **clear the way for** *the release of the hostages.* —see also **make way** (WAY¹ (22)) **9** [U] freedom to do exactly what one wants (esp. in the phrase **my/his/her, etc. way**): *If I had my way, these drug dealers would be shot!* | *He's very charming and always manages to* **get his own way.** **10** [U] forward movement; HEADWAY: *The ship was rapidly* **gathering way.** (=going faster) **11** [S] the stated condition, esp. of health: *I'm afraid he's* **in a bad way.** (=is ill) **12** [C] (esp. in names) a road or path: *a cycle way* | *Abercrombie Way* —see also HIGHWAY, PERMANENT WAY, RAILWAY, RUNWAY; see STREET (USAGE) **13 always the way** infml (esp. of

something bad) what always happens: *"The train was late." "That's always the way when you're in a hurry."* **14 by the way** (used to introduce a new subject in speech) in addition: *Oh by the way, have you heard from Bill lately?* —see USAGE **15 by way of: a** by going through: *We went by way of London.* **b** esp. BrE as a sort of or instead of: *We had some sandwiches by way of a meal.* **c** with the intention of: *By way of introducing himself he showed me his card.* **16 every which way** AmE infml in every direction; all over the place: *When the police arrived, the crowd started running every which way.* **17 give way (to): a** to admit defeat in an argument or fight: *My new evidence forced him to give way.* **b** to break under pressure; COLLAPSE: *The floor gave way under the heavy weight.* **c** BrE ‖ usu. **yield** AmE— to allow other traffic to go first: *You must give way when you come to this junction.* **d** to have its place taken by: *Steam trains gave way to electric trains.* **e** to allow oneself to show (esp. a feeling): *He gave way to tears.* **18 go out of the/one's way (to do)** to take the trouble (to do); make a special effort, esp. in spite of difficulties: *Although he was busy he went out of his way to help me.* | *She went out of her way to make things difficult for us.* **19 have a way with one** infml to have an attractive quality which persuades or pleases other people **20 have it ¹both ways** to gain advantage from each of two opposing opinions or actions: *You'll have to decide whether you want to lose weight or eat chocolates; you can't have it both ways!* **21 make one's way** to go: *I made my way home/towards the harbour/along the road/up the stairs.* **22 make way** to get out of someone's path; provide the necessary space: *Make way, there! I need to get through.* | *The old houses were knocked down to make way for a new office development.* **23 no way** infml (used to show strong refusal or opposition): *"Will you help me do this?" "No way; do it yourself!"* | *There's no way I'm agreeing to that!* **24 out of the way** unusual or not commonly known: *We did nothing out of the way on our holiday.* —see also OUT-OF-THE-WAY **25 put someone in the way of (doing) something** BrE old fash to give someone the chance of doing/getting something: *He put me in the way of a job.* **26 to ¹my way of thinking** in my opinion **27 under way** moving forward: *The great ship got under way.* | (fig.) *Our project is now well under way.* —see also WAYS, EACH WAY, RIGHT OF WAY, WAYS AND MEANS, **in the family way** (FAMILY), **pave the way** (PAVE), **pay one's way** (PAY¹), **see one's way (clear) to** (SEE¹) **28** AmE **way to go** to express satisfaction at or approval of something someone has done): *Way to go, team!*

▷ USAGE 1 **Way** is not usually used when you are thinking of a particular **road, path,** or **track** etc.: *There's a car outside parked in the* **road.** | *We followed a muddy* **path** *through the forest.* | *The shortest route to the village isn't by the main* **road** *but by a narrow, overgrown* **track.** —see also STREET (USAGE). 2 **By the way.** Although this expression seems to suggest that you are going to add unimportant information, in fact it is often used to introduce a subject that is really very important to you: **By the way,** *I wonder if we could discuss my salary some time?* | **By the way,** *do you think you could lend me £10?* —see also INCIDENTALLY (USAGE)◁

way² adv **1** [+adv/prep] far: *That happened way back in the 19th century.* | *Their profits were way below the original forecasts.* | *We're friends* **from way back.** (=have been friends a very long time) **2** [after n] near: *They live down Canterbury way.*

way·bill /ˈweɪˌbɪl/ n a paper showing details of goods or passengers being carried or delivered

way·far·er /ˈweɪˌfeərəʳ/ n esp. old use or lit a traveller on foot —**wayfaring** adj [A]

way·lay /weɪˈleɪ/ v -**laid** /ˈleɪd/ [T] to wait for and stop (someone going somewhere), esp. in order to attack them: *The travellers were waylaid by bandits.* | (fig.) *She waylaid me in the corridor and asked if she could speak to me in private.*

Wayne /weɪn/, **John** (1907–79) an American film actor whose films include *Stagecoach* and *True Grit*. The characters John Wayne played, esp. in WESTERNs, were often honest, strong, independent, and PATRIOTIC (=loving one's country). Because he played these characters, John Wayne was thought to have these qualities himself and to be an example of a good American: *He was the John Wayne of the American Marines.*

way of life /ˌ· · ˈ·/ n ways of
life **1** daily behaviour typical of a group of people, or
chosen by someone: *the Brit-
ish way of life* | *That family
have a very strange way of
life.* **2** the most important
thing in one's life: *Being a
doctor isn't a job, it's a way of
life.*

way-out /ˌ· ˈ·◂/ adj infml, becoming old-fash unusual or
strange, esp. in a modern
way: *way-out clothes/music*

John Wayne

ways /weɪz/ n **1** [P] customs
or habits: *We all have our
funny little ways.* —see also **mend one's ways** (MEND¹)
 2 [S] *esp. AmE for* WAY¹ (3): *We've a long ways to go yet.*

-ways see WORD FORMATION

ways and means /ˌ· · ˈ·/ n [P] **1** methods of doing or obtaining something, esp. unusual or mysterious methods:
*These addicts seem to have ways and means of getting the
drugs they need.* **2** means of obtaining the money that
is needed by a government to carry out its plans: *the Ways
and Means Committee of the House of Representatives*

way-side /ˈweɪsaɪd/ n [the +S] esp. old use the side of the
road or path: *a wayside inn* —see also **fall by the way-
side** (FALL¹)

way-ward /ˈweɪwəd‖-wərd/ adj usu. derog changeable and
difficult to guide or advise: *wayward behaviour* | *their
wayward son* – ~**ness** n [U]

WC /ˌdʌbəlju: ˈsi:/ n old-fash water closet; a TOILET which
is emptied by a flow of water from the pipes —see TOILET
(USAGE)

we /wi; *strong* wi:/ pron (*used as the subject of a sentence*)
 1 (plural of I) the people speaking; oneself and one or
more others: *We were all very excited when we heard the
news.* | *Shall we* (=you and I) *sit together, Mary?* | *Can
we* (=I and the others) *go now, sir?* **2** *fml* (used by a king
or queen in official language) I **3** (used by a writer or
speaker) you (the reader or listener) and I: *We saw in the
previous chapter how the king persuaded his nobles to stop
quarrelling* … | *We have all heard stories about people
being burgled.* **4** (used esp. to children and sick people)
you: *Now, we must be a brave giant, and stop crying.* | *And
how are we feeling today, Mr Jones?* (Many people do not
like this use of **we**) **5** *fml* people in general; human beings: *Do we have the right to destroy the world in which
we live?* —see also ROYAL WE

WEA /ˌdʌbəlju: i: ˈeɪ/ [the] Workers' Educational Association; a British group which arranges classes for adults,
esp. working-class people who may not have had a very
good education

weak /wi:k/ adj **1** not strong, esp. not strong enough to
work or last properly: *I still feel a bit weak after my ill-
ness.* | *The shelf is too weak to hold all those books.* | *Her
pulse is weak, she must be very ill.* | *a weak radio signal.* |
a weak heart | *weak eyes* **2** not strong or firm in charac-
ter; not determined or severe enough: *The teacher's so
weak that the children do what they like.* | *a weak and in-
decisive leader* | *too weak-willed to resist their arguments*
—see also WEAK-KNEED **3** *sometimes derog* containing a
lot of water; having little taste: *weak soup/tea* —compare
STRONG (6) **4** [(at, in)] not reaching a good standard; of
lower than average skill or ability: *She's weak in/at
French.* | *Her French is rather weak.* **5** lacking effective-
ness or persuasiveness: *weak arguments* | *The play was
well acted, but I thought the plot was a bit weak.* **6** [*no
comp.*] *tech* (of a verb) forming the past tense and past participle in a regular way, with the usual endings: *Stepped
is a weak form; swam and swum are strong.* —compare
STRONG (11) **7 weak at the knees** infml (of a person) not
well or strong, esp. after something surprising or unpleasant has happened – ~**ly** adv

weak-en /ˈwi:kən/ v [I;T] **1** to make or become weaker: *She
weakened as the illness grew worse.* | *The illness weakened
her heart.* | *These internal disputes have weakened the
government's position.* **2** to make or become less determined: *She asked so many times that in the end we
weakened and let her go.* | *None of these setbacks could
weaken her resolve to become a doctor.*

weaker sex /ˌ·· ˌ·/ n [the+S+sing./pl. v] pomp women in
general; most women would consider this offensive now

weak force /ˈ· ˌ·/ n [the] one of the four FUNDAMENTAL
FORCES, which causes RADIOACTIVITY

weak-kneed /ˌ· ˈ·◂/ adj infml derog habitually nervous
and lacking determination; cowardly; IRRESOLUTE

weak-ling /ˈwi:k-lɪŋ/ n derog a person who lacks physical
strength or strength of character

weak-ness /ˈwi:knəs/ n **1** [U] the fact or state of being
weak, esp. in mind, body, or character: *The president was
accused of weakness in dealing with the crisis.* **2** [C] an
imperfect part, esp. one that spoils the rest: *a structural
weakness in the aircraft* | *The only weakness of/in the plan
is its cost.* **3** [C] a fault in character; FAILING: *Drinking
is his weakness.* **4** [C (for)] a strong liking, esp. for something that is bad or slightly disapproved of: *I have a weakness for chocolate.* —compare STRENGTH

weal /wi:l/ n a raised usu. red mark on the skin where one
has been hit

Weald /wi:ld/ [the] an area in SE England in the counties
(COUNTY) of Kent, Surrey, and Sussex, famous for its fruit
and vegetable growing

wealth /welθ/ n **1** [U] a large amount of money and pos-
sessions: *How did he acquire his great wealth?* | *The coun-
try's wealth comes from its oil.* | *a man of wealth* **2** [S (of)]
fml or pomp a large number or amount: *a wealth of ex-
amples/of experience*

wealth-y /ˈwelθi/ adj (esp. of a person, family, or country)
rich

wean /wi:n/ v [T] to introduce (a baby or young animal) to
the habit of eating ordinary food instead of mother's milk
    wean sbdy. **from/off** sthg. *phr v* [T+obj/v-ing] to cause to
gradually leave (an interest, habit, companion, etc.,
that one disapproves of): *She tried to wean him (away)
from (taking) drugs.*
    wean sbdy. **on** sthg. *phr v* [T often pass.] to cause to
grow up under the influence of: *Today's generation is
being weaned on television.*

weap-on /ˈwepən/ n anything used to fight with, such as
a sword, gun, or bomb: *They used anything that came to
hand – stones, pieces of wood, bottles – as weapons.* |
nuclear/conventional weapons | (fig.) *The newspapers use
these sensational stories as a weapon in the bid to gain
readers.* —see also CHEMICAL WEAPON

weap-on-ry /ˈwepənri/ n [U] weapons: *nuclear weaponry*

wear¹ /weəʳ/ v wore /wɔːʳ/, worn /wɔ:n‖wɔ:rn/ **1** [T] to
have on one's body, esp. as clothing, but sometimes also
for protection, decoration, or other purposes: *He's wear-
ing a new coat.* | *She usually wears her hair up.* (=in a
raised style) | *She was wearing her diamonds/wearing an
expensive perfume.* | *He wore dark glasses to protect his
eyes from the strong sunlight.* | *Is it compulsory to wear
seat belts when you're driving?* —compare HAVE on; see
DRESS (USAGE) **2** [T] to have (a particular expression)
on the face: *She wore an angry frown.* **3** [I] to be reduced,
weakened, or damaged by continued use, rubbing, etc.:
I liked this shirt, but the collar has worn. —see also WEAR
away, WEAR **down**, WEAR **out** **4** [T+obj+adv/prep] to
produce by wear, use, rubbing, etc.: *You've worn a hole
in your sock.* | *The villagers had worn a path through the
fields.* **5** [I+adv] to last in the stated condition: *These
modern concrete buildings have worn badly.* (=no longer
look good or remain in good condition) | *Considering her
age, she has worn well.* (=still looks young) **6** [T *usu. in
questions and negatives*] infml, esp. BrE to allow or find
acceptable: *I was going to suggest Fiji for our holiday, but
I don't think father will wear it.* **7 wear one's heart on
one's sleeve** infml to show one's true feelings openly instead of hiding them **8 wear the trousers** BrE ‖ **pants**
AmE— infml to be in charge: *Who wears the trousers in
your house – you or your wife?* —see also WORN – ~**able**
adj
    wear (sthg.↔) **away** phr v [I;T] to (cause to) disappear
or be removed gradually through continued use, rubbing, etc.: *In the course of centuries, the wind has worn
the rocks away.*
    wear sthg./sbdy. ↔ **down** phr v [T] **1** to gradually
reduce the size of: *The constant rubbing wore down the
surface of the stone.* | *My shoes are badly worn down at
the heels.* **2** to lessen the strength or determination of,
by a long gradual process: *We wore down their opposition*

after several hours' argument. | *Months of illness wore her down.*

wear off *phr v* [I] (of a feeling, effect, etc., esp. an unpleasant one) to become less strong; to be reduced until it disappears: *The pain is wearing off.*

wear on *phr v* [I] to pass slowly in time: *The meeting wore on all afternoon.*

wear out *phr v* **1** [I;T (=**wear** sthg. ↔ **out**)] to (cause to) be reduced to nothing or to a useless state by long use: *Those thin shoes will wear out quickly.* **2** [T] (**wear** sbdy. ↔ **out**) to tire greatly; EXHAUST: *These children are wearing me out.* —see also OUTWORN, WORN-OUT

wear² *n* [U] **1** the act of wearing esp. clothes: *This suit only had a year's wear before it wore out.* **2** use which reduces, weakens, or spoils the material: *This carpet has had a lot of wear.* **3** damage resulting from continuous use: *These shoes I bought last week are already showing signs of wear.* **4** the quality of lasting in use: *There's a lot of wear in these tyres.* **5** (*often in comb.*) clothes of the stated type, or for the stated purpose: *men's wear* | *evening wear* | *holiday wear* | *footwear* (=shoes) | *swimwear* —see also **the worse for wear** (WORSE¹)

Wear /wɪəʳ/ [*the*] a river in NE England which flows through County Durham to the North Sea near Sunderland —see also TYNE AND WEAR

wear and tear /ˌ··ˈ·/ *n* [U] the damaging effects of ordinary use over a long period; WEAR² (3): *When you calculate the value of the car you must allow for wear and tear.* | (fig.) *the wear and tear of modern city life*

wear·ing /ˈweərɪŋ/ *adj* tiring: *I find him very wearing when he talks on and on.* | *It's a very wearing job.* —see also HARDWEARING

wear·i·some /ˈwɪərɪsəm/ *adj esp. fml or lit* which makes one feel tired, BORED, or annoyed; IRKSOME: *a wearisome day/task/child*

wear·y¹ /ˈwɪəri/ *adj* [(*of*)] **1** very tired, esp. after long work or a long journey: *I'm feeling weary.* | *a weary smile* | *weary travellers* | *I'm weary of all this arguing.* **2** *infml* which makes one tired: *a weary day* —**·ily** *adv* —**·iness** *n* [U]

weary² *v* [I (**of**);T (**with**)] *esp. fml or lit* to make or become weary: *He began to weary of the work.* | *You're wearying me with all these silly questions.*

wea·sel¹ /ˈwiːzəl/ *n* **1** a small thin furry animal with a pointed face which can kill other small animals. There is a well-known children's song called *Pop goes the Weasel.* **2** *AmE sl* a dishonest person

weasel

weasel² *v*

weasel out *phr v* [I (**of**)] *infml, esp. AmE* to escape or avoid a duty by clever dishonest means: *to weasel out of a responsibility*

weasel word /ˈ·· ˌ·/ *n* [*often* P] *AmE infml* a word used in place of some other word that would be more direct, honest, or clear: *He said she borrowed it but I think that was a weasel word for 'steal'.* | *With the election around the corner, politicians will only venture weasel words on that issue.*

weath·er¹ /ˈweðəʳ/ *n* [(*the*) U] **1** the condition of wind, temperature, rain, sunshine, snow, etc., at a certain time or over a period of time. British people often have conversations about the weather: *good/nice weather* | *The party will be held outdoors, weather permitting.* (=if the weather is fine) | *severe weather conditions* | *a period of hot weather* | *What will the weather be like tomorrow?* —compare CLIMATE **2 in all weathers** in every kind of weather, esp. in bad or difficult weather conditions such as storms or extreme heat **3 keep one's/a weather eye open (for)** to be ready (for what may happen, such as trouble) **4 under the weather** *infml* slightly ill —see also FAIR-WEATHER, **make heavy weather of something** (HEAVY¹)

weather² *v* **1** [T] to pass safely through (a storm or a difficult period): *Once this crisis had been weathered, the government's fortunes improved.* **2** [I;T] to change or be changed by being left in the air and weather over a period

of time: *Wood weathers better* (=is less damaged by rain, etc.) *if it is treated with creosote.*

weather-beat·en /ˈ·· ˌ··/ *adj* marked or damaged by the force of wind, sun, rain, etc.: *a weather-beaten face* (=brown and lined)

weath·er·board /ˈweðəbɔːd‖-ərbɔːrd/ *n* **1** [U] also **weath·er·board·ing** /-ˌbɔːdɪŋ‖-ˌbɔːr-/ ‖ also **clapboard** *AmE*— boards covering the outer walls of a house **2** [C] a board or set of boards fixed across the bottom of a door, to prevent floods from getting inside

weatherboard house /ˈ··· ˌ·/ a type of US home found esp. in New England with overlapping (OVERLAP) wooden boards on the outside —see colour picture on page 161

weather-bound /ˈ·· ·/ *adj* unable to move or take place because of bad weather

weath·er·cock /ˈweðəkɒk‖-ərkɑːk/ *n* a WEATHER VANE, sometimes in the shape of a COCK¹ (1)

weather eye /ˌ·· ˈ·/ *n* [*usu.* S] **1** an ability to know in advance how the weather will change **2** close and active awareness of a situation that one expects will change soon, esp. in the phrase **keep a weather eye out/open**

weather fore·cast /ˈ·· ˌ··/ *n* a description of likely future weather conditions, e.g. in a newspaper or on a radio broadcast — **-er** *n*

Weath·er·ill /ˈweðərˌɪl/, **Ber·nard** /ˈbɜːnəd‖ˈbɜːrnərd/ (1920–) a British Conservative politician, and Speaker of the House of Commons from 1983 to 1992

weath·er·man /ˈweðəmæn‖-ər-/ *n* **-men** /men/ a weather forecaster, esp. on television or radio: *According to the weatherman, we'll have snow tomorrow.*

weath·er·proof¹ /ˈweðəpruːf‖-ər-/ *adj* (esp. of a garment) which can keep out wind and rain

weatherproof² *v* [T] to make (a material) weatherproof

weather ship /ˈ·· ·/ *n* a ship at sea which reports on weather conditions

weather sta·tion /ˈ·· ˌ··/ *n* a place or building used for studying and recording weather conditions

weather strip /ˈ·· ˌ·/ *n AmE* a thin piece of INSULATION put around the edge of a door or window to keep cold air from coming inside —**ping** *n* [U]

weather vane /ˈ·· ·/ *n* a small metal apparatus fixed to the top of a building, which is blown round and so shows the direction of the wind

weave¹ /wiːv/ *v* **wove** /wəʊv/, **woven** /ˈwəʊvən/ **1** [I] to form threads into material by drawing one thread at a time under and over a set of longer threads stretched out on a LOOM **2** [T] to make by doing this: *woven fabric* | (fig.,*lit*) *He wove a fascinating story from a few forgotten incidents.* **3** [T+*obj*+*adv/prep*] to twist or wind: *He wove some branches together to form a roof.* **4** [T] to form by twisting parts together: *to weave a basket* | *These birds weave their nests out of sticks and feathers.* **5** (*past tense & participle* **weaved**) [I+*adv/prep*;T+*obj*+*adv/prep*] to move along or make (one's way) by turning and changing direction frequently: *The cyclist was weaving in and out between the cars.* | *He weaved his way through the crowd.* **6 get weaving** *BrE infml* **a** to become busy **b** to begin hurriedly

weave² *n* the way in which a material is woven and the pattern formed by this: *a loose/fine/herringbone weave*

weav·er /ˈwiːvəʳ/ *n* a person whose job is to weave cloth

web /web/ *n* **1** a net of thin threads made esp. by SPIDERs to catch insects: *The spider was spinning* (=making) *a web.* | (fig.) *a web of deceit* (=a set of lies) | (fig.) *a complex web of relationships* —see also COBWEB, and see picture at SPIDER **2** the skin filling the space between the toes of ducks and some other animals which use their feet for swimming

webbed /webd/ *adj* having a WEB (2) (between the toes): *webbed feet* | *webbed toes*

web·bing /ˈwebɪŋ/ *n* [U] strong woven material in narrow bands, used for supporting springs in seats, for belts, etc.

web-foot·ed /ˌ· ˈ··◂/ also **web-toed** /ˌ· ˈ·/— *adj* (of an animal) having webbed feet: *Ducks are web-footed.*

web off·set /ˌ· ˈ··/ *n* [U] a method of printing using one continuous roll of paper

Web·ster¹ /ˈwebstəʳ/, **Dan·iel** /ˈdænjəl/ (1782–1852) an American politician who believed in a strong central government and was called the "defender of the Constitution". He is also known for being a great speaker.

Webster², Noah (1758–1843) an American LEXICOGRAPHER (=writer of dictionaries). Some dictionaries are called "Webster's" even if they are not based on his work.

wed /wed/ *v* **wedded** *or* **wed** [I;T *not in progressive forms*] *old use or lit* (also used in newspapers) to marry: *They were wed in the spring.* | *"President's daughter to wed oil millionaire"* (title of newspaper story) —see also **with this ring I thee wed** (RING¹ (10))

we'd /wid; *strong* wiːd/*short for:* **1** we had: *We'd better go now.* **2** we would: *We'd rather stay.*

Wed. *written abbrev. for:* Wednesday

wed·ded /'wedɪd/ *adj* **1** [A] *fml or lit* having been legally married: *my* (**lawful**) **wedded husband/wife 2** [F+to] keen on; unable to give up (esp. an idea): *He's very much wedded to the idea of free trade.*

wed·ding /'wedɪŋ/ *n* a marriage ceremony, esp. with a party or meal after a church service: *Have you been invited to their wedding?*

▶ CULTURAL NOTE There are many types of wedding in Britain and the US depending on whether you are Christian, Moslem, Jewish, Hindu, etc. Many people get married in church. Other people get married at a **registry office** *BrE* ‖ office of the **justice of the peace** *AmE*, often followed by a party at home or in a hotel. —see also extra information on page 1406◀

wedding break·fast /'·· ˌ·-/ *n esp. BrE* a meal after a marriage ceremony, for the families and guests. Although it is called a breakfast, the meal is a LUNCH or dinner. —see also extra information on page 1406

wedding cake /'·· ·/ *n* [C;U] a cake made for a marriage ceremony. —see picture on page 1406

▶ CULTURAL NOTE A wedding cake in Britain is usu. white, often with three levels (TIERS), one on top of the other, and is cut by the BRIDE and GROOM at the wedding reception. What is left after the wedding is cut up and sent in small boxes to people who were not at the wedding. The top tier is sometimes kept until the first child is christened (CHRISTEN).◀

wedding chap·el /'·· ˌ·-/ a building used in the US for wedding ceremonies —see picture on page 1406

wedding dress /'·· ·/ *n* a long usu. white dress worn at a TRADITIONAL wedding —see also extra information on page 1406

Wedding March /'·· ·/ [*the*] a piece of music which is often played after a marriage ceremony, when the BRIDE and GROOM begin to walk down the AISLE (=path between seats) of the church. It can be played on other occasions to suggest a wedding.

wedding night /'·· ˌ·/ *n* the night following a couple's wedding, which in the past was usu. the first night that the couple had slept together and had sex

wedding pres·ent /'·· ˌ··/ *n* a gift given to two people who are getting married

wedding re·cep·tion /'·· ·ˌ··/ *also* **reception**— *n* a party held after a wedding, usu. by the married COUPLE or the BRIDE's parents —see extra information on page 1406

wedding ring /'·· ·/ *also* **wedding band** *old-fash*— *n* a usu. gold ring used in the marriage ceremony and worn on the third finger of the left hand to show that one is married —see picture at RING and see also extra information on page 1406

wedge¹ /wedʒ/ *n* **1** a piece of wood or other hard material with a V-shaped edge, one end being thin and the other quite wide, used esp. for making a space (to split or break something, e.g. a piece of wood) or filling a space (to hold two things together): *Put a wedge in the door so that it will stay open.* | (fig.) *He felt that the differences in their religions were* **driving a wedge between** *them.* (=separating them) **2** something shaped like this: *a wedge of chocolate cake* —see also **thin end of the wedge** (THIN¹ (10)) **3** a GOLF CLUB (2) with a metal head and an angled face, used esp. for hitting the ball out of a BUNKER

wedge² *v* [T] **1** to fix firmly with a wedge: *Wedge the door (open/shut).* **2** [+obj+adv/prep] to force into a narrow or limited space: *The people sitting close to me wedged me in/wedged me into the corner.*

Wedg·wood /'wedʒwʊd/ *n* [U] *tdmk* a type of English

CHINA, usu. having white figures or shapes on a background of blue, green, or black (named after **Josiah Wedgwood** (1730–95) who established the factory and first made the china)

wed·lock /'wedlɒk‖-lɑːk/ *n* [U] *old use* **1** the state of being married **2 out of wedlock** of unmarried parents: *children born out of wedlock*

Wednes·day /'wenzdi/ (*written abbrev.* **Wed.** *or* **Weds.**) *n* [C;U] the third day of the week, between Tuesday and Thursday: *He'll arrive on Wednesday.* | (*BrE infml & AmE*) *He'll arrive Wednesday.* | *She left last Wednesday.*| *We go shopping on Wednesdays.* | *My birthday is on a Wednesday this year.* —see also DAY (CULTURAL NOTE)

Weds. *written abbrev. for:* Wednesday

wee¹ /wiː/ *adj* [A] **1** *ScotE or infml* very small: *a wee child* **2 a wee bit** *infml* rather: *I'm afraid he's a wee bit drunk.* **3** *ScotE* **a wee dram** a glass of WHISKY **4** *ScotE and AmE* **wee hours** SMALL HOURS

wee² *also* **wee-wee** /'· ·/— *v* [I] *infml* (used esp. by or to children) to pass water from the body; URINATE — **wee, wee-wee** *n* [S]: *She wants to have/do a wee-wee.*

weed¹ /wiːd/ *n* **1** [C] an unwanted wild plant, esp. one which prevents crops or garden flowers from growing properly **2** [C] *BrE infml derog* (used esp. by children to other children) **a** a person who is physically weak and usu. very thin and tall **b** a person of weak character **3** [*the*+S] *infml* cigarettes or (something made of) tobacco **4** [U] *old-fash sl* CANNABIS; MARIJUANA

weed² *v* [I;T] to remove weeds from (a place where crops or flowers grow): *I spent the morning weeding (the garden).*

weed sbdy./sthg. ↔ **out** *phr v* [T] to get rid of (people or things of unacceptable quality) in order to improve something: *a series of tests to weed out incompetent operators from the workforce*

weed·kil·ler /'wiːdkɪlə^r/ *n* [U] a poison used for killing weeds

weeds /wiːdz/ *n* [P] *old use* black clothes worn at a funeral and sometimes for a period of time after that: *wearing her* **widow's weeds**

Weed Whacker /'wiːd ˌwakə^r/ *AmE tdmk* STRIMMER

weed·y /'wiːdi/ *adj infml derog* **1 a** thin and physically weak **b** weak in character **2** full of WEEDS¹ (1): *a weedy garden* —**iness** *n* [U]

Wee Free /ˌ· '·/ *n, adj infml, often derog* see FREE CHURCH OF SCOTLAND

week /wiːk/ *n* **1** a period of seven days (and nights), usu. measured in Britain from Monday to Sunday, but in the US and sometimes in Britain measured from Sunday to Saturday: *Wednesday is the third day of the week.* | *The flight to Accra goes twice a week.* | *I'll see you next week.*| *The training programme lasts three weeks.* **2** *also* **work·ing week**— the period of time during which one works in any seven days, for example in a factory or office. Most people in Britain work from Monday to Friday and work between 35 and 40 hours in total: *She works a 35-hour week.* | *The five-day week is usual in most firms.* **3 (Monday, Tuesday, etc.) week** *also* **a week on (Monday, Tuesday, etc.)—** *esp. BrE* a week after (the stated day): *She'll be here tomorrow week.* | *She's coming on Sunday week/a week on Sunday.* **4 (a) week last/next/ this/on (Monday, Tuesday, etc.)** a week before or after (the stated day): *It happened a week last Monday.* | *He's arriving two weeks next Saturday.* **5 week after week** *also* **week in week out—** continuously for many weeks: *He lay in bed week after week.*

week·day /'wiːkdeɪ/ *n* any day of the week except Sunday and usu. Saturday: *I only work on weekdays, not at weekends.*

week·end¹ /ˌwiːk'end, 'wiːkend‖'wiːkend/ *n* **1** Saturday and Sunday, esp. when considered as a holiday from work: *I don't work at weekends.* | *a weekend cottage* | *We're going for a* **long weekend** (=Saturday, Sunday, and also Friday and/or Monday) *to Paris.* **2** this period of time with the addition of Friday evening from the time of stopping work —see HOLIDAY (USAGE)

▷ USAGE In British English **at** is used with **weekend**: *I don't work* **at weekends**. | *What are you doing* **at the weekend?** In American English **on** is usually used: *I don't work* **weekends/on weekends**. | *What are you doing* **on the weekend?**◁

weekend² v [I+adv/prep] to spend the weekend: *We're weekending on the coast.*

week·end·er /ˌwiːkˈendəʳ‖ˈwiːkenˌ-/ n a person spending one or more weekends in a particular place: *They don't live here; they're only weekenders.*

week·ly¹ /ˈwiːkli/ adj, adv (happening or appearing) once a week or every week: *a weekly visit/magazine | the President's weekly radio talk | Are you paid weekly or monthly? | twice-weekly flights to Hong Kong*

weekly² n a magazine or newspaper which appears once a week

week·night /ˈwiːknaɪt/ n a night not at the weekend

wee·nie /ˈwiːni/ n AmE infml WIENER: *a weenie roast*

wee·ny /ˈwiːni/ BrE ‖ **weeney, ween·sie** /ˈwiːnzi/ AmE— adj infml extremely small —see also TEENY WEENY

weep /wiːp/ v **wept** /wept/ **1** [I (**over, for**);T] fml or lit to cry tears: *When he heard the news he broke down and wept. | She wept bitter tears over her lost youth.* —compare CRY¹ **2** [I] to lose liquid from a part of the body, esp. because of illness: *The wound is weeping.*

weep·ing /ˈwiːpɪŋ/ adj [A no comp.] (of a tree) with the branches hanging down: *a weeping willow*

weep·y /ˈwiːpi/ adj infml **1** tending to cry, or crying often; TEARFUL: *not very well, and feeling weepy* **2** (of a story, film, etc.) that makes one sad

Wee·ta·bix /ˈwiːtəbɪks/ n [U] tdmk a breakfast food popular in Britain, made with whole wheat and eaten in a bowl with milk

wee·vil /ˈwiːvəl/ n a small BEETLE which spoils grain, seeds, etc., by feeding on them

Wee Wil·lie Win·kie /ˌwiː ˌwɪli ˈwɪŋki/ a character in a NURSERY RHYME (=an old song or poem for children): *Wee Willie Winkie runs through the town, Upstairs and downstairs in his nightgown...*

weft /weft/ also **woof**— n [the+S] tech the threads of a material woven across the downward set of threads — compare WARP² (2)

weigh /weɪ/ v **1** [L+n] to have the stated weight: *It weighs six kilos. | I weigh less than I used to.* **2** [T] to find the weight of, esp. by using a machine: *Have you weighed yourself lately?* **3** [T (**against**)] to consider or compare carefully in order to form a judgment or make a decision: *He weighed the ideas in his mind. | You have to weigh the costs of the new system against the benefits it will bring.* —see also WEIGH up **4** [I ⊦ adv/prep, esp. with] fml to be important (to) or have influence (on): *Her evidence weighed quite strongly with the judge. | a new argument that weighed heavily in her favour* **5** [T] naut to raise (an ANCHOR)

  weigh sbdy./sthg. ↔ **down** phr v [T (**with**) often pass.] to make or cause to feel heavy (with a load): *I was weighed down with the shopping. | The branches of the trees were weighed down by snow. | (fig.) weighed down with grief/with debts*

  weigh in phr v [I] **1** [(**at**)] (of a BOXER or JOCKEY) to have one's weight tested before a fight or horse-race: *The champion weighed in at just under 13 stone.* **2** [(**with**)] infml to join in a fight or argument: *He weighed in (with information) to prove the point.*

  weigh on sthg./sbdy. phr v [T] to cause worry or great difficulty: *His responsibilities weighed on him. | The burden of debt weighs heavily on these developing countries.*

  weigh sthg. ↔ **out** phr v [T] to measure in amounts by weight: *The shopkeeper weighed out half a pound of coffee beans and ground them up.*

  weigh sthg./sbdy. **up** phr v [T] to (try to) form an opinion or judgment about, esp. by balancing opposing facts, influences, etc.: *We're just weighing up the advantages and disadvantages.*

weigh·bridge /ˈweɪˌbrɪdʒ/ n a machine for weighing vehicles and their loads, including a flat area onto which the vehicles are driven

weight¹ /weɪt/ n **1** [C;U] the heaviness of something, esp. as measured by a certain system; amount that something weighs: *Can you guess the weight of this sack? | It's two kilos in weight.* (=it weighs two kilos) | *She's* **lost weight/put on weight** (got thinner/fatter) *since I last saw her. | My husband has a bit of a* **weight problem.** **2** [C] a piece of metal that has a known heaviness and **a** can be balanced against something else in order to

measure its heaviness or **b** is lifted by people who want to develop large muscles or are competing in competitions —see also WEIGHT LIFTING **3** [C] (something with) a large amount of weight: *He's got a bad back so he can't lift weights.* **4** [U] a system of standard measures of weight: *metric weight* **5** [C (**on, off**)] (something that causes) a feeling of worry or anxiety: *The loss of the money has been a weight on my mind. | They've finally sold my house: that's a great weight off my mind.* **6** [U] the value, importance, or influence that someone or something has: *I don't* **attach any weight** *to these rumours.* (=I don't regard them as serious or believable) | *Don't worry what he thinks, his opinion doesn't* **carry much weight.** | *His declining health* **added weight** *to speculation that the king would soon abdicate.* **7 pull one's weight** to do one's full share of work: *My assistant hasn't been pulling her weight recently.* —see also PAPER-WEIGHT, **throw one's weight about** (THROW¹)

weight² v [T (**with**)] to put a weight on or add something heavy to: *Fishing nets are weighted.*

  weight sbdy./sthg. ↔ **down** phr v [T (**with**) usu. pass.] to load heavily; WEIGH **down**: *weighted down with her heavy bags*

weight·ed /ˈweɪtɪd/ adj [F (**in favour of, against**)] producing conditions favourable/unfavourable to a particular person or group: *These tests are weighted in favour of those people who have read the right books. | The voting system is weighted against the smaller parties.*

weight·ing /ˈweɪtɪŋ/ n [S;U] BrE something additional, esp. additional pay given because of the high cost of living in a certain area: *They got a London weighting of £1800 a year on top of their salaries.*

weight·less /ˈweɪtləs/ adj having no weight, e.g. when one is flying in space and free from the force of GRAVITY — ~ly adv — ~ness n [U]

weight lift·ing /ˈ· ˌ··/ also **weight training**— n [U] the sport or exercise of lifting specially shaped weights (WEIGHT¹ (26)) — -er n

Weight Watch·ers /ˈ· ˌ··/ tdmk a British and American organization that helps people who want to lose weight, esp. by dieting (DIET)

weight·y /ˈweɪti/ adj **1** heavy **2** fml important and serious: *weighty matters/decisions* —-ily adv —-iness n [U]

Weill /vaɪl/, **Kurt** /kɜːt‖kɜːrt/ (1900–50) a German COMPOSER (=writer of music) best known for *The Threepenny Opera*

Wei·mar /ˈvaɪmɑːʳ/ a city in what was formerly East Germany, a centre of industry and the arts, and the scene of the meeting which established the REPUBLICAN government (the **Weimar Republic**) in 1919

weir /wɪəʳ/ n **1** a wall-like structure across a river or stream which controls the flow of water **2** a wooden fence across a stream for catching fish

Weir, Peter (1944–) an Australian film DIRECTOR known esp. for the films *Gallipoli* and *Witness*

weird /wɪəd‖wɪərd/ adj **1** very strange; unnatural, mysterious, and/or frightening; EERIE: *It was a weird old house, full of creaks and groans.* **2** infml unusual and not sensible or acceptable; BIZARRE: *She has some weird ideas.* — ~ly adv — ~ness n [U]

weird·o /ˈwɪədəʊ‖ˈwɪər-/ also **weird·ie** /ˈwɪədi‖ˈwɪərdi/— n infml, sometimes derog a strange person, with unusual clothes, behaviour, etc. —**weirdo** adj [A] *a weirdo hair style...*

Weiss·mul·ler /ˈwaɪsmʌləʳ/, **John·ny** /ˈdʒɒni ‖ ˈdʒɑː-/ (1904–84) an American swimmer and film actor remembered esp. for playing the part of Tarzan

Wel·by /ˈwelbi/, **Mar·cus** /ˈmɑːkəs‖ˈmɑːr-/ a character from an American television show of the same name which was made in the 1970s. People often mention (Dr) Marcus Wellby when speaking of the perfect family doctor, always concerned and ready to be personally involved with his PATIENTS' problems.

welch /welʃ/ v [I (**on**)] to WELSH

Welch /weltʃ/, **Ra·quel** /ræˈkel/ (1940–) an American film star known for her beauty and her sexy figure

wel·come¹ /ˈwelkəm/ interj [(**to**)] (an expression of greeting to a guest or someone who has just arrived or returned): *Welcome to our home! | Welcome home/back!* (=when returning from another place) | *Welcome to England!*

welcome² *v* [T] **1** to greet (someone arriving in a new place) esp. with friendliness: *a welcoming smile* | *The Queen welcomed the President as he got off the plane.* **2** to be glad to accept; wish to have: *He doesn't welcome intrusions into his privacy.* | *I'd welcome any suggestions.*| *The college welcomes applications from people of all races.*

welcome³ *adj* **1** gladly accepted; received with pleasure: *a welcome suggestion* | *All suggestions will be welcome.*| *You are always welcome at our house.* | *He didn't* **make** *his guests very* **welcome.** (=did not receive them in a friendly way) **2** pleasant and likeable; AGREEABLE: *a welcome change* | *a welcome break from the pressures of work* **3** [F] freely allowed (to have or do) something, esp. when this is something that no one else wants: [+to] *If he wants that job he's welcome to it — I wouldn't take it for a million pounds!* [+to-v] *You're welcome to try, but you won't succeed.* **4 You're welcome** esp. AmE (a polite expression when thanked for something): *"Here's your pen." "Thank you!" "You're welcome."*

welcome⁴ *n* **1** a greeting given to someone when they arrive: *They gave us a* **warm welcome.** | (fig.) *Her suggestion received a rather unenthusiastic welcome.* **2 outstay/overstay one's welcome** to stay too long as a guest

welcome wag·on /'·· ,··/ *n AmE* a person, thing, or activity that welcomes someone to a new place: *The company is rolling out the welcome wagon for the new sales recruits.* | *She's the neighbourhood welcome wagon, she'll be over at the new people's house before they unpack their boxes.*

weld¹ /weld/ *v* [I;T (**to**, **TOGETHER**)] to join (usu. metals) or be joined by pressure or melting together when hot: *They welded a steel plate onto the plane's damaged wing.* | (fig.) *to weld a strong friendship* —compare FORGE¹ (2), SOLDER²

weld² *n* the part joined in welding: *a strong weld*

weld·er /'weldər/ *n* a person whose job is to make welded joints

wel·fare /'welfeər/ *n* [U] **1** health, comfort, and happiness; WELLBEING: *In making this decision, the court's main concern is for the welfare of the children.* **2** help provided for people with social problems, money difficulties, etc.: *The company's welfare officer deals with employees' personal problems.* | *welfare work* (=to improve life for poor people) **3** (in the US) (the system of) government money paid to people in special need: *Most of the families in this neighborhood are on* **welfare.** —see also FOOD STAMP, SOCIAL SECURITY; compare INCOME SUPPORT, SUPPLEMENTARY BENEFIT

welfare state /,·· '·||'·· ·/ *n* [C; *the*+S] (a country with) a system of social help provided by the state, esp. one which gives money to people who are poor or unemployed, provides medical treatment, etc.

wel·far·is·m /'welfeərizəm/ *n* [U] *AmE derog* a way of life in which one does not work and accepts money from the government in order to live and does not want this situation to change. Welfarism is a word used by people who think that there are too many government welfare programmes.

Welk /welk/, **Lawrence** (1902–92) an American band-leader who had a television programme in the 1950s and 1960s. He often said "a-one-and-a two-and-a" to give his band the beat before beginning to play.

wel·kin /'welkin/ *n* [*the*+S] *poet* the sky

well¹ /wel/ *adv* **better** /'betər/, **best** /best/ **1** in a good way; satisfactorily, kindly, successfully, etc.: *She sings very well.* | *He's always done his job extremely well.* | *a well-dressed young man* | *The party* **went well.** (=was successful) | *They* **speak** very **well of** *her* (=have a high opinion of her) *at school.* | *The business is* **doing well.** (=succeeding) | *She* **did** well (=gained a good profit) **out** *of the sale of her house.* | *She's been doing better at school since the new teacher arrived.* —opposites **badly, ill 2** thoroughly: *Wash it well before you dry it.* | *I'm* **well aware** *of the problems.* | *I know him quite well.* | *They were well beaten.* | *The pyramids are well worth seeing.*| (*BrE sl*) *He was well fed up.* (=extremely annoyed) **3** [+*adv/prep*] much; quite: *Profits were well above our original forecast.* | *He finished the exam well within the time allowed.* | *It's a popular hotel, so you'll need to make your reservations well in advance.* **4** justly, wisely, or properly: *I couldn't very well say no when there was no one else she could ask.* | *You did well to tell me.* (=it was a sensible thing to do) | *"Why wasn't she at the meeting?"*

"You **may well ask***!"* (=we were all wondering) **5 as well: a** in addition; also; too: *I'm going to London and my sister's coming as well.* **b** with as good a result: *The weather was so bad we* **might (just) as well** *have stayed at home.* **6 as well as** in addition to (being): *He was kind as well as sensible.* **7 (it's) just as well** (as a reply) it is fortunate (that); there's no harm done: *"We were too late to see the film." "Just as well; I hear it isn't very good."* **8 very well** *rather fml* (used as a form of agreement, but often with some degree of unwillingness): *"You ought to take a coat with you." "Oh very well, if I must."* **9 (all) well and good** esp. *BrE* not really good enough: *Dishwashers are all well and good, but washing-up by hand gets things cleaner.* **10 well and truly** *infml* completely: *George was well and truly drunk.* **11 Well done!** (said when someone has been successful): *You've passed your driving test — well done!* —see also WELL-DONE **12 well away: a** getting ahead: *We're well away on the rebuilding of the house.* **b** *infml, esp. BrE* starting to be drunk **13 well in with** having a good relationship (esp. with someone important or influential): *She's very well in with the sales director.* **14 well out of** *BrE infml* lucky to be free from: *She's well out of that marriage; they were never suited.* **15 well up in/on** esp. *BrE infml* well informed about: *She's well up in the latest fashions.* —see also **pretty well** (PRETTY²)

well² *interj* **1** an expression of surprise: *She's got a new job. Well, well!* **2** (used for introducing an expression of surprise, doubt, acceptance, etc.): *Well, really, what a stupid thing to do!* | *Well, I'm not sure.* | *Well, all right, I agree.* **3** (used when continuing a story): *Well, then she said ...* **4 oh well!** (used for showing cheerfulness when something bad has happened): *Oh well, I can't complain; it was my own fault.*

well³ *adj* **better, best 1** in good health: *She's been ill a lot recently but she's looking very well now/she's looking much better now.* | *I don't feel at all well today.* **2** [F] *esp. lit or old-fash* in an acceptable state; satisfactory; right: *All's well that ends well.* (proverb) **3 it's all very well** (an expression of dissatisfaction when comparing what is practical to what is suggested): *It's all very well for you to criticize, but could you have done any better yourself?*

well⁴ *n* **1** a place where water can be taken from underground: *The old well in the village had a wall round it and a bucket that could be lowered for water.* | *to* **sink a well** (=dig a hole to obtain water) *in order to irrigate the desert* | *well water* —see also WISHING WELL **2** an OIL WELL **3** an enclosed space in a building running straight up and down, for example for a LIFT² (2) to travel in —see also STAIRWELL **4** *BrE* the space in front of the judge in a law court

well⁵ *v* [I+*adv/prep*] (of liquid) to flow or start to flow: *Blood* **welled (out)** *from the cut.* | *She was so angry that tears* **welled (up)** *in her eyes*

we'll /wil; *strong* wiːl/ *short for:* **1** we will **2** we shall

well-ad·jus·ted /,·· ·'··◂/ *adj* (of a person) fitting in well with society and being emotionally healthy

well-ad·vised /,·· ·'·◂/ *adj* sensible; wise: *a well-advised plan* [F+*to-v*] *You would be well-advised to see the doctor about that pain.*

well-ap·point·ed /,·· ·'··◂/ *adj fml* having all the necessary furniture, services, equipment, etc.: *a well-appointed hotel*

well-bal·anced /,·· '··◂/ *adj* **1** (of a person) sensible and not controlled by unreasonable feelings; STABLE **2** (of a meal or way of eating) containing the right amounts of what is good for the body: *a well-balanced diet*

well-be·haved /,·· ·'·◂/ *adj* (usu. of children) behaving in a socially acceptable and polite way: *The children were very well-behaved on the train.*

well-be·ing /,wel'biːɪŋ||'wel,biːɪŋ/ *n* [U] personal and physical comfort, esp. good health and happiness: *The warm sunny weather always gives me a* **sense of wellbeing.**

well-born /,·· '·◂/ *adj fml* born of an UPPER-CLASS family

well-bred /,·· '·◂/ *adj old-fash* (typical of someone) coming from a family of high social class, esp. in having good manners

well-brought-up /,·· · '·◂/ *adj* (usu. of children) very polite and having good manners: *That little boy has been very well-brought-up.*

well-cho·sen /,·· '··◂/ *adj* chosen with care: *He replied to* *the vote of thanks with* **a few well-chosen words.** (=a short but suitable speech)

well-con·nect·ed /ˌ·ˌ·ˈ·-◄/ *adj* knowing people of power and social importance, esp. being related to them

well-de·fined /ˌ·ˌ·-◄/ *adj* clear in form or nature; easily recognizable: *The trees are well-defined in the picture.* | *well-defined limits*

well-dis·posed /ˌ·ˌ·ˈ·-◄/ *adj* [(towards)] tending to be friendly, sympathetic, or favourable (towards a person or idea): *a well-disposed nature* | *The management is not well-disposed towards technical innovation.*

well-done /ˌ·ˈ·-◄/ *adj* (of food, esp. meat) cooked for quite a long time, so that it is cooked all the way through — compare RARE²; see also **Well done!** (WELL¹)

well-dressed /ˌ·ˈ·-◄/ *adj* wearing attractive, stylish, and usu. expensive clothes

Welles /welz/, **Or·son** /ˈɔːsən‖ˈɔːr/ (1915–85) an American actor, director, and producer, whose famous works include his radio production of *The War of the Worlds* and his film *Citizen Kane*

well-earned /ˌ·ˈ·-◄/ *adj* much deserved: *a well-earned rest after so much hard work*

well-es·tab·lished /ˌ·ˌ·ˈ·-◄/ *adj* established for a number of years and so well known and respected: *a well-established firm of solicitors*

well-fa·voured /ˌ·ˈ·-◄/ *adj old-fash* (of a person) having an attractive appearance

well-fed /ˌ·ˈ·-◄/ *adj* **1** eating good, healthy food **2** fat; PLUMP

well-found /ˌ·ˈ·-◄/ *adj tech* (esp. of a ship) having all the necessary equipment; WELL-APPOINTED

well-found·ed /ˌ·ˈ·-◄/ *adj* based on facts or good judgment: *Our suspicions were well-founded; she turned out to be a thief.*

well-groomed /ˌ·ˈ·-◄/ *adj* having a very neat clean appearance, as if special care has been taken: *a well-groomed horse/woman/lawn*

well-ground·ed /ˌ·ˈ·-◄/ *adj* **1** [F (in)] fully instructed or trained: *The soldiers were well-grounded in the skills needed to survive in the desert.* **2** well-founded

well-heeled /ˌ·ˈ·-◄/ *adj infml* rich

well-hung /ˌ·ˈ·-◄/ *adj taboo apprec sl* **1** (of a man) having a large sex organ **2** *rare* (of a woman) having large breasts

wel·lie /ˈweli/ *n BrE infml* a WELLINGTON —see also GREEN WELLIE BRIGADE

well-in·formed /ˌ·ˌ·-◄/ *adj* **1** knowing a lot about several subjects **2** having good information about a particular subject; having good general knowledge: *According to a well-informed source, one of the President's leading advisers is going to resign.*

wel·ling·ton /ˈwelɪŋtən/ also **wellington boot** /ˌ···ˈ·/, **welly, wellie** *infml* ‖ **rubber boot** *AmE*— *n esp. BrE* a rubber boot which keeps water from the feet and lower part of the legs —see picture at SHOE

Wellington¹ the capital city of New Zealand, on the North Island, the country's second-largest city and a main port

Wellington², **Duke of** (1769–1852) a British soldier and politician best known for defeating Napoleon at Waterloo and serving as PRIME MINISTER (1828–30)

well-in·ten·tioned /ˌ·ˌ·-◄/ *adj* acting with kind, friendly, or sensible intentions, though often with unfortunate or unwanted results: *a well-intentioned effort to help*

well-kept /ˌ·ˈ·-◄/ *adj* **1** well looked after or cared for: *a well-kept garden* **2** (of a secret) known only to very few people

well-known /ˌ·ˈ·-◄/ *adj* known by many people: *a well-known fact/face/saying* | *It is well-known that too much sugar is bad for you.* | *one of the best-known opera singers of recent years* —see FAMOUS (USAGE)

well-lined /ˌ·ˈ·-◄/ *adj infml* **1** full of money: *well-lined pockets* **2** (of the stomach) full of food

well-mean·ing /ˌ·ˈ·-◄/ *adj* well-intentioned: *a well-meaning person/effort* —see also **mean well** (MEAN²)

well-meant /ˌ·ˈ·-◄/ *adj* said or done for a good or kind purpose though not with a good result: *Her help was well-meant, but it just made the job take longer.* —see also **mean well** (MEAN²)

We'll Meet A·gain /ˌ·ˌ·ˈ·/ a sad song thought of in connection with the singer Vera Lynn about people meeting again after being separated, and popular esp. during the Second World War

well-nigh /ˈ·ˈ·/ *adv fml BrE or AmE sl* almost: *well-nigh impossible*

well-off /ˌ·ˈ·-◄/ *adj* **better-off, best-off** **1** rich: *The government claims that some people are better-off than they were five years ago.* [also *n*, *the* + P] something which only the well-off can afford **2** [F (for)] having quite a lot: *We're quite well-off for good shops in this neighbourhood.* **3** [F] fortunate: *The trouble with you is* **you don't know when you're well off.** (=you're more fortunate than you know) —opposite **badly-off**; see also OFF¹ (10)

well-oiled /ˌ·ˈ·-◄/ *adj sl* drunk

well-paid /ˌ·ˈ·-◄/ *adj* (used of work, etc.) offering good payment: *a well-paid job* | *The work isn't very well paid.*

well-pre·served /ˌ·ˌ·-◄/ *adj apprec or euph* (of a person who is old or no longer young) showing few of the usual signs of age, esp. still in good physical condition

well-pro·por·tioned /ˌ·ˌ·-◄/ *adj apprec* having an attractive size or shape; having good PROPORTIONS

well-read /ˌwel ˈred◄/ *adj* having read a lot of books and gained a lot of useful information, esp. in many different subjects

well-round·ed /ˌ·ˈ·-◄/ *adj* **1** (of a person) having a full, pleasantly curved shape; SHAPELY **2** (esp. of a person's experience) full of different types of activity; complete and varied: *a well-rounded education* | *The new manager has a well-rounded background in the banking industry.*

Wells /welz/, **H G** (1866–1946) an English writer and social thinker whose books include *The Time Machine, The War of the Worlds*, and *Outline of History*

well-set /ˌ·ˈ·-◄/ *adj becoming rare* strong and with good muscles: *The young man was short but well-set.*

well-spok·en /ˌ·ˈ·-◄/ *adj* having an educated and socially acceptable way of speaking

well·spring /ˈwelˌsprɪŋ/ *n* [(of)] *esp. lit* a never-ending supply

well-thought-of /ˌ·ˈ· ·-◄/ *adj* (of a person) liked and admired generally

well-thought-out /ˌ·ˌ·ˈ·-◄/ *adj* considered in detail: *a well-thought-out plan of campaign*

well-thumbed /ˌ·ˈ·-◄/ *adj* (of a book, its pages, etc.) showing signs of having been well used, thoroughly read, esp. by being dirty, creased (CREASE²(1)), etc.: *a few well-thumbed paperbacks*

well-timed /ˌ·ˈ·-◄/ *adj* said or done at the most suitable time; OPPORTUNE: *well-timed advice*

well-to-do /ˌ·ˌ·ˈ·-◄/ *adj infml* rich; AFFLUENT: [also *n*, *the* + P] *luxury homes for the well-to-do*

well-tried /ˌ·ˈ·-◄/ *adj* often used before and known to work well: *well-tried methods*

well-turned /ˌ·ˈ·-◄/ *adj* (of a phrase) carefully formed and expressed in a pleasing way: *a well-turned compliment*

well-versed /ˌ·ˈ·-◄/ *adj* knowing a lot about something: *She's well-versed in office politics.*

well-wish·er /ˈ·ˌ·-/ *n* a person giving good wishes to another: *Crowds of well-wishers gathered outside the hospital, waiting for a report on the President's operation.*

well-worn /ˌ·ˈ·-◄/ *adj* **1** worn or used for a long time **2** (of a phrase) with little meaning, because used too often; HACKNEYED: *a well-worn cliché*

wel·ly /ˈweli/ *n BrE* **1** [C] *infml* a WELLINGTON **2** [U] *sl* effort; power

welsh, welch /welʃ/ *v* [I (on)] *derog* **1** to avoid payment: *He welshed on his debts.* **2** to fail to fulfil a promise: *She welshed on her promises.* — ~**er** *n*

▷ USAGE This verb is considered offensive by Welsh people.◁

Welsh *n* **1** [*the*+P] the people of Wales **2** [U] the CELTIC language of the people of Wales: *Do you speak Welsh?* — **Welsh** *adj* : *His voice has a distinct Welsh lilt.*

Welsh dres·ser /ˌ·ˈ··/ *BrE* ‖ **hutch** *AmE*— *n* a piece of furniture consisting of drawers and cupboards up to around waist level, and then shelves to a height of about six feet, often used to DISPLAY plates, cups, etc.

Welsh Guards /ˌ· ˈ·/ [the + P] a REGIMENT (=large division of men) in the British army used for ceremonies and previously to protect the king or queen. The Welsh Guards was formerly made up of men from Wales.

Welsh Na·tion·al·ist Par·ty /ˌ· ˈ···· ˌ··/ PLAID CYMRU

Welsh Na·tion·al·ists /ˌ· ˈ····/ n [P] Welsh people who want their rule to be independent from the government in London —see also PLAID CYMRU

Welsh National Op·e·ra /ˌ· ˌ··· ˈ···/ an OPERA company based in, and occasionally touring, Wales which is partly supported by government money

Welsh Of·fice /ˈ· ˌ··/ [the] a British government department responsible for certain services, such as health, in Wales

Welsh rare·bit /ˌwelʃ ˈreəbɪt‖-ˈreər-/ also **welsh rab·bit** /ˌ· ˈ··/— n a small meal of cheese melted on bread, sometimes with other things added, such as milk and beer

Welsh Wa·ter /ˌ· ˈ··/ a water company in Wales that deals with the supply of water to people and businesses and the removal and treatment of SEWAGE

welt /welt/ n **1** a piece of leather round the edge of a shoe to which the top and bottom are stitched **2** a raised mark on the skin where one has been hit, esp. with a whip

wel·ter /ˈweltəʳ/ n [S+of] a disordered mixture: *The researchers were buried under a welter of data.*

wel·ter·weight /ˈweltəweɪt‖-ər-/ n a BOXER (1) heavier than a LIGHTWEIGHT but lighter than a MIDDLEWEIGHT

Wem·bley /ˈwembli/ a place in London with a large STADIUM where important sports events such as the FA CUP final are held every year. There is also a large hall there used for popular music concerts.

wench[1] /wentʃ/ n old use or lit a girl or young woman, esp. in a country area: *A serving wench brought us our ale.*

wench[2] v [I] old use to have sex with many women, such as PROSTITUTES

wend /wend/ v **wend one's way** esp. lit to move or travel over a distance, esp. slowly: (fig.) *The new law is currently wending its way through Parliament.*

Wen·dy /ˈwendi/ one of the Darling children who were visited by Peter Pan in the story *Peter Pan* by J M Barrie —see also PETER PAN and see colour picture on page 619

wen·dy house /ˈ·· ˌ·/ BrE‖**play house** AmE— n a small house for children to play in, often made of cloth and about 1–2 metres high

Wen·dy's /ˈwendiz/ a FAST-FOOD restaurant in the US which serves mainly HAMBURGERS

Wens·ley·dale /ˈwenzlideɪl/ n [U] a not very strong white cheese made originally in Yorkshire

went /went/ past tense of GO

We Plough the Fields and Scat·ter /ˌ· ˌ· ˌ· · ˈ··/ a religious song (HYMN) sung in Britain at Harvest Festival

wept /wept/ past tense & participle of WEEP

were /wəʳ; strong wɜːʳ/ negative short form **weren't** /wɜːnt ‖ ˈwɜːrənt, wɜːrnt/ past tense of BE

we're /wɪəʳ; strong wiːəʳ/ short for: we are

were·wolf /ˈweəwulf, ˈwɪə-‖ˈweər-, ˈwɪər-/ n -**wolves** /wulvz/ (in stories) a person who sometimes turns into a WOLF, esp. when there is a full moon

wert /wɜːt‖wɜːrt/ thou wert old use or bibl (when talking to one person) you were

We Shall O·ver·come /ˌ· · ˌ·· ˈ·/ a song which was popular during the CIVIL RIGHTS MOVEMENT in the US, when it was often sung at meetings and marches. It is still sung by groups who are fighting against unfair treatment.

Wes·ley /ˈwezli, ˈwes-/, **John** (1703–91) an Englishman who established METHODISM and whose writings and teachings became the principles of the Methodist Church

Wes·ley·an /ˈwezliən, ˈwes-/ n, adj (a member) of the branch of the PROTESTANT church established by John Wesley —see also METHODISM

Wes·sex /ˈwesɪks/ one of the ANGLO-SAXON kingdoms of England including Hampshire, Dorset, Wiltshire, Berkshire, Somerset, and Devon. Thomas Hardy used the name Wessex for the SW counties (COUNTY) in his books.

Wessex Wa·ter /ˌ··· ˈ··/ a water company in SW England that deals with the supply of water to people and businesses and the removal and treatment of SEWAGE

west[1] /west/ (abbrev. W) n (often cap.) **1** [the+S;U] the direction towards which the sun sets; the direction which is on the left of a person facing north: *I'm lost — which direction is West?* | *A strange light appeared in the west.* | *Heathrow Airport is a few kilometres to the west of London.* **2** [the+S] the western part of a country: *The rain will spread to the West later.* —see NORTH[2] (USAGE)

west[2] adj [A] **1** (sometimes cap.) in the west or facing the west: *You enter the church through the west door.* | *They live in West Germany/West Beirut.* **2** (of a wind) coming from the west: *a gentle west wind*

west[3] adv (often cap.) **1** towards the west: *The room faces west, so we get the evening sun.* | *The plane flew west.* | *Brest is (a long way) west of Paris.* **2 go west** BrE humor **a** to die **b** to be damaged or ruined **3 Go west young man** a phrase used when advising someone to go somewhere new to start a new and better life (originally in the American West)

West[1] n [the] **1** (the people of) the western part of the world, esp. western Europe and North America: *Leaders of the West are meeting Soviet leaders in Geneva today.* | *an improvement in East-West relations* **2** also **American West** the western part of the US, including the states of Washington, Oregon, California, Arizona, New Mexico, Colorado, Utah, Nevada, Idaho, Wyoming, Montana, and parts of Texas. States east of these are called the MIDWEST. Associations with the American West include the WILD WEST, COWBOYS, and NATIVE AMERICANS. —compare MIDWEST, PACIFIC NORTHWEST, WEST COAST, WILD WEST

West[2], **Mae** /meɪ/ (1892–1980) an American actress who was a SEX SYMBOL of the 1930s, and is remembered for the phrase "Come up and see me sometime"

West[3], **Tim·o·thy** /ˈtɪməθi/ (1934–) an English actor who appeared in *The Day of the Jackal* and *The Thirty-Nine Steps* among many other cinema and television performances

West Bank /ˈ· ·/ [the] the land W of the Jordan River and the Dead Sea between Israel and Jordan, which is occupied (OCCUPY) by the Israelis but which the Palestinian Arabs, together with the Gaza Strip, consider to be their land. After the 1967 war, the UN Security Council asked the Israelis to leave this area. —compare EAST BANK

west·bound /ˈwestbaʊnd/ adj travelling or leading towards the west: *westbound traffic* | *the westbound side of the motorway*

West Coast /ˈ· ˌ·/ [the] the western coastal states of the US, esp. California, but also Oregon and Washington State. The West Coast, because it mainly means California, is connected with good weather, sunny BEACHes, a sense of freedom, and people who do not have a CONVENTIONAL life. People from Oregon and Washington State are often thought of as deep-thinking nature-lovers. —compare EAST COAST, WEST, WILD WEST; see also CALIFORNIA, PACIFIC NORTHWEST

West Coun·try /ˈ· ˌ··/ [the] the south-west of England

West End /ˌ· ˈ·◂/ [the] the western part of central London considered a fashionable place, where large or important shops, theatres, etc., are: *a West End show* —see colour map on page 817

west·er·ly /ˈwestəli‖-ərli/ adj **1** towards or in the west: *We set off in a westerly direction.* **2** (of a wind) coming from the west: *a light westerly breeze*

west·ern[1] /ˈwestən‖-ərn/ adj [no comp.] (often cap.) of or belonging to the west part of the world or of a country: *The Russian ballet is making a tour of Western Europe.* | *Western values* —see NORTH[2] (USAGE)

western[2] n also **cowboy film** BrE ‖also **cowboy movie** AmE— (often cap.) a film about life in the American WEST (2) in the past, esp. about COWBOYS, horses, and gunfights. They are not usu. based on fact. —see WILD WEST; see also COUNTRY AND WESTERN

Western Aus·tra·li·a /ˌ··· ˌ·· ·ˈ···/ the largest state of Australia, whose capital is Perth

West·ern·er /ˈwestənəʳ‖-tər-/ n **1** someone who lives in or comes from the WEST (1) **2** AmE someone who lives in or comes from the WEST (2)

Western Front /ˌ··· ˈ·/ [the] areas of France and Belgium where many battles of the First World War were fought

Western Isles /ˌ··· ˈ·/ [the + P] a REGION in NW Scotland consisting of the Outer Hebrides islands of Harris, Lewis, N and S Uist, and Barra

west·ern·ize also **-ise** *BrE* /ˈwestənaɪz‖-ər-/ *v* [T] to cause or influence (esp. African or Asian people and countries) to have or copy the customs and behaviour typical of America and Europe: *Although she's a Muslim, she's very westernized in her dress.* —**ization** /ˌwestənaɪˈzeɪʃ*ə*n‖-ərnə-/ *n* [U]

Western medi·cine /ˌ··ˈ···‖ˌ··ˈ···/ *n* [U] the science and practice of medicine that is standard in the West — compare ALTERNATIVE MEDICINE

west·ern·most /ˈwestənməʊst‖-tər-/ *adj* [no comp.] furthest west: *the westernmost parts of Scotland*

West Ger·ma·ny /ˌ·ˈ····/ also **Federal Republic of Germany** a former country in W Europe, established in 1949 and joined with East Germany after the fall of the Berlin Wall in 1989–90 —**West German** *n, adj*

West Gla·mor·gan /ˌwest gləˈmɔːgən‖-ˈmɔːr-/ a COUNTY in S Wales which includes the city of Swansea

West Ham /ˌ·ˈ·/ also **the Hammers** *infml*— a British football team based in the area of the same name in E London

West In·di·an /ˌ·ˈ····/ *adj* of or from the West Indies: *West Indian cooking*

West In·dies /ˌwest ˈɪndiz/ [*the* + P] the islands lying between SE North America and N South America including the Bahamas, Cuba, Jamaica, Puerto Rico, Barbados, Dominica, etc.

West·ing·house /ˈwestɪŋhaʊs/ an American company that makes many different products, esp. connected with electronics and lighting

West·land Af·fair /ˈwestlənd əˌfeəʳ/ [*the*] a disagreement in 1986 among members of the British government about the sale of a company called Westland, which made HELICOPTERS, to non-British owners, and also about secret government information being made public. Michael Heseltine, an important minister, left the government over this affair.

West Lo·thi·an /ˌ·ˈ····/ a former COUNTY in central Scotland, now part of Lothian REGION

West Mid·lands /ˌ·ˈ··/ [*the* +P] a former METROPOLITAN COUNTY in central England

West·min·ster /ˈwestmɪnstəʳ, westˈmɪnstəʳ◂/ **1** the main part of central London containing Westminster Abbey, the Houses of Parliament, Buckingham Palace and other important historic buildings **2** the HOUSES OF PARLIAMENT: *There's concern at Westminster about the closure of…*

Westminster Ab·bey /ˌ···ˈ···/ a very large GOTHIC church in Westminster, London. Almost all English kings and queens since William I have been crowned (CROWN) in the Abbey and many famous people are buried there —see colour map on page 817

Westminster Abbey

Westminster School /ˌ···ˈ·/ a PUBLIC school in London

West·mor·land /ˈwestmələnd‖-mɔːr-/ a former COUNTY of NW England, now part of Cumbria

West Point /ˌ·ˈ·/ a US military post on the Hudson River, N of New York City, where the **United States Military Academy** is based —compare SANDHURST

West Ri·ding /ˌ·ˈ··/ [*the*] a former COUNTY of central N England, now mainly contained in the present county of West Yorkshire

West Side Sto·ry /ˌ·· ·ˈ··/ *n* a musical play, also made into a film, about life in the streets of New York by Leonard Bernstein

West Sus·sex /ˌ·ˈ··/ a COUNTY in S England

West Vir·gin·i·a /ˌ·· ·ˈ···/ *written abbrev.* **WV** a mountainous state of the US in the E central part of the country —see colour map on pages 1374–5

west·ward /ˈwestwəd‖-wərd/ *adj* going towards the west: *a westward journey* | *in a westward direction*

west·wards /ˈwestwədz‖-wərdz/ also **westward**— *adv* towards the west: *We sailed westwards.* —see also WEST³

West York·shire /ˌ·ˈ···/ a COUNTY in NE England

wet¹ /wet/ *adj* **1** covered with liquid or in a liquid state; not dry: *I can't go out until my hair's dry; it's still wet from being washed.* | *wet ground* | *wet paint* (=which has not yet dried) | *I went out in the rain and got wet through.* (=extremely wet) **2** rainy: *wet weather* | *a wet day* | *We can't go out, it's too wet.* **3** *BrE infml derog* (of a person) lacking strength of character and unwilling to take firm or forceful action; weak: *Don't be so wet! Just tell them you refuse to do it.* **4 (still) wet behind the ears** *infml* very young and without experience – **~ly** *adv* – **~ness** *n* [U]

wet² *n* **1** [*the*+S] rainy weather: *What a horrible day! It's good to get in out of the wet.* **2** [*the*+S] wet ground, esp. after rain: *Come and walk on the dry road, instead of going through the wet.* **3** [C] *BrE infml* a politically MODERATE¹ (3) person in the British Conservative Party: *a leading wet*

wet³ *v* **wet** *or* **wetted** [T] **1** to make wet: *Wet your finger and hold it up; the side that dries is the side the wind's blowing from.* **2** to make (oneself, one's bed, or one's clothes) wet by passing water from the body uncontrollably **3 wet one's whistle** *humor* to have a drink, esp. of alcohol, when one is thirsty

▷ USAGE In British English the past tense and past participle are usually **wetted** except in phrases like **wet the bed** or **wet oneself**: *Billy's wet the bed again!*◁

wet·back /ˈwetbæk/ *n derog, AmE sl* a person from Mexico who is in the US illegally (considered offensive). The name comes from the fact that many Mexicans cross the Rio Grande River between the two countries in order to avoid IMMIGRATION officials at the border —see also ILLEGAL ALIEN

wet blan·ket /ˌ· ·ˈ··‖ˌ· ·ˌ··/ *n infml derog* a person who discourages others or prevents them from enjoying themselves: *Can't we stay a bit longer? Don't be such a wet blanket!*

wet dream /ˌ· ·ˈ·/ *n* a sexually exciting dream resulting in a male ORGASM

wet-look /ˈ· ·/ *adj* [A] (esp. of a garment) having a shiny surface, as if wet: *a wet-look leather coat*

wet nurse /ˈ· ·/ *n* a woman employed to give breast milk to another woman's baby

wet-nurse *v* [T] **1** to act as a wet nurse to **2** *derog* to treat with too much care; MOLLYCODDLE

wet suit /ˈ· ·/ *n* a usu. rubber garment worn by underwater swimmers, surfers (SURF²), etc., which allows some water to go through, but keeps them warm by fitting close to the body

wet·ting /ˈwetɪŋ/ *n infml* being wetted unpleasantly by rain, sea, etc.: *She got a real wetting when she fell in the harbour.*

wetting a·gent /ˈ·· ˌ··/ *n* a chemical substance which, when spread on a solid surface, makes it hold liquid

wetting so·lu·tion /ˈ·· ·ˌ··/ *n* [U] a liquid which is put on CONTACT LENSES

we've /wiv; *strong* wiːv/ *short for:* we have

Wex·ford /ˈweksfəd‖-fərd/ a COUNTY in the SE Republic of Ireland, with a county town of the same name

whack¹ /wæk/ *v* [T] *infml* to hit with a noisy blow

whack² *n infml* **1** (the noise made by) a hard blow **2** [*usu. sing.*] *BrE* a (fair or equal) share: *Have you all had your whack?* —see also **top whack** (TOP¹) **3** [*usu. sing.*] *BrE* a try; attempt: *If you can't open it, let me* **have a whack at it.**

whacked /wækt/ also **whacked out** /ˌ· ·ˈ·/— *adj* [F] *BrE infml* very tired: *I'm completely whacked.*

whack·ing¹ /ˈwækɪŋ/ *adj, adv infml* very (big): *a whacking (great) orange*

whacking² *n infml, esp. BrE* a beating

whack·y /ˈwæki/ *adj* WACKY

whale /weɪl/ *n* **1** an extremely large animal which lives in the sea and looks like a fish but is a MAMMAL. So many whales have been killed that they are in danger of dying out. People who are concerned about the environment sometimes wear BADGES which say "Save the Whales": *The blue whale is the world's largest living animal.* **2 a whale of a time** *infml* a very enjoyable time: *We had a whale of a time at the party.*

whale·bone /ˈweɪlbəʊn/ n [U] a material taken from the upper jaw of whales, used in former times for keeping things stiff and in their proper shape: *a whalebone corset*

whal·er /ˈweɪləʳ/ n **1** someone who hunts whales at sea **2** a ship or boat from which whales are hunted

whal·ing /ˈweɪlɪŋ/ n [U] the business of hunting whales and treating them in order to obtain oil and other materials

wham /wæm/ n *infml* (the sound made by) a hard, heavy blow

wharf /wɔːf‖wɔːrf/ n **wharfs** or **wharves** /wɔːvz‖wɔːrvz/ a place, usu. like a wide stone wall built on the edge of the sea or river, where ships can be tied up to unload goods

what¹ /wɒt‖waːt, wʌt/ *predeterminer, determiner, pron* **1 a** (used in questions about an unknown thing or person, or kind of thing or person): *What are you doing?* | *What colour is it?* | *What time will you arrive?* | *"What do you do?" "I'm a teacher."* | *What's your new boss like?* (=give me a description of him/her) **b** (used in asking someone to repeat or explain something they have said): *"I got up at 4 o'clock this morning." "What?|What did you say?|*(shows surprise) *You did what?"* **2** the thing or things that: *I believed what he told me.* | *She told me what to do.* | *He pointed to what looked like a tree.* | *Show me what you bought.* | *I gave them what books I've had.* (=the books I had, although I did not have many) (not *what book I had*) | *We're very grateful for what you did.* | *The President is determined to resist what he regards as blackmail by the terrorists.* | *What worries me is how we're going to pay for all this.* **3** (shows surprise, pleasure, annoyance, or other strong feeling): *What a strange thing to say!* | *What a pity!* (compare *How sad!*) | *What beautiful weather!* | *What a fool that man is!* **4** *infml* (used to introduce a suggestion or a piece of information) something: *I'll tell you what – let's go swimming.* | *Guess what! Jane's getting married.* **5 what (...) for?** *infml* a why?: *"I'm going to Paris." "What for?"* **b** for which purpose?: *What's this thing for?* (=tell me its purpose) **6 what have you** *infml* anything (else) like that: *The abandoned office was full of documents, books, and what have you.* **7 what if ?** (esp. in making suggestions) what will happen if ?: *What if we move the picture over here? Do you think it'll look better?* **8 what it takes** the qualities necessary to be successful: *Do you think she's got what it takes?* **9 what 'of it?** why should I care? why is that important? **10 what's his/her/their/its name** also **what d'you call him/her/them/it**– *infml* (used when speaking about a person or thing whose name one cannot remember): *Mary's gone out with what's his name – you know, the boy with the red car.* –compare WHATCH-AMACALLIT **11 what's more** and this is more important: *The new system is cheaper, and what's more, it's better.* **12 what's what** *infml* the true state of things: *You can't fool him; he knows what's what.* **13 what the ... ?** (used with various words, such as **hell, devil, blazes,** etc. when asking angry or surprised questions) (=what): *What the hell do you want?* | *What the devil did they do that for?* –see also **what about** (ABOUT¹); see HOW (USAGE), WHICH (USAGE)

what² *adv* **1** (used esp. in questions when no answer is expected) in what way; to what degree: *What do you care about it?* (=I don't think you care at all) | *We may be a little late, but what does it matter?* **2 what with** (used for introducing the cause of something, esp. something bad): *What with all this work and so little sleep at nights, I don't think I can go on much longer.*

what·cha·ma·call·it /ˈwɒtʃəməkɔːlɪt ‖ ˈwɑt-, ˈwʌt-/ n *infml* (used when speaking about a thing whose name one cannot remember): *I broke the whatchamacallit off the car door.* | *Pass me that whatchamacallit–there.* –see also DOODAH, DOOHICKEY, THINGAMAJIG; compare **what's his/her/their/its name** (WHAT¹ (10))

what·ev·er¹ /wɒtˈevəʳ‖wɑːt-, wʌt-/ also **what·so·ev·er** /ˌwɒtsəʊˈevəʳ‖ˌwɑːt-, ˌwʌt-/fml or lit– *determiner, pron* **1** any(thing) at all that: *Goats eat whatever (food) they can find.* **2** no matter what; without considering what: *Whatever I suggest, he always disagrees.* | *Don't keep him waiting* **whatever you do.** (=it is very important that you don't keep him waiting) | *She refuses, for whatever reason.* (=the reason why is not important) | *The building must be saved, whatever the cost.*

whatever² *pron* **1** *infml* anything (else) like that: *Anyone seen carrying bags, boxes, or whatever, was stopped by the*

police. **2** (shows surprise) what: *Look at that strange animal! Whatever is it?* | *Joe's getting married? Whatever next!* **3** *infml* (used when replying to an offer or suggestion, esp. to show a lack of interest): *"Shall I call you tonight or tomorrow?" "Whatever."* (=I don't care which)

whatever³ also **what·so·ev·er** /ˌwɒtsəʊˈevəʳ‖ˌwɑːt-, ˌwʌt-/– *adj* [after *n*; *in questions or negatives*] at all: *I have no money whatever.*

what for /ˌ· ˈ·/ n [U] *infml, esp. BrE* punishment: *If she finds out what you've done she'll* **give you what for!**

what·not /ˈwɒtnɒt‖ˈwɑːtnɑːt, ˈwʌt-/ n **1** [U] *infml* anything (else): *carrying his bags and whatnot* **2** [C] a piece of furniture with open shelves, used, esp. in Victorian times, for showing small decorations

whats·it /ˈwɒtsɪ̩t‖ˈwɑːts-, ˈwʌts-/ n *infml* a small object, such as a small piece of machinery, whose proper name one cannot remember: *I can't unfasten the whatsit; will you try?*

What's On /ˌ· ˈ·/ any of several magazines produced in different towns and cities, which gives details of entertainment and similar events for the current week or month

wheat /wiːt/ n [U] **1** a plant from whose grain flour is made: *a field of wheat* **2** the grain from this plant: *This bread is made from wheat.* –see picture at CEREAL **3 (to separate) the wheat from the chaff** (to separate) the good or important parts from the bad or worthless parts

wheat germ /ˈ· ·/ n [U] the centre of the wheat grain, containing much of the goodness and food value

Wheat·ies /ˈwiːtiːz/ n [P] *tdmk* a breakfast CEREAL (2) made of WHEAT
► CULTURAL NOTE Wheaties advertises by using images of healthy and strong people playing sports. People sometimes make jokes about people being strong or not strong enough by saying that they did or did not eat their Wheaties.◄

wheat·meal /ˈwiːtmiːl/ n [U] *esp. BrE* a flour made from esp. whole grains of wheat. Wheatmeal bread is brown bread but may contain white flour as well as whole wheat flour —**wheatmeal** *adj* [A] : *wheatmeal bread*

whee /wiː/ *interj* (used to express joy, esp. to children, and often when moving quickly, for example when riding on a swing)

whee·dle /ˈwiːdl/ v [I;T+*obj*+*adv/prep*] *derog* to (try to) persuade (someone) by pleasant but insincere behaviour and words: *She wheedled him into taking her with him.*
wheedle sthg. ↔ **out** *phr v* [T (of)] to obtain from someone by insincerely pleasant persuading: *I wheedled a promise/the information out of her.*

wheel¹ /wiːl/ n **1** [C] a circular object with an outer frame which turns round an inner part to which it is joined (the HUB), and is used for turning machinery, making vehicles move, etc.: *Most cars have four wheels, but this one has only three.* **2** [*the*+S] the STEERING WHEEL of a car or the wheel used to guide a ship: *I'm rather tired; will you* **take the wheel?** (=drive instead of me) | *My sister was* **at the wheel.** (=was driving) **3** [C] a movement by which a group of marching soldiers turns quickly to the left or right: *Platoon, right wheel!* **4 the wheel is come full circle** *quote* a phrase from Shakespeare's play *King Lear*, sometimes used when a number of connected events have ended in the same way that they began, esp. regarding a particular person's fortune (FORTUNE (3)) **5 wheels within wheels** facts or reasons which influence people's behaviour but which are hidden or only partly known or understood **6** -**wheeler** /wiːləʳ/a vehicle or other moving object with the stated number or type of wheels: *His car is a three-wheeler.* –see also WHEELS, **oil the wheels** (OIL²), **put one's shoulder to the wheel** (SHOULDER¹), **put a spoke in someone's wheel** (SPOKE²)

wheel² v **1** [T] to move (a wheeled object), esp. by pushing it with the hands: *The nurse wheeled the trolley up to the bed.* **2** [I (ROUND, AROUND, ABOUT)] to turn or change direction suddenly: *She wheeled round to face her accusers.* **3** [I] (of birds) to fly round and round in circles: *The vultures were wheeling overhead.* **4 wheel and deal** [I] *infml, often derog* to make deals, esp. in business or politics, in a skilful and perhaps dishonest way –see also WHEELER-DEALER
wheel sbdy./sthg. ↔ **out** *phr v* [T] *infml, esp. BrE* to produce in order to gain a desired result, esp. in a

dishonest or insincere way: *To back up these claims, they wheeled out their familiar arguments.*

wheel·bar·row /ˈwiːlˌbærəʊ‖-rəʊ, -rə/ also **barrow**— *n* a small cart with one wheel at the front, two legs, and two handles at the back for pushing: *The gardener put the dead plants in his wheelbarrow.*

wheel·base /ˈwiːlbeɪs/ *n* the distance between the front and back AXLE on a vehicle: *This truck is the long-wheelbase model.*

wheel·chair /ˈwiːltʃeəʳ/ *n* a chair with large wheels which can be turned by the user, used esp. by people who are unable to walk: *The injured pilot spent the rest of his life in a wheelchair.* —compare BATH CHAIR, and see picture at CHAIR

wheel clamp /ˈ· ·/ ‖**Denver boot** *AmE infml*— *n* a metal apparatus which the police fasten to a car's wheel if it is parked in the wrong place. The owner of the car must pay a lot of money to have it removed —see also YELLOW LINE —**wheel-clamp** *v* [I;T] : *I've just been wheel-clamped!*

wheel clamp

wheeled /wiːld/ *adj (often in comb.)* having wheels: *wheeled vehicles | a two-wheeled cart*

wheeler-deal·er /ˌ·· ˈ··/ *n infml often derog* someone who is skilled at making profitable or successful deals, esp. in business or politics —see also **wheel and deal** (WHEEL²) —**ing** *n* [U]

wheel·house /ˈwiːlhaʊs/ *n* **-houses** /ˌhaʊzʒz/ the place on a ship where the captain stands at the WHEEL¹ (2)

wheel·ie /ˈwiːli/ *n infml* an act of balancing a cycle on its back wheel while riding it

wheelie bin /ˈ·· ˌ·/ *n BrE* a large RUBBISH BIN on wheels

wheels /wiːlz/ *n* [P] *sl* a car or similar vehicle: *Are these your new wheels, man?*

wheel·wright /ˈwiːlraɪt/ *n* (esp. in former times) a person who makes and repairs wheels, esp. the wooden wheels for horse-drawn carts

wheeze¹ /wiːz/ *v* [I] to make a rough whistling sound because of difficulty in breathing: *By the time he reached the top of the stairs he was panting and wheezing.* | (fig.) *The old engine wheezed up the slope.*

wheeze² *n* **1** an act or sound of wheezing **2** *BrE infml* a clever and amusing trick or idea

wheez·y /ˈwiːzi/ *adj* that wheezes, esp. habitually: *a wheezy chest* —**ily** *adv* —**iness** *n* [U]

whelk /welk/ *n* a sea animal which lives in a shell, and is sometimes used as food

whelp /welp/ *n* a young animal, esp. a dog or wild animal of the dog or cat family

when¹ /wen/ *adv, conj* **1** at what time; at the time that: *When will they come? | Do you know when they're coming? | She'll tell us when to open it. | I jumped up when she called. | Things were different when I was a child. | Fire the rockets when I give the signal. | When completed, the new railway will run for 250 miles.* **2** considering that: *Why do you want a new job when you've got such a good one already?* **3** even though; in spite of the fact that: *They kept trying when they must have known it was hopeless.*

when² *pron* **1** (in questions) what time: **Since when** *has he had a beard?* **2** which time: *next May, by when the new house should be finished*

whence /wens/ *adv, pron old use* (from) where: *Whence came this man? | They returned to the land (from) whence they came.* —compare WHITHER

  ▷ USAGE Some people think that **from whence** is bad English, and that **whence** is better alone.◁

when·ev·er /wenˈevəʳ/ *adv, conj* **1** at whatever time: *Whenever I come here it rains! | Come whenever you like. | I'd like to see you whenever (it's) convenient.* **2** (shows surprise) when: *Whenever did you find time to do all that?*

where /weəʳ/ *adv, conj* at, to, or from what/which place, position, or situation; at or to the place that: *Where do*

you live? | Where are you going? | I asked her where she was going. | Where did you get that book (from)? | Where will all this trouble lead? (=what result will it have?) | This is the building where I work. | I told him where to put it.| Sit where you like. | The crisis has reached a point where the receiver will have to be called in. | Where possible (=whenever it is possible), we use fresh local ingredients.*

where·a·bouts¹ /ˌweərəˈbaʊts◂‖ˈweərəbaʊts/ *adv* (used in questions when an exact answer is not expected) where; in or to what place: *Whereabouts did I leave my bag? | Whereabouts in Scotland do they live?*

where·a·bouts² /ˈweərəbaʊts/ *n* [U+*sing.|pl. v*] *fml* the place where a person or thing is: *The escaped prisoner's whereabouts is/are still unknown.*

where·as /weərˈæz/ *conj* **1** (used to show an opposite or different fact, situation, etc.) but: *They want a house, whereas we would rather live in a flat. | Whereas we want a flat, they would rather live in a house.* **2** *law* (used at the beginning of a sentence, esp. in official papers) since; because of the fact that

where·at /weərˈæt/ *adv, conj old use* **1** WHEREUPON **2** at which; where

where·by /weəˈbaɪ‖weəʳ-/ *adv fml* **1** by means of which: *a system whereby we can calculate future costs* **2** according to which: *a law whereby all children are to receive cheap milk*

where·fore /ˈweəfɔːʳ‖ˈweəʳ-/ *adv, conj old use* **1** why: *Wherefore comest thou?* **2** for that reason; therefore

where·fores /ˈweəfɔːz‖ˈweəʳfɔːrz/ *n* see WHY³

where·in /weərˈɪn/ *adv, conj fml or old use* in what; in which: *Wherein lies the difficulty? | the grave wherein he lies*

where·of /weərˈɒv‖weərˈʌv, -ˈɑːv/ *adv, conj fml or old use* of what; of which

where·on /weərˈɒn‖weərˈɔːn, -ˈɑːn/ *adv, conj fml or old use* **1** on which: *the table whereon lay the food* **2** whereupon

where·so·ev·er /ˌweəsəʊˈevəʳ‖ˈweərsəʊˌevər/ *conj, adv lit for* WHEREVER (1)

where·to /weəˈtuː‖weəʳ-/ also **where·un·to** /weərˈʌntʊ, ˌweərʌnˈtuː‖weərˈʌntuː/*old use*— *adv, conj fml or old use* to what place; to which

where·u·pon /ˌweərəˈpɒn‖ˈweərəpɑːn, -pɔːn/ *conj* at once or soon after and because of which; at which point; as a result of which: *One of the men insulted another, whereupon a fight broke out.*

wher·ev·er /weərˈevəʳ/ *adv* **1** to or at whatever place, position, or situation: *Wherever you go, I go too. | Sleep wherever you like. | Wherever possible (=whenever it is possible) the jobs are given to local people.* **2** (shows surprise) where: *Wherever did you get that idea?*

where·with·al /ˈweəwɪðɔːl‖ˈweəʳ-/ *n (the+S) sometimes humor* the necessary means, esp. money: *I'd like a new car but I lack the wherewithal (to pay for it).*

whet /wet/ *v* **-tt-** [T] **1** *fml or lit* to sharpen: *He whetted his knife on the stone.* **2 whet someone's appetite** (of a taste or short experience) to make someone wish for more: *Going to France for the day has whetted her appetite.*

wheth·er /ˈweðəʳ/ *conj* **1** if ... or not: *He asked me whether she was coming. | I couldn't decide whether to do it. | It was uncertain whether she would recover. | The decision whether to see her was mine alone. | I worry about whether I hurt her feelings. | I wonder whether or not we should tell her. | I wonder whether we should tell her or not.* **2** a no matter if ... (or) ... : *I will go, whether you come with me or stay at home.* **b** (used to introduce two or more possibilities) I don't know if: *I'm sure we'll see each other again soon, whether here or in New York.* | **Whether by accident or design** (=through luck or on purpose) *they met.*

  ▷ USAGE **If** can be used instead of **whether** in meaning 1. But we must use **whether** (not **if**), **a** before infinitives: *The question is whether to go or stay,* **b** after prepositions: *It depends on whether he's mine or not,* **c** after nouns: *It's your decision whether you go or stay,* **d** with *or not* in sentences like this: *I asked him whether or not he was coming.* —see also IF (USAGE)◁

whet·stone /ˈwetstəʊn/ *n* a stone used for sharpening cutting tools

whew /hjuː/ *interj* PHEW

whey /weɪ/ n [U] the watery part of sour milk after the solid part has been removed —compare CURD

which[1] /wɪtʃ/ *determiner, pron* **1** (used in questions, when a choice is to be made) what particular one or ones: *Which shoes shall I wear, the red ones or the brown ones?* | *Which of these books is yours?* | *Ask him which (one) he wants.* (not *Ask him which does he want.*) | *She comes from either Los Angeles or San Francisco, I can't remember which.* **2** (shows what thing or things is/are meant): *Did you see the letter which/that came today?* | *This is the book which/that I told you about.* **3** (used esp. in written language, after a COMMA, to add more information to a sentence) **a** (about a thing or things): *The train, which takes only two hours to get there, is quicker than the bus, which takes three.* **b** (about the first part of the sentence): *She said she'd been waiting for an hour, which was true.* (=and this was true) | *The police arrived, after which* (=and after this) *the situation became calmer.* | *She may have missed her train,* **in which case** (=if this is true) *she won't arrive for another hour.* **4 which is which?** what is the difference between the two: *The twins look so alike that I can't tell which is which.*

▷ USAGE Compare **which** and **what**. 1 **Which** is used when a choice is to be made from a known set of things or people: **Which** *colour do you want, red or blue?* | **Which** *member of the family got most money when the old man died?* **What** is used when the choice is from an unknown set: **What** *colour was it?* | **What** *are you eating?* 2 **Which** can be followed by *of*, but **what** cannot: **Which** *of the girls/books do you like best?* —see also THAT (USAGE)◁

Which? a British magazine which tests and reports on all the different kinds of a particular product in order to help people decide which one to buy —compare CONSUMER REPORTS

which·ev·er /wɪtʃˈevəʳ/ *determiner, pron* **1** any (one) of the set that: *Take whichever seat you like.* | *Choose whichever of them you like best.* **2** no matter which: *It has the same result, whichever way you do it.*

whick·er /ˈwɪkəʳ/ v [I] to NEIGH (=make the sound which horses make) gently —**whicker** n

Whicker, Al·an /ˈælən/ (1925–) a British broadcaster best known for his unusual travel programmes, esp. the *Whicker's World* documentaries (DOCUMENTARY[2]) made and repeated over more than 30 years

whiff /wɪf/ n **1** [S (**of**)] a short-lasting smell or movement of air: *Something good must be cooking; I got/caught a whiff of it through the window.* | (fig.) *a whiff of scandal* **2** [C (**of**); *usu. pl.*] an act of breathing in (air, smoke, etc.)

whif·fy /ˈwɪfi/ *adj BrE infml* having a bad smell; smelly: *The dog is a bit whiffy.*

Whig /wɪg/ n, adj (a member) of a British political party of the 18th and early 19th centuries which supported the power of Parliament and wanted to limit royal power, and later became the Liberal Party

while[1] /waɪl/ n [S] a period of time, esp. a short one: *Just wait (for) a while and then I'll help you.* | *She's been gone quite a while.* (=a fairly long time) | *He telephoned a little while ago.* | *We thought he was at work when* **all the while** *he'd been at the cricket match.* —see also **once in a while** (ONCE[1]), **worth one's while** (WORTH[1])

while[2] *also* **whilst** /waɪlst/*esp. BrE*— *conj* **1** during the time that: *They arrived while we were having dinner.* | *While she read the paper, I cleaned up the kitchen.* | *He got malaria while travelling in Africa.* | *They got married while still at the university.* **2** although: *While I understand what you say, I can't agree with you.* **3** but; WHEREAS: *Their country has plenty of oil, while ours has none.*

while[3] v

while sthg. ↔ **away** *also* **wile** sthg. ↔ **away**— *phr v* [T] to pass (time) in a fairly interesting or pleasantly lazy way: *He whiled away the hours of waiting by reading a book.*

While shep·herds watched their flocks by night /ˌ· ˌ·· ˌ· · ˌ·· ˈ·/ a well-known HYMN (=religious song) which is sung at Christmas

whim /wɪm/ n a sudden idea or wish, often one that is not reasonable or sensible: *Government policy changes at the president's whim/at the whim of the president.* [+*to-v*] *a*

sudden whim to buy a cream cake | *I bought it* **on a whim.** | *Her grandparents* **indulged** *her every* **whim.** (=allowed her to have or do whatever she wanted)

whim·per /ˈwɪmpəʳ/ v **1** [I] (esp. of a frightened animal or person) to make small weak cries: *The little dog whimpered when I tried to bathe its wounds.* **2** [I;T] to speak or say in a weak trembling voice as if about to cry: *"Don't hurt me!" he whimpered.* —**whimper** n

whim·si·cal /ˈwɪmzɪkəl/ *adj* amusingly strange; with strange ideas: *a whimsical poem/smile* – ~ **ly** /ˈwɪmzɪkli/ *adv* – ~**ity** /ˌwɪmzɪˈkælɨti/ n [C;U]

whim·sy /ˈwɪmzi/ n **1** [U] a tendency to think or behave strangely, esp. making odd things seem humorous **2** [C] a strange act or idea

whine /waɪn/ v [I] **1** to make a long high sad sound: *The dog whined at the door, asking to be let out.* **2** *derog* to complain (too much) in an unnecessarily sad voice, usu. about something unimportant: *I wish you'd stop whining!* —**whine** n : *the whine of the aircraft's jet engines*

whin·er /ˈwaɪnəʳ/ n *derog* a person who complains. esp. habitually and in an unnecessarily sad voice

whinge, winge— /wɪndʒ/ v [I] *infml derog, esp. AustrE & BrE* to complain, esp. continually and in an annoying way

whin·ny /ˈwɪni/ v [I] to NEIGH (=make the sound which horses make) gently —**whinny** n

whip[1] /wɪp/ n **1** a long piece of rope or leather fastened to a handle, used esp. for driving animals or punishing people: *He cracked his whip and the horses began to trot.* **2** (in the British system of government) **a** a member of Parliament who is responsible for making other members of his or her party attend at voting time **b** an order given to members of Parliament to attend and vote —see also THREE-LINE WHIP **3** (in the American system of government) a member of Congress who is elected by his or her party to help the FLOOR LEADER and who helps persuade other members of his or her party to support bills that are important to the party **4** a sweet food made of beaten eggs and other foods (esp. fruit) whipped together

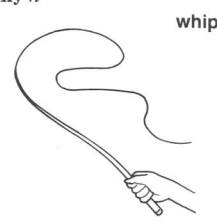

whip[2] v **-pp-** **1** [T] to beat with a whip **2** [I+*adv/prep*; T+*obj+adv/prep*] to move quickly or suddenly: *The wind whipped* (=blew fiercely) *across the plain.* | *He whipped out his gun.* | *She whipped off her shoes.* | *I'm just going to whip across the road to the bank.* **3** [T (UP)] to beat (esp. cream or the white part of an egg) until stiff: *whipped cream* —see also WHISK[2] (3), BEAT[1] (2) **4** [T] *infml* to defeat completely; beat: *Their team really whipped ours at basketball.* **5** [T] *BrE infml* to steal: *Someone's whipped my pen!* **6** [T] to cause (a TOP[4]) to spin by means of a piece of string fixed to a stick **7 whip someone/something into shape** *infml* to bring into the desired state by firm and forceful action: *The new coach soon whipped the team into shape.*

whip sthg. ↔ **up** *phr v* [T] **1** to cause (feelings) to appear, become stronger, etc.: *She tried to whip up some interest in the idea.* **2** to make or produce quickly or in a hurry: *It's not much of a meal; I just whipped it up in a few minutes.*

whip·cord /ˈwɪpkɔːd‖-kɔːrd/ n [U] **1** a strong type of cord **2** a strong woollen material

whip hand /ˈ· ·/ n [*the*+S] a position of power and advantage: *Don't let them do whatever they want; make sure you keep the whip hand.*

whip·lash /ˈwɪplæʃ/ n **1** [C] the blow (LASH) from a whip **2** [C;U] *also* **whiplash in·ju·ry** /ˈ·· ˈ···/— harm done to the body by the sudden violent movement of the head and neck, such as may happen in a car accident

whip·per·snap·per /ˈwɪpəˌsnæpəʳ‖ˈwɪpər-/ n *old-fash infml* a usu. young or small person who behaves in a too confident or important way: *Don't talk to me like that, you young whippersnapper!*

whip·pet /ˈwɪpɨt/ n a small thin racing dog like a GREYHOUND

whip·ping /ˈwɪpɪŋ/ n a beating, esp. as a punishment

whipping boy /'··· ·/ n someone who gets most of the blame and/or punishment for other people's mistakes or wrongdoing —compare SCAPEGOAT

whipping cream /'·· ·/ n [U] a type of cream which can be beaten until stiff

whip-poor-will /'wɪpʊə‚wɪl‖'wɪpər-/ n a small North American bird with a cry like its name

whip-py /'wɪpi/ adj (of a rod, stem, etc.) which bends or springs back easily

whip-round /'· ·/ n infml, esp. BrE a collection of money among a group of people, for example in a place of work, to give to one member: We're having a whip-round for old Fred, who's leaving the firm.

Whip-snade /'wɪpsneɪd/ an open-air ZOO in Bedfordshire, England, where the animals are given a lot of freedom, and kept in natural surroundings

whir /wɜːr/ see WHIRR

whirl¹ /wɜːl‖wɜːrl/ v 1 [I;T+obj+adv|prep] to (cause to) move round and round very fast: The dancers whirled around the floor. | The letter was picked up by the wind and whirled into the air. | (fig.) After meeting so many new people, my head was whirling. 2 [I+adv|prep;T+obj+adv|prep] to (cause to) move away in a hurry: The car whirled them off to the wedding.

whirl² n 1 [S] the act or sensation of whirling : (fig.) My head's in a whirl (=my mind is confused); I must sit down and think. 2 [C (of) usu. sing.] very fast movement or activity, esp. of a rather confused sort: a whirl of activity | the frenzied social whirl at Christmas time 3 **give something a whirl** infml to try something, even though one is not sure that it will be successful, enjoyable, etc.: It's an interesting suggestion and I think we ought to give it a whirl.

whir-li-gig /'wɜːli‚gɪg‖'wɜːr-/ n 1 a toy which spins; spinning TOP 2 a ROUNDABOUT¹ (2)

whirl-pool /'wɜːlpuːl‖'wɜːrl-/ n a place with circular currents of water in a sea or river, which can pull objects down into it

whirl-wind¹ /'wɜːl‚wɪnd‖'wɜːrl-/ also **tornado**‖also **twister** AmE infml— n a tall pipe-shaped body of air moving forward while whirling at high speed: The school was seriously damaged by a whirlwind. —see STORM (USAGE)

whirlwind² adj happening very quickly or suddenly: a whirlwind romance | a whirlwind tour

whirl-y-bird /'wɜːli‚bɜːd‖'wɜːrli‚bɜːrd/ n sl for HELICOPTER

whirr ‖ also **whir** esp. AmE /wɜːr/ v -rr- [I] to make a regular sound like something turning and beating against the air: the whirring sound of the helicopter blades —**whirr, whir** n : the whirr of the sewing machine

whisk¹ /wɪsk/ n 1 [usu. sing.] a quick light sweeping movement: The cow brushed away the flies with a whisk of its tail. 2 a small brush consisting of a bunch of feathers, hair, etc., tied to a handle, esp. a FLYWHISK 3 a small hand-held apparatus for beating eggs, whipping cream, etc.

whisk² v [T] 1 to move or remove with a quick sweeping movement: The horse whisked its tail/whisked away the flies with its tail. 2 [+obj+adv|prep] to move or remove quickly or by taking suddenly: She whisked the cups away. | The President was whisked off to the airport in his limousine. 3 to beat (esp. eggs), esp. with a WHISK¹ (3)

Whis-kas /'wɪskəz/ n [U] tdmk a type of cat food sold in Britain

whisk broom /'· ·/ n AmE a small hand-held brush usu. made from BROOM (2), used for brushing clothes or sweeping dust into a DUSTPAN

whis-ker /'wɪskər/ n 1 any of the long stiff hairs that grow near the mouth of a cat, rat, etc. —see also WHISKERS 2 **by a whisker** infml, esp. BrE by a very small amount; only just: He won the race by a whisker.

whis-kered /'wɪskəd‖-ərd/ adj having whiskers

whis-kers /'wɪskəz‖-ərz/ n [P] hair growing on the sides of a man's face or on his chin —**kery** adj

whis-key /'wɪski/ n [U] whisky made in Ireland or the US

whis-ky /'wɪski/ BrE ‖ **whiskey** AmE— n 1 [U] a SPIRIT (=strong alcoholic drink) made from malted (MALT) grain, such as BARLEY, produced esp. in Scotland 2 [C] a glass of whisky

whis-per¹ /'wɪspər/ v 1 [I;T] to speak or say very quietly, so that only a person close by can hear: The children were whispering in the corner. | She whispered a warning to me and then disappeared. | "Listen!" she whispered. 2 [I] (of the wind, leaves, etc.) to make a soft sound: The wind was whispering in the roof. 3 [T often pass.] to suggest (something) or pass (information) secretly: [+that] It's whispered that he may resign. — —er n

whisper² n 1 speech produced by whispering: She said it **in a whisper**, so I couldn't hear. 2 [usu. sing.] a soft windy sound: the whisper of the wind in the roof 3 infml a piece of information passed secretly from one person to another; RUMOUR: [+(that)] I've heard a whisper that he's going to resign. —see also STAGE WHISPER

whispering cam-paign /'··· ·‚·/ n an attack made against someone's position or good name by passing on unfavourable information about him/her (which may or may not be true) from one person to another —compare SMEAR CAMPAIGN

whist /wɪst/ n [U] a card game for four players in two pairs, in which each pair tries to win the largest number of TRICKS —compare BRIDGE³

whist drive /'· ·/ n a meeting to play whist between several pairs of partners who change opponents

whis-tle¹ /'wɪsəl/ n 1 a simple (musical) instrument for making a high sound by forcing air or steam through it 2 a high sound made by forcing air or steam through a whistle, through the lips, or through a bird's beak: He gave a loud whistle of surprise. —see also WOLF WHISTLE, **blow the whistle on** (BLOW¹), **wet one's whistle** (WET³)

whistle

whistle² v 1 [I] to make a high clear sound **a** by forcing air through a narrow hole formed by the lips, to make music or as a signal to draw attention: She whistled to her dog and it came running. **b** by forcing air or steam through a WHISTLE¹ (1): The referee whistled and the game began. | The old steam train whistled as it approached the station. 2 [T] to produce (music) by doing this: He whistled "God save the Queen". 3 [I+adv|prep] to move with a whistling sound: The wind whistled in the chimney. | A bullet whistled past my head. 4 **whistle for it** infml to ask for something, esp. payment, with no chance of success: "He wants his £5 back." "He'll have to whistle for it; I've got no money left." 5 **whistle in the dark** to put on a show of courage when one is afraid

whis-tle-blow-er /'wɪsəl‚bləʊər/ n esp. AmE a person who makes known (secret) information about illegal, immoral, or wrongful practices in an organization, often at some risk to themselves: whistleblowers in the nuclear energy industry | The scandal was brought to light by a whistleblower at the Pentagon. —see also **blow the whistle on** (BLOW¹ (20)) —**whistleblowing** n [U]

Whis-tler /'wɪslər/, **James Ab-bot Mc-Neill** /dʒeɪmz ˈæbət məkˈniːl/ (1834–1903) an American painter most famous for a picture known as Whistler's Mother

whistle-stop /'··· ·/ n AmE 1 (a town that is) a REQUEST STOP for a train 2 an appearance, esp. by a politician, on a whistle-stop tour: The vice president made a whistle-stop in Topeka before continuing his tour of Kansas and Nebraska.

whistle-stop tour /‚··· '·/ n a touring visit, esp. by a politician, with many short stops, esp. in small places

whit /wɪt/ n [S usu. in negatives] fml or old use (by) a small amount: He cares not a whit for public opinion.

Whit n [C;U] esp. BrE WHITSUN: the Whit weekend

Whit-ak-er's Al-ma-nack /‚wɪtəkəz ˈɔːlmənæk‖-kərz ˈɔːl-, ‚æl-/ a yearly book of information about Britain first produced in 1868 by **Joseph Whitaker** (1820–95), a London seller and producer of books

Whit-bread /'wɪtbred/ n tdmk a make of British beer

white¹ /waɪt/ adj 1 of the colour of milk, salt, and snow: white paint | white rice | white hair (=as of a very old person)

▶ CULTURAL NOTE White is usu. thought of as the colour of purity and VIRGINITY. Babies are dressed in white at CHRISTENINGS and BRIDES usu. wear white dresses at weddings that take place in church. People often wear white in the summer. ◀

2 pale in colour: *Her face was white with anger|fear.* |
white wine **3** [*no comp.*] **a** (of a person) of a pale-skinned
race **b** [A] of or for white people: *a white neighbourhood*
—compare BLACK¹ (2) **4** [*no comp.*] (of coffee) with milk
or cream —opposite **black 5 white as a sheet** *infml* pale
with fear or illness — ~**ness** *n* [U]

white² *n* **1** [U] the colour which is white: *a bride dressed
in white* (=wearing white clothes) **2** [C] a person of a
pale-skinned race: *There were both blacks and whites at
the meeting.* —see also POOR WHITE **3** [C (**of**)] the white
part of the eye **4** [C;U (**of**)] the part of an egg surrounding the YOLK (=yellow part), which is colourless, but
white after cooking: *Beat three egg whites until stiff.* —see
also WHITES, BLACK AND WHITE

white ant /ˌ· ˈ·/ *n* a TERMITE

white·bait /ˈwaɪtbeɪt/ *n* [U] very small young fish of several
types, eaten as food

white blood cell /ˌ· ˈ· ·/ also **leucocyte** *med*, **white
cor·pus·cle** /ˌ· ˈ···, ˌ· ·ˈ··/— *n* any of the cells in the blood
which fight against infection —compare RED BLOOD CELL

white·board /ˈwaɪtbɔːd‖-bɔːrd/ *n* a white smooth surface
used esp. in classrooms for writing and drawing on with
special pens —compare BLACKBOARD

white bread /ˌ· ˈ·/ *n* [U] bread made from white flour

white·cap /ˈwaɪtkæp/ *n* a WHITE HORSE

White·chap·el /ˈwaɪtˌtʃæpəl/ an area of the EAST END of
London. It is remembered as the area where Jack the Ripper committed (COMMIT) his murders.

white Christ·mas /ˌ· ˈ···/ *n* a Christmas Day when there is
snow on the ground, thought by many people to be attractive and TRADITIONAL. There is a well-known popular
song called *White Christmas*, sung by Bing Crosby.

White Cliffs of Do·ver /ˌ· ·· ˈ··/, **The** *n* **1** the first bit of
England that can be seen when crossing the English
Channel from France: *just 35 minutes from the White
Cliffs of Dover* **2** a song sung by Vera Lynn during the
Second World War:
> *There'll be bluebirds over*
> *The white cliffs of Dover*
> *Tomorrow,*
> *Just you wait and see.*

white-col·lar /ˌ· ˈ···◂/ *adj* [A] of or being people who work
in offices or at professional jobs, rather than doing hard
or dirty work with their hands: *white-collar workers* | *a
white-collar union* —compare BLUE-COLLAR, PINK-COLLAR

white-collar crime /ˈ· ·· ˌ·/ *n* a crime committed (COMMIT)
by a person who works in an office or professional job:
Fraud and embezzlement are usu. white-collar crimes.

whited sep·ul·chre /ˌwaɪtɪd ˈsepəlkər/ *n bibl or humor*
someone who gives the appearance of being good, but is
evil; HYPOCRITE

white dwarf /ˌ· ˈ·/ *n tech* a hot star, near the end of its life,
more solid but less bright than the sun —compare RED
GIANT

white el·e·phant /ˌ· ˈ···/ *n* something that is useless and
unwanted, esp. something that is big and/or costs a lot
of money

white elephant sale /ˌ· ˈ··· ˌ·/ *n AmE old-fash for* JUMBLE
SALE

white flag /ˌ· ˈ·/ *n* a sign that one accepts defeat: *They
walked towards the enemy waving the white flag to show
that they were surrendering.*

white flight /ˌ· ˈ·/ *n* [U] *AmE* large numbers of middle-class
white people leaving an area, usu. because (of fears that)
black families are coming to live there

white flour /ˌ· ˈ·/ *n* [U] wheat flour from which the BRAN
and WHEAT GERM have been removed —compare
WHOLEMEAL

white goods /ˈ· ˌ·/ *n* [P] **1** LINEN for the house e.g. sheets,
TOWELS, TABLECLOTHS, etc.: *There's a white goods sale on
at Greens.* **2** large, usu. white objects for the house e.g.
cookers, washing machines, REFRIGERATORS, etc.

White·hall /ˈwaɪthɔːl, ˌwaɪtˈhɔːl/ **1** the street in London in
or near which most of the British government offices
stand **2** the British government itself, esp. the government departments rather than Parliament or the Prime
Minister: *disagreement between Whitehall and Downing
Street about how to deal with this matter*

White Hart Lane /ˌ· ·· ˈ·/ the name of the ground at which

the London football team Tottenham Hotspur play

white heat /ˌ· ˈ·/ *n* [U] the very high temperature at which
a metal turns white, usu. after being red —see also
WHITE-HOT

white hope /ˌ· ˈ·/ *n* [*usu. sing.*] *sometimes humor or derog*
the person who is expected to bring great success: *our
great white hope for the future* | *the white hope of the
Republican Party*

white horse /ˌ· ˈ·/ *BrE*‖also **whitecap**— *n* a wave at sea
with a white top

white-hot /ˌ· ˈ·◂/ *adj* (of metal) so hot that it shines white
—compare RED-HOT; see also WHITE HEAT

the White House

White House /ˈ· ·/ [*the*] **1** the official Washington, D.C.
home of the President of the United States: *Ill-health
could force him to make an early departure from the White
House.* —see colour map on pages 1374–5 **2** the President
and his advisers: *The White House confirmed today that
the President will be visiting Britain.*

White·house /ˈwaɪt-haʊs/, **Mary** (1910–) a British
woman known for protesting about television
programmes, magazines, and plays that have a lot of sex,
violence, NUDITY, or bad language in them

white knight /ˌ· ˈ·/ *n* a person or organization that puts
money into a business company to save it from being
taken over by another company

white lead /ˌwaɪt ˈled/ *n* [U] a poisonous compound of lead
with CARBON and oxygen, formerly used in house paint

white lie /ˌ· ˈ·/ *n* a harmless lie, e.g. one told so as not to
hurt someone else

white light·ning /ˌ· ˈ···/ *n* [U] *AmE sl* MOONSHINE (2)

white ma·gic /ˌ· ˈ···/ *n* [U] magic used for good purposes
—compare BLACK MAGIC

white man's bur·den /ˌ· · ˈ···/ [*the*] the duty that white people believed in the past that they had to manage the affairs of less developed peoples until they had enough education to manage their own affairs. The expression
comes from a poem by Rudyard Kipling, and was used
esp. in the 19th century.

white meat /ˈ· ·/ *n* [U] **1** the very pale-coloured meat from
some parts of a cooked bird, such as the breast of a
chicken **2** certain types of pale-coloured meat, esp. VEAL
and PORK —compare RED MEAT

white met·al /ˌ· ˈ···/ *n* [C;U] any silvery-coloured mixture
of metals, containing tin

whit·en /ˈwaɪtn/ *v* [I;T] to make or become (more) white:
I must whiten my tennis shoes.

White Nile /ˌ· ˈ·/ [*the*] a river which rises at Lake Victoria
in E Africa and flows to join the Blue Nile at Khartoum
in Sudan, and through Egypt to the Mediterranean Sea

whit·en·ing /ˈwaɪtənɪŋ/ also **whit·en·er** /ˈwaɪtənər/
whiting— *n* [U] white material, powder, or liquid, which
is used for giving a clean white colour: *She put whitening on her tennis shoes.*

white·out /ˈwaɪtaʊt/ *n* a weather condition in which there
is very heavy cloud or snow so that one can see nothing
and everything appears white

White Out /ˈ· ·/ *n* [U] *AmE, tdmk* a white liquid used to
paint out mistakes in writing, typing, etc.

White Pag·es /ˌ· ˈ···/ [*the*] (in the US) a book (DIRECTORY)
of all of the names of people in a particular area who have
telephones, and their telephone numbers and usu. addresses: *Look her up in the local white pages.* —compare
YELLOW PAGES

white pa·per /ˌ·ˈ··/ n an official report from the British government, usu. explaining the government's ideas and plans concerning a particular subject before it suggests a new law in parliament: *a new white paper on education* —compare GREEN PAPER

white pep·per /ˌ·ˈ·/ n [U] PEPPER¹ (1a) made from crushed seeds from which the dark outer covering has been removed

White Rab·bit /ˌ·ˈ··/ [*the*] a character from *Alice's Adventures in Wonderland* by Lewis Carroll. He keeps looking at his watch because he is late, and disappearing down rabbit holes. —see also ALICE IN WONDERLAND

whites /waɪts/ n [P] **1** white clothing, sheets, etc., which are separated from other items when washing (used esp. in advertisements for washing powders) **2** *esp. BrE* white clothing, esp. as worn for sports, such as long white trousers used in cricket

white sale /ˈ·ˌ·/ n *AmE* a sale of TOWELS, sheets, etc.: *Robinson's has advertised a white sale this weekend.*

white sauce /ˌ·ˈ·‖ˈ·ˌ·/ n [U] a thick white liquid cooked with flour, poured over certain types of food

white slav·e·ry /ˌ·ˈ···/ n [U] *old-fash euph* the practice or business of taking girls to a foreign country and forcing them to be PROSTITUTES (**white slaves**) there

white spir·it /ˌ·ˈ··/ n [U] *esp. BrE* a strong liquid made from petrol, used for making paint thinner, for removing marks on clothes, etc.

white su·prem·a·cy /ˌ·ˈ·ˌ··/ n [U] the belief that white people are better than people of other races, esp. black people, and that other races should be kept at a lower level of society —compare CIVIL RIGHTS —**cist** n

white-tie /ˌ·ˈ·◄/ adj (of parties and other social occasions) at which the men wear white BOW TIES and TAILS: *a white-tie dinner* —compare BLACK-TIE, and see picture at EVENING DRESS

white trash /ˌ·ˈ·/ also **poor white trash**— n [U] *AmE derog infml* white people who are poor and uneducated; the lowest social class of whites

white·wash¹ /ˈwaɪtwɒʃ‖-wɔːʃ, -wɑːʃ/ n **1** [U] a white liquid mixture made from LIME, used esp. for covering walls **2** [C;U] *derog* an attempt to hide a mistake or bad action so that the person who is responsible will not be blamed or punished: *That whole affair was a whitewash.* | *The report was simply a whitewash.*

whitewash² v [T] **1** to cover with whitewash: *whitewashed cottages* **2** *derog* to prevent (something bad) from being noticed or make (what is bad) seem good or harmless: *The report attempts to whitewash recent events, but we all know the minister was seriously at fault.*

white·wa·ter /ˌwaɪtˈwɔːtər◄‖-ˈwɔːt-, -ˈwɑːt-/ n [U] *AmE for* RAPIDS

white wat or raft ing /ˌ· ·ˈ·/ n [U] a dangerous sport, sailing by RAFT¹ (1) (=a flat type of boat with little or no protection for those in it) down a river which is white because of the fast water striking rocks (RAPIDS). It is a popular sport in the US.

white wed·ding /ˌ·ˈ··/ n *esp. BrE* a wedding at which the BRIDE (=woman being married) wears a long white dress —see also extra information on page 1406

whith·er /ˈwɪðər/ adv *old use* **1** to which (place): *the place whither he went* **2** to what place: *Whither are you going?* —compare WHENCE

whit·ing¹ /ˈwaɪtɪŋ/ n **whiting** or **whitings** a sea fish used for food

whiting² n [U] WHITENING

whit·low /ˈwɪtləʊ/ also **felon**— n an infected piece of skin near a nail on the finger or toe

Whit·man /ˈwɪtmən/, **Walt** /wɔːlt/ (1819–1892) an American writer remembered for his poetry which celebrates nature and the value of freedom

Whit Mon·day /ˌ·ˈ··/ the day after Whitsun or Whit Sunday

Whit·sun /ˈwɪtsən/ also **Whit** *esp. BrE*— n [C;U] **1** also **Whit Sun·day** /ˌ·ˈ··/— the seventh Sunday after Easter which celebrates the coming down from heaven of the HOLY GHOST **2** also **Whit·sun·tide** /ˈwɪtsəntaɪd/— the period around this day

Whit·ting·ton /ˈwɪtɪŋtən/, **Dick** (1358–1423) a young man from London who, according to the story, ran away from his job, but then thought he heard the words "Turn again, Whittington, Lord Mayor of London" in the sound of some bells. He went back, and later became Lord Mayor of London. He is often pictured with his cat. The story of Dick Whittington is often performed in Britain as a PANTOMIME.

whit·tle /ˈwɪtl/ v [T (DOWN, AWAY)] **1** to cut (wood) to a smaller size by taking off small thin pieces **2** to reduce by a continuous and gradual process: *Bad financial management has whittled away the company's profits.* | *We've whittled down the list of candidates to five.* — **whittler** n

whizz¹, whiz /wɪz/ v *-zz-* [I+adv/prep] *infml* to move very fast, often making a noisy sound as if rushing through the air: *Cars were whizzing past.* | (fig.) *The days seemed to whizz by.*

whizz², whiz n **1** [S] a whizzing sound **2** [C *usu. sing.*] *infml* someone who is very fast, clever, or skilled in the stated activity: *a whizz at cards*

whizz kid, whiz kid /ˈ· ·/ n *infml, usu. apprec* a person who is very successful at an early age, esp. in business, usu. because of great natural skill and cleverness

who /huː/ pron (used esp. as the subject of a verb) **1** (used in questions) what person or people: *Who's that woman over there?* | *Who are they?* | *Who told you that?* | *Did they find out who stole the money?* | *Who did you stay with?* — see USAGE **2** (shows what person or people is/are meant): *Do you know the people who/that live here?* | *A postman is a man who/that delivers letters.* | *The official who/that used to deal with your business has moved to another branch.* **3** (used esp. in written language, after a COMMA, to add more information about a person or people): *I discussed it with my brother, who is a lawyer.*

▷ USAGE 1 Except in very formal language, **who** can be used instead of **whom** as an object in questions: **Who** *did you see?* | **Whom** *(fml) did you see?* | **Who** *was she dancing with?/With* **whom** *(fml) was she dancing?* 2 When a word like *family* or *team* is followed by a plural verb, use **who**: *a family* **who** *quarrel among themselves* | *a team* **who** *practise together.* When such verbs are followed by a singular verb, use **which**: *a family* **which** *has always lived here* | *a team* **which** *wins most of its matches.* —see also THAT (USAGE)◁

Who, Dr see DR WHO

Who, The a British popular music group, successful in the 1960s and 1970s

WHO /ˌdʌbəljuː eɪtʃ ˈəʊ/ abbrev. for: WORLD HEALTH ORGANIZATION

whoa /wəʊ, həʊ/ interj (a call to a horse to) stop

who'd /huːd/ short for: **1** who had **2** who would

who·dun·it, whodunnit /ˌhuːˈdʌnɪt/ n *infml* a story, film, etc., about a crime mystery, esp. concerned with finding out who was the criminal

who·ev·er /huːˈevər/ pron **1** anyone at all: *I'll take whoever wants to go.* **2** no matter who: *Whoever it is, I don't want to see them/him.* **3** (shows surprise) who: *Whoever can be phoning us at this time of night?*

whole¹ /həʊl/ adj **1** [A] all (the); the full amount of: *When I broke my leg, I spent a whole month/three whole weeks in bed.* | *I spent the whole morning in bed today.* | *He sat next to me in the car and slept the whole way.* | *She drank two whole bottles of wine.* | *Are you telling me the whole truth?* | (*infml, esp. AmE*) *The storm caused* **a whole lot of** (=a great deal of) *damage.* **2** not divided or broken up; complete: *I ordered a whole bottle of wine, waiter, not a half bottle.* | *He swallowed the cake whole, without chewing it at all.* | *The police found a whole human skeleton.* —see also WHOLLY, **go the whole hog** (HOG¹)

whole² n **1** [(*the*) S (**of**)] the complete amount, thing, etc.: *The whole of* (=all) *the morning was wasted.* | *There are some areas of poverty, but the country* **as a whole** *is fairly prosperous.* **2** [C *usu. sing.*] the sum of the parts: *Two halves make a whole.* **3 on the whole** generally; considering everything: *On the whole, I'm satisfied with her progress.*

whole·food /ˈhəʊlfuːd/ n [C;U] (a) food that is in a simple natural form, without anything removed or added. Wholefood is considered healthier than PROCESSED FOOD: *Brown rice and unrefined sugar are wholefoods.*

whole·heart·ed /ˌhəʊlˈhɑːtɪd◄/ adj with all one's feelings, interest, sincerity, etc.: *whole-hearted support/attention/sympathy* | *a whole-hearted effort* — ~**ly** adv

whole·meal /ˈhəʊlmiːl/ also **whole wheat** /ˌ· ˈ·◄/— adj [A] (made from flour) containing all the grain; made without removing the covering of the grain. Wholemeal flour is used esp. by people interested in eating healthy foods: *wholemeal flour* | *wholemeal bread* (=a type of brown bread)

whole note /ˈ· ·/ n AmE for SEMIBREVE —see picture at NOTATION

whole num·ber /ˌ· ˈ··/ n an INTEGER

whole·sale[1] /ˈhəʊlseɪl/ n [U] the business of selling goods in large quantities, esp. to shopkeepers —compare RETAIL[1]

wholesale[2] adj, adv **1** of, being, or employed in the sale of goods in large quantities and usu. at low prices: *a wholesale supplier of office machinery* | *He buys the materials/sells the products wholesale.* | *They cost $50 in the stores, but the wholesale price is $35.* **2** (usu. of something bad) on a large scale; widespread; INDISCRIMINATE: *wholesale slaughter*

whole·sal·er /ˈhəʊlˌseɪləʳ/ n a businessman who sells goods wholesale

whole·some /ˈhəʊlsəm/ adj apprec **1** good for the body or likely to produce good health: *wholesome food* **2** having a good or desirable moral effect: *Films like that are not wholesome entertainment for young children.* — ~ **ness** n [U]

whole wheat /ˈ· ·/ adj WHOLEMEAL

who'll /huːl/ short for: who will

whol·ly /ˈhəʊl-li/ adv completely: *You were not wholly to blame for the accident.* | *a wholly improper suggestion*

whom /huːm/ pron (the object form of **who**, used esp. in formal speech or writing): *Whom did you see?* | *I wouldn't appoint a man whom I didn't trust.* | *The minister, to whom I spoke recently/whom I spoke to recently, agrees with me.* | *She brought with her three friends, none of whom I had ever met before.* —see THAT (USAGE), WHO (USAGE)

whomp /wɒmp ‖ waːmp/ v [T] AmE sl **1** to hit very hard: *I'm going to whomp you if you do that again.* **2** to defeat: *The Bears really whomped the Redskins in last night's game.*

whoop /wuːp, huːp/ v [I] **1** to make a loud esp. joyful cry **2 whoop it up** infml to enjoy oneself a lot —**whoop** n : *whoops of victory*

whoo·pee[1] /wʊˈpiː/ interj a cry of joy

whoo·pee[2] /ˈwʊpiː/ n **make whoopee** infml **a** BrE to go out enjoying oneself **b** AmE to have sex

whoopee cush·ion /ˈ·· ˌ··/ n a CUSHION which makes a rude noise when you sit on it, used when playing jokes on people

whoop·ing cough /ˈhuːpɪŋ kɒf‖-kɔːf/ n [U] a disease that is caught esp. by children, in which each attack of coughing is followed by a long noisy drawing in of the breath

whoops /wʊps/ interj OOPS

whoosh[1] /wʊʃ‖wuːʃ/ n [usu. sing.] a soft sound, like air rushing out of something

whoosh[2] v [I+adv/prep] infml to move quickly with a rushing sound: *The express train whooshed past.*

whop /wɒp‖waːp/ v -**pp**- [T] infml, esp. AmE to beat or defeat

whop·per /ˈwɒpəʳ‖ˈwaː-/ n infml **1** something unusually or surprisingly big: *Did you catch that fish? What a whopper!* **2** a big lie: *He told a real whopper to excuse his lateness.*

whop·ping /ˈwɒpɪŋ‖ˈwaː-/ adj, adv [A] infml very (big): *a whopping (great) lie*

whore /hɔːʳ/ n esp. old use or derog **1** a PROSTITUTE **2** a woman whose sexual behaviour is regarded as immoral

who're /ˈhuːəʳ/ short for: who are

whore·house /ˈhɔːhaʊs‖ˈhɔːr-/ n -**houses** /ˌhaʊzɪz/ esp. old use or derog a BROTHEL

whorl /wɜːl‖wɔːrl/ n **1** a circular arrangement, esp. of leaves or flowers on a stem **2** the shape which a line makes when going round in a circle and continuing outward from the centre and not joining up, esp. on some fingers (a type of FINGERPRINT) or in the growth of some seashells; SPIRAL

whor·tle·ber·ry /ˈwɜːtlˌberi‖ˈwɜːr-/ n BrE for BILBERRY

who's /huːz/ short for: **1** who is: *Who's he talking about?* **2** who has: *Who's he brought to dinner?* **3** infml who does: *Who's he mean?*

whose /huːz/ determiner, pron **1** (used in questions) of whom (the one) belonging to which person or persons: *Whose house is this?* | *Whose is this car?* | *Whose are these shoes?* | *We never discovered whose (money) it was.* **2** (used for showing relationship) **a** of whom: *That's the man whose house was burned down.* **b** of which: *a new computer, whose low cost will make it very attractive to students*

who·so·ev·er /ˌhuːsəʊˈevəʳ/ also **who·so** /ˈhuːsəʊ/— pron old use for WHOEVER (1,2)

Who's Who /ˌ· ˈ·/ n a book which contains information about the lives and achievements of important people, usu. in a particular field: *a guest list that read like a Who's Who of show business*

who've /huːv/ short for: who have: *People who've been there say it's marvellous.*

why[1] /waɪ/ adv, conj **1** for what reason: *Why did you do it?* | *Why (should we) bother waiting any longer?* | *They asked him why he did it.* (not *They asked him why did he do it.*) | *I can't think why she said that.* | *Is there any reason why* (=a reason for which) *you can't come?* | *I can't see why it shouldn't work.* (=I think it probably will work) **2 why not?** (used for making suggestions): *Why not make one for yourself instead of buying one?* | *Why don't you ask him yourself?*

why[2] interj esp. AmE or old-fash (used for expressing surprise or slight impatience or annoyance): *I'm looking for my glasses; why, I was wearing them all the time!*

why[3] n the why(s) and (the) wherefore(s) (of) the reason(s) and explanation (for)

WI[1] /ˌdʌbəljuː ˈaɪ/ abbrev. for: WOMEN'S INSTITUTE

WI[2] written abbrev. for: WISCONSIN

wick /wɪk/ n **1** a piece of twisted thread in a candle, which burns as the WAX melts **2** a length of material in an oil lamp which draws up oil while burning **3 get on someone's wick** BrE infml to annoy someone, esp. continually

wick·ed /ˈwɪkɪd/ adj **1** extremely bad; morally wrong; evil: *wicked cruelty* | *a wicked man* | (fig.) *It's a wicked waste of money.* **2** infml playful in a rather troublesome or bad way; MISCHIEVOUS: *He had a wicked twinkle in his eye.* — ~ **ly** adv — ~ **ness** n [U]

▷ USAGE When used of people, **wicked** is very strong, and rather old-fashioned. **Evil** is a more common word. A noisy, disobedient child would not be called **wicked** or **evil**, but **naughty**.◁

wicked step·moth·er /ˌ··· ˈ···/ a standard character in fairy stories etc., who is wicked and jealous, and treats her stepchildren (STEPCHILD) very badly

wicked witch /ˌ·· ˈ·/ n a standard character in fairy stories etc., a SYMBOL of evil in the form of a WITCH: *I always thought my history teacher looked like a wicked witch.*

Wicked Witch of the West /ˌ··· ˌ· · · ˈ·/ [the] a character in the children's story *The Wizard of Oz*, who is evil and ugly

wick·er /ˈwɪkəʳ/ adj [A] made of wickerwork: *a wicker basket*

wick·er·work /ˈwɪkəwɜːk‖ˈwɪkərwɜːrk/ n [U] (objects made from) thin woven branches, REEDs, etc.: *wickerwork furniture*

wick·et /ˈwɪkɪt/ n (in cricket) **1 a** either of two sets of three sticks (STUMPS), with two small pieces of wood (BAILS) on top, at which the ball is bowled (BOWL) **b** also **pitch**— the stretch of grass between these two structures **2** one turn of a player to hit the ball: *England have lost three wickets.* (=three of their players have been dismissed) | *Sussex won by seven wickets.* (=with seven players left who have not completed, or yet started, their turn) —see also STICKY WICKET

wicket gate /ˈ·· ˌ·/ n old use a small gate or door which is part of a larger one

wicket keep·er /ˈ·· ˌ··/ n a cricket player who stands behind the WICKET (1a) to catch the ball —see picture at CRICKET

Wick·low /ˈwɪkləʊ/ a COUNTY in the E Republic of Ireland

wide[1] /waɪd/ adj **1** measuring a large amount from side to side or edge to edge: *a wide road* | *The gate isn't wide enough to get the car through.* [after *n*] *a plank six inches wide* **2** covering or including a large range of things; EXTENSIVE: *She has wide interests/experience.* | *The library has books on a wide variety/selection of subjects.* **3** also **wide o·pen** /ˌ· ˈ··/— fully open: *wide eyes* **4 wide of the mark** not at all suitable, correct, etc.: *His guess was wide of the mark.* —see also WIDELY, WIDTH

▷ USAGE Compare **wide** and **broad**. **Wide** is the more common word, and can be used to describe most objects, openings, and measurements from side to side. **Broad** can be used to describe very large, flat areas: *a* **broad/wide** *river*, or to suggest strength: **broad** *shoulders* | *a* **broad** *beam of wood supporting the whole building.* It is also used in literary or poetic writing: *I gazed on the* **broad** *acres which lay before me.*◁

wide² *adv* **1** to a great distance from side to side: *He stood with his legs wide apart.* | *"Open wide," said the dentist.* (=open your mouth completely) **2** [(**of**)] (in sport) far away from the right point: *The ball went wide (of the goal).*

wide³ *n* (in cricket) a ball that is bowled (BOWL) wide of the WICKET (1a)

wide-an·gle /ˌ· ˈ··◂/ *adj* [A] (of the LENS in a camera) able to give a wider than usual view

wide-a·wake /ˌ· · ˈ· ◂/ *adj* **1** fully awake **2** *apprec* showing fully active senses; ALERT; WATCHFUL

wide boy /ˈ· ·/ *n BrE derog infml* a cleverly dishonest person, esp. a businessman

wide-eyed /ˌ· ˈ·◂/ *adj* **1** with eyes fully open because of great surprise **2** showing a willingness to accept or admire things without questioning; NAIVE: *wide-eyed innocence*

wide·ly /ˈwaɪdli/ *adv* **1** over a wide area or range of things: *She has travelled widely.* (=to many different places) | *widely known* | *He is widely read/has read widely.* (=many types of book) | *It's widely believed* (=by many people) *that the government will lose the election.* **2** to a large degree: *widely different opinions*

wid·en /ˈwaɪdn/ *v* [I;T] to make or become wider: *They're widening the road.* —compare BROADEN, NARROW²

wide-rang·ing /ˌ· ˈ··◂/ *adj* covering a large range of subjects or things: *wide-ranging interests* | *a wide-ranging array of products*

wide·spread /ˈwaɪdspred/ *adj* existing, happening, etc., in many places or among many people: *The disease is becoming more widespread.* | *There is widespread public concern about this problem.*

wid·geon /ˈwɪdʒən/ *n* **widgeon** *or* **widgeons** a type of duck which lives on freshwater lakes and pools

wid·get /ˈwɪdʒɪt/ *n AmE infml* an imaginary product, used when talking about products generally and not any particular one. *If A turns out 70 widgets per hour and B makes 1.2 widgets per minute, who has a better rate of production?*

wid·ow /ˈwɪdəʊ/ *n* **1** a woman whose husband has died, and who has not married again —compare DIVORCÉE **2** *infml or humor* a woman whose husband is often away at the stated activity: *a golf widow* —see also GRASS WIDOW

wid·owed /ˈwɪdəʊd/ *adj* having become a widow or widower: *She was widowed at the age of 25.* | *her widowed mother*

wid·ow·er /ˈwɪdəʊəʳ/ *n* a man whose wife has died, and who has not married again

wid·ow·hood /ˈwɪdəʊhʊd/ *n* [U] the state or period of being a widow

Widow Twan·key /ˌ· ˈwɪdəʊ ˈtwæŋki/ an amusing female character in the British children's PANTOMIME *Aladdin*, usu. played by a man dressed in women's clothes

width /wɪdθ/ *n* **1** [C;U] size from side to side: *What is its*

width? | *The garden is six metres in width.* —compare BREADTH, HEIGHT, LENGTH¹ **2** [C] a piece of material of the full width that the material had when it was actually made: *We need four widths of curtain material to cover the windows.*

wield /wiːld/ *v* [T] **1** to have and/or use (power, influence, etc.): *She wields a lot of influence.* **2** *old use or lit* to hold and use (a weapon) — **~er** *n*

wie·ner /ˈwiːnəʳ/ also **wie·nie, wee·nie** /ˈwiːni/ *n AmE* **1** a FRANKFURTER **2** *sl* a fool **3** *sl* a PENIS

Wie·sen·thal /ˈwiːzəntɑːl/, **Simon** (1908–) a Jewish man who has tried to find Nazi war criminals since the end of the Second World War and tried to bring them to justice

wife /waɪf/ *n* **wives** /waɪvz/ the woman to whom a man is married: *Have you met my wife?* | *his ex-wife* | *a good wife and mother*

▶ CULTURAL NOTE The TRADITIONAL view of a good wife is of a woman who spends all her time looking after her home, her children and her husband and does not go out to work and who is good at things like cooking, sewing, etc.; many people, esp. women, now think that this idea is old-fashioned and that if a woman does not like doing these kinds of things and wants to work outside her home it does not mean that she is a bad wife. —see WOMAN (USAGE)◀

wife·ly /ˈwaɪfli/ also **wife·like** /-laɪk/— *adj apprec fml or humor* having qualities that are thought to be typical of a good wife: *wifely concern*

Wife of Bath /ˌ· · ˈ·/ [*the*] a character in Geoffrey Chaucer's poem *The Canterbury Tales*, who enjoys talking about sex in a humorous way

wife swap·ping /ˈ· ··/ *n* [U] the exchanging of wives or husbands for a short time for sexual relations with different partners. This is not considered usual or acceptable behaviour by most people, but is sometimes mentioned in jokes and humorous television programmes.

wig¹ /wɪg/ *n* an artificial covering of hair for the whole head, used to hide one's real hair or lack of hair. In England judges wear old-fashioned white wigs in court: *The actress wore a black wig over her blond hair.* —compare TOUPEE; see also BEWIGGED, BIGWIG

wig² *v*

wig out *phr v* [I] *AmE sl* to become (slightly) mad: *Their mother wigged out after the accident and had to be shut up for a while.*

Wig·an /ˈwɪgən/ a town in NW England

wig·ging /ˈwɪgɪŋ/ *n* [*usu. sing.*] *BrE infml* an act of talking angrily to someone who has done something wrong

wig·gle /ˈwɪgəl/ *v* [I;T] *infml* to move in small side-to-side, up-and-down, or turning movements: *He wiggled his toes.* —**wiggle** *n* : *with a wiggle of her hips*

wight /waɪt/ *n old use* a person

Wight see ISLE OF WIGHT

Wight·man Cup /ˈwaɪtmən kʌp/ [*the*] a yearly tennis competition between the best women players from the US and Britain

Wig·town·shire /ˈwɪgtaʊnʃəʳ, -tən-/ a former COUNTY in SW Scotland, now part of Dumfries and Galloway REGION

wig·wam /ˈwɪgwæm‖-wɑːm/ *n* a round hut of the type formerly used by some Native Americans —compare TEPEE

Wil·ber·force /ˈwɪlbəfɔːs‖-bərfɔːrs/, **William** (1759–1833) an English politician who worked to end SLAVERY in the British Empire

wild¹ /waɪld/ *adj* **1** living or growing in natural conditions and having natural qualities; not bred, grown, or produced by humans; not TAME or CULTIVATED: *a wild elephant/rabbit* | *Some wild flowers are growing in a corner of the garden.* | *wild land* (=not lived in or cultivated) | *wild honey* **2** (esp. of a person or animal) violent and uncontrollable in behaviour: *a wild dog* | *He had a wild look in his eyes.* **3** (of natural forces) violent; strong: *a wild wind* | *It's a wild night tonight.* (=with very strong wind, rain, etc.) **4** showing strong uncontrolled feelings: *wild with anger/with grief* | *His speech was greeted with wild applause.* **5** showing lack of thought, order, or direction: *a wild idea* | *I'll make a* **wild guess.** (=because I don't know the facts) | *a wild throw* **6** *infml apprec, old-fash* extremely good, esp. in an exciting way: *That was a really wild party last night!* **7** [F+**about**]

Widow Twankey

extremely eager for or excited about, often to an unreasonable degree: *My son's wild about racing cars.* **8** (of cards in card games) having no fixed value but rather one determined by the player or the rules of the game: *Are jokers wild in this game?* – ~ **ness** *n* [U] – ~ **ly** *adv* : *The mob ran wildly through the town.* | *a wildly in-accurate estimate*

wild² *n* **1 in the wild** in the natural state in which an animal usually lives: *Most of these animals are in zoos now – there are very few still living in the wild.* **2 the wilds** a distant natural area with few people: *He lives somewhere out in the wilds of Scotland.*

wild³ *adv infml* **1 go wild** to be filled with strong feeling, esp. eagerness, joy, or anger: *The critics went wild over his new play.* **2 run wild** to behave as one likes, without control: *They let their children run wild.*

wild boar /ˌ· ¹·/ *n* a large fierce hairy European wild pig that is often hunted. The wild boar is no longer found in Britain.

wild card /¹· ˌ·/ *n* **1** (in card games) a card which can represent any other card in points or value: *You can only get five of a kind if you're using wild cards.* –see also WILD¹ (8) **2** a person or thing whose behaviour in a future situation cannot be known or guessed at very well, esp. an UNSEEDED (=unranked) player in a sports contest **3** *tech* a character which can represent any other in some computer and WORD-PROCESSING commands: *Use the asterisk as a wild card in directory searches.*

wild·cat /¹waɪldkæt/ *n* **1** a naturally wild cat, esp. one that looks like a pet cat, but is very fierce **2** *infml* a person, esp. a woman, who shows sudden violent bad temper

wildcat strike /ˌ·· ¹·/ *n* a sudden unofficial stopping of work

Wilde /waɪld/, **Oscar** (1854–1900) an Irish WRITER best known for his play *The Importance of Being Earnest* and his story *The Picture of Dorian Gray*. Many of the clever and funny things he said in conversations are still famous. He was sent to prison for two years because he was HOMOSEXUAL and this was not allowed in Britain at that time.

wil·de·beest /¹wɪldᵻbiːst/ *n* **wildebeest** *or* **wildebeests** a GNU

Wild·er /¹waɪldəʳ/, **Billy** (1906–) an American film DIREC-TOR whose films include *Sunset Boulevard* and *Some Like It Hot*

Wilder, Lau·ra In·galls /¹lɔːrə ¹ɪŋgəlz/ (1867–1957) an American writer famous for her books about her child-hood, as an early settler in the Midwest. *Little House on the Prairie*, based on her books, became a popular tele-vision series in the 1970s.

Wilder, Thorn·ton /¹θɔːntən‖¹θɔːrn-/ (1897–1975) an Ameri-can writer known esp. for his plays *Our Town* and *The Skin of Our Teeth*

wil·der·ness /¹wɪldənᵻs‖-dər-/ *n* **1** [*the*+S] *old use or bibl* an area of land with little natural life, esp. a desert; in the Bible Christ goes into the wilderness alone to pray and while he is there he is tempted (TEMPT) by the devil **2** an area in its natural state where there are no signs of humans: *We went camping in the beautiful wilderness of West Virginia.* | *The mountain lion rarely leaves the wilderness.* **3** [C (**of**)] *usu. derog* any place where there is no sign of human presence or control: *That garden's a wilderness.* | *The city has become a lawless wilderness.* **4** [*the*+S] the state of being away from power or from the centre of an activity, esp. out of political life: *Churchill spent many years in the political wilderness before being called back to become prime minister.* **5 a voice crying in the wilderness** *phrase from the Bible* a call or warn-ing that nobody takes any notice of: *I'm afraid I'm just a voice crying in the wilderness.*

wilderness ar·e·a /¹··· ˌ···/ *n AmE* an area of public land, often within a National Forest, on which no development (e.g. roads or buildings) is permitted in order to keep it in its natural state: *The Weimanuche Wilderness Area* | *Does Arkansas have any wilderness areas?*

wild·fire /¹waɪldfaɪəʳ/ *n* **like wildfire** quickly and uncon-trollably: *The news spread like wildfire.*

wild·fowl /¹waɪldfaʊl/ *n* [U] birds that are shot for sport, esp. ones that live near water, such as ducks

wild-goose chase /ˌ· ¹· ·/ *n infml* a useless search or chase after something that does not exist or cannot be found:

We went to look for him at the library, but it was a com-plete wild-goose chase; he'd been at home all the time. | *She sent me on a wild-goose chase.*

wild·life /¹waɪldlaɪf/ *n* [U] animals and plants which live and grow in natural conditions: *a naturalist studying the wildlife of the area* | *a wildlife park*

wild oats /ˌ· ¹·/ *n* **sow one's wild oats** to behave wildly while young, esp. having many sexual partners, although expecting to live a quiet life in future. In the past it used to be considered a good or usual thing for a man to have several sexual partners before he got mar-ried, but a very bad thing for a woman. Today men and women are still judged differently by society but it is now more acceptable for a woman to have the same amount of sexual experience as a man.

wild rice /ˌ· ¹·/ *n* [U] the seed of a wild grass which grows in parts of North America and China

Wild West /ˌ· ¹·/ *the* the western US in former times before law and order was properly established –see also NATIVE AMERICAN, WESTERN and see colour picture on page 358

▶ CULTURAL NOTE The wild west is a very popular subject for films, called WESTERNS, which usu. tell the story of fights between COWBOYS and INDIANS or fights between the SHERIFF of a town and bad cowboys. These films do not give a true picture of what life was like in the wild west but for most people this is how they imagine the wild west used to be. ◀

wiles /waɪlz/ *n* [P] *fml or lit* tricks and deceit, used esp. as a way of persuading –see also WILY

wil·ful *BrE* ‖ **willful** *AmE* /¹wɪlfəl/ *adj* **1** *derog* showing a strong unreasonable determination to do what one wants, in spite of other people: *a wilful child* | *wilful dis-regard of our advice* **2** [A] (esp. of something bad) done on purpose: *wilful neglect/murder* – ~ **ly** *adv* – ~ **ness** *n* [U]

wi·li·ness /¹waɪlinᵻs/ *n* [U] the quality of being WILY

will¹ /wɪl/ *v* 3rd person sing. **will**, short form **'ll**, negative short form **won't** [*modal*+*to*-*v*] **1** (used for expressing the simple future tense): *They say that it will rain tomor-row.* | *The wedding will take place in July.* | *What time will she arrive/will she be arriving?* | *I will have finished the job by that time.* | *We'll see you next week.* | *New recruits will report to the sergeant at 9 a.m.* (=this is what they must do) **2** to be willing to; be ready to: *I won't go!* | *We can't find anyone who will take the job.* | *The door won't shut.* | *Will you have some tea?* (=a polite way of offering something) | *The doctor will see you now.* **3** (used when asking someone to do something): *Will you phone me later, please?* | *Shut the door, will you?* | *You won't tell him, will you?* (=I hope not) **4** (shows what al-ways happens): *Accidents will happen.* | *Oil will float on water.* | *He will ask silly questions.* | *Boys will be boys.* (=one must expect boys to behave in the way they typi-cally do) **5** (used like **can**, to show what is possible): *This car will hold five people comfortably.* **6** (used like **must**, to show what is likely): *That will be the postman at the door now.* **7 I will** the answer to a question in the marriage service "Will you take this woman/man to be your lawful wedded wife/husband?", by which one agrees formally to be married –see also WOULD; see NOT (USAGE), SHALL (USAGE)

will² *n* **1** [C;U] the power of the mind to make decisions and act in accordance with them, sometimes in spite of difficulty or opposition: *Do you believe in* **free will/free-dom of the will?** (=the power to decide freely what one will do) | *You must have an* **iron will** (=a very strong will) *to have given up smoking after all those years.* | *Even small children can have very strong wills.* **2** [U] what is wished or intended (by the stated person): *Her death is God's will/the will of God.* | *In a democracy, the govern-ment is supposed to reflect the will of the people.* [+*to*-*v*] *She seems to have lost the will to live.* (=the desire to stay alive) | *The prisoner was forced to sign a confession* **against his will.** | *She donated the money* **of her own free will.** (=because she wanted to, and not because she was asked or forced to) **3** [S] a strong determination to act in a particular way; intention: **Where there's a will, there's a way.** (old saying=if you really want something you will find a way of getting it) | *They set to work* **with a will.** (=with eager interest) | *He tries hard but,* **with the best will in the world** (=however good his inten-tions may be), *he'll never make a good teacher.* **4** [U] the stated feeling towards other people: *She bears him no ill will for speaking out against her proposals.* **5** [C] an official statement of the way someone wants their property to be shared out after they die: *Have you made your will yet?* **6 at will** *fml* as one wishes **7 -willed** /wɪld/ having a will of the stated strength: *strong-willed | weak-willed*

will³ *v* **1** [T] to (try to) make (something) happen, esp. by power of the mind: [+*obj+to-v*] *We were all at the side of the racetrack, willing her to win.* [+*that*] *God has willed that the Earth (should) turn once a day.* **2** [T (**to**)] to leave (possessions or money) in a WILL² (5) to be given after one's death: [+*obj(i)+obj(d)*] *Grandfather willed me his watch|willed his watch to me.* **3** [I;T] *old use* to wish: *She is going to leave, whether you will or no|not.*

Wil·liam /ˈwɪljəm/, **Prince** (1982–) the first child of the Prince and Princess of Wales

William and Ma·ry /ˌ··· ˈ··/ *adj* (of furniture or other articles) belonging to the period when William III was king and his wife Mary was queen (the late 17th century)

William Hill /ˌ··· ˈ·/ one of a group of BETTING SHOPs owned by the **William Hill Organization**, branches of which are found in many towns and cities in Britain

Wil·liam of Or·ange /ˌ··· ˈ··/ also **William III** /ˌwɪljəm ðə ˈθɜːd ‖ -ˈθɜːrd/— (1650–1702) the king of England, Scotland and Ireland from 1689–1702. His wife, Queen Mary II had equal power and people usu. talk about the REIGN of **William and Mary**.

Wil·liams /ˈwɪljəmz/, **Hank** (1923–53) an American popular music singer who, in spite of his short life, had a great influence on American COUNTRY AND WESTERN music

Williams, Ralph Vaughan see VAUGHAN WILLIAMS

Williams, Robin (1952–) an American actor and COMEDIAN whose films include *Good Morning Vietnam* and *Dead Poets Society* —see colour picture on page 553

Williams, Shir·ley /ˈʃɜːli‖ˈʃɜːrli/ (1930–) an English politician and former Labour MINISTER of Education who left Labour to help establish the Social Democratic Party (SDP) in 1981

Williams, Ted /ted/ (1918–) a BASEBALL player famous for being a good hitter. Many BATs have his name on them as a kind of advertisement.

Williams, Tennessee (1911–83) an American writer whose plays arc mainly about people with emotional problems and are set in the Southern States. His plays include *The Glass Menagerie, A Streetcar Named Desire,* and *Cat On A Hot Tin Roof*

William the Con·quer·or /ˌ··· ˈ···/ also **William I** /ˌwɪljəm ðə ˈfɜːst ‖ -ˈfɜːrst/— (1027–87) the DUKE of Normandy who became king of England after defeating King Harold at the Battle of Hastings in 1066. He gave a lot of power to other Normans and built many castles to control the English. He changed the organization of society and the rules about who owned the land. —see also HASTINGS, DOMESDAY BOOK, NORMAN CONQUEST

wil·lie also **willy** /ˈwɪli/ *n BrE euph sl for* PENIS

wil·lies /ˈwɪliz/ *n* **give someone the willies** *infml* to make someone frightened and uncomfortable, e.g. by being strange or dark: *This place|That person|The way he speaks gives me the willies.*

will·ing /ˈwɪlɪŋ/ *adj* **1** [F] regarding favourably the possibility of doing something; ready: *If the management is willing, the talks can be held today.*[+*to-v*] *Are you willing to help?* **2** *apprec* acting eagerly and without being forced: *a willing helper|volunteer* **3** [A] done or given gladly and without being forced: *willing help* — ~ **ly** *adv* — ~ **ness** *n* [U]: *willingness to help*

will-o'-the-wisp /ˌ··· ˈ·/ *n* **1** a bluish moving light seen at night over wet ground because of the burning of waste gases from decayed plants **2** something undependable, esp. an aim that cannot be reached: *chasing the will-o'-the-wisp of perfection*

wil·low /ˈwɪləu/ *n* **1** [C] also **willow tree** /ˈ·· ·/— a type of tree which grows near water, with long thin branches —see picture at TREE **2** [U] the wood from this tree —see also **the crack of leather on willow** (LEATHER)

willow pat·tern /ˈ·· ˌ··/ *n* [U] a set of pictures, usu. in blue and white and usu. including a willow tree and a river, which represent a Chinese story and are used to decorate plates, cups, etc.

wil·low·y /ˈwɪləui/ *adj* (of a woman) pleasantly tall, thin, and graceful; SLENDER

will·pow·er /ˈwɪlˌpauəʳ/ *n* [U] strength of WILL² (1); ability to control one's own actions and desires: *She managed to stop smoking by sheer will power.*

wil·ly-nil·ly /ˌwɪli ˈnɪli/ *adv* regardless of whether it is wanted or not: *The new law will be passed willy-nilly* (=whether or not we want it) *so we will have to consider how it affects us.*

Wil·son /ˈwɪlsən/, **Sir Harold** (1916–) an English Labour politician who was PRIME MINISTER from 1964 to 1970 and 1974 to 1976

Wilson, Wood·row /ˈwudrəu/ (1856–1924) an American Democratic politician who was president of the US from 1913 to 1921 and led the country into the First World War. He helped to form the League of Nations.

wilt¹ /wɪlt/ *v* **1** [I;T] **a** (of a plant) to become less fresh, bend, and start to die: *The flowers are wilting from lack of water.* **b** to cause (a plant) to become less fresh, bend, and start to die —compare WITHER **2** [I] (of a person) to become tired and weaker: *I'm wilting in this heat.*

wilt² *v* **thou wilt** *old use or bibl* (when talking to one person) you will

Wilt·shire /ˈwɪltʃəʳ/ a COUNTY in SW England which contains the towns of Trowbridge and Salisbury

wil·y /ˈwaɪli/ *adj* clever in using tricks, esp. in order to get what one wants; CRAFTY: *a wily fox|negotiator* —see also WILES — ~ **iness** *n* [U]

Wimbledon

Wim·ble·don /ˈwɪmbəldən/ an important tennis competition which takes place every summer at the All England Club, in the part of London called Wimbledon. Wimbledon is considered to be typically English and rather old-fashioned and is an important social occasion as well as being a sporting event. It is TRADITIONAL to eat strawberries (STRAWBERRY) and cream and drink CHAMPAGNE or PIMMS. People often joke about the fact that it often rains during Wimbledon: *her first Wimbledon final | Rain has delayed the start of play at Wimbledon.*

wimp¹ /wɪmp/ *n infml derog* a weak or useless person, esp. a man —**wimpy, wimpish** *adj*

wimp² *n* (a computer featuring) windows, ICONs (2), MENUs (2), and pointers, which make it easier for an unfamiliar user to learn to use a computer: *a wimp interface*

Wim·pey /ˈwɪmpi/ a large British building company, best known to most people for their private houses often built in large groups or ESTATEs (2)

wim·ple /ˈwɪmpəl/ *n* a covering of cloth over the head and arranged round the neck and face, formerly worn by women in the MIDDLE AGES, and now by some NUNs

Wim·py /ˈwɪmpi/ *n BrE tdmk* a HAMBURGER (1) sold at a **Wimpy Bar** restaurant

Wim·sey /ˈwɪmzi/, **Lord Peter** the DETECTIVE who is the main character in the books by Dorothy L Sayers. He is an UPPER-CLASS man who is always very polite to people, but manages to SOLVE crimes.

win¹ /wɪn/ *v* **won** /wʌn/, *present participle* **winning** **1** [I;T] to be the best or first in (a battle, competition, race, etc.); defeat one's opponent (in): *We won by scoring in the last minute. | I never win at cards|at tennis. | He won the race. | Who do you think will win the election? | I won my bet. | The winning team was given a silver cup.* | (fig.) *OK, you win* (=I admit that you are right, you have persuaded me, etc.) *—we'll do it your way.* —opposite **lose** **2** [T] to gain or receive as a result of victory or success in any kind of competition: *She won third place|a bronze medal.* | *His horse came first and he won a lot of money.* | *Do you think he will win the Republican nomination?* **3** [T] to gain by effort, ability, quality, etc.: *I can't win his friendship, though I've tried.* | *Their proposals for redeveloping the area have won the approval of the city council.* | *a campaign to win the support of the younger voters* [+*obj*(*i*)+*obj*(*d*)] *By her hard work she won herself a place at university.* **4 win hands 'down** to win easily **5 win someone's heart** to gain someone's love or strong approval **6 win the day** to be successful or gain victory: *In the end, the arguments of the environmentalists won the day.* —see also WINNER, WINNING, WINNING POST, WINNINGS

▷ USAGE Compare **win, beat,** and **defeat**. You can **win** a **game,** and after the event you can say *I've* **won**! You can also **win** a **prize,** or **win** a **victory**. A nation can **win** a **war**. When you win a game, you **beat** the other player or the other team (**defeat** can be used formally): *We* **beat** *their team by ten points.* When a nation wins a war it **defeats** its enemies (**beat** can be used informally): *The Americans* **defeated** *the British in 1781.* — see also GAIN (USAGE)◁

win sthg./sbdy. ↔ **back** *phr v* [T] to get back (something that has been lost), esp. through effort or struggle: *How can I win back her love|their support?*

win sbdy. **over/round** *phr v* [T (**to**)] to gain the support of, often by persuading: *He disagrees at the moment, but I'm sure we can win him round|over to our point of view.*

win through/out *phr v* [I] to succeed, esp. after some time or in spite of difficulties

win² *n* a victory or success (esp. in sport): *This season we've had three wins and two defeats.* | *Forecasters are predicting a Labour win at the by-election.* | *She had a big win in the lottery.* (=won a lot of money)

wince /wins/ *v* [I (**at**)] to move back suddenly, often making a twisted expression with the face, (as if) drawing away from something painful or unpleasant: *She winced as she touched the cold body.* | *He winced at her angry words.* —see also JUMP¹ (3), START¹ (11) —**wince** *n* [S]

win·cey·ette /ˌwinsiˈet/ *n* [U] *BrE* a fairly light material with a soft surface, used esp. for night clothes

winch¹ /wintʃ/ *n* a machine for pulling up objects by means of a rope or chain that is wound around a turning part

winch² *v* [T] to pull or lift with a winch: *They winched the car out of the ditch.*

Win·ches·ter /ˈwintʃ‚stəʳ‖-tʃes-/ a city in S England with a famous CATHEDRAL and PUBLIC SCHOOL. The local government for Hampshire is based there.

wind¹ /wind/ *n* **1** [C;U] moving air; a current of air, esp. one moving strongly or quickly: *the east wind* | *a 70-mile-an-hour wind* | *We couldn't play tennis because there was too much wind.* | *The clothes on the washing line flapped in the wind.* | *A sudden gust of wind blew the door shut.* | *High|strong winds made driving conditions dangerous* | (fig.) *the winds of change|controversy* —see USAGE **2** [U] breath or breathing: *It took him a while to* **get his wind** (=breathe properly or regularly) *after running so fast.* —see also SECOND WIND, WINDPIPE **3** [U] *esp. BrE* (the condition of having) air or gas in the stomach: *Cabbage gives me wind.* | *Small babies often get wind.* **4** [U] *infml derog* words without meaning: *That speech was just a load of wind.* —see also WINDBAG **5** [*the*+S+*sing.|pl. v*] the group of WIND INSTRUMENT players in a band: *the wind section of an orchestra* **6 get/have wind of** *infml* to hear or know about (something secret or private), esp. accidentally or unofficially: *The police have got wind of a robbery planned for tonight.* **7 in wind and limb** *BrE fml or pomp* in all parts of one's body: *The horse was* **sound in wind and limb.** (=completely healthy) **8 put/get the wind up** *infml* to make/become frightened or anxious: *These new police tactics have really put the wind up the local drug dealers.* **9 see/find out which way the 'wind blows** to find out what the situation is before taking action **10** (**something**) **in the wind** (something, esp. that is secret or not generally known) about to happen/being done **11 take the wind out of someone's sails** *infml* to take away someone's confidence or advantage, esp. by saying or doing something unexpected —see also WINDY, **break wind** (BREAK¹), (**sail**) **close to the wind** (CLOSE³), **throw caution to the winds** (THROW¹)

▷ USAGE **Wind** is a general word for a moving current of air. A **breeze** is usually a pleasant, gentle wind: *There's a nice breeze down by the sea.* A **gust** is a strong, sudden rush of air: *A gust of wind blew the door shut.* A **gale** is a very strong wind: *Our chimney was blown down in a gale.* —see also STORM (USAGE)◁

wind² /wind/ *v* [T] **1** to cause to be breathless or have difficulty in breathing: *He was winded by a sudden blow to the stomach.* **2** *tech* to smell the presence of (esp. a hunted animal): *The hounds winded a fox.*

wind³ /waind/ *v* **wound** /waund/ **1** [T] to turn round and round with a number of circular movements: *She was winding the handle.* **2** [T (UP)] to tighten the working parts of by turning round and round: *The clock's stopped; you'd better wind it (up).* **3** [T+*obj*+*adv|prep*] *BrE* ‖ **roll** *AmE* to move by turning: *I wound down the car window.* **4** [T+*obj*+*adv|prep*] to turn or twist (something) repeatedly, esp. round an object: *The nurse wound a bandage round my wounded arm.* | *She wound the wool into a ball.* | *I wound a scarf round my neck.* **5** [I+*adv|prep*] to follow a twisting course, with many changes of direction: *The path winds through the woods and up the side of the mountain.* —see also WINDING

wind down *phr v* **1** [T] (**wind sthg.** ↔ **down**) to bring to an end gradually; cause to be no longer in operation: *The company is winding down its business in Hong Kong.* —compare WIND **up** (1) **2** [I] (of a person) to rest and become calmer or less active after work or excitement

wind up *phr v* **1** [T (**with**)] (**wind sthg.** ↔ **up**) to bring to an end: *We wound up the meeting with a vote of thanks to the chairman.* | *The company is losing a lot of money, so it's being wound up.* —compare WIND **down** **2** [I;L] *infml* to get into the stated usu. unpleasant condition or place as an accidental or unintentional result of one's actions or behaviour: [+*v-ing*] *I wound up paying for it myself.* (=In the end it was me that had to pay.) [+*adj*] *He wound up drunk.* [+*adv|prep*] *You'll wind up in hospital if you drive so fast.* | *If you keep working at this rate you could wind up with a heart attack.* **3** [T] (**wind sbdy.** ↔ **up**) *BrE infml* to annoy or deceive (someone) playfully: *Don't take any notice – she's just trying to wind you up.* —see also WIND³ (2), WOUND-UP

wind⁴ /waind/ *n* a bend or turn: *Give the handle a few more winds.*

wind⁵ /waind/ *v* **winded** *or* **wound** /waund/ [T] *lit* to blow (a horn)

wind·bag /ˈwindbæg/ *n infml derog* a person who talks too much, esp. about uninteresting things —see also WIND¹ (4)

wind-blown /ˈwindbləun/ *adj* having the appearance (as if) caused by the action of wind: *windblown hair|landscapes*

wind·break /ˈwindbreik/ *n* a fence, wall, line of trees, etc., intended to prevent the wind coming through with its full force

wind·break·er /ˈwindbreikəʳ/ *n AmE for* WINDCHEATER

wind·cheat·er /ˈwind‚tʃiːtəʳ/ *BrE* ‖ **windbreaker** *AmE*— *n old-fash* a short coat usu. fastened closely at wrists and neck, which is intended to keep out the wind

Win·der·mere /ˈwindəmiəʳ‖-dər-/ a lake in the part of NW England known as the Lake District

wind·fall /ˈwindfɔːl/ *n* **1** a piece of fruit that has fallen off a tree: *These apples are windfalls, but they're good.* **2** an unexpected lucky gift or gain, esp. money from someone who has died: *a windfall of £100 from a distant relative* | *windfall profits*

wind gauge /ˈwind geidʒ/ *n* an instrument which measures the strength of the wind

wind·ing /ˈwaindiŋ/ *adj* having a twisting turning shape: *a winding path* | *winding stairs* —see also WIND³ (5)

winding sheet /ˈwaindiŋ ʃiːt/ *n* a SHROUD¹ (1)

wind in·stru·ment /ˈwind ‚instrǝmǝnt/ *n* a musical instrument played by blowing air through it: *Trumpets and clarinets are wind instruments.* —see pictures at BRASS and WOODWIND

Wind in the Wil·lows /ˌwind in ðə ˈwiləuz/, **The** a popular children's story by Kenneth Grahame, whose characters are all animals who live on the river bank. The main characters are Mole, Ratty, Toad, and Badger.

wind·jam·mer /ˈwind‚dʒæməʳ/ *n* a large sailing ship, esp. of a type that was used for trade in the 19th century

The Wind in the Willows

wind·lass /ˈwɪndləs/ n a machine for pulling or moving objects by means of a turning part, often with a handle

sail   propeller   **windmills**

windmill   windmill

windmills/wind turbines

wind·mill /ˈwɪndˌmɪl/ n 1 a a building or structure with large sails or similar parts which are turned round by the wind, used esp. for crushing grain b also **wind turbine**– a similar machine used to produce power for electricity: *windmill farms in California* 2 ‖ also **pinwheel** *AmE*– a toy consisting of a stick with usu. four small curved pieces at the end which turn round when blown –see also **tilt at windmills** (TILT)

win·dow /ˈwɪndəʊ/ n 1 a a usu. glass-filled opening in the wall of a building, in a vehicle etc., to let in light and air: *the bedroom windows* | *It's cold in here; shut the window.* | *She sat looking out of the window.* | *The car has a heated rear window.* b a piece of glass in a window; WINDOW-PANE: *The burglars smashed the window to get into the house.* | *a stained-glass window* | *a window cleaner* | *goods displayed in a shop window* –see also BAY WINDOW, FRENCH WINDOWS, SASH WINDOW, and see pictures at CAR and HOUSE 2 *tech* a one of a number of areas into which a computer's SCREEN can be divided, each of which is used to show a particular type of information b a part of the Earth's ATMOSPHERE through which radio waves can pass to or from space c a short period of time that is the only one that can be used for a particular activity: *a launch window for a space rocket* 3 a transparent area on the front of an envelope, through which the address can be seen on the letter inside

window box /ˈ·· ·/ n a box full of earth in which plants can be grown outside a window

window clean·er /ˈ·· ˌ··/ n a person whose job is cleaning windows.

▶CULTURAL NOTE In Britain, window cleaners are often mentioned in jokes because people imagine that they see a lot of strange or interesting things while they are doing their work, such as people with no clothes on.◀

window dres·ser /ˈ·· ˌ··/ n someone whose job is window dressing

window dress·ing /ˈ·· ˌ··/ n [U] 1 the art or practice of arranging goods in a shop window to give a good effect and attract customers 2 *usu. derog* something that is intended to attract people to an idea or activity, esp. by showing only what is favourable: *All these films and glossy pamphlets about the new house-building programme are just window dressing; it's going to cost the taxpayer a lot of money.*

win·dow·ing /ˈwɪndəʊɪŋ/ n [U] *tech* the designing (DESIGN) of computer PROGRAMS in a way that lets a person use them by means of windows (2a)

win·dow·pane /ˈwɪndəʊpeɪn/ n a single whole piece of glass in a window

window seat /ˈ·· ˌ·/ n 1 a seat inside a room below a window esp. a BAY window 2 a seat next to the window in a bus, plane, etc.

window shade /ˈ·· ˌ·/ n *AmE for* BLIND³ (1) –see picture at KITCHEN

window-shop /ˈ·· ·/ v -pp- [I] to look at the goods shown in shop windows without necessarily intending to buy: *I like going window-shopping.* – ~**per** n

win·dow·sill /ˈwɪndəʊˌsɪl/ n a flat shelf at the base of a window, on the inside or outside –see picture at HOUSE

wind·pipe /ˈwɪndpaɪp/ also **trachea** *med*– n the tube which forms an air passage from the throat to the top of the lungs –see picture at RESPIRATORY

Wind·scale /ˈwɪndskeɪl/ the former name of Sellafield NUCLEAR POWER STATION –see SELLAFIELD

wind·screen /ˈwɪndskriːn/ *BrE* ‖ **windshield** *AmE*– n a piece of glass or transparent material across the front of a car, TRUCK, etc., which the driver looks through –see picture at CAR

windscreen wash·er /ˈ·· ˌ··/ n an apparatus consisting of a water bottle, a pipe and a small JET¹(3) through which the water is forced onto a car windscreen for cleaning it while driving

windscreen wip·er /ˈ·· ˌ··/ n a movable arm which clears rain from a windscreen –see picture at CAR

wind·shield /ˈwɪndʃiːld/ n 1 a piece of transparent material fixed at the front of a motorcycle 2 *AmE* a windscreen –see picture at CAR

wind·sock /ˈwɪndsɒk‖-sɑːk/ n a piece of material shaped like a tube coming to a point at one end, fastened to a pole at airports to show the direction of the wind

Wind·sor /ˈwɪnzəʳ/ a town in S England on the river Thames famous for its castle –see also WINDSOR CASTLE, WINDSORS

Windsor Cas·tle /ˌ·· ˈ··/ one of the official homes of the British royal family, which is in the town of Windsor

Windsor Great Park /ˌ·· ˈ· ˌ·/ the large park in which Windsor Castle stands

Wind·sors /ˈwɪndzəz‖-zərz/ [the + P] the family name of the British Royal Family, used esp. by newspapers

Windsor Sa·fa·ri Park /ˌ·· ·ˈ·· ˌ·/ a ZOO near Windsor in S England where many of the animals are given the freedom of large enclosed areas which people may drive through

wind·storm /ˈwɪndstɔːm‖-ɔːrm/ n a weather condition of strong wind, with little or no rain

windsurfing

wind-surf·ing /ˈwɪnd ˌsɜːfɪŋ‖-ˌsɜːrf-/ n [U] the sport of riding on SAILBOARDs –see also SURF² – -**er** n

wind·swept /'wɪndswept/ *adj* **1** (of a place) open to the wind, esp. when there are no trees or buildings nearby: *a windswept moor* | *the windswept ruins of an ancient city* **2** (of a person, their hair, etc.) untidy (as if) blown by the wind: *She looked windswept when she came in out of the storm.*

wind tun·nel /'wɪnd ˌtʌnl/ *n* an artificial enclosed passage through which air is forced at fixed speeds to test aircraft and their parts

wind tur·bine /'wɪnd ˌtɜːbaɪn‖-ˌtɜːrbɪ̥n, -baɪn/ *n* a WINDMILL (1b) —see picture at WINDMILL

wind·ward[1] /'wɪndwəd‖-wərd/ *adj, adv esp. naut* **1** against the direction of the wind; towards the direction from which the wind is blowing: *We steered windward|a windward course.* **2** facing the wind: *the windward side of the wall* —opposite **leeward**

windward[2] *n* [U] *esp. naut* the side or direction from which the wind is blowing: *We steered a course to windward.*

Windward Is·lands /'·· ˌ·/ [*the*+P] a group of islands in the West Indies which includes Martinique, Grenada and St. Lucia

wind·y /'wɪndi/ *adj* **1** with a lot of wind: *a windy day* | *a windy hillside* **2** *esp. lit* (of a person or speech) full of fine-sounding but meaningless words, esp. when praising oneself **3** causing air or gas in the stomach **4** *old-fash infml, esp. BrE* frightened or nervous **—ily** *adv* **—iness** *n* [U]

Windy Cit·y /ˌ·· '··/ [*the*] CHICAGO

wine[1] /waɪn/ *n* [C;U] **1** (an) alcoholic drink made from GRAPES: *a glass of white|red wine* | *the wines of California|Bordeaux* | *my favourite wine* | *a wine glass* | *Would you like to taste the wine, sir?* (=drink a small quantity to test it for quality) **2** (an) alcoholic drink made from the stated fruit, plant, etc.: *apple wine* —see also TABLE WINE **3 wine, women, and song** *often humor* the pleasant life that represents the supposed usual enjoyment of men

wine[2] *v* **wine and dine** to entertain or be entertained with a meal and wine: *We wined and dined (them) until late into the night.*

wine bar /'· ·/ *n BrE* a type of BAR[1] (3) that serves mainly wine and also usu. provides light meals. Wine bars are very different from pubs and usu. aim to have a more fashionable image. They are popular esp. with MIDDLE-CLASS, professional men and women.

wine cool·er /'· ˌ··/ *n AmE* a drink made with wine, fruit juice, CARBONATED water

wine lake /'· ·/ *n* a very large amount of wine made by wine-producing countries that is additional to what is needed and is stored to prevent prices falling: *the EC wine lake*

wine vin·e·gar /ˌ· '···/ *n* [U] a type of VINEGAR made from sour wine, used in cooked dishes and sauces

Win·frey /'wɪnfri/, **O·prah** /'əʊprə/ (1954–) an American television personality who has a daily programme in which people discuss many different subjects. She has also appeared in films.

Oprah Winfrey

wing[1] /wɪŋ/ *n* **1 a** a movable limb which a bird, insect, etc., uses for flying: *The birds spread their wings and flew away.* | *a butterfly with beautiful markings on its wings* —see pictures at BIRD, CAR, and INSECT **b** the meat covering the wing bone of a chicken, duck, etc., used as food **2** one of the large flat structures that stand out from each side of a plane and support it in flight —see picture at AIRCRAFT **3** a part of something, esp. of a building, which stands out from the main or central part: *a campaign to raise money for a new hospital wing* | *the west wing of the house* **4** *BrE* ‖ **fender** *AmE—* the side part of a car that covers the wheels: *a wing mirror* —see picture at CAR **5** (in sport) the position or player on the far right or left of the field **6** a group within a political party or similar organization, whose members have aims or opinions that are different from

those of the main body of the organization: *The Senator is on the liberal wing of the Republican Party.* | *the political wing of the IRA* —see also LEFT WING, RIGHT WING **7 Oh for the wings of a dove** a song by Mendelssohn which is sung in a very high voice, usu. by a young boy **8 on the wing** *esp. lit* (of a bird) flying **9 take wing** *esp. lit* to fly (away): *The sudden noise frightened the birds, and they took wing.* **10 under someone's wing** being protected, helped, etc., by someone: *to take someone under one's wing* —see also WINGS, **clip someone's wings** (CLIP[3]), **spread one's wings** (SPREAD[1]) **– ~less** *adj*

wing[2] *v* **1** [I+adv|prep] to fly (as if) on wings: *The plane came winging down towards the coast.* **2** [T] to wound in the arm or wing **3 wing it** *AmE, sl* to do something without planning: *"What cities are you going to see on holiday?" "I don't know – I'm just going to wing it and do what I feel like."* | *I didn't have time to prepare for the meeting so I'll have to wing it.*

wing com·mand·er /'· ·ˌ··/ *n* a rank in the Royal Air Force —see TABLE 3

wing·ding /'wɪŋˌdɪŋ/ *n AmE becoming old-fash* a lively party

winge /wɪndʒ/ *n* [I] see WHINGE

winged /wɪŋd/ *adj* (*often in comb.*) having wings, esp. of the stated number or type

wing·er /'wɪŋəʳ/ *n* **1** (in games like football) a player in the area on the far left or right of the field —see also WING[1] (5) **2 -winger** a person who belongs to the stated group (RIGHT WING or LEFT WING) in a political party: *Republican right-wingers*

wing nut /'· ·/ also **butterfly nut—** *n* a NUT (2) with sides which one can hold while turning it

wings /wɪŋz/ *n* [P] **1** (either of) the sides of a stage, where an actor is hidden from view **2** a sign which a pilot can wear, to show he or she can fly an aircraft: *Have you got your wings yet?* **3 in the wings** not yet publicly known about but ready and able to take action when the time is right

wing·span /'wɪŋspæn/ also **wing·spread** /-spred/— *n* the distance from the end of one wing to the end of the other, when both are stretched out: *the eagle's huge wingspan* | *an aircraft with a wingspan of 50 metres*

wing·tips /'wɪŋtɪps/ *n* [P] *AmE* men's shoes with a decorative pattern of small holes in raised pieces of leather

wink[1] /wɪŋk/ *v* **1** [I(at);T] to close and open (one eye) quickly, usu. as a signal between people, esp. of amusement or a shared secret: *He winked at her, and she knew he was only pretending to be angry.* **2** [I;T] *BrE* ‖ **blink** *AmE—* to flash or cause (a light) to flash on and off: *The driver's winking his lights; he must be turning this way.* **wink at sthg.** *phr v* [T] to pretend not to notice (something bad or illegal), in a way that suggests approval: *The officials winked at the trucks carrying the illegal supplies.*

wink[2] *n* **1** [C] a winking movement of the eye: *She gave him a saucy wink|a conspiratorial wink.* **2** [S *usu. in negatives*] even a short period of sleep: *I didn't get a wink of sleep|didn't sleep a wink last night.* (=did not sleep at all) —see also FORTY WINKS, **a nod's as good as a wink** (NOD[2])

wink·ers /'wɪŋkəz‖-ərz/ *BrE* ‖ **blinkers** *AmE— n* [P] *infml* the small usu. orange lights on a car which flash either on the right or left to show that it will move towards that direction

win·kle[1] /'wɪŋkəl/ also **periwinkle—** *n* a small sea animal that lives in a shell and that people sometimes eat

winkle[2] *v*
winkle sthg./sbdy. out *phr v* [T (**of**)] *infml, esp. BrE* to get or remove slowly and with difficulty: *At last I winkled the truth out of him.* | *We'll winkle him out of there.*

Winkle, Rip Van see RIP VAN WINKLE

winkle-pick·er /'·· ˌ··/ *n* [C *usu. pl.*] *infml BrE* a type of man's shoe with very pointed toes which was fashionable in the late 1950s —see PAIR (USAGE)

Win·ne·ba·go /ˌwɪnɪ'beɪɡəʊ/ *n AmE tdmk* a kind of MOTOR HOME

win·ner /'wɪnəʳ/ *n* **1** a person or animal that has won something: *a Nobel Prize winner* | *the winner of last year's Kentucky Derby* | *The winners received a cup and the losers were given medals.* **2** *infml apprec* something that is (expected to be) successful: *That idea's a real winner.* |

The company is **onto a winner** *with this new car.*

Win·nie the Pooh /ˌwɪni ðə ˈpuː/ also **Pooh, Pooh Bear**— the main character in children's books written by A.A. Milne. Winnie the Pooh is a bear who is not very clever or brave, but is very cheerful and helpful and has lots of friends, including Piglet, Eeyore, and Tigger. He likes inventing songs and poems and his favourite food is HONEY.

win·ning /ˈwɪnɪŋ/ adj very pleasing or attractive; charming: *His winning ways made him popular with everyone.* | *a winning smile*

winning post /ˈ·· ˌ·/ [the] esp. BrE (in horse racing) a post marking the place where a race finishes

win·nings /ˈwɪnɪŋz/ n [P] money which has been won in a game, by betting (BET) on a race, etc.

Win·ni·peg /ˈwɪnɪpeg/ **1** a city in W Canada **2** a large lake in W Canada

win·now /ˈwɪnəʊ/ v [T] to blow the outer part (HUSKs) from (grain)

wi·no /ˈwaɪnəʊ/ n pl **winos** sl an ALCOHOLIC, esp. one who has no home and lives on the streets

win·some /ˈwɪnsəm/ adj old-fash apprec pleasant and attractive, esp. in a fresh, childlike way: *a winsome girl* — **~ly** adv — **~ness** n [U]

win·ter¹ /ˈwɪntər/ n [C;U] the season between autumn and spring, when it is cold. In northern countries the winter months are December, January and February and it often snows during this time: *It usually snows here in winter.* | **in the depths of winter** (=the coldest time) | *a cold winter* | *last winter* | *winter clothes* —see colour picture on page 1212

winter² v [I+adv/prep] to spend the winter: *These birds winter in a warm country.*

win·ter·ize /ˈwɪntəraɪz/ v [T] AmE to prepare for winter weather conditions: *winterize your house/car/wardrobe*

winter of dis·con·tent /ˌ··· ···ˈ·/ [the] the winter of 1978–79 when many British workers refused to work in protest against the Labour government's ideas on limiting pay rises. The Labour Party lost power after this. The phrase comes from the opening line of Shakespeare's play *Richard III.* —see also SUMMER OF DISCONTENT

winter sol·stice /ˌ··· ˈ···/ [the] the day, usu. around December 22nd, on which the sun is above the TROPIC OF CAPRICORN and as far to the S as possible, so that places in the N HEMISPHERE, like Britain, have the shortest day of the year and places in the S hemisphere have the longest day of the year. The winter solstice is not usually celebrated in Britain or the US. —compare EQUINOX, SUMMER SOLSTICE

winter sports /ˌ··· ˈ·/ n [P] sports which take place on snow or ice such as skiing (SKI) or sledging (SLEDGE)

Winter's Tale /ˌ··· ˈ·/, **The** a play by William Shakespeare written in 1610 or 1611

win·ter·time /ˈwɪntətaɪm‖-ər-/ n [(the) U] the winter season; the time of winter weather: *Heating bills are highest in (the) wintertime.*

win·try /ˈwɪntri/ also **win·ter·y** /ˈwɪntəri/— adj like winter, esp. cold or snowy: *wintry clouds* | *a wintry scene* | (fig.) *a wintry smile* (=rather unhappy or unfriendly)

wipe¹ /waɪp/ v [T] **1** to rub (a surface or object), e.g. with a cloth or against another surface, in order to remove dirt, liquid, etc.: *to wipe the table with a damp cloth* | *Wipe your feet/shoes (on the mat) before you come in.* | *Wipe your nose (on/with your handkerchief).* | *Wipe your face/the blackboard clean.* | (fig.) *The whole nation is likely to be* **wiped off the map/wiped off the face of the Earth** (=completely destroyed) *in the event of another world war.* **2** [+obj+adv/prep] to remove by doing this: *She wiped the tears away.* | *Wipe the crumbs off the table onto the floor.* | (fig.) *Tell him how much he'll have to pay; that'll* **wipe the smile off his face.** (=make him less pleased or satisfied) **3** **wipe the floor with someone** infml to defeat someone completely in a competition or argument, making them feel shame —see CLEAN (USAGE) —**wiper** n

wipe sthg. ↔ **out** phr v [T often pass.] **1** to destroy or remove completely: *The entire population was wiped out by the terrible disease.* | *The cost of the new building will wipe out all the company's profits this year.* **2** sl to make very tired; EXHAUST —see also WIPED OUT

wipe sthg. ↔ **up** phr v **1** [T] to remove (liquid or dirt that has been dropped) with a cloth: *She wiped up the milk she had spilled.* **2** [I;T] BrE old-fash to dry (dishes, plates, etc., that have been washed) with a cloth

wipe² n **1** a wiping movement: *Give the baby's nose a good wipe.* **2** a type of cloth used for wiping

wiped out /ˌ· ˈ·/ adj [F] sl **1** extremely tired; EXHAUSTED **2** under the effects of drugs —see also WIPE out

wire¹ /waɪər/ n **1** [C;U] (a length of) thin metal in the form of a thread: *a wire fence* | *The string wasn't strong enough, so we used wire.* —see also BARBED WIRE **2** [C;U] a piece of metal like this, usu. covered with plastic, used for carrying electricity from one place to another **3** [C] AmE for TELEGRAM —see also LIVE WIRE, WIRING, WIRY

wire² v [T] **1** [(UP)] to connect up wires in (something, esp. an electrical system): *Is the house wired up yet?* | *Are you wired for receiving cable TV?* **2** [(to, TOGETHER)] to fasten with wire(s) **3** [(to)] AmE to send a TELEGRAM to: *Wire me if you can't come.* [+obj(i)+obj(d)] *He wired me the results of the negotiations.* **4** [T] to send (money) electronically, by telling one bank to make the money available at another bank far away: *I'll wire you the money in New York.* | *Can your bank wire the deposit?*

wired /waɪəd ‖ waɪərd/ adj **1** connected or fastened with wires **2** AmE infml very excited or TENSE¹ (1)

wire-haired /ˌ·ˈ·◂‖ˈ·· ·/ adj (of a dog) having stiff smooth hair, not soft or wool-like: *a wire-haired terrier*

wire·less¹ /ˈwaɪələs‖ˈwaɪər-/ n [C;U] old-fash, esp. BrE (a) radio: *listening to the wireless*

wireless² adj [A] tech without (using) wires; connected by radio: *wireless telegraphy*

wire net·ting /ˌ· ˈ··/ n [U] a material made of wires woven together into a network, with quite large spaces between them, used esp. for fences

wire-tap /ˈwaɪətæp‖ˈwaɪər-/ n an act of wire-tapping or an electrical connection for wire-tapping

wire-tap·ping /ˈ· ˌ··/ n [U] listening secretly to other people's telephone conversations by an unofficial or illegal connection

wire wool /ˌ· ˈ·/ n [U] very fine wire woven together and arranged in a round fairly solid piece, e.g. used for cleaning pans —compare STEEL WOOL

wire-worm /ˈwaɪəwɜːm‖ˈwaɪərwɜːrm/ n a wormlike creature which is the young of an insect and destroys plants by eating them

wir·ing /ˈwaɪərɪŋ/ n [(the) U] the arrangement of wires that form the electrical system in a building; network of wires: *We're having this old wiring replaced.* | *faulty wiring*

Wir·ral /ˈwɪrəl/ [the] a thick finger of land between the mouths of the rivers Dee and Mersey in NW England

wir·y /ˈwaɪəri/ adj rather thin, but with strong muscles: *his wiry athletic body* —**iness** n [U]

Wis·con·sin /wɪˈskɒnsən‖-ˈskɑːn-/ written abbrev. **WI**— a STATE in the N central US, known for producing the most milk, cheese, and butter —see colour map on pages 1374–5

Wis·den /ˈwɪzdən/ a yearly book about cricket, giving all match results, players' SCOREs, etc. Its full name is *Wisden's Cricketers' Almanack.*

wis·dom /ˈwɪzdəm/ n [U] rather fml **1** the quality of being wise; good sense and judgment: *a man of great wisdom* | *I would question the wisdom of borrowing such a large sum of money.* (=I think it is an unwise thing to do) **2** knowledge gained through learning or experience: *the wisdom of the ancients* | *folk wisdom* | *According to (the)* **received/conventional wisdom** *in these matters* (=what is generally believed to be true) *the voters usually make their choice on the basis of domestic issues.*

wisdom tooth /ˈ··· ·/ n any of the four large back teeth in humans, which do not usu. appear until the rest of the body has stopped growing. They sometimes have to be removed —see picture at TEETH

wise¹ /waɪz/ adj **1** rather fml apprec having or showing good sense and judgment, and the ability to understand and decide on the right action: *a wise man/decision/precaution* [F+to-v] *You were wise to leave when you did.* | *It was wise of you to do so.* | *You'll understand when you're* **older and wiser. 2** **a word to the wise** saying just a slight suggestion is enough for a clever person (usu. used to suggest that a clever person should be able to realize what the speaker means without it actually being said) **3 get wise to** *infml* to learn to understand the methods or behaviour of (esp. someone dishonest): *I've got wise to him and his game.* (=cheating) **4 none the wiser** *infml* knowing no more, after being told: *He explained it all to me, but I was none the wiser!* **5 wise after the event** understanding what should have been done to prevent a bad situation that has now happened: *If we had waited another week we could have bought the car more cheaply. Well, it's easy to be wise after the event.* —see also STREETWISE — ~**ly** *adv* : *He wisely refrained from having any more to drink.* | *The money has been wisely invested.*

▷ USAGE In ordinary speech, a person is usually described as **sensible** rather than **wise**.◁

wise² *v*

wise up *phr v* [I;T (=**wise** sbdy. ↔ **up**)] *infml, esp. AmE* to (cause to) learn or become conscious of the true situation or true nature of someone or something

wise³ *n* [S] **1** *old use* a way; manner: *It happened* **in this wise.** (=like this) | *They are* **in no wise** *to blame.* **2 -wise: a** in the manner of; like: *to walk crabwise* **b** in the position or direction of: *lengthwise* | *Turn the handle clockwise.* **c** in connection with; with regard to: *taxwise*

▷ USAGE Many new adverbs are formed, especially in American English, by adding **-wise** to nouns, with the meaning "in connection with": *The company must try to improve its position taxwise/saleswise/moneywise/profitwise.* Some people do not like this use.◁

Wise, Ernie see MORECAMBE AND WISE

wise·a·cre /ˈwaɪzeɪkəʳ/ *n AmE infml* WISE GUY

wise·crack¹ /ˈwaɪzkræk/ *n infml* a clever joking remark or reply

wisecrack² *v* [I] *infml* to make a wisecrack or wisecracks: *his jovial, wisecracking manner*

wise guy /ˈ· ·/ *n infml derog* someone who thinks they can supply information which shows that they know more than others, but which is in fact of no use: *OK, wise guy; if you're so clever, what's the right answer?*

wise men /ˌ· ˈ·/ also **three wise men, three kings**— [the] according to the Bible, the three wise men or kings who followed the star to where Jesus had just been born, and brought gifts of gold, FRANKINCENSE and MYRRH —see also NATIVITY

wish¹ /wɪʃ/ *v* [*not usu. in progressive forms*] **1** [T+(*that*); *obj*] to want (a particular situation) to exist, when this is impossible either at the present time or at any time: *I wish (that) I had never met you!* | *I wish I were a bird.* | *The party was awful, and we all wished we had never gone to it.* —see HOPE¹ (USAGE) **2** [I (**for**)] to want and try to cause a particular thing, esp. when it can only happen by magic; make a WISH² (3) in FAIRYTALEs and stories somebody is often given three wishes by a FAIRY, GENIE etc. which means that they have three chances to ask for anything they want and it will happen or appear: *You have everything you could wish for.* **3** [I;T] *fml* to want: *The newspapers here can print whatever they wish.* | *I don't think I ought to, but I will if you wish/if you so wish.* [+to-v] *I wish to make a complaint.* | *You can change the office round if you wish to.* [+obj+to-v] *Is there anything else you wish me to bring you?* **4** [T+obj(i)+obj(d)] to hope that (someone) will have (something), esp. expressed as a greeting: *We wish you a merry Christmas/good luck/a safe journey!* **5** [T+obj+adj/adv| prep] *fml* to want (something or someone) to be: *Do you wish your coffee black or white, sir?* | *We wished her anywhere except in our house!* | *She says she wishes herself dead.* **6 wish someone joy of something** *infml BrE* (used when someone has chosen the wrong thing or person) to hope that someone will enjoy something more than seems likely **7 wish someone well** to hope that someone will have success, good luck, etc. **8 wish you were here** a phrase that is supposed to be commonly written on holiday POSTCARDs, now mainly written as a joke

▷ USAGE In British English it is common in informal situations to use *was* instead of *were* in sentences like *I wish I were a bird.* But in American English it would be considered bad English to use *was* in this type of sentence.◁

wish sbdy./sthg. **on/upon** sbdy. *phr v* [T] to give or pass

on (a difficult or unwanted person, responsibility, etc.) to (someone else), in order to avoid trouble for oneself: *She's a difficult person; I* **wouldn't wish her on my worst enemy.**

wish² *n* [(**for**)] **1** a feeling of wanting something, esp. something that is at present impossible; hope or desire: *The whole world shares the wish for these peace talks to succeed.* | *Please respect my wishes and do as I ask.* | *They have deliberately gone against my wishes.* [+to-v] *She had expressed a wish* (=said she wanted) *to see the gardens.* | *I have no wish to appear rude, but ...* [+that] *His last wish* (=before he died) *was that he could see his grandchildren again.* | (in greetings) *We sent our* **best wishes** *for her birthday.* (=a wish that she would have a happy birthday) —see HOPE² (USAGE) **2** a thing wished for; object of hope or desire: *She wanted a new bike for Christmas and she got her wish.* | *May all your wishes come true!* **3** an attempt to make a particular desired thing or situation happen, esp. when it can only happen by magic, expressed in a special way or silently; act of wishing (WISH¹ (2)): *He closed his eyes and* **made a wish.**

wish·bone /ˈwɪʃbəʊn/ *n* a V-shaped bone in the breast of a chicken or other farm bird. After the bird has been cooked, the ends of the wishbone are pulled apart by two people, and the one who gets the longer piece can make a wish.

wishful think·ing /ˌ·· ˈ··/ *n* [U] the false belief that something is true or will happen simply because one wishes it: *Their hopes of a peace settlement are nothing more than wishful thinking.*

wishing well /ˈ·· ·/ *n* a well or pool of water which people believe will make a wish come true if they throw a coin into it

wish list /ˈ· ·/ *n infml* a list of things one wants, esp. from a business deal

wish·y-wash·y /ˈwɪʃi ˌwɒʃi‖-ˌwɔːʃi, -ˌwɑːʃi/ *adj derog* **1** (of drinks, soup, etc.) thin and without strength; WATERY: *wishy-washy tea* **2** without determination or clear aims and principles: *wishy-washy ideas* | *He's a wishy-washy liberal.*

wisp /wɪsp/ *n* [(**of**)] **1** a thin or delicate untidy piece: *a wisp of hair* | *wisps of grass* **2** a small thin twisting bit (of smoke or steam) —see picture at PIECE —**wispy** *adj*

wis·te·ri·a /wɪˈstɪəriə/ *n* a climbing plant with purple or white flowers

wist·ful /ˈwɪstfəl/ *adj* thoughtful and rather sad, esp. because of desires which may not be satisfied or memories of past happiness which may not return: *wistful reminiscences of her lost youth* — ~**ly** *adv* — ~**ness** *n* [U]

wit¹ /wɪt/ *n* **1** [U] *apprec* the ability to say things which are both clever and amusing at the same time: *conversation sparkling with wit* **2** [C] a person who has this ability: *Oscar Wilde was a famous wit.* **3** [U] also **wits** *pl.*— power of thought; INTELLIGENCE: *It is surely not beyond the wit of the government to solve this simple problem.* (=it should be possible for them to do it) | *He hadn't the wit to say no.* | (fig.) *The explosion frightened me* **out of my wits.** (=very much) —see also HALF-WIT **4 at one's wits end** *infml* made so worried by difficulties that one does not know what to do next **5 have/keep one's wits about one** to be ready to think quickly and act sensibly according to what may happen **6 -witted** /ˈwɪtɪd/ having the stated type of ability or understanding: *quick-witted* —see also WITTY, **live by/on one's wits** (LIVE¹)

wit² *v* **to wit** *old use or law* that is (to say); NAMELY

witch /wɪtʃ/ *n* **1** a woman who has magic powers, esp. one who can make bad things happen to people, such as an illness or accident. —see also WICKED WITCH and see picture on page 1211

witch

▶ CULTURAL NOTE The typical image of a witch is of a very ugly old woman dressed in black and with a pointed hat, riding through the air on a BROOMSTICK. From the 14th to the 17th century, the fear of witchcraft was so great that many women were killed because they were believed, usu. wrongly, to be witches. ◀

2 *derog* an unpleasant and ugly woman   **3** *old-fash* a woman who seems to have unusual power in attracting men —see also BEWITCH

witch·craft /ˈwɪtʃkrɑːft‖-kræft/ *n* [U] the performing of magic to make esp. bad things happen

witch·doc·tor /ˈwɪtʃˌdɒktəʳ‖-ˌdɑːk-/ *n derog* (in some non-Western societies) a man who is believed to have magical powers and be able to cure people; a MEDICINE MAN or SHAMAN.

▶CULTURAL NOTE In Britain and the US the typical image of a witchdoctor is either a black African man with very few clothes and a painted face or body or a Native American with a painted face and a COSTUME with lots of feathers. Both types of men are seen as quite frightening figures. These images are very offensive to people who come from societies where there are shamans, such as African and Native American people. ◀

Witches' Sab·bath /ˌ·ˈ·· ˈ··/ *n* a midnight meeting of humans with magic powers e.g. WITCHes, SORCERERs, and evil spirits, attended by the Devil, believed in the past to be held once a year as a FESTIVAL or ORGY

witch-ha·zel, wych-hazel /ˈ· ˌ··/ *n* [C;U] (a tree which produces) a liquid used for treating small wounds on the skin

witch-hunt /ˈ· ·/ *n derog* a planned attempt, often based on false information, to remove from power or from membership of a group those people whose political opinions are disapproved of or regarded as dangerous

witch·ing hour /ˈ·· ˌ·/ *[the]* an important moment, esp. at night, when something special is to happen

with /wɪð, wɪθ/ *prep* **1** in the presence or company of; near, beside, or among: *I'm staying with* (=at the house of) *a friend.* | *Leave your dog with me.* | *All you do to make the soup is mix the powder with boiling water.* | *Who was that man you were with last night?* **2 a** having or possessing: *a book with a green cover* | *a well-known bank with over 200 branches* | *a child with a dirty face* | *The equipment comes (complete) with instructions and a guarantee.* | *With a few exceptions, it's a very friendly group of people.* **b** showing (a quality): *They fought with courage.* | *I read your letter with great interest.* **c** including: *With a tip, the meal cost $30 for two.* —opposite **without 3** by means of; using: *You eat it with a spoon.* | *Cut it with the scissors.* | *What will you buy with the money?* | *This photo was taken with a cheap camera.* **4** (shows the idea of filling, covering, or containing): *I filled it with sugar.* | *It was covered with dirt.* **5** concerning; in regard to or in the case of: *Be careful with that glass.* | *Be gentle with the baby.* | *He's in love with you.* | *She has a lot of influence with the president.* | *Be patient with them.* | *Britain's trade with Japan* | *What's wrong/the matter with you?* | *I'm very pleased with my new car.* | *I agree/disagree with his suggestion.* | **The trouble with** *this job* (=the thing that is unsatisfactory about it) *is that the pay is too low.* **6** in support of; in favour of: *Some opposition MPs voted with the government.* | *You're either with me or against me.* **7** against: *Stop fighting with your brother.* | *Have a race with me.* | *We're competing with foreign businesses.* **8** in the same direction as: *We sailed with the wind/with the tide.* **9** at the same time and rate as: *With the dark nights comes the bad weather.* | *This wine improves with age.* **10** (used in comparisons): *It's like comparing chalk with cheese.* | *The window is level with the street.* | *Compared with other children of the same age, he's very tall.* **11** (shows separation): *She doesn't want to part with the money.* | *The new system represents a complete break with tradition.* **12** in spite of: *With all his faults, I still like him.* | **With the best will** (=intention) **in the world,** *I can't do it if they won't provide the money.* **13** because of or considering the fact of: *They were trembling with fear.* | *The grass was wet with rain.* | *With John away* (=because John is away), *we've got more room.* | *With our luck* (=considering our usual bad luck), *we'll probably miss the plane.* | *With profits up by 60%, the company has had another excellent year.* **14** (used in expressing wishes or commands strongly): *Down with school!* | *Off to bed with you!* | *Away with old ideas!* | *On with the show!* **15 with me/you** (*usu. in questions and negatives*) following my/your argument: *Are you still with me?* | *I'm not with you; you're going too fast.* **16 with that** also **at that**— when that had been done; then: *He gave a little wave and with that he was gone.* —see also **what with** (WHAT[2])

▷ USAGE Note how **by** is used before people or things that do a job, while **with** is used before the things that are used to do the job, in sentences like this: *He was murdered by his enemies.* | *He was shot with an arrow.* | *He was killed by a blow to the head with an axe.*◁

with·al /wɪðˈɔːl/ *adv old use* besides; together with this

with·draw /wɪðˈdrɔː, wɪθ-/ *v* **-drew** /ˈdruː/, **-drawn** /ˈdrɔːn/ [(**from**)] **1** [T] to take away or take back: *She withdrew £50 from her bank account.* | *The drug, which is suspected of having serious side effects, has been withdrawn from the market.* | (fig.) *to withdraw a remark/an allegation/an offer* **2** [I;T] to (cause to) move away or move back: *The two men withdrew from the room* (=went outside) *while the meeting voted for which should be chairman.* | *The general withdrew his army as it was suffering so many casualties.* **3** [I;T] to (cause to) not take part in an activity: *She withdrew from the election.* | *He withdrew his horse from the race.* —see also WITHDRAWN

with·draw·al /wɪðˈdrɔːəl, wɪθ-/ *n* [(**from**)] **1** [U] the act of withdrawing or state of being withdrawn: *withdrawal of financial support for his scheme* **2** [C] an example of this: *He's made several withdrawals* (=of money) *from his account recently.* | *a gradual withdrawal of troops from the war zone* **3** withdrawal symptoms

withdrawal symp·toms /·ˈ·· ˌ··/ also **withdrawal**— *n* [P] the painful or unpleasant effects which are the result of breaking or stopping a habit, esp. the taking of a drug: *Withdrawal symptoms associated with giving up smoking include a cough, stomach pains, bad temper, and sleepiness.* —see also DRUG ABUSE

with·drawn /wɪðˈdrɔːn, wɪθ-/ *adj* habitually quiet and often seeming more concerned with one's own thoughts than with other people

with·er /ˈwɪðəʳ/ *v* [I (AWAY);T] to become or cause (esp. a plant) to become reduced in size, colour, strength, etc.: *The flowers withered in the cold.* | *The cold withered the leaves.* | (fig.) *withered hopes* —compare WILT[1] (1)

with·er·ing /ˈwɪðərɪŋ/ *adj* intended to make someone feel uncertain, ashamed, or completely without confidence: *a withering look/remark* | *She dismissed her opponents' plans with withering scorn.* **– –ly** *adv*

with·ers /ˈwɪðəz‖-ərz/ *n* [P] the high part above a horse's shoulders —see picture at HORSE

with·hold /wɪðˈhəʊld, wɪθ-/ *v* **-held** /ˈheld/ [T (**from**)] to keep (back) on purpose; refuse to give: *I withheld payment until they had fulfilled the contract.* | *He was accused of withholding information about terrorist offences from the police.*

with·hold·ing tax /·ˈ·· ˌ·/ *n* [C;U] *AmE* money taken out of a person's wages to pay income tax: *state and federal withholding tax*

with·in /wɪðˈɪn‖wɪðˈɪn, wɪθˈɪn/ *adv, prep* **1** not beyond; not more than: *He'll arrive within an hour/within the hour.* | *The climbers got to within 20 metres of the top of the mountain.* | *The 5% price rise is well within* (=is lower than) *the limits set by the government.* | (fig.) *Try to keep within* (=not break) *the law.* **2** inside (a place, group, etc.); enclosed or contained by: *The children must remain within the school grounds during the lunch break.* | *There are serious differences of opinion within the party.* | *an attempt to reform the system from within* | *"This building to be sold. Enquire within."* (on a notice) —opposite **outside**; see INSIDE (USAGE)

with-it /ˈ· ·/ *adj old-fash* fashionable in clothes, modern in ways of thinking, etc.

with·out /wɪðˈaʊt‖wɪðˈaut, wɪθˈaʊt/ *adv, prep* **1** not having; lacking: *Don't go out without a coat.* | *We couldn't have done it without John.* | *There's no milk, so you'll have to drink your tea without.* | *This is* **without doubt** (=certainly) *a big improvement.* | *[+v-ing] left without telling me.* | *Ticket inspectors check train tickets to make sure people do not travel without paying.* | *Without wishing to appear ungrateful* (=I don't want to seem ungrateful, but) *I think their wedding present could have been a bit more generous.* **2** *old use* outside: *The army is encamped without* (=outside) *(the city walls).* —see also DO **without,** GO **without**

with·stand /wɪðˈstænd, wɪθ-/ *v* **-stood** /ˈstʊd/ [T] **1** to oppose successfully: *They withstood the enemy's attack.* **2** to remain unharmed or unchanged by: *Children's furniture must be able to withstand rough treatment.* | *a*

building that has **withstood the test of time** (=still looks good, even though it is now old)

wit·less /'wɪtləs/ adj derog (as if) lacking in ability to think; silly: *He was scared witless.* | *a witless idea* – **~ly** adv – **~ness** n [U]

wit·ness¹ /'wɪtɹ̩s/ n 1 [(of)] also **eyewitness**– someone who is present when something happens, esp. a crime or an accident: *a witness of the accident* | *Police have appealed for witnesses to come forward.* 2 someone who tells in a court of law what they saw happen or what they know about a person: *the chief witness for the prosecution* 3 [(to)] someone who is present at the writing of an official paper and signs it to show that they have seen the writer sign it: *a witness to the will*

witness² v [T] 1 to see or notice (something) by being present when it happens: *Did anyone witness the accident?* | *The problems we are now witnessing in these areas are the consequences of years of neglect.* | *The 1980s have witnessed* (=have been a time of) *increasing unemployment.* 2 to be present as a WITNESS¹ (3) at the making of: *Will you witness my signature?* 3 to be a sign or proof of: *His tears witnessed the shame he felt.* | *The economic situation is clearly beginning to improve – witness the big rise in company profits this year.* (=this is a fact that proves the statement)
 witness to sthg. *phr v* [T] 1 to tell and prove (what happened), esp. in a court of law: [+*v-ing*] *She witnessed to having seen the man enter the building.* 2 to WITNESS² (3)

witness box /'··· ·/ BrE ‖ **stand, witness stand** AmE– n the raised area, enclosed at the sides, where witnesses stand in court when being questioned –see colour picture on page 751

Witt·gen·stein /'vɪtgənʃtaɪn/, **Lud·wig** /'lʊdvɪg‖-wɪg/ (1889–1951) an Austrian PHILOSOPHER, whose works include *Philosophical Investigations*

wit·ti·cis·m /'wɪtɹ̩sɪzəm/ n a witty remark

wit·ty /'wɪti/ adj apprec having or showing a quick clever mind and an amusing way of expressing thoughts: *a witty speaker* | *a witty remark* –**tily** adv –**tiness** n [U]

wives /waɪvz/ pl. of WIFE

wizard

wiz·ard /'wɪzəd‖-ərd/ n 1 (esp. in stories) a man who has magic powers, usu. shown in stories as an old man with a pointed hat and a long CLOAK who uses a MAGIC WAND to do SPELLs –compare SORCERER, WITCH 2 [(at)] apprec a person with unusual, almost magical, abilities: *He's a real wizard at playing the piano.* | *a computer/financial wizard*

Wizard of Oz /ˌ··· · '·/, **The** a children's book by L Frank Baum, later made into a film. It tells the story of a girl from Kansas called Dorothy who, with her dog Toto, is carried by a storm to the magic land of Oz. They travel along the Yellow Brick Road to the Emerald City to meet the Wizard of Oz, who can get them home again. On the way, Dorothy and Toto are joined by the Scarecrow, the Cowardly Lion, and the Tin Man. –see colour picture on page 685

wiz·ard·ry /'wɪzədri‖-ər-/ n [U] 1 the performing of magic 2 apprec wonderful ability: *his football wizardry*

wiz·ened /'wɪzənd/ adj smaller in size and dried up, with lines in the skin, esp. as a result of age: *wizened apples* | *a wizened old lady*

wk written abbrev. for: week

woad /wəʊd/ n [U] a blue DYE (=colouring substance), esp. used in ancient times for colouring the body

wob·ble /'wɒbəl‖'wɑː-/ v [I;T] to move unsteadily from side to side: *You're making the table wobble/wobbling the table with your foot.* | *His fat thighs wobbled as he ran along.* | (fig.) *His voice wobbled when he sang.* –**wobble** n

wob·bly¹ /'wɒbli‖'wɑː-/ adj tending to wobble; SHAKY: *wobbly handwriting* | *a wobbly jelly*

wobbly² n infml **throw a wobbly** to suddenly behave in a very emotional way, for example by showing strong anger or fear

Wo·be·gon /'wəʊbɪgɒn‖-gɔːn/, **Lake** LAKE WOBEGON

Wode·house /'wʊdhaʊs/, **P G** (1881–1975) an English writer who wrote many funny NOVELs. His best-known stories are about a rich and rather stupid young man called Bertie Wooster and his clever MANSERVANT Jeeves.

Wo·den /'wəʊdn/ see ODIN

wodge /wɒdʒ‖wɑːdʒ/ n BrE infml a thick piece or lump of something which has been broken or cut off the whole

woe /wəʊ/ n fml or lit 1 [U] great sorrow: *a heart full of woe* | (fig.) *If she comes to you with* **tales/a tale of woe** (=says how great her troubles are), *just ignore her.* 2 [C usu. pl.] a cause of trouble; problem: *financial woes* 3 **woe betide** esp. lit or humor (used in making threats) there will be trouble for: *We will be leaving at 8 o'clock sharp, and woe betide anyone who is late!*

woe·be·gone /'wəʊbɪgɒn‖-gɔːn/ adj esp. lit very sad in appearance

woe·ful /'wəʊfəl/ adj 1 esp. lit very sad; MOURNFUL or PATHETIC: *woeful eyes* 2 (of something bad) very great; DEPLORABLE: *a woeful lack of understanding* – **~ly** adv : *The education service has been woefully neglected.*

wog /wɒg‖wɑːg/ n BrE taboo derog a foreigner, esp. of a dark-skinned race (considered extremely offensive)

Wo·gan /'wəʊgən/, **Ter·ry** /'teri/ (1938–   ) an Irish television and radio PRESENTER, best known for his INTERVIEWs (=recorded conversations) with famous people

wok /wɒk‖wɑːk/ n a deep round pan used in Chinese cooking to cook things quickly in hot oil by stir-frying (STIR-FRY). Many people in Britain and the US own a wok and use it to cook both Chinese and Western food. –see picture at PAN

woke /wəʊk/ past tense of WAKE

wok·en /'wəʊkən/ past participle of WAKE

Wo·king /'wəʊkɪŋ/ a town in Surrey, SE England, thought of by many people as a fashionably expensive home for rich people

wold /wəʊld/ also **wolds** pl.– n (usu. cap. as part of a name) an area of hilly open country: *the Yorkshire Wolds*

Wolds /wəʊldz/ also **the Wolds**– n an area of low CHALK hills in Lincolnshire and Humberside in E England

wolf¹ /wʊlf/ n **wolves** /wʊlvz/ 1 a wild animal of the dog family which hunts other animals in a group (PACK). Wolves are no longer found in Britain, but are found in North America. 2 infml a man who charms women so as to use them for his own pleasure 3 **a wolf in sheep's clothing** a person who seems friendly or harmless but is hiding evil intentions 4 **keep the wolf from the door** to earn just enough money to eat and live –see also BIG BAD WOLF, LONE WOLF, **cry wolf** (CRY¹) – **~ish** adj

wolf² v [T (DOWN)] infml to eat quickly, swallowing large amounts: *He wolfed his meal down.*

Wolf Cub /'· ·/ n an old name for a CUB SCOUT

Wolfe /wʊlf/, **James** (1727–59) a British GENERAL who led the army which took Quebec from the French and gave the British control of Canada

Wolfe, Tom /tɒm‖tɑːm/ (1931–   ) an American writer known for his lively writing style in books such as *The Right Stuff* and *Bonfire of the Vanities*

wolf·hound /'wʊlfhaʊnd/ n a very large dog, originally used for hunting wolves

wol·fram /'wʊlfrəm/ n [U] TUNGSTEN

wolf whis·tle /'· ˌ··/ n a way of whistling a high note followed by a falling note, which men sometimes use in the street to express admiration for an attractive woman who is passing. It is not considered polite to do this and many women find it offensive.

Woll·stone·craft /ˈwʊlstəkrɑːft‖-kræft/, **Mary** (1759–97) an English writer who wrote in favour of social and educational rights for women

Wol·sey /ˈwʊlzi/, **Thomas** (about 1475–1530) an English CARDINAL and politician who lost power after failing to persuade the Catholic Church to agree to King Henry VIII's DIVORCE from Katharine of Aragon

Wol·ver·hamp·ton /ˌwʊlvəˈhæmptən, ˈwʊlvəhæmptən‖-vər-/ an industrial town in central England, NW of Birmingham

wom·an /ˈwʊmən/ n women /ˈwɪmɪn/ 1 [C] a fully grown human female: *"Is your doctor a man or a woman?" "I've got a woman doctor."* | *married women* 2 [U] *fml* women in general 3 [C] a female servant or other worker: *He's got a daily woman who comes in and cleans his room.* 4 **woman of the world** *apprec* an experienced woman who knows how people behave 5 **women and children first** an instruction that women and children should be saved before the men in a fire, when a ship is sinking, etc. 6 **-woman: a** a woman who lives in or is from the stated place: *a Frenchwoman* | *a countrywoman* **b** a woman who has the stated job, skill, etc.: *a businesswoman* | *a spokeswoman* —see also OLD WOMAN, **monstrous regiment of women** (MONSTROUS)

▷ USAGE 1 It is usu. considered offensive to talk about a man's wife or girlfriend as his **woman.** 2 Note the fixed phrase **women and children:** *The* **women and children** *hid in the caves for safety.* —see also FEMALE (USAGE), GENTLEMAN (USAGE), GIRL (USAGE)◁

Woman a popular British magazine for women, established for many years and popular esp. with older women

wom·an·hood /ˈwʊmənhʊd/ n [U] the condition or period of being a woman —compare MANHOOD

wom·an·ish /ˈwʊmənɪʃ/ adj usu. derog (of a man) like a woman in character, behaviour, appearance, etc.; EFFEMINATE: *a womanish walk*

wom·an·ize also **-ise** BrE /ˈwʊmənaɪz/ v [I] usu. derog (of a man) to habitually pay attention to many women for sexual purposes —**izer** n

wom·an·kind /ˈwʊmənkaɪnd/ n [U+sing./pl.v] women considered together as a group —compare MANKIND

wom·an·ly /ˈwʊmənli/ adj apprec having or showing qualities that are regarded as typical of or suitable to a woman: *She showed a womanly concern for their health.* —compare MANLY —**liness** n [U]

Woman's Hour /ˈ·· ˌ·/ a British radio programme with news, INTERVIEWs with famous people, etc., which deals esp. with subjects of particular interest to women

Woman's Own /ˌ·· ˈ·/ a popular British magazine for women, established for many years and popular esp. with older women

Woman's Realm /ˌ·· ˈ·/ a British magazine for women, established for many years and popular esp. with older women

Woman's Week·ly /ˌ·· ˈ·/ a British magazine for women, established for many years and popular esp. with older women

womb /wuːm/ n an organ inside female MAMMALs where the young can develop

wom·bat /ˈwɒmbæt‖ˈwɑːm-/ n an Australian animal like a small bear, whose young live in a pocket of skin on its body

Wom·ble /ˈwɒmbəl‖ˈwɑːm-/ n one of the characters in the British children's television programme *The Wombles*, about creatures who are said to live on Wimbledon Common in London

wom·en·folk /ˈwɪmɪnfəʊk/ n [P] infml women, esp. one's female relatives

Women in Love /ˌ·· ˈ·/ a NOVEL by D H Lawrence about difficult relationships between men and women

Women's In·sti·tute /ˌ·· ˈ···/ [the + sing./pl. v] a British organization for women, esp. in country areas, who meet for different kinds of social and CULTURAL activities. Although the Women's Institute has members of all ages, it is seen as rather old-fashioned and concerned mainly with activities related to the home such as cooking, sewing etc. People imagine a typical member of the Women's Institute to be an older middle-class woman who does not have a job and is quite CONSERVATIVE.

women's lib /ˌ·· ˈ·/ also **women's lib·e·ra·tion** /ˌ·· ···ˈ···/ fml – n [U] old-fash the women's movement. Women's lib is associated esp. with the idea of women burning their BRAS to show that they are free, which some women did in the 1960s when the movement began. —**women's lib·ber** n

women's move·ment /ˈ·· ˌ··/ [the] (all the women who join in making) a united effort to improve the social and political position of women and to end sexual DISCRIMINATION —compare MEN'S MOVEMENT

women's room /ˈ·· ·/ also **ladies' room** n esp. AmE euph a public TOILET for women

women's stud·ies /ˈ·· ˌ··/ n [P] studies, such as history or literature, concerned with women's changing position in society

won /wʌn/ past tense & participle of WIN

won·der¹ /ˈwʌndər/ v 1 [I (about);T+wh-;obj] to express a wish to know, in words or silently: *"Does she know we're here?" "I'm just wondering."* (=I don't know) | *I wonder what really happened.* | *What are they going to do now, I wonder?* | *I was just wondering how to do it.* | *His opponents* **wonder out loud/wonder aloud** *whether he is capable of doing the job.* | (in polite requests) *I wonder if I can/could have some more tea.* 2 [I (at);T+(that);obj] to be surprised and want to know (why): *"She left home." "I don't wonder, after the way he treated her."* | *The fact that she left home is not to be wondered at.* | *I wonder he dares to show his face here again after the way he behaved!* 3 [I (about);T+if/whether;obj] to suggest or think (something) that is not so; doubt: *"Does she mean it?" "I wonder."* | *He says such stupid things that sometimes I wonder if/whether he's got any brains at all!* – ~**ingly** adv

▷ USAGE 1 If you **wonder why** ... /who ... /whether ... etc., you ask yourself a question: *I* **wonder** *why she did that?* 2 Compare **wonder** and **admire.** You can **wonder at** (=be very much surprised by) both good and bad things: *The country boy* **wondered at** *all the high buildings in the city.* You can **admire** good things (=look at them with pleasure and respect) without being surprised by them: *I have always* **admired** *the poetry of T. S. Eliot.* 3 **Wonder** can be used to soften requests: *I* **wonder if** ... , or for more serious or difficult requests *I* **was wondering if** ... , can be used: *I* **wonder if** *you could post this letter for me?* | *I* **was wondering if** *you could let me stay for a few days.*◁

wonder² n 1 [U] a feeling of strangeness, surprise, etc., usu. combined with admiration, that is produced by something unusually fine or beautiful, or by something unexpected or new to one's experience: *We were filled with wonder at the sight of the beautiful mountains.* | *The children gazed in wonder when they saw snow for the first time.* 2 [C] something that causes this feeling, esp. a wonderfully made object: *The temple of Diana and the hanging gardens of Babylon were two of the Seven Wonders of the World in ancient times.* | *technological wonders* —see also SEVEN WONDERS OF THE WORLD 3 [C] apprec a wonderful person, esp. one who is able to do things that need great skill, cleverness, or effort: *He's a wonder, the way he arranges everything without any help.* 4 **do/work wonders** to bring unexpectedly good results: *She looked so tired before, but her holiday has worked wonders/done wonders (for her).* 5 **it's a wonder (that)** it's surprising: *It's a wonder you recognized me after all these years.* 6 **(it's) no wonder/little wonder/small wonder** it is not surprising; naturally: *It's no wonder you've got a headache when you drank so much last night.* 7 **Wonders will never cease** esp. humor (used for expressing surprise when the opposite of what one expects happens) —see also CHINLESS WONDER

wonder³ adj [A] unusually good of its kind: *a new wonder drug which they hope will cure cancer*

Wonder, Ste·vie /ˈstiːvi/ (1950–) a black American popular music singer, songwriter, and musician. Born blind, he started recording with the record company Motown in the 1960s and has been successful and influential ever since. He is also known for his political support for other black people in the US and Africa, and for encouraging good relations between people of different races.

Won·der·bread /ˈwʌndərbred‖-ər-/ n [U] tdmk a kind of white, soft bread sold in the US

won·der·ful /ˈwʌndəfəl‖-dər-/ adj unusually good; causing great pleasure or admiration: *a wonderful performance* |

wonderful news | We're having a wonderful time. — **-ly** *adv*

won·der·land /ˈwʌndəlænd‖-ər-/ *n* **1** [U] FAIRYLAND **2** [C *usu. sing.*] a place which is unusually beautiful, rich, etc. —see also ALICE IN WONDERLAND

won·der·ment /ˈwʌndəmənt‖-dər-/ *n* [U] *esp. lit* WONDER² (1): *The children listened in/with wonderment as he told his strange tale.*

won·drous /ˈwʌndrəs/ *adj poet* wonderful: *wondrous beauty*

won·ky /ˈwɒŋki‖ˈwaːŋki/ *adj BrE infml* unsteady and likely to break, fall, or fail: *a wonky table leg | He's got a rather wonky heart.*

wont¹ /wəʊnt‖wɔːnt/ *adj* [F+to-v] *fml* likely (to do or happen); in the habit of: *He is wont to express himself rather forcefully on that subject.* —see also WONTED

wont² *n* [S] *fml* (the stated person's) habit or custom: *She spoke for too long,* **as is her wont.**

won't /wəʊnt/ *short for:* will not

wont·ed /ˈwəʊntɪd‖ˈwɔːn-/ *adj* [A] *fml* customary: *He drove with his wonted carelessness.*

won·ton /ˌwɒnˈtɒn‖ˈwaːntaːn/ *n* [U] a Chinese food made of small filled cases of DOUGH eaten esp. in soup: *wonton soup*

woo /wuː/ *v* [T] **1** *esp. old use* (of a man) to try to persuade (a woman) into love and marriage. The TRADITIONAL and old-fashioned way for a man to woo a woman is for him to buy her flowers, chocolates and other presents, to write love letters to her and to take her to expensive restaurants. Many men (esp. young men) no longer do this and some women (esp. FEMINISTS) disapprove of this type of behaviour because they think that by behaving in this way men are not treating women as equals. **2** (esp. in newspapers) to make efforts to gain (the support of): *Politicians try to woo the voters before an election.* — **~er** *n*

wood /wʊd/ *n* **1** [U] the substance of which the trunks and branches of trees are made, which is cut and used for various purposes, such as burning, making paper or furniture, etc.: *Put some more wood on the fire. | The box is made of wood. | a polished wood floor | soft woods such as pine and hard woods such as ebony | He cut it against the grain of the wood.* **2** [C] also **woods** *pl.*— a place where trees grow thickly, smaller than a forest: *We went for a ride in the wood(s).* **3** [C] any of the set of four GOLF CLUBS² with wooden heads used for hitting a ball long distances —compare IRON¹ (3) **4** [*the*+S] *tech* barrels: *sherry* **from the wood** (=not from a bottle) **5 out of the wood** *BrE* free from danger, difficulty, etc.: *The situation's improving but we're not out of the wood yet.* —see also DEAD WOOD, **not see the wood for the trees** (SEE¹)

Wood¹, Grant (1892–1942) an American painter famous esp. for the painting AMERICAN GOTHIC —see colour picture on page 1016

Wood², Sir Henry (1869–1944) an English CONDUCTOR who started the yearly Promenade Concerts in London —see PROMENADE CONCERT

Wood³, Victoria (1953–) an English COMEDIAN known for her one-woman shows on stage and her television shows

wood al·co·hol /ˌ· ·ˈ···/ *n* [U] METHYL ALCOHOL

wood·bine /ˈwʊdbaɪn/ *n* [U] **1** *esp. poet for* HONEYSUCKLE **2** *AmE for* VIRGINIA CREEPER

wood·block /ˈwʊdblɒk‖-blaːk/ *n* **1** also **woodcut**— a piece of wood with a shape cut on it for printing **2** a block of wood used in making the floor of a room, sometimes in a pattern

wood·carv·ing /ˈwʊdkaːvɪŋ‖-kaːr-/ *n* **1** [U] the act of shaping wood with special tools esp. as an art form **2** [C] a work of art produced by shaping wood with sharp tools

wood·chuck /ˈwʊdtʃʌk/ *n* GROUNDHOG

wood·cock /ˈwʊdkɒk‖-kaːk/ *n* **woodcock** *or* **woodcocks** a brown woodland bird with a long thin beak, sometimes shot for food

wood·craft /ˈwʊdkraːft‖-kræft/ *n* [U] the skill of living in or finding one's way through woods and forests

wood·cut /ˈwʊdkʌt/ *n* **1** a picture which has been made by pressing down the shaped surface of a piece of wood on DYE (=a colouring substance) and then onto paper **2** a WOODBLOCK (1)

wood·cut·ter /ˈwʊdˌkʌtər/ *n* a man whose job is to cut down trees in a forest

wood·ed /ˈwʊdɪd/ *adj* having woods; covered with growing trees: *a densely wooded hillside*

wood·en /ˈwʊdn/ *adj* **1** made of wood: *a wooden bed/spoon* **2** awkwardly stiff; unbending: *wooden movements | The actress gave a rather wooden performance.* —compare CARDBOARD² (2) — **~ly** *adv* — **~ness** *n* [U]

Wooden, John (1910–) an American college BASKETBALL COACH (=teacher) who is considered to have been one of the best coaches of the game

wood·en·head·ed /ˌwʊdn'hedɪd◄/ *adj* stupid; slow in thought and understanding

Wooden Horse of Troy /ˌ··· ·· · ˈ·/ see TROJAN HORSE

wooden spoon /ˌ·· ˈ·/ *n* [*the*+S] *BrE infml* an imaginary prize supposed to be given to the person or team that finishes last in a competition

wood·land /ˈwʊdlənd, -lænd/ also **woodlands** *pl.*— *n* [U] wooded country; an area of land covered with growing trees: *large areas of woodland | birds of the woodland(s) | woodland birds*

wood·louse /ˈwʊdlaʊs/ *esp. BrE* ‖ also **pill bug** *AmE*— **-lice** /laɪs/ a very small insect-like animal with 14 legs which lives under wood, stones, etc.

wood·peck·er /ˈwʊdˌpekər/ *n* a bird with a long beak, which can make holes in trees and pull out insects. Woodpeckers can be heard hitting the trees with their beaks again and again. —see picture at BIRD

wood·pile /ˈwʊdpaɪl/ *n* a pile of firewood —see also **nigger in the woodpile** (NIGGER (2))

wood pulp /ˈ· ·/ *n* [U] broken bits of the soft parts of wood, used for making paper

wood·shed /ˈwʊdʃed/ *n* a place for storing wood for burning, esp. near a house

woods·man /ˈwʊdzmən/ *n* **-men** /mən/ a man who works in a wood or forest, protecting and/or cutting down trees

Wood·stock /ˈwʊdstɒk‖-staːk/ a popular music FESTIVAL in the town of Woodstock near New York in 1969 which attracted thousands of young people. Woodstock is often seen as representing the HIPPIE movement of the 1960s and early 1970s. —see picture at HIPPY

wood·sy /ˈwʊdzi/, **woodsie** *n AmE* a party in a wooded area, usu. arranged by and for young people, that takes place at night and may include camping

woodwind instruments

clarinet   oboe   flute

bassoon

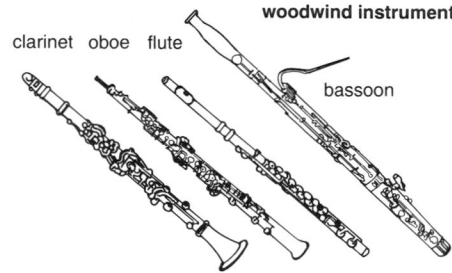

wood·wind /ˈwʊdˌwɪnd/ *n* [*the*+S+*sing./pl. v*] (the musicians who play) the set of tube-shaped wooden or metal instruments in an ORCHESTRA which are played by blowing, and most of which have a single or double REED (2): *The woodwind is/are too loud. | The flute and the oboe are woodwind instruments.* —compare BRASS (2)

wood·work /ˈwʊdwɜːrk‖-wɜːrk/ *n* [U] **1** the skill of making wooden objects, esp. furniture; CARPENTRY **2** objects produced by this **3** *infml* the parts of a house that are made of wood: *dry rot in the woodwork* **4** *infml* the GOAL-POSTS and CROSSBAR in football

wood·worm /ˈwʊdwɜːm‖-wɜːrm/ *n* **-worm 1** [C] the small soft wormlike young larvae (LARVA) of certain BEETLES, which make holes in wood; they can cause serious damage to buildings: *Have you treated it for woodworm?* **2** [U] the condition in which damage is done by these creatures

wood·y /ˈwʊdi/ *adj* **1** of or like wood: *plants with woody stems* **2** of or with woods; WOODED: *a woody valley*

woof¹ /wʊf/ *n, interj infml* (a word used for describing) the sound (BARK²) made by a dog

woof² /wuːf‖wʊf, wuːf/ *n* WEFT

woof·er /ˈwuːfəʳ‖ˈwu-/ *n* a LOUDSPEAKER that gives out deep sounds —compare TWEETER

Wook·ey Hole /ˌwʊki ˈhəʊl/ a popular TOURIST place in SW England with a CAVE where, according to an old story, a WITCH used to live

wool /wʊl/ *n* [U] **1** the soft thick hair which sheep and some goats have on their bodies **2** thick thread or cloth made from this: *a ball of knitting wool* | *a wool suit* **3** **pull the wool over someone's eyes** to trick someone by hiding the facts —see also COTTON WOOL, DYED-IN-THE-WOOL, WIRE WOOL

Woolf /wʊlf/, **Virginia** (1882–1941) an English writer and CRITIC who was an important member of the BLOOMSBURY GROUP and is admired by FEMINISTS. She is best known for her NOVELS *To The Lighthouse* and *The Waves*.

wool·gath·er·ing /ˈwʊlˌɡæðərɪŋ/ *n* [U] thinking of other things instead of what is being done, esp. when this leads to not hearing other people or doing things wrong; being ABSENT-MINDED

Wool·ie's /ˈwʊliz/ see WOOLWORTH'S

wool·len ‖ usu. **woolen** *AmE* /ˈwʊlən/ *adj* **1** made of wool: *a woollen coat* **2** [A] of the production or sale of materials made of wool: *woollen manufacturers*

wool·lens ‖ usu. **woolens** *AmE* /ˈwʊlənz/ *n* [P] clothes made of wool, esp. knitted (KNIT) —see also WOOLLY²

wool·ly¹ ‖ also **wooly** *AmE* /ˈwʊli/ *adj* **1** of or like wool, esp. with a soft surface: *woolly socks* **2** *derog* (of people or their thoughts) showing a lack of clear thinking: *His ideas are a bit woolly.* —**liness** *n* [U]

woolly² ‖ also **wooly** *AmE n* [usu. pl.] *infml, esp. BrE* a garment made of wool, esp. knitted (KNIT): *winter woollies*

woolly-head·ed /ˌ·· ˈ···◂/ also **woolly-minded**— *adj derog* tending not to think clearly or have firm ideas

woolly lib·e·ral /ˌ·· ˈ···/ *n esp. BrE derog* a LEFT-WING person who is considered to be rather weak and whose ideas are not clear or LOGICAL. People who describe other people as woolly liberals are usually RIGHT-WING and disapprove of their ideas.

wool·sack /ˈwʊlsæk/ *n* [the+S] **1** the seat in the British parliament on which the Lord Chancellor sits in the House of Lords **2** the position of being Lord Chancellor

Wool·wich /ˈwʊlɪdʒ, -ɪtʃ/ **1** an area of E London on the river Thames, best known for the Thames Barrier built across the river there **2** [the] a British BUILDING SOCIETY, branches of which are found in many towns and cities in Britain

Wool·worth's /ˈwʊlwəθs‖-wərθs/ also **Woolie's** *BrE infml*— one of a group of shops, found in many British and American towns, selling many different kinds of goods at low prices

Woos·ter /ˈwʊstəʳ, ˈwuː-/, **Ber·tie** /ˈbɜːti‖ˈbɜːr-/ a character in many stories of P G Wodehouse. He is wealthy and not very clever, depending on his servant Jeeves to get him out of trouble.

woo·zy /ˈwuːzi/ *adj infml* **1** having an unsteady feeling in the head; DIZZY **2** unclear; confused —**ziness** *n* [U]

wop /wɒp‖wɑːp/ *n taboo derog* a foreigner, esp. an Italian (considered extremely offensive)

Worces·ter /ˈwʊstəʳ/ a city in the W of England, near S Wales, famous for its CHINA. The local government for Worcestershire is based there.

Worces·ter·shire /ˈwʊstəʃəʳ ‖ -tər-/ a COUNTY in SW England

Worces·ter sauce /ˌ·· ˈ·/ *BrE* ‖ **Worcestershire sauce** /ˌ··· ˈ·/ *AmE n* [U] a dark strong-tasting liquid made from VINEGAR, SPICES, and SOY, put on food to give an additional taste

word¹ /wɜːd‖wɜːrd/ *n* **1** [C] (a written representation of) one or more sounds which can be spoken to represent an idea, object, action, etc.; the smallest unit of spoken language which has meaning and can stand alone: *"Good" and "goodness" are words, but "-ness" is not a word.* | *How do you pronounce this word?* | *I was trying to tell her what it was, but I couldn't think of the word (for it).* | *What's the French word for "dog"?* | *Sometimes it is hard to put your feelings into words.* (=to express them

clearly) | *I couldn't* **find words** *to describe it.* (=it was too wonderful, strange, etc.) | *Tell me what happened* **in your own words.** (=not copying what anyone else has said) | **Words fail me!** (=I can't describe or answer that, esp. because of surprise or shock) | *Tired/angry/pleased* **isn't the word for** *the way I feel.* (=that word doesn't describe the strength of feeling) | *He's a man* **of few words.** (=he doesn't say much) | *I know the tune of the song, but I don't* **know the words.** **2** [S] a short remark or statement: **In a word,** *no.* | *I don't* **believe a word of** *it.* (=I don't believe it at all) | *This is secret information so don't* **say/breathe a word** (=say anything) *about this to anyone.* | *The headmistress always* **has/gets the final/last word** (=makes the last decision) *on matters of school policy.* **3** [S] also **words** *pl.*— a short speech or conversation: *Can I have a few words with you/a word with you?* | *A word in your ear ...* (=Let me give you some advice or information...) | *We exchanged a few words.* | *A word of praise from you would be much appreciated.* | *(euph) I hear that words passed between them/that they* **had words.** (=that they had an argument) **4** [U (of)] a message or piece of news: *There's been no word from her for weeks.* | *Word of his success soon got around.* (=spread) [+that] *The word is that the election will be in June.* | *He* **sent word** *that he wanted to see me.* **5** [the+S] the right word; PASSWORD: *He* **gave the word** *and they let him in.* **6** [C usu. sing.] an order: *On the word of command/On his word they all moved forward.* —see also **say the word** (SAY¹) **7** [S] a promise: *I give you my* **word (of honour)** *I'll go.* | *I* **kept my word** *to her.* | *You can trust him; he's a man* **of his word.** (=always keeps promises) —see also **be as good as one's word** (GOOD¹) **8 by word of mouth** by speaking and not by writing: *The orders were passed on by word of mouth.* **9 from the word go** from the beginning **10 get a word in edgeways** *infml* to get a chance to speak: *He talks so much that no one else can get a word in edgeways.* **11 in other words** expressing the same thing in different words; which is the same as saying: *Your performance in the exam did not reach the required standard — in other words, you failed.* **12 (not) in so many words** (not) expressed with that meaning but only suggested: *"Did she say she liked him?" "Not in so many words, (but...)"* **13 put words in(to) someone's mouth: a** to tell someone what to say **b** *derog* to suggest or claim, falsely, that someone has said a particular thing **14 take someone at their word** to act on the belief that someone means what they said: *He says call in on him any time, but he doesn't expect you to take him at his word.* **15 take someone's word for it** to accept what someone says as correct: *I can't give you the exact figures; you'll just have to take my word for it.* **16 take the words out of someone's mouth** to say something that someone else was going to say, before they have had time or a chance to speak **17 (upon) my word!** *old-fash* (an expression of surprise) **18 word for word: a** in exactly the same words: *Tell me what she said, word for word.* **b** also **word by word**— giving a word in a foreign language for each word, rather than giving the meaning of whole phrases and sentences: *a word-for-word translation* —see also FOUR-LETTER WORD, GOOD WORD, LAST WORD, PLAY ON WORDS, **a word to the wise** (WISE), **eat one's words** (EAT)

word² *v* [T+*obj*+*adv/prep*] to express in words: *She worded the explanation well.* | *a carefully worded contract*

word blind·ness /ˈ· ˌ··/ *n* [U] DYSLEXIA

word·ing /ˈwɜːdɪŋ‖ˈwɜːr-/ *n* [U] the words and phrases chosen to express something: *The exact wording of a legal contract can be extremely important.*

word·less /ˈwɜːdləs‖ˈwɜːrd-/ *adj* without words; silent or unspoken: *Her look was a wordless question.* —**~ly** *adv* —**~ness** *n* [U]

word-per·fect /ˌ· ˈ··/ *BrE* ‖ **letter-perfect** *AmE*— *adj* repeating or remembering every word with complete correctness: *She rehearsed the speech until she was word-perfect.*

Word·per·fect /ˌwɜːdˈpɜːfɪkt‖ˌwɜːrdˈpɜːr-/ *n* [U] *tdmk* a kind of computer SOFTWARE used for word processing

word·play /ˈwɜːdpleɪ‖ˈwɜːrd-/ *n* [U] joking about word meanings; punning (PUN)

word pro·ces·sor /ˈ· ˌ···/ *n* a small computer used esp. for ordinary office jobs, such as typing letters and reports, storing information, etc. —**ing** *n* [U]

Word·star /ˈwɜːdstɑːʳ‖ˈwɜːrd-/ n [U] tdmk a kind of computer SOFTWARE used for word processing

Words·worth /ˈwɜːdzwəθ‖ˈwɜːrdzwəːrθ/, **William** (1770–1850) an English ROMANTIC poet whose poems are mainly about the beauty of nature and often describe the COUNTRYSIDE of the Lake District in NW England where he went to live. His most famous book of poetry is *Lyrical Ballads* (written with Samuel Coleridge) and his most famous poems include *Daffodils* and *The Prelude*.

word·y /ˈwɜːdi‖ˈwɜːrdi/ adj derog using or containing more words than are needed; VERBOSE: *a wordy explanation* —**·ily** adv —**·iness** n [U]: *Avoid wordiness in your exam answers.*

wore /wɔːʳ/ past tense of WEAR

work¹ /wɜːk‖wɜːrk/ n 1 [U] activity in which effort of the body or mind is used to produce something or gain a result, rather than for amusement: *skilled/unskilled work* | *She put a lot of (hard) work into writing that report.* | *Work on the new tunnel will begin in January.* | *The pupils complained that their teacher set them too much work.* | *He has been highly praised for the work he has done in genetic engineering.* 2 [U] (the nature or place of) a job or business: *"What's your work/What work do you do?" "I'm a reporter."/"I work in television."/"I do freelance work/repair work."* | *I go to work by train.* | *Hurry up! You'll be late for work.* | *school-leavers looking for work* (=trying to find jobs) | *What time do you get home from work?* | *Are your employers insured for accidents (happening) at work?* | *Foreigners need a work **permit*** (=official permission to work) *to get employment in the country.* —see JOB (USAGE) 3 [U] the subject, material, etc. one is working on: *I hear you've changed jobs; is the work more interesting at the new place?* | *I'm taking some work home to do this evening.* | *Don't stay inside to do your sewing; bring your work out with you.* 4 [U] what is produced by work, esp. of the hands: *This mat is my own work.* (=I made it) | (fig.) *This savage murder is clearly the work of a madman.* 5 [C usu. pl.] an object produced by writing, painting, etc.: *Shakespeare's works include plays and poems.* 6 [U] tech force multiplied by distance 7 **all in a/the day's work** as expected; which can be done without great difficulty; not unusual 8 **all work and no play makes Jack a dull boy** saying a person who spends all his time working will be a dull and uninteresting companion 9 **at work** (on) doing something, esp. work: *Danger; men at work (on this road)!* 10 **go/set to work** (on) to start doing something 11 **have one's ˈwork cut out** to have something difficult to do, esp. in the time allowed: *He's got/He'll have his work cut out to finish that by Friday.* 12 **in work/out of work** having a job/unemployed 13 **-work: a** work done using the stated materials or tools: *woodwork* **b** something produced by doing such work: *paintwork* —see also WORKS, DIRTY WORK, DONKEY WORK, LIFE WORK, PIECE OF WORK, SOCIAL WORK, WORKS **make short work of** (SHORT¹)

▷ USAGE **Work** can be used as a general word for all activities of the mind or body: *I'm at work on a new poem.* | *Digging the garden is hard work.* For tiring and unpleasant work, **labour** or (less common and more formal) **toil** can be used: *Clearing the field of stones took ten days of backbreaking labour/toil.* If the work is tiring, uninteresting, and not respected, **drudgery** can be used.◁

work² v 1 [I (**at, on**)] to do an activity which uses effort, esp. as one's job: *She works in a factory/for the council/as a bus driver.* | *I'm working on a new book.* | *I spent the whole weekend working in the garden.* | *He's still not very good at speaking English, but he's working at it.* (=trying hard) | *The builders worked closely with the architect in the construction of the offices.* —see also WORKING 2 [I] (of a plan, machine, or moving part) to operate in the proper way; perform the expected job without failing: *Does this light work?* | *The clock hasn't been working since I dropped it on the floor.* | *Your idea won't work in practice.* | *It works by electricity.* | *Can you explain to me how the banking system works?* —compare GO¹ (8) 3 [T+obj +adv/prep] to make (a person) do work: *They work us too hard in this office.* 4 [T] to make (a machine) operate: *Working these heavy presses is very tiring.* | *How do you work the gears on this bike?* | *It's worked by electricity.* 5 [T+obj+adv/prep] to make (one's way) by work or effort: *He worked his way to the front of the crowd.* | *She worked her way through college.* (=paid for herself to go to college

by working) 6 [I+adj/adv/prep; T+obj+adj/adv/prep] to (cause to) reach a state or position by small movements: *This little screw has worked (itself) loose.* | (fig.) *He worked himself into a temper.* | (fig.) *They're gradually working round to our point of view.* 7 [T] to produce (an effect): *This medicine works wonders/miracles.* 8 [T] infml to arrange, esp. unofficially: *How did you work it? Two days extra holiday!* | *I'll try and work it so that we can all go together.* 9 [I+adv/prep] to produce a particular effect or result: *She found that her lack of experience worked against her in trying to get a job.* 10 [T often pass.] to stitch: *a baby's dress worked by hand* 11 [I] tech for FERMENT¹ (1) 12 **work one's fingers to the bone** to work very hard 13 **work to rule** BrE to obey the rules of one's work so exactly that one causes inconvenience to others, in order to support a claim for more money, shorter working hours, etc. —see also WORKER, WORK-TO-RULE

▷ USAGE To make this word stronger you can use **hard**: *He worked hard/very hard/very hard indeed*◁

work sthg. ↔ **in** phr v [T(**to**)] to include, by a clever arrangement of words: *I'll try to work in a mention of the help you gave.* | *He worked a mention of her into his speech.*

work sthg. ↔ **off** phr v [T] to get rid of, by work or activity: *He worked off his anger by chopping some logs.* | *I have three years to work off the debt.*

work on sthg. phr v [T] to give one's attention to doing or trying to do: *"Have you drawn up that list of names yet?" "No, but I'm working on it."*

work out phr v 1 [T] (**work** sthg. ↔ **out**) to find by reasoning or calculating: *Have you worked out the answer/the sum yet?* [+wh-] *Try and work out how much it will all cost.* | *The police couldn't work out how the thieves had entered the building.* [+that] *She'd worked out that it would cost over £100.* 2 [I] to have a good result; be successful for a long time: *I hope the new job works out for you.* | *My affair with her was fun while it lasted, but I could see it was never going to work out.* 3 [I+adv/prep] to have a result; develop; TURN **out** (6): *I wonder how their ideas worked out in practice?* | *We didn't plan it like that but it worked out very well.* 4 [T] (**work** sthg. ↔ **out**) to plan or decide: *I've drawn up the main outlines, and we'll work out the details later* [+wh-] *I can't work out how to do it.* | *a carefully worked-out plan* 5 [I(**at**);L+adj] to reach a (stated) result or amount by being calculated: *The sum won't/doesn't work out.* (=I can't find the answer to it) | *The cost works out at about $20 per person.* | *If we go by plane it will work out rather expensive.* 6 [I] infml to exercise to improve physical fitness: *She's working out in the gym.* —see also WORKOUT 7 [T] (**work** sthg. ↔ **out**) to complete the use of (esp. a mine): *The mine was worked out years ago.*

work sbdy. ↔ **over** phr v [T] sl to attack violently

work up phr v 1 [T] (**work** sbdy. ↔ **up**) to excite the feelings, esp. anger, tears, etc., of: *The politician worked the crowd up until they were shouting and cheering.* | *He'd worked himself up into a terrible state about the coming exam.* —see also WORKED UP 2 [T] (**work** sthg. ↔ **up**) to cause oneself to have; develop: *I've worked up quite a thirst playing tennis.* | *I'm afraid I can't work up much enthusiasm for this scheme.* 3 [I (**to**)] to move or develop (towards): *She's working up to what she wants to say.* 4 [T (**into**)] (**work** sthg. ↔ **up**) to complete (a study) gradually: *I'm hoping to work up these notes into a book.*

wor·ka·ble /ˈwɜːkəbəl‖ˈwɜːr-/ adj 1 which can be put into effect; usable: *a workable timetable/system* 2 (of a substance) which can be shaped with the hands: *workable clay for making pots*

work·a·day /ˈwɜːkədeɪ‖ˈwɜːr-/ adj [A] ordinary and/or dull: *this workaday world*

work·a·hol·ic /ˌwɜːkəˈhɒlɪk◀‖ˌwɜːrkəˈhɔː-/ n infml, often derog a person who likes to work too hard or is unable to stop working and does not have time in their life for anything else, such as personal relationships: *She's a complete workaholic – her job is her whole life!* —**ism** /ˈwɜːkəhɒlɪzəm ‖ ˈwɜːrkəhɔː-/ n [U]

work·bag /ˈwɜːkbæg‖ˈwɜːrk-/ n a bag for tools and objects used in activities with the hands, such as sewing

work·bas·ket /ˈwɜːkˌbɑːskʌt‖ˈwɜːrk-ˌbæs-/ also **work·box** /ˈwɜːkbɒks ‖ ˈwɜːrkbɑːks/ ‖also **sewing basket, sewing kit** AmE— n a small stiff container, usu. woven, for small sewing objects such as needles and thread

work·bench /ˈwɜːkbentʃ ‖ ˈwɜːrk-/ n (a table with) a hard surface for working on with tools: *a carpenter at his workbench*

work·book /ˈwɜːkbʊk‖ˈwɜːrk-/ *n* a school book with questions and exercises. The answers are usu. written in the book by the student.

work·day /ˈwɜːkdeɪ‖ˈwɜːrk-/ also **working day**— *n* **1** the amount of time during which one works each day. In Britain and the US most people start work at about 9 o'clock and finish at about 5 o'clock. **2** a day which is not a holiday

worked up /ˌ· ˈ·◄/ *adj* [F (**about**)] very excited and showing strong feelings, esp. when worried: *He gets very worked up about going to school and leaves the house crying every day.* —see also WORK **up** (1)

work·er /ˈwɜːkəʳ‖ˈwɜːr-/ *n* **1** a person or animal that works, esp. in the stated job: *unskilled workers | office/farm workers* **2** *apprec* someone who works very hard: *She's a real worker; she gets twice as much done as anyone else.* **3** someone who works with their hands rather than their mind; WORKING-CLASS person

work eth·ic /ˈ· ˌ··/ *n esp. AmE* belief in the moral value of work: *The Americans have a strong work ethic, but the Japanese have an even stronger one.*

work ex·pe·ri·ence /ˈ· ·ˌ···/ *n* [U] experience of work in general or of a particular type of work: *She's very well qualified but she hasn't got much work experience.*

work·force /ˈwɜːkfɔːs‖ˈwɜːrkfɔːrs/ *n* [*the*+S+*sing./pl. v*] the people who work in a factory or in industry generally, considered as a group: *a workforce of 3500 | The whole workforce is/are out on strike.* —compare STAFF

work·horse /ˈwɜːkhɔːs‖ˈwɜːrkhɔːrs/ *n* **1** someone who does most of the work in the group to which they belong, esp. work that is difficult or uninteresting **2** a vehicle, machine, etc., that is very useful, esp. in performing ordinary continuous jobs

work·house /ˈwɜːkhaʊs‖ˈwɜːrk-/ (*the*) (in Britain in former times) a place for the poor to live when they had no employment, esp. when they were too old to work. Conditions in workhouses were very bad and people were very afraid of having to go there. People now think of workhouses in connection with the Victorians and with writers such as Charles Dickens who described what they were like in order to try and improve the situation of poor people.

work·ing /ˈwɜːkɪŋ‖ˈwɜːr-/ *adj* [A] **1** of, used for, or including work: *The visiting minister had a working breakfast with the head of government. | working clothes* **2** (of a person) having a job; who works, esp. with the hands: *What has the government done for ordinary working people?* **3** (of time) spent in work: *during working hours* **4** (of an idea) useful as a base for planning how to do something: *a working theory/hypothesis*

working cap·i·tal /ˌ·· ˈ···/ *n* the money readily available to a company for the daily running of a business

working class /ˌ·· ˈ·◄/ also **working classes** *pl.*, **lower class**— *n* [*the*+S+*sing./pl. v*.] the social class to which people belong who work with their hands, e.g. in factories or mines —see also BLUE-COLLAR, MIDDLE CLASS, UPPER CLASS and see also extra information on page 1258 —**working-class** *adj*

▷ USAGE **Working class** can be used in any of the following patterns: **a** with a singular or plural verb: *The* **working class** *doesn't/don't support this political party.* **b** in a plural form: *The* **working classes** *are angry about unemployment.* **c** as an adjective: *This is a* **working-class** *area. | Most of the people in this area are* **working-class**. **Lower class**, **middle class**, and **upper class** can also be used in these patterns.◁

working day /ˌ·· ˈ·◄‖ˈ·· ·/ *n* a WORKDAY

working girl /ˈ·· ˌ·/ *n euph* a PROSTITUTE

working knowl·edge /ˌ·· ˈ··/ *n* [S (**of**)] enough practical knowledge to do something: *I have a working knowledge of car engines and can do most repairs.*

working life /ˌ·· ˈ·/ *n* the part of a person's life that is spent at work: *He's worked for that company for all his working life.* (=it is his first and only job) *| Major changes in the working lives of ordinary people*

working lunch /ˌ·· ˈ·/ also **business lunch**— *n* a LUNCH where people meet to discuss business, etc.

working ma·jor·i·ty /ˌ·· ·ˈ···/ *n* a degree of support in an organization or law-making body which is large enough to insure success of its proposals —see also PARLIAMENTARY MAJORITY

working men's club /ˈ·· · ˌ·/ *n* a place found in some towns, esp. towns in industrial areas, where WORKING-CLASS men go to drink, meet friends, or for entertainment, and which is similar to a PUB

working moth·er /ˌ·· ˈ··/ *n* a woman with children who also has a job, esp. one outside the home

working or·der /ˌ·· ˈ··/ *n* [**in, into**+U] the state of working well, with no trouble

working par·ty /ˈ·· ˌ··/ *n* a committee, e.g. in a business organization or a parliament, which examines a particular matter and reports what it finds

work·ings /ˈwɜːkɪŋz‖ˈwɜːr-/ *n* [P] **1** the way in which something works or operates: *I shall never understand the inner workings of an engine/of his mind.* **2** the parts of a mine which have been dug out

working week /ˌ·· ˈ·/ *n* a WEEK (2)

work·load /ˈwɜːkləʊd‖ˈwɜːrk-/ *n* the amount of work that a person or machine is expected to do in a particular period of time: *She has a very heavy workload.*

work·man /ˈwɜːkmən‖ˈwɜːrk-/ *n* **-men** /mən/ **1** a man who works with his hands, esp. in a particular skill or trade: *The workmen fixed the water system.* **2 a bad workman (always) blames his tools** *saying* careless or unskilled people who produce bad work will blame their materials or tools rather than admit that the fault is theirs

work·man·like /ˈwɜːkmənlaɪk‖ˈwɜːrk-/ *adj apprec* having or showing the qualities of a good workman: *workmanlike methods | a very workmanlike job*

work·man·ship /ˈwɜːkmənʃɪp‖ˈwɜːrk-/ *n* [U] (signs of) skill in making things: *Look at the workmanship on this carved desk.*

work·mate /ˈwɜːkmeɪt‖ˈwɜːrk-/ *n* someone who one works with, usu. in a factory job —compare COLLEAGUE

workmen's com·pen·sa·tion /ˌ·· ···ˈ··/ also **workmen's comp** /-ˈkɒmp‖-ˈkɑːmp/— *n* [U] *AmE* payment (COMPENSATION) from one's employer for suffering harm at work or because of one's work. In the US, employers have INSURANCE to pay for such accidents, but it is still very difficult to get workmen's compensation, and sometimes a court of law is involved: *He received workmen's comp when the machinery hurt his knee. | You should apply for workmen's comp if you think that those fumes are the cause of your lung problems.*

work of art /ˌ·· · ˈ·/ *n* **works of art** **1** a piece of excellent art, e.g. a painting, SCULPTURE, etc. **2** something that can be compared to the best art esp. because of its beauty, detail, etc.: *My new car is a work of art. | This meal is a work of art.*

work·out /ˈwɜːkaʊt‖ˈwɜːr-/ *n infml* a period of physical exercise, e.g. when training for a sport —see also WORK out (6)

work·peo·ple /ˈwɜːkˌpiːpəl‖ˈwɜːrk-/ *n* [P] *BrE* workers who are employed, esp. in a factory

work·place /ˈwɜːkpleɪs‖ˈwɜːrk-/ *n* [C;*the*+S] the room or building in which workers perform their work: *the enforcement of health and safety precautions at the workplace*

work·room /ˈwɜːkrʊm, -ruːm‖ˈwɜːrk-/ *n* a room which is specially kept for working in, esp. on a certain sort of work: *a photographic workroom*

works /wɜːks‖wɜːrks/ *n* **1** [*the*+P] the moving parts (of a machine) —see also **a spanner in the works** (SPANNER) **2** [C] (*often in comb.*) an industrial place of work; factory: *a dye works | the works canteen* —see also GASWORKS, WAXWORKS **3** [*the*+P] *infml* everything: *The whole works — rod, line, basket, everything fell into the water. | OK, give me the works.* (=tell me everything) **4 give someone the works** *sl* to attack someone violently, physically, or with words —see also CLERK OF WORKS, PUBLIC WORKS

work·shop /ˈwɜːkʃɒp‖ˈwɜːrkʃɑːp/ *n* **1** a room or area, e.g. in a factory or business, where heavy repairs and jobs on machines are done: *I'll have to send the broken sewing machine away to the workshop.* **2** an occasion when a group of people meet and work together in order to share and develop ideas about a particular subject or activity: *a drama workshop | a two-day workshop on management techniques*

work·shy /'· ·/ adj derog not liking work and habitually trying to avoid it

work·sta·tion /'wɜːkˌsteɪʃən‖'wɜːrk-/ n an area in which a single person can work in an office, consisting e.g. of a desk with a small computer that is usu. connected to a large central computer

work-stud·y /'· ˌ·/ n [U] the skill or practice of making work more productive in less time by examining the way things are done by workers and suggesting improvement

work-study pro·gram /ˌ· ·· ˌ·/ n AmE a system of allowing students to work part-time in order to gain experience and earn money

work sur·face /'· ˌ·/ n a worktop

work·top /'wɜːktɒp‖'wɜːrktɑːp/ ‖ usu. **counter, countertop** AmE— n a flat surface on top of a piece of kitchen furniture, used for doing work on, such as preparing a meal —see picture at KITCHEN

work-to-rule /ˌ· · '·/ n BrE a form of working which reduces activity or production because careful attention is paid to every point in the rules, even when unnecessary, done in order to support a claim for more money, etc. —compare GO-SLOW; see also **work to rule** (WORK²)

world /wɜːld‖'wɜːrld/ n 1 [the] the body in space on which we live; the Earth: *the richest man in the world* | *the world's tallest building* | *She has sailed round the world.* (compare *A satellite goes round the Earth.*) | *English is a world language — it is spoken* all over the world. (=in many parts of the world) | a **world-famous** *musician* (=known all over the world) 2 [C] a PLANET or star system, esp. one which may contain life: *a strange creature from another world* 3 [the+S] a group of living things: *the animal world* 4 [the+S] a part or area of the world that has a particular character: *the developing world* | *This country has the lowest taxes in the industrialized world.* 5 [the+S] a particular area of human activity: *the world of football/show business* | *a well-known character in the business world* 6 [the+S] people generally; the public: *Keep quiet; we don't want the whole world to know about it.* | *The world waited anxiously for the results of the peace talks.* 7 [the+S] human life and its affairs: *He's very young and inexperienced, and doesn't know about the ways of the world.* | *She has brought four children into the world.* (=given birth to four children) | *a man/woman of the world* (=with plenty of experience of life) 8 [the+S] fml material standards and principles, rather than those of the spirit: *monks renouncing things of the world* 9 [(the) S+of] a large number or amount: *There's a world of difference between thinking about it and doing it!* | *The medicine did me a/the world of good.* (=made me feel much better) 10 all the world to very important to: *My family is/means all the world to me.* 11 for all the world as if/like exactly as if/like: *He goes around giving orders to everyone, for all the world as if he owns the company!* 12 in the world (in a question expressing surprise): *Where in the world* (=wherever) *could he be?* | *What in the world* (=whatever) *are you doing?* 13 not for the world certainly not: *I wouldn't hurt her for the world.* 14 not long for this world euph or humor about to die 15 out of this world infml unusually good; wonderful 16 worlds apart completely different: *Their ways of life are worlds apart.* 17 world without end (in prayers) for ever —see also FREE WORLD, NEW WORLD, OLD WORLD, THIRD WORLD, best of both worlds/of all possible worlds (BEST³), dead to the world (DEAD¹), all the world's a stage (STAGE), think the world of (THINK of), on top of the world (TOP¹)

World Al·ma·nac /ˌ· '···/ AmE tdmk any of a number of large books printed yearly in the US by different PUBLISHERS, which give short accounts of the year's news events and also contain much information in many different fields of knowledge such as politics, history, sports, entertainment, prizes, medicine, etc.

World Bank /ˌ· '·/ also **International Bank for Reconstruction and Development**— [the] a United Nations organization which lends money for development purposes and gives technical help to governments doing large-scale pieces of work

world-beat·er /'· ˌ·/ n a person or thing that is thought to be able to compete successfully with anyone/anything in the world: *This runner/new invention is a world-beater.*

world-class /ˌ· '·◂/ adj among the best in the world: *That cricketer is world-class.*

World Coun·cil of Church·es /ˌ· ˌ··· '··/ [the] an international organization of all types of Protestant and certain other churches, with its main offices in Geneva

World Cup /ˌ· '·/ [the] the most important football competition, which happens every four years and where countries are each represented by their national team: *Brazil won the World Cup* | *the 1990 World Cup*

world-fa·mous /ˌ· '···◂/ adj internationally well-known: *a world-famous event/singer* | *You must know him. He's world-famous.*

World Health Or·gan·i·za·tion /ˌ· '· ···ˌ··/ also **WHO**— [the] an international organization, started by the United Nations in 1948, which works to improve the health of people of all nations e.g. by education, by encouraging IMMUNIZATION, etc.

world·ly /'wɜːldli‖'wɜːr-/ adj 1 [A] of the material world: *all my worldly goods* (=everything I own) | *worldly success* 2 often derog concerned with or experienced in the ways of society; not SPIRITUAL —opposite **unworldly** —compare OTHERWORLDLY —-liness n [U]

worldly-wise /ˌ··· '·◂‖'·· ·/ adj experienced in the ways of society: *I'm too worldly-wise to expect too much of human nature.*

world mu·sic /'· ˌ··/ n [U] fashionable music which is not from Europe or the US and which is different in style from Western POP MUSIC. World music includes SALSA, REGGAE and many types of African music.

world pow·er /ˌ· '··/ n a nation which has great power and influence, and whose trade, politics, etc., have an effect on many other parts of the world

World Se·ries /ˌ· '···◂/ [the] a set of games played each year to decide which is the top US BASEBALL team. It is opened by the president of the US, who throws the first ball. —see also BASEBALL and see colour picture on page 950

World Ser·vice /ˌ· '··/ [the] see BBC WORLD SERVICE

world·shak·ing /'wɜːldˌʃeɪkɪŋ‖'wɜːrld-/ adj EARTH-SHATTERING

World Trade Cen·ter /ˌ· '· ˌ··/ [the] two buildings in Manhattan, New York City, which were the tallest in the world when they were built in the early 1970s by the New York Port Authority —see colour map on page 1376

world war /ˌ· '·◂/ n a war involving many countries in different parts of the world, esp. the 1914–18 and 1939–45 wars —see also FIRST WORLD WAR, SECOND WORLD WAR

World War I /ˌwɜːld wɔː 'wʌn‖ˌwɜːrld wɔːr-/ see FIRST WORLD WAR

World War II /ˌwɜːld wɔː 'tuː‖ˌwɜːrld wɔːr-/ see SECOND WORLD WAR

world-wear·y /ˌ· '···◂/ adj tired of life: *world-weary cynicism* —-iness n [U]

world·wide /ˌwɜːld'waɪd◂‖ˌwɜːr-/ adj, adv in or over all the world: *French cheeses are famous worldwide.* | *cars with a worldwide reputation for reliability*

World Wide Fund for Na·ture /ˌ· · ˌ· · '··/ [the] an international organization (CHARITY), formerly called the **World Wildlife Fund**, which raises money for CONSERVATION

worm¹ /wɜːm‖wɜːrm/ n 1 a small thin creature with no bones or limbs, like a round tube of flesh, esp. an EARTH-WORM: *I accidentally cut a worm in half with my spade.* | *Many birds eat worms.* | *This dog has worms.* (=which live inside the body) —see also GLOW-WORM, HOOKWORM, SILKWORM, SLOWWORM, TAPEWORM, WOODWORM 2 derog a weak and worthless, cowardly, etc. person: *You miserable worm!* 3 tech the curving line round a SCREW¹ (1) 4 even a worm will turn BrE saying even the most quiet and humble person will refuse to allow himself or herself to be treated badly beyond a certain point —see also can of worms (CAN²)

worm² v [T] 1 [+obj+adv/prep, esp. into] a to move gradually by twisting or effort: *We wormed our way through the crack in the wall.* b derog to make (oneself) accepted, gradually and perhaps by dishonest means: *He wormed himself into her affections.* 2 to remove living worms from the body of (e.g. a dog), esp. by chemical means
worm sthg. ↔ out phr v [T (of)] to obtain by questioning, esp. over a period of time: *We eventually managed to worm the secret out (of her).*

worm cast /'· ·/ n a tubelike pile of earth left on the surface of the ground by an EARTHWORM

worm-eat·en /ˈ· ˌ··/ *adj* **1** full of holes, esp. (of furniture) from WOODWORM **2** *infml derog* old and no longer usable; WORN-OUT

worm gear /ˈ· ·/ also **worm wheel**— *n* a GEAR¹ (1) with an arrangement inside curving round and round

worm·hole /ˈwɜːmhəʊl‖ˈwɜːrm-/ *n* **1** a hole in the ground left by a worm **2** a hole in wood made by WOODWORM

worm·wood /ˈwɜːmwʊd‖ˈwɜːrm-/ *n* [U] a plant with a bitter taste, used in making ABSINTH (=an alcoholic drink) and some medicines

Wormwood Scrubs /ˌ·· ˈ·/ also **The Scrubs** *infml*— a prison in W London

worm·y /ˈwɜːmi‖ˈwɜːrmi/ *adj* **1** of or like a worm **2** containing worms: *a wormy apple* **3** with holes made by worms; WORM-EATEN

worn /wɔːn‖wɔːrn/ *past participle of* WEAR

worn-out /ˌ· ˈ·◄/ *adj* **1** completely finished by continued use; no longer usable: *worn-out shoes* **2** [F] very tired: *She was worn-out after three sleepless nights.* —compare OUTWORN

wor·ried /ˈwʌrid‖ˈwɜːrid/ *adj* [(about)] experiencing worry; anxious: *a worried look/frown* | *She seems very worried about something.* | *We were* **worried sick** (=very worried) *when the children didn't come home.* [F+(that)] *They are worried (that) the hijackers will make further demands.* — ~**ly** *adv*

wor·ri·some /ˈwʌrisəm‖ˈwɜːri-/ *adj* which troubles one or makes one anxious

wor·ry¹ /ˈwʌri‖ˈwɜːri/ *v* **1** [T] to make anxious or uncomfortable; cause worry to: *The increasingly poor quality of his work is beginning to worry his teachers.* | *Heights don't worry me.* | *What worries me most is the possibility of a nuclear accident.* | *a very worrying situation/new development* **2** [I (about, over);T *obj*] to be anxious (about), esp. over a period of time: *Worrying about your health can make you ill.* | *Don't worry!* [+*wh*-] *Don't worry how much you spend.* (=it doesn't matter) [+*that*] *The teacher worried that the exam might be too difficult for her students.* | (*BrE*) *"I'm afraid I can't come after all." "Ah well,* **not to worry.**" (=it doesn't really matter) **3** [T] (esp. of a dog) to chase and bite (an animal): *The dog was found worrying sheep, and had to be shot.* —-**rier** *n* — ~**ingly** *adv*
worry at sthg./sbdy. *phr v* [T] to keep attempting to deal with something, using great effort: *She worried at the problem until she found an answer.*

worry² *n* **1** [U] an uncomfortable feeling in the mind caused by a mixture of fear and uncertainty; anxiety: *lines of worry on her face* **2** [C] a person or thing that causes this feeling: *It's a worry to me having to leave the children alone in the house.* | *We have no money worries.* | *The profit and loss figures have prompted worries over/about the company's future.*

worry beads /ˈ·· ·/ *n* [P] a string of BEADs (= small stones or wooden balls) which are turned over and over in one's hands to keep one calm in a difficult or worrying situation

wor·ry·wart /ˈwʌriwɔːt‖ˈwɜːriwɔːrt/ *n infml, esp. AmE* a person who worries a lot about unimportant things

worse¹ /wɜːs‖wɜːrs/ *adj* **1** (*comparative of* BAD) of lower quality; not as good, pleasant, or satisfactory (as someone or something else): *It wasn't a particularly good performance, although it could have been much/far worse.* | *He may be late or,* **worse still,** *he may not come at all.* | *Last year's harvest was bad, but this year's may be even worse.* | *The car broke down when I was driving home from work, and* **to make matters worse** (=this made the situation even more unpleasant) *it was pouring with rain.* **2** [F] (*comparative of* ill) more ill (than before): *I'm afraid she's getting steadily worse.* **3 none the worse (for)** not harmed (by): *The children got lost in the forest, but seemed none the worse (for it) when they arrived home in the morning.* **4 the worse for wear** spoilt/not improved by time and use or work: *The defeated challenger looked somewhat the worse for wear after the big fight.* **5 worse luck** *BrE infml* unfortunately: *He reached the food before I did, worse luck!* —compare BETTER¹; see also **go from bad to worse** (BAD¹)

worse² *n* [U] something worse: *We thought that the situation was as bad as it could be, but worse was to follow.* |

I'm afraid there's been a **change for the worse.** (=a bad change) —compare BETTER³

worse³ *adv* (*comparative of* BADLY) **1** in a worse way: *They said they had fixed the car, but it's now running even worse than before.* **2** to a worse degree: *It's hurting worse than before.* —compare BETTER²
▷ USAGE Some people think that **worse** should not be used as an adverb in sentences like *He's behaving* **worse** *this year than last year* and that it is better to say *in a* **worse** *way.*◁

wors·en /ˈwɜːsən‖ˈwɜːr-/ *v* [I;T] to make or become worse; (cause to) DETERIORATE: *The situation/crisis has worsened.* | *The rain has worsened our difficulties.* | *the worsening economic crisis* —compare BETTER⁴ (1)

wor·ship¹ /ˈwɜːʃɪp‖ˈwɜːr-/ *n* [U] **1** strong usu. religious feelings of love, respect, and admiration, esp. when shown to God or a god: *They bowed their heads in worship.* | *Some societies practise ancestor worship.* **2** the act of showing this: *They joined together in worship.* **3** a religious service: *They attended divine worship.* —see also HERO WORSHIP

worship² *v BrE* **-pp-**‖**-p-** *AmE* **1** [I;T] to show worship or great honour (to): *His followers* **worshipped at his feet.** | *Let us bow down and worship God.* | (fig.) *She worships her elder brother/***worships the ground he walks on.** (=admires him (too) greatly) **2** [I] to attend a church service: *We worship regularly at that church.* — ~**per** *n*

Worship *n esp. BrE* (used as a title for addressing or speaking of certain officials, esp. a MAYOR or a MAGISTRATE): *Good morning,* **Your Worship.** | *Pray silence for* **His Worship** *the mayor of Brighton!*

wor·ship·ful /ˈwɜːʃɪpfəl‖ˈwɜːr-/ *adj* [A] *esp. BrE* (used as a respectful form of address): *the Worshipful Mayor of Brighton* | *the Worshipful Company of Goldsmiths*

worst¹ /wɜːst‖wɜːrst/ *adj* (*superlative of* BAD) more bad, unpleasant, or unsatisfactory than anyone or anything else: *the worst airline disaster in history* | *It was the worst winter for 50 years.* | *a criminal of the worst kind* | *Who* **came off worst** (=was defeated) *in the argument?*

worst² *n* **1** worst [*the*+C] the most bad person, thing, state, or part: *I've seen bad work, but this is the worst.* | *The worst of it is that I could have prevented the accident if I had got there five minutes earlier.* | *to expect/fear/be prepared for the worst* | *The worst of the winter is probably over now.* **2 at (the) worst** if one thinks of it in the worst way: *He's a fool at (the) best, and at (the) worst he's a criminal.* **3 do one's worst** to do as much harm as one can (esp. suggesting that very little harm can be done): *We've harvested all the crops, so now the weather can do its worst.* **4 get the worst of (it)** to be defeated **5 if the worst comes to the worst** if the worst possible situation actually happens; if there is no better way: *If the worst comes to the worst, we can always go by bus tomorrow.*

worst³ *adv* (*superlative of* BADLY) most badly: *The others weren't very good but she played (the) worst of anybody.* (=worse than all the rest) | *It's the old and the poor who suffer worst when subsidies are cut.* | *the worst-dressed man in the office*

worst⁴ *v* [T *usu. pass.*] *old use* to defeat: *We were worsted in battle.*

worst case sce·na·ri·o /ˌ· ˈ· ·ˌ···/ *n* a situation under consideration in which the worst possible events may happen

wor·sted /ˈwʊstɪd/ *n* [U] wool cloth: *a worsted suit*

worth¹ /wɜːθ‖wɜːrθ/ *prep* (esp. after **be**) **1** having the stated value: *It's worth much more than I paid for it.* | *a piece of land worth £44,500* | *How much is your car worth?* | *The agreement wasn't* **worth the paper it was written on.** (=was completely worthless) **2** having possessions of the stated value: *She's worth at least $1,000,000.* **3** deserving of: *We may not succeed, but it's worth a try.* [+*v-ing*] *It isn't worth waiting for him.* | *The food's not worth eating.* | *It's well worth making the effort to learn how to do it.* | *It's such a minor detail that it's hardly worth mentioning.* **4 for all one is worth** with all possible effort: *He tried and tried for all he was worth, but it still wouldn't work.* **5 for what it's worth** though I'm not sure it's of value: *Here's the article I promised you, for what it's worth.* —compare **such as it is/they are** (SUCH¹) **6 not worth the candle** *infml, esp. BrE* not worth the effort **7 worth it** useful; worth the trouble: *Don't lock the door; it isn't worth it.* **8 worth one's salt** *infml* worthy of respect or of being so called: *No poet worth his salt would have used a terrible rhyme like that.* **9 worth one's/someone's while** worthwhile to one/someone: *If you'll tell me when the night watchman will be off duty, I'll* **make it worth your while.** (=pay you)

worth² *n* [U] value: *jewels of great worth | After his unkindness, I know the true worth of his friendship.* (=it is worthless) | *The storm did thousands of pounds' worth of damage.* (=did damage worth thousands of pounds)

worth·less /ˈwɜːθləs‖ˈwɜːrθ-/ *adj* **1** of no value: *The jewels he sold us turned out to be completely worthless.* —see VALUABLE (USAGE) **2** (of a person) of bad character; with no good qualities: *a worthless member of society* — ~ **ly** *adv* — ~ **ness** *n* [U]

worth·while /ˌwɜːθˈwaɪl◂‖ˌwɜːrθ-/ *adj* deserving the effort needed, the time or money spent, etc.: *a worthwhile charity to contribute to | We had a long wait, but it was worthwhile because we got the tickets.*

wor·thy¹ /ˈwɜːði‖ˈwɜːrði/ *adj* **1** [A] deserving respect or serious consideration: *a worthy opponent | worthy aims | She proved herself a worthy successor to the former champion.* **2** [F+of/to-v] deserving: *worthy of admiration | a performance worthy to be remembered* **3** *derog* having honourable and valuable qualities, but often not very exciting or interesting: *a worthy man* **4 -worthy** deserving: *blameworthy | praiseworthy | The bank didn't consider him creditworthy because he was very irresponsible with money.* —**thily** *adv* —**thiness** *n* [U]

worthy² *n, fml, sometimes humor* a person of importance: *local worthies*

wot /wɒt‖wɑːt/ *v* -**tt**- [I (**of**)] *BrE old use or humor* to know: *other times and places which we wot not of*

wot·cher /ˈwɒtʃəʳ‖ˈwɑː-/ *interj BrE old-fash sl* (esp. in southeastern England) HELLO

would /wʊd/ *v 3rd person sing.* **would,** *short form,* **'d,** *negative short form* **wouldn't** [*modal+to-v*] **1 a** (used instead of **will** to describe what someone has said, asked, etc.): *They said they would/they'd meet us at 10.30.* (their actual words were: *"We will meet you at 10.30."*) | *I knew she would be annoyed.* **b** (used instead of **will** with a past tense verb or when showing what is likely or possible): *I'd be surprised if he came. | Any fall in the price of oil would have serious consequences for our economy. | What would you do if you won a million pounds? | They couldn't find any one who would* (=was willing to) *take the job. | He said there had been a serious accident, but wouldn't give* (=refused to give) *any details.* **2 a** (shows what always happened): *We used to work in the same office and we would often have coffee together.* **b** (shows that one is annoyed at something that always happens or is typical): *That's exactly like him — he would lose the key!* **3 would rather** (expressing a choice): *Which would you rather do, go to the cinema or stay at home? | I'd rather not say what I think. | I'd rather you didn't tell him.* **4 would that** *fml or lit* (expressing a strong wish) if only … : *Would that we had seen her before she died.* **5 would you** (expressing a polite request): *Would you please lend me your pencil? | Shut the door, would you?* —see LIKE (USAGE), NOT (USAGE), SHOULD (USAGE), USE (USAGE)

would-be /ˈ· ·/ *adj* [A] which one wants or intends to be, but is not: *a would-be musician | She managed to escape from her would-be attacker.* —compare WANNABE

would·n't /ˈwʊdnt/ *short for:* would not

wouldst /wʊdst/ **thou wouldst** *old use or bibl* (when talking to one person) you would

wound¹ /waʊnd/ *past tense & participle of* WIND³ʼ⁵

wound² /wuːnd/ *n* [(**in**)] a damaged place in the body, usu. a hole or tear through the skin, esp. one made intentionally by a weapon, such as a gun or knife: *The president received/sustained a serious stomach wound/a serious wound in the stomach. | It's only a flesh wound.* (=not deep) | *a bullet wound | The wound is healing fast.* | (fig.) *You'll only* **open old wounds** (=remind someone of an unpleasant and hurtful experience, situation, etc.) *if you bring up that subject.* | (fig.) *a wound to her pride* —see also **rub salt into the/someone's wound(s)** (RUB¹)

wound³ /wuːnd/ *v* [T] to cause a wound to: *The bullet wounded his arm. | He wounded her in the arm. | Was he seriously/badly wounded?*

▷ USAGE Compare **wound, injure,** and **hurt** when used of bodily damage. You can be **wounded** or receive a **wound** from any attack in which a gun or sharp instrument such as a sword or knife is used. You can be **injured** or receive an **injury, a** when any other weapon such as a heavy stick or bomb is used, **b** in an accident: *He was seriously* **injured** *in a car crash.* Both **wound** and **injure** are more serious than **hurt:** *She slipped and* **hurt** *her knee.*◁

wound·ed /ˈwuːndʒd/ *adj* hurt; suffering from a wound: *wounded survivors* [(also *n, the*+P)] *The wounded were taken off to hospital.* | (fig.) *wounded pride*

Wounded Knee /ˌ·· ˈ·/, **Battle of** the last big battle against the Native Americans, in 1890, at Wounded Knee Creek in South Dakota, in which American soldiers killed nearly 200 Sioux, including women and children

wound-up /ˌwaʊnd ˈʌp◂/ *adj* anxiously excited

wove /wəʊv/ *past tense of* WEAVE

wov·en /ˈwəʊvən/ *past participle of* WEAVE

wow¹ /waʊ/ *interj infml* (an expression of surprise and admiration): *Wow! What a fantastic dress!*

wow² *n* [S] *sl* a great success

wow³ *v* [T] *sl* to cause surprise and admiration in (someone): *His new show really wowed the critics.*

wow⁴ *n* [U] faulty rising and falling sounds in a machine for playing recorded sound, caused by an unevenness in the speed of the motor —compare FLUTTER² (5a)

WP /ˌdʌbəljuː ˈpiː/ *abbrev. for:* word processing; word processor

WPC /ˌdʌbəljuː piː ˈsiː/ *n BrE* Woman Police Constable; a female member of the police force having the lowest rank. Since 1990 British police forces have stopped using this title: *W.P.C. Jenkins | Two W.P.Cs were attacked.* —see also P.C.

WRAC /ræk/ [(*the*)] Women's Royal Army Corps; a women's branch of the British Army

wrack¹ /ræk/ *n* [U] RACK³ʼ⁴

wrack² *n* [U] a type of SEAWEED

WRAF /ræf/ [(*the*)] Women's Royal Air Force; the women's branch of the British Royal Air Force

wraith /reɪθ/ *n lit* an exact image of a person, esp. seen just before or just after their death

wran·gle¹ /ˈræŋgəl/ *v* [I (**with, over**)] to argue, esp. angrily, noisily, and over a long period

wrangle² *n* an angry or noisy argument, esp. one that continues for a long time: *We are involved in another wrangle with the management over our pay.*

wran·gler /ˈræŋgləʳ/ *n* **1** a person who wrangles or is wrangling **2** *AmE* a COWBOY, esp. one who looks after horses

Wrangler *tdmk* a company which makes JEANS which are widely sold in Britain and the US, and are called **Wranglers:** *a pair of Wranglers | Wrangler jeans*

wrap¹ /ræp/ *v* -**pp**- [T] **1** [(UP, **in**)] to cover (something) in a material folded around: *I put the book in a box and wrapped it up in brown paper before I posted it. | The shop assistant offered to wrap the shoes, but I wanted to wear them at once.* | (fig.) *He wrapped* (=hid) *his meaning in a lot of pseudo-scientific jargon.* —see also GIFT-WRAP **2** [+*adv/prep*, esp. (**a**)**round**] to fold (a material) over: *I wrapped the rug around the sick man's legs to keep him warm. | She had a bandage wrapped round her finger.*
  wrap up *phr v* **1** [I] to wear warm clothes: *Wrap up well — it's cold outside!* **2** [T] (**wrap sthg.** ↔ **up**) *infml* to complete (a business arrangement, a meeting, etc.): *Now the trade agreement is wrapped up all we have to do is wait for the first orders.* **3** [I *usu. imperative*] *infml* to be quiet; SHUT up **4 wrapped up in** giving all one's love or attention to: *She's so wrapped up in him she can't see his faults.* | *wrapped up in one's own thoughts*

wrap² *n* **1** *esp. AmE* a garment which is used as a covering, esp. round a woman's shoulders **2 under wraps** *infml* kept secret from the public: *The plans for the new space mission are still under wraps.*

wrap·per /ˈræpəʳ/ *n* a piece of paper which forms a loose cover: *a book's wrapper*

wrap·ping /ˈræpɪŋ/ *also* **wrappings** *pl.— n* [C;U] material used for folding round and covering something: *I undid the wrapping(s) and looked inside.*

wrapping pa·per /ˈ·· ˌ·· / n [U] paper, usu. covered in attractive patterns, for wrapping presents

wrath /rɒθ‖ræθ/ n [U] fml or lit strong fierce anger esp. based on the desire to punish someone for harm done to oneself: *the wrath of God* | *Management incurred the wrath of the union by breaking the agreement.* —~ful adj —~fully adv

Wray /reɪ/, **Fay** (1907–) an American film actress famous esp. for appearing in the film *King Kong*

wreak /riːk/ v [T (on)] esp. lit to do (violence) or express (strong feelings) violently: *We shall wreak a terrible vengeance on our enemies.* | *These floods are* **wreaking havoc** (=causing destruction and confusion) *in low-lying areas.*

wreath /riːθ/ n **wreaths** /riːðz, riːθs/ **1** an arrangement of flowers or leaves, esp. in a circle, such as one given at a funeral or hung on the front door at Christmas in celebration of the season: *She laid a wreath on his grave.* **2** a circle of leaves or flowers placed on the head or round the neck of someone to honour them: *a laurel wreath* **3** [(of)] esp. lit a curl of smoke, mist, gas, etc.

wreathe /riːð/ v esp. lit **1** [T] to circle round and cover completely: *Mist wreathed the hilltops.* | (fig.) *Her face was* **wreathed in smiles.** (=She was smiling very happily) **2** [I+adv/prep] (of smoke, mist, gas, etc.) to move gently in circles: *The fog wreathed round the street light.*

wreck[1] /rek/ n **1** [C] a ship lost at sea or (partly) destroyed on rocks: *the wreck of an old Spanish galleon* | *Divers have found a hoard of gold in the wreck.* —see also SHIP-WRECK **2** [U] the state of being ruined or destroyed: *the wreck of all her hopes* **3** [C] infml something ruined or (partly) destroyed: *Have you seen that old wreck he drives around in!* **4** [C] a person whose health or spirits have been destroyed: *He's been a complete wreck since his illness.* | *This job is turning me into a* **nervous wreck.**

wreck[2] v [T] **1** [often pass.; not in progressive forms] **a** to cause (a ship) to be destroyed: *The ship was wrecked on the rocks.* **b** to cause (the people on a ship) to be in a SHIP-WRECK: *We were wrecked off the coast of Africa.* **2** to bring to a ruined or unusable state; destroy: *The weather has completely wrecked our plans.*

wreck·age /ˈrekɪdʒ/ n [U] the broken parts of a destroyed thing: *The wreckage of the aircraft was spread over a five-mile area.* | (fig.) *trying to put together the wreckage of my life/of our marriage*

wreck·er /ˈrekəʳ/ n **1** a person who destroys, esp. (in former times) one who tried to cause a ship to be caught on rocks in order to be able to steal from it **2** a person whose job is to bring out goods from ships which have been wrecked, so that they will not be lost **3** AmE a vehicle used for moving other vehicles when these have stopped working, or after accidents

wren /ren/ n a very small brown European and North American bird

Wren[1] n infml a member of the WRNS

Wren[2], **Sir Chris·to·pher** /ˈkrɪstəfəʳ/ (1632–1723) an English ARCHITECT who built many churches in London, including St Paul's Cathedral, and other buildings in Britain such as the Sheldonian Theatre in Oxford

St. Paul's Cathedral

wrench[1] /rentʃ/ v [T] **1** [+obj +adv/prep] to pull hard and often violently with a twisting or turning movement: *He wrenched the gun from/out of her hands.* | *I wrenched the door open.* | *She wrenched the lid off.* **2** to twist and damage (a joint of the body): *I fell and wrenched my ankle.* **3** to cause great suffering of the mind or very painful feelings: *a heart-wrenching story*

wrench[2] n **1** an act of twisting and pulling something hard and perhaps violently **2** damage to a joint of the body by twisting: *I've given my knee a bad wrench.* **3** [usu. sing.] something, esp. a separation, that causes great suffering of the mind or very painful feelings: *the wrench of leaving one's family* **4** a also **monkey wrench** AmE for SPANNER **b** BrE a SPANNER with jaws that can be moved so as to be close together or far apart —see picture at TOOL

wrest /rest/ v [T+obj+adv/prep, esp. **from, out of**] **1** to pull (away) violently: *He wrested it from her hands.* **2** esp. lit to obtain with difficulty: *We wrested victory from the jaws of defeat.* | *The farmers in this area have to struggle to wrest a living from the infertile soil.*

wres·tle /ˈresəl/ v [I (with);T] **1** to fight by trying to hold or throw one's opponent: *She wrestled with her attacker.* | *She wrestled him to the ground.* | (fig.) *wrestling with a difficult examination paper* **2** to fight (someone) like this as a sport (**wrestling**) —compare BOX³ (1) —**-tler** n

wres·tling /ˈreslɪŋ/ n [U] a sport in which two people fight in a ring, trying to hold or throw each other against the ropes or onto the floor. In Britain it is thought of as a working-class sport. Because the winners have often been secretly agreed on before the MATCHes, the sport is treated as entertainment rather than a real competition.

wretch /retʃ/ n **1** an unfortunate or unhappy person: *poor homeless wretches* **2** often humor a bad or useless person: *You wretch! You're late again.*

wretch·ed /ˈretʃɪd/ adj **1 a** very unhappy; in very low spirits: *He's in bed with a bad cold, feeling pretty wretched.* | *I feel wretched about having to disappoint her.* **b** causing unhappiness, discomfort, etc.: *a wretched life/headache* **2** extremely bad: *What wretched weather!* **3** [A] (used to express annoyance): *I can't find my wretched keys.* | *Why can't that wretched child behave himself?* **4 wretched refuse** *quote* a phrase taken from the words written on the Statue of Liberty in New York Harbor —see STATUE OF LIBERTY —~ly adv —~ness n [U]

wrig·gle[1] /ˈrɪgəl/ v **1** [I] to twist from side to side with short quick movements, either in one place or when moving along: *He wriggled uncomfortably on the hard chair.* | (fig.) *The prosecution have got a pretty strong case against him – he'll be lucky to wriggle free this time!* **2** [T] to move (a part of the body) in this way; WIGGLE: *Wriggle your toes.*

wriggle out of sthg. *phr v* [T] infml to escape (a difficult situation or responsibility) by clever tricks, by pretending, etc.: *You know you're to blame, so don't try to wriggle out of it.* [+v-ing] *I'd hoped to wriggle out of telling her.*

wriggle[2] n a wriggling movement

Wright[1] /raɪt/, **Frank Lloyd** (1869–1959) an American ARCHITECT known for his use of modern materials and methods, in buildings such as the Guggenheim Museum in New York

Wright[2], **Or·ville** /ˈɔːvɪl ‖ ˈɔːr-/ (1871–1948) an American AVIATOR who worked with his brother **Wilbur Wright** (1867–1912) building GLIDERs and other aircraft. The **Wright Brothers** are famous for making the first powered flight in their aircraft in 1903, at Kitty Hawk, North Carolina.

Wright[3], **Peter** (1917–) an English INTELLIGENCE AGENT who became famous for writing a book called *Spycatcher* in 1987 about the secret service. The British government tried to stop PUBLICATION of the book but were unsuccessful. —see also SPYCATCHER

Wrig·leys /ˈrɪgliz/ n [U] tdmk a type of CHEWING GUM made by the firm of Wrigley

wring /rɪŋ/ v **wrung** /rʌŋ/ [T] **1 a** to twist (esp. the neck, causing death): *to kill a chicken by wringing its neck* | (humor) *I'll wring your neck if you don't behave!* **b** to press hard on (esp. a person's hand): *He wrung my hand warmly.* (=when shaking hands in greeting) | *It's no use wringing your hands in sorrow.* | (fig.) *The baby's sufferings wrung its mother's heart.* (=made her extremely unhappy) **2** [(OUT, from)] to twist and/or press (wet clothes) to remove water, or to remove (water) by doing this: *Wring those wet things out.* | (fig.) *Her torturers wrung the truth out of her in the end.* **3 wringing wet** extremely wet, so that a lot of water can be pressed out

wring·er /ˈrɪŋəʳ/ n a machine, often part of a WASHING MACHINE, with ROLLERs (=tube-shaped parts) which press water from clothes, sheets, etc. that are passed through them —compare MANGLE²

wrin·kle[1] /ˈrɪŋkəl/ n **1** a small line or fold, esp. on the skin owing to age, worry, tiredness, etc.: *wrinkles round her eyes* | *wrinkled stockings* —compare CRINKLE² **2** infml a useful suggestion or trick: *Ask him; he knows all the wrinkles.* (=knows the best ways of doing something) —**-kly** adj

wrinkle² /v/ **1** [T (UP)] to cause to form into lines, folds, etc., esp. for a short time: *She wrinkled her nose at the bad smell.* **2** [I] (esp. of the skin) to form into lines, folds, etc.: *The skin round her eyes wrinkled when she smiled.*

wrink·ly /ˈrɪŋkli/ *n* **-ies** *infml derog* a young person's name for an old or older person

wrist /rɪst/ *n* the joint between the hand and the lower part of the arm —see also LIMP-WRISTED, and see picture at HAND

wrist·band /ˈrɪstbænd/ *n* **1** a loose CUFF **2** a band used for fastening something, such as a watch, to the wrist

wrist·let /ˈrɪstlɪt/ *n* a band worn round the wrist

wrist·watch /ˈrɪstwɒtʃ‖-wɑːtʃ, -wɔːtʃ/ *n* a watch made to be fastened on the wrist with a STRAP (=band) of metal or leather or other material

wrist·y /ˈrɪsti/ *adj apprec* (esp. in sport) having or showing strong movement of the wrist: *a wristy player/stroke*

writ¹ /rɪt/ *n* an official legal paper telling someone to do or not to do a particular thing: *The High Court has issued a writ forbidding her to communicate with him.* | *a writ of habeas corpus* —see also HOLY WRIT

writ² *adj* **writ large** *esp. lit or pomp* made more clearly noticeable; on a larger or grander scale

write /raɪt/ *v* **wrote** /rəʊt/, **written** /ˈrɪtn/ **1** [I;T] to make (marks that represent letters or words) by using a tool held in the hand, esp. with a pen or pencil on paper: *The children are learning to write.* | *She always writes with a pen/writes in ink.* | *Write the address on the envelope.* —compare DRAW¹ (1) **2** [T] to think of and record, esp. on paper; be the AUTHOR of: *to write a letter* | *Have you finished writing that report yet?* | *Charlotte Brontë wrote "Jane Eyre".* | *Elgar wrote two symphonies.* | *to write a computer program* | *a written statement* **3** [T] to make or complete (something) by putting words on it: [+obj(i)+obj(d)] *He wrote me a cheque for £15.* **4** [I] to be a writer of books, plays, etc.: *He writes for the stage.* **5** [I;T (to)] to produce and send (a letter): *She writes to me every day.* | *I wish you'd write more often.* [+obj(i)+obj(d)] *He writes me a letter every day/He writes a letter to me every day.* [+v-ing] *He wrote asking me to come.* [+to-v] *He wrote to ask me to come.* [+that] *He wrote that he'd be coming on Tuesday.* **6** [T] *esp. AmE* to produce and send a letter to (someone): *He writes me every day.* [+obj+that] *George wrote me that he couldn't come.* **7 be written on/all over** to be clearly showing because of the expression on: *Guilt was written all over his face.* **8 nothing to write home about** *infml* nothing special; not as good as it might be: *The food here isn't anything to write home about.* (=isn't very good)
  write away *phr v* [I (for)] to write to (someone) to ask them for something, esp. a product; WRITE off (3)
  write back *phr v* [I] to reply in a letter: *I received his letter two weeks ago, but I forgot to write back.* [+v-ing/to-v/that] *She wrote back (saying/to say) that she couldn't come.*
  write sthg. ↔ **down** *phr v* [T] to record in writing, esp. in order to remember: *Write your idea down while it's clear in your mind.* | *to write down a telephone number*
  write in *phr v* **1** [I (for)] to send a letter to a firm, asking for something or giving an opinion: *We wrote in for a free book, but the firm never replied.* **2** [T] (**write** sbdy./sthg. ↔ **in**) *AmE* **a** to vote for (someone) by writing their name on the voting paper **b** to add (a name) to a list in an election —see also WRITE-IN
  write off *phr v* **1** [T (as)] (**write** sthg. ↔ **off**) to accept as lost, useless, or as a failure: *I may have been beaten in this fight, but don't write me off yet — I'll be back!* | *She'd been written off as a failure at the age of eleven.* **2** [T] (**write** sthg. ↔ **off**) to remove (esp. a debt) from the records or accounts; CANCEL: *The company has written off £2m of the development costs of this project.* **3** [I (for)] to send a letter to a distant place, esp. in order to buy something one cannot get near home: *She wrote off for the book because the local shop didn't have it.* **4** [T] (**write** sthg. ↔ **off**) *esp. BrE* ‖ **total** sthg. *AmE* to damage (esp. a car) so badly that it cannot be repaired —see also WRITE-OFF
  write sbdy./sthg. ↔ **out** *phr v* [T] **1** to write in full: *The policeman was writing out his report.* | *Do it in rough before you write it out properly.* **2** to write (something formal): [+obj(i)+obj(d)] *Shall I write you out a receipt, sir?* **3** [(of)] to remove (a character) from a continuing set of stories or plays: *When the actor died, the character*

he played in the soap opera had to be written out.
  write up *phr v* **1** [T] (=**write** sthg. **up**) to write (again) in a complete and useful form: *I'm going to write up my notes.* **2** [T] (**write** sthg. ↔ **up**) to write a report on (goods, a play, an event, etc.), esp. giving a judgment: *I see they've written our play up in the local newspaper.* —see also WRITE-UP

write-in /ˈ· ·/ *n AmE* a vote given by writing the name of the person voted for —see also WRITE **in** (2)

write-off /ˈ· ·/ *n* **1** *esp. BrE* something which has been so badly damaged that it cannot be repaired: *The car was a write-off after the accident.* **2** something, esp. a debt, that has been removed from the records or accounts —see also WRITE **off**

writ·er /ˈraɪtəʳ/ *n* a person who writes, esp. as a way of earning money; AUTHOR: *He is a writer but he doesn't make enough money to live from his books.* | *a software writer* | *a sports writer* | *one of the President's speech writers*

writer's cramp /ˌ·· ˈ·/ *n* [U] stiffness of the hand after writing for a long time

write-up /ˈ· ·/ *n infml* a written report, esp. one that describes and gives a judgment about goods, a play, etc.: *The concert got a good write-up in the local newspaper.* —see also WRITE **up** (2)

writhe /raɪð/ *v* [I] to twist the body (as if) in great pain: *He was writhing on the ground in agony.*

writ·ing /ˈraɪtɪŋ/ *n* [U] **1** handwriting: *I can't read the doctor's writing.* **2** written work or form: *a piece of writing* | *You say you'll lend us the money; can I have that* **in writing?** (=in written form, so as to make it official) **3** the activity of writing, esp. books: *Writing is his life.* **4 the writing is on the wall** a business or an organization will not continue to exist for much longer: *With the current poor economic climate, the writing is on the wall for many companies.* —see also WRITINGS

writing desk /ˈ·· ·/ *n* a desk, esp. with a place for writing materials such as paper and pens

writing pa·per /ˈ·· ˌ··/ also **notepaper**— *n* [U] paper for writing letters on, usu. smooth and of quite good quality, which can be bought in various standard sizes

writ·ings /ˈraɪtɪŋz/ *n* [P] works of literature or other written material, produced by the stated person: *Darwin's scientific writings*

writ·ten /ˈrɪtn/ *past participle of* WRITE: *a written request*

WRNS /ˌdʌbəljuː ɑːr en ˈes/ [*the +sing./pl. v*] Women's Royal Naval Service; the women's branch of the British Royal Navy

wrong¹ /rɒŋ‖rɔːŋ/ *adj* **1** not correct; not in accordance with the facts or the truth: *This sum is wrong.* | *the wrong answer* | *You're doing it the wrong way.* | *We must be on the wrong road.* | *No, you're wrong; she didn't say that.* | *The clock's wrong; it's 2 o'clock, not 3 o'clock.* **2** [F] **a** evil; against moral standards: *Telling lies is wrong.* **b** against correct socially acceptable behaviour: [+to-v] *You were wrong not to have mentioned it.* **3** [F (with)] not satisfactory in condition, health, results, working, etc.: *You look upset; is anything wrong?* | *The car won't start. What's wrong with it?* (=What's the problem/trouble?) | *The baby won't stop crying — I hope there's nothing wrong with him.* (=I hope he is not ill) **4** not suitable: *This is the wrong time to make a visit.* | *He's a good actor, but this is the wrong part for him.* | *We got on the wrong bus* (=not the one we intended to catch) *by mistake.* **5 get (hold of) the wrong end of the stick** *infml* to misunderstand **6 on/from the wrong side of the tracks** *esp. AmE* in/from the less respectable part of a town or society, esp. (the part lived in by) poor people **7 on the wrong foot** unprepared: *I'm afraid you rather* **caught me on the wrong foot**, *asking for it at such short notice.* —opposite **right** (for 1, 2, 4); see also **get out of bed on the wrong side** (BED) — **~ly** *adv* : *We believe he was wrongly convicted of the murder.* (=he was not guilty) | *They believe,* **rightly or wrongly** (=whether or not they are right to believe this) *that they have been badly treated.*

wrong² *adv* **1** wrongly: *You've spelt the word wrong.* **2 get it/someone wrong** to misunderstand something/someone: *Don't get me wrong; I'm not really criticizing you, but …* **3 go wrong: a** to make a mistake, e.g. in following a path or method: *The sum hasn't worked out, but I can't see where I went wrong.* **b** to begin to fail or experience trouble: *The party was going well until my* *parents arrived, then everything went wrong.* **c** to stop working properly: *The car's gone wrong.* | *Something's* **gone wrong with** *the car.* **d** *old-fash* to act badly, immorally, etc.: *I'm not surprised she's gone wrong after mixing with such bad company.*

wrong³ *n* **1** [U] action or behaviour that is not morally right or correct: *She's too young to know right from wrong.* | *She seems to think he* **can do no wrong. 2** [C] *fml* a seriously bad or unjust action: *There are rights and wrongs on both sides of the dispute.* | *Two wrongs do not make a right.* (proverb) **3 in the wrong** mistaken or deserving blame: *Which of the two drivers was in the wrong?* —opposite **in the right**

▷ USAGE Compare **wrong** and **fault**. **Wrong** is a formal word for a particular bad or unjust act: *He committed a great* **wrong. Fault** is used, **a** of something bad in a person's character: *One of his* **faults** *is that he's always late,* **b** of a person's responsibility for bad results: *It's your* **fault** *we lost the watch.*◁

wrong⁴ *v* [T] to be unfair to or cause difficulty, suffering, etc., to: *I wronged him by|in saying he had lied.* (=because he had not)

wrong·do·ing /ˈrɒŋˌduːɪŋ‖ˌrɔːŋˈduːɪŋ/ *n* [C;U] (an example of) bad, evil, or illegal behaviour: *They found no evidence of wrongdoing.* | *to commit a wrongdoing* —**-er** *n*

wrong-foot /ˌ·ˈ·/ *vb* [T] **1** (in tennis, etc.) to play in a way that causes (one's opponent) to move in the wrong direction and lose their balance **2** to surprise (someone) into a disadvantageous position: *The prime minister was unexpectedly wrong-footed during yesterday's debate when the opposition parties produced evidence of a cover-up.*

wrong·ful /ˈrɒŋfəl‖ˈrɔːŋ-/ *adj* **1** unjust: *wrongful dismissal from a job* **2** illegal: *wrongful imprisonment* — **~ly** *adv*

wrong·head·ed /ˌrɒŋˈhedɪd◂‖ˌrɔːŋ-/ *adj* **1** *derog* sticking in a determined way to a wrong idea or course of action: *wrongheaded students who think they can cure the world's evils by destroying society* **2** mistaken: *a wrongheaded idea* — **~ly** *adv* — **~ness** *n* [U]

wrote /rəʊt/ *past tense of* WRITE

wroth /rɒθ‖rɔːθ/ *adj* [F] *old use, bibl, or poet* very angry

wrought /rɔːt/ *adj* [(of)] *old use or lit* made or done: *carefully wrought works of literature* | *wrought by hand* | *wrought of stone*

wrought i·ron /ˌ·ˈ···◂/ *n* [U] iron shaped into a useful form or pleasing pattern: *a wrought-iron gate*

wrought-up /ˌ·ˈ·◂/ *adj* very nervous and excited – compare OVERWROUGHT

wrung /rʌŋ/ *past tense & participle of* WRING

WRVS /ˌdʌbəljuː ɑː viː ˈes ‖ -ɑːr-/ [*the +sing.|pl. v*] Women's Royal Voluntary Service; a voluntary organization of women who help others less able to look after themselves, esp. known for their "Meals on Wheels" travelling food service to the ill and old

wry /raɪ/ *adj* (esp. of an expression on the face) showing a mixture of amusement and displeasure, dislike, or disbelief: *a wry smile|wry humour* — **~ly** *adv*

wt *written abbrev. for:* weight

Wu-hsien, Wuxian /ˌwuːˈsjen/ see SUZHOU

wuss /wʊs/ *n AmE, sl, derog* a weak or useless person; WIMP

Wuth·er·ing Heights /ˌwʌðərɪŋ ˈhaɪts/ a NOVEL by Emily Brontë. It is a ROMANTIC and sad love story, set on the Yorkshire Moors, about the love between the two main characters, Catherine and Heathcliffe. —see colour picture on page 1145

WV *written abbrev. for:* WEST VIRGINIA

WWF /ˌdʌbəljuː dʌbəljuː ˈef/ *n* [(*the*) U] *abbrev. for:* WORLD WIDE FUND FOR NATURE

WW I *written abbrev. for:* World War I, the FIRST WORLD WAR

WW II *written abbrev. for:* World War II, the SECOND WORLD WAR

WY *written abbrev. for:* WYOMING

Wych·er·ley /ˈwɪtʃəli‖-ər-/, **William** (1640–1716) an English writer of RESTORATION plays including *The Country Wife*

wych-ha·zel /ˈwɪtʃ ˌheɪzəl/ *n* [C;U] WITCH-HAZEL

Wyc·liffe /ˈwɪklɪf/, **John** (1328?–84) an English religious reformer (REFORM) who believed that the Bible, not the church, was the true authority, and worked on translating the Bible into English

Wye /waɪ/ *n* [*the*] a river in Wales and England

Wy·eth /ˈwaɪəθ/, **Andrew** (1917–) an American painter whose best known picture is *Christina's World*. His son **Jamie** is also a painter.

Wyke·ham·ist /ˈwɪkəmɪst/ *n* a pupil or former pupil of Winchester College

Wynd·ham /ˈwɪndəm/, **John** (1903–69) an English writer of SCIENCE FICTION books, including *The Day of the Triffids* and *The Midwich Cuckoos*

Wy·nette /wɪˈnet/, **Tam·my** /ˈtæmi/ (1942–) an American popular music singer whose many songs include *Stand by Your Man* and *D-I-V-O-R-C-E*

Wy·o·ming /waɪˈəʊmɪŋ/ *written abbrev.* **WY**– a US state in the Rocky Mountains with the smallest population of any state. It produces minerals and wool. —see colour map on pages 1374–5

WYSIWYG /ˈwɪziwɪg/ *adj* What You See Is What You Get; of a computer system where what is printed out is exactly what is shown on the SCREEN

Wyss /waɪs/, **Jo·hann** /ˈjəʊhæn ‖ -hɑːn/ (1743–1818) a Swiss writer best known for his very popular children's book *The Swiss Family Robinson*

wy·vern /ˈwaɪvən‖-ərn/ *n* an imaginary animal that looks like a two-legged winged DRAGON

X, x /eks/ **X's, x's** *or* **Xs, xs** **1** the 24th letter of the English alphabet **2** the ROMAN NUMERAL (number) for 10 **3** (a mark written esp. on a letter or card, meaning) a kiss **4** **X marks the spot** a phrase that appears, in stories about PIRATEs, on maps showing where TREASURE is buried

x *n* [U] (in MATHEMATICS) a quantity that is unknown until a calculation has been made: *If 3x=6, x=2.* —see picture at EQUATION

X *n* a person or thing whose name is not made known to the public: *At the trial, Mrs X, one of the witnesses, was allowed to keep her face covered.* | *ingredient X*

Xan·a·du /'zænədu:/ an unreal place of wonderful beauty (from the name of a place in the poem *Kubla Khan* by S T Coleridge)

X-cer·tif·i·cate /'eks sə₁tɪfɪkət‖-sər-/ *adj* X-RATED

X chro·mo·some /'eks ₁krəʊməsəʊm/ *n* a CHROMOSOME which exists in pairs in female cells and singly in male cells, and which, after union of male and female, will produce a female when combined with another of its own type, and a male when combined with a Y CHROMOSOME

xen·on /'zenɒn‖'zi:nɑːn, 'ze-/ *n* [U] a rare gas sometimes used in photography to produce short flashes of light

xen·o·pho·bi·a /₁zenə'fəʊbiə/ *n* [U] unreasonable fear and dislike of strange or foreign people, customs, etc. — compare RACISM —**phobic** *adj*

Xen·o·phon /'zenəfən, -fɒn‖-faːn/ (about 430–355 BC) a Greek HISTORIAN whose most famous work, the *Anabasis*, told the story of the RETREAT after the battle of Cunaxa, in which he took part

xe·rox /'zɪərɒks, 'ze-‖'zɪəraːks, 'ziː-/ *v, n* [T] *tdmk* (*often cap.*) (to make) a photographic copy of (printed or written matter) on a special electric copying machine; PHOTOCOPY

Xer·xes /'zɜːksiːz‖'zɜːr-/ (about 519–465 BC) a king of Persia who unsuccessfully tried to CONQUER Greece

X-film /'eks fɪlm/ *n* a film that is X-RATED

Xho·sa /'kɔːsə, 'kəʊ-‖'kəʊsə/ *n* **1** [C;U] (a member of) a S African Bantu people **2** [U] the Bantu language spoken by these people

Xiaoping see DENG XIAOPING

X·mas /'krɪsməs, 'eksməs/ *n* [C;U] *infml* CHRISTMAS; mainly used in writing, for example on shop signs and Christmas cards

X-OPEN /₁eks 'əʊpən/ an institution set up by large computer makers to set international standards for SOFTWARE that will run on many different systems

X-rat·ed /'eks ₁reɪt‡d/ also **X-certificate**— *adj* **1** (of a film) given, or deserving, a CERTIFICATE meaning that it is suitable only for people over the age of 18 to watch, usu. because of the sex or violence it contains: *an X-rated movie* **2** *infml* involving sex, violence, or bad language

x-ray /'eks reɪ/ *v* [T] (*often cap.*) to photograph, examine, or treat by means of X-rays: *They x-rayed her leg to find out if the bone was broken.*

X-ray *n* **1** [*usu. pl.*] a powerful unseen beam of light which can pass through substances that are not transparent, and which is used for photographing conditions inside the body, for treating certain diseases, and for various purposes in industry: *an X-ray machine* **2** a photograph taken using this: *The doctor examined the X-rays, to see if they showed anything wrong with her lungs.* **3** a medical examination made using this: *He had to go to the hospital for an X-ray.*

X-Win·dows /'eks wɪndəʊz/ *n tdmk* a type of computer WINDOWING that is expected to become an international standard for window SOFTWARE. It was developed at MIT under the control of X-OPEN.

xy·lo·phone /'zaɪləfəʊn/ *n* a musical instrument made up of a set of flat wooden or metal bars of different lengths, each of which gives out a different musical note, played by striking with two small hammers

Y, y /waɪ/ **Y's, y's** or **Ys, ys** the 25th letter of the English alphabet

yacht

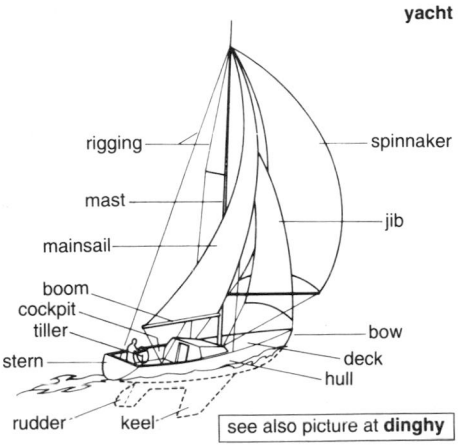

rigging — spinnaker
mast — jib
mainsail —
boom
cockpit
tiller — bow
stern — deck
— hull
rudder   keel | see also picture at **dinghy** |

yacht /jɒt‖jɑːt/ n **1** a light sailing boat, esp. one used for racing —compare DINGHY **2** a large often motor-driven boat used for pleasure. Yachts are often thought of in connection with very rich people.

yacht·ing /'jɒtɪŋ‖'jɑːtɪŋ/ n [U] (the act of) sailing, travelling, or racing in a yacht: *They go yachting most weekends.*

yachts·man /'jɒtsmən‖'jɑːts-/ n **yachts·wom·an** /-ˌwʊmən/ fem.— n -men /mən/ a person who owns or sails a yacht

Yah-boo /ˌjɑː'buː/ also **yah-boo sucks** /ˌ· · '·/— BrE interj used to express dislike or disrespect for someone, or to make fun of them

ya·hoo /jɑː'huː/ n (sometimes cap.) a rough, noisy, or bad-mannered UPPER-CLASS British person: *the stockbroker yahoos who swarm to Covent Garden for Pavarotti*

Yah·weh /'jɑːweɪ/ a Hebrew name for God

yak¹ /jæk/ n a long-haired cowlike animal of central Asia

yak² v -kk- [I (ON)] infml derog to talk continuously about unimportant things; CHATTER

Yale¹ /jeɪl/ an American university in New Haven, Connecticut. It is one of the oldest and most respected American universities: *Politicians are often graduates of Harvard and Yale.*

Yale² n tdmk a type of lock often used on outside doors, having a special sort of key

y'all /jɔːl/ pron AmE, infml you all; used mainly by people in the south of the US: *"Do y'all want to come over for lunch?"* | *"It's been so nice seeing y'all again!"*

Yal·ta /'jæltə‖'jɔːl-/ a port and holiday place on the Black Sea in Russia. The **Yalta Conference** was held here in 1945 between Churchill, Roosevelt, and Stalin, when certain European borders were decided on and the beginnings of the United Nations were agreed. —see picture on page 752

yam /jæm/ n **1** a tropical climbing plant grown for its root, which is eaten as a vegetable **2** AmE for SWEET POTATO

Yam·a·ha /'jæməhɑː/ **1** tdmk a motorcycle made by the Japanese company Yamaha **2** the company which also makes musical instruments, electronic musical KEY-BOARDs etc.

Ya·ma·ni /jə'mɑːni/, **Sheik Ah·med Za·ki** /'ɑːmed 'zɑːki/ (1930–) a Saudi Arabian politician

yam·mer /'jæmər/ v [I (ON)] infml derog to talk noisily and continuously

yang /jæŋ/ n [U] the male principle in Chinese PHILOSOPHY which is active, light and POSITIVE and which combines

with YIN (=the female principle) to form the whole world. There should be a balance of yin and yang in everything. —see picture at YIN

yank¹ /jæŋk/ v [I;T] infml to pull suddenly and sharply: *He yanked the nail|the tooth out.* | *He yanked (on) the rope.*

yank² n infml a sudden sharp pull

Yank n BrE derog for YANKEE (1)

Yan·kee /'jæŋki/ n infml **1** esp. BrE a citizen of the United States of America **2** AmE a person born or living in the northern or northeastern parts of the US. This word is connected with the American CIVIL WAR, when northerners (Yankees) fought southerners (REBELS).

Yankee Doo·dle /ˌ·· '··/ of a song which became popular with American soldiers during the American Revolutionary War. The song was probably originally British and made fun of the Americans:
> *Yankee Doodle went to town,*
> *Riding on a pony.*
> *Stuck a feather in his hat,*
> *And called it macaroni.*

yap /jæp/ v -pp- [I] derog **1** (esp. of a small dog) to make short sharp excited noises (sharp BARKs) **2** [(ON, AWAY)] infml to talk noisily about unimportant things —**yap** n

yard¹ /jɑːd‖jɑːrd/ n **1** (written abbrev. **yd**) a unit of length —see TABLE 2 **2** also **yards**— infml a great length or quantity: *His estimate was yards out.* (=wrong by a great deal) **3** naut a long pole that supports a square sail

yard² n **1** (often in comb.) an enclosed or partly enclosed area next to a building or group of buildings: *a churchyard* **2** AmE a BACKYARD (2) or a front garden (**front yard**): *You can play in our yard.* | *Play in the front yard today because the grass is shorter.* —see picture at HOUSE **3** (usu. in comb.) an area enclosed for a special purpose, activity, or business: *a shipyard* | *a coalyard*

Yard [the] infml for SCOTLAND YARD

yard·age /'jɑːdɪdʒ‖'jɑːr-/ n tech [C;U] the size of something measured in yards or square yards: *a large yardage of sail*

yard·arm /'jɑːd-ɑːm‖'jɑːrd-ɑːrm/ n either end of the pole (YARD¹ (3)) that supports a square sail

yard line /'· ·/ n (in American football) any of the lines drawn on the field to mark each yard: *The ball is at the 10-yard line.*

yard sale /'· ·/ n AmE for GARAGE SALE

yard·stick /'jɑːdˌstɪk‖'jɑːrd-/ n [(of)] a standard of measurement or comparison: *Is profit the only yardstick of success?*

yar·mul·ke /'jɑːmʊlkə‖'jɑːr-/ n a small circular cap worn by male Jews in the SYNAGOGUE and by some male Jews all the time

yarn¹ /jɑːn‖jɑːrn/ n **1** [U] esp. AmE a long continuous usu. cotton or woollen thick thread used in KNITTING, making cloth, mats, etc. **2** [C] infml a story of adventures, travels, etc., esp. that is exaggerated (EXAGGERATE) or untrue: *The old sea captain would often* **spin us a yarn** *about his adventures.*

yarn² v [I] infml to tell YARNs¹ (2)

yash·mak /'jæʃmæk/ n a piece of cloth worn across the face by some Muslim women

Yat-Sen Sun see SUN YAT-SEN

yaw /jɔː/ v [I] tech (of a ship, aircraft, etc.) to make a turn to the side, esp. out of the proper course —compare PITCH¹ (5), ROLL¹ (6) —**yaw** n [C;U]

yawl /jɔːl/ n **1** a sailing boat with at least two sails, one of which is set well back **2** a small boat carried on a ship

yawn¹ /jɔːn/ v [I] **1** to open the mouth wide and breathe in deeply, as when tired or uninterested **2** to be or become wide open: *The hole yawned before him.* | *a yawning chasm* | (fig.) *yawning gaps in the law*

yawn² n **1** an act of yawning **2** [usu. sing.] infml derog a dull uninteresting thing or person: *The party was a big yawn.*

yaws /jɔːz/ n [U] a tropical skin disease

Y chro·mo·some /'waɪ ˌkrəʊməsəʊm/ n a CHROMOSOME which exists singly in male cells, and which, after union of male and female, will produce a male when combined with an X CHROMOSOME

yd written abbrev. for: YARD(s)¹ (1)

ye¹ /jiː/ *pron old use* (used esp. when addressing more than one person, usu. only as the subject of a sentence) you

ye² *determiner* (a word used esp. in the names of PUBS and shops, in order to make them seem old and historical) the: *Ye Olde Dog and Duck* (pub sign)

yea¹ /jeɪ/ *adv old use* yes —opposite **nay**; see also AYE²

yea² *n* a vote or voter in favour of an idea, plan, law, etc. —opposite **nay**; see also AYE³

yeah /jeə/ *adv infml* yes

year /jɪəʳ, jɜːʳ‖jɪər/ *n* **1** a measure of time equal to about 365¼ days, which is the amount of time it takes for the Earth to travel completely round the sun **2** also **calendar year**— a period of 365 or 366 days divided into 12 months beginning on January 1st and ending on December 31st: *last year's budget | early/late in the year | It's been a good year for films.* (=There have been a lot of good films this year.) | *The lease expires in the year 2010.* **3** a period of 365 days measured from any point: *She has worked here for about four years. | I arrived here two years ago today. | a three-year-old child | a ten-year business plan* **4** a period of (about) a year in the life of an organization: *The school year is broken up with many holidays. | second-year students* (=in the second year of a course) **5 all the year round** during the whole year **6 year after year** continuously for many years **7 year in year out** regularly each year, without ever changing: *They go to the same campsite year in year out.* —see also YEARS, FINANCIAL YEAR, LEAP YEAR, LIGHT YEAR, NEW YEAR, SCHOOL YEAR

year·book /ˈjɪəbʊk, ˈjɜː-‖ˈjɪər-/ *n AmE* a book printed once a year giving facts and information about the year just past: *Look! There's my photo in the school yearbook.*

▶CULTURAL NOTE In American HIGH SCHOOLS, students usu. buy a yearbook at the end of the school year, esp. their final year. The yearbook includes a small photograph of every student, and usu. has informal photographs of students, groups, parties, and school activities as well. It is customary to have the yearbook signed by friends and teachers. Often the yearbook is designed by a group of students. ◀

year dot /ˌ·ˈ·/ *n* [*the*+S] *BrE infml, often derog* a very long time ago: *They've lived here since the year dot.*

year·ling /ˈjɪəlɪŋ, ˈjɜː-‖ˈjɪər-/ *n* an animal, esp. a young horse, between one and two years old

year·long /ˌjɪəˈlɒŋ◂, ˌjɜː-‖ˌjɪərˈlɔːŋ◂/ *adj* [A] lasting for a year or all through the year: *She came back after a yearlong absence.*

year·ly /ˈjɪəli, ˈjɜː-‖ˈjɪərli/ *adj, adv* (happening, appearing, etc.) every year or once a year: *a yearly pay award | a five-yearly medical examination* (=once every five years)

yearn /jɜːn‖jɜːrn/ *v* [I (**for**)] *esp. lit* to have a strong, loving, or sad desire: *He yearned for her return/for her to return.* [+*to-v*] *They yearned to return home.*

yearn·ing /ˈjɜːnɪŋ‖ˈjɜːr-/ *n* [C;U (**for**/*to-v*)] *esp. lit* (a) strong usu. sad desire: *a yearning for/to travel | an actor's yearning for recognition*

years /jɪəz, jɜːz‖jɪərz/ *n* [P] **1** *fml or lit* age, esp. old age: *He is very healthy for a man of his years.* **2** *infml* a long time: *I haven't seen her for years. | It happened years ago.*

yeast /jiːst/ *n* [U] a form of very small plant life that is used for producing alcohol in beer and wine and for making bread rise —~**y** *adj*: *a yeasty taste*

yeast ex·tract /ˌ·ˈ···/ *n* a food made from yeasts, which is used both to give taste and to supply many B VITAMINS

Yeats /jeɪts/, **W B** (1865–1939) an Irish poet, considered to be one of the most important Irish writers. He also wrote stories and plays and was active in Irish politics.

yell /jel/ *v* [I;T (**OUT, at**)] to shout or say very loudly, esp. in fear, anger, or excitement: *Don't yell at me like that! | He yelled (out) orders at everyone.* —**yell** *n* : *The new-born baby let out a yell.*

yel·low¹ /ˈjeləʊ/ *adj* **1** of a colour like that of butter, gold, or the YOLK (=middle part) of an egg

▶CULTURAL NOTE The colour yellow is associated with COWARDICE. ◀

2 having the light brown skin of some east Asian people (may be considered offensive) **3** also **yellow-bel·lied** /ˈ··ˌ··/— *derog sl* not brave; cowardly —**yellow** *n* [U]

yellow² *v* [I;T] to make or become yellow: *The paper had yellowed with age.*

yellow a·lert /ˌ···ˈ·/ *n* [C;U] (a condition of readiness to deal with) a situation of great danger. It is less serious than RED ALERT.

yellow brick road /ˌ···ˈ·/ [*the*] a road which leads to a place where a person can find something good (from the story *The Wizard of Oz* by L Frank Baum, in which Dorothy and her friends have to follow the yellow brick road to find the WIZARD who will help them)

yellow card /ˌ··ˈ·/ *n* a yellow card held up by a football REFEREE to show that a player is to be booked (BOOK² (3))

yellow fe·ver /ˌ··ˈ··/ *n* [U] a dangerous tropical disease in which the skin turns rather yellow

yellow line /ˌ··ˈ·/ *n* (in Britain) a line of yellow paint at the edge of a street or road next to the PAVEMENT (1), which shows that parking of vehicles is not allowed at certain times. A **double yellow line** means that there are more restrictions than a **single yellow line**

Yellow Pag·es /ˌ··ˈ··/ [*the*+P] *tdmk* a book that contains the telephone numbers and addresses of firms and similar organizations in an area, divided up according to the kind of business they do: *Can you find a plumber in the Yellow Pages?* —compare PHONE BOOK, THOMSON DIRECTORY, WHITE PAGES

Yellow Riv·er /ˌ··ˈ··/ [*the*] a long river in N China, known for the terrible floods which have caused many deaths and much damage, and the yellow SILT (=loose sand and soil) that it carries

Yellow Sea /ˌ··ˈ·/ [*the*] a sea that joins with the Pacific Ocean, between the E coast of China and Korea

Yel·low·stone Na·tion·al Park /ˌjeləʊstəʊn ˌnæʃənəl ˈpɑːk‖ -ˈpɑːrk/ [*the*] a large national park mostly in Wyoming, US, known for its hot springs and GEYSERS, esp. one called Old Faithful which is a big tourist attraction

yelp /jelp/ *v* [I] to make a short sharp high cry of pain, excitement, etc.: *The dog yelped and ran off.* —**yelp** *n*

Yelt·sin /ˈjeltsɪn, Bor·is /ˈbɒrɪs‖ˈbɔː-/ (1931–) a Russian politician who became president of the Russian parliament in 1990 and was involved, with Mikhail Gorbachev, with changing Russian society and politics

Yem·en /ˈjemən/ a country, bordered by the Red Sea, Saudi Arabia, and the Gulf of Aden, which until 1990 was split into two countries, **North Yemen** or the **Yemen Arab Republic**, and **South Yemen** or the **People's Democratic Republic of Yemen**, since then known as the **Republic of Yemen**; capital San'a; population 10,168,000 (1989) —**Yemeni** *adj, n*

yen¹ /jen/ *n* **yen** the standard unit of money in Japan

yen² *n* [S (**for**/*to-v*)] a strong desire: *a yen for/to travel*

yeo·man /ˈjəʊmən/ *n* -**men** /mən/ *BrE, esp. lit* a farmer who owns and works his own land

yeoman of the guard /ˌ···· ˈ·/ *n* (in Britain) a member of a military unit who attend the Queen at certain ceremonies and act as keepers at the Tower of London. They are also called **Beefeaters** and they wear a special uniform, which often appears on SOUVENIRS of London.

yeo·man·ry /ˈjəʊmənri/ *n* [*the*+S+*sing./pl. v*] *BrE, esp. lit* country landowners

yeoman ser·vice /ˌ··ˈ··/ *n* [U] great and loyal service, help, or support

yer /jəʳ/ *determiner* (used in writing to represent a nonstandard way of saying) your

yes¹ /jes/ *adv* **1** (used as an answer expressing agreement or willingness): *"Is this book a dictionary?" "Yes, it is." | "Is there anything you need?" "Yes, there is." | "Would you like to go to the cinema?" "Yes, please/Yes, I would." | We can ask them, but I doubt if they'll say yes.* —opposite **no 2** (used when partly agreeing, but going on to state a different opinion): *"This system is too expensive for the company to afford." "Yes, that's true, but …"* **3** (used for showing that one has heard a command or call, and will obey or is paying attention): *"Go and close the door." "Yes, sir." | "Michael!" "Yes?"* (=What do you want?) **4 yes and no** (used to show that one partly agrees and partly disagrees) —see NO (USAGE)

yes² *n* a vote, voter, or reply in favour of an idea, plan, law, etc.: *a yes vote*

ye·shi·va, yeshivah /jəˈʃiːvə/ *n* **yeshivas, yeshivoth** /-vəs/ a school where Jewish students are taught religious and other subjects, or may train to became RABBIS (=religious leaders)

yes-man /'jes mæn/ n -men /men/ derog someone who always agrees with their employer, leader, etc., in order to gain favour and appear in a good light so that they will succeed at work

Yes, Min·is·ter /ˌ· ˈ· ˌ···/ a British COMEDY programme first shown in the 1980s. The two main characters are a government minister called Jim Hacker and a CIVIL SERVANT called Sir Humphrey Appleby.

yes/no ques·tion /ˌ· ˈ· ˌ···/ n a question which can be answered with yes or no and (in English) begins with a verb

yes·ter·day /'jestədi‖-ər-/ adv, n 1 [U] (on) the day before this one: It was only yesterday that I saw him. | She came to tea the day before yesterday. | Is that yesterday's newspaper? | He left yesterday afternoon. 2 [C usu. pl.] a short time ago: I wasn't born yesterday. (=I'm not a fool) —see DAY (USAGE)

yes·ter·year /'jestəjɪəʳ, -jɜːʳ‖'jestərjɪər/ n [U] esp. poet the recent past: the songs of yesteryear

yet¹ /jet/ adv 1 [in questions and negatives] up until now or then; by a particular time; already: Has John arrived yet? | Not yet. | She hasn't answered yet. | John hasn't done much work yet, but Anne has already finished. | He wouldn't let me see it because he hadn't yet finished. 2 in the future; in spite of the way things seem now:We may win yet. | The plan could (even) yet succeed. 3 even; still: yet another reason | a yet worse mistake 4 in spite of that; but: a simple yet very effective system | strange yet true 5 fml at this time as at earlier times; still: He is yet a child. | I have yet to hear the story. (=I have still not heard it) 6 as yet (in questions and negatives) up to this moment: We have not succeeded as yet. | As yet, we have received no answer. —see ALREADY (USAGE), JUST (USAGE), STILL (USAGE)

yet² conj but even so; but: She felt sad yet at the same time relieved that it was time to leave. | She's a funny girl, (and/but) yet you can't help liking her.

yeti

yet·i /'jeti/ also **abominable snowman**— n a large hairy manlike animal supposed to live in the Himalaya mountains

Yev·tu·shen·ko /ˌjevtuː'ʃeŋkəʊ ‖ ˌjeftə-/, **Yev·ge·ny** /jev'geɪni/ (1933–   ) a Russian poet whose works, such as Babi Yar, caused CONTROVERSY by criticizing Russian society

yew /juː/ n [C;U] (the wood of) a tree with small EVERGREEN leaves (=leaves that are always green) and small red berries

Y-fronts /'waɪ frʌnts/ n [P] BrE men's UNDERPANTS with a sewn part in front in the shape of an upside-down Y

YHA /ˌwaɪ eɪtʃ 'eɪ/ [the] Youth Hostels Association; the organization which runs the YOUTH HOSTELS in Britain and has ties with similar organizations around the world, so that members can stay in hostels wherever they go

the symbol for the Youth Hostels Association

yid /jɪd/ n taboo derog a Jew (considered extremely offensive)

Yid·dish /'jɪdɪʃ/ n [U] a language spoken by Jews, esp. in eastern Europe, often in addition to the language of the country in which they live

yield¹ /jiːld/ v 1 [T] to produce, bear, or provide, esp. as a result of work or effort: That tree yields plenty of fruit. | His business yields big profits. | Their long search failed to yield any clues. | high-yielding investments/cereal crops 2 [I;T (UP, to)] fml or lit to give up control (of); SURRENDER: We were forced to yield. | We yielded (up) our position to the enemy. 3 [I] to bend, break, etc., because of a strong force: The shelf is beginning to yield under that heavy weight. 4 [I (to)] AmE‖give way BrE (a traffic sign) to allow other traffic to go first: You must yield to traffic from the left.

yield² n that which is produced or the amount that is produced: The trees gave a high yield (of fruit) this year. | yields on bonds/securities

yield·ing /'jiːldɪŋ/ adj 1 able to bend; not stiff or fixed 2 likely to agree with others or accept their wishes; COMPLIANT

yin /jɪn/ n [U] the female principle in Chinese PHILOSOPHY which is inactive, dark and NEGATIVE and which combines with YANG (=the male principle) to form the whole world. There should be a balance of yin and yang in everything.

the symbol for yin-yang

yip·pee /jɪ'piː‖'jɪpi/ interj infml (a cry of delight, happiness, success, etc.)

YMCA /ˌwaɪ em es iː 'eɪ/ Young Men's Christian Association; an organization in many countries which provides places to stay and sports centres for young people, esp. in large cities, and is also concerned with their spiritual well-being —see also YWCA

yob /jɒb‖jɑːb/ also **yob·bo** /'jɒbəʊ‖'jɑː-/— n BrE derog a rude or troublesome young man; LOUT

yodeller

Yodelayeeyoddelooo!

yo·del¹ /'jəʊdl/ v BrE -ll- ‖ -l- AmE [I,T] to sing (a song or piece of music) with many fast changes between the natural voice and a very high voice

yodel² n a song, piece of music, or cry sung or made by yodelling

yo·ga /'jəʊgə/ n [U] 1 a Hindu PHILOSOPHY which teaches control of the mind, senses, and body in order to reach union with God 2 a branch of yoga (e.g. hatha yoga) which consists of a system of exercises to gain control over the mind and esp. the body. In British society yoga is usu. done as a way of keeping fit, and is thought of by some people as slightly strange because of its connections with eastern PHILOSOPHY and MEDITATION.

yog·hurt , **yogurt**, **yoghourt** /'jɒgət‖'jəʊgərt/ n [U] milk that has turned thick and slightly acid through the action of certain bacteria, often eaten with fruit. Yoghurt is usu. thought of as a health food.

yo·gi /'jəʊgi/ n a person who practises yoga, esp. one who teaches it to others

Yogi Bear /ˌ·· '·/ an American CARTOON character on children's television, a bear who is always hungry and always trying to steal food from people

yoke¹ /jəʊk/ n 1 [C] a wooden bar used for joining two animals, esp. cattle, together in order to pull heavy loads, farm vehicles, etc. 2 [C] a frame fitted across a person's shoulders for carrying two equal loads 3 [the+S (of)] lit power, control, etc.: They were brought under the yoke of the king. 4 [the+S (of)] lit something that binds people or things together: the yoke of marriage

yoke² v [T (TOGETHER)] to join (as if) with a yoke: *Yoke the oxen together.*

yo·kel /ˈjəʊkəl/ n humor or derog a simple or foolish country person —compare VILLAGE IDIOT

yokel

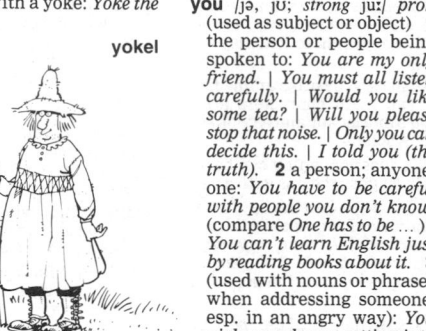

Yo·ko·ha·ma /ˌjəʊkəʊˈhɑːmə/ a city and port on Tokyo Bay, Japan

yolk /jəʊk‖jəʊk, jelk/ n [C;U] the yellow part in the centre of an egg, which is surrounded by the WHITE² (4)

Yom Kip·pur /ˌjɒm ˈkɪpər, -kɪˈpʊər‖ˌjəʊm-/ n [C,U] a Jewish holiday, the DAY OF ATONEMENT

yon·der /ˈjɒndər‖ˈjɑːn-/ also **yon** /jɒn ‖ jɑːn/— adj, adv old use or dial at a place or in a direction shown, suggested, or in view; over there: *Climb yonder* (=that) *hill and you will see the city.* | *There's a river (over) yonder.*

yonks /jɒŋks‖jɑːŋks/ n [U] BrE infml a very long time: *I haven't seen him for yonks; he's gone to live in Canada.*

yoo-hoo /ˌjuː ˈhuː/ interj infml (said to attract the attention of someone, esp. when you are in their view but they cannot see you)

YOP /jɒp‖jɑːp/ Youth Opportunities Programme; a British government programme which arranged work experience for people leaving school at the age of 16, to provide them with training and a small amount of money. YOP was replaced in 1983 by YTS.

yore /jɔːr/ n [U] lit time long past: *Brave knights courted fair ladies* **in days of yore.**

Yor·ick /ˈjɒrɪk ‖ ˈjɔː-/ a character in William Shakespeare's play *Hamlet*. He had been the king's JESTER but is dead, and the grave-diggers find and play with his SKULL when they are digging Ophelia's grave. When Hamlet finds the skull he says "Alas! poor Yorick. I knew him, Horatio". This line is very well known although it is often said as "Alas! poor Yorick. I knew him well." —see colour picture on page 1146

York /jɔːk ‖ jɔːrk/ a city in North Yorkshire, England, known for its chocolate factories and national railway MUSEUM, and the large CATHEDRAL called **York Minister**

York, Duke of see Prince ANDREW

York·shire /ˈjɔːkʃər‖ˈjɔːr-/ a former COUNTY in NE England, now divided into North, West, and South Yorkshire, and Humberside: *a Yorkshire accent*

York·shire·man /ˈjɔːkʃəmən‖ˈjɔːrkʃər-/ , **York·shire·wom·an** /-ˌwʊmən/ fem.— n -**men** /mən/ a person who comes or whose parents come from the former county of Yorkshire

Yorkshire Moors /ˌ·· ˈ·/ [the + P] a general name used by some people when talking about areas of MOOR in Yorkshire, esp. including the North York Moors

Yorkshire pud·ding /ˌ·· ˈ··/ n [C;U] a baked mixture of flour, milk, and egg, usu. served with or before BEEF esp. as part of a Sunday dinner

Yorkshire Rip·per /ˌ·· ˈ··/ [the] the name given by some newspapers to Peter Sutcliffe, who murdered 13 women in the late 1970s and early 1980s —see also Peter SUTCLIFFE

Yorkshire Tel·e·vi·sion /ˌ·· ˈ····, ˌ·· ··ˈ··/ one of the British television companies controlled by the ITC, sending out programmes to Yorkshire and Humberside

Yorkshire ter·ri·er /ˌ·· ˈ···/ n a type of small dog with long straight silky hair which is grey or brown —see picture at DOG

Yorkshire Wa·ter /ˌ·· ˈ··/ a water company in N England that deals with the supply of water to people and businesses and the removal and treatment of SEWAGE

York·town /ˈjɔːktaʊn ‖ ˈjɔːrk-/ a town in Virginia, US where the last battle of the American Revolutionary War and the SURRENDER of the British to the Americans took place in 1781

Yo·sem·i·te Na·tion·al Park /jəʊˌsemɪti ˌnæʃənəl ˈpɑːk ‖ -ˈpɑːrk/ a park in California, US, known for its beautiful lakes, waterfalls, and large REDWOOD trees

you /jə, jʊ; strong juː/ pron (used as subject or object) **1** the person or people being spoken to: *You are my only friend.* | *You must all listen carefully.* | *Would you like some tea?* | *Will you please stop that noise.* | *Only you can decide this.* | *I told you (the truth).* **2** a person; anyone; one: *You have to be careful with people you don't know.* (compare *One has to be ...*) | *You can't learn English just by reading books about it.* **3** (used with nouns or phrases when addressing someone, esp. in an angry way): *You girls are always getting into trouble.* | *You fool!* | *You in the corner; come here!*

Yosemite National Park

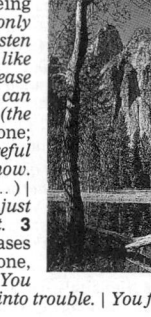

you'd /jəd, jʊd; strong juːd/ short for: **1** you had **2** you would

you'll /jəl, jʊl; strong juːl/ short for: **1** you will **2** you shall

young¹ /jʌŋ/ adj **younger** /ˈjʌŋgər/, **youngest** /ˈjʌŋgᵻst/ **1** in an early stage of life, growth, development, etc.; recently born or begun: *a young girl|plant|country* | *the younger generation* | *my younger brother* —opposite **old 2** of, for, or having the qualities of a young person: *He may be 55, but he's young at heart.* (=in his behaviour, opinions, etc.) | *That hat is too young for you.*

young² n **1** [the+P] young people considered as a group —see CHILD (USAGE) **2** [P] young animals: *The lion fought to protect her young.* | *the young of the elephant*

Young, Brig·ham /ˈbrɪgəm/ (1801–77) an American leader of the Mormon religion who directed the settlement at Salt Lake City, Utah. A university there is named after him.

Young, Cy /saɪ/ (1867–1955) a BASEBALL player famous for his PITCHING (=throwing). Each year the **Cy Young Award** is given to the best pitchers in the American and National Leagues.

young·er /ˈjʌŋgər/ adj [A; after n; no comp] being the son or daughter of someone with the same name: *William Pitt the younger was a prime minister of England.* —compare ELDER¹

young la·dy /ˌ· ˈ···/ n old-fash (said to or about a younger person by an older person) a GIRLFRIEND: *When are we going to meet your young lady then?* —compare LADY FRIEND

young man /ˌ· ˈ·/ n old-fash (said to or about a younger person by an older person) a BOYFRIEND: *Was that your young man I saw you with last night?*

young of·fen·der /ˌ· ·ˈ··/ n (in Britain) a criminal of any kind who is not an adult in the eyes of the law, and who may be sent to one of several types of **young offenders' institution**

Young Pre·tend·er /ˌ· ·ˈ··/ [the] another name for Charles Edward STUART

young·ster /ˈjʌŋstər/ n a young person, esp. a boy

Young Turk /ˌ· ˈ·/ n a member of a political party or other organization who wants great changes to be made

your /jər; strong jɔːr‖jər; strong jʊər, jɔːr/ determiner (possessive form of YOU) **1** of or belonging to you: *It's your book, not mine.* | *Was that your idea?* | *I told him your problem.* | *You must all come and bring your husbands.* | *It's your own fault if you've spent all your money!* **2** belonging to any person; one's: *If you are facing north, east is on your right.* **3** infml (used to show that something is well known or familiar): *Your typical postage stamp is square.* | *He was your archetypal English gentleman.*

you're /jər; strong jɔːr‖jər; strong jʊər, jɔːr/ short for: you are

yours /jɔːz‖jʊərz, jɔːrz/ pron **1** (possessive form of YOU) of the person or people spoken to: *This is our room, and yours* (=your room) *is at the end of the passage.* | *Yours is|are green.* | *Isn't she a friend of yours?* **2** (usu. cap.) (written at the end of a letter): **Yours faithfully/Yours truly** (=used to end a formal letter that begins *Dear Sir(s)|Madam*, etc.) | **Yours sincerely** (=used to end a less formal letter that begins *Dear Mr Smith, Dear Miss Jones*, etc.) | *Yours, Joe Baker.* **3 yours truly** /ˌ· ˈ··/

infml I; me; myself: *They all went out, leaving yours truly to clear up the mess.*

▷ USAGE In British English, **Yours sincerely** is the most common way of ending a letter to someone whose name you know. **Yours faithfully** is used when writing to someone whose name you do not know. In American English **Sincerely yours, Sincerely** and **Yours truly** are commonly used. In informal letters many other endings are possible, such as **Yours** and **Best wishes.**◁

your·self /jə'self‖jər-/ *pron* **-selves** /'selvz/ **1** (*reflexive form of* YOU): *You'll hurt yourself if you play with the scissors.| Buy yourself some shoes.* **2** (*strong form of* YOU): *You yourself said so. | You and Mary said so yourselves.* **3** *infml* (in) your usual state of mind or body: *Are you very tired? You don't seem yourself today. | I'll forgive you; I know you weren't yourself when you said that.* **4 (all) by yourself a** alone; without help: *Did you make this by yourself?* **b** alone; without anyone else: *Did you come here all by yourself?* **5 to yourself** for your private use; not shared; *a bedroom to yourself* —see also DO-IT-YOURSELF

▷ USAGE 1 Reflexive pronouns like **yourself, themselves**, etc. are used with verbs that need a reflexive object: *Are you enjoying* **yourself**? but with some verbs they can be left out with no change of meaning: *Let's go and wash* **(ourselves).** 2 They are also used after prepositions in sentences like *Mary looked at* **herself** *in the mirror*, but not after prepositions that show position or direction in space: *She shut the door behind* **her** (not **herself**).◁

youth /juːθ/ *n* **youths** /juːðz‖juːðz, juːθs/ **1** [U] the period of being young, esp. the period between being a child and being fully grown; early life: *In (his) youth, he had shown great promise.* **2** [C] *often derog* a young person, esp. a male TEENAGER: *a gang of youths* —see CHILD (USAGE) **3** [(the) S (of)+sing./pl. v] young men and women considered as a group: *The youth of the country is/are being ignored by politicians. | youth unemployment* (=among young people) **4** [S;U] the quality or state of being young: *He lost his youth a long time ago. | a product which claims to restore youth*

youth club /'· ·/ *n* a meeting place for young people where they can talk, drink coffee, play games, etc. and often connected with a church or COMMUNITY CENTRE

youth cul·ture /'· ·/ *n* [U] the interests and activities of young people, esp. the music, films, sports, or other entertainments they enjoy

youth·ful /'juːθfəl/ *adj* **1** (having the qualities) typical of youth: *youthful enthusiasm | She's over 50 but has a youthful complexion* **2** young or relatively young: *the youthful prime minister* — **~ly** *adv* — **~ness** *n* [U]

youth hos·tel /'· ·/ *n* a place in which members of the Youth Hostel Association, esp. young people walking around country areas on holiday, can stay for a small payment. The beds are usu. in dormitories (DORMITORY). Youth hostels are not common in the US. — **~ler** *n* — **~ling** *n* [U] : *I used to go youth-hostelling in my school vacations.*

Youth Op·por·tu·ni·ties Pro·gramme /,· ···'··· ,··/ see YOP

Youth Train·ing /,· '··/ see YT

Youth Train·ing Scheme /,· '·· ,·/ see YTS

you've /jəv; *strong* juːv/ *short for:* you have

yowl /jaʊl/ *v* [I] (esp. of a cat or dog) to make a long loud cry, esp. of pain or sadness — **yowl** *n*

yo·yo /'jəʊjəʊ/ *n* **-yos** a toy made of a thick circular piece of wood, plastic, etc., that can be made to run up and down a string tied to it

Y·pres /'iːprə/ a town in S Belgium known as the scene of three great battles of the First World War during which hundreds of thousands of soldiers died. It was known as **Wipers** by the British soldiers there.

YT /,waɪ 'tiː/ Youth Training; a British government SCHEME, run by the CAREERS OFFICE, which arranges TRAINING for young people without a job and provides a small payment for them while they are working or training. YT is COMPULSORY (=you have to do it) if you have not got a job and are aged between 16 and 18

YTS /,waɪ tiː 'es/ Youth Training Scheme; a British government programme which organized TRAINING for people leaving school at 16 and gave them a small amount of money. YTSs have now been replaced by Youth Training (YT)

Yuc·a·tán /,jʊkə'tɑːn‖,juːkə'tæn/ [*the*] a PENINSULA which lies in Mexico, Belize, and Guatemala and sticks out into the Gulf of Mexico. It was the centre of the Maya civilization.

yuc·ca /'jʌkə/ *n* a plant with long pointed leaves on a woody stem, with large white flowers

yuck, yuk /jʌk/ *interj infml* (an expression of extreme dislike)

yuck·y /'jʌki/ *adj infml derog* extremely unpleasant: *yucky food | a yucky colour*

Yu·go /'juːgəʊ/ *n tdmk* a make of car from the former Yugoslavia, based on old Fiat models and known esp. for being cheap

Yu·go·sla·vi·a /,juːgəʊ'slɑːviə/ a country in SE Europe formerly (1929–1990) consisting of a FEDERATION of six REPUBLICS; capital Belgrade. Since 1990 it has been divided into separate republics by declarations of independence.

Yu·kon /'juːkɒn‖-kɑːn/ [*the*] **1** a TERRITORY in NW Canada, which was the SITE of the Klondike gold rush in the 1890s **2** a river in NE North America

yule /juːl/ *n* [U] *old use (sometimes cap.)* CHRISTMAS

yule log /'· ·/ *n* **1** a log of wood burnt on the evening before Christmas **2** a cake made to look like this

yule·tide /'juːltaɪd/ *n* [U] *esp. poet or pomp (sometimes cap.)* CHRISTMAS: *Yuletide greetings*

yum·my /'jʌmi/ *adj infml* tasting very good; DELICIOUS

yuppie

yup·pie , yuppy /'jʌpi/ *n sometimes derog* (from abbrev. of Young Upwardly-mobile Professional) a young person in a professional job with a high income, esp. one who enjoys spending money and having a fashionable way of life. In Britain, yuppies are seen as young people who earn a lot of money without necessarily working very hard, usu. on the financial markets in the City. They typically drive Porsche cars and use car PHONES, PERSONAL ORGANIZERS, and other modern expensive goods and are more concerned about enjoying their lifestyle than having a family or helping others in society. In the US, yuppies are thought of as being slightly older and as being insensitive, AMBITIOUS, and too interested in material goods.

yuppie flu /,·· '·/ *n* [U] *derog* see ME

Yves St Laurent see Saint-LAURENT

YWCA /,waɪ dʌbəljuː siː 'eɪ/ Young Women's Christian Association; an organization in many countries which provides places to stay and sports centres for young women, esp. in large cities, and is also concerned with their spiritual well-being —see also YMCA

Z

Z, z /zed‖zi:/ **Z's, z's** *or* **Zs, zs** **1** the 26th and last letter of the English alphabet **2 catch some Z's** *AmE, sl* to go to sleep: *I'm going to catch some Z's.*

zab·a·glio·ne /ˌzæbəl'jəʊni‖ˌzɑ:-/ *n* [U] an Italian sweet dish made from a mixture of egg, sugar, and wine

Za·greb /'zɑːgreb/ capital city of Croatia

Za·ïre /zaɪ'ɪəʳ‖zɑ:-/ a country in central Africa, formerly known as the **Belgian Congo**; capital Kinshasa; population 35,330,000 (1990) —**Zaïrean, Zaïrian, Zaïrese** /ˌzaɪˌ'ri:z◂/ *adj, n*

Zam·be·zi, **Zambesi** /zæm'bi:zi/ [*the*] a large river in S central Africa which includes the Victoria Falls and the Kariba Dam

Zam·bi·a /'zæmbiə/ a country in S central Africa, an independent member of the British Commonwealth since 1964, and rich in minerals, esp. copper. Its former name was **Northern Rhodesia**; capital Lusaka; population 7,804,000 (1989). —**Zambian** *adj, n*

Zam·en·hof /'zæmənhɒf‖'zɑ:mənhəʊf/, **Laz·a·rus** /'læzərəs/ (1859–1917) a Polish teacher and student of human language who invented the artificial international language Esperanto

za·ny /'zeɪni/ *adj* foolish in an amusing or ABSURD way: *Michael made us all laugh with his zany tricks.*

Zan·zi·bar /'zænzˌbɑ:ʳ/ a TERRITORY in E Africa which joined with Tanganyika to form Tanzania in 1964; capital Zanzibar

zap¹ /zæp/ *n* [U] *infml apprec* liveliness; ENERGY – –**py** *adj* : *a zappy poster|English teacher|lesson*

zap² *v infml* **1** [T] to attack or destroy, esp. in a computer game or VIDEO **2** [I+*adv/prep*; T+*obj/adv/prep*] to (cause to) move quickly or forcefully: *She zapped (the car) from a standstill to 70 miles per hour in 10 seconds.* | (fig.) *I'll have to zap through the work to make the deadline.* **3** [T] *AmE* to cook in a MICROWAVE oven: *Zap that for about two minutes on high, will you?* **4** [T] to operate a television REMOTE CONTROL —see also ZAPPER

Za·pa·ta /zə'pɑːtə/, **E·mi·li·a·no** /eˌmi:li'ɑːnəʊ/ (about 1879–1919) a Mexican fighter against the government, who led an army of Mexican Indians in a largely successful attempt to take back land taken away from them by the authorities, but who was later killed

Zap·pa /'zæpə/, **Frank** (1940–93) an American singer and songwriter of the 1960s and 1970s who, along with his band the **Mothers of Invention**, was associated with the HIPPIE movement

zap·per /'zæpəʳ/ *n AmE infml* REMOTE CONTROL (2)

Zar·a·thus·tra /ˌzærə'θuːstrə/ see ZOROASTER

Zat·o·pek /'zætəpek/, **Em·il** /'emi:l/ (1922–) a Czech ATHLETE who broke several world records and won many races in the 1948 and 1952 OLYMPIC GAMES

Z Cars /'zed kɑːz‖-kɑːrz/ a British television SERIES shown in the 1960s and 70s about the police force

zeal /zi:l/ *n* [U] *fml* eagerness; keenness: *religious/ revolutionary zeal*

zeal·ot /'zelət/ *n usu. derog* someone who is too eager in their beliefs and tries to make other people share them: *religious zealots*

zeal·ous /'zeləs/ *adj fml, usu. apprec* eager; keen: *zealous missionaries* | *She is always zealous in performing her duties.* – ~**ly** *adv* – ~**ness** *n* [U]

ze·bra /'zi:brə, 'ze-‖'zi:brə/ *n* -**bra** *or* -**bras** an African animal that looks like a horse with broad black or dark brown and white lines all over its body

zebra cross·ing /ˌ·· '··/ *n* (in Britain) a place on a busy street, painted with black and white lines to show that PEDESTRIANS (=people walking in the street) have the right to cross before vehicles —compare PELICAN CROSSING and see picture at ZEBRA

zed /zed/ *BrE* ‖ **zee** /zi:/*AmE* – *n* (the name of) the letter Z

Zee·brug·ge /zeɪ'brʊgə, ziː-/ a sea port in N Belgium, a main crossing point for ferries (FERRY¹) to Britain, remembered as the port which the ferry **Herald of Free Enterprise** had just left when she sank in March 1987 with heavy loss of life

Zef·fi·rel·li /ˌzefˌ'reli/, **Fran·co** /'fræŋkəʊ/ (1923–) an Italian director of film, theatre and OPERA productions. His films include *Jesus of Nazareth* and *Romeo and Juliet.*

Zeiss /zaɪs/ *tdmk* a German company making LENSes for glasses, microscopes, and other OPTICAL instruments

zeit·geist /'zaɪtgaɪst/ [*the*] *Ger* (*often cap.*) the general spirit of a period in history, as shown in people's ideas and beliefs

Zen /zen/ also **Zen Buddhism** *n* [U] a Japanese form of Buddhism stating that one must look inside oneself for understanding rather than depend on holy writings, and aiming for ENLIGHTENMENT (2) through MEDITATION (=practice of emptying the mind of thought or fixing the attention on one matter)

zen·ith /'zenˌθ‖'zi:-/ *n* **1** [*the*+S] the point in the sky directly above a person looking from Earth **2** [C *usu. sing.*] the highest or greatest point of development, hope, fortune, etc.: *Opera reached its zenith at the turn of the century.*

zeph·yr /'zefəʳ/ *n poet* a soft gentle west wind

zeppelin

zep·pe·lin /'zepəlɪn/ *n* a large AIRSHIP used by the Germans in the First World War

Zer·matt /'zɜːmæt‖zeəʳ'mɑːt/ a holiday RESORT in the Swiss Alps, popular for climbing and winter sports

ze·ro¹ /'zɪərəʊ‖'zi:rəʊ/ *n* -**ros** *or* -**roes** **1** (the name of) the sign 0 and of the number it stands for **2** the point between + and – on a scale; on the CELSIUS scale, the temperature at which water freezes: *It was five degrees below zero last night.* | *sub-zero temperatures* —see also ABSOLUTE ZERO **3** (often written 0) nothing; no size or quantity: *Our population has reached zero growth.* (=it is not growing any more) | *zero value*

▷ USAGE In saying a number, zero is generally used for 0 in science. **O**, pronounced "Oh", is generally used after a decimal point, as in 1.04, and in telephone numbers. A British speaker might use **nought**, esp. before and after a decimal point, as in 0.06; and might use **nil**, esp. in sports results: *The teams drew* **nil-nil**. An American speaker would usu. use **zero** or **0** in either of these situations, or, in sports results **nothing** or **none**: *Their team won, five to nothing.*◁

ze·ro² *v*

zero in on sthg. *phr v* [T] **1** to aim gunfire or similar weapons directly at **2** to aim one's attention directly towards

zero cou·pon bond /ˌ··· '·· ˌ·/ *n AmE* a BOND¹(3) sold at a DISCOUNT which does not pay interest but which can be exchanged for its full value after a stated time. Zero coupon bonds have tax advantages in some situations.

zero hour /'·· ·/ *n* [U] the hour at which an action or esp.

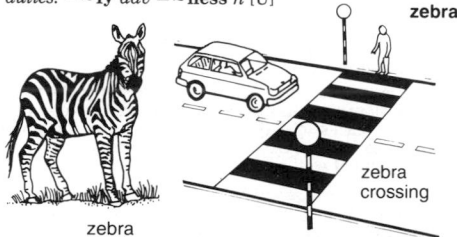

zebra

zebra
crossing

zebra

military operation is planned to begin: *Zero hour is fixed for midnight.*

zero-sum game /ˌ··ˈ· ˌ·/ *n AmE* a situation in which a balance is achieved between something (such as money) received and something given away: *Diplomatic negotiators often aim at a zero-sum game, where they don't give away any more than they get.*

zest /zest/ *n* **1** [S;U] (a quality of) being pleasantly exciting and interesting; SPICE¹ (2): *The danger of being caught gave|added a certain zest to the affair.* **2** [S;U] (a feeling of) being eager: *a zest for life* **3** [U] *BrE* ‖ **peel** *AmE*— the outer skin of an orange or LEMON used for giving a special taste to food, esp. when it is grated (GRATE) and used in making cakes — **~ful** *adj* — **~fully** *adv*

Zeus /zjuːs‖zuːs/ (in Greek MYTHOLOGY) the king and father of the gods, like the Roman **Jupiter**

Zhao Zi-yang /ˌdʒaʊ ˌdzɜːˈjæŋ‖-ˈjɑːŋ/ (1918–) a Chinese politician, PRIME MINISTER from 1980 and secretary of the Chinese Communist Party 1987–89. His LIBERAL views led to his DOWNFALL after the Tiananmen Square MASSACRE in Beijing in 1989.

Zhivago, Doctor see DOCTOR ZHIVAGO

Zhong-shan see SUN ZHONG-SHAN

Zhou En-lai /ˌdʒaʊ ˌenˈlaɪ/ (1898–1976) a Chinese politician, also known as **Chou En-lai**, who was PRIME MINISTER from 1949 to 1976

Zia ul-Haq /ˌzɪə ʊl ˈhæk‖-ˈhɑːk/, **General Mohammad** (1924–88) the president of Pakistan from 1977 until his death. He introduced a period of FUNDAMENTALIST Islamic rule and led the COUP against Zulfiqar Ali Bhutto in 1977.

Zieg-feld /ˈzɪgfeld, ˈziːg-/, **Flor-enz** /ˈflɒrənz‖ˈflɔː-/ (1869–1932) an American theatre producer who arranged a REVUE every year called **the Follies**, from 1907 to 1931

zig-zag¹ /ˈzɪgzæg/ *n* a line shaped like a row of z's: *a zigzag path* —see picture at PATTERN

zigzag² *v* **-gg-** [I] to go in a zigzag: *The path zigzags up the hill.*

zilch /zɪltʃ/ *adj, n AmE, infml* zero; none; nothing: *How much money is left?" "Zilch."* | *"Did we have any enquiries?" "Zilch."*

zil-lion /ˈzɪljən/ also **zillions** *pl.*— *n* [(of)] *infml* an extremely large number: *zillions of mosquitoes*

Zim-ba-bwe /zɪmˈbɑːbweɪ/ a country in S central Africa, officially called the **Republic of Zimbabwe**, which as Rhodesia was a British COLONY (1) until it declared its independence in 1965. It became a legally independent member of the British Commonwealth in 1980; capital Harare; population 9,122,000 (1989). —**Zimbabwean** *n, adj*

Zim-mer /ˈzɪməʳ/ also **Zimmer frame** /ˈ·· ˌ·/ *n BrE tdmk* a type of frame used to help esp. old or ill people to walk: *I'm not that old! I don't need a Zimmer frame yet!* compare WALKER (2)

zinc /zɪŋk/ *n* [U] a bluish-white metal that is a simple substance (ELEMENT) used in the production of other metals, and to PLATE (=cover) metal objects with a protective surface

zing /zɪŋ/ *n* [U] *AmE infml* liveliness; ZIP¹ (2)

Zin-ne-man /ˈzɪnəmən/, **Fred-e-rick** /ˈfredərɪk/ (1907–) an American film director, born in Austria, famous for films such as *High Noon* and *The Day of the Jackal*

Zi-on /ˈzaɪn/ **1** the name given to a Jewish homeland, either Israel or an imagined nation where Jews could live in peace **2** *poet* heaven

Zi-on-is-m /ˈzaɪənɪzəm/ *n* [U] the political movement to establish and develop an independent state of Israel for the Jews —**ist** *adj, n* : *a group of young Zionists*

zip /zɪp/ *n* **1** [C] also **zip fas-ten-er** /ˌ·ˈ····/ *esp. BrE* ‖ **zip-per** *esp. AmE*— a fastener made of two sets of metal or plastic teeth and a sliding piece that joins the edges of an opening in material by drawing the teeth together — see picture at FASTENER **2** [U] *infml apprec* liveliness; ENERGY **3** [S] *infml* a zipping (ZIP² (3)) sound: *We heard the zip of a bullet.* **4** [S] *AmE, infml* zero; nothing; none: *We beat them 10 to zip.* | *"How much money have you got left." "Zip."*

zip² *v* **-pp-** **1** [T+*obj*+*adj*] to put into the stated condition with a zip: *He zipped the bag open|shut.* **2** [I+*adv*|*prep*;T+*obj*+*adv*|*prep*] to (cause to) move very quickly and forcefully: *We zipped through customs.* | *They zipped the order through.* | *The minutes simply zipped past.* **3** [I+*adv*|*prep*] to travel with a hissing (HISS) sound: *The bullet zipped through the air.*

zip sthg./sbdy. **↔ up** *phr v* [T] to fasten (something or a person) into something) with a zip: *Will you zip me up|zip up my dress?* —opposite **unzip**

zip code /ˈ· ·/ *n AmE for* POSTCODE

zip-per /ˈzɪpəʳ/ *n esp. AmE* a zip —see picture at FASTENER

zip-py /ˈzɪpi/ *adj infml apprec* lively and ENERGETIC

zit /zɪt/ *n infml, esp. AmE* a spot on the skin; PIMPLE

zith-er /ˈzɪðəʳ/ *n* a flat musical instrument with 30–40 strings, played with the fingers or with a PLECTRUM (=small piece of plastic)

zizz /zɪz/ *n* [S] *BrE infml* a short sleep: *Father's having/taking a zizz after lunch.*

zodiac

Aquarius
21 Jan - 19 Feb

Pisces
20 Feb - 20 Mar

Aries
21 Mar - 20 Apr

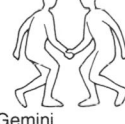

Taurus
21 Apr - 22 May

Gemini
23 May - 21 June

Cancer
22 June - 22 July

Leo
23 July - 22 Aug

Virgo
23 Aug - 22 Sept

Libra
23 Sept - 22 Oct

Scorpio
23 Oct - 21 Nov

Sagittarius
22 Nov - 22 Dec

Capricorn
23 Dec - 20 Jan

the signs of the zodiac

zo-di-ac /ˈzəʊdiæk/ *n* **1** [*the*] an imaginary belt through space along which the sun, the moon, and the nearest PLANETs appear to travel and which is divided into 12 equal parts (SIGNS), each named after a group (CONSTELLATION) of stars which were once in them: *Which sign of the zodiac were you born under?* —see USAGE **2** [C] a circular representation of this with pictures and names for each of the 12 signs of the zodiac, esp. as used by people who believe in the influence of the stars on people's character and fate —see also HOROSCOPE — **~al** /zəʊˈdaɪəkəl/ *adj*

▷ USAGE The signs of the **zodiac** are used in **astrology**. The signs are: **Aquarius, Pisces, Aries, Taurus, Gemini, Cancer, Leo, Virgo, Libra, Scorpio, Sagittarius,** and **Capricorn.**◁

Zo-la /ˈzəʊlə/, **Em-ile** /ˈemiːl/ (1840–1902) a French writer of NOVELs such as *Nana* and *Germinal* which describe French life in a natural and very detailed way

zom·bie , **-bi** /ˈzɒmbi‖ˈzɑːm-/ n 1 *derog* someone who moves very slowly, behaves in a lifeless way, etc. 2 (according to certain African and Caribbean religions) a dead person who is made to move by magic

zon·al /ˈzəʊnl/ adj of or arranged in zones — ~ly adv

zone[1] /zəʊn/ n 1 a division or area marked off from others by particular qualities or activities: *a war|danger|time zone | an economic zone* 2 *tech* any of the five divisions of the Earth's surface according to temperature, marked by imaginary lines running round it from east to west: *the* **torrid zone**, *the two* **temperate zones** *and the two* **frigid zones**

zone[2] v [T] 1 to divide into ZONES[1] (1) 2 [(as, for)] to give a special purpose to (an area in a town, etc.): *This part of the town has been zoned as a shopping area|for industrial development.*

zon·ing /ˈzəʊnɪŋ/ n [U] the choosing of areas to be developed for different purposes when planning a town

zonked /zɒŋkt‖zɑːŋkt/ adj [(F OUT)] sl 1 under the influence of alcohol or a drug 2 extremely tired; exhausted (EXHAUST)

zoo /zuː/ also **zoological gar·dens** /ˌ·····ˈ··/ [P] *fml*— n **zoos** a park where many kinds of wild animals are kept for show: *We took the children to the zoo to see the monkeys.*

zo·ol·o·gist /zuːˈɒlədʒɪst, zəʊˈɒ-‖-ˈɑːl-/ n a person who studies zoology

zo·ol·o·gy /zuːˈɒlədʒi, zəʊˈɒ-‖-ˈɑːl-/ n [U] the scientific study of the different kinds of animals, and of where and how they live —**gical** /ˌzuːəˈlɒdʒɪkəl◂, ˌzəʊə-‖-ˈlɑː-/ adj

zoom[1] /zuːm/ v [I] 1 [+adv|prep] *infml* to go quickly with a loud noise: *Jack went zooming past in his new car.* 2 *infml* to increase suddenly and quickly: *The cost of living has zoomed.* 3 [+adv|prep, esp. IN (on), OUT] (of a cinema camera) to move quickly between a distant and a close view: *The camera zoomed in on the child's face.*

zoom[2] n [S] (the deep low sound of) the fast movement of a vehicle

zoom lens /ˈ· ˌ·/ n a photographic LENS (=curved glass) that can move in from a distant to a close view while keeping what is being photographed in FOCUS (=clear)

zoot suit /ˈzuːt suːt/ n a suit consisting of a JACKET with wide shoulders, and wide trousers with narrow TURN-UPS, worn in the 1940s and 50s by people who liked JAZZ music

Zor·o·as·ter /ˌzɒrəʊˈæstər‖ˈzɔːrəʊæstər/ (about 628–about 551 BC) a Persian religious teacher and PROPHET, also called **Zarathustra**, who started Zoroastrianism

Zor·o·as·tri·a·nis·m /ˌzɒrəʊˈæstriənɪzəm‖ˌzɔːr-/ n [U] an ancient Persian religion which believes that the forces of good and evil are always fighting but that good will win in the end, helped by man. The religion is practised by the Parsees in India and Iran.

Zor·ro /ˈzɒrəʊ ‖ ˈzɔː-/ a character in a series of American films who wore a black MASK and CLOAK, and protected people from crime. He rode a horse and is known esp. for writing a letter Z in the air with his sword.

Zorro

zuc·chi·ni /zuˈkiːni/ n -ni or -nis *AmE, It for* COURGETTE — see picture at VEGETABLE

Zu·lu /ˈzuːluː/ adj of the language or people of Zululand in South Africa

Zul·u·land /ˈzuːluːlænd/ a HOMELAND of the Zulu people in South Africa

Zu·ñi, Zuni /ˈzuːni/ n a Native American people of western New Mexico, known for their fine usu. silver jewellery, and for their dances and dress during their religious celebrations

Zü·rich /ˈzʊərɪk/ a city in Switzerland; a world banking centre

zwie·back /ˈzwiːbæk‖ˈzwaɪ-/ n [U] *AmE tdmk* a kind of hard dry bread which has been baked twice, often given to babies when they are getting their first teeth: *Willa Jean blew bubbles filled with wet Zwieback crumbs and laughed delightedly.*

ZZ top /ˌziː ˌziː ˈtɒp‖-ˈtɑːp/ an American popular music group whose two main singers have very long hair and beards, and wear SUNGLASSES

zzz

zzz (used in pictures for showing that someone is asleep or snoring (SNORE))

1 Numbers

How numbers are spoken

Numbers over 20

21	twenty-one
22	twenty-two
32	thirty-two
99	ninety-nine

Numbers over 100

101	a/one hundred (and) one
121	a/one hundred (and) twenty-one
200	two hundred
232	two hundred (and) thirty-two
999	nine hundred (and) ninety-nine

Note: In British English the "and" is always used: *two hundred and thirty-two*. But in American English it is often left out: *two hundred thirty-two*.

Numbers over 1000

1001	a/one thousand (and) one
1121	one thousand one hundred (and) twenty-one
2000	two thousand
2232	two thousand two hundred (and) thirty-two
9999	nine thousand nine hundred (and) ninety-nine

Ordinal numbers

20th	twentieth
21st	twenty-first
25th	twenty-fifth
90th	ninetieth
99th	ninety-ninth
100th	hundredth
101st	hundred and first
225th	two hundred (and) twenty-fifth

Dates

1624	sixteen twenty-four
1903	nineteen-oh-three
1987	nineteen eighty-seven

What numbers represent

Numbers are often used on their own to show:

Price	*It cost eight seventy-five* (= 8 pounds 75 pence or 8 dollars 75 cents: £8.75 or $8.75).
Time	*We left at two twenty-five* (= 25 minutes after 2 o'clock).
Age	*She's forty-six* (= 46 years old).|*He's in his sixties* (= between 60 and 69 years old).
Size	*This shirt is a thirty-eight* (= size 38).

Temperature	*The temperature fell to minus fourteen* (= −14°).|*The temperature was in the mid-thirties* (= about 34–36°).
The score in a game	*Becker won the first set six-three* (= by six games to three: 6–3).
Something marked with the stated number	*She played two nines and an eight* (= playing cards marked with these numbers).
A set or group of the stated number	*The teacher divided us into fours* (= groups of 4).|*You can buy cigarettes in tens or twenties* (= in packets containing 10 or 20)

Numbers and grammar

Numbers can be used as:

Determiners	*Five people were hurt in the accident.*| *the three largest companies in the US*| *several hundred cars*
Pronouns	*We invited a lot of people but only twelve came/only twelve of them came.*|*Do exercise five on page nine.*
Nouns	*Six can be divided by two and three.*| *Three twos make six.*

See also NUMBER (USAGE)

2 Weights and measures

The words in **dark type** are the ones that are most commonly used in general speech.

METRIC
Units of length

	1 **millimetre**	= 0.03937 inch	
10 mm	= 1 **centimetre**	= 0.3937 inch	
10 cm	= 1 decimetre	= 3.937 inches	
10 dm	= 1 **metre**	= 39.37 inches	
10 m	= 1 decametre	= 10.94 yards	
10 dam	= 1 hectometre	= 109.4 yards	
10 hm	= 1 **kilometre**	= 0.6214 mile	

Units of weight

	= 1 **milligram**	= 0.015 grain	
10 mg	= 1 centigram	= 0.154 grain	
10 cg	= 1 decigram	= 1.543 grains	
10 dg	= 1 **gram**	= 15.43 grains	= 0.035 ounces
10 g	= 1 decagram	= 0.353 ounce	
10 dag	= 1 hectogram	= 3.527 ounces	
10 hg	= 1 **kilogram**	= 2.205 pounds	
1000 kg	= 1 **tonne** (metric ton)	= 0.984 (long) ton = 2204.62 pounds	

Units of capacity

	1 millilitre	= 0.00176 pint	
10 ml	= 1 centilitre	= 0.0176 pint	
10 cl	= 1 decilitre	= 0.176 pint	
10 dl	= 1 **litre**	= 1.76 pints	= 0.22 UK gallon
10 l	= 1 decalitre	= 2.20 gallons	
10 dal	= 1 hectolitre	= 22.0 gallons	
10 hl	= 1 kilolitre	= 220.0 gallons	

Square measure

1 square millimetre = 0.00155 square inch
100 mm^2= 1 square centimetre = 0.1550 square inch
10 cm^2 = 1 square metre = 1.196 square yards
100 m^2 = 1 are = 119.6 square yards
100 ares = 1 **hectare** = 2.471 acres
100 ha = 1 square kilometre = 247.1 acres

Cubic measure

1 cubic centimetre = 0.06102 cubic inch
1000 cm^3 = 1 cubic decimetre = 0.03532 cubic foot
1000 dm^3 = 1 cubic metre = 1.308 cubic yards

Circular measure

1 microradian = 0.206 seconds
1000 μrad = 1 milli- = 3.437 minutes
radian
1000 mrad = 1 radian = 57.296
degrees = 180/$_\mu$ degrees

Metric prefixes

	Abbreviation	Factor
tera-	T	10^{12}
giga-	G	10^{9}
mega-	M	10^{6}
kilo-	k	10^{3}
hecto-	h	10^{2}
deca-	da	10^{1}
deci-	d	10^{-1}
centi-	c	10^{-2}
milli-	m	10^{-3}
micro-	μ	10^{-6}
nano-	n	10^{-9}
pico-	p	10^{-12}
femto-	f	10^{-15}
atto-	a	10^{-18}

BRITISH AND AMERICAN
Units of length

	1 **inch**	= 2.54 cm
12 inches	= 1 **foot**	= 0.3048 m
3 feet	= 1 **yard**	= 0.9144 m
5½ yards	= 1 rod, pole, or perch	= 5.029 m
22 yards	= 1 chain	= 20.12 m
10 chains	= 1 furlong	= 0.2012 km
8 furlongs	= 1 **mile**	= 1.609 km
6076.12 feet	= 1 nautical mile	= 1852 m

Units of weight

	1 grain	= 64.8 mg
	1 dram	= 1.772 g
16 drams	= 1 **ounce**	= 28.35 g
16 ounces	= 1 **pound**	= 0.4536 kg
14 pounds	= 1 stone	= 6.350 kg
2 stones	= 1 quarter	= 12.70 kg
4 quarters	= 1 (long) hundredweight	= 50.80 kg
20 hundredweight	= 1 (long) **ton**	= 1.016 tonnes
100 pounds	= 1 (short) hundredweight	= 45.36 kg

2000 pounds = 1 (short) **ton** = 0.9072 tonnes

The short hundredweight and ton are more common in the US.

Units of capacity

	1 fluid ounce	= 28.41 cm^3
5 fluid ounces	= 1 gill	= 0.1421 dm^3
4 gills	= 1 **pint**	= 0.5683 dm^3
2 pints	= 1 **quart**	= 1.137 dm^3
4 quarts	= 1 (UK) **gallon**	= 4.546 dm^3
231 cubic inches	= 1 (US) **gallon**	= 3.785 dm^3
8 gallons	= 1 bushel	= 36.369 dm^3

Square measure

	1 square inch	= 645.16 mm^2
144 square inches	= 1 square foot	= 0.0929 m^2
9 square feet	= 1 square yard	= 0.8361 m^2
4840 square yards	= 1 acre	= 4047 m^2
640 acres	= 1 square mile	= 259 ha

Cubic measure

	1 cubic inch	= 16.39 cm^3
1728 cubic inches	= 1 cubic foot	= 0.02832 m^3
		= 28.32 dm^3
27 cubic feet	= 1 cubic yard	= 0.7646 m^3
		= 764.6 dm^3

Circular measure

	1 second	= 4.860 $_\mu$rad
60 seconds	= 1 minute	= 0.2909 $_\mu$rad
60 minutes	= 1 degree	= 17.45 $_\mu$rad
		= $_\mu$/180 rad
45 degrees	= 1 oxtant	= $_\mu$/4 rad
60 degrees	= 1 sextant	= $_\mu$/3 rad
90 degrees	= 1 quadrant or 1 right angle	= $_\mu$/2 rad
360 degrees	= 1 circle or 1 circumference	= 2$_\mu$ rad
1 grade or gon	= 1/100th of a right angle	= $_\mu$/200 rad

US dry measure

1 pint = 0.9689 UK pint = 0.5506 dm^3
1 bushel = 0.9689 UK bushel = 35.238 dm^3

US liquid measure

1 fluid ounce = 1.0408 UK fluid ounces
= 0.0296 dm^3
16 fluid ounces = 1 pint = 0.8327 UK pint
= 0.4732 dm^3
8 pints = 1 gallon = 0.8327 UK gallon
= 3.7853 dm^3

Temperature

$$^\circ Fahrenheit = \left(\frac{9}{5}\,^\circ C\right) + 32$$

$$^\circ Celsius = \frac{5}{9}\left(^\circ F - 32\right)$$

3 Military ranks

Royal Navy	US Navy	RAF	USAF
Admiral of the Fleet	Fleet Admiral	Marshal of the Royal Air Force	General of the Airforce
Admiral	Admiral	Air Chief Marshal	General
Vice-Admiral	Vice-Admiral	Air Marshal	Lieutenant General
Rear-Admiral	Rear Admiral	Air Vice Marshal	Major General
Commodore	Commodore	Air Commodore	Brigadier General
Captain	Captain	Group Captain	Colonel
Commander	Commander	Wing Commander	Lieutenant Colonel
Lieutenant-Commander	Lieutenant Commander	Squadron Leader	Major
Lieutenant	Lieutenant	Flight Lieutenant	Captain
Sub-Lieutenant	Lieutenant Junior Grade	Flying Officer	First Lieutenant
Midshipman	Ensign	Pilot Officer	Second Lieutenant
–	Chief Warrant Officer	–	Chief Warrant Officer
Fleet Chief Petty Officer	Warrant Officer	Warrant Officer	Chief Master Sergeant
–	Master Chief Petty Officer	–	Senior Master Sergeant
–	Senior Chief Petty Officer	Flight Sergeant	Master Sergeant
Chief Petty Officer	Chief Petty Officer	Chief Technician	Technical Sergeant
Petty Officer	Petty Officer 1st Class	Sergeant	Staff Sergeant
–	Petty Officer 2nd Class	Corporal	Airman 1st Class
Leading Seaman	Petty Officer 3rd Class	Junior Technician	–
Able Seaman	Seaman	Senior Aircraftman	Airman 2nd Class
Ordinary Seaman	Seaman Apprentice	Leading Aircraftman	Airman 3rd Class
Junior Seaman	Seaman Recruit	Aircraftman	Airman Basic

British Army	US Army	Royal Marines	US Marine Corps
Field-Marshal	General of the Army	General	General
General	General	Lieutenant-General	Lieutenant General
Lieutenant-General	Lieutenant General	Major-General	Major General
Major-General	Major General	Brigadier	Brigadier General
Brigadier	Brigadier General	Colonel	Colonel
Colonel	Colonel	Lieutenant-Colonel	Lieutenant Colonel
Lieutenant-Colonel	Lieutenant Colonel	Major	Major
Major	Major	Captain	Captain
Captain	Captain	Lieutenant	1st Lieutenant
Lieutenant	1st Lieutenant	2nd Lieutenant	2nd Lieutenant
2nd Lieutenant	2nd Lieutenant	–	Chief Warrant Officer
	Chief Warrant Officer	–	–
Warrant Officer 1st Class	Warrant Officer	Warrant Officer 1st Class	Warrant Officer
Warrant Officer 2nd Class	–	Warrant Officer 2nd Class	–
Staff Sergeant	Sergeant Major	Colour Sergeant	Sergeant Major
–	–	–	Master Gunnery Sergeant
Sergeant	Master Sergeant		Master Sergeant
–	1st Sergeant	Sergeant	1st Sergeant
–	Sergeant 1st Class	–	Gunnery Sergeant
–	Staff Sergeant	–	Staff Sergeant
–	Sergeant	–	Sergeant
Corporal	Corporal	–	Corporal
Lance Corporal	Private 1st Class	Corporal	Lance Corporal
Private	Private	–	Private 1st Class
		Lance Corporal	Private
		Marine	

4 Word formation

In English there are many word beginnings (prefixes) and word endings (suffixes) that can be added to a word to change its meaning or its word class. The most common ones are shown here, with examples of how they are used in the process of word formation. Many more are listed on the pages that follow.

Verb formation

The endings **-ize** and **-ify** can be added to many nouns and adjectives to form verbs, like this:

-ize

American Americanize
legal legalize
modern modernize
popular popularize

They want to make the factory more **modern**. *They want to* **modernize** *the factory.*

-ify

beauty beautify
liquid liquefy
pure purify
simple simplify

These tablets make the water **pure**. *They* **purify** *the water.*

Adverb formation

The ending **-ly** can be added to most adjectives to form adverbs, like this:

-ly

easy easily
main mainly
quick quickly
stupid stupidly

His behaviour was **stupid**. *He behaved* **stupidly**.

Noun formation

The endings **-er**, **-ment**, and **-ation** can be added to many verbs to form nouns, like this:

-er

drive driver
fasten fastener
open opener
teach teacher

John **drives** *a bus. He is a bus* **driver**.
A can **opener** *is a tool for* **opening** *cans.*

-ment

amaze amazement
develop development
pay payment
retire retirement

Children **develop** *very quickly. Their* **development** *is very quick.*

-ation

admire admiration
associate association
examine examination
organize organization

The doctor **examined** *me carefully. He gave me a careful* **examination**.

The endings **-ity** and **-ness** can be added to many adjectives to form nouns, like this:

-ity -ty

cruel cruelty
odd oddity
pure purify
stupid stupidity

Don't be so **cruel**. *I hate* **cruelty**.

-ness

dark darkness
deaf deafness
happy happiness
kind kindness

It was very **dark**. *The* **darkness** *made it impossible to see.*

Adjective formation

The endings **-y**, **-ic**, **-ical**, **-ful**, and **-less** can be added to many nouns to form adjectives, like this:

-y

bush bushy
dirt dirty
hair hairy
smell smelly

There was an awful **smell** *in the room. The room was very* **smelly**.

-ic -ical

atom atomic
biology biological
grammar grammatical
poetry poetic

This book contains exercises on **grammar**. *It contains* **grammatical** *exercises.*

-ful

pain painful
hope hopeful
care careful

His broken leg caused him a lot of **pain**. *It was very* **painful**.

-less

pain painless
hope hopeless
care careless

The operation didn't cause her any **pain**. *It was* **painless**.

The ending **-able** can be added to many verbs to form adjectives, like this:

-able

wash washable
love lovable
debate debatable
break breakable

*You can **wash** this coat, It's **washable**.*

Opposites

The following prefixes can be used in front of many words to produce an opposite meaning. Note, however, that the words formed in this way are not always EXACT opposites, and may have a slightly different meaning.

un-

happy unhappy
fortunate unfortunate
wind unwind
block unblock

*I'm not very **happy**. In fact I'm very **unhappy**.*

in-

efficient inefficient

im-

possible impossible

il-

literate illiterate

ir-

regular irregular

*It's just not **possible** to do that. It's **impossible**.*

dis-

agree disagree
approve disapprove
honest dishonest

*I don't **agree** with everything you said. I **disagree** with the last part.*

de-

centralize decentralize
increase decrease
ascend descend
Inflate doflate

Increase *means to make or become larger in amount or number.* ***Decrease*** *means to make or become smaller in amount or number.*

non-

sense nonsense
payment nonpayment
resident nonresident
conformist nonconformist

*The hotel serves meals to **residents** (= people who are staying in the hotel) only. **Nonresidents** are not allowed in.*

u.
acu
ing

-en /ən, ˌ
crown|wo
become, or
dark)|*to rip*
strength)

-ence /əns, ə
exists)|*refer*

-ency /ənsi, ən

-ent /ənt, ənt/
residents

-er¹ /ə^r/ (forma
tives and ad
fast, but hers

-er² (*in nouns*
a dancer (=
diners (= pe
——*s: a scre*

a-¹ /ə/ **1** in the stated condition or way: *alive* (= living) |*aloud*|*with nerves all atingle* (= tingling) **2** *lit or old use* in, to, at, or on: *abed* (= in bed)|*afar* (= far away)

a-² /eɪ, æ, ɔ/ (showing an opposite or the absence of something) not; without: *amoral* (= not moral)|*atypically* (= not typically)

aero- /eə rəu, eərə/ concerning the air or aircraft: *aerodynamics* (= science of movement through air)|*an aeroengine*

Afro- /æfrəu/ **1** of Africa; African: *an Afro-American* (= a black American person) **2** African and: *Afro-Asian* (= of both Africa and Asia)

after- /ɑːftəʳ|æf-/ coming or happening afterwards: *aftercare* (= care given afterwards)|*a bottle of aftershave* (= liquid used on the face after shaving)

agro- /ægrəu/ also **agri** /ægrɪ/ – concerning farming: *agrobiology*|*agribusiness*

all- /ɔːl/ **1** consisting or made only of: *an all-male club*|*an all-wool dress* **2** for the whole of: *All-India Railways*|*an all-day event*|*an all-night party* (= lasting all night)|*an all-night cafe* (= staying open all night)

ambi- /æmbɪ/ both; double: *ambidextrous* (= using both hands equally well)|*ambiguous* (= having two meanings)

an- /ɔn, æn/ (*the form used for* A-² *before a vowel sound*) not; without: *anarchy* (= without government)|*anoxia* (= condition caused by lack of oxygen)

-andr- /ændr/ *tech* concerning males or men: *androgynous plants* (= plants which are both male and female)|*polyandry* (= having more than one husband at the same time)

Anglo- /æŋgləu/ (*sometimes not cap.*) **1** of England or Britain: *an anglophile* (= someone who loves Britain) **2** English or British and: *an Anglo-Scottish family*|*an improvement in Anglo-American relations*

ante- /ænti/ before: *to antedate* (= be earlier than)|*antenatal* (= before birth) – compare ANTI-, POST-, PRE-

anthropo- /ænθrəu, -pə/ *tech* like or concerning human beings: *anthropomorphic* (= having human form or qualities)

anti- /ænti|ænti, æntaɪ/ also **ant-** /ænt/ **1** opposed to; against: *antinuclear* (= opposing the use of atomic weapons and power)|*anti-American* **2** opposite of: *an anticlimax* (= an unexciting ending instead of the expected CLIMAX)|*antimatter* (= made of material completely opposite in kind to the ordinary material in the universe) **3** acting to prevent the stated thing: *antifreeze* (= a liquid added to prevent freezing)|*antiseptic* (= to stop bacteria) – compare ANTE-, PRO-
■ USAGE In informal spoken English **anti** is sometimes used as a preposition: *She's very anti the present government.*|*My father's very anti pop music.* – see also PRO- (USAGE)

arch- /ɑːtʃ, ɑːk|ɑːr-/ of the highest class or rank; chief; main: *an archbishop* (= a chief BISHOP)|*our archenemy* (= our main or worst enemy)|*the company's archrivals* (= main competitors)

astro- /æstrəu, æstrə/ concerning the stars, the PLANETS, or space: *an astronaut* (= someone who travels in space)|*astrophysics* (= science of the stars)

Austro- /ɒstrəu|ɔː-, ɑː-/ **1** Australian and: *Austro-Malayan* **2** Austrian and: *the Austro-Italian border*

auto- /ɔːtəu, ɔːtə/ **1** of or by oneself: *an autobiography* (= book about one's own life, written by oneself) **2** working by itself without human operation: *an auto-pump*

be- /bɪ/ **1** (*in verbs*) to treat as the stated thing: *Don't belittle him.* (= say he is unimportant)|*She befriended me.* (= became my friend) **2** *esp. lit* (*in adjectives*) wearing the stated thing: *a bespectacled boy* (= wearing glasses) **3** *esp. lit or old use* (*in verbs*) completely; thoroughly: *to besmear* (= make very dirty)

bi- /baɪ/ two; twice; double: *bilingual* (= speaking two languages)|*to bisect* (= cut in two) – compare SEMI (3); see also DI-, TRI-
■ USAGE Expressions like **biweekly** can be confusing, because they can mean either "twice in one week/month/year" or "once in two weeks/months/years",

depending on the situation in which they are used.

biblio- /bɪbliəu, bɪbliə/ concerning books: *a bibliophile* (= someone who likes books)

bio- /baɪəu, baɪə/ concerning living things: *biochemistry* (= study of the chemistry of living things)

by-, bye- /baɪ/ less important: *a by-product* (= something made in addition to the main product)|*a by-election* (= one held between regular elections)

cardio- /kɑːdiəu, kɑːdiə|kɑːr-/ also **cardi-** /kɑːdi|kɑːr-/ – *med* concerning the heart: *a cardiograph* (= instrument that measures movements of the heart)

centi- /sentɪ/ also **cent-** /sent/ – **1** 100: *a centipede* (= creature with 100 legs) **2** 100th part of the stated unit: *a centimetre* (= 0.01 metres)

chrono- /krɒnəu, krɒnə|krɑː-/ also **chron-** /krɒn|krɑːn/ – concerning time: *a chronometer* (= instrument for measuring time very exactly)

cine- /sɪni/ *esp. BrE* concerning films or the film industry: *a cinecamera* (= for making films)

circum- /sɜːkəm|sɜːr-/ all the way round something: *to circumnavigate* (= sail round) *the world*|*to circumvent* (= avoid by finding a way round)

co- /kəu/ **1** together; with: *to coexist* (= exist together or at the same time)|*coeducation* (= of boys and girls together) **2** doing something with someone else **a** as an equal: *my coauthor* (= someone who wrote the book with me) **b** with less responsibility; ASSISTANT: *the copilot* (= someone who helps the pilot)

col- /kəl, kɒl|kəl, kɑː-/ (*the form used for* CON- *before* l): *to collaborate* (= work together)

com- /kəm, kɒm|kə, kɑːm/ (*the form used for* CON- *before* b, m, *or* p): *compassion* (= sympathy)

con- /kən, kɒn|kən, kɑːn/ together; with: *a confederation*|*to conspire* (= plan together)

contra- /kɒntrə|kɑːn-/ **1** acting to prevent the stated thing: *contraceptive devices* (= against CONCEPTION) **2** opposite: *plants in contradistinction to animals*

cor- /kə, kɒl|kə, kɔː, kɑː/ (*the form used for* CON- *before* r): *to correlate* (= connect together)

counter- /kauntəʳ/ **1** the opposite of: *a counterproductive thing to do* (= producing results opposite to those intended) **2** matching: *my counterpart in the American system* (= someone in the American system who has the same job as mine) **3** done or given in return, esp. so as to oppose the original one: *proposals and counter proposals* **4** acting to prevent the stated thing: *a counterinsurgency strategy* (= to prevent INSURGENTS)

cross- /krɒs|krɔːs/ **1** going from one side to the other; across; *a cross-Channel ferry* (= sailing from Britain to France) **2** going between the stated things and joining them: *cross-cultural influences*

crypto- /krɪptəu, krɪptə/ *fml derog* secret or hidden: *a crypto-Communist*

de- /diː, dɪ/ **1** (*in verbs and nouns*) (showing an opposite): *a depopulated area* (= which all or most of the population has left)|*deindustrialization* (= becoming less industrial) **2** (*esp. in verbs*) to remove or remove from the stated thing: *to debone a fish* (= remove its bones)|*to dethrone a king* (= remove him from power) **3** (*esp. in verbs*) to make less; reduce: *to devalue the currency*

deca- /dekə/ also **dec-** /dek/ – ten: *a decade* (= period of 10 years)|*the decathlon* (= sporting competition with 10 different events)

deci- /desɪ/ a 10th part of the stated unit: *a decilitre* (= 0.1 litres)

demi- /demi/ **1** half: *a demisemiquaver* (= very short musical note) **2** partly the stated thing: *a demigod* (= partly human and partly a god)

derm- /dɜːm|dɜːrm/ *med* concerning the skin: *dermatitis* (= painful skin condition)

di- /daɪ, dɪ/ two; twice; double: *A diphthong is a vowel made up of two sounds.* – see also BI-

dis- /dɪs/ **1** (showing an opposite or negative): *I disapprove.* (= do not approve)|*his dishonesty* (= lack of honesty)|*with a discontented look* **2** (shows the stopping or removing of the stated condition): *Disconnect the machine from the electricity supply.* (= so that it is no longer connected)|*Disinfect the wound.* **3** (*esp. in verbs*) to take away; remove: *a dismasted ship*

down- /daʊn/ **1** so as to be lower: *to downgrade a job* (= make it lower in importance)|*a downpour* (= heavy rain) **2** (*esp. in adverbs and adjectives*) at or towards the bottom or end: *downstairs*|*downriver* (= nearer to its mouth) **3** (*esp. in adverbs and adjectives*) at or towards the lower or worse part: *down-market* (= meeting the demand of the lower social groups) – compare UP-

electro- /ɪlektrəʊ, trə/ *tech* **1** concerning or worked by electricity: *to electrocute* (= kill by electricity)|*an electro-magnet* **2** electric and: *electro-chemical*

em- /em, ɪm/ (*the form used for* EN- *before* b, m, *or* p): *an embittered man* (= made bitter)

en- /en, ɪn/ (*esp. in verbs*) **1** to cause to become; make: *to enlarge*|*to enrich* **2** to put into the stated condition: *the endangering of life*

equi- /ekwɪ̸, iːkwɪ̸/ equal or equally: *equidistant*|*an equilateral triangle* (= with equal sides)

Euro- /jʊərəʊ/ **1 a** European, esp. western European: *Eurocommunism* **b** European and: *Euro-American relations* **2** of the EEC: *the Europarliament*

ex- /eks/ former (and still living): *my ex-wife*|*the ex-minister*|*an ex-England cricketer* – compare LATE[1] (3, 4)

extra- /ekstrə/ outside, beyond: *extragalactic* (= outside our GALAXY)|*extramarital sex* (= between people who are not married to each other)

fore- /fɔːʳ/ **1** in advance; before: *to forewarn* **2** placed at the front: *her forenames*|*a horse's forelegs* **3** the front part of the stated thing: *his strong forearms*

foster- /fɒstəʳ‖fɔː-, fɑː-/ giving or receiving parental care although not of the same family: *a foster-mother*|*a foster-son*|*a foster-home*|*Danny is my foster-brother.* (= we have different parents, but he is being brought up with me in my family)

Franco- /fræŋkəʊ/ **1** of France: French; *a Francophile* (= someone who loves France) **2** French and: *the Franco-Belgian border*

geo- /dʒiːəʊ, dʒɪə/ *tech* concerning the Earth or its surface: *geophysics*|*geopolitical*

Greco-, Graeco- /griːkəʊ, grekəʊ/ **1** of ancient Greece, Greek **2** ancient Greek and: *Greco-Roman art*

gyn- /gaɪn/ *tech, esp. med* concerning women: *gynaecology* (= treatment of women's diseases)

hemo- /hiːmə, hemə/ *AmE for* HAEMO-

he- /hiː/ (of an animal) male: *a he-goat*

hecto- /hektəʊ/ 100 times the stated unit: *a hectometre* (= 100 metres)

haemo-, hemo- /hiːmə, hemə/ *med* concerning the blood: *a hemorrhage* (= bleeding)

hetero- /hetərəʊ, -rə/ *fml or tech* other; opposite; different: *heterosexual* (= attracted to the opposite sex)

homo- /həʊməʊ, homə‖həʊməʊm hɑ-/ *fml or tech* same: *homosexual* (= attracted to the same sex)|*homographs* (= words spelt the same way)

hydro- /haɪdrəʊ, haɪdrə/ **1** concerning or using water: *hydroelectricity* (= produced by water power)|*hydrotherapy* (= treatment of disease using water) **2** concerning or containing HYDROGEN: *hydrocarbons*

hyper- /haɪpəʳ/ more than usual, esp. too much: *hypersensitive* (= too sensitive)|*hyperactive children*|*an economy suffering from hyperinflation*

hypo- /haɪpəʊ, haɪpə/ *tech* less than usual, esp. too little: *dying of hyopothermia* (= too low body temperature)

il- /ɪ/ (*the form used for* IN- *before* l): *illogical* (= not logical)

im- /ɪm/ (*the form used for* IN- *before* b, m, *or* p): *immobilize*|*impossible*

in- /ɪn/ (*esp. in adjectives and nouns*) (showing a negative, an opposite, or a lack) not: *insensitive* (= not sensitive) *inattention* (= lack of attention) – see UN- (USAGE)

Indo- /ɪndəʊ/ **1** of India; Indian **2** Indian and: *the Indo-Pakistan border*

infra- /ɪnfrə/ *tech* below in a range; beyond: *the infrared end of the spectrum* – compare ULTRA- (1)

inter- /ɪntəʳ/ between; among (a group): *interdepartmental* (= betweeen departments)|*to intermarry* (= marry someone of another race, religion, etc.)

intra- /ɪntrə/ *fml or tech* **1** inside; within: *intradepartmental* (= within a department)|*intracranial pressure* (= inside the head) **2** into: *an intravenous injection* (= into a VEIN)

intro- /ɪntrə/ into, esp. into the inside: *introspection* (= examining one's own feelings)

ir- /ɪ/ (*the form used for* IN- *before* r) not: *irregular* (= not regular)

iso- /aɪsəʊ, aɪsə/ *tech* the same all through or in every part; equal: *an isotherm* (= line joining places of equal temperature)

Italo- /ɪtæləʊ/ **1** of Italy; Italian **2** Italian and: *the Italo-Austrian border*

kilo- /kɪlə/ 1000 times the stated unit: *a kilogram* (= 1000 grams)

macro- /mækrəʊ/ *esp. tech* large, esp. concerning a whole system rather than particular parts of it: *macroeconomics* (= the study of large money systems, e.g. a country's) – compare MICRO-

mal- /mæl/ bad or badly: *a malformed* (= wrongly shaped) *limb*|*She maltreats her children.* (= treats them cruelly)

matri- /meɪtri, mætrɪ̸/ **1** concerning mothers: *matricide* (= killing one's mother) **2** concerning women: *a matriarchal society* (= controlled by women) – compare PATRI-

mega- /megə/ **1** a million times the stated unit: *a 100-megaton bomb* **2** *sl* unusually large or great: *Hollywood megastars*|*The film is set to earn megabucks.* (= an extremely large amount of money)

meta- /metə/ *esp. tech* beyond the ordinary or usual: *metaphysical* (= beyond ordinary physical things)

micro- /maɪkrəʊ, maɪkrə/ *esp. tech* extremely small: *a microcomputer*|*microelectronics* (= using extremely small electrical parts) – compare MACRO-, MINI-

mid- /mɪd/ middle: *She's in her mid-20s.* (= is about 25 years old)|*in mid-July*|*a cold midwinter night*|*at the midpoint of our holiday*

milli- /mɪlɪ̸/ 1000th part of the stated unit: *a millilitre* (= 0.001 litres)

mini- /mɪni/ *infml* very small compared with others of its kind: *a minibreak* (= a short holiday)|*a miniskirt* (= very short) – compare MICRO-

mis- /mɪs/ **1** bad or badly: *misfortune* (= bad luck)|*to misbehave* **2** wrong or wrongly: *a miscalculation*|*to misunderstand* **3** (showing an opposite or the lack of something): *I mistrust* (= don't trust) *him.*

mock- /mɒk‖mɑːk/ only pretendingly: *a mock-serious expression on her face*

mono- /mɒnəʊ, mɒnə‖mɑː-/ one; single: *a monoplane* (= plane with only one wing on each side)|*a monolingual dictionary* (= dealing with only one language)

multi- /mʌltɪ̸/ more than one; many: *multicoloured* (= with many colours)|*a multistorey office block*

neo- /niːəʊ, niːə/ (*esp. in nouns and adjectives*) a recent or later kind of the stated former system, style, etc.; new: *neoclassical architecture* (= copying that of ancient Greece and Rome)|*neocolonialism* (= the control of other countries by large modern states)

neuro- /njʊərəʊ‖nʊərə/ also **neur-** /njʊər‖nʊər/ – *med* concerning the nerves: *a neurosurgeon* (= who specializes in the body's nervous system)

k...
socie...

penta- /pen...

phono- /fəʊnə...
strong fɒn, fɒ...
ing the voice or...
sounds) **2** co...
animal hearin...

photo- /fəʊtəʊ, fə...
tive paper (= ...
concerning ph...
photographs in...

physio- /fɪziəʊ, fɪ...
nature and livi...
body works) **2**...
using exercises...

politico- /pəlɪtɪkəʊ...

poly- /pɒlɪ‖pɑːlɪ/...
more SYLLABLE...
husband at the...

post- /pəʊst/ later...
postpone (= ma...

pre- /priː/ **1** bef...
advance: *prear...*

pro- /prəʊ/ **1** in fa...
pro-abortion lo...
the place of: ...
■ USAGE In in...
times used as a...
ent government...

proto- /prəʊtəʊ, pr...
time or order, a...
develop from it;...
which all the g...
developed

pseudo- /sjuːdəʊ...
pseudo-intellect...
says astrology's...

psycho- /saɪkəʊ, s...

Word endings

tele- /telɪ/ 1 over a long distance: tele**pathy** (= sending of thought messages)|tele**shopping** (= using a computer in one's home to order goods) 2 by or for television: a tele**play**|a tele**recording**

theo- /θɪə/ also **the-** /θiː/ – tech concerning God or gods: **theo**logy (= study of)

thermo- /θɜːməʊ, θɜːm-/ also **therm-** /θɜːm/ — tech concerning heat: a **thermo**stat (= for controlling temperature)|**thermo**stable (= that does not change when heated)

trans- /trænz, trænz/ 1 on or to the far side of: across: **trans**atlantic flights|the **trans**-Siberian railway 2 between: INTER-: **trans**-racial fostering 3 (showing a change): to **trans**form|the **trans**mutation of base metal into gold

tri- /traɪ/ three; three times: **tri**lingual (= speaking three languages)|**tri**angle (= a shape with three sides and three angles) – see also BI-

ultra- /ʌltrə/ 1 tech above in a range; beyond: **ultra**sound (= too high to hear) – compare INFRA- 2 infml very; extremely: an **ultra**modern building|**ultra**cautious|**ultra**sensitive

un- /ʌn/ 1 (esp. in adjectives and adverbs) (showing a negative, a lack, or an opposite state): **un**fair (= not fair)|**un**happy|**un**fortunately|**un**belief (= lack of belief) 2 (esp. in verbs) (showing an opposite): The pipe's blocked, we must **un**block it (= remove what is blocking it)|to **un**dress (= take one's clothes off)

USAGE Compare **un-**, **in-** and **non-**, which all mean 'not'. The difference between them is the degree to which they suggest the idea of something opposite. **Non-** is usually just negative rather than something opposite (for example, **non**alcoholic drinks contain no alcohol), but **un-** is often used to suggest an opposite quality. Compare: He has applied for a **non**scientific job (= not connected with science) in the Civil Service.|It was very **un**scientific of you to measure your results not to scientific principles. Of the three prefixes, **in-** tends most often to suggest opposite qualities. Compare: their **in**human (= very cruel) treatment of political prisoners|The archaeologists discovered both human and **non**-human bones.

under- /ʌndə/ 1 too little: **under**development|**under**cooked cabbage 2 going underneath: an **under**pass 3 inner; beneath others: **under**garments 4 less important or lower in rank: a head gardener and three **under**-gardeners

uni- /juːnɪ/ one; single: **uni**directional

up- /ʌp/ 1 so as to be higher: **up**grade a job (= make it higher in importance) 2 (esp. in adverbs and adjectives) at or towards the top or beginning: **up**hill|**up**river (= nearer to where the river starts) 3 (esp. in verbs) so as to be out of place or upside down: an **up**rooted tree|She **up**ended the bucket.4 (esp. in adjectives and adverbs) at or towards the higher or better part: **up**market (= meeting the demand of the higher social groups) – compare down-

vice- /vaɪs/ the person next in official rank below the stated person, who has the power to represent them or act in place of them: the **Vice**-President of the USA|the **vice**-captain of the cricket team

---

-ability /əbɪləti/ also **-ibility**— (in nouns formed from adjectives ending in -able- and -ible-): manage**ability**|suit**ability**

USAGE This ending is commonly used with words that mean "that can be ——ed" (-ABLE(1)), but is much less usual with words that mean "having a quality" (-ABLE(2)) – you cannot say comfort**ability**

-able /əbəl/ also **-ible**— (in adjectives) 1 that can be ——ed: wash**able** (= that can be washed)|unbreak**able** (= that cannot be broken) 2 having the stated quality or condition: knowledge**able** (= knowing a lot)|comfort**able**——**-ably**, **-ibly** (in adverbs): unbeliev**ably**

-ade /eɪd/ (in [U] nouns) a usu. sweetened drink made from the stated fruit: orange**ade** (= drink made from orange juice)

-age /ɪdʒ/ (nouns) 1 the action or result of ——ing: allow for shrink**age** (= getting smaller)|several break**ages** (= things broken) 2 the cost of ——ing: Post**age** is extra. 3 the state or rank of a ——: a peer**age** (= noble rank)

-aholic /əhɒlɪk|əhɔː-, əhɑː-/ infml (in nouns and infml) (a person) who cannot stop doing or using the stated thing: a work**aholic** (= who loves working and cannot stop)|a comput**aholic**

-al /əl, əl/ also **-ial**— (in adjectives) of or concerning: coast**al** waters (= near the coast)|politic**al** ——s (in nouns) the action of ——ing: her arriv**al**

-an /ən, ən/ also **-ian**— 1 (in adjectives and nouns) (someone or something) of, from, or connected with—: an Americ**an** (= person from America)|the pre-Tolstoy**an** novel 2 (in nouns) someone skilled in or studying the stated subject: a histori**an** (= someone who studies history)

-ana /ɑːnə|ænə/ (in nouns) -IANA: Americ**ana**

-ance, -ence (in nouns) action, state, or quality of ——ing or of being—: his sudden appear**ance** (= he appeared suddenly)|her brilli**ance** (= she is brilliant)|several perform**ances**

-ancy, -ency /ənsi, ənsi/ (in nouns) the state or quality of ——ing or of being—: expect**ancy** (= state of expecting)|hesit**ancy**|complac**ency** (= being COMPLACENT)

-ant /ənt, ənt/ also **-ent**— (in nouns and adjectives) someone or something that ——s: a serv**ant** (= someone who serves others)|disinfect**ant** (= substance for killing germs)|expect**ant** (= expecting)|pleas**ant** (= pleasing)

-ar /ə, aːʳ/ 1 (in nouns) (the form used for -er in certain words): a begg**ar** (= person who begs) 2 (in adjectives) of or concerning——s: muscul**ar** strength (= strength of muscles)|molecul**ar**—see also -ULAR

-archy /aːki, aːkɪ|aːrki/ tech government; rule: an**archy** (= no government)|mon**archy** (= with one ruler)

-ard /əd|ərd/ (in nouns) someone with the stated usu. bad quality; someone who is usu. or always ——: a drunk**ard**

-arian /eəriən| (in adjectives and nouns) (of or for) someone who is connected with or believes in the stated thing: a veget**arian** restaurant (= for people who do not eat meat)|a libr**arian** (= someone who works in a library)—see also -GENARIAN

-ary /əri, ən|eri/ (in adjectives) of or concerning—: that is a ——: planet**ary** bodies (= that are PLANETS)|custom**ary**

-ary² (in nouns) 1 someone connected with a ——: the benefici**aries** of the will (= people who profit from it)|a function**ary** (= someone with duties) 2 a thing or place connected with or containing——: a libr**ary** (= containing books)|an ov**ary** (= containing eggs)

-ate /ɪt, eɪt/ 1 (in adjectives) full of or showing the stated quality: very affection**ate** (= showing love) 2 (in verbs) to cause to become ——: to activ**ate** (= make active)|to regul**ate** (= make regular) 3 (in nouns) a group of people with certain duties: the elector**ate** (= people who elect; voters)|an inspector**ate** 4 (in nouns) the job, rank, or degree of a ——: She was awarded her doctor**ate** (= the degree of doctor) 5 tech (in nouns) a chemical salt formed from the stated acid: phosph**ate**

-athon /əθɒn|əθɑːn/ (in nouns) an event in which the stated thing is done for a very long time, esp. to collect money: a swim**athon**|a talk**athon**

-ation /eɪʃən/ (in nouns) the act, state, or result of ——ing: an examin**ation** (= examining)|the contents|the combin**ation** of several factors

-ative /ətɪv|eɪtɪv/ (in adjectives) liking or tending to ——, or showing a liking for: talk**ative** (= liking to talk a lot)|argument**ative** (= enjoying arguments)|imagin**ative** (= showing imagination)

-ator /eɪtəʳ/ (in nouns) someone or something that ——s: a narr**ator** (= someone who tells a story)|a gener**ator**

non- /nɒn‖nɑːn/ 1 (esp. in adjectives and nouns) (showing a negative) not: a nonalcoholic drink|a nonsmoker (= someone who does not smoke)|a non-stick frying pan (= which food does not stick to) – see un- (USAGE) 2 infml (esp. in nouns) not deserving the stated name: a non-event (= something dull)|It was a really bad book – a non-story with non-characters.

nor'- /nɔː'‖-/ lit or tech (used esp. by sailors): north: nor'east|nor'west

omni- /ɒmni‖ɑːm-/ esp. fml or tech everything or every-where: all: an omnivore (= animal that eats all sorts of food)

osteo- /ɒstiəʊ, ɒstiə‖ɑːs-/ med concerning bones: osteo-arthritis (= disease of the joints)

out- /aʊt/ 1 (in nouns and adjectives formed from verbs and phrasal verbs followed by out): an outbreak of flu (from break out)|outspoken comments (from speak out)|with out-stretched hands (from stretch out) 2 (in nouns and adjectives) outside; beyond: an outhouse (= small additional building)|outlying areas (= far from the centre) 3 (in verbs) a beyond; further: She outlived her brother (= he died before her)|He's outgrown his clothes (= become too big for them) b so as to be better than or defeat: I can out-argue you any day.

over- /əʊvə'/ 1 too much: overpopulation|overcooked cabbage 2 above; beyond; across: overhanging branches|the overland route (= not by sea or air) 3 outer; covering: an overcoat 4 additional: working overtime (= beyond the usual time)

paleo-, palaeo- /pæliəʊ‖peɪliə/ tech extremely ancient, before historical times: paleobotany

pan- /pæn/ (sometimes cap.) including all: pan-African unity|Pan-Arabism (= political union of all Arabs)

para- /pærə/ 1 beyond; the paranormal (= strange unnatural events) 2 very similar to; (as if) copying: terrorists wearing paramilitary uniforms|paratyphoid 3 connected with and helping; para-: medical workers such as ambulance drivers

patri- /pætri, peɪtri/ 1 concerning fathers: patricide (= killing one's father) 2 concerning men: a patriarchal society (= controlled by men) – compare matri-

penta- /pentə/ five: a pentagon (= shape with five sides)

phono- /fəʊnəʊ, fəʊnə‖faː-/ also phon- /fən; fəʊn‖faː-/ 1 concerning sound or speech: phonetics (= science of speech sounds) 2 concerning sound: a phonoreceptor (= animal hearing organ)

photo- /fəʊtəʊ, fəʊtə/ 1 tech concerning light: photosensi-tive paper (= that changes when light acts on it) 2 concerning photography: photojournalism (= use of photographs in reporting news)

physio- /fɪziəʊ, fɪziə/ also physi- /fɪzi/ – 1 tech concerning nature and living things: physiology (study of how the body works) 2 physical: physiotherapy (= treatment using exercises, etc., rather than medicines)

politico- /pəlɪtɪkəʊ/ political and: politico-scientific

poly- /pɒli‖pɑːli/ many: polysyllabic (= with three or more syllables)|polygundry (= having more than one husband at the same time)

post- /pəʊst/ later than; after: postwar (= after a war)|to postpone (= make later) – compare ante-, pre-

pre- /priː/ 1 before: prewar (= before a war) 2 in advance: prearranged – compare ante-, post-

pro- /prəʊ/ 1 in favour of; supporting; pro-American|the pro-abortion lobby – compare anti- 2 tech acting in the place of: the pro-vice-chancellor ■ USAGE In informal spoken English pro is some-times used as a preposition: She's very pro the pres-ent government. – see also anti- (USAGE)

proto- /prəʊtəʊ, prəʊtə/ also prot- /prəʊt/ – esp. tech first in time or order, and esp. having others come after it or develop from it; original: the huge protogalaxy from which all the galaxies in the present-day universe developed

pseudo- /sjuː‖suː/ derog or tech not real; false: pseudo-intellectuals (= who pretend to be clever)|He says astrology's just a pseudoscience.

psycho- /saɪkəʊ, saɪkə‖saɪk-/ tech concern-ing the mind, as opposed to the body: psychotherapy (= treatment of the mind)

quadri- /kwɒdri‖kwɑː-/ also quadru- /kwɒdru‖kwɑː-/, quadra- /kwɒdrə‖kwɑː-/ four: quadrilateral (= with four straight sides)|a quadruped (= an animal with four legs)

quasi- /kweɪzaɪ, kwɑːzi/ 1 in some ways; partly: the chairman's quasi-judicial role (= acting in some ways like a judge) 2 derog pseudo-; quasi-scientific ideas

radio- /reɪdiəʊ/ also radi- /reɪdi/ – 1a concerning waves of force, e.g. light, sound, or radio waves: radiopaque (= which waves will not pass through) b using radio waves: a radiotelephone (= working with-out wires)|radiopaging (= calling people by radio) 2 concerning RADIOACTIVITY: radiochemistry (= study of radioactive chemicals)

re- /riː/ 1 again: to rebroadcast a radio play 2 again in a new and better way; to rewrite a letter 3 back to a former state: After years of separa-tion they were finally reunited. ■ USAGE When re- is used with the meanings shown here, it is pronounced /riː/. But it comes in many other words, such as rebuke and respond, where it does not have a separate meaning of its own, and in them it is usually pronounced /rɪ/ (or /rɪ/ before a vowel). Com-pare recover (= to get better) /rɪˈkʌvə'/ and re-cover (= to cover again) /ˌriːˈkʌvə'/.

retro- /retrəʊ, retrə/ 1 back towards the past: retroactive legislation (= which has an effect on things already done)|in retrospect 2 back towards an earlier and worse state: a retrograde step|to retrogress 3 back-wards: a retrorocket (= that fires backwards, oppo-site to the direction of travel)

Romano- /rəˈmɑːnəʊ/ 1 of ancient Rome: Roman 2 ancient Roman and: Romano-British art

Russo- /rʌsəʊ/ 1 of Russia; Russian: a Russophile (= someone who loves Russia) 2 Russian and: Russo-American trade

self- /self/ 1 by means of oneself or itself: He's self-taught (= He taught himself).|self-propelled 2 of, to, with, for, or in oneself or itself: a self-addressed envelope (= which one addresses to oneself)|a self-portrait (= a picture of oneself, drawn, painted, etc. by oneself)|self-restraint

semi- /semi/ 1 exactly half: a semicircle 2 partly but not completely: in the semidarkness|a semi-invalid|semi-literate people 3 happening, appearing, etc. twice in the stated period: a semiweekly visit|a semi-annual publication – compare bi-

she- /ʃiː/ female: a she-goat|a she-devil (= evil woman)

Sino- /saɪnəʊ/ 1 of China; Chinese: Sinology (= study of China) 2 Chinese and: Sino-Japanese trade

socio- /səʊsiəʊ, -siə; səʊʃiəʊ, -ʃiə/ esp. tech 1 concerning society: social; sociology (= study of society) 2 social and: sociopolitical

step- /step/ related not by birth but through a parent who has remarried: my stepfather (= not my real father, but a man who has married my mother)|her stepchildren

sub- /sʌb/ 1 under; below: subzero temperatures|sub-soil (= beneath the surface) 2 less important or of pow-er of or lower rank than: a subcommittee|a subtenant 3 part of the stated bigger whole: a subsection 4 derog similar to, but not as good as or not real: dreary rows of sub-Victorian villas 5 esp. tech almost: subtropical heat

super- /suːpə'‖suː-/ more, larger, greater, or more pow-erful than usual: a supertanker (= a ship that can carry extremely large loads)|superglue|super-rich film stars|superheated steam

sym- /sɪm/ (the form used for syn- before b, m, or p): sympathy

syn- /sɪn/ together; sharing; a synthesis (= combining of separate things)

techno- /teknəʊ/ concerning TECHNOLOGY: technocracy (= rule by skilled specialists)|technophobia (= esp. fear of computers)

tele- /teli, telɪ/ 1 at or over a long distance: a telescope (= for seeing a long way)|telecommunications|tele-

(= machine that produces electricity)

-bound /baund/ (*in adjectives*) limited, kept in, or controlled in the stated way: *a fog-bound aircraft/airport* (= unable to operate because of FOG)|*We were snowbound and couldn't get out of the house.* – see also BOUND[5]

-cide /saɪd/ (*in nouns*) -ICIDE: *genocide* (= killing a whole race of people) ——**-cidal** (*in adjectives*) ——**-cidally** (*in adverbs*)

-cracy /krəsi/ (*in nouns*) -OCRACY: *bureaucracy* (= government by officials who are not elected)

-craft /krɑːft‖kræft/ (*in nouns*) **1** a vehicle of the stated kind: *a spacecraft/a hovercraft/several aircraft* **2** skill of the stated kind: *statecraft* (= skill in the art of government)|*stagecraft* (= skill in acting or directing plays)

-crat /kræt/ (*in nouns*) -OCRAT

-cy /si/ (*in nouns*) **1** the state or quality of being ——: *privacy* (= state of being private)|*accuracy*|*bankruptcy* **2** the rank or position of a ——: *a baronetcy* (the rank of a BARONET)

-d /d, t/ (*the form used for* -ED *after* e): *baked*

-dom /dəm/ **1** (*in* [U] *nouns*) the state of being ——: *freedom* **2** (*in* [C] *nouns*) **a** the rank of a ——: *He was rewarded with a dukedom.* (= was made a DUKE, a high noble rank) **b** an area ruled by a ——: *a kingdom* **3** (*in* [U] *nouns*) *infml* all the people who share the same set of interests, have the same job, etc.: *officialdom* (= all officials)|*yuppiedom*

-drome /drəum/ *rather old fash* (*in nouns*) a large place for the stated purpose: *an aerodrome* (= an airport)

-ean /ɪən/ (*in adjectives and nouns*) -AN: *Mozartean* (– of or like Mozart)

-ectomy /ektəmi/ *tech* (*in nouns*) the removing of the stated body part by an operation: *an appendectomy* (= removing the APPENDIX)

-ed /d, ɪd, t/ **1** (forms the regular past tense and past participle of verbs. The past participle form is often used as an adjective.): *I want, I wanted, I have wanted*|*I show, I showed, I have shown*|*walked*|*echoed*| *a wanted criminal* **2** (*in adjectives*) having a ——: *a bearded man* (= a man with a beard)|*a kind-hearted woman*
■ USAGE **-ed** or **-d** added to the end of a verb to make the past tense or past participle (*failed, loved*) have the sound /d/ except: **a** after verbs ending with the sounds /p, k, f, θ, s, ʃ, tʃ/. Here **-ed** is pronounced /t/, as in *matched* /mætʃt/. **b** after verbs ending with the sounds /t, d/. Here **-ed** is pronounced /ɪd/ in British English and /əd/ in American English, as in *needed* /'niːdɪd/. see also -ING (USAGE)

-ee /iː/ (*in nouns*) **1** someone who is ——ed: *the payee* (= someone who is paid)|*a trainee*|*an employee* **2** someone who is —— or who ——s: *an absentee* (= someone who is absent)|*an escapee* (= someone who escapes)

-eer /ɪəʳ/ *often derog* **1** (*in nouns*) someone who does or makes a ——: *an auctioneer* (= someone who runs AUCTION sales)|*a profiteer* (= someone who makes unfair profits)|*a racketeer* **2** (*in verbs*) to perform actions connected with——s: *to profiteer*|*electioneer-*

·/ **1** (*in adjectives*) made of ——: *a golden* oden seats **2** (*in verbs*) to (cause to) be, have ——: *to darken* (= make or become ·en*|to strengthen* (= have or give more

(*in nouns*) -ANCE: *its existence* (= it e|*occurrence*

nouns) -ANCY: *a tendency*

ectives and nouns*) -ANT: *different*|

nparative of many short adjec-ot, hotter|dry, drier|My car is es faster.* – see also -EST (1)

who——s or who is ——ing: ances or is dancing)|*the* ·er*) **2** something that driving in screws) **3**

someone who makes ——s: *a hatter* (= someone who makes hats) **4** someone who lives in or comes from ——: *a Londoner* (= someone from London)|*the villagers* (= people who live in the village) **5** someone skilled in or studying the stated subject: *a geographer* (= someone who studies GEOGRAPHY) **6** something that has ——s: *a three-wheeler car* (= with three wheels) – see also -AR, -OR
■ USAGE In expressions like "She is a **dancer**", words ending in **-er** usually suggest that the person who performs the action of the verb does it professionally: One can, however, say "He's a very keen **footballer**/a very good **dancer**" without suggesting that he does it professionally.

-ery /əri, əri/ *also* **-ry**— (*in nouns*)**1a** the art, behaviour, or condition of a —— or of being ——: *slavery* (= being a slave)|*bravery* (= being brave) **b** a collection of——s: *modern machinery* (= machines)|*in all her finery* (= fine clothes) **2** a place where the stated thing lives or is done, made, or sold: *a rookery* (= where birds called ROOKs live)|*a bakery* (= where bread is baked)|*an oil refinery*

-es /ɪz/ (*the form used for* -s *when added to a word ending with* s, z, ch, *or* y): *glasses*|*buzzes*|*watches*|*ladies*

-ese /iːz/ **1** (*in nouns and adjectives*) (the people or language) belonging to the stated country or place: *The Viennese* (= people from Vienna) *are so charming.*|*learning Japanese* (= the language of Japan|*Chinese music* **2** *usu. derog* (*in nouns*) language or words limited to the stated group: *journalese* (= language used in newspapers)|*officialese* (= language used in official or legal writing)

-esque /esk/ (*in adjectives*) **1** in the manner or style of: *Kafkaesque* (= in the style of the writer Franz Kafka, or like the situations or characters in his books) **2** like a ——: *picturesque* (= pleasing to look at)

-ess /es, ɪs/ (*in nouns*) a female ——: *an actress* (= a female actor)|*a waitress*|*two lionesses*
■ USAGE Many people do not like the use of female forms such as **authoress** and **poetess**. They prefer to use the same word for both men and women: *Sylvia Plath, the well-known American* **poet**|*Iris Murdoch is the* **author** *of many novels.*

-est /ɪst/ **1** (forms the SUPERLATIVE of many shorter adjectives and adverbs: *cold, colder, coldest*|*dry, drier, driest*|*Our soap washes whitest.* – see also ER-[1] **2** *also* **-st**— *old use or bibl* (forms the second person singular of verbs): *thou goest*

-eth /ɪθ/ *also* **-th**— *old use or bibl* (forms the third person singular of verbs): *he goeth*

-ette /et/ (*in nouns*) **1** a small ——: *a kitchenette* (– small kitchen)|(*infml*) *a snackette* (= a very small meal) **2** a female ——: *an usherette* (= female USHER) **3** not real ——; IMITATION: *flanelette*|*chairs covered with leatherette*

-ey /i/ (*in adjectives*) (*the form used for* -Y *esp. after* y): *clayey soil*

-fashion /fæʃən/ (*in adverbs*) in the way of a ——; like a ——: *They ate Indian-fashion, using their fingers.*

-fold /fəuld/ (*in adjectives and adverbs*) of or by the stated number of times or kinds: *A window has a twofold purpose – it allows light into the room and lets people see out.*|*The value of the house has increased fourfold.* (= it is now worth four times as much as before)

-free /friː/ (*in adjectives and adverbs*) without ——: *a salt-free diet*|*a trouble-free journey*|*We bought the cigarettes duty-free.*|*They live in the house rent-free.*

-friendly /frendli/ (*in adjectives*) not difficult for ——s to use; helpful to ——s: *a user-friendly computer*|*a customer-friendly shopping environment*

-ful[1] /fəl/ (*in adjectives*) **1** full of ——s: *an eventful day* **2** having the quality of ——; causing ——: *restful colours*|*Is it painful?* – **-fully** (*in adverbs*): *shouting cheerfully*

-ful[2] /ful/ (*in nouns*) **1** the amount of a substance needed to fill the stated container: *two cupfuls of milk*|*He smoked a whole packetful of cigarettes.* **2** as much as

can be carried by, contained in, etc. the stated part of the body: *carrying an armful of flowers*|*She drank a few mouthfuls of tea.* **3** a place or space filled with people or things: *a shelf-ful of books*|*a roomful of people*
■ USAGE The plural of nouns ending in -**ful** can be formed in either of two ways. Both **basketfuls** and **basketsful** are correct, but the second is rather old-fashioned now.

-fy /faɪ/ *(in verbs)* -IFY

-gamy /gəmi/ *esp. tech (in* [U] *nouns)* marriage to the stated number or kind of people: *bigamy* (= being married to two people)|*monogamy* – -**gamous** *(in adjectives)*

-genarian /dʒənəˈriən/ *(in nouns and adjectives)* (someone) who is the stated number of DECADES (= periods of 10 years) old: *an octogenarian* (= between 80 and 89 years old)

-gon /gɒn; *strong* gɒn‖gən; *strong* gɑːn/ *(in nouns)* a shape with the stated number of sides and angles: *a hexagon* (= with six sides)|*a polygon* (= with many sides)

-gram /ɡræm/ *(in nouns)* a message delivered as an amusing surprise: *On his birthday we sent him a kissagram.* (= an unknown girl who was paid to deliver him a message and kiss him)

-head /hed/ *(in nouns)* **1** the top of a ——: *a pithead* (= the top of a coalmine) **2** the point of origin of a ——; SOURCE: *a fountainhead*

-high /haɪ/ *(in adjectives)* having the stated height: *The wall was about chest-high.* (as high as one's chest)|*a 7000-metre-high mountain*

-hood /hʊd/ *(in nouns)* the state or time of being (a) ——: *childhood*|*manhood*|*likelihood*

-i /i/ *(plural* -**is** /iːz/) *(in nouns and adjectives)* (a person or the language) of the stated place, esp. in Asia: *two Pakistanis*|*speakers of Nepali*|*the Israeli army*

-ial /iəl/ *(in adjectives)* -AL (1): *a managerial job* (= with the duties of a manager)

-ian /iən/ *(in adjectives and nouns)* -AN: *Dickensian characters* (= like those in Dickens's books)|*a librarian* (= someone who works in a library)

-iana /iɑːnə‖iænə/ also -**ana**— *(in nouns)* a collection of objects, papers, etc., connected with ——: *Churchilliana*|*Shakespeariana*

-ibility /əˈbɪlɪti/ *(in nouns)* -ABILITY: *invincibility*

-ible /əbəl/ *(in adjectives)* -ABLE: *irreversible*

-ic /ɪk/ **1** *(in adjectives)* of, like, or connected with ——: *photographic* (= of photography)|*an alcoholic drink* (= containing alcohol)|*polysyllabic* (= containing several SYLLABLES)|*pelvic* (= of the PELVIS)|*Byronic* (= like or connected with the poet Byron) **2** *(in nouns)* someone on whom the stated thing has an effect: *an alcoholic* (= someone who cannot stop drinking alcohol) — -**ically** /kli/ *(in adverbs)*: *photographically*
■ USAGE There are many adjectives which end in -**ic** and -**ical**. Some can end only in -**ic**: *energetic*|*idealistic*|*tragic*. Some can end only in -**ical**: *grammatical*|*hysterical*|*musical*. A few can take either ending without changing their meaning: *geometric*|*geometrical*|*magic*|*magical*|*poetic*|*poetical*. Some others can take either ending, but with a difference in meaning: *economic* and *economical*|*historic* and *historical*.

-ical /ɪkəl/ *(in adjectives)* -IC (1): *historical* (= of history)|*satirical* – -**ically** (in adverbs): *historically*

-ician /ɪʃən/ *(in nouns)* a skilled worker who deals with ——: *a beautician* (= someone who gives beauty treatments)|*a technician*

-icide /ɪsaɪd/ also -**cide**— *(in nouns)* killer; killing: *insecticide* (= chemical substance for killing insects)|*suicide* (= act of killing oneself) – -**cidal** *(in adjectives)* – -**icidally** *(in adverbs)*

-ics /ɪks/ *(in nouns)* **1** the scientific study or use of ——: *linguistics* (= the study of language)|*electronics* (= the study or making of apparatus that uses CHIPS, TRANSISTORS, etc.)|*acoustics* **2** the actions typically done by ——*s*: *athletics* (= running, jumping, throwing, etc.)|*acrobatics* **3** qualities or events connected with ——: *the acoustics* (= sound qualities) *of the hall*
■ USAGE Words ending in -**ics** usually take a singular verb when they mean a school subject or an area of study: **Acoustics** *is the study of how sound behaves.*|*European* **politics** *is his special subject.* In other cases they usually take a plural verb: *The* **acoustics** *of this hall are terrible.*|*His* **politics** *are left of centre.*

-ide /aɪd/ *tech (in nouns)* a chemical compound: *cyanide*|*sulphide*

-ie /i/ *infml (in nouns)* -Y (1): *dearie*

-iform /ɪfɔːm‖ɪfɔːrm/ *tech (in adjectives)* in the shape of a ——; like a ——: *cruciform* (= cross-shaped)

-ify /ɪfaɪ/ also -**fy**— *(in verbs)* **1** to make or become ——: *to purify* (= make or become pure)|*to clarify* (= make or become clear) **2** to fill with ——: *to terrify* (= fill with terror) **3** *infml, often humor or derog* **a** to make ——*s*: *to speechify* (= make speeches, use fine-sounding words) **b** to cause to be like or typical of a —— or the ——: *Frenchified* (= like the French)

-in /ɪn/ *(in nouns)* an activity in which a group of people do something together for a purpose: *a sit-in* (= where people sit in a place to prevent its usual activity)|*a teach-in*

-ine /aɪn/ *esp. fml or tech* **1** of or concerning ——*s*: *equine* (= of horses) **2** made of; like: *crystalline*

-ing /ɪŋ/ **1** (forms the present participle of verbs): *They're dancing.*|*to go dancing*|*a dancing bear* —see USAGE **2** *(in* [U] *nouns)* the action or process of the stated verb: *She hates swimming.*|*No Parking* (on a notice, = do not park here) **3** *(in* [C] *nouns)* **a** a case or example of the stated verb: *to hold a meeting* **b** a product or result of the stated verb: *a beautiful painting* **4** *(in nouns)* something used to —— or used for making ——*s*: *a silk lining*|*ten metres of shirting* (= cloth for shirts)
■ USAGE 1 Adjectives which end in -**ing** show that the noun they describe is the doer or subject of the verb they are formed from: *a* **frightening** *film* (= it frightens people)|*She's an* **interesting** *writer.* (= she interests me)|*It was an* **exciting** *game.* (= it made people feel excited). Adjectives which end in -**ed** show that the noun they describe is the object of the verb they are formed from: *a* **frightened** *child* (= someone or something has frightened him/her)|*an* **interested** *audience* (= the play/concert interested them)|*an* **excited** *crowd* (= the game made them feel excited). **2** When adjectives ending in -**ing** are used in certain combinations, different STRESS patterns give different meanings. Compare: *a* **'sleeping** ˌ*car* (= a special railway carriage where people can sleep) and *a* ˌ**sleeping** '*dog* (= a dog which is sleeping); *a* **'singing** ˌ*bird* (= a special kind of bird which can sing) and *a* ˌ**singing** '*bird* (= a bird which is singing at this moment).

-ion /ən/ *(in nouns)* the act, state, or result of ——*ing*: *the completion* (= completing) *of the task*|*his election* [f] *he was elected) to the post*|*several volcanic erup*[…]

-ise /aɪz/ *esp. BrE (in verbs)* -IZE – -**isation** /[…]

-ish /ɪʃ/ **1** *(in nouns and adjectives)* (the [language) belonging to the stated countr[y]: *Are the* **British** (= people from Britain) *un*[…] *speak Turkish* (= the language of T[…] *Swedish.* (= from Sweden)|*Spanish* f[…] Spain) **2** *often derog (in adjectives)* typ[…] like a ——: *foolish behaviour* (= typica[…] *be so childish!* (Don't behave in a wa[…] adult.) —compare CHILDLIKE|*sno*[…] adjectives) to some degree ——; rat[…] *youngish* (= not very young, but r[…] *reddish hair* **4** *infml (in adject*[…] number; APPROXIMATELY: *Co*[…] about 8 o'clock)|*He's fortyish*[…]

-ism /ɪzəm/ *(in nouns)* **1** (a m[…] on) the stated principle[…] *socialism*|*Buddhism* **2**[…] cess of——*ing* or of b[…]

(= he CRITICIZES it)|*her witticisms* (= funny or WITTY remarks) **3** the state or quality of being (a) ——: *heroism* (= being a HERO; bravery)|*magnetism* (= being MAGNETIC) **4** illness caused by too much ——: *alcoholism* **5** the practice of making unfair differences between people because of ——: *sexism* (= making unfair differences between men and women)|*racism*|*heightism* (= against people who are very tall or short)

-ist /ɪst/ **1** (*in nouns and adjectives*) (a follower) of the stated religion or set of principles or ideas: *a Buddhist*| *a Scottish Nationalist*|*her socialist views*|*He's very rightist* (= supports the political RIGHT WING (1)) — compare -ITE (1) **2** (*in nouns*) someone who studies, produces, plays, or operates (a) ——: *a linguist* (= someone who studies or learns languages)|*a novelist* (= someone who writes NOVELS)|*a guitarist* (= someone who plays the GUITAR)|*a machinist* (= someone who operates a machine) —see also -OLOGIST **3** (*in nouns and adjectives*) (someone) making unfair differences between people because of ——: *a very sexist remark* (= making unfair differences between men and women)

-ite /aɪt/ (*in nouns and adjectives*) **1** *something derog* (a follower or supporter) of the stated movement or person: *a group of Trotskyites* (= followers of Trotsky's political ideas)|*the Pre-Raphaelites*|*his Reaganite opinions* —compare -IST (1) **2** (someone) belonging to the stated place or tribe: *a Brooklynite* (= someone from Brooklyn)|*the Israelites in the Bible*

-itis /aɪtɪs/ (*in* [U] *nouns*) **1** a diseased or infected condition of the ——: *tonsillitis* (= infection of the TONSILS) **2** *humor* the condition of having too much of or being too keen on ——: *televisionitis* (= watching too much television)

-itude /ɪtjuːd‖ɪtuːd/ also **-tude**— *often pomp* (*in nouns*) the state or degree of being ——: *certitude* (= being certain)|*exactitude*

-ity /ɪti/ also **-ty**— (*in nouns*) the quality or an example of being ——: *with great regularity* (= regularly)|*such stupidities* (= stupid actions or remarks)

-ive /ɪv/ (*in nouns and adjectives*) (someone or something that ——s or can ——: *an explosive* (= substance that can explode)|*a detective* (= someone who tries to discover facts about crimes)|*the adoptive parents* (= who ADOPT a child)

-ize also **-ise** *esp. BrE* /aɪz/ (*in verbs*) **1** to cause to be (more) ——; make ——: *to modernize our procedures* (= make them (more) modern)|*Americanized spelling* (= spelling changed into the American system from another system)|*to privatize* (= put back into private ownership) **2** to become (—): *The liquid crystallized.* (= turned into CRYSTALS) **3** *sometimes derog* to speak in the stated way: *to soliloquize* (= speak a SOLILOQUY, to oneself)|*to sermonize* (= speak solemnly, as if in a SERMON) **4** to put into the stated place: *to hospitalize a patient* – *-ization* (*in nouns*): (a) *civilization*

■ USAGE 1 -ize is very often used to make new [T] verbs from nouns and adjectives, such as **containerize** (= pack goods in large containers), **hospitalize**, and **finalize**. Some people do not approve of -ize being used so much in this way. 2 the form -ise is commoner in British English than in American English. But when it is joined on to a word part which is not actually a word, as in **surprise** (**surpr-** is not a word), -ise is usually the only spelling in American English as well as in British English. The following words *must* be spelt with -ise: **advertise, advise, chastise, circumcise, comprise, compromise, despise, devise, disguise, exercise, excise, improvise, incise, merchandise, revise, supervise, surmise, surprise.**

-kin /kɪn/ also **-kins** /kɪnz/ – *infml, old-fash or humor* (*in nouns*) (used esp. to children) a small and usu. charming ——: *a lambkin*|*a little babykins*

-latry /tech, often derog (*in* [U] *nouns*) worship of ——: *Mariolatry* (= worship of the Virgin Mary)

-less /ləs/ (*in adjectives*) **1** without (a) ——: *a childless couple* (= who have no children)|*It's quite harmless* (= will not harm you)|*He was hatless.* (= wore no hat)|*endless complaints* (= that never end) **2** that never ——s or cannot be ——ed: *a tireless helper* (= who never gets tired)|*on countless occasions* (= too many to be counted)

-let /lɪt/ (*in nouns*) **1** a small kind of ——: *a booklet* (= small usu. paper-covered book)|*a piglet* (= young pig) **2** a band worn on the stated part of the body: *an anklet* (= worn on the ankle)

-like /laɪk/ (*in adjectives*) like, typical of, or suitable to a ——: *a jelly-like substance*|*childlike simplicity*|*ladylike behaviour*

-ling /lɪŋ/ *esp. old use* (*in nouns*) a small, young, or unimportant ——: *a duckling* (= young duck)|*minor Prussian princelings* (= unimportant princes)

-lived /lɪvd/ (*in adjectives*) lasting or living the stated length of time: *Her enthusiasm was short-lived.* (= did not last long)|*to come from a long-lived family*

-logist /lədʒɪst/ (*in nouns*) -OLOGIST: *genealogist*

-logue ‖also **-log** *AmE* /lɒg‖lɔːg, lɑːg/ (*in nouns*) something spoken; talk: *a monologue* (= speech by one person)

-logy /lədʒi/ (*in nouns*) -OLOGY: *genealogy*

-ly /li/ **1** (*in adverbs*) in the stated way: *He did it very cleverly.* (= in a clever way)|*slowly* **2** (*in adverbs*) from the stated point of view: *Politically (speaking)* (= from a political point of view) *it was a rather unwise remark.*|*a financially sound proposal* **3** (*in adjectives and adverbs*) (happening) at regular periods of a ——: *an hourly check* (= done every hour)|*They visit monthly.* (= once a month) **4** (*in adjectives*) like a —— in manner, nature, or appearance: *with queenly grace*|*a motherly woman* (showing the love, kindness, etc. of a mother)

-manship /mənʃɪp/ (*in* [U] *nouns*) the art or skill of a person of the stated type: *seamanship*|*statesmanship*|*horsemanship* (= skill at horse-riding)

-ment /mənt/ (*in nouns*) **1** the act, cause, means, or result of ——ing: *the need for strong government* (= strong governing)|*the replacement* (= replacing) *of obsolete machinery*|*some interesting new developments* **2** the condition of being ——ed: *his confinement* (= being shut up) *in prison* – **-mental** (*in adjectives*): *governmental*

-meter /miːtə/, mɪtə/ (*in nouns*) an instrument for measuring: *an altimeter* (– for measuring the height at which an aircraft is flying)

-metre *BrE*‖**-meter** *AmE* /miːtə/, mɪtə/ (*in nouns*) the stated part of a metre or a number of metres: *a millimetre*

-monger /mʌŋgə/‖mɑːŋ-, mʌŋ-/ (*in nouns*) **1** someone who sells ——: *a fishmonger* (= someone who sells fish, esp. in a shop) **2** *usu. derog* someone who likes to spread or encourage the stated unpleasant thing: *the rumourmongers* (= people who spread perhaps untrue stories about other people)|*a warmonger*

-most /məʊst/ (*in adjectives*) nearest to ——; most towards ——: *the northernmost town in Sweden* (= the town that is furthest to the north)|*the topmost branches of the tree*

-nd (forms written ORDINAL numbers with 2): *the 2nd* (= second) *of March*|*her 22nd birthday*

-ness /nɪs/ (*in nouns*) the condition, quality, or degree of being ——: *loudness*|*sadness*|*warm-heartedness*|*the many kindnesses you've done me*

-nik /nɪk/ *infml* (*in nouns*) a person who is connected with or keen on ——: *a computernik* (= someone who works with or is very keen on computers)|*a peacenik* (= someone who supports peace)

-ocracy /ɒkrəsi‖ɑː-/ also **-cracy**— (*in nouns*) **1** government by the stated (sort of) people or according to the stated principle: *democracy* (= government by the people)|*mobocracy* **2** a society or country governed in this way: *the Western democracies* (= countries governed by their people)|*a meritocracy* (= governed

(...)adjectives*) having the stated thing as the (...)tant or effective condition, influence, etc.: (...)rowth

by the people with most ability) **3** the usu. powerful social class made up of ——s: *the aristocracy* (= people with noble titles)|(*AustrE*) *the squattocracy* (= rich farmers)

-ocrat /əkræt/ also **-crat**— (*in nouns*) **1** a believer in the stated principle of government: *a democrat* (= someone who believes in government by the people) **2** a member of a usu. powerful or governing social class or group: *a technocrat* (= scientist who controls organizations, etc.) – **-ocratic** (*in adjectives*) – **-ocratically** (*in adverbs*)

-oid /ɔɪd/ *esp. tech* (*in adjectives*) like ——; in the form of ——: *humanoid creatures* (= similar to humans)| *ovoid* (= egg-shaped)

-ologist /ɒlədʒɪst‖ɑː-/ also **-logist**— (*in nouns*) a person who studies or specializes in the stated branch of science: *a biologist*

-ology /ɒlədʒi‖ɑː-/ also **-logy**— (*in nouns*) **1** the scientific study of ——: *geology* (= the study of rocks and the Earth)|*climatology* (= the study of CLIMATE)| *Egyptology* (= the study of ancient Egypt)|(*infml*) *futurology* (= the practice of trying to say how the future will develop) **2** qualities relating to the stated science: *The geology of north Devon is particularly interesting.* (= it has interesting rocks, etc.) – **-ological** (*in adjectives*) – **-ologically** /kli/ (*in adverbs*): *geologically interesting*

-or /ə'/ (*in nouns*) (*the form used for* -ER *in certain words*): *an actor* (= someone who acts)|*an inventor*

-ory¹ /əri‖ɔːri, əri/ (*in nouns*) a place or thing used for ——*ing*: *an observatory* (= where people look at things, esp. the stars)|*a directory* (= book giving lists of information)

-ory² (*in adjectives*) that ——s: *an explanatory note* (= that gives an explanation)|*a congratulatory telegram* (= that CONGRATULATES)

-osis /əusɪs/ **-oses** (*in nouns*) **1** *tech* a diseased condition: *silicosis* (= a lung disease)|*neuroses* (= disorders of the mind) **2** a condition or process: *a metamorphosis* (= change from one state to another) – **-otic** /ɒtɪk‖ɑː-/ (*in adjectives*): *neurotic*|*hypnotic* – **-otically** /kli/ (*in adverbs*)

-ous /əs/ (*in adjectives*) causing or having ——: *dangerous* (= full of danger)|*spacious* (= with much space)

-phile /faɪl/ also **-phil** /fɪl/ – (*in nouns*) a person who likes ——: *a bibliophile* (= someone who likes books)|*an Anglophile* (= someone who likes England or Britain)

-philia /fɪliə/ (*in nouns*) **1** a liking for ——: *Francophilia* (= a liking for France) **2** *tech* a diseased or unhealthy tendency towards or liking for ——: *haemophilia* (= a tendency to bleed)|*necrophilia* (= a sexual attraction to dead bodies)

-philiac /fɪliæk/ *tech* (*in nouns*) a person suffering from ——PHILIA (2): *a necrophiliac*

-phobe /fəub/ (*in nouns*) a person who dislikes or hates ——: *an Anglophobe* (= someone who hates England or Britain)|*a xenophobe* (= someone who hates foreigners)

-phobia /fəubiə/ (*in nouns*) **1** a dislike or hatred of ——: *Anglophobia* (= dislike of England or Britain) **2** *tech* a diseased or unhealthy dislike or fear of ——: *claustrophobia* (= fear of being in a small enclosed space)| *aquaphobia* (= fear of water)

-phobic /fəubɪk/ *tech* (*in adjectives and nouns*) (of or being) a person suffering from ——PHOBIA (2): *He's* (*a*) *claustrophobic.* – **-phobically** /kli/ (*in adverbs*)

-phone /fəun/ **1** (*in nouns*) an apparatus connected with sound and/or hearing, esp. a musical instrument: *earphones* (= for listening to a radio, etc.)|*a saxophone* **2** *tech* (*in adjectives and nouns*) (of or being) a person who speaks the stated language: *Francophone nations* (= where French is spoken)

-proof /pruːf/ (*in adjectives*) treated or made so as not to be harmed by ——s or so as to give protection against ——s: *a bulletproof car*|*an ovenproof dish* (= that cannot be harmed by heat) **2** (*in verbs*) to treat or make in this way: *to soundproof a room* (= so that sound cannot get into or out of it)

-rd (forms written ORDINAL numbers with 3): *the 3rd* (= third) *of June*|*his 53rd birthday*

-ridden /rɪdn/ (*in adjectives*) **1** suffering from the effect of too much ——: *her guilt-ridden dreams* (= she was feeling very guilty) **2** too full of ——s: *mosquito-ridden swamps*

-ry /ri/ (*in nouns*) -ERY: *his sheer wizardry* (= magical skill)

-s /z, s/ **1** (forms the plural of nouns): *a cat and two dogs* **2** (forms the third person singular of the present tense of most verbs): *he plays*|*she sits* **3** *esp. AmE* (*in adverbs*) during (the) ——: *Do you work Sundays?* (= regularly each Sunday)|*Summers we go to the seaside.*

■ USAGE When -s, -'s, and -s' are added to the end of a word (*dogs, comes, John's*) they have the sound /z/ except **a** after words ending with the sounds /p, t, k, f, θ/. Here they are pronounced /s/ as in *cats* /kæts/. **b** after words ending with the sounds /s, z, ʃ, ʒ, tʃ, dʒ/. Here -s is added when the word ends in *-e* (*roses*) and -es when it does not (*pushes*). After these words, both -s and -es are pronounced /ɪz/: *roses* /'rəuzɪz/; *pushes* /'puʃɪz/. The possessive ending -'s has the same sound as -s, but is never spelt -es. Compare *churches* (plural), *church's* (possessive).

-'s 1 (forms the possessive case of singular nouns, and of plural nouns that do not end in -s): *my sister's husband*|*Mary's generosity*|*yesterday's lesson*|*the children's bedroom*|*the man in the corner's coat* (= the coat belonging to the man in the corner) **2** *BrE* the shop or home of ——: *I bought it at the baker's.* (= at the baker's shop)|*I met him at Mary's.* (= at Mary's house) —see -s (USAGE)

-s' (forms the possessive case of plural nouns): *the girls' dresses* (= the dresses belonging to the girls) —see -s (USAGE)

-scape /skeɪp/ (*in nouns*) a wide view of the stated area, as in a picture: *the impressive cityscape of New York*|*some old Dutch seascapes* (= pictures of the sea)

-ship /ʃɪp/ (*in nouns*) **1a** the position of being a ——: *Full membership* (= being a full member) *of the club costs $35.*|*She was offered the professorship.* (= the job of PROFESSOR) **b** the time during which this lasts: *their long friendship* (= they were friends for a long time)|*during his premiership* **2** the art or skill of a ——: *her peerless musicianship* (= skill in performing or judging music)|*a work of great scholarship* —see also -MANSHIP **3** the whole group of ——s: *a magazine with a readership of 9000* (= with 9000 readers)|*The whole membership of the club is*|*are coming to the meeting.* **4** (forms part of certain titles): *your ladyship*

-smith /smɪθ/ (*in nouns*) a maker of ——s: *a gunsmith* (= someone who makes guns)|(fig.) *a wordsmith* (= someone who works with words, e.g. a JOURNALIST) —see also SMITH

-some¹ /səm/ (*in adjectives*) **1** causing or producing ——: *a troublesome boy* (= who causes trouble) **2** liking to ——: *a quarrelsome woman* (= who likes to quarrel)|*frolicsome* **3** able to be ——*ed*; that one would like to ——: *a cuddlesome baby* (= that one would like to hold in one's arms)

-some² (*in nouns*) a group of the stated number, esp. of players: *a golf foursome* (= four people playing GOLF together)

-speak /spiːk/ *often derog* (*in nouns*) the special language, esp. slang words, used in the stated business or activity: *oilspeak* (= language used in the oil industry) *computerspeak*

-sphere /sfɪə'/ *tech* (*in nouns*) the air surrounding Earth at a particular height: *the stratosphere*

-spoken /spəukən/ (*in adjectives*) speaking —— *softly-spoken girl* (= who speaks quietly)

-st 1 (forms written ORDINAL numbers with ——: (= first) *prize*|*my 21st birthday* **2** /st/ *old* ——-EST (2): *thou dost* (= you do)

-ster /stə'/ (*in nouns*) **1** a person who is —— (= a young person) **2** a person who is co—— deals with, or uses ——s: *a trickster* (=

plays deceiving tricks)|*a gangster* (= a member of a GANG)|*a pollster* (= someone who carries out POLLS)

-th /θ/ **1** (forms ORDINAL numbers, except with 1, 2, or 3): *the 17th of June*|*a fifth of the total* —see also -ND, -RD, -ST **2** *old use or bibl* -ETH: *he doth* (= does)

-tion /ʃən/ (*in nouns*) -ION

-tude /tjuːd|tuːd/ (*in nouns*) -ITUDE: *disquietude* (= anxiety)|*pulchritude*

-ty /ti/ (*in nouns*) -ITY: *certainty* (= being certain)

-ular /jŭlər/ (*in adjectives*) of or concerning ——s: *glandular fever* (= having an effect on GLANDS|*tubular steel* (= in the form of tubes)

-ule /juːl/ *esp. tech* (*in nouns*) a small ——: *a granule* (= small grain)|*a spherule* (= small SPHERE)

-ure /jər/ (*in nouns*) the act or condition of ——*ing*: *the closure* (= closing) *of the factory*|*exposure*

-ville /vɪl/ *old-fash or humor sl, esp. AmE* (*in nouns, formed from adjectives* + s) a place or thing that is ——: *This party is really dullsville.* (= it is very dull)

-ward /wəd|wərd/ (*in adjectives*) towards the stated direction or place: *our homeward journey* (= our journey towards home)|*a downward movement*

-wards /wədz|wərdz/ |also **-ward** *esp. AmE*— (*in adverbs*) towards the stated direction or place: *We're travelling northwards.* (= towards the north)|*The plane plunged earthwards.*|(*esp. AmE*) *moving gradually downward*

-ware /weər/ (*in* |U| *nouns*) **1** articles made of the stated material, esp. for use in the home: *glassware* (= glass bowls, glasses, etc.)|*silverware* (= silver dishes, knives, etc.) **2** articles used in the stated place for the preparation or serving of food: *ovenware* (= dishes for use in the OVEN)|*tableware* (= plates, glasses, knives, etc.) **3** things used in operating a computer: *software* (= PROGRAMS)|(*infml*) *liveware* (= people who operate computers)

-ways /weɪz/ (*in adverbs*) in the stated direction: *leaning sideways* (= leaning to the side)

-wright /raɪt/ (*in nouns*) a maker of ——s: *a wheelwright* (= someone who makes wheels)|*a playwright* (= someone who writes plays)

-y¹, -ey /i/ (*in adjectives*) **1** full of or covered with ——: *dirty hands* (= covered with dirt)|*a hairy chest* **2** tending to ——; that ——s: *curly hair* (= hair that curls)|*feeling sleepy* **3** like or typical of ——: *a cold wintry day* (= typical of winter)|*his horsy appearance* (= he looks like a horse) **4** fond of or interested in —— s: *a horsy woman* (= who is keen on horses) – **-ily** (*in adverbs*) – **-iness** (*in nouns*)

-y² (*in nouns*) **1** also **-ie**— (used, esp. when speaking to children, to make a word or name less formal, and often also to show fondness): *Where's little Johnny?* (= John|*my daddy* (= father)|*What a nice doggy!* (= dog)|(*BrE*) *wellies* (= WELLINGTONS) **2** an act or the action of ——*ing*: *the expiry date* (= date when something EXPIRES)

5 The Longman Defining Vocabulary

Words used in the definitions in this dictionary

All the definitions in this dictionary have been written using the words in this list. If a definition includes a word that is *not* in the list, that word is shown in SMALL CAPITAL LETTERS.

The Defining Vocabulary has been carefully chosen after a thorough study of all the well-known frequency lists of English words. Furthermore, only the most common and "central" meanings of the words in the list have actually been used in definitions. We have also used a special computer program that checks every entry to ensure that words from outside the Defining Vocabulary do not appear in definitions.

Word class restrictions

For some words in the list, a word class label such as *n* or *adj* is shown. This means that this particular word is used in definitions *only* in the word class shown. So **anger**, for example, is used only as a noun and not as a verb. But if no word class is shown for a word, it can be used in any of its usual word classes: **answer**, for example, is used in definitions both as a noun and as a verb.

Compound words

Definitions occasionally include compound words formed from words in the Defining Vocabulary, but this is only done if the meaning is completely clear. For example, the word **businessman** (formed from **business** and **man**) is used in some definitions.

Prefixes and suffixes

The main list is followed by a list of common prefixes and suffixes. These can be added to words in the main list to form derived words, provided the meaning is completely clear. For example, the word **nervousness** (formed by adding **-ness** to **nervous**) is used in some definitions.

Phrasal verbs

Phrasal verbs formed by combining words in the Defining Vocabulary (for example, **put up with**) are NOT used in definitions in the dictionary, except in a very small number of cases where the phrasal verb is extremely common and there is no common equivalent. So, for example, **give up** (as in *give up smoking*) and **take off** (as in *the plane took off*) are occasionally used.

Proper names

The Defining Vocabulary does not include the names of actual places, nationalities, religions, and so on, which are occasionally mentioned in definitions.

A	adult	almost	anywhere	attack
	advance *n, v*	alone	apart	attempt
a	advantage	along	apparatus	attend
ability	adventure *n*	aloud	appear	attendance
able	adverb	alphabet	appearance	attention
about	advertise	already	apple	attitude
above *adv. prep*	advertisement	also	appoint	attract
abroad	advice	although	approval	attractive
absence	advise	altogether *adv*	approve	aunt
absent *adj*	affair	always	arch *n*	authority
accept	afford	among	area	autumn
acceptable	afraid	amount *n*	argue	available
accident	after *adv, conj, prep*	amuse	argument	average *adj, n*
accordance	afternoon	amusement	arm	avoid
according (to)	afterwards	amusing *adj*	armour *n*	awake *adj*
account	again	an	arms	away *adv*
ache	against	ancient *adj*	army	awkward
achieve	age *n*	and	around	
acid	ago	anger *n*	arrange	**B**
across	agree	angle *n*	arrangement	baby
act	agreement	angry	arrival	back *adj, adv, n*
action *n*	ahead	animal	arrive	background
active *adj*	aim	ankle	art	backward(s) *adv*
activity	air *n*	annoy	article	bacteria
actor, actress	aircraft	annoyance	artificial	bad *adj*
actual	airport	another	as	bag *n*
add	alcohol	answer	ashamed	bake
addition	alike	ant	ash	balance
address	alive	anxiety	aside *adv*	ball *n*
adjective	all *adv.*	anxious	ask	banana
admiration	determiner,	any	asleep	band *n*
admire	predeterminer,	anyhow	association	bank *n*
admit	pron	anyone	at	bar *n, v*
admittance	allow	anything	atom	bare *adj*

barrel
base *n, v*
basket
bath *n*
bathe *v*
battle *n*
be
beak
beam *n*
bean
bear
beard *n*
beat *n, v*
beautiful
beauty
because
become
bed *n*
bee
beer
before
beg
begin
beginning
behave
behaviour
behind *adv, prep*
belief
believe
bell
belong
below *adv, prep*
belt *n*
bend
beneath
berry
beside(s)
best *adj, adv, n*
better *adj, adv*
between
beyond *adv, prep*
bicycle *n*
big *adj*
bill *n*
bind *v*
bird
birth
birthday
bit
bite
bitter *adj*
black *adj, n*
blade
blame
bleed
bless
blind
block
blood *n*
blow
blue
board *n*
boat *n*
body
boil *v*
bomb

bone *n*
book *n*
boot *n*
border
boring
born
borrow
both
bottle *n*
bottom *n*
bowels
bowl *n*
box *n*
boy
brain *n*
branch
brass
brave *adj*
bread
breadth
break *v*
breakfast *n*
breast *n*
breath
breathe
breed
brick *n*
bridge *n*
bright *adj*
bring
broad *adj*
broadcast
brother
brown *adj, n*
brush
bucket *n*
build *v*
building
bullet
bunch *n*
burial
burn
burst
bury
bus *n*
bush *n*
business
busy
but *conj*
butter *n*
button *n*
buy *v*
by

C

cage *n*
cake *n*
calculate
calculator
call
calm *adj*
camera
camp *n, v*
can *n, v*
candle
cap *n*

capital *n*
captain *n*
car
card *n*
cardboard
care
careful
careless
carriage
carry
cart *n*
case *n*
castle *n*
cat
catch *v*
cattle
cause
celebrate
cell
cement *n*
cent
centimetre
central
centre *n*
century
ceremony
certain *adj,*
    determiner
chain
chair *n*
chairperson
chalk *n*
chance *n*
change
character
charge
charm
chase *v*
cheap
cheat
check
cheek *n*
cheer
cheerful
cheese
chemical
chemistry
cheque
chest
chicken *n*
chief
child, children
childhood
chimney
chin
chocolate
choice *n*
choose
church *n*
cigarette
cinema
circle *n*
circular *adj*
citizen
city
civilization

claim
class *n*
clay
clean *adj, v*
clear *adj, v*
clerk
clever
cliff
climb *v*
clock *n*
clockwork
close *adj, adv, v*
cloth
clothes, clothing
cloud *n*
club *n*
coal
coast *n*
coat *n*
coffee
coin *n*
cold
collar *n*
collect *v*
college
colour
comb
combination
combine *v*
come
comfort
comfortable
command
committee
common *adj*
companion
company
compare *v*
comparison
compete
competition
competitor
complain
complaint
complete
compound *n*
computer
concern *v*
concerning
concert
condition *n*
confidence
confident
confuse
connect
conscience
conscious
consider
consist
consonant *n*
contain
contents *n*
context
continue
continuous
contract *n*

control
convenient
conversation
cook
cool *adj*
copper
copy
cord *n*
corn
corner *n*
correct *adj*
cost
cotton
cough
could
council
count *v*
country *n*
courage
course *n*
court *n*
cover
cow *n*
coward
cowardly
crack *n, v*
crash *n, v*
cream *n*
creature
creep *v*
cricket
crime
criminal
critisise
critisize
crop *n*
cross *n, v*
crowd *n*
cruel
cruelty
crush *v*
cry
cultivate
cup *n*
cupboard
cure
curl
current
curse
curtain *n*
curve
custom *n*
customer
cut
cycle *v*

D

daily *adj, adv*
damage
dance
danger
dangerous
dare *v*
daring
dark
date *n*

daughter
day
dead *adj*
deal
dear *adj*
death
debt
decay
deceit
deceive
decide
decimal
decision
declaration
declare
decorate
decoration
decrease
deep *adj*
deer
defeat
defence
defend
definite
degree
delay
deliberate
deliberately
delicate
delight
deliver
demand
department
depend
dependent
depth
descend
describe
description
descriptive
desert *n*
deserve
desirable
desire
desk
destroy
destruction
detail *n*
determination
determined
develop
devil *n*
diamond
dictionary
die *v*
difference
different
difficult
difficulty
dig *v*
dinner
dip *v*
direct
direction
dirt
dirty *adj*

disappoint
discourage
discouragement
discover
discovery
discuss
discussion
dish *n*
dismiss
distance *n*
distant
ditch *n*
divide *v*
division
do *v*
doctor *n*
document
dog *n*
dollar
door
doorway
dot *n*
double *adj, adv,*
   predeterminer, v
doubt
down *adj, adv, prep*
drag *v*
draw *v*
drawer
dream
dress *n, v*
drink
drive *v*
drop
drown
drug *n*
drum *n*
drunk
dry
duck *n*
dull *adj*
during
dust *n*
duty

E

each
eager
ear
early
earn
earth *n*
east
eastern
easy
eat
economic
edge *n*
educate
education
effect *n*
effective
effort
egg *n*
eight(h)
either

elastic
elbow *n*
elect *v*
election
electric
electricity
electronic
elephant
else
embarrass
emotion
employ *v*
employer
employment
empty *adj, v*
enclose
enclosure
encourage
encouragement
end
enemy
engine
engineer *n*
English
enjoy
enjoyment
enough
enter
entertain
entertainment
entrance *n*
envelope
environment
equal *adj, n, v*
equality
equipment
escape
especially
establish
establishment
even *adj, adv*
evening
event
ever
every
everyone
everything
everywhere
evil
exact *adj*
examine
examination
example
excellent
except *conj, prep*
exchange
excite
excited
exciting
excuse
exercise
exist
existence
expect
expensive
experience

explain
explanation
explode
explosion
explosive
express *v*
expression
extreme
eye
eyelid

F

face
fact
factory
fail *v*
failure
faint *adj, v*
fair *adj*
fairy
faith
faithful *adj*
fall
false *adj*
fame
familiar *adj*
family
famous
fancy *adj*
far
farm
farmer
farmyard
fashion *n*
fashionable
fast *adj, adv*
fasten
fat
fate
father *n*
fault
favour *n*
favourable
favourite *adj*
fear
feather *n*
feature
feed *v*
feel *v*
feeling(s)
fellow *n*
female
fence *n*
fever
few
field *n*
fierce
fifth
fight
figure *n*
fill *v*
film
final
finally
financial
find *v*

fine *adj*
finger *n*
finish
fire
fireplace
firm *adj, n*
first *adv, determiner*
fish
fisherman
fit *adj, v*
five
fix *v*
flag *n*
flame
flash *n, v*
flat
flesh
flight
float *v*
flood
floor *n*
flour
flow
flower *n*
fly *n, v*
fold
follow
fond
food
fool *n*
foolish
foot *n*
football
footpath
footstep
for *prep*
forbid
force
forehead
foreign
foreigner
forest
forget
forgive
fork *n*
form
formal
former
formerly
fort
fortune
fortunate
forward(s) *adv*
four(th)
fox *n*
frame *n*
free
freedom
freeze *v*
frequent *adj*
fresh
friend
friendly
frighten
frightening
from

front *adj, n*
fruit *n*
fulfil
full *adj*
fun
funeral
funny
fur *n*
furnish
furniture
further *adj, adv*
future

G
gain *v*
game *n*
garage *n*
garden
garment
gas *n*
gate *n*
gather *v*
general
generous
gentle
gentleman
get
gift
girl
give *v*
glad
glass *adj, n*
glory *n*
glue
go *v*
goat
god, God
gold
golden
good
goodbye
goods
govern
government
grace
graceful
gradual
grain
gram
grammar
grand *adj*
grandfather
grandmother
grass *n*
grateful
grave *n*
great
green
greet
greeting
grey *adj, n*
grief
grieve
ground *n*
group *n*
grow

growth
guard
guess
guest
guidance
guide
guilt
gun *n*

H
habit
habitual
hair
hairy
half
hall
hammer *n*
hand
handkerchief
handle
hang *v*
happen *v*
happy
hard
harden
hardly
hardship
harm
harmful
harmless
hasty
hat
hate *v*
hatred
have
he
head *adj, n*
health
healthy
hear
heart
heat
heaven
heavy *adj*
heel
height
help
helpful
hen
her(s)
here
herself
hide *v*
high *adj, adv*
hill
him
himself
hire
his
history
hit
hold
hole
holiday
hollow *adj*
holy

home *adv, n*
honest
honesty
honour *n*
honourable
hook *n*
hope
hopeful
hopeless
horizon
horn
horse *n*
hospital
host *n*
hot *adj*
hotel
hour
hourly
house *n*
how *adv*
human
humorous
humour
hundred(th)
hunger *n*
hungry
hunt *v*
hurry
hurt *v*
husband *n*
hut

I
I
ice *n*
icy
idea
if
ignore
ill *adj*
image
imaginary
imagination
imagine
immediate
importance
important
improve
improvement
in *adv, prep*
include
including
income
increase
independent
indoor(s)
industrial
industry
infect
infection
infectious
influence
influential
inform
information
ink *n*

inner
inquire
inquiry
insect
inside
instead
institution
instruct
instruction
instrument
insurance
insure
intend
intention
interest
interesting
international *adj*
interrupt
interruption
into
introduce
introduction
invent
invention
invitation
invite
involve
inwards
iron *adj, n*
island
it *pron*
its
itself

J
jaw *n*
jealous
jealousy
jelly
jewel
jewellery
job
join
joint
joke
journey *n*
joy
judge
judgment
juice
jump
just
justice

K
keen
keep *v*
key *n*
kick
kill *v*
kilo
kilogram
kilometre
kind
king
kingdom

kiss
kitchen
knee *n*
kneel
knife *n*
knock
knot
know *v*
knowledge

L
labour *n*
lack
ladder *n*
lady
lake
lamb
lamp
land
language
large
last *adv,*
    determiner, v
late
lately
laugh
laughter
law
lawyer
lay *v*
lazy
lead /led/ *n*
lead /li:d/ *v*
leaf *n*
lean *v*
learn
least
leather
leave *v*
left
leg *n*
legal
lend
length
less *adv,*
    determiner,
    pron
lesson
let *v*
letter
level *adj, adv, n*
library
lid
lie
life
lift
light
lightning
like *prep, v*
likely
limb
limit
line *n*
lion
lip
liquid

list *n*
listen *v*
literature
litre
little
live *v*
load
loaf *n*
local *adj*
lock
lodging(s)
log *n*
lonely
long *adj, adv*
look
loose *adj*
lord *n*
lose
loss
lot
loud
love
low *adj*
lower *v*
loyal
loyalty
luck *n*
lump *n*
lung

M

machine *n*
machinery
mad
magazine
magic
magician
mail
main *adj*
make *v*
male
man *n*
manage
manager
manner
many
map *n*
march
mark
market *n*
marriage
marry
mass *n*
master *n*
mat
match
material
matter
may *v*
me
meal
mean *v*
meaning *n*
means
measure
meat

medical *adj*
medicine
meet *v*
meeting
melt
member
memory
mend *v*
mental
mention *v*
merry
message
messenger
metal *n*
method
metre
metric
microscope
middle *adj, n*
might *v*
mile
military *adj*
milk
million(th)
mind
mine *n, pron*
mineral
minister *n*
minute *n*
mirror *n*
miss *v*
mist *n*
mistake
mix *v*
mixture
model *n*
modern *adj*
moment
money
monkey *n*
month
monthly *adj, adv*
moon *n*
moral *adj*
morals
more
morning
most
mother *n*
motor *adj, n*
mountain
mouse
mouth *n*
move *v*
much
mud
multiply
murder
muscle *n*
music
musician
must *v*
my
myself
mysterious
mystery

N

nail
name
narrow *adj*
nasty
nation
national *adj*
nature
naval
navy
near *adj, adv, prep*
nearly
neat
necessary
neck
need
needle *n*
negative
neighbour
neighbourhood
neither
nerve *n*
nervous
nest *n*
net *n*
network *n*
never
new
news
newspaper
next *adj, adv*
nice
night
nine
ninth
no *adv, determiner*
noble *adj*
nobleman
noise *n*
none *pron*
nonsense
no one
nor
north
northern
nose *n*
not
note
nothing
notice
noun
now
nowhere
number *n*
nurse
nut
nylon

O

obedience
obedient
obey
object *n*
obtain

occasion *n*
ocean
o'clock
odd
of
off *adv, prep*
offence
offend
offensive *adj*
offer
office
officer
official
often
oil
old
old-fashioned
on *adv, prep*
once *adv*
one
oneself
onion
only
open *adj, v*
operate
operation
opinion
opponent
oppose
opposite
opposition
or
orange
order
ordinary
organ
organization
origin
other
otherwise
ought
our(s)
ourselves
out *adj, adv*
outdoor(s)
outer
outside
over *adv, prep*
owe
owing to
own *determiner, pron, v*
oxygen

P

pack *v*
packet
page *n*
pain *n*
painful
paint
painting
pair *n*
palace
pale *adj*

pan *n*
paper *n*
parallel *adj, n*
parcel *n*
parent *n*
park
parliament
part *n*
participle
particular *adj*
partner *n*
party *n*
pass *v*
passage
passenger
past
pastry
path
patience
patient *adj*
pattern *n*
pause
pay
payment
peace
peaceful
pen *v*
pence
pencil *n*
people *n*
pepper *n*
per
perfect *adj*
perform
perhaps
period *n*
permanent
permission
permit *v*
person
personal
persuade
pet *n*
petrol
photograph
photography
phrase *n*
physical
piano *n*
pick *v*
picture *n*
piece *n*
pig *n*
pile
pilot
pin
pink *adj, n*
pipe *n*
pity
place
plain *adj, n*
plan
plane *n*
plant
plastic
plate *n*

play
pleasant
please
pleased
pleasure *n*
plenty *pron*
plural
pocket *n*
poem
poet
poetry
point
pointed
poison
poisonous
pole *n*
police *n*
polish
polite
political
politician
politics
pool *n*
poor
popular
popularity
population
port *n*
position *n*
positive
possess
possession
possible *adj*
possibly
possibility
post
pot *n*
potato
pound *n*
pour
powder *n*
power *n*
powerful
practical
practice
practise
praise
pray
prayer
precious *adj*
prefer
preparation
prepare
presence
present *adj, n*
preserve *v*
president
press *v*
pressure *n*
pretend
pretty *adj*
prevent
previous
price *n*
prickly
pride *n*

priest
prince
principle
print
prison
prisoner
private *adj*
prize *n*
probably *adj*
probability
problem
process *n*
procession
produce *v*
product
production
profession
profit *n*
programme
promise
pronounce
pronunciation
proof *n*
proper
property
proposal
protect
protection
protective
protest
proud
prove
provide
provision(s)
public
pull
pump
punish
punishment
pupil
pure
purple
purpose *n*
push
put

Q

quality
quantity
quarrel
quarter *n*
queen *n*
question
quick *adj*
quiet *adj, n*
quite

R

rabbit *n*
race
radio *n*
railway
rain
raise *v*

range *n*
rank *n*
rapid *adj*
rare
rat *n*
rate *n*
rather
raw *adj*
reach
react
reaction
read *v*
ready *adj*
real
realize
really
reason
reasonable
receive
recent
recently
recognition
recognize
record *n, v*
red
reduce
reduction
refusal
refuse *v*
regard
regular *adj*
related
relative
relation
relax
religion
religious
remain
remark *n*
remember
remind
remove *v*
rent
repair
repeat *v*
replace
reply
report
represent
representative
republic
request
respect
respectful
responsible
rest
restaurant
restrict
result
return *n, v*
reward
rice
rich
rid
ride
right *adj, adv, n*

ring
ripe
rise *v*
risk
river
road
rob
rock *n*
rod
roll *v*
roof *n*
room *n*
root *n*
rope *n*
rose
rough *adj*
round *adj, adv, prep*
row *n, v*
royal *adj*
rub *v*
rubber
rude
ruin
rule
ruler
run
rush

S

sad
safe *adj*
safety
sail
sale
salt *adj, n*
same
sand *n*
satisfaction
satisfactory
satisfy
save *v*
say *v*
scale *n*
scatter *v*
scene
scenery
school *n*
science
scientific
scientist
scissors
screw
sea
search
season *n*
seat
second *adv, determiner, n, pron*
secrecy
secret
secretary
see *v*
seed *n*
seem

seize
sell *v*
send
sensation
sense *n*
senseless
sensible
sensitive
sentence *n*
separate *adj, v*
serious
servant
serve
service *n*
set *n, v*
settle *v*
seven(th)
several
severe
sew
sex *n*
sexual
shade
shadow *n*
shake
shall
shame *n*
shape
share
sharp *adj*
she
sheep
sheet
shelf
shell *n*
shelter
shield *n*
shine *v*
ship *n*
shirt
shock *n, v*
shoe *n*
shoot *v*
shop
shopkeeper
shore *n*
short *adj*
shot *n*
should
shoulder *n*
shout
show *n, v*
shut
sick *adj*
side *adj, n*
sideways
sight *n*
sign
signal
signature
silence *n*
silent
silk
silly *adj*
silver
similar

similarity
simple
since
sincere
sing
single *adj*
singular
sink *v*
sister
sit
situation
six(th)
size *n*
skilful
skill
skin *n*
skirt *n*
sky *n*
slave *n*
sleep
slide *v*
slight *adj*
slip *v*
slippery
slope
slow
small
smell
smile
smoke
smooth *adj*
snake *n*
snow
so
soap *n*
social *adj*
society
sock *n*
soft
soil *n*
soldier *n*
solemn
solid
some *determiner, pron*
somehow
someone
something
sometimes
somewhere
son
song
soon
sore *adj*
sorrow *n*
sorry
sort *n*
soul
sound *n, v*
soup
sour *adj*
south
southern
space *n*
spacecraft
spade

speak
spear *n*
special *adj*
specialist
specific
speech
speed *n*
spell *v*
spend
spin *v*
spirit *n*
spite *n*
splendid
split *v*
spoil *v*
spoon *n*
sport *n*
spot *n*
spread *v*
spring
square *adj, n*
stage *n*
stair
stamp
stand *v*
standard
star *n*
start
state
statement
station *n*
stay
steady *adj*
steal *v*
steam *n*
steel *n*
steep *adj*
stem *n*
step
stick
sticky
stiff *adj*
still *adj, adv*
sting
stitch
stomach *n*
stone *n*
stop
store
storm *n*
story
straight *adj, adv*
strange
stranger
stream *n*
street
strength
stretch
strike *v*
string *n*
stroke *n*
strong
structure *n*
struggle
student
study

stupid
style *n*
subject *n*
substance
subtract
succeed
success
successful
such
suck *v*
sudden
suffer
sugar *n*
suggest
suit
suitable
sum *n*
summer *n*
sun *n*
supper
supply *n, v*
support
suppose
sure *adj*
surface *n*
surprise
surround *v*
swallow *v*
swear
sweep *v*
sweet
swell *v*
swim
swing
sword
sympathetic
sympathy
system

T

table *n*
tail *n*
take *v*
talk
tall
taste
tax
taxi *n*
tea
teach
team *n*
tear /teə^r/ *v*
tear /tɪə^r/ *n*
technical
telephone
television
tell
temper *n*
temperature
temple
tend
tendency
tender *adj*
tennis
tense *n*

tent
terrible
terror
test
than
thank
that *conj, determiner, pron*
the
theatre
their(s)
them
themselves
then *adv*
there
therefore
these
they
thick *adj*
thief
thin *adj*
thing
think *v*
third
thirst *n*
thirsty
this *determiner, pron*
those
though
thought
thousand(th)
thread *n*
threat
threaten
three
throat
through *adv, prep*
throw
thumb *n*
thunder
thus
ticket *n*
tidy *adj, v*
tie
tiger
tight *adj*
time *n*
timetable *n*
tin
tire *v*
title *n*
to
tobacco
today
toe *n*
together
tomorrow
tongue
tonight
too
tool *n*
tooth
top *adj, n*
touch

tour
tourist
towards
tower *n*
town
toy *n*
track
trade *n*
traffic *n*
train
translate
transparent
trap
travel
treat *v*
treatment
tree
tremble *v*
tribe
trick *n, v*
trip *n*
tropical
trouble
trousers
true *adj*
trunk
truth
trust
try *v*
tube
tune *n*
turn
twice
twist
type *n*
typical
tyre

U

ugly
uncle
under *prep*
understand
undo
uniform *n*
union
unit
unite
universal
universe
university
until
up *adj, adv, prep*
upper *adj*
upright *adj, adv*
upset *v*
upside down
upstairs *adj, adv*
urge
urgent
us
use
useful
useless
usual

V

valley
valuable *adj*
value *n*
variety
various
vary
vegetable
vehicle
verb
very *adv*
victory
view *n*
village
violence
violent
visit
voice *n*
vote
vowel
voyage *n*

W

wages
waist
wait *v*
waiter
wake *v*
walk
wall *n*
wander
want *v*
war *n*
warm *adj, v*
warmth
warn
wash
waste
watch
water
wave
way
we
weak
wealth
weapon
wear *v*
weather *n*
weave *v*
wedding

week
weekly *adj, adv*
weigh
weight *n*
welcome
well *adj, adv, n*
west
western *adj*
wet *adj*
what
whatever
wheat
wheel *n*
when *adv, conj*
whenever
where
whether
which
whichever
while *conj*
whip
whisper
whistle
white
who
whoever
whole
why
wicked
wide *adj, adv*
widespread
width
wife
wild *adj, adv*
will
willing
win *v*
wind /wɪnd/*n*
wind /waɪnd/*v*
window
wine *n*
wing *n*
winter *n*
wire *n*
wise *adj*
wisdom
wish
with
within *prep*
witness *n*
without *prep*
woman

wonder *n, v*
wood
wooden
wool
woollen
word *n*
work
world
worm *n*
worry
worse
worst
worship
worth
worthy (of)
would
wound *n, v*
wrap *v*
wreck
wrist
write
wrong *adj, adv, n*
wrongdoing

Y

yard
year
yearly
yellow *adj, n*
yes
yesterday
yet
you
young
your(s)
yourself
youth

Z

zero

Prefixes and suffixes that can be used with words in the Defining Vocabulary

-able	dis-	-ful	-ion	-ize	-ness	-ship
-al	-ed	-ible	ir-	-less	non-	-th
-an	-en	-ic	-ish	-like	-or	un-
-ance	-ence	-ical	-ist	-ly	-ous	-ward(s
-ar	-er	im-	-ity	-ment	re-	-work
-ate	-ery	in-	-ive	mid-	-ry	-y
-ation	-ess	-ing	-ization	mis-	self-	

6 Irregular verbs

verb	past tense	past participle
abide	abided, abode	abided
arise	arose	arisen
awake	awoke, awakened	awoken
be	see Table 7	
bear	bore	borne
beat	beat	beaten, beat
become	became	become
befall	befell	befallen
beget	begot (also begat bibl)	begotten
begin	began	begun
behold	beheld	beheld
bend	bent	bent
bereave	bereft, bereaved	bereft, bereaved
beseech	besought, beseeched	besought, beseeched
beset	beset	beset
bestride	bestrode	bestridden
bet	bet, betted	bet, betted
betake	betook	betaken
bethink	bethought	bethought
bid	bade, bid	bid, bidden
bind	bound	bound
bite	bit	bitten
bleed	bled	bled
bless	blessed, blest	blessed, blest
blow	blew	blown
break	broke	broken
breed	bred	bred
bring	brought	brought
broadcast	broadcast	broadcast
build	built	built
burn	burned, burnt	burned, burnt
burst	burst	burst
buy	bought	bought
can	see dictionary entry	
cast	cast	cast
catch	caught	caught
chide	chided, chid	chid, chidden
choose	chose	chosen
cleave	cleaved, cleft, clove	cleaved, cleft, cloven
cling	clung	clung
come	came	come
cost	cost	cost
could	see dictionary entry	
creep	crept	crept
cut	cut	cut
deal	dealt /delt/	dealt
dig	dug	dug
dive	dived, (AmE) dove	dived
do	did	done
draw	drew	drawn
dream	dreamed, dreamt	dreamed, dreamt
drink	drank	drunk
drive	drove	driven
dwell	dwelt, dwelled	dwelt, dwelled
eat	ate	eaten
fall	fell	fallen
feed	fed	fed
feel	felt	felt
fight	fought	fought
find	found	found
flee	fled	fled
fling	flung	flung
fly	flew	flown
forbear	forbore	forborne
forbid	forbade, forbad	forbidden
forecast	forecast	forecast
foresee	foresaw	foreseen
foretell	foretold	foretold
forget	forgot	forgotten
forgive	forgave	forgiven
forgo	forwent	forgone
forsake	forsook	forsaken
forswear	forswore	forsworn
freeze	froze	frozen
gainsay	gainsaid	gainsaid
get	got	got (also gotten AmE)
gird	girded, girt	girded, girt
give	gave	given
go	went	gone
grind	ground	ground
grow	grew	grown
hamstring	hamstrung	hamstrung
hang	hung, hanged	hung, hanged
have	had	had
hear	heard	heard
heave	heaved, hove	heaved, hove
hew	hewed	hewn, hewed
hide	hid	hidden, hid
hit	hit	hit
hold	held	held
hurt	hurt	hurt
keep	kept	kept
kneel	knelt, (esp. AmE) kneeled	knelt, (esp. AmE) kneeled
knit	knitted, knit	knitted, knit
know	knew	known
lay	laid	laid
lead	led	led
lean	leaned, (esp. BrE) leant	leaned, (esp. BrE) leant
leap	leapt, (esp. AmE) leaped	leapt, (esp. AmE) leaped
learn	learned, (esp. BrE) learnt	learned, (esp. BrE) learnt
leave	left	left
lend	lent	lent
let	let	let
lie	lay	lain
light	lit, lighted	lit, lighted
lose	lost	lost
make	made	made
may	see dictionary entry	
mean	meant	meant
meet	met	met
might	see dictionary entry	
miscast	miscast	miscast
mislay	mislaid	mislaid
mislead	misled	misled
misspell	misspelt, misspelled	misspelt, misspelled

verb	past tense	past participle	verb	past tense	past participle
misspend	misspent	misspent	sing	sang	sung
mistake	mistook	mistaken	sink	sank, sunk	sunk
misunderstand	misunderstood	misunderstood	sit	sat	sat
mow	mowed	mown, mowed	slay	slew	slain
outbid	outbid	outbid	sleep	slept	slept
outdo	outdid	outdone	slide	slid	slid
outgrow	outgrew	outgrown	sling	slung	slung
outrun	outran	outrun	slink	slunk	slunk
outshine	outshone	outshone	slit	slit	slit
overbear	overbore	overborne	smell	(esp. BrE) smelt,	(esp. BrE) smelt,
overcast	overcast	overcast		(esp. AmE)	(esp. AmE)
overcome	overcame	overcome		smelled	smelled
overdo	overdid	overdone	smite	smote	smitten
overhang	overhung	overhung	sneak	sneaked (also snuck	sneaked (also
overrun	overran	overrun		AmE)	snuck AmE)
oversee	oversaw	overseen	sow	sowed	sown, sowed
oversleep	overslept	overslept	speak	spoke	spoken
overtake	overtook	overtaken	speed	sped, speeded	sped, speeded
overthrow	overthrew	overthrown	spell	(esp. BrE) spelt,	(esp. BrE) spelt,
partake	partook	partaken		(esp. AmE)	(esp. AmE)
pay	paid	paid		spelled	spelled
prove	proved	proved (also	spend	spent	spent
		proven AmE)	spill	(esp. BrE) spilt,	(esp. BrE) spilt,
put	put	put		(esp. AmE) spilled	(esp. AmE) spilled
read	read /red/	read /red/	spin	spun, span	spun
rebind	rebound	rebound	spit	spat (also spit AmE)	spat (also spit
rebuild	rebuilt	rebuilt			AmE)
recast	recast	recast	split	split	split
redo	redid	redone	spoil	spoiled, spoilt	spoiled, spoilt
relay	relaid	relaid	spread	spread	spread
remake	remade	remade	spring	sprang (also sprung	sprung
rend	rent	rent		AmE)	
repay	repaid	repaid	stand	stood	stood
rerun	reran	rerun	steal	stole	stolen
reset	reset	reset	stick	stuck	stuck
retell	retold	retold	sting	stung	stung
rewind	rewound	rewound	stink	stank, stunk	stunk
rewrite	rewrote	rewritten	strew	strewed	strewn, strewed
rid	rid, ridded	rid, ridded	stride	strode	stridden
ride	rode	ridden	strike	struck	struck
ring	rang	rung	string	strung	strung
rise	rose	risen	strive	strove, strived	striven, strived
run	ran	run	swear	swore	sworn
saw	sawed	sawn, sawed	sweep	swept	swept
say	said	said	swell	swelled	swollen, swelled
see	saw	seen	swim	swam	swum
seek	sought	sought	swing	swung	swung
sell	sold	sold	take	took	taken
send	sent	sent	teach	taught	taught
set	set	set	tear	tore	torn
sew	sewed	sewn, sewed	tell	told	told
shake	shook	shaken	think	thought	thought
shall	see dictionary		thrive	thrived, throve	thrived
	entry		throw	threw	thrown
shave	shaved	shaved	thrust	thrust	thrust
shear	sheared	shorn, sheared	tread	trod	trodden, trod
shed	shed	shed	unbend	unbent	unbent
shine	shone, shined	shone, shined	unbind	unbound	unbound
shoe	shod	shod	undergo	underwent	undergone
shoot	shot	shot	understand	understood	understood
should	see dictionary		undertake	undertook	undertaken
	entry		undo	undid	undone
show	showed	shown, showed	unwind	unwound	unwound
shrink	shrank, shrunk	shrunk	uphold	upheld	upheld
shut	shut	shut	upset	upset	upset

verb	past tense	past participle
wake	woke, waked	woken, waked
waylay	waylaid	waylaid
wear	wore	worn
weave	wove	woven
wed	wedded, wed	wedded, wed
weep	wept	wept
wet	wetted, wet	wetted, wet
will	*see dictionary entry*	
win	won	won
wind /waɪnd/	wound	wound
withdraw	withdrew	withdrawn
withhold	withheld	withheld
withstand	withstood	withstood
would	*see dictionary entry*	
wring	wrung	wrung
write	wrote	written

7 The verb "be"

present

	I	you	she/he/it	we/they
	I am I'm	you are you're	she is, he is, it is she's, he's, it's	we are, they are we're, they're
questions	am I?	are you?	is she? is he? is it?	are we? are they?
negatives	I am not I'm not aren't I?	you are not you're not you aren't	she is not, he is not, it is not she's not, he's not, it's not she isn't, he isn't, it isn't	we are not, they are not we're not, they're not we aren't, they aren't

present participle: being

past

	I	you	she/he/it	we/they
	I was	you were	she was, he was, it was	we were, they were
questions	was I?	were you?	was she? was he?, was it?	were we? were they?
negatives	I was not I wasn't	you were not you weren't	she was not, he was not, it was not she wasn't, he wasn't, it wasn't	we were not, they were not we weren't, they weren't

past participle: been